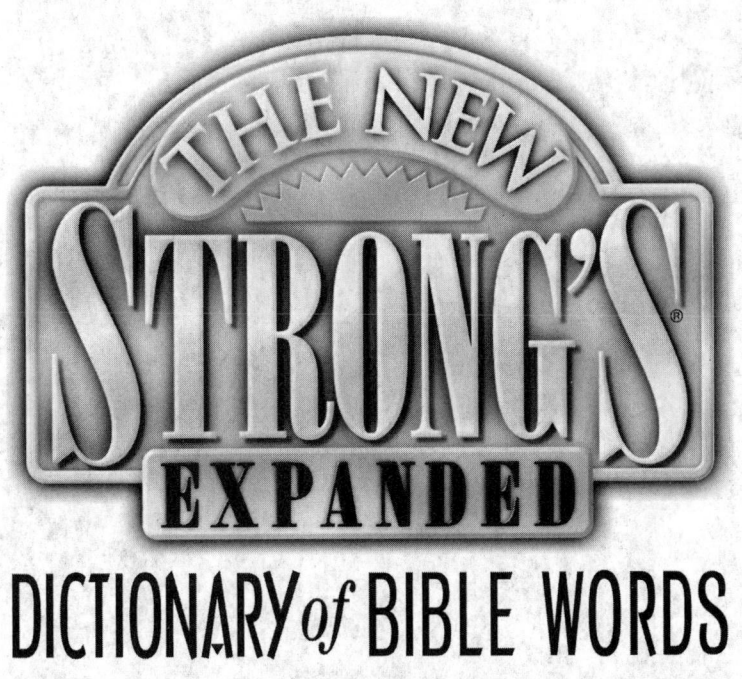

THE NEW STRONG'S EXPANDED

DICTIONARY of BIBLE WORDS

JAMES STRONG, LL.D., S.T.D.

Introduction by John R. Kohlenberger, III

THOMAS NELSON PUBLISHERS
Nashville

Published in Nashville, Tennessee, by Thomas Nelson Inc.

The publisher wishes to acknowledge the editorial and composition services of John R.
Kohlenberger III and Multnomah Graphics. The publisher further acknowledges the invaluable contribution of Robert P. Kendall in adapting material from W. E. Vine's *Complete
Expository Dictionary of Old and New Testament Words* and incorporating cross-references
to other lexicons into the Hebrew and Greek dictionaries.

Strong, James, 1822–1894.
    The new Strong's expanded dictionary of Bible words / James Strong.
    Includes index.
    ISBN: 0-7852-4676-2
    1. Hebrew language—Dictionaries—English. 2. Greek language, biblical—
Dictionaries—English. 3. Bible. O.T.—Dictionaries—Hebrew. 4. Bible. N.T.—
Dictionaries—Greek. I. Title.

Printed in the United States of America
9 — 06

WORDS OMITTED FROM THE ENGLISH INDEX

agone	2 Samuel 30.13	ago
bestead		placed, situated [see hardly bestead below]
cunningly	2 Peter 1.16	skillfully??
estate	numerous verses	style, station, manner
estates	Ezekiel 36.11 Mark 6.21	plural of estate
hardly bestead	Isaiah 8.21	greatly distressed
karnaim	Genesis 14.5	Ashteroth-Qarnayim, city in Og
liers [in wait]	Joshua 8.13, Judges 9.25, et al.	those lying in wait [apparently to ambush]
lign	Numbers 24.6	*trees of lign aloes*; aligned??
masteries	2 Timothy 2.5	upper hands, expert skills????
rovers	1 Chronicles 12.21	pirates, bandits, highwaymen
sap	Psalm 104.16	*trees full of sap*; vitality?
seatward	Exodus 37.9	*to the mercy seatward*; toward the mercy seat
selfsame	numerous verses	identical, very same
you-ward	2 Corinthians 1.12 2 Corinthians 13.3 Ephesians 3.2	toward you

Contents

Read this first!

How to Use *The New Strong's®* *Expanded Dictionary of Bible Words*

Strong's unique system of numbers continues to be *the* bridge between the original languages of the Bible and English translations for many Bible students. *The New Strong's® Expanded Dictionary of Bible Words* combines Nelson's exclusive English Index to the Biblical Languages with newly typeset, corrected, and greatly expanded print editions of *Strong's Hebrew and Aramaic Dictionary* and *Strong's Greek Dictionary* to offer a unique and valuable tool for biblical word studies.

1. What the Dictionary Is

The New Strong's® Expanded Dictionary of Bible Words is a fully integrated collection of three key Bible study tools. It is an essential companion to *The New Strong's® Exhaustive Concordance* or any other edition of this classic concordance. The English Index to the Biblical Languages contains every major word in the KJV in alphabetical order, with a list of every Hebrew, Aramaic, and Greek word that each English word translates. This unique index shows at a glance the range of meanings of each English word and provides a key to the biblical language dictionaries. The Introduction to the English Index follows on page v. *The Hebrew and Aramaic Dictionary* contains a wealth of information about the original languages of the Old Testament. It is keyed to the English Index by Strong's numbering system, as well as by the complete list of KJV renderings within each dictionary entry. The Introduction to *The Hebrew and Aramaic Dictionary* appears on page 290. *The Greek Dictionary* contains a wealth of information about the original language of the New Testament. It is also keyed to the English Index by Strong's numbering system, as well as by the complete list of KJV renderings within each dictionary entry. The Introduction to *The Greek Dictionary* appears on page 900.

2. Using the Dictionary Independently

To use this dictionary, look up any KJV word in the English Index. Within each entry is a listing of every Hebrew, Aramaic, and Greek word that the English word translates.

Because each original language word has a concise English definition, you immediately see the range of meaning of the English words. "Earnest," for example, is used as an adjective describing sincere emotions and is also used as a noun, as in "earnest money" or "pledge." Because each original language word is keyed to the Strong's numbering system, you can find further information in the *Hebrew and Aramaic* and *Greek Dictionaries*. If the Strong's number is not italicized (e.g., **1001**), consult the *Hebrew and Aramaic Dictionary*. If the Strong's number is italicized (e.g., *1001*), consult the *Greek Dictionary*. These dictionaries provide further definitions and explanations of the original languages. They also list every English word in the KJV that translates each original language word. These features of *The New Strong's® Expanded Dictionary of Bible Words* allow it to function as a complete dictionary and thesaurus to the original biblical languages and to the KJV.

3. Using the Dictionary with *The New Strong's® Exhaustive Concordance*

The New Strong's® Expanded Dictionary of Bible Words provides word meanings for the KJV and for the original biblical languages. Although its dictionaries do cite many biblical texts, it by no means replaces *The New Strong's® Exhaustive Concordance* as an exhaustive index to every appearance of every English word in the KJV. The English Index provides a quick and easy summary of the hundreds of thousands of contexts in *Strong's Exhaustive Concordance,* while the *Concordance* lists every context for every word of the KJV, allowing you to study the use of the word in the Bible itself. The Hebrew and Aramaic and Greek dictionaries duplicate the corrected and improved dictionaries of *The New Strong's® Exhaustive Concordance,* but do so in a more generous print size. Further, with both books open, you can do context research in the concordance and, without losing your place, consult the dictionaries of *The New Strong's® Expanded Dictionary of Bible Words*.

The publisher trusts you will soon find *The New Strong's® Expanded Dictionary of Bible Words* an invaluable and constant companion in your study of God's Word.

How to Use the English Index to the Biblical Languages

1. What the Index Is

The English Index to the Biblical Languages contains every major word in the KJV with a list of every Hebrew, Aramaic, and Greek word that each English word translates. Words that are omitted from this list include words that appear in the Appendix of Articles in the classic edition of *The New Strong's® Exhaustive Concordance* (such as "a," "and," and "the") and words that do not directly translate a Hebrew, Aramaic, or Greek word (such as "aileth," "letting," and "shouldest"). English words are listed in alphabetical order, exactly as they are spelled in the KJV.

Under each English entry is a listing of every Hebrew, Aramaic, and Greek word that the English word translates. These lists are organized in alphabetical order (which is also Strong's number order): Old Testament words first, then New Testament words. Each line has four elements: (1) the Strong's number; (2) the original language word in transliteration; (3) the total number of times the word is so translated, and (4) a brief definition. (See the enlarged example on page vi.)

(1) If the Strong's number is not italicized, it refers to an original word in the *Hebrew and Aramaic Dictionary*. If the Strong's number and the transliterated word are *italicized*, it refers to an original word in the *Greek Dictionary*.

(2) Words are transliterated exactly as in the dictionaries, according to the schemes outlined on pages 292–93 and 902–03. If more than one Strong's number is listed on an entry line (for example, 4697+1767 under "able"), in the interest of saving space, only the first word is transliterated. The additional word(s) are transliterated in the dictionaries.

(3) The total number of occurrences is given to show patterns of KJV usage and in case you wish to study the original language words in the order of their frequency. For example, Greek word *25* (*agapao*) is translated "love" 70 times in the KJV and may be a more significant or interesting word than *2309* (*thelo*), which is translated as "love" only once.

(4) The brief definition summarizes the fuller dictionary entries in *Strong's*. These definitions actually function as a dictionary to the vocabulary of the KJV, informing you that a "habergeon" is a "coat of mail" or that "unction" is a "special endowment of the Holy Spirit." Sometimes these definitions update the scholarship of the KJV, as in the case of "unicorn," which is defined as "wild bull." As is the case of the frequency numbers, the definition may also point out a key Hebrew, Aramaic, or Greek word that you may want to study in more detail by referring to the dictionaries.

2. Using the Index with the Dictionaries

Because the Index lists every Hebrew, Aramaic, and Greek word that is translated by any English word of the KJV, it functions as a concise dictionary and thesaurus of the biblical languages. Quickly scanning the entry for the word "love" shows that the word is used as general positive affection, deep compassion, fraternal affection, love for husbands, love for children, and greedy love of money. Reading the appropriate dictionary entries will enlarge on these definitions. Again, if a Strong's number is not italicized (e.g., 157), consult the *Hebrew and Aramaic Dictionary*. If a Strong's number is italicized (e.g., *26*), consult the *Greek Dictionary*. Each entry in the dictionaries also provides a complete list of KJV words that translate the original language word, following the :— symbol. Greek word *26* (*agape*), for example, lists four English words: charitably, charity, dear, and love. This shows the range of meaning the KJV translators assigned to *agape*. By returning to the Index and looking up each of these English words, you find even more original language words to study.

3. Using the Index with *The New Strong's® Exhaustive Concordance*

The English Index provides a quick and easily used summary of the hundreds of thousands of contexts in *The New Strong's® Exhaustive Concordance*, while the concordance lists every context for every word of the KJV. This allows you to study the use of the word in the Bible itself, which is the most important way to understand how a specific word is used in a specific context. Although Strong's Hebrew and Aramaic and Greek dictionaries offer definitions for each word of the original languages, these words do not have the sum total of every definition in every context. Greek word *26* (*agape*), for example, cannot mean "affection" and "love-feast" every time it occurs. It means "affection" in such contexts as Philemon 7 and "love-feast" in Jude 12. Similarly, the historical or etymological materials that *Strong's Dictionaries* often present at the beginning of an entry may show something of the origin of a word, but are not necessarily its *definition* in every biblical context. For example, when the Greek word *314* (*anaginosko*) is used in the New Testament, it means "to read," rather than "to know again," as *Strong's Dictionary* describes its origin.

In short, the wealth of materials contained in *The New Strong's® Expanded Dictionary of Bible Words* is truly maximized in conjunction with *The New Strong's® Exhaustive Concordance* when carefully applied to the study of God's Word.

An Example
from the English Index

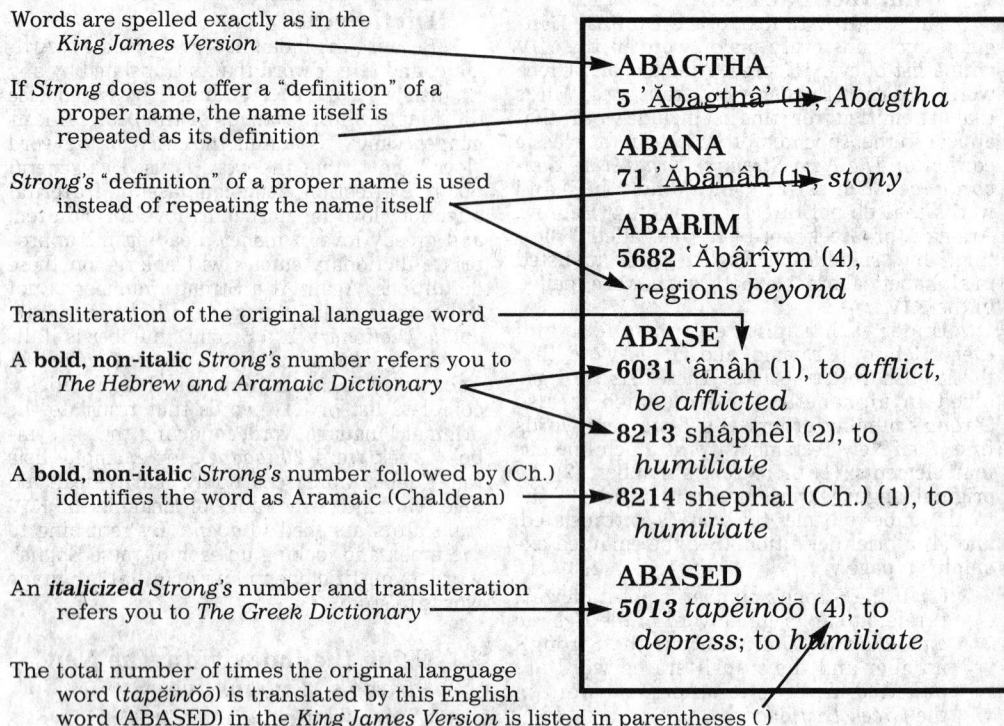

Words are spelled exactly as in the
  King James Version

If *Strong* does not offer a "definition" of a
  proper name, the name itself is
  repeated as its definition

Strong's "definition" of a proper name is used
  instead of repeating the name itself

Transliteration of the original language word

A **bold, non-italic** *Strong's* number refers you to
  The Hebrew and Aramaic Dictionary

A **bold, non-italic** *Strong's* number followed by (Ch.)
  identifies the word as Aramaic (Chaldean)

An ***italicized*** *Strong's* number and transliteration
  refers you to *The Greek Dictionary*

The total number of times the original language
  word (*tapĕinŏō*) is translated by this English
  word (ABASED) in the *King James Version* is listed in parentheses ( )

ABAGTHA
5 'Ăbagthâ' (1), *Abagtha*

ABANA
71 'Ăbânâh (1), *stony*

ABARIM
5682 'Ăbârîym (4),
  regions *beyond*

ABASE
6031 'ânâh (1), to *afflict,*
  be afflicted
8213 shâphêl (2), to
  humiliate
8214 shephal (Ch.) (1), to
  humiliate

ABASED
5013 tapĕinŏō (4), to
  depress; to *humiliate*

Words Omitted from the English Index

a	coloured	hers	one's	sunder	unperfect
about	condition	herself	onward	surely	unweighed
agone	counting	him	or	taker	unto
ailed	cunningly	himself	our	tapestry	up
aileth	dealer	his	ours	tend	upon
also	dealers	hurling	ourselves	tendeth	us
am	dealing	I	out	than	venomous
amounting	deals	in	parties	that	was
an	dearly	into	pertain	the	waxen
and	deputed	infallible	playedst	thee	we
apace	description	inflicted	playeth	thee-ward	weighing
appertained	deserve	its	practices	their	were
appertaineth	deserveth	itself	provokedst	theirs	what
are	determine	is	purposing	them	whatsoever
art	direction	it	quantity	themselves	which
as	dost	karnaim	ragged	then	who
battering	doth	letting	rests	thence	whom
be	drewest	liers	rovers	thenceforth	whom
became	duties	lign	sap	therefrom	whomsoever
becamest	easily	masteries	seatward	these	whose
become	ed	me	self	they	whoso
becometh	employment	meanest	selfsame	thine	whosoever
been	entreateth	mightest	selves	things'	with
belongest	estates	mine	shall	this	witty
belonging	exploits	mixt	shalt	those	ye
bestead	extendeth	my	she	thou	you
busied	folks	myself	so	though	your
but	for	no	soever	thus	yours
by	from	none	shouldest	thy	yourselves
caring	guiding	nor	slave	thyself	you-ward
cases	guilt	not	soundeth	titles	
causest	hadst	O	strongly	to	
causing	he	of	such	too	
closer	her	on	suits	toward	

ENGLISH INDEX TO THE BIBLICAL LANGUAGES

AARON
175 'Ahărôwn (315),
Aharon
2 Aarōn (4), Aaron

AARON'S
175 'Ahărôwn (30),
Aharon
2 Aarōn (1), Aaron

AARONITES
175 'Ahărôwn (2),
Aharon

ABADDON
3 Abaddōn (1),
destroying angel

ABAGTHA
5 'Ăbagthâ' (1), Abagtha

ABANA
71 'Ăbânâh (1), stony

ABARIM
5682 'Ăbârîym (4),
regions beyond

ABASE
6031 'ânâh (1), to afflict,
be afflicted
8213 shâphêl (2), to
humiliate
8214 shᵉphal (Ch.) (1), to
humiliate

ABASED
5013 tapĕinŏō (4), to
depress; to humiliate

ABASING
5013 tapĕinŏō (1), to
depress; to humiliate

ABATED
1639 gâra' (1), to
remove, lessen,
withhold
2637 châçêr (1), to lack;
to fail, want, make less
5127 nûwç (1), to vanish
away, flee
7043 qâlal (2), to be,
make light
7503 râphâh (1), to
slacken

ABBA
5 Abba (3), father

ABDA
5653 'Abdâ' (2), work

ABDEEL
5655 'Abdᵉ'êl (1), serving
God

ABDI
5660 'Abdîy (3),
serviceable

ABDIEL
5661 'Abdîy'êl (1),
servant of God

ABDON
5658 'Abdôwn (8),
servitude

ABED-NEGO
5664 'Ăbêd Nᵉgôw (1),
servant of -Nego
5665 'Ăbêd Nᵉgôw' (Ch.)
(14), servant of -Nego

ABEL
59 'Âbêl (2), meadow

62 'Âbêl Bêyth-Mă'akâh
(2), meadow of
Beth-Maakah
1893 Hebel (8),
emptiness or vanity
6 Abĕl (4), emptiness or
vanity

ABEL-BETH-MAACHAH
62 'Âbêl Bêyth-Mă'akâh
(2), meadow of
Beth-Maakah

ABEL-MAIM
66 'Âbêl Mayim (1),
meadow of water

ABEL-MEHOLAH
65 'Âbêl Mᵉchôwlâh (3),
meadow of dancing

ABEL-MIZRAIM
67 'Âbêl Mitsrayim (1),
meadow of Egypt

ABEL-SHITTIM
63 'Âbêl hash-Shiṭṭîym
(1), meadow of the
acacias

ABEZ
77 'Ebets (1), Ebets

ABHOR
887 bâ'ash (1), to be a
moral stench
1602 gâ'al (4), to detest;
to reject; to fail
2194 zâ'am (1), to be
enraged
3988 mâ'aç (1), to spurn;
to disappear
5006 nâ'ats (1), to scorn
8374 tâ'ab (1), to loathe
8581 tâ'ab (9), to loathe,
i.e. detest
655 apŏstugĕō (1), to
detest utterly, hate

ABHORRED
887 bâ'ash (2), to be a
moral stench
973 bâchal (1), to loathe,
detest
1602 gâ'al (1), to detest;
to reject; to fail
2194 zâ'am (1), to be
enraged
3988 mâ'aç (2), to spurn;
to disappear
5006 nâ'ats (2), to scorn
5010 nâ'ar (1), to reject
6973 qûwts (2), to be,
make disgusted
8262 shâqats (1), to
loathe, pollute
8581 tâ'ab (3), to loathe,
i.e. detest

ABHORREST
6973 qûwts (1), to be,
make disgusted
948 bdĕlussō (1), to
detest, abhor

ABHORRETH
2092 zâham (1), to
loathe, make loatheful
3988 mâ'aç (1), to spurn;
to disappear
5006 nâ'ats (1), to scorn

8581 tâ'ab (2), to loathe,
i.e. detest

ABHORRING
1860 dᵉrâ'ôwn (1),
aversion, loathing

ABI
21 'Ăbîy (1), fatherly

ABI-ALBON
45 'Ăbîy-'albôwn (1),
valiant, strong

ABI-EZER
44 'Ăbîy'ezer (2), helpful

ABI-EZRITE
33 'Abîy hâ-'Ezrîy (1),
father of the Ezrite

ABI-EZRITES
33 'Abîy hâ-'Ezrîy (2),
father of the Ezrite

ABIA
29 'Ăbîyâh (1),
worshipper of Jehovah
7 Abia (3), knowing

ABIAH
29 'Ăbîyâh (4),
worshipper of Jehovah

ABIASAPH
23 'Ăbîy'âçâph (1),
gatherer

ABIATHAR
54 'Ebyâthâr (29),
abundant, liberal
8 Abiathar (1),
abundant, liberal

ABIATHAR'S
54 'Ebyâthâr (1),
abundant, liberal

ABIB
24 'âbîyb (6), head of
grain; month of Abib

ABIDA
28 'Ăbîydâ' (1), knowing

ABIDAH
28 'Ăbîydâ' (1), knowing

ABIDAN
27 'Ăbîydân (5), judge

ABIDE
935 bôw' (1), to go or
come
1481 gûwr (2), to sojourn,
live as an alien
1692 dâbaq (1), to cling
or adhere
2342 chûwl (1), to wait
2583 chânâh (1), to
encamp for abode
3427 yâshab (31), to
dwell, remain; to settle
3557 kûwl (3), to keep in;
to maintain
3867 lâvâh (1), to unite;
to remain
3885 lûwn (5), to be
obstinate
5975 'âmad (2), to stand
6965 qûwm (1), to rise
7937 shâkar (1), to
become tipsy, to satiate
1961 ĕpimĕnō (3), to
remain; to persevere

3306 mĕnō (27), to stay,
remain
3887 paramĕnō (1), to be
permanent, persevere
4357 prŏsmĕnō (1), to
remain; to adhere to

ABIDETH
935 bôw' (1), to go or
come
3427 yâshab (4), to dwell,
to remain; to settle
3885 lûwn (3), to be
obstinate
5975 'âmad (2), to stand
3306 mĕnō (20), to stay,
remain

ABIDING
3427 yâshab (2), to dwell,
to remain; to settle
4723 miqveh (1),
confidence; collection
5596 çâphach (1), to
associate; be united
7931 shâkan (1), to reside
63 agraulĕō (1), to camp
out, live outdoors
1304 diatribō (1), to
remain, stay
3306 mĕnō (2), to stay,
remain

ABIEL
22 'Ăbîy'êl (3), possessor
of God

ABIEZER
44 'Ăbîy'ezer (5), helpful

ABIGAIL
26 'Ăbîygayil (17), source
of joy

ABIHAIL
32 'Ăbîyhayil (6),
possessor of might

ABIHU
30 'Ăbîyhûw' (12),
worshipper of Him

ABIHUD
31 'Ăbîyhûwd (1),
possessor of renown

ABIJAH
29 'Ăbîyâh (20),
worshipper of Jehovah

ABIJAM
38 'Ăbîyâm (5), seaman

ABILENE
9 Abilēnē (1), Abilene

ABILITY
1767 day (1), enough,
sufficient
3581 kôach (2), force,
might; strength
5381 nâsag (1), to reach
1411 dunamis (1), force,
power, miracle
2141 ĕupŏrĕō (1), to have
means, have ability
2479 ischus (1),
forcefulness, power

ABIMAEL
39 'Ăbîymâ'êl (2), father
of Mael

ABIMELECH
40 'Ăbîymelek (65), *father of the king*

ABIMELECH'S
40 'Ăbîymelek (2), *father of the king*

ABINADAB
41 'Ăbîynâdâb (13), *generous*, i.e. *liberal*

ABINOAM
42 'Ăbîynô'am (4), *gracious*

ABIRAM
48 'Ăbîyrâm (11), *lofty, high*

ABISHAG
49 'Ăbîyshag (5), *blundering*

ABISHAI
52 'Ăbîyshay (25), (poss.) *generous*

ABISHALOM
53 'Ăbîyshâlôwm (2), *friendly*

ABISHUA
50 'Ăbîyshûwa' (5), *prosperous*

ABISHUR
51 'Ăbîyshûwr (2), (poss.) *mason*

ABITAL
37 'Ăbîyṭal (2), *fresh*

ABITUB
36 'Ăbîyṭûwb (1), *good*

ABIUD
10 Abioud (2), *possessor of renown*

ABJECTS
5222 nêkeh (1), *smiter; attacker*

ABLE
2296 châgar (1), *to gird on a belt; put on armor*
2428 chayil (4), *army; wealth; virtue; strength*
3201 yâkôl (44), *to be able*
3202 yᵉkêl (Ch.) (4), *to be able*
3318 yâtsâ' (15), *to go, bring out*
3320 yâtsab (3), *to station, offer, continue*
3546 kᵉhal (Ch.) (2), *to be able*
3581 kôach (1), *force, might; strength*
4672+1767 mâtsâ' (2), *to find or acquire*
4979+3027 mâttânâh (1), *present; offering; bribe*
4991+3027 mattâth (2), *present*
5060+1767 nâga' (1), *to strike*
5375 nâsâ' (2), *to lift up*
5381 nâsag (6), *to reach*
5975 'âmad (6), *to stand*
6113 'âtsar (1), *to hold back; to maintain*
6113+3581 'âtsar (2), *to hold back; to maintain*
7272 regel (1), *foot; step*
1410 dunamai (41), *to be able or possible*

1415 dunatŏs (10), *powerful or capable*
1840 ĕxischuŏ (1), *to be entirely competent*
2192 ĕchō (1), *to have; hold; keep*
2425 hikanŏs (1), *ample; fit*
2427 hikanŏō (1), *to make competent*
2480 ischuō (6), *to have or exercise force*

ABNER
74 'Abnêr (62), *enlightening*

ABNER'S
74 'Abnêr (1), *enlightening*

ABOARD
1910 ĕpibainō (1), *to mount, embark, arrive*

ABODE
1961 hâyâh (2), *to exist,* i.e. *be or become*
2583 chânâh (3), *to encamp*
3427 yâshab (33), *to dwell, remain; to settle*
5975 'âmad (1), *to stand*
7931 shâkan (6), *to reside*
390 anastrĕphō (1), *to remain, to live*
835 aulizŏmai (1), *to pass the night*
1304 diatribō (4), *to remain, stay*
1961 ĕpimĕnō (1), *remain; to persevere*
2476 histēmi (1), *to stand, establish*
2650 katamĕnō (1), *reside, stay, live*
3306 mĕnō (12), *to stay, remain*
3438 mŏnē (1), *residence, dwelling place*
4160 pŏiĕō (1), *to make or do*
5278 hupŏmĕnō (1), *to undergo* (trials)

ABODEST
3427 yâshab (1), *to dwell, to remain; to settle*

ABOLISH
2498 châlaph (1), *to hasten away*

ABOLISHED
2865 châthath (1), *to break down*
4229 mâchâh (1), *to erase*
2673 katargĕō (3), *to be, render entirely useless*

ABOMINABLE
2194 zâ'am (1), *to be enraged*
6292 piggûwl (3), *unclean, fetid*
8251 shiqqûwts (2), *disgusting idol*
8262 shâqats (2), *to loathe, pollute*
8263 sheqets (2), *filthy idolatrous object*
8441 tôw'êbâh (4), *something disgusting*
8581 tâ'ab (6), *to loathe*

111 athĕmitŏs (1), *illegal; detestable*
947 bdĕluktŏs (1), *detestable, abominable*
948 bdĕlussō (1), *to detest, abhor*

ABOMINABLY
8581 tâ'ab (1), *to loathe*

ABOMINATION
887 bâ'ash (1), *to be a moral stench*
6292 piggûwl (1), *unclean, fetid*
8251 shiqqûwts (7), *disgusting idol*
8262 shâqats (2), *to loathe, pollute*
8263 sheqets (9), *filthy idolatrous object*
8441 tôw'êbâh (52), *something disgusting*
946 bdĕlugma (4), *detestable, abominable*

ABOMINATIONS
8251 shiqqûwts (13), *disgusting idol*
8441 tôw'êbâh (61), *something disgusting*
946 bdĕlugma (2), *detestable, abominable*

ABOUND
7227 rab (1), *great*
4052 pĕrissĕuō (12), *to superabound*
4121 plĕŏnazō (4), *to superabound*
4129 plēthunō (1), *to increase in numbers*
5248 hupĕrpĕrissĕuō (1), *to superabound*

ABOUNDED
4052 pĕrissĕuō (4), *to superabound*
4121 plĕŏnazō (1), *to superabound*

ABOUNDETH
7227 rab (1), *great*
4052 pĕrissĕuō (1), *to superabound*
4121 plĕŏnazō (1), *to superabound*

ABOUNDING
3513 kâbad (1), *to be rich, glorious*
4052 pĕrissĕuō (2), *to superabound*

ABOVE
4480 min (2), *from, out of*
4605 ma'al (55), *upward, above, overhead*
4791 mârôwm (7), *elevation; elation*
5921 'al (67), *above, over, upon, or against*
5922 'al (Ch.) (1), *above, over, upon, or against*
507 anō (5), *upward or on the top, heavenward*
509 anōthĕn (5), *from above; from the first*
511 anōtĕrŏs (1), *upper part; former part*
1883 ĕpanō (2), *over or on*
1909 ĕpi (5), *on, upon*
3844 para (4), *from; with; besides; on account of*

4012 pĕri (1), *about; around*
4117 plĕgma (1), *plait or braid of hair*
4253 prŏ (4), *before in time or space*
5228 hupĕr (13), *over; above; beyond*
5231 hupĕranō (2), *above, upward*

ABRAHAM
85 'Abrâhâm (160), *father of a multitude*
11 Abraam (68), *father of a multitude*

ABRAHAM'S
85 'Abrâhâm (14), *father of a multitude*
11 Abraam (5), *father of a multitude*

ABRAM
87 'Abrâm (54), *high father*

ABRAM'S
87 'Abrâm (7), *high father*

ABROAD
1980 hâlak (1), *to walk; live a certain way*
2351 chûwts (21), *outside, outdoors*
3318 yâtsâ' (1), *to go, bring out*
5074 nâdad (1), *to rove, flee; to drive away*
5203 nâṭash (1), *to disperse; to thrust off*
5310 nâphats (1), *to dash to pieces; to scatter*
6327 pûwts (4), *to dash in pieces; to disperse*
6340 pâzar (1), *to scatter*
6504 pârad (1), *to spread*
6524 pârach (1), *to break forth; to bloom*
6527 pâraṭ (5), *to scatter words,* i.e. *prate*
6555 pârats (3), *to break out*
6566 pâras (5), *to break apart, disperse, scatter*
6581 pâsâh (3), *to spread*
6584 pâshaṭ (1), *to strip*
7350 râchôwq (1), *remote, far*
7554 râqa' (2), *to pound*
7849 shâṭach (1), *to expand*
864 aphiknĕŏmai (1), *to go forth by rumor*
1096+5456 ginŏmai (1), *to be, become*
1232 diagnōrizō (1), *to tell abroad*
1255 dialalĕō (1), *to converse, discuss*
1287 diaskŏrpizō (2), *to scatter; to squander*
1289 diaspĕirō (3), *to scatter like seed*
1290 diaspŏra (1), *dispersion*
1310 diaphēmizō (2), *to spread news*
1330 diĕrchŏmai (1), *to traverse, travel through*

English

1519+1096 ĕis (1), *to* or *into*
1519+5318 ĕis (2), *to* or *into*
1632 ĕkchĕŏ (1), *to pour forth; to bestow*
1831 ĕxĕrchŏmai (4), *to issue; to leave*
4496 rhiptŏ (1), *to fling, toss; to lay out*
4650 skŏrpizŏ (2), *to dissipate, be liberal*

ABSALOM
53 'Ăbîyshâlôwm (102), *friendly*

ABSALOM'S
53 'Ăbîyshâlôwm (5), *friendly*

ABSENCE
666 apŏusia (1), *being away, absence*
817 atĕr (1), *apart from, without*

ABSENT
5641 çâthar (1), *to hide by covering*
548 apĕimi (7), *to be away, be absent*
553 apĕkdĕchŏmai (3), *to expect fully, await*

ABSTAIN
567 apĕchŏmai (6), *to hold oneself off*

ABSTINENCE
776 asitia (1), *state of food fasting*

ABUNDANCE
369+4557 'ayin (1), *there is no, none*
1995 hâmôwn (3), *noise, tumult; many, crowd*
2123 zìyz (1), *fulness of the breast*
3502 yithrâh (1), *wealth, abundance*
4342 makbîyr (1), *plenty*
6109 'otsmâh (1), *numerousness*
6283 'âthereth (1), *copiousness*
7227 rab (2), *great*
7230 rôb (35), *abundance*
7235 râbâh (2), *to increase*
7647 sâbâ' (1), *copiousness*
7962 shalvâh (1), *security, ease*
8228 shepha' (1), *abundance*
8229 shiph'âh (3), *copiousness*
8317 shârats (1), *to swarm, or abound*
100 hadrŏtēs (1), *liberality*
1411 dunamis (1), *force, power, miracle*
4050 pĕrissĕia (2), *superabundance*
4051 pĕrissĕuma (4), *superabundance*
4052 pĕrissĕuō (5), *to superabound*
5236 hupĕrbŏlē (1), *supereminence*

ABUNDANT
1419 gâdôwl (1), *great*
7227 rab (2), *great*
4052 pĕrissĕuō (2), *to superabound*
4055 pĕrissŏtĕrŏs (3), *more superabundant*
4056 pĕrissŏtĕrŏs (2), *more superabundantly*
4121 plĕŏnazŏ (1), *o superabound*
4183 pŏlus (1), *much*
5250 hupĕrplĕŏnazŏ (1), *to superabound*

ABUNDANTLY
1288 bârak (1), *to bless*
3381 yârad (1), *to descend*
5042 nâba' (1), *to gush forth; to utter*
6524 pârach (1), *to break forth; to flourish*
7227 rab (2), *great*
7230 rôb (4), *abundance*
7235 râbâh (1), *to increase*
7301 râvâh (2), *to slake thirst or appetites*
7937 shâkar (1), *to become tipsy, to satiate*
8317 shârats (6), *to swarm, or abound*
1519+4050 ĕis (1), *to or into*
1537+4053 ĕk (1), *out of*
4053 pĕrissŏs (1), *superabundant*
4054 pĕrissŏtĕrŏn (2), *superabundant way*
4056 pĕrissŏtĕrŏs (4), *more superabundantly*
4146 plŏusiŏs (2), *copiously, abundantly*

ABUSE
5953 'âlal (2), *to glean; to overdo*
2710 katachraŏmai (1), *to overuse*

ABUSED
5953 'âlal (1), *to glean; to overdo*

ABUSERS
733 arsĕnŏkŏitēs (1), *sodomite*

ABUSING
2710 katachraŏmai (1), *to overuse*

ACCAD
390 'Akkad (1), *Accad*

ACCEPT
1878 dâshên (1), *to be fat, thrive; to satisfy*
3947 lâqach (1), *to take*
5375 nâsâ' (8), *to lift up*
7306 rûwach (1), *to smell or perceive*
7521 râtsâh (13), *to be pleased with; to satisfy*
588 apŏdĕchŏmai (1), *welcome persons*

ACCEPTABLE
977 bâchar (1), *select, chose, prefer*
2656 chêphets (1), *pleasure; desire*
7522 râtsôwn (9), *delight*

8232 shephar (Ch.) (1), *to be beautiful*
587 apŏdĕktŏs (2), *agreeable, pleasant*
1184 dĕktŏs (2), *approved, favorable*
2101 ĕuarĕstŏs (4), *fully agreeable, pleasing*
2144 ĕuprŏsdĕktŏs (2), *approved, favorable*
5285 hupŏpnĕŏ (1), *to breathe gently*

ACCEPTABLY
2102 ĕuarĕstŏs (1), *quite agreeably*

ACCEPTANCE
7522 râtsôwn (1), *delight*

ACCEPTATION
594 apŏdŏchē (2), *acceptance, approval*

ACCEPTED
3190 yâṭab (2), *to be, make well*
5307 nâphal (2), *to fall*
5375 nâsâ' (3), *to lift up*
7521 râtsâh (7), *to be pleased with; to satisfy*
7522 râtsôwn (4), *delight*
7613 se'êth (1), *elevation; swelling* leprous scab
1184 dĕktŏs (3), *approved, favorable*
1209 dĕchŏmai (2), *to receive, welcome*
2101 ĕuarĕstŏs (1), *fully agreeable, pleasing*
2144 ĕuprŏsdĕktŏs (3), *approved, favorable*
5487 charitŏŏ (1), *one highly favored*

ACCEPTEST
2983 lambanŏ (1), *to take, receive*

ACCEPTETH
5375 nâsâ' (1), *to lift up*
7521 râtsâh (2), *to be pleased with; to satisfy*
2983 lambanŏ (1), *to take, receive*

ACCEPTING
4327 prŏsdĕchŏmai (1), *to receive; to await for*

ACCESS
4318 prŏsagōgē (3), *admission, access*

ACCHO
5910 'Akkôw (1), *to hem in*

ACCOMPANIED
2064+4862 ĕrchŏmai (1), *to go or come*
4311 prŏpĕmpŏ (1), *to escort or aid in travel*
4902 sunĕpŏmai (1), *to travel in company with*
4905 sunĕrchŏmai (1), *to go with*

ACCOMPANY
2192 ĕchŏ (1), *to have; hold; keep*

ACCOMPANYING
5973 'îm (1), *with*

ACCOMPLISH
3615 kâlâh (5), *to complete, prepare*

4390 mâlê' (1), *to fill*
6213 'âsâh (2), *to do or make*
6381 pâlâ' (1), *to be, make great, difficult*
6965 qûwm (1), *to rise*
7521 râtsâh (1), *to be pleased with; to satisfy*
8552 tâmam (1), *to complete, finish*
4137 plērŏŏ (1), *to fill, make complete*

ACCOMPLISHED
1961 hâyâh (1), *to exist, i.e. be or become*
3615 kâlâh (7), *to complete, prepare*
4390 mâlê' (6), *to fill*
8552 tâmam (1), *to complete, finish*
1822 ĕxartizŏ (1), *to finish out; to equip fully*
2005 ĕpitĕlĕŏ (1), *to terminate; to undergo*
4130 plēthō (4), *to fulfill, complete*
5055 tĕlĕŏ (4), *to end, i.e. complete, execute*

ACCOMPLISHING
2005 ĕpitĕlĕŏ (1), *to terminate; to undergo*

ACCOMPLISHMENT
1604 ĕkplērōsis (1), *completion, end*

ACCORD
5599 çâphîyach (1), *self-sown crop; freshet*
6310 peh (1), *mouth; opening*
830 authairĕtŏs (1), *self-chosen*
844 autŏmatŏs (1), *spontaneous, by itself*
3661 hŏmŏthumadŏn (11), *in togetherness*
4861 sumpsuchŏs (1), *united in spirit*

ACCORDING
413 'êl (2), *to, toward*
834 'âsher (1), *because, in order that*
1767 day (1), *enough, sufficient*
3605 kôl (1), *all, any*
3644 kemôw (2), *like, as*
3651 kên (1), *just; right, correct*
4481 min (Ch.) (1), *from or out of*
5921 'al (39), *above, over, upon, or against*
6310 peh (21), *mouth; opening*
6903 qebêl (Ch.) (1), *on account of, so as, since*
7272 regel (1), *foot; step*
2526 kathŏ (2), *precisely as, in proportion as*
2530 kathŏti (1), *as far or inasmuch as*
2531 kathŏs (5), *just or inasmuch as, that*
2596 kata (109), *down; according to*
4314 prŏs (3), *for; on, at; to, toward; against*
5613 hōs (2), *which, how*

ACCORDINGLY
5922 'al (Ch.) (1), *above, over, upon,* or *against*

ACCOUNT
2803 châshab (1), to *think, regard; to value*
2808 cheshbôwn (1), *contrivance; plan*
4557 miçpâr (1), *number*
6030 'ânâh (1), to *respond, answer*
6486 pᵉquddâh (1), *visitation; punishment*
1677 ĕllŏgĕō (1), to *charge to one's account*
2233 hēgĕŏmai (1), to *deem,* i.e. *consider*
3049 lŏgizŏmai (1), to *credit; to think, regard*
3056 lŏgŏs (8), *word, matter, thing; Word*

ACCOUNTED
2803 châshab (5), to *think, regard; to value*
5608 çâphar (1), to *enumerate; to recount*
1380 dŏkĕō (2), to *think, regard, seem good*
2661 kataxiŏō (2), to *deem entirely deserving*
3049 lŏgizŏmai (2), to *credit; to think, regard*

ACCOUNTING
3049 lŏgizŏmai (1), to *credit; to think, regard*

ACCOUNTS
2941 ța'am (Ch.) (1), *sentence, command*

ACCURSED
2763 charam (1), to *devote to destruction*
2764 chêrem (13), *doomed object*
7043 qâlal (1), to *be easy, trifling, vile*
7045 qᵉlâlâh (1), *vilification*
331 anathĕma (4), *excommunicated*

ACCUSATION
7855 sițnâh (1), *opposition*
156 aitia (3), *logical reason; legal crime*
2724 katēgŏria (3), *legal criminal charge*
2920 krisis (2), *decision; tribunal; justice*
4811 sukŏphantĕō (1), to *exact unlawfully, extort*

ACCUSE
3960 lâshan (1), to *calumniate, malign*
1908 ĕpērĕazō (1), to *insult, slander*
2722 katĕchō (11), to *hold down fast*
2723 katēgŏrĕō (2), to *bring a charge*
4811 sukŏphantĕō (1), to *exact unlawfully, extort*

ACCUSED
399+7170 'ăkal (Ch.) (2), to *eat*
1225 diaballō (1), to *malign by accusation*

1458 ĕgkalĕō (4), to *charge, criminate*
1722+2724 ĕn (1), *in; during; because of*
2722 katĕchō (4), to *hold down fast*
2723 katēgŏrĕō (2), to *bring a charge*

ACCUSER
2723 katēgŏrĕō (1), to *bring a charge*

ACCUSERS
1228 diabŏlŏs (2), *traducer,* i.e. *Satan*
2723 katēgŏrĕō (6), to *bring a charge*

ACCUSETH
2723 katēgŏrĕō (1), to *bring a charge*

ACCUSING
2722 katĕchō (1), to *hold down fast*

ACCUSTOMED
3928 limmûwd (1), *instructed one*

ACELDAMA
184 Akeldama (1), *field of blood*

ACHAIA
882 Achaïa (11), *Greece*

ACHAICUS
883 Achaïkŏs (1), *Achaïan*

ACHAN
5912 'Âkân (6), *troublesome*

ACHAR
5917 'Âkâr (1), *troublesome*

ACHAZ
881 Achaz (2), *possessor*

ACHBOR
5907 'Akbôwr (7), *Akbor*

ACHIM
885 Achĕim (2), cf. *Jehovah will raise*

ACHISH
397 'Âkîysh (21), *Akish*

ACHMETHA
307 'Achmᵉthâ' (1), *Ecbatana*

ACHOR
5911 'Âlôwr (5), *troubled*

ACHSA
5915 'Akçâh (1), *anklet*

ACHSAH
5915 'Akçâh (2), *anklet*
5919 'akshûwb (2), *asp, coiling serpent*

ACHSHAPH
407 'Akshâph (3), *fascination*

ACHZIB
392 'Akzîyb (4), *deceitful*

ACKNOWLEDGE
3045 yâda' (5), to *know*
5234 nâkar (6), to *acknowledge*
1921 ĕpiginōskō (4), to *acknowledge*

ACKNOWLEDGED
3045 yâda' (1), to *know*

5234 nâkar (1), to *acknowledge*
1922 ĕpignōsis (1), *acknowledgement*

ACKNOWLEDGEMENT
1922 ĕpignōsis (1), *acknowledgement*

ACKNOWLEDGING
1922 ĕpignōsis (3), *acknowledgement*

ACQUAINT
5532 çâkan (1), to *be familiar with*

ACQUAINTANCE
3045 yâda' (6), to *know*
4378 makkâr (2), *acquaintance*
1110 gnōstŏs (2), *well-known*
2398 idiŏs (1), *private* or *separate*

ACQUAINTED
3045 yâda' (1), to *know*
5532 çâkan (1), to *be familiar with*

ACQUAINTING
5090 nâhag (1), to *drive forth;* to *lead*

ACQUIT
5352 nâqâh (2), to *be, make clean*

ACRE
4618 ma'ănâh (1), *furrow, plow path*

ACRES
6776 tsemed (1), *acre* (i.e. a day's plowing)

ACT
5556 çol'âm (1), *destructive locust* kind
6467 pô'al (1), *act* or *work, deed*
1888 ĕpautŏphōrōᵢ (1), in *actual crime*

ACTIONS
5949 'ălîylâh (1), *opportunity, action*

ACTIVITY
2428 chayil (1), *wealth; virtue; valor; strength*

ACTS
1697 dâbâr (51), *word; matter; thing*
4640 Ma'say (4), *operative*
5949 'ălîylâh (1), *opportunity, action*
6467 pô'al (2), *act* or *work, deed*

ADADAH
5735 'Ăd'âdâh (1), *festival*

ADAH
5711 'Âdâh (8), *ornament*

ADAIAH
5718 'Ădâyâh (9), *Jehovah has adorned*

ADALIA
118 'Ădalyâ' (1), *Adalja*

ADAM
120 'âdâm (14), *human being; mankind*
121 'Âdâm (8), *Adam*

76 Adam (8), *first man*

ADAM'S
76 Adam (1), *first man*

ADAMAH
128 'Ădâmâh (1), *soil; land*

ADAMANT
8068 shâmîyr (2), *thorn;* (poss.) *diamond*

ADAMI
129 'Ădâmîy (1), *earthy*

ADAR
143 'Ădâr (8), (poss.) *fire; Adar*
144 'Ădâr (Ch.) (1), (poss.) *fire; Adar*
146 'Ădâr (1), *ample*

ADBEEL
110 'Adbᵉ'êl (2), *chastised of God*

ADD
3254 yâçaph (22), to *add* or *augment*
5414 nâthan (2), to *give*
5595 çâphâh (3), to *accumulate; to remove*
2007 ĕpitithēmi (2), to *impose*
2018 ĕpiphĕrō (1), to *inflict, bring upon*
2023 ĕpichŏrēgĕō (1), to *fully supply*
4369 prŏstithēmi (2), to *lay beside, annex*

ADDAN
135 'Addân (1), *firm*

ADDAR
146 'Addâr (1), *ample*

ADDED
3254 yâçaph (4), to *add* or *augment*
3255 yᵉçaph (Ch.) (1), to *add* or *augment*
4323 prŏsanatithēmi (1), to *add; to impart*
4369 prŏstithēmi (9), to *lay beside, annex, repeat*

ADDER
6620 pethen (2), *asp*
6848 tsepha' (1), *viper*
8207 shᵉphîyphôn (1), *cerastes* or *adder*

ADDERS'
5919 'akshûwb (1), *asp, coiling serpent*

ADDETH
3254 yâçaph (3), to *add* or *augment*
1928 ĕpidiatassŏmai (1), to *supplement*

ADDI
78 Addi (1), *finery*

ADDICTED
5021 tassō (1), to *arrange*

ADDITION
3914 lôyâh (1), *wreath*

ADDITIONS
3914 lôyâh (2), *wreath*

ADDON
114 'Addôwn (1), *powerful*

ADER
5738 'Eder (1),
arrangement

ADIEL
5717 'Ădîy'êl (3),
ornament of God

ADIN
5720 'Ădîyn (4),
voluptuous

ADINA
5721 'Ădîynâ' (1),
effeminacy

ADINO
5722 'ădîynôw (1), *his*
spear

ADITHAIM
5723 'Ădîythayim (1),
double prey

ADJURE
7650 shâba' (2), to *swear*
1844 ĕxŏrkizō (1), to
charge under oath
3726 hŏrkizō (2), to
solemnly enjoin

ADJURED
422 'âlâh (1), *imprecate,*
utter a curse
7650 shâba' (1), to *swear*

ADLAI
5724 'Adlay (1), *Adlai*

ADMAH
126 'Admâh (5), *earthy*

ADMATHA
133 'Admâthâ' (1),
Admatha

ADMINISTERED
1247 diakŏnĕō (2), to *act*
as a deacon

ADMINISTRATION
1248 diakŏnia (1),
attendance, aid, service

ADMINISTRATIONS
1248 diakŏnia (1),
attendance, aid, service

ADMIRATION
2295 thauma (1),
wonder, marvel
2296 thaumazō (1), to
wonder; to admire

ADMIRED
2296 thaumazō (1), to
wonder; to admire

ADMONISH
3560 nŏuthĕtĕō (3), to
caution or reprove

ADMONISHED
2094 zâhar (2), to
enlighten
5749 'ûwd (1), to *protest,*
testify; to restore
3867 parainĕō (1), to
recommend or advise
5537 chrēmatizō (1), to
utter an oracle

ADMONISHING
3560 nŏuthĕtĕō (1), to
caution or reprove

ADMONITION
3559 nŏuthĕsia (3), mild
rebuke or warning

ADNA
5733 'Adnâ' (2), *pleasure*

ADNAH
5734 'Adnâh (2), *pleasure*

ADO
2350 thŏrubĕō (1), to
disturb; clamor

ADONI-BEZEK
137 'Ădônîy-Bezeq (3),
lord of Bezek

ADONI-ZEDEK
139 'Ădônîy-Tsedeq (2),
lord of justice

ADONIJAH
138 'Ădônîyâh (25),
worshipper of Jehovah

ADONIKAM
140 'Ădônîyqâm (3),
high, lofty

ADONIRAM
141 'Ădônîyrâm (2), *lord*
of height

ADOPTION
5206 huiŏthĕsia (5),
adoption

ADORAIM
115 'Ădôwrayim (1),
double mound

ADORAM
151 'Ădôrâm (2), *Adoram*

ADORN
2885 kŏsmĕō (2), to
decorate; to snuff

ADORNED
5710 'âdâh (1), to
remove; to bedeck
2885 kŏsmĕō (3), to
decorate; to snuff

ADORNETH
5710 'âdâh (1), to
remove; to bedeck

ADORNING
2889 kŏsmŏs (2), *world*

ADRAMMELECH
152 'Adrammelek (3),
splendor of (the) king

ADRAMYTTIUM
98 Adramuttēnŏs (1),
Adramyttene

ADRIA
99 Adrias (1), *Adriatic*
Sea

ADRIEL
5741 'Adrîy'êl (2), *flock*
of God

ADULLAM
5725 'Ădullâm (8),
Adullam

ADULLAMITE
5726 'Ădullâmîy (3),
Adullamite

ADULTERER
5003 nâ'aph (3), to
commit adultery

ADULTERERS
5003 nâ'aph (5), to
commit adultery
3432 môichŏs (4), male
paramour

ADULTERESS
802+376 'ishshâh (1),
woman, wife
5003 nâ'aph (2), to
commit adultery

3428 môichalis (2),
adulteress

ADULTERESSES
5003 nâ'aph (2), to
commit adultery
3428 môichalis (1),
adulteress

ADULTERIES
5004 nî'ûph (2), *adultery*
5005 na'ăphûwph (1),
adultery
3430 môichĕia (2),
adultery

ADULTEROUS
5003 nâ'aph (1), to
commit adultery
3428 môichalis (3),
adulteress

ADULTERY
5003 nâ'aph (17), to
commit adultery
3428 môichalis (1),
adulteress
3429 môichaō (6), to
commit adultery
3430 môichĕia (2),
adultery
3431 môichĕuō (14), to
commit adultery

ADUMMIM
131 'Ădummîym (2), *red*
spots

ADVANCED
1431 gâdal (1), to *be*
great, make great
5375 nâsâ' (2), to *lift up*
6213 'âsâh (1), to *do or*
make

ADVANTAGE
5532 çâkan (1), to *be*
serviceable to
4053 pĕrissŏs (1),
superabundant
4122 plĕŏnĕktĕō (1), to
be covetous
5622 ŏphĕlĕia (1), *value,*
advantage

ADVANTAGED
5623 ŏphĕlĕō (1), to
benefit, be of use

ADVANTAGETH
3786 ŏphĕlŏs (1),
accumulate or benefit

ADVENTURE
5254 nâçâh (1), to *test,*
attempt
1325 didōmi (1), to *give*

ADVENTURED
7993 shâlak (1), to *throw*
out, down or away

ADVERSARIES
6696 tsûwr (1), to *cramp,*
i.e. confine; to harass
6862 tsar (21), *trouble;*
opponent
6887 tsârar (2), to *cramp*
7378 rîyb (1), to *hold a*
controversy; to defend
7853 sâţan (5), to *attack*
by accusation
7854 sâţân (1), *opponent*
480 antikĕimai (4), *be*
adverse to
5227 hupĕnantiŏs (1),
opposed; opponent

ADVERSARY
376+7379 'îysh (1), *man;*
male; someone
1166+4941 bâ'al (1), to *be*
master; to marry
6862 tsar (6), *trouble;*
opponent
6869 tsârâh (1), *trouble;*
rival-wife
6887 tsârar (1), to *cramp*
7854 sâţân (6), *opponent*
476 antidikŏs (5),
opponent
480 antikĕimai (1), *be*
adverse to

ADVERSITIES
6869 tsârâh (1), *trouble;*
rival-wife
7451 ra' (1), *bad; evil*

ADVERSITY
6761 tsela' (1), *limping*
6862 tsar (1), *trouble;*
opponent
6869 tsârâh (4), *trouble;*
rival-wife
7451 ra' (3), *bad; evil*
2558 kakŏuchĕō (1), to
maltreat; to torment

ADVERTISE
1540+241 gâlâh (1), to
denude; to reveal
3289 yâ'ats (1), to *advise*

ADVICE
1697 dâbâr (2), *word;*
matter; thing
2940 ţa'am (1),
intelligence; mandate
3289 yâ'ats (2), to *advise*
5779 'ûwts (1), to *consult*
6098 'êtsâh (1), *advice;*
plan; prudence
8458 tachbûlâh (1),
guidance; plan
1106 gnōmē (1),
cognition, opinion

ADVISE
3045 yâda' (1), to *know*
3289 yâ'ats (1), to *advise*
7200 râ'âh (1), to *see*

ADVISED
3289 yâ'ats (1), to *advise*
1012+5087 bŏulē (1),
purpose, plan, decision

ADVISEMENT
6098 'êtsâh (1), *advice;*
plan; prudence

ADVOCATE
3875 paraklētŏs (1),
intercessor, consoler

AENEAS
132 Ainĕas (2), (poss.)
praise

AENON
137 Ainōn (1), *springs*

AFAR
4801 merchâq (3),
distant place; from afar
7350 râchôwq (29),
remote, far
7368 râchaq (1), to
recede; remove
3112 makran (2), *at a*
distance, far away
3113 makrŏthĕn (13),
from a distance or afar

3467 muŏpazō (1), to *see indistinctly, be myopic*
4207 pŏrrhŏthĕn (2), *distantly, at a distance*

AFFAIRS
1697 dâbâr (2), *word; matter; thing*
5673 'ăbîydâh (Ch.) (2), *labor or business*
2596 kata (1), *down; according to*
4012 pĕri (2), *about; around*
4230 pragmatĕia (1), *transaction*

AFFECT
2206 zĕlŏŏ (2), to *have warmth* of feeling for

AFFECTED
2206 zĕlŏŏ (1), to *have warmth* of feeling for
2559 kakŏŏ (1), to *injure; to oppress; to embitter*

AFFECTETH
5953 'âlal (1), to *glean; to overdo*

AFFECTION
7521 râtsâh (1), to *be pleased with; to satisfy*
794 astŏrgŏs (2), *hard-hearted*
3806 pathŏs (1), *passion, concupiscence*
4698 splagchnŏn (1), *intestine; affection, pity*
5426 phrŏnĕō (1), to *be mentally disposed*

AFFECTIONATELY
2442 himĕirŏmai (1), to *long for, desire*

AFFECTIONED
5387 philŏstŏrgŏs (1), *lovingly devoted*

AFFECTIONS
3804 pathĕma (1), *passion; suffering*
3806 pathŏs (1), *passion, concupiscence*

AFFINITY
2859 châthan (3), to *become related*

AFFIRM
1226 diabĕbaiŏŏmai (2), to *confirm thoroughly*
5346 phĕmi (1), to *speak or say*

AFFIRMED
1340 diïschurizŏmai (2), to *asseverate*
5335 phaskō (1), to *assert a claim*

AFFLICT
3013 yâgâh (1), to *grieve; to torment*
3513 kâbad (1), to *be heavy, severe, dull*
3905 lâchats (1), to *press; to distress*
6031 'ânâh (28), to *afflict, be afflicted*
6887 tsârar (2), to *cramp*
7489 râ'a' (2), to *break to pieces*

AFFLICTED
1790 dak (1), *injured, oppressed*
3013 yâgâh (3), to *grieve; to torment*
4523 mâç (1), *disconsolate*
6031 'ânâh (21), to *afflict, be afflicted*
6040 'ŏnîy (1), *depression,* i.e. *misery*
6041 'ânîy (15), *depressed*
6862 tsar (1), *trouble; opponent*
6887 tsârar (2), to *cramp*
7043 qâlal (1), to *be easy, trifling, vile*
7489 râ'a' (3), to *break to pieces*
2346 thlibō (3), to *crowd, press, trouble*
2347 thlipsis (1), *pressure, trouble*
2553 kakŏpathĕō (1), to *undergo hardship*
5003 talaipōrĕō (1), to *be wretched*

AFFLICTEST
6031 'ânâh (1), to *afflict, be afflicted*

AFFLICTION
205 'âven (3), *trouble, vanity, wickedness*
3905 lâchats (3), to *press; to distress*
4157 mûw'âqâh (1), *pressure; distress*
6039 'ĕnûwth (1), *affliction*
6040 'ŏnîy (33), *depression,* i.e. *misery*
6862 tsar (3), *trouble; opponent*
6869 tsârâh (7), *trouble; rival-wife*
6887 tsârar (1), to *cramp*
7451 ra' (5), *bad; evil*
7667 sheber (2), *fracture; ruin*
2347 thlipsis (11), *pressure, trouble*
2552 kakŏpathĕia (1), *hardship, suffering*
2561 kakōsis (1), *maltreatment*
4797 sugchĕō (1), to *throw into disorder*

AFFLICTIONS
6031 'ânâh (1), to *afflict, be afflicted*
7451 ra' (1), *bad; evil*
2347 thlipsis (6), *pressure, trouble*
2553 kakŏpathĕō (1), to *undergo hardship*
3804 pathĕma (3), *passion; suffering*
4777 sugkakŏpathĕō (1), to *suffer hardship*

AFFORDING
6329 pûwq (1), to *issue; to furnish; to secure*

AFFRIGHT
3372 yârê' (1), to *fear; to revere*

AFFRIGHTED
270+8178 'âchaz (1), to *seize, grasp; possess*
926 bâhal (1), to *tremble; be, make agitated*
1204 bâ'ath (1), to *fear*
2865 châthath (1), to *break down*
6206 'ârats (1), to *awe; to dread; to harass*
1568 ĕkthambĕō (2), to *astonish utterly*
1719 ĕmphŏbŏs (2), *alarmed, terrified*

AFOOT
3978 pĕzĕuō (1), to *travel by land,* i.e. *on foot*
3979 pĕzĕi (1), *on foot*

AFORE
3808 lô' (1), *no, not*
6440 pânîym (2), *face; front*
6924 qedem (1), *before, anciently*
4270 prŏgraphō (1), to *write previously*
4279 prŏĕpaggĕllŏmai (1), to *promise from before*
4282 prŏĕtŏimazō (1), to *fit up in advance*

AFOREHAND
4301 prŏlambanō (1), to *take before*

AFORETIME
4481+6928+1836 min (Ch.) (1), *from or out of*
6440 pânîym (2), *face; front*
6924 qedem (1), *before, anciently*
7223 rî'shôwn (1), *first, in place, time or rank*
4218 pŏtĕ (1), *at some time, ever*
4270 prŏgraphō (1), to *write previously*

AFRAID
926 bâhal (3), to *tremble; be, make agitated; hasten, hurry anxiously*
1204 bâ'ath (10), to *fear*
1481 gûwr (6), to *sojourn, live as an alien*
1672 dâ'ag (3), to *be anxious, be afraid*
1763 dᵉchal (Ch.) (1), to *fear; be formidable*
2119 zâchal (1), to *crawl; glide*
2296 châgar (1), to *gird on a belt; put on armor*
2342 chûwl (1), to *dance, whirl; to writhe*
2727 chârag (1), to *be dismayed, tremble*
2729 chârad (20), to *shudder with terror*
2730 chârêd (1), *fearful*
2865 châthath (6), to *break down, either by violence, or by fear*
3025 yâgôr (5), to *fear*
3372 yârê' (78), to *fear; to revere*
3373 yârê' (3), *fearing; reverent*

AFFRIGHTED (cont.)
6206 'ârats (3), to *awe; to dread; to harass*
6342 pâchad (9), to *be startled; to fear*
7264 râgaz (1), to *quiver*
7297 râhâh (1), to *fear*
7493 râ'ash (1), to *undulate, quake*
8175 sâ'ar (3), to *storm; to shiver,* i.e. *fear*
1168 dĕiliaō (1), to *be timid, cowardly*
1630 ĕkphŏbŏs (1), *frightened out of one's wits*
1719 ĕmphŏbŏs (3), *alarmed, terrified*
5141 trĕmō (1), to *tremble or fear*
5399 phŏbĕō (29), to *fear, be frightened*

AFRESH
388 anastaurŏō (1), to *re-crucify*

AFTER
167 'âhal (1), to *pitch a tent*
310 'achar (492), *after*
311 'achar (Ch.) (3), *after*
314 'achârôwn (5), *late or last; behind; western*
413 'êl (4), *to, toward*
834 'âsher (2), *because, in order that*
870 'âthar (Ch.) (3), *after*
1767 day (2), *enough, sufficient*
1863 dardar (1), *thorn*
3602 kâkâh (4), *just so*
4480 min (1), *from, out of*
4481 min (Ch.) (1), *from or out of*
5921 'al (18), *above, over, upon, or against*
6256 'êth (1), *time*
6310 peh (1), *mouth; opening*
7093 qêts (10), *extremity; after*
7097 qâtseh (1), *extremity*
7272 regel (4), *foot; step*
516 axiōs (1), *appropriately, suitable*
1207 dĕutĕrŏprŏtŏs (1), *second-first*
1223 dia (3), *through, by means of; because of*
1230 diaginŏmai (1), to *have time elapse*
1377 diōkō (1), to *pursue; to persecute*
1534 ĕita (3), *then, moreover*
1567 ĕkzĕtĕō (2), to *seek out*
1722 ĕn (1), *in; during; because of*
1836 hĕxēs (1), *successive, next*
1872 ĕpakŏlŏuthĕō (1), to *accompany, follow*
1887 ĕpauriŏn (1), *to-morrow*
1894 ĕpĕidē (1), *when, whereas*
1899 ĕpĕita (3), *thereafter, afterward*
1905 ĕpĕrōtaō (1), to *inquire, seek*

English

1909 ĕpi (3), on, upon
1934 ĕpizētĕō (4), to search (inquire) for
1938 ĕpithumētēs (1), craver
1971 ĕpipŏthĕō (3), intensely crave
2089 ĕti (1), yet, still
2517 kathĕxēs (1), in a sequence
2569 kalŏpŏiĕō (3), to do well
2596 kata (58), down; according to
2614 katadiōkō (1), to search for, look for
2628 katakŏlŏuthĕō (1), to accompany closely
3195 mĕllō (2), to intend, i.e. be about to be
3326 mĕta (96), with, among; after, later
3693 ŏpisthĕn (2), at the back; after
3694 ŏpisō (22), behind, after, following
3753 hŏtĕ (3), when; as
3765 ŏukĕti (1), not yet, no longer
3779 hŏutō (2), in this way; likewise
4023 pĕriĕchō (1), to clasp; to encircle
4137 plērŏō (1), to fill, make complete
4329 prŏsdŏkia (1), apprehension
4459 pŏs (1), in what way?; how?; how much!
5225 huparchō (1), to come into existence
5613 hōs (3), which, how, i.e. in that manner
5615 hōsautōs (1), in the same way
5618 hōspĕr (1), exactly like

AFTERNOON
5186+3117 nâṭâh (1), to stretch or spread out

AFTERWARD
310 'achar (21), after
314 'achărôwn (2), late or last; behind; western
1208 dĕutĕrŏs (1), second; secondly
1534 ĕita (1), then, moreover
1899 ĕpeita (1), thereafter, afterward
2517 kathĕxēs (1), in a sequence
2547 kakĕithĕn (1), from that place (or time)
3347 mĕtĕpeita (1), thereafter
5305 hustĕrŏn (7), more lately, i.e. eventually

AFTERWARDS
268 'âchôwr (1), behind, backward; west
310 'achar (5), after
310+3651 'achar (2), after
314 'achărôwn (1), late or last; behind; western
1899 ĕpeita (1), thereafter, afterward

5305 hustĕrŏn (1), more lately, i.e. eventually

AGABUS
13 Agabŏs (2), locust

AGAG
90 'Ăgag (8), flame

AGAGITE
91 'Ăgâgîy (5), Agagite

AGAIN
310 'achar (1), after
322 'ăchôrannîyth (1), by turning around
1571 gam (2), also; even
1906 hêd (1), shout of joy
1946 hûwk (Ch.) (1), to go, come
3138 yôwreh (2), autumn rain showers
3254 yâçaph (49), to add or augment
3284 ya'ănâh (1), ostrich
5437 çâbab (1), to surround
5750 'ôwd (51), again; repeatedly; still; more
7725 shûwb (246), to turn back; to return
7999 shâlam (3), to reciprocate
8138 shânâh (1), to fold; to transmute
8145 shênîy (7), second; again
8579 tinyânûwth (Ch.) (1), second time
313 anagĕnnaō (2), to beget or bear again
321 anagō (2), to lead up; to bring out
326 anazaō (3), to recover life, live again
330 anathallō (1), to flourish; to revive
344 anakamptō (1), to turn back, come back
364 anamnēsis (1), recollection
375 anapĕmpō (2), to send up or back
386 anastasis (2), resurrection from death
450 anistēmi (15), to come back to life
456 anŏikŏdŏmĕō (2), to rebuild
467 antapŏdidōmi (2), to requite good or evil
470 antapŏkrinŏmai (1), to contradict or dispute
479 antikalĕō (1), to reciprocate
483 antilĕgō (1), to dispute, refuse
486 antilŏidŏrĕō (1), to rail in reply, retaliate
488 antimĕtrĕō (1), to measure in return
509 anōthĕn (2), from the first; anew
518 apaggĕllō (2), to announce, proclaim
523 apaitĕō (1), to demand back
560 apĕlpizō (1), to fully expect in return
591 apŏdidōmi (2), to give away

600 apŏkathistēmi (1), to reconstitute
618 apŏlambanō (1), to receive; be repaid
654 apŏstrĕphō (2), to turn away or back
1208 dĕutĕrŏs (3), second; secondly
1364 dis (2), twice
1453 ĕgĕirō (8), to waken, i.e. rouse
1458 ĕgkalĕō (1), to charge
1515 ĕirēnē (1), peace; health; prosperity
1880 ĕpanĕrchŏmai (1), return home
1994 ĕpistrĕphō (5), to revert, turn back to
3326 mĕta (1), with, among; after, later
3825 palin (141), anew, i.e. back; once more
4388 prŏtithĕmai (2), to place before
4762 strĕphō (2), to turn around or reverse
5290 hupŏstrĕphō (6), to return

AGAINST
413 'êl (144), to, toward
431 'ălûw (Ch.) (1), lo!
834 'âsher (1), because, in order that
4136 mûwl (19), in front of, opposite
4775 mârad (1), to rebel
5048 neged (33), over against or before
5227 nôkach (11), opposite, in front of
5704 'ad (3), as far (long) as; during; while; until
5921 'al (525), above, over, upon, or against
5922 'al (Ch.) (7), above, over, upon, or against
5971 'am (1), people; tribe; troops
5973 'îm (35), with
5978 'immâd (1), along with
5980 'ummâh (26), near, beside, along with
6440 pânîym (11), face; front
6640 tsᵉbûw (Ch.) (1), affair; matter of determination
6655 tsad (Ch.) (1), at or upon the side of; against
6903 qᵉbêl (Ch.) (1), in front of, before
6965 qûwm (1), to rise
7125 qîr'âh (41), to encounter, to happen
210 akōn (1), unwilling
368 anantirrhētŏs (1), indisputable
470 antapŏkrinŏmai (1), to contradict or dispute
471 antĕpō (1), to refute
481 antikru (1), opposite
483 antilĕgō (1), to dispute, refuse
495 antipĕran (1), on the opposite side

497 antistratĕuŏmai (1), to wage war against
561 apĕnanti (2), before or against
1519 ĕis (24), to or into
1690 ĕmbrimaŏmai (1), to blame, warn sternly
1693 ĕmmainŏmai (1), to rage at
1715 ĕmprŏsthĕn (1), in front of
1722 ĕn (1), in; during
1727 ĕnantiŏs (1), opposite
1909 ĕpi (38), on, upon
2018 ĕpiphĕrō (2), to inflict, bring upon
2019 ĕpiphōnĕō (1), to exclaim, shout
2596 kata (59), down; according to
2620 katakauchaŏmai (2), to exult against
2649 katamarturĕō (1), to testify against
2691 katastrēniaō (1), to be voluptuous against
2702 kataphĕrō (1), to bear down
2713 katĕnanti (4), directly opposite
2729 katischuō (1), to overpower, prevail
3326 mĕta (4), with, among; after, later
3844 para (2), from; with; besides; on account of
4012 pĕri (2), around
4314 prŏs (23), for; on, at; to, toward; against
4366 prŏsrĕgnumi (1), burst upon
5396 phluarĕō (1), to berate

AGAR
28 Agar (2), Hagar

AGATE
3539 kadkôd (1), (poss.) sparkling ruby
7618 shᵉbûw (2), agate

AGATES
3539 kadkôd (1), (poss.) sparkling ruby

AGE
582 'ĕnôwsh (1), man; person, human
1121 bên (3), son, descendant; people
1755 dôwr (2), dwelling
2207 zôqen (1), old age
2209 ziqnâh (1), old age
2465 cheled (2), fleeting time; this world
3117 yôwm (6), day; time period
3485 Yissâˢkâr (1), he will bring a reward
3624 kelach (2), maturity
7869 sêyb (1), old age
7872 sêybâh (6), old age
2244 hĕlikia (4), maturity
2250 hēmĕra (1), day; period of time
5046 tĕlĕiŏs (1), complete; mature
5230 hupĕrakmŏs (1), past the prime of youth

AGED
2204 zâqên (1), to be old
2205 zâqên (4), old
3453 yâshîysh (1), old man
4246 prěsbutēs (2), old man
4247 prěsbutis (1), old woman

AGEE
89 'Âgê' (1), Agee

AGES
165 aiōn (2), perpetuity, ever; world
1074 gěněa (2), generation; age

AGO
3117 yôwm (1), day; time period
6928 qadmâh (Ch.) (1), former time; formerly
7350 râchôwq (3), remote, far
575 apŏ (4), from, away
3819 palai (2), formerly; sometime since
4253 prŏ (1), before in time or space

AGONY
74 agōnia (1), anguish, anxiety

AGREE
1526 ěisi (1), they are
2132 ěunŏěŏ (1), to reconcile
2470 isŏs (1), similar
4160+3391+1106 pŏiěō (1), to make or do
4856 sumphōněŏ (3), to be harmonious

AGREED
3259 yâ'ad (1), to meet; to summon; to direct
800 asumphōnŏs (1), disagreeable
2470 isŏs (1), similar
3982 pěithō (1), to pacify or conciliate
4856 sumphōněŏ (2), to be harmonious
4934 suntithěmai (2), to consent, concur, agree

AGREEMENT
2374 chôzeh (1), beholder in vision
2380 châzûwth (1), revelation; compact
4339 mêyshâr (1), straightness; rectitude
4783 sugkatathěsis (1), accord with

AGREETH
3662 hŏmŏiazō (1), to resemble, be like
4856 sumphōněŏ (1), to be harmonious

AGRIPPA
67 Agrippas (12), wild-horse tamer

AGROUND
2027 ěpŏkěllō (1), to beach a ship vessel

AGUE
6920 qaddachath (1), inflammation

AGUR
94 'Âgûwr (1), one received

AH
162 'ăhâhh (8), Oh!, Alas!, Woe!
253 'âch (2), Oh!; Alas!
1945 hôwy (7), oh!, woe!
3758 ŏua (1), ah!; so!

AHA
253 'âch (7), Oh!; Alas!

AHAB
256 'Ach'âb (90), friend of (his) father

AHAB'S
256 'Ach'âb (2), friend of (his) father

AHARAH
315 'Achrach (1), after (his) brother

AHARHEL
316 'Ăcharchêl (1), safe

AHASAI
273 'Achzay (1), seizer

AHASBAI
308 'Ăchaçbay (1), Achasbai

AHASUERUS
325 'Ăchashvêrôwsh (30), Xerxes

AHASUERUS'
325 'Ăchashvêrôwsh (1), Xerxes

AHAVA
163 'Ahăvă' (3), Ahava

AHAZ
271 'Âchâz (41), possessor

AHAZIAH
274 'Ăchazyâh (37), Jehovah has seized

AHBAN
257 'Achbân (1), one who understands

AHER
313 'Achêr (1), Acher

AHI
277 'Ăchîy (2), brotherly

AHIAH
281 'Ăchiyâh (4), worshipper of Jehovah

AHIAM
279 'Ăchiy'âm (2), uncle

AHIAN
291 'Achyân (1), brotherly

AHIEZER
295 'Ăchîy'ezer (6), brother of help

AHIHUD
282 'Ăchîyhûwd (1), possessor of renown
284 'Ăchîychûd (1), mysterious

AHIJAH
281 'Ăchiyâh (20), worshipper of Jehovah

AHIKAM
296 'Ăchîyqâm (20), high, exalted

AHILUD
286 'Ăchîylûwd (5), brother of one born

AHIMAAZ
290 'Ăchîyma'ats (15), brother of anger

AHIMAN
289 'Ăchîyman (4), gift

AHIMELECH
288 'Ăchîymelek (16), brother of (the) king

AHIMELECH'S
288 'Ăchîymelek (1), brother of (the) king

AHIMOTH
287 'Ăchîymôwth (1), brother of death

AHINADAB
292 'Ăchîynâdâb (1), brother of liberality

AHINOAM
293 'Ăchîynô'am (7), brother of pleasantness

AHIO
283 'Achyôw (6), brotherly

AHIRA
299 'Ăchîyra' (5), brother of wrong

AHIRAM
297 'Ăchîyrâm (1), high, exalted

AHIRAMITES
298 'Ăchîyrâmîy (1), Achiramite

AHISAMACH
294 'Ăchîyçâmâk (3), brother of support

AHISHAHAR
300 'Achîyshachar (1), brother of (the) dawn

AHISHAR
301 'Ăchîyshâr (1), brother of (the) singer

AHITHOPHEL
302 'Ăchîythôphel (20), brother of folly

AHITUB
285 'Ăchîyṭûwb (15), brother of goodness

AHLAB
303 'Achlâb (1), fertile

AHLAI
304 'Achlay (2), wishful

AHOAH
265 'Ăchôwach (1), brotherly

AHOHITE
266 'Ăchôwchîy (4), Achochite
1121+266 bên (1), son, descendant; people

AHOLAH
170 'Ohŏlâh (5), her tent (idolatrous sanctuary)

AHOLIAB
171 'Ohŏlîy'âb (5), tent of (his) father

AHOLIBAH
172 'Ohŏlîybâh (6), my tent (is) in her

AHOLIBAMAH
173 'Ohŏlîybâmâh (8), tent of (the) height

AHUMAI
267 'Ăchûwmay (1), neighbor of water

AHUZAM
275 'Ăchuzzâm (1), seizure

AHUZZATH
276 'Ăchuzzath (1), possession

AI
5857 'Ay (34), ruin
5892 'îyr (1), city, town, unwalled-village

AIAH
345 'Ayâh (5), hawk

AIATH
5857 'Ay (1), ruin

AIDED
2388+3027 châzaq (1), to be strong; courageous

AIJA
5857 'Ay (1), ruin

AIJALON
357 'Ayâlôwn (7), deer-field

AIJELETH
365 'ayeleth (1), doe deer

AIN
5871 'Ayin (5), fountain

AIR
7307 rûwach (1), breath; wind; life-spirit
8064 shâmayim (21), sky; unseen celestial places
109 aēr (7), air, sky
3772 ŏuranŏs (10), sky; air; heaven

AJAH
345 'Ayâh (1), hawk

AJALON
357 'Ayâlôwn (3), deer-field

AKAN
6130 'Ăqân (1), crooked

AKKUB
6126 'Aqqûwb (8), insidious

AKRABBIM
6137 'aqrâb (2), scorpion

ALABASTER
211 alabastrŏn (3), alabaster

ALAMETH
5964 'Âlemeth (1), covering

ALAMMELECH
487 'Allammelek (1), oak of (the) king

ALAMOTH
5961 'Ălâmôwth (2), soprano

ALARM
7321 rûwa' (4), to shout for alarm or joy
8643 t'rûw'âh (6), battle-cry; clangor

English

ALAS
160 'ahăbâh (7), *affection, love*
188 'ôwy (1), *Oh!, Woe!*
253 'âch (1), *Oh!; Alas!*
994 bîy (1), *Oh that!*
1930 hôw (1), *oh! ah!*
1945 hôwy (2), *oh!, woe!*
3758 ŏua (5), *ah!; so!*

ALBEIT
2443 hina (1), *in order that*

ALEMETH
5964 'Ālemeth (3), *covering*

ALEXANDER
223 Alĕxandrŏs (5), *man-defender*

ALEXANDRIA
221 Alĕxandrĕus (3), *of Alexandria*

ALEXANDRIANS
221 Alĕxandrĕus (1), *of Alexandria*

ALGUM
418 'algûwmmîym (3), *Algum-wood*

ALIAH
5933 'Alvâh (1), *moral perverseness*

ALIAN
5935 'Alvân (1), *lofty*

ALIEN
1616 gêr (1), *foreigner*
5236 nêkâr (1), *foreigner*
5237 nokrîy (3), *foreign; non-relative*

ALIENATE
5674 'âbar (1), *to cross over; to transition*

ALIENATED
3363 yâqa' (2), *to be dislocated*
5361 nâqa' (3), *to feel aversion*
526 apallŏtriŏō (2), *to be excluded*

ALIENS
5237 nokrîy (1), *foreign; non-relative*
245 allŏtriŏs (1), *not one's own*
526 apallŏtriŏō (1), *to be excluded*

ALIKE
259 'echâd (1), *first*
834 'ăsher (1), *who, which, what, that*
1571 găm (1), *also; even*
3162 yachad (5), *unitedly*
7737 shâvâh (1), *to equalize; to resemble*

ALIVE
2416 chay (30), *alive; raw; fresh; life*
2418 chăyâ' (Ch.) (1), *to live*
2421 châyâh (34), *to live; to revive*
8300 sârîyd (1), *survivor; remainder*
326 anazaŏ (2), *to recover life, live again*
2198 zaŏ (15), *to live*

ALL
2227 zōŏpŏiĕŏ (1), *to (re-)vitalize, give life*

ALL
622 'âçaph (1), *to gather, collect*
1571 găm (1), *also; even*
3162 yachad (1), *unitedly*
3605 kôl (4194), *all, any*
3606 kôl (Ch.) (50), *all, any or every*
3632 kâlîyl (2), *whole, entire; complete; whole*
3885 lûwn (14), *to be obstinate with*
4393 mᵉlô' (9), *fulness*
4557 miçpâr (3), *number*
5973 'îm (2), *with*
7230 rôb (1), *abundance*
8552 tâmam (2), *to complete, finish*
537 hapas (39), *all, every one, whole*
1273 dianuktĕrĕuō (1), *to pass, spend the night*
2178 ĕphapax (1), *once for all*
2527 kathŏlŏu (1), *entirely, completely*
3122 malista (1), *in the greatest degree*
3364 ŏu mĕ (7), *not at all, absolutely not*
3367 mĕdĕis (1), *not even one*
3650 hŏlŏs (62), *whole or all, i.e. complete*
3654 hŏlŏs (2), *completely*
3745 hŏsŏs (6), *as much as*
3762 ŏudĕis (4), *none, nobody, nothing*
3779 hŏutō (1), *in this way; likewise*
3829 pandŏchĕiŏn (1), *public lodging-place*
3832 panŏiki (1), *with the whole family*
3833 panŏplia (1), *full armor*
3837 pantachŏu (1), *universally, everywhere*
3843 pantŏs (2), *entirely; at all events*
3956 pas (947), *all, any, every, whole*
4219 pŏtĕ (1), *at what time?*
4561 sarx (1), *flesh*

ALLEGING
3908 paratithēmi (1), *to present something*

ALLEGORY
238 allēgŏrĕō (1), *to allegorize*

ALLELUIA
239 allēlŏuïa (4), *praise Jehovah!*

ALLIED
7138 qârôwb (1), *near, close*

ALLON
438 'Allôwn (2), *oak*

ALLON-BACHUTH
439 'Allôwn Bâkûwth (1), *oak of weeping*

ALLOW
1097 ginōskō (1), *to know*
4327 prŏsdĕchŏmai (1), *to receive; to await for*
4909 sunĕudŏkĕō (1), *to assent to, feel gratified*

ALLOWANCE
737 'ărûchâh (1), *ration, portion of food*

ALLOWED
1381 dŏkimazō (1), *to test; to approve*

ALLOWETH
1381 dŏkimazō (1), *to test; to approve*

ALLURE
6601 pâthâh (1), *to be, make simple; to delude*
1185 dĕlĕazō (1), *to delude, seduce*

ALMIGHTY
7706 Shadday (48), *the Almighty God*
3841 pantŏkratōr (9), *Absolute sovereign*

ALMODAD
486 'Almôwdâd (2), *Almodad*

ALMON
5960 'Almôwn (1), *hidden*

ALMON-DIBLATHAIM
5963 'Almôn Diblâthây°mâh (2), *Almon toward Diblathajim*

ALMOND
8247 shâqêd (2), *almond tree or nut*

ALMONDS
8246 shâqad (6), *to be, almond-shaped*
8247 shâqêd (2), *almond tree or nut*

ALMOST
4592 mᵉ'aț (5), *little or few*
3195 mĕllō (1), *to intend, i.e. be about to be*
4975 schĕdŏn (3), *nigh, i.e. nearly*

ALMS
1654 ĕlĕĕmŏsunē (13), *benefaction*

ALMSDEEDS
1654 ĕlĕĕmŏsunē (1), *benefaction*

ALMUG
484 'almuggiym (3), *Almug-wood*

ALOES
174 'ăhâlîym (4), *aloe-wood sticks*
250 alŏĕ (1), *aloes*

ALONE
259 'echâd (4), *first*
905 bad (42), *apart, only, besides*
909 bâdad (9), *to be solitary, be alone*
2308 châdal (2), *to desist, stop; be fat*
4422 mâlaț (1), *to escape as if by slipperiness*

ALLOW
7503 râphâh (4), *to slacken*
7662 shᵉbaq (Ch.) (1), *to allow to remain*
7896 shîyth (1), *to place, put*
863 aphiēmi (6), *to leave; to pardon, forgive*
1439 ĕaō (3), *to let be, i.e. permit or leave alone*
2651 katamŏnas (2), *separately, alone*
3440 mŏnŏn (3), *merely, just*
3441 mŏnŏs (21), *single, only; by oneself*

ALONG
1980 hâlak (3), *to walk; live a certain way*

ALOOF
5048 neged (1), *over against or before*

ALOTH
1175 Bᵉ'âlôwth (1), *mistresses*

ALOUD
1419+3605 gâdôwl (1), *great*
1627 gârôwn (1), *throat*
1993 hâmâh (1), *to be in great commotion*
2429 chayil (Ch.) (3), *strength; loud sound*
5414+854+6963 nâthan (1), *to give*
6670 tsâhal (2), *to be cheerful; to sound*
6963+1419 qôwl (1), *voice or sound*
7311+1419 rûwm (1), *to be high; to rise or raise*
7321 rûwa' (1), *to shout for alarm or joy*
7442 rânan (5), *to shout for joy*
7452 rêa' (1), *crash; noise; shout*
7768 shâva' (1), *to halloo, call for help*
310 anabŏaō (1), *to cry out*

ALPHA
1 A (4), *first*

ALPHAEUS
256 Alphaiŏs (5), *Alphæus*

ALREADY
3528 kᵉbâr (5), *long ago, formerly, hitherto*
2235 ĕdē (18), *even now*
4258 prŏamartanō (1), *to sin previously*
5348 phthanō (1), *to be beforehand*

ALTAR
741 'ărî'êyl (3), *altar*
4056 madbach (Ch.) (1), *sacrificial altar*
4196 mizbêach (347), *altar*
1041 bōmŏs (1), *altar*
2379 thusiastēriŏn (21), *altar*

ALTARS
4196 mizbêach (52), *altar*

2379 thusiastērion (1), *altar*

ALTASCHITH
516 'Al tashchêth (4), *"Thou must not destroy"*

ALTER
2498 châlaph (1), to *hasten away; to pass*
8133 sh⁰nâ' (Ch.) (2), to *alter, change*
8138 shânâh (1), to *transmute*

ALTERED
5674 'âbar (1), to *cross over; to transition*
1096+2087 ginŏmai (1), to *be, become*

ALTERETH
5709 'ădâ' (Ch.) (2), to *pass on or continue*

ALTHOUGH
272 'ăchuzzâh (2), *possession*
3588 kîy (7), *for, that because*
2543 kaitŏi (1), *nevertheless*

ALTOGETHER
259 'echâd (1), *first*
1571 gam (1), *also; even*
3162 yachad (5), *unitedly*
3605 kôl (4), *all, any*
3617 kâlâh (3), *complete destruction*
3650 hŏlŏs (1), *whole or all, i.e. complete*
3843 pantŏs (2), *entirely; at all events*

ALUSH
442 'Âlûwsh (2), *Alush*

ALVAH
5933 'Alvâh (1), *moral perverseness*

ALVAN
5935 'Alvân (1), *lofty*

ALWAY
3605+3117 kôl (4), *all, any or every*
5331 netsach (1), *splendor; lasting*
5769 'ôwlâm (2), *eternity; ancient; always*
8548 tâmîyd (4), *constantly, regularly*
104 aĕi (8), *ever, always*
1275 diapantŏs (2), *constantly, continually*
3842 pantŏtĕ (1), *at all times*
3956+2250 pas (1), *all, any, every, whole*

ALWAYS
3605+3117 kôl (4), *all, any or every*
3605+6256 kôl (4), *all, any or every*
5331 netsach (2), *splendor; lasting*
5769 'ôwlâm (3), *eternity; ancient; always*
8548 tâmîyd (6), *constantly, regularly*
104 aĕi (3), *ever, always*

1223+3956 dia (3), *through, by means of*
1275 diapantŏs (3), *constantly, continually*
1539 hĕkastŏtĕ (1), at *every time*
1722+3956+2540 ĕn (2), *in; during; because of*
3839 pantĕ (1), *wholly*
3842 pantŏtĕ (29), *at all times*

AMAD
6008 'Am'âd (1), *people of time*

AMAL
6000 'Âmâl (1), *wearing effort; worry*

AMALEK
6002 'Ămâlêq (24), *Amalek*

AMALEKITE
6003 'Ămâlêqîy (3), *Amalekite*

AMALEKITES
6003 'Ămâlêqîy (24), *Amalekite*

AMAM
538 'Ămâm (1), *gathering-spot*

AMANA
549 'Ămânâh (1), *covenant*

AMARIAH
568 'Ămaryâh (14), *Jehovah has promised*

AMASA
6021 'Ămâsâ' (16), *burden*

AMASAI
6022 'Ămâsay (5), *burdensome*

AMASHAI
6023 'Ămashçay (1), *burdensome*

AMASIAH
6007 'Ămaçyâh (1), *Jehovah has loaded*

AMAZED
926 bâhal (2), to *tremble; be, make agitated*
2865 châthath (1), to *break down*
8074 shâmêm (1), to *devastate; to stupefy*
8539 tâmahh (1), to *be astounded*
1096+2285 ginŏmai (1), to *be, become*
1568 ĕkthambĕŏ (2), to *astonish utterly*
1605 ĕkplēssō (3), to *astonish*
1611 ĕkstasis (1), *astonishment*
1611+2983 ĕkstasis (1), *astonishment*
1839 ĕxistēmi (6), to *become astounded*
2284 thambĕō (2), to *astound, be amazed*

AMAZEMENT
1611 ĕkstasis (1), *astonishment*

4423 ptŏēsis (1), *something alarm*

AMAZIAH
558 'Ămatsyâh (40), *strength of Jehovah*

AMBASSADOR
6735 tsîyr (3), *hinge; herald or errand-doer*
4243 prĕsbĕuō (1), to *act as a representative*

AMBASSADORS
3887 lûwts (1), to *scoff; to interpret; to intercede*
4397 mal'âk (4), *messenger*
6735 tsîyr (2), *hinge; herald or errand-doer*
4243 prĕsbĕuō (1), to *act as a representative*

AMBASSAGE
4242 prĕsbĕia (1), *ambassadors*

AMBER
2830 chashmal (3), *bronze*

AMBUSH
693 'ârab (7), to *ambush, lie in wait*

AMBUSHES
693 'ârab (1), to *ambush, lie in wait*

AMBUSHMENT
3993 ma'ărâb (2), *ambuscade, ambush*

AMBUSHMENTS
693 'ârab (1), to *ambush, lie in wait*

AMEN
543 'âmên (22), *truly, "may it be so!"*
281 amēn (51), *surely; so be it*

AMEND
2388 châzaq (1), to *fasten upon; to seize*
3190 yâṭab (4), to *be, make well*
2192+2866 ĕchō (1), to *have; hold; keep*

AMENDS
7999 shâlam (1), to *be friendly; to reciprocate*

AMERCE
6064 'ânash (1), to *inflict a penalty, to fine*

AMETHYST
306 'achlâmâh (2), *amethyst*
271 amĕthustŏs (1), *amethyst*

AMI
532 'Âmîy (1), *skilled craftsman*

AMIABLE
3039 y⁰dîyd (1), *loved*

AMINADAB
284 Aminadab (3), *people of liberality*

AMISS
5753 'âvâh (1), to *be crooked*
7955 shâlâh (Ch.) (1), *wrong*

824 atŏpŏs (1), *improper; injurious; wicked*
2560 kakōs (1), *badly; wrongly; ill*

AMITTAI
573 'Ămittay (2), *veracious*

AMMAH
522 'Ammâh (1), *cubit*

AMMI
5971 'am (1), *people*

AMMI-NADIB
5993 'Ammîy Nâdîyb (1), *my people (are) liberal*

AMMIEL
5988 'Ammîy'êl (6), *people of God*

AMMIHUD
5989 'Ammîyhûwd (10), *people of splendor*

AMMINADAB
5992 'Ammîynâdâb (13), *people of liberality*

AMMISHADDAI
5996 'Ammîyshadday (5), *people of (the) Almighty*

AMMIZABAD
5990 'Ammîyzâbâd (1), *people of endowment*

AMMON
5983 'Ammôwn (91), *inbred*

AMMONITE
5984 'Ammôwnîy (9), *Ammonite*

AMMONITES
1121+5984 bên (7), *son, descendant; people*
5984 'Ammôwnîy (16), *Ammonite*

AMMONITESS
5984 'Ammôwnîy (4), *Ammonite*

AMNON
550 'Amnôwn (25), *faithful*

AMNON'S
550 'Amnôwn (3), *faithful*

AMOK
5987 'Âmôwq (2), *deep*

AMON
526 'Âmôwn (17), *skilled craftsman*
300 Amŏn (2), *skilled craftsman*

AMONG
413 'êl (7), *to, toward*
854 'êth (8), *with; among*
996 bêyn (33), *between*
997 bêyn (Ch.) (1), *between; "either...or"*
1460 gêv (1), *middle, inside, in, on, etc.*
1767 day (1), *enough, sufficient*
4480 min (4), *from, out of*
5921 'al (7), *above, over, upon, or against*
5973 'îm (8), *with*
7130 qereb (74), *nearest part, i.e. the center*

English

AMONGST
7310 reⱽvâyâh (1), satisfaction
8432 tâvek (142), center, middle
575 apŏ (1), from, away
1223 dia (1), through, by means of; because of
1519 ĕis (18), to or into
1537 ĕk (5), out, out of
1722 ĕn (115), in; during; because of
1909 ĕpi (4), on, upon
2596 kata (2), down; according to
3319 mĕsŏs (7), middle
3326 mĕta (5), with, among; after, later
3844 para (2), from; with; besides; on account of
4045 pĕripiptō (1), to fall into the hands of
4314 prŏs (19), for; on, at; to, toward; against
4315 prŏsabbatŏn (1), Sabbath-eve
5259 hupŏ (1), under; by means of; at

AMONGST
8432 tâvek (2), center, middle

AMORITE
567 ʼĔmôrîy (14), mountaineer

AMORITES
567 ʼĔmôrîy (73), mountaineer

AMOS
5986 ʼÂmôwç (7), burdensome
301 Amŏs (1), strong

AMOZ
531 ʼÂmôwts (13), strong

AMPHIPOLIS
295 Amphipŏlis (1), city surrounded by a river

AMPLIAS
291 Amplias (1), enlarged

AMRAM
2566 Chamrân (1), red
6019 ʼAmrâm (13), high people

AMRAM'S
6019 ʼAmrâm (1), high people

AMRAMITES
6020 ʼAmrâmîy (2), Amramite

AMRAPHEL
569 ʼAmrâphel (2), Amraphel

AMZI
557 ʼAmtsîy (2), strong

ANAB
6024 ʼĂnâb (2), fruit

ANAH
6034 ʼĂnâh (12), answer

ANAHARATH
588 ʼĂnâchărâth (1), gorge or narrow pass

ANAIAH
6043 ʼĂnâyâh (2), Jehovah has answered

ANAK
6061 ʼĂnâq (9), necklace chain

ANAKIMS
6062 ʼĂnâqîy (9), Anakite

ANAMIM
6047 ʼĂnâmîm (2), Anamim

ANAMMELECH
6048 ʼĂnammelek (1), Anammelek

ANAN
6052 ʼĂnân (1), cloud

ANANI
6054 ʼĂnânîy (1), cloudy

ANANIAH
6055 ʼĂnanyâh (2), Jehovah has covered

ANANIAS
367 Ananias (11), Jehovah has favored

ANATH
6067 ʼĂnâth (2), answer

ANATHEMA
331 anathĕma (1), excommunicated

ANATHOTH
6068 ʼĂnâthôwth (16), answers

ANCESTORS
7223 rîʼshôwn (1), first, in place, time or rank

ANCHOR
45 agkura (1), anchor

ANCHORS
45 agkura (2), anchor

ANCIENT
2204 zâqên (6), to be old, venerated
3453 yâshîysh (1), old man
5769 ʼôwlâm (6), eternity; ancient; always
6267 ʼattîyq (1), weaned; antique
6268 ʼattîyq (Ch.) (3), venerable, old
6917 qâdûwm (1), pristine hero
6924 qedem (8), East, eastern; antiquity; before, anciently

ANCIENTS
2204 zâqên (9), to be old, venerated
6931 qadmôwnîy (1), anterior time; oriental

ANCLE
4974 sphurŏn (1), ankle

ANCLES
657 ʼepheç (1), end; no further

ANDREW
406 Andrĕas (13), manly

ANDRONICUS
408 Andrŏnikŏs (1), man of victory

ANEM
6046 ʼÂnêm (1), two fountains

ANER
6063 ʼÂnêr (3), Aner

ANETHOTHITE
6069 ʼAnthôthîy (1), Antothite

ANETOTHITE
6069 ʼAnthôthîy (1), Antothite

ANGEL
4397 malʼâk (100), messenger
4398 malʼak (Ch.) (2), messenger
32 aggĕlŏs (95), messenger; angel

ANGEL'S
32 aggĕlŏs (2), messenger; angel

ANGELS
430 ʼĕlôhîym (1), the true God; gods; great ones
4397 malʼâk (10), messenger
8136 shinʼân (1), change, i.e. repetition
32 aggĕlŏs (80), messenger; angel
2465 isaggĕlŏs (1), angelic, like an angel

ANGELS'
47 ʼabbîyr (1), mighty

ANGER
639 ʼaph (173), nose or nostril; face; person
2195 zaʼam (1), fury, anger
2534 chêmâh (1), heat; anger; poison
3707 kâʼaç (42), to grieve, rage, be indignant
3708 kaʼaç (2), vexation, grief
5006 nâʼats (1), to scorn
5674 ʼâbar (1), to cross over; to transition
5678 ʼebrâh (1), outburst of passion
6440 pânîym (3), face; front
7307 rûwach (1), breath; wind; life-spirit
3709 ŏrgē (3), ire; punishment
3949 parŏrgizō (1), to enrage, exasperate

ANGERED
7107 qâtsaph (1), to burst out in rage

ANGLE
2443 chakkâh (2), fish hook

ANGRY
599 ʼânaph (13), be enraged, be angry
639 ʼaph (4), nose or nostril; face; person
1149 beⱽnaç (Ch.) (1), to be enraged, be angry
2194 zâʼam (2), to be enraged
2734 chârâh (10), to blaze up
3707 kâʼaç (2), to grieve, rage, be indignant
3708 kaʼaç (1), vexation, grief
4751+5315 mar (1), bitter; bitterness; bitterly

ANETHOTHITE
6225 ʼâshan (1), to envelope in smoke
7107 qâtsaph (2), to burst out in rage
3710 ŏrgizō (5), to become exasperated, enraged
3711 ŏrgilŏs (1), irascible, hot-tempered
5520 chŏlaŏ (1), irritable, enraged

ANGUISH
2342 chûwl (1), to dance, whirl; to writhe in pain
4689 mâtsôwq (1), confinement; disability
4691 meⱽtsûwqâh (1), trouble, anguish
6695 tsôwq (3), distress
6862 tsar (1), trouble; opponent
6869 tsârâh (5), trouble; rival-wife
7115 qôtser (1), shortness (of spirit)
7661 shâbâts (1), intanglement
2347 thlipsis (1), pressure, trouble
4730 stĕnŏchōria (1), calamity, distress
4928 sunŏchē (1), anxiety, distress

ANIAM
593 ʼĂnîyʼâm (1), groaning of (the) people

ANIM
6044 ʼĂnîym (1), fountains

ANISE
432 anēthŏn (1), dill seed for seasoning

ANNA
451 Anna (1), favored

ANNAS
452 Annas (4), Jehovah has favored

ANOINT
4886 mâshach (25), to rub or smear
5480 çûwk (5), to smear
218 alĕiphō (3), to oil with perfume, anoint
1472 ĕgchriō (1), to besmear, anoint
3462 murizō (1), to apply perfumed unguent to

ANOINTED
1101 bâlal (1), to mix
1121+3323 bên (1), son, descendant; people
4473 mimshach (1), with outstretched wings
4886 mâshach (43), to rub or smear with oil
4888 mishchâh (1), unction; gift
4899 mâshîyach (37), consecrated person; Messiah
5480 çûwk (2), to smear
218 alĕiphō (5), to oil with perfume, anoint
2025 ĕpichriō (1), to smear over, anoint

2025+1909 ĕpichriō (1), to
smear over, anoint
5548 chriō (5), to *smear*
or rub with oil

ANOINTEDST
4886 mâshach (1), to *rub*
or smear with oil

ANOINTEST
1878 dâshên (1), to
anoint; to satisfy

ANOINTING
4888 mishchâh (24),
unction; gift
8081 shemen (1), *olive*
218 aleíphō (1), to *oil*
with perfume, *anoint*
5545 chrisma (2), special
endowment

ANON
2112 ĕuthĕōs (1), *at once*
or soon
2117 ĕuthus (1), *at once,*
immediately

ANOTHER
250 'Ezrâchîy (22),
Ezrachite
251 'âch (1), *brother;*
relative
259 'echâd (35), *first*
269 'achôwth (6), *sister*
312 'achêr (58), *other,*
another, different; next
317 'ochŏrîy (Ch.) (5),
other, another
321 'ochŏrân (Ch.) (1),
other, another
376 'îysh (5), *man; male;*
someone
1668 dâ' (Ch.) (2), *this*
1836 dên (Ch.) (1), *this*
2088 zeh (10), *this or that*
2090 zôh (1), *this or that*
2114 zûwr (3), to *be*
foreign, strange
3671 kânâph (1), *edge or*
extremity; wing
5234 nâkar (2), to *treat*
as a foreigner
5997 'âmîyth (2),
comrade or kindred
7453 rêa' (20), *associate*
7468 re'ûwth (2), *female*
associate
8145 shênîy (7), *second;*
again
8264 shâqaq (1), to *seek*
greedily
240 allêlōn (70), *one*
another
243 allŏs (60), *different,*
other
245 allŏtriŏs (4), *not*
one's own
246 allŏphulŏs (1),
Gentile, foreigner
1438 hĕautŏu (7),
himself, herself, itself
1520 hĕis (2), *one*
2087 hĕtĕrŏs (44), *other*
or different
3588 hŏ (1), *"the," i.e. the*
definite article
3739 hŏs (6), *who, which*
4299 prŏkrima (1),
prejudice
4835 sumpathēs (1),
commiserative

ANOTHER'S
7453 rêa' (2), *associate;*
one close
240 allēlōn (2), *one*
another
2087 hĕtĕrŏs (1), *other or*
different

ANSWER
559 'âmar (9), to *say,*
speak
1696 dâbar (1), to *speak,*
say; to subdue
1697 dâbâr (7), *word;*
matter; thing
3045 yâda' (1), to *know*
4405 millâh (1), *word;*
discourse; speech
4617 ma'ăneh (7), *reply,*
answer
6030 'ânâh (60), to
respond, answer;
6600 pithgâm (Ch.) (2),
decree; report
7725 shûwb (12), to *turn*
back; to return
8421 tûwb (Ch.) (2), to
reply, answer
470 antapŏkrinŏmai (1),
to contradict or dispute
611 apŏkrinŏmai (12), to
respond
612 apŏkrisis (3),
response
626 apŏlŏgĕŏmai (4), to
give an account of self
627 apŏlŏgia (4), *plea or*
verbal defense
1906 ĕpĕrōtēma (1),
inquiry
2036 ĕpō (1), to *speak*
5538 chrēmatismŏs (1),
divine response

ANSWERABLE
5980 'ummâh (1), *near,*
beside, along with

ANSWERED
559 'âmar (90), to *say,*
speak
1697 dâbâr (4), *word;*
matter; thing
6030 'ânâh (175), to
respond, answer
6032 'ânâh (Ch.) (16), to
respond, answer
6039 'ênûwth (1),
affliction
7725 shûwb (2), to *turn*
back; to return
8421 tûwb (Ch.) (1), to
reply, answer
611 apŏkrinŏmai (201),
to respond
626 apŏlŏgĕŏmai (2), to
give an account of self

ANSWEREDST
6030 'ânâh (2), to
respond, answer

ANSWEREST
6030 'ânâh (2), to
respond, answer
611 apŏkrinŏmai (4), to
respond

ANSWERETH
6030 'ânâh (6), to
respond, answer
7725 shûwb (1), to *turn*
back; to return

611 apŏkrinŏmai (4), to
respond
4960 sustŏichĕō (1), to
correspond to

ANSWERING
488 antimĕtrĕō (1), to
measure in return
611 apŏkrinŏmai (29), to
respond
5274 hupŏlambanō (1),
to take up, i.e. continue

ANSWERS
8666 tᵉshûwbâh (2), *reply*
612 apŏkrisis (1),
response

ANT
5244 nᵉmâlâh (1), *ant*

ANTICHRIST
500 antichristŏs (4),
opponent of Messiah

ANTICHRISTS
500 antichristŏs (1),
opponent of Messiah

ANTIOCH
490 Antiŏchĕia (18),
Antiochia
491 Antiŏchĕus (1),
inhabitant of Antiochia

ANTIPAS
493 Antipas (1), *instead*
of father

ANTIPATRIS
494 Antipatris (1),
Antipatris

ANTIQUITY
6927 qadmâh (1), *priority*
in time; *before; past*

ANTOTHIJAH
6070 'Anthôthîyâh (1),
answers of Jehovah

ANTOTHITE
6069 'Anthôthîy (2),
Antothite

ANTS
5244 nᵉmâlâh (1), *ant*

ANUB
6036 'Ânûwb (1), *borne*

ANVIL
6471 pa'am (1), *time;*
step; occurence

ANY
259 'echâd (18), *first*
376 'îysh (25), *man*
1697 dâbâr (2), *thing*
1991 hêm (1), *wealth*
3254 yâçaph (2), to *add*
3605 kôl (175), *all, any*
3606 kôl (Ch.) (8), *all,*
any or every
3792 kᵉthâb (Ch.) (1),
writing, record or book
3972 mᵉûwmâh (12),
something; anything
4310 mîy (1), *who?*
5315 nephesh (3), *life;*
breath; soul; wind
5750 'ôwd (9), *again;*
repeatedly; still; more
5769 'ôwlâm (1), *eternity;*
ancient; always
1520 hĕis (2), *one*
1535 ĕitĕ (2), *if too*
1536 ĕi tis (52), *if any*
1538 hĕkastŏs (1), *each*

2089 ĕti (10), *yet, still*
3361 mē (1), *not; lest*
3362 ĕan mē (2), *if not*
3364 ŏu mē (2), *not at all*
3367 mēdĕis (5), *not even*
one
3370 Mēdŏs (2),
inhabitant of Media
3379 mēpŏtĕ (7), *not*
ever; if, or lest ever
3381 mēpōs (4), *lest*
somehow
3387 mētis (6), *whether*
any
3588 hŏ (1), *"the," i.e. the*
definite article
3762 ŏudĕis (12), *none,*
nobody, nothing
3763 ŏudĕpŏtĕ (2), *never*
at all
3765 ŏukĕti (4), *not yet,*
no longer
3956 pas (9), *all, any,*
every, whole
4218 pŏtĕ (4), *at some*
time, ever
4455 pŏpŏtĕ (3), *at no*
time
4458 -pōs (4), *particle*
used in composition
5100 tis (122), *some or*
any person or object
5150 trimēnŏn (1), *three*
months' space

APART
905 bad (6), *apart, only,*
besides
5079 niddâh (3), *time of*
menstrual impurity
5674 'âbar (1), to *cross*
over; to transition
6395 pâlâh (1), to
distinguish
659 apŏtithēmi (1), to *put*
away; get rid of
2596 kata (7), *down;*
according to

APELLES
559 Apĕllēs (1), *Apelles*

APES
6971 qôwph (2), *ape or*
monkey

APHARSACHITES
671 'Àpharçᵉkay (Ch.)
(2), *Apharsekite*

APHARSATHCHITES
671 'Àpharçᵉkay (Ch.)
(1), *Apharsekite*

APHARSITES
670 'Àphârᵉçay (Ch.) (1),
Apharesite

APHEK
663 'Àphêq (8), *fortress*

APHEKAH
664 'Àphêqâh (1), *fortress*

APHIAH
647 'Àphîyach (1), *breeze*

APHIK
663 'Àphêq (1), *fortress*

APHRAH
1036 Bêyth lᵉ-'Aphrâh
(1), *house of dust*

APHSES
6483 Pitstsêts (1),
dispersive

English

APIECE
259 'echád (1), *first*
5982+259 'ammûwd (1), *column, pillar*
303 ana (2), *each; in turn; among*

APOLLONIA
624 Apŏllōnia (1), *sun*

APOLLOS
625 Apŏllōs (10), *sun*

APOLLYON
623 Apŏlluŏn (1), *Destroyer*

APOSTLE
652 apŏstŏlŏs (19), *commissioner* of Christ

APOSTLES
652 apŏstŏlŏs (53), *commissioner* of Christ
5570 psĕudapŏstŏlŏs (1), *pretended preacher*

APOSTLES'
652 apŏstŏlŏs (5), *commissioner* of Christ

APOSTLESHIP
651 apŏstŏlē (4), office of *apostle*

APOTHECARIES
7543 râqach (1), to *perfume, blend spice*

APOTHECARIES'
4842 mirqachath (1), *unguent; unguent-pot*

APOTHECARY
7543 râqach (4), to *perfume, blend spice*

APPAIM
649 'Appayim (2), *two nostrils*

APPAREL
899 beged (4), *clothing; treachery* or *pillage*
1264 bᵉrôwm (1), *damask*
3830 lᵉbûwsh (8), *garment; wife*
3847 lâbash (1), to *clothe*
4254 machălâtsâh (1), *mantle, garment*
4403 malbûwsh (4), *garment, clothing*
8071 simlâh (2), *dress, mantle*
2066 ĕsthēs (3), to *clothe; dress*
2440 himation (1), to *put on clothes*
2441 himatismŏs (1), *clothing*
2689 katastŏlē (1), *costume* or *apparel*

APPARELLED
3847 lâbash (1), to *clothe*
2441 himatismŏs (1), *clothing*

APPARENTLY
4758 mar'eh (1), *appearance; vision*

APPEAL
1941 ĕpikalĕŏmai (2), to *invoke*

APPEALED
1941 ĕpikalĕŏmai (4), to *invoke*

APPEAR
1540 gâlâh (1), to *denude; uncover*
1570 gâlash (2), to *caper*
4286 machsôph (1), *peeling, baring*
6524 pârach (1), to *break forth; to bloom; to fly*
7200 râ'âh (24), to *see*
82 adēlŏs (1), *indistinct, not clear*
398 anaphainō (1), to *appear*
1718 ĕmphanizō (1), to *show forth*
2064 ĕrchŏmai (1), to *go or come*
3700 ŏptanŏmai (2), to *appear*
5316 phainō (9), to *show; to appear, be visible*
5318+5600 phanĕrŏs (1), *apparent, visible, clear*
5319 phanĕrŏō (9), to *render apparent*

APPEARANCE
4758 mar'eh (30), *appearance; vision*
5869 'ayin (1), *eye; sight; fountain*
1491 ĕidŏs (1), *form, appearance, sight*
3799 ŏpsis (1), *face; appearance*
4383 prŏsōpŏn (2), *face, presence*

APPEARANCES
4758 mar'eh (2), *appearance; vision*

APPEARED
1540 gâlâh (1), to *denude; uncover*
3318 yâtsâ' (1), to *go, bring out*
6437 pânâh (1), to *turn, to face*
7200 râ'âh (39), to *see*
1718 ĕmphanizō (1), to *show forth*
2014 ĕpiphainō (3), to *become visible*
3700 ŏptanŏmai (15), to *appear*
5316 phainō (5), to *show; to appear, be visible*
5319 phanĕrŏō (3), to *render apparent*

APPEARETH
1540 gâlâh (1), to *denude; uncover*
4758 mar'eh (1), *appearance; vision*
7200 râ'âh (3), to *see*
8259 shâqaph (1), to *peep or gaze*
5316 phainō (3), to *show; to appear, be visible*

APPEARING
602 apŏkalupsis (1), *disclosure, revelation*
2015 ĕpiphanĕia (5), *manisfestation*

APPEASE
3722+6440 kâphar (1), to *cover; to expiate*

APPEASED
7918 shâkak (1), to *lay a trap; to allay*
2687 katastĕllō (1), to *quell, quiet*

APPEASETH
8252 shâqaṭ (1), to *repose*

APPERTAIN
2969 yâ'âh (1), to *be suitable, proper*

APPETITE
2416 chay (1), *alive; raw; fresh; life*
5315 nephesh (2), *life; breath; soul; wind*
8264 shâqaq (1), to *seek greedily*

APPHIA
682 Apphia (1), *Apphia*

APPII
675 'Appiŏs (1), *Appius*

APPLE
380 'îyshôwn (2), *pupil, eyeball*
380+1323 'îyshôwn (1), *pupil, eyeball*
892 bâbâh (1), *pupil of the eye*
1323 bath (1), *daughter, descendant, woman*
8598 tappûwach (3), *apple*

APPLES
8598 tappûwach (3), *apple*

APPLIED
5414 nâthan (2), to *give*
5437 çâbab (1), to *surround*

APPLY
935 bôw' (2), to *go, come*
5186 nâṭâh (1), to *stretch or spread out*
7896 shîyth (1), to *place, put*

APPOINT
559 'âmar (1), to *say, speak*
977 bâchar (1), *select, chose, prefer*
3259 yâ'ad (2), to *meet; to summon; to direct*
5344 nâqab (1), to *specify, designate, libel*
5414 nâthan (4), to *give*
5975 'âmad (2), to *stand*
6485 pâqad (10), to *visit, care for, count*
6680 tsâvâh (4), to *constitute, enjoin*
7136 qârâh (1), to *bring about; to impose*
7760 sûwm (11), to *put*
7896 shîyth (2), to *place*
7971 shâlach (1), to *send away*
1303 diatithĕmai (1), to *put apart, i.e. dispose*
2525 kathistēmi (1), to *designate, constitute*
5087 tithēmi (2), to *place, put*

APPOINTED
559 'âmar (2), to *say*

APPEARANCE 561 'êmer (1), *something said*
1121 bēn (3), *son, people of a class or kind*
1696 dâbar (1), to *speak, say; to subdue*
2163 zâman (3), to *fix a time*
2296 châgar (3), to *gird on a belt; put on armor*
2706 chôq (1), *appointment; allotment*
2708 chuqqâh (1), to *delineate*
2710 châqaq (1), to *enact laws; to prescribe*
2764 chêrem (1), *doomed object*
3045 yâda' (1), to *know*
3198 yâkach (2), to *decide, justify*
3245 yâçad (1), *settle, consult, establish*
3259 yâ'ad (3), to *meet; to summon; to direct*
3677 keçe' (2), *full moon*
4150 môw'êd (20), *assembly, congregation*
4151 môw'âd (1), *ranking of troop*
4152 mûw'âdâh (1), *appointed place*
4487 mânâh (4), to *allot; to enumerate or enroll*
4662 miphqâd (1), *designated spot; census*
5324 nâtsab (1), to *station*
5414 nâthan (7), to *give*
5567 çâman (1), to *designate*
5975 'âmad (10), to *stand*
6213 'âsâh (2), to *do or make*
6485 pâqad (4), to *visit, care for, count*
6635 tsâbâ' (3), *army, military host*
6680 tsâvâh (4), to *constitute, enjoin*
6942 qâdâsh (1), to *be, make clean*
7760 sûwm (8), to *put*
7896 shîyth (1), to *place*
322 anadĕiknumi (1), to *indicate, appoint*
606 apŏkĕimai (1), to *be reserved; to await*
1299 diatassō (4), to *institute, prescribe*
1303 diatithĕmai (1), to *put apart, i.e. dispose*
1476 hĕdraiŏs (1), *immovable; steadfast*
1935 ĕpithanatiŏs (1), *doomed to death*
2476 histēmi (1), to *stand, establish*
2749 kĕimai (1), to *lie outstretched*
4160 pŏiĕō (1), to *do*
4287 prŏthĕsmiŏs (1), *designated day or time*
4384 prŏtassō (1), to *prescribe beforehand*
4929 suntassō (2), to *direct, instruct*
5021 tassō (3), to *assign or dispose*

5081 tēlaugōs (1), in a
far-shining manner
5087 tithēmi (3), to *put*

APPOINTETH
6966 qûwm (Ch.) (1), to
rise

APPOINTMENT
3259 yâ'ad (1), to *meet;*
to *summon;* to *direct*
3883 lûwl (1), *spiral* step
6310 peh (2), *mouth;*
opening

APPREHEND
2638 katalambanō (1), to
seize; to *understand*
4084 piazō (1), to *seize,*
arrest, or *capture*

APPREHENDED
2638 katalambanō (2), to
seize; to *possess;* to
understand
4084 piazō (1), to *seize,*
arrest, or *capture*

APPROACH
5066 nâgash (5), to *be,*
come, bring near
7126 qârab (12), to
approach, bring near
7138 qârôwb (1), *near,*
close
676 aprŏsitŏs (1),
unapproachable

APPROACHED
5066 nâgash (1), to *be,*
come, bring near
7126 qârab (1), to
approach, bring near

APPROACHETH
1448 ĕggizō (1), to
approach

APPROACHING
7132 qᵉrâbâh (1),
approach
1448 ĕggizō (1), to
approach

APPROVE
7520 râtsad (1), to *look*
askant; to *be jealous*
1381 dŏkimazō (2), to
test; to *approve*

APPROVED
584 apŏdĕiknumi (1), to
accredit
1384 dŏkimŏs (6),
acceptable, approved
4921 sunistaō (1), to
introduce (favorably)

APPROVEST
1381 dŏkimazō (1), to
test; to *approve*

APPROVETH
7200 râ'âh (1), to *see*

APPROVING
4921 sunistaō (1), to
introduce (favorably)

APRONS
2290 chăgôwr (1), *belt*
for the waist
4612 simikinthiŏn (1),
narrow *apron*

APT
6213 'âsâh (1), to *do*
1317 didaktikŏs (2),
instructive

AQUILA
207 Akulas (6), *eagle*

AR
6144 'Âr (6), *city*

ARA
690 'Ärâ' (1), *lion*

ARAB
694 'Ärâb (1), *ambush*

ARABAH
6160 'ărâbâh (2), *desert,*
wasteland

ARABIA
6152 'Äräb (6), *Arabia*
688 Arabia (2), *Arabia*

ARABIAN
6153 'ereb (1), *dusk*
6163 'Ärâbîy (3), *Arabian*

ARABIANS
6163 'Ärâbîy (5), *Arabian*
690 'Araps (1), *native of*
Arabia

ARAD
6166 'Ärâd (5), *fugitive*

ARAH
733 'Ârach (4),
way-faring

ARAM
758 'Arâm (7), *highland*
689 Aram (3), *high*

ARAM-NAHARAIM
763 'Äram Nahărayim
(1), *Aram of* (the) *two*
rivers

ARAM-ZOBAH
760 'Äram Tsôwbâh (1),
Aram of Coele-Syria

ARAMITESS
761 'Ärammîy (1),
Aramite

ARAN
765 'Ärân (2), *stridulous*

ARARAT
780 'Ärârạt (2), *Ararat*

ARAUNAH
728 'Äravnâh (9),
Aravnah or *Ornah*

ARBA
704 'Arba' (2), *four*

ARBAH
704 'Arba' (1), *four*

ARBATHITE
6164 'Arbâthîy (2),
Arbathite

ARBITE
701 'Arbîy (1), *Arbite*

ARCHANGEL
743 archaggĕlŏs (2),
chief angel

ARCHELAUS
745 Archĕlaŏs (1),
people-ruling

ARCHER
1869 dârak (1), to *walk,*
lead; to *string* a *bow*
7198 qesheth (1), *bow;*
rainbow

ARCHERS
1167+2671 ba'al (1),
master; husband
1869+7198 dârak (1), to
walk; to *string* a *bow*

2686 châtsats (1), to
distribute into ranks
3384 yârâh (3), to *throw,*
shoot an arrow
3384+376+7198 yârâh (1),
to *shoot* an arrow
3384+7198 yârâh (1), to
throw, shoot an arrow;
to *point;* to *teach*
7198 qesheth (2), *bow;*
rainbow
7228 rab (2), *archer*

ARCHES
361 'êylâm (15), *portico,*
porch

ARCHEVITES
756 'Arkᵉvay (Ch.) (1),
Arkevite

ARCHI
757 'Arkîy (1), *Arkite*

ARCHIPPUS
751 Archippŏs (2),
horse-ruler

ARCHITE
757 'Arkîy (5), *Arkite*

ARCTURUS
5906 'Ayish (2), Great
Bear constellation

ARD
714 'Ard (3), *fugitive*

ARDITES
716 'Ardîy (1), *Ardite*

ARDON
715 'Ardôwn (1), *roaming*

ARELI
692 'Ar'êlîy (2), *heroic*

ARELITES
692 'Ar'êlîy (1), *heroic*

AREOPAGITE
698 Arĕŏpagitēs (1),
Areopagite

AREOPAGUS
697 Arĕiŏs Pagŏs (1),
rock of Ares

ARETAS
702 Arĕtas (1), *Aretas*

ARGOB
709 'Argôb (5), *stony*

ARGUING
3198 yâkach (1), to *be*
correct; to *argue*

ARGUMENTS
8433 tôwkêchâh (1),
correction, refutation

ARIDAI
742 'Ărîyday (1), *Aridai*

ARIDATHA
743 'Ărîydâthâ' (1),
Aridatha

ARIEH
745 'Aryêh (1), *lion*

ARIEL
740 'Ärî'êl (5), *Lion of*
God

ARIGHT
3190 yâṭab (1), to *be,*
make well
3559 kûwn (1), to *render*
sure, proper
3651 kên (1), *just; right,*
correct

4339 mêyshâr (1),
straightness; rectitude

ARIMATHAEA
707 Arimathaia (4),
height

ARIOCH
746 'Äryôwk (7), *Arjok*

ARISAI
747 'Äriyçay (1), *Arisai*

ARISE
2224 zârach (3), to *rise;*
to *be bright*
5782 'ûwr (1), to *awake*
5927 'âlâh (2), to *ascend,*
be high, mount
5975 'âmad (1), to *stand*
6965 qûwm (106), to *rise*
6966 qûwm (Ch.) (3), to
rise
6974 qûwts (1), to *awake*
7721 sôw' (1), *rising*
305 anabainō (1), to *go*
up, rise
393 anatĕllō (1), to *cause*
to *arise*
450 anistēmi (14), to
stand up; to *come back*
to *life*
1453 ĕgĕirō (13), to
waken, i.e. *rouse*

ARISETH
2224 zârach (4), to *rise;*
to *be bright*
5927 'âlâh (1), to *ascend,*
be high, mount
6965 qûwm (2), to *rise*
450 anistēmi (1), to
stand up; to *come back*
to *life*
1096 ginŏmai (2), to *be,*
become
1453 ĕgĕirō (1), to
waken, i.e. *rouse*

ARISING
6965 qûwm (1), to *rise*

ARISTARCHUS
708 Aristarchŏs (5), *best*
ruling

ARISTOBULUS'
711 Aristŏbŏulŏs (1), *best*
counselling

ARK
727 'ârôwn (194), *box*
8392 têbâh (28), *box,*
basket
2787 kibōtŏs (6), *ark;*
chest or *box*

ARKITE
6208 'Arqîy (2), *tush*

ARM
248 'ezrôwa (2), *arm*
2220 zᵉrôwa (59), *arm;*
foreleg; force, power
2502 châlats (1), to
depart; to *equip*
3802 kâthêph (1),
side-piece
1023 brachiōn (3), *arm*
3695 hŏplizō (1), to *equip*

ARMAGEDDON
717 Armagĕddōn (1), *hill*
of the *rendezvous*

ARMED
2502 châlats (16), to
equip; to *present*

English

ARMENIA
2571 châmûsh (3),
able-bodied *soldiers*
3847 lâbash (3), to *clothe*
4043 mâgên (2), small
shield (*buckler*)
5401 nâshaq (3), to *kiss*;
to *equip* with weapons
5402 nesheq (1), military
arms, arsenal
7324 rûwq (1), to *pour*
out, i.e. *empty*
2528 kathŏplizō (1), to
equip fully with armor

ARMENIA
780 'Ărârat (2), *Ararat*

ARMHOLES
679+3027 'atstsîyl (2),
joint of the hand

ARMIES
1416 gᵉdûwd (1), *band* of
soldiers
2428 chayil (4), *army;*
wealth; virtue; valor
4264 machăneh (4),
encampment
4630 ma'ărâh (1), *open*
spot
4634 ma'ărâkâh (6), *row;*
pile; military *array*
6635 tsâbâ' (22), *army,*
military host
3925 parĕmbŏlē (1),
battle-array
4753 stratĕuma (3), body
of *troops*
4760 stratŏpĕdŏn (1),
body of *troops*

ARMONI
764 'Armônîy (1), *palatial*

ARMOUR
2185 zônôwth (1), *harlots*
2290 chăgôwr (1), *belt*
for the waist
2488 chălîytsâh (1), *spoil,*
booty of the dead
3627 kᵉlîy (11),
implement, thing
4055 mad (2), *vesture,*
garment; carpet
5402 nesheq (3), military
arms, arsenal
3696 hŏplŏn (2),
implement, or *utensil*
or *tool*
3833 panŏplia (1), *full*
armor

ARMOURBEARER
5375+3627 nâsâ' (18), to
lift up

ARMOURY
214 'ôwtsâr (1),
depository
5402 nesheq (3), military
arms, arsenal
8530 talpîyâh (1),
something *tall*

ARMS
1672 dâ'ag (1), *be*
anxious, be afraid
2220 zᵉrôwa' (24), *arm;*
foreleg; force, power
2684 chôtsen (1), *bosom*
43 agkalĕ (1), *arm*
1723 ĕnagkalizŏmai (2),
to *take into one's arms*

ARMY
1416 gᵉdûwd (4), *band* of
soldiers
2426 chêyl (1), *rampart,*
battlement
2426+6635 chêyl (1),
rampart, battlement
2428 chayil (52), *army;*
wealth; virtue; valor
2429 chayil (Ch.) (2),
army; strength
2502 châlats (1), to
deliver, equip
4634 ma'ărâkâh (7), *row;*
pile; military *array*
4675 matstsâbâh (1),
military *guard*
6635 tsâbâ' (7), *army,*
military host
4753 stratĕuma (3), body
of *troops*

ARNAN
770 'Arnân (1), *noisy*

ARNON
769 'Arnôwn (25),
brawling stream

AROD
720 'Ărôwd (1), *fugitive*

ARODI
722 'Ărôwdîy (1), *Arodite*

ARODITES
722 'Ărôwdîy (1), *Arodite*

AROER
6177 'Ărô'êr (16),
nudity of situation

AROERITE
6200 'Ărô'êrîy (1),
Aroërite

AROSE
2224 zârach (2), to *rise;*
to *be bright*
5927 'âlâh (2), to *ascend,*
be high, mount
5975 'âmad (1), to *stand*
6965 qûwm (107), to *rise*
6966 qûwm (Ch.) (1), to
rise
7925 shâkam (7), to *start*
early in the morning
305 anabainō (1), to *go*
up, rise
450 anistēmi (24), to
stand up; to *come back*
to life
906 ballō (1), to *throw*
1096 ginŏmai (11), to *be,*
become
1326 diĕgĕirō (2), to
arouse, stimulate
1453 ĕgĕirō (13), to
waken, i.e. *rouse*
1525 ĕisĕrchŏmai (1), to
enter

ARPAD
774 'Arpâd (4), *spread*
out

ARPHAD
774 'Arpâd (2), *spread*
out

ARPHAXAD
775 'Arpakshad (9),
Arpakshad
742 Arphaxad (1),
Arphaxad

ARRAY
631 'âçar (1), to *fasten;* to
join battle
3847 lâbash (2), to *clothe*
5844 'âṭâh (1), to *wrap,*
i.e. *cover, veil, clothe*
6186 'ârak (26), to *set in*
a *row,* i.e. *arrange,*
7896 shîyth (1), to *place*
2441 himatismŏs (1),
clothing

ARRAYED
3847 lâbash (4), to *clothe*
1746 ĕnduō (1), to *invest*
with clothing
4016 pĕriballō (6), to
wrap around, clothe

ARRIVED
2668 kataplĕō (1), to *sail*
down
3846 paraballō (1), to
reach a place; to *liken*

ARROGANCY
1347 gâ'ôwn (3),
ascending; majesty
6277 'âthâq (1), *impudent*

ARROW
1121+7198 bên (1),
people of a class or kind
2671 chêts (11), *arrow;*
shaft of a spear
2678 chitstsîy (4), *arrow*

ARROWS
1121 bên (1), *people* of a
class or kind
2671 chêts (36), *arrow;*
wound; shaft of a spear
2678 chitstsîy (1), *arrow*
2687 châtsâts (1), *gravel,*
grit
7565 resheph (1), *flame*

ARTAXERXES
783 'Artachshastâ' (Ch.)
(14), *Artaxerxes*

ARTAXERXES'
783 'Artachshastâ' (Ch.)
(1), *Artaxerxes*

ARTEMAS
734 Artĕmas (1), *gift* of
Artemis

ARTIFICER
2794 chôrêsh (1), skilled
fabricator worker
2796 chârâsh (1), skilled
fabricator or worker

ARTIFICERS
2796 chârâsh (2), skilled
fabricator or worker

ARTILLERY
3627 kᵉlîy (1),
implement, thing

ARTS
4021 pĕriĕrgŏs (1),
magic, sorcery

ARUBOTH
700 'Ărubbôwth (1),
Arubboth

ARUMAH
725 'Ărûwmâh (1), *height*

ARVAD
719 'Arvad (2), refuge for
the *roving*

ARVADITE
721 'Arvâdîy (2), *Arvadite*

ARZA
777 'artsâ' (1), *earthiness*

ASA
609 'Âçâ (57), *Asa*
760 Asa (2), *Asa*

ASA'S
609 'Âçâ (1), *Asa*

ASAHEL
760 'Ăram Tsôwbâh (1),
Aram of Coele-Syria
6214 'Ăsâh'êl (17), *God*
has made

ASAHIAH
6222 'Ăsâyâh (2),
Jehovah has made

ASAIAH
6222 'Ăsâyâh (6),
Jehovah has made

ASAPH
623 'Âçâph (44), *collector*

ASAPH'S
623 'Âçâph (1), *collector*

ASAREEL
840 'Ăsar'êl (1), *right* of
God

ASARELAH
841 'Ăsar'êlâh (1), *right*
toward God

ASCEND
5927 'âlâh (9), to *ascend,*
be high, mount
305 anabainō (4), to *go*
up, rise

ASCENDED
5927 'âlâh (10), to
ascend, be high, mount
305 anabainō (9), to *go*
up, rise

ASCENDETH
305 anabainō (2), to *go*
up, rise

ASCENDING
5927 'âlâh (2), to *ascend,*
be high, mount
305 anabainō (3), to *go*
up, rise

ASCENT
4608 ma'ăleh (2),
elevation; platform
5930 'ôlâh (1), *sacrifice*
wholly consumed in fire
5944 'ălîyâh (1), *upper*
things; second-story

ASCRIBE
3051 yâhab (1), to *give*
5414 nâthan (2), to *give*

ASCRIBED
5414 nâthan (2), to *give*

ASENATH
621 'Âçᵉnath (3), *Asenath*

ASER
768 Asēr (2), *happy*

ASH
766 'ôren (1), *ash* tree

ASHAMED
954 bûwsh (79), to be
ashamed; disappointed
1322 bôsheth (1), *shame*
2659 châphêr (4), to *be*
ashamed, disappointed
3637 kâlam (12), to *taunt*
or *insult*

ASHAN
153 aischunŏmai (5), *to feel shame* for oneself
422 anĕpaischuntŏs (1), *unashamed*
1788 ĕntrĕpō (2), *to respect; to confound*
1870 ĕpaischunŏmai (11), *to feel shame*
2617 kataischunō (7), *to disgrace or shame*

ASHAN
6228 'Âshân (4), *smoke*

ASHBEA
791 'Ashbêa' (1), *adjurer*

ASHBEL
788 'Ashbêl (3), *flowing*

ASHBELITES
789 'Ashbêlîy (1), *Ashbelite*

ASHCHENAZ
813 'Ashkᵉnaz (2), *Ashkenaz*

ASHDOD
795 'Ashdôwd (21), *ravager*

ASHDODITES
796 'Ashdôwdîy (1), *Ashdodite*

ASHDOTH-PISGAH
798+6449 'Ashdôwth hap-Piçgâh (3), *ravines of the Pisgah*

ASHDOTHITES
796 'Ashdôwdîy (1), *Ashdodite*

ASHER
836 'Âshêr (42), *happy*

ASHERITES
843 'Âshêrîy (1), *Asherite*

ASHES
665 'êpher (24), *ashes*
1878 dâshên (2), *to be fat, thrive; to fatten*
1880 deshen (8), *fat; fatness, ashes*
6083 'âphâr (2), *dust, earth, mud; clay,*
6368 pîyach (2), *powder dust or ashes*
4700 spŏdŏs (3), *ashes*
5077 tĕphrŏō (1), *to incinerate*

ASHIMA
807 'Äshîymâ' (1), *Ashima*

ASHKELON
831 'Ashqᵉlôwn (9), *Ashkelon*

ASHKENAZ
813 'Ashkᵉnaz (1), *Ashkenaz*

ASHNAH
823 'Ashnâh (2), *Ashnah*

ASHPENAZ
828 'Ashpᵉnaz (1), *Ashpenaz*

ASHRIEL
845 'Asrî'êlîy (1), *Asrielite*

ASHTAROTH
6252 'Ashtârôwth (11), *increases*

ASHTERATHITE
6254 'Ashtᵉrâthîy (1), *Ashterathite*

ASHTEROTH
6255 'Ashtᵉrôth Qarnayim (1), *Ashtaroth of (the) double horns*

ASHTORETH
6252 'Ashtârôwth (3), *increases*

ASHUR
804 'Ashshûwr (2), *successful*

ASHURITES
843 'Âshêrîy (2), *Asherite*

ASHVATH
6220 'Ashvâth (1), *bright*

ASIA
773 Asia (20), *Asia Minor*
775 Asiarchēs (1), *ruler in Asia*

ASIDE
2015 hâphak (1), *to turn about or over*
3943 lâphath (1), *to clasp; to turn aside*
5186 nâtâh (16), *to stretch or spread out*
5265 nâça' (1), *start on a journey*
5437 çâbab (2), *to surround*
5493 çûwr (4), *to turn off*
5844 'âṭâh (1), *to wrap, i.e. cover, veil, clothe*
6437 pânâh (1), *to turn, to face*
7750 sûwṭ (1), *become derelict*
7847 sâṭâh (5), *to deviate from duty, go astray*
402 anachōrĕō (3), *to retire, withdraw*
565 apĕrchŏmai (1), *to go off, i.e. depart*
659 apŏtithēmi (2), *to put away; get rid of*
863 aphiēmi (1), *to leave; to pardon, forgive*
1824 ĕxautēs (2), *instantly, at once*
2596 kata (1), *down; according to*
5087 tithēmi (1), *to place, put*
5298 hupŏchōrĕō (1), *to vacate down, i.e. retire*

ASIEL
6221 'Äsîy'êl (1), *made of God*

ASK
1156 bᵉ'â' (Ch.) (2), *to seek or ask*
1245 bâqash (1), *to search out*
1875 dârash (1), *to pursue or search*
7592 shâ'al (41), *to ask*
154 aitĕō (38), *to ask for*
523 apaitĕō (1), *to demand back*
1833 ĕxĕtazō (1), *to ascertain or interrogate*
1905 ĕpĕrōtaō (8), *to inquire, seek*

2065 ĕrōtaō (11), *to interrogate; to request*
4441 punthanŏmai (2), *to ask for information*

ASKED
1156 bᵉ'â' (Ch.) (1), *to seek or ask*
1245 bâqash (1), *to search out*
7592 shâ'al (49), *to ask*
7593 shᵉ'êl (Ch.) (3), *to ask*
154 aitĕō (4), *to ask for*
1905 ĕpĕrōtaō (45), *to inquire, seek*
2065 ĕrōtaō (11), *to interrogate; to request*
3004 lĕgō (1), *to say*
4441 punthanŏmai (4), *to ask for information*

ASKELON
831 'Ashqᵉlôwn (3), *Ashkelon*

ASKEST
7592 shâ'al (1), *to ask*
154 aitĕō (1), *to ask for*
1905 ĕpĕrōtaō (1), *to inquire, seek*

ASKETH
7592 shâ'al (5), *to ask*
154 aitĕō (5), *to ask for*
2065 ĕrōtaō (1), *to interrogate; to request*

ASKING
7592 shâ'al (3), *to ask*
350 anakrinō (2), *to interrogate, determine*
1905 ĕpĕrōtaō (1), *to inquire, seek*
2065 ĕrōtaō (1), *to interrogate; to request*

ASLEEP
3463 yâshên (2), *sleepy*
7290 râdam (2), *to stupefy*
879 aphupnŏō (1), *to drop (off) in slumber*
2518 kathĕudō (5), *to fall asleep*
2837 kŏimaō (6), *to slumber; to decease*

ASNAH
619 'Açnâh (1), *Asnah*

ASNAPPER
620 'Oçnappar (Ch.) (1), *Osnappar*

ASP
6620 pethen (1), *asp*

ASPATHA
630 'Açpâthâ' (1), *Aspatha*

ASPS
6620 pethen (3), *asp*
785 aspis (1), *serpent, (poss.) asp*

ASRIEL
844 'Asrîy'êl (2), *right of God*

ASRIELITES
845 'Asrî'êlîy (1), *Asrielite*

ASS
860 'âthôwn (16), *female donkey, ass*

2543 chămôwr (55), *male donkey or ass*
5601 çappîyr (1), *sapphire*
5895 'ayîr (2), *young robust donkey or ass*
6171 'ârôwd (1), *onager or wild donkey*
6501 pere' (3), *onager, wild donkey*
3678 ŏnariŏn (1), *little donkey*
3688 ŏnŏs (5), *donkey*
5268 hupŏzugiŏn (2), *donkey*

ASS'S
860 'âthôwn (1), *female donkey, ass*
2543 chămôwr (1), *male donkey or ass*
6501 pere' (1), *onager, wild donkey*
3688 ŏnŏs (1), *donkey*

ASSAULT
6696 tsûwr (1), *to cramp, i.e. confine; to harass*
3730 hŏrmē (1), *violent impulse, i.e. onset*

ASSAULTED
2186 ĕphistēmi (1), *to be present; to approach*

ASSAY
5254 nâçâh (1), *to test, attempt*

ASSAYED
2974 yâ'al (1), *to assent; to undertake, begin*
5254 nâçâh (1), *to test, attempt*
3985 pĕirazō (1), *to endeavor, scrutinize, entice, discipline*
3987 pĕiraō (1), *to attempt, try*

ASSAYING
3984+2983 pĕira (1), *attempt, experience*

ASSEMBLE
622 'âçaph (10), *to gather, collect*
1481 gûwr (1), *to sojourn, live as an alien*
2199 zâ'aq (2), *to call out, convene publicly*
3259 yâ'ad (1), *to meet; to summon; to direct*
5789 'ûwsh (1), *to hasten*
6908 qâbats (5), *to collect, assemble*

ASSEMBLED
622 'âçaph (4), *to gather, collect*
662 'âphaq (1), *to abstain*
1413 gâdad (1), *to gash, slash oneself*
2199 zâ'aq (1), *to call out, convene publicly*
3259 yâ'ad (3), *to meet; to summon; to direct*
6633 tsâbâ' (1), *to mass an army or servants*
6638 tsâbâh (1), *to array an army against*
6908 qâbats (1), *to collect, assemble*

English

ASSEMBLIES
6950 qâhal (11), to
convoke, gather
7284 rᵉgash (Ch.) (3), to
gather tumultuously
1096 ginŏmai (1), to be,
become
4863 sunagō (6), to
gather together
4871 sunalizō (1), to
accumulate
4905 sunĕrchŏmai (1), to
gather together

ASSEMBLIES
627 'ăçuppâh (1),
collection of sayings
4150 môw'êd (1),
assembly, congregation
4744 miqrâ' (2), public
meeting
5712 'êdâh (1),
assemblage; family
6116 'ătsârâh (1),
assembly

ASSEMBLING
6633 tsâbâ' (1), to mass
an army or servants
1997 ĕpisunagōgē (1),
meeting, gathering

ASSEMBLY
4150 môw'êd (3),
assembly, congregation
4186 môwshâb (1), seat;
site; abode
5475 çôwd (5), intimacy;
consultation; secret
5712 'êdâh (8),
assemblage; family
6116 'ătsârâh (9),
assembly
6951 qâhâl (17),
assemblage
6952 qᵉhillâh (1),
assemblage
1577 ĕkklēsia (3),
congregation
3831 panēguris (1),
mass-meeting
4864 sunagōgē (1),
assemblage

ASSENT
6310 peh (1), mouth;
opening

ASSENTED
4934 suntithĕmai (1), to
place jointly

ASSES
860 'âthôwn (17), female
donkey, ass
2543 chămôwr (40), male
donkey or ass
5895 'ayîr (2), young
robust donkey or ass
6167 'ărâd (Ch.) (1),
onager or wild donkey
6501 pere' (4), onager,
wild donkey

ASSHUR
804 'Ashshûwr (8),
successful

ASSHURIM
805 'Ăshûwrîy (1),
Ashurite

ASSIGNED
5414 nâthan (2), to give

ASSIR
617 'Aççîyr (5), prisoner

ASSIST
3936 paristēmi (1), to
stand beside, present

ASSOCIATE
7489 râ'a' (1), to break to
pieces; to make

ASSOS
789 Assŏs (2), Assus

ASSUR
804 'Ashshûwr (2),
successful

ASSURANCE
539 'âman (1), to be firm,
faithful, true; to trust
983 beṭach (1), safety,
security, trust
4102 pistis (1),
faithfulness; faith, belief
4136 plērŏphŏria (4), full
assurance

ASSURE
3983 pĕinaō (1), to
famish; to crave

ASSURED
571 'emeth (1), certainty,
truth, trustworthiness
6966 qûwm (Ch.) (1), to
rise
4104 pistŏō (1), to assure

ASSUREDLY
571 'emeth (1), certainty,
truth, trustworthiness
3045 yâda' (1), to know
3318 yâtsâ' (1), to go,
bring out
3588 kîy (3), for, that
because
8354 shâthâh (1), to
drink, imbibe
806 asphalōs (1), securely
4822 sumbibazō (1), to
unite; to infer, show

ASSWAGE
2820 châsak (1), to
refuse, spare, preserve

ASSWAGED
2820 châsak (1), to
refuse, spare, preserve
7918 shâkak (1), to lay a
trap; to allay

ASSYRIA
804 'Ashshûwr (118),
successful

ASSYRIAN
804 'Ashshûwr (13),
successful

ASSYRIANS
804 'Ashshûwr (10),
successful

ASTAROTH
6252 Ashtârôwth (1),
increases

ASTONIED
1724 dâham (1), to be
astounded
7672 shᵉbash (Ch.) (1), to
perplex, be baffled
8074 shâmêm (6), to
devastate; to stupefy
8075 shᵉmam (Ch.) (1), to
devastate; to stupefy
8429 tᵉvahh (Ch.) (1), to
amaze, take alarm

ASTONISHED
8074 shâmêm (14), to
devastate; to stupefy
8539 tâmahh (1), to be
astounded
1605 ĕkplēssō (10), to
astonish
1839 ĕxistēmi (6), to
become astounded
2284 thambĕō (2), to
astound, be amazed
4023+2285 pĕriĕchō (1),
to clasp; to encircle

ASTONISHMENT
8047 shammâh (14),
ruin; consternation
8074 shâmêm (1), to
devastate; to stupefy
8078 shimmâmôwn (2),
stupefaction, despair
8541 timmâhôwn (2),
consternation, panic
8653 tar'êlâh (1), reeling,
staggering
1611 ĕkstasis (1),
bewilderment, ecstasy,
astonishment

ASTRAY
5080 nâdach (1), to push
off, scattered
7683 shâgag (1), to stray
7686 shâgâh (2), to stray
8582 tâ'âh (13), to
vacillate, stray
4105 planaō (5), to roam,
wander from safety

ASTROLOGER
826 'ashshâph (Ch.) (1),
conjurer, enchanter

ASTROLOGERS
825 'ashshâph (2),
conjurer, enchanter
826 'ashshâph (Ch.) (5),
conjurer, enchanter
1895+8064 hâbar (1), to
be a horoscopist

ASUNDER
996 bêyn (1), between
673 apŏchōrizō (1), to
rend apart; to separate
1288 diaspaō (1), to sever
or dismember
1371 dichŏtŏmĕō (1), to
flog severely
2997 laschō (1), to crack
open
4249 prizō (1), to saw in
two
5563 chōrizō (2), to place
room between

ASUPPIM
624 'âçûph (2), stores of
goods

ASYNCRITUS
799 Asugkritŏs (1),
incomparable

ATAD
329 'âṭâd (2), buckthorn
tree

ATARAH
5851 'Ăṭârâh (1), crown

ATAROTH
5852 'Ăṭârôwth (5),
crowns

ATAROTH-ADAR
5853 'Aṭrôwth 'Addâr
(1), crowns of Addar

ATAROTH-ADDAR
5853 'Aṭrôwth 'Addâr
(1), crowns of Addar

ATE
398 'âkal (2), to eat
2719 katĕsthiō (1), to
devour

ATER
333 'Âṭêr (5), maimed

ATHACH
6269 'Ăthâk (1), lodging

ATHAIAH
6265 'Ăthâyâh (1),
Jehovah has helped

ATHALIAH
6271 'Ăthalyâh (17),
Jehovah has
constrained

ATHENIANS
117 Athēnaiŏs (1),
inhabitant of Athenæ

ATHENS
116 Athēnai (6), city
Athenæ
117 Athēnaiŏs (1),
inhabitant of Athenæ

ATHIRST
6770 tsâmê' (2), to thirst
1372 dipsaō (3), to thirst
for

ATHLAI
6270 'Athlay (1),
compressed

ATONEMENT
3722 kâphar (73), to
cover; to expiate
3725 kippûr (7),
expiation
2643 katallagē (1),
restoration

ATONEMENTS
3725 kippûr (1),
expiation

ATROTH
5855 'Aṭrôwth
Shôwphân (1), crowns
of Shophan

ATTAI
6262 'Attay (4), timely

ATTAIN
3201 yâkôl (1), to be able
5381 nâsag (1), to reach
7069 qânâh (1), to create;
to procure
2658 katantaō (2), to
attain or reach

ATTAINED
935 bôw' (4), to go or
come
5381 nâsag (1), to reach
2638 katalambanō (1), to
seize; to possess
2983 lambanō (1), to
take, receive
3877 parakŏlŏuthĕō (1),
to attend; trace out
5348 phthanō (2), to
anticipate or precede

ATTALIA
825 Attalĕia (1), Attaleia

ATTEND
6440 pânîym (1), *face; front*
7181 qâshab (9), to *prick up* the ears
2145 ĕuprŏsĕdrŏs (1), *diligent service*

ATTENDANCE
4612 ma'ămâd (2), *position; attendant*
4337 prŏsĕchō (2), to *pay attention to*

ATTENDED
995 bîyn (1), to *understand; discern*
7181 qâshab (1), to *prick up* the ears
4337 prŏsĕchō (1), to *pay attention to*

ATTENDING
4343 prŏskartĕrĕsis (1), *persistency*

ATTENT
7183 qashshâb (2), *hearkening*

ATTENTIVE
7183 qashshâb (3), *hearkening*
1582 ĕkkrĕmamai (1), to *listen closely*

ATTENTIVELY
8085 shâma' (1), to *hear intelligently*

ATTIRE
2871 tâbûwl (1), *turban*
7196 qishshûr (1), *girdle or sash* for women
7897 shîyth (1), *garment*

ATTIRED
6801 tsânaph (1), to *wrap*, i.e. *roll or dress*

AUDIENCE
241 'ôzen (7), *ear*
189 akŏē (1), *hearing; thing heard*
191 akŏuō (4), to *hear; obey*

AUGMENT
5595 çâphâh (1), to *scrape*; to *accumulate*

AUGUSTUS
828 Augŏustŏs (3), *revered one*

AUGUSTUS'
828 Augŏustŏs (1), *revered one*

AUL
4836 martsêa' (2), *awl for piercing*

AUNT
1733 dôwdâh (1), *aunt*

AUSTERE
840 austĕrŏs (2), *severe, harsh; exacting*

AUTHOR
159 aitiŏs (1), *causer*
747 archēgŏs (1), *chief leader; founder*

AUTHORITIES
1849 ĕxŏusia (1), *authority, power, right*

AUTHORITY
7235 râbâh (1), to *increase*
8633 tôqeph (1), *might*
831 authĕntĕō (1), to *have authority*
1413 dunastēs (1), *ruler or officer*
1849 ĕxŏusia (28), *authority, power, right*
1850 ĕxŏusiazō (1), to *control, master another*
2003 ĕpitagē (1), *injunction or decree*
2715 katĕxŏusiazō (2), to *wield full privilege over*
5247 hupĕrŏchē (1), *superiority*

AVA
5755 'Ivvâh (1), *overthrow, ruin*

AVAILETH
7737 shâvâh (1), to *level; to resemble; to adjust*
2480 ischuō (3), to *have or exercise force*

AVEN
206 'Âven (3), *idolatry*

AVENGE
5358 nâqam (8), to *avenge or punish*
5358+5360 nâqam (1), to *avenge or punish*
5414+5360 nâthan (1), to *give*
6485 pâqad (1), to *visit, care for, count*
1556 ĕkdikĕō (4), to *vindicate; retaliate*
4160+3588+1557 pŏiĕō (2), to *make or do*

AVENGED
3467 yâsha' (1), to *make safe, free*
5358 nâqam (9), to *avenge or punish*
5414+5360 nâthan (1), to *give*
8199 shâphaṭ (2), to *judge*
1556 ĕkdikĕō (1), to *vindicate; retaliate*
2919+3588+2917 krinō (1), to *decide; to try*

AVENGER
1350 gâ'al (6), to *redeem; to be the next of kin*
5358 nâqam (2), to *avenge or punish*
1558 ĕkdikŏs (1), *punisher, avenger*

AVENGETH
5414+5360 nâthan (2), to *give*

AVENGING
3467 yâsha' (2), to *make safe, free*
6544+6546 pâra' (1), to *absolve, begin*

AVERSE
7725 shûwb (1), to *turn back; to return*

AVIM
5761 'Avvîym (1), *Avvim*

AVIMS
5757 'Avvîy (1), *Avvite*

AVITES
5757 'Avvîy (2), *Avvite*

AVITH
5762 'Ăvîyth (2), *ruin*

AVOID
6544 pâra' (1), to *loosen; to expose, dismiss*
1223 dia (1), *through, by means of; because of*
1578 ĕkklinō (1), to *shun; to decline*
3868 paraitĕŏmai (1), to *deprecate, decline*
4026 pĕriistēmi (1), to *stand around; to avoid*

AVOIDED
5437 çâbab (1), to *surround*

AVOIDING
1624 ĕktrĕpō (1), to *turn away*
4724 stĕllō (1), to *repress, abstain* from

AVOUCHED
559 'âmar (2), to *say, speak*

AWAIT
1917 ĕpibŏulē (1), *plot, plan*

AWAKE
5782 'ûwr (20), to *awake*
6974 qûwts (11), to *awake*
1235 diagrēgŏrĕō (1), to *waken thoroughly*
1326 diĕgĕirō (1), to *arouse, stimulate*
1453 ĕgĕirō (2), to *waken*, i.e. *rouse*
1594 ĕknēphō (1), to *rouse* (oneself) *out*
1852 ĕxupnizō (1), to *waken, rouse*

AWAKED
3364 yâqats (4), to *awake*
6974 qûwts (4), to *awake*

AWAKEST
5782 'ûwr (1), to *awake*
6974 qûwts (1), to *awake*

AWAKETH
6974 qûwts (3), to *awake*

AWAKING
1096+1853 ginŏmai (1), to *be, become*

AWARE
3045 yâda' (2), to *know*
1097 ginōskō (2), to *know*
1492 ĕidō (1), to *know*

AWAY
310 'achar (1), *after*
1197 bâ'ar (16), to *be brutish, be senseless*
1272 bârach (1), to *flee suddenly*
1473 gôwlâh (7), *exile; captive*
1497 gâzal (4), to *rob*
1540 gâlâh (17), to *denude; uncover*
1541 gᵉlâh (Ch.) (1), to *reveal mysteries*
1546 gâlûwth (4), *captivity; exiles*
1589 gânab (1), to *thieve; to deceive*
1639 gâra' (1), to *shave, remove, lessen*
1870 derek (1), *road; course of life*
1898 hâgâh (2), to *remove, expel*
1920 hâdaph (1), to *push away or down; drive out*
2219 zârâh (1), to *toss about; to diffuse*
2763 charam (1), to *devote to destruction*
2846 châthâh (1), to *lay hold of; to take away*
2862 châthaph (1), to *clutch, snatch*
3212 yâlak (4), to *walk; to live; to carry*
3318 yâtsâ' (4), to *go, bring out*
3988 mâ'aç (1), to *spurn; to disappear*
4422 mâlaṭ (1), to *escape as if by slipperiness*
5074 nâdad (1), to *rove, flee; to drive away*
5077 nâdâh (1), to *exclude*, i.e. *banish*
5111 nûwd (Ch.) (1), to *flee*
5186 nâṭâh (1), to *stretch or spread out*
5265 nâça' (3), *start on a journey*
5493 çûwr (70), to *turn off*
5496 çûwth (1), to *stimulate; to seduce*
5674 'âbar (7), to *cross over; to transition*
5709 'ădâ' (Ch.) (3), to *remove; to bedeck*
5710 'âdâh (1), to *pass on or continue; to remove*
7311 rûwm (2), to *be high; to rise or raise*
7368 râchaq (3), to *recede; remove*
7617 shâbâh (7), to *transport into captivity*
7628 shᵉbîy (1), *exile; booty*
7673 shâbath (1), to *repose; to desist* from
7726 shôwbâb (1), *apostate*, i.e. *idolatrous*
7953 shâlâh (1), to *draw out or off*, i.e. *remove*
115 athĕtēsis (1), *cancellation*
142 airō (12), to *lift, to take up*
337 anairĕō (1), to *take away*, i.e. *abolish*
343 anakaluptō (1), to *unveil*
520 apagō (12), to *take away*
522 apairō (1), to *remove, take away*
565 apĕrchŏmai (15), to *go off*, i.e. *depart*
577 apŏballō (2), to *throw off*; fig. to *lose*
580 apŏbŏlē (1), *rejection, loss*
595 apŏthĕsis (1), *laying aside*
617 apŏkuliō (3), to *roll away, roll back*

English

628 apŏlŏuō (1), to *wash fully*
630 apŏluō (27), to *relieve, release*
645 apŏspaō (1), to *withdraw* with force
646 apŏstasia (1), *defection* from truth
649 apŏstĕllō (4), to *send out* on a mission
654 apŏstrĕphō (6), to *turn away* or *back*
657 apŏtassŏmai (1), to *say adieu*; to *renounce*
659 apŏtithēmi (1), to *put away*; get *rid of*
665 apŏtrĕpō (1), to *deflect, avoid*
667 apŏhĕrō (3), to *bear off, carry away*
683 apŏthĕŏmai (4), to *push off*; to *reject*
726 harpazō (2), to *seize*
851 aphairĕō (8), to *remove, cut off*
863 aphiēmi (4), to *leave*; to *pardon, forgive*
868 aphistēmi (2), *instigate* to revolt
1294 diastrĕphō (1), to *distort*
1544 ĕkballō (1), to *throw out*
1593 ĕknĕuō (1), to *quietly withdraw*
1599 ĕkpĕmpō (1), to *despatch, send out*
1601 ĕkpiptō (1), to *drop away*
1602 ĕkplĕō (1), to *depart* by ship
1808 ĕxairō (1), to *remove, drive away*
1813 ĕxalĕiphō (2), to *obliterate*
1821 ĕxapŏstĕllō (4), to *despatch*, or to *dismiss*
1831 ĕxĕrchŏmai (1), to *issue*; to *leave*
1854 ĕxō (1), *out, outside*
2210 zēmiŏō (1), to *experience detriment*
2673 katargĕō (6), to *be, render entirely useless*
3179 mĕthistēmi (1), to *move*
3334 mĕtakinĕō (1), to *be removed, shifted from*
3350 mĕtŏikĕsia (3), *expatriation, exile*
3351 mĕtŏikizō (1), to *transfer* as a *settler* or *captive*
3895 parapiptō (1), to *apostatize, fall away*
3911 paraphĕrō (1), to *carry off*; to *avert*
3928 parĕrchŏmai (5), to *go by*; to *perish*
4014 pĕriairĕō (3), to *cast off* anchor; to *expiate*
4879 sunapagō (2), to *take off together*
5217 hupagō (3), to *withdraw* or *retire*

AWE
1481 gûwr (1), to *sojourn, live as an alien*

6342 pâchad (1), to *be startled*; to *fear*
7264 râgaz (1), to *quiver*

AWOKE
3364 yâqats (6), to *awake*
1326 diĕgĕirō (1), to *arouse, stimulate*
1453 ĕgĕirō (1), to *waken*, i.e. *rouse*

AX
1270 barzel (1), *iron; iron implement*
1631 garzen (2), *axe*
4601 Ma'ăkâh (1), *depression*
4621 ma'ătsâd (1), *axe*
7134 qardôm (1), *axe*
513 axinē (1), *axe*

AXE
1631 garzen (2), *axe*
7134 qardôm (1), *axe*
513 axinē (1), *axe*

AXES
2719 chereb (1), *knife, sword*
3781 kashshîyl (1), *axe*
4037 magzêrâh (1), *cutting blade, ax*
4050 mᵉgêrâh (1), *stone cutting saw*
7134 qardôm (3), *axe*

AXLETREES
3027 yâd (2), *hand; power*

AZAL
682 'Âtsêl (1), *noble*

AZALIAH
683 'Ătsalyâhûw (2), *Jehovah has reserved*

AZANIAH
245 'Ăzanyâh (1), *heard by Jehovah*

AZARAEL
5832 'Äzar'êl (1), *God has helped*

AZAREEL
5832 'Äzar'êl (5), *God has helped*

AZARIAH
5838 'Äzaryâh (47), *Jehovah has helped*
5839 'Äzaryâh (Ch.) (1), *Jehovah has helped*

AZAZ
5811 'Âzâz (1), *strong*

AZAZIAH
5812 'Äzazyâhûw (3), *Jehovah has strengthened*

AZBUK
5802 'Azbûwq (1), *stern depopulator*

AZEKAH
5825 'Äzêqâh (7), *tilled*

AZEL
682 'Âtsêl (6), *noble*

AZEM
6107 'Etsem (2), *bone*

AZGAD
5803 'Azgâd (4), *stern troop*

AZIEL
5815 'Äzîy'êl (1), *strengthened of God*

AZIZA
5819 'Äzîyzâ' (1), *strengthfulness*

AZMAVETH
5820 'Azmâveth (8), *strong* (one) *of death*

AZMON
6111 'Atsmôwn (3), *bone-like*

AZNOTH-TABOR
243 'Aznôwth Tâbôwr (1), *flats of Tabor*

AZOR
107 Azōr (2), *helpful*

AZOTUS
108 Azōtŏs (1), *Azotus*, i.e. *Ashdod*

AZRIEL
5837 'Azrîy'êl (3), *help of God*

AZRIKAM
5840 'Azrîyqâm (6), *help of an enemy*

AZUBAH
5806 'Äzûwbâh (4), *forsaking*

AZUR
5809 'Azzûwr (2), *helpful*

AZZAH
5804 'Azzâh (3), *strong*

AZZAN
5821 'Azzân (1), *strong one*

AZZUR
5809 'Azzûwr (1), *helpful*

BAAL
1168 Ba'al (61), *master*
896 Baal (1), *master*

BAAL'S
1168 Ba'al (1), *master*

BAAL-BERITH
1170 Ba'al Bᵉrîyth (2), *Baal of* (the) *covenant*

BAAL-GAD
1171 Ba'al Gâd (3), *Baal of Fortune*

BAAL-HAMON
1174 Ba'al Hâmôwn (1), *possessor of a multitude*

BAAL-HANAN
1177 Ba'al Chânân (5), *possessor of grace*

BAAL-HAZOR
1178 Ba'al Châtsôwr (1), *possessor of a village*

BAAL-HERMON
1179 Ba'al Chermôwn (2), *possessor of Hermon*

BAAL-MEON
1186 Ba'al Mᵉ'ôwn (3), *Baal of* (the) *habitation*

BAAL-PEOR
1187 Ba'al Pᵉ'ôwr (6), *Baal of Peor*

BAAL-PERAZIM
1188 Ba'al Pᵉ'râtsîym (4), *possessor of breaches*

BAAL-SHALISHA
1190 Ba'al Shâlîshâh (1), *Baal of Shalishah*

BAAL-TAMAR
1193 Ba'al Tâmâr (1), *possessor of* (the) *palm-tree*

BAAL-ZEBUB
1176 Ba'al Zᵉbûwb (4), *Baal of* (the) *Fly*

BAAL-ZEPHON
1189 Ba'al Tsᵉphôwn (3), *Baal of winter*

BAALAH
1173 Ba'ălâh (5), *mistress*

BAALATH
1191 Ba'ălâth (3), office of *mistress*

BAALATH-BEER
1192 Ba'ălath Bᵉ'êr (1), *mistress of a well*

BAALE
1184 Ba'ălêy Yᵉhûwdâh (1), *masters of Judah*

BAALI
1180 Ba'ălîy (1), *my master*

BAALIM
1168 Ba'al (18), *master*

BAALIS
1185 Ba'ălîç (1), *in exultation*

BAANA
1195 Ba'ănâ' (2), *in affliction*

BAANAH
1195 Ba'ănâ' (10), *in affliction*

BAARA
1199 Bâ'ărâ' (1), *brutish*

BAASEIAH
1202 Ba'ăsêyâh (1), *in* (the) *work of Jehovah*

BAASHA
1201 Ba'shâ' (28), *offensiveness*

BABBLER
1167+3956 ba'al (1), *master; husband*
4691 spĕrmŏlŏgŏs (1), *gossip* or *trifler* in talk

BABBLING
7879 sîyach (1), *uttered contemplation*

BABBLINGS
2757 kĕnŏphōnia (2), *fruitless discussion*

BABE
5288 na'ar (1), *male child; servant*
1025 brĕphŏs (4), *infant*
3516 nēpiŏs (3), *infant; simple-minded* person

BABEL
894 Bâbel (2), *confusion*

BABES
5768 'ôwlêl (2), *suckling child*
8586 ta'ălûwl (1), *caprice* (as a fit *coming on*)
1025 brĕphŏs (1), *infant*

3516 nēpĭŏs (5), *infant;*
simple-minded person
BABYLON
894 Bâbel (247),
confusion
895 Bâbel (Ch.) (25),
confusion
897 Babulōn (12),
Babylon
BABYLON'S
894 Bâbel (8), *confusion*
BABYLONIANS
896 Bablîy (Ch.) (1),
Babylonian
1121+894 bên (3), *people*
of a class or kind
BABYLONISH
8152 Shin'âr (1), *Shinar*
BACA
1056 Bâkâ' (1), *Baca*
BACHRITES
1076 Bakrîy (1), *Bakrite*
BACK
268 'âchôwr (16), *behind,*
backward; west
310 'achar (1), *after*
322 'âchôrannîyth (1),
backwardly, by turning
1354 gab (1), *mounded*
or rounded: top or rim
1355 gab (Ch.) (1), *back*
1458 gav (7), *back*
1639 gâra' (1), *to shave,*
remove, lessen
1973 hâl°âh (1), *far*
away; thus far
2015 hâphak (2), *to turn*
about or over
2820 châsak (4), *to*
restrain or refrain
3607 kâlâ' (1), *to hold*
back or in; to prohibit
4185 mûwsh (1), *to*
withdraw
4513 mâna' (4), *to deny,*
refuse
5253 nâçag (1), *to retreat*
5437 çâbab (1), *to*
surround
5472 çûwg (3), *to go*
back, to retreat
5493 çûwr (2), *to turn off*
5637 çârar (1), *to be*
refractory, stubborn
6203 'ôreph (4), *nape or*
back of the neck
6437 pânâh (6), *to turn,*
to face
6544 pâra' (1), *to loosen;*
to expose, dismiss
7725 shûwb (70), *to turn*
back; to return
7926 sh°kem (2), *neck;*
spur of a hill
617 apŏkuliō (2), *to roll*
away, roll back
650 apŏstĕrĕō (1), *to*
deprive; to despoil
3557 nŏsphizŏmai (2), *to*
sequestrate
3577 nōtŏs (1), *back*
3694 ŏpisō (5), *behind,*
after, following
4762 strĕphō (1), *to turn*
quite around or reverse
5288 hupŏstĕllō (2), *to*
cower or shrink

5289 hupŏstŏlē (1),
shrinkage, timidity
5290 hupŏstrĕphō (3), *to*
turn under, behind
BACKBITERS
2637 katalalŏs (1),
slanderer
BACKBITETH
7270 râgal (1), *to*
reconnoiter; to slander
BACKBITING
5643 çêther (1), *cover,*
shelter
BACKBITINGS
2636 katalalia (1),
defamation, slander
BACKBONE
6096 'âtseh (1), *spine*
BACKS
268 'âchôwr (1), *behind,*
backward; west
1354 gab (1), *mounded*
or rounded: top or rim
1458 gav (1), *back*
6203 'ôreph (4), *nape of*
the neck
BACKSIDE
268 'âchôwr (1), *behind,*
backward; west
310 'achar (1), *after*
3693 ŏpisthĕn (1), *at the*
back; after
BACKSLIDER
5472 çûwg (1), *to go*
back, to apostatize
BACKSLIDING
4878 m°shûwbâh (7),
apostasy
5637 çârar (1), *to be*
refractory, stubborn
7726 shôwbâb (2),
apostate, i.e. idolatrous
7728 shôwbêb (2),
apostate, heathenish
BACKSLIDINGS
4878 m°shûwbâh (4),
apostasy
BACKWARD
268 'âchôwr (11), *behind,*
backward; west
322 'âchôrannîyth (6),
backwardly, by turning
1519+3588+3694 ĕis (1),
to or into
BAD
873 bi'ûwsh (Ch.) (1),
wicked, evil
7451 ra' (13), *bad; evil*
2556 kakŏs (1), *bad, evil*
4190 pŏnĕrŏs (1), *malice,*
wicked, bad; crime
4550 saprŏs (1), *rotten,*
i.e. worthless
BADE
559 'âmar (6), *to say,*
speak
1696 dâbar (1), *to speak,*
say; to subdue
6680 tsâvâh (3), *to*
constitute, enjoin
657 apŏtassŏmai (1), *to*
say adieu; to renounce
2036 ĕpō (3), *to speak*
2564 kalĕō (4), *to call*

BADEST
1696 dâbar (1), *to speak,*
say; to subdue
BADGERS'
8476 tachash (14), (poss.)
antelope
BADNESS
7455 rôa' (1), *badness*
BAG
3599 kîyç (4), *cup;* utility
bag
3627 k°lîy (2),
implement, thing
6872 ts°rôwr (3), *parcel;*
kernel or particle
1101 glōssŏkŏmŏn (2),
money purse
BAGS
2754 chârîyṭ (1), *pocket*
6696 tsûwr (1), *to cramp,*
i.e. confine; to harass
905 balantiŏn (1), *money*
pouch
BAHARUMITE
978 Bachărûwmîy (1),
Bacharumite
BAHURIM
980 Bachûrîym (5),
young men
BAJITH
1006 Bayith (1), *house;*
temple; family, tribe
BAKBAKKAR
1230 Baqbaqqar (1),
searcher
BAKBUK
1227 Baqbûwq (2), *bottle*
BAKBUKIAH
1229 Baqbuqyâh (3),
wasting of Jehovah
BAKE
644 'âphâh (6), *to bake*
1310 bâshal (1), *to boil*
up, cook; to ripen
5746 'ûwg (1), *to bake*
BAKED
644 'âphâh (2), *to bake*
1310 bâshal (1), *to boil*
up, cook; to ripen
BAKEMEATS
3978+4639+644 ma'ăkâl
(1), *food*
BAKEN
644 'âphâh (4), *to bake*
7246 râbak (1), *to soak*
bread in oil
8601 tûphîyn (1), *baked*
cake
BAKER
644 'âphâh (8), *to bake*
BAKERS
644 'âphâh (2), *to bake*
BAKERS'
644 'âphâh (1), *to bake*
BAKETH
644 'âphâh (1), *to bake*
BALAAM
1109 Bil'âm (57),
foreigner
903 Balaam (3), *foreigner*
BALAAM'S
1109 Bil'âm (3), *foreigner*

BALAC
904 Balak (1), *waster*
BALADAN
1081 Bal'ădân (2), *Bel* (is
his) *lord*
BALAH
1088 Bâlâh (1), *failure*
BALAK
1111 Bâlâq (42), *waster*
BALAK'S
1111 Bâlâq (1), *waster*
BALANCE
3976 mô'zên (7), *pair of*
balance scales
7070 qâneh (1), *reed*
BALANCES
3976 mô'zên (8), *pair of*
balance scales
3977 mô'zên (Ch.) (1),
pair of balance scales
BALANCINGS
4657 miphlâs (1), *poising*
BALD
1371 gibbêach (1), *bald*
forehead
1372 gabbachath (3),
baldness on forehead
5556 çol'âm (1),
destructive locust kind
7139 qârach (4), *to*
depilate, shave
7142 qêrêach (3), *bald*
on the back of the head
7144 qorchâh (1),
baldness
7146 qârachath (1), *bald*
spot; threadbare spot
BALDNESS
7144 qorchâh (9),
baldness
BALL
1754 dûwr (1), *circle; ball*
BALM
6875 ts°rîy (6), *balsam*
BAMAH
1117 Bâmâh (1),
elevation, high place
BAMOTH
1120 Bâmôwth (2),
heights
BAMOTH-BAAL
1120 Bâmôwth (1),
heights of Baal
BAND
613 'ĕçûwr (Ch.) (2),
manacles, chains
1416 g°dûwd (5), *band* of
soldiers
2428 chayil (2), *army;*
wealth; virtue; valor
5688 'ăbôth (1), *entwined*
things: a string, wreath
8193 sâphâh (1), *lip,*
language, speech
4686 spĕira (7), *tenth of a*
Roman Legion
BANDED
4160+4963 pŏiĕō (1), *to*
make or do
BANDS
102 'aggâph (7), *crowds*
of troops

English

BANI

612 'êçûwr (2), *manacles, chains*
631 'âçar (1), to *fasten*; to *join* battle
1416 gᵉdûwd (8), *band* of soldiers
2256 chebel (3), *company, band*
2683 chêtsen (1), *bosom*
2784 chartsubbâh (2), *fetter; pain*
4133 môwṭâh (2), *pole; ox-bow; yoke*
4147 môwçêr (6), *halter; restraint*
4189 môwshᵉkâh (1), *cord, band*
4264 machǎneh (2), *encampment*
5688 'ǎbôth (3), *entwined* things: a *string, wreath*
7218 rô'sh (2), *head*
1199 dĕsmŏn (3), *shackle; impediment*
2202 zĕuktĕria (1), *tiller-rope, band*
4886 sundĕsmŏs (1), *ligament; control*

BANI
1137 Bânîy (15), *built*

BANISHED
5080 nâdach (2), to *push off, scattered*

BANISHMENT
4065 maddûwach (1), *seduction, misleading*
8331 sharshâh (1), *chain*

BANK
5550 çôlᵉlâh (3), siege mound, i.e. *rampart*
8193 sâphâh (10), *lip; edge, margin*
5132 trapĕza (1), *table or stool*

BANKS
1415 gâdâh (3), *border, bank* of a river
1428 gidyâh (1), *border, bank* of a river

BANNER
1714 degel (1), *flag, standard, banner*
5251 nêç (2), *flag; signal; token*

BANNERS
1713 dâgal (3), to *be conspicuous*

BANQUET
3738 kârâh (1), to *dig*; to *plot*; to *bore, hew*
4797 mirzach (1), *cry of joy; revel or feast*
4960 mishteh (10), *drink; banquet or feast*
4961 mishteh (Ch.) (1), *drink; banquet or feast*
8354 shâthâh (1), to *drink, imbibe*

BANQUETING
3196 yayin (1), *wine; intoxication*

BANQUETINGS
4224 pŏtŏs (1), *drinking-bout*

BAPTISM
908 baptisma (22), *baptism*

BAPTISMS
909 baptismŏs (1), *baptism*

BAPTIST
907 baptizō (1), *baptize*
910 Baptistēs (13), *baptizer*

BAPTIST'S
910 Baptistēs (1), *baptizer*

BAPTIZE
907 baptizō (9), *baptize*

BAPTIZED
907 baptizō (57), *baptize*

BAPTIZEST
907 baptizō (1), *baptize*

BAPTIZETH
907 baptizō (2), *baptize*

BAPTIZING
907 baptizō (4), *baptize*

BAR
270 'âchaz (1), to *seize, grasp; possess*
1280 bᵉrîyach (4), *bolt; cross-bar* of a door
4132 môwṭ (2), *pole; yoke*

BAR-JESUS
919 Bariēsŏus (1), *son of Joshua*

BAR-JONA
920 Bariōnas (1), *son of Jonah*

BARABBAS
912 Barabbas (11), *son of Abba*

BARACHEL
1292 Bârak'êl (2), *God has blessed*

BARACHIAS
914 Barachias (1), *blessing of Jehovah*

BARAK
1301 Bârâq (13), *(flash of) lightning*
913 Barak (1), *(flash of) lightning*

BARBARIAN
915 barbarŏs (3), *foreigner, non-Greek*

BARBARIANS
915 barbarŏs (2), *foreigner, non-Greek*

BARBAROUS
915 barbarŏs (1), *foreigner, non-Greek*

BARBED
7905 sukkâh (1), *dart, harpoon*

BARBER'S
1532 gallâb (1), *barber*

BARE
2029 hârâh (1), to *conceive, be pregnant*
2308 châdal (1), to *desist, stop; be fat*
2342 chûwl (1), to *dance, whirl; to writhe* in pain
2554 châmaç (1), to *be violent; to maltreat*

BASE
2834 châsaph (4), to *drain* away or *bail* up
3205 yâlad (110), to *bear young*; to *father a child*
4910 mâshal (1), to *rule*
5190 nâṭal (1), to *lift*; to *impose*
5375 nâsâ' (34), to *lift up*
6181 'eryâh (4), *nudity*
6209 'ârar (1), to *bare*; to *demolish*
6544 pâra' (1), to *loosen*; to *expose, dismiss*
7146 qârachath (1), *bald* spot; *threadbare* spot
7287 râdâh (2), to *subjugate*; to *crumble*
7980 shâlaṭ (1), to *dominate*, i.e. to *govern*
399 anaphĕrō (1), to *take up*; to *lead up*
941 bastazō (4), to *lift, bear*
1080 gĕnnaō (1), to *procreate, regenerate*
1131 gumnŏs (1), *nude* or *not well clothed*
3140 marturĕō (9), to *testify; to commend*
4160 pŏiĕō (2), to *make or do*
5342 phĕrō (1), to *bear or carry*
5576 psĕudŏmarturĕō (2), to *offer false evidence*

BAREFOOT
3182 yâchêph (4), *not wearing sandals*

BAREST
4910 mâshal (1), to *rule*
5375 nâsâ' (1), to *lift up*
3140 marturĕō (1), to *testify; to commend*

BARHUMITE
1273 Barchûmîy (1), *Barchumite*

BARIAH
1282 Bârîyach (1), *Bariach*

BARK
5024 nâbach (1), to *bark*

BARKED
7111 qᵉtsâphâh (1), *fragment*

BARKOS
1302 Barqôwç (2), *Barkos*

BARLEY
8184 sᵉ'ôrâh (33), *barley*
2915 krithē (1), *barley*
2916 krithinŏs (2), *consisting of barley*

BARN
1637 gôren (1), *open area*
4035 mᵉgûwrâh (1), *fright; granary*
596 apŏthēkē (2), *granary, grain barn*

BARNABAS
921 Barnabas (29), *son of prophecy*

BARNFLOOR
1637 gôren (1), *open area*

BARNS
618 'âçâm (1), *barn*

BARREL
3537 kad (3), *jar, pitcher*

BARRELS
3537 kad (1), *jar, pitcher*

BARREN
4420 mᵉlêchâh (1), *salted land*, i.e. a *desert*
6115 'ôtser (1), *closure; constraint*
6135 'âqâr (11), *sterile, barren*
6723 tsîyâh (1), *arid desert*
7909 shakkuwl (2), *bereaved*
7921 shâkôl (2), to *miscarry*
692 argŏs (1), *lazy; useless*
4722 stĕgō (4), to *endure patiently*

BARRENNESS
4420 mᵉlêchâh (1), *salted land*, i.e. a *desert*

BARS
905 bad (1), *limb, member; bar; chief*
1280 bᵉrîyach (35), *bolt; cross-bar* of a door
4800 merchâb (1), *open space; liberty*

BARSABAS
923 Barsabas (2), *son of Sabas*

BARTHOLOMEW
918 Barthŏlŏmaiŏs (4), *son of Tolmai*

BARTIMAEUS
924 Bartimaiŏs (1), *son of the unclean*

BARUCH
1263 Bârûwk (26), *blessed*

BARZILLAI
1271 Barzillay (12), *iron-hearted*

BASE
1097+8034 bᵉlîy (1), *without, not yet*
3653 kên (2), *pedestal or station* of a basin
4350 mᵉkôwnâh (7), *pedestal; spot or place*
4369 mᵉkûnâh (1), *spot*
7034 qâlâh (1), to *be light*
8217 shâphâl (2), *depressed, low*
36 agĕnēs (1), *ignoble, lowly*
5011 tapĕinŏs (1), *humiliated, lowly*

BASER
60 agŏraiŏs (1), *people of the market place*

BASES
4350 mᵉkôwnâh (13), *pedestal; spot or place*
4369 mᵉkûnâh (1), *spot*

BASEST
8215 sh⁰phal (Ch.) (1),
low
8217 shâphâl (1),
depressed, low

BASHAN
1316 Bâshân (59), Bashan

BASHAN-HAVOTH-JAIR
1316+2334 Bâshân (1),
Bashan

BASHEMATH
1315 Bosmath (6),
fragrance

BASKET
1731 dûwd (2), pot,
kettle; basket
2935 ţene' (4), basket
3619 k⁰lûwb (2),
bird-trap; basket
5536 çal (12), basket
4553 sarganĕ (1), wicker
basket
4711 spuris (1), hamper
or lunch-receptacle

BASKETS
1731 dûwd (1), pot,
kettle; basket
1736 dûwday (1), basket
5536 çal (2), basket
5552 çalçillâh (1), twig
2894 kŏphinŏs (6), small
basket
4711 spuris (4), hamper
or lunch-receptacle

BASMATH
1315 Bosmath (1),
fragrance

BASON
3713 k⁰phôwr (2), bowl;
white frost
5592 çaph (2), dish
3537 niptĕr (1), basin for
washing

BASONS
101 'aggân (1), bowl
3713 k⁰phôwr (3), bowl;
white frost
4219 mîzrâq (11), bowl
for sprinkling
5592 çaph (2), dish

BASTARD
4464 mamzêr (2),
mongrel

BASTARDS
3541 nŏthŏs (1), spurious
or illegitimate son

BAT
5847 'ăţallêph (2),
mammal, bat

BATH
1324 bath (6), liquid
measure

BATH-RABBIM
1337 Bath Rabbîym (1),
city of Rabbah

BATH-SHEBA
1339 Bath-Sheba' (11),
daughter of an oath

BATH-SHUA
1340 Bath-Shûwa' (1),
daughter of wealth

BATHE
7364 râchats (18), to
lave, bathe

BATHED
7301 râvâh (1), to slake
thirst or appetites

BATHS
1324 bath (8), liquid
measure
1325 bath (Ch.) (1), liquid
measure

BATS
5847 'ăţallêph (1), bat

BATTERED
7843 shâchath (1), to
decay; to ruin

BATTLE
3593 kîydôwr (1), (poss.)
tumult, battle
4221 môach (1), bone
marrow
4264 machăneh (1),
encampment
4421 milchâmâh (143),
battle; war; fighting
4661 mappêts (1),
war-club
5402 nesheq (1), military
arms, arsenal
5430 çe'ôwn (1), military
boot
6635 tsâbâ' (5), army,
military host
6635+4421 tsâbâ' (1),
army, military host
7128 qe'râb (5), hostile
encounter
4171 pŏlĕmŏs (5),
warfare; battle; fight

BATTLEMENT
4624 ma'ăqeh (1),
parapet

BATTLEMENTS
5189 ne'îyshâh (1),
tendril plant shoot

BATTLES
4421 milchâmâh (6),
battle; war; fighting

BAVAI
942 Bavvay (1), Bavvai

BAY
249 'ezrâch (1), native
born
554 'âmôts (2), red
3956 lâshôwn (3),
tongue; tongue-shaped

BAZLITH
1213 Batslûwth (1),
peeling

BAZLUTH
1213 Batslûwth (1),
peeling

BDELLIUM
916 b⁰dôlach (2),
bdellium, amber; pearl

BEACON
8650 tôren (1), mast
pole; flag-staff pole

BEALIAH
1183 Be'alyâh (1),
Jehovah (is) master

BEALOTH
1175 Be'âlôwth (1),
mistresses

BEAM
708 'ereg (1), weaving;
braid; also shuttle

BEAM
3714 kâphîyç (1), girder,
beam
4500 mânôwr (4), frame
of a loom
5646 'âb (1), architrave
6982 qôwrâh (2), rafter;
roof
1385 dŏkŏs (6), stick or
plank

BEAMS
1356 gêb (1), well, cistern
3773 kârûthâh (3), hewn
timber beams
6763 tsêlâ' (1), side of a
person or thing
6982 qôwrâh (2), rafter;
roof
7136 qârâh (4), to bring
about; to impose

BEANS
6321 pôwl (2), beans

BEAR
1319 bâsar (4), to
announce (good news)
1677 dôb (10), bear
1678 dôb (Ch.) (1), bear
2398 châţâ' (2), to sin
3205 yâlad (16), to bear
young; to father a child
3212 yâlak (1), to walk;
to live; carry
3318 yâtsâ' (1), to go,
bring out
3557 kûwl (1), to keep in;
to measure
4910 mâshal (1), to rule
5187 ne'ţîyl (1), laden
5201 nâţar (1), to guard;
to cherish anger
5375 nâsâ' (100), to lift up
5445 çâbal (3), to carry
5749 'ûwd (1), to protest,
testify; to encompass
6030 'ânâh (2), to
respond, answer
6213 'âsâh (4), to do
7287 râdâh (1), to
subjugate; to crumble
7981 she'lêţ (Ch.) (1), to
dominate, i.e. govern
8323 sârar (1), to have,
exercise, get dominion
8382 tâ'am (1), to be
twinned, i.e. duplicate
8505 tâkan (1), to
balance, i.e. measure
142 airō (4), to lift, to
take up
399 anapherō (1), to take
up; to lead up
430 anechŏmai (4), put
up with, endure
503 antŏphthalmĕō (1),
to face into the wind
715 arktŏs (1), bear
(animal)
941 bastazō (11), to lift,
bear
1080 gĕnnaō (1), to
procreate, regenerate
3114 makrŏthumĕō (1),
to be forbearing, patient
3140 marturĕō (21), to
testify; to commend
4160 pŏiĕō (2), to do
5041 tĕknŏgŏnĕō (1), to
be a child bearer

BEAR
5297 hupŏpherō (1), to
bear from underneath
5342 pherō (4), to bear
5409 phŏrĕō (1), to wear
5576 psĕudŏmarturĕō
(4), to offer falsehood in
evidence

BEARD
2206 zâqân (14), beard
8222 sâphâm (1), beard

BEARDS
2206 zâqân (4), beard

BEARERS
5449 çabbâl (3), porter,
carrier

BEAREST
3205 yâlad (1), to bear
young; to father a child
941 bastazō (1), to lift,
bear
3140 marturĕō (1), to
testify; to commend
5088 tiktō (1), to produce
from seed

BEARETH
3205 yâlad (2), to bear
young; to father a child
4910 mâshal (1), to rule
5375 nâsâ' (7), to lift up
6030 'ânâh (2), to
respond, answer
6509 pârâh (1), to bear
fruit
6779 tsâmach (1), to
sprout
8382 tâ'am (1), to be
twinned, i.e. duplicate
1627 ĕkpherō (1), to bear
out; to produce
2592 karpŏphŏrĕō (1), to
be fertile
3140 marturĕō (3), to
testify; to commend
4722 stĕgō (1), to endure
patiently
4828 summarturĕō (1), to
testify jointly
5342 pherō (2), to bear or
carry
5409 phŏrĕō (1), to wear

BEARING
2232 zâra' (1), to sow
seed; to disseminate
3205 yâlad (3), to bear
young; to father a child
5375 nâsâ' (10), to lift up
941 bastazō (3), to lift,
bear
4064 pĕripherō (1), to
transport
4828 summarturĕō (2), to
testify jointly
4901 sunĕpimarturĕō (1),
to testify further jointly
5342 pherō (1), to bear or
carry

BEARS
1677 dôb (2), bear

BEAST
929 be'hêmâh (83),
animal, beast
1165 be'îyr (1), cattle,
livestock
2123 zîyz (1), moving
creature

English

BEAST'S

2416 chay (34), *alive; raw; fresh; life*
2423 chêyvâ' (Ch.) (6), wild *animal; monster*
5038 nᵉbêlâh (1), *carcase or carrion*
5315 nephesh (1), *life; breath; soul; wind*
5315+929 nephesh (1), *life; breath; soul; wind*
7409 rekesh (1), *relay of animals*
2226 zôôn (7), *living animal*
2342 thĕrĭŏn (40), *dangerous animal*
2934 ktĕnŏs (1), *domestic animal*

BEAST'S

2423 chêyvâ' (Ch.) (1), wild *animal; monster*

BEASTS

338 'iy (3), solitary wild creature that *howls*
929 bᵉhêmâh (51), *animal, beast*
1165 bᵉ'îyr (3), *cattle, livestock*
2123 zîyz (1), *moving creature*
2416 chay (42), *alive; raw; fresh; life*
2423 chêyvâ' (Ch.) (13), wild *animal; monster*
2874 ṭebach (1), *butchery*
2966 ṭᵉrêphâh (5), *torn prey*
3753 karkârâh (1), *cow-camel*
4806 mᵉrîy' (2), *stall-fed animal*
6728 tsîyîy (3), wild *beast*
2226 zôôn (16), *living animal*
2341 thĕrĭŏmachĕŏ (1), to *be a beast fighter*
2342 thĕrĭŏn (6), *dangerous animal*
2934 ktĕnŏs (3), *domestic animal*
4968 sphagiŏn (1), *offering for slaughter*
5074 tĕtrapŏus (2), *quadruped animal*

BEAT

1743 dûwk (1), to *pulverize in a mortar*
1792 dâkâ' (1), to *pulverize; be contrite*
1849 dâphaq (1), to *knock; to press severely*
1854 dâqaq (2), to *crush*
2040 hâraç (1), to *pull down; break, destroy*
2251 châbaṭ (2), to *knock out or off, thresh a tree*
3807 kâthath (4), to *bruise or strike, beat*
5221 nâkâh (4), to *strike, kill*
5422 nâthats (3), to *tear down*
7554 râqa' (1), to *pound*
7833 shâchaq (3), to *grind or wear away*
1194 dĕrō (5), to *flay*, i.e. to *scourge or thrash*

BEATEN

1643 geres (2), *grain*
1851 daq (1), *crushed; small or thin*
1986 hâlam (1), to *strike, beat, stamp, conquer*
2251 châbaṭ (1), to *knock out or off, thresh a tree*
2865 châthath (1), to *break down*
3795 kâthîyth (4), pure oil from *beaten* olives
3807 kâthath (3), to *bruise or strike, beat*
4347 makkâh (1), *blow; wound; pestilence*
4749 miqshâh (8), work molded by *hammering*
5060 nâga' (1), to *strike*
5062 nâgaph (1), to *strike*
5221 nâkâh (4), to *strike, kill*
5310 nâphats (1), to *dash to pieces; to scatter*
7820 shâchaṭ (5), to *hammer out*
1194 dĕrō (5), to *flay*, i.e. to *scourge or thrash*
4463 rhabdizō (1), to *strike with a stick*

BEATEST

2251 châbaṭ (1), to *knock out or off, thresh a tree*
5221 nâkâh (1), to *strike, kill*

BEATETH

1194 dĕrō (1), to *flay*, i.e. to *scourge or thrash*

BEATING

1986 hâlam (1), to *strike, beat, stamp, conquer*
1194 dĕrō (1), to *flay*, i.e. to *scourge or thrash*
5180 tuptō (1), to *strike, beat, wound*

BEAUTIES

1926 hâdâr (1), *magnificence*

BEAUTIFUL

2896 ṭôwb (1), *good; well*
2896+4758 ṭôwb (1), *good; well*
3303 yâpheh (7), *beautiful; handsome*
3303+8389 yâpheh (2), *beautiful; handsome*
4998 nâ'âh (1), to *be pleasant*, i.e. *beautiful*
6643 tsᵉbîy (1), *conspicuous splendor*
8597 tiph'ârâh (6), *ornament*
5611 hōraiŏs (4), *flourishing, beauteous*

BEAUTIFY

6286 pâ'ar (3), to *shake a tree*

BEAUTY

1926 hâdâr (3), *magnificence*
1927 hădârâh (4), *decoration, ornament*
1935 hôwd (1), *grandeur, majesty*
2530 châmad (1), to *delight* in; *lust for*
3308 yŏphîy (20), *beauty*
4758 mar'eh (1), *appearance; vision*
5276 nâ'êm (1), to *be agreeable*
5278 no'am (4), *delight, suitableness*
6287 pᵉ'êr (1), *fancy head-dress*
6643 tsᵉbîy (2), *conspicuous splendor*
6736 tsîyr (1), *carved idolatrous image*
8597 tiph'ârâh (10), *ornament*

BEBAI

893 Bêbay (6), *Bebai*

BECAUSE

413 'êl (3), *to, toward*
834 'ăsher (42), *because, in order that*
1115 biltîy (3), *except, without, unless, besides*
1558 gâlâl (4), *on account of, because of*
1697 dâbâr (1), *word; matter; thing*
1768 dîy (Ch.) (2), *that; of*
1870 derek (1), *road; course of life*
3027 yâd (2), *hand; power*
3282 ya'an (59), *because, for this reason*
3588 kîy (455), *for, that because*
3605 kôl (1), *all, any*
4480 min (2), *from, out of*
4481 min (Ch.) (1), *from or out of*
4616 ma'an (11), *on account of*
5668 'âbûwr (7), *on account of*
5921 'al (45), *above, over, upon, or against*
6118 'êqeb (2), *unto the end; for ever*
6119 'âqêb (1), *track, footprint*
6440 pânîym (67), *face; front*
6448 pâçag (1), to *contemplate*
8478 tachath (1), *bottom; underneath; in lieu of*
575 apŏ (1), *from, away*
1063 gar (5), *for, indeed, but, because*
1223 dia (54), *through, by means of; because of*
1360 diŏti (13), *on the very account that*
1537 ĕk (2), *out, out of*
1722 ĕn (3), *in; during; because of*
1893 ĕpĕi (7), *since*
1894 ĕpĕidĕ (2), *when, whereas*
1909 ĕpi (1), *on, upon*
2443 hina (1), *in order that*
2530 kathŏti (2), *as far or inasmuch as*
3704 hŏpŏs (1), *in the manner that*
3754 hŏti (184), *that; because; since*
4314 prŏs (2), *for; on, at; to, toward; against*
5484 charin (1), *on account of, because of*

BECHER

1071 Beker (5), *young bull camel*

BECHORATH

1064 Bᵉkôwrath (1), *primogeniture*

BECKONED

1269 dianĕuō (1), to *nod or express by signs*
2656 katanĕuō (1), to *make a sign or signal*
2678 katasĕiō (2), to *motion a signal or sign*
3506 nĕuō (2), *nod*, i.e. *signal*

BECKONING

2678 katasĕiō (2), to *motion a signal or sign*

BED

3326 yâtsûwa' (3), *bed; wing or lean-to*
3331 yâtsa' (1), to *strew*
4296 miṭṭah (23), *bed; sofa, litter or bier*
4702 matstsâ' (1), *couch*
4903 mishkab (Ch.) (6), *bed*
4904 mishkâb (29), *bed; sleep; intercourse*
6170 'ărûwgâh (1), *parterre, kind of garden*
6210 'eres (4), *canopy couch*
6210+3326 'eres (1), *canopy couch*
2825 klinē (8), *couch*
2845 kŏitē (2), *couch; conception*
2895 krabbatŏs (10), *sleeping mat*
4766 strŏnnumi (1), to *spread a couch*

BED'S

4296 miṭṭah (1), *bed; sofa, litter or bier*

BEDAD

911 Bᵉdad (2), *separation*

BEDAN

917 Bᵉdân (2), *servile*

BEDCHAMBER

2315+4296 cheder (3), *apartment, chamber*
2315+4904 cheder (3), *apartment, chamber*

BEDEIAH

912 Bêdᵉyâh (1), *servant of Jehovah*

BEDS

4296 miṭṭah (2), *bed; sofa, litter or bier*

4904 mishkâb (5), *bed;
sleep; intercourse*
6170 'ărûwgâh (1),
parterre, kind of garden
2825 klinē (1), *couch*
2895 krabbatŏs (1),
sleeping *mat*

BEDSTEAD
6210 'eres (1), *canopy
couch*

BEE
1682 dᵉbôwrâh (1), *bee*

BEELIADA
1182 Bᵉ'elyâdâ' (1), *Baal
has known*

BEELZEBUB
954 Bĕĕlzĕbŏul (7),
dung-god

BEER
876 Bᵉ'êr (2), *well, cistern*

BEER-ELIM
879 Bᵉ'êr 'Êlîym (1), *well
of heroes*

BEER-LAHAI-ROI
883 Bᵉ'êr la-Chay Rô'îy
(1), *well of a living
(One) my seer*

BEER-SHEBA
884 Bᵉ'êr Sheba' (34),
well of an oath

BEERA
878 Bᵉ'êrâ' (1), *well*

BEERAH
880 Bᵉ'êrâh (1), *well*

BEERI
882 Bᵉ'êrîy (2), *fountain*

BEEROTH
881 Bᵉ'êrôwth (6), *wells*

BEEROTHITE
886 Bᵉ'êrôthîy (4),
Beërothite

BEEROTHITES
886 Bᵉ'êrôthîy (1),
Beërothite

BEES
1682 dᵉbôwrâh (3), *bee*

BEESH-TERAH
1203 Bᵉ'eshtᵉrâh (1),
with Ashtoreth

BEETLE
2728 chargôl (1), *leaping
insect*

BEEVES
1241 bâqâr (7), *plowing
ox; herd*

BEFALL
579 'ânâh (1), to *meet*, to
happen
4672 mâtsâ' (1), to *find
or acquire; to occur,
meet or be present*
7122 qârâ' (4), to
encounter, to happen
7136 qârâh (2), to *bring
about; to impose*
4876 sunantaō (1), to
meet with; to occur

BEFALLEN
4672 mâtsâ' (3), to *find
or acquire; to occur*
4745 miqreh (1),
accident or fortune

7122 qârâ' (1), to
encounter, to happen
7136 qârâh (1), to *bring
about; to impose*
4876 sunantaō (1), to
meet with; to occur

BEFALLETH
4745 miqreh (2),
accident or fortune

BEFELL
935 bôw' (1), to *go, come*
4672 mâtsâ' (1), to *find
or acquire; to occur*
7136 qârâh (1), to *bring
about; to impose*
1096 ginŏmai (1), to *be,
become*
4819 sumbainō (1), to
concur, happen

BEFORE
413 'êl (8), *to, toward*
639 'aph (2), *nose or
nostril; face; person*
854 'êth (4), *with; by; at*
865 'ethmôwl (1),
heretofore, formerly
2958 tᵉrôwm (1), *not yet,
before*
2962 ṭerem (41), *not yet
or before*
3808 lô' (2), *no, not*
3942 liphnay (1),
anterior, in front of
4136 mûwl (1), *in front
of, opposite*
4551 maççâ' (1), *stone
quarry; projectile*
4608 ma'ăleh (1),
elevation; platform
5048 neged (70), *over
against or before*
5084 nâdân (1), *sheath*
5226 nêkach (1), *opposite*
5227 nôkach (1),
opposite, in front of
5703 'ad (1), *perpetuity;
ancient*
5704 'ad (1), *as far (long)
as; during; while; until*
5869 'ayin (8), *eye; sight;
fountain*
5921 'al (12), *above, over,
upon, or against*
5973 'îm (5), *with*
6440 pânîym (1110), *face;
front*
6471 pa'am (1), *time;
step; occurence*
6903 qᵉbêl (Ch.) (3), *in
front of, before*
6905 qâbâl (1), *in front of*
6924 qedem (10), *before,
anciently*
6925 qŏdâm (Ch.) (29),
before
6931 qadmôwnîy (1),
anterior time
7130 qereb (1), *nearest
part, i.e. the center*
7223 rî'shôwn (3), *first, in
place, time or rank*
561 apĕnanti (2),
opposite, before
575 apŏ (2), *from, away*
1519 ĕis (2), *to or into*
1715 ĕmprŏsthĕn (41), *in
front of*

1722 ĕn (1), *in; during;
because of*
1725 ĕnanti (1), *before*, in
presence of
1726 ĕnantiŏn (4), *in the
presence of*
1773 ĕnnuchŏn (1), *by
night*
1799 ĕnōpiŏn (63), *in the
face of, before*
1909 ĕpi (17), *on, upon*
2596 kata (2), *down;
according to*
2713 katĕnanti (1),
directly opposite
2714 katĕnōpiŏn (3),
directly in front of
3319 mĕsŏs (1), *middle*
3764 ŏudĕpō (1), *not
even yet*
3844 para (3), *from; with;
besides; on account of*
3908 paratithēmi (9), to
present something
3936 paristēmi (2), to
stand beside, present
4250 prin (7), *prior,
sooner, before*
4253 prŏ (43), *before in
time or space*
4254 prŏagō (15), to *lead
forward; to precede*
4256 prŏaitiaŏmai (1), to
previously charge
4257 prŏakŏuō (1), to
hear beforehand
4264 prŏbibazō (1), to
bring to the front
4267 prŏginōskō (1), to
know beforehand
4270 prŏgraphō (1), to
write previously
4275 prŏĕidō (1), to
foresee
4277 prŏĕpō (1), to *say
already, to predict*
4278 prŏĕnarchŏmai (1),
to *commence already*
4280 prŏĕrĕō (8), to *say
already, predict*
4281 prŏĕrchŏmai (4), to
go onward, precede
4282 prŏĕtŏimazō (1), to
fit up in advance
4283 prŏĕuaggĕlizŏmai
(1), to *announce in
advance*
4293 prŏkataggĕllō (3),
to *predict, promise,
foretell*
4295 prŏkĕimai (3), to *be
present to the mind*
4296 prŏkĕrussō (1), to
proclaim in advance
4299 prŏkrima (1),
prejudgment
4300 prŏkurŏō (1), to
ratify previously
4301 prŏlambanō (1), to
take before
4302 prŏlĕgō (2), to
predict, forewarn
4304 prŏmĕlĕtaō (1), to
premeditate
4308 prŏŏraō (1), to
notice previously
4309 prŏŏrizō (1), to
predetermine

4310 prŏpaschō (1), to
undergo previously
4313 prŏpŏrĕuŏmai (1),
to *precede as guide*
4314 prŏs (2), *for; on, at;
to, toward; against*
4315 prŏsabbatŏn (1),
Sabbath-eve
4363 prŏspiptō (5), to
prostrate oneself
4384 prŏtassō (1), to
prescribe beforehand
4386 prŏtĕrŏn (4),
previously
4391 prŏüparchō (1), to
be or do previously
4401 prŏchĕirŏtŏnĕō (1),
to *elect in advance*
4412 prōtŏn (1), *firstly*
4413 prōtŏs (2), *foremost*

BEFOREHAND
4271 prŏdēlŏs (2),
obvious, evident
4294 prŏkatartizō (1), to
prepare in advance
4303 prŏmarturŏmai (1),
to *witness beforehand*
4305 prŏmĕrimnaō (1), to
care in advance

BEFORETIME
865+832 'ethmôwl (1),
heretofore, formerly
6440 pânîym (5), *face;
front*
7223 rî'shôwn (1), *first, in
place, time or rank*
8543+8032 tᵉmôwl (2),
yesterday
4391 prŏüparchō (1), to
be or do previously

BEG
7592 shâ'al (2), to *ask*
1871 ĕpaitĕō (1), to *ask
for, beg*

BEGAN
2490 châlal (34), to
profane, defile
2974 yâ'al (1), to *assent;
to undertake, begin*
3246 yᵉçûd (1),
foundation; beginning)
5927 'âlâh (1), to *ascend,
be high, mount*
6751 tsâlal (1), to *shade;
to grow dark*
8271 shᵉrê' (Ch.) (1), to
unravel, commence
756 archŏmai (64), to
begin
2020 ĕpiphōskō (1), to
grow light
2192 ĕchō (1), to *have;
hold; keep*

BEGAT
3205 yâlad (176), to *bear
young; to father a child*
616 apŏkuĕō (1), to
generate, bring to being
1080 gĕnnaō (43), to
procreate, regenerate

BEGET
3205 yâlad (10), to *bear
young; to father a child*

BEGETTEST
3205 yâlad (2), to *bear
young; to father a child*

English

BEGETTETH
3205 yâlad (3), to bear young; to father a child

BEGGAR
34 'ebyôwn (1), destitute; poor
4434 ptôchŏs (2), pauper, beggar

BEGGARLY
4434 ptôchŏs (1), pauper, beggar

BEGGED
154 aitĕō (2), to ask for
4319 prŏsaitĕō (1), to solicit, beg

BEGGING
1245 bâqash (1), to search; to strive after
4319 prŏsaitĕō (2), to solicit, beg

BEGIN
2490 châlal (12), to profane, defile
8462 tᵉchillâh (1), original; originally
756 archŏmai (11), to begin
3195 mĕllō (1), to intend, i.e. be about to be

BEGINNEST
2490 châlal (1), to profane, defile

BEGINNING
227 'âz (3), at that time or place; therefore
1931 hûw' (2), he, she, it; this or that
5769 'ôwlâm (1), eternity; ancient; always
7218 rô'sh (12), head
7223 rî'shôwn (4), first
7225 rê'shîyth (18), first
8462 tᵉchillâh (14), original; originally
509 anōthĕn (1), from above; from the first
746 archē (39), first in rank; first in time
756 archŏmai (8), to begin
4412 prōtŏn (1), firstly
4413 prōtŏs (1), foremost

BEGINNINGS
7218 rô'sh (2), head
7221 rî'shâh (1), beginning
746 archē (1), first

BEGOTTEN
3205 yâlad (7), to bear young; to father a child
3318 yâtsâ' (1), to go, bring out
4138 môwledeth (1), lineage, offspring
313 anagĕnnaō (1), to beget or bear again
1080 gĕnnaō (7), to procreate, regenerate
3439 mŏnŏgĕnēs (6), sole, one and only
4416 prōtŏtŏkŏs (1), first-born

BEGUILE
2603 katabrabĕuō (1), to award a price against

BEGETTETH
3884 paralŏgizŏmai (1), to delude, deceive

BEGUILED
5230 nâkal (1), to act treacherously
5377 nâshâ' (1), to lead astray, to delude
7411 râmâh (2), to hurl; to shoot; to delude
1818 ĕxapataō (1), to seduce wholly, deceive

BEGUILING
1185 dĕlĕazō (1), to delude, seduce

BEGUN
2490 châlal (6), to profane, defile
756 archŏmai (1), to begin
1728 ĕnarchŏmai (2), to commence on, begin
2691 katastrēniaō (1), to be voluptuous against
4278 prŏenarchŏmai (2), to commence already

BEHALF
854 'êth (1), with; by; at
5973 'îm (1), with
8478 tachath (1), bottom; underneath; in lieu of
1909 ĕpi (1), on, upon
3313 mĕrŏs (2), division or share
4012 pĕri (1), about; around
5228 hupĕr (4), over; in behalf of

BEHAVE
2388 châzaq (1), to fasten upon; to seize
5234 nâkar (1), to care for, respect, revere
7292 râhab (1), to urge severely
7919 sâkal (1), to be circumspect
390 anastrĕphō (1), to remain, to live
807 aschēmŏnĕō (1), to be, act unbecoming

BEHAVED
1980 hâlak (1), to walk; live a certain way
7489 râ'a' (1), to be good for nothing
7737 shâvâh (1), to level, i.e. equalize
7919 sâkal (4), to be circumspect
812 ataktĕō (1), to be, act irregular
1096 ginŏmai (1), to be, become

BEHAVETH
807 aschēmŏnĕō (1), to be, act unbecoming

BEHAVIOUR
2940 ţa'am (2), taste; perception
2688 katastēma (1), demeanor
2887 kŏsmiŏs (1), orderly

BEHEADED
5493+7218 çûwr (1), to turn off

BEGUILED
6202 'âraph (1), to break the neck, to destroy
607 apŏkĕphalizō (4), to decapitate
3990 pĕlĕkizō (1), to remove the head

BEHELD
2370+934 chăzâ' (Ch.) (6), to gaze upon
5027 nâbaţ (2), to scan; to regard with favor
7200 râ'âh (23), to see
333 anathĕōrĕō (1), to look again
991 blĕpō (2), to look at
1492 ĕidō (10), to know
1689 ĕmblĕpō (3), to observe; to discern
2300 thĕaŏmai (2), to look closely at
2334 thĕōrĕō (4), to see; to discern

BEHEMOTH
930 bᵉhêmôwth (1), hippopotamus

BEHIND
268 'âchôwr (5), behind, backward; west
310 'achar (49), after
3498 yâthar (1), to remain or be left
5975 'âmad (1), to stand
2641 katalĕipō (1), to abandon
3693 ŏpisthĕn (4), at the back; after
3694 ŏpisō (6), behind, after, following
5278 hupŏmĕnō (1), to undergo (trials)
5302 hustĕrĕō (4), to be inferior; to fall short

BEHOLD
431 'ălûw (Ch.) (5), lo!
718 'ărûw (Ch.) (4), lo!, behold!
1887 hê' (1), Lo!, Look!
2005 hên (237), lo!; if!
2009 hinnêh (770), lo!; Look!
2205 zâqên (2), old, venerated
2209 ziqnâh (1), old age
2372 châzâh (7), to gaze at; to perceive
5027 nâbaţ (9), to scan; to regard with favor
6822 tsâphâh (6), to peer into the distance
7200 râ'âh (58), to see
7789 shûwr (5), to spy out, survey
7891 shîyr (1), to sing
816 atĕnizō (1), to gaze intently
991 blĕpō (3), to look at
1492 ĕidō (5), to know
1689 ĕmblĕpō (1), to observe; to discern
1896 ĕpĕidŏn (1), to regard
2029 ĕpŏptĕuō (2), to watch, observe
2334 thĕōrĕō (3), to see; to discern
2396 idĕ (24), surprise!, lo!, look!

BEGUILED
2400 idŏu (180), lo!, note!, see!
2657 katanŏĕō (2), to observe fully

BEHOLDEST
5027 nâbaţ (1), to scan; to regard with favor
991 blĕpō (3), to look at

BEHOLDETH
6437 pânâh (1), to turn, to face
7200 râ'âh (2), to see
2657 katanŏĕō (1), to observe fully

BEHOLDING
6822 tsâphâh (1), to peer; to observe, await
7200 râ'âh (2), to see
816 atĕnizō (2), to gaze intently
991 blĕpō (2), to look at
1689 ĕmblĕpō (1), to observe; to discern
2334 thĕōrĕō (4), to see; to discern
2657 katanŏĕō (1), to observe fully
2734 katŏptrizŏmai (1), to see reflected
3708 hŏraō (1), to stare, see clearly

BEHOVED
1163 dĕi (1), it is (was) necessary
3784 ŏphĕilō (1), to owe; to be under obligation

BEING
1961 hâyâh (4), to exist, i.e. be or become
5750 'ôwd (2), again; repeatedly; still; more
1096 ginŏmai (5), to be, become
1909 ĕpi (1), on, upon
2070 ĕsmĕn (1), we are
2192 ĕchō (1), to have; hold; keep
5225 huparchō (13), to come into existence
5605 ōdinō (1), to experience labor pains
5607 ōn (35), being, existence

BEKAH
1235 beqa' (1), half shekel

BEL
1078 Bêl (3), Bel (Baal)

BELA
1106 Bela' (13), gulp; destruction

BELAH
1106 Bela' (1), gulp; destruction

BELAITES
1108 Bal'îy (1), Belaite

BELCH
5042 nâba' (1), to gush forth; emit a foul odor

BELIAL
1100 bᵉlîya'al (16), wickedness, trouble
955 Bĕlial (1), worthlessness

BELIED
3584 kâchash (1), to *lie,
disown; to disappoint*

BELIEF
4102 pistis (1), *faith,
belief; conviction*

BELIEVE
539 'âman (19), to *be
firm, faithful, true*
544 apĕithĕō (1), to
disbelieve
569 apistĕō (2), to
disbelieve, disobey
571 apistŏs (4), *without
faith; untrustworthy*
4100 pistĕuō (109), to
have faith, i.e. *credit; to
entrust*
4100+1722 pistĕuō (1), to
have faith, i.e. *credit*
4100+1909 pistĕuō (1), to
have faith, i.e. *credit*
4102 pistis (1), *faith,
belief; conviction*
4103 pistŏs (2), *trustful;
reliable*

BELIEVED
539 'âman (21), to *be
firm, faithful, true*
540 'âman (Ch.) (1), to *be
firm, faithful, true*
544 apĕithĕō (6), to
disbelieve
569 apistĕō (3), to
disbelieve, disobey
569+4100 apistĕō (1), to
disbelieve, disobey
3982 pĕithō (3), to *rely by
inward certainty*
4100 pistĕuō (76), to *have
faith,* i.e. *credit*
4103 pistŏs (2),
trustworthy; reliable
4135 plĕrŏphŏrĕō (1), to
assure or convince

BELIEVERS
4100 pistĕuō (1), to *have
faith,* i.e. *credit*
4103 pistŏs (1),
trustworthy; reliable

BELIEVEST
4100 pistĕuō (8), to *have
faith,* i.e. *credit*

BELIEVETH
539 'âman (4), to *be firm,
faithful, true; to trust*
544 apĕithĕō (1), to
disbelieve
569 apistĕō (1), to
disbelieve, disobey
571 apistŏs (3), *without
faith; untrustworthy*
1537+4102 ĕk (1), *out of*
4100 pistĕuō (33), to *have
faith,* i.e. *credit*
4103 pistŏs (2),
trustworthy; reliable

BELIEVING
4100 pistĕuō (6), to *have
faith,* i.e. *credit*
4103 pistŏs (2),
trustworthy; reliable

BELL
6472 pa'ămôn (3), *bell*

BELLIES
1064 gastĕr (1), *stomach;
womb; gourmand*

BELLOW
6670 tsâhal (1), to *be
cheerful; to sound*

BELLOWS
4647 mappûach (1),
bellows

BELLS
4698 mᵉtsillâh (1), *small
bell*
6472 pa'ămôn (3), *bell*

BELLY
990 beţen (30), *belly;
womb; body*
1512 gâchôwn (2), *belly*
3770 kᵉrês (1), *paunch*
4577 mᵉ'âh (Ch.) (1),
bowels, belly
4578 mê'âh (3), *viscera;
anguish, tenderness*
6897 qôbâh (1), *abdomen*
2836 kŏilia (10),
abdomen, womb, heart

BELONG
1510 ĕimi (1), I *exist,* I *am*

BELONGED
4490 mânâh (1), *ration;
lot or portion*
1510 ĕimi (1), I *exist,* I *am*

BELONGETH
1510 ĕimi (1), I *exist,* I *am*

BELOVED
157 'âhab (6), to *have
affection, love*
1730 dôwd (29), *beloved,
friend; relative*
2530 châmad (3), to
delight in; lust for
3033 yᵉdîdûwth (1),
darling object
3039 yᵉdîyd (5), *loved*
4261 machmâd (1),
*object of affection or
desire*
25 agapaō (5), to *love*
27 agapētŏs (57), *beloved*

BELOVED'S
1730 dôwd (2), *beloved,
friend; relative*

BELSHAZZAR
1113 Bêlsha'tstsar (Ch.)
(8), *Belshatstsar*

BELTESHAZZAR
1095 Bêlţᵉsha'tstsar (2),
Belteshatstsar
1096 Bêlţᵉsha'tstsar
(Ch.) (8), *Belteshatstsar*

BEMOAN
5110 nûwd (5), to
deplore; to taunt

BEMOANED
5110 nûwd (1), to
deplore; to taunt

BEMOANING
5110 nûwd (1), to
deplore; to taunt

BEN
1122 Bên (1), *son*

BEN-AMMI
1151 Ben-'Ammîy (1),
son of my people

BEN-HADAD
1130 Ben-Hădad (18),
son of Hadad
1131 Binnûwy (7), *built*

BEN-HAIL
1134 Ben-Chayil (1), *son
of might*

BEN-HANAN
1135 Ben-Chânân (1),
son of Chanan

BEN-ONI
1126 Ben-'Ôwnîy (1), *son
of my sorrow*

BEN-ZOHETH
1132 Ben-Zôwchêth (1),
son of Zocheth

BENAIAH
1141 Bᵉnâyâh (42),
Jehovah has built

BENCHES
7175 qeresh (1), *slab or
plank; deck of a ship*

BEND
1869 dârak (7), to *tread,
trample; to string a bow*
3719 kâphan (1), to *bend*

BENDETH
1869 dârak (2), to *walk,
lead; to string a bow*

BENDING
7817 shâchach (1), to
sink or depress

BENE-BERAK
1138 Bunnîy (1), *built*

BENE-JAAKAN
1142 Bᵉnêy Ya'ăqân (2),
sons of Yaakan

BENEATH
4295 maţţâh (7), *below
or beneath*
8478 tachath (17),
bottom; underneath
2736 katō (3), *downwards*

BENEFACTORS
2110 ĕuĕrgĕtēs (1),
philanthropist

BENEFIT
1576 gᵉmûwl (1), *act;
service; reward*
3190 yâţab (1), to *be,
make well*
18 agathŏs (1), *good*
2108 ĕuĕrgĕsia (1),
beneficence
5485 charis (1),
gratitude; benefit given

BENEFITS
1576 gᵉmûwl (1), *act;
service; reward*
8408 tagmûwl (1),
bestowment

BENEVOLENCE
2133 ĕunŏia (1), *eagerly,
with a whole heart*

BENINU
1148 Bᵉnînûw (1), *our
son*

BENJAMIN
1144 Binyâmîyn (158),
son of (the) *right hand*
953 bĕbĕlŏō (4), to
desecrate, profane

BENJAMIN'S
1144 Binyâmîyn (4), *son
of* (the) *right hand*

BENJAMITE
1145 Ben-yᵉmîynîy (9),
son of (the) *right hand*

BENJAMITES
1145 Ben-yᵉmîynîy (8),
son of (the) *right hand*

BENO
1121 bên (2), *son,
descendant; people*

BENT
1869 dârak (7), to *walk,
lead; to string a bow*
8511 tâlâ' (1), to *suspend;
to be uncertain*

BEON
1194 Beᵉ'ôn (1), *Beon*

BEOR
1160 Beᵉ'ôwr (10), *lamp*

BERA
1298 Bera' (1), *Bera*

BERACHAH
1294 Bᵉrâkâh (3),
benediction, blessing

BERACHIAH
1296 Berekyâh (1),
blessing of Jehovah

BERAIAH
1256 Bᵉrâ'yâh (1),
Jehovah has created

BEREA
960 Bĕrŏia (3), *region
beyond the coast-line*

BEREAVE
2637 châcêr (1), to *lack;
to fail, want, make less*
3782+(7921) kâshal (1), to
totter, waver; to falter
7921 shâkôl (4), to
miscarry

BEREAVED
7909 shakkuwl (2),
bereaved
7921 shâkôl (3), to
miscarry

BEREAVETH
7921 shâkôl (1), to
miscarry

BERECHIAH
1296 Berekyâh (10),
blessing of Jehovah

BERED
1260 Bered (2), *hail*

BERI
1275 Bêrîy (1), *Beri*

BERIAH
1283 Bᵉrîy'âh (11), *in
trouble*

BERIITES
1284 Bᵉrîy'îy (1), *Beriite*

BERITES
1276 Bêrîy (1), *Berites*

BERITH
1286 Bᵉrîyth (1), *Berith*

BERNICE
959 Bĕrnikē (3),
victorious

BERODACH-BALADAN
1255 Bᵉrô'dak Bal'ădân (1), *Berodak-Baladan*

BEROTHAH
1268 Bêrôwthâh (1), *cypress-like*

BEROTHAI
1268 Bêrôwthâh (1), *cypress-like*

BEROTHITE
1307 Bêrôthîy (1), *Berothite*

BERRIES
1620 gargar (1), *berry*
1636 ĕlaia (1), *olive*

BERYL
8658 tarshîysh (7), (poss.) *topaz*
969 bĕrullŏs (1), *beryl*

BESAI
1153 Bᵉçay (2), *domineering*

BESEECH
577 'ânnâ' (8), *I ask you!*
2470+6440 châlâh (1), *to be weak, sick, afflicted*
4994 nâ' (26), *I pray!, please!, I beg you!*
1189 dĕŏmai (6), *to beg, petition, ask*
2065 ĕrŏtaō (4), *to interrogate; to request*
3870 parakalĕō (20), *to call, invite*

BESEECHING
2065 ĕrŏtaō (1), *to interrogate; to request*
3870 parakalĕō (2), *to call, invite*

BESET
3803 kâthar (1), *to enclose, besiege; to wait*
5437 çâbab (3), *to surround*
6696 tsûwr (1), *to cramp, i.e. confine; to harass*
2139 ĕupĕristatŏs (1), *entangling, obstructing*

BESIDE
310 'achar (1), *after*
413 'êl (2), *to, toward*
657 'epheç (3), *end; no further*
681 'êtsel (12), *side; near*
854 'êth (2), *with; by; at; among*
905 bad (45), *apart, only, besides*
1107 bil'ădêy (7), *except; without, besides*
1115 biltîy (3), *except, without, unless, besides*
2108 zûwlâh (6), *except; apart from; besides*
3027 yâd (1), *hand; power*
5921 'al (17), *above, over, upon, or against*
5973 'îm (4), *with*
5980 'ummâh (2), *near, beside, along with*
6654 tsad (3), *side; adversary*
846 autŏs (1), *he, she, it*
1839 ĕxistēmi (2), *to astound*
1909 ĕpi (3), *on, upon*

BESIDES
3105 mainŏmai (1), *to rave as a maniac*
4862 sun (1), *with or together*
5565 chōris (3), *separately, apart* from

BESIDES
905 bad (1), *apart, only, besides*
2108 zûwlâh (1), *except; apart from; besides*
5750 'ôwd (4), *again; repeatedly; still; more*
5921 'al (1), *above, over, upon, or against*
3063 lŏipŏn (1), *something remaining; finally*
4359 prŏsŏphĕilō (1), *to be indebted*

BESIEGE
6696 tsûwr (8), *to cramp, i.e. confine; to harass*
6887 tsârar (3), *to cramp*

BESIEGED
935+4692 bôw' (3), *to go or come*
4692 mâtsôwr (1), *siege-mound; distress*
4693 mâtsôwr (2), *limit, border*
5341 nâtsar (2), *to guard, protect, maintain*
5437 çâbab (1), *to surround*
6696 tsûwr (14), *to cramp, i.e. confine*

BESODEIAH
1152 Bᵉçôwdᵉyâh (1), *in* (the) *counsel of Jehovah*

BESOM
4292 maṭ'ăṭê' (1), *broom*

BESOR
1308 Bᵉsôwr (3), *cheerful*

BESOUGHT
1245 bâqash (2), *to search out*
2470 châlâh (5), *to be weak, sick, afflicted*
2603 chânan (4), *to implore*
1189 dĕŏmai (3), *to beg, petition, ask*
2065 ĕrŏtaō (9), *to interrogate; to request*
387 'parakalĕō (21), *to call, invite*

BEST
2173 zimrâh (1), *choice*
2459 cheleb (5), *fat; choice part*
2896 tôwb (8), *good; well*
3190 yâṭab (1), *to be, make well*
4315 mêyṭâb (6), *best*
5324 nâtsab (1), *to station*
6338 pâzaz (1), *to refine gold*
2909 krĕittōn (1), *stronger, i.e. nobler*
4413 prōtŏs (1), *foremost*

BESTIR
2782 chârats (1), *to be alert, to decide*

BESTOW
5414 nâthan (2), *to give*

5415 nᵉthan (Ch.) (2), *to give*
6213 'âsâh (1), *to do or make*
4060 pĕritithēmi (1), *to present*
4863 sunagō (2), *to gather together*
5595 psōmizō (1), *to nourish, feed*

BESTOWED
1580 gâmal (2), *to benefit or requite; to wean*
3240 yânach (2), *to allow to stay*
5414 nâthan (2), *to give*
6485 pâqad (1), *to visit, care for, count*
1325 didōmi (2), *to give*
2872 kŏpiaō (3), *to feel fatigue; to work hard*

BETAH
984 Beṭach (1), *safety, security, trust*

BETEN
991 Beṭen (1), *belly; womb; body*

BETH-ANATH
1043 Bêyth 'Ănâth (3), *house of replies*

BETH-ANOTH
1042 Bêyth 'Ănôwth (1), *house of replies*

BETH-ARABAH
1026 Bêyth hâ-'Ărâbâh (3), *house of the desert*

BETH-ARAM
1027 Bêyth hâ-Râm (1), *house of the height*

BETH-ARBEL
1009 Bêyth 'Arbê'l (1), *house of God's ambush*

BETH-AVEN
1007 Bêyth 'Âven (7), *house of vanity*

BETH-AZMAVETH
1041 Bêyth 'Azmâveth (1), *house of Azmaveth*

BETH-BAAL-MEON
1010 Bêyth Ba'al Mᵉ'ôwn (1), *house of Baal of* (the) *habitation*

BETH-BARAH
1012 Bêyth Bârâh (2), *house of* (the) *river ford*

BETH-BIREI
1011 Bêyth Bir'îy (1), *house of a creative one*

BETH-CAR
1033 Bêyth Kar (1), *house of pasture*

BETH-DAGON
1016 Bêyth-Dâgôwn (2), *house of Dagon*

BETH-DIBLATHAIM
1015 Bêyth Diblâthayim (1), *house of* (the) *two figcakes*

BETH-EL
1008 Bêyth-'Êl (66), *house of God*

BETH-ELITE
1017 Bêyth hâ-'Êlîy (1), *Beth-elite*

BETH-EMEK
1025 Bêyth hâ-'Êmeq (1), *house of the valley*

BETH-EZEL
1018 Bêyth hâ-'Êtsel (1), *house of the side*

BETH-GADER
1013 Bêyth-Gâdêr (1), *house of* (the) *wall*

BETH-GAMUL
1014 Bêyth Gâmûwl (1), *house of* (the) *weaned*

BETH-HACCEREM
1021 Bêyth hak-Kerem (2), *house of the vineyard*

BETH-HARAN
1028 Bêyth hâ-Rân (1), *house of the height*

BETH-HOGLA
1031 Bêyth Choglâh (1), *house of a partridge*

BETH-HOGLAH
1031 Bêyth Choglâh (2), *house of a partridge*

BETH-HORON
1032 Bêyth Chôwrôwn (14), *house of hollowness*

BETH-JESHIMOTH
1020 Bêyth ha-Yᵉshîy-môwth (3), *house of the deserts*

BETH-JESIMOTH
1020 Bêyth ha-Yᵉshîy-môwth (1), *house of the deserts*

BETH-LEBAOTH
1034 Bêyth Lᵉbá'ôwth (1), *house of lionesses*

BETH-LEHEM
1035 Bêyth Lechem (30), *house of bread*

BETH-LEHEM-JUDAH
1035 Bêyth Lechem (10), *house of bread*

BETH-LEHEMITE
1022 Bêyth hal-Lachmîy (4), *Beth-lechemite*

BETH-MAACHAH
1038 Bêyth Ma'ăkâh (2), *house of Maakah*

BETH-MARCABOTH
1024 Bêyth ham-Markâbôwth (2), *place of* (the) *chariots*

BETH-MEON
1010 Bêyth Ba'al Mᵉ'ôwn (1), *house of Baal of* (the) *habitation*

BETH-NIMRAH
1039 Bêyth Nimrâh (2), *house of* (the) *leopard*

BETH-PALET
1046 Bêyth Peleṭ (1), *house of escape*

BETH-PAZZEZ
1048 Bêyth Patstsêts (1), *house of dispersion*

BETH-PEOR
1047 Bêyth Peʻôwr (4), house of Peor

BETH-PHELET
1046 Bêyth Peleṭ (1), house of escape

BETH-RAPHA
1051 Bêyth Râphâʼ (1), house of (the) giant

BETH-REHOB
1050 Bêyth Reᶜchôwb (2), house of (the) street

BETH-SHAN
1052 Bêyth Sheʼân (3), house of ease

BETH-SHEAN
1052 Bêyth Sheʼân (6), house of ease

BETH-SHEMESH
1053 Bêyth Shemesh (21), house of (the) sun

BETH-SHEMITE
1030 Bêyth hash-Shimshîy (2), Beth-shimshite

BETH-SHITTAH
1029 Bêyth hash-Shiṭṭâh (1), house of the acacia

BETH-TAPPUAH
1054 Bêyth Tappûwach (1), house of (the) apple

BETH-ZUR
1049 Bêyth Tsûwr (4), house of (the) rock

BETHABARA
962 Bēthabara (1), ferry-house

BETHANY
963 Bēthania (11), date-house

BETHER
1336 Bether (1), section

BETHESDA
964 Bēthĕsda (1), house of kindness

BETHINK
7725+413+3820 shûwb (2), to turn back

BETHLEHEM
1035 Bêyth Lechem (1), house of bread
965 Bēthlĕĕm (8), house of bread

BETHPHAGE
967 Bēthphagē (3), fig-house

BETHSAIDA
966 Bēthsaïda (7), fishing-house

BETHUEL
1328 Beᶜthûwʼêl (10), destroyed of God

BETHUL
1329 Beᶜthûwl (1), Bethuel

BETIMES
7836 shâchar (3), to search for
7925 shâkam (2), to load up, i.e. to start early

BETONIM
993 Beᶜṭônîym (1), hollows

BETRAY
7411 râmâh (1), to hurl; to shoot; to delude
3860 paradidōmi (17), to hand over

BETRAYED
3860 paradidōmi (18), to hand over

BETRAYERS
4273 prŏdŏtēs (1), betraying

BETRAYEST
3860 paradidōmi (1), to hand over

BETRAYETH
3860 paradidōmi (3), to hand over

BETROTH
781 ʼâras (4), to engage for matrimony, betroth

BETROTHED
781 ʼâras (6), to engage for matrimony, betroth
2778 châraph (1), to spend the winter
3259 yâʻad (2), to engage for marriage

BETTER
2896 ṭôwb (75), good; well
3027 yâd (1), hand; power
3148 yôwthêr (1), moreover; rest; gain
3190 yâṭab (4), to be, make well
3504 yithrôwn (1), preeminence, gain
1308 diaphĕrō (3), to differ; to surpass
2570 kalŏs (5), good; beautiful; valuable
2573 kalŏs (1), well
2909 krĕittŏn (18), stronger, i.e. nobler
3081 lusitĕlĕi (1), it is advantageous
4052 pĕrissĕuō (1), to superabound
4284 prŏĕchŏmai (1), to excel
4851 sumphĕrō (1), to collect; advantage
5242 hupĕrĕchō (1), excel; superior
5543 chrēstŏs (1), employed, i.e. useful

BETTERED
5623 ōphĕlĕō (1), to benefit, be of use

BETWEEN
996 bêyn (190), between
997 bêyn (Ch.) (1), between; "either...or"
5921 ʼal (1), upon, against
5973 ʼîm (2), with
8432 tâvek (3), center, middle
1722 ĕn (1), in; during; because of
3307 mĕrizō (1), to apportion, bestow
3342 mĕtaxu (6), betwixt
4314 prŏs (2), for; on, at; to, toward; against

BETWIXT
996 bêyn (13), between
6293 pâgaʻ (1), to impinge

1537 ĕk (1), out, out of

BEULAH
1166 bâʻal (1), to be master; to marry

BEWAIL
1058 bâkâh (4), to weep, moan
2799 klaiō (1), to sob, wail
3996 pĕnthĕō (1), to grieve

BEWAILED
1058 bâkâh (1), to weep, moan
2875 kŏptō (2), to beat the breast

BEWAILETH
3306 yâphach (1), to breathe hard, gasp

BEWARE
6191 ʼâram (1), to be cunning; be prudent
8104 shâmar (9), to watch
991 blĕpō (6), to look at
4337 prŏsĕchō (7), to pay attention to
5442 phulassō (2), to watch, i.e. be on guard

BEWITCHED
940 baskainō (1), to fascinate, bewitch
1839 ĕxistēmi (2), to astound; to be insane

BEWRAY
1540 gâlâh (1), to denude; uncover

BEWRAYETH
5046 nâgad (1), to announce
7121 qârâʼ (1), to call out
1212+4160 dēlŏs (1), clear, plain, evident

BEYOND
1973 hâlᵉʼâh (5), far away; thus far
5674 ʼâbar (4), to cross over; to transition
5675 ʼâbar (Ch.) (7), region across
5676 ʼêber (21), opposite side; east
5921 ʼal (2), above, over
1900 ĕpĕkĕina (1), on the further side of, beyond
4008 pĕran (7), across, beyond
5228 hupĕr (1), over; above; beyond
5233 hupĕrbainō (1), to transcend
5238 hupĕrĕkĕina (1), beyond, still farther
5239 hupĕrĕktĕinō (1), to overreach
5249 hupĕrpĕrissōs (1), exceedingly

BEZAI
1209 Bêtsay (3), Betsai

BEZALEEL
1212 Beᶜtsalʼêl (9), in (the) protection of God

BEZEK
966 Bezeq (3), lightning

BEZER
1221 Betser (5), inaccessible spot

BICHRI
1075 Bikrîy (8), youthful

BID
559 ʼâmar (6), to say
1696 dâbar (2), to speak, say; to subdue
6942 qâdâsh (1), to be, make clean
479 antikalĕō (1), to invite in return
657 apŏtassŏmai (1), to say adieu; to renounce
2036 ĕpō (2), to speak
2564 kalĕō (2), to call
2753 kĕlĕuō (1), to order
3004 lĕgō (1), to say

BIDDEN
559 ʼâmar (1), to say
7121 qârâʼ (2), to call out
2564 kalĕō (10), to call
4367 prŏstassō (1), to arrange towards

BIDDETH
3004 lĕgō (1), to say

BIDDING
4928 mishmaʻath (1), royal court; obedience

BIDKAR
920 Bidqar (1), stabbing assassin

BIER
4296 miṭṭâh (1), bed; sofa, litter or bier
4673 sŏrŏs (1), funeral bier

BIGTHA
903 Bigthâʼ (1), Bigtha

BIGTHAN
904 Bigthân (1), Bigthan

BIGTHANA
904 Bigthân (1), Bigthana

BIGVAI
902 Bigvay (6), Bigvai

BILDAD
1085 Bildad (5), Bildad

BILEAM
1109 Bilʻâm (1), foreigner

BILGAH
1083 Bilgâh (3), desistance

BILGAI
1084 Bilgay (1), desistant

BILHAH
1090 Bilhâh (11), timid

BILHAN
1092 Bilhân (4), timid

BILL
5612 çêpher (4), writing
975 bibliŏn (1), scroll; certificate
1121 gramma (2), writing; education

BILLOWS
1530 gal (1), heap; ruins
4867 mishbâr (1), breaker

BILSHAN
1114 Bilshân (2), Bilshan

English

BIMHAL
1118 Bimhâl (1), *with pruning*

BIND
631 'âçar (13), to *fasten*; to *join* battle
2280 châbash (6), to *wrap* firmly, *bind*
3729 kᵉphath (Ch.) (1), to *fetter, bind*
6029 'ânad (1), to *lace fast, bind*
6887 tsârar (3), to *cramp*
7164 qâraç (1), to *hunch*
7194 qâshar (10), to *tie, bind*
7405 râkaç (2), to *tie, bind*
7573 râtham (1), to *yoke*
1195 dĕsmĕuō (1), to *enchain, tie on*
1210 dĕō (9), to *bind*
5265 hupŏdĕō (1), to *put on shoes or sandals*

BINDETH
247 'âzar (1), to *belt*
631 'âçar (1), to *fasten*; to *join* battle
2280 châbash (4), to *wrap* firmly, *bind*
6014 'âmar (1), to *gather grain into sheaves*
6887 tsârar (2), to *cramp*

BINDING
481 'âlam (1), to be *tongue-tied, be silent*
632 'ĕçâr (1), *obligation, vow, pledge*
681 'êtsel (1), *side; near*
8193 sâphâh (1), *lip, edge, margin*
1195 dĕsmĕuō (1), to *enchain, tie on*

BINEA
1150 Bin'â' (2), *Bina*

BINNUI
1131 Binnûwy (7), *built*

BIRD
1167+3671 ba'al (1), *master; owner; citizen*
5775 'ôwph (3), *bird*
5861 'ayiṭ (2), bird of prey (poss.) *hawk*
6833 tsippôwr (21), little hopping bird
3732 ŏrnĕŏn (1), *bird*

BIRD'S
6833 tsippôwr (1), little hopping bird

BIRDS
5775 'ôwph (6), winged bird
5861 'ayiṭ (1), bird of prey (poss.) *hawk*
6833 tsippôwr (10), little hopping bird
4071 pĕtĕinŏn (5), bird which *flies*
4421 ptĕnŏn (1), *bird*

BIRDS'
6853 tsᵉphar (Ch.) (1), *bird*

BIRSHA
1306 Birsha' (1), *with wickedness*

BIRTH
3205 yâlad (2), to *bear young*; to *father a child*
4351 mᵉkûwrâh (1), *origin*
4866 mishbêr (2), vaginal *opening*
5309 nephel (3), *abortive miscarriage*
7665 shâbar (1), to *burst*
8435 tôwlᵉdâh (1), *family descent, family record*
1079 gĕnĕtĕ (1), *birth*
1083 gĕnnēsis (2), *nativity*
5605 ōdinō (2), to *experience labor pains*

BIRTHDAY
3117+3205 yôwm (1), *day; time period*
1077 gĕnĕsia (2), *birthday* ceremonies

BIRTHRIGHT
1062 bᵉkôwrâh (9), *state of, rights of first born*
4415 prōtŏtŏkia (1), *primogeniture* rights

BIRZAVITH
1269 Birzôwth (1), *holes*

BISHLAM
1312 Bishlâm (1), *Bishlam*

BISHOP
1984 ĕpiskŏpē (1), *episcopate*
1985 ĕpiskŏpŏs (5), *overseer, supervisor*

BISHOPRICK
1984 ĕpiskŏpē (1), *episcopate*

BISHOPS
1985 ĕpiskŏpŏs (1), *overseer, supervisor*

BIT
4964 metheg (1), *bit*
5391 nâshak (2), to *strike*; to *oppress*

BITE
5391 nâshak (6), to *strike*; to *oppress*
1143 daknō (1), to *bite*

BITETH
5391 nâshak (2), to *strike*; to *oppress*

BITHIAH
1332 Bithyâh (1), *worshipper of Jehovah*

BITHRON
1338 Bithrôwn (1), *craggy* spot

BITHYNIA
978 Bithunia (2), *Bithynia*

BITS
5469 chalinŏs (1), *curb* or *head-stall*, i.e. *bit*

BITTEN
5391 nâshak (2), to *strike*; to *oppress*

BITTER
4751 mar (20), *bitter; bitterness; bitterly*
4784 mârâh (1), to *rebel* or *resist*; to *provoke*

BITTER
4805 mᵉrîy (1), *rebellion, rebellious*
4815 mᵉrîyrîy (1), *bitter*, i.e. *poisonous*
4843 mârar (2), to *be, make bitter*
4844 mᵉrôr (2), *bitter herb*
4846 mᵉrôrâh (2), *bitter bile; venom of a serpent*
8563 tamrûwr (2), *bitterness*
4087 pikrainō (4), to *embitter, turn sour*
4089 pikrŏs (2), *sharp, pungent*, i.e. *bitter*

BITTERLY
779 'ârar (1), to *execrate, place a curse*
4751 mar (3), *bitter; bitterness; bitterly*
4843 mârar (2), to *be, make bitter*
8563 tamrûwr (1), *bitterness*
4090 pikrŏs (2), *bitterly*, i.e. *violently*

BITTERN
7090 qippôwd (3), *bittern*

BITTERNESS
4470 memer (1), *sorrow*
4472 mamrôr (1), *bitterness, misery*
4751 mar (10), *bitter; bitterness; bitterly*
4814 mᵉrîyrûwth (1), *bitterness*
4843 mârar (4), to *be, make bitter*
4844 mᵉrôr (1), *bitter herb*
4088 pikria (4), *acridity, bitterness*

BIZJOTHJAH
964 bizyôwthᵉyâh (1), *contempts of Jehovah*

BIZTHA
968 Biztha' (1), *Biztha*

BLACK
380 'îyshôwn (1), *pupil, eyeball; middle*
3648 kâmar (1), to *shrivel with heat*
5508 çôchereth (1), (poss.) black *tile*
6937 qâdar (4), to *be dark-colored*
7835 shâchar (1), to *be dim or dark in color*
7838 shâchôr (6), *dusky, jet black*
7840 shᵉcharchôreth (1), *swarthy, dark*
3189 mĕlas (3), *black*

BLACKER
2821 châshak (1), to *be dark*; to *darken*

BLACKISH
6937 qâdar (1), to *be dark*-colored

BLACKNESS
3650 kimrîyr (1), *obscuration, eclipse*
6289 pâ'rûwr (2), *flush of anxiety*

BLASPHEMETH
6940 qadrûwth (1), *duskiness*
1105 gnŏphŏs (1), *gloom as of a storm, darkness*
2217 zŏphŏs (1), *gloom*

BLADE
3851 lahab (2), *flame of fire; flash of a blade*
7929 shikmâh (1), *shoulder*-bone
5528 chŏrtŏs (2), *pasture, herbage or vegetation*

BLAINS
76 'ăba'bû'âh (2), *pustule, skin eruption*

BLAME
2398 châṭâ' (2), to *sin*
299 amōmŏs (1), *unblemished, blameless*
3469 mōmaŏmai (1), to *carp at*, i.e. to *censure*

BLAMED
2607 kataginōskō (1), to *find fault with*
3469 mōmaŏmai (1), to *carp at*, i.e. to *censure*

BLAMELESS
5352 nâqâh (1), to *be, make clean*; to *be bare*
5355 nâqîy (2), *innocent*
273 amĕmptŏs (3), *irreproachable*
274 amĕmptōs (1), *faultlessly*
298 amōmētŏs (1), *unblamable*
338 anaitiŏs (1), *innocent*
410 anĕgklētŏs (4), *irreproachable*
423 anĕpilēptŏs (2), *not open to blame*

BLASPHEME
1288 bârak (2), to *bless*
5006 nâ'ats (2), to *scorn*
987 blasphēmĕō (6), to *speak impiously*

BLASPHEMED
1442 gâdaph (5), to *revile, blaspheme*
2778 châraph (1), to *spend the winter*
5006 nâ'ats (2), to *scorn*
5344 nâqab (1), to *specify, designate, libel*
987 blasphēmĕō (7), to *speak impiously*

BLASPHEMER
989 blasphēmŏs (1), *slanderous*

BLASPHEMERS
987 blasphēmĕō (1), to *speak impiously*
989 blasphēmŏs (1), *slanderous*

BLASPHEMEST
987 blasphēmĕō (1), to *speak impiously*

BLASPHEMETH
1442 gâdaph (1), to *revile, blaspheme*
5344 nâqab (2), to *specify, designate, libel*
987 blasphēmĕō (2), to *speak impiously*

BLASPHEMIES
5007 nᵉ'âtsâh (1), *scorn;*
to bloom
988 blasphēmia (5),
impious speech

BLASPHEMING
987 blasphēmĕō (1), to
speak impiously

BLASPHEMOUS
989 blasphēmŏs (2),
slanderous

BLASPHEMOUSLY
987 blasphēmĕō (1), to
speak impiously

BLASPHEMY
5007 nᵉ'âtsâh (2), *scorn;*
to bloom
987 blasphēmĕō (1), to
speak impiously
988 blasphēmia (11),
impious speech

BLAST
5397 nᵉshâmâh (3),
breath, life
7307 rûwach (4), *breath;*
wind; life-spirit

BLASTED
7709 shᵉdêmâh (1),
cultivated field
7710 shâdaph (3), to
scorch
7711 shᵉdêphâh (1),
blight; scorching

BLASTING
7711 shᵉdêphâh (5),
blight; scorching

BLASTUS
986 Blastŏs (1), (poss.) to
yield fruit

BLAZE
1310 diaphēmizō (1), to
spread news

BLEATING
6963 qôwl (1), *voice* or
sound

BLEATINGS
8292 shᵉrûwqâh (1),
whistling; scorn

BLEMISH
3971 mʼûwm (15),
blemish; fault
8400 tᵉballûl (1),
cataract in the eye
8549 tâmîym (44), *entire,*
complete; integrity
299 amōmŏs (2),
unblemished, blameless

BLEMISHES
3971 mʼûwm (1),
blemish; fault
3470 mōmŏs (1), *flaw* or
blot

BLESS
1288 bârak (115), to *bless*
2127 ĕulŏgĕō (10), to
invoke a benediction

BLESSED
833 ʼâshar (7), to *be*
honest, prosper
835 ʼesher (27), *how*
happy!
1288 bârak (175), to *bless*
1289 bᵉrak (Ch.) (4), to
bless

1293 bᵉrâkâh (3),
benediction, blessing
1757 ĕnĕulŏgĕō (2), to
confer a benefit, bless
2127 ĕulŏgĕō (30), to
invoke a benediction
2128 ĕulŏgĕtŏs (8),
adorable, praised
3106 makarizō (1), to
pronounce fortunate
3107 makariŏs (43),
fortunate, well off

BLESSEDNESS
3108 makarismŏs (3),
fortunate

BLESSEST
1288 bârak (3), to *bless*

BLESSETH
1288 bârak (8), to *bless*

BLESSING
1288 bârak (1), to *bless*
1293 bᵉrâkâh (51),
benediction, blessing
2127 ĕulŏgĕō (1), to
invoke a benediction
2129 ĕulŏgia (12),
benediction

BLESSINGS
1293 bᵉrâkâh (11),
benediction, blessing
2129 ĕulŏgia (1),
benediction

BLEW
8628 tâqaʼ (18), to *clatter,*
slap, drive, clasp
1920 ĕpiginŏmai (1), to
come up, happen
4154 pnĕō (3), to *breeze*
5285 hupŏpnĕō (1), to
breathe gently

BLIND
5786 ʻâvar (1), to *blind*
5787 ʻivvêr (26), *blind*
5788 ʻivvârôwn (1),
blindness
5956 ʻâlam (1), to *veil*
from sight, i.e. conceal
5185 tuphlŏs (52),
blindness; blind person

BLINDED
4456 pōrŏō (2), to *render*
stupid or *callous*
5186 tuphlŏō (3), to
cause blindness

BLINDETH
5786 ʻâvar (1), to *blind*

BLINDFOLDED
4028 pĕrikaluptō (1), to
cover eyes

BLINDNESS
5575 çanvêr (3),
blindness
5788 ʻivvârôwn (2),
blindness
4457 pōrōsis (2),
stupidity or *callousness*

BLOOD
1818 dâm (337), *blood;*
juice; life
5332 nêtsach (1), blood
(as if *red juice*)
129 haima (97), *blood*
130 haimatĕkchusia (1),
pouring of blood

131 haimŏrrhĕō (1), to
have a hemorrhage

BLOODGUILTINESS
1818 dâm (1), *blood;*
juice; life

BLOODTHIRSTY
582+1818 ʼenôwsh (1),
man; person, human

BLOODY
1818 dâm (15), *blood;*
juice; life
1420 dusĕntĕria (1),
dysentery

BLOOMED
6692 tsûwts (1), to
blossom, flourish

BLOSSOM
6524 pârach (4), to
bloom; to fly; to flourish
6525 perach (1), *calyx*
flower; bloom
6692 tsûwts (1), to
blossom, flourish

BLOSSOMED
6692 tsûwts (1), to
blossom, flourish

BLOSSOMS
5322 nêts (1), *flower*
6731 tsîyts (1), burnished
plate; bright flower

BLOT
3971 mʼûwm (2),
blemish; fault
4229 mâchâh (10), to
erase; to grease
1813 ĕxalĕiphō (1), to
obliterate

BLOTTED
4229 mâchâh (5), to
erase; to grease
1813 ĕxalĕiphō (1), to
obliterate

BLOTTETH
4229 mâchâh (1), to
erase; to grease

BLOTTING
1813 ĕxalĕiphō (1), to
obliterate

BLOW
2690 châtsar (1), to blow
the *trumpet*
4347 makkâh (1), *blow;*
wound; pestilence
5265 nâçaʼ (1), *start* on a
journey
5301 nâphach (3), to
inflate, blow hard
5380 nâshab (1), to *blow;*
to *disperse*
5398 nâshaph (2), to
breeze as the wind
6315 pûwach (2), to *blow,*
to *fan, kindle;* to *utter*
7321 rûwaʼ (1), to *shout*
8409 tigrâh (1), *strife, i.e.*
infliction
8628 tâqaʼ (23), to *clatter,*
slap, drive, clasp
8643 tᵉrûwʼâh (1),
battle-cry; clangor
4154 pnĕō (2), to *breeze*

BLOWETH
5301 nâphach (1), to
inflate, blow hard

5380 nâshab (1), to *blow;*
to *disperse*
8628 tâqaʼ (1), to *clatter,*
slap, drive, clasp
4154 pnĕō (1), to *breeze*

BLOWING
8628 tâqaʼ (2), to *clatter,*
slap, drive, clasp
8643 tᵉrûwʼâh (2),
battle-cry; clangor

BLOWN
5301 nâphach (1), to
inflate, blow hard
8628 tâqaʼ (3), to *clatter,*
slap, drive, clasp

BLUE
8504 tᵉkêleth (50), color
violet

BLUENESS
2250 chabbûwrâh (1),
weal, bruise

BLUNT
6949 qâhâh (1), to *be*
dull; be blunt

BLUSH
3637 kâlam (3), to *taunt*
or *insult*

BOANERGES
993 Bŏanĕrgĕs (1), *sons*
of commotion

BOAR
2386 chăzîyr (1), *hog,*
boar

BOARD
7175 qeresh (17), *slab* or
plank; deck of a ship

BOARDS
3871 lûwach (4), *tablet*
6763 tsêlâʼ (2), *side*
7175 qeresh (33), *slab*
7713 sᵉdêrâh (1), *row, i.e.*
rank of soldiers
4548 sanis (1), *planked*
timber, board

BOAST
559 ʼâmar (1), to *say*
1984 hâlal (6), to *boast*
3235 yâmar (1), to
exchange
3513 kâbad (1), to *be*
heavy, severe, dull
6286 pâʼar (1), to *shake* a
tree
2620 katakauchaŏmai
(1), to *exult against*
2744 kauchaŏmai (8), to
glory in; to boast

BOASTED
1431 gâdal (1), to *be*
great, make great
2744 kauchaŏmai (1), to
glory in; to boast

BOASTERS
213 alazōn (2), *braggart*

BOASTEST
1984 hâlal (1), to *boast*

BOASTETH
1984 hâlal (3), to boast
3166 mĕgalauchĕō (1), to
be *arrogant, egotistic*

BOASTING
2744 kauchaŏmai (1), to
glory in; to boast

BOASTINGS
2745 kauchēma (1), boast; brag
2746 kauchēsis (6), boasting; bragging
3004 lěgō (1), to say

BOASTINGS
212 alazŏnĕïa (1), boasting

BOAT
5679 'ăbârâh (1), crossing-place
4142 plŏiariŏn (2), small boat
4627 skaphē (3), skiff or yawl, i.e. life boat

BOATS
4142 plŏiariŏn (1), small boat

BOAZ
1162 Bô'az (24), Boaz

BOCHERU
1074 Bôk°rûw (2), first-born

BOCHIM
1066 Bôkîym (2), weepers

BODIES
1354 gab (1), mounded or rounded: top or rim
1472 g°vîyâh (7), dead body
1480 gûwphâh (1), corpse
1655 geshem (Ch.) (2), body
5038 n°bêlâh (2), carcase or carrion
6297 peger (6), carcase; corpse
4430 ptōma (3), corpse, carrion
4983 sōma (11), body

BODILY
4983 sōma (1), body
4984 sōmatikŏs (2), corporeal or physical
4985 sōmatikŏs (1), corporeally

BODY
990 beṭen (8), belly; womb; body
1320 bâsâr (2), flesh; body; person
1460 gêv (1), middle, inside, in, on, etc.
1465 gêvâh (1), back
1472 g°vîyâh (3), dead body
1480 gûwphâh (1), corpse
1655 geshem (Ch.) (3), body
3409 yârêk (1), leg or shank, flank; side
5038 n°bêlâh (4), carcase or carrion
5085 nidneh (Ch.) (1), sheath; body
5315 nephesh (9), life; breath; soul; wind
6106 'etsem (2), bone; body; substance
7607 sh°'êr (1), flesh, meat; kindred by blood
4954 sussōmŏs (1), fellow-member
4983 sōma (131), body
5559 chrōs (1), skin

BODY'S
4983 sōma (1), body

BOHAN
932 Bôhan (2), thumb

BOIL
1158 bâ'âh (1), to ask; be bulging, swelling
1310 bâshal (4), to boil up, cook; to ripen
7570 râthach (2), to boil, churn
7822 sh°chîyn (9), inflammation, ulcer

BOILED
1310 bâshal (2), to boil
7570 râthach (1), to boil, churn

BOILING
4018 m°bashsh°lâh (1), cooking hearth

BOILS
7822 sh°chîyn (2), inflammation, ulcer

BOISTEROUS
2478 ischurŏs (1), forcible, powerful

BOLD
982 bâṭach (1), to trust, be confident or sure
662 apŏtŏlmaō (1), to bring forth boldly
2292 tharrhĕō (2), to be bold
3954 parrhēsia (1), frankness, boldness
3955 parrhēsiazŏmai (2), to be frank, confident
5111 tŏlmaō (4), to be bold, courageous

BOLDLY
983 beṭach (1), safety, security, trust
2292 tharrhĕō (1), to be bold
3954 parrhēsia (3), frankness, boldness
3955 parrhēsiazŏmai (6), to be frank, confident
5111 tŏlmaō (1), to be bold, courageous
5112 tŏlmērŏtĕrŏn (1), with greater confidence

BOLDNESS
5797 'ôz (1), strength
3954 parrhēsia (9), frankness, boldness

BOLLED
1392 gib'ôl (1), calyx

BOLSTER
4763 m°ra'ăshâh (6), headpiece; head-rest

BOLT
5274 nâ'al (1), to fasten up, lock

BOLTED
5274 nâ'al (1), to fasten up, lock

BOND
632 'ĕçâr (7), obligation, vow, pledge
4148 mûwçâr (1), reproof, warning
4562 mâçôreth (1), band

BONDAGE
1199 dĕsmŏn (1), shackle; impediment
1401 dŏulŏs (6), slave, servant
4886 sundĕsmŏs (3), ligament; control

BONDAGE
3533 kâbash (2), to conquer, subjugate
5647 'âbad (1), to do, work, serve
5650 'ebed (10), servant
5656 'ăbôdâh (8), work
5659 'abdûwth (3), servitude
1397 dŏulĕïa (5), slavery, bondage
1398 dŏulĕuō (4), to serve as a slave
1402 dŏulŏō (4), to enslave
2615 katadŏulŏō (2), to enslave utterly

BONDMAID
8198 shiphchâh (1), household female slave
3814 paidiskē (1), female slave or servant

BONDMAIDS
519 'âmâh (2), female servant or slave

BONDMAN
5650 'ebed (5), servant
1401 dŏulŏs (1), slave, servant

BONDMEN
5647 'âbad (1), to do, work, serve
5650 'ebed (16), servant

BONDS
632 'ĕçâr (3), obligation, vow, pledge
4147 môwçêr (5), halter; restraint
254 halusis (1), fetter or manacle
1198 dĕsmiŏs (2), bound captive; one arrested
1199 dĕsmŏn (14), shackle; impediment or disability
1210 dĕō (1), to bind

BONDSERVANT
5656+5650 'ăbôdâh (1), work of any kind

BONDSERVICE
5647 'âbad (1), to do, work, serve

BONDWOMAN
519 'âmâh (4), maid-servant or female slave
3814 paidiskē (4), female slave or servant

BONDWOMEN
8198 shiphchâh (3), household female slave

BONE
1634 gerem (1), bone; self
6106 'etsem (14), bone; body; substance
7070 qâneh (1), reed
3747 ŏstĕŏn (1), bone

BONES
1633 gâram (1), to crunch the bones
1634 gerem (2), bone; self
1635 gerem (Ch.) (1), bone
6106 'etsem (89), bone; body; substance
3747 ŏstĕŏn (4), bone
4974 sphurŏn (1), ankle

BONNETS
4021 migbâ'âh (4), cap wrapped around head
6287 p°'êr (2), fancy head-dress

BOOK
1697 dâbâr (7), word; matter; thing
5609 ç°phar (Ch.) (3), book
5612 çêpher (136), writing
974 bibliaridiŏn (4), little scroll
975 bibliŏn (23), scroll; certificate
976 biblŏs (15), scroll

BOOKS
5609 ç°phar (Ch.) (1), book
5612 çêpher (2), writing
975 bibliŏn (4), scroll; certificate
976 biblŏs (1), scroll of writing

BOOTH
5521 çukkâh (2), tabernacle; shelter

BOOTHS
5521 çukkâh (8), tabernacle; shelter

BOOTIES
4933 m°shiççâh (1), plunder

BOOTY
957 baz (1), plunder, loot
4455 malqôwach (1), spoil, plunder
4953 mashrôwqîy (Ch.) (1), musical pipe

BOOZ
1003 Bŏŏz (3), Boöz

BORDER
1366 g°bûwl (136), boundary, border
1379 gâbal (2), to set a boundary line, limit
3027 yâd (1), hand; power
3411 y°rêkâh (1), recesses, far away
4526 miçgereth (6), margin; stronghold
7093 qêts (2), extremity; after
7097 qâtseh (2), extremity
8193 sâphâh (3), lip; edge, margin
2899 kraspĕdŏn (2), margin

BORDERS
1366 g°bûwl (20), boundary, border
1367 g°bûwlâh (1), boundary marker
1552 g°lîylâh (3), circuit or region

3027 yâd (1), *hand; power*
3671 kânâph (2), *edge* or *extremity; wing*
4526 miçgereth (7), *margin; stronghold*
5299 náphâh (1), *height*
7093 qêts (1), *extremity*
7097 qâtseh (1), *extremity*
8444 tôwtsâ'âh (1), *exit,* i.e. *boundary*
8447 tôwr (1), *succession, order*
2899 kraspĕdŏn (1), *margin*
3181 mĕthŏriŏs (1), *frontier* region
3725 hŏriŏn (1), *region, area, vicinity*

BORE
5344 nâqab (1), to *puncture, perforate*
7527 râtsa' (1), to *pierce*

BORED
5344 nâqab (1), to *puncture, perforate*

BORN
249 'ezrâch (11), *native born*
990 beţen (1), *belly; womb; body*
1121 bên (2), *son, descendant*
3205 yâlad (80), to *bear young; to father a child*
3209 yillôwd (4), *born*
3211 yâlîyd (6), *born; descendants*
4138 môwledeth (2), *offspring, family*
313 anagĕnnaŏ (1), to *beget or bear again*
1080 gĕnnaŏ (39), to *procreate, regenerate*
1084 gĕnnĕtŏs (2), *pertaining to birth*
1085 gĕnŏs (2), *kin,* offspring in kind
1626 ĕktrōma (1), *untimely birth*
5088 tiktō (3), to *produce* from seed

BORNE
3205 yâlad (3), to *bear young; to father a child*
5190 nâţal (1), to *lift; to impose*
5375 nâsâ' (14), to *lift up*
5445 çâbal (1), to *carry*
5564 çâmak (1), to *lean upon; take hold of*
6006 'âmaç (1), to *impose* a burden
142 airō (1), to *lift, to take up*
941 bastazō (4), to *lift, bear*
1418 dus- (2), *hard,* i.e. *with difficulty*
5409 phŏrĕō (1), to *wear*

BORROW
3867 lâvâh (1), to *borrow; to lend*
5670 'âbaţ (1), to *pawn; to lend; to entangle*
7592 shâ'al (4), to *ask*
1155 danĕizō (1), to *loan on interest; to borrow*

BORROWED
3867 lâvâh (1), to *borrow; to lend*
7592 shâ'al (2), to *ask*

BORROWER
3867 lâvâh (2), to *borrow; to lend*

BORROWETH
3867 lâvâh (1), to *borrow; to lend*

BOSCATH
1218 Botsqath (1), *swell* of ground

BOSOM
2243 chôb (1), *bosom*
2436 chêyq (32), *bosom, heart*
2683 chêtsen (1), *bosom*
6747 tsallachath (2), *bosom*
2859 kŏlpŏs (5), *lap* area

BOSOR
1007 Bŏsŏr (1), *lamp*

BOSSES
1354 gab (1), *mounded* or *rounded: top* or *rim*

BOTCH
7822 shechîyn (2), *inflammation, ulcer*

BOTH
413 'êl (1), *to, toward*
1571 gam (30), *also; even; "both...and"*
3162 yachad (1), *unitedly*
8147 shenayim (78), *two-fold*
8174 Sha'aph (2), *fluctuation*
297 amphŏtĕrŏs (14), *both*
1417 duŏ (2), *two*
1538 hĕkastŏs (1), *each* or *every*
2532 kai (45), *and; or; even; also*
5037 tĕ (39), *both or also*

BOTTLE
1228 baqbûk (2), *bottle*
2573 chêmeth (4), skin *bottle*
4997 nô'd (4), skin *bag*
5035 nebel (5), skin *bag*

BOTTLES
178 'ôwb (1), *wineskin; necromancer, medium*
2573 chêmeth (1), skin *bottle*
4997 nô'd (2), skin *bag*
5035 nebel (3), skin *bag*
779 askŏs (12), *leather bottle or bag*

BOTTOM
773 'ar'îyth (Ch.) (1), *bottom, dirt floor*
2436 chêyq (2), *bosom, heart*
3247 yeçôwd (10), *foundation*
4688 metsôwlâh (1), *deep* place
4699 metsullâh (1), *shade, deep*
7172 qarqa' (1), *floor*
7507 rephîydâh (1), *railing*

8328 sheresh (1), *root*
2736 katō (2), *downwards*

BOTTOMLESS
12 abussŏs (7), *deep place, abyss*

BOTTOMS
7095 qetseb (1), *shape; base*

BOUGH
534 'âmîyr (1), *top*
1121 bên (2), *son, descendant; people*
2793 chôresh (1), *wooded forest*
6288 pe'ôrâh (1), *foliage, branches*
7754 sôwk (2), *branch*

BOUGHS
5577 çançîn (1), *twig*
5589 çe'appâh (2), *twig*
5634 çar'appâh (1), *twig*
5688 'ăbôth (3), *entwined* things: *foliage*
6056 'ănaph (Ch.) (1), *bough, branch*
6057 'ânâph (3), *twig*
6288 pe'ôrâh (2), *foliage, branches*
6529 perîy (1), *fruit*
7105 qâtsîyr (3), *harvest; limb* of a tree
7730 sôwbek (1), *thicket*

BOUGHT
3739 kârâh (1), to *purchase* by bargaining
4736 miqnâh (7), *acquisition*
7069 qânâh (21), to *create; to procure*
7666 shâbar (1), to *deal* in cereal grain
59 agŏrazō (13), to *purchase; to redeem*
5608 ōnĕŏmai (1), to *purchase, buy*

BOUND
615 'âçîyr (2), *captive, prisoner*
631 'âçar (33), to *fasten; to join* battle
640 'âphad (1), to *fasten, gird*
1366 gebûwl (4), *boundary, border*
2280 châbash (4), to *wrap firmly, bind*
3256 yâçar (1), to *chastise; to instruct*
3729 kephath (Ch.) (3), to *fetter, bind*
4205 mázôwr (1), *sore* needing a bandage
6123 'âqad (1), to *tie the feet with thongs*
6616 pâthîyl (1), *twine, cord*
6887 tsârar (7), to *cramp*
7194 qâshar (4), to *tie, bind*
7576 râthaq (1), to *fasten, bind*
8244 sâqad (1), to *fasten, bind*
8379 ta'ăvâh (1), *limit,* i.e. *full extent*
332 anathĕmatizō (3), to *declare* or *vow an oath*

1196 dĕsmĕŏ (1), *shackle; bind*
1210 dĕŏ (28), to *bind*
2611 katadĕŏ (1), to *bandage a wound*
3784 ŏphĕilō (2), to *owe; to be under obligation*
4019 pĕridĕŏ (1), to *wrap around*
4029 pĕrikĕimai (1), to *enclose, encircle*
4385 prŏtĕinō (1), to *tie prostrate* for scourging
4887 sundĕŏ (1), to *be a fellow-prisoner*

BOUNDS
1366 gebûwl (1), *boundary, border*
1367 gebûwlâh (1), *boundary marker*
1379 gâbal (2), to *set a boundary*
2706 chôq (2), *appointment; allotment*
3734 hŏrŏthĕsia (1), *boundary-line*

BOUNTIFUL
2896 ţôwb (1), *good; well*
7771 shôwa' (1), *noble,* i.e. *liberal; opulent*

BOUNTIFULLY
1580 gâmal (4), to *benefit* or *requite; to wean*
2129 ĕulŏgia (1), *benediction*

BOUNTIFULNESS
572 haplŏtĕs (1), *sincerity; generosity*

BOUNTY
3027 yâd (1), *hand; power*
2129 ĕulŏgia (2), *benediction*

BOW
86 'abrêk (1), *kneel*
3721 kâphaph (2), to *curve, bow*
3766 kâra' (9), to *prostrate*
5186 nâţâh (6), to *stretch* or spread out
5791 'âvath (1), to *wrest, twist*
7198 qesheth (55), *bow, rainbow*
7812 shâchâh (17), to *prostrate* in homage
7817 shâchach (2), to *sink* or *depress*
2578 kamptō (3), to *bend*
4781 sugkamptō (1), to *afflict*
5115 tŏxŏn (1), *bow*

BOWED
3721 kâphaph (3), to *curve, bow*
3766 kâra' (11), to *prostrate; to make miserable*
5186 nâţâh (5), to *stretch* or spread out
5791 'âvath (1), to *wrest, twist*
6915 qâdad (13), to *bend*
7743 shûwach (1), to *sink*
7812 shâchâh (35), to *prostrate* in homage

English

BOWELS (continued)

7817 shâchach (4), to sink or depress
1120 gŏnupĕtĕō (1), to fall on the knee, kneel
2578 kamptō (1), to bend
2827 klinō (2), to slant or slope
4794 sugkuptō (1), to be completely overcome

BOWELS

4578 mê'âh (26), viscera; anguish, tenderness
7130 qereb (1), nearest part, i.e. the center
7358 rechem (2), womb
4698 splagchnŏn (9), intestine; affection, pity

BOWETH

3766 kâra' (2), to prostrate
7817 shâchach (1), to sink or depress

BOWING

5186 nâṭâh (2), to stretch or spread out
5087 tithēmi (1), to put

BOWL

1543 gullâh (3), fountain; bowl or globe
4219 mîzrâq (13), bowl for sprinkling
5602 çêphel (1), basin, bowl

BOWLS

1375 gᵉbîya' (8), goblet; bowl
1543 gullâh (3), fountain; bowl or globe
4219 mîzrâq (8), bowl for sprinkling
4518 mᵉnaqqîyth (3), sacrificial basin
5592 çaph (2), dish

BOWMEN

7411+7198 râmâh (1), to hurl; to shoot

BOWS

7198 qesheth (13), bow, rainbow

BOWSHOT

2909+7198 ṭâchâh (1), to stretch a bow

BOX

6378 pak (2), flask, jug
8391 t 'ashshûwr (2), cedar
211 alabastrŏn (4), alabaster, vase

BOY

3206 yeled (1), young male

BOYS

3206 yeled (1), young male
5288 na'ar (1), male child; servant

BOZEZ

949 Bôwtsêts (1), shining

BOZKATH

1218 Botsqath (1), swell of ground

BOZRAH

1224 Botsrâh (9), sheep-fold, animal pen

BRACELET

685 'ets'âdâh (1), bracelet

BRACELETS

2397 châch (1), ring for the nose or lips
6616 pâthîyl (2), twine, cord
6781 tsâmŷd (6), bracelet; lid
8285 shêrâh (1), wrist-band

BRAKE

1234 bâqa' (3), to cleave, break, tear open
1518 gîyach (1), to issue forth; to burst forth
1855 dᵉqaq (Ch.) (5), to crumble; crush
1961 hâyâh (1), to exist, i.e. be or become
3807 kâthath (1), to bruise or strike, beat
5310 nâphats (1), to dash to pieces; to scatter
5422 nâthats (12), to tear down
5423 nâthaq (3), to tear off
6555 pârats (4), to break out
6561 pâraq (1), to break off or crunch; to deliver
6565 pârar (2), to break up; to violate, frustrate
7323 rûwts (1), to run
7533 râtsats (1), to crack in pieces, smash
7665 shâbar (20), to burst
1284 diarrhēssō (2), to tear asunder
2608 katagnumi (2), to crack apart
2622 kataklaō (2), to divide in pieces
2806 klaō (9), to break bread
4937 suntribō (1), to crush completely

BRAKEST

7533 râtsats (1), to crack in pieces, smash
7665 shâbar (4), to burst

BRAMBLE

329 'âṭâd (3), buckthorn
942 batŏs (1), brier

BRAMBLES

2336 chôwach (1), thorn; hook; ring for the nose

BRANCH

534 'âmîyr (1), top
1121 bên (1), son, descendant; people
2156 zᵉmôwrâh (3), twig, vine branch
2158 zâmîyr (1), song
3127 yôwneqeth (1), sprout, new shoot
3712 kippâh (3), leaf
5342 nêtser (4), shoot of a plant; descendant
5929 'âleh (1), leaf; foliage
6057 'ânâph (1), twig
6780 tsemach (5), sprout, branch
6788 tsammereth (2), foliage

BRANCHES

905 bad (3), limb, member; bar; chief
1121 bên (1), son, descendant; people
1808 dâlîyâh (8), bough, branch
2156 zᵉmôwrâh (1), pruned twig, branch
3127 yôwneqeth (3), sprout, new shoot
3709 kaph (1), hollow of hand; paw; sole
5189 nᵉṭîyshâh (1), tendril plant shoot
5585 çâ'îyph (2), fissure of rocks; bough
5688 'ăbôth (1), entwined things; string or foliage
5929 'âleh (3), leaf; foliage
6056 'ănaph (Ch.) (3), bough, branch
6057 'ânâph (3), twig
6058 'ânêph (1), branching
6073 'ophe (1), bough
6288 pᵉ'ôrâh (4), foliage, branches
7070 qâneh (19), reed
7641 shibbôl (1), stream; ear of grain
7976 shilluchâh (1), shoot of a vine
8299 sârîyg (3), entwining tendril
902 baïŏn (1), palm twig
2798 kladŏs (9), twig or bough
2814 klēma (1), limb or shoot
4746 stŏibas (1), bough of a tree so employed

BRAND

181 'ûwd (1), poker stick for a fire

BRANDISH

5774 'ûwph (1), to cover, to fly; to faint

BRANDS

3940 lappîyd (1), flaming torch, lamp or flame

BRASEN

5178 nᵉchôsheth (27), copper; bronze
5473 chalkiŏn (1), copper dish or kettle

BRASS

5153 nâchûwsh (1), coppery, i.e. hard
5154 nᵉchûwshâh (7), copper; bronze
5174 nᵉchâsh (Ch.) (9), copper
5178 nᵉchôsheth (102), copper; bronze
5470 chalkĕŏs (1), copper
5474 chalkŏlibanŏn (2), burnished copper
5475 chalkŏs (3), copper

BRAVERY

8597 tiph'ârâh (1), ornament

BRAWLER

269 amachŏs (1), not quarrelsome

BRAWLERS

269 amachŏs (1), not quarrelsome

BRAWLING

4090 mᵉdân (2), contest or quarrel

BRAY

3806 kâthash (1), to pound in a mortar
5101 nâhaq (1), to bray; to scream from hunger

BRAYED

5101 nâhaq (1), to bray; to scream from hunger

BREACH

919 bedeq (1), gap
1234 bâqa' (2), to cleave, break, tear open
6555 pârats (1), to break out
6556 perets (10), break, gap
7667 sheber (5), fracture; ruin
8569 tᵉnûw'âh (1), enmity

BREACHES

919 bedeq (7), gap
1233 bᵉqîya' (1), fissure, breach
4664 miphrâts (1), haven, cove
6555 pârats (1), to break out
6556 perets (3), break, gap
7447 râçîyç (1), ruin; dew-drop
7667 sheber (1), fracture; ruin

BREAD

3899 lechem (236), food, bread
740 artos (72), loaf of bread

BREADTH

2947 ṭêphach (1), palm-breadth
2948 ṭôphach (3), palm-breadth
4800 merchâb (1), open space; liberty
6613 pᵉthay (Ch.) (2), width
7338 rachab (1), width, expanse
7341 rôchab (75), width
4114 platŏs (4), width

BREAK

215 'ôwr (1), to be luminous
1234 bâqa' (3), to cleave, break, tear open
1633 gâram (2), to crunch the bones
1758 dûwsh (1), to trample or thresh
1792 dâkâ' (3), to pulverize; be contrite
1854 dâqaq (3), to crush; crumble

1986 hâlam (1), to *strike, beat, stamp, conquer*
2000 hâmam (1), to *disturb, drive, destroy*
2040 hâraç (7), to *pull down; break, destroy*
2490 châlal (3), to *profane, defile*
3318 yâtsâ' (1), to *go, bring out*
5003 nâ'aph (1), to *commit adultery*
5106 nûw' (1), to *refuse, forbid, dissuade*
5214 nîyr (2), to *till the soil*
5310 nâphats (10), to *dash* to pieces
5422 nâthats (6), to *tear down*
5423 nâthaq (2), to *tear off*
5670 'âbaṭ (1), to *pawn;* to *entangle*
6202 'âraph (3), to *break the neck*, to *destroy*
6206 'ârats (1), to *awe;* to *dread;* to *harass*
6315 pûwach (2), to *blow*, to *fan, kindle;* to *utter*
6476 pâtsach (6), to *break out in sound*
6524 pârach (2), to *break forth;* to *bloom;* to *fly*
6555 pârats (7), to *break out*
6561 pâraq (3), to *break off or crunch;* to *deliver*
6562 pᵉraq (Ch.) (1), to *discontinue, stop*
6565 pârar (14), to *break up;* to *violate, frustrate*
6605 pâthach (1), to *open wide;* to *loosen, begin*
6743 tsâlach (1), to *push forward*
6746 tsᵉlôchîyth (1), *vial* or *salt-cellar*
7489 râ'a' (3), to *break to pieces*
7533 râtsats (1), to *crack in pieces, smash*
7665 shâbar (33), to *burst*
7702 sâdad (2), to *break ground*
827 augē (1), *radiance, dawn*
1358 diōrussō (2), to *penetrate burglariously*
2608 katagnumi (1), to *crack apart*
2806 klaō (2), to *break bread*
3089 luō (1), to *loosen*
4486 rhēgnumi (2), to *break, burst forth*
4919 sunthruptō (1), to *crush together*

BREAKER
6555 pârats (1), to *break out*
3848 parabatēs (1), *violator, lawbreaker*

BREAKEST
7665 shâbar (1), to *burst*

BREAKETH
1234 bâqa' (1), to *cleave, break, tear open*

1638 gâraç (1), to *crush, break;* to *dissolve*
1855 dᵉqaq (Ch.) (1), to *crumble; crush*
2040 hâraç (1), to *pull down; break, destroy*
5927 'âlâh (1), to *ascend, be high, mount*
6327 pûwts (1), to *dash in pieces;* to *disperse*
6555 pârats (3), to *break out*
6566 pâras (1), to *break apart, disperse, scatter*
7665 shâbar (5), to *burst*
7779 shûwph (1), to *gape*, i.e. *snap* at
7940 Sâkar (1), *recompense*

BREAKING
4290 machtereth (1), *burglary*
4866 mishbêr (1), *vaginal opening*
5927 'âlâh (1), to *ascend, be high, mount*
6524 pârach (2), to *break forth;* to *bloom;* to *fly*
6556 perets (3), *break, gap*
6565 pârar (2), to *break up;* to *violate, frustrate*
6979 qûwr (1), to *throw forth;* to *wall up*
7667 sheber (2), *fracture; ruin*
7670 shibrôwn (1), *ruin*
2800 klasis (2), *fracturing*
2806 klaō (1), to *break bread*
3847 parabasis (1), *violation, breaking*

BREAKINGS
7667 sheber (1), *fracture; ruin*

BREAST
2306 chădîy (Ch.) (1), *breast*
2373 châzeh (11), *animal breast meat*
7699 shad (3), *female breast*
4738 stēthŏs (3), *area of the human chest*

BREASTPLATE
2833 chôshen (25), *gorget*
8302 shiryôwn (1), *corslet, coat of mail*
2382 thōrax (2), *corslet, chest*

BREASTPLATES
2382 thōrax (3), *corslet, chest*

BREASTS
1717 dad (2), *female breast or bosom*
2373 châzeh (2), *animal breast meat*
3824 lêbâb (1), *heart*
5845 'ăṭîyn (1), *receptacle* for milk
7699 shad (19), *female breast*
4738 stēthŏs (2), *area of the human chest*

BREATH
5315 nephesh (1), *life; breath; soul; wind*
5396 nishmâ' (Ch.) (1), *breath, life*
5397 nᵉshâmâh (12), *breath, life*
7307 rûwach (27), *breath; wind; life*-spirit
4157 pnŏē (1), *breeze; breath*

BREATHE
3307 yâpheach (1), *puffing; breathing out*
5301 nâphach (1), to *inflate, blow hard*
5397 nᵉshâmâh (2), *breath, life*

BREATHED
5301 nâphach (1), to *inflate, blow hard*
5397 nᵉshâmâh (2), *breath, life*
1720 ĕmphusaō (1), to *blow at or on*

BREATHETH
5397 nᵉshâmâh (1), *breath, life*

BREATHING
7309 rᵉvâchâh (1), *relief*
1709 ĕmpnĕō (1), to *be animated by*

BRED
7311 rûwm (1), to *be high;* to *rise or raise*

BREECHES
4370 miknâç (5), *drawers concealing* the privates

BREED
1121 bên (1), *people* of a *class or kind*
8317 shârats (1), to *swarm*, or *abound*

BREEDING
4476 mimshâq (1), *possession*

BRETHREN
251 'âch (329), *brother; relative; member*
252 'ach (Ch.) (1), *brother; relative*
80 adĕlphŏs (225), *brother*
81 adĕlphŏtēs (1), *fraternity, brotherhood*
5360 philadĕlphia (1), *fraternal affection*
5361 philadĕlphŏs (1), *fraternal*
5569 psĕudadĕlphŏs (2), *pretended associate*

BRETHREN'S
251 'âch (1), *brother; relative; member*

BRIBE
3724 kôpher (2), *redemption*-price

BRIBERY
7810 shachad (1), to *bribe; gift*

BRIBES
7810 shachad (3), to *bribe; gift*

BRICK
3835 lâban (3), to *make bricks*
3843 lᵉbênâh (4), *brick*

BRICKKILN
4404 malbên (3), *brick-kiln*

BRICKS
3843 lᵉbênâh (4), *brick*

BRIDE
3618 kallâh (9), *bride; son's wife*
3565 numphē (5), *young married* woman

BRIDECHAMBER
3567 numphōn (3), *bridal room*

BRIDEGROOM
2860 châthân (8), *bridegroom*
3566 numphiŏs (15), *bridegroom*

BRIDEGROOM'S
3566 numphiŏs (1), *bridegroom*

BRIDLE
4269 machçôwm (1), *muzzle*
4964 metheg (3), *bit*
7448 reçen (4), *jaw restraint* of a horse
5469 chalinŏs (1), *bit or bridle*

BRIDLES
5469 chalinŏs (1), *bit or bridle*

BRIDLETH
5468 chalinagōgĕō (1), to *curb, hold in check*

BRIEFLY
346 anakĕphalaiŏmai (1), to *sum up*
1223+3641 dia (1), *through*, by means of

BRIER
2312 chêdeq (1), *prickly plant*
5544 çillôwn (1), *prickle*
5636 çarpâd (1), *stinging nettle*

BRIERS
1303 barqân (2), *thorn, biers*
5621 çârâb (1), *thistle*
8068 shâmîyr (8), *thorn;* (poss.) *diamond*
5146 tribŏlŏs (1), *thorny caltrop plant*

BRIGANDINE
5630 çiyrôn (1), *coat of mail*, scale armor

BRIGANDINES
5630 çiyrôn (1), *coat of mail*, scale armor

BRIGHT
216 'ôwr (1), *luminary; lightning; happiness*
925 bâhîyr (1), *shining, bright*
934 bôhereth (11), *whitish, bright* spot
1300 bârâq (1), *lightning; flash of lightning*

BRIGHTNESS

1305 bârar (1), to *brighten; purify*
2385 chăzîyz (1), *flash of lightning*
3851 lahab (1), *flame of fire; flash of a blade*
3974 mâ'ôwr (1), *luminary, light source*
4803 mârat (1), to *polish; to make bald*
4838 mâraq (1), to *polish; to sharpen; to rinse*
5051 nôgahh (1), *brilliancy*
6219 'âshôwth (1), *polished*
6247 'esheth (1), *fabric*
7043 qâlal (1), to *be, make light*
796 astrapē (1), *lightning; light's glare*
2986 lamprŏs (2), *radiant; clear*
5460 phŏtĕinŏs (1), *well-illuminated*

BRIGHTNESS

2096 zôhar (2), *brilliancy, shining*
2122 zîyv (Ch.) (2), *cheerfulness*
3314 yiph'âh (2), *splendor, beauty*
3368 yâqâr (1), *valuable*
5051 nôgahh (11), *brilliancy*
5054 nᵉgôhâh (1), *splendor, luster*
541 apaugasma (1), *effulgence, radiance*
2015 ĕpiphanĕia (1), *manisfestation*
2987 lamprŏtēs (1), *brilliancy*

BRIM

7097 qâtseh (1), *extremity*
8193 sâphâh (7), *lip; edge, margin*
507 anō (1), *upward or on the top, heavenward*

BRIMSTONE

1614 gophrîyth (7), *sulphur*
2303 thĕiŏn (7), *sulphur*
2306 thĕiŏdēs (1), *sulphurous yellow*

BRING

338 'îy (1), *solitary wild creature that howls*
503 'âlaph (1), *increase by thousands*
622 'âçaph (2), to *gather, collect*
858 'âthâh (Ch.) (2), to *arrive; go*
935 bôw' (248), to *go or come*
1069 bâkar (1), to *give the birthright*
1431 gâdal (1), to *be great, make great*
1518 gîyach (1), to *issue forth; to burst forth*
1876 dâshâ' (1), to *sprout new plants*
1980 hâlak (1), to *walk; live a certain way*
2142 zâkar (2), to *remember; to mention*

2342 chûwl (1), to *dance, whirl; to writhe in pain*
2381 Chăzîy'êl (1), *seen of God*
2986 yâbal (5), to *bring*
3051 yâhab (2), to *give*
3205 yâlad (17), to *bear young; to father a child*
3212 yâlak (3), to *walk; to live; to carry*
3254 yâçaph (1), to *add or augment*
3318 yâtsâ' (73), to *go, bring out*
3381 yârad (24), to *descend*
3513 kâbad (1), to *be heavy, severe, dull*
3533 kâbash (1), to *conquer, subjugate*
3665 kâna' (3), to *humiliate, vanquish*
3947 lâqach (17), to *take*
4608 ma'âleh (1), *elevation; platform*
4672 mâtsâ' (2), to *find or acquire; to occur*
5060 nâga' (3), to *strike*
5066 nâgash (14), to *be, come, bring near*
5080 nâdach (1), to *push off, scattered*
5107 nûwb (1), to (*make*) *flourish; to utter*
5375 nâsâ' (10), to *lift up*
5381 nâsag (1), to *reach*
5414 nâthan (11), to *give*
5437 çâbab (2), to *surround*
5647 'âbad (1), to *do, work, serve*
5674 'âbar (1), to *cross over; to transition*
5924 'êllâ' (Ch.) (3), *above*
5927 'âlâh (35), to *ascend, be high, mount*
6049 'ânan (1), to *cover, becloud; to act covertly*
6213 'âsâh (9), to *do or make*
6315 pûwach (1), to *blow, to fan, kindle; to utter*
6398 pâlach (1), to *slice; to break open; to pierce*
6509 pârâh (2), to *bear fruit*
6779 tsâmach (1), to *sprout*
6805 tsâ'ad (1), to *pace, step regularly*
7034 qâlâh (1), to *hold in contempt*
7126 qârab (36), to *approach, bring near*
7311 rûwm (1), to *be high; to rise or raise*
7392 râkab (1), to *ride*
7665 shâbar (1), to *burst*
7725 shûwb (72), to *turn back; to return*
7760 sûwm (1), to *put, place*
7817 shâchach (1), to *sink or depress*
7896 shîyth (1), to *place*
7971 shâlach (1), to *send away*
8045 shâmad (1), to *desolate*

8074 shâmêm (2), to *devastate; to stupefy*
8213 shâphêl (4), to *humiliate*
8317 shârats (3), to *wriggle, swarm*
71 agō (14), to *lead; to bring, drive; to weigh*
114 athĕtĕō (1), to *disesteem, neutralize*
321 anagō (2), to *lead up; to bring out; to sail*
363 anamimnĕskō (1), to *remind; to recollect*
518 apaggĕllō (2), to *announce, proclaim*
520 apagō (1), to *take away*
667 apŏphĕrō (1), to *bear off, carry away*
1295 diasōzō (1), to *cure, preserve, rescue*
1396 dŏulagōgĕō (1), to *enslave, subdue*
1402 dŏulŏō (1), to *enslave*
1521 ĕisagō (1), to *lead into*
1533 ĕisphĕrō (2), to *carry inward*
1625 ĕktrĕphō (1), to *cherish or train*
1627 ĕkphĕrō (1), to *bear out; to produce*
1863 ĕpagō (2), *inflict; charge*
2018 ĕpiphĕrō (1), to *inflict, bring upon*
2036 ĕpō (1), to *speak or say*
2097 ĕuaggĕlizō (2), to *announce good news*
2592 karpŏphŏrĕō (4), to *be fertile*
2609 katagō (3), to *lead down; to moor a vessel*
2615 katadŏulŏō (2), to *enslave utterly*
2673 katargĕō (1), to *be, render entirely useless*
3919 parĕisagō (1), to *lead in aside*
4160 pŏiĕō (6), to *do*
4311 prŏpĕmpō (3), to *send forward*
4317 prŏsagō (2), to *bring near*
4374 prŏsphĕrō (2), to *present to; to treat as*
5062 tĕssarakŏnta (1), *forty*
5088 tiktō (3), to *produce from seed*
5179 tupŏs (1), *shape, i.e. statue or resemblance*
5342 phĕrō (17), to *bear or carry*
5461 phōtizō (1), to *shine or to brighten* up

BRINGERS

539 'âman (1), to *be firm, faithful, true; to trust*

BRINGEST

935 bôw' (1), to *go, come*
1319 bâsar (3), to *announce* (good news)
1533 ĕisphĕrō (1), to *carry inward*

BRINGETH

935 bôw' (6), to *go or come*
1069 bâkar (1), to *give the birthright*
1319 bâsar (5), to *announce* (good news)
2142 zâkar (1), to *remember*
2659 châphêr (1), to *shame, reproach*
3318 yâtsâ' (18), to *go, bring out*
3381 yârad (2), to *descend*
3615 kâlâh (1), to *complete, prepare*
5060 nâga' (1), to *strike*
5107 nûwb (1), to (*make*) *flourish; to utter*
5148 nâchâh (2), to *guide*
5414 nâthan (3), to *give*
5927 'âlâh (3), to *ascend, be high, mount*
6213 'âsâh (3), to *do or make*
6331 pûwr (1), to *crush*
6445 pânaq (1), to *enervate, reduce vigor*
6779 tsâmach (1), to *sprout*
7725 shûwb (3), to *turn back; to return*
7737 shâvâh (1), to *level, equalize; to resemble*
7817 shâchach (1), to *sink or depress*
8213 shâphêl (1), to *humiliate*
399 anaphĕrō (1), to *take up; to lead up*
616 apŏkuĕō (1), to *bring into being*
1521 ĕisagō (1), to *lead into*
1544 ĕkballō (3), to *throw out*
2592 karpŏphŏrĕō (2), to *be fertile*
4160 pŏiĕō (7), to *do*
4393 prŏphĕrō (2), to *bear forward*
4992 sōtēriŏn (1), *defender or defence*
5088 tiktō (2), to *produce from seed*
5342 phĕrō (2), to *bear or carry*

BRINGING

935 bôw' (6), to *go, come*
2142 zâkar (1), to *remember; to mention*
3318 yâtsâ' (3), to *go, bring out*
5375 nâsâ' (3), to *lift up*
7725 shûwb (2), to *turn back; to return*
71 agō (1), to *lead; to bring, drive; to weigh*
163 aichmalōtizō (2), to *make captive*
1863 ĕpagō (1), *inflict; charge*
1898 ĕpĕisagōgē (1), *introduction*
4160 pŏiĕō (1), to *do*
5342 phĕrō (3), to *bear or carry*

BRINK
7097 qâtseh (1), *extremity*
8193 sâphâh (5), *lip;
edge, margin*

BROAD
7338 râchab (1), *width,
expanse*
7338+3027 râchab (1),
width, expanse
7339 rᵉchôb (3), *myriad*
7341 rôchab (21), *width*
7342 râchâb (5), *roomy,
spacious*
7554 râqa' (1), *to pound*
7555 riqqûa' (1), *thin*
metallic *plate*
2149 ĕuruchŏrŏs (1),
spacious, wide
4115 platunō (1), *to
widen*

BROADER
7342 râchâb (1), *roomy,
spacious*

BROIDED
4117 plĕgma (1), *plait* or
braid of hair

BROIDERED
7553 riqmâh (7),
embroidery
8665 tashbêts (1),
checkered stuff

BROILED
3702 ŏptŏs (1), *roasted,
broiled*

BROKEN
6 'âbad (1), *perish;
destroy*
1234 bâqa' (6), *to cleave,
break, tear open*
1638 gâraç (1), *to crush,
break; to dissolve*
1792 dâkâ' (3), *to
pulverize; be contrite*
1794 dâkâh (3), *to
collapse; contrite*
1854 dâqaq (1), *to crush;
crumble*
1986 hâlam (2), *to strike,
beat, stamp, conquer*
2040 hâraç (4), *to pull*
down; *break, destroy*
2490 châlal (1), *to
profane, defile*
2844 chath (6), *terror*
2865 châthath (6), *to
break down*
3807 kâthath (1), *to
bruise or strike*
4535 maççâch (1),
cordon; barrier; in turn
4790 mᵉrôwach (1),
bruised, pounded
5181 nâchath (2), *to sink,
descend; to press*
5218 nâkê' (3), *smitten;
afflicted*
5310 nâphats (1), *to dash
to pieces; to scatter*
5421 nâtha' (1), *to tear
out*
5422 nâthats (5), *to tear
down*
5423 nâthaq (7), *to tear
off*
5927 'âlâh (1), *to ascend,
be high, mount*

6105 'âtsam (1), *to be,
make powerful*
6209 'ârar (1), *to bare;* to
demolish
6331 pûwr (1), *to crush*
6480 pâtsam (1), *to rend,
tear* by earthquake
6524 pârach (2), *to break*
forth; *to bloom*
6531 perek (1), *severity*
6555 pârats (12), *to
break out*
6565 pârar (9), *to break
up; to violate, frustrate*
7280 râga' (1), *to stir up*
7462 râ'âh (1), *to tend a
flock,* i.e. *pasture it*
7465 rô'âh (1), *breakage*
7489 râ'a' (2), *to break to
pieces*
7533 râtsats (4), *to crack
in pieces, smash*
7616 shâbâb (1),
fragment, i.e. *ruin*
7665 shâbar (65), *to burst*
8406 tᵉbar (Ch.) (1), *to be
fragile*
1358 diŏrussō (2), *to
penetrate* burglariously
1575 ĕkklaō (3), *to
exscind, cut off*
1846 ĕxŏrussō (1), *to dig
out*
2608 katagnumi (1), *to
crack apart*
2801 klasma (2), *piece,
bit*
2806 klaō (3), *to break*
bread
3089 luō (6), *to loosen*
4917 sunthlaō (2), *to
dash together, shatter*
4937 suntribō (3), *to
crush completely*
4977 schizō (1), *to split
or sever*

BROKENFOOTED
7667+7272 sheber (1),
fracture; ruin

BROKENHANDED
7667+3027 sheber (1),
fracture; ruin

BROKENHEARTED
7665+3820 shâbar (1), *to
burst*
4937+2588 suntribō (1),
to crush completely

BROOD
3555 nŏssia (1), *hen's
brood*

BROOK
4323 mîykâl (1), *brook*
5158 nachal (37), *valley,
ravine;* mine *shaft*
5493 chĕimarrhŏs (1),
winter-torrent

BROOKS
650 'âphîyq (1), *valley;
stream; mighty, strong*
2975 yᵉ'ôr (4), Nile *River;*
Tigris *River*
5158 nachal (9), *valley,
ravine;* mine *shaft*

BROTH
4839 mârâq (2),
soup-broth

6564 pârâq (1),
fragments in soup

BROTHER
251 'âch (244), *brother;
relative; member*
1730 dôwd (1), *beloved,
friend; relative*
2992 yâbam (2), *to marry*
a brother's widow
2993 yâbâm (2),
husband's brother
7453 rêa' (1), *associate;
one close*
80 adĕlphŏs (109),
brother

BROTHER'S
251 'âch (25), *brother;
relative; member*
2994 yᵉbêmeth (3), dead
brother's widow, i.e.
sister-in-law
80 adĕlphŏs (7), *brother*

BROTHERHOOD
264 'achăvâh (1),
fraternity; brotherhood
81 adĕlphŏtēs (1),
fraternity, brotherhood

BROTHERLY
251 'âch (1), *brother;
relative; member*
5360 philadĕlphia (5),
fraternal affection

BROTHERS'
1730 dôwd (1), *beloved,
friend; relative*

BROUGHT
539 'âman (5), *to be firm,
faithful, true; to trust*
622 'âçaph (3), *to gather,
collect*
656 'âphêç (1), *to cease*
857 'âthâh (1), *to arrive;
go*
858 'âthâh (Ch.) (7), *to
arrive; go*
935 bôw' (264), *to go or
come*
1197 bâ'ar (1), *to be
brutish, be senseless*
1310 bâshal (1), *to boil
up, cook; to ripen*
1319 bâsar (2), *to
announce* (good news)
1431 gâdal (6), *to be
great, make great*
1468 gûwz (1), *to pass*
rapidly
1540 gâlâh (1), *to
denude; uncover*
1541 gᵉlâh (Ch.) (1), *to
reveal mysteries*
1589 gânab (1), *to thieve;
to deceive*
1809 dâlal (3), *to
slacken, dangle*
1820 dâmâh (2), *to be
silent; to fail, cease*
1946 hûwk (Ch.) (1), *to
go, come*
1961 hâyâh (2), *to exist,*
i.e. *be or become*
2254 châbal (2), *to bind*
by a *pledge; to pervert*
2342 chûwl (3), *to dance,
whirl; to writhe* in pain
2659 châphêr (3), *to be
ashamed, disappointed*

2986 yâbal (7), *to bring*
2987 yᵉbal (Ch.) (2), *to
bring*
3205 yâlad (12), *to bear
young; to father a child*
3212 yâlak (8), *to walk;
to live; to carry*
3218 yekeq (1), *young
locust*
3318 yâtsâ' (127), *to go,
bring out*
3381 yârad (17), *to
descend*
3467 yâsha' (2), *to make
safe, free*
3474 yâshar (1), *to be
straight; to make right*
3533 kâbash (3), *to
conquer, subjugate*
3665 kâna' (4), *to
humiliate, vanquish*
3766 kâra' (2), *to make
miserable*
3947 lâqach (8), *to take*
4161 môwtsâ' (2), *going
forth*
4355 mâkak (2), *to
tumble; to perish*
4551 maççâ' (1), *stone
quarry; projectile*
5060 nâga' (1), *to strike*
5066 nâgash (13), *to be,
come, bring near*
5090 nâhag (4), *to drive*
forth; *to carry away*
5148 nâchâh (2), *to guide*
5265 nâça' (3), *start* on a
journey
5375 nâsâ' (13), *to lift up*
5414 nâthan (3), *to give*
5437 çâbab (1), *to
surround*
5493 çûwr (1), *to turn* off
5674 'âbar (6), *to cross
over; to transition*
5927 'âlâh (65), *to
ascend, be high, mount*
5954 'âlal (Ch.) (4), *to go
in; to lead in*
6030 'ânâh (1), *to
respond, answer*
6213 'âsâh (3), *to do or
make*
6565 pârar (1), *to break
up; to violate, frustrate*
6819 tsâ'ar (1), *to be
small; be trivial*
6908 qâbats (1), *to
collect, assemble*
7126 qârab (27), *to
approach, bring near*
7127 qᵉrêb (Ch.) (1), *to
approach, bring near*
7136 qârâh (1), *to bring
about; to impose*
7235 râbâh (1), *to
increase*
7311 rûwm (1), *to be
high; to rise or raise*
7323 rûwts (1), *to run*
7392 râkab (1), *to ride*
7617 shâbâh (1), *to
transport* into captivity
7725 shûwb (39), *to turn
back; to return*
7760 sûwm (4), *to put,
place*
7817 shâchach (3), *to
sink or depress*

BROUGHTEST
7971 shâlach (1), to *send away*
8213 shâphêl (3), to *humiliate*
8239 shâphath (1), to *place* or *put*
8317 shârats (2), to *swarm, or abound*
71 agō (32), to *lead; to bring, drive; to weigh*
321 anagō (4), to *lead up; to bring out; to sail*
397 anatrĕphō (1), to *rear, care for*
654 apŏstrĕphō (1), to *turn away or back*
985 blastanō (1), to *yield fruit*
1080 gĕnnaō (1), to *procreate, regenerate*
1096 ginŏmai (2), to *be, become*
1325 didōmi (1), to *give*
1402 dŏulŏō (1), to *enslave*
1521 ĕisagō (7), to *lead into*
1533 ĕisphĕrō (2), to *carry inward*
1627 ĕkphĕrō (1), to *bear out; to produce*
1806 ĕxagō (6), to *lead forth, escort*
1850 ĕxŏusiazō (1), to *control, master another*
2018 ĕpiphĕrō (2), to *inflict, bring upon*
2049 ĕrēmŏō (2), to *lay waste*
2064 ĕrchŏmai (1), to *go*
2097 ĕuaggĕlizō (1), to *announce good news*
2164 ĕuphŏrĕō (1), to *be fertile, produce a crop*
2476 histēmi (1), to *stand, establish*
2601 katabibazō (1), to *cause to bring down*
2609 katagō (4), to *lead down; to moor a vessel*
2865 kŏmizō (1), to *provide for*
2989 lampō (1), to *radiate brilliancy*
3350 mĕtŏikĕsia (1), *exile, deportation*
3860 paradidōmi (1), to *hand over*
3920 parĕisaktŏs (1), *smuggled in, infiltrated*
3930 parĕchō (2), to *hold near, i.e. to present*
3936 paristēmi (1), to *stand beside, present*
4160 pŏiĕō (1), to *make*
4254 prŏagō (3), to *lead forward; to precede*
4311 prŏpĕmpō (4), to *send forward*
4317 prŏsagō (1), to *bring near*
4374 prŏsphĕrō (15), to *present to; to treat as*
4851 sumphĕrō (1), to *collect; to conduce*
4939 suntrŏphŏs (1), one *brought up with*
5013 tapĕinŏō (1), to *depress; to humiliate*

5044 tĕknŏtrŏphĕō (1), to *be a child-rearer*
5088 tiktō (4), to *produce from seed*
5142 trĕphō (1), to *nurse, feed, care for*
5342 phĕrō (17), to *bear or carry*
5461 phōtizō (1), to *shine or to brighten up*

BROUGHTEST
935 bôw' (4), to *go or come*
3318 yâtsâ' (7), to *go, bring out*
5927 'âlâh (2), to *ascend, be high, mount*

BROW
4696 mêtsach (1), *forehead*
3790 ŏphrus (1), eye-*brow*

BROWN
2345 chûwm (4), *sunburnt* or *swarthy*

BRUISE
1792 dâkâ' (1) to *pulverize; be contrite*
1854 dâqaq (1), to *crush; crumble*
7490 rᵉᵃ' (Ch.) (1), to *shatter, dash to pieces*
7667 sheber (2), *fracture; ruin*
7779 shûwph (2), to *gape, i.e. snap at*
4937 suntribō (1), to *crush completely*

BRUISED
1792 dâkâ' (1), to *pulverize; be contrite*
1854 dâqaq (1), to *crush; crumble*
4600 mâ'ak (1), to *press, to pierce, emasculate*
6213 'âsâh (2), to *do or make*
7533 râtsats (2), to *crack in pieces, smash*
2352 thrauō (1), to *crush*
4937 suntribō (1), to *crush completely*

BRUISES
2250 chabbûwrâh (1), *weal, bruise*

BRUISING
6213 'âsâh (1), to *do or make*
4937 suntribō (1), to *crush completely*

BRUIT
8052 shᵉmûw'âh (1), *announcement*
8088 shêma' (1), *something heard*

BRUTE
249 alŏgŏs (2), *irrational, not reasonable*

BRUTISH
1197 bâ'ar (11), to *be brutish, be senseless*

BUCKET
1805 dᵉlîy (1), *pail, bucket*

BUCKETS
1805 dᵉlîy (1), *pail, bucket*

BUCKLER
4043 mâgên (6), *small shield (buckler); skin*
5507 çôchêrâh (1), *surrounding shield*
6793 tsinnâh (3), *large shield; piercing cold*
7420 rômach (1), *iron pointed spear*

BUCKLERS
4043 mâgên (3), *small shield (buckler); skin*
6793 tsinnâh (2), *large shield; piercing cold*

BUD
4161 môwtsâ' (1), *going forth*
5132 nûwts (1), to *fly away, leave*
6524 pârach (2), to *break forth; to bloom*
6525 perach (1), *calyx flower; bloom*
6779 tsâmach (6), to *sprout*

BUDDED
5132 nûwts (1), to *fly away, leave*
6524 pârach (3), to *break forth; to bloom*
985 blastanō (1), to *yield fruit*

BUDS
6525 perach (1), *calyx flower; bloom*

BUFFET
2852 kŏlaphizō (2), to *strike*

BUFFETED
2852 kŏlaphizō (3), to *strike*

BUILD
1124 bᵉnâ' (Ch.) (6), to *build*
1129 bânâh (140), to *build; to establish*
456 anŏikŏdŏmĕō (2), to *rebuild*
2026 ĕpŏikŏdŏmĕō (2), to *rear up, build up*
3618 ŏikŏdŏmĕō (12), *construct; edification*

BUILDED
1124 bᵉnâ' (Ch.) (10), to *build*
1129 bânâh (36), to *build; to establish*
2680 kataskĕuazō (2), to *construct; to arrange*
3618 ŏikŏdŏmĕō (1), *construct; edification*
4925 sunŏikŏdŏmĕō (1), to *construct*

BUILDEDST
1129 bânâh (1), to *build; to establish*

BUILDER
5079 tĕchnitēs (1), *artisan, craftsman*

BUILDERS
1129 bânâh (9), to *build; to establish*
3618 ŏikŏdŏmĕō (5), *construct; edification*

BUILDEST
1129 bânâh (3), to *build; to establish*
3618 ŏikŏdŏmĕō (2), *construct; edification*

BUILDETH
1129 bânâh (7), to *build; to establish*
2026 ĕpŏikŏdŏmĕō (2), to *rear up, build up*

BUILDING
1124 bᵉnâ' (Ch.) (3), to *build*
1129 bânâh (15), to *build; to establish*
1140 binyâh (1), *structure*
1146 binyân (7), *edifice, building*
1147 binyân (Ch.) (1), *edifice, building*
4746 mᵉqâreh (1), *frame of timbers*
1739 ĕndŏmēsis (1), *structure*
2026 ĕpŏikŏdŏmĕō (1), to *rear up, build up*
2937 ktisis (1), *formation*
3618 ŏikŏdŏmĕō (1), *construct; edification*
3619 ŏikŏdŏmē (3), *structure; edification*

BUILDINGS
3619 ŏikŏdŏmē (3), *structure; edification*

BUILT
1124 bᵉnâ' (Ch.) (1), to *build*
1129 bânâh (155), to *build; to establish*
2026 ĕpŏikŏdŏmĕō (3), to *rear up, build up*
2680 kataskĕuazō (1), to *construct; to arrange*
3618 ŏikŏdŏmĕō (10), *construct; edification*

BUKKI
1231 Buqqîy (5), *wasteful*

BUKKIAH
1232 Buqqîyâh (2), *wasting of Jehovah*

BUL
945 Bûwl (1), *rain*

BULL
7794 shôwr (1), *bullock*
8377 tᵉ'ôw (1), *antelope*

BULLOCK
1121+1241 bên (3), *son, descendant*
1241 bâqâr (1), *plowing ox; herd*
5695 'êgel (1), bull-*calf*
6499 par (89), *bullock*
7794 shôwr (10), *bullock*

BULLOCK'S
6499 par (3), *bullock*

BULLOCKS
1241 bâqâr (4), *plowing ox; herd*
5695 'êgel (1), bull-*calf*
6499 par (36), *bullock*
7794 shôwr (1), *bullock*
8450 tôwr (Ch.) (3), *bull*

BULLS
47 'abbîyr (4), *mighty*

1241 bâqâr (1), *plowing ox; herd*
6499 par (2), *bullock*
5022 taurŏs (2), *bullock, ox*

BULRUSH
100 'agmôwn (1), *rush; rope of rushes*

BULRUSHES
1573 gôme' (2), *papyrus plant*

BULWARKS
2426 chêyl (1), *entrenchment, rampart*
2430 chêylâh (1), *entrenchment, rampart*
4685 mâtsôwd (1), *net or snare; besieging tower*
4692 mâtsôwr (1), *siege-mound; distress*
6438 pinnâh (1), *pinnacle; chieftain*

BUNAH
946 Bûwnâh (1), *discretion*

BUNCH
92 'ăguddâh (1), *band; bundle; knot; arch*

BUNCHES
1707 dabbesheth (1), *hump of a camel*
6778 tsammûwq (2), *lump of dried grapes*

BUNDLE
6872 tsᵉrôwr (3), *parcel; kernel or particle*
4128 plēthŏs (1), *large number, throng*

BUNDLES
6872 tsᵉrôwr (1), *parcel; kernel or particle*
1197 dĕsmē (1), *bundle*

BUNNI
1137 Bânîy (3), *built*

BURDEN
3053 yᵉhâb (1), *lot given*
4853 massâ (52), *burden, utterance*
4858 massâ'âh (1), *conflagration from the rising of smoke*
4864 mas'êth (1), *raising; beacon; present*
5445 çâbal (1), *to carry*
5448 çôbel (3), *load, burden*
5449 çabbâl (1), *porter, carrier*
6006 'âmaç (1), *to impose a burden*
922 barŏs (3), *load, abundance, authority*
1117 gŏmŏs (1), *cargo, wares or freight*
2599 katabarĕō (1), *to be a burden*
5413 phŏrtiŏn (2), *burden, task or service*

BURDENED
916 barĕō (1), *to weigh down, cause pressure*
2347 thlipsis (1), *pressure, trouble*

BURDENS
92 'ăguddâh (1), *band; bundle; knot; arch*
4853 massâ' (5), *burden, utterance*
4864 mas'êth (2), *raising; beacon; present*
4942 mishpâth (1), *pair of stalls for cattle*
5447 çêbel (1), *load; forced labor*
5449 çabbâl (5), *porter, carrier*
5450 çᵉbâlâh (6), *porterage; forced labor*
922 barŏs (1), *load, abundance, authority*
5413 phŏrtiŏn (3), *burden, task or service*

BURDENSOME
4614 ma'ămâçâh (1), *burdensomeness*
4 abarēs (1), *not burdensome*
1722+922 ĕn (1), *in; during; because of*
2655 katanarkaō (2), *to be a burden*

BURIAL
6900 qᵉbûwrâh (4), *sepulchre*
1779 ĕntaphiazō (1), *to enswathe for burial*

BURIED
6912 qâbar (96), *to inter, pile up*
2290 thaptō (7), *to celebrate funeral rites*
4916 sunthaptō (2), *to be buried with*

BURIERS
6912 qâbar (1), *to inter, pile up*

BURN
1197 bâ'ar (19), *to be brutish, be senseless*
1754 dûwr (1), *circle; ball; pile*
2734 chârâh (1), *to blaze*
2787 chârar (1), *to melt, burn, dry up*
3344 yâqad (3), *to burn*
3857 lâhaṭ (1), *to blaze*
4729 miqṭâr (1), *hearth*
5400 nâsaq (1), *to catch fire*
5927 'âlâh (2), *to ascend, be high, mount*
6702 tsûwth (1), *to blaze, set on fire*
6999 qâṭar (59), *to turn into fragrance by fire*
8313 sâraph (40), *to be, set on fire*
2370 thumiaō (1), *to offer aromatic fumes*
2545 kaiō (1), *to set on fire*
2618 katakaiō (4), *to consume wholly by burning*
4448 purŏō (2), *to be ignited, glow; inflamed*

BURNED
1197 bâ'ar (8), *to be brutish, be senseless*

2787 chârar (7), *to melt, burn, dry up*
3341 yâtsath (9), *to burn or set on fire*
3554 kâvâh (2), *to blister, be scorched*
3857 lâhaṭ (2), *to blaze*
5375 nâsâ' (2), *to lift up*
6866 tsârab (1), *to burn*
6999 qâṭar (19), *to turn into fragrance by fire*
8313 sâraph (33), *to be, set on fire*
8314 sârâph (1), *poisonous serpent*
8316 sᵉrêphâh (1), *cremation*
1572 ĕkkaiō (1), *to inflame deeply*
1714 ĕmprēthō (1), *to burn, set on fire*
2545 kaiō (3), *to set on fire*
2618 katakaiō (6), *to consume wholly by burning*
2740 kausis (1), *act of burning*
4448 purŏō (1), *to be ignited, glow; inflamed*

BURNETH
1197 bâ'ar (4), *to be brutish, be senseless*
2142 zâkar (1), *to remember; to mention*
3344 yâqad (1), *to burn*
3857 lâhaṭ (2), *to blaze*
4348 mikvâh (1), *burn*
5635 çâraph (1), *to cremate*
6919 qâdach (1), *to inflame*
6999 qâṭar (2), *to turn into fragrance by fire*
8313 sâraph (4), *to be, set on fire*
2545 kaiō (1), *to set on fire*

BURNING
784 'êsh (3), *fire*
1197 bâ'ar (6), *to be brutish, be senseless*
1513 gechel (1), *ember, hot coal*
1814 dâlaq (1), *to flame; to pursue*
1815 dᵉlaq (Ch.) (1), *to flame, burn*
2746 charchûr (1), *hot fever*
3344 yâqad (3), *to burn*
3345 yᵉqad (Ch.) (10), *to burn*
3346 yᵉqêdâ' (Ch.) (1), *consuming fire*
3350 yᵉqôwd (1), *burning, blazing*
3555 kᵉvîyâh (1), *branding, scar*
3587 kîy (1), *brand or scar*
3940 lappîyd (1), *flaming torch, lamp or flame*
4169 môwqᵉdâh (1), *fuel*
4348 mikvâh (4), *burn*
6867 tsârebeth (2), *conflagration*
6920 qaddachath (1), *inflammation*

6999 qâṭar (1), *to turn into fragrance by fire*
7565 resheph (1), *flame*
8316 sᵉrêphâh (9), *cremation*
2545 kaiō (6), *to set on fire*
2742 kausōn (1), *burning heat, hot day*
4451 purōsis (2), *ignition; conflagration, calamity*

BURNINGS
4168 môwqêd (1), *conflagration, burning*
4955 misrâphâh (2), *cremation*

BURNISHED
7044 qâlâl (1), *brightened, polished*

BURNT
398 'âkal (1), *to eat*
1197 bâ'ar (6), *to be brutish, be senseless*
3632 kâlîyl (1), *whole, entire; complete; whole*
4198 mâzeh (1), *exhausted, empty*
5927 'âlâh (1), *to ascend, be high, mount*
5928 'ălâh (Ch.) (1), *wholly consumed in fire*
5930 'ôlâh (284), *sacrifice wholly consumed in fire*
6999 qâṭar (24), *to turn into fragrance by fire*
8313 sâraph (36), *to be, set on fire*
8316 sᵉrêphâh (2), *cremation*
2618 katakaiō (2), *to consume wholly by burning*
3646 hŏlŏkautōma (3), *wholly-consumed*

BURST
1234 bâqa' (1), *to cleave, break, tear open*
5423 nâthaq (4), *to tear off*
6555 pârats (1), *to break out*
2997 laschō (1), *to crack open*
4486 rhēgnumi (2), *to break, burst forth*

BURSTING
4386 mᵉkittâh (1), *fracture*

BURY
6912 qâbar (33), *to inter, pile up*
1779 ĕntaphiazō (1), *to enswathe for burial*
2290 thaptō (4), *to celebrate funeral rites*
5027 taphē (1), *burial*

BURYING
6912 qâbar (2), *to inter, pile up*
1780 ĕntaphiasmŏs (2), *preparation for burial*

BURYINGPLACE
6913 qeber (7), *sepulchre*

BUSH
5572 çᵉneh (6), *bramble*
942 batŏs (5), *brier*

BUSHEL
3426 mŏdiŏs (3), dry
measure of volume

BUSHES
5097 nahălôl (1), pasture
7880 sîyach (2),
shrubbery

BUSHY
8534 taltal (1), wavy

BUSINESS
1697 dâbâr (8), word;
matter; thing
4399 mᵉlâ'kâh (12),
work; property
4639 ma'ăseh (1), action;
labor
6045 'inyân (2),
employment, labor
2398 idiŏs (1), private or
separate
4229 pragma (1), matter,
deed, affair
4710 spŏudē (1),
despatch; eagerness
5532 chrĕia (1), affair;
occasion, demand

BUSY
6213 'âsâh (1), to do or
make

BUSYBODIES
4020 pĕriĕrgazŏmai (1),
to meddle
4021 pĕriĕrgŏs (1),
busybody; magic

BUSYBODY
244 allotriĕpiskŏpŏs (1),
meddler, busybody

BUTLER
4945 mashqeh (8), butler;
drink; well-watered

BUTLERS
4945 mashqeh (1), butler;
drink; well-watered

BUTLERSHIP
4945 mashqeh (1), butler;
drink; well-watered

BUTTER
2529 chem'âh (10),
curds, milk or cheese
4260 machămâ'âh (1),
buttery; flattery

BUTTOCKS
4667 miphsâ'âh (1),
crotch area
8357 shêthâh (2), seat
i.e. buttock

BUY
3739 kârâh (1), to
purchase by bargaining
3947 lâqach (2), to take
7066 qᵉnâ' (Ch.) (1), to
purchase
7069 qânâh (24), to
create; to procure
7666 shâbar (14), to deal
in cereal grain
59 agŏrazō (13), to
purchase; to redeem
1710 ĕmpŏrĕuŏmai (1),
to trade, do business

BUYER
7069 qânâh (3), to create;
to procure

BUYEST
7069 qânâh (2), to create;
to procure

BUYETH
3947 lâqach (1), to take
59 agŏrazō (2), to
purchase; to redeem

BUZ
938 Bûwz (3), disrespect;
scorn

BUZI
941 Bûwzîy (1), Buzi

BUZITE
940 Bûwzîy (2), Buzite

BYWAYS
734+6128 'ôrach (1),
well-traveled road

BYWORD
4405 millâh (1), word;
discourse; speech
4912 mâshâl (1), pithy
maxim; taunt
4914 mᵉshôl (1), satire
8148 shᵉnîynâh (3), gibe,
verbal taunt

CAB
6894 qab (1), dry
measure of volume

CABBON
3522 Kabbôwn (1), hilly

CABINS
2588 chânûwth (1), vault
or cell

CABUL
3521 Kâbûwl (2), sterile

CAESAR
2541 Kaisar (21), Cæsar

CAESAR'S
2541 Kaisar (9), Cæsar

CAESAREA
2542 Kaisarĕia (17), of
Cæsar

CAGE
3619 kᵉlûwb (1),
bird-trap; basket
5438 phulakē (1),
guarding or guard

CAIAPHAS
2533 Kaïaphas (9), dell

CAIN
7014 Qayin (17), lance
2535 Kaïn (3), lance

CAINAN
7018 Qêynân (5), fixed
2536 Kaïnan (2), fixed

CAKE
1690 dᵉbêlâh (1), cake of
pressed figs
2471 challâh (7), cake
shaped as a ring
4580 mâ'ôwg (1), cake of
bread, provision
5692 'uggâh (3),
round-cake
6742 tsᵉlûwl (1), round
or flattened cake

CAKES
1690 dᵉbêlâh (2), cake of
pressed figs
2471 challâh (8), cake
shaped as a ring
3561 kavvân (2),
sacrificial wafer

3823 lâbab (1), to make
cakes
3834 lâbîybâh (3), fried
or turned cake
4682 matstsâh (4),
unfermented cake
5692 'uggâh (4),
round-cake
7550 râqîyq (1), thin
cake, wafer

CALAH
3625 Kelach (2), maturity

CALAMITIES
343 'êyd (1), misfortune,
ruin, disaster
1942 havvâh (1), desire;
craving
7451 ra' (1), bad; evil

CALAMITY
343 'êyd (16), misfortune,
ruin, disaster
1942 havvâh (3), desire;
craving

CALAMUS
7070 qâneh (3), reed

CALCOL
3633 Kalkôl (1),
sustenance

CALDRON
100 'agmôwn (1), rush;
rope of rushes
5518 çîyr (3), thorn; hook
7037 qallachath (2),
kettle

CALDRONS
1731 dûwd (1), pot,
kettle; basket
5518 çîyr (2), thorn; hook

CALEB
3612 Kâlêb (32), forcible

CALEB'S
3612 Kâlêb (4), forcible

CALEB-EPHRATAH
3613 Kâlêb 'Ephrâthâh
(1), Caleb-Ephrathah

CALF
1121+1241 bên (2), son,
descendant
5695 'êgel (21), calf
3447 mŏschŏpŏiĕō (1), to
fabricate a bullock-idol
3448 mŏschŏs (4), young
bullock

CALF'S
5695 'êgel (1), calf

CALKERS
2388+919 châzaq (2), to
fasten upon; to seize

CALL
559 'âmar (2), to say,
speak
833 'âshar (5), to go
forward; guide
2142 zâkar (3), to
remember; to mention
5493 çûwr (1), to turn off
5749 'ûwd (3), to
duplicate or repeat
7121 qârâ (131), to call
out
7725 shûwb (1), to turn
back; to return
8085 shâma' (2), to hear
intelligently

363 anamimnēskō (1), to
remind; to recollect
1941 ĕpikalĕŏmai (9), to
invoke
2564 kalĕō (17), to call
2840 kŏinŏō (2), to make
profane
2983 lambanō (1), to
take, receive
3004 lĕgō (4), to say
3106 makarizō (1), to
pronounce fortunate
3333 mĕtakalĕō (2), to
summon for, call for
3343 mĕtapĕmpō (2), to
summon or invite
3687 ŏnŏmazō (1), to
give a name
4341 prŏskalĕŏmai (2),
to call toward oneself
4779 sugkalĕō (1), to
convoke, call together
5455 phōnĕō (4), to emit
a sound

CALLED
559 'âmar (4), to say,
speak
935 bôw' (1), to go or
come
2199 zâ'aq (3), to call
out, announce
6817 tsâ'aq (2), to shriek;
to proclaim
7121 qârâ (380), to call
out
7123 qᵉrâ' (Ch.) (1), to
call out
7760 sûwm (1), to put,
place
8085 shâma' (1), to hear
intelligently
154 aitĕō (1), to ask for
363 anamimnēskō (1), to
remind; to recollect
1458 ĕgkalĕō (1), to
charge, criminate
1528 ĕiskalĕō (1), to
invite in
1941 ĕpikalĕŏmai (4), to
invoke
1951 ĕpilĕgŏmai (1), to
surname, select
2028 ĕpŏnŏmazō (1), to
be called, denominate
2036 ĕpō (1), to speak
2046 ĕrĕō (1), to utter
2564 kalĕō (103), to call
2822 klētŏs (11),
appointed, invited
2919 krinō (2), to decide;
to try, condemn, punish
3004 lĕgō (36), to say
3044 Linŏs (1), (poss.)
flax linen
3333 mĕtakalĕō (2), to
summon for, call for
3686 ŏnŏma (4), name
3687 ŏnŏmazō (1), to
give a name
3739+2076 hŏs (1), who,
which, what, that
3870 parakalĕō (1), to
call, invite
4316 prŏsagŏrĕuō (1), to
designate a name
4341 prŏskalĕŏmai (25),
to call toward oneself
4377 prŏsphōnĕō (2), to
address, exclaim

4779 sugkalĕō (5), to convoke, call together
4867 sunathrŏizō (1), to convene
5455 phōnĕō (16), to emit a sound
5537 chrēmatizō (2), to utter an oracle
5581 psĕudōnumŏs (1), untruly named

CALLEDST
6485 pâqad (1), to visit, care for, count
7121 qârâ' (3), to call out

CALLEST
3004 lĕgō (3), to say

CALLETH
7121 qârâ' (13), to call out
2564 kalĕō (6), to call
3004 lĕgō (4), to say
4341 prŏskalĕŏmai (1), to call toward oneself
4779 sugkalĕō (2), to convoke, call together
5455 phōnĕō (4), to emit a sound

CALLING
2142 zâkar (1), to remember; to mention
4744 miqrâ' (1), public meeting
7121 qârâ' (3), to call out
363 anamimnēskō (1), to remind; to recollect
1941 ĕpikalĕŏmai (2), to invoke
2564 kalĕō (1), to call
2821 klēsis (10), invitation; station in life
4341 prŏskalĕŏmai (2), to call toward oneself
4377 prŏsphōnĕō (2), to address, exclaim
5455 phōnĕō (1), to emit a sound

CALM
1827 dᵉmâmâh (1), quiet
8367 shâthaq (2), to subside
1055 galēnē (3), tranquillity, calm

CALNEH
3641 Kalneh (2), Calneh or Calno

CALNO
3641 Kalneh (1), Calneh or Calno

CALVARY
2898 kraniŏn (1), skull

CALVE
2342 chûwl (2), to dance, whirl; to writhe in pain

CALVED
3205 yâlad (1), to bear young; to father a child

CALVES
1121 bên (2), son, descendant
1121+1241 bên (1), son, descendant
5695 'ĕgel (10), bull calf
5697 'eglâh (2), cow calf
6499 par (1), bullock

3448 mŏschŏs (2), young bullock

CALVETH
6403 pâlaṭ (1), to slip out, i.e. escape; to deliver

CAME
857 'âthâh (4), to arrive; go
858 'âthâh (Ch.) (3), to arrive; go
935 bôw' (668), to go or come
1061 bikkûwr (1), first-fruits of the crop
1518 gîyach (1), to issue forth; to burst forth
1691 Diblayim (1), two cakes
1916 hâdôm (2), foot-stool
1946 hûwk (Ch.) (1), to go, come
1961 hâyâh (527), to exist, i.e. be or become
1980 hâlak (7), to walk; live a certain way
2015 hâphak (1), to turn about or over
3212 yâlak (6), to walk; to live; to carry
3318 yâtsâ' (106), to go, bring out
3329 yâtsîy' (1), issue forth, i.e. offspring
3381 yârad (42), to descend
3847 lâbash (3), to clothe
3996 mâbôw' (1), entrance; sunset; west
4161 môwtsâ' (1), going forth
4291 mᵉṭâ' (Ch.) (4), to arrive, to extend
4672 mâtsâ' (2), to find or acquire; to occur
5060 nâga' (5), to strike
5066 nâgash (27), to be, come, bring near
5182 nᵉchath (Ch.) (1), to descend; to depose
5312 nᵉphaq (Ch.) (3), to issue forth; to bring out
5437 çâbab (1), to surround
5559 çᵉliq (Ch.) (5), to ascend, go up
5674 'âbar (4), to cross over; to transition
5927 'âlâh (82), to ascend, be high, mount
5954 'âlal (Ch.) (4), to go in; to lead in
5957 'âlam (Ch.) (1), forever
6293 pâga' (1), to impinge
6473 pâ'ar (1), to open wide
6555 pârats (1), to break out
6743 tsâlach (5), to push forward
7122 qârâ' (1), to encounter, to happen
7126 qârab (20), to approach, bring near
7127 qᵉrêb (Ch.) (5), to approach, bring near
7131 qârêb (1), near

7725 shûwb (16), to turn back; to return
191 akŏuō (1), to hear; obey
305 anabainō (3), to go up, rise
565 apĕrchŏmai (1), to go off, i.e. depart
1096 ginŏmai (88), to be, become
1237 diadĕchŏmai (1), succeed, receive in turn
1448 ĕggizō (3), to approach
1525 ĕisĕrchŏmai (10), to enter
1531 ĕispŏrĕuŏmai (1), to enter
1607 ĕkpŏrĕuŏmai (1), to depart, be discharged
1831 ĕxĕrchŏmai (38), to issue; to leave
1904 ĕpĕrchŏmai (1), to supervene
1910 ĕpibainō (1), to mount, ascend
1994 ĕpistrĕphō (1), to revert, turn back to
1998 ĕpisuntrĕchō (1), to hasten together upon
2064 ĕrchŏmai (199), to go or come
2113 ĕuthudrŏmĕō (1), to sail direct
2186 ĕphistēmi (7), to be present; to approach
2240 hēkō (3), to arrive, i.e. be present
2597 katabainō (16), to descend
2658 katantaō (8), to arrive at; to attain
2718 katĕrchŏmai (6), to go, come down
2944 kuklŏō (1), to surround, encircle
2983 lambanō (1), to take, receive
3415 mnaŏmai (1), to bear in mind
3719 ŏrthrizō (1), to get up early in the morning
3854 paraginŏmai (16), to arrive; to appear
3918 parĕimi (1), to be present; to have come
3922 parĕisĕrchŏmai (1), to supervene
3928 parĕrchŏmai (1), to go by; to perish
4130 plēthō (1), to fulfill, complete
4334 prŏsĕrchŏmai (65), to come near, visit
4370 prŏstrĕchō (1), to hasten by running
4836 sumparaginŏmai (1), to convene
4863 sunagō (6), to gather together
4872 sunanabainō (2), to ascend in company
4905 sunĕrchŏmai (8), to gather together
5342 phĕrō (3), to bear or carry

CAMEL
1581 gâmâl (5), camel
2574 kamēlŏs (4), camel

CAMEL'S
1581 gâmâl (1), camel
2574 kamēlŏs (2), camel

CAMELS
327 'ăchastârân (2), mule
1581 gâmâl (44), camel

CAMELS'
1581 gâmâl (3), camel

CAMEST
935 bôw' (8), to go, come
1518 gîyach (1), to issue forth; to burst forth
1980 hâlak (3), to walk; live a certain way
3318 yâtsâ' (7), to go, bring out
3381 yârad (3), to descend
7126 qârab (1), to approach, bring near
7725 shûwb (1), to turn back; to return
1096 ginŏmai (1), to be, become
1525 ĕisĕrchŏmai (1), to enter
1831 ĕxĕrchŏmai (1), to issue; to leave
2064 ĕrchŏmai (1), to go or come

CAMON
7056 Qâmôwn (1), elevation

CAMP
2583 chânâh (3), to encamp
4264 machăneh (127), encampment
8466 tachănâh (1), encampment
3925 parĕmbŏlē (3), encampment

CAMPED
2583 chânâh (1), to encamp

CAMPHIRE
3724 kôpher (2), village; bitumen; henna

CAMPS
4264 machăneh (7), encampment

CAN
3045 yâda' (1), to know
3201 yâkôl (18), to be able
3202 yᵉkêl (Ch.) (2), to be able
1097 ginōskō (1), to know
1410 dunamai (65), to be able or possible
1492 ĕidō (2), to know
2480 ischuō (1), to have or exercise force

CANA
2580 Kana (4), Cana

CANAAN
3667 Kᵉna'an (90), humiliated
5478 Chanaanaiŏs (1), Kenaanite

CANAANITE
3669 Kᵉna'ănîy (12), Kenaanite; merchant
2581 Kananitēs (2), zealous

English

CANAANITES
3669 Kᵉna'ăniy (55),
Kenaanite; merchant

CANAANITESS
3669 Kᵉna'ăniy (1),
Kenaanite; merchant

CANAANITISH
3669 Kᵉna'ăniy (2),
Kenaanite; merchant

CANDACE
2582 Kandakē (1),
Candacë

CANDLE
5216 nîyr (8), lamp;
lamplight
3088 luchnŏs (8),
portable lamp

CANDLES
5216 nîyr (1), lamp;
lamplight

CANDLESTICK
4501 mᵉnôwrâh (34),
chandelier, lamp-stand
5043 nebrᵉshâ' (Ch.) (1),
lamp-stand
3087 luchnia (6),
lamp-stand

CANDLESTICKS
4501 mᵉnôwrâh (6),
chandelier, lamp-stand
3087 luchnia (6),
lamp-stand

CANE
7070 qâneh (2), reed

CANKER
1044 gaggraina (1),
ulcer, i.e. gangrene

CANKERED
2728 katiŏō (1), to
corrode, tarnish

CANKERWORM
3218 yekeq (6), young
locust

CANNEH
3656 Kanneh (1), Canneh

CANNOT
369 'ayin (1), there is no,
i.e., not exist, none
408 'al (2), not; nothing
518 'îm (1), whether?; if,
although; Oh that!
1077 bal (2), nothing; not
at all; lest
1097 bᵉlîy (1), without,
not yet; lacking;
1115 biltîy (1), not,
except, without, unless
3201 yâkôl (3), to be able
3308 yŏphîy (2), beauty
3808 lô' (57), no, not
176 akatagnōstŏs (1),
unblamable
180 akatapaustŏs (1),
unrefraining, unceasing
215 alalētŏs (1),
unspeakable
368 anantirrhētŏs (1),
indisputable
551 apĕirastŏs (1), not
temptable
761 asalĕutŏs (1),
immovable, fixed
893 apsĕudēs (1),
veracious, free of deceit
1492 ĕidō (2), to know

3361 mē (2), not; lest
3467 muōpazō (1), to see
indistinctly, be myopic
3756 ŏu (3), no or not

CANST
3201 yâkôl (6), to be able
3202 yᵉkêl (Ch.) (2), to be
able
1097 ginōskō (1), to know
1410 dunamai (9), to be
able or possible
1492 ĕidō (1), to know

CAPERNAUM
2584 Kapĕrnaŏum (16),
walled village which is
comfortable

CAPHTHORIM
3732 Kaphtôrîy (1),
Caphtorite

CAPHTOR
3731 Kaphtôr (3),
wreath-shaped island

CAPHTORIM
3732 Kaphtôrîy (1),
Caphtorite

CAPHTORIMS
3732 Kaphtôrîy (1),
Caphtorite

CAPPADOCIA
2587 Kappadŏkia (2),
Cappadocia

CAPTAIN
1167 ba'al (1), master;
husband; owner; citizen
2951 ṭiphçar (1), military
governor
5057 nâgîyd (5),
commander, official
5387 nâsîy' (12), leader;
rising mist, fog
5921 'al (1), above, over,
upon, or against
6346 pechâh (2), prefect,
officer
7101 qâtsîyn (2),
magistrate
7218 rô'sh (4), head
7227 rab (23), great
7229 rab (Ch.) (1), great
7990 shallîyṭ (Ch.) (1),
premier, sovereign
7991 shâlîysh (2), officer;
of the third rank
8269 sar (51), head
person, ruler
747 archēgŏs (1), chief
leader; founder
4755 stratēgŏs (3),
military governor
4759 stratŏpĕdarchēs (1),
military commander
5506 chiliarchŏs (18),
colonel

CAPTAINS
441 'allûwph (1), friend,
one familiar; chieftain
2951 ṭiphçar (1), military
governor
3733 kar (1), ram sheep;
battering ram
3746 kârîy (2),
life-guardsman
5057 nâgîyd (1),
commander, official
6346 pechâh (7), prefect,
officer

6347 pechâh (Ch.) (4),
prefect, officer
7101 qâtsîyn (1),
magistrate
7218 rô'sh (6), head
7991 shâlîysh (9), officer;
of the third rank
8269 sar (80), head
person, ruler
4755 stratēgŏs (2),
military governor
5506 chiliarchŏs (4),
colonel

CAPTIVE
1473 gôwlâh (4), exile;
captive
1540 gâlâh (24), to
denude; uncover
1546 gâlûwth (2),
captivity; exiles
6808 tsâ'âh (1), to
depopulate; imprison
7617 shâbâh (21), to
transport into captivity
7628 shᵉbîy (3), exile;
booty
162 aichmalōtĕuō (2), to
capture
163 aichmalōtizō (1), to
make captive
2221 zōgrĕō (1), to
capture or ensnare

CAPTIVES
1123+1547 bēn (Ch.) (1),
son
1473 gôwlâh (3), exile;
captive
1540 gâlâh (3), to
denude; uncover
1546 gâlûwth (3),
captivity; exiles
7617 shâbâh (16), to
transport into captivity
7628 shᵉbîy (8), exile;
booty
7633 shibyâh (8), exile;
captive
164 aichmalōtŏs (1),
captive

CAPTIVITY
1473 gôwlâh (28), exile;
captive
1540 gâlâh (9), to
denude; uncover
1546 gâlûwth (11),
captivity; exiles
1547 gâlûwth (Ch.) (3),
captivity; exiles
2925 ṭalṭêlâh (1),
overthrow or rejection
7622 shᵉbûwth (31),
exile; prisoners
7628 shᵉbîy (30), exile;
booty
7633 shibyâh (6), exile;
captive
161 aichmalōsia (2),
captivity
163 aichmalōtizō (2), to
make captive

CARBUNCLE
1304 bârᵉqath (3),
flashing gem (poss.)
emerald

CARBUNCLES
68+688 'eben (1), stone

CARCAS
3752 Karkaç (1), Karkas

CARCASE
1472 gᵉvîyâh (2), dead
body
4658 mappeleth (1),
down-fall; ruin; carcase
5038 nᵉbêlâh (29),
carcase or carrion
6297 peger (1), carcase;
corpse
4430 ptōma (1), corpse,
carrion

CARCASES
5038 nᵉbêlâh (7), carcase
or carrion
6297 peger (13), carcase;
corpse
2966 kōlŏn (1), corpse

CARCHEMISH
3751 Karkᵉmîysh (2),
Karkemish

CARE
983 beṭach (1), safety,
security, trust
1674 dᵉ'âgâh (1), anxiety
1697 dâbâr (1), word;
matter; thing
2731 chărâdâh (1), fear,
anxiety
7760+3820 sûwm (2), to
put, place
1959 ĕpimĕlĕŏmai (3), to
care for
3199 mĕlō (3), it is a care
or concern
3308 mĕrimna (3),
solicitude; worry
3309 mĕrimnaō (2), to be
anxious about
4710 spŏudē (2),
despatch; eagerness
5426 phrŏnĕō (1), to be
mentally disposed

CAREAH
7143 Qârêach (1), bald

CARED
1875 dârash (1), to
pursue or search
3199 mĕlō (2), it is a care
or concern

CAREFUL
1672 dâ'ag (1), be
anxious, be afraid
2729 chârad (1), to
hasten with anxiety
2818 chăshach (Ch.) (1),
to need
3309 mĕrimnaō (2), to be
anxious about
5426 phrŏnĕō (1), to be
mentally disposed
5431 phrŏntizō (1), be
anxious; to be careful

CAREFULLY
2470 châlâh (1), to be
weak, sick, afflicted
8085 shâma' (1), to hear
intelligently
1567 ĕkzētĕō (1), to seek
out
4708 spŏudaiŏtĕrŏs (1),
more speedily

CAREFULNESS
1674 dᵉ'âgâh (2), anxiety

275 amĕrimnŏs (1), *not anxious, free of care*
4710 spŏudē (1), *despatch; eagerness*

CARELESS
982 bâṭach (3), to *trust, be confident* or *sure*
983 beṭach (2), *safety, security, trust*

CARELESSLY
983 beṭach (3), *safety, security, trust*

CARES
3303 mĕn (3), not translated

CAREST
3199 mĕlō (3), *it is a care* or *concern*

CARETH
1875 dârash (1), to *pursue* or *search*
3199 mĕlō (2), *it is a care* or *concern*
3309 mĕrimnaō (4), to be *anxious* about

CARMEL
3760 Karmel (26), *planted field; garden*

CARMELITE
3761 Karmᵉlîy (5), *Karmelite*

CARMELITESS
3762 Karmᵉlîyth (2), *Karmelitess*

CARMI
3756 Karmîy (8), *gardener*

CARMITES
3757 Karmîy (1), *Karmite*

CARNAL
4559 sarkikŏs (9), *pertaining to flesh*
4561 sarx (2), *flesh*

CARNALLY
7902+2233 shᵉkâbâh (2), *lying* down
7903+2233 shᵉkôbeth (1), *sexual lying* down with
4561 sarx (1), *flesh*

CARPENTER
2796 chârâsh (1), *skilled fabricator* or *worker*
2796+6086 chârâsh (1), *skilled fabricator*
5045 tĕktōn (1), *craftsman* in wood

CARPENTER'S
5045 tĕktōn (1), *craftsman* in wood

CARPENTERS
2796 chârâsh (6), *skilled fabricator* or *worker*
2796+6086 chârâsh (2), *skilled fabricator*
6086 'êts (1), *wood, things made of wood*

CARPUS
2591 Karpŏs (1), (poss.) *fruit*

CARRIAGE
3520 kᵉbûwddâh (1), *magnificence, wealth*

3627 kᵉlîy (2), *implement, thing*

CARRIAGES
3627 kᵉlîy (1), *implement, thing*
5385 nᵉsûw'âh (1), *load, burden*
643 apŏskĕuazō (1), to *pack up baggage*

CARRIED
935 bôw' (10), to *go, come*
1473 gôwlâh (10), *exile; captive*
1540 gâlâh (35), to *denude; uncover*
1541 gᵉlâh (Ch.) (1), to *reveal mysteries*
1546 gâlûwth (3), *captivity; exiles*
1980 hâlak (1), to *walk; live a certain way*
2986 yâbal (3), to *bring*
3212 yâlak (1), to *walk; to live; to carry*
3318 yâtsâ' (3), to *go, bring out*
3947 lâqach (3), to *take*
4116 mâhar (1), to *hurry; promptly*
4131 môwṭ (1), to *slip, shake, fall*
5090 nâhag (3), to *drive; to lead, carry away*
5095 nâhal (1), to *conduct; to protect*
5186 nâṭâh (2), to *stretch* or *spread out*
5375 nâsâ' (15), to *lift up*
5376 nᵉsâ' (Ch.) (1), to *lift up*
5437 çâbab (3), to *surround*
5445 çâbal (1), to *carry*
5674 'âbar (1), to *cross over; to transition*
5927 'âlâh (3), to *ascend, be high, mount*
7392 râkab (3), to *ride*
7617 shâbâh (18), to *transport into captivity*
7725 shûwb (2), to *turn back; to return*
71 agō (1), to *lead; to bring, drive; to weigh*
339 anakathizō (1), to *sit up*
520 apagō (1), to *take away*
667 apŏhĕrō (4), to *bear off, carry away*
941 bastazō (1), to *lift, bear*
1580 ĕkkŏmizō (1), to *bear forth to burial*
1627 ĕkphĕrō (1), to *bear out; to produce*
1643 ĕlaunō (1), to *push*
3346 mĕtatithēmi (1), to *transport; to exchange*
3350 mĕtŏikĕsia (1), *exile, deportation*
4064 pĕriphĕrō (3), to *transport*
4216 pŏtamŏphŏrētŏs (1), *overwhelmed by a stream*
4792 sugkŏmizō (1), to *convey together*

4879 sunapagō (1), to *take off together*

CARRIEST
2229 zâram (1), to *gush water, pour forth*

CARRIETH
1589 gânab (1), to *thieve; to deceive*
5375 nâsâ' (1), to *lift up*
941 bastazō (1), to *lift, bear*

CARRY
935 bôw' (7), to *go* or *come*
1319 bâsar (1), to *announce* (good news)
1540 gâlâh (5), to *denude; uncover*
1980 hâlak (1), to *walk; live a certain way*
2904 ṭûwl (1), to *cast down or out, hurl*
2986 yâbal (1), to *bring*
2987 yᵉbal (Ch.) (1), to *bring*
3212 yâlak (3), to *walk; to live; to carry*
3318 yâtsâ' (18), to *go, bring out*
3381 yârad (2), to *descend*
3947 lâqach (2), to *take*
4853 massâ' (1), *burden, utterance*
5182 nᵉchath (Ch.) (1), to *descend; to depose*
5375 nâsâ' (18), to *lift up*
5445 çâbal (3), to *carry*
5674 'âbar (2), to *cross over; to transition*
5927 'âlâh (4), to *ascend, be high, mount*
6403 pâlaṭ (1), to *slip out, i.e. escape; to deliver*
7400 râkîyl (1), *scandal-monger*
7617 shâbâh (5), to *transport into captivity*
7725 shûwb (4), to *turn back; to return*
142 airō (1), to *lift, to take up*
941 bastazō (1), to *lift, bear*
1308 diaphĕrō (1), to *bear, carry; to differ*
1627 ĕkphĕrō (2), to *bear out; to produce*
3351 mĕtŏikizō (1), to *transfer as a captive*
4046 pĕripŏiĕŏmai (1), to *acquire; to gain*
5342 phĕrō (1), to *bear or carry*

CARRYING
1540 gâlâh (1), to *denude; uncover*
5375 nâsâ' (3), to *lift up*
7411 râmâh (1), to *hurl; to shoot; to delude*
1627 ĕkphĕrō (1), to *bear out; to produce*
3350 mĕtŏikĕsia (2), *exile, deportation*

CARSHENA
3771 Karshᵉnâ' (1), *Karshena*

CART
5699 'ăgâlâh (15), *wheeled vehicle*

CARVED
2405 châṭûbâh (1), *tapestry*
2707 châqah (1), to *carve; to delineate*
4734 miqla'ath (1), *bas-relief sculpture*
6456 pᵉçîyl (3), *idol*
6459 peçel (2), *idol*
6603 pittûwach (2), *sculpture; engraving*
7049 qâla' (3), to *sling* a *stone; to carve*

CARVING
2799 chărôsheth (2), *skilled work*

CARVINGS
4734 miqla'ath (1), *bas-relief sculpture*

CASE
1697 dâbâr (1), *word; matter; thing*
3602 kâkâh (1), *just so*
7725 shûwb (2), to *turn back; to return*
156 aitia (1), *logical reason; legal crime*
3364 ŏu mē (1), *not at all, absolutely not*

CASEMENT
822 'eshnâb (1), *latticed window*

CASIPHIA
3703 Kâçiphyâ' (2), *silvery*

CASLUHIM
3695 Kaçlûchîym (2), *Casluchim*

CASSIA
6916 qiddâh (2), *cassia*
7102 qᵉtsîy'âh (1), *cassia*

CAST
1299 bâraq (1), to *flash lightning*
1457 gâhar (1), to *prostrate* oneself
1602 gâ'al (1), to *detest; to reject; to fail*
1644 gârash (9), to *drive out; to expatriate*
1740 dûwach (1), to *rinse clean, wash*
1760 dâchâh (1), to *push down; to totter*
1920 hâdaph (2), to *push away or down; drive out*
1972 hâlâ' (1), to *remove or be remote*
2186 zânach (17), to *reject, forsake, fail*
2219 zârâh (1), to *toss about; to diffuse*
2490 châlal (1), to *profane, defile*
2904 ṭûwl (12), to *cast down or out, hurl*
3032 yâdad (3), to *throw lots*
3034 yâdâh (2), to *throw; to revere or worship*
3240 yânach (1), to *allow to stay*

3332 yâtsaq (10), to *pour out*

3333 y°tsûqâh (1), *poured* out into a mold

3381 yârad (3), to *descend*

3384 yârâh (4), to *throw, shoot an arrow*

3423 yârash (10), to *inherit; to impoverish*

3766 kâra' (1), to *prostrate*

3782 kâshal (3), to *totter, waver; to falter*

3874 lûwṭ (1), to *wrap up*

3988 mâ'aç (10), to *spurn; to disappear*

4048 mâgar (1), to *yield up, be thrown*

4054 migrâsh (1), *open country*

4131 môwṭ (1), to *slip, shake, fall*

4166 mûwtsâqâh (1), *casting* of metal; *tube*

4788 mârûwd (1), *outcast; destitution*

5060 nâga' (1), to *strike*

5077 nâdâh (1), to *exclude,* i.e. *banish*

5080 nâdach (4), to *push off, scattered*

5203 nâtash (1), to *disperse; to thrust* off

5221 nâkâh (1), to *strike, kill*

5307 nâphal (24), to *fall*

5375 nâsâ' (1), to *lift up*

5390 n°shîyqâh (1), *kiss*

5394 nâshal (1), to *divest, eject,* or *drop*

5414 nâthan (5), to *give*

5422 nâthats (3), to *tear down*

5437 çâbab (1), to *surround*

5499 ç°châbâh (2), *rag*

5549 çâlal (4), to *mound up; to exalt; to oppose*

5619 çâqal (1), to *throw large stones*

5927 'âlâh (2), to *ascend, be high, mount*

6080 'âphar (1), to *be dust*

6327 pûwts (2), to *dash in pieces; to disperse*

6437 pânâh (1), to *turn, to face*

6696 tsûwr (1), to *cramp,* i.e. *confine; to harass*

7290 râdam (1), to *stupefy*

7324 rûwq (1), to *pour out,* i.e. *empty*

7368 râchaq (1), to *recede; remove*

7412 r°mâh (Ch.) (11), to *throw; to set; to assess*

7760 sûwm (1), to *put, place*

7817 shâchach (4), to *sink or depress*

7843 shâchath (1), to *decay; to ruin*

7921 shâkôl (3), to *miscarry*

7933 sheken (4), *residence*

7971 shâlach (14), to *send away*

7993 shâlak (113), to *throw out, down*

7995 shalleketh (1), *felling* of trees

7998 shâlâl (1), *booty*

8210 shâphak (8), to *spill forth; to expend*

8213 shâphêl (1), to *humiliate*

8628 tâqa' (1), to *clatter, slap, drive, clasp*

114 athětĕŏ (1), to *disesteem, neutralize*

577 apŏballō (1), to *throw off;* fig. to *lose*

641 apŏrrhiptō (1), to *throw oneself into*

656 apŏsunagōgŏs (1), *excommunicated*

683 apŏthĕŏmai (2), to *push off; to reject*

906 ballō (81), to *throw*

1000 bŏlē (1), *throw* as a measure

1260 dialŏgizŏmai (1), to *deliberate*

1544 ĕkballō (51), to *throw out*

1601 ĕkpiptō (1), to *drop away*

1614 ĕktĕinō (1), to *stretch*

1620 ĕktithēmi (1), to *expose; to declare*

1685 ĕmballō (1), *throw in*

1911 ĕpiballō (2), to *throw upon*

1977 ĕpirrhiptō (1), to *throw upon*

2210 zēmiŏō (1), to *experience detriment*

2598 kataballō (2), to *throw down*

2630 katakrēmnizŏ (1), to *precipitate down*

2975 lagchanō (1), to *determine by lot*

3036 lithŏbŏlĕō (1), to *throw stones*

3679 ŏnĕidizō (1), to *rail at, chide, taunt*

3860 paradidōmi (1), to *hand over*

4016 pĕriballō (3), to *wrap around, clothe*

4406 prŏïmŏs (1), *autumnal* showering

4496 rhiptō (5), to *fling, toss; to lay out*

5011 tapĕinŏs (1), *humiliated, lowly*

5020 tartarŏō (1), to *incarcerate* in Tartaros

CASTAWAY

96 adŏkimŏs (1), *failing the test, worthless*

CASTEDST

5307 nâphal (1), to *fall*

CASTEST

2186 zânach (1), to *reject, forsake, fail*

6565 pârar (1), to *break up; to violate, frustrate*

7993 shâlak (1), to *throw out, down* or *away*

CASTETH

1920 hâdaph (1), to *push away or down; drive out*

3381 yârad (1), to *descend*

3384 yârâh (1), to *throw, shoot an arrow*

5307 nâphal (1), to *fall*

6884 tsâraph (1), to *fuse metal; to refine*

6979 qûwr (2), to *throw forth; to wall up*

7921 shâkôl (1), to *miscarry*

7993 shâlak (1), to *throw out, down or away*

8213 shâphêl (1), to *humiliate*

906 ballō (2), to *throw*

1544 ĕkballō (4), to *throw out*

CASTING

2866 chăthath (1), *dismay*

3445 yeshach (1), *hunger*

4165 mûwtsâq (1), *casting* of metal

5307 nâphal (1), to *fall*

7901 shâkab (1), to *lie down*

8210 shâphak (1), to *spill forth; to expend*

577 apŏballō (1), to *throw off;* fig. to *lose*

580 apŏbŏlē (1), *rejection, loss*

906 ballō (6), to *throw*

1544 ĕkballō (3), to *throw out*

1977 ĕpirrhiptō (1), to *throw upon*

2507 kathairĕō (1), to *lower, or demolish*

CASTLE

759 'armôwn (1), *citadel, high fortress*

4679 m°tsad (1), *stronghold*

4686 mâtsûwd (1), *net or capture; fastness*

3925 parĕmbŏlē (6), *encampment*

CASTLES

1003 bîyrânîyth (2), *fortress, citadel*

2918 ṭîyrâh (3), *fortress; hamlet*

4026 migdâl (1), *tower; rostrum*

CASTOR

1359 Diŏskŏurŏi (1), *twins of Zeus*

CATCH

1641 gârar (1), to *drag off roughly*

2414 châṭaph (3), to *seize as a prisoner*

2480 châlaṭ (1), to *snatch at, seizing*

2963 ṭâraph (2), to *pluck off or pull to pieces*

3920 lâkad (2), to *catch; to capture*

4672 mâtsâ' (1), to *find or acquire; to occur*

5367 nâqash (1), to *entrap* with a noose

8610 tâphas (1), to *manipulate,* i.e. *seize*

64 agrĕuō (1), to *entrap, catch*

2221 zōgrĕō (1), to *capture or ensnare*

2340 thērĕuō (1), to *carp at*

CATCHETH

6679 tsûwd (1), to *lie in wait; to catch*

726 harpazō (2), to *seize*

CATERPILLER

2625 chaçîyl (5), *locust*

CATERPILLERS

2625 chaçîyl (1), *locust*

3218 yekeq (3), *young locust*

CATTLE

926 bâhal (1), to *tremble; be, make agitated*

929 b°hêmâh (56), *animal, beast*

1165 b°'îyr (2), *cattle, livestock*

1241 bâqâr (1), *plowing ox; herd*

4399 m°lâ'kâh (1), *work; property*

4734 miqla'ath (1), *bas-relief sculpture*

4735 miqneh (57), *live-stock*

4806 m°rîy' (3), *stall-fed animal*

6629 tsô'n (13), *flock of sheep or goats*

7069 qânâh (1), to *create; to procure*

7716 seh (7), *sheep or goat*

2353 thrĕmma (1), *stock*

4165 pŏimainō (1), to *tend* as a shepherd

CAUGHT

270 'âchaz (4), to *seize, grasp; possess*

962 bâzaz (1), to *plunder, take booty*

1497 gâzal (1), to *rob*

2388 châzaq (8), to *fasten upon; to seize*

3920 lâkad (3), to *catch; to capture*

8610 tâphas (3), to *manipulate,* i.e. *seize*

726 harpazō (5), to *seize*

1949 ĕpilambanŏmai (2), to *seize*

2983 lambanō (3), to *take, receive*

4084 piazō (2), to *seize, arrest, or capture*

4815 sullambanō (1), to *seize (arrest, capture)*

4884 sunarpazō (4), to *snatch together*

CAUL

3508 yôthereth (11), *lobe or flap of the liver*

5458 ç°gôwr (1), *breast*

CAULS

7636 shâbîyç (1), *netting*

CAUSE

657 'epheç (1), *end; no further*

834 'ăsher (1), *because, in order that*
1697 dâbâr (6), *word; matter; thing*
1700 dibrâh (1), *because, on account of*
1779 dîyn (7), *judge; judgment; law suit*
1961 hâyâh (1), *to exist, i.e. be or become*
2600 chinnâm (15), *gratis, free*
3651 kên (1), *just; right, correct*
4616 ma'an (1), *on account of*
4941 mishpâṭ (12), *verdict; formal decree*
5252 nᵉçibbâh (1), *turn of affairs*
5414 nâthan (5), *to give*
5438 çibbâh (1), *turn of affairs*
5668 'âbûwr (1), *on account of*
7379 rîyb (23), *contest, personal or legal*
7387 rêyqâm (2), *emptily; ineffectually*
7945 shel (1), *on account of; whatsoever*
8267 sheqer (1), *untruth; sham*
156 aitia (9), *logical reason; legal crime*
158 aitiŏn (2), *reason, basis; crime*
846 autŏs (1), *he, she, it*
873 aphŏrizō (1), *to limit, exclude, appoint*
1223 dia (13), *because of, for the sake of*
1352 diŏ (2), *consequently, therefore*
1432 dōrĕan (1), *gratuitously, freely*
1500 ĕikē (1), *idly, i.e. without reason or effect*
1752 hĕnĕka (4), *on account of*
2289 thanatŏō (3), *to kill*
3056 lŏgŏs (1), *word, matter, thing*
4160 pŏiĕō (3), *to do*
5484 charin (3), *on account of, because of*

CAUSED
1961 hâyâh (1), *to exist, i.e. be or become*
5414 nâthan (7), *to give*
3076 lupĕō (1), *to distress; to be sad*
4160 pŏiĕō (2), *to do*

CAUSELESS
2600 chinnâm (2), *gratis, free*

CAUSES
182 'ôwdôwth (1), *on account of; because*
1697 dâbâr (2), *word; matter; thing*
7379 rîyb (1), *contest, personal or legal*
1752 hĕnĕka (1), *on account of*

CAUSETH
5414 nâthan (1), *to give*

2358 thriambĕuō (1), *to lead in triumphal procession*
2716 katĕrgazŏmai (1), *to finish; to accomplish*
4160 pŏiĕō (3), *to do*

CAUSEWAY
4546 mᵉçillâh (2), *main thoroughfare; viaduct*

CAVE
4631 mᵉ'ârâh (32), *dark cavern*
4693 spēlaiŏn (1), *cavern; hiding-place*

CAVE'S
4631 mᵉ'ârâh (1), *dark cavern*

CAVES
2356 chôwr (1), *cavity, socket, den*
4247 mᵉchillâh (1), *cavern, hole*
4631 mᵉ'ârâh (3), *dark cavern*
3692 ŏpē (1), *hole, i.e. cavern; spring of water*

CEASE
988 bâṭêl (1), *to desist from labor, cease*
989 bᵉṭêl (Ch.) (3), *to stop*
1820 dâmâh (1), *to be silent; to fail, cease*
1826 dâmam (1), *to stop, cease; to perish*
2308 châdal (12), *to desist, stop; be fat*
2790 chârash (1), *to be silent; to be deaf*
3254 yâçaph (1), *to add or augment*
3615 kâlâh (1), *to complete, consume*
4185 mûwsh (1), *to withdraw*
6565 pârar (1), *to break up; to violate, frustrate*
7503 râphâh (1), *to slacken*
7647 sâbâ' (1), *copiousness*
7673 shâbath (37), *to repose; to desist*
7725 shûwb (1), *to turn back; to return*
7918 shâkak (1), *to lay a trap; to allay*
8552 tâmam (1), *to complete, finish*
180 akatapaustŏs (1), *unrefraining, unceasing*
3973 pauō (4), *to stop, i.e. restrain, quit*

CEASED
989 bᵉṭêl (Ch.) (1), *to stop*
1826 dâmam (1), *to stop, cease; to perish*
1934+989 hăvâ' (Ch.) (1), *to be, to exist*
2308 châdal (6), *to desist, stop; be fat*
5117 nûwach (1), *to rest; to settle down*
5307 nâphal (1), *to fall*
5975 'âmad (1), *to stand*
6313 pûwg (1), *to be sluggish; be numb*

7673 shâbath (6), *to repose; to desist*
1257 dialĕipō (1), *to intermit, stop*
2270 hēsuchazō (1), *to refrain*
2664 katapauō (1), *to cause to desist*
2673 katargĕō (1), *to be, render entirely useless*
2869 kŏpazō (3), *to tire, i.e. to relax*
3973 pauō (7), *to stop, i.e. restrain, quit*

CEASETH
1584 gâmar (1), *to end; to complete; to fail*
1820 dâmâh (1), *to be silent; to fail, cease*
2308 châdal (1), *to desist, stop; be fat*
3615 kâlâh (1), *to cease, be finished, perish*
7673 shâbath (4), *to repose; to desist*
8367 shâthaq (1), *to subside*
3973 pauō (1), *to stop, i.e. restrain, quit*

CEASING
2308 châdal (1), *to desist, stop; be fat*
83 adĕlŏtēs (1), *uncertainty*
89 adialĕiptŏs (4), *without omission*
1618 ĕktĕnēs (1), *intent, earnest*

CEDAR
729 'âraz (1), *of cedar*
730 'erez (49), *cedar tree*
731 'arzâh (1), *cedar paneling*

CEDARS
730 'erez (24), *cedar tree*

CEDRON
2748 Kĕdrōn (1), *dusky place*

CELEBRATE
1984 hâlal (1), *to speak words of thankfulness*
2278 chăbereth (1), *consort, companion*
7673 shâbath (1), *to repose*

CELESTIAL
2032 ĕpŏuraniŏs (2), *above the sky, celestial*

CELLARS
214 'ôwtsâr (2), *depository*

CENCHREA
2747 Kĕgchrĕai (2), *millet*

CENSER
4289 machtâh (7), *pan for live coals*
4730 miqtereth (2), *incense coal-pan*
2369 thumiastēriŏn (1), *altar of incense*
3031 libanōtŏs (2), *censer for incense*

CENSERS
4289 machtâh (8), *pan for live coals*

CENTURION
1543 hĕkatŏntarchēs (17), *captain of a hundred*
2760 kĕnturiōn (3), *captain of a hundred*

CENTURION'S
1543 hĕkatŏntarchēs (1), *captain of a hundred*

CENTURIONS
1543 hĕkatŏntarchēs (3), *captain of a hundred*

CEPHAS
2786 Kēphas (6), *rock*

CEREMONIES
4941 mishpâṭ (1), *verdict; formal decree; justice*

CERTAIN
259 'echâd (9), *first*
376 'îysh (4), *man; male; someone*
582 'ĕnôwsh (8), *man; person, human*
592 'ănîyâh (2), *groaning*
1400 gᵉbar (Ch.) (2), *person; someone*
1697 dâbâr (2), *word; matter; thing*
3045 yâda' (3), *to know; fixed, sure*
3330 yatstsîyb (Ch.) (1), *fixed, sure*
3559 kûwn (2), *to render sure, proper*
6256 'êth (1), *time*
6422 palmôwnîy (1), *a certain one*
444 anthrōpŏs (2), *human being; mankind*
444+5100 anthrōpŏs (1), *human being; mankind*
790 astatĕō (1), *homeless, vagabond*
804 asphalēs (1), *secure; certain*
1212 dēlŏs (1), *clear, plain, evident*
1520 hĕis (5), *one*
4225 pŏu (2), *somewhere, i.e. nearly*
5100 tis (112), *some or any person or object*

CERTAINLY
389 'ak (1), *surely; only, however*
403 'âkên (1), *surely!, truly!; but*
3588 kîy (1), *for, that because*
3689 ŏntōs (1), *really, certainly*

CERTAINTY
3330 yatstsîyb (Ch.) (1), *fixed, sure*
3559 kûwn (1), *to render sure, proper*
7189 qôsheṭ (1), *reality*
803 asphalĕia (1), *security; certainty*
804 asphalēs (2), *secure; certain*

CERTIFIED
559 'âmar (1), *to say*
3064 Yᵉhûwdîy (1), *Jehudite*

English

CERTIFY
3046 yᵉda' (Ch.) (3), to
know
5046 nâgad (1), to
announce
1107 gnŏrizŏ (1), to
make known, reveal

CHAFED
4751 mar (1), bitter;
bitterness; bitterly

CHAFF
2842 châshash (2), dry
grass, chaff
4671 môts (8), chaff
5784 'ûwr (Ch.) (1), chaff
8401 teben (1), threshed
stalks of cereal grain
892 achurŏn (2), chaff of
grain

CHAIN
2002 hamnîyk (Ch.) (3),
necklace
5178 nᵉchôsheth (1),
copper; bronze
6059 'ânaq (1), to collar;
to fit out
6060 'ânâq (1), necklace
chain
7242 râbîyd (2), collar
spread around the neck
7659 shib'âthayim (1),
seven-fold
8333 sharshᵉrâh (1),
chain
254 halusis (3), fetter or
manacle

CHAINS
246 'ăziqqîym (2),
manacles, chains
685 'ets'âdâh (1), bracelet
2131 zîyqâh (3), burning
arrow; bond, fetter
2397 châch (2), ring for
the nose or lips
2737 chârûwz (1), strung
beads
3574 kôwshârâh (1),
prosperity
5178 nᵉchôsheth (2),
copper; bronze
5188 nᵉṭîyphâh (1),
pendant for the ears
5688 'ăbôth (3), entwined
things: string, wreath
6060 'ânâq (2), necklace
chain
7569 rattôwq (2), chain
8333 sharshᵉrâh (6),
chain
8337 shêsh (1), six; sixth
254 halusis (7), fetter or
manacle
1199 dĕsmŏn (1),
shackle; impediment
4577 sĕira (1), chain, as
binding or drawing

CHALCEDONY
5472 chalkĕdŏn (1),
copper-like, chalcedony

CHALCOL
3633 Kalkôl (1),
sustenance

CHALDAEANS
5466 Chaldaiŏs (1),
native or the region of
the lower Euphrates

CHALDEA
3778 Kasdîy (7),
astrologer

CHALDEAN
3777 Kesed (2), Kesed

CHALDEANS
3778 Kasdîy (48),
astrologer
3779 Kasday (Ch.) (17),
magian or astrologer

CHALDEANS'
3778 Kasdîy (1),
astrologer

CHALDEES
3778 Kasdîy (13),
astrologer

CHALDEES'
3778 Kasdîy (1),
astrologer

CHALKSTONES
68+1615 'eben (1), stone

CHALLENGETH
559 'âmar (1), to say

CHAMBER
2315 cheder (15),
apartment, chamber
2646 chuppâh (1), canopy
3326 yâtsûwa' (1), bed;
wing or lean-to
3957 lishkâh (14), room
5393 nishkâh (2), room,
cell
5944 'ălîyâh (6),
second-story room
5952 'allîyth (Ch.) (1),
second-story room
6763 tsêlâ' (3), side of a
person or thing
8372 tâ' (4), room
5253 hupĕrŏiŏn (3), third
story apartment

CHAMBERING
2845 kŏitē (1), couch;
conception

CHAMBERLAIN
5631 çârîyç (4), eunuch;
official of state
1909+3588+2846 ĕpi (1),
on, upon
3623 ŏikŏnŏmŏs (1),
overseer, manager

CHAMBERLAINS
5631 çârîyç (9), eunuch;
official of state

CHAMBERS
2315 cheder (8),
apartment, chamber
3326 yâtsûwa' (2), bed;
wing or lean-to of a
building
3957 lishkâh (31), room
in a building
5393 nishkâh (1), room,
cell
5944 'ălîyâh (6), upper
things; second-story
room
6763 tsêlâ' (8), side of a
person or thing
8372 tâ' (9), room
5009 tamĕiŏn (1), room

CHAMELEON
3581 kôach (1), large
lizard

CHAMOIS
2169 zemer (1), gazelle

CHAMPAIGN
6160 'ărâbâh (1), desert,
wasteland

CHAMPION
376+1143 'îysh (2), man;
male; someone
1368 gibbôwr (1),
powerful; great warrior

CHANAAN
5477 Chanaan (2),
humiliated

CHANCE
4745 miqreh (1),
accident or fortune
6294 pega' (1), casual
impact
7122 qârâ' (2), to
encounter, to happen
4795 sugkuria (1),
chance occurrence
5177 tugchanŏ (1), to
happen; perhaps

CHANCELLOR
1169+2942 bᵉ'êl (Ch.) (3),
master

CHANCETH
4745 miqreh (1),
accident or fortune

CHANGE
2015 hâphak (1), to
change, overturn
2487 chălîyphâh (4),
alternation, change
2498 châlaph (4), to
pierce; to change
4171 mûwr (5), to alter;
to barter, to dispose of
4254 machălâtsâh (1),
mantle, garment
7760 sûwm (1), to put,
place
8133 shᵉnâ' (Ch.) (1), to
alter, change
8138 shânâh (3), to fold,
i.e. duplicate; to
transmute
8545 tᵉmûwrâh (1),
barter, compensation
236 allassŏ (2), to make
different, change
3331 mĕtathĕsis (1),
transferral,
disestablishment
3337 mĕtallassŏ (1), to
exchange
3345 mĕtaschĕmatizŏ
(1), to transfigure or
disguise; to apply

CHANGEABLE
4254 machălâtsâh (1),
mantle, garment

CHANGED
2015 hâphak (2), to
change, overturn
2498 châlaph (6), to pass
on; to change
2664 châphas (1), to
seek; to mask
4171 mûwr (6), to alter;
to barter, to dispose of
5437 çâbab (2), to
surround
8132 shânâ' (3), to alter,
change

8133 shᵉnâ' (Ch.) (12), to
alter, change
8138 shânâh (3), to fold,
to transmute
236 allassŏ (4), to make
different, change
3328 mĕtaballŏ (1), to
turn about in opinion
3337 mĕtallassŏ (1), to
exchange
3339 mĕtamŏrphŏŏ (1),
to transform, i.e.
metamorphose
3346 mĕtatithĕmi (1), to
transport; to exchange

CHANGERS
2773 kᵉrmatistēs (1),
money-broker

CHANGERS'
2855 kŏllubistēs (1),
coin-dealer

CHANGES
2487 chălîyphâh (7),
alternation, change

CHANGEST
8138 shânâh (1), to fold,
to transmute

CHANGETH
4171 mûwr (1), to alter;
to barter, to dispose of
8133 shᵉnâ' (Ch.) (1), to
alter, change

CHANGING
8545 tᵉmûwrâh (1),
barter, compensation

CHANNEL
7641 shibbôl (1), stream;
ear of grain

CHANNELS
650 'âphîyq (3), valley;
stream; mighty, strong

CHANT
6527 pâraṭ (1), to scatter
words, i.e. prate

CHAPEL
4720 miqdâsh (1),
sanctuary of deity

CHAPITER
3805 kôthereth (12),
capital of a column
6858 tsepheth (1),
capital of a column

CHAPITERS
3805 kôthereth (12),
capital of a column
7218 rô'sh (4), head

CHAPMEN
582+8846 'ĕnôwsh (1),
man; person; human

CHAPT
2865 châthath (1), to
break down

CHARASHIM
2798 Chărâshîym (1),
skilled worker

CHARCHEMISH
3751 Karkᵉmîysh (1),
Karkemish

CHARGE
3027 yâd (1), hand; power
4931 mishmereth (46),
watch, sentry, post

CHARGEABLE
4941 mishpâṭ (1), *verdict;*
formal decree; justice
5414 nâthan (1), *to give*
5447 çêbel (1), *load;*
forced labor
5749 'ûwd (1), *to protest,*
testify
5921 'al (3), *above, over,*
upon, or against
6213 'âsâh (1), *to do or*
make
6485 pâqad (1), *to visit,*
care for, count
6486 pᵉquddâh (2),
visitation; punishment
6496 pâqîyd (1),
superintendent, officer
6680 tsâvâh (16), *to*
constitute, enjoin
7130 qereb (1), *nearest*
part, i.e. the center
7592 shâ'al (1), *to ask*
7650 shâba' (7), *to swear*
77 adapanōs (1), *free of*
charge
1263 diamarturŏmai (2),
to attest or protest
1458+2596 ĕgkalĕō (1), *to*
charge, criminate
1462 ĕgklēma (1),
accusation
1781 ĕntĕllŏmai (2), *to*
enjoin, give orders
1909 ĕpi (1), *on, upon*
2004 ĕpitassō (1), *to*
order, command
2476 histēmi (1), *to*
stand, establish
3049 lŏgizŏmai (1), *to*
take an inventory
3726 hŏrkizō (1), *to*
solemnly enjoin
3852 paraggĕlia (2),
mandate, order
3853 paraggĕllō (4), *to*
enjoin; to instruct

CHARGEABLE
3513 kâbad (2), *to be*
rich, glorious
1912 ĕpibarĕō (2), *to be*
severe toward
2655 katanarkaō (1), *to*
be a burden

CHARGED
559 'âmar (1), *to say*
5414 nâthan (1), *to give*
5674+5921 'âbar (1), *to*
cross over; to transition
6485 pâqad (3), *to visit,*
care for, count
6680 tsâvâh (23), *to*
constitute, enjoin
7650 shâba' (2), *to swear*
7760 sûwm (1), *to put,*
place
916 barĕō (1), *to weigh*
down, cause pressure
1291 diastĕllŏmai (6), *to*
distinguish
1690 ĕmbrimaŏmai (2),
to blame, warn sternly
1781 ĕntĕllŏmai (1), *to*
enjoin, give orders
2008 ĕpitimaō (5), *to*
rebuke, warn, forbid
3146 mastigŏō (1), *to*
punish by flogging
3853 paraggĕllō (3), *to*
enjoin; to instruct

CHARGEDST
5749 'ûwd (1), *to protest,*
testify; to encompass

CHARGER
7086 qᵉ'ârâh (13), *bowl*
4094 pinax (4), *plate,*
platter, dish

CHARGERS
105 'ăgarṭâl (2), *basin*
7086 qᵉ'ârâh (1), *bowl*

CHARGES
4931 mishmereth (4),
watch, sentry, post
1159 dapanaō (1), *to*
incur cost; to waste
3800 ŏpsōniŏn (1),
rations, stipend or pay

CHARGEST
6485 pâqad (1), *to visit,*
care for, count

CHARGING
1263 diamarturŏmai (1),
to attest or protest
3853 paraggĕllō (1), *to*
enjoin; to instruct

CHARIOT
668 'appiryôwn (1),
palanquin, carriage
4818 merkâbâh (23),
chariot
5699 'ăgâlâh (1),
wheeled vehicle
7393 rekeb (28), *vehicle*
for riding
7395 rakkâb (2),
charioteer
7398 rᵉkûwb (1), *vehicle*
ridden on
716 harma (3), *chariot,*
carriage

CHARIOTS
2021 hôtsen (1), *weapon*
4817 merkâb (1), *chariot;*
seat in chariot
4818 merkâbâh (20),
chariot
7393 rekeb (87), *vehicle*
for riding
7396 rikbâh (1), *chariot*
716 harma (1), *chariot,*
carriage
4480 rhĕda (1), *wagon*
for riding

CHARITABLY
2596+26 kata (1), *down;*
according to

CHARITY
26 agapē (28), *love;*
love-feast

CHARMED
3908 lachash (1),
incantation; amulet

CHARMER
2266+2267 châbar (1), *to*
fascinate by spells

CHARMERS
328 'aṭ (1), *gently, softly*
3907 lâchash (1), *to*
whisper a magic spell

CHARMING
2266+2267 châbar (1), *to*
fascinate by spells

CHARRAN
5488 Charrhan (2),
parched

CHASE
1760 dâchâh (1), *to push*
down; to totter
7291 râdaph (5), *to run*
after with hostility

CHASED
1272 bârach (1), *to flee*
suddenly
5074 nâdad (2), *to rove,*
flee; to drive away
5080 nâdach (1), *to push*
off, scattered
6679 tsûwd (1), *to lie in*
wait; to catch
7291 râdaph (8), *to run*
after with hostility

CHASETH
1272 bârach (1), *to flee*
suddenly

CHASING
1814 dâlaq (1), *to flame;*
to pursue

CHASTE
53 hagnŏs (3), *innocent,*
modest, perfect, pure

CHASTEN
3198 yâkach (1), *to*
decide, justify, convict
3256 yâçar (3), *to*
chastise; to instruct
6031 'ânâh (1), *to afflict,*
be afflicted
3811 paidĕuō (1), *to*
educate or discipline

CHASTENED
3198 yâkach (1), *to*
decide, justify, convict
3256 yâçar (2), *to*
chastise; to instruct
8433 tôwkêchâh (1),
chastisement
3811 paidĕuō (3), *to*
educate or discipline

CHASTENEST
3256 yâçar (1), *to*
chastise; to instruct

CHASTENETH
3256 yâçar (2), *to*
chastise; to instruct
4148 mûwçâr (1),
reproof, warning
3811 paidĕuō (2), *to*
educate or discipline

CHASTENING
4148 mûwçâr (3),
reproof, warning
3809 paidĕia (3),
disciplinary correction

CHASTISE
3256 yâçar (6), *to*
chastise; to instruct
3811 paidĕuō (2), *to*
educate or discipline

CHASTISED
3256 yâçar (5), *to*
chastise; to instruct

CHASTISEMENT
4148 mûwçâr (3),
reproof, warning
3809 paidĕia (1),
disciplinary correction

CHASTISETH
3256 yâçar (1), *to*
chastise; to instruct

CHATTER
6850 tsâphaph (1), *to coo*
or chirp as a bird

CHEBAR
3529 Kᵉbâr (8), *length*

CHECK
4148 mûwçâr (1),
reproof, warning

CHECKER
7639 sᵉbâkâh (1),
net-work balustrade

CHEDORLAOMER
3540 Kᵉdorlâ'ômer (5),
Kedorlaomer

CHEEK
3895 lᵉchîy (6), *jaw; area*
of the jaw
4973 mᵉthallᵉ'âh (1),
tooth
4600 siagōn (2), *cheek*

CHEEKS
3895 lᵉchîy (5), *jaw; area*
of the jaw

CHEER
3190 yâṭab (1), *to be,*
make well
8055 sâmach (1), *to be,*
make gleesome
2114 ĕuthumĕŏ (3), *to be*
cheerful
2293 tharsĕō (5), *to have*
courage; take heart!

CHEERETH
8055 sâmach (1), *to be,*
make gleesome

CHEERFUL
2896 ṭôwb (1), *good; well*
3190 yâṭab (1), *to be,*
make well
5107 nûwb (1), *to (make)*
flourish; to utter
2431 hilarŏs (1), *prompt*
or willing

CHEERFULLY
2115 ĕuthumŏs (1),
cheerful, encouraged

CHEERFULNESS
2432 hilarŏtēs (1),
cheerful readiness

CHEESE
1385 gᵉbînah (1), *curdled*
milk
8194 shâphâh (1), *cheese*

CHEESES
2757+2461 chârîyts (1),
slice, portion

CHELAL
3636 Kᵉlâl (1), *complete*

CHELLUH
3622 Kᵉlûwhay (1),
completed

CHELUB
3620 Kᵉlûwb (2),
bird-trap; basket

CHELUBAI
3621 Kᵉlûwbay (1),
forcible

CHEMARIMS
3649 kâmâr (1), *pagan*
priest

English

CHEMOSH
3645 Kᵉmôwsh (8), *powerful*

CHENAANAH
3668 Kᵉna‘ănâh (5), *humiliated*

CHENANI
3662 Kᵉnânîy (1), *planted*

CHENANIAH
3663 Kᵉnanyâh (3), *Jehovah has planted*

CHEPHAR-HAAMMONAI
3726 Kᵉphar hâ-'Ammôwnîy (1), *village of the Ammonite*

CHEPHIRAH
3716 Kᵉphîyrâh (4), *village*

CHERAN
3763 Kᵉrân (2), *Keran*

CHERETHIMS
3774 Kᵉrêthîy (1), *executioner*

CHERETHITES
3746 kârîy (1), *life-guardsman*
3774 Kᵉrêthîy (8), *executioner*

CHERISH
5532 çâkan (1), to be *familiar with*

CHERISHED
5532 çâkan (1), to be *familiar with*

CHERISHETH
2282 thalpō (2), to *foster, care for*

CHERITH
3747 Kᵉrîyth (2), *cut*

CHERUB
3742 kᵉrûwb (26), *cherub*
3743 Kᵉrûwb (2), *cherub*

CHERUBIM
3742 kᵉrûwb (2), *cherub*

CHERUBIMS
3742 kᵉrûwb (61), *cherub*
5502 chĕrŏubim (1), *cherubs or kerubim*

CHERUBIMS'
3742 kᵉrûwb (1), *cherub*

CHESALON
3693 Kᵉçâlôwn (1), *fertile*

CHESED
3777 Kesed (1), *Kesed*

CHESIL
3686 Kᵉçîyl (1), *stupid or silly*

CHESNUT
6196 'armôwn (2), *plane tree*

CHEST
727 'ârôwn (6), *box*

CHESTS
1595 genez (1), *treasury coffer*

CHESULLOTH
3694 Kᵉçullôwth (1), *fattened*

CHEW
5927 'âlâh (3), to *ascend, be high, mount*

CHEWED
3772 kârath (1), to *cut (off, down or asunder)*

CHEWETH
1641 gârar (1), to *chew*
5927 'âlâh (6), to *ascend, be high, mount*

CHEZIB
3580 Kᵉzîyb (1), *falsified*

CHICKENS
3556 nŏssiŏn (1), *birdling, chick-bird*

CHIDE
7378 rîyb (4), to *hold a controversy; to defend*

CHIDING
7379 rîyb (1), *contest, personal or legal*

CHIDON
3592 Kîydôwn (1), *dart, javelin*

CHIEF
1 'âb (3), *father*
441 'allûwph (1), *friend, chieftain, leader*
678 'âtsîyl (1), *extremity; noble*
1167 ba‘al (1), *master; husband; owner; citizen*
1368 gibbôwr (1), *powerful; great warrior*
3548 kôhên (2), one *officiating as a priest*
5051 nôgahh (1), *brilliancy*
5057 nâgîyd (1), *commander, official*
5059 nâgan (1), to *play; to make music*
5329 nâtsach (55), i.e. to *be eminent*
5387 nâsîy' (8), *leader; rising mist, fog*
6260 'attûwd (1), *he-goats; leaders of the people*
6438 pinnâh (2), *pinnacle; chieftain*
7217 rê'sh (Ch.) (1), *head*
7218 rô'sh (97), *head*
7223 rî'shôwn (3), *first*
7225 rê'shîyth (5), *first*
7229 rab (Ch.) (1), *great*
7725 shûwb (3), to *turn back; to return*
8269 sar (33), *head person, ruler*
204 akrŏgōniaiŏs (2), *corner, cornerstone*
749 archiĕrĕus (65), *high-priest, chief priest*
750 archipŏimēn (1), *head shepherd*
752 archisunagōgŏs (2), *director of the synagogue services*
754 architĕlōnēs (1), *chief tax-gatherer*
758 archōn (3), *first in rank or power*
775 Asiarchēs (1), *ruler in Asia*
2233 hēgĕŏmai (3), to *lead, i.e. command*
4410 prōtŏkathĕdria (2), *place of pre-eminence*

CHIEFEST
47 'abbîyr (1), *mighty*
1713 dâgal (1), to *be conspicuous*
4608 ma‘ăleh (1), *elevation; platform*
7218 rô'sh (1), *head*
7225 rê'shîyth (1), *first*
3390 mētrŏpŏlis (1), *main city*
4413 prōtŏs (1), *foremost*
5228+3029 hupĕr (2), *over; above; beyond*

CHIEFLY
3122 malista (2), *in the greatest degree*
4412 prōtŏn (1), *firstly*

CHILD
1121 bên (10), *son, descendant*
2029 hârâh (2), to *conceive, be pregnant*
2030 hâreh (12), *pregnant*
2056 vâlâd (1), *boy*
2233 zera' (2), *seed; fruit*
3173 yâchîyd (1), *only son; alone; beloved*
3205 yâlad (5), to *bear young; to father a child*
3206 yeled (39), *young male*
4392 mâlê' (1), *full; filling; fulness; fully*
5288 na‘ar (44), *male child; servant*
5290 nô'ar (1), *boyhood*
5768 'ôwlêl (1), *suckling child*
1025 brĕphŏs (1), *infant*
1471 ĕgkuŏs (1), *pregnant*
1722+1064+2192 ĕn (7), *in; during; because of*
3439 mŏnŏgĕnēs (1), *sole, one and only*
3516 nēpiŏs (4), *infant; simple-minded person*
3812 paidiŏthĕn (1), *from infancy*
3813 paidiŏn (28), *child; immature*
3816 pais (5), *child; slave or servant*
5043 tĕknŏn (5), *child*
5088 tiktō (1), *to produce from seed*
5207 huiŏs (3), *son*

CHILD'S
3206 yeled (2), *young male*
5290 nô'ar (1), *boyhood*
3813 paidiŏn (1), *child; immature*

CHILDBEARING
5042 tĕknŏgŏnia (1), *maternity, childbearing*

CHILDHOOD
3208 yaldûwth (1), *boyhood or girlhood*
5271 nâ'ûwr (1), *youth; juvenility; young people*

CHILDISH
3516 nēpiŏs (1), *infant; simple-minded person*

CHILDLESS
6185 'ărîyrîy (4), *barren of child*
7921 shâkôl (2), to *miscarry*
815 atĕknŏs (1), *childless*

CHILDREN
1121 bên (1523), *son, descendant*
1123 bên (Ch.) (4), *son*
1129 bânâh (2), to *build; to establish*
2945 taph (12), *family of children and women*
3205 yâlad (1), to *bear young; to father a child*
3206 yeled (31), *young male*
3211 yâlîyd (4), *born; descendants*
5288 na‘ar (7), *male child; servant*
5768 'ôwlêl (12), *suckling child*
6768 Tseleq (1), *fissure*
815 atĕknŏs (2), *childless*
1025 brĕphŏs (1), *infant*
3515 nēpiazō (1), to *act as a baby*
3516 nēpiŏs (2), *infant; simple-minded person*
3808 paidariŏn (1), *little boy*
3813 paidiŏn (17), *child; immature*
3816 pais (2), *child; slave or servant*
5027 taphē (2), *act of burial*
5040 tĕkniŏn (9), *infant, i.e. a darling*
5041 tĕknŏgŏnĕō (1), to *be a child bearer*
5043 tĕknŏn (70), *child*
5044 tĕknŏtrŏphĕō (1), to *be a child-rearer*
5206 huiŏthĕsia (1), *adoption*
5207 huiŏs (44), *son*
5388 philŏtĕknŏs (1), *loving one's child(ren)*

CHILDREN'S
1121 bên (16), *son, descendant*
3813 paidiŏn (1), *child; immature* Christian
5043 tĕknŏn (2), *child*

CHILEAB
3609 Kil'âb (1), *restraint of (his) father*

CHILION
3630 Kilyôwn (2), *pining, destruction*

CHILION'S
3630 Kilyôwn (1), *pining, destruction*

CHILMAD
3638 Kilmâd (1), *Kilmad*

CHIMHAM
3643 Kimhâm (4), *pining*

CHIMNEY
699 'ărubbâh (1), *window; chimney*

CHINNERETH
3672 Kinn⁰rôwth (4),
(poss.) *harp*-shaped

CHINNEROTH
3672 Kinn⁰rôwth (2),
(poss.) *harp*-shaped

CHIOS
5508 Chiŏs (1), *Chios*

CHISLEU
3691 Kiçlêv (2), *Hebrew
month*

CHISLON
3692 Kiçlôwn (1), *hopeful*

CHISLOTH-TABOR
3696 Kiçlôth Tâbôr (1),
flanks of Tabor

CHITTIM
3794 Kittîy (6), *islander*

CHIUN
3594 Kîyûwn (1), *deity*
(poss.) *Priapus or
Baal-peor*

CHLOE
5514 Chlŏĕ (1), *green*

CHODE
7378 rîyb (2), to *hold a
controversy; to defend*

CHOICE
970 bâchûwr (3), *male
youth; bridegroom*
977 bâchar (4), *select,
chose, prefer*
1249 bar (1), *beloved;
pure; empty*
1305 bârar (2), to
examine; select
4005 mibchâr (9), *select*
8321 sôrêq (1), *choice
vine stock*
1586 ĕklĕgŏmai (1), *select, choose, pick out*

CHOICEST
4055 mad (1), *vesture,
garment; carpet*
8321 sôrêq (1), *choice
vine stock*

CHOKE
4846 sumpnigŏ (2), to
drown; to crowd

CHOKED
638 apŏpnigŏ (3), to *stifle
or choke*
4155 pnigŏ (1), to *throttle
or strangle; to drown*
4846 sumpnigŏ (2), to
drown; to crowd

CHOLER
4843 mârar (2), to *be,
make bitter*

CHOOSE
972 bâchîyr (1), *selected
one*
977 bâchar (53), *select,
chose, prefer*
1254 bârâ' (2), to *create;
fashion*
1262 bârâh (1), to *feed*
6901 qâbal (1), to *take*
138 hairĕŏmai (1), to
prefer, choose

CHOOSEST
977 bâchar (2), *select,
chose, prefer*

CHOOSETH
977 bâchar (3), *select,
chose, prefer*

CHOOSING
138 hairĕŏmai (1), to
prefer, choose

CHOP
6566 pâras (1), to *break
apart, disperse, scatter*

CHOR-ASHAN
3565 Kôwr 'Âshân (1),
furnace of smoke

CHORAZIN
5523 Chŏrazin (2),
Chorazin

CHOSE
977 bâchar (24), *select,
chose, prefer*
1586 ĕklĕgŏmai (4), to
select, choose, pick out
1951 ĕpilĕgŏmai (1), to
surname, select

CHOSEN
970 bâchûwr (21), *male
youth; bridegroom*
972 bâchîyr (8), *selected
one*
977 bâchar (58), *select,
chose, prefer*
1305 bârar (2), to
examine; select
4005 mibchâr (4), *select*
138 hairĕŏmai (1), to
prefer, choose
140 hairĕtizŏ (1), to
make a choice
1586 ĕklĕgŏmai (15), to
select, choose, pick out
1588 ĕklĕktŏs (7),
selected; chosen
1589 ĕklŏgĕ (1),
selection, choice
4400 prŏchĕirizŏmai (1),
to *purpose*
4401 prŏchĕirŏtŏnĕŏ (1),
to *elect in advance*
4758 stratŏlŏgĕŏ (1), to
enlist in the army
5500 chĕirŏtŏnĕŏ (1), to
select or appoint

CHOZEBA
3578 Kŏzĕbâ' (1),
fallacious

CHRIST
5477 Chanaan (1),
humiliated
5547 Christŏs (551),
Anointed One

CHRIST'S
5547 Christŏs (15),
Anointed One

CHRISTIAN
5546 Christianŏs (2),
follower of Christ

CHRISTIANS
5546 Christianŏs (1),
follower of Christ

CHRISTS
5580 psĕudŏchristŏs (2),
spurious Messiah

CHRONICLES
1697+3117 dâbâr (38),
word; matter; thing

CHRYSOLITE
5555 chrusŏlithŏs (1),
yellow chrysolite

CHRYSOPRASUS
5556 chrusŏprasŏs (1),
*greenish-yellow
chrysoprase*

CHUB
3552 Kùwb (1), *Kub*

CHUN
3560 Kùwn (1),
established

CHURCH
1577 ĕkklĕsia (80),
congregation

CHURCHES
1577 ĕkklĕsia (36),
congregation
2417 hiĕrŏsulŏs (1),
temple-despoiler

CHURL
3596 kîylay (2),
begrudging

CHURLISH
7186 qâsheh (1), *severe*

CHURNING
4330 mîyts (1), *pressure*

CHUSHAN-RISHATHAIM
3573 Kùwshan
Rish'âthâyim (4),
*Cushan of double
wickedness*

CHUZA
5529 Chŏuzas (1),
Chuzas

CIELED
2645 châphâh (1), to
cover; to veil, to encase
5603 çâphan (2), to *hide
by covering; to roof*
7824 shâchîyph (1),
board, panel

CIELING
5604 çippûn (1),
wainscot, paneling

CILICIA
2791 Kilikia (8), *Cilicia*

CINNAMON
7076 qinnâmôwn (3),
cinnamon spice
2792 kinamōmŏn (1),
cinnamon

CINNEROTH
3672 Kinn⁰rôwth (1),
(poss.) *harp*-shaped

CIRCLE
2329 chûwg (1), *circle*

CIRCUIT
2329 chûwg (1), *circle*
5437 çâbab (1), to
surround
8622 t⁰qûwphâh (1),
revolution, course

CIRCUITS
5439 çâbîyb (1), *circle;
neighbor; environs*

CIRCUMCISE
4135 mûwl (5), to
circumcise
5243 nâmal (1), to *be
circumcised*
4059 pĕritĕmnō (4), to
circumcise

CIRCUMCISED
4135 mûwl (23), to
circumcise
203 akrŏbustia (1),
uncircumcised
4059 pĕritĕmnō (13), to
circumcise
4061 pĕritŏmĕ (1),
circumcision; Jews

CIRCUMCISING
4135 mûwl (1), to
circumcise
4059 pĕritĕmnō (1), to
circumcise

CIRCUMCISION
4139 mûwlâh (1),
circumcision
4061 pĕritŏmĕ (35),
circumcision; Jews

CIRCUMSPECT
8104 shâmar (1), to
watch

CIRCUMSPECTLY
199 akribŏs (1), *exactly,
carefully*

CIS
2797 Kis (1), *bow*

CISTERN
953 bôwr (4), *pit hole,
cistern, well*

CISTERNS
877 bô'r (1), *well, cistern*

CITIES
5892 'îyr (419), *city, town,
unwalled-village*
7141 Qôrach (1), *ice*
8179 sha'ar (2), *opening,
i.e. door or gate*
4172 pŏlis (19), *town*

CITIZEN
4177 pŏlitĕs (2), *citizen*

CITIZENS
4177 pŏlitĕs (1), *citizen*

CITY
4062 madhêbâh (1), *gold
making*
5892 'îyr (650), *city, town,
unwalled-village*
5982 'ammûwd (1),
column, pillar
7149 qiryâ' (Ch.) (6), *city*
7151 qiryâh (32), *city*
7176 qereth (5), *city*
7179 qash (1), *dry straw*
8179 sha'ar (1), *opening,
i.e. door or gate*
3390 mĕtrŏpŏlis (1),
main city
4172 pŏlis (143), *town*
4173 pŏlitarchĕs (2),
magistrate, city official

CLAD
3680 kâçâh (1), to *cover*
5844 'âţâh (1), to *wrap,
i.e. cover, veil, clothe*

CLAMOROUS
1993 hâmâh (1), to *be in
great commotion*

CLAMOUR
2906 kraugĕ (1), *outcry*

CLAP
4222 mâchâ' (2), to *strike
the hands together*

English

CLAPPED
5606 çâphaq (2), to *clap the hands*
8628 tâqa' (2), to *clatter, slap, drive, clasp*

CLAPPED
4222 mâchâ' (1), to *strike the hands together*
5221 nâkâh (1), to *strike, kill*

CLAPPETH
5606 çâphaq (1), to *clap the hands*

CLAUDA
2802 Klaudē (1), *Claude*

CLAUDIA
2803 Klaudia (1), *Claudia*

CLAUDIUS
2804 Klaudiŏs (3), *Claudius*

CLAVE
1234 bâqa' (6), to *cleave, break, tear open*
1692 dâbaq (6), to *cling or adhere*
2388 châzaq (1), to *fasten upon; to seize; to be strong; courageous*
2853 kŏllaō (1), to *glue together*

CLAWS
6541 parçâh (2), split *hoof*

CLAY
2563 chômer (11), *clay; dry measure*
2635 chăçaph (Ch.) (9), *clay*
2916 ţîyţ (3), *mud or clay*
4423 meleţ (1), *smooth clay cement floor*
4568 ma'ăbeh (2), *compact part of soil*
5671 'abţîyţ (1), *something pledged, i.e. (collect.) pawned goods*
4081 pĕlŏs (6), *lump of clay*

CLEAN
656 'âphêç (1), to *cease*
1249 bar (3), *beloved; pure; empty*
1305 bârar (1), to *brighten; purify*
2134 zak (2), *pure; clear*
2135 zâkâh (4), to *be translucent*
2141 zâkak (2), to *be transparent; clean, pure*
2548 châmîyts (1), *salted provender or fodder*
2889 ţâhôwr (49), *pure, clean, flawless*
2891 ţâhêr (41), to *be pure, unadulterated*
5355 nâqîy (1), *innocent*
6565 pârar (1), to *break up; to violate, frustrate*
8552 tâmam (3), to *complete, finish*
2511 katharizō (5), to *cleanse*
2513 katharŏs (10), *clean, pure*
2889 kŏsmŏs (3), *world*
3689 ŏntŏs (1), *really, certainly*

CLEANNESS
1252 bôr (4), *purity, cleanness*
5356 niqqâyôwn (1), *clearness; cleanness*

CLEANSE
1305 bârar (1), to *brighten; purify*
2135 zâkâh (1), to *be translucent*
2398 châţâ' (7), to *sin*
2891 ţâhêr (15), to *be pure, unadulterated*
5352 nâqâh (3), to *be, make clean; to be bare*
2511 katharizō (6), to *cleanse*

CLEANSED
2135 zâkâh (1), to *be translucent*
2891 ţâhêr (23), to *be pure, unadulterated*
2893 ţohŏrâh (1), *purification; purity*
3722 kâphar (1), to *cover; to expiate*
5352 nâqâh (1), to *be, make clean; to be bare*
6663 tsâdaq (1), to *be, make right*
2511 katharizō (9), to *cleanse*

CLEANSETH
2891 ţâhêr (1), to *be pure, unadulterated*
8562 tamrûwq (1), *scouring, i.e. soap*
2511 katharizō (1), to *cleanse*

CLEANSING
2893 ţohŏrâh (8), *purification; purity*
2512 katharismŏs (2), *ablution; expiation*

CLEAR
216 'ôwr (1), *luminary; lightning; happiness*
1249 bar (1), *beloved; pure; empty*
2135 zâkâh (1), to *be translucent*
3368 yâqâr (1), *valuable*
5352 nâqâh (3), to *be, make clean; to be bare*
5355 nâqîy (1), *innocent*
6663 tsâdaq (1), to *be, make right*
6703 tsach (1), *dazzling, i.e. sunny, bright*
53 hagnŏs (1), *innocent, modest, perfect, pure*
2513 katharŏs (1), *clean, pure*
2929 krustallizō (1), to *appear as ice*
2986 lamprŏs (1), *radiant; clear*

CLEARER
6965 qûwm (1), to *rise*

CLEARING
5352 nâqâh (1), to *be, make clean; to be bare*
627 apŏlŏgia (1), *plea or verbal defense*

CLEARLY
1305 bârar (1), to *brighten; purify*
1227 diablēpō (2), see *clearly*
2529 kathŏraō (1), to *distinctly apprehend*
5081 tēlaugōs (1), *plainly*

CLEARNESS
2892 ţôhar (1), *brightness; purification*

CLEAVE
1234 bâqa' (3), to *cleave, break, tear open*
1692 dâbaq (18), to *cling or adhere; to catch*
1693 dᵉbaq (Ch.) (1), to *stick; to be united*
1695 dâbêq (1), *adhering, sticking to*
3867 lâvâh (1), to *unite*
5596 çâphach (1), to *associate; be united*
8156 shâça' (1), to *split or tear; to upbraid*
2853 kŏllaō (1), to *glue together*
4347 prŏskŏllaō (3), to *glue to, i.e. to adhere*

CLEAVED
1692 dâbaq (3), to *cling or adhere; to catch*

CLEAVETH
1234 bâqa' (2), to *cleave, break, tear open*
1692 dâbaq (6), to *cling or adhere; to catch*
3332 yâtsaq (1), to *pour out*
6398 pâlach (1), to *slice; to break open; to pierce*
6821 tsâphad (1), to *adhere, join*
8157 sheça' (1), *fissure, split*
2853 kŏllaō (1), to *glue together*

CLEFT
1234 bâqa' (1), to *cleave, break, tear open*
8156 shâça' (1), to *split or tear; to upbraid*

CLEFTS
1233 bᵉqîya' (1), *fissure, breach*
2288 chăgâv (3), *rift, cleft in rocks*
5366 nᵉqârâh (1), *fissure*

CLEMENCY
1932 ĕpiĕikĕia (1), *mildness, gentleness*

CLEMENT
2815 Klēmēs (1), *merciful*

CLEOPAS
2810 Klĕŏpas (1), *renown father*

CLEOPHAS
2832 Klōpas (1), cf. *friend of (his) father*

CLIFF
4608 ma'ăleh (1), *elevation; platform*

CLIFFS
6178 'ârûwts (1), *feared; horrible place or chasm*

CLIFT
5366 nᵉqârâh (1), *fissure*

CLIFTS
5585 çâ'îyph (1), *fissure of rocks; bough*

CLIMB
5927 'âlâh (4), to *ascend, be high, mount*

CLIMBED
5927 'âlâh (1), to *ascend, be high, mount*
305 anabainō (1), to *go up, rise*

CLIMBETH
305 anabainō (1), to *go up, rise*

CLIPPED
1639 gâra' (1), to *shave, remove, lessen*

CLODS
1487 gûwsh (1), *mass of earth, dirt clod*
4053 migrâphâh (1), *clod of cultivated dirt*
7263 regeb (2), *lump of clay*
7702 sâdad (2), to *harrow a field*

CLOKE
4598 mᵉ'îyl (1), *outer garment or robe*
1942 ĕpikaluma (1), *pretext, covering*
2440 himatiōn (2), to *put on clothes*
4392 prŏphasis (2), *pretext, excuse*
5341 phĕlŏnēs (1), *outer garment, mantle, cloak*

CLOSE
681 'êtsel (1), *side; near*
1443 gâdar (1), to *build a stone wall*
1692 dâbaq (1), to *cling or adhere; to catch*
4526 miçgereth (2), *margin; stronghold*
5641 çâthar (1), to *hide by covering*
5956 'âlam (1), to *veil from sight, i.e. conceal*
6113 'âtsar (1), to *hold back; to maintain*
6862 tsar (1), *trouble; opponent*
788 assŏn (1), *more nearly, i.e. very near*
4601 sigaō (1), to *keep silent*

CLOSED
2115 zûwr (1), to *press together, tighten*
3680 kâçâh (1), to *cover*
5437 çâbab (1), to *surround*
5462 çâgar (2), to *shut up; to surrender*
5640 çâtham (1), to *stop up; to keep secret*
6105 'âtsam (1), to *be, make powerful*
6113 'âtsar (1), to *hold back; to maintain*
2576 kammuō (2), to *close or shut the eyes*

4428 ptussō (1), to *fold*,
i.e. *furl* or *roll* a scroll

CLOSEST
8474 tachârâh (1), to *vie*
with a rival

CLOSET
2646 chuppâh (1), *canopy*
5009 tamĕiŏn (1), *room*

CLOSETS
5009 tamĕiŏn (1), *room*

CLOTH
899 beged (9), *clothing;*
treachery or *pillage*
4346 makbâr (1),
netted-cloth
8071 simlâh (2), *dress,*
mantle
4470 rhakŏs (2), *piece* of
cloth
4616 sindōn (3), *byssos,*
i.e. bleached *linen*

CLOTHE
3847 lâbash (12), to
clothe
294 amphiĕnnumi (2), to
enrobe, clothe

CLOTHED
3680 kâçâh (1), to *cover*
3736 karbêl (1), to *gird*
or *clothe*
3830 lᵉbûwsh (1),
garment; wife
3847 lâbash (39), to
clothe
3848 lᵉbash (Ch.) (3), to
clothe
294 amphiĕnnumi (2), to
enrobe, clothe
1463 ĕgkŏmbŏŏmai (1),
to *wear, be clothed*
1737 ĕndiduskŏ (1), to
clothe
1746 ĕnduō (6), to *invest*
with clothing, i.e. to
dress
1902 ĕpĕnduŏmai (2), to
clothe
2439 himatizŏ (2), to
dress, clothe
4016 pĕriballō (14), to
wrap around, clothe

CLOTHES
899 beged (69), *clothing;*
treachery or *pillage*
1545 gᵉlôwm (1),
clothing, fabric
4055 mad (1), *vesture,*
garment; carpet
5497 çûwth (1), *clothing*
8008 salmâh (3), *clothing*
8071 simlâh (6), *dress,*
mantle
2440 himatiŏn (12), to
put on clothes
3608 ŏthŏniŏn (5), strips
of *linen bandage*
4683 sparganŏŏ (2), to
wrap with cloth
5509 chitōn (1), *tunic* or
shirt

CLOTHEST
3847 lâbash (1), to *clothe*

CLOTHING
899 beged (1), *clothing;*
treachery or *pillage*

3830 lᵉbûwsh (9),
garment; wife
4374 mᵉkaççeh (1),
covering
8071 simlâh (2), *dress,*
mantle
8516 talbôsheth (1),
garment
1742 ĕnduma (1),
apparel, outer *robe*
2066 ĕsthēs (2), to *clothe*
4749 stŏlē (1),
long-fitting *gown*

CLOTHS
899 beged (4), *clothing;*
treachery or *pillage*

CLOUD
5645 'âb (9), *thick*
clouds; thicket
5743 'ûwb (1), to darkly
becloud
6051 'ânân (75), *nimbus*
cloud
6053 'ânânâh (1),
cloudiness
6205 'ârâphel (1), *gloom,*
darkness
3507 nĕphĕlē (18), *cloud*
3509 nĕphŏs (1), *cloud*

CLOUDS
2385 chăzîyz (1), *flash* of
lightning
3709 kaph (1), hollow of
hand; paw; sole of foot
5387 nâsîy' (1), *leader;*
rising *mist, fog*
5645 'âb (20), *thick*
clouds; thicket
6050 'ănan (Ch.) (1),
nimbus cloud
6051 'ânân (5), *nimbus*
cloud
6053 'ânânâh (1),
cloudiness
7834 shachaq (11),
firmament, clouds
3507 nĕphĕlē (8), *cloud*

CLOUDY
6051 'ânân (6), *nimbus*
cloud

CLOUTED
2921 ţâlâ' (1), to *be*
spotted or *variegated*

CLOUTS
5499 çᵉchâbâh (2), *rag*

CLOVEN
8156 shâça' (1), to *split*
or *tear;* to *upbraid*
1266 diamĕrizŏ (1), to
distribute

CLOVENFOOTED
8156+8157 shâça' (1), to
split or *tear;* to *upbraid*
8156+8157+6541 shâça'
(2), to *split* or *tear*

CLUSTER
811 'eshkôwl (5), *bunch*
of *grapes*

CLUSTERS
811 'eshkôwl (4), *bunch*
of *grapes*
6778 tsammûwq (2),
lump of *dried* grapes
1009 bŏtrus (1), *bunch,*
cluster of grapes

CNIDUS
2834 Knidŏs (1), *Cnidus*

COAL
1513 gechel (2), *ember,*
hot coal
7531 ritspâh (1), hot
stone; pavement
7815 shᵉchôwr (1), *soot*

COALS
1513 gechel (16), *ember,*
hot coal
6352 pechâm (3), black
coal, charcoal
7529 retseph (1), red-hot
stone for baking
7565 resheph (2), *flame*
439 anthrakia (2), fire
bed of burning *coals*
440 anthrax (1), live *coal*

COAST
1366 gᵉbûwl (47),
boundary, border
2256 chebel (4),
company, band
2348 chôwph (1), *cove,*
sheltered bay
3027 yâd (5), *hand; power*
5299 nâphâh (1), *height;*
sieve
7097 qâtseh (1), *extremity*
3864 parathalassiŏs (1),
by the lake
3882 paraliŏs (1),
maritime; seacoast

COASTS
1366 gᵉbûwl (23),
boundary, border
1367 gᵉbûwlâh (5), *region*
1552 gᵉlîylâh (1), *circuit*
or *region*
2348 chôwph (1), *cove,*
sheltered bay
3027 yâd (1), *hand; power*
3411 yᵉrêkâh (3), *far*
away places
7097 qâtseh (1), *extremity*
7098 qâtsâh (1),
termination; fringe
3313 mĕrŏs (3), *division*
or *share*
3725 hŏriŏn (10), *region,*
area, vicinity
5117 tŏpŏs (1), *place*
5561 chōra (1), *territory*

COAT
3801 kᵉthôneth (16),
garment that covers
4598 mᵉ'îyl (1), *outer*
garment or *robe*
8302 shiryôwn (3),
corslet, coat of mail
1903 ĕpĕndutēs (1), outer
garment, coat
5509 chitōn (4), *tunic* or
shirt

COATS
3801 kᵉthôneth (7),
garment that covers
5622 çarbal (Ch.) (2),
cloak
5509 chitōn (5), *tunic* or
shirt

COCK
220 alĕktōr (12), *rooster*

COCKATRICE
6848 tsepha' (1), *hissing*
viper

COCKATRICES
6848 tsepha' (1), *hissing*
viper

COCKCROWING
219 alektŏrŏphōnia (1),
rooster-crowing

COCKLE
890 bo'shâh (1), *weed*

COFFER
712 'argâz (3), *box, chest*

COFFIN
727 'ârôwn (1), *box*

COGITATIONS
7476 ra'yôwn (Ch.) (1),
mental *conception*

COLD
2779 chôreph (1),
autumn (and winter)
6793 tsinnâh (1), large
shield; piercing cold
7119 qar (2), *cool; quiet;*
cool-headed
7120 qôr (1), *cold*
7135 qârâh (5), *coolness,*
cold
5592 psuchŏs (3),
coolness, cold
5593 psuchrŏs (4), *chilly,*
cold
5594 psuchō (1), to *chill,*
grow cold

COLHOZEH
3626 Kol-Chôzeh (2),
every seer

COLLAR
6310 peh (1), *mouth;*
opening

COLLARS
5188 nᵉţîyphâh (1),
pendant for the ears

COLLECTION
4864 mas'êth (2), *raising;*
beacon; present
3048 lŏgia (1),
contribution, collection

COLLEGE
4932 mishneh (2),
duplicate copy; double

COLLOPS
6371 pîymâh (1), *obesity*

COLONY
2862 kŏlōnia (1), *colony*

COLORS
6320 pûwk (1), *stibium*

COLOSSE
2857 Kŏlŏssai (1),
colossal

COLOSSIANS
2858 Kŏlŏssaĕus (1),
inhabitant of Colossæ

COLOUR
5869 'ayin (11), *eye;*
sight; fountain
4392 prŏphasis (1),
pretext, excuse

COLOURS
2921 ţâlâ' (1), to *be*
spotted or *variegated*
6446 paç (5), *long*
-sleeved tunic

English

COLT
6648 tseba' (3), *dye*
7553 riqmâh (2), *variegation* of color

COLT
1121 bên (1), *son, descendant*
5895 'ayîr (2), *young robust donkey or ass*
4454 pôlŏs (12), *young donkey*

COLTS
1121 bên (1), *son, descendant*
5895 'ayîr (2), *young robust donkey or ass*

COME
270 'âchaz (1), to *seize, grasp; possess*
314 'achărôwn (8), *late or last; behind; western*
635 'Eçtêr (1), *Esther*
835 'esher (3), *how happy!*
857 'âthâh (12), to *arrive*
858 'âthâh (Ch.) (3), to *arrive; go*
935 bôw' (681), to *go, come*
1869 dârak (1), to *walk, lead;* to *string* a bow
1934 hăvâ' (Ch.) (3), to *be, to exist*
1961 hâyâh (131), to *exist,* i.e. *be or become*
1980 hâlak (7), to *walk; live a certain way*
3045 yâda' (3), to *know*
3051 yâhab (1), to *give*
3205 yâlad (1), to *bear young;* to *father a child*
3212 yâlak (72), to *walk;* to *l¡ve;* to *carry*
3318 yâtsâ' (84), to *go, bring out*
3381 yârad (57), to *descend*
4279 mâchar (8), *tomorrow; hereafter*
4291 mᵉtâ' (Ch.) (1), to *arrive,* to *extend*
4609 ma'ălâh (1), *thought arising*
4672 mâtsâ' (8), to *find* or *acquire;* to *occur*
5060 nâga' (13), to *strike*
5066 nâgash (28), to *be, come, bring near*
5181 nâchath (2), to *sink, descend*
5185 nâchêth (1), *descending*
5312 nᵉphaq (Ch.) (1), to *issue forth;* to *bring out*
5506 çᵉchôrâh (1), *traffic*
5674 'âbar (14), to *cross over;* to *transition*
5927 'âlâh (104), to *ascend, be high, mount*
6213 'âsâh (1), to *do or make*
6264 'âthîyd (1), *prepared; treasure*
6631 tse'ĕtsâ' (1), *produce, children*
6743 tsâlach (1), to *push forward*
6923 qâdam (5), to *anticipate, hasten*

7122 qârâ' (4), to *encounter,* to *happen*
7125 qîr'âh (1), to *encounter,* to *happen*
7126 qârab (33), to *approach, bring near*
7131 qârêb (2), *near*
7136 qârâh (2), to *bring about;* to *impose*
7138 qârôwb (1), *near, close*
7725 shûwb (30), to *turn back;* to *return*
8175 sâ'ar (1), to *storm;* to *shiver,* i.e. *fear*
8622 tᵉqûwphâh (1), *revolution, course*
191 akŏuō (1), to *hear; obey*
305 anabainō (7), to *go up, rise*
565 apérchŏmai (3), to *go off,* i.e. *depart*
576 apŏbainō (1), to *eventuate, become*
864 aphiknĕŏmai (1), to *go forth* by rumor
1096 ginŏmai (43), to *be, become*
1204 dĕurŏ (8), *hither!; hitherto*
1205 dĕutĕ (12), *come hither!*
1224 diabainō (1), to *pass by, over, across*
1330 diĕrchŏmai (1), to *traverse, travel through*
1448 ĕggizō (9), to *approach*
1511 ĕinai (8), to *exist*
1525 ĕisérchŏmai (18), to *enter*
1531 ĕispŏrĕuŏmai (1), to *enter*
1607 ĕkpŏrĕuŏmai (3), to *depart, be discharged*
1684 ĕmbainō (2), to *embark;* to *reach*
1764 ĕnistēmi (1), to *be present*
1831 ĕxérchŏmai (24), to *issue;* to *leave*
1834 ĕxēgĕŏmai (1), to *tell, relate again*
1880 ĕpanérchŏmai (1), *return home*
1904 ĕpérchŏmai (8), to *supervene*
1910 ĕpibainō (1), to *ascend, embark, arrive*
1975 ĕpipŏrĕuŏmai (1), to *go, come to*
2049 ĕrēmŏō (1), to *lay waste*
2064 ĕrchŏmai (290), to *go or come*
2186 ĕphistēmi (2), to *be present;* to *approach*
2240 hēkō (24), to *arrive,* i.e. *be present*
2597 katabainō (20), to *descend*
2638 katalambanō (1), to *seize;* to *possess*
2647 kataluō (1), to *halt for the night*
2658 katantaō (3), to *arrive at;* to *attain*

2673 katargĕō (1), to *be, render entirely useless*
2718 katérchŏmai (2), to *go, come down*
3195 mĕllō (16), to *intend,* i.e. *be about to*
3854 paraginŏmai (15), to *arrive;* to *appear*
3918 parĕimi (6), to *be present;* to *have come*
3928 parérchŏmai (1), to *go by;* to *perish*
3936 paristēmi (1), to *stand beside, present*
4137 plērŏō (1), to *fill, make complete*
4301 prŏlambanō (1), to *take before*
4331 prŏsĕggizō (1), to *approach near*
4334 prŏsérchŏmai (6), to *come near, visit*
4365 prŏspŏrĕuŏmai (1), to *come towards*
4845 sumplērŏō (2), to *be complete, fulfill*
4905 sunérchŏmai (14), to *go with*
4940 suntugchanō (1), to *come together*
5290 hupŏstrĕphō (1), to *turn under, behind*
5302 hustĕrĕō (3), to *be inferior;* to *fall short*
5348 phthanō (4), to *be anticipate or precede*
5562 chōrĕō (1), to *pass, enter;* to *hold, admit*

COMELINESS
1926 hâdâr (3), *magnificence*
1935 hôwd (1), *grandeur, majesty*
2157 ĕuschēmŏsunē (1), *decorousness*

COMELY
2433 chîyn (1), *graceful beauty*
3190 yâṭab (1), to *be, make well*
3303 yâpheh (1), *beautiful; handsome*
4998 nâ'âh (1), to *be pleasant or suitable*
5000 nâ'veh (7), *suitable or beautiful*
8389 tô'ar (1), *outline, figure or appearance*
8597 tiph'ârâh (1), *ornament*
2158 ĕuschēmōn (2), *decorous, proper; noble*
4241 prĕpō (1), to *be suitable or proper*

COMERS
4334 prŏsérchŏmai (1), to *come near, visit*

COMEST
935 bôw' (22), to *go or come*
2199 zâ'aq (1), to *call out, announce*
7126 qârab (2), to *approach, bring near*
2064 ĕrchŏmai (3), to *go or come*

COMETH
857 'âthâh (3), to *arrive*
935 bôw' (89), to *go, come*
1961 hâyâh (1), to *exist,* i.e. *be or become*
1980 hâlak (2), to *walk; live a certain way*
3318 yâtsâ' (19), to *go, bring out*
3381 yârad (1), to *descend*
4672 mâtsâ' (1), to *occur, meet or be present*
5034 nâbêl (1), to *wilt;* to *fall away*
5060 nâga' (1), to *strike*
5414 nâthan (1), to *give*
5674 'âbar (1), to *cross over;* to *transition*
5927 'âlâh (10), to *ascend, be high, mount*
6293 pâga' (1), to *impinge*
6437 pânâh (1), to *turn, to face*
6627 tsâ'âh (2), human *excrement*
6631 tse'ĕtsâ' (1), *produce, children*
7131 qârêb (5), *near*
7698 sheger (1), *what comes forth*
7725 shûwb (3), to *turn back;* to *return*
305 anabainō (1), to *go up, rise*
1096 ginŏmai (2), to *be, become*
1511 ĕinai (1), to *exist*
1607 ĕkpŏrĕuŏmai (2), to *depart, be discharged*
1831 ĕxérchŏmai (1), to *issue;* to *leave*
1999 ĕpisustasis (1), *insurrection*
2064 ĕrchŏmai (97), to *go or come*
2186 ĕphistēmi (1), to *be present;* to *approach*
2591 Karpŏs (1), (poss.) *fruit*
2597 katabainō (3), to *descend*
3854 paraginŏmai (3), to *arrive;* to *appear*
4334 prŏsérchŏmai (1), to *come near, visit*
4905 sunérchŏmai (1), to *gather together*

COMFORT
1082 bâlag (2), to *be comforted*
4010 mablîygîyth (1), *desolation*
5162 nâcham (33), to *be sorry;* to *pity, console*
5165 nechâmâh (1), *consolation*
5582 çâ'ad (3), to *support*
7502 râphad (1), to *spread a bed;* to *refresh*
2174 ĕupsuchĕō (1), to *feel encouraged*
2293 tharsĕō (3), to *have courage; take heart!*
3870 parakalĕō (9), to *call, invite*
3874 paraklēsis (6), *imploring, exhortation*

3888 paramuthĕŏmai (2), to *console*
3889 paramuthia (1), *consolation*
3890 paramuthiŏn (1), *consolation*
3931 parēgŏria (1), *consolation, comfort*

COMFORTABLE
4496 mᵉnûwchâh (1), *peacefully; consolation*
5150 nichûwm (1), *consoled; solace*

COMFORTABLY
5921+3820 'al (4), *above, over, upon, or against*
5921+3824 'al (1), *above, over, upon, or against*

COMFORTED
5162 nâcham (20), to *be sorry; to pity, console*
3870 parakalĕō (13), to *call, invite*
3888 paramuthĕŏmai (2), to *console*
4837 sumparakalĕō (1), to *console jointly*

COMFORTEDST
5162 nâcham (1), to *be sorry; to pity, console*

COMFORTER
5162 nâcham (3), to *be sorry; to pity, console*
3875 paraklētŏs (4), *intercessor, consoler*

COMFORTERS
5162 nâcham (5), to *be sorry; to pity, console*

COMFORTETH
5162 nâcham (3), to *be sorry; to pity, console*
3870 parakalĕō (2), to *call, invite*

COMFORTLESS
3737 ŏrphanŏs (1), *parentless, orphaned*

COMFORTS
5150 nichûwm (1), *consoled; solace*
8575 tanchûwm (1), *compassion, solace*

COMING
857 'âthâh (1), to *arrive*
935 bôw' (19), to *go, come*
1980 hâlak (1), to *walk; live a certain way*
3318 yâtsâ' (2), to *go, bring out*
3381 yârad (2), to *descend*
3996 mâbôw' (1), *entrance; sunset; west*
4126 môwbâ' (1), *entrance*
5182 nᵉchath (Ch.) (1), to *descend; to depose*
5674 'âbar (1), to *cross over; to transition*
7122 qârâ' (1), to *encounter, to happen*
7272 regel (1), *foot; step*
305 anabainō (2), to *go up, rise*
602 apŏkalupsis (1), *disclosure, revelation*

1525 ĕisĕrchŏmai (3), to *enter*
1529 ĕisŏdŏs (1), *entrance*
1531 ĕispŏrĕuŏmai (1), to *enter*
1660 ĕlĕusis (1), *advent, coming*
1831 ĕxĕrchŏmai (1), to *issue; to leave*
1904 ĕpĕrchŏmai (1), to *supervene*
2064 ĕrchŏmai (27), to *go or come*
2186 ĕphistĕmi (1), to *be present; to approach*
2597 katabainō (1), to *descend*
3854 paraginŏmai (1), to *arrive; to appear*
3952 parŏusia (22), *advent, coming*
4334 prŏsĕrchŏmai (3), *to come near, visit*

COMINGS
4126 môwbâ' (1), *entrance*

COMMAND
559 'âmar (2), to *say*
6310 peh (1), *mouth; opening*
6680 tsâvâh (84), to *constitute, enjoin*
1781 ĕntĕllŏmai (4), to *enjoin, give orders*
2004 ĕpitassō (1), to *order, command*
2036 ĕpō (3), to *speak*
2753 kĕlĕuō (1), to *order, direct*
3853 paraggĕllō (8), to *enjoin; to instruct*

COMMANDED
559 'âmar (25), to *say*
560 'ămar (Ch.) (12), to *say, speak*
1696 dâbar (4), to *speak, say; to subdue*
4480+2941 min (1), *from or out of*
4687 mitsvâh (2), *command*
6680 tsâvâh (333), to *constitute, enjoin*
7761+2942 sûwm (Ch.) (3), to *put, place*
1291 diastĕllŏmai (1), to *enjoin*
1299 diatassō (6), to *institute, prescribe*
1781 ĕntĕllŏmai (6), to *enjoin, give orders*
2004 ĕpitassō (4), to *order, command*
2036 ĕpō (5), to *speak*
2750 kĕiria (1), *swathe of cloth*
2753 kĕlĕuō (20), to *order, direct*
3853 paraggĕllō (11), to *enjoin; to give instruction*
4367 prŏstassō (6), to *enjoin*
4483 rhĕō (1), to *utter, i.e. speak or say*

COMMANDEDST
6680 tsâvâh (4), to *constitute, enjoin*

COMMANDER
6680 tsâvâh (1), to *constitute, enjoin*

COMMANDEST
6680 tsâvâh (2), to *constitute, enjoin*
2753 kĕlĕuō (1), to *order, direct*

COMMANDETH
559 'âmar (3), to *say, speak*
6680 tsâvâh (6), to *constitute, enjoin*
2004 ĕpitassō (3), to *order, command*
3853 paraggĕllō (1), to *enjoin; to instruct*

COMMANDING
6680 tsâvâh (1), to *constitute, enjoin*
1299 diatassō (1), to *institute, prescribe*
2753 kĕlĕuō (1), to *order, direct*

COMMANDMENT
559 'âmar (2), to *say*
565 'imrâh (1), *something said*
1697 dâbâr (15), *word; matter; thing*
1881 dâth (2), royal *edict or statute*
2941 ţa'am (Ch.) (2), *sentence, command*
2942 ţᵉ'êm (Ch.) (2), *judgment; account*
3318 yâtsâ' (1), to *go, bring out*
3982 ma'ămar (2), *edict, command*
4406 millâh (Ch.) (1), *word, command*
4662 miphqâd (1), *appointment*
4687 mitsvâh (43), *command*
6310 peh (37), *mouth; opening*
6673 tsav (1), *injunction*
6680 tsâvâh (9), to *constitute, enjoin*
1291 diastĕllŏmai (1), to *enjoin*
1297 diatagma (1), *authoritative edict*
1781 ĕntĕllŏmai (2), to *enjoin, give orders*
1785 ĕntŏlē (42), *prescription, regulation*
2003 ĕpitagē (6), *injunction or decree*
2753 kĕlĕuō (2), to *order, direct*
3852 paraggĕlia (1), *mandate, order*
3853 paraggĕllō (1), to *enjoin; to instruct*

COMMANDMENTS
1697 dâbâr (5), *word; matter; thing*
2706 chôq (1), *appointment; allotment*
4687 mitsvâh (130), *command*

6490 piqqûwd (2), *mandate of God, Law*
1778 ĕntalma (3), *precept, command*
1781 ĕntĕllŏmai (1), to *enjoin, give orders*
1785 ĕntŏlē (27), *prescription, regulation*
3852 paraggĕlia (1), *mandate, order*

COMMEND
3908 paratithēmi (2), to *present something*
4921 sunistaō (5), to *set together*

COMMENDATION
4956 sustatikŏs (2), *recommendatory*

COMMENDED
1984 hâlal (2), to *speak words of thankfulness*
7623 shâbach (1), to *address in a loud tone*
1867 ĕpainĕō (1), to *applaud, commend*
3908 paratithēmi (1), to *present something*
4921 sunistaō (1), to *set together*

COMMENDETH
3936 paristēmi (1), to *stand beside, present*
4921 sunistaō (3), to *set together*

COMMENDING
4921 sunistaō (1), to *set together*

COMMISSION
2011 ĕpitrŏpē (1), *permission*

COMMISSIONS
1881 dâth (1), royal *edict or statute*

COMMIT
1556 gâlal (2), to *roll; to commit*
2181 zânâh (11), to *commit adultery*
4560 mâçar (1), to *set apart; apostatize*
4603 mâ'al (4), to *act treacherously*
5003 nâ'aph (6), to *commit adultery*
5414 nâthan (1), to *give*
5753 'âvâh (2), to *be crooked*
6213 'âsâh (14), to *do or make*
6313 pûwg (1), to *be sluggish; be numb*
6466 pâ'al (1), to *do, make or practice*
6485 pâqad (2), to *visit, care for, count*
7760 sûwm (1), to *put, place*
2038 ĕrgazŏmai (1), to *toil*
2416 hiĕrŏsulĕō (1), to *be a temple-robber*
3429 mŏichaō (2), to *commit adultery*
3431 mŏichĕuō (10), to *commit adultery*

3908 paratithēmi (3), to present something
4100 pistēuō (2), to have faith, to entrust
4160 pŏiĕō (2), to make
4203 pŏrnĕuō (3), to indulge unlawful lust
4238 prassō (2), to execute, accomplish

COMMITTED
1961 hâyâh (2), to exist, i.e. be or become
2181 zânâh (5), to commit adultery
2398 châtâ' (6), to sin
4600 mâ'ak (6), to pierce, emasculate, handle
5003 nâ'aph (5), to commit adultery
5414 nâthan (5), to give
5753 'âvâh (2), to be crooked
6213 'âsâh (28), to do or make
6485 pâqad (4), to visit, care for, count
7561 râsha' (1), to be, do, declare wrong
8581 tâ'ab (1), to loathe, i.e. detest
764 asĕbĕō (1), to be, act impious or wicked
1325 didōmi (1), to give
1439 ĕaō (1), to let be, i.e. permit or leave alone
3431 mŏichĕuō (1), to commit adultery
3860 paradidōmi (2), to hand over
3866 parathēkē (1), trust, deposit entrusted
3872 parakatathēkē (2), deposit, trust
3908 paratithēmi (1), to present something
4100 pistēuō (5), to have faith; to entrust
4160 pŏiĕō (4), to make
4203 pŏrnĕuō (4), to indulge unlawful lust
4238 prassō (3), to execute, accomplish
5087 tithēmi (1), to place

COMMITTEST
2181 zânâh (1), to commit adultery

COMMITTETH
5003 nâ'aph (4), to commit adultery
5800 'âzab (1), to loosen; relinquish; permit
6213 'âsâh (4), to do or make
3429 mŏichaō (4), to commit adultery
3431 mŏichĕuō (2), to commit adultery
4160 pŏiĕō (3), to make or do
4203 pŏrnĕuō (1), to indulge unlawful lust

COMMITTING
5003 nâ'aph (1), to commit adultery
6213 'âsâh (1), to do or make

COMMODIOUS
428 anĕuthĕtŏs (1), inconvenient

COMMON
776 'erets (1), earth, land, soil; country
1121 bên (1), people of a class or kind
2455 chôl (2), profane, common, not holy
2490 châlal (1), to profane, defile
7227 rab (1), great
7230 rôb (1), abundance
442 anthrōpinŏs (1), human
1219 dēmŏsiŏs (1), public; in public
2839 kŏinŏs (8), common, i.e. profane
2840 kŏinŏō (1), to make profane
4183 pŏlus (1), much, many
4232 praitōriŏn (1), governor's court-room

COMMONLY
1310 diaphēmizō (1), to spread news
3654 hŏlōs (1), altogether

COMMONWEALTH
4174 pŏlitĕia (1), citizenship

COMMOTION
7494 ra'ash (1), bounding, uproar

COMMOTIONS
181 akatastasia (1), disorder, riot

COMMUNE
559 'âmar (1), to say
1696 dâbar (4), to speak, say; to subdue
1697 dâbâr (1), word; matter; thing
5608 çâphar (1), to enumerate; to recount
7878 sîyach (1), to ponder, muse aloud

COMMUNED
1696 dâbar (14), to speak, say; to subdue
1255 dialalĕō (1), to converse, discuss
3656 hŏmilĕō (2), to converse, talk
4814 sullalĕō (1), to talk together, i.e. converse

COMMUNICATE
2841 kŏinōnĕō (1), to share or participate
2842 kŏinōnia (1), benefaction; sharing
2843 kŏinōnikŏs (1), liberal
4790 sugkŏinōnĕō (1), to co-participate in

COMMUNICATED
394 anatithēmai (1), propound, set forth
2841 kŏinōnĕō (1), to share or participate

COMMUNICATION
1697 dâbâr (1), word; matter; thing

7879 sîyach (1), uttered contemplation
148 aischrŏlŏgia (1), vile conversation
2842 kŏinōnia (1), benefaction; sharing
3056 lŏgŏs (2), word, matter, thing; Word

COMMUNICATIONS
3056 lŏgŏs (1), word, matter, thing
3657 hŏmilia (1), associations

COMMUNING
1696 dâbar (2), to speak, say; to subdue

COMMUNION
2842 kŏinōnia (4), benefaction; sharing

COMPACT
2266 châbar (1), to fascinate by spells

COMPACTED
4822 sumbibazō (1), to drive together

COMPANIED
4905 sunĕrchŏmai (1), to gather together

COMPANIES
736 'ŏr°châh (1), caravan
1416 g°dûwd (1), band of soldiers
1979 hălîykâh (1), walking; procession
4256 machălŏqeth (1), section or division
4264 machăneh (1), encampment
6951 qâhâl (1), assemblage
7218 rô'sh (7), head
4849 sumpŏsiŏn (1), group

COMPANION
2270 châbêr (2), associate, friend
2278 chăbereth (1), consort, companion
4828 mêrêa' (3), close friend
7453 rêa' (3), associate; one close
7462 râ'âh (2), to associate as a friend
4791 sugkŏinōnŏs (1), co-participant
4904 sunĕrgŏs (1), fellow-worker

COMPANIONS
2269 chăbar (Ch.) (1), associate, friend
2270 châbêr (5), associate, friend
2271 chabbâr (1), partner
3675 k°nâth (Ch.) (8), colleague
4828 mêrêa' (1), close friend
7453 rêa' (1), associate; one close
7464 rĕ'âh (2), female associate
2844 kŏinōnŏs (1), associate, partner
4898 sunĕkdēmŏs (1), fellow-traveller

COMPANIONS'
7453 rêa' (1), associate; one close

COMPANY
736 'ŏr°châh (1), caravan
1323 bath (1), daughter, descendant, woman
1416 g°dûwd (3), band of soldiers
1995 hâmôwn (1), noise, tumult; many, crowd
2199 zâ'aq (1), to convene publicly
2256 chebel (2), company, band
2267 cheber (1), society, group; magic spell;
2274 chebrâh (1), association
2416 chay (1), alive; raw; fresh; life
2428 chayil (1), army; wealth, virtue; valor; strength
3862 lahăqâh (1), assembly
4246 m°chôwlâh (1), round-dance
4264 machăneh (5), encampment
5712 'êdâh (13), assemblage; crowd
6635 tsâbâ' (1), army, military host
6951 qâhâl (16), assemblage
7218 rô'sh (5), head
7285 regesh (1), tumultuous crowd
7462 râ'âh (1), to associate as a friend
8229 shiph'âh (2), copiousness
2398 idiŏs (1), private or separate
2828 klisia (1), party or group
2853 kŏllaō (1), to glue together
3461 murias (1), ten-thousand
3588+4012 hŏ (1), "the"
3658 hŏmilŏs (1), multitude
3792 ŏchlŏpŏiĕō (1), to raise a disturbance
3793 ŏchlŏs (7), throng
4012 pĕri (1), about; around
4128 plēthŏs (1), large number, throng
4874 sunanamignumi (3), to associate with
4923 sunŏdia (1), traveling company

COMPARABLE
5577 çançîn (1), twig

COMPARE
4911 mâshal (1), to use figurative language
6186 'ârak (1), to set in a row, i.e. arrange
3846 paraballō (1), to reach a place; to liken
4793 sugkrinō (1), to combine

COMPARED
1819 dâmâh (1), to resemble, liken
6186 'ârak (1), to set in a row, i.e. arrange,
7737 shâvâh (2), to resemble; to adjust

COMPARING
4793 sugkrinō (2), to combine

COMPARISON
3644 kᵉmôw (1), like, as; for; with
3850 parabŏlē (1), fictitious narrative

COMPASS
247 'âzar (1), to belt
2329 chûwg (1), circle
3749 karkôb (2), rim, ledge, or top margin
3803 kâthar (2), to enclose, besiege; to wait
4230 mᵉchûwgâh (1), compass
4524 mêçab (1), around, surround
5362 nâqaph (3), to surround or circulate
5437 çâbab (22), to surround
5439 çâbîyb (2), circle; environs; around
5849 'âṭar (1), to encircle, enclose in; to crown
4013 pĕriagō (1), to walk around
4022 pĕriĕrchŏmai (1), to stroll, vacillate, veer
4033 pĕrikuklŏō (1), to blockade completely

COMPASSED
661 'âphaph (5), to surround
2328 chûwg (1), to describe a circle
5362 nâqaph (4), to surround or circulate
5437 çâbab (28), to surround
5849 'âṭar (1), to encircle, enclose in; to crown
2944 kuklŏō (3), to surround, encircle
4029 pĕrikĕimai (2), to enclose, encircle

COMPASSEST
2219 zârâh (1), to toss about; to diffuse

COMPASSETH
5437 çâbab (4), to surround
6059 'ânaq (1), to collar; to fit out

COMPASSING
5362 nâqaph (2), to surround or circulate
5437 çâbab (1), to surround

COMPASSION
2550 châmal (5), to spare, have pity on
7349 rachûwm (5), compassionate
7355 râcham (8), to be compassionate

COMPASSION
7356 racham (2), compassion; womb
1653 ĕlĕĕŏ (3), to give out compassion
3356 mĕtriŏpathĕō (1), to deal gently
3627 ŏiktĕirō (1), to exercise pity
4697 splagchnizŏmai (12), to feel sympathy
4834 sumpathĕō (1), to commiserate
4835 sumpathēs (1), commiserative

COMPASSIONS
7355 râcham (1), to be compassionate
7356 racham (1), compassion; womb

COMPEL
597 'ânaç (1), to insist, compel
5647 'âbad (1), to do, work, serve
29 aggarĕuō (2), to press into public service
315 anagkazō (1), to necessitate, compel

COMPELLED
5080 nâdach (1), to push off, scattered
6555 pârats (1), to break out
29 aggarĕuō (1), to press into public service
315 anagkazō (3), to necessitate, compel

COMPELLEST
315 anagkazō (1), to necessitate, compel

COMPLAIN
596 'ânan (1), complain
1058 bâkâh (1), to weep, moan
7378 rîyb (1), to hold a controversy; to defend
7878 sîyach (1), to ponder, muse aloud

COMPLAINED
596 'ânan (1), complain
7878 sîyach (1), to ponder, muse aloud

COMPLAINERS
3202 mĕmpsimŏirŏs (1), discontented

COMPLAINING
6682 tsᵉvâchâh (1), screech of anguish

COMPLAINT
7878 sîyach (9), to ponder, muse aloud

COMPLAINTS
157 aitiama (1), thing charged

COMPLETE
8549 tâmîym (1), entire, complete; integrity
4137 plērŏō (2), to fill, make complete

COMPOSITION
4971 mathkôneth (2), proportion

COMPOUND
4842 mirqachath (1), unguent; unguent-pot

COMPOUNDETH
7543 râqach (1), to perfume, blend spice

COMPREHEND
3045 yâda' (1), to know
2638 katalambanō (1), to possess; to understand

COMPREHENDED
3557 kûwl (1), to measure; to maintain
346 anakĕphalaiŏmai (1), to sum up
2638 katalambanō (1), to possess; to understand

CONANIAH
3562 Kôwnanyâhûw (1), Jehovah has sustained

CONCEAL
2790 chârash (1), to be silent; to be deaf
3582 kâchad (2), to destroy; to hide
3680 kâçâh (2), to cover
5641 çâthar (1), to hide

CONCEALED
3582 kâchad (2), to destroy; to hide

CONCEALETH
3680 kâçâh (2), to cover

CONCEIT
4906 maskîyth (1), carved figure
5869 'ayin (4), eye; sight; fountain

CONCEITS
3844+1438 para (2), from; with; besides

CONCEIVE
2029 hârâh (3), to conceive, be pregnant
2030 hâreh (4), pregnant
2232 zâra' (1), to sow seed; to disseminate
3179 yâcham (4), to conceive
2602 katabŏlē (1), conception, beginning
4815 sullambanō (1), to conceive; to aid

CONCEIVED
2029 hârâh (1), to conceive, be pregnant
2030 hâreh (33), pregnant
2232 zâra' (1), to sow seed; to disseminate
2803 châshab (1), to plot; to think, regard
3179 yâcham (2), to conceive
3254 yâçaph (1), to add or augment
1080 gĕnnaō (1), to procreate, regenerate
2845+2192 kŏitē (1), couch; conception
4815 sullambanō (4), to conceive; to aid
5087 tithēmi (1), to place

CONCEIVING
2030 hâreh (1), pregnant

CONCEPTION
2032 hêrôwn (3), pregnancy

CONCERN
4012 pĕri (2), about; around

CONCERNETH
1157 bᵉ'ad (1), at, beside, among, behind, for

CONCERNING
413 'êl (15), to, toward
854 'êth (1), with; by; at; among
5921 'al (78), above, over, upon, or against
5922 'al (Ch.) (6), above, over, upon, or against
6655 tsad (Ch.) (1), at the side of; against
1519 ĕis (5), to or into
2596 kata (5), down; according to
3754 hŏti (1), that; because; since
4012 pĕri (44), about; around
4314 prŏs (1), for; on, at; to, toward; against
5228 hupĕr (1), over; above; beyond

CONCISION
2699 katatŏmē (1), mutilation, cutting

CONCLUDE
3049 lŏgizŏmai (1), to credit; to think, regard

CONCLUDED
2919 krinō (1), to decide; to try, condemn, punish
4788 sugklĕiō (2), to net fish; to lock up persons

CONCLUSION
5490 çôwph (1), termination; end

CONCORD
4857 sumphōnēsis (1), accordance, agreement

CONCOURSE
1993 hâmâh (1), to be in great commotion
4963 sustrŏphē (1), riotous crowd

CONCUBINE
6370 pîylegesh (22), concubine

CONCUBINES
3904 lᵉchênâh (Ch.) (3), concubine
6370 pîylegesh (14), concubine

CONCUPISCENCE
1939 ĕpithumia (3), longing

CONDEMN
7561 râsha' (11), to be, do, declare wrong
8199 shâphaṭ (1), to judge
2607 kataginōskō (2), to condemn
2618 katakaiō (1), to consume wholly by burning
2632 katakrinō (7), to judge against
2633 katakrisis (1), act of sentencing adversely
2919 krinō (1), to decide; to try, condemn, punish

English

CONDEMNATION
2631 *katakrima* (3),
adverse sentence
2633 *katakrisis* (1), act of
sentencing adversely
2917 *krima* (5), *decision*
2920 *krisis* (2), *decision;*
tribunal; justice
5272 *hupŏkrisis* (1),
deceit, hypocrisy

CONDEMNED
3318+7563 *yâtsâ'* (1), to
go, bring out
6064 *'ânash* (2), to *inflict*
a penalty, to fine
7561 *râsha'* (1), to *be, do,*
declare wrong
176 *akatagnōstŏs* (1),
unblamable
843 *autŏkatakritŏs* (1),
self-condemned
1519+2917 *ĕis* (1), to or
into
2613 *katadikazō* (4), to
condemn
2632 *katakrinō* (8), to
judge against
2919 *krinō* (2), to *decide;*
to *try, condemn, punish*

CONDEMNEST
2632 *katakrinō* (1), to
judge against

CONDEMNETH
7561 *râsha'* (2), to *be, do,*
declare wrong
2632 *katakrinō* (1), to
judge against
4314 *prŏs* (1), *for; on, at;*
to, toward; against

CONDEMNING
7561 *râsha'* (1), to *be, do,*
declare wrong
2919 *krinō* (1), to *decide;*
to *try, condemn, punish*

CONDESCEND
4879 *sunapagō* (1), to
take off together

CONDITIONS
4314 *prŏs* (1), *for; on, at;*
to, toward; against

CONDUCT
5674 *'âbar* (1), to *cross*
over; to transition
7971 *shâlach* (1), to *send*
away
4311 *prŏpĕmpō* (1), to
send forward

CONDUCTED
5674 *'âbar* (1), to *cross*
over; to transition
2525 *kathistēmi* (1), to
designate, constitute

CONDUIT
8585 *tᵉ'âlâh* (4),
irrigation channel;
bandage or plaster

CONEY
8227 *shâphân* (2), *rock-*
rabbit, (poss.) *hyrax*

CONFECTION
7545 *rôqach* (1),
aromatic, fragrance

CONFECTIONARIES
7543 *râqach* (1), to
perfume, blend spice

CONFEDERACY
1285 *bᵉrîyth* (1),
compact, agreement
7195 *qesher* (2), *unlawful*
alliance

CONFEDERATE
1167+1285 *ba'al* (1),
master; owner; citizen
1285+3772 *bᵉrîyth* (1),
compact, agreement
5117 *nûwach* (1), to *rest;*
to *settle* down

CONFERENCE
4323 *prŏsanatithēmi* (1),
to *add;* to *consult*

CONFERRED
1961+1697 *hâyâh* (1), to
exist, i.e. *be or become*
4323 *prŏsanatithēmi* (1),
to *add;* to *consult*
4814 *sullalĕō* (1), to *talk*
together, i.e. *converse*
4820 *sumballō* (1), to
converse, consult

CONFESS
3034 *yâdâh* (11), to
revere or worship
1843 *ĕxŏmŏlŏgĕō* (5), to
acknowledge or agree
3670 *hŏmŏlŏgĕō* (12), to
acknowledge, agree

CONFESSED
3034 *yâdâh* (3), to *throw;*
to *revere or worship*
1843 *ĕxŏmŏlŏgĕō* (1), to
acknowledge or agree
3670 *hŏmŏlŏgĕō* (3), to
acknowledge, agree

CONFESSETH
3034 *yâdâh* (1), to *throw;*
to *revere or worship*
3670 *hŏmŏlŏgĕō* (2), to
acknowledge, agree

CONFESSING
3034 *yâdâh* (1), to *throw;*
to *revere or worship*
1843 *ĕxŏmŏlŏgĕō* (2), to
acknowledge or agree

CONFESSION
3034 *yâdâh* (2), to *throw;*
to *revere or worship*
8426 *tôwdâh* (2),
expressions of thanks
3670 *hŏmŏlŏgĕō* (1), to
acknowledge, agree
3671 *hŏmŏlŏgia* (1),
confession

CONFIDENCE
982 *bâṭach* (4), to *trust,*
be confident or sure
983 *beṭach* (1), *safety,*
security, trust
985 *biṭchâh* (1), *trust*
986 *biṭṭâchôwn* (2), *trust*
3689 *keçel* (1), *loin;*
back; viscera; trust
3690 *kiçlâh* (1), *trust*
4009 *mibṭâch* (8),
security; assurance
2292 *tharrhĕō* (1), to
exercise courage
3954 *parrhēsia* (6),
frankness, boldness
3982 *pĕithō* (6), to *rely*
4006 *pĕpŏithēsis* (5),
reliance, trust

CONFIDENCES
4009 *mibṭâch* (1),
security; assurance

CONFIDENT
982 *bâṭach* (2), to *trust,*
be confident or sure
2292 *tharrhĕō* (2), to
exercise courage
3982 *pĕithō* (3), to *rely*
5287 *hupŏstasis* (1),
essence; assurance

CONFIDENTLY
1340 *diïschurizŏmai* (1),
to *asseverate*

CONFIRM
553 *'âmats* (1), to *be*
strong; be courageous
1396 *gâbar* (1), to *be*
strong; to prevail
2388 *châzaq* (2), to *bind,*
restrain, conquer
3559 *kûwn* (1), to *set up:*
establish, fix, prepare
4390 *mâlĕ'* (1), to *fill; be*
full
6965 *qûwm* (4), to *rise*
950 *bĕbaiŏō* (2), to
stabilitate, keep strong
2964 *kurŏō* (1), to *ratify,*
validate a treaty

CONFIRMATION
951 *bĕbaiōsis* (2),
confirmation

CONFIRMED
2388 *châzaq* (1), to *bind,*
restrain, conquer
3559 *kûwn* (2), to *render*
sure, proper or
prosperous
5975 *'âmad* (2), to *stand*
6965 *qûwm* (2), to *rise*
950 *bĕbaiŏō* (2), to
stabilitate, keep strong
1991 *ĕpistērizō* (1), to
re-establish, strengthen
2964 *kurŏō* (1), to *ratify,*
validate a treaty
3315 *mĕsitĕuō* (1), to
ratify as surety, confirm
4300 *prŏkurŏō* (1), to
ratify previously

CONFIRMETH
6965 *qûwm* (3), to *rise*

CONFIRMING
950 *bĕbaiŏō* (1), to
stabilitate, keep strong
1991 *ĕpistērizō* (2), to
re-establish, strengthen

CONFISCATION
6065 *'ănash* (Ch.) (1),
fine, penalty, mulct

CONFLICT
73 *agōn* (2), *contest,*
struggle

CONFORMABLE
4832 *summŏrphŏs* (1),
similar, conformed to

CONFORMED
4832 *summŏrphŏs* (1),
similar, conformed to
4964 *suschēmatizō* (1),
to *conform*

CONFOUND
1101 *bâlal* (2), to *mix;*
confuse
2865 *châthath* (1), to
break down
2617 *kataischunō* (2), to
disgrace or shame

CONFOUNDED
954 *bûwsh* (21), be
ashamed; disappointed
2659 *châphêr* (6), to *be*
ashamed, disappointed
3001 *yâbêsh* (9), to *dry*
up; to wither
3637 *kâlam* (11), to *taunt*
or insult
2617 *kataischunō* (1), to
disgrace or shame
4797 *sugchĕō* (2), to
throw into disorder

CONFUSED
7494 *ra'ash* (1),
bounding, uproar
4797 *sugchĕō* (1), to
throw into disorder

CONFUSION
954 *bûwsh* (1), be
ashamed, disappointed
1322 *bôsheth* (7), *shame*
2659 *châphêr* (2), to *be*
ashamed, disappointed
3637 *kâlam* (1), to *taunt*
or insult
3639 *kᵉlimmâh* (6),
disgrace, scorn
7036 *qâlôwn* (1), *disgrace*
8397 *tebel* (2), confused
mixture
8414 *tôhûw* (3), *waste,*
desolation, formless
181 *akatastasia* (2),
disorder, riot
4799 *sugchusis* (1),
riotous disturbance

CONGEALED
7087 *qâphâ'* (1), to
thicken, congeal

CONGRATULATE
1288 *bârak* (1), to *bless*

CONGREGATION
482 *'êlem* (1), *silence*
2416 *chay* (2), *alive; raw;*
fresh; life
4150 *môw'êd* (147),
assembly, congregation
5712 *'êdâh* (123),
assemblage; crowd
6951 *qâhâl* (85),
assemblage
6952 *qᵉhillâh* (1),
assemblage
4865 *sunagōnizŏmai* (1),
to *be a partner*

CONGREGATIONS
4150 *môw'êd* (1),
assembly, congregation
4721 *maqhêl* (2),
assembly

CONIAH
3659 *Konyâhûw* (3),
Jehovah will establish

CONIES
8226 *sâphan* (2), to
conceal

CONONIAH
3562 Kôwnanyâhûw (2), *Jehovah has sustained*

CONQUER
3528 nikaō (1), to *subdue, conquer*

CONQUERING
3528 nikaō (1), to *subdue, conquer*

CONQUERORS
5245 hupĕrnikaō (1), to gain a decisive *victory*

CONSCIENCE
4893 sunĕidēsis (31), moral *consciousness*

CONSCIENCES
4893 sunĕidēsis (1), moral *consciousness*

CONSECRATE
2763 charam (1), to *devote* to destruction
4390+3027 mâlê' (10), to *fill; be full*
5144 nâzar (1), to *devote*
6942 qâdâsh (2), to be, make clean

CONSECRATED
4390+3027 mâlê' (7), to *fill; be full*
6942 qâdâsh (4), to be, make clean
6944 qôdesh (1), *sacred* place or thing
1457 ĕgkainizō (1), to *inaugurate*
5048 tĕlĕiŏō (1), to *perfect, complete*

CONSECRATION
4394 millû' (7), *fulfilling; setting; consecration*
5145 nezer (2), *set apart; dedication*

CONSECRATIONS
4394 millû' (4), *fulfilling; setting; consecration*

CONSENT
14 'âbâh (4), to be *acquiescent*
225 'ûwth (3), to *assent*
376 'îysh (1), *man; male*
3820 lêb (1), *heart*
7926 shᵉkem (2), *neck; spur* of a hill
4334 prŏsĕrchŏmai (1), to *assent* to
4852 sumphēmi (1), to *assent* to
4859 sumphōnŏs (1), *agreeing; agreement*

CONSENTED
225 'ûwth (1), to *assent; agree*
8085 shâma' (1), to *hear*
1962 ĕpinĕuō (1), to *assent, give consent*
4784 sugkatatithĕmai (1), to *accord* with

CONSENTEDST
7521 râtsâh (1), to be *pleased with; to satisfy*

CONSENTING
4909 sunĕudŏkĕō (2), to *assent* to, *feel gratified*

CONSIDER
559 'âmar (1), to *say*
995 bîyn (20), to *understand; discern*
3045 yâda' (4), to *know*
5027 nâbaṭ (5), to *scan; to regard* with favor
6448 pâçag (1), to *contemplate*
7200 râ'âh (15), to *see*
7725 shûwb (1), to *turn back; to return*
7760 sûwm (2), to *put*
7760+3820 sûwm (4), to *put, place*
7760+3820+5921 sûwm (2), to *put, place*
7919 sâkal (2), to be or *act circumspect*
357 analŏgizŏmai (1), to *contemplate*
1260 dialŏgizŏmai (1), to *deliberate*
1492 ĕidō (1), to *know*
2334 thĕōrĕō (1), to *see; to discern*
2648 katamanthanō (1), to *note carefully*
2657 katanŏĕō (4), to *observe fully*
3539 nŏiĕō (1), to *exercise* the *mind*

CONSIDERED
995 bîyn (1), to *understand; discern*
2803 châshab (1), to *think, regard; to value*
5414 nâthan (1), to *give*
7200 râ'âh (4), to *see*
7760+3820 sûwm (2), to *put, place*
7896+3820 shîyth (1), to *place, put*
7920 sᵉkal (Ch.) (1), to be or *act circumspect*
8085 shâma' (1), to *hear*
2657 katanŏĕō (2), to *observe fully*
4894 sunĕidō (1), to *understand*
4920 suniēmi (1), to *comprehend*

CONSIDEREST
7200 râ'âh (1), to *see*
2657 katanŏĕō (1), to *observe fully*

CONSIDERETH
995 bîyn (1), to *understand; discern*
2161 zâmam (1), to *plan*
3045 yâda' (2), to *know*
7200 râ'âh (2), to *see*
7725 shûwb (1), to *turn back; to return*
7919 sâkal (2), to be or *act circumspect*

CONSIDERING
995 bîyn (2), to *understand; discern*
333 anathĕōrĕō (1), to *look again*
4648 skŏpĕō (1), to *watch out for*, i.e. to *regard*

CONSIST
4921 sunistaō (1), to *set together*

CONSISTETH
2076 ĕsti (1), he (she or it) *is; they are*

CONSOLATION
8575 tanchûwm (1), *compassion, solace*
3874 paraklēsis (14), *imploring, solace*

CONSOLATIONS
8575 tanchûwm (3), *compassion, solace*

CONSORTED
4845 sumplērŏō (1), to be *complete, fulfill*

CONSPIRACY
7195 qesher (9), unlawful *alliance*
4945 sunōmŏsia (1), *plot, conspiracy*

CONSPIRATORS
7194 qâshar (1), to *tie, bind*

CONSPIRED
5320 Naphtûchîym (1), *Naphtuchim*
7194 qâshar (18), to *tie, bind*

CONSTANT
2388 châzaq (1), to *fasten* upon; to *seize*

CONSTANTLY
5331 netsach (1), *splendor; lasting*
1226 diabĕbaiŏŏmai (1), to *confirm thoroughly*
1340 diïschurizŏmai (1), to *asseverate*

CONSTELLATIONS
3685 Kᵉçîyl (1), *constellation Orion*

CONSTRAIN
315 anagkazō (1), to *necessitate, compel*

CONSTRAINED
2388 châzaq (1), to *fasten* upon; to *seize*
315 anagkazō (3), to *necessitate, compel*
3849 parabiazŏmai (2), to *compel* by entreaty

CONSTRAINETH
6693 tsûwq (1), to *oppress, distress*
4912 sunĕchō (1), to *hold together*

CONSTRAINT
317 anagkastōs (1), *compulsorily*

CONSULT
3289 yâ'ats (1), to *advise*

CONSULTATION
4824 sumbŏuliŏn (1), *advisement*

CONSULTED
3272 yᵉ'aṭ (Ch.) (1), to *counsel*
3289 yâ'ats (8), to *advise*
4427 mâlak (1), to *reign* as king
7592 shâ'al (1), to *ask*
1011 bŏulĕuō (1), to *deliberate; to resolve*
4823 sumbŏulĕuō (1), to *recommend, deliberate*

CONSULTER
7592 shâ'al (1), to *ask*

CONSULTETH
1011 bŏulĕuō (1), to *deliberate; to resolve*

CONSUME
398 'âkal (9), to *eat*
402 'oklâh (1), *food*
1086 bâlâh (1), to *wear out, decay; consume*
1497 gâzal (1), to *rob*
2000 hâmam (1), to *disturb, drive, destroy*
2628 châçal (1), to *eat off, consume*
3423 yârash (1), to *inherit; to impoverish*
3615 kâlâh (23), to *complete, consume*
4529 mâçâh (1), to *dissolve, melt*
4743 mâqaq (4), to *melt; to flow, dwindle, vanish*
5486 çûwph (4), to *terminate*
5487 çûwph (Ch.) (1), to *come to an end*
5595 çâphâh (1), to *scrape; to accumulate*
8046 shᵉmad (Ch.) (1), to *desolate*
8552 tâmam (2), to *complete, finish*
355 analiskō (2), *destroy*
1159 dapanaō (1), to *incur cost; to waste*

CONSUMED
398 'âkal (21), to *eat*
622 'âçaph (1), to *gather*
1846 dâ'ak (1), to be *extinguished; to expire*
3615 kâlâh (37), to *complete, consume*
4127 mûwg (1), to *soften, flow down, disappear*
5486 çûwph (1), to *terminate*
5595 çâphâh (5), to *scrape; to accumulate*
6244 'âshêsh (3), to *fail*
6789 tsâmath (1), to *extirpate, root out*
8552 tâmam (24), to *complete, finish*
355 analiskō (1), *destroy*

CONSUMETH
398 'âkal (2), to *eat*
1086 bâlâh (1), to *wear out, decay; consume*
7503 râphâh (1), to *slacken*

CONSUMING
398 'âkal (2), to *eat*
2654 katanaliskō (1), to *consume utterly*

CONSUMMATION
3617 kâlâh (1), *complete destruction*

CONSUMPTION
3617 kâlâh (2), *complete destruction*
3631 killâyôwn (1), *pining, destruction*
7829 shachepheth (2), *wasting disease*

English

CONTAIN
1004 bayith (1), *house; temple; family, tribe*
3557 kûwl (3), *to keep in; to maintain*
5375 nâsâ' (1), *to lift up*
1467 ĕgkratĕuŏmai (1), *to exercise self-restraint*
5562 chōrĕō (1), *to pass, enter; to hold, admit*

CONTAINED
3557 kûwl (2), *to keep in; to maintain*
4023 pĕriĕchō (1), *to encircle; to contain*

CONTAINETH
3557 kûwl (1), *to keep in; to maintain*

CONTAINING
5562 chōrĕō (1), *to pass, enter; to hold, admit*

CONTEMN
3988 mâ'aç (1), *to spurn; to disappear*
5006 nâ'ats (1), *to scorn*

CONTEMNED
936 bûwz (1), *to disrespect, scorn*
959 bâzâh (1), *to disesteem, ridicule*
5006 nâ'ats (1), *to scorn*
7034 qâlâh (1), *to hold in contempt*

CONTEMNETH
3988 mâ'aç (1), *to spurn; to disappear*

CONTEMPT
937 bûwz (7), *disrespect, scorn*
963 bizzâyôwn (1), *disesteem, disrespect*
1860 dᵉrâ'ôwn (1), *object of loathing*
7043 qâlal (1), *to be easy, trifling, vile*

CONTEMPTIBLE
959 bâzâh (3), *to disesteem, ridicule*
1848 ĕxŏuthĕnĕō (1), *to treat with contempt*

CONTEMPTUOUSLY
937 bûwz (1), *disrespect*

CONTEND
1624 gârâh (3), *to provoke to anger*
1777 dîyn (1), *to judge; to strive or contend for*
3401 yârîyb (1), *contentious; adversary*
7378 rîyb (7), *to hold a controversy; to defend*
8474 tachârâh (1), *to vie with a rival*
1864 ĕpagōnizŏmai (1), *to struggle for, fight for*

CONTENDED
4695 matstsûwth (1), *quarrel, contention*
7378 rîyb (4), *to hold a controversy; to defend*
1252 diakrinō (1), *to decide; to hesitate*

CONTENDEST
7378 rîyb (1), *to hold a controversy; to defend*

CONTENDETH
3401 yârîyb (1), *contentious; adversary*
7378 rîyb (1), *to hold a controversy; to defend*
8199 shâphaṭ (1), *to judge*

CONTENDING
1252 diakrinō (1), *to decide; to hesitate*

CONTENT
14 'âbâh (1), *to be acquiescent*
2974 yâ'al (7), *to assent; to undertake, begin*
3190+5869 yâṭab (1), *to be, make well*
8085 shâma' (1), *to hear intelligently*
714 arkĕō (4), *to avail; be satisfactory*
842 autarkēs (1), *contented*
2425+3588+4160 hikanŏs (1), *ample; fit*

CONTENTION
4066 mâdôwn (3), *contest or quarrel*
4683 matstsâh (1), *quarrel*
7379 rîyb (2), *contest, personal or legal*
73 agōn (1), *contest, struggle*
2052 ĕrithĕia (1), *faction, strife, selfish ambition*
3948 parŏxusmŏs (1), *incitement; dispute*

CONTENTIONS
4079 midyân (4), *contest or quarrel*
2054 ĕris (2), *quarrel, i.e. wrangling*

CONTENTIOUS
4066 mâdôwn (3), *contest or quarrel*
1537+2052 ĕk (1), *out of*
5380 philŏnĕikŏs (1), *disputatious*

CONTENTMENT
841 autarkeia (1), *contentedness*

CONTINUAL
1115+5627 biltîy (1), *not, except, without, unless*
2956 ṭârad (1), *to drive on*
8548 tâmîyd (27), *constantly, regularly*
88 adialĕiptŏs (1), *permanent, constant*
1519+5056 ĕis (1), *to or into*

CONTINUALLY
1980 hâlak (3), *to walk; live a certain way*
1980+7725 hâlak (1), *walk; live a certain way*
3605+3117 kôl (10), *all, any or every*
6256 'êth (1), *time*
8411 tᵉdîyrâ' (Ch.) (2), *constantly, faithfully*
8544 tᵉmûwnâh (1), *something fashioned*
8548 tâmîyd (52), *constantly, regularly*

1275 diapantŏs (1), *constantly, continually*
1519+1336 ĕis (2), *to or into*
1725 ĕnanti (1), *before, in presence of*
4342 prŏskartĕrĕō (3), *to be constantly diligent*

CONTINUANCE
539 'âman (2), *to be firm; to be permanent*
3117 yôwm (1), *day; time period*
5769 'ôwlâm (1), *eternity; ancient; always*
5281 hupŏmŏnē (1), *endurance, constancy*

CONTINUE
309 'âchar (1), *to remain; to delay*
1961 hâyâh (2), *to exist, i.e. be or become*
3427 yâshab (2), *to dwell, to remain; to settle*
3885 lûwn (1), *to be obstinate*
4900 mâshak (1), *to draw out; to be tall*
5975 'âmad (4), *to stand*
6965 qûwm (3), *to rise*
7931 shâkan (1), *to reside*
1265 diamĕnō (2), *to stay constantly*
1696 ĕmmĕnō (1), *remain; to persevere*
1961 ĕpimĕnō (5), *to remain; to persevere*
2476 histēmi (1), *to stand, establish*
3306 mĕnō (7), *to stay, remain*
3887 paramĕnō (1), *to be permanent, persevere*
4160 pŏiĕō (2), *to do*
4342 prŏskartĕrĕō (1), *to persevere*
4357 prŏsmĕnō (1), *to remain; to adhere to*
4839 sumparamĕnō (1), *to remain in company*

CONTINUED
1961 hâyâh (3), *to exist, i.e. be or become*
2388 châzaq (1), *to fasten upon; to seize*
3254 yâçaph (2), *to add or augment*
3427 yâshab (3), *to dwell, to remain; to settle*
5125 nûwn (1), *to be perpetual*
5975 'âmad (1), *to stand*
7235 râbâh (1), *to increase*
1096 ginŏmai (1), *to be, become*
1265 diamĕnō (1), *to stay constantly*
1273 dianuktĕrĕuō (1), *to pass, spend the night*
1300 diatĕlĕō (1), *to persist, continue*
1304 diatribō (2), *to remain, stay*
1696 ĕmmĕnō (1), *remain; to persevere*
1961 ĕpimĕnō (2), *to remain; to persevere*

2523 kathizō (1), *to seat down, dwell*
3306 mĕnō (2), *to stay, remain*
3905 paratĕinō (1), *prolong, extend*
4342 prŏskartĕrĕō (3), *to persevere*

CONTINUETH
5975 'âmad (1), *to stand*
1696 ĕmmĕnō (1), *to remain; to persevere*
3306 mĕnō (1), *to stay, remain*
3887 paramĕnō (1), *to be permanent, persevere*
4357 prŏsmĕnō (1), *to remain; to adhere to*

CONTINUING
1641 gârar (1), *to ruminate; to saw*
3306 mĕnō (1), *to stay, remain*
4342 prŏskartĕrĕō (2), *to persevere; to adhere*

CONTRADICTING
483 antilĕgō (1), *to dispute, refuse*

CONTRADICTION
485 antilŏgia (2), *dispute, disobedience*

CONTRARIWISE
5121 tŏunantiŏn (3), *on the contrary*

CONTRARY
2016 hephek (2), *reverse, perversion*
7147 qᵉrîy (7), *hostile encounter*
480 antikĕimai (2), *be adverse to*
561 apĕnanti (1), *opposite, against*
1727 ĕnantiŏs (6), *opposite*
3844 para (3), *from; with; besides; on account of*
3891 paranŏmĕō (1), *transgress, violate law*
5227 hupĕnantiŏs (1), *opposed; opponent*

CONTRIBUTION
2842 kŏinōnia (1), *benefaction; sharing*

CONTRITE
1792 dâkâ' (1), *to be contrite, be humbled*
1793 dakkâ' (2), *contrite, humbled*
1794 dâkâh (1), *to collapse; contrite*
5223 nâkeh (1), *maimed; dejected*

CONTROVERSIES
7379 rîyb (1), *contest, personal or legal*

CONTROVERSY
7379 rîyb (12), *contest, personal or legal*
3672 hŏmŏlŏgŏumĕnōs (1), *confessedly*

CONVENIENT
2706 chôq (1), *appointment; allotment*
3477 yâshâr (2), *straight*

433 anēkŏ (2), *be proper, fitting*
2119 ĕukairĕŏ (1), to *have opportunity*
2121 ĕukairŏs (1), *opportune, suitable*
2520 kathēkŏ (1), *becoming, proper*
2540 kairŏs (1), *occasion, set or proper*

CONVENIENTLY
2122 ĕukairŏs (1), *opportunely*

CONVERSANT
1980 hâlak (2), to *walk; live a certain way*

CONVERSATION
1870 derek (2), *road; course* of life
390 anastrĕphŏ (2), to *remain,* to live
391 anastrŏphē (13), *behavior*
4175 pŏlitĕuma (1), *citizenship*
4176 pŏlitĕuŏmai (1), to *behave as a citizen*
5158 trŏpŏs (1), *deportment, character*

CONVERSION
1995 ĕpistrŏphē (1), moral *revolution*

CONVERT
7725 shûwb (1), to *turn* back; to *return*
1994 ĕpistrĕphŏ (1), to *revert, turn back to*

CONVERTED
2015 hâphak (1), to *turn* about or over
7725 shûwb (1), to *turn* back; to *return*
1994 ĕpistrĕphŏ (6), to *revert, turn back to*
4762 strĕphŏ (1), to *turn* around or *reverse*

CONVERTETH
1994 ĕpistrĕphŏ (1), to *revert, turn back to*

CONVERTING
7725 shûwb (1), to *turn* back; to *return*

CONVERTS
7725 shûwb (1), to *turn* back; to *return*

CONVEY
5674 'âbar (1), to *cross* over; to *transition*
7760 sûwm (1), to *put*

CONVEYED
1593 ĕknĕuŏ (1), to quietly *withdraw*

CONVICTED
1651 ĕlĕgchŏ (1), to *confute, admonish*

CONVINCE
1651 ĕlĕgchŏ (1), to *confute, admonish*
1827 ĕxĕlĕgchŏ (1), to *punish*

CONVINCED
3198 yâkach (1), to *be correct; to argue*

1246 diakatĕlĕgchŏmai (1), to *prove downright*
1651 ĕlĕgchŏ (2), to *confute, admonish, rebuke*

CONVINCETH
1651 ĕlĕgchŏ (1), to *confute, admonish*

CONVOCATION
4744 miqrâ' (15), *public meeting*

CONVOCATIONS
4744 miqrâ' (3), *public meeting*

COOK
2876 ṭabbâch (2), *butcher, cook*

COOKS
2876 ṭabbâch (1), *butcher, cook*

COOL
7307 rûwach (1), *breath; wind; life-spirit*
2711 katapsuchŏ (1), to *refresh, cool off*

COOS
2972 Kōs (1), *Cos*

COPIED
6275 'âthaq (1), to *grow old;* to *transcribe*

COPING
2947 ṭêphach (1), *palm-breadth*

COPPER
5178 n°chôsheth (1), *copper; bronze*

COPPERSMITH
5471 chalkĕus (1), *copper-worker*

COPULATION
7902 sh°kâbâh (3), *lying down*

COPY
4932 mishneh (2), *duplicate copy; double*
6572 parshegen (3), *transcript*
6573 parshegen (Ch.) (4), *transcript*

COR
3734 kôr (1), dry *measure*

CORAL
7215 râ'mâh (2), *high in value,* (poss.) *coral*

CORBAN
2878 kŏrban (1), *votive offering* or *gift*

CORD
2256 chebel (4), *company, band*
2339 chûwṭ (1), *string; measuring tape; line*
3499 yether (1), *remainder; small rope*

CORDS
2256 chebel (12), *company, band*
4340 mêythâr (8), *tent-cord; bow-string*
5688 'ăbôth (5), *entwined things*
4979 schŏiniŏn (1), *rushlet, i.e. grass-withe*

CORE
2879 Kŏrĕ (1), *ice*

CORIANDER
1407 gad (2), *coriander*

CORINTH
2882 Kŏrinthŏs (6), *Corinthus*

CORINTHIANS
2881 Kŏrinthiŏs (4), *inhabitant of Corinth*

CORINTHUS
2882 Kŏrinthŏs (1), *Corinthus*

CORMORANT
6893 qâ'ath (2), *pelican*
7994 shâlâk (2), *bird of prey* (poss.) *pelican*

CORN
1098 b°liyl (1), *feed, fodder*
1121 bên (1), *son, descendant*
1250 bâr (9), cereal *grain*
1637 gŏren (1), open *area*
1643 geres (2), *grain*
1715 dâgân (37), *grain*
3759 karmel (1), *planted field; garden produce*
5669 'âbûwr (2), *kept over; stored grain*
6194 'ârêm (1), *heap, mound; sheaf*
7054 qâmâh (7), *stalk of cereal grain*
7383 rîyphâh (1), *grits cereal*
7668 sheber (7), *grain*
7688 shâgach (1), to *glance sharply at*
2848 kŏkkŏs (1), *kernel*
4621 sitŏs (2), *grain, especially wheat*
4702 spŏrimŏs (3), *field planted with seed*
4719 stachus (3), *head of grain*

CORNELIUS
2883 Kŏrnēliŏs (10), *Cornelius*

CORNER
2106 zâvîyth (1), *angle, corner* (as *projecting*)
3671 kânâph (1), *edge or extremity; wing*
3802 kâthêph (2), *shoulder-piece; wall*
4742 m°quts'âh (1), *angle*
6285 pê'âh (5), *direction; region; extremity*
6434 pên (1), *angle*
6437 pânâh (1), to *turn, to face*
6438 pinnâh (17), *pinnacle; chieftain*
204 akrŏgōniaiŏs (2), *corner, cornerstone*
1137 gōnia (6), *angle; cornerstone*

CORNERS
2106 zâvîyth (1), *angle, corner* (as *projecting*)
3671 kânâph (2), *edge or extremity; wing*
4740 maqtsôwa' (1), *angle*
4742 m°quts'âh (6), *angle*

6284 pâ'âh (1), to *blow away*
6285 pê'âh (11), *region; extremity*
6438 pinnâh (6), *pinnacle; chieftain*
6471 pa'am (3), *time; step; occurence*
6763 tsêlâ' (2), *side*
7098 qâtsâh (1), *termination; fringe*
7106 qâtsa' (1), to *strip off, i.e.* (partially) *scrape*
746 archē (2), *first in rank; first in time*
1137 gōnia (2), *angle; cornerstone*

CORNET
7162 qeren (Ch.) (4), *horn*
7782 shôwphâr (3), *curved ram's horn*

CORNETS
4517 m°na'na' (1), *rattling instrument*
7782 shôwphâr (1), *curved ram's horn*

CORNFLOOR
1637+1715 gŏren (1), open *area*

CORPSE
4430 ptôma (1), *corpse, carrion*

CORPSES
1472 g°vîyâh (2), *dead body*
6297 peger (2), *carcase; corpse*

CORRECT
3198 yâkach (1), to *be correct; to argue*
3256 yâçar (6), to *chastise; to instruct*

CORRECTED
3256 yâçar (1), to *chastise; to instruct*
3810 paidĕutēs (1), *teacher or discipliner*

CORRECTETH
3198 yâkach (2), to *be correct; to argue*

CORRECTION
3198 yâkach (1), to *be correct; to argue*
4148 mûwçâr (8), *reproof, warning*
7626 shêbeṭ (1), *stick; clan, family*
8433 tôwkêchâh (1), *correction*
1882 ĕpanŏrthōsis (1), *rectification, correction*

CORRUPT
1605 gâ'ar (1), to *chide, reprimand*
2254 châbal (1), to *bind by a pledge; to pervert*
2610 chânêph (1), to *soil, be defiled*
4167 mûwq (1), to *blaspheme, scoff*
4743 mâqaq (1), to *melt; to flow, dwindle, vanish*
7843 shâchath (11), to *decay; to ruin*
7844 sh°chath (Ch.) (1), to *decay; to ruin*

English

853 aphanizō (2), to
consume (becloud)
1311 diaphthĕirō (1), to
ruin, to pervert
2585 kapēlĕuō (1), to
retail, i.e. to adulterate
2704 kataphthĕirō (1), to
spoil entirely
4550 saprŏs (6), rotten,
i.e. worthless
5351 phthĕirō (4), to
spoil; to deprave

CORRUPTED
7843 shâchath (11), to
decay; to ruin
4595 sēpō (1), to putrefy,
rot
5351 phthĕirō (2), to
spoil; to deprave

CORRUPTERS
7843 shâchath (2), to
decay; to ruin

CORRUPTETH
1311 diaphthĕirō (1), to
ruin, to pervert

CORRUPTIBLE
862 aphthartŏs (1),
undecaying, immortal
5349 phthartŏs (6),
perishable, not lasting

CORRUPTING
7843 shâchath (1), to
decay; to ruin

CORRUPTION
1097 bᵉ¹y (1), without,
not yet; lacking;
4889 mashchîyth (2),
destruction; corruption
4893 mishchâth (1),
disfigurement
7845 shachath (4), pit;
destruction
1312 diaphthŏra (6),
decay, corruption
5356 phthŏra (7), ruin;
depravity, corruption

CORRUPTLY
2254 châbal (1), to bind
by a pledge; to pervert
7843 shâchath (1), to
decay; to ruin

COSAM
2973 Kōsam (1), Cosam

COST
2600 chinnâm (2), free
1160 dapanē (1),
expense, cost

COSTLINESS
5094 timiŏtēs (1),
expensiveness

COSTLY
3368 yâqâr (4), valuable
4185 pŏlutĕlēs (1),
extremely expensive
4186 pŏlutimŏs (1),
extremely valuable

COTES
220 ʾăvêrâh (1), stall, pen

COTTAGE
4412 mᵉlûwnâh (1), hut
5521 çukkâh (1),
tabernacle; shelter

COTTAGES
3741 kârâh (1), meadow

COUCH
3326 yâtsûwaʾ (1), bed;
wing or lean-to
4904 mishkâb (1), bed;
sleep
6210 ʾeres (2), canopy
couch
7742 sûwach (1), to muse
pensively
2826 klinidiŏn (2), pallet
or little couch

COUCHED
3766 kâraʾ (1), to
prostrate
7257 râbats (1), to
recline, repose, brood

COUCHES
6210 ʾeres (1), canopy
couch
2895 krabbatŏs (1),
sleeping mat

COUCHETH
7257 râbats (1), to
recline, repose, brood

COUCHING
7257 râbats (1), to
recline, repose, brood

COUCHINGPLACE
4769 marbêts (1), resting
place

COULD
3045 yâdaʾ (2), to know
3201 yâkôl (46), to be able
3202 yᵉkêl (Ch.) (1), to be
able
3546 kᵉhal (Ch.) (1), to be
able
5074 nâdad (1), to rove,
flee; to drive away
5234 nâkar (1), to
acknowledge
5346 Neqeb (1), dell
102 adunatŏs (1), weak,
impossible
1410 dunamai (29), to be
able or possible
1415 dunatŏs (1),
powerful or capable
2192 ĕchō (3), to have;
hold; keep
2480 ischuō (7), to have
or exercise force
2489 Iōanna (1),
Jehovah-favored
5342 phĕrō (1), to bear or
carry

COULDEST
3201 yâkôl (1), to be able
2480 ischuō (1), to have
or exercise force

COULDST
3202 yᵉkêl (Ch.) (1), to be
able

COULTER
855 ʾêth (1), digging
implement

COULTERS
855 ʾêth (1), digging
implement

COUNCIL
7277 rigmâh (1), throng
4824 sumbŏuliŏn (2),
deliberative body
4892 sunĕdriŏn (20),
tribunal

COUNCILS
4891 sunĕgĕirō (2), to
raise up with

COUNSEL
1697 dâbâr (1), word;
matter; thing
3245 yâçad (2), settle,
consult
3289 yâʿats (21), to advise
4431 mᵉlak (Ch.) (1),
counsel, advice
5475 çôwd (6), intimacy;
consultation; secret
5843 ʿêṭâʾ (Ch.) (1),
prudence
6098 ʿêtsâh (80), advice;
plan; prudence
8458 tachbûlâh (2),
guidance; plan
1011 bŏulĕuō (1), to
deliberate; to resolve
1012 bŏulē (9), purpose,
plan, decision
4823 sumbŏulĕuō (4), to
recommend, deliberate
4824 sumbŏuliŏn (5),
deliberative body

COUNSELED
3289 yâʿats (1), to advise

COUNSELLED
3289 yâʿats (3), to advise

COUNSELLOR
3289 yâʿats (10), to advise
6098 ʿêtsâh (1), advice;
plan; prudence
1010 bŏulĕutēs (2),
adviser, councillor
4825 sumbŏulŏs (1),
adviser

COUNSELLORS
1884 dᵉthâbâr (Ch.) (2),
skilled in law; judge
1907 haddâbâr (Ch.) (4),
vizier, high official
3272 yᵉʿaṭ (Ch.) (2), to
counsel
3289 yâʿats (12), to advise
6098 ʿêtsâh (1), advice;
plan; prudence

COUNSELS
4156 môwʿêtsâh (6),
purpose, plan
6098 ʿêtsâh (2), advice;
plan; prudence
8458 tachbûlâh (3),
guidance; plan
1012 bŏulē (1), purpose,
plan, decision

COUNT
1961 hâyâh (1), to exist,
i.e. be or become
2803 châshab (3), to
think; to compute
3699 kâçaç (1), to
estimate, determine
4487 mânâh (1), to allot;
to enumerate or enroll
5414 nâthan (1), to give
5608 çâphar (4), to
inscribe; to enumerate
515 axiŏō (1), to deem
entitled or fit, worthy
2192 ĕchō (2), to have;
hold; keep
2233 hēgĕŏmai (7), to
deem, i.e. consider

3049 lŏgizŏmai (1), to
credit; to think, regard
3106 makarizō (1), to
esteem fortunate
5585 psēphizō (1), to
compute, estimate

COUNTED
2803 châshab (18), to
think; to compute
5608 çâphar (2), to
inscribe; to enumerate
6485 pâqad (3), to visit,
care for, count
515 axiŏō (2), to deem
entitled or fit, worthy
1075 gĕnĕalŏgĕō (1),
trace in genealogy
2192 ĕchō (2), to have;
hold; keep
2233 hēgĕŏmai (3), to
deem, i.e. consider
2661 kataxiŏō (2), to
deem entirely deserving
3049 lŏgizŏmai (4), to
credit; to think, regard
4860 sumpsēphizō (1), to
compute jointly

COUNTENANCE
639 ʾaph (1), nose or
nostril; face; person
1921 hâdar (1), to favor
or honor; to be proud
2122 ziyv (Ch.) (4),
cheerfulness
4758 marʾeh (8),
appearance; vision
5869 ʿayin (1), eye; sight;
fountain
6440 pânîym (30), face
8389 tôʾar (1), outline,
figure or appearance
2397 idĕa (1), sight
3799 ŏpsis (1), face;
appearance
4383 prŏsōpŏn (3), face,
presence
4659 skuthrōpŏs (1),
gloomy or mournful

COUNTENANCES
4758 marʾeh (2),
appearance; vision

COUNTERVAIL
7737 shâvâh (1), to
resemble; to adjust

COUNTETH
2803 châshab (2), to
think; to compute
5585 psēphizō (1), to
compute, estimate

COUNTRIES
776 ʾerets (48), earth,
land, soil; country
5316 nepheth (1), height
5561 chōra (1), space of
territory

COUNTRY
127 ʾădâmâh (1), soil;
land
249 ʾezrâch (5), native
born
339 ʾîy (1), dry land;
coast; island
776 ʾerets (91), earth,
land, soil; country
1552 gᵉlîylâh (1), circuit
or region

2256 chebel (1), *company, band*
4725 mâqôwm (1), *general locality, place*
6521 pᵉrâzîy (1), *rustic*
7704 sâdeh (17), *field*
68 agrŏs (8), *farmland, countryside*
589 apŏdēmĕō (4), *visit a foreign land*
1085 gĕnŏs (1), *kin, offspring in kind*
1093 gĕ (2), *soil, region, whole earth*
3968 patris (8), *hometown*
4066 pĕrichŏrŏs (4), *surrounding country*
5561 chōra (15), *space of territory*

COUNTRYMEN
1085 gĕnŏs (1), *kin, offspring in kind*
4853 sumphulĕtēs (1), *of the same country*

COUPLE
2266 châbar (5), *to fascinate by spells*
6776 tsemed (4), *paired yoke*
8147 shᵉnayim (1), *two-fold*

COUPLED
2266 châbar (7), *to fascinate by spells*
8382 tâ'am (2), *to be twinned, i.e. duplicate*
8535 tâm (2), *morally pious; gentle, dear*

COUPLETH
2279 chôbereth (2), *joint*

COUPLING
2279 chôbereth (2), *joint*
4225 machbereth (8), *junction*

COUPLINGS
4226 mᵉchabbᵉrâh (1), *joiner*

COURAGE
553 'âmats (9), *to be strong; be courageous*
2388 châzaq (8), *to be strong; courageous*
3824 lêbâb (1), *heart*
7307 rûwach (1), *breath; wind; life-spirit*
2294 tharsŏs (1), *boldness, courage*

COURAGEOUS
533+3820 'ammîyts (1), *strong; mighty; brave*
553 'âmats (2), *to be strong; be courageous*
2388 châzaq (2), *to be strong; courageous*

COURAGEOUSLY
2388 châzaq (1), *to be strong; courageous*

COURSE
4131 môwṭ (1), *to slip, shake, fall*
4256 machălôqeth (19), *section or division*
4794 mᵉrûwtsâh (2), *race*
165 aiōn (1), *perpetuity, ever; world*

1408 drŏmŏs (3), *career, course of life*
2113 ĕuthudrŏmĕō (1), *to sail direct*
2183 ĕphēmĕria (2), *rotation or class*
3313 mĕrŏs (1), *division or share*
4144 plŏŏs (2), *navigation, voyage*
5143 trĕchō (1), *to run or walk hastily; to strive*
5164 trŏchŏs (1), *wheel; circuitous course of life*

COURSES
2487 chălîyphâh (1), *alternation, change*
2988 yâbâl (1), *stream*
4255 machlᵉqâh (Ch.) (1), *section or division*
4256 machălôqeth (14), *section or division*
4546 mᵉçillâh (1), *main thoroughfare; viaduct*

COURT
1004 bayith (1), *house; temple; family, tribe*
2681 châtsîyr (1), *court or abode*
2691 châtsêr (114), *enclosed yard*
5835 'ăzârâh (2), *enclosure; border*
5892 'îyr (1), *city, town, unwalled-village*
833 aulĕ (1), *palace; house; courtyard*

COURTEOUS
5391 philŏphrōn (1), *kind, well-disposed*

COURTEOUSLY
5364 philanthrōpōs (1), *fondly to mankind*
5390 philŏphrŏnōs (1), *friendliness of mind*

COURTS
2691 châtsêr (24), *enclosed yard*

COUSIN
4773 suggĕnēs (1), *relative; countryman*

COUSINS
4773 suggĕnēs (1), *relative; countryman*

COVENANT
1285 bᵉrîyth (264), *compact, agreement*
1242 diathēkē (17), *contract; devisory will*

COVENANTBREAKERS
802 asunthĕtŏs (1), *untrustworthy*

COVENANTED
3772 kârath (2), *to make an agreement*
2476 histēmi (1), *to stand, establish*
4934 suntithĕmai (1), *to consent, concur, agree*

COVENANTS
1242 diathēkē (3), *contract; devisory will*

COVER
2645 châphâh (1), *to cover; to veil, to encase*

3680 kâçâh (50), *to cover*
4374 mᵉkaççeh (1), *covering*
5258 nâçak (4), *to pour a libation; to anoint*
5526 çâkak (5), *to fence in; cover over; protect*
5844 'âṭâh (5), *to wrap, i.e. cover, veil, clothe*
7159 qâram (1), *to cover*
7779 shûwph (1), *to gape, to overwhelm*
2572 kaluptō (2), *to cover*
2619 katakaluptō (1), *cover with a veil*
4028 pĕrikaluptō (1), *to cover eyes*

COVERED
1104 bâla' (1), *to swallow; to destroy*
2645 châphâh (7), *to cover; to veil, to encase*
2926 ṭâlal (1), *to cover, roof*
3271 yâ'aṭ (1), *to clothe, cover*
3680 kâçâh (61), *to cover*
3728 kâphash (1), *to tread down*
3780 kâsâh (1), *to grow fat*
3813 lâ'aṭ (1), *to muffle, cover*
4374 mᵉkaççeh (1), *covering*
5526 çâkak (8), *to fence in; cover over; protect*
5603 çâphan (3), *to hide by covering; to roof*
5743 'ûwb (1), *to darkly becloud*
5844 'âṭâh (3), *to wrap, i.e. cover, veil, clothe*
5848 'âṭaph (1), *to shroud, clothe*
6632 tsâb (1), *covered cart*
6823 tsâphâh (5), *to sheet over with metal*
7159 qâram (1), *to cover*
1943 ĕpikaluptō (1), *to forgive*
2572 kaluptō (2), *to cover*
2596 kata (1), *down*
2619 katakaluptō (2), *cover with a veil*
4780 sugkaluptō (1), *to conceal altogether*

COVEREDST
3680 kâçâh (1), *to cover*

COVEREST
3680 kâçâh (1), *to cover*
5844 'âṭâh (1), *to wrap, i.e. cover, veil, clothe*

COVERETH
3680 kâçâh (20), *to cover*
4374 mᵉkaççeh (2), *covering*
5526 çâkak (2), *to fence in; cover over; protect*
5844 'âṭâh (1), *to wrap, i.e. cover, veil, clothe*
5848 'âṭaph (1), *to shroud, i.e. clothe*
2572 kaluptō (1), *to cover*

COVERING
168 'ôhel (1), *tent*

3680 kâçâh (2), *to cover*
3681 kâçûwy (2), *covering*
3682 kᵉçûwth (6), *cover; veiling*
3875 lôwṭ (1), *veil*
4372 mikçeh (16), *covering*
4539 mâçâk (7), *veil; shield*
4540 mᵉçukkâh (1), *covering*
4541 maççêkâh (2), *cast image); woven coverlet*
4817 merkâb (1), *chariot; seat in chariot*
5526 çâkak (2), *to fence in; cover over; protect*
5643 çêther (1), *cover, shelter*
5844 'âṭâh (1), *to wrap, i.e. cover, veil, clothe*
6781 tsâmîyd (1), *bracelet; lid*
6826 tsippûwy (3), *encasement with metal*
4018 pĕribŏlaiŏn (1), *mantle, veil*

COVERINGS
4765 marbad (2), *coverlet, covering*

COVERS
7184 qâsâh (3), *jug*

COVERT
4329 mêyçâk (1), *covered portico*
4563 miçtôwr (1), *refuge, hiding place*
5520 çôk (1), *hut of entwined boughs; lair*
5521 çukkâh (1), *tabernacle; shelter*
5643 çêther (5), *cover, shelter*

COVET
183 'âvâh (1), *to wish for, desire*
2530 châmad (3), *to delight in; lust for*
1937 ĕpithumĕō (2), *to long for*
2206 zēlŏō (2), *to have warmth of feeling for*

COVETED
2530 châmad (1), *to delight in; lust for*
1937 ĕpithumĕō (1), *to long for*
3713 ŏrĕgŏmai (1), *to reach out after, long for*

COVETETH
183 'âvâh (1), *to wish for, desire*
1214 bâtsa' (1), *to plunder; to finish*

COVETOUS
1214 bâtsa' (1), *to plunder; to finish*
866 aphilargurŏs (1), *not greedy*
4123 plĕŏnĕktēs (4), *eager for gain, greedy*
4124 plĕŏnĕxia (1), *fraudulence, extortion*
5366 philargurŏs (2), *avaricious*

COVETOUSNESS
1215 betsa' (10), *plunder; unjust gain*
866 aphilargurŏs (1), *not greedy*
4124 plĕŏnĕxia (8), *fraudulence, avarice*

COVOCATION
4744 miqrâ' (1), *public meeting*

COW
5697 'eglâh (1), cow *calf*
6510 pârâh (2), *heifer*
7794 shôwr (2), *bullock*

COW'S
1241 bâqâr (1), *plowing ox; herd*

COZ
6976 Qôwts (1), *thorns*

COZBI
3579 Kozbîy (2), *false*

CRACKLING
6963 qôwl (1), *voice or sound*

CRACKNELS
5350 niqqud (1), *crumb, morsel; biscuit*

CRAFT
4820 mirmâh (1), *fraud*
1388 dŏlŏs (1), *wile, deceit, trickery*
2039 ĕrgasia (1), *occupation; profit*
3313 mĕrŏs (1), *division or share*
3673 hŏmŏtĕchnŏs (1), *fellow-artificer*
5078 tĕchnē (1), *trade, craft; skill*

CRAFTINESS
6193 'ôrem (1), *stratagem, craftiness*
3834 panŏurgia (4), *trickery or sophistry*

CRAFTSMAN
2976 yâ'ash (1), *to despond, despair*
5079 tĕchnitēs (1), *skilled craftsman*

CRAFTSMEN
2796 chârâsh (5), skilled *fabricator or worker*
5079 tĕchnitēs (2), *skilled craftsman*

CRAFTY
6175 'ârûwm (2), *cunning; clever*
6191 'âram (1), to *be cunning; be prudent*
3835 panŏurgŏs (1), *shrewd, clever*

CRAG
8127 shên (1), *tooth; ivory; cliff*

CRANE
5483 çûwç (2), *horse; bird swallow*

CRASHING
7667 sheber (1), *fracture; ruin*

CRAVED
154 aitĕō (1), *to ask for*

CRAVETH
404 'âkaph (1), *to urge*

CREATE
1254 bârâ' (8), *to create; fashion*

CREATED
1254 bârâ' (33), *to create; fashion*
2936 ktizō (12), *to fabricate, create*

CREATETH
1254 bârâ' (1), *to create; fashion*

CREATION
2937 ktisis (6), *formation*

CREATOR
1254 bârâ' (3), *to create; fashion*
2936 ktizō (1), *to fabricate, create*
2939 ktistēs (1), *founder*

CREATURE
2416 chay (6), *alive; raw; fresh; life*
5315 nephesh (9), *life; breath; soul; wind*
8318 sherets (1), *swarm, teeming mass*
2937 ktisis (11), *formation*
2938 ktisma (2), *created product*

CREATURES
255 'ôach (1), *creature that howls;*
2416 chay (9), *alive; raw; fresh; life*
2938 ktisma (2), *created product*

CREDITOR
1167+4874+3027 ba'al (1), *master; owner; citizen*
5383 nâshâh (1), *to lend or borrow*
1157 danĕistēs (1), *money lender*

CREDITORS
5383 nâshâh (1), *to lend or borrow*

CREEK
2859 kŏlpŏs (1), *lap area; bay*

CREEP
7430 râmas (2), *to glide swiftly, i.e. crawl*
8317 shârats (3), *to wriggle, swarm*
8318 sherets (2), *swarm, teeming mass*
1744+1519 ĕndunō (1), *to sneak in, creep in*

CREEPETH
7430 râmas (9), *to glide swiftly, i.e. crawl*
7431 remes (1), *any rapidly moving animal*
8317 shârats (4), *to wriggle, swarm*

CREEPING
7431 remes (15), *any rapidly moving animal*
8318 sherets (11), *swarm, teeming mass*
2062 hĕrpĕtŏn (3), *reptile*

CREPT
3921 parĕisdunō (1), *to slip in secretly*

CRESCENS
2913 Krēskēs (1), *growing*

CRETE
2914 Krētē (5), *Cretë*

CRETES
2912 Krēs (1), *inhabitant of Crete*

CRETIANS
2912 Krēs (2), *inhabitant of Crete*

CREW
5455 phōnĕō (5), *to emit a sound*

CRIB
18 'êbûwç (3), *manger or stall*

CRIED
2199 zâ'aq (31), *to call out, announce*
2200 z'ĕ'iq (Ch.) (1), *to make an outcry, shout*
2980 yâbab (1), *to bawl, cry out*
5414 nâthan (1), *to give*
6817 tsâ'aq (29), *to shriek; to proclaim*
7121 qârâ' (54), *to call out*
7123 q'râ' (Ch.) (3), *to call out*
7321 rûwa' (2), *to shout for alarm or joy*
7768 shâva' (10), *to halloo, call for help*
310 anabŏaō (2), *to cry out*
349 anakrazō (5), *to scream aloud*
863 aphiēmi (1), *to leave; to pardon, forgive*
994 bŏaō (3), *to shout for help*
2019 ĕpiphōnĕō (2), *to exclaim, shout*
2896 krazō (43), *to call aloud*
2905 kraugazō (6), *to clamor, shout*
5455 phōnĕō (5), *to emit a sound*

CRIES
995 bŏē (1), *to call for aid*

CRIEST
2199 zâ'aq (2), *to call out, announce*
6817 tsâ'aq (1), *to shriek; to proclaim*
7121 qârâ' (2), *to call out*

CRIETH
2199 zâ'aq (1), *to call out, announce*
5414+6963 nâthan (1), *to give*
6817 tsâ'aq (2), *to shriek; to proclaim*
7121 qârâ' (4), *to call out*
7442 rânan (3), *to shout for joy*
7768 shâva' (2), *to halloo, call for help*
2896 krazō (4), *to call aloud*

CRIME
2154 zimmâh (1), *bad plan*
1462 ĕgklēma (1), *accusation*

CRIMES
4941 mishpâṭ (1), *verdict; formal decree; justice*
156 aitia (1), *logical reason; legal crime*

CRIMSON
3758 karmîyl (3), *carmine, deep red*
8144 shânîy (1), *crimson dyed stuffs*
8438 tôwlâ' (1), *maggot worm; crimson-grub*

CRIPPLE
5560 chŏlŏs (1), *limping, crippled*

CRISPING
2754 chârîyṭ (1), *pocket*

CRISPUS
2921 Krispŏs (2), *crisp*

CROOKBACKT
1384 gibbên (1), *hunch-backed*

CROOKED
1281 bârîyach (1), *fleeing, gliding serpent*
1921 hâdar (1), *to favor or honor; to be high*
4625 ma'ăqâsh (1), *crook in a road*
5753 'âvâh (1), *to be crooked*
5791 'âvath (2), *to wrest, twist*
6121 'âqôb (2), *fraudulent; tracked*
6128 'ăqalqal (1), *crooked*
6129 'ăqallâthôwn (1), *crooked*
6140 'âqash (1), *to knot or distort; to pervert*
6141 'iqqêsh (1), *distorted, warped, false*
6618 p'thaltôl (1), *tortuous, perverse*
4646 skŏliŏs (2), *crooked; perverse*

CROP
4760 mur'âh (1), *craw or crop of a bird*
6998 qâṭaph (1), *to strip off, pick off*

CROPPED
6998 qâṭaph (1), *to strip off, pick off*

CROSS
4716 staurŏs (28), *pole or cross*

CROSSWAY
6563 pereq (1), *rapine; fork in roads*

CROUCH
7812 shâchâh (1), *to prostrate in homage*

CROUCHETH
1794 dâkâh (1), *to collapse; contrite*

CROW
5455 phōnĕō (7), *to emit a sound*

CROWN
2213 zêr (10), border molding on a building
3804 kether (3), royal headdress
5145 nezer (11), royal chaplet
5850 'ăṭârâh (20), crown
6936 qodqôd (7), crown of the head
4735 stĕphanŏs (15), chaplet, wreath

CROWNED
3803 kâthar (1), to enclose, besiege; to wait
4502 minnᵉzâr (1), prince
5849 'âṭar (2), to encircle, enclose in; to crown
4737 stephanŏō (2), to adorn with a wreath

CROWNEDST
4737 stephanŏō (1), to adorn with a wreath

CROWNEST
5849 'âṭar (1), to encircle, enclose in; to crown

CROWNETH
5849 'âṭar (1), to encircle, enclose in; to crown

CROWNING
5849 'âṭar (1), to encircle, enclose in; to crown

CROWNS
5850 'ăṭârâh (3), crown
1238 diadēma (3), crown or diadem
4735 stĕphanŏs (3), chaplet, wreath

CRUCIFIED
4362 prŏspēgnumi (1), to fasten to a cross
4717 staurŏō (31), to crucify
4957 sustaurŏō (5), to crucify with

CRUCIFY
388 anastaurŏō (1), to re-crucify
4717 staurŏō (13), to crucify

CRUEL
393 'akzâr (3), violent, deadly; brave
394 'akzârîy (8), terrible, cruel
395 'akzᵉrîyûwth (1), fierceness, cruelty
2555 châmâç (1), violence; malice
2556 châmêts (1), to be fermented; be soured
7185 qâshâh (2), to be tough or severe
7186 qâsheh (1), severe

CRUELLY
6233 'ôsheq (1), injury; fraud; distress

CRUELTY
2555 châmâç (4), violence; malice
6531 perek (1), severity

CRUMBS
5589 psichiŏn (3), little bit or morsel

CRUSE
1228 baqbûk (1), bottle
6746 tsᵉlôchîyth (1), vial or salt-cellar
6835 tsappachath (7), flat saucer

CRUSH
1792 dâkâ' (1), to pulverize; be contrite
2115 zûwr (1), to press together, tighten
7533 râtsats (1), to crack in pieces, smash
7665 shâbar (1), to burst

CRUSHED
1792 dâkâ' (2), to pulverize; be contrite
2000 hâmam (1), to disturb, drive, destroy
2116 zûwreh (1), trodden on
3807 kâthath (1), to bruise, strike, beat
3905 lâchats (1), to press; to distress
7533 râtsats (1), to crack in pieces, smash

CRY
602 'ânaq (3), to shriek, cry out in groaning
1993 hâmâh (1), to be in great commotion
2199 zâ'aq (25), to call out, announce
2201 za'aq (18), shriek, outcry, lament
5414+6963 nâthan (1), to give
6030 'ânâh (2), to respond, answer
6165 'ârag (1), to long for, pant for
6463 pâ'âh (1), to scream in childbirth
6670 tsâhal (3), to be cheerful; to sound
6682 tsᵉvâchâh (2), screech of anguish
6817 tsâ'aq (15), to shriek; to proclaim
6818 tsa'âqâh (19), shriek, wail
6873 tsârach (1), to whoop
6963 qôwl (1), voice or sound
7121 qârâ' (37), to call out
7321 rûwa' (5), to shout for alarm or joy
7440 rinnâh (12), shout
7442 rânan (1), to shout for joy
7768 shâva' (8), to call for help
7769 shûwa' (1), call
7773 sheva' (1), call
7775 shav'âh (11), call
8173 shâ'a' (1), to fondle, please or amuse (self)
994 bŏaō (2), to shout for help
2896 krazō (3), to call
2905 kraugazō (1), to clamor, shout
2906 kraugē (3), outcry

CRYING
603 'ănâqâh (1), shrieking, groaning
2201 za'aq (2), shriek, outcry, lament
4191 mûwth (1), to die; to kill
6682 tsᵉvâchâh (1), screech of anguish
6818 tsa'âqâh (2), shriek, wail
7121 qârâ' (1), to call out
7771 shôwa' (1), call
8663 tᵉshû'âh (1), crashing or clamor
310 anabŏaō (1), to cry out
994 bŏaō (6), to shout for help
1916 ĕpibŏaō (1), to cry out loudly
2896 krazō (9), to call
2906 kraugē (2), outcry

CRYSTAL
2137 zᵉkûwkîyth (1), transparent glass
7140 qerach (1), ice; hail; rock crystal
2929 krustallizō (1), to appear as ice
2930 krustallŏs (2), rock crystal

CUBIT
520 'ammâh (35), cubit
1574 gômed (1), measurement of length
4083 pēchus (2), measure of time or length

CUBITS
520 'ammâh (197), cubit
521 'ammâh (Ch.) (4), cubit
4088 pikria (2), acridity, bitterness

CUCKOW
7828 shachaph (2), gull

CUCUMBERS
4750 miqshâh (1), cucumber field
7180 qishshû' (1), cucumber

CUD
1625 gêrâh (11), cud

CUMBERED
4049 pĕrispaō (1), to be distracted

CUMBERETH
2673 katargĕō (1), to be, render entirely useless

CUMBRANCE
2960 ṭôrach (1), burden

CUMI
2891 kŏumi (1), rise!

CUMMIN
3646 kammôn (3), cummin
2951 kuminŏn (1), dill or fennel

CUNNING
542 'âmân (1), expert artisan, craftsman
995 bîyn (1), to understand; discern
1847 da'ath (1), understanding

CURSE
2450 châkâm (10), wise, intelligent, skillful
2803 châshab (11), to plot; to think, regard
3045 yâda' (4), to know
4284 machăshâbâh (3), contrivance; plan

CUP
1375 gᵉbîya' (4), goblet; bowl
3563 kôwç (29), cup; (poss.) owl
3599 kîyç (1), cup; utility bag
5592 çaph (1), dish
4221 pŏtēriŏn (31), drinking-vessel

CUPBEARER
4945 mashqeh (1), butler; drink; well-watered

CUPBEARERS
4945 mashqeh (2), butler; drink; well-watered

CUPS
101 'aggân (1), bowl
3563 kôwç (1), cup
4518 mᵉnaqqîyth (1), sacrificial basin
7184 qâsâh (1), jug
4221 pŏtēriŏn (2), drinking-vessel

CURDLED
7087 qâphâ' (1), to thicken, congeal

CURE
1455 gâhâh (1), to heal
7495 râphâ' (1), to cure, heal
2323 thĕrapĕuō (2), to relieve disease

CURED
8585 tᵉ'âlâh (1), bandage or plaster
2323 thĕrapĕuō (3), to relieve disease

CURES
2392 iasis (1), curing

CURIOUS
4284 machăshâbâh (1), contrivance; plan
4021 pĕriĕrgŏs (1), meddlesome, busybody

CURIOUSLY
7551 râqam (1), variegation; embroider

CURRENT
5674 'âbar (1), to cross over; to transition

CURSE
423 'âlâh (9), imprecation: curse
779 'ârar (15), to execrate, place a curse
1288 bârak (3), to bless
2764 chêrem (4), doomed object
3994 mᵉ'êrâh (4), execration, curse
5344 nâqab (4), to specify, designate, libel
6895 qâbab (7), to stab with words
7043 qâlal (17), to be easy, trifling, vile

English

CURSED
7045 qᵉlâlâh (24), *vilification*
7621 shᵉbûw'âh (1), *sworn oath*
8381 ta'âlâh (1), *imprecation*
332 anathēmatizō (3), to *declare* or *vow* an *oath*
2652 katanathĕma (1), *imprecation*
2653 katanathĕmatizō (1), to *imprecate*
2671 katara (3), *imprecation, execration*
2672 kataraŏmai (4), to *execrate, curse*

CURSED
779 'ârar (44), to *execrate, place a curse*
1288 bârak (1), to *bless*
2764 chêrem (3), *doomed object*
5344 nâqab (1), to *specify, designate, libel*
6895 qâbab (1), to *stab* with words
7043 qâlal (17), to be *easy, trifling, vile*
1944 ĕpikataratŏs (3), *execrable, cursed*
2671 katara (1), *imprecation, execration*
2672 kataraŏmai (1), to *execrate, curse*

CURSEDST
422 'âlâh (1), *imprecate, utter a curse*
2672 kataraŏmai (1), to *execrate, curse*

CURSES
423 'âlâh (5), *imprecation: curse*
7045 qᵉlâlâh (3), *vilification*

CURSEST
779 'ârar (1), to *execrate, place a curse*

CURSETH
779 'ârar (2), to *execrate, place a curse*
7043 qâlal (6), to be *easy, trifling, vile*
2551 kakŏlŏgĕō (2), to *revile, curse*

CURSING
423 'âlâh (4), *imprecation: curse*
3994 mᵉ'êrâh (1), *execration, curse*
7045 qᵉlâlâh (4), *vilification*
685 ara (1), *imprecation, curse*
2671 katara (2), *imprecation, execration*

CURSINGS
7045 qᵉlâlâh (1), *vilification*

CURTAIN
1852 dôq (1), *fine, thin* cloth
3407 yᵉrîy'âh (23), *drapery*
4539 mâçâk (1), *veil; shield*

CURTAINS
3407 yᵉrîy'âh (31), *drapery*

CUSH
3568 Kûwsh (8), *Cush*

CUSHAN
3572 Kûwshân (1), *Cushan*

CUSHI
3569 Kûwshîy (10), *Cushite*

CUSTODY
3027 yâd (4), *hand; power*
6486 pᵉquddâh (1), *visitation; punishment*

CUSTOM
1870 derek (1), *road; mode* of action
1983 hălâk (Ch.) (3), *toll, duty* on goods at a road
2706 chôq (2), *appointment; allotment*
4941 mishpâṭ (2), *verdict; formal decree; justice*
1480 ĕthizō (1), *customary, required*
1485 ĕthŏs (2), *usage*
3588+1486 hŏ (1), "*the*" i.e. the definite article
4914 sunēthĕia (2), *usage, custom*
5056 tĕlŏs (2), *conclusion* of an act or state
5058 tĕlōniŏn (3), *tax-gatherer's booth*

CUSTOMS
2708 chuqqâh (2), to *delineate*
1485 ĕthŏs (5), *usage*

CUT
1214 bâtsa' (3), to *plunder; to finish*
1219 bâtsar (1), to be *inaccessible*
1254 bârâ' (2), to *create; fashion*
1413 gâdad (5), to *gash, slash oneself*
1438 gâda' (21), to *fell a* tree; to *destroy*
1494 gâza: (2), to *shear; shave; destroy*
1504 gâzar (8), to *cut down; to destroy*
1505 gᵉzar (Ch.) (2), to *quarry rock*
1629 gâraz (1), to *cut off*
1820 dâmâh (5), to be *silent; to fail, cease*
1826 dâmam (5), to *stop, cease; to perish*
2404 châṭab (1), to *chop* or *carve* wood
2498 châlaph (1), to *pierce; to change*
2672 châtsab (1), to *cut* stone or *carve* wood
2686 châtsats (1), to *curtail*
3582 kâchad (10), to *destroy; to hide*
3683 kâçach (2), to *cut off*
3772 kârath (175), to *cut* (off, down or asunder)
4135 mûwl (2), to *circumcise*

5243 nâmal (4), to be *circumcised*
5352 nâqâh (2), to be, *make clean; to be bare*
5362 nâqaph (1), to *strike; to surround*
5408 nâthach (7), to *dismember, cut up*
5648 'ăbad (Ch.) (2), to *do, work, serve*
5927 'âlâh (1), to *ascend, be high, mount*
6780 tsemach (1), *sprout, branch*
6789 tsâmath (7), to *extirpate, destroy*
6990 qâṭaṭ (1), to *destroy*
6998 qâṭaph (2), to *strip* off, *pick off*
7059 qâmaṭ (1), to *pluck,* i.e. *destroy*
7082 qâçaç (1), to *lop off*
7088 qâphad (1), to *roll together*
7094 qâtsab (1), to *clip,* or *chop*
7096 qâtsâh (1), to *cut* off; to *destroy*
7112 qâtsats (10), to *chop* off; to *separate*
7113 qᵉtsats (Ch.) (1), to *chop off, lop off*
7167 qâra' (1), to *rend*
7787 sûwr (1), to *saw*
8295 sâraṭ (1), to *gash* oneself
8456 tâzaz (1), to *lop off*
581 apŏgĕnŏmĕnŏs (1), *deceased*
609 apŏkŏptō (6), *mutilate* the genitals
851 aphairĕō (1), to *remove, cut off*
1282 diapriō (2), to be *furious*
1371 dichŏtŏmĕō (2), to *flog severely*
1581 ĕkkŏptō (7), to *cut* off; to *frustrate*
2875 kŏptō (2), to *beat* the breast
4932 suntĕmnō (1), to *cut* short, i.e. *do speedily*

CUTH
3575 Kûwth (1), *Cuth* or *Cuthah*

CUTHAH
3575 Kûwth (1), *Cuth* or *Cuthah*

CUTTEST
7114 qâtsar (1), to *curtail, cut short*

CUTTETH
1234 bâqa' (1), to *cleave, break, tear open*
3772 kârath (1), to *cut* (off, down or asunder)
6398 pâlach (1), to *slice; to break* open; to *pierce*
7096 qâtsâh (1), to *cut* off; to *destroy*
7112 qâtsats (1), to *chop* off; to *separate*
7167 qâra' (1), to *rend*

CUTTING
1824 dᵉmîy (1), *quiet, peacefulness*

2799 chărôsheth (2), *skilled work*
7096 qâtsâh (1), to *cut* off; to *destroy*
2629 katakŏptō (1), to *mangle, cut up*

CUTTINGS
1417 gᵉdûwd (1), *furrow ridge*
8296 sereṭ (2), *incision*

CYMBAL
2950 kumbalŏn (1), *cymbal*

CYMBALS
4700 mᵉtsêleth (13), *pair* of *cymbals*
6767 tsᵉlâtsal (3), *whirring*

CYPRESS
8645 tirzâh (1), (poss.) *cypress*

CYPRUS
2954 Kuprŏs (8), *Cyprus*

CYRENE
2957 Kurēnē (4), *Cyrenë*

CYRENIAN
2956 Kurēnaiŏs (2), *inhabitant of Cyrene*

CYRENIANS
2956 Kurēnaiŏs (1), *inhabitant of Cyrene*

CYRENIUS
2958 Kurēniŏs (1), *Quirinus*

CYRUS
3566 Kôwresh (15), *Koresh*
3567 Kôwresh (Ch.) (8), *Koresh*

DABAREH
1705 Dâbᵉrath (1), *Daberath*

DABBASHETH
1708 Dabbesheth (1), *hump of a camel*

DABERATH
1705 Dâbᵉrath (2), *Daberath*

DAGGER
2719 chereb (3), *knife, sword*

DAGON
1712 Dâgôwn (11), *fish-god*

DAGON'S
1712 Dâgôwn (1), *fish-god*

DAILY
3117 yôwm (20), *day; time period*
3117+259 yôwm (1), *day; time period*
3119 yôwmâm (2), *daily*
3605+3117 kôl (11), *all, any* or *every*
8548 tâmîyd (7), *constantly, regularly*
1967 ĕpiŏusiŏs (2), *for subsistence, i.e. needful*
2184 ĕphēmĕrŏs (1), *diurnal, i.e. daily*
2522 kathēmĕrinŏs (1), *quotidian, i.e. daily*

2596+1538+2250 *kata* (1), *down; according to*
2596+2250 *kata* (15), *down; according to*
2596+3956+2250 *kata* (1), *down; according to*
3956+2250 *pas* (1), *all, any, every, whole*

DAINTIES
4303 maṭ'am (1), *delicacy*
4516 man'am (1), *delicacy eaten*
4574 ma'ădân (1), *delicacy; pleasure*

DAINTY
4303 maṭ'am (1), *delicacy*
8378 ta'ăvâh (1), *longing; delight*
3045 liparŏs (1), *costly, rich*

DALAIAH
1806 Dᵉlâyâh (1), *Jehovah has delivered*

DALE
6010 'êmeq (2), broad *depression* or valley

DALMANUTHA
1148 Dalmanŏutha (1), *Dalmanutha*

DALMATIA
1149 Dalmatia (1), *Dalmatia*

DALPHON
1813 Dalphôwn (1), *dripping*

DAM
517 'êm (5), *mother*

DAMAGE
2257 chăbal (Ch.) (1), *harm, wound*
2555 châmăç (1), *violence; malice*
5142 nᵉzaq (Ch.) (1), to *suffer, inflict loss*
5143 nêzeq (1), *injure, loss*
2209 zēmia (1), *detriment; loss*
2210 zēmiŏō (1), to *experience detriment*

DAMARIS
1152 Damaris (1), *gentle*

DAMASCENES
1159 dapanaō (1), to *incur cost; to waste*

DAMASCUS
1833 dᵉmesheq (1), *damask fabric*
1834 Dammeseq (44), *Damascus*
1154 Damaskŏs (15), *Damascus*

DAMNABLE
684 apōlĕia (1), *ruin or loss*

DAMNATION
684 apōlĕia (1), *ruin or loss*
2917 krima (7), *decision*
2920 krisis (3), *decision; tribunal; justice*

DAMNED
2632 katakrinō (2), to *judge against*

2919 krinō (1), to *decide; to try, condemn, punish*

DAMSEL
3207 yaldâh (1), *young female*
5291 na'ărâh (24), *female child; servant*
7356 racham (1), *womb; maiden*
2877 kŏrasiŏn (6), *little girl*
3813 paidiŏn (4), *child: boy or girl; immature*
3814 paidiskē (4), *female slave or servant*

DAMSEL'S
5291 na'ărâh (8), *female child; servant*

DAMSELS
5291 na'ărâh (2), *female child; servant*
5959 'almâh (1), *lass, young woman*

DAN
1835 Dân (71), *judge*

DAN-JAAN
1842 Dân Ya'an (1), *judge of purpose*

DANCE
2342 chûwl (1), to *dance, whirl; to writhe*
4234 mâchôwl (4), (round) *dance*
7540 râqad (3), to *spring about wildly or for joy*

DANCED
2342 chûwl (1), to *dance, whirl; to writhe* in pain; *to wait; to pervert*
3769 kârar (1), to *dance in whirling motion*
3738 ŏrchĕŏmai (4), to *dance*

DANCES
4246 mᵉchôwlâh (5), round-*dance*

DANCING
2287 châgag (1), to *observe a festival*
3769 kârar (1), to *dance in whirling motion*
4234 mâchôwl (1), (round) *dance*
4246 mᵉchôwlâh (2), round-*dance*
7540 râqad (1), to *spring about wildly or for joy*
5525 chŏrŏs (1), round *dance; dancing*

DANDLED
8173 shâ'a' (1), to *fondle, please* or *amuse* (self)

DANGER
1777 ĕnŏchŏs (5), *liable*
2793 kindunĕuō (2), to *undergo peril*

DANGEROUS
2000 ĕpisphalēs (1), *insecure, unsafe*

DANIEL
1840 Dânîyê'l (29), *judge of God*
1841 Dânîyê'l (Ch.) (50), *judge of God*

1158 Daniēl (2), *judge of God*

DANITES
1839 Dânîy (4), *Danite*

DANNAH
1837 Dannâh (1), *Dannah*

DARA
1873 Dâra' (1), *Dara*

DARDA
1862 Darda' (1), *pearl of knowledge*

DARE
5111 tŏlmaō (4), to be *bold; to dare*

DARIUS
1867 Dârᵉyâvêsh (10), *Darejavesh*
1868 Dârᵉyâvêsh (Ch.) (15), *Darejavesh*

DARK
651 'âphêl (1), *dusky, dark*
653 'ăphêlâh (1), *duskiness, darkness*
2420 chîydâh (5), *puzzle; conundrum; maxim*
2821 châshak (5), to be *dark; to darken*
2822 chôshek (7), *darkness; misery*
2824 cheshkâh (1), *darkness, dark*
2841 chashrâh (1), *gathering of clouds*
3544 kêheh (5), *feeble; obscure*
4285 machshâk (3), *darkness; dark place*
5399 nesheph (1), *dusk, dawn*
5939 'ălâṭâh (1), *dusk*
6205 'ărâphel (2), *gloom, darkness*
6751 tsâlal (1), to *shade; to grow dark*
6937 qâdar (4), to be *dark-colored*
7087 qâphâ' (1), to *thicken, congeal*
850 auchmērŏs (1), *obscure, dark*
4652 skŏtĕinŏs (1), *dark, very dark*
4653 skŏtia (2), *dimness*

DARKEN
2821 châshak (1), to be *dark; to darken*

DARKENED
2821 châshak (7), to be *dark; to darken*
3543 kâhâh (1), to *grow dull, fade; to be faint*
6150 'ârab (1), to *grow dusky at sundown*
6272 'âtham (1), be *desolated* by scorching
6937 qâdar (1), to be *dark-colored*
4654 skŏtizō (8), to be, *become dark*

DARKENETH
2821 châshak (1), to be *dark; to darken*

DARKISH
3544 kêheh (1), *feeble; obscure*

DARKLY
1722+135 ĕn (1), *in; during; because of*

DARKNESS
652 'ôphel (6), *dusk, darkness*
653 'ăphêlâh (6), *duskiness, darkness*
2816 chăshôwk (Ch.) (1), *dark, darkness*
2821 châshak (1), to be *dark; to darken*
2822 chôshek (69), *darkness; misery*
2825 chăshêkâh (5), *darkness; misery*
3990 ma'ăphêl (1), *opaque, dark*
3991 ma'phêlᵉyâh (1), *opaqueness, darkness*
4285 machshâk (4), *darkness; dark place*
5890 'êyphâh (2), *covering* of darkness
6205 'ărâphel (13), *gloom, darkness*
2217 zŏphŏs (2), *gloom*
4652 skŏtĕinŏs (2), *dark, very dark*
4653 skŏtia (13), *dimness*
4655 skŏtŏs (31), *darkness*
4656 skŏtŏō (1), to *make dark*, i.e. *blind*

DARKON
1874 Darqôwn (2), *Darkon*

DARLING
3173 yâchîyd (2), *only son; alone; beloved*

DART
2671 chêts (1), *arrow; wound; shaft* of a spear
4551 maççâ' (1), *stone quarry; projectile*
1002 bŏlis (1), *javelin, projectile*

DARTS
7626 shêbeṭ (1), *stick; clan, family*
7973 shelach (1), *spear; shoot of growth*
8455 tôwthâch (1), *stout club*
956 bĕlŏs (1), *spear or arrow*

DASH
5062 nâgaph (1), to *strike*
5310 nâphats (2), to *dash* to pieces; *to scatter*
7376 râṭash (1), to *dash down*
4350 prŏskŏptō (2), to *trip up; to strike*

DASHED
7376 râṭash (4), to *dash down*
7492 râ'ats (1), to *break in pieces; to harass*

DASHETH
5310 nâphats (1), to *dash* to pieces; *to scatter*

English

DATHAN

6327 pûwts (1), to *dash in pieces; to disperse*

DATHAN

1885 Dâthân (10), *Dathan*

DAUB

2902 ṭûwach (1), to *whitewash*

DAUBED

2560 châmar (1), to *glow; to smear*
2902 ṭûwach (6), to *whitewash*

DAUBING

2915 ṭîyach (1), *plaster, whitewash coating*

DAUGHTER

1004 bayith (1), *house; temple; family, tribe*
1121 bên (1), *son, descendant*
1323 bath (270), *daughter, descendant*
3618 kallâh (13), *bride; son's wife*
2364 thugatêr (24), *female child*
2365 thugatriŏn (2), *little daughter*
3565 numphê (3), young *married woman*

DAUGHTER'S

1323 bath (3), *daughter, descendant, woman*

DAUGHTERS

1121 bên (244), *son, descendant*
3618 kallâh (3), *bride*
2364 thugatêr (5), *female child, or descendant*
5043 tĕknŏn (1), *child*

DAVID

1732 Dâvîd (1019), *loving*
1138 Dabid (58), *loving*

DAVID'S

1732 Dâvîd (53), *loving*
1138 Dabid (1), *loving*

DAWN

1306 diaugazō (1), to *dawn, shine through*
2020 ĕpiphôskō (1), to *grow light*

DAWNING

5399 nesheph (2), *dusk, dawn*
5927 'âlâh (1), to *ascend, be high, mount*
6079 'aph'aph (1), *morning ray*
6437 pânâh (1), to *turn, to face*

DAY

215 'ôwr (1), to *be luminous*
216 'ôwr (1), *luminary; lightning; happiness*
1242 bôqer (4), *morning*
3117 yôwm (1250), *day; time period*
3118 yôwm (Ch.) (4), *day; time period*
3119 yôwmâm (53), *daily*
4283 mochŏrâth (2), *tomorrow, next day*
5399 nesheph (1), *dusk, dawn*

7837 shachar (6), *dawn*
737 arti (1), just *now; at once*
827 augē (1), *radiance, dawn*
839 auriŏn (1), *to-morrow*
1773 ĕnnuchŏn (1), *by night*
1887 ĕpauriŏn (8), *to-morrow*
2250 hēmĕra (200), *day; period of time*
3574 nuchthĕmĕrŏn (1), *full day*
3588+2596+2250 hŏ (2), *"the," definite article*
4594 sēmĕrŏn (38), *this day, today, now*
4594+2250 sēmĕrŏn (1), *this day, today, now*
4595 sēpō (1), to *putrefy, rot*
5459 phōsphŏrŏs (1), *morning-star*
5610 hōra (1), *hour, i.e. a unit of time*

DAY'S

3117 yôwm (6), *day; time period*
2250 hēmĕra (1), *day; period of time*
4594 sēmĕrŏn (1), *this day, today, now*

DAYS

3117 yôwm (665), *day; time period*
3118 yôwm (Ch.) (9), *day; time period*
8543 tᵉmôwl (1), (day before) *yesterday*
1909 ĕpi (2), *on, upon*
2250 hēmĕra (154), *day; period of time*
5066 tĕtartaiŏs (1), of the *fourth day*

DAYS'

3117 yôwm (13), *day; time period*

DAYSMAN

3198 yâkach (1), to *decide, justify, convict*

DAYSPRING

7837 shachar (1), *dawn*
395 anatŏlē (1), *dawn of sun; east*

DAYTIME

3119 yôwmâm (8), *daily*

DEACON

1247 diakŏnĕō (2), to *act as a deacon*

DEACONS

1249 diakŏnŏs (3), *attendant, deacon(-ess)*

DEAD

1472 gᵉvîyâh (1), *dead body*
1478 gâva' (1), to *expire, die*
4191 mûwth (136), to *die; to kill*
4194 mâveth (7), *death; dead*
5038 nᵉbêlâh (7), *carcase or carrion*
5315 nephesh (8), *life; breath; soul; wind*

6297 peger (6), *carcase; corpse*
7496 râphâ' (7), *dead*
7703 shâdad (1), to *ravage*
581 apŏgĕnŏmĕnŏs (1), *deceased*
599 apŏthnēskō (29), to *die off*
2258 ēn (1), I *was*
2289 thanatŏō (1), to *kill*
2348 thnēskō (12), to *die, be dead*
2837 kŏimaō (1), to *slumber; to decease*
3498 nĕkrŏs (130), *corpse; dead*
3499 nĕkrŏō (2), to *deaden, i.e. to subdue*
4430 ptōma (3), *corpse, carrion*
4880 sunapŏthnēskō (1), to *decease with*
5053 tĕlĕutaō (3), to *finish life, i.e. expire*

DEADLY

4194 mâveth (1), *death; dead*
5315 nephesh (1), *life; breath; soul; wind*
2286 thanasimŏs (1), *poisonous, deadly*
2287 thanatēphŏrŏs (1), *fatal, i.e. bringing death*
2288 thanatŏs (2), *death*

DEADNESS

3500 nĕkrōsis (1), *death, deadness*

DEAF

2790 chârash (1), to *be silent; to be deaf*
2795 chêrêsh (9), *deaf*
2974 kōphŏs (5), *deaf or silent*

DEAL

1580 gâmal (2), to *benefit or requite; to wean*
6213 'âsâh (26), to *do*
6536 pâraç (1), to *split, distribute*
4054 pĕrissŏtĕrŏn (1), *more superabundantly*

DEALEST

6213 'âsâh (1), to *do*

DEALETH

6213 'âsâh (7), to *do*
4374 prŏsphĕrō (1), to *present to; to treat as*

DEALINGS

1697 dâbâr (1), *word; matter; thing*
4798 sugchraŏmai (1), to *have dealings with*

DEALT

1580 gâmal (2), to *benefit or requite; to wean*
2505 châlaq (2), to *be smooth; be slippery*
6213 'âsâh (18), to *do or make*
1793 ĕntugchanō (1), to *entreat, petition*
2686 katasŏphizŏmai (1), to *be crafty against*
3307 mĕrizō (1), to *apportion, bestow*

4160 pŏiĕō (2), to *do*

DEAR

3357 yaqqîyr (1), *precious*
26 agapē (1), *love*
27 agapētŏs (3), *beloved*
1784 ĕntimŏs (1), *valued, considered precious*
5093 timiŏs (1), *honored, esteemed, or beloved*

DEARTH

1226 batstsôreth (1), *drought*
7458 râ'âb (5), *hunger*
3042 limŏs (2), *scarcity, famine*

DEATH

4191 mûwth (82), to *die; to kill*
4192 Mûwth (1), "*To die for the son*"
4193 môwth (Ch.) (1), *death*
4194 mâveth (126), *death; dead*
6757 tsalmâveth (18), *shade of death*
7523 râtsach (1), to *murder*
8546 tᵉmûwthâh (1), *execution, death*
336 anairĕsis (5), *act of killing*
337 anairĕō (2), to *take away, i.e. abolish, murder*
520 apagō (1), to *take away*
599 apŏthnēskō (1), to *die off*
615 apŏktĕinō (6), to *kill outright; to destroy*
1935 ĕpithanatiŏs (1), *doomed to death*
2079 ĕschatŏs (1), *finally, i.e. at the extremity*
2288 thanatŏs (113), *death*
2289 thanatŏō (7), to *kill*
5054 tĕlĕutē (1), *deceasedness, death*

DEATHS

4194 mâveth (1), *death; dead*
4463 mâmôwth (2), *mortal disease, death*
2288 thanatŏs (1), *death*

DEBASE

8213 shâphêl (1), to *humiliate*

DEBATE

4683 matstsâh (1), *quarrel*
7378 rîyb (2), to *hold a controversy; to defend*
2054 ĕris (1), *quarrel, i.e. wrangling*

DEBATES

2054 ĕris (1), *quarrel, i.e. wrangling*

DEBIR

1688 Dᵉbîyr (14), *inmost part of the sanctuary*

DEBORAH

1683 Dᵉbôwrâh (10), *bee*

DEBT

3027 yâd (1), *hand; power*

5378 nâshâ' (1), to *lend*
on interest
5386 nᵉshîy (1), *debt*
1156 danĕiŏn (1), *loan;*
debt
3782 ŏphĕilĕ (1), *sum*
owed; *obligation*
3783 ŏphĕilĕma (1), *due;*
moral fault
3784 ŏphĕilō (1), to *owe;*
to *be under obligation*

DEBTOR
2326 chôwb (1), *debt*
3781 ŏphĕilĕtēs (2),
person *indebted*
3784 ŏphĕilō (1), to *owe;*
to *be under obligation*

DEBTORS
3781 ŏphĕilĕtēs (3),
person *indebted*
5533 chrĕŏphĕilĕtēs (2),
indebted person

DEBTS
4859 mashshâ'âh (1),
secured *loan*
3783 ŏphĕilĕma (1), *due;*
moral fault

DECAPOLIS
1179 Dĕkapŏlis (3),
ten-city region

DECAY
4131 môwṭ (1), to *slip,*
shake, fall

DECAYED
2723 chorbâh (1),
desolation, dry desert
3782 kâshal (1), to *totter,*
waver; to *falter*

DECAYETH
2717 chârab (1), to
parch; desolate, destroy
4355 mâkak (1), to
tumble in ruins
3822 palaiŏō (1), to
become worn out

DECEASE
1841 ĕxŏdŏs (2), *exit*, i.e.
death

DECEASED
7496 râphâ' (1), *dead*
5053 tĕlĕutaō (1), to
finish life, i.e. *expire*

DECEIT
4820 mirmâh (19), *fraud*
4860 mashshâ'ôwn (1),
dissimulation
7423 rᵉmîyâh (2),
remissness; treachery
8267 sheqer (1), *untruth*
8496 tôk (2), *oppression*
8649 tormâh (4), *fraud*
539 apatē (1), *delusion*
1387 dŏliŏō (1), to
practice deceit
1388 dŏlŏs (2), *wile,*
deceit, trickery
4106 planē (1),
fraudulence; straying

DECEITFUL
3577 kâzâb (1),
falsehood; idol
4820 mirmâh (8), *fraud*
6121 ʻâqôb (1),
fraudulent; tracked

6280 ʻâthar (1), to *be,*
make abundant
7423 rᵉmîyâh (4),
remissness; treachery
8267 sheqer (2), *untruth;*
sham
8501 tâkâk (1), to
dissever, i.e. *crush*
8649 tormâh (1), *fraud*
539 apatē (1), *delusion*
1386 dŏliŏs (1), *guileful,*
tricky

DECEITFULLY
898 bâgad (2), to *act*
covertly
2048 hâthal (1), to
deride, mock
4820 mirmâh (3), *fraud*
6231 ʻâshaq (1), to
oppress; to *defraud*
7423 rᵉmîyâh (3),
remissness; treachery
1389 dŏlŏō (1), to
adulterate, falsify

DECEITFULNESS
539 apatē (3), *delusion*

DECEITS
4123 mahăthallâh (1),
delusion
4820 mirmâh (1), *fraud*

DECEIVABLENESS
539 apatē (1), *delusion*

DECEIVE
2048 hâthal (1), to
deride, mock
3884 lûwlĕ' (1), *if not*
5377 nâshâ' (7), to *lead*
astray, to *delude*
6601 pâthâh (2), to *be,*
make simple; to *delude*
7952 shâlâh (1), to
mislead
538 apataō (1), to *cheat,*
delude
1818 ĕxapataō (3), to
seduce wholly, deceive
4105 planaō (10), to
wander; to *deceive*
4106 planē (1),
fraudulence; straying

DECEIVED
2048 hâthal (2), to
deride, mock
5377 nâshâ' (5), to *lead*
astray, to *delude*
6231 ʻâshaq (1), to
oppress; to *defraud*
6601 pâthâh (6), to *be,*
make simple; to *delude*
7411 râmâh (4), to *hurl;*
to *shoot;* to *delude*
7683 shâgag (1), to *stray;*
to *sin*
7686 shâgâh (1), to *stray,*
wander; to *transgress*
8582 tâ'âh (1), to
vacillate, reel or stray
538 apataō (2), to *cheat,*
delude
1818 ĕxapataō (1), to
seduce wholly, deceive
4105 planaō (10), to
wander; to *deceive*

DECEIVER
5230 nâkal (1), to *act*
treacherously

7686 shâgâh (1), to *stray,*
wander; to *transgress*
8591 tâ'a' (1), to *cheat;* to
maltreat
4108 planŏs (2), *roving;*
impostor or misleader

DECEIVERS
4108 planŏs (2), *roving;*
impostor or misleader
5423 phrĕnapatēs (1),
seducer, misleader

DECEIVETH
7411 râmâh (1), to *hurl;*
to *shoot;* to *delude*
538 apataō (1), to *cheat,*
delude
4105 planaō (3), to *roam,*
wander; to *deceive*
5422 phrĕnapataō (1), to
delude, deceive

DECEIVING
3884 paralŏgizŏmai (1),
to *delude, deceive*
4105 planaō (1), to *roam,*
wander; to *deceive*

DECEIVINGS
539 apatē (1), *delusion*

DECENTLY
2156 ĕuschēmŏnŏs (1),
fittingly, properly

DECIDED
2782 chârats (1), to *be*
alert, to *decide*

DECISION
2742 chârûwts (2),
diligent, earnest

DECK
3302 yâphâh (1), to *be*
beautiful
5710 ʻâdâh (1), to
remove; to *bedeck*

DECKED
5710 ʻâdâh (3), to
remove; to *bedeck*
7234 râbad (1), to *spread*
5558 chrusŏō (2), to
guild, bespangle

DECKEDST
5710 ʻâdâh (1), to
remove; to *bedeck*
6213 ʻâsâh (1), to *do*

DECKEST
5710 ʻâdâh (1), to
remove; to *bedeck*

DECKETH
3547 kâhan (1), to
officiate as a priest

DECLARATION
262 'achvâh (1),
utterance
6575 pârâshâh (1),
exposition
1335 diēgĕsis (1), *recital,*
written account

DECLARE
560 'âmar (Ch.) (1), to
say, speak
874 bâ'ar (1), to *explain*
952 bûwr (1), to *examine*
1696 dâbar (1), to *speak,*
say; to *subdue*
3045 yâda' (3), to *know*
5046 nâgad (46), to
announce

5608 çâphar (20), to
enumerate; to *recount*
7878 sîyach (1), to
ponder, muse aloud
8085 shâma' (1), to *hear*
intelligently
312 anaggĕllō (2), to
announce, report
518 apaggĕllō (2), to
announce, proclaim
1107 gnōrizō (3), to
make known, reveal
1213 dēlŏō (1), to *make*
plain by words
1334 diēgĕŏmai (1), to
relate fully, describe
1555 ĕkdiēgĕŏmai (1), to
narrate through wholly
1718 ĕmphanizō (1), to
show forth
1732 ĕndĕixis (2),
demonstration
2097 ĕuaggĕlizō (1), to
announce good news
2605 kataggĕllō (1), to
proclaim, promulgate
3853 paraggĕllō (1), to
enjoin; to *instruct*
5419 phrazō (2), to
indicate, to *expound*

DECLARED
559 'âmar (1), to *say,*
speak
1696 dâbar (1), to *speak,*
say; to *subdue*
3045 yâda' (3), to *know*
5046 nâgad (13), to
announce
5608 çâphar (4), to
enumerate; to *recount*
6567 pârash (1), to
separate; to *specify*
8085 shâma' (1), to *hear*
312 anaggĕllō (2), to
announce, report
394 anatithĕmai (1), to
set forth a declaration
518 apaggĕllō (1), to
announce, proclaim
1107 gnōrizō (1), to
make known, reveal
1213 dēlŏō (2), to *make*
plain by words
1229 diaggĕllō (1), to
herald thoroughly
1334 diēgĕŏmai (2), to
relate fully, describe
1834 ĕxēgĕŏmai (4), to
tell, relate again
2097 ĕuaggĕlizō (1), to
announce good news
3724 hŏrizō (1), to
appoint, decree, specify
5319 phanĕrŏō (1), to
render apparent

DECLARETH
5046 nâgad (4), to
announce

DECLARING
5046 nâgad (1), to
announce
1555 ĕkdiēgĕŏmai (1), to
narrate through wholly
1834 ĕxēgĕŏmai (1), to
tell, relate again
2605 kataggĕllō (1), to
proclaim, promulgate

DECLINE
5186 nâṭâh (3), to *stretch* or *spread out*
5493 çûwr (1), to *turn off*
7847 sâṭâh (1), to *deviate* from *duty, go astray*

DECLINED
5186 nâṭâh (3), to *stretch* or *spread out*
5493 çûwr (1), to *turn off*

DECLINETH
5186 nâṭâh (2), to *stretch* or *spread out*

DECREASE
4591 mâ'aṭ (1), to *be, make small* or *few*
1642 ĕlattŏō (1), to *lessen*

DECREASED
2637 châçêr (1), to *lack*; to *fail, want, make less*

DECREE
633 'ĕçâr (Ch.) (7), *edict, decree*
1504 gâzar (1), to *exclude; decide*
1510 gᵉzêrâh (Ch.) (2), *decree, decision*
1697 dâbâr (1), *word; matter; thing*
1881 dâth (9), royal *edict* or *statute*
1882 dâth (Ch.) (3), *Law; royal edict* or *statute*
2706 chôq (7), *appointment; allotment*
2710 châqaq (2), to *engrave*; to *enact laws*
2940 ṭa'am (1), *taste; intelligence; mandate*
2942 ṭᵉ'êm (Ch.) (13), *judgment; account*
3982 ma'ămar (1), *edict, command*
6599 pithgâm (1), *judicial sentence; edict*
1378 dŏgma (1), *law*

DECREED
1504 gâzar (1), to *destroy, exclude; decide*
2706 chôq (1), *appointment; allotment*
2782 chârats (1), to *be alert, to decide*
6965 qùwm (1), to *rise*
2919 krinō (1), to *decide*; to *try, condemn, punish*

DECREES
2711 chêqeq (1), *enactment, resolution*
1378 dŏgma (2), *law*

DEDAN
1719 Dᵉdân (11), *Dedan*

DEDANIM
1720 Dᵉdânîym (1), *Dedanites*

DEDICATE
2596 chânak (1), to *initiate* or *discipline*
6942 qâdâsh (3), to *be, make clean*

DEDICATED
2596 chânak (3), to *initiate* or *discipline*
2764 chêrem (1), *doomed* object

DEEDS (second column)
6942 qâdâsh (7), to *be, make clean*
6944 qôdesh (12), *sacred place* or *thing*
1457 ĕgkainizō (1), to *inaugurate*

DEDICATING
2598 chănukkâh (2), *dedication*

DEDICATION
2597 chănukkâ' (Ch.) (4), *dedication*
2598 chănukkâh (6), *dedication*
1456 ĕgkainia (1), Feast of *Dedication*

DEED
199 'ûwlâm (2), *however* or *on the contrary*
1697 dâbâr (3), *word; matter; thing*
3559 kûwn (1), to *set up; establish, fix, prepare*
4639 ma'ăseh (1), *action; labor*
2041 ĕrgŏn (6), *work*
2108 ĕuĕrgĕsia (1), *beneficence*
4162 pŏiēsis (1), *action*, i.e. *performance*
4334 prŏsĕrchŏmai (1), to *come near, visit*

DEEDS
1578 gᵉmûwlâh (1), *act; service; reward*
1697 dâbâr (2), *word; matter; thing*
4639 ma'ăseh (2), *action; labor*
5949 'ălîylâh (2), *opportunity, action*
6467 pô'al (2), *act* or *work, deed*
1411 dunamis (1), *force, power, miracle*
2041 ĕrgŏn (16), *work*
2735 katŏrthōma (1), *made fully upright*
3739+4238 hŏs (1), *who, which, what, that*
4234 praxis (3), *act; function*

DEEMED
5282 hupŏnŏĕō (1), to *think*; to *expect*

DEEP
4113 mahămôrâh (1), (poss.) *abyss, pits*
4278 mechqâr (1), *recess, unexplored* place
4615 ma'ămâq (2), *deep place*
4688 mᵉtsôwlâh (5), *deep place*
4950 mishqâ' (1), *clear pond* with *settled* water
5994 'ămîyq (Ch.) (1), *profound, unsearchable*
6009 'âmaq (5), to *be, make deep*
6013 'âmôq (8), *deep, profound*
6683 tsûwlâh (1), *watery abyss*
7290 râdam (2), to *stupefy*

DEEP (third column)
8257 shâqa' (1), to *be overflowed; to cease*
8328 sheresh (1), *root*
8415 tᵉhôwm (20), *abyss of the sea*, i.e. the *deep*
8639 tardêmâh (7), *trance, deep sleep*
12 abussŏs (2), *deep place, abyss*
899 bathŏs (3), *extent; mystery*, i.e. *deep*
901 bathus (2), *deep, profound*
1037 buthŏs (1), *deep sea*
2532+900 kai (1), *and; or; even; also*

DEEPER
6012 'âmêq (1), *deep, obscure*
6013 'âmôq (8), *deep, profound*

DEEPLY
6009 'âmaq (2), to *be, make deep*
389 anastĕnazō (1), to *sigh deeply*

DEEPNESS
899 bathŏs (1), *extent; mystery*, i.e. *deep*

DEEPS
4688 mᵉtsôwlâh (3), *deep place*
8415 tᵉhôwm (1), *abyss of the sea*, i.e. the *deep*

DEER
3180 yachmûwr (1), *deer*

DEFAMED
987 blasphēmĕō (1), to *speak impiously*

DEFAMING
1681 dibbâh (1), *slander, bad report*

DEFEAT
6565 pârar (2), to *break up; to violate, frustrate*

DEFENCE
1220 betser (1), *gold*
2646 chuppâh (1), *canopy*
4043 mâgên (2), *small shield (buckler); animal skin*
4686 mâtsûwd (1), *net* or *capture; fastness*
4692 mâtsôwr (2), *siege-mound; distress*
4869 misgâb (7), *refuge*
5526 çâkak (1), to *fence in; cover over; protect*
6738 tsêl (3), *shade; protection*
626 apŏlŏgĕŏmai (1), to *give an account*
627 apŏlŏgia (3), *plea* or *verbal defense*

DEFENCED
1219 bâtsar (5), to *be inaccessible*
4013 mibtsâr (4), *fortification; defender*

DEFEND
1598 gânan (7), to *protect*
3467 yâsha' (1), to *make safe, free*
7682 sâgab (2), to *be, make lofty; be safe*

DEFEND (fourth column)
8199 shâphaṭ (1), to *judge*

DEFENDED
5337 nâtsal (1), to *deliver*
292 amunōmai (1), to *protect, help*

DEFENDEST
5526 çâkak (1), to *fence in; cover over; protect*

DEFENDING
1598 gânan (1), to *protect*

DEFER
309 'âchar (2), to *remain; to delay*
748 'ârak (1), to *be, make long*

DEFERRED
309 'âchar (1), to *remain; to delay*
4900 mâshak (1), to *draw out; to be tall*
306 anaballŏmai (1), to *put off, adjourn*

DEFERRETH
748 'ârak (1), to *be, make long*

DEFIED
2194 zâ'am (1), to *be enraged*
2778 châraph (5), to *spend the winter*

DEFILE
1351 gâ'al (2), to *soil, stain; desecrate*
2490 châlal (2), to *profane, defile*
2930 ṭâmê' (25), to *be morally contaminated*
2936 ṭânaph (1), to *soil, make dirty*
733 arsĕnŏkŏitēs (1), *sodomite*
2840 kŏinŏō (6), to *make profane*
3392 miainō (1), to *contaminate*
5351 phthĕirō (1), to *spoil, ruin; to deprave*

DEFILED
1351 gâ'al (2), to *soil, stain; desecrate*
2490 châlal (5), to *profane, defile*
2610 chânêph (3), to *soil, be defiled*
2930 ṭâmê' (44), to *be morally contaminated*
2931 ṭâmê' (5), *foul; ceremonially impure*
2933 ṭâmâh (1), to *be ceremonially impure*
5953 'âlal (1), to *glean; to overdo*
6031 'ânâh (1), to *afflict, be afflicted*
6942 qâdâsh (1), to *be, make clean*
2839 kŏinŏs (1), *common*, i.e. *profane*
3392 miainō (4), to *contaminate*
3435 mŏlunō (3), to *soil, make impure*

DEFILEDST
2490 châlal (1), to *profane, defile*

DEFILETH
2490 châlal (1), to profane, defile
2610 chânêph (1), to soil, be defiled
2930 ṭâmê' (1), to be foul; be morally contaminated
2840 kôinôō (5), to make profane
4695 spilôō (1), to stain or soil

DEFRAUD
6231 'âshaq (1), to oppress; to defraud
650 apŏstĕrĕō (3), to despoil or defraud
4122 plĕŏnĕktĕō (1), to be covetous

DEFRAUDED
6231 'âshaq (2), to oppress; to defraud
650 apŏstĕrĕō (1), to despoil or defraud
4122 plĕŏnĕktĕō (1), to be covetous

DEFY
2194 zâ'am (2), to be enraged
2778 châraph (3), to spend the winter

DEGENERATE
5494 çûwr (1), turned off; deteriorated

DEGREE
898 bathmŏs (1), grade of dignity
5011 tapĕinŏs (2), humiliated, lowly

DEGREES
4609 ma'ălâh (24), thought arising

DEHAVITES
1723 Dahăvâ' (Ch.) (1), Dahava

DEKAR
1857 Deqer (1), stab

DELAIAH
1806 Dᵉlâyâh (6), Jehovah has delivered

DELAY
309 'âchar (1), to remain; to delay; to procrastinate
311 anabŏlē (1), putting off, delay
3635 ŏknĕō (1), to be slow, delay

DELAYED
954 bûwsh (1), to be disappointed; delayed
4102 mâhahh (1), to be reluctant

DELAYETH
5549 chrŏnizō (2), to take time, i.e. linger

DELECTABLE
2530 châmad (1), to delight in; lust for

DELICACIES
4764 strēnŏs (1), luxury, sensuality

DELICATE
6026 'ânag (1), to be soft or pliable
6028 'ânôg (3), luxurious
8588 ta'ănûwg (1), luxury; delight

DELICATELY
4574 ma'ădân (2), delicacy; pleasure
6445 pânaq (1), to enervate, reduce vigor
5172 truphē (1), luxury or debauchery

DELICATENESS
6026 'ânag (1), to be soft or pliable

DELICATES
5730 'êden (1), pleasure

DELICIOUSLY
4763 strēniaō (2), to be luxurious, live sensually

DELIGHT
1523 gîyl (1), rejoice
2530 châmad (1), to delight in; lust for
2531 chemed (1), delight
2654 châphêts (17), to be pleased with, desire
2655 châphêts (1), pleased with
2656 chêphets (3), pleasure; desire
2836 châshaq (1), to join; to love, delight
4574 ma'ădân (1), delicacy; pleasure
5276 nâ'êm (1), to be agreeable
6026 'ânag (6), to be soft or pliable
6027 ôneg (1), luxury
7521 râtsâh (2), to be pleased with
7522 râtsôwn (5), delight
8173 shâ'a' (4), to fondle, please or amuse (self)
dismay, i.e. stare
8191 sha'shûa' (4), enjoyment
8588 ta'ănûwg (1), luxury; delight
4913 sunēdŏmai (1), to rejoice in with oneself

DELIGHTED
2654 châphêts (10), to be pleased with, desire
5727 'âdan (1), to be soft or pleasant
6026 'ânag (1), to be soft or pliable

DELIGHTEST
7521 râtsâh (1), to be pleased with

DELIGHTETH
2654 châphêts (12), to be pleased with, desire
7521 râtsâh (2), to be pleased with

DELIGHTS
5730 'êden (1), pleasure
8191 sha'shûa' (3), enjoyment
8588 ta'ănûwg (2), luxury; delight

DELIGHTSOME
2656 chêphets (1), pleasure; desire

DELILAH
1807 Dᵉlîylâh (6), languishing

DELIVER
579 'ânâh (1), to meet, to happen
1350 gâ'al (1), to redeem; to be the next of kin
2502 châlats (5), to depart; to deliver
3467 yâsha' (3), to make safe, free
4042 mâgan (2), to rescue, to surrender
4422 mâlaṭ (17), to be delivered; be smooth
4672 mâtsâ' (1), to find or acquire; to occur
5186 nâṭâh (1), to stretch or spread out
5337 nâtsal (115), to deliver
5338 nᵉtsal (Ch.) (2), to extricate, deliver
5414 nâthan (78), to give
5462 çâgar (10), to shut up; to surrender
6299 pâdâh (3), to ransom; to release
6308 pâda' (1), to retrieve
6403 pâlaṭ (11), to escape; to deliver
6561 pâraq (1), to break off or crunch; to deliver
7725 shûwb (5), to turn back; to return
7804 shᵉzab (Ch.) (6), to leave; to free
8000 shᵉlam (Ch.) (1), to restore; be safe
8199 shâphaṭ (1), to judge
525 apallassō (1), to release; be reconciled
1325 didōmi (1), to give
1807 ĕxairĕō (2), to tear out; to select; to release
3860 paradidōmi (15), to hand over
4506 rhuŏmai (8), to rescue
5483 charizŏmai (2), to grant as a favor, rescue

DELIVERANCE
2020 hatstsâlâh (1), rescue, deliverance
3444 yᵉshûw'âh (2), deliverance; aid
6405 pallêṭ (1), escape
6413 pᵉlêyṭâh (5), escaped portion
8668 tᵉshûw'âh (5), rescue, deliverance
629 apŏlutrōsis (1), ransom in full
859 aphĕsis (1), pardon, freedom

DELIVERANCES
3444 yᵉshûw'âh (1), deliverance; aid

DELIVERED
2502 châlats (9), to depart; to deliver
3052 yᵉhab (Ch.) (1), to give

3205 yâlad (6), to bear young; to father a child
3467 yâsha' (8), to make safe, free
4042 mâgan (1), to rescue, to surrender
4422 mâlaṭ (16), to be delivered; be smooth
4560 mâçar (1), to set apart; apostatize
4672 mâtsâ' (1), to find or acquire; to occur
5234 nâkar (1), to acknowledge, care for
5337 nâtsal (58), to deliver
5414 nâthan (98), to give
5462 çâgar (6), to shut up; to surrender
5674 'âbar (1), to cross over; to transition
6299 pâdâh (2), to ransom; to release
6403 pâlaṭ (3), to slip out, i.e. escape; to deliver
6487 piqqâdôwn (2), deposit
7804 shᵉzab (Ch.) (2), to leave; to free
325 anadidōmi (1), to hand over, deliver
525 apallassō (1), to release; be reconciled
591 apŏdidōmi (2), to give away
1080 gĕnnaō (1), to procreate, regenerate
1325 didōmi (2), to give
1560 ĕkdŏtŏs (1), surrendered
1659 ĕlĕuthĕrŏō (1), to exempt, liberate
1807 ĕxairĕō (2), to tear out; to select; to release
1825 ĕxĕgĕirō (1), to resuscitate; release
1929 ĕpididōmi (2), to give over
2673 katargĕō (1), to be, render entirely useless
3860 paradidōmi (44), to hand over
4506 rhuŏmai (9), to rescue
5088 tiktō (5), to produce from seed

DELIVEREDST
5414 nâthan (1), to give
3860 paradidōmi (2), to hand over

DELIVERER
3467 yâsha' (2), to make safe, free
5337 nâtsal (1), to deliver
6403 pâlaṭ (5), to slip out, i.e. escape; to deliver
3086 lutrōtēs (1), redeemer, deliverer
4506 rhuŏmai (1), to rescue

DELIVEREST
5337 nâtsal (1), to deliver
6403 pâlaṭ (1), to slip out, i.e. escape; to deliver

DELIVERETH
2502 châlats (2), to depart; to deliver
5337 nâtsal (7), to deliver

English

DELIVERING
5414 nâthan (1), to *give*
6403 pâlaṭ (1), to *slip out*, i.e. *escape*; to *deliver*
6475 pâtsâh (1), to *rend*, i.e. *open*
7804 sheᵉzab (Ch.) (1), to *leave*; to *free*

DELIVERING
1807 ĕxairĕō (1), to *tear out*; to *select*; to *release*
3860 paradidōmi (2), to *hand over*

DELIVERY
3205 yâlad (1), to *bear young*; to *father a child*

DELUSION
4106 planē (1), *fraudulence*; *straying*

DELUSIONS
8586 ta'ălûwl (1), *caprice* (as a fit *coming on*)

DEMAND
7592 shâ'al (3), to *ask*
7595 sheᵉêlâ' (Ch.) (1), judicial *decision*

DEMANDED
559 'âmar (1), to *say*
7592 shâ'al (1), to *ask*
7593 sheᵉêl (Ch.) (1), to *ask*
1905 ĕpĕrōtaō (2), to *inquire, seek*
4441 punthanŏmai (2), to *ask* for information

DEMAS
1214 Dēmas (3), *Demas*

DEMETRIUS
1216 Dēmētriŏs (3), *Demetrius*

DEMONSTRATION
585 apŏdĕixis (1), *manifestation, proof*

DEN
1358 gôb (Ch.) (10), lion *pit*
3975 meᵉûwrâh (1), serpent's *hole* or *den*
4583 mâ'ôwn (2), *retreat* or asylum *dwelling*
4585 meᵉôwnâh (1), *abode*
4631 meᵉârâh (1), dark *cavern*
5520 çôk (1), *hut* of *entwined* boughs
4693 spēlaiŏn (3), *cavern; hiding-place*

DENIED
3584 kâchash (2), to *lie, disown*; to *disappoint*
4513 mâna' (1), to *deny, refuse*
533 aparnĕŏmai (2), *disown, deny*
720 arnĕŏmai (14), to *disavow, reject*

DENIETH
720 arnĕŏmai (4), to *disavow, reject*

DENOUNCE
5046 nâgad (1), to *announce*

DENS
695 'ereb (1), *hiding place; lair*

DEPARTED
935 bôw' (1), to *go, come*
1540 gâlâh (3), to *denude; uncover*
1980 hâlak (3), to *walk; live a certain way*
3212 yâlak (47), to *walk; to live; to carry*
3318 yâtsâ' (10), to *go, bring out*
4185 mûwsh (2), to *withdraw*
5074 nâdad (1), to *rove, flee*; to *drive away*
5265 nâça' (30), *start on a journey*
5493 çûwr (31), to *turn off*
5709 'ădâ' (Ch.) (1), to *pass on or continue*
5927 'âlâh (1), to *ascend, be high, mount*
321 anagō (2), to *lead up; to bring out; to sail*
402 anachōrĕō (8), to *retire, withdraw*
525 apallassō (1), to *release; be reconciled*
565 apĕrchŏmai (24), to *go off*, i.e. *depart*
630 apŏluō (1), to *relieve, release*; to *let die, pardon or divorce*
673 apŏchōrizō (2), to *rend apart; to separate*
868 aphistēmi (6), to *desist, desert*
1316 diachōrizŏmai (1), to *remove* (oneself)
1330 diĕrchŏmai (1), to *traverse, travel through*
1607 ĕkpŏrĕuŏmai (1), to *depart, be discharged*
1826 ĕxĕimi (1), *leave; escape*
1831 ĕxĕrchŏmai (22), to *issue; to leave*
2718 katĕrchŏmai (1), to *go, come down*
3327 mĕtabainō (3), to *depart, move from*
3332 mĕtairō (2), to *move on, leave*
3855 paragō (1), to *go along or away*
4198 pŏrĕuŏmai (6), to *go, come; to travel*
5562 chōrĕō (1), to *pass, enter; to hold, admit*
5563 chōrizō (1), to *part; to go away*

DEPARTETH
3212 yâlak (2), to *walk; to live; to carry*
4185 mûwsh (2), to *withdraw*
5493 çûwr (3), to *turn off*
672 apŏchōrĕō (1), to *go away, leave*

DEPARTING
3318 yâtsâ' (2), to *go, bring out*
5253 nâçag (1), to *retreat*
5493 çûwr (2), to *turn off*
672 apŏchōrĕō (1), to *go away, leave*
867 aphixis (1), *departure, leaving*
868 aphistēmi (1), to *desist, desert*

DEPART
1540 gâlâh (1), to *denude; uncover*
1980 hâlak (3), to *walk; live a certain way*
3212 yâlak (15), to *walk; to live; to carry*
3249 yâçûwr (1), *departing*
3318 yâtsâ' (3), to *go, bring out*
3363 yâqa' (1), to *be dislocated*
3868 lûwz (2), to *depart; to be perverse*
4185 mûwsh (8), to *withdraw*
5493 çûwr (42), to *turn off*
5927 'âlâh (2), to *ascend, be high, mount*
6852 tsâphar (1), to *return*
7971 shâlach (4), to *send away*
8159 shâ'âh (1), to *be nonplussed, bewildered*
321 anagō (1), to *lead up; to bring out; to sail*
360 analuō (1), to *depart*
565 apĕrchŏmai (4), to *go off*, i.e. *depart*
630 apŏluō (2), to *relieve, release*
672 apŏchōrĕō (1), to *go away, leave*
868 aphistēmi (4), to *desist, desert*
1607 ĕkpŏrĕuŏmai (2), to *depart, be discharged*
1633 ĕkchōrĕō (1), to *depart, go away*
1826 ĕxĕimi (1), *leave; escape*
1831 ĕxĕrchŏmai (7), to *issue; to leave*
3327 mĕtabainō (3), to *depart, move from*
4198 pŏrĕuŏmai (5), to *go, come; to travel*
5217 hupagō (1), to *withdraw or retire*
5562 chōrĕō (6), to *pass, enter; to hold, admit*

DENY
3584 kâchash (3), to *lie, disown*; to *disappoint, cringe*
4513 mâna' (1), to *deny, refuse*
7725 shûwb (1), to *turn back*; to *return*
483 antilĕgō (1), to *dispute, refuse*
533 aparnĕŏmai (11), *disown, deny*
720 arnĕŏmai (7), to *disavow, reject*

DENYING
720 arnĕŏmai (4), to *disavow, reject*

DEPARTURE
3318 yâtsâ' (1), to *go, bring out*
359 analusis (1), *departure*

DEPOSED
5182 neᵉchath (Ch.) (1), to *descend; to depose*

DEPRIVED
5382 nâshâh (1), to *forget*
6485 pâqad (1), to *visit, care for, count*
7921 shâkôl (1), to *miscarry*

DEPTH
6009 'âmaq (1), to *be, make deep*
6012 'âmêq (1), *deep, obscure*
8415 teᵉhôwm (5), *abyss* of the sea, i.e. the *deep*
899 bathŏs (3), *extent; mystery*, i.e. *deep*
3989 pĕlagŏs (1), deep or *open sea*

DEPTHS
4615 ma'ămâq (3), *deep place*
4688 meᵉtsôwlâh (2), *deep place*
6010 'êmeq (1), broad *depression* or valley
8415 teᵉhôwm (10), *abyss* of the sea, i.e. the *deep*
899 bathŏs (3), *extent; mystery*, i.e. *deep*

DEPUTIES
6346 pechâh (2), *prefect, officer*
446 anthupatŏs (1), Roman *proconsul*

DEPUTY
5324 nâtsab (1), to *station*
446 anthupatŏs (4), Roman *proconsul*

DERBE
1191 Dĕrbē (4), *Derbe*

DERIDE
7832 sâchaq (1), to *laugh; to scorn; to play*

DERIDED
1592 ĕkmuktĕrizō (2), to *sneer at, ridicule*

DERISION
3887 lûwts (1), to *scoff; to interpret; to intercede*
3932 lâ'ag (5), to *deride; to speak unintelligibly*
7047 qeleç (3), *laughing-stock*
7814 seᵉchôwq (5), *laughter; scorn*
7832 sâchaq (1), to *laugh; to scorn; to play*

DESCEND
3381 yârad (6), to *descend*
2597 katabainō (4), to *descend*

DESCENDED
3381 yârad (12), to *descend*
2597 katabainō (7), to *descend*

DESCENDETH
2718 katĕrchŏmai (1), to *go, come down*

DESCENDING
3381 yârad (1), to *descend*
2597 katabainō (7), to *descend*

DESCENT
35 agĕnĕalŏgĕtŏs (1), *unregistered* as to birth
1075 gĕnĕalŏgĕō (1), *trace in genealogy*
2600 katabasis (1), *declivity, slope*

DESCRIBE
3789 kâthab (4), to *write*

DESCRIBED
3789 kâthab (2), to *write*

DESCRIBETH
1125 graphō (1), to *write*
3004 lĕgō (1), to *say*

DESCRY
8446 tûwr (1), to *wander, meander* for trade

DESERT
1576 gᵉmûwl (1), *act; service; reward*
2723 chorbâh (1), *desolation, dry* desert
3452 yᵉshîymôwn (4), *desolation*
4057 midbâr (13), *desert; also speech; mouth*
6160 'ărâbâh (8), *desert, wasteland*
6728 tsîyîy (3), *desert-dweller; beast*
2048 ĕrēmŏs (12), *remote place, deserted place*

DESERTS
2723 chorbâh (2), *desolation, dry* desert
4941 mishpâṭ (1), *verdict; formal decree; justice*
6160 'ărâbâh (1), *desert, wasteland*
2047 ĕrēmia (1), place of *solitude, remoteness*
2048 ĕrēmŏs (1), *remote place, deserted place*

DESERVING
1576 gᵉmûwl (1), *act; service; reward*

DESIRABLE
2531 chemed (3), *delight*

DESIRE
15 'âbeh (1), *longing*
35 'abîyôwnâh (1), *caper-berry*
183 'âvâh (7), to *wish for, desire*
1156 bᵉâ' (Ch.) (1), to *seek or ask*
1245 bâqash (1), to *search out;* to *strive*
2530 châmad (4), to *delight in; lust for*
2532 chemdâh (3), *delight*

2654 châphêts (6), to *be pleased* with, *desire*
2655 châphêts (2), *pleased* with
2656 chêphets (9), *pleasure; desire*
2836 châshaq (1), to *join;* to *love, delight*
2837 chêsheq (1), *delight, desired thing*
3700 kâçaph (1), to *pine after;* to *fear*
4261 machmâd (3), *object of desire*
5315 nephesh (3), *life; breath; soul; wind*
5375+5315 nâsâ' (2), to *lift up*
7522 râtsôwn (3), *delight*
7592 shâ'al (3), to *ask*
7602 shâ'aph (1), to *be angry;* to *hasten*
8378 ta'ăvâh (14), *longing; delight*
8420 tâv (1), *mark, signature*
8669 tᵉshûwqâh (3), *longing*
154 aitĕō (5), to *ask* for
515 axiŏō (1), to *deem entitled* or *fit, worthy*
1934 ĕpizĕtĕō (2), to *demand,* to *crave*
1937 ĕpithumĕō (4), to *long* for
1939 ĕpithumia (3), *longing*
1971 ĕpipŏthĕō (1), *intensely crave*
1972 ĕpipŏthēsis (2), *longing* for
1974 ĕpipŏthia (1), *intense longing*
2065 ĕrōtaō (1), *interrogate;* to *request*
2107 ĕudŏkia (1), *delight, kindness, wish*
2206 zēlŏō (2), to *have warmth* of feeling for
2309 thĕlō (9), to *will;* to *desire;* to *choose*
3713 ŏrĕgŏmai (2), to *reach out after, long* for

DESIRED
183 'âvâh (5), to *wish for, desire*
559 'âmar (1), to *say, speak*
1156 bᵉâ' (Ch.) (2), to *seek or ask*
2530 châmad (5), to *delight in; lust for*
2532 chemdâh (1), *delight*
2654 châphêts (1), to *be pleased* with, *desire*
2656 chêphets (2), *pleasure; desire*
2836 châshaq (2), to *join;* to *love, delight*
3700 kâçaph (1), to *pine after;* to *fear*
7592 shâ'al (4), to *ask*
154 aitĕō (10), to *ask* for
1809 ĕxaitĕŏmai (1), to *demand*
1905 ĕpĕrōtaō (1), to *inquire, seek*

1934 ĕpizĕtĕō (1), to *demand,* to *crave*
1937 ĕpithumĕō (1), to *long* for
1939 ĕpithumia (1), *longing*
2065 ĕrōtaō (4), to *interrogate;* to *request*
2212 zētĕō (1), to *seek*
2309 thĕlō (1), to *will;* to *desire;* to *choose*
3870 parakalĕō (5), to *call, invite*

DESIREDST
7592 shâ'al (1), to *ask*
3870 parakalĕō (1), to *call, invite*

DESIRES
3970 ma'ăvay (1), *desire*
4862 mish'âlâh (1), *request*
2307 thĕlēma (1), *purpose; inclination*

DESIREST
2654 châphêts (2), to *be pleased* with, *desire*

DESIRETH
183 'âvâh (4), to *wish* for, *desire*
559 'âmar (1), to *say, speak*
2530 châmad (2), to *delight in; lust for*
2655 châphêts (1), *pleased* with
2656 chêphets (1), *pleasure; desire*
7592 shâ'al (1), to *ask*
7602 shâ'aph (1), to *be angry;* to *hasten*
8378 ta'ăvâh (3), *longing; delight*
1937 ĕpithumĕō (1), to *long* for
2065 ĕrōtaō (1), to *interrogate;* to *request*
2309 thĕlō (1), to *will;* to *desire;* to *choose*

DESIRING
154 aitĕō (2), to *ask* for
1937 ĕpithumĕō (1), to *long* for
1971 ĕpipŏthĕō (3), *intensely crave*
2212 zētĕō (2), to *seek*
2309 thĕlō (2), to *will;* to *desire;* to *choose*
3870 parakalĕō (2), to *call, invite*

DESIROUS
183 'âvâh (1), to *wish* for, *desire*
2309 thĕlō (3), to *will;* to *desire;* to *choose*
2442 himĕirŏmai (1), to *long for, desire*
2755 kĕnŏdŏxŏs (1), *self-conceited*

DESOLATE
490 'almânâh (2), *widow*
816 'âsham (6), to *be guilty;* to *be punished*
820 'ashmân (1), *uninhabited places*
910 bâdâd (1), *separate, alone*

1327 battâh (1), area of *desolation*
1565 galmûwd (2), *sterile, barren, desolate*
2717 chârab (5), to *parch* through drought; *desolate, destroy*
2723 chorbâh (7), *desolation, dry* desert
3173 yâchîyd (1), to *will;* to *only son; alone; beloved*
3341 yâtsath (1), to *burn* or *set on fire*
3456 yâsham (4), to *lie waste*
3582 kâchad (1), to *destroy;* to *hide*
4923 mᵉshammâh (2), *waste; object of horror*
5352 nâqâh (1), to *be, make clean;* to *be bare*
7722 shôw' (2), *tempest; devastation*
8047 shammâh (11), *ruin; consternation*
8074 shâmêm (43), to *devastate;* to *stupefy*
8076 shâmêm (8), *ruined, deserted*
8077 shᵉmâmâh (42), *devastation*
2048 ĕrēmŏs (4), *remote place, deserted place*
2049 ĕrēmŏō (2), to *lay waste*
3443 mŏnŏō (1), to *isolate,* i.e. *bereave*

DESOLATION
2721 chôreb (1), *ruined; desolate*
2723 chorbâh (5), *desolation, dry* desert
4875 mᵉshôw'âh (1), *ruin*
7584 sha'ăvâh (1), *rushing tempest*
7612 shê'th (1), *devastation*
7701 shôd (2), *violence, ravage, destruction*
7722 shôw' (4), *tempest; devastation*
8047 shammâh (12), *ruin; consternation*
8074 shâmêm (3), to *devastate;* to *stupefy*
8077 shᵉmâmâh (11), *devastation*
2049 ĕrēmŏō (2), to *lay waste*
2050 ĕrēmŏsis (3), *despoliation, desolation*

DESOLATIONS
2723 chorbâh (3), *desolation, dry* desert
4876 mashshûw'âh (1), *ruin*
8047 shammâh (1), *ruin; consternation*
8074 shâmêm (4), to *devastate;* to *stupefy*
8077 shᵉmâmâh (2), *devastation*

DESPAIR
2976 yâ'ash (2), to *despond, despair*
1820 ĕxapŏrĕŏmai (1), to *be utterly at a loss*

English

DESPAIRED
1820 ĕxapŏrĕŏmai (1), to
be utterly at a loss

DESPERATE
605 'ânash (1), to *be frail,
feeble*
2976 yâ'ash (1), to
despond, despair

DESPERATELY
605 'ânash (1), to *be frail,
feeble*

DESPISE
936 bûwz (4), to
disrespect, scorn
959 bâzâh (6), to *ridicule,
scorn*
2107 zûwl (1), to *treat
lightly*
3988 mâ'aç (9), to *spurn;
to disappear*
5006 nâ'ats (1), to *scorn*
7043 qâlal (1), to *be easy,
trifling, vile*
7590 shâ'ţ (2), *reject by
maligning*
114 athĕtĕō (1), to
disesteem, neutralize
1848 ĕxŏuthĕnĕō (3), to
treat with contempt
2706 kataphrŏnĕō (7), to
disesteem, despise
3643 ŏligŏrĕō (1), to
disesteem, despise
4065 pĕriphrŏnĕō (1), to
depreciate, contemn

DESPISED
937 bûwz (4), *disrespect,
scorn*
939 bûwzâh (1),
something scorned
959 bâzâh (26), to
ridicule, scorn
3988 mâ'aç (12), to
spurn; to disappear
5006 nâ'ats (6), to *scorn*
7034 qâlâh (1), to *be,
hold in contempt*
7043 qâlal (2), to *be easy,
trifling, vile*
7590 shâ'ţ (1), *reject by
maligning*
114 athĕtĕō (1), to
disesteem, set aside
818 atimazō (1), to
maltreat, dishonor
820 atimŏs (1), *without
honor*
1519+3762+3049 ĕis (1),
to or into
1848 ĕxŏuthĕnĕō (3), to
treat with contempt

DESPISERS
865 aphilagathŏs (1),
hostile to virtue
2707 kataphrŏntēs (1),
contemner, scoffer

DESPISEST
2706 kataphrŏnĕō (1), to
disesteem, despise

DESPISETH
936 bûwz (4), to
disrespect, scorn
959 bâzâh (4), to *ridicule,
scorn*
960 bâzôh (1), *scorned*
3988 mâ'aç (3), to *spurn;
to disappear*

5006 nâ'ats (1), to *scorn*
114 athĕtĕō (3), to
disesteem, set aside

DESPISING
2706 kataphrŏnĕō (1), to
disesteem, despise

DESPITE
7589 she'âţ (1), *contempt*
1796 ĕnubrizō (1), to
insult

DESPITEFUL
7589 she'âţ (2), *contempt*
5197 hubristēs (1),
maltreater

DESPITEFULLY
1908 ĕpĕrĕazō (2), to
insult, slander
5195 hubrizō (1), to
exercise violence

DESTITUTE
2638 châçêr (1), *lacking*
5800 'âzab (1), to *loosen;
relinquish; permit*
6168 'ârâh (1), to *empty,
pour out; demolish*
6199 'ar'âr (1), *naked;
poor*
8047 shammâh (1), *ruin;
consternation*
650 apŏstĕrĕō (1), to
deprive; to despoil
3007 lĕipō (1), to *fail or
be absent*
5302 hustĕrĕō (1), to *be
inferior; to fall short*

DESTROY
6 'âbad (38), *perish;
destroy*
7 'âbad (Ch.) (4), *perish;
destroy*
9 'âbêdâh (1), *destruction*
622 'âçaph (1), to *gather,
collect*
816 'âsham (1), to *be
guilty; to be punished*
1104 bâla' (7), to
swallow; to destroy
1641 gârar (1), to
ruminate; to saw
1792 dâkâ' (1), to *be
contrite, be humbled*
1820 dâmâh (1), to *be
silent; to fail, cease*
1949 hûwm (1), to *make
an uproar; agitate*
2000 hâmam (3), to
disturb, drive, destroy
2040 hâraç (1), to *pull
down; break, destroy*
2254 châbal (5), to
pervert, destroy
2255 châbal (Ch.) (2), to
ruin, destroy
2763 charam (14), to
devote to destruction
3238 yânâh (1), to *rage
or be violent*
3423 yârash (1), to
inherit; to impoverish
3615 kâlâh (1), to
complete, consume
3772 kârath (2), to *cut
(off, down or asunder)*
4049 me gar (Ch.) (1), to
overthrow, depose
4135 mûwl (3), to
circumcise

4191 mûwth (1), to *die; to
kill*
4229 mâchâh (2), to
erase; to grease
4889 mashchîyth (4),
destruction; corruption
5255 nâçach (1), to *tear
away*
5362 nâqaph (1), to
strike; to surround
5395 nâsham (1), to
destroy
5422 nâthats (4), to *tear
down*
5595 çâphâh (3), to
scrape; to remove
6789 tsâmath (4), to
extirpate, destroy
6979 qûwr (1), to *throw
forth; to wall up*
7665 shâbar (2), to *burst*
7703 shâdad (1), to
ravage
7722 shōw' (1), *tempest;
devastation*
7843 shâchath (68), to
decay; to ruin
7921 shâkôl (1), to
miscarry
8045 shâmad (40), to
desolate
8074 shâmêm (2), to
devastate; to stupefy
622 apŏllumi (19), to
destroy fully; to perish
1311 diaphthĕirō (1), to
ruin, to decay
2647 kataluō (6), to
demolish; to halt
2673 katargĕō (3), to *be,
render entirely useless*
3089 luō (2), to *loosen*
5351 phthĕirō (1), to
spoil, ruin; to deprave

DESTROYED
6 'âbad (17), *perish;
destroy*
7 'âbad (Ch.) (1), *perish;
destroy*
1104 bâla' (1), to
swallow; to destroy
1696 dâbar (1), to *speak,
say; to subdue*
1792 dâkâ' (1), to
pulverize; be contrite
1820 dâmâh (1), to *be
silent; to fail, cease*
1822 dummâh (1),
desolation
2026 hârag (1), to *kill,
slaughter*
2040 hâraç (3), to *pull
down; break, destroy*
2254 châbal (2), to
pervert, destroy
2255 châbal (Ch.) (3), to
ruin, destroy
2717 chârab (1), to
desolate, destroy
2718 chărab (Ch.) (1), to
demolish
2763 charam (23), to
devote to destruction
2764 chêrem (1),
extermination
3615 kâlâh (1), to *cease,
be finished, perish*
3772 kârath (2), to *cut
(off, down or asunder)*

3807 kâthath (3), to
bruise, strike, beat
4229 mâchâh (3), to
erase; to grease
5422 nâthats (1), to *tear
down*
5428 nâthash (1), to *tear
away, be uprooted*
5595 çâphâh (2), to
scrape; to remove
5642 çe thar (Ch.) (1), to
demolish
6658 tsâdâh (1), to
desolate
6789 tsâmath (1), to
extirpate, destroy
7321 rûwa' (1), to *shout*
7665 shâbar (7), to *burst*
7703 shâdad (1), to
ravage
7843 shâchath (21), to
decay; to ruin
8045 shâmad (43), to
desolate
8074 shâmêm (1), to
devastate; to stupefy
622 apŏllumi (7), to
destroy fully; to perish
1311 diaphthĕirō (1), to
ruin, to pervert
1842 ĕxŏlŏthrĕuō (1), to
extirpate
2507 kathairĕō (2), to
lower, or demolish
2647 kataluō (2), to
demolish; to halt
2673 katargĕō (2), to *be,
render entirely useless*
3645 ŏlŏthrĕuō (1), to
slay, destroy
4199 pŏrthĕō (2), to
ravage, pillage
5356 phthŏra (1), *ruin;
depravity, corruption*

DESTROYER
2717 chârab (1), to
desolate, destroy
6530 pe rîyts (1), *violent,
i.e. a tyrant*
7703 shâdad (1), to
ravage
7843 shâchath (3), to
decay; to ruin
3644 ŏlŏthrĕutēs (1),
serpent which destroys

DESTROYERS
2040 hâraç (1), to *pull
down; break, destroy*
4191 mûwth (1), to *die; to
kill*
7843 shâchath (1), to
decay; to ruin
8154 shâçâh (1), to
plunder

DESTROYEST
6 'âbad (1), *perish;
destroy*
7843 shâchath (1), to
decay; to ruin
2647 kataluō (2), to
demolish; to halt

DESTROYETH
6 'âbad (4), *perish;
destroy*
3615 kâlâh (1), to
complete, consume
4229 mâchâh (1), to
erase; to grease

7843 shâchath (2), to
decay; to ruin

DESTROYING
1104 bâla' (1), to
swallow; to destroy
2763 charam (5), to
devote to destruction
4889 mashchîyth (1),
destruction; corruption
4892 mashchêth (1),
destruction
6986 qeṭeb (1), *ruin*
7843 shâchath (5), to
decay; to ruin

DESTRUCTION
6 'âbad (1), *perish;
destroy*
10 'ăbaddôh (1),
perishing
11 'ăbaddôwn (5),
perishing
12 'abdân (1), *perishing*
13 'obdân (1), *perishing*
343 'êyd (7), *misfortune,
ruin, disaster*
1793 dakkâ' (1), *crushed,
destroyed; contrite*
2035 hărîyçûwth (1),
demolition, destruction
2041 hereç (1),
demolition, destruction
2256 chebel (1),
company, band
2475 chălôwph (1),
destitute *orphans*
2764 chêrem (2),
extermination
3589 kîyd (1), *calamity,
destruction*
4103 mᵉhûwmâh (3),
confusion or uproar
4288 mᵉchittâh (7), *ruin;
consternation*
4876 mashshûw'âh (1),
ruin
4889 mashchîyth (2),
destruction; corruption
6365 pîyd (2), *misfortune*
6986 qeṭeb (2), *ruin*
6987 qôṭeb (1),
extermination
7089 qᵉphâdâh (1), *terror*
7171 qerets (1),
extirpation
7591 shᵉ'îyâh (1),
desolation
7667 sheber (20),
fracture; ruin
7670 shibrôwn (1), *ruin*
7701 shôd (7), *violence,
ravage, destruction*
7722 shôw' (2), *tempest;
devastation*
7843 shâchath (1), to
decay; to ruin
7845 shachath (2), *pit;
destruction*
8045 shâmad (1), to
desolate
8395 tᵉbûwçâh (1), *ruin*
8399 tabliyth (1),
consumption
684 apōlĕia (5), *ruin or
loss*
2506 kathairĕsis (2),
demolition
3639 ŏlĕthrŏs (4), *death,
punishment*

4938 suntrimma (1),
complete *ruin*

DESTRUCTIONS
2723 chorbâh (1),
desolation, dry desert
7722 shôw' (1), *tempest;
devastation*
7825 shᵉchîyth (1), *pit*-fall

DETAIN
6113 'âtsar (2), to *hold
back; to maintain*

DETAINED
6113 'âtsar (1), to *hold
back; to maintain*

DETERMINATE
3724 hŏrizō (1), to
appoint, decree, specify

DETERMINATION
4941 mishpâṭ (1), *verdict;
formal decree; justice*

DETERMINED
559 'âmar (1), to *say*
2782 chârats (6), to *be
alert, to decide*
2852 châthak (1), to
decree
3289 yâ'ats (2), to *advise*
3615 kâlâh (5), to *cease,
be finished, perish*
7760 sûwm (1), to *put,
place*
1011 bŏulĕuō (1), to
deliberate; to resolve
1956 ĕpiluō (1), to
explain; to decide
2919 krinō (7), to *decide;
to try, condemn, punish*
3724 hŏrizō (3), to
appoint, decree, specify
4309 prŏŏrizō (1), to
predetermine
5021 tassō (1), to *assign
or dispose*

DETEST
8262 shâqats (1), to
loathe, pollute

DETESTABLE
8251 shiqqûwts (6),
disgusting idol

DEUEL
1845 Dᵉ'ûw'êl (4), *known
of God*

DEVICE
1902 higgâyôwn (1),
musical notation
2808 cheshbôwn (1),
contrivance; plan
4209 mᵉzimmâh (1),
plan; sagacity
4284 machăshâbâh (4),
contrivance; plan
1761 ĕnthumēsis (1),
deliberation; idea

DEVICES
2154 zimmâh (1), bad
plan
4156 môw'êtsâh (1),
purpose, plan
4209 mᵉzimmâh (5),
plan; sagacity
4284 machăshâbâh (8),
contrivance; plan
3540 nŏēma (1),
perception, purpose

DEVIL
1139 daimŏnizŏmai (7),
to *be demonized*
1140 daimŏniŏn (18),
demonic being
1142 daimŏn (1), evil
supernatural *spirit*
1228 diabŏlŏs (35),
traducer, i.e. *Satan*

DEVILISH
1141 daimŏniōdēs (1),
demon-like, of the devil

DEVILS
7700 shêd (2), *demon*
8163 sâ'îyr (2), *shaggy;
he-goat; goat idol*
1139 daimŏnizŏmai (6),
to *be demonized*
1140 daimŏniŏn (40),
demonic being
1142 daimŏn (4), evil
supernatural *spirit*

DEVISE
2790 chârash (3), to
engrave; to plow
2803 châshab (13), to
weave, fabricate

DEVISED
908 bâdâ' (1), to *invent;
to choose*
1819 dâmâh (1), to
resemble, liken
2161 zâmam (3), to *plan*
2803 châshab (5), to *plot;
to think, regard*
4284 machăshâbâh (1),
contrivance; plan
4679 sŏphizō (1), to
make wise

DEVISETH
2790 chârash (2), to
engrave; to plow
2803 châshab (4), to *plot;
to think, regard*
3289 yâ'ats (2), to *advise*

DEVOTE
2763 charam (1), to
devote to destruction

DEVOTED
2763 charam (1), to
devote to destruction
2764 chêrem (5),
doomed object

DEVOTIONS
4574 sĕbasma (1), *object
of worship*

DEVOUR
398 'âkal (57), to *eat*
399 'ăkal (Ch.) (2), to *eat*
402 'oklâh (2), *food*
7462 râ'âh (1), to *tend* a
flock, i.e. *pasture* it
7602 shâ'aph (1), to *be
angry; to hasten*
2068 ĕsthiō (1), to *eat*
2666 katapinō (1), to
devour by swallowing
2719 katĕsthiō (6), to
devour

DEVOURED
398 'âkal (42), to *eat*
399 'ăkal (Ch.) (2), to *eat*
402 'oklâh (1), *food*
1104 bâla' (2), to
swallow; to destroy

3898 lâcham (1), to *fight*
a *battle,* i.e. *consume*
2719 katĕsthiō (5), to
devour

DEVOURER
398 'âkal (1), to *eat*

DEVOUREST
398 'âkal (1), to *eat*

DEVOURETH
398 'âkal (6), to *eat*
1104 bâla' (2), to
swallow; to destroy
3216 yâla' (1), to *blurt* or
utter inconsiderately
2719 katĕsthiō (1), to
devour

DEVOURING
398 'âkal (5), to *eat*
1105 bela' (1), *gulp;
destruction*

DEVOUT
2126 ĕulabēs (3),
circumspect, pious
2152 ĕusĕbēs (3), *pious*
4576 sĕbŏmai (3), to
revere, i.e. *adore*

DEW
2919 ṭal (30), *dew,
morning mist*
2920 ṭal (Ch.) (5), *dew,
morning mist*

DIADEM
4701 mitsnepheth (1),
turban
6797 tsânîyph (2),
head-dress, turban
6843 tsᵉphîyrâh (1),
encircling crown

DIAL
4609 ma'ălâh (2),
thought arising

DIAMOND
3095 yahălôm (3), (poss.)
onyx
8068 shâmîyr (1), *thorn;*
(poss.) *diamond*

DIANA
735 Artĕmis (5), *prompt*

DIBLAIM
1691 Diblayim (1), *two
cakes*

DIBLATH
1689 Diblâh (1), *Diblah*

DIBON
1769 Dîybôwn (9), *pining*

DIBON-GAD
1769 Dîybôwn (2), *pining*

DIBRI
1704 Dibrîy (1), *wordy*

DID
1580 gâmal (2), to *benefit
or requite; to wean*
1961 hâyâh (1), to *exist,*
i.e. *be or become*
2052 Vâhêb (1), *Vaheb*
5648 'ăbad (Ch.) (1), to
do, *work, serve*
6213 'âsâh (327), to *do or
make*
6313 pûwg (1), to *be
sluggish; be numb*
7965 shâlôwm (2), *safe;
well; health, prosperity*

English

15 agathŏpŏiĕō (1), to be
a well-doer
91 adikĕō (1), to do
wrong
1731 ĕndĕiknumi (1), to
show, display
3000 latrĕuō (1), to
minister to God
4160 pŏiĕō (54), to make
or do
4238 prassō (1), to
execute, accomplish

DIDDEST
387 anastatŏō (1), to
disturb, cause trouble

DIDST
6213 'âsâh (14), to do or
make
6466 pâ'al (1), to do,
make or practice

DIDYMUS
1324 Didumŏs (3), twin

DIE
1478 gâva' (8), to expire,
die
4191 mûwth (255), to die;
to kill
4194 mâveth (7), death;
dead
8546 tᵉmûwthâh (1),
execution, death
599 apŏthnĕskō (40), to
die off
622 apŏllumi (1), to
destroy fully; to perish
684 apŏlĕia (1), ruin or
loss
4880 sunapŏthnĕskō (2),
to decease with
5053 tĕlĕutaō (3), to
finish life, i.e. expire

DIED
1478 gâva' (3), to expire,
die
4191 mûwth (154), to die;
to kill
4194 mâveth (7), death;
dead
5038 nᵉbêlâh (1), carcase
or carrion
5307 nâphal (1), to fall
599 apŏthnĕskō (32), to
die off
5053 tĕlĕutaō (2), to
finish life, i.e. expire

DIEST
4191 mûwth (1), to die; to
kill

DIET
737 'ărûchâh (2), ration,
portion of food

DIETH
4191 mûwth (16), to die;
to kill
4194 mâveth (4), death;
dead
5038 nᵉbêlâh (4), carcase
or carrion
599 apŏthnĕskō (2), to
die off
5053 tĕlĕutaō (3), to
finish life, i.e. expire

DIFFER
1252 diakrinō (1), to
decide; to hesitate

DIFFERENCE
914 bâdal (3), to divide,
separate, distinguish
6395 pâlâh (1), to
distinguish
1252 diakrinō (2), to
decide; to hesitate
1293 diastŏlĕ (2),
variation, distinction
3307 mĕrizō (1), to
disunite, differ

DIFFERENCES
1243 diairĕsis (1),
distinction or variety

DIFFERETH
1308 diaphĕrō (2), to
bear, carry; to differ

DIFFERING
1313 diaphŏrŏs (1),
varying; surpassing

DIG
2658 châphar (3), to
delve, to explore
2672 châtsab (1), to cut
stone or carve wood
2864 châthar (5), to
break or dig into
3738 kârâh (2), to dig; to
plot; to bore, hew
4626 skaptō (2), to dig

DIGGED
2658 châphar (13), to
delve, to explore
2672 châtsab (3), to cut
stone or carve wood
2864 châthar (2), to
break or dig into
3738 kârâh (8), to dig; to
plot; to bore, hew
5365 nâqar (3), to bore;
to gouge
5737 'âdar (2), to hoe a
vineyard
6131 'âqar (1), to pluck
up; to hamstring
2679 kataskaptō (1), to
destroy, be ruined
3736 ŏrussō (3), to
burrow, i.e. dig out
4626 skaptō (1), to dig

DIGGEDST
2672 châtsab (1), to cut
stone or carve wood

DIGGETH
2658 châphar (1), to
delve, to explore
3738 kârâh (2), to dig; to
plot; to bore, hew

DIGNITIES
1391 Ĕpaphrŏditŏs (2),
devoted to Venus

DIGNITY
1420 gᵉdûwlâh (1),
greatness, grandeur
4791 mârôwm (1),
elevation; haughtiness
7613 sᵉ'êth (2), elevation;
swelling scab

DIKLAH
1853 Diqlâh (2), Diklah

DILEAN
1810 Dil'ân (1), Dilan

DILIGENCE
4929 mishmâr (1), guard;
deposit; usage; example

2039 ĕrgasia (1),
occupation; profit
4704 spŏudazō (2), to
make effort
4710 spŏudĕ (6),
despatch; eagerness

DILIGENT
2742 chârûwts (5),
diligent, earnest
3190 yâṭab (1), to be,
make well
3966 mᵉ'ôd (1), very,
utterly
4106 mâhîyr (1), skillful
4704 spŏudazō (2), to
make effort
4705 spŏudaiŏs (1),
prompt, energetic
4707 spŏudaiŏtĕrŏs (1),
more earnest

DILIGENTLY
149 'adrazdâ' (Ch.) (1),
carefully, diligently
995 bîyn (1), to
understand; discern
3190 yâṭab (2), to be,
make well
3966 mᵉ'ôd (4), very,
utterly
5172 nâchash (1), to
prognosticate
7182 qesheb (1),
hearkening
7836 shâchar (2), to
search for
8150 shânan (1), to
pierce; to inculcate
199 akribōs (2), exactly,
carefully
1567 ĕkzētĕō (1), to seek
out
1960 ĕpimĕlōs (1),
carefully, diligently
4706 spŏudaiŏtĕrŏn (1),
more earnestly
4709 spŏudaiōs (1),
earnestly, promptly

DIM
2821 châshak (1), to be
dark; to darken
3513 kâbad (1), to be
heavy, severe, dull
3543 kâhâh (3), to grow
dull, fade; to be faint
3544 kêheh (1), feeble;
obscure
6004 'âmam (1), to
overshadow
6965 qûwm (1), to rise
8159 shâ'âh (1), to
inspect, consider

DIMINISH
1639 gâra' (6), to shave,
remove, lessen
4591 mâ'aṭ (2), to be,
make small or few

DIMINISHED
1639 gâra' (2), to shave,
remove, lessen
4591 mâ'aṭ (3), to be,
make small or few

DIMINISHING
2275 hĕttēma (1), failure
or loss

DIMNAH
1829 Dimnâh (1),
dung-heap

DIMNESS
4155 mûw'âph (1),
obscurity; distress
4588 mâ'ûwph (1),
darkness, gloom

DIMON
1775 Dîymôwn (2),
Dimon

DIMONAH
1776 Dîymôwnâh (1),
Dimonah

DINAH
1783 Dîynâh (7), justice

DINAH'S
1783 Dîynâh (1), justice

DINAITES
1784 Dîynay (Ch.) (1),
Dinaite

DINE
398 'âkal (1), to eat
709 aristaō (2), to eat a
meal

DINED
709 aristaō (1), to eat a
meal

DINHABAH
1838 Dinhâbâh (2),
Dinhabah

DINNER
737 'ărûchâh (1), ration,
portion of food
712 aristŏn (3), breakfast
or lunch; feast

DIONYSIUS
1354 Diŏnusiŏs (1),
reveller

DIOTREPHES
1361 Diŏtrĕphĕs (1),
Zeus-nourished

DIP
2881 ṭâbal (9), to dip
911 baptō (1), to
overwhelm, cover

DIPPED
2881 ṭâbal (6), to dip
4272 mâchats (1), to
crush; to subdue
911 baptō (2), to
overwhelm, cover
1686 ĕmbaptō (1), to wet

DIPPETH
1686 ĕmbaptō (2), to wet

DIRECT
3384 yârâh (1), to point;
to teach
3474 yâshar (3), to be
straight; to make right
3559 kûwn (1), to set up:
establish, fix, prepare
3787 kâshêr (1), to be
straight or right
5414 nâthan (1), to give
6186 'ârak (1), to set in a
row, i.e. arrange,
2720 katĕuthunō (2), to
direct, lead, direct

DIRECTED
3559 kûwn (1), to set up:
establish, fix, prepare
6186 'ârak (1), to set in a
row, i.e. arrange,
8505 tâkan (1), to
balance, i.e. measure

DIRECTETH
3474 yâshar (1), to *be straight;* to *make right*
3559 kûwn (2), to *set up: establish, fix, prepare*

DIRECTLY
413+5227 'êl (1), *to, toward*
1903 hâgîyn (1), (poss.) *suitable* or *turning*

DIRT
2916 tîyṭ (2), *mud* or *clay*
6574 parshᵉdôn (1), *crotch* or *anus*

DISALLOW
5106 nûw' (1), to *refuse, forbid, dissuade*

DISALLOWED
5106 nûw' (3), to *refuse, forbid, dissuade*
593 apŏdŏkimazŏ (2), to *repudiate, reject*

DISANNUL
6565 pârar (2), to *break up;* to *violate, frustrate*
208 akurŏŏ (1), to *invalidate, nullify*

DISANNULLED
3722 kâphar (1), to *placate* or *cancel*

DISANNULLETH
114 athĕtĕŏ (1), to *neutralize* or *set aside*

DISANNULLING
115 athĕtēsis (1), *cancellation*

DISAPPOINT
6923 qâdam (1), to *anticipate, hasten*

DISAPPOINTED
6565 pârar (1), to *break up;* to *violate, frustrate*

DISAPPOINTETH
6565 pârar (1), to *break up;* to *violate, frustrate*

DISCERN
995 bîyn (2), to *understand; discern*
3045 yâda' (3), to *know*
5234 nâkar (4), to *acknowledge*
7200 râ'âh (1), to *see*
8085 shâma' (2), to *hear intelligently*
1252 diakrinŏ (1), to *decide;* to *hesitate*
1253 diakrisis (1), *estimation*
1381 dŏkimazŏ (1), to *test;* to *approve*

DISCERNED
995 bîyn (1), to *understand; discern*
5234 nâkar (2), to *acknowledge*
350 anakrinŏ (1), to *interrogate, determine*

DISCERNER
2924 kritikŏs (1), *discriminative*

DISCERNETH
3045 yâda' (1), to *know*

DISCERNING
1252 diakrinŏ (1), to *decide;* to *hesitate*
1253 diakrisis (1), *estimation*

DISCHARGE
4917 mishlachath (1), *mission; release; army*

DISCHARGED
5310 nâphats (1), to *dash* to *pieces;* to *scatter*

DISCIPLE
3100 mathĕtĕuŏ (1), to *become a student*
3101 mathētēs (27), *pupil, student*
3102 mathētria (1), *female pupil, student*

DISCIPLES
3928 limmûwd (1), *instructed one*
3101 mathētēs (240), *pupil, student*

DISCIPLES'
3101 mathētēs (1), *pupil, student*

DISCIPLINE
4148 mûwçâr (1), *reproof, warning*

DISCLOSE
1540 gâlâh (1), to *denude; uncover*

DISCOMFITED
1949 hûwm (3), to *make an uproar; agitate*
2000 hâmam (2), to *put in commotion*
2522 châlash (1), to *prostrate, lay low*
2729 chârad (1), to *shudder with terror*
3807 kâthath (1), to *bruise, strike, beat*
4522 maç (1), *forced labor*

DISCOMFITURE
4103 mᵉhûwmâh (1), *confusion* or *uproar*

DISCONTENTED
4751+5315 mar (1), *bitter; bitterness; bitterly*

DISCONTINUE
8058 shâmaṭ (1), to *let alone, desist, remit*

DISCORD
4066 mâdôwn (1), *contest* or *quarrel*
4090 mᵉdân (1), *contest* or *quarrel*

DISCOURAGE
5106 nûw' (1), to *refuse, forbid, dissuade*

DISCOURAGED
2865 châthath (1), to *break down*
4549 mâçaç (1), to *waste;* to *faint*
5106 nûw' (1), to *refuse, forbid, dissuade*
7114 qâtsar (1), to *curtail, cut short*
7533 râtsats (1), to *crack in pieces, smash*

120 athumĕŏ (1), to *be disheartened*

DISCOVER
1540 gâlâh (10), to *denude; uncover*
2834 châsaph (1), to *drain* away or *bail up*
6168 'ârâh (1), to *be, make bare;* to *empty*

DISCOVERED
1540 gâlâh (18), to *denude; uncover*
3045 yâda' (1), to *know*
6168 'ârâh (1), to *be, make bare;* to *empty*
398 anaphainŏ (1), to *appear*
2657 katanŏĕŏ (1), to *observe fully*

DISCOVERETH
1540 gâlâh (1), to *denude; uncover*
2834 châsaph (1), to *drain* away or *bail up*

DISCOVERING
6168 'ârâh (1), to *be, make bare;* to *empty*

DISCREET
995 bîyn (2), to *understand; discern*
4998 sŏphrŏn (1), *self-controlled*

DISCREETLY
3562 nŏunĕchŏs (1), *prudently*

DISCRETION
2940 ṭa'am (1), *taste; intelligence; mandate*
4209 mᵉzimmâh (4), *plan; sagacity*
4941 mishpâṭ (2), *verdict; formal decree; justice*
7922 sekel (1), *intelligence; success*
8394 tâbûwn (1), *intelligence; argument*

DISDAINED
959 bâzâh (1), to *ridicule, scorn*
3988 mâ'aç (1), to *spurn;* to *disappear*

DISEASE
1697 dâbâr (1), *word; matter; thing*
2483 chŏlîy (7), *malady; anxiety; calamity*
4245 machăleh (1), *sickness*
3119 malakia (3), *enervation, debility*
3553 nŏsĕma (1), *ailment, disease*

DISEASED
2456 châlâ' (2), to *be sick*
2470 châlâh (2), to *be weak, sick, afflicted*
770 asthĕnĕŏ (1), to *be feeble*
2560+2192 kakŏs (2), *badly; wrongly; ill*

DISEASES
4064 madveh (2), *sickness*
4245 machăleh (1), *sickness*

4251 machlûy (1), *disease*
8463 tachălûw' (2), *malady, disease*
769 asthĕnĕia (1), *feebleness* of *body*
3554 nŏsŏs (6), *malady, disease*

DISFIGURE
853 aphanizŏ (1), to *consume* (*becloud*)

DISGRACE
5034 nâbêl (1), to *be foolish* or *wicked*

DISGUISE
2664 châphas (2), to *let be sought;* to *mask*
8138 shânâh (1), to *transmute*

DISGUISED
2664 châphas (5), to *let be sought;* to *mask*

DISGUISETH
5643 çêther (1), *cover, shelter*

DISH
5602 çêphel (1), *basin, bowl*
6747 tsallachath (1), *bowl*
5165 trubliŏn (2), *bowl*

DISHAN
1789 Dîyshân (5), *antelope*

DISHES
7086 qᵉ'ârâh (3), *bowl*

DISHON
1788 dîyshôn (7), *antelope*

DISHONEST
1215 betsa' (2), *plunder; unjust gain*

DISHONESTY
152 aischunĕ (1), *shame* or *disgrace*

DISHONOUR
3639 kᵉlimmâh (3), *disgrace, scorn*
6173 'arvâh (Ch.) (1), *nakedness*
7036 qâlôwn (1), *disgrace*
818 atimazŏ (2), to *maltreat, dishonor*
819 atimia (4), *disgrace*

DISHONOUREST
818 atimazŏ (1), to *maltreat, dishonor*

DISHONOURETH
5034 nâbêl (1), to *wilt;* to *be foolish* or *wicked*
2617 kataischunŏ (2), to *disgrace* or *shame*

DISINHERIT
3423 yârash (1), to *inherit;* to *impoverish*

DISMAYED
926 bâhal (1), to *tremble; hurry anxiously*
2844 chath (1), *terror*
2865 châthath (26), to *break down*
8159 shâ'âh (2), to *be bewildered*

English

DISMAYING
4288 mᵉchittâh (1), *ruin; consternation*

DISMISSED
6362 pâṭar (1), to *burst through; to emit*
630 apŏluŏ (2), to *relieve, release; to divorce*

DISOBEDIENCE
543 apeîthĕia (3), *disbelief*
3876 parakŏĕ (3), *disobedience*

DISOBEDIENT
4784 mârâh (2), to *rebel or resist; to provoke*
506 anupŏtaktŏs (1), *insubordinate*
544 apeîthĕŏ (4), to *disbelieve*
545 apeîthĕs (6), *willful disobedience*

DISOBEYED
4784 mârâh (1), to *rebel or resist; to provoke*

DISORDERLY
812 ataktĕŏ (1), to *be, act irregular*
814 ataktŏs (2), *morally irregularly*

DISPATCH
1254 bârâ' (1), to *create; fashion*

DISPENSATION
3622 ŏikŏnŏmia (4), *administration*

DISPERSE
2219 zârâh (7), to *toss about; to diffuse*
6327 pûwts (1), to *dash in pieces; to disperse*

DISPERSED
2219 zârâh (1), to *toss about; to diffuse*
5310 nâphats (1), to *dash to pieces; to scatter*
6327 pûwts (2), to *dash in pieces; to disperse*
6340 pâzar (1), to *scatter*
6504 pârad (1), to *spread or separate*
6555 pârats (1), to *break out*
1287 diaskŏrpizŏ (1), to *scatter; to squander*
1290 diaspŏra (1), *dispersion*
4650 skŏrpizŏ (1) to *dissipate*

DISPERSIONS
8600 tᵉphôwtsâh (1), *dispersal*

DISPLAYED
5127 nûwç (1), to *vanish away, flee*

DISPLEASE
2734 chârâh (1), to *blaze up*
6213+7451+5869 'âsâh (1), to *do or make*
7489+5869 râ'a' (3), to *be good for nothing*

DISPLEASED
599 'ânaph (1), *be enraged, be angry*

DISQUIET
7264 râgaz (1), to *quiver*

DISQUIETED
1993 hâmâh (4), to *be in great commotion*
7264 râgaz (2), to *quiver*

DISQUIETNESS
5100 nᵉhâmâh (1), *snarling, growling*

DISSEMBLED
3584 kâchash (1), to *lie, disown; to disappoint*
8582 tâ'âh (1), to *vacillate, reel or stray*
4942 sunupŏkrinŏmai (1), to *act hypocritically*

DISSEMBLERS
5956 'âlam (1), to *veil from sight, i.e. conceal*

DISSEMBLETH
5234 nâkar (1), to *treat as a foreigner*

DISSENSION
4714 stasis (3), one *leading an uprising*

DISSIMULATION
505 anupŏkritŏs (1), *sincere, genuine*
5272 hupŏkrisis (1), *deceit, hypocrisy*

DISSOLVE
8271 shᵉrê' (Ch.) (1), to *unravel, commence*

DISSOLVED
4127 mûwg (3), to *soften, flow down, disappear*
4743 mâqaq (1), to *melt; to flow, dwindle, vanish*
6565 pârar (1), to *break up; to violate, frustrate*
2647 kataluŏ (1), to *demolish; to halt*
3089 luŏ (2), to *loosen*

DISSOLVEST
4127 mûwg (1), to *soften, flow down, disappear*

DISSOLVING
8271 shᵉrê' (Ch.) (1), to *free, separate*

DISTAFF
6418 pelek (1), *spindle-whorl; crutch*

DISTANT
7947 shâlab (1), to *make equidistant*

DISTIL
5140 nâzal (1), to *drip, or shed by trickling*
7491 râ'aph (1), to *drip*

DISTINCTION
1293 diastŏlê (1), *variation, distinction*

DISTINCTLY
6567 pârash (1), to *separate; to specify*

DISTRACTED
6323 pûwn (1), to *be perplexed*

DISTRACTION
563 apĕrispastŏs (1), *undistractedly*

DISTRESS
4689 mâtsôwq (1), *confinement; disability*
4691 mᵉtsûwqâh (1), *trouble, anguish*
4712 mêtsar (1), *trouble*
6693 tsûwq (5), to *oppress, distress*
6696 tsûwr (2), to *cramp, i.e. confine; to harass*
6862 tsar (4), *trouble; opponent*
6869 tsârâh (8), *trouble; rival-wife*
6887 tsârar (5), to *cramp*
7451 ra' (1), *bad; evil*
318 anagkê (3), *constraint; distress*
4730 stĕnŏchôria (1), *calamity, distress*
4928 sunŏchê (1), *anxiety, distress*

DISTRESSED
3334 yâtsar (4), to *be in distress*
5065 nâgas (2), to *exploit; to tax, harass*
6696 tsûwr (1), to *cramp, i.e. confine; to harass*
6887 tsârar (2), to *cramp*
6973 qûwts (1), to *be, make disgusted*
4729 stĕnŏchôrĕŏ (1), to *hem in closely*

DISTRESSES
4691 mᵉtsûwqâh (5), *trouble, anguish*
6862 tsar (1), *trouble; opponent*
4730 stĕnŏchôria (2), *calamity, distress*

DISTRIBUTE
2505 châlaq (1), to *be smooth; be slippery*
5157 nâchal (1), to *inherit*
5414 nâthan (1), to *give*
1239 diadidômi (1), to *divide up, distribute*
2130 ĕumĕtadŏtŏs (1), *liberal, generous*

DISTRIBUTED
2505 châlaq (2), to *be smooth; be slippery*
5157 nâchal (1), to *inherit*
1239 diadidômi (1), to *divide up, distribute*
3307 mĕrizŏ (2), to *apportion, bestow*

DISTRIBUTETH
2505 châlaq (1), to *be smooth; be slippery*

DISTRIBUTING
2841 kŏinōnĕŏ (1), to *share or participate*

DISTRIBUTION
1239 diadidômi (1), to *divide up, distribute*
2842 kŏinōnia (1), *benefaction; sharing*

DITCH
4724 miqvâh (1), *water reservoir*
7745 shûwchâh (1), *chasm*
7845 shachath (2), *pit; destruction*

DISPLEASURE
2534 chêmâh (3), *heat; anger; poison*
2740 chârôwn (1), *burning of anger*
7451 ra' (1), *bad; evil*

DISPOSED
7760 sûwm (2), to *put, place*
1014 bŏulŏmai (1), to *be willing, desire*
2309 thĕlŏ (1), to *will; to desire; to choose*

DISPOSING
4941 mishpâṭ (1), *verdict; formal decree; justice*

DISPOSITION
1296 diatagê (1), *putting into effect*

DISPOSSESS
3423 yârash (2), to *inherit; to impoverish*

DISPOSSESSED
3423 yârash (2), to *inherit; to impoverish*

DISPUTATION
4803 suzêtêsis (1), *discussion, dispute*

DISPUTATIONS
1253 diakrisis (1), *estimation*

DISPUTE
3198 yâkach (1), to *be correct; to argue*

DISPUTED
1256 dialĕgŏmai (3), to *discuss*
1260 dialŏgizŏmai (1), to *deliberate*
4802 suzĕtĕŏ (1), to *discuss, controvert*

DISPUTER
4804 suzĕtêtês (1), *sophist*

DISPUTING
1256 dialĕgŏmai (3), to *discuss*
4802 suzĕtĕŏ (1), to *discuss, controvert*
4803 suzêtêsis (1), *discussion, dispute*

DISPUTINGS
1261 dialŏgismŏs (1), *consideration; debate*
3859 paradiatribê (1), *meddlesomeness*

---

888 bᵉ'êsh (Ch.) (1), to *be displeased*
2198 zâ'êph (2), *angry, raging*
2734 chârâh (3), to *blaze up*
3415+5869 yâra' (1), to *fear*
6087 'âtsab (1), to *worry, have pain or anger*
7107 qâtsaph (3), to *burst out in rage*
7451+241 ra' (1), *bad; evil*
7489+5869 râ'a' (7), to *be good for nothing*
23 aganaktĕŏ (3), to *be indignant*
2371 thumŏmachĕŏ (1), to *be exasperated*

999 bŏthunŏs (2), *cistern, pit-hole*

DITCHES
1356 gêb (1), *well, cistern; pit*

DIVERS
582 'ĕnôwsh (1), *man; person, human*
2921 țâlâ' (1), to *be spotted* or *variegated*
3610 kil'ayim (1), *two different kinds of thing*
6446 paç (2), *long -sleeved* tunic
6648 tseba' (3), *dye*
7553 riqmâh (2), *variegation* of color
8162 sha'aṭnêz (1), *linen and woolen*
1313 diaphŏrŏs (1), *varying; surpassing*
4164 pŏikilŏs (8), *various* in character or kind
4187 pŏlutrŏpŏs (1), *in many ways*
5100 tis (2), *some* or *any*

DIVERSE
3610 kil'ayim (1), *two different kinds of thing*
8133 shᵉnâ' (Ch.) (5), to *alter, change*
8138 shânâh (2), to *duplicate; to transmute*

DIVERSITIES
1085 gĕnŏs (1), *kin,* offspring in kind
1243 diairĕsis (2), *distinction* or *variety*

DIVIDE
914 bâdal (5), to *divide, separate, distinguish*
1234 bâqa' (2), to *cleave, break, tear open*
1504 gâzar (2), to *destroy, divide*
2505 châlaq (17), to *be smooth; be slippery*
2673 châtsâh (3), to *cut* or *split* in two; to *halve*
5157 nâchal (3), to *inherit*
5307 nâphal (4), to *fall*
5312 nᵉphaq (Ch.) (2), to *issue forth; to bring out*
6385 pâlag (1), to *split*
6536 pâraç (4), to *break* in pieces; to *split*
6565 pârar (1), to *break up; to violate, frustrate*
1266 diamĕrizō (1), to *distribute*
3307 mĕrizō (1), to *apportion, bestow*

DIVIDED
914 bâdal (2), to *divide, separate, distinguish*
1234 bâqa' (2), to *cleave, break, tear open*
1334 bâthar (2), to *chop* up, *cut up*
1504 gâzar (1), to *destroy, divide*
2505 châlaq (21), to *be smooth; be slippery*
2673 châtsâh (8), to *cut* or *split* in two; to *halve*
5307 nâphal (2), to *fall*

5408 nâthach (1), to *dismember, cut up*
5504 çachar (1), *profit* from trade
6385 pâlag (3), to *split*
6386 pᵉlag (Ch.) (1), *dis-united*
6504 pârad (2), to *spread* or *separate*
6537 pᵉraç (Ch.) (1), to *split* up
7280 râga' (1), to *settle, to stir up*
7323 rûwts (1), to *run*
1096 ginŏmai (1), to *be, become*
1244 diairĕō (1), *distribute, apportion*
1266 diamĕrizō (4), to *distribute*
2624 kataklērŏdŏtĕō (1), to *apportion an estate*
3307 mĕrizō (8), to *apportion, bestow*
4977 schizō (2), to *split* or *sever*

DIVIDER
3312 mĕristēs (1), *apportioner*

DIVIDETH
2672 châtsab (1), to *cut stone* or *carve* wood
6536 pâraç (5), to *break; to split, distribute*
7280 râga' (2), to *settle, to stir up*
873 aphŏrizō (1), to *limit, exclude, appoint*
1239 diadidōmi (1), to *divide up, distribute*

DIVIDING
1234 bâqa' (1), to *cleave, break, tear open*
2505 châlaq (1), to *be smooth; be slippery*
6387 pᵉlag (Ch.) (1), *half*-time unit
1244 diairĕō (1), *distribute, apportion*
3311 mĕrismŏs (1), *separation, distribution*
3718 ŏrthŏtŏmĕō (1), to *expound correctly*

DIVINATION
4738 miqçâm (2), *augury, divination*
7080 qâçam (1), to *divine magic*
7081 qeçem (8), *divination*
4436 Puthōn (1), *inspiration in soothsaying*

DIVINATIONS
7081 qeçem (1), *divination*

DIVINE
5172 nâchash (1), to *prognosticate*
7080 qâçam (5), to *divine magic*
7081 qeçem (1), *divination*
7181 qâshab (1), to *prick* up the ears
2304 thĕiŏs (2), *divinity*
2999 latrĕia (1), *worship, ministry service*

DIVINERS
7080 qâçam (7), to *divine magic*

DIVINETH
5172 nâchash (1), to *prognosticate*

DIVINING
7080 qâçam (1), to *divine magic*

DIVISION
2515 châluqqâh (1), *distribution, portion*
6304 pᵉdûwth (1), *distinction; deliverance*
1267 diamĕrismŏs (1), *disunion*
4978 schisma (3), *dissension, i.e. schism*

DIVISIONS
4256 machălŏqeth (8), *section* or *division*
4653 miphlaggâh (1), *classification, division*
6391 pᵉluggâh (3), *section*
6392 pᵉluggâh (Ch.) (1), *section*
1370 dichŏstasia (2), *dissension*
4978 schisma (2), *dissension, i.e. schism*

DIVORCE
3748 kᵉrîythûwth (1), *divorce*

DIVORCED
1644 gârash (3), to *drive* out; to *divorce*
630 apŏluō (1), to *relieve, release; to divorce*

DIVORCEMENT
3748 kᵉrîythûwth (3), *divorce*
647 apŏstasiŏn (3), *marriage divorce*

DIZAHAB
1774 Dîy zâhâb (1), *of gold*

DO
1167 ba'al (1), *master; husband; owner; citizen*
1580 gâmal (1), to *benefit* or *requite; to wean*
3190 yâṭab (2), to *be, make well*
3318 yâtsâ' (1), to *go, bring out*
4640 Ma'say (1), *operative*
5647 'âbad (17), to *do, work, serve*
5648 'âbad (Ch.) (5), to *do, work, serve*
5674 'âbar (1), to *cross* over; to *transition*
5953 'âlal (2), to *glean; to overdo*
6213 'âsâh (617), to *do*
6466 pâ'al (6), to *do*
6467 pô'al (1), *act* or *work, deed*
14 agathŏĕrgĕō (1), to *do good work*
15 agathŏpŏiĕō (6), to *be a well-doer*
17 agathŏpŏiŏs (1), *virtuous one*

91 adikĕō (2), to *do wrong*
1107 gnōrizō (1), to *make known, reveal*
1286 diasĕiō (1), to *intimidate*
1398 dŏulĕuō (1), to *serve as a slave*
1754 ĕnĕrgĕō (1), to *be active, efficient, work*
2005 ĕpitĕlĕō (1), to *terminate; to undergo*
2038 ĕrgazŏmai (2), to *toil*
2140 ĕupŏiïa (1), *beneficence, doing good*
2192 ĕchō (1), to *have; hold; keep*
2480 ischuō (1), to *have* or *exercise force*
2554 kakŏpŏiĕō (2), to *injure; to sin, do wrong*
2698 katatithĕmi (1), to *place down*
2716 katĕrgazŏmai (3), to *finish; to accomplish*
3930 parĕchō (1), to *hold near, i.e. to present*
4160 pŏiĕō (199), to *do*
4238 prassō (15), to *execute, accomplish*
4704 spŏudazō (2), to *make effort*
4982 sōzō (1), to *deliver; to protect*

DOCTOR
3547 nŏmŏdidaskalŏs (1), *Rabbi*

DOCTORS
1320 didaskalŏs (1), *instructor*
3547 nŏmŏdidaskalŏs (1), *Rabbi*

DOCTRINE
3948 leqach (4), *instruction*
4148 mûwçâr (1), *reproof, warning*
8052 shᵉmûw'âh (1), *announcement*
1319 didaskalia (15), *instruction*
1322 didachē (28), *instruction*
3056 lŏgŏs (1), *word, matter, thing*

DOCTRINES
1319 didaskalia (4), *instruction*
1322 didachē (1), *instruction*

DODAI
1739 dâveh (1), *menstrual; fainting*

DODANIM
1721 Dôdânîym (2), *Dodanites*

DODAVAH
1735 Dôwdâvâhûw (1), *love of Jehovah*

DODO
1734 Dôwdôw (5), *loving*

DOEG
1673 Dô'êg (6), *anxious*

DOER
6218 'âsôwr (3), group of ten
2557 kakŏurgŏs (1), criminal, evildoer
4163 pŏiĕtēs (3), performer; poet

DOERS
6213 'âsâh (2), to do or make
6466 pâ'al (1), to do, make or practice
4163 pŏiĕtēs (2), performer; poet

DOEST
5648 'âbad (Ch.) (1), to do, work, serve
6213 'âsâh (18), to do or make
6466 pâ'al (1), to do, make or practice
7965 shâlôwm (1), safe; well; health, prosperity
4160 pŏiĕō (14), to do
4238 prassō (1), to execute, accomplish

DOETH
1580 gâmal (1), to benefit or requite; to wean
5648 'âbad (Ch.) (1), to do, work, serve
6213 'âsâh (44), to do
7760 sûwm (1), to put, place
15 agathŏpŏiĕō (1), to be a well-doer
91 adikĕō (1), to do wrong
2554 kakŏpŏiĕō (1), to injure; to sin, do wrong
4160 pŏiĕō (34), to do
4238 prassō (3), to execute, accomplish
4374 prŏsphĕrō (1), to present to; to treat as

DOG
3611 keleb (14), dog; male prostitute
2965 kuōn (1), dog

DOG'S
3611 keleb (2), dog; male prostitute

DOGS
3611 keleb (16), dog; male prostitute
2952 kunariŏn (4), small dog
2965 kuōn (4), dog

DOING
854 'êth (1), with; by; at; among
4640 Ma'say (1), operative
5949 'ălîylâh (1), opportunity, action
6213 'âsâh (14), to do or make
15 agathŏpŏiĕō (2), to be a well-doer
16 agathŏpŏiïa (1), virtue, doing good
92 adikĕma (1), wrong done
1096 ginŏmai (2), to be, become
1398 dŏulĕuō (1), to serve as a slave

2041 ĕrgŏn (1), work
2109 ĕuĕrgĕtĕō (1), to be philanthropic
2554 kakŏpŏiĕō (1), to injure; to sin, do wrong
2569 kalŏpŏiĕō (1), to do well
4160 pŏiĕō (8), to do

DOINGS
4611 ma'ălâl (35), act, deed
4640 Ma'say (3), operative
5949 'ălîylâh (13), opportunity, action

DOLEFUL
255 'ôach (1), creature that howls;
5093 nihyâh (1), lamentation

DOMINION
1166 bâ'al (1), to be master; to marry
1196 Ba'ănâh (1), in affliction
3027 yâd (2), hand; power
4474 mimshâl (2), ruler; dominion, rule
4475 memshâlâh (10), rule; realm or a ruler
4896 mishtâr (1), jurisdiction, rule
4910 mâshal (7), to rule
4915 môshel (2), empire; parallel
7287 râdâh (9), to subjugate
7300 rûwd (1), to ramble free or disconsolate
7980 shâlat (1), to dominate, i.e. govern
7985 shŏltân (Ch.) (11), official
2634 katakuriĕuō (1), to control, subjugate
2904 kratŏs (4), vigor, strength
2961 kuriĕuō (4), to rule, be master of
2963 kuriŏtēs (2), rulers, masters

DOMINIONS
7985 shŏltân (Ch.) (1), official
2963 kuriŏtēs (1), rulers, masters

DONE
466 'Ĕlîyphᵉlêhûw (1), God of his distinction
1254 bârâ' (1), to create; fashion
1580 gâmal (1), to benefit or requite; to wean
1639 gâra' (1), to shave, remove, lessen
1697 dâbâr (1), word; matter; thing
1961 hâyâh (2), to exist, i.e. be or become
3254 yâçaph (1), to add or augment
3615 kâlâh (9), to complete, prepare
5414 nâthan (1), to give
5647 'âbad (1), to do, work, serve

5648 'âbad (Ch.) (4), to do, work, serve
5953 'âlal (3), to glean; to overdo
6213 'âsâh (318), to do or make
6466 pâ'al (21), to do, make or practice
7760 sûwm (1), to put, place
8552 tâmam (2), to complete, finish
91 adikĕō (3), to do wrong
1096 ginŏmai (61), to be, become
1796 ĕnubrizō (1), to insult
2673 katargĕō (4), to be, render entirely useless
2716 katĕrgazŏmai (2), to finish; to accomplish
4160 pŏiĕō (52), to do
4238 prassō (6), to execute, accomplish

DOOR
1004 bayith (1), house; temple; family, tribe
1817 deleth (21), door; gate
4201 mᵉzûwzâh (2), door-post
4947 mashqôwph (1), lintel
5592 çaph (11), dish
6607 pethach (114), opening; door
6907 qubba'ath (2), goblet, cup
8179 sha'ar (1), opening, i.e. door or gate
2374 thura (28), entrance, i.e. door, gate
2377 thurŏrŏs (2), doorkeeper

DOORKEEPER
5605 çâphaph (1), to wait at (the) threshold

DOORKEEPERS
7778 shôw'êr (2), janitor, door-keeper

DOORS
1817 deleth (48), door; gate
5592 çaph (2), dish
6607 pethach (11), opening; door
8179 sha'ar (1), opening, i.e. door or gate
2374 thura (9), entrance, i.e. door, gate

DOPHKAH
1850 Dophqâh (2), knock

DOR
1756 Dôwr (6), dwelling

DORCAS
1393 Dŏrkas (2), gazelle

DOTE
2973 yâ'al (1), to be or act foolish

DOTED
5689 'âgab (6), to lust sensually

DOTHAN
1886 Dôthân (3), Dothan

DOTING
3552 nŏsĕō (1), to be sick, be ill

DOUBLE
3717 kâphal (2), to fold together; to repeat
3718 kephel (3), duplicate, double
4932 mishneh (8), duplicate copy; double
8147 shᵉnayim (5), two-fold
1362 diplŏus (2), two-fold
1374 dipsuchŏs (2), vacillating
3588+1362 hŏ (1), "the," i.e. the definite article

DOUBLED
3717 kâphal (3), to fold together; to repeat
8138 shânâh (1), to fold, i.e. duplicate

DOUBLETONGUED
1351 dilŏgŏs (1), insincere

DOUBT
551 'omnâm (1), verily, indeed, truly
142+5590 airō (1), to lift, to take up
639 apŏrĕō (1), be at a mental loss, be puzzled
686 ara (1), then, so, therefore
1063 gar (1), for, indeed, but, because
1252 diakrinō (2), to decide; to hesitate
1280 diapŏrĕō (1), to be thoroughly puzzled
1365 distazō (1), to waver in opinion
3843 pantŏs (1), at all events; in no event

DOUBTED
639 apŏrĕō (1), be at a mental loss, be puzzled
1280 diapŏrĕō (2), to be thoroughly puzzled
1365 distazō (1), to waver in opinion

DOUBTETH
1252 diakrinō (1), to decide; to hesitate

DOUBTFUL
1261 dialŏgismŏs (1), consideration; debate
3349 mĕtĕōrizō (1), to be anxious

DOUBTING
639 apŏrĕō (1), be at a mental loss, be puzzled
1252 diakrinō (2), to decide; to hesitate
1261 dialŏgismŏs (1), consideration; debate

DOUBTLESS
518 'îm (1), whether?; if, although; Oh that!
3588 kîy (1), for, that because
1065 gĕ (1), particle of emphasis
1211 dē (1), now, then; indeed, therefore

3304 měnŏungĕ (1), *so then at least*

DOUBTS
7001 qᵉtar (Ch.) (2), *riddle*

DOUGH
1217 bâtsêq (4), *fermenting dough*
6182 'ărîyçâh (4), *ground-up meal*

DOVE
3123 yôwnâh (14), *dove*
4058 pĕristĕra (4), *pigeon, dove*

DOVE'S
1686 dibyôwn (1), (poss.) *vegetable or root*

DOVES
3123 yôwnâh (5), *dove*
4058 pĕristĕra (5), *pigeon, dove*

DOVES'
3123 yôwnâh (2), *dove*

DOWN
935 bôw' (11), *to go or come*
1288 bârak (1), *to bless*
1438 gâda' (9), *to fell a tree; to destroy*
1457 gâhar (1), *to prostrate, bow down*
1760 dâchâh (1), *to push down; to totter*
2040 hâraç (22), *to pull down; break, destroy*
2904 ṭûwl (1), *to cast down or out, hurl*
3212 yâlak (1), *to walk; to live; to carry*
3281 Ya'lâm (1), *occult*
3332 yâtsaq (1), *to pour out*
3381 yârad (339), *to descend*
3665 kâna' (3), *to humiliate, vanquish*
3766 kâra' (9), *to prostrate*
3782 kâshal (4), *to totter, waver, stumble*
3996 mâbôw' (2), *entrance; sunset; west; towards*
4174 môwrâd (3), *descent, slope*
4295 maṭṭâh (1), *below or beneath*
4535 maççâch (1), *cordon; military barrier*
4606 mê'al (Ch.) (1), *setting of the sun*
4769 marbêts (2), *resting place*
5117 nûwach (1), *to rest; to settle down*
5128 nûwa' (1), *to waver*
5181 nâchath (4), *to sink, descend; to lead down*
5182 nᵉchath (Ch.) (2), *to descend; to depose*
5183 nachath (1), *descent; quiet*
5186 nâṭâh (8), *to stretch or spread out*
5242 Nᵉmûw'êlîy (2), *Nemuelite*

5243 nâmal (1), *to be circumcised*
5307 nâphal (9), *to fall*
5422 nâthats (29), *to tear down*
5456 çâgad (4), *to prostrate oneself*
5493 çûwr (1), *to turn off*
6131 'âqar (1), *to pluck up; to hamstring*
6201 'âraph (1), *to drip*
6915 qâdad (5), *to bend*
7250 râba' (2), *to lay down*
7252 reba' (1), *prostration for sleep*
7257 râbats (13), *to recline, repose, brood*
7323 rûwts (1), *to run*
7491 râ'aph (1), *to drip*
7503 râphâh (2), *to slacken*
7665 shâbar (1), *to burst*
7673 shâbath (1), *to repose; to desist*
7743 shûwach (1), *to sink*
7812 shâchâh (20), *to prostrate in homage*
7817 shâchach (12), *to sink or depress*
7821 shᵉchîyṭâh (1), *slaughter*
7901 shâkab (40), *to lie down*
7971 shâlach (2), *to send away*
8045 shâmad (2), *to desolate*
8058 shâmaṭ (2), *to jostle; to let alone*
8213 shâphêl (7), *to humiliate*
8214 shᵉphal (Ch.) (1), *to humiliate*
8231 shâphar (1), *to be, make fair*
8257 shâqa' (1), *to be overflowed; to cease*
8497 tâkâh (1), *to strew, i.e. encamp*
345 anakĕimai (2), *to recline at a meal*
347 anaklinō (7), *to lean back, recline*
377 anapiptō (10), *lie down, lean back*
387 anastatŏō (1), *to disturb, cause trouble*
1308 diaphĕrō (1), *to bear, carry; to differ*
1581 ĕkkŏptō (5), *to cut off; to frustrate*
1931 ĕpiduō (1), *to set*
2504 kagō (1), *and also*
2506 kathairĕsis (1), *demolition*
2507 kathairĕō (6), *to lower, or demolish*
2521 kathēmai (4), *to sit down; to remain, reside*
2523 kathizō (14), *to seat down, dwell*
2524 kathiĕmi (4), *to lower, let down*
2596 kata (3), *down; according to*
2597 katabainō (64), *to descend*

2598 kataballō (2), *to throw down*
2601 katabibazō (2), *to cause to bring down*
2609 katagō (5), *to lead down; to moor a vessel*
2621 katakĕimai (1), *to lie down; to recline*
2625 kataklinō (2), *to take a place at table*
2630 katakrēmnizō (1), *to precipitate down*
2647 kataluō (3), *to halt for the night*
2662 katapatĕō (1), *to trample down; to reject*
2667 katapiptō (1), *to fall down*
2673 katargĕō (1), *to be, render entirely useless*
2679 kataskaptō (1), *to destroy, be ruined*
2701 katatrĕchō (1), *to hasten, run*
2718 katĕrchŏmai (6), *to go, come down*
2736 katō (5), *downwards*
2778 kēnsŏs (1), *enrollment*
2875 kŏptō (2), *to beat the breast*
3879 parakuptō (3), *to lean over*
3935 pariĕmi (1), *to neglect; to be weakened*
4098 piptō (2), *to fall*
4496 rhiptō (2), *to fling, toss; to lay out*
4776 sugkathizō (1), *to give, take a seat with*
4781 sugkamptō (1), *to afflict*
4782 sugkatabainō (1), *to descend with*
5011 tapĕinŏs (1), *humiliated, lowly*
5294 hupŏtithēmi (1), *to hazard; to suggest*
5465 chalaō (5), *to lower as into a void*

DOWNSITTING
3427 yâshab (1), *to dwell, to remain; to settle*

DOWNWARD
4295 maṭṭâh (5), *below or beneath*

DOWRY
2065 zebed (1), *gift*
4119 môhar (3), *wife-price*

DRAG
4365 mikmereth (2), *fishing-net*

DRAGGING
4951 surō (1), *to trail, drag, sweep*

DRAGON
8577 tannîyn (6), *sea-serpent; jackal*
1404 drakōn (13), *fabulous kind of serpent*

DRAGONS
8568 tannâh (1), *female jackal*
8577 tannîyn (15), *sea-serpent; jackal*

DRAMS
150 'ădarkôn (2), *daric*
1871 darkᵉmôwn (4), *coin*

DRANK
4960 mishteh (2), *drink; banquet or feast*
8354 shâthâh (8), *to drink, imbibe*
8355 shᵉthâh (Ch.) (3), *to drink, imbibe*
4095 pinō (5), *to imbibe, drink*

DRAUGHT
4280 machărâ'âh (1), *privy sink, latrine*
61 agra (2), *haul of fish in a net*
856 aphĕdrōn (2), *privy or latrine*

DRAVE
1644 gârash (3), *to drive out; to expatriate*
3423 yârash (2), *to impoverish; to ruin*
5071 nᵉdâbâh (1), *abundant gift*
5090 nâhag (4), *to drive forth; to lead*
5394 nâshal (1), *to divest, eject, or drop*
556 apĕlaunō (1), *to dismiss, eject*
1856 ĕxōthĕō (1), *to expel; to propel*

DRAW
748 'ârak (1), *to be, make long*
1518 gîyach (1), *to issue forth; to burst forth*
1802 dâlâh (1), *to draw out water); to deliver*
2502 châlats (1), *to pull off; to strip; to depart*
2834 châsaph (1), *to drain away or bail up*
3318 yâtsâ' (1), *to go, bring out*
4900 mâshak (11), *to draw out; to be tall*
5423 nâthaq (1), *to tear off*
5498 çâchab (3), *to trail along*
6329 pùwq (1), *to issue; to furnish; to secure*
7324 rûwq (8), *to pour out, i.e. empty*
7579 shâ'ab (9), *to bale up water*
8025 shâlaph (4), *to pull out, up or off*
501 antlĕō (3), *dip water*
502 antlēma (1), *bucket for drawing water*
645 apŏspaō (1), *unsheathe a sword*
1670 hĕlkuō (4), *to drag, draw, pull in*
4334 prŏsĕrchŏmai (1), *to come near, visit*
5288 hupŏstĕllō (1), *to cower or shrink*
5289 hupŏstŏlē (1), *shrinkage, timidity*

DRAWER
7579 shâ'ab (1), *to bale up water*

English

DRAWERS
7579 shā'ab (3), to *bale up water*

DRAWETH
4900 mâshak (2), to *draw out; to be tall*
7503 râphâh (1), to *slacken*

DRAWING
4857 mash'âb (1), *water trough* for cattle
1096 ginŏmai (1), to *be, become*

DRAWN
3318 yâtsâ' (1), to *go, bring out*
3947 lâqach (1), to *take*
4900 mâshak (2), to *draw out; to be tall*
5080 nâdach (1), to *push off, scattered*
5203 nâṭash (1), to *disperse; to thrust off*
5423 nâthaq (3), to *tear off*
5498 çâchab (1), to *trail along*
6267 'attîyq (1), *weaned; antique*
6605 pâthach (2), to *open wide; to loosen, begin*
6609 pᵉthîchâh (1), *drawn sword*
7579 shā'ab (1), to *bale up water*
7725 shûwb (1), to *turn back; to return*
8025 shâlaph (5), to *pull out, up or off*
8388 tâ'ar (5), to *delineate; to extend*
385 anaspaō (1), to *take up or extricate*
1828 ĕxĕlkō (1), to *drag away, i.e. entice*

DREAD
367 'êymâh (1), *fright*
2844 chath (1), *terror*
3372 yârê' (1), to *fear; to revere*
4172 môwrâ' (1), *fearful*
6206 'ârats (2), to *awe; to dread; to harass*
6343 pachad (3), *sudden alarm, fear*

DREADFUL
1763 dᵉchal (Ch.) (2), to *fear; be formidable, awesome*
3372 yârê' (5), to *fear; to revere*
3374 yir'âh (1), *fear; reverence*
6343 pachad (1), *sudden alarm, fear*

DREAM
2472 chălôwm (44), *dream; dreamer*
2492 châlam (1), to *dream*
2493 chêlem (Ch.) (21), *dream*
1798 ĕnupniŏn (1), *dream, vision*
3677 ŏnar (6), *dream*

DREAMED
2492 châlam (19), to *dream*

DREAMER
1167+2472 ba'al (1), *master; owner; citizen*
2492 châlam (3), to *dream*

DREAMERS
2492 châlam (1), to *dream*
1797 ĕnupniazŏmai (1), to *dream*

DREAMETH
2492 châlam (2), to *dream*

DREAMS
2472 chălôwm (19), *dream; dreamer*
2493 chêlem (Ch.) (1), *dream*
1797 ĕnupniazŏmai (1), to *dream*

DREGS
6907 qubba'ath (2), *goblet, cup*
8105 shemer (1), *settlings* of wine, *dregs*

DRESS
5647 'âbad (2), to *do, work, serve*
6213 'âsâh (7), to *do or make*

DRESSED
6213 'âsâh (6), to *do or make*
1090 gĕŏrgĕō (1), to *till the soil*

DRESSER
289 ampĕlŏurgŏs (1), *vineyard caretaker*

DRESSERS
3755 kôrêm (1), *vinedresser*

DRESSETH
3190 yâṭab (1), to *be, make well*

DREW
748 'ârak (2), to *be, make long*
1802 dâlâh (2), to *draw out water); to deliver*
1869 dârak (1), to *walk, lead; to string a bow*
3318 yâtsâ' (1), to *go, bring out*
4871 mâshâh (3), to *pull out*
4900 mâshak (6), to *draw out; to be tall*
7579 shā'ab (4), to *bale up water*
7725 shûwb (2), to *turn back; to return*
8025 shâlaph (15), to *pull out, up or off*
307 anabibazō (1), *haul up a net*
501 antlĕō (1), *dip water*
645 apŏspaō (1), *unsheathe a sword*
868 aphistēmi (1), to *desist, desert*
1670 hĕlkuō (4), to *drag, draw, pull in*

DREAMED
2020 ĕpiphōskō (1), to *grow light*
4264 prŏbibazō (1), to *bring to the front*
4317 prŏsagō (1), to *bring near*
4334 prŏsĕrchŏmai (1), to *come near, visit*
4358 prŏsŏrmizō (1), to *moor to, i.e. land at*
4685 spaō (2), to *draw a sword*
4951 surō (3), to *trail, drag, sweep*

DRIED
1809 dâlal (1), to *slacken, dangle*
2717 chârab (9), to *parch; desolate, destroy*
2787 chârar (1), to *melt, burn, dry up*
3001 yâbêsh (22), to *dry up; to wither*
3002 yâbêsh (1), *dry*
6704 tsîcheh (1), *parched*
7033 qâlâh (1), to *toast, scorch*
3583 xĕrainō (3), to *shrivel, to mature*

DRIEDST
3001 yâbêsh (1), to *dry up; to wither*

DRIETH
3001 yâbêsh (3), to *dry up; to wither*

DRINK
1572 gâmâ' (1), to *swallow*
4469 mamçâk (1), *mixed-wine*
4945 mashqeh (2), *butler; drink; well-watered*
4960 mishteh (3), *drink; banquet* or *feast*
5257 nᵉçîyk (1), *libation; molten image; prince*
5261 nᵉçak (Ch.) (1), *libation*
5262 neçek (59), *libation; cast idol*
5435 çôbe' (1), *wine*
7937 shâkar (2), to *become tipsy, to satiate*
7941 shêkâr (21), *liquor*
8248 shâqâh (42), to *quaff, i.e. to irrigate*
8249 shiqqûv (1), *draught, drink*
8250 shiqqûwy (1), *beverage; refreshment*
8353 shêth (Ch.) (1), *six; sixth*
8354 shâthâh (161), to *drink, imbibe*
8355 shᵉthâh (Ch.) (1), to *drink, imbibe*
4095 pinō (50), to *imbibe, drink*
4188 pŏma (1), *beverage, drink*
4213 pŏsis (3), *draught, drink*
4222 pŏtizō (9), to *furnish drink, irrigate*
4608 sikĕra (1), *intoxicant*
4844 sumpinō (1), to *partake a beverage*

DRIED
2020 ĕpiphōskō (1), to *grow light*
5202 hudrŏpŏtĕō (1), to *drink water exclusively*

DRINKERS
8354 shâthâh (1), to *drink, imbibe*

DRINKETH
6231 'âshaq (1), to *overflow*
8354 shâthâh (8), to *drink, imbibe*
4095 pinō (7), to *imbibe, drink*

DRINKING
4945 mashqeh (2), *butler; drink; well-watered*
8354 shâthâh (12), to *drink, imbibe*
8360 shᵉthîyâh (1), *manner of drinking*
4095 pinō (6), to *imbibe, drink*

DRINKS
4188 pŏma (1), *beverage, drink*

DRIVE
1644 gârash (12), to *drive out; to divorce*
1920 hâdaph (2), to *push away or down; drive out*
2957 ṭᵉrad (Ch.) (2), to *expel, drive on*
3423 yârash (30), to *impoverish; to ruin*
5080 nâdach (5), to *push off, scattered*
5086 nâdaph (1), to *disperse, be windblown*
5090 nâhag (2), to *drive forth; to carry away*
6327 pûwts (1), to *dash in pieces; to disperse*
1929 ĕpididōmi (1), to *give over*

DRIVEN
1644 gârash (5), to *drive out; to divorce*
1760 dâchâh (2), to *push down; to totter*
1920 hâdaph (1), to *push away or down; drive out*
2957 ṭᵉrad (Ch.) (2), to *expel, drive on*
3423 yârash (2), to *impoverish; to ruin*
5080 nâdach (23), to *push off, scattered*
5086 nâdaph (4), to *disperse, be windblown*
5437 çâbab (2), to *surround*
5472 çûwg (1), to *go back, to retreat*
5590 çâ'ar (1), to *rush upon; to toss about*
7617 shâbâh (1), to *transport into captivity*
416 anemizō (1), to *toss with the wind*
1308 diaphĕrō (1), to *bear, carry; to differ*
1643 ĕlaunō (2), to *push*
5342 phĕrō (1), to *bear or carry*

DRIVER
5065 nâgas (1), to *exploit; to tax, harass*

7395 rakkâb (1), *charioteer*

DRIVETH
2342 chûwl (1), to *dance, whirl;* to *writhe*
5086 nâdaph (1), to *disperse, be windblown*
5090 nâhag (1), to *drive* forth; to *carry away*
1544 ĕkballō (1), to *throw out*

DRIVING
1644 gârash (1), to *drive* out; to *divorce*
3423 yârash (1), to *impoverish;* to *ruin*
4491 minhâg (2), chariot-*driving*

DROMEDARIES
1070 beker (1), young bull *camel*
7409 rekesh (1), *relay* of animals on a post-route
7424 rammâk (1), brood *mare*

DROMEDARY
1072 bikrâh (1), young she-*camel*

DROP
4752 mar (1), *drop* in a bucket
5140 nâzal (1), to *drip,* or *shed* by trickling
5197 nâṭaph (7), to *fall in drops*
6201 'âraph (2), to *drip*
7491 râ'aph (4), to *drip*

DROPPED
1982 hêlek (1), *wayfarer, visitor; flowing*
5197 nâṭaph (5), to *fall in drops*
5413 nâthak (1), to *flow* forth, *pour* out

DROPPETH
1811 dâlaph (1), to *drip*

DROPPING
1812 deleph (2), *dripping*
5197 nâṭaph (1), to *fall in drops*

DROPS
96 'egel (1), *reservoir*
5197 nâṭaph (1), to *fall in drops*
7447 râçîyç (1), *ruin;* dew-*drop*
2361 thrŏmbŏs (1), *clot* of blood

DROPSY
5203 hudrōpikŏs (1), to *suffer edema*

DROSS
5509 çîyg (8), *refuse, scoria*

DROUGHT
1226 batstsôreth (1), *drought*
2721 chôreb (3), *parched; ruined*
2725 chărâbôwn (1), parching *heat*
6710 tsachtsâchâh (1), *dry desert* place
6723 tsîyâh (2), arid *desert*

6774 tsimmâ'ôwn (1), *desert*
8514 tal'ûwbâh (1), *dehydration*

DROVE
1272 bârach (1), to *flee* suddenly
1644 gârash (3), to *drive* out; to *divorce*
3423 yârash (2), to *impoverish;* to *ruin*
4264 machăneh (1), *encampment*
5380 nâshab (1), to *blow;* to *disperse*
5425 nâthar (1), to *jump;* to *terrify; shake* off
5739 'êder (3), *muster, flock*
1544 ĕkballō (1), to *throw out*

DROVES
5739 'êder (1), *muster, flock*

DROWN
7857 shâṭaph (1), to *gush;* to *inundate*
1036 buthizō (1), to *sink;* to *plunge*

DROWNED
2823 châshôk (1), *obscure*
8248 shâqâh (2), to *quaff,* i.e. to *irrigate*
2666 katapinō (1), to *devour by swallowing*
2670 katapŏntizō (1), to *submerge, be drowned*

DROWSINESS
5124 nûwmâh (1), *sleepiness*

DRUNK
7301 râvâh (1), to *slake* thirst or appetites
7910 shikkôwr (2), *intoxicated*
7937 shâkar (4), to *become tipsy,* to *satiate*
8354 shâthâh (15), to *drink, imbibe*
8355 shᵉthâh (Ch.) (1), to *drink, imbibe*
3182 mĕthuskō (2), to *become drunk*
3184 mĕthuō (1), to *get drunk*
4095 pinō (2), to *imbibe, drink*

DRUNKARD
5435 çôbe' (2), *wine*
7910 shikkôwr (2), *intoxicated*
3183 mĕthusŏs (1), *drunkard*

DRUNKARDS
5435 çôbe' (1), *wine*
7910 shikkôwr (3), *intoxicated*
8354+7941 shâthâh (1), to *drink, imbibe*
3183 mĕthusŏs (1), *drunkard*

DRUNKEN
5435 çôbe' (1), *wine*
7301 râvâh (1), to *slake* thirst or appetites

7910 shikkôwr (6), *intoxicated*
7937 shâkar (13), to *become tipsy,* to *satiate*
7943 shikkârôwn (2), *intoxication*
8354 shâthâh (3), to *drink, imbibe*
3182 mĕthuskō (1), to *become drunk*
3184 mĕthuō (5), to *get drunk*
4095 pinō (1), to *imbibe, drink*

DRUNKENNESS
7302 râveh (1), *sated, full* with drink
7943 shikkârôwn (2), *intoxication*
8358 shᵉthîy (1), *intoxication*
3178 mĕthē (3), *intoxication*

DRUSILLA
1409 Drŏusilla (1), *Drusilla*

DRY
954 bûwsh (1), be *ashamed; disappointed*
2717 chârab (3), to *parch, desolate, destroy*
2720 chârêb (3), *parched; ruined*
2721 chôreb (3), *parched; ruined*
2724 chârâbâh (8), *desert, dry* land
3001 yâbêsh (9), to *dry* up; to *wither*
3002 yâbêsh (7), *dry*
3004 yabbâshâh (14), *dry* ground
3006 yabbesheth (2), *dry* ground
5424 netheq (1), *scurf,* i.e. diseased skin
6703 tsach (1), *dazzling,* i.e. *sunny, bright*
6707 tsᵉchîychâh (1), *parched desert* region
6723 tsîyâh (10), arid *desert*
6724 tsîyôwn (2), *desert*
6774 tsimmâ'ôwn (1), *desert*
6784 tsâmaq (1), to *dry* up, *shrivel* up
504 anudrŏs (2), *dry, arid*
3584 xērŏs (2), *scorched; arid; withered*

DRYSHOD
5275 na'al (1), *sandal*

DUE
1167 ba'al (1), *master; husband; owner; citizen*
1697 dâbâr (1), *word; matter; thing*
2706 chôq (2), *appointment; allotment*
4941 mishpâṭ (1), *verdict; formal decree; justice*
514 axiŏs (1), *deserving, comparable or suitable*
2398 idiŏs (3), *private or separate*
3784 ŏphĕilō (2), to *owe;* to *be under obligation*

DUES
3782 ŏphĕilē (1), *sum* owed; *obligation*

DUKE
441 'allûwph (20), *friend,* one *familiar; chieftain*

DUKES
441 'allûwph (13), *friend,* one *familiar; chieftain*
5257 nᵉçîyk (1), *libation; molten image; prince*

DULCIMER
5481 çûwmpôwnᵉyâh (Ch.) (3), *bagpipe*

DULL
917 barĕŏs (2), *heavily, with difficulty*
3576 nōthrŏs (1), *lazy; stupid*

DUMAH
1746 Dûwmâh (4), *silence; death*

DUMB
481 'âlam (7), to be *tongue-tied, be silent*
483 'illêm (6), *speechless*
1748 dûwmâm (1), *silently*
216 alalŏs (3), *mute, not able to speak*
880 aphōnŏs (3), *mute, silent; unmeaning*
2974 kōphŏs (8), *deaf* or *silent*
4623 siōpaō (1), to *be quiet*

DUNG
830 'ashpôth (4), *heap of rubbish; Dung gate*
1557 gâlâl (1), *dung pellets*
1561 gêlel (4), *dung; dung* pellets
1828 dômen (6), *manure, dung*
2716+(6675) chere' (2), *excrement*
2755 chărêy-yôwnîym (1), *excrements of doves* or a *vegetable*
6569 peresh (7), *excrement*
6832 tsᵉphûwa' (1), *excrement*
906+2874 ballō (1), to *throw*
4657 skubalŏn (1), *what* is *thrown* to the *dogs*

DUNGEON
953 bôwr (13), *pit hole, cistern, well; prison*

DUNGHILL
830 'ashpôth (2), *heap of rubbish; Dung gate*
4087 madmênâh (1), *dunghill*
5122 nᵉvâlûw (Ch.) (3), to *be foul; sink*
2874 kŏpria (1), *manure* or *rubbish pile*

DUNGHILLS
830 'ashpôth (1), *heap of rubbish; Dung gate*

English

DURA
1757 Dûwrâ' (Ch.) (1), *circle* or *dwelling*

DURABLE
6266 'âthîyq (1), *venerable* or *splendid*
6276 'âthêq (1), *enduring value*

DURETH
2076 ěsti (1), he (she or it) *is*; they *are*

DURST
3372 yârê' (1), to *fear*; to *revere*
5111 tôlmaō (7), to be *bold*; to *dare*

DUST
80 'âbâq (5), *fine dust*; *cosmetic powder*
1854 dâqaq (1), to *crush*; *crumble*
6083 'âphâr (91), *dust, earth, mud*; *clay,*
7834 shachaq (1), *firmament, clouds*
2868 kŏniŏrtŏs (5), *blown dust*
5522 chŏŏs (2), loose *dirt*

DUTY
1697 dâbâr (2), *word; matter; thing*
3784 ŏphěilō (2), to *owe; to fail in duty*

DWARF
1851 daq (1), *crushed; small* or *thin*

DWELL
1481 gûwr (11), to *sojourn, live as an alien*
1752 dûwr (1), *remain*
1753 dûwr (Ch.) (3), to *reside, live in*
2073 zᵉbûwl (1), *residence, dwelling*
2082 zâbal (1), to *reside*
3427 yâshab (210), to *dwell, to remain*
3488 yᵉthîb (Ch.) (1), to *sit* or *dwell*
3885 lûwn (1), to be *obstinate*
4186 môwshâb (1), *seat; site; abode*
5975 'âmad (1), to *stand*
7931 shâkan (69), to *reside*
7932 shᵉkan (Ch.) (1), to *reside*
1774 ĕnŏikěō (2), to *inhabit, live with*
2521 kathēmai (1), to *sit down; to remain, reside*
2730 katŏikěō (19), to *reside, live in*
3306 měnō (2), to *stay, remain*
3611 ŏikěō (4), to *reside, inhabit, remain*
4637 skēnŏō (4), to *occupy; to reside*
4924 sunŏikěō (1), to *reside together* as a family

DWELLED
3427 yâshab (6), to *dwell, to remain; to settle*

DWELLERS
7931 shâkan (1), to *reside*
2730 katŏikěō (2), to *reside, live in*

DWELLEST
3427 yâshab (14), to *dwell, to remain*
7931 shâkan (3), to *reside*
2730 katŏikěō (1), to *reside, live in*
3306 měnō (1), to *stay, remain*

DWELLETH
1481 gûwr (1), to *sojourn, live as an alien*
3427 yâshab (17), to *dwell, to remain*
4908 mishkân (1), *residence*
7931 shâkan (9), to *reside*
8271 shᵉrê' (Ch.) (1), to *free, separate; to reside*
1774 ĕnŏikěō (2), to *inhabit, live with*
2730 katŏikěō (7), to *reside, live in*
3306 měnō (9), to *stay, remain*
3611 ŏikěō (4), to *reside, inhabit, remain*

DWELLING
168 'ôhel (3), *tent*
2073 zᵉbûwl (1), *residence, dwelling*
3427 yâshab (17), to *dwell, to remain*
4070 mᵉdôwr (Ch.) (4), *dwelling*
4186 môwshâb (5), *seat; site; abode*
4349 mâkôwn (2), *basis; place*
4583 mâ'ôwn (6), *retreat or asylum dwelling*
4585 mᵉ'ôwnâh (1), *abode*
4908 mishkân (4), *residence*
5116 nâveh (3), *at home; lovely; home*
7931 shâkan (1), to *reside*
1460 ĕgkatŏikěō (1), *reside, live among*
2730 katŏikěō (3), to *reside, live in*
2731 katŏikěsis (1), *residence*
3611 ŏikěō (1), to *reside, inhabit, remain*

DWELLINGPLACE
4186 môwshâb (1), *seat; site; abode*
790 astatěō (1), *homeless, vagabond*

DWELLINGPLACES
4186 môwshâb (2), *seat; site; abode*
4908 mishkân (3), *residence*

DWELLINGS
4033 mâgûwr (2), *abode*
4186 môwshâb (8), *seat; site; abode*
4908 mishkân (6), *residence*
5116 nâveh (1), *at home; lovely; home*

DWELT
1753 dûwr (Ch.) (2), to *reside, live in*
2583 chânâh (2), to *encamp*
3427 yâshab (189), to *dwell, to remain*
4186 môwshâb (2), *seat; site; abode*
7931 shâkan (11), to *reside*
1774 ĕnŏikěō (1), to *inhabit, live with*
2730 katŏikěō (12), to *reside, live in*
3306 měnō (2), to *stay, remain*
3940 parŏikia (1), *foreign residence*
4039 pěriŏikěō (1), to be *a neighbor*
4637 skēnŏō (1), to *occupy; to reside*

DYED
2556 châmêts (1), to be *fermented; be soured*
2871 ṭâbûwl (1), *turban*

DYING
1478 gâva' (1), to *expire, die*
599 apŏthnēskō (4), to *die off*
3500 někrōsis (1), *death, deadness*

EACH
259 'echâd (10), *first*
376 'îysh (5), *man; male; someone*
802 'ishshâh (2), *woman, wife; women, wives*
905 bad (1), *limb, member; bar; chief*
240 allēlōn (2), *one another*
303 ana (1), *each; in turn; among*
1538 hěkastŏs (2), *each or every*

EAGLE
5404 nesher (19), *large bird of prey*
7360 râchâm (2), *kind of vulture*
105 aětŏs (2), *eagle, vulture*

EAGLE'S
5403 nᵉshar (Ch.) (1), *large bird of prey*
5404 nesher (1), *large bird of prey*

EAGLES
5404 nesher (5), *large bird of prey*
105 aětŏs (2), *eagle, vulture*

EAGLES'
5403 nᵉshar (Ch.) (1), *large bird of prey*
5404 nesher (1), *large bird of prey*

EAR
24 'âbîyb (1), *head of grain; month of Abib*
238 'âzan (33), to *listen*
241 'ôzen (63), *ear*

EARED
5647 'âbad (1), to *do, work, serve*

EARING
2758 chârîysh (2), *plowing; plowing season*

EARLY
1242 bôqer (3), *morning*
6852 tsâphar (1), to *return*
7836 shâchar (6), to *search for*
7837 shachar (2), *dawn*
7925 shâkam (62), to *start early*
8238 shᵉpharphar (Ch.) (1), *dawn*
260+4404 hama (1), *at the same time, together*
3719 ŏrthrizō (1), to *get up early in the morning*
3721 ŏrthriŏs (1), *up at day-break*
3722 ŏrthrŏs (3), *dawn, daybreak*
4404 prōï (3), *at dawn; day-break watch*
4405 prōïa (1), *day-dawn, early morn*
4406 prōïmŏs (1), *autumnal showering*

EARNEST
603 apŏkaradŏkia (2), *intense anticipation*
728 arrhabōn (3), *pledge, security*
1972 ěpipŏthēsis (1), *longing for*
4056 pěrissŏtěrōs (1), *more superabundantly*
4710 spŏudē (1), *eagerness, earnestness*

EARNESTLY
2734 chârâh (1), to *blaze up*
3190 yâṭab (1), to *be, make well*
816 atěnizō (3), to *gaze intently*
1617 ěktěněstěrŏn (1), *more earnest*
1864 ěpagōnizŏmai (1), to *struggle for, fight for*
1971 ěpipŏthěō (1), *intensely crave*
2206 zēlŏō (1), to *have warmth of feeling for*
4335 prŏsěuchē (1), *prayer; prayer chapel*

EARNETH
7936 sâkar (1), to *hire*

EARRING
5141 nezem (5), *nose-ring*

EARRING
5621 ōtiŏn (5), *earlet, ear (-lobe)*

EARED
5647 'âbad (1), to *do, work, serve*

EAR
8085 shâma' (1), to *hear intelligently*
3775 ŏus (13), *ear; listening*
4719 stachus (2), *head of grain*

EARRINGS
3908 lachash (1), *incantation; amulet*
5141 nezem (9), *nose-ring*
5694 'âgîyl (2), *ear-ring*

EARS
24 'âbîyb (1), *head of grain;* month of *Abib*
241 'ôzen (100), *ear*
3759 karmel (3), *planted field;* garden *produce*
4425 mᵉlîylâh (1), *cut-off head* of cereal grain
7641 shibbôl (13), *stream;* ear of grain
189 akŏē (4), *hearing; thing heard*
191 akŏuō (1), to *hear; obey*
3775 ŏus (24), *ear; listening*
4719 stachus (3), *head of grain*

EARTH
127 'ǎdâmâh (52), *soil; land*
772 'ǎra' (Ch.) (20), *earth, ground, land*
776 'erets (710), *earth, land, soil; country*
778 'ǎraq (Ch.) (1), *earth*
2789 cheres (1), piece of earthenware *pottery*
3007 yabbesheth (Ch.) (1), *dry* land
6083 'âphâr (7), *dust, earth, mud; clay,*
1093 gē (186), *soil, region,* whole *earth*
1919 ĕpigĕiŏs (1), *worldly, earthly*
2709 katachthŏniŏs (1), *infernal*
3625 ŏikŏumĕnē (1), *Roman empire*
3749 ŏstrakinŏs (1), *made of clay*

EARTHEN
2789 cheres (8), piece of earthenware *pottery*
3335 yâtsar (1), to *form; potter;* to *determine*
3749 ŏstrakinŏs (1), *made of clay*

EARTHLY
1537+3588+1093 ĕk (1), *out, out of*
1919 ĕpigĕiŏs (4), *worldly, earthly*

EARTHQUAKE
7494 ra'ash (6), *vibration, uproar*
4578 sĕismŏs (10), *gale storm; earthquake*

EARTHQUAKES
4578 sĕismŏs (3), *gale storm; earthquake*

EARTHY
5517 chŏikŏs (4), *dusty, dirty,* i.e. *terrene*

EASE
2896 ṭôwb (1), *good; well*
3427 yâshab (1), to *dwell,* to *remain;* to *settle*

4496 mᵉnûwchâh (1), *peacefully; consolation*
5162 nâcham (1), to *be sorry;* to *pity, console*
5375 nâsâ' (1), to *lift up*
7043 qâlal (2), to *be easy, trifling, vile*
7280 râga' (1), to *settle,* i.e. *quiet;* to *wink*
7599 shâ'an (2), to *loll,* i.e. *be peaceful*
7600 sha'ǎnân (6), *secure; haughty*
7946 shal'ǎnân (1), *tranquil*
7961 shâlêv (2), *carefree; security,* at *ease*
373 anapauō (1), to *repose;* to *refresh*

EASED
1980 hâlak (1), to *walk;* live *a certain way*
425 anĕsis (1), *relaxation; relief*

EASIER
7043 qâlal (1), to *be easy, trifling, vile*
2123 ĕukŏpōtĕrŏs (7), *better for toil*

EAST
2777 charçûwth (1), *pottery*
4161 môwtsâ' (1), *going forth*
4217 mizrâch (33), place of *sunrise; east*
4217+8121 mizrâch (2), place of *sunrise; east*
6921 qâdîym (61), *east; eastward;* east wind
6924 qedem (42), *east, eastern; antiquity*
6926 qidmâh (3), *east;* on the *east,* in front
6930 qadmôwn (1), *eastern*
6931 qadmôwnîy (4), *oriental, eastern*
395 anatŏlē (9), *dawn* of sun; *east*

EASTER
3957 pascha (1), *Passover* events

EASTWARD
1870+6921 derek (1), *road;* course of life
4217 mizrâch (19), place of *sunrise; east*
4217+8121 mizrâch (1), place of *sunrise; east*
6921 qâdîym (7), *East; eastward;* east wind
6924 qedem (11), *east, eastern; antiquity*
6926 qidmâh (1), *east;* on the *east,* in front

EASY
7043 qâlal (1), to *be easy, trifling, vile*
2138 ĕupĕithēs (1), *compliant, submissive*
2154 ĕusēmŏs (1), *significant*
5543 chrēstŏs (1), *employed,* i.e. *useful*

EAT
398 'âkal (497), to *eat*

399 'ǎkal (Ch.) (1), to *eat*
402 'oklâh (2), *food*
1262 bârâh (4), to *feed*
2490 châlal (1), to *profane, defile*
2939 tᵉ'am (Ch.) (2), to *feed*
3898 lâcham (5), to *fight a battle,* i.e. *consume*
3899 lechem (1), *food, bread*
6310 peh (1), *mouth; opening*
7462 râ'âh (2), to *tend* a flock, i.e. *pasture* it
1089 gĕuŏmai (1), to *taste;* to *eat*
2068 ĕsthiō (39), to *eat*
2719 katĕsthiō (1), to *devour*
3335 mĕtalambanō (1), *to participate*
3542+2192 nŏmē (1), *pasture, feeding*
4906 sunĕsthiō (4), to *take food with*
5315 phagō (88), to *eat*

EATEN
398 'âkal (86), to *eat*
935+413+7130 bôw' (2), to *go or come*
1197 bâ'ar (2), to *be brutish, be senseless*
2490 châlal (1), to *profane, defile*
7462 râ'âh (1), to *tend* a flock, i.e. *pasture* it
977 bibrōskō (1), to *eat*
1089 gĕuŏmai (2), to *taste;* to *eat*
2068 ĕsthiō (1), to *eat*
2719 katĕsthiō (1), to *devour*
2880 kŏrĕnnumi (1), to *cram,* i.e. *glut or sate*
4662 skōlĕkŏbrōtŏs (1), *diseased with maggots*
5315 phagō (5), to *eat*

EATER
398 'âkal (3), to *eat*

EATERS
2151 zâlal (1), to *be loose* morally, *worthless*

EATEST
398 'âkal (3), to *eat*

EATETH
398 'âkal (31), to *eat*
1104 bâla' (1), to *swallow;* to *destroy*
2068 ĕsthiō (13), to *eat*
4906 sunĕsthiō (1), to *take food with*
5176 trōgō (5), to *gnaw or chew,* i.e. to *eat*

EATING
398 'âkal (13), to *eat*
400 'ôkel (4), *food*
3894 lâchûwm (1), *flesh* as food
1035 brōsis (1), *food; rusting corrosion*
2068 ĕsthiō (6), to *eat*
5176 trōgō (1), to *gnaw or chew,* i.e. to *eat*
5315 phagō (1), to *eat*

EBAL
5858 'Êybâl (8), *bare, bald*

EBED
5651 'Ebed (6), *servant*

EBED-MELECH
5663 'Ebed Melek (6), *servant of a king*

EBEN-EZER
72 'Eben hâ-'êzer (3), *stone of the help*

EBER
5677 'Êber (13), *regions beyond*

EBIASAPH
43 'Ebyâçâph (3), *Ebjasaph*

EBONY
1894 hôben (1), *ebony*

EBRONAH
5684 'Ebrônâh (2), *Ebronah*

EDAR
5740 'Êder (1), *flock*

EDEN
5731 'Êden (20), *pleasure*

EDER
5740 'Êder (3), *flock*

EDGE
5310 nâphats (1), to *dash* to pieces; to *scatter*
6310 peh (34), *mouth; opening*
6440 pânîym (1), *face; front*
6697 tsûwr (1), *rock*
6949 qâhâh (3), to *be dull; be blunt*
7097 qâtseh (8), *extremity*
8193 sâphâh (5), *lip; edge, margin*
4750 stŏma (2), *mouth; edge*

EDGES
6366 pêyâh (1), *edge*
7098 qâtsâh (1), *termination; fringe*
7099 qetsev (1), *limit, borders*
1366 distŏmŏs (1), *double-edged*

EDIFICATION
3619 ŏikŏdŏmē (4), *edification*

EDIFIED
3618 ŏikŏdŏmĕō (2), to *construct, edify*

EDIFIETH
3618 ŏikŏdŏmĕō (3), to *construct, edify*

EDIFY
3618 ŏikŏdŏmĕō (2), to *construct, edify*
3619 ŏikŏdŏmē (1), *edification*

EDIFYING
3618 ŏikŏdŏmĕō (1), to *construct, edify*
3619 ŏikŏdŏmē (7), *edification*

EDOM
123 'Ĕdôm (87), *red*

EDOMITE
130 'Ĕdômîy (6), *Edomite*

English

EDOMITES
130 'Ĕdômîy (12),
Edomite

EDREI
154 'edre'îy (8), mighty

EFFECT
1697 dâbâr (1), word;
matter; thing
5106 nûw' (1), to refuse,
forbid, dissuade
5656 'ăbôdâh (1), work of
any kind
6213 'âsâh (1), to do or
make
6565 pârar (1), to break
up; to violate, frustrate
208 akuróō (2), to
invalidate, nullify
1601 ĕkpiptō (1), to drop
away
2673 katargĕō (4), to be,
render entirely useless
2758 kĕnóō (1), to make
empty

EFFECTED
6743 tsâlach (1), to push
forward

EFFECTUAL
1753 ĕnĕrgĕia (2),
efficiency, energy
1754 ĕnĕrgĕō (2), to be
active, efficient, work
1756 ĕnĕrgēs (2), active,
operative

EFFECTUALLY
1754 ĕnĕrgĕō (2), to be
active, efficient, work

EFFEMINATE
3120 malakŏs (1), soft;
catamite homosexual

EGG
2495 challâmùwth (1),
(poss.) purslain plant
5609 ŏŏn (1), egg

EGGS
1000 bêytsâh (6), egg

EGLAH
5698 'Eglâh (2), heifer

EGLAIM
97 'Eglayim (1), double
pond

EGLON
5700 'Eglôwn (13),
vituline

EGYPT
4713 Mitsrîy (1), Mitsrite
4714 Mitsrayim (585),
double border
125 Aiguptŏs (24),
Ægyptus

EGYPTIAN
4713 Mitsrîy (18), Mitsrite
4714 Mitsrayim (2),
double border
124 Aiguptiŏs (3),
inhabitant of Ægyptus

EGYPTIAN'S
4713 Mitsrîy (4), Mitsrite

EGYPTIANS
4713 Mitsrîy (7), Mitsrite
4714 Mitsrayim (88),
double border
124 Aiguptiŏs (2),
inhabitant of Ægyptus

EHI
278 'Êchîy (1), Echi

EHUD
261 'Êchûwd (10), united

EIGHT
8083 shᵉmôneh (74),
eight; eighth
3638 ŏktō (6), eight

EIGHTEEN
7239+8083 ribbôw (1),
myriad
8083+6240 shᵉmôneh
(18), eight; eighth
1176+2532+3638 dĕka (3),
ten

EIGHTEENTH
8083+6240 shᵉmôneh
(11), eight; eighth

EIGHTH
8066 shᵉmîynîy (28),
eight, eighth
8083 shᵉmôneh (4),
eight; eighth
3590 ŏgdŏŏs (5), eighth
3637 ŏktaĕmĕrŏs (1),
eighth-day

EIGHTIETH
8084 shᵉmônîym (1),
eighty; eightieth

EIGHTY
8084 shᵉmônîym (3),
eighty; eightieth

EITHER
176 'ôw (7), or, whether;
desire
376 'îysh (3), man; male;
someone
518 'îm (1), whether?; if,
although; Oh that!
1571 gam (1), also; even;
"both...and"
3588 kîy (1), for, that
because
8145 shênîy (1), second;
again
2228 ē (9), or; than

EKER
6134 'Êqer (1),
naturalized citizen

EKRON
6138 'Eqrôwn (22),
eradication

EKRONITES
6139 'Eqrôwnîy (2),
Ekronite

EL-BETH-EL
416 'Êl Bêyth-'Êl (1), God
of Bethel

EL-ELOHE-ISRAEL
415 'Êl 'ĕlôhêy Yisrâ'êl
(1), mighty God of Israel

EL-PARAN
364 'Êyl Pâ'rân (1), oak
of Paran

ELADAH
497 'El'âdâh (1), God has
decked

ELAH
425 'Êlâh (17), oak

ELAM
5867 'Êylâm (28), distant

ELAMITES
5962 'Almîy (Ch.) (1),
Elamite
1639 Ĕlamitēs (1),
distant ones

ELASAH
501 'El'âsâh (2), God has
made

ELATH
359 'Êylôwth (5), grove
(of palms)

ELDAAH
420 'Eldâ'âh (2), God of
knowledge

ELDAD
419 'Eldâd (2), God has
loved

ELDER
1419 gâdôwl (8), great
2205+3117 zâqên (1), old,
venerated
7227 rab (1), great
3187 mĕizōn (1), larger,
greater
4245 prĕsbutĕrŏs (7),
elderly; older; presbyter
4850 sumprĕsbutĕrŏs (1),
co-presbyter

ELDERS
2205 zâqên (113), old,
venerated
7868 sîyb (Ch.) (5), to
become aged
4244 prĕsbutĕriŏn (2),
order of elders
4245 prĕsbutĕrŏs (58),
elderly; older; presbyter

ELDEST
1060 bᵉkôwr (5),
firstborn, i.e. oldest son
1419 gâdôwl (6), great
2205 zâqên (1), old,
venerated
7223 rî'shôwn (1), first, in
place, time or rank
4245 prĕsbutĕrŏs (1),
elderly; older; presbyter

ELEAD
496 'El'âd (1), God has
testified

ELEALEH
500 'El'âlê' (5), God (is)
going up

ELEASAH
501 'El'âsâh (4), God has
made

ELEAZAR
499 'El'âzâr (71), God (is)
helper
1648 Ĕlĕazar (2), God (is)
helper

ELECT
972 bâchîyr (4), selected
one
1588 ĕklĕktŏs (13),
selected; chosen

ELECT'S
1588 ĕklĕktŏs (3),
selected; chosen

ELECTED
4899 sunĕklĕktŏs (1),
co-elected

ELECTION
1589 ĕklŏgē (6),
selection, choice

ELEMENTS
4747 stŏichĕiŏn (4),
elements, elementary

ELEPH
507 'Eleph (1), thousand

ELEVEN
259+6240 'echâd (9), first
505+3967 'eleph (3),
thousand
6249+6240 ashtêy (6),
eleven; eleventh
1733 hĕndĕka (6), eleven

ELEVENTH
259+6240 'echâd (4), first
6249+6240 'ashtêy (12),
eleven; eleventh
1734 hĕndĕkatŏs (3),
eleventh

ELHANAN
445 'Elchânân (4), God
(is) gracious

ELI
5941 'Êlîy (32), lofty
2241 ēli (1), my God

ELI'S
5941 'Êlîy (1), lofty

ELIAB
446 'Êlîy'âb (20), God of
(his) father

ELIAB'S
446 'Êlîy'âb (1), God of
(his) father

ELIADA
450 'Elyâdâ' (3), God (is)
knowing

ELIADAH
450 'Elyâdâ' (1), God (is)
knowing

ELIAH
452 'Êlîyâh (2), God of
Jehovah

ELIAHBA
455 'Elyachbâ' (2), God
will hide

ELIAKIM
471 'Elyâqîym (12), God
of raising
1662 Ĕliakĕim (3), God of
raising

ELIAM
463 'Êlîy'âm (2), God of
(the) people

ELIAS
2243 Hēlias (30), God of
Jehovah

ELIASAPH
460 'Êlyâçâph (6), God
(is) gatherer

ELIASHIB
475 'Elyâshîyb (17), God
will restore

ELIATHAH
448 'Êlîy'âthâh (2), God
of (his) consent

ELIDAD
449 'Êlîydâd (1), God of
(his) love

ELIEL
447 'Ĕlîy'êl (10), *God of (his) God*

ELIENAI
462 'Ĕlîy'êynay (1), *Elienai*

ELIEZER
461 'Ĕlîy'ezer (14), *God of help*
1663 Ĕlîĕzĕr (1), *God of help*

ELIHOENAI
454 'Elyᵉhôw'êynay (1), *toward Jehovah (are) my eyes*

ELIHOREPH
456 'Ĕlîychôreph (1), *God of autumn*

ELIHU
453 'Ĕlîyhûw (11), *God of him*

ELIJAH
452 'Ĕlîyâh (69), *God of Jehovah*

ELIKA
470 'Ĕlîyqâ' (1), *God of rejection*

ELIM
362 'Êylîm (6), *palm-trees*

ELIMELECH
458 'Ĕlîymelek (4), *God of (the) king*

ELIMELECH'S
458 'Ĕlîymelek (2), *God of (the) king*

ELIOENAI
454 'Elyᵉhôw'êynay (8), *toward Jehovah (are) my eyes*

ELIPHAL
465 'Ĕlîyphâl (1), *God of judgment*

ELIPHALET
467 'Ĕlîyphelet̬ (2), *God of deliverance*

ELIPHAZ
464 'Ĕlîyphaz (15), *God of gold*

ELIPHELEH
466 'Ĕlîyphᵉlêhûw (2), *God of his distinction*

ELIPHELET
467 'Ĕlîyphelet̬ (6), *God of deliverance*

ELISABETH
1665 Ĕlisabĕt (8), *God of (the) oath*

ELISABETH'S
1665 Ĕlisabĕt (1), *God of (the) oath*

ELISEUS
1666 Ĕlissaiŏs (1), *Elisha*

ELISHA
477 'Ĕlîyshâ' (58), *Elisha*

ELISHAH
473 'Ĕlîyshâh (3), *Elishah*

ELISHAMA
476 'Ĕlîyshâmâ' (17), *God of hearing*

ELISHAPHAT
478 'Ĕlîyshâphât̬ (1), *God of judgment*

ELISHEBA
472 'Ĕlîysheba' (1), *God of (the) oath*

ELISHUA
474 'Ĕlîyshûwa' (2), *God of supplication (or of riches)*

ELIUD
1664 Ĕliŏud (2), *God of majesty*

ELIZAPHAN
469 'Ĕlîytsâphân (4), *God of treasure*

ELIZUR
468 'Ĕlîytsûwr (5), *God of (the) rock*

ELKANAH
511 'Elqânâh (20), *God has obtained*

ELKOSHITE
512 'Elqŏshîy (1), *Elkoshite*

ELLASAR
495 'Ellâçâr (2), *Ellasar*

ELMODAM
1678 Ĕlmŏdam (1), *Elmodam*

ELMS
424 'êlâh (1), *oak*

ELNAAM
493 'Elna'am (1), *God (is his) delight*

ELNATHAN
494 'Elnâthân (7), *God (is the) giver*

ELOI
1682 ĕlŏï (1), *my God*

ELON
356 'Êylôwn (7), *oak-grove*

ELON-BETH-HANAN
358 'Êylôwn Bêyth Chânân (1), *oak-grove of (the) house of favor*

ELONITES
440 'Êlôwnîy (1), *Elonite*

ELOQUENT
376+1697 'îysh (1), *man; male; someone*
995 bîyn (1), *to understand; discern*
3052 lŏgiŏs (1), *fluent, i.e. an orator*

ELOTH
359 'Êylôwth (3), *grove (of palms)*

ELPAAL
508 'Elpa'al (3), *God (is) act*

ELPALET
467 'Ĕlîyphelet̬ (1), *God of deliverance*

ELSE
369 'ayin (1), *there is no, i.e. not exist, none*
518 'îm (1), *whether?; if, although; Oh that!*
3588 kîy (3), *for, that because*

5750 'ôwd (13), *again; repeatedly; still; more*
1490 ĕi dĕ mĕ(gĕ) (8), *but if not*
1893 ĕpĕi (2), *since*
2087 hĕtĕrŏs (1), *other or different*
2532 kai (1), *and; or; even; also*

ELTEKEH
514 'Eltᵉqê' (2), *Eltekeh*

ELTEKON
515 'Eltᵉqôn (1), *God (is) straight*

ELTOLAD
513 'Eltôwlad (2), *God (is) generator*

ELUL
435 'Ĕlûwl (1), *Elul*

ELUZAI
498 'El'ûwzay (1), *God (is) defensive*

ELYMAS
1681 Ĕlumas (1), *Elymas*

ELZABAD
443 'Elzâbâd (2), *God has bestowed*

ELZAPHAN
469 'Ĕlîytsâphân (2), *God of treasure*

EMBALM
2590 chânat̬ (1), *to embalm; to ripen*

EMBALMED
2590 chânat̬ (3), *to embalm; to ripen*

EMBOLDENED
3618 ŏikŏdŏmĕŏ (1), *to construct, edify*

EMBOLDENETH
4834 mârats (1), *to be pungent or vehement*

EMBRACE
2263 châbaq (8), *to clasp the hands, embrace*

EMBRACED
2263 châbaq (3), *to clasp the hands, embrace*
782 aspazŏmai (2), *to salute, welcome*

EMBRACING
2263 châbaq (1), *to clasp the hands, embrace*
4843 sumpĕrilambanŏ (1), *to embrace*

EMBROIDER
7660 shâbats (1), *to interweave*

EMBROIDERER
7551 râqam (2), *variegation; embroider*

EMERALD
5306 nôphek (3), *(poss.) garnet*
4664 smaragdinŏs (1), *of emerald*
4665 smaragdŏs (1), *green emerald*

EMERALDS
5306 nôphek (1), *(poss.) garnet*

EMERODS
2914 t̬ᵉchôr (2), *piles, tumor*
6076 'ôphel (6), *tumor; fortress*

EMIMS
368 'Êymîym (3), *terrors*

EMINENT
1354 gab (3), *mounded or rounded: top or rim*
8524 tâlal (1), *to elevate*

EMMANUEL
1694 Ĕmmanŏuēl (1), *God with us*

EMMAUS
1695 Ĕmmaŏus (1), *Emmaüs*

EMMOR
1697 Ĕmmŏr (1), *male donkey or ass*

EMPIRE
4438 malkûwth (1), *rule; dominion*

EMPLOY
935+6440 bôw' (1), *to go or come*

EMPLOYED
5921 'al (1), *above, over, upon, or against*
5975 'âmad (1), *to stand*

EMPTIED
1238 bâqaq (2), *to depopulate, ruin*
1809 dâlal (1), *to slacken, dangle*
6168 'ârâh (2), *to be, make bare; to empty*
7324 rûwq (2), *to pour out, i.e. empty*
7386 rêyq (1), *empty; worthless*

EMPTIERS
1238 bâqaq (1), *to depopulate, ruin*

EMPTINESS
922 bôhûw (1), *ruin, desolation*

EMPTY
950 bûwqâh (1), *empty, pillaged*
1238 bâqaq (3), *to depopulate, ruin*
6437 pânâh (1), *to turn, to face*
6485 pâqad (3), *to visit, care for, count*
7324 rûwq (5), *to pour out, i.e. empty*
7385 rîyq (5), *emptiness; worthless thing; in vain*
7386 rêyq (2), *empty; worthless*
7387 rêyqâm (12), *emptily; ineffectually*
8414 tôhûw (1), *waste, desolation, formless*
2756 kĕnŏs (4), *empty; vain; useless*
4980 schŏlazŏ (1), *to take a holiday*

EMULATION
3863 parazēlŏŏ (1), *to excite to rivalry*

English

EMULATIONS
2205 zēlŏs (1), zeal,
ardor; jealousy, malice

EN-DOR
5874 'Êyn-Dô'r (3),
fountain of dwelling

EN-EGLAIM
5882 'Êyn 'Eglayim (1),
fountain of two calves

EN-GANNIM
5873 'Êyn Gannîym (3),
fountain of gardens

EN-GEDI
5872 'Êyn Gedîy (6),
fountain of a kid

EN-HADDAH
5876 'Êyn Chaddâh (1),
fountain of sharpness

EN-HAKKORE
5875 'Êyn haq-Qôwrê'
(1), fountain of One
calling

EN-HAZOR
5877 'Êyn Châtsôwr (1),
fountain of a village

EN-MISHPAT
5880 'Êyn Mishpâṭ (1),
fountain of judgment

EN-RIMMON
5884 'Êyn Rimmôwn (1),
fountain of a
pomegranate

EN-ROGEL
5883 'Êyn Rôgêl (4),
fountain of a traveller

EN-SHEMESH
5885 'Êyn Shemesh (2),
fountain of (the) sun

EN-TAPPUAH
5887 'Êyn Tappûwach
(1), fountain of an
apple tree

ENABLED
1743 ĕndunamŏō (1), to
empower, strengthen

ENAM
5879 'Êynayim (1),
double fountain

ENAN
5881 'Êynân (5), having
eyes

ENCAMP
2583 chânâh (11), to
encamp for abode or
siege

ENCAMPED
2583 chânâh (33), to
encamp

ENCAMPETH
2583 chânâh (2), to
encamp

ENCAMPING
2583 chânâh (1), to
encamp

ENCHANTER
5172 nâchash (1), to
prognosticate

ENCHANTERS
6049 'ânan (1), to cover,
becloud; to act covertly

ENCHANTMENT
3908 lachash (1),
incantation; amulet
5172 nâchash (2), to
prognosticate

ENCHANTMENTS
2267 cheber (2), society,
group; magic spell
3858 lahaṭ (1), blaze;
magic
3909 lâṭ (3), incantation;
secrecy; covertly
5172 nâchash (4), to
prognosticate

ENCOUNTERED
4820 sumballō (1), to
consider; to aid; to join

ENCOURAGE
2388 châzaq (4), to be
strong; courageousd,
restrain, conquer

ENCOURAGED
2388 châzaq (5), to be
strong; courageous

END
319 'achărîyth (21),
future; posterity
657 'epheç (1), end; no
further
1104 bâla' (1), to
swallow; to destroy
1584 gâmar (1), to end;
to complete; to fail
1700 dibrâh (1), reason,
suit or style; because
2583 chânâh (1), to
encamp
2856 châtham (1), to
close up; to affix a seal
3318 yâtsâ' (1), to go,
bring out
3615 kâlâh (56), to
complete, prepare
4390 mâlê' (1), to fill; be
full
4616 ma'an (8), in order
that
5239 nâlâh (1), to
complete, attain
5331 netsach (2),
splendor; lasting
5486 çûwph (1), to
terminate
5490 çôwph (3),
termination; end
5491 çôwph (Ch.) (5), end
5704+5769+5703 'ad (1),
during; while; until
6118 'êqeb (2), on
account of
6285 pê'âh (1), direction;
region; extremity
6310 peh (3), mouth;
opening
7078 qenets (1),
perversion
7093 qêts (51), extremity;
after
7097 qâtseh (48),
extremity
7098 qâtsâh (4),
termination; fringe
7117 qᵉtsâth (3),
termination; portion
7118 qᵉtsâth (Ch.) (2),
termination; portion

7999 shâlam (2), to be
safe; complete
8503 taklîyth (2),
extremity
8537 tôm (1),
completeness
8552 tâmam (2), to
complete, finish
8622 tᵉqûwphâh (2),
revolution, course
165+3588+165 aiōn (1),
perpetuity, ever; world
206 akrŏn (1), extremity:
end, top
1519 ĕis (4), to or into
1545 ĕkbasis (1), exit,
way out
2078 ĕschatŏs (1),
farthest, final
3796 ŏpsĕ (1), late in the
day
4009 pĕras (1), extremity,
end, limit
4930 suntĕlĕia (6), entire
completion
5049 tĕlĕiŏs (1),
completely
5055 tĕlĕō (1), to end, i.e.
complete, conclude
5056 tĕlŏs (34),
conclusion

ENDAMAGE
5142 nᵉzaq (Ch.) (1), to
suffer, inflict loss

ENDANGER
2325 chùwb (1), to tie, to
owe, to forfeit

ENDANGERED
5533 çâkan (1), to
damage; to grow

ENDEAVOUR
4704 spŏudazō (1), to
make effort

ENDEAVOURED
2212 zētĕō (1), to seek
4704 spŏudazō (1), to
make effort

ENDEAVOURING
4704 spŏudazō (1), to
make effort

ENDEAVOURS
4611 ma'ălâl (1), act,
deed

ENDED
3615 kâlâh (7), to cease,
be finished, perish
7999 shâlam (2), to be
safe; be complete
8552 tâmam (5), to
complete, finish
1096 ginŏmai (1), to be,
become
4137 plĕrŏō (2), to fill,
make complete
4931 suntĕlĕō (4), to
complete entirely

ENDETH
2308 châdal (1), to desist,
stop; be fat

ENDING
5056 tĕlŏs (1), conclusion
of an act or state

ENDLESS
179 akatalutŏs (1),
permanent

562 apĕrantŏs (1),
without a finish

ENDOW
4117 mâhar (1), to wed a
wife by bargaining

ENDS
657 'epheç (13), end; no
further
1383 gablûth (2), twisted
chain or lace
3671 kânâph (2), edge or
extremity; wing
4020 migbâlâh (1),
border on garb
7097 qâtseh (7), extremity
7098 qâtsâh (17),
termination; fringe
7099 qetsev (4), limit,
borders
7218 rô'sh (2), head
2078 ĕschatŏs (1),
farthest, final
4009 pĕras (1), extremity,
end, limit
5056 tĕlŏs (1), conclusion
of an act or state

ENDUED
2064 zâbad (1), to confer,
bestow a gift
3045 yâda' (2), to know
1746 ĕnduō (1), to dress
1990 ĕpistēmōn (1),
intelligent, learned

ENDURE
1961 hâyâh (3), to exist,
i.e. be or become
3201 yâkôl (2), to be able
3427 yâshab (2), to dwell,
to remain; to settle
3885 lûwn (1), to be
obstinate
5975 'âmad (3), to stand
6440 pânîym (1), face;
front
6965 qùwm (1), to rise
7272 regel (1), foot; step
430 anĕchŏmai (2), put
up with, endure
2076 ĕsti (1), he (she or
it) is; they are
2553 kakŏpathĕō (2), to
undergo hardship
5278 hupŏmĕnō (5), to
undergo (trials)
5297 hupŏphĕrō (1), to
undergo hardship
5342 phĕrō (1), to bear or
carry

ENDURED
1961 hâyâh (1), to exist,
i.e. be or become
2594 kartĕrĕō (1), to be
steadfast or patient
3114 makrŏthumĕō (1),
to be forbearing, patient
5278 hupŏmĕnō (3), to
undergo (trials)
5297 hupŏphĕrō (1), to
undergo hardship
5342 phĕrō (1), to bear or
carry

ENDURETH
1097 bᵉlîy (1), without,
not yet; lacking;
5975 'âmad (4), to stand
3306 mĕnō (2), to stay,
remain

5278 hupŏmĕnō (3), to
undergo (trials)

ENDURING
5975 'âmad (1), to *stand*
3306 mĕnō (1), to *stay,*
remain
5281 hupŏmŏnē (1),
endurance, constancy

ENEMIES
341 'ôyêb (199),
adversary, enemy
6145 'âr (1), *foe*
6146 'âr (Ch.) (1), *foe*
6862 tsar (26), *trouble;*
opponent
6887 tsârar (9), to *cramp*
6965 qûwm (1), to *rise*
7790 shûwr (1), *foe as*
lying in wait
8130 sânê' (3), to *hate*
8324 shârar (5), *opponent*
2190 ĕchthrŏs (19),
adversary

ENEMIES'
341 'ôyêb (3), *adversary,*
enemy

ENEMY
340 'âyab (1), to *be*
hostile, be an enemy
341 'ôyêb (78),
adversary, enemy
6145 'âr (1), *foe*
6862 tsar (9), *trouble;*
opponent
6887 tsârar (5), to *cramp*
8130 sânê' (2), to *hate*
2190 ĕchthrŏs (11),
adversary

ENEMY'S
341 'ôyêb (1), *adversary,*
enemy
6862 tsar (2), *trouble;*
opponent

ENFLAMING
2552 châmam (1), to *be*
hot; to be in a rage

ENGAGED
6148 'ârab (1), to *intermix*

ENGINES
2810 chishshâbôwn (1),
machination, scheme
4239 mᵉchîy (1), *stroke of*
a battering-ram

ENGRAFTED
1721 ĕmphutŏs (1),
implanted

ENGRAVE
6605 pâthach (2), to *open*
wide; to plow, carve

ENGRAVEN
1795 ĕntupŏō (1), to
engrave, carve

ENGRAVER
2796 chârâsh (3), *skilled*
fabricator or worker

ENGRAVINGS
6603 pittûwach (5),
sculpture; engraving

ENJOIN
2004 ĕpitassō (1), to
order, command

ENJOINED
6485 pâqad (1), to *visit,*
care for, count

6965 qûwm (1), to *rise*
1781 ĕntĕllŏmai (1), to
enjoin, give orders

ENJOY
1086 bâlâh (1), to *wear*
out; consume, spend
1961 hâyâh (1), to *exist,*
i.e. be or become
3423 yârash (2), to
inherit; to impoverish
7200 râ'âh (4), to *see*
7521 râtsâh (3), to *be*
pleased with; to satisfy
619 apŏlausis (1), *full*
enjoyment, pleasure
2192+619 ĕchō (1), to
have; hold; keep
5177 tugchanō (1), to
take part in; to obtain

ENJOYED
7521 râtsâh (1), to *be*
pleased with; to satisfy

ENLARGE
6601 pâthâh (1), to *be,*
make simple; to delude
7235 râbâh (1), to
increase
7337 râchab (7), to
broaden
3170 mĕgalunō (1), to
increase or extol

ENLARGED
7337 râchab (8), to
broaden
3170 mĕgalunō (1), to
increase or extol
4115 platunō (2), to
widen

ENLARGEMENT
7305 revach (1), *room;*
deliverance

ENLARGETH
7337 râchab (2), to
broaden
7849 shâtach (1), to
expand

ENLARGING
7337 râchab (1), to
broaden

ENLIGHTEN
5050 nâgahh (1), to
illuminate

ENLIGHTENED
215 'ôwr (4), to *be*
luminous
5461 phōtizō (2), to *shine*
or to brighten up

ENLIGHTENING
215 'ôwr (1), to *be*
luminous

ENMITY
342 'êybâh (2), *hostility*
2189 ĕchthra (5),
hostility; opposition

ENOCH
2585 Chănôwk (9),
initiated
1802 Ĕnôch (3), *initiated*

ENOS
583 'Ĕnôwsh (6), *man;*
person, human
1800 Ĕnōs (1), *man*

ENOSH
583 'Ĕnôwsh (1), *man;*
person, human

ENOUGH
1767 day (6), *enough,*
sufficient
1952 hôwn (2), *wealth*
3027 yâd (1), *hand; power*
3605 kôl (1), *all, any or*
every
4672 mâtsâ' (1), to *find*
or acquire; to occur
7227 rab (7), *great*
7654 sob'âh (2), *satiety*
566 apĕchĕi (1), *it is*
sufficient
713 arkĕtŏs (1),
satisfactory, enough
714 arkĕō (1), to *avail; be*
satisfactory
2425 hikanŏs (1), *ample;*
fit
2880 kŏrĕnnumi (1), to
cram, i.e. glut or sate
4052 pĕrissĕuō (1), to
superabound

ENQUIRE
1158 bâ'âh (2), to *ask; be*
bulging, swelling
1239 bâqar (2), to
inspect, admire, care
for, consider
1240 bᵉqar (Ch.) (1), to
inspect, admire, care
for, consider
1875 dârash (32), to
pursue or search; to
seek or ask; to worship
7592 shâ'al (7), to *ask*
1231 diaginōskō (1),
ascertain exactly
1833 ĕxĕtazō (1), to
ascertain or interrogate
1934 ĕpizĕtĕō (1), to
search (inquire) for
2212 zĕtĕō (2), to *seek*
4441 punthanŏmai (1), to
ask for information
4802 suzĕtĕō (1), to
discuss, controvert

ENQUIRED
1245 bâqash (2), to
search; to strive after
1875 dârash (10), to
pursue or search
7592 shâ'al (15), to *ask*
7836 shâchar (1), to
search for
198 akribŏō (2), to
ascertain, find out
1567 ĕkzĕtĕō (1), to *seek*
4441 punthanŏmai (1), to
ask for information

ENQUIREST
1245 bâqash (1), to
search; to strive after

ENQUIRY
1239 bâqar (1), to
inspect, admire, care
1331 diĕrōtaō (1), to
question throughout

ENRICH
6238 'âshar (2), to *grow,*
make rich

ENRICHED
4148 plŏutizō (2), to
make wealthy

ENRICHEST
6238 'âshar (1), to *grow,*
make rich

ENSAMPLE
5179 tupŏs (1), *shape or*
resemblance; "type"
5262 hupŏdĕigma (1),
exhibit, specimen

ENSAMPLES
5179 tupŏs (3), *shape or*
resemblance; "type"

ENSIGN
226 'ôwth (1), *signal, sign*
5251 nêç (6), *flag; signal*
5264 nâçaç (1), to *gleam;*
to flutter a flag

ENSIGNS
226 'ôwth (1), *signal, sign*

ENSNARED
4170 môwqêsh (1), *noose*
for catching animals

ENSUE
1377 diōkō (1), to *pursue;*
to persecute

ENTANGLE
3802 pagidĕuō (1), to
ensnare, entrap

ENTANGLED
943 bûwk (1), to *be*
confused
1707 ĕmplĕkō (1), to
involve with
1758 ĕnĕchō (1), to *keep*
a grudge

ENTANGLETH
1707 ĕmplĕkō (1), to
involve with

ENTER
935 bôw (81), to *go or*
come
1980 hâlak (1), to *walk;*
live a certain way
5674 'âbar (1), to *cross*
over; to transition
1525 ĕisĕrchŏmai (63), to
enter
1529 ĕisŏdŏs (1),
entrance
1531 ĕispŏrĕuŏmai (1), to
enter

ENTERED
935 bôw' (38), to *go or*
come
305 anabainō (2), to *go*
up, rise
1524 ĕisĕimi (1), to *enter*
1525 ĕisĕrchŏmai (53), to
enter
1531 ĕispŏrĕuŏmai (3), to
enter
1684 ĕmbainō (7), to
embark; to reach
2064 ĕrchŏmai (2), to *go*
or come
3922 parĕisĕrchŏmai (1),
to supervene

ENTERETH
935 bôw' (9), to *go or*
come
5181 nâchath (1), to *sink,*
descend; to press down
1531 ĕispŏrĕuŏmai (5), to
enter
1535 ĕitĕ (4), *if too*

English

ENTERING
935 bôw' (15), to go, come
3996 mâbôw' (3),
  entrance; sunset; west
6607 pethach (17),
  opening; entrance way
1525 ĕisĕrchŏmai (4), to
  enter
1529 ĕisŏdŏs (1),
  entrance
1531 ĕispŏrĕuŏmai (4), to
  enter
1684 ĕmbainō (1), to
  embark; to reach
1910 ĕpibainō (1), to
  mount, arrive

ENTERPRISE
8454 tûwshîyâh (1),
  ability, undertaking

ENTERTAIN
5381 philŏnĕxia (1),
  hospitableness

ENTERTAINED
3579 xĕnizō (1), to be a
  host; to be a guest

ENTICE
5496 çûwth (1), to
  stimulate; to seduce
6601 pâṯhâh (7), to be,
  make simple; to delude

ENTICED
6601 pâthâh (2), to be,
  make simple; to delude
1185 dĕlĕazō (1), to
  delude, seduce

ENTICETH
6601 pâthâh (1), to be,
  make simple; to delude

ENTICING
3981 pĕithŏs (1),
  persuasive
4086 pithanŏlŏgia (1),
  persuasive language

ENTIRE
3648 hŏlŏklērŏs (1),
  entirely sound in body

ENTRANCE
935 bôw' (2), to go or
  come
2978 yeˈîthôwn (1), entry
3996 mâbôw' (3),
  entrance; sunset; west
6607 pethach (2),
  opening; entrance way
6608 pethach (1), opening
1529 ĕisŏdŏs (2),
  entrance

ENTRANCES
6607 pethach (1),
  opening; entrance way

ENTREAT
6293 pâga' (1), to impinge
2559 kakŏō (1), to injure;
  to oppress; to embitter

ENTREATED
818 atimazō (1), to
  maltreat, dishonor
2559 kakŏō (1), to injure;
  to oppress; to embitter
5195 hubrizō (3), to
  exercise violence
5530 chraŏmai (1), to
  employ or to act toward

ENTRIES
6607 pethach (1),
  opening; entrance way

ENTRY
872 beˈâh (1), entrance
3996 mâbôw' (6),
  entrance; sunset; west
6310 peh (1), mouth;
  opening
6607 pethach (7),
  opening; entrance way

ENVIED
7065 qânâ' (5), to be,
  make jealous, envious
7068 qin'âh (1), jealousy
  or envy

ENVIES
5355 phthŏnŏs (1),
  spiteful jealousy, envy

ENVIEST
7065 qânâ' (1), to be,
  make jealous, envious

ENVIETH
2206 zĕlŏō (1), to have
  warmth of feeling for

ENVIOUS
7065 qânâ' (4), to be,
  make jealous, envious

ENVIRON
5437 çâbab (1), to
  surround

ENVY
7065 qânâ' (3), to be,
  make zealous, jealous
  or envious
7068 qin'âh (7), jealousy
  or envy
2205 zēlŏs (1), zeal,
  ardor; jealousy, malice
2206 zēlŏō (2), to have
  warmth of feeling for
5355 phthŏnŏs (7),
  spiteful jealousy, envy

ENVYING
2205 zēlŏs (4), zeal,
  ardor; jealousy, malice
5354 phthŏnĕō (1), to be
  jealous of

ENVYINGS
2205 zēlŏs (1), zeal,
  ardor; jealousy, malice
5355 phthŏnŏs (1),
  spiteful jealousy, envy

EPAENETUS
1866 Ĕpainĕtŏs (1),
  praised

EPAPHRAS
1889 Ĕpaphras (3),
  devoted to Venus

EPAPHRODITUS
1891 Ĕpaphrŏditŏs (3),
  devoted to Venus

EPHAH
374 'êyphâh (34), dry
  grain measure
5891 'Êyphâh (5),
  obscurity

EPHAI
5778 'Ôwphay (1),
  birdlike

EPHER
6081 'Êpher (4), gazelle

EPHES-DAMMIM
658 'Epheç Dammîym
  (1), boundary of blood

EPHESIAN
2180 Ĕphĕsiŏs (1),
  Ephesian

EPHESIANS
2180 Ĕphĕsiŏs (5),
  Ephesian

EPHESUS
2181 Ĕphĕsŏs (17),
  Ephesus

EPHLAL
654 'Ephlâl (2), judge

EPHOD
641 'Êphôd (1), Ephod
642 'êphuddâh (2),
  plating
646 'êphôwd (49), ephod

EPHPHATHA
2188 ĕphphatha (1), be
  opened!

EPHRAIM
669 'Ephrayim (171),
  double fruit
2187 Ĕphraïm (1), double
  fruit

EPHRAIM'S
669 'Ephrayim (4),
  double fruit

EPHRAIMITE
673 'Ephrâthîy (1),
  Ephrathite or
  Ephraimite

EPHRAIMITES
669 'Ephrayim (5),
  double fruit

EPHRAIN
6085 'Ephrôwn (1),
  fawn-like

EPHRATAH
672 'Ephrâth (5),
  fruitfulness

EPHRATH
672 'Ephrâth (5),
  fruitfulness

EPHRATHITE
673 'Ephrâthîy (3),
  Ephrathite or
  Ephraimite

EPHRATHITES
673 'Ephrâthîy (1),
  Ephrathite or
  Ephraimite

EPHRON
6085 'Ephrôwn (13),
  fawn-like

EPICUREANS
1946 Ĕpikŏurĕiŏs (1),
  servant

EPISTLE
1992 ĕpistŏlē (13),
  written message

EPISTLES
1992 ĕpistŏlē (2), written
  message

EQUAL
1809 dâlal (1), to
  slacken, dangle
4339 mêyshâr (1),
  straightness; rectitude

EPHES
6186 'ârak (2), to set in a
  row, i.e. arrange,
6187 'êrek (1), pile,
  equipment, estimate
7737 shâvâh (3), to level,
  i.e. equalize
8505 tâkan (7), to
  balance, i.e. measure
2465 isaggĕlŏs (1),
  angelic, like an angel
2470 isŏs (4), similar
2471 isŏtēs (1), likeness;
  fairness

EQUALITY
2471 isŏtēs (2), likeness;
  fairness

EQUALLY
7947 shâlab (1), to make
  equidistant

EQUALS
4915 sunēlikiōtēs (1),
  alike, contemporary

EQUITY
3476 yôsher (1), right
3477 yâshâr (1), straight
3788 kishrôwn (1),
  success; advantage
4334 mîyshôwr (2), plain;
  justice
4339 mêyshâr (4),
  straightness; rectitude
5229 neˈkôchâh (1),
  integrity; truth

ER
6147 'Êr (10), watchful
2262 Ēr (1), watchful

ERAN
6197 'Êrân (1), watchful

ERANITES
6198 'Êrânîy (1), Eranite

ERASTUS
2037 Ĕrastŏs (3), beloved

ERE
2962 ṭerem (4), not yet or
  before
3808 lô' (4), no, not
4250 prin (1), prior,
  sooner, before

ERECH
751 'Erek (1), length

ERECTED
5324 nâtsab (1), to station

ERI
6179 'Êrîy (2), watchful

ERITES
6180 'Êrîy (1), Erite

ERR
7686 shâgâh (4), to stray,
  wander; to transgress
8582 tâ'âh (14), to
  vacillate, i.e. stray
4105 planaō (6), to roam,
  wander; to deceive

ERRAND
1697 dâbâr (3), word;
  matter; thing

ERRED
7683 shâgag (5), to stray;
  to sin
7686 shâgâh (2), to stray,
  wander; to transgress
8582 tâ'âh (2), to
  vacillate, i.e. stray

635 apŏplanaō (1), to
lead astray; to *wander*
795 astŏchĕō (2), *deviate*
or *wander* from truth

ERRETH
7686 shâgâh (1), to *stray,*
wander; to *transgress*
8582 tâ'âh (1), to
vacillate, i.e. *stray*

ERROR
4879 mᵉshûwgâh (1),
mistake
7684 shᵉgâgâh (2),
mistake
7944 shal (1), *fault*
7960 shâlûw (Ch.) (1),
fault, error
8432 tâvek (1), *center,
middle*
4106 planē (7),
fraudulence; straying

ERRORS
7691 shᵉgîy'âh (1), moral
mistake
8595 ta'tûa' (2), *fraud*
51 agnŏēma (1), *sin*
committed in ignorance

ESAIAS
2268 Hēsaïas (21),
Jehovah has saved

ESAR-HADDON
634 'Êçar-Chaddôwn (3),
Esar-chaddon

ESAU
6215 'Êsâv (84), *rough*
2269 Ēsau (3), *rough*

ESAU'S
6215 'Êsâv (12), *rough*

ESCAPE
3318 yâtsâ' (1), to *go,
bring out*
4422 mâlaṭ (22), to
escape; be delivered
4498+6 mânôwç (1),
fleeing; place of *refuge*
4655 miphlâṭ (1), *escape,
shelter*
5337 nâtsal (1), to
deliver; to *be snatched*
5674 'âbar (1), to *cross*
over; to *transition*
6403 pâlaṭ (2), to *slip out,*
i.e. *escape;* to *deliver*
6405 pallêṭ (1), *escape*
6412 pâlîyṭ (12), *refugee*
6413 pᵉlêyṭâh (9),
escaped portion
1309 diaphĕugō (1), to
escape, flee
1545 ĕkbasis (1), *exit,
way out*
1628 ĕkphĕugō (4), to
flee out, escape
5343 phĕugō (1), to *run
away;* to *vanish*
5343+575 phĕugō (1), to
run away; to *vanish*

ESCAPED
3318 yâtsâ' (1), to *go,
bring out*
4422 mâlaṭ (25), to
escape; be delivered
5337 nâtsal (1), to
deliver; to *be snatched*
6412 pâlîyṭ (8), *refugee*

6413 pᵉlêyṭâh (11),
escaped portion
7611 shᵉ'êrîyth (1),
remainder or residual
668 apŏphĕugō (3), to
escape from
1295 diasōzō (3), to *cure,
preserve, rescue*
1628 ĕkphĕugō (1), to
flee out, escape
1831 ĕxĕrchŏmai* (1), to
issue; to *leave*
5343 phĕugō (2), to *run
away;* to *vanish*

ESCAPETH
4422 mâlaṭ (3), to *escape;*
be *delivered;* be *smooth*
6412 pâlîyṭ (2), *refugee*
6413 pᵉlêyṭâh (1),
escaped portion

ESCAPING
6413 pᵉlêyṭâh (1),
escaped portion

ESCHEW
1578 ĕkklinō (1), to *shun;*
to *decline*

ESCHEWED
5493 çûwr (1), to *turn* off

ESCHEWETH
5493 çûwr (2), to *turn* off

ESEK
6230 'Êseq (1), *strife*

ESH-BAAL
792 'Eshba'al (2), *man of
Baal*

ESHBAN
790 'Eshbân (2), *vigorous*

ESHCOL
812 'Eshkôl (6), *bunch of
grapes*

ESHEAN
824 'Esh'ân (1), *support*

ESHEK
6232 'Êsheq (1),
oppression

ESHKALONITES
832 'Eshqᵉlôwnîy (1),
Ashkelonite

ESHTAOL
847 'Eshtâ'ôl (7), *entreaty*

ESHTAULITES
848 'Eshtâ'ûlîy (1),
Eshtaolite

ESHTEMOA
851 'Eshtᵉmôa' (5),
Eshtemoa or *Eshtemoh*

ESHTEMOH
851 'Eshtᵉmôa' (1),
Eshtemoa or *Eshtemoh*

ESHTON
850 'Eshtôwn (2), *restful*

ESLI
2069 Ēsli (1), *Esli*

ESPECIALLY
3966 mᵉ'ôd (1), *very,
utterly*
3122 malista (4), *in the
greatest degree*

ESPIED
7200 râ'âh (1), to *see*
8446 tûwr (1), to *wander,
meander*

ESPOUSALS
2861 chăthunnâh (1),
wedding
3623 kᵉlûwlâh (1),
bridehood

ESPOUSED
781 'âras (1), to *engage*
for matrimony, betroth
718 harmŏzō (1), to
betroth for marriage
3423 mnēstĕuō (3), to
betroth, be engaged

ESPY
6822 tsâphâh (1), to *peer;*
to *observe, await*
7270 râgal (1), to
reconnoiter; to *slander*

ESROM
2074 Ēsrōm (3),
court-yard

ESTABLISH
3322 yâtsag (1), to *place*
permanently
3427 yâshab (1), to *dwell,*
to *remain;* to *settle*
3559 kûwn (14), to *set up:
establish, fix, prepare*
5324 nâtsab (1), to *station*
5582 çâ'ad (1), to *support*
5975 'âmad (3), to *stand*
6965 qûwm (17), to *rise*
6966 qûwm (Ch.) (2), to
rise
2476 histēmi (3), to
stand, establish
4741 stērizō (1), to *turn
resolutely;* to *confirm*

ESTABLISHED
539 'âman (7), to *be firm,
faithful, true;* to *trust*
553 'âmats (1), to *be
strong; be courageous*
2388 châzaq (1), to
fasten upon; to *seize*
3245 yâçad (2), *settle,
establish a foundation*
3559 kûwn (44), to *set up:
establish, fix, prepare*
5564 çâmak (1), to *lean*
upon; *take hold of*
5975 'âmad (1), to *stand*
6965 qûwm (9), to *rise*
8627 tᵉqan (Ch.) (1), to
straighten up, *confirm*
950 bĕbaiŏō (1), to
stabilitate, keep strong
2476 histēmi (2), to
stand, establish
3549 nŏmŏthĕtĕō (1), to
be founded, enacted
4732 stĕrĕŏō (1), to *be,
become strong*
4741 stērizō (2), to *turn
resolutely;* to *confirm*

ESTABLISHETH
5975 'âmad (1), to *stand*
6965 qûwm (1), to *rise*
6966 qûwm (Ch.) (1), to
rise

ESTABLISHMENT
571 'emeth (1), *certainty,
truth, trustworthiness*

ESTATE
1700 dibrâh (1), *reason,
suit* or *style; because*

ESPOUSALS (dup heading)

3653 kên (5), *pedestal* or
station of a basin
8448 tôwr (1), *manner*
3588+4012 hŏ (1), "*the,*"
i.e. the definite article

ESTEEM
2803 châshab (1), to *plot;*
to *think, regard*
6186 'ârak (1), to *set in a
row,* i.e. *arrange,*
2233 hēgĕŏmai (2), to
deem, i.e. *consider*

ESTEEMED
2803 châshab (3), to *plot;*
to *think, regard*
5034 nâbêl (1), to *wilt;* to
fall away; to *be foolish*
6845 tsâphan (1), to
deny; to *protect;* to *lurk*
7043 qâlal (2), to *be,
make light*
1848 ĕxôuthĕnĕō (1), to
treat with contempt

ESTEEMETH
2803 châshab (1), to *plot;*
to *think, regard*
2919 krinō (2), to *decide;*
to *try, condemn, punish*
3049 lŏgizŏmai (1), to
credit; to *think, regard*

ESTEEMING
2233 hēgĕŏmai (1), to
lead; to *deem, consider*

ESTHER
635 'Eçtêr (52), *Esther*

ESTHER'S
635 'Eçtêr (3), *Esther*

ESTIMATE
6186 'ârak (2), to *set in a
row,* i.e. *arrange,*

ESTIMATION
6187 'êrek (23), *pile,
equipment, estimate*

ESTIMATIONS
6187 'êrek (1), *pile,
equipment, estimate*

ESTRANGED
2114 zûwr (4), to *be
foreign, strange*
5234 nâkar (1), to *treat
as a foreigner*

ETAM
5862 'Êyṭâm (5),
hawk-ground

ETERNAL
5769 'ôwlâm (1), *eternity;
ancient; always*
6924 qedem (1), *eastern;
antiquity; before*
126 aïdiŏs (1),
everduring, eternal
165 aiōn (2), *perpetuity;
ever; world*
166 aiōniŏs (42),
perpetual, long ago

ETERNITY
5703 'ad (1), *perpetuity;
ancient*

ETHAM
864 'Êthâm (4), *Etham*

ETHAN
387 'Êythân (8),
permanent

English

ETHANIM
388 Êythânîym (1), *permanent* brooks

ETHBAAL
856 'Ethba'al (1), *with Baal*

ETHER
6281 'Ether (2), *abundance*

ETHIOPIA
3568 Kûwsh (19), *Cush*
128 Aithiŏps (1), *inhabitant of Æthiop*

ETHIOPIAN
3569 Kûwshîy (8), *Cushite*

ETHIOPIANS
3569 Kûwshîy (12), *Cushite*
128 Aithiŏps (1), *inhabitant of Æthiop*

ETHNAN
869 'Ethnan (1), *gift* price of harlotry

ETHNI
867 'Ethnîy (1), *munificence, lavishness*

EUBULUS
2103 Êuboûlŏs (1), *good-willer*

EUNICE
2131 Êunîkē (1), *victorious*

EUNUCH
5631 çârîyç (2), *eunuch;* official of state
2135 ĕunoûchŏs (5), *castrated; impotent*

EUNUCHS
5631 çârîyç (15), *eunuch;* official of state
2134 ĕunŏuchizō (3), *to castrate*
2135 ĕunoûchŏs (2), *castrated; impotent*

EUODIAS
2136 Êuŏdia (1), *fine travelling*

EUPHRATES
6578 Pᵉrâth (19), *rushing*
2166 Êuphratēs (2), *Euphrates*

EUROCLYDON
2148 Êurŏkludōn (1), *wind from the east*

EUTYCHUS
2161 Êutuchŏs (1), *fortunate*

EVANGELIST
2099 ĕuaggĕlistēs (2), *preacher* of the gospel

EVANGELISTS
2099 ĕuaggĕlistēs (1), *preacher* of the gospel

EVE
2332 Chavvâh (2), *life-giver*
2096 Êua (2), *life-giver*

EVEN
227 'âz (1), *at that time* or *place; therefore*
389 'ak (2), *surely; only, however*

518 'îm (1), *whether?; if, although; Oh that!*
637 'aph (7), *also* or *yea; though*
853 'êth (25), not translated
1571 gam (50), *also; even; yea; though*
1887 hê' (1), *Lo!, Look!*
3588 kîy (7), *for, that because*
3602 kâkâh (5), *just so*
3651 kên (3), *just; right, correct*
4334 mîyshôwr (1), *plain; justice*
5704 'ad (3), *as far (long) as; during; while; until*
5705 'ad (Ch.) (2), *as far (long) as; during*
6153 'ereb (71), *dusk*
6664 tsedeq (1), *right*
7535 raq (1), *merely; although*
737 arti (1), just now; at once
891 achri (1), *until* or *up to*
1063 gar (1), *for, indeed, but, because*
1161 dĕ (3), *but, yet; and then*
2089 ĕti (1), *yet, still*
2193 hĕŏs (2), *until*
2504 kagō (7), *and also, even*
2509 kathapĕr (2), *exactly as*
2531 kathōs (24), *just or inasmuch as, that*
2532 kai (108), *and; or; even; also*
2548 kakĕinŏs (2), *likewise that* or *those*
3303 mĕn (1), not translated
3483 nai (4), *yes*
3676 hŏmōs (1), *at the same time, yet still*
3761 ŏudĕ (3), *neither, nor, not even*
3779 hŏutō (3), *in this way; likewise*
3796 ŏpsĕ (2), *late in the day*
3798 ŏpsiŏs (8), *late; early eve; later eve*
5037 tĕ (1), *both* or *also*
5613 hōs (5), *which, how,* i.e. *in that manner*
5615 hōsautōs (1), *in the same way*
5618 hōspĕr (2), *exactly like*

EVENING
6150 'ârab (2), *to grow dusky at sundown*
6153 'ereb (49), *dusk*
2073 hĕspĕra (2), *evening*
3798 ŏpsiŏs (5), *late; early eve; later eve*

EVENINGS
6160 'ârâbâh (1), *desert, wasteland*

EVENINGTIDE
6256+6153 'êth (2), *time*

EVENT
4745 miqreh (3), *accident* or *fortune*

EVENTIDE
6153 'ereb (1), *dusk*
6256+6153 'êth (2), *time*
2073 hĕspĕra (1), *evening*

EVER
753+3117 'ôrek (2), *length*
3605+3117 kôl (18), *all, any* or *every*
3808 lô' (1), *no, not*
3809 lâ' (Ch.) (1), *as nothing*
5331 netsach (23), *splendor; lasting*
5703 'ad (40), *perpetuity; ancient*
5704+5769 'ad (1), *as far (long) as; during; while*
5750 'ôwd (1), *again; repeatedly; still; more*
5757 'Avvîy (1), *Avvite*
5769 'ôwlâm (266), *ancient; always*
5769+5703 'ôwlâm (1), *ancient; always*
5865 'êylôwm (1), *forever*
5957 'âlam (Ch.) (11), *forever*
6783 tsᵉmîythûth (2), *perpetually*
6924 qedem (1), *eastern; antiquity; before*
8548 tâmîyd (3), *constantly, regularly*
104 aĕi (1), *ever, always*
165 aiōn (49), *perpetuity, ever; world*
166 aiōniŏs (1), *perpetual, long ago*
1336 diĕnĕkĕs (2), *perpetually, endless*
2250+165 hēmĕra (1), *day; period of time*
3364 ŏu mē (1), *not at all, absolutely not*
3745 hŏsŏs (3), *as much as*
3842 pantŏtĕ (6), *at all times*
3956+165 pas (1), *all, any, every, whole*
4218 pŏtĕ (1), *at some time, ever*
4253 prŏ (1), *before in time* or *space*

EVERLASTING
5703 'ad (2), *perpetuity; ancient*
5769 'ôwlâm (60), *ancient; always*
5957 'âlam (Ch.) (4), *forever*
6924 qedem (1), *eastern; antiquity; before*
126 aidiŏs (1), *everduring, eternal*
166 aiōniŏs (25), *perpetual, long ago*

EVERMORE
1755 dôwr (1), *dwelling*
3605+3117 kôl (2), *all, any* or *every*
5331 netsach (1), *splendor; lasting*
5703 'ad (1), *perpetuity; ancient*

5769 'ôwlâm (15), *ancient; always*
8548 tâmîyd (1), *constantly, regularly*
3588+165 hŏ (3), *"the,"* i.e. the definite article
3842 pantŏtĕ (2), *at all times*

EVERY
259 'echâd (5), *first*
376 'îysh (125), *man; male; someone*
802 'ishshâh (4), *woman, wife; women, wives*
1397 geber (1), *person, man*
3605 kôl (451), *all, any* or *every*
3606 kôl (Ch.) (4), *all, any* or *every*
3632 kâlîyl (1), *whole, entire; complete; whole*
5437 çâbab (26), *to surround*
7218 rô'sh (1), *head*
303 ana (2), *each; in turn; among*
376 anapĕrŏs (1), *maimed; crippled*
537 hapas (2), *all, every one, whole*
1330 diĕrchŏmai (1), *to traverse, travel through*
1538 hĕkastŏs (73), *each* or *every*
2596 kata (15), *down; according to*
3596 hŏdŏipŏrĕō (2), *to travel*
3650 hŏlŏs (2), *whole* or *all,* i.e. *complete*
3836 pantachŏthĕn (1), *from all directions*
3837 pantachŏu (6), *universally, everywhere*
3840 pantŏthĕn (1), *from, on all sides*
3956 pas (162), *all, any, every, whole*
5100 tis (2), *some* or *any person* or *object*
5101 tis (1), *who?, which?* or *what?*

EVI
189 'Êvîy (2), *desirous*

EVIDENCE
5612 çêpher (6), *writing*
1650 ĕlĕgchŏs (1), *proof, conviction*

EVIDENCES
5612 çêpher (2), *writing*

EVIDENT
5921+6440 'al (1), *above, over, upon,* or *against*
1212 dēlŏs (1), *clear, plain, evident*
1732 ĕndĕixis (1), *demonstration*
2612 katadēlŏs (1), *manifest, clear*
4271 prŏdēlŏs (1), *obvious, evident*

EVIDENTLY
4270 prŏgraphō (1), *to announce, prescribe*
5320 phanĕrŏs (1), *plainly,* i.e. *clearly*

EVIL
205 'âven (1), *trouble, vanity, wickedness*
1100 beﾃ（*lîya'al (1), wickedness, trouble*
1681 dibbâh (1), *slander, bad report*
7451 ra' (434), *bad; evil*
7455 rôa' (11), *badness, evil*
7462 râ'âh (1), to *associate with*
7489 râ'a' (24), to be *good for nothing*
92 adikēma (1), *wrong done*
987 blasphēmĕŏ (9), to *speak impiously*
988 blasphēmia (1), *impious speech*
1426 dusphēmia (1), *defamation, slander*
2549 kakia (1), *depravity; malignity*
2551 kakŏlŏgĕŏ (1), to *revile, curse*
2554 kakŏpŏiĕŏ (4), to *injure; to sin, do wrong*
2556 kakŏs (44), *bad, evil, wrong*
2557 kakŏurgŏs (1), *criminal, evildoer*
2559 kakŏŏ (3), to *injure; to oppress; to embitter*
2560 kakŏs (2), *badly; wrongly; ill*
2635 katalalĕŏ (4), to speak *slander*
2636 katalalia (1), *defamation, slander*
4190 pŏnĕrŏs (49), *malice, wicked, bad*
4190+4487 pŏnĕrŏs (1), *malice, wicked, bad*
5337 phaulŏs (4), *foul or flawed*, i.e. *wicked*

EVIL-MERODACH
192 'Ĕvîyl Merôdak (2), *Evil-Merodak*

EVILDOER
7489 râ'a' (1), to be *good for nothing*
2555 kakŏpŏiŏs (1), *bad-doer; criminal*

EVILDOERS
7489 râ'a' (9), to be *good for nothing*
2555 kakŏpŏiŏs (3), *bad-doer; criminal*

EVILFAVOUREDNESS
1697+7451 dâbâr (1), *word; matter; thing*

EVILS
7451 ra' (8), *bad; evil*
4190 pŏnĕrŏs (1), *malice, wicked, bad; crime*

EWE
3535 kibsâh (6), *ewe sheep*
7716 seh (1), *sheep or goat*

EWES
5763 'ûwl (1), to *suckle*, i.e. *give milk*
7353 râchêl (2), *ewe*

EXACT
5065 nâgas (3), to *exploit; to tax, harass*
5378 nâshâ' (2), to *lend on interest*
5383 nâshâh (2), to *lend or borrow*
4238 prassŏ (1), to *execute, accomplish*

EXACTED
3318 yâtsâ' (1), to *go, bring out*
5065 nâgas (1), to *exploit; to tax, harass*

EXACTETH
5382 nâshâh (1), to *forget*

EXACTION
4855 mashshâ' (1), *loan; interest* on a debt

EXACTIONS
1646 gerûshâh (1), *dispossession*

EXACTORS
5065 nâgas (1), to *exploit; to tax, harass*

EXALT
1361 gâbahh (3), to be *lofty; to be haughty*
5375 nâsâ' (2), to *lift up*
5549 çâlal (1), to *mound up; to exalt; to oppose*
7311 rûwm (17), to be *high; to rise or raise*
1869 ĕpairŏ (1), to *raise up, look up*
5312 hupsŏŏ (2), to *elevate; to exalt*

EXALTED
1361 gâbahh (5), to be *lofty; to be haughty*
5375 nâsâ' (8), to *lift up*
5927 'âlâh (2), to *ascend, be high, mount*
7311 rûwm (28), to be *high; to rise or raise*
7426 râmam (2), to *rise*
7682 sâgab (5), to be, *make lofty; be safe*
5229 hupĕrairŏmai (2), to *raise* oneself *over*
5251 hupĕrupsŏŏ (1), to *raise to the highest*
5311 hupsŏs (1), *altitude; sky; dignity*
5312 hupsŏŏ (10), to *elevate; to exalt*

EXALTEST
5549 çâlal (1), to *mound up; to exalt; to oppose*

EXALTETH
1361 gâbahh (1), to be *lofty; to be haughty*
7311 rûwm (3), to be *high; to rise or raise*
7682 sâgab (1), to be, *make lofty; be safe*
1869 ĕpairŏ (1), to *raise up, look up*
5229 hupĕrairŏmai (1), to *raise* oneself *over*
5312 hupsŏŏ (2), to *elevate; to exalt*

EXAMINATION
351 anakrisis (1), *judicial investigation*

EXAMINE
974 bâchan (1), to *test;* to *investigate*
1875 dârash (1), to *seek or ask;* to *worship*
350 anakrinō (1), to *interrogate, determine*
1381 dŏkimazō (1), to *test;* to *approve*
3985 pĕirazō (1), to *endeavor, scrutinize*

EXAMINED
350 anakrinō (4), to *interrogate, determine*
426 anĕtazō (2), to *investigate;* to *question*

EXAMINING
350 anakrinō (1), to *interrogate, determine*

EXAMPLE
1164 dĕigma (1), *specimen, example*
3856 paradĕigmatizō (1), to *expose to infamy*
5179 tupŏs (1), *shape, resemblance; "type"*
5261 hupŏgrammŏs (1), *copy, example, model*
5262 hupŏdĕigma (4), *exhibit; specimen*

EXAMPLES
5179 tupŏs (1), *shape, resemblance; "type"*

EXCEED
3254 yâçaph (2), to *add or augment*
4052 pĕrissĕuō (2), to *superabound*

EXCEEDED
1396 gâbar (1), to be *strong; to prevail*
1431 gâdal (2), to be *great, make great*

EXCEEDEST
3254 yâçaph (1), to *add or augment*

EXCEEDETH
3254 yâçaph (1), to *add or augment*

EXCEEDING
430 'ĕlôhîym (1), the true *God; gods; great ones*
1419 gâdôwl (1), *great*
2302 châdâh (1), to *rejoice, be glad*
2493 chêlem (Ch.) (1), *dream*
3493 yattîyr (Ch.) (1), *preeminent; very*
3499 yether (1), *remainder; small rope*
3966 meﾟôd (18), *very, utterly*
4605 ma'al (2), *upward, above, overhead*
5628 çârach (1), to *extend even to excess*
7235 râbâh (1), to *increase*
7235+3966 râbâh (1), to *increase*
7689 saggîy' (1), *mighty*
8057 simchâh (1), *blithesomeness or glee*
1519+5236 ĕis (1), to or *into*

EXCEEDINGLY
413+1524 'êl (1), to, *toward*
1419 gâdôwl (5), *great*
1419+3966 gâdôwl (1), *great*
3493 yattîyr (Ch.) (1), *preeminent; very*
3966 meﾟôd (9), *very, utterly*
4605 ma'al (4), *upward, above, overhead*
7227 rab (2), *great*
7235 râbâh (1), to *increase*
7235+3966 râbâh (1), to *increase*
8057 simchâh (1), *blithesomeness or glee*
1613 ĕktarassō (1), to *disturb wholly*
1630 ĕkphŏbŏs (1), *frightened out* of one's *wits*
4056 pĕrissŏtĕrŏs (3), *more superabundantly*
4057 pĕrissōs (1), *superabundantly*
4970 sphŏdra (1), *vehemently, much*
4971 sphŏdrōs (1), *very much*
5228+1537+4053 hupĕr (1), *over; above; beyond*
5401+3173 phŏbŏs (1), *alarm, or fright*

EXCEL
1368 gibbôwr (1), *powerful; great warrior*
3498 yâthar (1), to *remain or be left*
5329 nâtsach (1), i.e. to *be eminent*
4052 pĕrissĕuō (1), to *superabound*

EXCELLED
7227 rab (1), *great*

EXCELLENCY
1346 ga'ăvâh (3), *arrogance; majesty*
1347 gâ'ôwn (10), *ascending; majesty*
1363 gôbahh (1), *height; grandeur; arrogance*
1926 hâdâr (2), *magnificence*
3499 yether (2), *remainder; small rope*
3504 yithrôwn (1), *preeminence, gain*

EXAMINE
2596+5236 kata (1), *down; according to*
3029 lian (5), *very much*
3588+2316 hŏ (1), *"the,"* i.e. the definite article
4036 pĕrilupŏs (3), *intensely sad*
4970 sphŏdra (4), *vehemently, much*
5228 hupĕr (1), *over; above; beyond*
5235 hupĕrballō (3), to *surpass*
5248 hupĕrpĕrissĕuō (1), to *superabound*
5250 hupĕrplĕŏnazō (1), to *superabound*

English

EXCELLENT

7613 se'êth (2), *elevation; swelling* scab
7863 sîy' (1), *elevation*
5236 hupĕrbŏlē (1), *super-eminence*
5242 hupĕrĕchŏ (1), to *excel; be superior*
5247 hupĕrŏchē (1), *superiority*

EXCELLENT

117 'addîyr (4), *powerful; majestic*
977 bâchar (1), *select, chose, prefer*
1347 gâ'ôwn (1), *ascending; majesty*
1348 gê'ûwth (1), *ascending; majesty*
1420 gᵉdûwlâh (1), *greatness, grandeur*
1431 gâdal (1), to *be great, make great*
3368 yâqâr (1), *valuable*
3493 yattîyr (Ch.) (5), *preeminent; very*
3499 yether (1), *remainder;* small *rope*
5057 nâgîyd (1), *commander, official*
5716 'ădîy (1), *finery; outfit; headstall*
7119 qar (1), *cool; quiet;* cool-*headed*
7218 rô'sh (1), *head*
7230 rôb (1), *abundance*
7682 sâgab (1), to *be, make lofty; be safe*
7689 saggîy' (1), *mighty*
7991 shâlîysh (1), *officer; of the third* rank
8446 tûwr (1), to *wander, meander*
1308 diaphĕrŏ (2), to *differ; to surpass*
1313 diaphŏrŏs (2), *varying; surpassing*
2596+5236 kata (1), *down; according to*
2903 kratistŏs (2), *very honorable*
3169 mĕgalŏprĕpēs (1), *befitting greatness*
4119 plĕiŏn (1), *more*

EXCELLEST

5927 'âlâh (1), to *ascend, be high* mount

EXCELLETH

3504 yithrôwn (2), *preeminence, gain*
5235 hupĕrballŏ (1), to *surpass*

EXCEPT

369 'ayin (1), *there is no, i.e., not exist, none*
905 bad (1), *chief; apart, only, besides*
1115 biltîy (3), *not, except, without, unless*
3588 kîy (2), *for, that because*
3861 lâhên (Ch.) (3), *therefore; except*
3884 lûwlê' (3), *if not*
7535 raq (1), *merely; although*
1508 ĕi mē (7), *if not*
1509 ĕi mē ti (3), *if not somewhat*

2228 ē (1), *or; than*
3362 ĕan mē (33), *if not, i.e. unless*
3923 parĕisphĕrŏ (1), to *bear in alongside*
4133 plēn (1), *albeit, save that, rather, yet*

EXCEPTED

1622 ĕktŏs (1), *aside from, besides; except*

EXCESS

192 akrasia (1), *lack of control of self*
401 anachusis (1), *excessively pour out*
810 asōtia (1), *profligacy, debauchery*
3632 ŏinŏphlugia (1), *drunkenness*

EXCHANGE

4171 mûwr (1), to *alter; to barter, to dispose of*
8545 tᵉmûwrâh (2), *barter, compensation*
465 antallagma (2), *equivalent exchange*

EXCHANGERS

5133 trapĕzitēs (1), *money-broker*

EXCLUDE

1576 ĕklĕiŏ (1), to *shut out, exclude*

EXCLUDED

1576 ĕklĕiŏ (1), to *shut out, exclude*

EXCUSE

379 anapŏlŏgētŏs (1), *without excuse*
626 apŏlŏgĕŏmai (1), to *give an account*
3868 paraitĕŏmai (1), to *deprecate, decline*

EXCUSED

3868 paraitĕŏmai (2), to *deprecate, decline*

EXCUSING

626 apŏlŏgĕŏmai (1), to *give an account*

EXECRATION

423 'âlâh (2), *curse, oath, public agreement*

EXECUTE

1777 dîyn (1), to *judge; to strive or contend for*
5647 'âbad (1), to *do, work, serve*
6213 'âsâh (25), to *do or make*
8199 shâphaṭ (2), to *judge*
4160 pŏiĕŏ (2), to *do*

EXECUTED

5648 'ăbad (Ch.) (1), to *do, work, serve*
6213 'âsâh (15), to *do or make*
2407 hiĕratĕuŏ (1), to *be a priest*

EXECUTEDST

6213 'âsâh (1), to *do*

EXECUTEST

6213 'âsâh (1), to *do*

EXECUTETH

6213 'âsâh (5), to *do*

EXECUTING

6213 'âsâh (1), to *do*

EXECUTION

6213 'âsâh (1), to *do*

EXECUTIONER

4688 spĕkŏulatŏr (1), *life-guardsman*

EXEMPTED

5355 nâqîy (1), *innocent*

EXERCISE

1980 hâlak (1), to *walk; live a certain way*
6213 'âsâh (1), to *do or make*
778 askĕŏ (1), to *strive for one's best*
1128 gumnazŏ (1), to *train by exercise*
1129 gumnasia (1), *training of the body*
1850 ĕxŏusiazŏ (1), to *control, master another*
2634 katakuriĕuŏ (2), to *control, subjugate*
2715 katĕxŏusiazŏ (2), to *wield full privilege over*
2961 kuriĕuŏ (1), to *rule, be master of*

EXERCISED

6031 'ânâh (2), to *afflict, be afflicted*
1128 gumnazŏ (3), to *train by exercise*

EXERCISETH

4160 pŏiĕŏ (1), to *do*

EXHORT

3867 parainĕŏ (1), to *recommend or advise*
3870 parakalĕŏ (14), to *call, invite*

EXHORTATION

3870 parakalĕŏ (2), to *call, invite*
3874 paraklēsis (8), *imploring, exhortation*

EXHORTED

3870 parakalĕŏ (3), to *call, invite*

EXHORTETH

3870 parakalĕŏ (1), to *call, invite*

EXHORTING

3870 parakalĕŏ (3), to *call, invite*
4389 prŏtrĕpŏmai (1), to *encourage*

EXILE

1540 gâlâh (1), to *denude; uncover*
6808 tsâ'âh (1), to *tip over; to depopulate*

EXORCISTS

1845 ĕxŏrkistēs (1), *exorcist, i.e. conjurer*

EXPECTATION

4007 mabbâṭ (3), *expectation, hope*
8615 tiqvâh (7), *cord; expectancy*
603 apŏkaradŏkia (2), *intense anticipation*
4328 prŏsdŏkaŏ (1), to *anticipate; to await*

4329 prŏsdŏkia (1), *apprehension of evil*

EXPECTED

8615 tiqvâh (1), *cord; expectancy*

EXPECTING

1551 ĕkdĕchŏmai (1), to *await, expect*
4328 prŏsdŏkaŏ (1), to *anticipate; to await*

EXPEDIENT

4851 sumphĕrŏ (7), to *collect; to conduce*

EXPEL

1644 gârash (1), to *drive out; to expatriate*
1920 hâdaph (1), to *push away or down; drive out*

EXPELLED

3423 yârash (2), to *inherit; to impoverish*
5080 nâdach (1), to *push off, scattered*
1544 ĕkballŏ (1), to *throw out*

EXPENCES

5313 niphqâ' (Ch.) (2), *outgo, i.e. expense*

EXPERIENCE

5172 nâchash (1), to *prognosticate*
7200 râ'âh (1), to *see*
1382 dŏkimē (2), *test,* i.e. *trustiness*

EXPERIMENT

1382 dŏkimē (1), *test,* i.e. *trustiness*

EXPERT

3925 lâmad (1), to *teach, train*
6186 'ârak (3), to *set in a row,* i.e. *arrange*
7919 sâkal (1), to *be or act circumspect*
1109 gnŏstēs (1), *knower, expert*

EXPIRED

3615 kâlâh (1), to *cease, be finished, perish*
4390 mâlĕ' (3), to *fill; be full*
8666 tᵉshûwbâh (3), *recurrence; reply*
4137 plērŏŏ (1), to *fill, make complete*
5055 tĕlĕŏ (1), to *end,* i.e. *complete, execute*

EXPOUND

5046 nâgad (1), to *announce*

EXPOUNDED

5046 nâgad (1), to *announce*
1329 diĕrmĕnĕuŏ (1), to *explain thoroughly*
1620 ĕktithēmi (3), to *expose; to declare*
1956 ĕpiluŏ (1), to *explain; to decide*

EXPRESS

5481 charaktēr (1), *exact copy or representation*

EXPRESSED
5344 nâqab (5), to *specify, designate, libel*

EXPRESSLY
559 'âmar (1), to *say*
4490 rhētōs (1), *out-spoken, distinctly*

EXTEND
4900 mâshak (1), to *draw out; to be tall*
5186 nâṭâh (1), to *stretch or spread out*

EXTENDED
5186 nâṭâh (2), to *stretch or spread out*

EXTINCT
1846 dâ'ak (1), to *be extinguished; to expire*
2193 zâ'ak (1), to *extinguish*

EXTOL
5549 çâlal (1), to *mound up; to exalt; to oppose*
7311 rûwm (2), to *be high; to rise or raise*
7313 rûwm (Ch.) (1), *elation, arrogance*

EXTOLLED
5375 nâsâ' (1), to *lift up*
7318 rôwmâm (1), *exaltation, praise*

EXTORTION
6233 'ôsheq (1), *fraud; distress; unjust gain*
724 harpagē (1), *pillage; greediness; robbery*

EXTORTIONER
4160 mûwts (1), to *oppress*
5383 nâshâh (1), to *lend or borrow*
727 harpax (1), *rapacious; robbing*

EXTORTIONERS
727 harpax (3), *rapacious; robbing*

EXTREME
2746 charchûr (1), hot *fever*

EXTREMITY
6580 pash (1), *stupidity as a result of grossness*

EYE
5869 'ayin (73), *eye; sight; fountain*
5870 'ayin (Ch.) (1), *eye; sight*
3442 mŏnŏphthalmŏs (2), *one-eyed*
3788 ŏphthalmŏs (29), *eye*
5168 trumalia (2), *needle's eye*
5169 trupēma (1), *needle's eye*

EYE'S
5869 'ayin (1), *eye; sight; fountain*

EYEBROWS
1354+5869 gab (1), *rounded: top or rim; arch*

EYED
5770 'âvan (1), to *watch with jealousy*
5869 'ayin (1), *eye; sight; fountain*

EYELIDS
6079 'aph'aph (9), *fluttering eyelash*

EYES
5869 'ayin (417), *eye; sight; fountain*
5870 'ayin (Ch.) (5), *eye; sight*
3659 ŏmma (1), *eye*
3788 ŏphthalmŏs (70), *eye*

EYESALVE
2854 kŏllŏuriŏn (1), *poultice*

EYESERVICE
3787 ŏphthalmŏdŏulĕia (2), *service that needs watching*

EYESIGHT
5869 'ayin (1), *eye; sight; fountain*

EYEWITNESSES
845 autŏptēs (1), *eyewitness*
2030 ĕpŏptēs (1), *looker-on*

EZAR
687 'Etser (1), *treasure*

EZBAI
229 'Ezbay (1), *hyssop-like*

EZBON
675 'Etsbôwn (2), *Etsbon*

EZEKIAS
1478 Ĕzĕkias (2), *strengthened of Jehovah*

EZEKIEL
3168 Yᵉchezqê'l (2), *God will strengthen*

EZEL
237 'ezel (1), *departure*

EZEM
6107 'Etsem (1), *bone*

EZER
687 'Etser (4), *treasure*
5827 'Ezer (1), *help*
5829 'Êzer (4), *aid*

EZION-GABER
6100 'Etsyôwn (short (4), *backbone-like of a man*

EZION-GEBER
6100 'Etsyôwn (short (3), *backbone-like of a man*

EZNITE
6112 'Êtsen (1), *spear*

EZRA
5830 'Ezrâ' (26), *aid*

EZRAHITE
250 'Ezrâchîy (3), *Ezrachite*

EZRI
5836 'Ezrîy (1), *helpful*

FABLES
3454 muthŏs (5), *tale, fiction, myth*

FACE
600 'ănaph (Ch.) (1), *face*
639 'aph (19), *nose or nostril; face; person*
5869 'ayin (9), *eye; sight; fountain*
6440 pânîym (313), *face; front*
1799 ĕnôpiŏn (1), *in the face of, before*
3799 ŏpsis (1), *face; appearance*
4383 prŏsôpŏn (48), *face, presence*
4750 stŏma (4), *mouth; edge*

FACES
639 'aph (3), *nose or nostril; face; person*
6440 pânîym (62), *face; front*
4383 prŏsôpŏn (5), *face, presence*

FADE
5034 nâbêl (5), to *wilt; to fall away; to be foolish*
3133 marainō (1), to *pass away, fade away*

FADETH
5034 nâbêl (5), to *wilt; to fall away; to be foolish*
262 amarantinŏs (1), *fadeless*
263 amarantŏs (1), *perpetual, never fading*

FADING
5034 nâbêl (2), to *wilt; to fall away; to be foolish*

FAIL
235 'âzal (1), to *disappear*
656 'âphêç (1), to *cease*
1238 bâqaq (1), to *depopulate, ruin*
1584 gâmar (1), to *end; to complete; to fail*
1809 dâlal (1), to *slacken, dangle*
2637 châçêr (3), to *lack; to fail, want, make less*
2638 châçêr (1), *lacking*
3543 kâhâh (1), to *grow dull, fade; to be faint*
3576 kâzab (1), to *lie, deceive*
3584 kâchash (2), to *lie, disown; to disappoint*
3615 kâlâh (14), to *cease, be finished, perish*
3772 kârath (6), to *cut (off, down or asunder)*
3808+539 lô' (1), *no, not*
5307 nâphal (2), to *fall*
5405 nâshath (1), to *dry up*
5674 'âbar (2), to *cross over; to transition*
5737 'âdar (1), to *arrange as a battle*
5848 'âṭaph (1), to *shroud, to languish*
6461 paçaç (1), to *disappear*
6565 pârar (1), to *break up; to violate, frustrate*
7503 râphâh (4), to *slacken*

FACE *(7673 shâbath (2), to repose; to rest)*
7673 shâbath (2), to *repose; to rest*
7960 shâlûw (Ch.) (2), *fault, error*
8266 shâqar (1), to *cheat, i.e. be untrue in words*
1587 ĕklĕipō (3), to *die; to spot*
1952 ĕpilĕipō (1), to *be insufficient for*
2673 katargĕō (1), to *be, render entirely useless*
4098 piptō (1), to *fall*
5302 hustĕrĕō (1), to *be inferior; to fall short*

FAILED
6 'âbad (1), *perish; destroy*
2308 châdal (1), to *desist, stop; be fat*
3318 yâtsâ' (2), to *go, bring out*
3615 kâlâh (1), to *cease, be finished, perish*
5307 nâphal (4), to *fall*
5405 nâshath (1), to *dry up*
8552 tâmam (2), to *complete, finish*

FAILETH
6 'âbad (1), *perish; destroy*
369 'ayin (1), *there is no, i.e., not exist, none*
656 'âphêç (1), to *cease*
1602 gâ'al (1), to *detest; to reject; to fail*
2638 châçêr (1), *lacking*
3584 kâchash (1), to *lie, disown; to disappoint*
3615 kâlâh (4), to *cease, be finished, perish*
3782 kâshal (1), to *totter, waver; to falter*
5405 nâshath (1), to *dry up*
5737 'âdar (3), to *arrange as a battle*
5800 'âzab (2), to *loosen; relinquish; permit*
413 anĕklĕiptŏs (1), *not failing*
1601 ĕkpiptō (1), to *drop away*

FAILING
3631 killâyôwn (1), *pining, destruction*
674 apŏpsuchō (1), to *faint*

FAIN
1272 bârach (1), to *flee suddenly*
1937 ĕpithumĕō (1), to *long for*

FAINT
1738 dâvâh (1), to *be in menstruation cycle*
1739 dâveh (1), *menstrual; fainting*
1742 davvây (3), *sick; troubled, afflicted*
3286 yâ'aph (3), to *tire*
3287 yâ'êph (2), *exhausted*
3543 kâhâh (1), to *grow dull, fade; to be faint*

FAINTED

4127 mûwg (3), to *soften, flow down, disappear*
4549 mâçaç (1), to *waste; to faint*
5774 'ûwph (3), to *cover, to fly; to faint*
5848 'âṭaph (1), to *shroud, to languish*
5889 'âyêph (6), *languid*
5968 'âlaph (1), to *be languid, faint*
6296 pâgar (2), to *become exhausted*
7401 râkak (2), to *soften*
7503 râphâh (2), to *slacken*
1573 ĕkkakĕŏ (4), to *be weak, fail*
1590 ĕkluŏ (5), to *lose heart*

FAINTED

1961 hâyâh (1), to *exist, i.e. be or become*
3021 yâga' (1), to *be exhausted, to tire,*
3856 lâhahh (1), to *languish*
5848 'âṭaph (2), to *shroud, to languish*
5968 'âlaph (2), to *be languid, faint*
5969 'ulpeh (1), *mourning*
6313 pûwg (1), to *be sluggish; be numb*
1590 ĕkluŏ (1), to *lose heart*
2577 kamnŏ (1), to *tire; to faint, sicken*

FAINTEST

3811 lâ'âh (1), to *tire; to be, make disgusted*

FAINTETH

3286 yâ'aph (1), to *tire*
3615 kâlâh (2), to *cease, be finished, perish*
4549 mâçaç (1), to *waste; to faint*

FAINTHEARTED

3824+7401 lêbâb (1), *heart*
4127 mûwg (1), to *soften; to fear, faint*
7390+3824 rak (1), *tender; weak*

FAINTNESS

4816 môrek (1), *despondent fear*

FAIR

2091 zâhâb (1), *gold, golden colored*
2603 chânan (1), to *implore*
2889 ṭâhôwr (2), *pure, clean, flawless*
2896 ṭôwb (6), *good; well*
2896+4758 ṭôwb (1), *good; well*
2897+4758 Ṭôwb (1), *good*
2898 ṭûwb (1), *good; goodness; beauty*
3302 yâphâh (12), to *be beautiful*
3303 yâpheh (14), *beautiful; handsome*
3303+8389 yâpheh (1), *beautiful; handsome*

3304 yᵉphêh-phîyâh (1), *very beautiful*
3948 leqach (1), *instruction*
6320 pûwk (1), *stibium*
8209 sappîyr (Ch.) (2), *beautiful*
8597 tiph'ârâh (3), *ornament*
791 astĕiŏs (1), *handsome*
2105 ĕudia (1), *clear sky, i.e. fine weather*
2129 ĕulŏgia (1), *benediction*
2146 ĕuprŏsŏpĕŏ (1), to *make a good display*
2568 Kalŏi Limĕnĕs (1), *Good Harbors*

FAIRER

2896 ṭôwb (2), *good; well*
3302 yâphâh (1), to *be beautiful*

FAIREST

3303 yâpheh (3), *beautiful; handsome*

FAIRS

5801 'izzâbôwn (6), *trade, merchandise*

FAITH

529 'êmûwn (1), *trustworthiness; faithful*
530 'êmûwnâh (1), *fidelity; steadiness*
1680 ĕlpis (1), *expectation; hope*
3640 ŏligŏpistŏs (5), *lacking full confidence*
4102 pistis (238), *faithfulness; faith, belief*

FAITHFUL

529 'êmûwn (3), *trustworthiness; faithful*
530 'êmûwnâh (3), *fidelity; steadiness*
539 'âman (20), to *be firm, faithful, true*
540 'ăman (Ch.) (1), to *be firm, faithful, true*
571 'emeth (1), *certainty, truth, trustworthiness*
4103 pistŏs (53), *trustworthy; reliable*

FAITHFULLY

530 'êmûwnâh (5), *fidelity; steadiness*
571 'emeth (1), *certainty, truth, trustworthiness*
4103 pistŏs (1), *trustworthy; reliable*

FAITHFULNESS

530 'êmûwnâh (18), *fidelity; steadiness*
3559 kûwn (1), to *render sure, proper*

FAITHLESS

571 apistŏs (4), *without faith; untrustworthy*

FALL

2342 chûwl (2), to *dance, whirl; to writhe in pain*
3318 yâtsâ' (1), to *go, bring out*
3381 yârad (1), to *descend*

3782 kâshal (22), to *totter, waver; to falter*
3783 kishshâlôwn (1), *ruin*
3832 lâbaṭ (3), to *overthrow; to fall*
3872 Lûwchîyth (1), *floored*
4131 môwṭ (1), to *slip, shake, fall*
4383 mikshôwl (1), *stumbling-block*
4658 mappeleth (7), *down-fall; ruin; carcase*
5034 nâbêl (1), to *wilt; to fall away; to be foolish*
5064 nâgar (1), to *pour out; to deliver over*
5203 nâṭash (1), to *disperse; to thrust off*
5307 nâphal (149), to *fall*
5308 nᵉphal (Ch.) (3), to *fall*
5456 çâgad (2), to *prostrate oneself*
6293 pâga (8), to *impinge*
7264 râgaz (1), to *quiver*
7812 shâchâh (2), to *prostrate in homage*
7997 shâlal (1), to *drop or strip; to plunder*
868 aphistēmi (1), to *desist, desert*
1601 ĕkpiptŏ (4), to *drop away*
1706 ĕmpiptŏ (3), to *be entrapped by*
3895 parapiptŏ (1), to *apostatize, fall away*
3900 paraptŏma (2), *error; transgression*
4045 pĕripiptŏ (1), to *fall into the hands of*
4098 piptŏ (22), to *fall*
4417 ptaiŏ (1), to *trip up, stumble morally*
4431 ptŏsis (2), *downfall, crash*
4625 skandalŏn (1), *snare*

FALLEN

935 bôw' (1), to *go or come*
3782 kâshal (2), to *totter, waver; to falter*
4131+3027 môwṭ (1), to *slip, shake, fall*
4803 mâraṭ (2), to *polish; to make bald*
5307 nâphal (55), to *fall*
1601 ĕkpiptŏ (3), to *drop away*
1706 ĕmpiptŏ (1), to *be entrapped by*
1968 ĕpipiptŏ (1), to *embrace; to seize*
2064 ĕrchŏmai (1), to *go or come*
2667 katapiptŏ (2), to *fall down*
2702 kataphĕrŏ (1), to *bear down*
2837 kŏimaŏ (2), to *slumber; to decease*
4098 piptŏ (4), to *fall*

FALLEST

5307 nâphal (1), to *fall*

FALLETH

3918 layish (1), *lion*
5034 nâbêl (1), to *wilt; to fall away; to be foolish*
5307 nâphal (15), to *fall*
5308 nᵉphal (Ch.) (2), to *fall*
5456 çâgad (2), to *prostrate oneself*
7122 qârâ' (1), to *encounter, to happen*
1601 ĕkpiptŏ (2), to *drop away*
1911 ĕpiballŏ (1), to *throw upon*
4098 piptŏ (3), to *fall*

FALLING

1762 dᵉchîy (2), *stumbling fall*
3782 kâshal (1), to *totter, waver; to falter*
4131 môwṭ (1), to *slip, shake, fall*
5034 nâbêl (1), to *wilt; to fall away; to be foolish*
5307 nâphal (3), to *fall*
646 apŏstasia (1), *defection, rebellion*
679 aptaistŏs (1), *not stumbling, without sin*
2597 katabainŏ (1), to *descend*
4045 pĕripiptŏ (1), to *fall into the hands of*
4098 piptŏ (1), to *fall*
4248+1096 prēnēs (1), *headlong*
4363 prŏspiptŏ (1), to *prostrate oneself*

FALLOW

3180 yachmûwr (1), *kind of deer*
5215 nîyr (2), *freshly plowed land*

FALLOWDEER

3180 yachmûwr (1), *kind of deer*

FALSE

205 'âven (1), *trouble, vanity, wickedness*
2555 châmâç (2), *violence; malice*
3577 kâzâb (1), *falsehood; idol*
4820 mirmâh (2), *fraud*
7423 rᵉmîyâh (1), *remissness; treachery*
7723 shâv' (5), *ruin; guile; idolatry*
8267 sheqer (20), *untruth; sham*
1228 diabŏlŏs (2), *traducer, i.e. Satan*
4811 sukŏphantĕŏ (1), to *defraud, extort*
5569 psĕudadĕlphŏs (2), *pretended associate*
5570 psĕudapŏstŏlŏs (1), *pretended preacher*
5571 psĕudēs (1), *erroneous, deceitful*
5572 psĕudŏdidaskalŏs (1), *propagator of erroneous doctrine*
5573 psĕudŏlŏgŏs (4), *promulgating erroneous doctrine*

5575 psĕudŏmartur (3), bearer of untrue testimony
5576 psĕudŏmarturĕō (6), to offer falsehood
5577 psĕudŏmarturia (1), untrue testimony
5578 psĕudŏprŏphētĕs (6), pretended foreteller
5580 psĕudŏchristŏs (2), spurious Messiah

FALSEHOOD
4604 ma'al (1), sinful treachery
8267 sheqer (13), untruth; sham

FALSELY
3584 kâchash (1), to lie, disown; to disappoint
5921+8267 'al (1), above, over, upon, or against
7723 shâv' (1), ruin; guile; idolatry
8266 shâqar (2), to cheat, i.e. be untrue in words
8267 sheqer (12), untruth; sham
5574 psĕudŏmai (1), to utter an untruth
5581 psĕudŏnumŏs (1), untruly named

FALSIFYING
5791 'âvath (1), to wrest, twist

FAME
6963 qôwl (1), voice or sound
8034 shêm (4), appellation, i.e. name
8052 shᵉmûw'âh (2), announcement
8088 shêma' (3), something heard
8089 shôma' (4), report; reputation
189 akŏĕ (3), hearing; thing heard
1310 diaphēmizō (1), to spread news
2279 ēchŏs (1), roar; rumor
3056 lŏgŏs (1), word, matter, thing; Word
5345 phēmē (2), news, report

FAMILIAR
3045 yâda' (1), to know
7965 shâlôwm (1), safe; well; health, prosperity

FAMILIARS
7965 shâlôwm (1), safe; well; health, prosperity

FAMILIES
1004 bayith (2), house; temple; family, tribe
1004+1 bayith (2), house; temple; family, tribe
2945 ṭaph (1), family of children and women
4940 mishpâchâh (169), family, clan, people

FAMILY
504 'eleph (1), ox; cow or cattle
1004 bayith (1), house; temple; family, tribe

4940 mishpâchâh (120), family, clan, people
3965 patria (1), family, race, nation

FAMINE
3720 kâphân (2), hunger
7458 râ'âb (86), hunger
7459 rᵉ'âbôwn (3), famine
3042 limŏs (4), scarcity of food, famine

FAMINES
3042 limŏs (3), scarcity of food, famine

FAMISH
7329 râzâh (1), to make, become thin
7456 râ'êb (1), to hunger

FAMISHED
7456 râ'êb (1), to hunger
7458 râ'âb (1), hunger

FAMOUS
117 'addîyr (2), powerful; majestic
3045 yâda' (1), to know
7121 qârâ' (2), to call out
7148 qârîy' (1), called, i.e. select
8034 shêm (4), appellation, i.e. name

FAN
2219 zârâh (4), to toss about; to winnow
4214 mizreh (1), winnowing shovel
4425 ptuŏn (2), winnowing-fork

FANNERS
2114 zûwr (1), to be foreign, strange

FAR
1419 gâdôwl (1), great
2008 hênnâh (2), from here; from there
2186 zânach (1), to reject, forsake, fail
2486 châlîylâh (9), far be it!, forbid!
3966 mᵉ'ôd (3), very, utterly
4801 merchâq (15), distant place; from afar
5048 neged (3), over against or before
5079 niddâh (1), time of menstrual impurity
7350 râchôwq (59), remote, far
7352 rachîyq (Ch.) (1), far away; aloof
7368 râchaq (39), to recede; remove
7369 râchêq (2), remote, far
891 achri (2), until or up to
1519 ĕis (1), to or into
2193 hĕŏs (4), until
2436 hilĕŏs (1), God be gracious!, far be it!
3112 makran (6), at a distance, far away
3113 makrŏthĕn (1), from a distance or afar
3117 makrŏs (2), long, in place or time

4054 pĕrissŏtĕrŏn (1), in a superabundant way
4183 pŏlus (3), much, many
4206 pŏrrhō (2), forwards, at a distance
5231 hupĕranō (1), above, upward

FARE
7939 sâkâr (1), payment, salary; compensation
7965 shâlôwm (1), safe; well; health, prosperity
4517 rhônnumi (1), to strengthen

FARED
2165 ĕuphrainō (1), to rejoice, be glad

FAREWELL
657 apŏtassŏmai (2), to say adieu; to renounce
4517 rhônnumi (1), to strengthen
5463 chairō (1), to be cheerful

FARM
68 agrŏs (1), farmland, countryside

FARTHER
4008 pĕran (1), across, beyond
4260 prŏbainō (1), to advance
4281 prŏĕrchŏmai (1), to go onward, precede

FARTHING
787 assariŏn (1), assarius
2835 kŏdrantēs (2), quadrans

FARTHINGS
787 assariŏn (1), assarius

FASHION
1823 dᵉmûwth (1), resemblance, likeness
3559 kûwn (1), to set up; establish, fix, prepare
4941 mishpâṭ (2), verdict; formal decree; justice
8498 tᵉkûwnâh (1), structure; equipage
1491 ĕidŏs (1), form, appearance, sight
3778 hŏutŏs (1), this or that
4383 prŏsōpŏn (1), face, presence
4976 schēma (2), form or appearance
5179 tupŏs (1), shape, resemblance; "type"

FASHIONED
3335 yâtsar (3), to form; potter; to determine
3559 kûwn (2), to set up; establish, fix, prepare
6213 'âsâh (1), to do or make
4832 summŏrphŏs (1), similar, conformed to

FASHIONETH
3335 yâtsar (3), to form; potter; to determine

FASHIONING
4964 suschēmatizō (1), to conform to the same

FASHIONS
4941 mishpâṭ (1), verdict; formal decree; justice

FAST
629 'oçparnâ' (Ch.) (1), diligently
3966 mᵉ'ôd (1), very, utterly
6684 tsûwm (8), to fast from food
6685 tsôwm (16), fast from food
472 antĕchŏmai (1), to adhere to; to care for
805 asphalizō (1), to render secure
2722 katĕchō (3), to hold down fast
3521 nēstĕia (1), abstinence
3522 nēstĕuō (16), to abstain from food

FASTED
6684 tsûwm (12), to fast from food
3522 nēstĕuō (3), to abstain from food

FASTEN
2388 châzaq (1), to fasten upon; to seize
5414 nâthan (3), to give
8628 tâqa' (1), to clatter, slap, drive, clasp

FASTENED
270 'âchaz (3), to seize, grasp; possess
2388 châzaq (1), to fasten upon; to seize
2883 ṭâba' (1), to sink; to be drowned
3559 kûwn (1), to set up; establish, fix, prepare
5193 nâṭa' (1), to plant
5414 nâthan (1), to give
6775 tsâmad (1), to link, i.e. gird
6795 tsânach (1), to descend, i.e. drive down
8628 tâqa' (4), to clatter, slap, drive, clasp
816 atĕnizō (2), to gaze intently
2510 kathaptō (1), to seize upon

FASTENING
816 atĕnizō (1), to gaze intently

FASTEST
2522 kathēmĕrinŏs (1), quotidian, i.e. daily

FASTING
2908 ṭᵉvâth (Ch.) (1), hunger
6685 tsôwm (8), fast
777 asitŏs (1), without taking food
3521 nēstĕia (4), abstinence
3522 nēstĕuō (1), to abstain from food
3523 nēstis (2), abstinent from food

FASTINGS
6685 tsôwm (1), fast
3521 nēstĕia (3), abstinence

English

FAT

1254 bârâ' (1), to *create; fashion*
1277 bârîy' (6), *fatted* or *plump; healthy*
1878 dâshên (7), to *be fat, thrive*; to *fatten*
1879 dâshên (3), *fat; rich, fertile*
2459 cheleb (79), *fat; choice* part
2502 châlats (1), to *pull off*; to *strip*; to *depart*
2954 ṭâphash (1), to *be stupid*
3368 yâqâr (1), *valuable*
4220 mêach (1), *fat; rich*
4770 marbêq (1), *stall*
4806 merîy' (4), *stall-fed* animal
4924 mashmân (2), *fatness; rich* dish; *fertile* field; *robust* man
4945 mashqeh (1), *butler; drink; well-watered*
6309 peder (3), *suet*
6335 pûwsh (1), to *spread*; to *act proudly*
6371 pîymah (1), *obesity*
8080 shâman (3), to *be, make oily* or *gross*
8081 shemen (4), *olive oil, wood, lotions*
8082 shâmên (10), *rich; fertile*

FATFLESHED

1277 bârîy' (2), *fatted* or *plump; healthy*

FATHER

1 'âb (504), *father*
2 'ab (Ch.) (13), *father*
25 'Ăbîy Gib'ôwn (67), *founder of Gibon*
1121 bên (1), *son, descendant; people*
2524 châm (4), *father-in-law*
2589 channôwth (1), *supplication*
2859 châthan (20), to *become related*
540 apatôr (1), *of unrecorded paternity*
3962 patēr (344), *father*
3995 pĕnthĕrŏs (1), *wife's father*

FATHER'S

1 'âb (126), *father*
1730 dôwd (2), *beloved, friend; relative*
1733 dôwdâh (1), *aunt*
3962 patēr (17), *father*

FATHERLESS

369+1 'ayin (1), *there is no, i.e., not exist, none*
3490 yâthôwm (41), *child alone, fatherless child*
3737 ŏrphanŏs (1), *parentless, orphaned*

FATHERS

1 'âb (475), *father*
2 'ab (Ch.) (3), *father*
3962 patēr (52), *father*
3964 patralŏjas (1), *killing of father*
3967 patrikŏs (1), *ancestral, paternal*

FATHERS'

1 'âb (10), *father*
3962 patēr (1), *father*

FATHOMS

3712 ŏrguia (2), *measure of about six feet*

FATLING

4806 merîy' (1), *stall-fed* animal

FATLINGS

4220 mêach (1), *fat; rich*
4806 merîy' (2), *stall-fed* animal
4932 mishneh (1), *duplicate copy; double*
4619 sitistŏs (1), *grained,* i.e. *fatted*

FATNESS

1880 deshen (7), *fat; fatness, abundance*
2459 cheleb (4), *fat; choice* part
4924 mashmân (3), *fatness; fertile; robust*
8081 shemen (1), *olive oil, wood, lotions*
4096 piŏtēs (1), *oiliness,* i.e. *nourishing sap*

FATS

3342 yeqeb (2), wine-*vat,* wine-*press*

FATTED

75 'âbaç (1), to *feed; be fattened with feed*
4770 marbêq (1), *stall*
4618 sitĕutŏs (3), *fattened,* i.e. stall-fed

FATTER

1277 bârîy' (1), *fatted* or *plump; healthy*

FATTEST

4924 mashmân (2), *fatness; fertile; robust*

FAULT

2398 châṭâ' (1), to *sin*
3972 me'ûwmâh (1), *something; anything*
5771 'âvôn (2), *moral evil*
7564 rish'âh (1), *moral wrong*
7844 sheChath (Ch.) (2), to *decay;* to *ruin*
156 aitia (3), *logical reason; legal crime*
158 aitiŏn (2), *reason, basis; crime*
299 amōmŏs (1), *unblemished, blameless*
1651 ĕlĕgchŏ (1), to *confute, admonish*
2275 hēttēma (1), *failure* or *loss*
3201 mĕmphŏmai (3), to *blame*
3900 paraptōma (1), *error; transgression*

FAULTLESS

278 amĕtamĕlētŏs (1), *irrevocable*
299 amōmŏs (1), *unblemished, blameless*

FAULTS

2399 chêṭ' (1), *crime* or its *penalty*
264 hamartanō (1), to *miss the mark,* to *err*
3900 paraptōma (1), *error; transgression*

FAULTY

816 'âsham (1), to *be guilty;* to *be punished*
818 'âshêm (1), *bearing guilt, guilty*

FAVOUR

2580 chên (26), *graciousness; beauty*
2594 chănîynâh (1), *graciousness, kindness*
2603 chânan (8), to *implore*
2617 cheçed (3), *kindness, favor*
2655 châphêts (1), *pleased with*
2896 ṭôwb (2), *good; well*
3190 yâṭab (1), to *be, make well*
6440 pânîym (4), *face; front*
7520 râtsad (1), to *look askant;* to *be jealous*
7522 râtsôwn (15), *delight*
7965 shâlôwm (1), *safe; well; health, prosperity*
8467 techinnâh (1), *gracious entreaty*
5485 charis (6), *gratitude; benefit given*

FAVOURABLE

2603 chânan (1), to *implore*
7520 râtsad (3), to *look askant;* to *be jealous*

FAVOURED

2603 chânan (1), to *implore*
4758 mar'eh (7), *appearance; vision*
8389 tô'ar (2), *outline,* i.e. *figure* or *appearance*
5487 charitŏŏ (1), to *give special honor;* one *highly favored*

FAVOUREST

2654 châphêts (1), to *be pleased with, desire*

FAVOURETH

2654 châphêts (1), to *be pleased with, desire*

FEAR

367 'êymâh (5), *fright*
1481 gûwr (2), to *sojourn, live as an alien*
1674 de'âgâh (1), *anxiety*
1763 dechal (Ch.) (1), to *fear; be formidable, awesome*
2342 chûwl (2), to *dance, whirl;* to *writhe* in pain; to *wait;* to *pervert*
2731 chărâdâh (2), *fear, anxiety*
2844 chath (1), *terror*
3025 yâgôr (1), to *fear*
3372 yârê' (148), to *fear;* to *revere*

3373 yârê' (35), *fearing; reverent*
3374 yir'âh (41), *fear; reverence*
4032 mâgôwr (6), *fright, horror*
4034 megôwrâh (1), *affright, dread*
4172 môwrâ' (6), *fearful*
6206 'ârats (2), to *awe;* to *dread;* to *harass*
6342 pâchad (9), to *be startled;* to *fear*
6343 pachad (41), *sudden alarm, fear*
6345 pachdâh (1), *awe*
6440 pânîym (8), *face; front*
7267 rôgez (1), *disquiet; anger*
7374 reṭeṭ (1), *terror, panic*
7461 ra'ad (1), *shudder*
820 atimŏs (1), *dishonoured; without honor*
870 aphŏbŏs (3), *fearlessly*
1167 dĕilia (1), *timidity, cowardice*
1630+1510 ĕkphŏbŏs (1), *frightened out* of one's *wits*
2124 ĕulabĕia (1), *reverence; submission*
2125 ĕulabĕŏmai (1), to *have reverence*
5399 phŏbĕŏ (35), to *fear, be frightened;* to *revere*
5401 phŏbŏs (40), *alarm, or fright; reverence*
5401+2192 phŏbŏs (1), *fright; reverence*

FEARED

1481 gûwr (1), to *sojourn, live as an alien*
1763 dechal (Ch.) (1), to *fear; be formidable*
3372 yârê' (38), to *fear;* to *revere*
3373 yârê' (8), *fearing; reverent*
4172 môwrâ' (1), *fearful*
6206 'ârats (1), to *awe;* to *dread;* to *harass*
6342 pâchad (3), to *be startled;* to *fear*
8175 sâ'ar (1), to *storm;* to *shiver,* i.e. *fear*
2124 ĕulabĕia (1), *reverence; submission*
5399 phŏbĕŏ (17), to *fear, be* in *awe of, revere*
5399+5401 phŏbĕŏ (1), to *fear, be* in *awe of*

FEAREST

1481 gûwr (1), to *sojourn, live as an alien*
3372 yârê' (1), to *fear;* to *revere*
3373 yârê' (1), *fearing; reverent*

FEARETH

3372 yârê' (2), to *fear;* to *revere*
3373 yârê' (13), *fearing; reverent*

FEARFUL

6342 pâchad (1), *to be startled; to fear*
5399 phŏbĕō (4), *to fear, be in awe of, revere*

FEARFUL

3372 yârê' (2), *to fear; to revere*
3373 yârê' (2), *fearing; reverent*
4116 mâhar (1), *to hurry; promptly*
1169 dĕilŏs (3), *timid, i.e. faithless*
5398 phŏbĕrŏs (2), *frightful, i.e. formidable*
5400 phŏbĕtrŏn (1), *frightening thing*

FEARFULLY

3372 yârê' (1), *to fear; to revere*

FEARFULNESS

3374 yir'âh (1), *fear; reverence*
6427 pallâtsûwth (1), *affright, trembling fear*
7461 ra'ad (1), *shudder*

FEARING

3372 yârê' (1), *to fear; to revere*
2125 ĕulabĕōmai (1), *to have reverence*
5399 phŏbĕō (6), *to fear, be in awe of, revere*

FEARS

2849 chathchath (1), *terror, horror*
4035 mᵉgûwrâh (2), *fright; granary*
5401 phŏbŏs (1), *alarm, or fright; reverence*

FEAST

2282 chag (53), *solemn festival*
2287 châgag (4), *to observe a festival*
3899 lechem (1), *food, bread*
3900 lᵉchem (Ch.) (1), *food, bread*
4150 môw'êd (3), *assembly, congregation*
4960 mishteh (21), *drink; banquet or feast*
755 architriklinŏs (3), *director of the entertainment*
1408 drŏmŏs (2), *career, course of life*
1456 ĕgkainia (1), *Feast of Dedication*
1858 hĕŏrtazō (1), *to observe a festival*
1859 hĕŏrtē (26), *festival*
4910 sunĕuōchĕō (2), *to feast together*

FEASTED

6213+4960 'âsâh (1), *to do or make*

FEASTING

4960 mishteh (7), *drink; banquet or feast*

FEASTS

2282 chag (5), *solemn festival*
4150 môw'êd (19), *assembly, congregation*

FEATHERED

3671 kânâph (2), *edge or extremity; wing*

FEATHERS

84 'ebrâh (2), *pinion*
2624 chăçîydâh (1), *stork*
5133 nôwtsâh (3), *plumage*

FED

398 'âkal (5), *to eat*
1277 bârîy' (1), *fatted or plump; healthy*
2109 zùwn (1), *to nourish; feed*
2110 zûwn (Ch.) (1), *to nourish; feed*
2939 ţᵉ'am (Ch.) (1), *to feed*
3557 kûwl (3), *to keep in; to measure*
4806 mᵉrîy' (1), *stall-fed animal*
5095 nâhal (1), *to flow; to protect, sustain*
7462 râ'âh (10), *to tend a flock, i.e. pasture it*
1006 bŏskō (2), *to pasture a flock*
4222 pŏtizō (1), *to furnish drink, irrigate*
5142 trĕphō (1), *to nurse, feed, care for*
5526 chŏrtazō (1), *to supply food*

FEEBLE

535 'âmal (1), *to be weak; to be sick*
537 'ămêlâl (1), *languid, feeble*
2826 châshal (1), *to make unsteady*
3766 kâra' (1), *to make miserable*
3782 kâshal (4), *to totter, waver; to falter*
3808+3524 lô' (1), *no, not*
3808+6099 lô' (1), *no, not*
5848 'âṭaph (1), *to shroud; to languish*
6313 pûwg (1), *to be sluggish; be numb*
7503 râphâh (6), *to slacken*
772 asthĕnēs (1), *strengthless, weak*
3886 paraluō (1), *to be paralyzed or enfeebled*

FEEBLEMINDED

3642 ŏligŏpsuchŏs (1), *timid, faint-hearted*

FEEBLENESS

7510 riphyôwn (1), *slackness*

FEEBLER

5848 'âṭaph (1), *to shroud, to languish*

FEED

398 'âkal (8), *to eat*
1197 bâ'ar (1), *to be brutish, be senseless*

FED

2963 ţâraph (1), *to supply, provide food*
3557 kûwl (3), *to keep in; to measure*
3938 lâ'aṭ (1), *to swallow greedily, gulp*
7462 râ'âh (55), *to tend a flock, i.e. pasture it*
1006 bŏskō (3), *to pasture a flock*
4165 pŏimainō (4), *to tend as a shepherd*
5142 trĕphō (1), *to nurse, feed, care for*
5595 psōmizō (2), *to nourish, feed*

FEEDEST

398 'âkal (1), *to eat*
7462 râ'âh (1), *to tend a flock, i.e. pasture it*

FEEDETH

7462 râ'âh (5), *to tend a flock, i.e. pasture it*
4165 pŏimainō (1), *to tend as a shepherd*
5142 trĕphō (2), *to nurse, feed, care for*

FEEDING

7462 râ'âh (4), *to tend a flock, i.e. pasture it*
1006 bŏskō (3), *to pasture a flock*
4165 pŏimainō (2), *to tend as a shepherd*

FEEL

995 bîyn (1), *to understand; discern*
3045 yâda' (2), *to know*
4184 mûwsh (2), *to touch, feel*
4959 mâshash (1), *to feel of; to grope*
5584 psēlaphaō (1), *to verify by contac*

FEELING

524 apalgĕō (1), *become apathetic, callous*
4834 sumpathĕō (1), *to commiserate*

FEET

4772 margᵉlâh (5), *at the foot*
6471 pa'am (6), *time; step; occurence*
7166 qarçôl (2), *ankles*
7271 rᵉgal (Ch.) (7), *pair of feet*
7272 regel (151), *foot; step*
939 basis (1), *foot*
4228 pŏus (76), *foot*

FEIGN

5234 nâkar (1), *to treat as a foreigner*
5271 hupŏkrinŏmai (1), *to pretend*

FEIGNED

4820 mirmâh (1), *fraud*
4112 plastŏs (1), *artificial, fabricated*

FEIGNEDLY

8267 sheqer (1), *untruth; sham*

FEIGNEST

908 bâdâ' (1), *to invent; to choose*

FELIX

5344 Phēlix (8), *happy*

FELIX'

5344 Phēlix (1), *happy*

FELL

1961 hâyâh (7), *to exist, i.e. be or become*
3318 yâtsâ' (2), *to go, bring out*
3381 yârad (2), *to descend*
3766 kâra' (2), *to prostrate*
3782 kâshal (2), *to totter, waver; to falter*
5307 nâphal (122), *to fall*
5308 nᵉphal (Ch.) (5), *to fall*
5927 'âlâh (2), *to ascend, be high, mount*
6293 pâga' (4), *to impinge*
6298 pâgash (1), *to come in contact with*
6584 pâshaṭ (2), *to strip, i.e. unclothe, plunder*
7257 râbats (1), *to recline, repose, brood*
7812 shâchâh (2), *to prostrate*
634 apŏpiptō (1), *to fall off, drop off*
1096 ginŏmai (1), *to be, become*
1356 diŏpĕtēs (1), *sky-fallen*
1601 ĕkpiptō (1), *to drop away*
1706 ĕmpiptō (1), *to be entrapped by*
1968 ĕpipiptō (10), *to embrace; to seize*
2597 katabainō (1), *to descend*
4045 pĕripiptō (1), *to fall into the hands of*
4098 piptō (56), *to fall*
4363 prŏspiptō (6), *to prostrate oneself*

FELLED

5307 nâphal (1), *to fall*

FELLER

3772 kârath (1), *to cut (off, down or asunder)*

FELLEST

5307 nâphal (1), *to fall*

FELLING

5307 nâphal (1), *to fall*

FELLOES

2839 chishshùq (1), *wheel-spoke*

FELLOW

376 'îysh (1), *man; male; someone*
2270 châbêr (1), *associate, friend*
5997 'âmîyth (1), *comrade or kindred*
7453 rêa' (9), *associate; one close*

FELLOW'S

7453 rêa' (1), *associate; one close*

FELLOWCITIZENS

4847 sumpŏlitēs (1), *fellow citizen*

English

FELLOWDISCIPLES
4827 summathētēs (1),
co-learner

FELLOWHEIRS
4789 sugklēronŏmŏs (1),
participant in common

FELLOWHELPER
4904 sunĕrgŏs (1),
fellow-worker

FELLOWHELPERS
4904 sunĕrgŏs (1),
fellow-worker

FELLOWLABOURER
4904 sunĕrgŏs (2),
fellow-worker

FELLOWLABOURERS
4904 sunĕrgŏs (2),
fellow-worker

FELLOWPRISONER
4869 sunaichmalŏtŏs (2),
co-captive

FELLOWPRISONERS
4869 sunaichmalŏtŏs (1),
co-captive

FELLOWS
582 'ĕnŏwsh (1), *man;
person, human*
2269 chăbar (Ch.) (2),
associate, friend
2270 châbêr (3),
associate, friend
2273 chabrâh (Ch.) (1),
similar, associated
7453 rêa' (1), *associate;
one close*
7464 rê'âh (1), *female
associate*
435 anēr (1), *mar ; male*
2083 hĕtairŏs (1),
comrade, friend
3353 mĕtŏchŏs (1),
sharer, associate

FELLOWSERVANT
4889 sundŏulŏs (6),
*servitor of the same
master*

FELLOWSERVANTS
4889 sundŏulŏs (4),
*servitor of the same
master*

FELLOWSHIP
2266 châbar (1), *to
fascinate by spells*
8667+3027 tᵉsûwmeth
(1), *deposit, i.e. pledging*
2842 kŏinōnia (12),
benefaction; sharing
2844 kŏinōnŏs (1),
associate, partner
3352 mĕtŏchē (1),
something in common
4790 sugkŏinōnĕō (1), *to
co-participate*

FELLOWSOLDIER
4961 sustratiōtēs (1),
soldier together with

FELT
3045 yâda' (1), *to know*
4959 mâshash (2), *to feel
of; to grope*
1097 ginōskō (1), *to know*
3958 paschō (1), *to
experience pain*

FEMALE
802 'ishshâh (2), *woman,
wife; women, wives*
5347 nᵉqêbâh (19),
female, woman
2338 thēlus (3), *female*

FENCE
1447 gâdêr (1),
enclosure, wall or fence

FENCED
1211 betsel (1), *onion*
1219 bâtsar (15), *to be
inaccessible*
1443 gâdar (1), *to build a
stone wall*
4013 mibtsâr (12),
fortification; defender
4390 mâlê' (1), *to fill; be
full*
4692 mâtsôwr (1),
siege-mound; distress
4694 mᵉtsûwrâh (5),
rampart, fortification
5823 'âzaq (1), *to grub
over, dig*
7753 sûwk (1), *to shut in
with hedges*

FENS
1207 bitstsâh (1), *swamp,
marsh*

FERRET
604 'ănâqâh (1), *gecko*

FERRY
5679 'ăbârâh (1),
crossing-place

FERVENT
1618 ĕktĕnēs (1), *intent,
earnest*
2204 zĕō (2), *to be fervid
or earnest*
2205 zēlŏs (1), *zeal,
ardor; jealousy, malice*

FERVENTLY
1619 ĕktĕnōs (1),
intently, earnestly

FESTUS
5347 Phēstŏs (12), *festal*

FESTUS'
5347 Phēstŏs (1), *festal*

FETCH
935 bôw' (1), *to go or
come*
3318 yâtsâ' (1), *to go,
bring out*
3947 lâqach (20), *to take*
5375 nâsâ' (1), *to lift up*
5437 çâbab (1), *to
surround*
5670 'âbaṭ (1), *to pawn;
to lend; to entangle*
5927 'âlâh (1), *to ascend,
be high, mount*
7725 shûwb (1), *to turn
back; to return*
1806 ĕxagō (1), *to lead
forth, escort*

FETCHED
622 'âçaph (1), *to gather,
collect*
3318 yâtsâ' (1), *to go,
bring out*
3947 lâqach (10), *to take*
5375 nâsâ' (1), *to lift up*
5927 'âlâh (1), *to ascend,
be high, mount*

FETCHETH
5080 nâdach (1), *to push
off, scattered*

FETCHT
3947 lâqach (1), *to take*

FETTERS
2131 zîyqâh (1), *arrow;
bond, fetter*
3525 kebel (2), *fetter,
shackles*
5178 nᵉchôsheth (5),
copper; bronze
3976 pĕdĕ (3), *shackle
for the feet*

FEVER
6920 qaddachath (1),
inflammation
4445 purĕssō (2), *to burn
with a fever*
4446 purĕtŏs (6), *fever*

FEW
259 'echâd (3), *first*
4213 mizᵉâr (1), *fewness,
smallness*
4557 miçpâr (5), *number*
4591 mâ'aṭ (4), *to be,
make small or few*
4592 mᵉ'aṭ (24), *little or
few*
4962 math (4), *men*
7116 qâtsêr (1), *short*
1024 brachus (1), *little,
short*
3641 ŏligŏs (20), *puny,
small*
4935 suntŏmōs (1), *briefly*

FEWER
4592 mᵉ'aṭ (1), *little or
few*

FEWEST
4592 mᵉ'aṭ (1), *little or
few*

FEWNESS
4591 mâ'aṭ (1), *to be,
make small or few*

FIDELITY
4102 pistis (1),
faithfulness; faith, belief

FIELD
776 'erets (1), *earth,
land, soil; country*
1251 bar (Ch.) (8), *field*
2513 chelqâh (3),
flattery; allotment
7704 sâdeh (246), *field*
68 agrŏs (22), *farmland,
countryside*
5564 chōriŏn (3), *spot or
plot of ground*

FIELDS
2351 chûwts (2), *outside,
outdoors; countryside*
3010 yâgêb (1), *plowed
field*
7704 sâdeh (46), *field*
7709 shᵉdêmâh (4),
cultivated field
8309 shᵉrêmâh (1),
common
68 agrŏs (1), *farmland,
countryside*
5561 chōra (2), *space of
territory*

FIERCE
393 'akzâr (1), *violent,
deadly; brave*
2300 châdad (1), *to be,
make sharp; fierce*
2740 chârôwn (23),
burning of anger
2750 chŏrîy (3), *burning
anger*
3267 yâ'az (1), *to be
obstinate, be arrogant*
5794 'az (4), *strong,
vehement, harsh*
7826 shachal (3), *lion*
434 anĕmĕrŏs (1), *brutal,
savage*
2001 ĕpischuō (1), *to
insist stoutly*
4642 sklērŏs (1), *hard or
tough; harsh, severe*
5467 chalĕpŏs (1),
difficult, furious

FIERCENESS
2740 chârôwn (9),
burning of anger
7494 ra'ash (1),
bounding, uproar
2372 thumŏs (2),
passion, anger

FIERCER
7185 qâshâh (1), *to be
tough or severe*

FIERY
784 'êsh (1), *fire*
799 'eshdâth (1), *fire-law*
5135 nûwr (Ch.) (10), *fire*
8314 sârâph (5),
poisonous serpent
4442 pur (1), *fire*
4448 purŏō (1), *to be
ignited, glow*
4451 purŏsis (1), *ignition,
conflagration, calamity*

FIFTEEN
2568+6240 châmêsh (16),
five
6235+2568 'eser (1), *ten*
7657+2568 shib'îym (3),
seventy
1178 dĕkapĕntĕ (3),
fifteen
1440+4002 hĕbdŏ-
mēkŏnta (1), *seventy*

FIFTEENTH
2568+6240 châmêsh (17),
five
4003 pĕntĕkaidĕkatŏs
(1), *five and tenth*

FIFTH
2549 chămîyshîy (44),
fifth; fifth part
2567 châmash (1), *to tax
a fifth*
2568 châmêsh (6), *five*
2569 chômesh (1), *fifth
tax*
2570 chômesh (4),
abdomen, belly
3991 pĕmptŏs (4), *fifth*

FIFTIES
2572 chămishshîym (5),
fifty
4004 pĕntēkŏnta (2), *fifty*

FIFTIETH
2572 chămishshîym (4),
fifty

FIFTY

2572 chămishshîym (148), *fifty*
4002+3461 pĕntĕ (1), *five*
4004 pĕntēkŏnta (5), *fifty*

FIG

8384 tᵉʼên (24), *fig tree or fruit*
4808 sukē (16), *fig-tree*

FIGHT

3898 lâcham (85), to fight a *battle*, i.e. *consume*
4421 milchâmâh (5), *battle; war; fighting*
4634 maʼărâkâh (1), *row; pile;* military *array*
6633 tsâbâʼ (4), to *mass* an army or servants
73 agōn (1), *contest, struggle*
75 agōnizŏmai (2), to *struggle; to contend*
119 athlēsis (1), *struggle, contest*
2313 thĕŏmachĕō (1), to *resist deity*
2314 thĕŏmachŏs (1), *opponent of deity*
3164 machŏmai (1), to *war*, i.e. to *quarrel*
4170 pŏlĕmĕō (1), to *battle, make war*
4171 pŏlĕmŏs (1), *warfare; battle; fight*
4438 puktĕō (1), to *box as a sporting event*

FIGHTETH

3898 lâcham (3), to fight a *battle*, i.e. *consume*

FIGHTING

3898 lâcham (2), to fight a *battle*, i.e. *consume*
6213+4421 ʼâsâh (1), to *do or make*

FIGHTINGS

3163 machē (2), *controversy, conflict*

FIGS

6291 pag (1), *unripe* fig
8384 tᵉʼên (15), *fig tree or fruit*
3653 ŏlunthŏs (1), *unripe fig*
4810 sukŏn (4), *fig*

FIGURE

5566 çemel (1), *likeness*
8403 tabnîyth (1), *model, resemblance*
499 antitupŏn (1), *representative*
3345 mĕtaschēmatizō (1), to *transfigure*
3850 parabŏlē (2), *fictitious narrative*
5179 tupŏs (1), *shape, resemblance; "type"*

FIGURES

4734 miqlaʼath (1), *bas-relief sculpture*
499 antitupŏn (1), *representative*
5179 tupŏs (1), *shape, resemblance; "type"*

FILE

6477+6310 pᵉtsîyrâh (1), *bluntness*

FILL

4390 mâlêʼ (33), to *fill; be full*
4393 mᵉlôʼ (2), *fulness*
5433 çâbâʼ (1), to *quaff to satiety*
7301 râvâh (1), to *slake thirst or appetites*
7646 sâbaʼ (1), *fill to satiety*
7648 sôbaʼ (2), *satisfaction*
466 antanaplērŏō (1), to *fill up*
878 aphrōn (1), *ignorant; egotistic; unbelieving*
1072 gĕmizō (1), to *fill entirely*
2767 kĕrannumi (1), to *mingle*, i.e. to *pour*
4137 plērŏō (3), to *fill, make complete*
4138 plērōma (1), what *fills;* what is *filled*
5526 chŏrtazō (1), to *supply food*

FILLED

4390 mâlêʼ (74), to *fill; be full*
4391 mᵉlâʼ (Ch.) (1), to *fill; be full*
7059 qâmaṭ (1), to *pluck,* i.e. *destroy*
7301 râvâh (1), to *slake thirst or appetites*
7646 sâbaʼ (22), *fill to satiety*
1072 gĕmizō (7), to *fill entirely*
1705 ĕmpiplēmi (3), to *satisfy*
2767 kĕrannumi (1), to *mingle*, i.e. to *pour*
4130 plēthō (17), to *fulfill, complete*
4137 plērŏō (17), to *fill, make complete*
4138 plērōma (1), what *fills;* what is *filled*
4845 sumplērŏō (1), to be *complete, fulfill*
5055 tĕlĕō (1), to *end,* i.e. *complete, execute*
5526 chŏrtazō (11), to *supply food*

FILLEDST

4390 mâlêʼ (1), to *fill; be full*
7646 sâbaʼ (1), *fill to satiety*

FILLEST

4390 mâlêʼ (1), to *fill; be full*

FILLET

2339 chûwṭ (1), *string; measuring tape; line*

FILLETED

2836 châshaq (3), to *join; to love, delight*

FILLETH

4390 mâlêʼ (2), to *fill; be full*
5844 ʼâṭâh (1), to *wrap,* i.e. *cover, veil, clothe*
7646 sâbaʼ (2), *fill to satiety*

FILLETS

2838 châshûq (8), *fence-rail or rod*

FILLING

1705 ĕmpiplēmi (1), to *satisfy*

FILTH

6675 tsôwʼâh (1), *pollution*
4027 pĕrikatharma (1), *refuse, scum*
4509 rhupŏs (1), *dirt,* i.e. *moral depravity*

FILTHINESS

2932 ṭumʼâh (7), *ceremonial impurity*
5079 niddâh (2), *time of menstrual impurity*
5178 nᵉchôsheth (1), *copper; bronze*
6675 tsôwʼâh (2), *pollution*
151 aischrŏtēs (1), *obscenity*
168 akathartēs (1), state *of impurity*
3436 mŏlusmŏs (1), *contamination*
4507 rhuparia (1), moral *dirtiness*

FILTHY

444 ʼâlach (3), to *be or turn* morally *corrupt*
4754 mârâʼ (1), to *rebel; to lash* with whip; *flap*
5708 ʼêd (1), *periodical menstrual flux*
6674 tsôwʼ (2), *excrementitious, soiled*
147 aischrŏkĕrdŏs (1), *sordidly, greedily*
148 aischrŏlŏgia (1), *filthy speech*
150 aischrŏs (2), *shameful thing, base*
766 asĕlgĕia (1), *debauchery, lewdness*
4510 rhupŏō (2), to *become morally dirty*

FINALLY

3063 lŏipŏn (5), *finally*
5056 tĕlŏs (1), *conclusion*

FIND

2803 châshab (1), to *think, regard; to value*
4672 mâtsâʼ (100), to *find or acquire; to occur*
7912 shᵉkach (Ch.) (6), to *discover, find out*
2147 hĕuriskō (46), to *find*

FINDEST

4672 mâtsâʼ (2), to *find or acquire; to occur*

FINDETH

4672 mâtsâʼ (11), to *find or acquire; to occur*
2147 hĕuriskō (12), to *find*

FINDING

2714 chêqer (1), *examination*
4672 mâtsâʼ (2), to *find or acquire; to occur*

FINE

4131 plēktēs (1), *pugnacious*
421 anĕxichniastŏs (1), *unsearchable*
429 anĕuriskō (1), to *find out*
2147 hĕuriskō (4), to *find*

FINE

2212 zâqaq (1), to *strain, refine; extract, clarify*
2869 ṭâb (Ch.) (1), *good*
2896 ṭôwb (2), *good; well*
6668 tsâhab (1), to *be golden in color*
8305 sᵉrîyqâh (1), *linen cloth*
4585 sĕmidalis (1), fine *wheat flour*

FINER

6884 tsâraph (1), to *fuse* metal; to *refine*

FINEST

2459 cheleb (2), *fat; choice* part

FINGER

676 ʼetsbaʼ (19), *finger; toe*
1147 daktulŏs (5), *finger*

FINGERS

676 ʼetsbaʼ (11), *finger; toe*
677 ʼetsbaʼ (Ch.) (1), *finger; toe*
1147 daktulŏs (3), *finger*

FINING

4715 mitsrêph (2), *crucible*

FINISH

1214 bâtsaʼ (1), to *plunder; to finish*
3607 kâlâʼ (1), to *hold back or in; to prohibit*
3615 kâlâh (1), to *cease, be finished, perish*
535 apartismŏs (1), *completion*
1615 ĕktĕlĕō (2), to *complete fully, finish*
2005 ĕpitĕlĕō (1), to *terminate; to undergo*
4931 suntĕlĕō (1), to *complete entirely*
5048 tĕlĕiŏō (3), to *perfect, complete*

FINISHED

3319 yᵉtsâʼ (Ch.) (1), to *complete*
3615 kâlâh (19), to *cease, be finished, perish*
3635 kᵉlal (Ch.) (1), to *complete*
7999 shâlam (3), to *be safe; be complete*
8000 shᵉlam (Ch.) (2), to *complete, to restore*
8552 tâmam (4), to *complete, finish*
658 apŏtĕlĕō (1), to *bring to completion*
1096 ginŏmai (1), to *be, become*
1274 dianuō (1), to *accomplish thoroughly*
5048 tĕlĕiŏō (1), to *perfect, complete*
5055 tĕlĕō (8), to *end, complete, conclude*

English

FINISHER
5047 tĕlĕiŏtēs (1), completeness; maturity

FINS
5579 çᵉnappîyr (5), fin

FIR
1265 bᵉrôwsh (20), (poss.) cypress
1266 bᵉrôwth (1), (poss.) cypress

FIRE
215 'ôwr (1), to be luminous
217 'ûwr (4), flame; East
784 'êsh (375), fire
1200 bᵉ'êrâh (1), burning
3857 lâhaṭ (4), to blaze
5135 nûwr (Ch.) (8), fire
4442 pur (73), fire
4443 pura (2), fire
4447 purinŏs (1), fiery, i.e. flaming
4448 purŏō (1), to be ignited, glow
5394 phlŏgizō (2), to cause a blaze
5457 phōs (2), luminousness, light

FIREBRAND
181 'ûwd (1), poker stick for a fire
3940 lappîyd (1), flaming torch, lamp or flame

FIREBRANDS
181 'ûwd (1), poker stick for a fire
2131 zîyqâh (1), flash of fire
3940 lappîyd (1), flaming torch, lamp or flame

FIREPANS
4289 machtâh (4), pan for live coals

FIRES
217 'ûwr (1), flame; East

FIRKINS
3355 mĕtrētēs (1), liquid measure: 8-10 gallons

FIRM
1277 bârîy' (1), fatted or plump; healthy
3332 yâtsaq (2), to pour out
3559 kûwn (2), to set up: establish, fix, prepare
8631 tᵉqêph (Ch.) (1), to become, make mighty
949 bĕbaiŏs (1), stable, certain, binding

FIRMAMENT
7549 râqîya' (17), expanse

FIRST
259 'echâd (34), first
1061 bikkûwr (1), first-fruits of the crop
1069 bâkar (1), bear the first born
1073 bakkûrâh (1), first-ripe fruit of a fig
1121 bên (51), son, descendant
1323 bath (3), daughter, descendant, woman
2298 chad (Ch.) (4), one; single; first; at once

2490 châlal (1), to profane, defile
3138 yôwreh (1), autumn rain showers
4395 mᵉlê'âh (1), fulfilled; abundance
6440 pânîym (1), face; front
6933 qadmay (Ch.) (3), first
7218 rô'sh (6), head
7223 rî'shôwn (130), first, in place, time or rank
7224 rî'shônîy (1), first
7225 rê'shîyth (11), first
8462 tᵉchillâh (7), original; originally
509 anŏthĕn (1), from above; from the first
746 archē (4), first in rank; first in time
1207 dĕutĕrŏprōtŏs (1), second-first
1722+4413 ĕn (1), in; during; because of
3391 mia (7), one or first
3891 paranŏmĕō (1), to transgress, violate law
4272 prŏdidōmi (1), to give before
4276 prŏĕlpizō (1), to hope in advance of
4295 prŏkĕimai (1), to be present to the mind
4386 prŏtĕrŏn (3), previously
4412 prōtŏn (58), firstly
4413 prōtŏs (84), foremost
4416 prōtŏtŏkŏs (1), first-born

FIRSTBEGOTTEN
4416 prōtŏtŏkŏs (1), first-born

FIRSTBORN
1060 bᵉkôwr (101), firstborn
1062 bᵉkôwrâh (1), state of, rights of first born
1067 bᵉkîyrâh (6), first born, eldest daughter
1069 bâkar (1), bear the first born
4416 prōtŏtŏkŏs (7), first-born

FIRSTFRUIT
7225 rê'shîyth (1), first
536 aparchē (1), first-fruit

FIRSTFRUITS
1061 bikkûwr (13), first-fruits of the crop
7225 rê'shîyth (11), first
536 aparchē (7), first-fruit

FIRSTLING
1060 bᵉkôwr (8), firstborn, i.e. oldest son
1069 bâkar (1), bear the first born
6363 peṭer (4), firstling, first born

FIRSTLINGS
1060 bᵉkôwr (1), firstborn, i.e. oldest son
1062 bᵉkôwrâh (5), state of, rights of first born

FIRSTRIPE
1061 bikkûwr (1), first-fruits of the crop

1063 bikkûwrâh (3), early fig

FISH
1709 dâg (11), fish; fishes
1710 dâgâh (14), fish; fishes
1770 dîyg (1), to catch fish
5315 nephesh (1), life; breath; soul; wind
2486 ichthus (5), fish
3795 ŏpsariŏn (3), small fish

FISH'S
1710 dâgâh (1), fish; fishes

FISHER'S
1903 ĕpĕndutēs (1), outer garment, coat

FISHERMEN
231 haliĕus (1), one who fishes for a living

FISHERS
1728 davvâg (2), fisherman
1771 dayâg (1), fisherman
231 haliĕus (4), one who fishes for a living

FISHES
1709 dâg (8), fish; fishes
2485 ichthudiŏn (2), little fish
2486 ichthus (15), fish
3795 ŏpsariŏn (2), small fish

FISHHOOKS
5518+1729 çîyr (1), thorn; hook

FISHING
232 haliĕuō (1), to catch fish

FISHPOOLS
1295 bᵉrêkâh (1), reservoir, pool

FIST
106 'egrôph (2), clenched hand

FISTS
2651 chôphen (1), pair of fists

FIT
6257 'âthad (1), to prepare
6261 'ittîy (1), timely
433 anēkō (1), be proper, fitting
2111 ĕuthĕtŏs (2), appropriate, suitable
2520 kathēkō (1), becoming, proper

FITCHES
3698 kuççemeth (1), spelt
7100 qetsach (3), fennel-flower

FITLY
5921+655 'al (1), above, over, upon, or against
5921+4402 'al (1), above, over, upon, or against
4883 sunarmŏlŏgĕō (2), to render close-jointed

FITTED
3474 yâshar (1), to be straight; to make right

3559 kûwn (1), to render sure, proper
2675 katartizō (1), to repair; to prepare

FITTETH
6213 'âsâh (1), to do or make

FIVE
2568 châmêsh (271), five
3999 pĕntakis (1), five times
4000 pĕntakischiliŏi (16), five times a thousand
4001 pĕntakŏsiŏi (2), five hundred
4002 pĕntĕ (25), five

FIXED
3559 kûwn (4), to render sure, proper
4741 stērizō (1), to turn resolutely; to confirm

FLAG
260 'âchûw (1), bulrush or any marshy grass

FLAGON
809 'ăshîyshâh (2), cake of raisins

FLAGONS
809 'ăshîyshâh (2), cake of raisins
5035 nebel (1), skin-bag for liquids; vase; lyre

FLAGS
5488 çûwph (3), papyrus reed; reed

FLAKES
4651 mappâl (1), chaff; flap or fold of skin

FLAME
785 'êsh (Ch.) (1), fire
3632 kâlîyl (1), whole, entire; complete; whole
3827 labbâh (1), flame
3851 lahab (6), flame of fire; flash of a blade
3852 lehâbâh (12), flame; flash
4864 mas'êth (2), raising; beacon; present
7631 sᵉbîyb (Ch.) (2), flame tongue
7957 shalhebeth (3), flare, flame of fire
5395 phlŏx (6), flame; blaze

FLAMES
3851 lahab (2), flame of fire; flash of a blade
3852 lehâbâh (1), flame; flash

FLAMING
784 'êsh (1), fire
3852 lehâbâh (5), flame; flash
3857 lâhaṭ (1), to blaze
3858 lahaṭ (1), blaze; magic
5395 phlŏx (1), flame; blaze

FLANKS
3689 keçel (6), loin; back; viscera

FLASH
965 bâzâq (1), flash of lightning

FLAT
2763 charam (1), to
devote to destruction
8478 tachath (2), *bottom;*
underneath; in lieu of

FLATTER
2505 châlaq (1), to *be*
smooth; be slippery
6601 pâthâh (1), to *be,*
make simple; to delude

FLATTERETH
2505 châlaq (5), to *be*
smooth; be slippery
6601 pâthâh (1), to *be,*
make simple; to delude

FLATTERIES
2514 chălaqqâh (1),
smoothness; flattery
2519 chălaqlaqqâh (2),
smooth; treacherous

FLATTERING
2506 chêleq (1),
smoothness of tongue
2509 châlâq (2), *smooth,*
slippery of tongue
2513 chelqâh (2),
smoothness; flattery
3665 kâna' (2), to
humiliate, vanquish
2850 kŏlakĕia (1), *flattery*

FLATTERY
2506 chêleq (1),
smoothness of tongue
2513 chelqâh (1),
smoothness; flattery

FLAX
6593 pishteh (7), linen,
made of *carded* thread
6594 pishtâh (3), *flax;*
flax wick
3043 linŏn (1), flax *linen*

FLAY
6584 pâshaṭ (3), to *strip,*
i.e. *unclothe, flay*

FLAYED
6584 pâshaṭ (1), to *strip,*
i.e. *unclothe, flay*

FLEA
6550 par'ôsh (2), *flea*

FLED
1272 bârach (40), to *flee*
suddenly
5074 nâdad (8), to *rove,*
flee; to drive away
5127 nûwç (83), to *vanish*
away, *flee*
5132 nûwts (1), to *fly*
away, *leave*
1628 ĕkphĕugō (2), to
flee out, escape
2703 kataphĕugō (2), to
flee down
5343 phĕugō (11), to *run*
away; to shun

FLEDDEST
1272 bârach (1), to *flee*
suddenly
5127 nûwç (1), to *vanish*
away, *flee*

FLEE
1227 Baqbûwq (1),
gurgling *bottle*
1272 bârach (14), to *flee*
suddenly
3680 kâçâh (1), to *cover*

FLED column 2
4498 mânôwç (1), *fleeing;*
place of *refuge*
5074 nâdad (4), to *rove,*
flee; to drive away
5110 nûwd (1), to *waver;*
to *wander, flee*
5127 nûwç (62), to *vanish*
away, *flee*
5323 nâtsa' (1), to *go*
away
5756 'ûwz (1), to *save* by
fleeing
7368 râchaq (1), to
recede; remove
5343 phĕugō (15), to *run*
away; to shun

FLEECE
1488 gêz (2), shorn
fleece; mown *grass*
1492 gazzâh (7), wool
fleece

FLEEING
4499 mᵉnuwçâh (1),
retreat, fleeing
5127 nûwç (1), to *vanish*
away, *flee*
6207 'âraq (1), to *gnaw;* a
pain

FLEETH
1272 bârach (1), to *flee*
suddenly
5127 nûwç (4), to *vanish*
away, *flee*
5211 nîyç (1), *fugitive*
5775 'ôwph (1), *bird*
5343 phĕugō (2), to *run*
away; to shun

FLESH
829 'eshpâr (2),
measured *portion*
1320 bâsâr (253), *flesh;*
body; person
1321 bᵉsar (Ch.) (3),
flesh; body; person
2878 ṭibehâh (1),
butchery
3894 lâchûwm (1), *flesh*
7607 shᵉêr (7), *flesh,*
meat; kindred by blood
2907 krĕas (2), butcher's
meat
4561 sarx (143), *flesh*

FLESHHOOK
4207 mazlêg (2),
three-tined meat *fork*

FLESHHOOKS
4207 mazlêg (5),
three-tined meat *fork*

FLESHLY
4559 sarkikŏs (2),
pertaining to flesh

FLESHY
4560 sarkinŏs (1),
similar to flesh

FLEW
5774 'ûwph (1), to *cover,*
to *fly; to faint*
6213 'âsâh (1), to *do or*
make

FLIES
2070 zᵉbûwb (1), stinging
fly
6157 'ârôb (2), swarming
mosquitoes

FLIETH
1675 dâ'âh (1), to *fly*
rapidly, *soar*
5774 'ûwph (2), to *cover,*
to *fly; to faint*
5775 'ôwph (1), *bird*

FLIGHT
1272 bârach (1), to *flee*
suddenly
4498 mânôwç (1), *fleeing;*
place of *refuge*
4499 mᵉnuwçâh (1),
retreat, fleeing
5127 nûwç (1), to *vanish*
away, *flee*
7291 râdaph (1), to *run*
after with hostility
5437 phugē (2), *escape,*
flight, fleeing

FLINT
2496 challâmîysh (3),
flint, flinty rock
6864 tsôr (2), flint-stone
knife

FLINTY
2496 challâmîysh (1),
flint, flinty rock

FLOATS
1702 dôbᵉrâh (1), *raft,*
collection of logs

FLOCK
5739 'êder (16), *muster,*
flock
6629 tsô'n (83), *flock*
4167 pŏimnē (4), *flock*
4168 pŏimniŏn (5), *flock*

FLOCKS
2835 châsîph (1), small
company, flock
4735 miqneh (3), *stock*
4830 mir'îyth (1),
pasturage; flock
5739 'êder (16), *muster,*
flock
6251 'ashtᵉrâh (4), *flock*
of ewes
6629 tsô'n (54), *flock*

FLOOD
2229 zâram (1), to *gush*
water, *pour forth*
2230 zerem (1), *gush* of
water, *flood*
2975 yᵉ'ôr (6), Nile *River;*
Tigris *River*
3999 mabbûwl (13),
deluge
5104 nâhâr (8), *stream;*
Nile; Euphrates; Tigris
5158 nachal (3), *valley,*
ravine; mine *shaft*
7858 sheṭeph (1), *deluge,*
torrent
2627 kataklusmŏs (4),
inundation, flood
4182 pŏlupŏikilŏs (1),
many-sided
4215 pŏtamŏs (2),
current, brook
4216 pŏtamŏphŏrētŏs
(1), *overwhelmed by a*
stream

FLOODS
5104 nâhâr (10), *stream;*
Nile; Euphrates; Tigris
5140 nâzal (3), to *drip,* or
shed by trickling

FLIETH column 4
5158 nachal (2), *valley,*
ravine; mine *shaft*
7641 shibbôl (1), *stream;*
ear of grain
7858 sheṭeph (1), *deluge,*
torrent
4215 pŏtamŏs (2),
current, brook

FLOOR
1637 gôren (10), open
area
7136 qârâh (1), to *bring*
about; to impose
7172 qarqa' (6), *floor* of a
building or the sea
257 halôn (2),
threshing-*floor*

FLOORS
1637 gôren (1), open *area*

FLOTES
7513 raphçôdâh (1), log
raft

FLOUR
1217 bâtsêq (1),
fermenting *dough*
5560 çôleth (52), *fine*
flour
7058 qemach (4), *flour*
4585 sĕmidalis (1), fine
wheat *flour*

FLOURISH
5006 nâ'ats (1), to *scorn*
6524 pârach (9), to *break*
forth; to *bloom, flourish*
6692 tsûwts (3), to
blossom, flourish

FLOURISHED
6524 pârach (1), to *break*
forth; to *bloom, flourish*
330 anathallō (1), to
flourish; to revive

FLOURISHETH
6692 tsûwts (2), to
blossom, flourish

FLOURISHING
7487 ra'ânan (Ch.) (1),
prosperous
7488 ra'ănân (1),
verdant; prosperous

FLOW
2151 zâlal (1), to *be loose*
morally, *worthless*
3212 yâlak (2), to *walk;*
to *live; to carry*
5064 nâgar (1), to *pour*
out; to *deliver* over
5102 nâhar (5), to
sparkle; to flow
5140 nâzal (3), to *drip,* or
shed by trickling
4482 rhĕō (1), to *flow*
water

FLOWED
2151 zâlal (1), to *be loose*
morally, *worthless*
3212 yâlak (1), to *walk;*
to *live; to carry*
6687 tsûwph (1), to
overflow

FLOWER
582 'ĕnôwsh (1), *man;*
person, human
5328 nitstsâh (1), *blossom*
6525 perach (5), *calyx*
flower; bloom

English

6731 tsîyts (6), burnished *plate*; bright *flower*
6733 tsîytsâh (1), *flower*
438 anthŏs (4), flower *blossom*
5230 hupĕrakmŏs (1), *past the bloom of youth*

FLOWERS
4026 migdâl (1), *tower; rostrum*
5079 niddâh (2), time of menstrual *impurity*; idolatry
5339 nitstsân (1), *blossom*
6525 perach (9), *calyx flower; bloom*
6731 tsîyts (4), burnished *plate*; bright *flower*

FLOWETH
2100 zûwb (12), to *flow* freely, *gush*

FLOWING
2100 zûwb (9), to *flow* freely, *gush*
5042 nâba' (1), to *gush* forth; to *utter*
5140 nâzal (1), to *drip*, or *shed* by trickling
7857 shâṭaph (1), to *gush*; to *inundate*

FLUTE
4953 mashrôwqîy (Ch.) (4), musical *pipe*

FLUTTERETH
7363 râchaph (1), to *brood*; to *be relaxed*

FLUX
1420 dusĕntĕria (1), *dysentery*

FLY
82 'âbar (1), to *soar*
1675 dâ'âh (3), to *fly* rapidly, *soar*
2070 zᵉbûwb (1), *fly*
3286 yâ'aph (1), to *tire*
5774 'ûwph (13), to *cover*, to *fly*; to *faint*
5860 'îyṭ (1), to *swoop* down upon; to *insult*
6524 pârach (2), to *break* forth; to *bloom*; to *fly*
4072 pĕtŏmai (3), to *fly*

FLYING
3671 kânâph (1), *edge* or *extremity*; *wing*
5774 'ûwph (6), to *cover*, to *fly*; to *faint*
5775 'ôwph (2), *bird*
4072 pĕtŏmai (2), to *fly*

FOAL
1121 bên (1), *son, descendant*
5895 'ayîr (1), young donkey or *ass*
5207 huiŏs (1), *son*

FOALS
5895 'ayîr (1), young donkey or *ass*

FOAM
7110 qetseph (1), *rage* or *strife*

FOAMETH
875 aphrizō (1), to *froth* at the mouth

876 aphrŏs (1), *froth, foam*

FOAMING
875 aphrizō (1), to *froth* at the mouth
1890 ĕpaphrizō (1), to *foam upon*

FODDER
1098 bᵉlîyl (1), *feed, fodder*

FOES
341 'ôyêb (2), *adversary, enemy*
6862 tsar (2), *trouble; opponent*
8130 sânê' (1), to *hate*
2190 ĕchthrŏs (2), *adversary*

FOLD
1699 dôber (1), grazing *pasture*
4356 miklâ'âh (1), sheep or goat *pen*
5116 nâveh (3), *at home; lovely; home*
7257 râbats (1), to *recline, repose, brood*
833 aulē (1), *palace; house; sheepfold*
1667 hĕlissō (1), to *coil, roll up*, or *wrap*
4167 pŏimnē (1), *flock*

FOLDEN
5440 çâbak (1), to *entwine*

FOLDETH
2263 châbaq (1), to *clasp* the hands, *embrace*

FOLDING
1550 gâlîyl (2), *valve* of a folding door
2264 chibbûq (2), *folding*

FOLDS
1448 gᵉdêrâh (3), *enclosure* for flocks
4356 miklâ'âh (1), sheep or goat *pen*
5116 nâveh (1), *at home; lovely; home*

FOLK
3816 lᵉ'ôm (1), *community, nation*
5971 'am (2), *people; tribe; flock*

FOLLOW
310 'achar (5), *after*
935+310 bôw' (1), to *go* or *come*
1692 dâbaq (1), to *cling* or *adhere*; to *catch*
1961 hâyâh (3), to *exist*, i.e. *be* or *become*
1961+310 hâyâh (1), to *exist*, i.e. *be* or *become*
1980+310 hâlak (1), to *walk; live a certain way*
1980+7272 hâlak (1), to *walk; live a certain way*
3212+310 yâlak (8), to *walk; to live; to carry*
7272 regel (3), *foot; step*
7291 râdaph (11), to *run* after with hostility
190 akŏlŏuthĕō (30), to *accompany, follow*

1205+3694 dĕutĕ (1), *come hither!*
1377 diōkō (8), to *pursue; to persecute*
1811 ĕxakŏlŏuthĕō (1), to *imitate, obey*
1872 ĕpakŏlŏuthĕō (2), to *accompany, follow*
2071 ĕsŏmai (1), *will be*
2517 kathĕxēs (1), *in a sequence*
3326+5023 mĕta (1), *with, among; after, later*
3401 mimĕŏmai (4), to *imitate, i.e. model*
3877 parakŏlŏuthĕō (1), to *attend; trace out*
4870 sunakŏlŏuthĕō (1), to *follow, accompany*

FOLLOWED
310 'achar (16), *after*
1692 dâbaq (4), to *cling* or *adhere*; to *catch*
1961+310 hâyâh (2), to *exist*, i.e. *be* or *become*
1980+310 hâlak (7), to *walk; live a certain way*
3112+310 Yôwyâkîyn (1), *Jehovah will establish*
3212+310 yâlak (9), to *walk; to live; to carry*
3318+310 yâtsâ' (1), to *go, bring out*
6213 'âsâh (1), to *do* or *make*
7272 regel (1), *foot; step*
7291 râdaph (2), to *run* after with hostility
190 akŏlŏuthĕō (53), to *accompany, follow*
1096 ginŏmai (1), to *be, become*
1377 diōkō (2), to *pursue; to persecute*
1811 ĕxakŏlŏuthĕō (1), to *imitate, obey*
1872 ĕpakŏlŏuthĕō (1), to *accompany, follow*
2076+3326 ĕsti (1), he (she or it) *is*
2614 katadiōkō (1), to *search for, look for*
2628 katakŏlŏuthĕō (2), to *accompany closely*
4870 sunakŏlŏuthĕō (1), to *follow, accompany*

FOLLOWEDST
3212+310 yâlak (1), to *walk; to live; to carry*

FOLLOWERS
3402 mimētēs (7), *imitator, example*
4831 summimētēs (1), *co-imitator*

FOLLOWETH
310 'achar (1), *after*
935+310 bôw' (2), to *go* or *come*
1692 dâbaq (1), to *cling* or *adhere*; to *catch*
7291 râdaph (6), to *run* after with hostility
190 akŏlŏuthĕō (5), to *accompany, follow*

FOLLOWING
310 'achar (26), *after*
310+3651 'achar (1), *after*

312 'achêr (1), *other, another, different; next*
314 'achărôwn (1), *late* or *last; behind; western*
3212+310 yâlak (2), to *walk; to live; to carry*
190 akŏlŏuthĕō (3), to *accompany, follow*
1811 ĕxakŏlŏuthĕō (1), to *imitate, obey*
1836 hĕxēs (1), *successive, next*
1872 ĕpakŏlŏuthĕō (1), to *accompany, follow*
1887 ĕpauriŏn (2), *to-morrow*
1966 ĕpiŏusa (1), *ensuing*
2192 ĕchō (1), to *have; hold; keep*

FOLLY
200 'ivveleth (13), *silliness, foolishness*
3689 keçel (2), *loin; back; viscera; silliness*
3690 kiçlâh (1), *trust; silliness*
5039 nᵉbâlâh (10), moral *wickedness; crime*
5529 çekel (1), *silliness; dolts*
5531 çiklûwth (5), *silliness*
8417 tohŏlâh (1), *bluster, braggadocio*, i.e. *fatuity*
8604 tiphlâh (2), *frivolity, foolishness*
454 anŏia (1), *stupidity; rage*
877 aphrŏsunē (1), *senselessness*

FOOD
398 'âkal (1), to *eat*
400 'ôkel (16), *food*
402 'oklâh (1), *food*
944 bûwl (1), *produce*
3899 lechem (21), *food, bread*
3978 ma'ăkâl (5), *food, something to eat*
4361 makkôleth (1), *nourishment*
6718 tsayid (1), hunting *game; lunch, food*
7607 shᵉ'êr (1), *flesh, meat; kindred by blood*
1035 brōsis (1), *food; rusting corrosion*
1304 diatribō (1), to *remain, stay*
5160 trŏphē (2), *nourishment; rations*

FOOL
191 'ĕvîyl (11), *silly; fool*
3684 kᵉçîyl (34), *stupid* or *silly*
5030 nâbîy' (1), *prophet; inspired man*
5036 nâbâl (6), *stupid; impious*
5528 çâkal (1), to *be silly*
5530 çâkâl (3), *silly*
5536 çal (1), *basket*
876 aphrŏs (6), *froth, foam*
3474 mōrŏs (2), *heedless, moral blockhead*
3912 paraphrŏnĕō (1), to *be insane*

FOOL'S
191 'ĕvîyl (2), silly; fool
3684 kᵉçîyl (5), stupid or silly

FOOLISH
191 'ĕvîyl (6), silly; fool
196 'ĕvîlîy (1), silly, foolish
200 'ivveleth (1), silliness, foolishness
1198 ba'ar (1), brutishness; stupidity
1984 hâlal (2), to boast
2973 yâ'al (1), to be or act foolish
3684 kᵉçîyl (9), stupid or silly
3687 kᵉçîylûwth (1), silliness, stupidity
3688 kâçal (1), silly, stupid
5036 nâbâl (6), stupid; impious
5039 nᵉbâlâh (1), moral wickedness; crime
5528 çâkal (1), to be silly
5530 çâkâl (2), silly
6612 pᵉthîy (1), silly, i.e. seducible
8602 tâphêl (1), to plaster; frivolity
453 anŏĕtŏs (4), unintelligent, senseless
801 asunĕtŏs (2), senseless, dull; wicked
878 aphrōn (2), ignorant; egotistic; unbelieving
3471 mōrainō (1), to become insipid
3473 mōrŏlŏgia (1), buffoonery, foolish talk
3474 mōrŏs (7), heedless, moral blockhead

FOOLISHLY
200 'ivveleth (1), silliness, foolishness
1984 hâlal (1), to boast
2973 yâ'al (1), to be or act foolish
5034 nâbêl (1), to wilt; to fall away; to be foolish or wicked
5528 çâkal (5), to be silly
8604 tiphlâh (1), frivolity, foolishness
1722+877 ĕn (2), in; during; because of

FOOLISHNESS
200 'ivveleth (10), silliness, foolishness
5528 çâkal (1), to be silly
5531 çiklûwth (2), silliness
877 aphrŏsunē (1), senselessness
3472 mōria (5), absurdity, foolishness
3474 mōrŏs (1), heedless, moral blockhead

FOOLS
191 'ĕvîyl (7), silly; fool
1984 hâlal (2), to boast
2973 yâ'al (1), to be or act foolish
3684 kᵉçîyl (22), stupid or silly
5036 nâbâl (2), stupid; impious

453 anŏĕtŏs (1), unintelligent, senseless
781 asŏphŏs (1), unwise, foolish
878 aphrōn (2), ignorant; egotistic; unbelieving
3471 mōrainō (1), to become insipid
3474 mōrŏs (3), heedless, moral blockhead

FOOT
947 bûwç (2), to trample down; oppress
3653 kên (8), pedestal or station of a basin
4001 mᵉbûwçâh (1), trampling, oppression
4823 mirmâç (1), abasement
5541 çâlâh (1), to contemn, reject
7272 regel (61), foot; step
7273 raglîy (1), footman soldier
2662 katapatĕō (2), to trample down; to reject
3979 pĕzē; (1), on foot
4158 pŏdĕrēs (1), robe reaching the ankles
4228 pŏus (9), foot

FOOTBREADTH
3709+4096+7272 kaph (1), sole of foot

FOOTMEN
376+7273 'îysh (4), man; male; someone
7273 raglîy (7), footman soldier
7328 râz (Ch.) (1), mystery

FOOTSTEPS
6119 'âqêb (3), track, footprint; rear position
6471 pa'am (1), time; step; occurence

FOOTSTOOL
1916+7272 hădôm (6), foot-stool
3534 kebesh (1), footstool
5286 hupŏpŏdiŏn (1), under the feet
5286+3588+4228 hupŏpŏdiŏn (8), under the feet, i.e. a foot-rest

FORASMUCH
310 'achar (1), after
310+834 'achar (2), after
854+834 'êth (1), with; by; at; among
3282 ya'an (1), because, for this reason
3282+365 ya'an (2), because, for this reason
3282+834 ya'an (5), because, for this reason
3588 kîy (1), for, that because
3588+5921+3651 kîy (1), for, that because
3606+6903+1768 kôl (Ch.) (8), all, any or every
5704 'ad (1), as far (long) as; during; while; until
1487 ĕi (1), if, whether, that
1893 ĕpĕi (2), since

1894 ĕpĕidĕ (1), when, whereas
1895 ĕpĕidēpĕr (1), since indeed
5607 ōn (1), being, existence

FORBAD
6680 tsâvâh (1), to constitute, enjoin
1254 diakōluō (1), utterly prohibit or prevent
2967 kōluō (3), to stop

FORBARE
2308 châdal (3), to desist, stop; be fat

FORBEAR
1826 dâmam (1), to stop, cease; to perish
2308 châdal (15), to desist, stop; be fat
2820 châsak (1), to restrain or refrain
4900 mâshak (1), to draw out; to be tall
3361 mē (1), not; lest
4722 stĕgō (2), to endure patiently
5339 phĕidŏmai (1), to abstain; treat leniently

FORBEARANCE
463 anŏchē (2), tolerance, clemency

FORBEARETH
2308 châdal (1), to desist, stop; be fat
2310 châdêl (1), ceasing or destitute

FORBEARING
639 'aph (1), nose or nostril; face; person
3557 kûwl (1), to maintain
430 anĕchŏmai (2), put up with, endure
447 aniēmi (1), to slacken, loosen

FORBID
2486 châlîylâh (12), far be it!, forbid!
3607 kâlâ' (1), to hold back or in; to prohibit
2967 kōluō (9), to stop
3361+1096 mē (14), not; lest

FORBIDDEN
3808 lô' (1), no, not
6680 tsâvâh (1), to constitute, enjoin
2967 kōluō (1), to stop

FORBIDDETH
2967 kōluō (1), to stop

FORBIDDING
209 akōlutōs (1), in an unhindered manner
2967 kōluō (3), to stop

FORBORN
2308 châdal (1), to desist, stop; be fat

FORCE
153 'edra' (Ch.) (1), power
202 'ôwn (1), ability, power; wealth
1369 gᵉbûwrâh (1), force; valor; victory
1497 gâzal (1), to rob

2388 châzaq (1), to fasten upon; to seize
2394 chozqâh (2), vehemence, harshness
3027 yâd (2), hand; power
3533 kâbash (1), to conquer, subjugate
3581 kôach (3), force, might; strength
3893 lêach (1), fresh strength, vigor
6031 'ânâh (1), to afflict, be afflicted
726 harpazō (3), to seize
949 bĕbaiŏs (1), stable, certain, binding

FORCED
662 'âphaq (1), to abstain
3905 lâchats (1), to press; to distress
5080 nâdach (1), to push off, scattered
6031 'ânâh (4), to afflict, be afflicted

FORCES
2428 chayil (14), army; wealth; virtue; valor
3981 ma'ămâts (1), strength; resources
4581 mâ'ôwz (1), fortified place; defense

FORCIBLE
4834 mârats (1), to be pungent or vehement

FORCING
4330 mîyts (1), pressure
5080 nâdach (1), to push off, scattered

FORD
4569 ma'ăbâr (1), crossing-place

FORDS
4569 ma'ăbâr (3), crossing-place

FORECAST
2803 châshab (2), to plot; to think, regard

FOREFATHERS
4269 prŏgŏnŏs (1), ancestor

FOREFRONT
4136+6440 mûwl (1), in front of, opposite
4136+6640 mûwl (3), in front of, opposite
6440 pânîym (4), face; front
7218 rô'sh (1), head
8127 shên (1), tooth; ivory; cliff

FOREHEAD
639 'aph (1), nose or nostril; face; person
1371 gibbêach (1), bald forehead
1372 gabbachath (3), baldness on forehead
4696 mêtsach (9), forehead
3359 mĕtōpŏn (2), forehead

FOREHEADS
4696 mêtsach (2), forehead

3359 mĕtōpŏn (6), forehead

FOREIGNER
5237 nokrîy (1), foreign; non-relative; different
8453 tôwshâb (1), temporary dweller

FOREIGNERS
5237 nokrîy (1), foreign; non-relative; different
3941 parŏikŏs (1), strange; stranger

FOREKNEW
4267 prŏginōskō (1), to know beforehand

FOREKNOW
4267 prŏginōskō (1), to know beforehand

FOREKNOWLEDGE
4268 prŏgnōsis (2), forethought

FOREMOST
7223 ri'shôwn (3), first

FOREORDAINED
4267 prŏginōskō (1), to know beforehand

FOREPART
6440 pânîym (4), face; front
4408 prōra (1), prow, i.e. forward part of a vessel

FORERUNNER
4274 prŏdrŏmŏs (1), runner ahead

FORESAW
4308 prŏŏraō (1), to notice previously

FORESEEING
4375 prŏsphilēs (1), acceptable, pleasing

FORESEETH
7200 râ'âh (2), to see

FORESHIP
4408 prōra (1), prow, i.e. forward part of a vessel

FORESKIN
6188 'ârêl (1), to refrain from using
6190 'orlâh (8), prepuce or penile foreskin

FORESKINS
6190 'orlâh (5), prepuce or penile foreskin

FOREST
3293 ya'ar (37), honey in the comb
6508 pardêç (1), park, cultivated garden area

FORESTS
2793 chôresh (1), wooded forest
3293 ya'ar (1), honey in the comb
3295 ya'ărâh (1), honey in the comb

FORETELL
4302 prŏlĕgō (1), to predict, forewarn

FORETOLD
4280 prŏĕrĕō (1), to say already, predict
4293 prŏkataggĕllō (1), to predict, foretell

FOREWARN
5263 hupŏdĕiknumi (1), to exemplify, instruct

FOREWARNED
4277 prŏĕpō (1), to say already, to predict

FORFEITED
2763 charam (1), to devote to destruction

FORGAT
5382 nâshâh (1), to forget
7911 shâkach (7), to be oblivious of, forget

FORGAVE
3722 kâphar (1), to cover; to expiate
863 aphiĕmi (2), to leave; to pardon, forgive
5483 charizŏmai (4), to grant as a favor, pardon

FORGAVEST
5375 nâsâ' (2), to lift up

FORGED
2950 tâphal (1), to impute falsely

FORGERS
2950 tâphal (1), to impute falsely

FORGET
5382 nâshâh (2), to forget
7911 shâkach (48), to be oblivious of, forget
7913 shâkêach (2), oblivious, forgetting
1950 ĕpilanthanŏmai (2), to lose out of mind

FORGETFUL
1950 ĕpilanthanŏmai (1), to lose out of mind
1953 ĕpilēsmŏnē (1), negligence

FORGETFULNESS
5388 neshîyâh (1), oblivion

FORGETTEST
7911 shâkach (2), to be oblivious of, forget

FORGETTETH
7911 shâkach (2), to be oblivious of, forget
7913 shâkêach (1), oblivious, forgetting
1950 ĕpilanthanŏmai (1), to lose out of mind

FORGETTING
1950 ĕpilanthanŏmai (1), to lose out of mind

FORGIVE
3722 kâphar (1), to cover; to expiate
5375 nâsâ' (8), to lift up
5545 çâlach (18), to forgive
5546 çallâch (1), placable, tolerant
630 apŏluō (1), to relieve, release; to pardon
863 aphiĕmi (22), to leave; to pardon, forgive
5483 charizŏmai (3), to grant as a favor, pardon

FORGIVEN
3722 kâphar (1), to cover; to expiate

5375 nâsâ' (4), to lift up
5545 çâlach (13), to forgive
630 apŏluō (1), to relieve, release; to pardon
863 aphiĕmi (21), to leave; to pardon, forgive
5483 charizŏmai (2), to grant as a favor, pardon

FORGIVENESS
5547 çᵉlîychâh (1), pardon
859 aphĕsis (6), pardon, freedom

FORGIVENESSES
5547 çᵉlîychâh (1), pardon

FORGIVETH
5545 çâlach (1), to forgive
863 aphiĕmi (1), to leave; to pardon, forgive

FORGIVING
5375 nâsâ' (2), to lift up
5483 charizŏmai (2), to grant as a favor, pardon

FORGOT
7911 shâkach (1), to be oblivious of, forget

FORGOTTEN
5382 nâshâh (1), to forget
7911 shâkach (39), to be oblivious of, forget
7913 shâkêach (1), oblivious, forgetting
1585 ĕklanthanŏmai (1), to forget
1950 ĕpilanthanŏmai (3), to lose out of mind
3024+2983 lēthē (1), forgetfulness

FORKS
7969+7053 shâlôwsh (1), three; third; thrice

FORM
3335 yâtsar (1), to form; potter; to determine
4758 mar'eh (1), appearance; vision
4941 mishpâṭ (1), verdict; formal decree; justice
6440 pânîym (1), face; front
6699 tsûwrâh (2), rock; form as if pressed out
6755 tselem (Ch.) (1), idolatrous figure
7299 rêv (Ch.) (2), aspect, appearance
8389 tô'ar (3), outline, i.e. figure, appearance
8403 tabnîyth (3), model, resemblance
8414 tôhûw (2), waste, desolation, formless
3444 mŏrphē (3), shape, form; nature, character
3446 mŏrphōsis (2), appearance; semblance
5179 tupŏs (1), shape resemblance; "type"
5296 hupŏtupōsis (1), example, pattern

FORMED
2342 chûwl (5), to dance, whirl; to writhe in pain

3335 yâtsar (23), to form; potter; to determine
7169 qârats (1), to bite the lips, blink the eyes
3445 mŏrphŏō (1), to fashion, take on a form
4110 plasma (2), molded, what is formed
4111 plassō (1), to mold, i.e. shape or fabricate

FORMER
570 'emesh (1), last night
3138 yôwreh (2), autumn rain showers
3335 yâtsar (2), to form; potter; to determine
4175 môwreh (2), archer; teaching; early rain
6440 pânîym (1), face; front
6927 qadmâh (3), priority in time; before; past
6931 qadmôwnîy (2), anterior time; eastern
7223 ri'shôwn (32), first
4386 prŏtĕrŏn (2), previously
4387 prŏtĕrŏs (1), prior or previous
4413 prōtŏs (2), foremost

FORMETH
3335 yâtsar (2), to form; potter; to determine

FORMS
6699 tsûwrâh (2), rock; form as if pressed out

FORNICATION
2181 zânâh (3), to commit adultery
8457 taznûwth (1), harlotry
1608 ĕkpŏrnĕuō (1), to fornicate
4202 pŏrnĕia (24), sexual immorality
4203 pŏrnĕuō (7), to indulge unlawful lust

FORNICATIONS
8457 taznûwth (1), harlotry
4202 pŏrnĕia (2), sexual immorality

FORNICATOR
4205 pŏrnŏs (2), sexually immoral person

FORNICATORS
4205 pŏrnŏs (3), sexually immoral person

FORSAKE
2308 châdal (1), to desist, stop; be fat
5203 nâṭash (7), to disperse; to abandon
5800 'âzab (45), to loosen; relinquish
7503 râphâh (2), to slacken
646+575 apŏstasia (1), defection, rebellion
1459 ĕgkatalĕipō (1), to desert, abandon

FORSAKEN
488 'almân (1), discarded, forsaken
5203 nâṭash (6), to disperse; to abandon

5428 nâthash (1), to *tear away*, *be uprooted*
5800 'âzab (60), to *loosen; relinquish*
7971 shâlach (1), to *send away*
863 aphíëmi (2), to *leave; to pardon, forgive*
1459 ĕgkataleípō (4), to *desert, abandon*
2641 kataleípō (1), to *abandon*

FORSAKETH
5800 'âzab (5), to *loosen; relinquish; permit*
657 apŏtassŏmai (1), to *say adieu; to renounce*

FORSAKING
5805 'ăzûwbâh (1), *desertion, forsaking*
1459 ĕgkataleípō (1), to *desert, abandon*

FORSOMUCH
2530 kathŏti (1), *as far or inasmuch as*

FORSOOK
5203 nâṭash (2), to *disperse; to abandon*
5800 'âzab (16), to *loosen; relinquish*
863 aphíëmi (4), to *leave; to pardon, forgive*
1459 ĕgkataleípō (1), to *desert, abandon*
2641 kataleípō (1), to *abandon*

FORSOOKEST
5800 'âzab (2), to *loosen; relinquish; permit*

FORSWEAR
1964 ĕpíŏrkĕō (1), to *commit perjury*

FORT
1785 dâyêq (3), *battering-tower*
4581 mâ'ôwz (1), *fortified place; defense*
4686 mâtsûwd (1), *net or capture; fastness*
4869 misgâb (1), *high refuge*

FORTH
935 bôw' (1), to *go or come*
1310 bâshal (1), to *boil up, cook; to ripen*
1319 bâsar (1), to *announce (good news)*
1518 gîyach (4), to *issue forth; to burst forth*
1645 geresh (1), *produce, yield*
1876 dâshâ' (1), to *sprout new plants*
1921 hâdar (1), to *favor or honor; to be high*
2254 châbal (2), to *writhe in labor pain*
2315 cheder (1), *apartment, chamber*
2330 chûwd (4), to *propound a riddle*
2342 chûwl (4), to *dance, whirl; to writhe in pain*
2590 chânaṭ (1), to *embalm; to ripen*

2904 ṭûwl (3), to *cast down or out, hurl*
2986 yâbal (1), to *bring*
3205 yâlad (26), to *bear young; to father a child*
3209 yillôwd (1), *born*
3318 yâtsâ' (403), to *go, bring out*
3329 yâtsîy' (1), *issue forth*, i.e. *offspring*
4161 môwtsâ' (11), *going forth*
4163 môwtsâ'âh (3), *family descent*
4866 mishbêr (1), *vaginal opening*
5066 nâgash (2), to *be, come, bring near*
5107 nûwb (2), to *(make) flourish; to utter*
5132 nûwts (1), to *fly away, leave*
5221 nâkâh (1), to *strike, kill*
5265 nâça' (5), *start* on a journey
5312 nᵉphaq (Ch.) (7), to *issue forth; to bring out*
5375 nâsâ' (2), to *lift up*
5414 nâthan (1), to *give*
5608 çâphar (1), to *inscribe; to enumerate*
5674 'âbar (2), to *cross over; to transition*
5975 'âmad (1), to *stand*
6213 'âsâh (10), to *do or make*
6398 pâlach (1), to *slice; to break open; to pierce*
6440 pânîym (1), *face; front*
6509 pârâh (1), to *bear fruit*
6556 perets (1), *break, gap*
6566 pâras (1), to *break apart, disperse, scatter*
6605 pâthach (1), to *open wide; to loosen, begin*
6631 tse'ĕtsâ' (1), *produce, children*
6779 tsâmach (4), to *sprout*
7126 qârab (1), to *approach, bring near*
7737 shâvâh (1), to *level*, i.e. *equalize*
7971 shâlach (27), to *send away*
8317 shârats (5), to *swarm, or abound*
8444 tôwtsâ'âh (2), *exit, boundary; deliverance*
321 anagō (3), to *lead up; to bring out; to sail*
392 anatassŏmai (1), to *arrange*
584 apŏdĕiknumi (1), to *demonstrate*
616 apŏkuĕō (1), to *bring into being*
649 apŏstĕllō (11), to *send out on a mission*
669 apŏphthĕggŏmai (1), *declare, address*
985 blastanō (1), to *yield fruit*
1032 bruō (1), to *gush, pour forth*

1080 gĕnnaō (1), to *procreate, regenerate*
1544 ĕkballō (7), to *throw out*
1554 ĕkdidōmi (2), to *lease, rent*
1584 ĕklampō (1), to *be resplendent, shine*
1599 ĕkpĕmpō (1), to *despatch, send out*
1600 ĕkpĕtannumi (1), to *extend, spread out*
1607 ĕkpŏrĕuŏmai (4), to *depart, be discharged*
1614 ĕktĕinō (17), to *stretch*
1627 ĕkphĕrō (3), to *bear out; to produce*
1631 ĕkphuō (2), to *sprout up, put forth*
1632 ĕkchĕō (1), to *pour forth; to bestow*
1731 ĕndĕiknumi (1), to *show, display*
1754 ĕnĕrgĕō (2), to *be active, efficient, work*
1804 ĕxaggĕllō (1), to *declare, proclaim*
1806 ĕxagō (1), to *lead forth, escort*
1821 ĕxapŏstĕllō (4), to *despatch, or to dismiss*
1831 ĕxĕrchŏmai (32), to *issue; to leave*
1854 ĕxō (8), *out, outside*
1901 ĕpĕktĕinŏmai (1), to *stretch oneself forward*
1907 ĕpĕchō (1), to *retain; to detain*
1911 ĕpiballō (1), to *throw upon*
2164 ĕuphŏrĕō (1), to *be fertile, produce a crop*
2564 kalĕō (1), to *call*
2592 karpŏphŏrĕō (2), to *be fertile*
2604 kataggĕlĕus (1), *proclaimer*
2609 katagō (1), to *lead down; to moor a vessel*
3004 lĕgō (1), to *say*
3318 Mĕsŏpŏtamia (2), *between the Rivers*
3855 paragō (1), to *go along or away*
3860 paradidōmi (1), to *hand over*
3908 paratithĕmi (2), to *present something*
3928 parĕrchŏmai (2), *go by; to perish*
4160 pŏiĕō (14), to *do*
4198 pŏrĕuŏmai (1), to *go, come; to travel*
4254 prŏagō (2), to *lead forward; to precede*
4261 prŏballō (1), to *push to the front, germinate*
4270 prŏgraphō (1), to *announce, prescribe*
4295 prŏkĕimai (1), to *stand forth*
4311 prŏpĕmpō (1), to *send forward*
4388 prŏtithĕmai (1), to *place before, exhibit*
4393 prŏphĕrō (2), to *bear forward*

4486 rhĕgnumi (1), to *break, burst forth*
5087 tithĕmi (1), to *place*
5088 tiktō (9), to *produce from seed*
5319 phanĕrŏō (1), to *render apparent*
5348 phthanō (1), to *be beforehand, precede*

FORTHWITH
629 oçparnâ' (Ch.) (1), *with diligence*
2112 ĕuthĕŏs (7), *at once or soon*
2117 ĕuthus (1), *at once, immediately*
3916 parachrēma (1), *instantly, immediately*

FORTIETH
705 'arbâ'îym (4), *forty*

FORTIFIED
2388 châzaq (2), to *fasten upon; be strong*
4692 mâtsôwr (1), *siege-mound; distress*
5800 'âzab (1), to *loosen; relinquish; permit*

FORTIFY
553 'âmats (1), to *be strong; be courageous*
1219 bâtsar (2), to *be inaccessible*
2388 châzaq (1), to *fasten upon; be strong*
5800 'âzab (1), to *loosen; relinquish; permit*
6696 tsûwr (1), to *cramp*, i.e. *confine; to harass*

FORTRESS
4013 mibtsâr (4), *fortification; defender*
4581 mâ'ôwz (3), *fortified place; defense*
4686 mâtsûwd (6), *net or capture; fastness*
4693 mâtsôwr (2), *limit, border*

FORTRESSES
4013 mibtsâr (2), *fortification; defender*

FORTS
1785 dâyêq (3), *battering-tower*
4679 mᵉtsad (1), *stronghold*
4694 mᵉtsûwrâh (1), *rampart, fortification*
6076 'ôphel (1), *tumor; fortress*

FORTUNATUS
5415 Phŏrtŏunatŏs (2), *fortunate*

FORTY
702+7239 'arba (2), *four*
705 'arbâ'îym (126), *forty*
5062 tĕssarakŏnta (22), *forty*
5063 tĕssarakŏntaĕtĕs (2), *of forty years* of age

FORTY'S
705 'arbâ'îym (1), *forty*

FORUM
675 'Appiŏs (1), *Appius*

English

FORWARD
1973 hâlᵉâh (5), *far away; thus far*
1980 hâlak (1), to *walk; live a certain way*
3276 yâ'al (1), *to be valuable*
4605 ma'al (2), *upward, above, overhead*
5265 nâça' (18), *start on a journey*
5921 'al (3), *above, over, upon, or against*
6440 pânîym (4), *face; front*
6584 pâshaṭ (1), to *strip, i.e. unclothe, plunder*
6924 qedem (1), *eastern; antiquity; before*
2309 thĕlō (1), to *will; to desire; to choose*
4261 prŏballō (1), to *push to the front, germinate*
4281 prŏĕrchŏmai (1), to *go onward, precede*
4311 prŏpĕmpō (1), to *send forward*
4704 spŏudazō (1), to *make effort*
4707 spŏudaiŏtĕrŏs (1), *more earnest*

FORWARDNESS
4288 prŏthumia (1), *alacrity, eagerness*
4710 spŏudē (1), *despatch; eagerness*

FOUGHT
3898 lâcham (58), to fight *a battle, i.e. consume*
6633 tsâbâ' (1), to *mass an army or servants*
75 agōnizŏmai (1), to *struggle; to contend*
2341 thēriŏmachĕō (1), *to be a beast fighter*
4170 pŏlĕmĕō (2), to *battle, make war*

FOUL
2560 châmar (1), to *ferment, foam; to glow*
7515 râphas (1), to *trample, i.e. roil water*
169 akathartŏs (2), *impure; evil*
5494 chĕimōn (1), *winter season; stormy weather*

FOULED
4833 mirpâs (1), *muddied water*

FOULEDST
7515 râphas (1), to *trample, i.e. roil water*

FOUND
2713 châqar (2), to *examine, search*
4672 mâtsâ' (267), to *find or acquire; to occur*
7912 shᵉkach (Ch.) (11), *to discover, find out*
429 anĕuriskō (1), to *find out*
1096 ginŏmai (1), to be, *become*
2147 hĕuriskō (111), to *find*
2638 katalambanō (1), to *seize; to possess*

FOUNDATION
787 'ôsh (Ch.) (1), *foundation*
3245 yâçad (15), *settle, establish a foundation*
3247 yᵉçôwd (7), *foundation*
3248 yᵉçûwdâh (5), *foundation*
4143 mûwçâd (2), *foundation*
4527 maççad (1), *foundation*
2310 thĕmĕliŏs (12), *substruction*
2311 thĕmĕliŏō (1), to *erect; to consolidate*
2602 katabŏlē (10), *conception, beginning*

FOUNDATIONS
134 'eden (1), *base, footing*
787 'ôsh (Ch.) (2), *foundation*
803 'âshûwyâh (1), *foundation*
808 'âshîysh (1), (ruined) *foundation*
3245 yâçad (4), *settle, establish a foundation*
3247 yᵉçôwd (3), *foundation*
4146 môwçâdâh (13), *foundation*
4328 mᵉyuççâdâh (1), *foundation*
4349 mâkôwn (1), *basis; place*
8356 shâthâh (1), *basis*
2310 thĕmĕliŏs (4), *substruction*

FOUNDED
3245 yâçad (8), *settle, establish a foundation*
2311 thĕmĕliŏō (2), to *erect; to consolidate*

FOUNDER
6884 tsâraph (5), to *fuse metal; to refine*

FOUNDEST
4672 mâtsâ' (1), to *find or acquire; to occur*

FOUNTAIN
953 bôwr (1), pit *hole, cistern, well*
4002 mabbûwa' (1), *fountain, water spring*
4599 ma'yân (9), *fountain; source*
4726 mâqôwr (11), *flow*
5869 'ayin (7), *eye; sight; fountain*
4077 pēgē (4), *source or supply*

FOUNTAINS
4599 ma'yân (7), *fountain; source*
5869 'ayin (4), *eye; sight; fountain*
4077 pēgē (4), *source or supply*

FOUR
702 'arba' (258), *four*
703 'arba' (Ch.) (8), *four*
5064 tĕssarĕs (43), *four*
5066 tĕtartaiŏs (1), *of the fourth day*

FOURFOLD
706 'arba'tayim (1), *fourfold*
5073 tĕtraplŏŏs (1), *quadruple, i.e. four-fold*

FOURFOOTED
5074 tĕtrapŏus (3), *quadruped*

FOURSCORE
8084 shᵉmônîym (34), *eighty; eightieth*
3589 ŏgdŏĕkŏnta (2), *ten times eight*

FOURSQUARE
7243 rᵉbîy'îy (1), *fourth; fourth*
7251 râba' (8), to *be four sided, to be quadrate*
5068 tĕtragōnŏs (1), *four-cornered*

FOURTEEN
702+6240 'arba' (2), *four*
702+6246 'arba' (4), *four*
702+7657 'arba' (3), *four*
1180 dĕkatĕssarĕs (5), *fourteen*

FOURTEENTH
702+6240 'arba' (23), *four*
5065 tĕssarĕskaidĕkatŏs (2), *fourteenth*

FOURTH
702 'arba' (5), *four*
7243 rᵉbîy'îy (55), *fourth; fourth*
7244 rᵉbîy'ay (Ch.) (5), *fourth; fourth*
7253 reba' (2), *fourth part or side*
7255 rôba' (2), *quarter*
7256 ribbêa' (4), *fourth; fourth generation*
5067 tĕtartŏs (9), *fourth*

FOWL
1257 barbûr (1), *fowl*
5775 'ôwph (23), *bird*
5776 'ôwph (Ch.) (1), *bird*
5861 'ayiṭ (1), *bird of prey (poss.) hawk*
6833 tsippôwr (5), *little hopping bird*

FOWLER
3353 yâqûwsh (3), *snarer, trapper of fowl*

FOWLERS
3369 yâqôsh (1), to *ensnare, trap*

FOWLS
5775 'ôwph (36), *winged bird*
5776 'ôwph (Ch.) (1), *winged bird*
5861 'ayiṭ (3), *bird of prey (poss.) hawk*
6833 tsippôwr (1), *little hopping bird*
6853 tsᵉphar (Ch.) (3), *bird*
3732 ŏrnĕŏn (2), *bird*

FOURTH
5067 tĕtartŏs (1), *fourth*
5070 tĕtrakischiliŏi (5), *four times a thousand*
5071 tĕtrakŏsiŏi (2), *four hundred*
5072 tĕtramēnŏn (1), *four months' time*

(column)
4071 pĕtĕinŏn (9), *bird which flies*

FOX
7776 shûw'âl (1), *jackal*
258 alōpĕx (1), *fox*

FOXES
7776 shûw'âl (ó), *jackal*
258 alōpĕx (2), *fox*

FRAGMENTS
2801 klasma (7), *piece, bit*

FRAIL
2310 châdêl (1), *ceasing or destitute*

FRAME
3335 yâtsar (1), to *form; potter; to determine*
3336 yêtser (1), *form*
3559 kûwn (1), to *set up: establish, fix, prepare*
4011 mibneh (1), *building*
5414 nâthan (1), to *give*

FRAMED
3335 yâtsar (1), to *form; potter; to determine*
3336 yêtser (1), *form*
2675 katartizō (1), to *repair; to prepare*
4883 sunarmŏlŏgĕō (1), *to render close-jointed*

FRAMETH
3335 yâtsar (1), to *form; potter; to determine*
6775 tsâmad (1), to *link, i.e. gird*

FRANKINCENSE
3828 lᵉbôwnâh (15), *frankincense*
3030 libanŏs (2), *fragrant incense resin or gum*

FRANKLY
5435 Phrugia (1), *Phrygia*

FRAUD
8496 tôk (1), *oppression*
650 apŏstĕrĕō (1), to *deprive; to despoil*

FRAY
2729 chârad (3), to *shudder; to hasten*

FRECKLED
933 bôhaq (1), *white scurf, rash*

FREE
2600 chinnâm (1), *gratis, free*
2666 châphash (1), to *loose; free from slavery*
2670 chophshîy (16), *exempt, free*
5071 nᵉdâbâh (2), *abundant gift*
5081 nâdîyb (1), *magnanimous*
5082 nᵉdîybâh (1), *nobility, i.e. reputation*
5352 nâqâh (2), to be, *make clean; to be bare*
5355 nâqîy (1), *innocent*
6362 pâṭar (1), to *burst through; to emit*
6605 pâthach (1), to *open wide; to loosen, begin*
1658 ĕlĕuthĕrŏs (20), *not a slave*

1659 ĕlĕuthĕrŏō (6), *to exempt, liberate*
5486 charisma (2), *spiritual endowment*

FREED
3772 kârath (1), *to cut (off, down or asunder)*
1344 dikaiŏō (1), *show or regard as innocent*

FREEDOM
2668 chuphshâh (1), *liberty from slavery*
4174 pŏlitĕia (1), *citizenship*

FREELY
2600 chinnâm (1), *gratis, free*
5071 n°dâbâh (2), *abundant gift*
1432 dōrĕan (6), *gratuitously, freely*
3326+3954 mĕta (1), *with, among; after, later*
3955 parrhĕsiazŏmai (1), *to be confident*

FREEMAN
558 apĕlĕuthĕrŏs (1), *freedman*

FREEWILL
5069 n°dab (Ch.) (2), *be, give without coercion*
5071 n°dâbâh (15), *abundant gift*

FREEWOMAN
1658 ĕlĕuthĕrŏs (2), *not a slave*

FREQUENT
4056 pĕrissŏtĕrŏs (1), *more superabundantly*

FRESH
2319 châdâsh (1), *new, recent*
3955 l°shad (1), *juice; vigor; sweet or fat cake*
7488 ra'ănân (1), *new; prosperous*
1099 glukus (1), *sweet, fresh*

FRESHER
7375 rûwtăphash (1), *to be rejuvenated*

FRET
2734 chârâh (4), *to blaze up*
6356 p°chetheth (1), *mildewed garment hole*
7107 qâtsaph (1), *to burst out in rage*
7481 râ'am (1), *to crash thunder; to irritate*

FRETTED
7264 râgaz (1), *to quiver*

FRETTETH
2196 zâ'aph (1), *to be angry*

FRETTING
3992 mâ'ar (3), *to be painful; destructive*

FRIED
7246 râbak (2), *to soak bread in oil*

FRIEND
157 'âhab (4), *to have affection, love*

7451 ra' (1), *bad; evil*
7453 rêa' (27), *associate; one close*
7462 râ'âh (1), *to associate as a friend*
7463 rê'eh (3), *male advisor*
2083 hĕtairŏs (3), *comrade, friend*
3982 pĕithō (1), *to pacify or conciliate*
5384 philŏs (12), *friend; friendly*

FRIENDLY
3820 lêb (2), *heart*
7489 râ'a' (1), *to make, be good for nothing*

FRIENDS
157 'âhab (8), *to have affection, love*
441 'allûwph (2), *friend, one familiar; chieftain*
605+7965 'ânash (1), *to be frail, feeble*
4828 mêrêa' (3), *close friend*
4962 math (1), *men*
7453 rêa' (14), *associate; one close*
3588+3844 hŏ (1), "*the,*" i.e. the definite article
4674 sŏs (1), *things that are yours*
5384 philŏs (17), *friend; friendly*

FRIENDSHIP
7462 râ'âh (1), *to associate as a friend*
5373 philia (1), *fondness*

FRINGE
6734 tsîytsîth (2), *fore-lock of hair; tassel*

FRINGES
1434 g°dîl (1), *tassel; festoon*
6734 tsîytsîth (1), *fore-lock of hair; tassel*

FRO
235 'âzal (1), *to disappear*
7725 shûwb (1), *to turn back; to return*
7751 shûwṭ (8), *to travel, roam*
8264 shâqaq (1), *to seek greedily*
2831 kludŏnizŏmai (1), *to fluctuate back and forth on the waves*

FROGS
6854 ts°phardêa' (13), *frog, leaper*
944 batrachŏs (1), *frog*

FRONT
6440 pânîym (2), *face; front*

FRONTIERS
7097 qâtseh (1), *extremity*

FRONTLETS
2903 ṭôwphâphâh (3), *sign or symbolic box*

FROST
2602 chănâmâl (1), *aphis or plant-louse*
3713 k°phôwr (3), *bowl; white frost*

7140 qerach (3), *ice; hail; rock crystal*

FROWARD
2019 hăphakpak (1), *very perverse, crooked*
3868 lûwz (2), *to depart; to be perverse*
6141 'iqqêsh (6), *distorted, warped, false*
6143 'iqq°shûwth (2), *perversity*
6617 pâthal (3), *to struggle; to be tortuous*
8419 tahpûkâh (6), *perversity or fraud*
4646 skŏliŏs (1), *crooked; perverse*

FROWARDLY
7726 shôwbâb (1), *apostate, i.e. idolatrous*

FROWARDNESS
8419 tahpûkâh (3), *perversity or fraud*

FROZEN
3920 lâkad (1), *to catch; to capture*

FRUIT
4 'êb (Ch.) (3), *green plant*
1061 bikkûwr (2), *first-fruits of the crop*
2981 y°bûwl (3), *produce, crop; harvest*
3206 yeled (1), *young male*
3899 lechem (1), *food, bread*
3978 ma'ăkâl (1), *food, something to eat*
4395 m°lê'âh (1), *fulfilled; abundance*
5107 nûwb (1), *to (make) flourish; to utter*
5108 nôwb (2), *agricultural produce*
6509 pârâh (1), *to bear fruit*
6529 p°rîy (106), *fruit*
7920 s°kal (Ch.) (1), *to be or act circumspect*
8270 shôr (1), *umbilical cord; strength*
8393 t°bûw'âh (7), *income, i.e. produce*
8570 t°nûwbâh (1), *crop, produce*
175 akarpŏs (1), *barren, unfruitful*
1081 gĕnnēma (3), *offspring; produce*
2590 karpŏs (54), *fruit; crop*
2592 karpŏphŏrĕō (7), *to be fertile*
5052 tĕlĕsphŏrĕō (1), *to ripen fruit*
5352 phthinŏpōrinŏs (1), *autumnal*

FRUITFUL
1121+8081 bên (1), *people of a class or kind*
2233 zera' (1), *seed; fruit, plant, sowing-time*
3759 karmel (7), *planted field; garden produce*
6500 pârâ' (1), *to bear fruit*

6509 pârâh (21), *to bear fruit*
6529 p°rîy (2), *fruit*
2592 karpŏphŏrĕō (1), *to be fertile*
2593 karpŏphŏrŏs (1), *fruitbearing*

FRUITS
3 'êb (1), *green plant*
1061 bikkûwr (1), *first-fruits of the crop*
2173 zimrâh (1), *choice fruit*
3581 kôach (1), *force, might; strength*
4395 m°lê'âh (1), *fulfilled; abundance*
6529 p°rîy (7), *fruit*
8393 t°bûw'âh (6), *income, i.e. produce*
8570 t°nûwbâh (1), *crop, produce*
1081 gĕnnēma (2), *offspring; produce*
2590 karpŏs (12), *fruit; crop*
3703 ŏpōra (1), *ripe fruit*

FRUSTRATE
656 'âphêç (1), *to cease*
114 athĕtĕō (1), *to disesteem, neutralize*

FRUSTRATETH
6565 pârar (1), *to break up; to violate, frustrate*

FRYING
4802 marchesheth (1), *stew-pan*

FRYINGPAN
4802 marchesheth (1), *stew-pan*

FUEL
402 'oklâh (3), *food*
3980 ma'ăkôleth (2), *fuel for fire*

FUGITIVE
5128 nûwa' (2), *to waver*

FUGITIVES
1280 b°rîyach (1), *bolt; cross-bar of a door*
4015 mibrâch (1), *refugee*
5307 nâphal (1), *to fall*
6412 pâlîyṭ (1), *refugee*

FULFIL
3615 kâlâh (1), *to complete, consume*
4390 mâlê' (7), *to fill; be full*
6213 'âsâh (2), *to do or make*
378 anaplērŏō (1), *to complete; to occupy*
4137 plērŏō (6), *to fill, make complete*
4160 pŏiĕō (2), *to make or do*
5055 tĕlĕō (3), *to end, i.e. complete, execute*

FULFILLED
1214 bâtsa' (1), *to finish; to stop*
3615 kâlâh (2), *to complete, consume*
4390 mâlê' (20), *to fill; be full*
5487 çûwph (Ch.) (1), *to come to an end*

6213 'âsâh (1), to do
378 anaplērōō (1), to complete; accomplish
1096 ginōmai (3), to be, become
1603 ĕkplērōō (1), to accomplish, fulfill
4137 plērōō (45), to fill, make complete
4931 suntĕlĕō (1), to complete entirely
5048 tĕlĕiōō (2), to perfect, complete
5055 tĕlĕō (4), to end, i.e. complete, execute

FULFILLING
6213 'âsâh (1), to do or make
4138 plērōma (1), what fills; what is filled
4160 pŏiĕō (1), to do

FULL
3117 yôwm (10), day; time period
3624 kelach (1), maturity
3759 karmel (1), planted field; garden produce
4390 mâlê' (50), to fill; be full
4391 mᵉlâ' (Ch.) (1), to fill; be full
4392 mâlê' (58), full; filling; fulness; fully
4393 mᵉlô' (11), fulness
7227 rab (1), great
7235 râbâh (1), to increase
7646 sâba' (20), fill to satiety
7648 sôba' (3), satisfaction
7649 sâbêa' (2), satiated
7654 sob'âh (3), satiety
7999 shâlam (1), to be safe; be, make complete
8003 shâlêm (2), complete; friendly; safe
8537 tôm (1), completeness
8549 tâmîym (1), entire, complete; integrity
8552 tâmam (1), to complete, finish
1072 gĕmizō (1), to fill entirely
1073 gĕmō (11), to swell out, i.e. be full
1705 ĕmpiplēmi (1), to satisfy
2880 kŏrĕnnumi (1), to cram, i.e. glut or sate
3324 mĕstos (8), replete, full
3325 mĕstōō (1), to intoxicate
4130 plēthō (1), to fulfill, complete
4134 plērēs (17), replete, full, complete
4135 plērŏphŏrĕō (1), to fill completely
4136 plērŏphŏria (3), full assurance
4137 plērōō (9), to fill, make complete
4138 plērōma (1), what fills; what is filled
5046 tĕlĕiŏs (1), complete; mature

5460 phōtĕinŏs (4), well-illuminated
5526 chŏrtazō (1), to supply food until full

FULLER
1102 gnaphĕus (1), cloth-dresser

FULLER'S
3526 kâbaç (3), to wash

FULLERS'
3526 kâbaç (1), to wash

FULLY
3615 kâlâh (1), to complete, consume
4390 mâlê' (3), to fill; be full
4392 mâlê' (1), full; filling; fulness; fully
5046 nâgad (1), to announce
3877 parakŏlŏuthĕō (1), to attend; trace out
4135 plērŏphŏrĕō (3), to fill completely
4137 plērōō (1), to fill, make complete
4845 sumplērōō (1), to be complete, fulfill

FULNESS
4390 mâlê' (1), to fill; be full
4393 mᵉlô' (8), fulness
4395 mᵉlê'âh (1), fulfilled; abundance
7648 sôba' (1), satisfaction
7653 sib'âh (1), satiety
4138 plērōma (13), what fills; what is filled

FURBISH
4838 mâraq (1), to polish; to sharpen; to rinse

FURBISHED
4803 mâraṭ (5), to polish; to sharpen

FURIOUS
1167+2534 ba'al (1), master; owner; citizen
2534 chêmâh (4), heat; anger; poison
7108 qᵉtsaph (Ch.) (1), to become enraged

FURIOUSLY
2534 chêmâh (1), heat; anger; poison
7697 shiggâ'ôwn (1), craziness

FURLONGS
4712 stadiŏn (5), length of about 200 yards

FURNACE
861 'attûwn (Ch.) (10), fire furnace
3536 kibshân (4), smelting furnace
3564 kûwr (9), smelting furnace
5948 'ălîyl (1), (poss.) crucible
8574 tannûwr (2), fire-pot
2575 kaminŏs (4), furnace

FURNACES
8574 tannûwr (2), fire-pot

FURNISH
4390 mâlê' (1), to fill; be full
6059 'ânaq (1), to collar; to fit out
6186 'ârak (1), to set in a row, i.e. arrange,
6213+3627 'âsâh (1), to do or make

FURNISHED
5375 nâsâ' (1), to lift up
6186 'ârak (1), to set in a row, i.e. arrange,
1822 ĕxartizō (1), to finish out; to equip fully
4130 plēthō (1), to fulfill, complete
4766 strōnnumi (2), strew, spread a carpet

FURNITURE
3627 kᵉlîy (7), implement, thing
3733 kar (1), saddle bag

FURROW
8525 telem (1), bank or terrace

FURROWS
1417 gᵉdûwd (1), furrow ridge
4618 ma'ănâh (1), furrow, plow path
5869 'ayin (1), eye; sight; fountain
6170 'ărûwgâh (2), parterre, kind of garden
8525 telem (3), bank or terrace

FURTHER
3148 yôwthêr (1), moreover; rest; gain
3254 yâçaph (4), to add or augment
5750 'ôwd (2), again; repeatedly; still; more
6329 pùwq (1), to issue; to furnish; to secure
1339 diïstēmi (1), to remove, intervene
2089 ĕti (6), yet, still
4206 pŏrrhō (1), forwards, at a distance

FURTHERANCE
4297 prŏkŏpĕ (2), progress, advancement

FURTHERED
5375 nâsâ' (1), to lift up

FURTHERMORE
637 'aph (1), also or yea; though
5750 'ôwd (1), again; repeatedly; still; more
1161 dĕ (1), but, yet; and then
1534 ĕita (1), succession, then, moreover
3063 lŏipŏn (1), remaining; finally

FURY
2528 chĕmâ (Ch.) (2), anger
2534 chêmâh (67), heat; anger; poison
2740 chârôwn (1), burning of anger

GAAL
1603 Ga'al (9), loathing

GAASH
1608 Ga'ash (4), quaking

GABA
1387 Geba' (3), Geba

GABBAI
1373 Gabbay (1), collective

GABBATHA
1042 gabbatha (1), knoll

GABRIEL
1403 Gabrîy'êl (2), man of God
1043 Gabriēl (2), man of God

GAD
1410 Gâd (71), Gad
1045 Gad (1), Gad

GADARENES
1046 Gadarēnŏs (3), inhabitant of Gadara

GADDEST
235 'âzal (1), to disappear

GADDI
1426 Gaddîy (1), Gaddi

GADDIEL
1427 Gaddîy'êl (1), fortune of God

GADI
1424 Gâdîy (2), fortunate

GADITE
1425 Gâdîy (1), Gadite

GADITES
1425 Gâdîy (14), Gadite

GAHAM
1514 Gacham (1), flame

GAHAR
1515 Gachar (2), lurker

GAIN
1214 bâtsa' (9), to plunder; to finish; to stop
2084 zᵉban (Ch.) (1), to acquire by purchase
4242 mᵉchîyr (1), price, payment, wages
8393 tᵉbûw'âh (1), income, i.e. produce
8636 tarbîyth (1), percentage or bonus
2039 ĕrgasia (1), occupation; profit
2770 kĕrdainō (9), to gain; to spare
2771 kĕrdŏs (2), gain, profit
4122 plĕŏnĕktĕō (2), to be covetous
4200 pŏrismŏs (2), money-getting

GAINED
1214 bâtsa' (2), to plunder; to finish
1281 diapragmatĕuŏmai (1), to earn, make gain
2770 kĕrdainō (5), to gain; to spare
4160 pŏiĕō (1), to make or do
4333 prŏsĕrgazŏmai (1), to acquire besides

GAINS
2039 ĕrgasia (1), occupation; profit

GAINSAY
471 antĕpō (1), to *refute*
or *deny*

GAINSAYERS
483 antilĕgō (1), to
dispute, refuse

GAINSAYING
369 anantirrhĕtōs (1),
*without raising
objection*
483 antilĕgō (1), to
dispute, refuse
485 antilŏgia (1),
dispute, disobedience

GAIUS
1050 Gaïŏs (5), *Gaïus*

GALAL
1559 Gâlâl (3), *great*

GALATIA
1053 Galatia (4), *Galatia*
1054 Galatikŏs (2),
relating to *Galatia*

GALATIANS
1052 Galatēs (2),
inhabitant of Galatia

GALBANUM
2464 chelbᵉnâh (1),
fragrant resin gum

GALEED
1567 Gal'êd (2), *heap of
testimony*

GALILAEAN
1057 Galilaiŏs (3),
belonging to *Galilæa*

GALILAEANS
1057 Galilaiŏs (5),
belonging to *Galilæa*

GALILEE
1551 Gâlîyl (6), *circle* as
a special *circuit*
1056 Galilaia (66),
heathen *circle*

GALL
4845 mᵉrêrâh (1), bitter
bile of the gall bladder
4846 mᵉrôrâh (2), bitter
bile; venom of a serpent
7219 rô'sh (9), poisonous
plant; poison
5521 chŏlē (2), *gall* or
bile; bitterness

GALLANT
117 'addîyr (1), *powerful;
majestic*

GALLERIES
862 'attûwq (3), *ledge* or
offset
7298 rahaṭ (1), *ringlet* of
hair

GALLERY
862 'attûwq (1), *ledge* or
offset

GALLEY
590 'ŏnîy (1), *ship; fleet* of
ships

GALLIM
1554 Gallîym (2), *springs*

GALLIO
1058 Galliŏn (3), *Gallion*,
i.e. *Gallio*

GALLOWS
6086 'ēts (8), *wood,*
things made of *wood*

GAMALIEL
1583 Gamliy'êl (5),
reward of God
1059 Gamaliĕl (2),
reward of God

GAMMADIMS
1575 Gammâd (1),
warrior

GAMUL
1577 Gâmûwl (1),
rewarded

GAP
6556 perets (1), *break,
gap*

GAPED
6473 pâ'ar (1), to *open*
wide
6475 pâtsâh (1), to *rend,*
i.e. *open*

GAPS
6556 perets (1), *break,
gap*

GARDEN
1588 gan (39), *garden*
1593 gannâh (3), *garden,
grove*
1594 ginnâh (4), *garden,
grove*
2779 kēpŏs (5), *garden,
grove*

GARDENER
2780 kēpŏurŏs (1),
gardener

GARDENS
1588 gan (3), *garden*
1593 gannâh (9), *garden,
grove*

GAREB
1619 Gârêb (3), *scabby*

GARLANDS
4725 stĕmma (1), *wreath*

GARLICK
7762 shûwm (1), *garlic*

GARMENT
155 'addereth (4), *large;
splendid*
899 beged (36), *clothing;
treachery* or *pillage*
3801 kᵉthôneth (2),
garment that covers
3830 lᵉbûwsh (7),
garment; wife
3831 lᵉbûwsh (Ch.) (1),
garment
4055 mad (3), *vesture,
garment; carpet*
4594 ma'ăṭeh (1),
vestment, garment
7897 shîyth (1), *garment*
8008 salmâh (4), *clothing*
8071 simlâh (4), *dress,
mantle*
8162 sha'aṭnêz (1), *linen
and woolen*
8509 takrîyk (1), *wrapper*
or robe
1742 ĕnduma (2),
apparel, outer robe
2440 himatiŏn (15), to
put on clothes
4158 pŏdērēs (1), *robe
reaching the ankles*
4749 stŏlē (1),
long-fitting gown as a
mark of *dignity*

GARMENTS
899 beged (69), *clothing;
treachery* or *pillage*
3801 kᵉthôneth (3),
garment that covers
3830 lᵉbûwsh (2),
garment; wife
3831 lᵉbûwsh (Ch.) (1),
garment
4055 mad (1), *vesture,
garment; carpet*
4060 middâh (1), *portion;
vestment; tribute*
4063 medev (2), *dress,
garment*
8008 salmâh (4), *clothing*
8071 simlâh (2), *dress,
mantle*
2067 ĕsthēsis (1), *clothing*
2440 himatiŏn (15), to
put on clothes

GARMITE
1636 Garmîy (1), *strong*

GARNER
596 apŏthēkē (2),
granary, grain barn

GARNERS
214 'ôwtsâr (1),
depository
4200 mezev (1), *granary*

GARNISH
2885 kŏsmĕō (1), to
decorate; to snuff

GARNISHED
6823 tsâphâh (1), to
sheet over with metal
8235 shiphrâh (1),
brightness of skies
2885 kŏsmĕō (3), to
decorate; to snuff

GARRISON
4673 matstsâb (7), *spot;
office; military post*
4675 matstsâbâh (1),
military guard
5333 nᵉtsîyb (4), *military
post; statue*
5432 phrŏurĕō (1), to
post spies at gates

GARRISONS
4676 matstsêbâh (1),
column or *stone*
5333 nᵉtsîyb (5), *military
post; statue*

GASHMU
1654 Geshem (1), *rain
downpour*

GAT
622 'âçaph (1), to *gather,
collect*
935 bôw' (2), to *go* or
come
3212 yâlak (4), to *walk;
to live; to carry*
5927 'âlâh (7), to *ascend,
be high, mount*
6213 'âsâh (2), to *do* or
make
7392 râkab (1), to *ride*

GATAM
1609 Ga'tâm (3), *Gatam*

GATE
6607 pethach (4),
opening; door; entrance
8179 sha'ar (240),
opening, door or *gate*
8651 tᵉra' (Ch.) (1), *door*
2374 thura (1), *entrance,*
i.e. *door, gate*
4439 pulē (8), *gate*
4440 pulŏn (5), *gate-way,
door-way*

GATES
1817 deleth (14), *door;
gate*
5592 çaph (2), *dish*
6607 pethach (3),
opening; door, entrance
8179 sha'ar (112),
opening, door or *gate*
4439 pulē (2), *gate*
4440 pulŏn (11),
gate-way, door-way

GATH
1661 Gath (33),
wine-press or *vat*

GATH-HEPHER
1662 Gath-ha-Chêpher
(1), *wine-press of* (the)
well

GATH-RIMMON
1667 Gath-Rimmôwn (4),
wine-press of (the)
pomegranate

GATHER
103 'âgar (1), to *harvest*
622 'âçaph (36), to
gather, collect
1219 bâtsar (2), to *gather
grapes*
1413 gâdad (2), to *gash,
slash oneself*
1481 gûwr (3), to *sojourn,
live as an alien*
1716 dâgar (1), to *brood
over; to care for* young
2490 châlal (1), to
profane, defile
3259 yâ'ad (3), to *meet;
to summon; to direct*
3664 kânaç (5), to
collect; to enfold
3673 kânash (Ch.) (1), to
assemble
3950 lâqaṭ (13), to *pick
up, gather; to glean*
3953 lâqash (1), to *gather
the after* crop
4390 mâlē' (2), to *fill; be
full*
5619 çâqal (1), to *throw
large stones*
5756 'ûwz (3), to
strengthen
6908 qâbats (56), to
collect, assemble
6910 qᵉbûtsâh (1), *hoard,
gathering*
6950 qâhal (8), to
convoke, gather
7197 qâshash (4), to
assemble
346 anakĕphalaiŏmai
(1), to *sum up*
1996 ĕpisunagō (2), to
collect upon
4816 sullĕgō (6), to
collect, gather

GATHERED
4863 sunagō (11), to *gather together*
5166 trugaō (2), to *collect* the vintage

GATHERED
622 'âçaph (97), to *gather, collect*
626 'âçêphâh (1), (collect) *together*
717 'ârâh (1), to *pluck, pick fruit*
1219 bâtsar (1), to *gather* grapes
1481 gûwr (2), to *sojourn, live as an alien*
2199 zâ'aq (4), to *call out, announce*
3254 yâçaph (1), to *add or augment*
3259 yâ'ad (3), to *meet; to summon; to direct*
3664 kânaç (2), to *collect; to enfold*
3673 kânash (Ch.) (2), to *assemble*
3950 lâqaṭ (11), to *pick up, gather; to glean*
4390 mâlê' (1), to *fill; be full*
5413 nâthak (2), to *flow forth, pour* out
5596 çâphach (1), to *associate; be united*
6192 'âram (1), to *pile* up
6213 'âsâh (1), to *do or make*
6651 tsâbar (2), to *aggregate, gather*
6817 tsâ'aq (5), to *shriek; to proclaim*
6908 qâbats (57), to *collect, assemble*
6950 qâhal (19), to *convoke, gather*
6960 qâvâh (2), to *collect; to expect*
7035 qâlahh (1), to *assemble*
7197 qâshash (1), to *assemble*
7408 râkash (1), to *lay up,* i.e. *collect*
8085 shâma' (1), to *hear intelligently*
1865 epathrŏizō (1), to *accumulate, increase*
1996 episunagō (4), to *collect upon*
3792 ŏchlŏpŏiĕō (1), to *raise a disturbance*
4816 sullĕgō (2), to *collect, gather*
4863 sunagō (29), to *gather together*
4867 sunathrŏizō (1), to *convene*
4896 sunĕimi (1), to *assemble, gather*
4962 sustrĕphō (1), to *collect a bundle, crowd*
5166 trugaō (1), to *collect* the vintage

GATHERER
1103 bâlaç (1), to *pinch* sycamore figs

GATHEREST
1219 bâtsar (1), to *gather* grapes

GATHERETH
103 'âgar (2), to *harvest*
622 'âçaph (4), to *gather, collect*
3664 kânaç (2), to *collect; to enfold*
3950 lâqaṭ (1), to *pick up, gather; to glean*
6908 qâbats (4), to *collect, assemble*
1996 episunagō (1), to *collect upon*
4863 sunagō (3), to *gather together*

GATHERING
625 'ôçeph (2), fruit *harvest collection*
962 bâzaz (1), to *plunder, take booty*
3349 yiqqâhâh (1), *obedience*
4723 miqveh (1), *confidence; collection*
7197 qâshash (3), to *assemble*
1997 episunagōgē (1), *meeting, gathering*
4822 sumbibazō (1), to *drive together*
4863 sunagō (1), to *gather together*

GATHERINGS
3048 lŏgia (1), *contribution, collection*

GAVE
935 bôw' (1), to *go, come*
1696 dâbar (3), to *speak, say; to subdue*
3052 yᵉhab (Ch.) (4), to *give*
3254 yâçaph (1), to *add or augment*
3289 yâ'ats (2), to *advise*
5414 nâthan (252), to *give*
5462 çâgar (3), to *shut up; to surrender*
7121 qârâ' (3), to *call out*
7311 rûwm (4), to *be high; to rise or raise*
7725 shûwb (1), to *turn back; to return*
7760 sûwm (4), to *put, place*
7971 shâlach (1), to *send away*
437 anthŏmŏlŏgĕŏmai (1), to *give thanks*
591 apŏdidōmi (2), to *give away*
1291 diastĕllŏmai (1), to *distinguish*
1325 didōmi (77), to *give*
1433 dōrĕŏmai (1), to *bestow* gratuitously
1502 ĕikō (1), to *be weak,* i.e. *yield*
1781 ĕntĕllŏmai (1), to *enjoin, give orders*
1788 ĕntrĕpō (1), to *respect; to confound*
1907 ĕpĕchō (1), to *retain; to detain*
1929 ĕpididōmi (2), to *give over*
2010 ĕpitrĕpō (3), *allow, permit*
2702 kataphĕrō (1), to *bear down*

GAVEST
5414 nâthan (21), to *give*
7760 sûwm (1), to *put, place*
1325 didōmi (11), to *give*

GAY
2986 lamprŏs (1), *clear; magnificent*

GAZA
5804 'Azzâh (18), *strong*
1048 Gaza (1), *strong*

GAZATHITES
5841 'Azzâthîy (1), *Azzathite*

GAZE
7200 râ'âh (1), to *see*

GAZER
1507 Gezer (2), *portion, piece*

GAZEZ
1495 Gâzêz (2), *shearer*

GAZING
1689 ĕmblĕpō (1), to *observe; to discern*

GAZINGSTOCK
7210 rô'îy (1), *sight; spectacle*
2301 thĕatrizō (1), to *expose as a spectacle*

GAZITES
5841 'Azzâthîy (1), *Azzathite*

GAZZAM
1502 Gazzâm (2), *devourer*

GEBA
1387 Geba' (12), *Geba*

GEBAL
1381 Gᵉbâl (2), *mountain*

GEBER
1398 Geber (2), *(valiant) man*

GEBIM
1374 Gêbîym (1), *cisterns*

GEDALIAH
1436 Gᵉdalyâh (32), *Jehovah has become great*

GEDEON
1066 Gĕdĕōn (1), *warrior*

GEDER
1445 Geder (1), *wall or fence*

GEDERAH
1449 Gᵉdêrâh (1), *enclosure* for flocks

GEDERATHITE
1452 Gᵉdêrâthîy (1), *Gederathite*

GEDERITE
1451 Gᵉdêrîy (1), *Gederite*

GEDEROTH
1450 Gᵉdêrôwth (2), *walls*

GEDEROTHAIM
1453 Gᵉdêrôthayim (1), *double wall*

GEDOR
1446 Gᵉdôr (7), *enclosure*

GEHAZI
1522 Gêychăzîy (12), *valley of a visionary*

GELILOTH
1553 Gᵉlîylôwth (1), *circles*

GEMALLI
1582 Gᵉmalliy (1), *camel-driver*

GEMARIAH
1587 Gᵉmaryâh (5), *Jehovah has perfected*

GENDER
7250 râba' (1), to *lay down;* have sex
1080 gĕnnaō (1), to *procreate, regenerate*

GENDERED
3205 yâlad (1), to *bear young; to father a child*

GENDERETH
5674 'âbar (1), to *cross over; to transition*
1080 gĕnnaō (1), to *procreate, regenerate*

GENEALOGIES
3187 yâchas (6), to *enroll by family list*
1076 gĕnĕalŏgia (2), *genealogy, lineage*

GENEALOGY
3188 yachas (15), *family list*

GENERAL
8269 sar (1), *head person, ruler*
3831 panēguris (1), *mass-meeting*

GENERALLY
3605 kôl (1), *all, any or every*

GENERATION
1755 dôwr (50), *dwelling*
1859 dâr (Ch.) (2), *age; generation*
1074 gĕnĕa (30), *generation; age*
1078 genesis (1), *nativity, nature*
1081 gĕnnēma (4), *offspring; produce*
1085 gĕnŏs (1), *kin, offspring in kind*

GENERATIONS
1755 dôwr (73), *dwelling*
8435 tôwlᵉdâh (39), *family descent,* family *record*

1074 gĕnĕa (6), *generation; age*

GENNESARET
1082 Gĕnnēsarĕt (3), (poss.) *harp*-shaped

GENTILE
1672 Hĕllēn (2), *Greek (-speaking)*

GENTILES
1471 gôwy (30), foreign *nation; Gentiles*
1483 ĕthnikŏs (1), *as a Gentile*
1484 ĕthnŏs (93), *race; tribe; pagan*
1672 Hĕllēn (5), *Greek (-speaking)*

GENTLE
1933 ĕpiĕikēs (3), *mild, gentle*
2261 ēpiŏs (2), *affable,* i.e. *mild or kind*

GENTLENESS
6031 'ānâh (1), to *afflict, be afflicted*
6038 'ănâvâh (1), *modesty, clemency*
1932 ĕpiĕikĕia (1), *mildness, gentleness*
5544 chrēstŏtēs (1), *moral excellence*

GENTLY
3814 lâ'ṭ (1), *silently*

GENUBATH
1592 Gᵉnûbath (2), *theft*

GERA
1617 Gêrâ' (9), *cereal grain*

GERAHS
1626 gêrâh (5), *measure*

GERAR
1642 Gᵉrâr (10), *rolling country*

GERGESENES
1086 Gĕrgĕsēnŏs (1), *Gergesene*

GERIZIM
1630 Gᵉrîzîym (4), *rocky*

GERSHOM
1648 Gêrᵉshôwn (14), *refugee*

GERSHON
1647 Gêrᵉshôm (17), *refugee*

GERSHONITE
1649 Gerᵉshunnîy (3), *Gereshonite*

GERSHONITES
1649 Gerᵉshunnîy (9), *Gereshonite*

GESHAM
1529 Gêyshân (1), *lumpish*

GESHEM
1654 Geshem (3), *rain downpour*

GESHUR
1650 Gᵉshûwr (8), *bridge*

GESHURI
1651 Gᵉshûwrîy (2), *Geshurite*

GESHURITES
1651 Gᵉshûwrîy (5), *Geshurite*

GET
776 'erets (1), *earth, land, soil; country*
935 bôw' (8), to *go or come*
1214 bâtsa' (1), to *plunder; to finish*
1245 bâqash (1), to *search; to strive after*
1980 hâlak (1), to *walk; live a certain way*
3212 yâlak (17), to *walk; to live; to carry*
3318 yâtsâ' (7), to *go, bring out*
3381 yârad (9), to *descend*
3513 kâbad (1), to *be heavy, severe, dull*
3947 lâqach (5), to *take*
4422 mâlaṭ (1), to *escape as if by slipperiness*
4672 mâtsâ' (2), to *find or acquire; to occur*
5110 nûwd (1), to *waver; to wander, flee*
5111 nûwd (Ch.) (1), to *flee*
5265 nâça' (1), *start on a journey*
5381 nâsag (6), to *reach*
5674 'âbar (1), to *cross over; to transition*
5927 'âlâh (18), to *ascend, be high, mount*
6213 'âsâh (2), to *do or make*
6965 qûwm (1), to *rise*
7069 qânâh (8), to *create; to procure*
7426 râmam (1), to *rise*
7725 shûwb (1), to *turn back; to return*
1684 ĕmbainō (2), to *embark; to reach*
1826 ĕxĕimi (1), *leave; escape*
1831 ĕxĕrchŏmai (3), to *issue; to leave*
2147 hĕuriskō (1), to *find*
2597 katabainō (1), to *descend*
4122 plĕŏnĕktĕō (1), to *be covetous*
5217 hupagō (4), to *withdraw or retire*

GETHER
1666 Gether (2), *Gether*

GETHSEMANE
1068 Gĕthsēmanē (2), *oil-press*

GETTETH
3947 lâqach (1), to *take*
5060 nâga' (1), to *strike*
5927 'âlâh (1), to *ascend, be high, mount*
6213 'âsâh (1), to *do or make*
6329 pûwq (1), to *issue; to furnish; to secure*
7069 qânâh (3), to *create; to procure*

GETTING
6467 pô'al (1), *act or work, deed*
7069 qânâh (1), to *create; to procure*
7075 qinyân (1), *acquisition, purchase*

GEUEL
1345 Gᵉ'ûw'êl (1), *majesty of God*

GEZER
1507 Gezer (13), *portion, piece*

GEZRITES
1511 Gizrîy (1), *Gezerite; Girzite*

GHOST
1478 gâva' (9), to *expire, die*
5315 nephesh (2), *life; breath; soul; wind*
1606 ĕkpnĕŏ (3), to *expire*
1634 ĕkpsuchō (3), to *expire, die*
4151 pnĕuma (92), *spirit*

GIAH
1520 Gîyach (1), *fountain*

GIANT
1368 gibbôwr (1), *powerful; great warrior*
7497 râphâ' (7), *giant*

GIANTS
1368 gibbôwr (1), *powerful; great warrior*
5303 nᵉphîyl (2), *bully or tyrant*
7497 râphâ' (10), *giant*

GIBBAR
1402 Gibbâr (1), *Gibbar*

GIBBETHON
1405 Gibbᵉthôwn (6), *hilly spot*

GIBEA
1388 Gib'â' (1), *hill*

GIBEAH
1390 Gib'âh (48), *hillock*

GIBEATH
1394 Gib'ath (1), *hilliness*

GIBEATHITE
1395 Gib'âthîy (1), *Gibathite*

GIBEON
1391 Gib'ôwn (35), *hilly*

GIBEONITE
1393 Gib'ônîy (2), *Gibonite*

GIBEONITES
1393 Gib'ônîy (6), *Gibonite*

GIBLITES
1382 Giblîy (1), *Gebalite*

GIDDALTI
1437 Giddaltîy (2), *I have made great*

GIDDEL
1435 Giddêl (4), *stout*

GIDEON
1439 Gîd'ôwn (39), *warrior*

GIDEONI
1441 Gid'ônîy (5), *warlike*

GIDOM
1440 Gid'ôm (1), *desolation*

GIER
7360 râchâm (2), kind of *vulture*

GIFT
4503 minchâh (1), *tribute; offering*
4976 mattân (4), *present, gift*
4979 mâttânâh (5), *present; offering; bribe*
4991 mattâth (3), *present*
5379 nissê'th (1), *present*
7810 shachad (6), to *bribe; gift*
1390 dŏma (1), *present, gift*
1394 dŏsis (1), *gift*
1431 dōrĕa (11), *gratuity, gift*
1434 dōrēma (1), *bestowment, gift*
1435 dōrŏn (10), *sacrificial present*
5485 charis (1), *gratitude; benefit given*
5486 charisma (10), *spiritual endowment*

GIFTS
814 'eshkâr (1), *gratuity, gift; payment*
4503 minchâh (6), *tribute; offering*
4864 mas'êth (1), *tribute; reproach*
4976 mattân (1), *present, gift*
4978 mattᵉnâ' (Ch.) (3), *present, gift*
4979 mâttânâh (11), *present; offering; bribe*
5078 nêdeh (1), *bounty, reward for prostitution*
5083 nâdân (1), *present for prostitution*
7810 shachad (4), to *bribe; gift*
8641 tᵉrûwmâh (1), *tribute, present*
334 anathēma (1), *votive offering to God*
1390 dŏma (2), *present, gift*
1435 dōrŏn (9), *sacrificial present*
3311 mĕrismŏs (1), *distribution*
5486 charisma (7), *spiritual endowment*

GIHON
1521 Gîychôwn (6), *stream*

GILALAI
1562 Gîlălay (1), *dungy*

GILBOA
1533 Gilbôa' (8), *bubbling fountain*

GILEAD
1568 Gil'âd (100), *Gilad*

GILEAD'S
1568 Gil'âd (1), *Gilad*

GILEADITE
1569 Gil'âdîy (9), *Giladite*

GILEADITES
1569 Gil'âdîy (4), *Giladite*

GILGAL
1537 Gilgâl (39), *wheel*

GILOH
1542 Gîlôh (2), *open*

GILONITE
1526 Gîylônîy (2), *Gilonite*

GIMZO
1579 Gimzôw (1), *Gimzo*

GIN
4170 môwqêsh (1), *noose*
6341 pach (2), thin metallic *sheet; net*

GINATH
1527 Gîynath (2), *Ginath*

GINNETHO
1599 Ginn°thôwn (1), *gardener*

GINNETHON
1599 Ginn°thôwn (2), *gardener*

GINS
4170 môwqêsh (2), *noose*

GIRD
247 'âzar (4), to *belt*
640 'âphad (1), to *fasten, gird*
2290 châgôwr (1), *belt for the waist*
2296 châgar (16), to *gird on a belt; put on armor*
328 anazônnumi (1), to *gird, bind afresh*
2224 zônnumi (2), to *bind about*
4024 pěrizônnumi (2), to *fasten on one's belt*

GIRDED
247 'âzar (7), to *belt*
631 'âçar (1), to *fasten; to join battle*
2280 châbash (1), to *wrap firmly, bind*
2289 châgôwr (1), *belted around waist*
2296 châgar (18), to *gird on a belt; put on armor*
8151 shânaç (1), to *compress*
1241 diazônnumi (2), to *gird tightly, wrap*
4024 pěrizônnumi (2), to *fasten on one's belt*

GIRDEDST
2224 zônnumi (1), to *bind about*

GIRDETH
247 'âzar (1), to *belt*
631 'âçar (1), to *fasten; to join battle*
2296 châgar (2), to *gird on a belt; put on armor*

GIRDING
2296 châgar (1), to *gird on a belt; put on armor*
4228 machăgôreth (1), *girdle of sackcloth*

GIRDLE
73 'abnêṭ (6), *belt*
232 'êzôwr (13), *belt; band around waist*

GIRDLES
73 'abnêṭ (3), *belt*
232 'êzôwr (1), *belt; band around waist*
2289 châgôwr (1), *belted around waist*
2223 zônē (5), *belt, sash*

GIRLS
3207 yaldâh (1), *young female*

GIRT
247 'âzar (1), to *belt*
1241 diazônnumi (1), to *gird tightly, wrap*
4024 pěrizônnumi (2), to *fasten on one's belt*

GISPA
1658 Gishpâ' (1), *Gishpa*

GITTAH-HEPHER
1662 Gath-ha-Chêpher (1), *wine-press of* (the) *well*

GITTAIM
1664 Gittayim (2), *double wine-press*

GITTITE
1663 Gittîy (8), *Gittite*

GITTITES
1663 Gittîy (2), *Gittite*

GITTITH
1665 Gittîyth (3), *harp*

GIVE
1262 bârâh (1), to *feed*
1478 gâva' (3), to *expire, die*
1696 dâbar (1), to *speak, say; to subdue*
1961+413 hâyâh (1), to *exist, i.e. be or become*
3051 yâhab (24), to *give*
3052 y°hab (Ch.) (2), to *give*
3190 yâṭab (1), to *be, make well*
4900 mâshak (1), to *draw out; to be tall*
4991 mattâth (2), *present*
5066 nâgash (1), to *be, come, bring near*
5414 nâthan (482), to *give*
5415 n°than (Ch.) (2), to *give*
5441 çôbek (1), *copse or thicket*
5534 çâkar (1), to *shut up; to surrender*
6213 'âsâh (1), to *do or make*
7311 rûwm (1), to *be high; to rise or raise*
7725 shûwb (3), to *turn back; to return or restore*
7760 sûwm (5), to *put, place*
7761 sûwm (Ch.) (1), to *put, place*
7999 shâlam (1), to *be safe; be, make complete*
402 anachôrĕô (1), to *retire, withdraw*
591 apŏdidōmi (8), to *give away*
1096 ginŏmai (1), to *be, become*
1239 diadidōmi (1), to *divide up, distribute*
1325 didōmi (139), to *give*
1929 ĕpididōmi (5), to *give over*
2014 ĕpiphainō (1), to *become known*
2468 isthi (1), *be thou*
3330 mĕtadidōmi (1), to *share, distribute*
3844 para (1), *from; with; besides; on account of*
3860 paradidōmi (1), to *hand over*
3930 parĕchō (1), to *hold near, i.e. to present*
3936 paristēmi (1), to *stand beside, present*
4222 pŏtizō (3), to *furnish drink, irrigate*
4342 prŏskartĕrĕō (1), to *attend; to adhere*
4980 schŏlazō (1), to *devote oneself wholly to*
5461 phōtizō (1), to *shine or to brighten up*
5483 charizŏmai (1), to *grant as a favor*

GIVEN
1167 ba'al (2), *master; husband; owner; citizen*
1478 gâva' (1), to *expire, die*
1576 g°mûwl (1), *act; reward, recompense*
2505 châlaq (1), to *be smooth; be slippery*
2603 chânan (1), to *implore*
3052 y°hab (Ch.) (16), to *give*
3254 yâçaph (1), to *add or augment*
3289 yâ'ats (2), to *advise*
5221 nâkâh (3), to *strike, kill*
5301 nâphach (1), to *inflate, blow, scatter*
5375 nâsâ' (1), to *lift up*
5414 nâthan (253), to *give*
5462 çâgar (1), to *shut up; to surrender*
6213 'âsâh (1), to *do or make*
7760 sûwm (1), to *put, place*
7761 sûwm (Ch.) (1), to *put, place*

GIRDLE

GIRDLES

GIRL
3207 yaldâh (1), *young female*

GIRGASHITE
1622 Girgâshîy (1), *Girgashite*

GIRGASHITES
1622 Girgâshîy (5), *Girgashite*

GIRGASITE
1622 Girgâshîy (1), *Girgashite*

2290 châgôwr (5), *belt for the waist*
2805 chêsheb (8), *belt, waistband*
4206 mâzîyach (1), *leather belt*
2223 zônē (5), *belt, sash*

232 'êzôwr (1), *belt; band around waist*
2289 châgôwr (1), *belted around waist*
2223 zônē (1), *belt, sash*

5534 çâkar (1), to *shut up; to surrender*
6213 'âsâh (1), to *do or make*
7311 rûwm (1), to *be high; to rise or raise*
7725 shûwb (3), to *turn back; to return or restore*
7760 sûwm (5), to *put, place*
7761 sûwm (Ch.) (1), to *put, place*
7999 shâlam (1), to *be safe; be, make complete*
402 anachôrĕô (1), to *retire, withdraw*
591 apŏdidōmi (8), to *give away*
1096 ginŏmai (1), to *be, become*
1239 diadidōmi (1), to *divide up, distribute*
1325 didōmi (139), to *give*
1929 ĕpididōmi (5), to *give over*
2014 ĕpiphainō (1), to *become known*
2468 isthi (1), *be thou*
3330 mĕtadidōmi (1), to *share, distribute*
3844 para (1), *from; with; besides; on account of*
3860 paradidōmi (1), to *hand over*
3930 parĕchō (1), to *hold near, i.e. to present*
3936 paristēmi (1), to *stand beside, present*
4222 pŏtizō (3), to *furnish drink, irrigate*
4342 prŏskartĕrĕō (1), to *attend; to adhere*
4980 schŏlazō (1), to *devote oneself wholly to*
5461 phōtizō (1), to *shine or to brighten up*
5483 charizŏmai (1), to *grant as a favor*

1325 didōmi (123), to *give*
1377 diōkō (1), to *pursue; to persecute*
1402 dŏulŏō (1), to *enslave*
1433 dōrĕŏmai (2), to *bestow* gratuitously
1547 ĕkgamizō (1), to *marry off* a daughter
2227 zōŏpŏiĕō (1), to (re-) *vitalize, give life*
3860 paradidōmi (2), to *hand over*
3930 parĕchō (1), to *present, afford, exhibit*
3943 parŏinŏs (2), *tippling*
4272 prŏdidōmi (1), to *give before*
4337 prŏsĕchō (1), to *pay attention to*
4369 prŏstithēmi (1), to *lay beside, repeat*
5483 charizŏmai (5), to *grant as a favor*

GIVER
1395 dŏtēs (1), *giver*

GIVEST
5414 nâthan (7), to *give*
7971 shâlach (1), to *send away*

GIVETH
1478 gâva' (1), to *expire, die*
3052 y°hab (Ch.) (1), to *give*
5414 nâthan (77), to *give*
5415 n°than (Ch.) (3), to *give*
1325 didōmi (13), to *give*
3330 mĕtadidōmi (1), to *share, distribute*
3930 parĕchō (1), to *present, afford, exhibit*
5087 tithēmi (1), to *place*
5524 chŏrēgĕō (1), to *furnish, supply, provide*

GIVING
4646 mappâch (1), *expiring, dying*
5414 nâthan (5), to *give*
632 apŏnĕmō (1), *bestow, treat with respect*
1325 didōmi (3), to *give*
1394 dŏsis (1), *gift*
3004 lĕgō (1), to *say*
3548 nŏmŏthĕsia (1), *legislation, law*
3923 parĕisphĕrō (1), to *bear in alongside*

GIZONITE
1493 Gizôwnîy (1), *Gizonite*

GLAD
1523 gîyl (6), *rejoice*
1528 gîyr (Ch.) (4), *lime for plaster*
2302 châdâh (1), to *rejoice, be glad*
2868 ṭ°'êb (Ch.) (1), to *rejoice, be pleased*
2896 ṭôwb (2), *good; well*
7796 Sôwrêq (2), *vine*
7797 sûws (1), to *be bright, i.e. cheerful*
7996 Shalleketh (1), *felling of trees*

8056 sâmêach (49), *blithe* or *gleeful*
8190 Sha'ashgaz (1), *Shaashgaz*
21 agalliaō (2), to *exult*
2097 ĕuaggĕlizō (4), to *announce good news*
2165 ĕuphrainō (1), to *rejoice, be glad*
5463 chairō (14), to be *cheerful*

GLADLY
780 asmĕnōs (2), *with pleasure, gladly*
2234 hēdĕōs (3), *with pleasure, with delight*
2236 hēdista (2), *with great pleasure*

GLADNESS
1524 gîyl (1), *age, stage in life*
2304 chedvâh (1), *rejoicing, joy*
2898 ṭûwb (1), *good; goodness; gladness*
7440 rinnâh (1), *shout*
8057 simchâh (34), *blithesomeness* or *glee*
8342 sâsôwn (2), *cheerfulness; welcome*
20 agalliasis (3), *exultation, delight*
2167 ĕuphrŏsunē (1), *joyfulness, cheerfulness*
5479 chara (3), *calm delight, joy*

GLASS
7209 rᵉˀîy (1), *mirror*
2072 ĕsŏptrŏn (2), *mirror for looking into*
2734 katŏptrizŏmai (1), to *see reflected*
5193 hualinŏs (3), *pertaining to glass*
5194 hualŏs (2), *glass, crystal*

GLASSES
1549 gillâyôwn (1), *tablet for writing; mirror*

GLEAN
3950 lâqaṭ (7), to *pick up, gather; to glean*
5953 ʻâlal (3), to *glean; to overdo*

GLEANED
3950 lâqaṭ (5), to *pick up, gather; to glean*
5953 ʻâlal (1), to *glean; to overdo*

GLEANING
3951 leqeṭ (1), *gleaning after a harvest*
5955 ʻôlêlâh (4), *gleaning; gleaning-time*

GLEANINGS
3951 leqeṭ (1), *gleaning*

GLEDE
7201 râˀâh (1), bird of prey (poss. *vulture*)

GLISTERING
6320 pûwk (1), *stibium*
1823 ĕxastraptō (1), to be *radiant*

GLITTER
1300 bârâq (1), *lightning; flash of lightning*

GLITTERING
1300 bârâq (5), *lightning; flash of lightning*
3851 lahab (1), *flame of fire; flash of a blade*

GLOOMINESS
653 ˀăphêlâh (2), *duskiness, darkness*

GLORIEST
1984 hâlal (1), to *shine, flash, radiate*

GLORIETH
1984 hâlal (1), to *shine, flash, radiate*
2744 kauchaŏmai (2), to *glory in, rejoice in*

GLORIFIED
1922 hădar (Ch.) (1), to *magnify, glorify*
3513 kâbad (6), to be *heavy, severe, dull*; to be *rich, glorious*
6286 pâˀar (6), to *shake a tree*
1392 dŏxazō (34), to *render, esteem glorious*
1740 ĕndŏxazō (2), to *glorify*
4888 sundŏxazō (1), to *share glory with*

GLORIFIETH
3513 kâbad (1), to be *rich, glorious*

GLORIFY
3513 kâbad (7), to be *rich, glorious*
6286 pâˀar (1), to *shake a tree*
1392 dŏxazō (17), to *render, esteem glorious*

GLORIFYING
1392 dŏxazō (3), to *render, esteem glorious*

GLORIOUS
117 ˀaddîyr (1), *powerful; majestic*
142 ˀâdar (2), *magnificent; glorious*
215 ˀôwr (1), to be *luminous*
1921 hâdar (1), to *favor or honor*; to *be high or proud*
1926 hâdâr (1), *magnificence*
1935 hôwd (1), *grandeur, majesty*
3513 kâbad (5), to be *rich, glorious*
3519 kâbôwd (11), *splendor, wealth*
3520 kᵉbûwddâh (1), *magnificence, wealth*
6643 tsᵉbîy (5), *conspicuous splendor*
8597 tiphˀârâh (3), *ornament*
1223+1391 dia (1), *through, by means of*
1391 dŏxa (6), *glory; brilliance*
1392 dŏxazō (1), to *render, esteem glorious*

1722+1391 ĕn (3), *in; during; because of*
1741 ĕndŏxŏs (2), *splendid; noble*

GLORIOUSLY
3519 kâbôwd (1), *splendor, copiousness*

GLORY
155 ˀaddereth (1), *large; splendid*
1925 heder (1), *honor*
1926 hâdâr (7), *magnificence*
1935 hôwd (9), *grandeur, majesty*
1984 hâlal (12), to *shine, flash, radiate*
2892 ṭôhar (1), *brightness; purification*
3367 yᵉqâr (Ch.) (5), *glory, honor*
3513 kâbad (1), to be *rich, glorious*
3519 kâbôwd (155), *splendor, wealth*
6286 pâˀar (1), to *shake a tree*
6643 tsᵉbîy (7), *conspicuous splendor*
7623 shâbach (1), to *address; to pacify*
8597 tiphˀârâh (22), *ornament*
1391 dŏxa (146), *glory; brilliance*
1392 dŏxazō (3), to *render, esteem glorious*
2620 katakauchaŏmai (1), to *exult against*
2744 kauchaŏmai (18), to *glory in, rejoice in*
2745 kauchēma (3), *boast; brag*
2746 kauchēsis (1), *boasting; bragging*
2755 kĕnŏdŏxŏs (1), *self-conceited*
2811 klĕŏs (1), *renown, credited honor*

GLORYING
2744 kauchaŏmai (1), to *glory in, rejoice in*
2745 kauchēma (2), *boast; brag*
2746 kauchēsis (1), *boasting; bragging*

GLUTTON
2151 zâlal (2), to *be loose morally, worthless*

GLUTTONOUS
5314 phagŏs (2), *glutton*

GNASH
2786 châraq (2), to *grate, grind the teeth*

GNASHED
2786 châraq (1), to *grate, grind the teeth*
1031 bruchō (1), to *grate, grind teeth*

GNASHETH
2786 châraq (2), to *grate, grind the teeth*
5149 trizō (1), to *grate the teeth in frenzy*

GNASHING
1030 brugmŏs (7), *grinding of teeth*

GNAT
2971 kōnōps (1), *stinging mosquito*

GNAW
1633 gâram (1), to *crunch the bones*

GNAWED
3145 massaŏmai (1), to *chew, gnaw*

GO
236 ˀăzal (Ch.) (1), to *depart*
258 ˀâchad (1), to *unify, i.e. collect*
833 ˀâshar (2), to *go forward; guide*
935 bôwˀ (154), to *go, come*
1718 dâdâh (1), to *walk gently; lead*
1869 dârak (2), to *tread, trample; to walk, lead*
1946 hûwk (Ch.) (1), to *go, come*
1961 hâyâh (2), to *exist, i.e. be or become*
1980 hâlak (83), to *walk; live a certain way*
1982 hêlek (1), *wayfarer, visitor; flowing*
2498 châlaph (1), to *hasten away; to pass on*
2559 châmaq (1), to *depart, i.e. turn about*
3051 yâhab (4), to *give*
3212 yâlak (351), to *walk; to live; to carry*
3312 Yᵉphunneh (1), *he will be prepared*
3318 yâtsâˀ (185), to *go, bring out*
3381 yârad (73), to *descend*
3518 kâbâh (1), to *extinguish*
4161 môwtsâˀ (1), *going forth*
4609 maˀălâh (1), *thought arising*
4994 nâˀ (2), *I pray!, please!, I beg you!*
5066 nâgash (2), to *be, come, bring near*
5181 nâchath (1), to *sink, descend; to press down*
5186 nâṭâh (1), to *stretch or spread out*
5265 nâçaˀ (7), *start on a journey*
5362 nâqaph (2), to *strike; to surround*
5437 çâbab (7), to *surround*
5472 çûwg (1), to *go back, to retreat*
5493 çûwr (4), to *turn off*
5503 çâchar (1), to *travel round; to palpitate*
5674 ˀâbar (51), to *cross over; to transition*
5927 ˀâlâh (129), to *ascend, be high, mount*
5930 ˀôlâh (1), *sacrifice wholly consumed in fire*
6213 ˀâsâh (1), to *do*

English

6310 peh (1), *mouth; opening*
6485 pâqad (1), *to visit, care for, count*
6544 pâra' (1), *to absolve, begin*
6585 pâsa' (1), *to stride*
6805 tsâ'ad (1), *to pace, step regularly*
6806 tsa'ad (1), *pace or regular step*
6923 qâdam (1), *to hasten, meet*
7126 qârab (3), *to approach, bring near*
7368 râchaq (3), *to recede; remove*
7503 râphâh (4), *to slacken*
7686 shâgâh (2), *to stray, wander; to transgress*
7725 shûwb (15), *to turn back; to return*
7751 shûwţ (1), *to travel, roam*
7847 sâţâh (1), *to deviate from duty, go astray*
7971 shâlach (76), *to send away*
8582 tâ'âh (4), *to vacillate, reel or stray*
8637 tirgal (1), *to cause to walk*
33 agĕ (2), *to come on*
71 agō (6), *to lead; to bring, drive; to weigh*
305 anabainō (9), *to go up, rise*
565 apérchŏmai (25), *to go off, i.e. depart, withdraw*
630 apŏluō (13), *to relieve, release*
863 aphiēmi (1), *to leave; to pardon, forgive*
1330 diĕrchŏmai (4), *to traverse, travel through*
1524 ĕisĕimi (1), *to enter*
1525 ĕisĕrchŏmai (11), *to enter*
1607 ĕkpŏrĕuŏmai (1), *to depart, proceed, project*
1830 ĕxĕrĕunaō (1), *to explore*
1831 ĕxĕrchŏmai (14), *to issue; to leave*
1881 ĕpanistamai (2), *to stand up on, to attack*
1931 ĕpiduō (1), *to set*
1994 ĕpistrĕphō (1), *to revert, turn back to*
2064 ĕrchŏmai (2), *to go or come*
2212 zētĕō (1), *to seek*
2597 katabainō (2), *to descend*
3327 mĕtabainō (1), *to depart, move from*
3928 parĕrchŏmai (1), *to go by; to perish*
4043 pĕripatĕō (1), *to walk; to live a life*
4198 pŏrĕuŏmai (74), *to go, come; to travel*
4254 prŏagō (5), *to lead forward; to precede*
4281 prŏĕrchŏmai (2), *to go onward, precede*

4313 prŏpŏrĕuŏmai (2), *to precede*
4320 prŏsanabainō (1), *to be promoted*
4334 prŏsĕrchŏmai (1), *to come near, visit*
4782 sugkatabainō (1), *to descend with*
4905 sunĕrchŏmai (1), *to go with*
5217 hupagō (54), *to withdraw or retire*
5233 hupĕrbainō (1), *to transcend, to overreach*
5342 phĕrō (1), *to bear or carry*

GOAD
4451 malmâd (1), *ox-goad*

GOADS
1861 dorbôwn (2), *iron goad stick*

GOAT
689 'aqqôw (1), *ibex*
5795 'êz (9), *she-goat; goat's hair*
6842 tsâphîyr (3), *male goat*
8163 sâ'îyr (21), *shaggy; he-goat; goat idol*
8495 tayish (1), *buck or he-goat*

GOATH
1601 Gô'âh (1), *lowing, bellowing*

GOATS
3277 yâ'êl (3), *ibex animal*
5795 'êz (45), *she-goat; goat's hair*
6260 'attûwd (26), *he-goats; leaders*
6842 tsâphîyr (1), *he-goat*
8163 sâ'îyr (3), *shaggy; he-goat; goat idol*
8495 tayish (3), *he-goat*
2055 ĕriphiŏn (1), *goat*
2056 ĕriphŏs (1), *kid or goat*
5131 tragŏs (4), *he-goat*

GOATS'
5795 'êz (10), *she-goat; goat's hair*

GOATSKINS
122+1192 aigĕiŏs (1), *belonging to a goat*

GOB
1359 Gôb (2), *pit*

GOBLET
101 'aggân (1), *bowl*

GOD
136 'Ădônây (1), *the Lord*
401 'Ûkâl (1), *devoured*
410 'êl (217), *mighty; the Almighty*
426 'ĕlâhh (Ch.) (79), *God*
430 'ĕlôhîym (2340), *God; gods; great ones*
433 'ĕlôwahh (55), *the true God; god*
1008 Bêyth-'Êl (5), *house of God*
3068 Yᵉhôvâh (4), *Jehovah, the self-Existent or Eternal*

3069 Yᵉhôvîh (301), *Jehovah, (the) self-Existent or Eternal*
3609 Kil'âb (1), *restraint of (his) father*
4010 mablîygîyth (1), *desolation*
6697 tsûwr (2), *rock*
112 athĕŏs (1), *godless*
2312 thĕŏdidaktŏs (1), *divinely instructed*
2313 thĕŏmachĕō (1), *to resist deity*
2314 thĕŏmachŏs (1), *opponent of deity*
2315 thĕŏpnĕustŏs (1), *divinely breathed in*
2316 thĕŏs (1292), *deity; the Supreme Deity*
2318 thĕŏsĕbēs (1), *pious, devout, God-fearing*
2319 thĕŏstugēs (1), *impious, God-hating*
2962 kuriŏs (1), *supreme, controller, Mr.*
3361+1096 mē (15), *not; lest*
5377 philŏthĕŏs (1), *pious, i.e. loving God*
5537 chrēmatizō (1), *to utter an oracle*

GOD'S
410 'êl (2), *mighty; the Almighty*
430 'ĕlôhîym (7), *the true God; gods; great ones*
433 'ĕlôwahh (1), *the true God; god*
2316 thĕŏs (15), *deity; the Supreme Deity*

GOD-WARD
4136+430 mûwl (1), *in front of, opposite*
4314+2316 prŏs (2), *for; on, at; to, toward*

GODDESS
430 'ĕlôhîym (2), *god; gods; great ones*
2299 thĕa (3), *female deity, goddess*

GODHEAD
2304 thĕiŏs (1), *divinity*
2305 thĕiŏtēs (1), *divinity*
2320 thĕŏtēs (1), *divinity*

GODLINESS
2150 ĕusĕbĕia (14), *piety, religious*
2317 thĕŏsĕbĕia (1), *piety, worship of deity*

GODLY
430 'ĕlôhîym (1), *the true God; gods; great ones*
2623 châçîyd (1), *religiously pious, godly*
516+2316 axiŏs (1), *appropriately, suitable*
2152 ĕusĕbēs (1), *pious*
2153 ĕusĕbōs (2), *piously*
2316 thĕŏs (3), *deity; the Supreme Deity*
2596+2316 kata (3), *down; according to*

GODS
410 'êl (2), *mighty; the Almighty*
426 'ĕlâhh (Ch.) (14), *God*

430 'ĕlôhîym (214), *God; gods; judges, great ones*
1140 daimŏniŏn (1), *demonic being; god*
2316 thĕŏs (8), *deity; the Supreme Deity*

GOEST
935 bôw' (13), *to go or come*
1980 hâlak (5), *to walk; live a certain way*
3212 yâlak (13), *to walk; to live; to carry*
3318 yâtsâ' (7), *to go, bring out*
5927 'âlâh (1), *to ascend, be high, mount*
565 apérchŏmai (1), *to go off, i.e. depart*
5217 hupagō (5), *to withdraw or retire*

GOETH
732 'ârach (1), *to travel, wander*
925 bâhîyr (1), *shining, bright*
935 bôw' (14), *to go or come*
1869 dârak (1), *to tread, trample; to walk, lead*
1980 hâlak (19), *to walk; live a certain way*
3212 yâlak (2), *to walk; to live; to carry*
3318 yâtsâ' (31), *to go, bring out*
3381 yârad (5), *to descend*
3518 kâbâh (2), *to extinguish*
3996 mâbôw' (1), *entrance; sunset; west*
4609 ma'ălâh (1), *thought arising*
5186 nâţâh (1), *to stretch or spread out*
5493 çûwr (1), *to turn off*
5648 'âbad (Ch.) (1), *to do, work, serve*
5674 'âbar (6), *to cross over; to transition*
5927 'âlâh (10), *to ascend, be high, mount*
6437 pânâh (1), *to turn, to face*
7126 qârab (1), *to approach, bring near*
7847 sâţâh (1), *to deviate from duty, go astray*
305 anabainō (1), *to go up, rise*
565 apérchŏmai (1), *to go off, i.e. depart*
1525 ĕisĕrchŏmai (1), *to enter*
1607 ĕkpŏrĕuŏmai (3), *to depart, be discharged*
2212 zētĕō (1), *to seek*
3597 hŏdŏipŏria (1), *traveling*
4198 pŏrĕuŏmai (7), *to go/come; to travel*
4254 prŏagō (2), *to lead forward; to precede*
4334 prŏsĕrchŏmai (1), *to come near, visit*
5217 hupagō (9), *to withdraw or retire*

5562 chôrĕō (1), to *pass,
enter; to hold, admit*

GOG
1463 Gôwg (10), *Gog*
1136 Gōg (1), *Gog*

GOING
235 'āzal (1), to *disappear*
838 'āshshûwr (1), *step;
track*
935 bôw' (7), to *go or
come*
1980 hâlak (8), to *walk;
live a certain way*
3212 yâlak (5), to *walk;
to live; to carry*
3318 yâtsâ' (13), to *go,
bring out*
3381 yârad (3), to
descend
3996 mâbôw' (5),
entrance; sunset; west
4161 môwtsâ' (5), *going
forth*
4174 môwrâd (3),
descent, slope
4606 mê'al (Ch.) (1),
setting of the sun
4608 ma'ăleh (9),
elevation; platform
5362 nâqaph (1), to
strike; to surround
5674 'âbar (2), to *cross
over; to transition*
5927 'âlâh (4), to *ascend,
be high, mount*
5944 'ălîyâh (2), *upper
things; second-story*
6807 tsᵉ'âdâh (2),
stepping march
7751 shûwṭ (2), to *travel,
roam*
8444 tôwtsâ'âh (1), *exit,
boundary; deliverance*
8582 tâ'âh (1), to
vacillate, reel or stray
71 agō (1), to *lead; to
bring, drive; to weigh*
305 anabainō (2), to *go
up, rise*
565 apérchŏmai (1), to
go off, i.e. depart
1330 diérchŏmai (1), to
traverse, travel through
1607 ĕkpŏrĕuŏmai (1), to
depart, be discharged
2212 zētĕō (1), to *seek*
2597 katabainō (1), to
descend
4105 planaō (1), to *roam,
wander; to deceive*
4108 planŏs (1), *roving,
impostor or misleader*
4198 pŏrĕuŏmai (1), to
go/come; to travel
4254 prŏagō (2), to *lead
forward; to precede*
4260 prŏbainō (1), to
advance
4281 prŏĕrchŏmai (1), to
go onward, precede
5217 hupagō (1), to
withdraw or retire

GOINGS
838 'āshshûwr (2), *step;
track*
1979 hălîykâh (2),
walking; procession

4161 môwtsâ' (4), *going
forth*
4163 môwtsâ'âh (1),
family descent
4570 ma'gâl (2), *circular
track or camp rampart*
4703 mits'âd (1), *step;
companionship*
6471 pa'am (1), *time;
step; occurence*
6806 tsa'ad (1), *pace or
regular step*
8444 tôwtsâ'âh (12), *exit,
boundary; deliverance*

GOLAN
1474 Gôwlân (4), *captive*

GOLD
1220 betser (2), *gold*
1222 bᵉtsar (1), *gold*
1722 dᵉhab (Ch.) (14),
gold
2091 zâhâb (340), *gold,
golden colored*
2742 chârûwts (6),
mined gold; trench
3800 kethem (7), *pure
gold*
5458 çᵉgôwr (1), *breast;
gold*
6337 pâz (9), *pure gold*
5552 chrusĕŏs (3), *made
of gold*
5553 chrusiŏn (9), *golden
thing*
5554 chrusŏdaktuliŏs
(1), *gold-ringed*
5557 chrusŏs (13), *gold;
golden article*

GOLDEN
1722 dᵉhab (Ch.) (9), *gold*
2091 zâhâb (38), *gold,
golden colored*
3800 kethem (1), *pure
gold*
4062 madhêbâh (1), *gold
making*
5552 chrusĕŏs (15), *made
of gold*

GOLDSMITH
6884 tsâraph (3), to *fuse
metal; to refine*

GOLDSMITH'S
6885 Tsôrᵉphîy (1), *refiner*

GOLDSMITHS
6884 tsâraph (2), to *fuse
metal; to refine*

GOLGOTHA
1115 Golgŏtha (3), *skull
knoll*

GOLIATH
1555 Golyath (6), *exile*

GOMER
1586 Gômer (6),
completion

GOMORRAH
6017 'Ămôrâh (19),
(ruined) *heap*
1116 Gŏmŏrrha (1),
ruined *heap*

GOMORRHA
1116 Gŏmŏrrha (4),
ruined *heap*

GONE
230 'ăzad (Ch.) (2), *firm,
assured*

235 'āzal (2), to *disappear*
369 'ayin (4), *there is no,
i.e., not exist, none*
656 'âphêç (1), to *cease*
935 bôw' (10), to *go or
come*
1540 gâlâh (1), to
denude; uncover
1961 hâyâh (1), to *exist,
i.e. be or become*
1980 hâlak (22), to *walk;
live a certain way*
2114 zûwr (1), to *be
foreign, strange*
3212 yâlak (17), to *walk;
to live; to carry*
3318 yâtsâ' (31), to *go,
bring out*
3381 yârad (14), to
descend
4059 middad (1), *flight*
4161 môwtsâ' (2), *going
forth*
4185 mûwsh (1), to
withdraw
5128 nûwa' (1), to *waver*
5186 nâṭâh (1), to *stretch
or spread out*
5312 nᵉphaq (Ch.) (1), to
issue forth; to bring out
5362 nâqaph (2), to
surround or circulate
5437 çâbab (1), to
surround
5472 çûwg (1), to *go
back, to retreat*
5493 çûwr (2), to *turn off*
5674 'âbar (16), to *cross
over; to transition*
5927 'âlâh (22), to
ascend, be high, mount
6805 tsâ'ad (1), to *pace,
step regularly*
7725 shûwb (2), to *turn
back; to return*
7751 shûwṭ (1), to *travel,
roam*
7847 sâṭâh (2), to *deviate
from duty, go astray*
8582 tâ'âh (2), to
vacillate, reel or stray
305 anabainō (2), to *go
up, rise*
402 anachōrĕō (1), to
retire, withdraw
565 apérchŏmai (4), to
go off, i.e. depart
576 apŏbainō (1), to
disembark
1276 diapĕraō (1), to
cross over
1330 diérchŏmai (4), to
traverse, travel through
1339 diïstēmi (1), to
remove, intervene
1525 éisérchŏmai (1), to
enter
1578 ĕkklinō (1), to *shun;
to decline*
1607 ĕkpŏrĕuŏmai (1), to
depart, proceed, project
1826 ĕxĕimi (1), *leave;
escape*
1831 ĕxérchŏmai (11), to
issue; to leave
3985 pĕirazō (1), to
endeavor, scrutinize
4105 planaō (2), to *roam,
wander*

4198 pŏrĕuŏmai (3), to
go, come; to travel
4260 prŏbainō (1), to
advance
4570 sbĕnnumi (1), to
extinguish, snuff out
5055 tĕlĕō (1), to *end, i.e.
complete, execute*

GOOD
1319 bâsar (7), to
announce (good news)
1390 Gib'âh (1), *hillock*
1580 gâmal (1), to *benefit
or requite; to wean*
2492 châlam (1), to *be,
make plump; to dream*
2617 cheçed (1),
kindness, favor
2623 châçîyd (1),
religiously pious, godly
2869 ṭâb (Ch.) (1), *good*
2895 ṭôwb (6), to *be good*
2896 ṭôwb (363), *good;
well*
2898 ṭûwb (11), *good;
goodness; beauty,
gladness; welfare*
3190 yâṭab (20), to *be,
make well*
3191 yᵉṭab (Ch.) (1), to
be, make well
3276 yâ'al (1), to *be
valuable*
3474 yâshar (1), to *be
straight; to make right*
3788 kishrôwn (1),
success; advantage
3966 mᵉ'ôd (3), *very,
utterly*
5750 'ôwd (1), *again;
repeatedly; still; more*
6743 tsâlach (1), to *push
forward*
7368 râchaq (2), to
recede; remove
7522 râtsôwn (2), *delight*
7965 shâlôwm (1), *safe;
well; health, prosperity*
7999 shâlam (6), to *be
safe; be, make complete*
8232 shᵉphar (Ch.) (1), to
be beautiful
14 agathŏĕrgĕō (1), to *do
good work*
15 agathŏpŏiĕō (6), to *be
a well-doer*
18 agathŏs (98), *good*
515 axiŏō (1), to *deem
entitled or fit, worthy*
865 aphilagathŏs (1),
hostile to virtue
979 biŏs (1), *livelihood;
property*
2095 ĕu (1), *well*
2097 ĕuaggĕlizō (2), to
announce good news
2106 ĕudŏkĕō (1), to
think well, i.e. approve
2107 ĕudŏkia (3),
delight, kindness, wish
2108 ĕuĕrgĕsia (1),
beneficence
2109 ĕuĕrgĕtĕō (1), to *be
philanthropic*
2133 ĕunŏia (1), *eagerly,
with a whole heart*
2140 ĕupŏiïa (1),
beneficence, doing good

English

GOODLIER

2162 *ĕuphēmia* (1), *good repute*
2163 *ĕuphēmŏs* (1), *reputable*
2425 *hikanŏs* (1), *ample; fit*
2480 *ischuō* (1), *to have or exercise force*
2565 *kalliĕlaiŏs* (1), *cultivated olive*
2567 *kalŏdidaskalŏs* (1), *teacher of the right*
2570 *kalŏs* (78), *good; beautiful; valuable*
2573 *kalŏs* (3), *well,* i.e. *rightly*
2750 *kĕiria* (2), *swathe of cloth*
3112 *makran* (1), *at a distance, far away*
4851 *sumphĕrō* (1), *to collect; to conduce*
5358 *philagathŏs* (1), *promoter of virtue*
5542 *chrēstŏlŏgia* (1), *fair speech, plausibility*
5543 *chrēstŏs* (1), *employed,* i.e. *useful*
5544 *chrēstŏtēs* (1), *moral excellence*

GOODLIER

2896 *tôwb* (1), *good; well*

GOODLIEST

2896 *tôwb* (2), *good; well*

GOODLINESS

2617 *cheçed* (1), *kindness, favor*

GOODLY

117 *'addîyr* (1), *powerful; majestic*
145 *'eder* (1), *mantle; splendor*
155 *'addereth* (1), *large; splendid*
410 *'êl* (1), *mighty;* the *Almighty*
1926 *hâdâr* (1), *magnificence*
1935 *hôwd* (1), *grandeur, majesty*
2530 *châmad* (1), *to delight in; lust for*
2532 *chemdâh* (1), *delight*
2896 *tôwb* (11), *good; well*
4261 *machmâd* (1), *delightful*
4758 *mar'eh* (1), *appearance; vision*
6287 *p°'êr* (1), *fancy head-dress*
6643 *ts°bîy* (1), *conspicuous splendor*
7443 *renen* (1), *female ostrich*
8231 *shâphar* (1), *to be, make fair*
8233 *shepher* (1), *beauty*
2573 *kalŏs* (2), *well,* i.e. *rightly*
2986 *lamprŏs* (2), *radiant; magnificent*

GOODMAN

376 *'îysh* (1), *man; male; someone*
3611 *ŏikĕō* (5), *to reside, inhabit, remain*

GOODNESS

2617 *cheçed* (12), *kindness, favor*
2896 *tôwb* (16), *good; well*
2898 *tûwb* (13), *good; goodness; beauty*
19 *agathōsunē* (4), *virtue* or *beneficence*
5543 *chrēstŏs* (1), *employed,* i.e. *useful*
5544 *chrēstŏtēs* (4), *moral excellence*

GOODNESS'

2898 *tûwb* (1), *good; goodness; beauty*

GOODS

202 *'ôwn* (1), *ability, power; wealth*
2428 *chayil* (2), *army; wealth; virtue; valor*
2896 *tôwb* (2), *good; well*
2898 *tûwb* (3), *good; goodness; beauty*
4399 *m°lâ'kâh* (2), *work; property*
5232 *n°kaç* (Ch.) (2), *treasure, riches*
7075 *qinyân* (2), *purchase, wealth*
7399 *r°kûwsh* (12), *property*
18 *agathŏs* (2), *good*
3776 *ŏusia* (1), *wealth, property, possessions*
4147 *plŏutĕō* (1), *to be, become wealthy*
4632 *skĕuŏs* (2), *vessel, implement, equipment*
4674 *sŏs* (1), *things that are yours*
5223 *huparxis* (1), *property, wealth*
5224 *huparchŏnta* (7), *property or possessions*

GOPHER

1613 *gôpher* (1), (poss.) *cypress*

GORE

5055 *nâgach* (1), *to butt with bull's horns*

GORED

5055 *nâgach* (2), *to butt with bull's horns*

GORGEOUS

2986 *lamprŏs* (1), *radiant; magnificent*

GORGEOUSLY

4358 *miklôwl* (1), *perfection; splendidly*
1741 *ĕndŏxŏs* (1), *splendid; noble*

GOSHEN

1657 *Gôshen* (15), *Goshen*

GOSPEL

2097 *ĕuaggĕlizō* (24), *to announce good news*
2098 *ĕuaggĕliŏn* (73), *good message*
4283 *prŏĕuaggĕlizŏmai* (1), *to announce glad news in advance*

GOSPEL'S

2098 *ĕuaggĕliŏn* (3), *good message*

GOT

3318 *yâtsâ'* (2), *to go, bring out*
3423 *yârash* (1), *to inherit; to impoverish*
7069 *qânâh* (3), *to create; to procure*
7408 *râkash* (1), *to lay up,* i.e. *collect*

GOTTEN

622 *'âçaph* (1), *to gather, collect*
3254 *yâçaph* (1), *to add* or *augment*
4069 *maddûwa'* (1), *why?, what?*
4672 *mâtsâ'* (2), *to find* or *acquire; to occur*
5414 *nâthan* (1), *to give*
6213 *'âsâh* (8), *to do* or *make*
7069 *qânâh* (1), *to create; to procure*
7408 *râkash* (3), *to lay up,* i.e. *collect*
645 *apŏspaŏ* (1), *unsheathe; withdraw*

GOURD

7021 *qîyqâyôwn* (5), *gourd plant*

GOURDS

6498 *paqqû'âh* (1), *wild cucumber*

GOVERN

2280 *châbash* (1), *to wrap firmly, bind*
5148 *nâchâh* (1), *to guide*
6213 *'âsâh* (1), *to do*

GOVERNMENT

4475 *memshâlâh* (1), *rule; realm* or *a ruler*
4951 *misrâh* (2), *empire*
2963 *kuriŏtēs* (1), *rulers, masters*

GOVERNMENTS

2941 *kubĕrnēsis* (1), *directorship*

GOVERNOR

441 *'allûwph* (1), *friend, one familiar; chieftain*
4910 *mâshal* (3), *to rule*
5057 *nâgîyd* (3), *commander, official*
5387 *nâsiy'* (1), *leader; rising mist, fog*
5921 *'al* (1), *above, over, upon,* or *against*
6346 *pechâh* (10), *prefect, officer*
6347 *pechâh* (Ch.) (6), *prefect, officer*
6485 *pâqad* (5), *to visit, care for, count*
7989 *shallîyt* (1), *prince* or *warrior*
8269 *sar* (4), *head person, ruler*
755 *architriklinŏs* (2), *director of the entertainment*
1481 *ĕthnarchēs* (1), *governor of a district*
2116 *ĕuthunō* (1), *to straighten* or *level*
2230 *hēgĕmŏnĕuō* (3), *to act as ruler*

GOVERNOR'S

2232 *hēgĕmŏn* (15), *chief person*
2233 *hēgĕŏmai* (2), *to lead,* i.e. *command*

GOVERNOR'S

2232 *hēgĕmŏn* (1), *chief person*

GOVERNORS

441 *'allûwph* (2), *friend, one familiar; chieftain*
2710 *châqaq* (2), *to engrave; to enact laws*
4910 *mâshal* (1), *to rule*
5461 *çâgân* (5), *prfect of a province*
6346 *pechâh* (7), *prefect, officer*
8269 *sar* (2), *head person, ruler*
2232 *hēgĕmŏn* (2), *chief person*
3623 *ŏikŏnŏmŏs* (1), *overseer, manager*

GOZAN

1470 *Gôwzân* (5), *quarry*

GRACE

2580 *chên* (37), *graciousness; beauty*
8467 *t°chinnâh* (1), *gracious entreaty, supplication*
2143 *ĕuprĕpĕia* (1), *gracefulness*
5485 *charis* (127), *gratitude; benefit given*

GRACIOUS

2580 *chên* (2), *graciousness; beauty*
2587 *channûwn* (14), *gracious*
2589 *channôwth* (1), *supplication*
2603 *chânan* (11), *to implore*
5485 *charis* (1), *gratitude; benefit given*
5543 *chrēstŏs* (1), *employed,* i.e. *useful*

GRACIOUSLY

2603 *chânan* (3), *to implore*
2896 *tôwb* (1), *good; well*

GRAFF

1461 *ĕgkĕntrizō* (1), *to engraft*

GRAFFED

1461 *ĕgkĕntrizō* (5), *to engraft*

GRAIN

6872 *ts°rôwr* (1), *parcel; kernel* or *particle*
2848 *kŏkkŏs* (6), *kernel*

GRANDMOTHER

3125 *mammē* (1), *grandmother*

GRANT

5414 *nâthan* (12), *to give*
7558 *rishyôwn* (1), *permit*
1325 *didŏmi* (7), *to give*
2036 *ĕpō* (1), *to speak* or *say*

GRANTED

935 *bôw'* (1), *to go* or *come*
5414 *nâthan* (9), *to give*

6213 'âsâh (1), to *do* or
make
1325 didômi (3), to *give*
5483 charizômai (1), to
grant as a *favor*

GRAPE

1154 beçer (1),
immature, sour grapes
1155 bôçer (3),
immature, sour grapes
5563 çᵉmâdar (2), vine
blossom
6025 'ênâb (1), *grape*
cluster
6528 pereṭ (1), *stray* or
single berry

GRAPEGATHERER

1219 bâtsar (1), to *gather*
grapes

GRAPEGATHERERS

1219 bâtsar (2), to *gather*
grapes

GRAPEGLEANINGS

5955 'ôlêlâh (1),
gleaning; gleaning-time

GRAPES

891 bᵉ'ûshîym (2), *rotten*
fruit
1154 beçer (1),
immature, sour grapes
5563 çᵉmâdar (2), vine
blossom
6025 'ênâb (15), *grape*
cluster
4718 staphulē (3), *cluster*
of grapes

GRASS

1758 dûwsh (1), to
trample or *thresh*
1877 deshe' (7), *sprout;*
green *grass*
1883 dethe' (Ch.) (2),
sprout; green *grass*
2682 châtsîyr (17), *grass;*
leek plant
3418 yereq (1), *green*
grass or vegetation
6211 'âsh (5), *moth*
6212 'eseb (16), *grass,* or
any green, tender shoot
5528 chŏrtŏs (12),
pasture, herbage

GRASSHOPPER

697 'arbeh (1), *locust*
2284 châgâb (2), *locust*

GRASSHOPPERS

697 'arbeh (3), *locust*
1462 gôwb (2), *locust*
2284 châgâb (2), *locust*

GRATE

4345 makbêr (6), *grate,*
lattice

GRAVE

1164 bᵉ'îy (1), *prayer*
6603 pittûwach (1),
sculpture; engraving
6605 pâthach (3), to *open*
wide; to *loosen, begin*
6900 qᵉbûwrâh (4),
sepulchre
6913 qeber (19),
sepulchre
7585 shᵉ'ôwl (30), abode
of the *dead*
7845 shachath (1), *pit;*
destruction

86 ha₁dēs (1), *Hades,* i.e.
place of the dead
3419 mnēmĕiŏn (4),
place of interment
4586 sĕmnŏs (3),
honorable, noble

GRAVE'S

7585 shᵉ'ôwl (1), abode
of the *dead*

GRAVECLOTHES

2750 kĕiria (1), *swathe of*
cloth

GRAVED

6605 pâthach (2), to
loosen, plow, carve

GRAVEL

2687 châtsâts (2), *gravel,*
grit
4579 mê'âh (1), *belly*

GRAVEN

2672 châtsab (1), to *cut*
stone or *carve* wood
2710 châqaq (1), to
engrave; to *enact* laws
2790 chârash (1), to
engrave; to *plow*
2801 chârath (1), to
engrave
6456 pᵉçîyl (18), *idol*
6458 pâçal (1), to *carve,*
to *chisel*
6459 peçel (29), *idol*
6605 pâthach (2), to
loosen, plow, carve
5480 charagma (1),
mark, sculptured figure

GRAVES

6913 qeber (16),
sepulchre
3418 mnēma (1),
sepulchral *monument*
3419 mnēmĕiŏn (4),
place of interment

GRAVETH

2710 châqaq (1), to
engrave; to *enact* laws

GRAVING

2747 cheret (1), *chisel;*
style for writing
6603 pittûwach (2),
sculpture; engraving

GRAVINGS

4734 miqla'ath (1),
bas-relief *sculpture*

GRAVITY

4587 sĕmnŏtēs (2),
venerableness

GRAY

7872 sêybâh (5), old *age*

GRAYHEADED

7867 sîyb (2), to *become*
aged, i.e. to *grow gray*

GREASE

2459 cheleb (1), *fat;*
choice part

GREAT

410 'êl (1), *mighty;* the
Almighty
417 'elgâbîysh (3), *hail*
430 'ĕlôhîym (2), the true
God; gods; great ones
679 'atstsîyl (1), *joint* of
the hand

1004 bayith (1), *house;*
temple; family, tribe
1167 ba'al (1), *master;*
husband; owner; citizen
1241 bâqâr (1), *plowing*
ox; *herd*
1396 gâbar (2), to *be*
strong; to *prevail;* to
act insolently
1419 gâdôwl (413), *great*
1420 gᵉdûwlâh (3),
greatness, grandeur
1431 gâdal (33), to *be*
great, make great
1432 gâdêl (2), *large,*
powerful
1462 gôwb (1), *locust*
1560 gᵉlâl (Ch.) (2), *large*
stones
2030 hâreh (1), *pregnant*
2342 chûwl (1), to *dance,*
whirl; to *writhe* in pain
2750 chŏrîy (2), *burning*
anger
3244 yanshûwph (2), *bird*
3514 kôbed (1), *weight,*
multitude, vehemence
3515 kâbêd (8),
numerous; severe
3699 kâçaç (1), to
estimate, determine
3833 lâbîy' (3), *lion,*
lioness
3966 mᵉ'ôd (11), *very,*
utterly
4306 mâṭâr (1), *rain,*
shower of rain
4459 maltâ'âh (1),
grinder, molar tooth
4766 marbeh (1),
increasing; greatness
5006 nâ'ats (1), to *scorn*
6099 'âtsûwm (1),
powerful; numerous
6105 'âtsam (1), to *be,*
make powerful
6343 pachad (1), sudden
alarm, fear
7091 qippôwz (1),
arrow-snake
7227 rab (125), *great*
7229 rab (Ch.) (7), *great*
7230 rôb (7), *abundance*
7235 râbâh (9), to
increase
7236 rᵉbâh (Ch.) (1), to
increase
7239 ribbôw (1), *myriad,*
indefinite *large number*
7260 rabrab (Ch.) (8),
huge; domineering
7350 râchôwq (2),
remote, far
7451 ra' (1), *bad; evil*
7689 saggîy' (1), *mighty*
7690 saggîy' (Ch.) (3),
large
7991 shâlîysh (2), *officer;*
of the *third* rank
8514 tal'ûwbâh (1),
desiccation
1974 ĕpipŏthia (1),
intense longing
2245 hēlikŏs (2), *how*
much, how great
2425 hikanŏs (2), *ample;*
fit
3029 lian (1), *very much*

3112 makran (1), *at a*
distance, far away
3123 mallŏn (1), *in a*
greater degree
3166 mĕgalauchĕŏ (1), to
be arrogant, egotistic
3167 mĕgalĕiŏs (1), *great*
things, wonderful works
3170 mĕgalunŏ (1), to
increase or *extol*
3171 mĕgalŏs (1), *much,*
greatly
3173 mĕgas (149), *great,*
many
3175 mĕgistanĕs (2),
great person
3176 mĕgistŏs (1),
greatest or *very great*
3745 hŏsŏs (6), *as much*
as
3819 palai (1), *formerly;*
sometime since
3827 pampŏlus (1), *full*
many, i.e. *immense*
4080 pēlikŏs (1), *how*
much, how great
4118 plĕistŏs (1), *largest*
number or *very large*
4183 pŏlus (60), *much,*
many
4185 pŏlutĕlēs (2),
extremely expensive
4186 pŏlutimŏs (1),
extremely valuable
4214 pŏsŏs (1), *how*
much?; how much!
5082 tēlikŏutŏs (3), *so*
vast
5118 tŏsŏutŏs (5), *such*
great
5246 hupĕrŏgkŏs (2),
insolent, boastful

GREATER

1419 gâdôwl (20), *great*
1431 gâdal (3), to *be*
great, make great
1980 hâlak (1), to *walk;*
live a certain way
7227 rab (4), *great*
7235 râbâh (2), to
increase
3186 mĕizŏtĕrŏs (1), *still*
larger, greater
3187 mĕizŏn (34), *larger,*
greater
4055 pĕrissŏtĕrŏs (3),
more superabundant
4119 plĕiŏn (6), *more*

GREATEST

1419 gâdôwl (9), *great*
4768 marbîyth (1),
multitude; offspring
3173 mĕgas (2), *great,*
many
3187 mĕizŏn (9), *larger,*
greater

GREATLY

3966 mᵉ'ôd (49), *very,*
utterly
7227 rab (3), *great*
7230 rôb (1), *abundance*
7690 saggîy' (Ch.) (1),
large
1568 ĕkthambĕŏ (1), to
astonish utterly
1569 ĕkthambŏs (1),
utterly astounded

1971 ĕpĭpŏthĕō (3), *intensely crave*
3029 lian (4), *very much*
3171 mĕgalōs (1), *much, greatly*
4183 pŏlus (4), *much, many*
4970 sphŏdra (2), *high degree, much*
5479 chara (1), *calm delight, joy*

GREATNESS
1419 gâdôwl (1), *great*
1420 gᵉdûwlâh (7), *greatness, grandeur*
1433 gôdel (11), *magnitude, majesty*
4768 marbîyth (1), *multitude; offspring*
7230 rôb (9), *abundance*
7238 rᵉbûw (Ch.) (2), *increase*
3174 mĕgĕthŏs (1), *greatness*

GREAVES
4697 mitschâh (1), *shin-piece of armor*

GRECIA
3120 Yâvân (3), *effervescent*

GRECIANS
3125 Yᵉvânîy (1), *Jevanite*
1675 Hĕllēnistēs (3), *Hellenist or Greek-speaking Jew*

GREECE
3120 Yâvân (1), *effervescent*
1671 Hĕllas (1), *Hellas*

GREEDILY
8378 ta'ăvâh (1), *longing; delight*
1632 ĕkchĕō (1), *to pour forth; to bestow*

GREEDINESS
4124 plĕŏnĕxia (1), *extortion, avarice*

GREEDY
1214 bâtsa' (2), *to plunder; to finish*
3700 kâçaph (1), *to pine after; to fear*
5794+5315 'az (1), *strong, vehement, harsh*
146 aischrŏkĕrdēs (1), *sordid, greedy*
866 aphilargurŏs (1), *unavaricious*

GREEK
1672 Hĕllēn (7), *Greek (-speaking)*
1673 Hĕllēnikŏs (2), *Grecian* language
1674 Hĕllēnis (1), *Grecian woman*
1676 Hĕllēnisti (2), *Hellenistically, i.e. in the Grecian language*

GREEKS
1672 Hĕllēn (13), *Greek (-speaking)*
1674 Hĕllēnis (1), *Grecian woman*

GREEN
1877 deshe' (1), *sprout; green grass*
3387 yârôwq (1), *green plant*
3410 yarkâ' (Ch.) (1), *thigh*
3418 yereq (5), *green grass or vegetation*
3419 yârâq (1), *vegetable greens*
3768 karpaç (1), *byssus linen*
3892 lach (5), *fresh cut*
6291 pag (1), *unripe fig*
7373 râṭôb (1), *moist with sap*
7488 ra'ănân (18), *verdant; new*
5200 hugrŏs (1), *fresh and moist*
5515 chlōrŏs (3), *greenish, i.e. verdant*

GREENISH
3422 yᵉraqraq (2), *yellowishness*

GREENNESS
3 'êb (1), *green plant*

GREET
7592+7965 shâ'al (1), *to ask*
782 aspazŏmai (14), *to salute, welcome*

GREETETH
782 aspazŏmai (1), *to salute, welcome*

GREETING
5463 chairō (3), *salutation, "be well"*

GREETINGS
783 aspasmŏs (3), *greeting*

GREW
1431 gâdal (9), *to be great, make great*
1432 gâdêl (2), *large, powerful*
6509 pârâh (1), *to bear fruit*
6555 pârats (1), *to break out*
6779 tsâmach (2), *to sprout*
6780 tsemach (2), *sprout, branch*
7236 rᵉbâh (Ch.) (2), *to increase*
305 anabainō (1), *to go up, rise*
837 auxanō (6), *to grow, i.e. enlarge*
2064 ĕrchŏmai (1), *to go or come*

GREY
7872 sêybâh (1), *old age*

GREYHEADED
7872 sêybâh (1), *old age*

GREYHOUND
2223+4975 zarzîyr (1), *fleet animal (slender)*

GRIEF
2470 châlâh (2), *to be weak, sick, afflicted*
2483 chŏlîy (3), *malady; anxiety; calamity*

3013 yâgâh (1), *to grieve; to torment*
3015 yâgôwn (2), *affliction, sorrow*
3511 kᵉ'êb (2), *suffering; adversity*
3708 ka'aç (7), *vexation, grief*
4341 mak'ôb (2), *anguish; affliction*
4786 môrâh (1), *bitterness; trouble*
6330 pûwqâh (1), *stumbling-block*
7451 ra' (1), *bad; evil*
3076 lupĕō (1), *to distress; to be sad*
3077 lupē (1), *sadness, grief*
4727 stĕnazō (1), *to sigh, murmur, pray* inaudibly

GRIEFS
2483 chŏlîy (1), *malady; anxiety; calamity*

GRIEVANCE
5999 'âmâl (1), *wearing effort; worry*

GRIEVE
109 'âdab (1), *to languish, grieve*
3013 yâgâh (1), *to grieve; to torment*
6087 'âtsab (2), *to worry, have pain or anger*
3076 lupĕō (1), *to distress; to be sad*

GRIEVED
2342 chûwl (2), *to dance, whirl; to writhe* in pain
2470 châlâh (2), *to be weak, sick, afflicted*
2556 châmêts (1), *to be fermented; be soured*
2734 chârâh (1), *to blaze up*
3512 kâ'âh (1), *to despond; to deject*
3707 kâ'aç (1), *to grieve, rage, be indignant*
3735 kârâ' (Ch.) (1), *to grieve, be anxious*
3811 lâ'âh (1), *to tire; to be, make disgusted*
4784 mârâh (1), *to rebel or resist; to provoke*
4843 mârar (1), *to be, make bitter*
5701 'âgam (1), *to be sad*
6087 'âtsab (8), *to worry, have pain or anger*
6962 qûwṭ (3), *to detest*
6973 qûwts (1), *to be, make disgusted*
7114 qâtsar (1), *to curtail, cut short*
7489 râ'a' (4), *to break; to be good for nothing*
1278 diapŏnĕō (2), *to be worried*
3076 lupĕō (5), *to distress; to be sad*
4360 prŏsŏchthizō (2), *to be vexed with*
4818 sullupĕō (1), *to afflict jointly, sorrow at*

GRIEVETH
3811 lâ'âh (1), *to tire; to be, make disgusted*
4843 mârar (1), *to be, make bitter*

GRIEVING
3510 kâ'ab (1), *to feel pain; to grieve; to spoil*

GRIEVOUS
2342 chûwl (2), *to dance, whirl; to writhe* in pain
2470 châlâh (4), *to be weak, sick, afflicted*
3415 yâra' (1), *to fear*
3513 kâbad (1), *to be heavy, severe, dull*
3515 kâbêd (8), *severe, difficult, stupid*
4834 mârats (1), *to be vehement; to irritate*
5493 çûwr (1), *to turn off*
6089 'etseb (1), *earthen vessel; painful toil*
6277 'âthâq (1), *impudent*
7185 qâshâh (2), *to be tough or severe*
7186 qâsheh (3), *severe*
7451 ra' (2), *bad; evil*
7489 râ'a' (2), *to break; to be good for nothing*
8463 tachălûw' (1), *malady, disease*
926 barus (3), *weighty*
1418 dus- (2), *hard, i.e. with difficulty*
3077 lupē (1), *sadness, grief*
3636 ŏknērŏs (1), *irksome; lazy*
4190 pŏnērŏs (1), *malice, wicked, bad; crime*

GRIEVOUSLY
2342 chûwl (1), *to dance, whirl; to writhe* in pain
2399 chêṭ' (1), *crime or its penalty*
3513 kâbad (1), *to be heavy, severe, dull*
4604 ma'al (1), *sinful treachery*
4784 mârâh (1), *to rebel or resist; to provoke*
1171 dĕinōs (1), *terribly, i.e. excessively, fiercely*
2560 kakōs (1), *badly; wrongly; ill*

GRIEVOUSNESS
3514 kôbed (1), *weight, multitude, vehemence*
5999 'âmâl (1), *wearing effort; worry*

GRIND
2911 ṭᵉchôwn (1), *hand mill; millstone*
2912 ṭâchan (4), *to grind flour meal*
3039 likmaō (2), *to grind to powder*

GRINDERS
2912 ṭâchan (1), *to grind flour meal*

GRINDING
2913 ṭachănâh (1), *chewing, grinding*
229 alēthō (2), *to grind grain*

GRISLED
1261 bârôd (4), *spotted, dappled*

GROAN
584 'ânach (1), to *sigh, moan*
602 'ânaq (1), to *shriek, cry out in groaning*
5008 nâ'aq (2), to *groan*
4727 stĕnazō (3), to *sigh, murmur, pray* inaudibly

GROANED
1690 ĕmbrimaŏmai (1), to *blame, to sigh*

GROANETH
4959 sustĕnazō (1), to *moan jointly*

GROANING
585 'ănâchâh (4), *sighing, moaning*
603 'ănâqâh (1), *shrieking, groaning*
5009 nᵉ'âqâh (2), *groaning*
1690 ĕmbrimaŏmai (1), to *blame, to sigh*
4726 stĕnagmŏs (1), *sigh, groan*

GROANINGS
5009 nᵉ'âqâh (2), *groaning*
4726 stĕnagmŏs (1), *sigh, groan*

GROPE
1659 gâshash (2), to *feel about, grope around*
4959 mâshash (3), to *feel of; to grope*

GROPETH
4959 mâshash (1), to *feel of; to grope*

GROSS
6205 'ărâphel (2), *gloom, darkness*
3975 pachunō (2), to *fatten; to render callous*

GROUND
127 'ădâmâh (44), *soil; land*
776 'erets (97), *earth, land, soil; country*
2513 chelqâh (1), *smoothness; allotment*
2758 chârîysh (1), *plowing (season)*
2912 ţâchan (3), to *grind flour meal*
6083 'âphâr (1), *dust, earth, mud; clay*
7383 rîyphâh (1), *grits cereal*
7704 sâdeh (4), *field*
68 agrŏs (1), *farmland, countryside*
1093 gē (18), *soil, region, whole earth*
1474 ĕdaphizō (1), to *raze, dash to the ground*
1475 ĕdaphŏs (1), *soil, ground*
1477 hĕdraiōma (1), *basis, foundation*
5476 chamai (2), *toward the ground*
5561 chōra (1), *space of territory*

GROUNDED
4145 mûwçâdâh (1), *foundation*
2311 thĕmĕliŏō (2), to *erect; to consolidate*

GROVE
815 'êshel (1), *tamarisk tree*
842 'ăshêrâh (16), *happy; Astarte (goddess)*

GROVES
842 'ăshêrâh (24), *happy; Astarte (goddess)*

GROW
1342 gâ'âh (1), to *rise; to grow tall; be majestic*
1431 gâdal (1), to *be great, make great*
1711 dâgâh (1), to *become numerous*
3212 yâlak (1), to *walk; to live; to carry*
3318 yâtsâ' (1), to *go, bring out*
5599 çâphîyach (2), *self-sown crop; freshet*
5927 'âlâh (2), to *ascend, be high, mount*
6335 pûwsh (1), to *spread; to act proudly*
6509 pârâh (1), to *bear fruit*
6524 pârach (2), to *break forth; to bloom; flourish*
6779 tsâmach (9), to *sprout*
7235 râbâh (1), to *increase*
7680 sᵉgâ' (Ch.) (1), to *increase*
7685 sâgâh (1), to *enlarge, be prosperous*
7735 sûwg (1), to *hedge in, make grow*
7971 shâlach (1), to *send away*
837 auxanō (5), to *grow, i.e. enlarge*
1096 ginŏmai (2), to *be, become*
3373 mēkunō (1), to *enlarge, grow long*
4886 sundĕsmŏs (1), *ligament; control*

GROWETH
2498 châlaph (2), to *spring up; to change*
2583 chânâh (1), to *encamp*
3332 yâtsaq (1), to *pour out*
5599 çâphîyach (3), *self-sown crop; freshet*
5927 'âlâh (1), to *ascend, be high, mount*
6524 pârach (1), to *break forth; to bloom; flourish*
6779 tsâmach (1), to *sprout*
8025 shâlaph (1), to *pull out, up or off*
305 anabainō (1), to *go up, rise*
837 auxanō (1), to *grow, i.e. enlarge*

GROWN
648 'âphîyl (1), *unripe*
1431 gâdal (9), to *be great, make great*
5927 'âlâh (1), to *ascend, be high, mount*
6335 pûwsh (1), to *spread; to act proudly*
6779 tsâmach (4), to *sprout*
6965 qûwm (2), to *rise*
7236 rᵉbâh (Ch.) (3), to *increase*
837 auxanō (1), to *grow, i.e. enlarge*

GROWTH
3954 leqesh (2), *after crop, second crop*

GRUDGE
3885 lûwn (1), to *be obstinate*
5201 nâţar (1), to *guard; to cherish anger*
4727 stĕnazō (1), to *sigh, murmur, pray* inaudibly

GRUDGING
1112 gŏggusmŏs (1), *grumbling*

GRUDGINGLY
1537+3077 ĕk (1), *out, out of*

GUARD
2876 ţabbâch (29), *king's guard, executioner*
2877 ţabbâch (Ch.) (1), *king's guard, executioner*
4928 mishma'ath (2), *royal court; subject*
4929 mishmâr (3), *guard; deposit; usage; example*
7323 rûwts (14), to *run*
4759 stratŏpĕdarchēs (1), *military commander*

GUARD'S
2876 ţabbâch (1), *king's guard, executioner*

GUDGODAH
1412 Gudgôdâh (2), *cleft*

GUEST
2647 kataluō (1), to *halt for the night*

GUESTCHAMBER
2646 kataluma (2), *lodging-place*

GUESTS
7121 qârâ' (4), to *call out*
345 anakĕimai (2), to *recline at a meal*

GUIDE
441 'allûwph (4), *friend, one familiar; leader*
833 'âshar (1), to *go forward; guide*
1869 dârak (1), to *tread, trample; to walk, lead*
3289 yâ'ats (1), to *advise*
3557 kûwl (1), to *keep in; to measure*
5090 nâhag (1), to *drive forth; to lead*
5095 nâhal (3), to *flow; to conduct; to protect*

GROWN
5232 hupĕrauxanō (1), to *increase above*

GUIDE (cont.)
5148 nâchâh (4), to *guide*
7101 qâtsîyn (1), *magistrate, leader*
2720 katĕuthunō (1), to *direct, lead, direct*
3594 hŏdēgĕō (2), to *show the way, guide*
3595 hŏdēgŏs (2), *conductor, guide*
3616 ŏikŏdĕspŏtĕō (1), to *be the head of a family*

GUIDED
5090 nâhag (1), to *drive forth; to lead*
5095 nâhal (2), to *flow; to conduct; to protect*
5148 nâchâh (2), to *guide*

GUIDES
3595 hŏdēgŏs (2), *conductor, guide*

GUILE
4820 mirmâh (2), *fraud*
6195 'ormâh (1), *trickery; discretion*
7423 rᵉmîyâh (1), *remissness; treachery*
1388 dŏlŏs (7), *wile, deceit, trickery*

GUILTINESS
817 'âshâm (1), *guilt; fault; sin-offering*

GUILTLESS
5352 nâqâh (5), to *be, make clean; to be bare*
5355 nâqîy (4), *innocent*
338 anaitiŏs (1), *innocent*

GUILTY
816 'âsham (16), to *be guilty; to be punished*
7563 râshâ' (1), *morally wrong; bad person*
1777 ĕnŏchŏs (4), *liable*
3784 ŏphĕilō (1), to *owe; to be under obligation*
5267 hupŏdikŏs (1), *under sentence*

GULF
5490 chasma (1), *ch..sm or vacancy*

GUNI
1476 Gûwnîy (4), *protected*

GUNITES
1477 Gûwnîy (1), *Gunite*

GUR
1483 Gûwr (1), *cub*

GUR-BAAL
1485 Gûwr-Ba'al (1), *dwelling of Baal*

GUSH
5140 nâzal (1), to *drip, or shed by trickling*

GUSHED
2100 zûwb (3), to *flow freely, gush*
8210 shâphak (1), to *spill forth; to expend*
1632 ĕkchĕō (1), to *pour forth; to bestow*

GUTTER
6794 tsinnûwr (1), *culvert, water-shaft*

English

GUTTERS
7298 rahaṭ (2), *ringlet of hair*

HA
1889 he'âch (1), *aha!*

HAAHASHTARI
326 'ăchashtârîy (1), *courier*

HABAIAH
2252 Chăbayâh (2), *Jehovah has hidden*

HABAKKUK
2265 Chăbaqqûwq (2), *embrace*

HABAZINIAH
2262 Chăbatstsanyâh (1), *Chabatstsanjah*

HABERGEON
8302 shiryôwn (1), *corslet, coat of mail*
8473 tachărâ' (2), *linen corslet*

HABERGEONS
8302 shiryôwn (2), *corslet, coat of mail*

HABITABLE
8398 têbêl (1), *earth; world; inhabitants*

HABITATION
1628 gêrûwth (1), *(temporary) residence*
2073 z^ebûwl (3), *residence, dwelling*
2918 ṭiyrâh (1), *fortress; hamlet*
3427 yâshab (3), *to dwell, to remain; to settle*
4186 môwshâb (4), *seat; site; abode*
4349 mâkôwn (2), *basis; place*
4351 m^ekûwrâh (1), *origin*
4583 mâ'ôwn (9), *retreat or asylum dwelling*
4907 mishkan (Ch.) (1), *residence*
4908 mishkân (3), *residence*
5115 nâvâh (1), *to rest as at home*
5116 nâveh (21), *at home; lovely; home*
7931 shâkan (1), *to reside*
7932 sh^ekan (Ch.) (1), *to reside*
7933 sheken (1), *residence*
1886 ĕpaulis (1), *dwelling,residence*
2732 katŏikētēriŏn (2), *dwelling-place, home*
2733 katŏikia (1), *residence, dwelling*
3613 ŏikētēriŏn (1), *residence, home*

HABITATIONS
4186 môwshâb (8), *seat; site; abode*
4380 m^ekêrâh (1), *stabbing-sword*
4583 mâ'ôwn (1), *retreat or asylum dwelling*
4585 m^eôwnâh (1), *abode*
4908 mishkân (2), *residence*

HABOR
2249 Châbôwr (3), *united*

HACHALIAH
2446 Chăkalyâh (2), *darkness (of) Jehovah*

HACHILAH
2444 Chakîylâh (3), *dark*

HACHMONI
2453 Chakmôwnîy (1), *skillful*

HACHMONITE
2453 Chakmôwnîy (1), *skillful*

HAD
935 bôw' (1), *to go, come*
1961 hâyâh (104), *to exist, i.e. be or become*
2370 chăzâ' (Ch.) (1), *to gaze upon; to dream*
3426 yêsh (5), *there is*
3884 lûwlê' (1), *if not*
7760 sûwm (1), *to put*
1096 ginŏmai (1), *to be, become*
1510 ĕimi (8), *I exist, I am*
1746 ĕnduō (1), *to dress*
2192 ĕchō (106), *to have*
2722 katĕchō (1), *to hold down fast*
2983 lambanō (2), *to take, receive*
3844 para (1), *from; with; besides; on account of*
5607 ōn (1), *being, existence*

HADAD
1908 Hădad (13), *Hadad*
2301 Chădad (1), *fierce*

HADADEZER
1909 Hădad'ezer (9), *Hadad (is his) help*

HADADRIMMON
1910 Hădadrimmôwn (1), *Hadad-Rimmon*

HADAR
1924 Hădar (2), *magnificence*

HADAREZER
1928 Hădar'ezer (12), *Hadad is his help*

HADASHAH
2322 Chădâshâh (1), *new*

HADASSAH
1919 Hădaççâh (1), *Esther*

HADATTAH
2675 Châtsôwr Chădattâh (1), *new village*

HADID
2307 Châdîyd (3), *peak*

HADLAI
2311 Chadlay (1), *idle*

HADORAM
1913 Hădôwrâm (4), *Hadoram*

HADRACH
2317 Chadrâk (1), *Syrian deity*

HAFT
5325 nitstsâb (1), *handle of a sword or dagger*

HAGAB
2285 Chăgâb (1), *locust*

HAGABA
2286 Chăgâbâ' (1), *locust*

HAGABAH
2286 Chăgâbâ' (1), *locust*

HAGAR
1904 Hâgâr (12), *Hagar*

HAGARENES
1905 Hagrîy (1), *Hagrite*

HAGARITES
1905 Hagrîy (3), *Hagrite*

HAGERITE
1905 Hagrîy (1), *Hagrite*

HAGGAI
2292 Chaggay (11), *festive*

HAGGERI
1905 Hagrîy (1), *Hagrite*

HAGGI
2291 Chaggîy (2), *festive*

HAGGIAH
2293 Chaggîyâh (1), *festival of Jehovah*

HAGGITES
2291 Chaggîy (2), *festive*

HAGGITH
2294 Chaggîyîth (5), *festive*

HAI
5857 'Ay (2), *ruin*

HAIL
1258 bârad (1), *to rain hail*
1259 bârâd (26), *hail, hailstones*
5463 chairō (6), *salutation, "be well"*
5464 chalaza (4), *frozen ice crystals, i.e. hail*

HAILSTONES
68+417 'eben (3), *stone*
68+1259 'eben (2), *stone*

HAIR
1803 dallâh (1), *loose thread; loose hair*
4748 miqsheh (1), *curl of beautiful tresses*
4803 mâraṭ (2), *to polish; to make bald*
5145 nezer (1), *set apart; royal chaplet*
8177 s^e'ar (Ch.) (2), *hair*
8181 sê'âr (23), *tossed hair*
8185 sa'ărâh (5), *hairiness*
2359 thrix (9), *hair; single hair*
2863 kŏmaō (2), *to wear long hair*
2864 kŏmē (1), *long hair*
4117 plĕgma (1), *plait or braid of hair*
5155 trichinŏs (1), *made of hair*

HAIRS
8177 s^e'ar (Ch.) (1), *hair*
8181 sê'âr (1), *tossed hair*
8185 sa'ărâh (2), *hairiness*
2359 thrix (5), *hair*

HAIRY
1167+8181 ba'al (1), *master; owner; citizen*
8163 sâ'îyr (2), *shaggy; he-goat; goat idol*
8181 sê'âr (2), *tossed hair*

HAKKATAN
6997 Qâṭân (1), *small*

HAKKOZ
6976 Qôwts (1), *thorns*

HAKUPHA
2709 Chăqûwphâ' (2), *to bend, crooked*

HALAH
2477 Chălach (3), *Chalach*

HALAK
2510 Châlâq (2), *bare*

HALE
2694 katasurō (1), *to arrest judicially*

HALF
1235 beqa' (1), *half shekel*
2673 châtsâh (1), *to cut or split in two; to halve*
2677 chêtsîy (106), *half or middle, midst*
4275 mechĕtsâh (2), *halving, half*
4276 machătsîyth (14), *halving or the middle*
8432 tâvek (1), *center, middle*
2253 hēmithanēs (1), *entirely exhausted*
2255 hēmisu (5), *half*
2256 hēmiōriŏn (1), *half-hour*

HALHUL
2478 Chalchûwl (1), *contorted*

HALI
2482 Chălîy (1), *polished trinket, ornament*

HALING
4951 surō (1), *to trail, drag, sweep*

HALL
833 aulē (2), *palace; house; courtyard*
4232 praitōriŏn (6), *governor's court-room*

HALLOHESH
3873 Lôwchêsh (1), *enchanter*

HALLOW
6942 qâdâsh (15), *to be, make clean*

HALLOWED
4720 miqdâsh (1), *sanctuary of deity*
6942 qâdâsh (10), *to be, make clean*
6944 qôdesh (9), *sacred place or thing*
37 hagiazō (2), *to purify or consecrate*

HALOHESH
3873 Lôwchêsh (1), *enchanter*

HALT
6452 pâçach (1), to *hop, skip* over; to *hesitate*
6761 tsela' (1), *limping*
5560 chôlôs (4), *limping, crippled*

HALTED
6761 tsela' (2), *limping*

HALTETH
6761 tsela' (2), *limping*

HALTING
6761 tsela' (1), *limping*

HAM
1990 Hâm (1), *Ham*
2526 Châm (16), *hot*

HAMAN
2001 Hâmân (50), *Haman*

HAMAN'S
2001 Hâmân (3), *Haman*

HAMATH
2574 Chămâth (33), *walled*
2579 Chămath Rabbâh (1), *walled of Rabbah*

HAMATH-ZOBAH
2578 Chămath Tsôwbâh (1), *walled of Tsobah*

HAMATHITE
2577 Chămâthîy (2), *Chamathite*

HAMMATH
2575 Chammath (1), *hot springs*

HAMMEDATHA
4099 Mᵉdâthâ (5), *Medatha*

HAMMELECH
4429 Melek (2), *king*

HAMMER
1989 halmûwth (1), *hammer* or *mallet*
4717 maqqâbâh (1), *hammer*
4718 maqqebeth (1), *hammer*
6360 paṭṭîysh (3), *hammer* which *pounds*

HAMMERS
3597 kêylaph (1), *club* or sledge-hammer
4717 maqqâbâh (2), *hammer*

HAMMOLEKETH
4447 Môleketh (1), *queen*

HAMMON
2540 Chammôwn (2), *warm* spring

HAMMOTH-DOR
2576 Chammôth Dô'r (1), *hot* springs *of Dor*

HAMON-GOG
1996 Hămôwn Gôwg (2), *multitude of Gog*

HAMONAH
1997 Hămôwnâh (1), *multitude*

HAMOR
2544 Chămôwr (12), male donkey or *ass*

HAMOR'S
2544 Chămôwr (1), male donkey or *ass*

HAMUEL
2536 Chammûw'êl (1), *anger of God*

HAMUL
2538 Châmûwl (3), *pitied*

HAMULITES
2539 Châmûwlîy (1), *Chamulite*

HAMUTAL
2537 Chămûwṭal (3), *father-in-law of dew*

HANAMEEL
2601 Chănam'êl (4), *God has favored*

HANAN
2605 Chânân (12), *favor*

HANANEEL
2606 Chănan'êl (4), *God has favored*

HANANI
2607 Chănânîy (11), *gracious*

HANANIAH
2608 Chănanyâh (29), *Jehovah has favored*

HAND
405 'ekeph (1), *stroke, blow*
854 'êth (1), *with; by; at; among*
2026 hârag (1), to *kill, slaughter*
2651 chôphen (1), *pair of fists*
2947 ṭephach (1), *palm-breadth*
2948 ṭôphach (4), *palm-breadth*
3027 yâd (1086), *hand; power*
3028 yad (Ch.) (12), *hand; power*
3079 Yᵉhôwyâqîym (2), *Jehovah will raise*
3221 yâm (Ch.) (1), *sea; basin; west*
3225 yâmîyn (87), *right; south*
3227 yᵉmîynîy (1), *right*
3235 yâmar (1), to *exchange*
3325 Yitshârîy (1), *Jitsharite*
3709 kaph (52), *hollow of hand; paw; sole of foot*
4672 mâtsâ' (1), to *find or acquire*; to *occur*
7126 qârab (4), to *approach, bring near*
7138 qârôwb (5), *near, close*
8040 sᵉmô'wl (14), *north; left* hand
8041 sâma'l (1), to *use* the *left* hand or go *left*
8042 sᵉmâ'lîy (2), on the *left* side; *northern*
1448 ĕggizō (9), to *approach*
1451 ĕggus (6), *near, close*
1764 ĕnistēmi (1), to be *present*

HAMOR'S column continues:
2021 ĕpichĕirĕō (1), to *undertake, try*
2186 ĕphistēmi (1), to be *present*; to *approach*
5495 chĕir (87), *hand*
5496 chĕiragōgĕō (2), to *guide* a blind person by the hand
5497 chĕiragōgŏs (1), *conductor* of a blind person by the hand

HANDBREADTH
2947 ṭephach (2), *palm-breadth*
2948 ṭôphach (1), *palm-breadth*

HANDED
3027 yâd (1), *hand; power*

HANDFUL
4390+3709 mâlĕ' (3), to *fill; be full*
4393+7062 mᵉlô' (2), *fulness*
5995 'âmîyr (1), *bunch of* cereal new-cut grain
6451 piççâh (1), *abundance*
7061 qâmats (1), to *grasp* a handful
7062 qômets (1), *handful; abundance*

HANDFULS
4393+2651 mᵉlô' (1), *fulness*
6653 tsebeth (1), *lock of* stalks, *bundle* of grain
7062 qômets (1), *handful; abundance*
8168 shô'al (2), *palm of* hand; *handful*

HANDKERCHIEFS
4676 sŏudariŏn (1), *towel*

HANDLE
270 'âchaz (1), to *seize, grasp; possess*
4184 mûwsh (1), to *touch, feel*
4900 mâshak (1), to *draw out*; to *be tall*
6186 'ârak (1), to *set in a row*, i.e. *arrange*
8610 tâphas (5), to *manipulate*, i.e. *seize*
2345 thigganō (1), to *touch*
5584 psēlaphaō (1), to *manipulate*

HANDLED
8610+3709 tâphas (1), to *manipulate*, i.e. *seize*
821 atimŏō (1), to *maltreat, disgrace*
5584 psēlaphaō (1), to *manipulate*

HANDLES
3709 kaph (1), *hollow of* hand; *paw; sole* of foot

HANDLETH
5921 'al (1), *above, over, upon,* or *against*
8610 tâphas (2), to *manipulate*, i.e. *seize*

HANDLING
8610 tâphas (1), to *manipulate*, i.e. *seize*

HANDMAID
519 'âmâh (22), *female servant* or *slave*
8198 shiphchâh (22), household *female slave*
1399 dŏulē (1), *female slave*

HANDMAIDEN
1399 dŏulē (1), *female slave*

HANDMAIDENS
8198 shiphchâh (2), household *female slave*
1399 dŏulē (1), *female slave*

HANDMAIDS
519 'âmâh (1), *female servant* or *slave*
8198 shiphchâh (7), household *female slave*

HANDS
2651 chôphen (3), *pair of fists*
3027 yâd (274), *hand; power*
3028 yad (Ch.) (4), *hand; power*
3709 kaph (67), *hollow of hand; paw; sole* of foot
849 autŏchĕir (1), *self-handed, personally*
886 achĕirŏpŏïētŏs (3), *unmanufactured*
2902 kratĕō (2), to *seize*
4084 piazō (1), to *seize, arrest,* or *capture*
4475 rhapisma (1), *slap, strike*
5495 chĕir (90), *hand*
5499 chĕirŏpŏïētŏs (6), of *human construction*

HANDSTAVES
4731+3027 maqqêl (1), *shoot; stick; staff*

HANDWRITING
5498 chĕirŏgraphŏn (1), *document or bond*

HANDYWORK
4639+3027 ma'ăseh (1), *action; labor*

HANES
2609 Chânêç (1), *Chanes*

HANG
3363 yâqa' (2), to be *dislocated*; to *impale*
3381 yârad (1), to *descend*
5414 nâthan (3), to *give*
5628 çârach (2), to *extend even to excess*
8511 tâlâ' (1), to *suspend*; to *be uncertain*
8518 tâlâh (7), to *suspend, hang*
2910 krĕmannumi (2), to *hang*
3935 pariēmi (1), to *neglect*; to *be weakened*

HANGED
2614 chânaq (1), to *choke oneself*
3363 yâqa' (2), to be *dislocated*; to *impale*

4223 mᵉchâ' (Ch.) (1), to *strike; to impale*

8511 tâlâ' (1), to *suspend; to be uncertain*

8518 tâlâh (18), to *suspend, hang*

519 apagchŏmai (1), to *strangle oneself*

2910 krĕmannumi (4), to *hang*

4029 pĕrikĕimai (2), to *enclose, encircle*

HANGETH
8518 tâlâh (1), to *suspend, hang*

2910 krĕmannumi (1), to *hang*

HANGING
4539 mâçâk (17), *veil; shield*

8518 tâlâh (1), to *suspend, hang*

HANGINGS
1004 bayith (1), *house; temple; family, tribe*

7050 qela' (15), *slinging weapon; door screen*

HANIEL
2592 Chănnîy'êl (1), *favor of God*

HANNAH
2584 Channâh (13), *favored*

HANNATHON
2615 Channâthôn (1), *favored*

HANNIEL
2592 Chănnîy'êl (1), *favor of God*

HANOCH
2585 Chănôwk (5), *initiated*

HANOCHITES
2599 Chănôkîy (1), *Chanokite*

HANUN
2586 Chânûwn (11), *favored*

HAP
4745 miqreh (1), *accident or fortune*

HAPHRAIM
2663 Chăphârayîm (1), *double pit*

HAPLY
3863 lûw' (1), *if; would that!*

686 ara (2), *then, so, therefore*

3379 mĕpŏtĕ (2), *not ever; if, or lest ever*

3381 mĕpōs (1), *lest somehow*

HAPPEN
579 'ânâh (1), to *meet, to happen*

7136 qârâh (2), to *bring about; to impose*

4819 sumbainō (1), to *concur, happen*

HAPPENED
1961 hâyâh (1), to *exist, i.e. be or become*

7122 qârâ' (2), to *encounter, to happen*

7136 qârâh (2), to *bring about; to impose*

1096 ginŏmai (1), to *be, become*

4819 sumbainō (5), to *concur, happen*

HAPPENETH
4745 miqreh (1), *accident or fortune*

5060 nâga' (2), to *strike*

7136 qârâh (3), to *bring about; to impose*

HAPPIER
3107 makariŏs (1), *fortunate, well off*

HAPPY
833 'âshar (2), to *be honest, prosper*

835 'esher (16), how *happy!*

837 'ôsher (1), *happiness, blessedness*

7951 shâlâh (1), to *be tranquil, i.e. secure*

3106 makarizō (1), to *esteem fortunate*

3107 makariŏs (5), *fortunate, well off*

HARA
2024 Hârâ' (1), *mountainousness*

HARADAH
2732 Chărâdâh (2), *fear, anxiety*

HARAN
2039 Hârân (1), *mountaineer*

2309 chedel (6), *state of the dead, deceased*

2771 Chârân (12), *parched*

HARARITE
2043 Hărârîy (5), *mountaineer*

HARBONA
2726 Charbôwnâ' (1), *Charbona, Charbonah*

HARBONAH
2726 Charbôwnâ' (1), *Charbona, Charbonah*

HARD
280 'ăchîydâh (Ch.) (1), *enigma*

386 'êythân (1), *never-failing; eternal*

681 'êtsel (1), *side; near*

1692 dâbaq (4), to *cling or adhere; to catch*

2420 chîydâh (2), *puzzle; conundrum; maxim*

3332 yâtsaq (1), to *pour out*

3515 kâbêd (2), *severe, difficult, stupid*

5066 nâgash (1), to *be, come, bring near*

5221 nâkâh (1), to *strike, kill*

5564 çâmak (1), to *lean upon; take hold of*

5980 'ummâh (1), *near, beside, along with*

6277 'âthâq (1), *impudent*

6381 pâlâ' (5), to *be, make great, difficult*

7185 qâshâh (5), to *be tough or severe*

7186 qâsheh (6), *severe*

1421 dusĕrmĕnĕutŏs (1), *difficult to explain*

1422 duskŏlŏs (1), *impracticable, difficult*

1425 dusnŏĕtŏs (1), *difficult of perception*

4642 sklĕrŏs (5), *hard or tough; harsh, severe*

4927 sunŏmŏrĕō (1), to *border together*

HARDEN
533 'ammîyts (1), *strong; mighty; brave*

2388 châzaq (4), to *be obstinate; to bind*

5513 Çîynîy (1), *Sinite*

5539 çâlad (1), to *leap with joy*

7185 qâshâh (2), to *be tough or severe*

4645 sklĕrunō (3), to *indurate, be stubborn*

HARDENED
553 'âmats (1), to *be strong; be courageous*

2388 châzaq (9), to *be obstinate; to bind*

3513 kâbad (4), to *be heavy, severe, dull*

3515 kâbêd (3), *severe, difficult, stupid*

7185 qâshâh (8), to *be tough or severe*

7188 qâshach (2), to *be, make unfeeling*

8631 tᵉqêph (Ch.) (1), to *be obstinate*

4456 pōrŏō (3), to *render stupid or callous*

4645 sklĕrunō (2), to *indurate, be stubborn*

HARDENETH
5810 'âzaz (1), to *be stout; be bold*

7185 qâshâh (2), to *be tough or severe*

4645 sklĕrunō (1), to *indurate, be stubborn*

HARDER
2388 châzaq (1), to *be obstinate; to bind*

2389 châzâq (1), *strong; severe, hard, violent*

HARDHEARTED
7186+3820 qâsheh (1), *severe*

HARDLY
6031 'ânâh (1), to *afflict, be afflicted*

7185 qâshâh (2), to *be tough or severe*

1423 duskŏlŏs (3), *impracticably, with difficulty*

3425 mŏgis (1), *with difficulty*

3433 mŏlis (1), *with difficulty*

HARDNESS
4165 mûwtsâq (1), *casting of metal*

2553 kakŏpathĕō (1), to *undergo hardship*

4457 pōrōsis (1), *stupidity or callousness*

4641 sklĕrŏkardia (3), *hard-heartedness*

4643 sklĕrŏtēs (1), *stubbornness*

HARE
768 'arnebeth (2), *hare, rabbit*

HAREPH
2780 Chârêph (1), *reproachful*

HARETH
2802 Chereth (1), *forest*

HARHAIAH
2736 Charhăyâh (1), *fearing Jehovah*

HARHAS
2745 Charchaç (1), *sun*

HARHUR
2744 Charchûwr (2), *inflammation*

HARIM
2766 Chârîm (11), *snub-nosed*

HARIPH
2756 Chârîyph (2), *autumnal*

HARLOT
2181 zânâh (33), to *commit adultery*

6948 qᵉdêshâh (3), *sacred female prostitute*

4204 pŏrnē (4), *strumpet, i.e. prostitute; idolater*

HARLOT'S
2181 zânâh (2), to *commit adultery*

HARLOTS
2181 zânâh (2), to *commit adultery*

6948 qᵉdêshâh (1), *sacred female prostitute*

4204 pŏrnē (4), *strumpet, i.e. prostitute; idolater*

HARLOTS'
2181 zânâh (1), to *commit adultery*

HARM
1697+7451 dâbâr (1), *word; matter; thing*

2398 châtâ' (1), to *sin*

3415 yâra' (1), to *fear*

7451 ra' (4), *bad; evil*

7489 râ'a' (3), to *make, be good for nothing*

824 atŏpŏs (1), *improper; injurious; wicked*

2556 kakŏs (2), *bad, evil, wrong*

2559 kakŏō (1), to *injure; to oppress; to embitter*

4190 pŏnērŏs (1), *malice, wicked, bad; crime*

5196 hubris (1), *insult; injury*

HARMLESS
172 akakŏs (1), *innocent, blameless*

185 akĕraiŏs (2),
innocent

HARNEPHER
2774 Charnepher (1),
Charnepher

HARNESS
631 'âçar (1), to *fasten*; to
join battle
5402 nesheq (1), *military
arms, arsenal*
8302 shiryôwn (2),
corslet, coat of mail

HARNESSED
2571 châmûsh (1),
able-bodied *soldiers*

HAROD
5878 'Êyn Chărôd (1),
fountain of trembling

HARODITE
2733 Chărôdîy (1),
Charodite

HAROEH
7204 Rô'êh (1), *seer*

HARORITE
2033 Hărôwrîy (1),
mountaineer

HAROSHETH
2800 Chărôsheth (3),
skilled *worker*

HARP
3658 kinnôwr (25), *harp*
7030 qîythârôç (Ch.) (4),
lyre
2788 kithara (1), *lyre*

HARPED
2789 kitharizō (1), to
play a lyre

HARPERS
2790 kitharōįdŏs (2), one
who *plays a lyre*

HARPING
2789 kitharizō (1), to
play a lyre

HARPS
3658 kinnôwr (17), *harp*
2788 kithara (3), *lyre*

HARROW
7702 sâdad (1), to
harrow a field

HARROWS
2757 chârîyts (2),
threshing-sledge; slice

HARSHA
2797 Charshâ' (2),
magician

HART
354 'ayâl (9), *stag deer*

HARTS
354 'ayâl (2), *stag deer*

HARUM
2037 Hârûm (1), *high,
exalted*

HARUMAPH
2739 Chărûwmaph (1),
snub-nosed

HARUPHITE
2741 Chărûwphîy (1),
Charuphite

HARUZ
2743 Chârûwts (1),
earnest

HARVEST
7105 qâtsîyr (47),
harvest; limb of a tree
2326 thĕrismŏs (13),
harvest, crop

HARVESTMAN
7105 qâtsîyr (1), *harvest;
limb* of a tree
7114 qâtsar (1), to
curtail, cut short

HASADIAH
2619 Chăçadyâh (1),
Jehovah has favored

HASENUAH
5574 Çᵉnûw'âh (1),
pointed

HASHABIAH
2811 Chăshabyâh (15),
Jehovah has regarded

HASHABNAH
2812 Chăshabnâh (1),
inventiveness

HASHABNIAH
2813 Chăshabnᵉyâh (2),
thought of Jehovah

HASHBADANA
2806 Chashbaddânâh
(1), *considerate judge*

HASHEM
2044 Hâshêm (1), *wealthy*

HASHMONAH
2832 Chashmônâh (2),
fertile

HASHUB
2815 Chashshûwb (4),
intelligent

HASHUBAH
2807 Chăshûbâh (1),
estimation

HASHUM
2828 Chăshûm (5),
enriched

HASHUPHA
2817 Chăsûwphâ' (1),
nakedness

HASRAH
2641 Chaçrâh (1), *want*

HASSENAAH
5570 Çᵉnâ'âh (1), *thorny*

HASSHUB
2815 Chashshûwb (1),
intelligent

HAST
1961 hâyâh (2), to *exist*,
i.e. *be* or *become*
3426 yêsh (3), there *is* or
are
2076 ĕsti (1), he (she or
it) *is*; they *are*
2192 ĕchō (28), to *have;
hold; keep*
5224 huparchŏnta (1),
property or *possessions*

HASTE
213 'ûwts (1), to *be close,
hurry, withdraw*
924 bᵉhîylûw (Ch.) (1),
hastily, at once
926 bâhal (1), to *hasten,
hurry anxiously*
927 bᵉhal (Ch.) (3), to
terrify; hasten

1272 bârach (1), to *flee*
suddenly
2363 chûwsh (11), to
hurry; to be eager
2439 chîysh (1), to *hurry,
hasten*
2648 châphaz (5), to
hasten away, to fear
2649 chippâzôwn (3),
hasty flight
4116 mâhar (20), to
hurry; promptly
5169 nâchats (1), to *be
urgent*
4692 spĕudō (4), to *urge*
on diligently
4710 spŏudē (2),
despatch; eagerness

HASTED
213 'ûwts (2), to *be close,
hurry, withdraw*
926 bâhal (1), to *hasten,
hurry anxiously*
1765 dâchaph (2), to
urge; to hasten
2363 chûwsh (2), to
hurry; to be eager
2648 châphaz (2), to
hasten away, to fear
4116 mâhar (14), to
hurry; promptly
4692 spĕudō (1), to *urge*
on diligently

HASTEN
2363 chûwsh (4), to
hurry; to be eager
4116 mâhar (3), to *hurry;
promptly*
8245 shâqad (1), to *be
alert*, i.e. *sleepless*

HASTENED
213 'ûwts (2), to *be close,
hurry, withdraw*
926 bâhal (1), to *hasten,
hurry anxiously*
1765 dâchaph (1), to
urge; to hasten
4116 mâhar (2), to *hurry;
promptly*

HASTENETH
4116 mâhar (1), to *hurry;
promptly*

HASTETH
213 'ûwts (1), to *be close,
hurry, withdraw*
926 bâhal (1), to *hasten,
hurry anxiously*
2363 chûwsh (1), to
hurry; to be eager
2648 châphaz (1), to
hasten away, to fear
2907 tûws (1), to *pounce
or swoop upon*
4116 mâhar (3), to *hurry;
promptly*
7602 shâ'aph (1), to *be
angry; to hasten*

HASTILY
926 bâhal (1), to *hasten,
hurry anxiously*
4116 mâhar (2), to *hurry;
promptly*
4118 mahêr (2), *in a
hurry*
4120 mᵉhêrâh (1), *hurry;
promptly*
7323 rûwts (1), to *run*

5030 tachĕōs (1),
speedily, rapidly

HASTING
4106 mâhîyr (1), *skillful*
4692 spĕudō (1), to *urge*
on diligently

HASTY
213 'ûwts (2), to *be close,
hurry, withdraw*
926 bâhal (2), to *hasten,
hurry anxiously*
1061 bikkûwr (1),
first-fruits of the crop
2685 chătsaph (Ch.) (1),
to *be severe*
4116 mâhar (2), to *hurry;
promptly*
7116 qâtsêr (1), *short*

HASUPHA
2817 Chăsûwphâ' (1),
nakedness

HATACH
2047 Hăthâk (4), *Hathak*

HATCH
1234 bâqa' (1), to *cleave,
break, tear open*

HATCHETH
3205 yâlad (1), to *bear
young*; to *father a child*

HATE
7852 sâṭam (2), to
persecute
8130 sânê' (67), to *hate*
8131 sᵉnê' (Ch.) (1),
enemy
3404 misĕō (16), to
detest, to *love less*

HATED
7852 sâṭam (2), to
persecute
8130 sânê' (42), to *hate*
8135 sin'âh (2), *hate,
malice*
8146 sânîy' (1), *hated*
3404 misĕō (12), to
detest; to love less

HATEFUL
8130 sânê' (1), to *hate*
3404 misĕō (1), to *detest,
persecute; to love less*
4767 stugnētŏs (1),
hated, i.e. *odious*

HATEFULLY
8135 sin'âh (1), *hate,
malice*

HATERS
8130 sânê' (1), to *hate*
2319 thĕŏstugēs (1),
impious, God-hating

HATEST
8130 sânê' (5), to *hate*
3404 misĕō (1), to *detest,
persecute; to love less*

HATETH
7852 sâṭam (1), to
persecute
8130 sânê' (20), to *hate*
3404 misĕō (9), to *detest,
persecute; to love less*

HATH
413 'êl (1), *to, toward*
1167 ba'al (3), *master;
husband; owner; citizen*

English

HATHATH

1172 ba'ălâh (2), *mistress; female owner*
1933 hâvâ' (1), *to be, to exist*
1961 hâyâh (6), *to exist, i.e. be or become*
3426 yêsh (3), *there is or are*
4672 mâtsâ' (1), *to find or acquire; to occur, meet or be present*
2192 ĕchō (128), *to have; hold; keep*
5220 hupandrŏs (1), *married woman*
5224 huparchŏnta (2), *property or possessions*

HATHATH

2867 Chăthath (1), *dismay*

HATING

8130 sânê' (1), *to hate*
3404 misĕŏ (2), *to detest, persecute; to love less*

HATIPHA

2412 Chăṭîyphâ' (2), *robber*

HATITA

2410 Chăṭîyṭa' (2), *explorer*

HATRED

342 'êybâh (2), *hostility*
4895 masṭêmâh (2), *enmity*
8135 sin'âh (13), *hate, malice*
2189 ĕchthra (1), *hostility; opposition*

HATS

3737 karbᵉlâ' (Ch.) (1), *mantle*

HATTIL

2411 Chaṭṭîyl (2), *fluctuating*

HATTUSH

2407 Chaṭṭûwsh (5), *Chattush*

HAUGHTILY

7317 rôwmâh (1), *proudly*

HAUGHTINESS

1346 ga'ăvâh (2), *arrogance; majesty*
7312 rûwm (3), *elevation; elation*

HAUGHTY

1361 gâbahh (5), *to be lofty; to be haughty*
1363 gâbôah (1), *height; grandeur; arrogance*
1364 gâbôahh (1), *high; powerful; arrogant*
3093 yâhîyr (1), *arrogant*
4791 mârôwm (1), *elevation; haughtiness*
7311 rûwm (1), *to be high; to rise or raise*

HAUNT

1980 hâlak (1), *to walk; live a certain way*
3427 yâshab (1), *to dwell, to remain; to settle*
7272 regel (1), *foot; step*

HAURAN

2362 Chavrân (2), *cavernous*

HAVE

270 'âchaz (1), *to seize, grasp; possess*
383 'îythay (Ch.) (3), *there is*
935 bôw' (1), *to go, come*
1167 ba'al (1), *master; husband; owner; citizen*
1934 hăvâ' (Ch.) (2), *to be, to exist*
1961 hâyâh (87), *to exist, i.e. be or become*
3045 yâda' (2), *to know*
3318 yâtsâ' (3), *to go, bring out*
3426 yêsh (12), *there is*
3947 lâqach (1), *to take*
4672 mâtsâ' (1), *to find or acquire; to occur*
5307 nâphal (1), *to fall*
5375 nâsâ' (1), *to lift up*
5674 'âbar (1), *to cross over; to transition*
5921 'al (1), *above, over, upon, or against*
474 antiballō (1), *to exchange words*
568 apĕchō (4), *to be distant*
1096 ginŏmai (1), *to be, become*
1099 glukus (1), *sweet, fresh*
1526 ĕisi (1), *they are*
1699 ĕmŏs (1), *my*
1751 ĕnĕimi (1), *to be within*
2070 ĕsmĕn (1), *we are*
2071 ĕsŏmai (6), *will be*
2076 ĕsti (11), *he (she or it) is; they are*
2192 ĕchō (266), *to have; hold; keep*
2701 katatrĕchō (1), *to hasten, run*
2983 lambanō (1), *to take, receive*
3335 mĕtalambanō (1), *to accept and use*
3918 parĕimi (1), *to be present; to have come*
5224 huparchŏnta (1), *property or possessions*
5225 huparchō (1), *to come into existence*

HAVEN

2348 chôwph (2), *cove, sheltered bay*
4231 mâchôwz (1), *harbor*
3040 limēn (2), *harbor*

HAVENS

2568 Kalŏi Limĕnĕs (1), *Good Harbors*

HAVILAH

2341 Chăvîylâh (7), *circular*

HAVING

1167 ba'al (2), *master; husband; owner; citizen*
5414 nâthan (1), *to give*
1746 ĕnduō (1), *to dress*
2192 ĕchō (85), *to have; hold; keep*

HAVOCK

3075 lumainŏmai (1), *to insult, maltreat*

HAVOTH-JAIR

2334 Chavvôwth Yâ'îyr (2), *hamlets of Jair*

HAWK

5322 nêts (3), *flower; hawk*
8464 tachmâç (2), *unclean bird (poss.) owl*

HAY

2682 châtsîyr (2), *grass; leek plant*
5528 chŏrtŏs (1), *pasture, herbage or vegetation*

HAZAEL

2371 Chăzâ'êl (23), *God has seen*

HAZAIAH

2382 Chăzâyâh (1), *Jehovah has seen*

HAZAR-ADDAR

2692 Chătsar 'Addâr (1), *village of Addar*

HAZAR-ENAN

2703 Chătsar 'Êynôwn (1), *village of springs*
2704 Chătsar 'Êynân (3), *village of springs*

HAZAR-GADDAH

2693 Chătsar Gaddâh (1), *village of Fortune*

HAZAR-HATTICON

2694 Chătsar hat-Tîykôwn (1), *village of the middle*

HAZAR-SHUAL

2705 Chătsar Shûw'âl (4), *village of (the) fox*

HAZAR-SUSAH

2701 Chătsar Çûwçâh (1), *village of cavalry*

HAZAR-SUSIM

2702 Chătsar Çûwçîym (1), *village of horses*

HAZARDED

3860 paradidōmi (1), *to hand over*

HAZARMAVETH

2700 Chătsarmâveth (2), *village of death*

HAZAZON-TAMAR

2688 Chatsᵉtsôwn Tâmâr (1), *row of (the) palm-tree*

HAZEL

3869 lûwz (1), *nut-tree, (poss.) almond*

HAZELELPONI

6753 Tsᵉlelpôwnîy (1), *shade-facing*

HAZERIM

2699 Chătsêrîym (1), *yards*

HAZEROTH

2698 Chătsêrowth (6), *yards*

HAZEZON-TAMAR

2688 Chatsᵉtsôwn Tâmâr (1), *row of (the) palm-tree*

HAZIEL

2381 Chăzîy'êl (1), *seen of God*

HAZO

2375 Chăzow (1), *seer*

HAZOR

2674 Châtsôwr (18), *village*
2675 Châtsôwr Chădattâh (1), *new village*

HEAD

1270 barzel (2), *iron; iron implement*
1538 gulgôleth (1), *skull*
3852 lehâbâh (1), *flame; flash*
4763 mᵉra'ăshâh (1), *headpiece; head-rest*
6936 qoḏqôḏ (8), *crown of the head*
7217 rê'sh (Ch.) (11), *head*
7218 rô'sh (262), *head*
2775 kĕphalaiŏŏ (1), *to strike on the head*
2776 kĕphalē (55), *head*

HEADBANDS

7196 qishshûr (1), *girdle or sash for women*

HEADLONG

2630 katakrēmnizŏ (1), *to precipitate down*
4248 prēnēs (1), *head foremost, headlong*

HEADS

7217 rê'sh (Ch.) (1), *head*
7218 rô'sh (83), *head*
2776 kĕphalē (19), *head*

HEADSTONE

68+7222 'eben (1), *stone*

HEADY

4312 prŏpĕtēs (1), *falling forward headlong*

HEAL

7495 râphâ' (21), *to cure, heal*
1295 diasōzō (1), *to cure, preserve, rescue*
2323 thĕrapĕuō (10), *to relieve disease*
2390 iaŏmai (6), *to cure, heal*
2392 iasis (2), *curing*

HEALED

5414+7499 nâthan (1), *to give*
7495 râphâ' (31), *to cure, heal*
2323 thĕrapĕuō (25), *to relieve disease*
2390 iaŏmai (18), *to cure, heal*
4982 sōzō (3), *to deliver; to protect*

HEALER

2280 châbash (1), *to wrap firmly, bind*

HEALETH

7495 râphâ' (4), *to cure, heal*

HEALING

3545 kêhâh (1), *alleviation, i.e. a cure*
4832 marpê' (3), *cure; deliverance; placidity*
8585 tᵉâlâh (1), *bandage or plaster*

2322 thĕrăpĕia (2), *cure, healing; domestics*
2323 thĕrăpĕuō (3), *to relieve disease*
2386 iama (2), *cure*
2390 iaŏmai (1), *to cure, heal*
2392 iasis (1), *curing*

HEALINGS
2386 iama (1), *cure*

HEALTH
724 *'ărûwkâh* (4), *wholeness, health*
3444 y⁰shûw'âh (2), *aid; victory; prosperity*
4832 marpê' (5), *cure; deliverance; placidity*
7500 riph'ûwth (1), *cure, healing*
7965 shâlôwm (2), *safe; well; health, prosperity*
4491 rhiza (1), *root*
5198 hugiainō (1), *to have sound health*

HEAP
1530 gal (12), *heap; ruins*
2266 châbar (1), *to fascinate by spells*
2563 chômer (1), *clay; dry measure*
2846 châthâh (1), *to lay hold of; to pick up fire*
3664 kânaç (1), *to collect; to enfold*
4596 m⁰'îy (1), *pile of rubbish, ruin*
5067 nêd (6), *mound, heap, dam*
5595 çâphâh (1), *to scrape; to accumulate*
5856 'îy (1), *ruin; rubble*
6194 'ârêm (3), *heap, mound; sheaf*
6651 tsâbar (2), *to aggregate, gather*
7235 râbâh (1), *to increase*
7760 sûwm (1), *to put, place*
8510 têl (4), *mound*
2002 ĕpisōrĕuō (1), *to accumulate further*
4987 sōrĕuō (1), *to pile up, load up*

HEAPED
6651 tsâbar (1), *to aggregate, gather*
2343 thēsaurizō (1), *to amass or reserve, store*

HEAPETH
6651 tsâbar (1), *to aggregate, gather*
6908 qâbats (1), *to collect, assemble*

HEAPS
1530 gal (6), *heap; ruins*
2563 chômer (1), *clay; dry measure*
2565 chămôrâh (1), *heap*
5856 'îy (3), *ruin; rubble*
6194 'ârêm (6), *heap, mound; sheaf*
6632 tsâb (1), *lizard; covered cart*
8564 tamrûwr (1), *erection, i.e. pillar*

HEAR
238 'âzan (2), *to listen*
2045 hâshmâ'ûwth (1), *communication*
6030 'ânâh (28), *to respond, answer*
7181 qâshab (1), *to prick up the ears*
8085 shâma' (364), *to hear*
8086 sh⁰ma' (Ch.) (4), *to hear*
191 akŏuō (131), *to hear; obey*
1251 diakŏuŏmai (1), *to patiently listen*
1522 ĕisakŏuō (1), *to listen to*
3878 parakŏuō (2), *to disobey*

HEARD
6030 'ânâh (11), *to respond, answer*
7181 qâshab (1), *to prick up the ears*
8085 shâma' (376), *to hear*
8086 sh⁰ma' (Ch.) (4), *to hear*
189 akŏē (1), *hearing; thing heard*
191 akŏuō (239), *to hear; obey*
1522 ĕisakŏuō (4), *to listen to*
1873 ĕpakŏuō (1), *to hearken favorably to*
1874 ĕpakrŏaŏmai (1), *listen intently to*
4257 prŏakŏuō (1), *to hear beforehand*

HEARDEST
6030 'ânâh (1), *to respond, answer*
8085 shâma' (11), *to hear*

HEARER
202 akrŏatēs (2), *hearer*

HEARERS
191 akŏuō (2), *to hear; obey*
202 akrŏatēs (2), *hearer*

HEAREST
6030 'ânâh (1), *to respond, answer*
8085 shâma' (6), *to hear*
191 akŏuō (4), *to hear; obey*

HEARETH
8085 shâma' (29), *to hear*
191 akŏuō (22), *to hear; obey*

HEARING
241 'ôzen (5), *ear*
4926 mishmâ' (1), *report*
7182 qesheb (1), *hearkening*
8085 shâma' (6), *to hear*
8088 shēma' (1), *something heard*
189 akŏē (10), *hearing; thing heard*
191 akŏuō (13), *to hear; obey*
201 akrŏatēriŏn (1), *audience-room*

1233 diagnōsis (1), *magisterial examination*

HEARKEN
238 'âzan (5), *to listen*
7181 qâshab (21), *to prick up the ears*
8085 shâma' (119), *to hear*
191 akŏuō (6), *to hear; obey*
1801 ĕnōtizŏmai (1), *to take in one's ear*
5219 hupakŏuō (1), *to listen attentively*

HEARKENED
238 'âzan (1), *to listen*
7181 qâshab (5), *to prick up the ears*
8085 shâma' (74), *to hear*
3980 pĕitharchĕō (1), *to submit to authority*

HEARKENEDST
8085 shâma' (1), *to hear*

HEARKENETH
8085 shâma' (2), *to hear*

HEARKENING
8085 shâma' (1), *to hear*

HEART
1079 bâl (Ch.) (1), *heart, mind*
3820 lêb (479), *heart*
3821 lêb (Ch.) (1), *heart*
3823 lâbab (2), *to transport with love*
3824 lêbâb (207), *heart*
3825 l⁰bab (Ch.) (7), *heart*
3826 libbâh (2), *heart*
4578 mê'âh (1), *viscera; anguish, tenderness*
5315 nephesh (12), *life; breath; soul; wind*
7130 qereb (1), *nearest part, i.e. the center*
7907 sekvîy (1), *mind*
2588 kardia (101), *heart, i.e. thoughts or feelings*
4641 sklērŏkardia (2), *hard-heartedness*
5590 psuchē (1), *soul, vitality; heart, mind*

HEART'S
3820 lêb (1), *heart*
5315 nephesh (1), *life; breath; soul; wind*
2588 kardia (1), *heart, i.e. thoughts or feelings*

HEARTED
3820 lêb (8), *heart*

HEARTH
254 'âch (3), *fire-pot*
3344 yâqad (1), *to burn*
3595 kîyôwr (1), *dish; caldron; washbowl*
4168 môwqêd (1), *conflagration, burning*

HEARTILY
1537+5590 ĕk (1), *out, out of*

HEARTS
3820 lêb (21), *heart*
3824 lêbâb (22), *heart*
3826 libbâh (6), *heart*
5315 nephesh (2), *life; breath; soul; wind*

674 apŏpsuchō (1), *to faint*
2588 kardia (57), *heart, i.e. thoughts or feelings*
2589 kardiŏgnōstēs (2), *heart-knower*
4641 sklērŏkardia (1), *hard-heartedness*

HEARTS'
3820 lêb (1), *heart*

HEARTY
5315 nephesh (1), *life; breath; soul; wind*

HEAT
228 'ăzâ' (Ch.) (1), *to heat*
2527 chôm (9), *heat*
2534 chêmâh (1), *heat; anger; poison*
2535 chammâh (1), *heat of sun*
2552 châmam (2), *to be hot; to be in a rage*
2721 chôreb (6), *parched; ruined*
2750 chŏrîy (1), *burning anger*
3179 yâcham (1), *to conceive*
7565 resheph (1), *flame*
8273 shârâb (1), *glow of the hot air; mirage*
2329 thĕrmē (2), *warmth, heat*
2738 kauma (2), *scorching heat*
2741 kausŏō (2), *to set on fire*
2742 kausŏn (3), *burning heat, hot day*

HEATED
228 'ăzâ' (Ch.) (1), *to heat*
1197 bâ'ar (1), *to be brutish, be senseless*

HEATH
6176 'ărôw'êr (2), *juniper bush*

HEATHEN
1471 gôwy (143), *foreign nation; Gentiles*
1482 ĕthnikŏs (2), *Gentile*
1484 ĕthnŏs (5), *race; tribe; pagan*

HEAVE
7311 rûwm (1), *to be high; to rise or raise*
8641 t⁰rûwmâh (28), *sacrifice, tribute*

HEAVED
7311 rûwm (3), *to be high; to rise or raise*

HEAVEN
1534 galgal (1), *wheel; something round*
7834 shachaq (2), *firmament, clouds*
8064 shâmayim (285), *sky; unseen celestial places*
8065 shâmayin (Ch.) (35), *sky; unseen celestial places*
2032 ĕpŏuraniŏs (1), *above the sky, celestial*
3321 mĕsŏuranēma (3), *mid-sky, mid-heaven*

English

HEAVEN'S
3771 ŏuranŏthĕn (2), from the sky or heaven
3772 ŏuranŏs (248), sky; air; heaven

HEAVEN'S
3772 ŏuranŏs (1), sky; air; heaven

HEAVENLY
1537+3772 ĕk (1), out, out of
2032 ĕpŏuraniŏs (16), above the sky, celestial
3770 ŏuraniŏs (6), belonging to or coming from the sky or heaven

HEAVENS
6160 'ărâbâh (1), desert, wasteland
6183 'ărîyph (1), sky
8064 shâmayim (107), sky; unseen celestial places
8065 shâmayin (Ch.) (3), sky; unseen celestial places
3772 ŏuranŏs (19), sky; air; heaven

HEAVIER
3513 kâbad (3), to be heavy, severe, dull

HEAVILY
3513 kâbad (1), to be heavy, severe, dull
3517 kᵉbêdûth (1), difficulty
6957 qav (1), rule for measuring; rim

HEAVINESS
1674 dᵉ'âgâh (1), anxiety
3544 kêheh (1), feeble; obscure
5136 nûwsh (1), to be sick
6440 pânîym (1), face; front
8386 ta'ănîyâh (1), lamentation
8424 tûwgâh (3), depression; grief
8589 ta'ănîyth (1), affliction of self, fasting
85 adēmŏnĕŏ (1), to be in mental distress
2726 katēphĕia (1), sadness, dejection
3076 lupĕŏ (1), to distress; to be sad
3077 lupē (2), sadness, grief

HEAVY
3513 kâbad (16), to be heavy, severe, dull
3514 kôbed (2), weight, multitude, vehemence
3515 kâbêd (8), severe, difficult, stupid
4133 môwṭah (1), pole; ox-bow; yoke
4751 mar (1), bitter; bitterness; bitterly
5620 çar (2), peevish, sullen
7186 qâsheh (1), severe
7451 ra' (1), bad; evil
85 adēmŏnĕŏ (2), to be in mental distress
916 barĕŏ (3), to weigh down, cause pressure

926 barus (1), weighty

HEBER
2268 Cheber (10), community
5677 'Êber (2), regions beyond
1443 Ĕbĕr (1), regions beyond

HEBER'S
2268 Cheber (1), community

HEBERITES
2277 Chebrîy (1), Chebrite

HEBREW
5680 'Ibrîy (14), Eberite (i.e. Hebrew)
1444 Hĕbraïkŏs (1), Hebraïc or the Jewish language
1446 Hĕbrais (4), Hebrew or Jewish language
1447 Hĕbraïsti (6), Hebraistically or in the Jewish language

HEBREWESS
5680 'Ibrîy (1), Eberite (i.e. Hebrew)

HEBREWS
5680 'Ibrîy (17), Eberite (i.e. Hebrew)
1445 Hĕbraiŏs (3), Hebrew or Jew

HEBREWS'
5680 'Ibrîy (1), Eberite (i.e. Hebrew)

HEBRON
2275 Chebrôwn (72), seat of association

HEBRONITES
2276 Chebrôwnîy (6), Chebronite

HEDGE
1447 gâdêr (3), enclosure, wall or fence
4534 mᵉçûwkâh (1), thorn-hedge
4881 mᵉsûwkâh (2), thorn hedge
7753 sûwk (2), to shut in with hedges
5418 phragmŏs (1), fence or enclosing barrier

HEDGED
1443 gâdar (1), to build a stone wall
5526 çâkak (1), to entwine; to fence in
5418+4060 phragmŏs (1), fence or barrier

HEDGES
1447 gâdêr (1), enclosure, wall or fence
1448 gᵉdêrâh (4), enclosure for flocks
5418 phragmŏs (1), fence or enclosing barrier

HEED
238 'âzan (1), to listen
2095 zᵉhar (Ch.) (1), be admonished, be careful
5414+3820 nâthan (1), to give
5535 çâkath (1), to be silent

7181 qâshab (3), to prick up the ears
7182 qesheb (1), hearkening
7200 râ'âh (2), to see
8104 shâmar (35), to watch
433 anēkŏ (1), be proper, fitting
991 blĕpō (14), to look at
1907 ĕpĕchō (2), to detain; to pay attention
3708 hŏraō (5), to stare, see clearly; to discern
4337 prŏsĕchō (11), to pay attention to
4648 skŏpĕŏ (1), to watch out for, i.e. to regard

HEEL
6117 'âqab (1), to seize by the heel; to circumvent
6119 'âqêb (4), track, footprint; rear position
4418 ptĕrna (1), heel

HEELS
6119 'âqêb (2), track, footprint; rear position
6120 'âqêb (1), one who lies in wait
8328 sheresh (1), root

HEGAI
1896 Hêgê' (3), Hege or Hegai

HEGE
1896 Hêgê' (1), Hege or Hegai

HEIFER
5697 'eglâh (11), cow calf
6510 pârâh (6), heifer
1151 damalis (1), heifer

HEIFER'S
5697 'eglâh (1), cow calf

HEIGHT
1361 gâbahh (2), to be lofty; to be haughty
1363 gôbahh (8), height; grandeur; arrogance
1364 gâbôahh (2), high; powerful; arrogant
4791 mârôwm (9), elevation; elation
6967 qôwmâh (30), height
7218 rô'sh (1), head
7312 rûwm (2), elevation; elation
7314 rûwm (Ch.) (4), altitude, tallness
7419 râmûwth (1), heap of carcases
5311 hupsŏs (2), altitude; sky; dignity
5313 hupsōma (1), altitude; barrier

HEIGHTS
1116 bâmâh (1), elevation, high place
4791 mârôwm (1), elevation; elation

HEINOUS
2154 zimmâh (1), bad plan

HEIR
3423 yârash (9), to inherit; to impoverish
2816 klērŏnŏmĕŏ (1), to be an heir to, inherit

2818 klērŏnŏmŏs (8), possessor by inheritance

HEIRS
3423 yârash (1), to inherit; to impoverish
2816 klērŏnŏmĕŏ (1), to be an heir to, inherit
2818 klērŏnŏmŏs (7), possessor by inheritance
4789 sugklērŏnŏmŏs (2), participant in common

HELAH
2458 Chel'âh (2), rust

HELAM
2431 Chêylâm (2), fortress

HELBAH
2462 Chelbâh (1), fertility

HELBON
2463 Chelbôwn (1), fruitful

HELD
270 'âchaz (3), to seize, grasp; possess
631 'âçar (1), to fasten; to join battle
1102 bâlam (1), to muzzle, control
1826 dâmam (1), to be silent; to be astonished
2244 châbâ' (1), to secrete
2388 châzaq (6), to fasten upon; to seize
2790 chârash (10), to engrave; to plow
2814 châshâh (2), to hush or keep quiet
2820 châsak (2), to restrain or refrain
3447 yâshaṭ (2), to extend
3557 kûwl (1), to keep in; to measure
5582 çâ'ad (1), to support
6213 'âsâh (1), to do
6901 qâbal (1), to admit; to take
7311 rûwm (2), to be high; to rise or raise
8557 temeç (1), melting disappearance
2192 ĕchō (1), to have; hold; keep
2258 ēn (1), I was
2270 hēsuchazō (2), to refrain
2722 katĕchō (1), to hold down fast
2902 kratĕŏ (2), to seize
2983 lambanō (1), to take, receive
4160 pŏiĕō (1), to make
4601 sigaō (2), to keep silent
4623 siōpaō (4), to be quiet
4912 sunĕchō (1), to hold together

HELDAI
2469 Chelday (2), worldliness

HELEB
2460 Chêleb (1), fatness

HELED
2466 Chêled (1), *fleeting time; this world*

HELEK
2507 Chêleq (2), *portion*

HELEKITES
2516 Chelqîy (1), *Chelkite*

HELEM
2494 Chêlem (2), *dream*

HELEPH
2501 Cheleph (1), *change*

HELEZ
2503 Chelets (5), *strength*

HELI
2242 Hêli (1), *lofty*

HELKAI
2517 Chelqay (1), *apportioned*

HELKATH
2520 Chelqath (2), *smoothness*

HELKATH-HAZZURIM
2521 Chelqath hats-Tsûrîym (1), *smoothness of the rocks*

HELL
7585 sheʻôwl (31), *abode of the dead*
86 haˌdēs (10), *Hades, i.e. place of the dead*
1067 gĕenna (12), *valley of (the son of) Hinnom, fig. hell*
5020 tartaröō (1), *to incarcerate in Tartaros*

HELM
4079 pĕdaliŏn (1), *blade of an oar which steers*

HELMET
3553 kôwbaʻ (4), *helmet*
6959 qôwbaʻ (2), *helmet*
4030 pĕrikĕphalaia (2), *helmet*

HELMETS
3553 kôwbaʻ (2), *helmet*

HELON
2497 Chêlôn (5), *strong*

HELP
2388 châzaq (2), *to fasten upon; to seize*
3444 yeshûwʻâh (2), *deliverance; aid*
3447 yâshaṭ (1), *to extend*
3467 yâshaʻ (9), *to make safe, free*
5375 nâsâʼ (1), *to lift up*
5800 ʻâzab (2), *to loosen; relinquish; permit*
5826 ʻâzar (44), *to protect or aid*
5828 ʻêzer (21), *aid*
5833 ʻezrâh (24), *aid*
6965 qûwm (2), *to rise*
7125 qirʼâh (1), *to encounter, to happen*
8668 teshûwʻâh (5), *rescue, deliverance*
996 bŏêthĕia (1), *aid*
997 bŏêthĕō (5), *to aid or relieve*
1947 ĕpikŏuria (1), *assistance, aid*
4815 sullambanō (2), *to conceive; to aid*

4878 sunantilambanŏmai (1), *assist*

HELPED
3467 yâshaʻ (2), *to make safe, free*
5375 nâsâʼ (1), *to lift up*
5826 ʻâzar (18), *to protect or aid*
5833 ʻezrâh (1), *aid*
997 bŏêthĕō (1), *to aid or relieve*
4820 sumballō (1), *to aid; to join, attack*

HELPER
5826 ʻâzar (7), *to protect or aid*
998 bŏêthŏs (1), *succorer, helper*
4904 sunĕrgŏs (1), *fellow-worker*

HELPERS
5826 ʻâzar (4), *to protect or aid*
5833 ʻezrâh (1), *aid*
4904 sunĕrgŏs (2), *fellow-worker*

HELPETH
5826 ʻâzar (2), *to protect or aid*
4878 sunantilambanŏmai (1), *co-operate, assist*
4903 sunĕrgĕō (1), *to be a fellow-worker*

HELPING
3467 yâshaʻ (1), *to make safe, free*
5582 çâʻad (1), *to support*
4943 sunupŏurgĕō (1), *assist, join to help*

HELPS
484 antilēpsis (1), *relief, aid*
996 bŏêthĕia (1), *aid*

HELVE
6086 ʻêts (1), *wood, things made of wood*

HEM
7757 shûwl (5), *skirt; bottom edge*
2899 kraspĕdŏn (2), *margin*

HEMAM
1967 Hêymâm (1), *raging*

HEMAN
1968 Hêymân (16), *faithful*

HEMATH
2574 Chămâth (3), *walled*

HEMDAN
2533 Chemdân (1), *pleasant*

HEMLOCK
3939 laʼănâh (1), *poisonous wormwood*
7219 rôʼsh (1), *poisonous plant; poison*

HEMS
7757 shûwl (1), *skirt; bottom edge*

HEN
2581 Chên (1), *grace*
3733 ŏrnis (2), *hen*

HENA
2012 Hênaʼ (3), *Hena*

HENADAD
2582 Chênâdâd (4), *favor of Hadad*

HENCE
2088 zeh (14), *this or that*
3212 yâlak (1), *to walk; to live; to carry*
3318 yâtsâʼ (1), *to go, bring out*
1782 ĕntĕuthĕn (9), *hence, from here*
1821 ĕxapŏstĕllō (1), *to despatch, or to dismiss*
3326+5025 mĕta (1), *with, among; after, later*
5217 hupagŏ (1), *to withdraw or retire*

HENCEFORTH
3254 yâçaph (5), *to add or augment*
5750 ʻôwd (2), *again; repeatedly; still; more*
6258 ʻattâh (5), *at this time, now*
534 aparti (1), *henceforth, from now*
575+737 apŏ (2), *from, away*
575+3588+3568 apŏ (1), *from, away*
737 arti (1), *just now; at once*
2089 ĕti (1), *yet, still*
3063 lŏipŏn (4), *remaining; finally*
3371 mĕkĕti (4), *no further*
3568 nun (4), *now; the present or immediate*
3765 ŏukĕti (1), *not yet, no longer*

HENCEFORWARD
1973 hâlʼâh (1), *far away; thus far*
3371 mĕkĕti (1), *no further*

HENOCH
2585 Chănôwk (2), *initiated*

HEPHER
2660 Chêpher (9), *pit or shame*

HEPHERITES
2662 Chephrîy (1), *Chephrite*

HEPHZI-BAH
2657 Chephtsîy bâhh (2), *my delight (is) in her*

HERALD
3744 kârôwz (Ch.) (1), *herald*

HERB
1877 desheʼ (6), *sprout; green grass*
2682 châtsîyr (1), *grass; leek plant*
6212 ʻeseb (12), *grass, or any green, tender shoot*

HERBS
216 ʼôwr (1), *luminary; lightning; happiness*
219 ʼôwrâh (2), *luminousness, light*
3419 yârâq (3), *vegetable greens*

6212 ʻeseb (5), *grass, or any green, tender shoot*
1008 bŏtanē (1), *grazing herbage, vegetation*
3001 lachanŏn (4), *vegetable*

HERD
1241 bâqâr (14), *plowing ox; herd*
34 agĕlē (8), *drove, herd*

HERDMAN
951 bôwkêr (1), *herder, cattle-tender*

HERDMEN
5349 nôqêd (1), *owner or tender of sheep*
7462 râʻâh (6), *to tend a flock, i.e. pasture it*

HERDS
1241 bâqâr (30), *plowing ox; herd*
4735 miqneh (1), *live-stock*
5739 ʻêder (2), *muster, flock*

HERE
645 ʼêphôw (1), *then*
1988 hălôm (5), *hither, to here*
2005 hên (5), *lo!; if!*
2008 hênnâh (2), *from here; from there*
2009 hinnêh (12), *lo!; Look!*
2088 zeh (12), *this or that*
2236 zâraq (1), *to sprinkle, scatter*
3541 kôh (4), *thus*
4672 mâtsâʼ (1), *to find or acquire; to occur,*
6311 pôh (43), *here or hence*
8033 shâm (2), *where, there*
8552 tâmam (1), *to complete, finish*
848 hautŏu (1), *self*
1759 ĕnthadĕ (3), *here, hither*
3918 parĕimi (2), *to be present; to have come*
3936 paristēmi (1), *to stand beside, present*
4840 sumparĕimi (1), *to be at hand together*
5602 hŏdĕ (44), *here or hither*

HEREAFTER
268 ʼâchôwr (1), *behind, backward; west*
310 ʼachar (1), *after*
737 arti (1), *just now; at once*
2089 ĕti (1), *yet, still*
3195 mĕllō (1), *to intend, i.e. be about to*
3370 Mēdŏs (1), *inhabitant of Media*

HEREBY
2063 zôʼth (4), *this*
1537+5124 ĕk (1), *out, out of*
1722+5129 ĕn (8), *in; during; because of*

HEREIN
2063 zôʼth (1), *this*

HEREOF
5921+2063 'al (1), *above,
over, upon,* or *against*
1722+5129 ĕn (7), *in;
during; because of*

HEREOF
3778 hŏutŏs (1), *this* or
that
5026 tautē̦ (1), *(toward
or of) this*

HERES
2776 Chereç (1), *shining*

HERESH
2792 Cheresh (1),
magical craft; silence

HERESIES
139 hairĕsis (3), *party,
sect; disunion* or *heresy*

HERESY
139 hairĕsis (1), *party,
sect; disunion* or *heresy*

HERETICK
141 hairĕtikŏs (1),
schismatic, division

HERETOFORE
865 'ethmôwl (1),
heretofore, formerly
8543 tᵉmôwl (6),
yesterday
4258 prŏamartanō (1), *to
sin previously*

HEREUNTO
1519+5124 ĕis (1), *to* or
into

HEREWITH
2063 zô'th (2), *this*

HERITAGE
3425 yᵉrushâh (1),
conquest
4181 môwrâshâh (1),
possession
5157 nâchal (1), *to inherit*
5159 nachălâh (26),
occupancy
2819 klĕrŏs (1), *lot,
portion*

HERITAGES
5159 nachălâh (1),
occupancy

HERMAS
2057 Hĕrmas (1), *born of
god Hermes*

HERMES
2060 Hĕrmēs (1), *born of
god Hermes*

HERMOGENES
2061 Hĕrmŏgĕnēs (1),
born of god Hermes

HERMON
2768 Chermôwn (13),
abrupt

HERMONITES
2769 Chermôwnîym (1),
peaks of Hermon

HEROD
2264 Hērōdēs (40), *heroic*

HEROD'S
2264 Hērōdēs (4), *heroic*

HERODIANS
2265 Hērōdianŏi (3),
Herodians

HERODIAS
2266 Hērōdias (4), *heroic*

HERODIAS'
2266 Hērōdias (2), *heroic*

HERODION
2267 Hērōdiōn (1), *heroic*

HERON
601 'ănâphâh (2), (poss.)
parrot

HESED
2618 Cheçed (1), *favor*

HESHBON
2809 Cheshbôwn (38),
contrivance; plan

HESHMON
2829 Cheshmôwn (1),
opulent

HETH
2845 Chêth (14), *terror*

HETHLON
2855 Chethlôn (2),
enswathed

HEW
1414 gᵉdad (Ch.) (2), *to
cut down*
1438 gâda' (1), *to fell a
tree; to destroy*
2404 châṭab (1), *to chop
or carve wood*
2672 châtsab (2), *to cut
stone or carve wood*
3772 kârath (3), *to cut
(off, down or asunder)*
6458 pâçal (3), *to carve,
to chisel*

HEWED
1496 gâzîyth (5), *dressed
stone*
2672 châtsab (3), *to cut
stone or carve wood*
4274 machtsêb (1),
quarry stone
5408 nâthach (1), *to
dismember, cut up*
6458 pâçal (2), *to carve,
to chisel*
8158 shâçaph (1), *to
hack in pieces, i.e. kill*

HEWER
2404 châṭab (1), *to chop
or carve wood*

HEWERS
2404 châṭab (5), *to chop
or carve wood*
2672 châtsab (4), *to cut
stone or carve wood*

HEWETH
2672 châtsab (2), *to cut
stone or carve wood*
3772 kârath (1), *to cut
(off, down or asunder)*

HEWN
1438 gâda' (1), *to fell a
tree; to destroy*
1496 gâzîyth (5), *dressed
stone*
2672 châtsab (2), *to cut
stone or carve wood*
4274 machtsêb (2),
quarry stone
7060 qâmal (1), *to wither
off; to frustrate*
1581 ĕkkŏptō (3), *to cut
off; to frustrate*
2991 laxĕutŏs (1),
rock-quarried
2998 latŏmĕō (2), *to
quarry*

HERODIAS
2266 Hērōdias (2), *heroic*

HEZEKI
2395 Chizqîy (1), *strong*

HEZEKIAH
2396 Chizqîyâh (128),
*strengthened of
Jehovah*

HEZION
2383 Chezyôwn (1),
vision

HEZIR
2387 Chêzîyr (2),
protected

HEZRAI
2695 Chetsrôw (1),
enclosure

HEZRO
2695 Chetsrôw (1),
enclosure

HEZRON
2696 Chetsrôwn (17),
court-yard

HEZRON'S
2696 Chetsrôwn (1),
court-yard

HEZRONITES
2697 Chetsrôwnîy (2),
Chetsronite

HID
2244 châbâ' (25), *to
secrete*
2934 ṭâman (16), *to hide*
3582 kâchad (6), *to
destroy; to hide*
3680 kâçâh (2), *to cover*
4301 maṭmôwn (2),
secret storehouse
5641 çâthar (30), *to hide
by covering*
5956 'âlam (11), *to veil
from sight, i.e. conceal*
6845 tsâphan (8), *to hide;
to hoard or reserve*
8587 ta'ălummâh (1),
secret
613 apŏkruptō (5), *to
keep secret, conceal*
614 apŏkruphŏs (2),
secret, hidden things
1470 ĕgkruptō (2),
incorporate with, mix in
2572 kaluptō (1), *to cover
up*
2927 kruptŏs (3), *private,
unseen*
2928 kruptō (10), *to
conceal*
2990 lanthanō (2), *to lie
hid; unwittingly*
3871 parakaluptō (1), *to
veil, be hidden*
4032 pĕrikruptō (1), *to
conceal all around*

HIDDAI
1914 Hidday (1), *Hiddai*

HIDDEKEL
2313 Chiddeqel (2),
Tigris river

HIDDEN
2664 châphas (1), *to
seek; to mask*
2934 ṭâman (1), *to hide*
4301 maṭmôwn (1),
secret storehouse
4710 mitspûn (1), *secret*

HEZEKIAH
5341 nâtsar (1), *to guard;
to conceal, hide*
5640 çâtham (1), *to stop
up; to keep secret*
5956 'âlam (1), *to veil
from sight, i.e. conceal*
6381 pâlâ' (1), *to be,
make great, difficult*
6845 tsâphan (3), *to hide;
to hoard or reserve*
613 apŏkruptō (1), *to
keep secret, conceal*
2927 kruptŏs (3), *private,
unseen*
2928 kruptō (1), *to
conceal*
2990 lanthanō (1), *to lie
hid; unwittingly*

HIDE
2244 châbâ' (6), *to secrete*
2247 châbah (5), *to hide*
2934 ṭâman (5), *to hide*
3582 kâchad (10), *to
destroy; to hide*
3680 kâçâh (3), *to cover*
5127 nûwç (1), *to vanish
away, flee*
5641 çâthar (33), *to hide
by covering*
5785 ôwr (2), *skin,
leather*
5956 'âlam (8), *to veil
from sight, i.e. conceal*
6004 'âmam (2), *to
overshadow by
huddling together*
6845 tsâphan (5), *to hide;
to hoard or reserve*
2572 kaluptō (1), *to cover*
2928 kruptō (2), *to
conceal*

HIDEST
5641 çâthar (5), *to hide
by covering*
5956 'âlam (1), *to veil
from sight, i.e. conceal*

HIDETH
2244 châbâ' (1), *to secrete*
2821 châshak (1), *to be
dark; to darken*
2934 ṭâman (2), *to hide*
3680 kâçâh (1), *to cover*
5641 çâthar (5), *to hide
by covering*
5848 'âṭaph (1), *to
shroud, i.e. clothe*
5956 'âlam (2), *to veil
from sight, i.e. conceal*
6845 tsâphan (1), *to hide;
to hoard or reserve*
2928 kruptō (1), *to
conceal*

HIDING
2253 chebyôwn (1),
concealment, hiding
2934 ṭâman (1), *to hide*
4224 machăbê' (1),
refuge, shelter
5643 çêther (3), *cover,
shelter*

HIEL
2419 Chîy'êl (1), *living of
God*

HIERAPOLIS
2404 Hiĕrapŏlis (1), *holy
city*

HIGGAION
1902 higgâyôwn (1), *musical notation*

HIGH
376 'îysh (2), *man; male; someone*
753 'ôrek (1), *length*
1111 Bâlâq (1), *waster*
1116 bâmâh (99), *elevation, high place*
1361 gâbahh (4), *to be lofty; to be haughty*
1362 gâbâhh (3), *high; lofty*
1363 gôbahh (2), *height; grandeur; arrogance*
1364 gâbôahh (25), *high; powerful; arrogant*
1386 gabnôn (2), *peak of hills*
1419 gâdôwl (22), *great*
1870 derek (1), *road; course* of life
4546 meçillâh (1), *main thoroughfare; viaduct*
4605 ma'al (7), *upward, above, overhead*
4608 ma'âleh (1), *elevation; platform*
4791 mârôwm (33), *elevation; elation*
4796 Mârôwth (1), *bitter springs*
4869 misgâb (4), high *refuge*
5375 nâsâ' (1), *to lift up*
5920 'al (3), the *Highest God*
5943 'illay (Ch.) (9), the *supreme God*
5945 'elyôwn (37), *loftier, higher; Supreme God*
5946 'elyôwn (Ch.) (4), the *Supreme God*
6381 pâlâ' (1), *to be, make great, difficult*
6877 tserîyach (1), *citadel*
6967 qôwmâh (5), *height*
7218 rô'sh (3), *head*
7311 rûwm (25), *to be high; to rise or raise*
7312 rûwm (3), *elevation; elation*
7315 rôwm (1), *aloft, on high*
7319 rôwmemâh (1), *exaltation, i.e. praise*
7413 râmâh (4), *height; high seat* of idolatry
7682 sâgab (6), *to be, make lofty; be safe*
8192 shâphâh (1), *to bare*
8203 Shephatyâh (2), *Jehovah has judged*
8205 shephîy (7), *bare hill or plain*
8564 tamrûwr (1), *erection, i.e. pillar*
8643 terûw'âh (1), *battle-cry; clangor*
507 anō (1), *upward or on the top, heavenward*
749 archiĕrĕus (59), *high-priest, chief priest*
2032 ĕpŏuraniŏs (1), *above the sky, celestial*
2409 hiĕrĕus (1), *priest*
3173 mĕgas (2), *great, many*

5308 hupsēlŏs (9), *lofty* in place or character
5310 hupsistŏs (5), the *Supreme God*
5311 hupsŏs (3), *altitude; sky; dignity*
5313 hupsōma (1), *altitude; barrier*

HIGHER
1354 gab (1), *mounded or rounded: top or rim*
1361 gâbahh (4), *to be lofty; to be haughty*
1364 gâbôahh (5), *high; powerful; arrogant*
3201 yâkôl (1), *to be able*
5945 'elyôwn (4), *loftier, higher; Supreme God*
6706 tsechîyach (1), *glaring*
7311 rûwm (2), *to be high; to rise or raise*
511 anōtĕrŏs (1), *upper part; former part*
5242 hupĕrĕchō (1), *to excel; superior*
5308 hupsēlŏs (1), *lofty*

HIGHEST
1364 gâbôahh (1), *high; powerful; arrogant*
4791 mârôwm (1), *elevation; elation*
5945 'elyôwn (3), *loftier, higher; Supreme God*
6788 tsammereth (2), *foliage*
7218 rô'sh (1), *head*
4410 prōtŏkathĕdria (1), *pre-eminence* in council
4411 prōtŏklisia (1), *pre-eminence at meals*
5310 hupsistŏs (8), the *Supreme God*

HIGHLY
1537+4053 ĕk (1), *out of*
2371 thumŏmachĕō (1), *to be exasperated*
5251 hupĕrupsŏō (1), *to raise to the highest*
5252 hupĕrphrŏnĕō (1), *to esteem oneself overmuch*
5308 hupsēlŏs (1), *lofty* in place or character

HIGHMINDED
5187 tuphŏō (1), *to inflate with self-conceit*
5309 hupsēlŏphrŏnĕō (2), *to be lofty in mind*

HIGHNESS
1346 ga'ăvâh (1), *arrogance; majesty*
7613 se'êth (1), *elevation; swelling* leprous scab

HIGHWAY
4546 meçillâh (13), *main thoroughfare; viaduct*
4547 maçlûwl (1), *main thoroughfare*
3598 hŏdŏs (1), *road*

HIGHWAYS
734 'ôrach (1), *well-traveled road; manner of life*
2351 chûwts (1), *outside, outdoors; open market*

4546 meçillâh (6), *main thoroughfare; viaduct*
1327+3598 diĕxŏdŏs (1), *open square*
3598 hŏdŏs (2), *road*

HILEN
2432 Chîylên (1), *fortress*

HILKIAH
2518 Chilqîyâh (33), *portion* (of) *Jehovah*

HILKIAH'S
2518 Chilqîyâh (1), *portion* (of) *Jehovah*

HILL
1389 gib'âh (30), *hillock*
2022 har (34), *mountain or range* of hills
4608 ma'âleh (1), *elevation; platform*
7161 qeren (1), *horn*
697 Arĕiŏs Pagŏs (1), *rock of Ares*
1015 bŏunŏs (1), small *hill*
3714 ŏrĕinŏs (2), *Highlands* of Judæa
3735 ŏrŏs (3), *hill, mountain*

HILL'S
2022 har (1), *mountain or range* of hills

HILLEL
1985 Hillêl (2), *praising* (God)

HILLS
1389 gib'âh (39), *hillock*
2022 har (23), *mountain or range* of hills
2042 hârâr (2), *mountain*
1015 bŏunŏs (1), small *hill*

HIN
1969 hîyn (22), *liquid measure*

HIND
355 'ayâlâh (1), *doe* deer
365 'ayeleth (2), *doe* deer

HINDER
268 'âchôwr (3), *behind, backward; west*
309 'âchar (1), *to remain; to delay*
310 'achar (1), *after*
314 'achărôwn (1), *late or last; behind; western*
4513 mâna' (1), *to deny, refuse*
5490 çôwph (1), *termination; end*
6213+8442 'âsâh (1), *to do or make*
7725 shûwb (2), *to turn back; to return*
348 anakŏptō (1), *to beat back, i.e. check*
2967 kōluō (1), *to stop*
4403 prumna (2), *stern* of a ship
5100+1464+1325 tis (1), *some or any person*

HINDERED
989 betêl (Ch.) (1), *to stop*
1465 ĕgkŏptō (2), *to impede, detain*

1581 ĕkkŏptō (1), *to cut off; to frustrate*
2967 kōluō (1), *to stop*

HINDERETH
2820 châsak (1), *to restrain or refrain*

HINDERMOST
314 'achărôwn (1), *late or last; behind; western*
319 'achărîyth (1), *future; posterity*

HINDMOST
314 'achărôwn (1), *late or last; behind; western*
2179 zânab (2), *militarily attack* the rear position

HINDS
355 'ayâlâh (4), *doe* deer

HINDS'
355 'ayâlâh (3), *doe* deer

HINGES
6596 pôth (1), *hole; hinge; female genitals*
6735 tsîyr (1), *hinge*

HINNOM
2011 Hinnôm (13), *Hinnom*

HIP
7785 shôwq (1), lower *leg*

HIRAH
2437 Chîyrâh (2), *splendor*

HIRAM
2438 Chîyrâm (22), *noble*

HIRAM'S
2438 Chîyrâm (1), *noble*

HIRE
868 'ethnan (7), *gift price* of harlotry
4242 mechîyr (1), *price, payment, wages*
7936 sâkar (2), *to hire*
7939 sâkâr (8), *payment, salary; compensation*
3408 misthŏs (3), *pay for services*
3409 misthŏō (1), *to hire*

HIRED
7916 sâkîyr (11), man *at wages, hired hand*
7917 sekîyrâh (1), *hiring*
7936 sâkar (14), *to hire*
8566 tânâh (2), *to bargain* with a harlot
3407 misthiŏs (2), *hired-worker*
3409 misthŏō (1), *to hire*
3410 misthōma (1), *rented building*
3411 misthōtŏs (1), *wage-worker*

HIRELING
7916 sâkîyr (6), man *at wages, hired hand*
3411 misthōtŏs (2), *wage-worker*

HIRES
868 'ethnan (1), *gift price* of harlotry

HIREST
7806 shâzar (1), *to twist* a thread of straw

HISS
8319 shâraq (12), to *whistle* or *hiss*

HISSING
8292 sh^{e}rûwqâh (1), *whistling; scorn*
8322 sh^{e}rêqâh (7), *derision*

HIT
4672 mâtsâ' (2), to *find* or *acquire;* to *occur*

HITHER
1988 hălôm (6), *hither, to here*
2008 hênnâh (2), *from here; from there*
5066 nâgash (7), to *be, come, bring near*
6311 pôh (1), *here* or *hence*
1204 *dĕurŏ* (2), *hither!; hitherto*
1759 *ĕnthadĕ* (4), *here, hither*
3333 *mĕtakalĕō* (1), to *summon for, call for*
5602 *hōdĕ* (14), *here* or *hither*

HITHERTO
227 'âz (1), *at that time* or *place; therefore*
1973 hâl^{e}âh (2), *far away; thus far*
1988 hălôm (2), *hither, to here*
5704+2008 'ad (6), *as far (long) as; during*
5704+3541 'ad (2), *as far (long) as; during*
5704+6311 'ad (1), *as far (long) as; during*
5705+3542 'ad (Ch.) (1), *as far (long) as; during*
891+1204 *achri* (1), *until* or *up to*
2193+737 *hĕōs* (2), *until*
3768 *ŏupō* (1), *not yet*

HITTITE
2850 Chittîy (26), *Chittite*

HITTITES
2850 Chittîy (22), *Chittite*

HIVITE
2340 Chivvîy (9), *villager*

HIVITES
2340 Chivvîy (16), *villager*

HIZKIAH
2396 Chizqîyâh (1), *strengthened of Jehovah*

HIZKIJAH
2396 Chizqîyâh (1), *strengthened of Jehovah*

HO
1945 hôwy (3), *oh!, woe!*

HOAR
3713 k^{e}phôwr (2), *bowl;* white *frost*
7872 sêybâh (3), old *age*

HOARY
3713 k^{e}phôwr (1), *bowl;* white *frost*
7872 sêybâh (3), old *age*

HOBAB
2246 Chôbâb (2), *cherished*

HOBAH
2327 chôwbâh (1), *hiding* place

HOD
1963 hêyk (1), *how?*

HODAIAH
1939 Howday^{e}vâhûw (1), *majesty of Jehovah*

HODAVIAH
1938 Hôwdavyâh (3), *majesty of Jehovah*

HODESH
2321 Chôdesh (1), *new moon*

HODEVAH
1937 Hôwd^{e}vâh (1), *majesty of Jehovah*

HODIAH
1940 Hôwdîyâh (1), *Jewess*

HODIJAH
1940 Hôwdîyâh (5), *Jewess*

HOGLAH
2295 Choglâh (4), *partridge*

HOHAM
1944 Hôwhâm (1), *Hoham*

HOISED
1869 *ĕpairō* (1), to *raise up, look up*

HOLD
270 'âchaz (26), to *seize, grasp; possess*
816 'âsham (1), to *be guilty;* to *be punished*
1225 bitstsârôwn (1), *fortress*
2013 hâçâh (2), to *hush, be quiet*
2388 châzaq (35), to *fasten* upon; to *seize*
2790 chârash (16), to *engrave;* to *plow*
2814 châshâh (6), to *hush* or *keep quiet*
3447 yâshaṭ (1), to *extend*
3557 kûwl (1), to *keep in;* to *maintain*
3905 lâchats (1), to *press;* to *distress*
3943 lâphath (1), to *clasp;* to *turn* around
4013 mibtsâr (2), *fortification; defender*
4581 mâ'ôwz (1), *fortified* place; *defense*
4672 mâtsâ' (2), to *find* or *acquire;* to *occur*
4679 m^{e}tsad (2), *stronghold*
4686 mâtsûwd (7), *net* or *capture; fastness*
4692 mâtsôwr (1), *distress; fastness*
5253 nâçag (1), to *retreat*
5375 nâsâ' (1), to *lift up*
5381 nâsag (5), to *reach*
5553 çela' (1), craggy *rock; fortress*
5582 çâ'ad (1), to *support*
6076 'ôphel (1), *tumor; fortress*
6877 ts^{e}rîyach (3), *citadel*
6901 qâbal (1), to *admit;* to *take*
6965 qûwm (1), to *rise*
8551 tâmak (4), to *obtain, keep fast*
8610 tâphas (7), to *manipulate,* i.e. *seize*
472 *antĕchŏmai* (2), to *adhere to;* to *care for*
1949 *ĕpilambanŏmai* (5), to *seize*
2192 *ĕchō* (3), to *have; hold; keep*
2722 *katĕchō* (5), to *hold down fast*
2902 *kratĕō* (19), to *seize*
4601 *sigaō* (2), to *keep silent*
4623 *siōpaō* (5), to *be quiet*
5083 *tērĕō* (1), to *keep, guard, obey*
5084 *tērēsis* (1), *observance; prison*
5392 *phimŏō* (2), to *restrain to silence*
5438 *phulakē* (1), *guarding* or *guard*

HOLDEN
270 'âchaz (1), to *seize, grasp; possess*
2388 châzaq (1), to *fasten* upon; to *seize*
2814 châshâh (1), to *hush* or *keep quiet*
3920 lâkad (1), to *catch;* to *capture*
5564 çâmak (1), to *lean* upon; *take hold* of
5582 çâ'ad (1), to *support*
6213 'âsâh (2), to *do* or *make*
8551 tâmak (1), to *obtain, keep fast*
2902 *kratĕō* (2), to *seize*

HOLDEST
270 'âchaz (1), to *seize, grasp; possess*
2790 chârash (2), to *engrave;* to *plow*
2803 châshab (1), to *weave, fabricate*
8610 tâphas (1), to *manipulate,* i.e. *seize*
2902 *kratĕō* (1), to *seize*

HOLDETH
270 'âchaz (1), to *seize, grasp; possess*
2388 châzaq (2), to *fasten* upon; to *seize*
2790 chârash (2), to *engrave;* to *plow*
7760 sûwm (1), to *put, place*
8551 tâmak (2), to *obtain, keep fast*
2902 *kratĕō* (1), to *seize*

HOLDING
3557 kûwl (1), to *keep in;* to *measure*
8551 tâmak (1), to *obtain, keep fast*
472 *antĕchŏmai* (1), to *adhere to;* to *care for*
1907 *ĕpĕchō* (1), to *retain;* to *pay attention*
2192 *ĕchō* (2), to *have; hold; keep*
2902 *kratĕō* (3), to *seize*

HOLDS
4013 mibtsâr (11), *fortification; defender*
4581 mâ'ôwz (1), *fortified* place; *defense*
4679 m^{e}tsad (6), *stronghold*
4686 mâtsûwd (1), *net* or *capture; fastness*
4694 m^{e}tsûwrâh (1), *rampart, fortification*

HOLE
2356 chôwr (4), *cavity, socket, den*
4718 maqqebeth (1), *hammer*
5357 nâqîyq (1), *cleft, crevice*
6310 peh (6), *mouth; opening*

HOLE'S
6354 pachath (1), *pit*

HOLES
2356 chôwr (4), *cavity, socket, den*
4526 miçgereth (1), *margin; stronghold*
4631 m^{e}'ârâh (1), dark *cavern*
5344 nâqab (1), to *puncture, perforate*
5357 nâqîyq (2), *cleft, crevice*
5454 *phōlĕŏs* (2), *burrow, den hole*

HOLIER
6942 qâdâsh (1), to *be, make clean*

HOLIEST
39 *hagiŏn* (3), *sacred* thing, place or person

HOLILY
3743 *hŏsiōs* (1), *piously*

HOLINESS
6944 qôdesh (30), *sacred* place or thing
38 *hagiasmŏs* (5), state of *purity*
41 *hagiŏtēs* (1), state of *holiness*
42 *hagiōsunē* (3), quality of *holiness*
2150 *ĕusĕbĕia* (1), *piety, religious*
2412 *hiĕrŏprĕpēs* (1), *reverent*
3742 *hŏsiŏtēs* (2), *piety*

HOLLOW
3709 kaph (4), hollow of *hand; paw; sole* of foot
4388 maktêsh (1), *mortar; socket*
5014 nâbab (3), to *be hollow; be foolish*
8168 shô'al (1), *palm* of hand; *handful*
8258 sh^{e}qa'rûwrâh (1), *depression*

HOLON
2473 Chôlôwn (3), *sandy*

HOLPEN
2220 zᵉrôwa' (1), *arm; foreleg; force, power*
5826 'âzar (3), to *protect* or *aid*
482 antilambanŏmai (1), to *come to the aid*

HOLY
2623 châçîyd (5), religiously *pious, godly*
4720 miqdâsh (3), *sanctuary of deity*
6918 qâdôwsh (100), *sacred*
6922 qaddîysh (Ch.) (7), *sacred*
6942 qâdâsh (7), to *be, make clean*
6944 qôdesh (297), *sacred* place or thing
37 hagiazō (1), to *purify* or *consecrate*
39 hagiŏn (3), *sacred* thing, place or person
40 hagiŏs (162), *sacred, holy*
2413 hiĕrŏs (2), *sacred, set apart* for God
3741 hŏsiŏs (6), *hallowed, pious, sacred*

HOLYDAY
2287 châgag (1), to *observe* a festival
1859 hĕŏrtē (1), *festival*

HOMAM
1950 Hôwmâm (1), *raging*

HOME
168 'ôhel (1), *tent*
1004 bayith (26), *house; temple; family, tribe*
4725 mâqôwm (3), general *locality, place*
5115 nâvâh (1), to *rest* as at home
7725 shûwb (5), to *turn* back; to *return*
8432 tâvek (1), *center, middle*
1438 hĕautŏu (1), *himself, herself, itself*
1736 ĕndĕmĕō (1), to be *at home*
2398 idiŏs (2), *private* or *separate*
3614 ŏikia (1), *abode; family*
3624 ŏikŏs (4), *dwelling; family*
3626 ŏikŏurŏs (1), *domestically inclined*

HOMEBORN
249 'ezrâch (1), *native born*
1004 bayith (1), *house; temple; family, tribe*

HOMER
2563 chômer (10), *clay; dry measure*

HOMERS
2563 chômer (1), *clay; dry measure*

HONEST
2570 kalŏs (5), *good; valuable; virtuous*
4586 sĕmnŏs (1), *honorable, noble*

HONESTLY
2156 ĕuschēmŏnōs (2), *fittingly, properly*
2573 kalŏs (1), *well*, i.e. *rightly*

HONESTY
4587 sĕmnŏtēs (1), *venerableness*

HONEY
1706 dᵉbash (52), *honey*
3192 mĕli (4), *honey*

HONEYCOMB
3293 ya'ar (1), *honey* in the *comb*
3295+1706 ya'ărâh (1), *honey* in the *comb*
5317 nôpheth (4), *honey* from the comb
5317+6688 nôpheth (1), *honey* from the comb
6688+1706 tsûwph (1), *comb* of *dripping* honey
3193+2781 mĕlissiŏs (1), *honeybee* comb

HONOUR
1921 hâdar (2), to *favor* or *honor;* to *be high*
1922 hădar (Ch.) (1), to *magnify, glorify*
1923 hădar (Ch.) (2), *magnificence, glory*
1926 hâdâr (5), *magnificence*
1927 hădârâh (1), *ornament; splendor*
1935 hôwd (6), *grandeur, majesty*
3366 yᵉqâr (12), *wealth; costliness; dignity*
3367 yᵉqâr (Ch.) (2), *glory, honor*
3513 kâbad (22), to *be rich, glorious*
3515 kâbêd (1), *severe, difficult, stupid*
3519 kâbôwd (32), *splendor, wealth*
8597 tiph'ârâh (4), *ornament*
820 atimŏs (2), *dishonoured*
1391 dŏxa (6), *glory; brilliance*
5091 timaō (14), to *revere, honor*
5092 timē (31), *esteem; nobility; money*

HONOURABLE
142 'âdar (1), *magnificent; glorious*
1935 hôwd (2), *grandeur, majesty*
3368 yâqâr (1), *valuable*
3513 kâbad (13), to *be rich, glorious*
3519 kâbôwd (2), *splendor, wealth*
5375+6440 nâsâ' (4), to *lift up*
820 atimŏs (1), *dishonoured*
1741 ĕndŏxŏs (1), *noble; honored*
1784 ĕntimŏs (1), *valued, considered precious*
2158 ĕuschēmŏn (3), *decorous, proper; noble*

HONOURED
1921 hâdar (1), to *favor* or *honor;* to *be high*
1922 hădar (Ch.) (1), to *magnify, glorify*
3513 kâbad (5), to *be rich, glorious*
1392 dŏxazō (1), to *render, esteem glorious*
5092 timē (1), *esteem; nobility; money*

HONOUREST
3513 kâbad (1), to *be rich, glorious*

HONOURETH
3513 kâbad (4), to *be rich, glorious*
1392 dŏxazō (1), to *render, esteem glorious*
5091 timaō (3), to *revere, honor, show respect*

HONOURS
5091 timaō (1), to *revere, honor, show respect*

HOODS
6797 tsânîyph (1), *head-dress, turban*

HOOF
6541 parçâh (12), *split hoof*

HOOFS
6536 pâraç (1), to *break in pieces; to split*
6541 parçâh (5), *split hoof*

HOOK
100 'agmôwn (1), *rush; rope of rushes*
2397 châch (2), *ring* for the nose or lips
2443 chakkâh (1), *fish hook*
44 agkistrŏn (1), *fish hook*

HOOKS
2053 vâv (13), *hook*
2397 châch (2), *ring* for the nose or lips
6793 tsinnâh (1), *large shield; piercing cold*
8240 shâphâth (1), *two-pronged hook*

HOPE
982 bâṭach (1), to *trust, be confident* or *sure*
983 beṭach (1), *safety, security, trust*
986 biṭṭâchôwn (1), *trust*
2342 chûwl (1), to *dance, whirl;* to *wait;* to *pervert*
2620 châçâh (1), to *flee to;* to *confide in*
2976 yâ'ash (3), to *despond, despair*
3176 yâchal (19), to *wait;* to *be patient, hope*
3689 keçel (3), *loin; back; viscera; trust*
4009 mibṭâch (1), *security; assurance*
4268 machăçeh (2), *shelter; refuge*
4723 miqveh (4), *confidence; collection*
5093 timiŏs (1), *costly; honored, esteemed*

HONOURED
1921 hâdar (1), to *favor* or *honor;* to *be high*
1922 hădar (Ch.) (1), to *magnify, glorify*
3513 kâbad (5), to *be rich, glorious*
1392 dŏxazō (1), to *render, esteem glorious*
5092 timē (1), *esteem; nobility; money*

HONOUREST
3513 kâbad (1), to *be rich, glorious*

HONOURETH
3513 kâbad (4), to *be rich, glorious*
1392 dŏxazō (1), to *render, esteem glorious*
5091 timaō (3), to *revere, honor, show respect*

HONOURS
5091 timaō (1), to *revere, honor, show respect*

HOODS
6797 tsânîyph (1), *head-dress, turban*

HOOF
6541 parçâh (12), *split hoof*

HOOFS
6536 pâraç (1), to *break in pieces; to split*
6541 parçâh (5), *split hoof*

HOOK
100 'agmôwn (1), *rush; rope of rushes*
2397 châch (2), *ring* for the nose or lips
2443 chakkâh (1), *fish hook*
44 agkistrŏn (1), *fish hook*

HOOKS
2053 vâv (13), *hook*
2397 châch (2), *ring* for the nose or lips
6793 tsinnâh (1), *large shield; piercing cold*
8240 shâphâth (1), *two-pronged hook*

HOPE
982 bâṭach (1), to *trust, be confident* or *sure*
983 beṭach (1), *safety, security, trust*
986 biṭṭâchôwn (1), *trust*
2342 chûwl (1), to *dance, whirl;* to *wait;* to *pervert*
2620 châçâh (1), to *flee to;* to *confide in*
2976 yâ'ash (3), to *despond, despair*
3176 yâchal (19), to *wait;* to *be patient, hope*
3689 keçel (3), *loin; back; viscera; trust*
4009 mibṭâch (1), *security; assurance*
4268 machăçeh (2), *shelter; refuge*
4723 miqveh (4), *confidence; collection*

7663 sâbar (1), to *expect* with hope
7664 sêber (2), *expectation*
8431 tôwcheleth (6), *hope, expectation*
8615 tiqvâh (23), *cord; expectancy*
1679 ĕlpizō (7), to *expect* or *confide, hope for*
1680 ĕlpis (51), *hope; confidence*

HOPE'S
1679 ĕlpizō (1), to *expect* or *confide, hope for*

HOPED
982 bâṭach (1), to *trust, be confident* or *sure*
3176 yâchal (3), to *wait;* to *be patient, hope*
7663 sâbar (2), to *expect* with hope
1679 ĕlpizō (4), to *expect* or *confide, hope for*

HOPETH
1679 ĕlpizō (1), to *expect* or *confide, hope for*

HOPHNI
2652 Chophnîy (5), *pair of fists*

HOPING
560 apĕlpizō (1), to *fully expect* in return
1679 ĕlpizō (1), to *expect* or *confide, hope for*

HOR
2023 Hôr (12), *mountain*

HOR-HAGIDGAD
2735 Chôr hag-Gidgâd (2), *hole of the cleft*

HORAM
2036 Hôrâm (1), *high, exalted*

HOREB
2722 Chôrêb (17), *desolate*

HOREM
2765 Chŏrêm (1), *devoted*

HORI
2753 Chôrîy (4), *cave-dweller*

HORIMS
2752 Chôrîy (2), *cave-dweller*

HORITE
2752 Chôrîy (1), *cave-dweller*

HORITES
2752 Chôrîy (3), *cave-dweller*

HORMAH
2767 Chormâh (9), *devoted*

HORN
7161 qeren (28), *horn*
7162 qeren (Ch.) (5), *horn*
2768 kĕras (1), *horn*

HORNET
6880 tsir'âh (2), *wasp*

HORNETS
6880 tsir'âh (1), *wasp*

English

HORNS
3104 yôwbêl (3), *blast of a ram's horn*
7160 qâran (1), *to protrude out horns*
7161 qeren (46), *horn*
7162 qeren (Ch.) (5), *horn*
2768 kĕras (10), *horn*

HORONAIM
2773 Chôrônayim (4), *double cave-town*

HORONITE
2772 Chôrônîy (3), *Choronite*

HORRIBLE
2152 zal'âphâh (1), *glow; famine*
7588 shâ'ôwn (1), *uproar; destruction*
8186 sha'ărûwrâh (4), *something fearful*

HORRIBLY
8175 sâ'ar (1), *to storm; to shiver, i.e. fear*
8178 sa'ar (1), *tempest; terror*

HORROR
367 'êymâh (1), *fright*
2152 zal'âphâh (1), *glow; famine*
6427 pallâtsûwth (2), *affright, trembling fear*

HORSE
5483 çûwç (35), *horse*
2462 hippŏs (8), *horse*

HORSEBACK
5483 çûwç (1), *horse*
7392 râkab (2), *to ride*
7392+5483 râkab (2), *to ride*

HORSEHOOFS
6119+5483 'âqêb (1), *track, footprint*

HORSELEACH
5936 'ălûwqâh (1), *leech*

HORSEMAN
6571 pârâsh (1), *horse; chariot driver*
7395 rakkâb (1), *charioteer*

HORSEMEN
6571 pârâsh (56), *horse; chariot driver*
2460 hippĕus (2), *member of a cavalry*
2461 hippikŏn (1), *cavalry force*

HORSES
5483 çûwç (96), *horse*
5484 çûwçâh (1), *mare*
2462 hippŏs (7), *horse*

HORSES'
5483 çûwç (1), *horse*
2462 hippŏs (1), *horse*

HOSAH
2621 Chôçâh (5), *hopeful*

HOSANNA
5614 hōsanna (6), *"oh save!"*

HOSEA
1954 Hôwshêä' (3), *deliverer*

HOSEN
6361 paṭṭîysh (Ch.) (1), *garment*

HOSHAIAH
1955 Hôwshi'yâh (3), *Jehovah has saved*

HOSHAMA
1953 Hôwshâmâ' (1), *Jehovah has heard*

HOSHEA
1954 Hôwshêä' (11), *deliverer*

HOSPITALITY
5381 philŏnĕxia (1), *hospitableness*
5382 philŏxĕnŏs (3), *hospitable*

HOST
2426 chêyl (2), *rampart, battlement*
2428 chayil (28), *army; wealth; virtue; valor*
4264 machăneh (54), *encampment*
6635 tsâbâ' (100), *army, military host*
3581 xĕnŏs (1), *alien; guest or host*
3830 pandŏchĕus (1), *innkeeper*
4756 stratia (2), *army; celestial luminaries*

HOSTAGES
1121+8594 bên (2), *son, descendant; people*

HOSTS
2428 chayil (1), *army; wealth; virtue; valor*
4264 machăneh (4), *encampment*
6635 tsâbâ' (293), *army, military host*

HOT
228 'ăzâ' (Ch.) (1), *to heat*
784 'êsh (1), *fire*
2525 châm (1), *hot, sweltering*
2527 chôm (4), *heat*
2534 chêmâh (3), *heat; anger; poison*
2552 châmam (3), *to be hot; to be in a rage*
2734 chârâh (10), *to blaze up*
3179 yâcham (2), *to conceive*
7565 resheph (1), *flame*
2200 zĕstŏs (3), *hot, i.e. fervent*
2743 kautēriazŏ (1), *to brand or cauterize*

HOTHAM
2369 Chôwthâm (1), *seal*

HOTHAN
2369 Chôwthâm (1), *seal*

HOTHIR
1956 Hôwthîyr (2), *he has caused to remain*

HOTLY
1814 dâlaq (1), *to flame; to pursue*

HOTTEST
2389 châzâq (1), *strong; severe, hard, violent*

HOUGH
6131 'âqar (1), *to pluck up roots; to hamstring*

HOUGHED
6131 'âqar (3), *to pluck up roots; to hamstring*

HOUR
8160 shâ'âh (Ch.) (5), *immediately*
734 Artĕmas (1), *gift of Artemis*
2256 hēmiōriŏn (1), *half-hour*
5610 hōra (85), *hour, i.e. a unit of time*

HOURS
5610 hōra (3), *hour, i.e. a unit of time*

HOUSE
1004 bayith (1745), *house; temple; family*
1005 bayith (Ch.) (41), *house; temple; family*
1008 Bêyth-'Êl (5), *house of God*
1035 Bêyth Lechem (1), *house of bread*
5854 'Aṭrôwth Bêyth Yôw'âb (1), *crowns of (the) house of Joäb*
3609 ŏikĕiŏs (1), *of the household*
3613 ŏikētēriŏn (1), *residence, home*
3614 ŏikia (84), *abode; family*
3616 ŏikŏdĕspŏtĕō (1), *to be the head of a family*
3617 ŏikŏdĕspŏtēs (7), *head of a family*
3624 ŏikŏs (96), *dwelling; family*
3832 panŏiki (1), *with the whole family*

HOUSEHOLD
1004 bayith (47), *house; temple; family, tribe*
5657 'ăbuddâh (1), *service*
2322 thĕrapĕia (2), *cure, healing; domestics*
3609 ŏikĕiŏs (2), *of the household*
3610 ŏikĕtēs (1), *menial domestic servant*
3614 ŏikia (1), *abode; family*
3615 ŏikiakŏs (2), *relatives*
3624 ŏikŏs (3), *dwelling; family*

HOUSEHOLDER
3617 ŏikŏdĕspŏtēs (4), *head of a family*

HOUSEHOLDS
1004 bayith (7), *house; temple; family, tribe*

HOUSES
490 'almânâh (1), *widow*
1004 bayith (116), *house; temple; family, tribe*
1005 bayith (Ch.) (2), *house; temple; family*
4999 nâ'âh (1), *home, dwelling; pasture*

HOUSETOP
1406 gâg (2), *roof; top*
1430 dōma (5), *roof, housetop*

HOUSETOPS
1406 gâg (5), *roof; top*
1430 dōma (2), *roof, housetop*

HOW
335 'ay (1), *where?*
346 'ayêh (2), *where?*
349 'êyk (75), *how? or how!; where?*
434 'ĕlûwl (1), *good for nothing*
637 'aph (18), *also or yea; though*
834 'ăsher (26), *how, because, in order that*
1963 hêyk (2), *how?*
3588 kîy (11), *for, that because*
4069 maddûwa' (1), *why?, what?*
4100 mâh (59), *how?, how!; what, whatever*
4101 mâh (Ch.) (3), *how?, how!; what, whatever*
5704 'ad (47), *as far (long) as; during*
2193 hĕōs (6), *until*
2245 hēlikŏs (1), *how much, how great*
2531 kathōs (1), *just or inasmuch as, that*
3386 mētigĕ (1), *not to say (the rather still)*
3704 hŏpōs (4), *in the manner that*
3745 hŏsŏs (7), *as much as*
3754 hŏti (14), *that; because; since*
4012 pĕri (1), *about; around*
4080 pēlikŏs (2), *how much, how great*
4212 pŏsakis (2), *how many times*
4214 pŏsŏs (26), *how much?; how much!*
4219 pŏtĕ (1), *at what time?*
4459 pōs (96), *in what way?; how?; how much!*
4559 sarkikŏs (2), *pertaining to flesh*
5101 tis (11), *who?, which? or what?*
5613 hōs (19), *which, how, i.e. in that manner*

HOWBEIT
199 'ûwlâm (1), *however or on the contrary*
389 'ak (1), *surely; only, however*
657 'epheç (1), *end; no further*
3651 kên (1), *just; right, correct*
7535 raq (1), *merely; although*
235 alla (8), *but, yet, except, instead*

1161 dĕ (1), *but, yet*
3305 mĕntŏi (1), *however*

HOWL
3213 yâlal (27), to *howl, wail, yell*
3649 ŏlŏluzō (1), to *howl,* i.e. *shriek* or *wail*

HOWLED
3213 yâlal (1), to *howl, wail, yell*

HOWLING
3213 yâlal (5), to *howl, wail, yell*
3214 yᵉlêl (1), *howl, wail*

HOWLINGS
3213 yâlal (1), to *howl, wail, yell*

HOWSOEVER
1961+4101 hâyâh (1), to *exist,* i.e. *be* or *become*
3605+834 kôl (1), *all, any* or *every*
7535 raq (1), *merely; although*

HUGE
7230 rôb (1), *abundance*

HUKKOK
2712 Chuqqôq (1), *appointed*

HUKOK
2712 Chuqqôq (1), *appointed*

HUL
2343 Chûwl (2), *circle*

HULDAH
2468 Chuldâh (2), *weasel*

HUMBLE
3665 kâna' (2), to *humiliate, vanquish, subdue*
6031 'ânâh (4), to *afflict, be afflicted*
6041 'ânîy (5), *depressed*
7511 râphaç (1), to *trample; to prostrate*
7807+5869 shach (1), *sunk,* i.e. *downcast*
8213 shâphêl (2), to *humiliate*
8217 shâphâl (3), *depressed, low*
5011 tapĕinŏs (2), *humiliated, lowly*
5013 tapĕinŏō (5), to *depress; to humiliate*

HUMBLED
1792 dâkâ' (1), to be *contrite, be humbled*
3665 kâna' (13), to *humiliate, vanquish*
6031 'ânâh (7), to *afflict, be afflicted*
7743 shûwach (1), to *sink*
8213 shâphêl (4), to *humiliate*
8214 shᵉphal (Ch.) (1), to *humiliate*
5013 tapĕinŏō (1), to *depress; to humiliate*

HUMBLEDST
3665 kâna' (1), to *humiliate, vanquish*

HUMBLENESS
5012 tapĕinŏphrŏsunē (1), *modesty, humility*

HUMBLETH
3665 kâna' (2), to *humiliate, vanquish*
7817 shâchach (1), to *sink or depress*
8213 shâphêl (2), to *humiliate*
5013 tapĕinŏō (2), to *depress; to humiliate*

HUMBLY
6800 tsâna' (1), to *humiliate*
7812 shâchâh (1), to *prostrate in homage*

HUMILIATION
5014 tapĕinōsis (1), *humbleness, lowliness*

HUMILITY
6038 'ănâvâh (3), *condescension*
5012 tapĕinŏphrŏsunē (4), *modesty, humility*

HUMTAH
2457 chel'âh (1), *rust*

HUNDRED
520 'ammâh (1), *cubit*
3967 mê'âh (545), *hundred*
3969 mᵉ'âh (Ch.) (7), *hundred*
1250 diakŏsiŏi (8), *two hundred*
1540 hĕkatŏn (14), *hundred*
1541 hĕkatŏntaĕtēs (1), *centenarian*
3461 murias (1), *ten-thousand*
4001 pĕntakŏsiŏi (2), *five hundred*
5071 tĕtrakŏsiŏi (4), *four hundred*
5145 triakŏsiŏi (2), *three hundred*
5516 chi xi stigma (2), 666

HUNDREDFOLD
3967+8180 mê'âh (1), *hundred*
1540 hĕkatŏn (2), *hundred*
1542 hĕkatŏntaplasiōn (3), *hundred times*

HUNDREDS
3967 mê'âh (27), *hundred*
1540 hĕkatŏn (1), *hundred*

HUNDREDTH
3967 mê'âh (3), *hundred*

HUNGER
7456 râ'êb (5), to *hunger*
7457 râ'êb (8), *hungry*
3042 limŏs (3), *scarcity, famine*
3983 pĕinaō (8), to *famish; to crave*

HUNGERBITTEN
7457 râ'êb (1), *hungry*

HUNGERED
3983 pĕinaō (2), to *famish; to crave*

HUNGRED
3983 pĕinaō (9), to *famish; to crave*

HUNGRY
7456 râ'êb (25), to *hunger*
3983 pĕinaō (4), to *famish; to crave*
4361 prŏspĕinŏs (1), *intensely hungry*

HUNT
6679 tsûwd (11), to *lie in wait; to catch*
7291 râdaph (1), to *run after* with hostility

HUNTED
4686 mâtsûwd (1), *net or capture; fastness*

HUNTER
6718 tsayid (4), *hunting game; lunch, food*

HUNTERS
6719 tsayâd (1), *huntsman*

HUNTEST
6658 tsâdâh (1), to *desolate*
6679 tsûwd (1), to *lie in wait; to catch*

HUNTETH
6679 tsûwd (1), to *lie in wait; to catch*

HUNTING
6718 tsayid (2), *hunting game; lunch, food*

HUPHAM
2349 Chûwphâm (1), *protection*

HUPHAMITES
2350 Chûwphâmîy (1), *Chuphamite*

HUPPAH
2647 Chuppâh (1), *canopy*

HUPPIM
2650 Chuppîym (3), *canopies*

HUR
2354 Chûwr (16), *cell* of a *prison* or *white* linen

HURAI
2360 Chûwray (1), *linen*-worker

HURAM
2361 Chûwrâm (6), *noble*
2438 Chîyrâm (6), *noble*

HURI
2359 Chûwrîy (1), *linen*-worker

HURL
7993 shâlak (1), to *throw* out, down or away

HURLETH
8175 sâ'ar (1), to *storm;* to *shiver,* i.e. *fear*

HURT
1697 dâbâr (1), *word; matter; thing*
2248 chăbûwlâh (Ch.) (1), *crime, wrong*
2250 chabbûwrâh (1), *weal, bruise*
2255 chăbal (Ch.) (1), to *ruin, destroy*

2257 chăbal (Ch.) (2), *harm, wound*
3637 kâlam (2), to *taunt or insult*
5062 nâgaph (2), to *inflict* a disease
5142 nᵉzaq (Ch.) (1), to *suffer, inflict loss*
6031 'ânâh (1), to *afflict, be afflicted*
6087 'âtsab (1), to *worry, have pain or anger*
6485 pâqad (1), to *visit, care for, count*
7451 ra' (20), *bad; evil*
7489 râ'a' (7), to *break to pieces*
7665 shâbar (3), to *burst*
7667 sheber (4), *fracture; ruin*
91 adikĕō (10), to *do wrong*
984 blaptō (2), to *hinder,* i.e. to *injure*
2559 kakŏō (1), to *injure; to oppress; to embitter*
5196 hubris (1), *insult; injury*

HURTFUL
5142 nᵉzaq (Ch.) (1), to *suffer, inflict loss*
7451 ra' (1), *bad; evil*
983 blabĕrŏs (1), *injurious, harmful*

HURTING
7489 râ'a' (1), to *break to pieces*

HUSBAND
376 'îysh (66), *man; male; someone*
1167 ba'al (13), *master; husband; owner; citizen*
2860 châthân (2), *bridegroom*
435 anēr (38), *man; male*
5220 hupandrŏs (1), *married* woman

HUSBAND'S
376 'îysh (2), *man; male; someone*
2992 yâbam (2), to *marry* a dead brother's widow
2993 yâbâm (2), *husband's brother*

HUSBANDMAN
376+127 'îysh (1), *man; male; someone*
406 'ikkâr (2), *farmer*
5647 'âbad (1), to *do, work, serve*
1092 gĕōrgŏs (3), *farmer; tenant farmer*

HUSBANDMEN
406 'ikkâr (3), *farmer*
1461 gûwb (1), to *dig*
3009 yâgab (1), to *dig or plow*
1092 gĕōrgŏs (16), *farmer; tenant farmer*

HUSBANDRY
127 'ădâmâh (1), *soil; land*
1091 gĕōrgiŏn (1), *cultivable,* i.e. *farm*

HUSBANDS
376 'îysh (1), *man; male*

English

582 'ĕnôwsh (3), *man; person, human*
1167 ba'al (2), *master; husband; owner; citizen*
435 anēr (12), *man; male*
5362 philandrŏs (1), *affectionate as a wife to her husband*

HUSHAH
2364 Chûwshâh (1), *haste*

HUSHAI
2365 Chûwshay (14), *hasty*

HUSHAM
2367 Chûwshâm (4), *hastily*

HUSHATHITE
2843 Chûshâthîy (5), *Chushathite*

HUSHIM
2366 Chûwshîym (4), *those who hasten*

HUSK
2085 zâg (1), *grape skin*
6861 tsiqlôn (1), *tied up sack*

HUSKS
2769 kĕratiŏn (1), *pod*

HUZ
5780 'Ûwts (1), *consultation*

HUZZAB
5324 nâtsab (1), to *station*

HYMENAEUS
5211 Humĕnaiŏs (2), *one dedicated to the god of weddings*

HYMN
5214 humnĕō (1), to *celebrate God in song*

HYMNS
5215 humnŏs (2), *hymn or religious ode*

HYPOCRISIES
5272 hupŏkrisis (1), *deceit, hypocrisy*

HYPOCRISY
2612 chôneph (1), moral *filth*, i.e. *wickedness*
505 anupŏkritŏs (1), *sincere, genuine*
5272 hupŏkrisis (4), *deceit, hypocrisy*

HYPOCRITE
120+2611 'âdâm (1), *human being; mankind*
2611 chânêph (6), *soiled* (i.e. with sin), *impious*
5273 hupŏkritēs (3), *dissembler, hypocrite*

HYPOCRITE'S
2611 chânêph (1), *soiled* (i.e. with sin), *impious*

HYPOCRITES
120+2611 'âdâm (1), *human being; mankind*
2611 chânêph (2), *soiled* (i.e. with sin), *impious*
5273 hupŏkritēs (17), *dissembler, hypocrite*

HYPOCRITICAL
2611 chânêph (2), *soiled* (i.e. with sin), *impious*

HYSSOP
231 'êzôwb (10), *hyssop*
5301 hussōpŏs (2), *hyssop plant*

I-CHABOD
350 Îy-kâbôwd (1), *inglorious*

I-CHABOD'S
350 Îy-kâbôwd (1), *inglorious*

IBHAR
2984 Yibchar (3), *choice*

IBLEAM
2991 Yibleʿâm (3), *devouring people*

IBNEIAH
2997 Yibneʿyâh (1), *built of Jehovah*

IBNIJAH
2998 Yibnîyâh (1), *building of Jehovah*

IBRI
5681 'Ibrîy (1), *Eberite* (i.e. Hebrew)

IBZAN
78 'Ibtsân (2), *splendid*

ICE
7140 qerach (3), *ice; hail; rock crystal*

ICONIUM
2430 Ikŏniŏn (6), *image-like*

IDALAH
3030 Yid'ălâh (1), *Jidalah*

IDBASH
3031 Yidbâsh (1), *honeyed*

IDDO
112 'Iddôw (2), *Iddo*
3035 Yiddôw (1), *praised*
3260 Yeʿdîy (1), *appointed*
5714 'Iddôw (10), *timely*

IDLE
7423 remîyâh (1), *remissness; treachery*
7504 râpheh (2), *slack*
692 argŏs (6), *lazy; useless*
3026 lērŏs (1), *twaddle*, i.e. an *incredible* story

IDLENESS
6104 'atslûwth (1), *indolence*
8220 shiphlûwth (1), *remissness, idleness*
8252 shâqaṭ (1), to *repose*

IDOL
205 'âven (1), *trouble, vanity, wickedness*
457 'ĕlîyl (1), *vain idol*
4656 miphletseth (4), *terror idol*
5566 çemel (2), *likeness*
6089 'etseb (1), *earthen vessel; painful toil*
6090 'ôtseb (1), *fashioned idol; pain*
1494 ĕidōlŏthutŏn (1), *idolatrous offering*
1497 ĕidōlŏn (4), *idol*, or the *worship* of such

IDOL'S
1493 ĕidōlĕiŏn (1), *idol temple*

IDOLATER
1496 ĕidōlŏlatrēs (2), *image-worshipper*

IDOLATERS
1496 ĕidōlŏlatrēs (5), *image-worshipper*

IDOLATRIES
1495 ĕidōlŏlatrĕia (1), *image-worship*

IDOLATROUS
3649 kâmâr (1), pagan *priest*

IDOLATRY
8655 terâphîym (1), *healer*
1495 ĕidōlŏlatrĕia (3), *image-worship*
2712 katĕidōlŏs (1), *utterly idolatrous*

IDOLS
367 'êymâh (1), *fright*
410 'êl (1), *mighty; the Almighty*
457 'ĕlîyl (16), *vain idol*
1544 gillûwl (47), *idol*
2553 chammân (1), *sun-pillar*
6091 'âtsâb (16), *image, idol*
6736 tsîyr (1), *carved idolatrous image*
8251 shiqqûwts (1), *disgusting; idol*
8655 teráphîym (1), *healer*
1494 ĕidōlŏthutŏn (9), *idolatrous offering*
1497 ĕidōlŏn (7), *idol*, or the *worship* of such

IDUMAEA
2401 Idŏumaia (1), *Idumæa*, i.e. *Edom*

IDUMEA
123 'Ĕdôm (4), *red*

IF
176 'ôw (3), *or, whether*
194 'ûwlay (9), *if not*
432 'illûw (1), *if*
518 'îm (557), *whether?; if*
834 'ăsher (19), *who, which, what, that*
2005 hên (3), *lo!; if!*
2006 hên (Ch.) (11), *lo; whether, but, if*
3588 kîy (159), *for, that because*
3808 lô' (1), *no, not*
3863 lûw' (7), *if; would that!*
3883 lûwl (1), *spiral step*
3884 lûwlê (2), *if not*
6112 'Êtsen (1), *spear*
148 aischrŏlŏgia (3), *vile conversation*
1437 ĕan (216), *in case that, provided*
1477 hĕdraiōma (5), *basis, foundation*
1487 ĕi (305), *if, whether*
1489 ĕigĕ (5), *if indeed*
1490 ĕi dĕ mē(gĕ) (4), *but if not*
1499 ĕi kai (6), *if also*

1512 ĕi pĕr (4), *if perhaps*
1513 ĕi pōs (4), *if somehow*
1535 ĕitĕ (1), *if too*
2579 kan (5), *and if*
3379 mēpŏtĕ (1), *not ever; if*, or *lest ever*

IGAL
3008 Yig'âl (2), *avenger*

IGDALIAH
3012 Yigdalyâhûw (1), *magnified of Jehovah*

IGEAL
3008 Yig'âl (1), *avenger*

IGNOMINY
7036 qâlôwn (1), *disgrace*

IGNORANCE
7684 sheğâgâh (12), *mistake, transgression*
7686 shâgâh (1), to *transgress by mistake*
52 agnŏia (4), *ignorance*
56 agnŏsia (1), state of *ignorance*

IGNORANT
3808+3045 lô' (3), no, *not*
50 agnŏĕō (10), to *not know; not understand*
2399 idiōtēs (1), *not initiated; untrained*
2990 lanthanō (2), to *lie hid; unwittingly*

IGNORANTLY
1097+1847 belîy (1), *not yet; lacking*
7683 shâgag (1), to *sin through oversight*
50 agnŏĕō (2), to *not know; not understand*

IIM
5864 'Iyîym (2), *ruins*

IJE-ABARIM
5863 'Iyêy hâ-'Ăbârîym (2), *ruins of the passers*

IJON
5859 'Iyôwn (3), *ruin*

IKKESH
6142 'Îqqêsh (3), *perverse*

ILAI
5866 'Îylay (1), *elevated*

ILL
3415 yâra' (2), to *fear*
6709 tsachănâh (1), *stench*
7451 ra' (8), *bad; evil*
7489 râ'a' (3), to *be good for nothing*
2556 kakŏs (1), *bad, evil, wrong*

ILLUMINATED
5461 phōtizō (1), to *shine* or to *brighten* up

ILLYRICUM
2437 Illurikŏn (1), *Illyricum*

IMAGE
4676 matstsêbâh (3), *column or stone*
4906 maskîyth (1), *carved figure*
5566 çemel (2), *likeness*
6459 peçel (2), *idol*
6676 tsavva'r (Ch.) (1), *back of the neck*

6754 tselem (6), *phantom; idol*
6755 tselem (Ch.) (16), idolatrous *figure*
6816 tsa'tsûa' (1), *sculpture* work
8544 t^emûwnâh (1), something *fashioned*
8655 t^erâphîym (2), *healer*
1504 ĕikŏn (22), *likeness*
5481 charaktēr (1), exact copy or *representation*

IMAGE'S
6755 tselem (Ch.) (1), idolatrous *figure*

IMAGERY
4906 maskîyth (1), carved *figure*

IMAGES
457 'ĕlîyl (1), *vain idol*
1544 gillûwl (1), *idol*
2553 chammân (6), *sun*-pillar
4676 matstsēbâh (14), *column or stone*
6091 'âtsâb (1), *image, idol*
6456 p^eçîyl (2), *idol*
6754 tselem (9), *phantom; idol*
8655 t^erâphîym (5), *healer*

IMAGINATION
3336 yêtser (4), *form*
8307 sh^erîyrûwth (9), *obstinacy*
1271 dianŏia (1), *mind or thought*

IMAGINATIONS
3336 yêtser (1), *form*
4284 machăshâbâh (3), *contrivance; plan*
1261 dialŏgismŏs (1), *consideration; debate*
3053 lŏgismŏs (1), *reasoning; conscience*

IMAGINE
1897 hâgâh (2), to *murmur, ponder*
2050 hâthath (1), to *assail, verbally attack*
2554 châmaç (1), to be *violent; to maltreat*
2790 chârash (1), to be *silent; to be deaf*
2803 châshab (5), to *plot; to think, regard*
3191 mĕlĕtaō (1), to *plot, think about*

IMAGINED
2161 zâmam (1), to *plan*
2803 châshab (2), to *plot; to think, regard*

IMAGINETH
2803 châshab (1), to *plot; to think, regard*

IMLA
3229 Yimlâ' (2), *full*

IMLAH
3229 Yimlâ' (2), *full*

IMMANUEL
6005 'Immânûw'êl (2), *with us* (is) *God*

IMMEDIATELY
1824 ĕxautēs (3), *instantly, at once*
2112 ĕuthĕŏs (35), *at once or soon*
2117 ĕuthus (3), *at once, immediately*
3916 parachrēma (13), *instantly, immediately*

IMMER
564 'Immêr (10), *talkative*

IMMORTAL
862 aphthartŏs (1), *undecaying, immortal*

IMMORTALITY
110 athanasia (3), *deathlessness*
861 aphtharsia (2), *unending existence*

IMMUTABILITY
276 amĕtathĕtŏs (1), *unchangeable*

IMMUTABLE
276 amĕtathĕtŏs (1), *unchangeable*

IMNA
3234 Yimnâ' (1), *he will restrain*

IMNAH
3232 Yimnâh (2), *prosperity*

IMPART
3330 mĕtadidōmi (2), to *share, distribute*

IMPARTED
2505 châlaq (1), to be *smooth; be slippery*
3330 mĕtadidōmi (1), to *share, distribute*

IMPEDIMENT
3424 mŏgilalŏs (1), *hardly talking*

IMPENITENT
279 amĕtanŏētŏs (1), *unrepentant*

IMPERIOUS
7986 shalleteth (1), *dominant woman*

IMPLACABLE
786 aspŏndŏs (1), *not reconcilable*

IMPLEAD
1458 ĕgkalĕō (1), to *charge, criminate*

IMPORTUNITY
335 anaidĕia (1), *importunity, boldness*

IMPOSE
7412 r^emâh (Ch.) (1), to *throw; to set; to assess*

IMPOSED
1942 ĕpikaluma (1), *pretext, covering*

IMPOSSIBLE
101 adunatĕō (2), to be *impossible*
102 adunatŏs (6), *weak; impossible*
418 anĕndĕktŏs (1), *impossible*

IMPOTENT
102 adunatŏs (1), *weak; impossible*
770 asthĕnĕŏ (2), to be *feeble*
772 asthĕnēs (1), *strengthless, weak*

IMPOVERISH
7567 râshash (1), to *demolish*

IMPOVERISHED
1809 dâlal (1), to be *feeble; to be oppressed*
5533 çâkan (1), to *grow, make poor*
7567 râshash (1), to *demolish*

IMPRISONED
5439 phulakizō (1), to *incarcerate, imprison*

IMPRISONMENT
613 'ĕçûwr (Ch.) (1), *manacles, chains*
5438 phulakē (1), *watch; prison; haunt*

IMPRISONMENTS
5438 phulakē (1), *watch; prison; haunt*

IMPUDENT
2389+4696 châzâq (1), *severe, hard, violent*
5810 'âzaz (1), to be *stout; be bold*
7186+6440 qâsheh (1), *severe*

IMPUTE
2803 châshab (1), to *regard; to compute*
7760 sûwm (1), to *put, place*
3049 lŏgizŏmai (1), to *credit; to think, regard*

IMPUTED
2803 châshab (2), to *think, regard; compute*
1677 ĕllŏgĕō (1), to *charge to one's account*
3049 lŏgizŏmai (5), to *credit; to think, regard*

IMPUTETH
2803 châshab (1), to *think, regard; compute*
3049 lŏgizŏmai (1), to *credit; to think, regard*

IMPUTING
3049 lŏgizŏmai (1), to *credit; to think, regard*

IMRAH
3236 Yimrâh (1), *interchange*

IMRI
556 'amtsâh (2), *strength, force*

INASMUCH
1115 biltîy (1), *except, without, unless, besides*
3588 kîy (1), *for, that because*
2526 kathŏ (1), *precisely as, in proportion as*

INCENSE
3828 l^ebôwnâh (6), *frankincense*

6999 qâţar (58), to *turn into fragrance* by fire
7002 qiţţêr (1), *perfume*
7004 q^eţôreth (57), *fumigation*
2368 thumiama (4), *incense* offering
2370 thumiaō (1), to *offer aromatic fumes*

INCENSED
2734 chârâh (2), to *blaze*

INCLINE
5186 nâţâh (15), to *stretch* or spread out
7181 qâshab (1), to *prick up* the ears

INCLINED
5186 nâţâh (13), to *stretch* or spread out

INCLINETH
7743 shûwach (1), to *sink*

INCLOSE
6696 tsûwr (1), to *cramp, i.e. confine; to harass*

INCLOSED
1443 gâdar (1), to *build a stone wall*
3803 kâthar (1), to *enclose, besiege; to wait*
4142 mûwçabbâh (2), *backside; fold*
5274 nâ'al (1), to *fasten up, lock*
5362 nâqaph (1), to *surround or circulate*
5462 çâgar (1), to *shut up; to surrender*
4788 sugklĕiō (1), to *net fish; to lock up* persons

INCLOSINGS
4396 millû'âh (2), *setting*

INCONTINENCY
192 akrasia (1), *lack of control of self*

INCONTINENT
193 akratēs (1), *without self-control*

INCORRUPTIBLE
862 aphthartŏs (4), *undecaying, immortal*

INCORRUPTION
861 aphtharsia (4), *unending existence*

INCREASE
2981 y^ebûwl (10), *produce, crop; harvest*
3254 yâçaph (6), to *add or augment*
4768 marbîyth (3), *interest* on money
5107 nûwb (1), to (*make*) *flourish; to utter*
6555 pârats (1), to *break out*
7235 râbâh (18), to *increase*
7239 ribbôw (1), *myriad, indefinite large number*
7685 sâgâh (2), to *enlarge, be prosperous*
7698 sheger (4), what *comes forth*
8393 t^ebûw'âh (23), *income, i.e. produce*

8570 tᵉnûwbâh (2), *crop, produce*
8635 tarbûwth (6), *progeny, brood*
837 auxanō (4), to *grow,* i.e. *enlarge*
838 auxēsis (2), *growth, increase*
4052 pĕrissĕuō (1), to *superabound*
4121 plĕŏnazō (1), to *increase; superabound*
4298 prŏkŏptō (1), to *go ahead, advance*
4369 prŏstithēmi (1), to *lay beside, annex*

INCREASED
1431 gâdal (1), to *be great, make great*
3254 yâçaph (5), to *add* or *augment*
5927 'âlâh (3), to *ascend, be high, mount*
6105 'âtsam (4), to *be, make numerous*
6509 pârâh (3), to *bear fruit*
6555 pârats (4), to *break out*
7227 rab (2), *great*
7230 rôb (1), *abundance*
7231 râbab (3), to *increase; to multiply*
7235 râbâh (15), to *increase*
8317 shârats (1), to *swarm,* or *abound*
837 auxanō (3), to *grow,* i.e. *enlarge*
1743 ĕndunamŏō (1), to *empower, strengthen*
4052 pĕrissĕuō (1), to *superabound*
4147 plŏutĕō (1), to *be, become wealthy*
4298 prŏkŏptō (1), to *go ahead, advance*

INCREASEST
7235 râbâh (1), to *increase*

INCREASETH
553 'âmats (1), to *be strong; be courageous*
1342 gâ'âh (1), to *rise;* to *grow tall; be majestic*
3254 yâçaph (4), to *add* or *augment*
5927 'âlâh (1), to *ascend, be high, mount*
7235 râbâh (5), to *increase*
7679 sâgâ' (1), to *laud, extol*
837 auxanō (1), to *grow,* i.e. *enlarge*

INCREASING
837 auxanō (1), to *grow,* i.e. *enlarge*

INCREDIBLE
571 apistŏs (1), *without faith; incredible*

INCURABLE
369+4832 'ayin (1), *there is no,* i.e., *not exist*
605 'ânash (5), to *be frail, feeble*

INDEBTED
3784 ŏphĕilō (1), to *owe;* to *be under obligation*

INDEED
61 'ăbâl (2), *truly, surely; yet, but*
389 'ak (1), *surely; only, however*
546 'omnâh (2), *surely*
551 'omnâm (2), *verily, indeed, truly*
552 'umnâm (3), *verily, indeed, truly*
1571 gam (1), *also; even; yea; though*
230 alēthōs (6), *truly, surely*
235 alla (1), *but, yet, except, instead*
1063 gar (2), *for, indeed, but, because*
2532 kai (2), *and;* or; *even; also*
3303 mĕn (22), *indeed*
3689 ŏntōs (6), *really, certainly*

INDIA
1912 Hôdûw (2), *India*

INDIGNATION
2194 zâ'am (4), to *be enraged*
2195 za'am (20), *fury, anger*
2197 za'aph (2), *anger, rage*
2534 chêmâh (1), *heat; anger; poison*
3707 kâ'aç (1), to *grieve, rage, be indignant*
3708 ka'aç (1), *vexation, grief*
7110 qetseph (3), *rage* or *strife*
23 aganaktĕō (4), to *be indignant*
24 aganaktēsis (1), *indignation*
2205 zēlŏs (2), *zeal, ardor; jealousy, malice*
2372 thumŏs (1), *passion, anger*
3709 ŏrgē (1), *ire; punishment*

INDITING
7370 râchash (1), to *gush*

INDUSTRIOUS
6213+4399 'âsâh (1), to *do* or *make*

INEXCUSABLE
379 anapŏlŏgētŏs (1), *without excuse*

INFAMOUS
2931+8034 tâmê' (1), *foul; ceremonially impure*

INFAMY
1681 dibbâh (2), *slander, bad report*

INFANT
5764 'ûwl (1), *nursing babe*
5768 'ôwlêl (1), *suckling child*

INFANTS
5768 'ôwlêl (2), *suckling child*
1025 brĕphŏs (1), *infant*

INFERIOR
772 'ăra' (Ch.) (1), *earth, ground, land; inferior*
5307 nâphal (2), to *fall*
2274 hēttaō (1), to *rate lower, be inferior*

INFIDEL
571 apistŏs (2), *without faith; untrustworthy*

INFINITE
369+4557 'ayin (1), *there is no,* i.e., *not exist*
369+7093 'ayin (2), *there is no,* i.e., *not exist*

INFIRMITIES
769 asthĕnĕia (10), *feebleness; malady*
771 asthĕnēma (1), *failing, weakness*
3554 nŏsŏs (1), *malady, disease*

INFIRMITY
1738 dâvâh (1), to *be in menstruation cycle*
2470 châlâh (1), to *be weak, sick, afflicted*
4245 machăleh (1), *sickness*
769 asthĕnĕia (7), *feebleness; malady*

INFLAME
1814 dâlaq (1), to *flame;* to *pursue*

INFLAMMATION
1816 dalleqeth (1), *burning fever*
6867 tsârebeth (1), *conflagration*

INFLUENCES
4575 ma'ădannâh (1), *bond,* i.e. *group*

INFOLDING
3947 lâqach (1), to *take*

INFORM
3384 yârâh (1), to *point;* to *teach*

INFORMED
995 bîyn (1), to *understand; discern*
1718 ĕmphanizō (3), to *show forth*
2727 katēchĕō (2), to *indoctrinate*

INGATHERING
614 'âçîyph (2), *harvest, gathering in* of crops

INHABIT
3427 yâshab (8), to *dwell, to remain; to settle*
7931 shâkan (2), to *reside*

INHABITANT
1481 gûwr (1), to *sojourn, live as an alien*
3427 yâshab (31), to *dwell, to remain*
7934 shâkên (1), *resident; fellow-citizen*

INHABITANTS
1753 dûwr (Ch.) (2), to *reside, live in*
3427 yâshab (190), to *dwell, to remain*
7934 shâkên (2), *resident; fellow-citizen*

8453 tôwshâb (1), *temporary dweller*
2730 katŏikĕō (1), to *reside, live in*

INHABITED
1509 gᵉzêrâh (1), *desert, unfertile place*
3427 yâshab (29), to *dwell, to remain*
4186 môwshâb (1), *seat; site; abode*
7931 shâkan (1), to *reside*

INHABITERS
2730 katŏikĕō (2), to *reside, live in*

INHABITEST
3427 yâshab (1), to *dwell, to remain; to settle*

INHABITETH
3427 yâshab (1), to *dwell, to remain; to settle*
7931 shâkan (1), to *reside*

INHABITING
6728 tsîyîy (1), *desert-dweller; wild beast*

INHERIT
3423 yârash (21), to *inherit; to impoverish*
5157 nâchal (25), to *inherit*
5159 nachălâh (2), *occupancy*
2816 klērŏnŏmĕō (14), to *be an heir to, inherit*

INHERITANCE
2490 châlal (1), to *profane, defile*
2506 chêleq (1), *allotment*
3423 yârash (1), to *inherit; to impoverish*
3425 yᵉrushâh (2), *conquest*
4181 môwrâshâh (2), *possession*
5157 nâchal (18), to *inherit*
5159 nachălâh (189), *occupancy*
2817 klērŏnŏmia (14), *inherited possession*
2819 klērŏs (2), *lot, portion*
2820 klērŏō (2), to *allot*

INHERITANCES
5159 nachălâh (1), *occupancy*

INHERITED
3423 yârash (2), to *inherit; to impoverish*
5157 nâchal (3), to *inherit*
2816 klērŏnŏmĕō (1), to *be an heir to, inherit*

INHERITETH
5157 nâchal (1), to *inherit*

INHERITOR
3423 yârash (1), to *inherit; to impoverish*

INIQUITIES
1647+5771 Gêrᵉshôm (1), *refugee*
5758 'ivyâ' (Ch.) (1), *perverseness*
5766 'evel (1), *moral evil*
5771 'âvôn (47), *evil*

92 adikēma (1), *wrong done*
458 anŏmia (3), *violation of law, wickedness*
4189 pŏnēria (1), *malice, evil, wickedness*

INIQUITY
205 'âven (47), *trouble, vanity, wickedness*
1942 havvâh (1), *desire; craving*
5753 lâvâh (4), to *be crooked*
5766 'evel (35), moral *evil*
5771 'âvôn (170), moral *evil*
5932 'alvâh (1), *moral perverseness*
5999 'âmâl (1), *wearing effort; worry*
7562 resha' (1), *moral wrong*
93 adikia (6), *wrongfulness*
458 anŏmia (8), *violation of law, wickedness*
3892 paranŏmia (1), *transgression*

INJURED
91 adikĕō (1), to *do wrong*

INJURIOUS
5197 hubristēs (1), *maltreater, violent*

INJUSTICE
2555 châmâç (1), *violence; malice*

INK
1773 dᵉyôw (1), *ink*
3188 mĕlan (3), *black ink*

INKHORN
7083 qeçeth (3), *ink-stand*

INN
4411 mâlôwn (3), *lodgment* for night
2646 kataluma (1), *lodging-place*
3829 pandŏchĕiŏn (1), public *lodging-place*

INNER
2315 cheder (4), *apartment, chamber*
6441 pᵉnîymâh (1), *indoors, inside*
6442 pᵉnîymîy (30), *interior, inner*
2080 ĕsō (1), *inside, inner, in*
2082 ĕsŏtĕrŏs (1), *interior, inner*

INNERMOST
2315 cheder (2), *apartment, chamber*

INNOCENCY
2136 zâkûw (Ch.) (1), *purity; justice*
5356 niqqâyôwn (4), *clearness; cleanness*

INNOCENT
2600 chinnâm (1), *gratis, free*
2643 chaph (1), *pure, clean*

5352 nâqâh (5), to *be, make clean;* to *be bare*
5355 nâqîy (29), *innocent*
121 athŏŏs (2), *not guilty*

INNOCENTS
5355 nâqîy (2), *innocent*

INNUMERABLE
369+4557 'ayin (4), *there is no, i.e., not exist*
382 anarithmētŏs (1), *without number*
3461 murias (2), *ten-thousand*

INORDINATE
5691 'ăgâbâh (1), *love, amorousness*
3806 pathŏs (1), *passion, concupiscence*

INQUISITION
1245 bâqash (1), to *search;* to *strive after*
1875 dârash (2), to *pursue or search*

INSCRIPTION
1924 ĕpigraphō (1), to *inscribe, write upon*

INSIDE
1004 bayith (1), *house; temple; family, tribe*

INSOMUCH
1519 ĕis (1), to or into
5620 hŏstĕ (17), *thus, therefore*

INSPIRATION
5397 nᵉshâmâh (1), *breath, life*
2315 thĕŏpnĕustŏs (1), *divinely breathed in*

INSTANT
6621 petha' (2), *wink, i.e. moment; quickly*
7281 rega' (2), *very short space of time*
1945 ĕpikĕimai (1), to *rest upon; press upon*
2186 ĕphistēmi (1), to be *present;* to *approach*
4342 prŏskartĕrĕō (1), to *attend;* to *adhere*
5610 hōra (1), *hour, i.e. a unit of time*

INSTANTLY
1722+1616 ĕn (1), *in; during; because of*
4705 spŏudaiŏs (1), *prompt, energetic*

INSTEAD
8478 tachath (35), *underneath; in lieu of*

INSTRUCT
995 bîyn (1), to *understand; discern*
3250 yiççôwr (1), *reprover, corrector*
3256 yâçar (3), to *chastise;* to *instruct*
3925 lâmad (1), to *teach, train*
7919 sâkal (2), to *be or act circumspect*
4822 sumbibazō (1), to *unite;* to *show, teach*

INSTRUCTED
995 bîyn (2), to *understand; discern*

3045 yâda' (1), to *know*
3245 yâçad (1), *settle, consult, establish*
3256 yâçar (5), to *chastise;* to *instruct*
3384 yârâh (1), to *point;* to *teach*
3925 lâmad (2), to *teach, train*
7919 sâkal (1), to *be or act circumspect*
2727 katēchĕō (3), to *indoctrinate*
3100 mathĕtĕuō (1), to *become a student*
3453 muĕō (1), to *initiate*
4264 prŏbibazō (1), to *bring to the front*

INSTRUCTER
3913 lâṭash (1), to *sharpen;* to *pierce*

INSTRUCTERS
3807 paidagōgŏs (1), *tutor,* cf. *pedagogue*

INSTRUCTING
3811 paidĕuō (1), to *educate or discipline*

INSTRUCTION
4148 mûwçâr (30), *reproof, warning*
4561 môçâr (1), *admonition*
3809 paidĕia (1), *disciplinary correction*

INSTRUCTOR
3810 paidĕutēs (1), *teacher or discipliner*

INSTRUMENT
3627 kᵉlîy (2), *implement, thing*

INSTRUMENTS
1761 dachăvâh (Ch.) (1), *musical instrument*
3627 kᵉlîy (37), *implement, thing*
4482 mên (1), *part; musical chord*
7991 shâlîysh (1), *triangle instrument*
3696 hŏplŏn (2), *implement, or utensil*

INSURRECTION
5376 nᵉsâ' (Ch.) (1), to *lift up*
7285 regesh (1), *tumultuous crowd*
2721 katĕphistēmi (1), to *rush upon in an assault*
4714 stasis (1), one *leading an uprising*
4955 sustasiastēs (1), *fellow-insurgent*

INTEGRITY
8537 tôm (11), *prosperity; innocence*
8538 tummâh (5), *innocence*

INTELLIGENCE
995 bîyn (1), to *understand; discern*

INTEND
559 'âmar (2), to *say*
1014 bŏulŏmai (1), to be *willing, desire; choose*

3195 mĕllō (1), to *intend, i.e. be about to*

INTENDED
5186 nâṭâh (1), to *stretch or spread out*

INTENDEST
559 'âmar (1), to *say*

INTENDING
1011 bŏulĕuō (1), to *deliberate;* to *resolve*
2309 thĕlō (1), to *will;* to *desire;* to *choose*
3195 mĕllō (1), to *intend, i.e. be about to*

INTENT
1701 dibrâh (Ch.) (1), *because, on account of*
4616 ma'an (2), *on account of; in order*
5668 'âbûwr (1), *on account of; in order*
2443 hina (2), *in order that*
3056 lŏgŏs (1), *word, matter, thing*

INTENTS
4209 mᵉzimmâh (1), *plan; sagacity*
1771 ĕnnŏia (1), *moral understanding*

INTERCESSION
6293 pâga' (4), to *impinge*
1793 ĕntugchanō (4), to *entreat, petition*
5241 hupĕrĕntugchanō (1), to *intercede*

INTERCESSIONS
1783 ĕntĕuxis (1), *intercession*

INTERCESSOR
6293 pâga' (1), to *impinge*

INTERMEDDLE
6148 'ârab (1), to *intermix*

INTERMEDDLETH
1566 gâla' (1), to *be obstinate;* to *burst forth*

INTERMISSION
2014 hăphûgâh (1), *relaxation*

INTERPRET
6622 pâthar (4), to *interpret a dream*
1329 dĭĕrmēnĕuō (4), to *explain thoroughly*

INTERPRETATION
4426 mᵉlîytsâh (1), *aphorism, saying*
6591 pᵉshar (Ch.) (30), *interpretation*
6592 pêsher (1), *interpretation*
6623 pithrôwn (5), *interpretation*
7667 sheber (1), *solution of a dream*
1329 dĭĕrmēnĕuō (1), to *explain thoroughly*
1955 ĕpilusis (1), *interpretation*
2058 hĕrmēnĕia (2), *translation*
2059 hĕrmēnĕuō (3), to *translate*
3177 mĕthĕrmēnĕuō (1), to *translate*

English

INTERPRETATIONS
6591 pᵉshar (Ch.) (1), *interpretation*
6623 pithrŏwn (1), *interpretation*

INTERPRETED
6622 pâthar (3), to *interpret* a dream
8638 tirgam (1), to *translate, interpret*
2059 hĕrmĕnĕuō (1), to *translate*
3177 mĕthĕrmĕnĕuō (6), to *translate*

INTERPRETER
3887 lûwts (2), to *scoff; to interpret; to intercede*
6622 pâthar (1), to *interpret* a dream
1328 diĕrmĕnĕutēs (1), *explainer, translator*

INTERPRETING
6591 pᵉshar (Ch.) (1), *interpretation*

INTREAT
2470 châlâh (3), to *be weak, sick, afflicted*
6279 'âthar (6), *intercede*
6293 pâga' (2), to *impinge*
6419 pâlal (1), to *intercede, pray*
2065 ĕrōtaō (1), to *interrogate; to request*
3870 parakaleō (2), to *call, invite*

INTREATED
2470 châlâh (1), to *be weak, sick, afflicted*
2589 channôwth (1), *supplication*
2603 chânan (1), to *implore*
6279 'âthar (12), *intercede* in prayer
2138 ĕupĕithēs (1), *compliant, submissive*
3862 paradŏsis (1), *precept; tradition*
3870 parakaleō (1), to *call, invite*

INTREATIES
8469 tachănûwn (1), *earnest prayer, plea*

INTREATY
3874 paraklēsis (1), *imploring, exhortation*

INTRUDING
1687 ĕmbatĕuō (1), to *intrude on*

INVADE
935 bôw' (1), to *go or come*
1464 gûwd (1), to *attack*

INVADED
935 bôw' (1), to *go or come*
6584 pâshat (4), to *strip, i.e. unclothe, plunder*

INVASION
6584 pâshat (1), to *strip, i.e. unclothe, plunder, flay*

INVENT
2803 châshab (1), to *weave, fabricate*

INVENTED
2803 châshab (1), to *weave, fabricate*

INVENTIONS
2810 chishshâbôwn (1), *machination, scheme*
4209 mᵉzimmâh (1), *plan; sagacity*
4611 ma'ălâl (2), *act, deed*
5949 'ălîylâh (1), *opportunity, action*

INVENTORS
2182 ĕphĕurĕtēs (1), *contriver, inventor*

INVISIBLE
517 aŏratŏs (5), *invisible, not seen*

INVITED
7121 qârâ' (3), to *call* out

INWARD
1004 bayith (7), *house; temple; family, tribe*
2315 cheder (2), *apartment, chamber*
2910 tûwchâh (2), inmost *thought*
5475 çôwd (1), *intimacy; consultation; secret*
6441 pᵉnîymâh (2), *indoors, inside*
6442 pᵉnîymîy (1), *interior, inner*
7130 qereb (5), *nearest part, i.e. the center*
2080 ĕsō (1), *inside, inner, in*
2081 ĕsōthĕn (2), *from inside; inside*
4698 splagchnŏn (1), *intestine; affection, pity or sympathy*

INWARDLY
7130 qereb (1), *nearest part, i.e. the center*
1722+2927 ĕn (1), *in; during; because of*
2081 ĕsōthĕn (1), *from inside; inside*

INWARDS
7130 qereb (19), *nearest part, i.e. the center*

IPHEDEIAH
3301 Yiphdᵉyâh (1), *Jehovah will liberate*

IR
5893 'Îyr (1), *city, town, unwalled-village*

IR-NAHASH
5904 'Îyr Nâchâsh (1), *city of a serpent*

IR-SHEMESH
5905 'Îyr Shemesh (1), *city of (the) sun*

IRA
5896 'Îyrâ' (6), *wakefulness*

IRAD
5897 'Îyrâd (2), *fugitive*

IRAM
5902 'Îyrâm (2), *city-wise*

IRI
5901 'Îyrîy (1), *urbane*

IRIJAH
3376 Yir'îyâyh (2), *fearful of Jehovah*

IRON
1270 barzel (72), *iron; iron implement*
3375 Yir'ôwn (1), *fearfulness*
6523 parzel (Ch.) (19), *iron*
4603 sidĕrĕŏs (5), made *of iron*
4604 sidĕrŏs (1), *iron*

IRONS
7905 sukkâh (1), *dart, harpoon*

IRPEEL
3416 Yirpᵉ'êl (1), *God will heal*

IRU
5902 'Îyrâm (1), *city-wise*

ISAAC
3327 Yitschâq (104), *laughter*
3446 Yischâq (4), *he will laugh*
2464 Isaak (20), *he will laugh*

ISAAC'S
3327 Yitschâq (4), *laughter*

ISAIAH
3470 Yᵉsha'yâh (32), *Jehovah has saved*

ISCAH
3252 Yiçkâh (1), *observant*

ISCARIOT
2469 Iskariōtēs (11), *inhabitant of Kerioth*

ISH-BOSHETH
378 'Îysh-Bôsheth (11), *man of shame*

ISH-TOB
382 'Îysh-Ţôwb (2), *man of Tob*

ISHBAH
3431 Yishbach (1), *he will praise*

ISHBAK
3435 Yishbâq (2), *he will leave*

ISHBI-BENOB
3430 Yishbôw bᵉ-Nôb (1), *his dwelling (is) in Nob*

ISHI
376 'îysh (1), *man; male; someone*
3469 Yish'îy (5), *saving*

ISHIAH
3449 Yishshîyâh (1), *Jehovah will lend*

ISHIJAH
3449 Yishshîyâh (1), *Jehovah will lend*

ISHMA
3457 Yishmâ' (1), *desolate*

ISHMAEL
3458 Yishmâ'ê'l (47), *God will hear*

ISHMAEL'S
3458 Yishmâ'ê'l (1), *God will hear*

ISHMAELITE
3458 Yishmâ'ê'l (1), *God will hear*

ISHMAELITES
3459 Yishmâ'ê'lîy (2), *Jishmaëlite*

ISHMAIAH
3460 Yishma'yâh (1), *Jehovah will hear*

ISHMEELITE
3459 Yishmâ'ê'lîy (1), *Jishmaëlite*

ISHMEELITES
3459 Yishmâ'ê'lîy (4), *Jishmaëlite*

ISHMERAI
3461 Yishmᵉray (1), *preservative*

ISHOD
379 'Îyshhôwd (1), *man of renown*

ISHPAN
3473 Yishpân (1), *he will hide*

ISHUAH
3438 Yishvâh (1), *he will level*

ISHUAI
3440 Yishvîy (1), *level*

ISHUI
3440 Yishvîy (1), *level*

ISLAND
336 'îy (1), *not*
338 'îy (1), solitary wild creature that *howls*
3519 nēsiŏn (1), small *island*
3520 nēsŏs (6), *island*

ISLANDS
338 'îy (1), solitary wild creature that *howls*
339 'îy (6), dry *land; coast; island*

ISLE
339 'îy (3), *coast; island*
3520 nēsŏs (3), *island*

ISLES
339 'îy (27), dry *land; coast; island*

ISMACHIAH
3253 Yiçmakyâhûw (1), *Jehovah will sustain*

ISMAIAH
3460 Yishma'yâh (1), *Jehovah will hear*

ISPAH
3472 Yishpâh (1), *he will scratch*

ISRAEL
3478 Yisrâ'êl (2477), *he will rule (as) God*
3479 Yisrâ'êl (Ch.) (8), *he will rule (as) God*
3481 Yisrᵉ'êlîy (1), *Jisreëlite*
2474 Israēl (70), *he will rule (as) God*
2475 Israēlitēs (5), descendants *of Israel*

ISRAEL'S
3478 Yisrâ'êl (10), *he will rule* (as) *God*

ISRAELITE
1121+3478 bên (1), *son, descendant; people*
3481 Yisrᵉ'êlîy (1), *Jisreëlite*
2475 Israêlitēs (2), descendants of *Israel*

ISRAELITES
3478 Yisrâ'êl (16), *he will rule* (as) *God*
2475 Israêlitēs (2), descendants of *Israel*

ISRAELITISH
3482 Yisrᵉ'êlîyth (3), *Jisreëlitess*

ISSACHAR
3485 Yissâˢkâr (43), *he will bring a reward*
2466 Isachar (1), *he will bring a reward*

ISSHIAH
3449 Yishshîyâh (2), *Jehovah will lend*

ISSUE
2100 zûwb (16), *to flow freely, gush*
2101 zôwb (11), *flux or discharge*
2231 zirmâh (1), *emission* of semen
3318 yâtsâ' (3), *to go, bring out*
4138 môwledeth (1), *offspring, family*
4726 mâqôwr (1), *flow*
6849 tsᵉphî'âh (1), *outcast* thing, *offshoots*
131 haimŏrrhĕō (1), *to have a hemorrhage*
4511 rhusis (3), *flux*
4690 spĕrma (1), *seed, offspring*

ISSUED
3318 yâtsâ' (4), *to go, bring out*
5047 nᵉgad (Ch.) (1), *to flow*
1607 ĕkpŏrĕuŏmai (2), *to depart, be discharged*

ISSUES
8444 tôwtsâ'âh (2), *exit, boundary; source*

ISUAH
3440 Yishvîy (1), *level*

ISUI
3440 Yishvîy (1), *level*

ITALIAN
2483 Italikŏs (1), *belonging to Italia*

ITALY
2482 Italia (4), *Italia*

ITCH
2775 chereç (1), *itch; sun*

ITCHING
2833 knēthō (1), *to tickle, feel an itch*

ITHAI
863 'Ittay (1), *near*

ITHAMAR
385 'Îythâmâr (21), *coast* of the *palm*-tree

ITHIEL
384 'Îythîy'êl (3), *God has arrived*

ITHMAH
3495 Yithmâh (1), *orphanage*

ITHNAN
3497 Yithnân (1), *extensive*

ITHRA
3501 Yithrâ' (1), *wealth*

ITHRAN
3506 Yithrân (3), *excellent*

ITHREAM
3507 Yithrᵉ'âm (2), *excellence of people*

ITHRITE
3505 Yithrîy (4), *Jithrite*

ITHRITES
3505 Yithrîy (1), *Jithrite*

ITTAH-KAZIN
6278 'Êth Qâtsîyn (1), *time of a judge*

ITTAI
863 'Ittay (8), *near*

ITURAEA
2434 hilasmŏs (1), *atonement, expiator*

IVAH
5755 'Ivvâh (3), *overthrow, ruin*

IVORY
8127 shên (10), *tooth; ivory; cliff*
8143 shenhabbîym (2), *elephant's ivory tusk*
1661 ĕlĕphantinŏs (1), *of ivory*

IZEHAR
3324 Yitshâr (1), *olive oil; anointing*

IZEHARITES
3325 Yitshârîy (1), *Jitsharite*

IZHAR
3324 Yitshâr (8), *olive oil; anointing*

IZHARITES
3325 Yitshârîy (3), *Jitsharite*

IZRAHIAH
3156 Yizrachyâh (2), *Jehovah will shine*

IZRAHITE
3155 Yizrâch (1), *Ezrachite or Zarchite*

IZRI
3342 yeqeb (1), wine-*vat*, wine-*press*

JAAKAN
3292 Ya'ăqân (1), *Jaakan*

JAAKOBAH
3291 Ya'ăqôbâh (1), *heel*-catcher

JAALA
3279 Ya'ălâ' (1), *to be valuable*

JAALAH
3279 Ya'ălâ' (1), *to be valuable*

JAALAM
3281 Ya'lâm (4), *occult*

JAANAI
3285 Ya'ănay (1), *responsive*

JAARE-OREGIM
3296 Ya'ărêy 'Orᵉgîym (1), *woods of weavers*

JAASAU
3299 Ya'ăsûw (1), *they will do*

JAASIEL
3300 Ya'ăsîy'êl (1), *made of God*

JAAZANIAH
2970 Ya'ăzanyâh (4), *heard of Jehovah*

JAAZER
3270 Ya'ăzêyr (2), *helpful*

JAAZIAH
3269 Ya'ăzîyâhûw (2), *emboldened of Jehovah*

JAAZIEL
3268 Ya'ăzîy'êl (1), *emboldened of God*

JABAL
2989 Yâbâl (1), *stream*

JABBOK
2999 Yabbôq (7), *pouring forth*

JABESH
3003 Yâbêsh (12), *dry*

JABESH-GILEAD
3003+1568 Yâbêsh (12), *dry*

JABEZ
3258 Ya'bêts (4), *sorrowful*

JABIN
2985 Yâbîyn (7), *intelligent*

JABIN'S
2985 Yâbîyn (1), *intelligent*

JABNEEL
2995 Yabnᵉ'êl (2), *built of God*

JABNEH
2996 Yabneh (1), *building*

JACHAN
3275 Ya'kân (1), *troublesome*

JACHIN
3199 Yâkîyn (8), *he* (or *it*) *will establish*

JACHINITES
3200 Yâkîynîy (1), *Jakinite*

JACINTH
5191 huakinthinŏs (1), *deep blue color*
5192 huakinthŏs (1), *blue* gem, (poss.) *zircon*

JACOB
3290 Ya'ăqôb (331), *heel*-catcher
2384 Iakōb (26), *heel*-catcher

JACOB'S
3290 Ya'ăqôb (17), *heel*-catcher

JAZEL *(continued from far right)*

2384 Iakōb (1), *heel*-catcher

JADA
3047 Yâdâ' (2), *knowing*

JADAU
3035 Yiddôw (1), *praised*

JADDUA
3037 Yaddûwa' (3), *knowing*

JADON
3036 Yâdôwn (1), *thankful*

JAEL
3278 Yâ'êl (6), *ibex animal*

JAGUR
3017 Yâgûwr (1), *lodging*

JAH
3050 Yâhh (1), *Jehovah,* (the) *self-Existent or Eternal One*

JAHATH
3189 Yachath (8), *unity*

JAHAZ
3096 Yahats (5), *threshing-floor*

JAHAZA
3096 Yahats (1), *threshing-floor*

JAHAZAH
3096 Yahats (2), *threshing-floor*

JAHAZIAH
3167 Yachzᵉyâh (1), *Jehovah will behold*

JAHAZIEL
3166 Yachăzîy'êl (6), *beheld of God*

JAHDAI
3056 Yehday (1), *Judaistic*

JAHDIEL
3164 Yachdîy'êl (1), *unity of God*

JAHDO
3163 Yachdôw (1), *his unity*

JAHLEEL
3177 Yachlᵉ'êl (2), *expectant of God*

JAHLEELITES
3178 Yachlᵉ'êlîy (1), *Jachleëlite*

JAHMAI
3181 Yachmay (1), *hot*

JAHZAH
3096 Yahats (1), *threshing-floor*

JAHZEEL
3183 Yachtsᵉ'êl (2), *God will allot*

JAHZEELITES
3184 Yachtsᵉ'êlîy (1), *Jachtseëlite*

JAHZERAH
3170 Yachzêrâh (1), *protection*

JAHZIEL
3185 Yachtsîy'êl (1), *allotted of God*

JAILER
1200 dĕsmŏphulax (1), *jailer*

JAIR
2971 Yâ'îyr (10), *enlightener*

JAIRITE
2972 Yâ'îrîy (1), *Jaïrite*

JAIRUS
2383 Iaĕïrŏs (2), *enlightener*

JAKAN
3292 Ya'ăqân (1), *Jaakan*

JAKEH
3348 Yâqeh (1), *obedient*

JAKIM
3356 Yâqîym (2), *he will raise*

JALON
3210 Yâlôwn (1), *lodging*

JAMBRES
2387 Iambrēs (1), *Jambres*

JAMES
2385 Iakōbŏs (41), *heel*-catcher

JAMIN
3226 Yâmîyn (6), *right; south*

JAMINITES
3228 Yᵉmîynîy (1), *Jeminite*

JAMLECH
3230 Yamlêk (1), *he will make king*

JANGLING
3150 mataiŏlŏgia (1), *babble, meaningless talk*

JANNA
2388 Ianna (1), *Janna*

JANNES
2389 Iannēs (1), *Jannes*

JANOAH
3239 Yânôwach (1), *quiet*

JANOHAH
3239 Yânôwach (2), *quiet*

JANUM
3241 Yânîym (1), *asleep*

JAPHETH
3315 Yepheth (11), *expansion*

JAPHIA
3309 Yâphîya' (5), *bright*

JAPHLET
3310 Yaphlêṭ (3), *he will deliver*

JAPHLETI
3311 Yaphlêṭîy (1), *Japhletite*

JAPHO
3305 Yâphôw (1), *beautiful*

JARAH
3294 Ya'râh (2), *honey* in the *comb*

JAREB
3377 Yârêb (2), *he will contend*

JARED
3382 Yered (5), *descent*
2391 Iarĕd (1), *descent*

JARESIAH
3298 Ya'ăreshyâh (1), *Jaareshjah*

JARHA
3398 Yarchâ' (2), *Jarcha*

JARIB
3402 Yârîyb (3), *contentious; adversary*

JARMUTH
3412 Yarmûwth (7), *elevation*

JAROAH
3386 Yârôwach (1), (born at the) new *moon*

JASHEN
3464 Yâshên (1), *sleepy*

JASHER
3477 yâshâr (2), *straight*

JASHOBEAM
3434 Yâshob'âm (3), *people will return*

JASHUB
3437 Yâshûwb (3), *he will return*

JASHUBI-LEHEM
3433 Yâshûbiy Lechem (1), *returner of bread*

JASHUBITES
3432 Yâshûbîy (1), *Jashubite*

JASIEL
3300 Ya'ăsîy'êl (1), *made of God*

JASON
2394 Iasŏn (5), *about to cure*

JASPER
3471 yâshᵉpheh (3), *jasper* stone
2393 iaspis (4), *jasper*

JATHNIEL
3496 Yathnîy'êl (1), *continued of God*

JATTIR
3492 Yattîyr (4), *redundant*

JAVAN
3120 Yâvân (7), *effervescent*

JAVELIN
2595 chănîyth (6), *lance, spear*
7420 rômach (1), iron *pointed* spear

JAW
3895 lᵉchîy (3), *jaw;* jaw-bone
4973 mᵉthallᵉ'âh (1), *tooth*

JAWBONE
3895 lᵉchîy (3), *jaw;* jaw-bone

JAWS
3895 lᵉchîy (4), *jaw;* jaw-bone
4455 malqôwach (1), *spoil, plunder*
4973 mᵉthallᵉ'âh (1), *tooth*

JAZER
3270 Ya'ăzêyr (11), *helpful*

JAZIZ
3151 Yâzîyz (1), *he will make prominent*

JEALOUS
7065 qânâ' (11), to be, make zealous, jealous
7067 qannâ' (4), *jealous*
7072 qannôw' (2), *jealous*
2206 zēlŏŏ (1), to have *warmth* of feeling for

JEALOUSIES
7068 qin'âh (1), *jealousy or envy*

JEALOUSY
7065 qânâ' (5), to be, make zealous, jealous
7068 qin'âh (23), *jealousy*
7069 qânâh (1), to *create;* to procure
2205 zēlŏs (1), *zeal, ardor; jealousy, malice*

JEARIM
3297 Yᵉ'ârîym (1), *forests*

JEATERAI
2979 Yᵉ'âthᵉray (1), *stepping*

JEBERECHIAH
3000 Yᵉberekyâhûw (1), *blessed of Jehovah*

JEBUS
2982 Yᵉbûwç (4), *trodden*

JEBUSI
2983 Yᵉbûwçîy (2), *Jebusite*

JEBUSITE
2983 Yᵉbûwçîy (14), *Jebusite*

JEBUSITES
2983 Yᵉbûwçîy (25), *Jebusite*

JECAMIAH
3359 Yᵉqamyâh (1), *Jehovah will rise*

JECHOLIAH
3203 Yᵉkolyâh (1), *Jehovah will enable*

JECHONIAS
2423 Iĕchŏnias (2), *Jehovah will establish*

JECOLIAH
3203 Yᵉkolyâh (1), *Jehovah will enable*

JECONIAH
3204 Yᵉkonyâh (7), *Jehovah will establish*

JEDAIAH
3042 Yᵉdâyâh (2), *praised of Jehovah*
3048 Yᵉda'yâh (11), *Jehovah has known*

JEDIAEL
3043 Yᵉdîy'ă'êl (6), *knowing God*

JEDIDAH
3040 Yᵉdîydâh (1), *beloved*

JEDIDIAH
3041 Yᵉdîydᵉyâh (1), *beloved of Jehovah*

JEDUTHUN
3038 Yᵉdûwthûwn (16), *laudatory*

JEEZER
372 'Îy'ezer (1), *helpless*

JEEZERITES
373 'Îy'ezrîy (1), *Iezrite*

JEGAR-SAHADUTHA
3026 Yᵉgar Sahădûwthâ' (Ch.) (1), *heap of the testimony*

JEHALELEEL
3094 Yᵉhallel'êl (1), *praising God*

JEHALELEL
3094 Yᵉhallel'êl (1), *praising God*

JEHDEIAH
3165 Yechdîyâhûw (2), *unity of Jehovah*

JEHEZEKEL
3168 Yᵉchezqê'l (1), *God will strengthen*

JEHIAH
3174 Yᵉchîyâh (1), *Jehovah will live*

JEHIEL
3171 Yᵉchîy'êl (14), *God will live*
3273 Yᵉ'îy'êl (2), *carried away of God*

JEHIELI
3172 Yᵉchîy'êlìy (2), *Jechiëlite*

JEHIZKIAH
3169 Yᵉchizqîyâh (1), *strengthened of Jehovah*

JEHOADAH
3085 Yᵉhôw'addâh (2), *Jehovah-adorned*

JEHOADDAN
3086 Yᵉhôw'addîyn (2), *Jehovah-pleased*

JEHOAHAZ
3059 Yᵉhôw'âchâz (21), *Jehovah-seized*
3099 Yôw'âchâz (1), *Jehovah-seized*

JEHOASH
3060 Yᵉhôw'âsh (17), *Jehovah-fired*

JEHOHANAN
3076 Yᵉhôwchânân (6), *Jehovah-favored*

JEHOIACHIN
3078 Yᵉhôwyâkîyn (10), *Jehovah will establish*

JEHOIACHIN'S
3112 Yôwyâkîyn (1), *Jehovah will establish*

JEHOIADA
3111 Yôwyâdâ' (52), *Jehovah-known*

JEHOIAKIM
3079 Yᵉhôwyâqîym (37), *Jehovah will raise*

JEHOIARIB
3080 Yᵉhôwyârîyb (2), *Jehovah will contend*

JEHONADAB
3082 Yᵉhôwnâdâb (3),
Jehovah-largessed

JEHONATHAN
3083 Yᵉhôwnâthân (3),
Jehovah-given

JEHORAM
3088 Yᵉhôwrâm (23),
Jehovah-raised

JEHOSHABEATH
3090 Yᵉhôwshab'ath (2),
Jehovah-sworn

JEHOSHAPHAT
3046 yᵉda' (Ch.) (1), to
know
3092 Yᵉhôwshâphâṭ (84),
Jehovah-judged

JEHOSHEBA
3089 Yᵉhôwsheba' (1),
Jehovah-sworn

JEHOSHUA
3091 Yᵉhôwshûw'a (1),
Jehovah-saved

JEHOSHUAH
3091 Yᵉhôwshûw'a (1),
Jehovah-saved

JEHOVAH
3068 Yᵉhôvâh (4), (the)
self-*Existent* or Eternal

JEHOVAH-JIREH
3070 Yᵉhôvâh Yir'eh (1),
Jehovah will see (to it)

JEHOVAH-NISSI
3071 Yᵉhôvâh Niççîy (1),
Jehovah (is) *my banner*

JEHOVAH-SHALOM
3073 Yᵉhôvâh Shâlôwm
(1), *Jehovah* (is) *peace*

JEHOZABAD
3075 Yᵉhôwzâbâd (4),
Jehovah-endowed

JEHOZADAK
3087 Yᵉhôwtsâdâq (2),
Jehovah-righted

JEHU
3058 Yêhûw' (57),
Jehovah (is) *He*

JEHUBBAH
3160 Yᵉchubbâh (1),
hidden

JEHUCAL
3081 Yᵉhûwkal (1), *potent*

JEHUD
3055 Yᵉhûd (1),
celebrated

JEHUDI
3065 Yᵉhûwdîy (4),
Jehudite

JEHUDIJAH
3057 Yᵉhûdîyâh (1),
celebrated

JEHUSH
3266 Yᵉ'ûwsh (1), *hasty*

JEIEL
3273 Yᵉ'îy'êl (11), *carried
away of God*

JEKABZEEL
3343 Yᵉqabtsᵉ'êl (1), *God
will gather*

JEKAMEAM
3360 Yᵉqam'âm (2),
people will rise

JEKAMIAH
3359 Yᵉqamyâh (2),
Jehovah will rise

JEKUTHIEL
3354 Yᵉqûwthîy'êl (1),
obedience of God

JEMIMA
3224 Yᵉmîymâh (1), *dove*

JEMUEL
3223 Yᵉmûw'êl (2), *day
of God*

JEOPARDED
2778 châraph (1), to
spend the *winter*

JEOPARDY
2793 kinduněuō (2), to
undergo peril

JEPHTHAE
2422 Iĕphthaĕ (1), *he will
open*

JEPHTHAH
3316 Yiphtâch (29), *he
will open*

JEPHUNNEH
3312 Yᵉphunneh (16), *he
will be prepared*

JERAH
3392 Yerach (2), *lunar
month*

JERAHMEEL
3396 Yᵉrachmᵉ'êl (8),
*God will be
compassionate*

JERAHMEELITES
3397 Yᵉrachmᵉ'êlîy (2),
Jerachmeëlite

JERED
3382 Yered (2), *descent*

JEREMAI
3413 Yᵉrêmay (1),
elevated

JEREMIAH
3414 Yirmᵉyâh (146),
Jehovah will rise

JEREMIAH'S
3414 Yirmᵉyâh (1),
Jehovah will rise

JEREMIAS
2408 Hiĕrĕmias (1),
Jehovah will rise

JEREMOTH
3406 Yᵉrîymôwth (5),
elevations

JEREMY
2408 Hiĕrĕmias (2),
Jehovah will rise

JERIAH
3404 Yᵉrîyâh (2),
Jehovah will throw

JERIBAI
3403 Yᵉrîybay (1),
contentious

JERICHO
3405 Yᵉrîychôw (57), *its
month,* or *fragrant*
2410 Hiĕrichō (7), *its
month* or *fragrant*

JERIEL
3400 Yᵉrîy'êl (1), *thrown
of God*

JERIJAH
3404 Yᵉrîyâh (1),
Jehovah will throw

JERIMOTH
3406 Yᵉrîymôwth (8),
elevations

JERIOTH
3408 Yᵉrîy'ôwth (1),
curtains

JEROBOAM
3379 Yârob'âm (102),
people will contend

JEROBOAM'S
3379 Yârob'âm (2),
people will contend

JEROHAM
3395 Yᵉrôchâm (10),
compassionate

JERUBBAAL
3378 Yᵉrubba'al (14),
Baal will contend

JERUBBESHETH
3380 Yᵉrubbesheth (1),
the idol will contend

JERUEL
3385 Yᵉrûw'êl (1),
founded of God

JERUSALEM
3389 Yᵉrûwshâlaim
(640), *founded peaceful*
3390 Yᵉrûwshâlêm (Ch.)
(26), *founded peaceful*
2414 Hiĕrŏsŏluma (61),
founded peaceful
2419 Hiĕrŏusalêm (81),
founded peaceful

JERUSALEM'S
3389 Yᵉrûwshâlaim (3),
founded peaceful

JERUSHA
3388 Yᵉrûwshâ' (1),
possessed

JERUSHAH
3388 Yᵉrûwshâ' (1),
possessed

JESAIAH
3470 Yᵉsha'yâh (2),
Jehovah has saved

JESHAIAH
3740 kêrâh (5), *purchase*

JESHANAH
3466 Yᵉshânâh (1), *old*

JESHARELAH
3480 Yᵉsar'êlâh (1), *right
towards God*

JESHEBEAB
3434 Yâshob'âm (1),
people will return

JESHER
3475 Yêsher (1), *right*

JESHIMON
3452 yᵉshîymôwn (5),
desolation

JESHISHAI
3454 Yᵉshîyshay (1), *aged*

JESHOHAIAH
3439 Yᵉshôwchâyâh (1),
Jehovah will empty

JESHUA
3442 Yêshûwa' (28), *he
will save*
3443 Yêshûwa' (Ch.) (2),
he will save

JESHURUN
3484 Yᵉshûrûwn (3),
upright

JESIAH
3449 Yishshîyâh (2),
Jehovah will lend

JESIMIEL
3450 Yᵉsiymâ'êl (1), *God
will place*

JESSE
3448 Yîshay (41), *extant*
2421 Iĕssai (5), *extant*

JESTING
2160 ĕutrapĕlia (1),
ribaldry

JESUI
3440 Yishvîy (1), *level*

JESUITES
3441 Yishvîy (1), *Jishvite*

JESURUN
3484 Yᵉshûrûwn (1),
upright

JESUS
846 autŏs (1), *he, she, it*
2424 Iēsŏus (967),
Jehovah-saved

JESUS'
2424 Iēsŏus (10),
Jehovah-saved

JETHER
3500 Yether (8),
remainder

JETHETH
3509 Yᵉthêyth (2), *Jetheth*

JETHLAH
3494 Yithlâh (1), *be high*

JETHRO
3503 Yithrôw (10), *his
excellence*

JETUR
3195 Yᵉṭûwr (3), *enclosed*

JEUEL
3262 Yᵉ'ûw'êl (1), *carried
away of God*

JEUSH
3266 Yᵉ'ûwsh (8), *hasty*

JEUZ
3263 Yᵉ'ûwts (1),
counselor

JEW
3064 Yᵉhûwdîy (10),
Jehudite
2453 Iŏudaiŏs (22),
belonging to Jehudah

JEWEL
3627 kᵉlîy (1),
implement, thing
5141 nezem (2),
nose-ring

JEWELS
2484 chelyâh (2), *trinket,
ornament*
3627 kᵉlîy (18),
implement, thing
5141 nezem (1),
nose-ring
5459 çᵉgullâh (1), *wealth*

JEWESS
2453 Iŏudaiŏs (2),
belonging to Jehudah

JEWISH
2451 Iŏudaïkŏs (1),
resembling a Judæan

JEWRY
3061 Yᵉhûwd (Ch.) (1),
celebrated
2449 Iŏudaia (2),
Judæan land

JEWS
3054 yâhad (1), to
become Jewish
3062 Yᵉhûwdâ'îy (Ch.)
(8), Jew
3064 Yᵉhûwdîy (65),
Jehudite
2450 Iŏudaïzō (1), to
Judaize, live as a Jew
2452 Iŏudaïkŏs (1), in a
Judæan manner
2453 Iŏudaiŏs (167),
belonging to Jehudah

JEWS'
3064 Yᵉhûwdîy (4),
Jehudite
3066 Yᵉhûwdîyth (4), in
the Jewish language
2453 Iŏudaiŏs (4),
belonging to Jehudah
2454 Iŏudaismŏs (2),
Jewish faith

JEZANIAH
3153 Yᵉzanyâh (2), heard
of Jehovah

JEZEBEL
348 'Îyzebel (21), chaste
2403 Iĕzabĕl (1), chaste

JEZEBEL'S
348 'Îyzebel (1), chaste

JEZER
3337 Yêtser (3), form

JEZERITES
3339 Yitsrîy (1),
formative

JEZIAH
3150 Yizzîyâh (1),
sprinkled of Jehovah

JEZIEL
3149 Yᵉzav'êl (1),
sprinkled of God

JEZLIAH
3152 Yizlîy'ah (1), he will
draw out

JEZOAR
3328 Yitschar (1), he will
shine

JEZRAHIAH
3156 Yizrachyâh (1),
Jehovah will shine

JEZREEL
3157 Yizrᵉ'ê'l (36), God
will sow

JEZREELITE
3158 Yizrᵉ'ê'lîy (8),
Jizreëlite

JEZREELITESS
3159 Yizrᵉ'ê'lîyth (5),
Jezreëlitess

JIBSAM
3005 Yibsâm (1), fragrant

JIDLAPH
3044 Yidlâph (1), tearful

JIMNA
3232 Yimnâh (1),
prosperity

JIMNAH
3232 Yimnâh (1),
prosperity

JIMNITES
3232 Yimnâh (1),
prosperity

JIPHTAH
3316 Yiphtâch (1), he
will open

JIPHTHAH-EL
3317 Yiphtach-'êl (2),
God will open

JOAB
3097 Yôw'âb (137),
Jehovah-fathered
5854 'Aṭrôwth Bêyth
Yôw'âb (1), crowns of
(the) house of Joâb

JOAB'S
3097 Yôw'âb (8),
Jehovah-fathered

JOAH
3098 Yôw'âch (11),
Jehovah-brothered

JOAHAZ
3098 Yôw'âch (1),
Jehovah-brothered

JOANNA
2489 Iōanna (3),
Jehovah-favored

JOASH
3101 Yôw'âsh (47),
Jehovah-fired
3135 Yôw'âsh (2),
Jehovah-hastened

JOATHAM
2488 Iōatham (2),
Jehovah (is) perfect

JOB
347 'Îyôwb (57),
persecuted
3102 Yôwb (1), Job
2492 Iōb (1), persecuted

JOB'S
347 'Îyôwb (1), persecuted

JOBAB
3103 Yôwbâb (9), howler

JOCHEBED
3115 Yôwkebed (2),
Jehovah-gloried

JOED
3133 Yôw'êd (1),
appointer

JOEL
3100 Yôw'êl (19),
Jehovah (is his) God
2493 Iōēl (1), Jehovah (is
his) God

JOELAH
3132 Yôw'ê'lâh (1),
furthermore

JOEZER
3134 Yôw'ezer (1),
Jehovah (is his) help

JOGBEHAH
3011 Yogbᵉhâh (2),
hillock

JOGLI
3020 Yoglîy (1), exiled

JOHA
3109 Yôwchâ' (2),
Jehovah-revived

JOHANAN
3076 Yᵉhôwchânân (3),
Jehovah-favored
3110 Yôwchânân (24),
Jehovah-favored

JOHN
2491 Iōannēs (131),
Jehovah-favored

JOHN'S
2491 Iōannēs (2),
Jehovah-favored

JOIADA
3111 Yôwyâdâ' (4),
Jehovah-known

JOIAKIM
3113 Yôwyâqîym (4),
Jehovah will raise

JOIARIB
3114 Yôwyârîyb (5),
Jehovah will contend

JOIN
2266 châbar (2), to
fascinate by spells
2859 châthan (1), to
become related
3254 yâçaph (1), to add
or augment
3867 lâvâh (2), to unite;
to remain; to borrow
5060 nâga' (1), to strike
5526 çâkak (1), to
entwine; to fence in
7126 qârab (1), to
approach, bring near
2853 kŏllaō (3), to glue
together

JOINED
977 bâchar (1), select,
chose, prefer
1692 dâbaq (2), to cling
or adhere; to catch
2266 châbar (8), to
fascinate by spells
2302 châdâh (1), to
rejoice, be glad
2338 chûwṭ (Ch.) (1), to
repair; lay a foundation
2859 châthan (1), to
become related
3161 yâchad (1), to be,
become one
3867 lâvâh (8), to unite;
to remain; to borrow
5208 nîychôwach (Ch.)
(1), pleasure
5595 çâphâh (1), to
scrape; to accumulate
6186 'ârak (1), to set in a
row, i.e. arrange,
6775 tsâmad (3), to link,
i.e. gird
7000 qâṭar (1), to enclose
7126 qârab (1), to
approach, bring near
7194 qâshar (1), to tie,
bind
2675 katartizō (1), to
repair; to prepare
2853 kŏllaō (3), to glue
together

JOGLI
4347 prŏskŏllaō (2), to
glue to, i.e. to adhere
4801 suzĕugnumi (2), to
conjoin in marriage
4883 sunarmŏlŏgeō (1),
to render close-jointed
4927 sunŏmŏrĕō (1), to
border together

JOINING
1692 dâbaq (1), to cling
or adhere; to catch

JOININGS
4226 mᵉchabbᵉrâh (1),
joiner, brace or cramp

JOINT
3363 yâqa' (1), to be
dislocated
4154 mûw'edeth (1),
dislocated
6504 pârad (1), to spread
or separate
860 haphē (1), fastening
ligament, joint

JOINT-HEIRS
4789 sugklērŏnŏmŏs (1),
participant in common

JOINTS
1694 debeq (2), joint
2542 chammûwq (1),
wrapping, i.e. drawers
7001 qᵉṭar (Ch.) (1),
riddle; vertebra
719 harmŏs (1),
articulation, body-joint
860 haphē (1), fastening
ligament, joint

JOKDEAM
3347 Yoqdᵉ'âm (1),
burning of (the) people

JOKIM
3137 Yôwqîym (1),
Jehovah will raise

JOKMEAM
3361 Yoqmᵉ'âm (1),
people will be raised

JOKNEAM
3362 Yoqnᵉ'âm (4),
people will be lamented

JOKSHAN
3370 Yoqshân (4),
insidious

JOKTAN
3355 Yoqṭân (6), he will
be made little

JOKTHEEL
3371 Yoqthᵉ'êl (2),
veneration of God

JONA
2495 Iōnas (1), dove

JONADAB
3082 Yᵉhôwnâdâb (4),
Jehovah-largessed
3122 Yôwnâdâb (8),
Jehovah-largessed

JONAH
3124 Yôwnâh (19), dove

JONAN
2494 Iōnan (1), Jehovah-
favored or a dove

JONAS
2495 Iōnas (12), dove

**JONATH-ELEM-
RECHOKIM**
3128 Yôwnath 'êlem
rᵉchôqîym (1), *dove of
(the) silence*

JONATHAN
3083 Yᵉhôwnâthân (81),
Jehovah-given
3129 Yôwnâthân (37),
Jehovah-given

JONATHAN'S
3129 Yôwnâthân (3),
Jehovah-given

JOPPA
3305 Yâphôw (3),
beautiful
2445 Iŏppē (10), *beautiful*

JORAH
3139 Yôwrâh (1), *rainy*

JORAI
3140 Yôwray (1), *rainy*

JORAM
3141 Yôwrâm (19),
Jehovah-raised
3088 Yᵉhôwrâm (7),
Jehovah-raised
2496 Iôram (2),
Jehovah-raised

JORDAN
3383 Yardên (182),
descender
2446 Iŏrdanēs (15),
descender

JORIM
2497 Iŏrĕim (1), (poss.)
Jehovah-raised

JORKOAM
3421 Yorqᵉ'âm (1),
*people will be poured
forth*

JOSABAD
3107 Yôwzâbâd (1),
Jehovah-endowed

JOSAPHAT
2498 Iōsaphat (2),
Jehovah-judged

JOSE
2499 Iŏsē (1), (poss.) *let
him add*

JOSEDECH
3087 Yᵉhôwtsâdâq (6),
Jehovah-righted

JOSEPH
3084 Yᵉhôwçêph (1), *let
him add or adding*
3130 Yôwçêph (193), *let
him add or adding*
2501 Iōsēph (33), *let him
add or adding*

JOSEPH'S
3130 Yôwçêph (20), *let
him add or adding*
2501 Iōsēph (2), *let him
add or adding*

JOSES
2500 Iōsēs (6), (poss.) *let
him add*

JOSHAH
3144 Yôwshâh (1), *Joshah*

JOSHAPHAT
3146 Yôwshâphâṭ (1),
Jehovah-judged

JOSHAVIAH
3145 Yôwshavyâh (1),
Jehovah-set

JOSHBEKASHAH
3436 Yoshbᵉqâshâh (2),
hard seat

JOSHUA
3091 Yᵉhôwshûw'a (215),
Jehovah-saved

JOSIAH
2977 Yô'shîyâh (53),
founded of Jehovah

JOSIAS
2502 Iōsias (2), *founded
of Jehovah*

JOSIBIAH
3143 Yôwshîbyâh (1),
*Jehovah will cause to
dwell*

JOSIPHIAH
3131 Yôwçiphyâh (1),
Jehovah (is) adding

JOT
2503 iōta (1), *iota*

JOTBAH
3192 Yoṭbâh (1),
pleasantness

JOTBATH
3193 Yoṭbâthâh (1),
pleasantness

JOTBATHAH
3193 Yoṭbâthâh (2),
pleasantness

JOTHAM
3147 Yôwthâm (24),
Jehovah (is) perfect

JOURNEY
1870 derek (23), *road;
course of life; mode of
action*
4109 mahălâk (3),
passage or a distance
4550 maçça' (1),
departure
5265 nâça' (12), *start on
a journey*
5575+7272 çanvêr (1),
blindness
589 apŏdēmĕō (2), *visit a
foreign land*
590 apŏdēmŏs (1),
foreign traveller
1279 diapŏrĕuŏmai (1),
to travel through
2137 ĕuŏdŏō (1), *to
succeeʼ in business*
3596 hŏdŏipŏrĕō (1), *to
travel*
3597 hŏdŏipŏria (1),
traveling
3598 hŏdŏs (6), *road*
4198 pŏrĕuŏmai (2), *to
go, come; to travel*

JOURNEYED
5265 nâça' (28), *start on
a journey*
6213+1870 'âsâh (1), *to
do or make*
3593 hŏdĕuŏ (1), *to travel*
4198 pŏrĕuŏmai (2), *to
go/come; to travel*
4922 sunŏdĕuō (1), *to
travel in company with*

JOURNEYING
4550 maçça' (1),
departure
5265 nâça' (1), *start on a
journey*
4197+4160 pŏrĕia (1),
journey; life's conduct

JOURNEYINGS
4550 maçça' (1),
departure
3597 hŏdŏipŏria (1),
traveling

JOURNEYS
4550 maçça' (9),
departure

JOY
1523 gîyl (2), *rejoice*
1524 gîyl (3), *age, stage
in life*
1525 gîylâh (1), *joy,
delight*
2304 chedvâh (1),
rejoicing, joy
2305 chedvâh (Ch.) (1),
rejoicing, joy
2898 ṭûwb (1), *good;
beauty, gladness*
4885 mâsôws (12), *delight*
7440 rinnâh (3), *shout*
7442 rânan (3), *to shout
for joy*
7796 Sôwrêq (1), *vine*
8055 sâmach (4), *to be,
make gleesome*
8056 sâmêach (2), *blithe
or gleeful*
8057 simchâh (43),
blithesomeness or glee
8342 sâsôwn (14),
cheerfulness; welcome
8643 tᵉrûw'âh (2),
battle-cry; clangor
20 agalliasis (2),
exultation, delight
21 agalliaō (1), *to exult*
2167 ĕuphrŏsunē (1),
joyfulness, cheerfulness
2744 kauchaŏmai (1), *to
glory in, rejoice in; to
boast*
3685 ŏninēmi (1), *to
gratify, derive pleasure*
5468 chalinagōgĕō (3), *to
curb, hold in check*
5479 chara (51), *calm
delight, joy*
5485 charis (1),
gratitude; benefit given

JOYED
5463 chairō (1), *to be
cheerful*

JOYFUL
1523 gîyl (4), *rejoice*
2896 ṭôwb (1), *good; well*
5937 'âlaz (2), *to jump for
joy*
5970 'âlats (1), *to jump
for joy*
7442 rânan (1), *to shout
for joy*
7445 rᵉnânâh (2), *shout
for joy*
8055 sâmach (2), *to be,
make gleesome*
8056 sâmêach (3), *blithe
or gleeful*

8643 tᵉrûw'âh (1),
*battle-cry; clangor of
trumpets*
5479 chara (1), *calm
delight, joy*

JOYFULLY
2416 chay (1), *alive; raw;
fresh; life*
3326+5479 mĕta (1), *with,
among; after, later*
5463 chairō (1), *to be
cheerful*

JOYFULNESS
8057 simchâh (1),
blithesomeness or glee
5479 chara (1), *calm
delight, joy*

JOYING
5463 chairō (1), *to be
cheerful*

JOYOUS
5947 'allîyz (3), *exultant;
reveling*
5479 chara (1), *calm
delight, joy*

JOZABAD
3107 Yôwzâbâd (9),
Jehovah-endowed

JOZACHAR
3108 Yôwzâkâr (1),
Jehovah-remembered

JOZADAK
3136 Yôwtsâdâq (5),
Jehovah-righted

JUBAL
3106 Yûwbâl (1), *stream*

JUBILE
3104 yôwbêl (21), *blast of
a ram's horn*
8643 tᵉrûw'âh (1),
battle-cry; clangor

JUCAL
3116 Yûwkal (1), *potent*

JUDA
2448 Iŏuda (1),
celebrated
2455 Iŏudas (7),
celebrated

JUDAEA
2449 Iŏudaia (41),
Judæan land
2453 Iŏudaiŏs (1),
belonging to Jehudah
2499 Iŏsē (1), (poss.) *let
him add*

JUDAH
3061 Yᵉhûwd (Ch.) (5),
celebrated
3063 Yᵉhûwdâh (806),
celebrated
3064 Yᵉhûwdîy (1),
Jehudite
2455 Iŏudas (1),
celebrated

JUDAH'S
3063 Yᵉhûwdâh (4),
celebrated

JUDAS
2455 Iŏudas (33),
celebrated

JUDE
2455 Iŏudas (1),
celebrated

English

JUDEA
3061 Yᵉhûwd (Ch.) (1), *celebrated*

JUDGE
430 'ĕlôhîym (1), *God; magistrates, judges*
1777 dîyn (14), *to judge; to strive or contend for*
1781 dayân (1), *judge; advocate*
1784 Dîynay (Ch.) (1), *Dinaite*
3198 yâkach (1), *to decide, justify, convict*
6416 pᵉlîyliy (1), *judicial*
8199 shâphaṭ (102), *to judge*
350 anakrinō (1), *to interrogate, determine*
1252 diakrinō (3), *to decide; to hesitate*
1348 dikastēs (3), *one who judges*
2919 krinō (45), *to decide; to try*
2922 kritēriŏn (1), *rule; tribunal; lawsuit*
2923 kritēs (13), *judge*

JUDGED
1777 dîyn (2), *to judge; to strive or contend for*
4941 mishpâṭ (1), *verdict; formal decree; justice*
5307 nâphal (1), *to fall*
6419 pâlal (1), *to intercede, pray*
8199 shâphaṭ (28), *to judge*
350 anakrinō (3), *to interrogate, determine*
2233 hēgĕŏmai (1), *to deem, i.e. consider*
2919 krinō (26), *to decide; to try, condemn, punish*

JUDGES
148 'ădargâzêr (Ch.) (2), *chief diviner*
430 'ĕlôhîym (4), *God; magistrates, judges*
1782 dayân (Ch.) (1), *judge*
6414 pâlîyl (3), *magistrate*
8199 shâphaṭ (38), *to judge*
2923 kritēs (4), *judge*

JUDGEST
8199 shâphaṭ (2), *to judge*
2919 krinō (6), *to decide; to try, condemn, punish*

JUDGETH
1777 dîyn (1), *to judge; to strive or contend for*
8199 shâphaṭ (5), *to judge*
350 anakrinō (1), *to interrogate, determine*
2919 krinō (10), *to try, condemn, punish*

JUDGING
8199 shâphaṭ (4), *to judge*
2919 krinō (2), *to decide; to try, condemn, punish*

JUDGMENT
1777 dîyn (1), *to judge; to strive or contend for*

1779 dîyn (9), *judge; judgment; law suit*
1780 dîyn (Ch.) (5), *judge; judgment*
2940 ṭa'am (1), *perception; mandate*
4055 mad (1), *vesture, garment; carpet*
4941 mishpâṭ (187), *verdict; decree; justice*
6415 pᵉlîylâh (1), *justice*
6417 pᵉlîylîyâh (1), *judgment*
6419 pâlal (1), *to intercede, pray*
6485 pâqad (2), *to visit, care for, count*
8196 shᵉphôwṭ (2), *sentence, punishment*
8199 shâphaṭ (2), *to judge*
8201 shepheṭ (2), *criminal sentence*
144 aisthēsis (1), *discernment*
968 bēma (10), *tribunal platform; judging place*
1106 gnōmē (3), *cognition, opinion*
1341 dikaiŏkrisia (1), *just sentence*
1345 dikaiōma (1), *statute or decision*
1349 dikē (1), *justice*
2250 hēmĕra (1), *day; period of time*
2917 krima (12), *decision*
2920 krisis (39), *decision; tribunal; justice*
2922 kritēriŏn (1), *rule; tribunal; lawsuit*
4232 praitōriŏn (5), *governor's court-room*

JUDGMENTS
4941 mishpâṭ (108), *verdict; decree; justice*
8201 shepheṭ (14), *criminal sentence*
1345 dikaiōma (1), *deed; statute or decision*
2917 krima (1), *decision*
2920 krisis (2), *decision; tribunal; justice*
2922 kritēriŏn (1), *rule; tribunal; lawsuit*

JUDITH
3067 Yᵉhûwdîyth (1), *Jewess*

JUICE
6071 'âçîyç (1), *expressed fresh grape-juice*

JULIA
2456 Iŏulia (1), *Julia*

JULIUS
2457 Iŏuliŏs (1), *Julius*

JUMPING
7540 râqad (1), *to spring about wildly or for joy*

JUNIA
2458 Iŏunias (1), *Junias*

JUNIPER
7574 rethem (4), *broom tree*

JUPITER
1356 diŏpĕtēs (1), *sky-fallen*

2203 Zĕus (2), *Jupiter or Jove*

JURISDICTION
1849 ĕxŏusia (1), *authority, dominion*

JUSHAB-HESED
3142 Yûwshab Cheçed (1), *kindness will be returned*

JUST
3477 yâshâr (1), *straight*
4941 mishpâṭ (1), *verdict; formal decree; justice*
6662 tsaddîyq (42), *just*
6663 tsâdaq (3), *to be, make right*
6664 tsedeq (8), *right*
8003 shâlêm (1), *complete; friendly; safe*
1342 dikaiŏs (33), *equitable, holy*
1738 ĕndikŏs (2), *equitable, deserved, just*

JUSTICE
4941 mishpâṭ (1), *verdict; formal decree; justice*
6663 tsâdaq (2), *to be, make right*
6664 tsedeq (10), *right*
6666 tsᵉdâqâh (15), *rightness*

JUSTIFICATION
1345 dikaiōma (1), *deed; statute or decision*
1347 dikaiōsis (2), *acquittal, vindication*

JUSTIFIED
6663 tsâdaq (12), *to be, make right*
1344 dikaiŏō (31), *show or regard as just*

JUSTIFIER
1344 dikaiŏō (1), *show or regard as just*

JUSTIFIETH
6663 tsâdaq (2), *to be, make right*
1344 dikaiŏō (2), *show or regard as just*

JUSTIFY
6663 tsâdaq (7), *to be, make right*
1344 dikaiŏō (4), *show or regard as just*

JUSTIFYING
6663 tsâdaq (2), *to be, make right*

JUSTLE
8264 shâqaq (1), *to seek greedily*

JUSTLY
4941 mishpâṭ (1), *verdict; formal decree; justice*
1346 dikaiŏs (2), *equitably*

JUSTUS
2459 Iŏustŏs (3), *just*

JUTTAH
3194 Yuṭṭâh (2), *extended*

KABZEEL
6909 Qabtsᵉ'êl (3), *God has gathered*

KADESH
6946 Qâdêsh (17), *sanctuary*

KADESH-BARNEA
6947 Qâdêsh Barnêa' (10), *Kadesh of (the) Wilderness of Wandering*

KADMIEL
6934 Qadmîy'êl (8), *presence of God*

KADMONITES
6935 Qadmônîy (1), *ancient*

KALLAI
7040 Qallay (1), *frivolous*

KANAH
7071 Qânâh (3), *reediness*

KAREAH
7143 Qârêach (13), *bald*

KARKAA
7173 Qarqa' (1), *ground-floor*

KARKOR
7174 Qarqôr (1), *foundation*

KARTAH
7177 Qartâh (1), *city*

KARTAN
7178 Qartân (1), *city-plot*

KATTATH
7005 Qaṭṭâth (1), *littleness*

KEDAR
6938 Qêdâr (12), *dusky*

KEDEMAH
6929 Qêdᵉmâh (2), *precedence*

KEDEMOTH
6932 Qᵉdêmôwth (4), *beginnings*

KEDESH
6943 Qedesh (11), *sanctum*

KEDESH-NAPHTALI
6943+5321 Qedesh (1), *sanctum*

KEEP
1692 dâbaq (3), *to cling or adhere; to catch*
1961 hâyâh (1), *to exist, i.e. be or become*
2287 châgag (12), *to observe a festival*
2820 châsak (1), *to refuse, spare, preserve*
3533 kâbash (1), *to conquer, subjugate*
3607 kâlâ' (1), *to hold back or in; to prohibit*
4513 mâna' (1), *to deny, refuse*
4931 mishmereth (4), *watch, sentry, post*
5201 nâṭar (3), *to guard; to cherish anger*
5341 nâtsar (26), *to guard, protect*
5647 'âbad (1), *to do, work, serve*
5737 'âdar (2), *to arrange as a battle*

6113 'âtsar (1), to *hold back*; to *maintain, rule*
6213 'âsâh (30), to *do* or *make*
6485 pâqad (1), to *visit, care for, count*
6942 qâdâsh (1), to *be, make clean*
7069 qânâh (1), to *create; to procure*
7368 râchaq (1), to *recede; remove*
8104 shâmar (186), to *watch*
1301 diatērĕō (1), to *observe* strictly
1314 diaphulassō (1), to *protect, guard carefully*
1858 hĕŏrtazō (1), to *observe a festival*
2722 katĕchō (3), to *hold down fast*
2853 kŏllaō (1), to *glue together*
3557 nŏsphizŏmai (1), to *sequestrate, embezzle*
4160 pŏiĕō (2), to *do*
4238 prassō (1), to *execute, accomplish*
4601 sigaō (2), to *keep silent*
4874 sunanamignumi (1), to *associate with*
4912 sunĕchō (1), to *hold together*
5083 tērĕō (32), to *keep, guard, obey*
5299 hupōpiazō (1), to *beat up*; to *wear out*
5432 phrŏurĕō (1), to *hem in, protect*
5442 phulassō (13), to *watch,* i.e. *be on guard*

KEEPER
5201 nâṭar (1), to *guard*; to *cherish* anger
5341 nâtsar (1), to *guard, protect, maintain*
7462 râ'âh (1), to *tend* a flock, i.e. *pasture* it
8104 shâmar (13), to *watch*
8269 sar (3), *head person, ruler*
1200 dĕsmŏphulax (2), *jailer*

KEEPERS
5201 nâṭar (1), to *guard*; to *cherish* anger
8104 shâmar (15), to *watch*
3626 ŏikŏurŏs (1), *domestically inclined*
5083 tērĕō (1), to *keep, guard, obey*
5441 phulax (3), *watcher or sentry*

KEEPEST
8104 shâmar (3), to *watch*
5442 phulassō (1), to *watch,* i.e. *be on guard*

KEEPETH
2820 châsak (1), to *refuse, spare, preserve*
4513 mâna' (1), to *deny, refuse*
5307 nâphal (1), to *fall*

5341 nâtsar (7), to *guard, protect, maintain*
7462 râ'âh (1), to *tend* a flock, i.e. *pasture* it
7623 shâbach (1), to *address*; to *pacify*
8104 shâmar (18), to *watch*
4160 pŏiĕō (1), to *do*
5083 tērĕō (10), to *keep, guard, obey*
5442 phulassō (1), to *watch,* i.e. *be on guard*

KEEPING
5341 nâtsar (1), to *guard, protect, maintain*
7462 râ'âh (1), to *tend* a flock, i.e. *pasture* it
8104 shâmar (7), to *watch*
5084 tērēsis (1), *observance; prison*
5442 phulassō (1), to *watch,* i.e. *be on guard*

KEHELATHAH
6954 Qᵉhêlâthâh (2), *convocation*

KEILAH
7084 Qᵉˈîylâh (18), *citadel*

KELAIAH
7041 Qêlâyâh (1), *insignificance*

KELITA
7042 Qᵉlîyṭâ' (3), *maiming*

KEMUEL
7055 Qᵉmûw'êl (3), *raised of God*

KENAN
7018 Qêynân (1), *fixed*

KENATH
7079 Qᵉnâth (2), *possession*

KENAZ
7073 Qᵉnaz (11), *hunter*

KENEZITE
7074 Qᵉnizzîy (3), *Kenizzite*

KENITE
7014 Qayin (2), *lance*
7017 Qêynîy (4), *Kenite*

KENITES
7017 Qêynîy (8), *Kenite*

KENIZZITES
7074 Qᵉnizzîy (1), *Kenizzite*

KEPT
631 'âçar (1), to *fasten*; to *join* battle
680 'âtsal (1), to *select; refuse; narrow*
1639 gâra' (1), to *shave, remove, or withhold*
1692 dâbaq (1), to *cling or adhere*; to *catch*
2287 châgag (1), to *observe* a festival
2790 chârash (2), to *engrave; to plow*
2820 châsak (2), to *refuse, spare, preserve*
3607 kâlâ' (1), to *hold back or in*; to *prohibit*

4513 mâna' (2), to *deny, refuse*
4931 mishmereth (6), *watch, sentry, post*
5201 nâṭar (1), to *guard*; to *cherish* anger
5202 nᵉṭar (Ch.) (1), to *retain*
5341 nâtsar (4), to *guard, protect, maintain*
5641 çâthar (2), to *hide by covering*
5648 'âbad (Ch.) (1), to *do, work, serve*
6113 'âtsar (2), to *hold back*; to *maintain, rule*
6213 'âsâh (18), to *do* or *make*
6942 qâdâsh (1), to *be, make clean*
7462 râ'âh (3), to *tend* a flock, i.e. *pasture* it
7673 shâbath (1), to *repose*; to *desist*
8104 shâmar (70), to *watch*
71 agō (1), to *lead*; to *bring, drive*; to *weigh*
650 apŏstĕrĕō (1), to *deprive*; to *despoil*
1006 bŏskō (1), to *pasture* a flock
1096 ginŏmai (1), to *be, become*
1301 diatērĕō (1), to *observe* strictly
2192 ĕchō (1), to *have; hold; keep*
2343 thēsaurizō (1), to *amass* or *reserve, store*
2377 thurōrŏs (2), *doorkeeper*
2621 katakĕimai (1), to *lie down* in bed
2902 kratĕō (1), to *seize*
2967 kōluō (1), to *stop*
3557 nŏsphizŏmai (1), to *sequestrate, embezzle*
3930 parĕchō (1), to *hold near,* i.e. to *present*
4160 pŏiĕō (1), to *do*
4601 sigaō (2), to *keep silent*
4933 suntērĕō (1), to *protect*
5083 tērĕō (15), to *keep, guard, obey*
5288 hupŏstĕllō (1), to *conceal (reserve)*
5432 phrŏurĕō (3), to *hem in, protect*
5442 phulassō (8), to *watch,* i.e. *be on guard*

KERCHIEFS
4556 miçpachath (2), *scurf, rash*

KEREN-HAPPUCH
7163 Qeren Hap-pûwk (1), *horn of cosmetic*

KERIOTH
7152 Qᵉrîyôwth (3), *buildings*

KERNELS
2785 chartsan (1), *sour, tart grape*

KEROS
7026 Qêyrôç (2), *ankled*

KETTLE
1731 dûwd (1), *pot, kettle; basket*

KETURAH
6989 Qᵉṭûwrâh (4), *perfumed*

KEY
4668 maphtêach (2), *opening; key*
2807 klĕis (4), *key*

KEYS
2807 klĕis (2), *key*

KEZIA
7103 Qᵉtsîy'âh (1), *cassia*

KEZIZ
7104 Qᵉtsîyts (1), *abrupt*

KIBROTH-HATTAAVAH
6914 Qibrôwth hat-Ta'ăvâh (5), *graves of the longing*

KIBZAIM
6911 Qibtsayim (1), *double heap*

KICK
1163 bâ'aṭ (1), *kick*
2979 laktizō (2), to *recalcitrate, kick back*

KICKED
1163 bâ'aṭ (1), *kick*

KID
1423 gᵉdîy (8), *young male goat*
1423+5795 gᵉdîy (5), *young male goat*
5795 'êz (1), *she-goat; goat's hair*
8163 sâ'îyr (26), *shaggy; he-goat; goat idol*
8166 sᵉ'iyrâh (2), *she-goat*
2056 ĕriphŏs (1), *kid or goat*

KIDNEYS
3629 kilyâh (18), *kidney; mind, heart, spirit*

KIDRON
6939 Qidrôwn (11), *dusky place*

KIDS
1423 gᵉdîy (4), *young male goat*
5795 'êz (1), *she-goat; goat's hair*
8163 sâ'îyr (2), *shaggy; he-goat; goat idol*

KILL
2026 hârag (17), to *kill, slaughter*
2076 zâbach (3), to *(sacrificially) slaughter*
2491 châlâl (2), *pierced* to death, one *slain*
2873 ṭâbach (1), to *kill, butcher*
4191 mûwth (24), to *die; to kill*
5221 nâkâh (4), to *strike, kill*
5362 nâqaph (1), to *strike*; to *surround*
7523 râtsach (4), to *murder*
7819 shâchaṭ (22), to *slaughter; butcher*

KILLED
337 *anairĕō* (6), *to abolish, murder*
615 *apŏktĕinō* (28), *to kill outright; to destroy*
1315 *diachĕirizŏmai* (1), *to lay hands upon*
2380 *thuō* (3), *to kill; to butcher; to sacrifice*
4969 *sphazō* (1), *to slaughter or to maim*
5407 *phŏnĕuō* (8), *to commit murder*

KILLED
2026 hârag (3), *to kill, slaughter*
2076 zâbach (1), *to (sacrificially) slaughter*
2873 ṭâbach (3), *to kill, butcher*
3076 Yᵉhôwchânân (1), *Jehovah-favored*
4191 mûwth (6), *to die; to kill*
5221 nâkâh (3), *to strike, kill*
7523 râtsach (1), *to murder*
7819 shâchaṭ (15), *to slaughter; butcher*
337 *anairĕō* (3), *to take away, murder*
615 *apŏktĕinō* (22), *to kill outright; to destroy*
2289 *thanatŏō* (2), *to kill*
2380 *thuō* (5), *to kill; to butcher; to sacrifice*
5407 *phŏnĕuō* (2), *to commit murder*

KILLEDST
2026 hârag (2), *to kill, slaughter*

KILLEST
615 *apŏktĕinō* (2), *to kill outright; to destroy*

KILLETH
2026 hârag (1), *to kill, slaughter*
4191 mûwth (2), *to die; to kill*
5221 nâkâh (13), *to strike, kill*
6991 qâṭal (1), *to put to death*
7819 shâchaṭ (3), *to slaughter; butcher*
615 *apŏktĕinō* (3), *to kill outright; to destroy*

KILLING
2026 hârag (1), *to kill, slaughter*
7523 râtsach (1), *to murder*
7819 shâchaṭ (1), *to slaughter; butcher*
7821 shᵉchîyṭâh (1), *slaughter*
615 *apŏktĕinō* (1), *to kill outright; to destroy*

KIN
1320 bâsâr (2), *flesh; body; person*
7138 qârôwb (1), *near, close*
7607 shᵉʾêr (2), *flesh, meat; kindred* by blood
4773 *suggĕnēs* (1), blood relative; countryman

KINAH
7016 Qîynâh (1), *dirge*

KIND
2896 ṭôwb (1), *good; well*
4327 mîyn (29), *sort*, i.e. species
1085 *gĕnŏs* (3), *kin, offspring in kind*
5100 *tis* (1), *some* or *any* person or object
5449 *phusis* (1), *genus* or *sort*
5541 *chrēstĕuŏmai* (1), *to show oneself useful*
5543 *chrēstŏs* (2), *employed*, i.e. *useful*

KINDLE
215 *ʾôwr* (1), *to be luminous*
1197 bâʾar (4), *to be brutish, be senseless*
1814 dâlaq (2), *to flame; to pursue*
2787 chârar (1), *to melt, burn, dry up*
3341 yâtsath (8), *to burn or set on fire*
3344 yâqad (1), *to burn*
6919 qâdach (1), *to inflame*
6999 qâṭar (1), *to turn into fragrance* by fire

KINDLED
1197 bâʾar (9), *to be brutish, be senseless*
2734 chârâh (43), *to blaze up*
3341 yâtsath (4), *to burn or set on fire*
3648 kâmar (1), *to shrivel with heat*
5400 nâsaq (1), *to catch fire*
6919 qâdach (3), *to inflame*
8313 sâraph (1), *to be, set on fire*
381 *anaptō* (2), *to kindle, set on fire*
681 *haptō* (1), *to set on fire*

KINDLETH
3857 lâhaṭ (1), *to blaze*
5400 nâsaq (1), *to catch fire*
381 *anaptō* (1), *to kindle, set on fire*

KINDLY
2617 cheçed (5), *kindness, favor*
2896 ṭôwb (2), *good; well*
5921+3820 ʾal (1), *above, over, upon, or against*
5387 *philŏstŏrgŏs* (1), *fraternal, devoted*

KINDNESS
2617 cheçed (40), *kindness, favor*
2896 ṭôwb (1), *good; well*
5360 *philadĕlphia* (2), *fraternal affection*
5363 *philanthrŏpia* (1), *benevolence*
5544 *chrēstŏtēs* (4), *moral excellence*

KINDRED
250 ʾEzrâchîy (1), *Ezrachite*
1353 gᵉullâh (1), *blood relationship*
4130 môwdaʾath (1), *distant relative*
4138 môwledeth (11), *lineage, family*
4940 mishpâchâh (6), *family, clan, people*
1085 *gĕnŏs* (3), *kin*
4772 *suggĕnĕia* (3), *relatives; one's people*
5443 *phulē* (2), *race or clan*

KINDREDS
4940 mishpâchâh (3), *family, clan, people*
3965 patria (1), *family, group, race*, i.e. *nation*
5443 *phulē* (4), *race or clan*

KINDS
2177 zan (5), *form or sort*
4327 mîyn (1), *sort*, i.e. species
4940 mishpâchâh (2), *family, clan, people*
1085 *gĕnŏs* (2), *kin, offspring in kind*

KINE
504 ʾeleph (4), *ox; cow or cattle*
1241 bâqâr (2), *plowing ox; herd*
6510 pârâh (18), *heifer*

KING
4427 mâlak (43), *to reign as king*
4428 melek (1957), *king*
4430 melek (Ch.) (140), *king*
935 *basilĕus* (86), *sovereign*

KING'S
4410 mᵉlûwkâh (2), *realm, rulership*
4428 melek (259), *king*
4430 melek (Ch.) (18), *king*
4467 mamlâkâh (1), *royal dominion*
935 *basilĕus* (2), *sovereign*
937 *basilikŏs* (1), *befitting the sovereign*

KINGDOM
4410 mᵉlûwkâh (18), *realm, rulership*
4437 malkûw (Ch.) (45), *dominion*
4438 malkûwth (47), *rule; dominion*
4467 mamlâkâh (61), *royal dominion*
4468 mamlâkûwth (8), *royal dominion*
932 *basilĕia* (155), *rule; realm*

KINGDOMS
4437 malkûw (Ch.) (2), *dominion*
4438 malkûwth (1), *rule; dominion*
4467 mamlâkâh (49), *royal dominion*

KINGDOMS
932 *basilĕia* (5), *rule; realm*

KINGLY
4437 malkûw (Ch.) (1), *dominion*

KINGS
4428 melek (283), *king*
4430 melek (Ch.) (13), *king*
935 *basilĕus* (29), *sovereign*
936 *basilĕuō* (1), *to rule*

KINGS'
4428 melek (3), *king*
933 *basilĕiŏn* (1), *royal palace*
935 *basilĕus* (1), *sovereign*

KINSFOLK
7138 qârôwb (1), *near, close*
4773 *suggĕnēs* (1), blood relative; countryman

KINSFOLKS
1350 gâʾal (1), *to redeem; to be the next of kin*
3045 yâdaʿ (1), *to know*
4773 *suggĕnēs* (1), blood relative; countryman

KINSMAN
1350 gâʾal (12), *to be the next of kin*
3045 yâdaʿ (1), *to know*
7607 shᵉʾêr (1), *flesh, meat; kindred* by blood
4773 *suggĕnēs* (2), blood relative; countryman

KINSMAN'S
1350 gâʾal (1), *to redeem; to be the next of kin*

KINSMEN
1350 gâʾal (1), *to redeem; to be the next of kin*
7138 qârôwb (1), *near, close*
4773 *suggĕnēs* (5), blood relative; countryman

KINSWOMAN
4129 môwdaʾ (1), *distant relative*
7607 shᵉʾêr (2), *flesh, meat; kindred* by blood

KINSWOMEN
7608 shaʾărâh (1), *female kindred* by blood

KIR
7024 Qîyr (5), *fortress*

KIR-HARASETH
7025 Qîyr Cheres (1), *fortress of earthenware*

KIR-HARESETH
7025 Qîyr Cheres (1), *fortress of earthenware*

KIR-HARESH
7025 Qîyr Cheres (1), *fortress of earthenware*

KIR-HERES
7025 Qîyr Cheres (2), *fortress of earthenware*

KIRIATHAIM
7156 Qiryâthayim (3), *double city*

7741 Shâvêh
Qiryâthayim (1), *plain of a double city*

KIRIOTH
7152 Qᵉrîyôwth (1), *buildings*

KIRJATH
7157 Qiryath Yᵉ'ârîym (1), *city of forests*

KIRJATH-ARBA
7153 Qiryath 'Arba' (6), *city of Arba* or *of the four* (giants)

KIRJATH-ARIM
7157 Qiryath Yᵉ'ârîym (1), *city of forests* or *of towns*

KIRJATH-BAAL
7154 Qiryath Ba'al (2), *city of Baal*

KIRJATH-HUZOTH
7155 Qiryath Chûtsôwth (1), *city of streets*

KIRJATH-JEARIM
7157 Qiryath Yᵉ'ârîym (18), *city of forests*

KIRJATH-SANNAH
7158 Qiryath Çannâh (1), *city of branches* or *of a book*

KIRJATH-SEPHER
7158 Qiryath Çannâh (4), *city of branches* or *of a book*

KIRJATHAIM
7156 Qiryâthayim (3), *double city*

KISH
7027 Qîysh (20), *bow*

KISHI
7029 Qîyshîy (1), *bowed*

KISHION
7191 Qishyôwn (1), *hard ground*

KISHON
7028 Qîyshôwn (5), *winding*
7191 Qishyôwn (1), *hard ground*

KISON
7028 Qîyshôwn (1), *winding*

KISS
5401 nâshaq (9), *to kiss*
2705 kataphileō (1), *to kiss earnestly*
5368 phileō (3), *to be a friend, to kiss*
5370 philēma (7), *kiss*

KISSED
5401 nâshaq (21), *to kiss*
2705 kataphileō (5), *to kiss earnestly*

KISSES
5390 nᵉshîyqâh (2), *kiss*

KITE
344 'ayâh (2), *hawk*

KITHLISH
3798 Kithlîysh (1), *wall of a man*

KITRON
7003 Qitrôwn (1), *fumigative*

KITTIM
3794 Kittîy (2), *islander*

KNEAD
3888 lûwsh (2), *to knead*

KNEADED
3888 lûwsh (3), *to knead*

KNEADINGTROUGHS
4863 mish'ereth (2), *kneading-trough*

KNEE
1290 berek (1), *knee*
1119 gŏnu (3), *knee*

KNEEL
1288 bârak (2), *to bless*

KNEELED
1288 bârak (1), *to bless*
1289 bᵉrak (Ch.) (1), *to bless*
1120 gŏnupĕtĕō (1), *to fall on the knee, kneel*
5087+1119 tithēmi (5), *to place, put*

KNEELING
3766 kâra' (1), *to prostrate*
1120 gŏnupĕtĕō (2), *to fall on the knee, kneel*

KNEES
755 'arkûbâh (Ch.) (1), *knees*
1290 berek (24), *knee*
1291 berek (Ch.) (1), *knee*
1119 gŏnu (4), *knee joint*

KNEW
1847 da'ath (1), *knowledge*
3045 yâda' (83), *to know*
3046 yᵉda' (Ch.) (2), *to know*
5234 nâkar (9), *to acknowledge*
50 agnŏĕō (1), *to not know; understand*
1097 ginōskō (30), *to know*
1492 ĕidō (27), *to know*
1912 ĕpibarĕō (1), *to be severe toward*
1921 ĕpiginōskō (13), *to acknowledge*
4267 prŏginōskō (1), *to know beforehand*

KNEWEST
3045 yâda' (5), *to know*
3046 yᵉda' (Ch.) (1), *to know*
1097 ginōskō (1), *to know*
1492 ĕidō (3), *to know*

KNIFE
2719 chereb (2), *knife, sword*
3979 ma'ăkeleth (3), *knife*
7915 sakkîyn (1), *knife*

KNIT
2270 châber (1), *associate, friend*
3162 yachad (1), *unitedly*
7194 qâshar (1), *to tie, bind*
1210 dĕō (1), *to bind*

4822 sumbibazō (2), *to drive together*

KNIVES
2719 chereb (3), *knife, sword*
3979 ma'ăkeleth (1), *knife*
4252 machălâph (1), *butcher knife*

KNOCK
2925 krŏuō (4), *to rap, knock*

KNOCKED
2925 krŏuō (1), *to rap, knock*

KNOCKETH
1849 dâphaq (1), *to knock; to press severely*
2925 krŏuō (3), *to rap, knock*

KNOCKING
2925 krŏuō (1), *to rap, knock*

KNOP
3730 kaphtôr (10), *capital; button or disk*

KNOPS
3730 kaphtôr (6), *capital; button or disk*
6497 peqa' (3), *ornamental semi-globe*

KNOW
995 bîyn (1), *to understand; discern*
1847 da'ath (4), *knowledge*
3045 yâda' (429), *to know*
3046 yᵉda' (Ch.) (15), *to know*
5234 nâkar (9), *to acknowledge*
50 agnŏĕō (2), *to not know; not understand*
1097 ginōskō (92), *to know*
1110 gnōstŏs (1), *well-known*
1231 diaginōskō (1), *ascertain exactly*
1492 ĕidō (176), *to know*
1921 ĕpiginōskō (8), *to acknowledge*
1987 ĕpistamai (9), *to be acquainted with*
2467 isēmi (2), *to know*
4267 prŏginōskō (1), *to know beforehand*
4892 sunĕdriŏn (1), *head Jewish tribunal*

KNOWEST
1847 da'ath (1), *knowledge*
3045 yâda' (66), *to know*
1097 ginōskō (5), *to know*
1492 ĕidō (15), *to know*
1921 ĕpiginōskō (1), *to acknowledge*
2589 kardiŏgnōstēs (1), *heart-knower*

KNOWETH
854 'êth (1), *with; by; at; among*
3045 yâda' (59), *to know*
3046 yᵉda' (Ch.) (1), *to know*

5234 nâkar (1), *to acknowledge*
1097 ginōskō (16), *to know*
1492 ĕidō (22), *to know*
1921 ĕpiginōskō (2), *to acknowledge*
1987 ĕpistamai (1), *to comprehend*
2589 kardiŏgnōstēs (1), *heart-knower*

KNOWING
3045 yâda' (2), *to know*
50 agnŏĕō (1), *to not know; not understand*
1097 ginōskō (5), *to know*
1492 ĕidō (38), *to know*
1921 ĕpiginōskō (2), *to acknowledge*
1987 ĕpistamai (3), *to comprehend*

KNOWLEDGE
998 bîynâh (3), *understanding*
1843 dēa' (2), *knowledge*
1844 dê'âh (6), *knowledge*
1847 da'ath (82), *knowledge*
3045 yâda' (19), *to know*
4093 maddâ' (4), *intelligence*
5234 nâkar (2), *to treat as a foreigner*
5869 'ayin (1), *eye; sight; fountain*
7922 sekel (1), *intelligence; success*
56 agnōsia (1), *state of ignorance*
1097 ginōskō (1), *to know*
1108 gnōsis (28), *knowledge*
1492 ĕidō (1), *to know*
1921 ĕpiginōskō (3), *to acknowledge*
1922 ĕpignōsis (16), *full discernment*
1990 ĕpistēmōn (1), *intelligent, learned*
4907 sunĕsis (1), *intelligence, intellect*

KNOWN
3045 yâda' (105), *to know*
3046 yᵉda' (Ch.) (24), *to know*
5234 nâkar (2), *to acknowledge*
319 anagnōrizŏmai (1), *to make oneself known*
1097 ginōskō (46), *to know*
1107 gnōrizō (16), *to make known, reveal*
1110 gnōstŏs (11), *well-known*
1232 diagnōrizō (1), *to tell abroad*
1492 ĕidō (6), *to know*
1921 ĕpiginōskō (4), *to acknowledge*
3877 parakŏlŏuthĕō (1), *to attend; trace out*
4135 plērŏphŏrĕō (1), *to assure or convince*
5318 phanĕrŏs (3), *apparent, visible, clear*

English

KOA
6970 Qôwa' (1), *curtailment*

KOHATH
6955 Qᵉhâth (32), *allied*

KOHATHITES
6956 Qŏhâthîy (15), *Kohathite*

KOLAIAH
6964 Qôwlâyâh (2), *voice of Jehovah*

KORAH
7141 Qôrach (37), *ice*

KORAHITE
7145 Qorchîy (1), *Korchite*

KORAHITES
7145 Qorchîy (1), *Korchite*

KORATHITES
7145 Qorchîy (1), *Korchite*

KORE
6981 Qôwrê' (3), *crier*
7145 Qorchîy (1), *Korchite*

KORHITES
7145 Qorchîy (4), *Korchite*

KOZ
6976 Qôwts (4), *thorns*

KUSHAIAH
6984 Qûwshâyâhûw (1), *entrapped of Jehovah*

LAADAH
3935 La'dâh (1), *Ladah*

LAADAN
3936 La'dân (7), *Ladan*

LABAN
3837 Lâbân (51), *white*

LABAN'S
3837 Lâbân (4), *white*

LABOUR
213 'ûwts (1), to *be close, hurry, withdraw*
1518 gîyach (1), to *issue forth; to burst forth*
3018 yᵉgîya' (12), *toil, work; produce, property*
3021 yâga' (8), to *be exhausted, to tire,*
3023 yâgêa' (1), *tiresome*
3027 yâd (1), *hand; power*
3205 yâlad (2), to *bear young; to father a child*
4399 mᵉlâ'kâh (1), *work; property*
4639 ma'âseh (1), *action; labor*
5445 çâbal (1), to *carry*
5647 'âbad (2), to *do, work, serve*
5656 'ăbôdâh (1), *work of any kind*
5998 'âmal (2), to *work severely, put forth effort*
5999 'âmâl (25), *wearing effort; worry*
6001 'âmêl (1), *toiling; laborer; sorrowful*
6089 'etseb (1), *earthen vessel; painful toil*
6213 'âsâh (2), to *do*

6468 pᵉ'ullâh (2), *work, deed*
2038 ĕrgazŏmai (1), to *toil*
2041 ĕrgŏn (1), *work*
2872 kŏpiaō (11), to *feel fatigue; to work hard*
2873 kŏpŏs (8), *toil; pains*
4704 spŏudazō (1), to *make effort*
4904 sunĕrgŏs (1), *fellow-worker*
5389 philŏtimĕŏmai (1), to *be eager or earnest*

LABOURED
3021 yâga' (4), to *be exhausted, to tire,*
3022 yâgâ' (1), *earnings, i.e. the product of toil*
5998 'âmal (5), to *work severely, put forth effort*
6001 'âmêl (1), *toiling; laborer; sorrowful*
6213 'âsâh (1), to *do or make*
7712 shᵉdar (Ch.) (1), to *endeavor, strive*
2872 kŏpiaō (5), to *feel fatigue; to work hard*
4866 sunathlĕō (1), to *wrestle with*

LABOURER
2040 ĕrgatēs (2), *toiler, worker*

LABOURERS
2040 ĕrgatēs (8), *toiler, worker*
4904 sunĕrgŏs (1), *fellow-worker*

LABOURETH
5998 'âmal (1), to *work severely, put forth effort*
6001 'âmêl (2), *toiling; laborer; sorrowful*
2872 kŏpiaō (2), to *feel fatigue; to work hard*

LABOURING
5647 'âbad (1), to *do, work, serve*
75 agōnizŏmai (1), to *struggle; to contend*
2872 kŏpiaō (1), to *feel fatigue; to work hard*
2873 kŏpŏs (1), *toil; pains*

LABOURS
3018 yᵉgîya' (3), *toil, work; produce, property*
4639 ma'âseh (3), *action; labor*
6089 'eteb (1), *earthen vessel; painful toil; mental pang*
6092 'âtsêb (1), *hired workman*
2873 kŏpŏs (5), *toil; pains*

LACE
6616 pâthîyl (4), *twine, cord*

LACHISH
3923 Lâchîysh (24), *Lakish*

LACK
1097 bᵉlîy (3), *without, not yet; lacking;*
2637 châçêr (4), to *lack; to fail, want, make less*

4270 machçôwr (1), *impoverishment*
7326 rûwsh (1), to *be destitute*
1641 ĕlattŏnĕō (1), to *fall short, have too little*
3007 lĕipō (1), to *fail or be absent*
5302 hustĕrĕō (1), to *be inferior; to fall short*
5303 hustĕrēma (1), *deficit; poverty; lacking*
5332 pharmakĕus (1), *magician, sorcerer*

LACKED
2637 châçêr (2), to *lack; to fail, want, make less*
2638 châçêr (1), *lacking*
5737 'âdar (2), to *arrange as a battle*
6485 pâqad (1), to *visit, care for, count*
170 akairĕŏmai (1), to *fail of a proper occasion*
1729 ĕndĕēs (1), *lacking; deficient in; needy*
3361+2192 mē (1), *not; lest*
5302 hustĕrĕō (2), to *be inferior; to fall short*

LACKEST
3007 lĕipō (1), to *fail or be absent*
5302 hustĕrĕō (1), to *be inferior; to fall short*

LACKETH
2638 châçêr (3), *lacking*
6485 pâqad (1), to *visit, care for, count*
3361+3918 mē (1), *not; lest*

LACKING
5737 'âdar (1), to *arrange as a battle*
6485 pâqad (2), to *visit, care for, count*
7038 qâlat (1), to *be maim*
7673 shâbath (1), to *repose; to desist*
5303 hustĕrēma (3), *deficit; poverty; lacking*

LAD
5288 na'ar (32), *male child; servant*
3808 paidariŏn (1), *little boy*

LAD'S
5288 na'ar (1), *male child; servant*

LADDER
5551 çullâm (1), *stair-case*

LADE
2943 tâ'an (1), to *load a beast*
6006 'âmaç (1), to *impose a burden*
5412 phŏrtizō (1), to *overburden*

LADED
5375 nâsâ' (1), to *lift up*
6006 'âmaç (2), to *impose a burden*
2007 ĕpitithēmi (1), to *impose*

LADEN
3515 kâbêd (1), *severe, difficult, stupid*
5375 nâsâ' (2), to *lift up*
4987 sōrĕuō (1), to *pile up, load up*
5412 phŏrtizō (1), to *overburden*

LADETH
3515 kâbêd (1), *severe, difficult, stupid*

LADIES
8282 sârâh (2), *female noble*

LADING
6006 'âmaç (1), to *impose a burden*
5414 phŏrtŏs (1), *cargo of a ship*

LADS
5288 na'ar (1), *male child; servant*

LADY
1404 gᵉbereth (2), *mistress, noblewoman*
2959 Kuria (2), *Lady*

LAEL
3815 Lâ'êl (1), *belonging to God*

LAHAD
3854 lahag (1), *mental application*

LAHAI-ROI
883 Bᵉ'êr la-Chay Rô'îy (2), *well of a living (One) my seer*

LAHMAM
3903 Lachmâç (1), *food-like*

LAHMI
3902 Lachmîy (1), *foodful*

LAID
935 bôw' (1), to *go or come*
2470 châlâh (1), to *be weak, sick, afflicted*
2630 châçan (1), to *hoard, store up*
2934 tâman (2), to *hide*
3052 yᵉhab (Ch.) (1), to *give*
3240 yânach (1), to *allow to stay*
3241 Yânîym (8), *asleep*
3318 yâtsâ' (2), to *go, bring out*
3332 yâtsaq (1), to *pour out*
3369 yâqôsh (1), to *ensnare, trap*
3384 yârâh (1), to *point; to teach*
3515 kâbêd (1), *numerous; severe*
3647 kâmaç (1), to *store away*
5060 nâga' (1), to *strike*
5182 nᵉchath (Ch.) (1), to *descend; to depose*
5186 nâtâh (1), to *stretch or spread out*
5324 nâtsab (1), to *station*
5375 nâsâ' (4), to *lift up*
5414 nâthan (13), to *give*

5446 çᵉbal (Ch.) (1), to *raise*
5493 çûwr (1), to *turn* off
5564 çâmak (6), to *lean* upon; *take hold* of
5674 'âbar (1), to *cross* over; *to transition*
5927 'âlâh (1), to *ascend, be high, mount*
6293 pâga' (1), to *impinge*
6485 pâqad (2), to *visit, care for, count*
6486 pᵉquddâh (1), *visitation; punishment*
6845 tsâphan (3), to *hide; to hoard or reserve; to deny; to protect; to lurk*
7737 shâvâh (3), to *level,* i.e. *equalize*
7760 sûwm (38), to *put, place*
7896 shîyth (8), to *place, put*
7901 shâkab (17), to *lie down*
7971 shâlach (6), to *send away*
8371 shâthath (1), to *place,* i.e. *array; to lie*
8610 tâphas (1), to *manipulate,* i.e. *seize*
347 anaklinō (1), to *lean back, recline*
606 apŏkĕimai (3), to *be reserved; to await*
659 apŏtithēmi (1), to *put away; get rid of*
906 ballō (3), to *throw*
1096 ginŏmai (1), to *be, become*
1462 ĕgklēma (2), *accusation*
1911 ĕpiballō (7), to *throw upon*
1945 ĕpikĕimai (2), to *rest upon; press upon*
2007 ĕpitithēmi (13), to *impose*
2071 ĕsŏmai (1), *will be*
2698 katatithēmi (1), to *place down*
2749 kĕimai (6), to *lie outstretched*
3049 lŏgizŏmai (1), to *credit; to think, regard*
4369 prŏstithēmi (1), to *lay beside, annex*
5087 tithēmi (29), to *place, put*
5294 hupŏtithēmi (1), to *hazard; to suggest*
5342 phĕrō (1), to *bear*

LAIDST
7760 sûwm (1), to *put*

LAIN
3045+4904 yâda' (1), to *know*
5414+7903 nâthan (1), to *give*
7901 shâkab (2), to *lie down*
2749 kĕimai (1), to *lie outstretched*

LAISH
3919 Layish (7), *lion*

LAKE
3041 limnē (10), *pond; lake*

LAKUM
3946 Laqqûwm (1), (poss.) *fortification*

LAMA
2982 lama (2), *why?*

LAMB
2924 ṭâleh (2), *lamb*
3532 kebes (44), *young ram*
3535 kibsâh (5), *ewe sheep*
3733 kar (1), *ram sheep; battering ram*
3775 keseb (3), *young ram sheep*
3776 kisbâh (1), *young ewe sheep*
6629 tsŏ'n (1), *flock of sheep or goats*
7716 seh (17), *sheep or goat*
286 amnŏs (4), *lamb*
721 arniŏn (27), *lamb, sheep*

LAMB'S
721 arniŏn (2), *lamb, sheep*

LAMBS
563 'immar (Ch.) (3), *lamb*
1121+6629 bên (2), *son, descendant; people*
2922 ṭᵉlâ' (1), *lamb*
3532 kebes (60), *young ram*
3535 kibsâh (3), *ewe sheep*
3733 kar (9), *ram sheep; battering ram*
3775 keseb (1), *young ram sheep*
704 arēn (1), *male lamb*
721 arniŏn (1), *lamb, sheep*

LAME
5223 nâkeh (2), *maimed; dejected*
6452 pâçach (1), to *hop, skip over; to hesitate*
6455 piççêach (14), *lame*
5560 chōlŏs (10), *limping, crippled*

LAMECH
3929 Lemek (11), *Lemek*
2984 Lamĕch (1), *Lemek*

LAMENT
56 'âbal (2), to *bewail*
421 'âlâh (1), to *bewail, mourn*
578 'ânâh (1), to *groan, lament*
5091 nâhâh (1), to *bewail; to assemble*
5594 çâphad (9), to *tear the hair, wail*
6969 qûwn (4), to *chant or wail at a funeral*
8567 tânâh (1), to *ascribe praise,* i.e. *celebrate*
2354 thrēnĕō (1), to *bewail, lament*
2875 kŏptō (1), to *beat the breast*

LAMENTABLE
6088 'ătsab (Ch.) (1), to *afflict; be afflicted*

LAMENTATION
592 'ănîyâh (1), *groaning*
1058 bâkâh (1), to *weep, moan*
4553 miçpêd (3), *lamentation, howling*
5092 nᵉhîy (3), *elegy*
7015 qîynâh (14), *dirge*
2355 thrēnŏs (1), *wailing, funeral song*
2870 kŏpĕtŏs (1), *mourning*

LAMENTATIONS
7015 qîynâh (3), *dirge*

LAMENTED
56 'âbal (1), to *bewail*
5091 nâhâh (1), to *bewail; to assemble*
5594 çâphad (4), to *tear the hair, wail*
6969 qûwn (3), to *chant or wail at a funeral*
2354 thrēnĕō (1), to *bewail, lament*
2875 kŏptō (1), to *beat the breast*

LAMP
3940 lappîyd (3), *flaming torch, lamp or flame*
5216 nîyr (9), *lamp; lamplight*
2985 lampas (1), *lamp, lantern, torch*

LAMPS
3940 lappîyd (5), *flaming torch, lamp or flame*
5216 nîyr (26), *lamp; lamplight*
2985 lampas (6), *lamp, lantern, torch*

LANCE
3591 kîydôwn (1), *dart, javelin*

LANCETS
7420 rômach (1), *iron pointed spear*

LAND
127 'ădâmâh (123), *soil; land*
249 'ezrâch (2), *native born*
776 'erets (1505), *earth, land, soil; country*
3004 yabbâshâh (1), *dry ground*
7704 sâdeh (7), *field*
68 agrŏs (1), *farmland, countryside*
1093 gē (42), *soil, region, whole earth*
3584 xêrŏs (1), *scorched; arid; withered*
5561 chōra (3), *space of territory*
5564 chōriŏn (2), *spot or plot of ground*

LANDED
2609 katagō (1), to *lead down; to moor a vessel*
2718 katĕrchŏmai (1), to *go/come down*

LANDING
2609 katagō (1), to *lead down; to moor a vessel*

LANDMARK
1366 gᵉbûwl (4), *boundary, border*

LANDMARKS
1367 gᵉbûwlâh (1), *boundary marker*

LANDS
127 'ădâmâh (3), *soil; land*
776 'erets (34), *earth, land, soil; country, nation*
7704 sâdeh (4), *field*
68 agrŏs (3), *farmland, countryside*
5564 chōriŏn (1), *spot or plot of ground*

LANES
4505 rhumē (1), *alley or crowded avenue*

LANGUAGE
1697 dâbâr (1), *word; matter; thing*
3937 lâ'az (1), to *speak in a foreign tongue*
3956 lâshôwn (9), *tongue; tongue-shaped*
3961 lishshân (Ch.) (1), *nation*
8193 sâphâh (7), *lip, language, speech*
1258 dialĕktŏs (1), *known language*

LANGUAGES
3956 lâshôwn (1), *tongue; tongue-shaped*
3961 lishshân (Ch.) (6), *nation*

LANGUISH
535 'âmal (5), to *be weak; to be sick*

LANGUISHED
535 'âmal (1), to *be weak; to be sick*

LANGUISHETH
535 'âmal (8), to *be weak; to be sick*

LANGUISHING
1741 dᵉvay (1), *sickness*

LANTERNS
5322 phanŏs (1), *light; lantern,* i.e. *torch*

LAODICEA
2993 Laŏdikĕia (5), *Laodicea*

LAODICEANS
2994 Laŏdikĕus (2), *inhabitant of Laodicea*

LAP
899 beged (1), *clothing; treachery or pillage*
2436 chêyq (1), *bosom, heart*
2684 chôtsen (1), *bosom*

LAPIDOTH
3941 Lappîydôwth (1), *flaming torch, lamp*

LAPPED
3952 lâqaq (2), to *lick or lap*

LAPPETH
3952 lâqaq (2), to *lick or lap*

English

LAPWING
1744 dûwkîyphath (2), hoopoe; (poss.) grouse

LARGE
4800 merchâb (5), open space; liberty
7304 râvach (1), to revive; to have ample room
7337 râchab (2), to broaden
7342 râchâb (5), roomy, spacious
2425 hikanŏs (1), ample; fit
3173 mĕgas (2), great, many
4080 pēlikŏs (1), how much, how great
5118 tŏsŏutŏs (1), such great

LARGENESS
7341 rôchab (1), width

LASCIVIOUSNESS
766 asĕlgĕia (6), licentiousness

LASEA
2996 Lasaia (1), Lasæa

LASHA
3962 Lesha' (1), boiling spring

LASHARON
8289 Shârôwn (1), plain

LAST
314 'achărôwn (20), late or last; behind; western
318 'ochŏreyn (Ch.) (1), at last, finally
319 'achărîyth (10), future; posterity
6119 'âqêb (1), track, footprint; rear position
2078 ĕschatŏs (48), farthest, final
4218 pŏtĕ (1), at some time, ever
5305 hustĕrŏn (4), more lately, i.e. eventually

LASTED
1961 hâyâh (1), to exist, i.e. be or become

LASTING
5769 'ôwlâm (1), eternity; ancient; always

LATCHET
8288 sᵉrôwk (1), sandal thong
2438 himas (3), strap; lash

LATE
309 'âchar (1), to delay; to procrastinate
865 'ethmôwl (1), formerly; yesterday
3568 nun (1), now; the present or immediate

LATELY
4373 prŏsphatōs (1), recently

LATIN
4513 Rhōmaïkŏs (2), Latin

LATTER
314 'achărôwn (8), late or last; behind; western
319 'achărîyth (20), future; posterity
320 'achărîyth (Ch.) (1), later, end
3954 leqesh (2), after crop, second crop
4456 malqôwsh (8), spring rain
2078 ĕschatŏs (1), farthest, final
3797 ŏpsimŏs (1), later, i.e. vernal showering
5305 hustĕrŏn (1), more lately, i.e. eventually

LATTICE
822 'eshnâb (1), latticed window
2762 cherek (1), window lattice
7639 sᵉbâkâh (1), net-work balustrade

LAUD
1867 ĕpainĕō (1), to applaud, commend

LAUGH
3932 lâ'ag (4), to deride; to speak unintelligibly
6711 tsâchaq (3), to laugh; to scorn
6712 tsᵉchôq (1), laughter; scorn
7832 sâchaq (8), to laugh; to scorn; to play
1070 gĕlaō (2), to laugh

LAUGHED
3932 lâ'ag (3), to deride; to speak unintelligibly
6711 tsâchaq (3), to laugh; to scorn
6712 tsᵉchôq (1), laughter; scorn
7832 sâchaq (3), to laugh; to scorn; to play
2606 katagĕlaō (3), to laugh down, i.e. deride

LAUGHETH
7832 sâchaq (1), to laugh; to scorn; to play

LAUGHING
7814 sᵉchôwq (1), laughter; scorn

LAUGHTER
7814 sᵉchôwq (6), laughter; scorn
1071 gĕlōs (1), laughter

LAUNCH
1877 ĕpanagō (1), to put out to sea; to return

LAUNCHED
321 anagō (4), to bring out; to sail away

LAVER
3595 kîyôwr (15), caldron; washbowl

LAVERS
3595 kîyôwr (5), caldron; washbowl

LAVISH
2107 zûwl (1), to treat lightly

LAW
1881 dâth (6), royal edict or statute
1882 dâth (Ch.) (9), Law; royal edict or statute
2524 châm (4), father-in-law
2545 chămôwth (11), mother-in-law
2706 chôq (4), appointment; allotment
2710 châqaq (1), to engrave; to enact laws; to prescribe
2859 châthan (32), to become related
2860 châthân (5), relative by marriage
2994 yᵉbêmeth (2), sister-in-law
3618 kallâh (17), bride; son's wife
4687 mitsvâh (1), command
4941 mishpâṭ (2), verdict; formal decree; justice
8451 tôwrâh (206), precept or statute
60 agŏraiŏs (1), people of the market place
458 anŏmia (1), violation of law, wickedness
459 anŏmŏs (3), without Jewish law
460 anŏmōs (1), lawlessly
1772 ĕnnŏmŏs (1), legal, or subject to law
2917 krima (1), decision
2919 krinō (2), to decide; to try, condemn, punish
3544 nŏmikŏs (1), expert in the (Mosaic) law
3547 nŏmŏdidaskalŏs (3), a Rabbi
3548 nŏmŏthĕsia (1), legislation, law
3549 nŏmŏthĕtĕō (1), to be given law
3551 nŏmŏs (192), law
3565 numphē (3), young married woman
3891 paranŏmĕō (1), to transgress, violate law
3994 pĕnthĕra (3), wife's mother, mother-in-law
3995 pĕnthĕrŏs (1), wife's father
4160+458 pŏiĕō (1), to make or do

LAWFUL
4941 mishpâṭ (7), verdict; formal decree; justice
6662 tsaddîyq (1), just
7990 shallîyṭ (Ch.) (1), premier, sovereign
1772 ĕnnŏmŏs (1), legal, or subject to law
1832 ĕxĕsti (12), it is right, it is proper
1833 ĕxĕtazō (17), to ascertain or interrogate

LAWFULLY
3545 nŏmimōs (2), agreeably to the rules

LAWGIVER
2710 châqaq (6), to engrave; to enact laws

LAW
3550 nŏmŏthĕtēs (1), legislator, lawgiver

LAWLESS
459 anŏmŏs (1), without Jewish law

LAWS
1881 dâth (3), royal edict or statute
1882 dâth (Ch.) (2), Law; royal edict or statute
8451 tôwrâh (12), precept or codified statute
8541 timmâhôwn (1), consternation, panic
3551 nŏmŏs (2), law

LAWYER
3544 nŏmikŏs (3), expert in the (Mosaic) law

LAWYERS
3544 nŏmikŏs (5), expert in the (Mosaic) law

LAY
3241 Yânîym (10), asleep
3331 yâtsa' (1), to strew as a surface
3885 lûwn (1), to be obstinate
4422 mâlaṭ (1), to be delivered; be smooth
5117 nûwach (1), to rest; to settle down
5186 nâṭâh (1), to stretch or spread out
5307 nâphal (4), to fall
5414 nâthan (20), to give
5493 çûwr (1), to turn off
5564 çâmak (12), to lean upon; take hold of
6651 tsâbar (1), to aggregate, gather
6845 tsâphan (2), to hide; to hoard or reserve
7126 qârab (1), to approach, bring near
7257 râbats (3), to recline, repose, brood
7258 rebets (1), place of repose
7760 sûwm (26), to put, place
7871 shîybâh (1), residence
7896 shîyth (5), to place, put
7901 shâkab (45), to lie down
7902 shᵉkâbâh (2), lying down
7931 shâkan (1), to reside
7971 shâlach (8), to send away
659 apŏtithēmi (2), to put away; get rid of
1458 ĕgkalĕō (1), to charge, criminate
1474 ĕdaphizō (1), to dash to the ground
1911 ĕpiballō (2), to throw upon
1945 ĕpikĕimai (2), to rest upon; press upon
1949 ĕpilambanŏmai (2), to seize
2007 ĕpitithēmi (7), to impose
2343 thēsaurizō (1), to amass or reserve, store

2476 histēmi (1), *to stand, establish*
2621 katakĕimai (5), *to lie down; to recline*
2749 kĕimai (1), *to lie outstretched*
2827 klinō (2), *to slant or slope*
5087 tithēmi (13), *to place*

LAYEDST
5087 tithēmi (1), *to place*

LAYEST
7760 sûwm (1), *to put*

LAYETH
5381 nâsag (1), *to reach*
5414 nâthan (1), *to give*
6845 tsâphan (2), *to hide; to hoard or reserve*
7760 sûwm (5), *to place*
7896 shîyth (1), *to place*
7971 shâlach (1), *to send away*
2007 ĕpitithēmi (1), *to impose*

LAYING
2934 ţâman (1), *to hide*
597 apŏthēsaurizō (1), *to store treasure away*
659 apŏtithēmi (1), *to put away; get rid of*
863 aphiēmi (1), *to leave; to pardon, forgive*
1748 ĕnĕdrĕuō (1), *to lurk*
1917 ĕpibŏulē (1), *plot, plan*
1936 ĕpithĕsis (3), *imposition*
2598 kataballō (1), *to throw down*
4160 pŏiĕō (1), *to make or do*

LAZARUS
2976 Lazarŏs (15), *God (is) helper*

LEAD
833 'âshar (1), *to go forward; guide*
1869 dârak (2), *to tread, trample; to walk, lead*
1980 hâlak (1), *to walk; live a certain way*
2986 yâbal (1), *to bring*
3212 yâlak (2), *to walk; to live; to carry*
3318 yâtsâ' (1), *to go, bring out*
5090 nâhag (9), *to drive forth; to lead, carry*
5095 nâhal (2), *to flow; to conduct; to protect*
5148 nâchâh (16), *to guide*
5777 'ôwphereth (9), *mineral lead*
7218 rô'sh (1), *head*
71 agō (1), *to lead; to bring, drive; to weigh*
162 aichmalōtĕuō (1), *to capture*
520 apagō (2), *to take away*
1236 diagō (1), *to pass time, conduct one's life*
1533 ĕisphĕrō (2), *to carry inward*
1806 ĕxagō (1), *to lead forth, escort*

3594 hŏdēgĕō (3), *to show the way, i.e. lead*
4013 pĕriagō (1), *to take around as a companion*
5497 chĕiragōgŏs (1), *conductor of the blind*

LEADER
5057 nâgîyd (3), *commander, official*

LEADERS
833 'âshar (1), *to go forward; guide*
5057 nâgîyd (1), *commander, official*
3595 hŏdēgŏs (1), *conductor, guide*

LEADEST
5090 nâhag (1), *to drive forth; to lead away*

LEADETH
1869 dârak (1), *to tread, trample; to walk, lead*
3212 yâlak (3), *to walk; to live; to carry*
5090 nâhag (1), *to drive forth; to lead away*
5095 nâhal (1), *to flow; to conduct; to protect*
71 agō (1), *to lead; to bring, drive; to weigh*
399 anaphĕrō (1), *to take up; to lead up*
520 apagō (2), *to take away*
1806 ĕxagō (1), *to lead forth, escort*
4863 sunagō (1), *to gather together*
5342 phĕrō (1), *to bear or carry*

LEAF
5929 'âleh (11), *leaf; foliage*

LEAGUE
1285 bᵉrîyth (17), *compact, agreement*
2266 châbar (1), *to fascinate by spells*
3772 kârath (1), *to cut (off, down or asunder)*

LEAH
3812 Lê'âh (29), *weary*

LEAH'S
3812 Lê'âh (5), *weary*

LEAN
1800 dal (1), *weak, thin; humble, needy*
5564 çâmak (2), *to lean upon; take hold of*
7329 râzâh (1), *to make, become thin*
7330 râzeh (2), *thin, lean*
7534 raq (1), *emaciated, lank*
8172 shâ'an (4), *to support, rely on*

LEANED
5564 çâmak (1), *to lean upon; take hold of*
8172 shâ'an (4), *to support, rely on*
377 anapiptō (1), *lie down, lean back*

LEANETH
2388 châzaq (1), *to fasten upon; to seize*
8127 shên (1), *tooth; ivory; cliff*

LEANFLESHED
1851+1320 daq (2), *crushed; small or thin*
7534 raq (1), *emaciated, lank*

LEANING
7514 râphaq (1), *to recline*
345 anakĕimai (1), *recline at a meal*

LEANNESS
3585 kachash (1), *emaciation; hypocrisy*
7332 râzôwn (2), *thinness*
7334 râzîy (1), *thinness*

LEANNOTH
6030 'ânâh (1), *to sing, shout*

LEAP
1801 dâlag (2), *to spring up, ascend*
2178 zan (Ch.) (1), *sort, kind*
4422 mâlaţ (1), *to escape as if by slipperiness*
5425 nâthar (1), *to jump; to be agitated*
5927 'âlâh (1), *to ascend, be high, mount*
7520 râtsad (1), *to look askant; to be jealous*
7540 râqad (1), *to spring about wildly or for joy*
4640 skirtaō (1), *to jump*

LEAPED
1801 dâlag (2), *to spring up, ascend*
5927 'âlâh (1), *to ascend, be high, mount*
6452 pâçach (1), *to hop, skip over; to limp*
242 hallŏmai (1), *to jump up; to gush up*
2177 ĕphallŏmai (1), *spring upon, leap upon*
4640 skirtaō (2), *to jump*

LEAPING
1801 dâlag (1), *to spring up, ascend*
6339 pâzaz (1), *to solidify by refining; to spring*
242 hallŏmai (1), *to jump up; to gush up*
1814 ĕxallŏmai (1), *to spring forth*

LEARN
502 'âlaph (1), *to learn; to teach*
3925 lâmad (17), *to teach, train*
3129 manthanō (13), *to learn*
3811 paidĕuō (1), *to educate or discipline*

LEARNED
3045+5612 yâda' (3), *to know*
3925 lâmad (5), *to teach, train*
3928 limmûwd (2), *instructed one*

5172 nâchash (1), *to prognosticate*
3129 manthanō (10), *to learn*
3811 paidĕuō (1), *to educate or discipline*

LEARNING
3948 leqach (4), *instruction*
5612 çêpher (2), *writing*
1121 gramma (1), *writing; education*
1319 didaskalia (1), *instruction*
3129 manthanō (1), *to learn*

LEASING
3577 kâzâb (2), *falsehood; idol*

LEAST
176 'ôw (1), *or, whether; desire*
389 'ak (1), *surely; only, however*
4591 mâ'aţ (1), *to be, make small or few*
6810 tsâ'îyr (4), *little in number; few in age*
6994 qâţŏn (1), *to be, make diminutive*
6996 qâţân (10), *small, least, youngest*
7535 raq (1), *merely; although*
1646 ĕlachistŏs (9), *least*
1647 ĕlachistŏtĕrŏs (1), *far less*
1848 ĕxŏuthĕnĕō (1), *to treat with contempt*
2534 kaigĕ (1), *and at least (or even, indeed)*
2579 kan (1), *and if*
3398 mikrŏs (6), *small, little*

LEATHER
5785 'ôwr (1), *skin, leather*

LEATHERN
1193 dĕrmatinŏs (1), *made of leather hide*

LEAVE
2308 châdal (3), *to desist, stop; be fat*
3241 Yânîym (14), *asleep*
3322 yâtsag (1), *to place*
3498 yâthar (7), *to remain or be left*
3499 yether (1), *remainder; small rope*
5157 nâchal (1), *to inherit*
5203 nâţash (5), *to disperse; to thrust off*
5414 nâthan (2), *to give*
5800 'âzab (30), *to loosen; relinquish*
6168 'ârâh (1), *to be, make bare; to empty*
7503 râphâh (1), *to slacken*
7592 shâ'al (1), *to ask*
7604 shâ'ar (13), *to leave, remain*
7662 shᵉbaq (Ch.) (3), *to allow to remain*
8338 shâwshâw (1), *(poss.) to annihilate*

English

LEAVED
447 aniēmi (1), to *desert, desist* from
657 apŏtassŏmai (2), to *say adieu;* to *renounce*
782 aspazŏmai (1), to *give salutation*
863 aphiēmi (11), to *leave;* to *pardon, forgive*
1459 ĕgkataleipō (1), to *desert, abandon*
1544 ĕkballō (1), to *throw out*
2010 ĕpitrĕpō (2), *allow, permit*
2641 kataleipō (6), to *abandon*

LEAVED
1817 deleth (1), *door; gate*

LEAVEN
2557 châmêts (5), *ferment, yeasted*
4682 matstsâh (1), *unfermented cake*
7603 sᵉʼôr (4), yeast-cake for *fermentation*
2219 zumē (13), *ferment*

LEAVENED
2557 châmêts (11), *ferment, yeasted*
7603 sᵉʼôr (1), yeast-cake for *fermentation*
2220 zumŏŏ (2), to *cause to ferment*

LEAVENETH
2220 zumŏŏ (2), to *cause to ferment*

LEAVES
1817 deleth (3), *door; gate*
2529 chem'âh (1), *curds, milk* or *cheese*
2964 ṭereph (1), *fresh torn prey*
6074 'ŏphîy (Ch.) (3), *foliage*
6763 tsêlâ' (1), *side*
7050 qela' (1), *slinging weapon; door screen*
5444 phullŏn (6), *leaf*

LEAVETH
5800 'âzab (2), to *loosen; relinquish; permit*
863 aphiēmi (2), to *leave; to pardon, forgive*

LEAVING
863 aphiēmi (3), to *leave; to pardon, forgive*
2641 kataleipō (1), to *abandon*
5277 hupŏlimpanō (1), to *leave behind*

LEBANA
3848 lᵉbash (Ch.) (1), to *clothe*

LEBANAH
3848 lᵉbash (Ch.) (1), to *clothe*

LEBANON
3844 Lᵉbânôwn (71), *white snow mountain*

LEBAOTH
3822 Lᵉbâ'ôwth (1), *lionesses*

LEBBAEUS
3002 Lĕbbaiŏs (1), *Lebbæus*

LEBONAH
3829 Lᵉbôwnâh (1), *frankincense*

LECAH
3922 Lêkâh (1), *journey*

LED
833 âshar (1), to *go forward; guide*
935 bôw' (2), to *go*
1869 dârak (2), to *tread, trample; to walk, lead*
2986 yâbal (1), to *bring*
3212 yâlak (13), to *walk; to live; to carry*
5090 nâhag (4), to *drive forth; to lead away*
5148 nâchâh (6), to *guide*
5437 câbab (3), to *surround*
71 agō (11), to *lead; to bring, drive; to weigh*
162 aichmalōtĕuō (1), to *capture*
163 aichmalōtizō (1), to *make captive*
321 anagō (2), to *lead up; to bring out*
520 apagō (8), to *take away*
1521 ĕisagō (1), to *lead into*
1806 ĕxagō (3), to *lead forth, escort*
4879 sunapagō (1), to *take off together*
5496 chĕiragōgĕō (2), to *guide* a blind person

LEDDEST
3318 yâtsâ' (2), to *go, bring out*
5148 nâchâh (2), to *guide*
1806 ĕxagō (1), to *lead forth, escort*

LEDGES
3027 yâd (2), *hand; power*
7948 shâlâb (3), *interval*

LEEKS
2682 châtsîyr (1), *grass; leek plant*

LEES
8105 shemer (4), *settlings of wine, dregs*

LEFT
2308 châdal (7), to *desist, stop; be fat*
2790 chârash (1), to *be silent; to be deaf*
3240 yânach (8), to *allow to stay*
3241 Yânîym (3), *asleep*
3498 yâthar (47), to *remain or be left*
3499 yether (3), *remainder; small rope*
3615 kâlâh (3), to *cease, be finished, perish*
3885 lûwn (1), to *be obstinate with*
4672 mâtsâ' (2), to *find or acquire; to occur*
5203 nâṭash (7), to *disperse; to thrust off*
5414 nâthan (1), to *give*

5493 çûwr (1), to *turn off*
5800 'âzab (43), to *loosen; relinquish*
5975 'âmad (2), to *stand*
6275 'âthaq (1), to *remove; to grow old*
7604 shâ'ar (65), to *leave, remain*
7611 shᵉ'êrîyth (1), *remainder* or *residual*
7662 shᵉbaq (Ch.) (1), to *allow to remain*
7673 shâbath (1), to *repose; to desist*
7971 shâlach (1), to *send away*
8040 sᵉmô'wl (55), *north; left hand*
8041 sâma'l (4), to *use the left hand or go left*
8042 sᵉmâ'lîy (9), on the *left side; northern*
8300 sârîyd (3), *survivor; remainder*
620 apŏlĕipō (3), to *leave behind; to forsake*
710 aristĕrŏs (3), *left hand*
863 aphiēmi (36), to *leave; to pardon, forgive*
1439 ĕaō (1), to *let be, i.e. permit or leave alone*
1459 ĕgkataleipō (1), to *desert, abandon*
2176 ĕuōnumŏs (10), *left; at the left hand; south*
2641 kataleipō (15), to *abandon*
3973 pauō (2), to *stop, i.e. restrain, quit*
4051 pĕrissĕuma (1), *superabundance*
4052 pĕrissĕuō (1), to *superabound*
5275 hupŏlĕipō (1), to *remain, survive*

LEFTEST
5800 'âzab (1), to *loosen; relinquish; permit*

LEFTHANDED
334+3027+3225 'iṭṭêr (2), *impeded* (as to the right hand), *left-handed*

LEG
7640 shôbel (1), lady's *garment train*

LEGION
3003 lĕgĕōn (3), *legion*

LEGIONS
3003 lĕgĕōn (1), *legion*

LEGS
3767 kârâ' (9), *leg*
6807 tsᵉ'âdâh (1), *march; ankle-chain*
7272 regel (1), *foot; step*
7785 shôwq (4), *lower leg*
8243 shâq (Ch.) (1), *shank, or whole leg*
4628 skĕlŏs (3), *leg*

LEHABIM
3853 Lᵉhâbîym (2), *flames*

LEHI
3896 Lechîy (3), *jaw-bone*

LEISURE
2119 ĕukairĕō (1), to *have leisure*

LEMUEL
3927 Lᵉmûw'êl (2), (belonging) *to God*

LEND
3867 lâvâh (4), to *unite; to remain; to lend*
5383 nâshâh (2), to *lend or borrow*
5391 nâshak (3), to *strike; to oppress*
5414 nâthan (1), to *give*
5670 'âbaṭ (2), to *pawn; to lend; to entangle*
1155 danĕizō (3), to *loan on interest; to borrow*
5531 chraō (1), to *loan, lend*

LENDER
3867 lâvâh (2), to *unite; to borrow; to lend*

LENDETH
3867 lâvâh (3), to *unite; to borrow; to lend*
5383 nâshâh (1), to *lend or borrow*

LENGTH
319 'achărîyth (1), *future; posterity*
753 'ôrek (70), *length*
3372 mĕkŏs (3), *length*
4218 pŏtĕ (1), at *some time, ever*

LENGTHEN
748 'ârak (2), to *be, make long*

LENGTHENED
748 'ârak (1), to *be, make long*

LENGTHENING
754 'arkâ' (Ch.) (1), *length*

LENT
5383 nâshâh (2), to *lend or borrow*
5391 nâshak (1), to *strike; to oppress*
7592 shâ'al (4), to *ask*

LENTILES
5742 'âdâsh (4), *lentil bean*

LEOPARD
5245 nᵉmar (Ch.) (1), *leopard*
5246 nâmêr (4), *leopard*
3917 pardalis (1), *leopard, panther*

LEOPARDS
5246 nâmêr (2), *leopard*

LEPER
6879 tsâra' (13), to *be stricken with leprosy*
3015 lĕprŏs (4), *leper*

LEPERS
6879 tsâra' (1), to *be stricken with leprosy*
3015 lĕprŏs (5), *leper*

LEPROSY
6883 tsâra'ath (35), *leprosy*
3014 lĕpra (1), *leprosy*

LEPROUS
6879 tsâra' (6), to *be stricken with leprosy*

LESHEM
3959 Leshem (2), *jacinth* stone

LESS
657 'epheç (1), *end; no further*
4295 maṭṭâh (1), *below or beneath*
4591 mâ'aṭ (4), *to be, make small or few*
6996 qâṭân (3), *small, least, youngest*
253 alupŏtĕrŏs (1), *more without grief*
820 atimŏs (1), *without honor*
1640 ĕlassŏn (1), *smaller*
1647 ĕlachistŏtĕrŏs (1), *far less*
2276 hēttŏn (1), *worse; less*
3398 mikrŏs (2), *small, little*

LESSER
6996 qâṭân (2), *small, least, youngest*
7716 seh (1), *sheep or goat*

LEST
1077 bal (1), *nothing; not at all; lest*
1115 biltîy (3), *not, except, without, unless*
3808 lô' (12), *no, not*
6435 pên (120), *lest, not*
3361 mē (13), *not; lest*
3379 mĕpŏtĕ (20), *not ever; if, or lest ever*
3381 mĕpŏs (12), *lest somehow*

LET
3212 yâlak (1), *to walk; to live; to carry*
3240 yânach (3), *to allow to stay*
3381 yârad (7), *to descend*
5117 nûwach (1), *to rest; to settle down*
5186 nâṭâh (1), *to stretch or spread out*
5414 nâthan (3), *to give*
6544 pâra' (1), *to loosen*
7503 râphâh (2), *to slacken*
7725 shûwb (1), *to turn back; to return*
7971 shâlach (2), *to send away*
630 apŏluō (10), *to relieve, release*
863 aphiēmi (16), *to leave; to pardon, forgive*
1439 ĕaō (4), *to let be, i.e. permit or leave alone*
1554 ĕkdidōmi (4), *to lease, rent*
1832 ĕxĕsti (1), *it is right, it is proper*
1929 ĕpididōmi (1), *to give over*
2010 ĕpitrĕpō (1), *allow, permit*
2524 kathiĕmi (1), *to lower, let down*
2722 katĕchō (1), *to hold down fast*
2967 kōluō (1), *to stop*

LESHEM — column 2
5465 chalaō (5), *to lower as into a void*

LETTER
104 'iggĕrâ' (Ch.) (3), *epistle, letter*
107 'iggereth (4), *epistle, letter*
5406 nishtĕvân (2), *written epistle*
5407 nishtĕvân (Ch.) (3), *written epistle*
5612 çêpher (13), *writing*
6600 pithgâm (Ch.) (1), *decree; report*
1121 gramma (6), *writing; education*
1989 ĕpistĕllō (1), *to communicate by letter*
1992 ĕpistŏlē (3), *written message*

LETTERS
107 'iggereth (6), *epistle, letter*
5612 çêpher (16), *writing*
1121 gramma (3), *writing; education*
1992 ĕpistŏlē (6), *written message*

LETTEST
8257 shâqa' (1), *to be overflowed; to cease*
630 apŏluō (1), *to relieve, release*

LETTETH
6362 pâṭar (1), *to burst through; to emit*
2722 katĕchō (1), *to hold down fast*

LETUSHIM
3912 Lĕṭûwshîm (1), *oppressed ones*

LEUMMIM
3817 Lĕ'ummîym (1), *communities*

LEVI
3878 Lêvîy (64), *attached*
3017 Lĕuï (5), *attached*
3018 Lĕuïs (3), *attached*

LEVIATHAN
3882 livyâthân (5), *serpent (crocodile)*

LEVITE
3881 Lêvîyîy (26), *Levite*
3019 Lĕuïtēs (2), *descendants of Levi*

LEVITES
3878 Lêvîy (1), *attached*
3879 Lêvîy (Ch.) (4), *attached*
3881 Lêvîyîy (259), *Levite*
3019 Lĕuïtēs (1), *descendants of Levi*

LEVITICAL
3020 Lĕuïtikŏs (1), *relating to the Levites*

LEVY
4522 maç (4), *forced labor*
5927 'âlâh (1), *to ascend, be high, mount*
7311 rûwm (1), *to be high; to rise or raise*

LEWD
2154 zimmâh (2), *bad plan*

LEWD — column 3
4190 pŏnērŏs (1), *malice, wicked, bad; crime*

LEWDLY
2154 zimmâh (1), *bad plan*

LEWDNESS
2154 zimmâh (14), *bad plan*
4209 mĕzimmâh (1), *plan; sagacity*
5040 nablûwth (1), *female genitals*
4467 rhaᵢdiŏurgēma (1), *crime, legal fraction*

LIAR
376+3576 'îysh (1), *man; male; someone*
391 'akzâb (1), *deceit; treachery*
3576 kâzab (2), *to lie, deceive*
8267 sheqer (1), *untruth; sham*
5583 psĕustēs (8), *falsifier*

LIARS
907 bad (2), *brag or lie; liar, boaster*
3576 kâzab (1), *to lie, deceive*
3584 kâchash (1), *to lie, disown; to disappoint*
5571 psĕudēs (2), *erroneous, deceitful*
5583 psĕustēs (2), *falsifier*

LIBERAL
1293 bĕrâkâh (1), *benediction, blessing*
5081 nâdîyb (3), *generous*
572 haplŏtēs (1), *sincerity; generosity*

LIBERALITY
572 haplŏtēs (1), *sincerity; generosity*
5485 charis (1), *graciousness*

LIBERALLY
6059 'ânaq (1), *to collar; to fit out*
574 haplŏs (1), *bountifully, generously*

LIBERTINES
3032 Libĕrtinŏs (1), *Freedman*

LIBERTY
1865 dĕrôwr (7), *freedom; clear, pure*
2670 chophshîy (1), *exempt from bondage*
7342 râchâb (1), *roomy, spacious*
425 anĕsis (1), *relaxation; relief*
630 apŏluō (2), *to relieve, release; to pardon*
859 aphĕsis (1), *pardon, freedom*
1657 ĕlĕuthĕria (11), *freedom*
1658 ĕlĕuthĕrŏs (1), *unrestrained*
1849 ĕxŏusia (1), *authority, power, right*
2010 ĕpitrĕpō (1), *to allow*

LIBNAH
3841 Libnâh (18), *storax-tree*

LIBNI
3845 Libnîy (5), *white*

LIBNITES
3864 Lûwbîy (2), *dry region*

LIBYA
6316 Pûwṭ (2), *Put, person*
3033 Libuē (1), *south region*

LIBYANS
3864 Lûwbîy (1), *dry region*
6316 Pûwṭ (1), *Put, person*

LICE
3654 kên (6), *stinging bug*

LICENCE
2010 ĕpitrĕpō (1), *allow, permit*
5117 tŏpŏs (1), *place*

LICK
3897 lâchak (4), *to lick*
3952 lâqaq (1), *to lick*

LICKED
3897 lâchak (1), *to lick*
3952 lâqaq (2), *to lick*
621 apŏlĕichō (1), *to lick off clean*

LICKETH
3897 lâchak (1), *to lick*

LID
1817 deleth (1), *door; gate*

LIE
391 'akzâb (1), *deceit; treachery*
693 'ârab (2), *to ambush, lie in wait*
2583 chânâh (2), *to encamp*
3576 kâzab (12), *to lie, deceive*
3584 kâchash (1), *to lie, disown; to disappoint*
3885 lûwn (2), *to be obstinate*
4769 marbêts (1), *reclining or resting place*
5203 nâṭash (1), *to disperse; to abandon*
5307 nâphal (1), *to fall*
5414+7903 nâthan (3), *to give*
6658 tsâdâh (1), *to desolate*
7250 râba' (2), *to lay down; have sex*
7257 râbats (15), *to recline, repose, brood*
7258 rebets (1), *place of repose*
7693 shâgal (1), *to copulate*
7901 shâkab (59), *to lie down*
8266 shâqar (5), *to cheat, i.e. be untrue in words*
8267 sheqer (8), *untruth; sham*
893 apsĕudēs (1), *veracious, free of deceit*
2621 katakĕimai (1), *to lie down; to recline*

English

LIED
2749 *kĕimai* (1), to *lie* outstretched
3180 *mĕthŏdĕia* (1), *trickery, scheming*
3582 *xĕstēs* (1), *vessel*
5574 *pseŭdŏmai* (11), to *utter an untruth*
5579 *pseŭdŏs* (7), *falsehood*

LIED
3576 *kâzab* (2), to *lie, deceive*
3584 *kâchash* (1), to *lie, disown*; to *disappoint*
5574 *pseŭdŏmai* (1), to *utter an untruth*

LIEN
7693 *shâgal* (1), to *copulate* with
7901 *shâkab* (2), to *lie down*

LIES
907 *bad* (3), *brag* or *lie*; *liar, boaster*
1697+3576 *dâbâr* (1), *word; matter; thing*
1697+8267 *dâbâr* (1), *word; matter; thing*
3576 *kâzab* (22), to *lie, deceive*
3585 *kachash* (4), *emaciation; hypocrisy*
7723 *shâv'* (1), *ruin; guile; idolatry*
8267 *sheqer* (17), *untruth; sham*
8383 *t°'ûn* (1), *toil*
5573 *pseŭdŏlŏgŏs* (1), *promulgating erroneous doctrine*

LIEST
5307 *nâphal* (1), to *fall*
7901 *shâkab* (4), to *lie down*

LIETH
3318 *yâtsâ'* (3), to *go, bring out*
3584 *kâchash* (1), to *lie, disown*; to *disappoint*
4904 *mishkâb* (1), *bed; sleep; intercourse*
5564 *çâmak* (1), to *lean upon*; *take hold of*
6437 *pânâh* (1), to *turn, to face*
7257 *râbats* (2), to *recline, repose, brood*
7901 *shâkab* (20), to *lie down*
8172 *shâ'an* (1), to *support, rely on*
906 *ballō* (1), to *throw*
991 *blĕpō* (1), to *look at*
2192 *ĕchō* (1), to *have; hold; keep*
2749 *kĕimai* (2), to *lie* outstretched

LIEUTENANTS
323 *'ăchashdarpan* (4), *satrap*

LIFE
2416 *chay* (143), *alive; raw; fresh; life*
2417 *chay* (Ch.) (1), *alive; life*
2421 *châyâh* (10), to *live; to revive*

2425 *châyay* (1), to *live; to revive*
3117 *yôwm* (3), *day; time period*
3117+5921 *yôwm* (1), *day; time period*
5315 *nephesh* (90), *life; breath; soul; wind*
6106 *'etsem* (1), *bone; body; substance*
72 *agōgē* (1), *mode of living, way of life*
895 *apsuchŏs* (1), *lifeless, i.e. inanimate*
979 *biŏs* (5), *present state of existence*
981 *biōsis* (1), *mode of living*
982 *biōtikŏs* (3), *relating to the present existence*
2198 *zaō* (1), to *live*
2222 *zōē* (132), *life*
2227 *zōŏpŏiĕō* (2), to *(re-) vitalize, give life*
4151 *pnĕuma* (1), *spirit*
5590 *psuchē* (36), *soul, vitality; heart, mind*

LIFETIME
2416 *chay* (1), *alive; raw; fresh; life*
2198 *zaō* (1), to *live*
2222 *zōē* (1), *life*

LIFT
5127 *nûwç* (1), to *vanish away, flee*
5130 *nûwph* (3), to *quiver, vibrate, rock*
5375 *nâsâ'* (66), to *lift up*
5414 *nâthan* (1), to *give*
6030 *'ânâh* (1), to *respond, answer*
6670 *tsâhal* (1), to *be cheerful; to sound*
6965 *qûwm* (3), to *rise*
7311 *rûwm* (18), to *be high; to rise or raise*
352 *anakuptō* (1), to *straighten up*
461 *anŏrthŏō* (1), to *straighten up*
1458 *ĕgkalĕō* (1), to *charge, criminate*
1869 *ĕpairō* (4), to *raise up, look up*
5312 *hupsŏō* (1), to *elevate; to exalt*

LIFTED
935 *bôw'* (1), to *go or come*
1361 *gâbahh* (7), to *be lofty; to be haughty*
1431 *gâdal* (1), to *be great, make great*
1802 *dâlâh* (1), to *draw out water); to deliver*
5130 *nûwph* (1), to *quiver, vibrate, rock*
5191 *n°ṭal* (Ch.) (2), to *raise; to repent*
5264 *nâçaç* (1), to *gleam; to flutter a flag*
5375 *nâsâ'* (92), to *lift up*
5423 *nâthaq* (1), to *tear off*
5782 *'ûwr* (3), to *awake*
5927 *'âlâh* (1), to *ascend, be high, mount*

6075 *'âphal* (1), to *swell; be elated*
7213 *râ'am* (1), to *rise*
7311 *rûwm* (15), to *be high; to rise or raise*
7313 *rûwm* (Ch.) (2), *elation, arrogance*
7426 *râmam* (2), to *rise*
142 *airō* (4), to *lift, to take up*
352 *anakuptō* (2), to *straighten up*
450 *anistēmi* (1), to *stand up; to come back to life*
1453 *ĕgĕirō* (3), to *waken, i.e. rouse*
1869 *ĕpairō* (10), to *raise up, look up*
5188 *tuphō* (1), to *make a smoke*
5312 *hupsŏō* (5), to *elevate; to exalt*

LIFTER
7311 *rûwm* (1), to *be high; to rise or raise*

LIFTEST
5375 *nâsâ'* (1), to *lift up*
5414 *nâthan* (1), to *give*
7311 *rûwm* (2), to *be high; to rise or raise*

LIFTETH
4754 *mârâ'* (1), to *rebel; to lash with whip; flap*
5375 *nâsâ'* (2), to *lift up*
5749 *'ûwd* (1), to *duplicate or repeat*
5927 *'âlâh* (2), to *ascend, be high, mount*
7311 *rûwm* (4), to *be high; to rise or raise*

LIFTING
1348 *gê'ûwth* (1), *ascending; majesty*
1466 *gêvâh* (1), *exaltation; arrogance*
4607 *mô'al* (1), *raising of the hands*
4864 *mas'êth* (1), *raising; beacon; present*
5375 *nâsâ'* (2), to *lift up*
5782 *'ûwr* (1), to *awake*
7311 *rûwm* (2), to *be high; to rise or raise*
7427 *rômêmûth* (1), *exaltation*
1869 *ĕpairō* (1), to *raise up, look up*

LIGHT
215 *'ôwr* (1), to *be luminous*
216 *'ôwr* (126), *luminary; lightning; happiness*
217 *'ûwr* (1), *flame; East*
219 *'ôwrâh* (2), *luminousness, light*
3313 *yâpha'* (1), to *shine*
3974 *mâ'ôwr* (15), *luminary, light source*
4237 *mechĕzâh* (2), *window*
5051 *nôgahh* (1), *brilliancy*
5094 *n°hîyr* (Ch.) (3), *illumination*
5105 *n°hârâh* (1), *daylight*

5117 *nûwach* (1), to *rest; to settle down*
5216 *nîyr* (4), *lamp; lamplight*
5927 *'âlâh* (2), to *ascend, be high, mount*
6348 *pâchaz* (2), to *be unimportant*
7031 *qal* (1), *rapid, swift*
7034 *qâlâh* (1), to *be light*
7043 *qâlal* (7), to *be, make light*
7052 *q°lôqêl* (1), *insubstantial* food
7136 *qârâh* (1), to *bring about; to impose*
7837 *shachar* (1), *dawn*
272 *amĕlĕō* (1), to *be careless of, neglect*
681 *haptō* (1), to *set on fire*
1645 *ĕlaphrŏs* (2), *light, i.e. easy*
2014 *ĕpiphainō* (1), to *become visible*
2017 *ĕpiphauō* (1), to *illuminate, shine on*
2545 *kaiō* (1), to *set on fire*
2989 *lampō* (1), to *radiate brilliancy*
3088 *luchnŏs* (5), *lamp or other illuminator*
4098 *piptō* (1), to *fall*
5338 *phĕggŏs* (3), *brilliancy, radiance*
5457 *phōs* (65), *luminousness, light*
5458 *phōstēr* (1), *celestial luminary*
5460 *phōtĕinŏs* (4), *well-illuminated*
5461 *phōtizō* (4), to *shine or to brighten up*
5462 *phōtismŏs* (2), *light; illumination*

LIGHTED
3381 *yârad* (2), to *descend*
4672 *mâtsâ'* (1), to *find or acquire; to occur*
5307 *nâphal* (3), to *fall*
5927 *'âlâh* (2), to *ascend, be high, mount*
6293 *pâga'* (1), to *impinge*
6795 *tsânach* (2), to *descend, i.e. drive down*
681 *haptō* (2), to *set on fire*

LIGHTEN
215 *'ôwr* (2), to *be luminous*
5050 *nâgahh* (1), to *illuminate*
7043 *qâlal* (2), to *be, make light*
602 *apŏkalupsis* (1), *disclosure, revelation*
5461 *phōtizō* (1), to *shine or to brighten up*

LIGHTENED
215 *'ôwr* (1), to *be luminous*
5102 *nâhar* (1), to *sparkle; to be cheerful*
1546+4160 *ĕkbŏlē* (1), *jettison of cargo*

2893 kŏuphizō (1), to
unload, make lighter
5461 phōtizō (1), to shine
or to brighten up

LIGHTENETH
215 'ôwr (1), to be
luminous
797 astraptō (1), to flash
as lightning

LIGHTER
7043 qâlal (4), to be,
make light

LIGHTEST
5927 'âlâh (1), to ascend,
be high, mount

LIGHTETH
4672 mâtsâ' (1), to find
or acquire; to occur
5927 'âlâh (1), to ascend,
be high, mount
5461 phōtizō (1), to shine
or to brighten up

LIGHTING
5183 nachath (1),
descent; quiet
2064 ĕrchŏmai (1), to go
or come

LIGHTLY
4592 mᵉ'aṭ (1), little or
few
5034 nâbêl (1), to wilt; to
fall away; to be foolish
7034 qâlâh (1), to be light
7043 qâlal (3), to be,
make light
5035 tachu (1), without
delay, soon, suddenly

LIGHTNESS
6350 pachăzûwth (1),
frivolity
6963 qôwl (1), voice or
sound
1644 ĕlaphria (1),
fickleness

LIGHTNING
216 'ôwr (1), luminary;
lightning; happiness
965 bâzâq (1), flash of
lightning
1300 bârâq (5), lightning;
flash of lightning
2385 chăzîyz (2), flash of
lightning
796 astrapē (4),
lightning; light's glare

LIGHTNINGS
1300 bârâq (9), lightning;
flash of lightning
3940 lappîyd (1), flaming
torch, lamp or flame
796 astrapē (4),
lightning; light's glare

LIGHTS
216 'ôwr (1), luminary;
lightning; happiness
3974 mâ'ôwr (4),
luminary, light source
8261 shâqûph (1),
opening
2985 lampas (1), lamp,
lantern, torch
3088 luchnŏs (1), lamp
or other illuminator
5457 phōs (1),
luminousness, light

5458 phōstēr (1),
celestial luminary

LIGURE
3958 leshem (2), (poss.)
jacinth

LIKE
251 'âch (1), brother;
relative; member
1571 gam (2), also; even
1819 dâmâh (16), to
resemble, liken
1821 dᵉmâh (Ch.) (2), to
resemble; be like
1823 dᵉmûwth (2),
resemblance, likeness
1825 dimyôwn (1),
resemblance, likeness
1922 hădar (Ch.) (1), to
magnify, glorify
2088 zeh (1), this or that
2421 châyâh (1), to live;
to revive
2654 châphêts (2), to be
pleased with, desire
2803 châshab (1), to
think, regard; to value
3541 kôh (1), thus
3644 kᵉmôw (61), like,
as; for; with
3651 kên (7), just; right,
correct
4711 mâtsats (1), to suck
4911 mâshal (5), to use
figurative language
4915 môshel (1), empire;
parallel
5973 'îm (2), with
5974 'îm (Ch.) (1), with
7737 shâvâh (2), to
resemble; to adjust
407 andrizŏmai (1), to
act manly
499 antitupŏn (1),
representative
871 aphŏmŏiŏō (1), to be
like
1381 dŏkimazō (1), to
test; to approve
1503 eikō (2), to
resemble, be like
2470 isŏs (1), similar
2472 isŏtimŏs (1), of
equal value or honor
2504 kagō (1), and also
2532 kai (1), and; or
3663 hŏmŏiŏpathēs (2),
similarly affected
3664 hŏmŏiŏs (47),
similar
3665 hŏmŏiŏtēs (1),
resemblance, similarity
3666 hŏmŏiŏō (4), to
become like
3667 hŏmŏiōma (1),
form; resemblance
3779 hŏutō (2), in this
way; likewise
3945 parŏmŏiazō (2), to
resemble, be like
3946 parŏmŏiŏs (2),
similar, like
4832 summŏrphŏs (1),
similar, conformed to
5024 tauta (2), in the
same way
5108 tŏiŏutŏs (1), truly
this, i.e. of this sort
5613 hōs (10), which,
how, i.e. in that manner

5615 hōsautōs (2), in the
same way
5616 hōsĕi (6), as if
5618 hōspĕr (1), exactly
like

LIKED
7521 râtsâh (1), to be
pleased with; to satisfy

LIKEMINDED
2473 isŏpsuchŏs (1), of
similar spirit
3588+846+5426 hŏ (2),
"the," definite article

LIKEN
1819 dâmâh (4), to
resemble, liken
3666 hŏmŏiŏō (5), to
become like

LIKENED
1819 dâmâh (2), to
resemble, liken
3666 hŏmŏiŏō (4), to
become like

LIKENESS
1823 dᵉmûwth (19),
resemblance, likeness
8403 tabnîyth (5),
resemblance
8544 tᵉmûwnâh (5),
something fashioned
3666 hŏmŏiŏō (1), to
become like
3667 hŏmŏiōma (3),
form; resemblance

LIKETH
157 'âhab (1), to have
affection, love
2896 ṭôwb (2), good; well

LIKEWISE
1571 gam (15), also;
even; yea; though
2063 zō'th (2), this
3162 yachad (1), unitedly
3651 kên (14), just; right
36 agĕnēs (1), ignoble,
lowly
437 anthŏmŏlŏgĕŏmai
(1), respond in praise
2532 kai (11), and; or
3668 hŏmŏiŏs (29), in the
same way
3779 hŏutō (5), in this
way; likewise
3898 paraplēsiŏs (1), in a
manner near by
5615 hōsautōs (13), in
the same way

LIKHI
3949 Liqchîy (1), learned

LIKING
2492 châlam (1), to be,
make plump; to dream

LILIES
7799 shûwshan (8), white
lily; straight trumpet
2918 krinŏn (2), lily

LILY
7799 shûwshan (5), white
lily; straight trumpet

LIME
7875 sîyd (2), lime

LIMIT
1366 gᵉbûwl (1),
boundary, border

LIMITED
8428 tâvâh (1), to grieve,
bring pain

LIMITETH
3724 hŏrizō (1), to
appoint, decree, specify

LINE
2256 chebel (5),
company, band
2339 chûwṭ (1), string;
line
6616 pâthîyl (1), twine,
cord
6957 qav (14), rule;
musical string
8279 sered (1),
scribing-awl
8515 Tᵉla'ssar (1),
Telassar
8615 tiqvâh (1), cord;
expectancy
2583 kanŏn (1), rule,
standard

LINEAGE
3965 patria (1), family,
group, race, i.e. nation

LINEN
906 bad (23), linen
garment
948 bûwts (9), Byssus,
(poss.) cotton
4723 miqveh (4),
confidence; collection
5466 çâdîyn (2), shirt
6593 pishteh (9), linen,
from carded thread
8162 sha'aṭnêz (1), linen
and woolen
8336 shêsh (37), white
linen; white marble
1039 bussinŏs (4), linen
1040 bussŏs (2), white
linen
3043 linŏn (1), flax linen
3608 ŏthŏniŏn (5), strips
of linen bandage
4616 sindŏn (6), byssos,
i.e. bleached linen

LINES
2256 chebel (2),
company, band

LINGERED
4102 mâhahh (2), to be
reluctant

LINGERETH
691 argĕō (1), to delay,
grow weary

LINTEL
352 'ayîl (1), chief; ram;
oak tree
3730 kaphtôr (1), capital;
wreath-like button
4947 mashqôwph (2),
lintel

LINTELS
3730 kaphtôr (1), capital;
wreath-like button

LINUS
3044 Linŏs (1), (poss.)
flax linen

LION
738 'ărîy (56), lion
739 'ărîy'êl (2), Lion of
God

LION'S
3715 kᵉphîyr (16), walled
  village; young lion
3833 lâbîy' (9), lion,
  lioness
3918 layish (3), lion
7826 shachal (6), lion
3023 lĕôn (6), lion

LION'S
738 'ărîy (4), lion
3833 lâbîy' (1), lion,
  lioness
7830 shachats (1),
  haughtiness; dignity

LIONESS
3833 lâbîy' (1), lion,
  lioness

LIONESSES
3833 lâbîy' (1), lion,
  lioness

LIONLIKE
739 'ărîy'êl (2), Lion of
  God

LIONS
738 'ărîy (17), lion
744 'aryêh (Ch.) (8), lion
3715 kᵉphîyr (14), walled
  village; young lion
3833 lâbîy' (1), lion,
  lioness
3023 lĕôn (3), lion

LIONS'
738 'ărîy (1), lion
744 'aryêh (Ch.) (1), lion

LIP
822 'eshnâb (1), latticed
  window
8193 sâphâh (2), lip,
  language, speech

LIPS
2193 zâ'ak (1), to
  extinguish
8193 sâphâh (109), lip,
  language, speech
8222 sâphâm (3), beard
5491 chĕîlŏs (6), lip

LIQUOR
4197 mezeg (1),
  tempered wine
4952 mishrâh (1),
  steeped juice

LIQUORS
1831 dema' (1), juice

LISTED
2309 thĕlō (2), to will; to
  desire; to choose

LISTEN
8085 shâma' (1), to hear
  intelligently

LISTETH
2309 thĕlō (1), to will; to
  desire; to choose
3730+1014 hŏrmē (1),
  impulse, i.e. onset

LITTERS
6632 tsâb (1), lizard;
  covered cart

LITTLE
1851 daq (1), crushed;
  small or thin
2191 zᵉ'êyr (3), small,
  little
2192 zᵉ'êyr (Ch.) (1),
  small, little

3715 kᵉphîyr (16), walled

2835 châsîph (1), small
  company, flock
2945 ṭaph (32), family of
  children and women
3530 kibrâh (3), measure
  of length
3563 kôwç (2), cup;
  (poss.) owl
4591 mâ'aṭ (3), to be,
  make small or few
4592 mᵉ'aṭ (52), little or
  few
4704 mitstsᵉ'îyrâh (1),
  diminutive
4705 mits'âr (3), little;
  short time
5759 'ăvîyl (1), infant,
  young child
5768 'ôwlêl (1), suckling
  child
6810 tsâ'îyr (4), little in
  number; few in age
6819 tsâ'ar (1), to be
  small; be trivial
6966 qûwm (Ch.) (1), to
  rise
6995 qôṭen (2), little
  finger
6996 qâṭân (20), small,
  least, youngest
8102 shemets (2), inkling
8241 shetseph (1),
  outburst of anger
8585 tᵉ'âlâh (1), channel;
  bandage or plaster
974 bibliaridiŏn (4), little
  scroll
1024 brachus (6), little,
  short
1646 ĕlachistŏs (1), least
2365 thugatriŏn (1), little
  daughter
2485 ichthudiŏn (1), little
  fish
3357 mĕtriŏs (1),
  moderately, i.e. slightly
3397 mikrŏn (14), small
  space of time or degree
3398 mikrŏs (16), small,
  little
3640 ŏligŏpistŏs (5), little
  confidence
3641 ŏligŏs (9), puny,
  small
3813 paidiŏn (12), child;
  immature
4142 plŏiariŏn (2), small
  boat
5040 tĕkniŏn (9), infant,
  i.e. a darling Christian
5177 tugchanō (1), to
  take part in; to obtain

LIVE
2414 châṭaph (3), to seize
  as a prisoner
2416 chay (44), alive;
  raw; fresh; life
2418 chăyâ' (Ch.) (2), to
  live
2421 châyâh (110), to
  live; to revive
2425 châyay (15), to live;
  to revive
3117 yôwm (2), day; time
  period
7531 ritspâh (1), hot
  stone; pavement
390 anastrĕphō (2), to
  remain, to live

980 biŏō (1), to live life
1514 ĕirēnĕuō (2), to be,
  act peaceful
2068 ĕsthiō (1), to eat
2071+3118 ĕsŏmai (1),
  will be
2198 zaō (53), to live
2225 zōŏgŏnĕō (1), to
  rescue; be saved
4800 suzaō (3), to live in
  common with
5225 huparchō (1), to
  come into existence

LIVED
2416 chay (5), alive; raw;
  fresh; life
2421 châyâh (39), to live;
  to revive
2425 châyay (5), to live;
  to revive
326 anazaō (1), to
  recover life, live again
2198 zaō (4), to live
4176 pŏlitĕuŏmai (1), to
  behave as a citizen
5171 truphaō (1), to live
  indulgently

LIVELY
2416 chay (1), alive; raw;
  fresh; life
2422 châyeh (1), vigorous
2198 zaō (3), to live

LIVER
3516 kâbêd (14), liver

LIVES
2416 chay (5), alive; raw;
  fresh; life
2417 chay (Ch.) (1), alive;
  life
2421 châyâh (2), to live;
  to revive
5315 nephesh (18), life;
  breath; soul; wind
5590 psuchē (5), soul,
  vitality; heart, mind

LIVEST
2416 chay (1), alive; raw;
  fresh; life
3117 yôwm (1), day; time
  period
2198 zaō (2), to live

LIVETH
2416 chay (o1), alive;
  raw; fresh; life
2421 châyâh (1), to live;
  to revive
2425 châyay (2), to live;
  to revive
3117 yôwm (1), day; time
  period
2198 zaō (24), to live

LIVING
2416 chay (98), alive;
  raw; fresh; life
2417 chay (Ch.) (4), alive;
  life
2424 chayûwth (1), life,
  lifetime
979 biŏs (5), present
  state of existence
1236 diagō (1), to pass
  time or life
2198 zaō (34), to live

LIZARD
3911 lᵉṭâ'âh (1), kind of
  lizard

LO
718 'ărûw (Ch.) (1), lo!,
  behold!
1883 dethe' (Ch.) (1),
  sprout; green grass
1888 hê' (Ch.) (1), Lo!,
  Look!
2005 hên (13), lo!; if!
2009 hinnêh (103), lo!;
  Look!
2114 zûwr (1), to be
  foreign, strange
7200 râ'âh (3), to see
2395 iatrŏs (1), physician
2396 idĕ (2), surprise!,
  lo!, look!
2400 idŏu (29), lo!, note!,
  see!

LO-AMMI
3818 Lô' 'Ammîy (1), not
  my people

LO-DEBAR
3810 Lô' Dᵉbar (3),
  pastureless

LO-RUHAMAH
3819 Lô' Rûchâmâh (2),
  not pitied

LOADEN
6006 'âmaç (1), to impose
  a burden

LOADETH
6006 'âmaç (1), to impose
  a burden

LOAF
3603 kikkâr (2), round
  loaf; talent
740 artos (1), loaf of
  bread

LOAN
7596 shᵉ'êlâh (1), petition

LOATHE
3988 mâ'aç (1), to spurn;
  to disappear

LOATHETH
947 bûwç (1), to trample
  down; oppress
6973 qûwts (1), to be,
  make disgusted

LOATHSOME
887 bâ'ash (1), to be a
  moral stench
2214 zârâ' (1),
  disgusting, loathing
3988 mâ'aç (1), to spurn;
  to disappear
7033 qâlâh (1), to toast,
  scorch

LOAVES
3603 kikkâr (2), round
  loaf; talent
3899 lechem (5), food,
  bread
740 artos (22), loaf of
  bread

LOCK
4514 man'ûwl (1), bolt on
  door
6734 tsîytsîth (1),
  fore-lock of hair; tassel

LOCKED
5274 nâ'al (2), to fasten
  up, lock

LOCKS
4253 machlâphâh (2), *ringlet or braid,* of hair
4514 man'ûwl (5), *bolt on door*
6545 pera' (2), *hair as dishevelled*
6777 tsammâh (4), *veil*
6977 qᵉvutstsâh (2), *forelock of hair*

LOCUST
697 'arbeh (9), *locust*
5556 çol'âm (1), *destructive locust* kind
6767 tseᵉlâtsal (1), *cricket*

LOCUSTS
697 'arbeh (11), *locust*
1357 gêb (1), *locust swarm*
2284 châgâb (1), *locust*
200 akris (4), *locust*

LOD
3850 Lôd (4), *Lod*

LODGE
3885 lûwn (22), *to be obstinate*
4412 mᵉlûwnâh (1), *hut*
2647 kataluō (1), *to halt for the night*
2681 kataskēnŏō (2), *to remain, live*
3579 xĕnizō (1), *to be a host; to be a guest*

LODGED
3885 lûwn (12), *to be obstinate*
4411 mâlôwn (1), *lodging for night*
7901 shâkab (1), *to lie down*
835 aulizŏmai (1), *to pass the night*
2681 kataskēnŏō (1), *to remain, live*
3579 xĕnizō (4), *to be a host; to be a guest*
3580 xĕnŏdŏchĕō (1), *to be hospitable*

LODGEST
3885 lûwn (1), *to be obstinate*

LODGETH
3579 xĕnizō (1), *to be a host; to be a guest*

LODGING
3885 lûwn (1), *to be obstinate*
4411 mâlôwn (3), *lodgment for night*
3578 xĕnia (2), *place of entertainment*

LODGINGS
4411 mâlôwn (1), *lodgment for night*

LOFT
5944 'ălîyâh (1), *upper things; second-story*

LOFTILY
4791 mârôwm (1), *elevation; elation*

LOFTINESS
1363 gôbahh (1), *height; grandeur; arrogance*
1365 gabhùwth (1), *pride, arrogance*

LOFTY
1364 gâbôahh (2), *high; powerful; arrogant*
1365 gabhûwth (1), *pride, arrogance*
5375 nâsâ' (1), *to lift up*
7311 rûwm (3), *to be high; to rise or raise*
7682 sâgab (1), *to be, make lofty; be safe*

LOG
3849 lôg (5), *liquid measure*

LOINS
2504 châlâts (9), *loins, areas of the waist*
2788 chârêr (1), *arid, parched*
3409 yârêk (2), *leg or shank, flank; side*
3689 keçel (1), *loin; back; viscera*
4975 môthen (42), *loins*
3751 ŏsphus (8), *loin; belt*

LOIS
3090 Lŏïs (1), *Loïs*

LONG
748 'ârak (4), *to be, make long*
752 'ârôk (2), *long*
753 'ôrek (23), *length*
954 bûwsh (1), *to be delayed*
1419 gâdôwl (1), *great*
2442 châkâh (1), *to await; hope for*
3117 yôwm (16), *day; time period*
4101 mâh (Ch.) (1), *what?, how?, why?*
4900 mâshak (2), *to draw out; to be tall*
4970 mâthay (1), *when; when?, how long?*
5704 'ad (51), *as far (long) as; during*
5750 'ôwd (1), *again; repeatedly; still; more*
5769 'ôwlâm (3), *eternity; ancient; always*
5973 'îm (1), *with*
6256 'êth (1), *time*
6440 pânîym (1), *face; front*
7221 rî'shâh (1), *beginning*
7227 rab (11), *great*
7230 rôb (2), *abundance*
7235 râbâh (3), *to increase*
7350 râchôwq (3), *remote, far*
8615 tiqvâh (1), *cord; expectancy*
1909 ĕpi (1), *on, upon*
1909+4119 ĕpi (1), *on, upon*
1971 ĕpipŏthĕō (3), *intensely crave*
2118 ĕuthutēs (1), *rectitude, uprightness*
2193 hĕōs (7), *until*
2425 hikanŏs (6), *ample; fit*
2863 kŏmaō (2), *to wear long hair*
3114 makrŏthumĕō (3), *to be forbearing, patient*

LOFTY
3117 makrŏs (3), *long, in place or time*
3752 hŏtan (1), *inasmuch as, at once*
3756+3641 ŏu (1), *no or not*
3819 palai (1), *formerly; sometime since*
4183 pŏlus (4), *much, many*
4214 pŏsŏs (1), *how much?; how much!*
5118 tŏsŏutŏs (2), *such great*
5550 chrŏnŏs (4), *space of time, period*

LONGED
183 'âvâh (2), *to wish for, desire*
2968 yâ'ab (1), *to desire, long for*
3615 kâlâh (1), *to cease, be finished, perish*
8373 tâ'ab (2), *to desire*
1971 ĕpipŏthĕō (1), *intensely crave*
1973 ĕpipŏthĕtŏs (1), *yearned upon*

LONGEDST
3700 kâçaph (1), *to pine after; to fear*

LONGER
752 'ârôk (1), *long*
3254 yâçaph (1), *to add or augment*
5750 'ôwd (4), *again; repeatedly; still; more*
2089 ĕti (4), *yet, still*
3370 Mēdŏs (5), *inhabitant of Media*
4119 plĕiōn (1), *more*

LONGETH
183 'âvâh (1), *to wish for, desire*
2836 châshaq (1), *to join; to love, delight*
3642 kâmahh (1), *to pine after, long for*
3700 kâçaph (1), *to pine after; to fear*

LONGING
8264 shâqaq (1), *to seek greedily*
8375 ta'ăbâh (1), *desire*

LONGSUFFERING
750+639 'ârêk (4), *patient*
3114 makrŏthumĕō (1), *to be forbearing, patient*
3115 makrŏthumia (12), *forbearance; fortitude*

LONGWINGED
750+83 'ârêk (1), *patient*

LOOK
2342 chûwl (1), *to wait; to pervert*
2372 châzâh (3), *to gaze at; to perceive*
2376 chêzev (Ch.) (1), *sight, revelation*
4758 mar'eh (6), *appearance; vision*
5027 nâbaṭ (24), *to scan; to regard with favor*
5869 'ayin (3), *eye; sight*
6437 pânâh (13), *to turn, to face*

LOOKED
6440 pânîym (1), *face; front*
6485 pâqad (1), *to visit, care for, count*
6822 tsâphâh (2), *to peer into the distance*
6960 qâvâh (4), *to collect; to expect*
7200 râ'âh (53), *to see*
7210 rô'îy (1), *sight; spectacle*
7688 shâgach (1), *to glance sharply at*
7760 sûwm (2), *to put, place*
7789 shûwr (1), *to spy out, survey*
7896 shîyth (1), *to place, put*
8159 shâ'âh (4), *to inspect, consider*
8259 shâqaph (3), *to peep or gaze*
308 anablĕpō (1), *to look up; to recover sight*
352 anakuptō (1), *to straighten up*
553 apĕkdĕchŏmai (2), *to expect fully*
816 atĕnizō (2), *to gaze intently*
991 blĕpō (5), *to look at*
1492 ĕidō (1), *to know*
1551 ĕkdĕchŏmai (1), *to await, expect*
1914 ĕpiblĕpō (1), *to gaze at*
1980 ĕpiskĕptŏmai (1), *to inspect; to go to see*
2300 thĕaŏmai (1), *to look closely at*
3700 ŏptanŏmai (2), *to appear*
3706 hŏrasis (1), *vision*
3879 parakuptō (1), *to lean over to peer within*
4328 prŏsdŏkaō (5), *to anticipate; to await*
4648 skŏpĕō (2), *to watch out for, i.e. to regard*

LOOKED
5027 nâbaṭ (12), *to scan; to regard with favor*
6437 pânâh (18), *to turn, to face*
6440 pânîym (1), *face; front*
6960 qâvâh (8), *to collect; to expect*
6970 Qôwa' (1), *curtailment*
7200 râ'âh (55), *to see*
7805 shâzaph (1), *to scan*
8159 shâ'âh (1), *to inspect, consider*
8259 shâqaph (12), *to peep or gaze*
8559 Tâmâr (1), *palm tree*
308 anablĕpō (6), *to look up; to recover sight*
816 atĕnizō (4), *to gaze intently*
991 blĕpō (1), *to look at*
1492 ĕidō (7), *to know*
1551 ĕkdĕchŏmai (1), *to await, expect*
1689 ĕmblĕpō (2), *to observe; to discern*

1869 ĕpairō (1), to *raise up, look up*
2300 thĕaŏmai (1), to *look closely at*
4017 pĕriblĕpō (6), to *look all around*
4327 prŏsdĕchŏmai (1), to *receive; to await for*
4328 prŏsdŏkaō (2), to *anticipate; to await*

LOOKEST
5027 nâbaţ (1), to *scan; to regard with favor*
8104 shâmar (1), to *watch*

LOOKETH
995 bîyn (1), to *understand; discern*
4758+5869 mar'eh (1), *appearance; vision*
5027 nâbaţ (3), to *scan; to regard with favor*
6437 pânâh (8), to *turn, to face*
6440 pânîym (2), *face; front*
6822 tsâphâh (2), to *peer into the distance*
6960 qâvâh (1), to *collect; to expect*
7200 râ'âh (4), to *see*
7688 shâgach (2), to *glance sharply at*
7789 shûwr (1), to *spy out, survey*
8259 shâqaph (4), to *peep or gaze*
991 blĕpō (1), to *look at*
3879 parakuptō (1), to *lean over to peer within*
4328 prŏsdŏkaō (2), to *anticipate; to await*

LOOKING
6437 pânâh (9), to *turn, to face*
7209 rĕ'îy (1), *mirror*
8259 shâqaph (1), to *peep or gaze*
308 anablĕpō (3), to *look up; to recover sight*
816 atĕnizō (1), to *gaze intently*
872 aphŏraō (1), to *consider attentively*
991 blĕpō (1), to *look at*
1561 ĕkdŏchē (1), *expectation*
1689 ĕmblĕpō (2), to *observe; to discern*
1983 ĕpiskŏpĕō (1), to *ov .rsee; to beware*
233+ thĕŏrĕō (1), to *see; to discern*
4017 pĕriblĕpō (1), to *look all around*
4327 prŏsdĕchŏmai (3), to *receive; to await for*
4328 prŏsdŏkaō (2), to *anticipate; to await*
4329 prŏsdŏkia (1), *apprehension of evil*

LOOKINGGLASSES
4759 mar'âh (1), *vision; mirror*

LOOKS
5869 'ayin (3), *eye; sight; fountain*

6400 pelach (2), *slice*

LOOPS
3924 lûlâ'âh (13), *curtain loop*

LOOSE
2502 châlats (1), to *pull off; to strip; to depart*
5394 nâshal (1), to *divest, eject, or drop*
5425 nâthar (1), to *terrify; shake off; untie*
6605 pâthach (7), to *open wide; to loosen, begin*
7971 shâlach (3), to *send away*
8271 shĕrê' (Ch.) (1), to *free, separate; unravel*
3089 luō (15), to *loosen*

LOOSED
2118 zâchach (2), to *shove or displace*
2502 châlats (1), to *pull off; to strip; to depart*
4549 mâçaç (1), to *waste with disease; to faint*
5203 nâṭash (1), to *disperse; to thrust off*
5425 nâthar (1), to *terrify; shake off; untie*
6605 pâthach (5), to *open wide; to loosen, begin*
7368 râchaq (1), to *recede; remove*
8271 shĕrê' (Ch.) (1), to *free, separate; unravel*
321 anagō (2), to *lead up; to bring out; to sail*
447 aniēmi (2), to *slacken, loosen*
630 apŏluō (2), to *relieve, release; to pardon*
2673 katargĕō (1), to *be, render entirely useless*
3080 lusis (1), *divorce*
3089 luō (10), to *loosen*

LOOSETH
5425 nâthar (1), to *terrify; shake off; untie*
6605 pâthach (1), to *open wide; to loosen, begin*

LOOSING
142 airō (1), to *lift, to take up*
321 anagō (1), to *lead up; to bring out; to sail*
3089 luō (2), to *loosen*

LOP
5586 çâ'aph (1), to *dis-branch a tree*

LORD
113 'âdôwn (201), *sovereign, i.e. controller*
136 'Ădônây (430), the *Lord*
1376 gĕbîyr (2), *master*
3050 Yâhh (50), *Jehovah, self-Existent or Eternal*
3068 Yĕhôvâh (6394), *Jehovah, self-Existent*
4756 mârê' (Ch.) (4), *master*
7229 rab (Ch.) (1), *great*
7991 shâlîysh (3), *officer; of the third rank*
1203 dĕspŏtēs (4), *absolute ruler*

2961 kuriĕuō (1), to *rule, be master of*
2962 kuriŏs (694), *supreme, controller, Mr.*
4462 rhabbŏni (1), *my master*

LORD'S
113 'âdôwn (8), *sovereign, i.e. controller*
136 'Ădônây (1), the *Lord*
3068 Yĕhôvâh (108), *Jehovah, self-Existent*
2960 kuriakŏs (2), *belonging to the Lord*
2962 kuriŏs (15), *supreme, controller, Mr.*

LORDLY
117 'addîyr (1), *powerful; majestic*

LORDS
113 'âdôwn (4), *sovereign, i.e. controller*
1167 ba'al (2), *master; husband; owner; citizen*
5633 çeren (21), *axle; peer*
7261 rabĕbân (Ch.) (6), *magnate, noble*
7300 rûwd (1), to *ramble free or disconsolate*
7991 shâlîysh (1), *officer; of the third rank*
8269 sar (1), *head person, ruler*
2634 katakuriĕuō (1), to *control, subjugate, lord*
2961 kuriĕuō (1), to *rule, be master of*
2962 kuriŏs (3), *supreme, controller, Mr.*
3175 mĕgistanĕs (1), *great person*

LORDSHIP
2634 katakurieuō (1), to *subjugate, lord over*
2961 kuriĕuō (1), to *rule, be master of*

LOSE
6 'âbad (1), *perish; destroy*
622 'âçaph (1), to *gather, collect*
3772 kârath (1), to *cut (off, down or asunder)*
5307 nâphal (1), to *fall*
7843 shâchath (1), to *decay; to ruin*
622 apŏllumi (17), to *perish or lose*
2210 zēmiŏō (2), to *suffer loss*

LOSETH
622 apŏllumi (1), to *perish or lose*

LOSS
2398 châţâ' (1), to *sin*
7674 shebeth (1), *rest, interruption, cessation*
7921 shâkôl (2), to *miscarry*
580 apŏbŏlē (1), *rejection, loss*
2209 zēmia (3), *detriment; loss*
2210 zēmiŏō (2), to *suffer loss*

LOST
6 'âbad (9), to *perish*
9 'âbêdâh (4), *destruction*
5307 nâphal (2), to *fall*
7908 shĕkôwl (1), *bereavement*
7923 shikkûlîym (1), *childlessness*
358+1096 analŏs (1), *saltless, i.e. insipid*
622 apŏllumi (13), to *perish or lose*
3471 mōrainō (2), to *become insipid*

LOT
1486 gôwrâl (60), *lot, allotment*
2256 chebel (3), *company, band*
3876 Lôwţ (32), *veil*
2624 kataklĕrŏdŏtĕō (1), to *apportion an estate*
2819 klĕrŏs (2), *lot, portion*
2975 lagchanō (1), to *determine by lot*
3091 Lōt (3), *veil*

LOT'S
3876 Lôwţ (1), *veil*

LOTAN
3877 Lôwţân (5), *covering*

LOTAN'S
3877 Lôwţân (2), *covering*

LOTHE
3811 lâ'âh (1), to *tire; to be, make disgusted*
6962 qûwţ (3), to *detest*

LOTHED
1602 gâ'al (2), to *detest; to reject; to fail*
7114 qâtsar (1), to *curtail, cut short*

LOTHETH
1602 gâ'al (1), to *detest; to reject; to fail*

LOTHING
1604 gô'al (1), *abhorrence*

LOTS
1486 gôwrâl (16), *lot, allotment*
2819 klĕrŏs (6), *lot, portion*
2975 lagchanō (1), to *determine by lot*

LOUD
1419 gâdôwl (19), *great*
1993 hâmâh (1), to *be in great commotion*
2389 châzâq (1), *strong; severe, hard, violent*
5797 'ôz (1), *strength*
7311 rûwm (1), to *be high; to rise or raise*
8085 shâma' (2), to *hear*
3173 mĕgas (33), *great, many*

LOUDER
3966 mĕ'ôd (1), *very, utterly*

LOVE
157 'âhab (73), to *have affection, love*
160 'ahăbâh (34), *affection, love*

1730 dôwd (7), *beloved, friend; uncle, relative*
2836 châshaq (3), *to join; to love, delight*
5690 'egeb (1), *amative words, words of love*
5691 'ăgâbâh (1), *love, amorousness*
7355 râcham (1), *to be compassionate*
7474 ra'yâh (9), *female associate*
25 agapaō (70), *to love*
26 agapē (85), *love; love-feast*
2309 thĕlō (1), *to will; to desire; to choose*
5360 philadĕlphia (4), *fraternal affection*
5361 philadĕlphŏs (1), *fraternal*
5362 philandrŏs (1), *affectionate as a wife to her husband*
5363 philanthrōpia (1), *benevolence*
5365 philarguria (1), *avarice, greedy love of possessions*
5368 philĕō (10), *to be a friend, have affection*
5388 philŏtĕknŏs (1), *loving one's child(ren)*

LOVE'S
26 agapē (1), *love*

LOVED
157 'âhab (48), *to have affection, love*
160 'ahăbâh (7), *affection, love*
2245 châbab (1), *to cherish*
25 agapaō (37), *to love*
26 agapē (1), *love*
5368 philĕō (3), *to be a friend, have affection*

LOVEDST
157 'âhab (1), *to have affection, love*
25 agapaō (1), *to love*

LOVELY
157 'âhab (1), *to have affection, love*
4261 machmâd (1), *object of affection*
5690 'egeb (1), *amative words, words of love*
4375 prŏsphilês (1), *acceptable, pleasing*

LOVER
157 'âhab (2), *to have affection, love*
5358 philagathŏs (1), *promoter of virtue*
5382 philŏxĕnŏs (1), *hospitable*

LOVERS
157 'âhab (17), *to have affection, love*
158 'ahab (1), *affection, love*
5689 'âgab (1), *to lust sensually*
7453 rêa' (1), *associate; one close*
5367 philautŏs (1), *selfish*

5369 philĕdŏnŏs (1), *loving pleasure*
5377 philŏthĕŏs (1), *pious, i.e. loving God*

LOVES
159 'ôhab (1), *affection, love*
1730 dôwd (1), *beloved, friend; uncle, relative*
3039 yᵉdîyd (1), *loved*

LOVEST
157 'âhab (7), *to have affection, love*
25 agapaō (2), *to love*
5368 philĕō (3), *to be a friend, have affection*

LOVETH
157 'âhab (37), *to have affection, love*
25 agapaō (19), *to love*
5368 philĕō (6), *to be a friend, have affection*
5383 philŏprōtĕuō (1), *loving to be first*

LOVING
157 'âhab (1), *to have affection, love*
158 'ahab (1), *affection, love*
2896 ṭôwb (1), *good; well*

LOVINGKINDNESS
2617 cheçed (26), *kindness, favor*

LOVINGKINDNESSES
2617 cheçed (4), *kindness, favor*

LOW
120 'âdâm (1), *human being; mankind*
1809 dâlal (3), *to slacken, dangle*
3665 kâna' (2), *to humiliate, subdue*
3766 kâra' (1), *to prostrate*
4295 maṭṭâh (1), *below or beneath*
4355 mâkak (2), *to tumble in ruins*
6030 'ânâh (1), *to respond, answer*
6819 tsâ'ar (1), *to be small; be trivial*
7817 shâchach (3), *to sink or depress*
8213 shâphêl (11), *to humiliate*
8216 shêphel (1), *humble state or rank*
8217 shâphâl (5), *depressed, low*
8219 shᵉphêlâh (5), *lowland*
8482 tachtîy (2), *lowermost; depths*
5011 tapĕinŏs (3), *humiliated, lowly*
5013 tapĕinŏō (1), *depress; to humiliate*
5014 tapĕinōsis (2), *humbleness, lowliness*

LOWER
2637 châçêr (1), *to lack; to fail, want, make less*
8213 shâphêl (1), *to humiliate*

8217 shâphâl (4), *depressed, low*
8481 tachtôwn (5), *bottommost*
8482 tachtîy (4), *lowermost; depths*
1642 ĕlattŏō (2), *to lessen*
2737 katōtĕrŏs (1), *inferior, lower*

LOWEST
7098 qâtsâh (3), *termination; fringe*
8481 tachtôwn (2), *bottommost*
8482 tachtîy (4), *lowermost; depths*
2078 ĕschatŏs (2), *farthest, final*

LOWETH
1600 gâ'âh (1), *to bellow, i.e. low of a cow*

LOWING
1600 gâ'âh (1), *to bellow, i.e. low of a cow*
6963 qôwl (1), *voice or sound*

LOWLINESS
5012 tapĕinŏphrŏsunē (2), *modesty, humility*

LOWLY
6041 'ânîy (3), *depressed*
6800 tsâna' (1), *to humiliate*
8217 shâphâl (1), *depressed, low*
5011 tapĕinŏs (1), *humiliated, lowly*

LOWRING
4768 stugnazō (1), *to be overcast, somber*

LUBIM
3864 Lûwbîy (2), *dry region*

LUBIMS
3864 Lûwbîy (1), *dry region*

LUCAS
3065 Lŏukas (2), *Lucanus*

LUCIFER
1966 hêylêl (1), *Venus (i.e. morning star)*

LUCIUS
3066 Lŏukiŏs (2), *illuminative*

LUCRE
1215 betsa' (1), *plunder; unjust gain*
146 aischrŏkĕrdēs (2), *shamefully greedy*
147 aischrŏkĕrdōs (1), *sordidly, greedily*
866 aphilargurŏs (1), *unavaricious*

LUCRE'S
2771 kĕrdŏs (1), *gain, profit*

LUD
3865 Lûwd (4), *Lud*

LUDIM
3866 Lûwdîy (2), *Ludite*

LUHITH
3872 Lûwchîyth (2), *floored*

LUKE
3065 Lŏukas (2), *Lucanus*

LUKEWARM
5513 chliarŏs (1), *tepid*

LUMP
1690 dᵉbêlâh (2), *cake of pressed figs*
5445 phurama (5), *lump of clay; mass of dough*

LUNATICK
4583 sĕlēniazŏmai (2), *to be moon-struck*

LURK
6845 tsâphan (2), *to hide; to hoard; to lurk*

LURKING
3427 yâshab (1), *to dwell, to remain; to settle*
3993 ma'ărâb (1), *ambuscade, ambush*
4224 machăbê' (1), *refuge, shelter*

LUST
2530 châmad (1), *to delight in; lust for*
5315 nephesh (1), *life; breath; soul; wind*
8307 shᵉrîyrûwth (1), *obstinacy*
8378 ta'ăvâh (1), *longing; delight*
1511+1938 ĕinai (1), *to exist*
1937 ĕpithumĕō (2), *to long for*
1939 ĕpithumia (9), *longing*
3715 ŏrĕxis (1), *longing after, lust, desire*
3806 pathŏs (1), *passion, especially concupiscence*

LUSTED
183 'âvâh (2), *to wish for, desire*
1937 ĕpithumĕō (2), *to long for*

LUSTETH
183 'âvâh (4), *to wish for, desire*
1937 ĕpithumĕō (1), *to long for*
1971 ĕpipŏthĕō (1), *intensely crave*

LUSTING
8378 ta'ăvâh (1), *longing; delight*

LUSTS
1939 ĕpithumia (22), *longing*
2237 hēdŏnē (2), *delight; desire*

LUSTY
8082 shâmên (1), *rich; fertile*

LUZ
3870 Lûwz (7), *Luz*

LYCAONIA
3071 Lukaŏnia (2), *Lycaonia*

LYCIA
3073 Lukia (1), *Lycia*

LYDDA
3069 Ludda (3), *Lod*

LYDIA
3865 Lûwd (1), *Lud*
3070 *Ludia* (2), *Lydian* in Asia Minor

LYDIANS
3866 Lûwdîy (1), *Ludite*

LYING
3538 kᵉdab (Ch.) (1), *false, misleading*
3576 kâzab (1), to *lie, deceive*
3577 kâzâb (2), *falsehood; idol*
3584 kâchash (2), to *lie, disown; to disappoint*
3585 kachash (1), *emaciation; hypocrisy*
3586 kechâsh (1), *faithless*
4904 mishkâb (4), *bed; sleep; intercourse*
5307 nâphal (1), to *fall*
7252 reba' (1), *prostration* for sleep
7257 râbats (2), to *recline, repose, brood*
7723 shâv' (2), *ruin; guile; idolatry*
7901 shâkab (3), to *lie down*
8267 sheqer (21), *untruth; sham*
345 anakĕimai (1), to *recline* at a meal
906 ballō (1), to *throw*
1968 ĕpipiptō (1), to *embrace; to seize*
2749 kĕimai (4), to *lie* outstretched
5579 pseudŏs (2), *falsehood*

LYSANIAS
3078 Lusanias (1), *grief-dispelling*

LYSIAS
3079 Lusias (3), *Lysias*

LYSTRA
3082 Lustra (6), *Lystra*

MAACAH
4601 Ma'ăkâh (3), *depression*

MAACHAH
4601 Ma'ăkâh (18), *depression*

MAACHATHI
4602 Ma'ăkâthîy (1), *Maakathite*

MAACHATHITE
4602 Ma'ăkâthîy (4), *Maakathite*

MAACHATHITES
4602 Ma'ăkâthîy (4), *Maakathite*

MAADAI
4572 Ma'ăday (1), *ornamental*

MAADIAH
4573 Ma'adyâh (1), *ornament of Jehovah*

MAAI
4597 Mâ'ay (1), *sympathetic*

MAALEH-ACRABBIM
4610 Ma'ălêh 'Aqrabbîym (1), *Steep of Scorpions*

MAARATH
4638 Ma'ărâth (1), *waste*

MAASEIAH
4271 Machçêyâh (2), *refuge in Jehovah*
4641 Ma'ăsêyâh (23), *work of Jehovah*

MAASIAI
4640 Ma'say (1), *operative*

MAATH
3092 Maath (1), *Maath*

MAAZ
4619 Ma'ats (1), *closure*

MAAZIAH
4590 Ma'azyâh (2), *rescue of Jehovah*

MACEDONIA
3109 Makĕdŏnia (24), *Macedonia*
3110 Makĕdōn (4), *of Macedonia*

MACEDONIAN
3110 Makĕdōn (1), *of Macedonia*

MACHBANAI
4344 Makbannay (1), *Macbannite*

MACHBENAH
4343 Makbênâ' (1), *knoll*

MACHI
4352 Mâkîy (1), *pining*

MACHIR
4353 Mâkîyr (22), *salesman*

MACHIRITES
4354 Mâkîyrîy (1), *Makirite*

MACHNADEBAI
4367 Maknadbay (1), *what* (is) *like* (a) *liberal* (man)?

MACHPELAH
4375 Makpêlâh (6), *fold*

MAD
1984 hâlal (8), to *shine, flash, radiate; boast*
3856 lâhahh (1), to *languish*
7696 shâga' (7), to *rave* through insanity
1519+3130 ĕis (1), *to* or *into*
1693 ĕmmainŏmai (1), to *rage at*
3105 mainŏmai (4), to *rave; to act insane*

MADAI
4074 Mâday (2), *Madai*

MADE
1129 bânâh (3), to *build; to establish*
1443 gâdar (1), to *build a stone wall*
1961 hâyâh (1), to *exist,* i.e. *be* or *become*
2342 chûwl (1), to *dance, whirl; to writhe* in pain

2672 châtsab (1), to *cut* stone or *carve* wood
3322 yâtsag (2), to *place* permanently
3335 yâtsar (2), to *form; potter; to determine*
3627 kᵉlîy (1), *implement, thing*
3738 kârâh (2), to *dig; to plot; to bore, hew*
3772 kârath (50), to *cut* (off, down or asunder)
3835 lâban (1), to *make bricks*
4399 mᵉlâ'kâh (1), *work; property*
4639 ma'ăseh (2), *action; labor*
5221 nâkâh (1), to *strike, kill*
5414 nâthan (42), to *give*
5648 'ăbad (Ch.) (7), to *do, work, serve*
5975 'âmad (1), to *stand*
6087 'âtsab (5), to *fabricate* or *fashion*
6213 'âsâh (394), to *make*
6235 'eser (1), *ten*
6466 pâ'al (3), to *do, make* or *practice*
6555 pârats (1), to *break out*
6743 tsâlach (1), to *push forward*
7194 qâshar (1), to *tie, bind*
7236 rᵉbâh (Ch.) (1), to *increase*
7495 râphâ' (1), to *cure, heal*
7502 râphad (1), to *spread a bed; to refresh*
7543 râqach (1), to *perfume, blend spice*
7737 shâvâh (1), to *level; to resemble; to adjust*
7739 shᵉvâh (Ch.) (1), to *resemble*
7760 sûwm (50), to *put, place*
7761 sûwm (Ch.) (10), to *put, place*
7896 shîyth (5), to *place*
208 akurŏō (1), to *invalidate, nullify*
272 amĕlĕō (1), to *be careless of, neglect*
319 anagnōrizŏmai (1), to *make* oneself *known*
347 anaklinō (1), to *lean back, recline*
461 anŏrthŏō (1), to *strengthen, build*
591 apŏdidōmi (1), to *give away*
626 apŏlŏgĕŏmai (1), to *give an account*
770 asthĕnĕō (1), to *be feeble*
805 asphalizō (3), to *render secure*
871 aphŏmŏiŏō (1), to *assimilate closely*
886 achĕirŏpŏiētŏs (2), *unmanufactured*
1080 gĕnnaō (1), to *procreate, regenerate*
1096 ginŏmai (72), to *be, become*

1107 gnōrizō (9), to *make known, reveal*
1165 dĕigmatizō (1), to *expose to spectacle*
1215 dēmĕgŏrĕō (1), to *address an assembly*
1232 diagnōrizō (1), to *tell abroad*
1239 diadidōmi (2), to *divide up, distribute*
1295 diasōzō (1), to *cure, preserve, rescue*
1303 diatithĕmai (1), to *put apart,* i.e. *dispose*
1392 dŏxazō (1), to *render, esteem glorious*
1402 dŏulŏō (1), to *enslave*
1511 ĕinai (1), to *exist*
1517 ĕirēnŏpŏiĕō (1), to *harmonize, make peace*
1519 ĕis (2), *to* or *into*
1586 ĕklĕgŏmai (1), to *select, choose, pick out*
1642 ĕlattŏō (1), to *lessen*
1659 ĕlĕuthĕrŏō (4), to *exempt, liberate*
1743 ĕndunamŏō (1), to *empower, strengthen*
1770 ĕnnĕuō (1), to *gesture,* i.e. *signal*
1839 ĕxistēmi (1), to *astound; to be insane*
1861 ĕpaggĕllō (2), to *engage to do*
2005 ĕpitĕlĕō (1), to *terminate; to undergo*
2049 ĕrēmŏō (1), to *lay waste*
2090 hĕtŏimazō (4), to *prepare*
2092 hĕtŏimŏs (1), *ready, prepared*
2134 ĕunŏuchizō (2), to *castrate; to live unmarried*
2227 zōŏpŏiĕō (1), to (re-) *vitalize, give life*
2301 thĕatrizō (1), to *expose as a spectacle*
2390 iaŏmai (1), to *cure, heal*
2427 hikanŏō (2), to *make competent*
2525 kathistēmi (7), to *designate, constitute*
2559 kakŏō (1), to *injure; to oppress; to embitter*
2673 katargĕō (1), to *be, render entirely useless*
2680 kataskĕuazō (1), to *prepare thoroughly*
2721 katĕphistēmi (1), to *rush upon in an assault*
2722 katĕchō (1), to *hold down fast*
2749 kĕimai (1), to *lie* outstretched
2758 kĕnŏō (2), to *make empty*
2841 kŏinŏnĕō (1), to *share* or *participate*
3021 lĕukainō (1), to *whiten*
3076 lupĕō (5), to *distress; to be sad*
3182 mĕthuskō (1), to *become drunk*

3421 mnēmŏnĕuŏ (1), to
exercise memory
3447 mŏschŏpŏiĕŏ (1), to
fabricate a bull image
3471 mōrainō (1), to
become insipid
3489 nauagĕŏ (1), to be
shipwrecked
3666 hŏmŏiŏŏ (2), to
become like
3670 hŏmŏlŏgĕŏ (1), to
acknowledge, agree
3822 palaiŏŏ (1), to
make, become worn out
3903 paraskĕuazŏ (1), to
get ready, prepare
3982 pĕithō (1), to pacify
or conciliate
4087 pikrainō (1), to
embitter, turn sour
4147 plŏutĕŏ (2), to be,
become wealthy
4160 pŏiĕŏ (51), to make
4161 pŏiĕma (1), what is
made, product
4198 pŏrĕuŏmai (1), to
go, come; to travel
4222 pŏtizŏ (2), to
furnish drink, irrigate
4364 prŏspŏiĕŏmai (1), to
pretend as if about to
4483 rhĕŏ (1), to utter,
i.e. speak or say
4692 spĕudŏ (1), to urge;
to await eagerly
4732 stĕrĕŏŏ (1), to be,
become strong
4776 sugkathizŏ (1), to
give, take a seat in
company with
4832 summŏrphŏs (1),
similar, conformed to
4955 sustasiastēs (1),
fellow-insurgent
4982 sŏzŏ (9), to deliver;
to protect
5014 tapĕinōsis (1),
humbleness, lowliness
5048 tĕlĕiŏŏ (9), to
perfect, complete
5055 tĕlĕŏ (1), to end, i.e.
complete, execute
5087 tithēmi (3), to place
5293 hupŏtassŏ (2), to
subordinate; to obey
5319 phanĕrŏŏ (13), to
render apparent
5487 charitŏŏ (1), to give
special favor
5499 chĕirŏpŏiētŏs (6), of
human construction

MADEST
3045 yâda' (1), to know
3772 kârath (1), to cut
(off, down or asunder)
6213 'âsâh (1), to make
387 anastatŏŏ (1), to
disturb, cause trouble
1642 ĕlattŏŏ (1), to lessen

MADIAN
3099 Madian (1), contest
or quarrel

MADMANNAH
4089 Madmannâh (2),
dunghill

MADMEN
4086 Madmên (1),
dunghill

MADMENAH
4088 Madmênâh (1),
dunghill

MADNESS
1947 hôwlêlâh (4), folly,
delusion
1948 hôwlêlûwth (1),
folly, delusion
7697 shiggâ'ôwn (2),
craziness
454 anŏia (1), stupidity;
rage
3913 paraphrŏnia (1),
foolhardiness, insanity

MADON
4068 Mâdôwn (2), height

MAGBISH
4019 Magbîysh (1),
stiffening

MAGDALA
3093 Magdala (1), tower

MAGDALENE
3094 Magdalēnē (12), of
Magdala

MAGDIEL
4025 Magdîy'êl (2),
preciousness of God

MAGICIAN
2749 charṭôm (Ch.) (1),
horoscopist, magician

MAGICIANS
2748 charṭôm (11),
horoscopist, magician
2749 charṭôm (Ch.) (4),
horoscopist, magician

MAGISTRATE
3423+6114 yârash (1), to
inherit; to impoverish
758 archŏn (1), first

MAGISTRATES
8200 shᵉphaṭ (Ch.) (1), to
judge
746 archē (1), first in
rank; first in time
3980 pĕitharchĕŏ (1), to
submit to authority
4755 stratēgŏs (5),
military governor

MAGNIFICAL
1431 gâdal (1), to be
great, make great

MAGNIFICENCE
3168 mĕgalĕiŏtēs (1),
grandeur or splendor

MAGNIFIED
1431 gâdal (17), to be
great, make great
5375 nâsâ' (1), to lift up
3170 mĕgalunō (3), to
increase or extol

MAGNIFY
1431 gâdal (15), to be
great, make great
7679 sâgâ' (1), to laud,
extol
1392 dŏxazŏ (1), to
render, esteem glorious
3170 mĕgalunō (2), to
increase or extol

MAGOG
4031 Mâgôwg (4), Magog
3098 Magŏg (1), Magog

MAGOR-MISSABIB
*4036 Mâgôwr
miç-Çâbîyb* (1), affright
from around

MAGPIASH
4047 Magpîy'âsh (1),
exterminator of (the)
moth

MAHALAH
4244 Machlâh (1),
sickness

MAHALALEEL
4111 Mahălal'êl (7),
praise of God

MAHALATH
4257 Machălath (2),
sickness
4258 Machălath (2),
sickness

MAHALI
4249 Machlîy (1), sick

MAHANAIM
4266 Machănayim (13),
double camp

MAHANEH-DAN
4265 Machănêh-Dân (1),
camp of Dan

MAHARAI
4121 Mahăray (3), hasty

MAHATH
4287 Machath (3),
erasure

MAHAVITE
4233 Machăvîym (1),
Machavite

MAHAZIOTH
4238 Machăzîy'ôwth (2),
visions

**MAHER-SHALAL-
HASH-BAZ**
*4122 Mahêr Shâlâl
Châsh Baz* (2), hasting
is he to the booty, swift
to the prey

MAHLAH
4244 Machlâh (4),
sickness

MAHLI
4249 Machlîy (10), sick

MAHLITES
4250 Machlîy (2),
Machlite

MAHLON
4248 Machlôwn (3), sick

MAHLON'S
4248 Machlôwn (1), sick

MAHOL
4235 Mâchôwl (1),
(round) dance

MAID
519 'âmâh (5), female
servant or slave
1330 bᵉthûwlâh (4),
virgin maiden
1331 bᵉthûwlîym (2),
virginity
5291 na'ărâh (4), female
child; servant
5347 nᵉqêbâh (1), female,
woman
5959 'almâh (2), lass,
young woman

8198 shiphchâh (12),
household female slave
2877 kŏrasiŏn (2), little
girl
3814 paidiskē (2), female
slave or servant
3816 pais (1), child; slave
or servant

MAID'S
5291 na'ărâh (1), female
child; servant

MAIDEN
1330 bᵉthûwlâh (2),
virgin maiden
5291 na'ărâh (3), female
child; servant
8198 shiphchâh (2),
household female slave
3816 pais (1), child; slave
or servant

MAIDENS
1330 bᵉthûwlâh (3),
virgin maiden
5291 na'ărâh (13),
female child; servant
8198 shiphchâh (1),
household female slave
3814 paidiskē (1), female
slave or servant

MAIDS
519 'âmâh (3), female
servant or slave
1330 bᵉthûwlâh (3),
virgin maiden
5291 na'ărâh (2), female
child; servant
3814 paidiskē (1), female
slave or servant

MAIDSERVANT
519 'âmâh (13), female
servant or slave
8198 shiphchâh (3),
household female slave

MAIDSERVANT'S
519 'âmâh (1), female
servant or slave

MAIDSERVANTS
519 'âmâh (4), female
servant or slave
8198 shiphchâh (5),
household female slave

MAIDSERVANTS'
519 'âmâh (1), female
servant or slave

MAIL
7193 qasqeseth (2), fish
scales; coat of mail

MAIMED
2782 chârats (1), to be
alert, to decide
376 anapĕrŏs (2),
maimed; crippled
2948 kullŏs (4), crippled,
i.e. maimed

MAINSAIL
736 artĕmōn (1), foresail
or jib

MAINTAIN
2388 châzaq (1), to bind,
restrain, conquer
3198 yâkach (1), to be
correct; to argue
6213 'âsâh (6), to do or
make

English

MAINTAINED
4291 prŏïstēmi (2), to *preside; to practice*

MAINTAINED
6213 'âsâh (1), to *do or make*

MAINTAINEST
8551 tâmak (1), to *obtain, keep fast*

MAINTENANCE
2416 chay (1), *alive; raw; fresh; life*
4415 mᵉlach (Ch.) (1), to *eat salt*

MAJESTY
1347 gâ'ôwn (7), *ascending; majesty*
1348 gê'ûwth (2), *ascending; majesty*
1420 gᵉdûwlâh (1), *greatness, grandeur*
1923 hădar (Ch.) (1), *magnificence, glory*
1926 hâdâr (7), *magnificence*
1935 hôwd (4), *grandeur, majesty*
7238 rᵉbûw (Ch.) (3), *increase*
3168 mĕgalĕiŏtēs (1), *grandeur or splendor*
3172 mĕgalōsunē (3), *divinity, majesty*

MAKAZ
4739 Mâqats (1), *end*

MAKE
1124 bᵉnâ' (Ch.) (1), to *build*
1254 bârâ' (1), to *create; fashion*
1443 gâdar (2), to *build a stone wall*
2015 hâphak (1), to *char ge, overturn*
3331 yàtsa' (1), to *strew as a surface*
3335 yâtsar (1), to *form; potter; to determine*
3635 kᵉlal (Ch.) (2), to *complete*
3772 kârath (31), to *cut (off, down or asunder)*
3823 lâbab (1), *transport with love; to stultify*
5414 nâthan (64), to *give*
5674 'âbar (2), to *cross over; to transition*
6014 'âmar (1), to *gather grain into sheaves*
6213 'âsâh (238), to *make*
6381 pâlâ' (1), to *be, make great, wonderful*
7760 sûwm (65), to *put, place*
7761 sûwm (Ch.) (5), to *put, place*
7896 shîyth (9), to *place*
8074 shâmêm (1), to *devastate; to stupefy*
142 airō (1), to *lift, take up*
347 anaklinō (2), to *lean back, recline*
805 asphalizō (1), to *render secure*
1107 gnōrizō (6), to *make known, reveal*

1303 diatithĕmai (2), to *put apart, i.e. dispose*
1325 didōmi (2), to *give*
1510 ĕimi (1), I *exist, I am*
1519 ĕis (1), to *or into*
1659 ĕlĕuthĕrŏō (2), to *exempt, liberate*
1710 ĕmpŏrĕuŏmai (1), to *trade, do business*
1793 ĕntugchanō (1), to *entreat, petition*
2005 ĕpitĕlĕō (1), to *terminate; to undergo*
2090 hĕtŏimazō (6), to *prepare*
2116 ĕuthunō (1), to *straighten or level*
2146 ĕuprŏsōpĕō (1), to *make a good display*
2165 ĕuphrainō (3), to *rejoice, be glad*
2350 thŏrubĕō (1), to *disturb; clamor*
2433 hilaskŏmai (1), to *conciliate, to atone for*
2476 histēmi (1), to *stand, establish*
2511 katharizō (5), to *cleanse*
2525 kathistēmi (6), to *designate, constitute*
2625 kataklinō (1), to *recline, take a place*
2673 katargĕō (3), to *be, render entirely useless*
2675 katartizō (2), to *repair; to prepare*
2758 kĕnŏō (1), to *make empty*
2936 ktizō (1), to *fabricate, create*
3076 lupĕō (1), to *distress; to be sad*
3753 hŏtĕ (1), *when; as*
3856 paradĕigmatizō (1), to *expose to infamy*
3868 paraitĕŏmai (1), to *deprecate, decline*
4052 pĕrissĕuō (1), to *superabound*
4062 pĕritrĕpō (1), to *drive crazy*
4087 pikrainō (1), to *embitter, turn sour*
4115 platunō (1), to *widen*
4121 plĕŏnazō (1), to *increase; superabound*
4122 plĕŏnĕktĕō (2), to *be covetous*
4135 plērŏphŏrĕō (1), to *fill completely; assure*
4137 plērŏō (1), to *fill, make complete*
4160 pŏiĕō (48), to *make*
4170 pŏlĕmĕō (3), to *battle, make war*
4294 prŏkatartizō (1), to *prepare in advance*
4336 prŏsĕuchŏmai (3), to *supplicate, pray*
4400 prŏchĕirizŏmai (1), to *purpose*
4624 skandalizō (2), to *entrap, i.e. trip up*
4679 sŏphizō (1), to *be cleverly invented*
4692 spĕudō (2), to *urge on*

4766 strōnnumi (1), *strew, i.e. spread*
4820 sumballō (1), to *aid; to join, attack*
4921 sunistaō (1), to *set together, to introduce*
4931 suntĕlĕō (1), to *complete entirely*
5055 tĕlĕō (3), to *end, i.e. complete, execute*
5087 tithēmi (6), to *place*
5319 phanĕrŏō (2), to *render apparent*
5461 phōtizō (1), to *shine or to brighten up*

MAKER
3335 yâtsar (4), to *form; potter; to determine*
6213 'âsâh (13), to *make*
6466 pâ'al (1), to *make*
6467 pô'al (1), *act or work, deed*
1217 dēmiŏurgŏs (1), *worker, mechanic*

MAKERS
2796 chârâsh (1), *skilled fabricator or worker*

MAKEST
6213 'âsâh (6), to *make*
7760 sûwm (1), to *place*
7896 shîyth (1), to *place*
2744 kauchaŏmai (2), to *glory in, rejoice in*
4160 pŏiĕō (4), to *make*

MAKETH
3772 kârath (1), to *cut (off, down or asunder)*
5414 nâthan (2), to *give*
6213 'âsâh (23), to *make*
6466 pâ'al (1), to *make*
7706 Shadday (1), the *Almighty God*
7737 shâvâh (2), to *level, i.e. equalize*
7760 sûwm (6), to *place*
393 anatĕllō (1), to *cause to arise*
1252 diakrinō (1), to *decide; to hesitate*
1308 diaphĕrō (1), to *bear, carry; to differ*
1793 ĕntugchanō (3), to *entreat, petition*
2165 ĕuphrainō (1), to *rejoice, be glad*
2390 iaŏmai (1), to *cure, heal*
2525 kathistēmi (1), to *designate, constitute*
2617 kataischunō (1), to *disgrace or shame*
4160 pŏiĕō (6), to *make*
4977 schizō (1), to *split or sever*
5241 hupĕrĕntugchanō (1), to *intercede in behalf of*
5319 phanĕrŏō (1), to *render apparent*

MAKHELOTH
4721 maqhêl (2), *assembly*

MAKING
3772 kârath (1), to *cut (off, down or asunder)*
4639 ma'ăseh (2), *action; labor*

6213 'âsâh (1), to *make*
208 akurŏō (1), to *invalidate, nullify*
1189 dĕŏmai (1), to *beg, petition, ask*
1252 diakrinō (1), to *decide; to hesitate*
2350 thŏrubĕō (1), to *disturb; clamor*
4148 plŏutizō (1), to *make wealthy*
4160 pŏiĕō (7), to *make*
5567 psallō (1), to *play a stringed instrument*

MAKKEDAH
4719 Maqqêdâh (9), *herding-fold*

MAKTESH
4389 Maktêsh (1), *dell*

MALACHI
4401 Mal'âkîy (1), *ministrative*

MALCHAM
4445 Malkâm (2), *Malcam or Milcom*

MALCHI-SHUA
4444 Malkîyshûwa' (3), *king of wealth*

MALCHIAH
4441 Malkîyâh (9), *appointed by Jehovah*

MALCHIEL
4439 Malkîy'êl (3), *appointed by God*

MALCHIELITES
4440 Malkîy'êlîy (1), *Malkiëlite*

MALCHIJAH
4441 Malkîyâh (6), *appointed by Jehovah*

MALCHIRAM
4443 Malkîyrâm (1), *king of a high one*

MALCHUS
3124 Malchŏs (1), *king*

MALE
376 'îysh (2), *man; male*
2138 zâkûwr (1), *male*
2142 zâkâr (1), to *be male*
2145 zâkâr (37), *male*
730 arrhēn (4), *male*

MALEFACTOR
2555 kakŏpŏiŏs (1), *bad-doer; criminal*

MALEFACTORS
2557 kakŏurgŏs (3), *criminal, evildoer*

MALELEEL
3121 Malĕlĕēl (1), *praise of God*

MALES
2138 zâkûwr (2), *male*
2145 zâkâr (30), *male*

MALICE
2549 kakia (6), *depravity; malignity*

MALICIOUS
4190 pŏnĕrŏs (1), *malice, wicked, bad; crime*

MALICIOUSNESS
2549 kakia (2), *depravity; malignity*

MALIGNITY
2550 kakŏĕthĕia (1), mischievousness

MALLOTHI
4413 Mallôwthîy (2), loquacious

MALLOWS
4408 mallûwach (1), salt-purslain

MALLUCH
4409 Mallûwk (6), regnant

MAMMON
3126 mammōnas (4), wealth, riches

MAMRE
4471 Mamrê' (10), lusty

MAN
120 'âdâm (388), human being; mankind
375 'êyphôh (1), where?; when?; how?
376 'îysh (967), man; male; someone
376+2145 'îysh (1), man; male; someone
582 'ĕnôwsh (32), man; person, human
606 'ĕnâsh (Ch.) (8), man
935 bôw' (1), to go, come
1121 bên (3), son, descendant; people
1121+120 bên (1), son, descendant; people
1167 ba'al (5), master; husband; owner; citizen
1201 Ba'shâ' (1), offensiveness
1396 gâbar (1), to be strong; to prevail
1397 geber (54), person, man
1400 gᵉbar (Ch.) (2), person; someone
1538 gulgôleth (2), skull
2145 zâkâr (11), male
5315 nephesh (3), life; breath; soul; wind
5958 'elem (1), lad, young man
435 anēr (75), man; male
442 anthrōpinŏs (2), human
444 anthrōpŏs (347), human being; mankind
730 arrhēn (2), male
1520 hĕis (3), one
1538 hĕkastŏs (1), each or every
2478 ischurŏs (1), forcible, powerful
3367 mĕdĕis (33), not even one
3494 nĕanias (4), youth
3495 nĕaniskŏs (5), youth
3762 ŏudĕis (96), none, nobody, nothing
3956 pas (3), all, any, every, whole
5100 tis (40), some or any

MAN'S
120 'âdâm (17), human being; mankind
312 'achêr (1), other, another, different
376 'îysh (42), man; male; someone

582 'ĕnôwsh (3), man; person, human
606 'ĕnâsh (Ch.) (3), man
1167 ba'al (1), master; husband; owner; citizen
1397 geber (2), person, man
245 allŏtriŏs (4), not one's own
435 anēr (1), man; male
442 anthrōpinŏs (3), human
444 anthrōpŏs (10), human being; mankind
3494 nĕanias (1), youth
3762 ŏudĕis (1), none, nobody, nothing
5100 tis (3), some or any

MANAEN
3127 Manaēn (1), Manaën

MANAHATH
4506 Mânachath (3), rest

MANAHETHITES
2679 Chătsîy ham-Mᵉnûchôwth (1), midst of the resting-places
2680 Chătsîy ham-Mᵉnachtîy (1), Chatsi-ham-Menachtite

MANASSEH
4519 Mᵉnashsheh (141), causing to forget
4520 Mᵉnashshîy (2), Menashshite

MANASSEH'S
4519 Mᵉnashsheh (4), causing to forget

MANASSES
3128 Manassēs (3), causing to forget

MANASSITES
4519 Mᵉnashsheh (1), causing to forget
4520 Mᵉnashshîy (2), Menashshite

MANDRAKES
1736 dûwday (6), mandrake

MANEH
4488 mâneh (1), weight

MANGER
5336 phatnē (3), crib; stall

MANIFEST
1305 bârar (1), to examine; select
852 aphanēs (1), non-apparent, invisible
1212 dēlŏs (1), clear, plain, evident
1552 ĕkdēlŏs (1), wholly evident, clear
1717 ĕmphanēs (1), apparent, seen, visible
1718 ĕmphanizō (2), to show forth
4271 prŏdēlŏs (1), obvious, evident
5318 phanĕrŏs (7), apparent, visible, clear
5319 phanĕrŏō (23), to render apparent

MANIFESTATION
602 apŏkalupsis (1), disclosure, revelation
5321 phanĕrōsis (2), manifestation

MANIFESTED
5319 phanĕrŏō (10), to render apparent

MANIFESTLY
5319 phanĕrŏō (1), to render apparent

MANIFOLD
7227 rab (3), great
7231 râbab (1), to increase
4164 pŏikilŏs (2), various
4179 pŏllaplasiōn (1), very much more
4182 pŏlupŏikilŏs (1), multifarious

MANKIND
1320+376 bâsâr (1), flesh; body; person
2145 zâkâr (2), male
733 arsĕnŏkŏitēs (2), sodomite
5449+442 phusis (1), genus or sort

MANNA
4478 mân (14), manna, i.e. a "whatness?"
3131 manna (5), edible gum-like food

MANNER
734 'ôrach (1), road; manner of life
1571 gam (1), also; even; yea; though
1697 dâbâr (15), word; matter; thing
1699 dôber (1), grazing pasture
1823 dᵉmûwth (1), resemblance, likeness
1870 derek (8), road; course of life
1881 dâth (1), royal edict or statute
2177 zan (1), form or sort
3541 kôh (6), thus
3605 kôl (1), all, any or every
3651 kên (3), just; right, correct
3654 kên (1), stinging bug
4941 mishpât (36), verdict; decree; justice
8452 tôwrâh (1), custom
72 agōgē (1), mode of living, way of life
195 akribĕia (1), thoroughness
442 anthrōpinŏs (1), human
686 ara (3), then, so, therefore
981 biōsis (1), mode of living
1483 ĕthnikŏs (1), as a Gentile
1485 ĕthŏs (5), usage prescribed
1486 ĕthō (1), to be used by habit or convention
3592 hŏdĕ (1), this or that; these or those

3634 hŏiŏs (2), such or what sort of
3697 hŏpŏiŏs (2), what kind of, what sort of
3779 hŏutō (5), in this way; likewise
4012 pĕri (1), about; around
4169 pŏiŏs (1), what sort of?; which one?
4217 pŏtapŏs (6), of what possible sort?
4458 -pōs (1), particle used in composition
5158 trŏpŏs (2), deportment, character
5179 tupŏs (1), shape, resemblance; "type"
5615 hōsautōs (2), in the same way

MANNERS
2708 chuqqâh (1), to delineate
4941 mishpât (2), verdict; formal decree; justice
2239 ēthŏs (1), usage, i.e. moral habits
4187 pŏlutrŏpōs (1), in many ways
5159 trŏpŏphŏrĕō (1), to endure one's habits

MANOAH
4495 Mânôwach (18), rest

MANSERVANT
5650 'ebed (12), servant

MANSERVANT'S
5650 'ebed (1), servant

MANSERVANTS
5650 'ebed (1), servant

MANSIONS
3438 mŏnē (1), residence, dwelling place

MANSLAYER
7523 râtsach (2), to murder

MANSLAYERS
409 andrŏphŏnŏs (1), murderer

MANTLE
155 'addereth (5), large; splendid
4598 mᵉʻîyl (7), outer garment or robe
8063 sᵉmîykâh (1), rug

MANTLES
4595 ma'ătâphâh (1), cloak

MANY
1995 hâmôwn (3), noise, tumult; many, crowd
3513 kâbad (2), to be heavy, severe, dull
3605 kôl (1), all, any or every
7227 rab (196), great
7230 rôb (4), abundance
7231 râbab (6), to increase; to multiply
7233 rᵉbâbâh (1), myriad
7235 râbâh (27), to increase
7690 saggîy' (Ch.) (2), large
2425 hikanŏs (11), ample; fit

3745 hŏsŏs (31), *as much as*
4119 plěiŏn (14), *more*
4183 pŏlus (207), *much, many*
4214 pŏsŏs (11), *how much?; how much!*
5118 tŏsŏutŏs (6), *such great*

MAOCH
4582 Mâ'ôwk (1), *oppressed*

MAON
4584 Mâ'ôwn (7), *residence*

MAONITES
4584 Mâ'ôwn (1), *residence*

MAR
3510 kâ'ab (1), to feel *pain; to grieve; to spoil*
5420 nâthaç (1), *to tear up*
7843 shâchath (4), to *decay; to ruin*

MARA
4755 Mârâ' (1), *bitter*

MARAH
4785 Mârâh (5), *bitter*

MARALAH
4831 Mar'ălâh (1), (poss.) *earthquake*

MARANATHA
3134 maran atha (1), *Come, Lord!*

MARBLE
7898 shayith (1), wild *growth* of weeds
8336 shêsh (2), *white* linen; *white* marble
8338 shâwshâw (1), (poss.) to *annihilate*
3139 marmarŏs (1), sparkling *white marble*

MARCH
1980 hâlak (1), to *walk; live a certain way*
3212 yâlak (2), to *walk; to live; to carry*
6805 tsâ'ad (2), to *pace, step regularly*

MARCHED
5265 nâça' (1), *start on a journey*

MARCHEDST
6805 tsâ'ad (1), to *pace, step regularly*

MARCUS
3138 Markŏs (3), *Marcus*

MARESHAH
4762 Mar'êshâh (8), *summit*

MARINERS
4419 mallâch (4), *salt-water sailor*
7751 shûwṭ (1), to *travel, roam*

MARISHES
1360 gebe' (1), *reservoir; marsh*

MARK
226 'ôwth (1), *signal, sign*

995 bîyn (1), to *understand; discern*
3045 yâda' (3), to *know*
4307 maṭṭârâ' (3), *jail* (guard-house); *aim*
4645 miphgâ' (1), *object of attack, target*
6437 pânâh (1), to *turn, to face*
7181 qâshab (1), to *prick up the ears*
7200 râ'âh (1), to *see*
7760 sûwm (2), to *place*
7896 shîyth (1), to *place*
8104 shâmar (4), to *watch*
8420 tâv (2), *mark; signature*
3138 Markŏs (5), *Marcus*
4648 skŏpěŏ (2), to *watch out for*, i.e. to *regard*
4649 skŏpŏs (1), *goal*
5480 charagma (8), *mark, stamp*

MARKED
2856 châtham (1), to *close up; to affix a seal*
3799 kâtham (1), to *inscribe* indelibly
7181 qâshab (1), to *prick up the ears*
8104 shâmar (2), to *watch*
1907 ěpěchŏ (1), to *pay attention to*

MARKEST
8104 shâmar (1), to *watch*

MARKET
4627 ma'ărâb (4), *mercantile goods*
58 agŏra (2), *town-square, market*

MARKETH
8104 shâmar (1), to *watch*
8388 tâ'ar (2), to *delineate; to extend*

MARKETPLACE
58 agŏra (3), *town-square, market*

MARKETPLACES
58 agŏra (1), *town-square, market*

MARKETS
58 agŏra (4), *town-square, market*

MARKS
7085 qa'ăqa' (1), *incision or gash*
4742 stigma (1), *mark, scar* of service

MAROTH
4796 Mârôwth (1), *bitter springs*

MARRED
4893 mishchâth (1), *disfigurement*
7843 shâchath (3), to *decay; to ruin*
622 apŏllumi (1), to *destroy* fully

MARRIAGE
1984 hâlal (1), to *shine, flash, radiate*

5772 'ôwnâh (1), *marital cohabitation*
1061 gamiskŏ (1), to *espouse*
1062 gamŏs (9), *nuptials*
1547 ěkgamizŏ (3), to *marry off* a daughter
1548 ěkgamiskŏ (4), to *marry off* a daughter

MARRIAGES
2859 châthan (3), to *be related* by marriage

MARRIED
802 'ishshâh (3), *woman, wife; women, wives*
1166 bâ'al (7), to *be master; to marry*
1166+802 bâ'al (1), to *be master; to marry*
3427 yâshab (1), to *dwell, to remain; to settle*
3947 lâqach (4), to *take*
5375 nâsâ' (1), to *lift up*
1060 gaměŏ (9), to *wed*
1096 ginŏmai (3), to *be, become*

MARRIETH
1166 bâ'al (1), to *be master; to marry*
1060 gaměŏ (3), to *wed*

MARROW
2459 cheleb (1), *fat; choice* part
4221 môach (1), bone *marrow*
4229 mâchâh (1), to *erase; to grease*
8250 shiqqûwy (1), *beverage; refreshment*
3452 muělŏs (1), *marrow*

MARRY
802 'ishshâh (2), *woman, wife; women, wives*
1166 bâ'al (1), to *be master; to marry*
1961+376 hâyâh (1), to *exist*, i.e. *be* or *become*
2992 yâbam (1), to *marry* a dead brother's widow
1060 gaměŏ (16), to *wed*
1918 ěpigambrěuŏ (1), to *form an affinity with*

MARRYING
3427 yâshab (1), to *dwell, to remain; to settle*
1060 gaměŏ (1), to *wed*

MARS'
697 Arěiŏs Pagŏs (1), *rock of Ares*

MARSENA
4826 Marçěnâ' (1), *Marsena*

MART
5505 çâchar (1), *profit from trade*

MARTHA
3136 Martha (12), *mistress*, i.e. lady *lord*

MARTYR
3144 martus (2), *witness*

MARTYRS
3144 martus (1), *witness*

MARVEL
8539 tâmahh (1), to *be astounded*

2296 thaumazŏ (9), to *wonder; to admire*
2298 thaumastŏs (1), *wonderful, marvelous*

MARVELLED
8539 tâmahh (2), to *be astounded*
2296 thaumazŏ (21), to *wonder; to admire*

MARVELLOUS
6381 pâlâ' (16), to *be, make great, wonderful*
6382 pele' (1), *miracle*
6395 pâlâh (1), to *distinguish*
2298 thaumastŏs (6), *wonderful, marvelous*

MARVELLOUSLY
6381 pâlâ' (2), to *be, make great, wonderful*
8539 tâmahh (1), to *be astounded*

MARVELS
6381 pâlâ' (1), to *be, make great, wonderful*

MARY
3137 Maria (54), *rebelliously*

MASCHIL
4905 maskîyl (13), *instructional* poem

MASH
4851 Mash (1), *Mash*

MASHAL
4913 Mâshâl (1), *request*

MASONS
1443 gâdar (2), to *build a stone wall*
2672 châtsab (3), to *cut stone or carve wood*

MASREKAH
4957 Masrêqâh (2), *vineyard*

MASSA
4854 Massâ' (2), *burden*

MASSAH
4532 Maççâh (4), *testing*

MAST
2260 chibbêl (1), ship's *mast*
8650 tôren (1), mast ship *pole; flag-staff pole*

MASTER
113 'âdôwn (75), *sovereign*, i.e. *controller*
729 'áraz (2), of *cedar*
1167 ba'al (3), *master; husband; owner; citizen*
5782 'ûwr (1), to *awake*
7227 rab (1), *great*
8269 sar (1), *head person, ruler*
1320 didaskŏlŏs (47), *instructor*
1988 ěpistatēs (6), *commander*
2519 kathēgětēs (2), *teacher*
2942 kuběrnētēs (1), *helmsman, captain*
2962 kuriŏs (4), *supreme, controller, Mr.*
3617 ŏikŏděspŏtēs (2), *head of a family*

4461 rhabbi (8), *my master*

MASTER'S
113 'âdôwn (22), *sovereign, i.e. controller*
1167 ba'al (1), *master; husband; owner; citizen*
1203 děspŏtēs (1), *absolute ruler*

MASTERBUILDER
753 architěktōn (1), *architect, expert builder*

MASTERS
113 'âdôwn (5), *sovereign, i.e. controller*
1167 ba'al (1), *master; husband; owner; citizen*
1203 děspŏtēs (4), *absolute ruler*
1320 didaskalŏs (1), *instructor*
2519 kathēgētēs (1), *teacher*
2962 kuriŏs (8), *supreme, controller, Mr.*

MASTERS'
113 'âdôwn (1), *sovereign, i.e. controller*
2962 kuriŏs (1), *supreme, controller, Mr.*

MASTERY
1369 gᵉbûwrâh (1), *force; valor; victory*
6981 Qôwrê' (1), *crier*

MASTS
8650 tôren (1), *mast ship pole; flag-staff pole*

MATE
7468 rᵉ'ûwth (2), *female associate*

MATHUSALA
3103 Mathŏusala (1), *man of a dart*

MATRED
4308 Maṭrêd (2), *propulsive*

MATRI
4309 Maṭrîy (1), *rainy*

MATRIX
7358 rechem (5), *womb*

MATTAN
4977 Mattân (3), *present, gift*

MATTANAH
4980 Mattânâh (2), *present; sacrificial offering; bribe*

MATTANIAH
4983 Mattanyâh (16), *gift of Jehovah*

MATTATHA
3160 Mattatha (1), *gift of Jehovah*

MATTATHAH
4992 Mattattâh (1), *gift of Jehovah*

MATTATHIAS
3161 Mattathias (2), *gift of Jehovah*

MATTENAI
4982 Mattᵉnay (3), *liberal*

MATTER
1697 dâbâr (48), *word; matter; thing*
1836 dên (Ch.) (1), *this*
2659 châphêr (1), *to shame, reproach*
2941 ṭa'am (Ch.) (1), *sentence, command*
3602 kâkâh (1), *just so*
4405 millâh (1), *word; discourse; speech*
4406 millâh (Ch.) (4), *command, discourse*
6600 pithgâm (Ch.) (2), *decree; report*
1308 diaphěrō (1), *to bear, carry; to differ*
2596 kata (1), *down; according to*
3056 lŏgŏs (4), *word, matter, thing*
4229 pragma (3), *matter, deed, affair*
5208 hulē (1), *forest, i.e. wood fuel*

MATTERS
1419 gâdôwl (1), *great*
1697 dâbâr (15), *word; matter; thing*
4406 millâh (Ch.) (1), *word, command*

MATTHAN
3157 Matthan (2), *present, gift*

MATTHAT
3158 Matthat (2), *gift of Jehovah*

MATTHEW
3156 Matthaiŏs (5), *gift of Jehovah*

MATTHIAS
3159 Matthias (2), *gift of Jehovah*

MATTITHIAH
4993 Mattithyâh (8), *gift of Jehovah*

MATTOCK
4281 machărêshâh (1), (poss.) *pick-axe*
4576 ma'dêr (1), *hoe*

MATTOCKS
2719 chereb (1), *knife, sword*
4281 machărêshâh (1), (poss.) *pick-axe*

MAUL
4650 mêphîyts (1), *mallet-club*

MAW
6896 qêbâh (1), *paunch cavity; stomach*

MAY
194 'ûwlay (4), *if not; perhaps*
3201 yâkôl (11), *to be able*
1410 dunamai (9), *to be able or possible*
1832 ĕxěsti (1), *it is right, it is proper*
2481 isŏs (1), *perhaps*

MAYEST
3201 yâkôl (5), *to be able*
1410 dunamai (2), *to be able or possible*

1832 ĕxěsti (1), *it is right, it is proper*

MAZZAROTH
4216 Mazzârâh (1), *constellation*

ME-JARKON
4313 Mêy hay-Yarqôwn (1), *water of the yellowness*

MEADOW
260 'âchûw (2), *bulrush or any marshy grass*

MEADOWS
4629 ma'ăreh (1), *nude place, i.e. a common*

MEAH
3968 Mê'âh (2), *hundred*

MEAL
7058 qemach (9), *flour*
7058+5560 qemach (1), *flour*
224 alěurŏn (2), *flour*

MEALTIME
6256+400 'êth (1), *time*

MEAN
120 'âdâm (3), *human being; mankind*
2823 châshôk (1), *obscure*
5704+3541 'ad (1), *as far (long) as; during*
767 asēmŏs (1), *ignoble, i.e. ordinary*
1498 ĕiĕn (1), *might could, would*
2076 ĕsti (1), *he (she or it) is; they are*
2309+1511 thělō (1), *to will; to desire; to choose*
3342 mětaxu (2), *betwixt; meanwhile*
4160 pŏiĕō (1), *to make*

MEANETH
1819 dâmâh (1), *to resemble, liken*
2076 ĕsti (2), *he (she or it) is; they are*
2309+1511 thělō (1), *to will; to desire; to choose*

MEANING
998 bîynâh (1), *understanding*
1411 dunamis (1), *force, power, miracle*
3195 mĕllō (1), *to intend, i.e. be about to*

MEANS
1157 bᵉ'ad (1), *at, beside, among, behind, for*
3027 yâd (4), *hand; power*
4284 machăshâbâh (1), *contrivance; plan*
6903 qᵉbêl (Ch.) (1), *on account of, so as, since*
1096 ginŏmai (1), *to be, become*
3361 mē (1), *not; lest*
3364 ŏu mē (1), *not at all, absolutely not*
3843 pantōs (2), *entirely; at all events*
4458 -pōs (9), *particle used in composition*
4459 pōs (2), *in what way?; how?; how much!*

5158 trŏpŏs (2), *deportment, character*

MEANT
2803 châshab (1), *to think, regard; to value*
1498 ĕiĕn (2), *might could, would be*

MEARAH
4632 Mᵉ'ârâh (1), *cave*

MEASURE
374 'êyphâh (2), *dry grain measure*
520 'ammâh (1), *cubit*
2706 chôq (1), *appointment; allotment*
4055 mad (1), *vesture, garment; carpet*
4058 mâdad (7), *to measure*
4060 middâh (15), *measure; portion*
4884 mᵉsûwrâh (4), *liquid measure*
4941 mishpâṭ (2), *verdict; formal decree; justice*
4971 mathkôneth (1), *proportion*
5429 çᵉ'âh (3), *volume measure for grain*
5432 ça'çᵉ'âh (1), *moderation*
7991 shâlîysh (2), *three-fold measure*
8506 tôken (1), *fixed quantity*
280 amětrŏs (2), *immoderate*
3354 mětrĕō (3), *to admeasure*
3358 mětrŏn (13), *what is apportioned*
4053 pěrissŏs (1), *superabundant*
4057 pěrissŏs (1), *superabundantly*
5234 hupěrballŏntōs (1), *to a greater degree*
5236 hupěrbŏlē (2), *super-eminence*
5249 hupěrpěrissŏs (1), *beyond all measure*
5518 chŏinix (1), *about a dry quart measure*

MEASURED
4058 mâdad (40), *to measure*
4128 mûwd (1), *to shake*
488 antimětrĕō (2), *to measure in return*
3354 mětrĕō (3), *to admeasure*

MEASURES
374 'êyphâh (2), *dry grain measure*
3734 kôr (8), *dry measure*
4055 mad (1), *vesture, garment; carpet*
4060 middâh (12), *measure; portion*
4461 mêmad (1), *measurement*
5429 çᵉ'âh (6), *volume measure for grain*
943 batŏs (1), *measure for liquids*
2884 kŏrŏs (1), *dry bushel measure*

4568 satŏn (2), *measure of about 12 dry quarts*
5518 chŏinix (1), *about a dry quart measure*

MEASURING
4060 middâh (10), *measure; portion*
3354 mĕtrĕŏ (1), to *admeasure*

MEAT
396 'ăkîylâh (1), *food*
398 'ăkal (5), to *eat*
400 'ôkel (18), *food*
402 'oklâh (8), *food*
1262 bârâh (1), to *feed*
1267 bârûwth (1), *food*
1279 biryâh (3), *food*
2964 ţereph (3), *fresh torn prey*
3899 lechem (18), *food, bread*
3978 ma'ăkâl (22), *food, something to eat*
4202 mâzôwn (1), *food, provisions*
4203 mâzôwn (Ch.) (2), *food, provisions*
6595 path (1), *bit, morsel*
6598 pathbag (6), *dainty food*
6720 tsêydâh (1), *food, supplies*
1033 brōma (10), *food*
1034 brōsimŏs (1), *eatable*
1035 brōsis (7), *food; rusting corrosion*
4371 prŏsphagiŏn (1), *little fish*
4620 sitŏmĕtrŏn (1), *allowance or ration*
5132 trapĕza (1), *four-legged table*
5160 trŏphē (13), *nourishment; rations*
5315 phagŏ (1), *outer garment, i.e. a mantle*

MEATS
1033 brōma (6), *food*

MEBUNNAI
4012 Mᵉbunnay (1), *built up*

MECHERATHITE
4382 Mᵉkêrâthîy (1), *Mekerathite*

MEDAD
4312 Mêydâd (2), *affectionate*

MEDAN
4091 Mᵉdân (2), *contest or quarrel*

MEDDLE
1624 gârâh (4), to *provoke to anger*
6148 'ârab (2), to *intermix*

MEDDLED
1566 gâla' (1), to *be obstinate; to burst forth*

MEDDLETH
5674 'âbar (1), to *cross over; to transition*

MEDDLING
1566 gâla' (1), to *be obstinate; to burst forth*

MEDE
4075 Mâday (1), *Madian*

MEDEBA
4311 Mêydᵉbâ' (5), *water of quiet*

MEDES
4074 Mâday (9), *Madai*
4076 Mâday (Ch.) (4), *Madai*
3370 Mēdŏs (1), *inhabitant of Media*

MEDIA
4074 Mâday (6), *Madai*

MEDIAN
4077 Mâday (Ch.) (1), *Madian*

MEDIATOR
3316 mĕsitēs (6), *reconciler, intercessor*

MEDICINE
1456 gêhâh (1), *medicinal cure*
8644 tᵉrûwphâh (1), *remedy, healing*

MEDICINES
7499 rᵉphû'âh (2), *medicament, healing*

MEDITATE
1897 hâgâh (6), to *murmur, ponder*
7742 sûwach (1), to *muse pensively*
7878 sîyach (5), to *ponder, muse aloud*
3191 mĕlĕtaŏ (1), to *plot, think about*
4304 prŏmĕlĕtaŏ (1), to *premeditate*

MEDITATION
1900 hâgûwth (1), *musing, meditation*
1901 hâgîyg (1), *complaint, sighing*
1902 higgâyôwn (1), *musical notation*
7879 sîyach (1), *uttered contemplation*
7881 sîychâh (2), *reflection; devotion*

MEEK
6035 'ânâv (13), *needy; oppressed*
4235 pra₁ŏs (1), *gentle, i.e. humble*
4239 praüs (3), *mild, humble, gentle*

MEEKNESS
6037 'anvâh (1), *mildness; oppressed*
6038 'ănâvâh (1), *modesty, clemency*
4236 pra₁ŏtēs (9), *gentleness, humility*
4240 praütēs (3), *humility, meekness*

MEET
749 'ărak (Ch.) (1), to *suit*
1121 bên (1), *son, descendant; people*
3259 yâ'ad (8), to *meet; to summon; to direct*
3474 yâshar (1), to *be straight; to make right*
3476 yôsher (1), *right*
3477 yâshâr (1), *straight*

3559 kûwn (1), to *set up: establish, fix, prepare*
4672 mâtsâ' (2), to *find or acquire; to occur*
5828 'êzer (2), *aid*
6213 'âsâh (2), to *make*
6293 pâga' (5), to *impinge*
6298 pâgash (6), to *come in contact with*
6440 pânîym (3), *face; front*
6743 tsâlach (1), to *push forward*
7125 qîr'âh (70), to *encounter, to happen*
7136 qârâh (1), to *bring about; to impose*
7200 râ'âh (1), to *see*
514 axiŏs (4), *deserving, comparable or suitable*
528 apantaŏ (2), *encounter, meet*
529 apantēsis (4), *friendly encounter*
1163 dĕi (2), *it is (was) necessary*
1342 dikaiŏs (2), *equitable, holy*
2111 ĕuthĕtŏs (1), *appropriate, suitable*
2173 ĕuchrēstŏs (1), *useful, serviceable*
2425 hikanŏs (1), *ample; fit*
2427 hikanoŏ (1), to *make competent*
2570 kalŏs (2), *good; beautiful; valuable*
4876 sunantaŏ (1), to *meet with; to occur*
4877 sunantēsis (1), *meeting with*
5222 hupantēsis (1), *encounter; concurrence*

MEETEST
3477 yâshâr (1), *straight*
6293 pâga' (1), to *impinge*

MEETETH
6293 pâga' (2), to *impinge*
6298 pâgash (2), to *come in contact with*

MEETING
6116 'ătsârâh (1), *assembly*
7125 qîr'âh (1), to *encounter, to happen*

MEGIDDO
4023 Mᵉgiddôwn (11), *rendezvous*

MEGIDDON
4023 Mᵉgiddôwn (1), *rendezvous*

MEHETABEEL
4105 Mᵉhêyţab'êl (1), *bettered of God*

MEHETABEL
4105 Mᵉhêyţab'êl (2), *bettered of God*

MEHIDA
4240 Mᵉchîydâ' (2), *junction*

MEHIR
4243 Mᵉchîyr (1), *price*

MEHOLATHITE
4259 Mᵉchôlâthîy (2), *Mecholathite*

MEHUJAEL
4232 Mᵉchûwyâ'êl (2), *smitten of God*

MEHUMAN
4104 Mᵉhûwmân (1), *Mehuman*

MEHUNIM
4586 Mᵉ'ûwnîy (1), *Menite*

MEHUNIMS
4586 Mᵉ'ûwnîy (1), *Menite*

MEKONAH
4368 Mᵉkônâh (1), *base*

MELATIAH
4424 Mᵉlaţyâh (1), *Jehovah has delivered*

MELCHI
3197 Mĕlchi (2), *king*

MELCHI-SHUA
4444 Malkîyshûwa' (2), *king of wealth*

MELCHIAH
4441 Malkîyâh (1), *appointed by Jehovah*

MELCHISEDEC
3198 Mĕlchisĕdĕk (9), *king of right*

MELCHIZEDEK
4442 Malkîy-Tsedeq (2), *king of right*

MELEA
3190 Mĕlĕas (1), *Meleas*

MELECH
4429 Melek (2), *king*

MELICU
4409 Mallûwk (1), *regnant*

MELITA
3194 Mĕlitē (1), *Melita*

MELODY
2172 zimrâh (2), *song*
5059 nâgan (1), to *play; to make music*
5567 psallō (1), to *play a stringed instrument*

MELONS
20 'ăbaţţîyach (1), *melon*

MELT
3988 mâ'aç (1), to *spurn; to disappear*
4127 mûwg (4), to *soften, flow down, disappear*
4529 mâçâh (1), to *dissolve, melt*
4549 mâçaç (6), to *waste; to faint*
5413 nâthak (2), to *pour out; to liquefy, melt*
6884 tsâraph (1), to *fuse metal; to refine*
3089 luŏ (1), to *loosen*
5080 tēkō (1), to *liquefy, melt*

MELTED
2046 hittûwk (1), *melting*
4127 mûwg (3), to *soften, flow down, disappear*
4549 mâçaç (6), to *waste; to faint fear or grief*
5140 nâzal (1), to *drip, or shed by trickling*
5413 nâthak (2), to *pour out; to liquefy, melt*

MELTETH
1811 dâlaph (1), to *drip*
4549 mâçaç (3), to *waste*; to *faint*
5258 nâçak (1), to *pour* a libation
6884 tsâraph (1), to *fuse* metal; to *refine*
8557 temeç (1), *melting disappearance*

MELTING
2003 hâmâç (1), dry *twig* or *brushwood*

MELZAR
4453 Meltsâr (2), *court officer* (poss.) *butler*

MEMBER
3196 *mĕlŏs* (5), *limb* or part of the body

MEMBERS
3338 yâtsûr (1), *structure, human frame*
3196 *mĕlŏs* (29), *limb* or part of the body

MEMORIAL
234 'azkârâh (7), *remembrance-offering*
2143 zêker (5), *recollection; commemoration*
2146 zikrôwn (17), *commemoration*
3422 *mnēmŏsunŏn* (3), *memorandum*

MEMORY
2143 zêker (5), *commemoration*

MEMPHIS
4644 Môph (1), *Moph*

MEMUCAN
4462 Mᵉmûwkân (3), *Memucan* or *Momucan*

MEN
120 'âdâm (107), *human being; mankind*
376 'îysh (211), *man; male; someone*
582 'ĕnôwsh (491), *man; person, human*
606 'ĕnâsh (Ch.) (12), *man*
1121 bên (16), *son, descendant; people*
1167 ba'al (20), *master; husband; owner; citizen*
1368 gibbôwr (1), *powerful; great warrior*
1397 geber (6), *person, man*
1400 gᵉbar (Ch.) (18), *person; someone*
2145 zâkâr (1), *male*
2388 châzaq (1), to *be strong; courageous*
4962 math (14), *men*
4974 mᵉthôm (1), *completely*
407 *andrizŏmai* (1), to *act manly*
435 *anēr* (79), *man; male*
442 *anthrŏpinŏs* (1), *human*
444 *anthrŏpŏs* (192), *human being; mankind*
730 *arrhēn* (3), *male*
3495 *nĕaniskŏs* (5), *youth*

MERAIAH
4811 Mᵉrâyâh (1), *rebellion*

MERAIOTH
4812 Mᵉrâyôwth (7), *rebellious*

MERARI
4847 Mᵉrârîy (39), *bitter*

MERARITES
4848 Mᵉrârîy (1), *Merarite*

MERATHAIM
4850 Mᵉrâthayim (1), *double bitterness*

MERCHANDISE
4267 machănaq (1), *choking, strangling*
4627 ma'ărâb (4), *mercantile goods*
4819 markôleth (1), *mart, market*
5504 çachar (4), *profit from trade*
5505 çâchar (2), *profit from trade*
5506 çᵉchôrâh (1), *traffic*
6014 'âmar (2), to *gather grain into sheaves*
7404 rᵉkullâh (2), *peddled trade*
1117 gŏmŏs (2), *cargo, wares or freight*
1711 *ĕmpŏria* (1), *traffic, business trade*
1712 *ĕmpŏriŏn* (1), *emporium* marketplace

MERCHANT
3667 Kᵉna'an (3), *humiliated*
5503 çâchar (4), to *travel round; to palpitate*
7402 râkal (3), to *travel for trading*
1713 *ĕmpŏrŏs* (1), *tradesman, merchant*

MERCHANTMEN
5503 çâchar (1), to *travel round; to palpitate*
8446 tûwr (1), to *wander, meander* for trade

MERCHANTS
3669 Kᵉna'ănîy (1), *Kenaanite; merchant*
5503 çâchar (9), to *travel round; to palpitate*
7402 râkal (14), to *travel for trading*
1713 *ĕmpŏrŏs* (4), *tradesman, merchant*

MERCHANTS'
5503 çâchar (1), to *travel round; to palpitate*

MERCIES
2617 cheçed (9), *kindness, favor*
7356 racham (25), *compassion; womb*
7359 rᵉchêm (Ch.) (1), *pity*
3628 ŏiktirmŏs (4), *pity, compassion*
3741 hŏsiŏs (1), *hallowed, pious, sacred*

MEN'S
120 'âdâm (10), *human being; mankind*
582 'ĕnôwsh (2), *man; person, human*
444 *anthrŏpŏs* (4), *human being; mankind*
4283 prŏŭaggĕlizŏmai (1), to *announce* glad news *in advance*

MENAHEM
4505 Mᵉnachêm (8), *comforter*

MENAN
3104 Maïnan (1), *Maïnan*

MEND
2388 châzaq (1), to *fasten* upon; to *bind*

MENDING
2675 katartizō (2), to *repair; to prepare*

MENE
4484 menê' (Ch.) (2), *numbered*

MENPLEASERS
441 *anthrōparĕskŏs* (2), *man-courting, fawning*

MENSERVANTS
5650 'ebed (9), *servant*
3816 pais (1), *child; slave* or *servant*

MENSTEALERS
405 *andrapŏdistēs* (1), *enslaver, kidnapper*

MENSTRUOUS
1739 dâveh (1), *menstrual; fainting*
5079 niddâh (2), *time of menstrual impurity*

MENTION
2142 zâkar (18), to *remember; to mention*
3417 mnĕia (4), *recollection; recital*
3421 mnēmŏnĕuō (1), to *exercise memory*

MENTIONED
935 bôw' (1), to *go, come*
2142 zâkar (3), to *remember; to mention*
5927 'âlâh (1), to *ascend, be high, mount*
7121 qârâ' (1), to *call out*
8052 shᵉmûw'âh (1), *announcement*

MEONENIM
6049 'ânan (1), to *cover, becloud; to act covertly*

MEONOTHAI
4587 Mᵉ'ôwnôthay (1), *habitative*

MEPHAATH
4158 Môwpha'ath (4), *illuminative*

MEPHIBOSHETH
4648 Mᵉphîybôsheth (15), *dispeller of Shame*

MERAB
4764 Mêrâb (3), *increase*

MERCIES'
2617 cheçed (3), *kindness, favor*
7356 racham (1), *compassion; womb*

MERCIFUL
2551 chemlâh (1), *commiseration, pity*
2603 chânan (11), to *implore*
2616 châçad (2), to *reprove, shame*
2617 cheçed (5), *kindness, favor*
2623 châçîyd (3), *religiously pious, godly*
3722 kâphar (2), to *cover; to expiate*
7349 rachûwm (8), *compassionate*
7355 râcham (1), to *be compassionate*
1655 ĕlĕēmōn (2), *compassion*
2433 hilaskŏmai (1), to *conciliate, to atone for*
2436 hilĕŏs (1), God be *gracious!, far* be it!
3629 ŏiktirmōn (2), *compassionate*

MERCURIUS
2060 Hĕrmēs (1), *born of god Hermes*

MERCY
2603 chânan (16), to *implore*
2604 chănan (Ch.) (1), to *favor*
2617 cheçed (137), *kindness, favor*
3727 kappôreth (27), *lid, cover*
7355 râcham (31), to *be compassionate*
7356 racham (4), *compassion; womb*
448 anilĕŏs (1), *inexorable, merciless*
1653 ĕlĕĕŏ (27), to *give out compassion*
1656 ĕlĕŏs (28), *compassion*
3628 ŏiktirmŏs (1), *pity, compassion*
3629 ŏiktirmōn (1), *compassionate*

MERCYSEAT
2435 hilastēriŏn (1), *expiatory* place

MERED
4778 Mered (2), *rebellion*

MEREMOTH
4822 Mᵉrêmôwth (6), *heights*

MERES
4825 Mereç (1), *Meres*

MERIB-BAAL
4807 Mᵉrîyb Ba'al (3), *quarreller of Baal*
4810 Mᵉrîy Ba'al (1), *rebellion against Baal*

MERIBAH
4809 Mᵉrîybâh (6), *quarrel*

English

MERIBAH-KADESH
4809+6946 Mᵉrîybâh (1), quarrel

MERODACH
4781 Mᵉrôdâk (1), Merodak

MERODACH-BALADAN
4757 Mᵉrô'dak Bal'âdân (1), Merodak-Baladan

MEROM
4792 Mêrôwm (2), height

MERONOTHITE
4824 Mêrônôthîy (2), Meronothite

MEROZ
4789 Mêrôwz (1), Meroz

MERRILY
8056 sâmêach (1), blithe or gleeful

MERRY
1974 hillûwl (1), harvest celebration
2896 ṭôwb (7), good; well
3190 yâṭab (5), to be, make well
7832 sâchaq (2), to laugh; to scorn; to play
7937 shâkar (1), to become tipsy, to satiate
8055 sâmach (2), to be, make gleesome
8056 sâmêach (3), blithe or gleeful
2114 ĕuthumĕō (1), to be cheerful; keep courage
2165 ĕuphrainō (6), to rejoice, be glad

MERRYHEARTED
8056+3820 sâmêach (1), blithe or gleeful

MESECH
4902 Meshek (1), Meshek

MESHA
4331 Mêyshâ' (1), departure
4337 Mêyshâ' (1), safety
4338 Mêyshâ' (1), safety
4852 Mêshâ' (1), Mesha

MESHACH
4335 Mêyshak (1), Meshak
4336 Mêyshak (Ch.) (14), Meshak

MESHECH
4902 Meshek (8), Meshek

MESHELEMIAH
4920 Mᵉshelemyâh (4), ally of Jehovah

MESHEZABEEL
4898 Mᵉshêyzab'êl (3), delivered of God

MESHILLEMITH
4921 Mᵉshillêmîyth (1), reconciliation

MESHILLEMOTH
4919 Mᵉshillêmôwth (2), reconciliations

MESHOBAB
4877 Mᵉshôwbâb (1), returned

MESHULLAM
4918 Mᵉshullâm (25), allied

MESHULLEMETH
4922 Mᵉshullemeth (1), Meshullemeth

MESOBAITE
4677 Mᵉtsôbâyâh (1), found of Jehovah

MESOPOTAMIA
763 'Ăram Nahărayim (5), Aram of (the) two rivers
3318 Mĕsŏpŏtamia (2), between the Rivers

MESS
4864 mas'êth (2), raising; beacon; present

MESSAGE
1697 dâbâr (3), word; matter; thing
4400 mal'ăkûwth (1), message
31 aggĕlia (1), message
1860 ĕpaggĕlia (1), divine assurance
4242 prĕsbĕia (1), delegates

MESSENGER
1319 bâsar (1), to announce (good news)
4397 mal'âk (24), messenger
5046 nâgad (2), to announce
6680 tsâvâh (1), to constitute, enjoin
6735 tsîyr (1), hinge; herald or errand-doer
32 aggĕlŏs (4), messenger; angel
652 apŏstŏlŏs (1), commissioner of Christ

MESSENGERS
4397 mal'âk (74), messenger
6735 tsîyr (1), hinge; herald or errand-doer
32 aggĕlŏs (3), messenger; angel
652 apŏstŏlŏs (1), commissioner of Christ

MESSES
4864 mas'êth (1), raising; beacon; present

MESSIAH
4899 mâshîyach (2), consecrated; Messiah

MESSIAS
3323 Mĕssias (2), consecrated

MET
3259 yâ'ad (1), to meet; to summon; to direct
4672 mâtsâ' (3), to occur, meet or be present
6293 pâga' (4), to impinge
6298 pâgash (7), to come in contact with
6923 qâdam (2), to anticipate, meet
7122 qârâ' (2), to encounter, to happen
7125 qir'âh (3), to encounter, to happen
7135 qârâh (1), coolness; cold
7136 qârâh (4), to bring about; to impose

MESHULLAM *(cont.)*

296 amphŏdŏn (1), fork in the road
528 apantaō (5), encounter, meet
3909 paratugchanō (1), to chance near
4820 sumballō (1), to aid; to join, attack
4876 sunantaō (4), to meet with; to occur
5221 hupantaō (5), to meet, encounter

METE
4058 mâdad (3), to measure
3354 mĕtrĕō (3), to admeasure

METED
6978 qav-qav (2), stalwart
8505 tâkan (1), to balance, i.e. measure

METEYARD
4060 middâh (1), measure; portion

METHEG-AMMAH
4965 Metheg hâ-'Ammâh (1), bit of the metropolis

METHUSAEL
4967 Mᵉthûwshâ'êl (2), man who (is) of God

METHUSELAH
4968 Mᵉthûwshelach (6), man of a dart

MEUNIM
4586 Mᵉ'ûwnîy (1), Menite

MEZAHAB
4314 Mêy Zâhâb (2), water of gold

MIAMIN
4326 Mîyâmîn (2), from (the) right hand

MIBHAR
4006 Mibchâr (1), select, i.e. best

MIBSAM
4017 Mibsâm (3), fragrant

MIBZAR
4014 Mibtsâr (2), fortification; defender

MICAH
4316 Mîykâ' (1), who (is) like Jehovah?
4318 Mîykâh (22), who (is) like Jehovah?
4319 Mîykâhûw (4), who (is) like Jehovah?
4320 Mîykâyâh (1), who (is) like Jehovah?

MICAH'S
4318 Mîykâh (3), who (is) like Jehovah?

MICAIAH
4318 Mîykâh (1), who (is) like Jehovah?
4319 Mîykâhûw (1), who (is) like Jehovah?
4321 Mîykâyᵉhûw (16), who (is) like Jehovah?

MICE
5909 'akbâr (4), mouse

MICHA
4316 Mîykâ' (4), who (is) like Jehovah?

MICHAEL
4317 Mîykâ'êl (13), who (is) like God?
3413 Michaêl (2), who (is) like God?

MICHAH
4318 Mîykâh (3), who (is) like Jehovah?

MICHAIAH
4320 Mîykâyâh (3), who (is) like Jehovah?
4321 Mîykâyᵉhûw (2), who (is) like Jehovah?
4322 Mîykâyâhûw (2), who (is) like Jehovah?

MICHAL
4324 Mîykâl (18), rivulet

MICHMAS
4363 Mikmâç (2), hidden

MICHMASH
4363 Mikmâç (9), hidden

MICHMETHAH
4366 Mikmᵉthâth (2), concealment

MICHRI
4381 Mikrîy (1), salesman

MICHTAM
4387 Miktâm (6), poem

MIDDAY
4276+3117 machătsîyth (1), halving or middle
6672 tsôhar (1), window; noon time
2250+3319 hēmĕra (1), day; period of time

MIDDIN
4081 Middîyn (1), contest or quarrel

MIDDLE
2677 chêtsîy (1), half or middle, midst
2872 ṭabbûwr (1), summit
8432 tâvek (6), center, middle
8484 tîykôwn (9), central, middle
3320 mĕsŏtŏichŏn (1), partition wall

MIDDLEMOST
8484 tîykôwn (2), central, middle

MIDIAN
4080 Midyân (39), contest or quarrel

MIDIANITE
4084 Midyânîy (1), Midjanite

MIDIANITES
4080 Midyân (20), contest or quarrel
4084 Midyânîy (3), Midjanite
4092 Mᵉdânîy (1), Midjanite

MIDIANITISH
4084 Midyânîy (3), Midjanite

MIDNIGHT

2676+3915 châtsôwth (3), *middle* of the night
2677+3915 chêtsîy (3), *half* or *middle, midst*
8432+3915 tâvek (1), *center, middle*
3317 mĕsônuktiŏn (4), *midnight* watch
3319+3571 mĕsŏs (2), *middle*

MIDST

1459 gav (Ch.) (10), *middle*
2436 chêyq (1), *bosom, heart*
2673 châtsâh (1), to *cut* or *split* in two; to *halve*
2677 chêtsîy (8), *half* or *middle, midst*
2686 châtsats (1), to *curtail;* to *distribute*
2872 ṭabbûwr (1), *summit*
3820 lêb (12), *heart*
3824 lêbâb (1), *heart*
7130 qereb (73), *nearest* part, i.e. the *center*
8432 tâvek (209), *center, middle*
8484 tîykôwn (1), *central, middle*
3319 mĕsŏs (41), *middle*
3321 mĕsŏuranêma (3), mid-sky, mid-heaven
3322 mĕsŏō (1), to *be* at *midpoint*

MIDWIFE

3205 yâlad (3), to *bear* young; to *father a child*

MIDWIVES

3205 yâlad (7), to *bear* young; to *father a child*

MIGDAL-EL

4027 Migdal-'Êl (1), *tower of God*

MIGDAL-GAD

4028 Migdal-Gâd (1), *tower of Fortune*

MIGDOL

4024 Migdôwl (4), *tower*

MIGHT

202 'ôwn (2), *ability, power; wealth*
410 'êl (1), *mighty;* the *Almighty*
1369 gᵉbûwrâh (27), *force; valor; victory*
1370 gᵉbûwrâh (Ch.) (2), *power, strength*
2428 chayil (6), *army; wealth; virtue; strength*
3201 yâkôl (2), to *be able*
3581 kôach (7), *force, might; strength*
3966 mᵉ'ôd (2), *very, utterly*
5797 'ôz (2), *strength*
5807 'ĕzûwz (1), *forcibleness*
6108 'ôtsem (1), *power;* framework of the *body*
8632 tᵉqôph (Ch.) (1), *power*
1410 dunamai (6), to be *able* or *possible*
1411 dunamis (4), *force, power, miracle*

MIGHTIER

117 'addîyr (1), *powerful; majestic*
6099 'âtsûwm (7), *powerful; numerous*
6105 'âtsam (1), to *be, make powerful*
8623 taqqîyph (1), *powerful*
2478 ischurŏs (3), *forcible, powerful*

MIGHTIES

1368 gibbôwr (2), *powerful;* great *warrior*

MIGHTIEST

1368 gibbôwr (1), *powerful;* great *warrior*

MIGHTILY

2393 chezqâh (2), prevailing *power*
3966 mᵉ'ôd (2), *very, utterly*
1722+1411 ĕn (1), *in; during; because of*
1722+2479 ĕn (1), *in; during; because of*
2159 ĕutŏnōs (1), *intensely, cogently*
2596+2904 kata (1), *down; according to*

MIGHTY

46 'âbîyr (6), *mighty*
47 'abbîyr (4), *mighty*
117 'addîyr (5), *powerful; majestic*
193 'ûwl (1), *powerful; mighty*
352 'ayil (2), *chief; ram; oak tree*
376 'îysh (2), *man; male; someone*
386 'êythân (4), *never-failing; eternal*
410 'êl (5), *mighty;* the *Almighty*
430 'ĕlôhîym (2), the true *God;* great *ones*
533 'ammîyts (1), *strong; mighty; brave*
650 'âphîyq (1), *valley; stream; mighty, strong*
1121+410 bên (1), *son, descendant; people*
1219 bâtsar (1), to *be inaccessible*
1368 gibbôwr (135), *powerful;* great *warrior*
1369 gᵉbûwrâh (7), *force; valor; victory*
1396 gâbar (1), to *be strong;* to *prevail*
1397 geber (2), *person, man*
1401 gibbâr (Ch.) (1), *valiant man,* or *warrior*
1419 gâdôwl (7), *great*
2220 zᵉrôwa' (1), *arm; foreleg; force, power*
2388 châzaq (2), to *be strong; courageous*
2389 châzâq (20), *strong; severe, hard, violent*

MIGHTY (cont.)

2428 chayil (1), *army; wealth; virtue; strength*
3524 kabbîyr (5), *mighty; aged; mighty*
3966 mᵉ'ôd (1), *very, utterly*
5794 'az (3), *strong, vehement, harsh*
5797 'ôz (1), *strength*
5868 'ăyâm (1), (poss.) *strength*
6099 'âtsûwm (8), *powerful; numerous*
6105 'âtsam (4), to *be, make powerful*
6184 'ârîyts (1), *powerful* or *tyrannical*
6697 tsûwr (2), *rock*
7227 rab (5), *great*
7989 shallîyṭ (1), *prince* or *warrior*
8624 taqqîyph (Ch.) (2), *powerful*
972 biaiŏs (1), *violent*
1411 dunamis (14), *force, power, miracle*
1413 dunastēs (1), *ruler* or *officer*
1414 dunatĕŏ (1), to *be efficient, able, strong*
1415 dunatŏs (7), *powerful* or *capable*
1754 ĕnĕrgĕŏ (1), to *be active, efficient, work*
2478 ischurŏs (7), *forcible, powerful*
2479 ischus (1), *forcefulness, power*
2900 krataiŏs (1), *powerful, mighty*
3168 mĕgalĕiŏtēs (1), *grandeur* or *splendor*
3173 mĕgas (1), *great, many*
5082 tēlikŏutŏs (1), *so vast*

MIGRON

4051 Migrôwn (2), *precipice*

MIJAMIN

4326 Mîyâmîn (2), *from* (the) *right hand*

MIKLOTH

4732 Miqlôwth (4), *rods*

MIKNEIAH

4737 Miqnêyâhûw (2), *possession of Jehovah*

MILALAI

4450 Mîlălay (1), *talkative*

MILCAH

4435 Milkâh (11), *queen*

MILCH

3243 yânaq (1), to *suck;* to *give milk*
5763 'ûwl (2), to *suckle,* i.e. *give milk*

MILCOM

4445 Malkâm (3), *Malcam* or *Milcom*

MILDEW

3420 yêrâqôwn (5), *paleness; mildew*

MILE

3400 miliŏn (1), about 4,850 feet, Roman *mile*

MILETUM

3399 Milētŏs (1), *Miletus*

MILETUS

3399 Milētŏs (2), *Miletus*

MILK

2461 châlâb (42), *milk*
4711 mâtsats (1), to *suck*
1051 gala (5), *milk*

MILL

7347 rêcheh (1), *mill-stone*
3459 mulōn (1), *mill-house*

MILLET

1764 dôchan (1), *millet* cereal *grain*

MILLIONS

7233 rᵉbâbâh (1), *myriad* number

MILLO

4407 millôw' (10), *citadel*

MILLS

7347 rêcheh (1), *mill-stone*

MILLSTONE

7347 rêcheh (1), *mill-stone*
7393 rekeb (2), *upper millstone*
3037+3457 lithŏs (1), *stone*
3458 mulŏs (2), *grinder millstone*
3458+3684 mulŏs (2), *grinder millstone*

MILLSTONES

7347 rêcheh (2), *mill-stone*

MINCING

2952 ṭâphaph (1), to *trip* or *step*

MIND

3336 yêtser (1), *form*
3820 lêb (12), *heart*
3824 lêbâb (4), *heart*
5315 nephesh (11), *life; breath; soul; wind*
5973 'im (1), *with*
6310 peh (1), *mouth; opening*
7307 rûwach (6), *breath; wind; life-spirit*
363 anamimnēskŏ (1), to *remind;* to *recollect*
1106 gnōmē (2), *cognition, opinion*
1271 dianŏia (7), *mind* or *thought*
1771 ĕnnŏia (1), *moral understanding*
1878 ĕpanamimnēskŏ (1), to *remind* again of
3563 nŏus (15), *intellect, mind; understanding*
3661 hŏmŏthumadŏn (1), *unanimously*
3675 hŏmŏphrōn (1), *like-minded*
4288 prŏthumia (4), *alacrity, eagerness*
4290 prŏthumōs (1), *with alacrity, with eagerness*
4993 sōphrŏnĕŏ (2), to *be in a right state of mind*

4995 sōphrŏnismŏs (1), *self-discipline*
5012 tapĕinŏphrŏsunē (1), *modesty, humility*
5279 hupŏmimnĕskŏ (1), *to suggest to memory*
5426 phrŏnĕŏ (9), *to be mentally disposed*
5427 phrŏnēma (2), *inclination or purpose*
5590 psuchē (1), *soul, vitality; heart, mind*

MINDED
5973+3820 'îm (1), *with*
1011 bŏulĕuŏ (1), *to deliberate; to resolve*
1014 bŏulŏmai (3), *to be willing, desire*
1374 dipsuchŏs (2), *vacillating*
4993 sōphrŏnĕŏ (1), *to be in a right state of mind*
5426 phrŏnĕŏ (3), *to be mentally disposed*
5427 phrŏnēma (2), *mental inclination*

MINDFUL
2142 zâkar (6), *to remember; to mention*
3403 mimnēskŏ (3), *to remind or to recall*
3421 mnēmŏnĕuŏ (1), *to exercise memory*

MINDING
3195 mĕllŏ (1), *to intend, i.e. be about to*

MINDS
5315 nephesh (4), *life; breath; soul; wind*
1271 dianŏia (2), *mind or thought*
3540 nŏēma (4), *perception, i.e. purpose*
3563 nŏus (2), *intellect, mind; understanding*
5590 psuchē (2), *soul, vitality; heart, mind*

MINGLE
4537 mâcak (1), *to mix*
6151 'ărab (Ch.) (1), *to co-mingle, mix*

MINGLED
1101 bâlal (37), *to mix; confuse; to feed*
3610 kil'ayim (2), *two different kinds of thing*
3947 lâqach (1), *to take*
4537 mâcak (4), *to mix*
6148 'ârab (2), *to intermix*
6154 'êreb (4), *mixed or woven things*
3396 mignumi (4), *to mix, mingle*

MINIAMIN
4509 Minyâmîyn (3), *from (the) right hand*

MINISH
1639 gâra' (1), *to shave, remove, lessen*

MINISHED
4591 mâ'aṭ (1), *to be, make small or few*

MINISTER
1777 dîyn (1), *to judge; to strive or contend for*

8334 shârath (50), *to attend as a menial*
8335 shârêth (1), *service*
1247 diakŏnĕŏ (8), *to act as a deacon*
1248 diakŏnia (1), *attendance, aid, service*
1249 diakŏnŏs (14), *waiter; deacon (-ess)*
1325 didōmi (1), *to give*
2038 ĕrgazŏmai (1), *to toil*
3008 lĕitŏurgĕŏ (1), *to perform religious or charitable functions*
3011 lĕitŏurgŏs (2), *functionary in the Temple or Gospel*
3930 parĕchŏ (1), *to hold near, i.e. to present*
5256 hupĕrĕtĕŏ (1), *to be a subordinate*
5257 hupĕrĕtēs (3), *servant, attendant*
5524 chŏrēgĕŏ (1), *to furnish, supply, provide*

MINISTERED
8120 sheˤmash (Ch.) (1), *to serve*
8334 shârath (15), *to attend as a menial*
1247 diakŏnĕŏ (14), *to wait upon, serve*
2023 ĕpichŏrēgĕŏ (2), *to fully supply; to aid*
3008 lĕitŏurgĕŏ (1), *to perform religious or charitable functions*
3011 lĕitŏurgŏs (1), *functionary in the Temple or Gospel*
5256 hupĕrĕtĕŏ (1), *to be a subordinate*

MINISTERETH
2023 ĕpichŏrēgĕŏ (2), *to fully supply; to aid*

MINISTERING
5656 'ăbŏdâh (1), *work of any kind*
8334 shârath (1), *to attend as a menial*
1247 diakŏnĕŏ (1), *to wait upon, serve*
1248 diakŏnia (3), *attendance, aid, service*
2418 hiĕrŏurgĕŏ (1), *officiate as a priest*
3008 lĕitŏurgĕŏ (1), *to perform religious or charitable functions*
3010 lĕitŏurgikŏs (1), *engaged in holy service*

MINISTERS
6399 peˤlach (Ch.) (1), *to serve or worship*
8334 shârath (15), *to attend as a menial*
1249 diakŏnŏs (6), *attendant, deacon*
3011 lĕitŏurgŏs (2), *functionary in the Temple or Gospel*
5257 hupĕrĕtēs (2), *servant, attendant*

MINISTRATION
1248 diakŏnia (6), *attendance, aid, service*

3009 lĕitŏurgia (1), *service, ministry*

MINISTRY
3027 yâd (2), *hand; power*
5656 'ăbŏdâh (1), *work*
8335 shârêth (1), *service in the Temple*
1243 diakŏnia (16), *attendance, aid, service*
3009 lĕitŏurgia (2), *service, ministry*

MINNI
4508 Minnîy (1), *Minni*

MINNITH
4511 Minnîyth (2), *enumeration*

MINSTREL
5059 nâgan (2), *to play; to make music*

MINSTRELS
834 aulētēs (1), *flute-player*

MINT
2238 hēduŏsmŏn (2), *sweet-scented, mint*

MIPHKAD
4663 Miphqâd (1), *assignment*

MIRACLE
4159 môwphêth (1), *miracle; token or omen*
1411 dunamis (1), *force, power, miracle*
4592 sēmĕiŏn (7), *indication, sign, signal*

MIRACLES
226 'ôwth (2), *signal, sign*
4159 môwphêth (1), *miracle; token or omen*
6381 pâlâ' (1), *to be, make great, wonderful*
1411 dunamis (8), *force, power, miracle*
4592 sēmĕiŏn (15), *indication, sign, signal*

MIRE
1206 bôts (1), *mud*
1207 bitstsâh (1), *swamp, marsh*
2563 chômer (2), *clay; dry measure*
2916 ṭîyṭ (8), *mud or clay*
3121 yâvên (1), *mud, sediment*
7516 rephesh (1), *mud of the sea*
1004 bŏrbŏrŏs (1), *mud*

MIRIAM
4813 Miryâm (15), *rebelliously*

MIRMA
4821 Mirmâh (1), *fraud*

MIRTH
4885 mâsôws (3), *delight*
7797 sûws (1), *to be bright, i.e. cheerful*
8057 simchâh (8), *blithesomeness or glee*
8342 sâsôwn (3), *cheerfulness; welcome*

MIRY
1207 bitstsâh (1), *swamp, marsh*

2917 ṭîyn (Ch.) (2), *wet clay*
3121 yâvên (1), *mud, sediment*

MISCARRYING
7921 shâkôl (1), *to miscarry*

MISCHIEF
205 'âven (4), *trouble, vanity, wickedness*
611 'âçôwn (5), *hurt, injury*
1943 hôvâh (2), *ruin, disaster*
2154 zimmâh (3), *bad plan*
4827 mêra' (1), *wickedness*
5771 'âvôn (1), moral *evil*
5999 'âmâl (9), *wearing effort; worry*
7451 ra' (19), *bad; evil*
7489 râ'a' (1), *to be good for nothing*
4468 rhaˤdiŏurgia (1), *malignity, trickery*

MISCHIEFS
1942 havvâh (1), *desire; craving*
7451 ra' (2), *bad; evil*

MISCHIEVOUS
1942 havvâh (2), *desire; craving*
4209 meˤzimmâh (2), *plan; sagacity*
7451 ra' (1), *bad; evil*

MISERABLE
5999 'âmâl (1), *wearing effort; worry*
1652 ĕlĕĕinŏs (2), *worthy of mercy*

MISERABLY
2560 kakōs (1), *badly; wrongly; ill*

MISERIES
4788 mârûwd (1), *outcast; destitution*
5004 talaipōria (1), *calamity, distress*

MISERY
4788 mârûwd (1), *outcast; destitution*
5999 'âmâl (3), *wearing effort; worry*
6001 'âmêl (1), *toiling; laborer; sorrowful*
7451 ra' (1), *bad; evil*
5004 talaipōria (1), *calamity, distress*

MISGAB
4869 misgâb (1), *high refuge*

MISHAEL
4332 Mîyshâ'êl (8), *who (is) what God (is)?*

MISHAL
4861 Mish'âl (1), *request*

MISHAM
4936 Mish'âm (1), *inspection*

MISHEAL
4861 Mish'âl (1), *request*

MISHMA
4927 Mishmâ' (4), *report*

MISHMANNAH
4925 Mishmannâh (1), *fatness*

MISHRAITES
4954 Mishrâ'îy (1), *extension*

MISPERETH
4559 Miçpereth (1), *enumeration*

MISREPHOTH-MAIM
4956 Misrᵉphôwth Mayim (2), *burnings of water*

MISS
2398 châṭâ' (1), to *sin*
6485 pâqad (1), to *visit, care for, count*

MISSED
6485 pâqad (3), to *visit, care for, count*

MISSING
6485 pâqad (2), to *visit, care for, count*

MIST
108 'êd (1), *fog*
887 achlus (1), *dimness* of sight, i.e. *cataract*
2217 zŏphŏs (1), *gloom*

MISTRESS
1172 ba'ălâh (2), *mistress; female owner*
1404 gᵉbereth (7), *mistress, noblewoman*

MISUSED
8591 tâ'a' (1), to *cheat*; to *maltreat*

MITE
3016 lĕptŏn (1), *small coin*

MITES
3016 lĕptŏn (2), *small coin*

MITHCAH
4989 Mithqâh (2), *sweetness*

MITHNITE
4981 Mithnîy (1), *slenderness*

MITHREDATH
4990 Mithrᵉdâth (2), *Mithredath*

MITRE
4701 mitsnepheth (11), *royal/priestly turban*
6797 tsânîyph (2), *head-dress, turban*

MITYLENE
3412 Mitulēnē (1), *abounding in shell-fish*

MIXED
1101 bâlal (1), to *mix; confuse*; to *feed*
4107 mâhal (1), to *dilute* a mixture
4469 mamçâk (1), *mixed*-wine
6151 'ărab (Ch.) (3), to *co-mingle, mix*
6154 'êreb (2), *mixed or woven things*
4786 sugkĕrannumi (1), to *combine; assimilate*

MIXTURE
4538 meçek (1), *wine mixture with spices*
194 akratŏs (1), *undiluted*
3395 migma (1), *compound, mixture*

MIZAR
4706 Mits'âr (1), *little*

MIZPAH
4708 Mitspeh (5), *observatory*
4709 Mitspah (18), *observatory*

MIZPAR
4558 Miçpâr (1), *number*

MIZPEH
4708 Mitspeh (9), *observatory*
4709 Mitspah (14), *observatory*

MIZRAIM
4714 Mitsrayim (4), *double border*

MIZZAH
4199 Mizzâh (3), *terror*

MNASON
3416 Mnasŏn (1), *Mnason*

MOAB
4124 Môw'âb (165), *from mother's father*
4125 Môw'âbîy (2), *Moäbite or Moäbitess*

MOABITE
4125 Môw'âbîy (3), *Moäbite or Moäbitess*

MOABITES
4124 Môw'âb (16), *from mother's father*
4125 Môw'âbîy (3), *Moäbite or Moäbitess*

MOABITESS
4125 Môw'âbîy (6), *Moäbite or Moäbitess*

MOABITISH
4125 Môw'âbîy (1), *Moäbite or Moäbitess*

MOADIAH
4153 Môw'adyâh (1), *assembly of Jehovah*

MOCK
2048 hâthal (1), to *deride, mock*
3887 lûwts (1), to *scoff*; to *interpret; to intercede*
3932 lâ'ag (2), to *deride; to speak unintelligibly*
5953 'âlal (1), to *glean*; to *overdo*
6711 tsâchaq (2), to *scorn*; to make *sport of*
7046 qâlaç (1), to *disparage*, i.e. *ridicule*
7832 sâchaq (1), to *laugh*; to *scorn*; to *play*
1702 ĕmpaizō (3), *deride, ridicule*

MOCKED
2048 hâthal (4), to *deride, mock*
3931 lâ'ab (1), to *deride, mock*
3932 lâ'ag (2), to *deride; to speak unintelligibly*

MOCKER
3887 lûwts (1), to *scoff*; to *interpret; to intercede*

MOCKERS
2049 hâthôl (1), *derision, mockery*
3887 lûwts (1), to *scoff*; to *interpret; to intercede*
3934 lâ'êg (1), *buffoon; foreigner*
7832 sâchaq (1), to *laugh*; to *scorn*; to *play*
1703 ĕmpaiktēs (1), *derider; false teacher*

MOCKEST
3932 lâ'ag (1), to *deride; to speak unintelligibly*

MOCKETH
2048 hâthal (1), to *deride, mock*
3932 lâ'ag (3), to *deride; to speak unintelligibly*
7832 sâchaq (1), to *laugh*; to *scorn*; to *play*

MOCKING
6711 tsâchaq (1), to *scorn*; to make *sport of*
7048 qallâçâh (1), *ridicule*
1702 ĕmpaizō (2), to *deride, ridicule*
5512 chlĕuazō (1), *jeer at, sneer at*

MOCKINGS
1701 ĕmpaigmŏs (1), *derision, jeering*

MODERATELY
6666 tsᵉdâqâh (1), *rightness*

MODERATION
1933 ĕpiĕikēs (1), *mild, gentle*

MODEST
2887 kŏsmiŏs (1), *orderly*

MOIST
3892 lach (1), *fresh cut*, i.e. unused or undried

MOISTENED
8248 shâqâh (1), to *quaff*, i.e. to *irrigate*

MOISTURE
3955 lᵉshad (1), *juice; vigor*; sweet or fat *cake*
2429 hikmas (1), *dampness, dampness*

MOLADAH
4137 Môwlâdâh (4), *birth*

MOLE
8580 tanshemeth (1), (poss.) *tree-toad*

MOLECH
4432 Môlek (8), *king*

MOLES
2661 chăphôr (1), *hole*, i.e. a *burrowing rat*

MOLID
4140 Môwlîyd (1), *genitor*

MOLLIFIED
7401 râkak (1), to *soften*

MOLOCH
4432 Môlek (1), *king*
3434 Mŏlŏch (1), *king*

MOLTEN
3332 yâtsaq (6), to *pour out*
4541 maççêkâh (25), *cast image); libation*
4549 mâçaç (1), to *waste*; to *faint*
5258 nâçak (1), to *pour a libation*
5262 neçek (4), *libation; cast idol*
5413 nâthak (1), to *flow forth, pour out*
6694 tsûwq (1), to *pour out; melt*

MOMENT
7281 rega' (19), *very short space* of time
823 atŏmŏs (1), *indivisible* unit of time
3901 pararrhuĕō (1), to *flow by*
4743 stigmē (1), *point of time*, i.e. an *instant*

MONEY
3701 keçeph (112), *silver money*
3702 kᵉçaph (Ch.) (1), *silver money*
7192 qᵉsîyṭah (2), *coin of unknown weight*
694 argurиŏn (11), *silver; silver money*
2772 kĕrma (1), *coin*
2773 kĕrmatistēs (1), *money-broker*
3546 nŏmisma (1), *coin*
4715 statēr (1), *coin worth four day's wage*
5365 philarguria (1), *avarice*
5475 chalkŏs (2), *copper*
5536 chrēma (4), *wealth, price*

MONEYCHANGERS
2855 kŏllubistēs (2), *coin-dealer*

MONSTERS
8577 tannîyn (1), *sea-serpent; jackal*

MONTH
2320 chôdesh (215), *new moon; month*
3391 yerach (6), *lunar month*
3393 yᵉrach (Ch.) (1), *lunar month*
3376 mēn (4), *month; month's time*

MONTHLY
2320 chôdesh (1), *new moon; month*

English

MONTHS
2320 chôdesh (37), *new moon; month*
3391 yerach (5), *lunar month*
3393 yᵉrach (Ch.) (1), *lunar* month
3376 mên (14), *month; month's time*
5072 têtramênŏn (1), *four months' time*
5150 trimênŏn (1), *three months' space*

MONUMENTS
5341 nâtsar (1), to *guard, protect, maintain*

MOON
2320 chôdesh (9), *new moon; month*
3391 yerach (2), *lunar month*
3394 yârêach (26), *moon*
3842 lᵉbânâh (3), *white moon*
3561 nŏumênia (1), festival of *new moon*
4582 sêlênê (9), *moon*

MOONS
2320 chôdesh (11), *new moon; month*

MORASTHITE
4183 Mowrashtîy (2), *Morashtite*

MORDECAI
4782 Mordᵉkay (58), *Mordecai*

MORDECAI'S
4782 Mordᵉkay (2), *Mordecai*

MORE
637 'aph (1), *also* or *yea; though*
1058 bâkâh (1), to *weep, moan*
1490 gizbâr (Ch.) (3), *treasurer*
1980 hâlak (1), to *walk; live a certain way*
2351 chûwts (1), *outside, outdoors; open market; countryside*
3148 yôwthêr (3), *moreover; rest; gain*
3254 yâçaph (59), to *add* or *augment*
3499 yether (1), *remainder; small rope*
3513 kâbad (1), to *be heavy, severe, dull*
3651 kên (2), *just; right; correct*
4480 min (4), *from, out of*
4481 min (Ch.) (1), *from* or *out of*
5674 'âbar (1), to *cross over; to transition*
5720 'Ădîyn (1), *voluptuous*
5736 'âdaph (1), to *be redundant, have surplus*
5750 'ôwd (196), *again; repeatedly; still; more*
5922 'al (Ch.) (1), *above, over, upon,* or *against*
5973 'îm (1), *with*

6105 'âtsam (2), to *be, make numerous*
6440 pânîym (1), *face; front*
7138 qârôwb (1), *near, close*
7227 rab (14), *great*
7230 rôb (1), *abundance*
7231 râbab (2), to *increase*
7235 râbâh (11), to *increase*
7608 sha'ărâh (1), female *kindred by blood*
7725 shûwb (1), to *turn back; to return*
8145 shênîy (3), *second; again*
197 akribĕstĕrŏn (4), *more exactly*
243 allŏs (1), *different, other*
316 anagkaiŏs (1), *necessary*
414 anĕktŏtĕrŏs (6), *more bearable*
1065 gĕ (1), particle of *emphasis*
1308 diaphĕrō (2), to *differ; to surpass*
1508 ĕi mē (1), *if not*
1617 ĕktĕnĕstĕrŏn (1), *more intently*
1833 ĕxĕtazō (1), to *ascertain* or *interrogate*
2001 ĕpischuō (7), to *insist stoutly*
2089 ĕti (39), *yet, still*
2115 ĕuthumŏs (1), *cheerful, encouraged*
3122 malista (1), *in the greatest degree*
3123 mallŏn (47), *in a greater degree*
3185 mĕizŏn (1), in *greater degree*
3187 mĕizŏn (1), *larger, greater*
3370 Mēdŏs (3), *inhabitant of Media*
3745 hŏsŏs (1), *as much as*
3761 ŏudĕ (1), *neither, nor, not even*
3765 ŏukĕti (17), *not yet, no longer*
3844 para (2), *from; with; besides; on account of*
4053 pĕrissŏs (2), *superabundant*
4054 pĕrissŏtĕrŏn (1), *more superabundant*
4055 pĕrissŏtĕrŏs (10), *more superabundant*
4056 pĕrissŏtĕrŏs (10), *more superabundantly*
4057 pĕrissŏs (1), *superabundantly*
4065 pĕriphrŏnĕō (1), to *depreciate, contemn*
4119 plĕiōn (25), *more*
4179 pŏllaplasiōn (1), *very much more*
4325 prŏsdapanaō (1), to *expend additionally*
4369 prŏstithēmi (2), to *lay beside, repeat*
4707 spŏudaiŏtĕrŏs (2), *more prompt*

5112 tŏlmĕrŏtĕrŏn (1), *more daringly*
5228 hupĕr (4), *over; above; beyond*
5245 hupĕrnikaō (1), to *gain* a decisive *victory*

MOREH
4176 Môwreh (3), *archer; teaching; early rain*

MOREOVER
518 'îm (1), *whether?; if, although; Oh that!*
637 'aph (2), *also* or *yea; though*
1571 gam (25), *also; even; yea; though*
3148 yôwthêr (1), *moreover; rest; gain*
3254 yâçaph (1), to *add* or *augment*
5750 'ôwd (6), *again; repeatedly; still; more*
1161 dĕ (12), *but, yet; and then*
2089 ĕti (1), *yet, still*
2532 kai (1), *and; or; even; also*

MORESHETH-GATH
4182 Môwresheth Gath (1), *possession of Gath*

MORIAH
4179 Môwrîyâh (2), *seen of Jehovah*

MORNING
216 'ôwr (1), *luminary; lightning; happiness*
1242 bôqer (187), *morning*
4891 mishchâr (1), *dawn*
5053 nôgahh (Ch.) (1), *dawn*
6843 tsᵉphîyrâh (2), *mishap*
7836 shâchar (1), to *search for*
7837 shachar (12), *dawn*
7904 shâkâh (1), to *roam because of lust*
7925 shâkam (1), to *start early in the morning*
3720 ŏrthrinŏs (1), *matutinal, i.e. early*
4404 prōi (6), *at dawn; day-break watch*
4405 prōïa (3), *day-dawn, early morn*
4407 prōïnŏs (1), *matutinal, i.e. early*

MORROW
1242 bôqer (7), *morning*
4279 mâchar (45), *tomorrow; hereafter*
4283 mochŏrâth (28), *tomorrow, next day*
839 auriŏn (14), *to-morrow*
1836 hĕxēs (1), *successive, next*
1887 ĕpauriŏn (8), *to-morrow*

MORSEL
3603 kikkâr (1), *round loaf; talent*
6595 path (8), *bit, morsel*
1035 brōsis (1), *food; rusting corrosion*

MORSELS
6595 path (1), *bit, morsel*

MORTAL
582 'ĕnôwsh (1), *man; person, human*
2349 thnētŏs (5), *liable to die,* i.e. *mortal*

MORTALITY
2349 thnētŏs (1), *liable to die,* i.e. *mortal*

MORTALLY
5315 nephesh (1), *life; breath; soul; wind*

MORTAR
4085 mᵉdôkâh (1), *mortar for bricks*
4388 maktêsh (1), *mortar; socket*

MORTER
2563 chômer (4), *clay; dry measure*
6083 'âphâr (2), *dust, earth, mud; clay,*

MORTGAGED
6148 'ârab (1), to *intermix; to give* or *be security*

MORTIFY
2289 thanatŏō (1), to *kill*
3499 nĕkrŏō (1), to *deaden,* i.e. to *subdue*

MOSERA
4149 Môwçêrâh (1), *corrections*

MOSEROTH
4149 Môwçêrâh (2), *corrections*

MOSES
4872 Môsheh (749), *drawing out of the water*
4873 Môsheh (Ch.) (1), *drawing out of the water*
3475 Môsĕus (77), *drawing out of the water*

MOSES'
4872 Môsheh (16), *drawing out of the water*
3475 Môsĕus (3), *drawing out of the water*

MOST
2429 chayil (Ch.) (1), *army; strength*
2896 tôwb (1), *good; well*
3524 kabbîyr (1), *mighty; aged; mighty*
3800 kethem (1), *pure gold*
4581 mâ'ôwz (1), *fortified place; defense*
4971 mathkôneth (1), *proportion*
5920 'al (2), *the Highest God*
5943 'illay (Ch.) (9), *the supreme God*
5945 'elyôwn (25), *loftier, higher; Supreme God*
5946 'elyôwn (Ch.) (3), *the Supreme God*

6579 partam (1), *grandee, noble*
6944 qôdesh (48), *sacred* place or thing
7230 rôb (1), *abundance*
8077 shᵉmâmâh (1), *devastation*
8563 tamrûwr (1), *bitterness*
40 hagiŏs (1), *sacred, holy*
2236 hēdista (1), *with great pleasure*
2903 kratistŏs (4), *very honorable*
3122 malista (1), *in the greatest degree*
4118 plĕistŏs (1), *very large,* i.e. *the most*
4119 plĕiŏn (3), *more*
5310 hupsistŏs (5), *highest;* the *Supreme* God

MOTE
2595 karphŏs (6), *dry twig* or *straw*

MOTH
6211 'âsh (7), *moth*
4597 sēs (3), *moth* insect

MOTHEATEN
4598 sētŏbrŏtŏs (1), *moth-eaten*

MOTHER
517 'êm (143), *mother*
2545 chămôwth (11), *mother-in-law*
2859 châthan (1), to *become related* by marriage,
282 amētōr (1), *of unknown maternity*
3384 mētēr (76), *mother*
3994 pĕnthĕra (6), *wife's mother*

MOTHER'S
517 'êm (67), *mother*
3384 mētēr (7), *mother*

MOTHERS
517 'êm (3), *mother*
3384 mētēr (2), *mother*
3389 mētralŏ͵as (1), *matricide*

MOTHERS'
517 'êm (1), *mother*

MOTIONS
3804 pathēma (1), *passion; suffering*

MOULDY
5350 niqqud (2), *crumb, morsel; biscuit*

MOUNT
55 'âbak (1), to *coil* upward
1361 gâbahh (1), to *be lofty;* to *be haughty*
2022 har (222), *mountain* or *range* of hills
2042 hârâr (1), *mountain*
4674 mutstsâb (1), *station,* military *post*
5550 çôlᵉlâh (5), military siege *mound, rampart*
5927 'âlâh (4), to *ascend, be high, mount*
7311 rûwm (1), to *be high;* to *rise* or *raise*

3735 ŏrŏs (21), *hill, mountain*

MOUNTAIN
2022 har (104), *mountain* or *range* of hills
2042 hârâr (2), *mountain*
2906 tûwr (Ch.) (2), *rock* or *hill*
3735 ŏrŏs (28), *hill, mountain*

MOUNTAINS
2022 har (155), *mountain* or *range* of hills
2042 hârâr (8), *mountain*
3735 ŏrŏs (13), *hill, mountain*

MOUNTED
7426 râmam (1), to *rise*

MOUNTING
4608 ma'ăleh (1), *elevation; platform*

MOUNTS
5550 çôlᵉlâh (3), military siege *mound, rampart*

MOURN
56 'âbal (15), to *bewail*
57 'âbêl (3), *lamenting*
578 'ânâh (1), to *groan, lament*
584 'ânach (1), to *sigh, moan*
1897 hâgâh (4), to *murmur, utter a sound*
5098 nâham (2), to *growl, groan*
5110 nûwd (1), to *deplore;* to *taunt*
5594 çâphad (9), to *tear* the hair, *wail*
6937 qâdar (2), to *mourn* in *dark* garments
7300 rûwd (1), to *ramble*
2875 kŏptō (1), to *beat* the breast
3996 pĕnthĕō (5), to *grieve*

MOURNED
56 'âbal (10), to *bewail*
1058 bâkâh (2), to *weep, moan*
5594 çâphad (6), to *tear* the hair, *wail*
2354 thrēnĕō (2), to *bewail, lament*
3996 pĕnthĕō (2), to *grieve*

MOURNER
56 'âbal (1), to *bewail*

MOURNERS
57 'âbêl (2), *lamenting*
205 'âven (1), *trouble, vanity, wickedness*
5594 çâphad (1), to *tear* the hair, *wail*

MOURNETH
56 'âbal (8), to *bewail*
57 'âbêl (1), *lamenting*
1669 dâ'ab (1), to *pine, feel sorrow*
5594 çâphad (1), to *tear* the hair, *wail*

MOURNFULLY
6941 qᵉdôrannîyth (1), *in sackcloth*

MOURNING
56 'âbal (2), to *bewail*
57 'âbêl (2), *lamenting*
60 'êbel (24), *lamentation*
205 'âven (1), *trouble, vanity, wickedness*
585 'ănâchâh (1), *sighing, moaning*
1086 bâlâh (1), to *wear out, decay; consume*
1899 hegeh (1), *muttering; mourning*
1993 hâmâh (1), to *be in great commotion*
3382 Yered (1), *descent*
4553 miçpêd (6), *lamentation, howling*
4798 marzêach (1), *cry of lamentation*
6937 qâdar (4), to *mourn* in *dark* garments
6969 qûwn (1), to *chant* or *wail* at a funeral
8386 ta'ănîyâh (1), *lamentation*
3602 ŏdurmŏs (2), *lamentation*
3997 pĕnthŏs (2), *grief, mourning, sadness*

MOUSE
5909 'akbâr (2), *mouse*

MOUTH
1627 gârôwn (1), *throat*
2441 chêk (14), area of *mouth*
5716 'ădîy (2), *finery; outfit; headstall*
6310 peh (326), *mouth; opening*
6433 pûm (Ch.) (5), *mouth*
8651 tᵉra' (Ch.) (1), *door; palace*
3056 lŏgŏs (1), *word, matter, thing*
4750 stŏma (69), *mouth; edge*

MOUTHS
6310 peh (12), *mouth; opening*
6433 pûm (Ch.) (1), *mouth*
1993 ĕpistŏmizō (1), to *silence*
4750 stŏma (4), *mouth; edge*

MOVE
2782 chârats (1), to *be alert,* to *decide*
5110 nûwd (1), to *waver;* to *wander, flee*
5128 nûwa' (1), to *waver*
5130 nûwph (1), to *quiver, vibrate, rock*
6328 pûwq (1), to *waver*
6470 pâ'am (1), to *tap;* to *impel* or *agitate*
7264 râgaz (2), to *quiver*
8318 sherets (1), *swarm, teeming* mass
2795 kinĕō (2), to *stir, move, remove*
3056+4160 lŏgŏs (1), *word, matter, thing*

MOVEABLE
5128 nûwa' (1), to *waver*

MOVED
1607 gâ'ash (3), to *agitate* violently, *shake*
1949 hûwm (1), to *make an uproar; agitate*
1993 hâmâh (1), to *be in great commotion*
2111 zûwâ' (1), to *shake* with fear, *tremble*
2782 chârats (1), to *be alert,* to *decide*
4131 môwt (19), to *slip, shake, fall*
4132 môwt (3), *pole; yoke*
5074 nâdad (1), to *rove, flee;* to *drive* away
5120 nûwt (1), to *quake*
5128 nûwa' (5), to *waver*
5425 nâthar (1), to *jump;* to *be agitated*
5496 çûwth (4), to *stimulate;* to *seduce*
5648 'âbad (Ch.) (1), to *do, work, serve*
7043 qâlal (1), to *be, make light, swift*
7264 râgaz (5), to *quiver*
7363 râchaph (1), to *brood;* to *be relaxed*
7430 râmas (1), to *glide* swiftly, *move, swarm*
7493 râ'ash (2), to *undulate, quake*
23 aganaktĕō (1), to *be indignant*
383 anasĕiō (1), to *excite, stir up*
761 asalĕutŏs (1), *immovable, fixed*
2125 ĕulabĕŏmai (1), to *have reverence*
2206 zēlŏō (2), to *have warmth of feeling for*
2795 kinĕō (2), to *stir, move, remove*
3334 mĕtakinĕō (1), to *be removed, shifted from*
4525 sainō (1), to *shake;* to *disturb*
4531 salĕuō (1), to *waver,* i.e. *agitate, rock, topple*
4579 sĕiō (1), to *vibrate;* to *agitate*
4697 splagchnizŏmai (5), to *feel sympathy,* to *pity*
5342 phĕrō (1), to *bear* or *carry*

MOVEDST
5496 çûwth (1), to *stimulate;* to *seduce*

MOVER
2795 kinĕō (1), to *stir, move, remove*

MOVETH
1980 hâlak (1), to *walk; live a certain way*
2654 châphêts (1), to *be pleased* with, *desire*
7430 râmas (5), to *glide* swiftly, i.e. *crawl, move, swarm*
8317 shârats (1), to *wriggle, swarm*

MOVING
5205 nîyd (1), *motion* of the lips in speech
7169 qârats (1), to *bite* the lips, *blink* the eyes

English

MOWER
7430 râmas (1), to *glide swiftly, crawl, move*
8318 sherets (1), *swarm, teeming mass*
2796 kinēsis (1), *stirring, motion*

MOWER
7114 qâtsar (1), to *curtail, cut short*

MOWINGS
1488 gêz (1), shorn *fleece;* mown *grass*

MOWN
1488 gêz (1), shorn *fleece;* mown *grass*

MOZA
4162 Môwtsâ' (5), *going forth*

MOZAH
4681 Môtsâh (1), *drained*

MUCH
634 'Êçar-Chaddôwn (1), *Esar-chaddon*
637 'aph (15), *also or yea; though*
834 'âsher (2), *how, because, in order that*
1431 gâdal (2), to *be great, make great*
1571 gam (2), *also; even; yea; though*
1767 day (2), *enough, sufficient*
1931 hûw' (1), *he, she, it; this or that*
2479 chalchâlâh (1), *writhing* in childbirth
3254 yâçaph (1), to *add or augment*
3498 yâthar (1), to *remain or be left*
3515 kâbêd (2), *numerous; severe*
3524 kabbîyr (2), *mighty; aged; mighty*
3605 kôl (1), *all, any*
3966 mᵉ'ôd (9), *very, utterly*
4276 machătsîyth (1), *halving* or the *middle*
4767 mirbâh (1), *great quantity*
5704 'ad (2), *as far (long) as; during; while; until*
6079 'aph'aph (1), *fluttering eyelash*
6581 pâsâh (4), to *spread*
7114 qâtsar (1), to *curtail, cut short*
7225 rê'shîyth (1), *first*
7227 rab (38), *great*
7230 rôb (7), *abundance*
7235 râbâh (31), to *increase*
7335 râzam (1), to *twinkle* the eye
7690 saggîy' (Ch.) (4), *large*
23 aganaktĕō (2), to be *indignant*
1280 diapŏrĕō (1), to *be thoroughly puzzled*
2425 hikanŏs (6), *ample*
2470 isŏs (1), *similar*
2579 kan (1), *and (or even) if*

3123 mallŏn (3), *in a greater degree*
3366 mĕdĕ (1), *but not, not even; nor*
3383 mĕtĕ (1), *neither or nor; not even*
3386 mĕtigĕ (1), *not to say (the rather still)*
3433 mŏlis (1), *with difficulty*
3588 hŏ (2), *"the,"* i.e. the definite article
3745 hŏsŏs (4), *as much as*
3761 ŏudĕ (4), *neither, nor, not even*
4055 pĕrissŏtĕrŏs (1), *more superabundant*
4056 pĕrissŏtĕrŏs (1), *more superabundantly*
4124 plĕŏnĕxia (2), *extortion, avarice*
4180 pŏlulŏgia (1), *prolixity, wordiness*
4183 pŏlus (73), *much, many*
4214 pŏsŏs (11), *how much?; how much!*
5118 tŏsŏutŏs (7), *such great*
5248 hupĕrpĕrissĕuō (2), to *super-abound*

MUFFLERS
7479 ra'ălâh (1), long *veil*

MULBERRY
1057 bâkâ' (4), (poss.) *balsam tree*

MULE
6505 pered (6), *mule*
6506 pirdâh (3), *she-mule*

MULES
3222 yêm (1), *warm spring*
6505 pered (8), *mule*
7409 rekesh (2), *relay of animals on a post-route*

MULES'
6505 pered (1), *mule*

MULTIPLIED
1995 hâmôwn (1), *noise, tumult; many, crowd*
6280 'âthar (1), to *be, make abundant*
7231 râbab (3), to *increase*
7235 râbâh (29), to *increase*
7680 sᵉgâ' (Ch.) (2), to *increase*
4129 plēthunō (8), to *increase*

MULTIPLIEDST
7235 râbâh (1), to *increase*

MULTIPLIETH
3527 kâbar (1), to *augment; accumulate*
7235 râbâh (2), to *increase*

MULTIPLY
7227 rab (1), *great*
7231 râbab (1), to *increase*
7233 rᵉbâbâh (1), *myriad number*

7235 râbâh (41), to *increase*
4129 plēthunō (2), to *increase*

MULTIPLYING
7235 râbâh (1), to *increase*
4129 plēthunō (1), to *increase*

MULTITUDE
527 'âmôwn (4), *throng* of people, *crowd*
582 'ĕnôwsh (1), *man; person, human*
628 'açpᵉçûph (1), *assemblage*
1995 hâmôwn (55), *noise, tumult; many, crowd*
2416 chay (1), *alive; raw; fresh; life*
4392 mâlê' (1), *full; filling; fulness; fully*
4393 mᵉlô' (2), *fulness*
4768 marbîyth (1), *multitude; offspring*
5519 çâk (1), *crowd*
5712 'êdâh (1), *assemblage; crowd*
6154 'êreb (1), *mixed or woven things*
6951 qâhâl (3), *assemblage*
7227 rab (7), *great*
7230 rôb (68), *abundance*
7379 rîyb (1), *contest*
7393 rekeb (1), *upper millstone*
8229 shiph'âh (1), *copiousness*
3461 murias (1), *ten-thousand*
3793 ŏchlŏs (59), *throng*
4128 plēthŏs (29), *large number, throng*

MULTITUDES
1995 hâmôwn (2), *noise, tumult; many, crowd*
3793 ŏchlŏs (20), *throng*
4128 plēthŏs (1), *large number, throng*

MUNITION
4685 mâtsôwd (1), *net or snare; besieging tower*
4694 mᵉtsûwrâh (1), *rampart; fortification*

MUNITIONS
4679 mᵉtsad (1), *stronghold*

MUPPIM
4649 Muppîym (1), *wavings*

MURDER
2026 hârag (1), to *kill, slaughter*
7523 râtsach (3), to *murder*
5407 phŏnĕuō (1), to *commit murder*
5408 phŏnŏs (4), *slaying; murder*

MURDERER
2026 hârag (1), to *kill, slaughter*
7523 râtsach (13), to *murder*

7235 râbâh (41), to *increase*
4129 plēthunō (2), to *increase*

443 anthrŏpŏktŏnŏs (3), *killer of humans*
5406 phŏnĕus (3), *murderer*

MURDERERS
2026 hârag (1), to *kill, slaughter*
5221 nâkâh (1), to *strike, kill*
7523 râtsach (1), to *murder*
3389 mētralō¡as (1), *matricide*
3964 patralō¡as (1), *parricide*
4607 sikariŏs (1), *dagger-man*
5406 phŏnĕus (4), *murderer*

MURDERS
5408 phŏnŏs (4), *slaying; murder*

MURMUR
3885 lûwn (7), to *be obstinate with* words
1111 gŏgguzō (2), to *grumble, mutter*

MURMURED
3885 lûwn (7), to *be obstinate with* words
7279 râgan (3), to *grumbling rebel*
1111 gŏgguzō (6), to *grumble, mutter*
1234 diagŏgguzō (2), to *complain throughout*
1690 ĕmbrimaŏmai (1), to *blame, warn sternly*

MURMURERS
1113 gŏggustēs (1), *grumbler*

MURMURING
1112 gŏggusmŏs (2), *grumbling*

MURMURINGS
8519 tᵉlûwnâh (8), *grumbling*
1112 gŏggusmŏs (1), *grumbling*

MURRAIN
1698 deber (1), *pestilence, plague*

MUSE
7878 sîyach (1), to *ponder, muse aloud*

MUSED
1260 dialŏgizŏmai (1), to *deliberate*

MUSHI
4187 Mûwshîy (8), *sensitive*

MUSHITES
4188 Mûwshîy (2), *Mushite*

MUSICAL
7705 shiddâh (1), *wife* (as mistress of the house)
7892 shîyr (2), *song; singing*

MUSICIAN
5329 nâtsach (55), i.e. to *be eminent*

MUSICIANS
3451 mŏusikŏs (1), *minstrel, musician*

MUSICK
2170 zᵉmâr (Ch.) (4), instrumental *music*
4485 mangîynâh (1), *satire, mocking*
5058 nᵉgîynâh (1), stringed *instrument*
7892 shîyr (7), *song; singing*
4858 sumphōnia (1), *concert* of instruments

MUSING
1901 hâgîyg (1), *complaint, sighing*

MUST
318 anagkē (1), *constraint; distress*
1163 hina (63), *it is (was) necessary*
2192 ĕchō (1), *to have; hold; keep*
2443 hina (1), in order that
3784 ŏphĕilō (1), *to owe; to be under obligation*

MUSTARD
4615 sinapi (5), *mustard*

MUSTERED
6633 tsâbâ' (2), *to mass* an army or servants

MUSTERETH
6485 pâqad (1), *to visit, care for, count*

MUTH-LABBEN
4192 Mûwth (1), "*To die for the son*"

MUTTER
1897 hâgâh (1), *to murmur, utter a sound*

MUTTERED
1897 hâgâh (1), *to murmur, utter a sound*

MUTUAL
1722+240 ĕn (1), *in; during; because of*

MUZZLE
2629 châcam (1), *to muzzle; block*
5392 phimŏŏ (2), *to muzzle; silence*

MYRA
3460 Mura (1), *Myra*

MYRRH
3910 lôṭ (2), *sticky gum* resin (poss.) *ladanum*
4753 môr (12), *myrrh*
4666 smurna (2), *myrrh*
4669 smurnizō (1), *to mix with myrrh*

MYRTLE
1918 hădaç (6), *myrtle*

MYSIA
3463 muriŏi (2), *ten thousand*

MYSTERIES
3466 mustēriŏn (5), *secret*

MYSTERY
3466 mustēriŏn (22), *secret*

NAAM
5277 Na'am (1), *pleasure*

NAAMAH
5279 Na'ămâh (5), *pleasantness*

NAAMAN
5283 Na'ămân (15), *pleasantness*
3497 Nĕĕman (1), *pleasantness*

NAAMAN'S
5283 Na'ămân (1), *pleasantness*

NAAMATHITE
5284 Na'ămâthîy (4), *Naamathite*

NAAMITES
5280 Na'âmîy (1), *Naamanite*

NAARAH
5292 Na'ărâh (3), female *child; servant*

NAARAI
5293 Na'ăray (1), *youthful*

NAARAN
5295 Na'ărân (1), *juvenile*

NAARATH
5292 Na'ărâh (1), female *child; servant*

NAASHON
5177 Nachshôwn (1), *enchanter*

NAASSON
3476 Naassōn (3), *enchanter*

NABAL
5037 Nâbâl (18), *dolt*

NABAL'S
5037 Nâbâl (4), *dolt*

NABOTH
5022 Nâbôwth (22), *fruits*

NACHON'S
5225 Nâkôwn (1), *prepared*

NACHOR
5152 Nâchôwr (1), *snorer*
3493 Nachōr (1), *snorer*

NADAB
5070 Nâdâb (20), *liberal*

NAGGE
3477 Naggai (1), (poss.) *brilliancy*

NAHALAL
5096 Nahălâl (1), *pasture*

NAHALIEL
5160 Nachălîy'êl (2), *valley of God*

NAHALLAL
5096 Nahălâl (1), *pasture*

NAHALOL
5096 Nahălâl (1), *pasture*

NAHAM
5163 Nacham (1), *consolation*

NAHAMANI
5167 Nachămânîy (1), *consolatory*

NAHARAI
5171 Nachăray (1), *snorer*

NAHARI
5171 Nachăray (1), *snorer*

NAHASH
5176 Nâchâsh (9), *snake*

NAHATH
5184 Nachath (5), *quiet*

NAHBI
5147 Nachbîy (1), *occult*

NAHOR
5152 Nâchôwr (15), *snorer*

NAHOR'S
5152 Nâchôwr (2), *snorer*

NAHSHON
5177 Nachshôwn (9), *enchanter*

NAHUM
5151 Nachûwm (1), *comfortable*

NAIL
3489 yâthêd (8), tent *peg*

NAILING
4338 prŏsēlŏŏ (1), *to nail* to something

NAILS
2953 ṭᵉphar (Ch.) (2), finger-*nail; claw*
4548 maçmêr (4), *peg*
4930 masmᵉrâh (1), *pin* on the end of a goad
6856 tsippôren (1), *nail; point* of a pen
2247 hēlŏs (2), *stud,* i.e. *spike* or *nail*

NAIN
3484 Naïn (1), cf. a *home, dwelling; pasture*

NAIOTH
5121 Nâvîyth (6), *residence*

NAKED
4636 ma'ărôm (1), *bare, stripped*
5783 'ûwr (1), *to* (*be*) *bare*
5903 'êyrôm (9), *naked; nudity*
6168 'ârâh (1), *to be, make bare; to empty*
6174 'ârôwm (16), *nude; partially stripped*
6181 'eryâh (1), *nudity*
6544 pâra' (3), *to loosen; to expose, dismiss*
1130 gumnētĕuō (1), *go poorly clad, be in rags*
1131 gumnŏs (14), *nude or poorly clothed*

NAKEDNESS
4589 mâ'ôwr (1), *nakedness; exposed*
4626 ma'ar (1), *bare place; nakedness*
5903 'êyrôm (1), *naked; nudity*
6172 'ervâh (50), *nudity; disgrace; blemish*
1132 gumnŏtēs (3), *nudity or poorly clothed*

NAME
559 'âmar (2), *to say*
8034 shêm (735), *appellation*
8036 shum (Ch.) (8), *name*

NAHARI (continued)
2564 *kalĕŏ* (1), *to call*
3686 *ŏnŏma* (170), *name*

NAME'S
8034 shêm (19), *appellation,* i.e. name
3686 *ŏnŏma* (11), *name*

NAMED
559 'âmar (1), *to say*
1696 dâbar (1), *to speak, say; to subdue*
5344 nâqab (1), *to specify, designate, libel*
7121 qârâ' (5), *to call out*
7121+8034 qârâ' (1), *call out*
8034 shêm (4), *appellation,* i.e. name
8034+7121 shêm (1), *appellation,* i.e. name
8036 shum (Ch.) (1), *name*
2564 *kalĕŏ* (2), *to call*
3004 *lĕgō* (2), *to say*
3686 *ŏnŏma* (28), *name*
3687 *ŏnŏmazō* (7), *to give a name*

NAMELY
1722 *ĕn* (1), *in; during; because of*

NAMES
8034 shêm (82), *appellation,* i.e. name
8036 shum (Ch.) (3), *name*
3686 *ŏnŏma* (11), *name*

NAMETH
3687 *ŏnŏmazō* (1), *to give a name*

NAOMI
5281 No'ŏmîy (20), *pleasant*

NAOMI'S
5281 No'ŏmîy (1), *pleasant*

NAPHISH
5305 Nâphîysh (2), *refreshed*

NAPHTALI
5321 Naphtâlîy (49), *my wrestling*

NAPHTUHIM
5320 Naphtûchîym (1), *Naphtuchim*

NAPKIN
4676 sŏudariŏn (3), *towel*

NAPTHTUHIM
5320 Naphtûchîym (1), *Naphtuchim*

NARCISSUS
3488 Narkissŏs (1), *stupefaction*

NARROW
213 'ûwts (1), *to be close, hurry, withdraw*
331 'âṭam (4), *to close*
3334 yâtsar (1), *to be in distress*
6862 tsar (2), *trouble; opponent*
2346 *thlibō* (1), *to crowd, press, trouble*

NARROWED
4052 migrâ'âh (1), *ledge or offset*

NARROWER
6887 tsârar (1), to *cramp*

NARROWLY
8104 shâmar (1), to *watch*

NATHAN
5416 Nâthân (42), *given*
3481 Nathan (1), *given*

NATHAN-MELECH
5419 Neᵗhan-Melek (1), *given of (the) king*

NATHANAEL
3482 Nathanaël (6), *given of God*

NATION
249 'ezrâch (1), *native born*
524 'ummâh (Ch.) (1), *community, clan, tribe*
1471 gôwy (105), *foreign nation; Gentiles*
3816 leᵗôm (1), *community, nation*
5971 'am (2), *people; tribe; troops*
246 allŏphulŏs (1), *Gentile, foreigner*
1074 gĕnĕa (1), *generation; age*
1085 gĕnŏs (2), *kin, offspring in kind*
1484 ĕthnŏs (24), *race; tribe; pagan*

NATIONS
523 'ummâh (1), *community, clan, tribe*
524 'ummâh (Ch.) (7), *community, clan, tribe*
776 'erets (1), *earth, land, soil; nation*
1471 gôwy (266), *foreign nation; Gentiles*
3816 leᵗôm (9), *community, nation*
5971 'am (14), *people; tribe; troops*
1484 ĕthnŏs (37), *race; tribe; pagan*

NATIVE
4138 môwledeth (1), *lineage, native country*

NATIVITY
4138 môwledeth (6), *lineage, native country*
4351 meᵏûwrâh (1), *origin*

NATURAL
3893 lêach (1), *fresh strength, vigor*
1083 gĕnnēsis (1), *nativity*
2596+6449 kata (2), *down; according to*
5446 phusikŏs (3), *instinctive, natural*
5591 psuchikŏs (4), *physical* and *brutish*

NATURALLY
1103 gnēsiŏs (1), *genuine, true*
5447 phusikōs (1), *instinctively, naturally*

NATURE
1078 genesis (1), *nativity, nature*

5449 *phusis* (10), *genus or sort; disposition*

NAUGHT
7451 ra' (2), *bad; evil*

NAUGHTINESS
1942 havvâh (1), *desire; craving*
7455 rôa' (1), *badness, evil*
2549 kakia (1), *depravity; malignity; trouble*

NAUGHTY
1100 beᶫîya'al (1), *wickedness, trouble*
1942 havvâh (1), *desire; craving*
7451 ra' (1), *bad; evil*

NAUM
3486 Naŏum (1), *comfortable*

NAVEL
8270 shôr (2), umbilical *cord; strength*
8306 shârîyr (1), *sinew*
8326 shôrer (1), umbilical *cord*

NAVES
1354 gab (1), *mounded: top, rim; arch, bulwarks*

NAVY
590 'ŏnîy (6), *ship; fleet of ships*

NAY
408 'al (8), *not; nothing*
1571 gam (2), *also; even*
3808 lô' (17), *no, not*
6440 pânîym (1), *face; front*
235 alla (4), *but, yet*
3304 mĕnŏungĕ (1), *so then at least*
3756 ŏu (8), *no or not*
3780 ŏuchi (5), *not indeed*

NAZARENE
3480 Nazōraiŏs (1), *inhabitant of Nazareth*

NAZARENES
3480 Nazōraiŏs (1), *inhabitant of Nazareth*

NAZARETH
3478 Nazarĕth (29), *Nazareth or Nazaret*

NAZARITE
5139 nâzîyr (9), *prince; separated Nazirite*

NAZARITES
5139 nâzîyr (3), *prince; separated Nazirite*

NEAH
5269 Nê'âh (1), *motion*

NEAPOLIS
3496 Nĕapŏlis (1), *new town*

NEAR
413 'êl (1), *to, toward*
681 'êtsel (3), *side; near*
3027 yâd (2), *hand; power*
5060 nâga' (4), to *strike*
5066 nâgash (58), *to be, come, bring near*
5921 'al (1), *above, over, upon, or against*
5973 'îm (1), *with*

7126 qârab (54), *to approach, bring near*
7127 qeᵗrêb (Ch.) (5), *to approach, bring near*
7131 qârêb (2), *near*
7132 qeᵗrâbâh (1), *approach*
7138 qârôwb (42), *near, close*
7200 râ'âh (1), *to see*
7607 sheᵗ'êr (4), *flesh, meat; kindred* by blood
7608 sha'ărâh (1), *female kindred* by blood
316 anagkaiŏs (1), *necessary*
1448 ĕggizō (10), *to approach*
1451 ĕggus (4), *near, close*
4139 plēsiŏn (1), *neighbor, fellow*
4317 prŏsagō (1), to *bring near*
4334 prŏsĕrchŏmai (3), *to come near, visit*

NEARER
7138 qârôwb (1), *near, close*
1452 ĕggutĕrŏn (1), *nearer, closer*

NEARIAH
5294 Neᵗ'aryâh (3), *servant of Jehovah*

NEBAI
5109 Nôwbay (1), *fruitful*

NEBAIOTH
5032 Neᵗbâyôwth (2), *fruitfulnesses*

NEBAJOTH
5032 Neᵗbâyôwth (3), *fruitfulnesses*

NEBALLAT
5041 Neᵗballâṭ (1), *foolish secrecy*

NEBAT
5028 Neᵗbâṭ (25), *regard*

NEBO
5015 Neᵗbôw (13), *Nebo*

NEBUCHADNEZZAR
5019 Neᵗbûwkadne'tstsar (29), *Nebukadnetstsar*
5020 Neᵗbûwkadnetstsar (Ch.) (31), *Nebukadnetstsar*

NEBUCHADREZZAR
5019 Neᵗbûwkadne'tstsar (31), *Nebukadnetstsar*

NEBUSHASBAN
5021 Neᵗbûwshazbân (1), *Nebushazban*

NEBUZAR-ADAN
5018 Neᵗbûwzar'ădân (15), *Nebuzaradan*

NECESSARY
2706 chôq (1), *appointment; allotment*
316 anagkaiŏs (5), *necessary*
318 anagkē (1), *constraint; distress*
1876 ĕpanagkĕs (1), *necessarily*
4314+3588+5532 prŏs (1), *for; on, at; to, toward*

NECESSITIES
318 anagkē (2), *constraint; distress*
5532 chrĕia (1), *demand, requirement*

NECESSITY
316 anagkaiŏs (1), *necessary*
318 anagkē (6), *constraint; distress*
2192+318 ĕchō (1), to *have; hold; keep*
5532 chrĕia (2), *demand, requirement*

NECHO
5224 Neᵏôw (3), *Neko*

NECK
1621 gargeᵗrôwth (4), *throat*
1627 gârôwn (1), *throat*
4665 miphreketh (1), *vertebra of the neck*
6202 'âraph (3), *to break the neck, to destroy*
6203 'ôreph (12), *nape or back of the neck*
6676 tsavva'r (Ch.) (5), *back of the neck*
6677 tsavvâ'r (30), *back of the neck*
5137 trachēlŏs (6), *throat or neck; life*

NECKS
1627 gârôwn (1), *throat*
6203 'ôreph (6), *nape or back of the neck*
6677 tsavvâ'r (10), *back of the neck*
5137 trachēlŏs (1), *throat or neck; life*

NECROMANCER
1875+4191 dârash (1), *to seek or ask; to worship*

NEDABIAH
5072 Neᵗdabyâh (1), *largess of Jehovah*

NEED
2637 châçêr (1), to *lack; to fail, want, make less*
2638 châçêr (1), *lacking*
2818 châshach (Ch.) (1), *to need*
4270 machçôwr (1), *impoverishment*
6878 tsôrek (1), *need*
1163 dĕi (1), *it is (was) necessary*
2121 ĕukairŏs (1), *opportune, suitable*
2192+5532 ĕchō (8), to *have; hold; keep*
3784 ŏphĕilō (1), *to owe; to be under obligation*
5532 chrĕia (26), *demand, requirement*
5535 chrĕ̩zō (4), *to have necessity, be in want of*

NEEDED
2192+5532 ĕchō (1), to *have; hold; keep*
4326 prŏsdĕŏmai (1), *to require additionally*

NEEDEST
2192+5532 ĕchō (1), to *have; hold; keep*

NEEDETH
422 anĕpaischuntŏs (1), *unashamed*
2192+318 ĕchō (1), *to have; hold; keep*
2192+5532 ĕchō (1), *to have; hold; keep*
5532 chrĕia (1), *demand, requirement*
5535 chrĕ¡zō (1), *to have necessity, be in want of*

NEEDFUL
2819 chashchûwth (1), *necessity*
316 anagkaiŏs (1), *necessary*
318 anagkē (1), *constraint; distress*
1163 dĕi (1), *it is (was) necessary*
2006 ĕpitēdĕiŏs (1), *requisite, needful*
5532 chrĕia (1), *demand, requirement*

NEEDLE
4476 rhaphis (2), *sewing needle*

NEEDLE'S
4476 rhaphis (1), *sewing needle*

NEEDLEWORK
4639+7551 ma'ăseh (1), *action; labor*
7551 râqam (5), *variegation; embroider*
7553 riqmâh (3), *variegation* of color; *embroidery*

NEEDS
318 anagkē (3), *constraint; distress*
3843 pantōs (1), *entirely; at all events*

NEEDY
34 'ebyôwn (35), *destitute; poor*
1800 dal (2), *weak, thin; humble, needy*
7326 rûwsh (1), *to be destitute*

NEESINGS
5846 'ătîyshâh (1), *sneezing*

NEGINAH
5058 nᵉgîynâh (1), *stringed instrument*

NEGINOTH
5058 nᵉgîynâh (6), *stringed instrument*

NEGLECT
272 amĕlĕō (2), *to be careless of, neglect*
3878 parakŏuō (2), *to disobey*

NEGLECTED
3865 parathĕōrĕō (1), *to overlook or disregard*

NEGLECTING
857 aphĕidia (1), *austerity, asceticism*

NEGLIGENT
7952 shâlah (1), *to mislead*
272 amĕlĕō (1), *to be careless of, neglect*

NEHELAMITE
5161 Nechĕlâmîy (3), *dreamed*

NEHEMIAH
5166 Nᵉchemyâh (8), *consolation of Jehovah*

NEHILOTH
5155 Nᵉchîylâh (1), *flute*

NEHUM
5149 Nᵉchûwm (1), *comforted*

NEHUSHTA
5179 Nᵉchushtâ' (1), *copper*

NEHUSHTAN
5180 Nᵉchushtân (1), *copper serpent*

NEIEL
5272 Nᵉ'îy'êl (1), *moved of God*

NEIGHBOUR
5997 'âmîyth (7), *comrade or kindred*
7138 qârôwb (2), *near, close*
7453 rêa' (74), *associate; one close*
7468 rᵉ'ûwth (2), *female associate*
7934 shâkên (6), *resident; fellow-citizen*
4139 plēsiŏn (16), *neighbor, fellow*

NEIGHBOUR'S
5997 'âmîyth (2), *comrade or kindred*
7453 rêa' (26), *associate; one close*

NEIGHBOURS
7138 qârôwb (3), *near, close*
7453 rêa' (2), *associate; one close*
7934 shâkên (11), *resident; fellow-citizen*
1069 gĕitôn (4), *neighbour*
4040 pĕriŏikŏs (1), *neighbor*

NEIGHBOURS'
7453 rêa' (1), *associate; one close*

NEIGHED
6670 tsâhal (1), *to be cheerful; to sound*

NEIGHING
4684 matshâlâh (1), *whinnying*

NEIGHINGS
4684 matshâlâh (1), *whinnying*

NEITHER
369 'ayin (40), *there is no, i.e., not exist, none*
408 'al (66), *not; nothing*
518 'îm (5), *whether?; if, although; Oh that!*
1077 bal (3), *nothing; not at all; lest*
1115 biltîy (4), *not, except, without, unless*
1571 gam (5), *also; even*
3608 kele' (2), *prison*

3804 kether (1), *royal headdress*
3808 lô' (475), no, *not*
3809 lâ' (Ch.) (3), *as nothing*
4480 min (2), *from, out of*
2228 ē (4), *or; than*
3361 mē (5), *not; lest*
3366 mēdĕ (34), *but not, not even; nor*
3383 mētĕ (19), *neither or nor; not even*
3756 ŏu (12), *no or not*
3761 ŏudĕ (67), *neither, nor, not even*
3763 ŏudĕpŏtĕ (1), *never at all*
3777 ŏutĕ (39), *not even*

NEKEB
5346 Neqeb (1), *dell*

NEKODA
5353 Nᵉqôwdâ' (4), *distinction*

NEMUEL
5241 Nᵉmûw'êl (3), *day of God*

NEMUELITES
5242 Nᵉmûw'êlîy (1), *Nemuelite*

NEPHEG
5298 Nepheg (4), *sprout*

NEPHEW
5220 neked (2), *offspring*

NEPHEWS
1121 bên (1), *son, descendant; people*
1549 ĕkgŏnŏn (1), *grandchild*

NEPHISH
5305 Nâphîysh (1), *refreshed*

NEPHISHESIM
5300 Nᵉphûwshᵉçîym (1), *expansions*

NEPHTHALIM
3508 Nĕphthalĕim (2), *my wrestling*

NEPHTOAH
5318 Nephtôwach (2), *spring*

NEPHUSIM
5304 Nᵉphîyçîym (1), *expansions*

NEPTHALIM
3508 Nĕphthalĕim (1), *my wrestling*

NER
5369 Nêr (16), *lamp*

NEREUS
3517 Nērĕus (1), *wet*

NERGAL
5370 Nêrgal (1), *Nergal*

NERGAL-SHAREZER
5371 Nêrgal Shar'etser (3), *Nergal-Sharetser*

NERI
3518 Nēri (1), *light of Jehovah*

NERIAH
5374 Nêrîyâh (10), *light of Jehovah*

NERO
3505 Nĕrōn (1), *Nero*

NEST
7064 qên (12), *nest; nestlings; chamber*
7077 qânan (3), *to nestle*

NESTS
7077 qânan (2), *to nestle*
2682 kataskēnōsis (2), *perch or nest*

NET
2764 chêrem (5), *doomed object*
4364 makmâr (1), *hunter's snare-net*
4685 mâtsôwd (2), *net or snare; besieging tower*
4686 mâtsûwd (2), *net or capture; fastness*
7568 resheth (20), *hunting net; network*
293 amphiblēstrŏn (2), *fishing net which is cast*
1350 diktuŏn (6), *drag net*
4522 sagēnē (1), *seine*

NETHANEEL
5417 Nᵉthan'êl (14), *given of God*

NETHANIAH
5418 Nᵉthanyâh (20), *given of Jehovah*

NETHER
7347 rêcheh (1), *mill-stone*
8481 tachtôwn (5), *bottommost*
8482 tachtîy (9), *lowermost; depths*

NETHERMOST
8481 tachtôwn (1), *bottommost*

NETHINIMS
5411 Nâthîyn (17), ones *given to duty*
5412 Nᵉthîyn (Ch.) (1), ones *given to duty*

NETOPHAH
5199 Nᵉtôphâh (2), *distillation*

NETOPHATHI
5200 Nᵉtôphâthîy (1), *Netophathite*

NETOPHATHITE
5200 Nᵉtôphâthîy (8), *Netophathite*

NETOPHATHITES
5200 Nᵉtôphâthîy (2), *Netophathite*

NETS
2764 chêrem (4), *doomed object*
4364 makmâr (1), *hunter's snare-net*
4365 mikmereth (1), *fishing-net*
7638 sâbâk (1), *netting*
1350 diktuŏn (6), *drag net*

NETTLES
2738 chârûwl (3), *bramble, thorny weed*
7057 qimmôwsh (2), *prickly plant*

NETWORK
4640+7568 Ma'say (2), *operative*
7639 sᵉbâkâh (5), *net-work balustrade*

NETWORKS
2355 chôwr (1), *white linen*
7639 sᵉbâkâh (2), *net-work balustrade*

NEVER
369 'ayin (2), *there is no, i.e., not exist, none*
408 'al (1), *not; nothing*
1253 bôr (1), *vegetable lye as soap; flux*
1755 dôwr (1), *dwelling*
3808 lô' (17), *no, not*
165 aiōn (1), *perpetuity, ever; world*
3361 mē (1), *not; lest*
3364 ŏu mē (1), *not at all, absolutely not*
3368 mēdĕpŏtĕ (1), *not even ever*
3756 ŏu (5), *no or not*
3762 ŏudĕis (1), *none, nobody, nothing*
3763 ŏudĕpŏtĕ (14), *never at all*
3764 ŏudĕpō (2), *not even yet*

NEVERTHELESS
61 'ăbâl (2), *truly, surely; yet, but*
389 'ak (11), *surely; only, however*
403 'âkên (1), *surely!, truly!; but*
657 'epheç (1), *end; no further*
1297 bᵉram (Ch.) (1), *however, but*
1571 gam (3), *also; even*
3588 kîy (4), *for, that because*
7535 raq (5), *merely; although*
235 alla (10), *but, yet, except, instead*
1161 dĕ (11), *but, yet; and then*
2544 kaitŏigĕ (1), *although really*
3305 mĕntŏi (1), *however*
4133 plēn (8), *albeit, save that, rather, yet*

NEW
1069 bâkar (1), *bear the first born*
1278 bᵉrîy'âh (1), *creation*
2319 châdâsh (50), *new, recent*
2320 chôdesh (20), *new moon; month*
2323 chădath (Ch.) (1), *new*
2961 țârîy (1), *fresh*
8492 tîyrôwsh (11), *fresh squeezed grape-juice*
46 agnaphŏs (2), *new, unshrunk cloth*
1098 glĕukŏs (1), *sweet wine*
2537 kainŏs (44), *freshness, i.e. new*
3501 nĕŏs (11), *new*

3561 nŏumēnia (1), *festival of new moon*
4372 prŏsphatŏs (1), *lately made, i.e. new*

NEWBORN
738 artigĕnnētŏs (1), *new born; young convert*

NEWLY
6965 qûwm (1), *to rise*
7138 qârôwb (1), *near, close*

NEWNESS
2538 kainŏtēs (2), *renewal, newness*

NEWS
8052 shᵉmûw'âh (1), *announcement*

NEXT
312 'achêr (2), *other, another, different; next*
4283 mochŏrâth (3), *tomorrow, next day*
4932 mishneh (7), *duplicate copy; double*
7138 qârôwb (5), *near, close*
839 auriŏn (1), *to-morrow*
1206 dĕutĕraiŏs (1), *on the second day*
1836 hĕxēs (2), *successive, next*
1887 ĕpauriŏn (7), *to-morrow*
1966 ĕpiŏusa (3), *ensuing*
2064 ĕrchŏmai (1), *to go or come*
2087 hĕtĕrŏs (2), *other or different*
2192 ĕchō (3), *to have; hold; keep*
3342 mĕtaxu (1), *betwixt; meanwhile*

NEZIAH
5335 Nᵉtsîyach (2), *conspicuous*

NEZIB
5334 Nᵉtsîyb (1), *station*

NIBHAZ
5026 Nibchaz (1), *Nibchaz*

NIBSHAN
5044 Nibshân (1), *Nibshan*

NICANOR
3527 Nikanŏr (1), *victorious*

NICODEMUS
3530 Nikŏdēmŏs (5), *victorious among his people*

NICOLAITANES
3531 Nikŏlaïtēs (2), *adherent of Nicolaüs*

NICOLAS
3532 Nikŏlaŏs (1), *victorious over the people*

NICOPOLIS
3533 Nikŏpŏlis (2), *victorious city*

NIGER
3526 Nigĕr (1), *black*

NIGH
4952 mishrâh (1), *steeped juice*
5060 nâga' (3), *to strike*
5066 nâgash (12), *to be, come, bring near*
7126 qârab (32), *to approach, bring near*
7138 qârôwb (4), *near, close*
7607 shᵉ'êr (1), *flesh, meat; kindred by blood*
7934 shâkên (1), *resident; fellow-citizen*
1448 ĕggizō (21), *to approach*
1451 ĕggus (18), *near, close*
3844 para (2), *from; with; besides; on account of*
3897 paraplēsiŏn (1), *almost*
4314 prŏs (1), *for; on, at; to, toward; against*

NIGHT
956 bûwth (Ch.) (1), *to lodge over night*
2822 chôshek (1), *darkness; misery*
3915 layil (208), *night; adversity*
3916 leylᵉyâ' (Ch.) (4), *night*
5399 nesheph (3), *dusk, dawn*
6153 'ereb (4), *dusk*
6916 qiddâh (1), *cassia bark*
8464 tachmâç (2), *unclean bird (poss.) owl*
1273 dianuktĕrĕuō (1), *to pass, spend the night*
3571 nux (60), *night*
3574 nuchthēmĕrŏn (1), *full day*

NIGHTS
3915 layil (15), *night; adversity*
3571 nux (3), *night*

NIMRAH
5247 Nimrâh (1), *clear water*

NIMRIM
5249 Nimrîym (2), *clear waters*

NIMROD
5248 Nimrôwd (4), *Nimrod*

NIMSHI
5250 Nimshîy (5), *extricated*

NINE
8672 têsha' (44), *nine; ninth*
1767 ĕnnĕa (1), *nine*
1768 ĕnnĕnĕkŏntaĕnnĕa (4), *ninety-nine*

NINETEEN
8672+6240 têsha' (3), *nine; ninth*

NINETEENTH
8672+6240 têsha' (4), *nine; ninth*

NINETY
8673 tish'îym (20), *ninety*

1768 ĕnnĕnĕkŏntaĕnnĕa (4), *ninety-nine*

NINEVE
3535 Ninĕuï (1), *Nineveh*

NINEVEH
5210 Nîynᵉvêh (17), *Nineveh*
3536 Ninĕuïtēs (1), *inhabitant of Nineveh*

NINEVITES
3536 Ninĕuïtēs (1), *inhabitant of Nineveh*

NINTH
8671 tᵉshîy'îy (18), *ninth*
8672 têsha' (6), *nine; ninth*
1766 ĕnnatŏs (10), *ninth*

NISAN
5212 Nîyçân (2), *Nisan*

NISROCH
5268 Niçrôk (2), *Nisrok*

NITRE
5427 nether (2), *mineral potash for washing*

NOADIAH
5129 Nôw'adyâh (2), *convened of Jehovah*

NOAH
5146 Nôach (44), *rest*
5270 Nô'âh (4), *movement*
3575 Nŏĕ (3), *rest*

NOAH'S
5146 Nôach (2), *rest*

NOB
5011 Nôb (6), *fruit*

NOBAH
5025 Nôbach (3), *bark*

NOBLE
3358 yaqqîyr (Ch.) (1), *precious*
6579 partam (1), *grandee, noble*
2104 ĕugĕnēs (2), *high in rank; generous*
2908 krĕissŏn (2), *better, i.e. greater advantage*

NOBLEMAN
937 basilikŏs (2), *befitting the sovereign*
2104+444 ĕugĕnēs (1), *high in rank; generous*

NOBLES
117 'addîyr (7), *powerful; majestic*
678 'âtsîyl (1), *extremity; noble*
1281 bârîyach (1), *fleeing, gliding serpent*
1419 gâdôwl (1), *great*
2715 chôr (13), *noble, i.e. in high rank*
3513 kâbad (1), *to be rich, glorious*
5057 nâgîyd (1), *commander, official*
5081 nâdîyb (4), *magnanimous*
6579 partam (1), *grandee, noble*

NOD
5113 Nôwd (1), *vagrancy*

NODAB
5114 Nôwdâb (1), *noble*

NOE
3575 Nŏĕ (5), *rest*

NOGAH
5052 Nôgahh (2), *brilliancy*

NOHAH
5119 Nôwchâh (1), *quietude*

NOISE
1949 hûwm (2), to *make an uproar; agitate*
1993 hâmâh (4), to *be in great commotion*
1995 hâmôwn (4), *noise, tumult; many, crowd*
1998 hemyâh (1), *sound, tone*
6476 pâtsach (1), to *break out in sound*
6963 qôwl (48), *voice or sound*
7267 rôgez (1), *disquiet; anger*
7452 rêa' (1), *crash; noise; shout*
7588 shâ'ôwn (8), *uproar; destruction*
8085 shâma‘ (2), to *hear intelligently*
8643 t°rûw'âh (1), *battle-cry; clangor*
8663 t°shû'âh (1), *crashing or clamor*
2350 thŏrubĕŏ (1), to *disturb; clamor*
4500 rhŏizēdŏn (1), *with a crash, with a roar*
5456 phōnē (1), *voice, sound*

NOISED
191 akŏuŏ (1), to *hear; obey*
1096+5408 ginŏmai (1), to *be, become*
1255 dialalĕŏ (1), to *converse, discuss*

NOISOME
1942 havvâh (1), *desire; craving*
7451 ra‘ (2), *bad; evil*
2556 kakŏs (1), *bad, evil, wrong*

NON
5126 Nûwn (1), *perpetuity*

NOON
6672 tsôhar (11), *window: noon time*
3314 mĕsĕmbria (1), *midday; south*

NOONDAY
6672 tsôhar (10), *window: noon time*

NOONTIDE
6256+6672 'êth (1), *time*

NOPH
5297 Nôph (7), *Noph*

NOPHAH
5302 Nôphach (1), *gust*

NORTH
4215 m°zâreh (1), north *wind*
6828 tsâphôwn (128), *north, northern*

1005 borrhas (2), north
5566 chŏrŏs (1), *north-west* wind

NORTHERN
6828 tsâphôwn (1), *north, northern*
6830 ts°phôwnîy (1), *northern*

NORTHWARD
6828 tsâphôwn (24), *north, northern*

NOSE
639 'aph (11), *nose or nostril; face; person*
2763 charam (1), to *devote to destruction*

NOSES
639 'aph (1), *nose or nostril; face; person*

NOSTRILS
639 'aph (13), *nose or nostril; face; person*
5156 n°chîyr (1), *pair of nostrils*
5170 nachar (1), *snorting*

NOTABLE
2380 châzûwth (2), striking *appearance*
1110 gnōstŏs (1), *well-known*
1978 ĕpisēmŏs (1), *eminent, prominent*
2016 ĕpiphanēs (1), *conspicuous*

NOTE
2710 châqaq (1), to *engrave; to enact* laws
1978 ĕpisēmŏs (1), *eminent, prominent*
4593 sēmĕiŏŏ (1), to *mark for avoidance*

NOTED
7559 râsham (1), to *record*

NOTHING
369 'ayin (23), *there is no, i.e., not exist, none*
408 'al (3), *not; nothing*
657 'ephec (2), *end; no further*
1099 b°lîymâh (1), *nothing whatever*
1115 biltîy (3), *not, except, without, unless*
1697 dâbâr (2), *word; matter; thing*
2600 chinnâm (2), *gratis, free*
3605 kôl (1), *all, any or every*
3808 lô' (25), no, *not*
3809 lâ' (Ch.) (1), *as nothing*
4591 mâ‘aṭ (1), to *be, make small or few*
7535 raq (1), *merely; although*
8414 tôhûw (1), *waste, desolation, formless*
114 athĕtĕŏ (1), to *disesteem, neutralize*
3361 mē (1), *not; lest*
3367 mēdĕis (27), *not even one*
3385 mēti (2), *whether at all*

3756 ŏu (4), no or not
3762 ŏudĕis (66), *none, nobody, nothing*
3777 ŏutĕ (1), *not even*

NOTICE
5234 nâkar (1), to *acknowledge*
4293 prŏkataggĕllō (1), to *predict, promise*

NOTWITHSTANDING
389 'ak (6), *surely; only, however*
657 'ephec (1), *end; no further*
7535 raq (2), *merely; although*
235 alla (1), *but, yet, except, instead*
4133 plēn (4), *albeit, save that, rather, yet*

NOUGHT
205 'âven (1), *trouble, vanity, wickedness*
369 'ayin (1), *there is no, i.e., not exist, none*
408+3972 'al (1), *not; nothing*
434 'ĕlûwl (1), *good for nothing*
656 'âphēc (1), to *cease*
657 'ephec (1), *end; no further*
659 'êpha' (1), *nothing*
2600 chinnâm (6), *gratis, free*
3808 lô' (1), no, *not*
3808+1697 lô' (1), no, *not*
3808+1952 lô' (1), no, *not*
5034 nâbêl (1), to *wilt; to fall away; to be foolish*
6331 pûwr (1), to *crush*
6544 pâra' (1), to *loosen; to expose, dismiss*
6565 pârar (2), to *break up; to violate, frustrate*
8045 shâmad (1), to *desolate*
8414 tôhûw (2), *waste, desolation, formless*
557 apĕlĕgmŏs (1), *refutation, discrediting*
1432 dōrĕan (3), *gratuitously, freely*
1847 ĕxŏudĕnŏŏ (1), to *be treated with contempt*
1848 ĕxŏuthĕnĕŏ (3), to *treat with contempt*
2049 ĕrēmŏŏ (1), to *lay waste*
2647 kataluŏ (1), to *demolish*
2673 katargĕŏ (2), to *be, render entirely useless*
3762 ŏudĕis (1), *none, nobody, nothing*

NOURISH
1431 gâdal (2), to *be great, make great*
2421 châyâh (1), to *live; to revive*
3557 kûwl (2), to *keep in; to maintain*

NOURISHED
1431 gâdal (1), to *be great, make great*

2421 châyâh (1), to live; to revive
3557 kûwl (1), to *keep in; to measure*
7235 râbâh (1), to *increase*
397 anatrĕphō (2), to *rear, care for*
1789 ĕntrĕphō (1), to *educate; to be trained*
5142 trĕphō (3), to *nurse, feed, care for*

NOURISHER
3557 kûwl (1), to *keep in; to measure*

NOURISHETH
1625 ĕktrĕphō (1), to *cherish or train*

NOURISHING
1431 gâdal (1), to *be great, make great*

NOURISHMENT
2023 ĕpichŏrēgĕō (1), to fully *supply; to aid*

NOVICE
3504 nĕŏphutŏs (1), *young convert*

NOW
116 ĕdayin (Ch.) (2), *then*
227 'âz (1), *at that time or place; therefore*
645 'êphôw (10), *then*
1768 dîy (Ch.) (1), *that; of*
2008 hênnâh (1), *from here; from there*
2088 zeh (3), *this or that*
3117 yôwm (4), *day; time period*
3528 k°bâr (4), *long ago, formerly, hitherto*
3588 kîy (2), *for, that because*
3705 k°'an (Ch.) (14), *now*
4994 nâ (172), *I pray!, please!, I beg you!*
6254 'Asht°râthîy (1), *Ashterathite*
6258 'attâh (401), *at this time, now*
6288 p°'ôrâh (3), *foliage, branches*
6471 pa‘am (5), *time; step; occurence*
737 arti (25), *just now; at once*
1160 dapanē (2), *expense, cost*
1161 dĕ (160), *but, yet; and then*
1211 dē (1), *now, then; indeed, therefore*
2235 ēdē (3), *even now*
2236 hēdista (38), *with great pleasure*
2532 kai (5), *and; or; even; also*
3063 lŏipŏn (2), *remaining; finally*
3568 nun (127), *now; the present or immediate*
3570 nuni (20), *just now, indeed, in fact*
3765 ŏukĕti (5), *not yet, no longer*
3767 ŏun (12), *certainly; accordingly*

English

NUMBER
2714 chêqer (1), examination
3187 yâchas (1), to enroll by family list
4373 mikçâh (1), valuation of a thing
4487 mânâh (7), to allot; to enumerate or enroll
4507 Mᵉnîy (1), Apportioner, i.e. Fate
4510 minyân (Ch.) (1), enumeration, number
4557 miçpâr (108), number
4557+3187 miçpâr (1), number
4662 miphqâd (2), designated spot; census
5608 çâphar (10), to inscribe; to enumerate
5736 'âdaph (1), to be redundant
6485 pâqad (14), to visit, care for, count
705 arithmĕō (1), enumerate or count
706 arithmŏs (18), reckoned number
1469 ĕgkrinō (1), to count among
2639 katalĕgō (1), to enroll, put on a list
3793 ŏchlŏs (2), throng

NUMBERED
4483 mᵉnâ' (Ch.) (1), to count, appoint
4487 mânâh (7), to allot; to enumerate or enroll
4557 miçpâr (1), number
5608 çâphar (11), to inscribe; to enumerate
6485 pâqad (102), to visit, care for, count
705 arithmĕō (2), to enumerate or count
2674 katarithmĕō (1), to be numbered among
3049 lŏgizŏmai (1), to credit; to think, regard
4785 sugkatapsēphizō (1), to number with

NUMBEREST
5608 çâphar (1), to inscribe; to enumerate
6485 pâqad (2), to visit, care for, count

NUMBERING
5608 çâphar (1), to inscribe; to enumerate
5610 çᵉphâr (1), census

NUMBERS
4557 miçpâr (1), number
5615 çᵉphôrâh (1), numeration
6486 pᵉquddâh (1), visitation; punishment

NUN
5126 Nûwn (29), perpetuity

NURSE
539 'âman (2), to be firm, faithful, true; to trust
3243 yânaq (7), to suck; to give milk
5162 trŏphŏs (1), nurse-mother

NURSED
539 'âman (1), to be firm, faithful, true; to trust
5134 nûwq (1), to suckle

NURSING
539 'âman (2), to be firm, faithful, true; to trust
3243 yânaq (1), to suck; to give milk

NURTURE
3809 paidĕia (1), disciplinary correction

NUTS
93 'ĕgôwz (1), nut
992 bôṭen (1), pistachio

NYMPHAS
3564 Numphas (1), nymph-born

OAK
424 'êlâh (11), oak
427 'allâh (1), oak
437 'allôwn (3), oak

OAKS
352 'ayil (1), chief; ram; oak tree
437 'allôwn (5), oak

OAR
4880 mâshôwṭ (1), oar

OARS
4880 mâshôwṭ (1), oar
7885 shayiṭ (1), oar

OATH
423 'âlâh (14), curse, oath
7621 shᵉbûw'âh (26), sworn oath
7650 shâba' (7), to swear
332 anathĕmatizō (1), to declare or vow an oath
3727 hŏrkŏs (7), sacred restraint, i.e. an oath
3728 hŏrkōmŏsia (4), asseveration on oath

OATH'S
3727 hŏrkŏs (2), sacred restraint, i.e. an oath

OATHS
7621 shᵉbûw'âh (2), sworn oath
3727 hŏrkŏs (2), sacred restraint, i.e. an oath

OBADIAH
5662 'Ôbadyâh (20), serving Jehovah

OBAL
5745 'Ôwbâl (1), Obal

OBED
5744 'Ôwbêd (9), serving
5601 Obēd (3), serving

OBED-EDOM
5654 'Ôbêd 'Ĕdôwm (20), worker of Edom

OBEDIENCE
5218 hupakŏē (11), compliance, submission
5293 hupŏtassō (1), to subordinate; to obey

OBEDIENT
8085 shâma' (8), to hear intelligently
5218 hupakŏē (2), compliance, submission
5219 hupakŏuō (2), to heed or conform

OBEISANCE
7812 shâchâh (9), to prostrate in homage

OBEY
3349 yiqqâhâh (1), obedience
4928 mishma'ath (1), obedience; royal subject
8085 shâma' (40), to hear intelligently
8086 shᵉma' (Ch.) (1), to hear intelligently
544 apĕithĕō (3), to disbelieve
3980 pĕitharchĕō (3), to submit to authority
3982 pĕithō (5), to pacify or conciliate; to assent
5218 hupakŏē (1), compliance, submission
5219 hupakŏuō (13), to heed or conform
5255+1036 hupēkŏŏs (1), to listen attentively

OBEYED
8085 shâma' (34), to hear
3982 pĕithō (2), to pacify or conciliate; to assent
5219 hupakŏuō (5), to heed or conform

OBEYEDST
8085 shâma' (2), to hear

OBEYETH
8085 shâma' (3), to hear

OBEYING
8085 shâma' (2), to hear
5218 hupakŏē (1), compliance, submission

OBIL
179 'Ôwbîyl (1), mournful

OBJECT
2723 katēgŏrĕō (1), to bring a charge

OBLATION
4503 minchâh (5), tribute; offering
4541 maççêkâh (1), libation; woven coverlet
7133 qorbân (11), sacrificial present
8641 tᵉrûwmâh (17), sacrifice, tribute
8642 tᵉrûwmîyâh (1), sacrificial offering

OBLATIONS
4503 minchâh (1), sacrificial offering
4864 mas'êth (1), raising; beacon; present
7133 qorbân (1), sacrificial present
8641 tᵉrûwmâh (2), sacrifice, tribute

OBOTH
88 'Ôbôth (4), water-skins

OBSCURE
380 'îyshôwn (1), pupil, eyeball; middle

OBSCURITY
652 'ôphel (1), dusk, darkness
2822 chôshek (2), darkness; misery

OBSERVATION
3907 paratērēsis (1), careful observation

OBSERVE
5172 nâchash (1), to prognosticate
5341 nâtsar (1), to guard, protect, maintain
6049 'ânan (1), to cover, becloud; to act covertly
6213 'âsâh (3), to do or make
7789 shûwr (1), to spy out, survey
8104 shâmar (41), to watch
3906 paratērĕō (1), to note insidiously
4160 pŏiĕō (1), to make
5083 tērĕō (3), to keep, guard, obey
5442 phulassō (1), to watch, i.e. be on guard

OBSERVED
6049 'ânan (2), to cover, becloud; to act covertly
6213 'âsâh (1), to do or make
7789 shûwr (1), to spy out, survey
8104 shâmar (3), to watch
8107 shimmûr (2), observance
4933 suntērĕō (1), to preserve in memory
5442 phulassō (1), to watch, i.e. be on guard

OBSERVER
6049 'ânan (1), to cover, becloud; to act covertly

OBSERVERS
6049 'ânan (1), to cover, becloud; to act covertly

OBSERVEST
8104 shâmar (1), to watch

OBSERVETH
8104 shâmar (1), to watch

OBSTINATE
553 'âmats (1), to be strong; be courageous
7186 qâsheh (1), severe

OBTAIN
1129 bânâh (1), to build; to establish
2388 châzaq (1), to fasten upon; to seize
5381 nâsag (1), to reach
6329 pûwq (1), to issue; to furnish; to secure
1653 ĕlĕĕō (2), to give out compassion
2013 ĕpitugchanō (1), to attain, obtain
2638 katalambanō (1), to seize; to possess
2983 lambanō (2), to take, receive

4047 pĕripŏiēsis (1), *acquisition*
5177 *tugchanō* (3), to *take part in; to obtain*

OBTAINED
5375 nâsâ' (5), to *lift up*
7592 shâ'al (1), to *ask*
1653 ĕlĕĕŏ (6), to *give out compassion*
2013 *ĕpitugchanō* (4), to *attain, obtain*
2147 hĕuriskō (1), to *find*
2816 klĕrŏnŏmĕō (1), to *be an heir to, inherit*
2820 klĕrŏō (1), to *allot*
2902 kratĕō (1), to *seize*
2932 ktaŏmai (1), to *get,* i.e. *acquire*
2975 *lagchanō* (2), to *determine by lot*
3140 marturĕō (3), to *testify; to commend*
5177 *tugchanō* (2), to *take part in; to obtain*

OBTAINETH
6329 pûwq (2), to *issue; to furnish; to secure*

OBTAINING
4047 pĕripŏiēsis (1), *acquisition*

OCCASION
1556 gâlal (1), to *roll; to commit*
4672 mâtsâ' (2), to *find or acquire; to occur*
5308 nᵉphal (Ch.) (1), to *fall*
5931 'illâh (Ch.) (3), *pretext, legal grounds*
8385 ta'ănâh (2), *opportunity; purpose*
874 aphŏrmē (6), *opportunity, pretext*
1223 dia (1), *through, by means of; because of*
4625 skandalŏn (2), *snare*

OCCASIONED
5437 çâbab (1), to *surround*

OCCASIONS
5949 'ălîylâh (2), *opportunity, action*
8569 tᵉnûw'âh (1), *enmity*

OCCUPATION
4399 mᵉlâ'kâh (1), *work; property*
4639 ma'ăseh (2), *action; labor*
5078 tĕchnē (1), *trade, craft; skill*

OCCUPIED
5414 nâthan (3), to *give*
5503 çâchar (1), to *travel round; to palpitate*
6213 'âsâh (1), to *do or make*
6213+4399 'âsâh (1), to *do or make*
4043 pĕripatĕō (1), to *walk; to live a life*

OCCUPIERS
6148 'ârab (1), to *intermix*

OCCUPIETH
378 anaplĕrŏō (1), to *complete; to occupy*

OCCUPY
6148 'ârab (1), to *intermix*
4231 pragmatĕuŏmai (1), to *trade, do business*

OCCURRENT
6294 pega' (1), *casual impact*

OCRAN
5918 'Okrân (5), *muddler*

ODD
5736 'âdaph (1), to *be redundant*

ODED
5752 'Ôwdêd (3), *reiteration*

ODIOUS
887 bâ'ash (1), to *smell bad; be a moral stench*
8130 sânê' (1), to *hate*

ODOUR
3744 ŏsmē (2), *fragrance; odor*

ODOURS
1314 besem (2), *spice; fragrance; balsam*
5207 nîchôwach (1), *pleasant; delight*
5208 nîychôwach (Ch.) (1), *pleasure*
2368 thumiama (2), *incense offering*

OFF
5921 'al (65), *above, over, upon, or against*
114 athĕtĕō (1), to *neutralize or set aside*
554 apĕkduŏmai (2), to *divest wholly oneself*
568 apĕchō (1), to *be distant*
575 apŏ (13), *from, away*
595 apŏthĕsis (1), *laying aside*
609 apŏkŏptō (8), *mutilate the genitals*
631 apŏmassŏmai (1), to *scrape away, wipe off*
659 apŏtithēmi (3), to *put away; get rid of*
660 apŏtinassō (1), to *brush off, shake off*
851 aphairĕō (2), to *remove, cut off*
1537 ĕk (1), *out, out of*
1562 ĕkduō (1), to *divest*
1575 ĕkklaō (4), to *exscind, cut off*
1581 ĕkkŏptō (4), to *cut off; to frustrate*
1601 ĕkpiptō (2), to *drop away*
1621 ĕktinassō (3), to *shake violently*
3089 luō (1), to *loosen*
3112 makran (1), *at a distance, far away*
4048 pĕrirrhēgnumi (1), to *tear completely away*
4496 rhiptō (1), to *fling, toss; to lay out*

OFFENCE
816 'âsham (1), to *be guilty; to be punished*
4383 mikshôwl (2), *stumbling-block*
266 hamartia (1), *sin*

677 aprŏskŏpŏs (3), *faultless*
3900 paraptōma (5), *error; transgression*
4348 prŏskŏmma (1), *occasion of apostasy*
4349 prŏskŏpē (1), *occasion of sin*
4625 skandalŏn (5), *snare*

OFFENCES
2399 chĕṭ' (1), *crime or its penalty*
3900 paraptōma (2), *error; transgression*
4625 skandalŏn (4), *snare*

OFFEND
816 'âsham (4), to *be guilty; to be punished*
898 bâgad (1), to *act treacherously*
2254 châbal (1), to *pervert, destroy*
4383 mikshôwl (1), *stumbling-block*
4417 ptaiō (3), to *trip up, stumble morally*
4624 skandalizŏ (14), to *entrap,* i.e. *trip up*
4625 skandalŏn (1), *snare*

OFFENDED
816 'âsham (2), to *be guilty; to be punished*
819 'ashmâh (1), *guiltiness*
2398 châṭâ' (4), to *sin*
6586 pâsha' (1), to *break away from authority*
264 hamartanō (1), to *miss the mark, to sin*
4624 skandalizŏ (16), to *entrap,* i.e. *trip up*

OFFENDER
2398 châṭâ' (1), to *sin*
91 adikĕō (1), to *do wrong*

OFFENDERS
2400 chaṭṭâ' (1), *criminal, guilty*

OFFER
2076 zâbach (20), to *(sacrificially) slaughter*
2077 zebach (1), *animal flesh; sacrifice*
5066 nâgash (4), to *be, come, bring near*
5130 nûwph (3), to *quiver, vibrate, rock*
5186 nâṭâh (1), to *stretch or spread out*
5190 nâṭal (1), to *lift; to impose*
5258 nâçak (2), to *pour a libation*
5260 nᵉçak (Ch.) (1), to *pour out a libation*
5375 nâsâ' (1), to *lift up*
5414 nâthan (2), to *give*
5927 'âlâh (34), to *ascend, be high, mount*
6213 'âsâh (41), to *do or make*
6999 qâṭar (1), to *turn into fragrance by fire*

7126 qârab (79), to *approach, bring near*
7127 qᵉrêb (Ch.) (2), to *approach, bring near*
7311 rûwm (14), to *be high; to rise or raise*
7819 shâchaṭ (1), to *slaughter; butcher*
399 anaphĕrō (3), to *lead up; to offer sacrifice*
1325 didōmi (2), to *give*
1929 ĕpididōmi (1), to *give over*
3930 parĕchō (1), to *hold near,* i.e. to *present*
4374 prŏsphĕrō (10), to *present to; to treat as*

OFFERED
1684 dᵉbach (Ch.) (1), to *sacrifice an animal*
2076 zâbach (17), to *(sacrificially) slaughter*
2398 châṭâ' (1), to *sin*
4639 ma'ăseh (1), *action; labor*
5066 nâgash (2), to *be, come, bring near*
5068 nâdab (1), to *volunteer; to present*
5069 nᵉdab (Ch.) (1), *be, give without coercion*
5130 nûwph (2), to *quiver, vibrate, rock*
5927 'âlâh (38), to *ascend, be high, mount*
6213 'âsâh (6), to *do or make*
6999 qâṭar (2), to *turn into fragrance by fire*
7126 qârab (16), to *approach, bring near*
7127 qᵉrêb (Ch.) (1), to *approach, bring near*
7133 qorbân (1), *sacrificial present*
7311 rûwm (2), to *be high; to rise or raise*
8641 tᵉrûwmâh (1), *sacrifice, tribute*
321 anagō (1), to *lead up; to bring out; to sail*
399 anaphĕrŏ (1), to *lead up; to offer sacrifice*
1494 ĕidōlŏthutŏn (8), *idolatrous offering*
4374 prŏsphĕrō (14), to *present to; to treat as*
4689 spĕndō (2), to *pour out as a libation*

OFFERETH
2076 zâbach (1), to *(sacrificially) slaughter*
2398 châṭâ' (1), to *sin*
5066 nâgash (1), to *be, come, bring near*
5926 'illĕg (1), *stuttering, stammering*
5927 'âlâh (2), to *ascend, be high, mount*
7126 qârab (9), to *approach, bring near*

OFFERING
817 'âsham (1), *guilt; fault; sin-offering*
2076 zâbach (1), to *(sacrificially) slaughter*
4503 minchâh (147), *tribute; offering*

English

OMEGA
5598 Ō (4), last letter of
the Greek alphabet

OMER
6016 'ômer (5), *sheaf* of
grain; dry *measure*

OMERS
6016 'ômer (1), *sheaf* of
grain; dry *measure*

OMITTED
863 aphiëmi (1), to *leave;*
to *pardon, forgive*

OMNIPOTENT
3841 pantŏkratŏr (1),
Absolute *sovereign*

OMRI
6018 'Omrîy (18), *heaping*

ONAM
208 'Ôwnâm (4), *strong*

ONAN
209 'Ôwnân (8), *strong*

ONCE
227 'âz (1), *at that time*
or *place; therefore*
259 'echâd (15), *first*
996 bêyn (1), *between;*
"*either...or*"
3162 yachad (1), *unitedly*
4118 mahêr (1), *in a
hurry*
5750 'ôwd (1), *again;
repeatedly; still; more*
6471 pa'am (10), *time;
step; occurence*
6471+259 pa'am (1),
time; step; occurence
530 hapax (15), *once for
all*
2178 ĕphapax (5), *upon
one occasion*
3366 mēdĕ (1), *but not,
not even; nor*
3826 pamplēthĕi (1), *in
full multitude*
4218 pŏtĕ (2), *at some
time, ever*

ONE
259 'echâd (658), *first*
376 'îysh (173), *man;
male; someone*
428 'êl-leh (2), *these* or
those
492 'almônîy (1), *certain
so and so, whoever*
802 'ishshâh (8), *woman,
wife; women, wives*
1397 geber (1), *person,
man*
1571 gam (1), *also; even*
1668 dâ' (Ch.) (2), *this*
1836 dên (Ch.) (1), *this*
2063 zô'th (1), *this*
2088 zeh (10), *this* or *that*
2297 chad (1), *one*
2298 chad (Ch.) (5), *one;
single; first; at once*
3605 kôl (1), *all, any*
3627 kᵉlîy (1),
implement, thing
3671 kânâph (1), *edge* or
extremity; wing
5315 nephesh (1), *life;
breath; soul; wind*
6918 qâdôwsh (2), *sacred*
240 allēlōn (77), *one
another*

243 allŏs (4), *different,
other*
1438 hĕautŏu (6),
himself, herself, itself
1515 ĕirēnē (1), *peace;
health; prosperity*
1520 hĕis (231), *one*
2087 hĕtĕrŏs (1), *other* or
different
3303 mĕn (2), *not
translated*
3391 mia (56), *one* or *first*
3442 mŏnŏphthalmŏs
(2), *one-eyed*
3661 hŏmŏthumadŏn
(12), *unanimously*
3675 hŏmŏphrŏn (1),
like-minded
3739 hŏs (1), *who, which,
what, that*
3956 pas (2), *all, any,
every, whole*
4861 sumpsuchŏs (1),
similar in sentiment
5100 tis (35), *some* or
any person or object
5129 tŏutŏị (1), *in this
person or thing*

ONES
1121 bên (1), *son,
descendant; people*

ONESIMUS
3682 Ŏnēsimŏs (4),
profitable

ONESIPHORUS
3683 Ŏnēsiphŏrŏs (2),
profit-bearer

ONIONS
1211 betsel (1), *onion*

ONLY
259 'echâd (2), *first*
389 'ak (33), *surely; only,
however*
905 bad (35), *apart, only,
besides*
910 bâdâd (1), *separate,
alone*
2108 zûwlâh (1), *except;
apart from; besides*
3162 yachad (2), *unitedly*
3173 yâchîyd (7), *only
son; alone; beloved*
3535 kibsâh (1), *ewe
sheep*
3697 kâçam (1), *to shear,
clip*
7535 raq (52), *merely;
although*
1520 hĕis (1), *one*
3439 mŏnŏgĕnēs (9),
sole, one and only
3440 mŏnŏn (62), *merely;
just*
3441 mŏnŏs (24), *single,
only; by oneself*

ONO
207 'Ôwnôw (5), *strong*

ONYCHA
7827 shᵉchêleth (1),
scale or shell, mussel

ONYX
7718 shôham (11), (poss.)
pale green beryl stone

OPEN
1540 gâlâh (6), *to
denude; uncover*

3605 kôl (1), *all, any* or
every
4725 mâqôwm (1),
general locality, place
5869 'ayin (1), *eye; sight;
fountain*
6358 pâṭûwr (4), *opened;
bud*
6363 peṭer (1), *firstling;
first born*
6440 pânîym (13), *face;
front*
6475 pâtsâh (3), *to rend,
i.e. open*
6491 pâqach (10), *to
open the eyes*
6555 pârats (1), *to break
out*
6566 pâras (1), *to break
apart, disperse, scatter*
6605 pâthach (49), *to
open wide; to loosen*
6606 pᵉthach (Ch.) (1), *to
open*
6610 pithchôwn (1), *act
of opening the mouth*
8365 shâtham (2), *to
unveil, i.e. open*
71 agō (1), *to lead; to
bring, drive; to weigh*
343 anakaluptō (1), *to
unveil*
455 anŏigō (21), *to open
up*
1722+457 ĕn (1), *in;
during; because of*
3856 paradĕigmatizō (1),
to expose to infamy
4271 prŏdēlŏs (1),
obvious, evident

OPENED
1540 gâlâh (3), *to
denude; uncover*
3738 kârâh (1), *to dig; to
plot; to bore, hew*
6473 pâ'ar (3), *to open
wide*
6475 pâtsâh (7), *to rend,
i.e. open*
6491 pâqach (7), *to open
the eyes*
6589 pâsaq (1), *to
dispart, i.e., spread*
6605 pâthach (51), *to
open wide; to loosen*
6606 pᵉthach (Ch.) (1), *to
open*
380 anaptussō (1), *to
unroll a scroll*
455 anŏigō (53), *to open
up*
1272 dianŏigō (6), *to
open thoroughly*
4977 schizō (1), *to split
or sever*
5136 trachēlizō (1), *to lay
bare*

OPENEST
6605 pâthach (2), *to open
wide; to loosen, begin*

OPENETH
1540 gâlâh (3), *to
denude; uncover*
6363 peṭer (7), *firstling;
first born*
6491 pâqach (2), *to open
the eyes*

6589 pâsaq (1), *to
dispart, i.e., spread*
6605 pâthach (4), *to open
wide; to loosen, begin*
455 anŏigō (3), *to open up*
1272 dianŏigō (1), *to
open thoroughly*

OPENING
4668 maphtêach (1),
opening; key
4669 miphtâch (1),
utterance of lips
6491 pâqach (1), *to open
the eyes*
6495 pᵉqach-qôwach (1),
jail-delivery; salvation
6605 pâthach (1), *to open
wide; to loosen, begin*
6610 pithchôwn (1), *act
of opening the mouth*
1272 dianŏigō (1), *to
open thoroughly*

OPENINGS
6607 pethach (1),
opening; door, entrance

OPENLY
5879 'Êynayim (1),
double fountain
1219 dēmŏsiŏs (1),
public; in public
1717 ĕmphanēs (1),
apparent in self, seen
1722+3588+5318 ĕn (3),
in; during; because of
1722+3954 ĕn (2), *in;
during; because of*
3954 parrhēsia (4),
frankness, boldness
5320 phanĕrŏs (2),
plainly, i.e. clearly

OPERATION
4639 ma'ăseh (2), *action;
labor*
1753 ĕnĕrgĕia (1),
efficiency, energy

OPERATIONS
1755 ĕnĕrgēma (1),
effect, activity

OPHEL
6077 'Ŏphel (5), *fortress*

OPHIR
211 'Ôwphîyr (13), *Ophir*

OPHNI
6078 'Ophnîy (1), *Ophnite*

OPHRAH
6084 'Ophrâh (8), *female
fawn*

OPINION
1843 dêa' (3), *knowledge*

OPINIONS
5587 çâ'îph (1), *divided
in mind; sentiment*

OPPORTUNITY
170 akairĕŏmai (1), *to
fail of a proper occasion*
2120 ĕukairia (2),
favorable occasion
2540 kairŏs (2),
occasion, set time

OPPOSE
475 antidiatithĕmai (1),
be disputatious

English

OPPOSED
498 antitassŏmai (1),
oppose, resist

OPPOSEST
7852 sâṭam (1), to
persecute

OPPOSETH
480 antikĕimai (1), to be
an opponent

OPPOSITIONS
477 antithĕsis (1),
opposition

OPPRESS
1792 dâkâ' (1), to
pulverize; be contrite
3238 yânâh (5), to
suppress; to maltreat
3905 lâchats (5), to press;
to distress
6206 'ârats (1), to awe; to
dread; to harass
6231 'âshaq (9), to
oppress; to defraud
7703 shâdad (1), to
ravage
2616 katadunastĕuō (1),
to oppress, exploit

OPPRESSED
1790 dak (3), injured,
oppressed
2541 châmôwts (1),
violent
3238 yânâh (3), to
suppress; to maltreat
3905 lâchats (7), to press;
to distress
5065 nâgas (2), to
exploit; to tax, harass
6217 'âshûwq (1), used
tyranny
6231 'âshaq (11), to
oppress; to defraud
6234 'oshqâh (1),
anguish, trouble
7533 râtsats (6), to crack
in pieces, smash
2616 katadunastĕuō (1),
to oppress, exploit
2669 katapŏnĕō (1), to
harass, oppress

OPPRESSETH
3905 lâchats (1), to press;
to distress
6231 'âshaq (3), to
oppress; to defraud
6887 tsârar (1), to cramp

OPPRESSING
3238 yânâh (3), to
suppress; to maltreat

OPPRESSION
3238 yânâh (1), to
suppress; to maltreat
3906 lachats (7), distress
4939 mispâch (1),
slaughter
6115 'ôtser (1), closure;
constraint
6125 'âqâh (1), constraint
6233 'ôsheq (12), injury;
fraud; distress
7701 shôd (1), violence,
ravage, destruction

OPPRESSIONS
4642 ma'ăshaqqâh (1),
oppression

OPPRESSOR
376+2555 'îysh (1), man;
male; someone
3238 yânâh (1), to
suppress; to maltreat
4642 ma'ăshaqqâh (1),
oppression
5065 nâgas (5), to
exploit; to tax, harass
6184 'ârîyts (1), powerful
or tyrannical
6216 'âshôwq (1), tyrant
6231 'âshaq (2), to
oppress; to defraud
6693 tsûwq (2), to
oppress, distress

OPPRESSORS
3905 lâchats (1), to press;
to distress
5065 nâgas (2), to
exploit; to tax, harass
6184 'ârîyts (2), powerful
or tyrannical
6231 'âshaq (2), to
oppress; to defraud
7429 râmaç (1), to tread
upon

ORACLE
1687 dᵉbîyr (16), inmost
part of the sanctuary
1697 dâbâr (1), word;
matter; thing

ORACLES
3051 lŏgiŏn (4),
utterance of God

ORATION
1215 dēmēgŏrĕō (1), to
address an assembly

ORATOR
3908 lachash (1),
incantation; amulet
4489 rhētŏr (1), legal
advocate

ORCHARD
6508 pardêç (1), park,
cultivated garden area

ORCHARDS
6508 pardêç (1), park,
cultivated garden area

ORDAIN
3245 yâçad (1), settle,
establish a foundation
7760 sûwm (1), to put,
place
8239 shâphath (1), to
place or put
1299 diatassō (1), to
institute, prescribe
2525 kathistēmi (1), to
designate, constitute

ORDAINED
3245 yâçad (1), settle,
establish a foundation
3559 kûwn (1), to set up:
establish, fix, prepare
4483 mᵉnâ' (Ch.) (1), to
count, appoint
5414 nâthan (2), to give
5975 'âmad (1), to stand
6186 'ârak (2), to set in a
row, i.e. arrange,
6213 'âsâh (3), to do or
make
6965 qûwm (1), to rise

ORDAINETH
6466 pâ'al (1), to do,
make or practice

ORDER
631 'âçar (1), to fasten; to
join battle
1700 dibrâh (1), reason,
suit or style; because
3027 yâd (2), hand; power
3559 kûwn (3), to set up:
establish, fix, prepare
4634 ma'ărâkâh (1),
arrangement, row; pile
4941 mishpâṭ (5), verdict;
formal decree; justice
5468 çeder (1), to
arrange, order
6186 'ârak (19), to set in
a row, i.e. arrange,
6187 'êrek (1), pile,
equipment, estimate
6471 pa'am (1), time;
step; occurence
6680 tsâvâh (3), to
constitute, enjoin
7947 shâlab (1), to make
equidistant
8626 tâqan (1), to
straighten; to compose
1299 diatassō (3), to
institute, prescribe
1930 ĕpidiŏrthŏō (1), to
arrange additionally
2517 kathĕxēs (3), in a
sequence, subsequent
5001 tagma (1), series or
succession
5010 taxis (10),
succession; kind

ORDERED
3559 kûwn (1), to set up:
establish, fix, prepare
4634 ma'ărâkâh (1),
arrangement, row; pile
6186 'ârak (2), to set in a
row, i.e. arrange,

ORDERETH
7760 sûwm (1), to put,
place

ORDERINGS
6486 pᵉquddâh (1),
visitation; punishment

ORDERLY
4748 stŏichĕō (1), to
follow, walk; to conform

ORDINANCE
2706 chôq (6),
appointment; allotment
2708 chuqqâh (12), to
delineate
3027 yâd (1), hand; power
4931 mishmereth (3),
watch, sentry, post
4941 mishpâṭ (5), verdict;
formal decree; justice
1296 diatagē (1),
institution
2937 ktisis (1), formation

ORDINANCES
2706 chôq (3),
appointment; allotment
2708 chuqqâh (10), to
delineate
4687 mitsvâh (1),
command
4941 mishpâṭ (6), verdict;
formal decree; justice
1345 dikaiōma (3),
statute or decision
1378 dŏgma (2), law
1379 dŏgmatizō (1), to
submit to a certain rule
3862 paradŏsis (1),
precept; tradition

ORDINARY
2706 chôq (1),
appointment; allotment

OREB
6157 'ârôb (6), swarming
mosquitoes

OREN
767 'Ôren (1), ash tree

ORGAN
5748 'ûwgâb (3),
reed-instrument

ORGANS
5748 'ûwgâb (1),
reed-instrument

ORION
3685 Kᵉçîyl (3),
constellation Orion

ORNAMENT
642 'êphuddâh (1),
plating
2481 chălîy (1), polished
trinket, ornament
3880 livyâh (2), wreath
5716 'ădîy (2), finery;
outfit; headstall

ORNAMENTS
5716 'ădîy (9), finery;
outfit; headstall
5914 'ekeç (1), anklet,
bangle
6287 pᵉ'êr (1), fancy
head-dress
6807 tsᵉ'âdâh (1), march;
ankle-chain
7720 sahărôn (2), round
pendant or crescent

ORNAN
771 'Ôrnân (11), strong

ORPAH
6204 'Orpâh (2), mane

ORPHANS
3490 yâthôwm (1), child alone, fatherless child

OSEE
5617 Hōsēē (1), deliverer

OSHEA
1954 Hôwshêä' (2), deliverer

OSPRAY
5822 'oznîyâh (2), (poss.) sea-eagle

OSSIFRAGE
6538 pereç (2), kind of eagle

OSTRICH
5133 nôwtsâh (1), plumage

OSTRICHES
3283 yâ'ên (1), ostrich

OTHER
251 'âch (1), brother; relative; member
259 'echâd (32), first
269 'achôwth (1), sister
312 'achêr (99), other, another, different; next, more
317 'ochŏrîy (Ch.) (1), other, another
321 'ochŏrân (Ch.) (3), other, another
428 'êl-leh (3), these or those
2063 zō'th (2), this
2088 zeh (16), this or that
3541 kôh (1), thus
3671 kânâph (1), edge or extremity; wing
5048 neged (2), over against or before
5676 'êber (25), opposite side; east
6311 pôh (5), here or hence
7453 rêa' (2), associate; one close
7605 she'âr (1), remainder
8145 shênîy (36), second; again
237 allachôthēn (1), from elsewhere
240 allēlōn (5), one another
243 allŏs (51), different, other
244 allotriĕpiskŏpŏs (1), meddler, busybody
245 allŏtriŏs (2), not one's own
492 antiparĕrchŏmai (2), to go along opposite
846 autŏs (1), he, she, it
1520 hêis (7), one
1565 ĕkĕinŏs (2), that one
1622 ĕktŏs (1), aside from, besides; except
2084 hĕtĕrŏglōssŏs (1), foreigner
2085 hĕtĕrŏdidaskalĕō (1), to instruct differently
2087 hĕtĕrŏs (34), other or different
2548 kakĕinŏs (2), likewise that or those

3062 lŏipŏi (16), remaining ones
3739 hŏs (2), who, which, what, that
4008 pĕran (12), across, beyond

OTHERS
312 'achêr (9), other, another, different; next
428 'êl-leh (1), these
243 allŏs (29), different, other
245 allŏtriŏs (1), not one's own
2087 hĕtĕrŏs (11), other or different
3062 lŏipŏi (9), remaining ones
3588 hŏ (2), "the," i.e. the definite article
3739 hŏs (1), who, which

OTHERWISE
176 'ôw (1), or, whether
3808 lô' (1), no, not
243 allŏs (1), different, other
247 allōs (1), differently
1490 ĕi dĕ mē(gĕ) (3), but if not
1893 ĕpĕi (4), since
2085 hĕtĕrŏdidaskalĕō (1), to instruct differently
2088 hĕtĕrŏs (1), differently, otherly

OTHNI
6273 'Otnîy (1), forcible

OTHNIEL
6274 'Othnîy'êl (7), force of God

OUCHES
4865 mishbetsâh (8), reticulated setting

OUGHT
1697 dâbâr (2), word; matter; thing
3972 me'ûwmâh (6), something; anything
4465 mimkâr (1), merchandise
1163 dĕi (29), it is (was) necessary
3762 ŏudĕis (1), none, nobody, nothing
3784 ŏphĕilō (15), to owe; to be under obligation
5100 tis (8), some or any
5534 chrē (1), it needs (must or should) be

OUGHTEST
1163 dĕi (3), it is (was) necessary

OUTCAST
5080 nâdach (1), to push off, scattered

OUTCASTS
1760 dâchâh (3), to push down; to totter
5080 nâdach (4), to push off, scattered

OUTER
2435 chîytsôwn (1), outer wall side; exterior; secular
1857 ĕxōtĕrŏs (3), exterior, outer

OUTGOINGS
4161 môwtsâ' (1), going forth
8444 tôwtsâ'âh (7), exit, boundary; deliverance

OUTLANDISH
5237 nokrîy (1), foreign; non-relative

OUTLIVED
748+3117+310 'ârak (1), to be, make long

OUTMOST
7020 qîytsôwn (1), terminal, end
7097 qâtseh (2), extremity

OUTRAGEOUS
7858 sheteph (1), deluge, torrent

OUTRUN
4370+5032 prŏstrĕchō (1), to hasten by running

OUTSIDE
2351 chûwts (2), outside, outdoors; open market
7097 qâtseh (3), extremity
1623 hĕktŏs (1), sixth
1855 ĕxōthĕn (2), outside, external (-ly)

OUTSTRETCHED
5186 nâtâh (3), to stretch or spread out

OUTWARD
2435 chîytsôwn (8), outer wall side; exterior
5869 'ayin (1), eye; sight; fountain
1722+3588+5318 ĕn (1), in; during; because of
1854 ĕxō (1), out, outside
1855 ĕxōthĕn (2), outside, external (-ly)
4383 prŏsōpŏn (1), face, presence

OUTWARDLY
1722+5318 ĕn (1), in; during; because of
1855 ĕxōthĕn (1), outside, external (-ly)

OUTWENT
4281 prŏĕrchŏmai (1), to go onward, precede

OVEN
8574 tannûwr (10), fire-pot
2823 klibanŏs (2), earthen pot

OVENS
8574 tannûwr (1), fire-pot

OVER
413 'êl (19), to, toward
1157 be'ad (1), up to or over against
1541 ge'lâh (Ch.) (1), to reveal mysteries
1591 genêbâh (1), something stolen
1869 dârak (1), to tread, trample; to walk, lead
2498 châlaph (1), to hasten away; to pass on
3148 yôwthêr (1), moreover; rest; gain
4136 mûwl (14), in front of, opposite
4480 min (1), from, out of

4605 ma'al (3), upward, above, overhead
5048 neged (27), over against or before
5226 nêkach (1), opposite
5227 nôkach (9), opposite, in front of
5414 nâthan (1), to give
5462 çâgar (2), to shut up; to surrender
5534 çâkar (1), to shut up; to surrender
5674 'âbar (171), to cross over; to transition
5736 'âdaph (3), to have surplus
5764 'ûwl (2), nursing babe
5848 'âtaph (1), to shroud, i.e. clothe
5921 'al (406), above, over, upon, or against
5922 'al (Ch.) (12), above, over, upon, or against
5924 'êllâ' (Ch.) (1), above
5927 'âlâh (1), to ascend, be high, mount
5975 'âmad (1), to stand
5980 'ummâh (23), near, beside, along with
6440 pânîym (2), face; front
6743 tsâlach (1), to push forward
6903 qebêl (Ch.) (1), in front of, before
7235 râbâh (2), to increase
481 antikru (1), opposite of
495 antipĕran (1), on the opposite side
561 apĕnanti (2), opposite, before
1224 diabainō (1), to pass by, over, across
1276 diapĕraō (5), to cross over
1277 diaplĕō (1), to sail through, across
1330 diĕrchŏmai (4), to traverse, travel through
1537 ĕk (3), out, out of
1608 ĕkpŏrnĕuō (1), to be utterly unchaste
1722 ĕn (1), in; during; because of
1883 ĕpanō (6), over or on
1909 ĕpi (49), on, upon
1924 ĕpigraphō (1), to inscribe, write upon
2596 kata (2), down; according to
2634 katakuriĕuō (1), to control, lord over
2713 katĕnanti (4), directly opposite
3346 mĕtatithēmi (1), to transport; to exchange
3860 paradidōmi (2), to hand over
3928 parĕrchŏmai (1), to go by; to perish
4008 pĕran (3), across, beyond
4012 pĕri (2), about; around
4052 pĕrissĕuō (1), to superabound

4121 plĕŏnazō (1), to
superabound
4291 prŏïstēmi (1), to
preside; to practice
5055 tĕlĕō (1), to end, i.e.
complete, execute
5228 hupĕr (1), over;
above; beyond
5231 hupĕranō (1),
above, upward
5240 hupĕrĕkchunō (1),
to overflow

OVERCAME
2634 katakuriĕuō (1), to
control, lord over
3528 nikaō (2), to
subdue, conquer

OVERCHARGE
1912 ĕpibarĕō (1), to be
severe toward

OVERCHARGED
925 barunō (1), to
burden; to grieve

OVERCOME
1464 gûwd (2), to attack
1986 hâlam (1), to strike,
beat, stamp, conquer
2476 chălûwshâh (1),
defeat
3201 yâkôl (1), to be able
3898 lâcham (2), to fight
a battle
5674 'âbar (1), to cross
over; to transition
7292 râhab (1), to urge
severely, i.e. importune
2274 hĕttaō (2), to rate
lower, be inferior
3528 nikaō (10), to
subdue, conquer

OVERCOMETH
3528 nikaō (11), to
subdue, conquer

OVERDRIVE
1849 dâphaq (1), to
knock; to press severely

OVERFLOW
6687 tsûwph (1), to
overflow
7783 shûwq (2), to
overflow
7857 shâṭaph (10), to
gush; to inundate

OVERFLOWED
7857 shâṭaph (1), to
gush; to inundate
2626 katakluzō (1), to
deluge, flood

OVERFLOWETH
4390 mâlê' (1), to fill; be
full

OVERFLOWING
1065 bᵉkîy (1), weeping
2230 zerem (1), gush of
water, flood
7857 shâṭaph (8), to
gush; to inundate
7858 sheṭeph (1), deluge,
torrent

OVERFLOWN
3332 yâtsaq (1), to pour
out
4390 mâlê' (1), to fill; be
full

7857 shâṭaph (1), to
gush; to inundate

OVERLAID
2645 châphâh (4), to
cover; to veil, to encase
5968 'âlaph (1), to be
languid, faint
6823 tsâphâh (28), to
sheet over with metal
7901 shâkab (1), to lie
down
4028 pĕrikaluptō (1), to
cover eyes; to plait

OVERLAY
2902 ṭûwach (1), to
whitewash
6823 tsâphâh (12), to
sheet over with metal

OVERLAYING
6826 tsippûwy (2),
encasement with metal

OVERLIVED
748+3117+310 'ârak (1),
to be, make long

OVERMUCH
4055 pĕrissŏtĕrŏs (1),
more superabundant

OVERPASS
5674 'âbar (1), to cross
over; to transition

OVERPAST
5674 'âbar (2), to cross
over; to transition

OVERPLUS
5736 'âdaph (1), to have
surplus

OVERRAN
5674 'âbar (1), to cross
over; to transition

OVERRUNNING
5674 'âbar (1), to cross
over; to transition

OVERSEE
5329 nâtsach (1), i.e. to
be eminent

OVERSEER
6485 pâqad (2), to visit,
care for, count
6496 pâqîyd (4),
superintendent, officer
7860 shôṭêr (1), to write;
official who is a scribe

OVERSEERS
5329 nâtsach (2), i.e. to
be eminent
6485 pâqad (2), to visit,
care for, count
6496 pâqîyd (1),
superintendent, officer
1985 ĕpiskŏpŏs (1),
overseer, supervisor

OVERSHADOW
1982 ĕpiskiazō (2), to
cast a shade upon

OVERSHADOWED
1982 ĕpiskiazō (3), to
cast a shade upon

OVERSIGHT
4870 mishgeh (1), error
5414 nâthan (1), to give
5921 'al (2), above, over,
upon, or against
6485 pâqad (4), to visit,
care for, count

6486 pᵉquddâh (2),
visitation; punishment
1983 ĕpiskŏpĕō (1), to
oversee; to beware

OVERSPREAD
5310 nâphats (1), to dash
to pieces; to scatter

OVERSPREADING
3671 kânâph (1), edge or
extremity; wing

OVERTAKE
5066 nâgash (2), to be,
come, bring near
5381 nâsag (14), to reach
2638 katalambanō (1), to
seize; to possess

OVERTAKEN
5381 nâsag (1), to reach
4301 prŏlambanō (1), to
take before

OVERTAKETH
5381 nâsag (1), to reach

OVERTHREW
2015 hâphak (4), to
change, overturn
4114 mahpêkâh (3),
destruction
5286 nâ'ar (1), to growl
5287 nâ'ar (1), to tumble
about
390 anastrĕphō (1), to
remain, to live
2690 katastrĕphō (2), to
upset, overturn

OVERTHROW
1760 dâchâh (1), to push
down; to totter
2015 hâphak (5), to
change, overturn
2018 hăphêkâh (1),
destruction, demolition
2040 hâraç (2), to pull
down; break, destroy
4073 mᵉdachphâh (1),
ruin
4114 mahpêkâh (2),
destruction
5186 nâṭâh (1), to stretch
or spread out
5307 nâphal (2), to fall
5422 nâthats (1), to tear
down
396 anatrĕpō (1), to
overturn, destroy
2647 kataluō (1), to
demolish
2692 katastrŏphê (1),
catastrophical ruin

OVERTHROWETH
2040 hâraç (1), to pull
down; break, destroy
5557 çâlaph (4), to
wrench; to subvert

OVERTHROWN
2015 hâphak (4), to
change, overturn
2040 hâraç (2), to pull
down; break, destroy
3782 kâshal (2), to totter,
waver; to falter
4114 mahpêkâh (1),
destruction
5307 nâphal (3), to fall
5791 'âvath (1), to wrest,
twist

8045 shâmad (1), to
desolate
8058 shâmaṭ (1), to
jostle; to let alone
2693 katastrŏnnumi (1),
to prostrate, i.e. slay

OVERTOOK
1692 dâbaq (3), to cling
or adhere; to catch
5381 nâsag (7), to reach

OVERTURN
2015 hâphak (1), to
change, overturn
5754 'avvâh (1),
overthrow, ruin

OVERTURNED
2015 hâphak (1), to
change, overturn

OVERTURNETH
2015 hâphak (3), to
change, overturn

OVERWHELM
5307 nâphal (1), to fall

OVERWHELMED
3680 kâçâh (2), to cover
5848 'âṭaph (5), to
shroud, i.e. clothe
7857 shâṭaph (1), to
gush; to inundate

OWE
3784 ŏphĕilō (1), to owe;
to be under obligation

OWED
3781 ŏphĕilĕtĕs (1),
person indebted
3784 ŏphĕilō (2), to owe;
to be under obligation

OWEST
3784 ŏphĕilō (3), to owe;
to be under obligation
4359 prŏsŏphĕilō (1), to
be indebted

OWETH
3784 ŏphĕilō (1), to owe;
to be under obligation

OWL
1323+3284 bath (2),
daughter, descendant
3244 yanshûwph (3), bird
3563 kôwç (3), cup;
(poss.) owl
3917 lîylîyth (1), night
spectre (spirit)
7091 qippôwz (1),
arrow-snake

OWLS
1323+3284 bath (6),
daughter, descendant

OWN
249 'ezrâch (15), native
born
3548 kôhên (2), one
officiating as a priest
5315 nephesh (1), life;
breath; soul; wind
7522 râtsôwn (1), delight
830 authairĕtŏs (1),
self-chosen
846 autŏs (1), he, she, it
848 hautŏu (15), self
849 autŏchĕir (1),
self-handed, personally
1103 gnēsiŏs (2),
genuine, true

1438 hĕautŏu (24), *himself, herself, itself*
1683 ĕmautŏu (2), *myself*
1699 ĕmŏs (2), *my*
2398 idiŏs (76), *private or separate*
2596 kata (1), *down; according to*
4572 sĕautŏu (2), *of yourself*

OWNER
113 'âdôwn (1), *sovereign, i.e. controller*
1167 ba'al (10), *master; husband; owner; citizen*
7069 qânâh (1), *to create; to procure*
3490 nauklĕrŏs (1), *ship captain*

OWNERS
1167 ba'al (4), *master; husband; owner; citizen*
2962 kuriŏs (1), *supreme, controller, Mr.*

OWNETH
2076 ĕsti (1), he (she or it) *is;* they *are*

OX
441 'allûwph (1), *friend, one familiar; chieftain, leader*
1241 bâqâr (3), *plowing ox; herd*
7794 shôwr (53), *bullock*
8377 t°'ôw (1), *antelope*
1016 bŏus (4), *ox, cattle*

OXEN
441 'allûwph (1), *friend, one familiar; chieftain*
504 'eleph (2), *ox; cow or cattle*
1241 bâqâr (74), *plowing ox; herd*
5091 nâhâh (1), *to bewail; to assemble*
6499 par (2), *bullock*
7794 shôwr (8), *bullock*
8450 tôwr (Ch.) (4), *bull*
1016 bŏus (4), *ox, cattle*
5022 taurŏs (2), *bullock, ox*

OZEM
684 'Òtsem (2), *strong*

OZIAS
3604 Ŏzias (2), *strength of Jehovah*

OZNI
244 'Ozniy (1), *having (quick) ears*

OZNITES
244 'Ozniy (1), *having (quick) ears*

PAARAI
6474 Pa'ăray (1), *yawning*

PACATIANA
3818 Pakatianĕ (1), *Pacatianian*

PACES
6806 tsa'ad (1), *pace or regular step*

PACIFIED
3722 kâphar (1), to *placate or cancel*
7918 shâkak (1), to *lay a trap; to allay*

PACIFIETH
3240 yânach (1), to *allow to stay*
3711 kâphâh (1), to *tame or subdue*

PACIFY
3722 kâphar (1), to *cover; to placate*

PADAN
6307 Paddân (1), *table-land of Aram*

PADAN-ARAM
6307 Paddân (10), *table-land of Aram*

PADDLE
3489 yâthêd (1), tent *peg*

PADON
6303 Pâdôwn (2), *ransom*

PAGIEL
6295 Pag'îy'êl (5), *accident of God*

PAHATH-MOAB
6355 Pachath Môw'âb (6), *pit of Moăb*

PAI
6464 Pâ'ûw (1), *screaming*

PAID
3052 y°hab (Ch.) (1), to *give*
5414 nâthan (1), to *give*
591 apŏdidōmi (2), to *give away*

PAIN
2256 chebel (1), *company, band*
2342 chûwl (6), to *dance, whirl; to writhe in pain*
2427 chîyl (3), *throe of painful childbirth*
2470 châlâh (1), to *be weak, sick, afflicted*
2479 chalchâlâh (4), *writhing in childbirth*
3510 kâ'ab (1), to feel *pain; to grieve; to spoil*
3511 k°'êb (1), *suffering; adversity*
4341 mak'ôb (2), *anguish; affliction*
5999 'âmâl (1), *wearing effort; worry*
4192 pŏnŏs (2), *toil, i.e. anguish*

PAINED
2342 chûwl (3), to *dance, whirl; to writhe in pain*
3176 yâchal (1), to *wait; to be patient, hope*
928 basanizō (1), to *torture, torment*

PAINFUL
5999 'âmâl (1), *wearing effort; worry*

PAINFULNESS
3449 mŏchthŏs (1), *sadness*

PAINS
4712 mêtsar (1), *trouble*
6735 tsîyr (1), *hinge; trouble*
4192 pŏnŏs (1), *toil, i.e. anguish*

5604 ōdin (1), *pang of childbirth; agony*

PAINTED
4886 mâshach (1), to *rub or smear with oil*
7760+6320 sûwm (1), to *put, place*

PAINTEDST
3583 kâchal (1), to *paint the eyes with stibnite*

PAINTING
6320 pûwk (1), *stibium*

PAIR
2201 zĕugŏs (1), *team, pair*
2218 zugŏs (1), *coupling, yoke*

PALACE
643 'appeden (1), *pavilion or palace-tent*
759 'armôwn (4), *citadel, high fortress*
1002 bîyrâh (17), *palace, citadel*
1004 bayith (1), *house; temple; family, tribe*
1055 bîythân (3), *large house*
1964 hêykâl (8), *palace; temple; hall*
1965 hêykal (Ch.) (4), *palace; temple*
2038 harmôwn (1), *high castle or fortress*
2918 țîyrâh (1), *fortress; hamlet*
833 aulĕ (7), *palace; house; courtyard*
4232 praitōriŏn (1), *court-room or palace*

PALACES
759 'armôwn (27), *citadel, high fortress*
1964 hêykâl (3), *palace; temple; hall*
2918 țîyrâh (1), *fortress; hamlet*

PALAL
6420 Pâlâl (1), *judge*

PALE
2357 châvar (1), to *blanch with shame*
5515 chlōrŏs (1), *greenish, verdant*

PALENESS
3420 yêrâqôwn (1), *paleness; mildew*

PALESTINA
6429 P°lesheth (3), *migratory*

PALESTINE
6429 P°lesheth (1), *migratory*

PALLU
6396 Pallûw' (4), *distinguished*

PALLUITES
6384 Pallû'îy (1), *Palluïte*

PALM
3709 kaph (2), *hollow of hand; paw; sole of foot*
8558 tâmâr (12), *palm tree*

PALMS
3709 kaph (4), *hollow of hand; paw; sole of foot*
4474 rhapizō (1), to *slap, rap, strike*
4475 rhapisma (1), *slap, strike*
5404 phŏinix (1), *palm-tree*

PALSIES
3886 paraluŏ (1), to *be paralyzed or enfeebled*

PALSY
3885 paralutikŏs (10), *lame person*
3886 paraluŏ (3), to *be paralyzed or enfeebled*

PALTI
6406 Palțîy (1), *delivered*

PALTIEL
6409 Palțîy'êl (1), *deliverance of God*

PALTITE
6407 Palțîy (1), *Paltite*

PAMPHYLIA
3828 Pamphulia (5), *every-tribal, i.e. heterogeneous*

PAN
3595 kîyôwr (1), *caldron; washbowl*
4227 machăbath (6), *metal pan for baking in*
4958 masrêth (1), *pan*

PANGS
2256 chebel (2), *company, band*
2427 chîyl (2), *throe of painful childbirth*
6735 tsîyr (3), *hinge; herald, trouble*
6887 tsârar (2), to *cramp*

PANNAG
6436 Pannag (1), *food, (poss.) pastry*

PANS
2281 châbêth (1), *griddle-cake*
5518 çîyr (1), *thorn; hook*
6517 pârûwr (1), *skillet*
6745 tsêlâchâh (1), *flattened out platter*

PANT
7602 shâ'aph (1), to *be angry; to hasten*

PANTED
7602 shâ'aph (1), to *be angry; to hasten*
8582 tâ'âh (1), to *vacillate, i.e. reel*

PANTETH
5503 çâchar (1), to *travel round; to palpitate*

OWNER (col 4)

PALMERWORM
1501 gâzâm (3), *kind of locust*

8560 tômer (2), *palm trunk*
8561 timmôr (17), *palm-like pilaster*
4475 rhapisma (1), *slap, strike*
5404 phŏinix (1), *palm-tree*

English

PAPER
6165 'ârag (2), to *long for, pant* for

PAPER
6169 'ârâh (1), *bulrushes, reeds*
5489 *chartēs* (1), *sheet* of papyrus paper

PAPHOS
3974 *Paphŏs* (2), *Paphus*

PAPS
7699 shad (1), *female breast*
3149 *mastŏs* (3), *female breast; chest* area

PARABLE
4912 mâshâl (17), *pithy maxim; taunt*
3850 *parabŏlē* (31), *fictitious narrative*
3942 *parŏimia* (1), *illustration; adage*

PARABLES
4912 mâshâl (1), *pithy maxim; taunt*
3850 *parabŏlē* (15), *fictitious narrative*

PARADISE
3857 *paradĕisŏs* (3), *park*

PARAH
6511 Pârâh (1), *heifer*

PARAMOURS
6370 pîylegesh (1), *concubine; paramour*

PARAN
6290 Pâ'rân (11), *ornamental*

PARBAR
6503 Parbâr (2), *Parbar* or *Parvar*

PARCEL
2513 chelqâh (5), *allotment*
5564 *chōriŏn* (1), *spot* or *plot* of ground

PARCHED
2788 chârêr (1), *arid, parched*
7039 qâlîy (6), *roasted ears of cereal grain*
8273 shârâb (1), *glow* of the hot air; *mirage*

PARCHMENTS
3200 *mĕmbrana* (1), sheep-*skin* for writing

PARDON
3722 kâphar (1), to *cover; to expiate*
5375 nâsâ' (3), to *lift up*
5545 çâlach (11), to *forgive*
5547 ç°lîychâh (1), *pardon*

PARDONED
5545 çâlach (2), to *forgive*
7521 râtsâh (1), to *be pleased with; to satisfy*

PARDONETH
5375 nâsâ' (1), to *lift up*

PARE
6213 'âsâh (1), to *do* or *make*

PARENTS
1118 gŏnĕus (19), *parents*

3962 *patēr* (1), *father*
4269 *prŏgŏnŏs* (1), *ancestor*

PARLOUR
3957 lishkâh (1), *room*
5944 'ălîyâh (4), *upper things; second-story*

PARLOURS
2315 cheder (1), *apartment, chamber*

PARMASHTA
6534 Parmashtâ' (1), *Parmashta*

PARMENAS
3937 Parmĕnas (1), *constant*

PARNACH
6535 Parnak (1), *Parnak*

PAROSH
6551 Par'ôsh (5), *flea*

PARSHANDATHA
6577 Parshandâthâ' (1), *Parshandatha*

PART
2505 châlaq (3), to *be smooth; be slippery*
2506 chêleq (19), *allotment*
2513 chelqâh (1), *flattery; allotment*
2673 châtsâh (1), to *cut* or *split in two; to halve*
2677 chêtsîy (3), *half* or *middle, midst*
4481 min (Ch.) (5), *from* or *out of*
4490 mânâh (1), *ration; lot* or *portion*
4940 mishpâchâh (2), *family, clan, people*
5337 nâtsal (1), to *deliver; snatched* away
6418 pelek (7), *spindle-whorl; crutch*
6447 paç (Ch.) (2), *palm* of the hand
6504 pârad (1), to *spread* or *separate*
6626 pâthath (1), to *break, crumble*
7117 q°tsâth (1), *termination; portion*
2819 klērŏs (2), *lot, portion*
3307 *merizō* (1), to *apportion, share*
3310 *meris* (5), *portion, share, participation*
3313 *merŏs* (17), *division* or *share*
3348 *mĕtĕchō* (1), to *share* or *participate*
4119 *plĕiōn* (1), *more*
4403 *prumna* (1), *stern* of a ship

PARTAKER
2506 chêleq (1), *smoothness; allotment*
2841 *kŏinōnĕō* (2), to *share* or *participate*
2844 *kŏinōnŏs* (1), *associate, partner*
3335 *mĕtalambanō* (1), to *participate*
3348 *mĕtĕchō* (2), to *share* or *participate*

4777 *sugkakŏpathĕō* (1), to *suffer hardship with*
4791 *sugkŏinōnŏs* (1), *co-participant*

PARTAKERS
482 *antilambanŏmai* (1), to *succor; aid*
2841 *kŏinōnĕō* (3), to *share* or *participate*
2844 *kŏinōnŏs* (4), *associate, partner*
3310 *mĕris* (1), *portion, share, participation*
3335 *mĕtalambanō* (1), to *participate*
3348 *mĕtĕchō* (3), to *share* or *participate*
3353 *mĕtŏchŏs* (4), *sharer, associate*
4790 *sugkŏinōnĕō* (1), to *co-participate in*
4791 *sugkŏinōnŏs* (1), *co-participant*
4829 *summĕrizŏmai* (1), to *share jointly*
4830 *summĕtŏchŏs* (2), *co-participant*

PARTAKEST
1096+4791
Bêlţ°sha'tstsar (Ch.) (1), *Belteshatstsar*

PARTED
2505 châlaq (2), to *be smooth; be slippery*
2673 châtsâh (1), to *cut* or *split in two; to halve*
6504 pârad (2), to *spread* or *separate*
1266 *diamĕrizō* (6), to *have dissension*
1339 *diïstēmi* (1), to *remove, intervene*

PARTETH
6504 pârad (1), to *spread* or *separate*
6536 pâraç (2), to *break in pieces; to split*

PARTHIANS
3934 Parthŏs (1), *inhabitant of Parthia*

PARTIAL
5375+6440 nâsâ' (1), to *lift up*
1252 *diakrinō* (1), to *decide; to hesitate*

PARTIALITY
87 *adiakritŏs* (1), *impartial*
4346 *prŏsklisis* (1), *favoritism*

PARTICULAR
3313 *mĕrŏs* (1), *division* or *share*
3588+1520 hŏ (1), *"the,"* i.e. the definite article

PARTICULARLY
1520+1538+2596 hĕis (1), *one*
2596+3313 kata (1), *down; according to*

PARTING
517 'êm (1), *mother*

PARTITION
5674 'âbar (1), to *cross over; to transition*

5418 phragmŏs (1), *fence* or *enclosing barrier*

PARTLY
7118 q°tsâth (Ch.) (1), *termination; portion*
1161 dĕ (1), *but, yet*
3313+5100 mĕrŏs (1), *division* or *share*
5124+3303 tŏutŏ (1), *that thing*

PARTNER
2505 châlaq (1), to *be smooth; be slippery*
2844 kŏinōnŏs (2), *associate, partner*

PARTNERS
2844 kŏinōnŏs (1), *associate, partner*
3353 mĕtŏchŏs (1), *sharer, associate*

PARTRIDGE
7124 qôrê' (2), *calling partridge*

PARTS
905 bad (1), *limb, member; bar*
1335 bether (2), *section, piece*
1506 gezer (1), *portion, piece*
1697 dâbâr (1), *word; matter; thing*
2506 chêleq (6), *smoothness; allotment*
2677 chêtsîy (1), *half* or *middle, midst*
3027 yâd (3), *hand; power*
3411 y°rêkâh (2), *recesses, far places*
5409 nêthach (1), *fragment*
6310 peh (1), *mouth; opening*
7098 qâtsâh (1), *termination; fringe*
2825 klinē (1), *couch*
3313 mĕrŏs (6), *division* or *share*

PARUAH
6515 Pârûwach (1), *blossomed*

PARVAIM
6516 Parvayim (1), *Parvajim*

PAS-DAMMIM
6450 Paç Dammîym (1), *dell of bloodshed*

PASACH
6457 Pâçak (1), *divider*

PASEAH
6454 Pâçêach (3), *limping*

PASHUR
6583 Pashchûwr (14), *liberation*

PASS
935 bôw' (3), to *go* or *come*
1980 hâlak (1), to *walk; live a certain way*
2498 châlaph (2), to *hasten away; to pass on*
2499 chălaph (Ch.) (4), to *have time pass by*
3615 kâlâh (1), to *cease, be finished, perish*

PASSAGE

4569 ma'ăbâr (1), *crossing*-place
5674 'âbar (153), to *cross over; to transition*
5709 'ădâ' (Ch.) (1), to *pass on or continue*
6213 'âsâh (5), to *do or make*
6452 pâçach (2), to *hop, skip over; to hesitate*
390 anastrĕphō (1), to *remain, to live*
1224 diabainō (1), to *pass by, over, across*
1276 diapĕraō (1), to *cross over*
1279 diapŏrĕuŏmai (1), to *travel through*
1330 diĕrchŏmai (7), to *traverse, travel through*
3928 parĕrchŏmai (19), to *go by; to perish*
5230 hupĕrakmŏs (1), *past the bloom of youth*

PASSAGE

1552 gᵉlîylâh (1), *circuit or region*
4569 ma'ăbâr (2), *crossing*-place
5674 'âbar (1), to *cross over; to transition*

PASSAGES

4569 ma'ăbâr (4), *crossing*-place
5676 'êber (1), *opposite side; east*

PASSED

1431 gâdal (1), to *be great, make great*
2498 châlaph (2), to *hasten away; to pass on*
5674 'âbar (117), to *cross over; to transition*
5709 'ădâ' (Ch.) (1), to *pass on or continue*
5710 'ădâh (1), to *pass on or continue; to remove*
6437 pânâh (1), to *turn, to face*
6452 pâçach (1), to *hop, skip over; to hesitate*
492 antiparĕrchŏmai (2), to *go along opposite*
565 apĕrchŏmai (1), to *go off, i.e. depart*
1224 diabainō (1), to *pass by, over, across*
1276 diapĕraō (3), to *cross over*
1330 diĕrchŏmai (11), to *traverse, travel through*
1353 diŏdĕuō (1), to *travel through*
3327 mĕtabainō (2), to *depart, move from*
3855 paragō (6), to *go along or away*
3899 parapŏrĕuŏmai (4), to *travel near*
3928 parĕrchŏmai (3), to *go by; to perish, neglect*
4281 prŏĕrchŏmai (1), to *go onward, precede*

PASSEDST

5674 'âbar (1), to *cross over; to transition*

PASSENGERS

5674 'âbar (4), to *cross over; to transition*
5674+1870 'âbar (1), to *cross over; to transition*

PASSEST

5674 'âbar (5), to *cross over; to transition*

PASSETH

1980 hâlak (4), to *walk; live a certain way*
2498 châlaph (1), to *hasten away; to pass on*
5674 'âbar (28), to *cross over; to transition*
3855 paragō (2), to *go along or away*
3928 parĕrchŏmai (1), to *go by; to perish*
5235 hupĕrballō (1), to *surpass*
5242 hupĕrĕchō (1), to *excel; superior*

PASSING

5674 'âbar (7), to *cross over; to transition*
1330 diĕrchŏmai (2), to *traverse, travel through*
2064 ĕrchŏmai (1), to *go, come*
3881 paralĕgŏmai (1), to *sail past*
3928 parĕrchŏmai (1), to *go by; to perish*

PASSION

3958 paschō (1), to *experience pain*

PASSIONS

3663 hŏmŏiŏpathēs (2), *similarly affected*

PASSOVER

6453 Peçach (48), *Passover*
3957 pascha (28), *Passover events*

PASSOVERS

6453 Peçach (1), *Passover*

PAST

369 'ayin (1), *there is no, i.e., not exist, none*
5493 çûwr (2), to *turn off*
5674 'âbar (8), to *cross over; to transition*
6924 qedem (1), *eastern; antiquity; before*
7223 ri'shôwn (1), *first*
7291 râdaph (1), to *run after with hostility*
7725 shûwb (1), to *turn back; to return*
8032 shilshôwm (9), *day before yesterday*
421 anĕxichniastŏs (1), *untraceable*
524 apalgĕō (1), *become apathetic*
565 apĕrchŏmai (2), to *go off, i.e. depart*
1096 ginŏmai (2), to *be, become*
1230 diaginŏmai (1), to *have time elapse*
1330 diĕrchŏmai (1), to *traverse, travel through*
3819 palai (1), *formerly; sometime since*

PASTOR

7462 râ'âh (1), to *tend a flock, i.e. pasture it*

PASTORS

7462 râ'âh (7), to *tend a flock, i.e. pasture it*
4166 pŏimēn (1), *shepherd*

PASTURE

4829 mir'eh (11), *pasture; haunt*
4830 mir'îyth (8), *pasturage; flock*
3542 nŏmĕ (1), *pasture, i.e. the act of feeding*

PASTURES

3733 kar (2), *ram sheep*
4829 mir'eh (1), *pasture; haunt*
4830 mir'îyth (1), *pasturage; flock*
4945 mashqeh (1), *butler; drink; well-watered*
4999 nâ'âh (5), *home, dwelling; pasture*
7471 rᵉ'îy (1), *pasture*

PATARA

3959 Patara (1), *Patara*

PATE

6936 qodqôd (1), *crown of the head*

PATH

734 'ôrach (9), *road; manner of life*
4546 mᵉçillâh (1), *main thoroughfare; viaduct*
4570 ma'gâl (3), *circular track or camp rampart*
4934 mish'ôwl (1), *narrow passage*
5410 nâthîyb (8), (beaten) *track, path*
7635 shâbîyl (1), *track or passage-way*

PATHROS

6624 Pathrôwç (5), *Pathros*

PATHRUSIM

6625 Pathrûçîy (2), *Pathrusite*

PATHS

734 'ôrach (16), *road; manner of life*
4546 mᵉçillâh (1), *main thoroughfare; viaduct*
4570 ma'gâl (6), *circular track or camp rampart*
5410 nâthîyb (14), (beaten) *track, path*
7635 shâbîyl (1), *track or passage-way*
5147 tribŏs (3), *rut, or worn track*

PATHWAY

1870+5410 derek (1), *road; course of life*

PATIENCE

3114 makrŏthumĕō (3), to be *forbearing, patient*
3115 makrŏthumia (2), *forbearance; fortitude*
5281 hupŏmŏnĕ (29), *endurance, constancy*

PATIENT

750 'ârêk (1), *patient*
420 anĕxikakŏs (1), *forbearing*
1933 ĕpiĕikēs (1), *mild, gentle*
3114 makrŏthumĕō (3), to be *forbearing, patient*
5278 hupŏmĕnŏ (1), to *undergo, bear* (trials)
5281 hupŏmŏnĕ (2), *perseverence*

PATIENTLY

2342 chûwl (1), to *dance, whirl; to wait; to pervert*
6960 qâvâh (1), to *collect; to expect*
3114 makrŏthumĕō (1), to be *forbearing, patient*
3116 makrŏthumōs (1), *with long, enduring temper, i.e. leniently*
5278 hupŏmĕnŏ (2), to *undergo, bear* (trials)

PATMOS

3963 Patmŏs (1), *Patmus*

PATRIARCH

3966 patriarchēs (2), *progenitor or patriarch*

PATRIARCHS

3966 patriarchēs (2), *progenitor or patriarch*

PATRIMONY

1+5921 'âb (1), *father*

PATROBAS

3969 Pᵃtrŏbas (1), *father's life*

PATTERN

4758 mar'eh (1), *appearance; vision*
8403 tabnîyth (9), *structure; model*
8508 toknîyth (1), *admeasurement*
5179 tupŏs (2), *shape, resemblance; "type"*
5296 hupŏtupōsis (1), *example, pattern*

PATTERNS

5262 hupŏdĕigma (1), *exhibit; specimen*

PAU

6464 Pâ'ûw (1), *screaming*

PAUL

3972 Paulŏs (157), *little*

PAUL'S

3972 Paulŏs (6), *little*

PAULUS

3972 Paulŏs (1), *little*

English

PAVED
3840 libnâh (1),
transparency
7528 râtsaph (1), to
tessellate, embroider

PAVEMENT
4837 martsepheth (1),
pavement, stone base
7531 ritspâh (7), *hot
stone; pavement*
3037 lithŏs (1), *stone*

PAVILION
5520 çôk (1), *hut of
entwined* boughs
5521 çukkâh (2),
tabernacle; shelter
8237 shaphrûwr (1),
tapestry or canopy

PAVILIONS
5521 çukkâh (3),
tabernacle; shelter

PAW
3027 yâd (2), *hand; power*

PAWETH
2658 châphar (1), to
delve, to *explore*

PAWS
3709 kaph (1), hollow of
hand; paw; sole of foot

PAY
5414 nâthan (2), to *give*
5414+4377 nâthan (1), to
give
5415 nᵉthan (Ch.) (1), to
give
5927 'âlâh (1), to *ascend,
be high, mount*
7725 shûwb (1), to *turn*
back; to *return*
7999 shâlam (19), to *be
safe; be, make complete*
8254 shâqal (4), to
suspend in trade
586 apŏdĕkatŏŏ (1), to
tithe, give a tenth
591 apŏdidōmi (7), to
give away
5055 tĕlĕŏ (2), to *end,
discharge* (a debt)

PAYED
7999 shâlam (1), to *be
safe; be, make complete*
1183 dĕkatŏŏ (1), to *give
or take a tenth*

PAYETH
7999 shâlam (1), to *be
safe; be, make complete*

PAYMENT
591 apŏdidōmi (1), to
give away

PEACE
1826 dâmam (1), to *be
silent; to be astonished*
2013 hâçâh (2), to *hush,
be quiet*
2790 chârash (26), to *be
silent; to be deaf*
2814 châshâh (9), to
hush or keep quiet
6963 qôwl (1), *voice or
sound*
7962 shalvâh (1),
security, ease
7965 shâlôwm (169),
safe; well; health, peace

PEACEABLE
7961 shâlêv (1), *careless,
carefree; security*
7965 shâlôwm (2), *safe;
well; health, peace*
7999 shâlam (1), to *be
safe; be, make complete*
8003 shâlêm (1),
complete; friendly; safe
1516 ĕirēnikŏs (2),
pacific, peaceful
2272 hēsuchiŏs (1), *still,
undisturbed*

PEACEABLY
7962 shalvâh (2),
security, ease
7965 shâlôwm (9), *safe;
well; health, peace*
1518 ĕirēnŏpŏiŏs (1),
peaceable

PEACEMAKERS
1518 ĕirēnŏpŏiŏs (1),
peaceable

PEACOCKS
7443 renen (1), female
ostrich
8500 tukkîy (2), (poss.)
peacock

PEARL
3135 margaritēs (2), *pearl*

PEARLS
1378 gâbîysh (1), *crystal*
3135 margaritēs (7), *pearl*

PECULIAR
5459 çᵉgullâh (5), *wealth*
1519+4047 ĕis (1), *to or
into*
4041 pĕriŏusiŏs (1),
special, one's very own

PEDAHEL
6300 Pᵉdah'êl (1), *God
has ransomed*

PEDAHZUR
6301 Pᵉdâhtsûwr (5),
Rock has ransomed

PEDAIAH
6305 Pᵉdâyâh (8),
Jehovah has ransomed

PEDIGREES
3205 yâlad (1), to *bear
young;* to *father a child*

PEELED
4178 môwrâṭ (2),
obstinate, independent
4803 mâraṭ (1), to *polish;*
to *make bald*

PEEP
6850 tsâphaph (1), to *coo
or chirp* as a bird

PEEPED
6850 tsâphaph (1), to *coo
or chirp* as a bird

PEKAH
6492 Peqach (11), *watch*

PEKAHIAH
6494 Pᵉqachyâh (3),
Jehovah has observed

PEKOD
6489 Pᵉqôwd (2),
punishment

PELAIAH
6411 Pᵉlâyâh (3),
*Jehovah has
distinguished*

PELALIAH
6421 Pᵉlalyâh (1),
Jehovah has judged

PELATIAH
6410 Pᵉlaṭyâh (5),
Jehovah has delivered

PELEG
6389 Peleg (7),
earthquake

PELET
6404 Peleṭ (2), *escape*

PELETH
6431 Peleth (2), *swiftness*

PELETHITES
6432 Pᵉlêthîy (7), *courier*
or official *messenger*

PELICAN
6893 qâ'ath (3), *pelican*

PELONITE
6397 Pᵉlôwnîy (3),
separate

PEN
2747 cheret (1), *chisel;
style* for writing
5842 'êṭ (4), *stylus; reed
pen*
7626 shêbeṭ (1), *stick;
clan, family*
2563 kalamŏs (1), *reed;
pen*

PENCE
1220 dēnariŏn (5),
denarius

PENIEL
6439 Pᵉnûw'êl (1), *face of
God*

PENINNAH
6444 Pᵉninnâh (3), *round
pearl*

PENKNIFE
8593 ta'ar (1), *knife;
razor; scabbard*

PENNY
1220 dēnariŏn (9),
denarius

PENNYWORTH
1220 dēnariŏn (2),
denarius

PENTECOST
4005 pĕntēkŏstē (3), the
festival of *Pentecost*

PENUEL
6439 Pᵉnûw'êl (7), *face of
God*

PENURY
4270 machçôwr (1),
impoverishment
5303 hustĕrēma (1),
deficit; poverty; lacking

PEOPLE
376 'îysh (1), *man; male;
someone*
523 'ummâh (1),
community, clan, tribe
528 'Âmôwn (1), *Amon*
582 'ĕnôwsh (1), *man;
person, human*
1121 bên (1), *son,
descendant; people*
1471 gôwy (11), *foreign
nation; Gentiles*
3816 lᵉ'ôm (24),
community, nation
5712 'êdâh (1),
assemblage; family
5971 'am (1827), *people;
tribe; troops*
5972 'am (Ch.) (15),
people, nation
1218 dēmŏs (4), *public,
crowd*
1484 ĕthnŏs (2), *race;
tribe; pagan*
2992 laŏs (138), *people;
public*
3793 ŏchlŏs (83), *throng*

PEOPLE'S
5971 'am (2), *people;
tribe; troops*
2992 laŏs (2), *people;
public*

PEOPLES
2992 laŏs (2), *people;
public*

PEOR
6465 Pe'ôwr (4), *gap*

PEOR'S
6465 Pe'ôwr (1), *gap*

PERADVENTURE
194 'ûwlay (23), *if not;
perhaps*
3863 lûw' (1), *if; would
that!*
6435 pên (1), *lest, not
ever; if, or lest ever*
3379 mēpŏtĕ (1), *not
ever; if, or lest ever*
5029 tacha (1), *shortly,*
i.e. *possibly*

PERAZIM
6559 Pᵉrâtsîym (1),
breaks

PERCEIVE
995 bîyn (1), to
understand; discern
3045 yâda' (7), to *know*
7200 râ'âh (1), to *see*
8085 shâma' (1), to *hear
intelligently*
991 blĕpō (1), to *look at*
1097 ginôskō (2), to *know*
1492 ĕidō (3), to *know*
2334 thĕōrĕō (4), to *see;*
to *discern*

2638 *katalambanō* (1), to
seize; to possess
3539 *nŏiĕō* (2), to
exercise the mind
3708 *hŏraō* (1), to stare,
see clearly; to discern

PERCEIVED
238 'āzan (1), to listen
995 bîyn (3), to
understand; discern
3045 yâda' (11), to know
5234 nâkar (1), to
acknowledge
7200 râ'âh (4), to see
8085 shâma' (1), to hear
intelligently
143 aisthanŏmai (1), to
apprehend
1097 ginōskō (7), to know
1921 ĕpiginŏskō (3), to
become fully
acquainted with
2147 hĕuriskō (1), to find
2638 katalambanō (1), to
possess; to understand
2657 katanŏĕō (1), to
observe fully

PERCEIVEST
3045 yâda' (1), to know
2657 katanŏĕō (1), to
observe fully

PERCEIVETH
995 bîyn (1), to
understand; discern
2938 ţâ'am (1), to taste;
to perceive, experience
7789 shûwr (1), to spy
out, survey

PERCEIVING
1492 ĕidō (3), to know

PERDITION
684 apŏlĕia (8), ruin or
loss

PERES
6537 pᵉraç (Ch.) (1), to
split up

PERESH
6570 Peresh (1),
excrement

PEREZ
6557 Perets (3), breech

PEREZ-UZZA
6560 Perets 'Uzzâ' (1),
break of Uzza

PEREZ-UZZAH
6560 Perets 'Uzzâ' (1),
break of Uzza

PERFECT
1584 gâmar (1), to end;
to complete; to fail
1585 gᵉmar (Ch.) (1), to
complete
3559 kûwn (1), to render
sure, proper
3632 kâlîyl (3), whole,
entire; complete; whole
3634 kâlal (1), to
complete
4357 miklâh (1), wholly,
solidly
7999 shâlam (1), to be
safe; be, make complete
8003 shâlêm (15),
complete; friendly; safe

8503 taklîyth (1),
extremity
8535 tâm (9), morally
pious; gentle, dear
8537 tôm (1), prosperity
8549 tâmîym (18), entire,
complete; integrity
8552 tâmam (2), to
complete, finish
195 akrihĕia (1),
exactness
197 akribĕstĕrŏn (1),
more exactly
199 akribōs (1), exactly,
carefully
739 artiŏs (1), complete,
thorough, capable
2005 ĕpitĕlĕō (1), to
terminate; to undergo
2675 katartizō (5), to
repair; to prepare
3647 hŏlŏklĕria (1),
wholeness
4137 plĕrŏō (1), to fill,
make complete
5046 tĕlĕiŏs (17),
complete; mature
5048 tĕlĕiŏō (13), to
perfect, complete

PERFECTED
3634 kâlal (1), to
complete
5927+724 'âlâh (1), to
ascend, be high, mount
8003 shâlêm (1),
complete; friendly; safe
2675 katartizō (1), to
repair; to prepare
5048 tĕlĕiŏō (4), to
perfect, complete

PERFECTING
2005 ĕpitĕlĕō (1), to
terminate; to undergo
2677 katartismŏs (1),
complete furnishing

PERFECTION
3632 kâlîyl (1), whole,
entire; complete; whole
4359 miklâl (1),
perfection of beauty
4512 minleh (1), wealth
8502 tiklâh (1),
completeness
8503 taklîyth (2),
extremity
8537 tôm (1),
completeness
2676 katartisis (1),
thorough equipment
5050 tĕlĕiōsis (1),
completion; verification
5051 tĕlĕiŏtēs (1),
consummator, perfecter
5052 tĕlĕsphŏrĕō (1), to
ripen fruit

PERFECTLY
998 bîynâh (1),
discernment
197 akribĕstĕrŏn (3),
more exactly
199 akribōs (1), exactly,
carefully
1295 diasōzō (1), to cure,
preserve, rescue
2675 katartizō (1), to
repair; to prepare

PERFECTNESS
5047 tĕlĕiŏtēs (1),
completeness; maturity

PERFORM
5414 nâthan (1), to give
6213 'âsâh (12), to do or
make
6633 tsâbâ' (1), to mass
an army or servants
6965 qûwm (13), to rise
7999 shâlam (4), to be
safe; be, make complete
591 apŏdidōmi (1), to
give away
2005 ĕpitĕlĕō (2), to
terminate; to undergo
2716 katĕrgazŏmai (1),
to finish; to accomplish
4160 pŏiĕō (2), to do

PERFORMANCE
2005 ĕpitĕlĕō (1), to
terminate; to undergo
5050 tĕlĕiōsis (1),
completion; verification

PERFORMED
1214 bâtsa' (1), to
plunder; to finish
6213 'âsâh (5), to do or
make
6965 qûwm (11), to rise
7999 shâlam (1), to be
safe; be, make complete
1096 ginŏmai (1), to be,
become
2005 ĕpitĕlĕō (1), to
terminate; to undergo
5055 tĕlĕō (1), to end, i.e.
complete, execute

PERFORMETH
1584 gâmar (1), to end;
to complete; to fail
6965 qûwm (1), to rise
7999 shâlam (2), to be
safe; be, make complete

PERFORMING
6381 pâlâ' (2), to be,
make great, wonderful

PERFUME
7004 qᵉţôreth (3),
fumigation

PERFUMED
5130 nûwph (1), to
quiver, vibrate, rock
6999 qâţar (1), to turn
into fragrance by fire

PERFUMES
7547 raqqûach (1),
scented ointment

PERGA
4011 Pĕrgĕ (3), tower

PERGAMOS
4010 Pĕrgamŏs (2),
fortified

PERHAPS
686 ara (1), then, so,
therefore
3381 mēpōs (1), lest
somehow
5029 tacha (1), shortly,
i.e. possibly

PERIDA
6514 Pᵉrûwdâ' (1),
dispersion

PERIL
2794 kindunŏs (1),
danger, risk

PERILOUS
5467 chalĕpŏs (1),
difficult, i.e. dangerous

PERILS
2794 kindunŏs (8),
danger, risk

PERISH
6 'âbad (73), perish;
destroy
7 'âbad (Ch.) (2), perish;
destroy
8 'ôbêd (2), wretched;
destruction
1478 gâva' (1), to expire,
die
1820 dâmâh (2), to be
silent; to fail, cease
3772 kârath (1), to cut
(off, down or asunder)
5307 nâphal (1), to fall
5486 çûwph (1), to
terminate
5595 çâphâh (2), to
scrape; to remove
5674 'âbar (1), to cross
over; to transition
6544 pâra' (1), to loosen;
to expose, dismiss
7843 shâchath (1), to
decay; to ruin
622 apŏllumi (25), to
destroy fully; to perish
853 aphanizō (1), to
disappear, be destroyed
1311 diaphthĕirō (1), to
ruin, to decay
1510+1519+604 ĕimi (1), I
exist, I am
2704 kataphthĕirō (1), to
spoil entirely
5356 phthŏra (1), ruin;
depravity, corruption

PERISHED
6 'âbad (17), perish;
destroy
1478 gâva' (1), to expire,
die
8045 shâmad (1), to
desolate
599 apŏthnēskō (1), to
die off
622 apŏllumi (5), to
destroy fully; to perish
4881 sunapŏllumi (1), to
destroy, be slain with

PERISHETH
6 'âbad (6), perish;
destroy
622 apŏllumi (3), to
destroy fully; to perish

PERISHING
5674 'âbar (1), to cross
over; to transition

PERIZZITE
6522 Pᵉrîzzîy (5), of the
open country

PERIZZITES
6522 Pᵉrîzzîy (18), of the
open country

PERJURED
1965 ĕpiŏrkŏs (1),
forswearer, perjurer

PERMISSION
4774 suggnōmē (1), *concession*

PERMIT
2010 ĕpitrĕpō (2), *allow, permit*

PERMITTED
2010 ĕpitrĕpō (2), *allow, permit*

PERNICIOUS
684 apŏlĕia (1), *ruin or loss*

PERPETUAL
5331 netsach (4), *splendor; lasting*
5769 'ôwlâm (22), *eternity; always*
8548 tâmîyd (2), *constantly, regularly*

PERPETUALLY
3605+3711 kôl (2), *all, any or every*
5703 'ad (1), *perpetuity*

PERPLEXED
943 bûwk (2), to *be confused*
639 apŏrĕō (1), *be at a* mental *loss, be puzzled*
1280 diapŏrĕō (2), to *be thoroughly puzzled*

PERPLEXITY
3998 mᵉbûwkâh (2), *perplexity, confusion*
640 apŏria (1), state of *quandary, perplexity*

PERSECUTE
1814 dâlaq (1), to *flame;* to *pursue*
7291 râdaph (14), to *run after* with hostility
7921+310 shâkôl (1), to *miscarry*
1377 diōkō (8), to *pursue;* to *persecute*
1559 ĕkdiōkō (1), to *expel or persecute*

PERSECUTED
4783 murdâph (1), *persecuted*
7291 râdaph (5), to *run after* with hostility
1377 diōkō (13), to *pursue;* to *persecute*
1559 ĕkdiōkō (1), to *expel or persecute*

PERSECUTEST
1377 diōkō (6), to *pursue;* to *persecute*

PERSECUTING
1377 diōkō (1), to *pursue;* to *persecute*

PERSECUTION
7291 râdaph (1), to *run after* with hostility
1375 diōgmŏs (5), *persecution*
1377 diōkō (3), to *pursue;* to *persecute*
2347 thlipsis (1), *pressure, trouble*

PERSECUTIONS
1375 diōgmŏs (5), *persecution*

PERSECUTOR
1376 diōktēs (1), *persecutor*

PERSECUTORS
1814 dâlaq (1), to *flame;* to *pursue*
7291 râdaph (7), to *run after* with hostility

PERSEVERANCE
4343 prŏskartĕrēsis (1), *perseverance*

PERSIA
6539 Pâraç (27), *Paras*
6540 Pâraç (Ch.) (2), *Paras*

PERSIAN
6523 parzel (Ch.) (1), *iron*
6542 Parçîy (1), *Parsite*

PERSIANS
6539 Pâraç (1), *Paras*
6540 Pâraç (Ch.) (4), *Paras*

PERSIS
4069 Pĕrsis (1), *Persis*

PERSON
120 'âdâm (2), *human being; mankind*
376 'îysh (3), *man; male; someone*
376+120 'îysh (1), *man; male; someone*
1167 ba'al (1), *master; husband; owner; citizen*
5315 nephesh (14), *life; breath; soul; wind*
6440 pânîym (10), *face; front*
4383 prŏsōpŏn (5), *face, presence*
5287 hupŏstasis (1), *essence; assurance*

PERSONS
120 'âdâm (3), *human being; mankind*
376 'îysh (8), *man; male; someone*
582 'ĕnôwsh (2), *man; person, human*
4962 math (1), *men*
5315 nephesh (12), *life; breath; soul; wind*
5315+120 nephesh (4), *life; breath; soul; wind*
6440 pânîym (11), *face; front*
678 aprŏsōpŏlĕptŏs (2), *without prejudice*
4380 prŏsōpŏlĕptĕō (1), to *show partiality*
4381 prŏsōpŏlĕptēs (1), *exhibiting partiality*
4382 prŏsōpŏlĕpsia (4), *favoritism*
4383 prŏsōpŏn (2), *face, presence*

PERSUADE
5496 çûwth (3), to *stimulate; to seduce*
6601 pâthâh (3), to *be, make simple; to delude*
3982 pĕithō (3), to *assent* to evidence

PERSUADED
5496 çûwth (1), to *stimulate; to seduce*

PERSUADEST
3982 pĕithō (1), to *assent* to evidence

PERSUADETH
5496 çûwth (1), to *stimulate; to seduce*
374 anapĕithō (1), to *incite, persuade*

PERSUADING
3982 pĕithō (2), to *assent* to evidence

PERSUASION
3988 pĕismŏnē (1), *persuadableness*

PERTAINED
1961 hâyâh (1), to *exist*

PERTAINETH
1961 hâyâh (1), to *exist*
3627 kᵉlîy (1), *implement, thing*
3348 mĕtĕchō (1), to *share or participate*

PERTAINING
4012 pĕri (1), *about*

PERUDA
6514 Pᵉrûwdâ' (1), *dispersion*

PERVERSE
1942 havvâh (1), *desire; craving*
2015 hâphak (1), to *change, pervert*
3399 yâraṭ (1), to *be rash*
3868 lûwz (1), to *depart;* to *be perverse*
3891 lᵉzûwth (1), *perverseness*
5753 'âvâh (2), to *be crooked*
5773 'av'eh (1), *perversity*
6140 'âqash (2), to *knot or distort;* to *pervert*
6141 'iqqêsh (4), *distorted, warped, false*
8419 tahpûkâh (1), *perversity or fraud*
1294 diastrĕphō (4), to *be morally corrupt*
3859 paradiatribē (1), *meddlesomeness*

PERVERSELY
5753 'âvâh (2), to *be crooked*
5791 'âvath (1), to *wrest, twist*

PERVERSENESS
3868 lûwz (1), to *depart;* to *be perverse*
4297 muṭṭeh (1), *distortion; iniquity*
5558 çeleph (2), *distortion; viciousness*
5766 'evel (1), moral *evil*
5999 'âmâl (1), *wearing effort; worry*

PERVERT
5186 nâṭâh (2), to *stretch or spread out*

PERVERTED
2015 hâphak (1), to *change, pervert*
5186 nâṭâh (1), to *stretch or spread out*
5753 'âvâh (2), to *be crooked*
7725 shûwb (1), to *turn back; to return*

PERVERTETH
5186 nâṭâh (1), to *stretch or spread out*
5557 çâlaph (2), to *wrench; to subvert*
6140 'âqash (1), to *knot or distort;* to *pervert*
654 apŏstrĕphō (1), to *turn away or back*

PERVERTING
1294 diastrĕphō (1), to *be morally corrupt*

PESTILENCE
1698 deber (47), *pestilence, plague*

PESTILENCES
3061 lŏimŏs (2), *plague; disease; pest*

PESTILENT
3061 lŏimŏs (1), *plague; disease; pest*

PESTLE
5940 'ĕlîy (1), *mortar pestle*

PETER
4074 Pĕtrŏs (157), *piece of rock*

PETER'S
4074 Pĕtrŏs (4), *piece of rock*

PETHAHIAH
6611 Pᵉthachyâh (4), *Jehovah has opened*

PETHOR
6604 Pᵉthôwr (2), *Pethor*

PETHUEL
6602 Pᵉthûw'êl (1), *enlarged of God*

PETITION
1159 bâ'ûw (Ch.) (2), *request; prayer*
7596 shᵉ'êlâh (10), *petition*

PETITIONS
4862 mish'âlâh (1), *request*
155 aitēma (1), *thing asked, request*

PEULTHAI
6469 Pᵉ'ull'thay (1), *laborious*

PHALEC
5317 Phalĕk (1),
earthquake

PHALLU
6396 Pallûw' (1),
distinguished

PHALTI
6406 Palṭiy (1), *delivered*

PHALTIEL
6409 Palṭiy'êl (1),
deliverance of God

PHANUEL
5323 Phanŏuêl (1), *face
of God*

PHARAOH
6547 Par'ôh (221), *Paroh*
5328 Pharaŏ (3), *Pharaoh*

PHARAOH'S
6547 Par'ôh (46), *Paroh*
5328 Pharaŏ (2), *Pharaoh*

PHARAOH-HOPHRA
6548 Par'ôh Chophra'
(1), *Paroh-Chophra*

PHARAOH-NECHO
6549 Par'ôh Nᵉkôh (1),
Paroh-Nekoh (or -Neko)

PHARAOH-NECHOH
6549 Par'ôh Nᵉkôh (4),
Paroh-Nekoh (or -Neko)

PHARES
5329 Pharĕs (3), *breech*

PHAREZ
6557 Perets (12), *breech*

PHARISEE
5330 Pharisaiŏs (10),
separatist

PHARISEE'S
5330 Pharisaiŏs (2),
separatist

PHARISEES
5330 Pharisaiŏs (86),
separatist

PHARISEES'
5330 Pharisaiŏs (1),
separatist

PHAROSH
6551 Par'ôsh (1), *flea*

PHARPAR
6554 Parpar (1), *rapid*

PHARZITES
6558 Partsîy (1), *Partsite*

PHASEAH
6454 Pâçêach (1), *limping*

PHEBE
5402 Phŏibē (2), *bright*

PHENICE
5403 Phŏinikē (2),
palm-country
5405 Phŏinix (1),
palm-tree

PHENICIA
5403 Phŏinikē (1),
palm-country

PHICHOL
6369 Pîykôl (3), *mouth of
all*

PHILADELPHIA
5359 Philadĕlphĕia (2),
fraternal

PHILEMON
5371 Philēmōn (2),
friendly

PHILETUS
5372 Philētŏs (1), *amiable*

PHILIP
5376 Philippŏs (33), *fond
of horses*

PHILIP'S
5376 Philippŏs (3), *fond
of horses*

PHILIPPI
5375 Philippŏi (8),
Philippi

PHILIPPIANS
5374 Philippēsiŏs (1),
native of Philippi

PHILISTIA
6429 Pᵉlesheth (3),
migratory

PHILISTIM
6430 Pᵉlishtîy (1),
Pelishtite

PHILISTINE
6430 Pᵉlishtîy (33),
Pelishtite

PHILISTINES
6430 Pᵉlishtîy (250),
Pelishtite

PHILISTINES'
6430 Pᵉlishtîy (4),
Pelishtite

PHILOLOGUS
5378 Philŏlŏgŏs (1),
argumentative, learned

PHILOSOPHERS
5386 philŏsŏphŏs (1), *one
fond of wise things*, i.e.
philosopher

PHILOSOPHY
5385 philŏsŏphia (1),
wise things

PHINEHAS
6372 Pîynᵉchâç (24),
mouth of a serpent

PHINEHAS'
6372 Pîynᵉchâç (1),
mouth of a serpent

PHLEGON
5393 Phlĕgōn (1), *blazing*

PHRYGIA
5435 Phrugia (4), *Phrygia*

PHURAH
6513 Pûrâh (1), *foliage*

PHUT
6316 Pûwṭ (2), *Put*

PHUVAH
6312 Pûw'âh (1), *blast*

PHYGELLUS
5436 Phugĕllŏs (1),
fugitive

PHYLACTERIES
5440 phulaktēriŏn (1),
guard-case

PHYSICIAN
7495 râphâ' (1), to *cure,
heal*
2395 iatrŏs (5), *physician*

PHYSICIANS
7495 râphâ' (4), to *cure,
heal*

2395 iatrŏs (2), *physician*

PI-BESETH
6364 Pîy-Beçeth (1),
Pi-Beseth

PI-HAHIROTH
6367 Piy ha-Chîrôth (4),
mouth of the gorges

PICK
5365 nâqar (1), to *bore;
to gouge*

PICTURES
4906 maskîyth (2),
carved figure
7914 sᵉkîyâh (1),
conspicuous object

PIECE
95 'ăgôwrâh (1), *coin*
829 'eshpâr (2), *portion*
915 bâdâl (1), *part*
1335 bether (1), *piece*
2513 chelqâh (3),
flattery; allotment
3603 kikkâr (2), round
loaf; talent
4060 middâh (7),
measure; portion
4749 miqshâh (1), work
molded by *hammering*
5409 nêthach (2),
fragment
6400 pelach (6), *slice*
6595 path (2), *bit, morsel*
1406 drachmē (2), *coin*
1915 ĕpiblēma (4), *patch*
3313 mĕrŏs (1), *division
or share*
4138 plērōma (1), what
fills; what is *filled*

PIECES
1506 gezer (1), *portion,
piece*
1917 haddâm (Ch.) (2),
bit, piece
5409 nêthach (9),
fragment
6595 path (3), *bit, morsel*
7168 qera' (3), *rag, torn
pieces*
7518 rats (1), *fragment*
1288 diaspaŏ (1), to *sever
or dismember*
1406 drachmē (1), *coin*

PIERCE
4272 mâchats (1), to
crush; to subdue
5344 nâqab (2), to
puncture, perforate
1330 diĕrchŏmai (1), to
traverse, travel through

PIERCED
738 'ărîy (1), *lion*
1856 dâqar (1), to *stab,
pierce*
4272 mâchats (1), to
crush; to subdue
5365 nâqar (1), to *bore;
to gouge*
1574 ĕkkĕntĕō (2), to
pierce or impale
3572 nussō (1), to *pierce,
stab*
4044 pĕripĕirō (1), to
penetrate entirely

PIERCETH
5344 nâqab (1), to
puncture, perforate

PIERCING
1281 bârîyach (1),
fleeing, gliding serpent
1338 diiknĕŏmai (1),
penetrate, pierce

PIERCINGS
4094 madqârâh (1),
wound

PIETY
2151 ĕusĕbĕŏ (1), to *put
show piety toward*

PIGEON
1469 gôwzâl (1), *young of
a bird*
3123 yôwnâh (1), *dove*

PIGEONS
3123 yôwnâh (9), *dove*
4058 pĕristĕra (1),
pigeon, dove

PILATE
4091 Pilatŏs (55), *firm*

PILDASH
6394 Pildâsh (1), *Pildash*

PILE
4071 mᵉdûwrâh (2), *pile*

PILEHA
6401 Pilchâ' (1), *slicing*

PILGRIMAGE
4033 mâgûwr (4), *abode*

PILGRIMS
3927 parepidēmŏs (2),
resident foreigner

PILLAR
4676 matstsêbâh (10),
column or stone
4678 matstsebeth (4),
stock of a tree
5324 nâtsab (1), to *station*
5333 nᵉtsîyb (1), military
post; statue
5982 'ammûwd (29),
column, pillar
4769 stulŏs (2),
supporting pillar; leader

PILLARS
547 'ômᵉnâh (1), *column*
4552 miç'âd (1),
balustrade for stairs
4676 matstsêbâh (2),
column or stone
4690 mâtsûwq (1),
column; hilltop
5982 'ammûwd (79),
column, pillar
8490 tîymârâh (2),
column, i.e. cloud
4769 stulŏs (2),
supporting pillar; leader

PILLED
6478 pâtsal (2), to *peel*

PILLOW
3523 kᵉbîyr (2), matrass,
quilt of animal hair
4344 prŏskĕphalaiŏn (1),
cushion pillow

PILLOWS
3704 keçeth (2), cushion
or pillow
4763 mᵉra'ăshâh (2),
headpiece; head-rest

PILOTS
2259 chôbêl (4), *sailor*

PILTAI
6408 Pilṭay (1), *Piltai*

PIN
3489 yâthêd (3), tent *peg*

PINE
2100 zûwb (1), to *waste away*
4743 mâqaq (4), to *melt*; to *flow, dwindle, vanish*
6086+8081 'êts (1), *wood*
8410 tidhâr (2), *lasting* tree (poss.) *oak*

PINETH
3583 xērainō (1), to *shrivel*, to *mature*

PINING
1803 dallâh (1), *loose hair; indigent, needy*

PINNACLE
4419 ptĕrugiŏn (2), *winglet,* i.e. *extremity*

PINON
6373 Pîynôn (2), *Pinon*

PINS
3489 yâthêd (10), tent *peg*

PIPE
2485 châlîyl (3), *flute*
836 aulŏs (1), *flute*

PIPED
2490 châlal (1), to *play* the flute
832 aulĕō (3), to play the *flute*

PIPERS
834 aulētēs (1), *flute-player*

PIPES
2485 châlîyl (3), *flute* instrument
4166 mûwtsâqâh (1), *tube*
5345 neqeb (1), *bezel, gem mounting*
6804 tsantârâh (1), *tube, pipe*

PIRAM
6502 Pir'âm (1), *wildly*

PIRATHON
6552 Pir'âthôwn (1), *chieftaincy*

PIRATHONITE
6553 Pir'âthôwnîy (5), *Pirathonite*

PISGAH
6449 Piçgâh (5), *cleft*

PISIDIA
4099 Pisidia (2), *Pisidia*

PISON
6376 Pîyshôwn (1), *dispersive*

PISPAH
6462 Piçpâh (1), *dispersion*

PISS
7890 shayin (2), *urine*

PISSETH
8366 shâthan (6), to *urinate* as a male

PIT
875 bᵉ'êr (3), *well, cistern*
953 bôwr (41), pit *hole, cistern, well; prison*
1360 gebe' (1), *reservoir*

1475 gûwmmâts (1), *pit*
6354 pachath (8), *pit* for catching animals
7585 shᵉ'ôwl (3), abode of the *dead*
7743+7882 shûwach (1), to *sink*
7745 shûwchâh (2), *chasm*
7816 shᵉchûwth (1), *pit*
7845 shachath (14), *pit; destruction*
7882 shîychâh (1), *pit*-fall
999 bŏthunŏs (1), *cistern, pit-hole*
5421 phrĕar (5), *cistern* or water *well; abyss*

PITCH
167 'âhal (1), to pitch a *tent*
2203 zepheth (3), *asphalt*
2583 chânâh (11), to *encamp*
3724 kôpher (1), *village; bitumen; henna*
6965 qûwm (1), to *rise*
8628 tâqa' (1), to *clatter, slap, drive, clasp*

PITCHED
167 'âhal (1), to pitch a *tent*
2583 chânâh (70), to *encamp*
5186 nâṭâh (8), to *stretch* or spread out
8628 tâqa' (2), to *clatter, slap, drive, clasp*
4078 pēgnumi (1), to *set up* a tent

PITCHER
3537 kad (10), *jar, pitcher*
2765 kĕramiŏn (2), *earthenware* vessel

PITCHERS
3537 kad (4), *jar, pitcher*
5035 nebel (1), *skin-bag* for liquids; *vase; lyre*

PITHOM
6619 Pîthôm (1), *Pithom*

PITHON
6377 Pîythôwn (2), *expansive*

PITIED
2347 chûwç (1), to be *compassionate*
2550 châmal (4), to *spare, have pity on*
7356 racham (1), *compassion; womb*

PITIETH
4263 machmâl (1), *delight*
7355 râcham (2), to be *compassionate*

PITIFUL
7362 rachmânîy (1), *compassionate*
2155 ĕusplagchnŏs (1), *compassionate*
4184 pŏlusplagchnŏs (1), *extremely compassionate*

PITS
953 bôwr (1), pit *hole, cistern, well; prison*

1356 gêb (1), *well, cistern; pit*
7745 shûwchâh (1), *chasm*
7825 shᵉchîyth (1), *pit-fall*
7882 shîychâh (1), *pit*-fall

PITY
2347 chûwç (6), to be *compassionate*
2550 châmal (14), to *spare, have pity on*
2551 chemlâh (1), *commiseration, pity*
2603 chânan (3), to *implore*
2617 cheçed (1), *kindness, favor*
5110 nûwd (1), to *console, deplore;* to *taunt*
7355 râcham (1), to be *compassionate*
7356 racham (1), *compassion; womb*
1653 ĕlĕĕō (1), to give out *compassion*

PLACE
870 'âthar (Ch.) (5), *after*
1004 bayith (7), *house; temple; family, tribe*
1367 gᵉbûwlâh (1), *region*
3027 yâd (7), *hand; power*
3241 Yânîym (1), *asleep*
3427 yâshab (2), to *dwell,* to *remain;* to *settle*
3653 kên (1), *pedestal* or *station* of a basin
4349 mâkôwn (11), *basis; place*
4612 ma'ămâd (1), *position; attendant*
4634 ma'ărâkâh (1), *arrangement, row; pile*
4724 miqvâh (1), *water reservoir*
4725 mâqôwm (373), general *locality, place*
4800 merchâb (1), *open space; liberty*
5182 nᵉchath (Ch.) (1), to *descend;* to *depose*
5414 nâthan (3), to *give*
5977 'ômed (6), fixed *spot*
6607 pethach (1), *opening; door*
7675 shebeth (1), *abode* or *locality*
7760 sûwm (1), to *place*
7931 shâkan (5), to *reside*
8414 tôhûw (1), *waste, desolation, formless*
8478 tachath (17), *bottom; underneath*
201 akrŏatēriŏn (1), *audience-room*
402 anachōrĕō (1), to *retire, withdraw*
1502 ĕikō (1), to *be weak,* i.e. *yield*
1564 ĕkĕithĕn (1), *from there*
1786 ĕntŏpiŏs (1), local *resident*
3692 ŏpē (1), *hole,* i.e. *cavern; spring* of water
3699 hŏpŏu (1), *at whichever* spot
4042 pĕriŏchē (1), *passage* of Scripture

5117 tŏpŏs (74), *place*
5562 chōrĕō (1), to *pass, enter;* to *hold, admit*
5564 chōriŏn (2), *spot* or *plot* of ground
5602 hŏdĕ (2), *here*

PLACED
776 'erets (1), *earth, land, soil; country*
3240 yânach (2), to *allow to stay*
3427 yâshab (5), to *dwell,* to *remain;* to *settle*
3947 lâqach (1), to *take*
5414 nâthan (1), to *give*
5975 'âmad (1), to *stand*
7760 sûwm (1), to *place*
7931 shâkan (2), to *reside*

PLACES
168 'ôhel (1), *tent*
1004 bayith (9), *house; temple; family, tribe*
2723 chorbâh (1), *desolation, dry* desert
3027 yâd (1), *hand; power*
4585 mᵉ'ôwnâh (1), *abode*
4725 mâqôwm (20), general *locality, place*
5439 çâbîyb (1), *circle; environs; around*
8478 tachath (1), *bottom; underneath;* in *lieu of*
3837 pantachŏu (1), *universally, everywhere*
5117 tŏpŏs (7), *place*

PLAGUE
4046 maggêphâh (20), *pestilence; defeat*
4347 makkâh (2), *blow; wound; pestilence*
5061 nega' (64), *infliction, affliction; leprous spot*
5063 negeph (7), *infliction* of disease
3148 mastix (2), *flogging* device
4127 plēgĕ (2), *stroke; wound; calamity*

PLAGUED
4046 maggêphâh (1), *pestilence; defeat*
5060 nâga' (3), to *strike*
5062 nâgaph (2), to *inflict* a disease

PLAGUES
1698 deber (1), *pestilence, plague*
4046 maggêphâh (1), *pestilence; defeat*
4347 makkâh (8), *blow; wound; pestilence*
5061 nega' (1), *infliction, affliction; leprous spot*
3148 mastix (2), *flogging device*
4127 plēgĕ (10), *stroke; wound; calamity*

PLAIN
58 'âbêl (1), *meadow*
436 'êlôwn (7), *oak*
874 bâ'ar (1), to *explain*
1236 biq'â (Ch.) (1), wide level *valley*
1237 biq'âh (7), wide level *valley*

3603 kikkâr (13), *tract* or region; round *loaf*
4334 mîyshôwr (14), *plain; justice*
5228 nâkôach (1), *equitable, correct*
5549 çâlal (1), to *mound* up; to *exalt;* to *oppose*
6160 'ărâbâh (22), *desert, wasteland*
7737 shâvâh (1), to *level,* i.e. *equalize*
8219 sh⁰phêlâh (3), *lowland,*
8535 tâm (1), morally *pious; gentle, dear*
3723 ŏrthŏs (1), *correctly, rightly*
5117+3977 tŏpŏs (1), *place*

PLAINLY
559 'âmar (1), to *say*
874 bâ'ar (1), to *explain*
1540 gâlâh (1), to *denude; uncover*
5046 nâgad (1), to *announce*
6568 p⁰rash (Ch.) (1), to *specify, translate*
6703 tsach (1), *dazzling,* i.e. *sunny, bright*
1718 ĕmphanizō (1), to *show forth*
3954 parrhēsia (4), *frankness, boldness*

PLAINNESS
3954 parrhēsia (1), *frankness, boldness*

PLAINS
436 'êlôwn (2), *oak*
4334 mîyshôwr (1), *plain; justice*
6160 'ărâbâh (20), *desert, wasteland*
8219 sh⁰phêlâh (2), *lowland,*

PLAISTER
1528 gîyr (Ch.) (1), *lime for plaster*
2902 tûwach (1), to *whitewash*
4799 mârach (1), to *apply by rubbing*
7874 sîyd (2), to *plaster, whitewash* with lime

PLAISTERED
2902 tûwach (2), to *whitewash*

PLAITING
1708 ĕmplŏkē (1), *braiding* of the hair

PLANES
4741 maqtsŭ'âh (1), wood-carving *chisel*

PLANETS
4208 mazzâlâh (1), *constellations*

PLANKS
5646 'âb (1), *architrave*
6086 êts (1), *wood,* things made of *wood*
6763 tsêlâ' (1), *side*

PLANT
4302 maṭṭâ' (1), something *planted*
5193 nâṭa' (31), to *plant*

5194 neṭa' (3), *plant; plantation; planting*
5414 nâthan (1), to *give*
7880 sîyach (1), *shrubbery*
8362 shâthal (2), to *transplant*
5451 phuṭĕia (1), *shrub* or *vegetable*

PLANTATION
4302 maṭṭâ' (1), something *planted*

PLANTED
5193 nâṭa' (21), to *plant*
8362 shâthal (8), to *transplant*
4854 sumphutŏs (1), closely *united* to
5452 phuṭĕuō (8), to *implant,* i.e. to *instill* doctrine

PLANTEDST
5193 nâṭa' (2), to *plant*

PLANTERS
5193 nâṭa' (1), to *plant*

PLANTETH
5192 nêṭel (2), *burden*
5452 phuṭĕuō (3), to *implant,* i.e. to *instill*

PLANTING
4302 maṭṭâ' (2), something *planted*

PLANTINGS
4302 maṭṭâ' (1), something *planted*

PLANTS
4302 maṭṭâ' (1), something *planted*
5189 n⁰ṭîyshâh (1), *tendril* plant shoot
5194 neṭa' (2), *plant; plantation; planting*
5195 nâṭîya' (1), *plant*
7973 shelach (1), *spear; shoot* of growth
8291 sarûwq (1), choice *grapevine*
8363 sh⁰thîyl (1), *sucker* plant

PLAT
2513 chelqâh (2), *smoothness; flattery*

PLATE
6731 tsîyts (3), burnished *plate;* bright *flower*

PLATES
3871 lûwach (1), *tablet*
5633 çeren (1), *axle; peer*
6341 pach (2), thin metallic *sheet; net*

PLATTED
4120 plĕkō (3), to *twine* or *braid*

PLATTER
3953 parŏpsis (2), side-dish receptacle
4094 pinax (2), *plate, platter, dish*

PLAY
5059 nâgan (4), to *play;* to make music
6711 tsâchaq (1), to *laugh;* to *make sport* of

7832 sâchaq (5), to *laugh;* to *scorn;* to *play*
8173 shâ'a' (1), to *fondle, please* or *amuse* (self)
3815 paizō (1), to *indulge in (sexual) revelry*

PLAYED
5059 nâgan (4), to *play;* to *make music*
7832 sâchaq (3), to *laugh;* to *scorn;* to *play*

PLAYER
5059 nâgan (1), to *play;* to *make music*

PLAYERS
2490 châlal (1), to *play* the flute
5059 nâgan (1), to *play;* to *make music*

PLAYING
5059 nâgan (1), to *play;* to *make music*
7832 sâchaq (2), to *laugh;* to *scorn;* to *play*

PLEA
1779 dîyn (1), *judge; judgment; law suit*

PLEAD
1777 dîyn (2), to *judge;* to *strive* or *contend for*
3198 yâkach (3), to be *correct;* to *argue*
7378 rîyb (23), to *hold a controversy;* to *defend*
8199 shâphaṭ (9), to *judge*

PLEADED
7378 rîyb (2), to *hold a controversy;* to *defend*
8199 shâphaṭ (1), to *judge*

PLEADETH
7378 rîyb (1), to *hold a controversy;* to *defend*
8199 shâphaṭ (1), to *judge*

PLEADINGS
7379 rîyb (1), *contest,* personal or legal

PLEASANT
2530 châmad (3), to *delight* in; *lust for*
2531 chemed (2), *delight*
2532 chemdâh (11), *delight*
2580 chên (1), *graciousness; beauty*
2656 chêphets (1), *pleasure; desire*
2896 ṭôwb (2), *good; well*
3303 yâpheh (1), *beautiful; handsome*
4022 meged (3), *valuable*
4261 machmâd (5), *delightful*
4262 machmûd (3), *desired; valuable*
4999 nâ'âh (1), *home, dwelling; pasture*
5116 nâveh (1), *at home; lovely; home*
5273 nâ'îym (8), *delightful; sweet*
5276 nâ'êm (5), to be *agreeable*
5278 no'am (2), *agreeableness, delight*
6027 'ôneg (1), *luxury*
6148 'ârab (1), to *intermix*

6643 ts⁰bîy (1), *conspicuous* splendor
8191 sha'shûa' (2), *enjoyment*
8378 ta'ăvâh (1), *longing; delight*
8588 ta'ănûwg (1), *luxury; delight*

PLEASANTNESS
5278 no'am (1), *agreeableness*

PLEASE
2654 châphêts (5), to be *pleased* with, *desire*
2655 châphêts (1), *pleased* with
2894 ṭûw' (3), to *sweep away*
2895 ṭowb (6), to be *good*
2896 ṭôwb (2), *good; well*
3190 yâṭab (2), to be, *make well*
3477+5869 yâshâr (1), *straight*
5606 çâphaq (1), to be *enough;* to *vomit*
7451+5869 ra' (1), *bad; evil*
7521 râtsâh (3), to be *pleased with;* to *satisfy*
700 arĕskō (11), to *seek to please*
701 arĕstŏs (1), *agreeable; desirable; fit*
2001+1511 ĕpischuō (1), to *insist stoutly*
2100 ĕuarĕstĕō (1), to *gratify entirely, please*

PLEASED
2654 châphêts (8), to be *pleased* with, *desire*
2895 ṭowb (1), to be *good*
2896+5869 ṭôwb (1), *good; well*
2974 yâ'al (1), to *assent;* to *undertake, begin*
3190 yâṭab (2), to be, *make well*
3190+5869 yâṭab (10), to be, *make well*
3477+5869 yâshâr (7), *straight*
7451+5869 ra' (1), *bad; evil*
7521 râtsâh (4), to be *pleased with;* to *satisfy*
8232 sh⁰phar (Ch.) (1), to be *beautiful*
700 arĕskō (5), to *seek to please*
701 arĕstŏs (1), *agreeable; desirable; fit*
1380 dŏkĕō (2), to *think, regard, seem good*
2100 ĕuarĕstĕō (2), to *gratify entirely, please*
2106 ĕudŏkĕō (12), to *think well,* i.e. *approve*
2309 thĕlō (2), to *will;* to *desire;* to *choose*
4909 sunĕudŏkĕō (2), to *assent to, feel gratified*

PLEASETH
2654 châphêts (1), to be *pleased* with, *desire*
2896+5869 ṭôwb (2), *good; well*

English

PLEASING
2896+6440 ṭôwb (1),
good; well
3190+5869 yâṭab (1), to
be, make well
3477+5869 yâshâr (1),
straight

PLEASING
2896 ṭôwb (1), *good; well*
6148 'ârab (1), to *give or be security*
699 arĕskĕia (1),
complaisance, amiable
700 arĕskō (2), to *seek to please*
701 arĕstŏs (1),
agreeable; desirable; fit

PLEASURE
185+5315 'avvâh (1),
longing
2654 châphêts (3), to *be pleased* with, *desire*
2655 châphêts (2),
pleased with
2656 chêphets (16),
pleasure; desire
2837 chêsheq (1),
delight, desired thing
2896 ṭôwb (2), *good; well*
5315 nephesh (3), *life; breath; soul; wind*
5730 'êden (1), *pleasure*
6148 'ârab (1), to *give or be security*
7470 r°'ûwth (Ch.) (1),
desire
7521 râtsâh (6), to *be pleased with; to satisfy* a debt
7522 râtsôwn (5), *delight*
8057 simchâh (1),
blithesomeness or glee
2106 ĕudŏkĕō (6), to *think well,* i.e. *approve*
2107 ĕudŏkia (4),
delight, kindness, wish
2237 hēdŏnē (1), *delight; desire*
2307 thĕlēma (1), *decree; inclination*
3588+1380 hŏ (1), *"the,"* i.e. the definite article
4684 spatalaō (1), to *live in luxury*
4909 sunĕudŏkĕō (1), to *assent to, feel gratified*
5171 truphaō (1), to *indulge in luxury*
5485 charis (2),
gratitude; benefit given

PLEASURES
5273 nâ'îym (2),
delightful; sweet
5719 'âdîyn (1),
voluptuous
5730 'êden (1), *pleasure*
2237 hēdŏnē (2), *delight; desire*
5569 psĕudadĕlphŏs (1),
pretended associate

PLEDGE
2254 châbal (10), to *bind by a pledge; to pervert*
2258 châbôl (4), *pawn, pledge* as security
5667 'ăbôwṭ (4), *pledged* item
6161 'ărubbâh (1), as *security; bondsman*

6162 'ărâbôwn (3), *pawn, security pledge*

PLEDGES
6148 'ârab (2), to *give or be security*

PLEIADES
3598 Kîymâh (2), *cluster* of stars, *Pleiades*

PLENTEOUS
1277 bârîy' (1), *fatted or plump; healthy*
3498 yâthar (2), to *remain or be left*
7227 rab (3), *great*
7235 râbâh (1), to *increase*
7647 sâbâ' (2),
copiousness
8082 shâmên (1), *rich; fertile*
4180 pŏlulŏgia (1),
prolixity, wordiness

PLENTEOUSNESS
4195 môwthar (1), *gain; superiority*
7647 sâbâ' (1),
copiousness

PLENTIFUL
3759 karmel (3), *planted field; garden produce*
5071 n°dâbâh (1),
abundant gift

PLENTIFULLY
3499 yether (1),
remainder; small rope
7230 rôb (1), *abundance*
2164 ĕuphŏrĕō (1), to *be fertile, produce a crop*

PLENTY
398 'âkal (1), to *eat*
4723 miqveh (1),
confidence; collection
7230 rôb (3), *abundance*
7235 râbâh (1), to *increase*
7646 sâba' (2), *fill* to satiety
7647 sâbâ' (4),
copiousness
8443 tôw'âphâh (1),
treasure; speed

PLOTTETH
2161 zâmam (1), to *plan*

PLOUGH
723 arŏtrŏn (1), *plow*

PLOW
2790 chârash (6), to *engrave; to plow*
722 arŏtriŏō (1), to *plough, make furrows*

PLOWED
2790 chârash (5), to *engrave; to plow*

PLOWERS
2790 chârash (1), to *engrave; to plow*

PLOWETH
722 arŏtriŏō (1), to *plough, make furrows*

PLOWING
2790 chârash (2), to *engrave; to plow*
5215 nìyr (1), *freshly plowed* land

722 arŏtriŏō (1), to *plough, make furrows*

PLOWMAN
2790 chârash (2), to *engrave; to plow*

PLOWMEN
406 'ikkâr (2), *farmer*

PLOWSHARES
855 'êth (3), *digging implement*

PLUCK
717 'ârâh (1), to *pluck, pick fruit*
1497 gâzal (2), to *rob*
3318 yâtsâ' (1), to *go, bring out*
3615 kâlâh (1), to *cease, be finished, perish*
5255 nâçach (1), to *tear away*
5375 nâsâ' (1), to *lift up*
5423 nâthaq (2), to *tear off*
5428 nâthash (10), to *tear away, be uprooted*
5493 çûwr (1), to *turn off*
6131 'âqar (1), to *pluck up roots; to hamstring*
6998 qâṭaph (1), to *strip off, pick off*
8045 shâmad (1), to *desolate*
726 harpazō (2), to *seize*
1544 ĕkballō (1), to *throw out*
1807 ĕxairĕō (1), to *tear out; to select; to release*
1808 ĕxairō (1), to *remove, drive away*
5089 tillō (2), to *pull off* grain heads

PLUCKED
1497 gâzal (2), to *rob*
3318 yâtsâ' (1), to *go, bring out*
4803 mâraṭ (3), to *polish; to make bald*
4804 m°raṭ (Ch.) (1), to *pull off, tear off*
5255 nâçach (1), to *tear away*
5337 nâtsal (2), to *be snatched away*
5423 nâthaq (1), to *tear off*
5428 nâthash (4), to *tear away, be uprooted*
6132 'âqar (Ch.) (1), to *pluck up roots*
7993 shâlak (1), to *throw out, down or away*
8025 shâlaph (1), to *pull out, up or off*
1288 diaspaō (1), to *sever or dismember*
1610 ĕkrizŏō (2), to *uproot*
1846 ĕxŏrussō (1), to *dig out*
5089 tillō (1), to *pull off* grain heads

PLUCKETH
2040 hâraç (1), to *pull down; break, destroy*

PLUCKT
2965 ṭârâph (1), *freshly picked vegetation*

722 arŏtriŏō (1), to *plough, make furrows*

PLOWMAN
2790 chârash (2), to *engrave; to plow*

PLUMBLINE
594 'ănâk (4),
plumb-*line, plummet*

PLUMMET
68+913 'eben (1), *stone*
4949 mishqeleth (2),
plummet weight

PLUNGE
2881 ṭâbal (1), to *dip*

POCHERETH
6380 Pôkereth
Ts°bâyîym (2), *trap of gazelles*

POETS
4163 pŏiētēs (1),
performer; poet

POINT
19 'ibchâh (1),
brandishing of a sword
184 'âvâh (1), to *extend* or *mark* out
1980 hâlak (1), to *walk; live a certain way*
6856 tsippôren (1), *nail; point* of a style or pen
8376 tâ'âh (2), to *mark off,* i.e. *designate*
2079 ĕschatŏs (1), *finally,* i.e. *at the extremity*
3195 mĕllō (1), to *intend,* i.e. *be about to*

POINTED
2742 chârûwts (1),
threshing-sledge

POINTS
5980 'ummâh (1), *near, beside, along with*

POISON
2534 chêmâh (5), *heat; anger; poison*
7219 rô'sh (1), *poisonous plant; poison*
2447 iŏs (2), *corrosion; venom*

POLE
5251 nêç (2), *flag; signal; token*

POLICY
7922 sekel (1),
intelligence; success

POLISHED
1305 bârar (1), to *brighten; purify*
2404 châṭab (1), to *chop or carve wood*
7044 qâlâl (1),
brightened, polished

POLISHING
1508 gizrâh (1), *figure, appearance; enclosure*

POLL
1494 gâzaz (1), to *shear; shave; destroy*
1538 gulgôleth (1), *skull*
3697 kâçam (1), to *shear, clip*

POLLED
1548 gâlach (3), to *shave; to lay waste*

POLLS
1538 gulgôleth (6), *skull*

POLLUTE
2490 châlal (8), to *profane, defile*

2610 chânêph (1), to *soil, be defiled*
2930 ţâmê' (2), to *be morally contaminated*

POLLUTED
947 bûwç (2), to *trample down; oppress*
1351 gâ'al (7), to *soil, stain; desecrate*
2490 châlal (13), to *profane, defile*
2610 chânêph (3), to *soil, be defiled*
2930 ţâmê' (12), to *be morally contaminated*
2931 ţâmê' (1), *foul; ceremonially impure*
6121 'âqôb (1), *fraudulent; tracked*
2840 kŏinŏŏ (1), to *make profane*

POLLUTING
2490 châlal (2), to *profane, defile*

POLLUTION
2931 ţâmê' (1), *foul; ceremonially impure*

POLLUTIONS
234 alisgĕma (1), *ceremonially polluted*
3393 miasma (1), *foulness, corruption*

POLLUX
1359 Diŏskŏurŏi (1), *twins of Zeus*

POMEGRANATE
7416 rimmôwn (10), *pomegranate*

POMEGRANATES
7416 rimmôwn (22), *pomegranate*

POMMELS
1543 gullâh (3), *fountain; bowl or globe*

POMP
1347 gâ'ôwn (5), *ascending; majesty*
7588 shâ'ôwn (1), *uproar; destruction*
5325 phantasia (1), vain *show,* i.e. *pomp*

PONDER
6424 pâlaç (2), to *weigh mentally*

PONDERED
4820 sumballō (1), to *consider; to aid; to join, attack*

PONDERETH
6424 pâlaç (1), to *weigh mentally*
8505 tâkan (2), to *balance,* i.e. *measure*

PONDS
98 'ăgam (2), *marsh; pond; pool*
99 'âgêm (1), *sad*

PONTIUS
4194 Pŏntiŏs (4), *bridged*

PONTUS
4195 Pŏntŏs (3), *sea*

POOL
98 'ăgam (2), *marsh; pond; pool*

1295 bᵉrêkâh (15), *reservoir, pool*
2861 kŏlumbēthra (5), *pond*

POOLS
98 'ăgam (2), *marsh; pond; pool*
1293 bᵉrâkâh (1), *benediction, blessing*
1295 bᵉrêkâh (1), *reservoir, pool*
4723 miqveh (1), *confidence; collection*

POOR
34 'ebyôwn (25), *destitute; poor*
1800 dal (44), *weak, thin; humble, needy*
1803 dallâh (4), *indigent, needy*
2489 chêlᵉkâ' (3), *unhappy wretch*
3423 yârash (2), to *impoverish; to ruin*
4134 mûwk (4), to *be impoverished*
4270 machçôwr (1), *impoverishment*
4542 miçkên (4), *indigent, needy*
6033 'ănâh (Ch.) (1), to *afflict, be afflicted*
6035 'ânâv (1), *needy; oppressed*
6035+6041 'ânâv (3), *needy; oppressed*
6041 'ânîy (56), *depressed*
7326 rûwsh (21), to *be destitute*
3993 pĕnēs (1), *poor*
3998 pĕnichrŏs (1), *needy, impoverished*
4433 ptōchĕuō (1), to *become indigent, poor*
4434 ptōchŏs (31), *pauper, beggar*

POORER
4134 mûwk (1), to *be impoverished*

POOREST
1803 dallâh (1), *indigent, needy*

POPLAR
3839 libneh (1), *whitish tree,* (poss.) *storax*

POPLARS
3839 libneh (1), *whitish tree,* (poss.) *storax*

POPULOUS
527 'âmôwn (1), *crowd*
7227 rab (1), *great*

PORATHA
6334 Pôwrâthâ' (1), *Poratha*

PORCH
197 'ûwlâm (33), *vestibule, portico*
4528 miçdᵉrôwn (1), *colonnade or portico*
4259 prŏauliŏn (1), *vestibule,* i.e. *alley-way*
4440 pulōn (1), *gate-way, door-way*
4745 stŏa (3), *colonnade or interior piazza*

PORCHES
197 'ûwlâm (1), *vestibule, portico*
4745 stŏa (1), *colonnade or interior piazza*

PORCIUS
4201 Pŏrkiŏs (1), *swinish*

PORT
8179 sha'ar (1), *opening,* i.e. *door or gate*

PORTER
7778 shôw'êr (4), *janitor, door-keeper*
2377 thurŏrŏs (2), *gate-warden, doorkeeper*

PORTERS
7778 shôw'êr (31), *janitor, door-keeper*
8179 sha'ar (1), *opening,* i.e. *door or gate*
8652 târâ' (Ch.) (1), *doorkeeper*

PORTION
270 'âchaz (2), to *seize, grasp; possess*
1697 dâbâr (4), *word; matter; thing*
2256 chebel (2), *company, band*
2505 châlaq (1), to *be smooth; be slippery*
2506 chêleq (36), *allotment*
2508 chălâq (Ch.) (3), *part, portion*
2513 chelqâh (6), *allotment*
2706 chôq (3), *appointment; allotment*
4490 mânâh (4), *ration; lot or portion*
4521 mᵉnâth (4), *allotment*
6310 peh (2), *mouth; opening*
6598 pathbag (5), *dainty food*
7926 shᵉkem (1), *neck; spur of a hill*
3313 mĕrŏs (3), *division or share*
4620 sitŏmĕtrŏn (1), *allowance or ration*

PORTIONS
2256 chebel (2), *company, band*
2506 chêleq (4), *allotment*
4256 machălôqeth (1), *section or division*
4490 mânâh (6), *ration; lot or portion*
4521 mᵉnâth (3), *allotment*

POSSESS
423 'âlâh (2), *public agreement*
2631 chăçan (Ch.) (1), to *take possession*
3423 yârash (93), to *inherit; to impoverish*
5157 nâchal (5), to *inherit*
2932 ktaŏmai (3), to *get*

POSSESSED
270 'âchaz (1), to *seize, grasp; possess*

2631 chăçan (Ch.) (1), to *take possession*
3423 yârash (19), to *inherit; to impoverish*
7069 qânâh (3), to *create; to procure*
1139 daimŏnizŏmai (11), to *be demon-possessed*
2192 ĕchō (2), to *have; hold; keep*
2722 katĕchō (1), to *hold down fast*
5224 huparchŏnta (1), *property or possessions*

POSSESSEST
3423 yârash (1), to *inherit; to impoverish*

POSSESSETH
3423 yârash (1), to *inherit; to impoverish*
5224 huparchŏnta (1), *property or possessions*

POSSESSING
2722 katĕchō (1), to *hold down fast*

POSSESSION
270 'âchaz (1), to *seize, grasp; possess*
272 'ăchuzzâh (64), *possession*
3423 yârash (6), to *inherit; to impoverish*
3424 yᵉrêshâh (2), *occupancy*
3425 yᵉrushâh (11), *conquest*
4180 môwrâsh (1), *possession*
4181 môwrâshâh (6), *possession*
4735 miqneh (3), *live-stock*
4736 miqnâh (1), *acquisition*
5157 nâchal (1), to *inherit*
5159 nachălâh (1), *occupancy*
7272 regel (1), *foot; step*
2697 kataschĕsis (2), *occupancy, possession*
2933 ktēma (1), *estate; wealth, possessions*
4047 pĕripŏiēsis (1), *acquisition*

POSSESSIONS
270 'âchaz (3), to *seize, grasp; possess*
272 'ăchuzzâh (2), *possession*
4180 môwrâsh (1), *possession*
4639 ma'ăseh (1), *action; labor*
4735 miqneh (2), *live-stock*
2933 ktēma (3), *estate; wealth, possessions*
5564 chōriŏn (1), *spot or plot of ground*

POSSESSOR
7069 qânâh (2), to *create; to procure*

POSSESSORS
7069 qânâh (1), to *create; to procure*
2935 ktētōr (1), *land owner*

English

POSSIBLE
102 adunatŏs (1), *weak; impossible*
1410 dunamai (1), *to be able* or *possible*
1415 dunatŏs (13), *capable; possible*

POST
352 'ayîl (4), *chief; ram; oak* tree
4201 mᵉzûwzâh (4), *door-post*
4947 mashqôwph (1), *lintel*
7323 rûwts (2), *to run*

POSTERITY
310 'achar (4), *after*
319 'achărîyth (3), *future; posterity*
1755 dôwr (1), *dwelling*
7611 shᵉ'êrîyth (1), *remainder* or *residual*

POSTS
352 'ayîl (17), *chief; ram; oak* tree
520 'ammâh (1), *cubit*
4201 mᵉzûwzâh (15), *door-post*
5592 çaph (3), *dish*
7323 rûwts (6), *to run*

POT
610 'âçûwk (1), oil-*flask*
1731 dûwd (1), *pot, kettle; basket*
3627 kᵉlîy (1), *implement, thing*
4715 mitsrêph (2), *crucible*
5518 çîyr (12), *thorn; hook*
6517 pârûwr (2), *skillet*
6803 tsintseneth (1), *vase, receptacle*
4713 stamnŏs (1), *jar* or earthen *tank*

POTENTATE
1413 dunastēs (1), *ruler* or *officer*

POTI-PHERAH
6319 Pôwṭîy Phera' (3), *Poti-Phera*

POTIPHAR
6318 Pôwṭîyphar (2), *Potiphar*

POTS
1375 gᵉbîya' (1), *goblet; bowl*
1731 dûwd (1), *pot, kettle; basket*
5518 çîyr (9), *thorn; hook*
8240 shâphâth (1), *hook; hearth*
3582 xĕstēs (2), *vessel; measure*

POTSHERD
2789 cheres (4), *piece of* earthenware *pottery*

POTSHERDS
2789 cheres (1), *piece of* earthenware *pottery*

POTTAGE
5138 nâzîyd (6), *boiled* soup or stew

POTTER
3335 yâtsar (8), *to form; potter; to determine*
2763 kĕramĕus (1), *potter*
2764 kĕramikŏs (1), *made of clay*

POTTER'S
3335 yâtsar (7), *to form; potter; to determine*
2763 kĕramĕus (2), *potter*

POTTERS
3335 yâtsar (1), *to form; potter; to determine*

POTTERS'
3335 yâtsar (1), *to form; potter; to determine*
6353 pechâr (Ch.) (1), *potter*

POUND
4488 mâneh (2), fixed *weight*
3046 litra (2), 12 oz. measure, i.e. a *pound*
3414 mna (4), certain *weight*

POUNDS
4488 mâneh (2), fixed *weight*
3414 mna (5), certain *weight*

POUR
2212 zâqaq (1), to *strain, refine; extract, clarify*
3332 yâtsaq (13), *to pour out*
5042 nâba' (1), to *gush forth; to utter*
5064 nâgar (2), to *pour out; to deliver over*
5140 nâzal (2), to *drip*, or *shed* by trickling
5258 nâçak (6), to *pour* a libation; to *anoint*
5414 nâthan (1), to *give*
7324 rûwq (1), to *pour out*, i.e. *empty*
8210 shâphak (33), to *spill forth; to expend*
1632 ĕkchĕō (3), to *pour forth; to bestow*

POURED
2229 zâram (1), to *gush* water, *pour forth*
3251 yâçak (1), to *pour*
3332 yâtsaq (13), *to pour*
5064 nâgar (1), to *pour out; to deliver over*
5258 nâçak (10), to *pour* a libation; to *anoint*
5413 nâthak (13), to *flow forth, pour out*
6168 'ârâh (2), to *empty, pour out; demolish*
6694 tsûwq (2), to *pour out; melt*
7324 rûwq (1), to *pour out*, i.e. *empty*
8210 shâphak (25), to *spill forth*
8211 shephek (2), *ash-heap, dump*
906 ballō (1), to *throw*
1632 ĕkchĕō (9), to *pour forth; to bestow*
2708 katachĕō (2), to *pour down* or *out*

POUREDST
2767 kĕrannumi (1), to *mingle*, i.e. *to pour*

POUREDST
8210 shâphak (1), to *spill forth; to expend*

POURETH
1811 dâlaph (1), *to drip*
5042 nâba' (2), to *gush forth; to utter*
5064 nâgar (1), to *pour out; to deliver over*
8210 shâphak (6), to *spill forth; to expend*
906 ballō (1), to *throw*

POURING
8210 shâphak (1), to *spill forth; to expend*

POURTRAY
2710 châqaq (1), to *engrave; to enact laws*

POURTRAYED
2707 châqah (2), to *carve; to delineate*
2710 châqaq (1), to *engrave; to enact* laws

POVERTY
2639 cheçer (1), *lack; destitution*
3423 yârash (3), to *impoverish; to ruin*
4270 machçôwr (1), *impoverishment*
7389 rêysh (7), *poverty*
4432 ptōchĕia (3), *indigence, poverty*

POWDER
80 'âbâq (1), *fine dust; cosmetic powder*
1854 dâqaq (2), to *crush; crumble*
6083 'âphâr (3), *dust, earth, mud; clay*
3039 likmaō (2), to *grind to powder*

POWDERS
81 'âbâqâh (1), *cosmetic powder*

POWER
410 'êl (3), *mighty*; the *Almighty*
1369 gᵉbûwrâh (9), *force; valor; victory*
2220 zᵉrôwa' (3), *arm; foreleg; force, power*
2428 chayil (9), *army; wealth; virtue; strength*
2429 chayil (Ch.) (1), *army; strength; loud sound*
2632 chêçen (Ch.) (2), *strength, powerful rule*
3027 yâd (13), *hand; power*
3028 yad (Ch.) (1), *hand; power*
3201 yâkôl (1), to *be able*
3581 kôach (47), *force, might; strength*
3709 kaph (1), *hollow of hand; paw; sole of foot*
4475 memshâlâh (1), *rule; realm* or a *ruler*
4910 mâshal (2), to *rule*
5794 'az (1), *strong, vehement, harsh*
5797 'ôz (11), *strength*

POWER
5808 'izzûwz (1), *forcible; army*
6184 'ârîyts (1), *powerful* or *tyrannical*
7786 sûwr (1), to *rule, crown*
7980 shâlaṭ (3), to *dominate*, i.e. *govern*
7981 shᵉlêṭ (Ch.) (1), to *dominate*, i.e. *govern*
7983 shiltôwn (2), *potentate*
7989 shallîyṭ (1), *prince* or *warrior*
8280 sârâh (2), to *prevail, contend*
8592 ta'ătsûmâh (1), *might*
8617 tᵉqûwmâh (1), *resistfulness*
8633 tôqeph (1), *might*
746 archē (1), *first in rank; first in time*
1325 didōmi (2), to *give*
1410 dunamai (1), to *be able* or *possible*
1411 dunamis (71), *force, power, miracle*
1415 dunatŏs (1), *powerful* or *capable; possible*
1849 ĕxŏusia (61), *authority, power, right*
1850 ĕxŏusiazō (3), to *control, master another*
2479 ischus (2), *forcefulness, power*
2904 kratŏs (6), *vigor, strength*
3168 mĕgalĕiŏtēs (1), *grandeur* or *splendor*

POWERFUL
3581 kôach (1), *force, might; strength*
1756 ĕnĕrgēs (1), *active, operative*
2478 ischurŏs (1), *forcible, powerful*

POWERS
1411 dunamis (6), *force, power, miracle*
1849 ĕxŏusia (8), *authority, power, right*

PRACTISE
5953 'âlal (1), to *glean; to overdo*
6213 'âsâh (3), to *do* or *make*

PRACTISED
2790 chârash (1), to *engrave; to plow*
6213 'âsâh (1), to *do*

PRAETORIUM
4232 praitōriŏn (1), *governor's court-room*

PRAISE
1288 bârak (1), to *bless*
1974 hillûwl (1), harvest *celebration*
1984 hâlal (92), to *praise; thank; boast*
2167 zâmar (4), to *play music*
3034 yâdâh (52), to *revere* or *worship*
4110 mahălâl (1), *fame, good reputation*

7623 shâbach (4), to *address*; to *pacify*
7624 sh°bach (Ch.) (2), to *adulate*, i.e. *adore*
8416 t°hillâh (52), *laudation; hymn*
8426 tôwdâh (5), expressions of *thanks*
133 ainĕsis (1), *thank*-offering. *praise*
134 ainĕō (3), to *praise*
136 ainŏs (2), *praise*
1391 dŏxa (4), *glory; brilliance*
1867 ĕpainĕō (3), to *applaud, commend*
1868 ĕpainŏs (12), *laudation*
5214 humnĕō (1), to *celebrate in song*

PRAISED
1288 bârak (1), to *bless*
1984 hâlal (19), to *praise; thank; boast*
3034 yâdâh (1), to *throw; to revere or worship*
7623 shâbach (1), to *address*
7624 sh°bach (Ch.) (3), to *adulate*, i.e. *adore*
2127 ĕulŏgĕō (1), to *invoke a benediction*

PRAISES
1984 hâlal (1), to *praise; thank; boast*
8416 t°hillâh (5), *laudation; hymn*
8426 tôwdâh (1), expressions of *thanks*
703 arĕtē (1), *excellence, virtue*

PRAISETH
1984 hâlal (1), to *praise; thank; boast*

PRAISING
1984 hâlal (4), to *praise; thank; boast*
134 ainĕō (6), to *praise*

PRANSING
1725 dâhar (1), to *prance*

PRANSINGS
1726 dahăhar (2), *gallop*

PRATING
8193 sâphâh (2), *lip, language, speech*
5396 phluarĕō (1), to *berate*

PRAY
577 'ânnâ' (2), *oh now!, I ask you!*
2470 châlâh (3), to be *weak, sick, afflicted*
2603 chânan (1), to *implore*
3863 lûw' (1), *if; would that!*
4994 nâ' (195), *I pray!, please!, I beg you!*
6279 'âthar (1), *intercede*
6293 pâga' (1), to *impinge*
6419 pâlal (34), to *intercede, pray*
6739 ts°lâ' (Ch.) (1), *pray*
7592 shâ'al (2), to *ask*
7878 sîyach (1), to *ponder, muse aloud*

1189 dĕŏmai (7), to *beg, petition, ask*
2065 ĕrōtaō (10), to *interrogate; to request*
2172 ĕuchŏmai (2), to *wish for; to pray*
3870 parakalĕō (4), to *call, invite*
4336 prŏsĕuchŏmai (42), to *supplicate, pray*

PRAYED
6419 pâlal (30), to *intercede, pray*
6739 ts°lâ' (Ch.) (1), *pray*
1189 dĕŏmai (3), to *beg, petition, ask*
2065 ĕrōtaō (4), to *interrogate; to request*
3870 parakalĕō (2), to *call, invite*
4336 prŏsĕuchŏmai (25), to *supplicate, pray*

PRAYER
2470 châlâh (1), to be *weak, sick, afflicted*
3908 lachash (1), *incantation; amulet*
6279 'âthar (1), *intercede in prayer*
6419 pâlal (2), to *intercede, pray*
7878 sîyach (1), to *ponder, muse aloud*
7879 sîyach (1), *uttered contemplation*
8605 t°phillâh (75), *intercession*
1162 dĕēsis (7), *petition, request*
1783 ĕntĕuxis (1), *intercession*
2171 ĕuchĕ (1), *wish, petition*
4335 prŏsĕuchē (21), *prayer; prayer chapel*
4336 prŏsĕuchŏmai (1), to *supplicate, pray*

PRAYERS
8605 t°phillâh (2), *intercession*
1162 dĕēsis (5), *petition, request*
4335 prŏsĕuchē (15), *prayer; prayer chapel*
4336 prŏsĕuchŏmai (2), to *supplicate, pray*

PRAYEST
4336 prŏsĕuchŏmai (2), to *supplicate, pray*

PRAYETH
6419 pâlal (4), to *intercede, pray*
4336 prŏsĕuchŏmai (3), to *supplicate, pray*

PRAYING
1156 b°'â' (Ch.) (1), to *seek or ask*
6419 pâlal (5), to *intercede, pray*
1189 dĕŏmai (2), to *beg, petition, ask*
4336 prŏsĕuchŏmai (12), to *supplicate, pray*

PREACH
1319 bâsar (1), to *announce* (good news)
7121 qârâ' (2), to *call out*

1229 diaggĕllō (1), to *herald thoroughly*
2097 ĕuaggĕlizō (18), to *announce good news*
2605 kataggĕllō (4), to *proclaim, promulgate*
2784 kĕrussō (22), to *herald*
2980 lalĕō (1), to *talk*

PREACHED
1319 bâsar (1), to *announce* (good news)
189 akŏē (1), *hearing; thing heard*
1256 dialĕgŏmai (1), to *discuss*
2097 ĕuaggĕlizō (22), to *announce good news*
2605 kataggĕllō (6), to *proclaim, promulgate*
2784 kĕrussō (20), to *herald*
2907 krĕas (1), *meat*
2980 lalĕō (4), to *talk*
3954 parrhēsia (1), *frankness, boldness*
4137 plĕrŏō (1), to *fill, make complete*
4283 prŏĕuaggĕlizŏmai (1), to *announce glad news in advance*
4296 prŏkĕrussō (2), to *proclaim in advance*

PREACHER
6953 qôheleth (7), *assembler* i.e. *lecturer*
2783 kĕrux (3), *herald*
2784 kĕrussō (1), to *herald*

PREACHEST
2784 kĕrussō (1), to *herald*

PREACHETH
2097 ĕuaggĕlizō (1), to *announce good news*
2784 kĕrussō (2), to *herald*

PREACHING
7150 q°rìy'âh (1), *proclamation*
1256 dialĕgŏmai (1), to *discuss*
2097 ĕuaggĕlizō (6), to *announce good news*
2782 kĕrugma (8), *proclamation*
2784 kĕrussō (8), to *herald*
2980 lalĕō (1), to *talk*
3056 lŏgŏs (1), *word, matter, thing; Word*

PRECEPT
4687 mitsvâh (1), *command*
6673 tsav (4), *injunction*
1785 ĕntŏlē (2), *prescription, regulation*

PRECEPTS
4687 mitsvâh (3), *command*
6490 piqqûwd (21), *mandate* of God, *Law*

PRECIOUS
2530 châmad (3), to *delight in; lust for*

2532 chemdâh (1), *delight*
2580 chên (1), *graciousness; beauty*
2667 chôphesh (1), *carpet*
2896 tôwb (4), *good; well*
3365 yâqar (8), to be *valuable; to make rare*
3366 y°qâr (4), *wealth; costliness; dignity*
3368 yâqâr (25), *valuable*
4022 meged (5), *valuable*
4030 migdânâh (3), *preciousness*, i.e. a *gem*
4901 meshek (1), *sowing; possession*
5238 n°kôth (2), *valuables*
927 barutimŏs (1), *highly valuable*
1784 ĕntimŏs (2), *valued, considered precious*
2472 isŏtimŏs (1), *of equal value or honor*
4185 pŏlutĕlēs (1), *extremely expensive*
5092 timē (1), *esteem; nobility; money*
5093 timiŏs (11), *costly; honored, esteemed*

PREDESTINATE
4309 prŏŏrizō (2), to *predetermine*

PREDESTINATED
4309 prŏŏrizō (2), to *predetermine*

PREEMINENCE
4195 môwthar (1), *gain; superiority*
4409 prōtĕuō (1), to be *first*
5383 philŏprōtĕuō (1), *loving to be first*

PREFER
5927 'âlâh (1), to *ascend, be high, mount*

PREFERRED
5330 n°tsach (Ch.) (1), to *become chief*
8138 shânâh (1), to *fold, to transmute*
1096 ginŏmai (3), to *be, become*

PREFERRING
4285 prŏēgĕŏmai (1), to *show deference*
4299 prŏkrima (1), *prejudgment, partiality*

PREMEDITATE
3191 mĕlĕtaō (1), to *plot, think about*

PREPARATION
3559 kûwn (2), to *set up; establish, fix, prepare*
2091 hĕtŏimasia (1), *preparation*
3904 paraskĕuē (6), *readiness*

PREPARATIONS
4633 ma'ărâk (1), *mental disposition, plan*

PREPARE
631 'âçar (1), to *fasten; to join battle*
3559 kûwn (41), to *set up; establish, fix, prepare*

4487 mânâh (1), to *allot*; to *enumerate* or enroll
6186 'ârak (2), to set in a row, i.e. *arrange*,
6213 'âsâh (9), to *do* or *make*
6437 pânâh (4), to *turn*, to *face*
6942 qâdâsh (7), to *be, make clean*
2090 hĕtŏimazō (11), to *prepare*
2680 kataskĕuazō (3), to *prepare thoroughly*
3903 paraskĕuazō (1), to *get ready, prepare*

PREPARED
2164 z^{e}man (Ch.) (1), to *agree, conspire*
2502 châlats (2), to *deliver, equip*
3559 kûwn (53), to *set up; establish, fix, prepare*
3739 kârâh (1), to *purchase* by bargaining
4487 mânâh (4), to *allot*; to *enumerate* or enroll
6186 'ârak (2), to set in a row, i.e. *arrange*,
6213 'âsâh (13), to *do* or *make*
6437 pânâh (1), to *turn*, to *face*
7543 râqach (1), to *perfume, blend spice*
2090 hĕtŏimazō (18), to *prepare*
2092 hĕtŏimōs (1), *ready, prepared*
2675 katartizō (1), to *repair; to prepare*
2680 kataskĕuazō (2), to *prepare thoroughly*
4282 prŏĕtŏimazō (1), to *fit up in advance*

PREPAREDST
6437 pânâh (1), to *turn*, to *face*

PREPAREST
3559 kûwn (1), to *set up; establish, fix, prepare*
6186 'ârak (1), to set in a row, i.e. *arrange*,
6213 'âsâh (1), to *do* or *make*

PREPARETH
3559 kûwn (3), to *set up; establish, fix, prepare*

PREPARING
6213 'âsâh (1), to *do* or *make*
2680 kataskĕuazō (1), to *prepare thoroughly*

PRESBYTERY
4244 prĕsbutĕriŏn (1), *order of elders*

PRESCRIBED
3789 kâthab (1), to *write*

PRESCRIBING
3792 k^{e}thâb (Ch.) (1), *writing, record or book*

PRESENCE
5048 neged (8), *over against* or *before*
5869 'ayin (9), *eye; sight; fountain*

5921 'al (1), *above, over, upon,* or *against*
6440 pânîym (76), *face; front*
6925 qŏdâm (Ch.) (1), *before*
561 apĕnanti (1), *before* or *against*
1715 ĕmprŏsthĕn (1), *in front of*
1799 ĕnōpiŏn (9), *in the face of, before*
2714 katĕnōpiŏn (1), *directly in front of*
3952 parŏusia (2), *coming; presence*
4383 prŏsōpŏn (7), *face, presence*

PRESENT
814 'eshkâr (1), *gratuity, gift; payment*
1293 b^{e}râkâh (3), *benediction, blessing*
3320 yâtsab (5), to *station, offer, continue*
3557 kûwl (1), to *keep in; to measure*
4503 minchâh (22), *tribute; offering*
4672 mâtsâ' (17), to *find* or *acquire; to occur*
5307 nâphal (3), to *fall*
5324 nâtsab (1), to *station*
5975 'âmad (6), to *stand*
7810 shachad (2), to *bribe; gift*
7862 shay (1), *gift*
7964 shillûwach (1), *daughter's dower*
8670 t^{e}shûwrâh (1), *gift*
737 arti (2), *just now; at once*
1736 ĕndēmĕō (2), to *be at home*
1764 ĕnistēmi (5), to *be present*
2186 ĕphistēmi (1), to *be present; to approach*
2476 histēmi (1), to *stand, establish*
3306 mĕnō (1), to *stay, remain*
3568 nun (4), *now; the present or immediate*
3854 paraginŏmai (1), to *arrive; to appear*
3873 parakĕimai (2), to *be at hand*
3918 parĕimi (14), to *be present; to have come*
3936 paristēmi (7), to *stand beside, present*
4840 sumparĕimi (1), to *be now present*

PRESENTED
3320 yâtsab (4), to *station, offer, continue*
3322 yâtsag (1), to *place*
4672 mâtsâ' (3), to *find meet* or *be present*
5066 nâgash (1), to *be, come, bring near*
5307 nâphal (1), to *fall*
5414 nâthan (1), to *give*
5975 'âmad (1), to *stand*
7126 qârab (2), to *approach, bring near*
7200 râ'âh (1), to *see*

3936 paristēmi (2), to *stand beside, present*
4374 prŏsphĕrō (1), to *present to; to treat as*

PRESENTING
5307 nâphal (1), to *fall*

PRESENTLY
3117 yôwm (2), *day; time period*
1824 ĕxautēs (1), *instantly, at once*
3916 parachrēma (1), *instantly, immediately*
3936 paristēmi (1), to *stand beside, present*

PRESENTS
4030 migdânâh (1), *preciousness, i.e. a gem*
4503 minchâh (6), *tribute; offering*
7862 shay (2), *gift*
7964 shillûwach (1), *daughter's dower*

PRESERVE
2421 châyâh (4), to *live; to revive*
3498 yâthar (1), to *remain or be left*
4241 michyâh (1), *preservation of life*
4422 mâlaṭ (1), to *escape as if by slipperiness*
5341 nâtsar (11), to *guard, protect*
7760 sûwm (1), to *put*
8104 shâmar (9), to *watch*
2225 zōŏgŏnĕō (1), to *rescue; to preserve*
4982 sōzō (1), to *deliver; to protect*

PRESERVED
3467 yâsha' (4), to *make safe, free*
5336 nâtsîyr (1), *delivered*
5337 nâtsal (1), to *deliver; to be snatched*
8104 shâmar (6), to *watch*
4933 suntērĕō (2), to *preserve in memory*
5083 tērĕō (2), to *keep, guard, obey*

PRESERVER
5314 nâphash (1), to *be refreshed*

PRESERVEST
2421 châyâh (1), to *live; to revive*
3467 yâsha' (1), to *make safe, free*

PRESERVETH
2421 châyâh (1), to *live; to revive*
5341 nâtsar (1), to *guard, protect, maintain*
8104 shâmar (6), to *watch*

PRESIDENTS
5632 çârêk (Ch.) (5), *emir, high official*

PRESS
1660 gath (1), wine-*press* or *vat*
6333 pûwrâh (1), *wine-press trough*

598 apŏthlibō (1), to *crowd, press up* against
1377 diōkō (1), to *pursue; to persecute*
3793 ŏchlŏs (5), *throng*, i.e. crowd or mob

PRESSED
1765 dâchaph (1), to *urge; to hasten*
4600 mâ'ak (1), to *press*
5781 'ûwq (2), to *pack, be pressed*
6484 pâtsar (2), to *stun or dull*
6555 pârats (2), to *break out*
6693 tsûwq (1), to *oppress, distress*
7818 sâchaṭ (1), to *tread out, i.e. squeeze grapes*
916 barĕō (1), to *weigh down, cause pressure*
1945 ĕpikĕimai (1), to *rest upon; press upon*
1968 ĕpipiptō (1), to *embrace; to seize*
4085 piĕzō (1), to *pack down firm*
4912 sunĕchō (1), to *hold together, compress*

PRESSES
3342 yeqeb (2), wine-*vat*, wine-*press*

PRESSETH
5181 nâchath (1), to *sink, descend; to press down*
971 biazō (1), to *crowd oneself* into

PRESSFAT
3342 yeqeb (1), wine-*vat*, wine-*press*

PRESUME
2102 zûwd (1), to *be insolent*
4390 mâlê' (1), to *fill; be full*

PRESUMED
6075 'âphal (1), to *swell; be elated*

PRESUMPTUOUS
2086 zêd (1), *arrogant, proud*
5113 tŏlmētēs (1), *daring (audacious)* man

PRESUMPTUOUSLY
2087 zâdôwn (2), *arrogance, pride*
2102 zûwd (3), to *be insolent*
3027 yâd (1), *hand; power*

PRETENCE
4392 prŏphasis (3), *pretext, excuse*

PREVAIL
1396 gâbar (5), to *act insolently*
2388 châzaq (2), to *bind, restrain, conquer*
3201 yâkôl (13), to *be able*
3898 lâcham (1), to *fight a battle*
5810 'âzaz (1), to *be stout; be bold*
6113 'âtsar (1), to *hold back; to maintain, rule*

6206 'ârats (1), to *awe*; to *dread*; to *harass*
8630 tâqaph (2), to *overpower*
2729 katischuō (1), to *overpower, prevail*
5623 ōphĕlĕō (2), to *benefit, be of use*

PREVAILED
553 'âmats (1), to *be strong; be courageous*
1396 gâbar (9), to *be strong; to prevail*
2388 châzaq (8), to *bind, restrain, conquer*
3201 yâkôl (9), to *be able*
3202 yᵉkêl (Ch.) (1), to *be able*
3513 kâbad (1), to *be heavy, severe, dull*
5810 'âzaz (2), to *be stout; be bold*
7186 qâsheh (1), *severe*
2480 ischuō (3), to *have or exercise force*
2729 katischuō (1), to *overpower, prevail*
3528 nikaō (1), to *subdue, conquer*

PREVAILEST
8630 tâqaph (1), to *overpower*

PREVAILETH
7287 râdâh (1), to *subjugate; to crumble*

PREVENT
6923 qâdam (6), to *anticipate, hasten*
5348 phthanō (1), to *anticipate or precede*

PREVENTED
6923 qâdam (8), to *anticipate, hasten*
4399 prŏphthanō (1), to *anticipate*

PREVENTEST
6923 qâdam (1), to *anticipate, hasten*

PREY
400 'ôkel (2), *food*
957 baz (17), *plunder, loot*
961 bizzâh (4), *booty, plunder*
962 bâzaz (9), to *plunder, take booty*
2863 chetheph (1), *robber or robbery*
2963 târaph (1), to *pluck off or pull to pieces*
2964 tereph (18), *fresh torn prey*
4455 malqôwach (6), *spoil, plunder*
5706 'ad (3), *booty*
7997 shâlal (1), to *drop or strip; to plunder*
7998 shâlâl (11), *booty*

PRICE
3365 yâqar (1), to *be valuable; to make rare*
3701 keçeph (3), *silver money*
4242 mᵉchîyr (11), *price, payment, wages*
4377 meker (1), *merchandise; value*

4736 miqnâh (2), *acquisition*
4901 meshek (1), *sowing; possession*
6187 'êrek (1), *pile, equipment, estimate*
7939 sâkâr (2), *payment, salary; compensation*
4185 pŏlutĕlēs (1), *extremely expensive*
4186 pŏlutimŏs (1), *extremely valuable*
5092 timē (7), *esteem; nobility; money*

PRICES
5092 timē (1), *esteem; nobility; money*

PRICKED
8150 shânan (1), to *pierce; to inculcate*
2669 katapŏnĕō (1), to *harass, oppress*

PRICKING
3992 mâ'ar (1), to *be painful; destructive*

PRICKS
7899 sêk (1), *brier of a hedge*
2759 kĕntrŏn (2), *sting; goad*

PRIDE
1344 gê'âh (1), *arrogance, pride*
1346 ga'ăvâh (9), *arrogance; majesty*
1347 gâ'ôwn (20), *ascending; majesty*
1348 gê'ûwth (2), *ascending; majesty*
1363 gôbahh (2), *height; grandeur; arrogance*
1466 gêvâh (3), *arrogance, pride*
2087 zâdôwn (6), *arrogance, pride*
2103 zûwd (Ch.) (1), to *be proud*
7407 rôkeç (1), *snare as of tied meshes*
7830 shachats (1), *haughtiness; dignity*
212 alazŏnĕia (1), *boasting*
5187 tuphŏō (1), to *inflate with self-conceit*
5243 hupĕrēphania (1), *haughtiness, arrogance*

PRIEST
3547 kâhan (2), to *officiate as a priest*
3548 kôhên (423), one *officiating as a priest*
3549 kâhên (Ch.) (1), one *officiating as a priest*
748 archiĕratikŏs (1), *high-priestly*
749 archiĕrĕus (53), *high-priest, chief priest*
2409 hiĕrĕus (16), *priest*

PRIEST'S
3547 kâhan (20), to *officiate as a priest*
3548 kôhên (17), one *officiating as a priest*
3550 kᵉhunnâh (4), *priesthood*

749 archiĕrĕus (4), *high-priest, chief priest*
2405 hiĕratĕia (1), *priestly office*
2407 hiĕratĕuō (1), to *be a priest*

PRIESTHOOD
3550 kᵉhunnâh (9), *priesthood*
2405 hiĕratĕia (1), *priestly office*
2406 hiĕratĕuma (2), *priestly order*
2420 hiĕrōsunē (4), *priestly office*

PRIESTS
3548 kôhên (300), one *officiating as a priest*
3549 kâhên (Ch.) (6), one *officiating as a priest*
3649 kâmâr (1), *pagan priest*
749 archiĕrĕus (67), *high-priest, chief priest*
2409 hiĕrĕus (15), *priest*

PRIESTS'
3548 kôhên (8), one *officiating as a priest*

PRINCE
5057 nâgîyd (8), *commander, official*
5081 nâdîyb (4), *grandee or tyrant*
5387 nâsîy' (56), *leader; rising mist, fog*
7101 qâtsîyn (2), *magistrate; leader*
7333 râzôwn (1), *dignitary*
8269 sar (19), *head person, ruler*
8323 sârar (1), to *have, exercise, get dominion*
747 archēgŏs (2), *chief leader; founder*
758 archōn (8), *first*

PRINCE'S
5081 nâdîyb (1), *grandee or tyrant*
5387 nâsîy' (2), *leader; rising mist, fog*

PRINCES
324 ăchashdarpan (Ch.) (9), *satrap*
2831 chashmân (1), (poss.) *wealthy*
3548 kôhên (1), one *officiating as a priest*
5057 nâgîyd (1), *commander, official*
5081 nâdîyb (10), *grandee or tyrant*
5257 nᵉçîyk (3), *libation; molten image; prince*
5387 nâsîy' (40), *leader; rising mist, fog*
5461 çâgân (1), *prefect of a province*
6579 partam (1), *grandee, noble*
7101 qâtsîyn (2), *magistrate; leader*
7227 rab (2), *great*
7261 rabrᵉbân (Ch.) (2), *magnate, noble*
7336 râzan (5), *honorable*

7991 shâlîysh (1), *officer; of the third rank*
8269 sar (190), *head person, ruler*
758 archōn (3), *first*
2232 hēgĕmōn (1), *chief*

PRINCESS
8282 sârâh (1), *female noble*

PRINCESSES
8282 sârâh (1), *female noble*

PRINCIPAL
1 'âb (1), *father*
117 'addîyr (3), *powerful; majestic*
3548 kôhên (1), one *officiating as a priest*
5257 nᵉçîyk (1), *libation; molten image; prince*
7218 rô'sh (5), *head*
7225 rê'shîyth (1), *first*
7795 sôwrâh (1), *row*
8269 sar (2), *head person, ruler*
8291 sarûwq (1), *choice grapevine*

PRINCIPALITIES
4761 mar'âshâh (1), *headship, dominion*
746 archē (6), *first in rank; first in time*

PRINCIPALITY
746 archē (2), *first in rank; first in time*

PRINCIPLES
746 archē (1), *first in rank; first in time*
4747 stŏichĕiŏn (1), *basic principles*

PRINT
2707 châqah (1), to *carve; to delineate*
5414 nâthan (1), to *give*
5179 tupŏs (2), *shape, resemblance; "type"*

PRINTED
2710 châqaq (1), to *engrave; to enact laws*

PRISCA
4251 Priska (1), *ancient*

PRISCILLA
4252 Priskilla (5), *little Prisca*

PRISED
3365 yâqar (1), to *be valuable; to make rare*

PRISON
631 'âçar (2), to *fasten; to join battle*
1004+612 bayith (3), *house; temple; family*
1004+3608 bayith (7), *house; temple; family*
1004+5470 bayith (8), *house; temple; family*
1004+6486 bayith (1), *house; temple; family*
3608 kele' (4), *prison*
4115 mahpeketh (2), *stocks for punishment*
4307 maṭṭârâ' (13), *jail (guard-house); aim*
4525 maçgêr (3), *prison; craftsman*

4929 mishmâr (1), *guard; deposit; usage; example*
6115 'ôtser (1), *closure; constraint*
6495 pᵉqach-qôwach (1), *jail-delivery; salvation*
1200 dĕsmŏphulax (2), *jailer*
1201 dĕsmōtēriŏn (4), *dungeon, jail*
3612 ŏikēma (1), *jail cell*
3860 paradidōmi (2), *to hand over*
5084 tērēsis (1), *observance; prison*
5438 phulakē (33), *night watch; prison; haunt*

PRISONER
615 'âçîyr (1), *captive, prisoner*
616 'aççîyr (1), *captive, prisoner*
1198 dĕsmiŏs (11), *bound captive; one arrested*

PRISONERS
615 'âçîyr (8), *captive, prisoner*
616 'aççîyr (3), *captive, prisoner*
631 'âçar (2), to *fasten; to join battle*
7628 shᵉbîy (2), *exile; booty*
1198 dĕsmiŏs (3), *bound captive; one arrested*
1202 dĕsmōtēs (2), *captive*

PRISONS
5438 phulakē (3), *night watch; prison; haunt*

PRIVATE
2398 idiŏs (1), *private or separate*

PRIVATELY
2596+2398 kata (8), *down; according to*

PRIVILY
652 'ôphel (1), *dusk, darkness*
2934 ṭâman (3), to *hide*
3909 lâṭ (1), *incantation; secrecy; covertly*
5643 çêther (1), *cover, shelter*
6845 tsâphan (1), to *hide; to protect; to lurk*
8649 tormâh (1), *fraud*
2977 lathra (3), *privately, secretly*
3918 parĕimi (1), to *be present; to have come*
3922 parĕisĕrchŏmai (1), *to supervene stealthily*

PRIVY
2314 châdar (1), to *enclose; to beset*
3045 yâda' (1), to *know*
8212 shophkâh (1), *penis*
4894 sunĕidō (1), to *understand*

PRIZE
1017 brabĕiŏn (2), *prize in the public games*

PROCEED
3254 yâçaph (2), to *add or augment*

3318 yâtsâ' (8), to *go, bring out*
1607 ĕkpŏrĕuŏmai (3), to *proceed, project*
1831 ĕxĕrchŏmai (1), to *issue; to leave*
4298 prŏkŏptō (1), to *go ahead, advance*

PROCEEDED
3254 yâçaph (1), to *add or augment*
3318 yâtsâ' (2), to *go, bring out*
4161 môwtsâ' (1), *going forth*
1607 ĕkpŏrĕuŏmai (3), to *proceed, project*
1831 ĕxĕrchŏmai (1), to *issue; to leave*
4369 prŏstithēmi (1), to *annex, repeat*

PROCEEDETH
3318 yâtsâ' (6), to *go, bring out*
4161 môwtsâ' (1), *going forth*
1607 ĕkpŏrĕuŏmai (3), to *proceed, project*
1831 ĕxĕrchŏmai (1), to *issue; to leave*

PROCEEDING
1607 ĕkpŏrĕuŏmai (1), to *proceed, project*

PROCESS
7093 qêts (1), *extremity; after*
7227 rab (1), *great*
7235 râbâh (1), to *increase*

PROCHORUS
4402 Prŏchŏrŏs (1), *before the dance*

PROCLAIM
5674 'âbar (1), to *cross over; to transition*
6942 qâdâsh (1), to *be, make clean*
7121 qârâ' (21), to *call out*

PROCLAIMED
2199 zâ'aq (1), to *call out, announce*
5674 'âbar (1), to *cross over; to transition*
7121 qârâ' (11), to *call out*
8085 shâma' (1), to *hear*
2784 kĕrussō (1), to *herald*

PROCLAIMETH
7121 qârâ' (1), to *call out*

PROCLAIMING
7121 qârâ' (1), to *call out*
2784 kĕrussō (1), to *herald*

PROCLAMATION
3745 kᵉraz (Ch.) (1), to *proclaim*
5674+6963 'âbar (4), to *cross over; to transition*
6963 qôwl (1), *voice or sound*
7121 qârâ' (1), to *call out*
7440 rinnâh (1), *shout*
8085 shâma' (1), to *hear*

PROCURE
6213 'âsâh (2), to *make*

PROCURED
6213 'âsâh (2), to *make*

PROCURETH
1245 bâqash (1), to *search out*

PRODUCE
7126 qârab (1), to *approach, bring near*

PROFANE
2455 chôl (4), *profane, common, not holy*
2490 châlal (18), to *profane, defile*
2491 châlâl (3), *pierced to death, one slain*
2610 chânêph (1), to *soil, be defiled*
952 bĕbēlŏs (5), *irreligious, profane*
953 bĕbēlŏō (2), to *desecrate, profane*

PROFANED
2490 châlal (15), to *profane, defile*

PROFANENESS
2613 chănûphâh (1), *impiety, ungodliness*

PROFANETH
2490 châlal (1), to *profane, defile*

PROFANING
2490 châlal (2), to *profane, defile*

PROFESS
5046 nâgad (1), to *announce*
3670 hŏmŏlŏgĕō (2), to *acknowledge, declare*

PROFESSED
3670 hŏmŏlŏgĕō (1), to *acknowledge, declare*
3671 hŏmŏlŏgia (1), *acknowledgment*

PROFESSING
1861 ĕpaggĕllō (2), to *assert*
5335 phaskō (1), to *assert a claim*

PROFESSION
3671 hŏmŏlŏgia (4), *acknowledgment*

PROFIT
1215 betsa' (3), *plunder; unjust gain*
3148 yôwthêr (1), *moreover; rest; gain*
3276 yâ'al (18), to *be valuable*
3504 yithrôwn (5), *preeminence, gain*
4195 môwthar (1), *gain; superiority*
7737 shâvâh (1), to *resemble; to adjust*
3786 ŏphĕlŏs (2), *accumulate or benefit*
4851 sumphĕrō (4), to *collect; advantage*
5539 chrēsimŏs (1), *useful, valued*
5622 ŏphĕlĕia (1), *value, advantage*

5623 ŏphĕlĕō (4), to *benefit, be of use*

PROFITABLE
3276 yâ'al (1), to *be valuable*
3504 yithrôwn (1), *preeminence, gain*
5532 çâkan (2), to *be serviceable to*
6743 tsâlach (1), to *push forward*
2173 ĕuchrēstŏs (2), *useful, serviceable*
4851 sumphĕrō (3), to *conduce; advantage*
5624 ŏphĕlimŏs (3), *advantageous, useful*

PROFITED
7737 shâvâh (1), to *resemble; to adjust*
4298 prŏkŏptō (1), to *go ahead, advance*
5623 ŏphĕlĕō (4), to *benefit, be of use*

PROFITETH
3276 yâ'al (1), to *be valuable*
5532 çâkan (1), to *be serviceable to*
5623 ŏphĕlĕō (3), to *benefit, be of use*
5624+2076 ŏphĕlimŏs (1), *useful, valuable*

PROFITING
4297 prŏkŏpē (1), *progress, advancement*

PROFOUND
6009 'âmaq (1), to *be, make deep*

PROGENITORS
2029 hârâh (1), to *conceive, be pregnant*

PROGNOSTICATORS
3045 yâda' (1), to *know*

PROLONG
748 'ârak (12), to *be, make long*
3254 yâçaph (1), to *add or augment*
5186 nâṭâh (1), to *stretch or spread out*

PROLONGED
748 'ârak (5), to *be, make long*
754+3052 'arkâ' (Ch.) (1), *length*
4900 mâshak (3), to *draw out; to be tall*

PROLONGETH
748 'ârak (1), to *be, make long*
3254 yâçaph (1), to *add or augment*

PROMISE
562 'ômer (1), *something said*
1697 dâbâr (6), *word; matter; thing*
1860 ĕpaggĕlia (40), *divine assurance*
1861 ĕpaggĕllō (3), to *assert*
1862 ĕpaggĕlma (1), *self-committal*

PROMISED
559 'âmar (5), to *say*
1696 dâbar (29), to
speak, say; to *subdue*
1843 ĕxŏmŏlŏgĕō (1), to
acknowledge or *agree*
1861 ĕpaggĕllō (10), to
assert
3670 hŏmŏlŏgĕō (1), to
acknowledge, agree
4279 prŏĕpaggĕllŏmai
(1), to *promise before*

PROMISEDST
559 'âmar (1), to *say*
1696 dâbar (2), to *speak*

PROMISES
1860 ĕpaggĕlia (12),
divine *assurance*
1862 ĕpaggĕlma (1),
self-committal

PROMISING
2421 châyâh (1), to *live;*
to *revive*

PROMOTE
1431 gâdal (1), to *make
great, enlarge*
3513 kâbad (3), to *be
rich, glorious*
7311 rûwm (1), to *be
high;* to *rise* or *raise*

PROMOTED
1431 gâdal (1), to *make
great, enlarge*
5128 nûwa' (3), to *waver*
6744 tsᵉlach (Ch.) (1), to
advance; promote

PROMOTION
7311 rûwm (2), to *be
high;* to *rise* or *raise*

PRONOUNCE
981 bâṭâ' (1), to *babble,
speak rashly*
1696 dâbar (1), to *speak*

PRONOUNCED
1691 Diblayim (2), *two
cakes*
1696 dâbar (11), to *speak*
7126 qârab (1), to
approach, bring near

PRONOUNCING
981 bâṭâ' (1), to *babble,
speak rashly*

PROOF
1382 dŏkimē (3), *test,* i.e.
trustiness
1732 ĕndĕixis (1),
demonstration
4135 plērŏphŏrĕō (1), to
assure or *convince*

PROOFS
5039 tĕkmĕriŏn (1),
criterion of certainty

PROPER
5459 çᵉgullâh (1), *wealth*
791 astĕiŏs (1),
handsome
2398 idiŏs (2), *private* or
separate

PROPHECIES
4394 prŏphētĕia (2),
prediction

PROPHECY
4853 massâ' (2), *burden,
utterance*

5016 nᵉbûw'âh (3),
prediction
5030 nâbîy' (1), *prophet;
inspired man*
4394 prŏphētĕia (14),
prediction
4397 prŏphētikŏs (1),
prophetic

PROPHESIED
5012 nâbâ' (40), to speak
as a *prophet*
5013 nᵉbâ' (Ch.) (1), to
speak as a *prophet*
4395 prŏphētĕuō (9), to
foretell events, *divine*

PROPHESIETH
5012 nâbâ' (3), to speak
as a *prophet*
4395 prŏphētĕuō (4), to
foretell events, *divine*

PROPHESY
2372 châzâh (2), to *gaze
at; have a vision*
5012 nâbâ' (66), to speak
as a *prophet*
5197 nâṭaph (5), to *speak*
by inspiration
4395 prŏphētĕuō (14), to
foretell events, *divine*

PROPHESYING
5012 nâbâ' (2), to speak
as a *prophet*
5017 nᵉbûw'âh (Ch.) (1),
inspired *teaching*
4394 prŏphētĕia (2),
prediction
4395 prŏphētĕuō (1), to
foretell events, *divine*

PROPHESYINGS
4394 prŏphētĕia (1),
prediction

PROPHET
5012 nâbâ' (2), to speak
as a *prophet*
5029 nᵉbîy' (Ch.) (2),
prophet
5030 nâbîy' (164),
prophet; inspired man
5197 nâṭaph (1), to *speak*
by inspiration
4396 prŏphētēs (67),
foreteller
5578 pseudŏprŏphētēs
(4), *pretended foreteller*

PROPHET'S
5030 nâbîy' (1), *prophet;
inspired* man
4396 prŏphētēs (1),
foreteller

PROPHETESS
5031 nᵉbîy'âh (6),
prophetess
4398 prŏphētis (2),
female foreteller

PROPHETS
2374 chôzeh (1),
beholder in vision
5029 nᵉbîy' (Ch.) (2),
prophet
5030 nâbîy' (147),
prophet; inspired man
4396 prŏphētēs (80),
foreteller
4397 prŏphētikŏs (1),
prophetic

5578 pseudŏprŏphētēs
(7), *pretended foreteller*

PROPITIATION
2434 hilasmŏs (2),
atonement
2435 hilastēriŏn (1),
expiatory place

PROPORTION
4626 ma'ar (1), vacant
space
6187 'êrek (1), *pile,
equipment, estimate*
356 analŏgia (1),
proportion

PROSELYTE
4339 prŏsēlutŏs (2),
convert, i.e. *proselyte*

PROSELYTES
4339 prŏsēlutŏs (2),
convert, i.e. *proselyte*

PROSPECT
6440 pânîym (6), *face;
front*

PROSPER
3787 kâshêr (1), to *be
straight* or *right*
6743 tsâlach (37), to *push
forward*
7919 sâkal (7), to *be* or
act circumspect
7951 shâlâh (3), to *be
secure* or *successful*
2137 ĕuŏdŏō (1), to
succeed in business

PROSPERED
1980 hâlak (1), to *walk;
live a certain way*
6743 tsâlach (6), to *push
forward*
6744 tsᵉlach (Ch.) (2), to
advance; promote
7919 sâkal (1), to *be* or
act circumspect
7965 shâlôwm (1), *safe;
well; health, prosperity*
7999 shâlam (1), to *be
safe; be, make complete*
2137 ĕuŏdŏō (1), to
succeed in business

PROSPERETH
6743 tsâlach (1), to *push
forward*
6744 tsᵉlach (Ch.) (1), to
advance; promote
7919 sâkal (1), to *be* or
act circumspect
2137 ĕuŏdŏō (1), to
succeed in business

PROSPERITY
2896 ṭôwb (6), *good; well*
6743 tsâlach (1), to *push
forward*
7961 shâlêv (2), *careless,
carefree; security*
7962 shalvâh (3),
security, ease
7965 shâlôwm (4), *safe;
well; health, prosperity*

PROSPEROUS
6743 tsâlach (5), to *push
forward*
7965 shâlôwm (1), *safe;
well; health, prosperity*
7999 shâlam (1), to *be
safe; be, make complete*

2137 ĕuŏdŏō (1), to
succeed in business

PROSPEROUSLY
6743 tsâlach (2), to *push
forward*

PROSTITUTE
2490 châlal (1), to
profane, defile

PROTECTION
5643 çêther (1), *cover,
shelter*

PROTEST
5749 'ûwd (2), to *protest*
3513 nē (1), *as sure as*

PROTESTED
5749 'ûwd (3), to *protest*

PROTESTING
5749 'ûwd (1), to *protest*

PROUD
1341 gê' (2), *haughty,
proud*
1343 gê'eh (8), *arrogant,
haughty*
1346 ga'ăvâh (1),
arrogance; majesty
1347 gâ'ôwn (1),
ascending; majesty
1349 ga'ăyôwn (1),
haughty, arrogant
1362 gâbâhh (2), *high;
lofty*
1364 gâbôahh (1), *high;
powerful; arrogant*
1419 gâdôwl (1), *great*
2086 zêd (12), *arrogant,
proud*
2087 zâdôwn (3),
arrogance, pride
2102 zûwd (1), to *seethe,
to be insolent*
2121 zêydôwn (1),
boiling, raging wave
3093 yâhîyr (1), *arrogant*
7293 rahab (2), *bluster*
7295 râhâb (1), *insolent*
7311 rûwm (1), to *be
high;* to *rise* or *raise*
7342 râchâb (3), *roomy,
spacious*
5187 tuphŏō (1), to
inflate with self-conceit
5244 hupĕrēphanŏs (5),
haughty, arrogant

PROUDLY
1346 ga'ăvâh (1),
arrogance; majesty
1348 gê'ûwth (1),
ascending; majesty
1364 gâbôahh (1), *high;
powerful; arrogant*
1431 gâdal (1), to *be
great, make great*
2102 zûwd (4), to *seethe;
to be insolent*
7292 râhab (1), to *urge,
embolden*

PROVE
974 bâchan (1), to *test;* to
investigate
5254 nâçâh (14), to *test,
attempt*
584 apŏdĕiknumi (1), to
demonstrate
1381 dŏkimazō (6), to
test; to *approve*

English

3936 paristēmi (1), to stand beside, present
3985 pĕirazō (1), to endeavor, scrutinize

PROVED
974 bâchan (6), to test; to investigate
5254 nâçâh (5), to test, attempt
1381 dŏkimazō (3), to test; to approve
4256 prŏaitiaŏmai (1), to previously charge

PROVENDER
1098 bᵉlîyl (1), feed, fodder
1101 bâlal (1), to mix; confuse; to feed
4554 miçpôw' (5), fodder, animal feed

PROVERB
2420 chîydâh (1), puzzle; conundrum; maxim
4911 mâshal (4), to use figurative language
4912 mâshâl (12), pithy maxim; taunt
3850 parabŏlē (1), fictitious narrative
3942 parŏimia (2), illustration; adage

PROVERBS
4911 mâshal (2), to use figurative language
4912 mâshâl (5), pithy maxim; taunt
3942 parŏimia (2), illustration; adage

PROVETH
5254 nâçâh (1), to test, attempt

PROVIDE
2372 châzâh (1), to gaze at; to perceive
3559 kûwn (2), to set up: establish, fix, prepare
6213 'âsâh (1), to do
7200 râ'âh (7), to see
2532 kai (1), and; or
3936 paristēmi (1), to stand beside, present
4160 pŏiĕō (1), to do
4306 prŏnŏĕō (2), to look out for beforehand

PROVIDED
3559 kûwn (1), to set up: establish, fix, prepare
6213 'âsâh (1), to do
7200 râ'âh (2), to see
2090 hĕtŏimazō (1), to prepare
4265 prŏblĕpō (1), to furnish in advance

PROVIDENCE
4307 prŏnŏia (1), provident care, supply

PROVIDETH
3559 kûwn (2), to set up: establish, fix, prepare

PROVIDING
4306 prŏnŏĕō (1), to look out for beforehand

PROVINCE
4082 mᵉdîynâh (20), governmental region

4083 mᵉdîynâh (Ch.) (5), governmental region
1885 ĕparchia (2), Roman præfecture

PROVINCES
4082 mᵉdîynâh (29), governmental region
4083 mᵉdîynâh (Ch.) (1), governmental region

PROVING
1381 dŏkimazō (1), to test; to approve
4822 sumbibazō (1), to infer, show, teach

PROVISION
1697 dâbâr (1), word; matter; thing
3557 kûwl (1), to measure; to maintain
3559 kûwn (1), to set up: establish, fix, prepare
3740 kêrâh (1), purchase
3899 lechem (1), food, bread
6679 tsûwd (1), to lie in wait; to catch
6718 tsayid (2), hunting game; lunch, food
6720 tsêydâh (2), food, supplies
4307 prŏnŏia (1), provident care, supply

PROVOCATION
3708 ka'aç (4), vexation, grief
4784 mârâh (1), to rebel or resist; to provoke
4808 mᵉrîybâh (1), quarrel
3894 parapikrasmŏs (2), irritation

PROVOCATIONS
3708 ka'aç (1), vexation, grief
5007 nᵉ'âtsâh (2), scorn; to bloom

PROVOKE
4784 mârâh (2), to rebel or resist; to provoke
4843 mârar (1), to be, make bitter
5006 nâ'ats (2), to scorn
7264 râgaz (1), to quiver
653 apŏstŏmatizō (1), to question carefully
2042 ĕrĕthizō (1), to stimulate, provoke
3863 parazēlŏō (4), to excite to rivalry
3893 parapikrainō (1), to embitter alongside
3948 parŏxusmŏs (1), incitement to good
3949 parŏrgizō (1), to enrage, exasperate

PROVOKED
3707 kâ'aç (4), to grieve, rage, be indignant
4784 mârâh (4), to rebel or resist; to provoke
5006 nâ'ats (3), to scorn
5496 çûwth (1), to stimulate; to seduce
7265 rᵉgaz (Ch.) (1), to quiver
2042 ĕrĕthizō (1), to stimulate, provoke

3947 parŏxunō (1), to exasperate

PROVOKETH
5674 'âbar (1), to cross over; to transition

PROVOKING
3707 kâ'aç (1), to grieve, rage, be indignant
4784 mârâh (1), to rebel or resist; to provoke
4292 prŏkalĕŏmai (1), to irritate

PRUDENCE
6195 'ormâh (1), trickery; discretion
7922 sekel (1), intelligence; success
5428 phrŏnēsis (1), moral insight, understanding

PRUDENT
995 bîyn (8), to understand; discern
6175 'ârûwm (8), cunning; clever
6191 'âram (1), to be cunning; be prudent
7080 qâçam (1), to divine magic
7919 sâkal (2), to be or act circumspect
4908 sunĕtŏs (4), sagacious, learned

PRUDENTLY
7919 sâkal (1), to be or act circumspect

PRUNE
2168 zâmar (2), to trim or a vine

PRUNED
2167 zâmar (1), to play music

PRUNINGHOOKS
4211 mazmêrâh (4), pruning-knife

PSALM
2172 zimrâh (2), song
4210 mizmôwr (58), poem set to music
5568 psalmŏs (2), psalm; book of the Psalms

PSALMIST
2158 zâmîyr (1), song

PSALMS
2158 zâmîyr (1), song
2167 zâmar (2), to play music
5567 psallō (1), to play a stringed instrument
5568 psalmŏs (5), psalm; book of the Psalms

PSALTERIES
3627 kᵉlîy (1), implement, thing
5035 nebel (13), skin-bag for liquids; vase; lyre

PSALTERY
3627 kᵉlîy (1), implement, thing
5035 nebel (8), skin-bag for liquids; vase; lyre
6460 pᵉçanţêrîyn (Ch.) (4), lyre instrument

PTOLEMAIS
4424 Ptŏlĕmaïs (1), of Ptolemy

PUA
6312 Pûw'âh (1), blast

PUAH
6312 Pûw'âh (2), blast
6326 Pûw'âh (1), brilliancy

PUBLICAN
5057 tĕlōnēs (6), collector of revenue

PUBLICANS
754 architĕlōnēs (1), chief tax-gatherer
5057 tĕlōnēs (16), collector of revenue

PUBLICK
3856 paradĕigmatizō (1), to expose to infamy

PUBLICKLY
1219 dēmŏsiŏs (2), public; in public

PUBLISH
1319 bâsar (2), to announce (good news)
7121 qârâ' (1), to call out
8085 shâma' (11), to hear
2784 kērussō (2), to herald

PUBLISHED
559 'âmar (1), to say
1319 bâsar (1), to announce (good news)
1540 gâlâh (2), to reveal
1696 dâbar (1), to speak
8085 shâma' (1), to hear
1096 ginŏmai (1), to be, become
1308 diaphĕrō (1), to bear, carry; to differ
2784 kērussō (3), to herald

PUBLISHETH
8085 shâma' (4), to hear

PUBLIUS
4196 Pŏpliŏs (2), popular

PUDENS
4227 Pŏudēs (1), modest

PUFFED
5448 phusiŏō (6), to inflate, i.e. make proud

PUFFETH
6315 pûwach (2), to blow, to fan, kindle; to utter
5448 phusiŏō (1), to inflate, i.e. make proud

PUHITES
6336 Pûwthîy (1), hinge

PUL
6322 Pûwl (4), Pul, i.e. a person or tribe

PULL
2040 hâraç (3), to pull down; break, destroy
3318 yâtsâ' (1), to go, bring out
5422 nâthats (2), to tear down
5423 nâthaq (2), to tear off
6584 pâshaţ (1), to strip, i.e. unclothe, plunder

7725 shûwb (1), to *turn back*; to *return*
385 anaspaō (1), to *take up* or *extricate*
1544 ĕkballō (3), to *throw out*
2507 kathairĕō (1), to *lower*, or *demolish*

PULLED
935 bôw' (1), to *go, come*
4026 migdâl (1), *tower; rostrum*
5256 nᵉçach (Ch.) (1), to *tear away*
5414 nâthan (1), to *give*
5428 nâthash (1), to *tear away, be uprooted*
6582 pâshach (1), to *tear in pieces*
1288 diaspaō (1), to *sever* or *dismember*

PULLING
726 harpazō (1), to *seize*
2506 kathairĕsis (1), *demolition*

PULPIT
4026 migdâl (1), *tower; rostrum*

PULSE
2235 zêrôa' (2), *vegetable*

PUNISH
3256 yâçar (1), to *chastise; to instruct*
5221 nâkâh (1), to *strike, kill*
6064 'ânash (1), to *inflict a penalty, to fine*
6485 pâqad (27), to *visit, care for, count*
7489 râ'a' (1), to *break to pieces*
2849 kŏlazō (1), to *chastise, punish*

PUNISHED
2820 châsak (1), to *restrain* or *refrain*
5358 nâqam (2), to *avenge* or *punish*
6064 'ânash (4), to *inflict a penalty, to fine*
6485 pâqad (4), to *visit, care for, count*
1349+5099 dikē (1), *justice*
2849 kŏlazō (1), to *chastise, punish*
5097 timōrĕō (2), to *avenge*

PUNISHMENT
2399 chêṭ' (1), *crime* or *its penalty*
2403 chaṭṭâ'âh (3), *offence; sin offering*
5771 'âvôn (9), *moral evil*
6066 'ônesh (1), *fine*
1557 ĕkdikēsis (1), *retaliation, punishment*
2009 ĕpitimia (1), *penalty*
2851 kŏlasis (1), *infliction, punishment*
5098 timōria (1), *penalty, punishment*

PUNISHMENTS
5771 'âvôn (2), moral *evil*

PUNITES
6324 Pûwnîy (1), *turn*

PUNON
6325 Pûwnôn (2), *perplexity*

PUR
6332 Pûwr (3), *lot* cast

PURCHASE
1350 gâ'al (1), to *redeem*; to *be the next of kin*
4736 miqnâh (6), *acquisition*
4046 pĕripŏiĕŏmai (1), to *acquire; to gain*

PURCHASED
7069 qânâh (5), to *create*; to *procure*
2932 ktaŏmai (2), to *get*, i.e. *acquire*
4046 pĕripŏiĕŏmai (1), to *acquire; to gain*
4047 pĕripŏiēsis (1), *acquisition*

PURE
1249 bar (2), *beloved; pure; empty*
1305 bârar (3), to *brighten; purify*
1865 dᵉrôwr (1), *freedom; clear, pure*
2134 zak (9), *pure; clear*
2135 zâkâh (1), to *be innocent*
2141 zâkak (1), to *be transparent; clean, pure*
2561 chemer (1), *fermenting wine*
2888 Ṭabbath (2), *Tabbath*
2889 ṭâhôwr (40), *pure, clean, flawless*
2891 ṭâhêr (2), to *be pure, unadulterated*
3795 kâthîyth (1), pure *oil from beaten olives*
5343 nᵉqê' (Ch.) (1), *clean, pure*
5462 çâgar (8), to *shut up; to surrender*
6337 pâz (1), *pure gold*
6884 tsâraph (2), to *fuse metal; to refine*
53 hagnŏs (4), *innocent, modest, perfect, pure*
1506 ĕilikrinēs (1), *tested as genuine*, i.e. *pure*
2513 katharŏs (16), *clean, pure*

PURELY
1252 bôr (1), *purity, cleanness*

PURENESS
1252 bôr (1), *purity, cleanness*
2890 ṭᵉhôwr (1), *purity*
54 hagnŏtēs (1), *blamelessness, purity*

PURER
2141 zâkak (1), to *be transparent; clean, pure*
2889 ṭâhôwr (1), *pure, clean, flawless*

PURGE
1305 bârar (2), to *brighten; purify*
2212 zâqaq (1), to *strain, refine; extract, clarify*
2398 châṭâ' (1), to *sin*

2891 ṭâhêr (1), to *be pure, unadulterated*
3722 kâphar (4), to *cover; to expiate*
6884 tsâraph (1), to *fuse metal; to refine*
1245 diakatharizō (2), to *cleanse perfectly*
1571 ĕkkathairō (2), to *cleanse thoroughly*
2511 katharizō (1), to *cleanse*

PURGED
1740 dûwach (1), to *rinse clean, wash*
2891 ṭâhêr (4), to *be pure, unadulterated*
3722 kâphar (5), to *cover; to expiate*
2508 kathairō (1), to *prune dead wood*
2511 katharizō (1), to *cleanse*
2512 katharismŏs (1), *ablution; expiation*
4160+2512 pŏiĕō (1), to *make* or *do*

PURGETH
2508 kathairō (1), to *prune dead wood*

PURGING
2511 katharizō (1), to *cleanse*

PURIFICATION
2403 chaṭṭâ'âh (2), *offence; sin offering*
2893 ṭohŏrâh (2), *ceremonial purification*
8562 tamrûwq (2), *scouring, perfumery*
49 hagnismŏs (1), *purification*
2512 katharismŏs (1), *ablution; expiation*

PURIFICATIONS
4795 mârûwq (1), *rubbing*

PURIFIED
1305 bârar (1), to *brighten; purify*
2212 zâqaq (1), to *strain, refine; extract, clarify*
2398 châṭâ' (3), to *sin*
2891 ṭâhêr (3), to *be pure, unadulterated*
6942 qâdâsh (1), to *be, make clean*
48 hagnizō (2), *sanctify*; to *cleanse in ritual*
2511 katharizō (1), to *cleanse*

PURIFIER
2891 ṭâhêr (1), to *be pure, unadulterated*

PURIFIETH
2398 châṭâ' (1), to *sin*
48 hagnizō (1), *sanctify*; to *cleanse in ritual*

PURIFY
2398 châṭâ' (7), to *sin*
2891 ṭâhêr (3), to *be pure, unadulterated*
48 hagnizō (3), *sanctify*; to *cleanse in ritual*
2511 katharizō (1), to *cleanse*

PURIFYING
2403 chaṭṭâ'âh (1), *offence; sin offering*
2892 ṭôhar (2), *ceremonial purification*
2893 ṭohŏrâh (3), *ceremonial purification*
8562 tamrûwq (1), *scouring, perfumery*
48 hagnizō (1), *sanctify*; to *cleanse in ritual*
2511 katharizō (1), to *cleanse*
2512 katharismŏs (2), *ablution; expiation*
2514 katharŏtēs (1), *cleanness*

PURIM
6332 Pûwr (5), *lot* cast

PURITY
47 hagnĕia (2), *moral chastity, purity*

PURLOINING
3557 nŏsphizŏmai (1), to *embezzle*

PURPLE
710 'argᵉvân (1), *purple*
713 'argâmân (38), *purple*
4209 pŏrphura (5), *red-blue color*
4210 pŏrphurŏus (3), *bluish-red*
4211 pŏrphurŏpōlis (1), *trader in bluish-red cloth*

PURPOSE
559 'âmar (2), to *say*
1697 dâbâr (1), *word; matter; thing*
2656 chêphets (3), *pleasure; desire*
2803 châshab (2), to *plot*; to *think, regard*
4284 machăshâbâh (3), *contrivance; plan*
4639 ma'ăseh (1), *action; labor*
6098 'êtsâh (2), *advice; plan; prudence*
6640 tsᵉbûw (Ch.) (1), *determination*
7385 rîyq (1), *emptiness; worthless thing; in vain*
7997 shâlal (1), to *drop* or *strip; to plunder*
1011 bŏulĕuō (2), to *deliberate; to resolve*
1013 bŏulēma (1), *resolve, willful choice*
4286 prŏthĕsis (8), *setting forth*

PURPOSED
2161 zâmam (2), to *plan*
2803 châshab (4), to *plot*; to *think, regard*
3289 yâ'ats (5), to *advise*
3335 yâtsar (1), to *form; potter; to determine*
6440 pânîym (1), *face; front*
7760 sûwm (1), to *put, place*
1096+1106 ginŏmai (1), to *be, become*
4160 pŏiĕō (1), to *do*
4388 prŏtithĕmai (2), to *propose, determine*

English

5087 tithēmi (1), to *place*

PURPOSES
2154 zimmâh (1), *plan*
4284 machăshâbâh (3), *contrivance; plan*
8356 shâthâh (1), *basis*

PURPOSETH
4255 prŏairĕŏmai (1), to *propose, intend, decide*

PURSE
3599 kîyç (1), *cup;* utility *bag*
905 balantiŏn (3), money *pouch*
2223 zōnē (1), *belt, sash*

PURSES
2223 zōnē (1), *belt, sash*

PURSUE
3212 yâlak (1), to *walk;* to *live;* to *carry*
7291 râdaph (28), to *run after* with hostility

PURSUED
1692 dâbaq (1), to *cling* or *adhere;* to *catch*
1814 dâlaq (2), to *flame;* to *pursue*
7291 râdaph (35), to *run after* with hostility

PURSUER
7291 râdaph (1), to *run after* with hostility

PURSUERS
7291 râdaph (5), to *run after* with hostility

PURSUETH
7291 râdaph (7), to *run after* with hostility

PURSUING
310 'achar (2), *after*
7291 râdaph (4), to *run after* with hostility
7873 sîyg (1), *withdrawal* into a private place

PURTENANCE
7130 qereb (1), *nearest* part, i.e. the *center*

PUSH
5055 nâgach (6), to *butt*
5056 naggâch (2), act of *butting*
7971 shâlach (1), to *send away*

PUSHED
5055 nâgach (1), to *butt*

PUSHING
5055 nâgach (1), to *butt*

PUT
622 'âçaph (2), to *gather, collect*
935 bôw' (10), to *go, come*
1197 bâ'ar (13), to *be brutish, be senseless*
1396 gâbar (1), to *be strong;* to *prevail*
1644 gârash (2), to *drive out;* to *divorce*
1645 geresh (1), *produce, yield*
1846 dâ'ak (6), to *be extinguished;* to *expire*
1911 hâdâh (1), to *stretch forth* the hand

1921 hâdar (1), to *favor* or *honor;* to *be high*
2026 hârag (1), to *kill, slaughter*
2280 châbash (2), to *wrap firmly, bind*
2296 châgar (1), to *gird* on a belt; *put on* armor
2330 chûwd (4), to *propound* a riddle
2502 châlats (1), to *pull* off; to *strip;* to *depart*
3240 yânach (5), to *allow* to *stay*
3254 yâçaph (5), to *add* or *augment*
3318 yâtsâ' (2), to *go, bring out*
3322 yâtsag (2), to *place*
3381 yârad (2), to *descend*
3455 yâsam (1), to *put*
3518 kâbâh (3), to *extinguish*
3637 kâlam (1), to *taunt* or *insult*
3722 kâphar (1), to *cover;* to *expiate*
3847 lâbash (41), to *clothe*
3947 lâqach (1), to *take*
4191 mûwth (3), to *die;* to *kill*
4229 mâchâh (3), to *touch,* i.e. reach to
4916 mishlôwach (1), *sending out*
5056 naggâch (1), act of *butting*
5079 niddâh (2), time of menstrual *impurity*
5114 Nôwdâb (3), *noble*
5148 nâchâh (1), to *guide*
5186 nâṭâh (1), to.*stretch* or spread out
5365 nâqar (2), to *bore;* to *gouge*
5381 nâsag (1), to *reach*
5394 nâshal (2), to *divest, eject,* or *drop*
5411 Nâthîyn (1), ones *given* to duty
5414 nâthan (187), to *give*
5493 çûwr (19), to *turn off*
5564 çâmak (5), to *lean* upon; *take hold* of
5595 çâphâh (1), to *scrape;* to *remove*
5596 çâphach (1), to *associate;* be *united*
5674 'âbar (4), to *cross* over; to *transition*
5786 'âvar (3), to *blind*
5927 'âlâh (3), to *ascend,* be high, *mount*
6006 'âmaç (1), to *impose* a burden
6186 'ârak (1), to set in a row, i.e. *arrange,*
6213 'âsâh (1), to *do*
6316 Pûwṭ (2), *Put*
6319 Pôwṭîy Phera' (2), *Poti-Phera*
6584 pâshaṭ (6), to *strip,* i.e. *unclothe, plunder*
6605 pâthach (1), to *open* wide; to *loosen, begin*
6695 tsôwq (1), *distress*

7368 râchaq (4), to *recede; remove*
7392 râkab (2), to *ride*
7673 shâbath (2), to *repose;* to *desist*
7725 shûwb (7), to *turn back;* to *return*
7760 sûwm (150), to *put*
7896 shîyth (11), to *put*
7971 shâlach (45), to *send* away
7972 shᵉlach (Ch.) (1), to *send* away
7973 shelach (1), *spear; shoot* of growth
8214 shᵉphal (Ch.) (1), to *humiliate*
115 athĕtēsis (1), *cancellation*
142 airō (1), to *lift,* to *take up*
337 anairĕō (2), to *take away,* i.e. *abolish*
363 anamimnēskō (1), to *remind;* to *recollect*
506 anupŏtaktŏs (1), *independent*
520 apagō (1), to *take away*
554 apĕkduŏmai (1), to *divest wholly* oneself
595 apŏthĕsis (1), *laying aside*
615 apŏktĕinō (6), to *kill* outright; to *destroy*
630 apŏluō (13), to *relieve, release*
654 apŏstrĕphō (1), to *turn away* or *back*
659 apŏtithēmi (2), to *put away; get rid of*
683 apōthĕŏmai (2), to *push off;* to *reject*
863 aphiēmi (2), to *leave;* to *pardon, forgive*
906 ballō (14), to *throw*
1096 ginŏmai (1), to *be, become*
1252 diakrinō (1), to *decide;* to *hesitate*
1325 didōmi (5), to *give*
1544 ĕkballō (4), to *throw out*
1614 ĕktĕinō (3), to *stretch*
1677 ĕllŏgĕō (1), *attribute*
1688 ĕmbibazō (1), to *transfer*
1746 ĕnduō (16), to *dress*
1749 ĕnĕdrŏn (1), *ambush*
1808 ĕxairō (1), to *remove, drive away*
1911 ĕpiballō (1), to *throw upon*
2007 ĕpitithēmi (9), to *impose*
2289 thanatŏō (7), to *kill*
2507 kathairĕō (1), to *lower,* or *demolish*
2673 katargĕō (2), to *be, render entirely useless*
3004 lĕgō (1), to *say*
3089 luō (1), to *loosen*
3179 mĕthistēmi (1), to *move*
3856 paradĕigmatizō (1), to *expose to infamy*

3860 paradidōmi (1), to *hand over*
3908 paratithēmi (2), to *present*
3982 pĕithō (1), to *pacify* or *conciliate*
4016 pĕriballō (1), to *wrap around, clothe*
4060 pĕritithēmi (5), to *present*
4160 pŏiĕō (3), to *do*
4374 prŏsphĕrō (1), to *present to;* to *treat as*
5087 tithēmi (15), to *place, put*
5279 hupŏmimnēskō (4), to *suggest to memory*
5293 hupŏtassō (9), to *subordinate;* to *obey*
5294 hupŏtithēmi (1), to *hazard;* to *suggest*
5392 phimŏō (1), to *restrain to silence*
5562 chōrĕō (2), to *pass, enter;* to *hold, admit*

PUTEOLI
4223 Pŏtiŏlŏi (1), *little wells*

PUTIEL
6317 Pûwṭîy'êl (1), *contempt of God*

PUTRIFYING
2961 ṭârîy (1), *fresh*

PUTTEST
4916 mishlôwach (2), *presentation; seizure*
5414 nâthan (1), to *give*
5596 çâphach (1), to *associate;* be *united*
7673 shâbath (1), to *repose;* to *desist*
7760 sûwm (2), to *put, place*

PUTTETH
2590 chânaṭ (1), to *embalm;* to *ripen*
5414 nâthan (4), to *give*
5844 'âṭâh (1), to *wrap,* i.e. *cover, veil, clothe*
6605 pâthach (1), to *open* wide; to *loosen, begin*
7760 sûwm (5), to *put*
7971 shâlach (2), to *send* away
8213 shâphêl (1), to *humiliate*
630 apŏluō (1), to *relieve, release; divorce*
649 apŏstĕllō (1), to *send out on a mission*
906 ballō (2), to *throw*
1544 ĕkballō (1), to *throw out*
1631 ĕkphuō (2), to *sprout up, put forth*
1911 ĕpiballō (2), to *throw upon*
5087 tithēmi (2), to *place, put*

PUTTING
5414 nâthan (1), to *give*
7760 sûwm (1), to *put, place*
7971 shâlach (2), to *send* away
555 apĕkdusis (1), *divestment, removal*

595 apŏthĕsis (1), *laying aside*
659 apŏtithēmi (1), *to put away; get rid of*
1745 ĕndusis (1), *investment*
1746 ĕnduō (1), *to dress*
1878 ĕpanamimnēskō (1), *to remind again of*
1936 ĕpithĕsis (1), *imposition*
2007 ĕpitithēmi (2), *to impose*
4261 prŏballō (1), *to push to the front, germinate*
5087 tithēmi (1), *to place, put*
5279 hupŏmimnēskō (1), *to suggest to memory*

PYGARG
1787 Dîyshôwn, (1), *antelope*

QUAILS
7958 sᵉlâv (4), *quail bird*

QUAKE
7264 râgaz (1), *to quiver*
7493 râ'ash (1), *to undulate, quake*
1790 ĕntrŏmŏs (1), *terrified*
4579 sĕiō (1), *to vibrate; to agitate*

QUAKED
2729 chârad (1), *to shudder*
7264 râgaz (1), *to quiver*

QUAKING
2731 chărâdâh (1), *fear, anxiety*
7494 ra'ash (1), *vibration, uproar*

QUARREL
579 'ânâh (1), *to meet, to happen*
5359 nâqâm (1), *revenge*
1758 ĕnĕchō (1), *to keep a grudge*
3437 mŏmphē (1), *blame*

QUARRIES
6456 pᵉçîyl (2), *idol*

QUARTER
5676 'ēber (1), *opposite side; east*
6285 pē'âh (4), *region; extremity*
7098 qâtsâh (2), *termination; fringe*
3836 pantachŏthĕn (1), *from all directions*

QUARTERS
1366 gᵉbûwl (1), *boundary, border*
3411 yᵉrêkâh (1), *far away places*
3671 kânâph (1), *edge or extremity; wing*
7098 qâtsâh (1), *termination; fringe*
7307 rûwach (1), *breath; wind; life*-spirit
1137 gōnia (1), *angle; cornerstone*
5117 tŏpŏs (2), *place*

QUARTUS
2890 Kŏuartŏs (1), *fourth*

QUATERNIONS
5069 tĕtradiŏn (1), *squad of four Roman soldiers*

QUEEN
1377 gᵉbîyrâh (6), *mistress*
4427 mâlak (2), *to reign as king*
4433 malkâ' (Ch.) (2), *queen*
4436 malkâh (33), *queen*
4446 mᵉleketh (5), *queen*
7694 shêgâl (2), *queen*
938 basilissa (4), *queen*

QUEENS
4436 malkâh (2), *queen*
8282 sârâh (1), *female noble*

QUENCH
3518 kâbâh (8), *to extinguish*
7665 shâbar (1), *to burst*
4570 sbĕnnumi (3), *to extinguish, snuff out*

QUENCHED
1846 dâ'ak (1), *to be extinguished; to expire*
3518 kâbâh (9), *to extinguish*
8257 shâqa' (1), *to be overflowed; to cease*
762 asbĕstŏs (2), *not extinguished*
4570 sbĕnnumi (4), *to extinguish, snuff out*

QUESTION
1458 ĕgkalĕŏ (1), *to bring crimination*
2213 zētēma (2), *debate, dispute*
2214 zētēsis (1), *dispute or its theme*
2919 krinō (2), *to decide; to try, condemn, punish*
3056 lŏgŏs (1), *word, matter, thing; Word*
4802 suzētĕō (2), *to discuss, controvert*

QUESTIONED
1875 dârash (1), *to seek or ask; to worship*
1905 ĕpĕrōtaō (1), *to inquire, seek*
4802 suzētĕō (1), *to discuss, controvert*

QUESTIONING
4802 suzētĕō (2), *to discuss, controvert*

QUESTIONS
1697 dâbâr (2), *word; matter; thing*
2420 chîydâh (2), *puzzle; conundrum; maxim*
1905 ĕpĕrōtaō (1), *to inquire, seek*
2213 zētēma (3), *debate, dispute*
2214 zētēsis (5), *dispute*

QUICK
2416 chay (3), *alive; raw; fresh; life*
4241 michyâh (2), *preservation of life*
2198 zaō (4), *to live*

QUICKEN
2421 châyâh (12), *to live*

2227 zōŏpŏiĕō (1), *to (re-) vitalize, give life*

QUICKENED
2421 châyâh (2), *to live*
2227 zōŏpŏiĕō (2), *to (re-) vitalize, give life*
4806 suzōŏpŏiĕō (2), *to reanimate conjointly*

QUICKENETH
2227 zōŏpŏiĕō (5), *to (re-) vitalize, give life*

QUICKENING
2227 zōŏpŏiĕō (1), *to (re-) vitalize, give life*

QUICKLY
3966 mᵉ'ôd (1), *very*
4116 mâhar (3), *to hurry*
4118 mahêr (8), *in a hurry*
4120 mᵉhêrâh (10), *hurry; promptly*
1722+5034 ĕn (2), *in; during; because of*
5030 tachĕŏs (2), *speedily, rapidly*
5032 tachiŏn (1), *more rapidly, more speedily*
5035 tachu (12), *without delay, soon, suddenly*

QUICKSANDS
4950 surtis (1), *sand drawn by the waves*

QUIET
2790 chârash (1), *to be silent; to be deaf*
4496 mᵉnûwchâh (1), *peacefully; consolation*
5117 nûwach (1), *to rest; to settle down*
5183 nachath (1), *descent; quiet*
7282 râgêa' (1), *restful, i.e. peaceable*
7599 shâ'an (2), *to loll, i.e. be peaceful*
7600 sha'ănân (2), *secure; haughty*
7961 shâlêv (1), *carefree; security, at ease*
8003 shâlêm (1), *complete; friendly; safe*
8252 shâqat (15), *to repose*
8367 shâthaq (1), *to subside*
2263 ērĕmŏs (1), *tranquil, peaceful*
2270 hēsuchazō (1), *to refrain*
2272 hēsuchiŏs (1), *still, undisturbed*
2687 katastĕllō (2), *to quell, quiet*

QUIETED
1826 dâmam (1), *to be silent; to stop, cease*
5117 nûwach (1), *to rest; to settle down*

QUIETETH
8252 shâqat (1), *to repose*

QUIETLY
7987 shᵉlîy (1), *privacy*

QUIETNESS
5183 nachath (1), *quiet*
7961 shâlêv (1), *carefree; security, at ease*

2227 zōŏpŏiĕō (1), *to (re-) vitalize, give life*

QUICKENED
7962 shalvâh (1), *security, ease*
8252 shâqat (4), *to repose*
8253 sheqet (1), *tranquillity*
1515 ĕirēnē (1), *peace; health; prosperity*
2271 hēsuchia (1), *stillness*

QUIT
1961 hâyâh (1), *to exist, i.e. be or become*
5352 nâqâh (1), *to be bare, i.e. extirpated*
5355 nâqîy (2), *innocent*
407 andrizŏmai (1), *to act manly*

QUITE
3615 kâlâh (1), *to cease, be finished, perish*
5080 nâdach (1), *to push off, scattered*
6181 'eryâh (1), *nudity*

QUIVER
827 'ashpâh (6), *quiver*
8522 tᵉlîy (1), *quiver*

QUIVERED
6750 tsâlal (1), *to tinkle, to rattle together*

RAAMAH
7484 Ra'mâh (5), *horse's mane*

RAAMIAH
7485 Ra'amyâh (1), *Jehovah has shaken*

RAAMSES
7486 Ra'mᵉçêç (1), *Rameses or Raamses*

RAB-MAG
7248 Rab-Mâg (2), *chief Magian*

RAB-SARIS
7249 Rab-Çârîyç (3), *chief chamberlain*

RAB-SHAKEH
7262 Rabshâqêh (8), *chief butler*

RABBAH
7237 Rabbâh (13), *great*

RABBATH
7237 Rabbâh (2), *great*

RABBI
4461 rhabbi (7), *my master*

RABBITH
7245 Rabbîyth (1), *multitude*

RABBONI
4462 rhabbŏni (1), *my master*

RABSHAKEH
7262 Rabshâqêh (8), *chief butler*

RACA
4469 rhaka (1), *O empty one, i.e. worthless*

RACE
734 'ôrach (1), *road; manner of life*
4793 mêrôwts (1), *running foot-race*
73 agōn (1), *contest, struggle*

English

4712 stadiŏn (1), *length of about 200 yards*

RACHAB
4477 Rhachab (1), *proud*

RACHAL
7403 Râkâl (1), *merchant*

RACHEL
7354 Râchêl (41), *ewe*
4478 Rhachêl (1), *ewe*

RACHEL'S
7354 Râchêl (5), *ewe*

RADDAI
7288 Radday (1), *domineering*

RAFTERS
7351 rᵉchîyṭ (1), *panel*

RAGAU
4466 Rhagau (1), *friend*

RAGE
1984 hâlal (2), to *boast*
2195 za'am (1), *fury*
2197 za'aph (2), *anger*
2534 chêmâh (2), *heat; anger; poison*
5678 'ebrâh (2), *outburst*
7264 râgaz (5), to *quiver*
7266 rᵉgaz (Ch.) (1), *violent anger*
7267 rôgez (1), *disquiet; anger*
7283 râgash (1), to *be tumultuous*
5433 phruassō (1), to *make a tumult*

RAGED
1993 hâmâh (1), to *be in great commotion*

RAGETH
5674 'âbar (1), to *cross over; to transition*

RAGING
1348 gê'ûwth (1), *ascending; majesty*
1993 hâmâh (1), to *be in great commotion*
2197 za'aph (1), *anger, rage*
66 agriŏs (1), *wild (country)*
2830 kludōn (1), *surge, raging*

RAGS
899 beged (1), *clothing; treachery or pillage*
4418 mâlâch (2), *rag or old garment*
7168 qera' (1), *rag, torn pieces*

RAGUEL
7467 Rᵉ'ûw'êl (1), *friend of God*

RAHAB
7294 Rahab (3), *boaster*
7343 Râchâb (5), *proud*
4460 Rhaab (2), *proud*

RAHAM
7357 Racham (1), *pity*

RAHEL
7354 Râchêl (1), *ewe*

RAIL
2778 châraph (1), to *spend the winter*

RAILED
5860 'îyṭ (1), to *swoop down upon; to insult*
987 blasphēmĕō (2), to *speak impiously*

RAILER
3060 lŏidŏrŏs (1), *verbal abuser*

RAILING
988 blasphēmia (1), *impious speech*
989 blasphēmŏs (1), *slanderous*
3059 lŏidŏria (1), *slander*

RAILINGS
988 blasphēmia (1), *impious speech*

RAIMENT
899 beged (12), *clothing; treachery or pillage*
3682 kᵉçûwth (1), *cover; veiling*
3830 lᵉbûwsh (1), *garment; wife*
4055 mad (1), *vesture, garment; carpet*
4254 machălâtsâh (1), *mantle, garment*
4403 malbûwsh (3), *garment, clothing*
7553 riqmâh (1), *variegation of color*
8008 salmâh (5), *clothing*
8071 simlâh (11), *dress*
1742 ĕnduma (5), *apparel, outer robe*
2066 ĕsthēs (1), to *clothe*
2440 himatiŏn (12), to *put on clothes*
2441 himatismŏs (2), *clothing*
4629 skĕpasma (1), *clothing; covering*

RAIN
1653 geshem (30), *rain*
3138 yôwreh (1), *autumn rain showers*
3384 yârâh (2), to *throw, shoot an arrow*
4175 môwreh (3), *archer; teaching; early rain*
4305 mâṭar (11), to *rain*
4306 mâṭâr (37), *rain, shower of rain*
4456 malqôwsh (6), *spring rain*
8164 sâ'îyr (1), *shower*
1026 brĕchō (2), to *make wet; to rain*
1026+5205 brĕchō (1), to *make wet; to rain*
1028 brŏchē (2), *rain*
5205 huĕtŏs (5), *rain; rain shower*

RAINBOW
2463 iris (2), *rainbow*

RAINED
1656 gôshem (1), *rain downpour*
4305 mâṭar (6), to *rain*
1026 brĕchō (2), to *make wet; to rain*

RAINY
5464 çagrîyd (1), *pouring rain*

RAISE
5375 nâsâ' (2), to *lift up*
5549 çâlal (2), to *mound up; to exalt*
5782 'ûwr (6), to *awake*
6965 qûwm (30), to *rise*
450 anistēmi (8), to *rise; to come to life*
1453 ĕgĕirō (8), to *waken, i.e. rouse*
1817 ĕxanistēmi (2), to *beget, raise up*
1825 ĕxĕgĕirō (1), to *resuscitate; release*

RAISED
1361 gâbahh (1), to *be lofty; to be haughty*
5782 'ûwr (12), to *awake*
5927 'âlâh (3), to *ascend, be high, mount*
5975 'âmad (1), to *stand*
6209 'ârar (1), to *bare; to demolish*
6965 qûwm (10), to *rise*
6966 qûwm (Ch.) (1), to *rise*
386 anastasis (1), *resurrection from death*
450 anistēmi (6), to *rise; to come to life*
1326 diĕgĕirō (1), to *arouse, stimulate*
1453 ĕgĕirō (45), to *waken, i.e. rouse*
1825 ĕxĕgĕirō (1), to *resuscitate; release*
1892 ĕpĕgĕirō (1), to *excite against; stir up*
4891 sunĕgĕirō (1), to *raise up with*

RAISER
5674 'âbar (1), to *cross over; to transition*

RAISETH
2210 zâqaph (2), to *lift up, comfort*
5975 'âmad (1), to *stand*
6965 qûwm (2), to *rise*
7613 sᵉ'êth (1), *elevation; swelling leprous scab*
1453 ĕgĕirō (1), to *waken, i.e. rouse*

RAISING
5872 'Êyn Gedîy (1), *fountain of a kid*
4160+1999 pŏiĕō (1), to *do*

RAISINS
6778 tsammûwq (4), *lump of dried grapes*

RAKEM
7552 Reqem (1), *versi-color*

RAKKATH
7557 Raqqath (1), *beach (as expanded shingle)*

RAKKON
7542 Raqqôwn (1), *thinness*

RAM
352 'ayîl (89), *chief; ram*
7410 Râm (7), *high*

RAM'S
3104 yôwbêl (1), *blast of a ram's horn*

RAMA
4471 Rhama (1), *height*

RAMAH
7414 Râmâh (36), *height*

RAMATH
7418 Râmôwth-Negeb (1), *heights of (the) South*

RAMATH-LEHI
7437 Râmath Lechîy (1), *height of (a) jaw-bone*

RAMATH-MIZPEH
7434 Râmath ham-Mitspeh (1), *height of the watch-tower*

RAMATHAIM-ZOPHIM
7436 Râmâthayim Tsôwphîym (1), *double height of watchers*

RAMATHITE
7435 Râmâthîy (1), *Ramathite*

RAMESES
7486 Ra'mᵉçêç (4), *Rameses or Raamses*

RAMIAH
7422 Ramyâh (1), *Jehovah has raised*

RAMOTH
3406 Yᵉrîymôwth (1), *elevations*
7216 Râ'môwth (6), *heights*
7418 Râmôwth-Negeb (1), *heights of (the) South*

RAMOTH-GILEAD
7433 Râmôth Gil'âd (19), *heights of Gilad*

RAMPART
2426 chêyl (2), *rampart, battlement*

RAMS
352 'ayîl (61), *chief; ram*
1798 dᵉkar (Ch.) (3), *male sheep*
3733 kar (2), *ram sheep; battering ram*
6260 'attûwd (2), *he-goats; leaders*

RAMS'
352 'ayîl (5), *chief; ram*
3104 yôwbêl (4), *blast of a ram's horn*

RAN
1272 bârach (1), to *flee suddenly*
1980 hâlak (2), to *walk; live a certain way*
3331 yâtsa' (1), to *strew as a surface*
3332 yâtsaq (1), to *pour out*
5064 nâgar (1), to *pour out; to deliver over*
6379 pâkâh (1), to *pour, trickle*
6584 pâshaṭ (1), to *strip, i.e. unclothe, plunder*
7323 rûwts (30), to *run*
7519 râtsâ' (1), to *run; to delight in*
7857 shâṭaph (1), to *gush; to inundate*

1530 ĕispēdaō (1), to *rush in*
1532 ĕistrĕchō (1), to *hasten inward*
1632 ĕkchĕō (1), to *pour forth; to bestow*
2027 ĕpŏkĕllō (1), to *beach* a ship vessel
2701 katatrĕchō (1), to *hasten, run*
3729 hŏrmaō (4), to *dash* or *plunge, stampede*
4063 pĕritrĕchō (1), to *traverse, run about*
4370 prŏstrĕchō (1), to *hasten by running*
4390 prŏtrĕchō (1), to *run ahead,* i.e. to *precede*
4890 sundrŏmē (1), (riotous) *concourse*
4936 suntrĕchō (2), to *rush together*
5143 trĕchō (6), to *run or walk hastily; to strive*

RANG
1949 hûwm (2), to *make an uproar; agitate*

RANGE
3491 yâthûwr (1), *gleaning*

RANGES
3600 kîyr (1), portable cooking *range*
7713 sᵉdêrâh (3), *row,* i.e. *rank* of soldiers; *story*

RANGING
8264 shâqaq (1), to *seek*

RANK
1277 bârîy' (2), *fatted* or *plump; healthy*
4634 ma'ărâkâh (1), *row; pile;* military *array*
5737 'âdar (1), to *arrange; hoe* a vineyard

RANKS
734 'ôrach (1), *road; manner of life*
6471 pa'am (2), *time; step; occurence*
4237 prasia (1), arranged *group*

RANSOM
3724 kôpher (8), *village; redemption-price*
6299 pâdâh (1), to *ransom; to release*
6306 pidyôwm (1), *ransom; payment*
487 antilutrŏn (1), *redemption-price*
3083 lutrŏn (2), *redemption-price*

RANSOMED
1350 gâ'al (2), to *redeem; to be the next of kin*
6299 pâdâh (1), to *ransom; to release*

RAPHA
7498 Râphâ' (2), *giant*

RAPHU
7505 Râphûw' (1), *cured*

RARE
3358 yaqqîyr (Ch.) (1), *precious*

RASE
6168 'ârâh (1), to *be, make bare; demolish*

RASH
926 bâhal (1), to *tremble; hasten, hurry anxiously*
4116 mâhar (1), to *hurry; promptly*

RASHLY
4312 prŏpĕtēs (1), *falling forward headlong*

RASOR
8593 ta'ar (1), *knife; razor; scabbard*

RATE
1697 dâbâr (5), *word; matter; thing*

RATHER
408 'al (2), *not; nothing*
977 bâchar (1), *select, chose, prefer*
2228 ē (3), *or; than*
2309 thĕlō (1), to *will;* to *desire; to choose*
3123 mallôn (34), *in a greater degree*
3304 mĕnŏungĕ (1), *so then at least*
4056 pĕrissŏtĕrōs (1), *more superabundantly*
4133 plēn (2), *rather, yet*

RATTLETH
7439 rânâh (1), to *whiz, rattle*

RATTLING
7494 ra'ash (1), *vibration, bounding*

RAVEN
6158 'ôrêb (6), *dusky-hue raven*

RAVENING
2963 țâraph (3), to *pluck off* or *pull to pieces*
724 harpagē (1), *pillage; greediness; robbery*
727 harpax (1), *rapacious; robbing*

RAVENOUS
5861 'ayiț (2), bird of prey (poss.) *hawk*
6530 pᵉrîyts (1), *violent*

RAVENS
6158 'ôrêb (4), *dusky-hue raven*
2876 kŏrax (1), *crow* or *raven*

RAVIN
2963 țâraph (1), to *pluck off* or *pull to pieces*
2966 țᵉrêphâh (1), *torn prey*

RAVISHED
3823 lâbab (2), *transport* with love; to *stultify*
6031 'ânâh (1), to *afflict, be afflicted*
7686 shâgâh (2), to *stray, wander;* to *transgress*
7693 shâgal (2), to *copulate* with

RAW
2416 chay (6), *alive; raw; fresh; life*
4995 nâ' (1), *uncooked*

RAZOR
4177 môwrâh (3), *razor*
8593 ta'ar (2), *knife; razor; scabbard*

REACH
1272 bârach (1), to *flee suddenly*
1961 hâyâh (1), to *exist,* i.e. *be* or *become*
4229 mâchâh (1), to *touch,* i.e. reach to
5060 nâga' (5), to *strike*
5381 nâsag (2), to *reach*
2185 ĕphiknĕŏmai (1), to *extend to, reach to*
5342 phĕrō (2), to *bear* or *carry*

REACHED
4291 mᵉțâ' (Ch.) (2), to *arrive,* to *extend*
5060 nâga' (1), to *strike*
6293 pâga' (1), to *impinge*
6642 tsâbaț (1), to *hand out food*
190 akŏlŏuthĕō (1), to *accompany, follow*
2185 ĕphiknĕŏmai (1), to *extend to, reach to*

REACHETH
4291 mᵉțâ' (Ch.) (1), to *arrive,* to *extend*
5060 nâga' (4), to *strike*
6293 pâga' (5), to *impinge*
7971 shâlach (1), to *send away*

REACHING
5060 nâga' (3), to *strike*
1901 ĕpĕktĕinŏmai (1), to *stretch* oneself forward

READ
7121 qârâ' (35), to *call out*
7123 qᵉrâ' (Ch.) (7), to *call out*
314 anaginōskō (28), to *read* aloud in public

READEST
314 anaginōskō (2), to *read* aloud in public

READETH
7121 qârâ' (1), to *call out*
314 anaginōskō (3), to *read* aloud in public

READINESS
2092 hĕtŏimŏs (1), *ready, prepared*
4288 prŏthumia (2), *alacrity, eagerness*

READING
4744 miqrâ' (1), *public meeting*
7121 qârâ' (2), to *call out*
320 anagnōsis (3), act of public *reading*

READY
631 'âçar (4), to *fasten;* to *join battle*
1951 hûwn (1), to *be, act light*
2363 chûwsh (1), to *hurry; to be eager*
2896 țôwb (1), *good; well*
3559 kûwn (17), to *set up: establish, fix, prepare*
4106 mâhîyr (2), *skillful*

4116 mâhar (2), to *hurry; promptly*
4131 môwṭ (1), to *slip, shake, fall*
4672 mâtsâ' (1), to *find* or *acquire; to occur*
5750 'ôwd (1), *again; repeatedly; still; more*
6257 'âthad (1), to *prepare*
6263 'ăthîyd (Ch.) (1), *prepared*
6264 'âthîyd (4), *prepared; treasure*
7126 qârab (1), to *approach, bring near*
7138 qârôwb (1), *near, close*
8003 shâlêm (1), *complete; friendly; safe*
1451 ĕggus (1), *near, close*
2090 hĕtŏimazō (10), to *prepare*
2092 hĕtŏimŏs (15), *ready, prepared*
2093 hĕtŏimōs (3), *in readiness*
2130 ĕumĕtadŏtŏs (1), *liberal, generous*
3195 mĕllō (4), to *intend,* i.e. *be about to*
3903 paraskĕuazō (3), to *get ready, prepare*
4288 prŏthumia (1), *alacrity, eagerness*
4289 prŏthumŏs (3), *alacrity, eagerness*
4689 spĕndō (1), to *pour out as a libation*

REAIA
7211 Rᵉ'âyâh (1), *Jehovah has seen*

REAIAH
7211 Rᵉ'âyâh (3), *Jehovah has seen*

REALM
4437 malkûw (Ch.) (3), *dominion*
4438 malkûwth (4), *rule; dominion*

REAP
7114 qâtsar (18), to *curtail, cut short*
2325 thĕrizō (13), to *harvest, reap a crop*

REAPED
7114 qâtsar (1), to *curtail, cut short*
270 amaō (1), *reap, mow down grain*
2325 thĕrizō (2), to *harvest, reap a crop*

REAPER
7114 qâtsar (1), to *curtail, cut short*

REAPERS
7114 qâtsar (7), to *curtail, cut short*
2327 thĕristēs (2), *harvester, reaper*

REAPEST
7114 qâtsar (1), to *curtail, cut short*
2325 thĕrizō (1), to *harvest, reap a crop*

REAPETH
7114 qâtsar (1), to *curtail, cut short*
2325 thĕrizō (3), to *harvest, reap a crop*

REAPING
7114 qâtsar (1), to *curtail, cut short*
2325 thĕrizō (2), to *harvest, reap a crop*

REAR
6965 qûwm (3), to *rise*
1453 ĕgĕirō (1), to *waken*, i.e. *rouse*

REARED
5324 nâtsab (1), to *station*
6965 qûwm (9), to *rise*

REASON
413 'êl (1), *to, toward*
1697 dâbâr (1), *word; matter; thing*
2808 cheshbôwn (1), *intelligent plan*
2940 ṭa'am (1), *taste; intelligence; mandate*
3198 yâkach (3), to *be correct*; to *argue*
4480 min (5), *from, out of*
4486 manda' (Ch.) (1), *wisdom* or *intelligence*
5921 'al (2), *above, over, upon*, or *against*
5973 'îm (1), *with*
6440 pânîym (9), *face; front*
6903 q^{e}bêl (Ch.) (1), *on account of, so as, since*
8199 shâphaṭ (1), to *judge*
701 arĕstŏs (1), *agreeable; desirable; fit*
1223 dia (5), *through*, by means of; *because* of
1260 dialŏgizŏmai (5), to *deliberate*
1537 ĕk (3), *out, out of*
1752 hĕnĕka (1), *on account of*
3056 lŏgŏs (2), *word, matter, thing; Word*

REASONABLE
3050 lŏgikŏs (1), *rational, logical*

REASONED
1256 dialĕgŏmai (4), to *discuss*
1260 dialŏgizŏmai (5), to *deliberate*
3049 lŏgizŏmai (1), to *credit*; to *think, regard*
4802 suzētĕō (1), to *discuss, controvert*
4817 sullŏgizŏmai (1), to *reckon together*

REASONING
8433 tôwkêchâh (1), *correction, refutation*
1260 dialŏgizŏmai (1), to *deliberate*
1261 dialŏgismŏs (1), *consideration; debate*
4802 suzētĕō (1), to *discuss, controvert*
4803 suzētēsis (1), *discussion, dispute*

REASONS
8394 tâbûwn (1), *intelligence; argument*

REBA
7254 Reba' (2), *fourth*

REBECCA
4479 Rhĕbĕkka (1), *fettering* (by beauty)

REBEKAH
7259 Ribqâh (28), *fettering* (by beauty)

REBEKAH'S
7259 Ribqâh (2), *fettering* (by beauty)

REBEL
4775 mârad (9), to *rebel*
4784 mârâh (4), to *rebel* or *resist*; to *provoke*
5493 çûwr (1), to *turn* off

REBELLED
4775 mârad (12), to *rebel*
4784 mârâh (16), to *rebel* or *resist*; to *provoke*
6586 pâsha' (5), to *break* away from authority
6856 tsippôren (1), *nail; point* of a style or pen

REBELLEST
4775 mârad (2), to *rebel*

REBELLION
4776 m^{e}rad (Ch.) (1), *rebellion*
4779 mârâd (Ch.) (1), *rebellious*
4805 m^{e}rîy (4), *rebellion, rebellious*
5627 çârâh (2), *apostasy; crime; remission*
6588 pesha' (1), *revolt*

REBELLIOUS
4775 mârad (1), to *rebel*
4779 mârâd (Ch.) (2), *rebellious*
4780 mardûwth (1), *rebelliousness*
4784 mârâh (9), to *rebel* or *resist*; to *provoke*
4805 m^{e}rîy (17), *rebellion, rebellious*
5637 çârar (6), to *be refractory, stubborn*

REBELS
4775 mârad (1), to *rebel*
4784 mârâh (1), to *rebel* or *resist*; to *provoke*
4805 m^{e}rîy (1), *rebellion, rebellious*

REBUKE
1605 gâ'ar (7), to *chide, reprimand*
1606 g^{e}'ârâh (12), *chiding, rebuke*
2781 cherpâh (2), *contumely, disgrace*
3198 yâkach (8), to *be correct*; to *argue*
4045 mig'ereth (1), *reproof* (i.e. a curse)
8433 tôwkêchâh (4), *refutation, proof*
298 amōmētŏs (1), *unblemished*
1651 ĕlĕgchō (4), to *admonish, rebuke*
1969 ĕpiplēssō (1), to *upbraid, rebuke*
2008 ĕpitimaō (6), to *rebuke, warn, forbid*

REBUKED
1605 gâ'ar (4), to *chide, reprimand*
3198 yâkach (1), to *be correct*; to *argue*
7378 rîyb (1), to *hold a controversy*; to *defend*
1651 ĕlĕgchō (1), to *admonish, rebuke*
2008 ĕpitimaō (17), to *rebuke, warn, forbid*
2192+1649 ĕchō (1), to *have; hold; keep*

REBUKER
4148 mûwçâr (1), *reproof, warning*

REBUKES
8433 tôwkêchâh (3), *correction, refutation*

REBUKETH
1605 gâ'ar (1), to *chide, reprimand*
3198 yâkach (3), to *be correct*; to *argue*

REBUKING
1606 g^{e}'ârâh (1), *chiding, rebuke*
2008 ĕpitimaō (1), to *rebuke, warn, forbid*

RECALL
7725 shûwb (1), to *turn* back; to *return*

RECEIPT
5058 tĕlōniŏn (3), *tax-gatherer's booth*

RECEIVE
1878 dâshên (1), to *fatten*; to *satisfy*
3557 kûwl (2), to *keep in*; to *measure*
3947 lâqach (35), to *take*
5162 nâcham (1), to *be sorry*; to *pity, console*
5375 nâsâ' (3), to *lift up*
6901 qâbal (3), to *admit*; to *take*
6902 q^{e}bal (Ch.) (1), to *acquire*
8254 shâqal (1), to *suspend* in trade
308 anablĕpō (7), to *look up*; to *recover sight*
568 apĕchō (1), to *be distant*
588 apŏdĕchŏmai (1), to *welcome; approve*
618 apŏlambanō (8), to *receive; be repaid*
1209 dĕchŏmai (24), to *receive, welcome*
1325 didōmi (1), to *give*
1523 ĕisdĕchŏmai (1), to *take into* one's *favor*
1926 ĕpidĕchŏmai (1), to *admit, welcome*
2210 zēmiŏō (1), to *experience detriment*
2865 kŏmizō (6), to *provide* for
2983 lambanō (61), to *take, receive*
3858 paradĕchŏmai (4), to *accept, receive*
3880 paralambanō (1), to *assume* an office
4327 prŏsdĕchŏmai (2), to *receive*; to *await for*
4355 prŏslambanō (4), to *welcome, receive*
5562 chōrĕō (5), to *pass, enter*; to *hold, admit*

RECEIVED
622 'âçaph (1), to *gather, collect*
1961 hâyâh (2), to *exist*, i.e. *be* or *become*
2388 châzaq (1), to *fasten* upon; to *seize*
2505 châlaq (1), to *be smooth; be slippery*
3947 lâqach (22), to *take*
4672 mâtsâ' (1), to *find* or *acquire*; to *occur*
6901 qâbal (3), to *admit*; to *take*
308 anablĕpō (8), to *look up*; to *recover sight*
324 anadĕchŏmai (2), to *entertain* as a guest
353 analambanō (3), to *take up, bring up*
354 analēpsis (1), *ascension*
568 apĕchō (1), to *be distant*
588 apŏdĕchŏmai (4), *welcome; approve*
618 apŏlambanō (1), to *receive; be repaid*
1183 dĕkatŏō (1), to *give* or *take a tenth*
1209 dĕchŏmai (16), to *receive, welcome*
1653 ĕlĕĕō (1), to give out *compassion*
2865 kŏmizō (3), to *provide* for, to *carry* off
2983 lambanō (56), to *take, receive*
3336 mĕtalēmpsis (1), *participation, sharing*
3549 nŏmŏthĕtĕō (1), to *be given law*
3880 paralambanō (13), to *assume* an office
4355 prŏslambanō (3), to *welcome, receive*
4687 spĕirō (4), to *scatter*, i.e. *sow* seed
4732 stĕrĕŏō (1), to *be, become strong*
5264 hupŏdĕchŏmai (4), to *entertain hospitably*
5274 hupŏlambanō (1), to *take up*, i.e. *continue*

RECEIVEDST
618 apŏlambanō (1), to *receive; be repaid*

RECEIVER
8254 shâqal (1), to *suspend* in trade

RECEIVETH
622 'âçaph (1), to *gather, collect*
3947 lâqach (4), to *take*
1209 dĕchŏmai (8), to *receive, welcome*
1926 ĕpidĕchŏmai (1), to *admit, welcome*

2983 lambanō (14), to take, receive
3335 mĕtalambanō (1), to participate
3858 paradĕchŏmai (1), to accept, receive
4327 prósdĕchŏmai (1), to receive; to await for

RECEIVING
3947 lâqach (1), to take
618 apŏlambanō (1), to receive; be repaid
2865 kŏmizō (1), to provide for, to carry off
2983 lambanō (1), to take, receive
3028 lēmpsis (1), act of receipt
3880 paralambanō (1), to assume an office
4356 prŏslēpsis (1), admission, acceptance

RECHAB
7394 Rêkâb (13), rider

RECHABITES
7397 Rêkâh (4), softness

RECHAH
7397 Rêkâh (1), softness

RECKON
2803 châshab (3), to think, regard; to value
5608 çâphar (1), to inscribe; to enumerate
6485 pâqad (1), to visit, care for, count
3049 lŏgizŏmai (2), to credit; to think, regard
4868 sunairō (1), to compute an account

RECKONED
2803 châshab (4), to think, regard; to value
3187 yâchas (12), to enroll by family list
7737 shâvâh (1), to resemble; to adjust
3049 lŏgizŏmai (4), to credit; to think, regard

RECKONETH
4868+3056 sunairō (1), to compute an account

RECKONING
2803 châshab (1), to think, regard; to value
6486 pᵉquddâh (1), visitation; punishment

RECOMMENDED
3860 paradidōmi (2), to hand over

RECOMPENCE
1576 gᵉmûwl (9), act; reward, recompense
7966 shillûwm (1), requital; retribution; fee
8005 shillêm (1), requital
8545 tᵉmûwrâh (1), barter, compensation
468 antapŏdŏma (2), requital, recompense
489 antimisthia (2), correspondence
3405 misthapŏdŏsia (3), requital, good or bad

RECOMPENCES
1578 gᵉmûwlâh (1), act; reward, recompense
7966 shillûwm (1), requital; retribution; fee

RECOMPENSE
1580 gâmal (2), to benefit or requite; to wean
5414 nâthan (9), to give
7725 shûwb (3), to return or restore
7999 shâlam (7), to be safe; to reciprocate
467 antapŏdidōmi (3), to require good or evil
591 apŏdidōmi (1), to give away

RECOMPENSED
5414 nâthan (1), to give
7725 shûwb (5), to return or restore
7999 shâlam (2), to be safe; to reciprocate
467 antapŏdidōmi (2), to require good or evil

RECOMPENSEST
7999 shâlam (1), to be safe; to reciprocate

RECOMPENSING
5414 nâthan (1), to give

RECONCILE
3722 kâphar (2), to placate or cancel
7521 râtsâh (1), to be pleased with; to satisfy
604 apŏkatallassō (2), to reconcile fully, reunite

RECONCILED
604 apŏkatallassō (1), to reconcile fully, reunite
1259 diallassō (1), to be reconciled
2644 katallassō (5), to change mutually

RECONCILIATION
2398 châṭâ' (1), to sin
3722 kâphar (4), to placate or cancel
2433 hilaskŏmai (1), to conciliate, to atone for
2643 katallagē (2), restoration

RECONCILING
3722 kâphar (1), to cover; to expiate
2643 katallagē (1), restoration
2644 katallassō (1), to change mutually

RECORD
1799 dikrôwn (Ch.) (1), official register
2142 zâkar (2), to remember; to mention
5749 'ûwd (3), to duplicate or repeat
7717 sâhêd (1), witness
3140 marturĕō (13), to testify; to commend
3141 marturia (7), evidence given
3143 marturŏmai (1), to witness
3144 martus (2), witness

RECORDED
3789 kâthab (1), to write

RECORDER
2142 zâkar (9), to remember; to mention

RECORDS
1799 dikrôwn (Ch.) (2), official register
2146 zikrôwn (1), commemoration

RECOUNT
2142 zâkar (1), to remember; to mention

RECOVER
622 'âçaph (4), to gather, collect
1082 bâlag (1), to be comforted
2421 châyâh (6), to live; to revive
2492 châlam (1), to be, make plump; to dream
4241 michyâh (1), preservation of life; sustenance
5337 nâtsal (3), to deliver; to be snatched
6113 'âtsar (1), to hold back; to maintain, rule
7069 qânâh (1), to create; to procure
7725 shûwb (1), to turn back; to return
366 ananēphō (1), to regain one's senses
2192+2573 ĕchō (1), to have; hold; keep

RECOVERED
2388 châzaq (1), to fasten upon; to seize
2421 châyâh (2), to live; to revive
5337 nâtsal (2), to deliver; to be snatched
5927 'âlâh (1), to ascend, be high, mount
7725 shûwb (5), to turn back; to return

RECOVERING
309 anablĕpsis (1), restoration of sight

RED
119 'âdam (9), to be red in the face
122 'âdôm (7), rosy, red
132 'admônîy (1), reddish, ruddy
923 bahaṭ (1), white marble
2447 chaklîyl (1), darkly flashing eyes; brilliant
2560 châmar (1), to ferment, foam; to glow
2561 chemer (1), fermenting wine
5488 çûwph (24), papyrus reed; reed
5489 Çûwph (1), reed
5492 çûwphâh (1), hurricane wind
2281 thalassa (2), sea or lake
4449 purrhazō (2), to redden
4450 purrhŏs (2), fire-like, flame-colored

REDDISH
125 'ădamdâm (6), reddish

REDEEM
1350 gâ'al (23), to redeem; be next of kin
1353 gᵉullâh (5), redemption
6299 pâdâh (24), to ransom; to release
6304 pᵉdûwth (1), distinction; deliverance
1805 ĕxagŏrazō (1), to buy up, ransom
3084 lutrŏō (1), to free by paying a ransom

REDEEMED
1350 gâ'al (24), to redeem; be next of kin
1353 gᵉullâh (2), redemption
6299 pâdâh (23), to ransom; to release
6302 pâdûwy (2), ransom
6306 pidyôwm (2), ransom payment
6561 pâraq (1), to break off or crunch; to deliver
7069 qânâh (1), to create; to procure
59 agŏrazō (3), to purchase; to redeem
1805 ĕxagŏrazō (1), to buy up, ransom
3084 lutrŏō (2), to free by paying a ransom
4160+3085 pŏiĕō (1), to make or do

REDEEMEDST
6299 pâdâh (1), to ransom; to release

REDEEMER
1350 gâ'al (18), to redeem; be next of kin

REDEEMETH
1350 gâ'al (1), to redeem; to be the next of kin
6299 pâdâh (1), to ransom; to release

REDEEMING
1353 gᵉullâh (1), redemption
1805 ĕxagŏrazō (2), to buy up, ransom

REDEMPTION
1353 gᵉullâh (5), redemption
6304 pᵉdûwth (2), distinction; deliverance
6306 pidyôwm (2), ransom payment
629 apŏlutrōsis (9), ransom in full
3085 lutrōsis (2), ransoming

REDNESS
2498 châlaph (1), to hasten away; to pass on

REDOUND
4052 pĕrissĕuō (1), to superabound

REED
7070 qâneh (21), reed
2563 kalamŏs (11), reed

REEDS
98 'âgam (1), marsh; pond; pool
7070 qâneh (6), reed

English

REEL
2287 châgag (1), to
observe a festival
5128 nûwa' (1), to waver

REELAIAH
7480 Re'êlâyâh (1),
fearful of Jehovah

REFINE
6884 tsâraph (1), to fuse
metal; to refine

REFINED
2212 zâqaq (3), to strain,
refine; extract, clarify
6884 tsâraph (2), to fuse
metal; to refine

REFINER
6884 tsâraph (1), to fuse
metal; to refine

REFINER'S
6884 tsâraph (1), to fuse
metal; to refine

REFORMATION
1357 diŏrthōsis (1),
Messianic restoration

REFORMED
3256 yâçar (1), to
chastise; to instruct

REFRAIN
662 'âphaq (2), to abstain
2413 châtam (1), to stop,
restrain
2820 châsak (1), to
restrain or refrain
4513 mâna' (2), to deny
7368 râchaq (1), to
recede; remove
868 aphistēmi (1), to
desist, desert
3973 pauō (1), to stop

REFRAINED
662 'âphaq (3), to abstain
2820 châsak (1), to
restrain or refrain
3601 kìyshôwr (1),
spindle
3607 kâlâ' (1), to hold
back; to prohibit, stop
6113 'âtsar (1), to hold
back; to maintain, rule

REFRAINETH
2820 châsak (1), to
restrain or refrain

REFRESH
5582 çâ'ad (1), to support
373 anapauō (1), to
repose; to refresh
1958+5177 ĕpimĕlĕia (1),
carefulness

REFRESHED
5314 nâphash (3), to be
refreshed
7304 râvach (2), to
revive; to have room
373 anapauō (3), to
repose; to refresh
404 anapsuchō (1), to
relieve
4875 sunanapauŏmai
(1), to recruit oneself

REFRESHETH
7725 shûwb (1), to return
or restore

REFRESHING
4774 margē'âh (1), place
of rest
403 anapsuxis (1),
revival, relief

REFUGE
2620 châçâh (1), to flee
to; to confide in
4268 machăçeh (15),
shelter; refuge
4498 mânôwç (4), fleeing;
place of refuge
4585 me'ôwnâh (1), abode
4733 miqlât (20), asylum,
place of protection
4869 misgâb (5), high
refuge
2703 kataphĕugō (1), to
flee down

REFUSE
3973 mâ'ôwç (1), refuse
3985 mâ'ên (10), to
refuse, reject
3986 mâ'ên (4),
unwilling, refusing
3987 mê'ên (1),
refractory, stubborn
3988 mâ'aç (3), to spurn;
to disappear
4549 mâçaç (1), to waste;
to faint
4651 mappâl (1), chaff;
flap or fold of skin
6544 pâra' (1), to loosen;
to expose, dismiss
3868 paraitĕŏmai (4), to
deprecate, decline

REFUSED
3985 mâ'ên (24), to
refuse, reject
3988 mâ'aç (5), to spurn;
to disappear
579 apŏblētŏs (1),
rejected
720 arnĕŏmai (2), to
disavow, reject
3868 paraitĕŏmai (1), to
deprecate, decline

REFUSEDST
3985 mâ'ên (1), to refuse,
reject

REFUSETH
3985 mâ'ên (5), to refuse,
reject
3988 mâ'aç (1), to spurn;
to disappear
5800 'âzab (1), to loosen;
relinquish; permit
6544 pâra' (2), to loosen;
to expose, dismiss

REGARD
995 bìyn (4), to
understand; discern
1875 dârash (1), to
pursue or search
2803 châshab (1), to
think, regard; to value
3820 lêb (3), heart
5027 nâbat (4), to scan;
to regard with favor
5375 nâsâ' (3), to lift up
5375+6440 nâsâ' (1), to
lift up
5869+2437+5921 'ayin (1),
eye; sight; fountain
5921+1700 'al (1), above,
over, upon, or against

6437 pânâh (3), to turn,
to face
7200 râ'âh (1), to see
7789 shûwr (1), to spy
out, survey
8104 shâmar (2), to
watch
8159 shâ'âh (1), to
inspect, consider
1788 ĕntrĕpō (1), to
respect; to confound
4337 prŏsĕchō (1), to pay
attention to
5426 phrŏnĕō (1), to be
mentally disposed

REGARDED
3820 lêb (1), heart
7181 qâshab (1), to prick
up the ears
7182 qesheb (1),
hearkening
7200 râ'âh (2), to see
7761+2942 sûwm (Ch.)
(1), to put, place
272 amĕlĕō (2), to be
careless of, neglect
1788 ĕntrĕpō (1), to
respect; to confound
1914 ĕpiblĕpō (1), to gaze
at

REGARDEST
995 bìyn (1), to
understand; discern
991 blĕpō (2), to look at

REGARDETH
995 bìyn (1), to
understand; discern
2803 châshab (1), to
think, regard; to value
3045 yâda' (1), to know
5234 nâkar (1), to
respect, revere
5375 nâsâ' (1), to lift up
6437 pânâh (1), to turn,
to face
7200 râ'âh (1), to see
7761+2942 sûwm (Ch.)
(1), to put, place
8085 shâma' (1), to hear
8104 shâmar (1), to
watch
5426 phrŏnĕō (2), to be
mentally disposed

REGARDING
7760 sûwm (1), to put,
place
3851 parabŏulĕuŏmai
(1), to misconsult, i.e.
disregard

REGEM
7276 Regem (1),
stone-heap

REGEM-MELECH
7278 Regem Melek (1),
king's heap

REGENERATION
3824 paliggĕnĕsia (2),
renovation; restoration

REGION
2256 chebel (3),
company, band
5299 nâphâh (1), height;
sieve
4066 pĕrichŏrŏs (6),
surrounding country
5561 chōra (4), territory

REGIONS
2825 klinē (2), couch
5561 chōra (1), territory

REGISTER
3791 kâthâb (2), writing,
record or book
5612 çêpher (1), writing

REHABIAH
7345 Rechabyâh (5),
Jehovah has enlarged

REHEARSE
7760 sûwm (1), to put,
place
8567 tânâh (1), to
commemorate

REHEARSED
1696 dâbar (1), to speak,
say; to subdue
5046 nâgad (1), to
announce
312 anaggĕllō (1), to
announce in detail
756 archŏmai (1), to
begin

REHOB
7340 Rechôb (10), myriad

REHOBOAM
7346 Rechab'âm (50),
people has enlarged

REHOBOTH
7344 Rechôbôwth (4),
streets

REHUM
7348 Rechûwm (8),
compassionate

REI
7472 Rê'îy (1), social

REIGN
4427 mâlak (117), to
reign as king
4437 malkûw (Ch.) (4),
dominion
4438 malkûwth (21),
rule; dominion
4467 mamlâkâh (2),
royal dominion
4468 mamlâkûwth (1),
royal dominion
4910 mâshal (3), to rule
6113 'âtsar (1), to hold
back; to rule, assemble
7287 râdâh (1), to
subjugate
757 archō (1), to rule, be
first in rank
936 basilĕuō (13), to rule
2231 hēgĕmŏnia (1),
rulership, leadership
4821 sumbasilĕuō (2), to
be co-regent

REIGNED
4427 mâlak (159), to
reign as king
4910 mâshal (3), to rule
7786 sûwr (1), to rule,
crown
936 basilĕuō (6), to rule

REIGNEST
4910 mâshal (1), to rule

REIGNETH
4427 mâlak (11), to reign
as king
936 basilĕuō (1), to rule
2192+932 ĕchō (1), to
have; hold; keep

REIGNING
4427 mâlak (1), to *reign as king*

REINS
2504 châlâts (1), *loins, areas of the waist*
3629 kilyâh (13), *kidney; mind, heart, spirit*
3510 nĕphrŏs (1), inmost *mind*

REJECT
3988 mâ'aç (1), to *spurn; to disappear*
114 athĕtĕŏ (2), to *disesteem, neutralize*
3868 paraitĕŏmai (1), to *deprecate, decline*

REJECTED
2310 châdêl (1), *ceasing or destitute*
3988 mâ'aç (17), to *spurn; to disappear*
96 adŏkimŏs (1), *failing the test, worthless*
114 athĕtĕŏ (1), to *disesteem, neutralize*
593 apŏdŏkimazŏ (7), to *repudiate, reject*
1609 ĕkptuŏ (1), to *spurn, scorn*

REJECTETH
14 agathŏĕrgĕŏ (1), to do *good work*

REJOICE
1523 gîyl (23), *rejoice*
1524 gîyl (2), *age, stage in life*
4885 mâsôws (1), *delight*
5937 'âlaz (8), to *jump for joy*
5947 'allîyz (3), *exultant; reveling*
5965 'âlaç (1), to *leap for joy, i.e. exult, wave*
5970 'âlats (4), to *jump for joy*
7442 rânan (11), to *shout for joy*
7797 sûws (14), to be *bright, i.e. cheerful*
7832 sâchaq (1), to *laugh; to scorn; to play*
8055 sâmach (70), to *be, make gleesome*
8056 sâmêach (5), *blithe or gleeful*
8057 simchâh (4), *blithesomeness or glee*
21 agalliaŏ (4), to *exult*
2165 ĕuphrainŏ (5), to *rejoice, be glad*
2744 kauchaŏmai (4), to *glory in, rejoice in*
2745 kauchĕma (1), *boast; brag*
4796 sugchairŏ (5), to *sympathize in gladness*
5463 chairŏ (24), to be *cheerful*

REJOICED
1523 gîyl (2), *rejoice*
2302 châdâh (1), to *rejoice, be glad*
5937 'âlaz (2), to *jump for joy*
6670 tsâhal (1), to be *cheerful*

7797 sûws (3), to be *bright, i.e. cheerful*
8055 sâmach (20), to *be, make gleesome*
8056 sâmêach (3), *blithe or gleeful*
8057 simchâh (1), *blithesomeness or glee*
21 agalliaŏ (4), to *exult*
2165 ĕuphrainŏ (1), to *rejoice, be glad*
4796 sugchairŏ (1), to *sympathize in gladness*
5463 chairŏ (8), to be *cheerful*

REJOICEST
5937 'âlaz (1), to *jump for joy*

REJOICETH
1523 gîyl (1), *rejoice*
4885 mâsôws (1), *delight*
5937 'âlaz (1), to *jump for joy*
5938 'âlêz (1), *exultant*
5970 'âlats (2), to *jump for joy*
7797 sûws (3), to be *bright, i.e. cheerful*
8055 sâmach (4), to *be, make gleesome*
2620 katakauchaŏmai (1), to *exult over*
4796 sugchairŏ (1), to *sympathize in gladness*
5463 chairŏ (3), to be *cheerful*

REJOICING
1524 gîyl (1), *age, stage in life*
1525 gîylâh (1), *joy, delight*
5947 'allîyz (1), *exultant; reveling*
5951 'ălîytsûwth (1), *exultation*
7440 rinnâh (3), *shout*
7832 sâchaq (2), to *laugh; to scorn; to play*
8055 sâmach (1), to *be, make gleesome*
8056 sâmêach (1), *blithe or gleeful*
8057 simchâh (2), *blithesomeness or glee*
8342 sâsôwn (1), *cheerfulness; welcome*
8643 t⁰rûw'âh (1), *battle-cry; clangor*
2745 kauchĕma (4), *boast; brag*
2746 kauchĕsis (4), *boasting; bragging*
5463 chairŏ (5), to be *cheerful*

REKEM
7552 Reqem (5), *versi-color*

RELEASE
2010 hănâchâh (1), *quiet*
8058 shâmaţ (2), to *let alone, desist, remit*
8059 sh⁰miţţâh (5), *remission of debt*
630 apŏluŏ (13), to *relieve, release*

RELEASED
630 apŏluŏ (4), to *relieve, release; to divorce*

RELIED
8172 shâ'an (3), to *support, rely on*

RELIEF
1248 diakŏnia (1), *attendance, aid, service*

RELIEVE
833 'âshar (1), to *go forward; guide; prosper*
2388 châzaq (1), to *bind, restrain, conquer*
7725 shûwb (3), to *turn back; to return*
1884 ĕparkĕŏ (2), to *help*

RELIEVED
1884 ĕparkĕŏ (1), to *help*

RELIEVETH
5749 'ûwd (1), to *protest, testify; to restore*

RELIGION
2356 thrĕskĕia (3), *observance, religion*
2454 Iŏudaismŏs (2), *Jewish faith*

RELIGIOUS
2357 thrĕskŏs (1), *ceremonious, pious*
4576 sĕbŏmai (1), to *revere, i.e. adore*

RELY
8172 shâ'an (1), to *support, rely on*

REMAIN
1481 gûwr (1), to *sojourn, live as an alien*
1961 hâyâh (1), to *exist, i.e. be or become*
3241 Yânîym (1), *asleep*
3427 yâshab (11), to *dwell, to remain*
3498 yâthar (13), to *remain or be left*
3885 lûwn (5), to be *obstinate with*
5117 nûwach (1), to *rest; to settle down*
5975 'âmad (3), to *stand*
6965 qûwm (1), to *rise*
7604 shâ'ar (15), to *leave, remain*
7611 sh⁰'êrîyth (1), *remainder or residual*
7931 shâkan (3), to *reside*
8245 shâqad (1), to be *alert, i.e. sleepless*
8300 sârîyd (8), *survivor; remainder*
3062 lŏipŏi (1), *remaining ones*
3306 mĕnŏ (8), to *remain*
4035 pĕrilĕipŏ (2), to *survive, be left, remain*
4052 pĕrissĕuŏ (1), to *superabound*

REMAINDER
3498 yâthar (4), to *remain or be left*
7611 sh⁰'êrîyth (2), *remainder or residual*

REMAINED
1961 hâyâh (1), to *exist, i.e. be or become*

REMAINEST
3427 yâshab (10), to *dwell, to remain*
3462 yâshên (1), to *sleep; to grow old, stale*
3498 yâthar (5), to *remain or be left*
5975 'âmad (4), to *stand*
7604 shâ'ar (23), to *leave, remain*
8277 sârad (1), to *escape or survive*
8300 sârîyd (1), *survivor; remainder*
1265 diamĕnŏ (1), to *stay constantly*
3306 mĕnŏ (3), to *remain*
4052 pĕrissĕuŏ (3), to *superabound*

REMAINEST
3427 yâshab (1), to *dwell, to remain; to settle*
1265 diamĕnŏ (1), to *stay constantly*

REMAINETH
3117 yôwm (1), *day; time period*
3427 yâshab (1), to *dwell, to remain; to settle*
3498 yâthar (4), to *remain or be left*
3885 lûwn (2), to be *obstinate with*
5736 'âdaph (4), to be *redundant*
5975 'âmad (1), to *stand*
7604 shâ'ar (8), to *leave, remain*
7931 shâkan (1), to *reside*
8300 sârîyd (3), *survivor; remainder*
620 apŏlĕipŏ (3), to *leave behind; to forsake*
3306 mĕnŏ (5), to *stay, remain*
3588+3063 hŏ (1), *"the,"* i.e. the definite article

REMAINING
3320 yâtsab (1), to *station, offer, continue*
3498 yâthar (1), to *remain or be left*
7931 shâkan (1), to *reside*
8300 sârîyd (9), *survivor; remainder*
3306 mĕnŏ (1), to *remain*

REMALIAH
7425 R⁰malyâhûw (11), *Jehovah has bedecked*

REMALIAH'S
7425 R⁰malyâhûw (2), *Jehovah has bedecked*

REMEDY
4832 marpê' (3), *cure; deliverance; placidity*

REMEMBER
2142 zâkar (120), to *remember; to mention*
6485 pâqad (1), to *visit, care for, count*
3403 mimnēskŏ (1), to *remind or to recall*
3415 mnaŏmai (9), to *bear in mind*
3421 mnēmŏnĕuŏ (16), to *exercise memory*
5279 hupŏmimnēskŏ (1), to *suggest to memory*

English

REMEMBERED
2142 zâkar (48), to
remember; to mention
2143 zêker (1),
commemoration
3415 mnaŏmai (6), to
recollect
3421 mnēmŏnĕuō (1), to
recall
5279 hupŏmimnēskō (1),
to remind oneself

REMEMBEREST
2142 zâkar (1), to
remember; to mention
3415 mnaŏmai (1), to
recollect

REMEMBERETH
2142 zâkar (3), to
remember; to mention
363 anamimnēskō (1), to
remind; to recollect
3421 mnēmŏnĕuō (1), to
recall

REMEMBERING
2142 zâkar (1), to
remember; to mention
3421 mnēmŏnĕuō (1), to
recall

REMEMBRANCE
2142 zâkar (13), to
remember; to mention
2143 zêker (11),
recollection
2146 zikrôwn (5),
commemoration
6485 pâqad (1), to visit,
care for, count
363 anamimnēskō (3), to
remind; to recollect
364 anamnēsis (5),
recollection
3415 mnaŏmai (3), to
recollect
3417 mnĕia (3),
recollection; recital
3418 mnēma (1),
sepulchral monument
5179 tupŏs (2), shape,
resemblance; "type"
5279 hupŏmimnēskō (2),
to remind oneself
5280 hupŏmnēsis (3),
reminding
5294 hupŏtithēmi (1), to
hazard; to suggest

REMEMBRANCES
2146 zikrôwn (1),
commemoration

REMETH
7432 Remeth (1), height

REMISSION
859 aphĕsis (9), pardon,
freedom
3929 parĕsis (1),
toleration, passing over

REMIT
863 aphiēmi (1), to leave;
to pardon, forgive

REMITTED
863 aphiēmi (1), to leave;
to pardon, forgive

REMMON
7417 Rimmôwn (1),
pomegranate

REMMON-METHOAR
7417 Rimmôwn (1),
pomegranate

REMNANT
310 'achar (1), after
319 'achărîyth (1), future;
posterity
3498 yâthar (4), to
remain or be left
3499 yether (14),
remainder; small rope
5629 çerach (1),
redundancy
6413 pᵉlêŷtâh (1),
escaped portion
7604 shâ'ar (1), to leave,
remain
7605 shᵉ'âr (11),
remainder
7611 shᵉ'êrîyth (44),
remainder or residual
8293 shêrûwth (1),
freedom
8300 sârîyd (2), survivor;
remainder
2640 katalĕimma (1),
few, remnant
3005 lĕimma (1),
remainder, remnant
3062 lŏipŏi (4),
remaining ones

REMOVE
1540 gâlâh (2), to
denude; uncover
1556 gâlal (1), to roll; to
commit
4185 mûwsh (4), to
withdraw
5110 nûwd (4), to waver;
to wander, flee
5253 nâçag (4), to retreat
5265 nâça' (1), start
5437 çâbab (2), to
surround
5472 çûwg (1), to go
back, to retreat
5493 çûwr (15), to turn off
7368 râchaq (5), to
recede; remove
7493 râ'ash (1), to
undulate, quake
2795 kinĕō (1), to stir,
move, remove
3179 mĕthistēmi (1), to
move
3327 mĕtabainō (2), to
depart, move from
3911 paraphĕrō (1), to
carry off; to avert

REMOVED
167 'âhal (1), to pitch a
tent
1540 gâlâh (3), to
denude; uncover
1556 gâlal (1), to roll; to
commit
2186 zânach (1), to
reject, forsake, fail
2189 za'ăvâh (6),
agitation,
maltreatment
3014 yâgâh (1), to push
away, be removed
3670 kânaph (1), to
withdraw
4131 môwṭ (5), to slip,
shake, fall

REMMON-METHOAR
7417 Rimmôwn (1),
pomegranate

4171 mûwr (1), to alter;
to barter, to dispose of
4185 mûwsh (2), to
withdraw
5074 nâdad (1), to rove,
flee; to drive away
5079 niddâh (2), time of
menstrual impurity
5110 nûwd (1), to waver;
to wander, flee
5128 nûwa' (1), to waver
5206 nîydâh (1), removal
5265 nâça' (26), start
5437 çâbab (1), to
surround
5493 çûwr (21), to turn off
5674 'âbar (1), to cross
over; to transition
6275 'âthaq (4), to remove
7368 râchaq (4), to recede
142 airō (2), to lift, to
take up
3179 mĕthistēmi (1), to
move
3346 mĕtatithēmi (1), to
transport; to exchange
3351 mĕtŏikizō (1), to
transfer as a settler

REMOVETH
5253 nâçag (1), to retreat
5265 nâça' (1), start
5493 çûwr (1), to turn off
5709 'ădâ' (Ch.) (1), to
pass on or continue
6275 'âthaq (1), to remove

REMOVING
1473 gôwlâh (2), exile;
captive
5493 çûwr (2), to turn off
3331 mĕtathĕsis (1),
transferral to heaven

REMPHAN
4481 Rhĕmphan (1),
Kijun (a pagan god)

REND
1234 bâqa' (3), to cleave,
break, tear open
6533 pâram (2), to tear,
be torn
7167 qâra' (11), to rend
4486 rhēgnumi (1), to
tear to pieces
4977 schizō (1), to split
or sever

RENDER
5415 nᵉthan (Ch.) (1), to
give
7725 shûwb (16), to turn
back; to return
7999 shâlam (7), to be
safe; be, make complete
467 antapŏdidōmi (1), to
requite good or evil
591 apŏdidōmi (8), to
give away

RENDERED
7725 shûwb (4), to turn
back; to return

RENDEREST
7999 shâlam (1), to be
safe; be, make complete

RENDERETH
7999 shâlam (1), to be
safe; be, make complete

RENDERING
591 apŏdidōmi (1), to
give away

RENDING
6561 pâraq (1), to break
off or crunch; to deliver

RENEW
2318 châdash (3), to be
new, renew; to rebuild
2498 châlaph (2), to
spring up; to change
340 anakainizō (1), to
restore, bring back

RENEWED
2318 châdash (2), to be
new, renew; to rebuild
2498 châlaph (1), to
spring up; to change
341 anakainŏō (2), to
renovate, renew
365 ananĕŏō (1), to
renovate, i.e. reform

RENEWEST
2318 châdash (2), to be
new, renew; to rebuild

RENEWING
342 anakainōsis (2),
renovation, renewal

RENOUNCED
550 apĕipŏmēn (1), to
disown

RENOWN
8034 shêm (7), name,
appellation

RENOWNED
1984 hâlal (1), to boast
7121 qârâ' (3), to call out

RENT
1234 bâqa' (5), to cleave,
break, tear open
2963 ṭâraph (1), to pluck
off or pull to pieces
5364 niqpâh (1), rope
6533 pâram (1), to tear,
be torn
6561 pâraq (1), to break
off or crunch; to deliver
7167 qâra' (43), to rend
8156 shâça' (2), to split
or tear; to upbraid
1284 diarrhēssō (3), to
tear asunder
4048 pĕrirrhēgnumi (1),
to tear all around
4682 sparassō (1), to
convulse with epilepsy
4977 schizō (5), to split
or sever
4978 schisma (2),
divisive dissension

RENTEST
7167 qâra' (1), to rend

REPAID
7999 shâlam (1), to be
safe; to reciprocate

REPAIR
918 bâdaq (1), to mend a
breach
2318 châdash (3), to be
new, renew; to rebuild
2388 châzaq (8), to
fasten upon; to seize
2393 chezqâh (1),
prevailing power
5975 'âmad (1), to stand

REPAIRED
1129 bânâh (2), to *build;* to *establish*
2388 châzaq (39), to *fasten* upon; to *seize*
2421 châyâh (1), to *live;* to *revive*
5462 çâgar (1), to *shut* up; to *surrender*
7495 râphâ' (1), to *cure, heal*

REPAIRER
1443 gâdar (1), to *build a stone wall*

REPAIRING
3247 yᵉçôwd (1), *foundation*

REPAY
7999 shâlam (5), to *be complete;* to *reciprocate*
457 anŏixis (1), act of *opening*
591 apŏdidōmi (1), to *give away*
661 apŏtinō (1), to *pay in full, make restitution*

REPAYETH
7999 shâlam (1), to *be complete;* to *reciprocate*

REPEATETH
8138 shânâh (1), to *fold,* i.e. *duplicate*

REPENT
5162 nâcham (19), to *be sorry;* to *pity, rue*
7725 shûwb (3), to *turn back;* to *return*
3338 mĕtamĕllŏmai (2), to *regret*
3340 mĕtanŏĕō (21), to *reconsider*

REPENTANCE
5164 nôcham (1), *ruefulness*
278 amĕtamĕlētŏs (1), *irrevocable*
3341 mĕtanŏia (24), *reversal*

REPENTED
5162 nâcham (17), to *be sorry;* to *pity, rue*
278 amĕtamĕlētŏs (1), *irrevocable*
3338 mĕtamĕllŏmai (3), to *regret*
3340 mĕtanŏĕō (11), to *reconsider*

REPENTEST
5162 nâcham (1), to *be sorry;* to *pity, rue*

REPENTETH
5162 nâcham (3), to *be sorry;* to *pity, rue*
3340 mĕtanŏĕō (2), to *reconsider*

REPENTING
5162 nâcham (1), to *be sorry;* to *pity, rue*

REPENTINGS
5150 nichûwm (1), *consoled; solace*

REPETITIONS
945 battŏlŏgĕō (1), to *prate tediously, babble*

REPHAEL
7501 Rᵉphâ'êl (1), *God has cured*

REPHAH
7506 Rephach (1), *support*

REPHAIAH
7509 Rᵉphâyâh (5), *Jehovah has cured*

REPHAIM
7497 râphâ' (6), *giant*

REPHAIMS
7497 râphâ' (2), *giant*

REPHIDIM
7508 Rᵉphîydîym (5), *balusters*

REPLENISH
4390 mâlê' (2), to *fill; be full*

REPLENISHED
4390 mâlê' (5), to *fill; be full*

REPLIEST
470 antapŏkrinŏmai (1), to *contradict* or *dispute*

REPORT
1681 dibbâh (3), *slander, bad report*
1697 dâbâr (2), *word; matter; thing*
5046 nâgad (1), to *announce*
8034 shêm (1), *name, appellation*
8052 shᵉmûw'âh (4), *announcement*
8088 shêma' (5), *something heard*
189 akŏē (2), *hearing; thing heard*
518 apaggĕllō (1), to *announce, proclaim*
1426 dusphēmia (1), *defamation, slander*
2162 ĕuphēmia (1), *good repute*
2163 ĕuphēmŏs (1), *reputable*
3140 marturĕō (6), to *testify;* to *commend*
3141 marturia (1), *evidence given*

REPORTED
559 'âmar (2), to *say*
7725 shûwb (1), to *turn back;* to *return*
8085 shâma' (2), to *hear*
191 akŏuō (1), to *hear*
312 anaggĕllō (1), to *announce, report*
518 apaggĕllō (1), to *announce, proclaim*
987 blasphēmĕō (1), to *speak impiously*
1310 diaphēmizō (1), to *spread news*
3140 marturĕō (2), to *testify;* to *commend*

REPROACH
2617 cheçed (1), *kindness, favor*
2659 châphêr (1), to *shame, reproach*
2778 châraph (10), to *spend the winter*

2781 cherpâh (65), *contumely, disgrace*
3637 kâlam (1), to *taunt* or *insult*
3639 kᵉlimmâh (1), *disgrace, scorn*
7036 qâlôwn (1), *disgrace*
819 atimia (1), *disgrace*
3679 ŏnĕidizō (2), to *rail at, chide, taunt*
3680 ŏnĕidismŏs (3), *with insult*
3681 ŏnĕidŏs (1), *notoriety, i.e. a taunt*

REPROACHED
2778 châraph (12), to *spend the winter*
3637 kâlam (1), to *taunt* or *insult*
3679 ŏnĕidizō (2), to *rail at, chide, taunt*

REPROACHES
1421 giddûwph (1), *vilification, scorn*
2781 cherpâh (1), *contumely, disgrace*
3679 ŏnĕidizō (1), to *rail at, chide, taunt*
3680 ŏnĕidismŏs (1), *with insult*
5196 hubris (1), *insult*

REPROACHEST
5195 hubrizō (1), to *exercise violence, abuse*

REPROACHETH
1442 gâdaph (1), to *revile, blaspheme*
2778 châraph (5), to *spend the winter*
2781 cherpâh (1), *contumely, disgrace*

REPROACHFULLY
2781 cherpâh (1), *contumely, disgrace*
5484+3059 charin (1), on *account of, because of*

REPROBATE
3988 mâ'aç (1), to *spurn;* to *disappear*
96 adŏkimŏs (3), *failing the test, worthless*

REPROBATES
96 adŏkimŏs (3), *failing the test, worthless*

REPROOF
1606 gᵉ'ârâh (2), *chiding, rebuke*
8433 tôwkêchâh (12), *correction, refutation*
1650 ĕlĕgchŏs (1), *proof, conviction*

REPROOFS
8433 tôwkêchâh (2), *correction, refutation*

REPROVE
3198 yâkach (16), to *be correct;* to *argue*
1651 ĕlĕgchō (3), to *confute, admonish*

REPROVED
1605 gâ'ar (1), to *chide, reprimand*
3198 yâkach (4), to *be correct;* to *argue*

8433 tôwkêchâh (2), *correction, refutation*
1651 ĕlĕgchō (3), to *confute, admonish*

REPROVER
3198 yâkach (2), to *be correct;* to *argue*

REPROVETH
3198 yâkach (3), to *be correct;* to *argue*
3256 yâçar (1), to *chastise;* to *instruct*

REPUTATION
3368 yâqâr (1), *valuable*
1380 dŏkĕō (1), to *think, regard, seem* good
1784 ĕntimŏs (1), *valued, considered precious*
2758 kĕnŏō (1), to *make empty*
5093 timiŏs (1), *costly; honored, esteemed*

REPUTED
2804 chăshab (Ch.) (2), to *regard*

REQUEST
782 'ăresheth (1), *longing for*
1245 bâqash (3), to *search;* to *strive after*
1246 baqqâshâh (8), *petition, request*
1697 dâbâr (2), *word; matter; thing*
7596 shᵉ'êlâh (3), *petition*
1162 dĕēsis (1), *petition, request*
1189 dĕŏmai (1), to *beg, petition, ask*

REQUESTED
1156 bᵉ'â' (Ch.) (1), to *seek* or *ask*
1245 bâqash (1), to *search;* to *strive after*
7592 shâ'al (3), to *ask*

REQUESTS
155 aitēma (1), *thing asked, request*

REQUIRE
977 bâchar (1), *select, chose, prefer*
1245 bâqash (10), to *search;* to *strive after*
1875 dârash (11), to *pursue* or *search*
3117 yôwm (1), *day; time period*
7592 shâ'al (3), to *ask*
7593 shᵉ'êl (Ch.) (1), to *ask*
154 aitĕō (1), to *ask for*
1096 ginŏmai (1), to *be, become*

REQUIRED
1245 bâqash (3), to *search;* to *strive after*
1875 dârash (2), to *pursue* or *search*
1961 hâyâh (1), to *exist,* i.e. *be* or *become*
3117 yôwm (3), *day; time period*
7592 shâ'al (4), to *ask*
155 aitĕma (1), *thing asked, request*

REQUIREST
523 apaitĕō (1), to demand back
1567 ĕkzētĕō (2), to seek out
2212 zētĕō (2), to seek
4238 prassō (1), to execute, accomplish

REQUIREST
559 'âmar (1), to say

REQUIRETH
1245 bâqash (1), to search; to strive after
7593 sheʾêl (Ch.) (1), to ask

REQUIRING
154 aitĕō (1), to ask for

REQUITE
1580 gâmal (1), to benefit or requite; to wean
5414 nâthan (1), to give
6213 'âsâh (1), to do or make
7725 shûwb (2), to turn back; to return
7999 shâlam (3), to be safe; to reciprocate
287+591 amŏibē (1), requital, recompense

REQUITED
7725 shûwb (1), to turn back; to return
7999 shâlam (1), to be safe; to reciprocate

REQUITING
7725 shûwb (1), to turn back; to return

REREWARD
314 'achărōwn (1), late or last; behind; western
622 'âçaph (5), to gather, collect

RESCUE
3467 yâsha' (1), to make safe, free
5337 nâtsal (1), to deliver; to be snatched
7725 shûwb (1), to turn back; to return

RESCUED
5337 nâtsal (1), to deliver; to be snatched
6299 pâdâh (1), to ransom; to release
1807 ĕxairĕō (1), to tear out; to select; to release

RESCUETH
5338 neʾtsal (Ch.) (1), to extricate, deliver

RESEMBLANCE
5869 'ayin (1), eye; sight; fountain

RESEMBLE
3666 hŏmŏiŏō (1), to become similar

RESEMBLED
8389 tôʾar (1), outline, figure or appearance

RESEN
7449 Reçen (1), bridle

RESERVE
5201 nâṭar (1), to guard; to cherish anger
7604 shâʾar (1), to be, make redundant

RESERVED
5083 tērĕō (1), to keep, guard, obey

RESERVED
680 'âtsal (1), to select; refuse; narrow
2820 châsak (2), to restrain or refrain
3498 yâthar (3), to remain or be left
3947 lâqach (1), to take
2641 katalĕipō (1), to have remaining
5083 tērĕō (7), to keep, guard, obey

RESERVETH
5201 nâṭar (1), to guard; to cherish anger
8104 shâmar (1), to watch

RESHEPH
7566 Resheph (1), flame

RESIDUE
319 'achărîyth (1), future; posterity
3498 yâthar (3), to remain or be left
3499 yether (8), remainder; small rope
7605 sheʾâr (4), remainder
7606 sheʾâr (Ch.) (2), remainder
7611 sheʾêrîyth (13), remainder or residual
2645 katalŏipŏs (1), remaining; rest
3062 lŏipŏi (1), remaining ones

RESIST
7853 sâṭan (1), to attack by accusation
436 anthistēmi (7), oppose, rebel
496 antipiptō (1), to oppose, resist
498 antitassŏmai (1), oppose, resist

RESISTED
436 anthistēmi (1), oppose, rebel
478 antikathistēmi (1), withstand, contest

RESISTETH
436 anthistēmi (1), oppose, rebel
498 antitassŏmai (3), oppose, resist

RESOLVED
1097 ginōskō (1), to know

RESORT
935 bôw' (1), to go, come
6908 qâbats (1), to collect, assemble
4848 sumpŏrĕuŏmai (1), to journey together
4905 sunĕrchŏmai (1), to gather together

RESORTED
3320 yâtsab (1), to station, offer, continue
2064 ĕrchŏmai (2), to go
4863 sunagō (1), to gather together
4905 sunĕrchŏmai (1), to gather together

RESPECT
3045 yâda' (1), to know
4856 massô' (1), partiality
5027 nâbaṭ (3), to scan; to regard with favor
5234 nâkar (3), to respect, revere
5375 nâsâ' (2), to lift up
6437 pânâh (6), to turn, to face
7200 râ'âh (4), to see
8159 shâ'âh (3), to inspect, consider
578 apŏblĕpō (1), to intently regard, pay attention
678 aprŏsōpŏlēptōs (1), without prejudice
1914 ĕpiblĕpō (1), to gaze at
2596 kata (1), down; according to
3313 mĕrŏs (2), division or share
3382 mĕrŏs (1), thigh
4380 prŏsōpŏlēptĕō (1), to show partiality
4382 prŏsōpŏlēpsia (3), favoritism

RESPECTED
5375 nâsâ' (1), to lift up

RESPECTER
4381 prŏsōpŏlēptēs (1), exhibiting partiality

RESPECTETH
6437 pânâh (1), to turn, to face
7200 râ'âh (1), to see

RESPITE
7309 reʾvâchâh (1), relief
7503 râphâh (1), to slacken

REST
1824 deʾmîy (1), quiet, peacefulness
1826 dâmam (1), to be silent; to be astonished; to stop, cease; to perish
2308 châdal (1), to desist, stop; be fat
2342 chûwl (1), to wait; to pervert
2790 chârash (1), to be silent; to be deaf
3498 yâthar (1), to remain or be left
3499 yether (65), remainder; small rope
4494 mânôwach (6), quiet spot, home
4496 meʾnûwchâh (16), peacefully; consolation
4771 margôwa' (1), resting place
5117 nûwach (44), to rest; to settle down
5118 nûwach (1), quiet
5183 nachath (4), descent; quiet
6314 pûwgâh (1), intermission, relief
7257 râbats (1), to recline, repose, brood
7280 râga' (5), to settle, i.e. quiet; to wink
7599 shâ'an (1), to loll, i.e. be peaceful
7604 shâ'ar (2), to be, make redundant
7605 sheʾâr (10), remainder
7606 sheʾâr (Ch.) (9), remainder
7611 sheʾêrîyth (3), remainder or residual
7673 shâbath (7), to repose; to desist
7677 shabbâthôwn (8), special holiday
7901 shâkab (2), to lie down
7931 shâkan (2), to reside
7954 sheʾlâh (Ch.) (1), to be secure, at rest
7965 shâlôwm (1), safe; well; health, prosperity
8058 shâmaṭ (1), to let alone, desist, remit
8172 shâ'an (2), to support, rely on
8252 shâqaṭ (15), to repose
8300 sârîyd (1), survivor; remainder
372 anapausis (4), recreation, rest
373 anapauō (6), to repose; to refresh
425 anĕsis (3), relaxation; relief
1515 ĕirēnē (1), peace; health; prosperity
1879 ĕpanapauŏmai (1), to settle on, rely on
1954 ĕpilŏipŏs (1), remaining, rest
1981 ĕpiskēnŏō (1), to abide with
2192+372 ĕchō (1), to have; hold; keep
2663 katapausis (9), abode for resting
2664 katapauō (2), to settle down
2681 kataskēnŏō (1), to remain, live
3062 lŏipŏi (13), remaining ones
4520 sabbatismŏs (1), sabbatism

RESTED
270 'âchaz (1), to seize, grasp; possess
1826 dâmam (1), to stop, cease; to perish
2583 chânâh (2), to encamp
5117 nûwach (7), to rest; to settle down
5118 nûwach (2), quiet
5564 çâmak (1), to lean upon; take hold of
7673 shâbath (4), to repose; to desist
7931 shâkan (1), to reside
8252 shâqaṭ (1), to repose
2270 hēsuchazō (1), to refrain

RESTEST
1879 ĕpanapauŏmai (1), to settle on, rely on

RESTETH
5117 nûwach (2), to rest
8172 shâ'an (1), to support, rely on

373 anapauō (1), to
repose; to refresh

RESTING
4496 m*nûwchâh (2),
peacefully; consolation
5118 nûwach (1), *quiet*
7258 rebets (1), place of
repose

RESTINGPLACE
7258 rebets (1), place of
repose

RESTITUTION
7999 shâlam (4), to *make*
complete; to reciprocate
8545 t*mûwrâh (1),
barter, compensation
605 apŏkatastasis (1),
reconstitution

RESTORE
5927 'âlâh (1), to *ascend,*
be high, mount
7725 shûwb (27), to
return or restore
7999 shâlam (8), to *make*
complete; to reciprocate
591 apŏdidōmi (1), to
give away
600 apŏkathistēmi (2), to
reconstitute
2675 katartizō (1), to
repair; to prepare

RESTORED
2421 châyâh (4), to *live;*
to *revive*
5414 nâthan (1), to *give*
7725 shûwb (16), to
return or restore
8421 tûwb (Ch.) (1), to
come back with answer
600 apŏkathistēmi (5), to
reconstitute

RESTORER
7725 shûwb (2), to *return*
or restore

RESTORETH
7725 shûwb (1), to *return*
or restore
600 apŏkathistēmi (1), to
reconstitute

RESTRAIN
1639 gâra' (1), to *shave,*
remove, lessen
2296 châgar (1), to *gird*
on a belt; *put on armor*

RESTRAINED
662 'âphaq (1), to *abstain*
1219 bâtsar (1), to *be*
inaccessible
3543 kâhâh (1), to *grow*
dull, fade; to be faint
3607 kâlâ' (2), to *hold*
back or in; to prohibit
4513 mâna' (1), to *deny,*
refuse
6113 'âtsar (1), to *hold*
back; to maintain, rule
2664 katapauō (1), to
cause to desist

RESTRAINEST
1639 gâra' (1), to *remove,*
lessen, or withhold

RESTRAINT
4622 ma'tsôwr (1),
hindrance

RESURRECTION
386 anastasis (39),
resurrection from death
1454 ĕgĕrsis (1),
resurgence from death
1815 ĕxanastasis (1),
rising from death

RETAIN
2388 châzaq (1), to
fasten upon; to *seize;*
3607 kâlâ' (1), to *hold*
back or in; to prohibit
6113 'âtsar (1), to *hold*
back; to maintain, rule
8551 tâmak (2), to
obtain, keep fast
2192 ĕchō (1), to *have;*
hold; keep
2902 kratĕō (1), to *seize*

RETAINED
2388 châzaq (2), to
fasten upon; to *seize*
6113 'âtsar (2), to *hold*
back; to maintain, rule
2722 katĕchō (1), to *hold*
down fast
2902 kratĕō (1), to *seize*

RETAINETH
2388 châzaq (1), to
fasten upon; to *seize*
8551 tâmak (2), to
obtain, keep fast

RETIRE
5756 'ûwz (1), to
strengthen; to save
7725 shûwb (1), to *return*
or restore

RETIRED
2015 hâphak (1), to
return, pervert
6327 pûwts (1), to *dash*
in *pieces; to disperse*

RETURN
3427 yâshab (1), to *dwell,*
to *remain; to settle*
6437 pânâh (1), to *turn,*
to *face*
7725 shûwb (242), to *turn*
back; to return
8666 t*shûwbâh (3),
recurrence; reply
344 anakamptō (1), to
turn back, come back
360 analuō (1), to *depart*
390 anastrĕphō (1), to
remain; to return
844 autŏmatŏs (1),
spontaneous; by itself
1994 ĕpistrĕphō (4), to
revert, turn back to
5290 hupŏstrĕphō (5), to
turn under, to return

RETURNED
5437 çâbab (2), to
surround
7725 shûwb (151), to *turn*
back; to return
8421 tûwb (Ch.) (2), to
reply
344 anakamptō (1), to
turn back, come back
390 anastrĕphō (1), to
remain; to return
1877 ĕpanagō (1), to *put*
out to sea; to return
1880 ĕpanĕrchŏmai (1),
return home

RESURRECTION *(col. 2)*
1994 ĕpistrĕphō (2), to
revert, turn back to
5290 hupŏstrĕphō (24), to
turn under, to return

RETURNETH
7725 shûwb (6), to *turn*
back; to return
8138 shânâh (1), to *fold,*
to transmute

RETURNING
7729 shûwbâh (1),
return, i.e. repentance
5290 hupŏstrĕphō (3), to
turn under, to return

REU
7466 R*'ûw (5), *friend*

REUBEN
7205 R*'ûwbên (72), *see*
ye a son
7206 R*'ûwbênîy (1),
Rebenite
4502 Rhŏubēn (1), *see ye*
a son

REUBENITE
7206 R*'ûwbênîy (1),
Rebenite

REUBENITES
7206 R*'ûwbênîy (16),
Rebenite

REUEL
7467 R*'ûw'êl (10), *friend*
of God

REUMAH
7208 R*'ûwmâh (1),
raised

REVEAL
1540 gâlâh (2), to
denude; to reveal
1541 g*lâh (Ch.) (1), to
reveal mysteries
601 apŏkaluptō (4),
disclose, reveal

REVEALED
1540 gâlâh (11), to
denude; to reveal
1541 g*lâh (Ch.) (2), to
reveal mysteries
601 apŏkaluptō (22),
disclose, reveal
602 apŏkalupsis (2),
disclosure, revelation
5537 chrēmatizō (1), to
utter an oracle

REVEALER
1541 g*lâh (Ch.) (1), to
reveal mysteries

REVEALETH
1540 gâlâh (3), to
denude; to reveal
1541 g*lâh (Ch.) (3), to
reveal mysteries

REVELATION
602 apŏkalupsis (10),
disclosure, revelation

REVELATIONS
602 apŏkalupsis (2),
disclosure, revelation

REVELLINGS
2970 kōmŏs (2),
carousal, reveling, orgy

REVENGE
5358 nâqam (1), to
avenge or punish

REVILEST *(col. 4)*
5360 n*qâmâh (2),
avengement
1556 ĕkdikĕō (1), to
vindicate; retaliate
1557 ĕkdikēsis (1),
vindication; retaliation

REVENGED
5358 nâqam (1), to
avenge or punish

REVENGER
1350 gâ'al (6), to *redeem;*
to *be the next of kin*
1558 ĕkdikŏs (1),
punisher, avenger

REVENGERS
1350 gâ'al (1), to *redeem;*
to *be the next of kin*

REVENGES
6546 par'âh (1),
leadership

REVENGETH
5358 nâqam (2), to
avenge or punish

REVENGING
5360 n*qâmâh (1),
avengement

REVENUE
674 'app*thôm (Ch.) (1),
revenue
8393 t*bûw'âh (2),
income, i.e. produce

REVENUES
8393 t*bûw'âh (3),
income, i.e. produce

REVERENCE
3372 yârê' (2), to *fear; to*
revere
7812 shâchâh (5), to
prostrate in homage
127 aidōs (1), *modesty;*
awe
1788 ĕntrĕpō (4), to
respect; to confound
5399 phŏbĕō (1), to *be in*
awe of, i.e. revere

REVERENCED
7812 shâchâh (1), to
prostrate in homage

REVEREND
3372 yârê' (1), to *fear; to*
revere

REVERSE
7725 shûwb (3), to *turn*
back; to return

REVILE
7043 qâlal (1), to *be easy,*
trifling, vile
3679 ŏnĕidizō (1), to *rail*
at, chide, taunt

REVILED
486 antilŏidŏrĕō (1), to
rail in reply, retaliate
937 basilikŏs (1),
befitting the sovereign
3058 lŏidŏrĕō (2), *vilify,*
insult
3679 ŏnĕidizō (1), to *rail*
at, chide, taunt

REVILERS
3060 lŏidŏrŏs (1), *verbal*
abuser

REVILEST
3058 lŏidŏrĕō (1), *vilify,*
insult

English

REVILINGS
1421 giddûwph (2), vilification, scorn

REVIVE
2421 châyâh (8), to live; to revive

REVIVED
2421 châyâh (4), to live; to revive
326 anazaō (2), to recover life, live again

REVIVING
4241 michyâh (2), preservation of life

REVOLT
5627 çârâh (2), apostasy; crime; remission
6586 pâsha' (1), to break away from authority

REVOLTED
5498 çâchab (1), to trail along
5627 çârâh (1), apostasy; crime; remission
6586 pâsha' (5), to break away from authority

REVOLTERS
5637 çârar (2), to be refractory, stubborn
7846 sêṭ (1), departure

REVOLTING
5637 çârar (1), to be refractory, stubborn

REWARD
319 'achărîyth (2), future; posterity
868 'ethnan (3), gift price of harlotry
1309 bᵉsôwrâh (1), glad tidings, good news
1576 gᵉmûwl (3), reward, recompense
1578 gᵉmûwlâh (1), reward, recompense
1580 gâmal (1), to benefit or requite; to wean
4864 mas'êth (1), tribute; reproach
4909 maskôreth (1), wages; reward
4991 mattâth (1), present
6118 'êqeb (3), unto the end; for ever
6468 pᵉ'ullâh (1), work, deed
6529 pᵉrîy (1), fruit
7725 shûwb (2), to turn back; to return
7809 shâchad (1), to bribe; gift
7810 shachad (7), to bribe; gift
7938 seker (1), wages, reward
7939 sâkâr (5), payment, salary; compensation
7966 shillûwm (1), requital; retribution; fee
7999 shâlam (6), to make complete; to reciprocate
8011 shillumâh (1), retribution
469 antapŏdŏsis (1), requital, reward
514 axiŏs (1), deserving, comparable or suitable

591 apŏdidōmi (6), to give away
2603 katabrabĕuō (1), to award the price
3405 misthapŏdŏsia (3), requital, good or bad
3408 misthŏs (24), pay

REWARDED
1580 gâmal (7), to benefit or requite; to wean
7760 sûwm (1), to place
7939 sâkâr (2), payment, salary; compensation
7999 shâlam (3), to make complete; to reciprocate
591 apŏdidōmi (1), to give away

REWARDER
3406 misthapŏdŏtēs (1), rewarder

REWARDETH
7725 shûwb (1), to turn back; to return
7936 sâkar (2), to hire
7999 shâlam (3), to make complete; to reciprocate

REWARDS
866 'êthnah (1), gift price of harlotry
5023 nᵉbizbâh (Ch.) (2), largess, gift
8021 shalmôn (1), bribe, gift

REZEPH
7530 Retseph (2), hot stone for baking

REZIA
7525 Ritsyâ' (1), delight

REZIN
7526 Rᵉtsîyn (10), delight

REZON
7331 Rᵉzôwn (1), prince

RHEGIUM
4484 Rhēgiŏn (1), Rhegium

RHESA
4488 Rhēsa (1), (poss.) Jehovah has cured

RHODA
4498 Rhŏdē (1), rose

RHODES
4499 Rhŏdŏs (1), rose

RIB
6763 tsêlâ' (1), side

RIBAI
7380 Rîybay (2), contentious

RIBBAND
6616 pâthîyl (1), twine, cord

RIBLAH
7247 Riblâh (11), fertile

RIBS
6763 tsêlâ' (2), side

RICH
1952 hôwn (1), wealth
3513 kâbad (1), to be rich, glorious
5381 nâsag (1), to reach
6223 'âshîyr (23), rich; rich person
6238 'âshar (13), to grow, make rich

7771 shôwa' (1), noble, i.e. liberal; opulent
4145 plŏusiŏs (28), wealthy; abounding
4147 plŏutĕō (11), to be, become wealthy
4148 plŏutizō (1), to make wealthy

RICHER
6238 'âshar (1), to grow, make rich

RICHES
1952 hôwn (9), wealth
1995 hâmôwn (1), noise, tumult; many, crowd
2428 chayil (11), army; wealth; virtue; valor
2633 chôçen (1), wealth, stored riches
3502 yithrâh (1), wealth, abundance
4301 maṭmôwn (1), secret storehouse
5233 nekeç (1), treasure
6239 'ôsher (37), wealth
7075 qinyân (1), purchase, wealth
7399 rᵉkûwsh (5), property
7769 shûwa' (1), call
4149 plŏutŏs (22), abundant riches
5536 chrēma (3), wealth

RICHLY
4146 plŏusiōs (2), copiously, abundantly

RID
5337 nâtsal (3), to deliver; to be snatched
6475 pâtsâh (2), to rend
7673 shâbath (1), to repose; to desist

RIDDANCE
3615 kâlâh (1), to cease, be finished, perish
3617 kâlâh (1), complete destruction

RIDDEN
7392 râkab (1), to ride

RIDDLE
2420 chîydâh (9), puzzle; conundrum; maxim

RIDE
7392 râkab (20), to ride

RIDER
7392 râkab (7), to ride

RIDERS
7392 râkab (5), to ride

RIDETH
7392 râkab (7), to ride

RIDGES
8525 telem (1), bank or terrace

RIDING
7392 râkab (10), to ride

RIE
3698 kuççemeth (2), spelt

RIFLED
8155 shâçaç (1), to plunder, ransack

RIGHT
541 'âman (1), to take the right hand road

571 'emeth (3), certainty, truth, trustworthiness
1353 gᵉullâh (1), blood relationship
3225 yâmîyn (136), right; south
3227 yᵉmîynîy (1), right
3231 yâman (4), to be right-handed
3233 yᵉmânîy (31), right
3474 yâshar (2), to be straight; to make right
3476 yôsher (2), right
3477 yâshâr (52), straight
3559 kûwn (4), to render sure, proper
3651 kên (3), just; right
3787 kâshêr (1), to be straight or right
3788 kishrôwn (1), success; advantage
4334 mîyshôwr (1), plain; justice
4339 mêyshâr (3), straightness; rectitude
4941 mishpâṭ (19), verdict; decree; justice
5227 nôkach (2), forward, in behalf of
5228 nâkôach (2), equitable, correct
5229 nᵉkôchâh (2), integrity; truth
6227 'âshân (1), smoke
6437 pânâh (1), to turn, to face
6440 pânîym (1), face; front
6664 tsedeq (3), right
6666 tsᵉdâqâh (9), rightness
1188 dĕxiŏs (53), right
1342 dikaiŏs (5), equitable, holy
1849 ĕxŏusia (2), authority, power, right
2117 ĕuthus (3), at once, immediately
3723 ŏrthōs (1), rightly
4993 sōphrŏnĕō (2), to be in a right state of mind

RIGHTEOUS
3477 yâshâr (8), straight
6662 tsaddîyq (166), just
6663 tsâdaq (8), to be, make right
6664 tsedeq (9), right
6666 tsᵉdâqâh (3), rightness
1341 dikaiŏkrisia (1), proper judgment
1342 dikaiŏs (39), equitable, holy
1343 dikaiŏsunē (1), equity, justification

RIGHTEOUSLY
4334 mîyshôwr (1), plain; justice
4339 mêyshâr (1), straightness; rectitude
6664 tsedeq (3), right
6666 tsᵉdâqâh (1), rightness
1346 dikaiŏs (2), equitably

RIGHTEOUSNESS
6663 tsâdaq (1), to be, make right

6664 tsedeq (78), *right*
6665 tsidqâh (Ch.) (1), *beneficence*
6666 tsᵉdâqâh (124), *rightness*
1343 dikaiŏsunē (91), *equity, justification*
1345 dikaiŏma (4), *equitable deed; statute*
1346 dikaiŏs (1), *equitably*
2118 ĕuthutēs (1), *rectitude, uprightness*

RIGHTEOUSNESS'
6664 tsedeq (1), *right*
6666 tsᵉdâqâh (1), *rightness*
1343 dikaiŏsunē (2), *equity, justification*

RIGHTEOUSNESSES
6666 tsᵉdâqâh (3), *rightness*

RIGHTLY
3588 kîy (1), *for, that because*
3723 ŏrthōs (3), *rightly*

RIGOUR
6531 perek (5), *severity*

RIMMON
7417 Rimmôwn (14), *pomegranate*

RIMMON-PAREZ
7428 Rimmôn Perets (2), *pomegranate of* (the) *breach*

RING
2885 ṭabba'ath (9), *ring; signet ring* for sealing
1146 daktuliŏs (1), *finger-ring*
5554 chrusŏdaktuliŏs (1), *gold-ringed*

RINGLEADER
4414 prōtŏstatēs (1), *leader, ring leader*

RINGS
1354 gab (2), *mounded or rounded: top or rim*
1550 gâlîyl (2), *curtain ring*
2885 ṭabba'ath (39), *ring; signet ring* for sealing

RINGSTRAKED
6124 'âqôd (7), *striped, streaked animals*

RINNAH
7441 Rinnâh (1), *shout*

RINSED
7857 shâṭaph (3), *to inundate, cleanse*

RIOT
810 asŏtia (2), *profligacy, debauchery*
5172 truphē (1), *luxury or debauchery*

RIOTING
2970 kōmŏs (1), *carousal, reveling, orgy*

RIOTOUS
2151 zâlal (2), *to be loose morally, worthless*
811 asŏtōs (1), *with debauchery*

RIP
1234 bâqa' (1), *to cleave, break, tear open*

RIPE
1310 bâshal (2), *to boil up, cook; to ripen*
187 akmazŏ (1), *to be mature, be ripe*
3583 xērainō (1), *to shrivel, to mature*

RIPENING
1580 gâmal (1), *to benefit or requite; to wean*

RIPHATH
7384 Rîyphath (2), *Riphath*

RIPPED
1234 bâqa' (3), *to cleave, break, tear open*

RISE
2224 zârach (1), *to rise; to be bright*
5927 'âlâh (6), *to ascend, be high, mount*
6965 qûwm (76), *to rise*
6966 qûwm (Ch.) (1), *to rise*
7925 shâkam (5), *to load up,* i.e. *to start early*
8618 tᵉqôwmēm (1), *opponent*
305 anabainō (1), *to go up, rise*
386 anastasis (1), *resurrection from death*
393 anatĕllō (2), *to cause to arise*
450 anistēmi (23), *to rise; to come back to life*
1453 ĕgĕirō (23), *to waken,* i.e. *to rouse*
1881 ĕpanistamai (2), *to stand up on*

RISEN
1342 gâ'âh (1), *to rise; to grow tall; be majestic*
2224 zârach (2), *to rise; to be bright*
3318 yâtsâ' (1), *to go, bring out*
6965 qûwm (16), *to rise*
393 anatĕllō (1), *to cause to arise*
450 anistēmi (6), *to rise; to come back to life*
1453 ĕgĕirō (22), *to waken,* i.e. *to rouse*
4891 sunĕgĕirō (2), *to raise up with*

RISEST
6965 qûwm (2), *to rise*

RISETH
2224 zârach (2), *to rise; to be bright*
5927 'âlâh (1), *to ascend, be high, mount*
6965 qûwm (9), *to rise*
7837 shachar (1), *dawn*
1453 ĕgĕirō (1), *to waken,* i.e. *rouse*

RISING
510 'alqûwm (1), *resistlessness*
2225 zerach (1), *rising of light, dawning*

4217 mizrâch (8), *place of sunrise; east*
5927 'âlâh (1), *to ascend, be high, mount*
6965 qûwm (1), *to rise*
7012 qîymâh (1), *arising*
7613 sᵉ'êth (7), *elevation; swelling*
7836 shâchar (1), *to search for*
7925 shâkam (14), *to load up, to start early*
305 anabainō (1), *to rise*
386 anastasis (1), *resurrection from death*
393 anatĕllō (1), *to cause to arise*
450 anistēmi (1), *to rise; to come back to life*

RISSAH
7446 Riççâh (2), *ruin*

RITES
2708 chuqqâh (1), *to delineate*

RITHMAH
7575 Rithmâh (2), *broom tree*

RIVER
180 'ûwbâl (3), *stream*
2975 yᵉ'ôr (35), *Nile River; Tigris River*
3105 yûwbal (1), *stream*
5103 nᵉhar (Ch.) (14), *river; Euphrates River*
5104 nâhâr (66), *stream; Nile; Euphrates; Tigris*
5158 nachal (46), *valley*
4215 pŏtamŏs* (6), *current, brook*

RIVER'S
2975 yᵉ'ôr (3), *Nile River; Tigris River*
5104 nâhâr (1), *stream; Nile; Euphrates; Tigris*

RIVERS
650 'âphîyq (10), *valley; stream; mighty, strong*
2975 yᵉ'ôr (15), *Nile River; Tigris River*
5103 nᵉhar (Ch.) (9), *river; Euphrates River*
5104 nâhâr (22), *stream; Nile; Euphrates; Tigris*
5158 nachal (8), *valley*
6388 peleg (8), *small irrigation channel*
6390 pᵉlaggâh (1), *gully*
8585 tᵉ'âlâh (1), *irrigation channel*
4215 pŏtamŏs* (3), *current, brook*

RIZPAH
7532 Ritspâh (4), *hot stone; pavement*

ROAD
6584 pâshaṭ (1), *to strip,* i.e. *unclothe, plunder*

ROAR
1993 hâmâh (6), *to be in great commotion*
5098 nâham (2), *to growl, groan*
6873 tsârach (1), *to whoop*
7481 râ'am (2), *to crash thunder; to irritate*

7580 shâ'ag (12), *to rumble or moan*

ROARED
1993 hâmâh (1), *to be in great commotion*
7580 shâ'ag (4), *to rumble or moan*

ROARETH
1993 hâmâh (1), *to be in great commotion*
7580 shâ'ag (1), *to rumble or moan*
3455 mukaŏmai* (1), *to roar*

ROARING
1897 hâgâh (1), *to murmur, utter a sound*
5098 nâham (1), *to growl, groan*
5099 naham (2), *snarl, growl*
5100 nᵉhâmâh (1), *snarling, growling*
7580 shâ'ag (2), *to rumble or moan*
7581 shᵉ'âgâh (6), *rumbling or moan*
2278 ēchĕō* (1), *to reverberate, ring out*
5612 ōruŏmai* (1), *to roar*

ROARINGS
7581 shᵉ'âgâh (1), *rumbling or moan*

ROAST
1310 bâshal (1), *to boil up, cook; to ripen*
6740 tsâlâh (1), *to roast*
6748 tsâlîy (3), *roasted*

ROASTED
1310 bâshal (1), *to boil up, cook; to ripen*
6740 tsâlâh (1), *to roast*
7033 qâlâh (1), *to toast*

ROASTETH
740 'Ărî'êl (1), *Lion of God*
2760 chârak (1), *to catch*

ROB
962 bâzaz (3), *to plunder, take booty*
1497 gâzal (2), *to rob*
6906 qâba' (1), *to defraud, rob*
7921 shâkôl (1), *to miscarry*
8154 shâçâh (1), *to plunder*

ROBBED
962 bâzaz (4), *to plunder, take booty*
1497 gâzal (1), *to rob*
5100 nᵉhâmâh (1), *snarling, growling*
5749 'ûwd (1), *to encompass, restore*
6906 qâba' (2), *to defraud, rob*
7909 shakkuwl (2), *bereaved*
8154 shâçâh (1), *to plunder*
4813 sulaŏ* (1), *to despoil, rob*

ROBBER
6530 pᵉrîyts (1), *violent*

English

ROBBERS
6782 tsammîym (2), *noose, snare*
3027 lēₐstēs (2), *brigand*

ROBBERS
962 bâzaz (1), to *plunder, take booty*
6530 pᵉrîyts (3), *violent*
7703 shâdad (2), to *ravage*
2417 hiĕrŏsulŏs (1), *temple-despoiler*
3027 lēₐstēs (2), *brigand*

ROBBERY
1498 gâzêl (3), *robbery, stealing*
6503 Parbâr (1), *Parbar or Parvar*
7701 shôd (2), *violence, ravage, destruction*
725 harpagmŏs (1), *plunder*

ROBBETH
1497 gâzal (1), to *rob*

ROBE
145 'eder (1), *mantle; splendor*
155 'addereth (1), *large; splendid*
3301 Yiphdᵉyâh (1), *Jehovah will liberate*
4598 mᵉ'îyl (17), *outer garment or robe*
2066 ĕsthēs (1), to *clothe*
2440 himatiŏn (2), to *put on clothes*
4749 stŏlē (1), *long-fitting gown*
5511 chlamus (2), *military cloak*

ROBES
899 beged (4), *clothing; treachery or pillage*
4598 mᵉ'îyl (2), *outer garment or robe*
4749 stŏlē (5), *long-fitting gown*

ROBOAM
4497 Rhŏbŏam (2), *people has enlarged*

ROCK
2496 challâmîysh (1), *flint, flinty rock*
4581 mâ'ôwz (1), *fortified place; defense*
5553 çela' (44), *craggy rock; fortress*
5558 çeleph (2), *distortion; viciousness*
6697 tsûwr (56), *rock*
4073 pĕtra (13), *mass of rock*

ROCKS
3710 kêph (2), *hollow rock*
5553 çela' (10), *craggy rock; fortress*
6697 tsûwr (7), *rock*
4073 pĕtra (3), *mass of rock*
5138+5117 trachus (1), *uneven, jagged, rocky*

ROD
2415 chôṭer (2), *twig; shoot of a plant*
4294 maṭṭeh (42), *tribe; rod, scepter; club*

ROD
4731 maqqêl (2), *shoot; stick; staff*
7626 shêbeṭ (34), *stick; clan, family*
4464 rhabdŏs (6), *stick, rod*

RODE
7392 râkab (15), to *ride*

RODS
4294 maṭṭeh (8), *tribe; rod, scepter; club*
4731 maqqêl (6), *shoot; stick; staff*
4463 rhabdizŏ (1), to *strike with a stick*

ROE
3280 ya'ălâh (1), *ibex*
6643 tsᵉbîy (6), *gazelle*

ROEBUCK
6643 tsᵉbîy (4), *gazelle*

ROEBUCKS
6643 tsᵉbîy (1), *gazelle*

ROES
6643 tsᵉbîy (3), *gazelle*
6646 tsᵉbîyâh (2), *gazelle*

ROGELIM
7274 Rŏgᵉlîym (2), *fullers as tramping the cloth*

ROHGAH
7303 Rôwhăgâh (1), *outcry*

ROLL
1549 gillâyôwn (1), *tablet for writing; mirror*
1556 gâlal (4), to *roll; to commit*
4039 mᵉgillâh (14), *roll, scroll*
4040 mᵉgillâh (Ch.) (7), *roll, scroll*
6428 pâlash (1), to *roll in dust*
617 apŏkuliŏ (1), to *roll away, roll back*

ROLLED
1556 gâlal (6), to *roll; to commit*
617 apŏkuliŏ (3), to *roll away, roll back*
1507 hĕilissŏ (1), to *roll, coil or wrap*
4351 prŏskuliŏ (2), to *roll towards*

ROLLER
2848 chittûwl (1), *bandage for a wound*

ROLLETH
1556 gâlal (1), to *roll*

ROLLING
1534 galgal (1), *wheel; something round*

ROLLS
5609 çᵉphar (Ch.) (1), *book*

ROMAMTI-EZER
7320 Rôwmamtîy 'Ezer (2), *I have raised up a help*

ROMAN
4514 Rhŏmaiŏs (5), *Roman; of Rome*

ROMANS
4514 Rhŏmaiŏs (7), *Roman; of Rome*

ROME
4516 Rhŏmē (15), *strength*

ROOF
1406 gâg (11), *roof; top*
2441 chêk (5), *area of mouth*
6982 qôwrâh (1), *rafter; roof*
4721 stĕgē (3), *roof*

ROOFS
1406 gâg (2), *roof; top*

ROOM
4725 mâqôwm (3), *general locality, place*
4800 merchâb (1), *open space; liberty*
7337 râchab (2), to *broaden*
8478 tachath (11), *bottom; underneath*
473 anti (1), *instead of, because of*
508 anŏgĕŏn (1), *dome or a balcony*
1240 diadŏchŏs (1), *successor in office*
4411 prŏtŏklisia (1), *pre-eminence at meals*
5117 tŏpŏs (5), *place*
5253 hupĕrō̥ŏn (1), *upper room*
5362 philandrŏs (1), *affectionate as a wife to her husband*

ROOMS
7064 qên (1), *nest; nestlings; chamber*
8478 tachath (2), *bottom; underneath; in lieu of*
4411 prŏtŏklisia (4), *pre-eminence at meals*

ROOT
5428 nâthash (2), to *tear away, be uprooted*
8327 shârash (7), to *root, insert; to uproot*
8328 sheresh (17), *root*
1610 ĕkrizŏŏ (2), to *uproot*
4491 rhiza (15), *root*

ROOTED
5255 nâçach (1), to *tear away*
5423 nâthaq (1), to *tear off*
5428 nâthash (1), to *tear away, be uprooted*
6131 'âqar (1), to *pluck up roots; to hamstring*
8327 shârash (1), to *root, insert; to uproot*
1610 ĕkrizŏŏ (1), to *uproot*
4492 rhizŏŏ (2), to *root; to become stable*

ROOTS
5428 nâthash (1), to *tear away, be uprooted*
6132 'ăqar (Ch.) (1), to *pluck up roots*
8328 sheresh (13), *root*

ROUND
8330 shôresh (Ch.) (3), *root*
1610 ĕkrizŏŏ (1), to *uproot*
4491 rhiza (1), *root*

ROPE
5688 'ăbôth (1), *entwined things: a string, wreath*

ROPES
2256 chebel (3), *band*
5688 'ăbôth (2), *entwined things: a string, wreath*
4979 schŏiniŏn (1), *withe or tie or rope*

ROSE
2224 zârach (3), to *rise; to be bright*
2261 chăbatstseleth (2), *meadow-saffron*
5927 'âlâh (2), to *ascend, be high, mount*
6965 qûwm (71), to *rise*
7925 shâkam (29), to *load up, to start early*
305 anabainŏ (1), to *go up, rise*
450 anistēmi (18), to *rise; to come back to life*
1453 ĕgĕirŏ (3), to *waken, i.e. rouse*
1817 ĕxanistēmi (1), to *beget, raise up*
4911 sunĕphistēmi (1), to *resist or assault jointly*

ROSH
7220 Rô'sh (1), *head*

ROT
5307 nâphal (3), to *fall*
7537 râqab (2), to *decay by worm-eating*

ROTTEN
4418 mâlâch (2), *rag or old garment*
5685 'âbash (1), to *dry up*
7538 râqâb (1), *decay by caries*
7539 riqqâbôwn (1), *decay by caries*

ROTTENNESS
4716 maq (1), *putridity, stench*
7538 râqâb (4), *decay by caries*

ROUGH
386 'êythân (1), *never-failing; eternal*
5569 çâmâr (1), *shaggy*
7186 qâsheh (1), *severe*
7406 rekeç (1), *ridge*
8163 sâ'îyr (1), *shaggy; he-goat; goat idol*
8181 sê'âr (1), *tossed hair*
5138 trachus (1), *uneven, jagged, rocky, reefy*

ROUGHLY
5794 'az (1), *strong, vehement, harsh*
7186 qâsheh (5), *severe*

ROUND
1754 dûwr (1), *circle; ball; pile*
2636 chaçpaç (1), to *peel; to be scale-like*
3803 kâthar (2), to *enclose, besiege; to wait*

4524 mêçab (3), *divan couch; around*
5362 nâqaph (4), to *strike; to surround*
5437 çâbab (7), to *surround*
5439 çâbîyb (254), *circle; environs; around*
5469 çahar (1), *roundness*
5696 'âgôl (6), *circular*
5921 'al (2), *above, over*
7720 sahârôn (1), *round pendant or crescent*
2943 kuklôthĕn (10), *from the circle*
2944 kuklŏō (2), to *surround, encircle*
3840 pantôthĕn (1), *from, on all* sides
4015 pĕriastraptō (2), to *shine around*
4017 pĕriblĕpō (5), to *look all around*
4026 pĕriistēmi (1), to *stand around; to avoid*
4033 pĕrikuklŏō (1), to *blockade completely*
4034 pĕrilampō (2), to *shine all around*
4038 pĕrix (1), all *around*
4039 pĕriŏikĕō (1), to be *a neighbor*
4066 pĕrichōrŏs (9), *surrounding country*

ROUSE
6965 qûwm (1), to *rise*

ROW
2905 ṭûwr (14), *row, course* built into a *wall*
4635 ma'ăreketh (2), *pile* of loaves, *arrangement*
5073 nidbâk (Ch.) (1), *layer, row*

ROWED
2864 châthar (1), to *row*
1643 ĕlaunō (1), to *push*

ROWERS
7751 shûwṭ (1), to *travel, roam*

ROWING
1643 ĕlaunō (1), to *push*

ROWS
2905 ṭûwr (12), *row, course* built into a *wall*
2918 ṭîyrâh (1), *fortress; hamlet*
4634 ma'ărâkâh (1), *arrangement, row; pile*
5073 nidbâk (Ch.) (1), *layer, row*
8447 tôwr (1), *succession*

ROYAL
4410 mᵉlûwkâh (4), *realm, rulership*
4428 melek (2), *king*
4430 melek (Ch.) (1), *king*
4438 malkûwth (13), *rule; dominion*
4467 mamlâkâh (4), *royal dominion*
8237 shaphrûwr (1), *tapestry or canopy*
934 basilĕiŏs (1), *royal, kingly* in nature
937 basilikŏs (2), *befitting the sovereign*

RUBBING
5597 psōchō (1), to *rub* out grain kernels

RUBBISH
6083 'âphâr (2), *dust, earth, mud; clay,*

RUBIES
6443 pânîyn (6), (poss.) *round pearl*

RUDDER
4079 pēdaliŏn (1), *blade*

RUDDY
119 'âdam (1), to *red* in the face
132 'admônîy (3), *reddish, ruddy*

RUDE
2399 idiōtēs (1), not *initiated; untrained*

RUDIMENTS
4747 stŏichĕiŏn (2), *elementary* truths

RUE
4076 pēganŏn (1), *rue*

RUFUS
4504 Rhŏuphŏs (2), *red*

RUHAMAH
7355 râcham (1), to *be compassionate*

RUIN
4072 midcheh (1), *overthrow, downfall*
4288 mᵉchittâh (1), *ruin; consternation*
4383 mikshôwl (1), *obstacle; enticement*
4384 makshêlâh (1), *enticement*
4654 mappâlâh (2), *ruin*
4658 mappeleth (2), *down-fall; ruin; carcase*
6365 pîyd (1), *misfortune*
4485 rhēgma (1), *ruin*

RUINED
2040 hâraç (2), to *pull* down; *break, destroy*
3782 kâshal (1), to *totter, waver; to falter*

RUINOUS
4654 mappâlâh (1), *ruin*
5327 nâtsâh (2), to *be desolate, to lay waste*

RUINS
2034 hărîyçâh (1), *demolished, ruins*
4383 mikshôwl (1), *obstacle; enticement*
2679 kataskaptō (1), to *destroy, be ruined*

RULE
4427 mâlak (1), to *reign* as *king*
4475 memshâlâh (4), *rule; realm* or a *ruler*
4623 ma'tsâr (1), *self-control*
4910 mâshal (25), to *rule*
7287 râdâh (10), to *subjugate; to crumble*
7980 shâlaṭ (3), to *dominate,* i.e. *govern*
7981 shᵉlêṭ (Ch.) (1), to *dominate,* i.e. *govern*

7990 shallîyṭ (Ch.) (1), *premier, sovereign*
8323 sârar (3), to *have, exercise, get dominion*
746 archē (1), *first*
757 archō (1), to *rule, be first* in rank
1018 brabĕuō (1), to *govern; to prevail*
2233 hēgĕŏmai (3), to *lead,* i.e. *command*
2583 kanōn (4), *rule, standard*
4165 pŏimainō (4), to *tend* as a *shepherd*
4291 prŏïstēmi (2), to *preside; to practice*

RULED
4474 mimshâl (1), *ruler; dominion, rule*
4910 mâshal (5), to *rule*
5401 nâshaq (1), to *kiss; to equip* with weapons
7287 râdâh (3), to *subjugate; to crumble*
7990 shallîyṭ (Ch.) (1), *premier, sovereign*
8199 shâphaṭ (1), to *judge*

RULER
834+5921 'ăsher (1), *who, which, what, that*
4910 mâshal (13), to *rule*
5057 nâgîyd (19), *commander, official*
5387 nâsîy' (3), *leader; rising mist, fog*
6485 pâqad (2), to *visit, care for, count*
7101 qâtsîyn (2), *magistrate; leader*
7287 râdâh (1), to *subjugate; to crumble*
7860 shôṭêr (1), to *write; official* who is a *scribe*
7981 shᵉlêṭ (Ch.) (4), to *dominate,* i.e. *govern*
7989 shallîyṭ (1), *prince* or *warrior*
7990 shallîyṭ (Ch.) (2), *premier, sovereign*
8269 sar (10), *head person, ruler*
752 archisunagōgŏs (6), *director of the synagogue* services
755 architriklinŏs (1), *director of the entertainment*
758 archōn (9), *first*
2525 kathistēmi (6), to *designate, constitute*

RULER'S
4910 mâshal (1), to *rule*
758 archōn (1), *first*

RULERS
4043 mâgên (1), small *shield (buckler)*
4910 mâshal (4), to *rule*
5057 nâgîyd (1), *commander, official*
5387 nâsîy' (3), *leader; rising mist, fog*
5461 çâgân (16), *prefect*
6485 pâqad (1), to *visit, care for, count*
7101 qâtsîyn (2), *magistrate; leader*
7218 rô'sh (2), *head*

7336 râzan (1), *honorable*
7984 shiltôwn (Ch.) (2), *official*
8269 sar (21), *ruler*
752 archisunagōgŏs (2), *director of the synagogue services*
758 archōn (14), *first*
2232 hēgĕmōn (2), *chief*
2888 kŏsmŏkratōr (1), *world-ruler*
4178 pŏllakis (2), *many times,* i.e. *frequently*

RULEST
4910 mâshal (2), to *rule*

RULETH
4910 mâshal (7), to *rule*
7300 rûwd (1), to *ramble*
7980 shâlaṭ (4), to *dominate,* i.e. *govern*
4291 prŏïstēmi (2), to *preside; to practice*

RULING
4910 mâshal (2), to *rule*
4291 prŏïstēmi (1), to *preside; to practice*

RUMAH
7316 Rûwmâh (1), *height*

RUMBLING
1995 hâmôwn (1), *noise, tumult; many, crowd*

RUMOUR
8052 shᵉmûw'âh (8), *announcement*
3056 lŏgŏs (1), *word, matter, thing*

RUMOURS
189 akŏē (2), *hearing; thing heard*

RUMP
451 'alyâh (5), fat *tail*

RUN
935 bôw' (1), to *go, come*
1556 gâlal (1), to *roll; to commit*
1980 hâlak (3), to *walk; live a certain way*
2100 zûwb (1), to *flow freely, gush*
3212 yâlak (1), to *walk; to live; to carry*
3381 yârad (6), to *descend*
6293 pâga' (1), to *impinge*
6805 tsâ'ad (1), to *pace*
7323 rûwts (36), to *run*
7325 rûwr (1), to *emit a fluid*
7751 shûwṭ (6), to *travel, roam*
8264 shâqaq (2), to *seek*
4936 suntrĕchō (1), to *rush together*
5143 trĕchō (8), to *run* or *walk hastily; to strive*

RUNNEST
7323 rûwts (1), to *run*

RUNNETH
935 bôw' (1), to *go, come*
3381 yârad (2), to *descend*
7310 rᵉvâyâh (1), *satisfaction*
7323 rûwts (4), to *run*

English

RUNNING
1632 ĕkchĕō (1), *to pour
forth; to bestow*
5143 trĕchō (2), *to run*

RUNNING
1980 hâlak (1), *to walk*
2100 zûwb (2), *to
discharge; waste away*
2416 chay (7), *alive; raw*
4794 mᵉrûwtsâh (2), *race*
4944 mashshâq (1), rapid
traversing motion
5140 nâzal (1), *to drip*
7323 rûwts (6), *to run*
1998 ĕpisuntrĕchō (1), *to
hasten together upon*
4370 prŏstrĕchō (2), *to
hasten by running*
5143 trĕchō (1), *to run*
5240 hupĕrĕkchunō (1),
to overflow
5295 hupŏtrĕchō (1), *to
run under*

RUSH
100 'agmôwn (2), *rush*
1573 gôme' (1), *papyrus*
7582 shâ'âh (1), *to moan*

RUSHED
6584 pâshaṭ (2), *to strip*
3729 hŏrmaō (1), *to dash*

RUSHES
1573 gôme' (1), *papyrus*

RUSHETH
7857 shâṭaph (1), *to gush*

RUSHING
7494 ra'ash (3), *uproar*
7582 shâ'âh (1), *to moan*
7588 shâ'ôwn (2), *uproar*
5342 phĕrō (1), *to bear*

RUST
1035 brōsis (2), *food; rust*
2447 iŏs (1), *corrosion*

RUTH
7327 Rûwth (12), *friend*
4503 Rhŏuth (1), *friend*

SABACHTHANI
4518 sabachthani (2),
thou hast left me

SABAOTH
4519 sabaōth (2), *armies*

SABBATH
7673 shâbath (1), *to
repose; to desist*
7676 shabbâth (73), *day
of rest*
7677 shabbᵊâthôwn (3),
special holiday
4315 prŏsabbatŏn (1),
Sabbath-eve
4521 sabbatŏn (59), *day
of repose*

SABBATHS
4868 mishbâth (1),
cessation; destruction
7676 shabbâth (34), *day
of rest*

SABEANS
5433 çâbâ' (1), *to quaff*
5436 Çᵉbâ'îy (1), *Sebaite*
7614 Shᵉbâ' (1), *Sheba*
7615 Shᵉbâ'îy (1),
Shebaïte

SABTA
5454 Çabtâ' (1), *Sabta or
Sabtah*

SABTAH
5454 Çabtâ' (1), *Sabta or
Sabtah*

SABTECHA
5455 Çabtᵉkâ' (1),
Sabteca

SABTECHAH
5455 Çabtᵉkâ' (1),
Sabteca

SACAR
7940 Sâkar (2),
recompense

SACK
572 'amtêchath (5), *sack*
8242 saq (4), *bag*

SACK'S
572 'amtêchath (3), *sack*

SACKBUT
5443 çabbᵉkâ' (Ch.) (4),
lyre musical instrument

SACKCLOTH
8242 saq (41), coarse
cloth or *sacking; bag*
4526 sakkŏs (4),
sack-cloth

SACKCLOTHES
8242 saq (1), coarse cloth
or *sacking; bag*

SACKS
572 'amtêchath (6), *sack*
3672 Kinnᵉrôwth (1),
(poss.) *harp*-shaped
8242 saq (1), *bag*

SACKS'
572 'amtêchath (1), *sack*

SACRIFICE
2076 zâbach (48), *to
(sacrifically) slaughter*
2077 zebach (102),
animal *flesh; sacrifice*
2282 chag (2), solemn
festival
4503 minchâh (5),
tribute; offering
6213 'âsâh (1), *to make*
7133 qorbân (1),
sacrificial *present*
1494 ĕidōlŏthutŏn (3),
idolatrous offering
2378 thusia (17), *sacrifice*
2380 thuō (4), *to sacrifice*

SACRIFICED
2076 zâbach (29), *to
(sacrifically) slaughter*
6213 'âsâh (1), *to make*
1494 ĕidōlŏthutŏn (2),
idolatrous offering
2380 thuō (1), *to kill; to
butcher; to sacrifice*

SACRIFICEDST
2076 zâbach (1), *to
(sacrifically) slaughter*

SACRIFICES
1685 dᵉbach (Ch.) (1),
animal *sacrifice*
2077 zebach (53), animal
flesh; sacrifice
2282 chag (1), solemn
festival
2378 thusia (12),
sacrifice, offering

SACRIFICETH
2076 zâbach (6), *to
(sacrifically) slaughter*

SACRIFICING
2076 zâbach (2), *to
(sacrifically) slaughter*

SACRILEGE
2416 hiĕrŏsulĕō (1), *to be
a temple-robber*

SAD
2196 zâ'aph (1), *to be
angry*
3510 kâ'ab (1), *to feel
pain; to grieve; to spoil*
3512 kâ'âh (1), *to
despond; to deject*
5620 çar (1), *sullen*
7451 ra' (2), *bad; evil*
7489 râ'a' (1), *to be good
for nothing*
4659 skuthrōpŏs (2),
gloomy, mournful
4768 stugnazŏ (1), *to be
overcast; somber*

SADDLE
2280 châbash (3), *to
wrap firmly, bind*
4817 merkâb (1), *chariot;
seat in chariot*

SADDLED
2280 châbash (10), *to
wrap firmly, bind*

SADDUCEES
4523 Saddŏukaiŏs (14),
of Tsadok

SADLY
7451 ra' (1), *bad; evil*

SADNESS
7455 rôa' (1), *badness*

SADOC
4524 Sadōk (1), *just*

SAFE
983 beṭach (2), *safety*
3467 yâsha' (1), *to make
safe, free*
6403 pâlaṭ (1), *to slip out,
i.e. escape; to deliver*
7682 sâgab (2), *to be safe*
7965 shâlôwm (3), *safe*
809 aschēmōn (1),
inelegant, indecent
1295 diasōzō (2), *to cure,
preserve, rescue*
5198 hugiainō (1), *to
have sound health*

SAFEGUARD
4931 mishmereth (1),
watch, sentry, post

SAFELY
983 beṭach (17), *safety*
7965 shâlôwm (1), *safe*
806 asphalōs (2), *securely*

SAFETY
983 beṭach (9), *safety*
3468 yesha' (3), *liberty,
deliverance, prosperity*
7951 shâlâh (1), *to be
secure or successful*
8668 tᵉshûw'âh (4),
rescue, deliverance
803 asphalĕia (2),
security; certainty

SAFFRON
3750 karkôm (1), *crocus*

SAID
559 'âmar (2772), *to say*

SAID
560 'ămar (Ch.) (41), *to
say*
1696 dâbar (85), *to say*
1697 dâbâr (8), *word;
matter; thing*
4448 mâlal (1), *to speak*
4449 mᵉlal (Ch.) (1), *to
speak, say*
5002 nᵉ'ûm (9), *oracle*
6030 'ânâh (1), *to respond*
7121 qârâ' (1), *to call out*
669 apŏphthĕggŏmai (1),
declare, address
2036 ĕpō (756), *to speak*
2046 ĕrĕō (21), *to utter*
2063 ĕruthrŏs (3), *red*
2980 lalĕō (7), *to talk*
3004 lĕgō (200), *to say*
4280 prŏĕrĕō (4), *to say
already, predict*
4483 rhĕō (15), *to utter*
5346 phēmi (48), *to make
known one's thoughts*

SAIDST
559 'âmar (20), *to say*
1696 dâbar (1), *to speak*
2046 ĕrĕō (1), *to utter*

SAIL
5251 nêç (2), *flag; signal*
321 anagō (1), *to sail*
636 apŏplĕō (1), *to set
sail, sail away*
3896 paraplĕō (1), *to sail
near*
4126 plĕō (2), *to travel in
a ship*
4632 skĕuŏs (1), *vessel,
implement, equipment*

SAILED
321 anagō (2), *to lead
up; to sail away*
636 apŏplĕō (3), *to set
sail, sail away*
1020 braduplŏĕō (1), *to
sail slowly*
1277 diaplĕō (1), *to sail
through, across*
1602 ĕkplĕō (3), *to depart
by ship*
3881 paralĕgŏmai (1), *to
sail past*
4126 plĕō (2), *to travel in
a ship*
5284 hupŏplĕō (2), *to sail
under the lee of*

SAILING
1276 diapĕraō (1), *to
cross over*
4126 plĕō (1), *to travel in
a ship*
4144 plŏŏs (1),
navigation, voyage

SAILORS
3492 nautēs (1), *sailor*

SAINT
6918 qâdôwsh (3), *sacred*
40 hagiŏs (1), *holy*

SAINTS
2623 châçîyd (19),
religiously pious, godly
6918 qâdôwsh (9), *sacred*
6922 qaddîysh (Ch.) (6),
sacred
6944 qôdesh (1), *sacred*
40 hagiŏs (60), *holy*

SAINTS'
40 hagiŏs (1), *holy*

SAITH
559 'âmar (581), to *say*
1696 dâbar (7), to *speak*
5001 nâ'am (10), to *utter*
as an oracle
5002 nᵉ'ûm (353), *oracle*
6310 peh (1), *mouth*
2036 ĕpō (1), to *speak*
2980 lalĕō (2), to *talk*
3004 lĕgō (297), to *say*
5346 phēmi (5), to *make known* one's thoughts

SAKE
182 'ôwdôwth (1), on *account of; because*
1558 gâlâl (3), on *account of, because of*
1697 dâbâr (2), *word; matter; thing*
4616 ma'an (45), *on account of*
5668 'âbûwr (15), on *account of*
7068 qin'âh (1), *jealousy*
7945 shel (1), on *account of; whatsoever*
8478 tachath (2), *bottom; underneath; in lieu of*
1722 ĕn (1), *because of*
1752 hĕnĕka (14), *on account of*

SAKES
1558 gâlâl (1), on *account of, because of*
1697 dâbâr (1), *matter*
1701 dibrâh (Ch.) (1), *because, on account of*
5668 'âbûwr (1), on *account of*
5921 'al (3), *above, over*
6616 pâthîyl (6), *twine*

SALA
4527 Sala (1), *spear*

SALAH
7974 Shelach (6), *spear*

SALAMIS
4529 Salamis (1), *surge*

SALATHIEL
7597 Shᵉ'altîy'êl (1), *I have asked God*
4528 Salathiĕl (3), *I have asked God*

SALCAH
5548 Çalkâh (2), *walking*

SALCHAH
5548 Çalkâh (2), *walking*

SALE
4465 mimkâr (3), *merchandise*

SALEM
8004 Shâlêm (2), *peaceful*
4532 Salĕm (2), *peaceful*

SALIM
4530 Salĕim (1), (poss.) *waver*

SALLAI
5543 Çallûw (2), *weighed*

SALLU
5543 Çallûw (3), *weighed*

SALMA
8007 Salmâ' (4), *clothing*

SALMON
6756 Tsalmôwn (1), *shady*
8009 Salmâh (1), *clothing*
8012 Salmôwn (1), *investiture*
4533 Salmōn (3), *investiture*

SALMONE
4534 Salmōnē (1), (poss.) *surge on the shore*

SALOME
4539 Salōmē (2), *peace*

SALT
4416 mᵉlach (Ch.) (2), *salt*
4417 melach (27), *salt*
4420 mᵉlêchâh (1), *salted* land, i.e. a *desert*
5898 'Îyr ham-Melach (1), *city of* (the) *salt*
217 halas (8), *salt*
251 hals (1), *salt*
252 halukŏs (1), *salty*

SALTED
4414 mâlach (1), to *salt*
233 halizō (3), to *salt*

SALTNESS
1096+358 ginŏmai (1), to *be, become*

SALTPITS
4417 melach (1), *salt*

SALU
5543 Çallûw (1), *weighed*

SALUTATION
783 aspasmŏs (6), *greeting*

SALUTATIONS
783 aspasmŏs (1), *greeting*

SALUTE
1288 bârak (4), to *bless*
7592+7965 shâ'al (1), to *ask*
7965 shâlôwm (2), *safe; well; health, prosperity*
782 aspazŏmai (32), to *give salutation*

SALUTED
1288 bârak (1), to *bless*
7592+7965 shâ'al (3), to *ask*
782 aspazŏmai (5), to *give salutation*

SALUTETH
782 aspazŏmai (5), to *give salutation*

SALVATION
3444 yᵉshûw'âh (65), *deliverance; aid*
3467 yâsha' (3), to *make safe, free*
3468 yesha' (32), *liberty, deliverance, prosperity*
4190 môwshâ'âh (1), *deliverance*
8668 tᵉshûw'âh (17), *rescue, deliverance*
4991 sōtēria (40), *rescue*
4992 sōtēriŏn (5), *defender or defence*

SAMARIA
8111 Shōmᵉrown (109), *watch-station*

8115 Shomrayin (Ch.) (2), *watch-station*
4540 Samarĕia (13), *watch-station*

SAMARITAN
4541 Samarĕitēs (3), *inhabitant of Samaria*

SAMARITANS
8118 Shômᵉrônîy (1), *Shomeronite*
4541 Samarĕitēs (6), *inhabitant of Samaria*

SAME
428 'êl-leh (1), *these*
1459 gav (Ch.) (1), *middle*
1791 dêk (Ch.) (1), *this*
1797 dikkên (Ch.) (1), *this*
1931 hûw' (73), *this*
1933 hâvâ' (1), to *be*
1992 hêm (4), *they*
2063 zō'th (1), *this*
2088 zeh (9), *this or that*
6106 'etsem (6), *selfsame*
8478 tachath (1), *bottom*
846 autŏs (87), *he, she, it*
1565 ĕkĕinŏs (24), *that*
2532 kai (1), *even; also*
3673 hŏmŏtĕchnŏs (1), *of the same trade*
3748 hŏstis (1), *whoever*
3761 ŏudĕ (1), *neither*
3778 hŏutŏs (37), *this*
4954 sussōmŏs (1), *fellow-member*
5023 tauta (3), *these*
5026 tautē₁ (5), (*toward or of) this*
5126 tŏutŏn (2), to *this*
5129 tŏutō₁ (1), in *this*
5615 hōsautōs (1), in the *same way*

SAMGAR-NEBO
5562 Çamgar Nᵉbôw (1), *Samgar-Nebo*

SAMLAH
8072 Samlâh (4), *mantle*

SAMOS
4544 Samŏs (1), *Samus*

SAMOTHRACIA
4543 Samŏthra₁kē (1), *Samos of Thrace*

SAMSON
8123 Shimshôwn (35), *sunlight*
4546 Sampsōn (1), *sunlight*

SAMSON'S
8123 Shimshôwn (3), *sunlight*

SAMUEL
8050 Shᵉmûw'êl (135), *heard of God*
4545 Samŏuēl (3), *heard of God*

SANBALLAT
5571 Çanballaṭ (10), *Sanballat*

SANCTIFICATION
38 hagiasmŏs (5), state of *purity*

SANCTIFIED
6942 qâdâsh (46), to *be, make clean*
37 hagiazō (16), to *purify*

SANCTIFIETH
37 hagiazō (4), to *purify*

SANCTIFY
6942 qâdâsh (63), to *be, make clean*
37 hagiazō (6), to *purify*

SANCTUARIES
4720 miqdâsh (5), *sanctuary of deity*

SANCTUARY
4720 miqdâsh (64), *sanctuary of deity*
6944 qôdesh (68), *sacred*
39 hagiŏn (4), *sacred*

SAND
2344 chôwl (23), *sand*
285 ammŏs (5), *sand*

SANDALS
4547 sandaliŏn (2), *sandal*

SANG
6030 'ânâh (2), to *sing*
7442 rânan (1), to *shout for joy*
7891 shîyr (7), to *sing*
5214 humnĕō (1), to *celebrate God in song*

SANK
3381 yârad (1), to *descend*
6749 tsâlal (1), to *settle*

SANSANNAH
5578 Çançannâh (1), *bough*

SAPH
5593 Çaph (1), *dish*

SAPHIR
8208 Shâphîyr (1), *beautiful*

SAPPHIRA
4551 Sapphĕirē (1), *sapphire or lapis-lazuli*

SAPPHIRE
5601 çappîyr (8), *sapphire*
4552 sapphĕirŏs (1), *sapphire or lapis-lazuli*

SAPPHIRES
5601 çappîyr (3), *sapphire*

SARA
4564 Sarrha (1), *princess*

SARAH
8283 Sârâh (36), *princess*
8294 Serach (1), *superfluity*
4564 Sarrha (2), *princess*

SARAH'S
8283 Sârâh (2), *princess*
4564 Sarrha (1), *princess*

SARAI
8297 Sâray (16), *dominative*

SARAI'S
8297 Sâray (1), *dominative*

SARAPH
8315 Sâraph (1), *burning one, serpent*

SARDINE
4555 sardinŏs (1), *sard*

English

SARDIS
4554 Sardĕis (3), *Sardis*

SARDITES
5625 Çardîy (1), *Seredite*

SARDIUS
124 'ôdem (3), *ruby*
4556 sardiŏs (1), *sardian*

SARDONYX
4557 sardŏnux (1),
 sard-onyx

SAREPTA
4558 Sarĕpta (1),
 refinement

SARGON
5623 Çargôwn (1),
 Sargon

SARID
8301 Sârîyd (2), *survivor*

SARON
4565 Sarōn (1), *plain*

SARSECHIM
8310 Sarçᵉkîym (1),
 Sarsekim

SARUCH
4562 Sarŏuch (1), *tendril*

SAT
3427 yâshab (94), to *dwell*
8497 tâkâh (1), to *camp*
339 anakathizō (2), to *sit up*
345 anakĕimai (6), to *recline* at a meal
347 anaklinō (1), to *lean back, recline*
377 anapiptō (4), *lie down, lean back*
2516 kathĕzŏmai (4), to *sit down, be seated*
2521 kathēmai (43), to *sit down; to remain*
2523 kathizō (21), to *seat down, dwell*
2621 katakĕimai (3), to *lie down; recline*
2625 kataklinō (1), to *recline, take a place*
3869 parakathizō (1), to *sit down near, beside*
4775 sugkathēmai (2), to *seat oneself with*
4873 sunanakĕimai (8), to *recline with*

SATAN
7854 sâtân (18), *opponent*
4567 Satanas (34),
 accuser, i.e. the *Devil*

SATAN'S
4567 Satanas (1),
 accuser, i.e. the *Devil*

SATEST
3427 yâshab (2), to *settle*

SATIATE
7301 râvâh (1), to *slake*
7646 sâba' (1), to *fill*

SATIATED
7301 râvâh (1), to *slake*

SATISFACTION
3724 kôpher (2),
 redemption-price

SATISFIED
4390 mâlê' (1), to *fill*
7301 râvâh (1), to *slake*
7646 sâba' (36), *fill*

7649 sâbêa' (3), *satiated*

SATISFIEST
7646 sâba' (1), to *fill*

SATISFIETH
7646 sâba' (2), to *fill*
7654 sob'âh (1), *satiety*

SATISFY
4390 mâlê' (1), to *fill*
7301 râvâh (1), to *slake*
7646 sâba' (7), to *fill*
5526 chŏrtazō (1), to *supply food*

SATISFYING
7648 sôba' (1),
 satisfaction
4140 plēsmŏnē (1),
 gratification

SATISFED
7649 sâbêa' (1), *satiated*

SATYR
8163 sâ'îyr (1), *shaggy; he-goat; goat* idol

SATYRS
8163 sâ'îyr (1), *shaggy; he-goat; goat* idol

SAUL
7586 Shâ'ûwl (367), *asked*
4569 Saulŏs (23), *asked*

SAUL'S
7586 Shâ'ûwl (31), *asked*

SAVE
389 'ak (1), *surely; only*
518 'îm (1), *Oh that!*
657 'epheç (1), *end; no further*
1107 bil'ădêy (4), *except*
1115 biltîy (2), *except*
1115+518 biltîy (1), *not, except, without, unless*
2108 zûwlâh (6), *except*
2421 châyâh (21), to *live; to revive*
2425 châyay (1), to *live; to revive*
3444 yᵉshûw'âh (1), *deliverance; aid*
3467 yâsha' (106), to *make safe, free*
3588+518 kîy (12), *for, that because*
3861 lâhên (Ch.) (2), *therefore, except*
7535 raq (3), *although*
8104 shâmar (1), to *watch*
235 alla (2), *except*
1295 diasōzō (1), to *cure, preserve, rescue*
1508 ĕi mē (18), *if not*
2228 ē (1), *or; than*
3844 para (1), *besides*
4133 plēn (1), *save that*
4982 sōzō (41), to *deliver*

SAVED
2421 châyâh (8), to *live; to revive*
3467 yâsha' (35), to *make safe, free*
4422 mâlaṭ (1), to *escape*
5337 nâtsal (1), to *deliver*
8104 shâmar (1), to *watch*
1295 diasōzō (1), to *cure, preserve, rescue*

4982 sōzō (53), to *deliver*
4991 sōtēria (2), *rescue*
5442 phulassō (1), to *watch*, i.e. *be on guard*

SAVEST
3467 yâsha' (3), to *make safe, free*

SAVETH
3467 yâsha' (7), to *make safe, free*

SAVING
518 'îm (1), *Oh that!*
657 'epheç (1), *end; no further*
2421 châyâh (1), to *live; to revive*
3444 yᵉshûw'âh (2), *deliverance; aid*
3468 yesha' (1), *liberty, deliverance, prosperity*
1508 ĕi mē (2), *if not*
3924 parĕktŏs (1), *besides*
4047 pĕripŏiēsis (1), *preservation*
4991 sōtēria (1), *rescue*

SAVIOUR
3467 yâsha' (13), to *make safe, free*
4990 sōtēr (24), *Deliverer*

SAVIOURS
3467 yâsha' (2), to *make safe, free*

SAVOUR
6709 tsachănâh (1), *stench*
7381 rêyach (46), *odor*
2175 ĕuōdia (2), *aroma*
3471 mōrainō (2), to *become insipid*
3744 ŏsmē (4), *fragrance*

SAVOUREST
5426 phrŏnĕō (2), to *be mentally disposed*

SAVOURS
5208 nîychôwach (Ch.) (1), *pleasure*

SAVOURY
4303 maṭ'am (6), *delicacy*

SAW
2370 châzâ (Ch.) (9), to *gaze upon; to dream*
2372 châzâh (8), to *gaze at; to perceive*
4883 massôwr (1), *saw*
7200 râ'âh (306), to *see*
7805 shâzaph (1), to *scan*
991 blĕpō (9), to *look at*
1492 ĕidō (188), to *know*
1689 ĕmblĕpō (1), to *observe; to discern*
2147 hĕuriskō (1), to *find*
2300 thĕaŏmai (8), to *look closely at*
2334 thĕōrĕō (9), to *see*
3708 hŏraō (4), to *stare, see clearly; to discern*

SAWED
1641 gârar (1), to *saw*

SAWEST
2370 châzâ (Ch.) (7), to *gaze upon; to dream*
2372 châzâh (1), to *gaze at; to perceive*
7200 râ'âh (6), to *see*
1492 ĕidō (7), to *know*

SAWN
4249 prizō (1), to *saw* in *two*

SAWS
4050 mᵉgêrâh (3), *saw*

SAY
559 'âmar (573), to *say*
560 'âmar (Ch.) (2), to *say*
1696 dâbar (28), to *speak*
1697 dâbâr (1), *word*
4405 millâh (2), *word*
471 antĕpō (1), to *refute*
2036 ĕpō (66), to *speak*
2046 ĕrĕō (39), to *utter*
2980 lalĕō (6), to *talk*
3004 lĕgō (293), to *say*
3056 lŏgŏs (1), *word*
5335 phaskō (1), to *assert* a claim
5346 phēmi (6), to *make known* one's thoughts

SAYEST
559 'âmar (18), to *say*
2036 ĕpō (1), to *speak*
3004 lĕgō (20), to *say*

SAYING
559 'âmar (916), to *say*
560 'âmar (Ch.) (2), to *say*
1697 dâbâr (20), *word*
2420 chîydâh (1), *puzzle; conundrum; maxim*
2036 ĕpō (18), to *speak*
2981 lalia (1), *talk*
3004 lĕgō (380), to *say*
3007 lĕipō (5), to *fail*
3056 lŏgŏs (33), *word*
3058 lŏidŏrĕō (1), to *vilify, insult*
4487 rhēma (6), *utterance; matter*
5335 phaskō (1), to *assert*

SAYINGS
561 'êmer (2), *saying*
1697 dâbâr (5), *word*
2420 chîydâh (2), *puzzle; conundrum; maxim*
6310 peh (1), *mouth*
3004 lĕgō (1), to *say*
3056 lŏgŏs (16), *word*
4487 rhēma (3),
 utterance; matter

SCAB
1618 gârâb (1), *itching*
4556 miçpachath (3),
 scurf, rash
5597 çappachath (3),
 skin mange

SCABBARD
8593 ta'ar (1), *scabbard*

SCABBED
3217 yallepheth (2), *scurf*

SCAFFOLD
3595 kîyôwr (1), *caldron*

SCALES
650+4043 'âphîyq (1),
 valley; stream; mighty
6425 peleç (1), *balance*
7193 qasqeseth (7), *fish scales; coat of mail*
3013 lĕpis (1), *flake, scale*

SCALETH
5927 'âlâh (1), to *ascend, be high, mount*

SCALL
5424 netheq (14), *scurf*

SCALP
6936 qodqôd (1), *crown of the head*

SCANT
7332 râzôwn (1), *thinness*

SCAPEGOAT
5799 'ăzâ'zêl (4), *goat of departure; scapegoat*

SCARCE
3433 mŏlis (2), *with difficulty*

SCARCELY
3433 mŏlis (2), *with difficulty*

SCARCENESS
4544 miçkênûth (1), *indigence, poverty*

SCAREST
2865 châthath (1), *to break down*

SCARLET
711 'argᵉvân (Ch.) (3), *purple*
8144 shânîy (9), *crimson*
8144+8438 shânîy (33), *crimson dyed stuffs*
8529 tâla' (1), *to dye crimson*
2847 kŏkkinŏs (6), *crimson*

SCATTER
921 bᵉdar (Ch.) (1), *to scatter*
967 bâzar (2), *to scatter*
2210 zâqaph (1), *to lift up*
2219 zârâh (11), *to diffuse*
2236 zâraq (2), *to sprinkle, scatter*
5128 nûwa' (1), *to waver*
5310 nâphats (1), *to dash*
6284 pâ'âh (1), *to blow away*
6327 pûwts (18), *to dash*

SCATTERED
2219 zârâh (6), *to diffuse*
4900 mâshak (2), *to draw out; to be tall*
5310 nâphats (2), *to dash*
6327 pûwts (34), *to dash*
6340 pâzar (7), *to scatter*
6504 pârad (2), *to spread*
6555 pârats (1), *to break out*
6566 pâras (3), *to scatter*
1262 dialuō (1), *to break up*
1287 diaskŏrpizō (4), *to scatter; to squander*
1289 diaspĕirō (3), *to scatter like seed*
1290 diaspŏra (2), *dispersion*
4496 rhiptō (1), *to fling*
4650 skŏrpizō (1), *to dissipate*

SCATTERETH
2219 zârâh (2), *to diffuse*
6327 pûwts (3), *to dash in pieces; to disperse*
6340 pâzar (2), *to scatter*
4650 skŏrpizō (3), *to dissipate*

SCATTERING
5311 nephets (1), *storm which disperses*

SCENT
2143 zêker (1), *commemoration*
7381 rêyach (2), *odor*

SCEPTRE
7626 shêbeṭ (9), *stick*
8275 sharbîyṭ (4), *ruler's rod*
4464 rhabdŏs (2), *stick*

SCEPTRES
7626 shêbeṭ (1), *stick*

SCEVA
4630 Skĕuas (1), *left-handed*

SCHISM
4978 schisma (1), *divisive dissension*

SCHOLAR
6030 'ânâh (1), *to respond*
8527 talmîyd (1), *pupil*

SCHOOL
4981 schŏlē (1), *lecture hall, i.e. school*

SCHOOLMASTER
3807 paidagōgŏs (2), *tutor, cf. pedagogue*

SCIENCE
4093 maddâ' (1), *intelligence*
1108 gnōsis (1), *knowledge*

SCOFF
7046 qâlaç (1), *to disparage, i.e. ridicule*

SCOFFERS
1703 ĕmpaiktēs (1), *derider; false teacher*

SCORCH
2739 kaumatizō (1), *to burn, scorch, sear*

SCORCHED
2739 kaumatizō (3), *to burn, scorch, sear*

SCORN
959 bâzâh (1), *to scorn*
3887 lûwts (1), *to scoff*
3933 la'ag (2), *scoffing*
4890 mischâq (1), *laughing-stock*
2606 katagĕlaō (3), *to laugh down, i.e. deride*

SCORNER
3887 lûwts (11), *to scoff*

SCORNERS
3887 lûwts (3), *to scoff*
3945 lâtsats (1), *to scoff*

SCORNEST
3887 lûwts (1), *to scoff*
7046 qâlaç (1), *to disparage, i.e. ridicule*

SCORNETH
3887 lûwts (2), *to scoff; to interpret; to intercede*
7832 sâchaq (2), *to scorn*

SCORNFUL
3887 lûwts (1), *to scoff*
3944 lâtsôwn (2), *scoffing*

SCORNING
3933 la'ag (2), *scoffing*
3944 lâtsôwn (1), *scoffing*

SCORPION
4651 skŏrpiŏs (2), *scorpion*

SCORPIONS
6137 'aqrâb (6), *scorpion*
4651 skŏrpiŏs (3), *scorpion*

SCOURED
4838 mâraq (1), *to polish*

SCOURGE
7752 shôwṭ (4), *lash*
7885 shayiṭ (1), *oar*
3147 mastizō (1), *to whip*
3164 machŏmai (5), *to war, i.e. to quarrel*
5416 phragĕlliŏn (1), *lash*

SCOURGED
1244 biqqôreth (1), *due punishment*
3146 mastigŏō (1), *to punish by flogging*
5417 phragĕllŏō (2), *to whip, i.e. to lash*

SCOURGES
7850 shôṭêṭ (1), *goad, flogging device*

SCOURGETH
3146 mastigŏō (1), *to punish by flogging*

SCOURGING
3148 mastix (1), *flogging device*

SCOURGINGS
3148 mastix (1), *flogging device*

SCRABBLED
8427 tâvâh (1), *to mark*

SCRAPE
1623 gârad (1), *to rub off*
5500 çâchâh (1), *to sweep away*
7096 qâtsâh (1), *to cut off*

SCRAPED
7096 qâtsâh (1), *to cut off*
7106 qâtsa' (1), *to scrape*

SCREECH
3917 lîylîyth (1), *night spectre (spirit)*

SCRIBE
5608 çâphar (42), *to inscribe; to enumerate*
5613 çâphêr (Ch.) (6), *scribe, recorder*
1122 grammatĕus (4), *secretary, scholar*

SCRIBE'S
5608 çâphar (2), *to inscribe; to enumerate*

SCRIBES
5608 çâphar (6), *to inscribe; to enumerate*
1122 grammatĕus (62), *secretary, scholar*

SCRIP
3219 yalqûwṭ (1), *pouch*
4082 pēra (6), *wallet*

SCRIPTURE
3791 kâthâb (1), *writing*
1124 graphē (31), *document, i.e. holy Writ*

SCRIPTURES
1121 gramma (1), *writing*

1124 graphē (20), *document, i.e. holy Writ*

SCROLL
5612 çêpher (1), *writing*
975 bibliŏn (1), *scroll*

SCUM
2457 chel'âh (5), *rust*

SCURVY
1618 gârâb (2), *itching*

SCYTHIAN
4658 Skuthēs (1), *Scythene*

SEA
3220 yâm (291), *sea*
3221 yâm (Ch.) (2), *sea*
1724 ĕnaliŏs (1), *marine*
2281 thalassa (93), *sea*
3864 parathalassiŏs (1), *by the lake*
3882 paraliŏs (1), *maritime; seacoast*
3989 pĕlagŏs (1), *open sea*

SEAFARING
3220 yâm (1), *sea; basin*

SEAL
2368 chôwthâm (5), *seal*
2856 châtham (6), *to close up; to affix a seal*
4972 sphragizō (4), *to stamp with a signet*
4973 sphragis (11), *stamp impressed*

SEALED
2856 châtham (14), *to close up; to affix a seal*
2857 chătham (Ch.) (1), *to affix a seal*
2696 katasphragizō (1), *to seal closely*
4972 sphragizō (20), *to stamp with a signet*

SEALEST
2856 châtham (1), *to close up; to affix a seal*

SEALETH
2856 châtham (3), *to close up; to affix a seal*

SEALING
4972 sphragizō (1), *to stamp with a signet*

SEALS
4973 sphragis (5), *stamp*

SEAM
729 arrhaphŏs (1), *without seam*

SEARCH
1239 bâqar (1), *to inspect, admire*
1240 bᵉqar (Ch.) (4), *to inspect, admire*
1875 dârash (4), *to pursue or search*
2658 châphar (3), *to delve, to explore*
2664 châphas (8), *to seek; to let be sought*
2665 chêphes (1), *secret trick, plot*
2713 châqar (11), *to examine, search*
2714 chêqer (3), *examination*

4290 machtereth (1), *burglary*
8446 tûwr (9), to *meander*
1833 ĕxĕtazō (1), to *ascertain* or *interrogate*
2045 ĕrĕunaō (2), to *seek*, i.e. to *investigate*

SEARCHED
2664 châphas (3), to *seek*
2713 châqar (7), to *examine* intimately
2714 chêqer (1), *examination*
4959 mâshash (2), to *feel*
7270 râgal (1), to *reconnoiter; to slander*
8446 tûwr (4), to *meander*
350 anakrinō (1), to *interrogate, determine*
1830 ĕxĕrĕunaō (1), to *explore*

SEARCHEST
1875 dârash (1), to *search*
2664 châphas (1), to *seek*

SEARCHETH
1875 dârash (2), to *search*
2713 châqar (3), to *examine intimately*
2045 ĕrĕunaō (3), to *seek*

SEARCHING
2664 châphas (2), to *seek*
2714 chêqer (2), *examination*
8446 tûwr (1), to *meander*
2045 ĕrĕunaō (1), to *seek*

SEARCHINGS
2714 chêqer (1), *examination*

SEARED
2743 kautēriazō (1), to *brand* or *cauterize*

SEAS
3220 yâm (24), *sea*
1337 dithalassŏs (1), *having two seas*

SEASON
2165 zᵉmân (1), *time*
2166 zᵉmân (Ch.) (1), *time, appointed*
3117 yôwm (3), *day; time*
4150 môw' êd (10), *place of meeting*
4414 mâlach (1), to *disappear* as dust
6256 'êth (14), *time*
171 akairōs (1), *inopportunely*
741 artuō (1), to *spice*
2121 ĕukairŏs (1), *opportune, suitable*
2540 kairŏs (11), *set or proper* time
3641 ŏligŏs (1), *puny*
4340 prŏskairŏs (1), *temporary*
5550 chrŏnŏs (3), *time*
5610 hōra (3), *hour*

SEASONED
741 artuō (2), to *spice*

SEASONS
2166 zᵉmân (Ch.) (1), *time, appointed*
4150 môw'êd (2), *place of meeting; assembly*
6256 'êth (2), *time*
2540 kairŏs (4), *set or proper* time

5550 chrŏnŏs (1), *time*

SEAT
3678 kiççê' (7), *throne*
4186 môwshâb (7), *seat*
7674 shebeth (1), *rest*
7675 shebeth (2), *abode*
8499 tᵉkûwnâh (1), *something arranged*
968 bēma (10), *tribunal platform; judging place*
2362 thrŏnŏs (3), *throne*
2515 kathĕdra (1), *bench*

SEATED
5603 çâphan (1), to *roof*

SEATS
2362 thrŏnŏs (4), *throne*
2515 kathĕdra (2), *bench*
4410 prŏtŏkathĕdria (4), *pre-eminence* in council

SEBA
5434 Çᵉbâ' (4), *Seba*

SEBAT
7627 Shᵉbâṭ (1), *Shebat*

SECACAH
5527 Çᵉkâkâh (1), *enclosure*

SECHU
7906 Sêkûw (1), *Seku*

SECOND
4932 mishneh (12), *double; second*
8138 shânâh (3), to *fold*, i.e. *duplicate*
8145 shênîy (99), *second*
8147 shᵉnayim (10), *two*-fold
8578 tinyân (Ch.) (1), *second*
8648 tᵉrêyn (Ch.) (1), *two*
1207 dĕutĕrŏprŏtŏs (1), *second-first*
1208 dĕutĕrŏs (42), *second; secondly*

SECONDARILY
1208 dĕutĕrŏs (1), *second; secondly*

SECRET
328 'aṭ (1), *gently, softly*
2934 ṭâman (1), to *hide*
4565 miçtâr (8), *covert hiding place*
5475 çôwd (8), *secret*
5640 çâtham (1), to *repair; to keep secret*
5641 çâthar (4), to *hide*
5642 çᵉthar (Ch.) (1), to *demolish*
5643 çêther (15), *cover*
5956 'âlam (2), to *conceal*
6383 pil'îy (1), *remarkable*
6596 pôth (1), *hole; hinge*
6845 tsâphan (2), to *hide*
7328 râz (Ch.) (6), *mystery*
8368 sâthar (1), to *break out as an eruption*
614 apŏkruphŏs (1), *secret, hidden things*
2926 kruptē (1), *hidden*
2927 kruptŏs (10), *private*
2928 kruptō (1), to *conceal*
2931 kruphē (1), *in secret*
4601 sigaō (1), to *keep silent*

5009 tamĕiŏn (1), *room*

SECRETLY
1589 gânab (1), to *deceive*
2244 châbâ' (1), to *secrete*
2644 châphâ' (1), to *act covertly*
2790 chârash (1), to *engrave; to plow*
2791 cheresh (1), *magical craft; silence*
3909 lâṭ (1), *secrecy*
4565 miçtâr (2), *covert hiding place*
5643 çêther (9), *cover*
6845 tsâphan (1), to *hide*
2928 kruptō (1), to *conceal*
2977 lathra (1), *secretly*

SECRETS
4016 mâbûsh (1), *male genitals*
5475 çôwd (2), *secret*
7328 râz (Ch.) (3), *mystery*
8587 ta'ălummâh (2), *secret*
2927 kruptŏs (2), *private*

SECT
139 hairĕsis (5), *sect*

SECUNDUS
4580 Sĕkŏundŏs (1), *second*

SECURE
982 bâṭach (4), to *trust*
983 beṭach (1), *security*
987 baṭṭûchôwth (1), *security*
4160+275 mûwts (1), to *oppress*

SECURELY
983 beṭach (2), *safety, security, trust*

SECURITY
2425 hikanŏs (1), *ample*

SEDITION
849 'eshtaddûwr (Ch.) (2), *rebellion*
4714 stasis (3), one leading an *uprising*

SEDITIONS
1370 dichŏstasia (1), *dissension*

SEDUCE
635 apŏplanaō (1), to *lead astray; to wander*
4105 planaō (2), to *deceive*

SEDUCED
2937 ṭâ'âh (1), to *lead astray*
8582 tâ'âh (1), to *stray*

SEDUCERS
1114 gŏēs (1), *imposter*

SEDUCETH
8582 tâ'âh (1), to *stray*

SEDUCING
4108 planŏs (1), *roving*

SEE
2009 hinnêh (2), *Look!*
2370 chăzâ' (Ch.) (4), to *gaze upon; to dream*
2372 châzâh (15), to *gaze at; to perceive*

2374 chôzeh (2), *beholder* in vision
4758 mar'eh (1), *appearance; vision*
5027 nâbaṭ (4), to *scan; to regard* with favor
7200 râ'âh (346), to *see*
7789 shûwr (4), to *spy out, survey*
308 anablĕpō (1), to *look up; to recover sight*
542 apĕidō (1), to *see fully*
991 blĕpō (46), to *look at*
1227 diablĕpō (2), to *see clearly, recover vision*
1492 ĕidō (79), to *know*
1689 ĕmblĕpō (1), to *observe; to discern*
2300 thĕaŏmai (4), to *look closely at*
2334 thĕōrĕō (17), to *see*
2396 idĕ (1), *lo!, look!*
2400 idŏu (3), *lo!, see!*
2477 histŏrĕō (1), to *visit*
3467 muōpazō (1), to *see indistinctly, be myopic*
3700 ŏptanŏmai (29), to *appear*
3708 hŏraō (11), to *stare, see clearly; to discern*
5461 phōtizō (1), to *shine or to brighten* up

SEED
2233 zera' (218), *seed*
2234 zᵉra' (Ch.) (1), *posterity, progeny*
6507 pᵉrûdâh (1), *kernel*
4687 spĕirō (4), to *scatter, i.e. sow* seed
4690 spĕrma (41), *seed*
4701 spŏra (1), *sowing*
4703 spŏrŏs (5), *seed*

SEED'S
2233 zera' (1), *seed; fruit*

SEEDS
4690 spĕrma (3), *seed*

SEEDTIME
2233 zera' (1), *seed; fruit*

SEEING
310 achar (1), *after*
518 'im (1), *whether?; if*
1768 dîy (Ch.) (1), *that; of*
3282 ya'an (1), *because*
3588 kîy (9), *for, that*
6493 piqqêach (1), *clear-sighted*
7200 râ'âh (16), to *see*
990 blemma (1), *vision*
991 blĕpō (8), to *look at*
1063 gar (1), *for, indeed, but, because*
1492 ĕidō (2), to *know*
1512 ĕi pĕr (1), *if perhaps*
1893 ĕpĕi (4), *since*
1894 ĕpĕidē (2), *whereas*
1897 ĕpĕipĕr (1), *since*
2334 thĕōrĕō (1), to *see*
3708 hŏraō (1), to *stare, see clearly; to discern*
3754 hŏti (1), *that; since*
4275 prŏĕidō (1), to *foresee*

SEEK
1239 bâqar (3), to *inspect, admire*

SEEKEST
1245 bâqash (112), to search out; to strive
1556 gâlal (1), to roll
1875 dârash (56), to seek
2713 châqar (1), to search
7125 qîr'âh (1), to encounter, to happen
7836 shâchar (8), to search for
8446 tûwr (1), to wander
327 anazētĕŏ (1), to search out
1567 ĕkzētĕŏ (2), to seek out
1934 ĕpizētĕŏ (6), to search (inquire) for
2212 zētĕŏ (48), to seek

SEEKEST
1245 bâqash (7), to search out; to strive
2212 zētĕŏ (2), to seek

SEEKETH
579 'ânâh (1), to meet
1243 baqqârâh (1), looking after
1245 bâqash (19), to search out; to strive
1875 dârash (6), to seek
2658 châphar (1), to delve
7836 shâchar (1), to search for
1567 ĕkzētĕŏ (1), to seek out
1934 ĕpizētĕŏ (3), to search (inquire) for
2212 zētĕŏ (9), to seek

SEEKING
1875 dârash (2), to seek
2212 zētĕŏ (12), to seek

SEEM
3191 yᵉṭab (Ch.) (1), to be, make well
4591 mâ'aṭ (1), to be, make small or few
4758 mar'eh (1), appearance; vision
5869 'ayin (2), eye; sight
7034 qâlâh (1), to be light
7185 qâshâh (1), to be tough or severe
1380 dŏkĕŏ (5), to seem

SEEMED
5869 'ayin (4), eye; sight
1380 dŏkĕŏ (6), to think, regard, seem good
5316 phainŏ (1), to lighten; to appear

SEEMETH
5869 'ayin (18), eye; sight
6440 pânîym (2), face
7200 râ'âh (1), to see
1380 dŏkĕŏ (5), to seem

SEEMLY
5000 nâ'veh (2), suitable

SEEN
2370 chăzâ' (Ch.) (3), to gaze upon; to dream
2372 châzâh (9), to gaze at; to perceive
7200 râ'âh (162), to see
7210 rŏ'îy (2), sight
7805 shâzaph (1), to scan
991 blĕpŏ (9), to look at
1492 ĕidŏ (33), to know
2300 thĕaŏmai (8), to look closely at

SELED
5540 Çeled (1), exultation

SELEUCIA
4581 Sĕlĕukĕia (1), of Seleucus

SELFWILL
7522 râtsôwn (1), delight

SELFWILLED
829 authadēs (2), self-pleasing, arrogant

SELL
4376 mâkar (24), to sell
7666 shâbar (3), to deal
1710 ĕmpŏrĕuŏmai (1), to trade, do business
4453 pŏlĕŏ (7), to barter

SELLER
4376 mâkar (3), to sell
4211 pŏrphurŏpŏlis (1), female trader in bluish-red cloth

SELLERS
4376 mâkar (1), to sell

SELLEST
4376 mâkar (1), to sell

SELLETH
4376 mâkar (5), to sell
7666 shâbar (1), to deal
4453 pŏlĕŏ (1), to barter

SELVEDGE
7098 qâtsâh (2), termination; fringe

SEM
4590 Sĕm (1), name

SEMACHIAH
5565 Çᵉmakyâhûw (1), supported of Jehovah

SEMEI
4584 Sĕmĕï (1), famous

SENAAH
5570 Çᵉnâ'âh (2), thorny

SENATE
1087 gĕrŏusia (1), Jewish Sanhedrin

SENATORS
2205 zâqên (1), old, venerated

SEND
935 bôw' (1), to go, come
5042 nâba' (1), to gush
5130 nûwph (1), to rock
5414 nâthan (6), to give
7136 qârâh (1), to bring about; to impose
7971 shâlach (157), to send away
7972 shᵉlach (Ch.) (1), to send away
630 apŏluŏ (6), to relieve, release; divorce
649 apŏstĕllŏ (23), to send out on a mission
906 ballŏ (3), to throw
1032 bruŏ (1), to gush
1544 ĕkballŏ (3), to throw out
1821 ĕxapŏstĕllŏ (1), to despatch, or to dismiss
3343 mĕtapĕmpŏ (2), to summon or invite
3992 pĕmpŏ (25), to send

SENDEST
7971 shâlach (6), to send away

SENDETH
5414 nâthan (2), to give
7971 shâlach (8), to send away
649 apŏstĕllŏ (4), to send out on a mission
1026 brĕchŏ (1), to make wet; to rain

SENDING
4916 mishlôwach (3), sending out
4917 mishlachath (1), mission; release; army
7971 shâlach (9), to send away
3992 pĕmpŏ (1), to send

SENEH
5573 Çeneh (1), thorn

SENIR
8149 Shᵉnîyr (2), peak

SENNACHERIB
5576 Çanchêrîyb (13), Sancherib

SENSE
7922 sekel (1), intelligence; success

SENSES
145 aisthĕtĕriŏn (1), judgment, sense

SENSUAL
5591 psuchikŏs (2), physical and brutish

SENT
1980 hâlak (1), to walk
2904 ṭûwl (1), to cast down or out, hurl
3947 lâqach (1), to take
5414 nâthan (5), to give
5674 'âbar (2), to cross over; to transition
6680 tsâvâh (1), to constitute, enjoin
7725 shûwb (1), to return
7964 shillûwach (1), divorce; dower
7971 shâlach (459), to send away
7972 shᵉlach (Ch.) (12), to send away
375 anapĕmpŏ (4), to send up or back
628 apŏlŏuŏ (2), to wash fully
630 apŏluŏ (6), to release; divorce
640 apŏria (1), state of quandary, perplexity
649 apŏstĕllŏ (104), to send out on a mission
652 apŏstŏlŏs (2), commissioner of Christ
657 apŏtassŏmai (1), to say adieu; to renounce
863 aphiēmi (2), to leave
1524 ĕisĕimi (1), to enter
1544 ĕkballŏ (1), to throw out
1599 ĕkpĕmpŏ (2), to despatch, send out
1821 ĕxapŏstĕllŏ (10), to despatch, or to dismiss
3343 mĕtapĕmpŏ (4), to summon or invite

SEER
2374 chôzeh (11), beholder in vision
7200 râ'âh (10), to see

SEER'S
7200 râ'âh (1), to see

SEERS
2374 chôzeh (5), beholder in vision
7200 râ'âh (1), to see

SEEST
2372 châzâh (2), to gaze at; to perceive
7200 râ'âh (27), to see
7210 rŏ'îy (1), sight; spectacle
991 blĕpŏ (5), to look at
2334 thĕŏrĕŏ (1), to see

SEETH
2372 châzâh (2), to gaze at; to perceive
7200 râ'âh (27), to see
7210 rŏ'îy (1), sight; spectacle
991 blĕpŏ (11), to look at
2334 thĕŏrĕŏ (9), to see
3708 hŏraŏ (1), to stare

SEETHE
1310 bâshal (8), to boil

SEETHING
1310 bâshal (1), to boil
5301 nâphach (2), to inflate, blow, kindle

SEGUB
7687 Sᵉgûwb (3), aloft

SEIR
8165 Sê'îyr (39), rough

SEIRATH
8167 Sᵉ'îyrâh (1), roughness

SEIZE
3423 yârash (1), to inherit; to impoverish
3451 yᵉshîymâh (1), desolation
3947 lâqach (1), to take
2722 katĕchŏ (1), to hold down fast

SEIZED
2388 châzaq (1), to seize

SELA
5554 Çela' (1), craggy rock; fortress

SELA-HAMMAHLEKOTH
5555 Çela' ham-machlᵉqôwth (1), rock of the divisions

SELAH
5542 Çelâh (74), suspension of music
5554 Çela' (1), craggy rock; fortress

SEEKEST
2334 thĕŏrĕŏ (2), to see
2529 kathŏraŏ (1), to see clearly
3700 ŏptanŏmai (8), to appear
3708 hŏraŏ (32), to stare, see clearly; to discern
3780 ŏuchi (1), not indeed
4308 prŏŏraŏ (1), to notice previously
5316 phainŏ (2), to lighten; be visible

3992 pĕmpō (49), to *send*
4842 sumpĕmpō (2), to *dispatch with*
4882 sunapŏstĕllō (1), to *despatch with*

SENTENCE
1697 dâbâr (3), *word*
4941 mishpâṭ (2), *verdict; formal decree; justice*
6310 peh (1), *mouth*
6599 pithgâm (1), *judicial sentence; edict*
7081 qeçem (1), *divination*
610 apŏkrima (1), *decision or sentence*
1948 ĕpikrinō (1), to *adjudge, decide*
2919 krinō (1), to *decide*

SENTENCES
280 'ăchîydâh (Ch.) (1), *enigma*
2420 chîydâh (1), *puzzle*

SENTEST
7971 shâlach (4), to *send away*

SENUAH
5574 Çᵉnûw'âh (1), *pointed*

SEORIM
8188 Sᵉ'ôrîym (1), *barley*

SEPARATE
914 bâdal (7), to *divide*
1508 gizrâh (7), *figure, appearance; enclosure*
2505 châlaq (1), to *be smooth; be slippery*
3995 mibdâlâh (1), *separation; separate*
5139 nâzîyr (1), *prince; separated Nazirite*
5144 nâzar (4), to *set apart, devote*
6381 pâlâ' (1), to *be, make great, difficult*
6504 pârad (2), to *spread*
873 aphŏrizō (5), to *limit, exclude, appoint*
5562 chŏrĕō (3), to *pass, enter; to hold, admit*

SEPARATED
914 bâdal (17), to *divide*
5139 nâzîyr (1), *prince; separated Nazirite*
5144 nâzar (1), to *set apart, devote*
6395 pâlâh (2), to *distinguish*
6504 pârad (8), to *spread*
873 aphŏrizō (4), to *limit, exclude, appoint*

SEPARATETH
5144 nâzar (3), to *set apart, devote*
6504 pârad (2), to *spread*

SEPARATING
5144 nâzar (1), to *set apart, devote*

SEPARATION
914 bâdal (1), to *divide*
5079 niddâh (14), time of *menstrual impurity*
5145 nezer (11), *set apart; dedication*

SEPHAR
5611 Çᵉphâr (1), *census*

SEPHARAD
5614 Çᵉphârâd (1), *Sepharad*

SEPHARVAIM
5617 Çᵉpharvayim (6), *Sepharvajim*

SEPHARVITES
5616 Çᵉpharvîy (1), *Sepharvite*

SEPULCHRE
6900 qᵉbûwrâh (5), *sepulchre*
6913 qeber (14), *sepulchre*
3418 mnēma (4), *sepulchral monument*
3419 mnēmĕiŏn (26), *place of interment*
5028 taphŏs (5), *grave*

SEPULCHRES
6913 qeber (12), *sepulchre*
3419 mnēmĕiŏn (3), *place of interment*
5028 taphŏs (1), *grave*

SERAH
8294 Serach (2), *superfluity*

SERAIAH
8304 Sᵉrâyâh (20), *Jehovah has prevailed*

SERAPHIMS
8314 sârâph (2), *saraph*

SERED
5624 Çered (2), *trembling*

SERGIUS
4588 Sĕrgiŏs (1), *Sergius*

SERJEANTS
4465 rhabdŏuchŏs (2), *constable*

SERPENT
5175 nâchâsh (25), *snake*
8314 sârâph (3), *poisonous serpent*
8577 tannîyn (2), *sea-serpent; jackal*
3789 ŏphis (8), *snake*

SERPENT'S
5175 nâchâsh (2), *snake*

SERPENTS
2119 zâchal (1), to *crawl*
5175 nâchâsh (4), *snake*
8577 tannîyn (1), *sea-serpent; jackal*
2062 hᵉrpĕtŏn (1), *reptile*
3789 ŏphis (6), *snake*

SERUG
8286 Sᵉrûwg (5), *tendril*

SERVANT
5288 na'ar (30), *servant*
5647 'âbad (1), to *serve*
5649 'ăbad (Ch.) (1), *servant*
5650 'ebed (363), *servant*
7916 sâkîyr (8), man at *wages, hired hand*
8334 shârath (4), to *attend*
1248 diakŏnia (2), *attendance, aid, service*
1249 diakŏnŏs (3), *attendant, deacon*

1401 dŏulŏs (66), *servant*
1402 dŏulŏō (1), to *enslave*
2324 thĕrapōn (1), *menial attendant*
3610 ŏikĕtēs (3), *menial domestic servant*
3816 pais (8), *servant*

SERVANT'S
5650 'ebed (8), *servant*
1401 dŏulŏs (1), *servant*

SERVANTS
582 'ĕnôwsh (1), *man*
5288 na'ar (21), *servant*
5647 'âbad (4), to *serve*
5649 'ăbad (Ch.) (6), *servant*
5650 'ebed (367), *servant*
5657 'ăbuddâh (1), *service*
8334 shârath (1), to *attend as a menial*
341 anakainŏō (1), to *renovate, renew*
1249 diakŏnŏs (2), *attendant, deacon*
1401 dŏulŏs (55), *servant*
1402 dŏulŏō (2), to *enslave*
3407 misthiŏs (2), *hired-worker*
3610 ŏikĕtēs (1), *menial domestic servant*
3816 pais (1), *servant*
5257 hupĕrĕtēs (4), *servant, attendant*

SERVANTS'
5650 'ebed (4), *servant*

SERVE
5647 'âbad (162), to *serve*
5656 'ăbôdâh (1), *work*
5975+6440 'âmad (1), to *stand*
6399 pᵉlach (Ch.) (7), to *serve or worship*
8334 shârath (4), to *attend as a menial*
1247 diakŏnĕō (7), to *wait upon, serve*
1398 dŏulĕuō (13), to *serve as a slave*
3000 latrĕuō (13), to *minister to God*

SERVED
1580 gâmal (1), to *benefit or requite; to wean*
5647 'âbad (61), to *serve*
5975+6440 'âmad (1), to *stand*
6213 'âsâh (1), to *do*
8334 shârath (4), to *attend as a menial*
1247 diakŏnĕō (1), to *wait upon, serve*
1398 dŏulĕuō (1), to *serve as a slave*
3000 latrĕuō (2), to *minister to God*
5256 hupĕrĕtĕō (1), to *be a subordinate*

SERVEDST
5647 'âbad (1), to *serve*

SERVEST
6399 pᵉlach (Ch.) (2), to *serve or worship*

SERVETH
5647 'âbad (2), to *serve*
5656 'ăbôdâh (1), *work*
1247 diakŏnĕō (2), to *wait upon, serve*
1398 dŏulĕuō (1), to *serve as a slave*

SERVICE
3027 yâd (2), *hand; power*
5647 'âbad (4), to *serve*
5656 'ăbôdâh (98), *work*
5673 'ăbîydâh (Ch.) (1), *labor or business*
6402 polchân (Ch.) (1), *worship*
6635 tsâbâ' (4), *army, military host*
8278 sᵉrâd (4), *stitching*
8334 shârath (3), to *attend as a menial*
1248 diakŏnia (3), *attendance, aid, service*
1398 dŏulĕuō (3), to *serve as a slave*
2999 latrĕia (5), *worship, ministry service*
3000 latrĕuō (1), to *minister to God*
3009 lĕitŏurgia (3), *service, ministry*

SERVILE
5656 'ăbôdâh (12), *work*

SERVING
5647 'âbad (2), to *serve*
1248 diakŏnia (1), *attendance, aid, service*
1398 dŏulĕuō (3), to *serve as a slave*
3000 latrĕuō (1), to *minister to God*

SERVITOR
8334 shârath (1), to *attend as a menial*

SERVITUDE
5656 'ăbôdâh (2), *work*

SET
530 'ĕmûwnâh (5), *fidelity; steadiness*
631 'âçar (1), to *fasten*
935 bôw' (1), to *go, come*
1129 bânâh (2), to *build*
1197 bâ'ar (1), to *be brutish, be senseless*
1379 gâbal (1), to *set a boundary line, limit*
1431 gâdal (2), to *be great, make great*
2211 zᵉqaph (Ch.) (1), to *impale by hanging*
2232 zâra' (1), to *sow seed; to disseminate*
2706 chôq (1), *appointment; allotment*
2710 châqaq (1), to *engrave; to enact laws*
3051 yâhab (1), to *give*
3240 yânach (8), to *allow to stay*
3245 yâçad (1), *settle, consult, establish*
3259 yâ'ad (3), to *meet; to summon; to direct*
3320 yâtsab (5), to *station, offer, continue*
3322 yâtsag (8), to *place*
3332 yâtsaq (1), to *pour out*

3335 yâtsar (1), to *form*
3341 yâtsath (1), to *burn*
3427 yâshab (13), to *settle*
3488 yᵉthîb (Ch.) (2), to *sit*
3559 kûwn (6), to *set up*
3635 kᵉlal (Ch.) (4), to *complete*
3966 mᵉᵉôd (2), *very*
4142 mûwçabbâh (1), *backside; fold*
4150 môwᵉêd (10), *place of meeting*
4390 mâlê' (5), to *fill*
4394 millû' (4), *fulfilling; setting; consecration*
4427 mâlak (1), to *reign as king*
4483 mᵉnâ' (Ch.) (3), to *count, appoint*
4487 mânâh (1), to *allot*
4853 massâ' (1), *burden*
5079 niddâh (1), time of menstrual *impurity*
5117 nûwach (2), to *rest; to settle* down
5128 nûwa' (1), to *waver*
5183 nachath (1), *descent; quiet*
5258 nâçak (2), to *pour*
5265 nâça' (16), *start*
5324 nâtsab (18), to *station*
5329 nâtsach (4), to be *eminent*
5375 nâsâ' (9), to *lift up*
5414 nâthan (103), to *give*
5473 çûwg (1), to *hem in*
5496 çûwth (1), to *stimulate; to seduce*
5526 çâkak (1), to *entwine; to fence in*
5564 çâmak (1), to *lean* upon; *take hold of*
5774 'ûwph (1), to *cover, to fly; to faint*
5927 'âlâh (2), to *ascend, be high, mount*
5975 'âmad (44), to *stand*
6186 'ârak (1), to set in a *row*, i.e. *arrange*,
6187 'êrek (1), *pile, equipment, estimate*
6213 'âsâh (3), to *do*
6395 pâlâh (1), to *distinguish*
6485 pâqad (7), to *care*
6496 pâqîyd (1), *superintendent, officer*
6584 pâshaṭ (1), to *strip*
6605 pâthach (1), to *open*
6845 tsâphan (1), to *hide*
6965 qûwm (28), to *rise*
6966 qûwm (Ch.) (11), to *rise*
7311 rûwm (7), to *rise*
7313 rûwm (Ch.) (1), *elation, arrogance*
7392 râkab (2), to *ride*
7660 shâbats (1), to *interweave*
7682 sâgab (1), to *be, make lofty; be safe*
7725 shûwb (1), to *return*
7737 shâvâh (1), to *level*
7760 sûwm (129), to *put*
7761 sûwm (Ch.) (2), to *put, place*
7896 shîyth (22), to *place*
7931 shâkan (3), to *reside*

7947 shâlab (1), to *make equidistant*
7971 shâlach (5), to *send away*
8239 shâphath (2), to *put*
8371 shâthath (1), to *place*, i.e. *array; to lie*
8427 tâvâh (1), to *mark* out; *imprint*
321 anagō (1), to *lead* up; to *bring out*
345 anakĕimai (1), to *recline at a meal*
377 anapiptō (1), *lie down, lean back*
392 anatassŏmai (1), to *arrange*
461 anŏrthŏō (1), to *strengthen, build*
584 apŏdĕiknumi (1), to *demonstrate*
630 apŏluō (2), to *relieve, release; divorce*
649 apŏstĕllō (1), to *send out* on a mission
816 atĕnizō (1), to *gaze*
968 bēma (1), *tribunal platform; judging place*
1299 diatassō (1), to *institute, prescribe*
1325 didōmi (1), to *give*
1369 dichazō (1), to *sunder*, i.e. *alienate*
1416 dunō (1), to *have the sun set*
1847 ĕxŏudĕnŏō (1), to *be treated with contempt*
1848 ĕxŏuthĕnĕō (3), to *treat with contempt*
1913 ĕpibibazō (3), to *cause to mount*
1930 ĕpidiŏrthŏō (1), to *set in order*
1940 ĕpikathizō (1), to *seat upon*
2007 ĕpitithēmi (3), to *impose*
2064 ĕrchŏmai (1), to *go*
2350 thŏrubĕō (1), to *clamor; start a riot*
2476 histēmi (11), to *stand, establish*
2521 kathēmai (1), to *sit down; to remain, reside*
2523 kathizō (6), to *seat down, dwell*
2525 kathistēmi (1), to *designate, constitute*
2749 kĕimai (6), to *lie outstretched*
3908 paratithēmi (9), to *present something*
4060 pĕritithēmi (1), to *present*
4270 prŏgraphō (1), to *announce, prescribe*
4295 prŏkĕimai (4), to be *present to the mind*
4388 prŏtithĕmai (1), to *place before*
4741 stērizō (1), to *turn resolutely; to confirm*
4776 sugkathizō (1), to *give, take a seat with*
4900 sunĕlaunō (1), to *drive together*
4972 sphragizō (2), to *stamp* with a signet

5002 taktŏs (1), *appointed* or *stated*
5021 tassō (1), to *arrange, assign*
5087 tithēmi (5), to *place*
5394 phlŏgizō (1), to *cause a blaze, ignite*
5426 phrŏnĕō (1), to *be mentally disposed*

SETH
8352 Shêth (7), *put*
4589 Sēth (1), *put*

SETHUR
5639 Çᵉthûwr (1), *hidden*

SETTER
2604 kataggĕlĕus (1), *proclaimer*

SETTEST
4916 mishlôwach (3), *sending* out
5324 nâtsab (1), to *station*
7760 sûwm (1), to *put*
7896 shîyth (1), to *place*

SETTETH
3320 yâtsab (1), to *station, offer, continue*
3427 yâshab (1), to *dwell, to remain; to settle*
3559 kûwn (1), to *set up: establish, fix, prepare*
3857 lâhaṭ (1), to *blaze*
5265 nâça' (2), *start*
5375 nâsâ' (1), to *lift up*
5496 çûwth (1), to *stimulate; to seduce*
5927 'âlâh (2), to *ascend, be high, mount*
5975 'âmad (2), to *stand*
6966 qûwm (Ch.) (2), to *rise*
7034 qâlâh (1), to be *light*
7311 rûwm (1), to *raise*
7760 sûwm (1), to *put*
7918 shâkak (1), to *lay a trap; to allay*
2007 ĕpitithēmi (1), to *impose*
2476 histēmi (1), to *stand*
5394 phlŏgizō (1), to *cause a blaze*, i.e. *ignite*

SETTING
5414 nâthan (1), to *give*
1416 dunō (1), to *have the sun set*
3326 mĕta (1), *with*

SETTINGS
4396 millû'âh (1), *setting*

SETTLE
3427 yâshab (1), to *settle*
5835 'ăzârâh (6), *enclosure; border*
5975 'âmad (1), to *stand*
2311 thĕmĕliŏō (1), to *erect; to consolidate*
5087 tithēmi (1), to *place*

SETTLED
2883 ṭâba' (1), to *sink*
4349 mâkôwn (1), *place*
5324 nâtsab (1), to *station*
5975 'âmad (1), to *stand*
7087 qâphâ' (1), to *thicken, congeal*
8252 shâqaṭ (1), to *repose*
1476 hĕdraiŏs (1), *immovable; steadfast*

SETTLEST
5181 nâchath (1), to *sink*

SEVEN
3598 Kîymâh (1), *cluster of stars, the Pleiades*
7651 sheba' (346), *seven*
7655 shib'âh (Ch.) (6), *satiety*
7658 shib'ânâh (1), *seven*
7659 shib'âthayim (1), *seven-fold*
2033 hĕpta (80), *seven*
2034 hĕptakis (4), *seven times*
2035 hĕptakischiliŏi (1), *seven times a thousand*

SEVENFOLD
7659 shib'âthayim (6), *seven-fold*

SEVENS
7651 sheba' (2), *seven*

SEVENTEEN
7651+6240 sheba' (9), *seven*
7657+7651 shib'îym (1), *seventy*

SEVENTEENTH
7651+6240 sheba' (6), *seven*

SEVENTH
7637 shᵉbîy'îy (96), *seventh*
7651 sheba' (13), *seven*
1442 hĕbdŏmŏs (9), *seventh*
2035 hĕptakischiliŏi (1), *seven times a thousand*

SEVENTY
7657 shib'îym (58), *seventy*
1440 hĕbdŏmēkŏnta (2), *seventy*
1441 hĕbdŏmēkŏntakis (1), *seventy times*

SEVER
914 bâdal (1), to *divide, separate, distinguish*
6395 pâlâh (2), to *distinguish*
873 aphŏrizō (1), to *limit, exclude, appoint*

SEVERAL
2669 chôphshûwth (2), *prostration by sickness*
2398 idiŏs (1), *private*

SEVERALLY
2398 idiŏs (1), *private*

SEVERED
914 bâdal (2), to *divide*
6504 pârad (1), to *spread*

SEVERITY
663 apŏtŏmia (2), *rigor, severity*

SEW
8609 tâphar (2), to *sew*

SEWED
8609 tâphar (1), to *sew*

SEWEST
2950 ṭâphal (1), to *impute* falsely

SEWETH
1976 ĕpirrhaptō (1), to *stitch upon*

English

SHAALABBIN
8169 Sha'albîym (1),
fox-holes

SHAALBIM
8169 Sha'albîym (2),
fox-holes

SHAALBONITE
8170 Sha'albônîy (2),
Shaalbonite

SHAAPH
8174 Sha'aph (2),
fluctuation

SHAARAIM
8189 Sha'ărayim (2),
double gates

SHAASHGAZ
8190 Sha'ashgaz (1),
Shaashgaz

SHABBETHAI
7678 Shabbᵉthay (3),
restful

SHACHIA
7634 Shobyâh (1),
captivation

SHADE
6783 tsᵉmîythûth (1),
perpetually

SHADOW
2927 țᵉlal (Ch.) (1), to
cover with shade
6738 tsêl (47), *shade*
6752 tsêlel (1), *shade*
6757 tsalmâveth (16),
shade of death
644 apŏskiasma (1),
shading off
4639 skia (7), *shade*

SHADOWING
6751 tsâlal (1), to *shade*;
to *grow dark*
6767 tsᵉlâtsal (1),
whirring of wings
2683 kataskiazō (1), to
cover, overshadow

SHADOWS
6752 tsêlel (3), *shade*

SHADRACH
7714 Shadrak (1),
Shadrak
7715 Shadrak (Ch.) (14),
Shadrak

SHADY
6628 tse'el (2), *lotus* tree

SHAFT
2671 chêts (1), *shaft*
3409 yârêk (3), *shank*

SHAGE
7681 Shâgê' (1), *erring*

SHAHAR
7837 shachar (1), *dawn*

SHAHARAIM
7842 Shachărayim (1),
double dawn

SHAHAZIMAH
7831 Shachatsôwm (1),
proudly

SHAKE
2554 châmaç (1), to *be
violent*; to *maltreat*
4571 mâ'ad (1), to *waver*
5128 nûwa' (2), to *waver*
5130 nûwph (5), to
quiver, vibrate, rock

5287 nâ'ar (4), to *tumble*
5426 nᵉthar (Ch.) (1), to
tear off; to *shake off*
6206 'ârats (2), to *dread*
6342 pâchad (1), to *fear*
7264 râgaz (1), to *quiver*
7363 râchaph (1), to
brood; to *be relaxed*
7493 râ'ash (14), to *quake*
660 apŏtinassō (1), to
brush off, shake off
1621 ĕktinassō (2), to
shake violently
4531 salĕuō (1), to *waver*
4579 sĕiō (2), to *agitate*

SHAKED
5128 nûwa' (1), to *waver*

SHAKEN
1607 gâ'ash (1), to *agitate*
5086 nâdaph (1), to
disperse, be windblown
5110 nûwd (1), to *waver*
5128 nûwa' (3), to *waver*
5287 nâ'ar (2), to *tumble*
6327 pùwts (1), to *dash*
7477 râ'al (1), to *reel*
4531 salĕuō (11), to *waver*
4579 sĕiō (4), to *agitate*

SHAKETH
2342 chûwl (2), to *writhe*
4131 môwț (1), to *shake*
5130 nûwph (2), to *rock*
5287 nâ'ar (1), to *tumble*
7264 râgaz (1), to *quiver*

SHAKING
4493 mânôwd (1), *nod*
5363 nôqeph (2),
threshing of olives
7494 ra'ash (3),
vibration, bounding
8573 tᵉnûwphâh (2),
undulation of offerings

SHALEM
8003 shâlêm (1),
complete; friendly; safe

SHALIM
8171 Sha'ălîym (1), *foxes*

SHALISHA
8031 Shâlîshâh (1),
trebled land

SHALLECHETH
7996 Shalleketh (1),
felling of trees

SHALLUM
7967 Shallûwm (27),
retribution

SHALLUN
7968 Shallûwn (1),
retribution

SHALMAI
8014 Salmay (1), *clothed*
8073 Shamlay (1), *clothed*

SHALMAN
8020 Shalman (1),
Shalman

SHALMANESER
8022 Shalman'eçer (2),
Shalmaneser

SHAMA
8091 Shâmâ' (1), *obedient*

SHAMBLES
3111 makĕllŏn (1),
butcher's stall

SHAME
954 bûwsh (9), be
ashamed
955 bûwshâh (4), *shame*
1317 boshnâh (1),
shamefulness
1322 bôsheth (20), *shame*
2616 châçad (1), to
reprove, shame
2659 châphêr (4), to *be
ashamed*
2781 cherpâh (3),
contumely, disgrace
3637 kâlam (6), to *taunt*
3639 kᵉlimmâh (20),
disgrace, scorn
3640 kᵉlimmûwth (1),
disgrace, scorn
6172 'ervâh (1), *disgrace*
7036 qâlôwn (13),
disgrace
8103 shimtsâh (1),
scornful whispering
149 aischrŏn (3),
shameful thing
152 aischunē (5), *shame*
808 aschēmŏsunē (1),
indecency; shame
818 atimazō (1), to
maltreat, dishonor
819 atimia (1), *disgrace*
1788 ĕntrĕpō (1), to
respect; to confound
1791 ĕntrŏpē (2), *shame*
2617 kataischunō (1), to
disgrace or shame
3856 paradĕigmatizō (1),
to *expose to infamy*

SHAMED
937 bûwz (1), *disrespect*
954 bûwsh (1), to *be
ashamed*
3001 yâbêsh (1), to *dry
up*; to *wither*
8106 Shemer (1),
settlings of wine, *dregs*

SHAMEFACEDNESS
127 aidōs (1), *modesty*

SHAMEFUL
1322 bôsheth (1), *shame*
7022 qîyqâlôwn (1),
disgrace

SHAMEFULLY
3001 yâbêsh (1), to *dry
up*; to *wither*
818 atimazō (1), to
maltreat, dishonor
821 atimŏō (1), to
maltreat, disgrace
5195 hubrizō (1), to
exercise violence, abuse

SHAMELESSLY
1540 gâlâh (1), to *denude*

SHAMER
8106 Shemer (2),
settlings of wine, *dregs*

SHAMETH
3637 kâlam (1), to *taunt*

SHAMGAR
8044 Shamgar (2),
Shamgar

SHAMHUTH
8049 Shamhûwth (1),
desolation

SHAMIR
8053 Shâmûwr (1),
observed
8069 Shâmîyr (3), *thorn*
or (poss.) *diamond*

SHAMMA
8037 Shammâ' (1),
desolation

SHAMMAH
8048 Shammâh (8),
desolation

SHAMMAI
8060 Shammay (6),
destructive

SHAMMOTH
8054 Shammôwth (1),
ruins

SHAMMUA
8051 Shammûwa' (4),
renowned

SHAMMUAH
8051 Shammûwa' (1),
renowned

SHAMSHERAI
8125 Shamshᵉray (1),
sun-like

SHAPE
1491 ĕidŏs (2), *form,
appearance, sight*

SHAPEN
2342 chûwl (1), to *dance,
whirl*; to *writhe* in pain

SHAPES
3667 hŏmŏiōma (1), *form*

SHAPHAM
8223 Shâphâm (1), *baldly*

SHAPHAN
8227 shâphân (30), *hyrax*

SHAPHAT
8202 Shâphât (8), *judge*

SHAPHER
8234 Shepher (2), *beauty*

SHARAI
8298 Shâray (1), *hostile*

SHARAIM
8189 Sha'ărayim (1),
double gates

SHARAR
8325 Shârâr (1), *hostile*

SHARE
4282 machăresheth (1),
(poss.) *hoe*

SHAREZER
8272 Shar'etser (2),
Sharetser

SHARON
8289 Shârôwn (6), *plain*

SHARONITE
8290 Shârôwnîy (1),
Sharonite

SHARP
2299 chad (4), *sharp*
sword
2303 chaddûwd (1),
pointed, jagged
2742 chârûwts (2),
threshing-sledge
3913 lâțash (1), to
sharpen; to *pierce*
6697 tsûwr (2), *rock*
6864 tsôr (1), flint-*stone*
knife

8127 shên (2), *tooth*
8150 shânan (4), to *pierce*
3691 ŏxus (7), *sharp*

SHARPEN
3913 lâṭash (1), to
sharpen; to pierce
5324 nâtsab (1), to *station*

SHARPENED
2300 châdad (3), *to be,
make sharp; severe*
8150 shânan (1), to
pierce; to inculcate

SHARPENETH
2300 châdad (2), *to be,
make sharp; severe*
3913 lâṭash (1), to
sharpen; to pierce

SHARPER
5114 tŏmŏtĕrŏs (1), *more
keen*

SHARPLY
2394 chozqâh (1),
vehemence, harshness
664 apŏtŏmōs (1),
abruptly, peremptorily

SHARPNESS
664 apŏtŏmōs (1),
abruptly, peremptorily

SHARUHEN
8287 Shârûwchen (1),
abode of pleasure

SHASHAI
8343 Shâshay (1), *whitish*

SHASHAK
8349 Shâshaq (2),
pedestrian

SHAUL
7586 Shâ'ûwl (7), *asked*

SHAULITES
7587 Shâ'ûwlîy (1),
Shalite

SHAVE
1548 gâlach (12), to *shave*
5674+8593 'âbar (1), to
cross over; to transition
3587 xuraō (1), to *shave*

SHAVED
1494 gâzaz (1), to *shave*
1548 gâlach (3), to *shave*

SHAVEH
7740 Shâvêh (1), *plain*
7741 Shâvêh
Qiryâthayim (1), *plain
of a double city*

SHAVEN
1548 gâlach (5), to *shave*
3587 xuraō (2), to *shave*

SHAVSHA
7798 Shavshâ' (1), *joyful*

SHEAF
485 'ǎlummâh (2), *sheaf*
5995 'âmîyr (1), *bunch*
6016 'ômer (6), *measure*

SHEAL
7594 Shᵉ'âl (1), *request*

SHEALTIEL
7597 Shᵉ'altîy'êl (9), *I
have asked God*

SHEAR
1494 gâzaz (4), to *shear*

SHEAR-JASHUB
7610 Shᵉ'âr Yâshûwb (1),
remnant will return

SHEARER
2751 kĕirō (1), to *shear*

SHEARERS
1494 gâzaz (3), to *shear*

SHEARIAH
8187 Shᵉ'aryâh (2),
Jehovah has stormed

SHEARING
1044 Bêyth 'Êqed (1),
house of (the) *binding*
1044+7462 Bêyth 'Êqed
(1), *house of* (the)
binding
1494 gâzaz (1), to *shear*

SHEATH
5084 nâdân (1), *sheath*
8593 ta'ar (6), *scabbard*
2336 thēkē (1), *scabbard*

SHEAVES
485 'ǎlummâh (3), *sheaf*
5995 'âmîyr (2), *bunch*
6016 'ômer (2), *measure*
6194 'ârêm (1), *sheaf*

SHEBA
7614 Shᵉbâ' (22), *Sheba*
7652 Sheba' (10), *seven*

SHEBAH
7656 Shib'âh (1), *seventh*

SHEBAM
7643 Sᵉbâm (1), *spice*

SHEBANIAH
7645 Shᵉbanyâh (7),
Jehovah has prospered

SHEBARIM
7671 Shᵉbârîym (1), *ruins*

SHEBER
7669 Sheber (1), *crushing*

SHEBNA
7644 Shebnâ' (9), *growth*

SHEBUEL
7619 Shᵉbûw'êl (3),
*captive (or returned) of
God*

SHECANIAH
7935 Shᵉkanyâh (2),
Jehovah has dwelt

SHECHANIAH
7935 Shᵉkanyâh (8),
Jehovah has dwelt

SHECHEM
7927 Shᵉkem (45), *ridge*
7928 Shekem (17),
shoulder

SHECHEM'S
7927 Shᵉkem (2), *ridge*

SHECHEMITES
7930 Shikmîy (1),
Shikmite

SHED
5064 nâgar (1), to *pour*
7760 sûwm (1), to *put*
8210 shâphak (35), to
spill forth; to expend;
1632 ĕkchĕō (11), to *pour*

SHEDDER
8210 shâphak (1), to *spill
forth; to expend*

SHEDDETH
8210 shâphak (2), to *spill*

SHEDDING
130 haimatĕkchusia (1),
pouring of blood

SHEDEUR
7707 Shᵉdêy'ûwr (5),
spreader of light

SHEEP
3532 kebes (2), *young
ram*
3775 keseb (9), *young
ram sheep*
6629 tsô'n (111), *flock of
sheep or goats*
6792 tsônê' (2), *flock*
7353 râchêl (2), *ewe*
7716 seh (16), *sheep*
4262 prŏbatikŏs (1),
Sheep Gate
4263 prŏbatŏn (39), *sheep*

SHEEP'S
4263 prŏbatŏn (1), *sheep*

SHEEPCOTE
5116 nâveh (2), *at home;
lovely; home*

SHEEPCOTES
1448+6629 gᵉdêrâh (1),
enclosure for flocks

SHEEPFOLD
833+4263 aulē (1), *house;
courtyard; sheepfold*

SHEEPFOLDS
1488+6629 gêz (1), *shorn
fleece; mown grass*
4356+6629 miklâ'âh (1),
sheep or goat pen
4942 mishpâth (1), *pair
of stalls for cattle*

SHEEPMASTER
5349 nôqêd (1), *owner or
tender of sheep*

SHEEPSHEARERS
1494 gâzaz (2), to *shear;
shave; destroy*
1494+6629 gâzaz (1), to
shear; shave; destroy

SHEEPSKINS
3374 mēlōtē (1),
sheep-skin

SHEET
3607 ŏthŏnē (2), *linen
sail cloth*

SHEETS
5466 câdîyn (2), *shirt*

SHEHARIAH
7841 Shᵉcharyâh (1),
Jehovah has sought

SHEKEL
1235 beqa' (1), *half
shekel*
8255 sheqel (41),
standard weight

SHEKELS
8255 sheqel (45),
standard weight

SHELAH
7956 Shêlâh (10), *request*
7974 Shelach (1), *spear*

SHELANITES
8024 Shêlânîy (1),
Shelanite

SHELEMIAH
8018 Shelemyâh (10),
*thank-offering of
Jehovah*

SHELEPH
8026 Sheleph (2), *extract*

SHELESH
8028 Shelesh (1), *triplet*

SHELOMI
8015 Shᵉlômîy (1),
peaceable

SHELOMITH
8013 Shᵉlômôwth (4),
pacifications
8019 Shᵉlômîyth (5),
peaceableness

SHELOMOTH
8013 Shᵉlômôwth (1),
pacifications

SHELTER
4268 machǎceh (2),
shelter; refuge

SHELUMIEL
8017 Shᵉlûmîy'êl (5),
peace of God

SHEM
8035 Shêm (17), *name*

SHEMA
8087 Shema' (6), *heard*

SHEMAAH
8094 Shᵉmâ'âh (1),
annunciation

SHEMAIAH
8098 Shᵉma'yâh (40),
Jehovah has heard

SHEMARIAH
8114 Shᵉmaryâh (4),
Jehovah has guarded

SHEMEBER
8038 Shem'êber (1),
illustrious

SHEMER
8106 Shemer (2),
settlings of wine, dregs

SHEMIDA
8061 Shᵉmîydâ' (2),
name of knowing

SHEMIDAH
8061 Shᵉmîydâ' (1),
name of knowing

SHEMIDAITES
8062 Shᵉmîydâ'îy (1),
Shemidaite

SHEMINITH
8067 shᵉmîynîyth (3),
(poss.) *eight*-stringed
lyre

SHEMIRAMOTH
8070 Shᵉmîyrâmôwth
(4), *name of heights*

SHEMUEL
8050 Shᵉmûw'êl (3),
heard of God

SHEN
8129 Shên (1), *crag*

SHENAZAR
8137 Shen'atstsar (1),
Shenatstsar

8149 Shᵉnîyr (2), *peak*

English

SHEPHAM
8221 Sh^ephâm (2), *bare*

SHEPHATIAH
8203 Sh^ephaṭyâh (13), *Jehovah has judged*

SHEPHERD
7462 râ'âh (27), to *tend* a flock, i.e. *pasture* it
7462+6629 râ'âh (1), to *tend* a flock
7473 rô'îy (1), *shepherd*
750 archipŏimēn (1), *head shepherd*
4166 pŏimēn (13), *shepherd*

SHEPHERD'S
7462 râ'âh (1), to *tend* a flock, i.e. *pasture* it
7473 rô'îy (1), *shepherd*

SHEPHERDS
7462 râ'âh (31), to *tend* a flock, i.e. *pasture* it
7462+6629 râ'âh (2), to *tend* a flock
4166 pŏimēn (4), *shepherd*

SHEPHERDS'
7462 râ'âh (1), to *tend* a flock, i.e. *pasture* it

SHEPHI
8195 Sh^ephôw (1), *baldness*

SHEPHO
8195 Sh^ephôw (1), *baldness*

SHEPHUPHAN
8197 Sh^ephûwphâm (1), *serpent-like*

SHERAH
7609 She'ĕrâh (1), *kindred* by blood

SHERD
2789 cheres (1), *pottery*

SHERDS
2789 cheres (1), *pottery*

SHEREBIAH
8274 Shêrêbyâh (8), *Jehovah has brought heat*

SHERESH
8329 Sheresh (1), *root*

SHEREZER
8272 Shar'etser (1), *Sharetser*

SHERIFFS
8614 tiphtay (Ch.) (2), *lawyer, officer*

SHESHACH
8347 Shêshak (2), *Sheshak*

SHESHAI
8344 Shêshay (3), *whitish*

SHESHAN
8348 Shêshân (4), *lily*

SHESHBAZZAR
8339 Shêshbatstsar (4), *Sheshbatstsar*

SHETH
8352 Shêth (2), *put*, i.e. *substituted*

SHETHAR
8369 Shêthâr (1), *Shethar*

SHETHAR-BOZNAI
8370 Sh^ethar Bôwz^enay (4), *Shethar-Bozenai*

SHEVA
7724 Sh^evâ' (2), *false*

SHEW
1319 bâsar (3), to *announce* (good news)
1540 gâlâh (5), to *reveal*
1971 hakkârâh (1), *respect*, i.e. partiality
2324 chăvâ' (Ch.) (13), to *show*
2331 châvâh (5), to *show*
3045 yâda' (12), to *know*
3313 yâpha' (1), to *shine*
5046 nâgad (37), to *announce*
5414 nâthan (5), to *give*
5608 çâphar (5), to *inscribe*; to *enumerate*
6213 'âsâh (21), to *do*
6754 tselem (1), *phantom*; *idol*
7200 râ'âh (27), to *see*
7760 sûwm (1), to *put*
7896 shîyth (1), to *place*
8085 shâma' (3), to *hear*
312 anaggĕllō (4), to *announce* in detail
322 anadĕiknumi (1), to *indicate, appoint*
518 apaggĕllō (5), to *announce, proclaim*
1165 dĕigmatizō (1), to *exhibit, expose*
1166 dĕiknuō (20), to *show, make known*
1325 didōmi (3), to *give*
1334 diēgĕŏmai (1), to *relate fully, describe*
1731 ĕndĕiknumi (7), to *show, display*
1754 ĕnĕrgĕō (2), to be *active, efficient, work*
1804 ĕxaggĕllō (1), to *declare, proclaim*
1925 ĕpidĕiknumi (6), to *exhibit, call attention to*
2097 ĕuaggĕlizō (1), to *announce good news*
2146 ĕuprŏsōpĕō (1), to *make a good display*
2151 ĕusĕbĕō (1), to *put religion into practice*
2605 kataggĕllō (3), to *proclaim, promulgate*
2698 katatithēmi (1), to *place down, to deposit*
3004 lĕgō (1), to *say*
3056 lŏgŏs (1), *word, matter, thing; Word*
3377 mēnuō (1), to *report, declare*
3936 paristēmi (1), to *stand beside, present*
4392 prŏphasis (1), *pretext, excuse*
5263 hupŏdĕiknumi (2), to *exemplify*
5319 phanĕrŏō (1), to *render apparent*

SHEWBREAD
3899+4635 lechem (4), *food, bread*
3899+6440 lechem (6), *food, bread*
4635 ma'ăreketh (3), *pile* of loaves, *arrangement*
6440 pânîym (1), *face*
740+4286 artos (3), *loaf* of bread
4286+740 prŏthĕsis (1), *setting forth*

SHEWED
1540 gâlâh (2), to *reveal*
3045 yâda' (5), to *know*
3190 yâṭab (1), to be, *make well*
3384 yârâh (1), to *throw*
5046 nâgad (18), to *announce*
5186 nâṭâh (1), to *stretch*
5414 nâthan (1), to *give*
6213 'âsâh (17), to *do*
6567 pârash (1), to *separate*; to *disperse*
7200 râ'âh (37), to *see*
7760 sûwm (1), to *put*
8085 shâma' (4), to *hear*
312 anaggĕllō (2), to *announce* in detail
518 apaggĕllō (6), to *announce, proclaim*
1096 ginŏmai (1), to be
1166 dĕiknuō (8), to *show, make known*
1213 dēlŏō (1), to *make plain* by words
1325+1717+1096 didōmi (1), to *give*
1718 ĕmphanizō (1), to *show forth*
1731 ĕndĕiknumi (1), to *show, display*
1925 ĕpidĕiknumi (1), to *exhibit, call attention to*
3170 mĕgalunō (1), to *increase or extol*
3377 mēnuō (1), to *report, declare*
3700 ŏptanŏmai (1), to *appear*
3930 parĕchō (1), to *hold near*, i.e. to *present*
3936 paristēmi (1), to *stand beside, present*
4160 pŏiĕō (4), to *make*
4293 prŏkataggĕllō (2), to *predict, promise*
5268 hupŏzugiŏn (1), *donkey*
5319 phanĕrŏō (4), to *render apparent*

SHEWEDST
5414 nâthan (1), to *give*
7200 râ'âh (1), to *see*

SHEWEST
6213 'âsâh (1), to *do*
1166 dĕiknuō (1), to *show*
4160 pŏiĕō (1), to *make*

SHEWETH
1540+241 gâlâh (2), to *denude; uncover*
2331 châvâh (1), to *show*
5046 nâgad (6), to *announce*
6213 'âsâh (2), to *do*
7200 râ'âh (3), to *see*
1166 dĕiknuō (2), to *show*
1658 ĕlĕuthĕrŏs (2), *unrestrained*

SHEWING
263 'achăvâh (Ch.) (1), *solution*
5608 çâphar (1), to *inscribe*; to *enumerate*
6213 'âsâh (2), to *do*
6692 tsûwts (1), to *twinkle*, i.e. *glance*
323 anadĕixis (1), act of public *exhibition*
584 apŏdĕiknumi (1), to *demonstrate*
1731 ĕndĕiknumi (2), to *show, display*
1925 ĕpidĕiknumi (2), to *exhibit, call attention to*
3930 parĕchō (1), to *hold near*, i.e. to *present*

SHIBBOLETH
7641 shibbŏl (1), *stream; ear* of grain

SHIBMAH
7643 S^ebâm (1), *spice*

SHICRON
7942 Shikk^erôwn (1), *drunkenness*

SHIELD
3591 kîydôwn (2), *dart*
4043 mâgên (33), small *shield* (buckler)
6793 tsinnâh (9), large *shield; piercing cold*
2375 thurĕŏs (1), large door-shaped *shield*

SHIELDS
4043 mâgên (15), small *shield* (buckler)
6793 tsinnâh (1), large *shield; piercing cold*
7982 sheleṭ (7), *shield*

SHIGGAION
7692 Shiggâyôwn (1), *dithyramb or poem*

SHIGIONOTH
7692 Shiggâyôwn (1), *dithyramb or poem*

SHIHON
7866 Shî'yôwn (1), *ruin*

SHIHOR
7883 Shîychôwr (1), *dark*, i.e. *turbid*

SHIHOR-LIBNATH
7884 Shîychôwr Libnâth (1), *darkish whiteness*

SHILHI
7977 Shilchîy (2), *armed*

SHILHIM
7978 Shilchîym (1), *javelins or sprouts*

SHILLEM
8006 Shillêm (2), *requital*

SHILLEMITES
8016 Shillêmîy (1), *Shilemite*

SHILOAH
7975 Shilôach (1), *small stream*

SHILOH
7886 Shîylôh (1), *tranquil*
7887 Shîylôh (32), *tranquil*

SHILONI
8023 Shîlônîy (1), *Shiloni*

SHILONITE
7888 Shiylôwnîy (5), *Shilonite*

SHILONITES
7888 Shiylôwnîy (1), *Shilonite*

SHILSHAH
8030 Shilshâh (1), *triplication*

SHIMEA
8092 Shim'â' (4), *annunciation*

SHIMEAH
8039 Shim'âh (1), *obedient*
8092 Shim'â' (1), *annunciation*
8093 Shim'âh (2), *annunciation*

SHIMEAM
8043 Shim'âm (1), *obedient*

SHIMEATH
8100 Shim'âth (2), *annunciation*

SHIMEATHITES
8101 Shim'âthiy (1), *Shimathite*

SHIMEI
8096 Shim'iy (41), *famous*
8097 Shim'iy (1), *Shimite*

SHIMEON
8095 Shim'ôwn (1), *hearing*

SHIMHI
8096 Shim'iy (1), *famous*

SHIMI
8096 Shim'iy (1), *famous*

SHIMITES
8097 Shim'iy (1), *Shimite*

SHIMMA
8092 Shim'â' (1), *annunciation*

SHIMON
7889 Shîymôwn (1), *desert*

SHIMRATH
8119 Shimrâth (1), *guardship*

SHIMRI
8113 Shimriy (3), *watchful*

SHIMRITH
8116 Shimrîyth (1), *female guard*

SHIMROM
8110 Shimrôwn (1), *guardianship*

SHIMRON
8110 Shimrôwn (4), *guardianship*

SHIMRON-MERON
8112 Shimrôwn Mᵉr'ôwn (1), *guard of lashing*

SHIMRONITES
8117 Shimrônîy (1), *Shimronite*

SHIMSHAI
8124 Shimshay (Ch.) (4), *sunny*

SHINAB
8134 Shin'âb (1), *father has turned*

SHINAR
8152 Shin'âr (7), *Shinar*

SHINE
215 'ôwr (11), *to be luminous*
1984 hâlal (1), *to shine*
2094 zâhar (1), *to enlighten*
3313 yâpha' (4), *to shine*
5050 nâgahh (3), *to illuminate*
5774 'ûwph (1), *to cover*
6245 'âshath (1), *to be sleek; to excogitate*
6670 tsâhal (1), *to be cheerful; to sound*
826 augazō (1), *to beam forth*
1584 ĕklampō (1), *to be resplendent, shine*
2989 lampō (3), *to radiate brilliancy*
5316 phainō (3), *to shine*

SHINED
215 'ôwr (1), *to be luminous*
1984 hâlal (2), *to shine*
3313 yâpha' (2), *to shine*
5050 nâgahh (1), *to illuminate*
2989 lampō (2), *to radiate brilliancy*
4015 pĕriastraptō (1), *to envelop in light, shine*

SHINETH
166 'âhal (1), *to be bright*
215 'ôwr (2), *to be luminous*
2989 lampō (1), *to radiate*
5316 phainō (5), *to shine*

SHINING
5051 nôgahh (6), *brilliancy*
796 astrapē (1), *lightning; light's glare*
797 astraptō (1), *to flash*
4034 pĕrilampō (1), *to shine all around*
4744 stilbō (1), *to gleam*
5316 phainō (1), *to shine*

SHIP
591 'ŏnîyâh (4), *ship*
5600 çᵉphîynâh (1), *sea-going vessel*
6716 tsîy (1), *ship*
3490 nauklērŏs (1), *ship captain*
3491 naus (1), *boat*
4142 plŏiariŏn (2), *small boat*
4143 plŏiŏn (58), *ship*

SHIPHI
8230 Shiph'îy (1), *copious*

SHIPHMITE
8225 Shiphmîy (1), *Shiphmite*

SHIPHRAH
8236 Shiphrâh (1), *brightness of skies*

SHIPHTAN
8204 Shiphtân (1), *judge-like*

SHIPMASTER
7227+2259 rab (1), *great*
2942 kubĕrnētēs (1), *helmsman, captain*

SHIPMEN
582+591 'ĕnôwsh (1), *man; person, human*
3492 nautēs (2), *sailor*

SHIPPING
4143 plŏiŏn (1), *ship*

SHIPS
591 'ŏnîyâh (26), *ship*
6716 tsîy (3), *ship*
4142 plŏiariŏn (1), *small boat*
4143 plŏiŏn (8), *boat*

SHIPWRECK
3489 nauagĕō (2), *to be shipwrecked*

SHISHA
7894 Shîyshâ' (1), *whiteness*

SHISHAK
7895 Shîyshaq (7), *Shishak*

SHITRAI
7861 Shiṭray (1), *magisterial*

SHITTAH
7848 shiṭṭâh (1), *acacia*

SHITTIM
7848 shiṭṭâh (27), *acacia*
7851 Shiṭṭiym (5), *acacia*

SHIVERS
4937 suntribō (1), *to crush completely*

SHIZA
7877 Shîyzâ' (1), *Shiza*

SHOA
7772 Shôwa' (1), *rich*

SHOBAB
7727 Shôwbâb (4), *rebellious*

SHOBACH
7731 Shôwbâk (2), (poss.) *thicket*

SHOBAI
7630 Shôbay (2), *captor*

SHOBAL
7732 Shôwbâl (9), *overflowing*

SHOBEK
7733 Shôwbêq (1), *forsaking*

SHOBI
7629 Shôbîy (1), *captor*

SHOCHO
7755 Sôwkôh (1), *hedged*

SHOCHOH
7755 Sôwkôh (2), *hedged*

SHOCK
1430 gâdîysh (1), *stack of sheaves, shock of grain*

SHOCKS
1430 gâdîysh (1), *stack of sheaves, shock of grain*

SHOCO
7755 Sôwkôh (1), *hedged*

SHOD
5274 nâ'al (2), *to fasten up, to put on sandals*

SHOE
5265 hupŏdĕō (2), *to put on shoes or sandals*

SHOE
5275 na'al (9), *sandal*

SHOE'S
5266 hupŏdĕma (1), *sandal*

SHOELATCHET
8288+5275 sᵉrôwk (1), sandal *thong*

SHOES
4515 man'âl (1), *bolt on gate*
5275 na'al (11), *sandal*
5266 hupŏdĕma (9), *sandal*

SHOHAM
7719 Shôham (1), *beryl*

SHOMER
7763 Shôwmêr (2), *keeper*

SHONE
2224 zârach (1), *to rise; to be bright*
7160 qâran (3), *to shine*
4015 pĕriastraptō (1), *to envelop in light, shine*
4034 pĕrilampō (1), *to shine all around*
5316 phainō (1), *to shine*

SHOOK
1607 gâ'ash (3), *to agitate violently, shake*
5287 nâ'ar (1), *to tumble*
7264 râgaz (1), *to quiver*
7493 râ'ash (2), *to quake*
8058 shâmaṭ (1), *to jostle*
660 apŏtinassō (1), *to brush off, shake off*
1621 ĕktinassō (2), *to shake violently*
4531 salĕuō (1), *to waver*

SHOOT
1272 bârach (1), *to flee*
1869 dârak (1), *to tread; to string a bow*
3034 yâdâh (1), *to throw*
3384 yârâh (10), *to throw, shoot an arrow*
5414 nâthan (2), *to give*
6362 pâṭar (1), *to burst through; to emit*
7971 shâlach (1), *to send away*
4261 prŏballō (1), *to push to the front, germinate*

SHOOTERS
3384 yârâh (1), *to throw, shoot an arrow*

SHOOTETH
3318 yâtsâ' (1), *to go, bring out*
7971 shâlach (1), *to send away*
4160 pŏiĕō (1), *to do*

SHOOTING
5927 'âlâh (1), *to ascend, be high, mount*

SHOPHACH
7780 Shôwphâk (2), *poured*

English

SHOPHAN
5855 'Aṭrôwth Shôphân (1), crowns of Shophan

SHORE
2348 chôwph (2), cove
7097 qâtseh (1), extremity
8193 sâphâh (6), edge
123 aigialŏs (6), beach
4358 prŏsŏrmizō (1), to moor to, i.e. land at
5491 chĕilŏs (1), lip

SHORN
7094 qâtsab (1), to clip
2751 kĕirō (3), to shear

SHORT
2465 cheled (1), fleeting
7114 qâtsar (1), to curtail
7138 qârôwb (2), near
3641 ŏligŏs (2), small
4932 suntĕmnō (2), to cut short, i.e. do speedily
4958 sustĕllō (1), to draw together, i.e. enwrap
5302 hustĕrĕō (2), to be inferior; to fall short
5610 hōra (1), hour

SHORTENED
7114 qâtsar (5), to curtail
2856 kŏlŏbŏō (4), shorten

SHORTER
7114 qâtsar (2), to curtail

SHORTLY
4116 mâhar (1), to hurry
4120 mᵉhêrâh (1), hurry
7138 qârôwb (1), near
1722+5034 ĕn (4), in; during; because of
2112 ĕuthĕŏs (1), at once
5030 tachĕŏs (4), speedily
5031 tachinŏs (1), soon
5032 tachiŏn (2), more rapidly, more speedily

SHOSHANNIM
7799 shûwshan (2), white lily; straight trumpet

SHOSHANNIM-EDUTH
7802 Shûwshan 'Êdûwth (1), lily (or trumpet) of assemblage

SHOT
3384 yârâh (7), to shoot
5927 'âlâh (1), to ascend, be high, mount
7232 râbab (2), to shoot
7819 shâchaṭ (1), to slaughter; butcher
7971 shâlach (5), to send away

SHOULD
1163 dĕi (3), it is (was) necessary
3195 mĕllō (25), to intend, i.e. be about to
3784 ŏphĕilō (1), to owe

SHOULDER
2220 zᵉrôwa' (2), arm
3802 kâthêph (9), shoulder-piece; wall
7785 shôwq (13), lower leg
7926 shᵉkem (12), neck
7929 shikmâh (1), shoulder-bone

SHOULDERPIECES
3802 kâthêph (4), shoulder-piece; wall

SHOULDERS
3802 kâthêph (13), shoulder-piece; wall
7926 shᵉkem (5), neck
5606 ōmŏs (2), shoulder

SHOUT
1959 hêydâd (1), acclamation, shout
6030 'ânâh (1), to shout
6670 tsâhal (1), to be cheerful; to sound
6681 tsâvach (1), to screech exultingly
7321 rûwa' (12), to shout
7442 rânan (6), to shout
7768 shâva' (1), to halloo, call for help
8643 tᵉrûw'âh (9), battle-cry; clangor
2019 ĕpiphōnĕō (1), to exclaim, shout
2752 kĕlĕuma (1), cry of incitement

SHOUTED
7321 rûwa' (11), to shout
7442 rânan (1), to shout
7452 rêa' (1), shout
8643 tᵉrûw'âh (1), battle-cry; clangor

SHOUTETH
7442 rânan (1), to shout

SHOUTING
1959 hêydâd (4), shout of joy
7321 rûwa' (1), to shout
7440 rinnâh (1), shout
8643 tᵉrûw'âh (8), battle-cry; clangor

SHOUTINGS
8663 tᵉshû'âh (1), crashing or clamor

SHOVEL
7371 rachath (1), winnowing-fork

SHOVELS
3257 yâ' (9), shove

SHOWER
1653 geshem (3), rain
3655 ōmbrŏs (1), storm

SHOWERS
1653 geshem (2), rain
2230 zerem (1), flood
7241 râbîyb (6), rain

SHRANK
5384 nâsheh (2), rheumatic or crippled

SHRED
6398 pâlach (1), to slice

SHRINES
3485 naŏs (1), shrine

SHROUD
2793 chôresh (1), forest

SHRUBS
7880 sìyach (1), shrubbery

SHUA
7770 Shûwa' (1), halloo
7774 Shûw'â' (1), wealth

SHUAH
7744 Shûwach (2), dell

SHOBACH
7746 Shûwchâh (1), chasm
7770 Shûwa' (2), halloo

SHUAL
7777 Shûw'âl (2), jackal

SHUBAEL
2619 Châçadyâh (3), Jehovah has favored

SHUHAM
7748 Shûwchâm (1), humbly

SHUHAMITES
7749 Shûwchâmîy (2), Shuchamite

SHUHITE
7747 Shuchîy (5), Shuchite

SHULAMITE
7759 Shûwlammîyth (2), peaceful

SHUMATHITES
8126 Shûmâthîy (1), Shumathite

SHUN
4026 pĕriistēmi (1), to avoid, shun

SHUNAMMITE
7767 Shûwnammîyth (8), Shunammitess

SHUNEM
7766 Shûwnêm (3), quietly

SHUNI
7764 Shûwnîy (2), quiet

SHUNITES
7765 Shûwnîy (1), Shunite

SHUNNED
5288 hupŏstĕllō (1), to cower or shrink

SHUPHAM
8197 Shᵉphûwphâm (1), serpent-like

SHUPHAMITES
7781 Shûwphâmîy (1), Shuphamite

SHUPPIM
8206 Shuppîym (3), serpents

SHUR
7793 Shûwr (6), wall

SHUSHAN
7800 Shûwshan (21), lily

SHUSHAN-EDUTH
7802 Shûwshan 'Êdûwth (1), lily (or trumpet) of assemblage

SHUT
332 'âṭar (1), to close up
1479 gûwph (1), to shut
2902 ṭûwach (1), to whitewash
3607 kâlâ' (4), to stop
5274 nâ'al (1), to lock
5462 çâgar (55), to shut
5463 çᵉgar (Ch.) (1), to close up
5526 çâkak (1), to entwine; to fence in
5640 çâtham (2), to stop
6113 'âtsar (16), to hold
6887 tsârar (1), to cramp

SHOPHAN
7092 qâphats (3), to draw together, to leap; to die
8173 shâ'a' (1), to fondle, please or amuse (self)
608 apŏklĕiō (1), to close
2623 katakĕiō (2), to incarcerate, lock up
2808 klĕiō (13), to close
4788 sugklĕiō (1), to net fish; to lock up persons

SHUTHALHITES
8364 Shûthalchîy (1), Shuthalchite

SHUTHELAH
7803 Shûwthelach (4), crash of breakage

SHUTTETH
331 'âṭam (1), to close
5462 çâgar (1), to shut
5640 çâtham (1), to stop
6095 'âtsâh (1), to close
6105 'âtsam (1), to be, make powerful
2808 klĕiō (3), to shut

SHUTTING
5462 çâgar (1), to shut

SHUTTLE
708 'ereg (1), shuttle

SIA
5517 Çîy'â' (1), congregation

SIAHA
5517 Çîy'â' (1), congregation

SIBBECAI
5444 Çibbᵉkay (2), thicket-like

SIBBECHAI
5444 Çibbᵉkay (2), thicket-like

SIBBOLETH
5451 Çibbôleth (1), ear of grain

SIBMAH
7643 Sᵉbâm (4), spice

SIBRAIM
5453 Çibrayim (1), double hope

SICHEM
7927 Shᵉkem (1), ridge

SICK
605 'ânash (1), to be frail
1739 dâveh (1), menstrual; fainting
2470 châlâh (34), to be weak, sick, afflicted
2483 chŏlîy (1), malady
8463 tachălûw' (1), malady, disease
732 arrhōstŏs (4), infirmed, ill
770 asthĕnĕō (17), to be feeble
772 asthĕnēs (6), weak
2192+2560 ĕchō (8), to have; hold; keep
2577 kamnō (1), to sicken
3885 paralutikŏs (11), lame person
4445 purĕssō (2), to burn with a fever

SICKLE
2770 chermêsh (2), sickle
4038 maggâl (2), sickle

1407 drĕpanŏn (8), gathering *hook*

SICKLY
732 arrhŏstŏs (1), *infirmed, ill*

SICKNESS
1739 dâveh (1), *menstrual; fainting*
2483 chŏlîy (11), *malady*
4245 machăleh (3), *sickness*
769 asthĕnĕia (1), *feebleness* of body
3554 nŏsŏs (3), *malady*

SICKNESSES
2483 chŏlîy (1), *malady*
8463 tachălûw' (1), *malady, disease*
3554 nŏsŏs (2), *malady*

SIDDIM
7708 Siddîym (3), *flats*

SIDE
2296 châgar (1), to *gird*
2348 chôwph (1), *cove*
3027 yâd (5), *hand; power*
3225 yâmîyn (4), *right*
3409 yârêk (7), *side*
3411 yᵉrêkâh (2), *far away places*
3541 kôh (2), *thus*
3802 kâthêph (29), *side-piece*
4217 mizrâch (2), *east*
4975 môthen (4), *loins*
5048 neged (2), *beside*
5437 çâbab (1), to *surround*
5439 çâbîyb (26), *circle*
5675 'ăbar (Ch.) (7), region *across*
5676 'êber (56), *opposite*
6285 pê'âh (50), *direction*
6311 pôh (2), *here*
6654 tsad (20), *side*
6753 Tsᵉlelpôwnîy (2), *shade-facing*
6763 tsêlâ' (22), *side*
6921 qâdîym (1), *East; eastward; east wind*
6924 qedem (3), *East, eastern; antiquity*
6954 Qᵉhêlâthâh (1), *convocation*
7023 qîyr (2), *side-wall*
7097 qâtseh (1), *extremity*
7307 rûwach (5), *breath; wind; life*-spirit
7859 sᵉṭar (Ch.) (1), *side*
8040 sᵉmô'wl (1), *left*
8193 sâphâh (3), *edge*
492 antiparĕrchŏmai (2), to go along opposite
1188 dĕxiŏs (2), *right*
1782 ĕntĕuthĕn (2), on both sides
3313 mĕrŏs (1), *division*
3840 pantŏthĕn (1), *from, on all sides*
3844 para (15), *besides*
4008 pĕran (13), *across*
4125 plĕura (5), *side*

SIDES
3411 yᵉrêkâh (19), *far away places*
3802 kâthêph (4), *shoulder*-piece; *wall*
5676 'êber (4), *opposite*

6285 pê'âh (1), *direction*
6654 tsad (9), *side*
6763 tsêlâ' (4), *side*
7023 qîyr (2), *side-wall*
7253 reba' (3), *fourth*
7307 rûwach (1), *breath; wind; life*-spirit

SIDON
6721 Tsîydôwn (2), *fishery*
4605 Sidōn (12), *fishery*

SIDONIANS
6722 Tsîydônîy (5), *Tsidonian*

SIEGE
4692 mâtsôwr (13), *siege-mound; distress*
6696 tsûwr (3), to *cramp*

SIEVE
3531 kᵉbârâh (1), *sieve*
5299 nâphâh (1), *sieve*

SIFT
5128 nûwa' (1), to *waver*
5130 nûwph (1), to *quiver, vibrate, rock*
4617 siniazō (1), to *shake in a sieve*

SIFTED
5128 nûwa' (1), to *waver*

SIGH
584 'ânach (7), to *sigh*

SIGHED
584 'ânach (1), to *sigh*
389 anastĕnazō (1), to *sigh deeply*
4727 stĕnazō (1), to *sigh*

SIGHEST
584 'ânach (1), to *sigh*

SIGHETH
584 'ânach (1), to *sigh*

SIGHING
585 'ănâchâh (5), *sighing*
603 'ănâqâh (2), *shrieking, groaning*

SIGHS
585 'ănâchâh (1), *sighing*

SIGHT
2379 chăzôwth (Ch.) (2), *view, visible sight*
4758 mar'eh (18), *appearance; vision*
5048 neged (2), *before*
5869 'ayin (218), *sight*
6440 pânîym (39), *face*
7200 râ'âh (1), to *see*
308 anablĕpō (15), to *look up; to recover sight*
309 anablĕpsis (1), *restoration of sight*
991 blĕpō (2), to *look at*
1491 ĕidŏs (1), *sight*
1715 ĕmprŏsthĕn (3), in *front of*
1726 ĕnantiŏn (1), in the *presence of*
1799 ĕnōpiŏn (21), *before*
2335 thĕōria (1), *sight*
2714 katĕnōpiŏn (2), *directly in front of*
3705 hŏrama (1), *supernatural spectacle*
3706 hŏrasis (1), *appearance, vision*
3788 ŏphthalmŏs (1), *eye*
3844 para (1), *from; with; besides; on account of*

5324 phantazō (1), to *appear; spectacle, sight*

SIGHTS
5400 phŏbētrŏn (1), *frightening* thing

SIGN
226 'ôwth (33), *sign*
4159 môwphêth (8), *miracle; token or omen*
4864 mas'êth (1), *beacon*
5251 nêç (1), *flag; signal*
6725 tsîyûwn (1), *guiding pillar, monument*
7560 rᵉsham (Ch.) (1), to *record*
3902 parasēmŏs (1), *labeled, marked*
4592 sēmĕiŏn (29), *sign*

SIGNED
7560 rᵉsham (Ch.) (4), to *record*

SIGNET
2368 chôwthâm (8), *signature-ring, seal*
2858 chôthemeth (1), *signet ring seal*
5824 'izqâ' (Ch.) (2), *signet or signet-ring*

SIGNETS
2368 chôwthâm (1), *signature-ring, seal*

SIGNIFICATION
880 aphōnŏs (1), *mute, silent; unmeaning*

SIGNIFIED
4591 sēmainō (2), to *indicate, make known*

SIGNIFIETH
1213 dēlŏō (1), to *make plain by words*

SIGNIFY
1213 dēlŏō (1), to *make plain by words*
1229 diaggĕllō (1), to *herald thoroughly*
1718 ĕmphanizō (1), to *show forth*
4591 sēmainō (1), to *indicate, make known*

SIGNIFYING
1213 dēlŏō (1), to *make plain by words*
4591 sēmainō (3), to *indicate, make known*

SIGNS
226 'ôwth (27), *sign*
852 'âth (Ch.) (3), *sign*
1770 ĕnnĕuŏ (1), to *signal*
4591 sēmainō (17), to *indicate, make known*
4592 sēmĕiŏn (5), *sign*

SIHON
5511 Çîychôwn (37), *tempestuous*

SIHOR
7883 Shîychôwr (3), *dark, i.e. turbid*

SILAS
4609 Silas (13), *sylvan*

SILENCE
481 'âlam (1), to *be silent*
1745 dûwmâh (2), *silence*
1747 dûwmîyâh (1), *silently; quiet, trust*

1820 dâmâh (1), to *be silent; to fail, cease*
1824 dᵉmîy (2), *quiet*
1826 dâmam (6), to *be silent; to be astonished*
1827 dᵉmâmâh (1), *quiet*
2013 hâçâh (3), to *hush*
2790 chârash (5), to *be silent; to be deaf*
2814 châshâh (2), to *hush*
2271 hēsuchia (3), *stillness*
4601 sigaō (3), to *keep silent*
4602 sigē (2), *silence*
5392 phimŏō (2), to *restrain to silence*

SILENT
1748 dûwmâm (1), *silently*
1826 dâmam (4), to *be silent; to be astonished*
1947 hôwlêlâh (1), *folly*
2013 hâçâh (1), to *hush*
2790 chârash (2), to *be silent; to be deaf*

SILK
4897 meshîy (2), *silk*
8336 shêsh (1), *white linen; white marble*
2596 kata (1), *down; according to*

SILLA
5538 Çillâ' (1), *embankment*

SILLY
6601 pâthâh (2), to *be, make simple; to delude*
1133 gunaikariŏn (1), *little, i.e. foolish woman*

SILOAH
7975 Shilôach (1), *rill*

SILOAM
4611 Silōam (3), *rill*

SILVANUS
4610 Silŏuanŏs (4), *sylvan*

SILVER
3701 keçeph (280), *silver*
3702 kᵉçaph (Ch.) (12), *silver money*
7192 qᵉsîyṭah (1), *coin*
693 argurĕŏs (3), *made of silver*
694 arguriŏn (9), *silver*
696 argurŏs (5), *silver*
1406 drachmē (1), *silver coin*

SILVERLINGS
3701 keçeph (1), *silver*

SILVERSMITH
695 argurŏkŏpŏs (1), *worker of silver*

SIMEON
8095 Shim'ôwn (43), *hearing*
8099 Shim'ôniy (1), *Shimonite*
4826 Sumĕōn (6), *hearing*

SIMEONITES
8099 Shim'ôniy (1), *Shimonite*

SIMILITUDE
1823 dᵉmûwth (2), *resemblance, likeness*

English

8403 tabnîyth (2), *model, resemblance*
8544 tᵉmûwnâh (4), *something fashioned*
3665 hŏmŏiŏtēs (1), *resemblance, similarity*
3667 hŏmŏiōma (1), *form; resemblance*
3669 hŏmŏiōsis (1), *resemblance, likeness*

SIMILITUDES
1819 dâmâh (1), to *liken*

SIMON
4613 Simōn (67), *hearing*

SIMON'S
4613 Simōn (7), *hearing*

SIMPLE
6612 pᵉthîy (17), *silly*
6615 pᵉthayûwth (1), *silliness*, i.e. *seducible*
172 akakŏs (1), *innocent*
185 akĕraiŏs (1), *innocent*

SIMPLICITY
6612 pᵉthîy (1), *silly*
8537 tôm (1), *innocence*
572 haplŏtēs (3), *sincerity*

SIMRI
8113 Shimriy (1), *watchful*

SIN
817 'âshâm (3), *guilt*
819 'ashmâh (2), *guiltiness*
2398 châțâ' (68), to *sin*
2399 chêț' (22), *crime*
2401 chățâ'âh (8), *offence*
2402 chațțâ'âh (Ch.) (2), *offence, and penalty*
2403 chațțâ'âh (215), *offence; sin offering*
2409 chațțâyâ' (Ch.) (1), *expiation, sin offering*
5512 Çîyn (6), *Sin*
5771 'âvôn (1), moral *evil*
6588 pesha' (1), *revolt*
7686 shâgâh (1), to *stray*
264 hamartanŏ (15), to *miss the mark*, to *err*
265 hamartēma (1), *sin*
266 hamartia (91), *sin*
361 anamartētŏs (1), *sinless*

SINA
4614 Sina (2), *Sinai*

SINAI
5514 Çîynay (35), *Sinai*
4614 Sina (2), *Sinai*

SINCE
227 'âz (3), *therefore*
310 'achar (2), *after*
518 'îm (1), *whether?; if, although; Oh that!*
1767 day (3), *enough, sufficient*
2008 hênnâh (1), *from here; from there*
3588 kîy (1), *for, that*
4480 min (12), *from*
4480+227 min (1), *from*
4481 min (Ch.) (1), *from*
5750 'ôwd (2), *more*
575 apŏ (9), *from, away*
575+3739 apŏ (3), *from*
1537 ĕk (1), *out, out of*
1893 ĕpĕi (1), *since*

SINCERE
97 adŏlŏs (1), *pure*
1506 ĕilikrinēs (1), *pure*

SINCERELY
8549 tâmîym (2), *entire*
55 hagnŏs (1), *purely*

SINCERITY
8549 tâmîym (1), *integrity*
861 aphtharsia (2), *genuineness*
1103 gnēsiŏs (1), *genuine*
1505 ĕilikrinĕia (3), *purity, sincerity*

SINEW
1517 gîyd (3), *tendon*

SINEWS
1517 gîyd (4), *tendon*
6207 'âraq (1), to *gnaw*

SINFUL
2398 châțâ' (1), to *sin*
2400 chațțâ' (1), *guilty*
2401 chățâ'âh (1), *offence or sacrifice*
266 hamartia (1), *sin*
268 hamartōlŏs (4), *sinner; sinful*

SING
1984 hâlal (2), to *speak praise; thank*
2167 zâmar (33), to *play music*
5414+6963 nâthan (1), to *give*
6030 'ânâh (4), to *sing*
6031 'ânâh (2), to *afflict*
7440 rinnâh (1), *shout*
7442 rânan (25), to *shout*
7788 shûwr (1), to *travel*
7891 shîyr (32), to *sing*
7892 shîyr (1), *singing*
103 a₁dō (1), to *sing*
5214 humnĕō (1), to *celebrate* God in song
5567 psallō (4), to *play a stringed instrument*

SINGED
2761 chărak (Ch.) (1), to *scorch, singe*

SINGER
5329 nâtsach (1), i.e. to *be eminent*
7891 shîyr (1), to *sing*

SINGERS
2171 zammâr (Ch.) (1), *musician*
7891 shîyr (35), to *sing*
7892 shîyr (2), *singing*

SINGETH
7891 shîyr (1), to *sing*

SINGING
2158 zâmîyr (1), *song*
7440 rinnâh (9), *shout*
7442 rânan (2), to *shout for joy*
7445 rᵉnânâh (1), *shout for joy*
7891 shîyr (5), to *sing*
7892 shîyr (4), *singing*
103 a₁dō (2), to *sing*

SINGLE
573 haplŏus (2), *single*

SINGLENESS
572 haplŏtēs (2), *sincerity*
858 aphĕlŏtēs (1), *simplicity; sincerity*

SINGULAR
6381 pâlâ' (1), to *be, make great, difficult*

SINIM
5515 Çîynîym (1), *Sinim*

SINITE
5513 Çîynîy (2), *Sinite*

SINK
2883 țâba' (2), to *sink*
8257 shâqa' (1), to *be overflowed; to abate*
1036 buthizō (1), to *sink*
2670 katapŏntizō (1), to *submerge, be drowned*
5087 tithēmi (1), to *place*

SINNED
2398 châțâ' (102), to *sin*
264 hamartanŏ (15), to *miss the mark*, to *sin*
4258 prŏamartanŏ (2), to *sin previously*

SINNER
2398 châțâ' (8), to *sin*
2403 chațțâ'âh (1), *offence; sin offering*
268 hamartōlŏs (12), *sinner; sinful*

SINNERS
2400 chațțâ' (16), *guilty*
268 hamartōlŏs (30), *sinner; sinful*
3781 ŏphĕilĕtēs (1), *person indebted*

SINNEST
2398 châțâ' (1), to *sin*

SINNETH
2398 châțâ' (13), to *sin*
6213 'âsâh (1), to *do*
7683 shâgag (1), to *sin*
264 hamartanŏ (7), to *sin*

SINNING
2398 châțâ' (2), to *sin*

SINS
819 'ashmâh (2), *guiltiness*
2399 chêț' (8), *crime*
2403 chațțâ'âh (1), *offence; sin offering*
2408 chățîy (Ch.) (1), *sin*
6588 pesha' (2), *revolt*
265 hamartēma (3), *sin*
266 hamartia (78), *sin*
3900 paraptōma (3), *error; transgression*

SION
6726 Tsîyôwn (1), *capital*
7865 Siy'ôn (1), *peak*
4622 Siōn (7), *capital*

SIPHMOTH
8224 Siphmôwth (1), *Siphmoth*

SIPPAI
5598 Çippay (1), *bason-like*

SIR
113 'âdôwn (1), *sovereign*, i.e. *controller*
2962 kuriŏs (11), *supreme, controller, Mr.*

SIRAH
5626 Çîrâh (1), *departure*

SIRION
8304 Sᵉrâyâh (2), *Jehovah has prevailed*

SIRS
435 anēr (6), *man; male*
2962 kuriŏs (1), *supreme, controller, Mr.*

SISAMAI
5581 Çiçmay (2), *Sismai*

SISERA
5516 Çîyçᵉrâ' (21), *Sisera*

SISTER
269 'achôwth (91), *sister*
1733 dôwdâh (1), *aunt*
2994 yᵉbêmeth (2), *sister-in-law*
79 adĕlphē (15), *sister*

SISTER'S
269 'achôwth (5), *sister*
79 adĕlphē (1), *sister*
431 anĕpsiŏs (1), *cousin*

SISTERS
269 'achôwth (11), *sister*
79 adĕlphē (8), *sister*

SIT
3427 yâshab (65), to *dwell*, to *settle*
3488 yᵉthîb (Ch.) (2), to *sit*
5414 nâthan (1), to *give*
5437 çâbab (1), to *surround*
7674 shebeth (1), *rest*
347 anaklinō (6), to *recline*
377 anapiptō (5), *lie down, lean back*
2521 kathēmai (12), to *sit down; to remain*
2523 kathizō (15), to *seat down, dwell*
2621 katakĕimai (1), to *lie down*
2625 kataklinō (2), to *recline, take a place*
4776 sugkathizō (1), to *give, take a seat with*
4873 sunanakĕimai (1), to *recline with at meal*

SITH
518 'îm (1), *whether?; if, although; Oh that!*

SITNAH
7856 Sițnâh (1), *opposition*

SITTEST
3427 yâshab (6), to *settle*
2521 kathēmai (1), to *sit*

SITTETH
1716 dâgar (1), to *brood over; to care for young*
3427 yâshab (25), to *settle*
345 anakĕimai (2), to *recline at a meal*
2521 kathēmai (10), to *sit down; or reside*
2523 kathizō (3), to *seat down, dwell*

SITTING
3427 yâshab (15), to *settle*
4186 môwshâb (2), *seat*
7257 râbats (1), to *recline*
1910 ĕpibainō (1), to *mount, ascend*

2516 kathĕzŏmai (2), to
sit down, be seated
2521 kathēmai (21), to
sit down; to reside
2523 kathizō (1), to *seat
down, dwell*

SITUATE
3427 yâshab (2), to *settle*
4690 mâtsûwq (1),
column; hilltop

SITUATION
4186 môwshâb (1), *site*
5131 nôwph (1), *elevation*

SIVAN
5510 Çîyvân (1), *Sivan*

SIX
8337 shêsh (185), *six;
sixth*
8353 shêth (Ch.) (1), *six;
sixth*
1803 hĕx (11), *six*
1812 hĕxakŏsiŏi (1), *six
hundred*
5516 chi xi stigma (1), 666

SIXSCORE
3967+6242 mê'âh (1),
hundred
8147+6240+7239
shenayim (1), *two*-fold

SIXTEEN
8337+6240 shêsh (22),
six; sixth
1440+1803
hĕbdŏmēkŏnta (1),
seventy

SIXTEENTH
8337+6240 shêsh (3), *six;
sixth*

SIXTH
8337 shêsh (2), *six; sixth*
8338 shâwshâw (1),
(poss.) to *annihilate*
8341 shâshâh (1), to
divide into sixths
8345 shishshîy (26), *sixth*
8353 shêth (Ch.) (1), *six;
sixth*
1623 hĕktŏs (14), *sixth*

SIXTY
8346 shishshîym (11),
sixty
1835 hĕxēkŏnta (3), *sixty*

SIXTYFOLD
1835 hĕxēkŏnta (1), *sixty*

SIZE
4060 middâh (3),
measure; portion
7095 qetseb (2), *shape*

SKIES
7834 shachaq (5), *clouds*

SKILFUL
995 bîyn (1), to *discern*
2451 chokmâh (1),
wisdom
2796 chârâsh (1), skilled
fabricator or worker
3045 yâda' (2), to *know*
3925 lâmad (1), to *teach*
7919 sâkal (1), to *be or
act circumspect*

SKILFULLY
3190 yâṭab (1), to *be,
make well*

SKILFULNESS
8394 tâbûwn (1),
intelligence; argument

SKILL
995 bîyn (1), to *discern*
3045 yâda' (4), to *know*
7919 sâkal (2), to *be or
act circumspect*

SKIN
1320 bâsâr (1), *flesh*
1539 geled (1), *skin*
5785 'ôwr (71), *skin*
1193 dĕrmatinŏs (1),
made of leather *hide*

SKINS
5785 'ôwr (20), *skin*

SKIP
7540 râqad (1), to *spring*

SKIPPED
7540 râqad (2), to *spring*

SKIPPEDST
5110 nûwd (1), to *waver*

SKIPPING
7092 qâphats (1), to *leap*

SKIRT
3671 kânâph (12), *wing*

SKIRTS
3671 kânâph (2), *wing*
6310 peh (1), *mouth*
7757 shûwl (4), *skirt*

SKULL
1538 gulgôleth (2), *skull*
2898 kraniŏn (3), *skull*

SKY
7834 shachaq (2), *clouds*
3772 ŏuranŏs (5), *sky*

SLACK
309 'âchar (2), to *delay*
6113 'âtsar (1), to *hold
back; to maintain, rule*
7423 remîyâh (1),
remissness; treachery
7503 râphâh (3), to
slacken
1019 bradunō (1), to
delay, hesitate

SLACKED
6313 pûwg (1), to *be
sluggish; be numb*

SLACKNESS
1022 bradutēs (1),
tardiness, slowness

SLAIN
2026 hârag (31), to *kill*
2027 hereg (1), *kill*
2076 zâbach (2), to
(sacrificially) *slaughter*
2490 châlal (1), to
profane, defile
2491 châlâl (75), *slain*
2717 chârab (1), to
desolate, destroy
2873 ṭâbach (1), to *kill*
4191 mûwth (18), to *kill*
5062 nâgaph (2), to *strike*
5221 nâkâh (20), to *kill*
6992 qeṭal (Ch.) (4), to *kill*
7523 râtsach (3), to
murder
7819 shâchaṭ (5), to
slaughter; butcher
337 anairĕō (3), to *take
away, murder*
615 apŏktĕinō (7), to *kill*

1722+5408+599 ĕn (1), *in;
during; because of*
4968 sphagiŏn (1),
offering for slaughter
4969 sphazō (6), to
slaughter or to maim

SLANDER
1681 dibbâh (3), *slander*

SLANDERED
7270 râgal (1), to *slander*

SLANDERERS
1228 diabŏlŏs (1),
traducer, i.e. *Satan*

SLANDEREST
5414+1848 nâthan (1), to
give

SLANDERETH
3960 lâshan (1), to
calumniate, malign

SLANDEROUSLY
987 blasphēmĕō (1), to
speak impiously

SLANDERS
7400 râkîyl (2),
scandal-monger

SLANG
7049 qâla' (1), to *sling*

SLAUGHTER
2027 hereg (4), *kill*
2028 hărêgâh (5), *kill*
2873 ṭâbach (5), to *kill*
2875 Ṭebach (9),
massacre
2878 ṭibehâh (1),
butchery
4046 maggêphâh (3),
pestilence; defeat
4293 maṭbêach (1),
slaughter place
4347 makkâh (14), *blow;
wound; pestilence*
4660 mappâts (1),
striking to pieces
5221 nâkâh (5), to *kill*
6993 qeṭel (1), *death*
7524 retsach (1),
crushing; murder-cry
7819 shâchaṭ (1), to
slaughter; butcher
2871 kŏpē (1), *carnage*
4967 sphagē (3), *butchery*
5408 phŏnŏs (1), *slaying*

SLAVES
4983 sōma (1), *body*

SLAY
1194 Be'ôn (1), *Beon*
2026 hârag (38), to *kill*
2717 chârab (1), to
desolate, destroy
2763 charam (1), to
devote to destruction
2873 ṭâbach (1), to *kill,
butcher*
2875 Ṭebach (1),
massacre
4191 mûwth (43), to *kill*
5221 nâkâh (11), to *kill*
5221+5315 nâkâh (1), to
strike, kill
6991 qâṭal (2), to *put to
death*
6992 qeṭal (Ch.) (1), to *kill*
7819 shâchaṭ (9), to
slaughter; butcher

337 anairĕō (2), to *take
away, murder*
615 apŏktĕinō (3), to *kill*
2380 thuō (1), to *kill*
2695 katasphattō (1), to
slaughter, strike down

SLAYER
2026 hârag (1), to *kill*
5221 nâkâh (1), to *kill*
7523 râtsach (17), to
murder

SLAYETH
2026 hârag (2), to *kill*
2490 châlal (1), to
profane, defile
4191 mûwth (1), to *kill*
7523+5315 râtsach (1), to
murder

SLAYING
2026 hârag (3), to *kill*
4191 mûwth (1), to *kill*
5221 nâkâh (2), to *kill*
7819 shâchaṭ (1), to
slaughter; butcher

SLEEP
3462 yâshên (11), to
sleep; to grow old
3463 yâshên (4), *sleepy*
7290 râdam (3), to
stupefy
7901 shâkab (11), to *lie*
8139 shenâh (Ch.) (1),
sleep
8142 shênâh (24), *sleep*
8639 tardêmâh (4),
trance, deep sleep
1852 ĕxupnizō (1), to
waken, rouse
1853 ĕxupnŏs (1), *awake*
2518 kathĕudō (7), to *fall
asleep*
2837 kŏimaō (5), to
slumber; to decease
5258 hupnŏs (6), *sleep*

SLEEPER
7290 râdam (1), to
stupefy

SLEEPEST
3462 yâshên (1), to *sleep*
7901 shâkab (1), to *lie*
2518 kathĕudō (2), to *fall
asleep*

SLEEPETH
3463 yâshên (2), *sleepy*
7290 râdam (1), to
stupefy
2518 kathĕudō (3), to *fall
asleep*
2837 kŏimaō (1), to
slumber; to decease

SLEEPING
1957 hâzâh (1), to *dream*
3463 yâshên (1), *sleepy*
2518 kathĕudō (2), to *fall
asleep*
2837 kŏimaō (2), to
slumber; to decease

SLEIGHT
2940 kubĕia (1), *artifice*
or *fraud, deceit*

SLEPT
3462 yâshên (5), to *sleep*
3463 yâshên (1), *sleepy*
5123 nûwm (1), to
slumber
7901 shâkab (37), to *lie*

2518 kathĕudō (2), to fall
asleep
2837 kŏimaō (3), to
slumber; to decease

SLEW
2026 hârag (55), to kill
2076 zâbach (3), to
(sacrificially) slaughter
2126 Zîynâ' (1), well-fed
2490 châlal (1), to
profane, defile
2491 châlâl (3), slain
4191 mûwth (40), to kill
5221 nâkâh (57), to kill
5307 nâphal (1), to fall
6992 qᵉṭal (Ch.) (2), to kill
7819 shâchaṭ (21), to
slaughter; butcher
337 anairĕō (3), to take
away, murder
615 apŏktĕinō (4), to kill
1315 diachĕirizŏmai (1),
to lay hands upon
4969 sphazō (2), to
slaughter or to maim
5407 phŏnĕuō (1), to
commit murder

SLEWEST
5221 nâkâh (1), to kill

SLIDDEN
7725 shûwb (1), to return

SLIDE
4131 môwṭ (1), to slip
4571 mâ'ad (2), to waver

SLIDETH
5637 çârar (1), to be
refractory, stubborn

SLIGHTLY
7043 qâlal (2), to be,
make light

SLIME
2564 chêmâr (2), bitumen

SLIMEPITS
2564 chêmâr (1), bitumen

SLING
4773 margêmâh (1),
sling for stones
7049 qâla' (3), to sling
7050 qela' (4), sling

SLINGERS
7051 qallâ' (1), slinger

SLINGS
7050 qela' (1), sling

SLINGSTONES
68+7050 'eben (1), stone

SLIP
4131 môwṭ (1), to slip
4571 mâ'ad (3), to waver
3901 pararrhuĕō (1), to
flow by, to pass (miss)

SLIPPED
6362 pâṭar (1), to burst
through; to emit
8210 shâphak (1), to spill
forth; to expend

SLIPPERY
2513 chelqâh (1),
smoothness; flattery
2519 chălaqlaqqâh (2),
smooth; treacherous

SLIPPETH
4131 môwṭ (2), to slip
5394 nâshal (1), to drop

SLIPS
2156 zᵉmôwrâh (1), twig,
vine branch

SLOTHFUL
6101 'âtsal (1), to be slack
6102 'âtsêl (8), indolent
7423 rᵉmîyâh (2),
remissness; treachery
7503 râphâh (1), to
slacken
3576 nōthrŏs (1), lazy
3636 ŏknērŏs (2), lazy

SLOTHFULNESS
6103 'atslâh (2),
indolence

SLOW
750 'ârêk (10), patient
3515 kâbêd (1), stupid
692 argŏs (1), lazy
1021 bradus (2), slow

SLOWLY
1020 braduplŏĕō (1), to
sail slowly

SLUGGARD
6102 'âtsêl (6), indolent

SLUICES
7938 seker (1), wages

SLUMBER
5123 nûwm (5), to
slumber
8572 tᵉnûwmâh (4),
drowsiness, i.e. sleep
2659 katanuxis (1),
stupor, bewilderment

SLUMBERED
3573 nustazō (1), to fall
asleep; to delay

SLUMBERETH
3573 nustazō (1), to fall
asleep; to delay

SLUMBERINGS
8572 tᵉnûwmâh (1),
drowsiness, i.e. sleep

SMALL
1571 gam (1), also; even
1639 gâra' (1), to lessen
1851 daq (5), small
1854 dâqaq (5), to crush
3190 yâṭab (1), to be,
make well
4213 miz'âr (1), fewness
4592 mᵉ'aṭ (9), little
4705 mits'âr (2), little;
short time
4962 math (1), men
6694 tsûwq (1), to pour
out; melt
6810 tsâ'îyr (2), small
6819 tsâ'ar (1), to be
small; be trivial
6862 tsar (1), trouble;
opponent
6994 qâṭôn (2), to be,
make diminutive
6996 qâṭân (34), small
7116 qâtsêr (2), short
1646 ĕlachistŏs (2), least
2485 ichthudiŏn (1), little
fish
3398 mikrŏs (6), small
3641 ŏligŏs (3), small
3795 ŏpsariŏn (3), small
fish
4142 plŏiariŏn (1), small
boat

SMALLEST
6996 qâṭân (1), small
1646 ĕlachistŏs (1), least

SMART
7321+7451 rûwa' (1), to
shout for alarm or joy

SMELL
1314 besem (1), spice
7306 rûwach (5), to smell
7381 rêyach (10), odor
7382 rêyach (Ch.) (1),
odor
2175 ĕuōdia (1),
fragrance, aroma

SMELLED
7306 rûwach (2), to smell

SMELLETH
7306 rûwach (1), to smell

SMELLING
5674 'âbar (2), to cross
over; to transition
3750 ŏsphrēsis (1), smell

SMITE
1986 hâlam (1), to strike
3807 kâthath (1), to strike
4272 mâchats (2), to
crush; subdue
5062 nâgaph (9), to strike
5221 nâkâh (94), to strike
5307 nâphal (1), to fall
5596 çâphach (1), to
associate; be united
5606 çâphaq (1), to clap
6221 'Ăsîy'êl (2), made of
God
6375 pîyq (1), tottering
1194 dĕrō (1), to flay
3960 patassō (5), to strike
4474 rhapizō (1), to slap
5180 tuptō (3), to strike

SMITERS
5221 nâkâh (1), to strike

SMITEST
5221 nâkâh (1), to strike
1194 dĕrō (1), to flay

SMITETH
4272 mâchats (1), to
crush; to subdue
5221 nâkâh (11), to strike
5180 tuptō (1), to strike

SMITH
2796 chârâsh (2), skilled
fabricator or worker
2796+1270 chârâsh (1),
skilled fabricator

SMITHS
4525 maçgêr (4), prison;
craftsman

SMITING
5221 nâkâh (5), to strike

SMITTEN
1792 dâkâ' (1), to
pulverize; be contrite
3807 kâthath (1), to strike
5060 nâga' (1), to strike
5062 nâgaph (15), to
inflict; to strike
5221 nâkâh (43), to strike
4141 plēssō (1), to pound
5180 tuptō (1), to strike

SMOKE
6225 'âshan (5), to
envelope in smoke

4979 schŏiniŏn (1), rope

SMALLEST
6996 qâṭân (1), small
1646 ĕlachistŏs (1), least

6227 'âshân (24), smoke
7008 qîyṭôwr (3), fume
2586 kapnŏs (13), smoke

SMOKING
3544 kêheh (1), feeble;
obscure
6226 'âshên (2), smoky
6227 'âshân (1), smoke
5187 tuphŏō (1), to
inflate with self-conceit

SMOOTH
2509 châlâq (1), smooth
2511 challâq (1), smooth
2512 challûq (1), smooth
2513 chelqâh (2),
smoothness; flattery
3006 lĕiŏs (1), smooth

SMOOTHER
2505 châlaq (1), to be
smooth; be slippery
2513 chelqâh (1),
smoothness; flattery

SMOOTHETH
2505 châlaq (1), to be
smooth; be slippery

SMOTE
1986 hâlam (2), to strike
3766 kâra' (1), to
prostrate
4223 mᵉchâ' (Ch.) (2), to
strike; to impale
4277 mâchaq (1), to crush
4347 makkâh (1), blow
5060 nâga' (2), to strike
5062 nâgaph (6), to strike
5221 nâkâh (194), to
strike
5368 nᵉqash (Ch.) (1), to
knock; to be frightened
5606 çâphaq (1), to clap
8628 tâqa' (1), to slap
851 aphairĕō (1), to
remove, cut off
1194 dĕrō (1), to flay, i.e.
to scourge or thrash
1325+4475 didōmi (1), to
give
3817 paiō (4), to hit
3960 patassō (4), to strike
4474 rhapizō (1), to slap
5180 tuptō (4), to strike

SMOTEST
5221 nâkâh (1), to strike

SMYRNA
4667 Smurna (1), myrrh
4668 Smurnaiŏs (1),
inhabitant of Smyrna

SNAIL
2546 chômeṭ (1), lizard
7642 shablûwl (1), snail

SNARE
2256 chebel (1), band
3369 yâqôsh (1), to trap
4170 môwqêsh (14),
noose
4686 mâtsûwd (2), net
5367 nâqash (1), to
entrap with a noose
6315 pûwach (1), to blow,
to fan, kindle; to utter
6341 pach (17), net
6354 pachath (1), pit for
catching animals
6983 qôwsh (1), to set a
trap
7639 sᵉbâkâh (1), snare

1029 brŏchŏs (1), *noose*
3803 pagis (5), *trap; trick*

SNARED
3369 yâqôsh (5), to *trap*
4170 môwqêsh (1), *noose*
5367 nâqash (2), to *entrap* with a noose
6351 pâchach (1), to *spread a net*

SNARES
3353 yâqûwsh (1), *snarer*
4170 môwqêsh (6), *noose*
4685 mâtsôwd (1), *snare*
5367 nâqash (1), to *entrap* with a noose
6341 pach (6), *net*

SNATCH
1504 gâzar (1), to *destroy*

SNEEZED
2237 zârar (1), to *sneeze*

SNORTING
5170 nachar (1), *snorting*

SNOUT
639 'aph (1), *nose, nostril*

SNOW
7949 shâlag (1), to *be snow-white*
7950 sheleg (19), *white snow*
8517 tᵉlag (Ch.) (1), *snow*
5510 chiôn (3), *snow*

SNOWY
7950 sheleg (1), *white snow*

SNUFFDISHES
4289 machtâh (3), *pan for live coals*

SNUFFED
5301 nâphach (1), to *inflate, blow, expire*
7602 shâ'aph (1), to *be angry; to hasten*

SNUFFERS
4212 mᵉzammᵉrâh (5), *tweezer, trimmer*
4457 melqâch (1), *pair of tweezers or tongs*

SNUFFETH
7602 shâ'aph (1), to *be angry; to hasten*

SOAKED
7301 râvâh (1), to *slake*

SOBER
3524 nêphalĕŏs (2), *circumspect, temperate*
3525 nêphō (4), to *abstain* from wine
4993 sōphrŏnĕŏ (3), to *be in a right state of mind*
4994 sōphrŏnizō (1), to *discipline* or *correct*
4998 sōphrōn (2), *self-controlled*

SOBERLY
1519+4993 ĕis (1), to
4996 sōphrŏnōs (1), *with sound mind*

SOBERNESS
4997 sōphrŏsunē (1), *self-control, propriety*

SOBRIETY
4997 sōphrŏsunē (2), *self-control, propriety*

SOCHO
7755 Sôwkôh (1), *hedged*

SOCHOH
7755 Sôwkôh (1), *hedged*

SOCKET
134 'eden (1), *footing*

SOCKETS
134 'eden (52), *footing*

SOCOH
7755 Sôwkôh (2), *hedged*

SOD
1310 bâshal (1), to *boil*
2102 zûwd (1), to *seethe*

SODDEN
1310 bâshal (5), to *boil*
1311 bâshêl (1), *boiled*

SODERING
1694 debeq (1), *solder*

SODI
5476 Çôwdîy (1), *confidant*

SODOM
5467 Çᵉdôm (39), *volcanic* or *bituminous*
4670 Sŏdŏma (9), *volcanic* or *bituminous*

SODOMA
4670 Sŏdŏma (1), *volcanic* or *bituminous*

SODOMITE
6945 qâdêsh (1), *sacred male prostitute*

SODOMITES
6945 qâdêsh (3), *sacred male prostitute*

SOFT
4127 mûwg (1), to *soften*
7390 rak (3), *tender*
7401 râkak (1), to *soften*
3120 malakŏs (3), *soft*

SOFTER
7401 râkak (1), to *soften*

SOFTLY
328 'aṭ (3), *gently, softly*
3814 lâ'ṭ (1), *silently*
3909 lâṭ (1), *covertly*
5285 hupŏpnĕŏ (1), to *breathe gently*

SOIL
7704 sâdeh (1), *field*

SOJOURN
1481 gûwr (30), to *sojourn*
4033 mâgûwr (1), *abode*
1510+3941 ĕimi (1), I *exist,* I *am*

SOJOURNED
1481 gûwr (11), to *sojourn*
3939 parŏikĕŏ (1), to *reside* as a *foreigner*

SOJOURNER
1616 gêr (1), *foreigner*
8453 tôwshâb (7), *temporary dweller*

SOJOURNERS
1481 gûwr (1), to *sojourn*
8453 tôwshâb (2), *temporary dweller*

SOJOURNETH
1481 gûwr (15), to *sojourn*

SOJOURNING
1481 gûwr (1), to *sojourn*
4186 môwshâb (1), *seat*

3940 parŏikia (1), *foreign residence*

SOLACE
5965 'âlaç (1), to *leap* for joy, i.e. *exult, wave*

SOLD
935+4242 bôw' (1), to *go*
4376 mâkar (45), to *sell*
4465 mimkâr (5), *merchandise*
7666 shâbar (2), to *deal*
591 apŏdidŏmi (3), to *give away*
4097 pipraskŏ (9), to *sell*
4453 pōlĕŏ (14), to *barter*

SOLDIER
4757 stratiōtēs (4), *common warrior*
4758 stratŏlŏgĕŏ (1), to *enlist* in the army

SOLDIERS
1121 bên (1), *son, descendant; people*
2428 chayil (1), *army*
2502 châlats (1), to *equip*
6635 tsâbâ' (1), *army*
4753 stratĕuma (1), *body of troops*
4754 stratĕuŏmai (1), to *serve* in military
4757 stratiōtēs (21), *common warrior*

SOLDIERS'
4757 stratiōtēs (1), *common warrior*

SOLE
3709 kaph (12), *sole*

SOLEMN
2282 chag (3), *solemn festival*
2287 châgag (1), to *observe* a festival
4150 môw'êd (14), *assembly*
6116 'ătsârâh (10), *assembly*

SOLEMNITIES
4150 môw'êd (3), *assembly*

SOLEMNITY
2282 chag (1), *solemn festival*
4150 môw'êd (1), *assembly*

SOLEMNLY
5749 'ûwd (2), to *protest, testify;* to *encompass*

SOLES
3709 kaph (7), *sole* of foot

SOLITARILY
910 bâdâd (1), *separate*

SOLITARY
910 bâdâd (1), *separate*
1565 galmûwd (2), *sterile, barren, desolate*
3173 yâchîyd (1), *only son*
3452 yᵉshîymôwn (1), *desolation*
6723 tsîyâh (1), *desert*
2048 ĕrēmŏs (1), *remote place, deserted place*

SOLOMON
8010 Shᵉlômôh (271), *peaceful*

4672 Sŏlŏmōn (9), *peaceful*

SOLOMON'S
8010 Shᵉlômôh (22), *peaceful*
4672 Sŏlŏmōn (3), *peaceful*

SOME
259 'echâd (7), *first*
428 'êl-leh (3), *these*
582 'ĕnôwsh (3), *person*
1697 dâbâr (1), *thing*
4592 mᵉ'aṭ (2), *little*
7097 qâtseh (2), *extremity*
243 allôs (9), *other*
1520 hĕis (2), *one*
2087 hĕtĕrŏs (2), *other*
3381 mēpōs (1), *lest somehow*
3588 hŏ (7), "*the,*" i.e. the definite article
4218 pŏtĕ (1), *some time*
5100 tis (79), *some*

SOMEBODY
5100 tis (2), *some* or *any*

SOMETHING
4745 miqreh (1), *accident* or *fortune*
5100 tis (5), *some* or *any*

SOMETIME
4218 pŏtĕ (2), *some time*

SOMETIMES
4218 pŏtĕ (3), *some time*

SOMEWHAT
3544 kêheh (5), *feeble*
3972 mᵉûwmâh (1), *something; anything*
3313 mĕrŏs (1), *division*
5100 tis (6), *some* or *any*

SON
1121 bên (1798), *son, descendant; people*
1125 Ben-'Ăbîynâdâb (1), (the) *son of Abinadab*
1127 Ben-Geber (1), *son of* (the) *hero*
1128 Ben-Deqer (1), *son of piercing*
1133 Ben-Chûwr (1), *son of Chur*
1136 Ben-Cheçed (1), *son of kindness*
1247 bar (Ch.) (7), *son*
1248 bar (4), *son, heir*
2859 châthan (5), to *become related*
2860 châthan (7), *relative; bridegroom*
3025 yâgôr (1), to *fear*
3173 yâchîyd (1), *only son*
4497 mânôwn (1), *heir*
5209 nîyn (2), *progeny*
5220 neked (1), *offspring*
431 anĕpsiŏs (1), *cousin*
3816 pais (3), *child; slave*
5043 tĕknŏn (14), *child*
5048 tĕlĕiŏō (1), to *perfect, complete*
5207 huiŏs (304), *son*

SON'S
1121 bên (21), *son*
5220 neked (1), *offspring*

SONG
2176 zimrâth (3), *song*
4853 massâ' (3), *burden, utterance*

SONGS
5058 nᵉgîynâh (4),
instrument, poem
7892 shîyr (62), *song*
5603 ōįdē (5), religious
chant or ode

SONGS
2158 zâmîyr (3), *song*
5058 nᵉgîynâh (1),
instrument; poem
7438 rôn (1), *shout of
deliverance*
7440 rinnâh (1), *shout*
7892 shîyr (12), *song*
5603 ōįdē (2), religious
chant or ode

SONS
1121 bên (1024), *son*
1123 bên (Ch.) (3), *son*
2860 châthân (2),
relative; bridegroom
3206 yeled (3), *young
male*
3211 yâlîyd (2), *born;
descendants*
5043 tĕknŏn (6), *child*
5206 huiŏthĕsia (1),
placing as a son
5207 huiŏs (24), *son*

SONS'
1121 bên (26), *son*

SOON
834 'âsher (6), *because,
in order that*
1571 gam (1), *also; even*
2440 chîysh (1), *hurry*
4116 mâhar (3), to *hurry*
4120 mᵉhêrâh (1), *hurry*
4592 mᵉ'aṭ (2), *little*
4758 mar'eh (1),
appearance; vision
7116 qâtsêr (1), *short*
7323 rûwts (1), to *run*
1096 ginŏmai (1), to *be*
2112 ĕuthĕŏs (2), *soon*
3711 ŏrgilŏs (1),
irascible, hot-tempered
3752 hŏtan (2),
inasmuch as, at once
3753 hŏtĕ (2), *when; as*
3916 parachrēma (1),
instantly, immediately
5030 tachĕŏs (2),
speedily, rapidly

SOONER
5032 tachiŏn (1), *more
rapidly, more speedily*

SOOTHSAYER
7080 qâçam (1), to *divine
magic*

SOOTHSAYERS
1505 gᵉzar (Ch.) (4), to
determine by divination
6049 'ânan (2), to *cover,
becloud; to act covertly*

SOOTHSAYING
3132 mantĕuŏmai (1), to
utter spells, fortune-tell

SOP
5596 psōmiŏn (4), *morsel*

SOPATER
4986 Sōpatrŏs (1), *of a
safe father*

SOPE
1287 bôrîyth (2), *alkali
soap*

SOPHERETH
5618 Çôphereth (2),
female scribe

SORCERER
3097 magŏs (2), Oriental
scientist, i.e. magician

SORCERERS
3784 kâshaph (3), to
enchant
3786 kashshâph (1),
magician, sorcerer
5332 pharmakĕus (1),
magician, sorcerer
5333 pharmakŏs (1),
magician, sorcerer

SORCERESS
6049 'ânan (1), to *cover,
becloud; to act covertly*

SORCERIES
3785 kesheph (2), *sorcery*
3095 magĕia (1), *sorcery*
5331 pharmakĕia (2),
magic, witchcraft

SORCERY
3096 magĕuō (1), to
practice magic, sorcery

SORE
1419 gâdôwl (3), *great*
2388 châzaq (4), to
fasten upon; to *seize*
2389 châzâq (3), *severe*
2470 châlâh (2), to *be
weak, sick, afflicted*
3027 yâd (1), *hand; power*
3510 kâ'ab (2), to *feel
pain; to grieve; to spoil*
3513 kâbad (3), to *be
heavy, severe, dull*
3515 kâbêd (4), *severe*
3708 ka'aç (1), *vexation*
3966 mᵉ'ôd (22), *very*
4834 mârats (1), to *be
pungent* or *vehement*
5061 nega' (5), *infliction;
affliction; leprous spot*
5704+3966 'ad (1), *as far
(long) as; during*
7185 qâshâh (1), to *be
tough or severe*
7186 qâsheh (1), *severe*
7188 qâshach (1), to *be,
make unfeeling*
7235 râbâh (1), to
increase
7451 ra' (9), *bad; evil*
7690 saggîy' (Ch.) (1),
large
8178 sa'ar (1), *tempest;
terror*
23 aganaktĕō (1), to be
indignant
1568 ĕkthambĕō (1), to
astonish utterly
1630 ĕkphŏbŏs (1),
frightened out
1668 hĕlkŏs (1), *sore*
2425 hikanŏs (1), *ample*
2560 kakōs (1), *badly;
wrongly; ill*
3029 lian (1), *very much*
3173 mĕgas (1), *great*
4183 pŏlus (1), *much*
4970 sphŏdra (1), *much*

SOREK
7796 Sôwrêq (1), *vine*

SORELY
4843 mârar (1), to
embitter

SORER
5501 chĕirōn (1), *more
evil or aggravated*

SORES
4347 makkâh (1), *wound*
1668 hĕlkŏs (2), *sore*
1669 hĕlkŏō (1), to *be
ulcerous*

SORROW
17 'âbôwy (1), *want*
205 'âven (1), *trouble,
vanity, wickedness*
592 'ănîyâh (1), *groaning*
1669 dâ'ab (1), to *pine*
1670 dᵉ'âbâh (1), *pining*
1671 dᵉ'âbôwn (1), *pining*
1674 dᵉ'âgâh (1), *anxiety*
1727 dûwb (1), to *pine*
2342 chûwl (1), to *dance,
whirl; to writhe in pain*
2427 chîyl (2), *throe*
2490 châlal (1), to
profane, defile
3015 yâgôwn (12), *sorrow*
3511 kᵉ'êb (3), *suffering*
3708 ka'aç (4), *vexation*
4044 mᵉginnâh (1),
covering, veil
4341 mak'ôb (6), *anguish*
4620 ma'ătsêbâh (1),
anguish place
5999 'âmâl (2), *worry*
6089 'etseb (1), *painful
toil; mental pang*
6090 'ôtseb (2), *pain*
6093 'itstsâbôwn (2),
labor or pain
6094 'atstsebeth (2), *pain
or wound, sorrow*
6862 tsar (1), *trouble;
opponent*
7451 ra' (1), *bad; evil*
7455 rôa' (1), *badness*
8424 tûwgâh (1), *grief*
3076 lupĕō (1), to *be sad*
3077 lupē (10), *sadness*
3601 ŏdunē (1), *grief*
3997 pĕnthŏs (3), *grief*

SORROWED
3076 lupĕō (2), to *be sad*

SORROWETH
1672 dâ'ag (1), *be
anxious, be afraid*

SORROWFUL
1669 dâ'ab (1), to *pine*
1741 dᵉvay (1), *sickness*
2342 chûwl (1), to *dance,
whirl; to writhe in pain*
3013 yâgâh (1), to *grieve*
3510 kâ'ab (2), to *feel
pain; to grieve; to spoil*
7186 qâsheh (1), *severe*
253 alupŏtĕrŏs (1), *more
without grief*
3076 lupĕō (6), to *be sad*
4036 pĕrilupŏs (4),
intensely sad

SORROWING
3600 ŏdunaō (2), to *grieve*

SORROWS
2256 chebel (10),
company, band
4341 mak'ôb (5), *anguish*

SORELY
4843 mârar (1), to
embitter

SORRY
1672 dâ'ag (1), *be
anxious, be afraid*
2470 châlâh (1), to *be
weak, sick, afflicted*
5110 nûwd (1), to *console*
6087 'âtsab (1), to *worry*
3076 lupĕō (9), to *be sad*
4036 pĕrilupŏs (1),
intensely sad

SORT
1524 gîyl (1), *age, stage*
1697 dâbâr (1), *thing*
3660 kᵉnêmâ' (Ch.) (1),
so or thus
3671 kânâph (2), *edge*
516 axiŏs (1), *suitable*
3313 mĕrŏs (1), *division*
3697 hŏpŏiŏs (1), *what
kind of, what sort of*

SORTS
4358 miklôwl (1),
perfection; splendidly
4360 miklûl (1), *perfectly
splendid garment*

SOSIPATER
4989 Sōsipatrŏs (1), *of a
safe father*

SOSTHENES
4988 Sōsthĕnēs (2), *of
safe strength*

SOTAI
5479 Çôwṭay (2), *roving*

SOTTISH
5530 çâkâl (1), *silly*

SOUGHT
1156 bᵉ'â' (Ch.) (1), to
seek or ask
1158 bâ'âh (3), to *ask*
1245 bâqash (55), to
search; to strive after
1875 dârash (25), to *seek
or ask; to worship*
2713 châqar (1), to
examine, search
8446 tûwr (1), to *wander*
327 anazētĕō (1), to
search out
1567 ĕkzētĕō (1), to *seek*
1934 ĕpizētĕō (1), to
search (inquire) for
2212 zētĕō (36), to *seek*

SOUL
5082 nᵉdîybâh (1),
nobility, i.e. reputation
5315 nephesh (416), *soul*
5590 psuchē (39), *soul*

SOUL'S
5315 nephesh (1), *soul*

SOULS
5315 nephesh (58), *soul*
5397 nᵉshâmâh (1),
breath, life
5590 psuchē (19), *soul*

SOUND
1899 hegeh (1),
muttering; rumbling
1902 higgâyôwn (1),
musical notation

1993 hâmâh (3), to *be in great commotion*
4832 marpê' (1), *cure; deliverance; placidity*
5674 'âbar (2), to *cross over; to transition*
6310 peh (1), *mouth*
6963 qôwl (39), *sound*
7032 qâl (Ch.) (4), *sound*
7321 rûwa' (2), to *shout*
8085 shâma' (3), to *hear*
8454 tûwshîyâh (3), *ability, help*
8549 tâmîym (1), *entire, complete; integrity*
8629 têqa' (1), *blast* of a *trumpet*
8643 t°rûw'âh (1), *battle-cry; clangor*
2279 ēchŏs (2), *roar*
4537 salpizō (5), to *sound a trumpet blast*
4995 sōphrŏnismŏs (1), *self-control*
5198 hugiainō (8), to *have sound health*
5199 hugiēs (1), *well*
5353 phthŏggŏs (1), *utterance; musical*
5456 phōnē (8), *sound*

SOUNDED
2690 châtsar (3), to blow the *trumpet*
2713 châqar (1), to *search*
8628 tâqa' (2), to *clatter, slap, drive, clasp*
1001 bŏlizō (1), to *heave a weight*
1096 ginŏmai (1), to *be*
1837 ĕxēchĕŏmai (1), to *echo forth*, i.e. *resound*
4537 salpizō (7), to *sound a trumpet blast*

SOUNDING
1906 hêd (1), *shout of joy*
1995 hâmôwn (1), *noise*
2690 châtsar (1), to blow the *trumpet*
8085 shâma' (1), to *hear*
8643 t°rûw'âh (2), *battle-cry; clangor*
2278 ēchĕō (1), to *reverberate, ring out*

SOUNDNESS
4974 m°thôm (3), *wholesomeness*
3647 hŏlŏklēria (1), *wholeness*

SOUNDS
5353 phthŏggŏs (1), *utterance; musical*

SOUR
1155 bôçer (4), *immature, sour grapes*
5493 çûwr (1), to *turn off*

SOUTH
1864 dârôwm (17), *south; south wind*
2315 cheder (1), *apartment, chamber*
3220 yâm (1), *sea; west*
3225 yâmîyn (3), *south*
4057 midbâr (1), *desert*
5045 negeb (97), *South*
8486 têymân (14), *south; southward; south* wind
3047 lips (1), *southwest*

3314 mĕsēmbria (1), *midday; south*
3558 nŏtŏs (7), *south*

SOUTHWARD
5045 negeb (17), *south*
8486 têymân (7), *south*

SOW
2232 zâra' (28), to *sow seed; to disseminate*
4687 spĕirō (8), to *scatter*, i.e. *sow seed*
5300 hus (1), *swine*

SOWED
2232 zâra' (2), to *sow seed; to disseminate*
4687 spĕirō (8), to *scatter*, i.e. *sow seed*

SOWEDST
2232 zâra' (1), to *sow seed; to disseminate*

SOWER
2232 zâra' (2), to *sow seed; to disseminate*
4687 spĕirō (6), to *scatter*, i.e. *sow seed*

SOWEST
4687 spĕirō (3), to *scatter*, i.e. *sow seed*

SOWETH
2232 zâra' (2), to *sow seed; to disseminate*
4900 mâshak (1), to *draw out; to be tall*
7971 shâlach (3), to *send away*
4687 spĕirō (9), to *scatter*, i.e. *sow seed*

SOWING
2221 zêrûwa' (1), *plant*
2233 zera' (1), *seed; fruit, plant, sowing-time*

SOWN
2221 zêrûwa' (1), *plant*
2232 zâra' (14), to *sow seed; to disseminate*
4218 mizrâ' (1), *planted field*
4687 spĕirō (15), to *scatter*, i.e. *sow seed*

SPACE
1366 g°bûwl (2), *border*
3117 yôwm (3), *day; time*
4390 mâlê' (1), to *fill*
4725 mâqôwm (1), *place*
5750 'ôwd (1), *again*
7281 rega' (1), very *short space* of time
7305 revach (1), *room*
7350 râchôwq (1), *remote*
575 apŏ (1), *from, away*
1024 brachus (1), *short*
1292 diastēma (1), *interval* of time
1339 diïstēmi (1), to *remove, intervene*
1909 ĕpi (3), *on, upon*
4158 pŏdērēs (1), robe *reaching* the *ankles*
5550 chrŏnŏs (2), *space of time, period*

SPAIN
4681 Spania (2), *Spania*

SPAKE
559 'âmar (109), to *say*
560 'ămar (Ch.) (1), to *say*

981 bâţâ' (1), to *babble*
1696 dâbar (318), to *say*
4449 m°lal (Ch.) (2), to *speak, say*
5002 n°'ûm (1), *oracle*
6030 'ânâh (3), to *respond*
6032 'ănâh (Ch.) (14), to *respond, answer*
400 anaphōnĕō (1), to *exclaim*
483 antilĕgō (2), to *dispute, refuse*
626 apŏlŏgĕŏmai (1), to *give an account*
2036 ĕpō (30), to *speak*
2046 ĕrĕō (3), to *utter*
2551 kakŏlŏgĕō (1), to *revile, curse*
2980 lalĕō (72), to *talk*
3004 lĕgō (17), to *say*
4227 Pŏudēs (1), *modest*
4377 prŏsphōnĕō (3), to *address, exclaim*
4814 sullalĕō (1), to *talk together*, i.e. *converse*
5537 chrēmatizō (1), to *utter an oracle*

SPAKEST
559 'âmar (1), to *say*
1696 dâbar (8), to *speak*
1697 dâbâr (1), *word*

SPAN
2239 zereth (7), *span*
2949 ţippûch (1), *nursing, caring for*

SPANNED
2946 ţâphach (1), to *extend, spread out*

SPARE
2347 chûwç (14), to be *compassionate*
2550 châmal (13), to *spare, have pity on*
2820 châsak (3), to *refuse, spare, preserve*
5375 nâsâ' (3), to *lift up*
5545 çâlach (1), to *forgive*
8159 shâ'âh (1), to *inspect, consider*
4052 pĕrissĕuō (1), to *superabound*
5339 phĕidŏmai (4), to *treat leniently*

SPARED
2347 chûwç (2), to be *compassionate*
2550 châmal (4), to *spare, have pity on*
2820 châsak (3), to *refuse, spare, preserve*
5339 phĕidŏmai (4), to *treat leniently*

SPARETH
2550 châmal (1), to *spare, have pity on*
2820 châsak (3), to *refuse, spare, preserve*

SPARING
5339 phĕidŏmai (1), to *treat leniently*

SPARINGLY
5340 phĕidŏmĕnōs (2), *stingily, sparingly*

SPARK
5213 nîytsôwts (1), *spark*
7632 shâbîyb (1), *flame*

SPARKLED
5340 nâtsats (1), to *be bright*-colored

SPARKS
1121+7565 bên (1), *son, descendant; people*
2131 zîyqâh (2), *flash*
3590 kîydôwd (1), *spark*

SPARROW
6833 tsippôwr (2), little *hopping bird*

SPARROWS
4765 strŏuthiŏn (4), *little sparrow*

SPAT
4429 ptuō (1), to *spit*

SPEAK
559 'âmar (47), to *say*
560 'ămar (Ch.) (2), to *say*
1680 dâbab (1), to *move slowly*, i.e. *glide*
1696 dâbar (276), to *speak*
1897 hâgâh (3), to *murmur, utter a sound*
2790 chârash (1), to *engrave; to plow*
4405 millâh (1), *word; discourse; speech*
4448 mâlal (1), to *speak*
4449 m°lal (Ch.) (1), to *speak, say*
4911 mâshal (2), to *use figurative language*
5608 çâphar (2), to *recount an event*
5790 'ûwth (1), to *succor*
6030 'ânâh (5), to *answer*
6315 pûwach (1), to *utter*
7878 sîyach (4), to *ponder, muse aloud*
653 apŏstŏmatizō (1), to *question carefully*
669 apŏphthĕggŏmai (1), *declare, address*
987 blasphēmĕō (5), to *speak impiously*
1097 ginōskō (1), to *know*
2036 ĕpō (6), to *speak*
2046 ĕrĕō (2), to *utter*
2551 kakŏlŏgĕō (1), to *revile, curse*
2635 katalalĕō (3), to *speak slander*
2980 lalĕō (101), to *talk*
3004 lĕgō (30), to *say*
4354 prŏslalĕō (1), to *converse with*
5350 phthĕggŏmai (2), to *utter a clear sound*

SPEAKER
376+3956 'îysh (1), *man*
3056 lŏgŏs (1), *word*

SPEAKEST
1696 dâbar (11), to *speak*
2980 lalĕō (4), to *talk*
3004 lĕgō (2), to *say*

SPEAKETH
559 'âmar (7), to *say*
981 bâţâ' (1), to *babble*
1696 dâbar (22), to *say*
1897 hâgâh (1), to *murmur, utter a sound*
4448 mâlal (1), to *speak*
5046 nâgad (1), to *announce*

English

SPEAKING
6315 pûwach (5), to *utter*
6963 qôwl (1), *voice*
483 antilĕgō (1), to *dispute, refuse*
1256 dialĕgŏmai (1), to *discuss*
2036 ĕpō (2), to *speak*
2635 katalalĕō (2), to speak *slander*
2980 lalĕō (22), to *talk*
3004 lĕgō (4), to *say*

SPEAKING
1696 dâbar (37), to *speak*
2790 chârash (1), to *engrave; to plow*
4405 millâh (2), *word; discourse; speech*
4449 mᵉlal (Ch.) (1), to *speak, say*
226 alēthĕuō (1), to *be true*
987 blasphēmĕō (1), to *speak impiously*
988 blasphēmia (1), *impious speech*
2980 lalĕō (11), to *talk*
3004 lĕgō (1), to *say*
4180 pŏlulŏgia (1), *prolixity, wordiness*
4354 prŏslalĕō (1), to *converse with*
5350 phthĕggŏmai (1), to *utter a clear sound*
5573 psĕudŏlŏgŏs (1), *promulgating erroneous doctrine*

SPEAKINGS
2636 katalalia (1), *defamation, slander*

SPEAR
2595 chănîyth (34), *lance, spear*
3591 kîydôwn (5), *dart, javelin*
7013 qayin (1), *lance*
7420 rômach (3), iron *pointed spear*
3057 lŏgchē (1), *lance, spear*

SPEAR'S
2595 chănîyth (1), *lance, spear*

SPEARMEN
7070 qâneh (1), *reed*
1187 dĕxiŏlabŏs (1), *guardsman*

SPEARS
2595 chănîyth (6), *lance, spear*
6767 tsᵉlâtsal (1), *whirring of wings*
7420 rômach (9), iron *pointed spear*

SPECIAL
5459 çᵉgullâh (1), *wealth*
3756+3858+5177 ŏu (1), *no or not*

SPECIALLY
3122 malista (5), *particularly*

SPECKLED
5348 nâqôd (9), *spotted*
6641 tsâbûwa' (1), *hyena*
8320 sâruq (1), *bright red, bay colored*

SPECTACLE
2302 thĕatrŏn (1), *audience-room*

SPED
4672 mâtsâ' (1), to *find or acquire; to occur*

SPEECH
562 'ômer (2), something *said*
565 'imrâh (7), something *said*
1697 dâbâr (7), *word*
1999 hămullâh (1), *sound, roar, noise*
3066 Yᵉhûwdîyth (2), in the *Jewish language*
3948 leqach (1), *instruction*
4057 midbâr (1), *desert; also speech; mouth*
4405 millâh (4), *word; discourse; speech*
6310 peh (1), *mouth; opening*
8088 shêma' (1), something *heard*
8193 sâphâh (6), *lip, language, speech*
2981 lalia (3), *talk, speech*
3056 lŏgŏs (8), *word*
3072 Lukaŏnisti (1), in *Lycaonian language*
3424 mŏgilalŏs (1), *hardly talking*

SPEECHES
561 'êmer (2), something *said*
2420 chîydâh (1), *puzzle; conundrum; maxim*
4405 millâh (2), *word; discourse; speech*
2129 ĕulŏgia (1), *benediction*

SPEECHLESS
1769 ĕnnĕŏs (1), *speechless, silent*
2974 kŏphŏs (1), *silent*
5392 phimŏō (1), *torestrain to silence*

SPEED
553 'âmats (2), to *be strong; be courageous*
629 'oçparnâ' (Ch.) (1), *with diligence*
4116 mâhar (2), to *hurry*
4120 mᵉhêrâh (2), *hurry*
7136 qârâh (1), to *bring about; to impose*
5463 chairō (1), *salutation, "be well"*
5613+5033 hōs (1), *which, how, i.e. in that manner*

SPEEDILY
629 'oçparnâ' (Ch.) (4), *with diligence*
926 bâhal (1), to *hasten, hurry anxiously*
1980 hâlak (1), to *walk; live a certain way*
4116 mâhar (1), to *hurry; promptly*
4118 mahêr (4), in a *hurry*
4120 mᵉhêrâh (4), *hurry; promptly*

SPECTACLE (col3)
4422 mâlaṭ (1), to *escape as if by slipperiness*
5674 'âbar (1), to *cross over; to transition*
1722+5034 ĕn (1), in; *during; because of*

SPEEDY
926 bâhal (1), to *hasten, hurry anxiously*

SPEND
3615 kâlâh (4), to *cease, be finished, perish*
8254 shâqal (1), to *suspend in trade*
1159 dapanaō (1), to *incur cost; to waste*
5551 chrŏnŏtribĕō (1), to *procrastinate, linger*

SPENDEST
4325 prŏsdapanaō (1), to *expend additionally*

SPENDETH
6 'âbad (1), *perish; destroy*
1104 bâla' (1), to *swallow; to destroy*
6213 'âsâh (1), to *do*

SPENT
235 'âzal (1), to *disappear*
3615 kâlâh (4), to *complete, consume*
7286 râdad (1), to *conquer; to overlay*
8552 tâmam (3), to *complete, finish*
1159 dapanaō (2), to *incur cost; to waste*
1230 diaginŏmai (1), to *have time elapse*
1550 ĕkdapanaō (1), to *exhaust, be exhausted*
2119 ĕukairĕō (1), to *have opportunity*
2827 klinō (1), to *slant*
4160 pŏiĕō (1), to *do*
4298 prŏkŏptō (1), to *go ahead, advance*
4321 prŏsanaliskō (1), to *expend further*

SPEWING
7022 qîyqâlôwn (1), *disgrace*

SPICE
1313 bâsâm (1), *balsam*
1314 besem (2), *spice; fragrance; balsam*
7402 râkal (1), to *travel*
7543 râqach (1), to *perfume, blend spice*

SPICED
7544 reqach (1), *spice*

SPICERY
5219 nᵉkô'th (1), *gum, (poss.) styrax*

SPICES
1314 besem (22), *spice; fragrance; balsam*
5219 nᵉkô'th (1), *gum, (poss.) styrax*
5561 çam (3), *aroma*
759 arōma (4), *scented oils, perfumes, spices*

SPIDER
8079 sᵉmâmîyth (1), *lizard*

SPIDER'S
5908 'akkâbîysh (2), *web*-making *spider*

SPIED
7200 râ'âh (5), to *see*
7270 râgal (1), to *reconnoiter; to slander*

SPIES
871 'Äthârîym (1), *places to step*
7270 râgal (10), to *reconnoiter; to slander*
8104 shâmar (1), to *watch*
1455 ĕgkathĕtŏs (1), *spy*
2685 kataskŏpŏs (1), *reconnoiterer, i.e. a spy*

SPIKENARD
5373 nêrd (3), *nard*
3487+4101 nardŏs (2), oil from spike-*nard* root

SPILLED
7843 shâchath (1), to *decay; to ruin*
1632 ĕkchĕō (2), to *pour forth; to bestow*

SPILT
5064 nâgar (1), to *pour out; to deliver* over

SPIN
2901 ṭâvâh (1), to *spin* yarn
3514 nēthō (2), to *spin* yarn

SPINDLE
3601 kîyshôwr (1), *spindle or shank*

SPIRIT
178 'ôwb (7), *wineskin; necromancer, medium*
5397 nᵉshâmâh (2), *breath, life*
7307 rûwach (226), *breath; wind; life*-spirit
7308 rûwach (Ch.) (8), *breath; wind; life*-spirit
4151 pnĕuma (255), *spirit*
5326 phantasma (2), *spectre, apparition*

SPIRITS
178 'ôwb (9), *wineskin; necromancer, medium*
7307 rûwach (5), *breath; wind; life*-spirit
4151 pnĕuma (32), *spirit*

SPIRITUAL
7307 rûwach (1), *breath; wind; life*-spirit
4151 pnĕuma (1), *spirit*
4152 pnĕumatikŏs (25), *spiritual*

SPIRITUALLY
3588+4151 hŏ (1), *"the,"* i.e. the definite article
4153 pnĕumatikŏs (2), *non-physical*

SPIT
3417 yâraq (2), to *spit*
7536 rôq (1), *spittle, saliva*
7556 râqaq (1), to *spit*
1716 ĕmptuō (5), to *spit at*
4429 ptuō (2), to *spit*

SPITE
3708 ka'aç (1), *vexation*

SPITEFULLY
5195 hubrizō (2), *to exercise violence, abuse*

SPITTED
1716 ĕmptuō (1), *to spit at*

SPITTING
7536 rôq (1), *spittle*

SPITTLE
7388 rîyr (1), *saliva; broth*
7536 rôq (1), *spittle*
4427 ptusma (1), *saliva*

SPOIL
957 baz (4), *plunder, loot*
961 bizzâh (6), *plunder*
962 bâzaz (8), *to plunder*
1500 gᵉzêlâh (1), *robbery, stealing; things stolen*
2254 châbal (1), *to pervert, destroy*
2488 châlîytsâh (1), *spoil, booty of the dead*
2964 țereph (1), *fresh torn prey*
4882 mᵉshûwçâh (1), *spoilation, loot*
4933 mᵉshiççâh (3), *plunder*
5337 nâtsal (1), *to deliver; to be snatched*
6584 pâshaț (1), *to strip*
6906 qâba' (1), *to defraud, rob*
7701 shôd (5), *violence, ravage, destruction*
7703 shâdad (8), *to ravage*
7921 shâkôl (1), *to miscarry*
7997 shâlal (4), *to drop or strip; to plunder*
7998 shâlâl (62), *booty*
8154 shâçâh (3), *to plunder*
8155 shâçaç (1), *to plunder, ransack*
1283 diarpazō (4), *plunder, rob*
4812 sulagōgēō (1), *to take captive as booty*

SPOILED
957 baz (2), *plunder, loot*
958 bâzâ' (2), *to divide*
962 bâzaz (6), *to plunder*
1497 gâzal (7), *to rob*
5337 nâtsal (1), *to deliver; to be snatched*
6906 qâba' (1), *to defraud*
7701 shôd (3), *violence, ravage, destruction*
7703 shâdad (20), *to ravage*
7758 shôwlâl (2), *stripped; captive*
7997 shâlal (4), *to drop or strip; to plunder*
8154 shâçâh (3), *to plunder*
8155 shâçaç (3), *to plunder, ransack*
554 apĕkduŏmai (1), *to despoil*

SPOILER
7701 shôd (1), *violence, ravage, destruction*

SPOILERS
7703 shâdad (3), *to ravage*
7843 shâchath (2), *to decay; to ruin*
8154 shâçâh (2), *to plunder*

SPOILEST
7703 shâdad (1), *to ravage*

SPOILETH
1497 gâzal (1), *to rob*
6584 pâshaț (2), *to strip*
7703 shâdad (1), *to ravage*

SPOILING
7701 shôd (3), *violence, ravage, destruction*
7908 shᵉkôwl (1), *bereavement*
724 harpagē (1), *pillage*

SPOILS
698 'orŏbâh (1), *ambuscades*
7998 shâlâl (2), *booty*
205 akrŏthiniŏn (1), *best of the booty*
4661 skulŏn (1), *plunder*

SPOKEN
559 'âmar (15), *to say*
560 'ămar (Ch.) (1), *to say*
1696 dâbar (174), *to speak, say*
1697 dâbâr (2), *word*
6310 peh (1), *mouth*
312 anaggĕllō (1), *to announce, report*
369 anantirrhētŏs (1), *without objection*
483 antilĕgō (2), *to dispute, refuse*
987 blasphēmĕŏ (5), *to speak impiously*
2036 ĕpō (19), *to speak*
2046 ĕrĕō (4), *to utter*
2605 kataggĕllō (1), *to proclaim, promulgate*
2980 lalĕō (33), *to talk*
3004 lĕgō (7), *to say*
4280 prŏĕrĕō (2), *to say already, predict*
4369 prŏstithēmi (1), *to repeat*
4483 rhĕō (15), *to utter*

SPOKES
2840 chishshûr (1), *hub*

SPOKESMAN
1696 dâbar (1), *to speak*

SPOON
3709 kaph (12), *bowl; handle*

SPOONS
3709 kaph (12), *bowl; handle*

SPORT
6026 'ânag (1), *to be soft or pliable*
6711 tsâchaq (1), *to laugh; to make sport of*
7814 sᵉchôwq (1), *laughter; scorn*
7832 sâchaq (3), *to laugh; to scorn; to play*

SPORTING
6711 tsâchaq (1), *to laugh; to make sport of*
1792 ĕntruphaō (1), *to revel in, carouse*

SPOT
933 bôhaq (1), *white scurf, rash*
934 bôhereth (9), *whitish, bright spot*
3971 m'ûwm (3), *blemish; fault*
8549 tâmîym (6), *entire, complete; integrity*
299 amōmŏs (1), *unblemished, blameless*
784 aspilŏs (3), *unblemished*
4696 spilŏs (1), *stain or blemish, i.e. defect*

SPOTS
934 bôhereth (2), *whitish, bright spot*
2272 chăbarbûrâh (1), *streak, stripe*
4694 spilas (1), *ledge or reef of rock in the sea*
4696 spilŏs (1), *stain or blemish, i.e. defect*

SPOTTED
2921 țâlâ' (6), *to be spotted or variegated*
4695 spilŏŏ (1), *to soil*

SPOUSE
3618 kallâh (6), *bride; son's wife*

SPOUSES
3618 kallâh (2), *bride; son's wife*

SPRANG
305 anabainō (1), *to go up, rise*
393 anatĕllō (1), *to cause to arise*
1080 gĕnnaō (1), *to procreate, regenerate*
1530 ĕispēdaō (1), *to rush in*
1816 ĕxanatĕllō (1), *to germinate, spring forth*
4855 sumphuō (1), *to grow jointly*
5453 phuō (1), *to germinate or grow*

SPREAD
2219 zârâh (2), *to toss about; to diffuse*
3212 yâlak (2), *to walk; to live; to carry*
3318 yâtsâ' (1), *to go, bring out*
3331 yâtsa' (2), *to strew*
4894 mishțôwach (2), *spreading-place*
5186 nâțâh (6), *to stretch or spread out*
5203 nâțash (4), *to disperse; to thrust off*
5259 nâçak (1), *to interweave*
6327 pûwts (2), *to dash in pieces; to disperse*
6335 pûwsh (1), *to spread; to act proudly*
6555 pârats (1), *to break out*

SPORTING / SPREAD (right column continued)

6566 pâras (49), *to break apart, disperse, scatter*
6581 pâsâh (17), *to spread*
6584 pâshaț (2), *to strip*
6605 pâthach (1), *to open wide; to loosen, begin*
7286 râdad (1), *to conquer; to overlay*
7554 râqa' (4), *to pound*
7849 shâțach (3), *to expand*
1268 dianĕmō (1), *to spread information*
1310 diaphēmizō (1), *to spread news*
1831 ĕxĕrchŏmai (2), *to issue; to leave*
4766 strŏnnumi (3), *strew, i.e. spread*
5291 hupŏstrŏnnumi (1), *to strew underneath*

SPREADEST
4666 miphrâs (1), *expansion*

SPREADETH
4969 mâthach (1), *to stretch out*
5186 nâțâh (1), *to stretch or spread out*
6566 pâras (6), *to break apart, disperse, scatter*
6576 parshêz (1), *to expand*
6581 pâsâh (1), *to spread*
7502 râphad (1), *to spread a bed; to refresh*
7554 râqa' (2), *to pound*
7971 shâlach (1), *to send away*

SPREADING
4894 mishțôwach (1), *spreading-place*
5628 çârach (1), *to extend even to excess*
6168 'ârâh (1), *to pour out; demolish*
6524 pârach (1), *to break forth; to bloom; to fly*

SPREADINGS
4666 miphrâs (1), *expansion*

SPRIGS
2150 zalzal (1), *twig, shoot*
6288 pᵉ'ôrâh (1), *foliage, branches*

SPRING
1530 gal (1), *heap; ruins*
1876 dâshâ' (1), *to sprout new plants*
3318 yâtsâ' (1), *to go, bring out*
4161 môwtsâ' (2), *going forth*
4726 mâqôwr (2), *flow of liquids, or ideas*
5927 'âlâh (3), *to ascend, be high, mount*
6524 pârach (1), *to break forth; to bloom; to fly*
6779 tsâmach (10), *to sprout*
6780 tsemach (1), *sprout, branch*
985 blastanō (1), *to yield fruit*

English

SPRINGETH
3318 yâtsâ' (1), to *go,*
bring out
6524 pârach (1), to *break*
forth; to *bloom;* to *fly*
7823 shâchîyç (2),
after-growth

SPRINGING
2416 chay (1), *alive; raw;*
fresh; life
6780 tsemach (1), *sprout,*
branch
242 hallŏmai (1), to *jump*
up; to *gush up*
5453 phuŏ (1), to
germinate or *grow*

SPRINGS
794 'âshêdâh (3), *ravine*
1543 gullâh (4), *fountain;*
bowl or *globe*
4002 mabbûwa' (2),
fountain, water spring
4161 môwtsâ' (1), *going*
forth
4599 ma'yân (2),
fountain; source
4726 mâqôwr (1), *flow*
5033 nêbek (1), *fountain*

SPRINKLE
2236 zâraq (14), to
sprinkle, scatter
5137 nâzâh (17), to
splash or *sprinkle*

SPRINKLED
2236 zâraq (16), to
sprinkle, scatter
5137 nâzâh (6), to *splash*
or *sprinkle*
4472 rhantizŏ (3), to
asperse, sprinkle

SPRINKLETH
2236 zâraq (1), to
sprinkle, scatter
5137 nâzâh (1), to *splash*
or *sprinkle*

SPRINKLING
4378 prŏschusis (1),
affusion, sprinkling
4472 rhantizŏ (1), to
asperse, sprinkle
4473 rhantismŏs (2),
aspersion, sprinkling

SPROUT
2498 châlaph (1), to
spring up; to *pierce*

SPRUNG
6524 pârach (1), to *break*
forth; to *bloom;* to *fly*
6779 tsâmach (2), to
sprout
305 anabainŏ (1), to *go*
up, rise
393 anatĕllŏ (1), to *cause*
to arise
985 blastanŏ (1), to *yield*
fruit
1816 ĕxanatĕllŏ (1), to
germinate, spring forth
5453 phuŏ (1), to
germinate or *grow*

SPUE
6958 qôw' (2), to *vomit*
7006 qâyâh (1), to *vomit*
1692 ĕmĕŏ (1), to *vomit*

SPUED
6958 qôw' (1), to *vomit*

SPUN
2901 ţâvâh (1), to *spin*
yarn
4299 maţveh (1),
something spun

SPUNGE
4699 spŏggŏs (3), *sponge*

SPY
7200 râ'âh (2), to *see*
7270 râgal (7), to
reconnoiter; to *slander*
8446 tûwr (2), to *wander,*
meander
2684 kataskŏpĕŏ (1), to
inspect, spy on

SQUARE
7251 râba' (3), to *be four*
sided, to *be quadrate*

SQUARED
7251 râba' (1), to *be four*
sided, to *be quadrate*

SQUARES
7253 reba' (2), *fourth*

STABILITY
530 'ĕmûwnâh (1),
fidelity; steadiness

STABLE
3559 kûwn (1), to *set up:*
establish, fix, prepare
5116 nâveh (1), *at home;*
lovely; home

STABLISH
3559 kûwn (2), to *set up:*
establish, fix, prepare
5324 nâtsab (1), to *station*
6965 qûwm (3), to *rise*
4741 stĕrizŏ (6), to
confirm

STABLISHED
3559 kûwn (2), to *set up:*
establish, fix, prepare
5975 'âmad (1), to *stand*
950 bĕbaiŏŏ (1), to
stabilitate, keep strong

STABLISHETH
3559 kûwn (1), to *set up:*
establish, fix, prepare
950 bĕbaiŏŏ (1), to
stabilitate, keep strong

STACHYS
4720 Stachus (1), *head of*
grain

STACKS
1430 gâdîysh (1), *stack of*
sheaves, shock of grain

STACTE
5198 nâţâph (1), *drop;*
aromatic *gum resin*

STAFF
2671 chêts (1), *arrow;*
shaft of a spear
4132 môwţ (1), *pole; yoke*
4294 maţţeh (15), *tribe;*
rod, scepter; club
4731 maqqêl (7), *shoot;*
stick; staff
4938 mish'ênâh (11),
walking-stick
6086 'êts (3), *wood*
6418 pelek (1),
spindle-whorl; crutch
7626 shêbeţ (2), *stick*
4464 rhabdŏs (2), *stick,*
rod

STAGGER
5128 nûwa' (2), to *waver*
8582 tâ'âh (1), to
vacillate, i.e. *reel*

STAGGERED
1252 diakrinŏ (1), to
decide; to *hesitate*

STAGGERETH
8582 tâ'âh (1), to
vacillate, i.e. *reel*

STAIN
1350 gâ'al (1), to *redeem;*
to *be the next of kin*
1351 gâ'al (1), to *soil,*
stain; desecrate
2490 châlal (1), to
profane, defile

STAIRS
3883 lûwl (1), *spiral* step
4095 madrêgâh (1), *steep*
or *inaccessible* place
4608 ma'âleh (1),
platform; stairs
4609 ma'ălâh (5),
thought arising
304 anabathmŏs (2),
stairway step

STAKES
3489 yâthêd (2), tent *peg*

STALK
7054 qâmâh (1), *stalk* of
grain
7070 qâneh (2), *reed*

STALKS
6086 'êts (1), *wood*

STALL
4770 marbêq (2), *stall*
5336 phatnē (1), *stall*

STALLED
75 'âbaç (1), to *feed*

STALLS
723 'urvâh (3),
herding-place
7517 repheth (1), *stall*
for cattle

STAMMERERS
5926 'illêg (1), *stuttering,*
stammering

STAMMERING
3932 lâ'ag (1), to *deride;*
to *speak unintelligibly*
3934 lâ'êg (1), *buffoon;*
foreigner

STAMP
1854 dâqaq (1), to *crush*
7554 râqa' (1), to *pound*

STAMPED
1854 dâqaq (3), to *crush*
3807 kâthath (1), to
bruise, strike, beat
7429 râmaç (2), to *tread*
7512 rᵉphaç (Ch.) (2), to
trample; to *ruin*
7554 râqa' (1), to *pound*

STAMPING
8161 sha'ăţâh (1), *clatter*
of hoofs

STANCHED
2476 histēmi (1), to
stand, establish

STAND
539 'âman (1), to *be firm,*
faithful, true; to *trust*

1481 gûwr (1), to *sojourn*
1826 dâmam (1), to *stop,*
cease; to *perish*
3318 yâtsâ' (1), to *go,*
bring out
3320 yâtsab (22), to
station, offer, continue
5066 nâgash (1), to *be,*
come, bring near
5324 nâtsab (9), to *station*
5564 çâmak (1), to *lean*
upon; *take hold of*
5749 'ûwd (1), to *protest,*
testify; to *restore*
5975 'âmad (144), to
stand
5976 'âmad (1), to *shake*
6965 qûwm (31), to *rise*
6966 qûwm (Ch.) (2), to
rise
7126 qârab (1), to
approach, bring near
8617 tᵉqûwmâh (1),
resistfulness
450 anistēmi (2), to *rise;*
to *come back to life*
639 apŏrĕŏ (1), be at a
mental loss, be puzzled
1453 ĕgĕirŏ (1), to
waken, i.e. *rouse*
1510 ĕimi (1), I *exist,* I *am*
2476 histēmi (36), to
stand, establish
3306 mĕnŏ (1), to *stay*
3936 paristēmi (3), to
stand beside, present
4026 pĕriistēmi (1), to
stand around; to *avoid*
4739 stĕkŏ (1), to
persevere, be steadfast

STANDARD
1714 degel (10), *flag,*
standard, banner
5127 nûwç (1), to *vanish*
5251 nêç (7), *flag; signal*

STANDARD-BEARER
5264 nâçaç (1), to *gleam;*
to *flutter a flag*

STANDARDS
1714 degel (3), *flag,*
standard, banner

STANDEST
5975 'âmad (4), to *stand*
2476 histēmi (2), to *stand*

STANDETH
3559 kûwn (1), to *set up*
5324 nâtsab (4), to *station*
5975 'âmad (14), to *stand*
2476 histēmi (8), to *stand*
4739 stĕkŏ (1), to
persevere, be steadfast

STANDING
98 'ăgam (2), *marsh;*
pond; pool
3320 yâtsab (1), to
station, offer, continue
4613 mo'ŏmâd (1),
foothold
4676 matstsêbâh (2),
column or *stone*
5324 nâtsab (4), to *station*
5975 'âmad (12), to *stand*
5979 'emdâh (1), *station*
7054 qâmâh (5), *stalk*
2186 ĕphistēmi (1), to *be*
present; to *approach*

2192+4174 ĕchō (1), to
have; hold; keep
2476 histēmi (23), to
stand, establish
3936 paristēmi (1), to
stand beside, present
4921 sunistaō (1), to *set*
together; to stand near

STANK
887 bâ'ash (4), to *smell*
bad

STAR
3556 kôwkâb (2), *star*
792 astēr (11), *star*
798 astrŏn (1),
constellation; star
5459 phōsphŏrŏs (1),
morning-star

STARE
7200 râ'âh (1), to *see*

STARGAZERS
2374+3556 chôzeh (1),
beholder in vision

STARS
3556 kôwkâb (34), *star*
3598 Kîymâh (1), *cluster*
of stars, the *Pleiades*
792 astēr (13), *star*
798 astrŏn (3),
constellation; star

STATE
3027 yâd (2), *hand; power*
3651 kên (1), *just; right,*
correct
4612 ma'ămâd (1),
position; attendant
4971 mathkôneth (1),
proportion
5324 nâtsab (1), to *station*
6440 pânîym (1), *face;*
front
3588+2596 hŏ (1), *"the,"*
i.e. the definite article
3588+4012 hŏ (2), *"the,"*
i.e. the definite article

STATELY
3520 kᵉbûwddâh (1),
magnificence, wealth

STATION
4673 matstsâb (1), fixed
spot; office; post

STATURE
4055 mad (1), *vesture,*
garment; carpet
4060 middâh (4),
measure; portion
6967 qôwmâh (7), *height*
2244 hēlikia (5), *maturity*

STATUTE
2706 chôq (13),
appointment; allotment
2708 chuqqâh (20), to
delineate
7010 qᵉyâm (Ch.) (2),
edict arising in law

STATUTES
2706 chôq (73),
appointment; allotment
2708 chuqqâh (58), to
delineate
6490 piqqûwd (1),
mandate of God, *Law*

STAVES
905 bad (37), *limb,*
member; bar; chief

4133 môwṭâh (1), *pole;*
ox-bow; *yoke*
4294 maṭṭeh (1), *tribe;*
rod, scepter; club
4731 maqqêl (2), *shoot;*
stick; staff
4938 mish'ênâh (1),
walking-stick
3586 xulŏn (5), *timber,*
i.e. a *stick, club*
4464 rhabdŏs (2), *stick,*
rod

STAY
4102 mâhahh (1), to be
reluctant
4223 mᵉchâ' (Ch.) (1), to
strike; to arrest
4937 mish'ên (5),
support; protector
5564 çâmak (2), to *lean*
upon; *take hold* of
5702 'âgan (1), to *debar,*
withdraw
5975 'âmad (10), to *stand*
6117 'âqab (1), to *seize by*
the heel; to circumvent
6438 pinnâh (1),
pinnacle; chieftain
7503 râphâh (3), to
slacken
7901 shâkab (1), to *lie*
down
8172 shâ'an (5), to
support, rely on
8551 tâmak (1), to
obtain, keep fast

STAYED
309 'âchar (1), to *remain*
2342 chûwl (2), to *wait;*
to *pervert*
3176 yâchal (1), to *wait;*
to *be patient, hope*
3322 yâtsag (1), to *place*
3607 kâlâ' (3), to *hold*
back or in; to *prohibit*
5564 çâmak (1), to *lean*
upon; *take hold* of
5975 'âmad (9), to *stand*
6113 'âtsar (7), to *hold*
back; to *maintain*
7896 shîyth (1), to *place*
8156 shâça' (1), to *split*
or *tear; to upbraid*
8551 tâmak (1), to
obtain, keep fast
1907 ĕpĕchō (1), to
retain; to detain
2722 katĕchō (2), to *hold*
down fast

STAYETH
1898 hâgâh (1), to *remove*

STAYS
3027 yâd (4), *hand; power*

STEAD
8478 tachath (91), in *lieu*
of
5228 hupĕr (2), *in behalf*
of

STEADS
8478 tachath (1), in *lieu*
of

STEADY
530 'ĕmûwnâh (1),
fidelity; steadiness

STEAL
1589 gânab (11), to
thieve; to deceive
2813 klĕptō (10), to *steal*

STEALETH
1589 gânab (3), to *thieve*

STEALING
1589 gânab (2), to *thieve*

STEALTH
1589 gânab (1), to *thieve*

STEDFAST
539 'âman (2), to *be firm,*
faithful, true; to trust
3332 yâtsaq (1), to *pour*
out
7011 qayâm (Ch.) (1),
permanent
949 bĕbaiŏs (4), *stable,*
certain, binding
1476 hĕdraiŏs (2),
immovable; steadfast
4731 stĕrĕŏs (1), *solid,*
stable

STEDFASTLY
553 'âmats (1), to *be*
strong; be courageous
7760 sùwm (1), to *put*
816 atĕnizō (6), to *gaze*
intently
4342 prŏskartĕrĕō (1), to
be constantly diligent
4741 stērizō (1), to *turn*
resolutely; to confirm

STEDFASTNESS
4733 stĕrĕōma (1),
stability, firmness
4740 stērigmŏs (1),
stability; firmness

STEEL
5154 nᵉchûwshâh (3),
copper; bronze
5178 nᵉchôsheth (1),
copper; bronze

STEEP
4095 madrêgâh (1), *steep*
or *inaccessible* place
4174 môwrâd (1),
descent, slope
2911 krēmnŏs (3),
precipice, steep cliff

STEM
1503 geza' (1), *stump*

STEP
838 'âshshûwr (1), *step*
6587 pesa' (1), *stride, step*

STEPHANAS
4734 Stĕphanas (3),
crowned

STEPHANUS
4734 Stĕphanas (1),
crowned

STEPHEN
4736 Stĕphanŏs (7),
wreath

STEPPED
1684 ĕmbainō (1), to
embark; to reach

STEPPETH
2597 katabainō (1), to
descend

STEPS
838 'âshshûwr (5), *step*
1978 hâlîyk (1), *step*

4609 ma'ălâh (11),
thought arising
4703 mits'âd (2), *step*
6119 'âqêb (1), *track,*
footprint; rear position
6471 pa'am (4), *step*
6806 tsa'ad (11), *step*
2487 ichnŏs (3), *track*

STERN
4403 prumna (1), *stern*

STEWARD
376+834+5921 'îysh (1),
man; male; someone
834+5921 'ăsher (3), *who*
1121+4943 bên (1), *son,*
descendant; people
2012 ĕpitrŏpŏs (2),
manager, guardian
3621 ŏikŏnŏmĕō (1), to
manage a household
3622 ŏikŏnŏmia (3),
administration
3623 ŏikŏnŏmŏs (2),
overseer, manager

STEWARDS
8269 sar (1), *head, ruler*
3623 ŏikŏnŏmŏs (3),
overseer, manager

STEWARDSHIP
3622 ŏikŏnŏmia (3),
administration

STICK
1692 dâbaq (2), to *cling*
or *adhere; to catch*
3920 lâkad (1), to *catch;*
to *capture*
5181 nâchath (1), to *sink,*
descend; to press down
6086 'êts (9), *wood*
8205 shᵉphîy (1), *bare*
hill or plain

STICKETH
1695 dâbêq (1),
adhering, sticking to

STICKS
6086 'êts (5), *wood*
5484 charin (1), *on*
account of, because of

STIFF
6277 'âthâq (1), *impudent*
7185 qâshâh (1), to *be*
tough or *severe*
7186 qâsheh (1), *severe*

STIFFENED
7185 qâshâh (1), to *be*
tough or *severe*

STIFFHEARTED
2389+3820 châzâq (1),
strong; severe, hard

STIFFNECKED
7185+6203 qâshâh (2), to
be tough or *severe*
7186+6203 qâsheh (6),
severe
4644 sklērŏtrachēlŏs (1),
obstinate

STILL
1826 dâmam (6), to *be*
silent; to be astonished
1827 dᵉmâmâh (1), *quiet*
2790 chârash (1), to *be*
silent; to be deaf
2814 châshâh (2), to
hush or *keep quiet*

English

STILLED

4496 mᵉnûwchâh (1), *peacefully; consolation*
5265 nâça' (1), to *start*
5750 'ôwd (19), *still; more*
5975 'âmad (3), to *stand*
7503 râphâh (1), to *slacken*
7673 shâbath (2), to *repose; to desist*
8252 shâqaṭ (2), to *repose*
2089 ĕti (4), yet, still
2476 histēmi (4), to stand, establish
4357 prŏsmĕnŏ (1), to remain in a place
5392 phimŏŏ (1), to restrain to silence

STILLED

2013 hâçâh (1), to *hush*
2814 châshâh (1), to *hush or keep quiet*

STILLEST

7623 shâbach (1), to *pacify*

STILLETH

7623 shâbach (1), to *pacify*

STING

2759 kĕntrŏn (2), sting

STINGETH

6567 pârash (1), to *wound*

STINGS

2759 kĕntrŏn (1), sting

STINK

887 bâ'ash (4), to *smell bad*
889 bᵉ'ôsh (3), *stench*
4716 maq (1), *putridity, stench*

STINKETH

887 bâ'ash (1), to *smell bad*
3605 ŏzŏ (1), to stink

STINKING

887 bâ'ash (1), to *smell bad*

STIR

5782 'ûwr (13), to *awake*
5927 'âlâh (1), to *ascend, be high, mount*
6965 qûwm (1), to *rise*
329 anazŏpurĕŏ (1), to re-enkindle, fan a flame
1326 diĕgĕirŏ (2), to arouse, stimulate
5017 tarachŏs (2), disturbance, tumult

STIRRED

1624 gârâh (3), to *provoke to anger*
5375 nâsâ' (3), to *lift up*
5496 çûwth (2), to *stimulate; to seduce*
5782 'ûwr (5), to *awake*
5916 'âkar (1), to *disturb or afflict*
6965 qûwm (3), to *rise*
1892 ĕpĕgĕirŏ (1), to excite against, stir up
3947 parŏxunŏ (1), to exasperate
3951 parŏtrunŏ (1), stimulate to hostility

4531 salĕuō (1), to waver, i.e. *agitate, rock, topple*
4787 sugkinĕŏ (1), to *excite to sedition*
4797 sugchĕŏ (1), to *throw into disorder*

STIRRETH

1624 gârâh (3), to *provoke to anger*
5782 'ûwr (4), to *awake*
383 anasĕiŏ (1), to excite, stir up

STIRS

8663 tᵉshû'âh (1), *crashing or clamor*

STOCK

944 bûwl (1), *produce*
1503 geza' (2), *stump*
6086 'êts (2), *wood*
6133 'êqer (1), *naturalized citizen*
1085 gĕnŏs (2), kin

STOCKS

4115 mahpeketh (2), *stocks for punishment*
5465 çad (2), *stocks*
5914 'ekeç (1), *anklet*
6086 'êts (2), (of) *wood*
6729 tsîynôq (1), *pillory*
3586 xulŏn (1), (of) timber

STOICKS

4770 Stŏïkŏs (1), porch

STOLE

1589 gânab (4), to *thieve*
2813 klĕptŏ (2), to steal

STOLEN

1589 gânab (14), to *thieve*

STOMACH'S

4751 stŏmachŏs (1), stomach

STOMACHER

6614 pᵉthîygîyl (1), fine *mantle for holidays*

STONE

68 'eben (104), *stone*
69 'eben (Ch.) (6), *stone*
1496 gâzîyth (3), *dressed stone*
5619 çâqal (7), to *throw large stones*
6697 tsûwr (1), *rock*
6872 tsᵉrôwr (1), *parcel; kernel or particle*
7275 râgam (10), to *cast stones*
8068 shâmîyr (1), *thorn;* (poss.) *diamond*
2642 katalithazō (1), to stone to death
2991 laxĕutŏs (1), rock-quarried
3034 lithazŏ (4), to lapidate, to stone
3035 lithinŏs (3), made of stone
3036 lithŏbŏlĕŏ (1), to throw stones
3037 lithŏs (36), stone
4074 Pĕtrŏs (1), piece of rock
5586 psēphŏs (2), pebble stone

STONE'S

3037 lithŏs (1), stone

STONED

5619 çâqal (8), to *throw large stones*
7275 râgam (5), to *cast stones*
3034 lithazō (4), to lapidate, to stone
3036 lithŏbŏlĕŏ (5), to throw stones

STONES

68 'eben (136), *stone*
69 'eben (Ch.) (2), *stone*
810 'eshek (1), *testicle*
1496 gâzîyth (4), *dressed stone*
2106 zâvîyth (1), *angle, corner* (as projecting)
2687 châtsâts (1), *gravel*
2789 cheres (1), *piece of earthenware pottery*
5553 çela' (1), *craggy rock; fortress*
5619 çâqal (1), to *throw large stones*
6344 pachad (1), *male testicle*
6697 tsûwr (1), *rock*
3036 lithŏbŏlĕŏ (1), to throw stones
3037 lithŏs (16), stone

STONESQUARERS

1382 Gibliy (1), Gebalite

STONEST

3036 lithŏbŏlĕŏ (2), to throw stones

STONING

5619 çâqal (1), to *throw large stones*

STONY

68 'eben (2), *stone*
5553 çela' (1), *craggy rock; fortress*
4075 pĕtrŏdēs (4), rocky

STOOD

1826 dâmam (1), to *stop, cease; to perish*
3320 yâtsab (7), to *station, offer, continue*
3559 kûwn (1), to *set up*
4673 matstsâb (2), *fixed spot; office; post*
5324 nâtsab (19), to *station*
5568 çâmar (1), to *bristle*
5975 'âmad (189), to *stand*
5977 'ômed (1), *fixed spot*
6965 qûwm (15), to *rise*
6966 qûwm (Ch.) (4), to *rise*
450 anistēmi (7), to rise; to come back to life
2186 ĕphistēmi (5), to be present; to approach
2476 histēmi (60), to stand, establish
2944 kuklŏŏ (1), to surround, encircle
3936 paristēmi (14), to stand beside, present
4026 pĕriistēmi (1), to stand around; to avoid
4836 sumparaginŏmai (1), to convene; to appear in aid
4921 sunistaŏ (1), to set together

STOODEST

5324 nâtsab (1), to *station*
5975 'âmad (2), to *stand*

STOOL

3678 kiççê' (1), *throne*

STOOLS

70 'ôben (1), *potter's wheel; midwife's stool*

STOOP

7164 qâraç (1), to *hunch*
7812 shâchâh (1), to *prostrate in homage*
7817 shâchach (1), to *sink or depress*
2955 kuptō (1), to bend forward, stoop down

STOOPED

3486 yâshêsh (1), *gray-haired, aged*
3766 kâra' (1), to *prostrate*
6915 qâdad (2), to *bend*
2955 kuptō (2), to bend forward, stoop down
3879 parakuptō (1), to lean over to peer within

STOOPETH

7164 qâraç (1), to *hunch*

STOOPING

3879 parakuptō (2), to lean over to peer within

STOP

2629 châçam (1), to *muzzle; block*
5462 çâgar (1), to *shut up*
5640 çâtham (2), to *stop up; to repair*
6113 'âtsar (1), to *hold back; to maintain, rule*
7092 qâphats (1), to *draw together, to leap; to die*
5420 phrassō (1), to fence or enclose, to block up

STOPPED

2856 châtham (1), to *close up; to affix a seal*
3513 kâbad (1), to *be heavy, severe, dull*
5534 çâkar (2), to *shut up*
5640 çâtham (6), to *stop up; to repair*
8610 tâphas (1), to *manipulate, i.e. seize*
1998 ĕpisuntrĕchō (1), to hasten together upon
4912 sunĕchō (1), to hold together
5420 phrassō (2), to fence or enclose, to block up

STOPPETH

331 'âṭam (3), to *close*
7092 qâphats (1), to *draw together, to leap; to die*

STORE

214 'ôwtsâr (1), *depository*
686 'âtsar (3), to *store up*
1995 hâmôwn (2), *noise, tumult; many, crowd*
3462 yâshên (1), to *sleep; to grow old, stale*
4543 miçkᵉnâh (5), *storage-magazine*
4863 mish'ereth (2), *kneading-trough*

6487 piqqâdôwn (1),
deposit
7235 râbâh (1), *to*
increase
8498 tᵉkûwnâh (1),
structure; equipage
597 apóthēsaurizō (1), *to*
store *treasure away*
2343 thēsaurizō (2), *to*
amass, reserve, store up

STOREHOUSE
214 'ôwtsâr (1),
depository
5009 tamĕiŏn (1), *room*

STOREHOUSES
214 'ôwtsâr (2),
depository
618 'âçâm (1),
storehouse, barn
834 'âsher (1), *who,*
which, what, that
3965 ma'ăbûwç (1),
granary, barn
4543 miçkᵉnâh (1),
storage-magazine

STORIES
4609 ma'ălâh (1),
thought arising

STORK
2624 chăçîydâh (5), *stork*

STORM
2230 zerem (3), *flood*
5492 çûwphâh (3),
hurricane wind
5584 çâ'âh (1), *to rush*
5591 ça'ar (1), *hurricane*
7722 shôw' (1), *tempest;*
devastation
8178 sa'ar (1), *tempest*
8183 sᵉ'ârâh (1),
hurricane wind
2978 lailaps (2),
whirlwind; hurricane

STORMY
5591 ça'ar (4), *hurricane*

STORY
4097 midrâsh (2), *treatise*

STOUT
1433 gôdel (1),
magnitude, majesty
2388 châzaq (1), *to be*
strong; courageous
7229 rab (Ch.) (1), *great*

STOUTHEARTED
47+3820 'abbîyr (2),
mighty

STOUTNESS
1433 gôdel (1),
magnitude, majesty

STRAIGHT
3474 yâshar (9), *to be*
straight; to make right
4334 mîyshôwr (2), *plain;*
justice
5676 'êber (3), *opposite*
8626 tâqan (2), *to*
straighten; to compose
461 anŏrthóō (1), *to*
straighten up
2113 ĕuthudrŏmĕō (2), *to*
sail direct
2116 ĕuthunō (1), *to*
straighten or level
2117 ĕuthus (5), *at once,*
immediately

3717 ŏrthŏs (1), *straight*

STRAIGHTWAY
3651 kên (1), *just; right*
4116 mâhar (1), *to hurry*
6258 'attâh (1), *now*
6597 pith'ôwm (1),
instantly, suddenly
1824 ĕxautēs (1),
instantly, at once
2112 ĕuthĕōs (32), *at*
once or soon
2117 ĕuthus (2), *at once*
3916 parachrēma (3),
instantly, immediately

STRAIN
1368 diulizō (1), *to strain*
out

STRAIT
6862 tsar (3), *trouble*
6887 tsârar (3), *to cramp*
4728 stĕnŏs (3), *narrow*
4912 sunĕchō (1), *to hold*
together

STRAITEN
6693 tsûwq (1), *to oppress*

STRAITENED
680 'âtsal (1), *to select;*
refuse; narrow
3334 yâtsar (2), *to be in*
distress
4164 mûwtsaq (1),
distress
7114 qâtsar (1), *to*
curtail, cut short
4729 stĕnŏchōrĕō (2), *to*
hem in closely
4912 sunĕchō (1), *to hold*
together

STRAITENETH
5148 nâchâh (1), *to guide*

STRAITEST
196 akribĕstatŏs (1),
most exact, very strict

STRAITLY
547 apĕilē (1), *menace,*
threat
4183 pŏlus (2), *much*

STRAITNESS
4164 mûwtsaq (1),
distress
4689 mâtsôwq (4),
confinement; disability

STRAITS
3334 yâtsar (1), *to be in*
distress
4712 mêtsar (1), *trouble*

STRAKE
5465 chalaō (1), *to lower*
as into a *void*

STRAKES
6479 pᵉtsâlâh (1), *peeling*
8258 shᵉqa'rûwrâh (1),
depression

STRANGE
312 'achêr (1), *different*
1970 hâkar (1), (poss.) *to*
injure
2114 zûwr (22), *to be*
foreign, strange
3937 lâ'az (1), *to speak in*
a foreign tongue
5234 nâkar (1), *to treat*
as a foreigner
5235 neker (1), *calamity*

5236 nêkâr (16),
foreigner; heathendom
5237 nokrîy (20), *foreign;*
non-relative; different
6012 'âmêq (2), *obscure*
245 allŏtriŏs (2), *not*
one's own
1854 ĕxō (1), *out, outside*
2087 hĕtĕrŏs (1), *different*
3579 xĕnizō (3), *to be a*
guest; to be strange
3581 xĕnŏs (3), *alien*
3861 paradŏxŏs (1),
extraordinary

STRANGELY
5234 nâkar (1), *to treat*
as a foreigner

STRANGER
376+1616 'îysh (1), *man;*
male; someone
376+2114 'îysh (3), *man;*
male; someone
376+5237 'îysh (2), *man;*
male; someone
1121+5235 bên (3), *son,*
descendant; people
1121+5236 bên (2), *son,*
descendant; people
1616 gêr (69), *foreigner*
2114 zûwr (18), *to be*
foreign, strange
4033 mâgûwr (3), *abode*
5235 neker (1), *calamity*
5236 nêkâr (3), *foreigner*
5237 nokrîy (14), *foreign*
8453 tôwshâb (2),
temporary dweller
241 allŏgĕnēs (1),
foreign, i.e. not a Jew
245 allŏtriŏs (1), *not*
one's own
3581 xĕnŏs (4), *alien*
3939 parŏikĕō (1), *to*
reside as a foreigner
3941 parŏikŏs (1),
strange; stranger

STRANGER'S
1121+5236 bên (1), *son,*
descendant; people
1616 gêr (1), *foreigner*

STRANGERS
582+1616 'ĕnôwsh (1),
man; person, human
1121+5236 bên (6), *son,*
descendant; people
1481 gûwr (6), *to sojourn*
1616 gêr (18), *stranger*
2114 zûwr (26), *to be*
foreign, strange
4033 mâgûwr (1), *abode*
5236 nêkâr (3), *foreigner*
5237 nokrîy (2), *foreign*
8453 tôwshâb (1),
temporary dweller
245 allŏtriŏs (2), *not*
one's own
1722+3940 ĕn (1), *in;*
during; because of
1927 ĕpidĕmĕō (1), *to*
make oneself at home
3580 xĕnŏdŏchĕō (1), *to*
be hospitable
3581 xĕnŏs (6), *alien*
3927 parepidēmŏs (1),
resident foreigner
3941 parŏikŏs (1),
strange; stranger

5381 philŏnĕxia (1),
hospitableness to
strangers

STRANGERS'
2114 zûwr (1), *to be*
foreign, strange

STRANGLED
2614 chânaq (1), *to choke*
4156 pniktŏs (3), *animal*
choked to death

STRANGLING
4267 machănaq (1),
choking, strangling

STRAW
4963 mathbên (1), *straw*
8401 teben (15), *threshed*
stalks of grain

STRAWED
2219 zârâh (1), *to toss*
about; to winnow
1287 diaskŏrpizō (2), *to*
scatter; to squander
4766 strŏnnumi (2),
strew, i.e. spread

STREAM
650 'âphîyq (1), *valley;*
stream; mighty, strong
793 'eshed (1), *stream*
5103 nᵉhar (Ch.) (1),
river; Euphrates *River*
5158 nachal (7), *valley*
4215 pŏtamŏs (2),
current, brook

STREAMS
650 'âphîyq (1), *valley;*
stream; mighty, strong
2975 yᵉ'ôr (1), Nile *River;*
Tigris *River*
2988 yâbâl (1), *stream*
5104 nâhâr (2), *stream*
5140 nâzal (2), *to drip*
5158 nachal (4), *valley*
6388 peleg (1), *small*
irrigation channel

STREET
2351 chûwts (8), *outside,*
outdoors; open market
2351+6440 chûwts (1),
outside, outdoors
7339 rᵉchôb (22), *myriad*
7784 shûwq (1), *street*
4113 platĕia (3), *wide,*
open square
4505 rhumē (2), *alley* or
crowded avenue

STREETS
2351 chûwts (34),
outside, outdoors
7339 rᵉchôb (19), *myriad*
7784 shûwq (3), *street*
58 agŏra (1),
town-square, market
4113 platĕia (6), *wide,*
open square
4505 rhumē (1), *alley* or
crowded avenue

STRENGTH
193 'ûwl (1), *powerful;*
mighty
202 'ôwn (7), *ability,*
power; wealth
353 'ĕyâl (1), *strength*
360 'ĕyâlûwth (1), *power*
386 'êythân (2),
never-failing; eternal

English

556 'amtsâh (1), *strength, force*
905 bad (2), *limb, member; bar; chief*
1082 bâlag (1), *to be strengthened; invade*
1369 gᵉbûwrâh (17), *force; valor; victory*
1679 dôbe' (1), *leisurely*
2220 zᵉrôwa' (1), *arm; foreleg; force, power*
2388 châzaq (1), *to be strong; be courageous*
2391 chêzeq (1), *help*
2392 chôzeq (5), *power*
2394 chozqâh (1), *vehemence, harshness*
2428 chayil (11), *army; wealth; virtue; strength*
2633 chôçen (2), *wealth, stored riches*
3027 yâd (1), *hand; power*
3581 kôach (57), *force, might; strength*
4206 mâzîyach (2), *belt*
4581 mâ'ôwz (24), *fortified place; defense*
5326 nitsbâh (Ch.) (1), *firmness, haraness*
5331 netsach (2), *splendor; lasting*
5332 nêtsach (1), *blood (as if red juice)*
5797 'ôz (60), *strength*
5807 'ĕzûwz (2), *forcibleness*
6106 'etsem (1), *bone; body; substance*
6109 'otsmâh (2), *powerfulness*
6697 tsûwr (5), *rock*
7293 rahab (1), *bluster*
7296 rôhab (1), *pride*
8443 tôw'âphâh (3), *treasure; speed*
8510 têl (1), *mound*
8632 tᵉqôph (Ch.) (1), *power*
8633 tôqeph (1), *might*
772 asthénēs (1), *strengthless, weak*
1411 dunamis (7), *force, power, miracle*
1743 ĕndunamŏō (1), *to empower, strengthen*
1849 ĕxŏusia (1), *authority, power, right*
2479 ischus (4), *forcefulness, power*
2480 ischuŏ (1), *to have or exercise force*
2904 kratŏs (1), *vigor, strength*
4732 stĕrĕŏō (1), *to be, become strong*

STRENGTHEN
553 'âmats (7), *to be strong; be courageous*
1396 gâbar (2), *to be strong; to prevail*
2388 châzaq (14), *to be strong; courageous*
4581 mâ'ôwz (1), *fortified place; defense*
5582 çâ'ad (2), *to support*
5810 'âzaz (2), *to be stout; be bold*
6965 qûwm (1), *to rise*

4599 sthĕnŏō (1), *to strengthen*
4741 stērizō (2), *to turn resolutely; to confirm*

STRENGTHENED
553 'âmats (3), *to be strong; be courageous*
2388 châzaq (28), *to be strong; courageous*
2394 chozqâh (1), *vehemence, harshness*
5810 'âzaz (3), *to be stout; be bold*
1412 dunamŏō (1), *to enable, strengthen*
1743 ĕndunamŏō (1), *to empower, strengthen*
1765 ĕnischuō (1), *to invigorate oneself*
2901 krataiŏō (1), *increase in vigor*

STRENGTHENEDST
7292 râhab (1), *to urge, importune, embolden*

STRENGTHENETH
553 'âmats (2), *to be strong; be courageous*
1082 bâlag (1), *to be strengthened*
1396 gâbar (1), *to be strong; to prevail*
5582 çâ'ad (1), *to support*
5810 'âzaz (1), *to be stout; be bold*
1743 ĕndunamŏō (1), *to empower, strengthen*

STRENGTHENING
1765 ĕnischuō (1), *to invigorate oneself*
1991 ĕpistērizō (1), *to re-establish, strengthen*

STRETCH
5186 nâṭâh (28), *to stretch or spread out*
5628 çârach (1), *to extend even to excess*
6566 pâras (4), *to break apart, disperse, scatter*
7323 rûwts (1), *to run*
7971 shâlach (10), *to send away*
8311 sâra' (1), *to be deformed*
1614 ĕktĕinō (4), *to stretch*
5239 hupĕrĕktĕinō (1), *to extend inordinately*

STRETCHED
1457 gâhar (2), *to prostrate, bow down*
4058 mâdad (1), *to be extended*
4900 mâshak (1), *to draw out; to be tall*
5186 nâṭâh (47), *to stretch or spread out*
5203 nâṭash (1), *to disperse; to thrust off*
5628 çârach (1), *to extend even to excess*
6504 pârad (1), *to spread or separate*
6566 pâras (2), *to break apart, disperse, scatter*
7554 râqa' (1), *to pound*
7849 shâṭach (1), *to expand*

7971 shâlach (4), *to send away*
1600 ĕkpĕtannumi (1), *to extend, spread out*
1614 ĕktĕinō (7), *to stretch*
1911 ĕpiballō (1), *to throw upon*

STRETCHEDST
5186 nâṭâh (1), *to stretch*

STRETCHEST
5186 nâṭâh (1), *to stretch*

STRETCHETH
5186 nâṭâh (6), *to stretch*
6566 pâras (1), *to break apart, disperse, scatter*

STRETCHING
4298 muṭṭâh (1), *expansion, extending*
1614 ĕktĕinō (1), *to stretch*

STRICKEN
935 bôw' (7), *to go, come*
1856 dâqar (1), *to stab, pierce; to starve*
2498 châlaph (1), *to pierce; to change*
5060 nâga' (1), *to strike*
5061 nega' (1), *infliction, affliction; leprous spot*
5218 nâkê' (1), *smitten*
5221 nâkâh (3), *to strike, kill*
8628 tâqa' (1), *to slap*
4260 prŏbainō (2), *to advance*

STRIFE
1777 dîyn (1), *to judge; to strive or contend for*
1779 dîyn (1), *judge; judgment; law suit*
4066 mâdôwn (7), *contest or quarrel*
4683 matstsâh (1), *quarrel*
4808 mᵉrîybâh (5), *quarrel*
7379 rîyb (14), *contest*
485 antilŏgia (1), *dispute, disobedience*
2052 ĕrithĕia (4), *faction, strife, selfish ambition*
2054 ĕris (4), *quarrel, i.e. wrangling*
5379 philŏnĕikia (1), *dispute, strife*

STRIFES
4090 mᵉdân (1), *contest or quarrel*
2052 ĕrithĕia (1), *faction, strife, selfish ambition*
3055 lŏgŏmachia (1), *disputation*
3163 machē (1), *controversy, conflict*

STRIKE
2498 châlaph (1), *too pierce; to change*
4272 mâchats (1), *to crush; to subdue*
5060 nâga' (1), *to strike*
5130 nûwph (1), *to quiver, vibrate, rock*
5221 nâkâh (1), *to strike, kill*

5344 nâqab (1), *to puncture, perforate*
5414 nâthan (1), *to give*
6398 pâlach (1), *to pierce*
8628 tâqa' (2), *to slap*
906 ballō (1), *to throw*

STRIKER
4131 plēktēs (2), *pugnacious*

STRIKETH
5606 çâphaq (1), *to clap the hands*
8628 tâqa' (1), *to clatter, slap, drive, clasp*
3817 paiō (1), *to hit*

STRING
3499 yether (1), *remainder; small rope*
1199 dĕsmŏn (1), *shackle; impediment*

STRINGED
4482 mên (1), *part; musical chord*
5058 nᵉgîynâh (2), *stringed instrument*

STRINGS
4340 mêythâr (1), *tent-cord; bow-string*

STRIP
6584 pâshaṭ (7), *to strip*

STRIPE
2250 chabbûwrâh (1), *weal, bruise*

STRIPES
2250 chabbûwrâh (1), *weal, bruise*
4112 mahălummâh (1), *blow*
4347 makkâh (2), *blow; wound; pestilence*
5061 nega' (2), *infliction, affliction; leprous spot*
5221 nâkâh (2), *to strike, kill*
3468 mōlōps (1), *black eye or blow-mark, welt*
4127 plēgē (7), *stroke; wound; calamity*

STRIPLING
5958 'elem (1), *lad, young man*

STRIPPED
5337 nâtsal (2), *to deliver; to be snatched*
6584 pâshaṭ (6), *to strip*
7758 shôwlâl (1), *bare-foot; stripped*
1562 ĕkduō (2), *to divest*

STRIPT
6584 pâshaṭ (1), *to strip*

STRIVE
1777 dîyn (1), *to judge; to strive or contend for*
3401 yârîyb (1), *contentious; adversary*
5327 nâtsâh (2), *to quarrel, fight*
7378 rîyb (9), *to hold a controversy; to defend*
7379 rîyb (1), *contest*
75 agōnizŏmai (1), *to struggle; to contend*
118 athlĕō (2), *to contend in games*

2051 ĕrizō (1), to
wrangle, quarrel
3054 lŏgŏmachĕō (1), to
be disputatious
3164 machŏmai (1), to
quarrel, dispute
4865 sunagōnizōmai (1),
to struggle with

STRIVED
5389 philŏtimĕŏmai (1),
eager or earnest to do

STRIVEN
1624 gârâh (1), to
provoke to anger

STRIVETH
7378 rîyb (1), to hold a
controversy; to defend
75 agōnizōmai (1), to
struggle; to contend

STRIVING
75 agōnizōmai (1), to
struggle; to contend
464 antagōnizōmai (1),
to struggle against
4866 sunathlĕō (1), to
wrestle with

STRIVINGS
7379 rîyb (2), contest
3163 machē (1),
controversy, conflict

STROKE
3027 yâd (1), hand; power
4046 maggêphâh (1),
pestilence; defeat
4273 machats (1),
contusion
4347 makkâh (2), blow;
wound; pestilence
5061 nega' (3), infliction,
affliction; leprous spot
5607 çêpheq (1), satiety

STROKES
4112 mahălummâh (1),
blow

STRONG
47 'abbîyr (3), mighty
386 'êythân (5), never-
failing; eternal
410 'êl (1), mighty
533 'ammîyts (4), strong;
mighty; brave
553 'âmats (4), to be
strong; be courageous
559 'âmar (1), to say
650 'âphîyq (1), valley;
stream; mighty, strong
1219 bâtsar (1), to be
inaccessible
1225 bitstsârôwn (1),
fortress
1368 gibbôwr (5),
powerful; great warrior
1634 gerem (1), bone; self
2364 Chûwshâh (1), haste
2388 châzaq (47), to be
strong; courageous
2389 châzâq (26), strong;
severe, hard, violent
2393 chezqâh (1), power
2394 chozqâh (1),
vehemence, harshness
2428 chayil (5), army;
wealth; virtue; strength
2626 chăçîyn (1), mighty
2634 châçôn (1), strong

3524 kabbîyr (1), mighty;
aged; mighty
4013 mibtsâr (14),
fortification; defender
4581 mâ'ôwz (5), fortified
place; defense
4679 mᵉtsad (5),
stronghold
4686 mâtsûwd (2), net or
capture; fastness
4692 mâtsôwr (3),
siege-mound; distress
4694 mᵉtsûwrâh (1),
rampart, fortification
5553 çela' (1), craggy
rock; fortress
5794 'az (12), strong,
vehement, harsh
5797 'ôz (17), strength
5808 'izzûwz (1), forcible;
army
5810 'âzaz (1), to be
stout; be bold
6076 'ôphel (1), tumor;
fortress
6099 'âtsûwm (13),
powerful; numerous
6105 'âtsam (4), to be,
make powerful
6108 'ôtsem (1), power;
framework of the body
6110 'atstsûmâh (1),
defensive argument
6184 'ârîyts (1), powerful
or tyrannical
6339 pâzaz (1), to solidify
by refining; to spring
6697 tsûwr (1), rock
7682 sâgab (1), to be
safe, strong
7941 shêkâr (1), liquor
8624 taqqîyph (Ch.) (3),
powerful
8631 tᵉqêph (Ch.) (3), to
become, make mighty
1415 dunatŏs (3),
powerful or capable
1743 ĕndunamŏō (4), to
empower, strengthen
1753 ĕnĕrgĕia (1),
energy, power
2478 ischurŏs (11),
forcible, powerful
2901 krataiŏō (3),
increase in vigor
3173 mĕgas (1), great
3794 ŏchurōma (1),
fortress, stronghold
4608 sikĕra (1),
intoxicant
4731 stĕrĕŏs (2), solid
4732 stĕrĕŏō (1), to be,
become strong

STRONGER
553 'âmats (2), to be
strong; be courageous
555 'ômets (1), strength
1396 gâbar (1), to be
strong; to prevail
2388 châzaq (6), to be
strong; courageous
2389 châzâq (1), strong
2390 châzêq (1),
powerful; loud
5794 'az (1), strong
6105 'âtsam (1), to be,
make powerful
7194 qâshar (2), to tie,
bind

2478 ischurŏs (3),
forcible, powerful
STRONGEST
1368 gibbôwr (1),
powerful; great warrior
STROVE
1519 gîyach (Ch.) (1), to
rush forth
5327 nâtsâh (6), to
quarrel, fight
6229 'âsaq (1), to quarrel
7378 rîyb (3), to hold a
controversy; to defend
1264 diamachŏmai (1),
to fight fiercely
3164 machŏmai (2), to
war, quarrel, dispute
STROWED
2236 zâraq (1), to scatter
STRUCK
5062 nâgaph (2), to
inflict a disease; strike
5221 nâkâh (1), to strike
8138 shânâh (1), to fold
1325+4475 didōmi (1), to
give
3960 patassō (1), to strike
5180 tuptō (1), to strike
STRUGGLED
7533 râtsats (1), to crack
in pieces, smash
STUBBLE
7179 qash (16), dry straw
8401 teben (1), threshed
stalks of grain
2562 kalamē (1), stubble
STUBBORN
5637 çârar (4), to be
refractory, stubborn
7186 qâsheh (1), severe
STUBBORNNESS
6484 pâtsar (1), to stun
or dull
7190 qᵉshîy (1), obstinacy
STUCK
1692 dâbaq (1), to cling
or adhere; to catch
4600 mâ'ak (1), to press
2043 ĕrĕidō (1), to make
immovable
STUDIETH
1897 hâgâh (2), to
murmur, ponder
STUDS
5351 nᵉquddâh (1),
ornamental boss
STUDY
3854 lahag (1), mental
application
4704 spŏudazō (1), to
make effort
5389 philŏtimĕŏmai (1),
eager or earnest to do
STUFF
3627 kᵉlîy (14), thing
4399 mᵉlâ'kâh (1), work
4632 skĕuŏs (1), vessel
STUMBLE
3782 kâshal (15), to
stumble
5062 nâgaph (2), to
inflict a disease; strike
6328 pûwq (1), to waver

4350 prŏskŏptō (1), to
trip up; to strike
STUMBLED
3782 kâshal (3), to totter
8058 shâmaṭ (1), to
jostle; to let alone
4350 prŏskŏptō (1), to
trip up; to strike
4417 ptaiō (1), to trip up
STUMBLETH
3782 kâshal (1), to totter
4350 prŏskŏptō (3), to
trip up; to strike
STUMBLING
5063 negeph (1), trip
4625 skandalŏn (1),
snare
STUMBLINGBLOCK
4383 mikshôwl (7),
stumbling-block
4348 prŏskŏmma (2),
occasion of apostasy
4625 skandalŏn (3),
snare
STUMBLINGBLOCKS
4383 mikshôwl (1),
stumbling-block
4384 makshêlâh (1),
stumbling-block
STUMBLINGSTONE
3037+4348 lithŏs (2),
stone
STUMP
6136 'iqqar (Ch.) (3),
stock
SUAH
5477 Çûwach (1),
sweeping
SUBDUE
1696 dâbar (1), to subdue
3533 kâbash (3), to
conquer, subjugate
3665 kâna' (1), to
humiliate, subdue
7286 râdad (1), to
conquer; to overlay
8214 shᵉphal (Ch.) (1), to
humiliate
5293 hupŏtassō (1), to
subordinate; to obey
SUBDUED
3381 yârad (1), to
descend
3533 kâbash (5), to
conquer, subjugate
3665 kâna' (9), to
humiliate, subdue
3766 kâra' (2), to
prostrate
2610 katagōnizŏmai (1),
to overcome, defeat
5293 hupŏtassō (1), to
subordinate; to obey
SUBDUEDST
3665 kâna' (1), to
humiliate, subdue
SUBDUETH
1696 dâbar (1), to subdue
2827 chăshal (Ch.) (1), to
crush, pulverize
7286 râdad (1), to
conquer; to overlay
SUBJECT
1379 dŏgmatizō (1), to
submit to a certain rule

1777 ĕnŏchŏs (1), *liable*
3663 hŏmŏiŏpathēs (1), *similarly affected*
5293 hupŏtassō (14), *to subordinate; to obey*

SUBJECTED
5293 hupŏtassō (1), *to subordinate; to obey*

SUBJECTION
3533 kâbash (2), *to conquer, subjugate*
3665 kâna' (1), *to humiliate, subdue*
1396 dŏulagōgĕō (1), *to enslave, subdue*
5292 hupŏtagē (4), *subordination*
5293 hupŏtassō (6), *to subordinate; to obey*

SUBMIT
3584 kâchash (3), *to lie, disown; to cringe*
6031 'ânâh (1), *to afflict, be afflicted*
7511 râphaç (1), *to trample; to prostrate*
5226 hupĕikō (1), *to surrender, yield*
5293 hupŏtassō (6), *to subordinate; to obey*

SUBMITTED
3584 kâchash (1), *to lie, disown; to cringe*
5414+3027 nâthan (1), *to give*
5293 hupŏtassō (1), *to subordinate; to obey*

SUBMITTING
5293 hupŏtassō (1), *to subordinate; to obey*

SUBORNED
5260 hupŏballō (1), *to throw in stealthily*

SUBSCRIBE
3789 kâthab (2), *to write*

SUBSCRIBED
3789 kâthab (2), *to write*

SUBSTANCE
202 'ôwn (1), *ability, power; wealth*
1564 gôlem (1), *embryo*
1942 havvâh (1), *desire; craving*
1952 hôwn (7), *wealth*
2428 chayil (7), *wealth; virtue; valor; strength*
3351 yᵉqûwm (3), *living thing*
3426 yêsh (1), *there is*
3428 Yesheb'âb (1), *seat of (his) father*
3581 kôach (1), *force, might; strength*
4678 matstsebeth (2), *stock of a tree*
4735 miqneh (2), *stock*
6108 'ôtsem (1), *power; framework of the body*
7009 qîym (1), *opponent*
7075 qinyân (4), *acquisition, purchase*
7399 rᵉkûwsh (11), *property*
7738 shâvâh (1), *to destroy*

3776 ôusia (1), *wealth, property, possessions*
5223 huparxis (1), *property, possessions*
5224 huparchŏnta (1), *property or possessions*
5287 hupŏstasis (1), *essence; assurance*

SUBTIL
2450 châkâm (1), *wise, intelligent, skillful*
5341 nâtsar (1), *to conceal, hide*
6175 'ârûwm (1), *cunning; clever*

SUBTILLY
5230 nâkal (1), *to act treacherously*
6191 'âram (1), *to be cunning; be prudent*
2686 katasŏphizŏmai (1), *to be crafty against*

SUBTILTY
4820 mirmâh (1), *fraud*
6122 'oqbâh (1), *trickery*
6195 'ormâh (1), *trickery; discretion*
1388 dŏlŏs (2), *wile, deceit, trickery*
3834 panŏurgia (1), *trickery or sophistry*

SUBURBS
4054 migrâsh (110), *open country*
6503 Parbâr (1), *Parbar*

SUBVERT
5791 'âvath (1), *to wrest, twist*
396 anatrĕpō (1), *to overturn, destroy*

SUBVERTED
1612 ĕkstrĕphō (1), *to pervert, be warped*

SUBVERTING
384 anaskĕuazō (1), *to upset, trouble*
2692 katastrŏphē (1), *catastrophical ruin*

SUCCEED
6965 qûwm (1), *to rise*

SUCCEEDED
3423 yârash (3), *to impoverish; to ruin*

SUCCEEDEST
3423 yârash (2), *to impoverish; to ruin*

SUCCESS
7919 sâkal (1), *to be or act circumspect*

SUCCOTH
5523 Çukkôwth (18), *booths*

SUCCOTH-BENOTH
5524 Çukkôwth Bᵉnôwth (1), *brothels*

SUCCOUR
5826 'âzar (2), *to aid*
997 bŏēthĕō (1), *to aid*

SUCCOURED
5826 'âzar (1), *to aid*
997 bŏēthĕō (1), *to aid*

SUCCOURER
4368 prŏstatis (1), *assistant, helper*

SUCHATHITES
7756 Sûwkâthîy (1), *Sukathite*

SUCK
3243 yânaq (13), *to suck*
4680 mâtsâh (1), *to drain; to squeeze out*
5966 'âla' (1), *to sip up*
2337 thēlazō (4), *to suck*

SUCKED
3243 yânaq (1), *to suck*
2337 thēlazō (1), *to suck*

SUCKING
2461 châlâb (1), *milk*
3243 yânaq (3), *to suck*
5764 'ûwl (1), *babe*

SUCKLING
3243 yânaq (3), *to suck*

SUCKLINGS
3243 yânaq (3), *to suck*
2337 thēlazō (1), *to suck*

SUDDEN
6597 pith'ôwm (2), *instantly, suddenly*
160 aiphnidiŏs (1), *suddenly*

SUDDENLY
4116 mâhar (1), *to hurry*
4118 mahêr (1), *in a hurry*
6597 pith'ôwm (22), *instantly, suddenly*
6621 petha' (4), *wink, i.e. moment; quickly*
7280 râga' (2), *to settle, i.e. quiet; to wink*
7281 rega' (1), *very short space of time*
869 aphnō (3), *suddenly*
1810 ĕxaiphnēs (5), *suddenly, unexpectedly*
1819 ĕxapina (1), *unexpectedly*
5030 tachĕōs (1), *rapidly*

SUE
2919 krinō (1), *to decide; to try, condemn, punish*

SUFFER
3201 yâkôl (1), *to be able*
3240 yânach (3), *to allow to stay*
3803 kâthar (1), *to enclose, besiege; to wait*
5375 nâsâ' (5), *to lift up*
5414 nâthan (11), *to give*
430 anĕchŏmai (7), *put up with, endure*
818 atimazō (1), *to maltreat, dishonor*
863 aphiēmi (8), *to leave; to pardon, forgive*
1325 didōmi (2), *to give*
1377 diōkō (3), *to pursue; to persecute*
1439 ĕaō (2), *to let be, i.e. permit or leave alone*
2010 ĕpitrĕpō (6), *allow*
2210 zēmiŏō (1), *to experience detriment*
2553 kakŏpathĕō (1), *to undergo suffering*
2558 kakŏuchĕō (1), *to maltreat; to torment*
3805 pathētŏs (1), *doomed to pain*

3958 paschō (20), *to experience pain*
4722 stĕgō (1), *to endure patiently*
4778 sugkakŏuchĕō (1), *to endure persecution*
4841 sumpaschō (2), *to experience pain jointly*
5278 hupŏmĕnō (1), *to undergo, bear (trials)*
5302 hustĕrĕō (1), *to be inferior; to fall short*

SUFFERED
3240 yânach (2), *to allow to stay*
5203 nâṭash (1), *to disperse; to thrust off*
5375 nâsâ' (1), *to lift up*
5414 nâthan (7), *to give*
863 aphiēmi (6), *to leave; to pardon, forgive*
1439 ĕaō (5), *to let be, i.e. permit or leave alone*
2010 ĕpitrĕpō (4), *allow*
2210 zēmiŏō (1), *to suffer loss*
2967 kōluō (1), *to stop*
3958 paschō (17), *to experience pain*
4310 prŏpaschō (1), *to undergo hardship*
5159 trŏpŏphŏrĕō (1), *to endure one's habits*

SUFFEREST
1439 ĕaō (1), *to let be*

SUFFERETH
5414 nâthan (1), *to give*
971 biazō (1), *to crowd oneself into*
1439 ĕaō (1), *to let be*
3114 makrŏthumĕō (1), *to be forbearing, patient*

SUFFERING
2552 kakŏpathĕia (1), *hardship, suffering*
3804 pathēma (1), *passion; suffering*
3958 paschō (1), *to experience pain*
4330 prŏsĕaō (1), *permit further progress*
5254 hupĕchō (1), *to endure with patience*

SUFFERINGS
3804 pathēma (10), *passion; suffering*

SUFFICE
4672 mâtsâ' (2), *to find or acquire; to occur*
5606 çâphaq (1), *to be enough; to vomit*
7227 rab (3), *great*
713 arkĕtŏs (1), *enough*

SUFFICED
4672 mâtsâ' (1), *to find or acquire; to occur*
7646 sâba' (1), *fill to satiety*
7648 sôba' (1), *satisfaction*

SUFFICETH
714 arkĕō (1), *to avail; be satisfactory*

SUFFICIENCY
5607 çêpheq (1), *satiety*

English

841 autarkeia (1),
contentedness
2426 hikanŏtēs (1),
ability, competence

SUFFICIENT
1767 day (5), *enough*
7227 rab (1), *great*
713 arkĕtŏs (1), enough
714 arkĕŏ (2), to *avail; be satisfactory*
2425 hikanŏs (3), *ample*

SUFFICIENTLY
4078 madday (1),
sufficiently
7654 sob'âh (1), *satiety*

SUIT
2470 châlâh (1), to *be weak, sick, afflicted*
6187 'êrek (1), *pile, equipment, estimate*
7379 rîyb (1), *contest*

SUKKIIMS
5525 Çukkîy (1),
hut-dwellers

SUM
3724 kôpher (1),
redemption-price
4557 miçpâr (2), *number*
6485 pâqad (1), to *visit, care for, count*
6575 párâshâh (1),
exposition
7217 rê'sh (Ch.) (1), *head*
7218 rô'sh (9), *head*
8508 toknîyth (1),
consummation
8552 tâmam (1), to *complete, finish*
2774 kĕphalaiŏn (2),
principal; amount
5092 timē (1), *esteem; nobility; money*

SUMMER
4747 m°qêrâh (2),
cooling off, coolness
6972 qûwts (1), to *spend the harvest* season
7007 qâyiṭ (Ch.) (1),
harvest season
7019 qayits (20), *harvest*
2330 thĕrŏs (3), *summer*

SUMPTUOUSLY
2983 lambanŏ (1), to *take, receive*

SUN
216 'ôwr (1), *luminary*
2535 chammâh (4), *heat of sun*
2775 chereç (3), *itch; sun*
8121 shemesh (120), *sun*
8122 shemesh (Ch.) (1),
sun
2246 hēliŏs (30), *sun*

SUNDERED
6504 pârad (1), to *spread or separate*

SUNDRY
4181 pŏlumĕrŏs (1), *in many portions*

SUNG
7891 shîyr (1), to *sing*
103 a̤dō (2), to *sing*
5214 humnĕŏ (2), to *celebrate God in song*

SUNK
2883 ṭâba' (5), to *sink*
3766 kâra' (1), to *prostrate*
2702 kataphĕrō (1), to *bear down*

SUNRISING
4217 mizrâch (1), place of *sunrise; east*
4217+8121 mizrâch (9), place of *sunrise; east*

SUP
4041 m°gammâh (1),
accumulation
1172 dĕipnĕŏ (2), to *eat the principal meal*

SUPERFLUITY
4050 pĕrissĕia (1),
superabundance

SUPERFLUOUS
8311 sâra' (2), to *be deformed*
4053 pĕrissŏs (1),
superabundant

SUPERSCRIPTION
1923 ĕpigraphē (5),
superscription

SUPERSTITION
1175 dĕisidaimŏnia (1),
religion

SUPERSTITIOUS
1174 dĕisidaimŏnĕstĕrŏs (1), *more religious*

SUPPED
1172 dĕipnĕŏ (1), to *eat the principal meal*

SUPPER
1172 dĕipnĕŏ (1), to *eat the principal meal*
1173 dĕipnŏn (13),
principal meal

SUPPLANT
6117 'âqab (1), to *seize by the heel; to circumvent*

SUPPLANTED
6117 'âqab (1), to *seize by the heel; to circumvent*

SUPPLE
4935 mish'îy (1),
inspection

SUPPLIANTS
6282 'âthâr (1), *incense; worshipper*

SUPPLICATION
2420 chîydâh (1), *puzzle; conundrum; maxim*
2603 chánan (10), to *implore*
2604 chănan (Ch.) (1), to *favor*
6419 pâlal (1), to *intercede, pray*
8467 t°chinnâh (22),
supplication
1162 dĕēsis (4), *petition*

SUPPLICATIONS
8467 t°chinnâh (1),
supplication
8469 tachănûwn (17),
earnest prayer, plea
1162 dĕēsis (2), *petition*
2428 hikĕtēria (1),
entreaty, supplication

SUPPLIED
378 anaplērŏŏ (1), to *complete; to supply*
4322 prŏsanaplērŏŏ (1), to *furnish fully*

SUPPLIETH
2024 ĕpichŏrēgia (1),
contribution, aid
4322 prŏsanaplērŏŏ (1), to *furnish fully*

SUPPLY
378 anaplērŏŏ (1), to *complete; to supply*
2024 ĕpichŏrēgia (1),
contribution, aid
4137 plērŏŏ (1), to *fill, make complete*

SUPPORT
472 antĕchŏmai (1), to *adhere to; to care for*
482 antilambanŏmai (1), to *succor; aid*

SUPPOSE
559 'âmar (1), to *say*
1380 dŏkĕŏ (3), to *think, regard, seem good*
3049 lŏgizŏmai (2), to *credit; to think, regard*
3543 nŏmizŏ (1), to *deem*
3633 ŏiŏmai (1), to *imagine, opine*
5274 hupŏlambanŏ (2), to *assume, presume*

SUPPOSED
1380 dŏkĕŏ (2), to *think*
2233 hēgĕŏmai (1), to *deem, i.e. consider*
3543 nŏmizŏ (4), to *deem*
5282 hupŏnŏĕŏ (1), to *think; to expect*

SUPPOSING
1380 dŏkĕŏ (2), to *think*
3543 nŏmizŏ (4), to *deem*
3633 ŏiŏmai (1), to *imagine, opine*

SUPREME
5242 hupĕrĕchō (1), to *excel; be superior*

SUR
5495 Çûwr (1),
deteriorated

SURE
539 'âman (11), to *be firm, faithful, true*
546 'omnâh (1), *surely*
548 'ămânâh (1),
covenant
571 'emeth (1), *certainty, truth, trustworthiness*
982 bâṭach (1), to *trust, be confident or sure*
2388 châzaq (1), to *bind*
3045 yâda' (4), to *know*
3245 yâçad (1), *settle, consult, establish*
4009 mibṭach (1),
security; assurance
6965 qûwm (2), to *rise*
7011 qayâm (Ch.) (1),
permanent
7292 râhab (1), to *urge, embolden, capture*
8104 shâmar (1), to *watch*
804 asphalēs (1), *secure*

SWADDLED

805 asphalizŏ (3), to *render secure*
949 bĕbaiŏs (3), *stable, certain, binding*
1097 ginŏskŏ (2), to *know*
1492 ĕidŏ (3), to *know*
4103 pistŏs (1),
trustworthy; reliable
4731 stĕrĕŏs (1), *solid*

SURETIES
6148 'ârab (1), to *give or be security*

SURETISHIP
8628 tâqa' (1), to *clatter, slap, drive, clasp*

SURETY
389 'ak (1), *surely*
552 'umnâm (1), *verily*
3045 yâda' (1), to *know*
6148 'ârab (8), to *give or be security*
6161 'ărubbâh (1), as *security; bondsman*
230 alēthŏs (1), *surely*
1450 ĕgguŏs (1),
bondsman, guarantor

SURFEITING
2897 kraipalē (1),
debauch

SURMISINGS
5283 hupŏnŏia (1),
suspicion

SURNAME
3655 kânâh (1), to *address, give title*
1941 ĕpikalĕŏmai (6), to *invoke*
2564 kalĕŏ (1), to *call*

SURNAMED
3655 kânâh (1), to *address, give title*
1941 ĕpikalĕŏmai (5), to *invoke*
2007+3686 ĕpitithēmi (2), to *impose*

SURPRISED
270 'âchaz (1), to *seize*
8610 tâphas (2), to *seize*

SUSANCHITES
7801 Shûwshankîy (Ch.) (1), *Shushankite*

SUSANNA
4677 Sŏusanna (1), *lily*

SUSI
5485 Çûwçîy (1),
horse-like

SUSTAIN
3557 kûwl (4), to *maintain*

SUSTAINED
5564 çâmak (3), to *lean upon; take hold of*

SUSTENANCE
3557 kûwl (1), to *maintain*
4241 michyâh (1),
sustenance
5527 chŏrtasma (1), *food*

SWADDLED
2853 châthal (1), to *swathe, wrap in cloth*
2946 ṭâphach (1), to *nurse*

English

SWADDLING
4683 sparganŏō (2), to *wrap* with cloth

SWADDLINGBAND
2854 chăthullâh (1), *swathing* cloth to wrap

SWALLOW
1104 bâla' (13), to *swallow; to destroy*
1866 dᵉrôwr (2), *swallow*
3886 lûwa' (1), to *be rash*
5693 'âgûwr (2), *swallow*
7602 shâ'aph (4), to *be angry; to hasten*
2666 katapinō (1), to *devour by swallowing*

SWALLOWED
1104 bâla' (19), to *swallow; to destroy*
1105 bela' (1), *gulp*
3886 lûwa' (1), to *be rash*
7602 shâ'aph (1), to *be angry; to hasten*
2666 katapinō (4), to *devour by swallowing*

SWALLOWETH
1572 gâmâ' (1), to *swallow*
7602 shâ'aph (1), to *be angry; to hasten*

SWAN
8580 tanshemeth (2), (poss.) *water-hen*

SWARE
5375 nâsâ' (1), to *lift up*
7650 shâba' (70), to *swear*
3660 ŏmnuō (7), to *swear, declare on oath*

SWAREST
7650 shâba' (5), to *swear*

SWARM
5712 'êdâh (1), *assemblage; family*
6157 'ârôb (2), swarming *mosquitoes*

SWARMS
6157 'ârôb (5), swarming *mosquitoes*

SWEAR
422 'âlâh (2), *imprecate, utter a curse*
5375 nâsâ' (2), to *lift up*
7650 shâba' (43), to *swear*
3660 ŏmnuō (13), to *swear, declare on oath*

SWEARERS
7650 shâba' (1), to *swear*

SWEARETH
7650 shâba' (7), to *swear*
3660 ŏmnuō (4), to *swear, declare on oath*

SWEARING
422 'âlâh (2), *imprecate, utter a curse*
423 'âlâh (2), *imprecation: curse*

SWEAT
2188 zê'âh (1), *sweat*
3154 yeza' (1), *sweat*
2402 hidrōs (1), *sweat*

SWEEP
2894 ṭûw' (1), to *sweep away*

3261 yâ'âh (1), to *brush aside*
4563 sarŏō (1), to *sweep clean*

SWEEPING
5502 çâchaph (1), to *scrape off, sweep off*

SWEET
1314 besem (5), *spice; fragrance; balsam*
2896 ṭôwb (1), *good; well*
3190 yâṭab (1), to *be, make well*
4452 mâlats (1), to *be smooth; to be pleasant*
4477 mamtaq (2), *sweet*
4575 ma'ădannâh (1), *bond, i.e. group*
4840 merqâch (1), *spicy*
4966 mâthôwq (7), *sweet*
4985 mâthaq (5), to *relish; to be sweet*
5207 nîchôwach (43), *pleasant; delight*
5208 nîychôwach (Ch.) (2), *pleasure*
5273 nâ'îym (2), *delightful; sweet*
5276 nâ'êm (1), to *be agreeable*
5561 çam (16), *aroma*
5674 'âbar (2), to *cross over; to transition*
6071 'âçîyç (2), *expressed fresh grape-juice*
6148 'ârab (5), to *intermix*
6149 'ârêb (2), *agreeable*
8492 tîyrôwsh (1), *wine; squeezed grape-juice*
1099 glukus (3), *sweet*
2175 ĕuōdia (2), *fragrance, aroma*

SWEETER
4966 mâthôwq (2), *sweet*

SWEETLY
4339 mêyshâr (1), *straightness; rectitude*
4988 mâthâq (1), *sweet food*

SWEETNESS
4966 mâthôwq (2), *sweet*
4986 metheq (2), *pleasantness*
4987 môtheq (1), *sweetness*

SWEETSMELLING
2175 ĕuōdia (1), *fragrance, aroma*

SWELL
1216 bâtsêq (1), to *blister*
6638 tsâbâh (2), to *array an army against*
6639 tsâbeh (1), *swollen*

SWELLED
1216 bâtsêq (1), to *blister*

SWELLING
1158 bâ'âh (1), to *ask; be bulging, swelling*
1346 ga'ăvâh (1), *arrogance; majesty*
1347 gâ'ôwn (3), *ascending; majesty*
5246 hupĕrŏgkŏs (2), *insolent, boastful*

SWELLINGS
5450 phusiōsis (1), *haughtiness, arrogance*

SWEPT
1640 gâraph (1), to *sweep away*
5502 çâchaph (1), to *scrape off, sweep off*
4563 sarŏō (2), to *sweep clean*

SWERVED
795 astŏchĕō (1), *deviate*

SWIFT
16 'êbeh (1), *papyrus*
3753 karkârâh (1), *cow-camel*
4116 mâhar (3), to *hurry*
7031 qal (9), *rapid, swift*
7043 qâlal (1), to *be, make light (swift)*
7409 rekesh (1), *relay*
3691 ŏxus (1), *rapid, fast*
5031 tachinŏs (1), *soon, imminent*
5036 tachus (1), *prompt*

SWIFTER
7031 qal (1), *rapid, swift*
7043 qâlal (5), to *be, make light (swift)*

SWIFTLY
3288 yᵉ'âph (1), *utterly exhausted*
4120 mᵉhêrâh (1), *hurry*
7031 qal (2), *rapid, swift*

SWIM
6687 tsûwph (1), to *overflow*
7811 sâchâh (2), to *swim*
7813 sâchûw (1), *pond for swimming*
1579 ĕkkŏlumbaō (1), to *escape by swimming*
2860 kŏlumbaō (1), to *plunge into water*

SWIMMEST
6824 tsâphâh (1), *inundation*

SWIMMETH
7811 sâchâh (1), to *swim*

SWINE
2386 chăzîyr (2), *hog*
5519 chŏirŏs (14), *pig*

SWINE'S
2386 chăzîyr (4), *hog*

SWOLLEN
4092 pimprēmi (1), to *become inflamed*

SWOON
5848 'âṭaph (1), to *languish*

SWOONED
5848 'âṭaph (1), to *languish*

SWORD
1300 bârâq (1), *lightning; flash of lightning*
2719 chereb (380), *sword*
7524 retsach (1), *crushing; murder-cry*
7973 shelach (3), *spear*
3162 machaira (22), short *sword*
4501 rhŏmphaia (7), *sabre, cutlass*

SWORDS
2719 chereb (17), *sword*
6609 pᵉthîchâh (1), *drawn sword*
3162 machaira (6), short *sword*

SWORN
1167+7621 ba'al (1), *master; husband*
3027+5920+3676 yâd (1), *hand; power*
5375 nâsâ' (1), to *lift up*
7650 shâba' (42), to *swear*
3660 ŏmnuō (3), to *swear*

SYCAMINE
4807 sukaminŏs (1), *sycamore-fig tree*

SYCHAR
4965 Suchar (1), *liquor*

SYCHEM
4966 Suchĕm (2), *ridge*

SYCOMORE
8256 shâqâm (6), *sycamore tree*
4809 sukŏmōraia (1), *sycamore-fig tree*

SYCOMORES
8256 shâqâm (1), *sycamore tree*

SYENE
5482 Çᵉvênêh (2), the local *Seven*

SYNAGOGUE
656 apŏsunagōgŏs (2), *excommunicated*
752 archisunagōgŏs (7), *director of the synagogue services*
4864 sunagōgē (34), *assemblage*

SYNAGOGUE'S
752 archisunagōgŏs (2), *director of the synagogue services*

SYNAGOGUES
4150 môw'êd (1), *place of meeting; congregation*
656 apŏsunagōgŏs (1), *excommunicated*
4864 sunagōgē (22), *assemblage*

SYNTYCHE
4941 Suntuchē (1), *accident*

SYRACUSE
4946 Surakŏusai (1), *Syracuse*

SYRIA
758 'Arâm (66), *highland*
4947 Suria (8), (poss.) *rock*

SYRIA-DAMASCUS
758+1834 'Arâm (1), *highland*

SYRIA-MAACHAH
758 'Arâm (1), *highland*

SYRIACK
762 'Ărâmîyth (1), *in Araman*

SYRIAN
761 'Ărammîy (7), *Aramite*

SYRIANS

762 'Ărâmîyth (4), *in Araman*
4948 Surŏs (1), *native of Syria*

SYRIANS
758 'Ărâm (57), *highland*
761 'Ărammîy (4), *Aramite*

SYROPHENICIAN
4949 Surŏphŏinissa (1), *native of Phœnicia*

TAANACH
8590 Ta'ănâk (6), *Taanak or Tanak*

TAANATH-SHILOH
8387 Ta'ănath Shîlôh (1), *approach of Shiloh*

TABBAOTH
2884 Ţabbâ'ôwth (2), *rings*

TABBATH
2888 Ţabbath (1), *Tabbath*

TABEAL
2870 Ţâbe'êl (1), *pleasing (to) God*

TABEEL
2870 Ţâbe'êl (1), *pleasing (to) God*

TABERAH
8404 Tab'êrâh (2), *burning*

TABERING
8608 tâphaph (1), to *drum* on a tambourine

TABERNACLE
168 'ôhel (187), *tent*
4908 mishkân (114), *residence*
5520 çôk (1), *hut of entwined boughs*
5521 çukkâh (3), *tabernacle; shelter*
5522 çikkûwth (1), *idolatrous booth*
7900 sôk (1), *booth*
4633 skĕnē (15), *tent*
4636 skēnŏs (2), *tent*
4638 skēnōma (3), *dwelling:* the *Temple*

TABERNACLES
168 'ôhel (11), *tent*
4908 mishkân (5), *residence*
5521 çukkâh (9), *tabernacle; shelter*
4633 skĕnē (4), *tent*
4634 skĕnŏpēgia (1), *tabernacles, i.e. booths*

TABITHA
5000 Tabitha (2), *gazelle*

TABLE
3871 lûwach (4), *tablet*
4524 mêçab (1), *divan couch; around*
7979 shulchân (56), *table*
345 anakĕimai (1), to *recline at a meal*
4093 pinakidiŏn (1), wooden writing *tablet*
5132 trapĕza (9), four-legged *table* or *stool*

TABLES
3871 lûwach (34), *tablet*

TABLE
7979 shulchân (14), *table*
2825 klinē (1), *couch*
4109 plax (3), *tablet*
5132 trapĕza (4), four-legged *table* or *stool*

TABLETS
1004+5315 bayith (1), *house; temple; family*
3558 kûwmâz (2), *jewel*

TABOR
8396 Tâbôwr (10), *broken*

TABRET
8596 tôph (3), *tambourine*
8611 tôpheth (1), *smiting*

TABRETS
8596 tôph (5), *tambourine*

TABRIMON
2886 Ţabrimmôwn (1), *pleasing (to) Rimmon*

TACHES
7165 qereç (10), *knob*

TACHMONITE
8461 Tachkĕmônîy (1), *sagacious*

TACKLING
4631 skĕuē (1), *tackle*

TACKLINGS
2256 chebel (1), *company*

TADMOR
8412 Tadmôr (2), *palm*

TAHAN
8465 Tachan (2), *station*

TAHANITES
8470 Tachănîy (1), *Tachanite*

TAHAPANES
8471 Tachpanchêç (1), *Tachpanches*

TAHATH
8480 Tachath (6), *bottom*

TAHPANHES
8471 Tachpanchêç (5), *Tachpanches*

TAHPENES
8472 Tachpĕnêyç (3), *Tachpenes*

TAHREA
8475 Tachrêa' (1), (poss.) *earth, ground; low*

TAHTIM-HODSHI
8483 Tachtîym Chodshîy (1), *lower* (ones) *monthly*

TAIL
2180 zânâb (8), *tail*
3769 ŏura (1), *tail*

TAILS
2180 zânâb (2), *tail*
3769 ŏura (4), *tail*

TAKE
6 'âbad (1), to *perish*
270 'âchaz (12), to *seize*
622 'âçaph (3), to *gather*
680 'âtsal (1), to *select*
935 bôw' (1), to *go, come*
962 bâzaz (9), to *plunder*
1197 bâ'ar (4), to *be brutish, be senseless*
1497 gâzal (3), to *rob*

1692 dâbaq (1), to *cling* or *adhere;* to *catch*
1898 hâgâh (2), to *remove, expel*
1961 hâyâh (1), to *exist*
2095 zᵉhar (Ch.) (1), *be admonished, be careful*
2254 châbal (7), to *bind* by a *pledge;* to *pervert*
2388 châzaq (9), to *fasten* upon; to *seize*
2502 châlats (1), to *present, strengthen*
2834 châsaph (1), to *drain* away or *bail* up
2846 châthâh (3), to *lay hold* of; to *take away*
3051 yâhab (1), to *give*
3212 yâlak (1), to *carry*
3318 yâtsâ' (2), to *go, bring out*
3381 yârad (3), to *descend*
3423 yârash (3), to *inherit*
3615 kâlâh (1), to *complete, prepare*
3920 lâkad (19), to *catch*
3947 lâqach (367), to *take*
5253 nâçag (2), to *retreat*
5267 nᵉçaq (Ch.) (1), to *go up*
5312 nᵉphaq (Ch.) (1), to *issue forth;* to *bring out*
5337 nâtsal (1), to *deliver;* to *be snatched*
5375 nâsâ' (60), to *lift up*
5376 nᵉsâ' (Ch.) (1), to *lift up*
5381 nâsag (5), to *reach*
5414 nâthan (1), to *give*
5493 çûwr (45), to *turn* off
5496 çûwth (1), to *stimulate;* to *seduce*
5535 çâkath (1), to *be silent;* to *observe*
5674 'âbar (2), to *cross over;* to *transition*
5709 'ădâ' (Ch.) (1), to *pass* on or *continue*
5749 'ûwd (7), to *encompass, restore*
5927 'âlâh (4), to *ascend*
5978 'immâd (1), *with*
6213 'âsâh (1), to *do*
6331 pûwr (1), to *crush*
6679 tsûwd (1), to *catch*
6901 qâbal (1), to *admit*
6902 qᵉbal (Ch.) (1), to *acquire*
7061 qâmats (3), to *grasp*
7126 qârab (1), to *approach, bring near*
7200 râ'âh (2), to *see*
7311 rûwm (11), to *be high;* to *rise* or *raise*
7760 sûwm (2), to *put*
7896 shîyth (1), to *place*
7901 shâkab (2), to *lie*
7997 shâlal (4), to *drop* or *strip;* to *plunder*
8175 sâ'ar (1), to *storm;* to *shiver,* i.e. *fear*
8551 tâmak (2), to *obtain*
8610 tâphas (10), to *manipulate,* i.e. *seize*
142 airō (35), to *lift up*
353 analambanō (3), to *take up, bring up*
726 harpazō (3), to *seize*

851 aphairĕō (5), to *remove, cut off*
1209 dĕchŏmai (3), to *receive, accept*
1949 ĕpilambanŏmai (2), to *seize*
2507 kathairĕō (1), to *lower,* or *demolish*
2722 katĕchō (1), to *hold down fast*
2902 kratĕō (4), to *seize*
2983 lambanō (31), to *take, receive*
3335 mĕtalambanō (1), to *accept* and use
3880 paralambanō (5), to *associate with* oneself
3911 paraphĕrō (1), to *carry off;* to *avert*
4014 pĕriairĕō (1), to *unveil;* to *cast off*
4084 piazō (4), to *seize*
4355 prŏslambanō (1), to *take along, receive*
4648 skŏpĕō (1), to *watch out for,* i.e. to *regard*
4815 sullambanō (3), to *seize* (*arrest, capture*)
4838 sumparalambanō (2), to *take along*
4868 sunairō (1), to *compute an account*

TAKEN
247 'âzar (1), to *belt*
270 'âchaz (7), to *seize*
622 'âçaph (7), to *gather*
935 bôw' (1), to *go, come*
1197 bâ'ar (2), to *be brutish, be senseless*
1497 gâzal (5), to *rob*
1639 gâra' (4), to *remove, lessen,* or *withhold*
2254 châbal (1), to *bind* by a *pledge;* to *pervert*
2388 châzaq (5), to *fasten* upon; to *seize*
2502 châlats (1), to *pull* off; to *strip;* to *depart*
2974 yâ'al (2), to *assent;* to *undertake, begin*
3289 yâ'ats (2), to *advise*
3381 yârad (1), to *descend*
3427 yâshab (5), to *dwell*
3885 lûwn (1), to *be obstinate with*
3920 lâkad (42), to *catch*
3921 leked (1), *noose*
3947 lâqach (84), to *take*
4672 mâtsâ' (1), to *find*
5267 nᵉçaq (Ch.) (1), to *go up*
5312 nᵉphaq (Ch.) (2), to *issue forth;* to *bring out*
5337 nâtsal (3), to *deliver;* to *be snatched*
5375 nâsâ' (10), to *lift up*
5381 nâsag (1), to *reach*
5414 nâthan (1), to *give*
5493 çûwr (19), to *turn off*
5674 'âbar (1), to *cross over;* to *transition*
5709 'ădâ' (Ch.) (1), to *remove;* to *bedeck*
5927 'âlâh (9), to *ascend*
6001 'âmêl (1), *laborer*
6213 'âsâh (1), to *make*
6679 tsûwd (1), to *catch*
6813 tsâ'an (1), to *load*

7092 qâphats (1), to *draw together*, to *leap*; to *die*
7287 râdâh (1), to *subjugate*; to *crumble*
7311 rùwm (4), to *be high*; to *rise or raise*
7628 sh°bîy (2), *booty*
7725 shûwb (1), to *turn back*; to *return*
8610 tâphas (12), to *manipulate*, i.e. *seize*
142 airō (16), to *lift up*
259 halōsis (1), *capture*
353 analambanō (3), to *take up, bring up*
522 apairō (3), to *remove, take away*
642 apŏrphanizō (1), to *separate*
782 aspazŏmai (1), to *give salutation*
851 aphairĕō (1), to *remove*
1096 ginŏmai (1), to *be*
1723 ĕnagkalizŏmai (1), *take into one's arms*
1808 ĕxairō (1), to *remove, drive away*
1869 ĕpairō (1), to *raise*
2021 ĕpichĕirĕō (1), to *undertake, try*
2221 zōgrĕō (1), to *capture or ensnare*
2638 katalambanō (2), to *seize*; to *possess*
2639 katalĕgō (1), to *enroll, put on a list*
2983 lambanō (12), to *take, receive*
3880 paralambanō (5), to *associate with* oneself
4014 pĕriairĕō (3), to *unveil*; to *cast off*
4084 piazō (2), to *seize*
4355 prŏslambanō (1), to *take along; receive*
4815 sullambanō (2), to *seize (arrest, capture)*
4912 sunĕchō (3), to *hold together*

TAKEST
622 'âcaph (1), to *gather*
1980 hâlak (1), to *walk*
3947 lâqach (2), to *take*
5375 nâsâ' (1), to *lift up*
6001 'âmêl (1), *laborer*
8104 shâmar (1), to *watch*
142 airō (1), to *lift up*

TAKETH
270 'âchaz (2), to *seize*
1197 bâ'ar (1), to *be brutish, be senseless*
2254 châbal (1), to *bind by a pledge*; to *pervert*
2388 châzaq (4), to *fasten* upon; to *seize*
2862 châthaph (1), to *clutch, snatch*
3920 lâkad (5), to *catch*
3947 lâqach (11), to *take*
5190 nâtal (1), to *lift*; to *impose*
5337 nâtsal (1), to *deliver*; to *be snatched*
5375 nâsâ' (3), to *lift up*
5493 cûwr (2), to *turn off*
5710 'âdâh (1), to *pass on* or *continue*; to *remove*

5998 'âmal (2), to *work severely, put forth effort*
6908 qâbats (1), to *collect, assemble*
7953 shâlâh (1), to *draw out or off*, i.e. *remove*
8610 tâphas (1), to *manipulate*, i.e. *seize*
142 airō (11), to *lift up*
337 anairĕō (1), to *take away*, i.e. *abolish*
851 aphairĕō (1), to *remove, cut off*
1405 drassŏmai (1), to *grasp*, i.e. *entrap*
2018 ĕpiphĕrō (1), to *inflict, bring upon*
2638 katalambanō (1), to *seize; to possess*
2983 lambanō (4), to *take, receive*
3880 paralambanō (8), to *associate with oneself*
4301 prŏlambanō (1), to *take before; be caught*

TAKING
3947 lâqach (1), to *take*
4727 miqqâch (1), *reception*
8610 tâphas (1), to *manipulate*, i.e. *seize*
142 airō (1), to *lift up*
321 anagō (1), to *lead up; to bring out*
353 analambanō (1), to *take up, bring up*
1325 didōmi (1), to *give*
2983 lambanō (4), to *take*

TALE
1899 hegeh (1), *muttering*
4557 miçpâr (1), *number*
4971 mathkôneth (1), *proportion*
8506 tôken (1), *quantity*

TALEBEARER
1980+7400 hâlak (1), to *walk; live a certain way*
5372 nirgân (3), *slanderer*
7400 râkîyl (2), *scandal-monger*

TALENT
3603 kikkâr (10), *talent*
5006 talantiaiŏs (1), *weight* of 57-80 lbs.
5007 talantŏn (3), *weight*

TALENTS
3603 kikkâr (38), *talent*
3604 kikkêr (Ch.) (1), *talent weight*
5007 talantŏn (12), *weight* of 57-80 lbs.

TALES
7400 râkîyl (1), *scandal-monger*
3026 lērŏs (1), *twaddle*

TALITHA
5008 talitha (1), *young girl*

TALK
1696 dâbar (11), to *speak*
1697 dâbâr (2), *word*
1897 hâgâh (1), to *murmur, utter a sound*
5608 çâphar (1), to *recount* an event
6310 peh (1), *mouth*

7878 sîyach (5), to *ponder, muse aloud*
8193 sâphâh (1), *lip, language, speech*
2980 lalĕō (1), to *talk*
3056 lŏgŏs (1), *word, matter, thing*

TALKED
559 'âmar (1), to *say*
1696 dâbar (29), to *speak*
2980 lalĕō (8), to *talk*
3656 hŏmilĕō (2), to *talk*
4814 sullalĕō (1), to *talk*
4926 sunŏmilĕō (1), to *converse* mutually

TALKERS
3956 lâshôwn (1), *tongue*
3151 mataiŏlŏgŏs (1), *senseless talker*

TALKEST
1696 dâbar (2), to *speak*
2980 lalĕō (1), to *talk*

TALKETH
1696 dâbar (1), to *speak*
2980 lalĕō (1), to *talk*

TALKING
1696 dâbar (3), to *speak*
4405 millâh (1), *word; discourse; speech*
7879 sîyach (1), *uttered contemplation*
2980 lalĕō (1), to *talk*
3473 mōrŏlŏgia (1), *buffoonery, foolish talk*
4814 sullalĕō (2), to *talk together*, i.e. *converse*

TALL
6967 qôwmâh (2), *height*
7311 rùwm (3), to *be high*

TALLER
7311 rùwm (1), to *be high*

TALMAI
8526 Talmay (6), *ridged*

TALMON
2929 Ṭalmôwn (5), *oppressive*

TAMAH
8547 Temach (1), *Temach*

TAMAR
8559 Tâmâr (24), *palm*

TAME
1150 damazō (2), to *tame*

TAMED
1150 damazō (2), to *tame*

TAMMUZ
8542 Tammûwz (1), *Tammuz*

TANACH
8590 Ta'ănâk (1), *Taanak or Tanak*

TANHUMETH
8576 Tanchûmeth (2), *compassion, solace*

TANNER
1033 brōma (3), *food*

TAPHATH
2955 Ṭâphath (1), *dropping* (of ointment)

TAPPUAH
8599 Tappûwach (6), *apple*

TARAH
8646 Terach (2), *Terach*

TARALAH
8634 Tar'ălâh (1), *reeling*

TARE
1234 bâqa' (1), to *cleave, break, tear open*
7167 qâra' (1), to *rend*
4682 sparassō (1), to *convulse* with epilepsy
4952 susparassō (1), to *convulse* violently

TAREA
8390 Ta'ărêa' (1), (poss.) *earth, ground; low*

TARES
2215 zizaniŏn (8), *darnel*

TARGET
3591 kîydôwn (1), *dart*
6793 tsinnâh (2), large *shield; piercing cold*

TARGETS
6793 tsinnâh (3), large *shield; piercing cold*

TARPELITES
2967 Ṭarp°lay (Ch.) (1), *Tarpelite*

TARRIED
748 'ârak (2), to *be long*
2342 chûwl (1), to *wait*
3176 yâchal (1), to *wait*
3186 yâchar (1), to *delay*
3427 yâshab (6), to *dwell, to remain; to settle*
3885 lûwn (3), to *be obstinate with*
4102 mâhahh (1), to *be reluctant*
5116 nâveh (1), *at home*
5975 'âmad (1), to *stand*
1304 diatribō (2), to *stay*
1961 ĕpimĕnō (3), to *remain; to persevere*
3306 mĕnō (3), to *stay*
4160 pŏiĕō (1), to *do*
4328 prŏsdŏkaō (1), to *anticipate; to await*
4357 prŏsmĕnō (1), to *remain in a place*
5278 hupŏmĕnō (1), to *undergo, (trials)*
5549 chrŏnizō (1), to *take time*, i.e. *linger*

TARRIEST
3195 mĕllō (1), to *intend*, i.e. *be about to*

TARRIETH
3427 yâshab (1), to *dwell, to remain; to settle*
6960 qâvâh (1), to *expect*

TARRY
309 'âchar (4), to *remain; to delay*
1826 dâmam (1), to *stop, cease; to perish*
2442 châkâh (2), to *await; hope for*
3176 yâchal (2), to *wait*
3427 yâshab (13), to *dwell, to remain*
3559 kûwn (1), to *set up: establish, fix, prepare*
3885 lûwn (7), to *be obstinate with*

4102 mâhahh (3), *to be reluctant*
5975 'âmad (1), *to stand*
7663 sâbar (1), *to scrutinize; to expect*
1019 bradunō (1), *to delay, hesitate*
1551 ĕkdĕchŏmai (1), *to await, expect*
1961 ĕpimĕnŏ (4), *to remain; to persevere*
2523 kathizō (1), *to seat down, dwell*
3306 mĕnō (7), *to stay*
5549 chrŏnizō (1), *to take time,* i.e. *linger*

TARRYING
309 'âchar (2), *to remain*

TARSHISH
8659 Tarshîysh (24), *merchant vessel*

TARSUS
5018 Tarsĕus (2), *native of Tarsus*
5019 Tarsŏs (3), *flat*

TARTAK
8662 Tartâq (1), *Tartak*

TARTAN
8661 Tartân (2), *Tartan*

TASK
1697 dâbâr (1), *word; matter; thing*
2706 chôq (1), *appointment; allotment*

TASKMASTERS
5065 nâgas (5), *to exploit; to tax, harass*

TASKS
1697 dâbâr (1), *word; matter; thing*

TASTE
2441 chêk (4), *area of mouth*
2938 țâ'am (6), *to taste*
2940 ța'am (5), *taste*
1089 gĕuŏmai (7), *to taste*

TASTED
2938 țâ'am (2), *to taste*
2942 țᵉ'êm (Ch.) (1), *judgment; account*
1089 gĕuŏmai (5), *to taste; to eat*

TASTETH
2938 țâ'am (1), *to taste*

TATNAI
8674 Tattᵉnay (4), *Tattenai*

TATTLERS
5397 phluarŏs (1), *pratery*

TAUGHT
995 bîyn (1), *to understand; discern*
1696 dâbar (2), *to speak*
3045 yâda' (3), *to know*
3256 yâçar (2), *to instruct*
3384 yârâh (5), *to teach*
3925 lâmad (17), *to teach*
3928 limmûwd (1), *instructed one*
4000 mâbôwn (1), *instructing*
7919 sâkal (1), *to be or act circumspect*

8637 tirgal (1), *to cause to walk*
1318 didaktŏs (1), *instructed, taught*
1321 didaskō (36), *to teach*
1322 didachē (1), *instruction*
2258+1321 ēn (4), *I was*
2312 thĕŏdidaktŏs (1), *divinely instructed*
2727 katēchēō (1), *to indoctrinate*
3100 mathētĕuō (1), *to become a student*
3811 paidĕuō (1), *to educate or discipline*

TAUNT
1422 gᵉdûwphâh (1), *revilement, taunt*
8148 shᵉnîynâh (1), *gibe, verbal taunt*

TAUNTING
4426 mᵉlîytsâh (1), *aphorism, saying*

TAVERNS
4999 Tabĕrnai (1), *huts*

TAXATION
6187 'êrek (1), *estimate*

TAXED
6186 'ârak (1), *to arrange*
582 apŏgraphē (3), *census registration*

TAXES
5065 nâgas (1), *to exploit; to tax, harass*

TAXING
583 apŏgraphō (2), *enroll, take a census*

TEACH
502 'âlaph (1), *to teach*
2094 zâhar (1), *to enlighten*
3045 yâda' (5), *to know*
3046 yᵉda' (Ch.) (1), *know*
3384 yârâh (33), *to teach*
3925 lâmad (32), *to teach*
8150 shânan (1), *to pierce; to inculcate*
1317 didaktikŏs (2), *instructive*
1321 didaskō (26), *to teach*
2085 hĕtĕrŏdidaskalĕō (2), *to instruct differently*
2605 kataggĕllō (1), *to proclaim, promulgate*
2727 katēchēō (1), *to indoctrinate*
3100 mathētĕuō (1), *to become a student*
4994 sōphrŏnizō (1), *to train up*

TEACHER
995 bîyn (1), *to understand; discern*
3384 yârâh (1), *to teach*
1320 didaskalŏs (4), *instructor*

TEACHERS
3384 yârâh (3), *to teach*
3887 lûwts (1), *to scoff; to interpret; to intercede*
3925 lâmad (1), *to teach*

1320 didaskalŏs (6), *instructor*
2567 kalŏdidaskalŏs (1), *teacher of the right*
3547 nŏmŏdidaskalŏs (1), *Rabbi*
5572 psĕudŏdidaskalŏs (1), *propagator of erroneous doctrine*

TEACHEST
3925 lâmad (1), *to teach*
1321 didaskō (7), *to teach*

TEACHETH
502 'âlaph (1), *to teach*
3384 yârâh (3), *to teach*
3925 lâmad (5), *to teach*
7919 sâkal (1), *to be or act circumspect*
1318 didaktŏs (2), *taught*
1321 didaskō (3), *to teach*
2727 katēchēō (1), *to indoctrinate*

TEACHING
3384 yârâh (1), *to teach*
3925 lâmad (1), *to teach*
1319 didaskalia (1), *instruction*
1321 didaskō (21), *to teach*
3811 paidĕuō (1), *to educate or discipline*

TEAR
1234 bâqa' (1), *to cleave, break, tear open*
1758 dûwsh (1), *to trample or thresh*
2963 țâraph (5), *to pluck off or pull to pieces*
5498 çâchab (1), *to trail along*
6536 pâraç (1), *to break in pieces; to split*
6561 pâraq (1), *to break off or crunch; to deliver*
7167 qâra' (3), *to rend*

TEARETH
2963 țâraph (4), *to pluck off or pull to pieces*
4486 rhēgnumi (1), *to tear to pieces*
4682 sparassō (1), *to convulse with epilepsy*

TEARS
1058 bâkâh (1), *to weep*
1832 dim'âh (23), *tears*
1144 dakru (11), *teardrop*

TEATS
1717 dad (2), *female breast or bosom*
7699 shad (1), *breast*

TEBAH
2875 Țebach (1), *massacre*

TEBALIAH
2882 Țᵉbalyâhûw (1), *Jehovah has dipped*

TEBETH
2887 Țêbeth (1), *a month*

TEDIOUS
1465 ĕgkŏptō (1), *to impede, detain*

TEETH
4973 mᵉthallᵉ'âh (3), *tooth*
6374 pîyphîyâh (1), *tooth*

8127 shên (31), *tooth*
8128 shên (Ch.) (3), *tooth*
3599 ŏdŏus (10), *tooth*
3679 ŏnĕidizō (1), *to rail at, chide, taunt*

TEHAPHNEHES
8471 Tachpanchêç (1), *Tachpanches*

TEHINNAH
8468 Tᵉchinnâh (1), *supplication*

TEIL
424 'êlâh (1), *oak*

TEKEL
8625 tᵉqal (Ch.) (2), *to weigh in a scale*

TEKOA
8620 Tᵉqôwa' (6), *trumpet*

TEKOAH
8620 Tᵉqôwa' (1), *trumpet*
8621 Tᵉqôw'îy (2), *Tekoite*

TEKOITE
8621 Tᵉqôw'îy (3), *Tekoite*

TEKOITES
8621 Tᵉqôw'îy (2), *Tekoite*

TEL-ABIB
8512 Têl 'Âbîyb (1), *mound of green growth*

TEL-HARESHA
8521 Têl Charshâ' (1), *mound of workmanship*

TEL-HARSA
8521 Têl Charshâ' (1), *mound of workmanship*

TEL-MELAH
8528 Têl Melach (2), *mound of salt*

TELAH
8520 Telach (1), *breach*

TELAIM
2923 Tᵉlâ'îym (1), *lambs*

TELASSAR
8515 Tᵉla'ssar (1), *Telassar*

TELEM
2928 Telem (2), *oppression*

TELL
559 'âmar (29), *to say*
560 'âmar (Ch.) (5), *to say*
1696 dâbar (7), *to speak*
3045 yâda' (7), *to know*
5046 nâgad (69), *to announce*
5608 çâphar (12), *to recount an event*
8085 shâma' (2), *to hear*
226 alēthĕuō (1), *to be true*
312 anaggĕllō (2), *to announce, report*
518 apaggĕllō (6), *to announce, proclaim*
1334 diēgĕŏmai (2), *to relate fully, describe*
1492 ĕidō (9), *to know*
1583 ĕklalĕō (1), *to tell*
1650 ĕlĕgchŏs (1), *proof*
2036 ĕpō (28), *to speak*
2046 ĕrĕō (3), *to utter*
2980 lalĕō (3), *to talk*
3004 lĕgō (28), *to say*

4302 prŏlĕgō (1), to
predict, forewarn

TELLEST
5608 çâphar (1), to
recount an event

TELLETH
1696 dâbar (2), to *speak*
4487 mânâh (2), to *allot;*
to *enumerate* or enroll
5046 nâgad (2), to
announce
3004 lĕgō (1), to *say*

TELLING
1696 dâbar (1), to *speak*
4557 miçpâr (1), *number*
5608 çâphar (1), to
recount an event

TEMA
8485 Têymâ' (5), *Tema*

TEMAN
8487 Têymân (11), *south*

TEMANI
8489 Têymânîy (1),
Temanite

TEMANITE
8489 Têymânîy (6),
Temanite

TEMANITES
8489 Têymânîy (1),
Temanite

TEMENI
8488 Têymᵉnîy (1),
Temeni

TEMPER
7450 râçaç (1), to
moisten with drops

TEMPERANCE
1466 ĕgkratĕia (4),
self-control

TEMPERATE
1467 ĕgkratĕuŏmai (1),
to exercise self-restraint
1468 ĕgkratĕs (1),
self-controlled
4998 sōphrōn (1),
self-controlled

TEMPERED
1101 bâlal (1), to *mix*
4414 mâlach (1), to *salt*
4786 sugkĕrannumi (1),
to *combine, assimilate*

TEMPEST
2230 zerem (3), *flood*
5492 çûwphâh (1),
hurricane wind
5590 çâ'ar (1), to *rush*
upon; to *toss* about
5591 ça'ar (6), *hurricane*
7307 rûwach (1), *breath;*
wind; *life-spirit*
8183 sᵉ'ârâh (1),
hurricane wind
2366 thuĕlla (1), *blowing*
2978 lailaps (1),
whirlwind; hurricane
4578 sĕismŏs (1), *gale*
storm; earthquake
5492 chĕimazō (1), to *be*
battered in a storm
5494 chĕimōn (1), *winter*
season; stormy weather

TEMPESTUOUS
5490 çôwph (2),
termination; end

8175 sâ'ar (1), to *storm*
5189 tuphōnikŏs (1),
stormy

TEMPLE
1004 bayith (11), *house;*
temple; family, tribe
1964 hêykâl (68), *temple*
1965 hêykal (Ch.) (8),
palace; temple
2411 hiêrŏn (71), *sacred*
place; sanctuary
3485 naŏs (43), *temple*
3624 ŏikŏs (1), *dwelling*

TEMPLES
1964 hêykâl (2), *temple*
7451 ra' (5), *bad; evil*
3485 naŏs (2), *temple*

TEMPORAL
4340 prŏskairŏs (1),
temporary

TEMPT
974 bâchan (1), to *test*
5254 nâçâh (4), to *test*
1598 ĕkpĕirazō (3), to
test thoroughly
3985 pĕirazō (6), to
endeavor, scrutinize

TEMPTATION
4531 maççâh (1), *testing*
3986 pĕirasmŏs (15), *test*

TEMPTATIONS
4531 maççâh (3), *testing*
3986 pĕirasmŏs (5), *test*

TEMPTED
5254 nâçâh (8), to *test*
551 apĕirastŏs (1), *not*
temptable
1598 ĕkpĕirazō (1), to
test thoroughly
3985 pĕirazō (14), to
endeavor, scrutinize

TEMPTER
3985 pĕirazō (2), to
endeavor, scrutinize

TEMPTETH
3985 pĕirazō (1), to
endeavor, scrutinize

TEMPTING
3985 pĕirazō (7), to
endeavor, scrutinize

TEN
6218 'âsôwr (4), *ten*
6235 'eser (164), *ten*
6236 ăsar (Ch.) (4), *ten*
7231 râbab (1), to
multiply by the myriad
7233 rᵉbâbâh (13),
myriad
7239 ribbôw (2), *myriad*
7240 ribbôw (Ch.) (2),
myriad
1176 dĕka (24), *ten*
3461 murias (3), *ten*
thousand
3463 muriŏi (3), *ten*
thousand; innumerably

TEN'S
6235 'eser (1), *ten*

TENDER
3126 yôwnêq (1), *sucker*
plant; nursing infant
3127 yôwneqeth (1),
sprout, new shoot
7390 rak (10), *tender*
7401 râkak (2), to *soften*

527 hapalŏs (2), *tender*
3629 ŏiktirmōn (1),
compassionate
4698 splagchnŏn (1),
intestine; affection, pity

TENDERHEARTED
7390+3824 rak (1),
tender; weak
2155 ĕusplagchnŏs (1),
compassionate

TENDERNESS
7391 rôk (1), *softness*

TENONS
3027 yâd (6), *hand; power*

TENOR
6310 peh (2), *mouth*

TENS
6235 'eser (3), *ten*

TENT
167 'âhal (3), to pitch a
tent
168 'ôhel (89), *tent*
6898 qubbâh (1), *pavilion*

TENTH
4643 ma'ăsêr (4), *tithe,*
one-tenth
6218 'âsôwr (13), *ten*
6224 'ăsîyrîy (26), *tenth*
6237 'âsar (3), to *tithe*
6241 'issârôwn (28), *tenth*
1181 dĕkatĕ (2), *tenth*
1182 dĕkatŏs (3), *tenth*

TENTMAKERS
4635 skēnŏpŏiŏs (1),
manufacturer of tents

TENTS
168 'ôhel (50), *tent*
2583 chânâh (1), to
encamp
4264 machăneh (5),
encampment
4908 mishkân (1),
residence
5521 çukkâh (1),
tabernacle; shelter

TERAH
8646 Terach (11), *Terach*

TERAPHIM
8655 tᵉrâphîym (6),
healer

TERESH
8657 Teresh (2), *Teresh*

TERMED
559 'âmar (2), to *say*

TERRACES
4546 mᵉçillâh (1),
viaduct; staircase

TERRESTRIAL
1919 ĕpigĕiŏs (2),
worldly, earthly

TERRIBLE
366 'âyôm (3), *frightful*
367 'êymâh (2), *fright*
574 'emtânîy (Ch.) (1),
burly or *mighty*
1763 dᵉchal (Ch.) (1), to
fear; be formidable
2152 zal'âphâh (1), *glow*
3372 yârê' (30), to *fear*
6184 'ârîyts (13),
powerful or tyrannical
5398 phŏbĕrŏs (1),
frightful, i.e. formidable

TERRIBLENESS
3372 yârê' (1), to *fear*
4172 môwrâ' (1), *fearful*
8606 tiphletseth (1),
fearfulness

TERRIBLY
6206 'ârats (2), to *dread*

TERRIFIED
6206 'ârats (1), to *dread*
4422 ptŏĕō (2), to *be*
scared
4426 pturō (1), to *be*
frightened

TERRIFIEST
1204 bâ'ath (1), to *fear*

TERRIFY
1204 bâ'ath (2), to *fear*
2865 châthath (1), to
break down
1629 ĕkphŏbĕō (1), to
frighten utterly

TERROR
367 'êymâh (4), *fright*
928 behâlâh (1), *sudden*
panic, destruction
1091 ballâhâh (3),
sudden destruction
2283 châgâ' (1), *terror*
2847 chittâh (1), *terror*
2851 chittîyth (8), *terror*
4032 mâgôwr (1), *fright*
4172 môwrâ' (2), *fearful*
4288 mᵉchittâh (2), *ruin;*
consternation
4637 ma'ărâtsâh (1),
terrifying violent power
6343 pachad (1), *fear*
5401 phŏbŏs (3), *alarm,*
or fright; reverence

TERRORS
367 'êymâh (3), *fright*
928 behâlâh (1), *sudden*
panic, destruction
1091 ballâhâh (6),
sudden destruction
1161 bi'ûwthîym (2),
alarms, startling things
4032 mâgôwr (1), *fright*
4048 mâgar (1), to *yield*
up, be thrown
4172 môwrâ' (1), *fearful*

TERTIUS
5060 Tĕrtiŏs (1), *third*

TERTULLUS
5061 Tĕrtullŏs (2),
Tertullus

TESTAMENT
1242 diathēkē (11),
contract; devisory will
1248 diakŏnia (2),
attendance, aid, service

TESTATOR
1303 diatithĕmai (2), to
put apart, i.e. dispose

TESTIFIED
5749 'ûwd (7), to *protest,*
testify; to encompass
6030 'ânâh (3), to
respond, answer
1263 diamarturŏmai (6),
to attest earnestly
3140 marturĕō (6), to
testify; to commend
3142 marturiŏn (1),
something evidential

4303 prŏmarturŏmai (1), to *predict beforehand*

TESTIFIEDST
5749 'ûwd (2), to *protest, testify*; to *encompass*

TESTIFIETH
6030 'ânâh (1), to *respond, answer*
3140 marturĕō (4), to *testify*; to *commend*

TESTIFY
5749 'ûwd (6), to *protest, testify*; to *encompass*
6030 'ânâh (8), to *respond, answer*
1263 diamarturŏmai (4), to *attest earnestly*
3140 marturĕō (8), to *testify*; to *commend*
3143 marturŏmai (2), to *be witness*, i.e. to *obtest*
4828 summarturĕō (1), to *testify jointly*

TESTIFYING
1263 diamarturŏmai (1), to *attest earnestly*
1957 ĕpimarturĕō (1), to *corroborate*
3140 marturĕō (1), to *testify*; to *commend*

TESTIMONIES
5713 'êdâh (21), *testimony*
5715 'êdûwth (15), *testimony*

TESTIMONY
5713 'êdâh (1), *testimony*
5715 'êdûwth (40), *testimony*
8584 t'ûwdâh (3), *attestation, precept*
3140 marturĕō (3), to *testify*; to *commend*
3141 marturia (14), *evidence given*
3142 marturiŏn (15), *something evidential*

TETRARCH
5075 tĕtrarchĕō (3), to *be a tetrarch*
5076 tĕtrarchēs (4), *ruler of a fourth part*

THADDAEUS
2280 Thaddaiŏs (2), *Thaddæus*

THAHASH
8477 Tachash (1), (poss.) *antelope*

THAMAH
8547 Temach (1), *Temach*

THAMAR
2283 Thamar (1), *palm*

THANK
2192+5485 z'êyr (Ch.) (3), *small, little*
3029 y'dâ' (Ch.) (1), to *praise*
3034 yâdâh (4), to *throw*; to *revere or worship*
8426 tôwdâh (3), *thanks*
1843 ĕxŏmŏlŏgĕō (2), to *acknowledge*
2168 ĕucharistĕō (11), to *express gratitude*

5485 charis (3), *gratitude; benefit given*

THANKED
1288 bârak (1), to *bless*
2168 ĕucharistĕō (1), to *express gratitude*
5485 charis (1), *gratitude; benefit given*

THANKFUL
3034 yâdâh (1), to *throw*; to *revere or worship*
2168 ĕucharistĕō (1), to *express gratitude*
2170 ĕucharistŏs (1), *grateful, thankful*

THANKFULNESS
2169 ĕucharistia (1), *gratitude*

THANKING
3034 yâdâh (1), to *throw*; to *revere or worship*

THANKS
3029 y'dâ' (Ch.) (1), to *praise*
3034 yâdâh (32), to *throw*; to *revere, worship*
8426 tôwdâh (3), *thanks*
437 anthŏmŏlŏgĕŏmai (1), to *give thanks*
2168 ĕucharistĕō (26), to *express gratitude*
2169 ĕucharistia (5), *gratitude*
3670 hŏmŏlŏgĕō (1), to *acknowledge, agree*
5485 charis (4), *gratitude; benefit given*

THANKSGIVING
1960 huy'dâh (1), *choir*
3034 yâdâh (2), to *throw*; to *revere or worship*
8426 tôwdâh (16), *thanks*
2169 ĕucharistia (8), *gratitude; grateful*

THANKSGIVINGS
8426 tôwdâh (1), *thanks*
2169 ĕucharistia (1), *gratitude; grateful*

THANKWORTHY
5485 charis (1), *gratitude; benefit given*

THARA
2291 Thara (1), *Thara*

THARSHISH
8659 Tarshîysh (4), *merchant vessel*

THEATRE
2302 thĕatrŏn (2), *audience-room; show*

THEBEZ
8405 Têbêts (3), *whiteness*

THEFT
1591 g'nêbâh (2), *something stolen*

THEFTS
2804 Klaudiŏs (1), *Claudius*
2829 klŏpē (2), *theft*

THELASAR
8515 T'la'ssar (1), *Telassar*

THEOPHILUS
2321 Thĕŏphilŏs (2), *friend of God*

THERE
2008 hênnâh (1), *from here; from there*
8033 shâm (440), *there*
8536 tâm (Ch.) (2), *there*
847 autŏu (3), *in this*
1563 ĕkĕi (98), *there*
1564 ĕkĕithĕn (1), *from there*
1566 ĕkĕisĕ (2), *there*
1759 ĕnthadĕ (1), *here*
1927 ĕpidēmĕō (1), to *make oneself at home*
5602 hōdĕ (1), *here*

THEREABOUT
4012+5127 pĕri (1), *about*

THEREAT
1223+846 dia (1), *through*, by means of

THEREBY
2004 hên (2), *they*
5921 'al (2), *above, over*

THEREFORE
1571 gam (5), *also; even*
2006 hên (Ch.) (2), *lo; therefore, unless*
2063 zō'th (1), *this*
3588 kîy (2), *for, that*
3651 kên (170), *just; right, correct*
235 alla (3), *but, yet*
686 ara (6), *therefore*
1063 gar (1), *for, indeed*
1160 dapanē (1), *expense, cost*
1211 dē (1), *therefore*
1352 diŏ (9), *therefore*
1360 diŏti (1), *inasmuch as*
2532 kai (1), *and; or*
3747 ŏstĕŏn (1), *bone*
3757 hŏu (1), *at which*
3767 ŏun (255), *certainly*
5105 tŏigarŏun (1), *then*
5106 tŏinun (3), *then*
5124 tŏutŏ (1), *that thing*
5620 hōstĕ (9), *thus*

THEREIN
413 'êl (2), *to, toward*
1459 gav (Ch.) (1), *middle*
2004 hên (4), *they*
2007 hênnâh (1), *themselves*
4393 m'lô' (7), *fulness*
5921 'al (9), *above, over*
7130 qereb (2), *nearest*
8033 shâm (10), *there*
8432 tâvek (3), *center*
5125 tŏutŏis (1), *in these*

THEREINTO
1519+846 ĕis (1), *to*

THEREOF
8033 shâm (1), *there*
846 autŏs (26), *he, she, it*

THEREON
5921 'al (48), *above, over*
846 autŏs (2), *he, she, it*
1911 ĕpiballŏ (1), to *throw upon*
1913 ĕpibibazō (1), to *cause to mount*
1924 ĕpigraphō (1), to *inscribe, write upon*

1945 ĕpikĕimai (1), to *rest upon; press upon*
2026 ĕpŏikŏdŏmĕō (1), to *rear up, build up*

THEREOUT
8033 shâm (1), *where, there*

THERETO
5921 'al (8), *above, over*
1928 ĕpidiatassŏmai (1), to *appoint besides*

THEREUNTO
1519+846+5124 ĕis (1), to
1519+5124 ĕis (2), to
4334 prŏsĕrchŏmai (1), to *come near, visit*

THEREUPON
2026 ĕpŏikŏdŏmĕō (2), to *rear up, build up*

THEREWITH
854 'êth (1), *with; by; at*
5921 'al (2), *above, over*
1722+846 ĕn (2), *in*
1909+5125 ĕpi (1), *on*
5125 tŏutŏis (1), *in these*

THESSALONIANS
2331 Thĕssalŏnikĕus (5), of *Thessalonice*

THESSALONICA
2331 Thĕssalŏnikĕus (1), of *Thessalonice*
2332 Thĕssalŏnikē (5), *Thessalonice*

THEUDAS
2333 Thĕudas (1), *Theudas*

THICK
653 'ăphêlâh (1), *duskiness, darkness*
3515 kâbêd (1), *numerous; severe*
5441 çôbek (1), *thicket*
5645 'âb (2), *thick clouds*
5666 'ăbâh (1), to *be dense*
5672 'ăbîy (2), *density*
5687 'ăbôth (4), *dense*
5688 'ăbôth (4), *entwined*
6282 'âthâr (1), *incense; worshipper*
7341 rôchab (1), *width*

THICKER
5666 'ăbâh (2), to *be dense*

THICKET
5441 çôbek (1), *thicket*
5442 ç'bâk (1), *thicket*

THICKETS
2337 châvâch (1), *dell or crevice of rock*
5442 ç'bâk (2), *thicket*
5645 'âb (1), *thick clouds; thicket*

THICKNESS
5672 'ăbîy (2), *density*
7341 rôchab (2), *width*

THIEF
1590 gannâb (13), *stealer*
2812 klĕptēs (12), *stealer*
3027 lēįstēs (3), *brigand*

THIEVES
1590 gannâb (4), *stealer*
2812 klĕptēs (4), *stealer*
3027 lēįstēs (8), *brigand*

THIGH
3409 yârêk (19), leg or
shank, flank; side
7785 shôwq (1), lower leg
3382 mêrŏs (1), thigh

THIGHS
3409 yârêk (2), leg or
shank, flank; side
3410 yarkâ' (Ch.) (1),
thigh

THIMNATHAH
8553 Timnâh (1), portion

THIN
1809 dâlal (1), to
slacken, dangle
1851 daq (5), thin
4174 môwrâd (1),
descent, slope
7534 raq (1), emaciated

THING
562 'ômer (1), something
said
1697 dâbâr (182), thing
3627 kᵉlîy (11), thing
3651 kên (2), just; right
3972 mᵉ'ûwmâh (3),
something; anything
4399 mᵉlâ'kâh (2), work;
property
4406 millâh (Ch.) (9),
word, command
4859 mashshâ'âh (1),
secured loan
5315 nephesh (2), life;
breath; soul; wind
1520 hĕis (1), one
3056 lŏgŏs (2), word,
matter, thing
4110 plasma (1), molded
4229 pragma (2), matter
4487 rhēma (1), matter
5313 hupsōma (1), barrier

THINGS
1697 dâbâr (47), thing
4406 millâh (Ch.) (1),
word or subject
18 agathŏs (1), good
846 autŏs (1), he, she, it
3056 lŏgŏs (3), thing
4229 pragma (4), matter
4487 rhēma (2), thing
5023 tauta (1), these

THINK
559 'âmar (3), to say
995 bîyn (1), to
understand; discern
1819 dâmâh (1), to
consider, think
2142 zâkar (3), to
remember; to mention
2803 châshab (6), to
think, regard; to value
5452 çᵉbar (Ch.) (1), to
bear in mind, i.e. hope
5869 'ayin (2), eye; sight
6245 'âshath (1), to be
sleek; to excogitate
1380 dŏkĕō (22), to think
1760 ĕnthumĕŏmai (1),
ponder, reflect on
2233 hēgĕŏmai (2), to
deem, i.e. consider
3049 lŏgizŏmai (7), to
credit; to think, regard
3539 nŏiĕō (1), to
exercise the mind

3543 nŏmizō (4), to deem
or regard
3633 ŏiŏmai (1), to
imagine, opine
5252 hupĕrphrŏnĕō (1),
to esteem oneself
5282 hupŏnŏĕō (1), to
think; to expect
5316 phainō (1), to
lighten (shine)
5426 phrŏnĕō (4), to be
mentally disposed

THINKEST
2803 châshab (1), to
think, regard; to value
5869 'ayin (2), eye; sight
1380 dŏkĕō (1), to think
3049 lŏgizŏmai (1), to
think, regard
5426 phrŏnĕō (1), to be
mentally disposed

THINKETH
2803 châshab (1), to
think, regard; to value
7200 râ'âh (1), to see
8176 shâ'ar (1), to
estimate
1380 dŏkĕō (2), to think
3049 lŏgizŏmai (1), to
think, regard

THINKING
559 'âmar (1), to say
1931+1961 hûw' (1), this

THIRD
7969 shâlôwsh (9), three;
third; thrice
7992 shᵉlîyshîy (104),
third
8027 shâlash (2), to be
triplicate
8029 shillêsh (5), great
grandchild
8523 tᵉlîythay (Ch.) (2),
third
8531 tᵉlath (Ch.) (3),
tertiary, i.e. third rank
5152 tristĕgŏn (1), third
story place
5154 tritŏs (56), third
part; third time, thirdly

THIRDLY
5154 tritŏs (1), third part

THIRST
6770 tsâmê' (2), to thirst
6771 tsâmê' (1), thirsty
6772 tsâmâ' (16), thirst
6773 tsim'âh (1), thirst
1372 dipsaō (10), to thirst
1373 dipsŏs (1), thirst

THIRSTED
6770 tsâmê' (2), to thirst

THIRSTETH
6770 tsâmê' (2), to thirst
6771 tsâmê' (1), thirsty

THIRSTY
6770 tsâmê' (2), to thirst
6771 tsâmê' (7), thirsty
6772 tsâmâ' (1), thirst
6774 tsimmâ'ôwn (1),
desert
1372 dipsaō (3), to thirst

THIRTEEN
7969 shâlôwsh (2), three
7969+6240 shâlôwsh (13),
three; third; thrice

THIRTEENTH
7969+6240 shâlôwsh (11),
three; third; thrice

THIRTIETH
7970 shᵉlôwshîym (9),
thirty; thirtieth

THIRTY
7970 shᵉlôwshîym (161),
thirty; thirtieth
8533 tᵉlâthîyn (Ch.) (2),
thirty
5144 triakŏnta (9), thirty

THIRTYFOLD
5144 triakŏnta (2), thirty

THISTLE
1863 dardar (1), thorn
2336 chôwach (4), thorn

THISTLES
1863 dardar (1), thorn
2336 chôwach (1), thorn
5146 tribŏlŏs (1), thorny
caltrop plant

THITHER
1988 hălôm (1), hither
2008 hênnâh (3), from
here; from there
5704 'ad (1), until
8033 shâm (63), there
1563 ĕkĕi (8), thither
1904 ĕpĕrchŏmai (1), to
supervene
3854 paraginŏmai (1), to
arrive; to appear
4370 prŏstrĕchō (1), to
hasten by running

THITHERWARD
2008 hênnâh (1), from
here; from there
8033 shâm (1), there
1563 ĕkĕi (1), thither

THOMAS
2381 Thōmas (12), twin

THONGS
2438 himas (1), strap

THORN
2336 chôwach (2), thorn
4534 mᵉçûwkâh (1),
thorn-hedge
5285 na'âtsûwts (1),
brier; thicket
6975 qôwts (2), thorns
4647 skŏlŏps (1), thorn

THORNS
329 'âţâd (1), buckthorn
2312 chêdeq (1), prickly
2336 chôwach (3), thorn
5285 na'âtsûwts (1),
brier; thicket
5518 çîyr (4), thorn; hook
5544 çillôwn (1), prickle
6791 tsên (2), thorn
6975 qôwts (12), thorns
7063 qimmâshôwn (1),
prickly plant
7898 shayith (7), wild
growth of briers
173 akantha (14), thorn
174 akanthinŏs (2),
thorny

THOROUGHLY
3190 yâţab (1), to be,
make well
7495 râphâ' (1), to cure

THOUGHT
559 'âmar (9), to say

1672 dâ'ag (1), be
anxious, be afraid
1696 dâbar (1), to speak
1697 dâbâr (1), word;
matter; thing
1819 dâmâh (4), to think
2154 zimmâh (1), plan
2161 zâmam (5), to plan
2803 châshab (10), to
think, regard; to value
4093 maddâ' (1),
intelligence
4209 mᵉzimmâh (1), plan
4284 machăshâbâh (1),
contrivance; plan
5869 'ayin (3), eye; sight
6246 'ăshîth (Ch.) (1), to
purpose, plan
6248 'ashtûwth (1),
cogitation, thinking
6419 pâlal (1), to
intercede, pray
7454 rêa' (1), thought
7807 shach (1), sunk
8232+6925 shᵉphar (Ch.)
(1), to be beautiful
1260 dialŏgizŏmai (1), to
deliberate
1261 dialŏgismŏs (1),
consideration; debate
1380 dŏkĕō (5), to think
1760 ĕnthumĕŏmai (2),
ponder, reflect on
1911 ĕpiballō (1), to
throw upon
1963 ĕpinŏia (1),
thought, intention
2106 ĕudŏkĕō (1), to
think well, i.e. approve
2233 hēgĕŏmai (2), to
deem, i.e. consider
2919 krinō (1), to decide;
to try, condemn, punish
3049 lŏgizŏmai (1), to
credit; to think, regard
3309 mĕrimnaō (11), to
be anxious about
3540 nŏēma (1),
perception, i.e. purpose
3543 nŏmizō (1), to deem
4305 prŏmĕrimnaō (1), to
care in advance

THOUGHTEST
1819 dâmâh (1), to
consider, think

THOUGHTS
2031 harhôr (Ch.) (1),
mental conception
2711 chêqeq (1),
enactment, resolution
4180 môwrâsh (1),
possession
4209 mᵉzimmâh (2),
plan; sagacity
4284 machăshâbâh (24),
contrivance; plan
5587 çâ'îph (2), divided
in mind; sentiment
5588 çê'êph (1), divided
in mind; skeptic
6250 'eshtŏnâh (1),
thinking
7454 rêa' (1), thought
7476 ra'yôwn (Ch.) (5),
mental conception
8312 sar'aph (2),
cogitation
1261 dialŏgismŏs (8),
consideration; debate

1270 dianŏēma (1), *sentiment, thought*
1761 ĕnthumēsis (3), *deliberation; idea*
3053 lŏgismŏs (1), *reasoning; conscience*

THOUSAND
505 'eleph (436), *thousand*
506 'ălaph (Ch.) (3), *thousand*
7233 rᵉbâbâh (4), *myriad*
7239 ribbôw (5), *myriad*
7239+505 ribbôw (1), *myriad, large number*
7240 ribbôw (Ch.) (1), *myriad, large number*
1367 dischiliŏi (1), *two thousand*
2035 hĕptakischiliŏi (1), *seven times a thousand*
3461 murias (3), *ten thousand*
3463 muriŏi (3), *ten thousand*
4000 pĕntakischiliŏi (6), *five times a thousand*
5070 tĕtrakischiliŏi (5), *four times a thousand*
5153 trischiliŏi (1), *three times a thousand*
5505 chilias (21), *one thousand*
5507 chiliŏi (11), *thousand*

THOUSANDS
503 'âlaph (1), *increase by thousands*
505 'eleph (46), *thousand*
506 'ălaph (Ch.) (1), *thousand*
7232 râbab (1), *to shoot*
7233 rᵉbâbâh (7), *myriad*
7239 ribbôw (2), *myriad*
3461 murias (2), *ten thousand*
5505 chilias (1), *one thousand*

THREAD
2339 chûwṭ (4), *string*
6616 pâthîyl (1), *twine*

THREATEN
546 apĕilĕō (1), *to menace; to forbid*

THREATENED
546 apĕilĕō (1), *to menace; to forbid*
4324 prŏsapĕilĕō (1), *to menace additionally*

THREATENING
547 apĕilē (1), *menace*

THREATENINGS
547 apĕilē (2), *menace*

THREE
7969 shâlôwsh (377), *three; third; thrice*
7991 shâlîysh (1), *triangle, three*
7992 shᵉlîyshîy (4), *third*
8027 shâlash (6), *to be triplicate*
8032 shilshôwm (1), *day before yesterday*
8532 tᵉlâth (Ch.) (10), *three or third*
5140 trĕis (69), *three*

5145 triakŏsiŏi (2), *three hundred*
5148 triĕtia (1), *three years' period*
5150 trimēnŏn (1), *three months' space*
5151 tris (1), *three times*
5153 trischiliŏi (1), *three times a thousand*

THREEFOLD
8027 shâlash (1), *to be triplicate*

THREESCORE
7239 ribbôw (1), *myriad*
7657 shib'îym (38), *seventy*
8346 shishshîym (42), *sixty*
8361 shittîyn (Ch.) (4), *sixty*
1440 hĕbdŏmēkŏnta (3), *seventy*
1835 hĕxēkŏnta (4), *sixty*
5516 chi xi stigma (1), 666

THRESH
1758 dûwsh (3), *to thresh*
1869 dârak (1), *to tread*

THRESHED
1758 dûwsh (2), *to thresh*
2251 châbaṭ (1), *to thresh*

THRESHETH
248 alŏaō (1), *to tread*

THRESHING
1758 dûwsh (3), *to thresh*
1786 dayîsh (1), *threshing*-time
2742 chârûwts (2), *threshing-sledge*
4098 mᵉdushshâh (1), *down-trodden people*
4173 môwrag (3), *threshing sledge*

THRESHINGFLOOR
1637 gôren (17), *open area*

THRESHINGFLOORS
147 'iddar (Ch.) (1), *threshing-floor*
1637 gôren (1), *open area*

THRESHINGPLACE
1637 gôren (1), *open area*

THRESHOLD
4670 miphtân (8), *sill*
5592 çaph (6), *dish*

THRESHOLDS
624 'âçûph (1), *collection, stores*
5592 çaph (2), *dish*

THREW
5422 nâthats (1), *to tear down*
5619 çâqal (1), *to throw large stones*
8058 shâmaṭ (1), *to jostle*
906 ballō (2), *to throw*
4952 susparassō (1), *to convulse violently*

THREWEST
7993 shâlak (1), *to throw*

THRICE
7969+6471 shâlôwsh (4), *three; third; thrice*
5151 tris (11), *three times*

THROAT
1627 gârôwn (4), *throat*
3930 lôa' (1), *throat*
2995 larugx (1), *throat*
4155 pnigō (1), *to throttle*

THRONE
3678 kiççĕ' (120), *throne*
3764 korçĕ' (Ch.) (2), *throne*
968 bēma (1), *tribunal platform; judging place*
2362 thrŏnŏs (50), *throne*

THRONES
3678 kiççĕ' (4), *throne*
3764 korçĕ' (Ch.) (1), *throne*
2362 thrŏnŏs (4), *throne*

THRONG
2346 thlibō (1), *to crowd*
4912 sunĕchō (1), *to hold together*

THRONGED
4846 sumpnigō (1), *to drown; to crowd*
4918 sunthlibō (1), *to compress, i.e. to crowd*

THRONGING
4918 sunthlibō (1), *to compress, i.e. to crowd*

THROUGH
413 'êl (2), *to, toward*
1119 bᵉmôw (1), *in, with*
1157 bᵉ'ad (5), *through*
1234 bâqa' (3), *to cleave*
1811 dâlaph (1), *to drip*
1856 dâqar (2), *to pierce*
1870 derek (1), *road*
2864 châthar (1), *to break or dig into*
2944 ṭâ'an (1), *to stab*
3027 yâd (1), *hand; power*
4480 min (2), *from, out of*
5674 'âbar (10), *to cross*
5921 'al (5), *over, upon*
6440 pânîym (1), *face*
7130 qereb (5), *nearest part, i.e. the center*
7751 shûwṭ (1), *to travel*
8432 tâvek (7), *center*
303 ana (1), *through*
1223 dia (93), *through*
1224 diabainō (1), *to pass by, over, across*
1279 diapŏrĕuŏmai (1), *to travel through*
1330 diĕrchŏmai (8), *to traverse, travel through*
1350 diktuŏn (1), *drag net*
1358 diŏrussō (3), *to penetrate burglariously*
1537 ĕk (3), *out, out of*
1653 ĕlĕŏ (1), *to give out compassion*
1722 ĕn (37), *in; during*
1909 ĕpi (2), *on, upon*
2569 kalŏpŏiĕō (1), *to do well*
2596 kata (4), *down; according to*
2700 katatŏxĕuō (1), *shoot down*
4044 pĕripĕirō (1), *to penetrate entirely*
4063 pĕritrĕchō (1), *to traverse, run about*

THROUGHLY
7235 râbâh (1), *to increase*
1245 diakatharizō (2), *to cleanse perfectly*
1722+3956 ĕn (1), *in*
1822 ĕxartizō (1), *to finish out; to equip fully*

THROUGHOUT
5921 'al (2), *above, over*
1223 dia (3), *through*
1330 diĕrchŏmai (2), *to traverse, travel through*
1519 ĕis (6), *to or into*
1722 ĕn (5), *in; during*
1909 ĕpi (2), *on, upon*
2596 kata (8), *down; according to*

THROW
2040 hâraç (6), *to pull down; break, destroy*
5307 nâphal (1), *to fall*
5422 nâthats (1), *to tear down*
8058 shâmaṭ (1), *to jostle*

THROWING
3027 yâd (1), *hand; power*

THROWN
2040 hâraç (7), *to pull down; break, destroy*
5422 nâthats (3), *to tear down*
7411 râmâh (1), *to hurl*
7993 shâlak (1), *to throw*
906 ballō (1), *to throw*
2647 kataluō (3), *to demolish; to halt*
4496 rhiptō (1), *to toss*

THRUST
926 bâhal (1), *to be, make agitated; hasten*
1333 bâthaq (1), *to cut in pieces, hack up*
1644 gârash (6), *to drive out; to expatriate*
1760 dâchâh (1), *to push down; to totter*
1766 dâchaq (1), *to oppress*
1856 dâqar (8), *to stab*
1920 hâdaph (1), *to push away or down; drive out*
2115 zûwr (1), *to press*
2944 ṭâ'an (1), *to stab*
3238 yânâh (1), *to suppress; to maltreat*
3905 lâchats (1), *to press*
5074 nâdad (1), *to rove, flee; to drive away*
5080 nâdach (2), *to push off, scattered*
5365 nâqar (1), *to bore*
5414 nâthan (1), *to give*
8628 tâqa' (2), *to clatter, slap, drive, clasp*
683 apōthĕōmai (2), *to push off; to reject*
906 ballō (5), *to throw*
1544 ĕkballō (3), *to throw out*
1856 ĕxōthĕō (1), *to expel; to propel*
1877 ĕpanagō (1), *to put out to sea; to return*
2601 katabibazō (1), *to cause to bring down*

THRUSTETH
2700 *katatŏxĕuō* (1), to *shoot down*
3992 *pĕmpō* (2), to *send*

THRUSTETH
5086 nâdaph (1), to *disperse, be windblown*

THUMB
931 bôhen (6), *thumb*

THUMBS
931 bôhen (1), *thumb*
931+3027 bôhen (2), *thumb; big toe*

THUMMIM
8550 Tummîym (5), *perfections*

THUNDER
6963 qôwl (7), *sound*
7481 râ'am (2), to *crash thunder; to irritate*
7482 ra'am (6), *peal of thunder*
7483 ra'mâh (1), *horse's mane*
1027 brŏntē (3), *thunder*

THUNDERBOLTS
7565 resheph (1), *flame*

THUNDERED
7481 râ'am (3), to *crash thunder; to irritate*
1027+1096 brŏntē (1), *thunder*

THUNDERETH
7481 râ'am (3), to *crash thunder; to irritate*

THUNDERINGS
6963 qôwl (2), *sound*
1027 brŏntē (4), *thunder*

THUNDERS
6963 qôwl (3), *sound*
1027 brŏntē (4), *thunder*

THYATIRA
2363 *Thuatĕira* (4), *Thyatira*

THYINE
2367 *thuïnŏs* (1), of *citron*

TIBERIAS
5085 *Tibĕrias* (3), *Tiberius*

TIBERIUS
5086 *Tibĕriŏs* (1), (poss.) *pertaining to the river Tiberis or Tiber*

TIBHATH
2880 Ṭibchath (1), *slaughter*

TIBNI
8402 Tibnîy (3), *strawy*

TIDAL
8413 Tid'âl (2), *fearfulness*

TIDINGS
1309 bᵉsôwrâh (6), glad *tidings, good news*
1319 bâsar (16), to *announce* (good news)
1697 dâbâr (4), *word*
8052 shᵉmûw'âh (8), *announcement*
8088 shêma' (2), *something heard*
2097 ĕuaggĕlizō (6), to *announce good news*
3056 lŏgŏs (1), *word*
5334 phasis (1), *news*

TIE
631 'âçar (1), to *fasten*
6029 'ânad (1), to *bind*

TIED
631 'âçar (3), to *fasten*
5414 nâthan (1), to *give*
1210 dĕō (4), to *bind*

TIGLATH-PILESER
8407 Tiglath Pil'eçer (3), *Tiglath-Pileser*

TIKVAH
8616 Tiqvâh (2), *hope*

TIKVATH
8616 Tiqvâh (1), *hope*

TILE
3843 lᵉbênâh (1), *brick*

TILGATH-PILNESER
8407 Tiglath Pil'eçer (3), *Tiglath-Pileser*

TILING
2766 kĕramŏs (1), *clay roof tile*

TILL
5647 'âbad (4), to *work*
5704 'ad (90), *until*
5705 'ad (Ch.) (1), *until*
6440 pânîym (1), *face; front*
891 achri (5), *until, up to*
1519 ĕis (1), to or *into*
2193 hĕōs (41), *until*
3360 mĕchri (2), *until*

TILLAGE
5215 nîyr (1), *plowed land*
5656 'ăbôdâh (2), *work*

TILLED
5647 'âbad (2), to *work*

TILLER
5647 'âbad (1), to *work*

TILLEST
5647 'âbad (1), to *work*

TILLETH
5647 'âbad (2), to *work*

TILON
8436 Tûwlôn (1), *suspension*

TIMAEUS
5090 Timaiŏs (1), (poss.) *foul; impure*

TIMBER
636 'â' (Ch.) (3), *wood*
6086 'êts (23), *wood*

TIMBREL
8596 tôph (5), *tambourine*

TIMBRELS
8596 tôph (4), *tambourine*
8608 tâphaph (1), to *drum on a tambourine*

TIME
116 'ĕdayin (Ch.) (1), *then*
227 'âz (5), *at that time*
268 'âchôwr (1), *behind, backward; west*
570 'emesh (1), *yesterday evening*
1767 day (1), *enough*
2165 zᵉmân (1), *time*
2166 zᵉmân (Ch.) (6), *time, appointed*
3117 yôwm (55), *day*
3118 yôwm (Ch.) (2), *day*

TIME
4150 môw'êd (3), *assembly*
4279 mâchar (7), *tomorrow; hereafter*
5732 'iddân (Ch.) (7), *set time; year*
5769 'ôwlâm (1), *eternity*
6256 'êth (220), *time*
6258 'attâh (3), *now*
6440 pânîym (2), *front*
6471 pa'am (14), *time*
6635 tsâbâ' (2), *army*
7225 rê'shîyth (1), *first*
7227 rab (2), *great*
7674 shebeth (1), *rest*
8032 shilshôwm (1), *day before yesterday*
8462 tᵉchillâh (2), *original; originally*
8543 tᵉmôwl (1), *yesterday*
744 archaiŏs (3), *original*
1074 gĕnea (1), *age*
1208 dĕutĕrŏs (1), *second*
1597 ĕkpalai (1), *long ago*
1909 ĕpi (2), *on, upon*
2119 ĕukairĕō (2), to *have opportunity*
2121 ĕukairŏs (1), *opportune, suitable*
2235 ēdē (1), *even now*
2250 hēmĕra (4), *day*
2540 kairŏs (54), *set time*
3195 mĕllō (1), to *intend*
3379 mĕpŏtĕ (6), *never*
3568 nun (2), *now*
3598 hŏdŏs (1), *road*
3819 palai (1), *formerly*
4218 pŏtĕ (12), *ever*
4287 prŏthĕsmiŏs (1), *designated day or time*
4340 prŏskairŏs (1), *temporary*
4455 pôpŏtĕ (3), *at no time*
5119 tŏtĕ (4), *at the time*
5550 chrŏnŏs (28), *time*
5551 chrŏnŏtribĕō (1), to *procrastinate, linger*
5610 hōra (12), *hour*

TIMES
2165 zᵉmân (1), *time*
2166 zᵉmân (Ch.) (3), *time, appointed*
3027 yâd (1), *hand; power*
3117 yôwm (5), *day; time*
4150 môw'êd (1), *assembly*
4151 môw'âd (1), *troop*
4489 môneh (2), *instance*
5732 'iddân (Ch.) (6), *set time; year*
6256 'êth (22), *time*
6471 pa'am (42), *time*
8543 tᵉmôwl (2), *yesterday*
1074 gĕnea (1), *age*
1441 hĕbdŏmēkŏntakis (1), *seventy times*
2034 hĕptakis (4), *seven times*
2540 kairŏs (8), *set time*
3999 pĕntakis (1), *five times*
4218 pŏtĕ (3), *ever*
5151 tris (1), *three times*
5550 chrŏnŏs (8), *time*

TIMNA
8555 Timnâ' (4), *restraint*

TIMNAH
8553 Timnâh (3), *portion*
8555 Timnâ' (2), *restraint*

TIMNATH
8553 Timnâh (8), *portion*

TIMNATH-HERES
8556 Timnath Chereç (1), *portion of* (the) *sun*

TIMNATH-SERAH
8556 Timnath Chereç (2), *portion of* (the) *sun*

TIMNITE
8554 Timnîy (1), *Timnite*

TIMON
5096 Timōn (1), *valuable*

TIMOTHEOS
5095 Timŏthĕŏs (1), *dear to God*

TIMOTHEUS
5095 Timŏthĕŏs (18), *dear to God*

TIMOTHY
5095 Timŏthĕŏs (9), *dear to God*

TIN
913 bᵉdîyl (5), *tin*

TINGLE
6750 tsâlal (3), to *tinkle*

TINKLING
5913 'âkaç (1), to *put on anklets*
214 alalazō (1), to *clang*

TIP
8571 tᵉnûwk (8), *pinnacle, i.e. extremity*
206 akrŏn (1), *extremity*

TIPHSAH
8607 Tiphçach (2), *ford*

TIRAS
8493 Tîyrᵉyâ' (2), *fearful*

TIRATHITES
8654 Tir'âthîy (1), *gate*

TIRE
6287 pᵉ'êr (1), *head-dress*

TIRED
3190 yâṭab (1), to *be, make well; successful*

TIRES
6287 pᵉ'êr (1), *fancy head-dress*
7720 sahărôn (1), *round pendant or crescent*

TIRHAKAH
8640 Tirhâqâh (2), *Tirhakah*

TIRHANAH
8647 Tirchănâh (1), *Tirchanah*

TIRIA
8493 Tîyrᵉyâ' (1), *fearful*

TIRSHATHA
8660 Tirshâthâ' (5), *deputy or governor*

TIRZAH
8656 Tirtsâh (18), *delightsomeness*

TISHBITE
8664 Tishbîy (6), *Tishbite*

TITHE
4643 ma'ăsêr (11), *tithe*
6237 'âsar (1), to *tithe*

586 apŏdĕkatŏō (2), to
tithe

TITHES
4643 ma'ăsêr (16), *tithe*
6237 'âsar (2), to *tithe*
586 apŏdĕkatŏō (2), to
tithe, give a tenth
1181 dĕkatē (1), *tithe*
1183 dĕkatŏō (3), to *give*
or *take a tenth*

TITHING
4643 ma'ăsêr (1), *tithe*
6237 'âsar (1), to *tithe*

TITLE
6725 tsîyûwn (1), *guiding*
pillar, monument
5102 titlŏs (2), *title*

TITTLE
2762 kĕraia (2), *horn-like*

TITUS
5103 Titŏs (15), *Titus*

TIZITE
8491 Tîytsîy (1), *Titsite*

TOAH
8430 Tôwach (1), *humble*

TOB
2897 Ţôwb (2), *good*

TOB-ADONIJAH
2899 Ţôwb Ădônîyâhûw
(1), *pleasing* (to)
Adonijah

TOBIAH
2900 Ţôwbîyâh (15),
goodness of Jehovah

TOBIJAH
2900 Ţôwbîyâh (3),
goodness of Jehovah

TOCHEN
8507 Tôken (1), *quantity*

TOE
931 bôhen (6), *big toe*

TOES
676 'etsba' (2), *finger; toe*
677 'etsba' (Ch.) (2), *toe*
931 bôhen (1), *big toe*
931+7272 bôhen (2),
thumb; big toe

TOGARMAH
8425 Tôwgarmâh (4),
Togarmah

TOGETHER
259 'echâd (5), *first*
2298 chad (Ch.) (1), *one*
3162 yachad (125),
unitedly
6776 tsemed (1), *yoke*
240 allēlōn (1), *one*
another
260 hama (3), *together*
346 anakĕphalaiŏmai
(1), to *sum up*
1794 ĕntulissō (1), *wind*
up in, *enwrap*
1865 ĕpathrŏizō (1), to
accumulate, increase
1996 ĕpisunagō (6), to
collect upon
1997 ĕpisunagōgē (2),
meeting, gathering
1998 ĕpisuntrĕchō (1), to
hasten together upon
2086 hĕtĕrŏzugĕō (1), to
associate discordantly

2675 katartizō (1), to
prepare, equip
3674 hŏmŏu (3), *at the*
same place or time
4776 sugkathizō (2), to
give, take a seat with
4779 sugkalĕō (8), to
convoke, call together
4786 sugkĕrannumi (1),
to *combine, assimilate*
4789 sugklĕrŏnŏmŏs (1),
participant in common
4794 sugkuptō (1), to be
completely overcome
4801 suzĕugnumi (2), to
conjoin in marriage
4802 suzĕtĕō (1), to
discuss, controvert
4806 suzōŏpŏiĕō (2), to
reanimate conjointly
4811 sukŏphantĕō (1), to
defraud, i.e. exact
4816 sullĕgō (1), to *gather*
4822 sumbibazō (2), to
drive together, unite
4831 summimĕtēs (1),
co-imitator
4836 sumparaginŏmai
(1), to *convene*
4837 sumparakalĕō (1),
to *console jointly*
4851 sumphĕrō (1), to
collect; to conduce
4853 sumphulĕtēs (1),
native of the same
country
4854 sumphutŏs (1),
closely united to
4856 sumphōnĕō (1), to
be harmonious
4863 sunagō (31), to
gather together
4865 sunagōnizŏmai (1),
to *struggle with*
4866 sunathlĕō (1), to
wrestle with
4867 sunathrŏizō (3), to
convene
4873 sunanakĕimai (1),
to *recline with*
4883 sunarmŏlŏgĕō (2),
to *render close-jointed*
4886 sundĕsmŏs (1),
ligament; uniting
4888 sundŏxazō (1), to
share glory with
4890 sundrŏmē (1),
(riotous) *concourse*
4891 sunĕgĕirō (1), to
raise up with
4896 sunĕimi (1), to
assemble, gather
4897 sunĕisĕrchŏmai (1),
to *enter with*
4899 sunĕklĕktŏs (1),
chosen together with
4903 sunĕrgĕō (2), to be
a fellow-worker
4904 sunĕrgŏs (1),
fellow-worker
4905 sunĕrchŏmai (16),
to *gather together*
4911 sunĕphistēmi (1), to
resist or assault jointly
4925 sunŏikŏdŏmĕō (1),
to *construct*
4943 sunupŏurgĕō (1),
assist, join to help

4944 sunōdinō (1), to
sympathize

TOHU
8459 Tôchûw (1),
abasement

TOI
8583 Tô'ûw (3), *error*

TOIL
5999 'âmâl (1), *effort*
6093 'itstsâbôwn (1),
labor or pain
2872 kŏpiaō (2), to *feel*
fatigue; to *work hard*

TOILED
2872 kŏpiaō (1), to *feel*
fatigue; to *work hard*

TOILING
928 basanizō (1), to
torture, torment

TOKEN
226 'ôwth (10), *sign*
1730 ĕndĕigma (1), *plain*
indication
1732 ĕndĕixis (1),
indication
4592 sēmĕiŏn (1), *sign*
4953 sussēmŏn (1), *sign*
in common

TOKENS
226 'ôwth (4), *signal, sign*

TOLA
8439 Tôwlâ' (6), *worm*

TOLAD
8434 Tôwlâd (1), *posterity*

TOLAITES
8440 Tôwlâ'îy (1), *Tolaite*

TOLD
559 'âmar (13), to *say*
560 'ămar (Ch.) (1), to *say*
1540 gâlâh (2), to *reveal*
1696 dâbar (15), to *speak*
4487 mânâh (1), to *allot;*
to *enumerate or enroll*
5046 nâgad (152), to
announce
5608 çâphar (27), to
recount an event
8085 shâma' (2), to *hear*
8505 tâkan (1), to
balance, i.e. measure
312 anaggĕllō (4), to
announce, report
513 axinē (3), *axe*
518 apaggĕllō (17), to
announce, proclaim
1285 diasaphĕō (1), to
declare, tell
1334 diēgĕŏmai (2), to
relate fully, describe
1834 ĕxēgĕŏmai (1), to
tell, relate again
2036 ĕpō (13), to *speak*
2046 ĕrĕō (1), to *utter*
2980 lalĕō (10), to *talk*
3004 lĕgō (4), to *say*
3377 mēnuō (1), to *report*
4277 prŏĕpō (1), to *say*
already, *to predict*
4280 prŏĕrĕō (2), to *say*
already, *predict*
4302 prŏlĕgō (1), to
predict, forewarn

TOLERABLE
414 anĕktŏtĕrŏs (6),
more endurable

TOLL
4061 middâh (Ch.) (3),
tribute, tax money

TOMB
1430 gâdîysh (1), *stack*
3419 mnēmĕiŏn (2),
place of interment

TOMBS
3418 mnēma (2),
monument
3419 mnēmĕiŏn (3),
place of interment
5028 taphŏs (1), *grave*

TONGS
4457 melqâch (5), *tongs*
4621 ma'ătsâd (1), *axe*

TONGUE
762 'Ărâmîyth (2), in
Aramean
2013 hâçâh (1), to *hush*
2790 chârash (4), to be
silent; to be deaf
3956 lâshôwn (89),
tongue; tongue-shaped
1100 glōssa (24), *tongue*
1258 dialĕktŏs (5),
language
1447 Hĕbraïsti (3), in the
Jewish language

TONGUES
3956 lâshôwn (9), *tongue*
1100 glōssa (26), *tongue*
2084 hĕtĕrŏglōssŏs (1),
foreigner

TOOK
270 'âchaz (6), to *seize*
622 'âçaph (2), to *gather*
680 'âtsal (1), to *select*
935 bôw' (1), to *go, come*
1197 bâ'ar (1), to be
brutish, be senseless
1491 gâzâh (1), to *cut off*
1497 gâzal (1), to *rob*
1518 gîyach (1), to *issue*
forth; to *burst forth*
2388 châzaq (4), to
fasten upon; to seize
3318 yâtsâ' (1), to *bring*
out
3381 yârad (4), to
descend
3920 lâkad (43), to *catch*
3947 lâqach (359), to *take*
4185 mûwsh (1), to
withdraw
5265 nâça' (2), to *start*
5267 nᵉçaq (Ch.) (1), to
go up
5312 nᵉphaq (Ch.) (2), to
issue forth; to bring out
5375 nâsâ' (45), to *lift up*
5384 nâsheh (1),
rheumatic or crippled
5414 nâthan (1), to *give*
5493 çûwr (11), to *turn off*
5674 'âbar (2), to *cross*
over; to *transition*
5709 'ădâ' (Ch.) (1), to
remove
5927 'âlâh (3), to *ascend*
6901 qâbal (3), to *take*
6902 qᵉbal (Ch.) (1), to
acquire
7287 râdâh (1), to
subjugate; to crumble
7311 rûwm (2), to be
high; to rise or raise

English

TOOKEST
7673 shâbath (1), to
repose; to desist
7760 sûwm (1), to *put*
8610 tâphas (18), to
manipulate, i.e. *seize*
142 airō (18), to *take up*
337 anairĕō (1), to *take
away,* i.e. *abolish*
353 analambanō (3), to
take up, bring up
520 apagō (1), to *take
away*
589 apŏdēmĕō (2), *visit a
foreign land*
618 apŏlambanō (1), to
receive; be repaid
643 apŏskĕuazō (1), to
pack up baggage
657 apŏtassŏmai (1), to
say adieu; to renounce
941 bastazō (1), to *lift*
1011 bŏulĕuō (1), to
deliberate; to resolve
1209 dĕchŏmai (2), to
receive, welcome
1453 ĕgĕirō (1), to *waken*
1544 ĕkballō (1), to
throw out
1562 ĕkduō (2), to *divest*
1723 ĕnagkalizŏmai (1),
take into one's arms
1921 ĕpiginōskō (1), to
acknowledge
1949 ĕpilambanŏmai
(12), to *seize*
1959 ĕpimĕlĕŏmai (1), to
care for
2021 ĕpichĕirĕō (1), to
undertake, try
2192 ĕchō (1), to *have*
2507 kathairĕō (3), to
lower, or demolish
2902 kratĕō (11), to *seize*
2983 lambanō (57), to
take, receive
3348 mĕtĕchō (1), to
share or participate
3830 pandŏchĕus (1),
innkeeper
3880 paralambanō (16),
to *associate with*
4084 piazō (1), to *seize*
4160 pŏiĕō (1), to *make*
4327 prŏsdĕchŏmai (1),
to *receive; to await for*
4355 prŏslambanō (5), to
take along
4815 sullambanō (3), to
seize (arrest, capture)
4823 sumbŏulĕuō (2), to
recommend, deliberate
4838 sumparalambanō
(2), to *take along with*
4863 sunagō (3), to
gather together

TOOKEST
3947 lâqach (1), to *take*

TOOL
2719 chereb (1), *knife*
3627 kᵉlîy (1), *thing*

TOOTH
8127 shên (6), *tooth*
3599 ŏdŏus (1), *tooth*

TOOTH'S
8127 shên (1), *tooth*

TOP
1406 gâg (8), *roof; top*

1634 gerem (1), *bone; self*
5585 çâˈîyph (2), *bough*
6706 tsᵉchîyach (4),
exposed to the sun
6788 tsammereth (3),
foliage
6936 qodqôd (2), *crown*
7218 rô'sh (67), *head*
206 akrŏn (1), *extremity*
509 anōthĕn (3), *from
above; from the first*

TOPAZ
6357 piṭdâh (4), *topaz*
5116 tŏpazion (1), *topaz*

TOPHEL
8603 Tôphel (1),
quagmire

TOPHET
8612 Tôpheth (8), *smiting*
8613 Tophteh (1), place
of *cremation*

TOPHETH
8612 Tôpheth (1), *smiting*

TOPS
1406 gâg (2), *roof; top*
5585 çâˈîyph (1), *bough*
7218 rô'sh (8), *head*

TORCH
3940 lappîyd (1), *torch*

TORCHES
3940 lappîyd (1), *torch*
6393 pᵉlâdâh (1), *iron
armature*
2985 lampas (1), *torch*

TORMENT
928 basanizō (3), to
torture, torment
929 basanismŏs (6),
torture, agony
931 basanŏs (1), *torture*
2851 kŏlasis (1),
infliction, punishment

TORMENTED
928 basanizō (5), to
torture, torment
2558 kakŏuchĕō (1), to
maltreat; to torment
3600 ŏdunaō (2), to *grieve*

TORMENTORS
930 basanistēs (1),
torturer

TORMENTS
931 basanŏs (2), *torture*

TORN
1497 gâzal (1), to *rob*
2963 ṭâraph (4), to *pluck*
2966 ṭᵉrêphâh (8), *torn
prey*
5478 çûwchâh (1), *filth*
7665 shâbar (2), to *burst*
4682 sparassō (1), to
convulse with epilepsy

TORTOISE
6632 tsâb (1), *lizard*

TORTURED
5178 tumpanizō (1), to
beat to death

TOSS
1607 gâˈash (1), to
agitate violently, *shake*
6802 tsᵉnêphâh (1), *ball*

TOSSED
5086 nâdaph (1), to
disperse, be windblown

5287 nâˈar (1), to *tumble*
928 basanizō (1), to
torture, torment
2831 kludōnizŏmai (1),
to *fluctuate on waves*
4494 rhipizō (1), to *be
tossed about*
5492 chĕimazō (1), to *be
battered in a storm*

TOSSINGS
5076 nâdûd (1), *tossing*
and *rolling* on the bed

TOTTERING
1760 dâchâh (1), to *totter*

TOU
8583 Tôˈûw (2), *error*

TOUCH
5060 nâga' (31), to *strike*
680 haptŏmai (13), to
touch
2345 thigganō (2), to
touch
4379 prŏspsauō (1), to
lay a finger on

TOUCHED
5060 nâga' (24), to *strike*
5401 nâshaq (1), to *touch*
680 haptŏmai (21), to
touch
2609 katagō (1), to *lead
down; to moor a vessel*
4834 sumpathĕō (1), to
commiserate
5584 psēlaphaō (1), to
manipulate

TOUCHETH
5060 nâga' (37), to *strike*
7306 rûwach (1), to *smell*
680 haptŏmai (2), to
touch

TOUCHING
413 'êl (3), *to, toward*
5921 'al (1), *against*
1909 ĕpi (2), *on, upon*
2596 kata (3), *down;
according to*
4012 pĕri (11), *about*

TOW
5296 nᵉˈôreth (2), *tow*
6594 pishtâh (1), *flax*

TOWEL
3012 lĕntiŏn (2), *linen*

TOWER
969 bâchôwn (1), *assayer*
1431 gâdal (1), to *be
great, make great*
4024 Migdôwl (2), *tower*
4026 migdâl (34), *tower*
4692 mâtsôwr (1),
siege-mound; distress
4869 misgâb (2), *refuge*
6076 'ôphel (1), *fortress*
4444 purgŏs (4), *tower*

TOWERS
971 bachîyn (1),
siege-tower
975 bachan (1),
watch-tower
4026 migdâl (13), *tower*
6438 pinnâh (2), *pinnacle*

TOWN
5892 'îyr (3), *city, town*
7023 qîyr (2), *wall*
2968 kōmē (8), *town*

TOWNCLERK
1122 grammatĕus (1),
secretary, scholar

TOWNS
1323 bath (27), *outlying*
village
2333 chavvâh (4), *village*
2691 châtsêr (1), *village*
5892 'îyr (3), *city, town*
6519 pᵉrâzâh (1), *rural*
2968 kōmē (3), town
2969 kōmŏpŏlis (1),
unwalled city

TRACHONITIS
5139 Trachōnitis (1),
rough district

TRADE
582 'ĕnôwsh (2), *man;
person, human*
5503 çâchar (2), to *travel*
2038 ĕrgazŏmai (1), to
toil

TRADED
5414 nâthan (4), to *give*
2038 ĕrgazŏmai (1), to
toil

TRADING
1281 diapragmatĕuŏmai
(1), to *earn, make gain*

TRADITION
3862 paradŏsis (11),
Jewish *traditionary law*

TRADITIONS
3862 paradŏsis (2),
Jewish *traditionary law*

TRAFFICK
3667 Kᵉna'an (1),
humiliated
4536 miçchâr (1), *trade*
5503 çâchar (1), to *travel
round; to palpitate*
7404 rᵉkullâh (2),
peddled trade

TRAFFICKERS
3669 Kᵉna'ănîy (1),
Kenaanite; pedlar

TRAIN
2428 chayil (1), *army;
wealth; virtue; valor*
2596 chânak (1), to
initiate or discipline
7757 shûwl (1), *skirt*

TRAINED
2593 chânîyk (1), *trained*

TRAITOR
4273 prŏdŏtēs (1),
betraying

TRAITORS
4273 prŏdŏtēs (1),
betraying

TRAMPLE
7429 râmaç (2), to *tread*
2662 katapatĕō (1), to
trample down; to reject

TRANCE
1611 ĕkstasis (3),
bewilderment, ecstasy

TRANQUILITY
7963 shᵉlêvâh (Ch.) (1),
safety

TRANSFERRED
3345 mĕtaschēmatizō
(1), to *transfigure*

TRANSFIGURED
3339 mĕtamŏrphŏō (2), to *transform*

TRANSFORMED
3339 mĕtamŏrphŏō (1), to *transform*
3345 mĕtaschēmatizō (2), to *transfigure*

TRANSFORMING
3345 mĕtaschēmatizō (1), to *transfigure*

TRANSGRESS
898 bâgad (1), to *act treacherously*
4603 mâ'al (2), to *act treacherously*
5647 'âbad (1), to *do*
5674 'âbar (4), to *cross*
6586 pâsha' (3), to *break away from authority*
3845 parabainō (2), to *violate a command*
3848 parabatēs (1), *violator, lawbreaker*

TRANSGRESSED
898 bâgad (1), to *act treacherously*
4603 mâ'al (7), to *act treacherously*
5674 'âbar (12), to *cross*
6586 pâsha (13), to *break from authority*
3928 parĕrchŏmai (1), to *go by; to perish*

TRANSGRESSEST
5674 'âbar (1), to *cross*

TRANSGRESSETH
898 bâgad (1), to *act treacherously*
4603 mâ'al (1), to *act treacherously*
458+4160 anŏmia (1), *violation of law*
3845 parabainō (1), to *violate a command*

TRANSGRESSING
5674 'âbar (1), to *cross*
6586 pâsha' (1), to *break away from authority*

TRANSGRESSION
4604 ma'al (6), *treachery*
6586 pâsha' (1), to *break away from authority*
6588 pesha' (38), *revolt*
458 anŏmia (1), *violation of law, wickedness*
3845 parabainō (1), to *violate a command*
3847 parabasis (4), *violation, breaking*

TRANSGRESSIONS
6588 pesha' (46), *revolt*
3847 parabasis (2), *violation, breaking*

TRANSGRESSOR
898 bâgad (2), to *act treacherously*
6586 pâsha' (1), to *break away from authority*
3848 parabatēs (2), *violator, lawbreaker*

TRANSGRESSORS
898 bâgad (8), to *act treacherously*
5674 'âbar (1), to *cross*

6586 pâsha' (8), to *break away from authority*
459 anŏmŏs (2), *without Jewish law*
3848 parabatēs (1), *violator, lawbreaker*

TRANSLATE
5674 'âbar (1), to *cross*

TRANSLATED
3179 mĕthistēmi (1), to *move*
3346 mĕtatithēmi (2), to *transport; to exchange*

TRANSLATION
3331 mĕtathĕsis (1), *transferral* to heaven

TRANSPARENT
1307 diaphanēs (1), *appearing through*

TRAP
4170 môwqêsh (1), *noose*
4434 malkôdeth (1), *snare*
4889 mashchîyth (1), *bird snare; corruption*
2339 thēra (1), *hunting*

TRAPS
4170 môwqêsh (1), *noose*

TRAVAIL
2342 chûwl (2), to *dance, whirl; to writhe in pain*
2470 châlâh (1), to *be weak, sick, afflicted*
3205 yâlad (11), to *bear young; to father a child*
5999 'âmâl (3), *worry*
6045 'inyân (6), *labor; affair, care*
8513 tᵉlâ'âh (1), *distress*
3449 mŏchthŏs (2), *sadness*
5088 tiktō (1), to *produce from seed*
5604 ōdin (1), *pang*
5605 ōdinō (1), to *experience labor pains*

TRAVAILED
2342 chûwl (2), to *dance, whirl; to writhe in pain*
3205 yâlad (3), to *bear young; to father a child*

TRAVAILEST
5605 ōdinō (1), to *experience labor pains*

TRAVAILETH
2254 châbal (1), to *writhe in labor pain*
2342 chûwl (1), to *writhe in pain; to wait*
3205 yâlad (4), to *bear young; to father a child*
4944 sunōdinō (1), to *sympathize*

TRAVAILING
3205 yâlad (2), to *bear young; to father a child*
5605 ōdinō (1), to *experience labor pains*

TRAVEL
8513 tᵉlâ'âh (2), *distress*
4898 sunĕkdēmŏs (2), *fellow-traveller*

TRAVELERS
1980+5410 hâlak (1), to *walk*

TRAVELLED
1330 diĕrchŏmai (1), to *traverse, travel through*

TRAVELLER
734 'ôrach (1), *road*
1982 hêlek (1), *wayfarer*

TRAVELLETH
1980 hâlak (2), to *walk*

TRAVELLING
736 'ôrᵉchâh (1), *caravan*
6808 tsâ'âh (1), to *tip over; to depopulate*
589 apŏdēmĕō (1), *visit a foreign land*

TRAVERSING
8308 sârak (1), to *interlace*

TREACHEROUS
898 bâgad (6), to *act treacherously*
900 bôgᵉdôwth (1), *treachery*
901 bâgôwd (2), *treacherous*

TREACHEROUSLY
898 bâgad (23), to *act treacherously*

TREACHERY
4820 mirmâh (1), *fraud*

TREAD
947 bûwç (6), to *trample*
1758 dûwsh (1), to *trample or thresh*
1759 dûwsh (Ch.) (1), to *trample; destroy*
1869 dârak (14), to *tread*
1915 hâdak (1), to *crush*
6072 'âçaç (1), to *trample*
7429 râmaç (6), to *tread*
7760+4823 sûwm (1), to *put, place*
3961 patĕō (2), to *trample*

TREADER
1869 dârak (1), to *tread*

TREADERS
1869 dârak (1), to *tread*

TREADETH
1758 dûwsh (1), to *trample or thresh*
1869 dârak (4), to *tread*
7429 râmaç (2), to *tread*
248 alôaō (2), to *tread out grain*
3961 patĕō (1), to *trample*

TREADING
1318 bâshaç (1), to *trample down*
1869 dârak (1), to *tread*
4001 mᵉbûwçâh (1), *trampling, oppression*
4823 mirmâç (1), *abasement*

TREASON
7195 qesher (5), *unlawful alliance*

TREASURE
214 'ôwtsâr (11), *depository*
1596 gᵉnaz (Ch.) (2), *treasury storeroom*
2633 chôçen (2), *wealth*
4301 maṭmôwn (1), *secret storehouse*

TREASURED
686 'âtsar (1), to *store up*

TREASURER
1489 gizbâr (1), *treasurer*
5532 çâkan (1), to *minister to*

TREASURERS
686 'âtsar (1), to *store up*
1411 gᵉdâbâr (Ch.) (2), *treasurer*
1490 gizbâr (Ch.) (1), *treasurer*

TREASURES
214 'ôwtsâr (50), *depository*
1596 gᵉnaz (Ch.) (1), *treasury storeroom*
4301 maṭmôwn (1), *secret storehouse*
4362 mikman (1), *hidden-treasure*
6259 'âthûwd (1), *prepared*
8226 sâphan (1), to *conceal*
2344 thēsaurŏs (5), *wealth, what is stored*

TREASUREST
2343 thēsaurizō (1), to *amass or reserve*

TREASURIES
214 'ôwtsâr (7), *depository*
1595 genez (2), *treasury coffer*
1597 ginzak (1), *treasury storeroom*

TREASURY
214 'ôwtsâr (3), *depository*
1049 gazŏphulakiŏn (5), *treasure-house*
2878 kŏrban (1), *votive offering or gift*

TREATISE
3056 lŏgŏs (1), *word*

TREE
363 'îylân (Ch.) (6), *tree*
815 'êshel (2), *tamarisk*
6086 'êts (88), *wood*
65 agriĕlaiŏs (2), *wild olive* tree
1186 dĕndrŏn (17), *tree*
2565 kalliĕlaiŏs (1), *cultivated olive*
3586 xulŏn (10), *timber*
4808 sukē (16), *fig-tree*
4809 sukŏmŏraia (1), *sycamore-fig tree*

TREES
352 'ayil (2), *oak tree*
6086 'êts (77), *wood*
6097 'êtsâh (1), *timber*
1186 dĕndrŏn (9), *tree*

TREMBLE
2111 zûwa' (1), to *tremble*
2112 zûwa' (Ch.) (1), to *shake with fear*

4543 miçkᵉnâh (1), *storage-magazine*
1047 gaza (1), *treasure*
2343 thēsaurizō (2), to *amass or reserve*
2344 thēsaurŏs (13), *wealth, what is stored*

TREMBLED
2342 chûwl (2), to *writhe*
2648 châphaz (1), to *hasten away, to fear*
2729 chârad (6), to *shudder* with terror
2730 chârêd (2), *fearful*
6426 pâlats (1), to *quiver*
7264 râgaz (9), to *quiver*
7322 rûwph (1), to *quake*
7493 râ'ash (4), to *quake*
5425 phrissō (1), to *shudder* in *fear*

TREMBLED
2112 zûwa' (Ch.) (1), to *shake* with fear
2342 chûwl (2), to *writhe*
2729 chârad (5), to *shudder* with terror
2730 chârêd (2), *fearful*
7264 râgaz (2), to *quiver*
7364 râchats (1), to *bathe*
7493 râ'ash (5), to *quake*
1719+1096 ĕmphŏbŏs (1), *alarmed, terrified*
1790+1096 ĕntrŏmŏs (1), *terrified*
2192+5156 ĕchō (1), to *have; hold; keep*

TREMBLETH
2729 chârad (1), to *shudder* with terror
2730 chârêd (1), *fearful*
5568 çâmar (1), to *bristle*
7460 râ'ad (1), to *shudder*

TREMBLING
2729 chârad (1), to *shudder* with terror
2731 chărâdâh (4), *fear*
6427 pallâtsûwth (1), *trembling fear*
7268 raggâz (1), *timid*
7269 rogzâh (1), *trepidation*
7460 râ'ad (6), to *shudder* violently
7478 ra'al (1), *reeling*
7578 rᵉthêth (1), *terror*
8653 tar'êlâh (2), *reeling*
1096+1790 ginŏmai (1), to *be, become*
5141 trĕmō (3), to *tremble*
5156 trŏmŏs (4), *quaking* with *fear*

TRENCH
2426 chêyl (1), *entrenchment*
4570 ma'gâl (3), circular *track* or camp *rampart*
8565 tan (2), *jackal*
8585 tᵉâlâh (1), irrigation *channel*
5482 charax (1), *rampart*

TRESPASS
816 'âsham (2), to *be guilty; to be punished*
817 'âshâm (41), *guilt*
819 'ashmâh (11), *guiltiness*
2398 châṭâ' (1), to *sin*
4603 mâ'al (1), to *act treacherously*
4604 ma'al (18), *sinful treachery*
6588 pesha' (5), *revolt*
264 hamartanō (3), to *sin*

TRESPASSED
816 'âsham (2), to *be guilty; to be punished*
819 'ashmâh (1), *guiltiness*
4603 mâ'al (8), to *act treacherously*
4604 ma'al (3), *sinful treachery*

TRESPASSES
817 'âshâm (1), *guilt*
819 'ashmâh (1), *guiltiness*
4604 ma'al (1), *sinful treachery*
3900 paraptōma (9), *error; transgression*

TRESPASSING
819 'ashmâh (1), *guiltiness*
4603 mâ'al (1), to *act treacherously*

TRIAL
974 bâchan (1), to *test*
4531 maççâh (1), *testing*
1382 dŏkimē (1), *test*
1383 dŏkimiŏn (1), *testing; trustworthiness*
3984 pĕira (1), *attempt*

TRIBE
4294 maṭṭeh (160), *tribe*
7626 shêbeṭ (57), *clan*
5443 phulē (19), *clan*

TRIBES
4294 maṭṭeh (20), *tribe*
7625 shᵉbaṭ (Ch.) (1), *clan*
7626 shêbeṭ (84), *clan*
1429 dōdĕkaphulŏn (1), *twelve tribes*
5443 phulē (6), *clan*

TRIBULATION
6862 tsar (1), *trouble*
6869 tsârâh (2), *trouble*
2346 thlibō (1), to *trouble*
2347 thlipsis (18), *trouble*

TRIBULATIONS
6869 tsârâh (1), *trouble*
2347 thlipsis (3), *trouble*

TRIBUTARIES
4522 maç (4), *labor*

TRIBUTARY
4522 maç (1), *labor*

TRIBUTE
1093 bᵉlôw (Ch.) (3), *tax*
4060 middâh (1), *tribute*
4061 middâh (Ch.) (1), *tribute*
4371 mekeç (6), *assessment*, census-tax
4522 maç (12), *labor*
4530 miççâh (1), *liberally*
4853 massâ' (1), *burden*
6066 'ônesh (1), *fine*
1323 didrachmŏn (2), *double drachma*
2778 kēnsŏs (4), *enrollment*
5411 phŏrŏs (4), *tax, toll*

TRICKLETH
5064 nâgar (1), to *pour out; to deliver over*

TRIED
974 bâchan (4), to *test; to investigate*
976 bôchan (1), *trial*

TRESPASSED *(column 2 continues)*
6884 tsâraph (7), to *refine*
1381 dŏkimazō (1), to *test; to approve*
1384 dŏkimŏs (1), *acceptable, approved*
3985 pĕirazō (3), to *endeavor, scrutinize*
4448 purŏō (1), to *be ignited, glow*

TRIEST
974 bâchan (3), to *test*

TRIETH
974 bâchan (4), to *test; to investigate*
1381 dŏkimazō (1), to *test; to approve*

TRIMMED
6213 'âsâh (1), to *do*
2885 kŏsmĕō (1), to *snuff*

TRIMMEST
3190 yâṭab (1), to *be, make well*

TRIUMPH
5937 'âlaz (2), to *jump* for joy
5970 'âlats (1), to *jump* for joy
7321 rûwa' (3), to *shout*
7440 rinnâh (1), *shout*
7442 rânan (1), to *shout* for joy
7623 shâbach (1), to *address in a loud tone; to pacify*
2358 thriambĕuō (1), to *give victory, lead in triumphal procession*

TRIUMPHED
1342 gâ'âh (2), to *be exalted*

TRIUMPHING
7445 rᵉnânâh (1), *shout* for joy
2358 thriambĕuō (1), to *give victory, lead in triumphal procession*

TROAS
5174 Trōas (6), *plain of Troy*

TRODDEN
947 bûwç (3), to *trample*
1758 dûwsh (2), to *trample* or *thresh*
1869 dârak (7), to *tread*
4001 mᵉbûwçâh (2), *trampling, oppression*
4823 mirmâç (4), *abasement*
5541 çâlâh (2), to *contemn, reject*
7429 râmaç (2), to *tread*
2662 katapatĕō (3), to *trample down; to reject*
3961 patĕō (2), to *trample*

TRODE
1869 dârak (2), to *tread*
7429 râmaç (5), to *tread*
2662 katapatĕō (1), to *trample down; to reject*

TROGYLLIUM
5175 Trŏgulliŏn (1), *Trogyllium*

TROOP
92 'ăguddâh (2), *band*
1409 gâd (2), *fortune*

TROOP *(column 4)*
1416 gᵉdûwd (7), *band*
2416 chay (2), *alive; raw*

TROOPS
734 'ôrach (1), *road*
1416 gᵉdûwd (3), *band*

TROPHIMUS
5161 Trŏphimŏs (3), *nutritive*

TROUBLE
926 bâhal (2), to *tremble*
927 bᵉhal (Ch.) (2), to *terrify; hasten*
928 behâlâh (2), *sudden panic, destruction*
1091 ballâhâh (1), *sudden destruction*
1205 bᵉ'âthâh (2), *fear*
1804 dâlach (1), to *roil* water, *churn up*
2189 za'ăvâh (1), *agitation*
2960 ṭôrach (1), *burden*
4103 mᵉhûwmâh (4), *confusion or uproar*
5916 'âkar (4), to *disturb*
5999 'âmâl (3), *worry*
6040 'ŏnîy (3), *misery*
6862 tsar (17), *trouble*
6869 tsârâh (34), *trouble*
6887 tsârar (6), to *cramp*
7186+3117 qâsheh (1), *severe*
7267 rôgez (2), *disquiet*
7451 ra' (9), *bad; evil*
7561 râsha' (1), to *be, do, declare wrong*
8513 tᵉlâ'âh (1), *distress*
387 anastatŏō (1), to *disturb, cause trouble*
1613 ĕktarassō (1), to *disturb wholly*
1776 ĕnŏchlĕō (1), to *annoy, cause trouble*
2346 thlibō (1), to *trouble*
2347 thlipsis (3), *trouble*
2350 thŏrubĕō (1), to *disturb; clamor*
2553 kakŏpathĕō (1), to *undergo hardship*
2873 kŏpŏs (1), *toil; pains*
2873+3930 kŏpŏs (2), *toil*
3926 parĕnŏchlĕō (1), to *annoy, make trouble*
3930 parĕchō (1), to *hold near, i.e. to present*
4660 skullŏ (2), to *harass*
5015 tarassō (1), to *trouble, disturb*

TROUBLED
926 bâhal (12), to *tremble*
927 bᵉhal (Ch.) (6), to *terrify; hasten*
1089 bâlahh (1), to *terrify*
1204 bâ'ath (1), to *fear, be afraid*
1607 gâ'ash (1), to *agitate* violently, *shake*
1644 gârash (1), to *drive out; to divorce*
1993 hâmâh (2), to *be in great commotion*
2000 hâmam (1), to *put in commotion*
2560 châmar (3), to *ferment, foam*
5590 çâ'ar (1), to *rush upon; to toss about*

5753 'âvâh (1), to *be crooked*
5916 'âkar (4), to *disturb*
6031 'ânâh (1), to *afflict*
6470 pâ'am (4), to *impel or agitate*
7114 qâtsar (1), to *curtail, cut short*
7264 râgaz (3), to *quiver*
7481 râ'am (1), to *crash thunder; to irritate*
7515 râphas (1), to *trample*, i.e. *roil* water
1298 diatarassō (1), to disturb wholly
2346 thlibō (3), to crowd, press, trouble
2360 thrŏĕō (3), to frighten, be alarmed
5015 tarassō (14), to trouble, disturb
5015+1438 tarassō (1), to trouble, disturb
5182 turbazō (1), to make turbid

TROUBLEDST
1804 dâlach (1), to *roil* water, *churn up*

TROUBLER
5916 'âkar (1), to *disturb* or *afflict*

TROUBLES
6869 tsârâh (10), *trouble*
7451 ra' (1), *bad; evil*
5016 tarachē (1), mob disturbance; roiling

TROUBLEST
4660 skullō (1), to harass

TROUBLETH
598 'ânaç (Ch.) (1), to *distress*
926 bâhal (2), to *tremble*
1204 bâ'ath (1), to *fear, be afraid*
5916 'âkar (4), to *disturb*
3930+2873 parĕchō (1), to *hold near*
5015 tarassō (1), to trouble, disturb

TROUBLING
7267 rôgez (1), *disquiet; anger*
5015 tarassō (1), to trouble, disturb

TROUBLOUS
5916 'âkar (1), to *disturb* or *afflict*

TROUGH
8268 shôqeth (1), *watering-trough*

TROUGHS
7298 rahaṭ (1), *ringlet* of hair
8268 shôqeth (1), *watering-trough*

TROW
1380 dŏkĕō (1), to think, regard, seem good

TRUCEBREAKERS
786 aspŏndŏs (1), not reconcilable

TRUE
551 'omnâm (1), *verily, indeed, truly*

571 'emeth (18), *truth, trustworthiness*
3330 yatstsîyb (Ch.) (2), *fixed, sure*
3651 kên (5), *just; right*
6656 tsᵉdâ' (Ch.) (1), (*sinister*) *design*
227 alēthēs (22), true; genuine
228 alēthinŏs (27), truthful
1103 gnēsiŏs (1), genuine, true
2227 zōŏpŏiĕō (1), to (re-) vitalize, give life
3588+225 hŏ (1), "the," i.e. the definite article
4103 pistŏs (2), trustworthy; reliable

TRULY
199 'ûwlâm (4), *however*
389 'ak (3), *surely; only*
403 'âkên (2), *truly!*
530 'ĕmûwnâh (1), *fidelity; steadiness*
551 'omnâm (1), *truly*
571 'emeth (8), *certainty, truth, trustworthiness*
577 'ânnâ' (1), *oh now!*
3588 kîy (1), *for, that*
227 alēthēs (1), true
230 alēthōs (2), truly
686 ara (1), then, so
1161 dĕ (1), but, yet
1909+225 ĕpi (1), on, upon
3303 mĕn (12), truly

TRUMP
2689 châtsôtsᵉrâh (1), *trumpet*
7782 shôwphâr (1), *curved ram's horn*
4536 salpigx (2), trumpet

TRUMPET
3104 yôwbêl (1), *blast of a ram's horn*
7782 shôwphâr (47), *curved ram's horn*
8628 tâqa' (1), to *clatter, slap, drive, clasp*
4536 salpigx (7), trumpet
4537 salpizō (1), to sound a trumpet blast

TRUMPETERS
2689 châtsôtsᵉrâh (2), *trumpet*
2690 châtsar (1), to *blow* the *trumpet*
4538 salpistēs (1), trumpeter

TRUMPETS
2689 châtsôtsᵉrâh (24), *trumpet*
7782 shôwphâr (20), *curved ram's horn*
4536 salpigx (2), trumpet

TRUST
539 'âman (4), to *be firm, faithful, true; to trust*
982 bâṭach (61), to *trust, be confident or sure*
2342 chûwl (1), to *wait; to pervert*
2620 châçâh (32), to *confide in*
2622 châçûwth (1), *confidence*

3176 yâchal (2), to *wait; to be patient, hope*
4004 mibchôwr (1), *select*, i.e. *well fortified*
4009 mibṭâch (3), *security; assurance*
4268 machâçeh (1), *shelter; refuge*
1679 ĕlpizō (15), to confide, hope for
3892 paranŏmia (1), wrongdoing
3982 pĕithō (6), to rely by inward certainty
4006 pĕpŏithēsis (1), reliance, trust
4100 pistĕuō (3), to have faith, credit; to entrust

TRUSTED
539 'âman (1), to *trust*, to *be permanent*
982 bâṭach (18), to *trust, be confident or sure*
1556 gâlal (1), to *roll; to commit*
2620 châçâh (1), to *confide in*
7365 rᵉchats (Ch.) (1), to *attend upon, trust*
1679 ĕlpizō (2), to expect or confide, hope for
3982 pĕithō (3), to rely by inward certainty
4276 prŏĕlpizō (1), to hope in advance

TRUSTEDST
982 bâṭach (3), to *trust, be confident or sure*

TRUSTEST
982 bâṭach (6), to *trust, be confident or sure*

TRUSTETH
982 bâṭach (14), to *trust, be confident or sure*
2620 châçâh (2), to *confide in*
1679 ĕlpizō (1), to expect or confide, hope for

TRUSTING
982 bâṭach (1), to *trust, be confident or sure*

TRUSTY
539 'âman (1), to *be firm, faithful, true; to trust*

TRUTH
518+3808 'îm (1), *if, although; Oh that!*
529 'êmûwn (1), *trustworthiness; faithful*
530 'ĕmûwnâh (13), *fidelity; steadiness*
544 'ômen (1), *verity, faithfulness*
548 'ămânâh (2), *covenant*
551 'omnâm (3), *verily, indeed, truly*
571 'emeth (90), *certainty, truth*
3321 yᵉtsêb (Ch.) (1), to *speak surely*
3330 yatstsîyb (Ch.) (1), *fixed, sure*
3588+518 kîy (1), *for, that because*
7187 qᵉshôwṭ (Ch.) (2), *fidelity, truth*

7189 qôsheṭ (1), *reality*
225 alēthĕia (99), truth, truthfulness
226 alēthĕuō (8), to be true
227 alēthēs (1), true; genuine
230 alēthōs (7), truly, surely
3483 nai (1), yes
3689 ŏntōs (1), really, certainly

TRUTH'S
571 'emeth (1), *certainty, truth, trustworthiness*
225 alēthĕia (1), truth, truthfulness

TRY
974 bâchan (8), to *test; to investigate*
2713 châqar (1), to *examine, search*
5254 nâçâh (1), to *test, attempt*
6884 tsâraph (3), to *fuse* metal; to *refine*
1381 dŏkimazō (2), to test; to approve
3985 pĕirazō (1), to endeavor, scrutinize
4314+3986 prŏs (1), to, toward; against

TRYING
1383 dŏkimiŏn (1), testing; trustworthiness

TRYPHENA
5170 Truphaina (1), luxurious

TRYPHOSA
5173 Truphōsa (1), luxuriating

TUBAL
8422 Tûwbal (8), *Tubal*

TUBAL-CAIN
8423 Tûwbal Qayin (2), *offspring of Cain*

TUMBLED
2015 hâphak (1), to *change, overturn*

TUMULT
1993 hâmâh (1), to *be in great commotion*
1995 hâmôwn (4), *noise, tumult; many, crowd*
1999 hămullâh (1), *sound, roar, noise*
4103 mᵉhûwmâh (1), *confusion or uproar*
7588 shâ'ôwn (3), *uproar; destruction*
7600 sha'ănân (2), *secure; haughty*
2351 thŏrubŏs (4), disturbance

TUMULTS
4103 mᵉhûwmâh (1), *confusion or uproar*
181 akatastasia (2), disorder, riot

TUMULTUOUS
1121+7588 bên (1), *son, descendant; people*
1993 hâmâh (1), to *be in great commotion*

English

7588 shâ'ôwn (1), *uproar; destruction*

TURN
2015 hâphak (7), *to turn; to change, overturn*
2186 zânach (1), *to reject, forsake, fail*
5186 nâṭâh (17), *to stretch* or spread out
5414 nâthan (1), *to give*
5437 çâbab (14), *to surround*
5493 çûwr (27), *to turn* off
5627 çârâh (1), *apostasy; crime; remission*
5674 'âbar (2), *to cross over; to transition*
6437 pânâh (18), *to turn, to face*
6801 tsânaph (1), *to wrap*, i.e. *roll* or *dress*
7725 shûwb (152), *to turn back; to return*
7750 sûwṭ (2), *become derelict*
7760 sûwm (1), *to put, place*
7847 sâṭâh (1), *to deviate from duty, go astray*
8159 shâ'âh (1), *to inspect, consider*
8447 tôwr (2), *string or order*
344 anakamptō (1), *to turn back, come back*
576 apŏbainō (2), *to disembark*
654 apŏstrĕphō (5), *to turn away or back*
665 apŏtrĕpō (1), *to deflect, avoid*
1294 diastrĕphō (1), *to be morally corrupt*
1994 ĕpistrĕphō (10), *to revert, turn back to*
3329 mĕtagō (1), *to turn*
4762 strĕphō (4), *to turn* or *reverse* a course

TURNED
1750 dûwts (1), *to leap*
2015 hâphak (53), *to turn; to change*
3399 yâraṭ (1), *to be rash*
3943 lâphath (2), *to turn around or aside*
5186 nâṭâh (16), *to stretch* or spread out
5253 nâçag (1), *to retreat*
5414 nâthan (1), *to give*
5437 çâbab (31), *to surround*
5472 çûwg (10), *to go back, to retreat*
5493 çûwr (24), *to turn* off
6437 pânâh (36), *to turn, to face*
7725 shûwb (67), *to turn back; to return*
7734 sûwg (1), *to retreat*
7760 sûwm (1), *to put, place*
387 anastatŏō (1), *to disturb, cause trouble*
402 anachōrĕō (1), *to retire, withdraw*
654 apŏstrĕphō (2), *to turn away or back*
1096 ginŏmai (1), *to be, become*

1624 ĕktrĕpō (1), *to turn away*
1824 ĕxautēs (2), *instantly, at once*
1994 ĕpistrĕphō (11), *to revert, turn back to*
2827 klinō (1), *to slant or slope*
3179 mĕthistēmi (1), *to move*
3329 mĕtagō (1), *to turn*
3344 mĕtastrĕphō (1), *to transmute; corrupt*
4672 Sŏlŏmōn (1), *peaceful*
4762 strĕphō (12), *to turn* or *reverse* a course
5290 hupŏstrĕphō (2), *to turn under, behind*

TURNEST
6437 pânâh (1), *to turn, to face*
7725 shûwb (2), *to turn back; to return*

TURNETH
2015 hâphak (2), *to turn; to change, overturn*
5186 nâṭâh (2), *to stretch* or spread out
5437 çâbab (2), *to surround*
5493 çûwr (1), *to turn* off
5753 'âvâh (1), *to be crooked*
5791 'âvath (1), *to wrest, twist*
5844 'âṭâh (1), *to wrap*, i.e. *cover, veil, clothe*
6437 pânâh (4), *to turn, to face*
7725 shûwb (17), *to turn back; to return*
7760 sûwm (2), *to put, place*

TURNING
2015 hâphak (1), *to change, overturn*
2017 hôphek (1), *opposite-ness*
4142 mûwçabbâh (1), *transmutation*
4740 maqtsôwa' (5), *angle;* or *recess*
4878 mᵉshûwbâh (1), *apostasy*
7257 râbats (1), *to recline, repose, brood*
7725 shûwb (1), *to turn back; to return*
654 apŏstrĕphō (1), *to turn away or back*
1994 ĕpistrĕphō (2), *to revert, turn back to*
3346 mĕtatithēmi (1), *to transport; to exchange*
4762 strĕphō (1), *to turn* or *reverse* a course
5077 tĕphrŏō (1), *to incinerate*
5157 trŏpē (1), *turn*, i.e. *revolution (variation)*

TURTLE
8449 tôwr (2), *ring-dove*

TURTLEDOVE
8449 tôwr (3), *ring-dove*

TURTLEDOVES
8449 tôwr (6), *ring-dove*

5167 trugōn (1), *turtle-dove bird*

TURTLES
8449 tôwr (3), *ring-dove*

TUTORS
2012 ĕpitrŏpŏs (1), *manager, guardian*

TWAIN
8147 shᵉnayim (7), *two-fold*
1417 duŏ (10), *two*

TWELFTH
8147+6240 shᵉnayim (20), *two-fold*
1428 dōdĕkatŏs (1), *twelfth*

TWELVE
505 'eleph (1), *thousand*
8147 shᵉnayim (2), *two-fold*
8147+6240 shᵉnayim (107), *two-fold*
8648+6236 tᵉrêyn (Ch.) (2), *two*
1177 dĕkaduŏ (2), *twelve*
1427 dōdĕka (71), *twelve*
1429 dōdĕkaphulŏn (1), *twelve tribes*

TWENTIETH
6242 'esrîym (36), *twenty; twentieth*

TWENTY
6242 'esrîym (275), *twenty; twentieth*
6243 'esrîyn (Ch.) (1), *twenty; twentieth*
7239 ribbôw (3), *myriad, indefinite large number*
1501 ĕikŏsi (12), *twenty*

TWENTY'S
6242 'esrîym (1), *twenty; twentieth*

TWICE
4932 mishneh (3), *duplicate copy; double*
6471 pa'am (5), *time; step; occurence*
8147 shᵉnayim (5), *two-fold*
1364 dis (4), *twice*

TWIGS
3127 yôwneqeth (1), *sprout, new shoot*
3242 yᵉnîqâh (1), *sucker* or *sapling*

TWILIGHT
5399 nesheph (6), *dusk, dawn*
5939 'ălâṭâh (3), *dusk*

TWINED
7806 shâzar (21), *to twist a thread of straw*

TWINKLING
4493 rhipē (1), *instant*

TWINS
8380 tâ'ôwm (4), *twin, things doubled*
8382 tâ'am (2), *to be twinned*, i.e. *duplicate*

TWO
2677 chêtsîy (1), *half or middle, midst*
6471 pa'am (1), *time; step; occurence*

6771 tsâmê' (1), *thirsty*
8147 shᵉnayim (527), *two-fold*
8648 tᵉrêyn (Ch.) (1), *two*
296 amphŏdŏn (1), *fork in the road*
1250 diakŏsiŏi (7), *two hundred*
1332 diĕtēs (1), *of two years in age*
1333 diĕtia (2), *interval of two years*
1337 dithalassŏs (1), *having two seas*
1366 distŏmŏs (1), *double-edged*
1367 dischilïoi (1), *two thousand*
1417 duŏ (122), *two*

TWOEDGED
6310 peh (1), *mouth; opening*
6374 pîyphîyâh (1), *edge or tooth*
1366 distŏmŏs (2), *double-edged*

TWOFOLD
1366 distŏmŏs (1), *double-edged*

TYCHICUS
5190 Tuchikŏs (7), *fortunate*

TYRANNUS
5181 Turannŏs (1), *tyrant*

TYRE
6865 Tsôr (20), *rock*
6876 Tsŏrîy (5), *Tsorite*
5184 Turŏs (11), *rock*
5185 tuphlŏs (1), *blindness; blind person*

TYRUS
6865 Tsôr (22), *rock*

UCAL
401 'Ûkâl (1), *devoured*

UEL
177 'Ûw'êl (1), *wish of God*

ULAI
195 'Ûwlay (2), *Ulai* or *Eulus*

ULAM
198 'Ûwlâm (4), *solitary*

ULLA
5925 'Ullâ' (1), *burden*

UMMAH
5981 'Ummâh (1), *association*

UNACCUSTOMED
3808+3925 lô' (1), *no, not*

UNADVISEDLY
981 bâṭâ' (1), *to babble, speak rashly*

UNAWARES
1097+1847 bᵉlîy (1), *without, not yet*
3045 yâda' (1), *to know*
3820+3824 lêb (2), *heart*
7684 shᵉgâgâh (4), *mistake*
160 aiphnidiŏs (1), *suddenly*
2990 lanthanō (1), *to lie hid; unwittingly*

3920 *parĕisaktŏs* (1), *smuggled in, infiltrated*
3921 *parĕisdunō* (1), to *slip in secretly*

UNBELIEF
543 *apĕithĕia* (4), *disbelief*
570 *apistia* (12), *disbelief; disobedience*

UNBELIEVERS
571 *apistŏs* (4), *without faith; untrustworthy*

UNBELIEVING
544 *apĕithĕō* (1), to *disbelieve*
571 *apistŏs* (5), *without faith; untrustworthy*

UNBLAMEABLE
299 *amōmŏs* (2), *unblemished, blameless*

UNBLAMEABLY
274 *amĕmptŏs* (1), *faultlessly*

UNCERTAIN
82 *adēlŏs* (1), *indistinct, not clear*
83 *adēlŏtēs* (1), *uncertainty*

UNCERTAINLY
82 *adēlŏs* (1), *indistinct, not clear*

UNCHANGEABLE
531 *aparabatŏs* (1), *untransferable*

UNCIRCUMCISED
6189 *'ârĕl* (34), to *be uncircumcised*
6190 *'orlâh* (2), *prepuce or penile foreskin*
203+2192 *akrŏbustia* (1), *uncircumcised*
564 *apĕritmētŏs* (1), *uncircumcised*
1722+3588+203 *ĕn* (2), *in; during; because of*
1986 *ĕpispaŏmai* (1), to *efface the mark of circumcision*

UNCIRCUMCISION
203 *akrŏbustia* (16), *uncircumcised*

UNCLE
1730 *dôwd* (10), *beloved, friend; uncle, cousin*

UNCLE'S
1730 *dôwd* (1), *beloved, friend; uncle, cousin*
1733 *dôwdâh* (6), *aunt*

UNCLEAN
2930 *ţâmê'* (74), to *be morally contaminated*
2931 *ţâmê'* (78), *foul; ceremonially impure*
2932 *ţum'âh* (4), *ceremonial impurity*
5079 *niddâh* (2), *time of menstrual impurity*
6172 *'ervâh* (1), *nudity; disgrace; blemish*
6945 *qâdêsh* (1), *sacred male prostitute*
169 *akathartŏs* (28), *impure; evil*
2839 *kŏinŏs* (3), *common, i.e. profane*

2840 *kŏinŏō* (1), to *make profane*

UNCLEANNESS
2930 *ţâmê'* (1), to *be morally contaminated*
2932 *ţum'âh* (25), *ceremonial impurity*
5079 *niddâh* (1), *time of menstrual impurity*
6172 *'ervâh* (1), *nudity; disgrace; blemish*
7137 *qâreh* (1), *accidental occurrence*
167 *akatharsia* (10), *quality of impurity*
3394 *miasmŏs* (1), *act of moral contamination*

UNCLEANNESSES
2932 *ţum'âh* (1), *ceremonial impurity*

UNCLOTHED
1562 *ĕkduō* (1), to *divest*

UNCOMELY
807 *aschēmŏnĕō* (1), to *be, act unbecoming*
809 *aschēmōn* (1), *inelegant, indecent*

UNCONDEMNED
178 *akatakritŏs* (2), *without legal trial*

UNCORRUPTIBLE
862 *aphthartŏs* (1), *undecaying, immortal*

UNCORRUPTNESS
90 *adiaphthŏria* (1), *purity of doctrine*

UNCOVER
1540 *gâlâh* (22), to *denude; uncover*
6168 *'ârâh* (1), to *be, make bare; to empty*
6544 *pâra'* (3), to *loosen; to expose, dismiss*

UNCOVERED
1540 *gâlâh* (10), to *denude; uncover*
2834 *châsaph* (2), to *drain away or bail up*
6168 *'ârâh* (1), to *be, make bare; to empty*
177 *akatakaluptŏs* (2), *unveiled*
648 *apŏstĕgazō* (1), to *unroof, make a hole in a roof*

UNCOVERETH
1540 *gâlâh* (2), to *denude; uncover*
6168 *'ârâh* (1), to *be, make bare; to empty*

UNCTION
5545 *chrisma* (1), *special endowment of the Holy Spirit*

UNDEFILED
8535 *tâm* (2), *morally pious; gentle, dear*
8549 *tâmîym* (1), *entire, complete; integrity*
283 *amiantŏs* (4), *pure*

UNDER
413 *'êl* (2), *to, toward*
4295 *maţţâh* (1), *below or beneath*

5921 *'al* (9), *above, over, upon, or against*
8460 *t°chôwth* (Ch.) (4), *beneath, under*
8478 *tachath* (231), *bottom; underneath*
332 *anathĕmatizō* (2), to *declare or vow an oath*
506 *anupŏtaktŏs* (1), *independent*
1640 *ĕlassōn* (1), *smaller*
1722 *ĕn* (2), *in; during; because of*
1772 *ĕnnŏmŏs* (1), *legal, or subject to law*
1909 *ĕpi* (3), *on, upon*
2662 *katapatĕō* (2), to *trample down; to reject*
2709 *katachthŏniŏs* (1), *infernal*
2736 *katō* (1), *downwards*
5259 *hupŏ* (47), *under; by means of; at*
5270 *hupŏkatō* (8), *down under, i.e. beneath*
5273 *hupŏkritēs* (1), *dissembler, hypocrite*
5284 *hupŏplĕō* (2), to *sail under the lee of*
5293 *hupŏtassō* (4), to *subordinate; to obey*
5295 *hupŏtrĕchō* (1), to *run under*
5299 *hupōpiazō* (1), to *beat up; to wear out*

UNDERGIRDING
5269 *hupŏzŏnnumi* (1), to *gird under*

UNDERNEATH
4295 *maţţâh* (2), *below or beneath*
8478 *tachath* (1), *bottom; underneath; in lieu of*

UNDERSETTERS
3802 *kâthêph* (4), *shoulder-piece; wall*

UNDERSTAND
995 *bîyn* (44), to *understand; discern*
998 *bîynâh* (1), *understanding*
3045 *yâda'* (3), to *know*
7919 *sâkal* (9), to *be or act circumspect*
8085 *shâma'* (6), to *hear intelligently*
50 *agnŏĕō* (1), to *not know; not understand*
1097 *ginōskō* (3), to *know*
1107 *gnōrizō* (1), to *make known, reveal*
1492 *ĕidō* (1), to *know*
1987 *ĕpistamai* (1), to *comprehend*
3539 *nŏiĕō* (8), to *exercise the mind*
4920 *suniēmi* (13), to *comprehend*

UNDERSTANDEST
995 *bîyn* (2), to *understand; discern*
8085 *shâma'* (1), to *hear intelligently*
1097 *ginōskō* (1), to *know*

UNDERSTANDETH
995 *bîyn* (5), to *understand; discern*

7919 *sâkal* (1), to *be or act circumspect*
191 *akŏuō* (1), to *hear; obey*
1492 *ĕidō* (1), to *know*
4920 *suniēmi* (3), to *comprehend*

UNDERSTANDING
995 *bîyn* (33), to *understand; discern*
998 *bîynâh* (32), *understanding*
999 *bîynâh* (Ch.) (1), *understanding*
2940 *ţa'am* (1), *taste; intelligence; mandate*
3820 *lêb* (10), *heart*
3824 *lêbâb* (3), *heart*
4486 *manda'* (Ch.) (1), *wisdom or intelligence*
7306 *rûwach* (1), to *smell or perceive*
7919 *sâkal* (5), to *be or act circumspect*
7922 *sekel* (7), *intelligence; success*
7924 *sokl°thânûw* (Ch.) (3), *intelligence*
8085 *shâma'* (1), to *hear intelligently*
8394 *tâbûwn* (38), *intelligence; argument*
801 *asunĕtŏs* (3), *senseless, dull; wicked*
1271 *dianŏia* (3), *mind or thought*
3563 *nŏus* (7), *intellect, mind; understanding*
3877 *parakŏlouthĕō* (1), to *attend; trace out*
4907 *sunĕsis* (6), *understanding*
4920 *suniēmi* (2), to *understand*
5424 *phrēn* (2), *mind or cognitive faculties*

UNDERSTOOD
995 *bîyn* (11), to *understand; discern*
3045 *yâda'* (4), to *know*
7919 *sâkal* (2), to *be or act circumspect*
8085 *shâma'* (1), to *hear intelligently*
50 *agnŏĕō* (2), to *not know; not understand*
1097 *ginōskō* (4), to *know*
1425 *dusnŏētŏs* (1), *difficult of perception*
2154 *ĕusēmŏs* (1), *significant*
3129 *manthanō* (1), to *learn*
3539 *nŏiĕō* (1), to *exercise the mind*
4441 *punthanŏmai* (1), to *ask for information*
4920 *suniēmi* (7), to *understand*
5426 *phrŏnĕō* (1), to *be mentally disposed*

UNDERTAKE
6148 *'ârab* (1), to *intermix; to give or be security*

UNDERTOOK
6901 *qâbal* (1), to *admit; to take*

UNDO
5425 nâthar (1), to
terrify; shake off; untie
6213 'âsâh (1), to do or
make

UNDONE
6 'âbad (1), to perish;
destroy
1820 dâmâh (1), to be
silent; to fail, cease
5493 çûwr (1), to turn off

UNDRESSED
5139 nâzîyr (2), prince;
separated Nazirite

UNEQUAL
3808+8505 lô' (2), no, not

UNEQUALLY
2086 hĕtĕrŏzugĕō (1), to
associate discordantly

UNFAITHFUL
898 bâgad (1), to act
treacherously

UNFAITHFULLY
898 bâgad (1), to act
treacherously

UNFEIGNED
505 anupŏkritŏs (4),
sincere, genuine

UNFRUITFUL
175 akarpŏs (6), barren,
unfruitful

UNGIRDED
6605 pâthach (1), to open
wide; to loosen, begin

UNGODLINESS
763 asĕbĕia (4),
wickedness, impiety

UNGODLY
1100 bᵉlîya'al (4),
wickedness, trouble
3808+2623 lô' (1), no, not
5760 'ăvîyl (1), morally
perverse
7563 râshâ' (8), morally
wrong; bad person
763 asĕbĕia (3),
wickedness, impiety
764 asĕbĕō (2), to be, act
impious or wicked
765 asĕbĕs (8), impious
or wicked

UNHOLY
2455 chôl (1), profane,
common, not holy
462 anŏsiŏs (2), wicked,
unholy
2839 kŏinŏs (1),
common, i.e. profane

UNICORN
7214 rᵉ'êm (6), wild bull

UNICORNS
7214 rᵉ'êm (3), wild bull

UNITE
3161 yâchad (1), to be,
become one

UNITED
3161 yâchad (1), to be,
become one

UNITY
3162 yachad (1), unitedly
1775 hĕnŏtĕs (2),
unanimity, unity

UNJUST
205 'âven (1), trouble,
vanity, wickedness
5766 'evel (2), moral evil
5767 'avvâl (1), morally
evil
8636 tarbîyth (1),
percentage or bonus
91 adikĕō (1), to do
wrong
93 adikia (2),
wrongfulness
94 adikŏs (8), unjust,
wicked

UNJUSTLY
5765 'âval (1), to morally
distort
5766 'evel (1), moral evil

UNKNOWN
50 agnŏĕō (2), to not
know; not understand
57 agnŏstŏs (1), unknown

UNLADE
670 apŏphŏrtizŏmai (1),
to unload

UNLAWFUL
111 athĕmitŏs (1),
illegal; detestable
459 anŏmŏs (1), without
Jewish law

UNLEARNED
62 agrammatŏs (1),
illiterate, unschooled
261 amathēs (1),
ignorant
521 apaidĕutŏs (1),
stupid, uneducated
2399 idiŏtēs (3), not
initiated; untrained

UNLEAVENED
4682 matstsâh (51),
unfermented cake
106 azumŏs (9), made
without yeast; Passover

UNLESS
194 'ûwlay (1), if not;
perhaps
3884 lûwlê' (3), if not

UNLOOSE
3089 luŏ (3), to loosen

UNMARRIED
22 agamŏs (4),
unmarried

UNMERCIFUL
415 anĕlĕĕmōn (1),
merciless, ruthless

UNMINDFUL
7876 shâyah (1), to keep
in memory

UNMOVABLE
277 amĕtakinĕtŏs (1),
immovable

UNMOVEABLE
761 asalĕutŏs (1),
immovable, fixed

UNNI
6042 'Unnîy (3), afflicted

UNOCCUPIED
2308 châdal (1), to desist,
stop; be fat

UNPREPARED
532 aparaskĕuastŏs (1),
unready

UNPROFITABLE
5532 çâkan (1), to be
serviceable to
255 alusitĕlēs (1),
gainless, pernicious
512 anŏphĕlĕs (1), useless
888 achrĕiŏs (2), useless,
i.e. unmeritorious
889 achrĕiŏō (1), render
useless, i.e. spoil
890 achrēstŏs (1),
inefficient, detrimental

UNPROFITABLENESS
512 anŏphĕlĕs (1), useless

UNPUNISHED
5352 nâqâh (11), to be,
make clean; to be bare

UNQUENCHABLE
762 asbĕstŏs (2), not
extinguished

UNREASONABLE
249 alŏgŏs (1), irrational,
not reasonable
824 atŏpŏs (1), improper;
injurious; wicked

UNREBUKEABLE
423 anĕpilēptŏs (1), not
open to blame

UNREPROVEABLE
410 anĕgklētŏs (1),
irreproachable

UNRIGHTEOUS
205 'âven (2), trouble,
vanity, wickedness
2555 châmâç (1),
violence; malice
5765 'âval (1), to morally
distort
5767 'avvâl (1), morally
evil
94 adikŏs (4), unjust,
wicked

UNRIGHTEOUSLY
5766 'evel (1), moral evil

UNRIGHTEOUSNESS
3808+6664 lô' (1), no, not
5766 'evel (3), moral evil
93 adikia (16),
wrongfulness
458 anŏmia (1), violation
of law, wickedness

UNRIPE
1154 beçer (1),
immature, sour grapes

UNRULY
183 akataschĕtŏs (1),
unrestrainable
506 anupŏtaktŏs (2),
insubordinate
813 ataktŏs (1),
insubordinate

UNSATIABLE
1115+7654 biltîy (1), not,
except, without, unless

UNSAVOURY
6617 pâthal (1), to
struggle; to be tortuous
8602 tâphêl (1), to
plaster; be tasteless

UNSEARCHABLE
369+2714 'ayin (3), there
is no, i.e., not exist
419 anĕxĕrĕunētŏs (1),
inscrutable

UNDO
421 anĕxichniastŏs (1),
unsearchable

UNSEEMLY
808 aschēmŏsunē (1),
indecency; shame

UNSHOD
3182 mĕthuskŏ (1), to
intoxicate, become
drunk

UNSKILFUL
552 apĕirŏs (1), ignorant,
not acquainted with

UNSPEAKABLE
411 anĕkdiĕgētŏs (1),
indescribable
412 anĕklalētŏs (1),
unutterable
731 arrhētŏs (1),
inexpressible

UNSPOTTED
784 aspilŏs (1),
unblemished

UNSTABLE
6349 pachaz (1),
ebullition, turbulence
182 akatastatŏs (1),
inconstant, restless
793 astēriktŏs (2),
vacillating, unstable

UNSTOPPED
6605 pâthach (1), to open
wide; to loosen, begin

UNTAKEN
3361+348 mē (1), not; lest

UNTEMPERED
8602 tâphêl (5), to be
tasteless; frivolity

UNTHANKFUL
884 acharistŏs (2),
ungrateful

UNTIL
5704 'ad (288), as far
(long) as; during; until
891 achri (16), until or
up to
1519 ĕis (1), to or into
2193 hĕōs (35), until
3360 mĕchri (7), until, to
the point of

UNTIMELY
5309 nephel (3), abortive
miscarriage
3653 ŏlunthŏs (1), unripe
fig

UNTOWARD
4646 skŏliŏs (1), crooked;
perverse

UNWALLED
6519 pᵉrâzâh (1), rural,
open country
6521 pᵉrâzîy (1), rustic

UNWASHEN
449 aniptŏs (3), without
ablution, unwashed

UNWISE
3808+2450 lô' (2), no, not
453 anŏĕtŏs (1),
unintelligent, senseless
878 aphrōn (1), ignorant;
egotistic; unbelieving

UNWITTINGLY
1097+1847 bᵉlîy (2),
without, not yet

7684 sh^{e}gâgâh (1),
mistake, inadvertent
transgression

UNWORTHILY
371 anaxíŏs (2), in a
manner *unworthy*

UNWORTHY
370 anaxíŏs (1), *unfit,
unworthy*
3756+514 ŏu (1), *no or not*

UPBRAID
2778 châraph (1), to
spend the *winter*
3679 ŏnĕidizō (1), to *rail
at, chide, taunt*

UPBRAIDED
3679 ŏnĕidizō (1), to *rail
at, chide, taunt*

UPBRAIDETH
3679 ŏnĕidizō (1), to *rail
at, chide, taunt*

UPHARSIN
6537 p^{e}raç (Ch.) (1), to
split up

UPHAZ
210 'Ûwphâz (2), *Uphaz*

UPHELD
5564 çâmak (1), to *lean*
upon; *take hold* of

UPHOLD
5564 çâmak (5), to *lean*
upon; *take hold* of
8551 tâmak (3), to
obtain, keep fast

UPHOLDEN
5582 çâ'ad (1), to *support*
6965 qûwm (1), to *rise*

UPHOLDEST
8551 tâmak (1), to
obtain, keep fast

UPHOLDETH
5564 çâmak (3), to *lean*
upon; *take hold* of
8551 tâmak (1), to
obtain, keep fast

UPHOLDING
5342 phĕrō (1), to *bear or
carry*

UPPER
3730 kaphtôr (1), *capital;*
wreath-like *button*
4947 mashqôwph (1),
lintel
5942 'illîy (2), *higher*
5944 'ălîyâh (4), *upper
things; second-story*
5945 'elyôwn (8), *loftier,
higher; Supreme* God
7393 rekeb (1), *upper
millstone*
8222 sâphâm (1), *beard*
508 anŏgĕŏn (2), *dome
or a balcony*
510 anōtĕrikŏs (1), *more
remote* regions
5250 hupĕrplĕŏnazō (1),
to *superabound*
5253 hupĕrō̧ŏn (3), *room*
in the *third story*

UPPERMOST
5945 'elyôwn (1), *loftier,
higher; Supreme* God
4410 prōtŏkathĕdria (1),
pre-eminence in council

4411 prōtŏklisia (2),
pre-eminence at meals

UPRIGHT
3474 yâshar (1), to *be
straight;* to *make right*
3476 yôsher (1), *right*
3477 yâshâr (43), *straight*
4339 mêyshâr (1),
straightness; rectitude
4749 miqshâh (1), work
molded by *hammering*
5977 'ômed (2), fixed *spot*
6968 qôwm^{e}mîyûwth (1),
erectly, with head high
8535 tâm (1), morally
pious; gentle, dear
8537 tôm (2), *prosperity;
innocence*
8549 tâmîym (8), *entire,
complete; integrity*
8549+8552 tâmîym (1),
complete; integrity
8552 tâmam (2), to
complete, finish
3717 ŏrthŏs (1), *straight,
level*

UPRIGHTLY
3474 yâshar (1), to *be
straight;* to *make right*
3477 yâshâr (1), *straight*
4339 mêyshâr (3),
straightness; rectitude
8537 tôm (2), *prosperity;
innocence*
8549 tâmîym (4), *entire,
complete; integrity*
3716 ŏrthŏpŏdĕō (1), to
act *rightly*

UPRIGHTNESS
3476 yôsher (9), *right*
3477 yâshâr (1), *straight*
3483 yishrâh (1), *moral
integrity*
4334 mîyshôwr (1), *plain;
justice*
4339 mêyshâr (3),
straightness; rectitude
5228 nâkôach (1),
equitable, correct
5229 n^{e}kôchâh (1),
integrity; truth
8537 tôm (2), *prosperity;
innocence*

UPRISING
6965 qûwm (1), to *rise*

UPROAR
1993 hâmâh (1), to *be in
great commotion*
387 anastatŏō (1), to
disturb, cause trouble
2350 thŏrubĕō (1), to
clamor; start a riot
2351 thŏrubŏs (3),
commotion
4714 stasis (1), one
leading an *uprising*
4797 sugchĕō (1), to
throw into disorder

UPSIDE
5921+6440 'al (2), *above,
over, upon,* or *against*
389 anastĕnazō (1), to
sigh deeply

UPWARD
1361 gâbahh (1), to *be
lofty;* to *be haughty*

4605 ma'al (59), *upward,
above, overhead*
4791 mârôwm (1),
elevation; elation

UR
218 'Ûwr (5), *Ur*

URBANE
3779 hŏutō (1), *in this
way; likewise*

URGE
1758 ĕnĕchō (1), to *keep
a grudge*

URGED
509 'âlats (1), to *press,
urge*
6484 pâtsar (4), to *stun
or dull*
6555 pârats (1), to *break
out*

URGENT
2388 châzaq (1), to
fasten upon; to *seize*
2685 chătsaph (Ch.) (1),
to *be severe*

URI
221 'Ûwrîy (8), *fiery*

URIAH
223 'Ûwrîyâh (27), *flame
of Jehovah*

URIAH'S
223 'Ûwrîyâh (1), *flame
of Jehovah*

URIAS
3774 Ŏurias (1), *flame of
Jehovah*

URIEL
222 'Ûwrîy'êl (4), *flame
of God*

URIJAH
223 'Ûwrîyâh (11), *flame
of Jehovah*

URIM
224 'Ûwrîym (7), *lights*

US-WARD
413 'êl (1), *to, toward*
1519+2248 ĕis (2), *to or
into*

USE
559 'âmar (1), to *say*
3231 yâman (1), to *be
right-handed*
3947 lâqach (1), to *take*
4399 m^{e}lâ'kâh (1), *work;
property*
4911 mâshal (3), to *use
figurative language*
4912 mâshâl (1), *pithy
maxim; taunt*
5172 nâchash (1), to
prognosticate
5656 'ăbôdâh (1), *work*
7080 qâçam (1), to *divine
magic*
1838 hĕxis (1), *practice,
constant use*
1908 ĕpĕrĕazō (2), to
insult with threats
5195 hubrizō (1), to
exercise violence, abuse
5382 philŏxĕnŏs (1),
hospitable
5530 chraŏmai (7), to
furnish what is needed

USED
3928 limmûwd (1),
instructed one
6213 'âsâh (2), to *do or
make*
390 anastrĕphō (1), to
remain, to *live*
1247 diakŏnĕō (1), to
wait upon, serve
1387 dŏliŏō (1), to
practice deceit
1510 ĕimi (1), I *exist,* I am
3096 magĕuō (1), to
practice magic, sorcery
4238 prassō (1), to
execute, accomplish
5530 chraŏmai (3), to
furnish what is needed

USES
5532 chrĕia (1), *affair;
occasion, demand*

USEST
4941 mishpâṭ (1), *verdict;*
formal *decree; justice*

USETH
1696 dâbar (1), to *speak,
say;* to *subdue*
3348 mĕtĕchō (1), to
share or participate

USING
671 apŏchrēsis (1),
consumption, using up
2192 ĕchō (1), to *have;
hold; keep*

USURER
5383 nâshâh (1), to *lend
or borrow*

USURP
831 authĕntĕō (1), to
dominate

USURY
5378 nâshâ' (1), to *lend
on interest*
5383 nâshâh (5), to *lend
or borrow*
5391 nâshak (4), to
oppress through
finance
5392 neshek (11), *interest*
5110 tŏkŏs (2), *interest*
on money loaned

UTHAI
5793 'Ûwthay (2),
succoring

UTMOST
314 'achărôwn (2), *late
or last; behind; western*
7093 qêts (1), *extremity;
after*
7097 qâtseh (3), *extremity*
7112 qâtsats (3), to *chop
off;* to *separate*
4009 pĕras (1), *extremity,
end, limit*

UTTER
1696 dâbar (5), to *speak,
say;* to *subdue*
1897 hâgâh (1), to
*murmur, utter a sound;
ponder*

UTTERANCE

2435 chîytsôwn (12), outer *wall side; exterior*
2531 chemed (1), *delight*
3318 yâtsâ' (3), to *go, bring out*
3617 kâlâh (2), *complete destruction*
4448 mâlal (2), to *speak, say*
4911 mâshal (1), to *use figurative language*
5042 nâba' (4), to *gush forth; to utter*
5046 nâgad (3), to *announce*
5414 nâthan (4), to *give*
6030 'ânâh (1), to *respond, answer*
6315 pûwach (1), to *blow, to fan, kindle; to utter*
1325 didōmi (1), to *give*
2044 ĕreúgōmai (1), to *speak out*
2980 laléō (1), to *talk*

UTTERANCE

669 apŏphthĕggŏmai (1), *declare, address*
3056 lŏgŏs (4), *word, matter, thing*

UTTERED

1696 dâbar (1), to *speak, say; to subdue*
3318 yâtsâ' (1), to *go, bring out*
4008 mibṭâ' (2), *rash utterance*
5046 nâgad (2), to *announce*
5414 nâthan (5), to *give*
6475 pâtsâh (1), to *rend, i.e. open*
215 alalētŏs (1), *unspeakable*
2980 laléō (3), to *talk*
3004 lĕgō (1), to *say*

UTTERETH

502 'âlaph (1), to *learn; to teach*
559 'âmar (1), to *say*
1696 dâbar (1), to *speak, say; to subdue*
3318 yâtsâ' (2), to *go, bring out*
5042 nâba' (1), to *gush forth; to utter*
5414 nâthan (3), to *give*

UTTERING

1897 hâgâh (1), to *murmur, utter a sound*

UTTERLY

3605 kôl (1), *all, any or every*
3615 kâlâh (1), to *complete, prepare*
3632 kâlîyl (1), *whole, entire; complete; whole*
3966 me'ôd (2), *very, utterly*
7703 shâdad (1), to *ravage*
2618 katakaiō (1), to *consume wholly by burning*
2704 kataphthĕirō (1), to *spoil entirely*
3654 hŏlōs (1), *completely, altogether*

UTTERMOST

314 'achărôwn (1), *late or last; behind; western*
319 'achărîyth (1), *future; posterity*
657 'epheç (1), *end; no further*
3671 kânâph (1), *edge or extremity; wing*
7020 qîytsôwn (3), *terminal, end*
7097 qâtseh (10), *extremity*
7098 qâtsâh (3), *termination; fringe*
206 akrŏn (2), *extremity; end, top*
1231 diaginōskō (1), *ascertain exactly*
2078 ĕschatŏs (2), *farthest, final*
3838 pantĕlēs (1), *entire; completion*
4009 pĕras (1), *extremity, end, limit*
5056 tĕlŏs (1), *conclusion*

UZ

5780 'Ûwts (7), *consultation*

UZAI

186 'Ûwzay (1), *Uzai*

UZAL

187 'Ûwzâl (2), *Uzal*

UZZA

5798 'Uzzâ' (10), *strength*

UZZAH

5798 'Uzzâ' (4), *strength*

UZZEN-SHERAH

242 'Uzzên She'ĕrâh (1), *land of Sheerah*

UZZI

5813 'Uzzîy (11), *forceful*

UZZIA

5814 'Uzzîyâ' (1), *strength of Jehovah*

UZZIAH

5818 'Uzzîyâh (27), *strength of Jehovah*

UZZIEL

5816 'Uzzîy'êl (16), *strength of God*

UZZIELITES

5817 'Ozzîy'êlîy (2), *Uzziëlite*

VAGABOND

5110 nûwd (2), to *waver; to wander, flee*
4022 pĕriĕrchŏmai (1), to *stroll, vacillate, veer*

VAGABONDS

5128 nûwa' (1), to *waver*

VAIL

4304 miṭpachath (1), *cloak, woman's shawl*
4533 maçveh (3), *veil, cover*
4541 maççêkâh (1), *woven coverlet*
6532 pôreketh (25), *sacred screen, curtain*
6809 tsâ'îyph (3), *veil*
2571 kaluma (4), *veil, covering*

VAILS

7289 râdîyd (1), *veil*

VAIN

205 'âven (1), *trouble, vanity, wickedness*
1891 hâbal (5), to *be vain, be worthless*
1892 hebel (11), *emptiness or vanity*
2600 chinnâm (2), *gratis, free*
3576 kâzab (1), to *lie, deceive*
5014 nâbab (1), to *be hollow; be foolish*
7307 rûwach (2), *breath; wind; life-spirit*
7385 rîyq (8), *emptiness; worthless thing; in vain*
7386 rêyq (7), *empty; worthless*
7387 rêyqâm (1), *emptily; ineffectually*
7723 shâv' (22), *ruin; guile; idolatry*
8193 sâphâh (2), *lip, language, speech*
8267 sheqer (6), *untruth; sham*
8414 tôhûw (4), *waste, formless; in vain*
1432 dōrĕan (1), *gratuitously, freely*
1500 ĕikē (5), *idly, i.e. without reason or effect*
2755 kĕnŏdŏxŏs (1), *self-conceited*
2756 kĕnŏs (14), *empty; vain; useless*
2757 kĕnŏphōnia (2), *fruitless discussion*
2761 kĕnŏs (2), *vainly, i.e. to no purpose*
3150 mataiŏlŏgia (1), *meaningless talk*
3151 mataiŏlŏgŏs (1), *mischievous talker*
3152 mataiŏs (5), *profitless, futile; idol*
3154 mataiŏō (1), *wicked; idolatrous*
3155 matēn (2), to *no purpose, in vain*

VAINGLORY

2754 kĕnŏdŏxia (1), *self-conceit, vanity*

VAINLY

1500 ĕikē (1), *idly, i.e. without reason or effect*

VAJEZATHA

2055 Vay e zâthâ' (1), *Vajezatha*

VALE

6010 'êmeq (4), *broad depression or valley*
8219 she phêlâh (5), *lowland,*

VALIANT

47 'abbîyr (1), *mighty*
691 'er'êl (1), *hero, brave person*
1121+2428 bên (4), *son, descendant; people*
1368 gibbôwr (6), *powerful; great warrior*
1396 gâbar (1), to *be strong; to prevail*

VANISHED

2428 chayil (16), *army; wealth; virtue; valor*
3524 kabbîyr (1), *mighty; aged; mighty*
2478 ischurŏs (1), *forcible, powerful*

VALIANTEST

1121+2428 bên (1), *son, descendant; people*

VALIANTLY

2388 châzaq (1), to *be strong; courageous*
2428 chayil (5), *army; wealth; virtue; valor*

VALLEY

1237 biq'âh (9), *wide level valley*
1516 gay' (52), *gorge, valley*
5158 nachal (18), *valley, ravine; mine shaft*
6010 'êmeq (54), *broad depression or valley*
8219 she phêlâh (6), *lowland,*
5327 pharagx (1), *wadi ravine; valley*

VALLEYS

1237 biq'âh (4), *wide level valley*
1516 gay' (8), *gorge, valley*
5158 nachal (5), *valley, ravine; mine shaft*
6010 'êmeq (9), *broad depression or valley*
8219 she phêlâh (2), *lowland,*

VALOUR

2428 chayil (37), *army; wealth; virtue; valor*

VALUE

457 'ĕlîyl (1), *vain idol*
6186 'ârak (3), to *set in a row, i.e. arrange,*
1308 diaphĕrō (2), to *bear, carry; to differ*
5091 timaō (1), to *revere, honor, show respect*

VALUED

5541 çâlâh (2), to *contemn, reject*
5091 timaō (1), to *revere, honor, show respect*

VALUEST

6187 'êrek (1), *pile, equipment, estimate*

VANIAH

2057 Vanyâh (1), *Vanjah*

VANISH

4414 mâlach (1), to *disappear as dust*
6789 tsâmath (1), to *extirpate, root out*
854 aphanismŏs (1), *disappearance*
2673 katargĕō (1), to *be, render entirely useless*

VANISHED

5628 çârach (1), to *extend even to excess*
1096+855 ginŏmai (1), to *be, become*

VANISHETH
3212 yâlak (1), to *walk*;
to *live*; to *carry*
853 aphanizō (1), to
disappear, be destroyed

VANITIES
1892 hebel (12),
emptiness or *vanity*
3152 mataiòs (1),
profitless, futile; idol

VANITY
205 'âven (6), *trouble,
vanity, wickedness*
1892 hebel (49),
emptiness or *vanity*
7385 rîyq (2), *emptiness;
worthless* thing; *in vain*
7723 shâv' (22), *ruin;
guile; idolatry*
8414 tôhûw (4), *waste,
formless; in vain*
3153 mataiòtēs (3),
transientness; depravity

VAPORS
5387 nâsîy' (2), *leader;
rising mist, fog*

VAPOUR
108 'êd (1), *fog*
5927 'âlâh (1), to *ascend,
be high, mount*
822 atmis (2), *mist,
vapor; billows of smoke*

VAPOURS
5387 nâsîy' (1), *leader;
rising mist, fog*
7008 qîytôwr (1), *fume,*
i.e. smoke *cloud*

VARIABLENESS
3883 parallagē (1),
change or variation

VARIANCE
1369 dichazō (1), to
sunder, i.e. *alienate*
2054 éris (1), *quarrel,* i.e.
wrangling

VASHNI
2059 Vashnîy (1), *weak*

VASHTI
2060 Vashtîy (10), *Vashti*

VAUNT
6286 pâ'ar (1), to *shake* a
tree

VAUNTETH
4068 pĕrpĕrĕuŏmai (1),
to *boast, brag*

VEHEMENT
2759 chărîyshîy (1),
sultry, searing
3050 Yâhh (1), *Jehovah,*
(the) self-*Existent* or
Eternal One
1972 ĕpipŏthēsis (1),
longing for

VEHEMENTLY
1171 dĕinōs (1), *terribly,*
i.e. *excessively, fiercely*
1722+4 ĕn (1), *in; during;
because of*
2159 ĕutŏnōs (1),
intensely, cogently
4366 prŏsrēgnumi (2), to
burst upon

VEIL
7289 râdîyd (1), *veil*

2665 katapĕtasma (6),
door *screen*

VEIN
4161 môwtsâ' (1), *going
forth*

VENGEANCE
5358 nâqam (4), to
avenge or *punish*
5359 nâqâm (15), *revenge*
5360 nᵉqâmâh (19),
avengement
1349 dikē (2), *justice*
1557 ĕkdikēsis (4),
retaliation, punishment
3709 örgē (1), *ire;
punishment*

VENISON
6718 tsayid (7), *hunting
game; lunch, food*
6720 tsêydâh (1), *food,
supplies*

VENOM
7219 rô'sh (1), *poisonous
plant; poison*

VENT
6605 pâthach (1), to *open
wide;* to *loosen, begin*

VENTURE
8537 tôm (2), *prosperity;
innocence*

VERIFIED
539 'âman (3), to *be firm,
faithful, true;* to *trust*

VERILY
61 'âbâl (3), *truly, surely;
yet, but*
389 'ak (6), *surely; only,
however*
403 'âkên (2), *surely!,
truly!; but*
518 'îm (1), *whether?; if,
although; Oh that!*
518+3808 'îm (1), *Oh that!*
530 ĕmûwnâh (1),
fidelity; steadiness
559 'âmar (1), to *say*
7069 qânâh (1), to *create;
to procure*
230 alēthōs (1), *truly,
surely*
281 amēn (76), *surely; so
be it*
1063 gar (2), *for, indeed,
but, because*
1222 dēpŏu (1), *indeed
doubtless*
2532 kai (1), *and; or;
even; also*
3303 mēn (13), *verily*
3303+3767 mēn (1), *verily*
3304 mĕnŏungĕ (1), *so
then at least*
3483 nai (1), *yes*
3689 ŏntōs (1), *really,
certainly*

VERITY
571 'emeth (1), *certainty,
truth, trustworthiness*
225 alētheia (2), *truth,
truthfulness*

VERMILION
8350 shâshar (2), *red*

VERY
199 'ûwlâm (2), *however
or on the contrary*

430 'ĕlôhîym (1), the true
God; great ones
552 'umnâm (1), *verily,
indeed, truly*
651 'âphêl (1), *dusky,
dark*
898 bâgad (1), to *act
covertly*
899 beged (2), *clothing;
treachery or pillage*
1419 gâdôwl (1), *great*
1767 day (2), *enough,
sufficient*
1851 daq (1), *crushed;
small or thin*
1854 dâqaq (1), to *crush;
crumble*
1942 havvâh (1), *desire;
craving*
2088 zeh (2), *this or that*
3190 yâṭab (2), to *be,
make well;* be
successful
3304 yᵉphêh-phîyâh (1),
very beautiful
3453 yâshîysh (2), *old
man*
3559 kûwn (1), to *render
sure, proper*
3966 mᵉ'ôd (136), *very,
utterly*
4213 miz'âr (3), *fewness,
smallness*
4295 maṭṭâh (1), *below
or beneath*
4592 mᵉ'aṭ (1), *little or
few*
4605 ma'al (2), *upward,
above, overhead*
4801 merchâq (1),
distant place; from afar
5464 çagrîyd (1), *pouring
rain*
5690 'egeb (1), *amative
words, words of love*
5704 'ad (2), *as far (long)
as; during; while; until*
6106 'etsem (2), *bone;
substance; selfsame*
6621 petha' (1), *wink,* i.e.
moment; quickly
6985 qaṭ (1), *little,* i.e.
merely
7023 qîyr (1), *wall,
side-wall*
7230 rôb (1), *abundance*
7260 rabrab (Ch.) (1),
huge, domineering
7690 saggîy' (Ch.) (1),
large
85 adēmŏnĕŏ (2), to *be in
mental distress*
230 alēthōs (1), *truly,
surely*
662 apŏtŏlmaŏ (1), to
venture plainly
846 autŏs (5), *he, she, it*
927 barutimŏs (1), *highly
valuable*
957 bĕltiŏn (1), *better*
1565 ĕkĕinŏs (2), *that one*
1582 ĕkkrĕmamai (1), to
listen closely
1646 ĕlachistŏs (3), *least*
1888 ĕpautŏphōrŏi (1), *in
actual crime*
2236 hēdista (1), *with
great pleasure*

2532 kai (4), *and; or;
even; also*
2566 kalliŏn (1), *better*
2735 katŏrthōma (1),
made fully upright
3029 lian (2), *very much*
3827 pampŏlus (1), *full
many,* i.e. *immense*
4036 pĕrilupŏs (1),
intensely sad
4118 plĕistŏs (1), *very
large,* i.e. *the most*
4119 plĕiŏn (1), *more*
4184 pŏlusplagchnŏs (1),
*extremely
compassionate*
4185 pŏlutĕlēs (1),
extremely expensive
4186 pŏlutimŏs (1),
extremely valuable
4361 prŏspĕinŏs (1),
intensely hungry
4708 spŏudaiŏtĕrōs (1),
more speedily
4970 sphŏdra (4), *high
degree, much*
5228 hupĕr (2), *over;
above; beyond*

VESSEL
3627 kᵉlîy (33),
implement, thing
5035 nebel (1), skin-*bag*
for liquids; *vase; lyre*
4632 skĕuŏs (11), *vessel,
implement, equipment*

VESSELS
3627 kᵉlîy (129),
implement, thing
3984 mâ'n (Ch.) (7),
utensil, vessel
30 aggĕiŏn (2),
receptacle, vessel
4632 skĕuŏs (8), *vessel,
implement, equipment*

VESTMENTS
3830 lᵉbûwsh (1),
garment; wife
4403 malbûwsh (1),
garment, clothing

VESTRY
4458 meltâchâh (1),
wardrobe

VESTURE
3682 kᵉçûwth (1), *cover;
veiling*
3830 lᵉbûwsh (2),
garment; wife
2440 himatiŏn (2), to *put
on clothes*
2441 himatismŏs (2),
clothing
4018 pĕribŏlaiŏn (1),
thrown around

VESTURES
899 beged (1), *clothing;
treachery or pillage*

VEX
926 bâhal (1), to *tremble;
be, make agitated*
2000 hâmam (1), to *put in
commotion*
2111 zûwâ' (1), to *shake
with fear, tremble*
3013 yâgâh (1), to *grieve;
to torment*
3238 yânâh (2), to *rage
or be violent*

VEXATION

3707 kâ'aç (1), to *grieve,
rage, be indignant*
6213+7451 'âsâh (1), to
do or make
6887 tsârar (5), to *cramp*
6973 qûwts (1), to *be,
make anxious*
2559 kakôō (1), to *injure;
to oppress; to embitter*

VEXATION

2113 zᵉvâ'âh (1),
agitation, fear
4103 mᵉhûwmâh (1),
confusion or uproar
4164 mûwtsaq (1),
distress
7469 rᵉ'ûwth (7),
grasping after
7475 ra'yôwn (3), *desire,
chasing after*
7667 sheber (1), *fracture;
ruin*

VEXATIONS

4103 mᵉhûwmâh (1),
confusion or uproar

VEXED

926 bâhal (3), to *tremble;
be, make agitated*
1766 dâchaq (1), to
oppress
3238 yânâh (2), to *rage
or be violent*
3334 yâtsar (1), to *be in
distress*
4103 mᵉhûwmâh (1),
confusion or uproar
4843 mârar (2), to *be,
make bitter*
6087 'âtsab (1), to *worry,
have pain or anger*
6887 tsârar (1), to *cramp*
7114 qâtsar (1), to
curtail, cut short
7489 râ'a' (1), to *be good
for nothing*
7492 râ'ats (1), to *break
in pieces; to harass*
7561 râsha' (1), to *be, do,
declare wrong*
928 basanizō (1), to
torture, torment
1139 daimŏnizŏmai (1),
to *be exercised by a
demon*
2669 katapŏnĕō (1), to
harass, oppress
3791 ŏchlĕō (2), to
harass, be tormented
3958 paschō (1), to
experience pain

VIAL

6378 pak (1), *flask, small
jug*
5357 phialē (7), broad
shallow *cup*, i.e. a *phial*

VIALS

5357 phialē (5), broad
shallow *cup*, i.e. a *phial*

VICTORY

3467 yâsha' (1), to make
safe, free
5331 netsach (2),
splendor; lasting
8668 tᵉshûw'âh (3),
rescue, deliverance
3528 nikaō (1), to
subdue, conquer

3529 nikē (1), *conquest,
victory, success*
3534 nikŏs (4), *triumph,
victory*

VICTUAL

3557 kûwl (1), to
measure; to maintain
3978 ma'ăkâl (1), *food,
something to eat*
4202 mâzôwn (1), *food,
provisions*
6720 tsêydâh (2), *food,
supplies*

VICTUALS

400 'ôkel (3), *food*
737 'ărûchâh (1), *ration,
portion of food*
3557 kûwl (1), to
measure; to maintain
3899 lechem (2), *food,
bread*
4241 michyâh (1),
sustenance; quick
6718 tsayid (2), hunting
game; lunch, food
6720 tsêydâh (4), *food,
supplies*
7668 sheber (1), *grain*
1033 brōma (1), *food*
1979 ĕpisitismŏs (1), *food*

VIEW

5048 neged (2), *in front of*
7200 râ'âh (1), to *see*
7270 râgal (1), to
reconnoiter; to slander

VIEWED

995 bîyn (1), to
understand; discern
7370 râchash (1), to *gush*
7663 sâbar (2), to
scrutinize; to expect

VIGILANT

1127 grĕgŏrĕuō (1), to
watch, guard
3524 nĕphalĕŏs (1),
circumspect, temperate

VILE

959 bâzâh (2), to
disesteem, ridicule
2151 zâlal (2), to *be loose
morally, worthless*
2933 ṭâmâh (1), to be
ceremonially impure
5034 nâbêl (1), to *wilt; to
fall away; to be foolish*
5036 nâbâl (2), *stupid;
impious*
5039 nᵉbâlâh (1), moral
wickedness; crime
5240 nᵉmibzeh (1),
despised
7034 qâlâh (1), to *be,
hold in contempt*
7043 qâlal (4), to *be easy,
trifling, vile*
8182 shô'âr (1), *harsh or
horrid,* i.e. *offensive*
819 atimia (1), *disgrace*
4508 rhuparŏs (1),
shabby, dirty; wicked
5014 tapĕinōsis (1),
humbleness, lowliness

VILELY

1602 gâ'al (1), to *detest;
to reject; to fail*

VILER

5217 nâkâ' (1), to *smite,*
i.e. *drive away*

VILEST

2149 zullûwth (1), (poss.)
tempest

VILLAGE

2968 kŏmē (10), *hamlet,
town*

VILLAGES

1323 bath (12), *daughter,
outlying village*
2691 châtsêr (47), *yard;
walled village*
3715 kᵉphîyr (1), walled
village; young lion
3723 kâphâr (2), walled
village
3724 kôpher (1), *village;
bitumen; henna*
6518 pârâz (1), *chieftain*
6519 pᵉrâzâh (1), *rural,
open country*
6520 pᵉrâzôwn (2),
magistracy, leadership
6521 pᵉrâziy (1), *rustic*
2968 kŏmē (7), *hamlet,
town*

VILLANY

5039 nᵉbâlâh (2), moral
wickedness; crime

VINE

1612 gephen (44), grape
vine
2156 zᵉmôwrâh (1),
pruned *twig, branch*
3196 yayin (1), *wine;
intoxication*
3755 kôrêm (1),
vinedresser
5139 nâzîyr (2), *prince;
unpruned vine*
8321 sôrêq (3), *choice
vine stock*
288 ampĕlŏs (9), grape
vine

VINEDRESSERS

3755 kôrêm (4),
vinedresser

VINEGAR

2558 chômets (6), *vinegar*
3690 ŏxŏs (7), *sour* wine

VINES

1612 gephen (9), grape
vine
3754 kerem (3), *garden
or vineyard*

VINEYARD

3657 kannâh (1), *plant*
3754 kerem (44), *garden
or vineyard*
289 ampĕlŏurgŏs (1),
vineyard caretaker
290 ampĕlōn (23),
vineyard

VINEYARDS

3754 kerem (45), *garden
or vineyard*

VINTAGE

1208 bâtsôwr (1),
inaccessible
1210 bâtsîyr (7), *grape
crop, harvest*
3754 kerem (1), *garden
or vineyard*

VIOL

5035 nebel (2), skin-*bag
for liquids; vase; lyre*

VIOLATED

2554 châmaç (1), to *be
violent; to maltreat*

VIOLENCE

1497 gâzal (1), to *rob*
1498 gâzêl (1), *robbery,
stealing*
1499 gêzel (1), *violence*
1500 gᵉzêlâh (3), *robbery,
stealing; things stolen*
2554 châmaç (2), to *be
violent; to maltreat*
2555 châmaç (39),
violence; malice
4835 mᵉrûtsâh (1),
oppression
6231 'âshaq (1), to
violate; to overflow
970 bia (4), *force,
pounding violence*
971 biazō (1), to *crowd
oneself into*
1286 diasĕiō (1), to
intimidate, extort
1411 dunamis (1), *force,
power, miracle*
3731 hŏrmēma (1),
sudden *attack*

VIOLENT

1499 gêzel (1), *violence*
2555 châmaç (7),
violence; malice
6184 'ârîyts (1), *powerful
or tyrannical*
973 biastēs (1), *energetic,
forceful one*

VIOLENTLY

1497 gâzal (4), to *rob*
1500 gᵉzêlâh (1), *robbery,
stealing; things stolen*
2554 châmaç (1), to *be
violent; to maltreat*

VIOLS

5035 nebel (2), skin-*bag
for liquids; vase; lyre*

VIPER

660 'eph'eh (2), *asp*
2191 ĕchidna (1), *adder*

VIPER'S

660 'eph'eh (1), *asp*

VIPERS

2191 ĕchidna (4), *adder*

VIRGIN

1330 bᵉthûwlâh (24),
virgin
5959 'almâh (2), *lass,
young woman*
3933 parthĕnŏs (7), *virgin*

VIRGIN'S

3933 parthĕnŏs (1), *virgin*

VIRGINITY

1331 bᵉthûwlîym (8),
*virginity; proof of
female virginity*
3932 parthĕnia (1),
maidenhood, virginity

VIRGINS

1330 bᵉthûwlâh (14),
virgin
5959 'almâh (2), *lass,
young woman*
3933 parthĕnŏs (6), *virgin*

English

VIRTUE
703 arĕtē (4), *excellence, virtue*
1411 dunamis (3), *force, power, miracle*

VIRTUOUS
2428 chayil (3), *army; wealth; virtue; valor*

VIRTUOUSLY
2428 chayil (1), *army; wealth; virtue; valor*

VISAGE
600 'ănaph (Ch.) (1), *face*
4758 mar'eh (1), *appearance; vision*
8389 tô'ar (1), *outline, appearance*

VISIBLE
3707 hŏratŏs (1), *capable of being seen*

VISION
2376 chêzev (Ch.) (2), *sight, revelation*
2377 châzôwn (32), *sight; revelation*
2380 châzûwth (2), *striking appearance*
2384 chizzâyôwn (6), *dream; vision*
4236 machăzeh (4), *vision*
4758 mar'eh (14), *appearance; vision*
4759 mar'âh (3), *vision; mirror*
7203 rô'eh (1), *seer; vision*
3701 ŏptasia (2), *supernatural vision*
3705 hŏrama (12), *supernatural spectacle*
3706 hŏrasis (1), *appearance, vision*

VISIONS
2376 chêzev (Ch.) (9), *sight, revelation*
2377 châzôwn (3), *sight; revelation*
2378 châzôwth (1), *revelation*
2384 chizzâyôwn (3), *dream; vision*
4759 mar'âh (5), *vision; mirror*
7200 râ'âh (1), *to see*
3701 ŏptasia (1), *supernatural vision*
3706 hŏrasis (1), *appearance, vision*

VISIT
6485 pâqad (33), *to visit, care for, count*
1980 ĕpiskĕptŏmai (4), *to inspect, to go to see*

VISITATION
6486 pᵉquddâh (13), *visitation; punishment*
1984 ĕpiskŏpē (2), *episcopate*

VISITED
6485 pâqad (18), *to visit, care for, count*
1980 ĕpiskĕptŏmai (5), *to inspect; to go to see*

VISITEST
6485 pâqad (2), *to visit, care for, count*
1980 ĕpiskĕptŏmai (1), *to inspect; to go to see*

VISITETH
6485 pâqad (1), *to visit, care for, count*

VISITING
6485 pâqad (4), *to visit, care for, count*

VOCATION
2821 klēsis (1), *invitation; station in life*

VOICE
6963 qôwl (379), *voice or sound*
7032 qâl (Ch.) (3), *sound, music*
5456 phōnē (116), *voice, sound*
5586 psēphŏs (1), *pebble stone*

VOICES
6963 qôwl (2), *voice or sound*
5456 phōnē (15), *voice, sound*

VOID
6 'âbad (1), *perish; destroy*
922 bôhûw (2), *ruin, desolation*
1238 bâqaq (1), *to depopulate, ruin*
1637 gôren (2), *open area*
2638 châçêr (6), *lacking*
4003 mᵉbûwqâh (1), *emptiness, devastation*
5010 nâ'ar (1), *to reject*
6565 pârar (5), *to break up; to violate, frustrate*
7387 rêyqâm (1), *emptily; ineffectually*
677 aprŏskŏpŏs (1), *not led into sin*
2673 katargĕō (1), *to be, render entirely useless*
2758 kĕnŏō (2), *to make empty*

VOLUME
4039 mᵉgillâh (1), *roll, scroll*
2777 kĕphalis (1), *roll, scroll*

VOLUNTARILY
5071 nᵉdâbâh (1), *abundant gift*

VOLUNTARY
5071 nᵉdâbâh (2), *abundant gift*
7522 râtsôwn (1), *delight*
2309 thĕlō (1), *to will; to desire; to choose*

VOMIT
6892 qê' (4), *vomit*
6958 qôw' (3), *to vomit*
1829 ĕxĕrama (1), *vomit*

VOMITED
6958 qôw' (1), *to vomit*

VOMITETH
6958 qôw' (1), *to vomit*

VOPHSI
2058 Vophçîy (1), *additional*

VOW
5087 nâdar (9), *to promise, vow*
5088 neder (30), *promise to God; thing promised*
2171 ĕuchē (2), *wish, petition*

VOWED
5087 nâdar (16), *to promise, vow*
5088 neder (2), *promise to God; thing promised*

VOWEDST
5087 nâdar (1), *to promise, vow*

VOWEST
5087 nâdar (2), *to promise, vow*

VOWETH
5087 nâdar (1), *to promise, vow*

VOWS
5088 neder (30), *promise to God; thing promised*

VOYAGE
4144 plŏŏs (1), *navigation, voyage*

VULTURE
1676 dâ'âh (1), *kite*
1772 dayâh (1), *falcon*

VULTURE'S
344 'ayâh (1), *hawk*

VULTURES
1772 dayâh (1), *falcon*

WAFER
7550 râqîyq (3), *thin cake, wafer*

WAFERS
6838 tsappîychîth (1), *flat thin cake*
7550 râqîyq (4), *thin cake, wafer*

WAG
5110 nûwd (1), *to waver; to wander, flee*
5128 nûwa' (2), *to waver*

WAGES
2600 chinnâm (1), *gratis, free*
4909 maskôreth (3), *wages; reward*
6468 pᵉ'ullâh (1), *work, deed*
7936 sâkar (1), *to hire*
7939 sâkâr (6), *payment, salary; compensation*
3408 misthŏs (2), *pay for services, good or bad*
3800 ŏpsōniŏn (3), *rations, stipend or pay*

WAGGING
2795 kinĕō (2), *to stir, move, remove*

WAGON
5699 'ăgâlâh (1), *wheeled vehicle*

WAGONS
5699 'ăgâlâh (8), *wheeled vehicle*
7393 rekeb (1), *vehicle for riding*

WAIL
5091 nâhâh (1), *to bewail; to assemble*
5594 çâphad (1), *to tear the hair, wail*
2875 kŏptō (1), *to beat the breast*

WAILED
214 alalazō (1), *to wail; to clang*

WAILING
4553 miçpêd (6), *lamentation, howling*
5089 nôahh (1), *lamentation*
5092 nᵉhîy (4), *elegy*
5204 nîy (1), *lamentation*
2805 klauthmŏs (2), *lamentation, weeping*
3996 pĕnthĕō (2), *to grieve*

WAIT
693 'ârab (34), *to ambush, lie in wait*
695 'ereb (1), *hiding place; lair*
696 'ôreb (1), *hiding place; lair*
1748 dûwmâm (1), *silently*
1826 dâmam (1), *to stop, cease; to perish*
2342 chûwl (1), *to wait; to pervert*
2442 châkâh (6), *to await; hope for*
3027 yâd (1), *hand; power*
3176 yâchal (5), *to wait; to be patient, hope*
3993 ma'ărâb (1), *ambuscade, ambush*
6119 'âqêb (1), *track, footprint; rear position*
6633 tsâbâ' (1), *to mass an army or servants*
6658 tsâdâh (1), *to desolate*
6660 tsᵉdîyâh (2), *design, lying in wait*
6960 qâvâh (22), *to collect; to expect*
7663 sâbar (2), *to scrutinize; to expect*
7789 shûwr (1), *to spy out, survey*
8104 shâmar (4), *to watch*
362 anamĕnō (1), *to await in expectation*
553 apĕkdĕchŏmai (2), *to expect fully, await*
1096+1917 ginŏmai (1), *to be, become*
1747 ĕnĕdra (1), *ambush*
1748 ĕnĕdrĕuō (2), *to lurk*
1917 ĕpibŏulē (2), *plot, plan*
3180 mĕthŏdĕia (1), *trickery, scheming*
4037 pĕrimĕnō (1), *to await*
4160+1747 pŏiĕō (1), *to make or do*
4327 prŏsdĕchŏmai (1), *to receive; to await for*
4332 prŏsĕdrĕuō (1), *to attend as a servant*

English

WAITED
4342 prŏskartĕrĕō (1), to *persevere*

WAITED
1961+6440 hâyâh (1), to *exist*, i.e. *be* or *become*
2342 chûwl (1), to *wait;* to *pervert*
2442 châkâh (2), to *await; hope for*
3176 yâchal (6), to *wait;* to *be patient, hope*
5975 'âmad (5), to *stand*
6822 tsâphâh (1), to *observe, await*
6960 qâvâh (8), to *collect;* to *expect*
8104 shâmar (1), to *watch*
8334 shârath (1), to *attend* as a menial
1551 ĕkdĕchŏmai (2), to *await, expect*
4327 prŏsdĕchŏmai (2), to *receive;* to *await for*
4328 prŏsdŏkaō (2), to *anticipate;* to *await*
4342 prŏskartĕrĕō (1), to *persevere, be constant*

WAITETH
1747 dûwmîyâh (2), *silently; quiet, trust*
2442 châkâh (3), to *await; hope for*
3176 yâchal (1), to *wait;* to *be patient, hope*
8104 shâmar (2), to *watch*
553 apĕkdĕchŏmai (1), to *expect fully, await*
1551 ĕkdĕchŏmai (1), to *await, expect*

WAITING
6635 tsâbâ' (1), *army, military host*
8104 shâmar (1), to *watch*
553 apĕkdĕchŏmai (2), to *expect fully, await*
1551 ĕkdĕchŏmai (1), to *await, expect*
4327 prŏsdĕchŏmai (1), to *receive;* to *await for*
4328 prŏsdŏkaō (2), to *anticipate;* to *await*

WAKE
5782 'ûwr (1), to *awake*
6974 qûwts (2), to *awake*
1127 grēgŏrĕuō (1), to *watch, guard*

WAKED
5782 'ûwr (1), to *awake*

WAKENED
5782 'ûwr (1), to *awake*

WAKENETH
5782 'ûwr (1), to *awake*

WAKETH
5782 'ûwr (1), to *awake*
8245 shâqad (1), to *be alert*, i.e. *sleepless*

WAKING
8109 shᵉmûrâh (1), *eye-lid*

WALK
1869 dârak (2), to *tread, trample;* to *walk*

1979 hălîykâh (1), *walking; procession*
1980 hâlak (61), to *walk; live a certain way*
1981 hălak (Ch.) (1), to *walk; live a certain way*
3212 yâlak (79), to *walk;* to *live;* to *carry*
4108 mahlêk (1), *access; journey*
4109 mahălâk (1), *passage* or a *distance*
5437 çâbab (1), to *surround*
1704 ĕmpĕripatĕō (1), to *be occupied among*
4043 pĕripatĕō (55), to *walk;* to *live a life*
4198 pŏrĕuŏmai (4), to *go, come;* to *travel*
4748 stŏichĕō (4), to *follow, walk;* to *conform*

WALKED
1980 hâlak (67), to *walk; live a certain way*
1981 hălak (Ch.) (1), to *walk; live a certain way*
3212 yâlak (32), to *walk;* to *live;* to *carry*
3716 ŏrthŏpŏdĕō (1), to *act rightly*
4043 pĕripatĕō (19), to *walk;* to *live a life*
4198 pŏrĕuŏmai (1), to *go, come;* to *travel*

WALKEDST
4043 pĕripatĕō (1), to *walk;* to *live a life*

WALKEST
1980 hâlak (1), to *walk; live a certain way*
3212 yâlak (3), to *walk;* to *live;* to *carry*
4043 pĕripatĕō (2), to *walk;* to *live a life*
4748 stŏichĕō (1), to *follow, walk;* to *conform*

WALKETH
1980 hâlak (31), to *walk; live a certain way*
3212 yâlak (2), to *walk;* to *live;* to *carry*
1330 diĕrchŏmai (2), to *traverse, travel through*
4043 pĕripatĕō (5), to *walk;* to *live a life*

WALKING
1980 hâlak (10), to *walk; live a certain way*
1981 hălak (Ch.) (1), to *walk; live a certain way*
3212 yâlak (3), to *walk;* to *live;* to *carry*
4043 pĕripatĕō (12), to *walk;* to *live a life*
4198 pŏrĕuŏmai (4), to *go, come;* to *travel*

WALL
846 'ushsharnâ' (Ch.) (1), *wall*
1444 geder (2), *wall* or *fence*
1447 gâdêr (5), *enclosure*, i.e. *wall*
1448 gᵉdêrâh (1), *enclosure* for flocks
2346 chôwmâh (92), *wall*

2426 chêyl (1), *entrenchment*
2434 chayits (1), *wall*
2742 chârûwts (1), *mined gold; trench*
3796 kôthel (1), *house wall*
3797 kᵉthal (Ch.) (1), *house wall*
7023 qîyr (50), *wall, side-wall*
7791 shûwr (3), *wall*
7794 shôwr (1), *bullock*
5038 tĕichŏs (8), *house wall*
5109 tŏichŏs (1), *wall*

WALLED
1219 bâtsar (2), to *be inaccessible*
2346 chôwmâh (2), *wall*

WALLOW
5606 çâphaq (1), to *be enough;* to *vomit*
6428 pâlash (3), to *roll in dust*

WALLOWED
1556 gâlal (1), to *roll;* to *commit*
2947 kuliŏō (1), to *roll about*

WALLOWING
2946 kulisma (1), *wallowing* in *filth*

WALLS
846 'ushsharnâ' (Ch.) (1), *wall*
1447 gâdêr (1), *enclosure*, i.e. *wall*
2346 chôwmâh (39), *wall*
2426 chêyl (1), *rampart, battlement*
3797 kᵉthal (Ch.) (1), *house wall*
7023 qîyr (16), *wall, side-wall*
7791 shûwr (4), *wall*
8284 shârâh (1), *fortification*
5038 tĕichŏs (1), *house wall*

WANDER
5074 nâdad (1), to *rove, flee;* to *drive away*
5128 nûwa' (4), to *waver*
6808 tsâ'âh (1), to *tip over;* to *depopulate*
7462 râ'âh (1), to *tend* a flock, i.e. *pasture* it
7686 shâgâh (2), to *stray, wander;* to *transgress*
8582 tâ'âh (5), to *vacillate*, i.e. *reel, stray*

WANDERED
1980 hâlak (1), to *walk; live a certain way*
5128 nûwa' (3), to *waver*
7686 shâgâh (1), to *stray, wander;* to *transgress*
8582 tâ'âh (3), to *vacillate*, i.e. *reel, stray*
4022 pĕriĕrchŏmai (1), to *stroll, vacillate, veer*
4105 planaō (1), to *roam, wander* from safety

WANDERERS
5074 nâdad (1), to *rove, flee;* to *drive away*
6808 tsâ'âh (1), to *tip over;* to *depopulate*

WANDEREST
6808 tsâ'âh (1), to *tip over;* to *depopulate;* to *imprison;* to *lay down*

WANDERETH
5074 nâdad (5), to *rove, flee;* to *drive away*
8582 tâ'âh (1), to *vacillate*, i.e. *reel, stray*

WANDERING
1981 hălak (Ch.) (1), to *walk; live a certain way*
5074 nâdad (1), to *rove, flee;* to *drive away*
5110 nûwd (1), to *waver;* to *wander, flee*
8582 tâ'âh (1), to *vacillate*, i.e. *reel, stray*
4022 pĕriĕrchŏmai (1), to *stroll, vacillate, veer*
4107 planētēs (1), *roving, erratic* teacher

WANDERINGS
5112 nôwd (1), *exile*

WANT
657 'epheç (1), *end; no further*
1097 bᵉlîy (2), *without, not yet; lacking;*
2637 châçêr (4), to *lack;* to *fail, want, make less*
2638 châçêr (1), *lacking*
2639 cheçer (1), *lack; destitution*
2640 chôçer (3), *poverty*
3772 kârath (3), to *cut* (off, down or asunder)
3808 lô' (1), *no, not*
4270 machçôwr (7), *impoverishment*
6485 pâqad (1), to *visit, care for, count*
5302 hustĕrĕō (1), to *be inferior;* to *fall short* (be *deficient*)
5303 hustĕrēma (3), *deficit; poverty; lacking*
5304 hustĕrēsis (2), *penury, lack, need*

WANTED
2637 châçêr (1), to *lack;* to *fail, want, make less*
5302 hustĕrĕō (2), to *be inferior;* to *fall short*

WANTETH
2308 châdal (1), to *desist, stop; be fat*
2637 châçêr (2), to *lack;* to *fail, want, make less*
2638 châçêr (4), *lacking*

WANTING
2627 chaççîyr (Ch.) (1), *deficient, wanting*
2642 cheçrôwn (1), *deficiency*
3808 lô' (1), *no, not*
6485 pâqad (2), to *visit, care for, count*
3007 lĕipō (3), to *fail* or *be absent*

WANTON
8265 sâqar (1), to *ogle*,
i.e. *blink* coquettishly
2691 katastrēniaō (1), to
be voluptuous against
4684 spatalaō (1), to *live*
in luxury

WANTONNESS
766 asēlgĕia (2),
debauchery, lewdness

WANTS
4270 machçôwr (1),
impoverishment
5532 chrĕia (1), *affair;*
requirement

WAR
2428 chayil (1), *army;*
wealth; virtue; valor
2438 Chîyrâm (1), *noble*
3898 lâcham (9), to fight
a *battle*
3901 lâchem (1), *battle,*
war
4421 milchâmâh (151),
battle; war; fighting
4421+7128 milchâmâh
(1), *battle; war; fighting*
6635 tsâbâ' (41), *army,*
military host
6904 qôbel (1),
battering-ram
7128 qᵉrâb (3), hostile
encounter
7129 qᵉrâb (Ch.) (1),
hostile *encounter*
4170 pŏlĕmĕō (4), to
battle, make war
4171 pŏlĕmŏs (6),
warfare; battle; fight
4753 stratĕuma (1), body
of *troops*
4754 stratĕuŏmai (4), to
serve in military

WARD
4929 mishmâr (11),
guard; deposit; usage
4931 mishmereth (6),
watch, sentry, post
5474 çûwgar (1), animal
cage
6488 pᵉqîdûth (1),
supervision
5438 phulakē (1),
guarding or guard

WARDROBE
899 beged (2), *clothing;*
treachery or pillage

WARDS
4931 mishmereth (3),
watch, sentry, post

WARE
4377 meker (1),
merchandise; value
4465 mimkâr (1),
merchandise
4728 maqqâchâh (1),
merchandise, wares
1737 ĕndiduskō (1), to
clothe
4894 sunĕidō (1), to
understand or be aware
5442 phulassō (1), to
watch, i.e. be on guard

WARES
3627 kᵉlîy (1),
implement, thing

3666 kin'âh (1), *package,*
bundle
4639 ma'ăseh (2), *action;*
labor
5801 'izzâbôwn (1),
trade, merchandise

WARFARE
6635 tsâbâ' (2), *army,*
military host
4752 stratĕia (2),
warfare; fight
4754 stratĕuŏmai (1), to
serve in military

WARM
2215 zârab (1), to *flow*
away, be dry
2525 châm (1), *hot,*
sweltering
2527 chôm (1), *heat*
2552 châmam (4), to be
hot; to be in a rage
3179 yâcham (1), to
conceive

WARMED
2552 châmam (1), to be
hot; to be in a rage
2328 thĕrmainō (5), to
heat oneself

WARMETH
2552 châmam (2), to be
hot; to be in a rage

WARMING
2328 thĕrmainō (1), to
heat oneself

WARN
2094 zâhar (8), to
enlighten
3560 nŏuthĕtĕō (3), to
caution or reprove

WARNED
2094 zâhar (4), to
enlighten
5263 hupŏdĕiknumi (2),
to *exemplify*
5537 chrēmatizō (4), to
utter an oracle

WARNING
2094 zâhar (6), to
enlighten
5749 'ûwd (1), to
duplicate or repeat
3560 nŏuthĕtĕō (1), to
caution or reprove

WARP
8359 shᵉthîy (9), *warp* in
weaving

WARRED
3898 lâcham (7), to fight
a *battle*
6633 tsâbâ' (2), to *mass*
an army or servants

WARRETH
4754 stratĕuŏmai (1), to
serve in military

WARRING
3898 lâcham (2), to fight
a *battle*
497 antistratĕuŏmai (1),
destroy, wage war

WARRIOR
5431 çâ'an (1), *soldier*
wearing boots

WARRIORS
6213+4421 'âsâh (2), to
do or make

WARS
4421 milchâmâh (9),
battle; war; fighting
4171 pŏlĕmŏs (4),
warfare; battle; fight

WASH
3526 kâbaç (39), to *wash*
7364 râchats (36), to
lave, bathe
628 apŏlŏuō (1), to *wash*
fully
907 baptizō (1), *baptize*
1026 brĕchō (1), to *make*
wet; to rain
3538 niptō (11), to *wash,*
bathe

WASHED
1740 dûwach (2), to *rinse*
clean, wash
3526 kâbaç (7), to *wash*
7364 râchats (17), to
lave, bathe
7857 shâṭaph (2), to
inundate, cleanse
628 apŏlŏuō (1), to *wash*
fully
633 apŏniptō (1), to *wash*
off hands
907 baptizō (1), *baptize*
1026 brĕchō (1), to *make*
wet; to rain
3068 lŏuō (6), to *bathe; to*
wash
3538 niptō (6), to *wash,*
bathe
4150 plunō (1), to *wash*
or *launder* clothing

WASHEST
7857 shâṭaph (1), to
inundate, cleanse

WASHING
3526 kâbaç (1), to *wash*
4325 mayim (1), *water*
7364 râchats (1), to *lave,*
bathe
7367 rachtsâh (2),
bathing place
637 apŏplunō (1), to
rinse off, wash out
909 baptismŏs (2),
baptism
3067 lŏutrŏn (2),
washing, baptism

WASHINGS
909 baptismŏs (1),
baptism

WASHPOT
5518+7366 çîyr (2), *thorn;*
hook

WAST
1961 hâyâh (13), to *exist,*
i.e. *be or become*
2258 ēn (5), I *was*
5607 ōn (1), *being,*
existence

WASTE
1086 bâlâh (1), to *wear*
out, decay; consume
1110 bâlaq (2), to
annihilate, devastate
1326 bâthâh (1), *area of*
desolation

2717 chârab (13), to
desolate, destroy
2720 chârêb (6), *ruined;*
desolate
2721 chôreb (2),
parched; ruined
2723 chorbâh (14),
desolation, dry desert
3615 kâlâh (1), to
complete, prepare
3765 kirçêm (1), to *lay*
waste, ravage
4875 mᵉshôw'âh (2), *ruin*
5327 nâtsâh (1), to *be*
desolate, to lay waste
7489 râ'a' (1), to *be good*
for nothing
7582 shâ'âh (2), to *moan;*
to *desolate*
7703 shâdad (5), to
ravage
8047 shammâh (3), *ruin;*
consternation
8074 shâmêm (5), to
devastate; to stupefy
8077 shᵉmâmâh (1),
devastation
8414 tôhûw (1), *waste,*
desolation, formless
684 apŏlĕia (2), *ruin or*
loss

WASTED
1197 bâ'ar (1), to *be*
brutish, be senseless
2717 chârab (3), to
parch; desolate, destroy
2723 chorbâh (1),
desolation, dry desert
3615 kâlâh (1), to
complete, consume
7582 shâ'âh (1), to *moan;*
to *desolate*
7703 shâdad (2), to
ravage
7843 shâchath (1), to
decay; to ruin
8437 tôwlâl (1), *oppressor*
8552 tâmam (2), to
complete, finish
1287 diaskŏrpizō (2), to
scatter; to squander
4199 pŏrthĕō (1), to
ravage, pillage

WASTENESS
7722 shôw' (1), *tempest;*
devastation

WASTER
7843 shâchath (2), to
decay; to ruin

WASTES
2723 chorbâh (7),
desolation, dry desert

WASTETH
2522 châlash (1), to
prostrate, lay low
7703 shâdad (1), to
ravage
7736 shûwd (1), to
devastate

WASTING
7701 shôd (2), *violence,*
ravage, destruction

WATCH
821 'ashmûrâh (4), night
watch
4707 mitspeh (1),
military observatory

English

WATCHED
4929 mishmâr (4), *guard; deposit; usage; example*
4931 mishmereth (5), *watch, sentry, post*
6822 tsâphâh (5), to *observe, await*
8104 shâmar (5), to *watch*
8108 shomrâh (1), *watchfulness*
8245 shâqad (6), to *be on the lookout*
69 agrupnĕō (3), *to be sleepless, keep awake*
1127 grēgŏrĕuō (16), to *watch, guard*
2892 kŏustōdia (3), *sentry*
3525 nēphō (2), to *abstain from wine*
5438 phulakē (6), *night watch; prison; haunt*

WATCHED
6822 tsâphâh (1), to *observe, await*
8104 shâmar (2), to *watch*
8245 shâqad (2), to *be on the lookout*
1127 grēgŏrĕuō (2), to *watch, guard*
3906 paratērĕō (5), to *note insidiously*
5083 tērĕō (1), to *keep, guard, obey*

WATCHER
5894 'îyr (Ch.) (2), *watcher-angel*

WATCHERS
5341 nâtsar (1), to *guard, protect, maintain*
5894 'îyr (Ch.) (1), *watcher-angel*

WATCHES
821 'ashmûrâh (3), *night watch*
4931 mishmereth (2), *watch, sentry, post*

WATCHETH
6822 tsâphâh (1), to *observe, await*
6974 qûwts (1), to *awake*
1127 grēgŏrĕuō (1), to *watch, guard*

WATCHFUL
1127 grēgŏrĕuō (1), to *watch, guard*

WATCHING
6822 tsâphâh (2), to *observe, await*
8245 shâqad (1), to *be on the lookout*
69 agrupnĕō (1), *to be sleepless, keep awake*
1127 grēgŏrĕuō (1), to *watch, guard*
5083 tērĕō (1), to *keep, guard, obey*

WATCHINGS
70 agrupnia (2), *keeping awake*

WATCHMAN
6822 tsâphâh (14), to *peer into the distance*
8104 shâmar (1), to *watch*

WATCHMAN'S
6822 tsâphâh (1), to *peer into the distance*

WATCHMEN
5341 nâtsar (3), to *guard, protect, maintain*
6822 tsâphâh (5), to *peer into the distance*
8104 shâmar (4), to *watch*

WATCHTOWER
4707 mitspeh (1), *military observatory*
6844 tsâphîyth (1), *sentry*

WATER
1119 bᵉmôw (1), *in, with, by*
2222 zarzìyph (1), *pouring rain*
4325 mayim (308), *water*
4529 mâçâh (1), to *dissolve, melt*
7301 râvâh (1), to *slake thirst or appetites*
8248 shâqâh (9), to *quaff, i.e. to irrigate*
504 anudrŏs (2), *dry, arid*
5202 hudrŏpŏtĕō (1), to *drink water exclusively*
5204 hudōr (62), *water*

WATERCOURSE
4161+4325 môwtsâ' (1), *going forth*
8585 tᵉ'âlâh (1), *irrigation channel*

WATERED
3384 yârâh (1), to *point; to teach*
4945 mashqeh (1), *butler; drink; well-watered*
7302 râveh (2), *sated, full with drink*
8248 shâqâh (6), to *quaff, i.e. to irrigate*
4222 pŏtizō (1), to *furnish drink, irrigate*

WATEREDST
8248 shâqâh (1), to *quaff, i.e. to irrigate*

WATEREST
7301 râvâh (1), to *slake thirst or appetites*
7783 shùwq (1), to *overflow*

WATERETH
7301 râvâh (2), to *slake thirst or appetites*
8248 shâqâh (1), to *quaff, i.e. to irrigate*
4222 pŏtizō (2), to *furnish drink, irrigate*

WATERFLOOD
7641+4325 shibbôl (1), *stream; ear of grain*

WATERING
4325 mayim (1), *water*
7377 rîy (1), *irrigation*
4222 pŏtizō (1), to *furnish drink, irrigate*

WATERPOT
5201 hudria (1), *water jar, i.e. receptacle*

WATERPOTS
5201 hudria (2), *water jar, i.e. receptacle*

WATERS
4325 mayim (265), *water*
4215 pŏtamŏs (1), *current, brook, running water*
5204 hudōr (15), *water*

WATERSPOUTS
6794 tsinnûwr (1), *culvert, water-shaft*

WATERSPRINGS
4161+4325 môwtsâ' (2), *going forth*

WAVE
5130 nûwph (11), to *quiver, vibrate, rock*
8573 tᵉnûwphâh (19), *official undulation of sacrificial offerings*
2830 kludōn (1), *surge, raging*

WAVED
5130 nûwph (5), to *quiver, vibrate, rock*
8573 tᵉnûwphâh (1), *official undulation of sacrificial offerings*

WAVERETH
1252 diakrinō (1), to *decide; to hesitate*

WAVERING
186 aklinēs (1), *firm, unswerving*
1252 diakrinō (1), to *decide; to hesitate*

WAVES
1116 bâmâh (1), *elevation, high place*
1530 gal (14), *heap; ruins*
1796 dŏkìy (1), *dashing, pounding of surf*
4867 mishbâr (4), *breaker sea-waves*
2949 kuma (5), *bursting or toppling*
4535 salŏs (1), *billow, i.e. rolling motion of waves*

WAX
1749 dôwnag (4), *bees-wax*
2691 katastrēniaō (1), to *be voluptuous against*
3822 palaiŏō (2), to *make, become worn out*
4298 prŏkŏptō (1), to *go ahead, advance*
5594 psuchō (1), to *chill, grow cold*

WAXED
1980 hâlak (5), to *walk; live a certain way*
1096 ginŏmai (2), to *be, become*
2901 krataiŏō (2), *increase in vigor*
3955 parrhēsiazŏmai (1), to *be frank in utterance*
3975 pachunō (1), to *fatten; to render callous*
4147 plŏutĕō (1), to *be, become wealthy*

WAXETH
1095 gēraskō (1), to *be senescent, grow old*

WAXING
3982 pĕithō (1), to *pacify or conciliate; to assent*

WAY
734 'ôrach (18), *road; manner of life*
776 'erets (3), *earth, land, soil; country*
935 bôw' (1), to *go, come*
1870 derek (466), *road; course of life; mode*
2008 hênnâh (1), *from here; from there*
2088 zeh (1), *this or that*
3212 yâlak (6), to *walk; to live; to carry*
3541 kôh (1), *thus*
4498 mânôwç (1), *fleeing; place of refuge*
5265 nâça' (1), *start on a journey*
5410 nâthîyb (2), (beaten) *track, path*
7125 qir'âh (1), to *encounter, to happen*
7971 shâlach (1), to *send away*
8582 tâ'âh (2), to *vacillate, i.e. reel*
1545 ĕkbasis (1), *exit, way out*
1624 ĕktrĕpō (1), to *turn away*
1722 ĕn (1), *in; during; because of*
3112 makran (2), *at a distance, far away*
3319 mĕsŏs (2), *middle*
3598 hŏdŏs (81), *road*
3938 parŏdŏs (1), *by-road, i.e. a route*
4105 planaō (1), to *roam, wander from safety*
4206 pŏrrhō (1), *forwards*
4311 prŏpĕmpō (5), to *send forward*
5158 trŏpŏs (2), *deportment, character*

WAYFARING
732 'ârach (4), to *travel, wander*
1980+1870 hâlak (1), to *walk; live a certain way*
5674+734 'âbar (1), to *cross over; to transition*

WAYMARKS
6725 tsîyûwn (1), *guiding pillar, monument*

WAYS
734 'ôrach (8), *road; manner of life*
735 'ôrach (Ch.) (2), *road*
1870 derek (161), *road; course of life; mode of action*
1979 hălîykâh (2), *walking; procession or march; caravan*
4546 mᵉçillâh (1), *main thoroughfare; viaduct*
4570 ma'gâl (1), *circular track or camp rampart*
7339 rᵉchôb (1), *myriad*
296 amphŏdŏn (1), *fork in the road*
684 apŏlĕia (1), *ruin or loss*
3598 hŏdŏs (11), *road*

4197 pŏrĕia (1), *journey; life's daily conduct*

WAYSIDE
3027+4570 yâd (1), *hand; power*
3197+1870 yak (1), *hand or side*

WEAK
535 'âmal (1), *to be weak; to be sick*
536 'umlal (1), *sick, faint*
2470 châlâh (4), *to be weak, sick, afflicted*
2523 challâsh (1), *frail, weak*
3212 yâlak (2), *to walk; to live; to carry*
3782 kâshal (1), *to totter, waver; to falter*
7390 rak (1), *tender; weak*
7503 râphâh (1), *to slacken*
7504 râpheh (4), *slack*
102 adunatŏs (1), *weak; impossible*
770 asthĕnĕō (19), *to be feeble*
772 asthĕnēs (8), *strengthless, weak*

WEAKEN
2522 châlash (1), *to prostrate, lay low*

WEAKENED
6031 'ânâh (1), *to afflict, be afflicted*
7503 râphâh (2), *to slacken*

WEAKENETH
7503 râphâh (2), *to slacken*

WEAKER
1800 dal (1), *weak, thin; humble, needy*
772 asthĕnēs (1), *strengthless, weak*

WEAKNESS
769 asthĕnĕia (5), *feebleness; frailty*
772 asthĕnēs (2), *strengthless, weak*

WEALTH
1952 hôwn (5), *wealth*
2428 chayil (10), *army; wealth; virtue; valor*
2896 tôwb (3), *good; well*
3581 kôach (1), *force, might; strength*
5233 nekeç (4), *treasure, riches*
2142 ĕupŏria (1), *resources, prosperity*

WEALTHY
7310 rĕvâyâh (1), *satisfaction*
7961 shâlêv (1), *careless, carefree; security*

WEANED
1580 gâmal (12), *to benefit or requite*

WEAPON
240 'âzên (1), *spade; paddle*
3627 kĕlîy (4), *implement, thing*

5402 nesheq (1), *military arms, arsenal*
7973 shelach (2), *spear; shoot of growth*

WEAPONS
3627 kĕlîy (17), *implement, thing*
5402 nesheq (2), *military arms, arsenal*
3696 hŏplŏn (2), *implement, or utensil*

WEAR
1080 bĕlâ' (Ch.) (1), *to afflict, torment*
1961 hâyâh (1), *to exist, i.e. be or become*
3847 lâbash (4), *to clothe*
5034 nâbêl (1), *to wilt; to fall away; to be foolish*
5375 nâsâ' (2), *to lift up*
7833 shâchaq (1), *to grind or wear away*
2827 klinō (1), *to slant or slope*
5409 phŏrĕō (1), *to wear*

WEARETH
5409 phŏrĕō (1), *to wear*

WEARIED
3021 yâga' (5), *to be exhausted, to tire,*
3811 lâ'âh (5), *to tire; to be, make disgusted*
5888 'âyêph (1), *to languish*
2577 kamnō (1), *to tire; to faint, sicken*
2872 kŏpiaō (1), *to feel fatigue; to work hard*

WEARIETH
2959 țârach (1), *to overburden*
3021 yâga' (1), *to be exhausted, to tire,*

WEARINESS
3024 yĕgî'âh (1), *fatigue*
4972 mattĕlâ'âh (1), *what a trouble!*
2873 kŏpŏs (1), *toil; pains*

WEARING
5375 nâsâ' (1), *to lift up*
4025 pĕrithĕsis (1), *putting all around, i.e. decorating oneself with*
5409 phŏrĕō (1), *to wear*

WEARISOME
5999 'âmâl (1), *wearing effort; worry*

WEARY
3019 yâgîya' (1), *tired, exhausted*
3021 yâga' (7), *to be exhausted, to tire,*
3023 yâgêa' (2), *tiresome*
3286 yâ'aph (5), *to tire*
3287 yâ'êph (1), *exhausted*
3811 lâ'âh (10), *to tire; to be, make disgusted*
5354 nâqaț (1), *to loathe*
5774 'ûwph (1), *to cover, to fly; to faint*
5889 'âyêph (8), *languid*
6973 qûwts (2), *to be, make disgusted*
7646 sâba' (1), *fill to satiety*

1573 ĕkkakĕō (2), *to be weak, fail*
5299 hupōpiazō (1), *to beat up; to wear out*

WEASEL
2467 chôled (1), *weasel*

WEATHER
2091 zâhâb (1), *gold, piece of gold*
3117 yôwm (1), *day; time period*
2105 ĕudia (1), *clear sky, i.e. fine weather*
5494 chĕimōn (1), *winter season; stormy weather*

WEAVE
707 'ârag (2), *to plait or weave*

WEAVER
707 'ârag (2), *to plait or weave*

WEAVER'S
707 'ârag (4), *to plait or weave*

WEAVEST
707 'ârag (1), *to plait or weave*

WEB
1004 bayith (1), *house; temple; family, tribe*
4545 maççeketh (2), *length-wise threads*
6980 qûwr (1), *spider web*

WEBS
6980 qûwr (1), *spider web*

WEDDING
1062 gamōs (7), *nuptials*

WEDGE
3956 lâshôwn (2), *tongue; tongue-shaped*

WEDLOCK
5003 nâ'aph (1), *to commit adultery*

WEEDS
5488 çûwph (1), *papyrus reed; reed*

WEEK
7620 shâbûwa' (4), *seven-day week*
4521 sabbatŏn (9), *day of weekly repose*

WEEKS
7620 shâbûwa' (15), *seven-day week*

WEEP
1058 bâkâh (29), *to weep, moan*
1065 bĕkîy (2), *weeping*
1830 dâma' (1), *to weep*
2799 klaiō (15), *to sob, wail*

WEEPEST
1058 bâkâh (1), *to weep, moan*
2799 klaiō (2), *to sob, wail*

WEEPETH
1058 bâkâh (4), *to weep, moan*

WEEPING
1058 bâkâh (8), *to weep, moan*
1065 bĕkîy (21), *weeping*

2799 klaiō (9), *to sob, wail*
2805 klauthmŏs (6), *lamentation, weeping*

WEIGH
4948 mishqâl (2), *weight, weighing*
6424 pâlaç (2), *to weigh mentally*
8254 shâqal (2), *to suspend in trade*

WEIGHED
8254 shâqal (12), *to suspend in trade*
8505 tâkan (1), *to balance, i.e. measure*
8625 tĕqal (Ch.) (1), *to weigh in a balance*

WEIGHETH
8505 tâkan (2), *to balance, i.e. measure*

WEIGHT
68 'eben (4), *stone*
4946 mishqôwl (1), *weight*
4948 mishqâl (44), *weight, weighing*
6425 peleç (1), *balance, scale*
922 barŏs (1), *load, abundance, authority*
3591 ŏgkŏs (1), *burden, hindrance*
5006 talantiaiŏs (1), *weight of 57-80 lbs.*

WEIGHTIER
926 barus (1), *weighty*

WEIGHTS
68 'eben (6), *stone*

WEIGHTY
5192 nêțel (1), *burden*
926 barus (1), *weighty*

WELFARE
2896 tôwb (1), *good; well*
3444 yĕshûw'âh (1), *victory; prosperity*
7965 shâlôwm (5), *safe; well; health, prosperity*

WELL
71 'Âbânâh (1), *stony*
369 'ayin (1), *there is no, i.e., not exist, none*
375 'êyphôh (2), *where?; when?; how?*
875 bĕ'êr (21), *well, cistern*
883 Bĕ'êr la-Chay Rô'îy (1), *well of a living (One) my seer*
953 bôwr (6), *pit hole, cistern, well; prison*
995 bîyn (1), *to understand; discern*
2090 zôh (1), *this or that*
2654 châphêts (1), *to be pleased with, desire*
2895 țowb (9), *to be good*
2896 țôwb (20), *good; well*
2898 țûwb (2), *good; goodness; beauty, gladness, welfare*
3190 yâțab (35), *to be, make well*
3303 yâpheh (5), *beautiful; handsome*

English

WELL'S (cont.)

3651 kên (4), *just; right, correct*
3966 mᵉ'ôd (1), *very, utterly*
4599 ma'yân (2), *fountain; source*
4639 ma'ăseh (1), *action; labor*
4726 mâqôwr (1), *flow of liquids, or ideas*
5869 'ayin (9), *eye; sight; fountain*
5878 'Êyn Chărôd (1), *fountain of trembling*
6822 tsâphâh (1), *to peer into the distance*
7181 qâshab (1), *to prick up the ears*
7571 rethach (1), *boiling*
7965 shâlôwm (14), *safe; well; health, prosperity*
15 agathŏpŏiĕō (4), *to be a well-doer*
16 agathŏpŏiïa (1), *virtue, doing good*
17 agathŏpŏiŏs (1), *virtuous one*
18 agathŏs (1), *good*
957 bĕltĭŏn (1), *better*
1510+2101 ĕimi (1), *I exist, I am*
1921 ĕpiginōskō (1), *to acknowledge*
2095 ĕu (6), *well*
2100 ĕuarĕstĕō (1), *to gratify entirely, please*
2101 ĕuarĕstŏs (1), *fully agreeable, pleasing*
2106 ĕudŏkĕō (7), *to think well, i.e. approve*
2509 kathapĕr (1), *exactly as*
2532 kai (2), *and; or*
2569 kalŏpŏiĕō (1), *to do well*
2570 kalŏs (1), *good; beautiful; valuable*
2573 kalōs (33), *well, i.e. rightly*
3140 marturĕō (2), *to testify; to commend*
3184 mĕthuō (1), *to get drunk*
4077 pēgē (3), *source or supply*
4260 prŏbainō (2), *to advance*
4982 sōzō (1), *to deliver; to protect*
5421 phrĕar (2), *cistern or water well; abyss*

WELL'S
875 bᵉ'êr (6), *well, cistern*

WELLBELOVED
1730 dôwd (1), *beloved, friend; uncle, relative*
3039 yᵉdîyd (2), *loved*
27 agapētŏs (3), *beloved*

WELLFAVOURED
2896+2580 tôwb (1), *good; well*

WELLPLEASING
2101 ĕuarĕstŏs (2), *fully agreeable, pleasing*

WELLS
875 bᵉ'êr (3), *well, cistern*

953 bôwr (3), *pit hole, cistern, well; prison*
4599 ma'yân (3), *fountain; source*
5869 'ayin (1), *eye; sight; fountain*
4077 pēgē (1), *source or supply*

WELLSPRING
4726 mâqôwr (2), *flow*

WEN
2990 yabbêl (1), *having running sores*

WENCH
8198 shiphchâh (1), *household female slave*

WENT
236 'ăzal (Ch.) (6), *to depart*
935 bôw' (115), *to go*
980 Bachûrîym (1), *young men*
1718 dâdâh (1), *to walk gently; lead*
1961 hâyâh (4), *to exist, i.e. be or become*
1980 hâlak (93), *to walk; live a certain way*
3212 yâlak (281), *to walk; to live; to carry*
3318 yâtsâ' (216), *to go*
3381 yârad (64), *to descend*
3518 kâbâh (1), *to extinguish*
5066 nâgash (4), *to be, come, bring near*
5075 nᵉdad (Ch.) (1), *to depart*
5221 nâkâh (1), *to strike, kill*
5265 nâça' (13), *start on a journey*
5312 nᵉphaq (Ch.) (1), *to issue forth; to bring out*
5437 çâbab (6), *to surround*
5493 çûwr (1), *to turn off*
5674 'âbar (38), *to cross over; to transition*
5927 'âlâh (160), *to ascend, be high, mount*
5954 'ălal (Ch.) (3), *to go in; to lead in*
5974 'îm (Ch.) (1), *with*
6743 tsâlach (1), *to push*
6805 tsâ'ad (1), *to pace, step regularly*
6923 qâdam (2), *to anticipate, hasten*
7121 qârâ' (1), *to call out*
7126 qârab (2), *to approach, bring near*
7311 rûwm (1), *to be high; to rise or raise*
7683 shâgag (1), *to stray; to sin*
7725 shûwb (6), *to turn back; to return*
7751 shûwṭ (1), *to travel, roam*
8582 tâ'âh (6), *to vacillate, i.e. reel, stray*
305 anabainō (24), *to go up, rise*
402 anachōrĕō (1), *to retire, withdraw*

424 anĕrchŏmai (3), *to ascend*
549 apĕimi (1), *to go away*
565 apĕrchŏmai (54), *to go off, i.e. depart*
589 apŏdēmĕō (3), *visit a foreign land*
1279 diapŏrĕuŏmai (3), *to travel through*
1330 diĕrchŏmai (6), *to traverse, travel through*
1353 diŏdĕuō (1), *to travel through*
1524 ĕisĕimi (2), *to enter*
1525 ĕisĕrchŏmai (25), *to enter*
1531 ĕispŏrĕuŏmai (1), *to enter*
1607 ĕkpŏrĕuŏmai (7), *to depart, be discharged, proceed, project*
1681 Ĕlumas (1), *Elymas*
1684 ĕmbainō (2), *to embark; to reach*
1821 ĕxapŏstĕllō (2), *to despatch, or to dismiss*
1831 ĕxĕrchŏmai (86), *to issue; to leave*
1910 ĕpibainō (1), *to embark, arrive*
2021 ĕpichĕirĕō (1), *to undertake, try*
2064 ĕrchŏmai (11), *to go, come*
2212 zētĕō (1), *to seek*
2597 katabainō (13), *to descend*
2718 katĕrchŏmai (2), *to go, come down*
3596 hŏdŏipŏrĕō (1), *to travel*
3854 paraginŏmai (1), *to arrive; to appear*
3899 parapŏrĕuŏmai (1), *to travel near*
3987 pĕiraō (1), *to attempt, try*
4013 pĕriagō (4), *to walk around*
4105 planaō (1), *to roam, wander from safety*
4198 pŏrĕuŏmai (44), *to go, come; to travel*
4254 prŏagō (6), *to lead forward; to precede*
4281 prŏĕrchŏmai (4), *to go onward, precede*
4334 prŏsĕrchŏmai (3), *to come near, visit*
4344 prŏskĕphalaiŏn (1), *cushion pillow*
4848 sumpŏrĕuŏmai (3), *to journey together*
4897 sunĕisĕrchŏmai (2), *to enter with*
4905 sunĕrchŏmai (3), *to gather together*
5217 hupagō (5), *to withdraw or retire*
5221 hupantaō (1), *to meet, encounter*
5298 hupŏchōrĕō (1), *to vacate down, i.e. retire*

WENTEST
1980 hâlak (6), *to walk; live a certain way*
3212 yâlak (1), *to walk; to live; to carry*

3318 yâtsâ' (3), *to go, bring out*
5927 'âlâh (2), *to ascend, be high, mount*
7788 shûwr (1), *i.e. travel about*
1525 ĕisĕrchŏmai (1), *to enter*

WEPT
1058 bâkâh (57), *to weep, moan*
1145 dakruō (1), *to shed tears*
2799 klaiō (11), *to sob, wail*

WERT
1498 ĕiĕn (1), *might could, would, or should*

WEST
3220 yâm (51), *sea; basin; west*
3996+8121 mâbôw' (1), *entrance; sunset; west*
4628 ma'ărâb (10), *west*
1424 dusmē (5), *western*
3047 lips (1), *southwest*
5566 chōrŏs (1), *north-west wind*

WESTERN
3220 yâm (1), *sea; basin; west*

WESTWARD
3220 yâm (21), *sea; basin; west*
3996+8121 mâbôw' (1), *entrance; sunset; west*
4628 ma'ărâb (4), *west*

WET
6647 tsᵉba' (Ch.) (5), *to dip, be wet*
7372 râṭab (1), *to be moist*

WHALE
8565 tan (1), *jackal*
8577 tannîyn (1), *sea-serpent; jackal*

WHALE'S
2785 kētŏs (1), *huge fish*

WHALES
8577 tannîyn (1), *sea-serpent; jackal*

WHEAT
1250 bâr (5), *grain*
1715 dâgân (2), *grain*
2406 chiṭṭâh (29), *wheat*
2591 chinṭâ' (Ch.) (2), *wheat*
7383 rîyphâh (1), *grits cereal*
4621 sitŏs (12), *grain, especially wheat*

WHEATEN
2406 chiṭṭâh (1), *wheat*

WHEEL
212 'ôwphân (10), *wheel*
1534 galgal (3), *wheel; something round*
1536 gilgâl (1), *wheel*

WHEELS
70 'ôben (1), *potter's wheel; midwife's stool*
212 'ôwphân (24), *wheel*
1534 galgal (6), *wheel; something round*

1535 galgal (Ch.) (1),
wheel
6471 pa'am (1), *time;*
step; occurence

WHELP
1482 gûwr (3), *cub*

WHELPS
1121 bên (2), *son,*
descendant; people
1482 gûwr (3), *cub*
1484 gôwr (3), lion *cub*

WHEN
310 'achar (1), *after*
518 'îm (19), *whether?*
834 'ăsher (83), *who,*
what, that; when
1767 day (3), *enough,*
sufficient
1768 dîy (Ch.) (4), *that; of*
1961 hâyâh (4), *to exist*
3117 yôwm (7), *day; time*
3588 kîy (280), *for, that*
3644 kᵉmôw (1), *like, as*
4970 mâthay (14), *when;*
when?, how long?
5704 'ad (3), *as far (long)*
as; during; while; until
5750 'ôwd (2), *again;*
repeatedly; still; more
5921 'al (1), *above, over,*
upon, or against
6256 'êth (7), *time*
6310 peh (2), *mouth;*
opening
1437 ĕan (2),
indefiniteness
1875 ĕpan (3), *whenever*
1893 ĕpĕi (1), *since*
2259 hĕnika (2), *at which*
time, whenever
2531 kathōs (1), *just or*
inasmuch as, that
3326 mĕta (2), *with,*
among; after, later
3698 hŏpŏtĕ (1), *as soon*
as, when
3704 hŏpŏs (1), *in the*
manner that
3752 hŏtan (123),
inasmuch as, at once
3753 hŏtĕ (99), *when; as*
3756 ŏu (1), *no or not*
4218 pŏtĕ (13), *at some*
time, ever
5613 hōs (40), *which,*
how, i.e. in that manner
5618 hōspĕr (2), *exactly*
like

WHENCE
335 'ay (1), *where?*
370 'ayin (19), *where*
from?, whence?
1992 hêm (1), *they*
3606 hŏthĕn (4), *from*
which place or source
3739 hŏs (2), *who, which,*
what, that
4159 pŏthĕn (28), *from*
which; what

WHENSOEVER
3605 kôl (1), *all, any or*
every
3752 hŏtan (1),
inasmuch as, at once
5613+1437 hōs (1), *which,*
how, i.e. in that manner

WHERE
335 'ay (16), *where?*
346 'ayêh (45), *where?*
349 'êyk (1), *where?*
351 'êykôh (1), *where*
370 'ayin (2), *where*
from?, whence?
375 'êyphôh (9), *where?*
413 'êl (2), *to, toward*
575 'ân (2), *where from?*
645 'êphôw (5), *then*
657 'epheç (1), *end; no*
further
834 'ăsher (58), *where*
1768 dîy (Ch.) (1), *that; of*
3027 yâd (1), *hand; power*
5921 'al (2), *above, over,*
upon, or against
8033 shâm (20), *where*
8478 tachath (1), *bottom;*
underneath; in lieu of
8536 tâm (Ch.) (1), *there*
296 amphŏdŏn (1), *fork*
in the road
1330 dierchŏmai (1), *to*
traverse, travel through
1337 dithalassŏs (1),
having two seas
2596 kata (1), *down;*
according to
3606 hŏthĕn (2), *from*
which place or source
3699 hŏpŏu (58), *at*
whichever spot
3757 hŏu (21), *at which*
place, i.e. where
3837 pantachŏu (5),
universally, everywhere
3838 pantelēs (1), *entire;*
completion
4226 pŏu (37), *at what*
locality?
5101 tis (1), *who?,*
which? or what?

WHEREABOUT
834 'ăsher (1), *where,*
how, because

WHEREAS
518 'îm (1), *whether?; if,*
although; Oh that!
834 'ăsher (2), *because,*
in order that
1768 dîy (Ch.) (4), *that; of*
3588 kîy (5), *for, that*
because
6258 'attâh (2), *at this*
time, now
8478 tachath (1), *bottom;*
underneath; in lieu of
3699 hŏpŏu (2), *at*
whichever spot
3748 hŏstis (1), *whoever*

WHEREBY
834 'ăsher (17), *because,*
in order that
4100 mâh (1), *whatever;*
that which
4482 mên (1), *part;*
musical chord
3588 hŏ (1), "*the,*" i.e. the
definite article
3739 hŏs (1), *who, which,*
what, that

WHEREFORE
199 'ûwlâm (1), *however*
or on the contrary
3651 kên (18), *just; right,*
correct

3861 lâhên (Ch.) (1),
therefore; except
4069 maddûwa' (28),
why?, what?
4100 mâh (86), *what?,*
how?, why?, when?
686 ara (1), *therefore*
1161 dĕ (1), *but, yet*
1302 diati (4), *why?*
1352 diŏ (41),
consequently, therefore
1355 diŏpĕr (3), *on which*
very account
3606 hŏthĕn (4), *from*
which place or source
3767 ŏun (7), *certainly;*
accordingly
5101 tis (3), *who?,*
which? or what?
5105 tŏigarŏun (1),
consequently, then
5620 hŏstĕ (17), *thus,*
therefore

WHEREIN
834 'ăsher (70), *when,*
where, how, because
1459 gav (Ch.) (1), *middle*
2098 zûw (2), *this or that*
4100 mâh (15), *what?,*
how?, why?, when?
8033 shâm (1), *where*
3739 hŏs (1), *what, that*
3757 hŏu (3), *where*

WHEREINSOEVER
1722+3739+302 ĕn (1), *in;*
during; because of

WHEREINTO
824+8432 'Esh'ân (1),
support
834+413+8432 'ăsher (1),
when, where, how
1519+3739 ĕis (1), *to or*
into

WHEREOF
834 'ăsher (24), *where*
3739 hŏs (11), *who,*
which, what, that

WHEREON
834 'ăsher (2), *where,*
how, because
834+5921 'ăsher (13),
where, how, because
5921 'al (2), *above, over,*
upon, or against
5921+4100 'al (1), *above,*
over, upon, or against
1909+3739 ĕpi (4), *on,*
upon
3739 hŏs (1), *who, which,*
what, that

WHERESOEVER
834 'ăsher (1), *where,*
how, because
3605 kôl (1), *all, any*
3699 hŏpŏu (1), *at*
whichever spot

WHERETO
834 'ăsher (1), *where,*
how, because
4100 mâh (1), *what?,*
how?, why?, when?
1519+3739 ĕis (1), *to or*
into

WHEREUNTO
834 'ăsher (6), *where,*
how, because

3739 hŏs (6), *who, which,*
what, that
5101 tis (7), *who?,*
which? or what?

WHEREUPON
413 'êl (2), *to, toward*
5921 'al (1), *above, over,*
upon, or against
3606 hŏthĕn (3), *from*
which place or source

WHEREWITH
834 'ăsher (68), *when,*
where, how, because
1697 dâbâr (1), *word;*
matter; thing
4100 mâh (9), *what?,*
how?, why?, when?
1722+3739 ĕn (2), *in;*
during; because of
1722+5101 ĕn (3), *in;*
during; because of
3739 hŏs (9), *who, which*
3745 hŏsŏs (1), *as much*
as
5101 tis (1), *who?,*
which? or what?

WHEREWITHAL
5101 tis (1), *who?,*
which? or what?

WHET
3913 lâṭash (1), *to*
sharpen; to pierce
7043 qâlal (1), *to be,*
make light (sharp)
8150 shânan (2), *to*
pierce; to inculcate

WHETHER
176 'ôw (8), *or, whether*
335 'ay (1), *where?*
518 'îm (27), *whether?*
996 bêyn (4), "*either...or*"
2006 hên (Ch.) (2),
whether, but, if
3588 kîy (1), *for, that*
because
4100 mâh (1), *what?,*
how?, why?, when?
4480 min (3), *from, out of*
5704 'ad (1), *as far (long)*
as; during; while; until
5750 'ôwd (2), *again;*
repeatedly; still; more
1487 ĕi (22), *if, whether*
1535 ĕitĕ (31), *if too*
2273 ĕtŏi (1), *either...or*
3379 mĕpŏtĕ (1), *not*
ever; if, or lest ever
4220 pŏtĕrŏn (1), *which*
5037 tĕ (1), *both or also*
5101 tis (8), *who?,*
which? or what?

WHILE
518 'îm (1), *whether?; if,*
although; Oh that!
834 'ăsher (1), *when,*
where, how, because
3117 yôwm (7), *day; time*
3541 kôh (1), *thus*
3588 kîy (3), *for, that*
because
4705 mits'âr (1), *little;*
short time
5704 'ad (9), *during; while*
5750 'ôwd (7), *again;*
repeatedly; still; more
5751 'ôwd (Ch.) (1),
again; repeatedly; still

English

WHILES

7350 râchôwq (1), *remote, far*
2193 hěŏs (8), *until*
2250 hēměra (2), *day; period of time*
2540 kairŏs (1), *occasion*, i.e. *set time*
3153 mataiŏtēs (1), *transientness; depravity*
3397 mikrŏn (2), *small space of time or degree*
3641 ŏligŏs (2), *puny, small*
3752 hŏtan (1), *inasmuch as, at once*
3753 hŏtě (1), *when; as*
3819 palai (1), *formerly; sometime since*
4340 prŏskairŏs (1), *temporary*
5550 chrŏnŏs (3), *time*
5613 hŏs (4), *which, how,* i.e. *in that manner*

WHILES

5750 'ôwd (1), *again; repeatedly; still; more*
2193+3755 hěŏs (1), *until*

WHILST

834 'ăsher (1), *when, where, how, because*
5704 'ad (4), *as far (long) as; during; while; until*

WHIP

7752 shôwṭ (2), *lash*

WHIPS

7752 shôwṭ (4), *lash*

WHIRLETH

1980 hâlak (1), to *walk; live a certain way*

WHIRLWIND

5492 çûwphâh (10), *hurricane* wind
5590 çâ'ar (3), to *rush* upon, to *toss* about
5591 ça'ar (11), *hurricane* wind
7307+5591 rûwach (1), *breath; wind; life-spirit*
8175 sâ'ar (2), to *storm;* to *shiver,* i.e. *fear*

WHIRLWINDS

5492 çûwphâh (1), *hurricane* wind
5591 ça'ar (1), *hurricane*

WHISPER

3907 lâchash (1), to *whisper* a magic spell
6850 tsâphaph (1), to *coo* or *chirp* as a bird

WHISPERED

3907 lâchash (1), to *whisper* a magic spell

WHISPERER

5372 nirgân (1), *slanderer, gossip*

WHISPERERS

5588 psithuristēs (1), *maligning gossip*

WHISPERINGS

5587 psithurismŏs (1), *whispering, detraction*

WHIT

1697 dâbâr (1), *word; matter; thing*

3632 kâlîyl (1), *whole, entire; complete; whole*
3367 měděis (1), *not even*
3650 hŏlŏs (2), *whole* or *all,* i.e. *complete*

WHITE

1858 dar (1), *mother-of-pearl* or *alabaster*
2353 chûwr (2), *white* linen
2751 chôrîy (1), *white* bread
3835 lâban (4), to *be, become white*
3836 lâbân (29), *white*
6703 tsach (1), *dazzling*
6713 tsachar (1), *whiteness*
6715 tsâchôr (1), *white*
7388 rîyr (1), *saliva; broth*
2986 lamprŏs (2), *radiant; clear*
3021 lěukainō (2), to *whiten*
3022 lěukŏs (24), *bright white*

WHITED

2867 kŏniaō (2), to *whitewash*

WHITER

3835 lâban (1), to *be, become white*
6705 tsâchach (1), to *be dazzling* white

WHITHER

413 'êl (2), to, *toward*
575 'ân (20), *where from?, when?*
834 'ăsher (6), *when, where, how, because*
8033 shâm (3), *where*
3699 hŏpŏu (9), *at whichever* spot
3757 hŏu (2), *where*
4226 pŏu (10), *at what?*

WHITHERSOEVER

413+3605+834 'êl (1), *to, toward*
413+3605+834+8033 'êl (1), *to, toward*
575 'ân (1), *where from?*
834 'ăsher (2), *where, how, because*
1870+834 derek (1), *road; course* of life
3605+834 kôl (13), *all, any* or *every*
3605+834+8033 kôl (1), *all, any* or *every*
4725+834 mâqôwm (1), *general locality, place*
5921+834+8033 'al (1), *above, over, upon*
5921+3605+834 'al (1), *above, over, upon*
3699+302 hŏpŏu (4), *at whichever* spot
3699+1437 hŏpŏu (1), *at whichever* spot
3757+1437 hŏu (1), *at which place,* i.e. *where*

WHOLE

854+3605 'êth (13), *with; by; at; among*
2421 châyâh (1), to *live; to revive*

3117 yôwm (4), *day; time*
3605 kôl (115), *all, any*
3606 kôl (Ch.) (6), *all, any*
3632 kâlîyl (2), *whole*
4749 miqshâh (1), *work molded by hammering*
7495 râphâ' (2), to *heal*
8003 shâlêm (4), *complete; friendly; safe*
8549 tâmîym (4), *entire*
8552 tâmam (1), to *complete, finish*
537 hapas (3), *whole*
1295 diasōzō (1), to *cure*
2390 iaōmai (1), to *heal*
2480 ischuō (2), to *have* or *exercise force*
3390 mētrŏpŏlis (1), *main city, metropolis*
3646 hŏlŏkautōma (1), *wholly-consumed*
3648 hŏlŏklērŏs (1), *sound in the entire body*
3650 hŏlŏs (43), *whole*
3956 pas (10), *all, any*
3958 paschō (2), to *experience pain*
4982 sōzō (11), to *deliver; to protect*
5198 hugiainō (2), to *have sound health*
5199 hugiēs (13), *well, healthy; true*

WHOLESOME

4832 marpê' (1), *cure; deliverance; placidity*
5198 hugiainō (1), to *have sound health*

WHOLLY

3605 kôl (9), *all, any*
3615 kâlâh (1), to *complete, prepare*
3632 kâlîyl (4), *whole*
4390 mâlê' (6), to *fill*
5352 nâqâh (1), to *be, make clean; to be bare*
6942 qâdâsh (1), to *be, make clean*
7760 sûwm (1), to *put*
7965 shâlôwm (1), *safe; well; health, prosperity*
1510+1722 ĕimi (1), I *exist, I am*
3651 hŏlŏtělēs (1), *absolutely perfect*

WHORE

2181 zânâh (9), to *commit adultery*
6948 qᵉdêshâh (1), *sacred female prostitute*
4204 pŏrnē (4), *prostitute*

WHORE'S

2181 zânâh (1), to *commit adultery*

WHOREDOM

2181 zânâh (11), to *commit adultery*
2183 zânûwn (1), *adultery; idolatry*
2184 zᵉnûwth (7), *adultery, infidelity*
8457 taznûwth (3), *harlotry*

WHOREDOMS

2181 zânâh (2), to *commit adultery*
2183 zânûwn (11), *adultery; idolatry*
2184 zᵉnûwth (2), *adultery, infidelity*
8457 taznûwth (15), *harlotry,* physical or spiritual

WHOREMONGER

4205 pŏrnŏs (1), *debauchee, immoral*

WHOREMONGERS

4205 pŏrnŏs (4), *debauchee, immoral*

WHORES

2181 zânâh (2), to *commit adultery*

WHORING

2181 zânâh (19), to *commit adultery*

WHORISH

2181 zânâh (3), to *commit adultery*

WHY

4060 middâh (1), *measure*
4069 maddûwa' (41), *why?, what?*
4100 mâh (119), *what?, how?, why?, when?*
4101 mâh (Ch.) (2), *what?, how?, why?*
1063 gar (4), *for, indeed, but, because*
1302 diati (23), *why?*
2444 hinati (4), *why?*
3754 hŏti (23), *that; because; since*
5101 tis (66), *who?, which? or what?*

WICKED

205 'âven (6), *trouble, vanity, wickedness*
605 'ânash (1), to *be frail, feeble*
1100 bᵉlîya'al (5), *wickedness, trouble*
2154 zimmâh (2), *bad plan*
2162 zâmâm (1), *plot*
2617 cheçed (1), *kindness, favor*
4209 mᵉzimmâh (3), *plan; sagacity*
4849 mirsha'ath (1), *female wicked-doer*
5766 'evel (1), *evil*
5767 'avvâl (3), *evil*
6001 'âmêl (1), *toiling; laborer; sorrowful*
6090 'ôtseb (1), *idol; pain*
7451 ra' (26), *bad; evil*
7489 râ'a' (5), to *be good for nothing*
7561 râsha' (4), to *be, do, declare wrong*
7562 resha' (4), *wrong*
7563 râshâ' (252), *wrong; bad* person
113 athěsmŏs (2), *criminal*
459 anŏmŏs (2), *without* Jewish *law*
2556 kakŏs (1), *wrong*

4190 pŏnērŏs (17),
malice, wicked, bad
4191 pŏnērŏtĕrŏs (2),
more evil

WICKEDLY
4209 mᵉzimmâh (1),
plan; sagacity
5753 'âvâh (1), to *be
crooked*
5766 'evel (1), moral *evil*
7451 ra' (1), *bad; evil*
7489 râ'a' (5), to *be good
for nothing*
7561 râsha' (13), to *be,
do, declare wrong*
7564 rish'âh (1), *moral
wrong*

WICKEDNESS
205 'âven (2), *trouble,
vanity, wickedness*
1942 havvâh (3), *desire;
craving*
2154 zimmâh (4), *bad
plan*
5766 'evel (7), moral *evil*
5999 'âmâl (1), *wearing
effort; worry*
7451 ra' (59), *bad; evil*
7455 rôa' (3), *badness*
7561 râsha' (1), to *be, do,
declare wrong*
7562 resha' (25), *wrong*
7564 rish'âh (13), *wrong*
2549 kakia (1),
*depravity; malignity;
trouble*
4189 pŏnēria (6), *malice,
evil, wickedness*
4190 pŏnērŏs (1), *malice,
wicked, bad; crime*
5129+824 tŏutŏi (1), in
this person or thing

WIDE
2267 cheber (2), *society,
group; magic spell;*
4060 middâh (1),
measure; portion
6605 pâthach (3), to *open
wide; to loosen, begin*
7337 râchab (3), to
broaden
7342 râchâb (1), *roomy*
7342+3027 râchâb (2),
roomy, spacious
4116 platus (1), *wide*

WIDENESS
7341 rôchab (1), *width*

WIDOW
490 'almânâh (37), *widow*
5503 chēra (13), *widow*

WIDOW'S
490 'almânâh (4), *widow*
491 'almânûwth (1),
widow; widowhood

WIDOWHOOD
489 'almôn (1),
widowhood
491 'almânûwth (2),
widow; widowhood

WIDOWS
490 'almânâh (12), *widow*
5503 chēra (10), *widow*

WIDOWS'
5503 chēra (3), *widow*

WIFE
802 'ishshâh (301),
woman, wife
1166 bâ'al (1), to *be
master; to marry*
1753 dûwr (Ch.) (1), to
reside, live in
2994 yᵉbêmeth (3),
sister-in-law
1134 gunaikĕiŏs (1),
feminine
1135 gunē (80), *wife*

WIFE'S
802 'ishshâh (8), *woman,
wife; women, wives*
3994 pĕnthĕra (3), *wife's
mother*

WILD
338 'îy (3), solitary wild
creature that *howls*
689 'aqqôw (1), *ibex*
891 bᵉ'ûshîym (2), *rotten
fruit*
2123 zîyz (2), *fulness*
2416 chay (1), *alive; raw*
3277 yâ'êl (3), *ibex*
6167 'ărâd (Ch.) (1),
onager or wild donkey
6171 'ârôwd (1), *onager*
or wild donkey
6501 pere' (10), *onager,
wild* donkey
6728 tsîyîy (3), wild *beast*
7704 sâdeh (8), *field*
8377 tᵉ'ôw (2), *antelope*
65 agriĕlaiŏs (2), *wild*
olive tree
66 agriŏs (2), *wild*
2342 thēriŏn (3),
dangerous animal

WILDERNESS
3452 yᵉshîymôwn (2),
desolation
4057 midbâr (255),
desert; also *speech*
6160 'ărâbâh (4), *desert,
wasteland*
6166 'Ărâd (1), *fugitive*
6723 tsîyâh (2), *desert*
6728 tsîyîy (3), wild *beast*
8414 tôhûw (2), *waste,
desolation, formless*
2047 ĕrēmia (3), place of
solitude, remoteness
2048 ĕrēmŏs (32), *remote
place, deserted place*

WILES
5231 nêkel (1), *deceit*
3180 mĕthŏdĕia (1),
trickery, scheming

WILFULLY
1596 hĕkŏusiŏs (1),
voluntarily, willingly

WILILY
6195 'ormâh (1), *trickery;
discretion*

WILL
14 'âbâh (5), to *be
acquiescent*
165 'êhîy (3), *Where?*
2654 châphêts (2), to *be
pleased* with, *desire*
3045 yâda' (1), to *know*
5314 nâphash (1), to *be
refreshed*
5315 nephesh (3), *life;
breath; soul; wind*

6634 tsᵉbâ' (Ch.) (5), to
please
7470 rᵉ'ûwth (Ch.) (1),
desire
7522 râtsôwn (15), *delight*
210 akŏn (1), *unwilling*
1012 bŏulē (1), *purpose,
plan, decision*
1013 bŏulēma (1),
resolve, willful choice
1014 bŏulŏmai (12), to *be
willing, desire*
1106 gnŏmē (1), *opinion,
resolve*
1479 ĕthĕlŏthrēskĕia (1),
voluntary piety
2107 ĕudŏkia (2),
delight, kindness, wish
2133 ĕunŏia (1), *eagerly,
with a whole heart*
2307 thĕlēma (62),
purpose; decree
2308 thĕlēsis (1),
determination
2309 thĕlō (70), to *will;* to
desire; to *choose*
3195 mĕllō (6), to *intend,*
i.e. *be about to*

WILLETH
2309 thĕlō (1), to *will;* to
desire; to *choose*

WILLING
14 'âbâh (4), to *be
acquiescent*
2655 châphêts (1),
pleased with
5068 nâdab (3), to
volunteer
5071 nᵉdâbâh (2),
spontaneous gift
5081 nâdîyb (3),
magnanimous
830 authairĕtŏs (1),
self-chosen,voluntary
1014 bŏulŏmai (5), to *be
willing, desire*
2106 ĕudŏkĕŏ (2), to
think well, i.e. *approve*
2309 thĕlō (8), to *will;* to
desire; to *choose*
2843 kŏinōnikŏs (1),
liberal
4288 prŏthumia (1),
alacrity, eagerness
4289 prŏthumŏs (1),
alacrity, eagerness

WILLINGLY
2656 chêphets (1),
pleasure; desire
2974 yâ'al (1), to *assent;*
to *undertake, begin*
3820 lêb (1), *heart*
5068 nâdab (13), to
volunteer
5071 nᵉdâbâh (1),
spontaneous gift
5414 nâthan (1), to *give*
1596 hĕkŏusiŏs (1),
voluntarily, willingly
1635 hĕkōn (2), *voluntary*
2309 thĕlō (2), to *will*

WILLOW
6851 tsaphtsâphâh (1),
willow tree

WILLOWS
6155 'ârâb (5), *willow*

WILT
2309 thĕlō (21), to *will*

WIMPLES
4304 mitpachath (1),
cloak, shawl

WIN
1234 bâqa' (1), to *cleave*
2770 kĕrdainō (1), to
gain; to *spare*

WIND
7307 rûwach (82),
breath; wind; life-spirit
7308 rûwach (Ch.) (1),
breath; wind; life-spirit
416 anemizō (1), to *toss
with the wind*
417 anĕmŏs (20), *wind*
4151 pnĕuma (1), *spirit*
4154 pnĕō (1), to *breeze*
4157 pnŏē (1), *breeze;
breath*

WINDING
3583 kâchal (1), to *paint*
4141 mûwçâb (1), *circuit*
5437 çâbab (1), to
surround

WINDOW
2474 challôwn (13),
window; opening
6672 tsôhar (1), *window*
2376 thuris (2), *window*

WINDOWS
699 'ărubbâh (8),
window; chimney
2474 challôwn (18),
window; opening
3551 kav (Ch.) (1),
window
8121 shemesh (1), *sun*
8260 sheqeph (1),
loophole
8261 shâqûph (1),
opening

WINDS
7307 rûwach (11),
breath; wind; life-spirit
7308 rûwach (Ch.) (1),
breath; wind; life-spirit
417 anĕmŏs (11), *wind*

WINDY
7307 rûwach (1), *breath;
wind; life*-spirit

WINE
2561 chemer (1),
fermenting wine
2562 chămar (Ch.) (6),
wine
3196 yayin (135), *wine*
3342 yeqeb (1), wine-*vat*
4469 mamçâk (1),
mixed-wine
5435 çôbe' (1), *wine*
6025 'ênâb (1), *grape*
6071 'âçîyç (4), *expressed
fresh* grape-juice
7491 râ'aph (1), to *drip*
8492 tîyrôwsh (40), *wine,*
squeezed grape-juice
1098 glĕukŏs (1), *sweet*
wine
3631 ŏinŏs (32), *wine*
3632 ŏinŏphlugia (1),
drunkenness
3943 parŏinŏs (2),
tippling

English

WINEBIBBER
3630 ŏinŏpŏtēs (1), *tippler*

WINEBIBBERS
5433+3196 çâbâ' (1), *to become tipsy*

WINEFAT
1660 gath (1), wine-*press or vat*
5276 hupŏlēniŏn (1), *lower wine vat*

WINEPRESS
1660 gath (2), wine-*press or vat*
3342 yeqeb (7), wine-*vat,* wine-*press*
6333 pûwrâh (1), *wine-press* trough
3025 lēnŏs (4), *trough,* i.e. wine-*vat*
3025+3631 lēnŏs (1), *trough,* i.e. wine-*vat*

WINEPRESSES
1660 gath (1), wine-*press*
3342 yeqeb (3), wine-*press*

WINES
8105 shemer (2), *settlings* of wine, *dregs*

WING
3671 kânâph (13), *edge* or *extremity;* wing

WINGED
3671 kânâph (2), *edge* or *extremity;* wing

WINGS
34 'ebyôwn (1), *destitute; poor*
83 'êber (2), *pinion*
84 'ebrâh (1), *pinion*
1611 gaph (Ch.) (3), *wing*
3671 kânâph (60), *edge* or *extremity;* wing
6731 tsîyts (1), *wing*
4420 ptĕrux (5), *wing*

WINK
7169 qârats (1), to *blink*
7335 râzam (1), to *twinkle* the eye

WINKED
5237 hupĕrĕidō (1), to *not punish*

WINKETH
7169 qârats (2), to *blink*

WINNETH
3947 lâqach (1), to *take*

WINNOWED
2219 zârâh (1), to *winnow*

WINNOWETH
2219 zârâh (1), to *winnow*

WINTER
2778 châraph (2), to *spend the winter*
2779 chôreph (3), *autumn, ripeness* of age
5638 çᵉthâv (1), *winter*
3914 parachĕimazŏ (3), to *spend the winter*
3915 parachĕimasia (1), *wintering* over
5494 chĕimōn (4), *winter*

WINTERED
3916 parachrēma (1), *instantly, immediately*

WINTERHOUSE
2779 chôreph (1), *autumn* (and winter)

WIPE
4229 mâchâh (3), to *erase; to grease*
631 apŏmassŏmai (1), to *scrape away, wipe off*
1591 ĕkmassō (2), to *wipe dry*
1813 ĕxalĕiphō (2), to *obliterate*

WIPED
4229 mâchâh (1), to *erase; to grease*
1591 ĕkmassō (3), to *wipe dry*

WIPETH
4229 mâchâh (2), to *erase; to grease*

WIPING
4229 mâchâh (1), to *erase; to grease*

WIRES
6616 pâthîyl (1), *twine, cord*

WISDOM
998 bîynâh (2), *understanding*
2449 châkam (1), to *be wise*
2451 chokmâh (144), *wisdom*
2452 chokmâh (Ch.) (8), *wisdom*
2454 chokmôwth (4), *wisdom*
2942 ṭᵉ'êm (Ch.) (1), *judgment; account*
3820 lêb (6), *heart*
6195 'ormâh (1), *trickery; discretion*
7919 sâkal (2), to *be or act circumspect*
7922 sekel (3), *intelligence; success*
8394 tâbûwn (1), *intelligence; argument*
8454 tûwshîyâh (7), *undertaking*
4678 sŏphia (51), *wisdom*
5428 phrŏnēsis (1), *moral insight, understanding*

WISE
995 bîyn (3), to *understand; discern*
2445 chakkîym (Ch.) (14), *wise one*
2449 châkam (19), to *be wise*
2450 châkâm (122), *wise, intelligent, skillful*
2454 chokmôwth (1), *wisdom*
3198 yâkach (1), to *be correct; to argue*
3823 lâbab (1), *transport with love; to stultify*
6031 'ânâh (1), to *afflict, be afflicted*
6493 piqqêach (1), *clear-sighted*
7919 sâkal (12), to *be or act circumspect*
7922 sekel (1), *intelligence; success*

WINTERHOUSE
3097 magŏs (4), Oriental *scientist,* i.e. *magician*
3364 ŏu mē (1), *not* at all, absolutely *not*
3588+3838 hŏ (1), "*the,*" i.e. the definite article
3779 hŏutō (6), *in this way; likewise*
3843 pantŏs (1), *entirely; at all events*
4679 sŏphizō (1), to *make wise*
4680 sŏphŏs (21), *wise*
4920 suniēmi (1), to *comprehend*
5429 phrŏnimŏs (13), *sagacious* or *discreet*

WISELY
995 bîyn (1), to *understand; discern*
2449 châkam (2), to *be wise*
2451 chokmâh (2), *wisdom*
7919 sâkal (8), to *be or act circumspect*
5430 phrŏnimōs (1), *prudently, shrewdly*

WISER
2449 châkam (4), to *be wise*
2450 châkâm (2), *wise, intelligent, skillful*
4680 sŏphŏs (1), *wise*
5429 phrŏnimŏs (1), *sagacious* or *discreet*

WISH
2655 châphêts (1), *pleased with*
4906 maskîyth (1), *carved figure*
6310 peh (1), *mouth*
2172 ĕuchŏmai (3), to *wish for; to pray*

WISHED
7592 shâ'al (1), to *ask*
2172 ĕuchŏmai (1), to *wish for; to pray*

WISHING
7592 shâ'al (1), to *ask*

WIST
3045 yâda' (7), to *know*
1492 ĕidō (6), to *know*

WIT
3045 yâda' (2), to *know*
1107 gnōrizō (1), to *make known, reveal*
5613 hōs (1), *which, how*

WIT'S
2451 chokmâh (1), *wisdom*

WITCH
3784 kâshaph (2), to *enchant*

WITCHCRAFT
3784 kâshaph (1), to *enchant*
7081 qeçem (1), *divination*
5331 pharmakĕia (1), *magic, witchcraft*

WITCHCRAFTS
3785 kesheph (4), *magic, sorcery*

WITHAL
834+3605 'âsher (1), *who, which, what, that*
1992 hêm (1), *they*
2004 hên (3), *they*
3162 yachad (2), *unitedly*
5973 'îm (1), *with*
260 hama (3), *at the same time, together*

WITHDRAW
622 'âçaph (4), to *gather, collect*
3240 yânach (1), to *allow to stay*
3365 yâqar (1), to *be valuable; to make rare*
5493 çûwr (1), to *turn off*
7368 râchaq (1), to *recede*
7725 shûwb (1), to *turn back; to return*
868 aphistēmi (1), to *desist, desert*
4724 stĕllō (1), to *repress*

WITHDRAWEST
7725 shûwb (1), to *turn back; to return*

WITHDRAWETH
1639 gâra' (1), to *shave, remove, lessen*

WITHDRAWN
2502 châlats (1), to *pull off; to strip; to depart*
2559 châmaq (1), to *depart,* i.e. turn about
5080 nâdach (1), to *push off, scattered*
7725 shûwb (2), to *turn back; to return*
645 apŏspaō (1), *withdraw* with force

WITHDREW
5414+5437 nâthan (1), to *give*
7725 shûwb (1), to *turn back; to return*
402 anachōrĕō (2), to *retire, withdraw*
5288 hupŏstĕllō (1), to *cower* or *shrink*
5298 hupŏchōrĕō (1), to *vacate down,* i.e. *retire*

WITHER
3001 yâbêsh (8), to *wither*
5034 nâbêl (2), to *wilt*
7060 qâmal (1), to *wither*

WITHERED
3001 yâbêsh (11), to *wither*
6798 tsânam (1), to *blast*
3583 xērainō (9), to *shrivel, to mature*
3584 xērŏs (4), *withered*

WITHERETH
3001 yâbêsh (5), to *wither*
3583 xērainō (2), to *shrivel, to mature*
5352 phthinŏpōrinŏs (1), *autumnal*

WITHHELD
2820 châsak (3), to *restrain* or *refrain*
4513 mâna' (3), to *deny, refuse*

WITHHELDEST
4513 mâna' (1), to *deny, refuse*

WITHHOLD
3240 yânach (1), to *allow to stay*
3607 kâlâ' (2), to *hold*
4513 mâna' (5), to *deny*
6113 'âtsar (1), to *hold*

WITHHOLDEN
1219 bâtsar (1), to *be inaccessible*
2254 châbal (1), to *bind by a pledge; to pervert*
4513 mâna' (8), to *deny, refuse*

WITHHOLDETH
2820 châsak (1), to *restrain or refrain*
4513 mâna' (1), to *deny, refuse*
6113 'âtsar (1), to *hold back; to maintain*
2722 katĕchō (1), to *hold down fast*

WITHIN
413 'êl (2), *to, toward*
990 beṭen (2), *belly; womb; body*
996 bêyn (1), *between*
1004 bayith (23), *house; temple; family; tribe*
1157 bᵉ'ad (3), *up to or over against*
2315 cheder (1), *apartment, chamber*
2436 chêyq (1), *bosom, heart*
4481 min (Ch.) (1), *from or out of*
5704 'ad (2), *as far (long) as; during; while; until*
5705 'ad (Ch.) (1), *as far (long) as; during*
5750 'ôwd (4), *again; repeatedly; still; more*
5921 'al (8), *above, over, upon, or against*
5978 'immâd (1), *along with*
6440 pânîym (1), *face; front*
6441 pᵉnîymâh (10), *indoors, inside*
6442 pᵉnîymîy (1), *interior, inner*
7130 qereb (26), *nearest part, i.e. the center*
7146 qârachath (1), *bald spot; threadbare spot*
8432 tâvek (20), *center, middle*
8537 tôm (1), *completeness*
1223 dia (1), *through, by means of; because of*
1722 ĕn (13), *in; during; because of*
1737 ĕndidúskō (1), to *clothe*
1787 ĕntós (1), *inside, within*
2080 ĕsō (3), *inside, inner, in*
2081 ĕsōthĕn (10), *from inside; inside*
2082 ĕsōtĕrŏs (1), *interior, inner*
4314 prŏs (1), *for; on, at; to, toward; against*

WITHOUT
268 'âchôwr (1), *behind, backward; west*
369 'ayin (42), *there is no, i.e., not exist, none*
657 'epheç (3), *end; no further*
1097 bᵉlîy (16), *without, not yet; lacking;*
1107 bil'âdêy (4), *except, without, besides*
1115 biltîy (4), *not, except, without, unless*
1372 gabbachath (1), *baldness on forehead*
2351 chûwts (71), *outside, outdoors*
2435 chîytsôwn (5), *outer wall side; exterior*
2600 chinnâm (17), *gratis, free*
2963 ṭâraph (1), to *pluck off or pull to pieces*
3808 lô' (29), *no, not*
3809 lâ' (Ch.) (1), *as nothing*
4682 matstsâh (1), *unfermented cake*
5493 çûwr (1), to *turn off*
7387 rêyqâm (2), *emptily; ineffectually*
8267 sheqer (1), *untruth; sham*
8414 tôhûw (2), *waste, desolation, formless*
8549 tâmîym (50), *entire, complete; integrity*
35 agĕnĕalŏgĕtŏs (1), *unregistered as to birth*
77 adapanŏs (1), *free of charge*
87 adiakritŏs (1), *impartial*
88 adialĕiptŏs (1), *permanent, constant*
89 adialĕiptōs (4), *without omission*
112 athĕŏs (1), *godless*
175 akarpŏs (1), *barren, unfruitful*
186 aklinēs (1), *firm, unswerving*
194 akratŏs (1), *undiluted*
267 amarturŏs (1), *without witness*
275 amĕrimnŏs (1), *not anxious, free of care*
278 amĕtamĕlĕtŏs (1), *irrevocable*
280 amĕtrŏs (2), *immoderate*
282 amĕtōr (1), *of unknown maternity*
298 amōmĕtŏs (1), *unblemished*
299 amōmŏs (5), *unblemished, blameless*
361 anamartētŏs (1), *sinless*
369 anantirrhētŏs (1), *without raising objection*
379 anapŏlŏgĕtŏs (1), *without excuse*
427 anĕu (3), *without, apart from*
448 anilĕŏs (1), *inexorable, merciless*

459 anŏmōs (4), *without Jewish law*
460 anŏmŏs (2), *lawlessly, i.e. apart from Jewish Law*
504 anudrŏs (2), *dry, arid*
505 anupŏkritŏs (2), *sincere, genuine*
540 apatōr (1), *of unrecorded paternity*
563 apĕrispastōs (1), *undistractedly*
677 aprŏskŏpŏs (1), *faultless*
678 aprŏsōpŏlēptŏs (1), *without prejudice*
729 arrhaphŏs (1), *of a single piece, without seam*
772 asthĕnēs (1), *strengthless, weak*
784 aspilŏs (3), *unblemished*
794 astŏrgŏs (2), *hard-hearted*
801 asunĕtŏs (3), *senseless, dull; wicked*
815 atĕknŏs (2), *childless*
817 atĕr (1), *apart from, without*
820 atimŏs (2), *without honor*
866 aphilargurŏs (1), *not greedy*
870 aphŏbŏs (4), *fearlessly*
880 aphōnŏs (1), *mute, silent; unmeaning*
886 achĕirŏpŏiētŏs (2), *unmanufactured*
895 apsuchŏs (1), *lifeless, i.e. inanimate*
1432 dōrĕan (1), *gratuitously, freely*
1500 ĕikē (1), *idly, i.e. without reason or effect*
1618 ĕktĕnēs (1), *intent, earnest*
1622 ĕktŏs (1), *aside from, besides; except*
1854 ĕxō (23), *out, outside*
1855 ĕxōthĕn (6), *outside, external (-ly)*
2673 katargĕō (1), to *be, render entirely useless*
3361 mē (1), *not; lest*
3672 hŏmŏlŏgŏumĕnōs (1), *confessedly*
3924 parĕktŏs (1), *besides; apart from*
5565 chōris (36), *at a space, i.e. separately*

WITHS
3499 yether (3), *remainder; small rope*

WITHSTAND
2388 châzaq (2), to *bind, restrain, conquer*
3320 yâtsab (1), to *station, offer, continue*
5975 'âmad (4), to *stand*
7854 sâṭân (1), *opponent*
436 anthistēmi (1), *oppose, rebel*
2967 kōluō (1), to *stop*

WITHSTOOD
5975 'âmad (2), to *stand*

436 anthistēmi (4), *oppose, rebel*

WITNESS
5707 'êd (45), *witness; testimony*
5711 'Âdâh (1), *ornament*
5713 'êdâh (3), *testimony*
5715 'êdûwth (4), *testimony*
5749 'ûwd (5), to *protest, testify; to encompass*
6030 'ânâh (2), to *respond, answer*
8085 shâma' (1), to *hear intelligently*
267 amarturŏs (1), *without witness*
2649 katamarturĕō (4), to *testify against*
3140 marturĕō (28), to *testify; to commend*
3141 marturia (15), *evidence given*
3142 marturiŏn (4), *something evidential; the Decalogue*
3144 martus (8), *witness*
4828 summarturĕō (3), to *testify jointly*
4901 sunĕpimarturĕō (1), to *testify further jointly*
5576 psĕudŏmarturĕō (6), to *be an untrue testifier*
5577 psĕudŏmarturia (2), *untrue testimony*

WITNESSED
5749 'ûwd (1), to *protest, testify; to encompass*
3140 marturĕō (3), to *testify; to commend*

WITNESSES
5707 'êd (23), *witness; testimony*
3140 marturĕō (1), to *testify; to commend*
3144 martus (21), *witness*
5575 psĕudŏmartur (3), *bearer of untrue testimony*

WITNESSETH
1263 diamarturŏmai (1), to *attest or protest*
3140 marturĕō (1), to *testify; to commend*

WITNESSING
3140 marturĕō (1), to *testify; to commend*

WITTINGLY
7919 sâkal (1), to *be or act circumspect*

WIVES
802 'ishshâh (115), *woman, wife*
5389 nâshîyn (Ch.) (1), *women, wives*
7695 shêgâl (Ch.) (3), *queen*
1135 gunē (12), *woman; wife*

WIVES'
1126 graŏdēs (1), *old lady-like, i.e. silly*

WIZARD
3049 yiddᵉ'ônîy (2), *conjurer; ghost*

English

WIZARDS
3049 yidd^eʻônîy (9),
   conjurer; ghost

WOE
188 ʼôwy (22), *Oh!, Woe!*
190 ʼôwyâh (1), *Oh!, Woe!*
337 ʼîy (2), *alas!*
480 ʼal^elay (2), *alas!; woe!*
1929 hâhh (1), *ah!; woe!*
1945 hôwy (36), *oh!, woe!*
1958 hîy (1),
   lamentation, woe
3759 ŏuai (39), *woe!; woe*

WOEFUL
605 ʼânash (1), *to be frail,
   feeble*

WOES
3759 ŏuai (1), *woe!; woe*

WOLF
2061 z^eʼêb (4), *wolf*
3074 lukŏs (2), *wolf*

WOLVES
2061 z^eʼêb (3), *wolf*
3074 lukŏs (4), *wolf*

WOMAN
802 ʼishshâh (211),
   woman, wife
5291 naʻărâh (1), *female
   child; servant*
5347 n^eqêbâh (2), *female,
   woman*
1135 gunē (96), *woman;
   wife*
1658 ĕlĕuthĕrŏs (1), *not a
   slave*
2338 thēlus (1), *female*

WOMAN'S
802 ʼishshâh (7), *woman*

WOMANKIND
802 ʼishshâh (1), *woman,
   wife; women, wives*

WOMB
990 beṭen (31), *belly;
   womb; body*
4578 mê'âh (1), *viscera;
   anguish, tenderness*
7356 racham (1),
   compassion; womb
7358 rechem (20), *womb*
1064 gastēr (1), *stomach;
   womb; gourmand*
2836 kŏilia (11),
   abdomen, womb, heart
3388 mētra (2), *womb*

WOMBS
7358 rechem (1), *womb*
2836 kŏilia (1),
   abdomen, womb, heart

WOMEN
802 ʼishshâh (104),
   woman, wife
5347 n^eqêbâh (1), *female*
1133 gunaikariŏn (1),
   little woman
1135 gunē (33), *woman*
2338 thēlus (1), *female*
4247 prĕsbutis (1), *old
   woman*

WOMEN'S
802 ʼishshâh (1), *woman*

WOMENSERVANTS
8198 shiphchâh (3),
   household *female slave*

WON
2770 kĕrdainō (1), *to
   gain; to spare*

WONDER
4159 môwphêth (6),
   miracle; token or omen
6382 peleʼ (1), *miracle*
8539 tâmahh (3), *to be
   astounded*
2285 thambŏs (1),
   astonishment
2296 thaumazō (2), *to
   wonder; to admire*
4592 sēmĕiŏn (2),
   indication, sign, signal

WONDERED
4159 môwphêth (1),
   miracle; token or omen
8074 shâmêm (2), *to
   devastate; to stupefy*
1839 ĕxistēmi (1), *to
   astound*
2296 thaumazō (11), *to
   wonder; to admire*

WONDERFUL
6381 pâlâʼ (13), *to be,
   make great*
6382 peleʼ (3), *miracle*
6383 pilʼîy (1),
   remarkable
8047 shammâh (1), *ruin;
   consternation*
1411 dunamis (1), *force,
   power, miracle*
2297 thaumasiŏs (1),
   miracle, wondrous act
3167 mĕgalĕiŏs (1), *great
   things, wonderful works*

WONDERFULLY
5953 ʻâlal (1), *to glean; to
   overdo*
6381 pâlâʼ (1), *to be,
   make wonderful*
6382 peleʼ (1), *miracle*
6395 pâlâh (1), *to
   distinguish*

WONDERING
7583 shâʼâh (1), *to be
   astonished*
1569 ĕkthambŏs (1),
   utterly astounded
2296 thaumazō (1), *to
   wonder; to admire*

WONDEROUSLY
6381 pâlâʼ (1), *to be,
   make wonderful*

WONDERS
4159 môwphêth (19),
   miracle; token or omen
6381 pâlâʼ (9), *to be,
   make wonderful*
6382 peleʼ (7), *miracle*
8540 t^emahh (Ch.) (3),
   miracle
4592 sēmĕiŏn (1),
   indication, sign, signal
5059 tĕras (16), *omen or
   miracle sign*

WONDROUS
4652 miphlâ'âh (1),
   miracle
6381 pâlâʼ (14), *to be,
   make wonderful*

WONDROUSLY
6381 pâlâʼ (1), *to be,
   make wonderful*

WONT
1696 dâbar (1), *to speak,
   say; to subdue*
1980 hâlak (1), *to walk;
   live a certain way*
2370 chăzâʼ (Ch.) (1), *to
   gaze upon; to dream*
5056 naggâch (1), *act of
   butting*
5532 çâkan (1), *to be
   serviceable to*
1486 ĕthō (2), *to be used
   by habit*
2596+1485 kata (1),
   down; according to
3543 nŏmizō (1), *to deem*

WOOD
636 ʼâ (Ch.) (2), *tree;
   wood; plank*
2793 chôresh (4),
   wooded forest
3293 yaʻar (18), *honey in
   the comb*
6086 ʼêts (106), *wood*
3585 xulinŏs (2), *made of
   wood*
3586 xulŏn (3), *timber
   and its products*

WOODS
3264 yâʼôwr (1), *forest*

WOOF
6154 ʼêreb (9), *mixed or
   woven things*

WOOL
6015 ʻămar (Ch.) (1), *wool*
6785 tsemer (11), *wool*
2053 ĕriŏn (2), *wool*

WOOLLEN
6785 tsemer (5), *wool*
8162 shaʻaṭnêz (1), *linen
   and woollen*

WORD
562 ʼômer (2), *something
   said*
565 ʼimrâh (26),
   something said
1697 dâbâr (433), *word;
   matter; thing*
1699 dôber (2), *grazing
   pasture*
3983 mêʼmar (Ch.) (1),
   edict, command
4405 millâh (1), *word;
   discourse; speech*
4406 millâh (Ch.) (2),
   word, command
6310 peh (15), *mouth;
   opening*
6600 pithgâm (Ch.) (1),
   decree; report
518 apaggĕllō (2), *to
   announce, proclaim*
2036 ĕpō (1), *to speak*
3050 lŏgikŏs (1),
   rational, logical
3056 lŏgŏs (173), *word,
   matter, thing; Word*
4487 rhēma (28),
   utterance; matter

WORD'S
1697 dâbâr (1), *word;
   matter; thing*
3056 lŏgŏs (1), *word,
   matter, thing; Word*

WORDS
561 ʼêmer (42),
   something said
565 ʼimrâh (3),
   something said
1697 dâbâr (373), *word;
   matter; thing*
1703 dabbârâh (1), *word,
   instruction*
4405 millâh (21), *word;
   discourse; speech*
4406 millâh (Ch.) (5),
   word, command
3054 lŏgŏmachĕō (1), *to
   be disputatious*
3055 lŏgŏmachia (1),
   disputation
3056 lŏgŏs (48), *word,
   matter, thing; Word*
4086 pithanŏlŏgia (1),
   persuasive language
4487 rhēma (31),
   utterance; matter
5542 chrēstŏlŏgia (1),
   fair speech

WORK
731 ʼarzâh (1), *cedar
   paneling*
1697 dâbâr (1), *word;
   matter; thing*
3018 y^egîyaʻ (1), *toil,
   work; produce, property*
3027 yâd (1), *hand; power*
3336 yêtser (1), *form*
4399 m^elâʼkâh (125),
   work; property
4639 maʻăseh (113),
   action; labor
4640 Maʻsay (1),
   operative
4649 Muppîym (1),
   wavings
4749 miqshâh (5), *work
   molded by hammering*
5627 çârâh (1), *apostasy;
   crime; remission*
5647 ʻâbad (4), *to do,
   work, serve*
5656 ʻăbôdâh (10), *work*
5673 ʻăbîydâh (Ch.) (3),
   labor or business
5950 ʻălîylîyâh (2),
   execution, deed
6213 ʻâsâh (23), *to do*
6381 pâlâʼ (2), *to be,
   make wonderful*
6466 pâʻal (5), *to do,
   make or practice*
6467 pôʻal (28), *act or
   work, deed*
6468 p^eʻullâh (8), *work*
6603 pittûwach (1),
   sculpture; engraving
7553 riqmâh (5),
   variegation of color
7639 s^ebâkâh (2),
   reticulated ornament
1411 dunamis (1), *force,
   power, miracle*
1754 ĕnĕrgĕō (2), *to be
   active, efficient, work*
2038 ĕrgazŏmai (12), *to
   toil*
2039 ĕrgasia (1),
   occupation; profit
2040 ĕrgatēs (1), *toiler,
   worker*
2041 ĕrgŏn (45), *work*

2716 katĕrgazŏmai (1),
to *finish; to accomplish*
3056 lŏgŏs (2), *word,
matter, thing; Word*
3433+2480 mŏlis (1), *with
difficulty*
4229 pragma (1), *matter,
deed, affair*
4903 sunĕrgĕŏ (1), *to be
a fellow-worker*

WORK'S
2041 ĕrgŏn (1), *work*

WORKER
2790 chârash (1), *to
engrave; to plow*

WORKERS
2796 chârâsh (1), *skilled
fabricator or worker*
6213 'âsâh (1), *to do*
6466 pâ'al (19), *to do,
make or practice*
1411 dunamis (1), *force,
power, miracle*
2040 ĕrgatēs (3), *toiler,
worker*
4903 sunĕrgĕŏ (1), *to be
a fellow-worker*

WORKETH
5648 'âbad (Ch.) (1), *to
work, serve*
6213 'âsâh (6), *to do or
make*
6466 pâ'al (4), *to do,
make or practice*
1754 ĕnĕrgĕŏ (11), *to be
active, efficient, work*
2038 ĕrgazŏmai (7), *to
toil*
2716 katĕrgazŏmai (7),
to *finish; to accomplish*
4160 pŏiĕŏ (1), *to make
or do*

WORKFELLOW
4904 sunĕrgŏs (1),
fellow-worker

WORKING
4639 ma'âseh (1), *action;
labor*
6213 'âsâh (1), *to do or
make*
6466 pâ'al (1), *to do,
make or practice*
8454 tûwshîyâh (1),
ability, i.e. *direct help*
1753 ĕnĕrgĕia (6),
efficiency, energy
1755 ĕnĕrgēma (1),
effect, activity
2038 ĕrgazŏmai (4), *to
toil*
2716 katĕrgazŏmai (2),
to *finish; to accomplish*
4160 pŏiĕŏ (2), *to make
or do*
4903 sunĕrgĕŏ (1), *to be
a fellow-worker*

WORKMAN
542 'âmân (1), *expert
artisan, craftsman*
2796 chârâsh (5), *skilled
fabricator or worker*
2803 châshab (2), *to
weave, fabricate*
2040 ĕrgatēs (2), *toiler,
worker*

WORKMANSHIP
4399 mᵉlâ'kâh (5), *work;
property*
4639 ma'âseh (1), *action;
labor*
4161 pŏiēma (1), *what is
made, product*

WORKMEN
582+4399 'ĕnôwsh (1),
man; person, human
2796 chârâsh (1), *skilled
fabricator or worker*
6213+4399 'âsâh (7), *to
do or make*
2040 ĕrgatēs (1), *toiler,
worker*

WORKMEN'S
6001 'âmêl (1), *toiling;
laborer; sorrowful*

WORKS
1697 dâbâr (1), *word;
matter; thing*
4399 mᵉlâ'kâh (3), *work;
property*
4566 ma'bâd (1), *act,
deed*
4567 ma'bâd (Ch.) (1),
act, deed
4611 ma'ălâl (3), *act,
deed*
4639 ma'âseh (70),
action; labor
4640 Ma'say (2),
operative
4659 miph'âl (3),
performance, deed
5652 'ăbâd (1), *deed*
5949 'ălîylâh (3),
opportunity, action
6467 pô'al (2), *act or
work, deed*
6468 pᵉ'ullâh (1), *work,
deed*
2041 ĕrgŏn (104), *work*
4234 praxis (1), *act;
function*

WORKS'
2041 ĕrgŏn (1), *work*

WORLD
776 'erets (4), *earth,
land, soil; country*
2309 chedel (1), *state of
the dead, deceased*
2465 cheled (2), *fleeting
time; this world*
5769 'ôwlâm (4), *eternity;
ancient; always*
8398 têbêl (35), *earth;
world; inhabitants*
165 aiōn (37), *perpetuity,
ever; world*
166 aiōniŏs (3),
perpetual, long ago
1093 gē (1), *soil, region,
whole earth*
2889 kŏsmŏs (183), *world*
3625 ŏikŏumĕnē (14),
Roman empire

WORLD'S
2889 kŏsmŏs (1), *world*

WORLDLY
2886 kŏsmikŏs (2),
earthly, worldly

WORLDS
165 aiōn (2), *perpetuity,
ever; world*

WORM
5580 çâç (1), *garment
moth*
7415 rimmâh (5), *maggot*
8438 tôwlâ' (5), *maggot
worm; crimson-grub*
4663 skōlēx (3), *grub,
maggot or earth-worm*

WORMS
2119 zâchal (1), *to crawl;
glide*
7415 rimmâh (2), *maggot*
8438 tôwlâ' (3), *maggot
worm; crimson-grub*
4662 skōlēkŏbrŏtŏs (1),
diseased with maggots

WORMWOOD
3939 la'ănâh (7),
poisonous wormwood
894 apsinthŏs (2),
wormwood, bitterness

WORSE
2196 zâ'aph (1), *to be
angry*
5062 nâgaph (5), *to
inflict a disease*
7451 ra' (1), *bad; evil*
7489 râ'a' (5), *to be good
for nothing*
1640 ĕlassōn (1), *smaller*
2276 hēttŏn (1), *worse*
5302 hustĕrĕŏ (1), *to be
inferior; to fall short*
5501 chĕirŏn (10), *more
evil or aggravated*

WORSHIP
5457 çᵉgîd (Ch.) (8), *to
prostrate oneself*
6087 'âtsab (1), *to
fabricate or fashion*
7812 shâchâh (54), *to
prostrate in homage*
1391 dŏxa (1), *glory;
brilliance*
1479 ĕthĕlŏthrēskĕia (1),
voluntary piety
2151 ĕusĕbĕŏ (1), *to put
religion into practice*
3000 latrĕuŏ (3), *to
minister to God*
4352 prŏskunĕŏ (34), *to
prostrate oneself*
4352+1799 prŏskunĕŏ (1),
to prostrate oneself
4576 sĕbŏmai (3), *to
revere,* i.e. *adore*

WORSHIPPED
5457 çᵉgîd (Ch.) (2), *to
prostrate oneself*
7812 shâchâh (39), *to
prostrate in homage*
2323 thĕrapĕuŏ (1), *to
adore God*
4352 prŏskunĕŏ (24), *to
prostrate oneself*
4573 sĕbazŏmai (1), *to
venerate, worship*
4574 sĕbasma (1), *object
of worship*
4576 sĕbŏmai (2), *to
revere,* i.e. *adore*

WORSHIPPER
2318 thĕŏsĕbēs (1), *pious,
devout, God-fearing*
3511 nĕŏkŏrŏs (1),
temple servant

WORSHIPPERS
5647 'âbad (5), *to serve*
3000 latrĕuŏ (1), *to
minister to God*
4353 prŏskunētēs (1),
adorer

WORSHIPPETH
5457 çᵉgîd (Ch.) (2), *to
prostrate oneself*
7812 shâchâh (3), *to
prostrate in homage*
4576 sĕbŏmai (1), *to
revere,* i.e. *adore*

WORSHIPPING
7812 shâchâh (3), *to
prostrate in homage*
2356 thrēskĕia (1),
observance, religion
4352 prŏskunĕŏ (1), *to
prostrate oneself*

WORST
7451 ra' (1), *bad; evil*

WORTH
3644 kᵉmôw (1), *like, as;
for; with*
4242 mᵉchîyr (1), *price,
payment, wages*
4373 mikçâh (1),
valuation of a thing
4392 mâlê' (1), *full;
filling; fulness; fully*
7939 sâkâr (1), *payment,
salary; compensation*

WORTHIES
117 'addîyr (1), *powerful;
majestic*

WORTHILY
2428 chayil (1), *army;
wealth; virtue; valor*

WORTHY
376 'îysh (1), *man; male;
someone*
639 'aph (1), *nose or
nostril; face; person*
1121 bên (2), *son,
descendant; people*
2428 chayil (1), *army;
wealth; virtue; valor*
6994 qâṭôn (1), *to be,
make diminutive*
514 axiŏs (35), *deserving,
comparable or suitable*
515 axiŏŏ (5), *to deem
entitled or fit, worthy*
516 axiŏs (3),
appropriately, suitable
2425 hikanŏs (5), *ample;
fit*
2570 kalŏs (1), *good;
beautiful; valuable*
2661 kataxiŏŏ (4), *to
deem entirely deserving*
2735 katŏrthōma (1),
made fully upright

WOT
3045 yâda' (6), *to know*
1107 gnōrizō (1), *to
make known, reveal*
1492 ĕidŏ (3), *to know*

WOTTETH
3045 yâda' (1), *to know*

WOULD
14 'âbâh (41), *to be
acquiescent*
305 'achălay (1), *would
that!, Oh that!, If Only!*

English

2654 châphêts (1), *to be pleased* with, *desire*
2655 châphêts (1), *pleased* with
2974 yâ'al (3), *to assent; to undertake, begin*
3863 lûw' (6), *would that!*
5315 nephesh (1), *life; breath; soul; wind*
6634 tsᵉbâ' (Ch.) (5), *to please*
1096 ginŏmai (1), *to be, become*
2172 ĕuchŏmai (1), *to wish for; to pray*
2309 thĕlō (73), *to will; to desire; to choose*
3195 mĕllō (9), *to intend, i.e. be about to*
3785 ŏphĕlŏn (4), *I wish*

WOULDEST
3426 yêsh (1), *there is*
2309 thĕlō (4), *to will; to desire; to choose*

WOUND
2671 chêts (1), *arrow; wound; thunder-bolt*
4204 mâzôwr (1), *ambush*
4205 mâzôwr (2), *sore*
4272 mâchats (3), *to crush; to subdue*
4347 makkâh (8), *blow; wound; pestilence*
5061 nega' (1), *infliction, affliction; leprous spot*
6482 petsa' (2), *wound*
1210 dĕō (1), *to bind*
4127 plĕgē (3), *stroke; wound; calamity*
4958 sustĕllō (1), *to draw together, i.e. enwrap or enshroud a corpse*
5180 tuptō (1), *to strike, beat, wound*

WOUNDED
1214 bâtsa' (1), *to plunder; to finish*
1795 dakkâh (1), *mutilated by crushing*
1856 dâqar (1), *to stab, pierce; to starve*
2342 chûwl (2), *to dance, whirl; to writhe in pain*
2470 châlâh (3), *to be weak, sick, afflicted*
2490 châlal (3), *to profane, defile*
2491 châlâl (10), *pierced to death, one slain*
4272 mâchats (2), *to crush; to subdue*
4347 makkâh (1), *blow; wound; pestilence*
5218 nâkê' (1), *smitten; afflicted*
5221 nâkâh (3), *to strike, kill*
6481 pâtsa' (2), *to wound*
4127+2007 plĕgē (1), *stroke; wound*
4969 sphazō (1), *to slaughter or to maim*
5135 traumatizō (2), *to inflict a wound*

WOUNDEDST
4272 mâchats (1), *to crush; to subdue*

WOUNDETH
4272 mâchats (1), *to crush; to subdue*

WOUNDING
6482 petsa' (1), *wound*

WOUNDS
2250 chabbûwrâh (1), *weal, bruise*
3859 lâham (2), *to rankle*
4347 makkâh (6), *blow; wound; pestilence*
6094 'atstsebeth (1), *pain or wound, sorrow*
6482 petsa' (4), *wound*
5134 trauma (1), *wound*

WOVE
707 'ârag (1), *to plait or weave*

WOVEN
707 'ârag (3), *to plait or weave*
5307 huphantŏs (1), *knitted, woven*

WRAP
3664 kânaç (1), *to collect; to enfold*
5686 'âbath (1), *to pervert*

WRAPPED
1563 gâlam (1), *to fold*
2280 châbash (1), *to wrap firmly, bind*
3874 lûwṭ (2), *to wrap up*
4593 mâ'ôṭ (1), *sharp, thin-edged*
5440 çâbak (1), *to entwine*
5968 'âlaph (1), *to be languid, faint*
8276 sârag (1), *to entwine*
1750 ĕnĕilĕō (1), *to enwrap*
1794 ĕntulissō (3), *wind up in, enwrap*
4683 sparganŏō (2), *to strap or wrap*

WRATH
639 'aph (42), *nose or nostril; face; person*
2197 za'aph (1), *anger, rage*
2534 chêmâh (34), *heat; anger; poison*
2740 chârôwn (6), *burning of anger*
3707 kâ'aç (1), *to grieve, rage, be indignant*
3708 ka'aç (4), *vexation, grief*
5678 'ebrâh (31), *outburst of passion*
7107 qâtsaph (5), *to burst out in rage*
7109 qᵉtsaph (Ch.) (1), *rage*
7110 qetseph (23), *rage or strife*
7265 rᵉgaz (Ch.) (1), *to quiver*
7267 rôgez (1), *disquiet; anger*
2372 thumŏs (14), *passion, anger*
3709 ŏrgē (31), *ire; punishment*
3949 parŏrgizō (1), *to enrage, exasperate*

3950 parŏrgismŏs (1), *rage*

WRATHFUL
2534 chêmâh (1), *heat; anger; poison*
2740 chârôwn (1), *burning* of anger

WRATHS
2372 thumŏs (1), *passion, anger*

WREATH
7639 sᵉbâkâh (1), *reticulated ornament*

WREATHED
8276 sârag (1), *to entwine*

WREATHEN
5688 'ăbôth (8), *entwined things: a string, wreath*
7639 sᵉbâkâh (2), *reticulated ornament*

WREATHS
1434 gᵉdîl (1), *tassel; festoon*
7639 sᵉbâkâh (2), *reticulated ornament*

WREST
5186 nâṭâh (3), *to stretch or spread out*
6087 'âtsab (1), *to fabricate or fashion*
4761 strĕblŏō (1), *to pervert, twist*

WRESTLE
2076+3823 ĕsti (1), *he (she or it) is; they are*

WRESTLED
79 'âbaq (2), *grapple, wrestle*
6617 pâthal (1), *to struggle; to be tortuous*

WRESTLINGS
5319 naphtûwl (1), *struggle*

WRETCHED
5005 talaipōrŏs (2), *miserable, wretched*

WRETCHEDNESS
7451 ra' (1), *bad; evil*

WRING
4454 mâlaq (2), *to wring* a bird's neck
4680 mâtsâh (1), *to drain; to squeeze out*

WRINGED
4680 mâtsâh (1), *to drain; to squeeze out*

WRINGING
4330 mîyts (1), *pressure*

WRINKLE
4512 rhutis (1), *face wrinkle*

WRINKLES
7059 qâmaṭ (1), *to pluck, i.e. destroy*

WRITE
3789 kâthab (35), *to write*
3790 kᵉthab (Ch.) (1), *to write*
1125 graphō (50), *to write*
1924 ĕpigraphō (2), *to inscribe, write upon*
1989 ĕpistĕllō (1), *to communicate by letter*

WRITER
5608 çâphar (2), *to inscribe; to enumerate*

WRITER'S
5608 çâphar (2), *to inscribe; to enumerate*

WRITEST
3789 kâthab (2), *to write*

WRITETH
3789 kâthab (1), *to write*

WRITING
3789 kâthab (1), *to write*
3791 kâthâb (14), *writing, record or book*
3792 kᵉthâb (Ch.) (10), *writing, record or book*
4385 miktâb (8), *written thing*
975 bibliŏn (1), *scroll; certificate*
1125 graphō (1), *to write*
4093 pinakidiŏn (1), *wooden writing tablet*

WRITINGS
1121 gramma (1), *writing; education*

WRITTEN
3789 kâthab (138), *to write*
3790 kᵉthab (Ch.) (2), *to write*
3792 kᵉthâb (Ch.) (1), *writing, record or book*
7560 rᵉsham (Ch.) (2), *to record*
583 apŏgraphō (1), *enroll, take a census*
1123 graptŏs (1), *inscribed, written*
1125 graphō (134), *to write*
1449 ĕggraphō (2), *inscribe, write*
1722+1121 ĕn (1), *in; during; because of*
1924 ĕpigraphō (2), *to inscribe, write upon*
1989 ĕpistĕllō (2), *to communicate by letter*
4270 prŏgraphō (2), *to write previously; to announce, prescribe*

WRONG
2555 châmâç (3), *violence; malice*
3238 yânâh (1), *to suppress; to maltreat*
3808+4941 lô' (1), *no, not*
5627 çârâh (1), *apostasy; crime; remission*
5753 'âvâh (1), *to be crooked*
5792 'avvâthâh (1), *oppression*
6127 'âqal (1), *to wrest, be crooked*
6231 'âshaq (2), *to violate; to overflow*
7451 ra' (1), *bad; evil*
7563 râshâ' (1), *morally wrong; bad* person
91 adikĕō (11), *to do wrong*
92 adikēma (1), *wrong*
93 adikia (1), *wrongfulness*

WRONGED
91 adikĕō (2), to do wrong

WRONGETH
2554 châmaç (1), to be violent; to maltreat

WRONGFULLY
2554 châmaç (1), to be violent; to maltreat
3808+4941 lô' (1), no, not
8267 sheqer (4), untruth; sham
95 adikōs (1), unjustly

WROTE
3789 kâthab (34), to write
3790 kᵉthab (Ch.) (5), to write
1125 graphō (21), to write
4270 prŏgraphō (1), to write previously; to announce, prescribe

WROTH
2196 zá'aph (2), to be angry
2534 chêmâh (1), heat; anger; poison
2734 chârâh (13), to blaze up
3707 kâ'aç (1), to grieve, rage, be indignant
5674 'âbar (5), to cross over; to transition
7107 qâtsaph (22), to burst out in rage
7264 râgaz (1), to quiver
2373 thumŏō (1), to enrage
3710 ŏrgizō (3), to become exasperated

WROUGHT
1496 gâzîyth (1), dressed stone
1980 hâlak (2), to walk; live a certain way
2790 chârash (1), to engrave; to plow
4639 ma'ăseh (3), action; labor
4865 mishbᵉtsâh (1), reticulated setting
5647 'âbad (1), to do, work, serve
5648 'âbad (Ch.) (1), to work, serve
5656 'ăbôdâh (1), work
5927 'âlâh (1), to ascend, be high, mount
5953 'âlal (2), to glean; to overdo
6213 'âsâh (52), to do
6466 pâ'al (7), to do, make or practice
7194 qâshar (1), to tie, bind
7551 râqam (1), variegation; embroider
7760 sùwm (1), to put, place
1096 ginŏmai (2), to be, become
1754 ĕnĕrgĕō (2), to be active, efficient, work
2038 ĕrgazŏmai (7), to toil
2716 katĕrgazŏmai (6), to finish; to accomplish

4160 pŏiĕō (5), to make or do
4903 sunĕrgĕō (1), to be a fellow-worker

WROUGHTEST
6213 'âsâh (1), to make

WRUNG
4680 mâtsâh (4), to drain; to squeeze out

YARN
4723 miqveh (4), confidence; collection

YEA
432 'illûw (1), if
637 'aph (39), also or yea; though
834 'âsher (1), who, which, what, that
1571 gam (66), also; even; yea; though
3588 kîy (7), for, that because
235 alla (15), but, yet, except, instead
1161 dĕ (13), but, yet; and then
2089 ĕti (1), yet, still
2228 ē (1), or; than
2532 kai (5), and; or; even; also
3304 mĕnŏungĕ (1), so then at least
3483 nai (22), yes

YEAR
3117 yôwm (6), day; time period
8140 shᵉnâh (Ch.) (5), year
8141 shâneh (323), year
1763 ĕniautŏs (13), year
2094 ĕtŏs (3), year
4070 pĕrusi (2), last year; from last year

YEAR'S
3117 yôwm (3), day; time period
8141 shâneh (1), year

YEARLY
3117 yôwm (6), day; time period
8141 shâneh (3), year

YEARN
3648 kâmar (1), to shrivel with heat

YEARNED
3648 kâmar (1), to shrivel with heat

YEARS
3027 yâd (1), hand; power
3117 yôwm (3), day; time period
8027 shâlash (2), to be, triplicate
8140 shᵉnâh (Ch.) (2), year
8141 shâneh (466), year
1096+3173 ginŏmai (1), to be, become
1332 diĕtĕs (1), of two years in age
1333 diĕtia (2), interval of two years
1541 hĕkatŏntaĕtĕs (1), centenarian
1763 ĕniautŏs (2), year
2094 ĕtŏs (46), year

2250 hēmĕra (2), day; period of time
5063 tĕssarakŏntaĕtēs (2), of forty years of age
5148 triĕtia (1), triennium, three years

YEARS'
8141 shâneh (2), year

YELL
5286 nâ'ar (1), to growl

YELLED
5414+6963 nâthan (1), to give

YELLOW
3422 yᵉraqraq (1), yellowishness
6669 tsâhôb (3), golden in color

YES
3304 mĕnŏungĕ (1), so then at least
3483 nai (3), yes

YESTERDAY
570 'emesh (1), yesterday evening
865 'ethmôwl (1), heretofore, formerly
8543 tᵉmôwl (4), yesterday
5504 chthĕs (3), yesterday; in time past

YESTERNIGHT
570 'emesh (3), yesterday evening

YET
227 'âz (1), at that time or place; therefore
389 'ak (13), surely; only, however
559 'âmar (1), to say
637 'aph (1), also or yea
1297 bᵉram (Ch.) (2), however, but
1571 gam (14), also; even; yea; though
2962 ţerem (4), not yet or before
3588 kîy (14), for, that because
5704 'ad (4), as far (long) as; during; while; until
5728 'âden (2), till now, yet
5750 'ôwd (142), again; repeatedly; still; more
7535 raq (2), merely; although
188 akmēn (1), just now, still
235 alla (11), but, yet, except, instead
1063 gar (3), for, indeed, but, because
1065 gĕ (2), particle of emphasis
1161 dĕ (19), but, yet; and then
2089 ĕti (54), yet, still
2236 hēdista (2), with great pleasure
2532 kai (7), and; or; even; also
2539 kaipĕr (1), nevertheless
2579 kan (1), and (or even) if

2596 kata (2), down; according to
3195 mĕllō (1), to intend, i.e. be about to
3305 mĕntŏi (2), however
3364 ŏu mē (1), not at all, absolutely not
3369 mĕdĕpō (1), not even yet
3380 mĕpō (1), not yet
3764 ŏudĕpō (4), not even yet
3765 ŏukĕti (3), not yet, no longer
3768 ŏupō (21), not yet

YIELD
3254 yâçaph (1), to add or augment
5186 nâţâh (1), to stretch or spread out
5375 nâsâ' (1), to lift up
5414 nâthan (13), to give
5414+3027 nâthan (1), to give
6213 'âsâh (6), to do or make
1325 didōmi (1), to give
3936 paristēmi (4), to stand beside, present
3982 pĕithō (1), to assent to authority
4160 pŏiĕō (1), to make or do

YIELDED
1478 gâva' (1), to expire, die
1580 gâmal (1), to benefit or requite; to wean
3052 yᵉhab (Ch.) (1), to give
591 apŏdidōmi (1), to give away
863 aphiēmi (1), to leave; to pardon, forgive
1325 didōmi (1), to give
1634 ĕkpsuchō (1), to expire, die
3936 paristēmi (1), to stand beside, present

YIELDETH
5414 nâthan (1), to give
7235 râbâh (1), to increase
591 apŏdidōmi (1), to give away

YIELDING
2232 zâra' (3), to sow seed; to disseminate
4832 marpê' (1), cure; deliverance; placidity
6213 'âsâh (3), to do or make

YOKE
4132 môwţ (1), pole; yoke
4133 môwţâh (4), pole; ox-bow; yoke
5923 'ôl (39), neck yoke
6776 tsemed (7), paired yoke
2201 zĕugŏs (1), team
2218 zugŏs (5), coupling, yoke

YOKED
2086 hĕtĕrŏzugĕō (1), to associate discordantly

English

YOKEFELLOW
4805 suzugŏs (1), *colleague*

YOKES
4133 môwṭâh (4), *pole; ox-bow; yoke*

YONDER
1973 hâl°âh (1), *far away; thus far*
3541 kôh (2), *thus*
5676 'êber (1), *opposite side; east*
5704+3541 'ad (1), *as far (long) as; during; while; until*
1563 ĕkĕi (2), *there, thither*

YOUNG
667 'ephrôach (4), *brood of a bird*
970 bâchûwr (42), *male youth; bridegroom*
979 b°chûrôwth (1), *youth*
1121 bên (20), *son, descendant; people*
1121+1241 bên (34), *son, descendant; people*
1123 bên (Ch.) (1), *son*
1241 bâqâr (1), *plowing ox; herd*
1469 gôwzâl (2), *young of a bird*
1482 gûwr (1), *cub*
3127 yôwneqeth (1), *sprout, new shoot*
3206 yeled (10), *young male*
3242 y°nîqâh (1), *sucker or sapling*
3715 k°phîyr (25), *walled village; young lion*
3833 lâbîy' (1), *lion, lioness*
5288 na'ar (92), *male child; servant*
5288+970 na'ar (1), *male child; servant*
5291 na'ărâh (6), *female child; servant*
5763 'ûwl (3), *to suckle, i.e. give milk*
5958 'elem (1), *lad, young man*
6082 'ôpher (5), *dusty-colored fawn*
6499 par (1), *bullock*
6810+3117 tsâ'îyr (1), *young in value*
6996 qâṭân (1), *small, least, youngest*
7988 shilyâh (1), *fetus or infant baby*
1025 brĕphŏs (1), *infant*
2365 thugatriŏn (1), *little daughter*
3494 nĕanias (5), *youth, up to about forty years*
3495 nĕaniskŏs (10), *youth under forty*
3501 nĕŏs (4), *new*
3502 nĕŏssŏs (1), *young*
3678 ŏnariŏn (1), *little donkey*
3813 paidiŏn (10), *child; immature*
3816 pais (1), *child; slave or servant*

YOUNGER
6810 tsâ'îyr (7), *little, young*
6810+3117 tsâ'îyr (1), *little, young*
6996 qâṭân (14), *small, least, youngest*
1640 ĕlassŏn (1), *smaller*
3501 nĕŏs (8), *new*

YOUNGEST
6810 tsâ'îyr (3), *little, young*
6996 qâṭân (15), *small, least, youngest*

YOUTH
979 b°chûrôwth (2), *youth*
2779 chôreph (1), *autumn (and winter)*
3208 yaldûwth (2), *boyhood or girlhood*
5271 nâ'ûwr (46), *youth; juvenility; young people*
5288 na'ar (5), *male child; servant*
5290 nô'ar (2), *boyhood*
5934 'âlûwm (4), *adolescence; vigor*
6526 pirchach (1), *progeny, i.e. a brood*
6812 ts°'îyrâh (1), *juvenility*
7839 shachărûwth (1), *juvenescence, youth*
3503 nĕŏtēs (5), *youthfulness*

YOUTHFUL
3512 nĕŏtĕrikŏs (1), *juvenile, youthful*

YOUTHS
1121 bên (1), *son, descendant; people*
5288 na'ar (1), *male child; servant*

ZAANAIM
6815 Tsa'ănannîym (1), *removals*

ZAANAN
6630 Tsa'ănân (1), *sheep pasture*

ZAANANNIM
6815 Tsa'ănannîym (1), *removals*

ZAAVAN
2190 Za'ăvân (1), *disquiet*

ZABAD
2066 Zâbâd (8), *giver*

ZABBAI
2079 Zabbay (2), *Zabbai*

ZABBUD
2072 Zabbûwd (1), *given*

ZABDI
2067 Zabdîy (6), *giving*

ZABDIEL
2068 Zabdîy'êl (2), *gift of God*

ZABUD
2071 Zâbûwd (1), *given*

ZABULON
2194 Zaboulōn (3), *habitation*

ZACCAI
2140 Zakkay (2), *pure*

ZACCHAEUS
2195 Zakchaiŏs (3), *Zacchæus*

ZACCHUR
2139 Zakkûwr (1), *mindful*

ZACCUR
2139 Zakkûwr (8), *mindful*

ZACHARIAH
2148 Z°karyâh (4), *Jehovah has remembered*

ZACHARIAS
2197 Zacharias (11), *Jehovah has remembered*

ZACHER
2144 Zeker (1), *recollection; commemoration*

ZADOK
6659 Tsâdôwq (52), *just*

ZADOK'S
6659 Tsâdôwq (1), *just*

ZAHAM
2093 Zaham (1), *loathing*

ZAIR
6811 Tsâ'îyr (1), *little*

ZALAPH
6764 Tsâlâph (1), *Tsalaph*

ZALMON
6756 Tsalmôwn (2), *shady*

ZALMONAH
6758 Tsalmônâh (2), *shadiness*

ZALMUNNA
6759 Tsalmunnâ' (12), *shade has been denied*

ZAMZUMMIMS
2157 Zamzôm (1), *intriguing*

ZANOAH
2182 Zânôwach (5), *rejected*

ZAPHNATH-PAANEAH
6847 Tsophnath Pa'nêach (1), *Tsophnath-Paneäch*

ZAPHON
6829 Tsâphôwn (1), *boreal, northern*

ZARA
2196 Zara (1), *rising of light, dawning*

ZARAH
2226 Zerach (2), *rising of light, dawning*

ZAREAH
6881 Tsor'âh (1), *stinging wasp*

ZAREATHITES
6882 Tsor'îy (1), *Tsorite or Tsorathite*

ZARED
2218 Zered (1), *lined with shrubbery*

ZAREPHATH
6886 Tsâr°phath (3), *refinement*

ZARETAN
6891 Tsâr°thân (1), *Tsarethan*

ZARETH-SHAHAR
6890 Tsereth hash-Shachar (1), *splendor of the dawn*

ZARHITES
2227 Zarchîy (6), *Zarchite*

ZARTANAH
6891 Tsâr°thân (1), *Tsarethan*

ZARTHAN
6891 Tsâr°thân (1), *Tsarethan*

ZATTHU
2240 Zattûw' (1), *Zattu*

ZATTU
2240 Zattûw' (3), *Zattu*

ZAVAN
2190 Za'ăvân (1), *disquiet*

ZAZA
2117 Zâzâ' (1), *prominent*

ZEAL
7065 qânâ' (1), *to be, make zealous, jealous or envious*
7068 qin'âh (9), *jealousy or envy*
2205 zēlŏs (6), *zeal, ardor; jealousy, malice*

ZEALOUS
7065 qânâ' (2), *to be, make zealous*
2206 zēlŏō (1), *to have warmth of feeling for*
2207 zēlōtēs (5), *zealot*

ZEALOUSLY
2206 zēlŏō (2), *to have warmth of feeling for*

ZEBADIAH
2069 Z°badyâh (9), *Jehovah has given*

ZEBAH
2078 Zebach (12), *sacrifice*

ZEBAIM
6380 Pôkereth Ts°bâyîym (2), *trap of gazelles*

ZEBEDEE
2199 Zĕbĕdaiŏs (10), *Zebedæus*

ZEBEDEE'S
2199 Zĕbĕdaiŏs (2), *Zebedæus*

ZEBINA
2081 Z°bîynâ' (1), *gainfulness*

ZEBOIIM
6636 Tsĕbô'iym (2), *gazelles*

ZEBOIM
6636 Tsĕbô'iym (3), *gazelles*
6650 Ts°bô'iym (2), *hyenas*

ZEBUDAH
2081 Z°bîynâ' (1), *gainfulness*

ZEBUL
2083 Z°bûl (6), *dwelling*

ZEBULONITE
2075 Z^{e}bûwlônîy (2), *Zebulonite*

ZEBULUN
2074 Z^{e}bûwlûwn (44), *habitation*

ZEBULUNITES
2075 Z^{e}bûwlônîy (1), *Zebulonite*

ZECHARIAH
2148 Z^{e}karyâh (39), *Jehovah has remembered*

ZEDAD
6657 Ts^{e}dâd (2), *siding*

ZEDEKIAH
6667 Tsidqîyâh (61), *right of Jehovah*

ZEDEKIAH'S
6667 Tsidqîyâh (1), *right of Jehovah*

ZEEB
2062 Z^e'êb (6), *wolf*

ZELAH
6762 Tsela' (2), *limping*

ZELEK
6768 Tseleq (2), *fissure*

ZELOPHEHAD
6765 Ts^{e}lophchâd (11), *Tselophchad*

ZELOTES
2208 Zēlōtēs (2), *Zealot, partisan*

ZELZAH
6766 Tseltsach (1), *clear shade*

ZEMARAIM
6787 Ts^{e}mârayim (2), *double fleece*

ZEMARITE
6786 Ts^{e}mârîy (2), *Tsemarite*

ZEMIRA
2160 Z^{e}mîyrâh (1), *song*

ZENAN
6799 Ts^{e}nân (1), *Tsenan*

ZENAS
2211 Zēnas (1), *Jove-given*

ZEPHANIAH
6846 Ts^{e}phanyâh (10), *Jehovah has secreted*

ZEPHATH
6857 Ts^{e}phath (1), *watch-tower*

ZEPHATHAH
6859 Ts^{e}phâthâh (1), *watch-tower*

ZEPHI
6825 Ts^{e}phôw (1), *observant*

ZEPHO
6825 Ts^{e}phôw (2), *observant*

ZEPHON
6827 Ts^{e}phôwn (1), *watch-tower*

ZEPHONITES
6831 Ts^{e}phôwnîy (1), *Tsephonite*

ZER
6863 Tsêr (1), *rock*

ZERAH
2226 Zerach (19), *rising of light, dawning*

ZERAHIAH
2228 Z^{e}rachyâh (5), *Jehovah has risen*

ZERED
2218 Zered (3), lined with *shrubbery*

ZEREDA
6868 Ts^{e}rêdâh (1), *puncture*

ZEREDATHAH
6868 Ts^{e}rêdâh (1), *puncture*

ZERERATH
6888 Ts^{e}rêrâh (1), *puncture*

ZERESH
2238 Zeresh (4), *Zeresh*

ZERETH
6889 Tsereth (1), *splendor*

ZERI
6874 Ts^{e}rîy (1), *balsam*

ZEROR
6872 ts^{e}rôwr (1), *parcel; kernel* or *particle*

ZERUAH
6871 Ts^{e}rûw'âh (1), *leprous*

ZERUBBABEL
2216 Z^{e}rubbâbel (21), *from Babylon*
2217 Z^{e}rubbâbel (Ch.) (1), *from Babylon*

ZERUIAH
6870 Ts^{e}rûwyâh (26), *wounded*

ZETHAM
2241 Zêthâm (2), *seed*

ZETHAN
2133 Zéythân (1), *olive grove*

ZETHAR
2242 Zêthar (1), *Zethar*

ZIA
2127 Zîya' (1), *agitation*

ZIBA
6717 Tsîybâ' (16), *station*

ZIBEON
6649 Tsib'ôwn (8), *variegated*

ZIBIA
6644 Tsibyâ' (1), *female gazelle*

ZIBIAH
6645 Tsibyâh (2), *female gazelle*

ZICHRI
2147 Zikrîy (12), *memorable*

ZIDDIM
6661 Tsiddîym (1), *sides*

ZIDKIJAH
6667 Tsidqîyâh (1), *right of Jehovah*

ZIDON
6721 Tsîydôwn (20), *fishery*
6722 Tsîydônîy (1), *Tsidonian*

ZIDONIANS
6722 Tsîydônîy (10), *Tsidonian*

ZIF
2099 Zîv (2), *flowers*

ZIHA
6727 Tsîychâ' (3), *drought*

ZIKLAG
6860 Tsiqlâg (14), *Tsiklag* or *Tsikelag*

ZILLAH
6741 Tsillâh (3), *Tsillah*

ZILPAH
2153 Zilpâh (7), fragrant *dropping* as myrrh

ZILTHAI
6769 Tsill^{e}thay (2), *shady*

ZIMMAH
2155 Zimmâh (3), bad *plan*

ZIMRAN
2175 Zimrân (2), *musical*

ZIMRI
2174 Zimrîy (15), *musical*

ZIN
6790 Tsîn (10), *crag*

ZINA
2126 Zîynâ' (1), well-*fed*

ZION
6726 Tsîyôwn (152), permanent *capital* or *monument*

ZION'S
6726 Tsîyôwn (1), permanent *capital* or *monument*

ZIOR
6730 Tsîy'ôr (1), *small*

ZIPH
2128 Zìyph (10), *flowing*

ZIPHAH
2129 Zîyphâh (1), *flowing*

ZIPHIMS
2130 Zîyphîy (1), *Ziphite*

ZIPHION
6837 Tsiphyôwn (1), *watch-tower*

ZIPHITES
2130 Zìyphîy (2), *Ziphite*

ZIPHRON
2202 Ziphrôn (1), *fragrant*

ZIPPOR
6834 Tsippôwr (7), little *hopping bird*

ZIPPORAH
6855 Tsippôrâh (3), *bird*

ZITHRI
5644 Çithrîy (1), *protective*

ZIZ
6732 Tsîyts (1), *bloom*

ZIZA
2124 Zîyzâ' (2), *prominence*

ZIZAH
2125 Zìyzâh (1), *prominence*

ZOAN
6814 Tsô'an (7), *Tsoän*

ZOAR
6820 Tsô'ar (10), *little*

ZOBA
6678 Tsôwbâ' (2), *station*

ZOBAH
6678 Tsôwbâ' (11), *station*

ZOBEBAH
6637 Tsôbêbâh (1), *canopier*

ZOHAR
6714 Tsôchar (4), *whiteness*

ZOHELETH
2120 Zôcheleth (1), *serpent*

ZOHETH
2105 Zôwchêth (1), *Zocheth*

ZOPHAH
6690 Tsôwphach (2), *breath*

ZOPHAI
6689 Tsûwph (1), *honey-comb*

ZOPHAR
6691 Tsôwphar (4), *departing*

ZOPHIM
6839 Tsôphîym (1), *watchers*

ZORAH
6681 tsâvach (8), to *screech* exultingly

ZORATHITES
6882 Tsor'îy (1), *Tsorite* or *Tsorathite*

ZOREAH
6881 Tsor'âh (1), *stinging wasp*

ZORITES
6882 Tsor'îy (1), *Tsorite* or *Tsorathite*

ZOROBABEL
2216 Zŏrŏbabĕl (3), *from Babylon*

ZUAR
6686 Tsûw'âr (5), *small*

ZUPH
6689 Tsûwph (3), *honey-comb*

ZUR
6698 Tsûwr (5), *rock*

ZURIEL
6700 Tsûwrîy'êl (1), *rock of God*

ZURISHADDAI
6701 Tsûwrîyshadday (5), *rock of* (the) *Almighty*

ZUZIMS
2104 Zûwzîym (1), *prominent*

The New Strong's®
Expanded
Dictionary

of the Words in the

Hebrew Bible

---

with their Renderings in the King James Version

and with Additional Definitions
Adapted from W. E. Vine
and Cross-references to Other
Word Study Resources

read this first!

How to Use the Hebrew and Aramaic Dictionary

For many people Strong's unique system of numbers continues to be *the* bridge between the original languages of the Bible and the English of the *King James Version* (AV). *Strong's Hebrew and Aramaic Dictionary* is a fully integrated companion to *Strong's Concordance,* and its entries contain a wealth of information about the words of the Bible in their original language. In order to enhance the strategic importance of the dictionary for Bible students, significant features have been added in this new, expanded edition.

New Features

The dictionary is designed to provide maximum information so that your word studies are enriching and satisfying. The most significant enhancement is the expanded definitions, which come from the best of the standard word-study resources: *Vine's Complete Expository Dictionary of Old and New Testament Words, Brown-Driver-Briggs Hebrew and English Lexicon,* and *Girdlestone's Synonyms of the Old Testament.* The expanded definitions reveal the entire range of meanings so that the user can conduct more precise and accurate word studies. In addition, they help to convey the depth and richness of Hebrew and Aramaic words.

The second item that has been added is the frequency word counts, which appear in curly brackets {}. Frequency counts are provided for both the Hebrew words and the English words used in the AV. For example, the Hebrew word *ab* (entry #1) has {1211x} following it. This means that this word occurs 1211 times in the Hebrew text. Then after the :— symbol, a list of English translations and their occurrences are given. For example, "chief" {2x} means that this word is used twice in the AV as a translation of the Hebrew word *ab.*

For those wanting to conduct more advanced word studies, a cross-reference to other lexicons is given at the end of the definition. These lexicons are the *Theological Wordbook of the Old Testament,* by R. Laird Harris, Gleason L. Archer, Jr., and Bruce K. Waltke (Moody, 1980); and the *Brown-Driver-Briggs Hebrew and English Lexicon* (Hendrickson, 1999). These two lexicons are abbreviated in the definitions as TWOT and BDB.

Using the Dictionary to Do Word Studies

Careful Bible students do word studies, and *The New Strong's® Expanded Dictionary of Bible Words* with enhanced *Hebrew and Aramaic Dictionary* offers unique assistance. Consider the word "love" as found in the AV. By skimming the main concordance, you find these numbers for Hebrew and Aramaic words that the King James Bible translates with the English word "love": 157, 160, 2836, 7355, 1730, 7474, 5690, and 5691. Now for any one Bible reference in this entry there is only one Hebrew word cited and you may be interested only in establishing the precise meaning for just that word in that occurrence. If so, it will be very helpful for you to observe that same Hebrew word in *each* of its occurrences in the Bible. In that way, you develop an idea of its possible range of meanings, and you can help clarify what is most likely the precise meaning in the specific Bible reference you are studying.

Now see the *Dictionary* entry 157 itself, and notice that after the symbol :— all the words and word prefixes and suffixes are listed. These show you that this one Hebrew word, *'ahab,* is translated into several different but related words in the King James Bible: beloved, love, loved, lovely, lover, loving, like, befriend. This list tells you the range of uses of the one Hebrew word in the AV. This information can help you distinguish between the nuances of the meaning found where this and the other Hebrew words are translated by these same words and similar ones in the King James Bible.

These three ways of using the dictionary in conjunction with *Strong's Concordance* show you only a sampling of the many ways *The New Strong's® Expanded Dictionary of Bible Words* can enrich your study of the Bible. (See also *Getting the Most from Your New Strong's® Exhaustive Bible Concordance,* Nelson, 2000.) They also show why it is important that you take the time to become familiar with each feature in the dictionary as illustrated on the following page.

An Example
from the
Hebrew and Aramaic Dictionary

Strong's number, corresponding to the numbers at the beginning of each entry in the English Index.

An unnumbered cross-reference entry.

The word as it appears in the original Hebrew (or Aramaic) spelling.

The degree symbol denotes the presence of a textual variation. (See "Special Symbols")

The Hebrew (or Aramaic) word represented in English letters in **bold** type (the transliteration).

Strong's syllable-by-syllable pronunciation in *italics*, with the emphasized syllable marked by the accent.

Information regarding relationship to other Hebrew (or Aramaic) words, usually cited by Strong's numbers. Sometimes a word may refer to a Greek entry (shown by *italic* numbers) or it may come from another language.

צְאוֹן° **tse'ôn**. See 6629.

6628. צֶאֱל **tse'el**, *tseh´-el;* from an unused root mean. to *be slender;* the *lotus* tree:— shady tree.

6629. צֹאן **tsô'n**, *tsone;* or

צְאוֹן° **tse'ôwn** (Psa. 144:13) *tseh-one´;* from an unused root mean. to *migrate;* a collect. name for a flock (of sheep or goats); also fig. (of men):— (small) cattle, flock (+ -s), lamb (+ s), sheep ([-cote, -fold, -shearer, -herds]).

See "Special Symbols."

Occasional, helpful Scripture references.

Improved, consistent abbreviations. All abbreviations occur with their full spelling in the list of abbreviations.

Brief English definitions (shown by italics).

After the long dash (—), there is a complete, alphabetical listing of all renderings of this Hebrew (or Aramaic) word in the KJV. (See also "Special Symbols").

Note that Hebrew (or Aramaic) spelling variations are conveniently indented for easy comparison.

Plan of the Hebrew and Aramaic Dictionary

1. All the original words are presented in alphabetical order and are numbered for easy matching between this dictionary and *Strong's Concordance*. Many reference books also use these numbers created by Dr. Strong.

2. The number of times a Hebrew or Aramaic word occurs in the Hebrew Old Testament is given in curly brackets {} with an "x" inside of it.

3. After each word, the exact equivalent of each sound (phoneme) is given in English characters, according to the transliteration system given below, followed by the precise pronunciation, with the proper stress mark.

4. Next follows the etymology, root meaning, and common uses of the word, along with other important related details. In the case of proper nouns, the normal English spelling is given.

5. After the colon and dash (: —), all the different ways that the word appears in the King James Bible are listed in alphabetical order. The number surrounded by curly brackets {} refers to the number of times this word is translated in the AV. When the Hebrew or Aramaic word appears in English as a phrase, the main word of the phrase is used to alphabetize it.

6. The main new feature of the dictionary is the expanded word studies. These provide the full range of meaning, and they give the student all the various nuances of the word.

7. The information following "See" at the end of each entry provides cross-references to two other word study dictionaries, the *Theological Wordbook of the Old Testament* (TWOT) and the *Brown-Driver-Briggs Hebrew and English Lexicon* (BDB). The number for TWOT refers to the word number assigned by TWOT. However, the number for BDB refers to the page number, followed by the quadrant (e.g., 2d means page 2, quadrant d). The schema for quadrants is as follows: A   C
                                                          B   D

Transliteration and Pronunciation of the Hebrew and Aramaic

The following shows how the Hebrew words are transliterated into English in this Dictionary.

1. The Hebrew and Aramaic read *from right to left*. Both alphabets consist of 22 letters (and their variations), which are all regarded as *consonants*, although four consonants (א ה ו י) sometimes indicate vowel sounds. To help enunciation, vowels are primarily indicated by certain "points" or marks, mostly beneath the letters. Hebrew and Aramaic do not use *capitals, italics,* etc.

2. The Hebrew and Aramaic characters are as follows:

No.	Form	Name	Transliteration and Pronunciation
1.	א	'Aleph (*aw´-lef*)	', silent
2.	ב	Bêyth (*bayth*)	b
3.	ג	Gîymel (*ghee´-mel*)	g hard = γ
4.	ד	Dâleth (*daw´-leth*)	d
5.	ה	Hê' (*hay*)	h, often quiescent
6.	ו	Vâv (*vawv*) or Wâw (*waw*)	v or w, quiescent
7.	ז	Zayin (*zah´-yin*)	z, as in *zeal*
8.	ח	Chêyth (*khayth*)	German **ch** = χ (nearly *kh*)
9.	ט	Têyth (*tayth*)	ṭ = T
10.	י	Yôwd (*yode*)	y, often quiescent
11.	כ final ך	Kaph (*caf*)	k = ק
12.	ל	Lâmed (*law´-med*)	l
13.	מ final ם	Mêm (*mame*)	m
14.	נ final ן	Nûwn (*noon*)	n
15.	ס	Çâmek (*saw´-mek*)	ç = s sharp = שׂ
16.	ע	'Ayin (*ah´-yin*)	' peculiar [1]
17.	פ final ף	Phê' (*fay*)	ph = f = φ
	פ	Pê' (*pay*)	p
18.	צ, final ץ	Tsâdêy (*tsaw-day´*)	ts
19.	ק	Qôwph (*cofe*)	q = k = כ
20.	ר	Rêysh (*raysh*)	r
21.	שׂ	Sîyn (*seen*)	s sharp = ס = σ
	שׁ	Shîyn (*sheen*)	sh
22.	ת	Thâv (*thawv*)	th, as in *THin* = θ
	ת	Tâv (*tawv*)	t = ט = τ

---

[1] The letter *'Ayin*, because Westerners find it difficult to pronounce accurately (it is a deep guttural sound, like that made in *gargling*), is generally passed over silently in reading. We have represented it to the eye (but not exact- ly to the ear) by the Greek *rough breathing* mark (') in order to distinguish it from *'Aleph*, which is likewise treated as silent, being similarly represented by the Greek *smooth breathing* (').

3. The vowel points are as follows:

Form [2]	Name	Transliteration and Pronunciation
בָ	Qâmêts (*caw-mates*)	â, as in *All*
בַ	Pattach (*pat´-takh*)	a, as in *mAn*
בֲ	Shevâ'-Pattach (*she-vaw´ pat´-takh*)	ă, as in *hAt*
בֵ	Tsêrêy (*tsay-ray*)	ê, as in *thEy* = η
בֶ	Çegôwl (*seg-ole*)	e, as in *thEir*
		e, as in *mEn* = ε
בֱ	Shevâ'-Çegôwl (*she-vaw´ seg-ole*)	ě, as in *mEt*
בְ	Shevâ' (*she-vaw*) [3]	obscure, as in *avErage*
		silent, as *e* in *madE*
בִ	Chîyriq (*khee´-rik*)	î, as in *machIne* [4]
		i, as in *supplIant* (*misery, hit*)
בֹ	Chôwlem (*kho´-lem*) [5]	ô, as in *no* = ω
בָ	Short Qâmêts (*caw-mates*) [6]	o, as in *nor* = o
בָ	Shevâ-Qâmêts (*she-vaw´ caw-mates*)	ŏ, as in *not*
בוּ	Shûwrêq * (*shoo-rake*) [7]	û, as in *crUel*
בֻ	Qîbbûts * (*kib´-boots*) [7]	u, as in *fUll, rude*

4. A point in the heart of a letter is called *Dâgêsh´*, and is of two kinds, which must be carefully distinguished.

    a. Dâgêsh *lenè* occurs only in the letters ב, ג, ד, כ, פ, ת (technically vocalized B*e*gad´-K*e*phath), when they *begin* a clause or sentence, or are preceded by a consonant *sound;* and simply has the effect of removing their aspiration. [8]

    b. Dâgêsh *forte* may occur in any letter except א, ה, ח, ע or ר; it is equivalent to *doubling* the letter, and at the same time it removes the aspiration of a B*e*gad-K*e*phath letter. [9]

5. The *Maqqêph´* (־), like a *hyphen*, unites words only for purposes of pronunciation (by removing the primary accent from all except the last word), but it does not affect their meaning or grammatical construction.

Special Symbols

+ (*addition*) denotes a rendering in the A.V. of one or more Hebrew or Aramaic words in connection with the one under consideration. For example, in 2 Kgs. 4:41, No. 1697, דָּבָר (**dâbâr**) is translated as "harm," in connection with No. 7451. Literally, it is "bad thing."

× (*multiplication*) denotes a rendering in the A.V. that results from an idiom peculiar to the Hebrew or Aramaic. For example, in Psa. 132:15, the whole Hebrew phrase in which בָּרַךְ, **bârak** (1288) appears is a means of expressing a verb root emphatically, i. e. "blessing, I will bless" = "I will abundantly bless."

° (*degree*), attached to a Hebrew word, denotes a corrected vowel pointing which is different from the Biblical text. (This mark is set in Hebrew Bibles over syllables in which the vowels of the margin have been inserted instead of those which properly belong to the text.)

For example, see the difference between the Hebrew text and the scribes' marginal note in Ezek. 40:15 for No. 2978, translated "entrance."

( ) (*parentheses*), in the renderings from the A.V., denote a word or syllable which is sometimes given in connection with the principal word to which it is attached. In Num. 34:6, the only occurrence of "western" in the A. V., the underlying Hebrew word is יָם (**yâm**, No. 3220), which is usually translated "sea."

[ ] (*brackets*), in the rendering from the A.V., denote the inclusion of an additional word in the Hebrew or Aramaic. For example, No. 3117, יוֹם (**yôwm**), is translated as "birthday" in Gen. 40:20, along with No. 3205. So, two Hebrew words are translated by one English word.

Italics, at the end of a rendering from the A.V., denote an explanation of the variations from the usual form.

---

[2] The same Hebrew/Aramaic consonant (ב) is shown here in order to show the position of the vowel points, whether below, above, or in the middle of Hebrew or Aramaic consonants.

[3] Silent *Shevâ'* is not represented by any mark in our method of transliteration, since it is understood whenever there is no other vowel point.

[4] Chîyriq is long only when it is followed by a quiescent *yôwd* (either expressed or implied).

[5] Chôwlem is written *fully* only over *Vâv* or *Wâw* (וֹ), which is then quiescent (w); but when used "defectively" (without the *Vâv* or *Wâw*) it may be written either over the left-hand corner of the letter to which it belongs, or over the right-hand corner of the following one.

[6] Short *Qâmêts* is found only in *unaccented syllables ending with a consonant sound.*

[7] *Shûwrêq* is written only in the heart of *Vâv* or *Wâw*. Sometimes it is said to be "defectively" written (without the *Vâv* or *Wâw*), and then takes the form of *Qibbûts*, which in such cases is called *vicarious*.

[8] In our system of transliteration Dâgêsh *lenè* is represented only in the letters פ and ת, because elsewhere it does not affect the pronunciation.

[9] A point in the heart of ה is called *Mappîyq* (*mappeek*). It occurs only in the final vowel-less letter of a few words, and we have represented it by hh. A Dâgêsh *forte* in the heart of ו may easily be distinguished from the vowel *Shûwrêq* by noticing that in the former case the letter has a proper vowel point accompanying it.

It should be noted that both kinds of Dâgêsh are often omitted in writing (being *implied*), but (in the case at least of Dâgêsh *forte*) the word is usually pronounced the same as if it were present.

abb. = abbreviated
    abbreviation
abstr. = abstract
    abstractly
act. = active (voice)
    actively
acc. = accusative (case) [1]
adj. = adjective
    adjectivally
adv. = adverb
    adverbial
    adverbially
aff. = affix [2]
    affixed
affin. = affinity
alt. = alternate
    alternately
anal. = analogy
appar. = apparent
    apparently
arch. = architecture
    architectural
    architecturally
art. = article [3]
artif. = artificial
    artificially
Ass. = Assyrian
A.V. = Authorized Version
    (King James Version)
Bab. = Babylon
    Babylonia
    Babylonian
caus. = causative [4]
    causatively
cerem. = ceremony
    ceremonial
    ceremonially
Chald. = Chaldee
    (Aramaic)
    Chaldaism
    (Aramaism)
Chr. = Christian
collat. = collateral
    collaterally
collect. = collective
    collectively
comp. = compare [5]
    comparison
    comparative
    comparatively
concr. = concrete
    concretely
conjec. = conjecture
    conjectural
    conjecturally
conjug. = conjugation [6]
    conjugational
    conjugationally
conjunc. = conjunction
    conjunctional
    conjunctionally
constr. = construct [7]
    construction
    constructive
    constructively

contr. = contracted [8]
    contraction
correl. = correlated
    correlation
    correlative
    correlatively
corresp. = corresponding
    correspondingly
dat. = dative (case) [9]
def. = definite [10]
    definitely
demonstr. = demonstra-
    tive[11]
denom. = denominative [12]
    denominatively
der. = derived
    derivation
    derivative
    derivatively
desc. = descended
    descendant
    descendants
dimin. = diminutive [13]
dir. = direct
    directly
E. = East
    Eastern
eccl. = ecclesiastical
    ecclesiastically
e.g. = for example
Eg. = Egypt
    Egyptian
    Egyptians
ellip. = ellipsis [14]
    elliptical
    elliptically
emphat. = emphatic
    emphatically
equiv. = equivalent
    equivalently
err. = error
    erroneous
    erroneously
espec. = especially
etym. = etymology [15]
    etymological
    etymologically
euphem. = euphemism [16]
    euphemistic
    euphemistically
euphon. = euphonious [17]
    euphonically
extens. = extension [18]
    extensive
extern. = external
    externally
fem. = feminine (gender)
fig. = figurative
    figuratively
for. = foreign
    foreigner
freq. = frequentative
    frequentatively
fut. = future

gen. = general
    generally
    generic
    generical
    generically
Gr. = Greek
    Graecism
gut. = guttural [19]
Heb. = Hebrew
    Hebraism
i.e. = that is
ident. = identical
    identically
immed. = immediate
    immediately
imper. = imperative [20]
    imperatively
imperf. = imperfect [21]
impers. = impersonal
    impersonally
impl. = implied
    impliedly
    implication
incept. = inceptive [22]
    inceptively
incl. = including
    inclusive
    inclusively
indef. = indefinite
    indefinitely
ind. = indicative [23]
    indicatively
indiv. = individual
    individually
infer. = inference
    inferential
    inferentially
infin. = infinitive
inhab. = inhabitant
    inhabitants
ins. = inserted
intens. = intensive
    intensively
interch. = interchangeable
intern. = internal
    internally
interj. = interjection [24]
    interjectional
    interjectionally
interrog. = interrogative [25]
    interrogatively
intr. = intransitive [26]
    intransitively
invol. = involuntary
    involuntarily
irreg. = irregular
    irregularly
Isr. = Israelite
    Israelites
    Israelitish
Lat. = Latin
Levit. = Levitical
    Levitically

lit. = literal
    literally
marg. = margin
    marginal reading
masc. = masculine (gender)
mean. = meaning
ment. = mental
    mentally
metaph. = metaphorical
    metaphorically
mid. = middle (voice) [27]
modif. = modified
    modification
mor. = moral
    morally
mult. = multiplicative [28]
nat. = natural
    naturally
neg. = negative
    negatively
neut. = neuter (gender)
obj. = object
    objective
    objectively
obs. = obsolete
ord. = ordinal [29]
or. = origin
orig. = original
    originally
orth. = orthography [30]
    orthographical
    orthographically
Pal. = Palestine
part. = participle
pass. = passive (voice)
    passively
patron. = patronymic [31]
    patronymical
    patronymically
perh. = perhaps
perm. = permutation [32] (of
    adjacent letters)
pers. = person
    personal
    personally
Pers. = Persia
    Persian
    Persians
phys. = physical
    physically
plur. = plural
poet. = poetry
    poetical
    poetically
pos. = positive
    positively
pref. = prefix
    prefixed
prep. = preposition
    prepositional
    prepositionally
prim. = primitive
prob. = probable
    probably

prol. = prolonged [33]
    prolongation
pron. = pronoun
    pronominal
    pronominally
prop. = properly
prox. = proximate
    proximately
recip. = reciprocal
    reciprocally
redupl. = reduplicated [34]
    reduplication
refl. = reflexive [35]
    reflexively
reg. = regular
rel. = relative
    relatively
relig. = religion
    religious
    religiously
Rom. = Roman
second. = secondary
    secondarily
signif. = signification
    signifying
short. = shorter
    shortened
sing. = singular
spec. = specific
    specifically
streng. = strengthening
subdiv. = subdivision
    subdivisional
    subdivisionally
subj. = subjectively
    subjective
    subject
substit. = substituted
suff. = suffix
superl. = superlative [36]
    superlatively
symb. = symbolic
    symbolical
    symbolically
tech. = technical
    technically
term. = termination
tran. = transitive [37]
    transitively
transc. = transcription
transm. = transmutation [38]
transp. = transposed [39]
    transposition
typ. = typical
    typically
uncert. = uncertain
    uncertainly
var. = various
    variation
voc. = vocative (case) [40]
vol. = voluntary
    voluntarily

---

[1] often indicating the direct object of an action verb

[2] part of a word which, when attached to the beginning of the word is called a prefix; if attaching within a word, an infix; and if at the end, a suffix

[3] "the" is the definite article; "a" and "an" are indefinite articles

[4] expressing or denoting causation

[5] the comparative of an adjective or adverb expresses a greater degree of an attribute, e.g. "higher"; "more slowly"

[6] a systematic array of various verbal forms

[7] the condition in Hebrew and Aramaic when two adjacent nouns are combined semantically as follows, e.g. "sword" + "king" = "(the) sword of (the) king" or "(the) king's sword". These languages tend to throw the stress of the entire noun phrase toward the end of the whole expression.

[8] a shortened form of a word. It is made by omitting or combining some elements or by reducing vowels or syllables, e.g. "is not" becomes "isn't".

[9] often the indirect object of an action verb

[10] the definite article ("the")

[11] demonstrative pronouns which point (show), e.g. "this," "that"

[12] derived from a noun

[13] a grammatical form which expresses smallness and/or endearment

[14] a construction which leaves out understood words

[15] the historical origin of a word

[16] the use of a pleasant, polite, or harmless-sounding word or phrase to hide harsh, rude, or infamous truths, e.g. "to pass away" = "to die"

[17] a linguistic mechanism to make pronunciation easier, e.g. "an" before "hour" instead of "a"

[18] when a general term can denote an entire class of things

[19] speech sounds which are produced deep in the throat

[20] the mood which expresses a command

[21] used of a tense which expresses a continuous but unfinished action or state

[22] used of a verbal aspect which denotes the beginning of an action

[23] used of the mood which expresses a verbal action as actually occurring (not hypothetical)

[24] an exclamation which expresses emotion

[25] indicating a question

[26] referring to verbs which do not govern direct objects

[27] reflexive

[28] capable of multiplying or tending to multiply

[29] This shows the position or the order within a series, e.g. "second"; the corresponding cardinal number is "two".

[30] the written system of spelling in a given language

[31] a name derived from that of a paternal ancestor, often created by an affix in various languages

[32] a rearrangement

[33] lengthening a pronunciation

[34] the repetition of a letter or syllable to form a new, inflected word

[35] denoting an action by the subject upon itself

[36] expressing the highest degree of comparison of the quality indicated by an adjective or an adverb, e.g. "highest"; "most timely"

[37] expressing an action directed toward a person or a thing (the direct object)

[38] the change of one grammatical element to another

[39] switching word order

[40] an inflection which is used when one is addressing a person or a thing directly, e.g. "John, come here!"

HEBREW AND ARAMAIC DICTIONARY OF THE OLD TESTAMENT

א

1. אָב {1211x} ʾâb, *awb;* a prim. word; *father* in a lit. and immed., or fig. and remote application:—chief {2x}, (fore-{1x}) father {1205x} ([-less] {1x}), × patrimony {1x}, principal {1x}. comp. names in "Abi-".

Ab means "father; grandfather; forefather; ancestor." **(1)** Basically, *ab* relates to the familial relationship represented by the word "father." This is the word's significance in its first biblical appearance: "Therefore shall a man leave his father and his mother, and shall cleave unto his wife . . ." (Gen 2:24). **(2)** In poetical passages, the word is sometimes paralleled to *em,* "mother": "I have said to corruption, Thou art my father: to the worm, Thou art my mother, and my sister" (Job 17:14). The word is also used in conjunction with "mother" to represent one's parents (Lev 19:3). But unlike the word *em, ab* is never used of animals. **(3)** *Ab* also means "grandfather" and/or "great-grandfather," as in Gen 28:13: "I am the LORD God of Abraham thy [grand]father, and the God of Isaac. . . ." Such progenitors on one's mother's side were called "thy mother's father" (Gen 28:2).

(4) This noun may be used of any one of the entire line of men from whom a given individual is descended: "But he [Elijah] himself went a day's journey into the wilderness, and came and sat down under a juniper tree: and he requested for himself that he might die; and said, It is enough; now, O LORD, take away my life; for I am not better than my fathers" (1 Kin 19:4). In such use, the word may refer to the first man, a "forefather," **(4a)** a clan (Jer 35:6), **(4b)** a tribe (Josh. 19:47), **(4c)** a group with a special calling (1 Chr 24:19), **(4d)** a dynasty (1 Kin 15:3), or **(4e)** a nation (Josh 24:3). **(5)** Thus, "father" does not necessarily mean the man who directly sired a given individual. **(6)** This noun sometimes describes the adoptive relationship, especially when it is used of the "founder of a class or station," such as a trade: "And Adah bare Jabal: he was the father of such as dwell in tents, and of such as have cattle" (Gen 4:20). **(7)** *Ab* can be a title of respect, usually applied to an older person, as when David said to Saul: "Moreover, my father, see, yea, see the skirt of thy robe in my hand . . ." (1 Sa 24:11).

(8) The word is also applied to teachers: "And Elisha saw it, and he cried, My father, my father, the chariot of Israel, and the horsemen thereof . . ." (2 Kin 2:12). **(9)** In 2 Kin 6:21, the word is applied to the prophet Elisha. **(10)** In Judg 17:10 it is applied to a priest. **(11)** This word is also a title of respect when used of "one's husband": "Wilt thou not from this time cry unto me, My father, thou art the guide of my youth?" (Jer 3:4). **(12)** In Gen 45:8, the noun is used of an "advisor": "So now it was not you that sent me hither, but God: and he hath made me a father [advisor] to Pharaoh, and lord of all his house, and a ruler throughout all the land of Egypt." **(13)** In each case, the one described as "father" occupied a position or status and received the honor due to a "father." **(14)** In conjunction with *bayit* [1004 - "house"], the word *ab* may mean "family": "In the tenth day of this month they shall take to them every man a lamb, according to the house of their fathers . . ." (Ex 12:3). **(15)** Sometimes the plural of the word used by itself can represent "family": ". . . These are the heads of the fathers [households] of the Levites according to their families" (Ex 6:25).

(16) God is described as the "father" of Israel (Deut 32:6). **(16a)** He is the One who begot and protected them, the One they should revere and obey. **(16b)** Mal 2:10 tells us that God is the "father" of all people. **(16c)** He is especially the "protector" or "father" of the fatherless: "A father of the fatherless, and a judge of the widows, is God in his holy habitation" (Ps 68:5). **(17)** As the "father" of a king, God especially aligns Himself to that man and his kingdom: "I will be his father, and he shall be my son. If he commit iniquity, I will chasten him with the rod of men, and with the stripes of the children of men" (2 Sa 7:14). **(17a)** Not every king was a son of God—only those whom He adopted. **(17b)** In a special sense, the perfect King was God's adopted Son: "I will declare the decree: the LORD hath said unto me, Thou art my Son; this day have I begotten thee" (Ps 2:7). The extent, power, and duration of His kingdom are guaranteed by the Father's sovereignty (Ps 2:8–9). **(18)** On the other hand, one of the Messiah's enthronement names is "Eternal Father": ". . . And his name shall be called Wonderful, Counselor, The mighty God, The everlasting Father, The Prince of Peace" (Is 9:6). See: TWOT—4a; BDB—1a, 3a, 1078b.

2. אַב {9x} ʾab (Aram.), *ab;* corresp. to 1:— father {9x}. See: TWOT—2553; BDB—1078a, b.

3. אֵב {2x} ʾêb, *abe;* from the same as 24; a *green* plant:—greenness {1x}, fruit {1x}. See: TWOT—1a; BDB—1a, 1078a.

4. אֵב {3x} ʾêb (Aram.), *abe;* corresp. to 3:—
   fruit {3x}. See: TWOT—2554; BDB—
   1078a, 1081b.

5. אַבַגְתָא {1x} ʾĂbagthâʾ, *ab-ag-thaw';* of for.
   or.; *Abagtha,* a eunuch of Xerxes:—
   Abagtha. BDB—1b.

6. אָבַד {184x} ʾâbad, *aw-bad';* a prim. root;
   prop. to *wander* away, i.e. *lose* oneself;
   by impl. to *perish* (caus. *destroy*); :— break {1x},
   destroy {62x} (-uction {1x}), + not escape {1x},
   fail {2x}, lose {10x}, (cause to, make) perish
   {98x}, spendeth {1x}, × and surely {2x}, take
   {1x}, be undone {1x}, × utterly {2x}, be void of
   {1x}, have no way to flee {1x}.
   Basically *âbad* represents the disappearance of someone or something. **(1)** In its strongest sense the word means "to die or to cease
   to exist" (Lev 26:38). **(2)** bring to non-existence
   (Num 33:52; Deut 12:2–3). **(3)** to go to ruin or
   to be ruined (Ex 10:7; Num 21:29–30). **(4)** to
   succumb, focuses on the process rather than
   the conclusion (Num 17:12–13). **(5)** being carried off to death or destruction by some means
   (Num 6:33; Deut 4:26). **(6)** to disappear but not
   be destroyed, to be lost (Deut 22:3; Jer 50:6).
   (7) to go astray, in the sense of wandering (Deut
   26:5). **(8)** human qualities which are lessening
   or have lessened (Deut 32:28; Ps 146:4). Syn.:
   2763, 7843, 8045. Summary: This word refers
   to the death of the righteous or the wicked; to
   the downfall and dissolution of nations; to the
   desolation of countries; to the withering away
   of herbage and crops; to the fading away of
   strength, hope, wisdom, knowledge, and wealth.
   Syn: See: TWOT—2; BDB—1b, 1078b.

7. אֲבַד {7x} ʾăbad (Aram.), *ab-ad';* corresp. to
   6:— to destroy {5x}, to perish {2x}.
   Basically *abad* represents the disappearance of someone or something. **(1)** In its strongest sense the word means "to die or to cease
   to exist." The LORD warned Israel that disobedience and godlessness would be punished by
   their removal from the Promised Land and death
   in a foreign land: "And ye shall perish among
   the heathen, and the land of your enemies shall
   eat you up" (Lev 26:38). This sense may be further heightened by the use of the intensive stem
   so that the verb comes to mean "utterly destroy."
   The stem also changes the force of the verb from
   intransitive to transitive. So God told Israel
   "to utterly destroy" ("bring to non-existence")
   the false gods of Canaan: "[Utterly] destroy all
   their pictures and [utterly] destroy all their
   molten images" (Num 33:52). The force of this
   command was further heightened when He
   said: "Ye shall utterly destroy all the places,
   wherein the nations which ye shall possess
   served their gods . . . and destroy the names
   of them out of that place" (Deut 12:2–3). This

intensified sense is used of the destruction of
peoples (armies), too; as for Pharaoh's army,
"the LORD hath destroyed them unto this day"
(Deut 11:4).
   (2) A somewhat different emphasis of *abad*
is "to go to ruin" or "to be ruined." After the
second plague Pharaoh's counsellors told him
to grant Israel's request to leave because the nation was in ruins: ". . . knowest thou not yet that
Egypt is destroyed [ruined]?" (Ex 10:7—the first
biblical occurrence). In a similar sense Moab
is said "to be ruined" or laid waste: "Woe to
thee, Moab! Thou art undone, O people of Chemosh. . . . We have shot at them; Heshbon is
perished even unto Dibon, and we have laid them
waste even unto Nophah" (Num 21:29–30). **(3)**
Closely related to the immediately preceding
emphasis is that of "to succumb." This use of
abad focuses on the process rather than the
conclusion. The sons of Israel spoke to Moses
about the disastrous effects of everyone drawing near to God. They needed some mediators
(priests) who could focus on keeping ritualisti-
cally prepared so they would not die when they
approached God. They used the verb, therefore,
in the sense of the nation gradually perishing,
or "succumbing" to death: "Behold, we die, we
perish, we all perish. Whosoever cometh any
thing near unto the tabernacle of the LORD shall
die: shall we be consumed with dying?" (Num
17:12–13). God responds by establishing the
priesthood so "that there be no wrath any more
upon the children of Israel" (Num 18:5).
   (4) *Abad* can also speak of being carried off
to death or destruction by some means. The leaders of the rebellion against the Aaronic priesthood (Korah, Dathan, and Abiram) and their
families were swallowed up by the ground:
". . . and the earth closed upon them: and they
perished from among the congregation" (Num
16:33). This same nuance appears when God
says the people will "perish" from off the land
if they do not keep the covenant: "Ye shall soon
utterly perish from off the land whereunto ye go
over Jordan to possess it; ye shall not prolong
your days upon it, but shall utterly be destroyed" (Deut 4:26). As a nation they will be
destroyed as far as the land is concerned.
(5) The verb may mean to disappear but not be
destroyed, in other words "to be lost." God instructs Israel concerning lost possessions: "In
like manner shalt thou do with his ass; and so
shalt thou do with his raiment; and with all lost
things of thy brother's, which he hath lost, and
thou hast found, shalt thou do likewise: thou
mayest not hide thyself" (Deut 22:3). Israel is
called "lost sheep" whose "shepherds have
caused them to go astray" (Jer 50:6). **(6)** Another nuance of the verb is "to go astray" in the
sense of wandering. At the dedication of the

first fruits Israel is to recognize God's rights to the land, that He is the landowner and they are the temporary tenants, by confessing "a Syrian ready to perish was my father" (Deut 26:5).

(7) Finally, *abad* can be applied to human qualities which are lessening or have lessened: "For they are a nation void of counsel, neither is there any understanding in them" (Deut 32:28). The word can also be used of the failure of human wisdom as in Ps 146:4: as for men "his breath goeth forth, he returneth to his earth; in that very day his thoughts perish."

8. אֹבֵד {2x} ʾôbêd, o-bade'; act. of part. of 6; (concr.) *wretched* or (abstr.) *destruction:*—perish {2x}. See: TWOT—2a; BDB—1b, 2b.

9. אֲבֵדָה {4x} ʾăbêdâh, ab-ay-daw'; from 6; concr. something *lost*; abstr. *destruction,* i.e. Hades:—lost thing {3x}, that which was lost {1x}. *Abedah,* which is found 4 times, refers to a "thing which has been lost" (Ex 22:9). Syn.: comp. 10. See: TWOT—2b; BDB—2b.

10. אֲבַדֹּה {1x} ʾăbaddôh, ab-ad-do'; the same as 9, miswritten for 11; a *perishing:*—destruction {1x}. See: TWOT—2b; BDB—2b, c.

11. אֲבַדּוֹן {6x} ʾăbaddôwn, ab-ad-done'; intens. from 6; abstr. a *perishing;* concr. Hades:—destruction {6x}. The noun *abaddown* occurs 6 times and means "the place of destruction" (Job 26:6). See: TWOT—2d; BDB—2b.

12. אַבְדָן {1x} ʾabdân, ab-dawn'; from 6; a *perishing:*—destruction {1x}. *Abdan* occurs once with the meaning "destruction" (Est 9:5). See: TWOT—2c; BDB—2b.

13. אָבְדָן {2x} ʾobdân, ob-dawn'; from 6; a *perishing:*—destruction {2x}. A variant spelling *obdan* also occurs with the meaning "destruction" (Est 8:6; 9:5). See: TWOT—2c; BDB—2b.

14. אָבָה {54x} ʾâbâh, aw-baw'; a prim. root; to *breathe* after, i.e. (fig.) to be *accquiescent:*—consent {3x}, rest content {1x}, will {4x}, be willing {4x}, would {42x}.

This verb, which occurs 54 times, is sometimes associated with the noun *'ebyon,* "needy (person)." **(1)** This verb means "to consent to" in Deut 13:8: "Thou shalt not consent unto him, nor hearken unto him." Basically represents the inclination which leads towards action, rather than the volition which immediately precedes it. See: TWOT—3; BDB—2c.

15. אָבֶה {1x} ʾâbeh, aw-beh'; from 14; *longing:*—desire {1x}. See: TWOT—3; BDB—106b.

16. אֵבֶה {1x} ʾêbeh, ay-beh'; from 14 (in the sense of *bending* toward); the *papyrus:*—swift {1x}. See: TWOT—3c; BDB—3a.

17. אֲבוֹי {1x} ʾăbôwy, ab-o'ee; from 14 (in the sense of *desiring*); *want:*—sorrow {1x}. See: TWOT—3d; BDB—5a.

18. אֵבוּס {3x} ʾêbûwç, ay-booce'; from 75; a *manger* or *stall:*—crib {3x}. See: TWOT—10a; BDB—7b.

19. אִבְחָה {1x} ʾibchâh, ib-khaw'; from an unused root (appar. mean. to *turn*); *brandishing* of a sword:—point (of the sword) {1x}. See: TWOT—786b; BDB—5b.

20. אֲבַטִּיחַ {1x} ʾăbaṭṭîyach, ab-at-tee'-akh; of uncert. der.; a *melon* (only plur.):—melons {1x}. See: TWOT—234a; BDB—5b, 105c.

21. אֲבִי {1x} ʾĂbîy, ab-ee'; from 1; *fatherly; Abi,* Hezekiah's mother:—Abi {1x}. See: BDB—4a, 5b.

22. אֲבִיאֵל {3x} ʾĂbîyʾêl, ab-ee-ale'; from 1 and 410; *father* (i.e. *possessor*) *of God; Abiel,* the name of two Isr.:—Abiel {3x}. See: BDB—3d.

23. אֲבִיאָסָף {1x} ʾĂbîyʾâçâph, ab-ee-aw-sawf'; from 1 and 622; *father of gathering* (i.e. *gatherer*); *Abiasaph,* an Isr.:—Abiasaph {1x}. See: BDB—4a.

24. אָבִיב {8x} ʾâbîyb, aw-beeb'; from an unused root (mean. to *be tender*); *green,* i.e. a young *ear* of grain; hence, the name of the month *Abib* or Nisan:—Abib {6x}, in the ear {1x}, green ears of corn {1x}. See: TWOT—1b; BDB—1b.

25. אֲבִי גִבְעוֹן {2x} ʾĂbîy Gibʿôwn, ab-ee' ghib-one'; from 1 and 1391; *father* (i.e. *founder*) *of Gibon; Abi-Gibon,* perh. an Isr.:—father of Gibeon {2x}. See: BDB—149c.

26. אֲבִיגַיִל {17x} ʾĂbîygayil, ab-ee-gah'-yil, or short.

אֲבִיגַל ʾĂbîygal, ab-ee-gal'; from 1 and 1524; *father* (i.e. *source*) *of joy; Abigail* or *Abigal,* the name of two Israelitesses:—Abigal {17x}. See: BDB—1b, 4a, 5a.

27. אֲבִידָן {5x} ʾĂbîydân, ab-ee-dawn'; from 1 and 1777; *father of judgment* (i.e. *judge*); *Abidan,* an Isr.:—Abidan {5x}. See: BDB—4a.

28. אֲבִידָע {2x} ʾĂbîydâʿ, ab-ee-daw'; from 1 and 3045; *father of knowledge* (i.e. *knowing*); *Abida,* a son of Abraham by Keturah:—Abida, Abidah. {2x}. See: BDB—4a.

29. אֲבִיָּה {25x} ʾĂbîyâh, ab-ee-yaw'; or prol.

אֲבִיָּהוּ ʾĂbîyâhûw, ab-ee-yaw'-hoo; from 1 and 3050; *father* (i.e. *worshiper*) of

Jah; Abijah, the name of several Isr. men and two Israelitesses:—Abijah 20, Abiah 4, Abia 1; {25x}. See: BDB—4a, 5b.

30. אֲבִיהוּא {12x} **’Ăbîyhûw’,** *ab-ee-hoo’;* from 1 and 1931; *father* (i.e. *worshiper*) of *Him* (i.e. *God*); *Abihu,* a son of Aaron:—Abihu {12x}. See: BDB—4b.

31. אֲבִיהוּד {1x} **’Ăbîyhûwd,** *ab-ee-hood’;* from 1 and 1935; *father* (i.e. *possessor*) *of renown; Abihud,* the name of two Isr.:—Abihud {1x}. See: BDB—4b.

32. אֲבִיהַיִל {6x} **’Ăbîyhayil,** *ab-ee-hah’-yil;* or (more correctly)

אֲבִיחַיִל **’Ăbîychayil,** *ab-ee-khah’-yil;* from 1 and 2428; *father* (i.e. *possessor*) *of might; Abihail* or *Abichail,* the name of three Isr. and two Israelitesses:—Abihail {6x}. See: BDB—4b, 5b.

33. אֲבִי הָעֶזְרִי {3x} **’Abîy hâ-‘Ezrîy,** *ab-ee’-haw-ez-ree’;* from 44 with the art. ins.; *father of the Ezrite;* an *Abiezrite* or desc. of Abiezer:—Abiezrite {3x}. See: BDB—4c, 5b.

34. אֶבְיוֹן {35x} **’ebyôwn,** *eb-yone’;* from 14, in the sense of *want* (espec. in feeling); *destitute:*—beggar {1x}, needy {35x}, poor {24x}, poor man {1x}.
(1) This noun refers to someone who is poor in a material sense. Such a one may have lost the land of his inheritance: "But the seventh year thou shalt let it rest and lie still; that the poor of thy people may eat: and what they leave the beasts of the field shall eat" (Ex 23:11). He has come into difficult financial straits (Job 30:25) and perhaps lacks clothing (Job 31:19) or food (Ps 132:15). **(2)** Secondly *ebyown* may refer to the lack of social standing which causes a need for protection. The first biblical occurrence bears this emphasis. God guarantees protection for such a one: "Thou shalt not wrest the judgment of thy poor in his cause" (Ex 23:6). The godly man defends the needy and defenseless: "I was a father to the poor: and the cause which I knew not I searched out" (Job 29:16; cf. Pro 31:9; Rom 3:14–15). Divine provisions are encased in the Mosaic stipulations such as the seventh year reversion of ancestral hereditary lands (Ex 23:11), cancellation of loans (Deut 15:4), and special extension of loans (Deut 15:7, 9, 11).
(3) Thirdly, this noun sometimes describes one's spiritual condition before God: "Thus saith the LORD; For three transgressions of Israel, and for four, I will not turn away the punishment thereof; because they sold the righteous for silver, and the poor for a pair of shoes" (Amos 2:6). In this verse *ebyown* is in synonymous parallelism to "righteous," which means that it de-

scribes a moral quality. Syn.: 1800, 6041. See: TWOT—3a; BDB—2d, 5b.

35. אֲבִיוֹנָה {1x} **’abîyôwnâh,** *ab-ee-yo-naw’;* from 14; provocative of *desire;* the *caper* berry (from its *stimulative* taste):—desire {1x}. See: TWOT—3b; BDB—2d.

36. אֲבִיטוּב {1x} **’Ăbîytûwb,** *ab-ee-toob’;* from 1 and 2898; *father of goodness* (i.e. *good*); *Abitub,* an Isr.:—Abitub {1x}. See: BDB—4b.

37. אֲבִיטַל {2x} **’Ăbîytal,** *ab-ee-tal’;* from 1 and 2919; *father of dew* (i.e. *fresh*); *Abital,* a wife of King David:—Abital {2x}. See: BDB—4b.

38. אֲבִיָּם {5x} **’Ăbîyâm,** *ab-ee-yawm’;* from 1 and 3220; *father of* (the) *sea* (i.e. *seaman*); *Abijam* (or Abijah), a king of Judah:—Abijam {5x}. See: BDB—4a, 5b.

39. אֲבִימָאֵל {2x} **’Ăbîymâ’êl,** *ab-ee-maw-ale’;* from 1 and an elsewhere unused (prob. for.) word; *father of Mael* (appar. some Arab tribe); *Abimael,* a son of Joktan:—Abimael {2x}. See: BDB—4b.

40. אֲבִימֶלֶךְ {67x} **’Ăbîymelek,** *ab-ee-mel’-ek;* from 1 and 4428; *father of* (the) *king; Abimelek,* the name of two Philistine kings and of two Isr.:—Abimelech {67x}. See: BDB—4b.

41. אֲבִינָדָב {12x} **’Ăbîynâdâb,** *ab-ee-naw-dawb’;* from 1 and 5068; *father of generosity* (i.e. *liberal*); *Abinadab,* the name of four Isr.:—Abinadab {12x}. See: BDB—4c.

42. אֲבִינֹעַם {4x} **’Ăbîynô‘am,** *ab-ee-no’-am;* from 1 and 5278; *father of pleasantness* (i.e. *gracious*); *Abinoam,* an Isr.:—Abinoam {4x}. See: BDB—4c.

אֲבִינֵר **’Ăbîynêr.** See 74.

43. אֶבְיָסָף {3x} **’Ebyâçâph,** *eb-yaw-sawf’;* contr. from 23; *Ebjasaph,* an Isr.:—Ebiasaph {3x}. See: BDB—4a, 5b.

44. אֲבִיעֶזֶר {7x} **’Ăbîy‘ezer,** *ab-ee-ay’-zer;* from 1 and 5829; *father of help* (i.e. *helpful*); *Abiezer,* the name of two Isr.:—Abiezer {7x}. See: BDB—4c, 33b.

45. אֲבִי־עַלְבוֹן {1x} **’Ăbîy-‘albôwn,** *ab-ee al-bone’;* from 1 and an unused root of uncert. der.; prob. *father of strength* (i.e. *valiant*); *Abialbon,* an Isr.:—Abialbon {1x}. See: BDB—3d, 748a.

46. אָבִיר {6x} **’âbîyr,** *aw-beer’;* from 82; *mighty* (spoken only of God):—mighty (One) {6x}. See: TWOT—13c; BDB—7d.

47. אַבִּיר {17x} **’abbîyr,** *ab-beer’;* from 46:—bulls {4x}, strong (ones) {4x}, mighty

{3x}, stouthearted {2x}, valiant {2x}, angels {1x}, chiefest {1x}. See: TWOT—13d; BDB—7d.

48. אֲבִירָם {11x} ʾĂbîyrâm, ab-ee-rawm'; from 1 and 7311; father of height (i.e. lofty); Abiram, the name of two Isr.:—Abiram {11x}. See: BDB—4d.

49. אֲבִישָׁג {5x} ʾĂbîyshag, ab-ee-shag'; from 1 and 7686; father of error (i.e. blundering); Abishag, a concubine of David:—Abishag {5x}. See: BDB—4d.

50. אֲבִישׁוּעַ {5x} ʾĂbîyshûwaʿ, ab-ee-shoo'-ah; from 1 and 7771; father of plenty (i.e. prosperous); Abishua, the name of two Isr.:—Abishua {5x}. See: BDB—4d.

51. אֲבִישׁוּר {2x} ʾĂbîyshûwr, ab-ee-shoor'; from 1 and 7791; father of (the) wall (i.e. perh. mason); Abishur, an Isr.:—Abishur {2x}. See: BDB—4d.

52. אֲבִישַׁי {25x} ʾĂbîyshay, ab-ee-shah'ee; or (short.)

אַבְשַׁי ʾAbshay, ab-shah'ee; from 1 and 7862; father of a gift (i.e. prob. generous); Abishai, an Isr.:—Abishai {25x}. See: BDB—5a, 8a.

53. אֲבִישָׁלוֹם {111x} ʾĂbîyshâlôwm, ab-ee-shaw-lome'; or (short.)

אַבְשָׁלוֹם ʾAbshâlôwm, ab-shaw-lome'; from 1 and 7965; father of peace (i.e. friendly); Absalom, a son of David; also (the fuller form) a later Isr.:—Abishalom {2x} Absalom {109x}. See: BDB—5a, 8a.

54. אֶבְיָתָר {30x} ʾEbyâthâr, eb-yaw-thawr'; contr. from 1 and 3498; father of abundance (i.e. liberal); Ebjathar, an Isr.:—Abiathar {30x}. See: BDB—5a.

55. אָבַךְ {1x} ʾâbak, aw-bak'; a prim. root; prob. to coil upward:—mount up {1x}. See: TWOT—5; BDB—5b.

56. אָבַל {39x} ʾâbal, aw-bal'; a prim. root; to bewail:—lament {3x}, mourn {36x}.

(1) Abal is used in the simple, active verbal form primarily in poetry, and usually in a figurative sense. When it is used of mourning for the dead in a literal sense, the word is found in prose sections and in the reflexive form, indicating action back on the subject. To mourn, lament for the dead (1) in a literal sense over the dead (Gen 37:34). (2) When used in the figurative sense, abal expresses "mourning" by gates (Is 3:26), by the land (Is 24:4), and by pastures (Amos 1:2). (3) In addition to mourning for the dead, "mourning" may be over Jerusalem (Is 66:10), over sin (Ezra 10:6), or over God's judgment (Ex 33:4). (4) One may pretend to be a mourner (2 Sa 14:2) simply by putting

on mourning clothes. Syn: 5594 is more dramatic stressing wailing and tearing out the hair. See: TWOT—6; BDB—5b.

57. אָבֵל {8x} ʾâbêl, aw-bale'; from 56; lamenting:—mourn {8x}. This word is usually mourning (1) for the dead or (2) because of calamity. See: TWOT—6b; BDB—5c.

58. אָבֵל {1x} ʾâbêl, aw-bale'; from an unused root (mean. to be grassy); a meadow:—plain {1x}. See: TWOT—7a; BDB—5d.

59. אָבֵל {4x} ʾÂbêl, aw-bale'; from 58; a meadow; Abel, the name of two places in Pal.:—Abel {4x}. BDB—5d.

60. אֵבֶל {24x} ʾêbel, ay'-bel; from 56; lamentation:—mourning. This may refer to the rites associated with mourning. See: TWOT—6a; BDB—5c.

61. אֲבָל {11x} ʾăbâl, ab-awl'; appar. from 56 through the idea of negation; nay (i.e. truly or yet):—but {4x}, verily {3x}, indeed {2x}, nevertheless {2x}. See: TWOT—8; BDB—6a.

62. אָבֵל בֵּית־מַעֲכָה {2x} ʾÂbêl Bêyth-Măʿakâh, aw-bale' bayth ma-a-kaw'; from 58 and 1004 and 4601; meadow of Beth-Maakah; Abel of Beth-maakah, a place in Pal.:—Abel-beth-maachah {2x}. See: BDB—6a.

63. אָבֵל הַשִּׁטִּים {1x} ʾÂbêl hash-Shiṭṭîym, aw-bale' hash-shit-teem'; from 58 and the plur. of 7848, with the art. ins.; meadow of the acacias; Abel hash-Shittim, a place in Pal.:—Abel-shittim {1x}. See: BDB—6a, 1008d.

64. אָבֵל כְּרָמִים {1x} ʾÂbêl Kərâmîym, aw-bale' dker-aw-meem'; from 58 and the plur. of 3754; meadow of vineyards; Abel-Keramim, a place in Pal.:—plain of the vineyards {1x}. See: BDB—6a.

65. אָבֵל מְחוֹלָה {3x} ʾÂbêl Məchôwlâh, aw-bale' mekh-o-law'; from 58 and 4246; meadow of dancing; Abel-Mecholah, a place in Pal.:—Abel-meholah {3x}. See: BDB—6a, 562d, 563a.

66. אָבֵל מַיִם {1x} ʾÂbêl Mayim, aw-bale' mah'-yim; from 58 and 4325; meadow of water; Abel-Majim, a place in Pal.:—Abelmaim {1x}. See: BDB—6a.

67. אָבֵל מִצְרַיִם {1x} ʾÂbêl Mitsrayim, aw-bale' mits-rah'-yim; from 58 and 4714; meadow of Egypt; Abel-Mitsrajim, a place in Pal.:—Abel-mizraim {1x}. See: BDB—5c, 6a.

68. אֶבֶן {272x} ʾeben, eh'-ben; from the root of 1129 through the mean. to build; a stone:—+ carbuncle + 688 –{1x}, + mason + 7023 – {1x}, + plummet {1x}, [chalk-, hail- 5, head- {1x},

sling- {1x}] stone (-s {247x} – ny {2x}), (divers +68 – {3x}) weight (-s {7x}).

(1) Primarily, a construction material, **(2)** covers for wells (Gen 29:3ff.), **(3)** storage containers (Ex 7:19), **(4)** weights (Deut 25:13; Prov 11:1), **(5)** slingstones (1 Sa 17:49), **(6)** plumblines were suspended stones (Is 34:11), **(7)** pavement (2 Kin 16:17), **(8)** hailstones (Josh 10:11; Eze 13:11ff.), **(9)** tombs (Is 14:19), **(10)** bodies heaped with "stones" (Josh 7:26; 8:29; 2 Sa 18:17). **(11)** Worship of the carved "stone" figurines strictly forbidden to Israel (Lev 26:1). **(12)** Altars and memorials made of unhewn "stones" (Gen 28:18ff.; 31:45; Josh 4:5; 24:26–27). **(13)** Precious "stones" - onyx (Gen 2:12) and sapphire (Eze 1:26) **(14)** God is called the "stone of Israel" (Gen 49:24). **(15)** Viewed as messianic (Gen 28:18; Ps 118:22; Is 8:14; 28:16; Dan 2:34; Zec 4:7). Syn.: *Eben* is used almost exclusively for movable stone(s), *sela* (5553) a large immovable rock, and *sur* (6697), a cliff. See: TWOT—9; BDB—6b, 918d, 1078b.

69. אֶבֶן {8x} **ʾeben** (Aram.), *eh'-ben;* corresp. to 68:—stone(s) {8x}. See: TWOT—2556; BDB—1078b.

70. אֹבֶן {2x} **ʾôben**, *o'-ben;* from the same as 68; a *pair of stones* (only dual); a potter's *wheel* or a midwife's *stool* (consisting alike of two horizontal disks with a support between):—stools {1x}, wheels {1x}. See: TWOT—9a; BDB—7a.

71. אֲבָנָה {1x} **ʾĂbânâh**, *ab-aw-naw';* perh. fem. of 68; *stony; Abanah,* a river near Damascus:—Abana {1x}. See: BDB—7b. comp. 549.

72. אֶבֶן הָעֵזֶר {3x} **ʾEben hâ-ʿêzer**, *eh'-ben haw-e'-zer;* from 68 and 5828 with the art. ins.; *stone of the help; Eben-ha-Ezer,* a place in Pal.:—Ebenezer {3x}. See: BDB—7a.

73. אַבְנֵט {9x} **ʾabnêt**, *ab-nate';* of uncert. der.; a *belt:*—girdle(s) {9x}. These are the sashes of the high priest or other priests. See: TWOT—256a; BDB—7b, 126a.

74. אַבְנֵר {63x} **ʾAbnêr**, *ab-nare';* or (fully)

אֲבִינֵר **ʾĂbîynêr**, *ab-ee-nare';* from 1 and 5216; *father of light* (i.e. *enlightening*); *Abner,* an Isr.:—Abner {63x}. BDB—4c, 7b.

75. אָבַס {2x} **ʾâbaç**, *aw-bas';* a prim. root; to *fodder:*—fatted {1x}, stalled {1x}. See: TWOT—10; BDB—7b.

76. אֲבַעְבֻּעָה {2x} **ʾăbaʿbûʿâh**, *ab-ah-boo-aw';* (by redupl.) from an unused root (mean. to *belch* forth); an inflammatory *pustule* (as *eruption*):—blains {2x}. See: TWOT—217a; BDB—7b, 101b.

77. אָבֵץ {1x} **ʾEbets**, *eh'-bets;* from an unused root prob. mean. to *gleam; conspicuous; Ebets,* a place in Pal.:—Abez {1x}. See: BDB—7b.

78. אִבְצָן {2x} **ʾIbtsân**, *ib-tsawn';* from the same as 76; *splendid; Ibtsan,* an Isr.:—Ibzan {2x}. See: BDB—7b.

79. אָבַק {2x} **ʾâbaq**, *aw-bak';* a prim. root, prob. to *float* away (as vapor), but used only as denom. from 80; to *bedust,* i.e. *grapple:*—wrestled {2x}. See: TWOT—12; BDB—7c.

80. אָבָק {6x} **ʾâbâq**, *aw-bawk';* from root of 79; light *particles* (as *volatile*):—dust {5x}, powder {1x}. See: TWOT—11a; BDB—7b.

81. אֲבָקָה {1x} **ʾăbâqâh**, *ab-aw-kaw';* fem. of 80:—powders {1x}. See: TWOT—11b; BDB—7c.

82. אָבַר {1x} **ʾâbar**, *aw-bar';* a prim. root; to *soar:*—fly {1x}. See: TWOT—13b; BDB—7c.

83. אֵבֶר {3x} **ʾêber**, *ay-ber';* from 82; a *pinion:*—wings {2x}, winged {1x}. See: TWOT—13a; BDB—7c.

84. אֶבְרָה {4x} **ʾebrâh**, *eb-raw';* fem. of 83:—feathers {2x}, wings {2x}. See: TWOT—13a; BDB—7c.

85. אַבְרָהָם {175x} **ʾAbrâhâm**, *ab-raw-hawm';* contr. from 1 and an unused root (prob. mean. to *be populous*); *father of a multitude; Abraham,* the later name of Abram:—Abraham {175x}. See: BDB—4d, 7d.

86. אַבְרֵךְ {1x} **ʾabrêk**, *ab-rake';* prob. an Eg. word mean. *kneel:*—bow the knee {1x}. See: TWOT—14; BDB—7d.

87. אַבְרָם {61x} **ʾAbrâm**, *ab-rawm';* contr. from 48; *high father; Abram,* the original name of Abraham:—Abram {61x}. See: BDB—4d, 8a.

אֲבְשַׁי **ʾAbshay**. See 52.

אֲבְשָׁלוֹם **ʾAbshâlôwm**. See 53.

88. אֹבֹת {4x} **ʾÔbôth**, *o-both';* plur. of 178; *water- skins; Oboth,* a place in the Desert:—Oboth {4x}. See: BDB—15c.

89. אָגֵא {1x} **ʾÂgê**, *aw-gay';* of uncert. der. [comp. 90]; *Agë,* an Isr.:—Agee {1x}. See: BDB—8a.

90. אֲגַג {8x} **ʾĂgag**, *ag-ag';* or

אֲגָג **ʾĂgâg**, *Ag-awg';* of uncert. der. [comp. 89]; *flame; Agag,* a title of Amalekitish kings:—Agag {8x}. See: BDB—8a.

91. אֲגָגִי {5x} **ʾĂgâgîy**, *ag-aw-ghee';* patrial or patron. from 90; an *Agagite* or de-

scendent (subject) of Agag:—Agagite {5x}. See: BDB—8a.

92. אֲגֻדָּה {4x} **ʾăguddâh**, *ag-ood-daw';* fem. pass. part. of an unused root (mean. to *bind*); a *band, bundle, knot,* or *arch:*—troop {2x}, bunch {1x}, burdens {1x}. See: TWOT—15a; BDB—8a.

93. אֱגוֹז {1x} **ʾĕgôwz**, *eg-oze';* prob of Pers. or.; a *nut:*—nut {1x}. TWOT—16; BDB—8b.

94. אָגוּר {1x} **ʾÂgûwr**, *aw-goor';* pass. part. of 103; *gathered* (i.e. *received* among the sages); *Agur,* a fanciful name for Solomon:—Agur {1x}. See: BDB—8d.

95. אֲגוֹרָה {1x} **ʾăgôwrâh**, *ag-o-raw';* from the same as 94; prop. something *gathered,* i.e. perh. a *grain* or *berry;* used only of a small (silver) *coin:*—piece [of] silver {1x}. Payment. See: TWOT—23a; BDB—8d.

96. אֵגֶל {1x} **ʾegel**, *eh'-ghel;* from an unused root (mean. to *flow* down or together as drops); a *reservoir:*—drops {1x}. See: TWOT—17a; BDB—8b.

97. אֶגְלַיִם {1x} **ʾEglayim**, *eg-lah'-yim;* dual of 96; a *double pond; Eglajim,* a place in Moab:—Eglaim {1x}. See: BDB—8b.

98. אֲגַם {9x} **ʾăgam**, *ag-am';* from an unused root (mean. to *collect* as water); a *marsh;* hence, a *rush* (as growing in swamps); hence, a *stockade* of reeds:—pools {6x}, standing {2x}, reeds {1x}. See: TWOT—18a; BDB—8b.

99. אָגֵם {1x} **ʾâgêm**, *aw-game';* prob. from the same as 98 (in the sense of *stagnant* water); fig. *sad:*—pools {1x}. See: TWOT—18b; BDB—8c.

100. אַגְמוֹן {5x} **ʾagmôwn**, *ag-mone';* from the same as 98; a marshy *pool* [others from a different root, a *kettle*]; by impl. a *rush* (as growing there); collect. a rope of rushes:—rush {2x}, bulrush {1x}, caldron {1x}, hook {1x}. See: TWOT—19; BDB—8c.

101. אַגָּן {3x} **ʾaggân**, *ag-gawn';* prob. from 5059; a *bowl* (as *pounded* out hollow):—basins {1x}, cups {1x}, goblet {1x}. See: TWOT—20a; BDB—8c.

102. אַגָּף {7x} **ʾaggâph**, *ag-gawf';* prob. from 5062 (through the idea of *impending*); a *cover* or *heap;* i.e. (only plur.) *wings* of an army, or *crowds* of troops:—bands {7x}. See: TWOT—21a; BDB—8c, 1086d.

103. אָגַר {3} **ʾâgar**, *aw-gar';* a prim. root; to *harvest:*—gather {3x}. See: TWOT—22; BDB—8d.

104. אִגְּרָא {3x} **ʾiggᵉrâ** (Aram.), *ig-er-aw';* of Pers. or.; an *epistle* (as carried by

a state courier or postman):—letter {3x}. See: TWOT—2557; BDB—1078b.

105. אַגַרְטָל {2x} **ʾăgarṭâl**, *ag-ar-tawl';* of uncert. der.; a *basin:*—charger {1x}. See: TWOT—380a; BDB—8d, 173d.

106. אֶגְרֹף {2x} **ʾegrôph**, *eg-rofe';* from 1640 (in the sense of *grasping*); the *clenched* hand:—fist {2x}. See: TWOT—385a; BDB—8d, 175d.

107. אִגֶּרֶת {10x} **ʾiggereth**, *ig-eh'-reth;* fem. of 104; an *epistle:*—letter(s) {10x}. See: TWOT—23b; BDB—8d, 1078b.

108. אֵד {2x} **ʾêd**, *ade;* from the same as 181 (in the sense of *enveloping*); a *fog:*—mist {1x}, vapor {1x}. See: TWOT—38d; BDB—9a, 15d.

109. אָדַב {1x} **ʾâdab**, *aw-dab';* a prim. root; to *languish:*—grieve {1x}. See: TWOT—24; BDB—9a.

110. אַדְבְּאֵל {2x} **ʾAdbᵉʾêl**, *ad-beh-ale';* prob. from 109 (in the sense of *chastisement*) and 410; *disciplined of God; Adbeël,* a son of Ishmael:—Adbeel {2x}. See: BDB—9a.

111. אֲדַד {1x} **ʾĂdad**, *ad-ad';* prob. an orth. var. for 2301; *Adad* (or *Hadad*), an Edomite:—Hadad {1x}. See: BDB—9a, 212d.

112. אִדּוֹ {2x} **ʾIddôw**, *id-do';* of uncert. der.; *Iddo,* an Isr.:—Iddo {2x}. See: BDB—9a.

אֱדוֹם **ʾÉdôwm**. See 123.

אֱדוֹמִי **ʾÉdôwmîy**. See 30.

113. אָדוֹן {1x} **ʾâdôwn**, *aw-done';* or (short.)

אָדֹן {335x} **ʾâdôn**, *aw-done';* from an unused root (mean. to *rule*); *sovereign,* i.e. *controller* (human or divine):—Lord {31x}, lord {197x}, master(s) {105x}, owner {1x}, sir {1x};. comp. also names beginning with "Adoni-".

Adon (113), or *adonay* (136), "lord; master; Lord." The form *adon* appears 335 times, while the form *adonay* (used exclusively as a divine name) appears 439 times. **(1)** Basically, *adon* means "lord" or "master." It is distinguished from the Hebrew word *ba'al,* which signifies "possessor" or "owner." *Adon* basically describes the one who occupies the position of a "master" or "lord" over a slave or servant: "And the servant put his hand under the thigh of Abraham his master" (Gen 24:9). It is used of kings and their most powerful aides. Joseph told his brothers: "So now it was not you that sent me hither, but God: and he hath made me a father [i.e., an adviser] to Pharaoh, and lord of all his house, and a ruler throughout all the land of Egypt" (Gen 45:8; cf. 42:30). Only once is this word used in the sense of "owner" or "possessor" (1 Kin 16:24). **(2)** *Adon* is often used as a term of polite address. In some cases, the one

so named really occupies a position of authority. In Gen 18:12 (the first occurrence) Sarah called Abraham her "lord." On the other hand, this may be a purely honorary title by which the speaker intends to indicate his submission to the one so addressed. Jacob instructed his slaves to speak to "my lord Esau" (Gen 32:18); i.e., Jacob called his brother Esau "lord." In places where the speaker is addressing someone calling him "lord," the word virtually means "you."

(3) When applied to God, *adon* is used in several senses. **(3a)** It signifies His position as the one who has authority (like a master) over His people to reward the obedient and punish the disobedient: "Ephraim provoked him to anger most bitterly: therefore shall he leave his blood upon him, and his reproach shall his Lord return unto him" (Hos 12:14). In such contexts God is conceived as a Being who is sovereign ruler and almighty master. **(3b)** The word is often a title of respect, a term of direct address usually assuming a specific concrete lord-vassal or master-servant relationship (Ps 8:1). **(3c)** In some cases the word appears to be a title suggesting God's relationship to and position over Israel: "Three times in the year all thy males shall appear before the Lord God" (Ex 23:17). In such contexts *adon* is a formal divine name and should probably be transliterated if the proper emphasis is to be retained. Syn: *YHWH* (3068) sets forth His essential and unswerving principles of mercy and judgment, and presents Him as Father, a Friend, and a Moral Governor. *Yah* (3050), the shortened form of YHWH, is usually used when Yah is stressed as the One accomplishing a deed in contrast to no other. See: TWOT—27b; BDB—10d.

114. אַדּוֹן {1x} ʾ**Addôwn**, *ad-done';* prob. intens. for 113; *powerful; Addon,* appar. an Isr.:—Addon {1x}. See: BDB—11d.

115. אֲדוֹרַיִם {1x} ʾ**Ădôwrayim**, *ad-o-rah'-yim;* dual from 142 (in the sense of *eminence*); *double mound; Adorajim,* a place in Pal.:—Adoraim {1x}. See: BDB—12a.

116. אֱדַיִן {57x} ʾ**ĕdayin** (Aram.), *ed-ah'-yin;* of uncert. der.; *then* (of time):—then {55x}, now {1x}, time {1x}. See: TWOT—2558; BDB—1078c.

117. אַדִּיר {27x} ʾ**addîyr**, *ad-deer';* from 142; *wide* or (Gen) *large;* fig. *powerful:*—excellent {4x}, famous {2x}, gallant {1x}, glorious {1x}, goodly {1x}, lordly {1x}, mighty (-ier, one {5x}), noble {1x}, nobles {7x}, principal {3x}, worthy {1x};

(1) As a noun, ʾ*addîyr* is **(1a)** paralleled to "mighty" in Judg 5:13: "Then he made him that remaineth have dominion over the nobles among

the people: the LORD made me have dominion over the mighty." The word also occurs in Jer 14:3 and Jer 30:21. **(1b)** In 2 Chr 23:20 ʾ*addyr* is paralleled to "captains and governors." **(1c)** The word is applied to the Messiah; the Messiah is none other than God Himself: "But there the glorious LORD will be unto us a place of broad rivers" (Is 33:21). Syn.: ʾ*Addîyr* stresses the might of the person; whereas *chor* (2715) stresses rank. See: TWOT—28b; BDB—12b.

118. אֲדַלְיָא {1x} ʾ**Ădalyâ**, *ad-al-yaw';* of Pers. der.; *Adalja,* a son of Haman:—Adalia {1x}. See: BDB—9a.

119. אָדַם {10x} ʾ**âdam**, *aw-dam';* of unknown derivation; to *show blood* (in the face), i.e. *flush* or turn rosy:—dyed red {5x}, red {4x}, ruddy {1x}. See: TWOT—26b; BDB—10a.

120. אָדָם {552x} ʾ**âdâm**, *aw-dawm';* from 119; *ruddy,* i.e. a *human being* (an individual or the species, *mankind,* etc.):—Adam {13x}, + hypocrite {1x}, + common sort {1x}, X low, man {408x}, men {121x}, person(s) {8x}.

Adam means "man; mankind; people; someone (indefinite); *Adam* (the first man); or a city in the Jordan Valley (Josh 3:16)." **(1)** This noun is related to the verb *adom,* "to be red," and therefore probably relates to the original ruddiness of human skin. **(2)** The noun connotes "man" as the creature created in God's image, the crown of all creation. In its first appearance *adam* is used for mankind, or generic man: "And God said, Let us make man in our image, after our likeness" (Gen 1:26). In Gen 2:7 the word refers to the first "man," *Adam:* "And the LORD God formed man of the dust of the ground, and breathed into his nostrils the breath of life; and man became a living soul."

(3) Throughout Gen 2:5—5:5 there is a constant shifting and interrelationship between the generic and the individual uses. **(3a)** "Man" is distinguished from the rest of the creation insofar as he was created by a special and immediate act of God: he alone was created in the image of God (Gen 1:27). **(3b)** He consisted of two elements, the material and the nonmaterial (Gen 2:7). **(3c)** From the outset he occupied an exalted position over the rest of the earthly creation and was promised an even higher position (eternal life) if he obeyed God: "And God blessed them, and God said unto them, Be fruitful, and multiply, and replenish the earth, and subdue it: and have dominion over the fish of the sea, and over the fowl of the air, and over every living thing that moveth upon the earth" (Gen 1:28; cf. 2:16–17). **(3d)** In Gen 1 "man" is depicted as the goal and crown of creation, while in Gen 2 the world is shown to have been created as the scene of human activity. **(3e)** "Man" was in God's image with

reference to his soul and/or spirit. (He is essentially spiritual; he has an invisible and immortal aspect which is simple or indivisible.) Other elements of this image are his mind and will, intellectual and moral integrity (he was created with true knowledge, righteousness, and holiness), his body (this was seen as a fit organ to share immortality with man's soul and the means by which dominion over the creation was exercised), and dominion over the rest of the creation.

(4) The Fall greatly affected the nature of "man," but he did not cease to be in God's image (Gen 9:6). **(4a)** Fallen "man" occupies a new and lower position before God: "And God saw that the wickedness of man was great in the earth, and that every imagination of the thoughts of his heart was only evil continually" (Gen 6:5; cf. 8:21). **(4b)** No longer does "man" have perfect communion with the Creator; he is now under the curse of sin and death. **(4c)** Original knowledge, righteousness, and holiness are destroyed. **(4d)** Restoration to his proper place in the creation and relationship to the Creator comes only through spiritual union with the Christ, the second *Adam* (Rom 5:12–21). **(5)** In some later passages of Scripture *adam* is difficult to distinguish from *ish* (376)—man as the counterpart of woman and/or as distinguished in his maleness.

(6) Sometimes *adam* identifies a limited and particular "group of men": "Behold, waters rise up out of the north, and shall be an overflowing flood, and shall overflow the land [of the Philistines], and all that is therein; the city, and them that dwell therein: then the men [used in the singular] shall cry, and all the inhabitants of the land shall howl" (Jer 47:2). **(7)** When used of a particular group of individual "men," the noun appears in the phrase "sons of men": "And the LORD came down to see the city and the tower, which the children of men builded" (Gen 11:5). **(8)** The phrase "son of man" usually connotes a particular individual: "God is not a man [*ish*], that he should lie; neither the son of man, that he should repent" (Num 23:19; cf. Eze 2:1). The one notable exception is the use of this term in Dan 7:13–14: "I saw in the night visions, and, behold, one like the Son of man [*enosh* (582)] came with the clouds of heaven. . . . His dominion is an everlasting dominion, which shall not pass away." Here the phrase represents a divine being.

(9) *Adam* is also used in reference to any given man, or to anyone male or female: "When a man [anyone] shall have in the skin of his flesh a rising, a scab, or bright spot, and it be in the skin of his flesh like the plague of leprosy; then he shall be brought unto Aaron" (Lev 13:2). Syn.: Man is represented by four apparently in-

consistent aspects: As *ʾâdâm*, he is of the earth, earthy; as *ish* (376 – {967x}), he is endued with immaterial and personal existence; as *bachur* (970) he is the fully developed, vigorous, unmarried man in his prime; as *enosh* (582 – {32x}), he is weak or incurable; and as *geber* (1397 – {54x}), he is mighty and noble. Syn.: *ʾÂdâm* connotes man as the creature created in God's image, the crown of all creation. *Ish* (376) is used for man as the counterpart of woman and/or as distinguished in his maleness. *Geber* (1397) denotes a male as an antonym of a woman, many times suggesting strength, strong man. *Enosh* (582) sets forth a collective idea of man suggesting the frailty, vulnerability, and finitude of man as contrasted to God. See also: 376, 582, 1167, 1397, 1400, 4962. See: TWOT—25a; BDB—9a.

121. אָדָם {9x} *ʾÂdâm, aw-dawm'*; the same as 120; *Adam* the name of the first man, also of a place in Pal.:—*Adam* {9x}. See: BDB—9c.

122. אָדֹם {9x} *ʾâdôm, aw-dome'*; from 119; *rosy:*—red {8x}, ruddy {1x}. See: TWOT—26b; BDB—10b.

123. אֱדֹם {100x} *ʾÉdôm, ed-ome'*; or (fully)

אֱדוֹם *ʾÉdôwm, ed-ome'*; from 122; *red* [see Gen 25:25]; *Edom,* the elder twin-brother of Jacob; hence, the region (Idumæa) occupied by him:—Edom {87x}, Edomites {9x}, Idumea {4x}. See: BDB—10b.

124. אֹדֶם {3x} *ʾôdem, o'-dem*; from 119; *redness,* i.e. the *ruby, garnet,* or some other red gem:—sardius {3x}. See: TWOT—26c; BDB—10b.

125. אֲדַמְדָּם {6x} *ʾădamdâm, ad-am-dawm'*; redupl. from 119; *reddish:*—(somewhat) reddish {6x}. See: TWOT—26g; BDB—10c.

126. אַדְמָה {5x} *ʾAdmâh, ad-maw'*; contr. for 127; *earthy; Admah,* a place near the Dead Sea:—*Admah* {5x}. See: BDB—10a.

127. אֲדָמָה {225x} *ʾădâmâh, ad-aw-maw'*; from 119; *soil* (from its Gen *redness*) [the productive agent]:—country {1x}, earth {53x}, ground {43x}, husband [-man {2x}] (-ry {1x}), land(s) {125x}.

Initially this noun represents **(1)** arable "ground" (probably red in color) supporting water and plants (Gen 2:6); **(2)** source of Adam's body (Gen 2:7); **(3)** the actual soil itself (2 Kin 5:17); **(4)** ground (Ex 3:5); **(5)** property or possession (Zec 2:12); **(6)** a relationship exists between *adam,* "man," and the *ʾădâmâh.* If Adam were to remain obedient to God, the "ground" would give forth its fruit (Gen 2:6). Sin disrupted the harmony between man and the "ground,"

and the "ground" no longer responded to man's care. Increased human rebellion caused decreased fruitfulness of the "ground" (Gen 4:12, 14; cf. 8:21). In Abraham the promised redemption (Gen 3:15) took the form of the restoration of a proper relation between God and man and between man and the "ground" (Gen 28:14–15). Under Moses the fruitfulness of the "ground" depended on the obedience of God's people (cf. Deut 11:17). Syn.: ʾĂdâmâh, from its Gen redness is the productive agent; *erets* (776 – {1505x}) a territory or even the whole earth; *sadeh* (7704 – {7x}) a field, plot of land, or estate. See: TWOT—25b; BDB—9c.

128. אֲדָמָה {1x} ʾĂdâmâh, *ad-aw-maw'*; the same as 127; *Adamah*, a place in Pal.:—*Adamah* {1x}. See: BDB—10a.

129. אַדְמִי {1x} ʾĂdâmîy, *ad-aw-mee'*; from 127; *earthy*; *Adami*, a place in Pal.:—*Adami* {1x}. See: BDB—10a.

130. אֲדֹמִי {12x} ʾĔdômîy, *ed-o-mee'*; or (fully)

אֱדוֹמִי ʾĔdôwmîy, *ed-o-mee'*; patron. from 123; an *Edomite*, or desc. from (or inhab. of) Edom:—Edomite(s) {11x}, Syria {1x}. Syn.: See 726. See: BDB—10c.

131. אֲדֻמִּים {2x} ʾĂdummîym, *ad-oom-meem'*; plur. of 121; *red spots*; *Adummim*, a pass in Pal.:—Adummim {2x}. See: BDB—10c, 751c.

132. אַדְמֹנִי {3x} ʾadmônîy, *ad-mo-nee'*; or (fully)

אַדְמוֹנִי ʾadmôwnîy, *ad-mo-nee'*; from 119; *reddish* (of the hair or the complexion):—red {1x}, ruddy {2x}. See: TWOT—26h; BDB—10c.

133. אַדְמָתָא {1x} ʾAdmâthâ, *ad-maw-thaw'*; prob. of Pers. der.; *Admatha*, a Pers. nobleman:—*Admatha* {1x}. See: BDB—10c.

134. אֶדֶן {57x} ʾeden, *eh'-den*; from the same as 113 (in the sense of *strength*); a *basis* (of a building, a column, etc.):—socket(s) {56x}, foundations {1x}. See: TWOT—27a; BDB—10d.

אָדֹן ʾâdôn. See 113.

135. אַדָּן {1x} ʾAddân, *ad-dawn'*; intens. from the same as 134; *firm*; *Addan*, an Isr.:—*Addan* {1x}. See: BDB—11d.

136. אֲדֹנָי {434x} ʾĂdônây, *ad-o-noy'*; an emphat. form of 113; the *Lord* (used as a proper name of God only):—(my) Lord {431x}, lord {2x}, God {1x}. Syn.: See 113. See: TWOT—27b; BDB—10d.

In the form *adonay* the word means "Lord" par excellence or "Lord over all," even as it sometimes does in the form *adon* (cf. Deut 10:17, where God is called the "God of gods, and Lord of lords"; Josh 3:11, where He is called the "Lord

of all the earth"). The word *adonay* appears in Gen 15:2: "And Abram said, Lord God, what wilt thou give me, seeing I go childless, ..." This word frequently appears in Psalms (Ps 68:17; 86:3) and Isaiah (Isa. 29:13; 40:10).

137. אֲדֹנִי־בֶזֶק {3x} ʾĂdônîy-Bezeq, *ad-o"-nee-beh'-zek*; from 113 and 966; *lord of Bezek*; *Adoni-Bezek*; a Canaanitish king:—Adoni-bezek {1x}. See: BDB—11d.

138. אֲדֹנִיָּה {26x} ʾĂdônîyâh, *ad-o-nee-yaw'*; or (prol.)

אֲדֹנִיָּהוּ ʾĂdônîyâhûw, *ad-o-nee-yaw'-hoo*; from 113 and 3050; *lord* (i.e. worshipper) of Jah; *Adonijah*, the name of three Isr.:—Adonijah {26x}. See: BDB—11d.

139. אֲדֹנִי־צֶדֶק {2x} ʾĂdônîy-Tsedeq, *ad-o"-nee-tseh'-dek*; from 113 and 6664; *lord of justice*; *Adoni-Tsedek*, a Canaanitish king:—Adonizedec {2x}. See: BDB—11d.

140. אֲדֹנִיקָם {3x} ʾĂdônîyqâm, *ad-o-nee-kawm'*; from 113 and 6965; *lord of rising* (i.e. *high*); *Adonikam*, the name of one or two Isr.:—Adonikam {3x}. See: BDB—12a.

141. אֲדֹנִירָם {2x} ʾĂdônîyrâm, *ad-o-nee-rawm'*; from 113 and 7311; *lord of height*; *Adoniram*, an Isr.:—Adoniram {2x}. See: BDB—12a.

142. אָדַר {3x} ʾâdar, *aw-dar'*; a prim. root; to *expand*, i.e. *be great* or (fig.) *magnificent*:—glorious {2x}, honourable {1x}.

This verb occurs only twice and in a poetical usage. The word appears in Is 42:21: "The LORD is well pleased for his righteousness' sake; he will magnify the law, and make it honorable [ʾadar]." The word also appears in Ex 15:6; 11. See: TWOT—28; BDB—12a.

143. אֲדָר {8x} ʾĂdâr, *ad-awr'*; prob. of for. der.; perh. mean. *fire*; *Adar*, the 12th Heb. month:—Adar {8x}. See: BDB—12c, 1078d.

144. אֲדָר {1x} ʾĂdâr (Aram.), *ad-awr'*; corresp. to 143:—Adar {1x}. See: BDB—1078d.

145. אֶדֶר {2x} ʾeder, *eh'-der*; from 142; *amplitude*, i.e. (concr.) a *mantle*; also (fig.) *splendor*:—goodly {1x}, robe {1x}. ʾEder may refer to a "luxurious outer garment" (Mic 2:8). See: TWOT—28a; BDB—12a.

146. אַדָּר {1x} ʾAddâr, *ad-dawr'*; intens. from 142; *ample*; *Addar*, a place in Pal.; also an Isr.:—Adar {1x}, Addar {1x}. See: BDB—12a.

147. אִדַּר {1x} ʾiddar (Aram.), *id-dar'*; intens. from a root corresp. to 142; *ample*, i.e. a threshing-*floor*:—threshing-floors {1x}. See: TWOT—2560; BDB—1078d.

Hebrew

148. אֲדַרְגָּזַר {2x} ʾădargâzêr (Aram.), ad-ar″-gaw-zare′; from the same as 147 and 1505; a *chief diviner*, or *astrologer*:—judge(s) {2x}. See: TWOT—2561; BDB—1078d.

149. אֲדְרַזְדָּא {1x} ʾadrazdâ (Aram.), ad-raz-daw′; prob. of Pers. or.; *quickly* or *carefully*:—diligently {1x}. Correctly, exactly. See: TWOT—2562; BDB—1079a.

150. אֲדַרְכֹּן {2x} ʾădarkôn, ad-ar-kone′; of Pers. or.; a *daric* or Pers. coin:—drams {2x}. See: TWOT—28; BDB—12c, 204b.

151. אֲדֹרָם {2x} ʾĂdôrâm, ad-o-rawm′; contr. for 141; *Adoram* (or Adoniram), an Isr.:—Adoram {2x}. See: BDB—12a, c.

152. אַדְרַמֶּלֶךְ {3x} ʾAdrammelek, ad-ram-meh′-lek; from 142 and 4428; *splendor of* (the) *king*; *Adrammelek,* the name of an Ass. idol, also of a son of Sennacherib:—Adrammelech {3x}. See: BDB—12c.

153. אֶדְרָע {1} ʾedraʿ (Aram.), ed-raw′; an orth. var. for 1872; an *arm,* i.e. (fig.) *power:*—force {1x}. See: TWOT—2682b; BDB—1079a, 1089a.

154. אֶדְרֶעִי {8x} ʾedreʿîy, ed-reh′-ee; from the equiv. of 153; *mighty; Edrei,* the name of two places in Pal.:—Edrei {8x}. See: BDB—12c, 204c.

155. אַדֶּרֶת {12x} ʾaddereth, ad-deh′-reth; fem. of 117; something *ample* (as a *large* vine, a *wide* dress); also the same as 145:—mantle {5x}, garment {4x}, glory {1x}, goodly {1x}, robe {1x}.

ʾAddereth may mean "luxurious outer garment, mantle, cloak." This word appears in Gen 25:25 to mean "mantle." See: TWOT—28c; BDB—12b.

156. אָדַשׁ {1x} ʾâdash, aw-dash′; a prim. root; to *tread* out (grain):—thresh {1x}. See: TWOT—419; BDB—12c, 190c.

157. אָהַב {208x} ʾâhab, aw-hab′; or

אָהֵב ʾâhêb, aw-habe′; a prim. root; to *have affection* for (sexually or otherwise):—(be-) love {169x}, (-d) {5x}, -ly {1x}, -r(s) {19x}, -ing {1x}, like {1x}, friend(s) {12x}.

Ahab or *aheb* means "to love; like." Basically this verb is equivalent to the English "to love" in the sense of having a strong emotional attachment to and desire either to possess or to be in the presence of the object. **(1)** First, the word refers to the love a man has for a woman and a woman for a man. Such love is rooted in sexual desire, although as a rule it is desire within the bounds of lawful relationships: "And Isaac brought her into his mother Sarah's tent, and took Rebekah, and she became his wife; and he loved her" (Gen 24:67). **(2)** This word may

refer to an erotic but legal love outside marriage. Such an emotion may be a desire to marry and care for the object of that love, as in the case of Shechem's love for Dinah (Gen 34:3). **(3)** In a very few instances *ahab* (or *aheb*) may signify no more than pure lust—an inordinate desire to have sexual relations with its object (cf. 2 Sa 13:1). **(4)** Marriage may be consummated without the presence of love for one's marriage partner (Gen 29:30). **(5)** *Ahab* (or *aheb*) seldom refers to making love [usually this is represented *yada* (3045), "to know," or by *shakab* (7901), "to lie with"]. **(6)** The word does seem to have this added meaning, however, in 1 Kin 11:1: "But King Solomon loved many strange women, together with the daughter of Pharaoh" (cf. Jer 2:25). Hosea appears to use this nuance when he writes that God told him to "go yet, love a woman beloved of her friend, yet an adulteress" (3:1). **(7)** This is the predominant meaning of the verb when it appears in the causative stem (as a participle). **(8)** In every instance except one (Zec 13:6) *ahab* (or *aheb*) signifies those with whom one has made or intends to make love: "Go up to Lebanon, and cry; and lift up thy voice in Bashan, and cry from the passages: for all thy lovers are destroyed" (Jer 22:20; cf. Eze 16:33).

(9) *Ahab* (or *aheb*) is also used of the love between parents and their children. In its first biblical appearance, the word represents Abraham's special attachment to his son Isaac: "And he said, Take now thy son, thine only son Isaac, whom thou lovest . . ." (Gen 22:2). **(10)** *Ahab* (or *aheb*) may refer to the family love experienced by a daughter-in-law toward her mother-in-law (Ruth 4:15). This kind of love is also represented by the word *racham* (7356). **(11)** *Ahab* (or *aheb*) sometimes depicts a special strong attachment a servant may have toward a master under whose dominance he wishes to remain: "And if the servant shall plainly say, I love my master, my wife, and my children; I will not go out free . . ." (Ex 21:5). **(12)** Perhaps there is an overtone here of family love; he "loves" his master as a son "loves" his father (cf. Deut 15:16). This emphasis may be in 1 Sa 16:21, where we read that Saul "loved [David] greatly." Israel came "to love" and deeply admire David so that they watched his every move with admiration (1 Sa 18:16).

(13) A special use of this word relates to an especially close attachment of friends: "The soul of Jonathan was knit with the soul of David, and Jonathan loved him as his own soul" (1 Sa 18:1). In Lev 19:18: "Thou shalt love thy neighbor as thyself" (cf. Lev 19:34; Deut 10:19) *ahab* (or *aheb*) signifies this brotherly or friendly kind of love. **(14)** The word suggests, furthermore, that one seek to relate to his brother and

all men according to what is specified in the law structure God gave to Israel. This was to be the normal state of affairs between men. **(15)** This verb is used politically to describe the loyalty of a vassal or a subordinate to his lord—so Hiram of Tyre "loved" David in the sense that he was completely loyal (1 Kin 5:1). **(16)** The strong emotional attachment and desire suggested by *ahab* (or *aheb*) may also be fixed on objects, circumstances, actions, and relationships. Syn.: 1730; 7453. See: TWOT—29; BDB—12c.

158. אָהֵב {2x} ʾahab, ah′-hab; from 157; *affection* (in a good or a bad sense):—lovers {1x}, loving {1x}. See: TWOT—29a; BDB—13b.

159. אֹהַב {1x} ʾôhab, o′-hab; from 156; mean. the same as 158:—love {1x}. See: TWOT—29b; BDB—13b.

160. אֲהָבָה {40x} ʾahăbâh, ă-hab-aw; fem. of 158 and mean. the same:—love {40x}.
Ahabah means "love." This word represents several kinds of "love." **(1)** The first biblical occurrence of *ahabah* is in Gen 29:20; there the word deals with the "love" between man and wife as a general concept. **(2)** In Hos 3:1 the word is used of "love" as a sexual activity. **(3)** *Ahabah* means "love" between friends in 1 Sa 18:3: "Then Jonathan and David made a covenant because he loved him as his own soul." **(4)** The word refers to Solomon's "love" in 1 Kin 11:2 and **(5)** to God's "love" in Deut 7:8. Syn.: See 158. See: TWOT—29c; BDB—13b.

161. אֹהַד {2x} ʾÔhad, o′-had; from an unused root mean. to *be united; unity; Ohad,* an Isr.:—*Ohad* {2x}. See: BDB—13c.

162. אֲהָהּ {15x} ʾăhâhh, ă-haw′; appar. a prim. word expressing *pain* exclamatorily; *Oh!:*—Ah {8x}, Alas {6x}, O {1x}. See: TWOT—30; BDB—13c.

163. אֲהָוָא {3x} ʾAhăvâʾ, ă-hav-aw′; prob. of for. or.; *Ahava,* a river of Bab.:—*Ahava* {3x}. BDB—13c.

164. אֵהוּד {9x} ʾÊhûwd, ay-hood′; from the same as 161; *united; Ehud,* the name of two or three Isr.:—*Ehud* {9x}. See: BDB—13c.

165. אֵהִי {3x} ʾěhîy, e-hee′; appar. an orth. var. for 346; *where:*—will {3x}. [*which is often the rendering of the same Heb. form from 1961*]. See: TWOT—31; BDB—13c.

166. אָהַל {1x} ʾahal, aw-hal′; a prim. root; to *be clear:*—shineth {1x}. See: TWOT—33; BDB—14c.

167. אָהַל {3x} ʾâhal, aw-hal′; a denom. from 168; to *tent:*—pitch tent {2x} remove a tent {1x}. See: TWOT—32; BDB—14b.

168. אֹהֶל {345x} ʾôhel, o′-hel; from 166; a *tent* (as *clearly* conspicuous from a distance):—covering {1x}, (dwelling {2x}) (place [s] {2x}), home {1x}, tabernacle {198x}, tent(s) {141x}.
Ohel (168) means "tent; home; dwelling; habitation." **(1)** First, this word refers to the mobile structure called a "tent." This is its meaning in Gen 4:20: "And Adah bare Jabal: he was the father of such as dwell in tents, and of such as have cattle." These are what nomadic Bedouins normally live in. **(2)** "Tents" can also be used as housing for animals: "They smote also the tents of cattle and carried away sheep and camels in abundance" (2 Chr 14:15). **(3)** Soldiers lived in "tents" during military campaigns (1 Sa 17:54). **(4)** A "tent" was pitched on top of a house so everyone could see that Absalom went in to his father's concubines (2 Sa 16:22). This constituted an open rejection of David's dominion and a declaration that he (Absalom) was claiming the throne. **(5)** The word is a synonym for "home, dwelling," and "habitation." This emphasis is especially evident in Judg 19:9: "Behold, the day groweth to an end, lodge here, that thine heart may be merry; and tomorrow get you early on your way, that thou mayest go home." This meaning appears in the phrase "to your tents": "We have no part in David, neither have we inheritance in the son of Jesse: every man to his tents, O Israel" (2 Sa 20:1). The "tabernacle" ("tent") of David, therefore, is his dwelling place or palace (Is 16:5). **(6)** Similarly, the "tabernacle" ("tent") of the daughter of Zion is Israel's capital, or what Israel inhabits—Jerusalem (Lam 2:4).
(7) *Ohel* may represent those who dwell in the dwellings of a given area or who form a unit of people. Thus the "tents" of Judah are her inhabitants: "The LORD also shall save the tents of Judah first, that the glory of the house of David and the glory of the inhabitants of Jerusalem do not magnify themselves against Judah" (Zec 12:7; cf. Ps 83:6). **(8)** Bedouin "tents" today (as in the past) are constructed of strong black cloth of woven goat's hair. They are shaped variously. The women pitch them by stretching the cloth over poles and tying it down with cords of goat's hair or hemp. Wooden mallets are used to drive the tent pegs into the ground (Judg 4:21). Sometimes the structure is divided in order to separate families or to separate animals from people (2 Chr 14:15). The back of the "tent" is closed and the front open. The door is made by turning back the fold where the two ends of the cloth meet (Gen 18:1). The "tent" and all its contents are transported on the back of a single pack animal. Richer people cover the floor with mats of various materials. A chief or sheikh may have several "tents"—one for himself and his guest(s), another for his wives and other fe-

males in his immediate family, and still another for the animals (Gen 31:33).

(9) Before the construction of the tabernacle Moses pitched a "tent" outside the camp (Ex 33:7). There he met with God. The "tent" outside the camp persisted as a living institution for only a short period after the construction of the tabernacle and before the departure from Sinai (Num 11:16ff.; 12:4ff.). Eventually the ark of the covenant was moved into the tabernacle (Ex 40:21) where the LORD met with Moses and spoke to Israel (Ex 29:42). This structure is called the tent of meeting inasmuch as it contained the ark of the covenant and the tables of testimony (Num 9:15). As the tent of meeting it was the place where God met with His people through Moses (or the high priest) and revealed His will to them (1 Sa 2:22). Syn.: *Mishkan* (4908) stresses the dwelling place/residence; whereas *ʾôhel* stresses a specific dwelling place, a tent. See: TWOT—32a; BDB—13d.

169. אֹהֶל {1x} ʾÔhel, *o'-hel;* the same as 168; *Ohel,* an Isr.:—Ohel {1x}. See: BDB—13b.

170. אָהֳלָה {5x} ʾOhŏlâh, *ŏ-hol-aw';* in form a fem. of 168, but in fact for

אָהֳלָה ʾOhŏlâhh, *ŏ-hol-aw';* from 168; *her tent* (i.e. idolatrous *sanctuary); Oholah,* a symbol. name for Samaria:—Aholah {5x}. See: TWOT—32b; BDB—14b.

171. אָהֳלִיאָב {5x} ʾOhŏlîyʾâb, *ŏ''-hol-e-awb';* from 168 and 1; *tent of* (his) *father; Oholiab,* an Isr.:—Aholiab {5x}. See: BDB—14b, c.

172. אָהֳלִיבָה {6x} ʾOhŏlîybâh, *ŏ''-hol-ee-baw';* (similarly with 170) for

אָהֳלִיבָה ʾOhŏlîybâhh, *ŏ''-hol-e-baw';* from 168; *my tent* (is) *in her; Oholibah,* a symb. name for Judah:—Aholibah {6x}. See: BDB—14c.

173. אָהֳלִיבָמָה {8x} ʾOhŏlîybâmâh, *ŏ''-hol-ee-baw-maw';* from 168 and 1116; *tent of* (the) *height; Oholibamah,* a wife of Esau:—Aholibamah {8x}. See: BDB—14c.

174. אֲהָלִים {4x} ʾăhâlîym, *ă-haw-leem';* or (fem.)

אֲהָלוֹת ʾăhâlôwth, *ă-haw-loth'* (only used thus in the plur.); of for. or.; *aloe* wood (i.e. sticks):—aloes {3x}, trees of lign aloes {1x}. See: TWOT—34; BDB—14d.

175. אַהֲרוֹן {347x} ʾAhărôwn, *ă-har-one';* of uncert. der.; *Aharon,* the brother of Moses:—Aaron {345x}, Aaronites {2x}. See: BDB—14d.

176. אֹו {21x} ʾôw, *o;* presumed to be the "constr." or genitival form of

אַו ʾav, *av;* short. for 185; *desire* (and so prob. in Prov 31:4); hence, (by way of alternative) *or,* also *if:*—also, and, either, if, at the least, ✕ nor, or, otherwise, then, whether {21x}. See: TWOT—36; BDB—14d, 16b.

177. אוּאֵל {1x} ʾÛwʾêl, *oo-ale';* from 176 and 410; *wish of God; Uel,* an Isr.:—Uel {1x}. See: BDB—15a.

178. אֹוב {17x} ʾôwb, *obe;* from the same as 1 (appar. through the idea of *prattling* a father's name); prop. a *mumble,* i.e. a water-skin (from its hollow sound); hence, a *necromancer* (ventriloquist, as from a jar):—bottle(s) {1x}, familiar spirit(s) {16x}.

Owb means "spirit (of the dead); necromancer; pit." **(1)** The word usually represents the troubled spirit (or spirits) of the dead. This meaning appears unquestionably in Is 29:4: "Thy voice shall be, as of one that hath a familiar spirit, out of the ground, and thy speech shall whisper out of the dust." **(2)** Its second meaning, "necromancer," refers to a professional who claims to summon forth such spirits when requested (or hired) to do so: "Regard not them that have familiar spirits, neither seek after wizards" (Lev 19:31—first occurrence). These mediums summoned their "guides" from a hole in the ground. Saul asked the medium (witch) of Endor (1 Sa 28:8). **(3)** God forbade Israel to seek information by this means, which was so common among the pagans (Lev 19:31; Deut 18:11). Perhaps the pagan belief in manipulating one's basic relationship to a god (or gods) explains the relative silence of the Old Testament regarding life after death. Yet God's people believed in life after death, from early times (e.g., Gen 37:35; Is 14:15ff.)

(4) Necromancy was so contrary to God's commands that its practitioners were under the death penalty (Deut 13). **(5)** Necromancers' unusual experiences do not prove that they truly had power to summon the dead. For example, the medium of Endor could not snatch Samuel out of God's hands against His wishes. But in this particular incident, it seems that God rebuked Saul's apostasy, either through a revived Samuel or through a vision of Samuel. Mediums do not have power to summon the spirits of the dead, since this is reprehensible to God and contrary to His will. Syn.: 7307. TWOT—37a; BDB—15a.

179. אוֹבִיל {1x} ʾÔwbîyl, *o-beel';* prob. from 56; *mournful; Obil,* an Ishmael-ite:—Obil {1x}. See: BDB—6a.

180. אוֹבָל {3x} 'ûwbâl, oo-bawl'; or (short.)
אֲבָל 'ûbâl, oo-bawl'; from 2986 (in the
sense of 2988); a *stream*:—river {3x}.
See: TWOT—835g; BDB—6b, 385c.

181. אוּד {3x} 'ûwd, ood; from an unused root
mean. to *rake* together; a *poker* (for
turning or *gathering* embers):—firebrand(s) {2x},
brand {1x}. See: TWOT—38a; BDB—15c.

182. אוֹדוֹת {11x} 'ôwdôwth, o-dōth'; or (short.)
אֹדוֹת 'ôdôwth, o-dōth'(only thus in the
plur.); from the same as 181; *turn-
ings* (i.e. *occasions*); (adv.) on *account* of:—because
{5x}, cause(s) {2x}, concerning {2x}, [concerning]
thee {1x}, sake {1x}. See: TWOT—38b; BDB—15c.

183. אָוָה {26x} 'âvâh, aw-vaw'; a prim. root;
to *wish* for:—desire {17x}, lust {4x},
longed {3x}, covet {2x}. See: TWOT—40; BDB—
16a.

184. אָוָה {1x} 'âvâh, aw-vaw'; a prim. root; to
extend or *mark* out:—point out {1x}.
See: TWOT—41; BDB—16c, 1060d, 1063b.

185. אַוָּה {7x} 'avvâh, av-vaw'; from 183; *longing*:—desire {3x}, lust after {3x}, pleasure {1x}. See: TWOT—40b; BDB—16b.

186. אוּזַי {1x} 'Ûwzay, oo-zah'-ee; perh. by perm.
for 5813, *strong*; *Uzai*, an Isr.:—Uzai
{1x}. See: BDB—17a.

187. אוּזָל {2x} 'Ûwzâl, oo-zâwl'; of uncert. der.;
Uzal, a son of Joktan:—Uzal {2x}.
See: BDB—23d.

188. אוֹי {24x} 'ôwy, ō'-ee; prob. from 183 (in
the sense of *crying* out after); *lamentation*; also interj. *Oh!*:—woe {23x}, alas {1x}.
See: TWOT—42; BDB—17a.

189. אֱוִי {2x} 'Ĕvîy, ev-ee'; prob. from 183; *desirous*; *Evi*, a Midianitish chief:—Evi
{2x}. See: BDB—16c.

אוֹיֵב 'ôwyêb. See 341.

190. אוֹיָה {1x} 'ôwyâh, o-yaw'; fem. of 188:—
woe {1x}. See: BDB—17a.

191. אֱוִיל {1x} 'ĕvîyl, ev-eel'; from an unused root
(mean. to *be perverse*); (fig.) *silly*:—
fool(s) {20x}, (-ish) (man {6x}).
Primarily 'ĕvîyl describes one who (1) lacks
wisdom (Prov 24:7); (2) is morally undesirable
despising wisdom and discipline (Prov 1:7;
15:5); (3) mocks guilt (Prov 14:9), (4) is quarrelsome (Prov 20:3); (5) licentious (Prov 7:22); and
(6) refuses instruction (Prov 16:22). Syn.: The
fool's (a) only authority is himself (5034 - {94x}-
Ps 14:1; 53:1); (b) twists God's ways into his own
(191 - {18x}); (c) is insensitive to godly prodding
(3688 - 46x); and (d) lives by his own resources,

deserving pity (5528 - 8x). See: TWOT—44a; 17b;
BDB—17b.

192. אֱוִיל מְרֹדַךְ {2x} 'Ĕvîyl M'rôdak, ev-eel'
mer-o-dak'; of Aram. der. and
prob. mean. *soldier of Merodak*; *Evil-Merodak*,
a Bab. king:—Evil-merodach {2x}. See: BDB—
17b.

193. אוּל {2x} 'ûwl, ool; from an unused root
mean. to *twist*, i.e. (by impl.) *be strong*;
the *body* (as being *rolled* together); also *powerful*:—mighty {1x}, strength {1x}. See: TWOT—
45a; BDB—17c.

194. אוּלַי {11x} 'ûwlay, oo-lah'ee; or (short.)
אֻלַי 'ûlay, oo-lah'ee; from 176; *if not*; hence,
perhaps:—if (so be), may (be), peradventure, unless = {11x}.
Ulay (194) means "peradventure; perhaps;
suppose; if; less." (1) This word meaning "peradventure or perhaps" usually expresses a hope:
"Behold now, the LORD hath restrained me from
bearing: I pray thee, go in unto my maid; it may
be that I may obtain children by her" (Gen 16:2—
the first occurrence). (2) Elsewhere *ulay* expresses
fear or doubt: "Peradventure the woman will
not be willing to follow me unto this land; must
I needs bring thy son again unto the land from
whence thou camest?" (Gen 24:5). (3) If followed by another clause the word almost functions to introduce a protasis: "Peradventure there
be fifty righteous within the city: wilt thou also
destroy . . ." (Gen 18:24). (4) In Num 22:33 the
word has a different force: "And the ass saw me,
and turned from me these three times: unless
she had turned from me, surely now also I had
slain thee, and saved her alive." See: TWOT—
46; BDB—19c.

195. אוּלַי {2x} 'Ûwlay, oo-lah'ee; of Pers. der.;
the *Ulai* (or Eulæus), a river of Pers.:—
Ulai {2x}. See: BDB—19c, 47a.

196. אֱוִלִי {1x} 'ĕvîlîy, ev-ee-lee'; from 191; *silly*,
foolish; hence, (mor.) *impious*:—fool-
ish {1x}. See: TWOT—44b; BDB—17c.

197. אוּלָם {34x} 'ûwlâm, oo-lawm'; or (short.)
אֻלָם 'ûlâm, oo-lawm'; from 481 (in the
sense of *tying*); a *vestibule* (as *bound*
to the building):—porch(es) {34x}. See: TWOT—
45c; BDB—17c, 19d.

198. אוּלָם {4x} 'Ûwlâm, oo-lawm'; appar. from
481 (in the sense of *dumbness*); *solitary*; *Ulam*, the name of two Isr.:—Ulam {4x}.
BDB—17d, 19d.

199. אוּלָם {19x} 'ûwlâm, oo-lawm'; appar. a
var. of 194; *however* or *on the contrary*:—but {8x}, but truly {3x}, surely {2x}, very
deed {2x}, howbeit {1x}, wherefore {1x}, truly {1x},

not translated {1x}. See: TWOT—47; BDB—19d, 48a.

200. אִוֶּלֶת {25x} ʾ**ivveleth**, *iv-veh'-leth;* from the same as 191; *silliness:*—folly {13x}, foolishness {10x}, foolish {1x}, foolishly {1x}.

(1) This noun can mean "foolishness" in the sense of violating God's law, or "sin" (Ps 38:5). **(2)** The word also describes the activities and life-style of the man who ignores the instructions of wisdom (Prov 5:23). **(3)** In another nuance, the noun means "thoughtless." Hence *ivveleth* describes the way a young person is prone to act (Pro 22:15) and the way any fool or stupid person chatters (Prov 15:2). Syn.: 5039. See: TWOT—44c; BDB—17c.

201. אוֹמָר {3x} ʾ**Ôwmâr**, *o-mawr';* from 559; *talkative; Omar,* a grandson of Esau:—Omar {3x}. See: BDB—57b.

202. אוֹן {12x} ʾ**ôwn**, *ōne;* prob. from the same as 205 (in the sense of *effort,* but successful); *ability, power,* (fig.) *wealth:*—strength {7x}, might {2x}, force {1x}, goods {1x}, substance {1x}.

This noun generally means **(1)** vigour, generative power; **(2)** wealth; **(3)** physical strength (of men and behemoth). See: TWOT—49a; BDB—20b.

203. אוֹן {1x} ʾ**Ôwn**, *ōne;* the same as 202; *On,* an Isr.:—On {1x}. See: BDB—20b.

204. אוֹן {3x} ʾ**Ôwn**, *ōne;* or (short.);

אֹן ʾ**Ôn**, *ōne;* of Eg. der.; *On,* a city of Egypt:—On {3x}. See: BDB—20a, c, 58a.

205. אָוֶן {78x} ʾ**âven**, *aw-ven';* from an unused root perh. mean. prop. to *pant* (hence, to *exert* oneself, usually in vain; to *come to naught*); strictly *nothingness;* also *trouble, vanity, wickedness;* spec. an *idol:*—affliction {3x}, evil {1x}, false {1x}, idol {1x}, iniquity {47x}, mischief {3x}, mourners {1x} (-ing {1x}), naught {1x}, sorrow {1x}, unjust {1x}, unrighteous {2x}, vain {1x}, vanity {6x}, wicked (-ness {8x}). comp. 369.

Aven (205) means "iniquity; misfortune." **(1)** This noun is derived from a root meaning "to be strong." The first occurrence is in Num 23:21: "He hath not beheld iniquity in Jacob, neither hath he seen perverseness in Israel: the LORD his God is with him, and the shout of a king is among them." **(2)** The meaning of "misfortune" comes to expression in the devices of the wicked against the righteous. The psalmist expected "misfortune" to come upon him: "And if he come to see me, he speaketh vanity: his heart gathereth iniquity to itself; when he goeth abroad, he telleth it" (Ps 41:6). **(3)** *Aven* in this sense is synonymous with *ed* (343), "disaster" (Job 18:12). **(4)** In a real sense *aven* is part of human exis-

tence, and as such the word is identical with '*amal* (5999), "toil," as in Ps 90:10: "The days of our years are threescore years and ten; and if by reason of strength they be fourscore years, yet is their strength labor and sorrow; for it is soon cut off, and we fly away." **(5)** *Aven* in a deeper sense characterizes the way of life of those who are without God: "For the vile person will speak villany, and his heart will work iniquity, to practice hypocrisy, and to utter error against the LORD, to make empty the soul of the hungry, and he will cause the drink of the thirsty to fail" (Is 32:6).

(6) The being of man is corrupted by "iniquity." **(7)** Though all of mankind is subject to *aven* ("toil"), there are those who delight in causing difficulties and "misfortunes" for others by scheming, lying, and acting deceptively. The psalmist puts internalized wickedness this way: "Behold, he travaileth with iniquity, and hath conceived mischief, and brought forth falsehood" (Ps 7:14; cf. Job 15:35). **(8)** Those who are involved in the ways of darkness are the "workers of iniquity," the doers of evil or the creators of "misfortune" and disaster. **(9)** Synonyms for *aven* with this sense are *ra,* "evil," and *rasha,* "wicked," opposed to "righteousness" and "justice." They seek the downfall of the just (Ps 141:9). Between Ps 5:5 and 141:9 there are as many as 16 references to the workers of evil (cf. "The foolish shall not stand in thy sight: thou hatest all workers of iniquity"—Ps 5:5). In the context of Ps 5, the evil spoken of is falsehood, bloodshed, and deceit (v. 6).

(10) The qualitative aspect of the word comes to the best expression in the verbs with *aven.* The wicked work, speak, beget, think, devise, gather, reap, and plow *aven,* and it is revealed ("comes forth") by the misfortune that comes upon the righteous. **(11)** Ultimately when Israel's religious festivals (Is 1:13) and legislation (Is 10:1) were affected by their apostate way of life, they had reduced themselves to the Gentile practices and way of life. **(12)** The prophetic hope lay in the period after the purification of Israel, when the messianic king would introduce a period of justice and righteousness (Is 32) and the evil men would be shown up for their folly and ungodliness. Syn.: 2398, 5771, 7451, 7561. See: TWOT—48a; BDB—19d, 58a.

206. אָוֶן {3x} ʾ**Âven**, *aw'-ven;* the same as 205; *idolatry; Aven,* the contemptuous synonym of three places, one in Cæle-Syria, one in Egypt (On), and one in Pal. (Bethel):—Aven {3x}. See also 204, 1007. See: BDB—19d, 122b.

207. אוֹנוֹ {5x} ʾ**Ôwnôw**, *o-no';* or (short.)

אֹנוֹ ʾ**Ônôw**, *o-no';* prol. from 202; *strong; Ono,* a place in Pal.:—Ono {1x}. See: BDB—20c.

208. אוֹנָם {4x} ᵓÔwnâm, *o-nawm';* a var. of 209; *strong; Onam,* the name of an Edomite and of an Isr.:—Onam {4x}. See: BDB—20c.

209. אוֹנָן {8x} ᵓÔwnân, *o-nawn';* a var. of 207; *strong; Onan,* a son of Judah:—Onan {8x}. See: BDB—20c.

210. אוּפָז {2x} ᵓÛwphâz, *oo-fawz';* perh. a corruption of 211; *Uphaz,* a famous gold region:—Uphaz {2x}. See: BDB—20c.

211. אוֹפִיר {13x} ᵓÔwphîyr, *o-feer';* or (short.)

אֹפִיר ᵓÔphîyr, *o-feer';* and

אוֹפִר ᵓÔwphîr, *o-feer';* of uncert. der.; *Ophir,* the name of a son of Joktan, and of a gold region in the East:—Ophir {13x}. See: TWOT—50; BDB—20c.

212. אוֹפָן {36x} ᵓôwphân, *o-fawn';* or (short.)

אֹפָן ᵓôphân, *o-fawn';* from an unused root mean. to *revolve;* a *wheel:*—wheel(s) {35x}, fitly {1x}. See: TWOT—146a; BDB—66d.

אוֹפִר ᵓÔwphîr. See 211.

213. אוּץ {10x} ᵓûwts, *oots;* a prim. root; to *press;* (by impl.) to *be close, hurry, withdraw:*—haste {8x}, labour {1x}, narrow {1x}. See: TWOT—51; BDB—21a.

214. אוֹצָר {79x} ᵓôwtsâr, *o-tsawr';* from 686; a *depository:*—treasure(s) {61x}, treasury {10x}, storehouse(s) {3x}, cellars {2x}, armoury {1x}, garners {1x}, store {1x}. See: TWOT—154a; BDB—69d.

215. אוֹר {43x} ᵓôwr, *ore;* a prim. root; to *be* (caus. *make*) *luminous* (lit. and metaph.):—light {19x}, shine {14x}, enlighten {5x}, break of day {1x}, fire {1x}, give {1x}, glorious {1x}, kindle {1x}.

Owr (215) means (1) "to become light" in Gen 44:3: "As soon as the morning was light, the men were sent away, they and their asses," (2) become lighted up (of daybreak), (3) to give light in Num 8:2: "the seven lamps shall give light over against the candlestick," or (4) cause light to shine. See: TWOT—52; BDB—21a.

216. אוֹר {120x} ᵓôwr, *ore;* from 215; *illumination* or (concr.) *luminary* (in every sense, incl. *lightning, happiness,* etc.):—bright {1x}, clear {1x}, + day {2x}, light(s) {114x} (-ning), morning {1x}, sun {1x}.

Owr (216), the noun, means "light." (1) The first occurrence of *owr* is in the Creation account: "And God said, Let there be light: and there was light" (Gen 1:3). Here "light" is the opposite of "darkness." (2) The opposition of "light" and "darkness" is not a unique phenomenon. (2a) It occurs frequently as a literary device: "Woe unto them that call evil good, and good evil; that put darkness for light, and light for darkness;

that put bitter for sweet, and sweet for bitter!" (Is 5:20); and "In that day they shall roar against them like the roaring of the sea: and if one look unto the land, behold darkness and sorrow, and the light is darkened in the heavens thereof" (Is 5:30). (3) In Hebrew various antonyms of *owr* are used in parallel constructions: "The people that walked in darkness have seen a great light: they that dwell in the land of the shadow of death, upon them hath the light shined" (Is 9:2).

(4) The basic meaning of *owr* is "daylight" (Gen 1:3). (5) The "light" given by the heavenly bodies was also known as *or:* "Moreover the light of the moon shall be as the light of the sun, and the light of the sun shall be sevenfold, as the light of seven days, in the day that the LORD bindeth up the breach of his people, and healeth the stroke of their wound" (Is 30:26). (6) In the metaphorical use *owr* signifies life over against death: "For thou hast delivered my soul from death: wilt thou not deliver my feet from falling, that I may walk before God in the light of the living?" (Ps 56:13). (7) To walk in the "light" of the face of a superior (Prov 16:15), or of God (Ps 89:15), is an expression of a joyful, blessed life in which the quality of life is enhanced. (8) The believer is assured of God's "light," even in a period of difficulty; cf. "Rejoice not against me, O mine enemy: when I fall, I shall arise; when I sit in darkness, the LORD shall be a light unto me" (Mic 7:8; cf. Ps 23:4). Syn.: 3974; 7043. See: TWOT—52a; BDB—21c, 70b.

217. אוּר {6x} ᵓûwr, *oor;* from 215; *flame,* hence, (in the plur.) the *East* (as being the region of light):—fire(s) {5x}, light {1x}. Syn.: See also 224. See: TWOT—52d; BDB—22a.

218. אוּר {5x} ᵓÛwr, *oor;* the same as 217; *Ur,* a place in Chaldæa; also an Isr.:—Ur {5x}. See: BDB—22b, d.

219. אוֹרָה {4x} ᵓôwrâh, *o-raw';* fem. of 216; *luminousness,* i.e. (fig.) *prosperity;* also a plant (as being *bright*):—herbs {2x}, light {2x}. See: TWOT—52b; BDB—21d, 77a.

220. אֲוֵרָה {1x} ᵓăvêrâh, *av-ay-raw';* by transp. for 723; a *stall:*—cotes {1x}. See: TWOT—158b; BDB—22d, 71d.

221. אוּרִי {8x} ᵓÛwrîy, *oo-ree';* from 217; *fiery; Uri,* the name of three Isr.:—Uri {8x}. See: BDB—22b.

222. אוּרִיאֵל {4x} ᵓÛwrîyᵓêl, *oo-ree-ale';* from 217 and 410; *flame of God; Uriel,* the name of two Isr.:—Uriel {4x}. See: BDB—22b.

223. אוּרִיָּה {39x} ʾÛwrîyâh, *oo-ree-yaw'*; or (prol.)

אוּרִיָהוּ ʾÛwrîyâhûw, *oo-ree-yaw'-hoo;* from 217 and 3050; *flame of Jah; Urijah,* the name of one Hittite and five Isr.:—Uriah {39x}, Urijah {11x}. See: BDB—22c.

224. אוּרִים {7x} ʾÛwrîym, *oo-reem';* plur. of 217; *lights; Urim,* the oracular brilliancy of the figures in the high-priest's breastplate:—Urim {7x}. See: BDB—22a, 1070d.

אוֹרְנָה ʾOwrenâh. See 728.

225. אוּת {4x} ʾûwth, *ooth;* a prim. root; prop. to *come,* i.e. (impl.) to *assent:*—consent {1x}. See: TWOT—53; BDB—22d.

226. אוֹת {79x} ʾôwth, *ōth;* prob. from 225 (in the sense of *appearing*); a *signal* (lit. or fig.), as a *flag, beacon, monument, omen, prodigy, evidence,* etc.:—mark {1x}, miracles {2x}, ensign(s) {2x}, sign(s) {60x}, token(s) {14x}.

Owth means "sign; mark." **(1)** This word represents something by which a person or group is characteristically marked. This is its emphasis in Gen 4:15: "And the LORD set a mark upon Cain, lest any finding him should kill him." **(2)** In Ex 8:23 God promises to "put a division between my people and thy people: tomorrow shall this sign be" (cf. Ex 12:13). **(3)** Num 2:2 uses *owth* to represent a military banner, while Job 21:29 uses the word of the identifying banners of nomadic tribes. **(4)** Rahab asked her Israelite guests for a trustworthy "mark" which they stipulated to be the scarlet cord by which she lowered them out of her window and outside Jericho's walls (Josh 2:12, 18).

(5) The word means "sign" as a reminder of one's duty. This usage first appears in Gen 9:12: "This [the rainbow] is the token of the covenant which I make between me and you and every living creature" (cf. vv. 4–15). **(6)** A reminding token is represented by *owth:* "And it [the observance of the Feast of Unleavened Bread] shall be for a sign unto thee upon thine hand, and for a memorial between thine eyes, that the LORD's law may be in thy mouth" (Ex 13:9). **(7)** A "sign" eventually showing the truth of a statement is indicated by *owth:* "Certainly I will be with thee; and this shall be a token unto thee, that I have sent thee: When thou hast brought forth the people out of Egypt, ye shall serve God upon this mountain" (Ex 3:12). **(8)** In passages such as Ex 4:8 *owth* represents a miraculous "sign": "And it shall come to pass, if they will not believe thee, neither hearken to the voice of the first sign, that they will believe the voice of the latter sign." **(9)** "Signs" are attestations of the validity of a prophetic message, but they are not the highest or final test

of a prophet; he must speak in conformity to past revelation (cf. Deut 13:1–5).

(10) Several passages use *owth* of omens and/or indications of future events: "But if they say thus, Come up unto us; then we will go up: for the LORD hath delivered them into our hand: and this shall be a sign unto us" (1 Sa 14:10). **(11)** An *owth* can be a "warning sign": "The censers of these sinners against their own souls, let them make them broad plates for a covering of the altar: for they offered them before the LORD, therefore they are hallowed: and they shall be a sign unto the children of Israel" (Num 16:38). **(12)** The first occurrence of *owth* is in Gen 1:14. Here it refers to the stars, indicators of the time of day and seasons. Syn.: 4159. See: TWOT—41a; BDB—16d, 23a.

227. אָז {22x} ʾâz, *awz;* a demonstr. adv.; *at that time* or *place;* also as a conjunc., *therefore:*—beginning, even, for, from, hitherto, now, old, since, then, time, when, yet = {22x}. See: TWOT—54; BDB—23a.

228. אֲזָא {3x} ʾăzâ (Aram.), *az-zaw';* or

אֲזָה ʾăzâh (Aram.), *az-aw';* to *kindle;* (by impl.) to *heat:*—heated {2x}, hot {1x}. See: TWOT—2563; BDB—1079a.

229. אֶזְבַּי {1x} ʾEzbay, *ez-bah'ee;* prob. from 231; *hyssop-like; Ezbai,* an Isr.:—Ezbai {1x}. See: BDB—23c.

230. אַזַד {2x} ʾăzad (Aram.), *az-awd';* of uncert. der.; *firm:*—gone {2x}. See: TWOT—2564; BDB—1079a.

231. אֵזוֹב {10x} ʾêzôwb, *ay-zobe';* prob. of for. der.; *hyssop:*—hyssop {10x}. Hyssop is a plant used for religious and medicinal purposes. See: TWOT—55; BDB—23c.

232. אֵזוֹר {14x} ʾêzôwr, *ay-zore';* from 246; something *girt;* a *belt,* also a *band:*—girdle(s) {14x}. A waistcloth. See: TWOT—59a; BDB—25b.

233. אֲזַי {3x} ʾăzay, *az-ah'ee;* prob. from 227; *at that time:*—then {3x}. TWOT—54; BDB—23b.

234. אַזְכָּרָה {7x} ʾazkârâh, *az-kaw-raw';* from 2142; a *reminder;* spec. *remembrance-offering:*—memorial {7x}.

The noun *ʿazkarah* means "memorial offering" and **(1)** it occurs primarily in Leviticus. **(2)** "Memorials" were directed toward God. **(3)** A "memorial" portion of each meal offering was burnt on the altar (Lev 2:2, 9, 16), in other words a small portion in place of the whole amount. See: TWOT—551d; BDB—23c, 272b.

235. אָזַל {6x} ʾâzal, *aw-zal';* a prim. root; to *go away,* hence, to *disappear:*—gone {2x},

fail {1x}, gaddest about {1x}, to and fro {1x}, spent
{1x}. See: TWOT—56; BDB—23c, 1079b.

236. **אֲזַל** {7x} ʾăzal (Aram.), *az-al'*; the same as
235; to *depart:*—went (up) {6x}, go {1x}.
See: TWOT—2565; BDB—1079b.

237. **אֵזֶל** {1x} ʾezel, *eh'-zel;* from 235; *departure;*
Ezel, a memorial stone in Pal.:—*Ezel*
{1x}. See: BDB—23d.

238. **אָזַן** {41x} ʾâzan, *aw-zan';* a prim. root; prob.
to *expand;* but used only as a denom.
from 241; to *broaden out the ear* (with the hand),
i.e. (by impl.) to *listen:*—give ear {31x}, hearken
{6x}, hear {3x}, perceived by the ear {1x}. Syn.:
241, 6030, 7181, 8085. See: TWOT—57; BDB—
24b.

239. **אָזַן** {1x} ʾâzan, *aw-zan';* a prim. root [rather
ident. with 238 through the idea of
scales as if two ears]; to *weigh,* i.e. (fig.) *ponder:*—
gave good heed {1x}. See: TWOT—58; BDB—
24d, 1079b.

240. **אָזֵן** {1x} ʾâzên, *aw-zane';* from 238; a
spade or *paddle* (as having a *broad*
end):—weapon {1x}. See: TWOT—57b; BDB—
24c.

241. **אֹזֶן** {187x} ʾôzen, *o'-zen;* from 238; *broad-
ness,* i.e. (concr.) the *ear* (from its form
in man):—advertise +1540 –{1x}, audience {7x},
+ displeased {1x}, ear(s) {63x}, hear {1x}, hear
+ 8088 {1x}, hearing {5x}, reveal +1540 – {1x},
show +1540 –{6x}, tell + 1540 –{1x}.
   Ozen means "ear, audience; hearing." **(1)** It
mainly designates a part of the body. The first
occurrence is in Gen 20:8: "Abimelech rose early
in the morning, and called all his servants, and
told all these things in their ears: and the men
were sore afraid." **(2)** The "ear" was the place
for earrings (Gen 35:4); thus it might be pierced
as a token of perpetual servitude (Ex 21:6). **(3)**
Several verbs are found in relation to "ear": **(3a)**
(3b) "to inform" (Eze 24:26), **(3c)** "to pay attention" (Ps 10:17), **(3d)** "to listen" (Ps 78:1), **(3e)**
"to stop up" (Is 33:15), **(3f)** "to make deaf" (Is
6:10), and **(3g)** "to tingle" (1 Sa 3:11). **(4)** Animals are also said to have "ears" (Prov 26:17).
   (5) God is idiomatically said to have "ears":
"Hide not thy face from me in the day when I
am in trouble; incline thine ear unto me; . . .
when I call answer me speedily" (Ps 102:2). Elsewhere, "And Samuel heard all the words of the
people, and he rehearsed them in the ears of
the LORD" (1 Sa 8:21). **(5a)** The LORD "pierces"
(i.e., opens up) ears (Ps 40:6), **(5b)** implants ears
(Ps 94:9), and **(5c)** fashions ears (Prov 20:12) in
order to allow man to receive direction from
his Creator. **(5d)** As the Creator, He also is able
to hear and respond to the needs of His people
(Ps 94:9). **(6)** The LORD reveals His words to

the "ears" of his prophets: "Now the LORD had
told Samuel in his ear a day before Saul came,
saying . . ." (1 Sa 9:15).
   (7) Since the Israelites had not responded
to the prophetic message, they had made themselves spiritually deaf: "Hear now this, O foolish
people, and without understanding; which have
eyes, and see not; which have ears, and hear
not" (Jer 5:21). **(8)** After the Exile, the people
of God were to experience a spiritual awakening and new sensitivity to God's Word which,
in the words of Isaiah, is to be compared to the
opening of the "ears" (Is 50:5). Syn.: 238. See:
TWOT—57a; BDB—23d.

242. **אֹזֶן שֶׁאֱרָה** {1x} ʾUzzên Sheʾĕrâh, *ooz-zane'
sheh-er-aw';* from 238 and 7609;
plat of Sheerah (i.e. settled by him); *Uzzen-
Sheërah,* a place in Pal.:—Uzzen-sherah {1x}.
See: BDB—25a.

243. **אַזְנוֹת תָּבוֹר** {1x} ʾAznôwth Tâbôwr, *az-
nōth' taw-bore';* from 238
and 8396; *flats* (i.e. *tops*) *of* Tabor (i.e. situated
on it); *Aznoth-Tabor,* a place in Pal.:—Aznoth-
tabor {1x}. See: BDB—24d.

244. **אָזְנִי** {2x} ʾOznîy, *oz-nee';* from 241; *having* (quick) *ears; Ozni,* an Isr.; also an
Oznite (collect.), his desc.:—Ozni {1x}, Oznites
{1x}. See: BDB—24c.

245. **אֲזַנְיָה** {1x} ʾĂzanyâh, *az-an-yaw';* from 238
and 3050; *heard* by *Jah; Azanjah,*
an Isr.:—Azaniah {1x}. See: BDB—24c.

246. **אֲזִקִּים** {2x} ʾăziqqîym, *az-ik-keem';* a var.
for 2131; *manacles:*—chains {2x}.
See: TWOT—577b; BDB—25a, 279b.

247. **אָזַר** {16x} ʾâzar, *aw-zar';* a prim. root; to
belt:—gird (up) {14x}, bind about {1x},
compass about {1x}. See: TWOT—59; BDB—25a.

248. **אֶזְרוֹעַ** {2x} ʾezrôwaʿ, *ez-ro'-ă;* a var. for 2220;
the *arm:*—arm {2x}. See: TWOT—
583b; BDB—25b, 284b, 1089b.

249. **אֶזְרָח** {18x} ʾezrâch, *ez-rawkh';* from 2224
(in the sense of *springing up*); a spontaneous *growth,* i.e. *native* (tree or persons):—
born {8x}, country {5x}, land {1x}, homeborn {1x},
nation {1x}, bay tree {1x}.
   A baytree is native to the land of Israel. See:
TWOT—580b; BDB—25b, 280c.

250. **אֶזְרָחִי** {3x} ʾEzrâchîy, *ez-raw-khee';* patron. from 2246; an *Ezrachite* or
desc. of Zerach:—Ezrahite {3x}. See: BDB—280d.

251. **אָח** {629x} ʾâch, *awkh;* a prim. word; a
brother (used in the widest sense of
lit. relationship and metaph. affinity or resemblance [like 1]):—another {24x}, brethren {332x},
brother {269x}(-ly {1x}), kindred {1x}, like {1x},

other {1x}. Compare also the proper names beginning with "Ah-" or "Ahi-".

Ach (251) means "brother." **(1)** In its basic meaning, *ach* represents a "male sibling," a "brother." This is its meaning in the first biblical appearance: "And she again bare his brother Abel" (Gen 4:2). This word represents a full brother or a half-brother: "And he said to him, Go, I pray thee, see whether it be well with thy brethren" (Gen 37:14). **(2)** In another nuance, *ach* can represent a "blood relative." Abram's nephew is termed his "brother": "And he brought back all the goods, and also brought again his brother Lot, and his goods, and the women also, and the people" (Gen 14:16). This passage, however, might also reflect the covenantal use of the term whereby it connotes "ally" (cf. Gen 13:8). **(3)** In Gen 9:25, *ach* clearly signifies "relative": "Cursed be Canaan; a servant of servants shall he be unto his brethren." Laban called his cousin Jacob an ’*ach*: "And Laban said unto Jacob, Because thou art my brother, shouldest thou therefore serve me for nought?" (Gen 29:15). Just before this, Jacob described himself as an *ach* of Rachel's father (Gen 29:12). **(4)** Tribes may be called *achim*: "And [the tribe of] Judah said unto [the tribe of] Simeon his brother, Come up with me into my lot . . ." (Judg 1:3). **(5)** The word *ach* is used of a fellow tribesman: "With whomsoever thou findest thy gods, let him not live: before our brethren discern thou what is thine" (Gen 31:32). **(6)** Elsewhere it describes a fellow countryman: "And it came to pass in those days, when Moses was grown, that he went out unto his brethren, and looked on their burdens" (Ex 2:11). **(7)** In several passages, the word *ach* connotes "companion" or "colleague"—that is, a brother by choice. One example is found in 2 Kin 9:2: "And when thou comest thither, look out there Jehu the son of Jehoshaphat the son of Nimshi, and go in, and make him arise up from among his brethren, and carry him to an inner chamber" (cf. Is 41:6; Num 8:26). **(8)** Somewhat along this line is the covenantal use of the word as a synonym for "ally": "And Lot went out at the door unto them, and shut the door after him, and said, I pray you, brethren, do not so wickedly" (Gen 19:6–7). Notice this same use in Num 20:14 and 1 Kin 9:13. **(9)** *Ach* can be a term of polite address, as it appears to be in Gen 29:4: "And Jacob said unto them [shepherds whose identity he did not know], My brethren, whence be ye?" **(10)** The word *ach* sometimes represents someone or something that simply exists alongside a given person or thing: "And surely your blood of your lives will I require; at the hand of every beast will I require it, and at the hand of . . . every man's brother will I require the life

of man" (Gen 9:5–6). See: TWOT—62a; BDB—25b, 26a, 1079c.

252. אָח {1x} ’ach (Aram.), *akh;* corresp. to 251:—brother 1. See: TWOT—2566; BDB—1079c.

253. אָח {2x} ’âch, *awkh;* a var. for 162; *Oh!* (expressive of grief or surprise):—ah {1x}, alas {1x}. See: TWOT—60; BDB—25b.

254. אָח {3x} ’âch, *awkh;* of uncert. der.; a fire-pot or chafing-dish:—hearth {3x}. See: TWOT—66a; BDB—25b, 28d.

255. אֹחַ {1x} ’ôach, *o'-akh;* prob. from 253; a *howler* or lonesome wild animal:—doleful creatures {1x}. *Oach* may be a jackal or hyena. See: TWOT—65a; BDB—25b, 28d.

256. אַחְאָב {93x} ’Ach’âb, *akh-awb';* once (by contr.)

אֶחָב ’Echâb (Jer 29:22), *ekh-awb';* from 251 and 1; *brother* [i.e. *friend*] *of* (his) *father; Achab,* the name of a king of Israel and of a prophet at Bab.:—Ahab {93x}. See: BDB—25b, 26c.

257. אַחְבָּן {1x} ’Achbân, *akh-bawn';* from 251 and 995; *brother* (i.e. *possessor*) *of understanding; Achban,* an Isr.:—Ahban {1x}. See: BDB—25b, 26c.

258. אָחַד {1x} ’âchad, *aw-khad';* perh. a prim. root; to *unify,* i.e. (fig.) *collect* (one's thoughts):—go thee one way or other {1x}. See: TWOT—605; BDB—25c.

259. אֶחָד {951x} ’echâd, *ekh-awd';* a numeral from 258; prop. *united,* i.e. *one;* or (as an ord.) *first:*—an {7x}, another {35x}, any {18x}, a certain {9x}, eleven + 6240 –{13x}, every {10x}, first {36x}, once {13x}, one {687x}, other {30x}, some {7x}, together {1x},

Misc: a, alike, alone, altogether, anything, apiece, daily, each (one), few, + highway, a man, only, together = {86x}. Syn.: ’*Echâd* stresses unity/oneness but recognizes diversity within that oneness; whereas *pa'am* (6471 – {12x}) stresses a single occurrence such as a step. See: TWOT—61; BDB—25c, 31c, 1079c.

260. אָחוּ {3x} ’âchûw, *aw'-khoo;* of uncert. (perh. Egyp. der.); a *bulrush* or any marshy grass (particularly that along the Nile):—meadow {2x}, flag {1x}. See: TWOT—63; BDB—28a.

261. אֵחוּד {1x} ’Êchûwd, *ay-khood';* from 258; *united; Echud,* the name of three Isr.:—Ehud {1x}. See: BDB—26a.

262. אַחְוָה {1x} ’achvâh, *akh-vaw';* from 2331 (in the sense of 2324); an *utterance:*—declaration {1x}. See: TWOT—618a; BDB—28a, 296a.

263. אַחֲוָה {1x} ʾachăvâh (Aram.), akh-av-aw'; corresp. to 262; solution (of riddles):—shewing {1x}. See: TWOT—2722a; BDB—1079c, 1092b.

264. אַחֲוָה {1x} ʾachăvâh, akh-av-aw'; from 251; fraternity:—brotherhood {1x}. See: TWOT—62b; BDB—27c.

265. אָחוֹחַ {1x} ʾĂchôwach, akh-o'-akh; by redupl. from 251; brotherly; Achoach, an Isr.:—Ahoah {1x}. See: BDB—29a.

266. אֲחוֹחִי {5x} ʾĂchôwchîy, akh-o-khee'; patron. from 264; an Achochite or desc. of Achoach:—Ahohite {5x}. See: BDB—29a.

267. אֲחוּמַי {1x} ʾĂchûwmay, akh-oo-mah'-ee; perh. from 251 and 4325; brother (i.e. neighbour) of water; Achumai, an Isr.:—Ahumai {1x}. See: BDB—26c.

268. אָחוֹר {41x} ʾâchôwr, aw-khore'; or (short.)

אָחֹר ʾâchôr, aw-khore'; from 299; the hinder part; hence, (adv.) behind, backward; also (as facing north) the West:—back(s) {16x}, backward {11x}, behind {5x}, hinder parts {3x}, afterwards {1x}, back parts {1x}, backside {1x}, hereafter {1x}, time to come {1x}, without {1x}. Syn.: 322. See: TWOT—68d; BDB—30d.

269. אָחוֹת {114x} ʾachôwth, aw-khōth'; irreg. fem. of 251; a sister (used very widely [like 250], lit. and fig.):—(an- {6x}) other {1x}, sister(s) {106x}, together with + 802 – {1x}.

Achowth (269) means "sister." (1) The first occurrence is in Gen 4:22: "And Zillah, she also bare Tubal-cain, an instructor of every artificer in brass and iron: and the sister of Tubal-cain was Naamah." (2) The translation of "sister" for achowth is only the beginning. (2a) In Hebrew custom the word was a term employed to refer to the daughter of one's father and mother (Gen 4:22) or (2b) one's half-sister (Gen 20:12). (2c) It may also refer to one's aunt on the father's side (Lev 18:12; 20:19) or (2d) on the mother's side (Lev 18:13; 20:19).

(3) The use of achowth more generally denotes female relatives: "And they blessed Rebekah, and said unto her, Thou art our sister, be thou the mother of thousands of millions, and let thy seed possess the gate of those which hate them" (Gen 24:60). (4) This meaning lies behind the metaphorical use, where two divisions of a nation (Judah and Israel; Jer 3:7) and two cities (Sodom and Samaria; Eze 16:46) are portrayed as sisters—Hebrew names of geographical entities are feminine. (5) The more specialized meaning "beloved" is found only in Song 4:9: "Thou hast ravished my heart, my sister [or beloved], my spouse; thou hast ravished my heart with one of thine eyes, with one chain of thy neck." Here achowth is used as a term of endearment rather than a term for a blood relative. See: TWOT—62c; BDB—27d.

270. אָחַז {67x} ʾâchaz, aw-khaz'; a prim. root; to seize (often with the accessory idea of holding in possession):—hold {31x}, take {16x}, possess {5x}, caught {3x}, fastened {3x}, misc.: be affrighted, bar, come upon, fasten, handle, portion, (have or take) possess (-ion) = {9x}.

Achaz means to seize, grasp, hold fast, bolt (a door)." (1) The verb appears in Gen 25:26: "And his hand took hold on Esau's heel" (cf. Gen 22:13). (2) The meaning of "to bolt" (a door) appears in Neh 7:3: "Let them shut and bar the doors." (3) In 2 Chr 9:18, ʾachaz means "fastened." (4) Metaphorical sense: (4a) God seized Job by the neck (Job 16:12); (4b) He holds the psalmist's hand (Ps 73:23); (4c) pain seizes Israel's enemies (Ex 15:14–15); (4d) horror seizes people of the east (Job 18:20). Syn.: 2388; 4686. See: TWOT—64; BDB—28a.

271. אָחָז {41x} ʾĂchâz, aw-khawz'; from 270; possessor; Achaz, the name of a Jewish king and of an Isr.:—Ahaz {41x}. See: BDB—28c.

272. אֲחֻזָּה {66x} ʾăchuzzâh, akh-ooz-zaw'; fem. pass. part. from 270; something seized, i.e. a possession (espec. of land):—possession(s) {66x}.

Achuzzah (272) means "property; possession." (1) Essentially achuzzah is a legal term usually used of land, especially family holdings to be passed down to one's heirs. (1a) In Gen 17:13 Abram is promised the territory of Palestine as a familial or tribal possession until the indiscriminate future. (1b) In Gen 23:20 (cf. vv. 4, 9) the word bears a similar meaning. The difference appears to be that here no feudal responsibilities were attached to this "possession." However, the rather small lot belonged to Abraham and his descendants as a burial site: "And the field, and the cave that is therein, were made sure unto Abraham for a possession of a burying place by the sons of Heth" (Gen 23:20). (2) In Lev 25:45–46 non-Israelites could also be inheritable property, but a fellow Israelite could not. (3) The "inheritable property" of the Levites was not fields but the Lord Himself (Eze 44:28). See: TWOT—64a; BDB—28c.

273. אָחְזַי {1x} ʾAchzay, akh-zah'ee; from 270; seizer; Achzai, an Isr.:—Ahasai {1x}. BDB—28d, 403d.

274. אֲחַזְיָה {37x} ʾĂchazyâh, akh-az-yaw'; or (prol.)

אֲחַזְיָהוּ ʾĂchazyâhûw, akh-az-yaw'-hoo; from 270 and 3050; Jah has seized; Achazjah, the name of a Jewish and an Isr. king:—Ahaziah {37x}. See: BDB—28d, 306c.

Hebrew

275. אֲחֻזָּם {1x} ʾÂchuzzâm, akh-ooz-zawm'; from 270; seizure; Achuzzam, an Isr.:—Ahuzam {1x}. See: BDB—28d.

276. אֲחֻזַּת {1x} ʾÂchuzzath, akh-ooz-zath'; a var. of 272; possession; Achuzzath, a Philistine:—Ahuzzath {1x}. See: BDB—28d.

277. אָחִי {2x} ʾÂchîy, akh-ee'; from 251; brotherly; Achi, the name of two Isr.:—Ahi {1x}. See: BDB—26c

278. אֵחִי {1x} ʾÊchîy, ay-khee'; prob. the same as 277; Echi, an Isr.:—Ehi {1x}. See: BDB—29a.

279. אֲחִיאָם {2x} ʾÂchîyʾâm, akh-ee-awm'; from 251 and 517; brother of (the) mother (i.e. uncle); Achiam, an Isr.:—Ahiam {1x}. See: BDB—26c.

280. אֲחִידָה {1x} ʾăchîydâh (Aram.), akh-ee-daw'; corresp. to 2420, an enigma:—hard sentences {1x}. See: TWOT—2567; BDB—1079c, 1092a.

281. אֲחִיָה {24x} ʾÂchiyâh, akh-ee-yaw; or (prol.)

אֲחִיָהוּ ʾÂchîyâhûw, akh-ee-yaw'-hoo; from 251 and 3050; brother (i.e. worshiper) of Jah; Achijah, the name of nine Isr.:—Ahiah {4x}, Ahijah {20x}. See: BDB—26c.

282. אֲחִיהוּד {1x} ʾÂchîyhûwd, akh-ee-hood'; from 251 and 1935; brother (i.e. possessor) of renown; Achihud, an Isr.:—Ahihud {1x}. See: BDB—26d.

283. אַחְיוֹ {6x} ʾAchyôw, akh-yo'; prol. from 251; brotherly; Achio, the name of three Isr.:—Ahio {6x}. See: BDB—26d.

284. אֲחִיחֻד {1x} ʾÂchîychûd, akh-ee-khood'; from 251 and 2330; brother of a riddle (i.e. mysterious); Achichud, an Isr.:—Ahihud {1x}. See: BDB—26d.

285. אֲחִיטוּב {15x} ʾÂchîyṭûwb, akh-ee-toob'; from 251 and 2898; brother of goodness; Achitub, the name of several priests:—Ahitub {15x}. See: BDB—26d.

286. אֲחִילוּד {5x} ʾÂchîylûwd, akh-ee-lood'; from 251 and 3205; brother of one born; Achilud, an Isr.:—Ahilud {5x}. See: BDB—27a.

287. אֲחִימוֹת {1x} ʾÂchîymôwth, akh-ee-mōth'; from 251 and 4191; brother of death; Achimoth, an Isr.:—Ahimoth {1x}. See: BDB—27a.

288. אֲחִימֶלֶךְ {17x} ʾÂchîymelek, akh-ee-meh'-lek; from 251 and 4428; brother of (the) king; Achimelek, the name of an Isr. and of a Hittite:—Ahimelech {17x}. See: BDB—27a.

289. אֲחִימַן {4x} ʾÂchîyman, akh-ee-man'; or

אֲחִימָן ʾÂchîymân, akh-ee-mawn'; from 251 and 4480; brother of a portion (i.e. gift); Achiman, the name of an Anakite and of an Isr.:—Ahiman {4x}. See: BDB—27a.

290. אֲחִימַעַץ {15x} ʾÂchîymaʿats, akh-ee-mah'-ats; from 251 and the equiv. of 4619; brother of anger; Achimaats, the name of three Isr.:—Ahimaaz {15x}. See: BDB—27a, 591d.

291. אַחְיָן {1x} ʾAchyân, akh-yawn'; from 251; brotherly; Achjan, an Isr.:—Ahian {1x}. See: BDB—27b.

292. אֲחִינָדָב {1x} ʾÂchîynâdâb, akh-ee-naw-dawb'; from 251 and 5068; brother of liberality; Achinadab, an Isr.:—Ahinadab {1x}. See: BDB—27b.

293. אֲחִינֹעַם {7x} ʾÂchîynôʿam, akh-ee-no'-am; from 251 and 5278; brother of pleasantness; Achinoam, the name of two Israelitesses:—Ahinoam {7x}. See: BDB—27b.

294. אֲחִיסָמָךְ {3x} ʾÂchîyçâmâk, akh-ee-saw-mawk'; from 251 and 5564; brother of support; Achisamak, an Isr.:—Ahisamach {3x}. See: BDB—27b.

295. אֲחִיעֶזֶר {6x} ʾÂchîyʿezer, akh-ee-eh'-zer; from 251 and 5828; brother of help; Achiezer, the name of two Isr.:—Ahiezer {6x}. See: BDB—27b.

296. אֲחִיקָם {20x} ʾÂchîyqâm, akh-ee-kawm'; from 251 and 6965; brother of rising (i.e. high); Achikam, an Isr.:—Ahikam {20x}. See: BDB—27b.

297. אֲחִירָם {1x} ʾÂchîyrâm, akh-ee-rawm'; from 251 and 7311; brother of height (i.e. high); Achiram, an Isr.:—Ahiram {1x}. See: BDB—27b.

298. אֲחִירָמִי {1x} ʾÂchîyrâmîy, akh-ee-raw-mee'; patron. from 297; an Achiramite or desc. (collect.) of Achiram:—Ahiramites {1x}. See: BDB—27c.

299. אֲחִירַע {5x} ʾÂchîyraʿ, akh-ee-rah'; from 251 and 7451; brother of wrong; Achira, an Isr.:—Ahira {5x}. See: BDB—27c.

300. אֲחִישַׁחַר {1x} ʾÂchîyshachar, akh-ee-shakh'-ar; from 251 and 7837; brother of (the) dawn; Achishachar, an Isr.:—Ahishar {1x}. See: BDB—27c.

301. אֲחִישָׁר {1x} ʾÂchîyshâr, akh-ee-shawr'; from 251 and 7891; brother of (the) singer; Achishar, an Isr.:—Ahishar {1x}. See: BDB—27c.

302. אֲחִיתֹפֶל {20x} ʾÂchîythôphel, akh-ee-tho'-fel; from 251 and 8602; brother

of folly; *Achithophel,* an Isr.:—Ahithophel {20x}. See: BDB—27c.

303. אַחְלָב {1x} ʾ**Achlâb,** *akh-lawb';* from the same root as 2459; *fatness* (i.e. *fertile*); *Achlab,* a place in Pal.:—Ahlab {1x}. See: BDB—29a, 317b.

304. אֶחְלָי {2x} ʾ**Achlay,** *akh-lah'ee;* the same as 305; *wishful; Achlai,* the name of an Israelitess and of an Isr.:—Ahlai {2x}. See: BDB—29a.

305. אַחֲלַי {2x} ʾ**achălay,** *akh-al-ah'ee;* or

אַחֲלֵי ʾ**achălêy,** *akh-al-ay';* prob. from 253 and a var. of 3863; *would that!:—* O that {1x}, would God {1x}. See: TWOT—67a; BDB—25b.

306. אַחְלָמָה {2x} ʾ**achlâmâh,** *akh-law'-maw;* perh. from 2492 (and thus *dream-stone*); a gem, prob. the *amethyst:—*amethyst {2x}.

The identification is not certain but is a purple stone or perhaps a corundum or red or brown jasper. See: TWOT—67b; BDB—29a.

307. אַחְמְתָא {1x} ʾ**Achmᵉthâ,** *akh-me-thaw';* of Pers. der.; *Achmetha* (i.e. *Ecbatana*), the summer capital of Persia:—Achmetha {1x}. See: BDB—1079c.

308. אֲחַסְבַּי {1x} ʾ**Ăchaçbay,** *akh-as-bah'ee;* of uncert. der.; *Achasbai,* an Isr.:—Ahasbai {1x}. See: BDB—29b.

309. אָחַר {17x} ʾ**âchar,** *aw-khar';* a prim. root; to *loiter* (i.e. *be behind*); by impl. to *procrastinate:—*continue {1x}, defer {3x}, delay {1x}, hinder {1x}, sit up late {1x}, slack {2x}, stayed there {1x}, tarry {7x}.

Achar means "to tarry (Judg 5:28), remain behind/stayed there (Gen 32:4), delay." Other words derived from this verb are: "other," "after (wards)," "backwards." ʾ*Achar* appears in Ex 22:29 with the meaning "delay": "Thou shalt not delay to offer the first of thy ripe fruits, and of thy liquors: the firstborn of thy sons shalt thou give unto me." Syn.: 3427. See: TWOT—68; BDB—29b.

310. אַחַר {709x} ʾ**achar,** *akh-ar';* from 309; prop. the *hind* part; Gen used as an adv. or conjunc., *after* (in various senses):—after {454x}, follow {78x}, afterward(s) {46x}, behind {44x}, misc. {87x} = again, at, away from, back (from, -side), beside, by, forasmuch, from, hereafter, hinder end, + out (over) live, + persecute, posterity, pursuing, remnant, seeing, since, thence [-forth], when, with.

(1) As an adverb *achar* means "behind; after(wards)." **(1a)** One adverbial use of *achar* has a local-spatial emphasis that means "behind": "The singers went before, the players on instruments followed after" (Ps 68:25). **(1b)** Another adverbial usage has a temporal emphasis that

can mean "afterwards": "And I will fetch a morsel of bread, and comfort ye your hearts; after that ye shall pass on" (Gen 18:5). **(2)** As a preposition *achar* means "behind; after." **(2a)** *Achar* as a preposition can have a local-spatial significance, such as "behind": "And the man said, They are departed hence; for I heard them say, Let us go to Dothan" (Gen 37:17). As such, it can mean "follow after": "And also the king that reigneth over you [will] continue following the LORD your God" (1 Sa 12:14). **(2b)** *Achar* can signify "after" with a temporal emphasis: "And Noah lived after the flood three hundred and fifty years" (Gen 9:28, the first biblical occurrence of the word). **(2c)** This same emphasis may occur when *achar* appears in the plural (cf. Gen 19:6—local-spatial; Gen 17:8—temporal). **(3)** As a conjunction *achar* can mean "after" with a temporal emphasis: "And the days of Adam after he had begotten Seth were eight hundred years" (Gen 5:4). Syn.: see 309. See: TWOT—68b, 68c; BDB—29d, 30c, 405b, 1079d.

311. אֲחַר {3x} ʾ**achar** (Aram.), *akh-ar';* corresp. to 310; *after:—*hereafter {2x}, after {1x}. Ref. TWOT—2568; BDB—1079d.

312. אַחֵר {166x} ʾ**achêr,** *akh-air';* from 309; prop. *hinder;* Gen *next, other,* etc.:— other(s) {105x}, another {55x}, next {2x}, following {1x}, man's {1x}, men {1x}, strange {1x}.

Acher (312) means "following; different; other." **(1)** The first meaning of this word is temporal, and is seen in Gen 17:21: "But my covenant will I establish with Isaac, which Sarah shall bear unto thee at this set time in the next year" (i.e., the year "following"). **(2)** The first biblical occurrence of the word is in Gen 4:25: "And Adam [had relations with] his wife again; and she bare a son, and called his name Seth: For God, said she, hath appointed me another seed instead of Abel." **(3)** This meaning of "different" or "another" also appears in Lev 27:20: "And if he will not redeem the field, or if he have sold the field to another man, it shall not be redeemed any more." **(4)** In Is 28:11, *acher* defines tongue or language; hence it should be understood as "foreign": "For with stammering lips and another tongue will he speak to this people." **(5)** Finally, *acher* can mean "other." In this usage, the word distinguishes one thing from another without emphasizing any contrast. This is its meaning in Ex 20:3: "Thou shalt have no other gods before me." Syn: 259, 310, 7453. See: TWOT—68a; BDB—29c.

313. אַחֵר {1x} ʾ**Achêr,** *akh-air';* the same as 312; *Acher,* an Isr.:—Aher {1x}. See: BDB—31b.

314. אַחֲרוֹן {51x} **ʾachărôwn**, *akh-ar-one';* or (short.)

אַחֲרֹן *ʾachărôn*, *akh-ar-one';* from 309; *hinder;* Gen *late* or *last;* spec. (as facing the east) *western:*—last {20x}, after(ward)(s) {15x}, latter {6x}, end {2x}, utmost {2x}, following {1x}, hinder {1x}, hindermost {1x}, hindmost {1x}, rereward {1x}, uttermost {1x}.

Acharon (314) means "at the back; western; later; last; future." **(1)** *Acharon* has a local-spatial meaning. Basically, it means "at the back": "And he put the handmaids and their children foremost, and Leah and her children after, and Rachel and Joseph hindermost" (Gen 33:2—the first biblical appearance). **(2)** When applied elsewhere, the word means "western": "Every place whereon the soles of your feet shall tread shall be yours: from the wilderness and Lebanon, from the river, the river Euphrates, even unto the uttermost [western] sea shall your coast be" (Deut 11:24).

(3) Used temporally, *acharon* has several nuances. **(3a)** First, it means "last" as contrasted to the first of two things: "And it shall come to pass, if they will not believe thee, neither hearken to the voice of the first sign, that they will believe the voice of the latter sign" (Ex 4:8). **(3b)** Second, it can represent the "last" in a series of things or people: "Ye are my brethren, ye are my bones and my flesh: wherefore then are ye the last to bring back the king?" (2 Sa 19:12). **(3c)** The word also connotes "later on" and/or "afterwards": "But thou shalt surely kill him; thine hand shall be first upon him to put him to death, and afterwards the hand of all the people" (Deut 13:9). **(4)** Next the emphasis can be on the finality or concluding characteristic of a given thing: "Now these be the last words of David" (2 Sa 23:1). **(5)** *Acharon* connotes "future," or something that is yet to come: "So that the generation to come of your children that shall rise up after you, and the stranger that shall come from a far land, shall say, when they see the plagues of that land . . ." (Deut 29:22).

(6) The combination of "first" and "last" is **(6a)** an idiom of completeness: "Now the rest of the acts of Solomon, first and last, are they not written in the book of Nathan the prophet, and in the prophecy of Ahijah the Shilonite, and in the visions of Iddo the seer against Jeroboam the son of Nebat?" (2 Chr 9:29). **(6b)** Likewise the phrase expresses the sufficiency of the LORD, since He is said to include within Himself the "first" as well as the "last": "Thus saith the LORD the King of Israel, and his Redeemer the LORD of hosts; I am the first, and I am the last; and beside me there is no God" (Is 44:6; cf. 48:12). These verses affirm that there is no other

God, because all exists in Him. See: TWOT—68e; BDB—30d.

315. אַחְרַח {1x} **ʾAchrach**, *akh-rakh';* from 310 and 251; *after* (his) *brother; Achrach,* an Isr.:—Aharah {1x}. See: BDB—31b.

316. אַחְרְחֵל {1x} **ʾĂcharchêl**, *akh-ar-kale';* from 310 and 2426; *behind* (the) *intrenchment* (i.e. *safe*); *Acharchel,* an Isr.:—Aharhel {1x}. See: BDB—31c.

317. אָחֳרִי {6x} **ʾochŏrîy** (Aram.), *okh-or-ee';* from 311; *other:*—another {5x}, other {1x}. Syn.: 259, 312. See: TWOT—2568a; BDB—1079d.

318. אָחֳרֵין {1x} **ʾochŏrêyn** (Aram.), *okh-or-ane';* or (short.)

אָחֳרֵן *ʾochŏrên* (Aram.), *okh-or-ane';* from 317; *last:*—last one {1x}. See: TWOT—2568c; BDB—1079d.

319. אַחֲרִית {61x} **ʾachărîyth**, *akh-ar-eeth';* from 310; the *last* or *end,* hence, the *future;* also *posterity:*—end {31x}, latter {12x}, last {7x}, posterity {3x}, reward {2x}, hindermost {1x}, misc. {5x}.

Achariyth (319) means "hind-part; end; issue; outcome; posterity." **(1)** Used spatially, the word identifies the "remotest and most distant part of something": "If I take the wings of the morning, and dwell in the uttermost parts of the sea . . ." (Ps 139:9). **(2)** The most frequent emphasis of the word is "end," "issue," or "outcome." **(2a)** This nuance is applied to time in a superlative or final sense: "The eyes of the LORD thy God are always upon it, from the beginning of the year even unto the end of the year" (Deut 11:12). **(2b)** A slight shift of meaning occurs in Dan 8:23, where *achariyth* is applied to time in a relative or comparative sense: "And in the latter time of their kingdom, when the transgressors are come to the full, a king of fierce countenance, and understanding dark sentences, shall stand up." Here the word refers to a "last period," but not necessarily the "end" of history.

(3) In a different nuance, the word can mean "latter" or "what comes afterward": "O that they were wise, that they understood this, that they would consider their latter end!" (Deut 32:29). **(4)** In some passages, *achariyth* represents the "ultimate outcome" of a person's life. Num 23:10 speaks thus of death: "Who can count the dust of Jacob, and the number of the fourth part of Israel? Let me die the death of the righteous, and let my last end be like his!" **(5)** In other passages, *achariyth* refers to "all that comes afterwards." Passages such as Jer 31:17 use the word of one's "descendants" or "posterity" (KJV, "children"). In view of the parallelism

suggested in this passage, the first line should be translated "and there is hope for your posterity." **(6)** In Amos 9:1, *achariyth* is used of the "rest" (remainder) of one's fellows.

(7) Both conclusion and result are apparent in passages such as Is 41:22, where the word represents the "end" or "result" of a matter: "Let them bring them forth, and show us what shall happen: let them show the former things what they be, that we may consider them, and know the latter end of them; or declare us things for to come." **(8)** *Achariyth* indicates the "last" or the "least in importance": "Your mother shall be sore confounded; she that bare you shall be ashamed: behold. the hindermost of the nations shall be a wilderness, a dry land, and a desert" (Jer 50:12).

(9) The fact that *achariyth* used with "day" or "years" may signify either "a point at the end of time" or "a period of the end time" has created considerable debate on fourteen Old Testament passages. Some scholars view this use of the word as non-eschatological—that it merely means "in the day which follows" or "in the future." This seems to be its meaning in Gen 49:1 (its first occurrence in the Bible): "Gather yourselves together, that I may tell you that which shall befall you in the last days." Here the word refers to the entire period to follow. **(10)** On the other hand, Is 2:2 uses the word more absolutely of the "last period of time": "In the last days, . . . the mountain of the LORD's house shall be established [as the chief of the mountains]." **(11)** Some scholars believe the phrase sometimes is used of the "very end of time": "Now I am come to make thee understand what shall befall thy people in the latter days: for yet the vision is for many days" (Dan 10:14). This point, however, is much debated. Syn.: 3615; 7093; 7097. See: TWOT—68f; BDB—31a.

320. אַחֲרִית {1x} ʾachărîyth (Aram.), *akh-ar-eeth';* from 311; the same as 319; *later:*—latter {1x}. See: TWOT—2568b; BDB—1079d.

321. אָחֳרָן {5x} ʾochŏrân (Aram.), *okh-or-awn';* from 311; the same as 317; *other:*—other {3x}, another {2x}. See: TWOT—2568c; BDB—1079d.

אָחֳרֵן ʾochŏrên. See 318.

322. אַחֲרַנִית {7x} ʾachŏrannîyth, *akh-o-ran-neeth';* prol. from 268; *backwards:*—backward {6x}, again {1x}. See: TWOT—68d; BDB—30d.

323. אֲחַשְׁדַּרְפַּן {4x} ʾăchashdarpan, *akh-ash-dar-pan';* of Pers. der.; a satrap or governor of a main province (of Persia):—lieutenants {4x}. See: TWOT—69; BDB—31c.

324. אֲחַשְׁדַּרְפַּן {9x} ʾăchashdarpan (Aram.), *akh-ash-dar-pan';* corresp. to 323:—princes {9x}. See: TWOT—2569; BDB—1080a.

325. אֲחַשְׁוֵרוֹשׁ {31x} ʾĂchashvêrôwsh, *akh-ash-vay-rōsh';* or (short.)

אֲחַשְׁרֹשׁ ʾAchashrôsh, *akh-ash-rōsh'* (Esth. 10:1); of Pers. or.; *Achashverosh* (i.e. Ahasuerus or Artaxerxes, but in this case Xerxes), the title (rather than name) of a Pers. king:—Ahasuerus {31x}. See: BDB—31c.

326. אֲחַשְׁתָּרִי {1x} ʾăchashtârîy, *akh-ash-taw-ree';* prob. of Pers. der.; an *achastarite* (i.e. courier); the designation (rather than name) of an Isr.:—Haakashtari [*includ. the art.*] {1x}. See: BDB—31c.

327. אֲחַשְׁתָּרָן {2x} ʾăchastârân, *akh-ash-taw-rawn';* of Pers. or.; a *mule:*—camels {2x}. See: TWOT—70; BDB—31c.

328. אַט {6x} ʾat, *at;* from an unused root perh. mean. to *move softly;* (as a noun) a *necromancer* (from their soft incantations), (as an adv.) *gently:*—softly {3x}, charmers {1x}, gently {1x}, secret {1x}.
Isaiah 19:3 speaks of charmers, those who speak with soft voices and perhaps charm serpents. See: TWOT—72b; BDB—31c, 31d, 521b.

329. אָטָד {6x} ʾâtâd, *aw-tawd';* from an unused root prob. mean. to *pierce* or *make fast;* a *thorn*-tree (espec. the *buckthorn*):—bramble {3x}, Atad {2x}, thorns {1x}. See: TWOT—71a; BDB—31d.

330. אֵטוּן {1x} ʾêtûwn, *ay-toon';* from an unused root (prob. mean. to *bind*); prop. *twisted* (yarn), i.e. *tapestry:*—fine linen {1x}. See: TWOT—73b; BDB—32a.

331. אָטַם {8x} ʾâtam, *aw-tam';* a prim. root; to *close* (the lips or ears); by anal. to *contract* (a window by bevelled jambs):—narrow {4x}, stoppeth {3x}, shutteth {1x}. See: TWOT—73; BDB—31d.

332. אָטַר {1x} ʾâtar, *aw-tar';* a prim. root; to *close* up:—shut {1x}. See: TWOT—74; BDB—32a.

333. אָטֵר {5x} ʾÂtêr, *aw-tare';* from 332; *maimed; Ater,* the name of three Isr.:—Ater {5x}. See: BDB—32a.

334. אִטֵּר {2x} ʾittêr, *it-tare';* from 332; *shut up,* i.e. *impeded* (as to the use of the right hand):—lefthanded + 3025 {2x}. See: TWOT—74a; BDB—32a.

335. אַי {16x} ʾay, *ah'ee;* perh. from 370; *where?* hence, *how?:*—where {9x}, what {3x}, whence {4x}. See: TWOT—75; BDB—32a, 58b.

336. **אִי** {1x} ʾîy, *ee;* prob. ident. with 335 (through the idea of a *query*); *not:*—island {1x}. (Job 22:30). See: TWOT—77; BDB—33a.

337. **אִי** {2x} ʾîy, *ee;* short. from 188; *alas!:*—woe {2x}. See: TWOT—76; BDB—33a.

338. **אִי** {3x} ʾîy, *ee;* prob. ident. with 337 (through the idea of a *doleful* sound); a *howler* (used only in the plur.), i.e. any solitary wild creature:—wild beasts of the islands {3x}. See: TWOT—43a; BDB—17b.

339. **אִי** {36x} ʾîy, *ee;* from 183; prop. a *habitable* spot (as *desirable*); dry *land,* a *coast,* an *island:*—isle(s) {30x}, islands {5x}, country {1x}. See: TWOT—39a; BDB—15d, 33b.

340. **אָיַב** {1x} ʾâyab, *aw-yab´;* a prim. root; to *hate* (as one of an opposite tribe or party); hence, to *be hostile:*—enemy {1x}. See: TWOT—78; BDB—33b.

341. **אֹיֵב** {282x} ʾôyêb, *o-yabe´;* or (fully)

אוֹיֵב ʾôwyêb, *o-yabe´;* act. part. of 340; *hating;* an *adversary:*—enemy(s) {280x}, foes {2x}.

Oyeb means "enemy." In form, the word is an active infinitive (or more precisely, a verbal noun). **(1)** This word means "enemy," and is used in at least one reference to both individuals and nations: "In blessing I will bless thee, and in multiplying I will multiply thy seed as the stars of the heaven, and as the sand which is upon the sea shore; and thy seed shall possess the gate of his enemies" (Gen 22:17—the first occurrence). **(2)** "Personal foes" may be represented by this word: "If thou meet thine enemy's ox or his ass going astray, thou shalt surely bring it back to him again" (Ex 23:4). This idea includes "those who show hostility toward me": "But mine enemies are lively, and they are strong; and they that hate me wrongfully are multiplied" (Ps 38:19). **(3)** One might be an "enemy" of God: "The LORD will take vengeance on his adversaries, and he reserveth wrath for his enemies" (Nah 1:2). **(4)** God is the "enemy" of all who refuse to submit to His lordship: "But they rebelled, and vexed his holy Spirit: therefore he was turned to be their enemy" (Is 63:10). Syn.: *Tsar* (6862) is the general designation for enemy; *ʾôwyêb* is specific; *sone* (8130) stresses hatred; and *rodep* (7291) stresses persecution. Syn.: 6862, 6887, 8324. See: TWOT—78; BDB—33b.

342. **אֵיבָה** {5x} ʾêybâh, *ay-baw´;* from 340; *hostility:*—enmity {3x}, hatred {2x}. See: TWOT—78a; BDB—33c.

343. **אֵיד** {24x} ʾêyd, *ade;* from the same as 181 (in the sense of *bending* down); *oppression;* by impl. *misfortune, ruin:*—calamity {17x}, destruction {7x}.

(1) This word signifies a "disaster" or "calamity" befalling a nation or individual. When used of a nation, it represents a "political or military event": "To me belongeth vengeance, and recompense; their foot shall slide in due time: for the day of their calamity is at hand, and the things that shall come upon them make haste" (Deut 32:35—first occurrence). The prophets tend to use ʾeyd in the sense of national "disaster," while Wisdom writers use it for "personal tragedy." Syn.: 3589, 4288, 7667, 7701. See: TWOT—38c; BDB—15c, 33d.

344. **אַיָּה** {3x} ʾayâh, *ah-yaw´;* perh. from 337; the *screamer,* i.e. a *hawk:*—kite {2x}, vulture {1x}. See: TWOT—43b; BDB—17b, 33d.

345. **אַיָּה** {6x} ʾAyâh, *ah-yaw´;* the same as 344; *Ajah,* the name of two Isr.:—Aiah {5x}, Ajah {1x}. See: BDB—17b.

346. **אַיֵּה** {2x} ʾayêh, *ah-yay´;* prol. from 335; *where?:*—where {2x}. See: TWOT—75a; BDB—32c, 33d.

347. **אִיּוֹב** {58x} ʾÎyôwb, *ee-yobe´;* from 340; *hated* (i.e. *persecuted*); *Ijob,* the patriarch famous for his patience:—Job {58x}. See: BDB—33c.

348. **אִיזֶבֶל** {22x} ʾÎyzebel, *ee-zeh´-bel;* from 336 and 2083; *chaste; Izebel,* the wife of king Ahab:—Jezebel {22x}. See: BDB—33b.

349. **אֵיךְ** {10x} ʾêyk, *ake;* also

אֵיכָה ʾêykâh, *ay-kaw´;* and

אֵיכָכָה ʾêykâkâh, *ay-kaw´-kah;* prol. from 335; *how?* or *how!;* also *where:*—how, what, where = {10x}. See: TWOT—75b, c, d, e; BDB—32c, 32d, 33d.

350. **אִי־כָבוֹד** {2x} ʾÎy-kâbôwd, *ee-kaw-bode´;* from 336 and 3519; (there is) *no glory,* i.e. *inglorious; Ikabod,* a son of Phineas:—I-chabod {2x}. See: BDB—33b.

351. **אֵיכֹה** {1x} ʾêykôh, *ay-kō;* prob. a var. for 349, but not as an interrogative; *where:*—where {1x}. TWOT—75d; BDB—33d.

אֵיכָה ʾêykâh;

אֵיכָכָה ʾêykâkâh. See 349.

352. **אַיִל** {185x} ʾayîl, *ah´-yil;* from the same as 193; prop. *strength;* hence, anything *strong;* spec. a *chief* (politically); also a *ram* (from his strength); a *pilaster* (as a strong support); an *oak* or other strong tree:—ram(s) {156x}, post(s) {21x}, mighty (men) {4x}, trees {2x}, lintel {1x}, oaks {1x}.

The basic meaning of ʾayîl is strength; hence, also *ayil* means "ram." **(1)** *Ayil* represents a male sheep or "ram." The word first appears in Gen 15:9, where God told Abram: "Take me a heifer

of three years old, and a she goat of three years old, and a ram of three years old, and a turtledove, and a young pigeon." **(2)** These animals were often used in sacrificing (cf. Gen 22:13). **(3)** They were eaten (Gen 31:38), and the wool used to make clothing (cf. 2 Kin 3:4). **(4)** Consequently, as highly valuable animals, such "rams" were selected by Jacob to be part of a peace present sent to Esau (Gen 32:14).

(5) Many passages use *ayil* as a figure of despots or mighty men: "Then the dukes of Edom shall be amazed; the mighty men of Moab, trembling shall take hold upon them" (Ex 15:15). The king of Babylon deported Judah's kings, princes, and the "mighty of the land" (Eze 17:13). **(6)** In the first instance the word represents chiefs in the sense of head political figures, whereas in the second use it appears to signify lesser figures. An even more powerful figure is in view in Eze 31:11, where *ayil* represents a central, powerful, earthly figure who will ruthlessly destroy Assyria: "I have therefore delivered him into the hand of the mighty one of the heathen; he shall surely deal with him: I have driven him out for his wickedness." Syn.: *ʾAyîl* is the support upon which the rafters rest; whereas *mashshebah* (4676 – {32x}) refers to a "pillar" as **(1)** a personal memorial (2 Sa 18:18); **(2)** a monument (Gen 28:18); or **(3)** sacred stones or pillars (Ex 24:4). See also: 1368, 2389, 4676. See: TWOT d, e, f, g; BDB—17d, 18a, 18b, 33d.

353. אֱיָל {1x} ʾĕyâl, *eh-yawl'*; a var. of 352; *strength:*—strength {1x}. See: TWOT—79; BDB—33d.

354. אַיִל {11x} ʾayâl, *ah-yawl'*; an intens. form of 352 (in the sense of *ram*); a *stag* or male deer:—hart(s) {11x}. See: TWOT—45k; BDB—19d.

355. אַיָּלָה {8x} ʾayâlâh, *ah-yaw-law'*; fem. of 354; a *doe* or female deer:—hind(s) {8x}. See: TWOT—45l; BDB—19b.

356. אַיָּלוֹן {7x} ʾÊylôwn, *ay-lone'*; or (short.)

אַיָּלוֹן ʾÊlôwn, *ay-lone'*; or

אַיָּלוֹן ʾÊylôn, *ay-lone'*; from 352; *oak-grove; Elon*, the name of a place in Pal., and also of one Hittite, two Isr.:—Elon {7x}. See: BDB—19a.

357. אַיָּלוֹן {10x} ʾAyâlôwn, *ah-yaw-lone'*; from 354; *deer-field; Ajalon*, the name of five places in Pal.:—Aijalon {7x}, Ajalon {3x}. See: BDB—19c.

358. אֵילוֹן בֵּית חָנָן {1x} ʾÊylôwn Bêyth Chânân, *ay-lone' bayth chaw-nawn'*; from 356, 1004, and 2603; *oak-grove of* (the) *house of favor; Elon of Beth-chanan*, a place in Pal.:—Elon-beth-hanan {1x}. See: BDB—19a, 111c.

359. אֵילוֹת {8x} ʾÊylôwth, *ay-lōth'*; or

אֵילַת ʾÊylath, *ay-lath'*; from 352; *trees* or a *grove* (i.e. palms); *Eloth* or *Elath*, a place on the Red Sea:—Elath {5x}, Eloth {3x}. See: BDB—19a.

360. אֵילוֹת {1x} ʾĕyâlûwth, *eh-yaw-looth'*; fem. of 353; *power;* by impl. *protection:*—strength {1x}. See: TWOT—79a; BDB—33d.

361. אֵילָם {15x} ʾêylâm, *ay-lawm'*; or (short.)

אֵלָם ʾêlâm, *ay-lawm'*; or (fem.)

אֵלַמָּה ʾêlammâh, *ay-lam-maw'*; prob. from 352; a *pillar-space* (or colonnade), i.e. a *pale* (or portico):—arches {15x}. See: TWOT—45j; BDB—19a, 48a.

362. אֵילִם {6x} ʾÊylîm, *ay-leem'*; plur. of 352; *palm- trees; Elim*, a place in the desert:—Elim {1x}. See: BDB—18c.

363. אִילָן {6x} ʾîylân (Aram.), *ee-lawn'*; corresp. to 356; a *tree:*—tree {6x}. See: TWOT—2570; BDB—1079a, 1080a.

364. אֵיל פָּארָן {1x} ʾÊyl Pâʾrân, *ale paw-rawn'*; from 352 and 6290; *oak of Paran; El-Paran*, a portion of the district of Paran:—El-paran {1x}. See: BDB—18c.

אֵילֹן ʾÊylôn. See 356.

365. אַיֶּלֶת {3x} ʾayeleth, *ah-yeh'-leth;* the same as 355; a *doe:*—hind {2x}, Aijeleth {1x}. See: TWOT—45l; BDB—19b.

אַיִם ʾayim. See 368.

366. אָיֹם {3x} ʾâyôm, *aw-yome';* from an unused root (mean. to *frighten); frightful:*—terrible {3x}. See: TWOT—80a; BDB—33d.

367. אֵימָה {17x} ʾêymâh, *ay-maw';* or (short.)

אֵמָה ʾêmah, *ay-maw';* from the same as 366; *fright;* concr. an *idol* (as a bugbear):—terror(s) {7x}, fear {5x}, terrible {2x}, dread {1x}, horror {1x}, idols {1x}.

The basic meaning is to be in the presence of an object (God, army) that causes a deep-seated terror; or dread. Syn.: 2851. See: TWOT—80b; BDB—33d, 1080a.

368. אֵימִים {3x} ʾÊymîym, *ay-meem';* plur. of 367; *terrors; Emim*, an early Canaanitish (or Moabitish) tribe:—Emims {3x}. See: BDB—33d, 34a.

369. אַיִן {29x} ʾayin, *ah'-yin;* as if from a prim. root mean. to *be nothing* or *not exist;* a *non-entity;* Gen used as a neg. particle:—except {1x}, faileth {1x}, fatherless + 1 – {1x}, incurable + 4832 – {1x}, infinite {3x}, innumerable {4x}, neither {40x}, never {2x}, no {52x}, none {48x}, not {164x}, nothing {23x}, nought {1x}, without {42x}.

'Ayin may be used (1) absolutely and signify nonexistence (Gen 2:5); (2) preceded by the particle *im,* the word may mean not (Ex 17:7) or because (Jer 7:32), (3) or else (Gen 30:1; Ps 39:5); (4) without (Prov 15:22); (5) simple negation (Ps 135:17); (6) With a suffixed pronoun *'ayin* negates the existence of the one or thing so represented; with the suffixed pronoun "he," the word means he was no longer (Gen 5:24). Syn.: comp. 370, 1097, 3808. See: TWOT—81; BDB—33b, 34a.

370. אַיִן {17x} *'ayin, ah'-yin;* prob. ident. with 369 in the sense of *query* (comp. 336); *where?* (only in connection with prep. pref., *whence*):— whence {16x}, where {1x}. See: TWOT—75f; BDB—32d, 34a.

371. אִין {1x} *'iyn, een;* appar. a short. form of 369; but (like 370) interrog.; is it *not?:*— (is) there not {1x}. See: TWOT—81; BDB—35b.

372. אִיעֶזֶר {1x} *'Îy'ezer, ee-eh'-zer;* from 336 and 5828; *helpless; Iezer,* an Isr.:— Jeezer {1x}. See: BDB—4c.

373. אִיעֶזְרִי {1x} *'Îy'ezrîy, ee-ez-ree';* patron. from 372; an *Iezrite* or desc. of Iezer:—Jezerite {1x}. See: BDB—4d.

374. אֵיפָה {40x} *'êyphâh, ay-faw';* or (short.) אֵפָה *'êphâh, ay-faw';* of Eg. der.; an *ephah* or measure for grain; hence, a *measure* in Gen:—ephah {34x}, measure(s) {6x}. See: TWOT—82; BDB—35b.

375. אֵיפֹה {10x} *'êyphôh, ay-fo';* from 335 and 6311; *what place?;* also (of time) *when?;* or (of means) *how?:*—where {9x}, what {1x}. See: TWOT—75h; BDB—33a, 35c.

376. אִישׁ {1639x} *'îysh, eesh;* contr. for 582 [or perh. rather from an unused root mean. to *be extant*]; a *man* as an individual or a male person; often used as an adjunct to a more def. term (and in such cases frequently not expressed in translation):—man {1002x}, men {210x}, one {188x}, husband {69x}, any {27x}, misc.: also, another, a certain, + champion, consent, each, every (one), fellow, he, high (degree), him (that is, man [-kind], + none, people, person, + steward, what (man) soever, whoso = {143x}.

Iysh means "man; husband; mate; human being; human; somebody; each; every." The plural of this noun is usually *anashim* (582). (1) Basically, this word signifies "man" in correspondence to woman; a "man" is a person who is distinguished by maleness. This emphasis is in Gen 2:24 (the first biblical occurrence): "Therefore shall a man leave his father and his mother, and shall cleave unto his wife." Sometimes the phrase "man and woman" signifies anyone whatsoever, including children: "If an ox gore a man or a woman, that they die: then the ox shall be surely stoned" (Ex 21:28). (2) This phrase can also connote an inclusive group, including children: "And they utterly destroyed all that was in the city, both man and woman, young and old, and ox, and sheep, and ass, with the edge of the sword" (Josh 6:21). This idea is sometimes more explicitly expressed by the word series "men, women, and children": "Gather the people together, men, and women, and children, and thy stranger that is within thy gates" (Deut 31:12).

(3) *Iysh* is often used in marriage contexts (cf. Gen 2:24) meaning "husband" or "mate": "Take ye wives, and beget sons and daughters; and take wives for your sons, and give your daughters to husbands, that they may bear sons and daughters" (Jer 29:6). A virgin is described as a lass who has not known a "man" ("husband"): "And she went with her companions, and bewailed her virginity upon the mountains. And it came to pass at the end of two months, that she returned unto her father, who did with her according to his vow which he had vowed: and she knew no man" (Judg 11:38–39). (4) The sense "mate" appears in Gen 7:2, where the word represents male animals: "Of every clean beast thou shalt take to thee by sevens, the male and his female."

(5) One special nuance of *iysh* appears in passages such as Gen 3:6, where it means "husband," or one responsible for a wife or woman and revered by her: "[And she] gave also unto her husband with her: and he did eat." This emphasis is in Hos 2:16 where it is applied to God. (6) Sometimes this word connotes that the one so identified is a "man" par excellence. As such he is strong, influential, and knowledgeable in battle: "Be strong, and quit yourselves like men, O ye Philistines, that ye be not servants unto the Hebrews" (1 Sa 4:9). (7) In a few places *iysh* is used as a synonym of "father": "We are all sons of one man . . ." (Gen 42:11). (8) In other passages the word is applied to a son (cf. Gen 2:24). (9) In the plural the word can be applied to groups of men who serve or obey a superior. Pharaoh's men escorted Abraham: "And Pharaoh commanded his men concerning him: and they sent him away" (Gen 12:20). (10) In a similar but more general sense, the word may identify people who belong to someone or something: "For all these abominations have the men of the land done, which were before you, and the land is defiled" (Lev 18:27). (11) Infrequently (and in later historical literature) this word is used as a collective noun referring to an entire group: "And his servant said, . . . Should I set this before a hundred men?" (2 Kin 4:43).

(12) Many passages use *iysh* in the more general or generic sense of "man," a human being: "He that smiteth a man, so that he die, shall

be surely put to death" (Ex 21:12). Even if one strikes a woman or child and he or she dies, the attacker should be put to death. Again, notice Deut 27:15: "Cursed be the man that maketh any graven or molten image." **(12a)** This is the sense of the word when it is contrasted with animals: "But against any of the children of Israel shall not a dog move his tongue, against man or beast . . ." (Ex 11:7). **(12b)** The same nuance appears when man over against God is in view: "God is not a man, that he should lie . . ." (Num 23:19).

(13) Sometimes *iysh* is indefinite, meaning "somebody" or "someone" ("they"): "And I will make thy seed as the dust of the earth: so that if a man can number the dust of the earth, then shall thy seed also be numbered" (Gen 13:16). **(14)** In other passages the word suggests the meaning "each" (Gen 40:5). **(15)** Closely related to the previous nuance is the connotation "every" (Jer 23:35). comp. 802. Syn.: *ʾAdam* (120) connotes man as the creature created in God's image, the crown of all creation. *Iysh* (376) is used for man as the counterpart of woman and/or as distinguished in his maleness. *Geber* (1397) denotes a male as an antonym of a woman, many times suggesting strength, strong man. *Enosh* (582) sets forth a collective idea of man suggesting the frailty, vulnerability, and finitude of man as contrasted to God. *Bachur* (970) signifies the fully developed, vigorous, unmarried man is in his prime. See also: 120, 582, 1167, 1397, 1400, 4962. See: TWOT—83a; BDB—35c.

377. אִישׁ {1x} ʾiysh, *eesh;* denom. from 376; to *be a man,* i.e. act in a manly way:— shew yourselves men {1x}. See: TWOT—83a; BDB—84a, 1083b.

378. אִישׁ־בֹּשֶׁת {11x} ʾÎysh-Bôsheth, *eesh-bō'-sheth;* from 376 and 1322; *man of shame; Ish-Bosheth,* a son of King Saul:— Ish-bosheth {11x}. See: BDB—36b.

379. אִישׁהוֹד {1x} ʾÎyshhôwd, *eesh-hode';* from 376 and 1935; *man of renown; Is-hod,* an Isr.:—Ishod {1x}. See: BDB—36b.

380. אִישׁוֹן {6x} ʾîyshôwn, *ee-shone';* dimin. from 376; the *little man* of the eye; the *pupil* or *ball;* hence, the *middle* (of night):— apple {3x}, obscure {2x}, black {1x}.

The word *iyshown* means "little man," a diminutive form of the noun. Although it literally means "little man," it signifies the pupil of the eye and is so translated ("apple of his eye"). See: TWOT—83b; BDB—36b, 37c.

אִישׁ־חַי ʾÎysh-Chay. See 381.

381. אִישׁ־חַיִל ʾÎysh-Chayil, *eesh-khah'-yil;* from 376 and 2428; *man of might;* by defect. transc. (2 Sa 23:20)

אִישׁ־חַי {4x} ʾÎysh-Chay, *eesh-khah'ee;* as if from 376 and 2416; *living man; Ish-chail* (or *Ish-chai*), an Isr.:—a valiant man {1x}. See: BDB—35d.

382. אִישׁ־טוֹב {2x} ʾÎysh-Tôwb, *eesh-tobe';* from 376 and 2897; *man of Tob; Ish-Tob,* a place in Pal.:—Ish-tob {1x}. See: BDB—36a.

383. אִיתַי {17x} ʾîythay (Aram.), *ee-thah'ee;* corresp. to 3426; prop. *entity;* used only as a particle of affirmation, there *is:*—art thou, can, do ye, have, it be, there is (are), ✕ we will not = {17x}. See: TWOT—2572; BDB—1080a, 1083c.

384. אִיתִיאֵל {3x} ʾÎythîyʾêl, *eeth-ee-ale';* perh. from 837 and 410; *God has arrived; Ithiel,* the name of an Isr., also of a symb. person:—Ithiel {3x}. See: BDB—36b, 87b.

385. אִיתָמָר {21x} ʾÎythâmâr, *eeth-aw-mawr';* from 339 and 8558; *coast* of the *palm*-tree; *Ithamar,* a son of Aaron:—Ithamar {21x}. BDB—16a, 33b, 36b.

386. אֵיתָן {13x} ʾêythân, *ay-thawn';* or (short.) אֵתָן ʾêthân, *ay-thawn';* from an unused root (mean. to *continue*); *permanence;* hence, (concr.) *permanent;* spec. a *chieftain:*— strong {5x}, mighty {4x}, strength {2x}, hard {1x}, rough {1x}. See: TWOT—935a; BDB—36b, 450d.

387. אֵיתָן {8x} ʾÊythân, *ay-thawn';* the same as 386; *permanent; Ethan,* the name of four Isr.:—Ethan {8x}. See: BDB—451a.

388. אֵיתָנִים {1x} Êythânîym, *ay-thaw-neem';* plur. of 386; always with the art.; the *permanent* brooks; *Ethanim,* the name of a month:—Ethanim {1x}. See: BDB—450d.

389. אַךְ {22x} ʾak, *ak;* akin to 403; a particle of affirmation, *surely;* hence, (by limitation) *only:*—also, but, certainly, even, howbeit, least, nevertheless, notwithstanding, only, save, scarce, surely, surety, truly, verily, wherefore, yet = {22x}. See: TWOT—84; BDB—36c.

390. אַכַּד {1x} ʾAkkad, *ak-kad';* from an unused root prob. mean. to *strengthen;* a *fortress; Accad,* a place in Bab.:—Accad {1x}. See: BDB—37a.

391. אַכְזָב {2x} ʾakzâb, *ak-zawb';* from 3576; *falsehood;* by impl. *treachery:*—liar {1x}, lie {1x}. See: TWOT—970b; BDB—37a, 469d.

392. אַכְזִיב {4x} ʾAkzîyb, *ak-zeeb';* from 391; *deceitful* (in the sense of a winter-torrent which *fails* in summer); *Akzib,* the name

of two places in Pal.:—Achzib {4x}. See: BDB—37a, 469d.

393. אַכְזָר {4x} ʾakzâr, ak-zawr'; from an unused root (appar. mean. to act harshly); violent; by impl. deadly; also (in a good sense) brave:—cruel {3x}, fierce {1x}. See: TWOT—971a; BDB—37a, 470a.

394. אַכְזָרִי {8x} ʾakzârîy, ak-zaw-ree'; from 393; terrible:—cruel {7x}, one {1x}. See: TWOT—971b; BDB—37a, 470a.

395. אַכְזְרִיּוּת {1x} ʾakzᵉrîyûwth, ak-ze-ree-ooth'; from 394; fierceness:—cruel {1x}. See: TWOT—971c; BDB—37a, 470a.

396. אֲכִילָה {1x} ʾăkîylâh, ak-ee-law'; fem. from 398; something eatable, i.e. food:—meat {1x}. See: TWOT—85c; BDB—38b.

397. אָכִישׁ {21x} ʾÂkîysh, aw-keesh'; of uncert. der.; Akish, a Philistine king:—Achish {21x}. See: BDB—37a.

398. אָכַל {810} ʾâkal, aw-kal'; a prim. root; to eat (lit. or fig.):—eat (-er, up) {604x}, devour (-er, up), {111x}, consume {32x}, misc. {63x}.

Akal means "to eat, feed, consume, devour." (1) Essentially, this root refers to the "consumption of food by man or animals." In Gen 3:6, we read that Eve took of the fruit of the tree of the knowledge of good and evil and "ate" it. (2) The function of eating is presented along with seeing, hearing, and smelling as one of the basic functions of living (Deut 4:28). (3) "Eating," as every other act of life, is under God's control; He stipulates what may or may not be eaten (Gen 1:29). (3a) After the Flood, man was allowed to "eat" meat (Gen 9:3). (3b) But under the Mosaic covenant, God stipulated that certain foods were not to be "eaten" (Lev 11; Deut 14) while others were permissible. This distinction is certainly not new, inasmuch as it is mentioned prior to the Flood (Gen 7:2; cf. Gen 6:19). A comparison of these two passages demonstrates how the Bible can speak in general terms, with the understanding that certain limitations are included. Hence, Noah was commanded to bring into the ark two of every kind (Gen 6:19), while the Bible tells us that this meant two of every unclean and fourteen of every clean animal (Gen 7:2). Thus, Gen 9:3 implies that man could "eat" only the clean animals. (4) This verb is often used figuratively with overtones of destroying something or someone. (4a) So the sword, fire, and forest are said to "consume" men. (4b) The things "consumed" may include such various things as land (Gen 3:17), fields (Is 1:7), offerings (Deut 18:1), and a bride's purchase price (Gen 31:15). (5) Akal might also connote bearing the results of an action (Is 3:10).

(6) The word can refer not only (6a) to "eating" but (6b) to the entire concept "room and board" (2 Sa 9:11, 13), (6c) the special act of "feasting" (Eccl 10:16), or (6d) the entire activity of "earning a living" (Amos 7:12; cf. Gen 3:19). (7) In Dan 3:8 and 6:24, "to eat one's pieces" is to charge someone maliciously. (8) "To eat another's flesh," used figuratively, (8a) refers to tearing him to pieces or "killing him" (Ps 27:2), although akal may also be used literally, (8b) as when one "eats" human beings in times of serious famine (Lev 26:29). (9) Eccl 4:5 uses the expression, "eat one's own flesh," for allowing oneself to waste away.

(10) Abstinence from eating may indicate deep emotional upset, like that which overcame Hannah before the birth of Samuel (1 Sa 1:7). (11) It may also indicate the religious self-denial seen in fasting. (12) Unlike the pagan deities (Deut 32:37–38) God "eats" no food (Ps 50:13); although as a "consuming" fire (Deut 4:24), He is ready to defend His own honor and glory. (13) He "consumes" evil and the sinner. (14) He will also "consume" the wicked like a lion (Hos 13:8). (15) There is one case in which God literally "consumed" food—when He appeared to Abraham in the form of three "strangers" (Gen 18:8). (16) God provides many good things to eat, (16a) such as manna to the Israelites (Ex 16:32) and (16b) all manner of food to those who delight in the LORD (Is 58:14), (16c) even the finest food (Ps 81:16). (17) He puts the Word of God into one's mouth; by "consuming" it, it is taken into one's very being (Eze 3:2). Syn.: 1104. See: TWOT—85; v. BDB—37a, 1080b.

399. אֲכַל {7x} ʾăkal (Aram.), ak-al'; corresp. to 398:—devour {4x}, accused {2x}, eat {1x}. See: TWOT—2573; BDB—1080b.

400. אֹכֶל {44x} ʾôkel, o'-kel; from 398; food:—meat {18x}, food {16x}, eating {4x}, victuals {3x}, prey {2x}, mealtime + 6256 –{1x}.

Okel means "food." (1) Okel appears twice in Gen 41:35 with the sense of "food supply": "And let them gather all the food of those good years that come, and lay up corn under the hand of Pharaoh, and let them keep food in the cities." (2) The word refers to the "food" of wild animals in Ps 104:21: "The young lions roar after their prey, and seek their meat from God." (3) Okel is used for "food" given by God in Ps 145:15. (4) The word may also be used for "food" as an offering, as in Mal 1:12. Syn.: 3899, 6720. See: TWOT—85a; BDB—38a.

401. אֻכָל {1x} ʾÛkâl, oo-kawl'; or

אֻכָּל ʾUkkâl, ook-kawl'; appar. from 398; devoured; Ucal, a fancy name:—Ucal {1x}. See: BDB—38b.

402. אָכְלָה {18x} ʾoklâh, *ok-law'*; fem. of 401;
food:—meat {8x}, devour {3x}, fuel
{3x}, eat {2x}, consume {1x}, food {1x}. See:
TWOT—85b; BDB—38a.

403. אָכֵן {18x} ʾâkên, *aw-kane'*; from 3559
[comp. 3651]; *firmly;* fig. *surely;* also
(advers.) *but:*—surely {9x}, but {3x}, verily {2x},
truly {2x}, certainly {1x}, nevertheless {1x}. See:
TWOT—86; BDB—38c.

404. אָכַף {1x} ʾâkaph, *aw-kaf';* a prim. root;
appar. mean. to *curve* (as with a
burden); to *urge:*—craveth {1x}. See: TWOT—
87; BDB—38c.

405. אֶכֶף {1x} ʾekeph, *eh'-kef;* from 404; a *load;*
by impl. a *stroke* (others *dignity*):—
hand {1x}. See: TWOT—87a; BDB—38d.

406. אִכָּר {7x} ʾikkâr, *ik-kawr';* from an unused root mean. to *dig;* a *farmer:*—
husbandman {5x}, plowman {2x}. See: TWOT—
88a; BDB—38d.

407. אַכְשָׁף {3x} ʾAkshâph, *ak-shawf';* from
3784; *fascination; Acshaph,* a place
in Pal.:—Achshaph {3x}. See: BDB—38d, 506d.

408. אַל {12x} ʾal, *al;* a neg. particle [akin to
3808]; *not* (the qualified negation, used
as a deprecative); once (Job 24:25) as a noun,
nothing:—never {2x}, nay {1x}, neither {1x}, no
{1x}, none {1x}, nor {1x}, not {1x}, nothing {1x},
rather than {1x}, whither {1x}, nothing worth
{1x}. See: TWOT—90; BDB—39a, 1080b.

409. אַל {3x} ʾal (Aram.), *al;* corresp. to 408:—
not 3. See: TWOT—2574; BDB—1080b.

410. אֵל {245x} ʾêl, *ale;* short. from 352; *strength;*
as adj. *mighty;* espec. the *Almighty*
(but used also of any *deity*):—God {213x}, god
{16x}, power {4x}, mighty {5x}, goodly {1x}, great
{1x}, idols {1x}, Immanuel + 6005 — {2x}, might
{1x}, strong {1x}. comp. names in "-el."

El (410) means "god." **(1)** This term was the
most common general designation of deity in
the ancient Near East. **(2)** While it frequently
occurred alone, *el* was also combined with other
words to constitute a compound term for deity,
or to identify the nature and functions of the
"god" in some manner. Thus the expression "God,
the God of Israel" (Gen 33:20) identified the
specific activities of Israel's God. **(3)** In the ancient world, knowledge of a person's name was
believed to give one power over that person. A
knowledge of the character and attributes of
pagan "gods" was thought to enable the worshipers to manipulate or influence the deities
in a more effective way than they could have if
the deity's name remained unknown. To that
extent, the vagueness of the term *el* frustrated
persons who hoped to obtain some sort of power
over the deity, since the name gave little or no

indication of the god's character. This was particularly true for *El*, the chief Canaanite god.
The ancient Semites stood in mortal dread of
the superior powers exercised by the gods and
attempted to propitiate them accordingly. They
commonly associated deity with the manifestation and use of enormous power. Perhaps this
is reflected in the curious Hebrew phrase, "the
power [ʾel] of my hand" (Gen 31:29; cf. Deut
28:32).

(4) Some Hebrew phrases in the Psalms associated *el* with impressive natural features,
such as the cedar trees of Lebanon (Ps 80:10)
or mountains (Ps 36:6). In these instances, *el*
conveys a clear impression of grandeur or majesty. **(5)** Names with *el* as one of their components were common in the Near East in the
second millennium B.C. The names Methusael
(Gen 4:18) and Ishmael (Gen 16:11) come from
a very early period. **(6)** In the Mosaic period, *el*
was synonymous with the LORD who delivered
the Israelites from bondage in Egypt and made
them victorious in battle (Num 24:8). **(7)** This
tradition of the Hebrew *el* as a "God" who revealed Himself in power and entered into a covenant relationship with His people was prominent
in both poetry (Ps 7:11; 85:8) and prophecy (Is
43:12; 46:9). **(8)** The name of *el* was commonly
used by the Israelites to denote supernatural
provision or power. This was both normal and
legitimate, since the covenant between "God"
and Israel assured an obedient and holy people
that the creative forces of the universe would
sustain and protect at all times. Equally, if they
became disobedient and apostate, these same
forces would punish them severely. Syn.: 410
+ 7706, 426, 430, 433, 3069. See: TWOT—93a;
BDB—41d, 42b, 769b.

אֵל שַׁדָּי *El shadday* (410, 7706) means "God
Almighty." **(1)** This combination of *el* with a
qualifying term represents a religious tradition
among the Israelites that was probably in existence by the third millennium B.C. **(2)** A few
centuries later, *shadday* appeared in Hebrew
personal names such as Zurishaddai (Num 1:6)
and Ammishaddai (Num 1:12). **(3)** The earliest
Old Testament appearance of the appellation
as a title of deity ("God Almighty") is in Gen
17:1, where "God" identifies Himself in this
way to Abraham. Unfortunately, the name is
not explained in any manner; and even the directions "walk before me, and be thou perfect"
throw no light on the meaning of *shadday.*

(4) Scholars have attempted to understand the
word relating it to the Akkadian *shadu* ("mountain"), as though "God" had either revealed His
mighty power in association with mountain phenomena such as volcanic eruptions or that He
was regarded as strong and immutable, like the
"everlasting hills" of the blessing of Jacob (Gen

49:26). **(5)** Certainly the associating of deity with mountains was an important part of Mesopotamian religion. The "gods" were believed to favor mountaintop dwellings, and the Sumerians constructed their staged temple-towers or ziggurats as artificial mountains for worship. It was customary to erect a small shrine on the uppermost stage of the ziggurat so that the patron deity could descend from heaven and inhabit the temple. The Hebrews began their own tradition of mountain revelation just after the Exodus, but by this time the name *el shadday* had been replaced by the tetragrammaton of Yahweh (Ex 3:15, 6:3). **(6)** *El shadday* served as the patriarchs' covenant name for "God," and continued as such until the time of Moses, when a further revelation took place (Ex 6:3). **(7)** The Abrahamic covenant was marked by a degree of closeness between "God" and the human participants that was distinctive in Hebrew history. **(8)** "God Almighty" revealed Himself as a powerful deity who was able to perform whatever He asserted. But the degree of intimacy between *el shadday* and the patriarchs at various stages shows that the covenant involved God's care and love for this growing family that He had chosen, protected, and prospered. He led the covenant family from place to place, being obviously present with them at all times. His covenant formulations show that He was not preoccupied with cultic rites or orgiastic celebrations. Instead, He demanded a degree of obedience that would enable Abraham and his descendants to walk in His presence, and live blameless moral and spiritual lives (Gen 17:1). **(9)** The true covenantal service of *el shadday*, therefore, was not cultic or ritualistic, but moral and ethical in character. **(10)** In the early Mosaic era, the new redemptive name of "God" and the formulation of the Sinai covenant made *el shadday* largely obsolete as a designation of deity. Subsequently, the name occurs about 35 times in the Old Testament, most of which are in the Book of Job. **(11)** Occasionally, the name is used synonymously with the tetragrammaton of Yahweh (Ruth 1:21; Ps 91:1–2), to emphasize the power and might of "God" in characteristic fashion.

עֹלָם אֵל **El olam** (410, 5769) means "God of eternity; God the everlasting; God for ever." **(1)** The word *olam* has related forms in various ancient Near Eastern languages, all of which describe lengthy duration or distant time. The idea seems to be quantitative rather than metaphysical, expressing a period of time that could not be measured other than as lengthy duration. **(2)** Only in rare poetic passages such as Ps 90:2 are temporal categories regarded inadequate to describe the nature of God's existence as *el olam*. In such an instance, the Creator is deemed

to have been "from everlasting to everlasting"; but even this use of *olam* expresses the idea of continued, measurable existence rather than a state of being independent of temporal considerations.

(3) The name *el olam* was associated predominantly with Beer-sheba (Gen 21:25–34). The settlement of Beer-sheba means "well of the oath" (Gen 21:31). But it could also mean "well of the seven"—i.e., the seven lambs that were set apart as witnesses of the oath. Abraham planted a commemorative tree in Beer-sheba and invoked the name of the Lord as *el olam*. The fact that Abraham subsequently stayed many days in the land of the Philistines seems to imply that he associated continuity and stability with *el olam*, who was not touched by the vicissitudes of time. Although Beer-sheba may have been a place where the Canaanites worshiped originally, the area later became associated with the veneration of the God of Abraham. **(4)** At a subsequent period, Jacob journeyed to Beer-sheba and offered sacrifices to the God of Isaac his father. He did not offer sacrifices to *el olam* by name, however; and although he saw a visionary manifestation of God, he received no revelation that this was the God Abraham had venerated at Beer-sheba. Indeed, God omitted any mention of Abraham, stating that He was the God of Jacob's father. **(5)** Gen 21:33 is the only place in the Old Testament where the title *el olam* occurs. Is 40:28 is the only other instance where *olam* is used in conjunction with a noun meaning God.

411. אֵל {9x} ʾêl, *ale;* a demonstr. particle (but only in a plur. sense) *these* or *those:*— these {7x}, those {2x}. See: TWOT—92; BDB—41b.

412. אֵל {1x} ʾêl (Aram.), *ale;* corresp. to 411:— these {1x}. See: TWOT—2575; BDB—1080b.

413. אֵל {38x} ʾêl, *ale;* (but only used in the short. constr. form אֶל ʾel, *el*); a prim. particle; prop. denoting motion *towards*, but occasionally used of a quiescent position, i.e. *near, with* or *among;* often in general, *to:*—unto, with, against, at, into, in, before, to, of, upon, by, toward, hath, for, on, beside, from, where, after, within = {38x}. See: TWOT—91; BDB—39b.

414. אֵלָא {1x} ʾÊlâʾ, *ay-law';* a var. of 424; *oak; Ela*, an Isr.:—Elah {1x}. See: BDB—41d.

415. אֵל אֱלֹהֵי יִשְׂרָאֵל {1x} ʾÊl ʾĕlôhêy Yisrâʾêl, *ale el-o-hay' yis-raw-ale';* from 410, 430 and 3478; the *mighty God of Jisrael; El-Elohi-Jisrael*, the title given to a consecrated spot by Jacob:—El-elohe-israel {1x}. See: BDB—42d.

416. אֵל בֵּית־אֵל {1x} ʾÊl Bêyth-ʾÊl, *ale bayth-ale';* from 410 and 1008; the *God of Bethel; El-Bethel,* the title given to a consecrated spot by Jacob:—El-beth-el {1x}. See: BDB—42c.

417. אֶלְגָּבִישׁ {3x} ʾelgâbîysh, *el-gaw-beesh';* from 410 and 1378; *hail* (as if a *great pearl*):—hailstone + 68 {3x}. See: TWOT—89a; BDB—38d.

418. אַלְגּוּמִּים {3x} ʾalgûwmmîym, *al-goom-meem';* by transp. for 484; *sticks of algum wood:*—algum {2x}, algum tree {1x}. See: TWOT—89b; BDB—38d.

419. אֶלְדָּד {2x} ʾEldâd, *el-dâd';* from 410 and 1730; *God has loved; Eldad,* an Isr.:—Eldad {2x}. See: BDB—44d.

420. אֶלְדָּעָה {2x} ʾEldâʿâh, *el-daw-aw';* from 410 and 3045; *God of knowledge; Eldaah,* a son of Midian:—Eldaah {2x}. See: BDB—44d.

421. אָלָה {1x} ʾâlâh, *aw-law';* a prim. root [rather ident. with 422 through the idea of *invocation*]; to *bewail:*—lament {1x}. See: TWOT—95; BDB—46d, 1080c.

422. אָלָה {6x} ʾâlâh, *aw-law';* a prim. root; prop. to *adjure,* i.e. (usually in a bad sense) *imprecate:*—swear {4x}, curse {1x}, adjure {1x}. See: TWOT—94; BDB—46c, 1060d.

423. אָלָה {36x} ʾâlâh, *aw-law';* from 422; an *imprecation:*—curse {18x}, oath {14x}, execration {2x}, swearing {2x}.
Alah means "curse; oath." **(1)** In distinction from *arar* (779) ["to curse by laying an anathema on someone or something") and *qalal* (7043) ["to curse by abusing or by belittling"], *alah* basically refers to "the execution of a proper oath to legalize a covenant or agreement." **(2)** As a noun, *alah* refers to the "oath" itself: "Then shalt thou be clear from this my oath, when thou comest to my kindred; and if they give not thee one, thou shalt be clear from my oath" (Gen 24:41—the first occurrence). **(3)** The "oath" was a "curse" on the head of the one who broke the agreement. **(4)** This same sense appears in Lev 5:1, referring to a general "curse" against anyone who would give false testimony in a court case. **(5)** So *alah* functions as a "curse" sanctioning a pledge or commission, and it can close an agreement or covenant. **(6)** On the other hand, the word sometimes represents a "curse" against someone else, whether his identity is known or not. Syn.: *Arar* (779 - {63x}) - to curse by laying an anathema on someone or something; *qalal* (7043 - {83x}) and 7045 - {33x}) to curse by abusing or by belittling. See: TWOT—91a; BDB—46d.

424. אֵלָה {13x} ʾêlâh, *ay-law';* fem. of 352; an *oak* or other strong tree:—oak {11x}, elm {1x}, teil tree {1x}. See: TWOT—45h; BDB—18c.

425. אֵלָה {16x} ʾÊlâh, *ay-law';* the same as 424; *Elah,* the name of an Edomite, of four Isr., and also of a place in Pal.:—Elah {16x}. See: BDB—18d.

426. אֱלָהּ {95x} ʾĕlâhh (Aram.), *el-aw';* corresp. to 433; *God:*—God {79x}, god {16x}.
Elahh means "god." **(1)** This Aramaic word is the equivalent of the Hebrew *eloahh* (433). It is a general term for "God" in the Aramaic passages of the Old Testament, and it is a cognate form of the word *allah,* the designation of deity used by the Arabs. The word was used widely in the Book of Ezra, occurring no fewer than 43 times between Ezra 4:24 and 7:26. On each occasion, the reference is to the "God" of the Jewish people, whether the speaker or writer was himself Jewish or not. Thus the governor of the province "Beyond the River" (i.e., west of the river Euphrates) spoke to King Darius of the "house of the great God" (Ezra 5:8). So also Cyrus instructed Sheshbazzar, the governor, that the "house of God be builded" in Jerusalem (Ezra 5:15). **(2)** While the Persians were certainly not worshipers of the "God" of Israel, they accorded Him the dignity that befitted a "God of heaven" (Ezra 6:10). This was done partly through superstition; but the pluralistic nature of the newly-won Persian empire also required them to honor the gods of conquered peoples, in the interests of peace and social harmony.
(3) When Ezra himself used the word *elahh,* he frequently specified the God of the Jews. Thus he spoke of the "God of Israel" (5:1; 6:14), the "God of heaven" (5:12; 6:9) and "God of Jerusalem" (7:19); he also associated "God" with His house in Jerusalem (5:17; 6:3). **(4)** In the decree of Artaxerxes, Ezra was described as "the priest, the scribe of the God of heaven" (7:12, 21). This designation would have sounded strange coming from a pagan Persian ruler, had it not been for the policy of religious toleration exercised by the Achaemenid regime. **(5)** Elsewhere in Ezra, *elahh* is associated with the temple, both when it was about to be rebuilt (5:2, 13) and as a finished edifice, consecrated for divine worship (6:16). **(6)** In the only verse in the Book of Jeremiah that was written in Aramaic (10:11), the word *elahh* appears in plural form to describe "gods" that had not participated in the creation of the universe. Although such false "gods" were being worshiped by pagan nations (and perhaps worshiped by some of the Hebrews who were in exile in Babylo-

nia), these deities would ultimately perish because they were not eternal in nature.

(7) In the Book of Daniel, *elahh* was used both of heathen "gods" and the one true "God" of heaven. **(7a)** The Chaldean priests told Nebuchadnezzar: "And it is a rare thing that the king requireth, and there is none other that can show it before the king, except the gods, whose dwelling is not with flesh" (Dan 2:11). The Chaldeans referred to such "gods" when reporting that Shadrach, Meshach, and Abednego refused to participate in idol worship on the plain of Dura (Dan 3:12). The "gods" were enumerated by Daniel when he condemned Nebuchadnezzar's neglect of the worship of Israel's one true "God" (Dan 5:23). In Dan 3:25, the word refers to a divine being or messenger sent to protect the three Hebrews (Dan 3:28). In Dan 4:8–9, 18; and 5:11, the phrase "the spirit of the holy gods" appears. **(7b)** Elsewhere the references to *elahh* are to the living "God" whom Daniel worshiped. Syn.: 410 + 7706, 426, 430, 433, 3069. See: TWOT—2576; n.m. BDB—1080c.

427. אַלָּה {1x} ʾallâh, al-law'; a var. of 424:— oak {1x}. See: TWOT—100a; BDB—47c.

428. אֵלֶּה {20x} ʾêl-leh, ale'-leh; prol. from 411; *these* or *those*:—these, those, this, thus, who, so, such, some, same, other, which, another, whom, they, them = {20x}. See: TWOT—92; BDB—41c, 1080d.

429. אֵלֶּה {1x} ʾêlleh (Aram.), ale'-leh; corresp. to 428:—these {1x}. See: TWOT—2577; BDB—1080c.

אֱלֹהַּ ʾĕlôahh. See 433.

430. אֱלֹהִים {2606x} ʾĕlôhîym, el-o-heem'; plur. of 433; *gods* in the ordinary sense; but spec. used (in the plur. thus, espec. with the art.) of the supreme *God;* occasionally applied by way of deference to *magistrates;* and sometimes as a superlative:—God {2346x}, god {244x}, judge {5x}, GOD {1x}, goddess {2x}, great {2x}, mighty {2x}, angels {1x}, exceeding {1x}, Godward + 4136 –{1x}, godly {1x}.

Plural in number refers to **(1)** rulers, judges, either as divine, representatives at sacred places or as reflecting divine majesty and power; **(2)** divine, ones, superhuman beings including God and angels; **(3)** angels; cf. the sons of God, or sons of gods = angels; **(4)** gods, goddess. Syn.: See 410. See: TWOT—93c; BDB—43b, 218d, 238a.

431. אֲלוּ {5x} ʾălûw (Aram.), al-oo'; prob. prol. from 412; *lo!:*—behold {5x}. See: TWOT—2578; BDB—1080d, 1082d.

432. אִלּוּ {2x} ʾillûw, il-loo'; prob. from 408; *nay,* i.e. (softened) *if:*—but if {1x}, yea though {1x}. See: TWOT—96; BDB—47a.

433. אֱלוֹהַּ {57x} ʾĕlôwahh, el-o'-ah; rarely (short.)

אֱלֹהַּ ʾĕlôahh, el-o'-ah; prob. prol. (emphat.) from 410; a *deity* or the *Deity:*—God {52x}, god {5x}.

Eloahh (433) means "god." **(1)** This Hebrew name for "God" corresponds to the Aramaic *elahh* (426). The origin of the term is unknown, and it is used rarely in Scripture as a designation of deity. **(2)** *Eloahh* occurs 40 times in the Book of Job between 3:4 and 40:2, while in the remainder of the Old Testament it is used no more than 15 times. **(3)** Certain scholars regard the word as being a singular version of the common plural form *elohim* (430), a plural of majesty. **(4)** *Eloahh* is commonly thought to be vocative in nature, meaning "O God." But it is not clear why a special form for the vocative in an address to God should be needed, since the plural *elohim* is frequently translated as a vocative when the worshiper is speaking directly to God, as in Ps 79:1. There is an obvious general linguistic relationship between *eloahh* and *elohim,* but determining its precise nature is difficult.

(5) The word *eloahh* is predominant in poetry rather than prose literature, and this is especially true of the Book of Job. Some scholars have suggested that the author of Job deliberately chose a description for godhead that avoided the historical associations found in a phrase such as "the God of Bethel" (Gen 31:13) or "God of Israel" (Ex 24:10). But even the Book of Job is by no means historically neutral, since places and peoples are mentioned in introducing the narrative (cf. Job 1:1, 15, 17). Perhaps the author considered *eloahh* a suitable term for poetry and used it accordingly with consistency. **(6)** This is also apparently the case in Ps 18:31, where *eloahh* is found instead of el, as in the parallel passage of 2 Sa 22:32. *Eloahh* also appears as a term for God in Ps 50:22; 139:19; and Prov 30:5. **(7)** Although *eloahh* as a divine name is rarely used outside Job, its literary history extends from at least the second millennium B.C. (as in Deut 32:15) to the fifth century B.C. (as in Neh 9:17). Syn.: See 430. See: TWOT—93b; BDB—43a, 1080c.

434. אֱלִיל {1x} ʾĕlûwl, el-ool'; for 457; good for *nothing:*—thing of nought {1x}. See: TWOT—99a; BDB—47b.

435. אֱלוּל {1x} ʾĔlûwl, el-ool'; prob. of for. der.; *Elul,* the sixth Jewish month:—Elul {1x}. See: TWOT—97; BDB—47a.

436. אֵלוֹן {9x} ʾêlôwn, ay-lone'; prol. from 352; an *oak* or other strong tree:—plain {9x}.

This word means "large tree," usually an isolated tree in relation to places of worship. It may well be that these were all ancient cultic sites.

The word does not represent a particular genus or species of tree but, like the noun to which it is related, simply a "big tree": "Gaal spoke again and said, Look, men are coming down from the center of the land, and one company is coming from the direction of the Meonenim ["diviner's oak"]" (Judg 9:37). Judg 9:6 speaks of the "plain of the pillar" in Shechem where the men of Shechem and Beth-millo made Abimelech king. Syn.: See 356. See: TWOT—45i; BDB—18d.

437. אַלּוֹן {8x} ʾallôwn, al-lone'; a var. of 436:— oak {1x}. See: TWOT—100b; BDB—47c.

438. אַלּוֹן {2x} ʾAllôwn, al-lone'; the same as 437; Allon, an Isr., also a place in Pal.:—Allon {2x}. See: BDB—47d.

439. אַלּוֹן בָּכוּת {1x} ʾAllôwn Bâkûwth, al-lone' baw-kooth'; from 437 and a var. of 1068; oak of weeping; Allon-Bakuth, a monumental tree:—Allon-bachuth {1x}. See: BDB—18d, 47c, 113d.

440. אֵלוֹנִי {1x} ʾÊlôwnîy, ay-lo-nee'; or rather (short.)

אֵלֹנִי ʾÊlônîy, ay-lo-nee'; patron. from 438; an Elonite or desc. (collect.) of Elon:—Elonites {1x}. See: BDB—19a.

441. אַלּוּף {69x} ʾallûwph, al-loof'; or (short.)

אַלֻּף ʾallûph, al-loof'; from 502; familiar; a friend, also gentle; hence, a bullock (as being tame; applied, although masc., to a cow); and so, a chieftain (as notable, like neat cattle):—duke {57x}, guide {4x}, friends {2x}, governors {2x}, captains {1x}, governor {1x}, ox {2x}. See: TWOT—109b; BDB—48d, 49b.

442. אָלוּשׁ {2x} ʾÂlûwsh, aw-loosh'; of uncert. der.; Alush, a place in the desert:—Alush {2x}. See: BDB—47a.

443. אֶלְזָבָד {2x} ʾElzâbâd, el-zaw-bawd'; from 410 and 2064; God has bestowed; Elzabad, the name of two Isr.:—Elzabad {1x}. See: BDB—44d.

444. אָלַח {3x} ʾâlach, aw-lakh'; a prim. root; to muddle, i.e. (fig. and intr.) to turn (morally) corrupt:—become filthy {3x}. See: TWOT—98; BDB—47a.

445. אֶלְחָנָן {4x} ʾElchânân, el-khaw-nawn'; from 410 and 2603; God (is) gracious; Elchanan, an Isr.:—Elkanan {4x}. See: BDB—44d.

אֵלִי ʾÊlîy. See 1017.

446. אֱלִיאָב {21x} ʾÊlîyʾâb, el-ee-awb'; from 410 and 1; God of (his) father; Eliab, the name of six Isr.:—Eliab {21x}. See: BDB—45a.

447. אֱלִיאֵל {10x} ʾÊlîyʾêl, el-ee-ale'; from 410 repeated; God of (his) God; Eliel, the name of nine Isr.:—Eliel {10x}. See: BDB—45a.

448. אֱלִיאָתָה {2x} ʾÊlîyʾâthâh, el-ee-aw-thaw'; or (contr.)

אֱלִיָתָה ʾÊlîyâthâh, el-ee-yaw-thaw'; from 410 and 225; God of (his) consent; Eliathah, an Isr.:—Eliathah {2x}. See: BDB—45a, 46a.

449. אֱלִידָד {1x} ʾÊlîydâd, el-ee-dawd'; from the same as 419; God of (his) love; Elidad, an Isr.:—Elidad {1x}. See: BDB—44d, 45a.

450. אֶלְיָדָע {4x} ʾElyâdâʿ, el-yaw-daw'; from 410 and 3045; God (is) knowing; Eljada, the name of two Isr. and of an Aramaean leader:—Eliada {3x}, Eliadah {1x}. See: BDB—45a.

451. אַלְיָה {5x} ʾalyâh, al-yaw'; from 422 (in the orig. sense of strength); the stout part, i.e. the fat tail of the Oriental sheep:—rump {5x}. See: TWOT—95a; BDB—46d.

452. אֵלִיָּה {71x} ʾÊlîyâh, ay-lee-yaw'; or prol.

אֵלִיָּהוּ ʾÊlîyâhûw, ay-lee-yaw'-hoo; from 410 and 3050; God of Jehovah; Elijah, the name of the famous prophet and of two other Isr.:—Elijah {69x}, Eliah {2x}. See: BDB—45b.

453. אֱלִיהוּ {11x} ʾÊlîyhûw, el-ee-hoo'; or (fully)

אֱלִיהוּא ʾÊlîyhûwʾ, el-ee-hoo'; from 410 and 1931; God of him; Elihu, the name of one of Job's friends, and of three Isr.:—Elihu {11x}. See: BDB—45b.

454. אֶלְיְהוֹעֵינַי {9x} ʾElyᵉhôwʿêynay, el-ye-ho-ay-nah'ee; or (short.)

אֶלְיוֹעֵינַי ʾElyôwʿêynay, el-yo-ay-nah'ee; from 413 and 3068 and 5869; toward Jehovah (are) my eyes; Eljehoenai or Eljoenai, the name of seven Isr.:—Elihoenai {1x}, Elionai {8x}. See: BDB—41b.

455. אֱלִיַחְבָּא {2x} ʾElyachbâʾ, el-yakh-baw'; from 410 and 2244; God will hide; Eljachba, an Isr.:—Eliahbah {2x}. See: BDB—45b.

456. אֱלִיחֹרֶף {1x} ʾÊlîychôreph, el-ee-kho'-ref; from 410 and 2779; God of autumn; Elichoreph, an Isr.:—Elihoreph {1x}. See: BDB—45b.

457. אֱלִיל {20x} ʾĕlîyl, el-eel'; appar. from 408; good for nothing, by anal. vain or vanity; spec. an idol:—- idol {17x}, image {1x}, no value {1x}, things of nought {1x}.

Eliyl means "idol; gods; nought; vain." (1)

This disdainful word signifies an "idol" or "false god." **(2)** *Eliyl* first appears in Lev 19:4: "Turn ye not unto idols, nor make to yourselves molten gods." **(3)** In Lev 26:1 the *elilim* are what Israel is forbidden to make: "Ye shall make you no idols." The irony of this is biting not only with respect to the usual meaning of this word but also in view of its similarity to the usual word for God (*elohim;* cf. Ps 96:5): "For all the gods [*elohim*] of the people are idols [*elilim*] . . ." (1 Chr 16:26). **(4)** This word can mean "nought" or "vain." 1 Chr 16:26 might well be rendered: "For all the gods of the people are nought." This nuance appears clearly in Job 13:4: "But ye are forgers of lies; ye are all physicians of no value [physicians of vanity]." Jeremiah told Israel that their prophets were "prophesy [ing] unto you a false vision and divination, and a thing of nought . . .".

Gillulim (1544), "idols." **(5)** Of the 48 occurrences of this word, all but 9 appear in Ezekiel. This word for "idols" is a disdainful word and may originally have meant "dung pellets": "And I will destroy your high places, and cut down your images, and cast your carcases upon the carcases of your idols, and my soul shall abhor you" (Lev 26:30). Syn: This word and others for "idol" exhibit the horror and scorn that biblical writers felt toward them. In passages such as Is 66:3 the word for "idol," *awen* (205), means "uncanny or wickedness." Jer 50:38 evidences the word *emim* (367), which means "fright or horror." The word *elil* appears for "idol" in Lev 19:4; it means "nothingness or feeble." 1 Kin 15:13 uses the Hebrew word, *mipletset* (4656), meaning a "horrible thing, a cause of trembling." A root signifying to make an image or to shape something, *tsb* (6091) [a homonym of the root meaning "sorrow and grief"] is used in several passages (cf. 1Sa 31:9). See: TWOT—99a; BDB—47b.

458. אֱלִימֶלֶךְ {6x} ʾĔlîymelek, *el-ee-meh'-lek;* from 410 and 4428; *God of* (the) *king; Elimelek,* an Isr.:—Elimelech {6x}. See: BDB—45b.

459. אִלֵּין {5x} ʾilêyn (Aram.), *il-lane';* or short.

אִלֵּן ʾillên, *il-lane';* prol. from 412; *these:—* these {4x}, the {1x}. See: TWOT—2579; BDB—1080c, 1080d, 1088d.

460. אֶלְיָסָף {6x} ʾElyâçâph, *el-yaw-sawf';* from 410 and 3254; *God* (is) *gatherer; Eljasaph,* the name of two Isr.:—Eliasaph {6x}. See: BDB—45b.

461. אֱלִיעֶזֶר {14x} ʾĔliyʿezer, *el-ee-eh'-zer;* from 410 and 5828; *God of help; Eliezer,* the name of a Damascene and of ten Isr.:—Eliezer {14x}. See: BDB—45c.

462. אֱלִיעֵינַי {1x} ʾĔliyʿêynay, *el-ee-ay-nah'ee;* prob. contr. for 454; *Elienai,* an Isr.:—Elienai {1x}. See: BDB—41b.

463. אֱלִיעָם {2x} ʾĔliyʿâm, *el-ee-awm';* from 410 and 5971; *God of* (the) *people; Eliam,* an Isr.:—Eliam {2x}. See: BDB—45c.

464. אֱלִיפַז {15x} ʾĔlîyphaz, *el-ee-faz';* from 410 and 6337; *God of gold; Eliphaz,* the name of one of Job's friends, and of a son of Esau:—Eliphaz {15x}. See: BDB—45c.

465. אֱלִיפָל {1x} ʾĔlîyphâl, *el-ee-fawl';* from 410 and 6419; *God of judgment; Eliphal,* an Isr.:—Eliphal {1x}. See: BDB—45c.

466. אֱלִיפְלֵהוּ {2x} ʾĔlîyphʿlêhûw, *el-ee-fe-lay'-hoo;* from 410 and 6395; *God of his distinction; Eliphelehu,* an Isr.:—Elipheleh {2x}. See: BDB—45c.

467. אֱלִיפֶלֶט {9x} ʾĔlîyphelet, *el-ee-feh'-let;* or (short.)

אֶלְפֶּלֶט ʾĔlpelet, *el-peh'-let;* from 410 and 6405; *God of deliverance; Eliphelet* or *Elpelet,* the name of six Isr.:—Eliphalet {2x}, Eliphelet {6x}, Elpalet {1x}. See: BDB—45c, 46c.

468. אֱלִיצוּר {5x} ʾĔlîytsûwr, *el-ee-tsoor';* from 410 and 6697; *God of* (the) *rock; Elitsur,* an Isr.:—Elizur {5x}. See: BDB—45d.

469. אֱלִיצָפָן {6x} ʾĔlîytsâphân, *el-ee-tsaw-fawn';* or (short.)

אֶלְצָפָן ʾĔltsâphân, *el-tsaw-fawn';* from 410 and 6845; *God of treasure; Elitsaphan* or *Eltsaphan,* an Isr.:—Elizaphan {4x}, Elzaphan {2x}. See: BDB—45d, 46c.

470. אֱלִיקָא {1x} ʾĔlîyqâʾ, *el-ee-kaw';* from 410 and 6958; *God of rejection; Elika,* an Isr.:—Elika {1x}. See: BDB—45d.

471. אֱלְיָקִים {12x} ʾElyâqîym, *el-yaw-keem';* from 410 and 6965; *God of raising; Eljakim,* the name of four Isr.:—Eliakim {12x}. See: BDB—45d.

472. אֱלִישֶׁבַע {1x} ʾĔlîysheba‘, *el-ee-sheh'-bah;* from 410 and 7651 (in the sense of 7650); *God of* (the) *oath; Elisheba,* the wife of Aaron:—Elisheba {1x}. See: BDB—45d, 989d.

473. אֱלִישָׁה {3x} ʾĔlîyshâh, *el-ee-shaw';* prob. of for. der.; *Elishah,* a son of Javan:—Elishah {3x}. See: BDB—47a.

474. אֱלִישׁוּעַ {2x} ʾĔlîyshûwa‘, *el-ee-shoo'-ah;* from 410 and 7769; *God of supplication* (or *of riches*); *Elishua,* a son of King David:—Elishua {2x}. See: BDB—46a.

475. אֱלִישִׁיב {17x} ʾElyâshîyb, *el-yaw-sheeb';* from 410 and 7725; *God will*

restore; Eljashib, the name of six Isr.:—Eliashib {17x}. See: BDB—46a.

476. אֱלִישָׁמָע {17x} **ᵓĔlîyshâmâᶜ**, *el-ee-shaw-maw';* from 410 and 8085; *God of hearing; Elishama,* the name of seven Isr.:—Elishama {17x}. See: BDB—46a.

477. אֱלִישָׁע {58x} **ᵓĔlîyshâᶜ**, *el-ee-shaw';* contr. for 474; *Elisha,* the famous prophet:—Elisha {58x}. See: 46a.

478. אֱלִישָׁפָט {1x} **ᵓĔlîyshâphât**, *el-ee-shaw-fawt';* from 410 and 8199; *God of judgment; Elishaphat,* an Isr.:—Elishaphat {1x}. See: BDB—46a.

479. אִלֵּךְ {14x} **ᵓillêk** (Aram.), *il-lake';* prol. from 412; *these:*—these {10x}, those {4x}. See: TWOT—2580; BDB—1080d, 1088c.

480. אַלְלַי {2x} **ᵓalᶜlay**, *al-le-lah'ee;* by redupl. from 421; *alas!:*—woe {2x}. See: TWOT—101; BDB—47d.

481. אָלַם {9x} **ᵓâlam**, *aw-lam';* a prim. root; to *tie* fast; hence, (of the mouth) to be *tongue-tied:*—dumb {7x}, put to silence {1x}, binding {1x}. See: TWOT—102; BDB—47d.

482. אֵלֶם {1x} **ᵓêlem**, *ay'-lem;* from 481; *silence* (i.e. mute justice):—congregation {1x}.

In Ps 58:1 this word signifies either to bind into a sheaf or to be bound/dumb; a very suitable symbol of a congregation. Syn.: comp. 3128. See: TWOT—102b; BDB—48a.

אֵלָם **ᵓêlâm**. See 361.

אָלֻם **ᵓâlum**. See 485.

483. אִלֵּם {6x} **ᵓillêm**, *il-lame';* from 481; *speechless:*—dumb (man) {6x}. See: TWOT—102c; BDB—48a.

484. אַלְמֻגִּים {3x} **ᵓalmuggiym**, *al-moog-gheem';* prob. of for. der. (used thus only in the plur.); *almug* (i.e. prob. sandal-wood) sticks:—almug trees {3x}. Syn.: comp. 418. See: TWOT—89c; BDB—38d.

485. אַלֻּמָּה {5x} **ᵓălummâh**, *al-oom-maw';* or (masc.)

אָלֻם **ᵓâlum**, *aw-loom';* pass. part. of 481; something *bound;* a *sheaf:*—sheaf {5x}. See: TWOT—102a; BDB—48a.

486. אַלְמוֹדָד {2x} **ᵓAlmôwdâd**, *al-mo-dawd';* prob. of for. der.; *Almodad,* a son of Joktan:—Almodad {2x}. See: BDB—38d, 46b.

487. אַלַּמֶּלֶךְ {1x} **ᵓAllammelek**, *al-lam-meh'-lek;* from 427 and 4428; *oak of* (the) *king; Allammelek,* a place in Pal.:—Alammelech {1x}. See: BDB—47d.

488. אַלְמָן {1x} **ᵓalmân**, *al-mawn';* prol. from 481 in the sense of *bereavement; discarded* (as a divorced person):—forsaken {1x}. See: TWOT—103; BDB—48a.

489. אַלְמֹן {1x} **ᵓalmôn**, *al-mone';* from 481 as in 488; *bereavement:*—widowhood {1x}. See: TWOT—104; BDB—48a.

490. אַלְמָנָה {55x} **ᵓalmânâh**, *al-maw-naw';* fem. of 488; a *widow;* also a *desolate* place:—widow {53x}, desolate house {1x}, desolate palace {1x}.

Almanah means "widow." **(1)** The word represents a woman who, because of the death of her husband, has lost her social and economic position. The gravity of her situation was increased if she had no children. In such a circumstance she returned to her father's home and was subjected to the Levirate rule whereby a close male relative surviving her husband was to produce a child through her in her husband's behalf: "Then said Judah to Tamar his daughter-in-law, Remain a widow at thy father's house, till Shelah my son be grown" (Gen 38:11 the first occurrence of the word). These words constitute a promise to Tamar that the disgrace of being without both husband and child would be removed when Shelah was old enough to marry.

(2) Even if children had been born before her husband's death, a widow's lot was not a happy one (2 Sa 14:5). **(3)** Israel was admonished to treat "widows" and other socially disadvantaged people with justice, God Himself standing as their protector (Ex 22:21–24). **(4)** Wives whose husbands shut them away from themselves are sometimes called "widows": "And David came to his house at Jerusalem; and the king took the ten women his concubines, whom he had left to keep the house, and put them in ward, and fed them, but went not in unto them. So they were shut up unto the day of their death, living in widowhood" (2 Sa 20:3). **(5)** Destroyed, plundered Jerusalem is called a "widow" (Lam 1:1). Syn.: See also 489, 491. See: TWOT—105; BDB—48a.

491. אַלְמָנוּת {4x} **ᵓalmânûwth**, *al-maw-nooth';* fem. of 488; concr. a *widow;* abstr. *widowhood:*—widow {1x}, widowhood {3x}. See: TWOT—106; BDB—48b.

492. אַלְמֹנִי {3x} **ᵓalmôniy**, *al-mo-nee';* from 489 in the sense of *concealment; some* one (i.e. *so and so,* without giving the name of the person or place):—and such {2x}, a one {1x}. See: TWOT—107; BDB—48c.

493. אֶלְנַעַם {1x} **ᵓElnaᶜam**, *el-nah'-am;* from 410 and 5276; *God* (is his) *delight; Elnaam,* an Isr.:—Elnaam {1x}. See: BDB—46b.

Hebrew

494. אֶלְנָתָן {7x} ʾElnâthân, el-naw-thawn'; from 410 and 5414; God (is the) giver; Elnathan, the name of four Isr.:—Elnathan {7x}. See: BDB—46b.

495. אֶלָּסָר {2x} ʾEllâçâr, el-law-sawr'; prob. of for. der.; Ellasar, an early country of Asia:—Ellasar {2x}. See: BDB—48c.

496. אֶלְעָד {1x} ʾElʿâd, el-awd'; from 410 and 5749; God has testified; Elad, an Isr.:—Elead {1x}. See: BDB—46b.

497. אֶלְעָדָה {1x} ʾElʿâdâh, el-aw-daw'; from 410 and 5710; God has decked; Eladah, an Isr.:—Eladah {1x}. See: BDB—46b.

498. אֶלְעוּזַי {1x} ʾElʿûwzay, el-oo-zah'ee; from 410 and 5756 (in the sense of 5797); God (is) defensive; Eluzai, an Isr.:—Eluzai {1x}. See: BDB—46b.

499. אֶלְעָזָר {72x} ʾElʿâzâr, el-aw-zawr'; from 410 and 5826; God (is) helper; Elazar, the name of seven Isr.:—Eleazar {72x}. See: BDB—46b.

500. אֶלְעָלָא {5x} ʾElʿâlê, el-aw-lay'; or (more prop.)

אֶלְעָלֵה ʾElʿâlêh, el-aw-lay'; from 410 and 5927; God (is) going up; Elale or Elaleh, a place east of the Jordan:—Elealeh {5x}. See: BDB—46c.

501. אֶלְעָשָׂה {6x} ʾElʿâsâh, el-aw-saw'; from 410 and 6213; God has made; El-asah, the name of four Isr.:—Elasah {2x}, Eleasah {4x}. See: BDB—46c.

502. אָלַף {4x} ʾâlaph, aw-laf'; a prim. root, to associate with; hence, to learn (and caus. to teach):—teach {2x}, learn {1x}, utter {1x}. See: TWOT—108; BDB—48c.

503. אָלַף {1x} ʾâlaph, aw-laf'; denom. from 505; caus. to make a thousand-fold:—bring forth thousands {1x}. See: TWOT—109; BDB—48d.

504. אֶלֶף {8x} ʾeleph, eh'-lef; from 502; a family; also (from the sense of yoking or taming) an ox or cow:—kine {4x}, oxen {3x}, family {1x}.

Cattle signifies **(1)** the domesticated animal or the herd animal: oxen, sheep, goats, cows (Deut 7:13); **(2)** thousand (Gen 20:16); **(3)** group (Num 1:16); **(4)** leaders of a large group (Gen 36:15). Syn.: 1241, 6510. See: TWOT—108a; BDB—48c.

505. אֶלֶף {505x} ʾeleph, eh'-lef; prop. the same as 504; hence, (the ox's head being the first letter of the alphabet, and this eventually used as a numeral) a thousand:—thousand {500x}, eleven hundred + 3967 {3x}, variant {1x}, twelve hundred + 3967 {1x}. See: TWOT—109a; BDB—48d, 1081a.

506. אֲלַף {4x} ʾălaph (Aram.), al-af'; or

אֱלֶף ʾeleph (Aram.), eh'-lef; corresp. to 505:—thousand {4x}. See: TWOT—2581; BDB—1081a.

507. אֶלֶף {1x} ʾEleph, eh'-lef; the same as 505; Eleph, a place in Pal.:—Eleph {1x}. See: BDB—49b.

508. אֶלְפַּעַל {3x} ʾElpaʿal, el-pah'-al; from 410 and 6466; God (is) act; El-paal, an Isr.:—Elpaal {3x}. See: BDB—46c.

509. אָלַץ {1x} ʾâlats, aw-lats'; a prim. root; to press:—urge {1x}. See: TWOT—110; BDB—49b.

אֶלְצָפָן ʾEltsâphân. See 469.

510. אַלְקוּם {1x} ʾalqûwm, al-koom'; prob. from 408 and 6965; a non-rising (i.e. resistlessness):—rising up {1x}. See: TWOT—90; BDB—39a, 49b, 879c.

511. אֶלְקָנָה {21x} ʾElqânâh, el-kaw-naw'; from 410 and 7069; God has obtained; Elkanah, the name of several Isr.:—Elkanah {21x}. See: BDB—46c.

512. אֶלְקֹשִׁי {1x} ʾElqôshîy, el-ko-shee'; patrial from a name of uncert. der.; an El-koshite or native of Elkosh:—Elkoshite {1x}. See: BDB—49b.

513. אֶלְתּוֹלַד {2x} ʾEltôwlad, el-to-lad'; prob. from 410 and a masc. form of 8435 [comp. 8434]; God (is) generator; Eltolad, a place in Pal.:—Eltolad {2x} See: BDB—39a.

514. אֶלְתְּקָא {2x} ʾElteqê, el-te-kay'; or (more prop.)

אֶלְתְּקֵה ʾElteqêh, el-te-kay'; of uncert. der.; Eltekeh or Elteke, a place in Pal.: Eltekeh {2x}. See: BDB—49c.

515. אֶלְתְּקֹן {1x} ʾElteqôn, el-te-kone'; from 410 and 8626; God (is) straight; Eltekon, a place in Pal.:—Eltekon {1x}. See: BDB—49c.

516. אַל תַּשְׁחֵת {4x} ʾAl tashchêth, al tash-kayth'; from 408 and 7843; Thou must not destroy; prob. the opening words of a popular song:—Al-taschith {4x}. See: BDB—1008c.

517. אֵם {220x} ʾêm, ame; a prim. word; a mother (as the bond of the family); in a wide sense (both lit. and fig. [like 1]:—mother {214x}, dam {5x}, parting {1x}.

Em (517) means "mother; grandmother; step-mother." **(1)** The basic meaning of the word has to do with the physical relationship of the individual called "mother." This emphasis of the word is in Gen 2:24 (the first biblical appearance): "Therefore shall a man leave his father and his

mother, and shall cleave unto his wife." **(2)** *Em* sometimes represents an animal "mother": "Likewise shalt thou do with thine oxen, and with thy sheep: seven days it shall be with its [mother]; on the eighth day thou shalt give it me" (Ex 22:30). **(3)** The phrase "father and mother" is the biblical phrase for parents: "And he brought up Hadassah, that is, Esther, his uncle's daughter: for she had neither father nor mother [living]" (Est 2:7). **(4)** The "son of one's mother" is his brother (Gen 43:29), just as the "daughter of one's mother" is his sister (Gen 20:12). These phrases usually emphasize that the persons so represented are whole brothers or sisters, whereas the Hebrew words *ach,* (251 - "brother") and *achot,* (269 - "sister") meaning both whole and half siblings, leave the issue unclear.

(5) On the other hand, in Gen 27:29 this phrase appears to mean peoples more distantly related: "Let people serve thee, and nations bow down to thee: be lord over thy brethren, and let thy mother's sons bow down to thee: cursed be every one that curseth thee, and blessed be he that blesseth thee." **(6)** *Em* can represent blood relatives further removed than one's mother. In 1 Kin 15:10 the word means "grandmother": "And forty and one years reigned he in Jerusalem. And his [grand]mother's name was Maachah, the daughter of Abishalom." **(7)** This word can also mean "stepmother." When Joseph told his dream to his family, "his father rebuked him, and said unto him, What is this dream that thou hast dreamed? Shall I and thy [step]mother and thy brethren indeed come to bow down ourselves to thee to the earth?" (Gen 37:10; cf. 35:16ff., where we read that Rachel died). **(8)** The word can signify a mother-in-law, or the mother of one's wife: "And if a man take a wife and her mother, it is wickedness" (Lev 20:14).

(9) The woman through whom a nation originated is called its "mother"; she is the first or tribal "mother," an ancestress: "Thus saith the LORD God unto Jerusalem; Thy birth and thy nativity is of the land of Canaan; thy father was an Amorite, and thy mother a Hittite" (Eze 16:3). Even further removed physically is Eve, "the mother of all living" (Gen 3:20). **(10)** *Em* can represent all one's female forebears: "Let the iniquity of his fathers be remembered with the LORD; and let not the sin of his mother be blotted out" (Ps 109:14). **(11)** A group of people, a people, or a city may be personified and called a "mother." Hosea calls the priests (probably) the "mother" of Israel: "And the prophet also shall fall with thee in the night, and I will destroy thy mother" (Hos 4:5).

(12) The people of Israel, the northern kingdom, are the "mother" of Judah: "Where is the bill of your mother's divorcement, whom I have put away? or which of my creditors is it to whom I have sold you? Behold, for your iniquities have ye sold yourselves, and for your transgressions is your mother put away" (Is 50:1; cf. Hos 2:4, 7). **(13)** An important city may be called a "mother" of its citizens: "Thou seekest to destroy a city and a mother in Israel" (2 Sa 20:19). **(14)** The title "mother in Israel" was a title of respect in Deborah's day (Judg 5:7). **(15)** "The mother of a way" is the starting point for roads: "For the king of Babylon stood at the parting of the way, at the head of the two ways, to use divination" (Eze 21:21). Syn.: 2545. See: TWOT—115a; BDB—51a, 51c.

518. אִם {43x} *ʾîm, eem;* a prim. particle; used very widely as demonstr., *lo!;* interrog., *whether?;* or conditional, *if, although;* also *Oh that!, when;* hence, as a neg., *not:*—if, not, or, when, whether, surely, doubtless, while, neither, saving, verily = {43x}. See: TWOT—111; BDB—49c, 210b, 243d, 474c, 1090d, 1099a.

519. אָמָה {55x} *ʾâmâh, aw-maw';* appar. a prim. word; a *maid-servant* or female slave:—handmaid {22x}, maidservant {19x}, maid {8x}, bondwoman {4x}, bondmaids {2x}. See: TWOT—112; BDB—51a, 1046c.

אָמָה *ʾêmâh.* See 367.

520. אַמָּה {245x} *ʾammâh, am-maw';* prol. from 517; prop. a *mother* (i.e. *unit* of measure, or the *fore-arm* (below the elbow), i.e. a *cubit;* also a door-*base* (as a *bond* of the entrance):—cubit {242x}, measure {1x}, post {1x}, not translated {1x}.

Ammah (520) means "cubit." **(1)** It appears about 245 times in biblical Hebrew and in all periods, but especially in Ex 25—27; 37—38 (specifications of the tabernacle); 1 Kin 6—7 (the specifications of Solomon's temple and palace); and Eze 40—43 (the specifications of Ezekiel's temple). **(2)** In one passage, *ammah* means "pivot": "And the posts [literally, "sockets"] of the door moved at the voice of him that cried" (Is 6:4). **(3)** In almost every other occurrence, the word means "cubit," the primary unit of linear measurement in the Old Testament. **(4)** A "cubit" ordinarily was the distance from one's elbow to the tip of the middle finger. Since this distance varied from individual to individual, the "cubit" was a rather imprecise measurement. Yet the first appearance of *ammah* (Gen 6:15) refers to the measurement of Noah's ark, which implies that the word must refer to a more precise length than the ordinary "cubit." Syn.: 3967, 4060. See: TWOT—115c; BDB—51a, 52a, 52c, 1081a.

Hebrew

521. אָמָּה {4x} ’ammâh (Aram.), am-maw'; corresp. to 520:—cubit {4x}. See: TWOT—2582; BDB—51a, 1081a.

522. אַמָּה {1x} ’Ammâh, am-maw'; the same as 520; Ammah, a hill in Pal.:—Ammah {1x}. See: BDB—51a, 52a, 52c.

523. אֻמָּה {3x} ’ummâh, oom-maw'; from the same as 517; a collection, i.e. community of persons:—people {2x}, nation {1x}. See: TWOT—115e; BDB—52c, 1081a.

524. אֻמָּה {8x} ’ummâh (Aram.), oom-maw'; corresp. to 523:—nation {8x}. See: TWOT—2583; BDB—1081a.

525. אָמוֹן {1x} ’âmôwn, aw-mone'; from 539, prob. in the sense of training; skilled, i.e. an architect [like 542]:—one brought up {1x}. See: TWOT—116L; BDB—54c.

526. אָמוֹן {17x} ’Âmôwn, aw-mone'; the same as 525; Amon, the name of three Isr.:—Amon {17x}. See: BDB—51b, 54c.

527. אָמוֹן {3x} ’âmôwn, aw-mone'; a var. for 1995; a throng of people:—multitude {2x}, populous {1x}. See: TWOT—116L; BDB—54c.

528. אָמוֹן {2x} ’Âmôwn, aw-mone'; of Eg. der.; Amon (i.e. Ammon or Amn), a deity of Egypt (used only as an adjunct of 4996):—not translated {2x}. See: BDB—51b.

529. אֵמוּן {5x} ’êmûwn, ay-moon'; from 539; established, i.e. (fig.) trusty; also (abstr.) trustworthiness:—faithful {3x}, truth {1x}, faith {1x}. See: TWOT—116d; BDB—53c.

530. אֱמוּנָה {49x} ’ĕmûwnâh, em-oo-naw'; or (short.)

אֱמֻנָה ’ĕmûnâh, em-oo-naw'; fem. of 529; lit. firmness; fig. security; mor. fidelity:—faithfulness {18x}, truth {13x}, faithfully {5x}, office {5x}, faithful {3x}, faith {1x}, stability {1x}, steady {1x}, truly {1x}, verily {1x}. Emunah (530) means "firmness; faithfulness; truth; honesty; official obligation." **(1)** In Ex 17:12 (the first biblical occurrence), the word means "to remain in one place": "And his [Moses'] hands were steady until the going down of the sun." **(2)** Closely related to this use is that in Is 33:6: "And wisdom and knowledge shall be the stability of thy times." **(3)** In passages such as 1 Chr 9:22, emunah appears to function as a technical term meaning "a fixed position" or "enduring office": "All these which were chosen to be porters in the gates were two hundred and twelve. These were reckoned by their genealogy in their villages, whom David and Samuel the seer did ordain in their set [i.e., established] office." **(4)** The most frequent sense of emunah is "faithfulness," as illustrated by

1 Sa 26:23: "The LORD render to every man his righteousness and his faithfulness." The LORD repays the one who demonstrates that he does what God demands.

(5) Quite often, this word means "truthfulness," as when it is contrasted to false swearing, lying, and so on: "Run ye to and fro through the streets of Jerusalem, and see now, and know, and seek in the broad places thereof, if ye can find a man, if there be any that executeth judgment, that seeketh the truth [i.e., honesty]" (Jer 5:1; cf. Jer 5:2). Here emunah signifies the condition of being faithful to God's covenant, practicing truth, or doing righteousness. **(6)** On the other hand, the word can represent the abstract idea of "truth": "This is a nation that obeyeth not the voice of the Lord their God, nor receiveth correction: truth [emunah] is perished, and is cut off from their mouth" (Jer 7:28). These quotations demonstrate the two senses in which emunah means "true"—the personal sense, which identifies a subject as honest, trustworthy, faithful, truthful (Prov 12:22); and the factual sense, which identifies a subject as being factually true (cf. Prov 12:27), as opposed to that which is false.

(7) The essential meaning of emunah is "established" or "lasting," "continuing," "certain." **(7a)** So God says, "And in mercy shall the throne be established: and he shall sit upon it in truth in the tabernacle of David, judging, and seeking judgment, and hasting righteousness" (cf. 2 Sa 7:16; Is 16:5). **(7b)** Thus, the phrase frequently rendered "with lovingkindness and truth" should be rendered "with perpetual (faithful) lovingkindness" (cf. Josh 2:14). He who sows righteousness earns a "true" or "lasting" reward (Prov 11:18), a reward on which he can rely.

(8) In other contexts, emunah embraces other aspects of the concept of truth: "[The Lord] hath remembered his mercy and his truth toward the house of Israel" (Ps 98:3). Here the word does not describe the endurance of God but His "truthfulness"; that which He once said He has maintained. The emphasis here is on truth as a subjective quality, defined personally. **(9)** In a similar sense, one can both practice (Gen 47:29) and speak the "truth" (2 Sa 7:28). In such cases, it is not a person's dependability (i.e., others can act on the basis of it) but his reliability (conformity to what is true) that is considered. The first emphasis is subjective and the second objective. It is not always possible to discern which emphasis is intended by a given passage. See: TWOT—116e; BDB—53c.

531. אָמוֹץ {13x} ’Âmôwts, aw-mohts'; from 553; strong; Amots, an Isr.:—Amoz {13x}. See: BDB—55b.

532. אֱמִי {1x} ʾÂmîy, *aw-mee'*; an abbrev. for 526; *Ami*, an Isr.:—Ami {1x}. See: BDB—51b, 54c.

אֲמִינוֹן ʾĂmîynôwn. See 550.

533. אָמִיץ {6x} ʾammîyts, *am-meets'*; or (short.)

אָמִץ ʾammîts, *am-meets'*; from 553; *strong* or (abstr.) *strength:*—strong {4x}, mighty {1x}, courageous {1x}. See: TWOT—117d; BDB—55c.

534. אָמִיר {2x} ʾâmîyr, *aw-meer'*; appar. from 559 (in the sense of *self-exaltation*); a *summit* (of a tree or mountain:—bough {1x}, branch {1x}. See: TWOT—118d; BDB—57b, 1051c.

535. אָמַל {16x} ʾâmal, *aw-mal'*; a prim. root; to *droop;* by impl. to *be sick*, to *mourn:*—languish {14x}, feeble {1x}, weak {1x}. See: TWOT—114; BDB—51b.

536. אֻמְלַל {1x} ʾumlal, *oom-lal'*; from 535; *sick:*—weak {1x}. See: TWOT—114b; BDB—51c.

537. אֲמֵלָל {1x} ʾămêlâl, *am-ay-lawl'*; from 535; *languid:*—feeble {1x}. See: TWOT—114a; BDB—51c.

538. אָמָם {1x} ʾĂmâm, *am-awm'*; from 517; *gathering*-spot; *Amam*, a place in Pal.:—Amam {1x}. See: BDB—52c.

539. אָמַן {108x} ʾâman, *aw-man'*; a prim. root; prop. to *build up* or *support;* to *foster* as a parent or nurse; fig. to *render* (or *be*) *firm* or faithful, to *trust* or believe, to *be permanent* or quiet; mor. to *be true* or certain; once (Is 30:21; interch. for 541) to *go to the right hand:*—believe {44x}, assurance {1x}, faithful {20x}, sure {11x}, established {7x}, trust {5x}, verified {3x}, steadfast {2x}, continuance {2x}, father {2x}, bring up {4x}, nurse {2x}, be nursed {1x}, surely be {1x}, stand fast {1x}, fail {1x}, trusty {1x}.

Aman means "to be firm, endure, be faithful, be true, stand fast, trust, have belief, believe." **(1)** It appears in all periods of biblical Hebrew (about 96 times) and only in the causative and passive stems. **(2)** In the passive stem, *aman* has several emphases: **(2a)** it indicates that a subject is "lasting" or "enduring," which is its meaning in Deut 28:59: "Then the LORD will make thy plagues wonderful, and the plagues of thy seed, even great plagues, and of long continuance, and sore sicknesses, and of long continuance." It also signifies the element of being "firm" or "trustworthy." **(2b)** In Is 22:23, *aman* refers to a "firm" place, a place into which a peg will be driven so that it will be immovable. The peg will remain firmly anchored, even though it is pushed so hard that

it breaks off at the point of entry (Is 22:25). **(3)** The Bible also speaks of "faithful" people who fulfill their obligations (cf. 1 Sa 22:14; Prov 25:13). **(4)** The nuance meaning "trustworthy" also occurs: "He that is of a faithful spirit concealeth the matter" (Prov 11:13; cf. Is 8:2).

(5) An officebearer may be conceived as an "entrusted one": "He removeth away the speech of the trusty [entrusted ones], and taketh away the understanding of the aged" (Job 12:20). In this passage, *aman* is synonymously parallel (therefore equivalent in meaning) to "elders" or "officebearers." Thus, it should be rendered "entrusted ones" or "those who have been given a certain responsibility (trust)." Before receiving the trust, they are men "worthy of trust" or "trustworthy" (cf. 1 Sa 2:35; Neh 13:13). **(6)** In Gen 42:20 (the first biblical appearance of this stem), Joseph requests that his brothers bring Benjamin to him; "so shall your words be verified," or "be shown to be true" (cf. 1 Kin 8:26; Hos 5:9). **(7)** In Hos 11:12, *aman* contrasts Judah's actions ("faithful") with those of Ephraim and Israel ("deceit"). So here *aman* represents both "truthfulness" and "faithfulness" (cf. Ps 78:37; Jer 15:18). **(8)** The word may be rendered "true" in several passages (1 Kin 8:26; 2 Chr 1:9; 6:17).

(9) A different nuance of *aman* is seen in Deut 7:9: "the faithful God, which keepeth covenant and mercy. . . ." There is a good reason here to understand the word *aman* as referring to what God has done ("faithfulness"), rather than what He will do ("trustworthy"), because He has already proved Himself faithful by keeping the covenant. Therefore, the translation would become, "faithful God who has kept His covenant and faithfulness, those who love Him kept . . ." (cf. Is 47:7). **(10)** In the causative stem, *aman* means "to stand fast," or "be fixed in one spot," which is demonstrated by Job 39:24: "He [a war horse] swalloweth the ground with fierceness and rage: neither believeth he that it is the sound of the trumpet." **(11)** Even more often, this stem connotes a psychological or mental certainty, as in Job 29:24: "If I laughed on them, they believed it not."

(12) Considering something to be trustworthy is an act of full trusting or believing. This is the emphasis in the first biblical occurrence of *aman:* "And [Abram] believed in the LORD; and he counted it to him for righteousness" (Gen 15:6). The meaning here is that Abram was full of trust and confidence in God, and that he did not fear Him (v. 1). It was not primarily in God's words that he believed, but in God Himself. Nor does the text tell us that Abram believed God so as to accept what He said as "true" and "trustworthy" (cf. Gen

45:26), but simply that he believed in God. In other words, Abram came to experience a personal relationship to God rather than an impersonal relationship with His promises. **(13)** Thus, in Ex 4:9 the meaning is, "if they do not believe in view of the two signs," rather than, "if they do not believe these two signs." The focus is on the act of believing, not on the trustworthiness of the signs. **(14)** A more precise sense of *aman* does appear sometimes: "That they may believe that the LORD . . . hath appeared unto thee" (Ex 4:5; cf. 1 Kin 10:7). **(15)** In other instances, *aman* has a cultic use, by which the worshiping community affirms its identity with what the worship leader says (1 Chr 16:32). The "God of the amen" (2 Chr 20:20; Is 65:16) is the God who always accomplishes what He says; He is a "God who is faithful." Syn.: 529, 530, 982. See: TWOT—116; BDB—52d, 1081a.

540. אֲמַן {3x} ʾăman (Aram.), *am-an´;* corresp. to 539:—believe {1x}, sure {1x}, faithful {1x}. See: TWOT—2584; BDB—1081a.

541. אָמַן {1x} ʾâman, *aw-man´;* denom. from 3225; to take the *right hand* road:—turn to the right {1x}. Syn.: See 539. See: TWOT—872; BDB—54d, 411c, 412b.

542. אָמָן {1x} ʾâmân, *aw-mawn´;* from 539 (in the sense of *training);* an *expert:*—cunning workman {1x}. See: TWOT—116c; BDB—53b.

543. אָמֵן {30x} ʾâmên, *aw-mane´;* from 539; *sure;* abstr. *faithfulness;* adv. *truly:*—amen {27x}; truly {2x}, so be it {1x}.
    Amen (543), an adverb, means "truly; genuinely; *amen;* so be it." **(1)** This Hebrew word usually appears as a response to a curse that has been pronounced upon someone, as the one accursed accepts the curse upon himself. By so doing, he binds himself to fulfill certain conditions or else be subject to the terms of the curse (cf. Deut 29:15–26). **(2)** Although signifying a voluntary acceptance of the conditions of a covenant, the *amen* was sometimes pronounced with coercion. Even in these circumstances, the one who did not pronounce it received the punishment embodied in the curse. **(3)** So the *amen* was an affirmation of a covenant, which is the significance of the word in Num 5:22, its first biblical occurrence. **(4)** Later generations or individuals might reaffirm the covenant by voicing their *amen* (Neh 5:1–13; Jer 18:6). **(5)** In 1 Kin 1:36, *amen* is noncovenantal. It functions as an assertion of a person's agreement with the intent of a speech just delivered: "And Benaiah the son of Jehoiada answered the king, and said, *Amen:* the LORD God of my lord the king say so too." However, the context shows

that Benaiah meant to give more than just verbal assent; his *amen* committed him to carry out the wishes of King David. It was a statement whereby he obligated himself to do what David had indirectly requested of him (cf. Neh 8:6). Syn.: 539. See: TWOT—116b; BDB—53b.

544. אֹמֶן {1x} ʾômen, *oh-men´;* from 539; *verity:*—truth {1x}. See: TWOT—116a; BDB—53b.

545. אָמְנָה {1x} ʾomnâh, *om-naw´;* fem. of 544 (in the spec. sense of *training*); *tutelage:*—brought up {1x}. See: TWOT—116f; BDB—53d.

546. אָמְנָה {2x} ʾomnâh, *om-naw´;* fem. of 544 (in its usual sense); adv. *surely:*—indeed {2x}. See: TWOT—116g; BDB—53d.

547. אָמְנָה {1x} ʾômᵉnâh, *om-me-naw´;* fem. act. part. of 544 (in the orig. sense of *supporting*); a *column:*—pillar {1x}. See: TWOT—116; BDB—52d.

548. אֲמָנָה {2x} ʾămânâh, *am-aw-naw´;* fem. of 543; something *fixed,* i.e. a covenant, an *allowance:*—sure {1x}, portion {1x}. See: TWOT—116h; BDB—53d.

549. אֲמָנָה {2x} ʾĂmânâh, *am-aw-naw´;* the same as 548; *Amanah,* a mountain near Damascus:—Amana {1x}, variant for Abana {1x}. See: BDB—53d.

550. אַמְנוֹן {28x} ʾAmnôwn, *am-nohn´;* or

אֲמִינוֹן ʾĂmîynôwn, *am-ee-nohn´;* from 539; *faithful; Amnon* (or Aminon), a son of David:—Amnon {28x}. See: BDB—54c.

551. אָמְנָם {9x} ʾomnâm, *om-nawm´;* adv. from 544; *verily:*—truth {3x}, indeed {2x}, true {1x}, no doubt {1x}, surely {1x}, indeed {1x}. Syn.: 571. See: TWOT—116j; BDB—53d.

552. אֻמְנָם {5x} ʾumnâm, *oom-nawm´;* an orth. var. of 551: —indeed {3x}, very deed {1x}, surety {1x}. See: TWOT—116i; BDB—53d.

553. אָמַץ {41x} ʾâmats, *aw-mats´;* a prim. root; to be alert, phys. (on foot) or ment. (in courage):—strengthen {12x}, courage {9x}, strong {5x}, courageous {2x}, harden {2x}, speed {2x}, stronger {2x}, confirm {1x}, established {1x}, fortify {1x}, increaseth {1x}, steadfastly minded {1x}, obstinate {1x}, prevailed {1x}. Syn.: 1369, 2388, 2392, 2428, 4581, 5797. Ref. TWOT—117; BDB—54d.

554. אָמֹץ {2x} ʾâmôts, *aw-mohts´;* prob. from 553; of a *strong* color, i.e. *red* (others *fleet*):—bay {2x}. See: TWOT—117c; BDB—55b.

Hebrew

555. אֹמֶץ {1x} ʾômets, o'-mets; from 553; strength:—stronger {1x}. See: TWOT—117a; BDB—55b.

אֹמֶץ ʾammîts. See 533.

556. אַמְצָה {1x} ʾamtsâh, am-tsaw'; from 553; force:—strength {1x}. See: TWOT—117b; BDB—55b.

557. אַמְצִי {2x} ʾAmtsîy, am-tsee'; from 553; strong; Amtsi, an Isr.:—Amzi {2x}. See: BDB—55c.

558. אֲמַצְיָה {40x} ʾĂmatsyâh, am-ats-yaw'; or

אֲמַצְיָהוּ ʾĂmatsyâhûw, am-ats-yaw'-hoo; from 553 and 3050; strength of Jah; Amatsjah, the name of four Isr.:—Amaziah {40x}. See: BDB—55c.

559. אָמַר {5308x} ʾâmar, aw-mar'; a prim. root; to say (used with great latitude):—said {4874x}, speak {179x}, answer {99x}, command {30x}, tell {29x}, call {7x}, promised {6x}, misc. {84x} = appoint, avouch, bid, boast self, certify, challenge, charge, commandment, commune, consider, declare, demand, × desire, determine, × expressly, × indeed, × intend, name, × plainly, publish, report, require, × still, × suppose, talk, term, × that is, × think, use [speech], utter, × verily, × yet.

Amar means "to say, speak, tell, command, answer." (1) Amar refers to the simple act of communicating with the spoken word. Usually the word is used of direct speech ("say"), although it may be used of indirect speech as well ("speak"). (2) The usual subject of this verb is some self-conscious personality—man (Gen 2:23) or God (Gen 1:3—the first occurrence of the word). (3) Infrequently animals (Gen 3:1) or, in figures of speech such as personification, inanimate objects "say" something (Judg 9:8ff.). (4) This verb bears many connotations and in some passages is better translated accordingly. The KJV renders this verb "answer" 98 times ("say as a response").

(5) God speaks in Gen 9:8; 22:2; Ex 8:27. The force of God's speaking is more than merely making a statement: It is authoritative. (6) In addition to these frequently occurring connotations, amar is rendered with many words representing various aspects of spoken communication, such as (6a) "appoint" or "assign" (1 Kin 11:18), (6b) "mention" or "name" (Gen 43:27), (6c) "call" (Is 5:20), and (6d) "promise" (2 Kin 8:19). (7) Although not always so translated, this word can imply the act of thinking within oneself (Gen 44:28) and the intention to do something (Ex 2:14). (8) When used of divine speaking, this verb may refer to simple communication (Gen 1:26). (9) Often, however, there is a much fuller sense where God's saying effects the thing spoken (cf. Gen 1). (10) The phrase "thus says the Lord," so frequent in the prophets, has been analyzed as a message-formula. The Bible recognizes that behind the divine speaking is divine authority and power. Syn.: 1696, 5002. See: TWOT—118; BDB—59c, 1081a.

560. אֲמַר {71x} ʾămar (Aram.), am-ar'; corresp. to 559:—say {45x}, commanded {12x}, speak {4x}, tell {9x}, declare {1x}. Syn.: 1697, 4405. See 559. See: TWOT—2585; BDB—1081a.

561. אֵמֶר {49x} ʾêmer, ay'-mer; from 559; something said:—words {43x}, speeches {2x}, sayings {2x}, appointed {1x}, answer {1x}.

This noun appears 48 times. ʾEmer refers to "words" in Prov 2:1: "My son, if thou wilt receive my words, and hide my commandments with thee." Syn: Several other nouns are related to the verb ʾamar. ʾImrah (565) also means "word, speech," and it occurs 37 times. One occurrence of ʾimrah is in 2 Sa 22:31 (cf. Ps 18:30). The noun ʾomer (562) is found 6 times and means "word, speech, promise" (Ps 68:11; Hab 3:9). Maʾamar (3982) and meʾmar (3983) mean "word, command." Maʾamar occurs 3 times (Est 1:15; 2:22; 9:32), and meʾmar occurs twice (Ezra 6:9; Dan 4:17). ʿEmer simply refers to "words." Syn.: 373, 4405. See: TWOT—118a; BDB—57a.

562. אֹמֶר {6x} ʾômer, o'-mer; the same as 561:—word {2x}, speech {2x}, thing {1x}, promise {1x}. See: TWOT—118a; BDB—56d, 1051c.

563. אִמַּר {3x} ʾimmar (Aram.), im-mar'; perh. from 560 (in the sense of bringing forth); a lamb:—lamb {3x}. See: TWOT—2585; BDB—1081b.

564. אִמֵּר {10x} ʾImmêr, im-mare'; from 559; talkative; Immer, the name of five Isr.:—Immer {10x}. See: BDB—57b.

565. אִמְרָה {37x} ʾimrâh, im-raw'; or

אֶמְרָה ʾemrâh, em-raw'; fem. of 561, and mean. the same:—word {29x}, speech {7x}, commandment {1x}. Syn.: 561, 1697, 4405. See: TWOT—118b; BDB—57a, 57b.

566. אִמְרִי {2x} ʾImrîy, im-ree'; from 564; wordy; Imri, the name of two Isr.:—Imri {2x}. See: BDB—57c.

567. אֱמֹרִי {87x} ʾĔmôrîy, em-o-ree'; prob. a patron. from an unused name derived from 559 in the sense of publicity, i.e. prominence; thus, a mountaineer; an Emorite,

one of the Canaanitish tribes:—Amorite {87x}. See: TWOT—119; BDB—57b.

568. אֲמַרְיָה {16x} ʾĂmaryâh, am-ar-yaw'; or prol.

אֲמַרְיָהוּ ʾĂmaryâhûw, am-ar-yaw'-hoo; from 559 and 3050; *Jah has said* (i.e. promised); *Amarjah,* the name of nine Isr.:—Amariah {16x}. See: BDB—57c.

569. אַמְרָפֶל {2x} ʾAmrâphel, am-raw-fel'; of uncert. (perh. for.) der.; *Amraphel,* a king of Shinar:—Amraphel {2x}. See: BDB—57d.

570. אֶמֶשׁ {5x} ʾemesh, eh'-mesh; time *past,* i.e. *yesterday* or *last night:*—yesternight {3x}, former time {1x}, yesterday {1x}. See: TWOT—120; BDB—57d.

571. אֱמֶת {127x} ʾemeth, eh'-meth; contr. from 539; *stability;* fig. *certainty, truth, trustworthiness:*—truth {92x}, true {18x}, truly {7x}, right {3x}, faithfully {2x}, assured {1x}, assuredly {1x}, establishment {1x}, faithful {1x}, sure {1x}, verity {1x}.

Emeth means "truth; right; faithful." **(1)** In Zec 8:3, Jerusalem is called "a city of truth." **(2)** Elsewhere, *emeth* is rendered as the word "right": "Howbeit thou art just in all that is brought upon us; for thou hast done right, but we have done wickedly" (Neh 9:33). **(3)** Only infrequently (16 times) is *emeth* translated "faithful," as when Nehemiah is described as "a faithful man, and feared God above many" (Neh 7:2). Syn.: See: TWOT—116k; BDB—54a, 57d.

572. אַמְתַּחַת {15x} ʾamtêchath, am-taykh'-ath; from 4969; prop. something *expansive,* i.e. a flexible container for grain; a *bag:*—sack {15x}. See: TWOT—1265a; BDB—57d, 607c.

573. אֲמִתַּי {2x} ʾĂmittay, am-it-tah'ee; from 571; *veracious; Amittai,* an Isr.:—Amittai {2x}. See: BDB—54c, 57d.

574. אֶמְתָּנִי {1x} ʾemtânîy (Aram.), em-taw-nee'; from a root corresp. to that of 4975; well-*loined* (i.e. burly) or *mighty:*—terrible {1x}. See: TWOT—2571; BDB—1080a.

575. אָן {8x} ʾân, awn; or

אָנָה ʾânâh, aw-naw'; contr. from 370; *where?;* hence, *whither?, when?;* also *hither* and *thither:*—whither, how, where, whithersoever, hither = {8x}. See: TWOT—75g; BDB—33a, 57d.

576. אֲנָא {16x} ʾănâʾ (Aram.), an-aw'; or

אֲנָה ʾânâh (Aram.), an-aw'; corresp. to 589; *I:*—I {14x}, me, {2x}. See: TWOT—2586; BDB—1081b.

577. אַנָּא {13x} ʾânnâʾ, awn-naw'; or

אָנָּה ʾânnâh, awn-naw'; appar. contr. from 160 and 4994; *oh now!:*—I beseech thee {8x}, I pray thee {2x}, Oh {x1}, O {2x}. See: TWOT—122; BDB—58a, 58c.

אֲנָה ʾănâh. See 576.

אָנָה ʾânâh. See 575.

578. אָנָה {2x} ʾânâh, aw-naw'; a prim. root; to *groan:*—lament {1x}, mourn {1x}. See: TWOT—124; BDB—58b.

579. אָנָה {4x} ʾânâh, aw-naw'; a prim. root [perh. rather ident. with 578 through the idea of *contraction* in anguish]; to *approach;* hence, to *meet* in various senses:—deliver {1x}, befall {1x}, happen {1x}, seeketh a quarrel {1x}. See: TWOT—126; BDB—58c, 1099c.

אָנָּה ʾânnâh. See 577.

580. אֲנוּ {1x} ʾănûw, an-oo'; contr. for 587; *we:*—we {1x}. See: TWOT—128; BDB—58c, 59a.

אֲנוֹ ʾÔnôw. See 207.

581. אִנּוּן {4x} ʾinnûwn (Aram.), in-noon'; or (fem.)

אִנִּין ʾinnîy (Aram.), in-neen'; corresp. to 1992; *they:*—are {2x}, these {1x}, them {1x}. See: TWOT—2587; BDB—1081c.

582. אֱנוֹשׁ {564x} ʾĕnôwsh, en-oshe'; from 605; prop. a *mortal* (and thus differing from the more dignified 120); hence, a *man* in Gen (singly or collect.). It is often unexpressed in the English Version, espec. when used in apposition with another word.:—man {520x}, certain {10x}, husbands {3x}, some {3x}, merchantmen {2x}, persons {2x}, misc.: another, chap [-man], people, person, servant, some (X of them), + stranger, those – {24x}.

Enowsh means "man." **(1)** It occurs 25 times in biblical Aramaic and 42 times in biblical Hebrew. **(2)** Hebrew uses *enowsh* exclusively in poetical passages. The only apparent exception is 2 Chr 14:11, but this is a prayer and, therefore uses poetical words. **(3)** *Enowsh* never appears with the definite article and at all times except once (Ps 144:3) sets forth a collective idea, "man." **(4)** In most cases where the word occurs in Job and the Psalms it suggests the frailty, vulnerability, and finitude of "man" as contrasted to God: "As for man, his days are as grass: as a flower of the field, so he flourisheth" (Ps 103:15). As such "man" cannot be righteous or holy before God: "Shall mortal man be more just than God? Shall a man be more pure than his Maker?" (Job 4:17). **(5)** In the Psalms this word is used to indicate the enemy: "Arise, O LORD; let not man prevail: let the heathen

be judged in thy sight" (Ps 9:19). Here the parallelism shows that *enowsh* is synonymous with "nations," or the enemy. They are, therefore, presented as weak, vulnerable, and finite: "Put them in fear, O LORD: that the nations may know themselves to be but men" (Ps 9:20).

(6) *Enowsh* may connote "men" as weak but not necessarily morally weak: "Blessed is the man that doeth this, and the son of man that layeth hold of it" (Is 56:2). In this passage the *enowsh* is blessed because he has been morally strong. **(7)** In a few places the word bears no moral overtones and represents "man" in a sense parallel to Hebrew *adam*. **(8)** He is finite as contrasted to the infinite God: "I said, I would scatter them into corners, I would make the remembrance of them to cease from among men" (Deut. 32:26—the first biblical occurrence). Syn.: *Adam* (120) connotes man as the creature created in God's image, the crown of all creation. *Iysh* (376) is used for man as the counterpart of woman and/or as distinguished in his maleness. *Geber* (1397) denotes a male as an antonym of a woman, many times suggesting strength, strong man. *ʾĔnôwsh* (582) sets forth a collective idea of man suggesting the insignificance, frailty, vulnerability, and finitude of man as contrasted to God. *Bachur* (970) signifies the fully developed, vigorous, unmarried man *is* in his prime. See also: 376, 1167, 1397, 1400, 4962. See: TWOT—136a; BDB—60d, 1081d.

583. אֱנוֹשׁ {7x} ʾĔnôwsh, *en-ohsh';* the same as 582; *Enosh,* a son of Seth:—Enos {6x}, Enosh {1x}. See: BDB—60d.

584. אָנָה {12x} ʾânach, *aw-nakh';* a prim. root; to *sigh:*—sigh {10x}, groan {1x}, mourn {1x}. See: TWOT—127; BDB—58d.

585. אֲנָחָה {11x} ʾănâchâh, *an-aw-khaw';* from 584; *sighing:*—sighing {5x}, groanings {4x}, sighs {1x}, mourning {1x}. See: TWOT—127a; BDB—58d.

586. אֲנַחְנָא {4x} ʾănachnâ (Aram.), *an-akh'-naw;* or

אֲנַחְנָה ʾănachnâh (Aram.), *an-akh-naw';* corresp. to 587; *we:*—we {4x}. See: TWOT—2588; BDB—1081c.

587. אֲנַחְנוּ {6x} ʾănachnûw, *an-akh'-noo;* appar. from 595; *we:*—ourselves, us, we = {6x}. See: TWOT—128; BDB—58d, 59c.

588. אֲנָחֲרָת {1x} ʾĂnâchărâth, *an-aw-kha-rawth';* prob. from the same root as 5170; a *gorge* or narrow pass; *Anacharath,* a place in Pal.:—Anaharath. See: BDB—58d.

589. אֲנִי {13x} ʾăniy, *an-ee';* contr. from 595; *I:*—I, me, which, for I, mine = {13x}. See: TWOT—129; BDB—58d, 219a; 1081b.

590. אֳנִי {7x} ʾŏniy, *on-ee';* prob. from 579 (in the sense of *conveyance*); a *ship* or (collect.) a *fleet:*—navy {5x}, navy of ships {1x}, galley {1x}. See: TWOT—125a,b; BDB—58b.

591. אֳנִיָּה {32x} ʾŏnîyâh, *on-ee-yaw';* fem. of 590; a *ship:*—ship {31x}, shipman + 582 {1x}. See: TWOT—125b; BDB—58b.

592. אֲנִיָּה {2x} ʾănîyâh, *an-ee-yaw';* from 578; *groaning:*—lamentation {1x}, sorrow {1x}. See: TWOT—124a; BDB—58b.

אִנִּין ʾinnîyn. See 581.

593. אֲנִיעָם {1x} ʾĂnîyʿâm, *an-ee-awm';* from 578 and 5971; *groaning of* (the) *people; Aniam,* an Isr.:—Aniam {1x}. See: BDB—58b.

594. אֲנָךְ {4x} ʾănâk, *an-awk';* prob. from an unused root mean. to *be narrow;* according to most a plumb-*line,* and to others a *hook:*—plumb-line {1x}. See: TWOT—129.1; BDB—59d.

595. אָנֹכִי {3x} ʾânôkîy, *aw-no-kee'* (sometimes *aw-no'-kee*); a prim. pron.; *I:*—I {1x}, me {1x}, which {1x}. See: TWOT—130; BDB—59a, 59d.

596. אָנַן {2x} ʾânan, *aw-nan';* a prim. root; to *mourn,* i.e. *complain:*—complain {2x}. See: TWOT—131; BDB—59d.

597. אָנַס {1x} ʾânaç, *aw-nas';* to *insist:*—compel {1x}. See: TWOT—132; BDB—60a.

598. אֲנַס {1x} ʾănaç (Aram.), *an-as';* corresp. to 597; fig. to *distress:*—troubleth {1x}. See: TWOT—2589; BDB—1081c.

599. אָנַף {14x} ʾânaph, *aw-naf';* a prim. root; to *breathe* hard, i.e. *be enraged:*—angry {13x}, displeased {1x}. The verb appears in Is 12:1 and means angry: "O LORD, I will praise thee: though thou wast angry with me." Syn.: 639, 2734. See: TWOT—133; BDB—60a.

600. אֲנַף {2x} ʾănaph (Aram.), *an-af';* corresp. to 639 (only in the plur. as a sing.); the *face:*—face {1x}, visage {1x}. See: TWOT—2590; BDB—1081c.

601. אֲנָפָה {2x} ʾănâphâh, *an-aw-faw';* from 599; an unclean bird, perh. the *parrot* (from its *irascibility*):—heron {2x}. See: TWOT—133a; BDB—60b.

602. אָנַק {4x} ʾânaq, *aw-nak';* a prim. root; to *shriek:*—cry {3x}, groan {1x}. See: TWOT—134; BDB—60b.

603. אֲנָקָה {4x} ʾănâqâh, *an-aw-kaw';* from 602; *shrieking:*—sighing {2x}, crying out {1x}, groaning {1x}. See: TWOT—134a; BDB—60c.

604. אֲנָקָה {1x} ʾănâqâh, *an-aw-kaw'*; the same as 603; some kind of lizard, prob. the *gecko* (from its *wail*):—ferret {1x}. See: TWOT—134b; BDB—60c.

605. אָנַשׁ {9x} ʾânash, *aw-nash'*; a prim. root; to *be frail, feeble,* or (fig.) *melancholy:*—incurable {5x}, desperate {1x}, desperately wicked {1x}, woeful {1x}, sick {1x}. See: TWOT—135; BDB—60c.

606. אֱנָשׁ {25x} ʾĕnâsh (Aram.), *en-awsh';* or

     אֱנַשׁ ʾĕnash (Aram.), *en-ash';* corresp. to 582; a *man:*—man {23x}, whosoever + 3606 {2x}. See: TWOT—2591; BDB—1081d.

     אַנְתְּ ʾant. See 859.

607. אַנְתָּה {14x} ʾantâh (Aram.), *an-taw';* corresp. to 859; *thou:*—thou {13x}, thee {1x}. See: TWOT—2592; BDB—1082a.

608. אַנְתּוּן {1x} ʾantûwn (Aram.), *an-toon';* plur. of 607; *ye:*—ye {1x}. See: TWOT—2593; BDB—1082a.

609. אָסָא {58x} ʾÂçâ', *aw-saw';* of uncert. der.; *Asa,* the name of a king and of a Levite:—Asa {58x}. See: BDB—61d.

610. אָסוּךְ {1x} ʾăçûwk, *aw-sook';* from 5480; *anointed,* i.e. an oil-*flask:*—pot {1x}. See: TWOT—1474a; BDB—62a, 692a.

611. אָסוֹן {5x} ʾâçôwn, *aw-sone';* of uncert. der.; *hurt:*—mischief {3x}, mischief fellow {2x}. See: TWOT—138a; BDB—62a.

612. אֵסוּר {3x} ʾêçûwr, *ay-soor';* from 631; a *bond* (espec. *manacles* of a prisoner):—band {2x}, prison {1x}. See: TWOT—141a; BDB—64a, 1082a.

613. אֱסוּר {3x} ʾĕçûwr (Aram.), *es-oor';* corresp. to 612:—band {2x}, imprisonment {1x}. See: TWOT—2595a; BDB—1082b.

614. אָסִיף {2} ʾâçîyph, *aw-seef';* or

     אָסִף ʾâçiph, *aw-seef';* from 622; *gathered,* i.e. (abstr.) a *gathering* in of crops:—ingathering {2x}. See: TWOT—140b; BDB—63b.

615. אָסִיר {12x} ʾâçîyr, *aw-sere';* from 631; *bound,* i.e. a *captive:*—prisoner {10x}, bound {2x}. See: TWOT—141b; BDB—64a.

616. אַסִּיר {3x} ʾaççîyr, *as-sere';* for 615:—prisoner {3x}. See: TWOT—141c; BDB—64b.

617. אַסִּיר {5x} ʾAççîyr, *as-sere';* the same as 616; *prisoner; Assir,* the name of two Isr.:—Assir {5x}. See: BDB—64b.

618. אָסָם {2x} ʾâçâm, *aw-sawm';* from an unused root mean. to *heap* together; a

storehouse (only in the plur.):—barn {1x}, storehouse {1x}. See: TWOT—139a; BDB—62a.

619. אַסְנָה {1x} ʾAçnâh, *as-naw';* of uncert. der.; *Asnah,* one of the Nethinim:—Asnah {1x}. See: BDB—62a.

620. אָסְנַפַּר {1x} ʾOçnappar (Aram.), *os-nappar';* of for. der.; *Osnappar,* an Ass. king:—Asnapper {1x}. See: BDB—1082a.

621. אָסְנַת {3x} ʾÂçᵉnath, *aw-se-nath';* of Eg. der.; *Asenath,* the wife of Joseph:—Asenath {3x}. See: BDB—62a.

622. אָסַף {200x} ʾâçaph, *aw-saf';* a prim. root; to *gather* for any purpose; hence, to *receive, take away,* i.e. remove (destroy, leave behind, put up, restore, etc.):—together {51x}, gather {86x}, assemble {15x}, rereward {5x}, misc. {51x}.

Acaph means "to gather, gather in, take away." **(1)** Basically, *acaph* refers to "bringing objects to a common point." This may mean to "gather" or "collect" something such as food. The first occurrence is when God told Noah to "gather" food to himself (Gen 6:21). Eventually, the food was to go into the ark. **(2)** This verb can also refer to "gathering" food at harvest time, or "harvesting": "And six years thou shalt sow thy land, and shalt gather in the fruits thereof" (Ex 23:10). **(3)** Second Kings 22:4 refers not to a process of going out and getting something together, but to standing still as someone brings money to one. **(4)** Also notice Gen 29:22: "And Laban gathered together all the men of the place, and made a feast"; this verse similarly focuses on the end product of gathering. But here the "gatherer" does not physically handle what is "gathered." He is simply the impetus or active cause for a congregating of all those men. **(5)** God may "gather" a man to his fathers—i.e., cause him to die (2 Kin 22:20). Here the emphasis is on the end product, and God as the agent who "gathers."

(6) *Acaph* may represent not only the process of bringing things to a common location; the word may also represent "bringing" things to oneself. After the harvest is brought ("gathered") in from the threshing floor and wine vat, the Feast of Booths is to be celebrated (Deut 16:13). **(7)** In Deut 22:2, a man is to "gather" into his home (bring home and care for) a lost animal whose owner cannot be found. **(8)** In this manner, God "gathers" to Himself those abandoned by their family (Ps 27:10). **(9)** A special application of this nuance is to "receive hospitality": "When he went in he sat him down in a street of the city: for there was no man that took them into his house to lodging" (Judg 19:15). **(10)** "To gather in" also may mean "to be

consumed by"—God promises that His people "shall be no more consumed with hunger" (Eze 34:29). **(11)** It is used in this way the verb can mean "to bring into," as when Jacob "gathered up his feet into the bed" (Gen 49:33).

(12) *Acaph* can emphasize "withdrawal" or "removal" of something; the action is viewed from the perspective of one who loses something because someone has taken it ("gathered it in"). In Ps 85:3, the "gathering" represents this sort of "withdrawal away from" the speaker. Thus, anger "disappears": "Thou hast taken away all thy wrath." Compare also Rachel's statement at the birth of Joseph: "God hath taken away my reproach" (Gen 30:23). In this case, Rachel speaks of the "destruction" of her reproach. **(13)** "To gather one's soul" is "to lose" one's life (Judg 18:25). **(14)** God can also be the agent who "gathers" or "takes away" a soul: "Gather not my soul with sinners . . ." (Ps 26:9). **(15)** In this sense, *acaph* can mean "being cured" of a disease; "Would God my lord were with the prophet that is in Samaria! for he would recover him of his leprosy" (2 Kin 5:3). Syn.: ʾÂçaph is a near synonym to *qabats* (6908 – {136x}), differing by having a more extensive range of meanings. ʾÂçaph, duplicates all the meanings of *qabats*. See: TWOT—140; BDB—62a.

623. אָסָף {46x} ʾÂçâph, *aw-sawf'*; from 622; *collector; Asaph*, the name of three Isr., and of the family of the first:—Asaph {1x}. See: BDB—63a.

אָסִיף ʾâçîph. See 614

624. אָסֻף {3x} ʾâçûph, *aw-soof'*; pass. part. of 622; *collected* (only in the plur.), i.e. a *collection* (of offerings):—threshold {1x}, Asuppim {2x}. See: TWOT—140c; BDB—62b, 62c.

625. אֹסֶף {3x} ʾôçeph, *o'-sef*; from 622; a *collection* (of fruits):—the gathering {2x}, gather {1x}. See: TWOT—140a; BDB—63a.

626. אֲסֵפָה {1x} ʾăçêphâh, *as-ay-faw'*; from 622; a *collection* of people (only adv.):—together {1x}. See: TWOT—140d; BDB—63b.

627. אֲסֻפָּה {1x} ʾăçuppâh, *as-up-paw'*; fem. of 624.; a *collection* of (learned) men (only in the plur.):—assemblies {1x}. See: TWOT—140e; BDB—63b.

628. אֲסַפְסֻף {1x} ʾaçpᵉçûph, *as-pes-oof'*; by redupl. from 624; *gathered up together*, i.e. a promiscuous *assemblage* (of people):—mixed multitude {1x}. See: TWOT—140f; BDB—63c.

629. אָסְפַּרְנָא {7x} ʾoçparnâ' (Aram.), *os-par-naw'*; of Pers. der.; *diligently:*—speedily {4x}, speed {1x}, fast {1x}, forthwith {1x}. See: TWOT—2594; BDB—1082a.

630. אַסְפָּתָא {1x} ʾAçpâthâ', *as-paw-thaw'*; of Pers. der.; *Aspatha*, a son of Haman:—Aspatha {1x}. See: BDB—63c.

631. אָסַר {72x} ʾâçar, *aw-sar'*; a prim. root; to *yoke* or *hitch;* by anal. to *fasten* in any sense, to *join* battle:—bind {47x}, prison {4x}, (-er {2x}), tie {4x}, misc.: fast, gird, harness, hold, keep, make ready, order, prepare, put in bonds, set in array – {15x}.

Acar means "to bind, imprison, tie, gird, to harness." **(1)** The first use of *acar* in the Hebrew text is in Gen 39:20, which tells how Joseph was "imprisoned" after being wrongfully accused by Potiphar's wife. **(2)** The common word for "tying up" for security and safety, *acar* is often used to indicate the tying up of horses and donkeys (2 Kin 7:10). **(3)** Similarly, oxen are "harnessed" to carts (1 Sa 6:7, 10). **(4)** Frequently, *acar* is used to describe the "binding" of prisoners with cords and various fetters (Gen 42:24; Judg 15:10, 12–13). **(5)** Samson misled Delilah as she probed for the secret of his strength, telling her to "bind" him with bowstrings (Judg 16:7) and new ropes (Judg 16:11), none of which could hold him. **(6)** Used in an abstract sense, *acar* refers **(6a)** to those who are spiritually "bound" (Ps 146:7; Is 49:9; 61:1) or **(6b)** a man who is emotionally "captivated" by a woman's hair (Song 7:5). **(7)** Strangely, the figurative use of the term in the sense of obligation or "binding" to a vow or an oath is found only in Num 30, but it is used there a number of times (vv. 3, 5–6, 8–9, 11–12). See: TWOT—141; BDB—63c, 1082a.

632. אֵסָר {11x} ʾêçâr, *es-sawr'*; or

אִסָּר ʾiççâr, *is-sawr'*; from 631; an *obligation* or *vow* (of abstinence):—binding {1x}, bond {10x}. See: TWOT—141d; BDB—64b, 1082b.

633. אֱסָר {7x} ʾĕçâr (Aram.), *es-sawr';* corresp. to 632 in a legal sense; an *interdict:*—decree {7x}. See: TWOT—2595b; BDB—1082b.

634. אֵסַר־חַדֹּון {3x} ʾÊçar-Chaddôwn, *ay-sar' chad-dohn';* of for. der.; *Esarchaddon*, an Assy. king:—Esar-haddon {3x}. See: BDB—64d.

635. אֶסְתֵּר {55x} ʾEçtêr, *es-tare';* of Pers. der.; *Ester*, the Jewish heroine:—Esther {55x}. See: BDB—64d.

636. אָע {5x} ʾâʿ (Aram.), *aw;* corresp. to 6086; a *tree* or *wood:*—timber {3x}, wood {2x}. See: TWOT—2596; BDB—1082b.

637. אַף {17x} ʾaph, *af;* a prim. particle; mean. *accession* (used as an adv. or conjunc.); *also* or *yea;* adversatively *though:*—also, even, yet, moreover, yea, with, low, therefore, much = {17x}. This is a conjunction denoting addition, especially of something greater. See: TWOT—142; BDB—64d, 210b, 1082b.

638. אַף {4x} ʾaph (Aram.), *af;* corresp. to 637:—also {4x}. See: TWOT—2597; BDB—1082b.

639. אַף {276} ʾaph, *af;* from 599; prop. the *nose* or *nostril;* hence, the *face,* and occasionally a *person;* also (from the rapid breathing in passion) *ire:*—anger {172x}, wrath {42x}, face {22x}, nostrils {13x}, nose {12x}, angry {4x}, longsuffering + 750 {4x}, before {2x}, countenance {1x}, forbearing {1x}, forehead {1x}, snout {1x}, worthy {1x}.

Aph (639) means "nose; nostrils; face; wrath; anger." **(1)** The fundamental meaning of the word is "nose," as a literal part of the body. *Aph* bears this meaning in the singular, while the dual refers to the "nostrils" through which air passes in and out: "And the LORD God formed man of the dust of the ground, and breathed into his nostrils the breath of life" (Gen 2:7—the first biblical occurrence). **(2)** In other contexts *aph* in the dual represents the "entire face." God cursed Adam saying: "In the sweat of thy face shalt thou eat bread, till thou return unto the ground" (Gen 3:19). **(3)** This emphasis appears often with the phrase "to bow one's face to the ground": "And Joseph's brethren came, and bowed down themselves before him with their faces to the earth" (Gen 42:6). **(4)** The words "length of face or nostrils" constitute an idiom meaning "longsuffering" or "slow to anger." **(4a)** It is used both of God and of man: "The LORD, The LORD God, merciful and gracious, long-suffering, and abundant in goodness and truth" (Ex 34:6). **(4b)** The contrasting idiom, meaning "quick to anger," might literally mean "short of face/nostrils." It implies a changeable countenance, a capricious disposition.

(5) Prov 14:17 uses this idiom with a little stronger emphasis: "He that is soon angry dealeth foolishly: and a man of wicked devices is hated." The accuracy of this translation is supported by the parallelism of the phrase and "a man of evil devices." **(6)** Clearly *aph* must mean something evil in God's sight. **(7)** Finally, the dual form can mean "wrath" (only in 4 passages): "Surely the churning of milk bringeth forth butter, and the wringing of the nose bringeth forth blood: so the forcing of wrath bringeth forth strife" (Prov 30:33; cf. Ex 15:8). **(8)** The singular form means "nose" about 25 times. In Num 11:19–20 the word represents a human nose: "You [Israel] shall . . . eat [the meat God will supply] . . . a whole month, until it comes out of your nostrils and becomes loathsome to you." **(9)** Is 2:22 makes it clear that the word represents the place where the breath is: "Cease ye from man, whose breath of life is in his nostrils." **(10)** *Aph* is applied also to the "nose" of animals. In Job 40:24, God speaks of a large water animal: "He taketh it with his eyes: his nose pierceth through snares."

(11) The word can be used anthropomorphically of God. Certainly passages such as Deut 4:15–19 make it clear that God is a Spirit (cf. Jn 4:24) and has not a body like men. Yet, speaking figuratively, it may be said: "They shall teach Jacob thy judgments, and Israel thy law: they shall put incense before thee [literally, "in thy nostrils"], and whole burnt sacrifice upon thine altar" (Deut 33:10; cf. Ps 18:8, 15). **(12)** The idiom "high of nose" means "haughty" (cf. the English idiom "to have one's nose in the air"): "The wicked, through the pride of his countenance, will not seek after God" (Ps 10:4). **(13)** The singular form often means "anger" or "wrath." This meaning first appears in Gen 30:2: "And Jacob's anger was kindled against Rachel. . . ." **(14)** This meaning is applied to God as a figure of speech (anthropopathism) whereby He is attributed human emotions. Since God is infinite, eternal, and unchangeable and since anger is an emotion representing a change in one's reaction (cf. Num 25:4), God does not really become angry, He only appears to do so in the eyes of men (cf. Prov 29:8). **(15)** The Spirit of God can seize a man and move him to a holy "anger" (Judg 14:19; 1 Sa 11:6). Syn.: 3707. See: TWOT—133a; BDB—60a, 64d, 1081d.

640. אָפַד {2x} ʾâphad, *aw-fad';* a prim. root [rather a denom. from 646]; to *gird* on (the ephod):—bind {1x}, gird {1x}. See: TWOT—142.1; BDB—65d.

אֵפֹד ʾêphôd. See 646.

641. אֵפֹד {1x} ʾÊphôd, *ay-fode';* the same as 646 short.; *Ephod,* an Isr.:—Ephod {1x}. See: BDB—65d.

642. אֲפֻדָּה {3x} ʾêphuddâh, *ay-food-daw';* fem. of 646; a *girding* on (of the ephod); hence, Gen a *plating* (of metal):—ephod {2x}, ornament {1x}.

Ephuddah means "ephod; covering." This word is a feminine form of epod (or ephod). The word occurs 3 times, first in Ex 28:8: "And the curious girdle of the ephod, which is upon it, shall be of . . . gold, of blue, and purple, and scarlet, and fine twined linen." See: 142.1b; BDB—65d.

643. אַפֶּדֶן {1x} ʾappeden, ap-peh'-den; appar. of for. der.; a *pavilion* or palace-tent:—palace {1x}. See: TWOT—142.2; BDB—66a.

644. אָפָה {25x} ʾâphâh, aw-faw'; a prim. root; to *cook*, espec. to *bake:*—bake {13x}, baker {11x}, bakemeats + 4639 {1x}. See: TWOT—143; BDB—66a.

אֵפֹה ʾêphâh. See 374.

645. אֵפוֹ {15x} ʾêphôw, ay-fo'; or

אֵפוֹא ʾêphôwʾ, ay-fo'; from 6311; strictly a demonstr. particle, *here;* but used of time, *now* or *then:*—now {10x}, where {4x}, here {1x}. See: TWOT—144; BDB—66b.

646. אֵפוֹד {49x} ʾêphôwd, ay-fode'; rarely

אֵפֹד ʾêphôd, ay-fode'; prob. of for. der.; a *girdle;* spec. the *ephod* or high-priest's shoulder-piece; also Gen an *image:*—ephod {49x}.

Ephod is transliterated as "*ephod.*" (1) This word represents a close-fitting outer garment associated with worship. (1a) It was a kind of long vest, generally reaching to the thighs. (1b) The "*ephod*" of the high priest was fastened with a beautifully woven girdle (Ex 28:27–28) and had shoulder straps set in onyx stones, on which were engraved the names of the twelve tribes. (1c) Over the chest of the high priest was the breastplate, also containing twelve stones engraved with the tribal names. (1d) Rings attached it to the "*ephod.*" (1e) The Urim and Thummin were also linked to the breastplate. (2) Apparently, this "*ephod*" and attachments were prominently displayed in the sanctuary. David consulted the "*ephod*" to learn whether the people of Keilah would betray him to Saul (1 Sa 23:9–12); no doubt the Urim and Thummim were used. (3) The first biblical occurrence of the word refers to this high priestly *ephod:* "Onyx stones, and stones to be set in the *ephod,* and in the breastplate" (Ex 25:7). (4) So venerated was this "*ephod*" that replicas were sometimes made (Judg 8:27; 17:1–5) and even worshiped. (5) Lesser priests (1 Sa 2:28) and priestly trainees wore less elaborate "*ephods*" made of linen whenever they appeared before the altar. See: TWOT—142.1a; BDB—65b.

647. אֲפִיחַ {1x} ʾĂphîyach, af-ee'-akh; perh. from 6315; *breeze; Aphiach,* an Isr.:—Aphiah {1x}. See: BDB—66c.

648. אָפִיל {1x} ʾâphîyl, aw-feel'; from the same as 651 (in the sense of *weakness*); *unripe:*—grown up {1x}. See: TWOT—145d; BDB—66d.

649. אַפַּיִם {2x} ʾAppayim, ap-pah'-yim; dual of 639; *two nostrils; Appajim,* an Isr.:—Appaim {2x}. See: BDB—60b.

650. אָפִיק {19x} ʾâphîyq, aw-feek'; from 622; prop. *containing,* i.e. a *tube;* also a *bed* or *valley* of a stream; also a *strong* thing or a *hero:*—river {10x}, channel {3x}, stream {2x}, brooks {1x}, mighty {1x}, scales {1x}, strong {1x}. See: TWOT—149a; BDB—67d.

651. אָפֵל {1x} ʾâphêl, aw-fale'; from an unused root mean. to *set* as the sun; *dusky:*—very dark {1x}. See: TWOT—145b; BDB—66c.

652. אֹפֶל {9x} ʾôphel, o'fel; from the same as 651; *dusk:*—darkness {7x}, privily {1x}, obscurity {1x}. See: TWOT—145a; BDB—66c.

653. אֲפֵלָה {10x} ʾăphêlâh, af-ay-law'; fem. of 651; *duskiness,* fig. *misfortune;* concr. *concealment:*—darkness {6x}, gloominess {2x}, dark {1x}, thick {1x}. See: TWOT—145c; BDB—66c.

654. אֶפְלָל {2x} ʾEphlâl, ef-lawl'; from 6419; *judge; Ephlal,* an Isr.:—Ephlal {2x}. See: BDB—66d, 813d.

655. אֹפֶן {1x} ʾôphen, o'-fen; from an unused root mean. to *revolve;* a *turn,* i.e. a *season:*—fitly {1x}. See: TWOT—146b; BDB—67a.

אוֹפָן ʾôphân. See 212.

656. אָפֵס {5x} ʾâphêç, aw-face'; a prim. root; to *disappear,* i.e. *cease:*—fail {2x}, gone {1x}, end {1x}, brought to nought {1x}. See: TWOT—147; BDB—67a.

657. אֶפֶס {43x} ʾepheç, eh'-fes; from 656; *cessation,* i.e. an *end* (espec. of the earth); often used adv. *no further;* also (like 6466) the *ankle* (in the dual), as being the extremity of the leg or foot:—ends {13x}, no {4x}, none {3x}, not {3x}, nothing {2x}, without {2x}, else {2x}, beside {1x}, but {1x}, cause {1x}, howbeit {1x}, misc. {10x}.

Ephec means "end; not; nothing; only." (1) Basically, the noun indicates that a thing "comes to an end" and "is no more." (2) The idea of the "far reaches" of a thing is seen in passages such as Prov 30:4: "Who hath gathered the wind in his fists? Who hath bound the waters in a garment? Who hath established all the ends [boundaries] of the earth?" (cf. Ps 72:8). (3) In other contexts, *ephec* means the "territory" of the nations other than Israel: "With them he shall push the people together to the ends of the earth" (Deut 33:17). (4) More often, this word represents the peoples who live outside the territory of Israel: "Ask of me,

and I shall give thee the heathen for thine inheritance, and the [very ends] of the earth for thy possession" (Ps 2:8). **(5)** In Ps 22:27, the phrase, "the ends of the world," is synonymously parallel to "all the [families] of the nations." Therefore, "the ends of the earth" in such contexts represents all the peoples of the earth besides Israel.

(6) *Ephec* is used to express "non-existence" primarily in poetry, where it appears chiefly as a synonym of *ayin* ("none, nothing"). **(7)** In one instance, *ephec* is used expressing the "non-existence" of a person or thing and is translated "not" or "no": "Is there not yet any of the house of Saul, that I may show the kindness of God unto him?" (2 Sa 9:3). **(8)** In Is 45:6, the word means "none" or "no one": "That they may know from the rising of the sun, and from the west, that there is none beside me" (cf. v. 9). **(10)** In a few passages, *ephec* used as a particle of negation means "at an end" or "nothing": "And all her princes shall be nothing," or "unimportant" and "not exalted" to kingship (Is 34:12). **(11)** The force of this word in Is 41:12 is on the "non-existence" of those so described: "They that war against thee shall be as nothing, and as a thing of nought."

(12) This word can also mean "nothing" in the sense of "powerlessness" and "worthlessness": "All nations before him are as nothing; and they are counted to him less than nothing, and [meaningless]" (Is 40:17). **(13)** In Num 22:35 *ephec* means "nothing other than" or "only": "Go with the men: but only the word that I shall speak unto thee, that thou shall speak" (cf. Num 23:13). In such passages, *ephec* (with the Hebrew particle *ki*) qualifies the preceding phrase. **(14)** In 2 Sa 12:14, a special nuance of the word is represented by the English "howbeit." **(15)** In Is 52:4 *ephec* preceded by the preposition *be* ("by; because of") means "without cause": "And the Assyrian oppressed them without cause." Syn.: 319, 3615, 7093, 7097, 7098. See: TWOT—147a; BDB—67a, 67b.

658. אֶפֶס דַּמִּים {1x} ʾ**Epheç Dammîym**, *eh'-fes dam-meem';* from 657 and the plur. of 1818; *boundary of blood*-drops; *Ephes-Dammim*, a place in Pal.:—Ephesdammim {1x}. See: BDB—67c, 819d.

659. אֶפַע {1x} ʾ**êpha**ʿ, *eh'-fah;* from an unused root prob. mean. to *breathe;* prop. a *breath*, i.e. *nothing:*—of nought {1x}. See: TWOT—1791a; BDB—67c.

660. אֶפְעֶה {3x} ʾ**ephʿeh**, *ef-eh';* from 659 (in the sense of *hissing*); an *asp* or other venomous serpent:—viper {3x}. See: TWOT—1791b; BDB—67c, 821a.

661. אָפַף {5x} ʾ**âphaph**, *aw-faf';* a prim. root; to *surround:*—compass {5x}. See: TWOT—148; BDB—67c.

662. אָפַק {7x} ʾ**âphaq**, *aw-fak';* a prim. root; to *contain*, i.e. (reflex.) *abstain:*—refrain {5x}, forced {1x}, restrained {1x}. See: TWOT—149; BDB—67c.

663. אָפֵק {9x} ʾ**Âphêq**, *af-ake';* or

אָפִיק ʾ**Âphîyq**, *af-eek';* from 662 (in the sense of *strength*); *fortress; Aphek* (or *Aphik*), the name of three places in Pal.:—Aphek {8x}, Aphik {1x}. See: BDB—67d.

664. אֲפֵקָה {1x} ʾ**Âphêqâh**, *af-ay-kaw';* fem. of 663; *fortress; Aphekah*, a place in Pal.:—Aphekah {1x}. See: BDB—68a.

665. אֵפֶר {22x} ʾ**êpher**, *ay'-fer;* from an unused root mean. to *bestrew; ashes:*—ashes {22x}. Ref.: TWOT—150a; BDB—68a.

666. אֲפֵר {2x} ʾ**ăphêr**, *af-ayr';* from the same as 665 (in the sense of *covering*); a *turban:*—ashes {2x}. See: TWOT—151a; BDB—68b.

667. אֶפְרֹחַ {2x} ʾ**ephrôach**, *ef-ro'-akh;* from 6524 (in the sense of *bursting* the shell); the *brood* of a bird:—young one {2x}, young {2x}. See: TWOT—1813c; BDB—68b, 827b.

668. אַפִּרְיוֹן {1x} ʾ**appiryôwn**, *ap-pir-yone';* prob. of Eg. der.; a *palanquin:*—chariot {1x}. See: TWOT—151b; BDB—68b.

669. אֶפְרַיִם {180x} ʾ**Ephrayim**, *ef-rah'-yim;* dual of a masc. form of 672; *double fruit; Ephrajim*, a son of Joseph; also the tribe descended from him, and its territory:—Ephraim {176x}, Ephraimites {4x}. See: BDB—68b.

670. אֲפָרְסִי {1x} ʾ**Âphârʿçay** (Aram.), *af-aw-re-sah'ee;* of for. or. (only in the plur.); an *Apharesite* or inhab. of an unknown region of Assyria:—Apharsite {1x}. See: BDB—1082b.

671. אֲפַרְסְכַי {2x} ʾ**Âpharçʿkay** (Aram.), *af-ar-sek-ah'ee;* or

אֲפַרְסַתְכַי ʾ**Âpharçathkay** (Aram.), *af-ar-sath-kah'ee;* of for. or. (only in the plur.); an *Apharsekite* or *Apharsathkite*, an unknown Ass. tribe:—Apharsachites {2x}, Apharsathchites {1x}. See: BDB—1082b, 1082c.

672. אֶפְרָת {10x} ʾ**Ephrâth**, *ef-rawth';* or

אֶפְרָתָה ʾ**Ephrâthâh**, *ef-raw'-thaw;* from 6509; *fruitfulness; Ephrath*, another name for Bethlehem; once (Ps 132:6) perh. for *Ephraim;* also of an Isr. woman:—

Ephrath {5x}, Ephratah {5x}. See: BDB—68c, 68d.

673. אֶפְרָתִי {5x} 'Ephrâthîy, ef-rawth-ee'; patrial from 672; an Ephrathite or an Ephraimite:—Ephraimite {1x}, Ephrathite {4x}. See: BDB—68d.

674. אַפְּתֹם {1x} 'app°thôm (Aram.), ap-pe-thome'; of Pers. or.; revenue; others at the last:—revenue {1x}. See: TWOT—2601; BDB—1082c.

675. אֶצְבּוֹן {2x} 'Etsbôwn, ets-bone'; or

אֶצְבֹּן 'Etsbôn, ets-bone'; of uncert. der.; Etsbon, the name of two Isr.:—Ezbon. {2x}. See: BDB—69a.

676. אֶצְבַּע {32x} 'etsbac, ets-bah'; from the same as 6648 (in the sense of rasping); something to seize with, i.e. a finger; by anal. a toe:—finger {32x}. See: TWOT—1873a; BDB—69a, 840c, 1109c.

677. אֶצְבַּע {3x} 'etsbac (Aram.), ets-bah'; corresp. to 676:—finger {1x}, toe {2x}. See: TWOT—2602; BDB—1082c, 1109c.

678. אָצִיל {2x} 'âtsîyl, aw-tseel'; from 680 (in its second. sense of separation); an extremity (Is 41:9), also a noble:—nobles {1x}, chief men {1x}. See: TWOT—153b; BDB—69c.

679. אַצִּיל {3x} 'atstsîyl, ats-tseel'; from 680 (in its primary sense of uniting); a joint of the hand (i.e. knuckle); also (according to some) a party-wall (Eze 41:8):—armhole + 3027 {2x}, great {1x}. See: TWOT—153c; BDB—69c.

680. אָצַל {5x} 'âtsal, aw-tsal'; a prim. root; prop. to join; used only as a denom. from 681; to separate; hence, to select, refuse, contract:—take {2x}, reserved {1x}, kept {1x}, straitened {1x}. See: TWOT—153; BDB—69b.

681. אֵצֶל {58x} 'êtsel, ay'-tsel; from 680 (in the sense of joining); a side; (as a prep.) near:—by {21x}, beside {12x}, by . . . {10x}, near {3x}, at {2x}, with . . . {2x}, from . . . {1x}, against {1x}, close {1x}, to {1x}, toward {1x}, unto {1x}, with {1x}. Syn.: 905, 5921. See: TWOT—153a; BDB—69a.

682. אָצֵל {7x} 'Âtsêl, aw-tsale'; from 680; noble; Atsel, the name of an Isr., and of a place in Pal.:—Azal {1x}, Azel {6x}. See: BDB—69b, 69c.

683. אֲצַלְיָהוּ {2x} 'Ătsalyâhûw, ats-al-yaw'-hoo; from 680 and 3050 prol.; Jah has reserved; Atsaljah, an Isr.:—Azaliah {2x}. See: BDB—69c.

684. אֹצֶם {2x} 'Ôtsem, o'-tsem; from an unused root prob. mean. to be strong; strength (i.e. strong); Otsem, the name of two Isr.:—Ozem {2x}. See: BDB—69d.

685. אֶצְעָדָה {2x} 'etscâdâh, ets-aw-daw'; a var. from 6807; prop. a step-chain; by anal. a bracelet:—bracelet {1x}, chain {1x}. See: TWOT—1943e; BDB—69d, 858a.

686. אָצַר {5x} 'âtsar, aw-tsar'; a prim. root; to store up:—lay up in store {2x}, store up {1x}, make treasurer {1x}, treasured {1x}. See: TWOT—154; BDB—69d.

687. אֵצֶר {5x} 'Etser, ay'-tser; from 686; treasure; Etser, an Idumæan:—Ezer {5x}. See: BDB—69d.

688. אֶקְדָּח {1x} 'eqdâch, ek-dawkh'; from 6916; burning, i.e. a carbuncle or other fiery gem:—carbuncle {1x}. See: TWOT—1987b; BDB—70a, 869b.

689. אַקּוֹ {1x} 'aqqôw, ak-ko'; prob. from 602; slender, i.e. the ibex:—wild goat {1x}. See: TWOT—155; BDB—70a.

690. אֲרָא {1x} 'Ărâ', ar-aw'; prob. for 738; lion; Ara, an Isr.:—Ara {1x}. See: BDB—70b.

691. אֶרְאֵל {1x} 'er°êl, er-ale'; prob. for 739; a hero (collect.):—valiant one {1x}. See: TWOT—159a; BDB—70b, 72a.

692. אַרְאֵלִי {3x} 'Ar°êlîy, ar-ay-lee'; from 691; heroic; Areli (or an Arelite, collect.), an Isr. and his desc.:—Areli {2x}, Arelites {1x}. See: BDB—70b, 72a.

693. אָרַב {42x} 'ârab, aw-rab'; a prim. root; to lurk:—lay in wait {26x}, liers in wait {8x}, ambush {8x}. See: TWOT—156; BDB—70b, 936d.

694. אֲרָב {1x} 'Ărâb, ar-awb'; from 693; ambush; Arab, a place in Pal.:—Arab {1x}. See: BDB—70c.

695. אֶרֶב {2x} 'ereb, eh'-reb; from 693; ambuscade:—den {1x}, lie in wait {1x}. See: TWOT—156a; BDB—70c.

696. אֹרֶב {1x} 'ôreb, o'-reb; the same as 695:—wait {1x}. See: TWOT—156b; BDB—70c.

אַרְבֵּאל 'Arbê'l. See 1009.

697. אַרְבֶּה {24x} 'arbeh, ar-beh'; from 7235; a locust (from its rapid increase):—grasshopper {4x}, locust {20x}.

This noun, which occurs 24 times, refers to a kind of swarming "locust": "Stretch out thine hand over the land of Egypt for the locusts, that they may come up upon the land of Egypt, and eat every herb of the land" (Ex 10:12). Syn.: 1462, 2284, 5556. See: TWOT—2103a; BDB—70d, 916a.

Hebrew

698. אֲרֻבָּה {1x} ʾorŏbâh, or-ob-aw'; fem. of 696 (only in the plur.); ambuscades:—spoils {1x}. See: TWOT—156c; BDB—70c.

699. אֲרֻבָּה {9x} ʾărubbâh, ar-oob-baw'; fem. part. pass. of 693 (as if for lurking); a lattice; (by impl.) a window, dove-cot (because of the pigeon-holes), chimney (with its apertures for smoke), sluice (with openings for water):—chimney {1x}, windows {1x}. Syn.: 2474. See: TWOT—156d; BDB—70c.

700. אֲרֻבּוֹת {1x} ʾĂrubbôwth, ar-oob-both'; plur. of 699; Arubboth, a place in Pal.:—Aruboth {1x}. See: BDB—70d.

701. אַרְבִּי {1x} ʾArbîy, ar-bee'; patrial from 694; an Arbite or native of Arab:—Arbite {1x}. See: BDB—70c.

702. אַרְבַּע {316x} ʾarbaʿ, ar-bah'; masc.
אַרְבָּעָה ʾarbâʿâh, ar-baw-aw'; from 7251; four:—four {265x}, fourteen + 6240 {19x}, fourteenth + 6240 {23x}, fourth {5x}, forty {2x}, three score and fourteen + 7657 {2x}. See: TWOT—2106a; BDB—70d, 916d, 112c.

703. אַרְבַּע {8x} ʾarbaʿ (Aram.), ar-bah'; corresp. to 702:—four {8x}. See: TWOT—2986a; BDB—1082c, 1112c.

704. אַרְבַּע {2x} ʾArbaʿ, ar-bah'; the same as 702; Arba, one of the Anakim:—Arba {2x}. See: BDB—70d, 917b.

אַרְבָּעָה ʾarbâʿâh. See 702.

705. אַרְבָּעִים {136x} ʾarbâʿîym, ar-baw-eem'; multiple of 702; forty:—forty {132x}, fortieth {4x}. See: TWOT—2106b; BDB—70d, 917b.

706. אַרְבַּעְתַּיִם {1x} ʾarbaʿtayim, ar-bah-tah'-yim; dual of 702; fourfold:—fourfold {1x}. See: TWOT—2106a; BDB—916d.

707. אָרַג {13x} ʾârag, aw-rag'; a prim. root; to plait or weave:—weave {4x}, weaver {6x}, woven {3x}. See: TWOT—157; BDB—70d.

708. אֶרֶג {2x} ʾereg, eh'-reg; from 707; a weaving; a braid; also a shuttle:—beam {1x}, weaver's shuttle {1x}. See: TWOT—157a; BDB—71a.

709. אַרְגֹּב {5x} ʾArgôb, ar-gobe'; from the same as 7263; stony; Argob, a district of Pal.:—Argob {1x}. See: BDB—71a, 918d.

710. אַרְגְּוָן {1x} ʾargᵉvân, arg-ev-awn'; a var. for 713; purple:—purple {1x}. See: TWOT—157b; BDB—71a, 1082c.

711. אַרְגְּוָן {3x} ʾargᵉvân (Aram.), arg-ev-awn'; corresp. to 710:—scarlet {3x}. Ar-

gevan is possibly a deep reddish-purple. See: TWOT—2603; BDB—1082c.

712. אַרְגָּז {3x} ʾargâz, ar-gawz'; perh. from 7264 (in the sense of being suspended); a box (as a pannier):—coffer {3x}. See: TWOT—2112d; BDB—71a, 919c.

713. אַרְגָּמָן {38x} ʾargâmân, ar-gaw-mawn'; of for. or.; purple (the color or the dyed stuff):—purple {38x}. See: TWOT—157b; BDB—71a, 1082c.

714. אַרְדְּ {2x} ʾArd, ard; from an unused root prob. mean. to wander; fugitive; Ard, the name of two Isr.:—Ard {2x}. See: BDB—71b.

715. אַרְדּוֹן {1x} ʾArdôwn, ar-dohn'; from the same as 714; roaming; Ardon, an Isr.:—Ardon {1x}. See: BDB—71b.

716. אַרְדִּי {1x} ʾArdîy, ar-dee; patron. from 714; an Ardite (collect.) or desc. of Ard:—Ardites {1x}. See: BDB—71b.

717. אָרָה {2x} ʾârâh, aw-raw'; a prim. root; to pluck:—gather {1x}, pluck {1x}. See: TWOT—158; BDB—71c, 1082c.

718. אֲרוּ {5x} ʾărûw (Aram.), ar-oo'; prob. akin to 431; lo!:—behold {4x}, lo {1x}. See: TWOT—2604; BDB—1080d, 1082c.

719. אַרְוַד {2x} ʾArvad, ar-vad'; prob. from 7300; a refuge for the roving; Arvad, an island-city of Pal.:—Arvad {2x}. See: BDB—71c.

720. אָרוֹד {1x} ʾĂrôwd, ar-ode'; an orth. var. of 719; fugitive; Arod, an Isr.:—Arod {1x}. See: BDB—71b.

721. אַרְוָדִי {2x} ʾArvâdîy, ar-vaw-dee'; patrial from 719; an Arvadite or citizen of Arvad:—Arvadite {2x}. See: BDB—71c.

722. אֲרוֹדִי {2x} ʾĂrôwdîy, ar-o-dee'; patron. from 721; an Arodite or desc. of Arod:—Arodi {1x}, Arodites {1x}. See: BDB—71b.

723. אֻרְוָה {3x} ʾurvâh, oor-vaw'; or
אֲרָיָה ʾărâyâh, ar-aw-yah'; from 717 (in the sense of feeding); a herding-place for an animal:—stall {3x}. See: TWOT—158b; BDB—71d.

724. אֲרוּכָה {6x} ʾărûwkâh, ar-oo-kaw'; or
אֲרֻכָה ʾărûkâh, ar-oo-kaw'; fem. pass. part. of 748 (in the sense of restoring to soundness); wholeness (lit. or fig.):—health {4x}, perfected {1x}, made up {1x}. See: TWOT—162d; BDB—74a.

725. אֲרוּמָה {1x} **ʾĂrûwmâh**, *ar-oo-maw'*; a var. of 7316; *height; Arumah,* a place in Pal.:—Arumah {1x}. See: BDB—72b.

726. אֲרוֹמִי {1x} **ʾĂrôwmîy**, *ar-o-mee'*; a clerical err. for 130; an *Edomite* (as in the marg.):—Syrian {1x}. See: BDB—10c.

727. אָרוֹן {202x} **ʾârôwn**, *aw-rone'*; or

אָרֹן **ʾârôn**, *aw-rone';* from 717 (in the sense of *gathering*); a *box:*—ark {195x}, chest {6x}, coffin {1x}.

Aron (727)means "ark; coffin; chest; box." **(1)** In Gen 50:26, this word represents a coffin or sarcophagus: "So Joseph died, being a hundred and ten years old: and they embalmed him, and he was put in a coffin in Egypt." This coffin was probably quite elaborate and similar to those found in ancient Egyptian tombs. **(2)** During the reign of Joash (or Jehoash), when the temple was repaired, money for the work was deposited in a "chest" with a hole in its lid. The high priest Jehoida prepared this chest and put it at the threshold to the temple (2 Kin 12:9). **(3)** In most occurrences, *aron* refers to the "ark of the covenant." **(3a)** This piece of furniture functioned primarily as a container. **(3b)** As such the word is often modified by divine names or attributes. **(3b1)** The divine name first modifies *aron* in 1 Sa 3:3: "And ere the lamp of God went out in the temple of the LORD, where the ark of God was, and Samuel was laid down to sleep. . . ." **(3b2)** *Aron* is first modified by God's covenant name, *Yahweh,* in Josh 4:5. **(3b3)** Judg 20:27 is the first appearance of the "ark" as the ark of the covenant of *Elohim.* **(3b4)** First Samuel 5:11 uses the phrase "the ark of the God [*elohim*] of Israel," and 1 Chr 15:12 employs "the ark of the LORD [*Yahweh*] God [*elohim*] of Israel."

(4) Sometimes divine attributes replace the divine name: "Arise, O LORD, into thy rest; thou, and the ark of thy strength" (Ps 132:8). **(5)** Another group of modifiers focuses on divine redemption (cf. Heb. 8:5). Thus *aron* is often described as the "ark of the covenant" (Josh 3:6) or "the ark of the covenant of the LORD" (Num 10:33). **(6)** As such, the ark contained the memorials of God's great redemptive acts—the tablets upon which were inscribed the Ten Commandments, an omer or two quarts of manna, and Aaron's rod. **(7)** By Solomon's day, only the stone tablets remained in the ark (1 Kin 8:9). This chest was also called "the ark of the testimony" (Ex 25:22), which indicates that the two tablets were evidence of divine redemption. **(8)** Ex 25:10–22 tells us that this ark was made of acacia wood and measured 3¾ feet by 2¼ feet by 2¼ feet. It was gold-plated inside and outside, with a molding of gold. Each of its four feet had a golden ring

at its top, through which passed unremovable golden carrying poles. The golden cover or mercy seat (place of propitiatory atonement) had the same dimensions as the top of the ark. Two golden cherubim sat on this cover facing each other, representing the heavenly majesty (Eze 1:10) that surrounds the living God. **(9)** In addition to containing memorials of divine redemption, the ark represented the presence of God. To be before it was to be in God's presence (Num 10:35), although His presence was not limited to the ark (cf. 1 Sa 4:3–11; 7:2, 6). The ark ceased to have this sacramental function when Israel began to regard it as a magical box with sacred power (a palladium). **(10)** God promised to meet Moses at the ark (Ex 25:22). Thus, the ark functioned as a place where divine revelation was received (Lev 1:1; 16:2; Num 7:89). **(11)** The ark served as an instrument through which God guided and defended Israel during the wilderness wandering (Num 10:11). **(12)** Finally, it was upon this ark that the highest of Israel's sacraments, the blood of atonement, was presented and received (Lev 16:2ff.). See: TWOT—166a; BDB—75b.

728. אֲרַוְנָה {9x} **ʾĂravnâh**, *ar-av-naw';* or (by transp.)

אוֹרְנָה **ʾÔwrnâh**, *ore-naw';* or

אֲרַנְיָה **ʾArnîyah**, *ar-nee-yaw';* all by orth. var. for 771; *Aravnah* (or *Arnijah* or *Ornah*), a Jebusite:—Araunah {9x}. See: BDB—22d, 72b, 75d.

729. אָרַז {1x} **ʾâraz**, *aw-raz';* a prim. root; to *be firm;* used only in the pass. part. as a denom. from 730; of *cedar:*—made of cedar {1x}. See: TWOT—160c; BDB—72c, 72d.

730. אֶרֶז {73x} **ʾerez**, *eh-rez';* from 729; a *cedar* tree (from the tenacity of its roots):—cedar {67x}, cedar tree {6x}. See: TWOT—160a; BDB—72c.

731. אַרְזָה {1x} **ʾarzâh**, *ar-zaw';* fem. of 730; *cedar paneling:*—cedar work {1x}. See: TWOT—160b; BDB—72d.

732. אָרַח {5x} **ʾârach**, *aw-rakh';* a prim. root; to *travel:*—wayfaring man {4x}, goeth {1x}. See: TWOT—161; BDB—72d.

733. אָרַח {4x} **ʾĂrach**, *aw-rakh';* from 732; *way-faring; Arach,* the name of three Isr.:—Arah {4x}. See: BDB—73b.

734. אֹרַח {58x} **ʾôrach**, *o'-rakh;* from 732; a *well-trodden road* (lit. or fig.); also a *caravan:*—way {26x}, path {25x}, highway {1x}, wayfaring man + 5674 08802 {1x}, manner {1x}, race {1x}, ranks {1x}, traveller {1x}, troops {1x}.

Orach means "way; path; course; conduct; manner." In meaning this word parallels Hebrew derek (1870), which it often synonymously parallels. **(1)** Orach means "path" or "way" conceived as a marked-out, well-traveled course: "Dan shall be a serpent by the way, an adder in the path, that biteth the horse heels" (Gen 49:17). **(2)** In Judg 5:6 the word means "highway": "In the days of Shamgar . . . the highways were unoccupied, and the travelers walked through byways." **(3)** When the sun is likened to a "strong man" who rejoices "to run a race" (Ps 19:5), orach represents a race course rather than a highway or a primitive, snake-laden path.

(4) The man who makes his path straight goes directly on his journey, not turning aside for the beckoning harlot (Prov 9:15). So here the word represents the "course" one follows between his departure and arrival conceived in terms of small units, almost step by step. **(5)** In Ps. 8:8 the word represents the ocean currents: "The fowl of the air and the fish of the sea, and whatsoever passeth through the paths of the seas." **(6)** Orach signifies the ground itself as the path upon which one treads: "He pursued them, and passed safely; even by the way that he had not gone with his feet" (Is 41:3). **(7)** In Job 30:12 the word seems to represent an obstruction or dam: "They push away my feet, and they raise up against me the ways of their destruction."

(8) The word can refer to a recurring life event typical of an individual or a group. **(8a)** In its first biblical occurrence (Gen 18:11) it is used of "the manner of women" (menstruation). **(8b)** Job 16:22 mentions the "way whence I shall not return," or death, **(8c)** while other passages speak of life actions (Job 34:11; literally, "conduct") or life-style (Prov. 15:10: "Correction is grievous unto him that forsaketh the way"—prescribed life-style; Prov. 5:6: "Lest thou shouldest ponder the path [which is typified by] life"). **(8d)** Thus, orach sometimes figures a proper course of action or proceeding within a given realm—"the path of judgment" (Is 40:14). **(9)** The noun orchah, which occurs 3 times, represents a "wandering company" or a "caravan" (Gen 37:25). Syn.: 1870, 5410. See: TWOT—161a; BDB—73a.

735. אֹרַח {2x} ʾôrach (Aram.), o'-rakh; corresp. to 734; a road:—way {2x}. See: TWOT—2605; BDB—1082d.

736. אֹרְחָה {2x} ʾôreʹchâh, o-rekh-aw'; fem. act. part. of 732; a caravan:—(travelling) company {2x}. See: TWOT—161c; BDB—73c.

737. אֲרֻחָה {6x} ʾărûchâh, ar-oo-khaw'; fem. pass. part. of 732 (in the sense of

appointing); a ration of food:—allowance {2x}, diet {2x}, dinner {1x}, victuals {1x}. See: TWOT—161b; BDB—73c.

738. אֲרִי {80x} ʾărîy, ar-ee'; or (prol.)

אַרְיֵה ʾaryêh, ar-yay'; from 717 (in the sense of violence); a lion:—lion {79x}, untranslated variant {1x}. "lion."

(1) The word represents a "full-grown lion." **(2)** This word should be compared to: **(2a)** gur (1482- Gen 49:9), a suckling lion; **(2b)** shachal (7826- Hos 5:14), a young lion which no longer is a suckling; and **(2c)** kepir (3715- Judg 14:5), a young lion which no longer is a suckling and which hunts for its food independently. **(3)** The "lion" was a much-feared beast (Amos 3:12) found mostly in the Trans-jordan (Jer 49:19) and in the mountainous areas (Song 4:8). **(4)** The various characteristics of the "lion" make it a frequent figure **(4a)** of strength and power (Judg 14:18), **(4b)** of plundering (Gen 49:9), and **(4c)** of malicious scheming (Ps 10:9). Syn.: 738, 744, 3715, 3833, 3918. See: TWOT—158a; BDB—71c, 1082c.

739. אֲרִיאֵל {2x} ʾărîyʾêl, ar-ee-ale'; or

אֲרִאֵל ʾărîʾêl, ar-ee-ale'; from 738 and 410; lion of God, i.e. heroic:—lion-like men {2x}. See: TWOT—159a; BDB—72a.

740. אֲרִיאֵל {6x} ʾĂrîʾêl, ar-ee-ale'; the same as 739; Ariel, a symb. name for Jerusalem, also the name of an Isr.:—Ariel {6x}. See: BDB—72a, 73c.

741. אֲרִאֵיל {3x} ʾărîʾêyl, ar-ee-ale'; either by transp. for 739 or, more prob. an orth. var. for 2025; the altar of the temple:—altar {3x}. See: TWOT—159a; BDB—72a, 72b, 73c.

742. אֲרִידַי {1x} ʾĂrîyday, ar-ee-dah'-ee; of Pers. or.; Aridai, a son of Haman:—Aridai {1x}. See: BDB—71c.

743. אֲרִידָתָא {1x} ʾĂrîydâthâʾ, ar-ee-daw-thaw'; of Pers. or.; Aridatha, a son of Haman:—Aridatha {1x}. See: BDB—71c.

744. אַרְיֵה {10x} ʾaryêh (Aram.), ar-yay'; corresp. to 738:—lion {10x}. See: TWOT—2606; BDB—71d, 1082c, 1082d.

745. אַרְיֵה {1x} ʾAryêh, ar-yay'; the same as 738; lion; Arjeh, an Isr.:—Arieh {1x}. See: BDB—72a.

אֲרָיָה ʾărâyâh. See 723.

746. אַרְיוֹךְ {7x} ʾAryôwk, ar-yoke'; of for. or.; Arjok, the name of two Babylonians:—Arioch {7x}. See: BDB—73c.

747. אֲרִיסַי {1x} ʾĂriyçay, ar-ee-sah'-ee; of Pers. or.; Arisai, a son of Haman:—Arisai {1x}. See: BDB—1121a.

748. אָרַךְ {34x} 'ârak, *aw-rak';* a prim. root; to
be (caus. *make*) *long* (lit. or fig.):—
prolong {18x}, long {5x}, lengthen {3x}, draw
out {3x}, defer {2x}, tarried {1x}, . . . lived + 3117
0310 {2x}. See: TWOT—162; BDB—73c, 1082d.

749. אֲרַךְ {1x} 'ărak (Aram.), *ar-ak';* prop.
corresp. to 748, but used only in the
sense of *reaching* to a given point; to *suit:*—be
meet {1x}. See: TWOT—2607; BDB—1082d.

750. אָרֵךְ {15x} 'ârêk, *aw-rake';* from 748;
long:—slow {9x}, longsuffering +
639 {4x}, longwinged + 83 {1x}, patient {1x}.
See: TWOT—162b; BDB—74a, 1082d.

751. אֶרֶךְ {1x} 'Erek, *eh'-rek;* from 748;
length; Erek, a place in Bab.:—
Erech {1x}. See: BDB—74b, 1083a.

752. אָרֹךְ {3x} 'ârôk, *aw-roke';* from 748;
long:—long {2x}, longer {1x}. See:
TWOT—162c; BDB—74a.

753. אֹרֶךְ {95x} 'ôrek, *o'rek';* from 748;
length:—length {70x}, long {21x},
ever {2x}, as long as {1x}, high {1x}. *Orek* refers
to length without limits. See: TWOT—162a;
BDB—73d.

754. אַרְכָּא {1x} 'arkâ (Aram.), *ar-kaw';* or

אַרְכָה 'arkâh (Aram.), *ar-kaw';* from
749; *length:*—prolonged {1x}. See:
TWOT—2609; BDB—1082d.

755. אַרְכֻּבָה {1x} 'arkûbâh (Aram.), *ar-koo-
baw';* from an unused root cor-
resp. to 7392 (in the sense of *bending* the knee);
the *knee:*—knees {1x}. See: TWOT—2608;
BDB—1083a, 1085c.

אֲרֻכָה 'ărûkâh. See 724.

756. אַרְכְּוָי {1x} 'Ark°vay (Aram.), *ar-kev-
ah'ee;* patrial from 751; an *Arkevite* (collect.) or native of Erek:—Archevites
{1x}. See: BDB—1083a.

757. אַרְכִּי {6x} 'Arkîy, *ar-kee';* patrial from
another place (in Pal.) of similar
name with 751; an *Arkite* or native of Erek:—
Archi {1x}, Archite {5x}. See: BDB—74b.

758. אֲרָם {132x} 'Arâm, *arawm';* from the
same as 759; the *highland; Aram* or
Syria, and its inhab.; also the name of a son of
Shem, a grandson of Nahor, and of an Isr.:—
Syria {67x}, Syrians {56x}, *Aram* {7x}, Syriada-
mascus + 4601 {1x}, Syriamaachah + 4601 {1x}.
See: TWOT—163; BDB—74b, 591a.

759. אַרְמוֹן {32x} 'armôwn, *ar-mone';* from an
unused root (mean. to *be ele-
vated*); a *citadel* (from its *height*):—castle {1x},
palace {31x}. Syn.: 1002, 1003, 2038, 2918. See:
TWOT—164a; BDB—74d.

760. אֲרַם צוֹבָה {1x} 'Aram Tsôwbâh, *ar-am'
tso-baw';* from 758 and 6678;
Aram of Tsoba (or Cœle-Syria):—Aram-zobah
{1x}. See: BDB—74b.

761. אֲרַמִּי {1x} 'Ârammîy, *ar-am-mee';* patrial
from 758; an *Aramite* or Ara-
mæan:—Syrian {10x}, Aramitess {1x}. See:
BDB—74c, 248c, 942b.

762. אֲרָמִית {5x} 'Ărâmîyth, *ar-aw-meeth';*
fem. of 761; (only adv.) in *Aramæan:*—Syrian language {2x}, Syrian tongue
{2x}, Syriack {1x}. See: BDB—74c.

763. אֲרַם נַהֲרַיִם {6x} 'Ăram Naharayim, *aram' nah-har-ah'-yim;* from
758 and the dual of 5104; *Aram of* (the) *two
rivers* (Euphrates and Tigris) or Mesopotamia:—Aham-naharaim {1x}, Mesopotamia
{6x}. See: BDB—74b, 74c.

764. אַרְמֹנִי {1x} 'Armônîy, *ar-mo-nee';* from
759; *palatial; Armoni,* an Isr.:—
Armoni {1x}. See: BDB—74d.

765. אֲרָן {2x} 'Ărân, *ar-awn';* from 7442;
stridulous; Aran, an Edomite:—
Aran {2x}. See: BDB—75a.

766. אֹרֶן {1x} 'ôren, *o'-ren;* from the same as
765 (in the sense of *strength*); the
ash tree (from its toughness):—ash {1x}. See:
TWOT—165a; BDB—75a.

767. אֹרֶן {1x} 'Ôren, *o'-ren;* the same as 766;
Oren, an Isr.:—Oren {1x}. See:
BDB—75a.

אָרֹן 'ârôn. See 727.

768. אַרְנֶבֶת {2x} 'arnebeth, *ar-neh'-beth;* of
uncert. der.; the *hare:*—hare {2x}.
See: TWOT—123a; BDB—58a, 75c.

769. אַרְנוֹן {25x} 'Arnôwn, *ar-nohn';* or

אַרְנֹן 'Arnôn, *ar-nohn';* from 7442; a
brawling stream; the *Arnon,* a river
east of the Jordan; also its territory:—Arnon
{25x}. See: BDB—75a.

770. אַרְנָן {1x} 'Arnân, *ar-nawn';* prob. from
the same as 769; *noisy; Arnan,* an
Isr.:—Arnan {1x}. See: BDB—75a.

771. אָרְנָן {12x} 'Ornân, *or-nawn';* prob. from
766; *strong; Ornan,* a Jebusite:—
Ornan {12x}. Syn.: See 728. See: BDB—75a.

772. אֲרַע {21x} 'ăra' (Aram.), *ar-ah';* corresp.
to 776; the *earth;* by impl. (fig.)
low:—earth {20x}, interior {1x}. See: TWOT—
2610; BDB—1083a.

773. אַרְעִית {1x} 'ar'îyth (Aram.), *arh-eeth';*
fem. of 772; the *bottom:*—bottom
{1x}. See: TWOT—2611; BDB—1083a.

774. אַרְפָּד {6x} **ʾArpâd**, *ar-pawd′;* from 7502; *spread* out; *Arpad,* a place in Syria:—*Arpad* {4x}, Arphad {2x}. See: BDB—75d, 951c.

775. אַרְפַּכְשַׁד {9x} **ʾArpakshad**, *ar-pak-shad′;* prob. of for. or.; *Arpakshad,* a son of Noah; also the region settled by him:—Arphaxad {9x}. See: BDB—75d.

776. אֶרֶץ {2504x} **ʾerets**, *eh′-rets;* from an unused root prob. mean. to *be firm;* the *earth* (at large, or partitively a *land*):—land {1543x}, earth {712x}, country {140x}, ground {98x}, world {4x}, way {3x}, common {1x}, field {1x}, nations {1x}, wilderness + 4057 {1x}.

Erets (776) means "earth; land." **(1)** *Erets* may be translated "earth," the temporal scene of human activity, experience, and history. **(2)** The material world had a beginning when God "made the earth by His power," "formed it," and "spread it out" (Is 40:28; 42:5; 45:12, 18; Jer 27:5; 51:15). **(2a)** Because He did so, it follows that "the earth is the LORD's" (Ps 24:1; Deut 10:1; Ex 9:29; Neh 9:6). **(2b)** No part of it is independent of Him, for "the very ends of the earth are His possession," including "the mountains," "the seas," "the dry land," "the depths of the earth" (Ps 2:8; 95:4–5; Amos 4:13; Jonah 1:9). **(2c)** God formed the earth to be inhabited (Is 45:18). **(2d)** Having "authority over the earth" by virtue of being its Maker, He decreed to "let the earth sprout vegetation: of every kind" (Job 34:13; Gen 1:11). **(2e)** It was never to stop its productivity, for "while the earth stands, seedtime and harvest, and cold and heat, and summer and winter, and day and night shall not cease" (Gen 8:22). "The earth is full of God's riches" and mankind can "multiply and fill the earth and subdue it" (Ps 104:24; Gen 1:28; 9:1). **(2f)** Let no one think that the earth is an independent, self-contained mechanism, for "the LORD reigns" as He "sits on the vault of the earth" from where "He sends rain on the earth" (Ps 97:1; Is 40:22; 1 Kin 17:14; Ps 104:4). **(3)** As "the eyes of the LORD run to and fro throughout the earth," He sees that "there is not a just man on earth" (Eccl 7:20). At an early stage, God endeavored to "blot out man . . . from the face of the earth" (Gen 6:5–7). **(3a)** Though He relented and promised to "destroy never again all flesh on the earth," we can be sure that "He is coming to judge the earth" (Gen 7:16f.; Ps 96:13). **(3b)** At that time, "the earth shall be completely laid waste" so that "the exalted people of the earth fade away" (Jer 10:10; Joel 2:10; Is 33:3–6; Ps 75:8). **(3c)** But He also provides a way of escape for all who heed His promise: "Turn to me and be saved, all the ends of the earth" (Is 45:22). **(4)** What the Creator formed "in the beginning"

is also to have an end, for He will "create a new heaven and a new earth" (Is 65:17; 66:22). **(5)** The Hebrew word *erets* also occurs frequently in the phrase "heaven and earth" or "earth and heaven." **(5a)** In other words, the Scriptures teach that our terrestrial planet is a part of an all-embracing cosmological framework which we call the universe. **(5b)** Not the result of accident or innate forces, the unfathomed reaches of space and its uncounted components owe their origin to the LORD "who made heaven and earth" (Ps 121:2; 124:8; 134:3).

(6) Because God is "the possessor of heaven and earth," the whole universe is to reverberate in the praise of His glory, which is "above heaven and earth" (Gen 14:19, 22; Ps 148:13). "Shout, O heavens and rejoice, O earth": "let the heavens be glad and let the earth rejoice" (Ps 49:13; 96:11). Such adoration is always appropriate, for "whatever the LORD pleases, He does in heaven and in earth, in the seas and in all deeps" (Ps 135:6). **(7)** *Erets* does not only denote the entire terrestrial planet, but is also used of some of the earth's component parts. English words like land, country, ground, and soil transfer its meaning into our language. **(7a)** Quite frequently, it refers to an area occupied by a nation or tribe. So we read of "the land of Egypt," "the land of the Philistines," "the land of Israel," "the land of Benjamin," and so on (Gen 47:13; Zec 2:5; 2 Kin 5:2, 4; Judg 21:21). **(7b)** Israel is said to live "in the land of the LORD" (Lev 25:33f.; Hos 9:13). When the people arrived at its border, Moses reminded them that it would be theirs only because the LORD drove out the other nations to "give you their land for an inheritance" (Deut 4:38). **(7c)** Moses promised that God would make its soil productive, for "He will give rain for your land" so that it would be "a fruitful land," "a land flowing with milk and honey, a land of wheat and barley" (Deut 11:13–15; 8:7–9; Jer 2:7). **(8)** The Hebrew noun may also be translated "the ground" (Job 2:13; Amos 3:5; Gen 24:52; Eze 43:14). Syn.: 127, 1471. See: TWOT—167; BDB—75d, 1083a.

777. אַרְצָא {1x} **ʾartsâ**, *ar-tsaw′;* from 776; *earthiness; Artsa,* an Isr.:—Arza {1x}. See: BDB—76c.

778. אֲרַק {1x} **ʾăraq** (Aram.), *ar-ak′;* by transm. for 772; the *earth:*—earth {1x}. See: TWOT—2612; BDB—1083a.

779. אָרַר {63x} **ʾârar**, *aw-rar′;* a prim. root; to *execrate:*—curse {62x}, bitterly {1x}.

Arar (779) means "to curse." **(1)** The first occurrence is in Gen 3:14: "Thou [the serpent] art cursed above all cattle," and Gen 3:17: "Cursed is the ground for thy [Adam's] sake." **(2)** This form accounts for more than half of

the occurrences. It is a pronouncement of judgment on those who break covenant, as: "Cursed is the man who . . ." (twelve times in Deut 27:15–26). **(3)** "Curse" is usually parallel with "bless." The two "curses" in Gen 3 are in bold contrast to the two blessings ("And God blessed them . . .") in Gen 1. **(4)** The covenant with Abraham includes: "I will bless them that bless thee, and curse [different root] him that curseth thee . . ." (Gen 12:3). **(5)** Compare Jeremiah's "Cursed be the man that trusteth in man" and "Blessed is the man that trusteth in the LORD" (17:5, 7). **(6)** Pagans used the power of "cursing" to deal with their enemies, as when Balak sent for Balaam: "Come . . . , curse me this people" (Num 22:6). Israel had the ceremonial "water that causeth the curse" (Num 5:18ff.).

(7) God alone truly "curses." It is a revelation of His justice, in support of His claim to absolute obedience. Men may claim God's "curses" by committing their grievances to God and trusting in His righteous judgment (cf. Ps 109:26–31). **(8)** "Curse" in the Old Testament is summed up in the statement: "Cursed be the man that obeyeth not the words of this covenant" (Jer 11:3). **(9)** The New Testament responds: "Christ hath redeemed us from the curse of the law, being made a curse for us: for it is written, Cursed is every one that hangeth on a tree" (Gal 3:13). Syn.: 423, 6895, 7045. See: TWOT–168; BDB–76c.

780. אֲרָרַט {4x} **ˀĂrârat,** *ar-aw-rat';* of for. or.; Ararat (or rather Armenia):–Ararat {2x}, Armenia {2x}. See: BDB–76d.

781. אָרַשׂ {11x} **ˀâras,** *aw-ras';* a prim. root; to *engage* for matrimony:–betroth {10x}, espouse {1x}. See: TWOT–170; BDB–76d.

782. אֲרֶשֶׁת {1x} **ˀăresheth,** *ar-eh'-sheth;* from 781 (in the sense of *desiring* to possess); a *longing* for:–request {1x}. See: TWOT–171a; BDB–77a.

783. אַרְתַּחְשַׁשְׂתְּא {15x} **ˀArtachshastâˀ** (Aram.), *ar-takh-shas-taw';* or

אַרְתַּחְשַׁשְׂתְּא **ˀArtachshastˀ** (Aram.), *ar-takh-shast';* or by perm.

אַרְתַּחְשַׂסְתְּא **ˀArtachshaçtˀ** (Aram.), *ar-takh-shast';* of for. or.; Artachshasta (or Artaxerxes), a title (rather than name) of several Pers. kings:–Artaxerxes {15x}. See: BDB–77a, 1083a.

784. אֵשׁ {379x} **ˀêsh,** *aysh;* a prim. word; *fire* (lit. or fig.):–fire {373x}, burning {1x}, fiery {1x}, untranslated variant {1x}, fire + 800 {1x}, flaming {1x}, hot {1x}.

Esh (784) means "fire." **(1)** In its first biblical appearance this word, *esh* represents God's presence as "a torch of fire": "And it came to pass, that, when the sun went down, and it was dark, behold a smoking furnace, and a [flaming torch]" (Gen 15:17). **(2)** "Fire" was the instrument by which an offering was transformed into smoke, whose ascending heavenward symbolized God's reception of the offering (Lev 9:24). **(3)** God also consumed people with the "fire of judgment" (Num 11:1; Ps 89:46). **(4)** Various things were to be burnt as a sign of total destruction and divine judgment (Ex 32:20). **(5)** "Fire" often attended God's presence in theophanies (Ex 3:2). **(6)** Thus He is sometimes called a "consuming fire" (Ex 24:17). See: TWOT–172; BDB–77b, 1083b.

785. אֵשׁ {1x} **ˀêsh** (Aram.), *aysh;* corresp. to 784:–flame {1x}. See: TWOT–2614; BDB–1083b.

786. אִשׁ {2x} **ˀîsh,** *eesh;* ident. (in or. and formation) with 784; *entity;* used only adv., there *is* or *are:*–can {1x}, there {1x}. See: TWOT–173; BDB–78a.

787. אֹשׁ {3x} **ˀôsh** (Aram.), *ohsh;* corresp. (by transp. and abb.) to 803; a *foundation:*–foundation {3x}. See: TWOT–2613; BDB–1083b.

788. אַשְׁבֵּל {3x} **ˀAshbêl,** *ash-bale';* prob. from the same as 7640; *flowing; Ashbel,* an Isr.:–Ashbel {3x}. See: BDB–78a.

789. אַשְׁבֵּלִי {1x} **ˀAshbêlîy,** *ash-bay-lee';* patron. from 788; an *Ashbelite* (collect.) or desc. of Ashbel:–Ashbelites {1x}. See: BDB–78a.

790. אֶשְׁבָּן {1x} **ˀEshbân,** *esh-bawn';* prob. from the same as 7644; *vigorous; Eshban,* an Idumæan:–Eshban {1x}. See: BDB–78b.

791. אַשְׁבֵּעַ {1x} **ˀAshbêaˁ,** *ash-bay'-ah;* from 7650; *adjurer; Asbeä,* an Isr.:–Ashbea {1x}. See: BDB–78b.

792. אֶשְׁבַּעַל {2x} **ˀEshbaˁal,** *esh-bah'-al;* from 376 and 1168; *man of Baal; Eshbaal* (or Ishbosheth), a son of King Saul:–Eshbaal {2x}. See: BDB–36b, 78b.

793. אֶשֶׁד {1x} **ˀeshed,** *eh'-shed;* from an unused root mean. to *pour;* an *outpouring:*–stream {1x}. Syn.: 5104. See: TWOT–174a; BDB–78b.

794. אֲשֵׁדָה {6x} **ˀăshêdâh,** *ash-ay-daw';* fem. of 793; a *ravine:*–springs {3x}, variant {3x}. See: TWOT–174b; BDB–78b.

795. אַשְׁדּוֹד {17x} **ˀAshdôwd,** *ash-dode';* from 7703; *ravager; Ashdod,* a place in Pal.:–Ashdod {17x}. See: BDB–78b, 994c.

796. אַשְׁדּוֹדִי {5x} **ʾAshdôwdîy**, *ash-do-dee';* patrial from 795; an *Ashdodite* (often collect.) or inhab. of Ashdod:—Ashdodites {2x}, of Ashdod {3x}. See: BDB—78c.

797. אַשְׁדּוֹדִית {1x} **ʾAshdôwdîyth**, *ash-do-deeth';* fem. of 796; (only adv.) *in the language of Ashdod:*—in the speech of Ashdod {1x}. See: BDB—78c.

798. אַשְׁדּוֹת הַפִּסְגָּה {3x} **ʾAshdôwth hap-Piçgâh**, *ash-doth' hap-pis-gaw';* from the plur. of 794 and 6449 with the art. interposed; *ravines of the Pisgah; Ash-doth-Pisgah,* a place east of the Jordan:—Ash-doth-pisgah {3x}. See: BDB—820a.

799. אֶשְׁדָּת {1x} **ʾeshdâth**, *esh-dawth';* from 784 and 1881; a *fire-law:*—fiery {1x}. See: TWOT—174b; BDB—77d.

800. אֶשָּׁה {1x} **ʾeshshâh**, *esh-shaw';* fem. of 784; *fire:*—fire {1x}. See: TWOT—172; BDB—77d.

801. אִשֶּׁה {65x} **ʾishshâh**, *ish-shaw';* the same as 800, but used in a liturgical sense; prop. a *burnt-offering;* but occasionally of any *sacrifice:*—(offering, sacrifice), (made) by fire {65x}.

Ishshah means "fire offering." **(1)** Sixty-three of the 65 appearances of this word occur in the sacramental prescriptions of Exodus-Deuteronomy. The other two occurrences (Josh 13:14; 1 Sa 2:28) bear the same meaning and sacramental context. **(2)** All legitimate sacrifices had to be presented before God at His altar, and all of them involved burning to some degree. Thus they may all be called fire offerings (Ex 29:18). **(3)** The word *ishshah* first occurs in Ex 29:18: "And thou shalt burn the whole ram upon the altar: it is a burnt offering unto the LORD: it is a sweet savor, an offering made by fire unto the LORD." Syn.: 817, 4503, 5927, 5930, 7133, 8641. See: TWOT—172a; BDB—77d.

802. אִשָּׁה {780x} **ʾishshâh**, *ish-shaw';* fem. of 376 or 582; irreg. plur.

נָשִׁים **nâshîym**, *naw-sheem';* a *woman* (used in the same wide sense as 582) [*Often unexpressed in English.*]:—wife {425x}, woman {324x}, one {10x}, married {5x}, female {2x}, misc.: [adulter]ess, each, every, X many, + none, + together = {14x}.

Ishshah (802) means "woman; wife; betrothed one; bride; each." **(1)** This noun connotes one who is a female human being regardless of her age or virginity. **(1a)** Therefore, it appears in correlation to "man" (376 - *ish*): "She shall be called Woman, because she was taken out of Man" (Gen 2:23). **(1b)** This is its meaning in its first biblical usage: "And the

rib, which the LORD God had taken from man [120 - *adam*], made he a woman, and brought her unto the man" (Gen 2:22). **(1c)** The stress here is on identification of womanhood rather than a family role. **(2)** The stress on the family role of a "wife" appears in passages such as Gen 8:16: "Go forth of the ark, thou, and thy wife, and thy sons, and thy sons' wives with thee."

(3) In one special nuance the word connotes "wife" in the sense of a woman who is under a man's authority and protection; the emphasis is on the family relationship considered as a legal and social entity: "And Abram took Sarai his wife and Lot his brother's son, and all their substance that they had gathered . . ." (Gen 12:5). **(4)** In Lam 2:20 *ishshah* is a synonym for "mother": "Shall the women eat their [offspring, the little ones who were born healthy]?" **(5)** In Gen 29:21 (cf. Deut 22:24) it appears to connote "bride" or "betrothed one": "And Jacob said unto Laban, Give me my wife, for my days are fulfilled, that I may go in unto her." **(6)** Eccl 7:26 uses the word generically of "woman" conceived in general, or womanhood: "And I find more bitter than death the woman, whose heart is snares and nets" (cf. Gen 31:35). **(7)** This word is used only infrequently of animals: "Of every clean beast thou shalt take to thee by sevens, the male and his female: and of beasts that are not clean by two, the male and his female" (Gen 7:2). **(8)** This word can also be used figuratively describing foreign warriors and/or heroes as "women," in other words as weak, unmanly, and cowardly: "In that day shall Egypt be like unto women: and it shall be afraid and fear because of the shaking of the hand of the LORD of hosts" (Is 19:16). **(9)** In a few passages *ishshah* means "each" or "every": "But every woman shall borrow of her neighbor, and of her that sojourneth in her house" (Ex 3:22; cf. Amos 4:3). **(10)** A special use of this nuance occurs in passages such as Jer 9:20, where in conjunction with *reuwth* (7468 -"neighbor") it means "one" (female): "Yet hear the word of the LORD, O ye women, and let your ear receive the word of his mouth, and teach your daughters wailing, and every one her neighbor lamentation." See: TWOT—137a; BDB—61a, 78c, 84b, 1081d.

803. אֲשׁוּיָה {1x} **ʾăshûwyâh**, *ash-oo-yah';* fem. pass. part. from an unused root mean. to *found; foundation:*—foundation {1x}. See: TWOT—175a; BDB—78c.

804. אַשּׁוּר {151x} **ʾAshshûwr**, *ash-shoor';* or

אַשֻּׁר **ʾAshshûr**, *ash-shoor';* appar. from 833 (in the sense of *successful*); *Ashshur,* the second son of Shem; also his desc. and the country occupied by them (i.e. Assyria), its region and its empire:—Assyria

{118x}, Assyrian {19x}, Asshur {8x}, Assyrian + 1121 {5x}, Assur {1x}. Syn.: See 838. See: TWOT—176; BDB—78c.

805. אֲשׁוּרִי {1x} ʾĂshûwrîy, ash-oo-ree'; or

אַשּׁוּרִי ʾAshshûwrîy, ash-shoo-ree'; from a patrial word of the same form as 804; an Ashurite (collect.) or inhab. of Ashur, a district in Pal.:—Asshurim {1x}, Ashurites {1x}. See: BDB—78d, 79a.

806. אַשְׁחוּר {2x} ʾAshchûwr, ash-khoor'; prob. from 7835; black; Ashchur, an Isr.:—Ashur {2x}. See: BDB—79a, 1007b.

807. אֲשִׁימָא {1x} ʾĂshîymâʾ, ash-ee-maw'; of for. or.; Ashima, a deity of Hamath:—Ashima {1x}. See: BDB—79a, 92d.

אֲשֵׁירָה ʾăshêyrâh. See 842.

808. אָשִׁישׁ {1x} ʾâshîysh, aw-sheesh'; from the same as 784 (in the sense of pressing down firmly; comp. 803); a (ruined) foundation:—foundation {1x}. See: TWOT—185a; BDB—84b.

809. אֲשִׁישָׁה {4x} ʾăshîyshâh, ash-ee-shaw'; fem. of 808; something closely pressed together, i.e. a cake of raisins or other comfits:—flagon {1x}. See: TWOT—185a; BDB—84b.

810. אֶשֶׁךְ {1x} ʾeshek, eh'-shek; from an unused root (prob. mean. to bunch together); a testicle (as a lump):—stone {1x}. See: TWOT—177; BDB—79a.

811. אֶשְׁכּוֹל {9x} ʾeshkôwl, esh-kole'; or

אֶשְׁכֹּל ʾeshkôl, esh-kole'; prob. prol. from 810; a bunch of grapes or other fruit:—cluster {8x}, cluster of grapes {1x}. See: TWOT—178; BDB—79a.

812. אֶשְׁכֹּל {6x} ʾEshkôl, esh-kole'; the same as 811; Eshcol, the name of an Amorite, also of a valley in Pal.:—Eshcol {6x}. See: BDB—79b.

813. אַשְׁכְּנַז {3x} ʾAshkᵉnaz, ash-ken-az'; of for. or.; Ashkenaz, a Japhethite, also his desc.:—Ashkenaz {3x}. See: BDB—79b.

814. אֶשְׁכָּר {2x} ʾeshkâr, esh-kawr'; for 7939; a gratuity:—gift {1x}, present {1x}. See: BDB—79b, 1016d.

815. אֵשֶׁל {3x} ʾêshel, ay'-shel; from a root of uncert. signif.; a tamarisk tree; by extens. a grove of any kind:—grove {1x}, tree {2x}. A bona fide grove in contrast to the pagan grove, asherah (842). See: TWOT—179a; BDB—79b.

816. אָשַׁם {35x} ʾâsham, aw-sham'; or

אָשֵׁם ʾâshêm, aw-shame'; a prim. root; to be guilty; by impl. to be punished or perish:—guilty {14x}, desolate {6x}, offend {6x}, trespass {4x}, certainly {1x}, destroy {1x}, faulty {1x}, greatly {1x}, offence {1x}. See: TWOT—180; BDB—79c.

817. אָשָׁם {46x} ʾâshâm, aw-shawm'; from 816; guilt; by impl. a fault; also a sin-offering:—trespass offering {34x}, trespass {8x}, offering for sin {1x}, sin {2x}, guiltiness {1x}.
Asham means "guilt offering; offense; guilt; gift of restitution; gift of atonement." (1) The noun asham occurs 46 times in biblical Hebrew; 33 of its occurrences are in the Pentateuch. (2) The most frequent meaning of the word is "guilt offering": "And he shall bring his trespass [guilt] offering unto the LORD for his sin which he hath sinned" (Lev 5:6). (3) This specialized kind of sin offering (Lev 5:7) was to be offered when someone had been denied what was due to him. (4) The valued amount defrauded was to be repaid plus 20 percent (Lev 5:16; 6:5). (5) Ritual infractions and periods of leprosy and defilement took from God a commodity or service rightfully belonging to Him and required repayment plus restitution. (6) Every violation of property rights required paying full reparation and the restitution price (20 percent) to the one violated as well as presenting the guilt offering to God as the LORD of all (i.e., as a feudal lord over all). (7) If the offended party was dead, reparation and restitution were made to God (i.e. given to the priests; Num 5:5–10).
(8) Usually the "guilt offering" consisted of a ram (Lev 5:15) or a male lamb. (8a) The offerer presented the victim, laying his hands on it. (8b) The priest sprinkled its blood around the altar, burned the choice parts on the altar, and received the rest as food (Lev 7:2–7). (8c) When a cleansed leper made this offering, blood from the sacrifice was applied to the man's right ear, right thumb, and right big toe (Lev 14:14). (9) In some passages, asham is used of an offense against God and the guilt incurred by it: "And Abimelech said, What is this thou hast done unto us? One of the people might lightly have lain with thy wife, and thou shouldest have brought guiltiness upon us" (Gen 26:10—the first occurrence). There is an added sense here that the party offended would punish the perpetrator of the crime. (10) In two verses (Num 5:7–8), asham represents the repayment made to one who has been wronged: "Then they shall confess their sin which they have done: and he shall recompense his trespass with the principal thereof, and add unto it the fifth part thereof, and give it unto him against whom he hath trespassed." (10a) In the Hebrew the word is the value of the initial thing taken from the injured party, which value is to be returned to him, i.e., the reparation or

restitution itself. **(10b)** This basic idea is extended so that the word comes to mean a gift made to God to remove guilt (1 Sa 6:3), or atone for sin (Is 53:10) other than the specified offerings to be presented at the altar.

(11) The noun implies the condition of guilt incurred through some wrongdoing (Gen 26:10); *asham* refers **(12)** to the compensation given to satisfy an injured party [trespass offering or guilt offering] **(12a)** presented on the altar by the repentant offender **(12b)** after paying a compensation of six-fifths of the damage inflicted (Num 5:7– 8). The trespass offering was **(12c)** the blood sacrifice of a ram (Lev 5:18; Lev 7:5, 7; 14:12–13). **(13)** The most significant theological statement containing *asham* is Is 53:10, which says that the servant of Yahweh was appointed as an *asham* for sinful mankind; suggesting that His death furnished a 120-percent compensation for the broken law of God. **(14)** It also is offense against God and the guilt incurred thereby (Gen 26:10). Syn. 801, 4503, 5927, 5030, 7133, 8641. See: TWOT— 180b; BDB—79d.

818. אָשֵׁם {3x} ʾâshêm, *aw-shame′;* from 816; *guilty;* hence, *presenting a sin-offering:*—guilty {2x}, faulty {1x}. See: TWOT— 180a; BDB—79d.

819. אַשְׁמָה {19x} ʾashmâh, *ash-maw′;* fem. of 817; *guiltiness,* a *fault,* the *presentation of a sin-offering:*—trespass {13x}, sin {4x}, offend {1x}, trespass offering {1x}. See: TWOT—180c; BDB—80a.

אַשְׁמוּרָה ʾashmûwrâh. See 821.

820. אַשְׁמָן {1x} ʾashmân, *ash-mawn′;* prob. from 8081; a *fat* field:—desolate {1x}. See: TWOT—2410d; BDB—80b, 1032c.

821. אַשְׁמֻרָה {7x} ʾashmûrâh, *ash-moo-raw′;* or

אַשְׁמוּרָה ʾashmûwrâh, *ash-moo-raw′;* or

אַשְׁמֹרֶת ʾashmôreth, *ash-mo′-reth;* fem. from 8104; a night *watch:*—watch {5x}, night watch {2x}. Syn.: 4929, 4931, 6822, 8104, 8245. See: TWOT—2414e; BDB—80b, 1038a.

822. אֶשְׁנָב {2x} ʾeshnâb, *esh-nawb′;* appar. from an unused root (prob. mean. to *leave small spaces between two things*); a latticed *window:*—casement {1x}, lattice {1x}. See: TWOT—2418a; BDB—80b, 1039d.

823. אַשְׁנָה ʾAshnâh, *ash-naw′;* prob. a var. for 3466; *Ashnah,* the name of two places in Pal.:—*Ashnah* {2x}. See: BDB—80b.

824. אֶשְׁעָן {1x} ʾEshʿân, *esh-awn′;* from 8172; *support; Eshan,* a place in Pal.:—Eshean {1x}. See: BDB—80b, 1043d.

825. אַשָּׁף {2x} ʾashshâph, *ash-shawf′;* from an unused root (prob. mean. to *lisp,* i.e. *practice enchantment*); a *conjurer:*—astrologer {2x}.

Ashshaph means "enchanter." **(1)** The noun appears only twice in biblical Hebrew, and only in the Book of Daniel. **(2)** The vocation of *ashipu* is known from earliest times in the Akkadian (Old Babylonian) society. It is not clear whether the *ashipu* was an assistant to a particular order of Babylonian priests (*mashmashu*) or an order parallel in function to the *mashmashu* order. In either case, the *ashipu* offered incantations to deliver a person from evil magical forces (demons). The sick often underwent actual surgery while the incantations were spoken. **(3)** In the Bible, *ashshaph* first occurs in Dan 1:20: "And as for every matter of wisdom and understanding about which the king consulted them he found them ten times better than all the magicians and enchanters who were in his realm." See: TWOT— 181; BDB—80b, 1083b.

826. אָשַׁף {6x} ʾashshâph (Aram.), *ash-shawf′;* corresp. to 825:—astrologer {6x}. The ungodly one who attempts to determine the future from the alignment of the stars. See: TWOT—2615; BDB—1083b.

827. אַשְׁפָּה {6x} ʾashpâh, *ash-paw′;* perh. (fem.) from the same as 825 (in the sense of *covering*); a *quiver* or arrow-case:—quiver {6x}. See: TWOT—182a; BDB—80c, 251c, 1046a.

829. אֶשְׁפָּר {2x} ʾeshpâr, *esh-pawr′;* of uncert. der.; a measured *portion:*—piece {1x}, flesh {1x}. See: TWOT—182.1; BDB—80c, 1051c.

830. אַשְׁפֹּת {7x} ʾashpôth, *ash-pohth′;* or

אַשְׁפּוֹת ʾashpôwth, *ash-pohth′;* or (contr.)

שְׁפֹת shephôth, *shef-ohth′;* plur. of a noun of the same form as 827, from 8192 (in the sense of *scraping*); a heap of *rubbish* or *filth:*—dung {4x}, dunghill {3x}. See: TWOT— 2441b; BDB—80c, 1046b, 1052a.

831. אַשְׁקְלוֹן {12x} ʾAshqᵉlôwn, *ash-kel-one′;* prob. from 8254 in the sense of *weighing*-place (i.e. *mart*); *Ashkelon,* a place in Pal.:—Ashkelon {9x}, Askalon {3x}. See: BDB—80c.

832. אֶשְׁקְלוֹנִי {1x} ʾEshqᵉlôwnîy, *esh-kel-o-nee′;* patrial from 831; an *Ashkelonite* (collect.) or inhab. of Ashkelon:—Eshkalonites {1x}. See: BDB—80d.

833. אָשַׁר {16x} ʾâshar, *aw-shar′;* or

אָשֵׁר ʾâshêr, *aw-share′;* a prim. root; to *be straight* (used in the widest sense,

espec. to *be level, right, happy*); fig. to *go forward, be honest, prosper:*—blessed {7x}, lead {2x}, go {2x}, guide {1x}, happy {2x}, leaders {1x}, relieve {1x}. See: TWOT—183; BDB—80d.

834. אֲשֶׁר {111x} 'ăsher, *ash-er';* a prim. rel. pron. (of every gender and number); *who, which, what, that;* also (as adv. and conjunc.) *when, where, how, because, in order that,* etc.:—which, wherewith, because, when, soon, whilst, as if, as when, that, until, much, whosoever, whereas, wherein, whom, whose = {111x}. See: TWOT—184; BDB—81c, 84a, 455b, 606b, 758a, 774d, 775c, 979b, 979d, 980a, 1083d, 1087.

835. אֹשֶׁר {45x} 'esher, *eh'-sher;* from 833; *happiness;* only in masc. plur. constr. as interj., how *happy!:*—blessed {27x}, happy {18x}.

Esher (835) means "blessed; happy." **(1)** All but 4 of the 44 biblical occurrences of this noun are in poetical passages, with 26 occurrences in the Psalms and 8 in Proverbs. **(2)** Basically, this word connotes the state of "prosperity" or "happiness" that comes when a superior bestows his favor (blessing) on one. **(2a)** In most passages, the one bestowing favor is God Himself: "Happy art thou, O Israel: who is like unto thee, O people saved by the LORD" (Deut 33:29). **(2b)** The state that the blessed one enjoys does not always appear to be "happy": "Behold, happy is the man whom God correcteth: therefore despise not thou the chastening of the Almighty: for he maketh sore, and bindeth up" (Job 5:17–18). Eliphaz was not describing Job's condition as a happy one; it was "blessed," however, inasmuch as God was concerned about him. Because it was a blessed state and the outcome would be good, Job was expected to laugh at his adversity (Job 5:22). **(3)** God is not always the one who makes one "blessed." At least, the Queen of Sheba flatteringly told Solomon that this was the case (1 Kin 10:8). **(4)** One's status before God (being "blessed") is not always expressed in terms of the individual or social conditions that bring what moderns normally consider to be "happiness." **(5)** So although it is appropriate to render *esher* as "blessed," the rendering of "happiness" does not always convey its emphasis to modern readers. Syn.: 833, 1288, 1293. See: TWOT—183a; BDB—80d.

836. אָשֵׁר {43x} 'Âshêr, *aw-share';* from 833; *happy; Asher,* a son of Jacob, and the tribe descended from him, with its territory; also a place in Pal.:—*Asher* {43x}. See: BDB—81a.

837. אֹשֶׁר {1x} 'ôsher, *o'-sher;* from 833; *happiness:*—happy {1x}. See: TWOT—183b; BDB—81a.

838. אַשּׁוּר {9x} 'ăshshûwr, *aw-shoor';* or

אַשֻּׁר 'ăshshûr, *ash-shoor';* from 833 in the sense of *going;* a *step:*—going {6x}, step {3x}. See: TWOT—183d; BDB—78c, 81a, 1083d.

839. אָשֻׁר {1x} 'ăshûr, *ash-oor';* contr. for 8391; the *cedar* tree or some other light elastic wood:—Ashurite {1x}. See: BDB—81b.

840. אֲשַׂרְאֵל {1x} 'Ăsar'êl, *as-ar-ale';* by orth. var. from 833 and 410; *right of God; Asarel,* an Isr.:—Asareel {1x}. See: BDB—77b.

841. אֲשַׂרְאֵלָה {1x} 'Ăsar'êlâh, *as-ar-ale'-aw;* from the same as 840; *right toward God; Asarelah,* an Isr.:—Asarelah. comp. 3480 {1x}. See: BDB—77b.

842. אֲשֵׁרָה {40x} 'ăshêrâh, *ash-ay-raw';* or

אֲשֵׁירָה 'ăshêyrâh, *ash-ay-raw';* from 833; *happy; Asherah* (or Astarte) a Phœnician goddess; also an *image* of the same:—grove {40x}.

Asheyrah is transliterated "*Asherah,* Asherim (pl.)." **(1)** This noun first appears in the Bible in passages anticipating the settlement in Palestine. **(2)** The word's most frequent appearances, however, are usually in historical literature. Of its 40 appearances, 4 are in Israel's law code, 4 in Judges, 4 in prophetic books, and the rest are in 1 Kings and 2 Chronicles. **(3)** *Asheyrah* refers to a cultic object representing the presence of the Canaanite goddess *Asherah.* **(3a)** When the people of Israel entered Palestine, they were to have nothing to do with the idolatrous religions of its inhabitants. **(3b)** Rather, God said, "But ye shall destroy their altars, break their images, and cut down their groves [*asherim*]" (Ex 34:13). **(4)** This cult object was manufactured from wood (Judg 6:26; 1 Kin 14:15) and it could be burned (Deut 12:3). Some scholars conclude that it was a sacred pole set up near an altar to Baal. Since there was only one goddess with this name, the plural (*asherim*) probably represents her several "poles."

(5) *Asherah* signifies the name of the goddess herself: "Now therefore send, and gather to me all Israel unto mount Carmel, and the prophets of Baal four hundred and fifty, and the prophets of the groves [*asherah*] four hundred, which eat at Jezebel's table" (1 Kin 18:19). **(6)** The Canaanites believed that *Asherah* ruled the sea, was the mother of all the gods including Baal, and sometimes was his

deadly enemy. Apparently, the mythology of Canaan maintained that *Asherah* was the consort of Baal, who had displaced El as their highest god. Thus her sacred objects (poles) were immediately beside altars to Baal, and she was worshiped along with him. Syn.: comp. 6253. See: TWOT—183h; BDB—81b.

843. אֲשֵׁרִי {1x} ’**Âshêrîy**, *aw-shay-ree';* patron. from 836; an *Asherite* (collect.) or desc. of Asher:—Asherites {1x}. See: BDB—81b.

844. אַשְׂרִיאֵל {3x} ’**Asrîy’êl**, *as-ree-ale';* an orth. var. for 840; *Asriel*, the name of two Isr.:—Ashriel {2x}, Asriel {1x}. See: BDB—77b.

845. אַשְׂרִאֵלִי {1x} ’**Asrî’êlîy**, *as-ree-ale-ee';* patron. from 844; an *Asrielite* (collect.) or desc. of Asriel:—Asrielites {1x}. See: BDB—77b.

846. אֻשַּׁרְנָא {2x} ’**ushsharnâ** (Aram.), *oosh-ar-naw';* from a root corresp. to 833; a *wall* (from its uprightness):—wall {2x}. See: TWOT—2616; BDB—1083b.

847. אֶשְׁתָּאֹל {7x} ’**Eshtâ’ôl**, *esh-taw-ole';* or

אֶשְׁתָּאוֹל ’**Eshtâ’ôwl**, *esh-taw-ole';* prob. from 7592; *intreaty; Eshtaol,* a place in Pal.:—Eshtaol {1x}. See: BDB—84b.

848. אֶשְׁתָּאֻלִי {1x} ’**Eshtâ’ûlîy**, *esh-taw-oo-lee';* patrial from 847; an *Eshtaolite* (collect.) or inhab. of Eshtaol:—Eshtaulites {1x}. See: BDB—84b.

849. אֶשְׁתַּדּוּר {2x} ’**eshtaddûwr** (Aram.), *esh-tad-dure';* from 7712 (in a bad sense); *rebellion:*—sedition {2x}. See: TWOT—3021a; BDB—1083b, 1114c.

850. אֶשְׁתּוֹן {2x} ’**Eshtôwn**, *esh-tone';* prob. from the same as 7764; *restful; Eshton,* an Isr.:—Eshton {2x}. See: BDB—84c.

851. אֶשְׁתְּמֹעַ {6x} ’**Eshtᵉmôa‘**, *esh-tem-o'-ah;* or

אֶשְׁתְּמוֹעַ ’**Eshtᵉmôwa‘**, *esh-tem-o'-ah;* or

אֶשְׁתְּמֹה ’**Eshtᵉmôh**, *esh-tem-o';* from 8085 (in the sense of *obedience*); *Eshtemoa* or *Eshtemoh,* a place in Pal.:—Eshtemoa {5x}, Eshtemoh {1x}. See: BDB—84c, 1035d.

852. אָת {3x} ’**âth** (Aram.), *awth;* corresp. to 226; a *portent:*—sign {3x}. See: TWOT—2617; BDB—1079a, 1083c.

853. אֵת {22x} ’**êth**, *ayth;* appar. contr. from 226 in the demonstr. sense of *entity;* prop. *self* (but Gen used to point out more def. the obj. of a verb or prep., *even* or *namely*):—not translated {22x}. See: TWOT—186; BDB—84c, 1096b.

854. אֵת {24x} ’**êth**, *ayth;* prob. from 579; prop. *nearness* (used only as a prep. or an adv.), *near;* hence, Gen *with, by, at, among,* etc. [*Often with another prep. prefixed.*]:—against, among, before, by, for, from, in (-to), (out) of, with = {24x}. See: TWOT—187; BDB—85c.

855. אֵת {5x} ’**êth**, *ayth;* of uncert. der.; a *hoe* or other digging implement:—coulter {2x}, plowshare {3x}. See: TWOT—192a; BDB—87b, 88a.

אַתְּ ’**âttâ**. See 859.

אַתָּא ’**âthâ**. See 857.

856. אֶתְבַּעַל {1x} ’**Ethba‘al**, *eth-bah'-al;* from 854 and 1168; *with Baal; Ethbaal,* a Phœnician king:—Ethbaal {1x}. See: BDB—87a.

857. אָתָה {21x} ’**âthâh**, *aw-thaw';* or

אָתָא ’**âthâ**, *aw-thaw';* a prim. root [collat. to 225 contr.]; to *arrive:*—come {20x}, brought {1x}. See: TWOT—188; BDB—87b, 1083c.

858. אֲתָה {16x} ’**âthâh** (Aram.), *aw-thaw';* or

אֲתָא ’**âthâ** (Aram.), *aw-thaw';* corresp. to 857:—come {7x}, bring {9x}. See: TWOT—2618; BDB—1083c.

859. אַתָּה {1000's x} **attâh**, *at-taw';* or (short.);

אַתְּ ’**attâ**, *at-taw';* or

אַת ’**ath**, *ath;* fem. (irreg.) sometimes

אַתִּי ’**attîy**, *at-tee';* plur. masc.

אַתֶּם ’**attem**, *at-tem';* fem.

אַתֵּן ’**atten**, *at-ten';* or

אַתֵּנָה ’**attênâh**, *at-tay'-naw;* or

אַתֵּנָּה ’**attênnâh**, *at-tane'-naw;* a prim. pron. of the second pers.; *thou* and *thee,* or (plur.) *ye* and *you:*—thee, thou, ye, you = {1000's x}. See: TWOT—189; BDB—61c, 61d, 87b, 87c, 87d, 1082a.

860. אָתוֹן {34x} ’**âthôwn**, *aw-thone';* prob. from the same as 386 (in the sense of *patience*); a female *ass* (from its docility):—(she) ass {34x}. See: TWOT—190a; BDB—87c.

861. אַתּוּן {10x} ’**attûwn** (Aram.), *at-toon';* prob. from the corresp. to 784; prob. a *fire-place,* i.e. *furnace:*—furnace {10x}. See: TWOT—2619; BDB—1083c.

862. אַתּוּק {5x} ’**attûwq**, *at-tooke';* or

אַתִּיק ’**attîyq**, *at-teek';* from 5423 in the sense of *decreasing;* a *ledge* or offset in a building:—gallery {5x}. TWOT—191a; BDB—87d.

863. אִתַּי {9x} ʾIttay, it-tah'ee; or

אִיתַי ʾIythay, ee-thah'ee; from 854; near; Ittai or Ithai, the name of a Gittite and of an Isr.:—Ithai {1x}, Ittai {8x}. See: BDB—87a.

864. אֵתָם {4x} ʾÊtham, ay-thawm'; of Eg. der.; Etham, a place in the desert:— Etham {4x}. See: BDB—87c.

אַתֶּן ʾattem. See 859.

865. אֶתְמוֹל {8x} ʾethmôwl, eth-mole'; or

אִתְמוֹל ʾithmôwl, ith-mole'; or

אֶתְמוּל ʾethmûwl, eth-mool'; prob. from 853 or 854 and 4136; heretofore; def. yesterday:—time past + 8032 {2x}, herefore + 832 {1x}, beforetime + 8032 {1x}, yesterday {1x}, old {1x}, late {1x}, before {1x}. See: TWOT—2521; BDB—87c, 1069d.

866. אֶתְנָה {6x} ʾethnâh, eth-naw'; from 8566; a present (as the price of harlotry):—reward {6x}. See: TWOT—2524a; BDB—1071d, 1072c.

אֶתְנָה ʾattênâh or

אֶתְנָּה ʾattennâh. See 859.

867. אֶתְנִי {1x} ʾEthnîy, eth-nee'; perh. from 866; munificence; Ethni, an Isr.:— Ethni {1x}. See: BDB—87d.

868. אֶתְנַן {11x} ʾethnan, eth-nan'; the same as 866; a gift (as the price of harlotry or idolatry):—hire {8x}, reward {3x}. TWOT— 2529a; BDB—87d, 1071d, 1072c.

869. אֶתְנַן {1x} ʾEthnan, eth-nan'; the same as 868 in the sense of 867; Ethnan, an Isr.:—Ethnan {1x}. See: BDB—1071d, 1072c.

870. אֲתַר {8x} ʾăthar (Aram.), ath-ar'; from a root corresp. to that of 871; a place; (adv.) after:—after {3x}, place {5x}. TWOT— 2620; BDB—1079d, 1083c, 1084a, 1085d.

871. אֲתָרִים {1x} ʾĂthârîym, ath-aw-reem'; plur. from an unused root (prob. mean. to step); places; Atharim, a place near Pal.:—spies {1x}. See: BDB—87d.

ב

872. בְּאָה {1x} bᵉâh, bè-aw'; from 935; an entrance to a building:—entry {1x}. See: TWOT—212a, 99d.

873. בְּאוּשׁ {1x} bᵉûwsh (Aram.), be-oosh'; from 888; wicked:—bad {1x}. See: TWOT—2622a; BDB—1084a.

874. בָּאַר {3x} bâʾar, baw-ar'; a prim. root; to dig; by anal. to engrave; fig. to ex-

plain:—plain {1x}, plainly {1x}, declare {1x}. See: TWOT—194; BDB—91b.

875. בְּאֵר {37x} bᵉêr, bè-ayr'; from 874; a pit; espec. a well:—well {32x}, pit {3x}, slimepits {1x}, not translated {1x}.

Be'er means "pit; well." (1) This word appears 37 times in the Bible with no occurrences in the Old Testament prophetic books. (2) Be'er means a "well" in which there may be water. (2a) By itself the word does not always infer the presence of water. (2b) The word refers to the "pit" itself whether dug or natural: "And Abraham reproved Abimelech because of a well of water, which Abimelech's servants had violently taken away" (Gen 21:25). (2c) Such a "well" may have a narrow enough mouth that it can be blocked with a stone which a single strong man could move (Gen 29:2, 10). (2d) In the desert country of the ancient Near East a "well" was an important place and its water the source of deep satisfaction for the thirsty. This concept pictures the role of a wife for a faithful husband (Prov 5:15). (3) A "pit" may contain something other than water. In its first biblical appearance be'er is used of tar pits: "And the vale of Siddim was full of slimepits" (Gen 14:10). (4) A "pit" may contain nothing as does the "pit" which becomes one's grave (Ps 55:23, "pit of the grave"). (5) In some passages the word was to represent more than a depository for the body but a place where one exists after death (Ps 69:15). See: TWOT— 194a; BDB—91c.

876. בְּאֵר {2x} Bᵉêr, bè-ayr'; the same as 875; Beër, a place in the desert, also one in Pal.:—Beer {1x}. See: BDB—91d.

877. בֹּאר {2x} bôʾr, bore; from 874; a cistern:—cistern {2x}. Syn.: 953, 5869. See: TWOT—194d; BDB—92b.

878. בְּאֵרָא {1x} Bᵉêrâ, bè-ay-raw'; from 875; a well; Beëra, an Isr.:—Beera {1x}. See: BDB—92a.

879. בְּאֵר אֵלִים {1x} Bᵉêr ʾÊlîym, bè-ayr' ay-leem'; from 875 and the plur. of 410; well of heroes; Beër-Elim, a place in the desert:—Beer-elim {1x}. See: BDB—91d.

880. בְּאֵרָה {1x} Bᵉêrâh, bè-ay-raw'; the same as 878; Beërah, an Isr.:—Beerah {1x}. See: BDB—92a.

881. בְּאֵרוֹת {5x} Bᵉêrôwth, bè-ay-rohth'; fem. plur. of 875; wells; Beëroth, a place in Pal.:—Beeroth {1x}. See: BDB—92a.

882. בְּאֵרִי {2x} Bᵉêrîy, bè-ay-ree'; from 875; fountained; Beëri, the name of a Hittite and of an Isr.:—Beeri {2x}. See: BDB— 92b.

883. בְּאֵר לַחַי רֹאִי {3x} **Bᵉᵉr la-Chay Rôʼîy**, *bè-ayr′ lakh-ah′ee ro-ee′;* from 875 and 2416 (with pref.) and 7203; *well of a living* (One) *my seer; Beër-Lachai-Rô*, a place in the desert:—the well Lahairoi {2x}, Beerlahairoi {1x}. See: BDB—91d.

884. בְּאֵר שֶׁבַע {34x} **Bᵉᵉr Shebaᶜ**, *be-ayr′ sheh′-bah;* from 875 and 7651 (in the sense of 7650); *well of an oath; Beër-Sheba*, a place in Pal.:—Beer-shebah {34x}. See: BDB—92a, 989d.

885. בְּאֵרֹת בְּנֵי־יַעֲקָן {1x} **Bᵉᵉrôth Bᵉnêy-Yaᶜă-qan**, *bè-ay-roth′ be-nay′ yah-a-kan′;* from the fem. plur. of 875, and the plur. contr. of 1121, and 3292; *wells of* (the) *sons of Jaakan; Beëroth-Bene-Jaakan*, a place in the desert:—Beeroth of the children of Jaakan {1x}. See: BDB—92b, 785c.

886. בְּאֵרֹתִי {5x} **Bᵉᵉrôthîy**, *bè-ay-ro-thee′;* patrial from 881; a *Beërothite* or inhab. of Beëroth:—Beerothite {1x}. See: BDB—92a.

887. בָּאַשׁ {17x} **bâʼash**, *baw-ash′;* a prim. root; to *smell bad;* fig. to *be offensive* mor.:—stink {10x}, abhor {3x}, abomination {1x}, loathsome {1x}, stinking savour {1x}, utterly {1x} (inf. for emphasis). Syn.: 889, 8581. See: TWOT—195; BDB—1084a.

888. בְּאֵשׁ {1x} **bᵉᵉsh** (Aram.), *bè-aysh′;* corresp. to 887:—displease {1x}. See: TWOT—2622; BDB—1084a, 1094a.

889. בְּאֹשׁ {3x} **bᵉᵉôsh**, *bè-oshe′;* from 877; a *stench:*—stink {3x}. See: TWOT—195a; BDB—93b.

890. בָּאְשָׁה {1x} **boʼshâh**, *bosh-aw′;* fem. of 889; *stink-weed* or any other noxious or useless plant:—cockle {1x}. See: TWOT—195b; BDB—93b.

891. בְּאֻשִׁים {2x} **bᵉûshîym**, *bè-oo-sheem′;* plur. of 889; *poison-berries:*—wild grapes {2x}. See: TWOT—195c; BDB—93b.

892. בָּבָה {1x} **bâbâh**, *baw-baw′;* fem. act. part. of an unused root mean. to *hollow out;* something *hollowed* (as a *gate*), i.e. the *pupil* of the eye:—apple [of the eye] {1x}. See: TWOT—196; BDB—93b.

893. בֵּבַי {6x} **Bêbay**, *bay-bah′ee;* prob. of for. or.; *Bebai*, an Isr.:—Bebai {1x}. See: BDB—93c.

894. בָּבֶל {262x} **Bâbel**, *baw-bel′;* from 1101; *confusion; Babel* (i.e. Babylon), incl. Babylonia and the Bab. empire:—Babylon {257x}, Babylonian + 1121 {3x}, Babel {2x}. See: BDB—93c, 1084a.

895. בָּבֶל {25x} **Bâbel** (Aram.), *baw-bel′;* corresp. to 894:—Babylon {25x}. See: BDB—1084a.

896. בַּבְלִי {1x} **Bablîy** (Aram.), *bab-lee′;* patrial from 895; a *Babylonian:*—Babylonia {1x}. See: BDB—1084a.

897. בַּג {1x} **bag**, *bag;* a Pers. word; *food:*—spoil {1x}. See: TWOT—225a; BDB—93c, 103a.

898. בָּגַד {49x} **bâgad**, *baw-gad′;* a prim. root; to *cover* (with a garment); fig. to *act covertly;* by impl. to *pillage:*—treacherously {23x}, transgressor {10x}, transgress {3x}, deceitfully {2x}, treacherous dealer {3x}, treacherous {2x}, very {2x} (inf. for emphasis), unfaithful man {1x}, treacherous men {1x}, offend {1x}, unfaithfully {1x}. Syn.: 6586. See: TWOT—198; BDB—93c.

899. בֶּגֶד {217x} **beged**, *behg′-ed;* from 898; a *covering*, i.e. clothing; also *treachery* or *pillage:*—garment {107x}, clothes {69x}, cloth {13x}, raiment {12x}, apparel {4x}, robe {4x}, wardrobe {2x}, very {2x}, clothing {1x}, lap {1x}, rags {1x}, vestures {1x}.

Beged means "garment; covering; cloth; blanket; saddlecloth." **(1)** The word signifies any kind of "garment" or "covering," usually for human wear. **(2)** *Beged* first appears in Gen 24:53: "And the servant brought forth jewels of silver, and jewels of gold, and raiment, and gave them to Rebekah." **(2a)** Here the word represents "garments made of precious materials." **(2b)** The "garments" of widows, on the other hand, must have been quite common and valueless (Gen 38:14). **(2c)** Certainly mourners' "garments" must have been very plain, if not torn (2 Sa 14:2). **(3)** *Beged* sometimes refers to "outer garments." **(3a)** Thus in 2 Kin 7:15, the Syrian soldiers who fled from Jerusalem left behind their "clothes" and equipment; they left behind everything that would hinder their escape. **(3b)** Surely this did not include their essential "clothing." **(4)** In Judg 14:12, however, the word is distinguished from linen wrappings ("outer garments")—Samson promised the Philistines that if they would solve his riddle, he would give them "thirty linen sheets and thirty change of garments" (cf. Judg 17:10).

(5) The "holy garments" Moses was commanded to make for Aaron included everything he was to wear while officiating before the Lord: "A breastplate, and an ephod, and a robe, and an embroidered coat, a mitre, and a sash; and they shall make holy garments for Aaron" (Ex 28:4). **(6)** In passages such as Num 4:6, *beged* means "covering," in the sense of a large flat piece of cloth material to be laid over something: "And [they] shall put thereon the

covering of badgers' skins, and shall spread over it a cloth wholly of blue." **(7)** When put over people, such clothes were probably "blankets": "Now king David was old and stricken in years; and they covered him with clothes, but he gat no heat" (1 Kin 1:1). **(8)** When put over beasts, such coverings were "saddlecloths" (Eze 27:20). Syn.: 3801, 3847, 4403, 8008, 8071. See: TWOT—198a; BDB—93d.

900. בִּגְדוֹת {1x} **bôgᵉdôwth**, *bohg-ed-ōhth';* fem. plur. act. part. of 898; *treacheries:*—treacherous {1x}. TWOT—198b; BDB—93d.

901. בָּגוֹד {2x} **bâgôwd**, *baw-gode';* from 898; *treacherous:*—treacherous {2x}. See: TWOT—198c; BDB—93d.

902. בִּגְוַי {1x} **Bigvay**, *big-vah'ee;* prob. of for. or.; *Bigvai*, an Isr.:—Bigvai {1x}. See: BDB—94a.

903. בִּגְתָא {1x} **Bigthâ᾽**, *big-thaw';* of Pers. der.; *Bigtha*, a eunuch of Xerxes:—Bigtha {1x}. See: BDB—94a.

904. בִּגְתָן {2x} **Bigthân**, *big-thawn';* or

בִּגְתָנָא **Bigthânâ᾽**, *big-thaw'naw;* of similar der. to 903; *Bigthan* or *Bigthana*, a eunuch of Xerxes:—Bigthan {1x}, Bigthana {1x}. See: BDB—94b.

905. בַּד {56x} **bad**, *bad;* from 909; prop. *separation;* by impl. a *part* of the body, *branch* of a tree, *bar* for carrying; fig. *chief* of a city; espec. (with prep. pref.) as adv., *apart, only, besides:*—staves {37x}, beside {3x}, branches {3x}, alone {2x}, only {2x}, strength {2x}, apart {1x}, bars {1x}, each {1x}, except {1x}, beside him {1x}, like {1x}, themselves {1x}.

Bad (905) means "part; portion; limbs; piece of cloth; pole; shoot; alone; by themselves; only; apart from; besides; aside from." **(1)** First, *bad* means a "part or portion" of something. **(1a)** In Ex 30:34 it refers to the portion or amount of spices mixed together to make incense for the worship of God. **(1b)** In Job 18:13 the word represents the members or parts of the wicked (cf. Job 41:12—"limbs" of a crocodile). **(2)** Second, the word means a piece of cloth: **(2a)** "And thou shalt make them linen breeches to cover their nakedness" (Ex 28:42—first occurrence of this nuance). **(2b)** This word is always used of a priestly garment or at least of a garment worn by one who appears before God or His altar. **(3)** Third, *bad* can mean a long piece of wood or woody material. **(3a)** The ark, altars, and table of the Bread of the Presence were carried by staves passed through rings attached to these articles: "And thou shalt put the staves into the rings by the sides of the ark, that the ark may be borne with them" (Ex 25:14—first occurrence of this nuance). **(3b)** In Eze 19:14 *bad* is used of the "shoots" or limbs of a vine; "And fire is gone out of a rod of her branches" (cf. Eze 17:6). **(3c)** The gates of a city are *badim* (Job 17:16).

(4) Fourth, in most of its appearances (152x) this word is preceded by the preposition *le.* **(4a)** This use means "alone" (89x): "And the Lord God said, It is not good that the man should be alone; I will make him a help meet for him" (Gen 2:18—first occurrence of the word). **(4b)** In a second nuance the phrase identifies a unit by itself, a single unit: "And thou shalt couple five curtains by themselves, and six curtains by themselves" (Ex 26:9). **(4c)** Twice the word is used as an adverb of limitation meaning "only": "Lo, this only have I found, that God hath made man upright; but they have sought out many inventions" (Eccl 7:29). **(4d)** When followed by the preposition *min* (or *al*) the word functions as an adverb meaning "apart from" or "besides": "And the children of Israel journeyed from Rameses to Succoth, about six hundred thousand on foot that were men, beside children" (Ex 12:37). **(4e)** In Num 29:39 the translation "besides" is appropriate: "These things ye shall do unto the Lord in your set feasts, beside your vows, and your freewill offerings." **(4f)** In 33 passages the word is preceded by the preposition *min* but still means "besides." See: TWOT—201a; BDB—94b, 94c, 571c.

906. בַּד {23x} **bad**, *bad;* perh. from 909 (in the sense of *divided* fibres); flaxen *thread* or yarn; hence, a *linen* garment:—linen {23x}. Syn.: 948, 6593, 8336. See: TWOT—199; BDB—94b.

907. בַּד {6x} **bad**, *bad;* from 908; a *brag* or *lie;* also a *liar:*—lie {3x}, liar {2x}, parts {1x}. Syn.: 3576. See: TWOT—202a; BDB—94b, 95a.

908. בָּדָא {2x} **bâdâ᾽**, *baw-daw';* a prim. root; (fig.) to *invent:*—devise {1x}, feign {1x}. See: TWOT—200; BDB—94b.

909. בָּדַד {3x} **bâdad**, *baw-dad';* a prim. root; to *divide*, i.e. (reflex.) *be solitary:*—alone {3x}.

Badad means "to be isolated, be alone." One of its 3 appearances is in Ps 102:7: "I watch, and am as a sparrow alone upon the housetop." Syn.: 905. See: TWOT—201; BDB—94b.

910. בָּדָד {11x} **bâdâd**, *baw-dawd';* from 909; *separate;* adv. *separately:*—alone {7x}, solitary {2x}, only {1x}, desolate {1x}. See: TWOT—201b; BDB—94d.

911. בְּדַד {2x} **Bᵉdad**, *bed-ad';* from 909 {2x}. See: BDB—95a.

912. בְּדְיָה {1x} **Bêd°yâh**, *bay-dè-yaw';* prob. short. form 5662; *servant of Jehovah; Bedejah*, an Isr.:—Bedeiah {1x}. See: BDB—95a.

913. בְּדִיל {6x} **b°dîyl**, *bed-eel';* from 914; *alloy* (because *removed* by smelting); by anal. *tin*:—tin {5x}, plummet + 68 {1x}. Syn. 4949. See: TWOT—203c; BDB—95d.

914. בָּדַל {42x} **bâdal**, *baw-dal';* a prim. root; to *divide* (in var. senses lit. or fig., *separate, distinguish, differ, select,* etc.):—separate {25x}, divide {8x}, difference {4x}, asunder {2x}, severed {2x}, sever out {1x}, separation {1x}, utterly {1x} (inf. for emphasis). Syn.: 2673, 5144, 6504. See: TWOT—203; BDB—95a.

915. בָּדָל {1x} **bâdâl**, *baw-dawl';* from 914; a *part*:—piece {1x}. See: TWOT—203a; BDB—95c.

916. בְּדֹלַח {2x} **b°dôlach**, *bed-o'-lakh;* prob. from 914; something in *pieces*, i.e. *bdellium*, a (fragrant) gum (perh. *amber*); others a *pearl*:—bdellium {2x}. See: TWOT—203d; BDB—95d.

917. בְּדָן {2x} **B°dân**, *bed-awn';* prob. short. for 5658; *servile; Bedan*, the name of two Isr.:—Bedan {2x}. See: BDB—96a.

918. בָּדַק {1x} **bâdaq**, *baw-dak';* a prim. root; to *gap* open; used only as a denom. from 919; to *mend* a breach:—repair {1x}. See: TWOT—204; BDB—96a.

919. בֶּדֶק {10x} **bedeq**, *beh'-dek;* from 918; a *gap* or *leak* (in a building or a ship):—breach {8x}, calker + 2388 {2x}. See: TWOT—204a; BDB—96a.

920. בִּדְקַר {1x} **Bidqar**, *bid-car';* prob. from 1856 with prep. pref.; *by stabbing,* i.e. *assassin; Bidkar*, an Isr.:—Bidkar {1x}. See: BDB—96a.

921. בְּדַר {1x} **b°dar** (Aram.), *bed-ar';* corresp. (by transp.) to 6504; to *scatter*:—scatter {1x}. Syn.: 2219, 6340, 6566. See: TWOT—2623; BDB—1084a

922. בֹּהוּ {3x} **bôhûw**, *bo'-hoo;* from an unused root (mean. to *be empty*); a *vacuity,* i.e. (superficially) an undistinguishable *ruin*:—emptiness {1x}, void {2x}. See: TWOT—205a; BDB—96a.

923. בַּהַט {1x} **bahat**, *bah'-hat;* from an unused root (prob. mean. to *glisten*); white *marble* or perh. *alabaster*:—red [marble] {1x}. See: TWOT—206; BDB—96b.

924. בְּהִילוּ {1x} **b°hîylûw** (Aram.), *bè-heeloo';* from 927; a *hurry;* only adv. *hastily*:—in haste {1x}. See: TWOT—2624a; BDB—1084b.

925. בָּהִיר {1x} **bâhîyr**, *baw-here';* from an unused root (mean. to *be bright*); *shining*:—bright {1x}. See: TWOT—211b; BDB—97c.

926. בָּהַל {39x} **bâhal**, *baw-hal';* a prim. root; to *tremble* inwardly (or *palpitate*), i.e. (fig.) be (caus. *make*) (suddenly) *alarmed* or *agitated;* by impl. to *hasten* anxiously:—trouble {17x}, haste {4x}, afraid {3x}, vexed {3x}, amazed {2x}, hasty {2x}, affrighted {1x}, dismayed {1x}, hastily {1x}, thrust him out {1x}, rash {1x}, speedily {1x}, speedy {1x}, vex {1x}. Syn.: 6862, 6869. See: TWOT—207; BDB—96b, 1084b.

927. בְּהַל {11x} **b°hal** (Aram.), *bè-hal';* corresp. to 926; to *terrify, hasten*:—in haste {3x}, trouble {8x}. See: TWOT—2624; BDB—1084a.

928. בֶּהָלָה {4x} **behâlâh**, *beh-haw-law';* from 926; *panic, destruction*:—terror {2x}, trouble {2x}. See: TWOT—207a; BDB—96d.

929. בְּהֵמָה {189x} **b°hêmâh**, *bè-hay-maw';* from an unused root (prob. mean. to *be mute*); prop. a *dumb* beast; espec. any large quadruped or *animal* (often collect.):—beast {136x}, cattle {53x}.

Behemah means "beast; animal; domesticated animal; cattle; riding beast; wild beast." **(1)** In Ex 9:25, this word clearly embraces even the larger "animals," all the animals in Egypt: "And the hail smote throughout all the land of Egypt all that was in the field, both man and beast." **(1a)** This meaning is especially clear in Gen 6:7: "I will destroy man whom I have created from the face of the earth; both man, and beast, and the creeping thing, and the fowls of the air." **(1b)** In 1Kin 4:33, this word seems to exclude birds, fish, and reptiles: "He [Solomon] spake also of beasts, and of fowl, and of creeping things, and of fishes."

(2) The word *behemah* can be used of all the domesticated beasts or animals other than man: "And God said, Let the earth bring forth the living creature after his kind, cattle, and creeping thing, and [wild] beast of the earth after his kind" (Gen 1:24, first occurrence). **(2a)** Ps 8:7 uses *behemah* in synonymous parallelism with "oxen" and "sheep," as though it includes both: "All sheep and oxen, yea, and the beasts of the field." **(2b)** The word can, however, be used of cattle only: "Shall not their cattle and their substance and every beast of theirs be ours?" (Gen 34:23). **(3)** In a rare use of the word, it signifies a "riding animal," such as a horse or mule: "And I arose in the night, I and some few men with me; neither told I any man what my God had put in my heart to do

at Jerusalem: neither was there any beast with me, save the beast that I rode upon" (Neh 2:12). **(4)** Infrequently, *behemah* represents any wild, four-footed, undomesticated beast: "And thy carcase shall be meat unto all fowls of the air, and unto the beasts of the earth, and no man shall [frighten] them away" (Deut 28:26). Syn.: 1165, 2416, 4735, 6629, 6728. See: TWOT— 208a; BDB—96d.

930. בְּהֵמוֹת {1x} **bᵉhêmôwth**, *bè-hay-mōhth';* in form a plur. of 929, but really a sing. of Eg. der.; a *water-ox*, i.e. the *hippopotamus* or Nile-horse:—Behemoth {1x}. Could possibly be an extinct dinosaur. See: TWOT— 208b; BDB—97a.

931. בֹּהֶן {16x} **bôhen**, *bo'-hen;* from an unused root appar. mean. to *be thick;* the *thumb* of the hand or *great toe* of the foot:— thumb {9x}, great toe {7x}. See: TWOT—209a; BDB—97b.

932. בֹּהַן {2x} **Bôhan**, *bo'han;* an orth. var. of 931; *thumb, Bohan*, an Isr.:—*Bohan* {2x}. See: BDB—97b.

933. בֹּהַק {1x} **bôhaq**, *bo'-hak;* from an unused root mean. to *be pale;* white *scurf:*—freckled spot {1x}. *Bohaq* is a harmless eruption of the skin; a pimple. See: TWOT— 210a; BDB—97b.

934. בֹּהֶרֶת {13x} **bôhereth**, *bo-heh'-reth;* fem. act. part. of the same as 925; a *whitish* spot on the skin:—bright spot {13x}. See: TWOT—211a; BDB—97b.

935. בּוֹא {2577x} **bôwᵒ**, *bo;* a prim. root; to *go* or *come* (in a wide variety of applications):—come {1435x}, bring {487x}, . . . in {233x}, enter {125x}, go {123x}, carry {17x}, . . . down {23x}, pass {13x}, . . . out {12x}, misc. {109x}.

Bow' (935) means "to go in, enter, come, go." **(1)** First, this verb connotes movement in space from one place toward another. **(1a)** The meaning "go in" or "enter" appears in Gen 7:7, where it is said that Noah and his family "entered" the ark. **(1b)** In the causative stem, this verb can signify "cause to enter" or "bring into" (Gen 6:19) or "bring unto" (its meaning in its first biblical occurrence, Gen 2:19). **(1c)** In Gen 10:19, the verb is used more absolutely in the phrase "as thou goest unto Sodom." **(1d)** Interestingly, this verb can also mean "to come" and "to return." Abram and his family "came" to the land of Canaan (Gen 12:5), **(1e)** while in Deut 28:6 God blessed the godly who "go forth" (to work in the morning) and "return" (home in the evening). **(2)** Sometimes *bow'* refers to the "going down" or "setting" of the sun (Gen 15:12). **(3)** It can connote

dying, in the sense of "going to one's fathers" (Gen 15:15). **(4)** Another special use is the "going into one's wife" or "cohabitation" (Gen 6:4). *Bow'* can also be used of movement in time. For example, the prophets speak of the "coming" day of judgment (1 Sa 2:31). **(5)** Finally, the verb can be used of the "coming" of an event such as the sign predicted by a false prophet (Deut 13:2).

(6) There are three senses in which God is said "to come." **(6a)** God "comes" through an angel (Judg 6:11) or other incarnated being (cf. Gen 18:14). **(6a1)** He "appears" and speaks to men in dreams (Gen 20:3) and **(6a2)** in other actual manifestations (Ex 20:20). **(6a3)** For example, during the Exodus, God "appeared" in the cloud and fire that went before the people (Ex 19:9). **(6b)** Secondly, God promises to "come" to the faithful wherever and whenever they properly worship Him (Ex 20:24). **(6b1)** The Philistines felt that God had "come" into the Israelite camp when the ark of the covenant arrived (1 Sa 4:7). **(6b2)** This usage associated with formal worship may appear in Ps 24:7, where the gates of Zion are said to open as the King of glory "enters" Jerusalem. **(6b3)** Also, the Lord is "to return" ("come back") to the new temple described in Eze 43:2. **(6c)** Finally, there is a group of prophetic pictures of divine "comings." **(6c1)** This theme may have originated in the hymns sung of God's "coming" to aid His people in war (cf. Deut 33:2). **(6c2)** In the Psalms (e.g., 50:3) and prophets (e.g., Is 30:27), the Lord "comes" in judgment and blessing—a poetic figure of speech borrowed from ancient Near Eastern mythology (cf. Eze 1:4).

(7) *Bow'* also is used to refer to the "coming" of the Messiah. **(7a)** In Zec 9:9, the messianic king is pictured as "coming" on a foal of a donkey. **(7b)** Some of the passages pose especially difficult problems, such as Gen 49:10, which prophesies that the scepter will remain in Judah "until Shiloh come." **(7c)** Another difficult passage is Eze 21:27: "until he come whose right it is." **(8)** A very well-known prophecy using the verb *bow'* is that concerning the "coming" of the Son of Man (Dan 7:13). **(9)** Finally, there is the "coming" of the last day (Amos 8:2) and the Day of the Lord (Is 13:6). See: TWOT—212; BDB—97c.

936. בּוּז {12x} **bûwz**, *booz;* a prim. root; to *disrespect:*—despise {10x}, contemned {1x}, utterly (inf. for emphasis) {1x}. Syn.: 959, 3988. See: TWOT—213; BDB—100b.

937. בּוּז {11x} **bûwz**, *booz;* from 936; *disrespect:*—contempt {7x}, despised {2x}, contemptuously {1x}, shamed {1x}. See: TWOT— 213a; BDB—100b.

Hebrew

938. בּוּז {3x} **Bûwz**, *booz;* the same as 937; *Buz,* the name of a son of Nahor, and of an Isr.:—Buz {3x}. See: BDB—100c.

939. בּוּזָה {1x} **bûwzâh**, *boo-zaw';* fem. pass. part. of 936; something *scorned;* an obj. of *contempt:*—despised {1x}. See: TWOT—213b; BDB—100c.

940. בּוּזִי {2x} **Bûwzîy**, *boo-zee';* patron. from 938; a *Buzite* or desc. of Buz:—Buzite {2x}. See: BDB—100c.

941. בּוּזִי {1x} **Bûwzîy**, *boo-zee';* the same as 940; *Buzi,* an Isr.:—Buzi {1x}. See: BDB—100c.

942. בַּוַּי {1x} **Bavvay**, *bav-vah'ee;* prob. of Pers. or.; *Bavvai,* an Isr.:—Bavai {1x}. See: BDB—100c.

943. בּוּךְ {3x} **bûwk**, *book;* a prim. root; to *involve* (lit. or fig.):—perplexed {2x}, entangled {1x}. See: TWOT—214; BDB—100c.

944. בּוּל {2x} **bûwl**, *bool;* for 2981; *produce* (of the earth, etc.):—food {1x}, stock {1x}. See: TWOT—835d; BDB—100d, 385b.

945. בּוּל {1x} **Bûwl**, *bool;* the same as 944 (in the sense of *rain*); *Bul,* the eighth Heb. month:—Bul {1x}. See: TWOT—215; BDB—100d.

946. בּוּנָה {1x} **Bûwnâh**, *boo-naw';* from 995; *discretion; Bunah,* an Isr.:—Bunah {1x}. See: BDB—100d, 107b.

בּוּנִי **Bûwnîy**. See 1138.

947. בּוּס {12x} **bûwç**, *boos;* a prim. root; to *trample* (lit. or fig.):—tread . . . {9x}, polluted {2x}, loath {1x}. See: TWOT—216; BDB—100d.

948. בּוּץ {8x} **bûwts**, *boots;* from an unused root (of the same form) mean. to *bleach,* i.e. (intr.) *be white;* prob. *cotton* (of some sort):—fine linen {7x}, white linen {1x}. See: TWOT—219; BDB—101b.

949. בּוֹצֵץ {1x} **Bôwtsêts**, *bo-tsates';* from the same as 948; *shining; Botsets,* a rock near Michmash:—Bozez {1x}. See: BDB—130d.

950. בּוּקָה {1x} **bûwqâh**, *boo-kaw';* fem. pass. part. of an unused root (mean. to *be hollow*); *emptiness* (as adj.):—empty {1x}. See: TWOT—220a; BDB—101c.

951. בּוֹקֵר {1x} **bôwkêr**, *bo-kare';* prop. act. part. from 1239 as denom. from 1241; a *cattle-tender:*—herdsman {1x}. See: TWOT—274b; BDB—133c.

952. בּוּר {1x} **bûwr**, *boor;* a prim. root; to *bore,* i.e. (fig.) *examine:*—declare {1x}. See: TWOT—221; BDB—101c.

953. בּוֹר {69x} **bôwr**, *bore;* from 952 (in the sense of 877); a *pit hole* (espec. one used as a *cistern* or a *prison*):—pit {42x}, cistern {4x}, dungeon {11x}, well {9x}, dungeon + 1004 {2x}, fountain {1x}. Syn.: 875. See: TWOT—194e; BDB—92b, 92d, 101c, 694c, 710a.

954. בּוּשׁ {109x} **bûwsh**, *boosh;* a prim. root; prop. to *pale,* i.e. by impl. to *be ashamed;* also (by impl.) to *be disappointed,* or *delayed:*—ashamed {72x}, confounded {21x}, shame {9x}, all {2x} (inf. for emphasis), confusion {1x}, delayed {1x}, dry {1x}, long {1x}, shamed {1x}.

Buwsh means "to be ashamed, feel ashamed." **(1)** The word has overtones of being or feeling worthless. **(1)** *Buwsh* means "to be ashamed" in Is 1:29: "For they shall be ashamed of the oaks which ye have desired, and ye shall be confounded for the gardens that ye have chosen." Syn.: 1322, 2659, 3639, 7036. See: TWOT—222; BDB—101c.

955. בּוּשָׁה {4x} **bûwshâh**, *boo-shaw';* fem. part. pass. of 954; *shame:*—shame {4x}. See: TWOT—222a; BDB—102a.

956. בּוּת {1x} **bûwth** (Aram.), *booth;* appar. denom. from 1005; to *lodge* over night:—pass the night {1x}. See: TWOT—2629; BDB—1084c.

957. בַּז {25x} **baz**, *baz;* from 962; *plunder:*—prey {18x}, spoil {4x}, spoiled {2x}, booty {1x}. Syn.: 961, 962, 1497, 7998, 8154. See: TWOT—225a; BDB—102b, 103a.

958. בָּזָא {2x} **bâzâ'**, *baw-zaw';* a prim. root; prob. to *cleave:*—spoiled {2x}. Syn.: See 957. See: TWOT—223; BDB—102b.

959. בָּזָה {43x} **bâzâh**, *baw-zaw';* a prim. root; to *disesteem:*—despise {36x}, contemptible {3x}, contemned {1x}, disdained {1x}, vile person {1x}, scorn {1x}. Syn.: 936, 937, 3988. See: TWOT—224; BDB—102b.

960. בָּזֹה {1x} **bâzôh**, *baw-zo';* from 959; *scorned:*—despise {1x}. See: TWOT—224b; BDB—102b.

961. בִּזָּה {10x} **bizzâh**, *biz-zaw';* fem. of 957; *booty:*—prey {4x}, spoil {6x}. See: TWOT—225, 225b; BDB—102c, 103a.

962. בָּזַז {43x} **bâzaz**, *baw-zaz';* a prim. root; to *plunder:*—spoil {9x}, prey {9x}, spoiled {6x}, rob {6x}, take {6x}, take away {2x}, caught {1x}, gathering {1x}, robbers {1x}, took {1x}, utterly {1x}. Syn.: See 957. See: TWOT—225; BDB—102d.

963. בִּזָּיוֹן {1x} **bizzâyôwn**, *biz-zaw-yone';* from 959; *disesteem:*—contempt {1x}. See: TWOT—224a; BDB—102c.

964. בִּזְיוֹתְיָה {1x} **bizyôwthᵉyâh**, *biz-yo-thè-yaw'*; from 959 and 3050; *contempts of Jah; Bizjothjah*, a place in Pal.:—Bizjothjah {1x}. See: BDB—103a.

965. בָּזָק {1x} **bâzâq**, *baw-zawk'*; from an unused root mean. to *lighten*; a *flash* of lightning:—flash of lightning {1x}. See: TWOT—226a; BDB—103b.

966. בֶּזֶק {3x} **Bezeq**, *beh'-zek*; from 965; *lightning; Bezek*, a place in Pal.:—Bezek {3x}. See: BDB—103b.

967. בָּזַר {2x} **bâzar**, *baw-zar'*; a prim. root; to *disperse*:—scatter {2x}. See: TWOT—227; BDB—103b, 1084a.

968. בִּזְתָא {1x} **Biztháʼ**, *biz-thaw'*; of Pers. or.; *Biztha*, a eunuch of Xerxes:—Biztha {1x}. See: BDB—103b.

969. בָּחוֹן {1x} **bâchôwn**, *baw-khone'*; from 974; an *assayer* of metals:—tower {1x}. See: TWOT—230d; BDB—103d.

970. בָּחוּר {45x} **bâchûwr**, *baw-khoor'*; or

בָּחֻר **bâchûr**, *baw-khoor'*; pass. part. of 977; prop. *selected*, i.e. a *youth* (often collect.):—young man {42x}, the chosen {1x}, young {1x}, not translated {1x}. Syn.: 972, 977, 4005, 7206.

Bachur means "young man." **(1)** This word signifies the fully developed, vigorous, unmarried man. **(2)** In its first occurrence *bachur* is contrasted to *betulah* (1330), "virgin": "The sword without, and terror within, shall destroy both the young man and the virgin, the suckling also with the man of gray hairs" (Deut 32:25). **(3)** The strength of the "young man" is contrasted with the gray hair (crown of honor) of old men (Prov 20:29). **(4)** The period during which a "young man" is in his prime (could this be the period during which he is eligible for the draft—i.e., age 20-50?) is represented by the two nouns, *bechurim* (979) and *bechurot* (970). Syn.: ʼAdam (120) connotes man as the creature created in God's image, the crown of all creation. *Iysh* (376) is used for man as the counterpart of woman and/or as distinguished in his maleness. *Geber* (1397) denotes a male as an antonym of a woman, many times suggesting strength, strong man. *Enowsh* (582) sets forth a collective idea man suggesting the frailty, vulnerability, and finitude of man as contrasted to God. *Bâchûr* (970) signifies the fully developed, vigorous, unmarried man is in his prime. See also: 376, 582, 1167, 1397, 1400, 4962. See: TWOT—231a; BDB—104c.

בְּחוּרוֹת **bᵉchûwrôwth**. See 979.

בַּחוּרִים **Bachûwrîym**. See 980.

971. בָּחִין {1x} **bachîyn**, *bakh-een'*; another form of 975; a watch-*tower* of besiegers:—tower {1x}. See: TWOT—230c; BDB—103d.

972. בָּחִיר {13x} **bâchîyr**, *baw-kheer'*; from 977; *select*:—chosen {8x}, elect {4x}, chose {1x}.

Bachiyr means "chosen ones." It is used always of the Lord's "chosen ones": "Saul, whom the Lord did choose" (2 Sa 21:6); "ye children of Jacob, his chosen ones" (1 Chr 16:13). Syn.: See 970. See: TWOT—231c; BDB—104c.

973. בָּחַל {2x} **bâchal**, *baw-khal'*; a prim. root; to *loathe*:—abhor {1x}, gotten hastily {1x}. See: TWOT—229; BDB—103b, 103c.

974. בָּחַן {29x} **bâchan**, *baw-khan'*; a prim. root; to *test* (espec. metals); Gen and fig. to *investigate*:—try {19x}, prove {7x}, examine {1x}, tempt {1x}, trial {1x}. Syn.: 5254. See: TWOT—230; BDB—103c.

975. בַּחַן {1x} **bachan**, *bakh'-an*; from 974 (in the sense of keeping a *look-out*); a watch-*tower*:—tower {1x}. See: TWOT—230b; BDB—103d.

976. בֹּחַן {1x} **bôchan**, *bo'-khan*; from 974; *trial*:—tried {1x}. See: TWOT—230a; BDB—103d.

977. בָּחַר {172x} **bâchar**, *baw-khar'*; a prim. root; prop. to *try*, i.e. (by impl.) *select*:—choose {77x}, chosen {77x}, choice {6x}, choose . . . out {5x}, acceptable {1x}, appoint {1x}, excellent {1x}, chosen men {1x}, rather {1x}, require {1x}, not translated {1x}.

Bachar (977) means "to choose." **(1)** *Bachar* first occurs in the Bible in Gen 6:2: "They took them wives of all which they chose." **(2)** It is often used with a man as the subject: "Lot chose [for himself] all the plain of Jordan" (Gen 13:11). **(3)** In more than half of the occurrences, God is the subject of *bachar*, as in Num 16:5: "The Lord will show who are his, and who is holy; . . . even him whom he hath chosen will he cause to come near unto him." **(4)** Neh 9:7-8 describes God's "choosing" (election) of persons as far back as Abram: "Thou art the Lord the God, who didst choose Abram, and broughtest him forth out of Ur of the Chaldees, and gavest him the name of Abraham. **(5)** *Bachar* is used 30 times in Deuteronomy, all but twice referring to God's "choice" of Israel or something in Israel's life. "Because he loved thy fathers, therefore he chose their seed after them" (Deut 4:37). **(6)** Being "chosen" by God brings people into an intimate relationship with Him: "The children of the Lord your God: . . . the Lord hath chosen thee to be a

peculiar people unto himself, above all the nations that are upon the earth" (Deut 14:1–2).

(7) God's "choices" shaped the history of Israel; **(7a)** His "choice" led to their redemption from Egypt (Deut 7:7–8), **(7b)** sent Moses and Aaron to work miracles in Egypt (Ps 105:26–27), and **(7c)** gave them the Levites "to bless in the name of the Lord" (Deut 21:5). **(7d)** He "chose" their inheritance (Ps 47:4), including Jerusalem, where He dwelt among them (Deut 12:5; 2 Chr 6:5, 21). **(7e)** But "they have chosen their own ways, and . . . I also will choose their delusions, and will bring their fears upon them" (Is 66:3–4). **(8)** The covenant called men to respond to God's election: "I have set before you life and death . . . : therefore choose life" (Deut 30:19; cf. Josh 24:22). Syn.: 970, 972, 4005. See: TWOT–231; BDB–103d.

978. בַּחֲרוּמִי {1x} **Bachărûwmîy,** *bakh-ar-oo-mee';* patrial from 980 (by transp.); a *Bacharumite* or inhab. of Bachurim:–Baharumite {1x}. See: BDB–104d, 138c.

979. בְּחֻרוֹת {3x} **bᵉchûrôwth,** *bekh-oo-rothe';* or

בְּחוּרוֹת **bᵉchûwrôwth,** *bekh-oo-roth';* fem. plur. of 970; also (masc. plur.)

בְּחֻרִים **bᵉchûrîym,** *bekh-oo-reem'; youth* (collect. and abstr.):–young men {1x}, youth {2x}. See: TWOT–231b; BDB–104c.

980. בַּחֻרִים {5x} **Bachûrîym,** *bakh-oo-reem';* or

בַּחוּרִים **Bachûwrîym,** *bakh-oo-reem';* masc. plur. of 970; *young men; Bachurim,* a place in Pal.:–Bahurim {5x}. See: BDB–104c.

981. בָּטָא {4x} **bâṭâ',** *baw-taw';* or

בָּטָה **bâṭâh,** *baw-taw';* a prim. root; to *babble;* hence, to *vociferate* angrily:–pronounce {2x}, speak {1x}, speak unadvisely {1x}. See: TWOT–232; BDB–104d.

982. בָּטַח {120x} **bâṭach,** *baw-takh';* a prim. root; prop. to *hie* for refuge [but not so *precipitately* as 2620]; fig. to *trust, be confident* or *sure:*–trust {103x}, confidence {4x}, secure {4x}, confident {2x}, bold {1x}, careless {1x}, hope {1x}, hoped {1x}, ones {1x}, sure {1x}, women {1x}.

(1) *Betach* is a noun meaning "security, trust." One occurrence is in Isa. 32:17: "And the effect of righteousness, quietness and assurance [*betach*] for ever." **(2)** *Batach* as a verb means "to be reliant, trust, be unsuspecting." The word means "to trust" in Deut 28:52: "And he shall besiege thee in all thy gates, until thy high and fenced walls come down, wherein

thou trustedst, throughout all thy land." **(3)** *Betach* as an adjective means "secure." In two passages this word suggests trust and security: "And Gideon went up . . . and smote the host: for the host was secure [unsuspecting]" (Judg. 8:11; cf. Is 32:17). Syn.: 2620. See: TWOT–233; BDB–105a.

983. בֶּטַח {42x} **beṭach,** *beh'takh;* from 982; prop. a place of *refuge;* abstr. *safety,* both the fact (*security*) and the feeling (*trust*); often (adv. with or without prep.) *safely:*–safely {17x}, safety {9x}, carelessly {3x}, careless {2x}, safe {2x}, securely {2x}, assurance {1x}, boldly {1x}, care {1x}, confidence {1x}, hope {1x}, secure {1x}, surely {1x}.

(1) *Betach* as an adverb means "securely." **(2)** In its first occurrence *betach* emphasizes the status of a city which was certain of not being attacked: "Two of the sons . . . took each man his sword, and came upon the city boldly, and slew all the males" (Gen 34:25). Thus the city was unsuspecting regarding the impending attack. **(3)** In passages such as Prov 10:9 (cf. Prov 1:33) *betach* emphasizes a confidence and the absence of impending doom: "He that walketh uprightly walketh surely: but he that perverteth his ways shall be known [faces certain judgment]." **(4)** Israel dwells in security **(4a)** apart from any possible doom or danger because God keeps her completely safe (Deut 33:12, 28; cf. 12:10). **(4b)** This condition is contingent on their faithfulness to God (Lev 25:18–19). **(5)** In the eschaton, however, such absence of danger is guaranteed by the Messiah's presence (Jer 23:5–6). See: TWOT–233a; BDB–105b.

984. בֶּטַח {1x} **Beṭach,** *beh'-takh;* the same as 983; *Betach,* a place in Syria:–Betah {1x}. See: BDB–105c.

985. בִּטְחָה {1x} **biṭchâh,** *bit-khaw';* fem. of 984; *trust:*–confidence {1x}. See: TWOT–233b; BDB–105c.

986. בִּטָּחוֹן {3x} **biṭṭâchôwn,** *bit-taw-khone';* from 982; *trust:*–confidence {2x}, hope {1x}. See: TWOT–233c; BDB–105c.

987. בַּטֻּחוֹת {1x} **baṭṭûchôwth,** *bat-too-khōth';* fem. plur. from 982; *security:*–secure {1x}. See: TWOT–233c; BDB–105c.

988. בָּטֵל {1x} **bâṭêl,** *baw-tale';* a prim. root; to *desist* from labor:–cease {1x}. See: TWOT–235; BDB–105d, 1084b.

989. בְּטֵל {6x} **bᵉṭêl** (Aram.), *bet-ale';* corresp. to 988; to *stop:*–(cause, make to), cease {5x}, hinder {1x}. See: TWOT–2625; BDB–1084b.

Hebrew

990. בֶּטֶן {72x} **beten**, *beh'-ten;* from an unused root prob. mean. to *be hollow;* the *belly,* espec. the *womb;* also the *bosom* or *body* of anything:—belly {30x}, womb {31x}, body {8x}, within {2x}, born {1x}. Syn.: 7358. See: TWOT—236a; BDB—105d.

991. בֶּטֶן {1x} **Beten**, *beh'-ten;* the same as 990; *Beten,* a place in Pal.:—Beten {1x}. See: BDB—106b.

992. בֹּטֶן {1x} **bôten**, *bo'-ten;* from 990; (only in plur.) a *pistachio*-nut (from its form):—nuts {1x}. See: TWOT—237a; BDB—106b.

993. בְּטֹנִים {1x} **Bᵉtônîym**, *bet-o-neem';* prob. plur. from 992; *hollows: Betonim,* a place in Pal.:—Betonim {1x}. See: BDB—106b.

994. בִּי {12x} **bîy**, *bee;* perh. from 1158 (in the sense of *asking*); prop. a *request;* used only adv. (always with "my Lord"); *Oh that!; with leave,* or *if it please:*—O {7x}, Oh {4x}, alas {1x}. See: TWOT—238a; BDB—106c.

995. בִּין {170x} **bîyn**, *bene;* a prim. root; to *separate* mentally (or *distinguish*), i.e. (Gen) *understand:*—understand {62x}, understanding {32x}, consider {22x}, prudent {8x}, perceive {7x}, regard {6x}, discern {3x}, instruct {3x}, misc. {27x}.

Bîyn basically means to understand, be able, deal wisely, consider, pay attention to, regard, notice, discern, perceive, inquire. **(1)** *Bîyn* appears in Jer 9:12 with the meaning "to understand": "Who is the wise man, that may understand this?" **(2)** In Job 6:30 the word means "to discern," and in **(3)** Deut 32:7 it means "to consider." Syn.: 998, 7919. See: TWOT—239; BDB—106c.

996. בֵּין {32x} **bêyn**, *bane* (sometimes in the plur. masc. or fem.); prop. the constr. contr. form of an otherwise unused noun from 995; a *distinction;* but used only as a prep. *between* (repeated before each noun, often with other particles); also as a conj., *either . . . or:*—between, betwixt, asunder, within, between, out of, from = {32x}.

Beyn means "between; in the midst of; among; within; in the interval of." **(1)** This word nearly always (except in 1 Sa 17:4, 23) is a preposition meaning "in the interval of" or "between." **(2)** The word may represent "the area between" in general: "And it shall be for a sign unto thee upon thine hand, and for a memorial between thine eyes" (Ex 13:9). **(3)** Sometimes the word means "within," in the sense of a person's or a thing's "being in the area of": "The slothful man saith, There is a lion in the way; a lion is in the streets" (Prov

26:13). **(4)** In other places, *beyn* means "among": "Shall the companions make a banquet of him [Leviathan]? Shall they part him among [give each a part] the merchants?" (Job 41:6). **(5)** In Job 34:37, the word means "in the midst of," in the sense of "one among a group": "For he addeth rebellion unto his sin, he clappeth his hands among us."

(6) The area separating two particular objects is indicated in several ways. **(6a)** First, by repeating *beyn* before each object: "And God divided the light from the darkness" [literally, "between the light and between the darkness"] (Gen 1:4); that is, He put an interval or space between them. **(6b)** In other places (more rarely), this concept is represented by putting *beyn* before one object and the preposition *le* before the second object: "Let there be a firmament in the midst [*beyn*] of the waters, and let it divide the waters from [le] the waters" (Gen 1:6). **(6c)** In still other instances, this idea is represented **(6c1)** by placing *beyn* before the first object plus the phrase meaning "with reference to" before the second (Joel 2:17), or **(6c2)** by *beyn* before the first object and the phrase "with reference to the interval of" before the second (Is 59:2). **(7)** *Beyn* is used in the sense of "distinguishing between" in many passages: "Let there be lights in the firmament of the heaven to divide the day from [*ben*] the night" (Gen 1:14).

(8) Sometimes *beyn* signifies a metaphorical relationship. For example, "This is the token of the covenant which I make between [*beyn*] me and you and every living creature" (Gen 9:12). The covenant is a contractual relationship. **(9)** Similarly, the Bible speaks of an oath (Gen 26:28) and of goodwill (Prov 14:9) filling the metaphorical "space" between two parties. **(10)** This word is used to signify an "interval of days," or "a period of time": "Now that which was prepared for me was . . . once in ten days [literally, "at ten-day intervals"] store of all sorts of wine" (Neh 5:18). **(11)** In the dual form, *beyn* represents "the space between two armies": "And there went out a champion [literally, "a man between the two armies"] out of the camp of the Philistines, named Goliath" (1 Sa 17:4). In ancient warfare, a battle or even an entire war could be decided by a contest between two champions. See: TWOT—239a; BDB—107b, 108a, 126a, 1084b.

997. בֵּין {2x} **bêyn** (Aram.), *bane;* corresp. to 996:—among {1x}, between {1x}. See: TWOT—2626; BDB—1084b.

998. בִּינָה {38x} **bîynâh**, *bee-naw';* from 995; *understanding:*—understanding {32x}, wisdom {2x}, knowledge {1x}, meaning {1x}, perfectly {1x}, understand {1x}.

Hebrew

Biynah means "understanding." **(1)** *Biynah* appears 37 times and in all periods of biblical Hebrew, even though it belongs primarily to the sphere of wisdom and wisdom literature. **(2)** This noun represents the "act of understanding": "And in all matters of wisdom and understanding, that the king inquired of them, he found them ten times better than all the magicians" (Dan 1:20). **(3)** Elsewhere *biynah* signifies the faculty "understanding": "The spirit of my understanding causeth me to answer" (Job 20:3). **(4)** In other passages the object of knowledge, in the sense of what one desires to know, is indicated by *biynah:* "Keep therefore and do them [God's laws]: for this is your wisdom and your understanding in the sight of the nations, which shall hear all these statutes" (Deut 4:6; cf. 1 Chr 22:12). **(5)** God's law, therefore, is wisdom and "understanding"—what one should know. **(6)** This word is sometimes personified: "Yea, if thou criest after knowledge, and liftest up thy voice for understanding; if thou seekest her as silver, and searchest for her as for hid treasures . . ." (Prov 2:3–4). See also: 4905, 8394. See: TWOT—239b; BDB—108a, 1084b.

999. בִּינָה {1x} **bîynâh** (Aram.), *bee-naw';* corresp. to 998:—understanding {1x}. See: TWOT—2627; BDB—1084b.

1000. בֵּיצָה {1x} **bêytsâh**, *bay-tsaw';* from the same as 948; an *egg* (from its whiteness):—egg {1x}. See: TWOT—218a; BDB—101b.

1001. בִּירָא {1x} **bîyrâ** (Aram.), *bee-raw';* corresp. to 1002; a *palace:*—palace {1x}. See: TWOT—2628; BDB—1084c.

1002. בִּירָה {16x} **bîyrâh**, *bee-raw';* of for. or.; a *castle* or *palace:*—palace {16x}. Syn.: 1964. See: TWOT—240; BDB—108b, 1084c.

1003. בִּירָנִית {2x} **bîyrânîyth**, *bee-raw-neeth';* from 1002; a *fortress:*—castle {2x}. See: TWOT—240; BDB—108c.

1004. בַּיִת {2055X} **bayith**, *bah'-yith;* prob. from 1129 abb.; a *house* (in the greatest var. of applications, espec. *family,* etc.):—house {1881x}, household {54x}, home {25x}, within {22x}, temple {11x}, prison {16x}, place {16x}, family {3x}, families + 1 {2x}, dungeon {2x}, misc. {23x}.

Bayith means "house or building; home; household; land." **(1)** First, this noun denotes a fixed, established structure made from some kind of material. **(1a)** As a "permanent dwelling place" it is usually distinguished from a tent (2 Sa 16:21, cf. v. 22). **(1c)** This word can even be applied to a one-room dwelling: "And

he [Lot] said [to the two angels], Behold now, my lords, turn in, I pray you, into your servant's house" (Gen 19:2). **(1d)** *Bayith* is also distinguished from temporary booths or huts: "And Jacob journeyed to Succoth, and built him a house, and made booths for his cattle" (Gen 33:17). **(1e)** In Ps 132:3 the word means "dwelling-living-place" and is used in direct conjunction with "tent" (literally, "tent of my house"): "Surely I will not come into the tabernacle of my house, nor go up into my bed." **(1f)** A similar usage appears in 1 Chr 9:23 (literally, "the tent house"): "So they and their children had the oversight of the gates of the house of the Lord, namely, the house of the tabernacle, by wards."

(2) Second, in many passages (especially when the word is joined to the word God) *bayith* represents a place of worship or "sanctuary": "The first of the first fruits of thy land thou shalt bring into the house of the Lord thy God" (Ex 23:19). **(2a)** Elsewhere this noun signifies God's temple in Jerusalem: "And against the wall of the house he built chambers round about, against the walls of the house round about, both of the temple and of the oracle" (1 Kin 6:5). **(2b)** Sometimes the word has this meaning although it is not further defined (cf. Eze 41:7). **(3)** Third, *bayith* can signify rooms and/or wings of a house: "And let the king appoint officers in all the provinces of his kingdom, that they may gather together all the fair young virgins unto Shushan the palace, to the [harem] (literally, to the house of the women; Est 2:3)." **(3a)** In this connection *bayith* can also represent the inside of a building or some other structure as opposed to the outside: "Make thee an ark of gopher wood; rooms shalt thou make in the ark, and shalt pitch it within and without with pitch" (Gen 6:14—the first biblical occurrence).

(4) Fourth, *bayith* sometimes refers to the place where something or someone dwells or rests. So the underworld (Sheol) is termed a "home": "If I wait, the grave is mine house: I have made my bed in the darkness" (Job 17:13). **(4b)** An "eternal home" is one's grave: "Man goeth to his long home, and the mourners go about the streets" (Eccl 12:5). **(4c)** "House" can also mean "place" when used with "grave," as in Neh 2:3: "Let the king live for ever: why should not my countenance be sad, when the city, the place of my fathers' sepulchers. . . ." **(4d)** *Bayith* means a receptacle in Is 3:20. **(4e)** In 1 Kin 18:32 the "house of two seeds" is a container for seed: "And with the stones he built an altar in the name of the Lord: and he made a trench about the altar, as great as would contain [literally, "a house of"] two measures of seed." **(4f)** Houses for bars are supports: "And thou shalt overlay the boards with gold, and make

their rings of gold for places [literally, "houses"] for the bars" (Ex 26:29). **(4g)** Similarly, see "the places [house] of the two paths," a crossing of two paths, in Prov 8:2. **(4h)** The steppe is termed the "house of beasts": ". . . whose house I have made the wilderness, and the barren land his dwellings [house of beasts]" (Job 39:6).

(5) Fifth, *bayith* is often used of those who live in a house, i.e., a "household": "Come thou and all thy house into the ark" (Gen 7:1). **(5a)** In passages such as Josh 7:14 this word means "family": "And it shall be, that the tribe which the Lord taketh shall come according to the families thereof; and the family which the Lord shall take shall come by households [literally, by house or by those who live in a single dwelling]." **(5b)** In a similar nuance this noun means "descendants": "And there went a man of the house of Levi, and took to wife a daughter of Levi" (Ex 2:1). **(5c)** This word can be used of one's extended family and even of everyone who lives in a given area: "And the men of Judah came, and there they anointed David king over the house of Judah" (2 Sa 2:4). **(5d)** Gen 50:4, however, uses *bayith* in the sense of "a royal court" or all the people in a king's court: "And when the days of his mourning were past, Joseph spake unto the house of Pharaoh. . . ." **(5e)** The ideas "royal court" and "descendant" are joined in 1 Sa 20:16: "So Jonathan made a covenant with the house of David. . . ." **(5f)** In a few passages *bayith* means "territory" or "country": "Set the trumpet to thy mouth. He shall come as an eagle against the house of the Lord" (Hos 8:1; 9:15; Jer 12:7; Zec 9:8). See: TWOT—241; BDB—108c, 111b, 143d, 476c, 1084c.

1005. בַּיִת {44x} **bayith** (Aram.), *bah-yith;* corresp. to 1004:—house {44x}. See: TWOT—2629a; BDB—1084c.

1006. בַּיִת {1x} **Bayith**, *bah'-yith;* the same as 1004; *Bajith*, a place in Pal.:—Bajith {1x}. See: BDB—110c.

1007. בֵּית אָוֶן {1x} **Bêyth ʾÂven**, *bayth aw'-ven;* from 1004 and 205; *house of vanity; Beth-Aven*, a place in Pal.:—Beth-aven {1x}. See: BDB—110c.

1008. בֵּית־אֵל {70x} **Bêyth-ʾÊl**, *bayth-ale';* from 1004 and 410; *house of God; Beth-El*, a place in Pal.:—Beth-el {70x}. See: TWOT—241a; BDB—110d.

1009. בֵּית אַרְבֵּאל {1x} **Bêyth ʾArbêʾl**, *bayth ar-bale';* from 1004 and 695 and 410; *house of God's ambush; Beth-Arbel*, a place in Pal.:—Beth-Arbel {1x}. See: BDB—70d, 111a.

1010. בֵּית בַּעַל מְעוֹן {2x} **Bêyth Baʿal Mᵉʿôwn**, *bayth bah'-al mè-own';* from 1004 and 1168 and 4583; *house of Baal of* (the) *habitation of* [appar. by transp.]; or (short.)

בֵּית מְעוֹן **Bêyth Mᵉʿôwn**, *bayth mè-own'; house of habitation of* (Baal); *Beth-Baal-Meön*, a place in Pal.:—Beth-baal-meon {1x}, Bethmeon {1x}. Syn.: 1186 and 1194. See: BDB—111a, 112a.

1011. בֵּית בִּרְאִי {1x} **Bêyth Birʾîy**, *bayth bir-ee';* from 1004 and 1254; *house of a creative one; Beth-Biri*, a place in Pal.:—Beth-birei {1x}. See: BDB—111a, 111d, 135d, 740a.

1012. בֵּית בָּרָה {2x} **Bêyth Bârâh**, *bayth baw-raw';* prob. from 1004 and 5679; *house of* (the) *ford; Beth-Barah*, a place in Pal.:—Beth-barah {2x}. See: BDB—111a.

1013. בֵּית־גָּדֵר {1x} **Bêyth-Gâdêr**, *bayth-gaw-dare';* from 1004 and 1447; *house of* (the) *wall; Beth-Gader*, a place in Pal.:—Beth-gader {1x}. See: BDB—111b.

1014. בֵּית גָּמוּל {1x} **Bêyth Gâmûwl**, *bayth gaw-mool';* from 1004 and the pass. part. of 1576; *house of* (the) *weaned; Beth-Gamul*, a place E. of the Jordan:—Beth-gamul {1x}. See: BDB—111b.

1015. בֵּית דִּבְלָתָיִם {1x} **Bêyth Diblâthayim**, *bayth dib-law-thah'-yim;* from 1004 and the dual of 1690; *house of* (the) *two figcakes; Beth-Diblathajim*, a place E. of the Jordan:—Beth-diblathaim {1x}. See: BDB—111b, 179c.

1016. בֵּית־דָּגוֹן {2x} **Bêyth-Dâgôwn**, *bayth-daw-gohn';* from 1004 and 1712; *house of Dagon; Beth-Dagon*, the name of two places in Pal.:—Beth-dagon {2x}. See: BDB—111b.

1017. בֵּית הָאֱלִי {1x} **Bêyth hâ-ʾĔlîy**, *bayth haw-el-ee';* patrial from 1008 with the art. interposed; a *Beth-elite*, or inhab. of Bethel:—Bethelite {1x}. See: BDB—111a.

1018. בֵּית הָאֵצֶל {1x} **Bêyth hâ-ʾÊtsel**, *bayth haw-ay'-tsel;* from 1004 and 681 with the art. interposed; *house of the side; Beth-ha-Etsel*, a place in Pal.:—Beth-ezel {1x}. See: BDB—111a.

1019. בֵּית הַגִּלְגָּל {1x} **Bêyth hag-Gilgâl**, *bayth hag-gil gawl';* from 1004 and 1537 with the article interposed; *house of Gilgal* (or *rolling*); *Beth-hag-Gilgal*, a place in Pal.:—Beth-gilgal {1x}. See: BDB—111b.

1020. בֵּית הַיְשִׁמוֹת {4x} **Bêyth ha-Yᵉshîy-môwth**, *bayth hah-yesh-ee-mōth'*; from 1004 and the plur. of 3451 with the art. interposed; *house of the deserts; Beth-ha-Jeshimoth,* a town E. of the Jordan:—Beth-jeshimoth {4x}. See: BDB—111d.

1021. בֵּית הַכֶּרֶם {2x} **Bêyth hak-Kerem**, *bayth hak-keh'-rem;* from 1004 and 3754 with the art. interposed; *house of the vineyard; Beth-hak-Kerem,* a place in Pal.:—Beth-haccerem {2x}. See: BDB—111d.

1022. בֵּית הַלַּחְמִי {4x} **Bêyth hal-Lachmîy**, *bayth hal-lakh-mee';* patrial from 1035 with the art. ins.; a *Beth-lechemite,* or native of Bethlechem:—Bethlehemite {1x}. See: BDB—112a.

1023. בֵּית הַמֶּרְחָק {1x} **Bêyth ham-Merchâq**, *bayth ham-mer-khawk';* from 1004 and 4801 with the art. interposed; *house of the breadth; Beth-ham-Merchak,* a place in Pal.:—place that was far off {1x}. See: BDB—112a, 935d.

1024. בֵּית הַמַּרְכָּבוֹת {2x} **Bêyth ham-Markâbôwth**, *bayth ham-mar-kaw-both';* or (short.)

בֵּית מַרְכָּבֹת **Bêyth Markâbôwth**, *bayth mar-kaw-both';* from 1004 and the plur. of 4818 (with or without the art. interposed); *place of (the) chariots; Beth-ham-Markaboth* or *Beth-Markaboth,* a place in Pal.:—Beth-marcaboth {2x}. See: BDB—1121b.

1025. בֵּית הָעֵמֶק {1x} **Bêyth hâ-ꞌÉmeq**, *bayth haw-ay'-mek;* from 1004 and 6010 with the art. interposed; *house of the valley; Beth-ha-Emek,* a place in Pal.:—Beth-emek {1x}. See: BDB—112b.

1026. בֵּית הָעֲרָבָה {3x} **Bêyth hâ-ꞌĂrâbâh**, *bayth haw-ar-aw-baw';* from 1004 and 6160 with the art. interposed; *house of the Desert; Beth-ha-Arabah,* a place in Pal.:—Beth-arabah {3x}. See: BDB—112c.

1027. בֵּית הָרָם {1x} **Bêyth hâ-Râm**, *bayth haw-rawm';* from 1004 and 7311 with the art. interposed; *house of the height; Beth-ha-Ram,* a place E. of the Jordan:—Beth-aram {1x}. See: BDB—111b, 248b.

1028. בֵּית הָרָן {1x} **Bêyth hâ-Rân**, *bayth haw-rawn';* prob. for 1027; *Beth-ha-Ran,* a place E. of the Jordan:—Beth-haran {1x}. See: BDB—111c.

1029. בֵּית הַשִּׁטָּה {1x} **Bêyth hash-Shittâh**, *bayth hash-shit-taw';* from 1004 and 7848 with the art. interposed; *house of the acacia; Beth-hash-Shittah,* a place in Pal.:—Beth-shittah {1x}. See: BDB—112d.

1030. בֵּית הַשִּׁמְשִׁי {2x} **Bêyth hash-Shimshîy**, *bayth hash-shim-shee';* patrial from 1053 with the art. ins.; a *Beth-shimshite,* or inhab. of Bethshemesh:—Bethshemite {2x}. See: BDB—113a.

1031. בֵּית חָגְלָה {3x} **Bêyth Choglâh**, *bayth chog-law';* from 1004 and the same as 2295; *house of a partridge; Beth-Choglah,* a place in Pal.:—Beth-hoglah {2x}, Bethhogla {1x}. See: BDB—111c.

1032. בֵּית חוֹרוֹן {14x} **Bêyth Chôwrôwn**, *bayth kho-rone';* from 1004 and 2356; *house of hollowness; Beth-Choron,* the name of two adjoining places in Pal.:—Beth-horon {14x}. See: BDB—111c, 357b, 751c.

בֵּית חָנָן **Bêyth Chânân**. See 358.

1033. בֵּית כַּר {1x} **Bêyth Kar**, *bayth kar;* from 1004 and 3733; *house of pasture; Beth-Car,* a place in Pal.:—Beth-car {1x}. See: BDB—111d.

1034. בֵּית לְבָאוֹת {1x} **Bêyth Lᵉbâꞌôwth**, *bayth leb-aw-ōth';* from 1004 and the plural of 3833; *house of lionesses; Beth-Lebaoth,* a place in Pal.:—Beth-lebaoth {1x}. Syn.: 3822. See: BDB—111d.

1035. בֵּית לֶחֶם {411x} **Bêyth Lechem**, *bayth leh'-khem;* from 1004 and 3899; *house of bread; Beth-Lechem,* a place in Pal.:—Beth-lehem {31x}, Bethlemjudah + 3063 {10x}. See: BDB—111d.

1036. בֵּית לְעַפְרָה {1x} **Bêyth lᵉ-ꞌAphrâh**, *bayth lè-af-raw';* from 1004 and the fem. of 6083 (with prep. interposed); *house to (i.e. of) dust; Beth-le-Aphrah,* a place in Pal.:—house of Aphrah {1x}. See: BDB—112a, 780b.

1037. בֵּית מִלּוֹא {4x} **Bêyth Millôwꞌ**, *bayth mil-lo';* or

בֵּית מִלֹּא **Bêyth Millôꞌ**, *bayth mil-lo';* from 1004 and 4407; *house of (the) rampart; Beth-Millo,* the name of two citadels:—house of Millo {4x} [or left untranslated]. See: BDB—112a, 571c.

1038. בֵּית מַעֲכָה {2x} **Bêyth Maꞌăkâh**, *bayth mah-ak-aw';* from 1004 and 4601; *house of Maakah; Beth-Maakah,* a place in Pal.:—Beth-maachah {2x}. See: BDB—112a, 591.

1039. בֵּית נִמְרָה {2x} **Bêyth Nimrâh**, *bayth nim-raw';* from 1004 and the fem. of 5246; *house of (the) leopard; Beth-Nimrah,* a place east of the Jordan:—Beth-nimrah {2x}. Syn.: 5247. See: BDB—112b.

1040. בֵּית עֵדֶן {1x} **Bêyth ꞌÉden**, *bayth ay'-den;* from 1004 and 5730;

house of pleasure; Beth-Eden, a place in Syria:—Beth-eden {1x}. See: BDB—112b, 727a.

1041. בֵּית עַזְמָוֶת {1x}   **Bêyth ʿAzmâveth,** *bayth az-maw'-veth;* from 1004 and 5820; *house of Azmaveth,* a place in Pal.:—Beth-az-maveth {1x}. Syn.: 5820. See: BDB—112b.

1042. בֵּית עֲנוֹת {1x} **Bêyth ʿĂnôwth,** *bayth an-ōth';* from 1004 and a plur. from 6030; *house of replies; Beth-Anoth,* a place in Pal.:—Beth-anoth {1x}. See: BDB—112b, 779a.

1043. בֵּית עֲנָת {3x} **Bêyth ʿĂnâth,** *bayth an-awth';* an orth. var. for 1042; *Beth-Anath,* a place in Pal.:—Beth-anath {3x}. See: BDB—112c, 779a.

1044. בֵּית עֶקֶד {2x} **Bêyth ʾÊqed,** *bayth ay'-ked;* from 1004 and a der. of 6123; *house of* (the) *binding* (for sheep-shearing); *Beth-Eked,* a place in Pal.:—shearing house {1x}, not translated {1x}. See: BDB—112c, 785b.

1045. בֵּית עַשְׁתָּרוֹת {1x} **Bêyth ʿAshtârôwth,** *bayth ash-taw-rōth';* from 1004 and 6252; *house of Ashtoreths; Beth-Ashtaroth,* a place in Pal.:—house of Ashtaroth {1x}. Syn.: 1203, 6252. See: BDB—800a, 800b.

1046. בֵּית פֶּלֶט {2x} **Bêyth Pelet,** *bayth peh'-let;* from 1004 and 6412; *house of escape; Beth-Palet,* a place in Pal.:—Bethphelet {1x}, Bethpalet {1x}. See: BDB—112c.

1047. בֵּית פְּעוֹר {4x} **Bêyth Pᵉʿôwr,** *bayth pè-ore';* from 1004 and 6465; *house of Peor; Beth-Peor,* a place E. of the Jordan:—Beth-peor {4x}. See: BDB—112c.

1048. בֵּית פַּצֵּץ {1x} **Bêyth Patstsêts,** *bayth pats-tsates';* from 1004 and a der. from 6327; *house of dispersion; Beth-Patstsets,* a place in Pal.:—Beth-pazzez {1x}. See: BDB—112d, 823a.

1049. בֵּית צוּר {4x} **Bêyth Tsûwr,** *bayth tsoor';* from 1004 and 6697; *house of* (the) *rock; Beth-Tsur,* a place in Pal.:—Beth-zur {4x}. See: BDB—112d.

1050. בֵּית רְחוֹב {2x} **Bêyth Rᵉchôwb,** *bayth rè-khobe';* from 1004 and 7339; *house of* (the) *street; Beth-Rechob,* a place in Pal.:—Beth-rehob {1x}. See: BDB—112d.

1051. בֵּית רָפָא {1x} **Bêyth Râphâʾ,** *bayth raw-faw';* from 1004 and 7497; *house of* (the) *giant; Beth-Rapha,* an Isr.:—Beth-rapha {1x}. See: BDB—112d, 951a.

1052. בֵּית שְׁאָן {9x} **Bêyth Shᵉʾân,** *bayth shè-awn';* or

בֵּית שָׁן **Bêyth Shân,** *bayth shawn';* from 1004 and 7599; *house of ease; Beth-Shean* or *Beth-Shan,* a place in Pal.:—Beth-shean {6x}, Beth-Shan {3x}. See: BDB—112d, 983b, 1039c.

1053. בֵּית שֶׁמֶשׁ {21x} **Bêyth Shemesh,** *bayth sheh'-mesh;* from 1004 and 8121; *house of* (the) *sun; Beth-Shemesh,* a place in Pal.:—Beth-shemesh {21x}. See: BDB—112d, 746d.

1054. בֵּית תַּפּוּחַ {1x} **Bêyth Tappûwach,** *bayth tap-poo'-akh;* from 1004 and 8598; *house of* (the) *apple; Beth-Tappuach,* a place in Pal.:—Beth-tappuah {1x}. See: BDB—113a.

1055. בִּיתָן {3x} **bîythân,** *bee-thawn';* prob. from 1004; a *palace* (i.e. *large house*):—palace {3x}. See: TWOT—241c; BDB—113a.

1056. בָּכָא {1x} **Bâkâʾ,** *baw-kaw';* from 1058, *weeping; Baca,* a valley in Pal.:—Baca {1x}. See: BDB—113a.

1057. בָּכָא {4x} **bâkâʾ,** *baw-kaw';* the same as 1056; the *weeping* tree (some gum-distilling tree, perh. the *balsam*):—mulberry tree {4x}. *Baka'* is a shrub which drips sap when cut. See: TWOT—242; BDB—113a.

1058. בָּכָה {114x} **bâkâh,** *baw-kaw';* a prim. root; to *weep;* Gen to *bemoan:*—weep {98x}, bewail {5x}, sore {3x} (inf. for emphasis) mourned {2x}, all {1x} (inf), complain {1x}, lamentation {1x}, more {1x} (inf.), weep over {1x}, tears {1x}. See: TWOT—243; BDB—113b.

1059. בֶּכֶה {1x} **bekeh,** *beh'-keh;* from 1058; a *weeping:*—✗ sore {1x}. See: TWOT—243a; BDB—113d.

1060. בְּכוֹר {117x} **bᵉkôwr,** *bek-ore';* from 1069; *firstborn;* hence, *chief:*—firstborn {101x}, firstling {10x}, eldest {4x}, firstborn + 1121 {1x}, eldest son {1x}.

Bekowr means "firstborn." **(1)** The word represents the "firstborn" individual in a family (Gen 25:13); **(2)** the word can also represent the "firstborn" of a nation, collectively (Num 3:46). **(3)** The plural form of the word appears occasionally (Neh 10:36); in this passage, the word is applied to animals. **(4)** In other passages, the singular form of *bekowr* signifies a single "firstling" animal (Lev 27:26) or collectively the "firstborn" of a herd (Ex 11:5). **(5)** The "oldest" or "firstborn" son (Ex 6:14) had special privileges within the family. **(5a)** He received the special family blessing, which meant spiritual and social leadership

and a double portion of the father's possessions—or twice what all the other sons received (Deut 21:17). **(5b)** He could lose this blessing through misdeeds (Gen 35:22) or by selling it (Gen 25:29–34).

(6) God claimed all Israel and all their possessions as His own. **(6a)** As a token of this claim, Israel was to give Him all its "firstborn" (Ex 13:1–16). **(6b)** The animals were to be sacrificed, redeemed, or killed, while the male children were redeemed either by being replaced with Levites or by the payment of a redemption price (Num 3:40ff.). **(7)** Israel was God's "firstborn"; it enjoyed a privileged position and blessings over all other nations (Ex 4:22; Jer 31:9). **(8)** The "first-born of death" is an idiom meaning a deadly disease (Job 18:13); **(9)** the "first-born of the poor" is the poorest class of people (Is 14:30). See: TWOT—244a; BDB—114a.

1061. בִּכּוּר {18x} **bikkûwr**, *bik-koor';* from 1069; the *first-fruits* of the crop:—firstfruit {14x}, firstripe {2x}, firstripe figs {1x}, hasty fruit {1x}.

Bikkuwr (1061) means "first fruits." **(1)** The "first grain and fruit" harvested was to be offered to God (Num 28:26) in recognition of God's ownership of the land and His sovereignty over nature. **(2)** Bread of the "first fruits" was bread made of the first harvest grain, presented to God at Pentecost (Lev 23:20). **(3)** The "day of the first fruits" was Pentecost (Num 28:26). See: TWOT 244e; BDB—114c.

1062. בְּכוֹרָה {15x} **bᵉkôwrâh**, *bek-o-raw';* or (short.)

בְּכֹרָה **bᵉkôrâh**, *bek-o-raw';* fem. of 1060; the *firstling* of man or beast; abstr. *primogeniture:*—birthright {9x}, firstling {5x}, firstborn {1x}. See: TWOT—244c; BDB—114c.

1063. בִּכּוּרָה {2x} **bikkûwrâh**, *bik-koo-raw';* fem. of 1061; the *early* fig:—firstripe {1x}, firstripe fruit {1x}. See: TWOT—244f; BDB—114c.

1064. בְּכוֹרַת {1x} **Bᵉkôwrath**, *bek-o-rath';* fem. of 1062; *primogeniture; Bekorath,* an Isr.:—Bechorath {1x}. See: BDB—114c.

1065. בְּכִי {30x} **bᵉkîy**, *bek-ee';* from 1058; a *weeping;* by anal. a *dripping:*—weep {24x}, overflowing {1x}, sore {1x}, wept + 1058 08799 {3x}, wept + 6963 {1x}. Syn.: 1058, 7857. See: TWOT—243b; BDB—113d.

1066. בֹּכִים {2x} **Bôkîym**, *bo-keem';* plur. act. part. of 1058; (with the art.) the weepers; *Bo-kim,* a place in Pal.:—Bochim {2x}. See: BDB—114a.

1067. בְּכִירָה {6x} **bᵉkîyrâh**, *bek-ee-raw';* fem. from 1069; the *eldest* daughter:—firstborn {6x}. See: TWOT—244d; BDB—114c.

1068. בְּכִית {1x} **bᵉkîyth**, *bek-eeth';* from 1058; a *weeping:*—mourning {1x}. See: TWOT—243d; BDB—114a.

1069. בָּכַר {4x} **bâkar**, *baw-kar';* a prim. root; prop. to *burst* the womb, i.e. (caus.) *bear* or *make early fruit* (of woman or tree); also (as denom. from 1061) to *give the birthright:*—firstborn {1x}, new fruit {1x}, firstling {1x}, first child {1x}. See: TWOT—244; BDB—114a.

1070. בֶּכֶר {1x} **beker**, *beh'-ker;* from 1069 (in the sense of *youth*); a young *camel:*—dromedary {1x}. See: TWOT—244b; BDB—114c.

1071. בֶּכֶר {5x} **Beker**, *beh'-ker;* the same as 1070; *Beker,* the name of two Isr.:—Becher {5x}. See: BDB—114b.

1072. בִּכְרָה {1x} **bikrâh**, *bik-raw';* fem. of 1070; a young *she-camel:*—dromedary {1x}. See: TWOT—244b; BDB—114c.

בְּכֹרָה **bᵉkôrâh**. See 1062.

1073. בַּכֻּרָה {1x} **bakkûrâh**, *bak-koo-raw';* by orth. var. for 1063; a *first-ripe* fig:—firstripe {1x}. See: TWOT—244f; BDB—114c.

1074. בֹּכְרוּ {2x} **Bôkᵉrûw**, *bo-ker-oo';* from 1069; *first-born; Bokeru,* an Isr.:—Bocheru {2x}. See: BDB—114b.

1075. בִּכְרִי {8x} **Bikrîy**, *bik-ree';* from 1069; *youth-ful; Bikri,* an Isr.:—Bichri {8x}. See: BDB—114b.

1076. בַּכְרִי {1x} **Bakrîy**, *bak-ree';* patron. from 1071; a *Bakrite* (collect.) or desc. of Beker:—Bachrites {1x}. See: BDB—114b.

1077. בַּל {9x} **bal**, *bal;* from 1086; prop. a *failure;* by impl. *nothing;* usually (adv.) *not* at all; also *lest:*—none, not, nor, lest, nothing, not, neither, no = {9x}. See: TWOT—246d; BDB—114d, 115b.

1078. בֵּל {3x} **Bêl**, *bale;* by contr. for 1168; *Bel,* the Baal of the Babylonians:—Bel {3x}. See: BDB—114d, 128c.

1079. בַּל {1x} **bâl** (Aram.), *bawl;* from 1080; prop. *anxiety,* i.e. (by impl.) the *heart* (as its seat):—heart {1x}. See: TWOT—2630; BDB—1084b, 1084c.

1080. בְּלָא {1x} bᵉlâ᾽ (Aram.), bel-aw'; corresp. to 1086 (but used only in a ment. sense); to afflict:—wear out {1x}. See: TWOT—2631; BDB—1094c.

1081. בַּלְאֲדָן {2x} Balʼădân, bal-ad-awn'; from 1078 and 113 (contr.); Bel (is his) lord; Baladan, the name of a Bab. prince:—Baladan {1x}. See: BDB—114d, 597d.

1082. בָּלַג {4x} bâlag, baw-lag'; a prim. root; to break off or loose (in a favorable or unfavorable sense), i.e. desist (from grief) or invade (with destruction):—comfort {2x}, strength {1x}, strengthen {1x}. See: TWOT—245; BDB—114d.

1083. בִּלְגָּה {3x} Bilgâh, bil-gaw'; from 1082; desistance; Bilgah, the name of two Isr.:—Bilgah {3x}. See: BDB—114d.

1084. בִּלְגַּי {1x} Bilgay, bil-gah'-ee; from 1082; desistant; Bilgai, an Isr.:—Bilgai {1x}. See: BDB—114d.

1085. בִּלְדַּד {5x} Bildad, bil-dad'; of uncert. der.; Bildad, one of Job's friends:—Bildad {5x}. See: BDB—115a.

1086. בָּלָה {16x} bâlâh, baw-law'; a prim. root; to fail; by impl. to wear out, decay (caus. consume, spend):—wax old {9x}, become old {2x}, consume {2x}, waste {1x}, enjoy {1x}, non translated variant {1x}. Syn.: 398, 3615. See: TWOT—246; BDB—115a, 1084c.

1087. בָּלֶה {5x} bâleh, baw-leh'; from 1086; worn out:—old {5x}. See: TWOT—246a; BDB—115b.

1088. בָּלָה {1x} Bâlâh, baw-law'; fem. of 1087; failure; Balah, a place in Pal.:—Balah {1x}. See: BDB—115a.

1089. בָּלַהּ {1x} bâlahh, baw-lah'; a prim. root [rather by transp. for 926]; to palpitate; hence, (caus.) to terrify:—trouble {1x}. See: TWOT—247; BDB—117a.

1090. בִּלְהָה {11x} Bilhâh, bil-haw'; from 1089; timid; Bilhah, the name of one of Jacob's concubines; also of a place in Pal.:—Bilhah {11x}. See: BDB—117b.

1091. בַּלָּהָה {10x} ballâhâh, bal-law-haw'; from 1089; alarm; hence, destruction:—terror {10x}. Syn.: 928. See: TWOT—247a; BDB—117a.

1092. בִּלְהָן {4x} Bilhân, bil-hawn'; from 1089; timid; Bilhan, the name of an Edomite and of an Isr.:—Bilhan {4x}. See: BDB—117b.

1093. בְּלוֹ {3x} bᵉlôw (Aram.), bel-o'; from a root corresp. to 1086; excise (on articles consumed):—tribute {3x}. See: TWOT—2632; BDB—1084c.

1094. בְּלוֹא {3x} bᵉlôwʼ, bel-o'; or (fully)

בְּלוֹי bᵉlôwy, bel-o'-ee; from 1086; (only in plur. constr.) rags:—old {3x}. See: TWOT—246b; BDB—115b.

1095. בֵּלְטְשַׁאצַּר {2x} Bêlṭᵉshaʼtstsar, bale-tesh-ats-tsar'; of for. der.; Belteshatstsar, the Bab. name of Daniel:—Belteshazzar {2x}. See: BDB—117b, 1084d.

1096. בֵּלְטְשַׁאצַּר {8x} Bêlṭᵉshaʼtstsar (Aram.), bale-tesh-ats-tsar'; corresp. to 1095:—Belteshazzar {8x}. See: BDB—1084d.

1097. בְּלִי {14x} bᵉliy, bel-ee'; from 1086; prop. failure, i.e. nothing or destruction; usually (with prep.) without, not yet, because not, as long as, etc.:—not, without, un . . . , lack of, so that no, corruption = {14x}. See: TWOT—246e; BDB—115c, 116a.

1098. בְּלִיל {3x} bᵉliyl, bel-eel'; from 1101; mixed, i.e. (spec.) feed (for cattle):—fodder {1x}, corn {1x}, provender {1x}. See: TWOT—248a; BDB—117d.

1099. בְּלִימָה {1x} bᵉliymâh, bel-ee-mah'; from 1097 and 4100; (as indef.) nothing whatever:—nothing {1x}. See: TWOT—246f; BDB—116a.

1100. בְּלִיַּעַל {27x} bᵉliyaʻal, bel-e-yah'-al; from 1097 and 3276; without profit, worthlessness; by extens. destruction, wickedness (often in connection with 376, 802, 1121, etc.):—Belial {16x}, wicked {5x}, ungodly {3x}, evil {1x}, naughty {1x}, ungodly men {1x}.

Beliyaʻal means wickedness; wicked; destruction. (1) The basic meaning of this word appears in a passage such as Judg 20:13, where the sons of beliyaʻal are perpetrators of wickedness (they raped and murdered a man's concubine): "Now therefore deliver us the men, the children of Belial which are in Gibeah, that we may put them to death, and put away evil from Israel." (2) In its first appearance the word represents men who lead others into idolatry: "Certain men, the children of Belial, are gone out from among you, and have [seduced] the inhabitants of their city" (Deut 13:13). (3) In Deut 15:9 the word modifies Hebrew dabar, "word" or "matter." Israel is warned to avoid "wicked" words (thoughts) in their hearts. (4) Beliyaʻal is a synonym for rashaʼ (7563 - "wicked rebellious one") in Job 34:18. (5) In Nah 1:11 the wicked counselor plots evil against God. (6) The psalmist uses beliyaʻal as a synonym of death: "The cords of death encompassed me, and the floods of ungodly men terrified me" (Ps 18:4). Syn.: 7451, 7455, 7489. See: TWOT—246g; BDB—116a.

1101. בָּלַל {44x} bâlal, baw-lal'; a prim. root; to overflow (spec. with oil); by

impl. to *mix;* also (denom. from 1098) to *fodder:*—mingled {37x}, confound {2x}, anointed {1x}, mixed {1x}, give provender {1x}, tempered {1x}, non translated variant {1x}. Syn.: 4537, 6148. See: TWOT—248; BDB—117b, 117d.

1102. בָּלַם {1x} **bâlam**, *baw-lam';* a prim. root; to *muzzle:*—held {1x}. See: TWOT—249; BDB—117d.

1103. בָּלַס {1x} **bâlaç**, *baw-las';* a prim. root; to *pinch* sycamore figs (a process necessary to ripen them):—gatherer {1x}. See: TWOT—250; BDB—118a.

1104. בָּלַע {49x} **bâla**ᶜ, *baw-lah';* a prim. root; to *make away with* (spec. by *swallowing*); Gen to *destroy:*—swallow . . . {34x}, destroy {9x}, devour {3x}, covered {1x}, at . . . end {1x}.

Bala' means "to swallow, engulf." **(1)** *Bala*ᶜ is first used in Gen 41:7 in Pharaoh's dream of seven lean ears of grain "swallowing up" the seven plump ears. **(2)** While it is used of the normal physical swallowing of something quite frequently, such as Jonah's "being swallowed" by the great fish (Jonah 1:17), the word is used more often in the figurative sense, often implying destruction. **(2a)** Thus, the violent "overwhelm" the innocent (Prov 1:11–12); **(2b)** an enemy "swallows" those he conquers "like a dragon" (Jer 51:34); and **(2c)** the false prophet and priest "are swallowed up of wine" (Is 28:7). Syn.: 1572, 1866, 5693. See: TWOT—251; BDB—118a.

1105. בֶּלַע {2x} **bela**ᶜ, *beh'-lah;* from 1104; a *gulp;* fig. *destruction:*—devouring {1x}, swallowed {1x}. See: TWOT—251a; BDB—118c.

1106. בֶּלַע {14x} **Bela**ᶜ, *beh'-lah;* the same as 1105; *Bela,* the name of a place, also of an Edomite and of two Isr.:—*Bela* {13x}, Belah {1x}. See: BDB—118c, 118d, 858d.

1107. בִּלְעֲדֵי {17x} **bil'âdêy**, *bil-ad-ay';* or

בַּלְעֲדֵי **bal'âdêy**, *bal-ad-ay';* constr. plur. from 1077 and 5703, *not till,* i.e. (as prep. or adv.) *except, without, besides:*—beside {7x}, save {4x}, without {4x}, not in me {1x}, not {1x}. See: TWOT—246h; BDB—116b, 118d.

1108. בַּלְעִי {1x} **Bal'îy**, *bal-ee';* patron. from 1106: a *Belaite* (collect.) or desc. of Bela:—Belaites {1x}. See: BDB—118c.

1109. בִּלְעָם {61x} **Bil'âm**, *bil-awm';* prob. from 1077 and 5971; *not (of the) people,* i.e. *foreigner; Bilam,* a Mesopotamian prophet; also a place in Pal.:—Balaam {60x}, Bileam {1x}. See: TWOT—251b; BDB—118d.

1110. בָּלַק {2x} **bâlaq**, *baw-lak';* a prim. root; to *annihilate:*—(make) waste {2x}. TWOT—252; BDB—118d, 550b.

1111. בָּלָק {43x} **Bâlâq**, *baw-lawk';* from 1110; *waster; Balak,* a Moabitish king:—Balak {43x}. See: BDB—118d.

1112. בֵּלְשַׁאצַּר {1x} **Bêlsha'tstsar**, *bale-shats-tsar';* or

בֵּלְאשַׁצַּר **Bêl'shatstsar**, *bale-shats-tsar';* of for. or. (comp. 1095); *Belshatssar,* a Bab. king:—Belshazzar {1x}. See: BDB—128d, 1084d.

1113. בֵּלְשַׁאצַּר {7x} **Bêlsha'tstsar** (Aram.), *bale-shats-tsar';* corresp. to 1112:—Belshazzar {7x}. See: BDB—1084d.

1114. בִּלְשָׁן {2x} **Bilshân**, *bil-shawn';* of uncert. der.; *Bilshan,* an Isr.:—Bilshan {1x}. See: BDB—119a.

1115. בִּלְתִּי {30x} **biltîy**, *bil-tee';* constr. fem. of 1086 (equiv. to 1097); prop. a *failure of,* i.e. (used only as a neg. particle, usually with prep. pref.) *not, except, without, unless, besides, because not, until,* etc.:—but, except, save, nothing, lest, no, from, inasmuch, and not = {30x}. See: TWOT—246i; BDB—116c.

1116. בָּמָה {102x} **bâmâh**, *baw-maw';* from an unused root (mean. to *be high*); an *elevation:*—high place {100x}, heights {1x}, waves {1x}.

Bamah (1116) means "high place." **(1)** *Bamah* is used 102 times in biblical Hebrew, and the first occurrence is in Lev 26:30: "And I will destroy your high places, and cut down your images, and cast your carcases upon the carcases of your idols, and my soul shall abhor you." **(2)** Most of the uses are in the Books of Kings and Chronicles, with the sense of "cultic high place." The word is rarely used in the Pentateuch or in the poetic or prophetic literature. **(3)** *Bamah* refers to **(3a)** the heights of the clouds: "I will ascend above the heights [*bamah*] of the clouds; I will be like the most High" (Is 14:14), and **(3b)** the waves of the sea "[He] alone spreadeth out the heavens, and treadeth upon the waves [literally, "high places"] of the sea" (Job 9:8); **(3c)** *Bamah* can be understood idiomatically for authority: Ps. 18:33 (cf. 2 Sa 22:34; Hab 3:19): "He maketh my feet like hinds' feet, and setteth me upon my high places." **(4)** The word is used metaphorically to portray the Lord as providing for His people: "He made him ride on the high places of the earth, that he might eat the increase of the fields; and he made him to suck honey out of the rock, and oil out of the flinty rock" (Deut 32:13; cf. Is 58:14). **(5)** The idiom, "to ride upon the high places

of the earth," is a Hebraic way of expressing God's protection of His people. It expresses the exalted nature of Israel, whose God is the Lord. **(6)** Not every literal *bamah* was a cultic high place; the word may simply refer to a geographical unit; cf. "Therefore shall Zion for your sake be plowed as a field, and Jerusalem shall become heaps, and the mountain of the [temple] as the high places of the forest" (cf. Amos 4:13; Mic 3:12). **(7)** The Canaanites served their gods on these hills, where pagan priests presented the sacrifices to the gods: Israel imitated this practice (1 Kin 3:2), even when they sacrificed to the Lord. **(8)** The surrounding nations had high places dedicated to Chemosh (1 Kin 11:7), Baal (Jer 19:5), and other deities. **(9)** On the "high place," a temple was built and dedicated to a god: **(9a)** "[Jeroboam] made a house of high places, and **(9b)** made priests of the lowest of the people, which were not of the sons of Levi" (1 Kin 12:31). **(9c)** Cultic symbols were added as decoration; thus, the sacred pillars (842 - *asherah*) and sacred trees or poles (4676 - *matstsebah*) were associated with a temple: "For they also built them high places, and [sacred stones], and groves, on every high hill [1389 - *gib'ah*], and under every green tree" (1 Kin 14:23; cf. 2 Kin 16:4).

(10) Before the temple was built, Solomon worshiped the Lord at the great *bamah* of Gideon (1 Kin 3:4). **(10a)** This was permissible until the temple was constructed; however, **(10b)** history demonstrates that Israel soon adopted these "high places" for pagan customs. **(11)** The *bamah* was found in the cities of **(11a)** Samaria (2 Kin 23:19), and **(11b)** Judah (2 Chr 21:11), and even **(11c)** in Jerusalem (2 Kin 23:13). **(12)** The *bamah* was a place of cult prostitution: "[They] pant after the dust of the earth on the head of the poor, and turn aside the way of the meek: and a man and his father will go in unto the same maid, to profane my holy name: And they lay themselves down upon clothes laid to pledge by every altar, and they drink the wine of the condemned in the house of their god" (Amos 2:7–8). Syn.: 7413. See: TWOT—253; BDB—119a.

1117. בָּמָה {1x} **Bâmâh**, *baw-maw'*; the same as 1116; *Bamah*, a place in Pal.:— *Bamah* {1x}. Syn.: 1120. See: BDB—119d.

1118. בִּמְהָל {1x} **Bimhâl**, *bim-hawl'*; prob. from 4107 with prep. pref.; *with pruning; Bimhal*, an Isr.:—*Bimhal* {1x}. See: BDB—119d.

1119. בְּמוֹ {10x} **b^emôw**, *bem-o'*; prol. for prep. pref.; *in, with, by*, etc.:—with {3x}, in {2x}, into {1x}, through {1x}, for {1x}, at {1x}, non translated variant {1x}. Syn.: See: TWOT—193; prep (poetic form); BDB—91b, 119d.

1120. בָּמוֹת {4x} **Bâmôwth**, *baw-môth'*; plur. of 1116; *heights;* or (fully)

בָּמוֹת בַּעַל **Bâmôwth Ba'al**, *baw-môth' bah'-al;* from the same and 1168; *heights of Baal; Bamoth* or *Bamoth-Baal*, a place E. of the Jordan:—Bamoth {2x}, Baal {1x}, Bamothbaal {1x}. See: BDB—119d.

1121. בֵּן {4906x} **bên**, *bane;* from 1129; a *son* (as a *builder* of the family name), in the widest sense (of lit. and fig. relationship, incl. *grandson, subject, nation, quality* or *condition*, etc., [like 1, 251, etc.]):—son {2978x}, children {1568x}, old {135x}, first {51x}, man {20x}, young {18x}, young + 1241 {17x}, child {10x}, stranger {10x}, people {5x}, misc. {92x}.

Ben means "son," *bat* (1323) means "daughter." **(1)** These nouns are derived from the verb *banah*. They are actually different forms of the same noun. **(1a)** Basically, this noun represents one's immediate physical male or female offspring. For example, Adam "begat sons and daughters" (Gen 5:4). **(1b)** The special emphasis here is on the physical tie binding a man to his offspring. **(2)** The noun can also be used of an animal's offspring: "Binding his foal unto the vine, and his ass's colt unto the choice vine" (Gen 49:11). **(3)** Sometimes the word *ben*, which usually means "son," can mean "children" (both male and female). God told Eve that "in sorrow thou shalt bring forth children" (Gen 3:16—the first occurrence of this noun). **(4)** The words *ben* and *bat* can signify "descendants" in general—daughters, sons, granddaughters, and grandsons. Laban complained to Jacob that he had not allowed him "to kiss my sons and my daughters" (Gen 31:28; cf. v. 43).

(5) The phrase, "my son," may be used by a superior to a subordinate as a term of familiar address. Joshua said to Achan, "My son, give, I pray thee, glory to the Lord God of Israel" (Josh 7:19). **(6)** On the lips of the subordinate, "son" signifies conscious submission. Ben-hadad's servant Hazael took gifts to Elisha, saying, "Thy son Benhadad king of Syria hath sent me to thee" (2 Kin 8:9). **(7)** *Ben* can also be used in a formula expressing a unique and unbreakable relationship: "Thou art my Son; this day have I begotten thee" (Ps 2:7). **(8)** *Ben* often is used in this sense of a king's relationship to God (i.e., he is God's adopted son). **(9)** Sometimes the same word expresses Israel's relationship to God: "When Israel was a child, then I loved him, and called my son out of Egypt" (Hos 11:1). **(10)** The Bible also refers to the heavenly court as the "sons of God" (Job 1:6). **(10a)** God called the elders of Israel the "children" of the Most High" (Ps 82:6). **(10b)** In Gen 6:2, the phrase "sons of God" is variously understood as **(10b1)** members of the heavenly

court, **(10b2)** the spiritual disciples of God (the sons of Seth), and **(10b3)** the boastful among mankind.

(11) *Ben* may signify "young men" in general, regardless of any physical relationship to the speaker: "And [I] beheld among the simple ones, I discerned among the youths, a young man void of understanding" (Prov 7:7). **(12)** A city may be termed a "mother" and its inhabitants its "sons": "For he hath strengthened the bars of thy gates; he hath blessed thy children within thee" (Ps 147:13). **(13)** *Ben* is sometimes used to mean a single individual; thus Abraham ran to his flock and picked out a "son of a cow" (Gen 18:7). **(14)** The phrase "son of man" is used in this sense—God is asked to save the poor individuals, not the children of the poor (Ps 72:4). **(15)** *Ben* may also denote a member of a group. An example is a prophet who followed Elijah (1 Kin 20:35; cf. Amos 7:14). **(16)** This noun may also indicate someone worthy of a certain fate—e.g., "a stubborn and rebellious son" (Deut 21:18). **(17)** Used figuratively, "son of" can mean "something belonging to"—e.g., "the arrow [literally, "the son of a bow"] cannot make him flee" (Job 41:28). Syn.: 1247, 1248, 2860. See: TWOT—254; BDB—119d, 122b, 1085b.

1122. בֵּן {1x} **Bên,** *bane;* the same as 1121; *Ben,* an Isr.:—*Ben* {1x}. See: BDB—122a.

1123. בֵּן {11x} **bên** (Aram.), *bane;* corresp. to 1121:—children {6x}, son {3x}, young, of the captives + 1547 {1x}. See: TWOT—2639; BDB—1085b.

1124. בְּנָא {22x} **bᵉnâʾ** (Aram.), *ben-aw´;* or

בְּנָה **bᵉnâh** (Aram.), *ben-aw´;* corresp. to 1129; to *build:*—build {17x}, building {3x}, builded + 1934 {1x}, make {1x}. Syn.: 1129. See: TWOT—2633; BDB—1084d.

1125. בֶּן־אֲבִינָדָב {1x} **Ben-ʾĂbîynâdâb,** *ben-ab-ee´´-naw-dawb´;* from 1121 and 40; (the) *son of Abinadab; Ben-Abinadab,* an Isr.:—the son of Abinadab {1x}. See: BDB—122a.

1126. בֶּן־אוֹנִי {1x} **Ben-ʾÔwnîy,** *ben-o-nee´;* from 1121 and 205; *son of my sorrow; Ben-Oni,* the orig. name of Benjamin:—Ben-oni {1x}. See: BDB—122b.

1127. בֶּן־גֶּבֶר {1x} **Ben-Geber,** *ben-gheh´-ber;* from 1121 and 1397; *son of* (the) *hero; Ben-Geber,* an Isr.:—the son of Geber {1x}. See: BDB—122b.

1128. בֶּן־דֶּקֶר {1x} **Ben-Deqer,** *ben-deh´-ker;* from 1121 and a der. of 1856; *son of piercing* (or *of a lance*); *Ben-Deker,* an Isr.:—the son of Dekar {1x}. See: BDB—122b.

1129. בָּנָה {376x} **bânâh,** *baw-naw´;* a prim. root; to *build* (lit. and fig.):—build {340x}, build up {14x}, builder {10x}, made {3x}, built again + 8735 {2x}, repair {2x}, set up {2x}, have children + 8735 {1x}, obtain children + 8735 {1x}, surely {1x} (inf. for emphasis).

Banah means to build, establish, construct, rebuild. **(1)** In its basic meaning, *banah* appears in Gen 8:20, where Noah is said to have "constructed" an ark. **(2)** In Gen 4:17, *banah* means not only that Enoch built a city, but that he "founded" or "established" it. **(3)** This verb can also mean "to manufacture," or adding to an existing material to fashion a new object: **(3a)** as in Eze 27:5: "They have made all thy ship boards of fir trees." **(3b)** Somewhat in the same sense, we read that God "made" or "fashioned" Eve out of Adam's rib (Gen 2:22—the first biblical occurrence). **(3c)** In like manner, Asa began with the cities of Geba and Mizpah and "fortified" them (1 Kin 15:22). **(4)** *Banah* can also refer to "rebuilding" something that is destroyed. Joshua cursed anyone who would rise up and rebuild Jericho, the city that God had utterly destroyed (Josh 6:26). **(5)** Metaphorically or figuratively, the verb *banah* is used to mean "building one's house"—i.e., having children. Sarai said to Abram, "I pray thee, go in unto my maid; it may be that I may obtain children by her" (Gen 16:2). **(5a)** It was the duty of the nearest male relative to conceive a child with the wife of a man who had died childless (Deut 25:9); he thus helped "to build up the house" of his deceased relative. **(5b)** Used figuratively, "to build a house" may also mean "to found a dynasty" (2 Sa 7:27). Syn.: 1124. See: TWOT—255; BDB—124a, 1084d.

1130. בֶּן־הֲדַד {25x} **Ben-Hădad,** *ben-had-ad´;* from 1121 and 1908; *son of Hadad; Ben-Hadad,* the name of several Syrian kings:—Ben-hadad {25x}. See: BDB—122b.

1131. בִּנּוּי {7x} **Binnûwy,** *bin-noo´-ee;* from 1129; *built up; Binnui,* an Isr.:—Binnui {7x}. See: BDB—125a.

1132. בֶּן־זוֹחֵת {1x} **Ben-Zôwchêth,** *ben-zo-khayth´;* from 1121 and 2105; *son of Zocheth; Ben-Zocheth,* an Isr.:—Ben-zoketh {1x}. See: BDB—122b.

1133. בֶּן־חוּר {1x} **Ben-Chûwr,** *ben-khoor´;* from 1121 and 2354; *son of Chur; Ben-Chur,* an Isr.:—the son of Hur {1x}. See: BDB—122b, 301b.

1134. בֶּן־חַיִל {1x} **Ben-Chayil,** *ben-khah´-yil;* from 1121 and 2428; *son of might; Ben-Chail,* an Isr.:—Ben-hail {1x}. See: BDB—122c.

Hebrew

1135. בֶּן־חָנָן {1x} **Ben-Chânân**, *ben-khaw-nawnʼ;* from 1121 and 2605; *son of Chanan; Ben-Chanan,* an Isr.:—Ben-hanan {1x}. See: BDB—122c.

1136. בֶּן־חֶסֶד {1x} **Ben-Cheçed**, *ben-khehʼ-sed;* from 1121 and 2617; *son of kindness; Ben-Chesed,* an Isr.:—the son of Hesed {1x}. See: BDB—122c.

1137. בָּנִי {15x} **Bânîy**, *baw-neeʼ;* from 1129; *built; Bani,* the name of five Isr.:—Bani {15x}. See: BDB—125b.

1138. בֻּנִּי {3x} **Bunnîy**, *boon-neeʼ;* or (fuller)

בּוּנִי **Bûwnîy**, *boo-neeʼ;* from 1129; *built; Bunni or Buni,* an Isr.:—Bunni {3x}.

See: BDB—100d, 1ʼ25a, 125b.

1139. בְּנֵי־בְרַק {1x} **Bᵉnêy-Bᵉraq**, *ben-ayʼ-ber-akʼ;* from the plur. constr. of 1121 and 1300; *sons of lightning, Bene-berak,* a place in Pal.:—Bene-barak {1x}. See: BDB—122c, 140c.

1140. בִּנְיָה {1x} **binyâh**, *bin-yawʼ;* fem. from 1129; *a structure:*—building {1x}. See: TWOT—255; BDB—125b.

1141. בְּנָיָה {42x} **Bᵉnâyâh**, *ben-aw-yawʼ;* or (prol.)

בְּנָיָהוּ **Bᵉnâyâhûw**, *ben-aw-yawʼ-hoo;* from 1129 and 3050; *Jah has built; Benajah,* the name of twelve Isr.:—Benaiah {42x}. See: BDB—125c.

1142. בְּנֵי יַעֲקָן {2x} **Bᵉnêy Yaᵃăqân**, *ben-ayʼ yah-ak-awnʼ;* from the plur. of 1121 and 3292; *sons of Yaakan; Bene-Jaakan,* a place in the desert:—Bene-jaakan {2x}. See: BDB—122c, 785c.

1143. בֵּנַיִם {2x} **bênayim**, *bay-nahʼ-yim;* dual of 996; *a double interval,* i.e. the space between two armies:—champion {2x}.

Benayim literally means [a man] in the space between two armies; an army's representative, its champion. See: BDB—108a.

1144. בִּנְיָמִן {161x} **Binyâmîyn**, *bin-yaw-meneʼ;* from 1121 and 3225; *son of* (the) *right hand; Binjamin,* youngest son of Jacob; also the tribe descended from him, and its territory:—Benjamin {161x}. See: TWOT—254a; BDB—122c.

1145. בֶּן־יְמִינִי {18x} **Ben-yᵉmînîy**, *ben-yem-ee-neeʼ;* sometimes (with the art. ins.)

בֶּן־הַיְמִינִי **Ben-ha-yᵉmînîy**, *ben-hah-yem-ee-neeʼ;* with 376 ins. (1 Sa 9:1)

בֶּן־אִישׁ יְמִינִי **Ben-ʾÎysh Yᵉmîynîy**, *ben-eeshʼ yem-ee-neeʼ;* son of a man of Jemini; or short. (1 Sa 9:4; Est 2:5)

אִישׁ יְמִינִי **ʾÎysh Yᵉmîynîy**, *eesh yem-ee-neeʼ;* a man of Jemini, or (1 Sa 20:1) simply

יְמִינִי **Yᵉmînîy**, *yem-ee-neeʼ;* a Jeminite; (plur.

בְּנֵי יְמִינִי **Bᵉnîy Yᵉmîynîy**, *ben-ayʼ yem-ee-neeʼ;* patron. from 1144; a *Benjaminite,* or descendent of Benjamin:—Benjamite {16x}, of Benjamin {1x}, Benjamite + 1121 {1x}. See: BDB—122d, 412b.

1146. בִּנְיָן {7x} **binyân**, *bin-yawnʼ;* from 1129; an *edifice:*—building {7x}. Syn.: 1129. See: TWOT—255a; BDB—125c.

1147. בִּנְיָן {1x} **binyân** (Aram.), *bin-yawnʼ;* corresp. to 1146:—building {1x}. See: TWOT—2633a; BDB—1084d.

1148. בְּנִינוּ {1x} **Bᵉnîynûw**, *ben-ee-nooʼ;* prob. from 1121 with pron. suff.; *our son; Beninu,* an Isr.:—Beninu {1x}. See: BDB—123a.

1149. בְּנַס {1x} **bᵉnaç** (Aram.), *ben-asʼ;* of uncert. affin.; *to be enraged:*—be angry {1x}. See: TWOT—2634. See: BDB—1084d.

1150. בִּנְעָא {2x} **Binᶜâʾ**, *bin-awʼ;* or

בִּנְעָה **Binᶜâh**, *bin-awʼ;* of uncert. der.; *Bina or Binah,* an Isr.:—Binea {2x}. See: BDB—126a.

1151. בֶּן־עַמִּי {1x} **Ben-ᶜAmmîy**, *ben-am-meeʼ;* from 1121 and 5971 with pron. suff.; *son of my people; Ben-Ammi,* a son of Lot:—Ben-ammi {1x}. See: BDB—122c.

1152. בְּסוֹדְיָה {1x} **Bᵉçôwdᵉyâh**, *bes-o-deh-yawʼ;* from 5475 and 3050 with prep. pref.; *in* (the) *counsel of Jehovah; Besodejah,* an Isr.:—Besodeiah {1x}. See: BDB—126a, 691d.

1153. בְּסַי {2x} **Bᵉçay**, *bes-ahʼ-ee;* from 947; *domineering; Besai,* one of the Nethinim:—Besai {1x}. See: BDB—126a.

1154. בֶּסֶר {1x} **beçer**, *behʼ-ser;* from an unused root mean. to *be sour;* an *immature* grape:—unripe grape {1x}. See: TWOT—257; BDB—126a.

1155. בֹּסֶר {4x} **bôçer**, *boʼser;* from the same as 1154:—sour grape {4x}. See: TWOT—257a; BDB—126a.

1156. בְּעָא {12x} **bᵉᶜâʾ** (Aram.), *beh-awʼ;* or

בְּעָה **bᵉᶜâh** (Aram.), *beh-awʼ;* corresp. to 1158; to *seek* or *ask:*—seek {3x},

ask {3x}, desire {3x}, pray {3x}, request {3x}, make (petition) {1x}. See: TWOT—2635; BDB—1085a.

1157. בְּעַד {19x} **bᵉad,** *beh-ad';* from 5704 with prep. pref.; *in up to* or *over against;* gen. *at, beside, among, behind, for,* etc.:—at, for, by, over, upon, about, up, through = {19x}. See: TWOT—258a; BDB—126b.

1158. בָּעָה {5x} **bâʿâh,** *baw-aw';* a prim. root; to *gush* over, i.e. to *swell;* (fig.) to *desire* earnestly; by impl. to *ask:*—enquire {2x}, boil {1x}, sought up {1x}, swelling out {1x}.

Ba'ah basically means to conciliate the face of a person, and hence to pray with some prospect of success. Syn.: 1875, 7592. See: TWOT—259; BDB—126d, 1085a.

1159. בְּעוּ {1x} **bâʿûw** (Aram.), *baw-oo';* from 1156; a *request:*—petition {1x}. See: TWOT—2635a; BDB—1085a.

1160. בְּעוֹר {10x} **Bᵉôwr,** *beh-ore';* from 1197 (in the sense of *burning);* a *lamp; Beör,* the name of the father of an Edomitish king; also of that of Balaam:—Beor {10x}. See: BDB—129d.

1161. בְּעוּתִים {2x} **bîʿûwthîym,** *be-oo-theme';* masc. plur. from 1204; *alarms:*—terrors {2x}. See: TWOT—265b; BDB—130a.

1162. בֹּעַז {24x} **Bôʿaz,** *bo'-az;* from an unused root of uncert. mean.; *Boaz,* the ancestor of David; also the name of a pillar in front of the temple:—Boaz {24x}. See: BDB—126d.

1163. בָּעַט {2x} **bâʿat,** *baw-at';* a prim. root; to *trample* down, i.e. (fig.) *despise:*—kick {2x}. See: TWOT—261; BDB—127a.

1164. בְּעִי {1x} **bᵉîy,** *beh-ee';* from 1158; a *prayer:*—grave {1x}. See: TWOT—1577d; BDB—127a, 730d.

1165. בְּעִיר {6x} **bᵉîyr,** *beh-ere';* from 1197 (in the sense of *eating);* cattle:—beast {4x}, cattle {2x}. TWOT—264a; BDB—129c.

1166. בָּעַל {16x} **bâʿal,** *baw-al';* a prim. root; to *be master;* hence, (as denom. from 1167) to *marry:*—marry {8x}, husband {3x}, dominion {2x}, wife {1x}, married wife {1x}, Beulah {1x}. *Ba'al* basically means to exercise dominion over. See: TWOT—262; BDB—127a.

1167. בַּעַל {82x} **baʿal,** *bah'-al;* from 1166; a *master;* hence, a *husband,* or (fig.) *owner* (often used with another noun in modifications of this latter sense):—man {25x}, owner {14x}, husband {11x}, have {7x}, master {5x}, man given {2x}, adversary {1x}, archers

{1x}, babbler + 3956 {1x}, bird + 3671 {1x}, captain {1x}, confederate + 1285 {1x}, misc. {12x}.

Ba'al means "master; baal." **(1)** The word *ba'al* occurs 84 times in the Hebrew Old Testament, 15 times with the meaning of "husband" and 50 times as a reference to a deity. The first occurrence of the noun *ba'al* is in Gen 14:13: "And there came one that had escaped, and told Abram the Hebrew; for he dwelt in the plain of Mamre the Amorite, brother of Eshcol, and brother of Aner: and these were confederate with [literally, "*ba'al's* of a covenant with"] Abram." **(2)** The primary meaning of *ba'al* is "possessor." Isaiah's use of *ba'al* in parallel with *qanah* (7069) clarifies this basic significance of *ba'al:* "The ox knoweth his owner [7069 - *qanah*], and the ass his master's [*ba'al*] crib: but Israel does not know, my people doth not consider" (Is 1:3). **(3)** Man may be the owner [*ba'al*] of an animal (Ex 22:10), a house (Ex 22:7), a cistern (Ex 21:34), or even a wife (Ex 21:3). **(4)** A secondary meaning, "husband," is clearly indicated by the phrase *ba'al ha-ishshah* (literally, "owner of the woman"). For example: "If men strive, and hurt a woman with child, so that her fruit depart from her, and yet no mischief follow: he shall be surely punished, according as the woman's husband [*ba'al ha-ishshah*] will lay upon him; and he shall pay as the judges determine" (Ex 21:22).

(5) The meaning of *ba'al* is closely related to *ish* (376 - "man"), as is seen in the usage of these two words in one verse: "When the wife of Uriah heard that Uriah her husband [*ish*] was dead, she mourned for her husband [*ba'al*]" (2 Sa 11:26). **(6)** The word *ba'al* with another noun may signify a peculiar characteristic or quality: "And they said one to another, Behold, this master of dreams cometh" (Gen 37:19). **(7)** The word *ba'al* may denote any deity other than the God of Israel. **(7a)** *Baal* was a common name given to the god of fertility in Canaan. In the Canaanite city of Ugarit, *Baal* was especially recognized as the god of fertility. **(7b)** The Old Testament records that *Baal* was "the god" of the Canaanites. **(7c)** The Israelites worshiped *Baal* during **(7c1)** the time of the judges (Judg 6:25–32) and **(7c2)** of King Ahab. **(7c3)** Elijah stood as the opponent of the *Baal* priests at Mount Carmel (1 Kin 18:21ff.).

(8) Many cities made *Baal* a local god and honored him with special acts of worship: *Baal-peor* (Num 25:5), *Baal-berith* at Shechem (Judg 8:33), *Baal-zebub* (2 Kin 1:2–16) at Ekron, *Baal-zephon* (Num 33:7), and *Baal-hermon* (Judg 3:3). **(9)** Among the prophets, Jeremiah and Hosea mention *Baal* most frequently. **(9a)** Hosea pictured Israel as turning to the baals and only returning to the Lord after a time of despair (Hos 2:13, 17). **(9b)** He says that the

name of *Baal* will no longer be used, not even
with the meaning of "Lord" or "master," as the
association was contaminated by the idolatrous practices: "And it shall be at that day,
saith the Lord, that thou shalt call me Ishi; and
shalt call me no more Ba-a-li [*ba'al*]. For I will
take away the names of Ba-a-lim out of her
mouth, and they shall no more be remembered
by their name" (Hos 2:16–17). **(9c)** In Hosea's
and Jeremiah's time, the *ba'al* idols were still
worshiped, as the peoples sacrificed, built high
places, and made images of the *ba'alim* (plural). Syn.: 113. See: TWOT—262a; BDB -127b,
127d, 1085a.

1168. בַּעַל {80x} **Ba'al**, *bah'-al;* the same as
1167; *Baal,* a Phœnician deity:—
Baal {62x}, Baalim {18x}. See: TWOT—262a;
BDB—127c.

1169. בְּעֵל {3x} **b°êl** (Aram.), *beh-ale';* corresp. to 1167:—chancellor + 2942
{3x}. See: TWOT—2636; BDB—1085a.

1170. בַּעַל בְּרִית {2x} **Ba'al B°rîyth**, *bah'-al*
ber-eeth'; from 1168 and
1285; *Baal of* (the) *covenant; Baal-Berith,* a
special deity of the Shechemites:—Baal-berith
{2x}. See: BDB—127d.

1171. בַּעַל גָּד {3x} **Ba'al Gâd**, *bah'-al gawd;*
from 1168 and 1409; *Baal of*
Fortune; Baal-Gad, a place in Syria:—*Baal-
gad* {1x}. See: BDB—128a.

1172. בַּעֲלָה {2x} **ba'alâh**, *bah-al-aw';* fem. of
1167; a *mistress:*—mistress {2x},
hath (a familiar spirit) {2x}. See: TWOT—262b;
BDB—128b.

1173. בַּעֲלָה {5x} **Ba'alâh**, *bah-al-aw';* the same
as 1172; *Baalah,* the name of
three places in Pal.:—*Baalah* {5x}. See: BDB—
128b.

1174. בַּעַל הָמוֹן {1x} **Ba'al Hâmôwn**, *bah'-al*
haw-mone'; from 1167 and
1995; *possessor of a multitude; Baal-Hamon,* a
place in Pal.:—Baal-hamon {1x}. See: BDB—
128a.

1175. בְּעָלוֹת {2x} **B°'âlôwth**, *beh-aw-lōth';*
plur. of 1172; *mistresses; Beä-
loth,* a place in Pal.:—Bealoth {1x}, in Aloth
{1x}. See: BDB—128c.

1176. בַּעַל זְבוּב {4x} **Ba'al Z°bûwb**, *bah'-al*
zeb-oob'; from 1168 and 2070;
Baal of (the) *Fly; Baal-Zebub,* a special deity
of the Ekronites:—Baal-zebub {4x}. See: BDB—
127d.

1177. בַּעַל חָנָן {5x} **Ba'al Chânân**, *bah'-al khaw-
nawn';* from 1167 and 2603;
possessor of grace; Baal-Chanan, the name of

an Edomite, also of an Isr.:—Baal-hanan {5x}.
See: BDB—128a.

1178. בַּעַל חָצוֹר {1x} **Ba'al Châtsôwr**, *bah'-al*
khaw-tsore'; from 1167 and
a modif. of 2691; *possessor of a village; Baal-
Chatsor,* a place in Pal.:—Baal-hazor {1x}. See:
BDB—128a.

1179. בַּעַל חֶרְמוֹן {2x} **Ba'al Chermôwn**, *bah'-
al kher-mone';* from 1167
and 2768; *possessor of Hermon; Baal-
Chermon,* a place in Pal.:—Baal-hermon {2x}.
See: BDB—128a.

1180. בַּעֲלִי {1x} **Ba'ălîy**, *bah-al-ee';* from 1167
with pron. suff.; *my master; Ba-
ali,* a symb. name for Jehovah:—Baali {1x}. See:
BDB—127b.

1181. בַּעֲלֵי בָּמוֹת {1x} **Ba'ălêy Bâmôwth**,
bah-al-ay' baw-mōth';
from the plur. of 1168 and the plur. of 1116;
Baals of (the) *heights; Baale-Bamoth,* a place
E. of the Jordan:—lords of the high places {1x}.
See: BDB—127b.

1182. בְּעֶלְיָדָע {1x} **B°'elyâdâ'**, *beh-el-yaw-
daw';* from 1168 and 3045;
Baal has known; Beëljada, an Isr.:—Beeliada
{1x}. See: BDB—128c.

1183. בְּעַלְיָה {1x} **B°'alyâh**, *beh-al-yaw';* from
1167 and 3050; *Jah* (is) *master;
Bealjah,* an Isr.:—Bealiah {1x}. See: BDB—
128c.

1184. בַּעֲלֵי יְהוּדָה {1x} **Ba'ălêy Y°hûwdâh**,
bah-al-ay' yeh-hoo-daw';
from the plural of 1167 and 3063; *masters of
Judah; Baale-Jehudah,* a place in Pal.:—Baale
of Judah {1x}. See: BDB—128b.

1185. בַּעֲלִיס {1x} **Ba'ălîç**, *bah-al-ece';* prob.
from a der. of 5965 with prep.
pref.; *in exultation; Baalis,* an Ammonitish
king:—Baalis {1x}. See: BDB—128d.

1186. בַּעַל מְעוֹן {3x} **Ba'al M°'ôwn**, *bah-al
meh-one';* from 1168 and
4583; *Baal of* (the) *habitation* (of) [comp. 1010];
Baal-Meön, a place E. of the Jordan:—Baal-
meon {3x}. See: BDB—128b.

1187. בַּעַל פְּעוֹר {6x} **Ba'al P°'ôwr**, *bah'-al
peh-ore';* from 1168 and
6465; *Baal of Peor; Baal-Peör,* a Moabitish deity:—Baal-peor {6x}. See: BDB—128b.

1188. בַּעַל פְּרָצִים {4x} **Ba'al P°râtsîym**, *bah'-
al per-aw-tseem';* from
1167 and the plur. of 6556; *possessor of
breaches; Baal-Peratsim,* a place in Pal.:—
Baal-perazim {4x}. See: BDB—128b.

1189. בַּעַל צָפוֹן {3x} **Ba'al Ts°phôwn**, *bah'-al
tsef-one';* from 1168 and

6828 (in the sense of *cold*) [according to others an Eg. form of *Typhon,* the destroyer]; *Baal of winter; Baal-Tsephon,* a place in Egypt:— Baal-zephon {3x}. See: BDB—128b, 859d, 861b.

1190. בַּעַל שָׁלִשָׁה {1x} **Ba'al Shâlîshâh,** *bah'-al shaw-lee-shaw';* from 1168 and 8031; *Baal of Shalishah, Baal-Shalishah,* a place in Pal.:—Baal-shalisha {1x}. See: BDB—128b.

1191. בַּעֲלָת {3x} **Ba'ălâth,** *bah-al-awth';* a modif. of 1172; *mistress-ship; Baalath,* a place in Pal.:—Baalath {3x}. See: BDB—128c.

1192. בַּעֲלָת בְּאֵר {1x} **Ba'ălath B**ᵉᵉ**êr,** *bah-al-ath' beh-ayr';* from 1172 and 875; *mistress of a well; Baalath-Beër,* a place in Pal.:—Baalath-beer {1x}. See: BDB—127d, 128c, 928b.

1193. בַּעַל תָּמָר {1x} **Ba'al Tâmâr,** *bah'-al taw-mawr';* from 1167 and 8558; *possessor of* (the) *palm-tree; Baal-Tamar,* a place in Pal.:—Baal-tamar {1x}. See: BDB—128b, 1071c.

1194. בְּעֹן {1x} **B**ᵉᵉ**ôn,** *beh-ohn';* prob. a contr. of 1010; *Beön,* a place E. of the Jordan:—Beon {1x}. See: BDB—111a, 128d.

1195. בַּעֲנָא {3x} **Ba'ănâ',** *bah-an-aw';* the same as 1196; *Baana,* the name of four Isr.:—Baana {2x}, Baanah {1x}. See: BDB—128d.

1196. בַּעֲנָה {9x} **Ba'ănâh,** *bah-an-aw';* from a der. of 6031 with prep. pref.; *in affliction; Baanah,* the name of four Isr.:—Baanah {9x}. See: BDB—128d.

1197. בָּעַר {94x} **bâ'ar,** *baw-ar';* a prim. root; *to kindle,* i.e. *consume* (by fire or by eating); also (as denom. from 1198) *to be* (*-come*) *brutish:*—burn {41x}, . . . away {21x}, kindle {13x}, brutish {7x}, eaten {2x}, set {2x}, burn up {2x}, eat up {2x}, feed {1x}, heated {1x}, took {1x}, wasted {1x}. Syn.: 2787, 3341, 6999. 8313. See: TWOT—263; BDB—128d, 129c.

1198. בַּעַר {5x} **ba'ar,** *bah'-ar;* from 1197; prop. *food* (as *consumed*); i.e. (by exten.) of cattle *brutishness;* (concr.) *stupid:*—brutish {4x}, foolish {1x}. See: TWOT—264b; BDB—129d.

1199. בָּעֲרָא {1x} **Bâ'ărâ',** *bah-ar-aw';* from 1198; *brutish: Baara,* an Isr. woman:—Baara {1x}. See: BDB—129d.

1200. בְּעֵרָה {1x} **b**ᵉᵉ**êrâh,** *bè-ay-raw';* from 1197; a *burning:*—fire {1x}. Syn.: 784, 3857. See: TWOT 263a; BDB—129c.

1201. בַּעְשָׁא {28x} **Ba'shâ',** *bah-shaw';* from an unused root mean. *to stink; offensiveness; Basha,* a king of Israel:—Baasha {28x}. See: BDB—129d.

1202. בַּעֲשֵׂיָה {1x} **Ba'ăsêyâh,** *bah-as-ay-yaw';* from 6213 and 3050 with a prep. pref.; *in* (the) *work of Jah; Baasejah,* an Isr.:—Baaseiah {1x}. See: BDB—129d.

1203. בְּעֶשְׁתְּרָה {1x} **B**ᵉᵉ**esht**ᵉ**râh,** *beh-esh-ter-aw';* from 6251 (as sing. of 6252) with prep. pref.; *with Ashtoreth; Beësh-terah,* a place E. of the Jordan:—Beeshterah {1x}. See: BDB—129d.

1204. בָּעַת {16x} **bâ'ath,** *baw-ath';* a prim. root; *to fear:*—afraid {10x}, terrify {3x}, affrighted {1x}, trouble {2x}. Syn.: 2729, 3372, 6342. See: TWOT—265; BDB—129d.

1205. בְּעָתָה {2x} **b**ᵉᵉ**âthâh,** *beh-aw-thaw';* from 1204; *fear:*—trouble {2x}. See: TWOT—265a; BDB—130a.

1206. בֹּץ {1x} **bôts,** *botse;* prob. the same as 948; *mud* (as *whitish* clay):—mire {1x}. Syn.: 2916. See: TWOT—268a; BDB—130a, 130c.

1207. בִּצָּה {3x} **bitstsâh,** *bits-tsaw';* intens. from 1206; a *swamp:*—mire {1x}, fens {1x}, miry place {1x}. See: TWOT—268b; BDB—130c.

1208. בָּצוֹר {1x} **bâtsôwr,** *baw-tsore';* from 1219; *inaccessible,* i.e. *lofty:*—vintage {1x}. Syn.: 1210. See: TWOT—270f; BDB—131b.

1209. בֵּצָי {3x} **Bêtsay,** *bay-tsah'-ee;* perh. the same as 1153; *Betsai,* the name of two Isr.:—Bezai {3x}. See: BDB—130a.

1210. בָּצִיר {7x} **bâtsîyr,** *baw-tseer';* from 1219; *clipped,* i.e. the *grape crop:*—vintage {1x}. See: TWOT—270f; BDB—131b.

1211. בְּצֶל {1x} **betsel,** *beh'-tsel;* from an unused root appar. mean. *to peel;* an *onion:*—onion {1x}. See: TWOT—266a; BDB—130a.

1212. בְּצַלְאֵל {9x} **B**ᵉᵉ**tsal'êl,** *bets-al-ale';* prob. from 6738 and 410 with prep. pref.; *in* (the) *shadow* (i.e. *protection*) *of God; Betsalel,* the name of two Isr.:—Bezaleel {9x}. See: BDB—130b.

1213. בַּצְלוּת {2x} **Batslûwth,** *bats-looth';* or

בַּצְלִית **Batslîyth,** *bats-leeth';* from the same as 1211; a *peeling; Batsluth* or *Batslith,* an Isr.:—Bazluth {2x}. See: BDB—130b.

1214. בָּצַע {16x} **bâtsa'**, *baw-tsah';* a prim. root to *break* off, i.e. (usually) *plunder;* fig. to *finish,* or (intr.) *stop:*—cut me off {2x}, gained {2x}, given {2x}, greedy {2x}, coveteth {1x}, covetous {1x}, cut {1x}, finish {1x}, fulfilled {1x}, get {1x}, performed {1x}, wounded {1x}. See: TWOT—267; BDB—130b.

1215. בֶּצַע {23x} **betsa'**, *beh'-tsah;* from 1214; *plunder;* by extens. *gain* (usually unjust):—covetousness {10x}, gain {9x}, profit {3x}, lucre {1x}. See: TWOT—267a; BDB—130c.

1216. בָּצֵק {2x} **bâtsêq**, *baw-tsake';* a prim. root; perh. to *swell* up, i.e. *blister:*—swell {2x}. See: TWOT—269; BDB—130d.

1217. בָּצֵק {5x} **bâtsêq**, *baw-tsake';* from 1216; *dough* (as *swelling* by fermentation):—dough {4x}, flour {1x}. Syn.: 5560, 7058. See: TWOT—269a; BDB—130d.

1218. בָּצְקַת {2x} **Botsqath**, *bots-cath';* from 1216; a *swell* of ground; *Botscath,* a place in Pal.:—Bozcath {1x}, Boskath {1x}. See: BDB—130d.

1219. בָּצַר {38x} **bâtsar**, *baw-tsar';* a prim. root; to *clip* off; spec. (as denom. from 1210) to *gather* grapes; also to *be isolated* (i.e. *inaccessible* by height or fortification):—fenced {15x}, defenced {5x}, gather {4x}, grapegatherers {3x}, fortify {2x}, cut off {1x}, restrained {1x}, strong {1x}, mighty things {1x}, walled up {1x}, fenced up {1x}, walled {1x}, withholden {1x}, non translated variant {1x}. Syn.: 4013. See: TWOT—270; BDB—130d.

1220. בֶּצֶר {2x} **betser**, *beh'-tser;* from 1219; strictly a *clipping,* i.e. *gold* (as *dug* out):—gold {1x}, defence {1x}. See: TWOT—270a; BDB—131a.

1221. בֶּצֶר {5x} **Betser**, *beh'-tser;* the same as 1220, an *inaccessible* spot; *Betser,* a place in Pal.; also an Isr.:—Bezer {5x}. See: BDB—131a.

1222. בְּצָר {1x} **b°tsar**, *bets-ar';* another form for 1220; *gold:*—gold {1x}. See: TWOT—270a; BDB—131a.

1223. בָּצְרָה {1x} **botsrâh**, *bots-raw';* fem. from 1219; an *enclosure,* i.e. *sheepfold:*—Bozrah {1x}. See: TWOT—270b; BDB—131a.

1224. בָּצְרָה {9x} **Botsrâh**, *bots-raw';* the same as 1223; *Botsrah,* a place in Edom:—Bozrah {8x}, non translated variant {1x}. See: BDB—131b.

1225. בִּצָּרוֹן {1x} **bitstsârôwn**, *bits-tsaw-rone';* masc. intens. from 1219; a *fortress:*—stronghold {1x}. See: TWOT—270c; BDB—131b.

1226. בַּצֹּרֶת {2x} **batstsôreth**, *bats-tso'-reth;* fem. intens. from 1219; *restraint* (of rain), i.e. *drought:*—dearth {1x}, drought {1x}. See: TWOT—270d; BDB—131b.

1227. בַּקְבּוּק {2x} **Baqbûwq**, *bak-book';* the same as 1228; *Bakbuk,* one of the *Nethinim:*—Bakbuk {2x}. See: BDB—131c, 132d.

1228. בַּקְבֻּק {3x} **baqbûk**, *bak-book';* from 1238; a *bottle* (from the gurgling in *emptying*):—bottle {2x}, cruse {1x}. See: TWOT—273a; BDB—131c, 132d.

1229. בַּקְבֻּקְיָה {3x} **Baqbuqyâh**, *bak-book-yaw';* from 1228 and 3050; *emptying* (i.e. *wasting*) *of Jah; Bakbukjah,* an Isr.:—Bakbukiah {3x}. See: BDB—131c, 132d.

1230. בַּקְבַּקַּר {1x} **Baqbaqqar**, *bak-bak-kar';* redupl. from 1239; *searcher; Bakbakkar,* an Isr.:—Bakbakkar {1x}. See: BDB—131c.

1231. בֻּקִּי {5x} **Buqqîy**, *book-kee';* from 1238; *wasteful; Bukki,* the name of two Isr.:—Bukki {5x}. See: BDB—131c.

1232. בֻּקִּיָּה {2x} **Buqqîyâh**, *book-kee-yaw';* from 1238 and 3050; *wasting of Jah; Bukkijah,* an Isr.:—Bukkiah {2x}. See: BDB—131c.

1233. בְּקִיעַ {2x} **b°qîya'**, *bek-ee'-ah;* from 1234; a *fissure:*—breach {1x}, cleft {1x}. See: TWOT—271c; BDB—132c.

1234. בָּקַע {2x} **bâqa'**, *baw-kah';* a prim. root; to *cleave; gen.* to *rend, break, rip* or *open:*—cleave {10x}, . . . up {9x}, divide {5x}, rent {4x}, . . . out {3x}, break through {3x}, rend {3x}, breach {2x}, asunder {2x}, hatch {2x}, brake {1x}, burst {1x}, cleft {1x}, break forth {1x}, pieces {1x}, tare {1x}, tear {1x}, win {1x}.

Baqa (1234) means "to cleave, split, break open, break through." It is the origin of the name of the famous Beqa Valley (which means "valley" or "cleft") in Lebanon. **(1)** In its verbal forms, *baqa'* is found some 50 times in the Hebrew Old Testament. **(2)** The word is first used there in Gen 7:11, which states that the "fountains of the great deep [were] broken up," resulting in the Flood. **(3)** The everyday use of the verb is seen in references **(3a)** to "splitting" wood (Eccl 10:9) and **(3b)** the ground "splitting" asunder (Num 16:31). **(3c)** Serpents' eggs "split open" or "hatch out" their young (Is 59:5). **(4)** City walls are "breached" or "broken into" in order to take them captive (Jer 52:7). **(5)** One of the horrors of war was the "ripping open" of pregnant women by the enemy (2 Kin 8:12; 15:16). **(6)** Three times God is said "to split open" rocks or the ground in order to pro-

vide water for His people (Judg 15:19; Ps 74:15; Is 48:21).

(7) In the figurative sense, it is said that the light of truth will "break forth as the morning" (Is 58:8). **(8)** Using hyperbole or exaggeration, the historian who recorded the celebration for Solomon's coronation said that it was so loud "that the earth rent with the sound of them" (1 Kin 1:40). **(9)** As here, the KJV often renders *baqa'* by "rent." In other contexts, it may be translated "burst; clave (cleave); tear; divide; break." Syn.: 1692, 2673, 6536. See: TWOT— 271; BDB—131c.

1235. בֶּקַע {2x} **beqaᶜ**, *beh'-kah;* from 1234; a *section* (half) of a shekel, i.e. a *beka* (a weight and a coin):—bekah {1x}, half a shekel {1x}. See: TWOT—271a; BDB—132b.

1236. בִּקְעָא {1x} **biqᶜâʾ** (Aram.), *bik-aw';* corresp. to 1237:—plain {1x}. See: TWOT—2637; BDB—1085a.

1237. בִּקְעָה {20x} **biqᶜâh**, *bik-aw';* from 1234; prop. a *split,* i.e. a wide level *valley* between mountains:—plain {7x}, valley {13x}. See: TWOT—271b; BDB—132c, 1085a.

1238. בָּקַק {9x} **bâqaq**, *baw-kak';* a prim. root; to *pour* out, i.e. to *empty,* fig. to *depopulate;* by anal. to *spread* out (as a fruitful vine):—empty {5x}, make void {1x}, emptiers {1x}, fail {1x}, utterly (inf for emphasis). See: TWOT—273; BDB—132c.

1239. בָּקַר {7x} **bâqar**, *baw-kar;* a prim. root; prop. to *plow,* or (gen.) *break* forth, i.e. (fig.) to *inspect, admire, care for, consider:*—enquire {3x}, seek {3x}, search {1x}.

(1) *Baqar* means "to attend, bestow care on, seek with pleasure." **(2)** Although this verb is found only 7 times in biblical Hebrew, it occurs in early, middle, and late periods and in both prose and poetry. **(3)** In Lev 13:36 *baqar* means "to attend to": "If the scall be spread in the skin, the priest shall not seek for yellow hair." **(4)** The word implies "to seek with pleasure or delight" in Ps 27:4: ". . . to behold the beauty of the Lord, and *to inquire* in his temple." Syn.: 1875, 2664. See: TWOT—274; BDB—133a, 1085b.

1240. בְּקַר {5x} **bᵉqar** (Aram.), *bek-ar';* corresp. to 1239:—inquire {1x}, make search {4x}. See: TWOT—2638; BDB—1085a.

1241. בָּקָר {182x} **bâqâr**, *baw-kawr';* from 1239; a *beeve* or animal of the ox kind of either gender (as used for *plowing*); collect. a *herd:*—ox {78x}, herd {44x}, beeves {7x}, young {18x}, young + 1121 {17x}, bullock {6x}, bullock + 1121 {2x}, calf + 1121 {2x}, heifer {2x}, kine {2x}, bulls {1x}, cattle {1x}, cow's {1x}, great {1x}.

Baqar (1241) means "herd; cattle." **(1)** One meaning of the word is "cattle." **(1a)** Such beasts were slaughtered for food, and their hides were presented as offerings to God (Num 15:8). **(1b)** This meaning of *baqar* is in Gen 12:16 (the first biblical occurrence): "And he [Pharaoh] entreated Abram well for her [Sarah's] sake: and he had sheep, and oxen, and he asses." **(1c)** These were grazing beasts (1 Chr 27:29) and were eaten (1 Kin 4:23). **(1d)** These animals pulled carts (2 Sa 6:6) and plows (Job 1:14), and carried burdens on their backs (1 Chr 12:40). **(2)** *Baqar* often refers to a group of cattle or "herd" (both sexes), as it does in Gen 13:5: "And Lot also, which went with Abram, had flocks, and herds [in the Hebrew, this word appears in a singular form] and tents." **(3)** The word can represent a "small group of cattle" (not a herd; cf. Gen 47:16; Ex 22:1) or even a pair of oxen (Num 7:17). **(4)** A single ox is indicated either by some other Hebrew word or called an offspring of oxen (Gen 18:7). **(5)** *Baqar* also refers to statues of oxen: "It [the altar of burnt offerings] stood upon twelve oxen, three looking toward the north, and three looking toward the west, and three looking toward the south, and three looking toward the east" (1 Kin 7:25). Syn.: 6499, 7794. See: TWOT—274a; BDB—133a.

1242. בֹּקֶר {204x} **bôqer**, *bo'-ker;* from 1239; prop. *dawn* (as the *break* of day); gen. *morning:*—morning {190x}, morrow {7x}, day {3x}, days + 6153 {1x}, early {3x}.

Boqer (1242) means "morning." **(1)** This word means "morning," **(1a)** though not the period of time before noon. **(1b)** Rather it indicates the point of time at which night is changing to day or that time at the end of night: "And Moses stretched forth his rod over the land of Egypt, and the Lord brought an east wind upon the land all that day, and all that night; and when it was morning, the east wind brought the locusts" (Ex 10:13). **(2)** *Boqer* can represent the time just before the rising of the sun. In Judg 19:25 we read that the men of Gibeah raped and abused the Levite's concubine "all the night until the morning: and when the day began to spring, they let her go" (cf. Ruth 3:13). **(3)** In the ancient Near East the night was divided into three watches. **(3a)** The last period of the night was called the morning watch (Ex 14:24). **(3b)** It lasted from 2:00 A.M. until sunrise, and in such a context the word indicates this period of time.

(4) *Boqer* can mean "daybreak" or "dawn." In Ex 14:27 it is reported that the water of the Red Sea "returned to his [normal state] when the morning appeared [literally, "at the turning of the morning"]." **(5)** *Boqer* is used as a synonym of "dawn" in Job 38:12: "Hast thou commanded the morning since thy days; and

caused the dayspring to know his place?" **(6)** Sometimes *boqer* appears to mean "early morning," or shortly after daybreak: **(6a)** "And Joseph came in unto them in the morning, and looked upon them and, behold, they were sad" (Gen 40:6). **(6b)** Thus, Moses "rose up early in the morning" and went up to Mount Sinai; he arose before daybreak so he could appear before God in the "morning" as God had commanded (Ex 34:2, 4). **(6c)** In the "morning" Jacob saw that his bride was Leah rather than Rachel (Gen 29:25; cf. 1 Sa 29:10). **(7)** As the opposite of night the word represents the entire period of daylight. The psalmist prays that it is good "to show forth thy loving-kindness in the morning, and thy faithfulness every night" (Ps 92:2), in other words, to always be praising God (cf. Amos 5:8).

(8) In Ps 65:8 *boqer* represents a place, specifically, the place where the sun rises: "They also that dwell in the uttermost parts are afraid at thy tokens: thou makest the outgoings of the morning and evening to rejoice." **(9)** At least once the word appears to represent the resurrection: "Like sheep they [the ungodly] are laid in the grave; death shall feed on them; and the upright shall have dominion over them in the morning" (Ps 49:14). **(10)** *Boqer* can mean "morrow" or "next day." This meaning first appears in Ex 12:10, where God tells Israel not to leave any of the Passover "until the morning; and that which remaineth of it until the morning ye shall burn with fire" (cf. Lev 22:30). Syn.: 5399, 7837. See: TWOT—274c; BDB—133c.

1243. בַּקָּרָה {1x} **baqqârâh**, *bak-kaw-raw'*; intens. from 1239; a *looking after:*—seek out {1x}. See: TWOT—274d; BDB—134c.

1244. בִּקֹּרֶת {1x} **biqqôreth**, *bik-ko'-reth;* from 1239; prop. *examination,* i.e. (by impl.) *punishment:*—scourged {1x}. See: TWOT—274e; BDB—134c.

1245. בָּקַשׁ {225x} **bâqash**, *baw-kash';* a prim. root; to *search* out (by any method, spec. in worship or prayer); by impl. to *strive after:*—seek {189x}, require {14x}, request {4,x} seek out {4x}, enquired {3x}, besought {2x}, ask {2x}, sought for {2x}, begging {1x}, desire {1x}, get {1x}, inquisition {1x}, procureth {1x}.

Baqash means "to seek, search, consult." **(1)** Basically *baqash* means "to seek" to find something that is lost or missing, or, at least, whose location is unknown. **(1a)** In Gen 37:15 a man asks Joseph: "What seekest thou?" **(1b)** A special nuance of this sense is "to seek out of a group; to choose, select" something or someone yet undesignated, as in 1 Sa 13:14: "The Lord hath sought him a man after his own heart."

(1c) To seek one's face is "to seek" to come before him, or to have a favorable audience with him; all the world "was seeking" the presence of Solomon (1 Kin 10:24). **(1d)** In a similar sense one may "seek" God's face by standing before Him in the temple praying (2 Sa 21:1).

(2) The sense "seek to secure" emphasizes the pursuit of a wish or the accomplishing of a plan. **(2a)** Moses asked the Levites who rebelled against the unique position of Aaron and his sons: "Seek ye the priesthood also?" (Num 16:10). **(2b)** This usage may have an emotional coloring, such as, "to aim at, devote oneself to, and be concerned about." So God asks the sons of men (mankind): "How long will ye turn my glory into shame? How long will ye love vanity, and seek after [sin]?" (Ps 4:2). **(2c)** Cultically one may "seek" to secure God's favor or help: "And Judah gathered themselves together, to ask help of the Lord" (2 Chr 20:4). **(2d)** In such usages the intellectual element usually is in the background; there is no seeking after information. **(2e)** An exception to this is Judg 6:29: "And when they inquired [1875 - *darash*] and asked [1245 - *baqash*], they said, Gideon the son of Joash hath done this thing."

(3) Infrequently this verb is used of seeking information from God (Ex 33:7). **(3a)** In a similar sense one may "seek" God's face (2 Sa 21:1). Here *baqash* is clearly used of searching for information (a cognitive pursuit). **(3b)** Also, compare the pursuit of wisdom (Prov. 2:4). **(4)** This sense of "seeking to secure" may also be used of seeking one's life (5315 - *nepesh*). **(4a)** God told Moses to "go, return into Egypt: for all the men are dead which sought thy life" (Ex 4:19). **(4b)** *Baqash* may be used with this same nuance but without *nepesh*—so Pharaoh "sought to slay Moses" (Ex 2:15). **(5)** Only twice is this nuance applied to seeking to procure one's good as in Ps 122:9: "Because of the house of the LORD our God I will seek thy good" [usually *darash* (1875) is used of seeking one's good].

(6) About 20 times *baqash* means to hold someone responsible for something because the speaker has a (real or supposed) legal right to it. In Gen 31:39 (the first biblical occurrence of the verb) Jacob points out to Laban that regarding animals lost to wild beasts, "of my hand didst thou require it." **(7)** Only infrequently is *baqash* used of seeking out a place, or as a verb of movement toward a place. So Joseph "sought [a place] to weep; and he entered into his chamber, and wept there" (Gen 43:30). **(8)** Theologically, this verb can be used not only "to seek" a location before the Lord (to stand before Him in the temple and seek to secure His blessing), but it may also be used of a state of mind: "But if from thence thou shalt seek the LORD thy God, thou shalt find him, if

thou seek him [*darash*] with all thy heart and with all thy soul" (Deut 4:29). In instances such as this where the verb is used in synonymous parallelism with *darash*, the two verbs have the same meaning. Syn.: 1875, 7836. See: TWOT—276; BDB—134c.

1246. בַּקָּשָׁה {8x} **baqqâshâh**, *bak-kaw-shaw'*; from 1245; a *petition:*—request {8x}. See: TWOT—276a; BDB—135a.

1247. בַּר {8x} **bar** (Aram.), *bar;* corresp. to 1121; a *son, grandson,* etc.:—× old {1x}, son {7x}. See: TWOT—276a; BDB—1085b.

1248. בַּר {4x} **bar**, *bar;* borrowed (as a title) from 1247; the *heir* (apparent to the throne):—son {4x}. Syn.: 1121. See: TWOT—277; BDB—135a, 1085b.

1249. בַּר **bar**, *bar;* from 1305 (in its various senses); *beloved;* also *pure, empty:*—clean {3x}, pur {2x}, choice {1x}, clear {1x}. See: TWOT—288a; BDB—135a, 141a.

1250. בָּר {14x} **bâr**, *bawr;* or

בַּר **bar**, *bar;* from 1305 (in the sense of *winnowing*); *grain* of any kind (even while standing in the field); by extens. the open *country:*—corn {9x}, wheat {5x}. See: BDB—135a, 141b, 1085c.

1251. בַּר {8x} **bar** (Aram.), *bar;* corresp. to 1250; a *field:*—field {8x}. See: TWOT—2640; BDB—1085b, 1085c.

1252. בֹּר {6x} **bôr**, *bore;* from 1305; *purity:*—cleanness {4x}, pureness {1x}, never {1x}. See: TWOT—288d; BDB—101c, 141b.

1253. בֹּר {2x} **bôr**, *bore;* the same as 1252; vegetable *lye* (from its *cleansing*); used as a *soap* for washing, or a *flux* for metals:—purely {1x}, non translated variant {1x}. See: TWOT—288c; BDB—141b.

1254. בָּרָא {54x} **bârâʾ**, *baw-raw';* a prim. root; (absolutely) to *create;* (qualified) to *cut* down (a wood), *select, feed* (as formative processes):—create {42x}, creator {3x}, choose {2x}, make {2x}, cut down {2x}, dispatch {1x}, done {1x}, make fat {1x}.

Bara' means "to create, make." **(1)** This verb is of profound theological significance, since it has only God as its subject. **(1a)** Only God can "create" in the sense implied by *bara'*. **(1b)** The verb expresses creation out of nothing, an idea seen clearly in passages having to do with creation on a cosmic scale: "In the beginning God created the heaven and the earth" (Gen 1:1; cf. Gen 2:3; Is 40:26; 42:5). **(1c)** All other verbs for "creating" allow a much broader range of meaning; they have both divine and human subjects, and are used in contexts where bringing something or someone into existence is not

the issue. **(2)** Objects of the verb include **(2a)** the heavens and earth (Gen 1:1; Is 40:26; 42:5; 45:18; 65:17), **(2b)** man (Gen 1:27; 5:2; 6:7; Deut 4:32; Ps 89:47; Is 43:7; 45:12); **(2c)** Israel (Is 43:1; Mal 2:10); **(2d)** a new thing (Jer 31:22); **(2e)** cloud and smoke (Is 4:5); **(2f)** north and south (Ps 89:12); **(2g)** salvation and righteousness (Is 45:8); **(2h)** speech (Is 57:19); **(2i)** darkness (Is 45:7); **(2j)** wind (Amos 4:13); and **(2k)** a new heart (Ps 51:10).

(3) A careful study of the passages where *bara'* occurs shows that in the few non-poetic uses (primarily in Genesis), the writer uses scientifically precise language to demonstrate that God brought the object or concept into being from previously nonexistent material. **(4)** Especially striking is the use of *bara'* in Isaiah 40—65. **(4a)** Out of 49 occurrences of the verb in the Old Testament, 20 are in these chapters. **(4b)** Because Isaiah writes prophetically to the Jews in Exile, he speaks words of comfort based upon God's past benefits and blessings to His people. Isaiah especially wants to show that, since Yahweh is the Creator, He is able to deliver His people from captivity. The God of Israel has created all things: "I have made [6213 - *'asah*] the earth, and created [*bara'*] man upon it: I, even my hands, have stretched out the heavens, and all their host have I commanded" (Is 45:12). **(4c)** The gods of Babylon are impotent nonentities (Is 44:12–20; 46:1–7), and so **(4d)** Israel can expect God to triumph by effecting a new creation (43:16–21; 65:17–25).

(5) Though a precisely correct technical term to suggest cosmic, material creation from nothing, *bara'* is a rich theological vehicle for communicating the sovereign power of God, who originates and regulates all things to His glory. Syn.: "For thus saith the LORD that created [*bara*] the heavens; God himself that formed [*yatsar* - 3335] the earth and made [*asah* - 6213] it; he hath established [*kun* - 3559] it, he created [*bara*] it not in vain, he formed [*yatsar* - 3335] it to be inhabited: I am the LORD; and there is none else" (Is 45:18). The technical meaning of *bara* (to create out of nothing) may not hold in these passages; perhaps the verb was popularized in these instances for the sake of providing a poetic synonym. See: TWOT—278; BDB—135a, 135d.

1255. בְּרֹאדַךְ בַּלְאֲדָן {1x} **Bᵉrôʾdak Balʾădân**, *ber-o-dak' bal-ad-awn';* a var. of 4757; *Berodak-Baladan*, a Bab. king:—Berodach-baladan {1x}. See: BDB—135d, 597d.

בִּרְאִי **Birʾîy**. See 1011.

1256. בְּרָאיָה {1x} **Bᵉrâʾyâh**, *ber-aw-yaw';* from 1254 and 3050; *Jah has created;*

Berajah, an Isr.:—Beraiah {1x}. See: BDB—135c.

1257. בַּרְבֻּר {1x} **barbûr,** *bar-boor';* by redupl. from 1250; a *fowl* (as fattened on *grain*):—fowl {1x}. See: TWOT—288g; BDB—135d, 141b.

1258. בָּרַד {1x} **bârad,** *baw-rad';* a prim. root, to *hail:*—hail {1x}. See: TWOT—280; BDB—136a.

1259. בָּרָד {29x} **bârâd,** *baw-rawd';* from 1258; *hail:*—hail {27x}, hailstones +68 {2x}. See: TWOT—280a; BDB—135d.

1260. בֶּרֶד {1x} **Bered,** *beh'red;* from 1258; *hail; Bered,* the name of a place south of Pal., also of an Isr.:—Bered {1x}. See: BDB—136a.

1261. בָּרֹד {4x} **bârôd,** *baw-rode';* from 1258; *spotted* (as if with *hail*):—grisled {4x}. See: TWOT—280b; BDB—136a.

1262. בָּרָה {7x} **bârâh,** *baw-raw';* a prim. root; to *select;* also (as denom. from 1250) to *feed;* also (as equiv. to 1305) to *render clear* (Eccl 3:18):—eat {4x}, choose {1x}, give {1x}, cause to eat {1x}. See: TWOT—281; BDB—136a.

1263. בָּרוּךְ {26x} **Bârûwk,** *baw-rook';* pass. part. from 1288; *blessed; Baruk,* the name of three Isr.:—Baruch {26x}. See: BDB—138c, 140a.

1264. בְּרֹם {1x} **b⁽e⁾rôwm,** *ber-ome';* prob. of for. or.; *damask* (stuff of variegated *thread*):—rich apparel {1x}. See: TWOT—286a; BDB—140b.

1265. בְּרוֹשׁ {20x} **b⁽e⁾rôwsh,** *ber-ōsh';* of uncert. der.; a *cypress* (?) *tree;* hence, a *lance* or a *musical* instrument (as made of that wood):—fir tree {13x}, fir {7x}. See: TWOT—289a; BDB—137b, 141b.

1266. בְּרוֹת {1x} **b⁽e⁾rôwth,** *ber-ōth';* a var. of 1265; the *cypress* (or some elastic tree):—fir {1x}. See: TWOT—289a; BDB—137b, 141c.

1267. בָּרוּת {1x} **bârûwth,** *baw-rooth';* from 1262; *food:*—meat {1x}. See: TWOT—281b; BDB—136a, 137b.

1268. בֵּרוֹתָה {2x} **Bêrôwthâh,** *bay-ro-thaw';* or

בֵּרֹתַי **Bêrôthay,** *bay-ro-tha'-ee;* prob. from 1266; *cypress* or *cypresslike; Berothah* or *Berothai,* a place north of Pal.:—Berothah {1x}, Berothai {1x}. See: BDB—92d, 137b, 467b.

1269. בִּרְזוֹת {1x} **Birzôwth,** *beer-zoth';* prob. fem. plur. from an unused root

(appar. mean. to *pierce*); *holes; Birzoth,* an Isr.:—Birzavith {1x}. See: BDB—137b.

1270. בַּרְזֶל {76x} **barzel,** *bar-zel';* perh. from the root of 1269; *iron* (as *cutting*); by extens. an iron *implement:*—iron {73x}, (axe) head {2x}, smith + 2796 {1x}. See: TWOT—283a; BDB—137b, 1108d.

1271. בַּרְזִלַּי {12x} **Barzillay,** *bar-zil-lah'-ee;* from 1270; *iron*-hearted; *Barzillai,* the name of three Isr.:—Barzillai {12x}. See: BDB—137d.

1272. בָּרַח {65x} **bârach,** *baw-rakh';* a prim. root; to *bolt,* i.e. fig. to *flee* suddenly:—flee {52x}, . . .away {7x}, chased {1x}, fain {1x} (inf. for emphasis), flight {1x}, make haste {1x}, reach {1x}, shoot {1x}.

Barach means "to flee, pass through." **(1)** The word first appears in Gen 16:6, where it is said that Hagar "fled from her [Sarah's] face" as a result of Sarah's harsh treatment. **(2)** Men may "flee" from many things or situations. David "fled" from Naioth in Ramah in order to come to Jonathan (1 Sa 20:1). **(3)** Sometimes it is necessary to "flee" from weapons (Job 20:24). **(4)** In describing flight from a person, the Hebrew idiom "from the presence of" (literally, "from the face of") is often used (Gen 16:6, 8; 31:27; 35:1, 7). **(5)** In its figurative use, the word describes days "fleeing" away (Job 9:25) or frail man "fleeing" like a shadow (Job 14:2). **(6)** A rather paradoxical use is found in Song 8:14, in which "flee" must mean "come quickly": "Make haste [literally, "flee"], my beloved, and be thou like to a gazelle." Syn.: 5127. See: TWOT—284; BDB—137d.

1273. בַּרְחֻמִי {1x} **Barchûmîy,** *bar-khoo-mee';* by transp. for 978; a *Barchumite,* or native of *Bachurim:*—Barhumite {1x}. See: BDB—104d, 138c.

1274. בְּרִי {1x} **b⁽e⁾rîy,** *ber-ee';* from 1262; *fat:*—fat {1x}. See: TWOT—279a; BDB—135d, 138c.

1275. בֵּרִי {1x} **Bêrîy,** *bay-ree';* prob. by contr. from 882; *Beri,* an Isr.:—Beri {1x}. See: BDB—92d, 138c.

1276. בֵּרִי {1x} **Bêrîy,** *bay-ree';* of uncert. der. (only in the plur. and with the art.); the *Berites,* a place in Pal.:—Berites {1x}. See: BDB—138c.

1277. בָּרִיא {13x} **bârîy⁾,** *baw-ree';* from 1254 (in the sense of 1262); *fatted* or *plump:*—fat {5x}, rank {2x}, fatfleshed + 1320 {2x}, firm {1x}, fatter {1x}, fed {1x}, plenteous {1x}. Syn.: 1878, 2459. See: TWOT—279a; BDB—135d.

1278. בְּרִיאָה {1x} bᵉrîyʾâh, ber-ee-aw'; fem. from 1254; a *creation*, i.e. a *novelty:*—new thing {1x}. See: TWOT—278a; BDB—135c.

1279. בִּרְיָה {3x} biryâh, beer-yaw'; fem. from 1262; *food:*—meat {1x}. See: BDB—135d, 136a, 138c.

1280. בְּרִיחַ {41x} bᵉrîyach, ber-ee'-akh; from 1272; a *bolt:*—bar {40x}, fugitive {1x}. See: TWOT—284b; BDB—138a.

1281. בָּרִיחַ {3x} bârîyach, baw-ree'-akh; or (short.)

בָּרִחַ bâriach, baw-ree'-akh; from 1272; a *fugitive*, i.e. the *serpent* (as *fleeing*), and the constellation by that name:—crooked {1x}, nobles {1x}, piercing {1x}. See: TWOT—284a; BDB—138a.

1282. בָּרִיחַ {1x} Bârîyach, baw-ree'-akh; the same as 1281; *Bariach*, an Isr.:—Bariah {1x}. See: BDB—138a.

1283. בְּרִיעָה {11x} Bᵉrîyʿâh, ber-ee'-aw; appar. from the fem. of 7451 with prep. pref.; *in trouble; Beriah*, the name of four Isr.:—Beriah {11x}. See: BDB—140b.

1284. בְּרִיעִי {1x} Bᵉrîyʿîy, ber-ee-ee'; patron. from 1283; a *Beriite* (collect.) or desc. of Beriah:—Beerites {1x}. See: BDB—140b.

1285. בְּרִית {284x} bᵉrîyth, ber-eeth'; from 1262 (in the sense of *cutting* [like 1254]); a·*compact* (because made by passing between *pieces* of flesh):—covenant {264x}, league {17x}, confederacy {1x}, confederate {1x}, confederate + 1167 {1x}.

Beriyth means "covenant; league; confederacy." **(1)** The first occurrence of the word is in Gen 6:18: "But with thee [Noah] will I establish my covenant." **(2)** It is translated 15 times as "league": "Now therefore make ye a league with us" (Josh 9:6). **(2a)** These are all cases of political agreement within Israel (2 Sa 3:12–13, 21; 5:3) or **(2b)** between nations (1 Kin 15:19). **(2c)** In Judg 2:2: "And ye shall make no league with the inhabitants of this land." **(2d)** The command had been also given in Ex 23:32; 34:12–16; and Deut 7:2–6 ["covenant"]. **(3)** The word is used of "agreements between men," as **(3a)** Abraham and Abimelech (Gen 21:32): "Thus they made a covenant at Beer-sheba." **(3b)** David and Jonathan made a "covenant" of mutual protection that would be binding on David's descendants forever (1 Sa 18:3; 20:8, 16–18, 42). **(3c)** In these cases, there was "mutual agreement confirmed by oath in the name of the Lord." **(3d)** Sometimes there were also material pledges (Gen 21:28–31).

(4) Ahab defeated the Syrians: "So he made a covenant with [Ben-hadad], and sent him away" (1 Kin 20:34). **(5)** The king of Babylon "took of the king's seed [Zedekiah], and made a covenant with him, and hath taken an oath of him" (Eze 17:13). In such "covenants," the terms were imposed by the superior military power; they were not mutual agreements. **(6)** In Israel, the kingship was based on "covenant": "David made a league with them [the elders of Israel] in Hebron before the LORD" (2 Sa 5:3). **(6a)** The "covenant" was based on their knowledge that God had appointed him (2 Sa 5:2); **(6b)** thus they became David's subjects (cf. 2 Kin 11:4, 17).

(7) The great majority of occurrences of *beriyth* are of God's "covenants" with men, as in Gen 6:18 above. **(7a)** The verbs used are important: "I will establish my covenant" (Gen 6:18)—literally, "cause to stand" or "confirm." **(7b)** "I will make my covenant" (Gen 17:2). **(7c)** "He declared to you his covenant" (Deut 4:13). **(7d)** "My covenant which I commanded them . . ." (Josh 7:11). **(7e)** "I have remembered my covenant. Wherefore . . . I will bring you out from under the burdens of the Egyptians" (Ex 6:5–6). **(7f)** God will not reject Israel for their disobedience so as "to destroy them utterly, and to break my covenant with them" (Lev 26:44). **(7g)** "He will not . . . forget the covenant . . . which he sware unto them" (Deut 4:31). **(7h)** The most common verb is "to cut [*karat*] a covenant," which is always translated as in Gen 15:18: "The LORD made a covenant with Abram." This use apparently comes from the ceremony described in Gen 15:9–17 (cf. Jer 34:18), in which God appeared as "a smoking furnace, and a burning lamp [flaming torch] that passed between those pieces" (Gen 15:17). **(7i)** These verbs make it plain that God takes the sole initiative in covenant-making and fulfillment.

(8) The words of the "covenant" were written in a book (Ex 24:4, 7; Deut 31:24–26) and on stone tablets (Ex 34:28). **(9)** Men "enter into" (Deut 29:12) or "join" (Jer 50:5) God's "covenant." **(10)** They are to obey (Gen 12:4) and "observe carefully" all the commandments of the "covenant" (Deut 4:6). **(11)** But above all, the "covenant" calls Israel to "love the LORD thy God with all thine heart, and with all thy soul, and with all thy might" (Deut 6:5). **(12)** God's "covenant" is a relationship of love and loyalty between the Lord and His chosen people: **(12a)** "If ye will obey my voice indeed, and keep my covenant, then ye shall be a peculiar treasure unto me above all people . . . and ye shall be unto me a kingdom of priests, and a holy nation" (Ex 19:5–6). **(12b)** "All the commandments . . . shall ye observe to do, that ye may live, and multiply, and go in and possess the land which the LORD sware unto your

fathers" (Deut 8:1). **(13)** In the "covenant," man's response contributes to covenant fulfillment; yet man's action is not causative. God's grace always goes before and produces man's response.

(14) Occasionally, Israel "made a covenant before the LORD, to walk after the LORD, and to keep his commandments . . . , to perform the words of this covenant that were written in this book" (2 Kin 23:3). **(14a)** This is like their original promise: "All that the LORD hath spoken we will do" (Ex 19:8; 24:7). **(14b)** Israel did not propose terms or a basis of union with God. They responded to God's "covenant." **(15)** The use of "Old Testament" and "New Testament" as the names for the two sections of the Bible indicates that God's "covenant" is central to the entire book. **(16)** The Bible relates God's "covenant" purpose, that man be joined to Him in loving service and know eternal fellowship with Him through the redemption that is in Jesus Christ. Syn: "Covenant" is parallel or equivalent to the Hebrew words **(A)** *dabar* (1697 - "word"), **(B)** *hoq* (2706 - "statute"), **(C)** *piqqud* (6490 - "precepts"—Ps 119:94), **(D)** *'edah* (5715 - "testimony"—Ps 25:10), **(E)** *torah* (8451 - "law"—Ps 78:10), and **(F)** *checed* (2617 - "lovingkindness"—Ps 17:7). These words emphasize the authority and grace of God in making and keeping the "covenant," and the specific responsibility of man under the covenant. See: TWOT—282a; BDB—136b, 138c.

1286. בְּרִית {1x} **B°rîyth,** *ber-eeth';* the same as 1285; *Berith,* a Shechemitish deity:—Berith {1x}. See: BDB—42c, 136c.

1287. בֹּרִית {1x} **bôrîyth,** *bo-reeth';* fem. of 1253; vegetable *alkali:*—soap {1x}. See: TWOT—288e; BDB—138c, 141b.

1288. בָּרַךְ {330x} **bârak,** *baw-rak';* a prim. root; to *kneel;* by impl. to *bless* God (as an act of adoration), and (vice-versa) man (as a benefit); also (by euphem.) to *curse* (God or the king, as treason):—bless {302x}, salute {5x}, curse {4x}, blaspheme {2x}, blessing {2x}, praised {2x}, kneel down {2x}, congratulate {1x}, kneel {1x}, make to kneel {1x}, misc. {8x}.

Barak means "to kneel, bless, be blessed, curse." **(1)** *Barak* occurs first in Gen 1:22: "And God blessed them, saying, Be fruitful and multiply, . . ." **(2)** God's first word to man is introduced in the same way: "And God blessed them, and God said unto them, Be fruitful, and multiply" (v. 28). Thus the whole creation is shown to depend upon God for its continued existence and function (cf. Ps 104:27–30). **(3)** *Barak* is used again of man in Gen 5:2, at the beginning of the history of believing men,

and again after the Flood in Gen 9:1: "And God blessed Noah and his sons."

(4) The central element of God's covenant with Abram is: "I will bless thee . . . and thou shalt be a blessing: And I will bless them that bless thee . . . and in thee shall all families of the earth be blessed" (Gen 12:2–3). **(4a)** This "blessing" on the nations is repeated in Gen 18:18; 22:18; and 28:14 (cf. Gen 26:4; Jer 4:2). **(4b)** In all of these instances, God's blessing goes out to the nations through Abraham or his seed. **(4c)** The covenant promise called the nations to seek the "blessing" (cf. Is 2:2–4), but made it plain that the initiative in blessing rests with God, and that Abraham and his seed were the instruments of it. **(5)** God, either directly or through His representatives, is the subject of this verb over 100 times. **(6)** The Levitical benediction is based on this order: "On this wise ye shall bless the children of Israel . . . the Lord bless thee . . . and they shall put my name upon the children of Israel; and I will bless them" (Num 6:23–27).

(7) The passive form of *barak* is used in pronouncing God's "blessing on men," as through Melchizedek: "Blessed be Abram of the most high God" (Gen 14:19). **(8)** "Blessed be the LORD God of Shem" (Gen 9:26) is an expression of praise. **(9)** "Blessed be the most high God, which hath delivered thine enemies into thy hand" (Gen 14:20) is mingled praise and thanksgiving. **(10)** A common form of greeting was, "Blessed be thou of the LORD" (1 Sa 15:13; cf. Ruth 2:4); "Saul went out to meet [Samuel], that he might salute him" (1 Sa 13:10). **(11)** The simple form of the verb is used in 2 Chr 6:13: "He . . . kneeled down." **(12)** Six times the verb is used to denote profanity, as in Job 1:5: "It may be that my sons have sinned, and cursed God in their hearts." See: TWOT—285; BDB—138c, 1085b.

1289. בְּרַךְ {5x} **b°rak** (Aram.), *ber-ak';* corresp. to 1288:—bless {4x}, kneel {1x}. See: TWOT—2641; BDB—1085b.

1290. בֶּרֶךְ {25x} **berek,** *beh'-rek;* from 1288; a *knee:*—knee {1x}. See: TWOT—285a; BDB—139c.

1291. בְּרַךְ {1x} **berek** (Aram.), *beh'-rek;* corresp. to 1290:—knee {1x}. See: TWOT—2641a; BDB—1085c.

1292. בַּרַכְאֵל {2x} **Bârak°êl,** *baw-rak-ale';* from 1288 and 410, *God has blessed; Barakel,* the father of one of Job's friends:—Barachel {1x}. See: BDB—140a.

1293. בְּרָכָה {69x} **b°râkâh,** *ber-aw-kaw';* from 1288; *benediction;* by impl. *prosperity:*—blessing {61x}, blessed {3x}, present {3x}, liberal {1x}, pools {1x}.

Berakah means "blessing." **(1)** It is used in conjunction with the verb *barak* ("to bless") 71 times in the Old Testament. **(2)** The word appears most frequently in Genesis and Deuteronomy. **(3)** The first occurrence is God's blessing of Abram: "I will make of thee a great nation, and I will bless thee, and make thy name great; and thou shalt be a blessing [*berakah*]" (Gen 12:2). **(4)** When expressed by men, a "blessing" was a wish or prayer for a blessing that is to come in the future: "And [God] give thee the blessing of Abraham, to thee, and to thy seed with thee; that thou mayest inherit the land wherein thou art a stranger, which God gave unto Abraham" (Gen 28:4). **(4a)** This refers to a "blessing" that the patriarchs customarily extended upon their children before they died. **(4b)** Jacob's "blessings" on the tribes (Gen 49) and **(4c)** Moses' "blessing" (Deut 33:1ff.) are other familiar examples of this.

(5) Blessing was the opposite of a cursing (*qelalah*): "My father peradventure will feel me, and I shall seem to him as a deceiver; and I shall bring a curse upon me, and not a blessing" (Gen 27:12). **(6)** The blessing might also be presented more concretely in the form of a gift. For example, "Take, I pray thee, my blessing that is brought to thee; because God hath dealt graciously with me, and because I have enough. And he urged him, and he took it" (Gen 33:11). **(7)** When a "blessing" was directed to God, it was a word of praise and thanksgiving, as in: "Stand up and bless the LORD your God for ever and ever: and blessed be thy glorious name, which is exalted above all blessing and praise" (Neh 9:5). **(8)** The LORD's "blessing" rests on those who are faithful to Him: "A blessing, if ye obey the commandments of the LORD your God, which I command you this day" (Deut 11:27). His blessing brings **(8a)** righteousness (Ps 24:5), **(8b)** life (Ps. 133:3), **(8c)** prosperity (2 Sa 7:29), and **(8d)** salvation (Ps 3:8).

(9) The "blessing" is portrayed as a rain or dew: "I will make them and the places round about my hill a blessing; and I will cause the shower to come down in his season; there shall be showers of blessing" (Eze 34:26; cf. Ps 84:6). **(10)** In the fellowship of the saints, the LORD commands His "blessing": "[It is] as the dew of Hermon, and as the dew that descended upon the mountains of Zion: for there the Lord commanded the blessing, even life for evermore" (Ps 133:3). **(11)** In a few cases, the LORD made people to be a "blessing" to others. Abraham is a blessing to the nations (Gen 12:2). **(12)** His descendants are expected to become a blessing to the nations (Is 19:24; Zec 8:13). See: TWOT—285b; BDB—139c.

1294. בְּרָכָה {3x} **Bᵉrâkâh**, *ber-aw-kaw';* the same as 1293; *Berakah,* the name of an Isr., and also of a valley in Pal.:—Berachah {3x}. See: BDB—139d.

1295. בְּרֵכָה {17x} **bᵉrêkâh**, *ber-ay-kaw';* from 1288; a *reservoir* (at which camels *kneel* as a resting-place):—fishpools {1x}, pool {16x}. See: TWOT—285c; BDB—140a.

1296. בֶּרֶכְיָה {11x} **Berekyâh**, *beh-rek-yaw';* or

בֶּרֶכְיָהוּ **Berekyâhûw**, *beh-rek-yaw'-hoo;* from 1290 and 3050; *knee* (i.e. *blessing*) of *Jah; Berekjah,* the name of six Isr.:—Berachiah {1x}, Berechiah {10x}. See: BDB—140a.

1297. בְּרַם {5x} **bᵉram** (Aram.), *ber-am';* perh. from 7313 with prep. pref.; prop. *highly,* i.e. *surely;* but used adversatively, *however:*—but {2x}, yet {2x}, nevertheless {1x}. See: TWOT—2642; BDB—1085c.

1298. בֶּרַע {1x} **Beraᶜ**, *beh'-rah;* of uncert. der.; *Bera,* a Sodomitish king:—Bera {1x}. See: BDB—140b.

1299. בָּרַק {1x} **bâraq**, *baw-rak';* a prim. root; to *lighten* (lightning):—cast forth {1x}. See: TWOT—287; BDB—140b.

1300. בָּרָק {21x} **bârâq**, *baw-rawk';* from 1299; *lightning;* by anal. a *gleam;* concr. a *flashing* sword:—lightning {14x}, glittering {4x}, bright {1x}, glitter {1x}, glittering sword {1x}. See: TWOT—287a; BDB—140c.

1301. בָּרָק {13x} **Bârâq**, *baw-rawk';* the same as 1300; *Barak,* an Isr.:—Barak {13x}. See: BDB—140c.

1302. בַּרְקוֹס {2x} **Barqôwç**, *bar-kose';* of uncert. der.; *Barkos,* one of the Nethimim:—Barkos {2x}. See: BDB—140d.

1303. בַּרְקָן {2x} **barqân**, *bar-kwan';* from 1300; a *thorn* (perh. as burning *brightly*):—briers {2x}. See: TWOT—287e; BDB—140d.

1304. בָּרֶקֶת {3x} **bârᵉqath**, *baw-reh'-keth;* or

בָּרְכַת **bârᵉkath**, *baw-rek-ath';* from 1300; a *gem* (as *flashing*), perh. the *emerald:*—carbuncle {3x}. See: TWOT—287d; BDB—140c, 140d.

1305. בָּרַר {18x} **bârar**, *baw-rar';* a prim. root; to *clarify* (i.e. *brighten*), *examine, select:*—pure {5x}, choice {2x}, chosen {2x}, clean {2x}, clearly {1x}, manifest {1x}, bright {1x}, purge out {1x}, polished {1x}, purge {1x}, purified {1x}. Syn.: 2134, 2141. See: TWOT—288; BDB—140d, 1085c.

1306. בִּרְשַׁע {1x} **Birshaᶜ**, *beer-shah';* prob. from 7562 with a prep. pref.; *with*

wickedness; Birsha, a king of Gomorrah:—*Birsha* {1x}. See: BDB—141d.

1307. בֵּרֹתִי {1x} **Bêrôthîy**, *bay-ro-thee';* patrial from 1268; a *Berothite,* or inhab. of Berothai:—Berothite {1x}. See: BDB—92d, 141d.

1308. בְּשׂוֹר {3x} **Bᵉsôwr**, *bes-ore';* from 1319; *cheerful; Besor,* a stream of Pal.:—Besor {1x}. See: BDB—143a.

1309. בְּשׂוֹרָה {6x} **bᵉsôwrâh**, *bes-o-raw';* or (short.)

בְּשֹׂרָה **bᵉsôrâh**, *bes-o-raw';* fem. from 1319; glad *tidings;* by impl. *reward for good news:*—tidings {6x}. See: TWOT—291b; BDB—142d.

1310. בָּשַׁל {28x} **bâshal**, *baw-shal';* a prim. root; prop. to *boil* up; hence, to be *done* in cooking; fig. to *ripen:*—seethe {10x}, boil {6x}, sod {6x}, bake {2x}, ripe {2x}, roast {2x}. Syn.: 7570. See: TWOT—292; BDB—143a.

1311. בָּשֵׁל {2x} **bâshêl**, *baw-shale';* from 1310; *boiled:*—sodden {1x}, at all {1x} (inf. for emphasis). See: TWOT—292a; BDB—143b.

1312. בִּשְׁלָם {1x} **Bishlâm**, *bish-lawm';* of for. der.; *Bishlam,* a Pers.:—Bishlam {1x}. See: BDB—143b.

1313. בָּשָׂם {1x} **bâsâm**, *baw-sawm';* from an unused root mean. to be *fragrant;* [comp. 5561] the *balsam* plant:—spice {1x}. See: TWOT—290a; BDB—141d.

1314. בֶּשֶׂם {29x} **besem**, *beh'-sem;* or

בֹּשֶׂם **bôsem**, *bo'-sem;* from the same as 1313; *fragrance;* by impl. *spicery;* also the *balsam* plant:—spice {24x}, sweet odours {2x}, sweet {2x}, sweet smell {1x}. TWOT—290a; BDB—141d.

1315. בָּשְׂמַת {7x} **Bosmath**, *bos-math';* fem. of 1314 (the second form); *fragrance; Bosmath,* the name of a wife of Esau, and of a daughter of Solomon:—Bashemath {6x}, Basmath {1x}. See: BDB—142a.

1316. בָּשָׁן {60x} **Bâshân**, *baw-shawn';* of uncert. der.; *Bashan* (often with the art.), a region E. of the Jordan:—*Bashan* {59x}, Bashanhavothjair + 2334 {1x}. See: BDB—143b.

1317. בָּשְׁנָה {1x} **boshnâh**, *bosh-naw';* fem. from 954; *shamefulness:*—shame {1x}. See: TWOT—222b; BDB—102a, 143c.

1318. בָּשַׂס {1x} **bâshaç**, *baw-shas';* a prim. root; to *trample* down:—treading {1x}. See: TWOT—294; BDB—143c.

1319. בָּשַׂר **bâsar**, *baw-sar';* a prim. root; prop. to be *fresh,* i.e. *full (rosy,* (fig.) *cheerful);* to *announce* (glad news):—tidings {16x}, show forth {3x}, publish {3x}, messenger {1x}, preached {1x}. Syn.: 5046. See: TWOT—291; BDB—142a.

1320. בָּשָׂר {269x} **bâsâr**, *baw-sawr';* from 1319; *flesh* (from its *freshness*); by extens. *body, person;* also (by euphem.) the *pudenda* of a man:—flesh {256x}, body {2x}, fatfleshed + 1277 {2x}, leanfleshed + 1851 {2x}, kin {2x}, leanfleshed + 7534 {1x}, mankind + 376 {1x}, myself {1x}, nakedness {1x}, skin {1x}.

Basar means "flesh; meat." **(1)** The word means the "meaty part plus the skin" of men: "And the LORD God caused a deep sleep to fall upon Adam, and he slept: and he took one of his ribs, and closed up the flesh instead thereof" (Gen 2:21—the first occurrence). **(2)** This word can also be applied to the "meaty part" of animals (Deut 14:8). **(2a)** Gen 41:2 speaks of seven cows, sleek and "fat of flesh." **(2b)** In Num 11:33, *basar* means the meat or "flesh" of the quail that Israel was still chewing. Thus the word means "flesh," whether living or dead. **(3)** *Basar* often means the "edible part" of animals. **(3a)** Eli's sons did not know God's law concerning the priests' portion, so "when any man offered sacrifice, the priest's [Eli's] servant came, while the flesh was [boiling], with a [three-pronged fork] in his hand" (1 Sa 2:13). **(3b)** However, they insisted that "before they burnt the fat . . . , Give flesh to roast for the priest; for he will not have [boiled] flesh of thee, but raw" (literally, "living"—1 Sa 2:15). **(3c)** *Basar,* then, represents edible animal "flesh" or "meat," whether cooked (Dan 10:3) or uncooked. **(3d)** The word sometimes refers to "meat" that one is forbidden to eat (cf. Ex 21:28).

(4) This word may represent a part of the body. **(4a)** At some points, the body is viewed as consisting of two components, "flesh" and bones: "This is now bone of my bones, and flesh of my flesh: she shall be called Woman, because she was taken out of Man" (Gen 2:23). **(4b)** That part of the "fleshly" element known as the foreskin was to be removed by circumcision (Gen 17:11). **(4c)** In other passages, the elements of the body are the "flesh," the skin, and the bones (Lam 3:4). **(4d)** Num. 19:5 mentions the "flesh," hide, blood, and refuse of a heifer. **(4e)** In Job 10:11, we read: "Thou hast clothed me with skin and flesh, and hast [knit] me with bones and sinews." **(5)** Flesh sometimes means "blood relative": "And Laban said to him [Jacob], Surely thou art my bone and my flesh" (Gen 29:14). **(5a)** The phrase "your flesh" or "our flesh" standing alone may bear the same meaning: "Come, and let us sell him to the Ish-

maelites, and let not our hand be upon him; for he is our brother and our flesh" (Gen 37:27). **(5b)** The phrase *she'er basar* is rendered "near of kin" (Lev 18:6).

(6) About 50 times, "flesh" represents the "physical aspect" of man or animals as contrasted with the spirit, soul, or heart (the nonphysical aspect). **(6a)** In the case of men, this usage appears in Num 16:22: "O God, the God of the spirits of all flesh, shall one man sin, and wilt thou be wroth with all the congregation?" **(6b)** In such passages, then, *basar* emphasizes the "visible and structural part" of man or animal. **(7)** In a few passages, the word appears to mean "skin," or the part of the body that is seen: "By reason of the voice of my groaning my bones cleave to my skin" (Ps 102:5; 119:120). **(8)** In passages such as Lev. 13:2, the ideas "flesh" and "skin" are clearly distinguished. **(9)** The term "all flesh" has several meanings. **(9a)** It means "all mankind" in Deut 5:26: "For who is there of all flesh, that hath heard the voice of the living God?" **(9b)** In another place, this phrase refers to "all living creatures within the cosmos," or all men and animals (Gen 6:17). See: TWOT—291a; BDB—142b, 925b, 1085c.

1321. בְּשַׂר {3x} **bᵉsar** (Aram.), *bes-ar';* corresp. to 1320:—flesh {3x}. See: TWOT—2643; BDB—1085c.

בְּשֹׂרָה **bᵉsôrâh.** See 1309.

1322. בֹּשֶׁת {30x} **bôsheth,** *bo'-sheth;* from 954; *shame* (the feeling and the condition, as well as its cause); by impl. (spec.) an *idol:* —shame {20x}, confusion {7x}, ashamed {1x}, greatly {1x}, shameful thing {1x}.

Bosheth means "shame; shameful thing." **(1)** The 30 appearances of this noun are mostly in poetic materials—only 5 appearances are in historical literature. **(2)** This word means a "shameful thing" as a substitute for the name Baal: "For shame hath devoured the labor of our fathers from our youth" (Jer 3:24; cf. Jer 11:13; Hos 9:10). **(3)** This substitution also occurs in proper names: *Ish-bosheth* (2 Sa 2:8), the "man of shame," was originally Esh-baal (cf. 1 Chr 8:33), the "man of Baal." **(4)** This word represents both "shame and worthlessness": "Thou son of the perverse rebellious woman, do not I know that thou hast chosen the son of Jesse . . . unto the confusion of thy mother's nakedness" (1 Sa 20:30). **(5)** The "shame of one's face" (2 Chr 32:21) may well mean being red-faced or embarrassed. See: TWOT—222b; BDB—102a, 143c, 574c.

1323. בַּת **bath,** *bath;* from 1129 (as fem. of 1121); a *daughter* (used in the same wide sense as other terms of relationship, lit.

and fig.):—daughter {526x}, town {32x}, village {1x}2, owl + 3284 {8x}, first {3x}, apple {1x}, branches {1x}, children {1x}, company {1x}, daughter + 8676 {1x}, eye {1x}, old {1x}. For a discussion, see 1129. See: TWOT—254b; BDB—123a, 143c.

1324. בַּת {13x} **bath,** *bath;* prob. from the same as 1327; a *bath* or Heb. measure (as a means of *division*) of liquids:—bath {13x}. See: TWOT—298a; BDB—143d, 144c, 1085d.

1325. בַּת {2x} **bath** (Aram.), *bath;* corresp. to 1324:—bath {2x}. See: TWOT—2644; BDB—1085d.

1326. בָּתָה {1x} **bâthâh,** *baw-thaw';* prob. an orth. var. for 1327; *desolation:*—waste {1x}. See: TWOT—298c; BDB—144d.

1327. בַּתָּה {1x} **battâh,** *bat-taw';* fem. from an unused root (mean. to *break* in pieces); *desolation:*—desolate {1x}. See: TWOT—298b; BDB—144c.

1328. בְּתוּאֵל {10x} **Bᵉthûw'êl,** *beth-oo-ale';* appar. from the same as 1326 and 410; *destroyed of God; Bethuel,* the name of a nephew of Abraham, and of a place in Pal.:—Bethuel {1x}. Syn.: comp. 1329. See: BDB—143d.

1329. בְּתוּל {1x} **Bᵉthûwl,** *beth-ool';* for 1328; *Bethul* (i.e. *Bethuel*), a place in Pal.:—Bethuel {1x}. See: BDB—143d.

1330. בְּתוּלָה {50x} **bᵉthûwlâh,** *beth-oo-law';* fem. pass. part. of an unused root mean. to *separate;* a *virgin* (from her *privacy*); sometimes (by continuation) a *bride;* also (fig.) a *city* or *state:*—virgin {38x}, maid {7x}, maiden {5x}.

Bethuwlah (1330) means "maiden, virgin." **(1)** This word can mean "virgin," as is clear in Deut 22:17, where if a man has charged that "I found not thy daughter a maid," the father is to say, "And yet these are the tokens of my daughter's virginity [betulim]. The text continues: "And they shall spread the cloth before the elders of the city." The husband was to be chastised and fined (which was given to the girl's father), "because he hath brought up an evil name upon a virgin of Israel" (Deut 22:19). If she was found not to be a "virgin," she was to be stoned to death "because she hath wrought folly in Israel, to play the whore in her father's house" (Deut 22:21). **(2)** In several passages this word merely means a grown-up girl or a "maiden"; it identifies her age and marital status. The prophets who denounce Israel for playing the harlot also called her the *bethuwlah* of Yahweh, or the *bethuwlah* (daughter) of Israel (Jer 31:4, 21). **(3)** The other nations are also called *betuloth:* Is 23:12—

Zidon; Is 47:1—Babylon; Jer 46:11—Egypt.
(3a) These nations are hardly being commended for their purity! **(3b)** In Ugaritic literature the word is used frequently of the goddess Anat, the sister of Baal and hardly a virgin. **(3c)** What was true of her and figuratively of these nations (including Israel) was that she was a vigorous young woman at the height of her powers and not married. **(3d)** Thus *bethuwlah* is often used in parallelism with the Hebrew *bachur,* which signifies a young man, regardless of his virginity, who is at the height of his powers (Deut 32:25). **(3e)** In such contexts virility and not virginity is in view. **(3f)** Because of this ambiguity Moses described Rebekah as a young girl (5291 - *na'arah*) who was "very fair to look upon, a virgin [*betulah*], neither had any man known her" (Gen 24:16—the first occurrence of the word). **(4)** It is safe to say that all virgins are maidens, but not all maidens are virgins. Syn.: 5659. See: TWOT—295a; BDB—143d.

1331. בְּתוּלִים {10x} **bᵉthûwlîym,** *beth-oo-leem';* masc. plur. of the same as 1330; (collect. and abstr.) *virginity;* by impl. and concr. the *tokens* of it:—virginity {8x}, maid {2x}. See: TWOT—295b; BDB—144a.

1332. בִּתְיָה {1x} **Bithyâh,** *bith-yaw';* from 1323 and 3050; *daughter* (i.e. worshipper) *of Jah; Bithjah,* an Eg. woman:—Bithiah {1x}. See: BDB—124a, 143d.

1333. בָּתַק {1x} **bâthaq,** *baw-thak';* a prim. root; to *cut* in pieces:—thrust through {1x}. See: TWOT—296; BDB—144a.

1334. בָּתַר {2x} **bâthar,** *baw-thar';* a prim. root, to *chop* up:—divide {2x}. See: TWOT—297; BDB—144a.

1335. בֶּתֶר {3x} **bether,** *beh'-ther;* from 1334; a *section:*—part {2x}, piece {1x}. See: TWOT—297a; BDB—144a.

1336. בֶּתֶר {1x} **Bether,** *beh'-ther;* the same as 1335; *Bether,* a (craggy) place in Pal.:—*Bether* {1x}. See: BDB—144b.

1337. בַּת רַבִּים {1x} **Bath Rabbîym,** *bath rab-beem';* from 1323 and a masc. plur. from 7227; the *daughter* (i.e. *city*) *of Rabbah:*—Bath-rabbim {1x}. See: BDB—123d.

1338. בִּתְרוֹן {1x} **Bithrôwn,** *bith-rone';* from 1334; (with the art.) the *craggy* spot; *Bithron,* a place E. of the Jordan:—Bithron {1x}. See: BDB—144c.

1339. בַּת־שֶׁבַע {11x} **Bath-Shebaʿ,** *bath-sheh'-bah;* from 1323 and 7651 (in the sense of 7650); *daughter of an oath; Bath-Sheba,* the mother of Solomon:—Bath-sheba {11x}. See: BDB—124a.

1340. בַּת־שׁוּעַ {2x} **Bath-Shûwaʿ,** *bath-shoo'-ah;* from 1323 and 7771; *daughter of wealth; Bath-shuä,* the same as 1339:—Bath-shua {2x}. See: BDB—124a.

ג

1341. גֵּא {1x} **gêʾ,** *gay';* for 1343; *haughty:*—proud {1x}. See: TWOT—299a; BDB—144b.

1342. גָּאָה {7x} **gâʾâh,** *gaw-aw';* a prim. root; to *mount* up; hence, in gen. to *rise,* (fig.) be *majestic:*—triumph {2x}, gloriously {2x}, risen {1x}, grow up {1x}, increase {1x}.

Ga'ah means "to be proud, be exalted." The word appears in Ex 15:1 in the sense of "to be exalted": "I will sing to the LORD, for he hath triumphed gloriously: the horse and his rider hath he thrown into the sea." See: TWOT—299; BDB—144b, 1085d.

1343. גֵּאֶה {9x} **gêʾeh,** *gay-eh';* from 1342; *lofty;* fig. *arrogant:*—proud {9x}.

Ge'eh also means "proud" in its 9 occurrences, once in Is 2:12: "For the day of the LORD of hosts shall be upon every one that is proud and lofty." See: TWOT—299b; BDB—144b.

1344. גֵּאָה {1x} **gêʾâh,** *gay-aw';* fem. from 1342; *arrogance:*—pride {1x}. *Ge'ah* occurs once to mean "pride" (Prov 8:13). See: TWOT—299c; BDB—144d, 1085d.

1345. גְּאוּאֵל {1x} **Gᵉʾûwʾêl,** *gheh-oo-ale';* from 1342 and 410; *majesty of God; Geel,* an Isr.:—Geuel {1x}. See: BDB—145b.

1346. גַּאֲוָה {19x} **gaʾǎvâh,** *gah-av-aw';* from 1342; *arrogance* or *majesty;* by impl. (concr.) *ornament:*—pride {9x}, excellency {3x}, haughtiness {2x}, arrogancy {1x}, highness {1x}, proud {1x}, proudly {1x}, swelling {1x}.

The noun *ga'avah* which is found 19 times, also means "pride": "And all the people shall know, even Ephraim and the inhabitant of Samaria, that say in the pride and stoutness of heart . . ." (Is 9:9). See: TWOT—299d; BDB—144d.

1347. גָּאוֹן {49x} **gâʾôwn,** *gaw-ohn';* from 1342; the same as 1346:—pride {20x}, excellency {10x}, majesty {7x}, pomp {5x}, swelling {3x}, arrogancy {2x}, excellent {1x}, proud {1x}.

Ga'own means "pride." **(1)** This noun is a poetic word, which is found only in poetic books, the prophets (12 times in Isaiah), Moses' song (Ex 15:7), and Lev (26:19). **(2)** In a positive sense *ga'own,* like the verb, signifies "excellence" or "majesty." **(2a)** God's "majesty" was expressed in Israel's deliverance through the

Red Sea (Ex 15:7). **(2b)** Israel as the redeemed people, then, is considered to be an expression of God's "majesty": "He shall choose our inheritance for us, the excellency of Jacob whom he loved" (Ps 47:4). **(3)** The meaning of ga'own is here close to that of kabod (3519), "glory." **(4)** Related to "majesty" is the word ga'own attributed to nature as something mighty, luxuriant, rich, and thick. The poets use the word to refer to the proud waves (Job 38:11) or the thick shrubbery by the Jordan; cf. "If thou hast run with the footmen, and they have wearied thee, then how canst thou contend with horses? And if in the land of peace, wherein thou trustedst, they wearied thee, then how wilt thou do in the swelling [literally, "majesty"] of Jordan?" (Jer 12:5; cf. 49:19; 50:44).

(5) The majority of the uses of ga'own are negative in that they connote human "pride" as an antonym for humility (Prov 16:18). **(5a)** Proverbs puts ga'own together with arrogance, evil behavior, and perverse speech. **(5b)** In her independence from the LORD, Israel as a majestic nation, having been set apart by a majestic God, had turned aside and claimed its excellence as a prerogative earned by herself. **(5c)** The new attitude of insolence was not tolerated by God: "The Lord God hath sworn by himself, saith the LORD the God of hosts, I abhor the excellency of Jacob, and hate his palaces: therefore will I deliver up the city with all that is therein" (Amos 6:8). See: TWOT—299e; BDB—144d.

1348. גֵּאוּת {8x} gê'ûwth, gay-ooth'; from 1342; the same as 1346:—pride {2x}, majesty {2x}, proudly {1x}, raging {1x}, lifting up {1x}, excellent things {1x}.

Ge'uwth appears 8 times and refers to "majesty": "Let favor be showed to the wicked, yet will he not learn righteousness: in the land of uprightness will he deal unjustly, and will not behold the majesty of the LORD" (Is 26:10). See: TWOT—299f; BDB—145a.

1349. גַּאֲיוֹן {1x} ga'ăyôwn, gah-ăh-yone'; from 1342: haughty:—proud {1x}. Ga'ay-own, which means "pride," appears once in biblical Hebrew (Ps 123:4). See: TWOT—299g; BDB—145b.

1350. גָּאַל {104x} gâ'al, gaw-al'; a prim. root, to redeem (according to the Oriental law of kinship), i.e. to be the next of kin (and as such to buy back a relative's property, marry his widow, etc.):—redeem {50x}, redeemer {18x}, kinsman {13x}, revenger {7x}, avenger {6x}, ransom {2x}, at all {2x}, deliver {1x}, kinsfolks {1x}, kinsman's part {1x}, purchase {1x}, stain {1x}, wise {1x}.

Ga'al means "to redeem, deliver, avenge, act as a kinsman." **(1)** The first occurrence of ga'al is in Gen 48:16: "The angel which redeemed me [Jacob] from all evil . . ." **(2)** Its basic use had to do with the deliverance of persons or property that had been sold for debt, as **(2a)** in Lev 25:25: "If thy brother be waxen poor, and hath sold away some of his possession, and if any of his kin come to redeem it, then shall he redeem that which his brother sold." **(2b)** If he prospers, the man himself may "redeem" it (Lev 25:26). **(2c)** A poor man may sell himself to a fellow Israelite (Lev 25:39) or to an alien living in Israel (Lev 25:47). **(3)** The responsibility "to redeem" belonged to the nearest relative—brother, uncle, uncle's son, or a blood relative from his family (Lev 25:25, 48–49). **(4)** The person who "redeemed" the one in financial difficulties was known as a **(4a)** kinsman in Ruth 2:20. **(4b)** In Deut 19:6 the redeemer is called the "avenger of blood" whose duty it was to execute the murderer of his relative. **(4b1)** The verb occurs in this sense 12 times and is translated "revenger" (Num 35:19, 21, 24, 27) or **(4b2)** "avenger" (Num 35:12).

(5) The Book of Ruth is a beautiful account of the kinsman-redeemer. **(5a)** His responsibility is summed up in Ruth 4:5: "What day thou buyest the field of the hand of Naomi, thou must buy it also of Ruth the Moabitess, the wife of the dead, to raise up the name of the dead upon his inheritance." **(5b)** Thus the kinsman-redeemer was responsible for preserving the integrity, life, property, and family name of his close relative or for executing justice upon his murderer. **(6)** The greater usage of this word group is of God who promised: "I am the LORD . . . I will redeem you with a stretched out arm and with great judgments" (Ex 6:6; cf. Ps 77:15). **(6a)** Israel confessed: "Thou in thy mercy hast led forth the people which thou hast redeemed" (Ex 15:13). **(6b)** "And they remembered that God was their rock, and the high God their redeemer" (Ps 78:35).

(7) The Book of Isaiah evidences the word "Redeemer" used of God 13 times, all in chapters 41–63, and ga'al is used 9 times of God, **(7a)** first in 43:1: "Fear not; for I have redeemed thee, I have called thee by thy name; thou art mine." **(7b)** Ga'al is used of deliverance from Egypt (51:10; 63:9) and **(7c)** from captivity in Babylon (48:20; 52:3, 9; 62:12). **(7d)** Israel's "Redeemer" is **(7d1)** "the Holy One of Israel" (41:14), **(7d2)** "the creator of Israel, your King" (43:14–15), **(7d3)** "the LORD of hosts" (44:6), and **(7d4)** "the mighty One of Jacob" (49:26). **(7e)** Those who share His salvation are "the redeemed" (35:9). **(8)** The Book of Psalms often places spiritual redemption in parallel with physical redemption. **(8a)** For example: "Draw nigh unto my soul, and redeem it: deliver me because of mine enemies" (Ps 69:18). **(8b)** "Bless

the Lord, O my soul, and forget not all his benefits: . . . who redeemeth thy life from destruction; who crowneth thee with loving-kindness and tender mercies" (Ps 103:2, 4). Syn.: 6299. See: TWOT—300; BDB—145b.

1351. גָּאַל {11x} gâ'al, *gaw-al'*; a prim. root, [rather ident. with 1350, through the idea of *freeing*, i.e. *repudiating*]; to *soil* or (fig.) *desecrate*:—pollute {7x}, defile {3x}, stain {1x}. See: TWOT—301; BDB—146a.

1352. גֹּאֵל {1x} gô'el, *go'-el*; from 1351; *profanation*:—defile {1x}. See: TWOT—301a; BDB—146a.

1353. גְּאֻלָּה {14x} gᵉullâh, *gheh-ool-law'*; fem. pass. part. of 1350; *redemption* (incl. the right and the object); by impl. *relationship*:—redeem {5x}, redemption {5x}, again {1x}, kindred {1x}, redeem + 4672 {1x}, right {1x}.

Ge'ullah means "(right of) redemption." **(1)** This word is used in regard to deliverance of persons or property that had been sold for debt. **(1a)** The law required that the "right of redemption" of land and of persons be protected (Lev 25:24, 48). **(1b)** The redemption price was determined by the number of years remaining until the release of debts in the year of jubilee (Lev 25:27–28). **(2)** The word *ge'ullah* also occurs in Jer 32:7: "Behold, Hanameel the son of Shallum thine uncle shall come unto thee, saying, Buy thee my field that is in Anathoth: for the right of redemption is thine to buy it." See: TWOT—300b; BDB—145d.

1354. גַּב {13x} gab, *gab*; from an unused root mean. to *hollow* or *curve*; the *back* (as *rounded* [comp. 1460 and 1479]; by anal. the *top* or *rim*, a *boss*, a *vault*, *arch* of eye, *bulwarks*, etc.:—eminent place {3x}, rings {2x}, bodies {2x}, back {1x}, backs {1x}, bosses {1x}, eyebrows {1x}, naves {1x}, higher place {1x}. See: TWOT—303a; BDB—146a, 146b, 1085d.

1355. גַּב {1x} gab (Aram.), *gab*; corresp. to 1354:—back {1x}. See: TWOT—2645; BDB—1085d.

1356. גֵּב {3x} gêb, *gabe*; from 1461; a *log* (as *cut* out); also *well* or *cistern* (as *dug*):—beam {1x}, ditch {1x}, pit {1x}. See: TWOT—323a,b; BDB—146b, 155d.

1357. גֵּב {1x} gêb, *gabe*; prob. from 1461 [comp. 1462]; a *locust* (from its *cutting*):—locust {1x}. See: TWOT—304a; BDB—146a, 146d.

1358. גֹּב {10x} gôb (Aram.), *gobe*; from a root corresp. to 1461; a *pit* (for wild animals) (as *cut* out):—den {10x}. See: BDB—1085d.

1359. גֹּב {2x} Gôb, *gobe*; or (fully)

גּוֹב Gôwb, *gobe*; from 1461; *pit*; *Gob*, a place in Pal.:—Gob {2x}. See: BDB—146b, 146c, 1085d.

1360. גֶּבֶא {3x} gebe', *geh'-beh*; from an unused root mean. prob. to *collect*; a *reservoir*; by anal. a *marsh*:—marish {1x}, pit {2x}. See: TWOT—302a; BDB—146b.

1361. גָּבַהּ {42x} gâbahh, *gaw-bah'*; a prim. root; to *soar*, i.e. *be lofty*; fig. to *be haughty*:—exalt {9x}, . . . up {9x}, haughty {5x}, higher {4x}, high {3x}, above {1x}, height {1x}, proud {1x}, upward {1x}. See: TWOT—305; BDB—146d.

1362. גָּבָהּ {4x} gâbâhh, *gaw-bawh'*; from 1361; *lofty* (lit. or fig.):—high {2x}, proud {2x}.

Gabahh, as an adjective, means "to be high, exalted, lofty." **(1)** It may mean "to be high, lofty." **(1a)** In this sense, it is used of trees (Eze 19:11), **(1b)** the heavens (Job 35:5), and **(1c)** a man (1 Sa 10:23). **(2)** It may mean "to be exalted" in dignity and honor (Job 36:7). **(3)** Or it may simply mean "to be lofty," **(3a)** used in the positive sense of "being encouraged" (2 Chr. 17:6) or in **(3b)** the negative sense of "being haughty or proud" (2 Chr 26:16). Syn.: 1343, 2086. See: TWOT—305a; BDB—147a.

1363. גֹּבַהּ {17x} gôbahh, *go'-bah*; from 1361; *elation*, *grandeur*, *arrogance*:—height {9x}, high {3x}, pride {2x}, excellency {1x}, haughty {1x}, loftiness {1x}.

Gobahh, as a noun, means "height; exaltation; grandeur; haughtiness; pride." **(1)** This noun, which occurs 17 times in biblical Hebrew, refers to the "height" **(1a)** of things (2 Chr 3:4) and **(1b)** of men (1 Sa 17:4). **(2)** It may also refer **(2a)** to "exaltation" or "grandeur" (Job 40:10), and **(2b)** to "haughtiness" or "pride" (2 Chr 32:26). Syn.: 4791, 6967. See: TWOT—305b; BDB—147b.

1364. גָּבֹהַּ {37x} gâbôahh, *gaw-bo'-ah*; or (fully)

גָּבוֹהַּ gâbôwahh, *gaw-bo'-ah*; from 1361; *elevated* (or *elated*), *powerful*, *arrogant*:—high {24x}, higher {5x}, lofty {2x}, exceeding {1x}, haughty {1x}, height {1x}, highest {1x}, proud {1x}, proudly {1x}.

Gabowahh as an adjective means "high; exalted." **(1)** This word means "high, lofty, tall in dimension": "And the waters [of the flood] prevailed exceedingly upon the earth; and all the high hills, that were under the whole heaven, were covered" (Gen 7:19—the first occurrence). **(2)** When used of a man, *gabowahh* means "tall": Saul was "higher than any of the people" (1 Sa 9:2; cf. 16:7). **(3)** In Dan 8:2, *gabowahh* describes the length of a ram's horns:

"And the two horns were high; but one was higher than the other, and the higher came up last." **(4)** The word means "high or exalted in station": **(4a)** "Thus saith the Lord God; Remove the diadem, and take off the crown: this shall not be the same: exalt him that is low, and abase him that is high" (Eze 21:26). **(4b)** In Eccl 5:8, this connotation of "one of high rank" may be expressed in the translation "higher/highest." **(5)** *Gabowahh* may be used of a psychological state, such as "haughtiness": "Talk no more so exceeding proudly [this double appearance of the word emphasizes it]; let not arrogancy come out of your mouth" (1 Sa 2:3). Syn.: 1116, 4791, 6967. See: TWOT—305a; BDB—147a.

1365. גַּבְהוּת {2x} **gabhûwth,** *gab-hooth';* from 1361; *pride:*—loftiness {1x}, lofty {1x}. See: TWOT—305c; BDB—147b.

1366. גְּבוּל {241x} **gᵉbûwl,** *gheb-ool';* or (short.)

גְּבֻל **gᵉbûl,** *gheb-ool';* from 1379; prop. a *cord* (as *twisted*), i.e. (by impl.) a *boundary;* by extens. the *territory* inclosed:— border {158x}, coast {69x}, bound {5x}, landmark {4x}, space {2x}, limit {1x}, quarters {1x}, non translated variant {1x}.

Gebul (1366) means "boundary; limit; territory; closed area." **(1)** *Gebul* literally means "boundary" or "border." **(1a)** This meaning appears in Num 20:23, where it signifies the border or boundary of the entire land of Edom. **(1b)** Sometimes such an imaginary line was marked by a physical barrier: "Arnon is the border of Moab, between Moab and the Amorites" (Num 21:13). **(1c)** Sometimes *gebul* denoted ethnic boundaries, such as the borders of the tribes of Israel: "And unto the Reubenites and unto the Gadites I gave from Gilead even unto the river Arnon half the valley, and the border even unto the river Jabbok, which is the border of the children of Ammon" (Deut 3:16). **(1d)** In Gen 23:17, *gebul* represents the "border" of an individual's field or piece of ground: "And the field of Ephron, which was in Machpelah, which was before Mamre, the field, and the cave which was therein, and all the trees that were in the field, that were in all the borders round about, were made sure." **(1e)** Fields were delineated by "boundary marks," whose removal was forbidden by law (Deut 19:14; cf. Deut 27:17).

(2) *Gebul* can suggest the farthest extremity of a thing: "Thou hast set a bound that they may not pass over; that they turn not again to cover the earth" (Ps 104:9). **(3)** This word sometimes represents the concrete object marking the border of a thing or area (cf. Eze 40:12). **(3a)** The "border" of Ezekiel's altar is signified by *gebul* (Eze 43:13) and **(3b)** Jerusalem's "surrounding wall" is represented by this word (Is 54:12). **(4)** *Gebul* represents the territory within certain boundaries: "And the border of the Canaanites was from Sidon, as thou comest to Gerar, unto Gaza; as thou goest, unto Sodom, and Gomorrah, and Admah, and Zeboim, even unto Lasha" (Gen 10:19). **(5)** In Ex 34:24, Num 21:22, 1 Chr 21:12, and Ps 105:31–32, *gebul* is paralleled to the "territory" surrounding and belonging to a city. See: TWOT—307a; BDB—147c, 147d.

1367. גְּבוּלָה {10x} **gᵉbûwlâh,** *gheb-oo-law';* or (short.)

גְּבֻלָה **gᵉbûlâh,** *gheb-oo-law';* fem. of 1366; a *boundary, region:*—coast {5x}, bounds {2x}, place {1x}, border {1x}, landmark {1x}.

Gebulah, the feminine form of *gebul,* occurs 9 times and means "boundary" in such passages as Is 10:13, and "territory" or "area" in other passages, such as Num 34:2. See: TWOT—307b; BDB—148b.

1368. גִּבּוֹר {158x} **gibbôwr,** *ghib-bore';* or (short.)

גִּבֹּר **gibbôr,** *ghib-bore';* intens. from the same as 1397; *powerful;* by impl. *warrior, tyrant:*—mighty {63x}, mighty man {68x}, strong {4x}, valiant {3x}, . . . ones {4x}, mighties {2x}, man {2x}, valiant men {2x}, strong man {1x}, upright man {1x}, champion {1x}, chief {1x}, excel {1x}, giant {1x}, men's {1x}, mightiest {1x}, strongest {1x}.

Gibbor means "strong/mighty man" **(1)** The first occurrence of *gibbor* is in Gen 6:4: "There were giants in the earth in those days; and also after that, when the sons of God came in unto the daughters of men, and they bare children to them, the same became mighty men which were of old, men of renown." **(2)** In the context of battle, the word is better understood to refer to the category of warriors. **(2a)** The *gibbor* is the proven warrior; especially is this true when *gibbor* is used in combination with *chayil* (2428 - "strength"). **(2b)** The KJV gives a literal translation, "mighty men [*gibbor*] of valor [*chayil*]." **(3)** David, who had proven himself as a warrior, **(3a)** attracted "mighty men" to his band while he was being pursued by Saul (2 Sa 23). **(3b)** When David was enthroned as king, these men became a part of the elite military corps.

(4) The phrase *gibbor chayil* may also refer to a man of a high social class, the landed man who had military responsibilities. Saul came from such a family (1 Sa 9:1); so also Jeroboam (1 Kin 11:28). **(5)** The king symbolized the strength of his kingdom. **(5a)** He had to lead his troops in battle, and as commander he was expected to be a "mighty man." **(5b)** Early in

David's life, he was recognized as a "mighty man" (1 Sa 18:7). **(5c)** The king is described as "mighty": "Gird thy sword upon thy thigh, O most Mighty, with thy glory and thy majesty" (Ps 45:3). **(6)** The messianic expectation included the hope that the Messiah would be "mighty": "For unto us a child is born, unto us a son is given: and the government shall be upon his shoulder; and his name shall be called Wonderful, Counselor, The mighty God, The everlasting Father, The Prince of Peace" (Is 9:6).

(7) Israel's God was a mighty God (Is 10:21). **(7a)** He had the power to deliver: "The Lord thy God in the midst of thee is mighty; he will save, he will rejoice over thee with joy; he will rest in his love, he will joy over thee with singing" (Zeph 3:17). **(7b)** Jeremiah's moving confession (32:17ff.) bears out the might of God in creation (v. 17) and in redemption (vv. 18ff.). **(7c)** The answer to the emphatic question, "Who is this King of glory?" in Ps 24 is: "The Lord strong and mighty, the Lord mighty in battle" (v. 8). **(8)** Gibbor may be translated by the adjective "strong" in the following contexts: **(8a)** a "strong" man (1 Sa 14:52), **(8b)** a "strong" lion (Prov 30:30), **(8c)** a mighty hunter (Gen 10:9), and **(8d)** the mighty ones (Gen 6:1–4). See: TWOT—310b; BDB—150a.

1369. גְּבוּרָה {61x} **geḇûwrâh**, *gheb-oo-raw';* fem. pass. part. from the same as 1368; *force* (lit. or fig.); by impl. *valor, victory:*—might {27x}, strength {17x}, power {9x}, mighty acts {4x}, mighty {2x}, force {1x}, mastery {1x}.

The primary meaning of *gebuwrah* is power or strength. **(1)** Certain animals are known for their strength, such as **(1a)** horses (Ps 147:10) and **(1b)** crocodiles (Job 41:4). **(2)** Man demonstrates might **(2a)** in heroic acts (Judg 8:21) and **(2b)** in war (Is 3:25). **(3)** David's powerful regime is a kingship of *gebuwrah* (1 Chr 29:30). **(4)** Both physical strength and wisdom were necessary for leadership, these two qualities are joined together **(4a)** in Wisdom (Prov 8:14), and **(4b)** in the Spirit-filled Micah (Mic 3:8). **(5)** The Messiah's special role will be a demonstration of might and counsel (Is 11:2). **(6)** God's might is lauded **(6a)** in psalms of praise (Ps 65:6), or **(6b)** in the context of prayer (Ps 54:1); and **(6c)** is a manifestation of His wisdom (Job 12:13). In the plural *gebuwrah* denotes God's mighty deeds of the past (Deut 3:24). See: TWOT—310c; BDB—150b.

1370. גְּבוּרָה {2x} **geḇûwrâh** (Aram.), *gheb-oo-raw';* corresp. to 1369; *power:*—might {2x}. See: TWOT—2647b; BDB—1086a.

1371. גְּבַח {1x} **gibbêach**, *ghib-bay'-akh;* from an unused root mean. to *be high* (in the forehead); *bald* in the forehead:—forehead bald {1x}. See: TWOT—306a; BDB—147c.

1372. גַּבַּחַת {4x} **gabbachath**, *gab-bakh'-ath;* from the same as 1371; *baldness* in the forehead; by anal. a *bare spot* on the right side of cloth:—bald forehead {3x}, X without {1x}. See: TWOT—306b; BDB—147c.

1373. גַּבַּי {1x} **Gabbay**, *gab-bah'-ee;* from the same as 1354; *collective; Gabbai,* an Isr.: Gabbai {1x}. See: BDB—146c, 147c.

1374. גֵּבִים {1x} **Gêbîym**, *gay-beem';* plur. of 1356; *cisterns; Gebim,* a place in Pal.:—Gebim {1x}. See: BDB—147c, 155d.

1375. גְּבִיעַ {14x} **geḇîyaᶜ**, *gheb-ee'-ah;* from an unused root (mean. to *be convex*); a *goblet;* by anal. the *calyx* of a flower:—bowl {8x}, cup {5x}, pot {1x}. See: TWOT—309b; BDB—149b.

1376. גְּבִיר {2x} **geḇîyr**, *gheb-eer';* from 1396; a *master:*—lord {2x}. See: TWOT—310d; BDB—150c.

1377. גְּבִירָה {6x} **geḇîyrâh**, *gheb-ee-raw';* fem. of 1376; a *mistress:*—queen {1x}. See: TWOT—310d; BDB—150c.

1378. גָּבִישׁ {1x} **gâḇîysh**, *gaw-beesh';* from an unused root (prob. mean. to *freeze*); *crystal* (from its resemblance to *ice*):—pearl {1x}. See: TWOT—311a; BDB—150d.

1379. גָּבַל {1x} **gâḇal**, *gaw-bal';* a prim. root; prop. to *twist* as a rope; only (as a denom. from 1366) to *bound* (as by a line):—border {2x}; set bounds {2x}, set {1x}. See: TWOT—307; BDB—148b.

1380. גְּבַל {1x} **Geḇal**, *gheb-al';* from 1379 (in the sense of a *chain* of hills); a *mountain; Gebal,* a place in Phœnicia:—Gebal {1x}. See: BDB—148b.

1381. גְּבָל {1x} **Geḇâl**, *gheb-awl';* the same as 1380; *Gebal,* a region in Idumæa:—Gebal {1x}. See: BDB—148c.

1382. גִּבְלִי {1x} **Giḇlîy**, *ghib-lee';* patrial from 1380; a *Gebalite,* or inhab. of Gebal:—Giblites, stone-squarer {1x}. See: BDB—148c.

1383. גַּבְלֻת {2x} **gablûth**, *gab-looth';* from 1379; a twisted *chain* or *lace:*—the ends {2x}. See: TWOT—307c; BDB—148b.

1384. גִּבֵּן {1x} **gibbên**, *gib-bane';* from an unused root mean. to *be arched* or *contracted; hunch-backed:*—crookbackt {1x}. See: TWOT—308a; BDB—148c.

1385. גִּבְנָה {1x} **geḇînah**, *gheb-ee-naw';* fem. from the same as 1384; *curdled*

Hebrew

milk:—cheese {1x}. See: TWOT—308b; BDB—148c.

1386. גַּבְנֹן {2x} **gabnôn**, *gab-nohn'*; from the same as 1384; a *hump* or *peak* of hills:—high {2x}. See: TWOT—308c; BDB—148d.

1387. גֶּבַע {19x} **Geba°**, *gheh'-bah;* from the same as 1375, a *hillock; Geba,* a place in Pal.:—*Geba* {13x}, Gibeah {4x}, Gaba {2x}. See: BDB—148d.

1388. גִּבְעָא {1x} **Gib°â'**, *ghib-aw';* by perm. for 1389; a *hill; Giba,* a place in Pal.:—Gibeah {1x}. See: BDB—148d.

1389. גִּבְעָה {69x} **gib°âh**, *ghib-aw';* fem. from the same as 1387; a *hillock:*—hill {69x}. See: TWOT—309a; BDB—148d.

1390. גִּבְעָה {44x} **Gib°âh**, *ghib-aw';* the same as 1389; *Gibah;* the name of three places in Pal.:—Gibeah {1x}. See: BDB—149b.

1391. גִּבְעוֹן {37x} **Gib°ôwn**, *ghib-ohn';* from the same as 1387; *hilly; Gibon,* a place in Pal.:—Gibeon {37x}. See: BDB—149c.

1392. גִּבְעֹל {1x} **gib°ôl**, *ghib-ole';* prol. from 1375; the *calyx* of a flower:—bolled {1x}. See: TWOT—309d; BDB—149c.

1393. גִּבְעֹנִי {8x} **Gib°ôniy**, *ghib-o-nee';* patrial from 1391; a *Gibonite,* or inhab. of Gibon:—Gibeonite {8x}. See: BDB—149c.

1394. גִּבְעַת {1x} **Gib°ath**, *ghib-ath';* from the same as 1375; *hilliness; Gibath:*—Gibeath {1x}. See: BDB—149b.

1395. גִּבְעָתִי {1x} **Gib°âthîy**, *ghib-aw-thee';* patrial from 1390; a *Gibathite,* or inhab. of Gibath:—Gibeathite {1x}. See: BDB—149b.

1396. גָּבַר **gâbar**, *gaw-bar';* a prim. root; to be *strong;* by impl. to *prevail, act insolently:*—prevail {14x}, strengthen {3x}, great {2x}, confirm {1x}, exceeded {1x}, mighty {1x}, put {1x}, stronger {1x}, valiant {1x}.

Gabar means "to be strong." The root meaning "to be strong" appears in all Semitic languages as a verb or a noun, but the verb occurs only 25 times in the Old Testament. Job 21:7 contains an occurrence of *gabar:* "Wherefore do the wicked live, become old, yea, are mighty in power?" Syn.: 2388, 8630. See: TWOT—310; BDB—149c, 1085d.

1397. גֶּבֶר {68x} **geber**, *gheh'-ber;* from 1396; prop. a *valiant* man or *warrior;* gen. a *person* simply:—man {64x}, mighty {2x}, man child {1x}, every one {1x}. *Geber* means "man," **(1)** probably referring to a man strong enough to fulfill an assigned responsibility: 1 Chr 23:3: "Now the Levites were numbered

from the age of thirty years and upward: and their number by their polls, man by man, was thirty and eight thousand." **(2)** This word occurs 68 times in the Hebrew Old Testament, and its frequency of usage is higher (32 times, nearly half of all the occurrences) in the poetical books. **(3)** The word occurs first in Ex 10:11: "Not so: go now ye that are men, and serve the Lord; for that ye did desire." **(4)** The root meaning "to be strong" is no longer obvious in the usage of *geber,* since it is a synonym of *ish:* "Thus saith the Lord, Write ye this man [*ish*] childless, a man [*geber*] that shall not prosper in his days: for no man of his seed shall prosper, sitting upon the throne of David" (Jer 22:30).

(5) A *geber* denotes a "male," as an antonym of a "woman"; cf. "The woman [*ishshah*] shall not wear that which pertaineth unto a man, neither shall a man [*geber*] put on a woman's [*ishshah*] garment: for all that do so are abomination unto the Lord thy God" (Deut 22:5). **(6)** In standardized expressions of curse and blessing *geber* also functions as a synonym for *ish,* "man." The expression may begin with "Cursed be the man" (*geber;* Jer 17:5) or "Blessed is the man" (*geber;* Ps 34:8), but these same expressions also occur with *ish* (Ps 1:1; Deut 27:15). Syn: Other synonyms are *zakar* (2145 - "male" - Jer 30:6); *enos* (582 - "man" - Job 4:17); and *adam* (120 - "man" - Job 14:10). When compared to the weakness found in *enosh,* one can readily see that man is a marvelous combination of strength (*geber*) and weakness (*enosh*). Syn.: 120, 376, 582, 2145. See: TWOT—310a; BDB—149d.

1398. גֶּבֶר {1x} **Geber**, *gheh'-ber;* the same as 1397; *Geber,* the name of two Isr.:—Geber {1x}. See: BDB—150a.

1399. גֶּבֶר {1x} **g°bar**, *gheb-ar';* from 1396; the same as 1397; a person:—man {1x}. See: TWOT—310a; BDB—149d, 989d, 1086a.

1400. גְּבַר {21x} **g°bar** (Aram.), *gheb-ar';* corresp. to 1399:—certain {2x}, man {19x}. See: TWOT—2647a; BDB—1086a.

1401. גִּבָּר {1x} **gibbâr** (Aram.), *ghib-bawr';* intens. of 1400; *valiant,* or *warrior:*—mighty {1x}. See: TWOT—2647b; BDB—1086a.

1402. גִּבָּר {1x} **Gibbâr**, *ghib-bawr';* intens. of 1399; *Gibbar,* an Isr.:—Gibbar {1x}. See: BDB—150a.

גְּבֻרָה **g°bûrâh**. See 1369.

1403. גַּבְרִיאֵל {1x} **Gabrîy°êl**, *gab-ree-ale';* from 1397 and 410; *man of God; Gabriel,* an archangel:—Gabriel {1x}. See: BDB—150c.

1404. גְּבֶרֶת {9x} gᵉbereth, *gheb-eh'-reth;* fem. of 1376; *mistress:*—lady {2x}, mistress {9x}. See: TWOT—310e; BDB—150c.

1405. גִּבְּתוֹן {6x} Gibbᵉthôwn, *ghib-beth-one';* intens. from 1389; a *hilly* spot; Gibbethon, a place in Pal.:—Gibbethon {6x}. See: BDB—146d, 150d.

1406. גָּג {30x} gâg, *gawg;* prob. by redupl. from 1342; a *roof;* by anal. the *top* of an altar:—roof {12x}, housetop {8x}, top {6x}, . . . house {4x}. See: TWOT—312; BDB—150d.

1407. גַּד {2x} gad, *gad;* from 1413 (in the sense of *cutting*); *coriander* seed (from its furrows):—coriander {2x}. See: TWOT—313c; BDB—151a, 151b.

1408. גַּד {2x} Gad, *gad;* a var. of 1409; *Fortune,* a Bab. deity:—that troop {2x}. See: TWOT—313e; BDB—151c.

1409. גַּד {2x} gâd, *gawd;* from 1464 (in the sense of *distributing*); *fortune:*—troop {2x}. See: TWOT—313d; BDB—151c.

1410. גַּד {70x} Gâd, *gawd;* from 1464; *Gad,* a son of Jacob, incl. his tribe and its territory; also a prophet:—Gad {1x}. See: BDB—151a, 151c.

1411. גִּדְבָר {2x} gᵉdâbâr (Aram.), *ghed-aw-bawr';* corresp. to 1489; a *treasurer:*—treasurer {2x}. See: TWOT—2653; BDB—1086a, 1086b, 1089d.

1412. גֻּדְגֹּדָה {2x} Gudgôdâh, *gud-go'-daw;* by redupl. from 1413 (in the sense of *cutting*) *cleft; Gudgodah,* a place in the desert:—Gudgodah {2x}. See: TWOT—2653; BDB—151a, 151d, 211c.

1413. גָּדַד {8x} gâdad, *gaw-dad';* a prim. root [comp. 1464]; to *crowd;* also to *gash* (as if by *pressing* into):—cut {5x}, gather together {1x}, assemble by troop {1x}, gather {1x}.
The verb *gadad* means (1) to gather together against (Ps 94:21), (2) to make incisions into oneself as a religious act (Deut 14:1), (3) to roam about (Jer 30:23), or (4) to muster troops (Mic 5:1). See: TWOT—313; BDB—151a, 1086a.

1414. גְּדַד {2x} gᵉdad (Aram.), *ghed-ad';* corresp. to 1413; to *cut* down:—hew down {2x}. See: TWOT—2649; BDB—1086a.

גְּדֻדָה gᵉdûdâh. See 1417.

1415. גָּדָה {4x} gâdâh, *gaw-daw';* from an unused root (mean. to *cut* off); a *border* of a river (as *cut* into by the stream):—bank {1x}. See: TWOT—314a; BDB—152a.

גַּדָּה Gaddâh. See 2693.

1416. גְּדוּד {34x} gᵉdûwd, *ghed-ood';* from 1413; a *crowd* (espec. of soldiers):—band {13x}, troop {11x}, army {5x}, company {4x}, men {1x}.
Geduwd (1416) means "band (of raiders); marauding band; raiding party; army; units (of an army); troops; bandits; raid." (1) Basically, this word represents individuals or a band of individuals who raid and plunder an enemy. (1a) The units that perform such raids may be a group of outlaws ("bandits"), (1b) a special unit of any army, or (1c) an entire army. (2) Ancient peoples frequently suffered raids from their neighbors. (2a1) When the Amalekites "raided" Ziklag, looting and burning it while taking captive the wives and families of the men who followed David, he inquired of God, "Shall I pursue after this troop? shall I overtake them?" (1 Sa 30:8). (2a2) In this case, the "raiding band" consisted of the entire army of Amalek. (2b) This meaning of *geduwd* occurs for the first time in Gen 49:19: "A troop shall overcome him." Here the word is a collective noun referring to all the "band of raiders" to come. (3) When Job described the glory of days gone by, he said he "dwelt as a king in the army" (Job 29:25).
(4) When David and his followers were called a *geduwd,* they were being branded outlaws—men who lived by fighting and raiding (1 Kin 11:24). (5) In some passages, *geduwd* signifies a smaller detachment of troops or a military unit or division: (5a) "And Saul's son had two men that were captains of bands" (2 Sa 4:2). (5b) God sent against Jehoiakim "units" from the Babylonian army—"bands of the Chaldees, and bands of the Syrians, and bands of the Moabites, and bands of the children of Ammon" (2 Kin 24:2). (6) The word can also represent individuals who are members of such raiding or military bands. (6a) The individuals in the household of Izrahiah, the descendant of Issachar, formed a military unit, "and with them by their generations, after the house of their fathers, were bands of soldiers for war, six and thirty thousand men" (1 Chr 7:4). (6b) Bildad asks the rhetorical question concerning God, "Is there any number [numbering] of his armies?" (Job 25:3). See: TWOT—313a; BDB—151b.

1417. גְּדוּד {2x} gᵉdûwd, *ghed-ood';* or (fem.)
גְּדֻדָה gᵉdûdâh, *ghed-oo-daw';* from 1413; a *furrow* (as *cut*):—furrow {1x}, cutting {1x}. See: TWOT—313b; BDB—151b.

1418. גְּדוּדָה {1x} gᵉdûwdâh, *ghed-oo-daw';* fem. pass. part. of 1413; an *incision:*—cutting {1x}. See: TWOT—313b; BDB—151b.

1419. גָּדוֹל {529x} **gâdôwl**, *gaw-dole'*; or (short.)

גָּדֹל **gâdôl**, *gaw-dole'*; from 1431; *great* (in any sense); hence, *older;* also *insolent:*—great {397x}, high {22x}, greater {9x}, loud {9x}, greatest {9x}, elder {8x}, great man {8x}, mighty {7x}, eldest {6x}, misc. {44x}.

Gadol means "great." **(1)** The adjective *gadol* is the most frequently appearing word related to the verb *gadal* (1431). **(2)** *Gadol* is used **(2a)** of extended dimension (Gen 1:21), **(2b)** of number (Gen 12:2), **(2c)** of power (Deut 4:37), **(2d)** of punishment (Gen 4:13), and **(2e)** of value or importance (Gen 39:9). **(3)** The verb *gadal* (1431) and the related adjective *gadol* may each be used to make distinctive statements. **(3a)** In Hebrew one may say "he is great" both by using the verb alone and by using the pronoun and the adjective *gadol*. **(3a1)** The first sets forth a standing and existing condition—so Mal 1:5 could be rendered: "The Lord is magnified beyond the borders of Israel." **(3a2)** The second construction announces newly experienced information to the recipient, as in Is 12:6: "Great is the Holy One of Israel in the midst of thee." This information was known previously, but recent divine acts have made it to be experienced anew. The emphasis is on the freshness of the experience. See: TWOT—315d; BDB—152d.

1420. גְּדוּלָה {12x} **gᵉdûwlâh**, *ghed-oo-law'*; or (short.)

גְּדֻלָּה **gᵉdullâh**, *ghed-ool-law'*; or (less accurately)

גְּדוּלָּה **gᵉdûwllâh**, *ghed-ool-law'*; fem. of 1419; *greatness;* (concr.) *mighty acts:*—greatness {7x}, great things {3x}, majesty {1x}, dignity {1x}.

Geduwllah means "greatness; great dignity; great things." **(1)** This noun means "greatness" in Ps 71:21: "Thou shalt increase my greatness, and comfort me on every side." **(2)** *Geduwllah* may refer also to "great dignity" (Est 6:3) and **(3)** to "great things" (2 Sa 7:21). See: TWOT—315e; BDB—153c.

1421. גִּדּוּף {3x} **giddûwph**, *ghid-doof'*; or (short.)

גִּדֻּף **giddûph**, *ghid-doof'*; and (fem.)

גִּדּוּפָה **giddûwphâh**, *ghid-doo-faw'*; or

גִּדֻּפָה **giddûphâh**, *ghid-doo-faw'*; from 1422; *vilification:*—revilings {2x}, reproaches {1x}. See: TWOT—317b; BDB—154d.

1422. גְּדוּפָה {1x} **gᵉdûwphâh**, *ghed-oo-faw'*; fem. pass. part. of 1442; a *revile-ment:*—taunt {1x}. See: TWOT—317g; BDB—154d.

גְּדוֹר **Gᵉdôwr**. See 1446.

1423. גְּדִי {16x} **gᵉdîy**, *ghed-ee'*; from the same as 1415; a young *goat* (from *browsing*):—kid {16x}. See: TWOT—314b; BDB—152a.

1424. גָּדִי {2x} **Gâdîy**, *gaw-dee'*; from 1409; *fortunate; Gadi*, an Isr.:—Gadi {1x}. See: BDB—151d.

1425. גָּדִי {16x} **Gâdîy**, *gaw-dee'*; patron. from 1410; a *Gadite* (collect.) or desc. of Gad:—Gadites {16x}. See: BDB—151d.

1426. גַּדִּי {1x} **Gaddîy**, *gad-dee'*; intens. for 1424; *Gaddi*, an Isr.:—Gaddi {1x}. See: BDB—151d.

1427. גַּדִּיאֵל {1x} **Gaddîy'êl**, *gad-dee-ale'*; from 1409 and 410; *fortune of God; Gaddiel*, an Isr.:—Gaddiel {1x}. See: BDB—151d.

1428. גִּדְיָה {1x} **gidyâh**, *ghid-yaw'*; or

גַּדְיָה **gadyâh**, *gad-yaw'*; the same as 1415; a river *brink:*—bank {1x}. See: TWOT—314a; BDB—152a.

1429. גְּדִיָּה {1x} **gᵉdîyâh**, *ghed-ee-yaw'*; fem. of 1423; a young female *goat:*—kid {1x}. See: TWOT—314c; BDB—152a.

1430. גָּדִישׁ {3x} **gâdîysh**, *gaw-deesh'*; from an unused root (mean. to *heap* up); a *stack* of sheaves; by anal. a *tomb:*—shock {2x}, stack {1x}, tomb {1x}. See: TWOT—319a, 320a; BDB—155c.

1431. גָּדַל {x} **gâdal**, *gaw-dal'*; a prim. root; prop. to *twist* [comp. 1434], i.e. to *be* (caus. *make*) *large* (in various senses, as in body, mind, estate or honor, also in pride):—magnify {32x}, great {26x}, grow {14x}, nourish up {7x}, grow up {6x}, greater {5x}, misc. {25x}.

Gadal means "to become strong, grow up, be great or wealthy, evidence oneself as great (magnified), be powerful, significant, or valuable." **(1)** This verb can signify the increasing of size and age as with the maturing process of human life: "And the child grew, and was weaned" (Gen 21:8). **(2)** The word also depicts the "growing up" **(2a)** of animals (2 Sa 12:3) and **(2b)** plants (Is 44:14) and **(2c)** the maturing of animal horns (Dan 8:9) and **(2d)** other growing things. **(3)** In the intensive stem *gadal* indicates that this rearing has occurred: "I have nourished and brought up children" (Is 1:2). **(4)** This stem may also imply permission: "[He] shall let the locks of the hair of his head grow" (Num 6:5). **(5)** *Gadal* can represent the status of "being great or wealthy." Abraham's servant

reported: "And the Lord hath blessed my master greatly; and he is become great" (Gen 24:35)—here the word represents the conclusion of a process.

(6) In the intensive stem the verb sets forth a fact, as when God said: "And I will make of thee a great nation, and I will bless thee, and make thy name great" (Gen 12:2—the first biblical occurrence of the verb). **(7)** This word is sometimes used with the meaning "to be great, to evidence oneself as great": **(7a)** "And now, I beseech thee, let the power of my Lord be great, according as thou hast spoken" (Num 14:17). **(7b)** Moses is praying that God will demonstrate that He is truly great, even as He has said, and do so not by destroying His people. **(7c)** Such an act (destroying Israel) would make onlookers conclude that God was not able to accomplish what He had promised. **(7d)** If, however, He would bring Israel into Palestine, this would exhibit His greatness before the nations. **(7e)** This same sense appears in 2 Sa 7:22, except with the added overtone of "magnified," "praised as great": "Wherefore thou art great, O Lord God: for there is none like thee, neither is there any God besides thee, according to all that we have heard with our ears."

(8) Another emphasis of *gadal* is "to be great, powerful, important, or valuable." This nuance arises when the word is applied to kings. Pharaoh said to Joseph: "Thou shalt be over my house, and according unto thy word shall all my people be ruled: only in the throne will I be greater [more powerful and honored] than thou" (Gen 41:40). **(9)** The Messiah "shall stand and feed in the strength of the Lord, in the majesty of the name of the Lord his God; and they shall abide: for now shall he be great unto the ends of the earth" (Mic 5:4); He will be powerful to the ends of the earth. **(10)** The nuance "to be valuable" appears in 1 Sa 26:24 when David said to Saul: "And, behold, as thy life was much set by this day in mine eyes, so let my life be much set by in the eyes of the Lord, and let him deliver me out of all tribulation." **(10a)** In this statement the second use of the verb is in the intensive stem. **(10b)** Perhaps the force of this could be expressed if one were to translate: "So may my life be very highly valued."

(11) In the reflexive stem *gadal* may signify "to magnify oneself." **(11a)** God says: "Thus will I magnify myself, and sanctify myself; and I will be known in the eyes of many nations" (Eze 38:23). **(11b)** The context shows that He will bring judgment. **(11c)** In this way He "magnifies Himself," or shows Himself to be great and powerful. **(12)** On the other hand, a false statement of greatness and power is an empty boast. So *gadal* can mean "to boast":

"Shall the axe boast itself against him that heweth therewith? or shall the saw magnify itself against him that shaketh it?" (Is 10:15). **(13)** In the causative stem the verb may signify "to assume great airs": "If indeed ye will magnify yourselves against me, and plead against me my reproach . . ." (Job 19:5). **(14)** A nuance appears in Job 7:17, where *gadal* is in the intensive stem, suggesting an estimation of greatness: "What is man, that thou shouldest magnify him? and that thou shouldest set thine heart upon him?" (Ps 8:4). When man is so insignificant, why then does God esteem him so important? See: TWOT—315; BDB—152a.

1432. גָּדֵל {4x} **gâdêl**, *gaw-dale';* from 1431; *large* (lit. or fig.):—great {2x}, grew {2x}.

Another adjective *gadel* means "becoming great; growing up." This verbal adjective occurs 4 times, once in Gen 26:13: "And the man waxed great (1431), and went forward, and grew (1432) until he became very great (1431)." See: TWOT—315a; BDB—152c.

1433. גֹּדֶל {13x} **gôdel**, *go'-del;* from 1431; *magnitude* (lit. or fig.):—greatness {11x}, stout {1x}, stoutness {1x}.

Godel means "greatness" in terms **(1)** of size (Eze 31:7), **(2)** of divine power (Ps 79:11), **(3)** of divine dignity (Deut 32:3), **(4)** of divine majesty (Deut 3:24), **(5)** of divine mercy (Num 14:19), or **(6)** of the false greatness of one's heart (insolence; Is 9:9). See: TWOT—315b; BDB—152d.

1434. גְּדִל {2x} **gᵉdîl**, *ghed-eel';* from 1431 (in the sense of *twisting*); *thread,* i.e. a *tassel* or *festoon:*—fringe {1x}, wreath {1x}. See: TWOT—315c; BDB—152d.

1435. גִּדֵּל {4x} **Giddêl**, *ghid-dale';* from 1431; *stout; Giddel,* the name of one of the Nethinim, also of one of "Solomon's servants":—Giddel {1x}. See: BDB—153c.

גְּדֹל **gâdôl**. See 1419.

גְּדֻלָּה **gᵉdullâh**. See 1420.

1436. גְּדַלְיָה {32x} **Gᵉdalyâh**, *ghed-al-yaw';* or (prol.)

גְּדַלְיָהוּ **Gᵉdalyâhûw**, *ghed-al-yaw'-hoo;* from 1431 and 3050; *Jah has become great; Gedaljah,* the name of five Isr.:—Gedaliah {32x}. See: BDB—153c, 153d.

1437. גִּדַּלְתִּי {2x} **Giddaltîy**, *ghid-dal'-tee;* from 1431; *I have made great; Giddalti,* an Isr.:—Giddalti {2x}. See: BDB—153d.

1438. גָּדַע {x} **gâdaᶜ**, *gaw-dah';* a prim. root; to *fell* a tree; gen. to *destroy* anything:—cut . . . down {11x}, cut off {7x}, cut asunder {3x}, cut in sunder {2x}. See: TWOT—316; BDB—154b.

1439. גִּדְעוֹן {39x} Gîd'ôwn, *ghid-ohn';* from 1438; *feller* (i.e. *warrior*); *Gidon,* an Isr.:—Gideon {39x}. See: TWOT—316a; BDB—154c.

1440. גִּדְעֹם {1x} Gid'ôm, *ghid-ohm';* from 1438; a *cutting* (i.e. *desolation*); *Gidom,* a place in Pal.:—*Gidom* {1x}. See: BDB—154c.

1441. גִּדְעֹנִי {5x} Gid'ônîy, *ghid-o-nee';* from 1438; *warlike* [comp. 1439]; *Gidoni,* an Isr.:—Gideoni {5x}. See: BDB—154c.

1442. גָּדַף {7x} gâdaph, *gaw-daf';* a prim. root; to *hack* (with words), i.e. *revile:*—blaspheme {6x}, reproach {1x}. See: TWOT—317; BDB—154c.

גִּדֻּף giddûph, and

גִּדֻּפָה giddûphâh. See 1421.

1443. גָּדַר {10x} gâdar, *gaw-dar';* a prim. root; to *wall* in or around:—make {3x}, mason {2x}, repairer {1x}, close up {1x}, fenced up {1x}, hedged {1x}, inclosed {1x}. See: TWOT—318; BDB—154d.

1444. גֶּדֶר {4x} geder, *gheh'-der;* from 1443; a *circumvallation:*—wall {1x}. See: TWOT—318a; BDB—154d.

1445. גֶּדֶר {1x} Geder, *gheh'-der:* the same as 1444; *Geder,* a place in Pal.:—*Geder* {1x}. See: BDB—155a.

1446. גְּדֹר {7x} G'dôr, *ghed-ore';* or (fully)

גְּדוֹר G'dôwr, *ghed-ore';* from 1443; *inclosure; Gedor,* a place in Pal.; also the name of three Isr.:—Gedor {7x}. See: BDB—155b.

1447. גָּדֵר {12x} gâdêr, *gaw-dare';* from 1443; a *circumvallation;* by impl. an *inclosure:*—wall {7x}, hedge {4x}, fence {1x}. See: TWOT—318a; BDB—154d.

1448. גְּדֵרָה {10x} g'dêrâh, *ghed-ay-raw';* fem. of 1447; *inclosure* (espec. for flocks):—hedge {4x}, fold {3x}, wall {1x}, sheepfold {1x}, sheepcote {1x}. See: TWOT—318b; BDB—155a.

1449. גְּדֵרָה G'dêrâh, *ghed-ay-raw';* the same as 1448; (with the art.). *Gederah,* a place in Pal.:—*Gederah* {1x}. See: TWOT—318b; BDB—155b.

1450. גְּדֵרוֹת {2x} G'dêrôwth, *ghed-ay-rohth';* plur. of 1448; *walls; Gederoth,* a place in Pal.:—Gederoth {2x}. See: BDB—155b.

1451. גְּדֵרִי {1x} G'dêrîy, *ghed-ay-ree';* patrial from 1445; a *Gederite,* or inhab. of Geder:—Gederite {1x}. See: BDB—155b.

1452. גְּדֵרָתִי {1x} G'dêrâthîy, *ghed-ay-raw-thee';* patrial from 1449; a *Gederathite,* or inhab. of Gederah:—Gederathite {1x}. See: BDB—155b.

1453. גְּדֵרֹתַיִם {1x} G'dêrôthayim, *ghed-ay-ro-thah'-yim;* dual of 1448; *double wall; Gederothajim,* a place in Pal.:—Gederothaim {1x}. See: BDB—155b.

1454. גֵּה {1x} gêh, *gay;* prob. a clerical err. for 2088; *this:*—this {1x}. See: TWOT—528; BDB—155c.

1455. גָּהָה {1x} gâhâh, *gaw-haw';* a prim. root; to *remove* (a bandage from a wound, i.e. *heal* it):—cure {1x}. See: TWOT—321; BDB—155c.

1456. גֵּהָה {1x} gêhâh, *gay-haw';* from 1455; a *cure:*—medicine {1x}. See: TWOT—321a; BDB—155c.

1457. גָּהַר {3x} gâhar, *gaw-har';* a prim. root; to *prostrate* oneself:—stretch {2x}, cast himself down {1x}. See: TWOT—322; BDB—155c.

1458. גַּו {3x} gav, *gav;* another form for 1460; the *back:*—back {3x}. See: TWOT—326a; BDB—155c, 156a.

1459. גַּו {13x} gav (Aram.), *gav;* corresp. to 1460; the *middle:*—midst {10x}, within the same {1x}, wherein {1x}, therein {1x}. See: TWOT—2650; BDB—1086a.

1460. גֵּו {7x} gêv, *gave;* from 1342 [corresp. to 1354]; the *back;* by anal. the *middle:*—back {5x}, among {1x}, body {1x}. See: TWOT—326b; BDB—156a, 156b, 1086a.

1461. גּוּב {1x} gûwb, *goob;* a prim. root; to *dig:*—husbandman {1x}. See: TWOT—323; BDB—146a, 155c.

1462. גּוֹב {2x} gôwb, *gobe;* from 1461; the *locust* (from its *grubbing* as a larvae):—grasshopper {2x}. See: TWOT—304b; BDB—146d, 147c, 155c.

1463. גּוֹג {10x} Gôwg, *gohg;* of uncert. der.; *Gog,* the name of an Isr., also of some northern nation:—Gog {10x}. See: TWOT—324; BDB—155d.

1464. גּוּד {3x} gûwd, *goode;* a prim. root [akin to 1413]; to *crowd* upon, i.e. *attack:*—invade {1x}, overcome {2x}. See: TWOT—325; BDB—156a.

1465. גֵּוָה {1x} gêvâh, *gay-vaw';* fem. of 1460; the *back,* i.e. (by extens.) the *person:*—body {1x}. See: TWOT—326c; BDB—156b.

1466. גֵּוָה {3x} gêvâh, *gay-vaw';* the same as 1465; *exaltation;* (fig.) *arrogance:*—

lifting up {1x}, pride {2x}. See: TWOT—299h; BDB—145b, 156a.

1467. גֵּוָה {1x} **gêvâh** (Aram.), *gay-vaw';* corresp. to 1466:—pride {1x}. See: TWOT—2651; BDB—1085d, 1086b.

1468. גּוּז {2x} **gûwz**, *gooz;* a prim. root [comp. 1494]; prop. to *shear* off; but used only in the (fig.) sense of *passing* rapidly:—bring {1x}, cut off {1x}. See: TWOT—327; BDB—156d.

1469. גּוֹזָל {2x} **gôwzâl**, *go-zawl';* or (short.)

גֹּזָל **gôzâl**, *go-zawl';* from 1497; a *nestling* (as being comp. *nude* of feathers):—young {1x}, young pigeon {1x}. See: TWOT—337c; BDB—160a.

1470. גּוֹזָן {5x} **Gôwzân**, *go-zawn';* prob. from 1468; a *quarry* (as a place of *cutting* stones); *Gozan,* a province of Assyria:—Gozan {1x}. See: BDB—157a.

1471. גּוֹי {558x} **gôwy**, *go'-ee;* rarely (short.)

גֹּי **gôy**, *go'-ee;* appar. from the same root as 1465 (in the sense of *massing*); a foreign *nation;* hence, a *Gentile;* also (fig.) a *troop* of animals, or a *flight* of locusts:—nation {374x}, heathen {143x}, Gentiles {30x}, people {11x}.

Goy means "nation; people; heathen." **(1)** *Goy* refers to a "people or nation," usually with overtones of territorial or governmental unity/identity. **(1a)** This emphasis is in the promise formulas where God promised to make someone a great, powerful, numerous "nation" (Gen 12:2). **(1b)** Certainly these adjectives described the future characteristics of the individual's descendants as compared to other peoples (cf. Num 14:12). **(1c)** So *goy* represents a group of individuals who are considered as a unit with respect to origin, language, land, jurisprudence, and government. **(1d)** This emphasis is in Gen 10:5 (the first occurrence): "By these were the isles of the Gentiles divided in their lands; every one after his tongue, after their families, in their nations." **(1e)** Deut 4:6 deals not with political and national identity but with religious unity, its wisdom, insight, righteous jurisprudence, and especially its nearness to God: "Keep therefore and do them; for this is your wisdom and your understanding in the sight of the nations, which shall hear all these statutes, and say, Surely this great nation is a wise and understanding people." **(1f)** Certainly all this is viewed as the result of divine election (Deut 4:32ff.). **(1g)** Israel's greatness is due to the greatness of her God and the great acts He has accomplished in and for her.

(2) *Goy* is sometimes almost a derogatory name for non-Israelite groups, or the "heathen": "And I will scatter you among the heathen, and will draw out a sword . . ." (Lev 26:33). **(2a)** This negative connotation is not always present, however, when the word is used of the heathen: "For from the top of the rocks I see him, and from the hills I behold him: lo, the people shall dwell alone, and shall not be reckoned among the nations" (Num 23:9). **(3)** Certainly in contexts dealing with worship the *goyim* are the non-Israelites: "They feared the Lord, and served their own gods, after the manner of the nations whom they carried away from thence" (2 Kin 17:33). **(4)** In passages such as Deut 4:38 *goyim* specifically describes the early inhabitants of Canaan prior to the Israelite conquest. **(4a)** Israel was to keep herself apart from and distinct from the "heathen" (Deut 7:1) and **(4b)** was to be an example of true godliness before them (Deut 4:6).

(5) On the other hand, Israel was to be the means by which salvation was declared to the nations (heathen) as a blessing to all the nations (Gen 12:2) and **(5a)** as a holy "nation" and kingdom of priests (Ex 19:6), and **(5b)** the nations came to recognize God's sovereignty (Is 60). **(6)** So the Messiah is the light of the nations (Is 49:6). Syn: **(A)** The word *'am* (5971), "people, nation," suggests subjective personal interrelationships based on common familial ancestry and/or a covenantal union, while *goy* suggests a political entity with a land of its own: "Now therefore, I pray thee, if I have found grace in thy sight, show me thy way, that I may know thee, that I may find grace in thy sight: and consider that this nation is thy people" (Ex 33:13). **(B)** *Goy* may be used of a people, however, apart from its territorial identity: "And ye shall be unto me a kingdom of priests, and a holy nation" (Ex 19:6). Syn.: 5971. See: TWOT—326e; BDB—156c, 157a, 361d.

1472. גְּוִיָּה {13x} **gᵉvîyâh**, *ghev-ee-yaw';* prol. for 1465; a *body,* whether alive or dead:—body {9x}, corpse {2x}, carcase {2x}. See: TWOT—326d; BDB—156b, 157a.

1473. גּוֹלָה {42x} **gôwlâh**, *go-law';* or (short.)

גֹּלָה **gôlâh**, *go-law';* act. part. fem. of 1540; *exile;* concr. and collect. *exiles:*—captivity {26x}, carry away {7x}, captive {5x}, removing {2x}, remove {1x}, captivity + 3627 {1x}.

Golah means "exile; people exiled." **(1)** Ezra 2:1 uses the word of "people returning from the exile." **(2)** In other references, the word means "people in exile" (2 Kin 24:15). **(3)** In 1 Chr 5:22, *golah* refers to the era of the "exile." See: TWOT—350a; BDB—163c, 1086c.

1474. גּוֹלָן {4x} **Gôwlân**, *go-lawn';* from 1473; *captive; Golan,* a place E. of the Jordan:—Golan {4x}. See: BDB—157a.

1475. גּוּמָץ {1x} **gûwmmâts**, *goom-mawts';* of uncert. der.; a *pit:*—pit {1x}. See: TWOT—362a; BDB—170a.

1476. גּוּנִי {4x} **Gûwnîy**, *goo-nee';* prob. from 1598; *protected; Guni,* the name of two Isr.:—Guni {1x}. See: BDB—157b.

1477. גּוּנִי {1x} **Gûwnîy**, *goo-nee';* patron. from 1476; a *Gunite* (collect. with art. pref.) or desc. of Guni:—Gunites {1x}. See: BDB—157b.

1478. גָּוַע {25x} **gâva**', *gaw-vah';* a prim. root; to *breathe* out, i.e. (by impl.) *expire:*—die {12x}, give up the ghost {9x}, dead {1x}, perish {2x}, dead {1x}. See: TWOT—328; BDB—157b.

1479. גּוּף {1x} **gûwph**, *goof;* a prim. root; prop. to *hollow* or *arch,* i.e. (fig.) *close;* to *shut:*—shut {1x}. See: TWOT—329; BDB—157c.

1480. גּוּפָה {2x} **gûwphâh**, *goo-faw';* from 1479; a *corpse* (as *closed* to sense):—body {2x}. See: TWOT—329a; BDB—157c.

1481. גּוּר {98x} **gûwr**, *goor;* a prim. root; prop. to *turn* aside from the road (for a lodging or any other purpose), i.e. *sojourn* (as a guest); also to *shrink, fear* (as in a *strange* place); also to *gather* for hostility (as *afraid*):—sojourn {58x}, dwell {12x}, afraid {6x}, stranger {6x}, gather together {4x}, fear {3x}, abide {2x}, assemble {1x}, stand in awe {1x}, gathered {1x}, inhabitant {1x}, remain {1x}, sojourners {1x}, surely {1x}.

This verb means "to dwell or sojourn in a land as a client." The first occurrence of the word is in Gen 12:10, where it is reported that Abram journeyed to Egypt and dwelt there as a client. In Gen 21:23, Abraham makes a covenant with Abimelech, saying, "According to the kindness that I have done unto thee, thou shalt do unto me, and to the land wherein thou hast sojourned." Syn.: 3427, 7931, 8453. See: TWOT—330, 332; BDB—157c, 158c, 158d.

1482. גּוּר {7x} **gûwr**, *goor;* or (short.)

גֻּר **gur**, *goor;* perh. from 1481; a *cub* (as still *abiding* in the lair), espec. of the lion:—whelp {6x}, young one {1x}. See: TWOT—331b; BDB—158d.

1483. גּוּר {1x} **Gûwr**, *goor;* the same as 1482; *Gur,* a place in Pal.:—Gur {1x}. See: BDB—158a, 751c.

1484. גּוֹר {2x} **gôwr**, *gore;* or (fem.)

גֹּרָה **gôrâh**, *go-raw';* a var. of 1482:—whelp {1x}. See: TWOT—331a; BDB—158d, 177c.

1485. גּוּר־בַּעַל {1x} **Gûwr-Ba'al**, *goor-bah'-al;* from 1481 and 1168; *dwelling of Baal; Gur-Baal,* a place in Arabia:—Gurbaal {1x}. See: BDB—158a.

1486. גּוֹרָל {77x} **gôwrâl**, *go-rawl';* or (short.)

גֹּרָל **gôrâl**, *go-ral';* from an unused root mean. to *be rough* (as stone); prop. a *pebble,* i.e. a *lot* (small stones being used for that purpose); fig. a *portion* or *destiny* (as if determined by lot):—lot {1x}.

Goral means "lot." **(1)** *Goral* represents the "lot" which was cast to discover the will of God in a given situation: "And Aaron shall cast lots upon the two goats; one lot for the Lord, and the other lot for the scapegoat" (Lev 16:8—the first occurrence). **(2)** Exactly what casting the "lot" involved is not known. **(3)** Since the land of Palestine was allocated among the tribes by the casting of the "lot," these allotments came to be known as their lots: "This then was the lot of the tribe of the children of Judah by their families; even to the border of Edom" (Josh 15:1). **(4)** In an extended use the word *goral* represents the idea "fate" or "destiny": "And behold at eveningtide trouble; and before the morning he is not. This is the portion of them that spoil us, and the lot of them that rob us" (Is 17:14). **(5)** Since God is viewed as controlling all things absolutely, the result of the casting of the "lot" is divinely controlled: "The lot is cast into the lap; but the whole disposing thereof is of the Lord" (Prov 16:33). **(6)** Thus, providence (divine control of history) is frequently figured as one's "lot." See: TWOT—381a; BDB—174a.

1487. גּוּשׁ {1x} **gûwsh**, *goosh;* or rather (by perm.)

גִּישׁ **gîysh**, *gheesh;* of uncert. der.; a *mass* of earth:—clod {1x}. See: TWOT—333a; BDB—159a, 162c.

1488. גֵּז {4x} **gêz**, *gaze;* from 1494; a *fleece* (as *shorn*); also mown *grass:*—fleece {2x}, mowings {1x}, mown grass {1x}. See: TWOT—336a; BDB—159a, 159c.

1489. גִּזְבָּר {1x} **gizbâr**, *ghiz-bawr';* of for. der.; *treasurer:*—treasurer {1x}. See: TWOT—334; BDB—159b, 1086b.

1490. גִּזְבָּר {1x} **gizbâr** (Aram.), *ghiz-bawr';* corresp. to 1489:—treasurer {1x}. See: TWOT—2653; BDB—1086b.

1491. גָּזָה {1x} **gâzâh**, *gaw-zaw'*; a prim. root [akin to 1468]; to *cut* off, i.e. *portion* out:—take {1x}. See: TWOT—335; BDB—159b.

1492. גִּזָּה {7x} **gazzâh**, *gaz-zaw'*; fem. from 1494; a *fleece*:—fleece {7x}. See: TWOT—336b; BDB—159b, 159c.

1493. גִּזוֹנִי {1x} **Gizôwnîy**, *ghee-zo-nee'*; patrial from the unused name of a place appar. in Pal.; a *Gizonite* or inhab. of Gizoh:—Gizonite {1x}. See: BDB—159b.

1494. גָּזַז {15x} **gâzaz**, *gaw-zaz'*; a prim. root [akin to 1468]; to *cut* off; spec. to *shear* a flock or *shave* the hair; fig. to *destroy* an enemy:—shear {5x}, sheepshearer {3x}, shearers {3x}, cut off {1x}, poll {1x}, shave {1x}, cut down {1x}. Syn.: 5349. See: TWOT—336; BDB—159c.

1495. גָּזֵז {2x} **Gâzêz**, *gaw-zaze'*; from 1494; *shearer; Gazez*, the name of two Isr.:—*Gazez* {1x}. See: BDB—159c.

1496. גָּזִית {11x} **gâzîyth**, *gaw-zeeth'*; from 1491; something *cut*, i.e. *dressed* stone:—hewed, hewn stone {10x}, wrought {1x}. See: TWOT—335a; BDB—159b, 159d.

1497. גָּזַל {30x} **gâzal**, *gaw-zal'*; a prim. root; to *pluck* off; spec. to *flay, strip* or *rob*:—spoil {8x}, take away {8x}, rob {4x}, pluck {3x}, caught {1x}, consume {1x}, exercised {1x}, force {1x}, pluck off {1x}, torn {1x}, violence {1x}. See: TWOT—337; BDB—159d.

1498. גָּזֵל {4x} **gâzêl**, *gaw-zale'*; from 1497; *robbery*, or (concr.) *plunder*:—robbery {3x}, thing taken away by violence {1x}. See: TWOT—337a; BDB—160a.

1499. גֵּזֶל {2x} **gêzel**, *ghe'-zel;* from 1497; *plunder*, i.e. *violence*:—violence {1x}, violent perverting {1x}. See: BDB—160a.

גֹּזָל **gôzâl**. See 1469.

1500. גְּזֵלָה {5x} **gᵉzêlâh**, *ghez-ay-law';* fem. of 1498 and mean. the same:—violence {3x}, robbed {1x}, that {1x}. See: TWOT—337b; BDB—160a.

1501. גָּזָם {3x} **gâzâm**, *gaw-zawm';* from an unused root mean. to *devour;* a kind of *locust*:—palmer-worm {3x}. See: TWOT—338a; BDB—160b.

1502. גַּזָּם {2x} **Gazzâm**, *gaz-zawm';* from the same as 1501; *devourer; Gazzam*, one of the Nethinim:—*Gazzam* {2x}. See: BDB—160b.

1503. גֶּזַע {3x} **gezaᶜ**, *geh'-zah;* from an unused root mean. to *cut down* (trees); the *trunk* or *stump* of a tree (as felled or as planted):—stem {1x}, stock {2x}. See: TWOT—339a; BDB—160b.

1504. גָּזַר {13x} **gâzar**, *gaw-zar';* a prim. root; to *cut* down or off; (fig.) to *destroy, divide, exclude*, or *decide*:—cut off {6x}, divide {3x}, decree {2x}, cut down {1x}, snatch {1x}. See: TWOT—340; BDB—160b, 1086b.

1505. גְּזַר {6x} **gᵉzar** (Aram.), *ghez-ar';* corresp. to 1504; to *quarry; determine*:—cut out {2x}, soothsayer {4x}.

The Chaldean soothsayer (Dan 2:27; 4:7; 5:7, 11) was no doubt an astrologer, who pretended to do what astrologers in many countries and in various eras have professed to do, namely, to calculate the destinies of man by interpreting the movements and conjunctions of the heavenly bodies. Their name comes from this verb which is literally to cut. Whether their name was applied to them from their marking out the heavens into certain divisions for purposes of observation, or whether they derived it from the fact that they cut off or decided the fate of those who came to them for advice, is a matter which perhaps cannot now be determined. See: TWOT—2654; BDB—1086b.

1506. גֶּזֶר {2x} **gezer**, *gheh'-zer;* from 1504; something *cut* off; a *portion*:—part {1x}, piece {1x}. See: TWOT—340a; BDB—160c.

1507. גֶּזֶר {15x} **Gezer**, *gheh'-zer;* the same as 1506; *Gezer*, a place in Pal.:—Gazer {2x}, *Gezer* {13x}. See: BDB—160c.

1508. גִּזְרָה {8x} **gizrâh**, *ghiz-raw';* fem. of 1506; the *figure* or person (as if *cut* out); also an *inclosure* (as *separated*):—polishing {1x}, separate place {7x}. See: TWOT—340c; BDB—160d.

1509. גְּזֵרָה {1x} **gᵉzêrâh**, *ghez-ay-raw';* from 1504; a *desert* (as *separated*):—not inhabited {1x}. See: TWOT—340b; BDB—160c.

1510. גְּזֵרָה {2x} **gᵉzêrâh** (Aram.), *ghez-ay-raw';* from 1505 (as 1504); a *decree*:—decree {1x}. See: TWOT—2654a; BDB—1086b.

1511. גִּזְרִי {1x} **Gizrîy** (in the marg.), *ghiz-ree';* patrial from 1507; a *Gezerite* (collect.) or inhab. of Gezer; but better (as in the text) by transp.

גִּרְזִי **Girzîy**, *gher-zee';* patrial of 1630; a *Girzite* (collect.) or member of a native tribe in Pal.:—Gezrites {1x}. See: BDB—160c, 173d.

1512. גָּחוֹן {2x} **gâchôwn**, *gaw-khone';* prob. from 1518; the external *abdomen*,

belly (as the *source* of the fetus [comp. 1521]):— belly {1x}. See: TWOT—342a; BDB—161a.

גֶחְזִי **Gĕchăzîy.** See 1522.

גָחֹל **gachol.** See 1513.

1513. גֶחֶל {18x} **gechel,** *geh'-khel;* or (fem.)

גַחֶלֶת **gacheleth,** *gah-kheh'-leth;* from an unused root mean. to *glow* or *kindle;* an *ember:*—coals {17x}, coals of fire {1x}. See: TWOT—341a; BDB—160d.

1514. גַחַם {1x} **Gacham,** *gah'-kham;* from an unused root mean. to *burn; flame; Gacham,* a son of Nahor:—Gaham {1x}. See: BDB—161a.

1515. גַחַר {1x} **Gachar,** *gah'-khar;* from an unused root mean. to *hide; lurker; Gachar,* one of the Nethinim:—Gahar {2x}. See: BDB—161a.

גּוֹי **gôy.** See 1471.

1516. גַיְא {60x} **gay᾽,** *gah'-ee;* or (short.)

גַי **gay,** *gah'-ee;* prob. (by transm.) from the same root as 1466 (abb.); a *gorge* (from its *lofty* sides; hence, narrow, but not a gully or winter-torrent):—valley {60x}. Syn.: 1237, 5158, 6010. See: TWOT—343; BDB—161a, 360d, 361d.

1517. גִּיד {7x} **gîyd,** *gheed;* prob. from 1464; a *thong* (as *compressing*); by anal. a *tendon:*—sinew {7x}. See: TWOT—344a; BDB—161c.

1518. גִּיחַ {6x} **gîyach,** *ghee'-akh;* or (short.)

גֹּחַ **gôach,** *go'-akh;* a prim. root; to *gush* forth (as water), gen. to *issue:*—come forth {3x}, take {1x}, bring forth {1x}, draw up {1x}. See: TWOT—345; BDB—157a, 160d, 161c.

1519. גִּיחַ {1x} **gîyach** (Aram.), *ghee'-akh;* or (short.)

גּוּחַ **gûwach** (Aram.), *goo'-akh;* corresp. to 1518; to *rush* forth:—strive {1x}. See: TWOT—345; BDB—1086b.

1520. גִּיחַ {1x} **Gîyach,** *ghee'-akh;* from 1518; a *fountain; Giach,* a place in Pal.:—Giah {1x}. See: BDB—161d.

1521. גִּיחוֹן {6x} **Gîychôwn,** *ghee-khone';* or (short.)

גִּחוֹן **Gîchôwn,** *ghee-khone';* from 1518; *stream; Gichon,* a river of Paradise; also a valley (or pool) near Jerusalem:—Gihon {1x}. See: TWOT—345a; BDB—161d.

1522. גֵּיחֲזִי {12x} **Gêychăzîy,** *gay-khah-zee';* or

גֵּחֲזִי **Gêchăzîy,** *gay-khah-zee';* appar. from 1516 and 2372; *valley of a vi-*

sionary; Gechazi, the servant of Elisha:—Gehazi {12x}. See: BDB—160d, 161c, 162a.

1523. גִּיל {44x} **gîyl,** *gheel;* or (by perm.)

גּוּל **gûwl,** *gool;* a prim. root; prop. to *spin* round (under the influence of any violent emotion), i.e. usually *rejoice,* or (as *cringing*) *fear:*—rejoice {27x}, glad {10x}, joyful {4x}, joy {2x}, delight {1x}. See: TWOT—346; BDB—157a, 162a.

1524. גִּיל {10x} **gîyl,** *gheel;* from 1523; a *revolution* (of time, i.e. an *age*); also *joy:*—rejoice {3x}, joy {3x}, gladness {2x}, exceedingly {1x}, of your sort {1x}. Syn.: 5937, 7442, 8055. See: TWOT—346a,b; BDB—162b.

1525. גִּילָה {2x} **gîylâh,** *ghee-law';* or

גִּילַת **gîylath,** *ghee-lath';* fem. of 1524; *joy:*—joy {1x}, rejoicing {1x}. See: TWOT—346c; BDB—162b.

גִּילֹה **Gîylôh.** See 1542.

1526. גִּילֹנִי {2x} **Gîylônîy,** *ghee-lo-nee';* patrial from 1542; a *Gilonite* or inhab. of Giloh:—Gilonite {2x}. See: BDB—162b.

1527. גִּינַת {2x} **Gîynath,** *ghee-nath';* of uncert. der.; *Ginath,* an Isr.:—Ginath {2x}. See: BDB—162b. 171b.

1528. גִּיר {1x} **gîyr** (Aram.), *gheer;* corresp. to 1615; *lime:*—plaster {1x}. See: TWOT—2655; BDB—1086b.

1529. גֵּישָׁן {1x} **Gêyshân,** *gay-shawn';* from the same as 1487; *lumpish; Geshan,* an Isr.:—Geshan {1x}. See: BDB—162c.

1530. גַּל {1x} **gal,** *gal;* from 1556; something *rolled,* i.e. a *heap* of stone or dung (plural *ruins*), by anal. a *spring* of water (plur. *waves*):—heap {18x}, wave {4x}, spring {1x}, billow {1x}, of {1x}. See: TWOT—353a; BDB—162c, 164c.

1531. גֹּל {1x} **gôl,** *gole;* from 1556; a *cup* for oil (as *round*):—bowl {1x}. See: TWOT—353c; BDB—165a.

גְּלָא **gᵉlâ᾽.** See 1541.

1532. גַּלָּב {1x} **gallâb,** *gal-lawb';* from an unused root mean. to *shave;* a *barber:*—barber {1x}. See: TWOT—348; BDB—162c.

1533. גִּלְבֹּעַ {8x} **Gilbôaʿ,** *ghil-bo'-ah;* from 1530 and 1158; *fountain of ebullition; Gilboa,* a mountain of Pal.:—Gilboa {8x}. See: BDB—162c.

1534. גַּלְגַּל {11x} **galgal,** *gal-gal';* by redupl. from 1556; a *wheel;* by anal. a *whirlwind;* also *dust* (as *whirled*):—heaven

{1x}, rolling thing {1x}, wheel {8x}, whirlwind {1x}. See: TWOT—353i; BDB—162c, 165d.

1535. גַּלְגַּל {1x} **galgal** (Aram.), *gal-gal';* corresp. to 1534; a *wheel:—*wheel {1x}. See: TWOT—2657a; BDB—1086b, 1086c.

1536. גִּלְגָּל {1x} **gilgâl**, *ghil-gawl';* a var. of 1534:—wheel {1x}. See: TWOT—353j; BDB—162c, 166a.

1537. גִּלְגָּל {41x} **Gilgâl**, *ghil-gawl';* the same as 1536 (with the art. as a prop. noun); *Gilgal*, the name of three places in Pal.:—*Gilgal* {41x}. See: BDB—166a. See also 1019.

1538. גֻּלְגֹּלֶת {12x} **gulgôleth**, *gul-go'-leth;* by redupl. from 1556; a *skull* (as *round*); by impl. a *head* (in enumeration of persons):—poll {7x}, scull {2x}, every man {2x}, head {1x}. See: TWOT—353l; BDB—162c, 166b.

1539. גֶּלֶד {1x} **geled**, *ghe'-led;* from an unused root prob. mean. to *polish;* the (human) *skin* (as *smooth*):—skin {1x}. See: TWOT—349; BDB—162d.

1540. גָּלָה {188x} **gâlâh**, *gaw-law';* a prim. root; to *denude* (espec. in a disgraceful sense); by impl. to *exile* (captives being usually *stripped*); fig. to *reveal:—*uncover {34x}, discover {29x}, captive {28x}, carry away {22x}, reveal {16x}, open {12x}, captivity {11x}, shew {9x}, remove {6x}, appear {3x}, misc. {18x} = + advertise, bewray, bring, depart, disclose, exile, be gone, × plainly, publish, × shamelessly, × surely, tell.

Galah means "to leave, depart, uncover, reveal." **(1) Intransitively**, *galah* signifies "depart" or "leave." **(1a)** This meaning is seen clearly in 1 Sa 4:21: "And she named the child Ichabod, saying, The glory is departed from Israel." **(1b)** Thus Isaiah 24:11: "The mirth of the land is gone." **(1c)** One special use of this sense of the verb is "to go into exile." The first biblical occurrence of *galah* carries this nuance: "And the children of Dan set up the graven image: and Jonathan . . . and his sons were priests to the tribe of Dan until the day of the captivity of the land" (Judg 18:30), or until they lost control of the land and were forced to serve other gods. **(1d)** The best-known Old Testament captivity was the one brought by God through the kings of Assyria and Babylon (1 Chr 5:26; cf. Jer 29:1).

(1e) Although *galah* is not used in this sense in the law of Moses, the idea is clearly present. If Israel does not "observe to do all the words of this law that are written in this book, that thou mayest fear this glorious and fearful name, The Lord Thy God; . . . ye shall be plucked from off the land whither thou goest to possess it. And the Lord shall scatter thee among all people" (Deut 28:58, 63–64; cf. Lev 26:27, 33). **(1f)** This verb can also be used of the "exile of individuals," such as David (2 Sa 15:19). **(1g)** This word may signify "making oneself naked." Noah "drank of the wine, and was drunken; and he was uncovered within his tent" (Gen 9:21).

(2) The **transitive form** occurs less frequently, but has a greater variety of meanings. **(2a)** "To uncover" another person may mean "to have sexual relations with" him or her: "None of you shall approach to any [blood relative of his] to uncover their nakedness: I am the Lord" (Lev 18:6). **(2b)** Uncovering one's nakedness does not always, however, refer to sexual relations (cf. Ex 20:26). **(2c)** Another phrase, "to uncover someone's skirts," means to have sexual relations with a person (Deut 22:30). **(2d)** In Is 16:3, *galah* (in the intensive stem) signifies "betray": "Hide the outcasts [do not betray the fugitive]. . . ." **(2e)** This verb may also be used of "discovering" things, of "laying them bare" so that they become visible: "The foundations of the world were discovered at the rebuking of the Lord" (2 Sa 22:16). **(2f)** In a related sense Eze 23:18 speaks of "uncovering" harlotries, of "exposing" them constantly or leading a life of harlotry. **(2g)** God's "uncovering" of Himself means that He "revealed" Himself (Gen 35:7).

(2h) "To uncover someone's ears" is to tell him something: **(2h1)** "Now the LORD had told Samuel in his ear [literally, "had uncovered the ear"] a day before Saul came, saying, to Samuel . . ." (1 Sa 9:15). **(2h2)** In this case, the verb means not simply "to tell," but "to tell someone something that was not known." **(2h3)** Used in this sense, *galah* is applied to the "revealing" of secrets (Prov 11:13) and of one's innermost feelings. **(2h4)** Hence, Jer 11:20 should be translated: "For unto thee have I revealed my case." **(2i)** Thus *galah* can be used of "making something" openly known, or of "publicizing" it: "The copy of the writing for a commandment to be given in every province was published unto all people, that they should be ready against that day" (Est 3:14). **(2j)** Another nuance appears in Jer 32:11, where *galah*, in connection with a deed of purchase, means "not sealed or closed up." See: TWOT—350; BDB—162d, 1086c.

1541. גְּלָה {9x} **gᵉlâh** (Aram.), *ghel-aw';* or

גְּלָא **gᵉlâ'** (Aram.), *ghel-aw';* corresp. to 1540:—brought over {1x}, carry away {1x}, reveal {7x}. See: TWOT—2656; BDB—1086c.

גֻּלָה **gôlâh**. See 1473.

Hebrew

1542. גִּלֹה {2x} **Gîlôh**, *ghee-lo';* or (fully)

גִּילֹה **Gîylôh**, *ghee-lo';* from 1540; *open; Giloh,* a place in Pal.:—Giloh {2x}. See: BDB—162b, 163d.

1543. גֻּלָּה {14x} **gullâh**, *gool-law';* fem. from 1556; a *fountain, bowl* or *globe* (all as *round*):—bowl {5x}, pommel {3x}, spring {6x}. See: TWOT—353c; BDB—163d, 165a.

1544. גִּלּוּל {48x} **gillûwl**, *ghil-lool';* or (short.)

גִּלֻּל **gillûl**, *ghil-lool';* from 1556; prop. a *log* (as *round*); by impl. an *idol:*—idol {47x}, image {1x}. See: TWOT—353h; BDB—165c.

1545. גְלוֹם **gelôwm**, *ghel-ome';* from 1563; *clothing* (as *wrapped*):—clothes {1x}. See: TWOT—354a; BDB—166b.

1546. גָּלוּת {1x} **gâlûwth**, *gaw-looth';* fem. from 1540; *captivity;* concr. *exiles* (collect.):—

גְלוֹם {1x} **gelôwm**, *ghel-ome';* from 1563; *clothing* (as *wrapped*):—captivity {10x}, captive captives {3x}, them that are carried away captive {2x}. See: clothes {1x}. See: TWOT—354a; BDB—166b. TWOT—350b; BDB—163c.

1547. גָּלוּת {4x} **gâlûwth** (Aram.), *gaw-looth';* corresp. to 1546:—captivity {3x}, captive {1x}. Syn.: 1473, 7617. See: TWOT—2656a; BDB—1086c.

1548. גָּלַח {23x} **gâlach**, *gaw-lakh';* a prim. root; prop. to *be bald,* i.e. (caus.) to *shave;* fig. to *lay waste:*—poll {2x}, shave {17x}, shave off {4x}. See: TWOT—351; BDB—164a.

1549. גִּלָּיוֹן {2x} **gillâyôwn**, *ghil-law-yone';* or

גִּלְיוֹן **gilyôwn**, *ghil-yone';* from 1540; a *tablet* for writing (as *bare*); by anal. a *mirror* (as a *plate*):—glass {1x}, roll {1x}. See: TWOT—350c; BDB—163d.

1550. גָּלִיל {4x} **gâlîyl**, *gaw-leel';* from 1556; a *valve* of a folding door (as *turning*); also a *ring* (as *round*):—folding {2x}, ring {2x}. See: TWOT—353f; BDB—165b.

1551. גָּלִיל {6x} **Gâlîyl**, *gaw-leel';* or (prol.)

גָּלִילָה **Gâlîylâh**, *gaw-lee-law';* the same as 1550; a *circle* (with the art.); *Galil* (as a special *circuit*) in the North of Pal.:—Galilee {6x}. See: BDB—165b.

1552. גְּלִילָה {5x} **gelîylâh**, *ghel-ee-law';* fem. of 1550; a *circuit* or *region:*—border {3x}, coast {1x}, country {1x}. See: TWOT—353g; BDB—165b.

1553. גְּלִילוֹת {1x} **Gelîylôwth**, *ghel-ee-lowth';* plur. of 1552; *circles; Geliloth,*

a place in Pal.:—Geliloth {1x}. See: TWOT—353g; BDB—165c.

1554. גַּלִּים {2x} **Gallîym**, *gal-leem';* plur. of 1530; *springs; Gallim,* a place in Pal.:—Gallim {2x}. See: BDB—164d.

1555. גָּלְיָת {6x} **Golyath**, *gol-yath';* perh. from 1540; *exile; Goljath,* a Philistine:—Goliath {1x}. See: BDB—163d.

1556. גָּלַל {18x} **gâlal**, *gaw-lal';* a prim. root; to *roll* (lit. or fig.):—roll {9x}, roll . . . {3x}, seek occasion {1x}, wallow {1x}, trust {1x}, commit {1x}, remove {1x}, run down {1x}. See: TWOT—353; BDB—94a, 164b, 1086c.

1557. גָּלָל {1x} **gâlâl**, *gaw-lawl';* from 1556; *dung* (as in *balls*):—dung {1x}. See: TWOT—353d; BDB—165b.

1558. גָּלָל {10x} **gâlâl**, *gaw-lawl';* from 1556; a *circumstance* (as *rolled* around); only used adv., on *account* of:—because {4x}, . . . sake {4x}, because of thee {1x}, for {1x}. See: TWOT—352; BDB—164b.

1559. גָּלָל {3x} **Gâlâl**, *gaw-lawl';* from 1556, in the sense of 1560; *great; Galal,* the name of two Isr.:—Galal {3x}. See: BDB—165b.

1560. גְּלָל {2x} **gelâl** (Aram.), *ghel-awl';* from a root corresp. to 1556; *weight* or *size* (as if *rolled*):—great {2x}. See: TWOT—2657; BDB—1086c.

1561. גֵּלֶל {4x} **gêlel**, *gay'-lel;* a var. of 1557; *dung* (plur. *balls* of dung):—dung {4x}. See: TWOT—353d; BDB—165a.

1562. גִּלֲלַי {1x} **Gîlălay**, *ghe-lal-ah'-ee;* from 1561; *dungy; Gilalai,* an Isr.:—Gilalai {1x}. See: BDB—165b.

1563. גָּלַם {1x} **gâlam**, *gaw-lam';* a prim. root; to *fold:*—wrap together {1x}. See: BDB—166b.

1564. גֹּלֶם {1x} **gôlem**, *go'-lem;* from 1563; a *wrapped* (and unformed *mass,* i.e. as the *embryo*):—substance yet being unperfect {1x}. See: TWOT—354b; BDB—166b.

1565. גַּלְמוּד {4x} **galmûwd**, *gal-mood';* prob. by prol. from 1563; *sterile* (as *wrapped* up too hard); fig. *desolate:*—desolate {2x}, solitary {2x}. See: TWOT—354c; BDB—166c.

1566. גָּלַע {3x} **gâla'**, *gaw-lah';* a prim. root; to *be obstinate:*—intermeddle {1x}, meddle {2x}. See: TWOT—355; BDB—166c.

1567. גַּלְעֵד {2x} **Gal'êd**, *gal-ade';* from 1530 and 5707; *heap of testimony;*

Galed, a memorial cairn E. of the Jordan:— Galeed {2x}. See: BDB—165a, 166d.

1568. גִּלְעָד {134x} **Gil‘âd,** *ghil-awd';* prob. from 1567; *Gilad,* a region E. of the Jordan; also the name of three Isr.:—Gilead {101x}, Ramothgilead + 7433 {18x}, Jabeshgilead + 3003 {12x}, Gileadites {2x}. See: TWOT—356; BDB—166d, 928c.

1569. גִּלְעָדִי {11x} **Gil‘âdîy,** *ghil-aw-dee';* patron. from 1568; a *Giladite* or desc. of Gilad:—Gileadite {11x}. See: TWOT—356a; BDB—167c.

1570. גָּלַשׁ {2x} **gâlash,** *gaw-lash';* a prim. root; prob. to *caper* (as a goat):— appear {2x}. See: TWOT—357; BDB—167c.

1571. גַּם {34x} **gam,** *gam;* by contr. from an unused root mean. to *gather;* prop. *assemblage;* used only adv. *also, even, yea, though;* often repeated as correl. *both . . . and:*—also {5x}, as {3x}, even {2x}, again {1x}, and {1x}, misc. {22x}. See: TWOT—361a; BDB—167c, 168d, 210b.

1572. גָּמָא {2x} **gâmâ',** *gaw-maw';* a prim. root (lit. or fig.) to *absorb:*—swallow {1x}, drink {1x}. See: TWOT—358; BDB—167c.

1573. גֹּמֶא {4x} **gôme',** *go'-meh;* from 1572; prop. an *absorbent,* i.e. the *bulrush* (from its *porosity*); spec. the *papyrus:*—bulrush {2x}, rush {2x}. See: TWOT—358a; BDB—167d.

1574. גֹּמֶד {1x} **gômed,** *go'-med;* from an unused root appar. mean. to *grasp;* prop. a *span:*—cubit {1x}. See: TWOT—359a; BDB—167d.

1575. גַּמָּד {1x} **Gammâd,** *gam-mawd';* from the same as 1574; a *warrior* (as *grasping* weapons):—Gammadims {1x}. See: BDB—167d.

1576. גְּמוּל {19x} **g⁰mûwl,** *ghem-ool';* from 1580; *treatment,* i.e. an *act* (of good or ill); by impl. *service* or *requital:*—recompense {10x}, reward {3x}, benefit {2x}, given {1x}, serve + 1580 {1x}, deserve {1x}. See: TWOT—360a; BDB—168b.

1577. גָּמוּל {1x} **Gâmûwl,** *gaw-mool';* pass. part. of 1580; *rewarded; Gamul,* an Isr.:—Gamul {1x}. See also 1014.

1578. גְּמוּלָה {3x} **g⁰mûwlâh,** *ghem-oo-law';* fem. of 1576; mean. the same:— deed {1x}, recompense {1x}, such a reward {1x}. See: TWOT—360b; BDB—168c.

1579. גִּמְזוֹ {1x} **Gimzôw,** *ghim-zo';* of uncert. der.; *Gimzo,* a place in Pal.:— Gimzo {1x}. See: BDB—168a.

1580. גָּמַל {37x} **gâmal,** *gaw-mal';* a prim. root; to *treat* a person (well or ill),

i.e. *benefit* or *requite;* by impl. (of *toil*), to *ripen,* i.e. (spec.) to *wean:*—wean {10x}, reward {8x}, dealt bountifully {4x}, do {4x}, bestowed {2x}, recompense {2x}, weaned child {2x}, do good {1x}, requite {1x}, ripening {1x}, served {1x}, yielded {1x}.

Gamal means "to deal out, deal with, wean, ripen." **(1)** While the basic meaning of the word is "to deal out, with," the wide range of meaning can be seen in its first occurrence in the biblical text: "And the child grew, and was weaned" (Gen 21:8). **(2)** *Gamal* is used most frequently in the sense of "to deal out to," such as in Prov 31:12: "She will do him good and not evil." **(3)** The word is used twice in 1 Sa 24:17: "Thou hast rewarded me good, whereas I have rewarded thee evil." **(4)** The psalmist rejoices and sings to the Lord "because he hath dealt bountifully with me" (Ps 13:6). **(5)** This word can express ripening of grapes (Is 18:5) or **(6)** bearing ripe almonds (Num 17:8). See: TWOT—360; BDB—168a.

1581. גָּמָל {54x} **gâmâl,** *gaw-mawl';* appar. from 1580 (in the sense of *labor* or *burden-bearing*); a *camel:*—camel {54x}. See: TWOT—360d; BDB—168c.

1582. גְּמַלִּי {1x} **G⁰malliy,** *ghem-al-lee';* prob. from 1581; *camel-driver; Gemalli,* an Isr.:—Gemalli {1x}. See: BDB—168d.

1583. גַּמְלִיאֵל {5x} **Gamliy'êl,** *gam-lee-ale';* from 1580 and 410; *reward of God; Gamliel,* an Isr.:—Gamaliel {5x}. See: BDB—168c.

1584. גָּמַר {5x} **gâmar,** *gaw-mar';* a prim. root; to *end* (in the sense of *completion* or *failure*):—cease {1x}, fail {1x}, come to an end {1x}, perfect {1x}, perform {1x}. See: TWOT—363; BDB—170a, 1086c.

1585. גְּמַר {1x} **g⁰mar** (Aram.), *ghem-ar';* corresp. to 1584:—perfect {1x}. See: TWOT—2658; BDB—1086c.

1586. גֹּמֶר {6x} **Gômer,** *go'-mer;* from 1584; *completion; Gomer,* the name of a son of Japheth and of his desc.; also of a Hebrewess:—Gomer {6x}. See: BDB—170a.

1587. גְּמַרְיָה {5x} **G⁰maryâh,** *ghem-ar-yaw';* or

גְּמַרְיָהוּ **G⁰maryâhûw,** *ghem-ar-yaw'-hoo;* from 1584 and 3050; *Jah has perfected; Gemarjah,* the name of two Isr.:—Gemariah {1x}. See: BDB—170b.

1588. גַּן {42x} **gan,** *gan;* from 1598; a *garden* (as *fenced*):—garden {42x}. Syn.: 1593. See: TWOT—367a; BDB—111b, 170b, 171a.

Hebrew

1589. גָּנַב {39x} **gânab**, *gaw-nab';* a prim. root; to *thieve* (lit. or fig.); by impl. to *deceive:*—steal {30x}, steal away {7x}, carry away {1x}, brought {1x}. See: TWOT—364; BDB—170b.

1590. גַּנָּב {17x} **gannâb**, *gaw-nab';* from 1589; a *stealer:*—thief {1x}. See: TWOT—364b; BDB—170c.

1591. גְּנֵבָה {2x} **gᵉnêbâh**, *ghen-ay-baw';* from 1589; *stealing,* i.e. (concr.) something *stolen:*—theft {2x}. See: TWOT—364a; BDB—170c.

1592. גְּנֻבַת {2x} **Gᵉnûbath**, *ghen-oo-bath';* from 1589; *theft; Genubath,* an Edomitish prince:—*Genubath* {2x}. See: BDB—170c.

1593. גַּנָּה {12x} **gannâh**, *gan-naw';* fem. of 1588; a *garden:*—garden {12x}. Syn.: 1594. See: TWOT—367b; BDB—171a.

1594. גִּנָּה {4x} **ginnâh**, *ghin-naw';* another form for 1593:—garden {4x}. See: TWOT—367b; BDB—171a.

1595. גֶּנֶז {3x} **genez**, *gheh'-nez;* from an unused root mean. to *store; treasure;* by impl. a *coffer:*—chest {1x}, treasury {3x}. See: TWOT—365a; BDB—170d, 1086c.

1596. גְּנַז {3x} **gᵉnaz** (Aram.), *ghen-az';* corresp. to 1595; *treasure:*—treasure {3x}. See: TWOT—2659; BDB—1086c.

1597. גִּנְזַךְ {1x} **ginzak**, *ghin-zak';* prol. from 1595; a *treasury:*—treasury {1x}. See: TWOT—366; BDB—170d.

1598. גָּנַן {8x} **gânan**, *gaw-nan';* a prim. root; to *hedge* about, i.e. (gen.) *protect:*—defend {8x}. See: TWOT—367; BDB—170d.

1599. גִּנְּתוֹן {3x} **Ginnᵉthôwn**, *ghin-neth-ōne';* or

גִּנְּתוֹ **Ginnᵉthôw**, *ghin-neth-o';* from 1598; *gardener; Ginnethon* or *Ginnetho,* an Isr.:—Ginnetho {1x}, Ginnethon {2x}. See: BDB—171b.

1600. גָּעָה {2x} **gâ'âh**, *gaw-aw';* a prim. root; to *bellow* (as cattle):—low {2x}. See: TWOT—368; BDB—171d.

1601. גֹּעָה {1x} **Gô'âh**, *go-aw';* fem. act. part. of 1600; *lowing; Goah,* a place near Jerusalem:—Goath {1x}. See: BDB—171d.

1602. גָּעַל {10x} **gâ'al**, *gaw-al';* a prim. root; to *detest;* by impl. to *reject:*—abhor {5x}, lothe {3}, cast away {1x}, fail {1x}. See: TWOT—369; BDB—171d.

1603. גַּעַל {9x} **Ga'al**, *gah'-al;* from 1602; *loathing; Gaal,* an Isr.:—Gaal {9x}. See: BDB—172a.

1604. גֹּעַל {1x} **gô'al**, *go'-al;* from 1602; *abhorrence:*—loathing {1x}. See: TWOT—369a; BDB—172a.

1605. גָּעַר {14x} **gâ'ar**, *gaw-ar';* a prim. root; to *chide:*—rebuke {12x}, corrupt {1x}, reprove {1x}. See: TWOT—370; BDB—172a.

1606. גְּעָרָה {15x} **gᵉ'ârâh**, *gheh-aw-raw';* from 1605; a *chiding:*—rebuke {13x}, reproof {2x}. Syn.: 3198. See: TWOT—370a; BDB—172a.

1607. גָּעַשׁ {10x} **gâ'ash**, *gaw-ash';* a prim. root to *agitate* violently:—shake {5x}, move {3x}, trouble {1x}, toss themselves {1x}. See: TWOT—371; BDB—172b.

1608. גַּעַשׁ {4x} **Ga'ash**, *ga'-ash;* from 1607; a *quaking; Gaash,* a hill in Pal.:—Gaash {4x}. See: BDB—172b.

1609. גַּעְתָּם {3x} **Ga'tâm**, *gah-tawm';* of uncert. der.; *Gatam,* an Edomite:—Gatam {3x}. See: BDB—172b.

1610. גַּף {4x} **gaph**, *gaf;* from an unused root mean. to *arch;* the *back;* by extens. the *body* or self:—highest places {1x}, himself {1x}. See: TWOT—373a; BDB—172b, 172c.

1611. גַּף {3x} **gaph** (Aram.), *gaf;* corresp. to 1610; a *wing:*—wing {3x}. See: TWOT—2660; BDB—1086d.

1612. גֶּפֶן {55x} **gephen**, *gheh'-fen;* from an unused root mean. to *bend;* a *vine* (as *twining*), espec. the grape:—vine {54x}, tree {1x}. See: TWOT—372a; BDB—172b.

1613. גֹּפֶר {1x} **gôpher**, *go'-fer;* from an unused root, prob. mean. to *house in;* a kind of tree or wood (as used for *building*), appar. the *cypress:*—gopher {1x}. See: TWOT—374; BDB—172d.

1614. גָּפְרִית {7x} **gophrîyth**, *gof-reeth';* prob. fem. of 1613; prop. cypress-*resin;* by anal. *sulphur* (as equally inflammable):—brimstone {7x}. See: TWOT—375; BDB—172d.

1615. גִּר {1x} **gîr**, *gheer;* perh. from 3564; *lime* (from being *burned* in a kiln):—chalkstone {1x}. See: TWOT—347a; BDB—162c, 173a, 1086b.

1616. גֵּר {92x} **gêr**, *gare;* or (fully)

גּוּר **gêyr**, *gare;* from 1481; prop. a *guest;* by impl. a *foreigner:*—stranger {87x}, alien {1x}, sojourner {1x}, stranger + 376 {1x}, stranger + 4480 {1x}, strangers + 582 {1x}.

Geyr means "client; stranger." **(1)** A "client" was not simply a foreigner (5237 - *nakri*) or a stranger (2114 - *zar*). **(1a)** He was a permanent resident, once a citizen of another land, who

had moved into his new residence. **(1b)** Frequently he left his homeland under some distress, as when Moses fled to Midian (Ex 2:22). **(1c)** Whether the reason for his journey was to escape some difficulty or merely to seek a new place to dwell, he was one who sought acceptance and refuge. **(1d)** Consequently he might also call himself a *toshab* (8453), a settler. **(1e)** Neither the settler nor the "client" could possess land. **(1e1)** In the land of Canaan the possession of land was limited to members or descendants of the original tribal members. **(1e2)** Only they were full citizens who enjoyed all the rights of citizenry, which meant sharing fully in the inheritance of the gods and forefathers—the feudal privileges and responsibilities (cf. Eze 47:22).

(2) In Israel a *geyr*, like a priest, **(2a)** could possess no land and enjoyed the special privileges of the third tithe. **(2b)** Every third year the tithe of the harvest was to be deposited at the city gate with the elders and distributed among "the Levite, (because he hath no part nor inheritance with thee,) and the stranger, and the fatherless, and the widow, which are within thy gates" (Deut 14:29). **(3)** In the eschaton such "clients" were to be treated as full citizens: "And it shall come to pass, that ye shall divide it [the land] by lot for an inheritance unto you, and to the strangers that sojourn among you, which shall beget children among you: and they shall be unto you as born in the country among the children of Israel; they shall have inheritance with you among the tribes of Israel" (Eze 47:22). **(4)** Under the Mosaic law aliens were not slaves but were usually in the service of some Israelite whose protection they enjoyed (Deut 24:14). **(4a)** This, however, was not always the case. **(4b)** Sometimes a "client" was rich and an Israelite would be in his service (Lev 25:47).

(5) The *geyr* was to be treated (except for feudal privileges and responsibilities) as an Israelite, being responsible to and protected by the law: **(5a)** "Hear the causes between your brethren, and judge righteously between every man and his brother, and the stranger that is with him" (Deut 1:16); **(5b)** "ye shall therefore keep my statutes and my judgments, and shall not commit any of these abominations; neither any of your own nation, nor any stranger that sojourneth among you" (Lev 18:26); **(5c)** "ye shall have one manner of law, as well for the stranger, as for one of your own country: for I am the Lord your God" (Lev 24:22). **(6)** The *geyr* also enjoyed the Sabbath rest (Lev 25:6) and divine protection (Deut 10:18). **(7)** God commanded Israel to love the "client" as himself (Lev 19:34).

(8) The *geyr* could also be **(8a)** circumcised

(Ex 12:48) and **(8b)** enjoy all the privileges of the true religion: **(8b1)** the Passover (Ex 12:48–49), **(8b2)** the Atonement feast (Lev 16:29), **(8b3)** presenting offerings (Lev 17:8), and **(8b4)** all the feasts (Deut 16:11). **(8c)** He was also obligated to keep the purity laws (Lev 17:15). **(9)** Israel is told that God is the true owner of all the land and its people are but "clients" owing Him feudal obedience (Lev 19:34; Deut 10:19). **(10)** They are admonished to treat the client with justice, righteousness, and love because like Abraham (Gen 23:4) they were "clients" in Egypt (Ex 22:21). **(11)** In legal cases the "client" could appeal directly to God the great feudal Lord (Lev 24:22).

Syn: Two other nouns related to *geyr* are *megurim* (4033) and *gerut* (1628). *Megurim* refers to the "status or condition of being a client" (Gen 17:8) and to a "dwelling where one is a client" (Job 18:19). *Gerut* refers to a "place where clients dwell" (Jer 41:17). See: TWOT—330a; BDB—158a, 162c, 173a.

1617. אֵרָא {9x} **Gêrâ²**, *gay-raw'*; perh. from 1626; a *grain; Gera,* the name of six Isr.:—*Gera* {9x}. See: BDB—173a.

1618. גָּרָב {3x} **gârâb**, *gaw-rawb'*; from an unused root mean. to *scratch; scurf* (from *itching*):—scab {1x}, scurvy {2x}. See: TWOT—376a; BDB—173a.

1619. גָּרֵב {3x} **Gârêb**, *gaw-rabe'*; from the same as 1618; *scabby; Gareb,* the name of an Isr., also of a hill near Jerusalem:—*Gareb* {3x}. See: BDB—173a.

1620. גַּרְגַּר {1x} **gargar**, *gar-gar'*; by redupl. from 1641; a *berry* (as if a pellet of *rumination*):—berry {1x}. See: TWOT—386c; BDB—173a, 176b.

1621. גַּרְגְּרוֹת {4x} **garg°rôwth**, *gar-gher-owth'*; fem. plur. from 1641; the *throat* (as used in *rumination*):—neck {1x}. See: TWOT—386d; BDB—173a, 176b.

1622. גִּרְגָּשִׁי {7x} **Girgâshîy**, *ghir-gaw-shee'*; patrial from an unused name [of uncert. der.]; a *Girgashite,* one of the native tribes of Canaan:—Girgashite {6x}, Girgasite {1x}. BDB—See: 173a.

1623. גָּרַד {1x} **gârad**, *gaw-rad'*; a prim. root; to *abrade:*—scrape {1x}. See: TWOT—377; BDB—173b.

1624. גָּרָה {14x} **gârâh**, *gaw-raw'*; a prim. root; prop. to *grate,* i.e. (fig.) to *anger:*—stir up {6x}, meddle {4x}, contend {3x}, strive {1x}. See: TWOT—378; BDB—173b.

1625. גֵּרָה {11x} **gêrâh**, *gay-raw'*; from 1641; the *cud* (as *scraping* the throat):—

cud {11x}. See: TWOT—386a; BDB—173d, 176a.

1626. גֵּרָה {5x} **gêrâh**, *gay-raw'*; from 1641 (as in 1625); prop. (like 1620) a *kernel* (round as if *scraped*), i.e. a *gerah* or small weight (and coin):—*gerah* {5x}.

A *gerah*, was a weight, a 20th part of a shekel, equal to the weight of 16 barley grains or 4 to 5 carob beans. See: TWOT—386b; BDB—173d, 176a.

גֹּרָה **gôrâh**. See 1484.

1627. גָּרוֹן {8x} **gârôwn**, *gaw-rone'*; or (short.)

גָּרֹן **gârôn**, *gaw-rone'*; from 1641; the *throat* [comp. 1621] (as *roughened* by swallowing):—throat {4x}, neck {2x}, mouth {1x}, aloud {1x}. See: TWOT—378a; BDB—159a, 173c, 175c.

1628. גֵּרוּת {1x} **gêrûwth**, *gay-rooth'*; from 1481; a (temporary) *residence:*—habitation {1x}. See: TWOT—330b; BDB—158c, 173d.

1629. גָּרַז {1x} **gâraz**, *gaw-raz'*; a prim. root; to *cut* off:—cut off {1x}. See: TWOT—379; BDB—173d.

1630. גְּרִזִים {4x} **G⁽ᵉ⁾rîzîym**, *gher-ee-zeem'*; plur. of an unused noun from 1629 [comp. 1511], *cut up* (i.e. *rocky*); *Gerizim*, a mountain of Pal.:—Gerizim {4x}. See: BDB—173d.

1631. גַּרְזֶן {4x} **garzen**, *gar-zen'*; from 1629; an *axe:*—ax {4x}. See: TWOT—379a; BDB—173d.

1632. גָּרֹל {1x} **gârôl**, *gaw-role'*; from the same as 1486; *harsh:*—man of great {1x}. See: TWOT—381a; BDB—175a.

גֹּרָל **gôrâl**. See 1486.

1633. גָּרַם {3x} **gâram**, *gaw-ram'*; a prim. root; to *be spare* or *skeleton-like;* used only as a denom. from 1634; (caus.) to *bone*, i.e. *denude* (by extens. *crunch*) the bones:—gnaw the bones {1x}, break {2x}. See: TWOT—382b; BDB—175.

1634. גֶּרֶם {5x} **gerem**, *gheh'-rem;* from 1633; a *bone* (as the *skeleton* of the body); hence, *self*, i.e. (fig.) *very:*—bone {3x}, strong {1x}, top {1x}. See: TWOT—382a; BDB—175a, 1086d.

1635. גְּרֶם **gerem** (Aram.), *gheh'-rem;* corresp. to 1634; a *bone:*—bone {1x}. See: TWOT—382a; BDB—1086d.

1636. גַּרְמִי {1x} **Garmîy**, *gar-mee';* from 1634; *bony*, i.e. *strong:*—Garmite {1x}. See: BDB—175a.

1637. גֹּרֶן {36x} **gôren**, *go'-ren;* from an unused root mean. to *smooth;* a threshing-*floor* (as made *even*); by anal. any open *area:*—. threshingfloor {18x}, floor {11x}, place {2x}, barn {1x}, barnfloor {1x}, corn {1x}, cornfloor + 1715 {1x}, threshingplace {1x}. See: TWOT—383a; BDB—175b, 188d.

גָּרוֹן **gârôn**. See 1627.

1638. גָּרַס {2x} **gâraç**, *gaw-ras';* a prim. root; to *crush;* also (intr. and fig.) to *dissolve:*—break {1x}. See: TWOT—387; BDB—175c, 176b.

1639. גָּרַע {21x} **gâraʿ**, *gaw-rah';* a prim. root; to *scrape* off; by impl. to *shave, remove, lessen,* or *withhold:*—diminish {8x}, take {3x}, . . .away {2x}, restrain {2x}, abated {1x}, keep back {1x}, clipped {1x}, minish {1x}, small {1x}, withdraweth {1x}. See: TWOT—384; BDB—175c.

1640. גָּרַף {1x} **gâraph**, *gaw-raf';* a prim. root; to *bear* off violently:—sweep away {1x}. See: TWOT—385; BDB—175d.

1641. גָּרַר {5x} **gârar**, *gaw-rar';* a prim. root; to *drag* off roughly; by impl. to *bring up* the cud (i.e. *ruminate*); by anal. to *saw:*—catch {1x}, destroy {1x}, chew {1x}, saw {1x}, continuing {1x}. See: TWOT—386; BDB—176a.

1642. גְּרָר {10x} **G⁽ᵉ⁾râr**, *gher-awr';* prob. from 1641; a *rolling* country; *Gerar*, a Philistine city:—Gerar {1x}. See: BDB—176b.

1643. גֶּרֶשׂ {2x} **geres**, *gheh'-res;* from an unused root mean. to *husk;* a *kernel* (collect.), i.e. *grain:*—beaten corn {2x}. See: TWOT—387a; BDB—176c.

1644. גָּרַשׁ {47x} **gârash**, *gaw-rash';* a prim. root; to *drive* out from a possession; espec. to *expatriate* or *divorce:*—drive out {20x}, cast out {8x}, thrust out {6x}, drive away {2x}, put away {2x}, divorced {2x}, driven {1x}, expel {1x}, drive forth {1x}, surely {1x}, troubled {1x}, cast up {1x}, divorced woman {1x}.

Garash means "to drive out, cast out." **(1)** An early occurrence in the Old Testament is in Ex 34:11: "Behold, I drive out before thee the Amorite, and the Canaanite. . . ." **(2)** The word may be used of a divorced woman as in Lev 21:7—a woman that is "put away from her husband." See: TWOT—388; BDB—176c.

1645. גֶּרֶשׁ {1x} **geresh**, *gheh'-resh;* from 1644; *produce* (as if *expelled*):—put forth {1x}. See: TWOT—388a; BDB—177a.

1646. גְּרֻשָׁה {1x} **g⁽ᵉ⁾rûshâh**, *gher-oo-shaw';* fem. pass. part. of 1644; (abstr.) *dispossession:*—exaction {1x}. See: TWOT—388b; BDB—177a.

1647. גֵּרְשֹׁם {14x} **Gêrᵉshôm**, *gay-resh-ome';* for 1648; *Gereshom,* the name of four Isr.:—Gershom {14x}. See: BDB—177a.

1648. גֵּרְשׁוֹן {17x} **Gêrᵉshôwn**, *gay-resh-one';* or

גֵּרְשׁוֹם **Gêrᵉshôwm**, *gay-resh-ome';* from 1644; a *refugee; Gereshon* or *Gereshom,* an Isr.:—Gershon {17x}. See: TWOT—388b; BDB—177a.

1649. גֵּרְשֻׁנִּי {13x} **Gerᵉshunnîy**, *gay-resh-oon-nee';* patron. from 1648; a *Geres-honite* or desc. of Gereshon:—Gershonite, sons of Gershon {13x}. See: BDB—177b.

1650. גְּשׁוּר {9x} **Gᵉshûwr**, *ghesh-oor';* from an unused root (mean. to *join); bridge; Geshur,* a district of Syria:—Geshur {8x}, Geshurite {1x}. See: BDB—178a.

1651. גְּשׁוּרִי {6x} **Gᵉshûwrîy**, *ghe-shoo-ree';* patrial from 1650; a *Geshurite* (also collect.) or inhab. of Geshur:—Geshuri {2x}, Geshurites {4x}. See: BDB—178c.

1652. גָּשַׁם {1x} **gâsham**, *gaw-sham';* a prim. root; to *shower* violently:—(cause to) rain {1x}. See: TWOT—389; BDB—177d.

1653. גֶּשֶׁם {35x} **geshem**, *gheh'-shem;* from 1652; a *shower:*—rain {31x}, shower {4x}. See: TWOT—389a; BDB—177c, 1086d.

1654. גֶּשֶׁם {4x} **Geshem**, *gheh'-shem;* or (prol.)

גַּשְׁמוּ **Gashmûw**, *gash-moo';* the same as 1653; *Geshem* or *Gashmu,* an Arabian:—Geshem {3x}, Gashmu {1x}. See: BDB—177c, 177d.

1655. גֶּשֶׁם {5x} **geshem** (Aram.), *gheh'-shem;* appar. the same as 1653; used in a peculiar sense, the *body* (prob. for the [fig.] idea of a *hard* rain):—body {5x}. See: TWOT—2662; BDB—1086d.

1656. גֹּשֶׁם {1x} **gôshem**, *go'-shem;* from 1652; equiv. to 1653:—rained upon {1x}. See: TWOT—389; BDB—177d.

גַּשְׁמוּ **Gashmûw**. See 1654.

1657. גֹּשֶׁן {15x} **Gôshen**, *go'-shen;* prob. of Eg. or.; *Goshen,* the residence of the Isr. in Egypt; also a place in Pal.:—Goshen {15x}. See: TWOT—390; BDB—177d.

1658. גִּשְׁפָּא {1x} **Gishpâᵓ**, *ghish-paw';* of un-cert. der.; *Gishpa,* an Isr.:—Gispa {1x}. See: BDB—177d.

1659. גָּשַׁשׁ {2x} **gâshash**, *gaw-shash';* a prim. root; appar. to *feel* about:—grope {2x}. See: TWOT—391; BDB—178c.

1660. גַּת {5x} **gath**, *gath;* prob. from 5059 (in the sense of *treading* out grapes); a

wine-*press* (or vat for holding the grapes in pressing them):—winepress {3x}, press {1x}, winefat {1x}. See: TWOT—841a; BDB—178c, 387c.

1661. גַּת {33x} **Gath**, *gath;* the same as 1660; *Gath,* a Philistine city:—Gath {33x}. See: BDB—178c, 387d, 440c.

1662. גַּת־הַחֵפֶר **Gath-ha-Chêpher**, *gath-hah-khay'-fer;* or (abridged)

גִּתָּה־חֵפֶר **Gittâh-Chêpher**, *ghit-taw-khay'-fer;* from 1660 and 2658 with the art. ins.; *wine-press of* (the) *well; Gath-Chepher,* a place in Pal.:—Gath-kephr {1x}, Gittah-kephr {1x}. See: BDB—387d.

1663. גִּתִּי {10x} **Gittîy**, *ghit-tee';* patrial from 1661; a *Gittite* or inhab. of Gath:—Gittite {10x}. See: BDB—178c, 388a.

1664. גִּתַּיִם {2x} **Gittayim**, *ghit-tah'-yim;* dual of 1660; *double wine-press; Git-tajim,* a place in Pal.:—Gittaim {2x}. See: BDB—178c, 388a.

1665. גִּתִּית {3x} **Gittîyth**, *ghit-teeth';* fem. of 1663; a *Gittite* harp:—Gittith {3x}. See: BDB—178c, 388a.

1666. גֶּתֶר {2x} **Gether**, *gheh'-ther;* of uncert. der.; *Gether,* a son of Aram, and the region settled by him:—Gether {2x}. See: BDB—178c.

1667. גַּת־רִמּוֹן {4x} **Gath-Rimmôwn**, *gath-rim-mone';* from 1660 and 7416; *wine-press of* **(the)** *pomegranate; Gath-Rimmon,* a place in Pal.:—Gath-rimmon {4x}. See: BDB—387d.

ד

1668. דָּא {6x} **dâᵓ** (Aram.), *daw;* corresp. to 2088; *this:*—one {2x}, another {2x}, this {1x}. See: TWOT—2663; BDB—1086d.

1669. דָּאַב {3x} **dâᵓab**, *daw-ab';* a prim. root; to *pine:*—mourn {1x}, sorrow {1x}, sorrowful {1x}. See: TWOT—392; BDB—178a.

1670. דְּאָבָה {1x} **dᵉᵓâbâh**, *dèh-aw-baw';* from 1669; prop. *pining;* by anal. *fear:*—sorrow {1x}. See: TWOT—392a; BDB—178b.

1671. דְּאָבוֹן {1x} **dᵉᵓâbôwn**, *dèh-aw-bone';* from 1669; *pining:*—sorrow {1x}. See: TWOT—392b; BDB—178b.

1672. דָּאַג {7x} **dâᵓag**, *daw-ag';* a prim. root; *be anxious:*—afraid {3x}, sorrow {1x}, sorry {1x}, careful {1x}, take thought {1x}. See: TWOT—393; BDB—178b.

1673. דֹּאֵג {6x} **Dô°êg**, *do-ayg'*; or (fully)

דּוֹאֵג **Dôw°êg**, *do-ayg'*; act. part. of 1672; *anxious; Doëg*, an Edomite:—*Doeg* {6x}. See: BDB—178c.

1674. דְּאָגָה {6x} **d°âgâh**, *dèh-aw-gaw'*; from 1672; *anxiety:*—carefulness {2x}, fear {1x}, heaviness {1x}, sorrow {1x}, with care {1x}. See: TWOT—393a; BDB—178c.

1675. דָּאָה {4x} **dâ°âh**, *daw-aw'*; a prim. root; to *dart*, i.e. *fly* rapidly:—fly {4x}. See: TWOT—394; BDB—178d.

1676. דָּאָה {1x} **dâ°âh**, *daw-aw'*; from 1675; the *kite* (from its rapid *flight*):—vulture {1x}. See 7201. See: TWOT—394a; BDB—178d, 906b.

1677. דֹּב {12x} **dôb**, *dobe*; or (fully)

דּוֹב **dôwb**, *dobe*; from 1680; the *bear* (as slow):—bear {12x}. See: TWOT—396a; BDB—179a, 187b, 1087a.

1678. דֹּב {1x} **dôb** (Aram.), *dobe*; corresp. to 1677:—bear {1x}. See: TWOT—2664; BDB—1087a.

1679. דֹּבֶא {1x} **dôbe°**, *do'-beh*; from an unused root (comp. 1680) (prob. mean. to *be sluggish*, i.e. *restful*); *quiet:*—strength {1x}. See: TWOT—395a; BDB—179a.

1680. דָּבַב {1x} **dâbab**, *daw-bab'*; a prim. root (comp. 1679); to *move* slowly, i.e. *glide:*—cause to speak {1x}. See: TWOT—396; BDB—179a.

1681. דִּבָּה {9x} **dibbâh**, *dib-baw'*; from 1680 (in the sense of *furtive* motion); *slander:*— evil report {3x}, slander {3x}, infamy {2x}, slander {1x}. See: TWOT—396b; BDB—179a.

1682. דְּבוֹרָה {4x} **d°bôwrâh**, *deb-o-raw'*; or (short.)

דְּבֹרָה **d°bôrâh**, *deb-o-raw'*; from 1696 (in the sense of *orderly* motion); the *bee* (from its *systematic* instincts):—bee {1x}. See: TWOT—399f; BDB—184b.

1683. דְּבוֹרָה {10x} **D°bôwrâh**, *deb-o-raw'*; or (short.)

דְּבֹרָה **D°bôrâh**, *deb-o-raw'*; the same as 1682; *Deborah*, the name of two Hebrewesses:—*Deborah* {1x}. See: BDB—184b.

1684. דְּבַח {1x} **d°bach** (Aram.), *deb-akh'*; corresp. to 2076; to *sacrifice* (an animal):—offer sacrifice {1x}. See: TWOT—2665; BDB—1087a.

1685. דְּבַח {1x} **d°bach** (Aram.), *deb-akh'*; from 1684; a *sacrifice:*—sacrifice {1x}. See: TWOT—2665a; BDB—1087a.

1686. דִּבְיוֹן {1x} **dibyôwn**, *dib-yone'*; in the marg. for the textual reading

חֲרְיוֹן **cheryôwn**, *kher-yone'*; both (in the plur. only and) of uncert. der.; prob. some cheap vegetable, perh. a bulbous root:—dove's dung {1x}. See: BDB—179b.

1687. דְּבִיר {16x} **d°bîyr**, *deb-eer'*; or (short.)

דְּבִר **d°bîr**, *deb-eer'*; from 1696 (appar. in the sense of *oracle*); the *shrine* or innermost part of the sanctuary:—oracle {1x}. The place from which deity speaks. See: TWOT—399g; BDB—184b.

1688. דְּבִיר {14x} **D°bîyr**, *deb-eer'*; or (short.)

דְּבִר **D°bîr** (Josh 13:26 [but see 3810]), *deb-eer'*; the same as 1687; *Debir*, the name of an Amoritish king and of two places in Pal.:—*Debir* {14x}. See: BDB—184c, 529a.

1689. דִּבְלָה {1x} **Diblâh**, *dib-law'*; prob. an orth. err. for 7247; *Diblah*, a place in Syria:—Diblath {1x}. See: BDB—179c.

1690. דְּבֵלָה {5x} **d°bêlâh**, *deb-ay-law'*; from an unused root (akin to 2082) prob. mean. to *press* together; a *cake* of pressed figs:—cake of figs {3x}, lump {2x}. See: TWOT—397a; BDB—179b.

1691. דִּבְלַיִם {1x} **Diblayim**, *dib-lah'-yim*; dual from the masc. of 1690; *two cakes; Diblajim*, a symb. name:—Diblaim {1x}. See: BDB—179c.

דִּבְלָתָיִם **Diblâthayim**. See 1015.

1692. דָּבַק {54x} **dâbaq**, *daw-bak'*; a prim. root; prop. to *impinge*, i.e. *cling* or *adhere*; fig. to *catch* by pursuit:—cleave {32x}, follow hard {5x}, overtake {3x}, stick {3x}, keep fast {2x}, . . . together {2x}, abide {1x}, close {1x}, joined {1x}, pursued {1x}, take {1x}.

Dabaq means "to cling, cleave, keep close." **(1)** *Dabaq* yields the noun form for "glue" and also the more abstract ideas of "loyalty, devotion." **(2)** In Gen 2:24: "Therefore shall a man leave his father and his mother, and shall cleave unto his wife: and they shall be one flesh." This usage reflects the basic meaning of one object's (person's) being joined to another. **(3)** In this sense, Eleazar's hand "cleaved" to the sword as he struck down the Philistines (2 Sa 23:10). **(4)** Jeremiah's linen waistcloth "clung" to his loins, symbolic of Israel's "clinging" to God (Jer 13:11). **(5)** In time of war and siege, the resulting thirst and famine caused the tongue "to cleave" to the roof of the mouth of those who had been so afflicted. **(6)** The figurative use of *dabaq* in the sense of "loyalty" and "affection" is based on the physical closeness of the persons involved, such as **(6a)** a husband's

closeness to his wife (Gen 2:24), **(6b)** Shechem's affection for Dinah (Gen 34:3), or **(6c)** Ruth's staying with Naomi (Ruth 1:14). **(7)** "Cleaving" to God is equivalent to "loving" God (Deut 30:20). See: TWOT—398; BDB—179c, 1087a.

1693. דְּבַק {1x} **dᵉbaq** (Aram.), *deb-ak';* corresp. to 1692; to *stick* to:—cleave {1x}. See: TWOT—2666; BDB—1087a.

1694. דֶּבֶק {3x} **debeq**, *deh'-bek;* from 1692; a *joint;* by impl. *solder:*—joint {2x}, solder {1x}. See: TWOT—398a; BDB—180a.

1695. דָּבֵק {3x} **dâbêq**, *daw-bake';* from 1692; *adhering:*—cleave {1x}, joining {1x}, stick closer {1x}. See: TWOT—398?; BDB—180a.

1696. דָּבַר {1143x} **dâbar**, *daw-bar';* a prim. root; perh. prop. to *arrange;* but used fig. (of words), to *speak;* rarely (in a destructive sense) to *subdue:*—speak {840x}, say {118x}, talk {46x}, promise {31x}, tell {25x}, commune {20x}, pronounce {14x}, utter {7x}, command {4x} misc. {38x} = answer, appoint, bid, declare, destroy, give, name, rehearse, be spokesman, subdue, teach, think, use [entreaties], X well, X work.

Dabar means "to speak, say." **(1)** This verb focuses not only on the content of spoken verbal communication but also and especially on the time and circumstances of what is said. **(2)** Unlike *'amar* (559), "to say," *dabar* often appears without any specification of what was communicated. **(2a)** Those who "speak" are primarily persons (God or men) or organs of speech. **(2a1)** In Gen 8:15 (the first occurrence of this verb) God "spoke" to Noah, **(2a2)** while in Gen 18:5 one of the three men "spoke" to Abraham. **(3)** Exceptions to this generalization occur, for example **(3a)** in Job 32:7, where Elihu personifies "days" (a person's age) as that which has the right "to speak" first. **(3b)** In 2 Sa 23:2 David says that the Spirit of the Lord "spoke" to him; contrary to many (especially liberal) scholars, this is probably a reference to the Holy Spirit.

(4) Among the special meanings of this verb are **(4a)** "to say" (Dan 9:21), **(4b)** "to command" (2 Kin 1:9), **(4c)** "to promise" (Deut 6:3), **(4d)** "to commission" (Ex 1:17), **(4e)** "to announce" (Jer 36:31), **(4f)** "to order or command" (Deut 1:14), and **(4g)** "to utter a song" (Judg 5:12). **(4h)** Such secondary meanings are, however, quite infrequent. Syn.: *Amar* (559) usually focuses on the mode of revelation, whereas *dabar* focuses on the content. See: TWOT—399; BDB—180b.

1697. דָּבָר {1439x} **dâbâr**, *daw-baw';* from 1696; a *word;* by impl. a *matter* (as *spoken* of) or *thing;* adv. a *cause:*—word {807x},

thing {231x}, matter {63x}, acts {51x}, chronicles {38x}, saying {25x}, commandment {20x}, misc. {204x} = advice, affair, answer, X any such (thing), + because of, book, business, care, case, cause, certain rate, X commune (-ication), + concern [-ing], + confer, counsel, + dearth, decree, deed, X disease, due, duty, effect, + eloquent, errand, [evil favoured-] ness, + glory, + harm, hurt, + iniquity, + judgment, language, + lying, manner, message, [no] thing, oracle, X ought, X parts, + pertaining, + please, portion, + power, promise, provision, purpose, question, rate, reason, report, request, X (as hast) said, sake, sentence, + sign, + so, some [uncleanness], somewhat to say, + song, speech, X spoken, talk, task, + that, X there done, thought, + thus, tidings, what [-soever], + wherewith, which, work.

Dabar means "word, matter; something." **(1)** The noun *dabar* refers, first, to what is said, to the actual "word" itself; whereas *'emer* (561) is essentially oral communication (the act of speaking). **(2)** Before the dispersion from the tower of Babel all men spoke the same "words" or language (Gen 11:1). **(3)** This noun can also be used of the content of speaking. When God "did according to the word of Moses" (Ex 8:13), He granted his request. **(4)** The noun can connote "matter" or "affair," as in Gen 12:17, where it is reported that God struck Pharaoh's household with plagues "because of Sarai." **(5)** A rather specialized occurrence of this sense appears in references to **(5a)** records of the "events of a period" (1 Kin 14:19) or **(5b)** the activities of a particular person (1 Kin 11:41; cf. Gen 15:1).

(6) *Dabar* can be used as a more general term in the sense of **(6a)** "something"—so in Gen 24:66 the "all things" is literally "all of something(s)"; **(6b)** it is an indefinite generalized concept rather than a reference to everything in particular. **(7)** This noun also appears to have had almost a technical status in Israel's law procedures. Anyone who had a "matter" before Moses had a law case (Ex 18:16). **(8)** As a biblical phrase "the word of the Lord" is quite important; it occurs about 242 times. **(8a)** Against the background just presented it is important to note that "word" here may focus on the content (meaning) of what was said, **(8b)** but it also carries overtones of the actual "words" themselves. **(8c)** It was the "word of the Lord" that came to Abram in a vision after his victory over the kings who had captured Lot (Gen 15:1). **(8d)** In most cases this is a technical phrase referring expressly to prophetic revelation (about 225 times). **(8e)** It has been suggested that this phrase has judicial overtones although there are only 7 passages where this is certain (cf. Num 15:31).

(9) This noun is used twice of God's "affairs" in the sense of the care of the temple (1 Chr 26:32). (10) The "word" of God indicates God's thoughts and will. (10a) This should be contrasted with His name, which indicates His person and presence. (10b) Therefore, God's "word" is called "holy" only once (cf. Ps 105:42), while His name is frequently called "holy." Syn: Several other nouns related to the verb *dabar* occur infrequently. (A) *Dibrah* (1700), which occurs 5 times, means "cause, manner" (Job 5:8). (B) *Dabberet* (1703) means "word" once (Deut 33:3). (C) *Deborah* (1682) appears 5 times and refers to "honey bee" (Deut 1:44; Ps 118:12). (D) *Midbar* (4057) refers to "speaking" once (Song 4:3). (E) *Dabar* refers to what is said, the actual word itself; whereas *emer* (561) is essentially oral communication (the act of speaking). See: TWOT–399a; BDB–182a.

1698. דֶּבֶר {49x} **deber**, *deh'-ber;* from 1696 (in the sense of *destroying*); a *pestilence:*—pestilence {47x}, plagues {1x}, murrain {1x}.

Deber means "pestilence." (1) The meaning of *deber* is best denoted by the English word "pestilence" or "plague." (1a) A country might be quickly reduced in population by the "plague" (cf. 2 Sa 24:13ff.). (1b) The nature of the "plague" (bubonic or other) is often difficult to determine from the contexts, as the details of medical interest are not given or are scanty. (2) In the prophetical writings, the "plague" occurs with other disasters: famine, flood, and the sword: "When they fast, I will not hear their cry; and when they offer burnt offering and an oblation, I will not accept them: but I will consume them by the sword, and by the famine, and by the pestilence" (Jer 14:12). See: TWOT–399b; BDB–184a.

1699. דֹּבֶר {2x} **dôber**, *do'-ber;* from 1696 (in its original sense); a *pasture* (from its *arrangement* of the flock):—fold {1x}, manner {1x}. See: TWOT–399c; BDB–184a.

דְּבִר **deᵇbîr** or

דְּבִר **Deᵇbîr**. See 1687, 1688.

1699′. דִּבֵּר {1x} **dibbêr**, *dib-bare';* for 1697:—word {1x}. See: BDB–184c.

1700. דִּבְרָה {5x} **dibrâh**, *dib-raw';* fem. of 1697; a *reason, suit* or *style:*—cause {1x}, end {1x}, estate {1x}, order {1x}, regard {1x}. See: TWOT–399e; BDB–184a, 1087a.

1701. דִּבְרָה {1x} **dibrâh** (Aram.), *dib-raw';* corresp. to 1700:—intent {1x}, sake {1x}. See: TWOT–2667; BDB–1087a.

דְּבֹרָה **deᵇbôrâh** or

דְּבֹרָה **Deᵇbôrâh**. See 1682, 1683.

1702. דֹּבְרָה {1x} **dôbᵉrâh**, *do-ber-aw';* fem. act. part. of 1696 in the sense of *driving* [comp. 1699]; a *raft:*—float {1x}. See: TWOT–399d; BDB–184a.

1703. דַּבָּרָה {1x} **dabbârâh**, *dab-baw-raw';* intens. from 1696; a *word:*—word {1x}. See: TWOT–399j; BDB–184c.

1704. דִּבְרִי {1x} **Dibrîy**, *dib-ree';* from 1697; *wordy;* Dibri, an Isr.:—Dibri {1x}. See: BDB–184c.

1705. דָּבְרַת {3x} **Dâbᵉrath**, *daw-ber-ath';* from 1697 (perh. in the sense of 1699); *Daberath*, a place in Pal.:—Dabareh {1x}, Daberath {1x}. See: BDB–184b.

1706. דְּבַשׁ {54x} **deᵇbash**, *deb-ash';* from an unused root mean. to *be gummy; honey* (from its *stickiness*); by anal. *syrup:*—honey {52x}, honeycomb + 3295 {1x}, honeycomb + 6688 {1x}. See: TWOT–400a; BDB–185a.

1707. דַּבֶּשֶׁת {1x} **dabbesheth**, *dab-beh'-sheth;* intens. from the same as 1706; a sticky *mass*, i.e. the *hump* of a camel:—hunch of a camel {1x}. See: TWOT–400b; BDB–185c.

1708. דַּבֶּשֶׁת {1x} **Dabbesheth**, *dab-beh'-sheth;* the same as 1707; *Dabbesheth*, a place in Pal.:—Dabbesheth {1x}. See: BDB–185c.

1709. דָּג {20x} **dâg**, *dawg;* or (fully)

דָּאג **dâ'g** (Neh. 13:16), *dawg;* from 1711; a *fish* (as *prolific*); or perh. rather from 1672 (as *timid*); but still better from 1672 (in the sense of *squirming*, i.e. moving by the vibratory action of the tail); a *fish* (often used collect.):—fish {20x}. See: TWOT–401a; BDB–178d, 185c.

1710. דָּגָה {15x} **dâgâh**, *daw-gaw';* fem. of 1709, and mean. the same:—fish {1x}. See: TWOT–401b; BDB–185d.

1711. דָּגָה {1x} **dâgâh**, *daw-gaw';* a prim. root; to *move rapidly;* used only as a denom. from 1709; to *spawn*, i.e. *become numerous:*—grow {1x}. See: TWOT–401; BDB–185c.

1712. דָּגוֹן {13x} **Dâgôwn**, *daw-gohn';* from 1709; the *fish-god; Dagon*, a Philistine deity:—Dagon {13x}.

1713. דָּגַל {4x} **dâgal**, *daw-gal';* a prim. root; to *flaunt*, i.e. *raise a flag;* fig. to *be conspicuous:*—set up banner {3x}, chiefest {1x}. See: TWOT–402b; BDB–186a, 186b.

1714. דֶּגֶל {14x} **degel**, *deh'-gel;* from 1713; a *flag:*—banner {1x}, standard {13x}. See: TWOT–402a; BDB–186b.

1715. דָּגָן {40x} dâgân, daw-gawn'; from 1711; prop. increase, i.e. grain:—corn {37x}, wheat {2x}, cornfloor + 1637 {1x}. See: TWOT—403a; 186b.

1716. דָּגַר {2x} dâgar, daw-gar'; a prim. root, to brood over eggs or young:— gather {1x}, sit {1x}. See: TWOT—404; BDB—186c.

1717. דַּד {4x} dad, dad; appar. from the same as 1730; the breast (as the seat of love, or from its shape):—breast {2x}, teat {2x}. See: TWOT—405; BDB—186d.

1718. דָּדָה {2x} dâdâh, daw-daw'; a doubtful root; to walk gently:—went {1x}, go softly {1x}. See: TWOT—406; BDB—186d.

1719. דְּדָן {11x} Dᵉdân, ded-awn'; or (prol.)

דְּדָנֶה Dᵉdâneh (Eze 25:13), deh-daw'-neh; of uncert. der.; Dedan, the name of two Cushites and of their territory:— Dedan {11x}. See: BDB—186d, 187a, 922b.

1720. דְּדָנִים {1x} Dᵉdânîym, ded-aw-neem'; plur. of 1719 (as patrial); Dedanites, the desc. or inhab. of Dedan:—Dedanim {1x}. See: BDB—187a.

1721. דְּדָנִים {2x} Dôdânîym, do-daw-neem'; or (by orth. err.)

רֹדָנִים Rôdânîym (1 Chr 1:7), ro-daw-neem'; a plur. of uncert. der.; Dodanites, or desc. of a son of Javan:—Dodanim {1x}. See: BDB—187a, 922b, 922c.

1722. דְּהַב {23x} dᵉhab (Aram.), deh-hab'; corresp. to 2091; gold:—gold {14x} golden {9x}. See: TWOT—2668; BDB—1087a.

1723. דַּהֲוָא {1x} Dahăvâᵓ (Aram.), dah-hav-aw'; of uncert. der.; Dahava, a people colonized in Samaria:—Dehavites {1x}. See: BDB—1087a.

1724. דָּהַם {1x} dâham, daw-ham'; a prim. root (comp. 1740); to be dumb, i.e. (fig.) dumb-founded:—be astonied {1x}. See: TWOT—407; BDB—187a.

1725. דָּהַר {1x} dâhar, daw-har'; a prim. root; to curvet or move irregularly:— pransing {1x}. See: TWOT—408; BDB—187b.

1726. דַּהֲהַר {2x} dahăhar, dah-hah-har'; by redupl. from 1725; a gallop:— pransings {2x}. See: TWOT—408a; BDB—187b.

דֹּואֵג Dôwᵓêg. See 1673.

1727. דּוּב {1x} dûwb, doob; a prim. root; to mope, i.e. (fig.) pine:—cast sorrow {1x}. See: TWOT—409; BDB—187b.

דּוֹב dôwb. See 1677.

1728. דַּוָּג {2x} davvâg, dav-vawg'; an orth. var. of 1709 as a denom. 1771]; a fisherman:—fisher {2x}. See: TWOT—401d; BDB—186a, 187b.

1729. דּוּגָה {1x} dûwgâh, doo-gaw'; fem. from the same as 1728; prop. fishery, i.e. a hook for fishing:—fishhook + 5518 {1x}. See: TWOT—401e; BDB—186a, 187b.

1730. דּוֹד dôwd, dode; or (short.)

דֹּד {61x} dôd, dode; from an unused root mean. prop. to boil, i.e. (fig.) to love; by impl. a love-token, lover, friend; spec. an uncle:—See: TWOT—410a; BDB—186d, 187c.

1731. דּוּד {7x} dûwd, dood; from the same as 1730; a pot (for boiling); also (by resemblance of shape) a basket:—basket {3x}, caldron {1x}, kettle {1x}, seething pot {2x}. See: TWOT—410e; BDB—188b.

1732. דָּוִד {1076x} Dâvîd, daw-veed'; rarely (fully)

דָּוִיד Dâvîyd, daw-veed'; from the same as 1730; loving; David, the youngest son of Jesse:—David {1076x}. See: TWOT—410c; BDB—187d.

1733. דּוֹדָה {3x} dôwdâh, do-daw'; fem. of 1730; an aunt:—aunt {1x}, father's sister {1x}, uncle's wife {1x}. See: TWOT—410b; BDB—186d, 187d.

1734. דּוֹדוֹ {5x} Dôwdôw, do-do'; from 1730; loving; Dodo, the name of three Isr.:—Dodo {5x}. See: BDB—186d, 187d.

1735. דּוֹדָוָהוּ {1x} Dôwdâvâhûw, do-daw-vaw'-hoo; from 1730 and 3050; love of Jah; Dodavah, an Isr.:—Dodavah {1x}. See: BDB—187d.

1736. דּוּדַי {7x} dûwday, doo-dah'-ee; from 1731; a boiler or basket; also the mandrake (as aphrodisiac):—basket {1x}, mandrake {7x}. See: TWOT—410d; BDB—188b.

1737. דּוֹדַי {1x} Dôwday, do-dah'-ee; formed like 1736; amatory; Dodai, an Isr.:—Dodai {1x}. See: BDB—187d.

1738. דָּוָה {1x} dâvâh, daw-vaw'; a prim. root; to be sick (as if in menstruation):— infirmity {1x}. See: TWOT—411; BDB—188c.

1739. דָּוֶה {5x} dâveh, daw-veh'; from 1738; sick (espec. in menstruation):— faint {2x}, menstruous cloth {1x}, she that is sick {1x}, having sickness {1x}. See: TWOT—411b; BDB—188c.

1740. דּוּחַ {4x} dûwach, doo'-akh; a prim. root; to thrust away; fig. to cleanse:—

cast out {1x}, purge {1x}, wash {1x}. See: TWOT—412; BDB—188d.

1741. דְּוַי {2x} dᵉvay, *dev-ah'-ee;* from 1739; *sickness;* fig. *loathing:*—languishing {1x}, sorrowful {1x}. See: TWOT—411a; BDB—188c.

1742. דַּוָּי {3x} davvây, *dav-voy';* from 1739; *sick;* fig. *troubled:*—faint {3x}. See: TWOT—411d; BDB—188d.

דָּוִיד **Dâvîyd.** See 1732.

1743. דּוּךְ {1x} dûwk, *dook;* a prim. root; to *bruise* in a mortar:—beat {1x}. See: TWOT—413; BDB—188d.

1744. דּוּכִיפַת {2x} dûwkîyphath, *doo-kee-fath';* of uncert. der.; the *hoopoe* or else the *grouse:*—lapwing {2x}. See: TWOT—414; BDB—189a.

1745. דּוּמָה {2x} dûwmâh, *doo-maw';* from an unused root mean. to *be dumb* (comp. 1820); *silence;* fig. *death:*—silence {2x}. See: TWOT—415a; BDB—189a.

1746. דּוּמָה {4x} Dûwmâh, *doo-maw';* the same as 1745; *Dumah,* a tribe and region of Arabia:—Dumah {4x}. See: BDB—189a.

1747. דּוּמִיָּה {4x} dûwmîyâh, *doo-me-yaw';* from 1820; *stillness;* adv. *silently;* abstr. *quiet, trust:*—silence {1x}, silent {1x}, waiteth {2x}. See: TWOT—415b; BDB—189b.

1748. דּוּמָם {3x} dûwmâm, *doo-mawm';* from 1826; *still;* adv. *silently:*—dumb {1x}, silent {1x}, quietly wait {1x}. See: TWOT—415c; BDB—189b.

1749. דּוֹנַג {4x} dôwnag, *do-nag';* of uncert. der.; *wax:*—wax {4x}. See: TWOT—444a; BDB—200a.

1750. דּוּץ {1x} dûwts, *doots;* a prim. root; to *leap:*—turn into joy {1x}. See: TWOT—416; BDB—189b.

1751. דּוּק {1x} dûwq (Aram.), *dook;* corresp. to 1854; to *crumble:*—break into pieces {1x}. See: TWOT—2681; BDB—1089a.

1752. דּוּר {1x} dûwr, *dure;* a prim. root; prop. to *gyrate* (or move in a circle), i.e. to *remain:*—dwell {1x}. See: TWOT—418; BDB—189c, 1087b.

1753. דּוּר {7x} dûwr (Aram.), *dure;* corresp. to 1752; to *reside:*—dwell {5x}, inhabitant {2x}. See: TWOT—2669; BDB—1087b.

1754. דּוּר {3x} dûwr, *dure;* from 1752; a *circle, ball* or *pile:*—ball {1x}, burn

{1x}, round about {1x}. See: TWOT—418a; BDB—189c, 462a.

1755. דּוֹר dôwr, *dore;* or (short.)

דֹּר {167x} dôr, *dore;* from 1752; prop. a *revolution* of time, i.e. an *age* or *generation;* also a *dwelling:*—generation {133x}, all {18x}, many {6x}, age {2x}, ever {5x}, X evermore {1x}, never {1x}, posterity {1x}.

Dor means "generation." **(1)** In the Old Testament, the word *dor* occurs about 167 times; as many as 74 of these are in the repetition "*dor* plus *dor*," meaning "alway." **(2)** The first occurrence of the word is in Gen 6:9: "These are the generations of Noah [the account of Noah]: Noah was a just man and perfect in his generations, and Noah walked with God." **(3)** First the concrete meaning of "generation" is the "period during which people live": "And the Lord said unto Noah, Come thou and all thy house into the ark; for thee have I seen righteous before me in this generation" (Gen 7:1). **(4)** A "generation" may be described as **(4a)** "perverse" (Deut 32:5) or **(4b)** "righteous" (Ps 14:5).

(5) Close to this meaning is the temporal element of *dor:* A *dor* is roughly the period of time from one's birth to one's maturity, which in the Old Testament corresponds to a period of about 40 years (Num 14:33). **(6)** Abraham received the promise that four "generations" of his descendants were to be in Egypt before the Promised Land would be inherited. **(7)** Israel was warned to be faithful to the Lord, **(7a)** as the punishment for disobedience would extend to the fourth "generation" (Ex 20:5); **(7b)** but the Lord's love extends to a thousand "generations" of those who love Him (Deut 7:9). **(8)** The lasting element of God's covenantal faithfulness is variously expressed with the word *dor:* "Thy faithfulness is unto all generations: thou hast established the earth, and it abideth" (Ps 119:90)

(9) The use of *dor* in Isaiah 51 teaches the twofold perspective of "generation," with reference to the future as well as to the past. **(9a)** Isaiah spoke about the Lord's lasting righteousness and said that His deliverance is everlasting (literally, "generation of generations"—v. 8); **(9b)** but in view of Israel's situation, Isaiah petitioned the Lord to manifest His loving strength on behalf of Israel as in the past (literally, "generations forever"—v. 9). **(9c)** Thus, depending on the context, *dor* may refer to the past, the present, or the future. The psalmist recognized the obligation of one "generation" to the "generations" to come: "One generation shall praise thy works to another, and shall declare thy mighty acts" (Ps 145:4). **(10)** Even the grey-haired man has the opportunity to

instruct the youth (Ps 71:17–18). See: TWOT—418b; BDB—189c, 201b, 1087b.

1756. דּוֹר {7x} **Dôwr**, *dore* or (by perm.)

דֹּאר **Dô'r** (Josh. 17:11; 1 Kings 4:11), *dore;* from 1755; *dwelling; Dor,* a place in Pal.:—*Dor* {1x}. See: BDB—178d, 190b.

1757. דּוּרָא {1x} **Dûwrâ'** (Aram.), *doo-raw';* prob. from 1753; *circle* or *dwelling; Dura,* a place in Bab.:—Dura {1x}. See: BDB—1087b.

1758. דּוּשׁ {14x} **dûwsh**, *doosh;* or

דּוֹשׁ **dôwsh**, *dōsh;* or

דִּישׁ **dîysh**, *deesh;* a prim. root; to *trample* or *thresh:*—thresh {9x}, tread out {3x}, break {1x}, tear {1x}, vr grass {1x}. See: TWOT—419; BDB—190b.

1759. דּוּשׁ {1x} **dûwsh** (Aram.), *doosh;* corresp. to 1758; to *trample:*—tread down {1x}. See: TWOT—2670; BDB—1087c.

1760. דָּחָה {11x} **dâchâh**, *daw-khaw';* or

דָּחַח **dâchach** (Jer 23:12), *daw-khakh';* a prim. root; to *push* down:—outcast {3x}, thrust {1x}, sore {1x}, overthrow {1x}, chase {1x}, tottering {1x}, driven away {1x}, driven on {1x}, cast down {1x}. See: TWOT—420; BDB—190d, 191a, 1087c.

1761. דַּחֲוָה {1x} **dachăvâh** (Aram.), *dakh-av-aw';* from the equiv. of 1760; prob. a musical *instrument* (as being *struck*):—instrument of music {1x}. See: TWOT—2671; BDB—1087c.

1762. דְּחִי {2x} **dᵉchîy**, *deh-khee';* from 1760; a *push,* i.e. (by impl.) a *fall:*—falling {2x}. See: TWOT—420a; BDB—191a.

1763. דְּחַל {6x} **dᵉchal** (Aram.), *deh-khal';* corresp. to 2119; to *slink,* i.e. (by impl.) to *fear,* or (caus.) *be formidable:*—make afraid {1x}, dreadful {2x}, fear {2x}, terrible {1x}. See: TWOT—2672; BDB—1087c.

1764. דֹּחַן {1x} **dôchan**, *do'-khan;* of uncert. der.; *millet:*—millet {1x}. See: TWOT—422a; BDB—191a.

1765. דָּחַף {4x} **dâchaph**, *daw-khaf';* a prim. root; to *urge,* i.e. *hasten:*—hasten {3x}, press {1x}. See: TWOT—423; BDB—191b.

1766. דָּחַק {2x} **dâchaq**, *daw-khak';* a prim. root; to *press,* i.e. *oppress:*—thrust {1x}, vex {1x}. See: TWOT—424; 191b.

1767. דַּי {38x} **day**, *dahee;* of uncert. der.; *enough* (as noun or adv.), used chiefly with prep. in phrases:—enough {6x}, sufficient {5x}, from {5x}, when {3x}, since {3x}, able {3x}, misc. {13x}: according to, after ability, among, as oft as, more than enough, in, much as is sufficient, sufficiently, too much, very.

Day means "sufficiency; the required enough." **(1)** The word is translated variously according to the needs of a given passage. **(1a)** The meaning "sufficiency" is clearly manifested in Ex 36:7: "For the stuff they had was sufficient for all the work to make it, and too much." **(1b)** A different translation is warranted in Jer 49:9: "If thieves [come] by night, they will destroy till they have enough" (cf. Obad 5). **(1c)** In Prov 25:16 the word means only what one's digestive system can handle: "Hast thou found honey? Eat so much as is sufficient for thee, lest thou be filled therewith, and vomit it." **(1d)** Other passages use this word of money (Deut 15:8). **(1e)** In Jer 51:58 day preceded by the preposition be means "only for": "The people shall labor in vain [only for nothing], and the folk in the fire [only for fire], and they shall be weary." **(2)** The phrase "as long as there is need" signifies until there is no more required (Mal 3:10 - "that there shall not be room enough to receive it"). **(3)** The word first appears in Ex 36:5 and is preceded by the preposition min: "The people bring much more than enough for the service of the work, which the Lord commanded to make."

(4) There are many special uses of *day* where the basic meaning is in the background and the context dictates a different nuance. **(4a)** When preceded by the preposition ke, "as," the word usually means "according to": "The judge shall cause him to lie down, and to be beaten before his face, according to his fault, by a certain number" (Deut 25:2). **(4b)** Preceded by min, "from," the word sometimes means "regarding the need." This illuminates passages such as 1 Sa 7:16: "And he [Samuel] went from year to year [according to the need of each year; "annually"] in circuit to Beth-el" (cf. Is 66:23). **(4c)** In other places this phrase (day preceded by min) signifies "as often as": "Then the princes of the Philistines went forth: and it came to pass, after they went forth, that David behaved himself more wisely than all the servants of Saul" (1 Sa 18:30). See: TWOT—425; BDB—95a, 191b, 461d, 552a.

1768. דִּי {19x} **dîy** (Aram.), *dee;* appar. for 1668; *that,* used as rel., conjunc., and espec. (with prep.) in adv. phrases; also as prep. *of:*—as {1x}, but {1x}, for {1x}, forasmuch {1x}, now {1x}, of {2x}, seeing {1x}, than {1x}, that {2x}, therefore {1x}, until {1x}, what soever {1x}, when {2x}, which {1x}, whom {1x}, whose {1x}. See: TWOT—2673; BDB—1087c, 1096c, 1096d.

1769. דִּיבוֹן {1x} **Dîybôwn,** *dee-bome';* or (short.)

דִּיבֹן **Dîybôn,** *dee-bone';* from 1727; *pining; Dibon,* the name of three places in Pal.:—Dibon {1x}. See: BDB—192a. [*Also, with* 1410 *added,* Dibon-gad.]

1770. דִּיג {1x} **dîyg,** *deeg;* denom. from 1709; to *fish:*—fish {1x}. See: TWOT—401c; BDB—185d, 192a.

1771. דַּיָּג {2x} **dayâg,** *dah-yawg';* from 1770; a *fisherman:*—fisher {2x}, See: TWOT—401d; BDB—186a, 192a.

1772. דַּיָּה {12x} **dayâh,** *dah-yaw';* intens. from 1675; a *falcon* (from its *rapid* flight):—vulture {1x}. See: TWOT—394b; BDB—178d, 192a.

1773. דְּיוֹ {1x} **dᵉyôw,** *deh-yo';* of uncert. der.; *ink:*—ink {1x}. See: TWOT—411e; BDB—188d, 192a.

1774. דִּי זָהָב {1x} **Dîy zâhâb,** *dee zaw-hawb';* as if from 1768 and 2091; *of gold; Dizahab,* a place in the desert:—Dizahab {1x}. See: BDB—191d.

1775. דִּימוֹן {2x} **Dîymôwn,** *dee-mone';* perh. for 1769; *Dimon,* a place in Pal.:—Dimon {1x}. See: BDB—192a.

1776. דִּימוֹנָה {1x} **Dîymôwnâh,** *dee-mo-naw';* fem. of 1775; *Dimonah,* a place in Pal.:—Dimonah {1x}. See: BDB—192a.

1777. דִּין {24x} **dîyn,** *deen;* or (Gen 6:3)

דּוּן **dûwn,** *doon;* a prim. root [comp. 113]; to *rule;* by impl. to *judge* (as umpire); also to *strive* (as at law):—contend {1x}, execute (judgment) {1x}, judge {18x}, minister judgment {1x}, plead (the cause) {1x}, at strife {1x}, strive {1x}.

Diyn implies a settlement of what is right where there is a charge upon a person. *Diyn* is a judicial word marking the act whereby men's position and destiny are decided. *Shaphath* (8199) is an administrative word pointing to the mode in which men are to be governed and their affairs administered. See: TWOT—426; BDB—189b, 192a, 1088b.

1778. דִּין {2x} **dîyn** (Aram.), *deen;* corresp. to 1777; to *judge:*—judge {1x}, tread out {1x}. See: TWOT—2674; BDB—1088b.

1779. דִּין {20x} **dîyn,** *deen;* or (Job 19:29)

דּוּן **dûwn,** *doon;* from 1777; *judgement* (the suit, justice, sentence or tribunal); by impl. also *strife:*—cause {8x}, judgement {9x}, plea {2x}, strife {1x}. See: TWOT—426a; BDB—189b, 192c, 995a.

1780. דִּין {5x} **dîyn** (Aram.), *deen;* corresp. to 1779:—judgement {5x}. See: TWOT—2674?; BDB—1088b.

1781. דַּיָּן {2x} **dayân,** *dah-yawn';* from 1777; a *judge* or *advocate:*—judge {2x}. See: TWOT—426b; BDB—193a.

1782. דַּיָּן {1x} **dayân** (Aram.), *dah-yawn';* corresp. to 1781:—judge {1x}. See: TWOT—2674a; BDB—1088c.

1783. דִּינָה {8x} **Dîynâh,** *dee-naw';* fem. of 1779; *justice; Dinah,* the daughter of Jacob:—Dinah {8x}. See: BDB—192d.

1784. דִּינַי {1x} **Dîynay** (Aram.), *dee-nah'-ee;* patrial from an uncert. prim.; a *Dinaite* or inhab. of some unknown Ass. province:—Dinaite {1x}. See: BDB—1088c.

דִּיפַת **Dîyphath.** See 7384.

1785. דָּיֵק {6x} **dâyêq,** *daw-yake';* from a root corresp. to 1751; a *battering-tower:*—fort {6x}. See: TWOT—417a; BDB—189b, 193d.

1786. דַּיִשׁ {1x} **dayîsh,** *dah-yish';* from 1758; *threshing-*time:—threshing {1x}. See: TWOT—419a; BDB—190c, 193d.

1787. דִּישׁוֹן {7x} **Dîyshôwn,**

דִּישֹׁן **Dîyshôn,**

דִּשׁוֹן **Dîshôwn,** or

דִּשֹׁן **Dîshôn,** *dee-shone';* the same as 1788; *Dishon,* the name of two Edomites:—Dishon {7x}. See: BDB—190d, 193d.

1788. דִּישֹׁן {1x} **dîyshôn,** *dee-shone';* from 1758; the *leaper,* i.e. an *antelope:*—pygarg {1x}. See: TWOT—419c; BDB—190d, 193d.

1789. דִּישָׁן {5x} **Dîyshân,** *dee-shawn';* another form of 1787; *Dishan,* an Edomite:—Dishan {5x}. See: BDB—190d. 193d.

1790. דַּךְ {4x} **dak,** *dak;* from an unused root (comp. 1794); *crushed,* i.e. (fig.) *injured:*—afflicted {1x}, oppressed {3x}. See: TWOT—429a; BDB—194c.

1791. דֵּךְ {13x} **dêk** (Aram.), *dake;* or

דָּךְ **dâk** (Aram.), *dawk;* prol. from 1668; *this:*—the same {1x}, this {12x}. See: TWOT—2675; BDB—1080d, 1088c.

1792. דָּכָא {18x} **dâkâʾ,** *daw-kaw';* a prim. root (comp. 1794); to *crumble;* tran. to *bruise* (lit. or fig.):—break {3x}, break in pieces {3x}, crush {3x}, bruise {2x}, destroy {2x}, contrite {1x}, smite {1x}, oppress {1x}, beat

to pieces {1x}, humble {1x}. Syn.: 1854, 5310, 7489, 7533. See: TWOT—427; BDB—193d.

1793. אָכָּדַ {3x} **dakkâ'**, *dak-kaw';* from 1792; *crushed* (lit. *powder,* or fig. *contrite*):—contrite {2x}, destruction {1x}. This word means to dash into pieces or crush. See: TWOT—427a, b; BDB—194b.

1794. כָָּה דָ {3x} **dâkâh**, *daw-kaw';* a prim. root (comp. 1790, 1792); to *collapse* (phys. or ment.):—break (sore) {3x}, contrite {1x}, crouch {1x}. See: TWOT—428; BDB—194d.

1795. כָָּה דַ {1x} **dakkâh**, *dak-kaw';* from 1794 like 1793; *mutilated:*—+ wounded {1x}. See: TWOT—429b; BDB—194c.

1796. דְכִי {1x} **dŏkîy**, *dok-ee';* from 1794; a *dashing* of surf:—wave {1x}. See: TWOT—428a; BDB—194b.

1797. דִכֵּן {1x} **dikkên** (Aram.), *dik-kane';* prol. from 1791; *this:*—same {1x}, that {1x}, this {1x}. See: TWOT—2676; BDB—1088c.

1798. דְכַר {13} **dᵉkar** (Aram.), *dek-ar';* corresp. to 2145; prop. a *male,* i.e. of sheep:—ram {3x}. See: TWOT—2677a; BDB—1088d.

1799. דִכְרוֹן {3x} **dikrôwn** (Aram.), *dik-rone';* or

דָכְרָן **dokrân**, *dok-rawn'* (Aram.); corresp. to 2146; a *register:*—record {1x}. See: TWOT—2677b; BDB—1088d.

1800. דַל {48x} **dal**, *dal;* from 1809; prop. *dangling,* i.e. (by impl.) *weak* or *thin:*—lean {1x}, needy {2x}, poor (man) {43x}, weaker {2x}.

Dal is "one who is low, poor, reduced, helpless, weak." **(1)** The *dallim* (pl.) constituted the middle class of Israel—those who were physically deprived (in the ancient world the majority of people were poor). For example, the *dallim* may be viewed as the opposite of the rich (Ex 30:15; cf. Ruth 3:10; Prov 10:15). **(2)** In addition, the word may connote social poverty or lowliness. As such, *dal* describes those who are the counterparts of the great: "Ye shall do no unrighteousness in judgment: thou shalt not respect the person of the poor, nor honor the person of the mighty: but in righteousness shalt thou judge thy neighbor" (Lev 19:15; cf. Amos 2:7). **(3)** When Gideon challenged the Lord's summoning him to deliver Israel, he emphasized that his clan was too weak to do the job: "And he said unto him, Oh my Lord, wherewith shall I save Israel? behold, my family is poor in Manasseh" (Judg 6:15; cf. 2 Sa 3:1). **(4)** God commands that society protect the

poor, the lowly, and the weak: "Thou shalt not follow a multitude to do evil; neither shalt thou speak in a cause to decline after many to wrest judgment: neither shalt thou countenance a poor man in his cause" (Ex 23:2–3; cf. Lev 14:21; Is 10:2).

(5) He also warns that if men fail to provide justice, He will do so (Is 11:4). **(6)** In Gen 41:19 (the first biblical appearance of the word) *dal* is contrasted to "healthy" or "fat": "And behold, seven other kine came up after them, poor and very ill-favored and leanfleshed." **(6a)** Thus, *dal* indicates a physical condition and appearance of sickliness. **(6b)** It is used in this sense to describe Amnon's appearance as he longed for Tamar (2 Sa 13:4). **(7)** *Dal* is used (very infrequently) of spiritual poverty (in such cases it is sometimes paralleled to 'ebyon (34): "Therefore I said, Surely these are poor; they are foolish: for they know not the way of the Lord, nor the judgment of their God" (Jer 5:4). [Some scholars argue that here the word means "ignorance," and as the context shows, this is ignorance in the knowledge of God's word.] Syn: *Dal* is related to, but differs from, 'ani (6041 - which suggests affliction of some kind), 'ebyon (34 - which emphasizes need), and *rash* (7326 - which suggests destitution). See: TWOT—433a; BDB—194c, 195d.

1801. דָלַג {5x} **dâlag**, *daw-lag';* a prim. root; to *spring:*—leap {5x}. See: TWOT—430; BDB—194c.

1802. דָלָה {5x} **dâlâh**, *daw-law';* a prim. root (comp. 1809); prop. to *dangle,* i.e. to *let down* a bucket (for *drawing* out water); fig. to *deliver:*—draw out {3x}, enough {1x}, lift up {1x}. See: TWOT—431; BDB—194c.

1803. דַלָּה {8x} **dallâh**, *dal-law';* from 1802; prop. something *dangling,* i.e. a loose *thread* or *hair;* fig. *indigent:*—poor {5x}, poorest sort {1x}, pinning sickness {1x}, hair {1x}.

Dallah, related to *dal* (1800), means "poverty; dishevelled hair." **(1)** The word appears in 2 Kin 24:14: ". . . none remained, save the poorest sort of the people of the land," where *dallah* emphasizes the social lowliness and "poverty" of those people whom it describes. **(2)** In Song 7:5 the word refers to "dishevelled hair" in the sense of something that hangs down. See: TWOT—433c; BDB—195d.

1804. דָלַח {3x} **dâlach**, *daw-lakh';* a prim. root; to *roil* water:—trouble {3x}. See: TWOT—432; BDB—195c.

1805. דְלִי {2x} **dᵉlîy**, *del-ee';* or

דָלִי **dŏlîy**, *dol-ee';* from 1802; a *pail* or *jar* (for *drawing* water):—bucket {2x}. See: TWOT—431c; BDB—194d.

1806. דְּלָיָה {7x} D**e**lâyâh, del-aw-yaw'; or (prol.)

דְּלָיָהוּ D**e**lâyâhûw, del-aw-yaw'-hoo; from 1802 and 3050; Jah has delivered; Delajah, the name of five Isr.:—Dalaiah {1x}, Delaiah {6x}. See: BDB—195b.

1807. דְּלִילָה {6x} D**e**lîylâh, del-ee-law'; from 1809; languishing; Delilah, a Philistine woman:—Delilah {6x}. See: BDB—196a.

1808. דָּלִיָּה {8x} dâlîyâh, daw-lee-yaw'; from 1802; something dangling, i.e. a bough:—branch {8x}. See: TWOT—431d; BDB—194d.

1809. דָּלַל {9x} dâlal, daw-lal'; a prim. root (comp. 1802); to slacken or be feeble; fig. to be oppressed:—brought low {3x}, dried up {1x}, not equal {1x}, emptied {1x}, fail {1x}, impoverished {1x}, made thin {1x}.

Dalal means "to be low, hang down." (1) This verb appears always in poetical passages. (2) The word appears in Ps 79:8: "O remember not against us former iniquities: let thy tender mercies speedily prevent us; for we are brought very low." See: TWOT—433; BDB—195c.

1810. דִּלְעָן {1x} Dilân, dil-awn'; of uncert. der.; Dilan, a place in Pal.:—Dilean {1x}. See: 196a.

1811. דָּלַף {3x} dâlaph, daw-laf'; a prim. root; to drip; by impl. to weep:—drop through {1x}, melt {1x}, pour out {1x}. See: TWOT—434; BDB—196a.

1812. דֶּלֶף {2x} deleph, deh'-lef; from 1811; a dripping:—dropping {2x}. See: TWOT—434a; BDB—196a.

1813. דַּלְפוֹן {1x} Dalphôwn, dal-fone'; from 1811; dripping; Dalphon, a son of Haman:—Dalphon {1x}. See: BDB—196a.

1814. דָּלַק {9x} dâlaq, daw-lak'; a prim. root; to flame (lit. or fig.):—pursue {2x}, kindle {2x}, chase {1x}, persecute {1x}, persecutors {1x}, burning {1x}, inflame {1x}. See: TWOT—435; BDB—196a, 1088d.

1815. דְּלַק {1x} d**e**laq (Aram.), del-ak'; corresp. to 1814:—burn {1x}. See: TWOT—2678; BDB—1088d.

1816. דַּלֶּקֶת {1x} dalleqeth, dal-lek'-keth; from 1814; a burning fever:—inflammation {1x}. See: TWOT—435a; BDB—196b.

1817. דֶּלֶת {88x} deleth, deh'-leth; from 1802; something swinging, i.e. the valve of a door:—doors {69x}, gates {14x}, leaves {4x},

lid {1x}. See: TWOT—431a,e; BDB—194c, 194d, 195a, 196b. [In Ps 141:3, dâl, irreg.].

1818. דָּם {361x} dâm, dawm; from 1826 (comp. 119); blood (as that which when shed causes death) of man or an animal; by anal. the juice of the grape; fig. (espec. in the plur.) bloodshed (i.e. drops of blood):—blood {342x}, bloody {15x}, person + 5315 {1x}, bloodguiltiness {1x}, bloodthirsty + 582 {1x}, var. blood {1x}.

Dam means "blood." (1) Dam is used to denote the "blood" of animals, birds, and men (never of fish). (2) In Gen 9:4, "blood" is synonymous with "life": "But flesh with the life thereof, which is the blood thereof, shall ye not eat." (3) The high value of life as a gift of God led to the prohibition against eating "blood": "It shall be a perpetual statute for your generations throughout all your dwellings, that ye eat neither fat nor blood" (Lev 3:17). (4) Only infrequently does this word mean "blood-red," a color: "And they rose up early in the morning, and the sun shone upon the water, and the Moabites saw the water on the other side as red as blood" (2 Kin 3:22). (5) In two passages, dam represents "wine": "He washed his garments in wine, and his clothes in the blood of grapes" (Gen 49:11; cf. Deut 32:14).

(6) Dam bears several nuances. (6a) It can mean "blood shed by violence": "So ye shall not pollute the land wherein ye are: for blood it defileth the land: and the land cannot be cleansed of the blood that is shed therein" (Num 35:33). (6b) Thus it can mean "death": "So will I send upon you famine and evil beasts, and they shall bereave thee; and pestilence and blood shall pass through thee; and I will bring the sword upon thee" (Eze 5:17). (7) Next, dam may connote an act by which a human life is taken, or blood is shed: "If there arise a matter too hard for thee in judgment, between blood and blood [one kind of homicide or another] . . ." (Deut 17:8).

(8) To "shed blood" is to commit murder: "Whoso sheddeth man's blood, by man shall his blood be shed" (Gen 9:6). (8a) The second occurrence here means that the murderer shall suffer capital punishment. (8b) In other places, the phrase "to shed blood" refers to a nonritualistic slaughter of an animal: "What man soever there be of the house of Israel, that killeth an ox, or lamb . . . in the camp, or that killeth it out of the camp, and bringeth it not unto the door of the tabernacle of the congregation, to offer an offering unto the Lord before the tabernacle of the Lord; blood [guiltiness] shall be imputed unto that man" (Lev 17:3–4). (9) In judicial language, "to stand against one's blood" means to stand before a court and against the accused as a plaintiff, witness, or

judge: "Thou shalt not go up and down as a talebearer among thy people: neither shalt thou stand against the blood [i.e., act against the life] of thy neighbor" (Lev 19:16).

(10) The phrase, "his blood be on his head," signifies that the guilt and punishment for a violent act shall be on the perpetrator: "For everyone that curseth his father or his mother shall be surely put to death: he hath cursed his father or his mother; his blood [guiltiness] shall be upon him" (Lev 20:9). **(10a)** This phrase bears the added overtone that those who execute the punishment by killing the guilty party are not guilty of murder. **(10b)** So here "blood" means responsibility for one's dead: "And it shall be, that whosoever shall go out of the doors of thy house into the street, his blood shall be upon his head, and we will be guiltless: and whosoever shall be with thee in the house, his blood shall be on our head, if any hand be upon him" (Josh 2:19).

(11) Animal blood could take the place of a sinner's blood in atoning (covering) for sin: "For it is the blood that maketh an atonement for the soul" (Lev 17:11). **(11a)** Adam's sin merited death and brought death on all his posterity (cf. Rom 5:12); **(11b)** so the offering of an animal in substitution not only typified the payment of that penalty, but it symbolized that the perfect offering would bring life for Adam and all others represented by the sacrifice (cf. Heb 10:4). **(11c)** The animal sacrifice prefigured and typologically represented the blood of Christ, who made the great and only effective substitutionary atonement, and whose offering was the only offering that gained life for those whom He represented. **(12c)** The shedding of His "blood" seals the covenant of life between God and man (cf. Mt 26:28). See: TWOT—436; BDB—196b.

1819. דָּמָה {29x} **dâmâh**, *daw-maw'*; a prim. root; to *compare;* by impl. to *resemble, liken, consider:*—like {14x}, liken {5x}, thought {6x}, compared {1x}, devised {1x}, meaneth {1x}, similitudes {1x}. *Damah* (1819) means "to be like, resemble, be or act like, liken or compare, devise, balance or ponder." **(1)** This verb appears in biblical Hebrew about 29 times. Cognates of this word appear in biblical Aramaic, Akkadian, and Arabic. **(2)** *Damah* means "to be like" in Ps 102:6: "I am like a pelican of the wilderness: I am like an owl of the desert." See: TWOT—437; BDB—197d, 1088d.

1820. דָּמָה {16x} **dâmâh**, *daw-maw'*; a prim. root; to *be dumb* or *silent;* hence, to *fail* or *perish;* trans. to *destroy:*—cut off {3x}, cease {2x}, perish {2x}, bring to silence {2x}, liken {2x}, destroy {2x}, undone {1x}, utterly

{1x}, cut down {1x}. See: TWOT—438; BDB—198c.

1821. דְּמָה {2x} **dᵉmâh** (Aram.), *dem-aw';* corresp. to 1819; to *resemble:*—be like {1x}. See: TWOT—2679; BDB—1088d.

1822. דֻּמָּה {1x} **dummâh**, *doom-maw';* from 1820; *desolation;* concr. *desolate:*—like the destroyed {1x}. See: TWOT—439b; BDB—199a.

1823. דְּמוּת {25x} **dᵉmûwth**, *dem-ooth';* from 1819; *resemblance;* concr. *model, shape;* adv. *like:*—likeness {19x}, similitude {2x}, like {2x}, manner {1x}, fashion {1x}.

Demuwth means "likeness; shape; figure; form; pattern." **(1)** All but 5 of the 25 appearances of this word are in poetical or prophetical books of the Bible. **(2)** The word means "pattern," in the sense of the specifications from which an actual item is made: "And king Ahaz went to Damascus . . . and saw an altar that was at Damascus: and king Ahaz sent to Urijah the priest the fashion of the altar, and the pattern of it, according to all the workmanship thereof" (2 Kin 16:10). **(3)** *Demuwth* means "shape" or "form," the thing(s) made after a given pattern. **(3a)** In 2 Chr 4:3 the word represents the "shape" of a bronze statue: "And under it was the similitude of oxen, which did compass it round about: ten in a cubit, compassing the sea round about."

(3b) In such passages *demuwth* means more than just "shape" in general; it indicates the "shape" in particular. **(3c)** In Eze 1:10, for example, the word represents the "form" or "likeness" of the faces of the living creatures Ezekiel describes. **(3d)** In Eze 1:26 the word refers to what something seemed to be rather than what it was: "And above the firmament that was over their heads was the likeness of a throne." **(4)** *Demuwth* signifies the original after which a thing is patterned: **(4a)** "To whom then will ye liken God? or what likeness will ye compare unto him?" (Is 40:18). **(4b)** This significance is in its first biblical appearance: "And God said, Let us make man in our image, after our likeness . . ." (Gen 1:26). **(5)** In Ps 58:4 the word appears to function merely to extend the form but not the meaning of the preposition *ke:* "Their poison is like the poison of a serpent." See: TWOT—437a; BDB—198b.

1824. דְּמִי {4x} **dᵉmîy**, *dem-ee';* or

דֳּמִי **dŏmîy**, *dom-ee';* from 1820; *quiet:*—cutting off {1x}, rest {1x}, silence {2x}. See: TWOT—438a; BDB—198c.

1825. דִּמְיוֹן {1x} **dimyôwn**, *dim-yone';* from 1819; *resemblance:*—✕ like {1x}. See: TWOT—437b; BDB—198b.

Hebrew

1826. דָּמַם {30x} **dâmam**, *daw-mam';* a prim. root [comp. 1724, 1820]; to *be dumb;* by impl. to *be astonished,* to *stop;* also to *perish:*—silence {6x}, still {6x}, silent {x}4, cut off {3x}, cut down {2x}, rest {2x}, cease {2x}, forbear 1, peace {1x}, quieted {1x}, tarry {1x}, wait {1x}. See: TWOT—439; BDB—198d, 199b.

1827. דְּמָמָה {3x} **dᵉmâmâh**, *dem-aw-maw';* fem. from 1826; *quiet:*—calm {1x}, silence {1x}, still {1x}. See: TWOT—439a; BDB—199a.

1828. דֹּמֶן {6x} **dômen**, *do'-men;* of uncert. der.; *manure:*—dung {6x}. Syn.: 830, 1557, 2755, 6569, 6832. See: TWOT—441a; BDB—199b.

1829. דִּמְנָה {1x} **Dimnâh**, *dim-naw';* fem. from the same as 1828; a *dung-heap; Dimnah,* a place in Pal.:—Dimnah {1x}. See: BDB—199b.

1830. דָּמַע {2x} **dâmaʿ**, *daw-mah';* a prim. root; to *weep:*—× sore {1x}, weep {1x}. See: BDB—199c.

1831. דֶּמַע {1x} **demaʿ**, *dah'-mah;* from 1830; a *tear;* fig. *juice:*—liquor {1x}. Syn.: 4197, 4952. See: TWOT—442a; BDB—199c.

1832. דִּמְעָה {23x} **dimʿâh**, *dim-aw';* fem. of 1831; *weeping:*—tears {23x}. See: TWOT—442b; BDB—199c.

1833. דְּמֶשֶׁק {1x} **dᵉmesheq**, *dem-eh'-shek;* by orth. var. from 1834; *damask* (as a fabric of Damascus):—in Damascus {1x}. See: TWOT—433?; BDB—200a.

1834. דַּמֶּשֶׂק {45x} **Dammeseq**, *dam-meh'-sek;* or

דּוּמֶשֶׂק **Dûwmeseq**, *doo-meh'-sek;* or

דַּרְמֶשֶׂק **Darmeseq**, *dar-meh'-sek;* of for. or.; *Damascus,* a city of Syria:—Damascus {44x}, Syriadamascus {1x}. See: BDB—199d, 204b, 217a.

1835. דָּן {71x} **Dân**, *dawn;* from 1777; *judge; Dan,* one of the sons of Jacob; also the tribe descended from him, and its territory; likewise a place in Pal. colonized by them:—Dan {71x}. See: BDB—75a, 192d, 200a.

1836. דֵּן {57x} **dên** (Aram.), *dane;* an orth. var. of 1791; *this:*—this {38x}, these {3x}, thus {2x}, hereafter {1x}, that {1x}, misc. {12x} = aforetime, + after this manner, one . . . another, such, therefore, wherefore, which. See: TWOT—680; BDB—1080d, 1088d, 1096c.

דָּנִיֵּאל **Dânîʾêl**. See 1841.

1837. דַּנָּה {1x} **Dannâh**, *dan-naw';* of uncert. der.; *Dannah,* a place in Pal.:—Dannah {1x}. See: BDB—200a.

1838. דִּנְהָבָה {1x} **Dinhâbâh**, *din-haw-baw';* of uncert. der.; *Dinhabah,* an Edomitish town:—Dinhabah {2x}. See: BDB—200b.

1839. דָּנִי {5x} **Dânîy**, *daw-nee';* patron. from 1835; a *Danite* (often collect.) or desc. (or inhab.) of Dan:—Danites {4x}, of Dan {1x}. See: BDB—193a.

1840. דָּנִיֵּאל {29x} **Dânîyêʾl**, *daw-nee-yale';* in Eze.

דָּנִאֵל **Dânîʾêl**, *daw-nee-ale';* from 1835 and 410; *judge of God; Daniel* or *Danijel,* the name of two Isr.:—Daniel {29x}. See: BDB—193a, 200a, 200b.

1841. דָּנִיֵּאל {42x} **Dânîyêʾl** (Aram.), *daw-nee-yale';* corresp. to 1840; *Danijel,* the Heb. prophet:—Daniel {42x}. See: BDB—1088c.

1842. דָּן יַעַן {1x} **Dân Yaʿan**, *dawn yah'-an;* from 1835 and (appar.) 3282; *judge of purpose; Dan-Jaan,* a place in Pal.:—Dan-jaan {1x}. See: BDB—193a, 419a.

1843. דֵּעַ {2x} **dêaʿ**, *day'-ah;* from 3045; *knowledge:*—knowledge {2x}, opinion {3x}. Syn.: 1844, 1847. See: TWOT—848; BDB—200b, 395b.

1844. דֵּעָה {1x} **dêʿâh**, *day-aw';* fem. of 1843; *knowledge:*—knowledge {6x}. Syn.: 1847. See: TWOT—848b; BDB—200b, 395c.

1845. דְּעוּאֵל {4x} **Dᵉʿûwêl**, *deh-oo-ale';* from 3045 and 410; *known of God; Deel,* an Isr.:—Deuel {1x}. See: BDB—200b, 396a.

1846. דָּעַךְ {9x} **dâʿak**, *daw-ak';* a prim. root; to *be extinguished;* fig. to *expire* or *be dried up:*—be extinct {1x}, consumed {1x}, put out {6x}, quenched {1x}. Syn.: 2193, 3518. See: TWOT—445; BDB—200b.

1847. דַּעַת {93x} **daʿath**, *dah'-ath;* from 3045; *knowledge:*—knowledge {82x}, know {6x}, cunning {1x}, unwittingly 2 + 1097 {2x}, ignorantly + 1097 {1x}, unawares + 1097 {1x}.

Da'ath means "knowledge." **(1)** Several nouns are formed from *yada'* (3045) and the most frequently occurring is *da'ath* which appears 93 times in the Old Testament. **(2)** One appearance is in Gen 2:9: ". . . and the tree of knowledge of good and evil." **(2)** The word also appears in Ex 31:3. Syn.: 1843, 1844. See: TWOT—848c; BDB—200b, 395c.

1848. דְּפִי {1x} dŏphîy, dof'-ee; from an unused root (mean. to *push* over); a
stumbling-block:—slanderest {1x}. Syn.: 1681,
3960, 7270. See: TWOT—446a; BDB—200c.

1849. דָּפַק {3x} dâphaq, daw-fak'; a prim.
root; to *knock*; by anal. to *press*
severely:—beat {1x}, knock {1x}, overdrive {1x}.
See: TWOT—447; BDB—200c.

1850. דָּפְקָה {2x} Dophqâh, dof-kaw'; from
1849; a *knock*; *Dophkah*, a place
in the Desert:—Dophkah {2x}. See: BDB—
200c.

1851. דַּק {41x} daq, dak; from 1854; *crushed*,
i.e. (by impl.) *small* or *thin*:—thin
{5x}, small {5x}, leanfleshed + 1320 {2x}, dwarf
{1x}, little thing {1x}. See: TWOT—448a;
BDB—200c, 201a.

1852. דֹּק {1x} dôq, doke; from 1854; something *crumbling*, i.e. *fine* (as a *thin*
cloth):—curtain {1x}. See: TWOT—448b;
BDB—200c, 201a.

1853. דִּקְלָה {2x} Diqlâh, dik-law'; of for. or.;
Diklah, a region of Arabia:—
Diklah {1x}. See: BDB—200c.

1854. דָּקַק {13x} dâqaq, daw-kak'; a prim.
root [comp. 1915]; to *crush* (or
intr.) *crumble*:—beat small {2x}, powder {2x},
stamp {2x}, stamp small {2x}, bruise {2x}, small
{1x}, made dust {1x}, beat in pieces {1x}. See:
TWOT—448; BDB—200d, 1089c.

1855. דְּקַק {10x} dᵉqaq (Aram.), dek-ak'; corresp. to 1854; to *crumble* or
(trans.) *crush*:—break to pieces {1x}. See:
TWOT—2681; BDB—1089a.

1856. דָּקַר {1x} dâqar, daw-kar'; a prim. root; to
stab; by anal. to *starve*; fig. to *revile*:—thrust through {8x}, pierced {1x},
wounded {1x}, stricken through {1x}. See:
TWOT—449; BDB—201a.

1857. דֶּקֶר {1x} Deqer, deh'-ker; from 1856; a
stab; *Deker*, an Isr.:—Dekar {1x}.
See: BDB—201b.

1858. דַּר {1x} dar, dar; appar. from the same
as 1865; prop. a *pearl* (from its
sheen as rapidly *turned*); by anal. *pearl-stone*,
i.e. mother-of-pearl or alabaster:—white {1x}
Syn.: 3835, 3836, 6713. See: TWOT—454a;
BDB—201b, 204d.

1859. דָּר {4x} dâr (Aram.), dawr; corresp. to
1755; an *age*:—generation {1x}. See:
TWOT—2669a; BDB—1087b, 1089a.

דֹּר dôr. See 1755.

1860. דְּרָאוֹן dᵉrâʾôwn, der-aw-one'; or

דֵּרָאוֹן {2x} dêraʾôwn, day-raw-one';
from an unused root (mean. to
repulse); an obj. of *aversion*:—abhorring {1x},
contempt {1x}. See: TWOT—450a; BDB—201b.

1861. דָּרְבוֹן {1x} dorbôwn, dor-bone' [also
dor-bawn']; of uncert. der.; a
goad:—goad {2x}. See: TWOT—451a,b;
BDB—201c.

1862. דַּרְדַּע {1x} Dardaᶜ, dar-dah'; appar.
from 1858 and 1843; *pearl of
knowledge*; *Darda*, an Isr.:—Darda {1x}. See:
BDB—201c.

1863. דַּרְדַּר {2x} dardar, dar-dar'; of uncert.
der.; a *thorn*:—thistle {1x}. See:
TWOT—454e; BDB—201d 205a.

1864. דָּרוֹם {17x} dârôwm, daw-rome'; of uncert. der.; the *south*; poet. the
south wind:—south {1x}. See: TWOT—454d;
BDB—201d, 204.

1865. דְּרוֹר {8x} dᵉrôwr, der-ore'; from an unused root (mean. to *move rap-
idly*); *freedom*; hence, *spontaneity* of outflow,
and so *clear*:—liberty {7x}, pure {1x}. See:
TWOT—454b; BDB—204d.

1866. דְּרוֹר {2x} dᵉrôwr, der-ore'; the same as
1865, applied to a bird; the *swift*,
a kind of swallow:—swallow {2x}. See:
TWOT—454c; BDB—204d.

1867. דָּרְיָוֶשׁ {10x} Dârᵉyâvêsh, daw-reh-yaw-
vaysh'; of Pers. or.; *Darejavesh*,
a title (rather than name) of several Pers.
kings:—Darius {1x}. See: BDB—201d, 1089a.

1868. דָּרְיָוֶשׁ {15x} Dârᵉyâvêsh (Aram.), daw-
reh-yaw-vaysh'; corresp. to
1867:—Darius {15x}. See: BDB—1089a.

1869. דָּרַךְ {62x} dârak, daw-rak'; a prim.
root; to *tread*; by impl. to *walk*;
also to *string* a bow (by treading on it in bending):—tread {23x}, bend {8x}, bent {7x}, lead
{4x}, archer {2x}, tread down {2x}, come {1x},
go {2x}, treader {2x}, tread upon {2x}, walk {2x},
drew {1x}, lead forth {1x}, guide {1x}, tread out
{1x}, go over {1x}, shoot {1x}, thresh {1x}. See:
TWOT—453; BDB—201d.

1870. דֶּרֶךְ {705x} derek, deh'-rek; from 1869;
a *road* (as *trodden*); fig. a *course* of
life or *mode* of action, often adv.:—way {590x},
toward {31x}, journey {23x}, manner {8x}, misc.
{53x} = along, away, because of, + by, conversation, custom, eastward, passenger, through,
highway, pathway, wayside, whither, whithersoever.
Derek means "way (path, road, highway);
distance; journey; manner, conduct; condition;

destiny." **(1)** First, this word refers to a path, a road, or a highway. In Gen 3:24 (the first occurrence of the word) it means "path" or "route": "And he placed at the east of the garden of Eden cherubim, and a flaming sword which turned every [direction], to [guard] the way of the tree of life." **(2)** Sometimes, as in Gen 16:7, the word represents a pathway, road, or route: "And the angel of the Lord found her by a fountain of water in the wilderness, by the fountain in the way to Shur." **(3)** The actual road itself is represented in Gen 38:21: "Where is the [temple prostitute], that was openly by the wayside?" **(4)** In Num 20:17 the word means "highway," a well-known and well-traveled road: "We will go by the king's highway, we will not turn to the right hand nor to the left, until we have passed thy borders."

(5) This noun represents a "distance" (how far or how long) between two points: "And he set three days' journey [a distance of three days] betwixt himself and Jacob" (Gen 30:36). **(6)** In other passages *derek* refers to the action or process of "taking a journey": "And to his father he sent after this manner; ten asses laden with the good things of Egypt, and ten she asses laden with corn and bread and meat for his father by the way [on the journey]" (Gen 45:23). **(7)** In an extended nuance *derek* means "undertaking": "If thou turn away thy foot from the sabbath, from doing thy pleasure on my holy day; and call the sabbath a delight, the holy of the Lord, honorable; and shalt honor him, not doing thine own ways, nor finding thine own pleasure . . ." (Is 58:13). Cf. Gen 24:21: "And the man wondering at her held his peace, to wit whether the Lord had made his journey prosperous or not" (cf. Deut 28:29).

(8) In another emphasis this word connotes how and what one does, a "manner, custom, behavior, mode of life": "Our father is old, and there is not a man in the earth to come in unto us after the manner of all the earth" (Gen 19:31). **(9)** In 1 Kin 2:4 *derek* is applied to an activity that controls one, one's life-style: "If thy children take heed to their way, to walk before me in truth with all their heart and with all their soul, there shall not fail thee . . . a man on the throne of Israel." **(10)** In 1 Kin 16:26 *derek* is used of Jeroboam's attitude: "For he walked in all the way of Jeroboam the son of Nebat, and in his sin wherewith he made Israel to sin." **(11)** Deeds, or specific acts, may be connoted by this noun: "Lo, these are parts of his ways; but how little a portion is heard of him? But the thunder of his power who can understand?" (Job 26:14). **(12)** Derek refers to a "condition" in the sense of what has happened to someone. This is clear by the parallelism of Is 40:27: "Why

sayest thou, O Jacob, and speakest, O Israel, My way is hid from the Lord, and [the justice due to me is passed away] from my God?" **(13)** In one passage *derek* signifies the overall course and fixed path of one's life, or his "destiny": "O Lord, I know that the way of man is not in himself: it is not in man that walketh to direct his steps" (Jer 10:23). **(14)** This word sometimes seems to bear the meaning of "power" or "rulership": "Only acknowledge thine iniquity, that thou hast transgressed against the Lord thy God, and hast scattered thy ways to the strangers under every green tree" (Jer 3:13; cf. Job 26:14; 36:23; 40:19; Ps 67:2; 110:7; 119:37; 138:5; Prov 8:22; 19:16; 31:3; Hos 10:13; Amos 8:14). Some scholars, however, contest this explanation of these passages. Syn.: 734, 5410. See: TWOT–453a; BDB–202c, 1008b.

1871. דַּרְכְּמוֹן {4x} **darkᵉmôwn**, *dar-kem-one'*; of Pers. or.; a "*drachma*," or coin:–dram {1x}. Syn.: 150. See: TWOT–453c; BDB–204b.

1872. דְּרָע {1x} **dᵉrâʿ** (Aram.), *der-aw'*; corresp. to 2220; an *arm*:–arm {1x}. See: TWOT–2682a; BDB–1089a.

1873. דָּרַע {1x} **Dâraʿ**, *daw-rah'*; prob. contr. from 1862; *Dara,* an Isr.:–Dara {1x}. See: BDB–201d, 204c.

1874. דַּרְקוֹן {2x} **Darqôwn**, *dar-kone'*; of uncert. der.; *Darkon,* one of "Solomon's servants":–Darkon {1x}. See: BDB–204c.

1875. דָּרַשׁ {164x} **dârash**, *daw-rash'*; a prim. root; prop. to *tread* or *frequent;* usually to *follow* (for pursuit or search); by impl. to *seek* or *ask;* spec. to *worship:*–seek {84x}, enquire {43x}, require {12x}, search {7x}, misc. {18x}: ask, × at all, care for, × diligently, make inquisition, [necro-] mancer, question, seek for, seek out, × surely.

Darash means "to seek, inquire, consult, ask, require, frequent." **(1)** Occurring more than 160 times in the Old Testament, *darash* is first used in Gen 9:5: "And surely your blood of your lives will I require." It often has the idea of avenging an offense against God or the shedding of blood (see Eze 33:6). **(2)** One of the most frequent uses of this word is in the expression "to inquire of God," which sometimes **(2a)** indicates a private seeking of God in prayer for direction (Gen 25:22), and often **(2b)** it refers to the contacting of a prophet who would be the instrument of God's revelation (1 Sa 9:9; 1 Kin 22:8). **(3)** At other times this expression is found in connection with the use of the Urim and Thummim by the high priest as **(3a)** he sought to discover the will of God

by the throwing of these sacred stones (Num 27:21). **(3b)** Just what was involved is not clear, but it may be presumed that only yes-or-no questions could be answered by the manner in which these stones fell.

(4) Pagan people and sometimes even apostate Israelites "inquired of" heathen gods. **(4a)** Thus, Ahaziah instructed messengers: "Go, inquire of Baal-zebub the god of Ekron whether I shall recover of this disease" (2 Kin 1:2). **(4b)** In gross violation of the Mosaic law (Deut 18:10– 11), Saul went to the witch of Endor "to inquire of" her, which in this instance meant that she was to call up the spirit of the dead prophet Samuel. Saul went to the witch of Endor as a last resort, saying, "Seek me a woman that hath a familiar spirit, that I may go to her, and enquire of her" (1 Sa 28:7). **(5)** This word is often used to describe the "seeking" of the Lord in the sense of entering into covenantal relationship with Him. **(6)** The prophets often used *darash* as they called on the people to make an about-face in living and instead "seek ye the Lord while he may be found" (Is 55:6). See: TWOT—455; BDB—201d, 205a.

1876. דָּשָׁא {2x} **dâshâ²**, *daw-shaw';* a prim. root; to *sprout:*—bring forth {1x}, spring {1x}. See: TWOT—456; BDB—205d.

1877. דֶּשֶׁא {15x} **deshe²**, *deh'-sheh;* from 1876; a *sprout;* by anal. *grass:*—(tender) grass {8x}, green {1x}, (tender) herb {6x}. See: TWOT—456a; BDB—206a, 1089b.

1878. דָּשֵׁן {11x} **dâshên**, *daw-shane';* a prim. root; to *be fat;* tran. to *fatten* (or regard as fat); spec. to *anoint;* fig. to *satisfy;* denom. (from 1880) to *remove* (fat) *ashes* (of sacrifices):—accept {1x}, anoint {1x}, take away the ashes {1x}, receive his ashes from {1x}, made fat {6x}, wax fat {1x}. See: TWOT—457; BDB—206a.

1879. דָּשֵׁן {3x} **dâshên**, *daw-shane';* from 1878; *fat;* fig. *rich, fertile:*—fat {3x}. See: TWOT—457b; BDB—206c.

1880. דֶּשֶׁן {15x} **deshen**, *deh'-shen;* from 1878; the *fat;* abstr. *fatness,* i.e. (fig.) *abundance;* spec. the (fatty) *ashes* of sacrifices:—ashes {8x}, fatness {7x}. See: TWOT—457a; BDB—206b.

1881. דָּת {22x} **dâth**, *dawth;* of uncert. (perh. for.) der.: a royal *edict* or statute:—law {9x}, decree {9x}, commandment {2x}, manner {1x}, commission {1x}. Syn.: 1882, 4941, 8451. See: TWOT—458; BDB—206c, 1089b.

1882. דָּת {14x} **dâth** (Aram.), *dawth;* corresp. to 1881:—decree {3x}, law {11x}. See: TWOT—2683; BDB—1089b.

1883. דֶּתֶא {2x} **dethe²** (Aram.), *deh'-thay;* corresp. to 1877:—tender grass {2x}. See: TWOT—2684; BDB—1089b.

1884. דְּתָבָר {2x} **d²thâbâr** (Aram.), *deth-aw-bawr';* of Pers. or.; mean. one *skilled in law;* a *judge:*—counselor {2x}. See: TWOT—2685; BDB—1089b.

1885. דָּתָן {10x} **Dâthân**, *daw-thawn';* of uncert. der.; *Dathan,* an Isr.:—Dathan {10x}. See: BDB—206d.

1886. דֹּתָן {3x} **Dôthân**, *do'-thawn;* or (Chaldaizing dual)

דֹּתַיִן **Dôthayin** (Gen 37:17), *do-thah'-yin;* of uncert. der.; *Dothan,* a place in Pal.:—Dothan {3x}. See: BDB—206d.

הּ

1887. הֵא {2x} **hê²**, *hay;* a prim. particle; *lo!:*—behold {1x}, lo {1x}. See: TWOT—461; BDB—210c, 1089c.

1888. הֵא {2x} **hê²** (Aram.), *hay;* or

הָא **hâ²** (Aram.), *haw;* corresp. to 1887:—even {1x}, lo {1x}. See: TWOT—02687, 02688; BDB—1089c.

1889. הֶאָח {13x} **he²âch**, *heh-awkh';* from 1887 and 253; *aha!:*—ah, aha, ha {13x}. See: TWOT—462; BDB—210c.

הָאֲרָרִי **Hâ²rârîy**. See 2043.

1890. הַבְהָב {1x} **habhâb**, *hab-hawb';* by redupl. from 3051; *gift* (in sacrifice), i.e. *holocaust:*—offering {1x}. See: TWOT—849b; BDB—210c, 396d.

1891. הָבַל {5x} **hâbal**, *haw-bal';* a prim. root; to *be vain* in act, word, or expectation; spec. to *lead astray:*—become vain {4x}, make vain {1x}. See: TWOT—463; BDB—211a.

1892. הֶבֶל {73x} **hebel**, *heh'-bel;* or (rarely in the abs.)

הֲבֵל **hăbêl**, *hab-ale';* from 1891; *emptiness* or *vanity;* fig. Something *transitory* and *unsatisfactory;* often used as an adv.:—vanity {61x}, vain {11x}, altogether {1x}.

Hebel means "breath; vanity; idol." **(1)** All but 4 of its 73 occurrences are in poetry (37 in Ecclesiastes). **(2)** The word represents human "breath" as a transitory thing: "I loathe it; I would not live always: let me alone; for my days are vanity [literally, but a breath]" (Job 7:16). **(3)** *Hebel* means something meaningless and purposeless: "Vanity of vanities, saith the Preacher, vanity of vanities; all is vanity" (Eccl 1:2). Cotton candy is an excellent example; it appears to offer a lot, when in reality it disap-

pears when sampled. **(4)** This word signifies an "idol," which is unsubstantial, worthless, and vain: "They have moved me to jealousy with that which is not God; they have provoked me to anger with their vanities . . ." (Deut 32:21 — the first occurrence). See: TWOT—463a; BDB—210c.

1893. הֶבֶל {8x} **Hebel**, *heh'-bel;* the same as 1892; *Hebel,* the son of Adam:— Abel {8x}. See: BDB—211a.

1894. הֹבֶן {1x} **hôben**, *ho'-ben;* only in plur., from an unused root mean. to *be hard; ebony:*—ebony {1x}. See: TWOT—464; BDB—211b.

1895. הָבַר {1x} **hâbar**, *haw-bar';* a prim. root of uncert. (perh. for.) der.; to *be a horoscopist:*—astrologer {1x}. Syn.: 825, 826. See: TWOT—465; BDB—211b.

1896. הֵגֵא {4x} **Hêgê**, *hay-gay';* or (by perm.)

הֵגַי **Hêgay**, *hay-gah'-ee;* prob. of Pers. or.; *Hege* or *Hegai,* a eunuch of Xerxes:—Hegai {13}, Hege {1x}. See: BDB—211b, 212b.

1897. הָגָה {25x} **hâgâh**, *haw-gaw';* a prim. root [comp. 1901]; to *murmur* (in pleasure or anger); by impl. to *ponder:*—imagine {2x}, meditate {6x}, mourn {4x}, mutter {2x}, roar {1x}, ✕ sore {1x}, speak {4x}, study {2x}, talk {1x}, utter {2x}.

Hagah means "to meditate, moan, growl, utter, speak." **(1)** Found only 25 times in the Hebrew Old Testament, **(1a)** it seems to be an onomatopoetic term, reflecting the sighing and low sounds one may make while musing, at least as the ancients practiced it. **(1b)** This meaning is seen in its first occurrence in the text: "This book of the law shall not depart out of thy mouth; but thou shalt meditate therein day and night . . ." (Josh 1:8). **(2)** Perhaps the most famous reference "to meditating" on the law day and night is Ps 1:2.

(3) *Hagah* also expresses the "growl" of lions (Is 31:4) and the "mourning" of doves (Is 38:14). **(4)** When the word is used in the sense of "to mourn," it apparently emphasizes the sorrowful sounds of mourning, as seen in this parallelism: "Therefore will I howl for Moab, and I will cry out for all Moab; mine heart shall mourn for the men of Kir-heres" (Jer 48:31). **(5)** The idea that mental exercise, planning, often is accompanied by low talking seems to be reflected by Prov 24:1–2: "Be not thou envious against evil men, . . . for their heart studieth destruction, and their lips talk of mischief." Syn.: 2803, 7878. See: TWOT—467; BDB—211c.

1898. הָגָה {3x} **hâgâh**, *haw-gaw';* a prim. root; to *remove:*—stay {1x}, take away {2x}. See: TWOT—468; BDB—212a.

1899. הֶגֶה {3x} **hegeh**, *heh'-geh;* from 1897; a *muttering* (in sighing, thought, or as thunder):—mourning {1x}, sound {1x}, tale {1x}. See: TWOT—467a; BDB—211d.

1900. הָגוּת {1x} **hâgûwth**, *haw-gooth';* from 1897; *musing:*—meditation {1x}. See: TWOT—467b; BDB—212a.

1901. הָגִיג {2x} **hâgîyg**, *haw-gheeg';* from an unused root akin to 1897; prop. a *murmur,* i.e. *complaint:*—meditation {1x}, musing {1x}. See: TWOT—466a; BDB—211c.

1902. הִגָּיוֹן {4x} **higgâyôwn**, *hig-gaw-yone';* intens. from 1897; a *murmuring* sound, i.e. a musical notation (prob. similar to the modern *affettuoso* to indicate solemnity of movement); by impl. a *machination:*—device {1x}, Higgaion {1x}, meditation {1x}, solemn sound {1x}. See: TWOT—467c; BDB—212a.

1903. הָגִין {1x} **hâgîyn**, *haw-gheen';* of uncert. der.; perh. *suitable* or *turning:*—directly {1x}. See: TWOT—469a; BDB—212b.

1904. הָגָר {12x} **Hâgâr**, *haw-gawr';* of uncert. (perhaps for.) der.; *Hagar,* the mother of Ishmael:—Hagar {12x}. See: BDB—212b.

1905. הַגְרִי {3x} **Hagrîy**, *hag-ree';* or (prol.)

הַגְרִיא **Hagrîy**ʾ, *hag-ree';* perh. patron. from 1904; a *Hagrite* or member of a certain Arabian clan:—Hagarene {1x}, Hagarite {1x}, Haggeri {1x}. See: BDB—212b, 212c.

1906. הֵד {1x} **hêd**, *hade;* for 1959; a *shout:*—sounding again {1x}. See: TWOT—471b; BDB—212c, 212d.

1907. הַדָּבָר {4x} **haddâbâr** (Aram.), *had-daw-bawr';* prob. of for. origin; a *vizier:*—counselor {4x}. See: TWOT—2689; BDB—1089c.

1908. הֲדַד {12x} **Hădad**, *had-ad';* prob. of for. or. [comp. 111]; *Hadad,* the name of an idol, and of several kings of Edom:—Hadad {12x}. See: TWOT—471c; BDB—212d.

1909. הֲדַדְעֶזֶר {9x} **Hădadʿezer**, *had-ad-eh'-zer;* from 1908 and 5828; *Hadad (is his) help; Hadadezer,* a Syrian king:— Hadadezer {9x}. Syn.: comp. 1928. See: BDB—212d.

1910. הֲדַדְרִמּוֹן {1x} **Hădadrimmôwn**, *had-ad-rim-mone';* from 1908 and 7417; *Hadad-Rimmon,* a place in Pal.:—Hadad-rimmon {1x}. 213a. See: BDB—213a.

1911. הָדָה {1x} **hâdâh**, *haw-daw';* a prim. root [comp. 3034]; to *stretch forth* the hand:—put. {1x}. See: TWOT—472; BDB—213a.

1912. הֹדוּ {2x} **Hôdûw**, *ho'-doo;* of for. or.; *Hodu* (i.e. Hindû-stan):—India {2x}. See: BDB—213a.

1913. הֲדוֹרָם {4x} **Hădôwrâm**, *had-o-rawm';* or

הֲדֹרָם **Hădôrâm**, *had-o-rawm';* prob. of for. der.; *Hadoram,* a son of Joktan, and the tribe descended from him:—Hadoram {4x}. See: BDB—213a, 214c.

1914. הִדַּי {1x} **Hidday**, *hid-dah'ee;* of uncert. der.; *Hiddai,* an Isr.:—Hiddai {1x}. See: BDB—213b, 301b.

1915. הָדַךְ {1x} **hâdak**, *haw-dak';* a prim. root [comp. 1854]; to *crush* with the foot:—tread down {1x}. See: TWOT—473; BDB—213b. Syn.: 947, 1758, 1869, 7429.

1916. הֲדֹם {6x} **hădôm**, *had-ome';* from an unused root mean. to *stamp* upon; a foot-*stool:*—footstool + 7272 {6x}. Syn.: 3534. See: TWOT—474; BDB—213b.

1917. הַדָּם {2x} **haddâm** (Aram.), *had-dawm';* from a root corresp. to that of 1916; something *stamped* to pieces, i.e. a *bit:*—pieces {1x}. See: TWOT—2690; BDB—1089d.

1918. הֲדַס {6x} **hădaç**, *had-as';* of uncert. der.; the *myrtle:*—myrtle {2x}, myrtle tree {4x}. See: TWOT—475; BDB—213c.

1919. הֲדַסָּה {1x} **Hădaççâh**, *had-as-saw';* fem. of 1918; *Hadassah* (or Esther):—Hadassah {1x}. See: BDB—213c.

1920. הָדַף {1x} **hâdaph**, *haw-daf';* a prim root; to *push away* or down:—thrust {3x}, drive {3x}, cast out {2x}, expel {1x}, thrust away {1x}, cast away {1x}. Syn.: 1644, 5974, 5090. See: TWOT—476; BDB—213c.

1921. הָדַר {7x} **hâdar**, *haw-dar';* a prim. root; to *swell* up (lit. or fig., act. or pass.); by impl. to *favor* or *honour, be high* or *proud:*—honour {3x}, countenance {1x}, crooked places {1x}, glorious {1x}, put forth {1x}.

Hadar means "to honor, prefer, exalt oneself, behave arrogantly." **(1)** This verb, which appears 7 times in biblical Hebrew means "to honor" or "to prefer" in Ex 23:3: "Neither shalt thou countenance a poor man in his cause." **(2)** In Prov 25:6 *hadar* means "to exalt oneself" or "to behave arrogantly." See: TWOT—477; BDB—213d, 1089d.

1922. הֲדַר {3x} **hădar** (Aram.), *had-ar';* corresp. to 1921; to *magnify* (fig.):—

glorify {1x}, honour {2x}. See: TWOT—2691; BDB—1089d.

1923. הֲדַר {3x} **hădar** (Aram.), *had-ar';* from 1922; *magnificence:*—honour {2x}, majesty {1x}. See: TWOT—2691a; BDB—1089d.

1924. הֲדַר {1x} **Hădar**, *had-ar';* the same as 1926; *Hadar,* an Edomite:—Hadar {1x}. See: BDB—214c.

1925. הֶדֶר {1x} **heder**, *heh'-der;* from 1921; *honour;* used (fig.) for the *capital city* (Jerusalem):—glory {1x}. See: BDB—214a.

1926. הָדָר {30x} **hâdâr**, *haw-dawr';* from 1921; *magnificence,* i.e. ornament or splendor:—glory {7x}, majesty {7x}, honour {5x}, beauty {4x}, comeliness {3x}, excellency {2x}, glorious {1x}, goodly {1x}.

Hadar means "honor; splendor." **(1)** Its 30 appearances in the Bible are exclusively in poetic passages and in all periods. **(2)** *Hadar* refers to "splendor" in nature: "And ye shall take you on the first day the boughs of goodly trees [literally, trees of splendor or beauty] . . ." (Lev 23:40—the first occurrence). **(3)** This word is a counterpart to Hebrew words for "glory" and "dignity." **(3a)** Thus *hadar* means not so much overwhelming beauty as a combination of physical attractiveness and social position. **(3b)** The Messiah is said to have "no form nor [majesty]; and when we shall see him, there is no beauty that we should desire him" (Is 53:2). **(4)** Mankind is crowned with "glory and honor" in the sense of superior desirability (for God) and rank (Ps 8:5). **(5)** In Prov 20:29 *hadar* focuses on the same idea—an aged man's mark of rank and privilege is his gray hair. This reflects the theme present throughout the Bible that long life is a mark of divine blessing and results (often) when one is faithful to God, whereas premature death is a result of divine judgment.

(6) The ideas of glorious brilliance, preeminence, and lordship are included in *hadar* when it is applied to God: "Glory and honor are in his presence; strength and gladness are in his place" (1 Chr 16:27). **(6a)** Not only are these characteristics of His sanctuary (Ps 96:6) **(6b)** but He is clothed with them (Ps 104:1). **(7)** God gave David all good things: a crown of gold on his head, long life, and glory or "splendor" and majesty (Ps 21:3–5). **(8)** In the case of earthly kings their beauty or brilliance usually arises from their surroundings. So God says of Tyre: "They of Persia and of Lud and of Phut were in thine army, thy men of war: they hanged the shield and helmet in thee; they set forth thy comeliness [honor]. The men of Arvad with thine army were upon thy walls round about, and the Gammadim were in thy towers:

they hanged their shields upon thy walls round about; they have made thy beauty perfect" (Eze 27:10–11). **(9)** God, however, manifests the characteristic of "honor or splendor" in Himself. Syn.: 3519. See: TWOT—477b; BDB—214a.

1927. הֲדָרָה {5x} **hădârâh**, *had-aw-raw'*; fem. of 1926; *decoration:*—beauty {4x}, honour {1x}.

The noun *hadarah* means "majesty; splendor; exaltation; adornment." **(1)** This noun appears 5 times in the Bible. **(2)** The word implies "majesty or exaltation" in Prov 14:28: in the multitude of people *is* the king's honour: but in the want of people *is* the destruction of the prince. **(3)** *Hadarah* refers to "adornment" in Ps 29:2. See: TWOT—477c; BDB—214c.

1928. הֲדַרְעֶזֶר {12x} **Hădarᶜezer**, *had-ar-eh'-zer;* from 1924 and 5828; *Hadar* (i.e. *Hadad*, 1908) is his *help; Hadarezer* (i.e. Hadadezer, 1909), a Syrian king:—Hadarezer {12x}. See: BDB—214c.

1929. הָהּ {1x} **hâhh**, *haw;* a short. form of 162; *ah!* expressing grief:—woe worth {1x}. See: BDB—214c.

1930. הוֹ **hôw**, *ho;* by perm. from 1929; *oh!:*—alas {1x}. See: TWOT—479; BDB—214c.

1931. הוּא {38x} **hûwʾ**, *hoo;* of which the fem. (beyond the Pentateuch) is

הִיא **hîyʾ**, *he;* a prim. word, the third pers. pron. sing., *he* (*she* or *it*); only expressed when emphat. or without a verb; also (intens.) *self,* or (espec. with the art.) the *same;* sometimes (as demonstr.) *this* or *that;* occasionally (instead of copula) *as* or *are:*—he, as for her, him (-self), it, the same, she (herself), such, that (. . . it), these, they, this, those, which (is), who. {38x}. See: TWOT—480; BDB—214d, 223d, 1090a.

1932. הוּא {7x} **hûwʾ** (Aram.), *hoo;* or (fem.)

הִיא **hîyʾ** (Aram.), *he;* corresp. to 1931:—to be {2x}, it {2x}, this {2x}, one {1x}. See: TWOT—2693; BDB—1081c, 1090a.

1933. הָוָא {6x} **hâvâʾ**, *haw-vaw';* or

הָוָה **hâvâh**, *haw-vaw';* a prim. root [comp. 183, 1961] supposed to mean prop. to *breathe;* to *be* (in the sense of existence):—be thou {2x}, be {1x}, shall be {1x}, may be {1x}, hath {1x}. See: TWOT—484, 491; BDB—216d, 217c.

1934. הֲוָא {69x} **hăvâʾ** (Aram.), *hav-aw';* or

הֲוָה **hăvâh** (Aram.), *hav-aw';* corresp. to 1933; to *exist;* used in a great variety of applications (espec. in connection with

other words):—be {16x}, misc.: {52}: become, + behold, + came (to pass), + cease, + cleave, + consider, + do, + give, + have, + judge, + keep, + labour, + mingle (self), + put, + see, + seek, + set, + slay, + take heed, tremble, + walk, + would. See: TWOT—2692; BDB—1089d.

1935. הוֹד {24x} **hôwd**, *hode;* from an unused root; *grandeur* (i.e. an imposing form and appearance):—glory {9x}, honour {6x}, majesty {4x}, beauty {1x}, comeliness {1x}, glorious {1x}, goodly {1x}, honourable {1x}.

Howd means "splendor; majesty; authority." **(1)** All but 4 of its 24 biblical appearances occur in poetry. **(2)** The basic significance of "splendor and majesty" with overtones of superior power and position is attested in the application of this word to kings: **(2a)** "Therefore thus saith the LORD concerning Jehoiakim the son of Josiah king of Judah; They shall not lament for him, saying, Ah my brother! or, Ah sister! they shall not lament for him, saying, Ah lord! or, Ah his glory!" (Jer 22:18). **(2b)** This concept is equally prominent when the word is used of God: "Fair weather cometh out of the north: with God is terrible majesty" (Job 37:22).

(3) In many cases *howd* focuses on "dignity and splendor" with overtones of superior power and position but not to the degree seen in oriental kings: "And thou shalt put some of thine honor upon him, that all the congregation of the children of Israel may be obedient" (Num 27:20—the first occurrence of the word). **(4)** When used of the olive tree (Hos 14:6), *howd* focuses on its "splendor and dignity" as the most desired and desirable of the trees (cf. Judg 9:9–15). **(5)** The proud carriage of a war horse and seeming bravery in the face of battle lead God to say "The glory of his nostrils is terrible" (Job 39:20). **(6)** In every use of the word the one so described evokes a sense of amazement and satisfaction in the mind of the beholder. Syn.: 142, 3519, 6643. See: TWOT—482a; BDB—213a, 217a.

1936. הוֹד {1x} **Hôwd**, *hode;* the same as 1935; *Hod,* an Isr.:—Hod {1x}. See: BDB—217b.

1937. הוֹדְוָה {1x} **Hôwdᵉvâh**, *ho-dev-aw';* a form of 1938; *Hodevah* (or Hodevjah), an Isr.:—Hodevah {1x}. See: BDB—217b, 217c.

1938. הוֹדְוָיָה {3x} **Hôwdavyâh**, *ho-dav-yaw';* from 1935 and 3050; *majesty of Jah; Hodavjah,* the name of three Isr.:—Hodaviah {3x}. See: BDB—217b, 217c.

1939. הוֹדַיְוָהוּ {1x} **Howdayᵉvâhûw**, *ho-dah-yeh-vaw'-hoo;* a form of 1938;

Hodajvah, an Isr.:—Hodaiah {1x}. See: BDB—217c.

1940. הוֹדְיָה {1x} **Hôwdîyâh**, *ho-dee-yaw'*; a form for the fem. of 3064; a *Jewess:*—Hodiah {1x}. See: BDB—217c.

1941. הוֹדְיָה {5x} **Hôwdîyâh**, *ho-dee-yaw'*; a form of 1938; *Hodijah*, the name of three Isr.:—Hodijah {5x}. See: BDB—217c.

הָוָה **hâvâh**. See 1933.

הָוָה **hăvâh**. See 1934.

1942. הַוָּה {16x} **havvâh**, *hav-vaw'*; from 1933 (in the sense of eagerly *coveting* and *rushing* upon; by impl. of *falling*); *desire;* also *ruin:*—calamity {4x}, wickedness {3x}, perverse thing {1x}, mischief {1x}, noisome {1x}, iniquity {1x}, substance {1x}, naughtiness {1x}, naughty {1x}, mischievous {1x}. See: TWOT—483a; BDB—217c.

1943. הֹוָה {3x} **hôvâh**, *ho-vaw';* another form for 1942; *ruin:*—mischief {3x}. See: TWOT—483c; BDB—217d.

1944. הוֹהָם {1x} **Hôwhâm**, *ho-hawm';* of uncert. der.; *Hoham,* a Canaanitish king:—Hoham. {1x}. See: BDB—222d.

1945. הוֹי {52x} **hôwy**, *hoh'-ee;* a prol. form of 1930 [akin to 188]; *oh!:*—woe {36x}, Ah {7x}, Ho {4x}, O {3x}, Alas {2x}. See: TWOT—485; BDB—222d.

1946. הוּךְ {4x} **hûwk** (Aram.), *hook;* corresp. to 1981; to *go;* caus. to *bring:*—go up {1x}, came {1x}, brought again {1x}, go {1x}. See: TWOT—2695; BDB—1090b.

1947. הוֹלֵלָה {4x} **hôwlêlâh**, *ho-lay-law';* fem. act. part. of 1984; *folly:*—madness {4x}. See: TWOT—501a; BDB—239c.

1948. הוֹלֵלוּת {1x} **hôwlêlûwth**, *ho-lay-looth';* from act. part. of 1984; *folly:*—madness {1x}. See: TWOT—501b; BDB—239c.

1949. הוּם {6x} **hûwm**, *hoom;* a prim. root [comp. 2000]; to *make an uproar,* or *agitate* greatly:—rang again {2x}, make a noise {2x}, moved {1x}, destroy {1x}. See: TWOT—486; BDB—223a, 228d.

1950. הוֹמָם {1x} **Hôwmâm**, *ho-mawm';* from 2000; *raging; Homam,* an Edomitish chieftain:—Homam {1x}. comp. 1967. See: BDB—223b, 243a.

1951. הוּן {1x} **hûwn**, *hoon;* a prim. root; prop. to *be naught,* i.e. (fig.) to *be* (caus. act) *light:*—be ready {1x}. See: TWOT—487; BDB—223b.

1952. הוֹן {26x} **hôwn**, *hone;* from the same as 1951 in the sense of 202; *wealth;* by impl. *enough:*—riches {11x}, substance {7x}, wealth {5x}, enough {2x}, nought {1x}.

Hown (1952) means "wealth; substance; riches; possessions; enough." **(1)** The 26 occurrences of this word are almost wholly in wisdom literature, with 17 of them in the Book of Proverbs. **(2)** This word appears only in the singular form. **(3)** *Hown* usually refers to movable goods considered as "wealth": "But if he [the thief] be found, he shall restore seven-fold; he shall give all the substance of his house" (Prov 6:31; cf. Eze 27:12). **(4)** "Wealth" can be good and a sign of blessing: "Wealth and riches shall be in his [the righteous man's] house: and his righteousness endureth for ever" (Ps 112:3). **(5)** The creation is God's wealth: "I have rejoiced in the way of thy testimonies, as much as in all riches" (Ps 119:14). **(6)** In the Proverbs "wealth" is usually an indication of ungodliness: "The rich man's wealth is his strong city: the destruction of the poor is their poverty" (Prov 10:15). **(7)** This word can also represent any kind of concrete "wealth": ". . . If a man would give all the substance of his house for love, it would utterly be contemned" (Song 8:7). This is the significance of the word in its first occurrence: "Thou sellest thy people for nought and dost not increase thy wealth by their price" (Ps 44:12). **(9)** "Wealth" in general is meant in Prov 12:27: "The slothful man roasteth not that which he took in hunting: but the substance of a diligent man is precious." **(10)** Finally, *hown* means "enough" (only in Prov 30:15–16): "The horseleech hath two daughters, crying, Give, Give. There are three things that are never satisfied, yea, four things say not, It is enough: the grave; and the barren womb; the earth that is not filled with water; and the fire that saith not, It is enough." Syn.: 2428, 2633, 3502, 6239. See: TWOT—487a; BDB—223c.

1953. הוֹשָׁמָע {1x} **Hôwshâmâ**ᶜ, *ho-shaw-maw';* from 3068 and 8085; *Jehovah has heard; Hoshama,* an Isr.:—Hoshama {1x}. See: BDB—221d, 223c.

1954. הוֹשֵׁעַ {17x} **Hôwshêä**ᶜ, *ho-shay'-ah;* from 3467; *deliverer; Hosheä,* the name of five Isr.:—Hosea {3x}, Hoshea {3x}, Oshea {3x}. See: BDB—223c, 448a.

1955. הוֹשַׁעְיָה {3x} **Hôwsha**ᶜ**yâh**, *ho-shah-yaw';* from 3467 and 3050; *Jah has saved; Hoshajah,* the name of two Isr.:—Hoshaiah {3x}. See: BDB—448a.

1956. הוֹתִיר {2x} **Hôwthîyr**, *ho-theer';* from 3498; *he has caused to remain; Hothir,* an Isr.:—Hothir {2x}. See: BDB—223d, 452d.

Hebrew

1957. הָזָה {1x} **hâzâh**, *haw-zaw'*; a prim. root [comp. 2372]; to *dream:*—sleep {1x}. See: TWOT—489; BDB—223d.

1958. הִי {1x} **hîy**, *he;* for 5092; *lamentation:*—woe {1x}. Syn.: 188, 190, 337, 480, 1929, 1945. See: TWOT—490; BDB—223d.

הִיא **hîy**ʾ. See 1931, 1932.

1959. הֵידָד {7x} **hêydâd**, *hay-dawd'*; from an unused root (mean. to *shout*); *acclamation:*—shouting {1x}. See: TWOT—471a; BDB—212c, 223d.

1960. הִידָה {1x} **huy**ᵉ**dâh**, *hoo-yed-aw'*; from the same as 1959; prop. an *acclaim,* i.e. a *choir* of singers:—thanksgiving {1x}. Syn.: 8426. See: TWOT—847a; BDB—224a, 392d.

1961. הָיָה {75x} **hâyâh**, *haw-yaw;* a prim. root [comp. 1933]; to *exist,* i.e. *be* or *become, come to pass* (always emphat., and not a mere copula or auxiliary):—{75x} = beacon, X altogether, be (-come), accomplished, committed, like), break, cause, come (to pass), do, faint, fall, + follow, happen, X have, last, pertain, quit (one-) self, require, X use.

Hayah means "to become, occur, come to pass, be." **(1)** Often this verb indicates more than simple existence or identity (this may be indicated by omitting the verb altogether). **(1a)** Rather, the verb makes a strong statement about the being or presence of a person or thing. **(1b)** Yet the simple meaning "become" or "come to pass" appears often in the English versions. **(2)** The verb can be used to emphasize **(2a)** the presence of a person (e.g., God's Spirit—Judg 3:10), **(2c)** an emotion (e.g., fear—Gen 9:2), or **(2d)** a state of being (e.g., evil—Amos 3:6). **(2e)** In such cases, the verb indicates that their presence (or absence) is noticeable—it makes a real difference to what is happening. **(3)** On the other hand, in some instances *hayah* does simply mean "happen, occur." **(3a)** Here the focus is on the simple occurrence of the events—as seen, for example, in the statement following the first day of creation: "And so it happened" (Gen 1:7). **(3b)** In this sense, *hayah* is frequently translated "it came to pass." **(4)** The use of this verb with various particles colors its emphasis accordingly. **(4a)** In passages setting forth blessing or cursing, for example, this verb not only is used to specify the object of the action but also the dynamic forces behind and within the action. **(4b)** Gen 12:2, for example, records that God told Abram: ". . . I will bless thee, and make thy name great; and thou shalt be [*hayah*] a blessing." **(4c)** Abram was already blessed, so God's pronouncement conferred upon him a future blessedness. **(4d)** The use of *hayah* in such pas-

sages declares the actual release of power, so that the accomplishment is assured—Abram will be blessed because God has ordained it. **(5)** In another set of passages, *hayah* constitutes intent rather than accomplishment. Hence, the blessing becomes a promise and the curse a threat (cf. Gen 15:5). **(6)** Finally, in a still weaker use of *hayah,* the blessing or curse constitutes a wish or desire (cf. Ps 129:6). **(6a)** Even here the verb is somewhat dynamic, since the statement recognizes God's presence, man's faithfulness (or rebellion), and God's intent to accomplish the result pronounced. **(7)** In miracle accounts, *hayah* often appears at the climax of the story to confirm the occurrence of the event itself. **(7a)** Lot's wife looked back and "became" a pillar of salt (Gen 19:26); **(7b)** the use of *hayah* emphasizes that the event really occurred. **(7c)** This is also the force of the verb in Gen 1:3, in which God said, "Let there be light." He accomplished His word so that there was light. **(8)** The prophets use *hayah* to project God's intervention in the future. By using this verb, they emphasize not so much the occurrence of predicted events and circumstances as the underlying divine force that will effect them (cf. Is 2:2). **(9)** Legal passages use *hayah* in describing God's relationship to His covenant people, to set forth what is desired and intended (cf. Ex 12:16). **(10)** When covenants were made between two partners, the formulas usually included *hayah* (Deut 26:17–18; Jer 7:23). **(11)** One of the most debated uses of *hayah* occurs in Ex 3:14, where God tells Moses His name. He says: "I am [*hayah*] that I am [*hayah*]." **(11a)** Since the divine name Jehovah or Yahweh was well-known long before (cf. Gen 4:1), this revelation seems to emphasize that the God who made the covenant was the God who kept the covenant. **(11b)** So Ex 3:14 is more than a simple statement of identity: "I am that I am"; **(11c)** it is a declaration of divine control of all things (cf. Hos 1:9). See: TWOT—491; BDB—218b, 224a, 1089d.

1962. הַיָּה {2x} **hayâh**, *hah-yaw'*; another form for 1943; *ruin:*—calamity {2x}. See: TWOT—483b; BDB—217d, 228a.

1963. הֵיךְ {2x} **hêyk**, *hake;* another form for 349; *how?:*—how {1x}. See: TWOT—492; BDB—228a, 1089c.

1964. הֵיכָל {80x} **hêykâl**, *hay-kawl'*; prob. from 3201 (in the sense of *capacity*); a large public building, such as a *palace* or *temple:*—palace {10x}, temple {70x}.

Heykal (1964) means "palace; temple." **(1)** The word occurs 78 times from First Samuel to Malachi, most frequently in Ezekiel. **(2)** The

first usage pertains to the tabernacle at Shiloh (1 Sa 1:9). **(3)** The word "palace" in English versions may have one of three Hebrew words behind it: *heykal, bayit* (1004), or *'armon* (759). **(4)** The *heykal* with its 15 usages as "palace" refers to the palaces **(4a)** of Ahab (1 Kin 21:1), **(4b)** of the king of Babylon (2 Kin 20:18), and **(4c)** of Nineveh (Nah 2:6). **(5)** The "palace" was luxuriously decorated and the residents enjoyed the fulfillment of their pleasures; cf.: **(5a)** "And the wild beasts of the islands shall cry in their desolate houses, and dragons in their pleasant palaces: and her time is near to come, and her days shall not be prolonged" (Is 13:22). **(5b)** The psalmist compared beautiful girls to fine pillars in an ornate "palace": ". . . That our sons may be as plants grown up in their youth; that our daughters may be as corner stones, polished after the similitude of a palace" (Ps 144:12).

(6) Amos prophesied that the "songs of the temple" were to turn to wailing at the destruction of the northern kingdom (Amos 8:3). **(7)** *Heykal* with the meaning "temple" is generally clarified in the context by two markers that follow. **(7a)** The first marker is the addition "of the LORD": "And when the builders laid the foundation of the temple of the LORD, they set the priests in their apparel with trumpets, and the Levites the sons of Asaph with cymbals, to praise the LORD, after the ordinance of David king of Israel" (Ezra 3:10). **(7b)** The second marker is a form of the word *qodesh* (6944), "holy": "O God, the heathen are come into thine inheritance; thy holy temple have they defiled; they have laid Jerusalem on heaps" (Ps 79:1). **(8)** Sometimes the definite article suffices to identify the "temple in Jerusalem": "In the year that King Uzziah died I saw also the Lord sitting upon a throne, high and lifted up, and his train filled the temple" (Is 6:1), especially in a section dealing with the "temple" (Eze 41).

(9) The Old Testament also speaks about the heavenly *heykal*, the *heykal* of God. **(9a)** It is difficult to decide on a translation, whether "palace" or "temple." **(9b)** Most versions opt in favor of the "temple" idea: **(9b1)** "Hear, all ye people; hearken, O earth, and all that therein is: and let the Lord GOD be witness against you, the LORD from his holy temple" (Mic 1:2; cf. Ps 5:7; 11:4; Hab 2:20). **(9b2)** "In my distress I called upon the LORD, and cried to my God: and he did hear my voice out of his temple, and my cry did enter into his ears" (2 Sa 22:7). **(10)** However, since Scripture portrays the presence of the royal judgment throne in heaven, it is not altogether impossible that the original authors had a royal "palace" in mind. **(11)** The imagery of the throne, the "palace,"

and judgment seems to lie behind Ps 11:4–5. "The LORD is in his holy temple, the LORD's throne is in heaven: his eyes behold, his eyelids try, the children of men. The LORD trieth the righteous: but the wicked and him that loveth violence his soul hateth." See: TWOT–493; BDB–228a, 1090b.

1965. הֵיכַל {13x} **hêykal** (Aram.), *hay-kal';* corresp. to 1964:–palace {5x}, temple {8x}. See: TWOT–2694; BDB–1090b.

1966. הֵילֵל {1x} **hêylêl**, *hay-lale';* from 1984 (in the sense of *brightness*); the *morning-star:*–Lucifer {1x}. See: TWOT–499a; BDB–228d, 237d.

1967. הֵימָם {1x} **Hêymâm**, *hay-mawm';* another form for 1950; *Hemam,* an Idumæan:–Hemam {1x}. See: BDB–228d, 243a.

1968. הֵימָן {17x} **Hêymân**, *hay-mawn';* prob. from 539; *faithful; Heman,* the name of at least two Isr.:–Heman {17x}. See: BDB–54c, 228d.

1969. הִין {22x} **hîyn**, *heen;* prob. of Eg. or.; a *hin* or liquid measure:–hin {22x}. See: TWOT–494; BDB–228d.

1970. הָכַר {1x} **hâkar**, *haw-kar';* a prim. root; appar. to *injure:*–make self strange {1x}. See: TWOT–495; BDB–229a.

1971. הַכָּרָה {1x} **hakkârâh**, *hak-kaw-raw';* from 5234; *respect,* i.e. partiality:–shew {1x}. See: TWOT–1368e; BDB–229b, 648b.

הַל   **hal**. See 1973.

1972. הָלָא {1x} **hâlâ'**, *haw-law';* prob. denom. from 1973; to *remove* or be *remote:*–cast far off {1x}. See: TWOT–496; BDB–229b, 229c.

1973. הָלְאָה {16x} **hâl'âh**, *haw-leh-aw';* from the prim. form of the art. **[hal]**; to *the distance,* i.e. *far away;* also (of time) *thus far:*–beyond {5x}, forward {5x}, hitherto {2x}, back {1x}; thenceforth {1x}, henceforth {1x}, yonder {1x}. See: See: TWOT–496a; BDB–210b, 229b.

1974. הִלּוּל {2x} **hillûwl**, *hil-lool';* from 1984 (in the sense of *rejoicing*); a *celebration* of thanksgiving for harvest:–merry {1x}, praise {1x}.

Hilluwlim [plural], which occurs twice, means "praise" in Lev 19:24: "But in the fourth year all the fruit thereof shall be holy to praise the LORD *withal.* See: TWOT–500a; BDB–239b.

1975. הַלָּז {1x} **hallâz**, *hal-lawz';* from 1976; *this* or *that:*–this {4x}, that {2x},

other side + 5676 {1x}. See: TWOT—497; BDB—229c, 534c.

1976. הַלָּזֶה {2x} **hallâzeh,** *hal-law-zeh';* from the art. [see 1973] and 2088; *this very:*—this {1x}. See: TWOT—497; BDB—229d, 534c.

1977. הַלָּזוּ {1x} **hallêzûw,** *hal-lay-zoo';* another form of 1976; *that:*—this {1x}. See: TWOT—497; BDB—229d, 534c.

1978. הָלִיךְ {1x} **hâlîyk,** *haw-leek';* from 1980; a *walk,* i.e. (by impl.) a *step:*—step {1x}. *Haliyk* appears once with the meaning "steps" (Job 29:6). See: TWOT—498b; BDB—237b.

1979. הֲלִיכָה {7x} **hălîykâh,** *hal-ee-kaw';* fem. of 1978; a *walking;* by impl. a *procession* or *march,* a *caravan:*—ways {2x}, goings {2x}, companies {1x}, walk {1x}, way {1x}.
    Haliykah means "course; doings; traveling company; caravan; procession." **(1)** This noun occurs 6 times in the Old Testament. **(2)** This word conveys several nuances. **(2a)** In Nah 2:5 *haliykah* refers to a "course": "He shall recount his worthies: they shall stumble in their walk. . . ." **(2b)** The word means "doings" in Prov 31:27. **(2c)** It may also mean "traveling-company" or "caravan" as in Job 6:19 or a "procession" as in Ps 68:24. See: TWOT—498c; BDB—237b.

1980. הָלַךְ {500x} **hâlak,** *haw-lak';* akin to 3212; a prim. root; to *walk* (in a great variety of applications, lit. and fig.):—go {217x}, walk {156x}, come {16x}, . . . away {7x}, . . . along {6x}, misc. {98x} = (all) along, apace, behave (self), come, (on) continually, be conversant, depart, + be eased, enter, exercise (self), + follow, forth, forward, get, go (about, abroad, along, away, forward, on, out, up and down), + greater, grow, be wont to haunt, lead, march, × more and more, move (self), needs, on, pass (away), be at the point, quite, run (along), + send, speedily, spread, still, surely, + tale-bearer, + travel (-ler), walk (abroad, on, to and fro, up and down, to places), wander, wax, [way-] faring man, × be weak, whirl.
    Halak means "to go, walk, behave." **(1)** Essentially, this root refers to movement without any suggestion of direction in the sense of going, whether of **(1a)** man (Gen 9:23), **(1b)** beasts (Gen 3:14), or **(1c)** inanimate objects (Gen 2:14—the first occurrence of the word). **(2)** In cases other than men (where it means "to walk") *halak* may be translated "to go." **(2a)** It is used sometimes with a special emphasis on the end or goal of the action in mind; men are but flesh, "a wind that passeth [goes] away, and cometh not again" (Ps 78:39). **(2b)** Applied to

human existence the word suggests "going to one's death," as in Gen 15:2, when Abraham says: "O Lord GOD, what wilt thou give me, seeing I go [am going to my death] childless . . . ?" **(3)** This verb can also be used of one's behavior, or the way one "walks in life." **(3a)** So he who "walks" uprightly shall be blessed of God (Is 33:15). **(3b)** This does not refer to walking upright on one's feet but to living a righteous life.
    (4) This root is used in various other special ways. **(4a)** It may be used to emphasize that a certain thing occurred; **(4a1)** Jacob went and got the kid his mother requested, in other words, he actually did the action (Gen 27:14). **(4a2)** In Gen 8:3 the waters of the flood steadily receded from the surface of the earth. **(5)** Sometimes this verb implies movement away from, as in Gen 18:33, when the Lord "departed" from Abraham. **(6)** God is said to "walk" or "go in three senses. **(6a)** First, there are certain cases where He assumed some kind of physical form. **(6a1)** For example, Adam and Eve heard the sound of God "walking" to and fro in the garden of Eden (Gen 3:8). **(6a2)** He "walks" on the clouds (Ps 104:3) or in the heavens (Job 22:14); these are probably anthropomorphisms (God is spoken of as if He had bodily parts). **(6b)** Even more often God is said to accompany His people (Ex 33:14), **(6b1)** to go to redeem (deliver) them from Egypt (2 Sa 7:23), and **(6b2)** to come to save them (Ps 80:2). **(6c)** The idea of God's "going" ("walking") before His people in the pillars of fire and cloud (Ex 13:21) leads to the idea that His people must "walk" behind Him (Deut 13:5).
    (7) Quite often the people are said to have "walked" or to be warned against "walking behind" foreign gods (Deut 4:3). **(8)** Thus, the rather concrete idea of following God through the wilderness moves to "walking behind" Him spiritually. **(9)** Some scholars suggest that "walking behind" pagan gods (or even the true God) arose from the pagan worship where the god was carried before the people as they entered the sanctuary. **(10)** Men may also "walk . . . after the imagination of their evil heart," or act stubbornly (Jer 3:17). **(11)** The pious followed or practiced God's commands; they "walked" **(11a)** in righteousness (Is 33:15), **(11b)** in humility (Mic 6:8), and **(11c)** in integrity (Ps 15:2). **(12)** They also "walk with God" (Gen 5:22), and **(13)** they live in His presence, and "walk before" Him (Gen 17:1), in the sense of living responsibly before Him. See: TWOT—498; BDB—229d, 539d, 540b.

1981. הֲלַךְ {3x} **hălak** (Aram.), *hal-ak';* corresp. to 1980 [comp. 1946]; to *walk:*—walk {1x}. See: TWOT—2695; BDB—1090b.

1982. חֵלֶךְ {2x} **hêlek**, *hay'-lek;* from 1980; prop. a *journey,* i.e. (by impl.) a *wayfarer;* also a *flowing:*—× dropped {1x}, traveler {1x}. *Helek* occurs twice and means a "visitor" (2 Sa 12:4). See: TWOT—498a; BDB—237a.

1983. חֲלָךְ {3x} **hălâk** (Aram.), *hal-awk';* from 1981; prop. a *journey,* i.e. (by impl.) *toll* on goods at a road:—custom {3x}. See: TWOT—2695a; BDB—1090b.

1984. הָלַל {165x} **hâlal**, *haw-lal';* a prim. root; to *be clear* (orig. of sound, but usually of color); to *shine;* hence, to *make a show,* to *boast;* and thus to be (clamorously) *foolish;* to *rave;* caus. to *celebrate;* also to *stultify:*—praise {117x}, glory {14x}, boast {10x}, be mad {8x}, shine {3x}, foolish {3x}, be fools {2x}, commended {2x}, rage {2x}, celebrate {1x}, give {1x}, give in marriage {1x}, renowned {1x}.

Halal means "to praise, celebrate, glory, sing (praise), boast." **(1)** The meaning "to praise" is actually the meaning of the intensive form of the Hebrew verb *halal,* which in its simple active form means "to boast." **(2)** Found more than 160 times in the Old Testament, *halal* is used for the first time in Gen 12:15, where it is noted that because of Sarah's great beauty, the princes of Pharaoh "commended" her to Pharaoh. **(3)** While *halal* is often used simply to indicate "praise" of people, including the king (2 Chr 23:12) or the beauty of Absalom (2 Sa 14:25), the word is usually used in reference to the "praise" of God. **(4)** Indeed, not only all living things but all created things, including the sun and moon, are called upon **(4a)** "to praise" God (Ps 148:2–5, 13; 150:1). **(4b)** Typically, such "praise" is called for and expressed in the sanctuary, especially in times of special festivals (Is 62:9).

(5) The Hebrew name for the Book of Psalms is simply the equivalent for the word "praises" and is a bit more appropriate than "Psalms," which comes from the Greek and has to do with the accompaniment of singing with a stringed instrument of some sort. **(5a)** It is little wonder that the Book of Psalms contains more than half the occurrences of *halal* in its various forms. **(5b)** Psalms 113–118 are traditionally referred to as the "Hallel Psalms," because they have to do with praise to God for deliverance from Egyptian bondage under Moses. **(5b1)** Because of this, they are an important part of the traditional Passover service. **(5b2)** There is no reason to doubt that these were the hymns sung by Jesus and His disciples on Maundy Thursday when He instituted the Lord's Supper (Mt 26:30).

(6) The word *halal* is the source of "Hallelujah," a Hebrew expression of "praise" to God **(6a)** which has been taken over into virtually every language of mankind. **(6b)** The Hebrew "Hallelujah" is generally translated "Praise the LORD!" **(6c)** The Hebrew term is more technically translated "Let us praise Yah," **(6c1)** the term "Yah" being a shortened form of "Yahweh," the unique Israelite name for God. **(6c2)** The term "Yah" is found in the KJV rendering of Ps 68:4, reflecting the Hebrew text. **(7)** Most versions follow the traditional translation "Lord," a practice begun in Judaism before New Testament times when the Hebrew term for "Lord" was substituted for "Yahweh," although it probably means something like "He who causes to be." **(8)** The Greek approximation of "Hallelujah" is found 4 times in the New Testament in the form "Alleluia" (Rev 19:1, 3–4, 6). **(9)** Christian hymnody certainly would be greatly impoverished if the term "Hallelujah" were suddenly removed from our language of praise. Syn.: See: 1288, 3034. TWOT - 499, 500; BDB—237c, 237d, 239c.

1985. הִלֵּל {2x} **Hillêl**, *hil-layl';* from 1984; *praising* (namely God); *Hillel,* an Isr.:—Hillel {2x}. See: BDB—239b.

1986. הָלַם {9x} **hâlam**, *haw-lam';* a prim. root; to *strike* down; by impl. to *hammer, stamp, conquer, disband:*—smite {3x}, break down {2x}, break {1x}, beat down {1x}, beat {1x}, overcome {1x}. Syn.: 3807, 5060, 5062, 5221. See: TWOT—502; BDB—240c.

1987. הֶלֶם {1x} **Helem**, *heh'-lem;* from 1986; *smiter; Helem,* the name of two Isr.:—Helem {1x}. See: BDB—240c.

1988. הֲלֹם {11x} **hălôm**, *hal-ome';* from the art. [see 1973]; *hither:*—hither {6x}, hitherto {2x}, here {2x}, thither {1x}. See: TWOT—503; BDB—240d.

1989. הַלְמוּת {1x} **halmûwth**, *hal-mooth';* from 1986; a *hammer* (or *mallet*):—hammer {1x}. See: TWOT—502a; BDB—240d.

1990. הָם {1x} **Hâm**, *hawm;* of uncert. der.; *Ham,* a region of Pal.:—Ham {1x}. See: BDB—241a.

1991. הֵם {1x} **hêm**, *haym;* from 1993; *abundance,* i.e. *wealth:*—any of theirs {1x}. See: TWOT—505; BDB—241a.

1992. הֵם {44x} **hêm**, *haym;* or (prol.) הֵמָּה **hêmmâh**, *haym'-maw;* masc. plur. from 1931; *they* (only used when emphat.):—it, like, × (how, so) many (soever, more as) they (be), (the) same, × so, × such, their, them, these, they, those, which, who, whom, withal, ye = {44x}. See: TWOT—504; BDB—216d, 241a, 1090b.

Hebrew

1993. הָמָה {34x} **hâmâh**, *haw-maw'*; a prim. root [comp. 1949]; to *make a loud sound* (like the English "hum"); by impl. to *be in great commotion* or *tumult*, to *rage, war, moan, clamor:*—roar {8x}, noise {6x}, disquieted {4x}, sound {3x}, troubled {2x}, aloud {1x}, loud {1x}, clamorous {1x}, concourse {1x}, mourning {1x}, moved {1x}, raged {1x}, raging {1x}, tumult {1x}, tumultuous {1x}, uproar {1x}.

Hamah basically means "to make a noise, be tumultuous, roar, groan, bark, sound, moan." This verb occurs 34 times in biblical Hebrew. Psalm 83:2 contains one appearance: "For, lo, thine enemies make a tumult: and they that hate thee have lifted up the head." See: TWOT—505; BDB—242a.

1994. הִמּוֹ {11x} **himmôw** (Aram.), *him-mo';* or (prol.)

הִמּוֹן **himmôwn** (Aram.), *him-mone';* corresp. to 1992; *they:*—them {7x}, set + 3488 {1x}, are {1x}, those {1x}, men + 1400 {1x}. See: TWOT—2696; BDB—1090b.

1995. הָמוֹן {83x} **hâmôwn**, *haw-mone';* or

הָמֹן **hâmôn** (Eze 5:7), *haw-mone';* from 1993; a *noise, tumult, crowd;* also *disquietude, wealth:*—multitude {62x}, noise {4x}, tumult {4x}, abundance {3x}, many {3x}, store {2x}, company {1x}, multiplied {1x}, riches {1x}, rumbling {1x}, sounding {1x}.

Hamon means "multitude; lively commotion; agitation; tumult; uproar; commotion; turmoil; noise; crowd; abundance." **(1)** The word represents a "lively commotion or agitation": "Look down from heaven, and behold from the habitation of thy holiness and of thy glory: where is thy zeal and thy strength, the sounding of thy bowels and of thy mercies toward me?" (Is 63:15). **(2)** *Hamon* represents the stirring or agitation of a crowd of people: "When Joab sent the king's servant, and me thy servant, I saw a great tumult, but I knew not what it was" (2 Sa 18:29). **(3)** In Is 17:12 the word is synonymously parallel to *sha'on* (7588) "rushing": "Woe to the multitude of many people, which make a noise like the noise of the seas; and to the rushing of nations, that make a rushing like the rushing of mighty waters!" **(4)** Sometimes *hamon* represents the noise raised by an agitated crowd of people (a "tumult"): "And when Eli heard the noise of the crying, he said, "What meaneth the noise of this tumult [raised by the report that the battle was lost]?" (1 Sa 4:14).

(5) In Is 13:4 the word represents the mighty sound of a gathering army rather than the confused outcry of a mourning city: "The noise of a multitude in the mountains, like as of a great people; a tumultuous noise of the kingdoms of nations gathered together: the LORD of hosts mustereth the host of the battle." **(6)** A young lion eating his prey is not disturbed by the noise of a band of shepherds trying to scare him off (Is 31:4). **(7)** There are exceptions to the rule that the word represents the sound of a large number of people. **(7a)** In 1 Kin 18:41 *hamon* signifies the roar of a heavy downpour of rain (cf. Jer 10:13), and **(7b)** in Jer 47:3 it represents the tumult of chariots. **(8)** *Hamon* sometimes means a "multitude or crowd" from which a tumult may arise. **(9)** Frequently the word represents a large army: "And I will draw unto thee, to the river Kishon, Sisera, the captain of Jabin's army, with his chariots and his multitude . . ." (Judg 4:7; cf. 1 Sa 14:16).

(10) Elsewhere *hamon* represents a whole people: "And he dealt among all the people, even among the whole multitude of Israel . . ." (2 Sa 6:19). **(11)** Finally, any great throng, or a great number of people (Gen 17:4—the first occurrence) may be represented by this word. **(12)** A great number of things can be indicated by *hamon* "O LORD our God, all this store that we have prepared to build thee a house for thine holy name . . ." (1 Chr 29:16). **(13)** Abundance of possessions or wealth is indicated by *hamon*, as in: "A little that a righteous man hath is better than the riches of many wicked" (Ps 37:16; cf. Eccl 5:10—parallel to "silver" [money]; Is 60:5). **(14)** Finally, *hamon* refers to a group of people organized around a king, specifically, his courtiers: **(14a)** "Son of man, speak unto Pharaoh king of Egypt, and to his multitude [his train or royal retinue]; Whom art thou like in thy greatness?" (Eze 31:2). **(14b)** Thus in Ps 42:4 the word can represent a festival procession, a kind of train. Syn.: 527, 6951. See: TWOT—505a; BDB—242b.

הַמֹּלֶכֶת **ham-môleketh**. See 4447.

1996. הֲמוֹן גּוֹג {2x} **Hămôwn Gôwg**, *ham-one' gohg;* from 1995 and 1463; the *multitude of Gog;* the fanciful name of an emblematic place in Pal.:—Hamon-gog {2x}. See: BDB—155d, 242b.

1997. הֲמוֹנָה {1x} **Hămôwnâh**, *ham-o-naw';* fem. of 1995; *multitude; Hamonah*, the same as 1996:—Hamonah {1x}. See: BDB—242d.

הֲמוֹנֶךְ **hămûwnêk**. See 2002.

1998. הֶמְיָה {1x} **hemyâh**, *hem-yaw';* from 1993; *sound:*—noise {1x}. Syn.: 7452. See: TWOT—505b; BDB—242d.

1999. הֲמֻלָּה {2x} **hămullâh**, *ham-ool-law';* or (too fully)

הֲמוּלָּה **hămûwllâh** (Jer 11:16), *ham-ool-law';* fem. pass. part. of an

unused root mean. to *rush* (as rain with a windy roar); a *sound:*—speech {1x}, tumult {1x}. See: TWOT—506a; BDB—242d.

2000. הָמַם {13x} **hâmam,** *haw-mam';* a prim. root [comp. 1949, 1993]; prop. to *put in commotion;* by impl. to *disturb, drive, destroy:*—discomfit {5x}, destroy {3x}, vex {1x}, crush {1x}, break {1x}, consume {1x} trouble {1x}. See: TWOT—507; BDB—243a.

הָמוֹן **hâmôn.** See 1995.

2001. הָמָן {54x} **Hâmân,** *haw-mawn';* of for. der.; *Haman,* a Pers. vizier:—Haman {54x}. See: BDB—243b.

2002. הַמְנִיךְ {3x} **hamnîyk** (Aram.), *ham-neek';* but the text is

הֲמוּנֵךְ **hămûwnêk,** *ham-oo-nayk';* of for. or.; a *necklace:*—chain {3x}. See: TWOT—2697; BDB—1090c.

2003. הָמָס {1x} **hâmâç,** *haw-mawce';* from an unused root appar. mean. to *crackle;* a dry *twig* or *brushwood:*—melting {1x}. See: TWOT—508a; BDB—243b.

2004. הֵן {16x} **hên,** *hane;* fem. plur. from 1931; *they* (only used when emphat.):—therein {4x}, withal {3x}, which {2x}, they {2x}, for {1x}, like {1x}, them {1x}, thereby {1x}, wherein {1x}. See: TWOT—504; BDB—241d, 243b, 530a.

2005. הֵן {7x} **hên,** *hane;* a prim. particle; *lo!;* also (as expressing surprise) *if:*—behold, if, lo, though = {7x}. See: TWOT—510; BDB—243b, 530a, 1090c.

2006. הֵן {16x} **hên** (Aram.), *hane;* corresp. to 2005: *lo!* also *there* [-fore], [un-] *less, whether, but, if:*—if {2x}, or {2x}, whether {2x}. See: TWOT—2698; BDB—243d, 1090c, 1099a.

2007. הֵנָּה {26x} **hênnâh,** *hane'-naw;* prol. for 2004; *themselves* (often used emphat. for the copula, also in indirect relation):—× in, × such (and such things), their, (into) them, thence, therein, these, they (had), on this side, those, wherein = {26x}. See: TWOT—504; BDB—216d, 241b, 244d.

2008. הֵנָּה {14x} **hênnâh,** *hane'-naw;* from 2004; *hither* or *thither* (but used both of place and time):—here, hither [-to], now, on this (that) side, + since, this (that) way, thitherward, + thus far, to . . . fro, + yet = {14x}. See: TWOT—510b; BDB—244c.

2009. הִנֵּה {17x} **hinnêh,** *hin-nay';* prol. for 2005; *lo!:*—Behold, see, lo, here . . . I, and lo = {17x}. See: TWOT—510a; BDB—243d, 774b.

2010. הֲנָחָה {1x} **hănâchâh,** *han-aw-khaw';* from 5117; *permission* of rest, i.e.

quiet:—release {1x}. See: TWOT—1323d; BDB—244d, 629c.

2011. הִנֹּם {13x} **Hinnôm,** *hin-nome';* prob. of for. or.; *Hinnom,* appar. a Jebusite:—Hinnom {13x}. See: BDB—244d.

2012. הֵנַע {3x} **Hênaʿ,** *hay-nah';* prob. of for. der.; *Hena,* a place appar. in Mesopotamia:—Hena {3x}. See: BDB—245a.

2013. הָסָה {8x} **hâçâh,** *haw-saw';* a prim. root; to *hush:*—keep silence {3x}, hold your peace {2x}, hold your tongue {1x}, still {1x}, (keep) silence {1x}. See: TWOT—511; BDB—245a, 245b.

2014. הֲפֻגָה {1x} **hăphûgâh,** *haf-oo-gaw';* from 6313; *relaxation:*—intermission {1x}. See: TWOT—1740b; BDB—245b, 806b.

2015. הָפַךְ **hâphak,** *haw-fak';* a prim. root; to *turn about or over;* by impl. to *change, overturn, return, pervert:*—turn {57x}, overthrow {13x}, overturn {5x}, change {3x}, turn . . . {6x}, become {1x}, came {1x}, converted {1x}, gave {1x}, make {1x}, perverse {1x}, perverted {1x}, retired {1x}, tumbled {1x}.

Haphak means "to turn, overturn, change, transform, turn back." **(1)** Used for the first time in the biblical text in Gen 3:24, the Hebrew verb form there indicates reflexive action: ". . . A flaming sword which turned every way [NAB, "revolving"; NEB, "whirling"] . . ." **(2)** In its simplest meaning, *hapak* expresses the turning from one side to another, such as **(2a)** "turning" one's back (Josh 7:8), or **(2b)** "as a man wipeth a dish, wiping it, and turning it upside down" (2 Kin 21:13). **(2c)** Similarly, Hosea refers to Israel as being "a cake not turned" (Hos 7:8). **(3)** The meaning of "transformation" or "change" is vividly illustrated in the story of Saul's encounter with the Spirit of God. **(3a)** Samuel promised that Saul "shalt be turned into another man" (1 Sa 10:6), and **(3b)** when the Spirit came on him, "God gave him another heart" (1 Sa 10:9).

(3c) Other examples of change are the "changing" of Pharaoh's mind (Ex 14:5; literally, "the heart of Pharaoh . . . was turned"); **(3d)** the "turning" of Aaron's rod into a serpent (Ex 7:15); **(3e)** dancing "turned" to mourning (Lam 5:14); **(3f)** water "turned" into blood (Ex 7:17); and **(3g)** the sun "turned" to darkness and the moon to blood (Joel 2:31). **(4)** Ps 41:3 "the LORD will strengthen him upon the bed of languishing: thou wilt make all his bed in his sickness." In view of the poetic parallelism involved, restoration of health must be meant. **(5)** The KJV rendering of Is 60:5 sounds strange to our modern ears: "The abundance of the sea shall be converted unto thee . . ." simply means

the riches of the seas will be given back to thee. See: TWOT—512; BDB—245b.

2016. הֶפֶךְ {2x} **hephek**, *heh'-fek;* or

הֵפֶךְ **hêphek**, *hay'-fek;* from 2015; a *turn,* i.e. the *reverse:*—contrary {2x}. See: TWOT—512a; BDB—246a.

2017. הֹפֶךְ {1x} **hôphek**, *ho'-fek;* from 2015; an *upset,* i.e. (abstr.) *perversity:*—turning of things upside down {1x}. See: TWOT—512; BDB—246a.

2018. הַפֵכָה {1x} **hăphêkâh**, *haf-ay-kaw';* fem. of 2016; *destruction:*—overthrow {1x}. See: TWOT—512b; BDB—246b.

2019. הֲפַכְפַּךְ {1x} **hăphakpak**, *haf-ak-pak';* by redupl. from 2015; *very perverse:*—froward {1x}. See: TWOT—512c; BDB—246b.

2020. הַצָּלָה {1x} **hatstsâlâh**, *hats-tsaw-law';* from 5337; *rescue:*—deliverance {1x}. See: TWOT—1404a; BDB—246c, 665a.

2021. הֹצֶן {1x} **hôtsen**, *ho'-tsen;* from an unused root mean. appar. to *be sharp* or *strong; a weapon* of war:—chariot {1x}. See: TWOT—513; BDB—246c.

2022. הַר {546x} **har**, *har;* a short. form of 2042; a *mountain* or *range* of hills (sometimes used fig.):—mountain {261x}, mount {224x}, hill {59x}, hill country {1x}, promotion {1x}.

Har means "mountain range; mountainous region; mount." **(1)** In its first biblical appearance *har* refers to the "mountain range" upon which Noah's ark came to rest (Gen 8:4). **(2)** In the singular form the word can mean a "mountain range" or the "mountains" of a given area: **(2a)** ". . . And [he] set his face toward the mount Gilead" (Gen 31:21). **(2)** Jacob was fleeing from Laban toward the "mountains" where he thought to find protection. **(2c)** A further extension of this meaning applies this word to an area which is primarily mountainous; the word focuses on the territory in general rather than on the mountains in particular: "And they gave them the city of Arba the father of Anak, which city is Hebron, in the hill country of Judah, with the suburbs thereof round about it" (Josh 21:11). **(3)** The word can be used of particular "mountains": ". . . And he led the flock to the backside of the desert, and came to the mountain of God, even to Horeb" (Ex 3:1). **(3a)** In this particular instance "the mountain of God" refers to Horeb. **(3b)** Elsewhere it is Jerusalem: "Why leap ye, ye high hills? This is the hill which God desireth to dwell in; yea, the Lord will dwell in it for ever" (Ps 68:16). **(4)** *Har* signifies inhabitable sites situated on hills and/or mountainsides: **(4a)** "And at that time came Joshua, and cut off the Anakim from the mountains, from Hebron, from Debir, from Anab, and from all the mountains of Judah, and from all the mountains of Israel: Joshua destroyed them utterly with their cities" (Josh 11:21). **(4b)** In this regard, compare Deut 2:37: "Only unto the land of the children of Ammon thou camest not, nor unto any place of the river Jabbok, nor unto the cities in the mountains, nor unto whatsoever the Lord our God forbade us." **(4c)** A comparison of Judg 1:35 and Josh 19:41 shows that Mount Heres is the same as the city of Heres.

(5) In the poetical literature of the Old Testament, the view of the world held by men of that era finds its reflection. **(5a)** One can speak of the foundations of the mountains as rooted in the underworld (Deut 32:22), serving to support the earth as the "bars" of the earth (Jonah 2:6). **(5b)** Mountain peaks may be said to reach into the heavens where God dwells (Is 24:21; in Gen 11:4, the men who built the tower at Babel erroneously thought they were going to reach God's dwelling place). **(5c)** Although it would be wrong to conclude that God is setting forth this understanding of creation, yet He used it in explaining His word to men just as He used other contemporaneous ideas.

(6) Since "mountains" were associated with deity (Is 14:13), God chose to make great revelations on "mountains," concretely impressing the recipients with the solemnity and authority of the message (Deut 27; Josh 8:30–35). **(7)** At the same time such locations provided for better audibility and visibility (Judg 9:7; 2 Chr 13:4). **(8)** "Mountains" often serve as a symbol of strength (Zec 4:7) inasmuch as they carried mythological significance since many people thought of them as sacred areas (Jer 3:22–23), and they were the locations of strong fortresses (Josh 10:6). **(9)** Even the "mountains" tremble before the Lord; He is mightier than they are (Job 14:18). Syn.: 1389, 2042. See: TWOT—517a; BDB—219b, 223c, 246d, 249a, 251a.

2023. הֹר {1x} **Hôr**, *hore;* another form of 2022; *mountain; Hor,* the name of a peak in Idumæa and of one in Syria:—Hor {1x}. See: BDB—246d.

2024. הָרָא {1x} **Hârâ'**, *haw-raw';* perh. from 2022; *mountainousness; Hara,* a region of Media:—Hara {1x}. See: BDB—246d.

2025. הַרְאֵל {1x} **har'êl**, *har-ale';* from 2022 and 410; *mount of God;* fig. the *altar* of burnt-offering:—altar {1x}. Syn.: comp. 739. See: TWOT—159a; BDB—72b, 246d.

2026. הָרַג {167x} **hârag**, *haw-rag';* a prim. root; to *smite* with deadly intent:—

slay {100x}, kill {24x}, kill . . . {3x}, murder {2x}, destroyed {1x}, murder {1x}, out of hand {1x}, made {1x}, put {1x}, slain {31x}, slayer {1x}, surely {1x}.

Harag means "to kill, slay, destroy." **(1)** The fact that it is found in the Old Testament some 167 times reflects how commonly this verb was used to indicate the taking of life, whether animal or human. **(2)** *Harag* is found for the first time in the Old Testament in the Cain and Abel story (Gen 4:8; also vv. 14–15). **(2)** Rarely suggesting premeditated killing or murder, this term generally is used for the "killing" of animals, including sacrificially, and for ruthless personal violence of man against man. **(3)** *Harag* is not the term used in the sixth commandment (Ex 20:13; Deut 5:17). The word there is *rashach* (7523), and since it implies premeditated killing, the commandment is better translated: "Do not murder," as most modern versions have it. **(4)** The word *harag* often means wholesale slaughter, both in battle and after battle (Num 31:7–8; Josh 8:24; 2 Sa 10:18). **(5)** The word is only infrequently used of men's killing at the command of God. In such instances, the causative form of the common Hebrew verb for "to die" is commonly found. **(6)** In general, *harag* refers to violent "killing" and destruction, sometimes even referring to the "killing" of vines by hail (Ps 78:47). Syn.: 7523, 7819. See: TWOT—514; BDB—246d.

2027. הֶרֶג {1x} **hereg,** *heh'-reg;* from 2026; *slaughter:*—be slain {1x}, slaughter {4x}. See: TWOT—514a; BDB—247c.

2028. הֲרֵגָה {5x} **hărêgâh,** *har-ay-gaw';* fem. of 2027; *slaughter:*—slaughter {5x}. See: TWOT—514b; 247c.

2029. הָרָה {43x} **hârâh,** *haw-raw';* a prim. root; to *be* (or *become*) *pregnant, conceive* (lit. or fig.):—conceive {38x}, woman with child {2x}, with child {2x}, again {1x}, bare {1x}, progenitors {1x}. See: TWOT—515; BDB—247c.

2030. הָרֶה {16x} **hâreh,** *haw-reh';* or

הָרִי **hârîy** (Hos 14:1), *haw-ree';* from 2029; *pregnant:*— . . . with child {13x}, conceive {3x}. See: TWOT—515a; BDB—248a.

2031. הַרְהֹר {1x} **harhôr** (Aram.), *har-hor';* from a root corresp. to 2029; a mental *conception:*—thought {1x}. See: TWOT—2700; BDB—1090d.

2032. הֵרוֹן {3x} **hêrôwn,** *hay-rone';* or

הֵרָיוֹן **hêrâyôwn,** *hay-raw-yone';* from 2029; *pregnancy:*—conception {3x}. See: TWOT—515c; BDB—248a.

2033. הֲרוֹרִי {1x} **Hărôwrîy,** *har-o-ree';* another form for 2043; a *Harorite* or mountaineer:—Harorite {1x}. See: BDB—248b, 353d.

2034. הֲרִיסָה {1x} **hărîyçâh,** *har-ee-saw';* from 2040; something *demolished:*—ruin {1x}. See: TWOT—516b; BDB—249a.

2035. הֲרִיסוּת {1x} **hărîyçûwth,** *har-ee-sooth';* from 2040; *demolition:*—destruction {1x}. See: TWOT—516c; BDB—249a.

2036. הֹרָם {1x} **Hôrâm,** *ho-rawm';* from an unused root (mean. to *tower* up); *high; Horam,* a Canaanitish king:—Horam {1x}. See: BDB—248b.

2037. הָרֻם {1x} **Hârûm,** *haw-room';* pass. part. of the same as 2036; *high; Harum,* an Isr.:—Harum {1x}. See: BDB—248b.

2038. הַרְמוֹן {1x} **harmôwn,** *har-mone';* from the same as 2036; a *castle* (from its height):—palace {1x}. Syn.: 1002, 1964. See: BDB—248b.

2039. הָרָן {7x} **Hârân,** *haw-rawn';* perh. from 2022; *mountaineer; Haran,* the name of two men:—Haran {7x}. See: BDB—248c.

2040. הָרַס {43x} **hâraç,** *haw-ras';* a prim. root; to *pull* down or in pieces, *break, destroy:*—throw down {13x}, break down {9x}, overthrow {5x}, destroy {4x}, pull down {3x}, break through {2x}, ruined {2x}, beat down {1x}, pluck down {1x}, break {1x}, destroyers {1x}, utterly {1x}. Syn.: 5422. See: TWOT—516; BDB—248c.

2041. הֶרֶס {1x} **hereç,** *heh'-res;* from 2040; *demolition:*—destruction {1x}. See: TWOT—516a; BDB—249a, 256d.

2042. הָרָר {13x} **hârâr,** *haw-rawr';* from an unused root mean. to *loom* up; a *mountain:*—hill {2x}, mountain {10x}, mount {1x}. See: TWOT—517; BDB—249a.

2043. הֲרָרִי {5x} **Hărârîy,** *hah-raw-ree';* or

הָרָרִי **Hârârîy** (2 Sa 23:11), *haw-raw-ree';* or

הָאֲרָרִי **Hâ'rârîy** (2 Sa 23:34, last clause), *haw-raw-ree';* appar. from 2042; a *mountaineer:*—Hararite {5x}. See: BDB—76d, 210c, 251a.

2044. הָשֵׁם {1x} **Hâshêm,** *haw-shame';* perh. from the same as 2828; *wealthy; Hashem,* an Isr.:—Hashem {1x}. See: BDB—251c.

2045. הַשְׁמָעוּת {1x} **hâshmâ'ûwth,** *hashmaw-ooth';* from 8085; *announce-*

ment:—to cause to hear {1x}. See: TWOT—2412e; 251c, 1036a.

2046. הִתּוּךְ {1x} **hittûwk,** *hit-took';* from 5413; a *melting:*—is melted {1x}. See: TWOT—1442a; BDB—251c, 678a.

2047. הֲתָךְ {4x} **Hăthâk,** *hath-awk';* prob. of for. or.; *Hathak,* a Pers. eunuch:—Hatach {4x}. See: BDB—251c.

2048. הָתַל {10x} **hâthal,** *haw-thal';* a prim. root; to *deride;* by impl. to *cheat:*—mock {6x}, deceive {3x}, deal deceitfully {1x}. Syn.: 3931. See: TWOT—518; BDB—251c, 1068c.

2049. הָתֹל {1x} **hâthôl,** *haw-thole';* from 2048 (only in plur. collect.); a *derision:*—mocker {1x}. See: TWOT—518a; BDB—251c, 1068c.

2050. הָתַת {1x} **hâthath,** *haw-thath';* a prim. root; prop. to *break* in upon, i.e. to *assail:*—imagine mischief {1x}. See: TWOT—488; BDB—223c, 251d.

ו

2051. וְדָן {1x} **Vᵉdân,** *ved-awn';* perh. for 5730; *Vedan* (or Aden), a place in Arabia:—Dan also {1x}. See: BDB—246c.

2052. וָהֵב {1x} **Vâhêb,** *vaw-habe';* of uncert. der.; *Vaheb,* a place in Moab:—what he did {1x}. See: BDB—255a.

2053. וָו {13x} **vâv,** *vaw;* prob. a *hook* (the name of the sixth Heb. letter):—hook {13x}. See: TWOT—520; BDB—255b.

2054. וָזָר {1x} **vâzâr,** *vaw-zawr';* presumed to be from an unused root mean. to *bear* guilt; *crime:*—X strange {1x}. See: TWOT—521; BDB—255c.

2055. וַיְזָתָא {1x} **Vayᵉzâthâ',** *vah-yez-aw'-thaw;* of for. or.; *Vajezatha,* a son of Haman:—Vajezatha {1x}. See: BDB—255c.

2056. וָלָד {2x} **vâlâd,** *vaw-lawd';* for 3206; a *boy:*—child {2x}. See: BDB—255c, 409b.

2057. וַנְיָה {1x} **Vanyâh,** *van-yaw';* perh. for 6043; *Vanjah,* an Isr.:—Vaniah {1x}. See: BDB—255c.

2058. וָפְסִי {1x} **Vophçîy,** *vof-see';* prob. from 3254; *additional; Vophsi,* an Isr.:—Vophsi {1x}. See: BDB—255c.

2059. וַשְׁנִי {1x} **Vashnîy,** *vash-nee';* prob. from 3461; *weak; Vashni,* an Isr.:—Vashni {1x}. See: BDB—255c.

2060. וַשְׁתִּי {10x} **Vashtîy,** *vash-tee';* of Pers. or.; *Vashti,* the queen of Xerxes:—Vashti {10x}. See: BDB—255d.

ז

2061. זְאֵב {7x} **zᵉêb,** *zeh-abe';* from an unused root mean. to *be yellow;* a *wolf:*—wolf {7x}. See: TWOT—522; BDB—255b.

2062. זְאֵב {6x} **Zᵉêb,** *zeh-abe';* the same as 2061; *Zeëb,* a Midianitish prince:—Zeeb {6x}. See: BDB—255d.

2063. זֹאת {41x} **zô'th,** *zothe';* irreg. fem. of 2089; *this* (often used adv.):—hereby (-in, -with), it, likewise, the one (other, same), she, so (much), such (deed), that, therefore, these, this (thing), thus = {41x}. See: TWOT—528; BDB—256a, 260a.

2064. זָבַד {1x} **zâbad,** *zaw-bad';* a prim. root; to *confer:*—endue {1x}. See: TWOT—524; BDB—256a.

2065. זֶבֶד {1x} **zebed,** *zeh'-bed;* from 2064; a *gift:*—dowry {1x}. Syn.: 4119. See: TWOT—524a; BDB—256b.

2066. זָבָד {8x} **Zâbâd,** *zaw-bawd';* from 2064; *giver; Zabad,* the name of seven Isr.:—Zabad {8x}. See: BDB—256b.

2067. זַבְדִּי {61x} **Zabdîy,** *zab-dee';* from 2065; *giving; Zabdi,* the name of four Isr.:—Zabdi {1x}. See: BDB—256c.

2068. זַבְדִּיאֵל {2x} **Zabdîy'êl,** *zab-dee-ale';* from 2065 and 410; *gift of God; Zabdiel,* the name of two Isr.:—See: BDB—256c.

2069. זְבַדְיָה {9x} **Zᵉbadyâh,** *zeb-ad-yaw';* or

זְבַדְיָהוּ **Zᵉbadyâhûw,** *zeb-ad-yaw'-hoo;* from 2064 and 3050; *Jah has given; Zebadjah,* the name of nine Isr.:—Zebadiah {1x}. See: BDB—256c.

2070. זְבוּב {2x} **zᵉbûwb,** *zeb-oob';* from an unused root (mean. to *flit*); a *fly* (espec. one of a stinging nature):—fly {2x}. See: TWOT—523a; BDB—256a.

2071. זָבוּד {1x} **Zâbûwd,** *zaw-bood';* from 2064; *given; Zabud,* an Isr.:—Zabud {1x}. See: BDB—256b.

2072. זַבּוּד {1x} **Zabbûwd,** *zab-bood';* a form of 2071; *given; Zabbud,* an Isr.:—Zabbud {1x}. See: BDB—256b.

2073. זְבוּל {5x} **zᵉbûwl,** *ze-bool';* or

זְבֻל **zᵉbûl,** *zeb-ool';* from 2082; a *residence:*—dwell in {1x}, dwelling {1x}, habitation {3x}. See: TWOT—526a; BDB—259c.

2074. זְבוּלוּן {45x} **Zᵉbûwlûwn**, *zeb-oo-loon';*
or

זְבֻלוּן **Zᵉbûlûwn**, *zeb-oo-loon';* or

זְבוּלֻן **Zᵉbûwlûn**, *zeb-oo-loon';* from 2082;
habitation; Zebulon, a son of Ja-
cob; also his territory and tribe:—Zebulun
{45x}. See: TWOT—526b; BDB—259d.

2075. זְבוּלֹנִי {3x} **Zᵉbûwlôniy**, *zeb-oo-lo-nee';*
patron. from 2074; a *Zebulonite*
or desc. of Zebulun:—Zebulonite {1x}, Zebu-
lunite {1x}. See: BDB—259d.

2076. זָבַח {134x} **zâbach**, *zaw-bakh';* a prim.
root; to *slaughter* an animal (usu-
ally in sacrifice):—sacrifice {85x}, offer {39x},
kill {5x}, slay {5x}.
    Zabach means "to slaughter, sacrifice."
(1) This word is a common Semitic term for
sacrifice in general, although there are a number of other terms used in the Old Testament
for specific sacrificial rituals. **(2)** There is no
question that this is one of the most important
terms in the Old Testament; *zabach* is found
more than 130 times in its verbal forms and its
noun forms occur over 500 times. **(3)** The first
time the verb occurs is in **(3a)** Gen 31:54, where
"Jacob offered sacrifice upon the mount."
(3b) In Ex 20:24 the word is used in relation to
the kinds of sacrifices to be made. **(4)** While
there were grain and incense offerings prescribed as part of the Mosaic laws dealing with
sacrifice (see Lev 2), the primary kind of sacrifice was the blood offering which required the
slaughter of an animal (cf. Deut 17:1; 1 Chr
15:26).
    (4a) This blood was poured around the altar,
for the blood contained the life, as stated in
Lev 17:11 "For the life of the flesh *is* in the
blood: and I have given it to you upon the altar
to make an atonement for your souls: for it *is*
the blood *that* maketh an atonement for the
soul." **(4b)** Since the blood was the vehicle of
life, it belonged to God alone. **(4c)** Because the
blood is the life, and because it is given to God
in the process of pouring it about the altar,
it becomes the means of expiating sin, as an
offering for sin and not because it becomes a
substitute for the sinner. **(5)** *Zabach* is also used
as a term for "slaughter for eating." **(5a)** This
usage is closely linked with "slaughter for sacrifice" since all eating of flesh was sacrificial
among ancient Hebrews. **(5b)** The word carries
this meaning in 1 Kin 19:21: "And he returned
back from him, and took a yoke of oxen, and
slew them, and boiled their flesh . . . and gave
unto the people, and they did eat." See:
TWOT—525; BDB—256d, 1087a.

2077. זֶבַח {162x} **zebach**, *zeh'-bakh;* from
2076; prop. a *slaughter,* i.e. the

flesh of an animal; by impl. a *sacrifice* (the victim or the act):—sacrifice {155x}, offerings {6x},
offer {1x}.
    Zebach properly means **(1)** to slay an animal
for food, and accordingly rendered kill or slay.
(2) The idea of a sacrifice is mistakenly thought
to be performed solely by a priest. **(3)** A lay
offerer, the head of the family, could also
present and slay an animal before God's sanctuary (Deut 12:15, 21; 1 Sa 28:24; 2 Chr 18:2;
Eze 34:3). **(3a)** The family or nation, following
the priest's directions, offered the sacrifice
through their representatives and **(3b)** partook
of the flesh of the victims, entering thereby
into communion with God. **(4)** The various ceremonies connected with the *zebach* are described in Lev 17:5–7. **(4a)** A man brought an
unblemished animal to the door of the sacred
tent, **(4b)** pressed his hands on its head, and
(4c) slew it. **(4d)** The priest, **(4d1)** acting on
God's behalf, **(4d2)** took the blood, which represented the life of the animal (and therefore
the life of the offerer), and **(4d3)** poured it forth
on the altar as an atonement (Lev 3:2). **(4d4)**
He also burned the fat - to represent the fact
that the richness or goodness of animal life
proceeded from God, and was due to Him (Lev
3:4–5). **(4d5)** The sacrifice demonstrated that
without the shedding of blood there is no remission of sins (Lev 17:1; cf. Heb 9:22).
    (4e) A certain fixed portion of the flesh was
(4e1) then given to the priest, to be eaten by
himself and his family (Ex 29:28; Lev 7:31–35;
Deut 18:3), and **(4e2)** the rest was eaten by the
offerer and his household. **(4e3)** Because the
people shared in the eating, the *zebach* was a
communal meal in which the Lord hosted His
people (Zeph 1:7). **(5)** Whether the feast was
public or private, and whether the animal was
offered by the elders of the nation or by the
head of a family, these ceremonies were to symbolize the union between God and man, who
were thus made partakers of the same food.
(6) If it was impossible to perform the full rites
connected with the sacrifice through distance
from the tabernacle of the congregation, or
from the place that God should subsequently
choose to put His name, i.e., the temple, one
point at any rate was to be observed: the blood
of the slain animal was to be poured on the
earth and covered with dust (Lev 7:13).
    (7) The rites connected with the *zebach* were
designed to produce a moral effect on the children of Israel. They were **(7a)** reminded of
God's merciful disposition toward them,
(7b) stimulated to live in conformity with His
law, and **(7c)** were to deal mercifully with their
poorer brethren. **(8)** The pious Israelite would
be impressed **(8a)** that sin brought death into
the world, and that **(8b)** he himself had sinned.

His conscience would be stimulated through participating in **(8b1)** the death of the animal, **(8b2)** by the sprinkling of the blood, and **(8b3)** the burning of the fat. **(9)** He would thus have "a broken spirit" (Ps 51:17). **(10)** Through his sacrifice would be **(10a)** a strong call to righteousness (Ps 4:5), **(10b)** to obedience (1Sa 15:22), **(10c)** to joy (Ps 27:6), and **(10d)** to mercy (Hos 6:6). **(11)** Where the sacrifice had not this spirit, it lost all its value and significance. **(12)** *Zebach* was connected to covenant making, the sharing in food being a symbol of the oneness of the eaters (Gen 31:54; Ps 50:5).

(13) The prophets looked with condemnation on apostate Israel's sacrifices (Is 1:11). **(14)** Sacrifices, however, had their place **(15)** behind Israel's love for God (Hos 6:6), **(16)** less desired by God than obedience (1 Sa 15:22), and **(17)** a broken spirit and a contrite heart (Ps 51:16–17). **(18)** The Passover and the peace-offering were special kinds of *zebach*. **(19)** The "sacrifice" which was part of a covenant ritual involved the sprinkling of the blood on the people and upon the altar, which presumably symbolized God as the covenant partner (see Ex 24:6–8). **(20)** Another special "sacrifice" was "the sacrifice of the feast of the passover" (Ex 34:25). **(20a)** In this case the sacrificial lamb provided the main food for the passover meal, and **(20b)** its blood was sprinkled on the doorposts of the Israelite homes as a sign to the death angel. **(21)** The "sacrifice" of animals was in no way unique to Israelite religion, for sacrificial rituals generally are part of all ancient religious cults. **(21a)** Indeed, the mechanics of the ritual were quite similar, especially between Israelite and Canaanite religions. **(21b)** However, the differences are very clear in the meanings which the rituals had as they were performed either to capricious Canaanite gods or for the one true God who kept His covenant with Israel.

(22) The noun *zebach* is used of "sacrifices" to the one true God in Gen 46:1: "And Israel took his journey with all that he had . . . and offered sacrifices unto the God of his father Isaac" (cf. Ex 10:25; Neh 12:43). **(23)** The noun refers to "sacrifices" to other deities in Ex 34:15: "Lest thou make a covenant with the inhabitants of the land, and they go a whoring after their gods, and do sacrifice unto their gods, and one call thee, and thou eat of his sacrifice" (cf. Num 25:2; 2 Kin 10:19). **(24)** The idea of "sacrifice" certainly is taken over into the New Testament, for **(25)** Christ became "the Lamb of God, who takes away the sin of the world" (cf. Jn 1:29). **(26)** The writer of Hebrews makes much of the fact that with the "sacrifice" of Christ, no more sacrifices are necessary (cf. Heb 9). Syn.: The *zebach* (2077) or sacrifice was

utterly distinct from the *'olath* (5930) or ascending-offering, which was wholly burned or turned into smoke, and from the sin-offering (2403), which was partly burned and partly eaten by the priest. comp. 801, 2282, 4503, 7133, 8426. See: TWOT—525a; BDB—257b.

2078. זֶבַח {12x} **Zebach**, *zeh'-bakh;* the same as 2077; *sacrifice; Zebach,* a Midianitish prince:—Zebah {12x}. See: BDB—258a.

2079. זַבַּי {1x} **Zabbay**, *zab-bah'-ee;* prob. by orth. err. for 2140; *Zabbai* (or Zaccai), an Isr.:—Zabbai {1x}. See: BDB—256a, 259b.

2080. זְבִידָה {1x} **Z^ebîydâh**, *zeb-ee-daw';* fem. from 2064; *giving; Zebidah,* an Israelitess:—Zebudah {1x}. See: BDB—256b.

2081. זְבִינָא {1x} **Z^ebîynâ'**, *zeb-ee-naw';* from an unused root (mean. to *purchase*); *gainfulness; Zebina,* an Isr.:—Zebina {1x}. See: BDB—259b.

2082. זָבַל {1x} **zâbal**, *zaw-bal';* a prim. root; appar. prop. to *inclose,* i.e. to *reside:*—dwell with me {1x}. See: TWOT—526; BDB—259c.

2083. זְבֻל {6x} **Z^ebûl**, *zeb-ool';* the same as 2073; *dwelling; Zebul,* an Isr.:—Zebul {1x}. See: BDB - 259d, 560d. Syn.: comp. 2073.

זְבוּלוּן **Z^ebûlûwn**. See 2074.

2084. זְבַן {1x} **z^eban** (Aram.), *zeb-an';* corresp. to the root of 2081; to *acquire* by purchase:—gain {1x}. See: TWOT—2702; BDB—1091a.

2085. זָג {1x} **zâg**, *zawg;* from an unused root prob. mean. to *inclose;* the *skin* of a grape:—husk {1x}. See: TWOT—527a; BDB—260a.

2086. זֵד {1x} **zêd**, *zade';* from 2102; *arrogant:*—presumptuous {1x}, proud {13x}. See: TWOT—547a; BDB—260a, 267d.

2087. זָדוֹן {11x} **zâdôwn**, *zaw-done';* from 2102; *arrogance:*—presumptuously {2x}, pride {6x}, proud (man) {3x}. See: TWOT—547a; BDB—260a, 268a.

2088. זֶה {1x} **zeh**, *zeh;* a prim. word; the masc. demonstr. pron., *this* or *that:*—he, × hence, × here, it (-self), × now, × of him, the one . . . the other, × than the other, (× out of) the (self) same, such (an one) that, these, this (hath, man), on this side . . . on that side, × thus, very, which = {38x}. Syn.: 2063, 2090, 2097, 2098. See: TWOT—528; BDB—260a, 774b, 1086d, 1087c.

2089. זֶ {1x} **zeh** (1 Sa 17:34), *zeh;* by perm. for 7716; a *sheep:*—lamb {1x}. See: BDB—962a.

2090. זֹה {13x} **zôh**, *zo;* for 2088; *this* or *that:*—this {7x}, thus {3x}, that {1x}, what {1x}, another {1x}. See: BDB—262b, 1086d.

2091. זָהָב {ז!} **zâhâb**, *zaw-hawb';* from an unused root mean. to *shimmer; gold,* fig. something *gold-colored* (i.e. *yellow*), as *oil,* a *clear sky:*—gold {348x}, golden {40x}, fair weather {1x}.

   Zahab means "gold." **(1)** *Zahab* can refer to "gold ore," or "gold in its raw state." This is its meaning in its first biblical appearance: "The name of the first is Pison: that is it which compasseth the whole land of Havilah, where there is gold" (Gen 2:11). **(2)** The word can also be used of "gold" which has already been refined: "But he knoweth the way that I take: when he hath tried me, I shall come forth as gold" (Job 23:10). **(3)** "Gold" could be beaten (1 Kin 10:16) and **(4)** purified (Ex 25:11). **(5)** One can also speak of the best "gold" (2 Chr 3:5). **(6)** *Zahab* can be conceived of as an "object of wealth": "And Abram was very rich in cattle, in silver, and in gold" (Gen 13:2). **(6a)** As such, the emphasis is on "gold" as a valuable or precious commodity. **(6b)** Consequently, the word is used in comparisons: "The gold and the crystal cannot equal it: and the exchange of it shall not be for jewels of fine gold" (Job 28:17). **(7)** "Gold" was often one of the spoils of war: "But all the silver, and gold, and vessels of brass and iron, are consecrated unto the LORD: they shall come into the treasury of the LORD" (Josh 6:19). **(8)** "Gold" was bought and sold as an object of merchandise: "The merchants of Sheba and Raamah, they were thy merchants: they [paid for your wares] with chief of all spices, and with all precious stones, and gold" (Eze 27:22).

   (9) *Zahab* was used as a costly gift: "And Balaam answered and said unto the servants of Balak, If Balak would give me his house full of silver and gold, I [could not do anything] . . ." (Num 22:18). **(10)** This metal was used as a material to make jewelry and other valuable items: "And it came to pass, as the camels had done drinking, that the man took a golden earring of half a shekel weight, and two bracelets for her hands of ten shekels weight of gold . . ." (Gen 24:22). **(11)** Solomon's temple was adorned with "gold" (1 Kin 6:20–28). **(12)** Gold was used as money, being exchanged in various weights and values (according to its weight): "And he made three hundred shields of beaten gold; three pound of gold went to one shield . . ." (1 Kin 10:17; cf. 2 Sa 12:30). **(13)** "Gold" even existed in the form of "coins"

(Ezra 2:69). **(14)** *Zahab* is used for the color "gold": "What be these two olive branches which through the two golden pipes empty the golden oil out of themselves?" (Zec 4:12). See: TWOT—529a; BDB—262c, 1087a.

2092. זָהַם {1x} **zâham**, *zaw-ham';* a prim. root; to *be rancid,* i.e. (tran.) to *loathe:*—abhor {1x}. See: TWOT—530; BDB—263d.

2093. זַהַם {1x} **Zaham**, *zah'-ham;* from 2092; *loathing; Zaham,* an Isr.:—Zaham {1x}. See: BDB—263d.

2094. זָהַר {זָהַר} **zâhar**, *zaw-har';* a prim. root; to *gleam;* fig. to *enlighten* (by caution):—warn {18x}, admonish {2x}, teach {1x}, shine {1x}. See: TWOT—531, 532; BDB—263d, 264a, 1091a.

2095. זְהַר {1x} **zᵉhar** (Aram.), *zeh-har';* corresp. to 2094; (pass.) *be admonished:*—take heed {1x}. See: TWOT—2703; BDB—1091a.

2096. זֹהַר {2x} **zôhar**, *zo'-har;* from 2094; *brilliancy:*—brightness {2x}. See: TWOT—531a; BDB—264a.

2097. זוֹ {2x} **zôw**, *zo;* for 2088; *this* or *that:*—that {1x}, this {1x}. See: TWOT—528; BDB—262b, 264c.

2098. זוּ {15x} **zûw**, *zoo;* for 2088; *this* or *that:*—which {5x}, this {4x}, that {3x}, wherein {2x}, whom {1x}. See: TWOT—528; BDB—262b, 264c.

2099. זִו {2x} **Zîv**, *zeev';* prob. from an unused root mean. to *be prominent;* prop. *brightness* [comp. 2122], i.e. (fig.) the month of *flowers; Ziv* (corresp. to Ijar or May):—Zif {2x}. See: TWOT—533; BDB—264c.

2100. זוּב {42x} **zûwb**, *zoob;* a prim. root; to *flow* freely (as water), i.e. (spec.) to *have a* (sexual) *flux;* fig. to *waste* away; also to *overflow:*—flow {21x}, have an issue {14x}, gush out {3x}, pine away {1x}, hath {1x}, have {1x}, run {1x}. See: TWOT—534; BDB—264c.

2101. זוֹב {13x} **zôwb**, *zobe;* from 2100; a seminal or menstrual *flux:*—issue {13x}. See: TWOT—534a; BDB—264d.

2102. זוּד {10x} **zûwd**, *zood;* or (by perm.)

   זִיד **zîyd**, *zeed;* a prim. root; to *seethe;* fig. to *be insolent:*—deal proudly {4x}, presumptuously {3x}, presume {1x}, be proud {1x}, sod {1x}. See: TWOT—547; BDB—264d, 267c, 1091a.

2103. זוּד {1x} **zûwd** (Aram.), *zood;* corresp. to 2102; to *be proud:*—in pride {1x}. See: TWOT—2704; BDB—1091a.

Hebrew

2104. זוּזִים {1x} **Zûwzîym**, *zoo-zeem';* plur. prob. from the same as 2123; *prominent; Zuzites,* an aboriginal tribe of Pal.:—Zuzims {1x}. See: BDB—265c.

2105. זוֹחֵת **Zôwchêth**, *zo-khayth';* of uncert. or.; *Zocheth,* an Isr.:—Zoheth {1x}. See: BDB—265d.

2106. זָוִית {2x} **zâvîyth**, *zaw-veeth';* appar. from the same root as 2099 (in the sense of *prominence*); an *angle* (as *projecting*), i.e. (by impl.) a *corner-column* (or *anta*):—corner {1x}, cornerstone {1x}. See: TWOT—2704; BDB—265a, 265d.

2107. זוּל {2x} **zûwl**, *zool;* a prim. root [comp. 2151]; prob. to *shake* out, i.e. (by impl.) to *scatter* profusely; fig. to *treat lightly:*—lavish {1x}, despise {1x}. See: TWOT—538; BDB—266a.

2108. זוּלָה {16x} **zûwlâh**, *zoo-law';* from 2107; prob. *scattering,* i.e. *removal;* used adv. *except:*—beside . . . {7x}, save {5x}, only {2x}, but me {1x}, but {1x}. See: TWOT—537a; BDB—265d.

2109. זוּן {1x} **zûwn**, *zoon;* a prim. root; perh. prop. to *be plump,* i.e. (tran.) to *nourish:*—feed {1x}. See: BDB—266a, 402c, 1091b.

2110. זוּן {1x} **zûwn** (Aram.), *zoon;* corresp. to 2109:—feed {1x}. See: BDB—1091b.

2111. זוּעַ {3x} **zûwâ**, *zoo'-ah;* a prim. root; prop. to *shake* off, i.e. (fig.) to *agitate* (as with fear):—move {1x}, tremble {1x}, vex {1x}. See: TWOT—540; BDB—266a, 1091b.

2112. זוּעַ {2x} **zûwa** (Aram.), *zoo'-ah;* corresp. to 2111; to *shake* (with fear):—tremble {2x}. See: TWOT—2706; BDB—1091b.

2113. זְוָעָה {6x} **zᵉvâʿâh**, *zev-aw-aw';* from 2111; *agitation, fear:*—be removed {1x}, trouble {4x}, vexation {1x}. See: TWOT—540a; BDB—266b. Syn.: comp. 2189.

2114. זוּר {77x} **zûwr**, *zoor;* a prim. root; to *turn* aside (espec. for lodging); hence, to *be a foreign, strange, profane;* spec. (act. part.) to *commit adultery:*—stranger {45x}, strange {18x}, estranged {4x}, stranger + 376 {3x}, another {2x}, strange woman {2x}, gone away {1x}, fanners {1x}, another place {1x}. Syn.: 1616, 5236. See: TWOT—541; BDB—266b, 266d, 268b.

2115. זוּר {3x} **zûwr**, *zoor;* a prim. root [comp. 6695]; to *press* together, *tighten:*—close {1x}, crush {1x}, thrust together {1x}. See: TWOT—543; BDB—266d.

2116. זוּרֶה {1x} **zûwreh**, *zoo-reh';* from 2115; *trodden* on:—that which is crushed {1x}. See: TWOT—543; BDB—266d.

2117. זָזָא {1x} **Zâzâ**, *zaw-zaw';* prob. from the root of 2123; *prominent; Zaza,* an Isr.:—Zaza {1x}. See: BDB—265b, 267a.

2118. זָחַח {2x} **zâchach**, *zaw-khakh';* a prim. root; to *shove* or *displace:*—loose {2x}. See: TWOT—544; BDB—267b.

2119. זָחַל {3x} **zâchal**, *zaw-khal';* a prim. root; to *crawl;* by impl. to *fear:*—be afraid {1x}, serpent {1x}, worm {1x}. See: TWOT—545; BDB—267b, 267c, 1087c.

2120. זֹחֶלֶת {1x} **Zôcheleth**, *zo-kheh'-leth;* fem. act. part. of 2119; *crawling* (i.e. *serpent*); *Zocheleth,* a boundary stone in Pal.:—Zoheleth {1x}. See: BDB—267b.

2121. זֵידוֹן {1x} **zêydôwn**, *zay-dohn';* from 2102; *boiling* of water, i.e. *wave:*—proud {1x}. See: TWOT—547c; BDB—268a.

2122. זִיו {6x} **zîyv** (Aram.), *zeev;* corresp. to 2099; (fig.) *cheerfulness:*—brightness {4x}, countenance {2x}. See: TWOT—2707; BDB—1091b.

2123. זִיז {3x} **zîyz**, *zeez;* from an unused root appar. mean. to *be conspicuous; fulness* of the breast; also a moving *creature:*—abundance {1x}, wild beast {2x}. See: TWOT—535a, 536a; BDB—265a, 265c, 268d.

2124. זִיזָא {2x} **Zîyzâ**, *zee-zaw';* appar. from the same as 2123; *prominence; Ziza,* the name of two Isr.:—Ziza {1x}. See: BDB—265b, 268b.

2125. זִיזָה {1x} **Zîyzâh**, *zee-zaw';* another form for 2124; *Zizah,* an Isr.:—Zizah. See: BDB—265b, 268b.

2126. זִינָא {1x} **Zîynâ**, *zee-naw';* from 2109; *well-fed;* or perh. an orth. err. for 2124; *Zina,* an Isr.:—Zina {1x}. See: BDB—265b, 286b.

2127. זִיעַ {1x} **Zîya**, *zee'-ah;* from 2111; *agitation; Zia,* an Isr.:—Zia {1x}. See: BDB—266b, 268b.

2128. זִיף {10x} **Zîyph**, *zeef;* from the same as 2203; *flowing; Ziph,* the name of a place in Pal.; also of an Isr.:—Ziph {1x}. See: BDB—268b.

2129. זִיפָה {1x} **Zîyphâh**, *zee-faw';* fem. of 2128; a *flowing; Ziphah,* an Isr.:—Ziphah {1x}. See: BDB—268b.

2130. זִיפִי {3x} **Zîyphîy**, *zee-fee';* patrial from 2128; a *Ziphite* or inhab. of Ziph:—Ziphim {1x}, Ziphite {2x}. See: BDB—268b.

2131. זִיקָה {7x} **zîyqâh** (Isa. 50:11), *zee-kaw'* (fem.); and

זִק **zîq**, *zeek;* or

זֵק **zêq**, *zake;* from 2187; prop. what *leaps* forth, i.e. *flash* of fire, or a burning *arrow;* also (from the orig. sense of the root) a *bond:*—chain {3x}, spark {2x}, firebrand {1x}, fetter {1x}. See: TWOT—573; BDB—268b, 278a, 279b.

2132. זַיִת {38x} **zayith**, *zay'-yith;* prob. from an unused root [akin to 2099]; an *olive* (as yielding *illuminating* oil), the tree, the branch or the berry:—olive {17x}, olive tree {14x}, oliveyard {6x}, Olivet {1x}. See: TWOT—548; BDB—268b.

2133. זֵיתָן {1x} **Zêythân**, *zay-thawn';* from 2132; *olive* grove; *Zethan*, an Isr.:—Zethan {1x}. See: BDB—268d.

2134. זַךְ {11x} **zak**, *zak;* from 2141; *clear:*—clean {2x}, pure {9x}. See: TWOT—550a; BDB—269a, 269b.

2135. זָכָה {8x} **zâkâh**, *zaw-kaw';* a prim. root [comp. 2141]; to *be translucent;* fig. to *be innocent:*—be (make) clean {6x}, be clear {1x}, count pure {1x}. Syn.: See 2212, 2141, 2135. There are three roots closely connected together that all represent purity cleanness, or freedom from pollution, namely (1) *zaqaq* (2212 - Ps 12:6; Mal 3:3) (2) *zakak* (2141 - Job 8:6; 11:4), and (3) *zakah* (2135 - Job 15:14; Prov 20:9). These passages refer to moral purity and transparency of heart. They point to a character free from taint or sully as the object that man aims at, but which he fails to obtain by his own devices; and even at the best, that which seems perfectly pure in his sight is proved vile when seen in the light of God. See: TWOT—549; BDB—269a, 1091b.

2136. זָכוּ {1x} **zâkûw** (Aram.), *zaw-koo';* from a root corresp. to 2135; *purity:*—innocency {1x}. See: TWOT—2708; BDB—1091b.

2137. זְכוּכִית {1x} **z^ekûwkîyth**, *zek-oo-keeth;* from 2135; prop. *transparency,* i.e. *glass:*—crystal {1x}. See: TWOT—550b; BDB—269a, 269b.

2138. זָכוּר {4x} **zâkûwr**, *zaw-koor';* prop. pass. part. of 2142, but used for 2145; a *male* (of man or animals):—males {3x}, men-children {1x}. Syn.: 376, 2145. See: TWOT—551f; BDB—271d.

2139. זַכּוּר {10x} **Zakkûwr**, *zaw-koor';* from 2142; *mindful; Zakkur*, the name of seven Isr.:—Zaccur {8x}, Zacchur {1x}, var. trans. {1x}. See: TWOT—551f; BDB—271d.

2140. זַכָּי {3x} **Zakkay**, *zak-kah'-ee;* from 2141; *pure; Zakkai*, an Isr.:—Zaccai {3x}. See: BDB—269b.

2141. זָכַךְ {4x} **zâkak**, *zaw-kak';* a prim. root [comp. 2135]; to *be transparent* or *clean* (phys. or mor.):—be clean {2x}, make clean {1x}, be pure {1x}. Syn.: See 2135. See: TWOT—550; BDB—269a.

2142. זָכַר {233x} **zâkar**, *zaw-kar';* a prim. root; prop. to *mark* (so as to be recognized), i.e. to *remember;* by impl. to *mention;* also (as denom. from 2145) to *be male:*—remember {172x}, mention {21x}, remembrance {10x}, recorder {9x}, mindful {6x}, think {3x}, bring to remembrance {2x}, record {2x}, × burn {1x}, to burn incense {1x}, × earnestly {1x}, be male {2x}, recount {1x}, × still {1x}, × well {1x}.

Zakar means "to remember, think of, mention." **(1)** The group of words (the verb and the three nouns derived from it) is found throughout the Old Testament. **(2)** The first occurrence of *zakar* is in Gen 8:1 with God as the subject: **(2a)** "God remembered Noah . . . : and God made a wind to pass over the earth, and the waters assuaged." **(2b)** In Gen 9:15 God said to Noah: "And I will remember my covenant . . . ; and the waters shall no more become a flood to destroy all flesh." **(2c)** As in these two cases (cf. Gen 6:18), "remember" is used of God in respect to His covenant promises and is followed by an action to fulfill His covenant. **(2d)** God delivered Lot from Sodom because of His covenant with Abraham to bless all the nations through him (Gen 18:17–33): "God remembered Abraham, and sent Lot out of the midst of the overthrow" (Gen 19:29).

(3) This marks the history of Israel at every major point: "And I have also heard the groaning of the children of Israel, . . . and I have remembered my covenant. . . . and I will bring you out from under the burdens of the Egyptians . . ." (Ex 6:5–6). **(3a)** The promise "to remember" was repeated in the covenant at Sinai (Lev 26:40–45), **(3b)** God's remembrance was sung in the Psalms (98:3; 105:8, 42; 106:45), **(3c)** and the promise was repeated by the prophets in regard to restoration from captivity (Eze 16:60). **(3d)** The new covenant promise is: "I will forgive their iniquity, and I will remember their sin no more" (Jer 31:34). **(4)** Because of this God's people pray, **(4a)** as Moses: "Turn from thy fierce wrath. . . . Remember Abraham, Isaac, and Israel, thy servants, to whom thou swarest" (Ex 32:12–13); or **(4b)** Nehemiah: "Remember . . . the word that thou commandedst thy servant Moses" (Neh 1:8, quoting Lev 26:33); or **(4c)** the psalmist: "Remember not the sins of my youth, nor my transgressions: according to thy mercy remember

thou me" (Ps 25:7); or **(4d)** Jeremiah: "Remember, break not thy covenant with us" (Jer 14:21).

(5) Men also "remember." Joseph said to Pharaoh's butler: "But think on me . . . , and make mention of me unto Pharaoh" (Gen 40:14). **(5a)** Again, "to remember" means more than "to recall"; **(5b)** it means "to retain in thought" so as to tell someone who can take action (cf. Ps 20:7). **(6)** *Zakar* may have more specific connotations in certain circumstances: "Hear ye this, O house of Jacob, . . . which swear by the name of the Lord, . . . and make mention of the God of Israel . . ." (Is 48:1), **(6a)** pointing to the mention of God's name in worship. **(6b)** David appointed "Levites as ministers before the ark of the LORD, to invoke . . . the LORD . . ." (1 Chr 16:4). **(7)** The covenant commanded Israel to **(7a)** "remember this day, in which ye came out from Egypt" (Ex 13:3); **(7b)** to "remember the sabbath day . . ." (Ex 20:8); **(7c)** to "remember that thou wast a servant in the land of Egypt, and that the LORD thy God brought thee out thence through a mighty hand" (Deut 5:15 and often); and **(7d)** to "remember his marvelous works . . ." (Ps 105:5; cf. 1 Chr 16:15). **(8)** But "the children of Israel remembered not the LORD their God, who had delivered them out of the hands of all their enemies" (Judg 8:34; cf. Ps 78:42). See: TWOT—551; BDB—269c, 272c, 561b.

2143. זֵכֶר {23x} **zêker**, *zay'-ker*; or

     זֶכֶר **zeker**, *zeh'-ker*; from 2142; a *memento*, abstr. *recollection* (rarely if ever); by impl. *commemoration:*—remembrance {11x}, memorial {5x}, memory {5x}, remembered {1x}, scent {1x}.

Zeker means "remembrance; memorial." **(1)** Of His covenant name, YHWH ("LORD"), God said: ". . . This is my memorial unto all generations" (Ex 3:15; cf. Ps 30:4; 135:13). **(1a)** The name would recall His acts of covenant fulfillment. **(1b)** Moses was told to write an account of the war with Amalek "for a memorial [2146 - *zikkaron*] in a book, and rehearse it in the ears of Joshua: for I will utterly put out the remembrance [*zeker*] of Amalek from under heaven" (Ex 17:14). **(2)** The name would recall His acts of covenant fulfillment (Ex 17:14). See: TWOT—551a; BDB—271a, 271b.

2144. זֶכֶר {1x} **Zeker**, *zeh'-ker*; the same as 2143; *Zeker*, an Isr.:—Zeker {1x}. See: BDB—271a.

2145. זָכָר {1x} **zâkâr**, *zaw-kawr'*; from 2142; prop. *remembered*, i.e. a *male* (of man or animals, as being the most noteworthy sex):—male {67x}, man {7x}, child {4x}, mankind {2x}, him {1x}.

(1) *Zakar*, as a noun, means "male." **(1a)** It occurs 82 times and usually in early prose (Genesis through Deuteronomy), only 5 times in the biblical prophets, and never in biblical wisdom or poetical literature. **(1b)** *Zakar* emphasizes "maleness" as over against "femaleness"; this word focuses on the sex of the one so named. Thus, "God created man in his own image, in the image of God created he him; male and female created he them" (Gen 1:27). **(1c)** The word can be used not only of an "adult male" but also of a "male child" (Lev 12:7). **(1d)** *Zakar* is used collectively in many passages—in singular form, with a plural reference (Judg 21:11). **(1e)** In some contexts the word represents a "male animal": "And of every living thing of all flesh, two of every sort shalt thou bring into the ark, to keep them alive with thee; they shall be male and female" (Gen 6:19). **(2)** *Zakar*, the adjective, means "male." **(2a)** "Number all the firstborn of the males of the children of Israel from a month old and upward" (Num 3:40). **(2b)** The word appears in Jer 20:15: "A man child is born unto thee; making him very glad." See: TWOT—551e; BDB—271b, 1088d.

2146. זִכְרוֹן {24x} **zikrôwn**, *zik-rone'*; from 2142; a *memento* (or memorable thing, day or writing):—memorial {17x}, remembrance {6x}, records {1x}.

Zikrown means "memorial." **(1)** God gave the bronze plates covering the altar (Num 16:40) and the heap of stones at the Jordan (Josh 4:7, 20–24) as perpetual "memorials" for the sons of Israel. **(2)** The names of the twelve tribes of Israel were engraved on two stones that were attached to the ephod as "stones of memorial unto the children of Israel: and Aaron shall bear their names before the LORD" (Ex 28:12; cf. v. 29). **(3)** When Israel went into battle, and when they offered sacrifice, they were to blow trumpets "that they may be to you for a memorial before your God" (Num 10:9–10). See: TWOT—551b; BDB—272a, 1088d.

2147. זִכְרִי {12x} **Zikrîy**, *zik-ree'*; from 2142; *memorable*; *Zicri*, the name of twelve Isr.:—Zichri {12x}. See: BDB—271d.

2148. זְכַרְיָה {3x} **Zekaryâh**, *zek-ar-yaw'*; or

     זְכַרְיָהוּ **Zekaryâhûw**, *zek-ar-yaw'-hoo*; from 2142 and 3050; *Jah has remembered*; *Zecarjah*, the name of twenty-nine Isr.:—Zachariah or Zechariah {43x}. See: BDB—272a, 1091c.

2149. זַלּוּת {11x} **zullûwth**, *zool-looth'*; from 2151; prop. a *shaking*, i.e. perh. a *tempest:*—vilest {1x}. See: TWOT—554a; BDB—273a.

2150. זַלְזַל {1x} **zalzal**, *zal-zal';* by redupl. from 2151; *tremulous,* i.e. a *twig:*—sprig {1x}. See: TWOT—553a; BDB—272d.

2151. זָלַל {8x} **zâlal**, *zaw-lal';* a prim. root [comp. 2107]; to *shake* (as in the wind), i.e. to *quake;* fig. to *be loose* morally, *worthless* or *prodigal:*—flow down {2x}, vile {2x}, glutton {2x}, riotous eaters {1x}, riotous {1x}. See: TWOT—553; BDB—272d.

2152. זַלְעָפָה {3x} **zalʻâphâh**, *zal-aw-faw';* or

זִלְעָפָף **zilʻâphâph**, *zil-aw-faw';* from 2196; a *glow* (of wind or anger); also a *famine* (as *consuming*):—horrible {1x}, horror {1x}, terrible {1x}. See: TWOT—555a; BDB—273a.

2153. זִלְפָּה {7x} **Zilpâh**, *zil-paw;* from an unused root appar. mean. to *trickle,* as myrrh; fragrant *dropping; Zilpah,* Leah's maid:—Zilpah {7x}. See: BDB—273a.

2154. זִמָּה {29x} **zimmâh**, *zim-maw';* or

זַמָּה **zammâh**, *zam-maw';* from 2161; a *plan,* espec. a bad one:—lewdness {14x}, wickedness {4x}, mischief {3x}, lewd {2x}, heinous crime {1x}, wicked devices {1x}, lewdly {1x}, wicked mind {1x}, purposes {1x}, thought {1x}.

Zimmah means "loose conduct; lewdness." **(1)** The 29 occurrences of this noun are all in legal and poetical books of the Bible, except for a single occurrence in Judges. **(2)** This noun signifies "loose or infamous conduct" and is used most often with regard to illicit sexual conduct: "Thou shalt not uncover the nakedness of a woman and her daughter, . . . or her daughter's daughter, to uncover her nakedness; for they are her near kinswomen: it is wickedness" (Lev 18:17—the first occurrence). **(3)** Rejection of God's law or spiritual adultery may be represented by *zimmah* (Ps 119:150; cf. Eze 16:12–28). **(4)** A plan or scheme identified by the word is, therefore, a "harlotrous" plan (Ps 26:10). Syn: 2161, 4209. See: TWOT—556b; BDB—273b.

2155. זִמָּה {3x} **Zimmâh**, *zim-maw';* the same as 2154; *Zimmah,* the name of two Isr.:—Zimmah {3x}. See: BDB—273c.

2156. זְמוֹרָה {5x} **zᵉmôwrâh**, *zem-o-raw';* or

זְמֹרָה **zᵉmôrâh**, *zem-o-raw'* (fem.); and

זְמֹר **zᵉmôr**, *zem-ore'* (masc.); from 2168; a *twig* (as *pruned*):—branch {3x}, branches {1x}, slip {1x}. See: TWOT—559b; BDB—274d.

2157. זַמְזֹם {1x} **Zamzôm**, *zam-zome';* from 2161; *intriguing;* a *Zamzumite,* or native tribe of Pal.:—Zamzummim {1x}. See: BDB—273d.

2158. זָמִיר {6x} **zâmîyr**, *zaw-meer';* or

זָמִר **zâmir**, *zaw-meer';* and (fem.)

זְמִרָה **zᵉmîrâh**, *zem-ee-raw';* from 2167; a *song* to be accompanied with instrumental music:—psalmist {2x}, singing {1x}, song {3x}. See: TWOT—558b; BDB—274b.

2159. זָמִיר {1x} **zâmîyr**, *zaw-meer';* from 2168; a *twig* (as *pruned*):—branch {1x}. See: BDB—254d.

2160. זְמִירָה {1x} **Zᵉmîyrâh**, *zem-ee-raw';* fem. of 2158; *song; Zemirah,* an Isr.:—Zemira {1x}. See: BDB—275b.

2161. זָמַם {13x} **zâmam**, *zaw-mam';* a prim. root; to *plan,* usually in a bad sense:—thought {5x}, devise {3x}, consider {1x}, purpose {1x}, imagine {1x}, plot {1x}.

Zamam, the verb, means "to ponder, to cogitate." In Zec 8:14–15 the word appears to carry the sense of "to ponder": "For thus saith the Lord of hosts; As I thought (*zamam*) to punish you, when your fathers provoked me to wrath . . . and I repented not: So again have I thought (*zamam*) in these days to do well unto Jerusalem and to the house of Judah: fear ye not." Syn: 2154, 2803, 4209. See: TWOT—556; BDB—273a.

2162. זָמָם {1x} **zâmâm**, *zaw-mawm';* from 2161; a *plot:*—wicked device {1x}. See: TWOT—556a; BDB—273b.

2163. זָמַן {3x} **zâman**, *zaw-man';* a prim. root; to *fix* (a time):—appoint {3x}. See: TWOT—557; BDB—273d.

2164. זְמַן {1x} **zᵉman** (Aram.), *zem-an';* corresp. to 2163; to *agree* (on a time and place):—prepare {1x}. See: TWOT—2709; BDB—1091c.

2165. זְמָן {4x} **zᵉmân**, *zem-awn';* from 2163; an *appointed* occasion:—season {1x}, time {3x}. Syn.: 6256, 6471. See: TWOT—557a; BDB—273d, 1091c.

2166. זְמָן {11x} **zᵉmân** (Aram.), *zem-awn';* from 2165; the same as 2165:—season {2x}, time {9x}. See: TWOT—2709a; BDB—1091c.

2167. זָמַר {45x} **zâmar**, *zaw-mar';* a prim. root [perh. ident. with 2168 through the idea of *striking* with the fingers]; prop. to *touch* the strings or parts of a musical instrument, i.e. *play* upon it; to make *music,* accompanied by the voice; hence, to *celebrate* in song and music:—praise {26x}, sing {16x}, sing psalms {2x}, sing forth {1x}. Syn.: 1984,

3034, 7891. See: TWOT—558; BDB—274a, 1091c.

2168. זָמַר {3x} **zâmar**, *zaw-mar';* a prim. root [comp. 2167, 5568, 6785]; to *trim* (a vine):—prune {3x}. See: TWOT—559; BDB—274d.

2169. זֶמֶר {1x} **zemer**, *zeh'-mer;* appar. from 2167 or 2168; a *gazelle* (from its lightly *touching* the ground):—chamois {1x}. See: TWOT—560b; BDB—275a.

2170. זְמָר {4x} **zᵉmâr** (Aram.), *zem-awr';* from a root corresp. to 2167; instrumental *music:*—musick {1x}. See: TWOT—2710a; BDB—1091c.

זָמִיר **zâmîr**. See 2158.

זְמוֹר **zᵉmôr**. See 2156.

2171. זַמָּר {1x} **zammâr** (Aram.), *zam-mawr';* from the same as 2170; an instrumental *musician:*—singer {1x}. See: TWOT—2710b; BDB—1091c.

2172. זִמְרָה {4x} **zimrâh**, *zim-raw';* from 2167; a *musical* piece or *song* to be accompanied by an instrument:—melody {2x}, psalm {2x}. Syn.: 4210. See: TWOT—558a; BDB—274b.

2173. זִמְרָה {1x} **zimrâh**, *zim-raw';* from 2168; *pruned* (i.e. *choice*) fruit:—best fruit {1x}. Syn.: 6529. See: TWOT—560a; BDB—275a.

זִמְרָה **zᵉmîrâh**. See 2158.

זִמְרָה **zᵉmôrâh**. See 2156.

2174. זִמְרִי {15x} **Zimrîy**, *zim-ree';* from 2167; *musical; Zimri*, the name of five Isr., and of an Arabian tribe:—Zimri {15x}. See: BDB—275b.

2175. זִמְרָן {2x} **Zimrân**, *zim-rawn';* from 2167; *musical; Zimran*, a son of Abraham by Keturah:—Zimran {2x}. See: BDB—275b.

2176. זִמְרָת {3x} **zimrâth**, *zim-rawth';* from 2167; instrumental *music;* by impl. *praise:*—song {3x}. Syn.: 7892. See: TWOT—558a; BDB—274b.

2177. זַן {3x} **zan**, *zan;* from 2109; prop. *nourished* (or fully *developed*), i.e. a *form* or *sort:*—divers kinds {2x}, × all manner of store {1x}. See: TWOT—561; BDB—275b, 1091c.

2178. זַן {1x} **zan** (Aram.), *zan;* corresp. to 2177; *sort:*—kind {1x}. See: TWOT—2711; BDB—1091c.

2179. זָנָב {2x} **zânab**, *zaw-nab';* a prim. root mean. to *wag;* used only as a denom.

from 2180; to *curtail*, i.e. *cut* off the rear:—smite the hindmost {2x}. See: TWOT—562; BDB—275c.

2180. זָנָב {11x} **zânâb**, *zaw-nawb';* from 2179 (in the orig. sense of *flapping*); the *tail* (lit. or fig.):—tail {11x}. See: TWOT—562a; BDB—275b.

2181. זָנָה {93x} **zânâh**, *zaw-naw';* a prim. root [highly-*fed* and therefore *wanton*]; to *commit adultery* (usually of the female, and less often of simple fornication, rarely of involuntary ravishment); fig. to *commit idolatry* (the Jewish people being regarded as the spouse of Jehovah):—harlot {36x}, go a whoring {19x}, . . . whoredom {15x}, whore {11x}, commit fornication {3x}, whorish {3x}, harlot + 802 {2x}, commit {1x}, continually {1x}, great {1x}, whore's + 802 {1x}.

Zanah means "to go a whoring, commit fornication, be a harlot, serve other gods." **(1)** This is the regular term denoting prostitution throughout the history of Hebrew, with special nuances coming out of the religious experience of ancient Israel. **(2)** It is used for the first time in the text at the conclusion of the story of the rape of Dinah by Shechem, as her brothers excuse their revenge by asking: "Should he deal with our sister as with a harlot?" (Gen 34:31). **(3)** While the term means "to commit fornication," whether by male or by female, **(3a)** it is to be noted that it is almost never used to describe sexual misconduct on the part of a male in the Old Testament. **(3b)** Part of the reason lies in the differing attitude in ancient Israel concerning sexual activity by men and women. **(3b)** The main reason, however, is the fact that this term is used most frequently to describe "spiritual prostitution" **(3b1)** in which Israel turned from God to strange gods.

(3b2) Deut 31:16 illustrates this meaning: "And the LORD said unto Moses, Behold, thou shalt sleep with thy fathers; and this people will rise up, and go a whoring after the gods of the strangers of the land, whither they go to be among them, and will forsake me, and break my covenant which I have made with them." **(4)** *Zanah* became, then, the common term for spiritual backsliding. **(4a)** The act of harloting after strange gods was more than changing gods, however. This was especially true when Israel went after the Canaanite gods, for the worship of these pagan deities involved actual prostitution with cult prostitutes connected with the Canaanite shrines. **(4b)** In the Old Testament sometimes the use of the phrase "go a whoring after" gods **(4b1)** implies an individual's involvement with cult prostitutes. **(4b2)** An example might be in Ex 34:15–16:

"Lest thou make a covenant with the inhabitants of the land, and they go a whoring after their gods, and do sacrifice unto their gods. . . . And thou take of their daughters unto thy sons, and their daughters go a whoring after their gods, and make thy sons go a whoring after their gods." **(5)** The religious theory behind such activity at the Canaanite shrine was that such **(5a)** sexual activity with cult prostitutes, both male and female, **(5b)** who represented the gods and goddesses of the Canaanite fertility cult, **(5c)** would stimulate fertility in their crops and flocks. **(5d)** Such cult prostitutes were not designated as prostitutes but rather "holy ones" or "set-apart ones," **(5d1)** since the Semitic term for "holy" means, first of all, to be set apart for a special use. **(5d2)** This is illustrated in Deut 23:17: "There shall be a whore of the daughters of Israel, neither shall there be a "sodomite of the sons of Israel."

(5e) This theme of religious harlotry looms large in the prophets who denounce this backsliding in no uncertain terms. **(5e1)** Ezekiel minces no words as he openly calls both Judah and Israel "harlots" and vividly describes their backsliding in sexual terms (Eze 16:6–63; 23). **(5e2)** The Book of Hosea, in which Hosea's wife Gomer became unfaithful and most likely was involved in such cult prostitution, again illustrates not only Hosea's heartbreak but also God's own heartbreak because of the unfaithfulness of his wife, Israel. Israel's unfaithfulness appears in Hos 9:1: "Rejoice not, O Israel, for joy, as other people: for thou hast gone a whoring from thy God, thou hast loved a reward upon every cornfloor." See: TWOT–563; BDB–266a, 275c.

2182. זָנוֹחַ {5x} **Zânôwach**, *zaw-no'-akh;* from 2186; *rejected; Zanoach,* the name of two places in Pal.:—Zanoah {5x}. See: BDB–276c.

2183. זָנוּן {12x} **zânûwn**, *zaw-noon';* from 2181; *adultery;* fig. *idolatry:*—whoredom {12x}. Syn.: 8457. See: TWOT–563a; BDB–276.

2184. זְנוּת {9x} **z'nûwth**, *zen-ooth';* from 2181; *adultery,* i.e. (fig.) *infidelity, idolatry:*—whoredom {9x}. Syn.: 8457. See: TWOT–563b; BDB–276a.

2185. זֹנוֹת {1x} **zônôwth**, *zo-noth';* regarded by some as if from 2109 or an unused root, and applied to military *equipments;* but evidently the fem. plur. act. part. of 2181; *harlots:*—armour {1x}. See: BDB–275d.

2186. זָנַח {20x} **zânach**, *zaw-nakh';* a prim. root mean. to *push* aside, i.e. *reject, forsake, fail:*—cast . . . off {17x}, cast away {1x}, turn . . . away {1x}, removed . . . far off {1x}.

Syn.: 1644, 2904. See: TWOT–564; BDB–276b, 276c.

2187. זָנַק {1x} **zânaq**, *zaw-nak';* a prim. root; prop. to *draw together* the feet (as an animal about to dart upon its prey), i.e. to *spring* forward:—leap {1x}. See: TWOT–566; BDB–276c.

2188. זֵעָה {1x} **zê'âh**, *zay-aw';* from 2111 (in the sense of 3154); *perspiration:*—sweat {1x}. See: TWOT–857b; BDB–276c, 402c.

2189. זַעֲוָה {7x} **za'ăvâh**, *zah-av-aw';* by transp. for 2113; *agitation, maltreatment:*—✗ removed {6x}, trouble {1x}. See: TWOT–540a; BDB–266b, 276c.

2190. זַעֲוָן {2x} **Za'ăvân**, *zah-av-awn';* from 2111; *disquiet; Zaavan,* an Idumæan:—Zaavan {2x}. See: BDB–266b, 276c.

2191. זְעֵיר {5x} **z'êyr**, *zeh-ayr';* from an unused root [akin (by perm.) to 6819], mean. to *dwindle; small:*—little {5x}. See: TWOT–571a; BDB–277d, 1091d.

2192. זְעֵיר {1x} **z'êyr** (Aram.), *zeh-ayr';* corresp. to 2191:—little {1x}. See: TWOT–2712; BDB–1091d.

2193. זָעַךְ {1x} **zâ'ak**, *zaw-ak';* a prim. root; to *extinguish:*—be extinct {1x}. See: TWOT–567; BDB–276c.

2194. זָעַם {12x} **zâ'am**, *zaw-am';* a prim. root; prop. to *foam* at the mouth, i.e. to *be enraged:*—indignation {4x}, defy {3x}, abhor {2x}, angry {2x}, abominable {1x}. Syn.: 7110. See: TWOT–568; BDB–276d.

2195. זַעַם **za'am**, *zah'-am;* from 2194; strictly *froth* at the mouth, i.e. (fig.) *fury* (espec. of God's displeasure with sin):—angry {1x}, indignation {20x}, rage {1x}. See: TWOT–568a; BDB–276d.

2196. זָעַף {5x} **zâ'aph**, *zaw-af';* a prim. root; prop. to *boil* up, i.e. (fig.) to *be peevish* or *angry:*—fret {1x}, sad {1x}, worse liking {1x}, be wroth {2x}. See: TWOT–569; BDB–277a.

2197. זַעַף {6x} **za'aph**, *zah'-af;* from 2196; *anger:*—indignation {1x}, rage {2x}, raging {1x}, wrath {1x}. See: TWOT–569a; BDB–277a.

2198. זָעֵף {2x} **zâ'êph**, *zaw-afe';* from 2196; *angry:*—displeased {2x}. See: TWOT–569b; BDB–277a.

2199. זָעַק {73x} **zâ'aq**, *zaw-ak';* a prim. root; to *shriek* (from anguish or danger); by anal. (as a herald) to *announce* or *convene* publicly:—cry {50x}, cry out {11x}, assemble

{3x}, called {3x}, gathered together {2x}, gathered {2x}, company {1x}, proclaimed {1x}.

Za'aq means "to cry, cry out, call." **(1)** Its first occurrence is in the record of the suffering of the Israelite bondage in Egypt: "And the children of Israel sighed by reason of the bondage, and they cried [for help]" (Ex 2:23). **(2)** *Za'aq* is perhaps most frequently used to indicate the "crying out" for aid in time of emergency, **(2a)** especially "crying out" for divine aid. **(2b)** God often heard this "cry" for help in the time of the judges, as Israel found itself in trouble because of its backsliding (Judg 3:9, 15; 6:7; 10:10). **(3)** The word is used also in appeals to pagan gods (Judg 10:14; Jer 11:12; Jonah 1:5). **(4)** That *za'aq* means more than a normal speaking volume is indicated in appeals to the king (2 Sa 19:28). **(5)** The word may imply **(5a)** a "crying out" in distress (1 Sa 4:13), **(5b)** a "cry" of horror (1 Sa 5:10), or **(5c)** a "cry" of sorrow (2 Sa 13:19). **(6)** Used figuratively, it is said that "the stone shall cry out of the wall" (Hab 2:11) of a house that is built by means of evil gain. Syn.: 6817, 7124, 7440, 77678. See: TWOT−570; BDB−277a, 1091c.

2200. זְעֵק {1x} **zᵉʿîq** (Aram.), *zeh-eek'*; corresp. to 2199; to *make an outcry:—* cry {1x}. See: TWOT−2712; BDB−1091c.

2201. זַעַק {18x} **za'aq**, *zah'-ak;* and (fem.)

זְעָקָה **zᵉâqâh**, *zeh-aw-kaw';* from 2199; a *shriek* or *outcry:—*cry {17x}, crying {1x}. See: TWOT−570a; BDB−277c.

2202. זִפְרֹן {1x} **Ziphrôn**, *zi-frone';* from an unused root (mean. to *be fragrant*); *Ziphron,* a place in Pal.:—*Ziphron* {1x}. See: BDB−277d.

2203. זֶפֶת {3x} **zepheth**, *zeh'-feth;* from an unused root (mean. to *liquify*); *asphalt* (from its tendency to *soften* in the sun):— pitch {3x}. See: TWOT−572; BDB−278a.

זִק **zîq** or

זֵק **zêq**. See 2131.

2204. זָקֵן {27x} **zâqên**, *zaw-kane';* a prim. root; to *be old:—*aged man {1x}, old {26x}.

Zaqen means "old man; old woman; elder; old." **(1)** The first occurrence is in Gen 18:11: "Now Abraham and Sarah were old and well stricken in age; and it ceased to be with Sarah after the manner of women." **(2)** In Gen 19:4, the word "old" is used as an antonym of "young": **(2a)** "But before they lay down, the men of the city, even the men of Sodom, compassed the house round, both old and young [5288 - *na'ar*, "young man"], all the people from every quarter" (cf. Josh 6:21). **(2b)** A similar usage of *zaqen* and "young" appears in other

Bible references: "But [Rehoboam] forsook the counsel of the old men, which they had given him, and consulted with the young men [3206 - *yeled,* "boy; child"] that were grown up with him" (1 Kin 12:8). **(2c)** "Then shall the virgin rejoice in the dance, both young men [970 - *bachur*] and old together: for I will turn their mourning into joy, and will comfort them, and make them rejoice from their sorrow" (Jer 31:13).

(3) The "old man" is described as **(3a)** being advanced in days (Gen 18:11), **(3b)** as being satisfied with life or full of years. **(4)** A feminine form of *zaqen* refers to an "old woman" (2205 - *zeqenah*). **(5)** The word *zaqen* has a more specialized use with the sense of "elder" (more than 100 times). **(5a)** The "elder" was recognized by the people for his gifts of leadership, wisdom, and justice. He was set apart to administer justice, settle disputes, and guide the people of his charge. **(5b)** Elders are also known as officers (7860 - *shotrim*), heads of the tribes, and judges; notice the parallel usage: "Joshua called for all Israel, and for their elders, and for their heads, and for their judges, and for their officers, and said unto them; I am old and stricken in age" (Josh 23:2).

(6) The "elders" were consulted by the king, but the king could determine his own course of action (1 Kin 12:8). **(7)** In a given city, the governing council was made up of the "elders," who were charged with the well-being of the town: "And Samuel did that which the LORD spake, and came to Bethlehem. And the elders of the town trembled at his coming, and said, Comest thou peaceably?" (1 Sa 16:4). **(8)** The elders met in session **(8a)** by the city gate (Eze 8:1). **(8b)** The place of meeting became known as the "seat" or "assembly") of the elders (Ps 107:32). **(9)** The KJV gives various translations of *zaqen:* "old; elder; old man; ancient." **(9a)** Note that the KJV distinguishes between "elder" and "ancient"; **(9b)** whenever the word *zaqen* does not apply to age or to rule, the KJV uses the word "ancient." See: TWOT−574; BDB−278b.

2205. זָקֵן {178x} **zâqên**, *zaw-kane';* from 2204; *old:—*elders {115x}, old {23x}, old man {19x}, ancient {14x}, aged {3x}, eldest {1x}, ancient man {1x}, senators {1x}, old women {1x}.

(1) The word *zaqen* has a specialized use as elder **(1a)** recognized by the people for his gifts of leadership, wisdom, and justice; **(1b)** set apart to administer justice, settle disputes, and guide the people of his charge; **(1c)** known as officers (*shotrim* -7860), heads of the tribes, and judges (Josh 23:2); **(1d)** consulted by the king, but the king could determine his own course of action (1 Kin 12:8). **(2)** In a given

city, the governing council was made up of the elders who **(2a)** were charged with the well-being of the town (1 Sa 16:4) and **(2b)** met in session by the city gate (Eze 8:1), with the place of meeting known as the seat/council/assembly of the elders (Ps 107:32). Whenever the word *zaqen* does not apply to age or to rule, the KJV uses the word *ancient*. See: TWOT−574b; BDB−278C.

2206. זָקָן {19x} **zâqân**, *zaw-kawn';* from 2204; the *beard* (as indicating *age*):− beard.

Zaqan means "beard." **(1)** The word *zaqan* refers to a "beard" in Ps 133:2: "It is like the precious ointment upon the head, that ran down upon the beard, even Aaron's beard: that went down to the skirts of his garments." **(2)** The association of "old age" with a "beard" can be made, but should not be stressed. See: TWOT−574a; BDB−278a.

2207. זֹקֶן {1x} **zôqen**, *zo'-ken;* from 2204; old *age*:−age {1x}. See: TWOT−574c; BDB−279a.

2208. זָקֻן {4x} **zâqûn**, *zaw-koon';* prop. pass. part. of 2204 (used only in the plur. as a noun); *old* age:−old age {4x}. See: TWOT−574e; BDB−279a.

2209. זִקְנָה {6x} **ziqnâh**, *zik-naw';* fem. of 2205; old *age*:−old {3x}, old age {3x}. See: TWOT−574d; BDB−279a.

2210. זָקַף {2x} **zâqaph**, *zaw-kaf';* a prim. root; to *lift*, i.e. (fig.) *comfort*:− raise (up) {2x}. See: TWOT−575; BDB−279a, 1091d.

2211. זְקַף {1x} **zᵉqaph** (Aram.), *zek-af';* corresp. to 2210; to *hang*, i.e. *impale*:−set up {1x}. See: TWOT−2714; BDB−1091d.

2212. זָקַק {7x} **zâqaq**, *zaw-kak';* a prim. root; to *strain*, (fig.) *extract, clarify*:− fine {1x}, pour down {1x}, purge {1x}, purify {1x}, refine {3x}. Syn.: See 2135. See: TWOT−576; 279b; BDB−279b.

2213. זֵר {10x} **zêr**, *zare;* from 2237 (in the sense of *scattering*); a *chaplet* (as *spread* around the top), i.e. (spec.) a border *moulding*:−crown {10x}. See: TWOT−543a; BDB−267a, 279c.

2214. זָרָא {1x} **zârâ'**, *zaw-raw';* from 2114 (in the sense of *estrangement*) [comp. 2219]; *disgust*:−loathsome {1x}. See: TWOT−542a; BDB−266d, 279c.

2215. זָרַב {1x} **zârab**, *zaw-rab';* a prim. root; to *flow* away:−wax warm {1x}. See: TWOT−578; BDB−279c.

2216. זְרֻבָּבֶל {21x} **Zᵉrubbâbel**, *zer-oob-baw-bel';* from 2215 and 894; *descended of* (i.e. from) *Babylon*, i.e. born there; *Zerubbabel*, an Isr.:−Zerubbabel {21x}. See: TWOT−578a; BDB−279c, 1091d.

2217. זְרֻבָּבֶל {1x} **Zᵉrubbâbel** (Aram.), *zer-oob-baw-bel';* corresp. to 2216:−Zerubbabel {1x}. See: BDB−1091d.

2218. זֶרֶד {4x} **Zered**, *zeh'-red;* from an unused root mean. to *be exuberant* in growth; lined with *shrubbery; Zered*, a brook E. of the Dead Sea:−Zared {1x}, Zered {3x}. See: BDB−279c.

2219. זָרָה {39x} **zârâh**, *zaw-raw';* a prim. root [comp. 2114]; to *toss* about; by impl. to *diffuse, winnow*:−scatter {19x}, disperse {8x}, fan {4x}, spread {2x}, winnowed {2x}, cast away {1x}, scatter away {1x}, compass {1x}, strawed {1x}. Syn.: 967, 2236, 6340, 6566. See: TWOT−579; BDB−279d, 561d.

2220. זְרוֹעַ {91x} **zᵉrôwaᶜ**, *zer-o'-ah;* or (short.)

זְרֹעַ **zᵉrôaᶜ**, *zer-o'-ah;* and (fem.)

זְרוֹעָה **zᵉrôwᶜâh**, *zer-o-aw';* or

זְרֹעָה **zᵉrôᶜâh**, *zer-o-aw';* from 2232; the *arm* (as *stretched* out), or (of animals) the *foreleg;* fig. *force*:−arm {83x}, power {3x}, shoulder {2x}, holpen {1x}, mighty {1x}, strength {1x}.

Zeroaᶜ means "arm; power; strength; help." **(1)** *Zeroaᶜ* means "arm," a part of the body: **(1a)** "Blessed be he that enlargeth Gad: he dwelleth as a lion, and teareth the arm with the crown of the head" (Deut 33:20). **(1b)** The word refers to arms in Gen 49:24 (the first occurrence): "But his bow abode in strength, and the arms of his hands were made strong." The strength of his arms enabled him to draw the bow. **(2)** In some passages, *zeroaᶜ* refers especially to the forearm: "It shall be as when the harvestman gathereth the corn, and reapeth the ears with his arm" (Is 17:5). **(3)** Elsewhere, the word represents the shoulder: "And Jehu drew a bow with his full strength, and smote Jehoram between his arms" (2 Kin 9:24). **(4)** *Zeroaᶜ* connotes the "seat of strength": **(4a)** "He teacheth my hands to war, so that a bow of steel is broken by mine arms" (Ps 18:34). **(4b)** In Job 26:2, the poor are described as the arm that hath no strength. **(5)** God's strength is figured by anthropomorphisms (attributing to His human bodily parts), such as His "stretched out arm" (Deut 4:34) or His "strong arm" (Jer 21:5).

(6) In Is 30:30, the word seems to represent lightning bolts: "And the Lord shall cause his glorious voice to be heard, and shall show the lighting down of his arm, with the indignation of his anger, and with the flame of a devouring

fire, with scattering, and tempest, and hailstones" (cf. Job 40:9). **(7)** The arm is frequently a symbol of strength, both of man (1 Sa 2:31) and of God (Ps 71:18): "Now also when I am old and grayheaded, O God, forsake me not; until I have showed thy strength unto this generation, and thy power to every one that is to come." **(8)** In Eze 22:6 zeroaʻ may be translated "power": "Behold, the princes of Israel, every one were in thee to their power to shed blood." **(9)** Zeroaʻ is also translated "help": "Assur also is joined with them: they have helped the children of Lot" (Ps 83:8). **(10)** The word can represent political or military forces: "And the arms of the south shall not withstand, neither his chosen people, neither shall there be any strength to withstand" (Dan 11:15; cf. Eze 17:9). **(11)** In Num 6:19 zeroaʻ is used of an animal's shoulder: "And the priest shall take the sodden shoulder of the ram" (cf. Deut 18:3). See: TWOT—583a; BDB—283d, 1089a.

2221. זֵרוּעַ {2x} **zêrûwaᶜ**, *zay-roo'-ah;* from 2232; something *sown,* i.e. a *plant:*—sowing {1x}, thing that is sown {1x}. See: TWOT—582b; BDB—283b.

2222. זַרְזִיף {1x} **zarzîyph**, *zar-zeef';* by redupl. from an unused root mean. to *flow;* a *pouring rain:*—water {1x}. Syn.: 4325. See: TWOT—584a; BDB—280a, 284b.

זְרֻעָה **zᵉrôwᶜâh**. See 2220.

2223. זַרְזִיר {1x} **zarzîyr**, *zar-zeer';* by redupl. from 2115; prop. tightly *girt,* i.e. prob. a *racer,* or some fleet animal (as being *slender* in the waist):—+ greyhound {1x}. See: TWOT—543b; BDB—267a, 280a.

2224. זָרַח {1x} **zârach**, *zaw-rakh';* a prim. root; prop. to *irradiate* (or shoot forth beams), i.e. to *rise* (as the sun); spec. to *appear* (as a symptom of leprosy):—arise {8x}, rise {6x}, rise up {2}, shine {1x}, up {1x}. See: TWOT—580; BDB—280b.

2225. זֶרַח {1x} **zerach**, *zeh'-rakh;* from 2224; a *rising* of light:—rising {1x}. See: TWOT—580a; BDB—280b.

2226. זֶרַח {21x} **Zerach**, *zeh'-rakh;* the same as 2225; *Zerach,* the name of three Isr., also of an Idumæan and an Ethiopian prince:—Zarah {20x}, Zerah {1x}. See: BDB—280b.

2227. זַרְחִי {6x} **Zarchîy**, *zar-khee';* patron. from 2226; a *Zarchite* or desc. of Zerach:—Zarchite {6x}. See: BDB—280c.

2228. זְרַחְיָה {5x} **Zᵉrachyâh**, *zer-akh-yaw';* from 2225 and 3050; *Jah has risen; Zerachjah,* the name of two Isr.:—Zerahiah {1x}. See: BDB—280c.

2229. זָרַם {2x} **zâram**, *zaw-ram';* a prim. root; to *gush* (as water):—carry away as with a flood {1x}, pour out {1x}. See: TWOT—581; BDB—281a.

2230. זֶרֶם {9x} **zerem**, *zeh'-rem;* from 2229; a *gush* of water:—flood {1x}, overflowing {1x}, shower {1x}, storm {3x}, tempest {3x}. See: TWOT—581a; BDB—281b.

2231. זִרְמָה {2x} **zirmâh**, *zir-maw';* fem. of 2230; a *gushing* of fluid (semen):—issue {2x}. See: TWOT—581b; BDB—281b.

2232. זָרַע {56x} **zâraᶜ**, *zaw-rah';* a prim. root; to *sow;* fig. to *disseminate, plant, fructify:*—sow {47x}, yielding {3x}, sower {2x}, bearing {1x}, conceive {1x}, seed {1x}, set {1x}.

Zaraʻ means "to sow, scatter seed, make pregnant." **(1)** It occurs first in Gen 1:29 in the summary of the blessings of creation which God has given to mankind: "In the which is the fruit of a tree yielding seed." **(2)** In an agricultural society such as ancient Israel, zaraʻ would be most important and very commonly used, especially to describe the annual sowing of crops (Judg 6:3; Gen 26:12). **(3)** Used in the figurative sense, it is said that Yahweh "will sow" Israel in the land (Hos 2:23); in the latter days, Yahweh promises: "I will sow the house of Israel and the house of Judah with the seed of man, and with the seed of beast" (Jer 31:27). **(4)** Of great continuing comfort are the words, "They that sow in tears shall reap in joy" (Ps 126:5). The universal law of the harvest, sowing and reaping, applies to all areas of life and experience.

(5) In Num 5, which describes the law of trial by ordeal in the case of a wife accused of infidelity. **(5a)** If she was found innocent, it was declared: "She shall be free, and shall conceive [zaraʻ] seed [zeraʻ]" (Num 5:28). **(5b)** This phrase is literally: "She shall be acquitted and shall be seeded seed," or "She shall be made pregnant with seed." **(6)** An Old Testament name, Jezreel, has been connected with this root. Jezreel ("God sows") refers both to a city and valley near Mt. Gilboa (Josh 17:16; 2 Sa 2:9) and to the symbolically named son of Hosea (Hos 1:4). See: TWOT—582; BDB—281b, 1091d.

2233. זֶרַע {229x} **zeraᶜ**, *zeh'-rah;* from 2232; *seed;* fig. *fruit, plant, sowing-time, posterity:*—seed {221x}, child {2x}, carnally + 7902 {2x}, carnally {1x}, fruitful {1x}, seedtime {1x}, sowing time {1x}.

Zeraʻ means "seed; sowing; seedtime; harvest; offspring; descendant(s); posterity." **(1)** Zeraʻ refers to the process of scattering seed, or "sowing." **(1a)** This is the emphasis in Gen 47:24: "And it shall come to pass in the

increase, that ye shall give the fifth part unto Pharaoh, and four parts shall be your own, for seed of the field, and for your food." **(1b)** Num. 20:5: ". . . it is no place of seed, or of figs, or of vines, or of pomegranates; neither is there any water to drink." **(1c)** Eze 17:5 "He took also of the seed of the land, and planted it in a fruitful field;" **(1d)** A closely related emphasis occurs in passages such as Gen 8:22, where the word represents "sowing" as a regularly recurring activity: "While the earth remaineth, seedtime and harvest, and cold and heat . . . shall not cease."

(2) *Zera*‘ frequently means "seed." There are several nuances under this emphasis, **(2a)** the first being what is sown to raise crops for food. The Egyptians told Joseph: "Buy us and our land for bread, and we and our land will be servants unto Pharaoh: and give us seed, that we may live, and not die, that the land be not desolate" (Gen 47:19).

(2b) The word represents the product of a plant: "Let the earth bring forth grass, the herb yielding seed [food], and the fruit tree yielding fruit after his kind, whose seed is in itself" (Gen 1:11-the first biblical appearance). **(2c)** In this and other contexts *zera*‘ specifically refers to "grain seed," or "edible seed" (cf. Lev 27:30). **(2d)** This may be the meaning of the word in 1 Sa 8:15: "And he will take the tenth of your seed, and of your vineyards." **(3)** In other contexts the word represents an entire "crop or harvest": "For the seed [harvest] shall be prosperous; the vine shall give her fruit, and the ground shall give her increase, and the heavens shall give their dew" (Zec 8:12). **(4)** In Is 23:3 *zera*‘ and the usual Hebrew word for "harvest" (7105 - *qatsir*) are in synonymous parallelism. **(5)** *Zera*‘ sometimes means **(5a)** "semen," or a man's "seed": "And if any man's seed of copulation go out from him [if he has a seminal emission]" (Lev 15:16). **(5b)** A beast's "semen" can also be indicated by this word (Jer 31:27).

(6) *Zera*‘ often means "offspring." **(6a)** "And I will put enmity between thee [the devil] and the woman [Eve], and between thy seed and her seed" (Gen 3:15). **(6b)** This verse uses the word in several senses. **(6b1)** The first appearance means both the descendants of the snake and those of the spiritual being who used the snake (evil men). **(6b2)** The second appearance of the word refers to all the descendants of the woman and ultimately to a particular descendant (Christ). **(7)** In Gen 4:25 *zera*‘ appears not as a collective noun but refers to a particular and immediate "offspring"; upon the birth of Seth, Eve said: "God . . . hath appointed me another seed [offspring]." **(7a)** Gen 46:6 uses the word (in the singular) of one's entire family including children and grandchildren (cf. Gen

17:12). **(7b)** One's larger family, including all immediate relatives, is included in the word in passages such as 1 Kin 11:14. **(8)** The word is used of an entire nation of people in Est 10:3.

(9) *Zera*‘ is used of groups and individuals marked by a common moral quality. **(9a)** This usage was already seen in Gen 3:15. **(9b)** Is 65:23 mentions the "seed" of the blessed of God. The Messiah or Suffering Servant will see His "offspring," or those who believe in and follow Him (Is 53:10). **(10)** We also read about **(10a)** the followers of the righteous (Prov 11:21), **(10b)** the faithful "seed" (Jer 2:21), and **(10c)** godly "offspring." **(10d)** In each case this word represents those who are united by being typified by the modifier of *zera*‘. **(11)** Several other passages exhibit the same nuance except that *zera*‘ is modified by an undesirable quality. See: TWOT—582a; BDB—282a, 1091d.

2234. זְרַע {1x} **z^era^c** (Aram.), *zer-ah'*; corresp. to 2233; *posterity:*—seed {1x}. See: TWOT—2715; BDB—1091d.

זְרֹעַ **z^erôa^c**. See 2220.

זְרֹעַ {2x} **zêrôa^c**, *zay-ro'-ah;* or

2235. זֵרָעֹן **zêrâ^côn**, *zay-raw-ohn';* from 2232; something *sown* (only in the plur.), i.e. a *vegetable* (as food):—pulse {1x}. See: TWOT—582c; BDB—283b.

זֵרֹעָה **z^erô^câh**. See 2220.

2236. זָרַק **zâraq**, *zaw-rak';* a prim. root; to *sprinkle* (fluid or solid particles):— sprinkle {31x}, scatter {2x}, here and there {1x}, strowed {1x}. Syn.: 967, 5137.

Zaraq means "to throw; sprinkle; strew; toss; scatter abundantly." **(1)** Used 35 times in the text of the Hebrew Old Testament, **(1a)** in 26 of those times it expresses the "throwing" or "sprinkling" of blood against the sacrificial altar or on the people. **(1b)** Thus, it appears very often in Leviticus (1:5, 11; 3:2, 8, 13 et al.). **(2)** Ezekiel's version of "the New Covenant" includes the "sprinkling" of the water of purification (Eze 36:25). **(3)** In the first use of *zaraq* in the Old Testament, it describes the "throwing" of handsful of dust into the air which would settle down on the Egyptians and cause boils (Ex 9:8, 10). **(4)** In his reform, Josiah ground up the Canaanite idol images and "scattered, strewed," the dust over the graves of idol worshipers (2 Chr 34:4). **(5)** In Ezekiel's vision of the departure of God's glory from the temple, the man in linen takes burning coals and "scatters" them over Jerusalem (Eze 10:2). See: TWOT—585; BDB—284c.

2237. זָרַר **zârar**, *zaw-rar';* a prim. root [comp. 2114]; perh. to *diffuse*, i.e.

(spec.) to *sneeze:*—sneeze {1x}. See: TWOT—586; BDB—284b.

2238. זֶרֶשׁ {4x} **Zeresh**, *zeh'-resh;* of Pers. or.; *Zeresh,* Haman's wife:—Zeresh {4x}. See: BDB—284d.

2239. זֶרֶת {7x} **zereth**, *zeh'-reth;* from 2219; the *spread* of the fingers, i.e. a *span:*—span {1x}. See: TWOT—587; BDB—284d.

2240. זַתּוּא {4} **Zattûw'**, *zat-too';* of uncert. der.; *Zattu,* an Isr.:—Zattu {1x}. See: BDB—285c.

2241. זֵתָם {2} **Zêthâm**, *zay-thawm';* appar. a var. for 2133; *Zetham,* an Isr.:—Zetham {2}. See: BDB—268d, 285c.

2242. זֵתַר {1x} **Zêthar**, *zay-thar';* of Pers. or.; *Zethar,* a eunuch of Xerxes:—Zethar {1x}. See: BDB—285c.

ח

2243. חֹב {1x} **chôb**, *khobe;* by contr. from 2245; prop. a *cherisher,* i.e. the *bosom:*—bosom {1x}. Syn.: 2436, 2683. See: TWOT—589a; BDB—285a, 285c.

2244. חָבָא {33x} **châbâ'**, *khaw-baw';* a prim. root [comp. 2245]; to *secrete:*—✗ held {1x}, hide (self) {31x}, do secretly {1x}. Syn.: 2247, 2931, 5641, 5956. See: TWOT—588; BDB—285a.

2245. חָבַב {1x} **chabab**, *khaw-bab';* a prim. root [comp. 2244, 2247]; prop. to *hide* (as in the bosom), i.e. to *cherish* (with affection):—love {1x}. Syn.: 157, 160. See: TWOT—589; BDB—285c.

2246. חֹבָב {2x} **Chôbâb**, *kho-bawb';* from 2245; *cherished; Chobab,* father-in-law of Moses:—Hobab {2x}. See: BDB—285d.

2247. חָבָה {5x} **châbah**, *khaw-bah';* a prim. root [comp. 2245]; to *secrete:*—hide (self) {5x}. Syn.: 2244, 2931, 5641, 5956. See: TWOT—590; BDB—285d.

2248. חֲבוּלָה {1x} **chăbûwlâh** (Aram.), *khab-oo-law';* from 2255; prop. *over-thrown,* i.e. (morally) *crime:*—hurt {1x}. See: TWOT—2716b; BDB—1092a.

2249. חָבוֹר {1x} **Châbôwr**, *khaw-bore';* from 2266; *united; Chabor,* a river of Assyria:—Habor {3x}. See: BDB—289c.

2250. חַבּוּרָה {7x} **chabbûwrâh**, *khab-boo-raw';* or חַבֻּרָה **chabbûrâh**, *khab-boo-raw';* or חֲבֻרָה **chăbûrâh**, *khab-oo-raw';* from 2266; prop. *bound* (with stripes), i.e. a *weal* (or black-and-blue mark itself):—

stripe {3x}, hurt {1x}, wounds {1x}, blueness {1x}, bruise {1x}. Syn.: 2257. See: TWOT—598g; BDB—289a, 289c.

2251. חָבַט **châbat**, *khaw-bat';* a prim. root; to *knock* out or off:—beat out {2x}, beat off {1x}, beat down {1x}, threshed {1x}. Syn.: 1758. See: TWOT—591; BDB—286a.

2252. חֲבַיָּה {2x} **Chăbayâh**, *khab-ah-yaw';* or חֲבָיָה **Chăbâyâh**, *khab-aw-yaw';* from 2247 and 3050; *Jah has hidden; Chabajah,* an Isr.:—Habaiah {2x}. See: BDB—285d, 286a.

2253. חֶבְיוֹן {1x} **chebyôwn**, *kheb-yone';* from 2247; a *concealment:*—hiding {1x}. Syn.: 2934. See: BDB—285d, 286a.

2254. חָבַל {29x} **châbal**, *khaw-bal';* a prim. root; to *wind* tightly (as a rope), i.e. to *bind;* spec. by a *pledge;* fig. to *pervert, destroy;* also to *writhe* in pain (espec. of parturition):—destroy {7x}, take a pledge {5x} pledge {5x}, bands {2x}, brought forth {2x}, at all {1x}, corrupt {1x}, corruptly {1x}, offend {1x}, spoil {1x}, travaileth {1x}, very {1x}, withholden {1x}. Syn.: 6, 343, 1104, 1820, 2040, 2475, 2717, 3615, 3772, 4135, 5395, 7665. See: TWOT—592, 593, 594, 595; BDB—286b, 287b, 1091d.

2255. חֲבַל {6x} **chăbal** (Aram.), *khab-al';* corresp. to 2254; to *ruin:*—destroy {5x}, hurt {1x}. See: TWOT—2716; BDB—1091d.

2256. חֶבֶל {60x} **chebel**, *kheh'-bel;* or חֵבֶל **chêbel**, *khay'-bel;* from 2254; a *rope* (as *twisted*), espec. a measuring *line;* by impl. a *district* or *inheritance* (as *measured*); or a *noose* (as of *cords*); fig. a *company* (as if *tied* together); also a *throe* (espec. of parturition); also *ruin:*—sorrows {10x}, cord {16x}, line {7x}, coast {4x}, portion {4x}, region {3x}, lot {3x}, ropes {3x}, company {2x}, pangs {2x}, bands {1x}, country {1x}, destruction {1x}, pain {1x}, snare {1x}, tacklings {1x}.

Chebel means "cord; rope; tackle; measuring line; measurement; allotment; portion; region." **(1)** *Chebel* primarily means "cord" or "rope." "Then she let them down by a cord through the window: for her house *was* upon the town wall, and she dwelt upon the wall" (Josh 2:15). **(2)** The word is used of "tent ropes" in Is 33:20: "A tabernacle that shall not be taken down . . . neither shall any of the cords thereof be broken." **(3)** A ship's "tackle" is the meaning of *chebel* in Is 33:23. **(4)** Used figuratively, *chebel* emphasizes "being bound." In 1 Kin 20:31, we read that the Syrians who fled into Aphek proposed to put sackcloth on their heads as a sign of repentance for attacking Israel, and to put "ropes" about their necks as a sign of submission to Israel's authority.

(5) Snares used "cords" or "ropes," forming a web or a noose into which the prey stepped and was caught. In this manner, the wicked would be caught by God (Job 18:10).

(6) In many passages, death is pictured as a hunter whose trap has been sprung and whose quarry is captured by the "cords" of the trap: "the sorrows of hell compassed me about; the snares of death prevented me;" (2 Sa 22:6). **(7)** In other cases, the thing that "binds" is good: "I drew them with cords of a man, with bands of love" (Hos 11:4). **(8)** Eccl 12:6 pictures human life as being held together by a silver "cord." **(9)** A "cord" could be used as a "measuring line": "And he smote Moab, and measured them with a line, casting them down to the ground; even with two lines measured he to put to death, and with one full line to keep alive" (2 Sa 8:2). **(9a)** This meaning of *chebel* also occurs in Ps 78:55: ". . . And [He] divided them an inheritance by line." **(9b)** Compare Mic 2:5: "Therefore thou shalt have none that shall cast a cord by lot in the congregation of the Lord." **(10)** The act referred to by Micah appears in Ps 16:6 as an image of one's life in general: "The lines are fallen unto me in pleasant places; yea, I have a goodly heritage."

(11) *Chebel* also means "the thing measured or allotted": **(11a)** "For the LORD's portion is his people; Jacob is the lot of his inheritance" (Deut 32:9). Here the use is clearly figurative, **(11b)** but in 1 Chr 16:18 the "portion" of Israel's inheritance is a concrete "measured thing"; **(11c)** this nuance first appears in Josh 17:5. **(12)** In passages such as Deut 3:4, the word is used of a "region" or "a measured area": ". . . Threescore cities, all the region of Argob, the kingdom of Og in Bashan." **(12)** The word may refer to a group of people, describing them as that which is tied together—"a band": "Thou shalt meet a company of prophets coming down from the high place" (1 Sa 10:5). See: TWOT—592b, 595a; BDB—286c, 286d, 287a, 287c.

2257. חֲבַל {3x} **chăbal** (Aram.), *khab-al';* from 2255; *harm* (personal or pecuniary):—damage {1x}, hurt {2x}. See: BDB—1092a.

2258. חֲבֹל {4x} **chăbôl**, *khab-ole';* or (fem.)

חֲבֹלָה **chăbôlâh**, *khab-o-law';* from 2254; *a pawn* (as security for debt):—pledge {4x}. Syn.: 5567, 6162. See: TWOT—593a; BDB—287a.

2259. חֹבֵל **chôbêl**, *kho-bale';* act. part. from 2254 (in the sense of handling *ropes*); *a sailor:*—pilot {4x}, shipmaster + 7227 {1x}. See: TWOT—592c; BDB—287a.

2260. חִבֵּל {1x} **chibbêl**, *khib-bale';* from 2254 (in the sense of furnished with *ropes*); *a mast:*—mast {1x}. See: TWOT—592d; BDB—287a.

2261. חֲבַצֶּלֶת {2x} **chăbatstseleth**, *khab-ats-tseh'-leth;* of uncert. der.; prob. *meadow-saffron:*—rose {2x}. See: TWOT—596.1; BDB—287c.

2262. חֲבַצַּנְיָה {1x} **Chăbatstsanyâh**, *khab-ats-tsan-yaw';* of uncert. der.; *Chabatstsanjah*, a Rechabite:—Habazaniah {1x}. See: BDB—287c.

2263. חָבַק {13x} **châbaq**, *khaw-bak';* a prim. root; to *clasp* (the hands or in embrace):—embrace {12x}, fold {1x}. See: TWOT—597; BDB—287d.

2264. חִבֻּק {2x} **chibbûq**, *khib-book';* from 2263; *a clasping* of the hands (in idleness):—fold {2x}. See: TWOT—597a; BDB—287d.

2265. חֲבַקּוּק {2x} **Chăbaqqûwq**, *khab-ak-kook';* by redupl. from 2263; *embrace; Chabakkuk*, the prophet:—Habakkuk {2x}. See: BDB—287d.

2266. חָבַר {29x} **châbar**, *khaw-bar';* a prim. root; to *join* (lit. or fig.); spec. (by means of spells) to *fascinate:*—couple {8x}, join {8x}, couple together {4x}, join together {3x}, compact {1x}, charmer + 2267 {1x}, charming + 2267 {1x}, have fellowship {1x}, league {1x}, heap up {1x}. See: TWOT—598; BDB—251c, 287d, 1092a.

2267. חֶבֶר {7x} **cheber**, *kheh'-ber;* from 2266; *a society;* also a *spell:*—wide {2x}, enchantment {2x}, company {1x}, charmer + 2266 {1x}, charming + 2266 {1x}. *Cheber* means binding, fascination and is rendered "enchantment" (Is 47:9, 12) and "[serpent] charmer" (Ps 58:5). Syn.: 328, 825, 826, 1505, 3858, 3907, 3909, 5172, 6049, See: TWOT—598a; BDB—288c.

2268. חֶבֶר {11x} **Cheber**, *kheh'-ber;* the same as 2267; *community; Cheber*, the name of a Kenite and of three Isr.:—Heber {1x}. See: BDB—288c.

2269. חֲבַר {3x} **chăbar** (Aram.), *khab-ar';* from a root corresp. to 2266; an *associate:*—companion {1x}, fellow {2x}. See: TWOT—2717, 2717a; BDB—1092a.

2270. חָבֵר {12x} **châbêr**, *khaw-bare';* from 2266; an *associate:*—companion {7x}, fellow {4x}, knit together {1x}. Syn.: 2271, 4828, 7453, 7462. See: TWOT—598c; BDB—288d.

Hebrew

2271. חַבָּר {1x} **chabbâr**, *khab-bawr'*; from 2266; a *partner:*—companion {1x}. See: TWOT—598f; BDB—289a.

2272. חֲבַרְבֻּרָה {1x} **chăbarbûrâh**, *khab-ar-boo-raw'*; by redupl. from 2266; a *streak* (like a *line*), as on the tiger:—spot {1x}. See: TWOT—598h; BDB—289a.

2273. חַבְרָה {1x} **chabrâh** (Aram.), *khab-raw'*; fem. of 2269; an *associate:*—other {1x}. See: TWOT—2717b; BDB—1092a.

2274. חֶבְרָה {1x} **chebrâh**, *kheb-raw'*; fem. of 2267; *association:*—company {1x}. Syn.: 2256. See: TWOT—598b; BDB—288d.

2275. חֶבְרוֹן {71x} **Chebrôwn**, *kheb-rone'*; from 2267; seat of *association; Chebron,* a place in Pal., also the name of two Isr.:—Hebron {71x}. See: TWOT—598i; BDB—289b, 900c.

2276. חֶבְרוֹנִי {6x} **Chebrôwnîy**, *kheb-ro-nee'*; or

חֶבְרֹנִי **Chebrônîy**, *kheb-ro-nee'*; patron. from 2275; *Chebronite* (collect.), an inhab. of Chebron:—Hebronites {6x}. See: BDB—289c.

2277. חֶבְרִי {1x} **Chebrîy**, *kheb-ree'*; patron. from 2268; a *Chebrite* (collect.) or desc. of Cheber:—Heberites {1x}. See: BDB—288d.

2278. חֲבֶרֶת {1x} **chăbereth**, *khab-eh'-reth;* fem. of 2270; a *consort:*—companion {1x}. See: TWOT—598d; BDB—289a.

2279. חֹבֶרֶת {4x} **chôbereth**, *kho-beh'-reth;* fem. act. part. of 2266; a *joint:*—which coupleth {2x}, coupling {2x}. See: TWOT—598e; BDB—289a.

2280. חָבַשׁ {33x} **châbash**, *khaw-bash';* a prim. root; to *wrap* firmly (espec. a turban, compress, or *saddle*); fig. to *stop,* to *rule:*—saddle {13x}, bind up {9x}, bind {5x}, put {2x}, about {1x}, girded {1x}, govern {1x}, healer {1x}. See: TWOT—599; BDB—289c.

2281. חָבֵת {1x} **châbêth**, *khaw-bayth';* from an unused root prob. mean. to *cook* [comp. 4227]; something *fried,* prob. a griddle-*cake:*—pan {1x}. See: TWOT—600a; BDB—290a.

2282. חַג {62x} **chag,** *khag;* or

חָג **châg,** *khawg;* from 2287; a *festival,* or a *victim* therefore:—feast {56x}, sacrifice {3x}, feast days {2x}, solemnity {1x}.

Chag means "feast; festal sacrifice." **(1)** Biblical Hebrew attests it about 62 times and in all periods, except in the wisdom literature. **(2)** This word refers especially to a "feast ob-

served by a pilgrimage." That is its meaning in its first biblical occurrence, when Moses said to Pharaoh: "We will go with our young and with our old, with our sons and with our daughters, with our flocks and with our herds will we go; for we must hold a feast unto the LORD" (Ex 10:9). **(3)** *Chag* usually represents Israel's three annual "pilgrimage feasts," **(3a)** which were celebrated with processions and dances. **(3b)** These special feasts are distinguished from the sacred seasons ("festal assemblies"—Eze 45:17), the new moon festivals, and the Sabbaths (Hos 2:11). **(4)** There are two unique uses of *chag.* **(4a)** First, Aaron proclaimed a "feast to the LORD" at the foot of Mt. Sinai. This "feast" involved no pilgrimage but was celebrated with burnt offerings, communal meals, singing, and dancing. The whole matter was displeasing to God (Ex 32:5–7). **(4b)** In two passages, *chag* represents the "victim sacrificed to God" (perhaps during one of the three annual sacrifices): "Bind the [festal] sacrifice with cords, even unto the horns of the altar" (Ps 118:27; cf. Ex 23:18). Syn.: 2077. See: TWOT—602a; BDB—290b, 290d.

2283. חָגָא {1x} **chagâ>**, *khaw-gaw';* from an unused root mean. to *revolve* [comp. 2287]; prop. *vertigo,* i.e. (fig.) *fear:*—terror {1x}. Syn.: 2847, 2851. See: TWOT—602b; BDB—290b, 291b.

2284. חָגָב {5x} **chagâb**, *khaw-gawb';* of uncert. der.; a *locust:*—locusts {1x}, grasshopper {2x}, grasshoppers {2x}. See: TWOT—601a; BDB—290b.

2285. חָגָב {1x} **Châgâb**, *khaw-gawb';* the same as 2284; *locust; Chagab,* one of the Nethinim:—Hagab {1x}. See: BDB—290c.

2286. חֲגָבָא {2x} **Chăgâbâ>**, *khag-aw-baw';* or

חֲגָבָה **Chăgâbâh**, *khag-aw-baw';* fem. of 2285; *locust; Chagaba* or *Chagabah,* one of the Nethinim:—Hagaba {1x}, Hagabah {1x}. See: BDB—290c.

2287. חָגַג {16x} **châgag**, *khaw-gag';* a prim. root [comp. 2283, 2328]; prop. to *move* in a *circle,* i.e. (spec.) to *march* in a sacred procession, to *observe* a festival; by impl. to be *giddy:*—keep {8x}, . . . feast {3x}, celebrate {1x}, keep a solemn feast {1x}, dancing {1x}, holy day {1x}, reel to and fro {1x}. See: TWOT—602; BDB—290c.

2288. חֲגָו {3x} **chăgâv**, *khag-awv';* from an unused root mean. to *take refuge;* a *rift* in rocks:—cleft {3x}. Syn.: 1233, 5366. See: TWOT—603a; BDB—291c.

2289. חָגוֹר {3x} **châgôwr**, *khaw-gore';* from 2296; *belted:*—girded with {1x},

girdle {2x}, girdles {1x}. Syn.: 73, 232, 247, 2280, 2296. See: TWOT—604b; BDB—292a.

2290. חָגוֹר {6x} chăgôwr, khag-ore'; or

חֲגֹר chăgôr, khag-ore'; and (fem.)

חֲגוֹרָה chăgôwrâh, khag-o-raw'; or

חֲגֹרָה chăgôrâh, khag-o-raw'; from 2296; a belt (for the waist):—girdle {3x}, apron {1x}, armour {1x}, gird {1x}. See: TWOT—604a, 604c; BDB—292a.

2291. חַגִּי {3x} Chaggiy, khag-ghee'; from 2287; festive, Chaggi, an Isr.; also (patron.) a Chaggite, or desc. of the same:—Haggi {2x}, Haggites {1x}. See: BDB—291b.

2292. חַגַּי {11x} Chaggay, khag-gah'-ee; from 2282; festive; Chaggai, a Heb. prophet:—Haggai {11x}. See: BDB—291b, 1092a.

2293. חַגִּיָּה {1x} Chaggiyâh, khag-ghee-yaw'; from 2282 and 3050; festival of Jah; Chaggijah, an Isr.:—Haggiah {1x}. See: BDB—291b.

2294. חַגִּית {5x} Chaggiyîth, khag-gheeth'; fem. of 2291; festive; Chaggith, a wife of David:—Haggith {5x}. See: BDB—291b.

2295. חָגְלָה {4x} Choglâh, khog-law'; of uncert. der.; prob. a partridge; Choglah, an Israelitess:—Hoglah {4x}. Syn.: See also 1031. See: BDB—291c.

2296. חָגַר {43x} châgar, khaw-gar'; a prim. root; to gird on (as a belt, armor, etc.):—gird {31x}, appointed {3x}, gird on {3x}, gird up {2x}, be afraid {1x}, put {1x}, restrain {1x}, on every side {1x}. See: TWOT—604; BDB—291c.

2297. חַד {1x} chad, khad; abridged from 259; one:—one {1x}. See: TWOT—61; BDB—26a, 292b.

2298. חַד {14x} chad (Aram.), khad; corresp. to 2297; as card. one; as art. single; as an ord. first; adv. at once:—one {5x}, first {4x}, a {4x}, together {1x}. See: TWOT—2718; BDB—1079c, 1092a, 1096c.

2299. חַד {4x} chad, khad; from 2300; sharp:—sharp {1x}. See: TWOT—605a; BDB—292b.

2300. חָדַד {6x} châdad, khaw-dad'; a prim. root; to be (caus. make) sharp or (fig.) severe:—be fierce {1x}, sharpen {5x}. See: TWOT—605; BDB—292b, 292c.

2301. חֲדַד {1x} Chădad, khad-ad'; from 2300; fierce; Chadad, an Ishmaelite:—Hadad {1x}. See: BDB—292c.

2302. חָדָה {3x} châdâh, khaw-daw'; a prim. root; to rejoice:—make glad {1x}, be joined {1x}, rejoice {1x}. See: TWOT—607; BDB—292d.

2303. חַדּוּד {1x} chaddûwd, khad-dood'; from 2300; a point:—sharp {1x}. See: TWOT—605b; BDB—292c.

2304. חֶדְוָה {2x} chedvâh, khed-vaw'; from 2302; rejoicing:—gladness {1x}, joy {1x}. See: TWOT—607a; BDB—292d, 1092a.

2305. חֶדְוָה {1x} chedvâh (Aram.), khed-vaw'; corresp. to 2304:—joy {1x}. See: TWOT—2719; BDB—1092a.

2306. חֲדִי {1x} chădiy (Aram.), khad-ee'; corresp. to 2373; a breast:—breast {1x}. See: TWOT—2720; BDB—1092a.

2307. חָדִיד {3x} Châdîyd, khaw-deed'; from 2300; a peak; Chadid, a place in Pal.:—Hadid {3x}. See: BDB—292c.

2308. חָדַל {59x} châdal, khaw-dal'; a prim. root; prop. to be flabby, i.e. (by impl.) desist; (fig.) be lacking or idle:—cease {20x}, forbear {16x}, leave {5x}, left off {5x}, let . . . alone {2x}, forbare {3x}, endeth {1x}, failed {1x}, forborn {1x}, forsake {1x}, rest {1x}, unoccupied {1x}, wanteth {1x}, nontranslated variant {1x}.

Chadal means "to cease, come to an end, desist, forbear, lack." (1) The first occurrence of chadal is in Gen 11:8 where, after man's language was confused, "and they left off to build the city." (2) The basic meaning of chadal is "coming to an end." Thus, Sarah's capacity for childbearing had long since "ceased" before an angel informed her that she was to have a son (Gen 18:11). (3) The Mosaic law made provision for the poor, since they would "never cease out of the land" (Deut 15:11; cf. Mt 26:11). (4) In Ex 14:12 this verb is better translated "let us alone" for the literal "cease from us." Syn.: 988, 1826, 3615, 7606, 7673, 7676. See: TWOT—609; BDB—292d.

2309. חֶדֶל {1x} chedel, kheh'-del; from 2308; rest, i.e. the state of the dead:—world {1x}. The place of rest, cessation, forbearance (Is 38:11). Syn.: 7465, 8398. See: TWOT—609a; BDB—293b.

2310. חָדֵל {3x} châdêl, khaw-dale'; from 2308; vacant, i.e. ceasing or destitute:—he that forbeareth {1x}, frail {1x}, rejected {1x}. See: TWOT—609b; BDB—293b.

2311. חַדְלַי {1x} Chadlay, khad-lah'-ee; from 2309; idle; Chadlai, an Isr.:—Hadlai {1x}. See: BDB—293b.

2312. חֵדֶק {2x} chêdeq, khay'-dek; from an unused root mean. to sting; a

prickly plant:—brier {1x}, thorn {1x}. Syn.: 329, 1303, 2336, 5285, 5544, 5636, 6975, 7898, 8068. See: TWOT—611a; BDB—293b.

2313. חִדֶּקֶל {2x} **Chiddeqel**, *khid-deh'-kel;* prob. of for. or.; the *Chiddekel* (or Tigris) river:—Hiddekel {2x}. See: BDB—293c.

2314. חָדַר {1x} **châdar**, *khaw-dar';* a prim. root; prop. to *inclose* (as a room), i.e. (by anal.) to *beset* (as in a siege):—enter a privy chamber {1x}. See: TWOT—612; BDB—293c.

2315. חֶדֶר **cheder**, *kheh'-der;* from 2314; an *apartment* (usually lit.):—chamber {21x}, inner {4x}, bedchamber + 4296 {3x}, bedchamber + 4904 {3x}, inward parts {2x}, innermost parts {2x}, parlours {1x}, south {1x}, within {1x}. See: TWOT—612a; BDB—293c.

2316. חֲדַר {1x} **Chădar**, *khad-ar';* another form for 2315; *chamber; Chadar,* an Ishmaelite:—Hadar {1x}. See: BDB—293c.

2317. חַדְרָךְ {1x} **Chadrâk**, *khad-rawk';* of uncert. der.; *Chadrak,* a Syrian deity:—Hadrach {1x}. See: BDB—293d.

2318. חָדַשׁ {10x} **châdash**, *khaw-dash';* a prim. root; to *be new;* caus. to *rebuild:*—renew {7x}, repair {3x}. *Chadash* means "to renew." **(1)** This verb occurs in post-Mosaic literature (with the exception of Job 10:17). **(2)** The first appearance of *chadash* in the Bible is in 1 Sa 11:14: "Then said Samuel to the people, Come, and let us go to Gilgal, and renew the kingdom there." Syn: 2319, 2320.See: TWOT—613; BDB—293d.

2319. חָדָשׁ {53x} **châdâsh**, *khaw-dawsh';* from 2318; *new:*—fresh {1x}, new {48x}, new thing {4x}. *Chadash,* the adjective, means "new; renewed." **(1)** *Chadash* means "new" both in the sense of recent or fresh and in the sense of something not previously existing (a new king - Ex 1:8). **(1a)** The first nuance appears in Lev 23:16: "Even unto the morrow after the seventh sabbath shall ye number fifty days; and ye shall offer a new meat offering unto the LORD." **(1b)** The first biblical occurrence of *chadash* (Ex 1:8) demonstrates the second meaning: "Now there arose up a new king over Egypt, which knew not Joseph." **(1b1)** This second nuance occurs in Isaiah's discussion of the future salvation. **(1b2)** For example, in Is 42:10 a new saving act of God will bring forth a new song of praise to Him: "Sing unto the LORD a new song, and his praise from the end of the earth." **(1b3)** The Psalter uses the phrase "a new song" in this sense; a new saving act of God has occurred and a song responding to that act celebrates it. **(1b4)** The "new" is often contrasted to the former: "Be-

hold, the former things are come to pass, and new things do I declare: before they spring forth I tell you of them" (Is 42:9). **(1b5)** Jer 31:31–34 employs this same nuance speaking of the new covenant (cf. Eze 11:19; 18:31).

(2) A unique meaning appears in Lam 3:23, where *chadash* appears to mean "renewed"; just as God's creation is renewed and refreshed, so is His compassion and lovingkindness: "They are new every morning: great is thy faithfulness." This nuance is more closely related to the verb from which this word is derived. Syn: 2318, 2320. See: TWOT—613a; BDB—294a, 1092a.

2320. חֹדֶשׁ {276x} **chôdesh**, *kho'-desh;* from 2318; the *new* moon; by impl. a *month:*—month {254x}, new moon {20x}, monthly {1x}, another {1x}.

Chodesh means "new moon; month." **(1)** The word refers to the day on which the crescent reappears: "So David hid himself in the field: and when the new moon was come, the king sat him down to eat meat" (1 Sa 20:24). **(2)** Is 1:14 uses this word of the feast which occurred on that day: "Your new moons [festivals] and your appointed feasts my soul hateth" (cf. Num 28:14; 29:6). **(3)** *Chodesh* can refer to a "month," or the period from one new moon to another. The sense of a measure of time during which something happens occurs in Gen 38:24: "And it came to pass about three months after, that it was told Judah. . . . " **(4)** In a related nuance the word refers not so much to a measure of time as to a period of time, or a calendar month. These "months" are sometimes named (Ex 13:4) and sometimes numbered (Gen 7:11). Syn: 2318, 2319. See: TWOT—613b; BDB—294b.

2321. חֹדֶשׁ {1x} **Chôdesh**, *kho'-desh;* the same as 2320; *Chodesh,* an Israelitess:—Hodesh {1x}. See: BDB—295a.

2322. חֲדָשָׁה {1x} **Chădâshâh**, *khad-aw-shaw';* fem. of 2319; *new; Chadashah,* a place in Pal.:—Hadashah {1x}. See: BDB—295a.

2323. חֲדָת {1x} **chădath** (Aram.), *khad-ath';* corresp. to 2319; *new:*—new {1x}. See: TWOT—2721; BDB—1092a.

2324. חֲוָא {14x} **chăvâ'** (Aram.), *khav-aw';* corresp. to 2331; to *show:*—shew {14x}. See: BDB—1092b.

2325. חוּב {1x} **chûwb**, *khoob;* also

חָיַב **châyab**, *khaw-yab';* a prim. root; prop. perh. to *tie,* i.e. (fig. and refl.) to *owe,* or (by impl.) to *forfeit:*—make endanger {1x}. See: TWOT—614; BDB—295a.

2326. חוֹב {1x} **chôwb**, *khobe;* from 2325; *debt:*—debtor {1x}. See: TWOT—614a; BDB—295a.

2327. חוֹבָה {1x} **chôwbâh**, *kho-baw';* fem. act. part. of 2247; *hiding* place; *Chobah,* a place in Syria:—Hobah {1x}. See: BDB—295b.

2328. חוּג {1x} **chûwg**, *khoog;* a prim. root [comp. 2287]; to describe a *circle:*—compass {1x}. See: TWOT—615; BDB—295b.

2329. חוּג {3x} **chûwg**, *khoog;* from 2328; a *circle:*—circle {1x}, circuit {1x}, compass {1x}. See: TWOT—615a; BDB—295b.

2330. חוּד {4x} **chûwd**, *khood;* a prim. root; prop. to *tie* a knot, i.e. (fig.) to *propound* a riddle:—put forth {4x}. See: TWOT—616; BDB—295c.

2331. חָוָה {6x} **châvâh**, *khaw-vah';* a prim. root; [comp. 2324, 2421]; prop. to *live;* by impl. (intens.) to *declare* or *show:*—shew {6x}. See: TWOT—618; BDB—296a, 1092b.

2332. חַוָּה {2x} **Chavvâh**, *khav-vaw';* caus. from 2331; *life-giver; Chavvah* (or Eve), the first woman:—Eve {2x}. See: BDB—295c.

2333. חַוָּה {4x} **chavvâh**, *khav-vaw';* prop. the same as 2332 (*life-giving,* i.e. *living-place*); by impl. an encampment or *village:*—(small) town {4x}. See: TWOT—617a; BDB—295d.

2334. חַוּוֹת יָעִיר {3x} **Chavvôwth Yâ‘îyr**, *khav-vothe' yaw-eer';* from the plural of 2333 and a modif. of 3265; *hamlets of Jair,* a region of Pal.:—Bashanhavoth-jair {1x}, Havoth-jair {2x}. See: BDB—295d.

2335. חוֹזַי {1x} **Chôwzay**, *kho-zah'-ee;* from 2374; *visionary; Chozai,* an Isr.:—the seers {1x}. See: BDB—296a, 302c, 302d.

2336. חוֹחַ {11x} **chôwach**, *kho'-akh;* from an unused root appar. mean. to *pierce;* a *thorn;* by anal. a *ring* for the nose:—brambles {1x}, thistle(s) {5x}, thorn(s) {5x}. Syn.: 329, 1303, 2312, 5285, 5544, 5636, 6975, 7898, 8068. See: TWOT—620a, 620b; BDB—296a.

2337. חָוָח {1x} **châvâch**, *khaw-vawkh';* perh. the same as 2336; a *dell* or *crevice* (as if *pierced* in the earth):—thicket {1x}. See: TWOT—620a; BDB—296a.

2338. חוּט {1x} **chûwṭ** (Aram.), *khoot;* corresp. to the root of 2339, perhaps as a denom.; to *string* together, i.e. (fig.) to *repair:*—join {1x}. See: TWOT—2723; BDB—1092b.

2339. חוּט {7x} **chûwṭ**, *khoot;* from an unused root prob. mean. to *sew;* a *string;* by impl. a measuring *tape:*—cord {1x}, fillet {1x}, line {1x}, thread {4x}. See: TWOT—621a; BDB—296c, 1092b.

2340. חִוִּי {25x} **Chivvîy**, *khiv-vee';* perh. from 2333; a *villager;* a *Chivvite,* one of the aboriginal tribes of Pal.:—Hivite {25x}. See: BDB—295d, 296c.

2341. חֲוִילָה {7x} **Chăvîylâh**, *khav-ee-law';* prob. from 2342; *circular; Chavilah,* the name of two or three eastern regions; also perh. of two men:—Havilah {7x}. See: TWOT—622; BDB—296c.

2342. חוּל {62x} **chûwl**, *khool;* or

חִיל **chîyl**, *kheel;* a prim. root; prop. to *twist* or *whirl* (in a circular or spiral manner), i.e. (spec.) to *dance,* to *writhe* in pain (espec. of parturition) or fear; fig. to *wait,* to *pervert:*—pain {6x}, formed {5x}, bring forth {4x}, pained {4x}, tremble {4x}, travail {4x}, dance {2x}, calve {2x}, grieved {2x}, grievous {2x}, wounded {2x}, shake {2x}, misc. {23x} = bear, drive away, fear, great, hope, look, make, rest, shapen, (be) sorrow (-ful), stay, tarry, trust, wait carefully (patiently), See: TWOT—623; BDB—296d, 298c, 313d.

2343. חוּל {2x} **Chûwl**, *khool;* from 2342; a *circle; Chul,* a son of Aram; also the region settled by him:—Hul {2x}. See: BDB—299a.

2344. חוֹל {23x} **chôwl**, *khole;* from 2342; *sand* (as *round* or whirling particles):—sand {23x}. See: TWOT—623a; BDB—297c.

2345. חוּם {4x} **chûwm**, *khoom;* from an unused root mean. to *be warm,* i.e. (by impl.) *sunburnt* or *swarthy* (blackish):—brown {4x}. See: TWOT—625a; BDB—299b.

2346. חוֹמָה {133x} **chôwmâh**, *kho-maw';* fem. act. part. of an unused root appar. mean. to *join;* a *wall* of protection:—wall {131x}, walled {2x}.

Chowmah means "wall." **(1)** Its first occurrence is in Ex 14:22: "And the children of Israel went into the midst of the sea upon the dry ground: and the waters were a wall unto them on their right hand, and on their left." **(2)** It is rare in the Pentateuch, in the historical books, and in the poetical books. The most frequent use is in Nehemiah, where Nehemiah is in charge of the rebuilding of the "wall" of Jerusalem. **(3)** The primary meaning of *chowmah* is a "wall" around a city, since in ancient Israel people had to protect themselves by constructing such a well-fortified "wall" (cf. Lev 25:29-30). **(3a)** Stones were used in the construction of the "wall": "Now Tobiah the Ammonite was by him, and he said, Even that which they

build, if a fox go up, he shall even break down their stone wall" (Neh 4:3). **(3b)** The "wall" was also strengthened by thickness and other devices.

(3c) From Solomonic times double walls (casemate) served a strategic purpose in that they were easy to construct and could be filled in with rocks and dirt in the case of a siege. **(3d)** There was also another possibility during a siege: "And the city was broken up, and all the men of war fled by night by the way of the gate between two walls, which is by the king's garden: (now the Chaldees were against the city round about:)" (2 Kin 25:4). **(4)** In the case of war the enemy besieged a city and made efforts to breach the "wall" with a battering ram. **(4a)** The goal was to force a breach wide enough for the troops to enter into the city; "And Jehoash king of Israel took Amaziah king of Judah, the son of Jehoash the son of Ahaziah, at Beth-shemesh, and came to Jerusalem, and brake down the wall of Jerusalem from the gate of Ephraim unto the corner gate, four hundred cubits [about six hundred feet]" (2 Kin 14:13).

(4b) At the time of Nebuchadnezzar's invasion and victory over Jerusalem, he had the "walls" of the city demolished: "And they burnt the house of God, and brake down the wall of Jerusalem, and burnt all the palaces thereof with fire, and destroyed all the goodly vessels thereof" (2 Chr 36:19). **(4c)** For this reason Nehemiah had to help his unsuccessful compatriots to rebuild the "wall" about 135 years later: "Then said I unto them, Ye see the distress that we are in, how Jerusalem lieth waste, and the gates thereof are burned with fire: come, and let us build up the wall of Jerusalem, that we be no more a reproach" (Neh 2:17). **(5)** *Chowmah* also referred to any "wall," whether around buildings or parts of the city such as the temple precincts: "And behold a wall on the outside of the house round about, and in the man's hand a measuring reed of six cubits long by the cubit and a handbreadth: so he measured the breadth of the building, one reed; and the height, one reed" (Eze 40:5). See: TWOT—674c; BDB—299b, 327b.

2347. סוּח {24x} **chûwç**, *khoos;* a prim. root; prop. to *cover,* i.e. (fig.) to *compassionate:*—pity {7x}, regard {1x}, spare {16x}. See: TWOT—626; BDB—299b.

2348. חוֹף {7x} **chôwph**, *khofe;* from an unused root mean. to *cover;* a *cove* (as a *sheltered* bay):—haven {2x}, shore {2x}, coast {2x}, side {1x}. See: TWOT—710a; BDB—299c, 342b.

2349. חוּפָם {1x} **Chûwphâm**, *khoo-fawm';* from the same as 2348; *protec-*

tion: Chupham, an Isr.:—Hupham {1x}. See: BDB—299c.

2350. חוּפָמִי {1x} **Chûwphâmîy**, *khoo-faw-mee';* patron. from 2349; a *Chuphamite* or desc. of Chupham:—Huphamites {1x}. See: BDB—299c.

2351. חוּץ {164x} **chûwts**, *khoots;* or (short.)

חֻץ **chûts**, *khoots;* (both forms fem. in the plur.) from an unused root mean. to *sever;* prop. *separate* by a wall, i.e. *outside, outdoors:*—without {70x}, street {44x}, abroad {21x}, out {17x}, outside {2x}, fields {2x}, forth {2x}, highways {1x}, Kirjathhuzoth + 7155 {1x}, more {1x}, out of {1x}, outward {1x}, utter {1x}.

(1) *Chuts,* as a noun, means "street." **(1a)** A particular use of *chuts* denotes the place outside the houses in a city, or the "street." **(1a1)** The "street" was the place for setting up bazaars: "The cities, which my father took from thy father, I will restore; and thou shalt make streets for thee in Damascus, as my father made in Samaria" (1 Kin 20:34). **(1a2)** Craftsmen plied their trade on certain "streets" named after the guild—for example, the Bakers' Street: "Then Zedekiah the king commanded that they should commit Jeremiah into the court of the prison, and that they should give him daily a piece of bread out of the bakers' street, until all the bread in the city were spent" (Jer 37:21). **(1a3)** The absence of justice in the marketplace was an indication of the wickedness of the whole population of Jerusalem. Jeremiah was called to check in the "streets" to find an honest man: "Run ye to and fro through the streets of Jerusalem, and see now, and know, and seek in the broad places thereof, if ye can find a man, if there be any that executeth judgment, that seeketh the truth; and I will pardon it" (Jer 5:1). **(1b)** Other descriptions of the "streets" are given by the prophets. **(1b1)** Several mention that the "streets" were muddy: ". . . And to tread them down like the mire of the streets" (Is 10:6; cf. Mic 7:10; Zec 10:5). **(1b2)** Others make reference to the blood (Eze 28:23), **(1b3)** the famished (Lam 2:19), and **(1b4)** the dead (Nah 3:10) which filled the "streets" in times of war. **(1c)** The area outside a city was also known as the *chuts.* In this case it is better translated as "open country" or "field"; cf. "That our garners may be full, affording all manner of store, that sheep may bring forth thousands and ten thousands in our streets" (Ps 144:13; cf. Job 5:10; Prov 8:26). **(2)** *Chuts,* as an adverb, means "outside." **(2a)** The first occurrence of this word is in Gen 6:14: "Make thee an ark of gopher wood; rooms shalt thou make in the ark, and shalt pitch it within and without [*chuts*] with pitch." **(2b)** By *chuts* the general idea of "the outside"

is intimated. **(2b1)** "Thou shalt have a place also without the camp, whither thou shalt go forth abroad" (Deut 23:12). **(2b2)** The area could be "outside" a home, tent, city, or camp— hence the adverbial usage of "outside." **(2c)** The word is also connected with a preposition with the sense of "in, to, on, toward the outside": "If he rise again, and walk abroad upon his staff, then shall he that smote him be quit: only he shall pay for the loss of his time, and shall cause him to be thoroughly healed" (Ex 21:19). See: TWOT—627a; BDB—299c.

חֹק **chôwq.** See 2436.

חֻקֹּק **Chûwqôq.** See 2712.

2352. חֻר **chûwr,** *khoor;* or (short.)

חֻר **chûr,** *khoor;* from an unused root prob. mean. to *bore;* the *crevice* of a serpent; the *cell* of a prison:—hole {2x}. See: TWOT—758b; BDB—301b, 351a, 359d.

2353. חֻר **chûwr,** *khoor;* from 2357; *white* linen:—white {2x}. See: TWOT— 630a; BDB—301a.

2354. חֻר **Chûwr,** *khoor;* the same as 2353 or 2352; *Chur,* the name of four Isr. and one Midianite:—Hur {15x}. See: BDB—301a.

2355. חֹר **chôwr,** *khore;* the same as 2353; *white* linen:—network {1x}. Syn.: comp. 2715. See: TWOT—630a; BDB—301a.

2356. חֹר **chôwr,** *khore;* or (short.)

חֹר **chôr,** *khore;* the same as 2352; a *cavity, socket, den:*—cave {1x}, hole {6x}. See: TWOT—758a; BDB—351a, 359d.

2357. חָוַר **châvar,** *khaw-var';* a prim. root; to *blanch* (as with shame):— wax pale {1x}. See: TWOT—630; BDB—301a, 1092c.

2358. חִוָּר **chivvâr** (Aram.), *khiv-vawr';* from a root corresp. to 2357; *white:*—white {1x}. See: TWOT—2724; BDB—1092c.

חוֹרוֹן **Chôwrôwn.** See 1032.

חוֹרִי **chôwrîy.** See 2753.

2359. חוּרִי **Chûwrîy,** *khoo-ree';* prob. from 2353; *linen*-worker; *Churi,* an Isr.:—Huri {1x}. See: BDB—301b.

2360. חוּרַי **Chûwray,** *khoo-rah'ee;* prob. an orth. var. for 2359; *Churai,* an Isr.:—Hurai {1x}. See: BDB—213b. 301b.

2361. חוּרָם **Chûwrâm,** *khoo-rawm';* prob. from 2353; *whiteness,* i.e. noble; *Churam,* the name of an Isr. and two Syrians:—

Huram {13x}. Syn.: comp. 2438. See: BDB—27c, 301b.

2362. חַוְרָן **Chavrân,** *khav-rawn';* appar. from 2357 (in the sense of 2352); *cavernous; Chavran,* a region E. of the Jordan:—Hauran {1x}. See: BDB—301c.

2363. חוּשׁ **chûwsh,** *koosh;* a prim. root; to *hurry;* fig. to *be eager* with excitement or enjoyment:—make haste {19x}, ready {1x}. Syn.: 926, 4116. See: TWOT—631; BDB—301c, 301d.

2364. חוּשָׁה **Chûwshâh,** *khoo-shaw';* from 2363; *haste; Chushah,* an Isr.:— Hushah {1x}. See: BDB—302a.

2365. חוּשַׁי **Chûwshay,** *khoo-shah'-ee;* from 2363; *hasty; Chushai,* an Isr.:—Hushai {14x}. See: BDB—302a.

2366. חוּשִׁים **Chûwshîym,** *khoo-sheem';* or

חֻשִׁים **Chûshîym,** *khoo-sheem';* or

חֻשִׁם **Chûshîm,** *khoo-shim';* plur. from 2363; *hasters; Chushim,* the name of three Isr.:—Hushim {4x}. See: BDB—302a, 364d.

2367. חוּשָׁם **Chûwshâm,** *khoo-shawm';* or

חֻשָׁם **Chûshâm,** *khoo-shawm';* from 2363; *hastily; Chusham,* an Idumæan:—Husham {4x}. See: BDB—302a, 364d.

2368. חוֹתָם **chôwthâm,** *kho-thawm';* or

חֹתָם **chôthâm,** *kho-thawm';* from 2856; a *signature*-ring:—seal {5x}, signet {9x}. See: TWOT—780a; BDB—302a, 368a.

2369. חוֹתָם **Chôwthâm,** *kho-thawm';* the same as 2368; *seal; Chotham,* the name of two Isr.:—Hotham {1x}, Hothan {1x}. See: BDB—302a, 368b.

2370. חֲזָא **chăzâ'** (Aram.), *khaz-aw';* or

חֲזָה **chăzâh** (Aram.), *khaz-aw';* corresp. to 2372; to *gaze* upon; ment. to *dream, be usual* (i.e. *seem*):—see {17x}, saw + 1934 {6x}, beheld + 1934 {5x}, had {1x}, wont {1x}, beheld {1x}. See: TWOT—2725; BDB—1092c.

2371. חֲזָאֵל **Chăzâ'êl,** *khaz-aw-ale';* or

חֲזָהֵאל **Chăzâh'êl,** *khaz-aw-ale';* from 2372 and 410; *God has seen; Chazaël,* a king of Syria:—Hazael {28x}. See: BDB—302a, 303c.

2372. חָזָה **châzâh,** *khaw-zaw';* a prim. root; to *gaze* at; ment. to *perceive, contemplate* (with pleasure); spec. to *have a*

vision of:—see {38x}, behold {7x}, look {3x}, prophesy {2x}, provide {1x}.

Chazah, as a verb, means "to see, behold, select for oneself." It means **(1)** "to see or behold" in general (Prov 22:29), **(2)** "to see" in a prophetic vision (Num 24:4), and **(3)** "to select for oneself" (Ex 18:21—the first occurrence of the word). **(4)** In Lam 2:14 the word means "to see" in relation to prophets' visions: "Thy prophets have seen vain and foolish things for thee: and they have not discovered thine iniquity." Syn: 2377, 2384. See: TWOT—633; BDB—302a, 1092d.

2373. חָזֶה {13x} **châzeh**, *khaw-zeh';* from 2372; the *breast* (as most *seen* in front):—breast {13x}. Syn.: 1717, 2306, 7699. See: TWOT—634a; BDB—303d, 1092a.

2374. חֹזֶה {19x} **chôzeh**, *kho-zeh';* act. part. of 2372; a *beholder* in vision; also a *compact* (as *looked upon* with approval):—agreement {1x}, prophet {1x}, see that {3x}, seer {16x}, stargazer {1x}.

One who sees a vision, not with the eye of sense but with the spiritual and intellectual faculties. Usually found in passages that refer to visions vouchsafed by God. Syn.: 5030. See: TWOT—633; BDB—302c.

חֲזָהאֵל **Chăzâh᾽êl**. See 2371.

2375. חֲזוֹ {1x} **Chăzow**, *khaz-o';* from 2372; *seer; Chazo*, a nephew of Abraham:—Hazo {1x}. See: BDB—303d.

2376. חֵזֶו {13x} **chêzev** (Aram.), *khay'-zev;* from 2370; a *sight:*—look {1x}, vision {12x}. See: BDB—1092c.

2377. חָזוֹן {35x} **châzôwn**, *khaw-zone';* from 2372; a *sight* (ment.), i.e. a *dream, revelation,* or *oracle:*—vision {35x}.

Chazown means "vision." **(1)** None of the 35 appearances of this word appear before First Samuel, and most of them are in the prophetic books. **(2)** Chazown almost always signifies a means of divine revelation. **(2a)** First, it refers to the means itself, to a prophetic "vision" by which divine messages are communicated: "The days are prolonged, and every vision faileth" (Eze 12:22). **(2b)** Second, this word represents the message received by prophetic "vision": "Where there is no vision, the people perish: but he that keepeth the law, happy is he" (Prov 29:18). **(2c)** Finally, chazown can represent the entirety of a prophetic or prophet's message as it is written down: "The vision of Isaiah the son of Amoz . . ." (Is 1:1). **(2d)** Thus the word inseparably related to the content of a divine communication focuses on the means by which that message is received: "And the word of the LORD was precious in those days;

there was no open vision" (1 Sa 3:1—the first occurrence of the word). **(3)** In Is 29:7 this word signifies a non-prophetic dream. Syn: 2372, 2384. See: TWOT—633a; BDB—302d.

2378. חָזוֹת {1x} **châzôwth**, *khaw-zooth';* from 2372; a *revelation:*—vision {1x}. See: TWOT—633c; BDB—303a.

2379. חָזוֹת {2x} **chăzôwth** (Aram.), *khaz-oth';* from 2370; a *view:*—sight {2x}. See: TWOT—2725b; 1092d; BDB—1092d.

2380. חָזוּת {4x} **châzûwth**, *khaw-zooth';* from 2372; a *look;* hence, (fig.) striking *appearance, revelation,* or (by impl.) *compact:*—agreement {1x}, notable one {1x}, vision {2x}. See: TWOT—633d; BDB—303a.

2381. חֲזִיאֵל {1x} **Chăzîy᾽êl**, *khaz-ee-ale';* from 2372 and 410; *seen of God; Chaziel*, a Levite:—Haziel {1x}. See: BDB—303c.

2382. חֲזָיָה {1x} **Chăzâyâh**, *khaz-aw-yaw';* from 2372 and 3050; *Jah has seen; Chazajah*, an Isr.:—Hazaiah {1x}. See: BDB—303c.

2383. חֶזְיוֹן {1x} **Chezyôwn**, *khez-yone';* from 2372; *vision; Chezjon*, a Syrian:—Hezion {1x}. See: BDB—303c.

2384. חִזָּיוֹן {9x} **chizzâyôwn**, *khiz-zaw-yone';* from 2372; a *revelation*, espec. by *dream:*—vision {9x}.

Chizzayown means "vision." This noun, which occurs 9 times, refers **(1)** to a prophetic "vision" in Joel 2:28: "And it shall come to pass afterward, that I will pour out my spirit upon all flesh; and your sons and your daughters shall prophesy, your old men shall dream dreams, your young men shall see visions." Chizzayown refers **(2)** to divine communication in 2 Sa 7:17 (the first biblical occurrence) and **(3)** to an ordinary dream in Job 4:13. Syn: 2372, 2377. See: TWOT—633e; BDB—303b.

2385. חֲזִיז {3x} **chăzîyz**, *khaw-zeez';* from an unused root mean. to *glare;* a *flash* of lightning:—bright cloud {1x}, lightning {2x}. See: TWOT—635a; BDB—304a.

2386. חֲזִיר {7x} **chăzîyr**, *khaz-eer';* from an unused root prob. mean. to *inclose;* a *hog* (perh. as *penned*):—boar {1x}, swine {1x}. See: TWOT—637a; BDB—306b.

2387. חֵזִיר {2x} **Chêzîyr**, *khay-zeer';* from the same as 2386; perh. *protected; Chezir*, the name of two Isr.:—Hezir {2x}. See: BDB—306c.

2388. חָזַק {290x} **châzaq**, *khaw-zak';* a prim. root; to *fasten* upon; hence, to *seize, be strong* (fig. *courageous,* caus.

strengthen, cure, help, repair, fortify), obstinate; to *bind, restrain, conquer:*—strong {48x}, repair {47x}, hold {37x}, strengthened {28x}, strengthen {14x}, harden {13x}, prevail {10x}, encourage {9x}, take {9x}, courage {8x}, caught {5x}, stronger {5x}, hold {5x}, misc. {52x} = aid, amend, X calker, catch, cleave, confirm, be constant, constrain, continue, be established, fasten, force, fortify, help, lean, maintain, play the man, mend, become (wax) mighty, be recovered, retain, seize, be (wax) sore, be stout, be sure, be urgent, behave self valiantly, withstand.

Chazaq, as a verb, means "to be strong, strengthen, harden, take hold of." **(1)** The word first occurs in Gen 41:56: ". . . And the famine waxed sore in the land of Egypt." **(2)** In reference to Pharaoh, it means to brace up and strengthen and points to the hardihood with which he set himself to act in defiance against God and closed all the avenues to his heart to those signs and wonders which Moses wrought. **(2a)** Pharoah was responsible for his hard heart. Four times we read: "Pharaoh's heart was hardened" (Ex 7:13, 22; 8:19; 9:35). **(2b)** He hardened it. In Ex 9:34 Pharaoh's responsibility is made clear by the statement "he sinned yet more, and hardened his heart. . . ." **(2c)** God hardened it. The strong form of the verb is used in Ex 4:21: "I will harden his [Pharaoh's] heart." This statement is found 8 times.

(3) In the sense of personal strength *chazaq* is first used in Deut 11:8 in the context of the covenant: **(3a)** "Therefore shall ye keep all the commandments which I command you this day, that ye may be strong, and go in and possess the land." **(3b)** Moses was commanded to "charge Joshua, and encourage him" (Deut 3:28). **(3c)** The covenant promise accompanies the injunction to "be strong and of a good courage": ". . . For the LORD thy God, he it is that doth go with thee; he will not fail thee, nor forsake thee" (Deut 31:6). **(3d)** The same encouragement was given to the returned captives as they renewed the work of rebuilding the temple (Zec 8:9; 13; cf. Hag 2:4). **(4)** If in the above examples there is moral strength combined with physical, the latter is the sense of Judg 1:28: **(4a)** "And it came to pass, when Israel was strong, that they put the Canaanites to [forced labor]." **(4b)** Israel sinned and the Lord "strengthened Eglon the king of Moab against Israel" (Judg 3:12).

(5) The word is used in reference **(5a)** to a building: "The priests had not repaired the breaches of the house" (2 Kin 12:6), or **(5b)** to a city: "Moreover Uzziah built towers in Jerusalem . . . and fortified them" (2 Chr 26:9). **(6)** In battle *chazaq* means: "So David prevailed over the Philistine . . ." (1 Sa 17:50). **(7)** As the

prophet said, "For the eyes of the LORD run to and fro throughout the whole earth to show himself strong in the behalf of them whose heart is perfect toward him" (2 Chr 16:9). **(8)** To His Servant, the Messiah, **(8a)** God said: "I . . . will hold thine hand" (Is 42:6); and to **(8b)** Cyrus He said: ". . . Whose right hand I have holden . . ." (Is 45:1). **(9)** Other noteworthy uses of the word are: **(9a)** "Thou shalt relieve him [a poor Israelite] . . ." (Lev 25:35); and **(9b)** "[Saul] laid hold upon the skirt of his mantle, and it rent" (1 Sa 15:27). **(10)** In summary, **(10a)** this word group describes the physical and moral strength of man and society. **(10b)** God communicates strength to men, even to the enemies of His people as chastisement for His own. **(10c)** Men may turn their strength into stubbornness against God. See: TWOT—636; BDB—304a.

2389. חָזָק {56x} **châzâq,** *khaw-zawk';* from 2388; *strong* (usually in a bad sense, *hard, bold, violent*):—strong {26x}, mighty {20x}, sore {3x}, stronger {2x}, harder {1x}, hottest {1x}, impudent {1x}, loud {1x}, stiffhearted {1x}.

Chazaq, as an adjective, means "strong; mighty; heavy; severe; firm; hard." **(1)** First, the word means "firm" or "hard" in the sense that something is impenetrable. **(1a)** In Eze 3:8–9 the prophet's face is compared to rock; **(1b)** God has made him determined to his task just as Israel is determined not to listen to him: "Behold, I have made thy face [hard] against their faces, and thy forehead [hard] against their foreheads. As an adamant harder than flint have I made thy forehead." **(1c)** Job 37:18 uses *chazaq* of molten solidified metal. **(2)** Second, this word means "strong." In its basic meaning it refers to physical strength. God's hand (an anthropomorphism; cf. Deut 4:15, 19) as a symbol of His effecting His will among men is "strong": "And I am sure that the king of Egypt will not let you go, no, not by a mighty hand" (Ex 3:19—the first biblical occurrence). **(2a)** This word modifies a noun, specifying that it is the opposite of weak, or unable to effect anything (Num 13:18). **(2b)** Isaiah speaks of God's "sore and great and strong sword" (27:1). **(2c)** When Ezekiel wrote of "fat and strong" animals, he probably meant that they were well fed and healthy (34:16). **(3)** Third, *chazaq* means "heavy." **(3a)** When applied to a battle or war, it describes the event(s) as severe (1 Sa 14:52). **(3b)** The word is also used to indicate **(3b1)** a severe sickness (1 Kin 17:17) and **(3b2)** famine (1 Kin 18:2). See: TWOT—636a; BDB—305c.

2390. חָזֵק {3x} **châzêq,** *khaw-zake';* from 2388; *powerful:*—X wax louder {1x},

stronger {2x}. See: TWOT—636a; BDB—304a, 395d.

2391. חֵזֶק {1x} **chêzeq**, *khay'-zek;* from 2388; *help:*—strength {1x}. Syn.: 2392, 2482, 3581, 5797. See: TWOT—636b; BDB—305d.

2392. חֹזֶק {5x} **chôzeq**, *kho'-zek;* from 2388; *power:*—strength {5x}. See: TWOT—636c; BDB—305d.

2393. חֶזְקָה {5x} **chezqâh**, *khez-kaw';* fem. of 2391; *prevailing power:*—strengthen self {1x}, strength {2x}, (was) strong {2x}. See: TWOT—636b; BDB—395d.

2394. חָזְקָה {6x} **chozqâh**, *khoz-kaw';* fem. of 2392; *vehemence* (usually in a bad sense):—force {2x}, mightily {2x}, repair {1x}, sharply {1x}. See: TWOT—636d; BDB—306a.

2395. חִזְקִי {1x} **Chizqîy**, *khiz-kee';* from 2388; *strong; Chizki,* an Isr.:—Hezeki {1x}. See: BDB—306a.

2396. חִזְקִיָּה {87x} **Chizqîyâh**, *khiz-kee-yaw';* or

חִזְקִיָּהוּ **Chizqîyâhûw**, *khiz-kee-yaw'-hoo;* also

יְחִזְקִיָּה **Y°chizqîyâh**, *yekh-iz-kee-yaw';* or

יְחִזְקִיָּהוּ **Y°chizqîyâhûw**, *yekh-iz-kee-yaw'-hoo;* from 2388 and 3050; *strengthened of Jah; Chizkijah,* a king of Judah, also the name of two other Isr.:—Hezekiah {85x}, Hizkiah {1x}, Hizkijah {1x}. Syn.: comp. 3169. See: BDB—306a.

2397. חָח {8x} **châch**, *khawkh;* once (Eze 29:4)

חָחִי **châchîy**, *khakh-ee';* from the same as 2336; a *ring* for the nose (or lips):—bracelet {1x}, chain {2x}, hook {5x}. See: TWOT—620b; BDB—296b, 306c.

חָחִי **châchîy**. See 2397.

2398. חָטָא {238x} **châtâᵓ**, *khaw-taw';* a prim. root; prop. to *miss;* hence, (fig. and gen.) to *sin;* by infer. to *forfeit, lack, expiate, repent,* (caus.) *lead astray, condemn:*—sin {188x}, purify {11x}, cleanse {8x}, sinner {8x}, committed {6x}, offended {4x}, blame {2x}, done {2x}, fault {1x}, harm {1x}, loss {1x}, miss {1x}, offender {1x}, purge {1x}, reconciliation {1x}, sinful {1x}, trespass {1x}.

Chata' means sin; sin-guilt; sin purification; sin offering. *Chata',* as a verb, means "to miss, sin, be guilty, forfeit, purify." **(1)** The basic nuance of *chata'* is sin conceived as missing the road or mark; illustrated in Judg 20:16: **(1a)** "There were 700 left-handed Benjamite soldiers who "could sling stones at a hair

breadth, and not miss." **(1b)** The meaning is extended in Prov 19:2: "He who makes haste with his feet sinneth." **(1c)** The intensive form is used in Gen 31:39: "That which was torn of beasts I brought not unto thee; I bare the loss of it." **(2)** From this basic meaning comes the word's chief usage to indicate moral failure toward both God and men, and certain results of such wrongs. **(2a)** The first occurrence of the verb is in Gen 20:6, God's word to Abimelech after he had taken Sarah: "Yea, I know that thou didst this in the integrity of thy heart; for I also withheld thee from sinning against me: therefore suffered I thee not to touch her. (cf. Gen 39:9). **(2b)** Sin against God is defined in Josh 7:11: "Israel hath sinned, and they have also transgressed my covenant which I commanded them." **(2c)** Also note Lev 4:27: "And if any one of the common people sin through ignorance, while he doeth somewhat against any of the commandments of the Lord concerning things which ought not to be done, and be guilty."

(3) The verb may also refer to the result of wrongdoing, as in Gen 43:9: ". . . Then let me bear the blame for ever." **(4)** Deut 24:1–4, after forbidding adulterous marriage practices, concludes: ". . . For that is abomination before the LORD: and thou shalt not cause the land to sin." **(5)** Similarly, those who pervert justice are described as "those who by a word make a man out to be guilty" (Is 29:21). **(6)** This leads to the meaning in Lev 9:15: **(6a)** "And he . . . took the goat . . . and slew it, and offered it for sin." **(6b)** The effect of the offerings for sin is described in Ps 51:7: "Purge me with hyssop, and I shall be clean" (cf. Num 19:1–13). **(7)** Another effect is seen in the word of the prophet to evil Babylon: "You have sinned against your life" (Hab. 2:10). **(8)** The word is used concerning acts committed against men, as in **(8a)** Gen 42:22: "Spake I not unto you, saying, Do not sin against the child . . . ?" and **(8b)** 1 Sa 19:4: "Do not let the king sin against his servant David, since he has not sinned against you."

(9) Men are **(9a)** to turn from sin - a path/life-style, or act deviating from God's direction (1 Kin 8:35), **(9b)** to depart from sin (2 Kin 10:31), **(9c)** be concerned about it (Ps 38:18), and **(9d)** confess it (Num 5:7). **(10)** It also connotes the guilt or condition of sin (Gen 18:20), **(11)** means purification from sin (Num 8:7; 9:9), **(12)** the sin offering (Lev 4:1–5:13; 6:24–30) for **(12a)** some specific sin **(12b)** committed unwittingly, **(12c)** without intending to do it and **(12d)** perhaps even without knowing it at the time (Lev. 4:2; 5:15). Syn.: 205, 817, 599, 2403, 5674, 5771, 6588, 7451, 7563. See: TWOT—638; BDB—306c.

Hebrew

2399. חֵטְא {33x} **chêtᵓ**, *khate;* from 2398; a *crime* or its *penalty:*—faults {1x}, × grievously {1x}, offences {1x}, (punishment of) sin {30x}.

(1) This word means "sin" in the sense of missing the mark or the path. **(1a)** This may be sin against either a man (Gen 41:9—the first occurrence of the word) or **(1b)** God (Deut 9:18). **(2)** Second, it connotes the "guilt" of such an act (Num 27:3). The psalmist confessed that his mother was in the condition of sin and guilt (cf. Rom 5:12) when he was conceived (Ps 51:5). See: TWOT—638a; BDB—307d, 1092d.

2400. חַטָּא {18x} **chaṭṭâᵓ**, *khat-taw';* intens. from 2398; a *criminal,* or one accounted *guilty:*—offender {1x}, sinful {1x}, sinner {16x}.

(1) The noun *chatta',* with the form reserved for those who are typified with the characteristic represented by the root, is used both as an adjective (emphatic) and as a noun. **(2)** The word occurs 18 times. **(3)** Men are described as "sinners" (1 Sa 15:18) and as those who are liable to the penalty of an offense (1 Kin 1:21). **(4)** The first occurrence of the word is in Gen 13:13: "But the men of Sodom were wicked and sinners before the Lord exceedingly." See: TWOT—638b; 308b.

2401. חֲטָאָה {8x} **chăṭâᵓâh**, *khat-aw-aw';* fem. of 2399; an *offence,* or a *sacrifice* for it:—sin offering {1x}, sin {7x}. See: TWOT—638d; BDB—308b.

2402. חֲטָאָה {1x} **chaṭṭâᵓâh** (Aram.), *khat-taw-aw';* corresp. to 2401; an *offence,* and the *penalty* or *sacrifice* for it:—sin (offering) {1x}. See: TWOT—2726b; BDB—308b.

2403. חַטָּאָה {296x} **chaṭṭâᵓâh**, *khat-taw-aw';* or

חַטָּאת **chaṭṭâᵓth**, *khat-tawth';* from 2398; an *offence* (sometimes habitual *sinfulness*), and its penalty, occasion, sacrifice, or expiation; also (concr.) an *offender:*—sin {182x}, sin offering {116x}, punishment {3x}, purification for sin {2x}, purifying {1x}, sinful {1x}, sinner {1x}.

Chatta'th, as a noun, means "sin; sin-guilt; sin purification; sin offering." **(1)** The basic nuance of this word is "sin" conceived as missing the road or mark (155 times). **(2)** *Chatta'th* can refer to an offense against a man: "And Jacob was wroth, and chode with Laban: and Jacob answered and said to Laban, What is my trespass [6588 – *peshaᶜ*]? what is my sin, that thou hast so hotly pursued after me?" (Gen 31:36). **(2a)** It is such passages which prove that *chatta'th* is not simply a general word for "sin"; **(2b)** since Jacob used two different words, he

probably intended two different nuances. **(3)** For the most part this word represents a sin against God (Lev 4:14). **(3a)** Men are to return from "sin," which is a path, a life-style, or act deviating from that which God has marked out (1 Kin 8:35). **(3b)** They should depart from "sin" (2 Kin 10:31), **(3c)** be concerned about it (Ps 38:18), and **(3d)** confess it (Num 5:7). **(4)** The noun first appears in Gen 4:7, where Cain is warned that "sin lieth at the door." **(4a)** This citation may introduce a second nuance of the word—"sin" in general. **(4b)** Certainly such an emphasis appears in Ps 25:7, where the noun represents rebellious sin (usually indicated by *pêshaᶜ* - 6588): "Remember not the sins of my youth, nor my transgressions." **(5)** In a few passages the term connotes the guilt or condition of sin: "The cry of Sodom and Gomorrah is great, and . . . their sin is very grievous" (Gen 18:20). **(6)** The word means "purification from sin" in two passages: "And thus shalt thou do unto them, to cleanse them: Sprinkle water of purifying upon them" (Num 8:7; cf. 19:9). **(7)** *Chatta'th* means "sin offering" (135 times). **(7a)** The law of the "sin offering" is recorded in Lev 4- 5:13; 6:24–30. **(7b)** This was an offering for some specific "sin" committed unwittingly, without intending to do it and perhaps even without knowing it at the time (Lev 4:2; 5:15). **(7c)** Finally, several passages use this word for the idea of "punishment for sin" (Lev 20:20). Syn.: 801, 817, 2077, 4503, 5071, 5258, 5930, 6452, 7133, 8002, 8573. See: TWOT—638e; BDB—303b, 310d, 1092d.

2404. חָטַב {9x} **châtab**, *khaw-tab';* a prim. root; to *chop* or *carve* wood:—cut down {1x}, hew {1x}, hewer {1x}, hewers {5x}, polished {1x}. See: TWOT—639; BDB—310a.

2405. חֲטֻבָה {1x} **chătûbâh**, *khat-oo-baw';* fem. pass. part. of 2404; prop. a *carving;* hence, a *tapestry* (as figured):—carved {1x}. See: TWOT—640a; 310b; BDB—310b.

2406. חִטָּה {30x} **chittâh**, *khit-taw';* of uncert. der.; *wheat,* whether the grain or the plant:—wheat {29x}, wheaten {1x}. See: TWOT—691b; BDB—310b, 334d, 1093b.

2407. חַטּוּשׁ {5x} **Chaṭṭûwsh**, *khat-toosh';* from an unused root of uncert. signif.; *Chattush,* the name of four or five Isr.:—Hattush {5x}. See: BDB—310d.

2408. חֲטִי {1x} **chătîy** (Aram.), *khat-ee';* from a root corresp. to 2398; an *offence:*—sin {1x}. See: TWOT—2726a; BDB—1092d.

2409. חֲטָאָה {1x} **chaṭṭâyâᵓ** (Aram.), *khat-taw-yaw';* from the same as 2408; an

expiation:—sin offering {1x}. See: TWOT—2726b; BDB—1092d.

2410. חֲטִיטָא {2x} **Chătîyta**ɔ, *khat-ee-taw';* from an unused root appar. mean. to *dig* out; *explorer; Chatita,* a temple porter:—Hatita {2x}. See: BDB—310b.

2411. חַטִּיל {2x} **Chaṭṭîyl**, *khat-teel';* from an unused root appar. mean. to *wave; fluctuating; Chattil,* one of "Solomon's servants":—Hattil {2x}. See: BDB—310b.

2412. חֲטִיפָא {2x} **Chătîyphâ**ɔ, *khat-ee-faw';* from 2414; *robber; Chatipha,* one of the Nethinim:—Hatipha {1x}. See: BDB—310c.

2413. חָטַם {1x} **châtam**, *khaw-tam';* a prim. root; to *stop:*—refrain {1x}. Syn.: 2820. See: TWOT—641; BDB—310c.

2414. חָטַף {3x} **châtaph**, *khaw-taf';* a prim. root; to *clutch;* hence, to *seize* as a prisoner:—catch {3x}. Syn.: 3920. See: TWOT—642; BDB—310c.

2415. חֹטֶר {2x} **chôter**, *kho'-ter;* from an unused root of uncert. signif.; a *twig:*—rod {2x}. Syn.: 4294, 4731, 7626. See: TWOT—643a; BDB—310d.

2416. חַי {501x} **chay**, *khah'-ee;* from 2421; *alive;* hence, *raw* (flesh); *fresh* (plant, water, year), *strong;* also (as noun, espec. in the fem. sing. and masc. plur.) *life* (or living thing), whether lit. or fig.:—live {197x}, life {144x}, beast {76x}, alive {31x}, creature {15x}, running {7x}, living thing {6x}, raw {6x}, misc. {19x} = + age, appetite, company, congregation, maintenance, + merry, multitude, + (be) old, quick, springing, troop.

Chay, in its **(1) masculine noun form,** means "living thing; life." **(1a)** The use of this word occurs only in the oath formula "as X lives," literally, "by the life of X": "And he said, They were my brethren, even the sons of my mother: as the LORD liveth, if ye had saved them alive, I would not slay you" (Judg 8:19). **(1b)** This formula summons the power of a superior to sanction the statement asserted. **(1b1)** In Judg 8:19 God is the witness to Gideon's pledge to kill his enemies and this statement that they brought the penalty on themselves. **(1b2)** A similar use appears in Gen 42:15 except that the power summoned is Pharaoh's: "Hereby ye shall be proved: By the life of Pharaoh ye shall not go forth hence, except your youngest brother come hither." **(1bc)** In 1 Sa 1:26 Hannah employs a similar phrase summoning Eli himself to attest the truthfulness of her statement: "And she said, Oh my lord, as thy soul liveth, my lord, I am the woman that stood by thee here, praying unto the LORD." **(1c)** Only

God swears by His own power: "And the Lord said, I have pardoned according to thy word: But as truly as I live, all the earth shall be filled with the glory of the Lord" (Num 14:20–21).

(2) The **feminine form of the word,** *chayyah,* means "living being" and is especially used of animals. **(2a)** When so used, it usually distinguishes wild and undomesticated from domesticated animals; the word connotes that the animals described are untamed: **(2a1)** "And God remembered Noah, and every living thing, and all the cattle that was with him in the ark" (Gen 8:1). **(2a2)** Job 37:8 uses *chayyah* of rapacious beasts: "Then the beasts go into dens, and remain in their places." **(2a3)** This same word may also connote "evil beast": "Come now therefore, and let us slay him, and cast him into some pit, and we will say, Some evil beast hath devoured him" (Gen 37:20). **(2b)** In another nuance the word describes land animals as distinct from birds and fish: "Be fruitful, and multiply, and replenish the earth, and subdue it: and have dominion over the fish of the sea, and over the fowl of the air, and over every living thing that moveth upon the earth" (Gen 1:28). **(2c)** Infrequently *chayyah* represents a domesticated animal: "And the cities shall they have to dwell in; and the suburbs of them shall be for their cattle, and for their goods, and for all their beasts" (Num 35:3). **(2d)** Sometimes this word is used of "living beings" in general: "Also out of the midst thereof came the likeness of four living creatures: (Eze 1:5). In such passages the word is synonymous with the Hebrew word *nepesh* (5315).

(3) The **masculine plural of the noun** *chay, chayyim,* is a general word for the state of living as opposed to that of death. **(3a)** This meaning is in Deut 30:15: **(3a1)** "See, I have set before thee this day life and good, and death and evil." **(3a2)** Notice also Gen 27:46: "And Rebekah said to Isaac, I am weary of my life because of the daughters of Heth." **(3b)** In a second nuance the plural signifies "lifetime," or the days of one's life: ". . . And dust shalt thou eat all the days of thy life" (Gen 3:14). **(3c)** The phrase "the years of one's life" represents the same idea: "And Sarah was a hundred and seven and twenty years old: these were the years of the life of Sarah" (Gen 23:1). **(3d)** The "breath of life" in Gen 2:7 is the breath that brings "life": "And the LORD God formed man of the dust of the ground, and breathed into his nostrils the breath of life; and man became a living soul" (cf. Gen 6:17). **(3e)** The "tree of life" is the tree which gives one eternal, everlasting "life." Therefore, it is the tree whose fruit brings "life": "And out of the ground made the LORD God to grow every tree that is pleasant to the sight, and good for food; the tree of

life also in the midst of the garden . . ." (Gen 2:9). **(3f)** In another nuance this word suggests a special quality of "life," life as a special gift from God (a gift of salvation): "I call heaven and earth to record this day against you, that I have set before you life and death, blessing and cursing: therefore choose life, that both thou and thy seed may live" (Deut 30:19). **(3g)** The plural of the word can represent "persons who are alive," or living persons: "And he stood between the dead and the living; and the plague was stayed" (Num 16:48).

(4) *Chay,* as **a masculine adjective,** means "alive; living." **(4a)** Used adjectivally it modifies men, animals, and God, but never plants. **(4a1)** In Gen 2:7 the word used with the noun *nepesh* (5315 - "soul, person, being") means a "living" person: "And the Lord God formed man of the dust of the ground, and breathed into his nostrils the breath of life; and man became a living soul." **(4a2)** The same two words are used in Gen 1:21 but with a slightly different meaning: "And God created . . . every living creature that moveth, which the waters brought forth abundantly, after their kind." Here a living *nepesh* ("creature") is an animal.

(4b) Deut 5:26 refers to God as the "living" God, distinguishing Him from the lifeless gods/idols of the heathen. **(4c)** In a related nuance *chay* describes flesh (animal meat or human flesh) under the skin, or "raw flesh." **(4c1)** In Lev 13:10 one reads that leprosy involved seeing quick (alive), raw (*chay*) flesh: "And the priest shall see him: and, behold, if the rising be white in the skin, and it have turned the hair white, and there be quick raw flesh in the rising. . . ." **(4c2)** The same words (*bashar chay*) are applied to dead, raw (skinned) animal flesh: "Give flesh to roast for the priest; for he will not have [boiled] flesh of thee, but raw" (1 Sa 2:15). **(4d)** Applied to liquids, *chay* means "running"; it is used metaphorically describing something that moves: "And Isaac's servants digged in the valley, and found there a well of springing water" (Gen 26:19). **(4e)** The Song of Solomon uses the word in a figure of speech describing one's wife; she is "a well of living waters" (4:15). The emphasis is not on the fact that the water flows but on its freshness; it is not stagnant, and therefore is refreshing and pleasant when consumed.

Chay, as a **masculine adjective,** means alive/living and modifies **(1)** man **(1a)** as man (Gen 2:7), or **(1b)** his flesh (Lev 13:10); **(2)** God (Deut 5:26); or **(3)** animals (1 Sa 2:15). **(4)** Applied to liquids, *chay* means running, being used metaphorically to describe something that moves: **(4a)** a well of springing water (Gen 26:19); **(4b)** living, life-giving waters (Jer 2:13; 17:3; Zec 14:8); **(4c)** one's wife; "a well of living wa-

ters" (Song 4:15). The emphasis is not on the fact that the water flows but on its freshness; it is not stagnant, and therefore is refreshing and pleasant when consumed. The **feminine** form, *chayyah,* means "living being" and is especially used of animals: **(1)** wild, untamed, undomesticated (Gen 8:1); **(1a)** rapacious beasts (Job 37:8); **(1b)** evil beasts (Gen 37:20); **(1c)** land animals as distinct from birds and fish (Gen 1:28). Infrequently *chayyah* represents

(2) a domesticated animal (Num 35:3). **(3)** Sometimes this word is used of living beings in general (Eze 1:5). The **masculine plural** of *chay, chayyim,* is a general word for **(1)** the state of living as opposed to that of death (Deut 30:15; Gen 27:46) and **(2)** signifies lifetime, or the days of one's life or the years of one's life (Gen 3:14; 23:1). **(3)** The "breath of life" (Gen 2:7; 6:17) is the breath that brings life. **(4)** The "tree of life" is the tree that gives one eternal, everlasting life (Gen 2:9). **(5)** This word also suggests a special quality of life, life as a special gift from God (a gift of salvation - Deut 30:19). **(6)** The plural can represent alive or living persons (Num 16:48). See: TWOT—644a; BDB—310d, 311d, 312c, 312d, 313a, 1092d.

2417. חַי {7x} **chay** (Aram.), *khah'-ee;* from 2418; *alive;* also (as noun in plur.) *life:*—life {2x}, that liveth {1x}, living {4x}. See: TWOT—2727a; BDB—1092d.

2418. חֲיָא {6x} **chăyâ** (Aram.), *khah-yaw';* or

חֲיָה **chăyâh** (Aram.), *khah-yaw';* corresp. to 2421; to *live:*—live {5x}, keep alive {1x}. See: TWOT—2727; BDB—1092d.

2419. חִיאֵל {1x} **Chîyʼêl,** *khee-ale';* from 2416 and 410; *living of God; Chiel,* an Isr.:—Hiel {1x}. See: BDB—27d, 310d, 313c.

חָיַב **châyab.** See 2325.

2420. חִידָה {17x} **chîydâh,** *khee-daw';* from 2330; a *puzzle,* hence, a *trick, conundrum, sententious maxim:*—riddle {9x}, dark sayings {3x}, hard question {2x}, dark sentence {1x}, proverb {1x}, dark speech {1x}. See: TWOT—616a; BDB—295b, 310d.

2421. חָיָה {262x} **châyâh,** *khaw-yaw';* a prim. root [comp. 2331, 2421]; to *live,* whether lit. or fig.; caus. to *revive:*—keep (leave, make) alive, ✕ certainly, give (promise) life, (let, suffer to) live, nourish up, preserve (alive), quicken, recover, repair, restore (to life), revive, (✕ God) save (alive, life, lives), ✕ surely, be whole.

Chayah means "to live." **(1)** In the ground stem this verb connotes "having life": **(1a)** "And Adam lived a hundred and thirty years . . ." (Gen 5:3). **(1b)** A similar meaning appears in

Num 14:38 and Josh 9:21. **(2)** The intensive form of *chayah* means "to preserve alive": "Two of every sort shalt thou bring into the ark, to keep them alive with thee" (Gen 6:19). **(3)** This word may also mean "to bring to life" or "to cause to live": "I dwell . . . with him also that is of a contrite and humble spirit, to revive the spirit of the humble, and to revive the heart of the contrite ones" (Is 57:15). **(4)** "To live" is more than physical existence. **(4a)** According to Deut 8:3, "man doth not live by bread only, but by every word that proceedeth out of the mouth of the LORD doth man live." **(4a)** Moses said to Israel: "Love the LORD thy God . . . that thou mayest live and multiply" (Deut 30:16). See: TWOT—644; BDB—295c, 310d, 1092d.

2422. חָיֶה {1x} **châyeh**, *khaw-yeh';* from 2421; *vigorous:*—lively {1x}. See: TWOT—644e; BDB—313a.

2423. חֵיוָא {20x} **chêyvâ'** (Aram.), *khay-vaw';* from 2418; an *animal:*—beast {20x}. See: TWOT—2727b; BDB—1092d.

2424. חָיוּת {1x} **chayûwth**, *khah-yooth';* from 2421; *life:*—× living {1x}. See: TWOT—644g; BDB—313c.

2425. חָיַי {23x} **châyay**, *khaw-yah'-ee;* a prim. root [comp. 2421]; to *live;* caus. to *revive:*—live {21x}, save life {2x}. See: TWOT—644; BDB—310d.

2426. חֵיל {10x} **chêyl**, *khale;* or (short.)

חֵל **chêl**, *khale;* a collat. form of 2428; an *army;* also (by anal.) an *intrenchment:*—wall {2x}, rampart {2x}, host {2x}, trench {1x}, poor {1x}, bulwark {1x}, army {1x}. See: TWOT—623d; BDB—298a, 313d, 315d.

חִיל **chîyl**. See 2342.

2427. חִיל {6x} **chîyl**, *kheel;* and (fem.)

חִילָה **chîylâh**, *khee-law';* from 2342; a *throe* (espec. of childbirth):—pain {3x}, pang {2x}, sorrow {1x}. Syn.: 2342, 2479. See: TWOT—623b; 297d, 313d.

2428. חַיִל {243x} **chayil**, *khah'-yil;* from 2342; prob. a *force,* whether of men, means or other resources; an *army, wealth, virtue, valor, strength:*—army {56x}, man of valour {37x}, host {29x}, forces {14x}, valiant {13x}, strength {12x}, riches {11x}, wealth {10x}, power {9x}, substance {8x}, might {6x}, strong {5x}, misc. {33x} = able, activity, band of men (soldiers), company, goods, train, virtuous (-ly), war, worthy (-ily).

Chayil means strength; power; wealth; property; capable; valiant; army; troops; influential; upper-class people (courtiers). **(1)** First, this word signifies a faculty or "power," the ability to effect or produce something. **(1a)** The word is used of physical "strength" in the sense of power that can be exerted: "If the iron be blunt, and he do not whet the edge, then must he put to more strength" (Eccl 10:10). **(1b)** Quite often this word appears in a military context. Here it is the physical strength, power, and ability to perform in battle that is in view. This idea is used of men in 1 Sa 2:4: "The bows of the mighty men are broken, and they that stumbled are girded with strength" (cf. Ps 18:32, 39). **(1c)** Ps 33:17 applies the word to a war horse. **(1d)** An interesting use of *chayil* appears in Num 24:17–18, where Balaam prophesied the destruction of Moab and Edom at the hands of Israel: "And Edom shall be a possession, Seir also shall be a possession for his enemies; and Israel shall do valiantly" (v. 18). The idea here is dynamic; something is happening. **(1e)** One might also render this phrase: "Israel performs mightily." This translation of the word is somewhat inexact; a noun is translated as an adverb.

(2) Second, *chayil* means "wealth, property." **(2a)** This nuance of the word focuses on that which demonstrates one's ability, his wealth or goods; Levi, Simeon, and their cohorts attacked the Shechemites: "And all their wealth, and all their little ones, and their wives took they captive, and spoiled even all that was in the home" (Gen 34:29—the first biblical occurrence of the word). **(2b)** In Num 31:9 *chayil* includes all the possessions of the Midianites except the women, children, cattle, and flocks. Thus it seems to be a little narrower in meaning. **(2c)** When this nuance is used with the Hebrew word "to do or make," the resulting phrase means "to become wealthy or make wealth" (cf. Deut 8:18; Ruth 4:11). **(2d)** This is in marked contrast to the emphasis of the same construction in Num. 24:18. Joel 2:22 uses *chayil* in the sense of "wealth" or products of the ability of a tree to produce fruit.

(3) Third, several passages use the word in the sense of "able." **(3a)** In Gen 47:6 the ability to do a job well is in view. Pharaoh told Joseph: "The land of Egypt is before thee; in the best of the land make thy father and brethren to dwell; in the land of Goshen let them dwell: and if thou knowest any men of activity [capable men] among them, then make them rulers over my cattle." **(3b)** This word can also represent the domestic skills of a woman—Ruth is described as a woman of ability and, therefore, either potentially or actually a good wife (Ruth 3:11; Prov 12:4). **(3c)** When applied to men, *chayil* sometimes focuses on their ability to conduct themselves well in battle as well as being loyal to their commanders (1 Sa 14:52; 1 Kin 1:42). When used in such contexts, the word may be translated "valiant": "And there

was sore war against the Philistines all the days of Saul: and when Saul saw any strong man, or any valiant man, he took him unto him" (1 Sa 14:52; cf. Num 24:18; 1 Sa 14:48). **(4)** Fourth, this word sometimes means "army"; "And I will harden Pharaoh's heart, that he shall follow after them; and I will be honored upon Pharaoh, and upon all his host [army]" (Ex 14:4). **(4a)** The word can also refer to the army as troops in the sense of a combination of a lot of individuals. **(4b)** Under such an idea the word can represent the members of an army distributed to perform certain functions. Jehoshaphat "placed forces in all the fenced cities of Judah, and set garrisons in the land of Judah . . ." (2 Chr 17:2). **(4c)** This is also the emphasis in 1 Kin 15:20: "Ben-hadad . . . sent the captains of the hosts which he had against the cities of Israel." **(5)** Fifth, *chayil* sometimes represents the "upper class," who, as in all feudal systems, were at once soldiers, wealthy, and influential; **(5a)** Sanballat "spake before his brethren and the army of Samaria," i.e., in the royal court (Neh 4:2). **(5b)** The Queen of Sheba was accompanied by a large escort of upperclass people from her homeland: "And she came to Jerusalem with a very great train" (1 Kin 10:2). Syn.: 2426. See: TWOT—624a; BDB—298c, 313d, 1093a.

2429. חַיִל {7x} **chayil** (Aram.), *khah'-yil;* corresp. to 2428; an *army,* or *strength:*—aloud {3x}, army {2x}, power {1x}, most {1x}. See: TWOT—2728; BDB—1093a.

2430. חֵילָה {1x} **chêylâh,** *khay-law';* fem. of 2428; an *intrenchment:*—bulwark {1x}. See: TWOT—623e; BDB—298a.

2431. חֵילָם {2x} **Chêylâm,** *khay-lawm';* or

חֵלָאם **Chêlâ'm,** *khay-lawm';* from 2428; *fortress; Chelam,* a place E. of Pal.:—Helam {2x}. See: BDB—298a, 313d, 316a.

2432. חִילֵן {1x} **Chîylên,** *khee-lane';* from 2428; *fortress; Chilen,* a place in Pal.:—Hilen {1x}. See: BDB—298b.

2433. חִין {1x} **chîyn,** *kheen;* another form for 2580; *beauty:*—comely {1x}. See: TWOT—694c; BDB—313d, 336d.

2434. חַיִץ {1x} **chayits,** *khah'-yits;* another form for 2351; a *wall:*—wall {1x}. Syn.: 1444, 1447, 2346, 3796, 7791. See: TWOT—628a; BDB—300c, 313d.

2435. חִיצוֹן {25x} **chîytsôwn,** *khee-tsone';* from 2434; prop. the (outer) *wall side;* hence, *exterior;* fig. *secular* (as opposed to sacred):—utter {12x}, outward {7x}, without {5x}, outer {1x}. See: TWOT—627b; BDB—300b, 313d.

2436. חֵיק {39x} **chêyq,** *khake;* or

חֵק **chêq,** *khake;* and

חוֹק **chôwq,** *khoke;* from an unused root, appar. mean. to *inclose;* the bosom (lit. or fig.):—bosom {32x}, bottom {3x}, lap {1x}, midst {1x}, within {1x}, variant {1x}.

Cheq means "bosom; lap; base." **(1)** The word represents the "outer front of one's body" where beloved ones, infants, and animals are pressed closely: "Have I conceived all this people? have I begotten them, that thou shouldest say unto me, Carry them in thy bosom, as a nursing father beareth the sucking child" (Num 11:12). **(2)** In its first biblical appearance, *cheq* is used of a man's "bosom": "And Sarai said unto Abram, My wrong be upon thee: I have given my maid into thy bosom; and when she saw that she had conceived, I was despised in her eyes" (Gen 16:5). **(3)** The "husband of one's bosom" is **(3a)** a husband who is "held close to one's heart" or "cherished" (Deut 28:56). **(3b)** This figurative inward sense appears again in Ps 35:13: "My prayer returned into mine own bosom" (cf. Job 19:27). **(3c)** In 1 Kin 22:35, the word means the "inside" or "heart" of a war chariot.

(4) *Cheq* represents a fold of one's garment above the belt where things are hidden: "And the Lord said furthermore unto him [Moses], Put now thine hand into thy bosom" (Ex 4:6). **(5)** This word is rendered as "lap": **(5a)** "The lot is cast into the lap; but the whole disposing thereof is of the LORD" (Prov 16:33). **(5b)** Yet "bosom" may be used, even where "lap" is clearly intended: "But the poor man had nothing, save one little ewe lamb, which he had bought and nourished up: and it grew up together with him, and with his children; it did eat of his own meat, and drank of his own cup, and lay in his bosom" (2 Sa 12:3). **(6)** Finally, *cheq* means the "base of the altar," as described in Eze 43:13 (cf. Eze 43:17). Syn.: 2243, 2683, 6747. See: TWOT—629a; BDB—300c, 313d, 348d.

2437. חִירָה {2x} **Chîyrâh,** *khee-raw';* from 2357 in the sense of *splendor; Chirah,* an Adullamite:—Hirah {2x}. See: BDB—301b, 313d.

2438. חִירָם {24x} **Chîyrâm,** *khee-rawm';* or

חִירֹם **Chîyrôm,** *khee-rome';* another form of 2361; *Chiram* or *Chirom,* the name of two Tyrians:—Hiram {23x}, Huram {1x}. See: BDB—27c, 313d.

2439. חִישׁ {1x} **chîysh,** *kheesh;* another form of 2363; to *hurry:*—make haste {1x}. Syn.: 926, 2363, 2648, 4116. See: TWOT—631; BDB—301c.

2440. חִישׁ {1x} **chîysh**, *kheesh;* from 2439; prop. a *hurry;* hence, (adv.) *quickly:*— soon {1x}. Syn.: 4116. See: TWOT—631a; BDB—301d.

2441. חֵךְ {15x} **chêk**, *khake;* prob. from 2596 in the sense of *tasting;* prop. the *palate* or inside of the mouth; hence, the *mouth* itself (as the organ of speech, taste and kissing):—roof of the mouth {5x}, mouth {9x}, taste {1x}. See: TWOT—692a; BDB—313d, 335a.

2442. חָכָה {14x} **châkâh**, *khaw-kaw';* a prim. root [appar. akin to 2707 through the idea of *piercing*]; prop. to *adhere* to; hence, to *await:*—long {1x}, tarry {2x}, wait {11x}. See: TWOT—645; BDB—314a.

2443. חַכָּה {3x} **chakkâh**, *khak-kaw';* prob. from 2442; a *hook* (as *adhering*):— angle {2x}, hook {1x}. Syn.: 2053, 8240. See: TWOT—693c; BDB—341a, 335c.

2444. חֲכִילָה {3x} **Chakîylâh**, *khak-ee-law';* from the same as 2447; *dark; Chakilah,* a hill in Pal.:—Hachilah {3x}. See: BDB—314b.

2445. חַכִּים {14x} **chakkîym** (Aram.), *khak-keem';* from a root corresp. to 2449; *wise,* i.e. a *Magian:*—wise {14x}. See: TWOT—2729a; BDB—1093a.

2446. חֲכַלְיָה {2x} **Chăkalyâh**, *khak-al-yaw';* from the base of 2447 and 3050; *darkness* (of) *Jah; Chakaljah,* an Isr.:—Hachaliah {2x}. See: BDB—314b.

2447. חַכְלִיל {1x} **chaklîyl**, *khak-leel';* by redupl. from an unused root appar. mean. to *be dark;* darkly *flashing* (only of the eyes); in a good sense, *brilliant* (as stimulated by wine):—red {1x}. Syn.: 119, 122, 132, 2448. See: TWOT—646a; BDB—314b.

2448. חַכְלִלוּת {1x} **chaklîlûwth**, *khak-lee-looth';* from 2447; *flash* (of the eyes); in a bad sense, *blearedness:*—redness {1x}. See: TWOT—646b; BDB—314b.

2449. חָכַם {27x} **châkam**, *khaw-kam';* a prim. root, to *be wise* (in mind, word or act):—wise {19x}, wiser {4x}, wisely {2x}, teach wisdom {1x}, exceeding {1x}.

Chakam means "to be wise, act wisely, make wise, show oneself wise." **(1)** The word means "to be wise" in Prov 23:15: "My son, if thine heart be wise, my heart shall rejoice, even mine." **(2)** In Ps 119:98 *chakam* means "to make wise": "Thou through thy commandments hast made me wiser than mine enemies: for they are ever with me." **(3)** This word represents the discernment of good and evil, prudence in secular matters, skill in arts, and experience in Divine things. **(4)** It is moral rather than intel-lectual; it is the adaptation of what we know to what we have (and ought) to do. Syn.: 995, 2450, 2454, 7919. See: TWOT—647; BDB—314b.

2450. חָכָם {137x} **châkâm**, *khaw-kawm';* from 2449; *wise,* (i.e. intelligent, skillful or artful):—wise {109x}, wise man {13x}, cunning {6x}, cunning men {4x}, subtil {1x}, unwise {2x}, wiser {2x}.

Chakam, the adjective, means "wise; skillful; practical." **(1)** This word plus the noun *chakemah* and the verb "to be wise" signify an important element of the Old Testament religious point of view. **(1a)** Religious experience was not a routine, a ritual, or faith experience. **(1b)** It was viewed as a mastery of the art of living in accordance with God's expectations. **(1c)** In their definition, the words "mastery" and "art" signify that wisdom was a process of attainment and not an accomplishment. **(2)** *Chakam* appears 132 times in the Hebrew Old Testament and occurs most frequently in Job, Proverbs, and Ecclesiastes, for which reason these books are known as "wisdom literature." **(3)** The first occurrence of *chakam* is in Gen 41:8: "And it came to pass in the morning that his spirit was troubled; and he sent and called for all the magicians of Egypt, and all the wise men thereof: and Pharaoh told them his dream; but there was none that could interpret them unto Pharaoh."

(4) The *chakam* in secular usage signified a man who was a "skillful" craftsman. **(4a)** The manufacturers of the objects belonging to the tabernacle were known to be wise, or experienced in their crafts (Ex 36:4). **(4b)** Even the man who was skillful in making idols was recognized as a craftsman (Is 40:20; cf. Jer 10:9). **(4c)** The reason for this is to be found in the man's skill, craftsmanship, and not in the object which was being manufactured. **(4d)** Those who were experienced in life were known as "wise," but their wisdom is not to be confused with the religious usage. **(4e)** Cleverness and shrewdness characterized this type of wisdom. **(4e1)** Amnon consulted Jonadab, who was known as a shrewd man (2 Sa 13:3), and followed his plan of seducing his sister Tamar. **(4e2)** Joab hired a "wise" woman to make David change his mind about Absalom (2 Sa 14:2).

(5) Based on the characterization of wisdom as a skill, a class of counselors known as "wise men" arose. **(5a)** They were to be found in Egypt (Gen 41:8), in Babylon (Jer 50:35), in Tyre (Eze 27:9), in Edom (Obad 8), and in Israel. **(5b)** In pagan cultures the "wise" man practiced magic and divination: **(5b1)** "Then Pharaoh also called the wise men and the sorcerers: now the magicians of Egypt, they also did in like manner with their enchantments" (Ex 7:11); and **(5b2)** ". . . that frustrateth the tokens of the

liars, and maketh diviners mad; that turneth wise men backward, and maketh their knowledge foolish" (Is 44:25). **(6)** The religious sense of *chakam* excludes delusion, craftiness, shrewdness, and magic. **(6a)** God is the source of wisdom, as He is "wise": "Yet he also is wise, and will bring evil, and will not call back his words: but will arise against the house of the evildoers, and against the help of them that work iniquity" (Is 31:2).

(6b) The man or woman who, fearing God, lives in accordance with what God expects and what is expected of him in a God-fearing society is viewed as an integrated person. **(6c)** He is "wise" in that his manner of life projects the fear of God and the blessing of God rests upon him. **(6d)** Even as the craftsman is said to be skillful in his trade, the Old Testament *chakam* was learning and applying wisdom to every situation in life, and the degree in which he succeeded was a barometer of his progress on the road of wisdom. **(7)** The opposite of the *chakam* is the "fool" or wicked person, who stubbornly refuses counsel and depends on his own understanding: "For the turning away of the simple shall slay them, and the prosperity of fools shall destroy them" (Prov 1:32; cf. Deut 32:5–6; Prov 3:35). See: TWOT—647b; BDB—314c, 1093a.

2451. חָכְמָה {149x} **chokmâh**, *khok-maw';* from 2449; *wisdom* (in a good sense):—wisdom {145x}, wisely {2x}, skilful man {1x}, wits {1x}.

Chokmah, the noun, means "wisdom; experience; shrewdness." **(1)** Like *chakam,* most occurrences of this word are in Job, Proverbs, and Ecclesiastes. **(1a)** The *chakam* seeks after *chokmah,* "wisdom." **(1b)** Like *chakam,* the word *chokmah* can refer to technical skills or special abilities in fashioning something. **(1c)** The first occurrence of *chokmah* is in Ex 28:3: "And thou shalt speak unto all that are wisehearted, whom I have filled with the spirit of wisdom, that they may make Aaron's garments to consecrate him, that he may minister unto me in the priest's office." **(1c1)** This first occurrence of the word in the Hebrew Bible bears this out as well as the description of the workers on the tabernacle. **(1c2)** The artisan was considered to be endowed with special abilities given to him by God: "And he hath filled him with the spirit of God, in wisdom, in understanding, and in knowledge, and in all manner of workmanship" (Ex 35:31).

(2) *Chokmah* is the knowledge and the ability to make the right choices at the opportune time. **(2a)** The consistency of making the right choice is an indication of maturity and development. **(2b)** The prerequisite for "wisdom" is the fear of the Lord: "The fear of the Lord is

the beginning of knowledge: but fools despise wisdom and instruction" (Prov 1:7). **(2c)** "Wisdom" is viewed as crying out for disciples who will do everything to pursue her (Prov 1:20). **(2d)** The person who seeks *chokmah* diligently **(2d1)** will receive understanding: "For the LORD giveth wisdom: out of his mouth cometh knowledge and understanding" (Prov 2:6); **(2d2)** he will benefit in his life by walking with God: "That thou mayest walk in the way of good men, and keep the paths of the righteous" (Prov 2:20). **(3)** The advantages of "wisdom" are many: "For length of days, and long life, and peace, shall they add to thee. Let not mercy and truth forsake thee: bind them about thy neck; write them upon the table of thine heart: so shalt thou find favor and good understanding in the sight of God and man" (Prov 3:2–4).

(4) The prerequisite is a desire to follow and imitate God as He has revealed Himself in Jesus Christ, without self-reliance and especially not in a spirit of pride: "A wise man will hear, and will increase learning; and a man of understanding shall attain unto wise counsels: to understand a proverb, and the interpretation; the words of the wise, and their dark sayings. The fear of the Lord is the beginning of knowledge: but fools despise wisdom and instruction" (Prov 1:5–7). **(5)** The fruits of *chokmah* are many, and the Book of Proverbs describes the characters of the *chakam* and *chokmah.* **(6)** In New Testament terms the fruits of "wisdom" are the same as the fruits of the Holy Spirit; cf. **(6a)** "But the fruit of the Spirit is love, joy, peace, long-suffering, gentleness, goodness, faith, meekness, temperance: against such there is no law" (Gal. 5:22–23); **(6b)** "But the wisdom that is from above is first pure, then peaceable, gentle, and easy to be entreated, full of mercy and good fruits, without partiality, and without hypocrisy. And the fruit of righteousness is sown in peace of them that make peace" (Jas 3:17–18).

(7) The importance of "wisdom" explains **(7a)** why books were written about it. **(7b)** Songs were composed in celebration of "wisdom" (Job 28). **(7c)** Even "wisdom" is personified in Proverbs. **(7c1)** *Chokmah* as a person stands for that divine perfection of "wisdom" which is manifest in God's creative acts. **(7c2)** As a divine perfection it is visible in God's creative acts: "Doth not wisdom cry: and understanding put forth her voice? . . . I wisdom dwell with prudence, and find out knowledge of witty inventions. . . . The LORD possessed me in the beginning of his way, before his works of old. . . . Then I was by him, as one brought up with him: and I was daily his delight, rejoicing always before him. . . . Now therefore hearken unto me, O ye children: for blessed are they

that keep my ways" (Prov 8:1, 12, 22, 30, 32). See: TWOT—647a; BDB—315b.

2452. חָכְמָה {8x} **chokmâh** (Aram.), *khok-maw';* corresp. to 2451; *wisdom:*—wisdom {8x}. See: TWOT—2729b; BDB—1093a.

2453. חַכְמוֹנִי {2x} **Chakmôwnîy**, *khak-mo-nee';* from 2449; *skilful; Chakmoni*, an Isr.:—Hachmoni {1x}, Hachmonite {1x}. See: BDB—315d.

2454. חָכְמוֹת {5x} **chokmôwth**, *khok-mōth';* or

חַכְמוֹת **chakmôwth**, *khak-mōth';* collat. forms of 2451; *wisdom:*—wisdom {4x}, every wise [woman] {1x}. See: TWOT—647a; BDB—315b.

חֵל **chêl**. See 2426.

2455. חֹל {7x} **chôl**, *khole;* from 2490; prop. *exposed;* hence, *profane:*—common {2x}, profane {2x}, profane place {2x}, unholy {1x}.

Chol is that which is devoted to ordinary use in contrast to a sanctified, holy use. See: TWOT—623a, 661a; BDB—315d, 320d.

2456. חָלָא {1x} **châlâ'**, *khaw-law';* a prim. root [comp. 2470]; to *be sick:*—be diseased {1x}. See: TWOT—648; BDB—316a.

2457. חֶלְאָה {5x} **chel'âh**, *khel-aw';* from 2456; prop. *disease;* hence, *rust:*—scum {5x}. See: TWOT—649a; BDB—316a.

2458. חֶלְאָה {2x} **Chel'âh**, *khel-aw';* the same as 2457; *Chelah*, an Israelitess:—Helah {2x}. See: BDB—316a.

2459. חֶלֶב {92x} **cheleb**, *kheh'-leb;* or

חֵלֶב **chêleb**, *khay'-leb;* from an unused root mean. to *be fat; fat*, whether lit. or fig.; hence, the *richest* or *choice* part:—fat {79x}, fatness {4x}, best {5x}, finest {2x}, grease {1x}, marrow {1x}. See: TWOT—651a; BDB—316d.

2460. חֵלֶב {1x} **Chêleb**, *khay'-leb;* the same as 2459; *fatness; Cheleb*, an Isr.:—Heleb {1x}. See: BDB—317a.

2461. חָלָב {44x} **châlâb**, *khaw-lawb';* from the same as 2459; *milk* (as the *richness* of kine):—+ cheese {1x}, milk {42x}, sucking {1x}. See: TWOT—650a; BDB—316b.

2462. חֶלְבָּה {1x} **Chelbâh**, *khel-baw';* fem. of 2459; *fertility: Chelbah*, a place in Pal.:—Helbah {1x}. See: BDB—317a.

2463. חֶלְבּוֹן {1x} **Chelbôwn**, *khel-bone';* from 2459; *fruitful; Chelbon*, a place in Syria:—Helbon {1x}. See: BDB—317a.

2464. חֶלְבְּנָה {1x} **chelb°nâh**, *khel-ben-aw';* from 2459; *galbanam*, an odorous gum (as if *fatty*):—galbanum {1x}. See: TWOT—652; BDB—317b.

2465. חֶלֶד {5x} **cheled**, *kheh'-led;* from an unused root appar. mean. to *glide* swiftly; *life* (as a *fleeting* portion of time); hence, the *world* (as *transient*):—age {2x}, short time {1x}, world {2x}. This word stresses the transitory nature of things in this world which pass away. See: TWOT—653a; BDB—317b.

2466. חֵלֶד {1x} **Chêled**, *khay'-led;* the same as 2465; *Cheled*, an Isr.:—Heled {1x}. See: BDB—317c.

2467. חֹלֶד {1x} **chôled**, *kho'-led;* from the same as 2465; a *weasel* (from its *gliding* motion):—weasel {1x}. See: TWOT—654a; BDB—317c.

2468. חֻלְדָּה {2x} **Chuldâh**, *khool-daw';* fem. of 2467; *Chuldah*, an Israelitess:—Huldah {2x}. See: BDB—317c.

2469. חֶלְדַּי {2x} **Chelday**, *khel-dah'-ee;* from 2466; *worldliness; Cheldai*, the name of two Isr.:—Heldai {2x}. See: BDB—317c.

2470. חָלָה {75x} **châlâh**, *khaw-law';* a prim. root [comp. 2342, 2470, 2490]; prop. to *be rubbed* or *worn;* hence, (fig.) to *be weak, sick, afflicted;* or (caus.) to *grieve, make sick;* also to *stroke* (in flattering), *entreat:*—sick {34x}, beseech {6x}, be weak {4x}, grievous {4x}, be diseased {3x}, wounded {3x}, pray {3x}, intreat {3x}, grief {2x}, grieved {2x}, sore {2x}, pain {1x}, infirmity {1x}, intreated {1x}, laid {1x}, prayer {1x}, sorry {1x}, make suit {1x}, supplication {1x}, travail {1x}.

Chalah, as a verb, means "to be sick, weak." **(1)** It is found the first time near the end of the Book of Genesis when Joseph is told: "Behold, thy father is sick" (Gen 48:1). **(2)** A survey of the uses of *chalah* shows that there was a certain lack of precision in many of its uses, and that the context would be the deciding factor in its meaning. **(2a)** When Samson told Delilah that if he were tied up with bowstrings he would "be weak, and be as another man" (Judg 16:7), the verb obviously did not mean "become sick," unless being sick implied being less than normal for Samson. **(2b)** When Joram is described as being sick because of wounds suffered in battle (2 Kin 8:29), perhaps it would be better to say that he was weak. **(2c)** Sacrificial animals that are described as being lame or "sick" (Mal 1:8) are actually imperfect or not acceptable for sacrifice. **(3)** This word is sometimes used in the figurative sense of overexerting oneself, thus becoming "weak." **(3a)** This is seen in Jer 12:13: "They have put themselves

to pain." **(3b)** Song 2:5, "sick of/with love," probably means "weak with passion." See: TWOT—655; BDB—317c, 318c.

2471. חַלָּה {14x} **challâh**, *khal-law';* from 2490; a *cake* (as usually *punctured)*:—cake {14x}. Syn.: 4580, 5692, 6742. See: TWOT—660b; BDB—319c.

2472. חֲלוֹם {65x} **chălôwm**, *khal-ome';* or (short.)

חֲלֹם **chălôm**, *khal-ome';* from 2492; a *dream:*—dream {64x}, dreamer + 1167 {1x}.

Chalom, as a noun, means "dream." **(1)** The word means "dream." It is used of the ordinary dreams of sleep: "Then thou scarest me with dreams, and terrifiest me through visions" (Job 7:14). **(2)** The most significant use of this word, however, is with reference to prophetic "dreams" and/or "visions." **(2a)** Both true and false prophets claimed to communicate with God by these dreams and visions. **(2b)** Perhaps the classical passage using the word in this sense is Deut 13:1ff.: "If there arise among you a prophet, or a dreamer of dreams, and giveth thee a sign or a wonder, and the sign or the wonder come to pass. . . . " **(2c)** This sense, that a dream is a means of revelation, appears in the first biblical occurrence of *chalom:* "But God came to Abimelech in a dream by night" (Gen 20:3). Syn.: 2492. See: TWOT—663a; BDB—321c, 1093a.

2473. חֹלוֹן {3x} **Chôlôwn**, *kho-lone';* or (short.)

חֹלֹן **Chôlôn**, *kho-lone';* prob. from 2344; *sandy; Cholon*, the name of two places in Pal.:—Holon {3x}. See: BDB—298b, 322a.

2474. חַלּוֹן {31x} **challôwn**, *khal-lone';* a *window* (as *perforated)*:—window {31x}. Syn.: 699, 6672. See: TWOT—660c; BDB—319d.

2475. חֲלוֹף {1x} **chălôwph**, *khal-ofe';* from 2498; prop. *surviving;* by impl. (collect.) *orphans:*—destruction {1x}. Syn.: 343, 816, 1104, 1820, 1949, 2254, 2717, 3772, 4288, 5255, 6979, 7665. See: TWOT—666b; BDB—322b.

2476. חֲלוּשָׁה {1x} **chălûwshâh**, *khal-oo-shaw';* fem. pass. part. of 2522; *defeat:*—being overcome {1x}. See: TWOT—671b; BDB—325d.

2477. חֲלַח {3x} **Chălach**, *khal-akh';* prob. of for. or.; *Chalach*, a region of Assyria:—Halah {3x}. See: BDB—318d.

2478. חֲלְחוּל {1x} **Chalchûwl**, *khal-khool';* by redupl. from 2342; *contorted; Chalchul*, a place in Pal.:—Halhul {1x}. See: BDB—319a.

2479. חַלְחָלָה {4x} **chalchâlâh**, *khal-khaw-law';* fem. from the same as 2478; *writhing* (in childbirth); by impl. *terror:*—(great, much) pain {4x}. Syn.: 2342. See: TWOT—623f; BDB—298b, 319a.

2480. חָלַט {1x} **châlat**, *khaw-lat';* a prim. root; to *snatch* at:—catch {1x}. Syn.: 2414, 3920. See: TWOT—658; BDB—319a.

2481. חֲלִי {2x} **chălîy**, *khal-ee';* from 2470; a *trinket* (as *polished)*:—jewel {1x}, ornament {1x}. See: TWOT—657a; BDB—316a, 318d.

2482. חֲלִי {1x} **Chălîy**, *khal-ee';* the same as 2481; *Chali*, a place in Pal.:—Hali {1x}. See: BDB—318d.

2483. חֳלִי {24x} **chŏlîy**, *khol-ee';* from 2470; *malady, anxiety, calamity:*—sickness {12x}, disease {7x}, grief {4x}, sick {1x}.

Choliy means "sickness." **(1)** The use of this word in the description of the Suffering Servant in Is 53:3–4 is rendered "grief." **(2)** The meaning of "sickness" occurs in Deut 7:15: **(2a)** "And the Lord will take away from thee all sickness, and will put none of the evil diseases [4064 - *madweh*] of Egypt." **(2b)** *Choliy* is used metaphorically as a distress of the land in Hos 5:13. Syn.: 4245, 8463. See: TWOT—655a; BDB—318b.

2484. חֶלְיָה {1x} **chelyâh**, *khel-yaw';* fem. of 2481; a *trinket:*—jewel {1x}. See: TWOT—657b; BDB—318d.

2485. חָלִיל {4x} **châlîyl**, *khaw-leel';* from 2490; a *flute* (as *perforated)*:—pipe {4x}. See: TWOT—660d; BDB—319d.

2486. חָלִילָה {21x} **châlîylâh**, *khaw-lee'-law;* or

חָלִלָה **châlîlâh**, *khaw-lee'-law;* a directive from 2490; lit. *for a profaned* thing; used (interj.) *far be it!:*—God forbid {9x}, far be it {4x}, be . . . far {4x}, Lord forbid {3x}, misc. {1x}. See: TWOT—661c; BDB—321a.

2487. חֲלִיפָה {12x} **chălîyphâh**, *khal-ee-faw';* from 2498; *alternation:*—change {11x}, course {1x}. See: TWOT—666c; BDB—322b.

2488. חֲלִיצָה {2x} **chălîytsâh**, *khal-ee-tsaw';* from 2502; *spoil:*—armour {1x}, spoil {1x}. Syn.: 957, 961, 7998. See: TWOT—667a, 668a; BDB—322d.

2489. חֵלְכָא {4x} **chêlᵉkâᵓ**, *khay-lek-aw';* or

חֵלְכָה **chêlᵉkâh**, *khay-lek-aw';* appar. from an unused root prob. mean. to *be dark* or (fig.) *unhappy;* a *wretch*, i.e. *unfortunate:*—poor {2x}, variant {2x}. Syn.: 34,

1800, 1803, 4134, 4270, 4542, 6035. See: TWOT—659a; BDB—319a, 456c.

2490. חָלַל {141x} **châlal**, *khaw-lal';* a prim. root [comp. 2470]; prop. to *bore,* i.e. (by impl.) to *wound,* to *dissolve;* fig. to *profane* (a person, place or thing), to *break* (one's word), to *begin* (as if by an "opening wedge"); denom. (from 2485) to *play* (the flute):—begin {52x}, profane {36x}, pollute {23x}, defile {9x}, break {4x}, wounded {3x}, eat {2x}, slay {2x}, first {1x}, gather grapes {1x}, inheritance {1x}, men began {1x}, piped {1x}, players {1x}, prostitute {1x}, sorrow {1x}, stain {1x}, eat as common things {1x}.

Chalal (2490), means "to pollute, defile, profane, begin." **(1)** The most frequent use of this Hebrew root is in the sense of "to pollute, defile." **(1a)** This may be a ritual defilement, such as that resulting from contact with a dead body (Lev 21:4), or **(1b)** the ceremonial profaning of the sacred altar by the use of tools in order to shape the stones (Ex 20:25). **(1c)** Holy places may be profaned (Eze 7:24); **(1d)** the name of God (Eze 20:9) and **(1e)** even God Himself (Eze 22:26) may be profaned. **(1f)** The word is often used to describe the defilement which results from illicit sexual acts, such as harlotry (Lev 21:9) or violation of one's father's bed (Gen 49:4—the first occurrence). **(2)** In more than 50 instances, this root is used in the sense of "to begin." **(2a)** Perhaps the most important of such uses is found in Gen 4:26.

(2a1) There it is stated that after the birth of Seth, who was born to Adam and Eve after the murder of Abel by Cain, "then began men to call upon the name of the Lord." **(2a2)** One must ask whether the writer meant to say that it was not until the birth of Enosh, the son of Seth, that people "began" to call on the name of the Lord altogether, or whether he meant that this was the first time the name Yahweh was used. **(2a3)** In view of the accounts in Gen 1–3, neither of these seems likely. **(2a4)** Perhaps the writer is simply saying that in contrast to the apparent non-God-fearing attitude expressed by Cain, the generation beginning with Seth and his son Enosh was known for its God-fearing way of life. **(2a5)** Perhaps, in view of the passive intensive verb form used here, the meaning is something like this: "Then it was begun again to call on the name of the Lord." See: TWOT—660, 661; BDB—319b, 320a.

2491. חָלָל {94x} **châlâl**, *khaw-lawl';* from 2490; *pierced* (espec. to death); fig. *polluted:*—slay {78x}, wounded {10x}, profane {3x}, kill {2x}, slain man {1x}. See: TWOT—660a; BDB—319c, 321a.

חֲלִילָה **châlîlâh**. See 2486.

2492. חָלַם {29x} **châlam**, *khaw-lam';* a prim. root; prop. to *bind* firmly, i.e. (by impl.) to *be* (caus. to *make*) *plump;* also (through the fig. sense of *dumbness*) to *dream:*—dreamed {20x}, dreamer {4x}, dream {1x}, dreameth {2x}, be in good liking {1x}, recover {1x}.

Chalam, as a verb, means "to become healthy or strong; to dream." **(1)** The meaning, "to become healthy," applies only to animals though "to dream" is used of human dreams. **(2)** Gen 28:12, the first occurrence, tells how Jacob "dreamed" that he beheld a ladder to heaven. See: TWOT—662, 663; BDB—321b.

2493. חֵלֶם {22x} **chêlem** (Aram.), *khay'-lem;* from a root corresp. to 2492; a *dream:*—dream {22x}. See: TWOT—2730; BDB—1093a.

2494. חֵלֶם {1x} **Chêlem**, *khay'lem;* from 2492; a *dream; Chelem,* an Isr.:—Helem {1x}. comp. 2469. See: BDB—321b.

2495. חַלָּמוּת {1x} **challâmûwth**, *khal-law-mooth';* from 2492 (in the sense of *insipidity*); prob. *purslain:*—egg {1x}. Syn.: 1000. See: TWOT—664; BDB—321d.

2496. חַלָּמִישׁ {5x} **challâmîysh**, *khal-law-meesh';* prob. from 2492 (in the sense of *hardness*); *flint:*—flint {3x}, flinty {1x}, rock {1x}. Syn.: 6864. See: TWOT—665; BDB—321d.

2497. חֵלֹן {5x} **Chêlôn**, *khay-lone';* from 2428; *strong; Chelon,* an Isr.:—Helon {5x}. See: BDB—298b, 322a.

2498. חָלַף {1x} **châlaph**, *khaw-laf';* a prim. root; prop. to *slide* by, i.e. (by impl.) to *hasten* away, *pass on, spring* up, *pierce* or *change:*—change {10x}, pass {3x}, renew {3x}, strike through {2x}, grow up {2x}, abolish {1x}, sprout again {1x}, alter {1x}, pass away {1x}, cut off {1x}, go on {1x}, pass on {1x}, over {1x}.

Chalaph means "to pass on, pass away, change, overstep, transgress." **(1)** When used in the simple active form, *chalaph* occurs only in poetry (except for 1 Sa 10:3), and it has the meaning of "to pass on, through." **(2)** The word is typically used in narrative or prose **(2a)** with the meaning of "to change." **(2b)** With this meaning *chalaph* first occurs in the Old Testament in Gen 31:7: "Your father hath deceived me, and changed my wages ten times" (cf. Gen 31:41). **(3b)** *Chalaph* expresses the "sweeping on" **(3b1)** of a flood (Is 8:8), **(3b2)** of a whirlwind (Is 21:1), and **(3b3)** of God Himself (Job 9:11). **(4)** The word has the meaning of "to pass away or to vanish," with reference **(4a)** to days (Job 9:26), **(4b)** the rain (Song 2:11), and **(4c)** idols (Is 2:18). **(5)** Not only wages, but

garments are "changed" (Gen 35:2; Ps 102:26).
(6) "To change" is "to renew" strength (Is 40:31;
41:1); **(7)** a tree appears "to be renewed" when
it sprouts again (Job 14:7). See: TWOT—666;
BDB—322a, 1025c, 1093a.

2499. חֲלַף {4x} **chălaph** (Aram.), *khal-af';*
      corresp. to 2498; to *pass* on (of
time):—pass {4x}. See: TWOT—2731; BDB—
1093a.

2500. חֵלֶף {2x} **chêleph**, *khay'-lef;* from 2498;
      prop. *exchange;* hence, (as prep.)
instead of:—× for {2x}. See: TWOT—666a;
BDB—322b.

2501. חֵלֶף {1x} **Cheleph**, *kheh'-lef;* the same
as 2500; *change; Cheleph,* a place
in Pal.:—Heleph {1x}. See: BDB—322b.

2502. חָלַץ {44x} **châlats**, *khaw-lats';* a prim.
      root; to *pull* off; hence, (intens.) to
strip, (reflex.) to *depart;* by impl. to *deliver,*
equip (for fight); *present, strengthen:*—deliver
{15x}, arm {14x}, loose {2x}, armed men {2x},
prepared {2x}, take {2x}, army {1x}, make fat
{1x}, put off {1x}, delivered out {1x}, draw out
{1x}, armed soldiers {1x} withdrawn {1x}. See:
TWOT—667, 668; BDB—322c, 323a.

2503. חֶלֶץ {5x} **Chelets**, *kheh'-lets;* or

      חֵלֶץ **Chêlets**, *khay'-lets;* from 2502;
      perh. *strength; Chelets,* the name
of two Isr.:—Helez {5x}. See: BDB—323b.

2504. חֲלָץ {1x} **châlâts**, *khaw-lawts';* from 2502
      (in the sense of *strength*); only in
the dual; the *loins* (as the seat of vigor):—loins
{9x}, reins {1x}. Syn.: 3629, 4975. See: TWOT—
668 (668b); BDB—323b, 1093d.

2505. חָלַק {65x} **châlaq**, *khaw-lak';* a prim.
      root; to *be smooth* (fig.); by impl.
(as smooth stones were used for *lots*) to *apportion* or *separate:*—divide {40x}, flatter {6x},
part {5x}, distribute {4x}, dealt {2x}, smoother
{2x}, given {1x}, imparted {1x}, partner {1x},
portion {1x}, received {1x}, separate {1x}.
Chalaq, means "to divide, share, plunder,
assign, distribute." **(1)** It appears for the first
time in Gen 14:15, **(1a)** where it is said that
Abram "divided himself against them" as he
rescued his nephew Lot from the enemy.
(1b) Apparently, Abram was "assigning" different responsibilities to his troops as part of
his strategy. **(2)** The sense of "dividing" or "al-
lotting" is found in Deut 4:19, **(2a)** where the
sun, moon, and stars are said to have been "allotted" to all peoples by God. **(2b)** A similar
use is seen in Deut 29:26, where God is said
not to have "allotted" false gods to His people.
(3) *Chalaq* is used in the legal sense of "sharing" an inheritance in Prov 17:2. **(4)** The word
is used three times in reference to "sharing"

the spoils of war in 1 Sa 30:24. **(5)** This verb
describes the "division" of the people of Israel,
as one half followed Tibni and the other half
followed Omri (1 Kin 16:21). **(6)** The word *chalaq* is also important in the description of the
"dividing" of the land of Canaan among the
various tribes and clans (Num 26:52–55). Syn.:
2506, 2511, 2513. See: TWOT—669; BDB—
323c, 325a, 1093b.

2506. חֵלֶק {66x} **chêleq**, *khay'-lek;* from 2505;
      prop. *smoothness* (of the tongue);
also an *allotment:*—portion {40x}, part {22x},
flattering {1x}, flattery {1x}, inheritance {1x},
partaker {1x}.
Cheleq, as a noun, means "portion; territory." It has a variety of meanings, such as
(1) "booty" of war (Gen 14:24), **(2)** a "portion"
of food (Lev 6:17), **(3)** a "tract" of land (Josh
18:5), **(4)** a spiritual "possession" or blessing
(Ps 73:26), and **(5)** a chosen "pattern" or "life-
style" (Ps 50:18). Syn.: 2511, 2513. See:
TWOT—669a; BDB—324a, 325b.

2507. חֵלֶק {2x} **Chêleq**, *khay'-lek;* the same
      as 2506; *portion; Chelek,* an Isr.:—
Helek {2x}. See: BDB—324c.

2508. חֲלָק {3x} **chălâq** (Aram.), *khal-awk';*
      from a root corresp. to 2505; a
part:—portion {3x}. See: TWOT—2732a;
BDB—1093b.

2509. חָלָק {4x} **châlâq**, *khaw-lawk';* from
      2505; *smooth* (espec. of tongue):—
flattering {2x}, smooth {1x}, smoother {1x}.
Syn.: 2506, 2511, 2513. See: TWOT—670b;
BDB—325b.

2510. חָלָק {2x} **Châlâq**, *khaw-lawk';* the
      same as 2509; *bare; Chalak,* a
mountain of Idumæa:—Halak {2x}. See: BDB—
325b.

2511. חַלָּק {1x} **challâq**, *khal-lawk';* from
      2505; *smooth:*—smooth {1x}. Syn.:
2506, 2513. See: TWOT—670d; BDB—325b.

2512. חַלֻּק {1x} **challûq**, *khal-look';* from 2505;
      smooth:—smooth {1x}. See: TWOT—
670d; BDB—325c.

2513. חֶלְקָה {29x} **chelqâh**, *khel-kaw';* fem. of
2506; prop. *smoothness;* fig. *flat-
tery;* also an *allotment:*—portion {6x}, parcel
{5x}, piece {5x}, field {3x}, flattering {2x}, plat
{2x}, part {1x}, flattery {1x}, ground {1x}, places
{1x}, smooth {1x}, smooth things {1x}. See:
TWOT—670c; BDB—324c, 325c.

2514. חֲלַקָּה {1x} **chălaqqâh**, *khal-ak-kaw';*
      fem. from 2505; *flattery:*—flat-
teries {1x}. See: TWOT—670e; BDB—325c.

2515. חֲלֻקָּה {1x} **chăluqqâh,** *khal-ook-kaw';* fem. of 2512; a *distribution:*—division {1x}. See: TWOT—669c; BDB—324c.

2516. חֶלְקִי {1x} **Chelqîy,** *khel-kee';* patron. from 2507; a *Chelkite* or desc. of Chelek:—Helkites {1x}. See: BDB—324c.

2517. חֶלְקִי {1x} **Chelqay,** *khel-kah'ee;* from 2505; *apportioned; Chelkai,* an Isr.:—Helkai {1x}. See: BDB—324d.

2518. חִלְקִיָּה {34x} **Chilqîyâh,** *khil-kee-yaw';* or

חִלְקִיָּהוּ **Chilqîyâhûw,** *khil-kee-yaw'-hoo;* from 2506 and 3050; *portion* (of) *Jah; Chilhijah,* the name of eight Isr.:—Hilkiah {34x}. See: BDB—324d.

2519. חֲלַקְלַקָּה {4x} **chălaqlaqqâh,** *khal-ak-lak-kaw';* by redupl. from 2505; prop. something *very smooth;* i.e. a *treacherous* spot; fig. *blandishment:*—flatteries {2x}, slippery {2x}. See: TWOT—670f; BDB—325c.

2520. חֶלְקַת {2x} **Chelqath,** *khel-kath';* a form of 2513; *smoothness; Chelkath,* a place in Pal.:—Helkath {2x}. See: BDB—324d.

2521. חֶלְקַת הַצֻּרִים {1x} **Chelqath hats-Tsûrîym,** *khel-kath' hats-tsoo-reem';* from 2520 and the plur. of 6697, with the art. ins.; *smoothness of the rocks; Chelkath Hats-tsurim,* a place in Pal.:—Helkath-hazzurim {1x}. See: BDB—324d.

2522. חָלַשׁ {3x} **châlash,** *khaw-lash';* a prim. root; to *prostrate;* by impl. to *overthrow, decay:*—discomfit {1x}, waste away {1x}, weaken {1x}. See: TWOT—671; BDB—325d.

2523. חַלָּשׁ {1x} **challâsh,** *khal-lawsh';* from 2522; *frail:*—weak {1x}. Syn.: 535, 2470, 7390. See: TWOT—671a; BDB—325d.

2524. חָם {4x} **châm,** *khawm;* from the same as 2346; a *father-in-law* (as in affinity):—father in law {4x}. See: TWOT—674a; BDB—326a, 327a, 328d.

2525. חָם {2x} **châm,** *khawm;* from 2552; *hot:*—hot {1x}, warm {1x}. See: TWOT—677b; BDB—326a, 328d.

2526. חָם {16x} **Châm,** *khawm;* the same as 2525; *hot* (from the tropical habitat); *Cham,* a son of Noah; also (as a patron.) his desc. or their country:—Ham {16x}. See: BDB—325d, 328d.

2527. חֹם {14x} **chôm,** *khome;* from 2552; *heat:*—heat {9x}, to be hot {4x}, warm {1x}. Syn.: 2534, 2552. See: TWOT—677a; BDB—326a, 328b.

2528. חֱמָא {2x} **chĕmâ** (Aram.), *khem-aw';* or

חֲמָה **chămâh** (Aram.), *kham-aw';* corresp. to 2534; *anger:*—fury {1x}. See: TWOT—2733; BDB—1093b 1095c.

חֵמָא **chêmâ.** See 2534.

2529. חֶמְאָה {10x} **chem'âh,** *khem-aw';* or (short.)

חֵמָה **chêmâh,** *khay-maw';* from the same root as 2346; curdled *milk* or *cheese:*—butter {1x}. See: TWOT—672a; BDB—326a, 328a.

2530. חָמַד {21x} **châmad,** *khaw-mad';* a prim. root; to *delight* in:—desire {11x}, covet {4x}, delight {2x}, pleasant {1x}, beauty {1x}, lust {1x}, delectable things {1x}. See: TWOT—673; BDB—326b, 326d.

2531. חֶמֶד {6x} **chemed,** *kheh'-med;* from 2530; *delight:*—desirable {3x}, pleasant {3x}. See: TWOT—673a; BDB—326c.

2532. חֶמְדָּה {25x} **chemdâh,** *khem-daw';* fem. of 2531; *delight:*—pleasant {12x}, desire {4x}, beloved {3x}, goodly {2x}, precious {4x}. See: TWOT—673b; BDB—326c.

2533. חֶמְדָּן {1x} **Chemdân,** *khem-dawn';* from 2531; *pleasant; Chemdan,* an Idumæan:—Hemdan {1x}. See: BDB—326d.

2534. חֵמָה {124x} **chêmâh,** *khay-maw';* or (Dan. 11:44)

חֵמָא **chêmâ,** *khay-maw';* from 3179; *heat;* fig. *anger, poison* (from its *fever*): fury {67x}, wrath {34x}, poison {6x}, furious {4x}, displeasure {3x}, rage {2x}, anger {1x}, bottles {1x}, furious + 1167 {1x}, furiously {1x}, heat {1x}, indignation {1x}, wrathful {1x}, wroth {1x}.

Chemah means "wrath; heat; rage; anger." **(1)** The noun, as well as the verb *yacham* (3179), denotes a strong emotional state. **(1a)** The noun is used 124 times, predominantly in the poetic and prophetic literature, especially Ezekiel. **(1b)** The first usage of *chemah* takes place in the story of Esau and Jacob. Jacob is advised to go to Haran with the hope that Esau's "anger" will dissipate: "And tarry with him a few days, until thy brother's fury turn away" (Gen 27:44). **(2)** The word indicates a state of anger. **(2a)** Most of the usage involves God's "anger." His "wrath" is expressed against Israel's sin in the wilderness: "For I was afraid of the anger and hot displeasure, wherewith the Lord was wroth against you to destroy you" (Deut 9:19). **(2b)** The psalmist prayed for God's mercy in the hour of God's "anger": "O LORD, rebuke me not in thine anger, neither chasten me in thy hot displeasure" (Ps 6:1).

(2c) God's "anger" against Israel was ultimately expressed in the exile of the Judeans to Babylon: "The Lord hath accomplished his fury; he hath poured out his fierce anger, and hath kindled a fire in Zion, and it hath devoured the foundations thereof" (Lam 4:11). **(2d)** The metaphor "cup" denotes the judgment of God upon His people. **(2d1)** His "wrath" is poured out: "Therefore he hath poured upon him the fury of his anger, and the strength of battle: and it hath set him on fire round about, yet he knew not; and it burned him, yet he laid it not to heart" (Is 42:25); **(2d2)** and the "cup of wrath" is drunk: "Awake, awake, stand up, O Jerusalem, which hast drunk at the hand of the LORD the cup of his fury; thou hast drunken the dregs of the cup of trembling . . ." (Is 51:17). **(3)** Thus, God as the Almighty Potentate is angered by the sins and the pride of His people, as they are an insult to His holiness. **(3a)** In a derived sense, the rulers on earth are also described as those who are angered, but their "anger" is aroused from circumstances over which they have no control. **(3a1)** Naaman was angry with Elisha's advice (2 Kin 5:11–12); **(3a2)** Ahasuerus became enraged with Vashti's refusal to display her beauty before the men (Est 1:12). **(4)** *Chemah* also denotes man's reaction to everyday circumstances. **(4a)** Man's "rage" is a dangerous expression of his emotional state, as it inflames everybody who comes close to the person in rage. **(4a1)** "Wrath" may arise for many reasons. Proverbs speaks strongly against *chemah*, as jealousy (6:34); cf. "Wrath is cruel, and anger is outrageous; but who is able to stand before envy?" (Prov 27:4; cf. Eze 16:38). **(4a2)** The man in rage may be culpable of crime and be condemned: "Be ye afraid of the sword: for wrath bringeth the punishments of the sword, that ye may know there is a judgment" (Job 19:29). **(4a3)** The wise response to "rage" is a soft answer: "A soft answer turneth away wrath: but grievous words stir up anger" (Prov 15:1). **(5)** There are two special meanings of *chemah*: **(5a)** One is "heat," as in "the Spirit lifted me up, and took me away, and I went in bitterness, in the heat of my spirit; but the hand of the LORD was strong upon me" (Eze 3:14). **(5b)** The other is "poison," or "venom," as in Deut 32:33: "Their wine is the poison of dragons, and the cruel venom of asps." Syn: *Chemah* is associated with **(A)** *qin'ah* (7068), "jealousy," and also with **(B)** *naqam* (5358), "vengeance," as the angered person intends to save his name or avenge himself on the person who provoked him. In God's dealing with Israel He was jealous of His Holy name, for which reason He had to deal justly with idola-

trous Israel by avenging Himself: "That it might cause fury to come up to take vengeance; I have set her blood upon the top of a rock, that it should not be covered" (Eze 24:8); but He also avenges His people against their enemies: "God is jealous, and the LORD revengeth; the LORD revengeth, and is furious; the LORD will take vengeance on his adversaries and he reserveth wrath for his enemies" (Nah 1:2). Other synonyms of *chemah* are **(C)** *'ap* (639) "anger," (Deut 29:27); and **(D)** *qetseph*, "wrath (7110)," (Jer 21:5). comp. 2529. See: TWOT—860a; BDB—326b, 328a, 404b, 1095c.

2535. חֵמָה {5x} **chammâh**, *kham-maw'*; from 2525; *heat;* by impl. the *sun:*—heat {1x}, sun {5x}. See: TWOT—677c; BDB—328d.

2536. חַמּוּאֵל {1x} **Chammûw'êl**, *kham-moo-ale'*; from 2535 and 410; *anger of God; Chammuel,* an Isr.:—Hamuel {1x}. See: BDB—328a, 329b.

2537. חֲמוּטַל {3x} **Chămûwṭal**, *kham-oo-tal';* or

חֲמִיטַל **Chămîyṭal**, *kham-ee-tal';* from 2524 and 2919; *father-in-law of dew; Chamutal* or *Chamital,* an Israelitess:—Hamutal {3x}. See: BDB—327d, 328a.

2538. חָמוּל {3x} **Châmûwl**, *khaw-mool';* from 2550; *pitied; Chamul,* an Isr.:—Hamul {3x}. See: BDB—328b.

2539. חָמוּלִי {1x} **Châmûwlîy**, *khaw-moo-lee';* patron. from 2538: a *Chamulite* (collect.) or desc. of Chamul:—Hamulites {1x}. See: BDB—328b.

2540. חַמּוֹן {2x} **Chammôwn**, *kham-mone';* from 2552; *warm* spring; *Chammon,* the name of two places in Pal.:—Hammon {2x}. See: BDB—329a.

2541. חָמוֹץ {1x} **châmôwts**, *khaw-motse';* from 2556; prop. *violent;* by impl. a *robber:*—oppressed {1x}. See: TWOT—681a; BDB—330b.

2542. חַמּוּק {1x} **chammûwq**, *kham-mook';* from 2559; a *wrapping,* i.e. drawers:—joints {1x}. See: TWOT—682a; BDB—330b.

2543. חֲמוֹר {96x} **chămôwr**, *kham-ore';* or (short.)

חֲמֹר **chămôr**, *kham-ore';* from 2560; a male *ass* (from its dun *red*):—(he) ass {96x}. See: TWOT—685a; BDB—331a.

2544. חֲמוֹר {13x} **Chămôwr**, *kham-ore';* the same as 2543; *ass; Chamor,* a Canaanite:—Hamor {13x}. See: BDB—331c.

2545. חָמוֹת {11x} **chămôwth**, *kham-ōth';* or
(short.)

חָמֹת **chămôth**, *kham-ōth';* fem. of 2524;
a *mother-in-law:*—mother in law
{11x}. See: TWOT—674b; BDB—327b, 328a.

2546. חֹמֶט {1x} **chômet**, *kho'-met;* from an
unused root prob. mean. to *lie low;*
a *lizard* (as *creeping):*—{1x} snail. See:
TWOT—675a; BDB—328a.

2547. חָמְטָה {1x} **Chumtâh**, *khoom-taw';* fem.
of 2546; *low; Chumtah,* a place
in Pal.:—Humtah {1x}. See: BDB—328a.

2548. חָמִיץ {1x} **châmîyts**, *khaw-meets';* from
2556; *seasoned,* i.e. *salt* proven-
der:—clean {1x}. See: TWOT—679c; BDB—
330a.

2549. חֲמִישִׁי {45x} **chămîyshîy**, *kham-ee-shee';*
or

חֲמִשִּׁי **chamishshîy**, *kham-ish-shee';* ord.
from 2568; *fifth;* also a *fifth:*—
fifth {42x}, fifth part {3x}. Syn.: 2567, 2569. See:
TWOT—686d; BDB—332c.

2550. חָמַל {41x} **châmal**, *khaw-mal';* a prim.
root; to *commiserate;* by impl. to
spare:—pity {18x}, spare {18x}, have compassion {5x}. See: TWOT—676; BDB—328a, 328b.

2551. חֶמְלָה {2x} **chemlâh**, *khem-law';* from
2550; *commiseration:*—merciful
{1x}, pity {1x}. See: TWOT—676a; BDB—328b.

2552. חָמַם {13x} **châmam**, *khaw-mam';* a prim.
root; to *be hot* (lit. or fig.):—warm
{7x}, hot {3x}, heat {2x}, enflaming {1x}. See:
TWOT—677; BDB—328a, 328c.

2553. חַמָּן {8x} **chammân**, *kham-mawn';* from
2535; a *sun*-pillar:—idol {1x}, im-
age {8x}. Syn.: 4676. See: TWOT—677d; BDB—
329a.

2554. חָמַס {8x} **châmaç**, *khaw-mas';* a prim.
root; to *be violent;* by impl. to *maltreat:*—violence {2x}, violated {1x}, shake off
{1x}, wrongfully imagine {1x}, violently taken
away {1x}, wronged {1x}, made bare {1x}.
Chamac, as a verb, means "to treat violently." **(1)** This verb appears in Jer. 22:3 with
the meaning of "to do no violence": ". . . And
do no wrong, do no violence to the stranger,
the fatherless, nor the widow, neither shed innocent blood in this place." See: TWOT—678;
BDB—329b.

2555. חָמָס {60x} **châmâç**, *khaw-mawce';* from
2554; *violence;* by impl. *wrong;* by
meton. unjust *gain:*—violence {39x}, violent
{7x}, cruelty {4x}, wrong {3x}, false {2x}, cruel
{1x}, damage {1x}, injustice {1x}, oppressor +
376 {1x}, unrighteous {1x}.

Chamac, as a noun, means "violence; wrong;
maliciousness." **(1)** Basically *chamac* connotes
the disruption of the divinely established order
of things. **(2)** It has a wide range of nuances
within this legal sphere. **(2a)** The expression
"a witness in the case of violent wrongdoing"
means someone who bears witness in a case
having to do with such an offense (cf. Deut
19:16). **(2a1)** In this context the truthfulness
of the witness is not established except upon
further investigation (Deut 19:18). **(2a2)** Once
he was established as a false witness, the penalty for the crime concerning which he bore
false witness was to be executed against the
liar (cf. Deut 19:19). **(2b)** In Ex 23:1 Israel is
admonished: "Put not thine hand with the
wicked to be an unrighteous witness," i.e., a
witness who in accusing someone of a violent
crime intends to see the accused punished severely.

(3) *Chamac* perhaps connotes a "violent
wrongdoing" which has not been righted, the
guilt of which lies on an entire area (its inhabitants) disrupting their relationship with God
and thereby interfering with His blessings.
(3a) It is this latter sense which appears in the
phrase "the earth was full of violent wrongdoing": "The earth also was corrupt before
God, and the earth was filled with violence"
(Gen 6:11—the first occurrence of the word).
(3b) Thus, in Gen 16:5 Sarai summons God to
judge between Abram and herself because he
has not acted properly toward her keeping Hagar in submission: "My wrong [done me] be
upon thee: I have given my maid into thy bosom; and when she saw that she had conceived,
I was despised in her eyes: the LORD judge between me and thee." **(3c)** Abram as God's judge
(in God's stead) accepts the correctness of her
case and commits Hagar to Sarai's care to be
dealt with properly. See: TWOT—678a; BDB—
329c.

2556. חָמֵץ {8x} **châmêts**, *khaw-mates';* a prim.
root; to *be pungent;* i.e. in taste
(*sour,* i.e. lit. *fermented,* or fig. *harsh*), in color
(*dazzling*):—leavened {5x}, cruel {1x}, dyed
{1x}, grieved {1x}. See: TWOT—679, 680, 681;
BDB—329d, 330a.

2557. חָמֵץ {11x} **châmêts**, *khaw-mates';* from
2556; *ferment,* (fig.) *extortion:*—
leaven {5x}, leavened {1x}, leavened bread {5x}.
See: TWOT—679a; BDB—329d, 330a.

2558. חֹמֶץ {6x} **chômets**, *kho'-mets;* from 2556;
vinegar:—vinegar {6x}. See: TWOT—
679b; BDB—330a.

2559. חָמַק {2x} **châmaq**, *khaw-mak';* a prim.
root; prop. to *enwrap;* hence, to

depart (i.e. turn about):—go about {1x}, withdraw self {1x}. See: TWOT—682; BDB—330b.

2560. חָמַר {6x} **châmar**, *khaw-mar';* a prim. root; prop. to *boil* up; hence, to *ferment* (with scum); to *glow* (with redness); as denom. (from 2564) to *smear* with pitch:—troubled {3x}, red {1x}, daub {1x}, foul {1x}. See: TWOT—683, 683d, 685; BDB—330b, 330d, 331a.

2561. חֶמֶר {2x} **chemer**, *keh'-mer;* from 2560; *wine* (as *fermenting*):—✕ pure {1x}, red wine {1x}. See: TWOT—683a; BDB—330c, 1093b.

2562. חֲמַר {6x} **chămar** (Aram.), *kham-ar';* corresp. to 2561; *wine:*—wine {6x}. See: TWOT—2734; BDB—1093b.

חֲמֹר **chămôr**. See 2543.

2563. חֹמֶר {30x} **chômer**, *kho'mer;* from 2560; prop. a *bubbling* up, i.e. of water, a *wave;* of earth, *mire* or *clay* (cement); also a *heap;* hence, a *chomer* or dry measure:—clay {11x}, homer {11x}, mortar {4x}, mire {2x}, heap {2x}. Syn.: 2916. See: TWOT—683c; BDB—330c, 330d.

2564. חֵמָר {3x} **chêmâr**, *khay-mawr';* from 2560; *bitumen* (as *rising* to the surface):—slime {2x}, slimepit + 875 {1x}. See: TWOT—683b; BDB—330c.

2565. חֲמֹרָה {1x} **chămôrâh**, *kham-o-raw';* from 2560 [comp. 2563]; a *heap:*—heap {1x}. See: TWOT—684c; BDB—331a.

2566. חַמְרָן {1x} **Chamrân**, *kham-rawn';* from 2560; *red; Chamran,* an Idumæan:—Amran {1x}. See: BDB—331c.

2567. חָמַשׁ {1x} **châmash**, *khaw-mash';* a denom. from 2568; to *tax a fifth:*—take up the fifth part {1x}. Syn.: 2549, 2569. See: TWOT—686; BDB—332b.

2568. חָמֵשׁ {343x} **châmêsh**, *khaw-maysh';* masc.

חֲמִשָּׁה **chămishshâh**, *kham-ish-shaw';* a prim. numeral; *five:*—five {300x}, fifteenth + 6240 {16x}, fifteen + 6240 {15x}, fifth {6x}, fifteen + 7657 {3x}, variant {1x}. See: TWOT—686a; BDB—331c.

2569. חֹמֶשׁ {1x} **chômesh**, *kho'-mesh;* from 2567; a *fifth* tax:—fifth part {1x}. Syn.: 2549. See: TWOT—686b; BDB—332b.

2570. חֹמֶשׁ {4x} **chômesh**, *kho'-mesh;* from an unused root prob. mean. to *be stout;* the *abdomen* (as *obese*):—fifth rib {4x}. See: TWOT—687a; BDB—332d.

2571. חָמֻשׁ {4x} **châmûsh**, *khaw-moosh';* pass. part. of the same as 2570; *staunch,*

i.e. able-bodied *soldiers:*—armed {2x}, armed men {1x}, harnessed {1x}. See: TWOT—688a; BDB—332d.

חֲמִשָּׁה **chămishshâh**. See 2568.

חֲמִשִּׁי **chămishshîy**. See 2549.

2572. חֲמִשִּׁים {162x} **chămishshîym**, *kham-ish-sheem';* multiple of 2568; *fifty:*—fifty {151x}, fifties {6x}, fiftieth {4x}, fifty + 376 {1x}. See: TWOT—686c; BDB—332b.

2573. חֵמֶת {1x} **chêmeth**, *khay'-meth;* from the same as 2346; a skin *bottle* (as *tied* up):—bottle {1x}. Syn.: 1228, 4997, 5035. See: TWOT—689a; BDB—332d.

2574. חֲמָת {37x} **Chămâth**, *kham-awth';* from the same as 2346; *walled; Chamath,* a place in Syria:—Hamath {34x}, Hemath {3x}. See: TWOT—689a; BDB—333a.

חֲמֹת **chămôth**. See 2545.

2575. חַמַּת {1x} **Chammath**, *kham-math';* a var. for the first part of 2576; *hot* springs; *Chammath,* a place in Pal.:—Hammath {1x}. See: BDB—329a, 333b.

2576. חַמֹּת דֹּאר {1x} **Chammôth Dô'r**, *kham-moth' dore;* from the plur. of 2535 and 1756; *hot* springs *of Dor; Chammath-Dor,* a place in Pal.:—Hamath-Dor {1x}. See: BDB—329a, 329b.

2577. חֲמָתִי {2x} **Chămâthiy**, *kham-aw-thee';* patrial from 2574; a *Chamathite* or native of *Chamath:*—Hamathite {2x}. See: BDB—333b.

2578. חֲמָת צוֹבָה {1x} **Chămath Tsôwbâh**, *kham-ath' tso-baw';* from 2574 and 6678; *Chamath of Tsobah; Chamath-Tsobah;* prob. the same as 2574:—Hamath-Zobah {1x}. See: BDB—333a, 844b, 844c.

2579. חֲמַת רַבָּה {1x} **Chămath Rabbâh**, *kham-ath' rab-baw';* from 2574 and 7237; *Chamath of Rabbah; Chamath-Rabbah,* prob. the same as 2574:—Hamath the great {1x}. See: BDB—333a.

2580. חֵן {69x} **chên**, *khane;* from 2603; *graciousness,* i.e. subj. (*kindness, favor*) or obj. (*beauty*):—grace {38x}, favour {26x}, gracious {2x}, pleasant {1x}, precious {1x}, well-favoured + 2896 {1x}.

Chen, as a noun, means "favor; grace." **(1)** The Hebrew noun *chen* occurs 69 times, **(1a)** mainly in the Pentateuch and in the historical books through Samuel. **(1b)** The word's frequency increases in the poetic books, but it is rare in the prophetic books. **(1c)** The first occurrence is in Gen 6:8: "But Noah found grace in the eyes of the LORD." **(2)** The basic meaning of *chen* is "favor." **(2a)** Whatever is

"pleasant and agreeable" can be described by this word. When a woman is said to have *chen,* she is a "gracious" woman (Prov 11:16); **(2b)** or the word may have the negative association of being "beautiful without sense" (Prov 31:30). **(2c)** A person's speech may be characterized by "graciousness": "He that loveth pureness of heart, for the grace of his lips the king shall be his friend" (Prov 22:11; cf. Ps 45:2). **(3)** *Chen* also denotes the response to whatever is "agreeable." **(4)** The verbs used with "favor" are: **(4a)** "give favor" (Gen 39:21), **(4b)** "obtain favor" (Ex 3:21), and **(4c)** "find favor" (Gen 6:8). **(5)** The idioms are equivalent to the English verbs "to like" or "to love": "[She] said to him, Why have I found favor in your eyes, that you should take notice of me, when I am a foreigner?" (Ruth 2:10). See: TWOT—694a; BDB—333b, 336b.

2581. חֵן {1x} **Chên,** *khane;* the same as 2580; *grace; Chen,* a fig. name for an Isr.:—Hen {1x}. See: BDB—333b, 336d.

2582. חֲנָדָד {4x} **Chênâdâd,** *khay-naw-dawd';* prob. from 2580 and 1908; *favor of Hadad; Chenadad,* an Isr.:—Henadad {4x}. See: BDB—333b, 337b.

2583. חָנָה {143x} **chânâh,** *khaw-naw';* a prim. root [comp. 2603]; prop. to *incline;* by impl. to *decline* (of the slanting rays of evening); spec. to *pitch* a tent; gen. to *encamp* (for abode or siege):—pitch {78x}, encamp {47x}, camp {4x}, pitch . . . tent {4x}, abide {3x}, dwelt {2x}, lie {2x}, rested {2x}, grows to an end {1x}. See: TWOT—690; BDB—333b.

2584. חַנָּה {13x} **Channâh,** *khan-naw';* from 2603; *favored; Channah,* an Israelitess:—Hannah {13x}. See: BDB—333b, 336d.

2585. חֲנוֹךְ {16x} **Chănôwk,** *khan-oke';* from 2596; *initiated; Chanok,* an antediluvian patriarch:—Enoch {9x}, Hanoch {5x}, Henoch {2x}. See: BDB—335c.

2586. חָנוּן {11x} **Chânûwn,** *khaw-noon';* from 2603; *favored; Chanun,* the name of an Ammonite and of two Isr.:—Hanun {11x}. See: BDB—337a.

2587. חַנּוּן {13x} **channûwn,** *khan-noon';* from 2603; *gracious:*—gracious {13x}.

Channuwn, as an adjective, means "gracious." **(1)** One of the word's 13 occurrences is in Ex 34:6: "And the LORD passed by before him [Moses], and proclaimed, The LORD, The LORD God, merciful and gracious, long-suffering, and abundant in goodness and truth." **(2)** This adjective is used only of God and denotes the action that springs from His free and unmerited love to His creatures. See: TWOT—694d; BDB—337a.

2588. חָנוּת {1x} **chânûwth,** *khaw-nooth';* from 2583; prop. a *vault* or *cell* (with an arch); by impl. a *prison:*—cabins {1x}. See: TWOT—690a; BDB—333d.

2589. חַנּוֹת {2x} **channôwth,** *khan-nōth';* from 2603 (in the sense of *prayer*); *supplication:*—be gracious {1x}, intreated {1x}. See: TWOT—694; BDB—335d.

2590. חָנַט {5x} **chânaṭ,** *khaw-nat';* a prim. root; to *spice;* by impl. to *embalm;* also to *ripen:*—embalm {4x}, put forth {1x}. See: TWOT—691; 334c, 334d.

2591. חִנְטָא {2x} **chinṭâ'** (Aram.), *khint-taw';* corresp. to 2406; *wheat:*—wheat {2x}. See: TWOT—2735; BDB—1093b.

2592. חַנִּיאֵל {2x} **Chănnîy'êl,** *khan-nee-ale';* from 2603 and 410; *favor of God; Channiel,* the name of two Isr.:—Hanniel {1x}, Haniel {1x}. See: BDB—335a, 337a.

2593. חָנִיךְ {1x} **chânîyk,** *kaw-neek';* from 2596; *initiated;* i.e. *practiced:*—trained {1x}. See: TWOT—693a; BDB—335c.

2594. חֲנִינָה {1x} **chănîynâh,** *khan-ee-naw';* from 2603; *graciousness:*—favour {1x}. See: TWOT—694e; BDB—337a.

2595. חֲנִית {47x} **chănîyth,** *khan-eeth';* from 2583; a *lance* (for *thrusting,* like *pitching* a tent):—javelin {6x}, spear {41x}. Syn.: 3591, 7013, 7420. See: TWOT—690b; BDB—333d, 335a.

2596. חָנַךְ {5x} **chânak,** *khaw-nak';* a prim. root; prop. to *narrow* (comp. 2614); fig. to *initiate* or *discipline:*—dedicate {4x}, train up {1x}.

Chanak basically means "to initiate/ inaugurate/dedicate": **(1)** the altar (Num 7:10, 11), **(2)** the house of the Lord (2 Chr 7:5, 9), **(3)** the rebuilt temple (Ezr 6:16), **(4)** Jerusalem's wall (Neh 12:27), **(5)** Nebuchadnezzar's image (Dan 3:2). See: TWOT—693; BDB—335b.

2597. חֲנֻכָּא {4x} **chănukkâ'** (Aram.), *chan-ook-kaw';* corresp. to 2598; *consecration:*—dedication {4x}. See: TWOT—2736; BDB—1093b.

2598. חֲנֻכָּה {8x} **chănukkâh,** *khan-ook-kaw';* from 2596; *initiation,* i.e. *consecration:*—dedicating {2x}, dedication {6x}. See: TWOT—693b; BDB—335c, 1093b.

2599. חֲנֹכִי {1x} **Chănôkîy,** *khan-o-kee';* patron. from 2585; a *Chanokite* (collect.) or desc. of Chanok:—Hanochites {1x}. See: BDB—335c.

2600. חִנָּם {32x} **chinnâm,** *khin-nawm';* from 2580; *gratis,* i.e. devoid of cost, reason or advantage:—without cause {15x}, for

nought {6x}, causeless {2x}, in vain {2x}, free {1x}, without cost {1x}, freely {1x}, innocent {1x}, cost me nothing {1x}, for nothing {1x}, without wages {1x}.

Chinnam basically means "for nothing; for no purpose; useless; without a cause; for no reason." **(1)** This substantive is used chiefly as an adverb. It means "for nought": "And Laban said unto Jacob, Because thou art my brother, shouldest thou therefore serve me for nought? tell me, what shall thy wages be?" (Gen 29:15 — the first occurrence). **(2)** The word means "in vain," or "for no purpose": "Surely in vain the net is spread in the sight of any bird" (Prov 1:17). **(3)** Finally, it means "for no cause": "Wherefore then wilt thou sin against innocent blood, to slay David without a cause?" (1Sa 19:5). See: TWOT—694b; BDB—335d, 336c.

2601. חֲנַמְאֵל {4x} **Chănamᵉêl**, *khan-am-ale';* prob. by orth. var. for 2606; *Chanamel,* an Isr.:—Hanameel {4x}. See: BDB—335d.

2602. חֲנָמָל {1x} **chănâmâl**, *khan-aw-mawl';* of uncert. der.; perh. the *aphis* or plant-louse:—frost {1x}. See: TWOT—693.1; BDB—335d.

2603. חָנַן {78x} **chânan**, *khaw-nan';* a prim. root [comp. 2583]; prop. to *bend* or *stoop* in kindness to an inferior; to *favor, bestow;* caus. to *implore* (i.e. move to favor by petition):—mercy {16x}, gracious {13x}, merciful {12x}, supplication {10x}, favour {7x}, besought {4x}, pity {4x}, fair {1x}, favourable {1x}, favoured {1x}, misc. {9x} = intreat, have pity upon, pray, × very.

Chanan, as a verb, means "to be gracious, considerate; to show favor." **(1)** The first time in Gen 33:5: "The children which God hath graciously given thy servant." **(2)** Generally, this word implies the extending of "favor," often when it is neither expected nor deserved. **(2a)** *Chanan* may express "generosity," a gift from the heart (Ps 37:21). **(2b)** God especially is the source of undeserved "favor" (Gen 33:11), and He is asked repeatedly for such "gracious" acts as only He can do (Num 6:25; Gen 43:29). The psalmist prays: "Grant me thy law graciously" (Ps 119:29). **(3)** God's "favor" is especially seen in His deliverance from one's enemies or surrounding evils (Ps 77:9; Amos 5:15). **(4)** However, God extends His "graciousness" in His own sovereign way and will, to whomever He chooses (Ex 33:19). See: TWOT—694, 695; 335d, 337d, 1093b.

2604. חֲנַן {2x} **chănan** (Aram.), *khan-an';* corresp. to 2603; to *favor* or (caus.) to *entreat:*—shew mercy {1x}, make supplication {1x}. See: TWOT—2737; BDB—1093b.

2605. חָנָן {12x} **Chânân**, *khaw-nawn';* from 2603; *favor; Chanan,* the name of seven Isr.:—Canan {12x}. See: BDB—336d.

2606. חֲנַנְאֵל {4x} **Chănanᵉêl**, *khan-an-ale';* from 2603 and 410; *God has favored; Chananel,* prob. an Isr., from whom a tower of Jerusalem was named:—Hananeel {4x}. See: BDB—337a.

2607. חֲנָנִי {11x} **Chănânîy**, *khan-aw-nee';* from 2603; *gracious; Chanani,* the name of six Isr.:—Hanani {11x}. See: BDB—337b.

2608. חֲנַנְיָה {29x} **Chănanyâh**, *khan-an-yaw';* or

חֲנַנְיָהוּ **Chănanyâhûw**, *khan-an-yaw'-hoo;* from 2603 and 3050; *Jah has favored; Chananjah,* the name of thirteen Isr.:—Hananiah {29x}. See: BDB—337b, 1093b.

2609. חָנֵס {1x} **Chânêç**, *khaw-nace';* of Eg. der.; *Chanes,* a place in Egypt:—Hanes {1x}. See: BDB—337d.

2610. חָנֵף {11x} **chânêph**, *khaw-nafe';* a prim. root; to *soil,* espec. in a mor. sense:—pollute {4x}, defile {4x}, greatly {1x}, corrupt {1x}, profane {1x}. See: TWOT—696; BDB—337d.

2611. חָנֵף {13x} **chânêph**, *khaw-nafe';* from 2610; *soiled* (i.e. with sin), *impious:*—hypocrite {11x}, hypocritical {1x}. See: TWOT—696b; BDB—338a.

2612. חֹנֶף {1x} **chôneph**, *kho'-nef;* from 2610; *moral filth,* i.e. *wickedness:*—hypocrisy {1x}. See: TWOT—696a; BDB—338a.

2613. חֲנֻפָה {1x} **chănûphâh**, *khan-oo-faw';* fem. from 2610; *impiety:*—profaneness {1x}. See: TWOT—696c; BDB—338b.

2614. חָנַק {2x} **chânaq**, *khaw-nak';* a prim. root [comp. 2596]; to *be narrow;* by impl. to *throttle,* or (reflex.) to *choke* oneself to death (by a rope):—hang self {1x}, strangle {1x}. See: TWOT—697; BDB—338b.

2615. חַנָּתֹן {1x} **Channâthôn**, *khan-naw-thone';* prob. from 2603; *favored; Channathon,* a place in Pal.:—Hannathon {1x}. See: BDB—337b, 338b.

2616. חָסַד {3x} **châçad**, *khaw-sad';* a prim. root; prop. perh. to *bow* (the neck only [comp. 2603] in courtesy to an equal), i.e. to *be kind;* also (by euphem. [comp. 1288], but rarely) to *reprove:*—shew self merciful {2x}, put to shame {1x}.

Chacad is a practical exhibition of lovingkindness toward our fellowman, whose only claim may be misfortune and whom it is in our power to help, though perhaps at the expense

of time, money, convenience, and even religious or national prejudice. See: TWOT—698, 699; 338b, 340a. BDB—338b, 340a.

2617. חֶסֶד {248x} cheçed, *kheh'-sed;* from 2616; *kindness;* by impl. (toward God) *piety;* rarely (by opposition) *reproof,* or (subj.) *beauty:*—mercy {149x}, kindness {40x}, lovingkindness {30x}, goodness {12x}, kindly {5x}, merciful {4x}, favour {3x}, good {1x}, goodliness {1x}, pity {1x}, reproach {1x}, wicked thing {1x}.

Cheçed, as a noun, means "loving-kindness; steadfast love; grace; mercy; faithfulness; goodness; devotion." **(1)** This word is used 240 times in the Old Testament, and **(1a)** is especially frequent in the Psalter. **(1b)** The term is one of the most important in the vocabulary of Old Testament theology and ethics. **(2)** In general, one may identify three basic meanings of the word, which always interact: "strength," "steadfastness," and "love." Any understanding of the word that fails to suggest all three inevitably loses some of its richness. "Love" by itself easily becomes sentimentalized or universalized apart from the covenant. Yet "strength" or "steadfastness" suggests only the fulfillment of a legal or other obligation. **(3)** The word refers primarily to mutual and reciprocal rights and obligations between the parties of a relationship (especially Yahweh and Israel). **(3a)** But *cheçed* is not only a matter of obligation; **(3b)** it is also of generosity. **(3c)** It is not only a matter of loyalty, but also of mercy. **(3d)** The weaker party seeks the protection and blessing of the patron and protector, but he may not lay absolute claim to it. **(3e)** The stronger party remains committed to his promise, but retains his freedom, especially with regard to the manner in which he will implement those promises. **(4)** *Cheçed* implies personal involvement and commitment in a relationship beyond the rule of law. **(5)** Marital love is often related to *cheçed.* **(5a)** Marriage certainly is a legal matter, and there are legal sanctions for infractions. **(5b)** Yet the relationship, if sound, far transcends mere legalities. **(5c)** The prophet Hosea applies the analogy to Yahweh's *cheçed* to Israel within the covenant (e.g., 2:21). **(6)** Hence, "devotion" is sometimes the single English word best capable of capturing the nuance of the original. **(7)** Hebrew writers often underscored the element of steadfastness (or strength) by pairing *cheçed* with *'emet* (571 - "truth, reliability") and *'emunah* (530 - "faithfulness"). **(8)** Biblical usage frequently speaks of someone "doing," "showing," or "keeping" *cheçed.* **(9)** The concrete content of the word is especially evident when it is used in the plural. **(9a)** God's "mercies," "kindnesses," or "faith-

fulnesses" are His specific, concrete acts of redemption in fulfillment of His promise. **(9b)** An example appears in Is 55:3: ". . . And I will make an everlasting covenant with you, even the sure mercies of David." **(10)** *Cheçed* has both God and man as its subject. **(10a)** When man is the subject of *cheçed,* the word usually describes the person's kindness or loyalty to another; cf. 2 Sa 9:7: "And David said . . . I will surely show thee [Mephibosheth] kindness for Jonathan thy father's sake." **(10b)** Only rarely is the term applied explicitly to man's affection or fidelity toward God; **(10c)** the clearest example is probably Jer 2:2: "Go and cry in the ears of Jerusalem, saying, thus saith the LORD; I remember thee, the kindness of thy youth, the love of thine espousals, when thou wentest after me in the wilderness." **(10d)** Man exercises *cheçed* toward various units within the community—toward family and relatives, but also to friends, guests, masters, and servants. **(10e)** *Cheçed* toward the lowly and needy is often specified.

(11) The Bible prominently uses the term *cheçed* to summarize and characterize a life of sanctification within, and in response to, the covenant. **(11a)** Thus, Hos 6:6 states that God desires "mercy and not sacrifice" (i.e., faithful living in addition to worship). **(11b)** Similarly, Mic 6:8 features *cheçed* in the prophets' summary of biblical ethics: ". . . and what doth the LORD require of thee, but . . . to love mercy . . . ?" **(12)** Behind all these uses with man as subject, however, stand the repeated references to God's *cheçed.* **(12a)** It is one of His most central characteristics. **(12b)** God's loving-kindness is offered to His people, who need redemption from sin, enemies, and troubles. **(12c)** A recurrent refrain describing God's nature is "abounding/plenteous in *cheçed*" (Ex 34:6; Neh 9:17; Ps 103:8; Jonah 4:2). **(12d)** The entire history of Yahweh's covenantal relationship with Israel can be summarized in terms of *cheçed.* **(12e)** It is the one permanent element in the flux of covenantal history. **(12f)** Even the Creation is the result of God's *cheçed* (Ps 136:5-9). **(12g)** His love lasts for a "thousand generations" (Deut 7:9; cf. Deut 5:10 and Ex 20:6), indeed "forever" (especially in the refrains of certain psalms, such as Ps 136).

(13) Words used in synonymous parallelism with *cheçed* help to define and explain it. **(13a)** The word most commonly associated with *cheçed* is *'emet* (571 - "fidelity; reliability"): ". . . Let thy loving-kindness [*cheçed*] and thy truth [*'emet*] continually preserve me." **(13b)** *'Emunah* (530) with a similar meaning is also common: "He hath remembered his mercy [*cheçed*] and his truth [*'emunah*] toward the house of Israel." **(14)** This emphasis is

especially appropriate when God is the subject, because His *checed* is stronger and more
enduring than man's. **(14a)** Etymological investigation suggests that *checed's* primitive
significance may have been "strength" or "permanence." **(14b)** If so, a puzzling use of *checed*
in Is 40:6 would be explained: "All flesh is
grass, and all the goodliness thereof is as the
flower of the field."

(15) The association of *checed* with "covenant" **(15a)** keeps it from being misunder-
stood as mere providence or love for all
creatures; **(15b)** it applies primarily to God's
particular love for His chosen and covenanted
people. **(15c)** "Covenant" also stresses the reciprocity of the relationship; **(15d)** but since
God's *checed* is ultimately beyond the covenant, it will not ultimately be abandoned,
even when the human partner is unfaithful and
must be disciplined (Is 54:8, 10). **(16)** Since its
final triumph and implementation is eschatological, *checed* can imply the goal and end of
all salvation-history (Ps 85:7, 10; 130:7; Mic
7:20). See: TWOT—698a, 699a; BDB—338c,
340a.

2618. חֶסֶד {1x} **Cheçed,** *kheh'-sed;* the same
as 2617: *favor; Chesed,* an Isr.:—
Hesed {1x}. See: BDB—122c.

2619. חֲסַדְיָה {1x} **Chăçadyâh,** *khas-ad-yaw';*
from 2617 and 3050; *Jah has fa-
vored; Chasadjah,* an Isr.:—Hasadiah {1x}. The
proper noun *Chacadyah* (1Chr 3:20) is related
to *checed* (2617). The name of Zerubbabel's son
means "Yahweh is faithful/gracious," a fitting
summary of the prophet's message. See: BDB—
339d.

2620. חָסָה {37x} **châçâh,** *khaw-saw';* a prim.
root; to *flee* for protection [comp.
982]; fig. to *confide* in:—to trust {35x}, to make
a refuge {1x}, have hope {1x}. It is often used
where God is compared to a rock or a shield
or one with protective wings. See: TWOT—700;
BDB—340a.

2621. חֹסָה {5x} **Chôçâh,** *kho-saw';* from 2620;
hopeful; Chosah, an Isr.; also a
place in Pal.:—Hosah {5x}. See: BDB—340b.

2622. חָסוּת {1x} **châçûwth,** *khaw-sooth';* from
2620; *confidence:*—trust {1x}. See:
TWOT—700a; BDB—340b.

2623. חָסִיד {32x} **châçîyd,** *khaw-seed';* from
2616; prop. *kind,* i.e. (relig.) *pious*
(a saint):—saints {19x}, holy {3x}, merciful {3x},
godly {2x}, good {1x}, godly man {1x}, Holy One
{1x}, holy one {1x}, ungodly + 3808 {1x}.
Chaciyd, as an adjective, means "pious; devout; faithful; godly." **(1)** The adjective is often
used to describe the faithful Israelite.

(1a) God's *checed* provides the pattern, model,
and strength by which the life of the *chaciyd*
is to be directed. **(1b)** One reference to the
"godly" man appears in Ps 12:1: "Help, LORD;
for the godly man ceaseth; for the faithful fail
from among the children of men." **(1c)** Usually
a suffix or possessive pronoun referring to God
is attached to the word, indicating His special
attachment to those who pattern their lives after His: "O love the LORD, all ye his saints [lit-
erally, "His pious ones"]: for the LORD
preserveth the faithful, and plentifully rewardeth the proud doer" (Ps 31:23). **(2)** Following the Greek *hosios* and Latin *sanctus,* the
KJV often renders the word "saint"—which
must be understood in the sense of sanctification [dependent upon grace], not moralistically
[of native goodness]. See: TWOT—698b; BDB—
339c.

2624. חֲסִידָה {6x} **chăçîydâh,** *khas-ee-daw';*
fem. of 2623; the *kind* (mater-
nal) bird, i.e. a *stork:*—X feathers {1x}, stork
{5x}. See: TWOT—698c; BDB—339d.

2625. חָסִיל {6x} **chaçîyl,** *khaw-seel';* from
2628; the *ravager,* i.e. a *locust:*—
caterpillar {6x}. See: TWOT—701a; BDB—
340c.

2626. חָסִין {1x} **chăçîyn,** *khas-een';* from 2630;
prop. *firm,* i.e. (by impl.) *mighty:*—
strong {1x}. See: TWOT—703c; BDB—340d.

2627. חַסִּיר {1x} **chaççîyr** (Aram.), *khas-seer';*
from a root corresp. to 2637; *defi-
cient:*—wanting {1x}. Syn.: 47, 410, 533, 553,
1368, 2388, 2428, 2642, 5794. See: BDB—1093c.

2628. חָסַל {1x} **châçal,** *khaw-sal';* a prim.
root; to *eat* off:—consume {1x}.
Syn.: 3615. See: TWOT—701; BDB—340c.

2629. חָסַם {2x} **châçam,** *khaw-sam';* a prim.
root; to *muzzle;* by anal. to *stop*
the nose:—muzzle {1x}, stop {1x}. See: TWOT—
702; BDB—340c.

2630. חָסַן {1x} **châçan,** *khaw-san';* a prim.
root; prop. to (*be*) *compact;* by impl.
to *hoard:*—lay up {1x}. See: TWOT—703;
BDB—340d, 1093c.

2631. חֲסַן {2x} **chăçan** (Aram.), *khas-an';* corresp. to 2630; to *hold* in occu-
pancy:—possess {2x}. See: TWOT—2738; BDB—
1093c.

2632. חֱסֵן {2x} **chêçen** (Aram.), *khay'-sen;*
from 2631; *strength:*—power {2x}.
Syn.: 410, 2428, 3027, 3581, 5797. See: TWOT—
2738a; BDB—1093c.

2633. חֹסֶן {5x} **chôçen,** *kho'-sen;* from 2630;
wealth:—riches {1x}, strength {2x},
treasure {2x}. See: TWOT—703a; BDB—340d.

2634. חָסֹן {2x} ch**â**çôn, *khaw-sone';* from 2630; *powerful:*—strong {2x}. Syn.: 47, 533, 553, 1368, 2388, 2389, 5794, 5797. See: TWOT—703b; BDB—340d.

2635. חֲסַף {9x} ch**ă**çaph (Aram.), *khas-af';* from a root corresp. to that of 2636; a *clod:*—clay {9x}. Syn.: 2563, 2916, 4423. See: TWOT—2739; BDB—1093c.

2636. חַסְפַּס {1x} chaçpaç, *khas-pas';* redupl. from an unused root mean. appar. to *peel;* a *shred* or *scale:*—round thing {1x}. See: TWOT—704; BDB—341a, 1093c.

2637. חָסֵר {21x} ch**â**çêr, *khaw-sare';* a prim. root; to *lack;* by impl. to *fail, want, lessen:*—want {7x}, lack {6x}, fail {3x}, decreased {1x}, abated {1x}, have need {1x}, made lower {1x}, bereave {1x}. See: TWOT—705; BDB—341a, 1093c.

2638. חָסֵר {19x} ch**â**çêr, *khaw-sare';* from 2637; *lacking;* hence, *without:*—void {6x}, want {5x}, lack {4x}, fail {2x}, destitute {1x}, need {1x}. See: TWOT—705c; BDB—341c.

2639. חֶסֶר {2x} cheçer, *kheh'-ler;* from 2637; *lack;* hence, *destitution:*—poverty {1x}, want {1x}. See: TWOT—705a; BDB—341c.

2640. חֹסֶר {3x} ch**ô**çer, *kho'-ser;* from 2637; *poverty:*—in want of {3x}. See: TWOT—705b; BDB—341c.

2641. חַסְרָה {1x} Chaçr**â**h, *khas-raw';* from 2637; *want; Chasrah,* an Isr.:—Hasrah {1x}. See: BDB—341c.

2642. חֶסְרוֹן {1x} cheçrôwn, *khes-rone';* from 2637; *deficiency:*—that which is wanting {1x}. See: TWOT—705d; 341c.

2643. חַף {1x} chaph, *khaf;* from 2653 (in the mor. sense of *covered* from soil); *pure:*—innocent {1x}. Syn.: 5355. See: TWOT—711a; BDB—341d, 342c.

2644. חָפָא {1x} ch**â**ph**â**', *khaw-faw';* an orth. var. of 2645; prop. to *cover,* i.e. (in a sinister sense) to *act covertly:*—do secretly {1x}. See: TWOT—706; BDB—341d.

2645. חָפָה {12x} ch**â**ph**â**h, *khaw-faw';* a prim. root (comp. 2644, 2653); to *cover;* by impl. to *veil,* to *incase, protect:*—ceiled {x}, covered {7x}, overlaid {4x}. See: TWOT—707; BDB—341d.

2646. חֻפָּה {3x} chupp**â**h, *khoop-paw';* from 2645; a *canopy:*—chamber {1x}, closet {1x}, defence {1x}. See: TWOT—710b; BDB—342a, 342c,

2647. חֻפָּה {1x} Chupp**â**h, *khoop-paw';* the same as 2646; *Chuppah,* an Isr.:—Huppah {1x}. See: BDB—342a, 342c.

2648. חָפַז {9x} ch**â**phaz, *khaw-faz';* a prim. root; prop. to *start* up suddenly, i.e. (by impl.) to *hasten* away, to *fear:*—haste {3x}, to haste {3x}, make haste {2x}, tremble {1x}. See: TWOT—708; BDB—342a.

2649. חִפָּזוֹן {3x} chîpp**â**zôwn, *khip-paw-zone';* from 2648; *hasty flight:*—haste {3x}. See: TWOT—708a; BDB—342a.

2650. חֻפִּים {3x} Chuppîym, *khoop-peem';* plur. of 2646 [comp. 2349]; *Chuppim,* an Isr.:—Huppim {3x}. See: BDB—342a, 342c.

2651. חֹפֶן {6x} chôphen, *kho'-fen;* from an unused root of uncert. signif.; a *fist* (only in the dual):—hand {4x}, fist {1x}, handful + 4393 {1x}. See: TWOT—709a; BDB—342b.

2652. חָפְנִי {5x} Chophnîy, *khof-nee';* from 2651; perh. *pugilist; Chophni,* an Isr.:—Hophni {5x}. See: BDB—342b.

2653. חָפַף {1x} chôphaph, *khaw-faf';* a prim. root (comp. 2645, 3182); to *cover* (in protection):—cover {1x}. See: TWOT—710; BDB—342b.

2654. חָפֵץ {75x} ch**â**phêts, *khaw-fates';* a prim. root; prop. to *incline* to; by impl. (lit. but rarely) to *bend;* fig. to *be pleased* with, *desire:*—delight {39x}, please {14x}, desire {9x}, will {3x}, pleasure {3x}, favour {2x}, like {2x}, moveth {1x}, would {1x}, at all {1x}.

Chaphets (2654), as a verb, means "to take pleasure in, take care of, desire, delight in, have delight in." **(1)** *Chaphets* means "to delight in" in 2 Sa 15:26: "But if he thus say, I have no delight in thee; behold, here am I, let him do to me as seemeth good unto him." **(2)** There is no reference to what we call favoritism, **(2a)** i.e., the overlooking of the claims of some so as to gratify the wishes of special friends; **(2b)** it is simply recorded that pleasure was found in certain persons, whatever the ground of it might be. **(3)** It is not so much an intense pleasurable emotion as a favorable disposition, or the prompting of the heart to take a certain course of action from a sense of fitness. See: TWOT—712, 713; BDB—342c, 33c.

2655. חָפֵץ {11x} ch**â**phêts, *khaw-fates';* from 2654; *pleased* with:—desire {3x}, have pleasure {2x}, whosoever would {1x}, if it please {1x}, willing {1x}, favour {1x}, wish {1x}, delight {1x}.

Chaphets means delighting in, having pleasure in (Ps 35:27): "Let the Lord be magnified, which hath pleasure in the prosperity of his servant." See: TWOT—712a; BDB—343a.

2656. חֵפֶץ ch**ê**phets, *khay'-fets;* from 2654; *pleasure;* hence, (abstr.) *desire;*

concr. a *valuable* thing; hence, (by extens.) a *matter* (as something in mind):—pleasure {16x}, desire {12x}, delight {3x}, purpose {3x}, acceptable {1x}, delightsome {1x}, matter {1x}, pleasant {1x}, willingly {1x}.

Chephets, as a noun, means "pleasure; delight; desire; request; affair; thing." **(1)** This word often means "pleasure" or "delight": **(1a)** "Hath the LORD as great delight in burnt offerings and sacrifices, as in obeying the voice of the LORD?" (1 Sa 15:22—the first occurrence). **(1b)** Thus "the preacher [writer of Ecclesiastes] sought to find out acceptable [*chephets*] words: and that which was written was upright, even words of truth" (Eccl 12:10), words that were both true and aesthetically pleasing. **(2)** A good wife works with "hands of delight," or hands which delight in her work because of her love for her family; "she seeketh wool, and flax, and worketh willingly [in delight] with her hands" (Prov 31:13). **(2)** *Chephets* can mean not simply what one takes pleasure in or what gives someone delight but one's wish or desire: "Although my house be not so with God; yet he hath made with me an everlasting covenant, ordered in all things, and sure: for this is all my salvation, and all my desire, although he make it not to grow" (2 Sa 23:5).

(3) "To do one's desire" is to grant a request (1 Kin 5:8). **(4)** "Stones of desire" are precious stones (Is 54:12). **(5)** *Chephets* sometimes represents one's *affairs* as that in which one takes delight: **(5a)** "There is . . . a time to every purpose [literally, delight] under the heaven" (Eccl 3:1). **(5b)** In Is 58:13 the first occurrence of this word means "pleasure" or "delight," while the last occurrence indicates an affair or matter in which one delights: "If thou turn away thy foot from the sabbath, from doing thy pleasure on my holy day; and call the sabbath a delight, the holy of the LORD, honorable; and shalt honor him, not doing thine own ways, nor finding thine own pleasure, nor speaking thine own words." **(6)** Finally, in one passage this word means "affair" in the sense of a "thing" or "situation": "If thou seest the oppression of the poor, and violent perverting of judgment and justice in a province, marvel not at the matter" (Eccl 5:8). See: TWOT—712b; BDB—343a.

2657. חֶפְצִי בָהּ {2x} **Chephtsîy bâhh**, *khef-tsee′-baw;* from 2656 with suffixes; *my delight* (is) *in her; Cheptsi-bah,* a fanciful name for Pal.:—Hephzi-bah {2x}. See: BDB—343b.

2658. חָפַר {22x} **châphar**, *khaw-far′;* a prim. root; prop. to *pry* into; by impl. to *delve,* to *explore:*—dig {17x}, search out {3x}, paweth {1x}, seeketh {1x}. See: TWOT—714; BDB—343c.

2659. חָפֵר {17x} **châphêr**, *khaw-fare′;* a prim. root [perhaps rath. the same as 2658 through the idea of *detection*]: to *blush;* fig. to *be ashamed, disappointed;* caus. to *shame, reproach:*—be ashamed {4x}, be confounded {6x}, be brought to confusion {2x}, be brought unto shame {4x}, bring reproach {1x}. See: TWOT—715; BDB—344a.

2660. חֵפֶר {9x} **Chêpher**, *khay′-fer;* from 2658 or 2659; a *pit* or *shame; Chepher,* a place in Pal.; also the name of three Isr.:—Hepher {9x}. See: BDB—343d.

2661. חָפֹר {1x} **châphôr**, *khaf-ore′;* from 2658; a *hole;* only in connection with 6512, which ought rather to be joined as one word, thus

חֲפַרְפֵּרָה **chăpharpêrâh**, *khaf-ar-pay-raw′;* by redupl. from 2658; a *burrower,* i.e. prob. a *rat:*—+ mole {1x}. See: TWOT—714a; BDB—344a, 344b, 826c.

2662. חֶפְרִי {1x} **Chephrîy**, *khef-ree′;* patron. from 2660; a *Chephrite* (collect.) or desc. of *Chepher:*—Hepherites {1x}. See: BDB—343d.

2663. חֲפָרַיִם {1x} **Chăphârayim**, *khaf-aw-rah′-yim;* dual of 2660; *double pit; Chapharajim,* a place in Pal.:—Haphraim {1x}. See: BDB—343d.

חֲפַרְפֵּרָה **chăpharpêrâh**. See 2661.

2664. חָפַשׂ {23x} **châphas**, *khaw-fas′;* a prim. root; to *seek;* caus. to *conceal* oneself (i.e. let be sought), or *mask:*—search {11x}, disguise {7x}, search out {2x}, changed {1x}, diligent {1x}, hidden {1x}. See: TWOT—716; BDB—344b.

2665. חֵפֶשׂ {1x} **chêphes**, *khay′-fes;* from 2664; something *covert,* i.e. a *trick:*—search {1x}. See: TWOT—716a; BDB—344c.

2666. חָפַשׁ {1x} **châphash**, *khaw-fash′;* a prim. root; to *spread* loose; fig. to *manumit:*—be free {1x}. See: TWOT—717; BDB—344d.

2667. חֹפֶשׁ {1x} **chôphesh**, *kho′-fesh;* from 2666; something *spread* loosely, i.e. a *carpet:*—precious {1x}. See: TWOT—717a; BDB—344d.

2668. חֻפְשָׁה {1x} **chuphshâh**, *khoof-shaw′;* from 2666; *liberty* (from slavery):—freedom {1x}. See: TWOT—717b; BDB—344d.

2669. חָפְשׁוּת {3x} **chôphshûwth**, *khof-shooth′;* and

חָפְשִׁית **chophshîyth**, *khof-sheeth′;* from 2666; *prostration* by sickness

(with 1004, a *hospital*):—several {3x}. See: TWOT—717d; BDB—345a.

2670. חָפְשִׁי {17x} **chophshîy**, *khof-shee';* from 2666; *exempt* (from bondage, tax or care):—free {16x}, liberty {1x}.

2671. חֵץ {53x} **chêts**, *khayts;* from 2686; prop. a *piercer*, i.e. an *arrow;* by impl. a *wound;* fig. (of God) thunder-*bolt;* (by interchange for 6086) the *shaft* of a spear:—arrow {48x}, archers + 1167 {1x}, dart {1x}, shaft {1x}, wound {1x}, variant {1x}. See: TWOT—721b; BDB—345a, 346b.

חֻץ **chûts**. See 2351.

2672. חָצַב {25x} **châtsab**, *khaw-tsab';* or

חָצֵב **châtsêb**, *khaw-tsabe';* a prim. root; to *cut* or *carve* (wood, stone or other material); by impl. to *hew, split, square, quarry, engrave:*—dig {5x}, hew {4x}, hewers {4x}, hew out {4x}, mason {3x}, cut {1x}, divideth {1x}, graven {1x}, hewn {1x}, made {1x}. See: TWOT—718; BDB—345a.

2673. חָצָה {15x} **châtsâh**, *khaw-tsaw';* a prim. root [comp. 2686]); to *cut* or *split* in two; to *halve:*—divide {11x}, part {2x}, live out half {1x}, midst {1x}.

Chatsah, as a verb, means "to divide, reach unto." The word most commonly means "to divide," as in Ex 21:35: "Then they shall sell the live ox, and divide the money of it." See: TWOT—719; BDB—345b.

2674. חָצוֹר {19x} **Châtsôwr**, *khaw-tsore';* a collect. form of 2691; *village; Chatsor,* the name (thus simply) of two places in Pal. and of one in Arabia:—Hazor {19x}. See: BDB—347d.

2675. חָצוֹר חֲדַתָּה {1x} **Châtsôwr Chădattâh**, *khaw-tsore' khad-at-taw';* from 2674 and a Chaldaizing form of the fem. of 2319 [comp. 2323]; *new Chatsor,* a place in Pal.:—Hazor, Hadattah [*as if two places*] {1x}. See: BDB—347d.

2676. חָצוֹת {3x} **châtsôwth**, *khaw-tsoth';* from 2673; the *middle* (of the night):—midnight {3x}. See: TWOT—719a; BDB—345c, 346a.

2677. חֵצִי {125x} **chêtsîy**, *khay-tsee';* from 2673; the *half* or *middle:*—half {108x}, midst {8x}, part {4x}, midnight + 3915, middle {1x}.

Chetsiy, as a noun, means "half; halfway; middle." **(1)** First, the word is used to indicate "half" of anything. This meaning first occurs in Ex 24:6: "And Moses took half of the blood, and put it in basins; and half of the blood he sprinkled on the altar." **(2)** Second, *chetsiy* can mean "middle," as it does in its first biblical

appearance: "And it came to pass, that at midnight [literally, "the middle of the night"] the LORD smote all the first-born in the land of Egypt" (Ex 12:29). **(3)** In Ex 27:5, the word means "halfway": "And thou shalt put it under the compass of the altar beneath, that the net may be even to the midst [i.e., up to the middle] of the altar." See: TWOT—719b; BDB—345c, 346a.

2678. חִצִּי {5x} **chitstsîy**, *khits-tsee';* or

חֵצִי **chêtsîy**, *khay-tsee';* prol. from 2671; an *arrow:*—arrow {5x}. Syn.: 2671. See: TWOT—719c, 721b; BDB—345d.

2679. חֲצִי הַמְּנֻחוֹת {1x} **Chătsîy ham-Mᵉnû-chôwth**, *chat-tsee' ham-men-oo-khoth';* from 2677 and the plur. of 4496, with the art. interposed; *midst of the resting-places; Chatsi-ham-Menuchoth,* an Isr.:—half of the Manahethites {1x}. See: BDB—345d, 630a.

2680. חֲצִי הַמְּנַחְתִּי {1x} **Chătsîy ham-Mᵉnach-tîy**, *khat-see' ham-men-akh-tee';* patron. from 2679; a *Chatsi-ham-Menachtite* or desc. of Chatsi-ham-Menuchoth:—half of the Manahethites {1x}. See: BDB—345d, 630a.

2681. חָצִיר {1x} **châtsîyr**, *khaw-tseer';* a collat. form of 2691; a *court* or *abode:*—court {1x}. See: TWOT—723b; BDB—347d.

2682. חָצִיר {21x} **châtsîyr**, *khaw-tseer';* perh. orig. the same as 2681, from *greenness* of a courtyard; *grass;* also a *leek* (collect.):—grass {17x}, hay {2x}, herb {1x}, leek {1x}. See: TWOT—724a, 725a; BDB—348b.

2683. חֵצֶן {1x} **chêtsen**, *khay'-tsen;* from an unused root mean. to hold *firmly;* the *bosom* (as *comprised* between the arms):—bosom {1x}. Syn.: 2243, 2436, 6747. See: TWOT—720a; BDB—346a.

2684. חֹצֶן {2x} **chôtsen**, *kho'tsen;* a collat. form of 2683, and mean. the same:—arm {1x}, lap {1x}. See: TWOT—720b; BDB—346a.

2685. חֲצַף {2x} **chătsaph** (Aram.), *khats-af';* a prim. root; prop. to *shear* or cut close; fig. to *be severe:*—hasty {1x}, be urgent {1x}. See: TWOT—2740; BDB—1093c.

2686. חָצַץ {3x} **châtsats**, *khaw-tsats';* a prim. root [comp. 2673]; prop. to *chop* into, pierce or sever; hence, to *curtail,* to *distribute* (into ranks); as denom. from 2671, to *shoot* an arrow:—archer {1x}, ✕ bands {1x}, cut off in the midst {1x}. See: TWOT—721, 721c; BDB—346a, 346d.

2687. חָצָץ {3x} **châtsâts,** *khaw-tsawts';* from 2687; prop. something *cutting;* hence, *gravel* (as *grit*); also (like 2671) an *ar-row:*—arrow {1x}, gravel {1x}, stone {1x}. See: TWOT—721a; BDB—346b.

2688. חַצְצוֹן תָּמָר {1x} **Chatsᵉtsôwn Tâmâr,** *khats-ets-one' taw-mawr';* or

חַצְצֹן תָּמָר **Chatsătsôn Tâmâr,** *khats-ats-one' taw-mawr';* from 2686 and 8558; *division* [i.e. perh. *row*] *of* (the) *palm-tree; Chatsetson-tamar,* a place in Pal.:—Hazezon-tamar {1x}. See: BDB—346c.

2689. חֲצֹצְרָה {29x} **chătsôtsᵉrâh,** *khats-o-tser-aw';* by redupl. from 2690; a *trumpet* (from its *sundered* or quavering note):—trumpet {1x}, trumpets {24x}, trumpeter {4x}. See: TWOT—726a; BDB—346d, 348c.

2690. חָצַר {11x} **châtsar,** *khaw-tsar';* a prim. root; prop. to *surround* with a stockade, and thus *separate* from the open country; but used only in the redupl. form

חֲצֹצֵר **chătsôtsêr,** *khast-o-tsare';* or (2 Chr 5:12)

חֲצֹרֵר **chătsôrêr,** *khats-o-rare';* as denom. from 2689; to *trumpet,* i.e. blow on that instrument:—sounded {2x}, blow {1x}, sound {1x}, trumpeters {1x}, sounded {1x}, variant {5x}. See: TWOT—726b; BDB—348b.

2691. חָצֵר {189x} **châtsêr,** *khaw-tsare'* (masc. and fem.); from 2690 in its orig. sense; a *yard* (as *enclosed* by a fence); also a *hamlet* (as similarly *surrounded* with walls):—court {141x}, villages {47x}, towns {1x}.

Chatser means "court; enclosure." **(1)** This word is related to a common Semitic verb that has two meanings: **(1a)** "to be present," in the sense of living at a certain place (encampment, residence, court), and **(1b)** "to enclose, surround, press together." **(1c)** In some Hebrew dictionaries, the usage of *chatser* as "settled abode," "settlement," or "village" is separated from the meaning "court." But most modern dictionaries identify only one root with two related meanings. **(2)** The first biblical occurrence of *chatser* is in Gen 25:16: "These are the sons of Ishmael, and these are their names, by their towns, and by their castles; twelve princes according to their nations." **(2a)** Here *chatser* is related to the first meaning of the root; this occurs less frequently than the usage meaning "court." **(3)** The *chatser* ("settlement") was a place where people lived without an enclosure to protect them. The word is explained in Lev 25:31: "But the houses of the villages which have no wall round about them shall be counted as the fields of the country: they may

be redeemed, and they shall go out in the jubilee."

(3a) *Chatser* signifies the "settlements" of semi-nomadic peoples: the Ishmaelites (Gen 25:16), the Avim (Deut 2:23), and Kedar (Is 42:11). **(3b)** *Chatser* also denotes a "settlement" of people outside the city wall. The cities of Canaan were relatively small and could not contain the whole population. In times of peace, residents of the city might build homes and workshops for themselves outside the wall and establish a separate quarter. If the population grew, the king or governor often decided to enclose the new quarter by surrounding it with a wall and incorporating the section into the existing city, in order to protect the population from bandits and warriors. **(3c)** Jerusalem gradually extended its size westward; at the time of Hezekiah, it had grown into a large city. Huldah the prophetess lived in such a development, known in Hebrew as the *mishneh* (4932): ". . . she dwelt in Jerusalem in the college" (2 Kin 22:14).

(4) The Book of Joshua includes Israel's victories in Canaan's major cities as well as the suburbs: "Ain, Remmon, and Ether, and Ashan; four cities and their villages . . ." (19:7; cf. 15:45, 47; 21:12). **(5)** The predominant usage of *chatser* is "court," whether of a house, a palace, or the temple. **(5a)** Each house generally had a courtyard surrounded by a wall or else one adjoined several homes: "Nevertheless a lad saw them, and told Absalom: but they went both of them away quickly, and came to a man's house in Bahurim, which had a well in his court; whither they went down" (2 Sa 17:18). **(5b)** Solomon's palace had several "courts"—an outer "court," an "enclosed space" around the palace, and a "court" around which the palace was built. **(5c)** Similarly, the temple had various courts. The psalmist expressed his joy in being in the "courts" of the temple, where the birds built their nests (Ps 84:3); "For a day in thy courts is better than a thousand. I had rather be a doorkeeper in the house of my God, than to dwell in the tents of wickedness" (Ps 84:10). **(5d)** God's people looked forward to the thronging together of all the people in God's "courts": ". . . In the courts of the LORD's house, in the midst of thee, O Jerusalem" (Ps 116:19). See: TWOT—722a, 723a; BDB—346d, 347b.

2692. חֲצַר אַדָּר {1x} **Chătsar 'Addâr,** *khats-ar' addawr';* from 2691 and 146; (the) *village of Addar; Chatsar-Addar,* a place in Pal.:—Hazar-addar {1x}. See: BDB—347b.

2693. חֲצַר גַּדָּה {1x} **Chătsar Gaddâh,** *khats-ar' gad-daw';* from 2691 and a fem. of 1408; (the) *village of* (female) *Fortune;*

Chatsar-Gaddah, a place in Pal.:—Hazar-gaddah {1x}. See: BDB—151d, 347c.

2694. חֲצַר הַתִּיכוֹן {1x} **Chătsar hat-Tîykôwn,** *khats-ar' hat-tee-kone';* from 2691 and 8484 with the art. interposed; *village of the middle; Chatsar-hat-Tikon,* a place in Pal.:—Hazar-hatticon {1x}. See: BDB—347c, 1064a.

2695. חֶצְרוֹ {1x} **Chetsrôw,** *khets-ro';* by an orth. var. for 2696; *inclosure; Chetsro,* an Isr.:—Hezro {1x}, Hezrai {1x}. See: BDB—347d.

2696. חֶצְרוֹן {18x} **Chetsrôwn,** *khets-rone';* from 2691; *court-yard; Chetsron,* the name of a place in Pal.; also of two Isr.:— Hezron {18x}. See: BDB—348a.

2697. חֶצְרוֹנִי {2x} **Chetsrôwnîy,** *khets-ro-nee';* patron. from 2696; a *Chetsronite* or (collect.) desc. of Chetsron:—Hezronites {2x}. See: BDB—348a.

2698. חֲצֵרוֹת {6x} **Chătsêrowth,** *khats-ay-roth';* fem. plur. of 2691; *yards; Chats-eroth,* a place in Pal.:—Hazeroth {6x}. See: BDB—348a.

2699. חֲצֵרִים {1x} **Chătsêrîym,** *khats-ay-reem';* plur. masc. of 2691; *yards; Chats-erim,* a place in Pal.:—Hazerim {1x}. See: BDB—346d, 347b.

2700. חֲצַרְמָוֶת {2x} **Chătsarmâveth,** *khats-ar-maw'-veth;* from 2691 and 4194; *village of death; Chatsarmaveth,* a place in Arabia:—Hazarmaveth {1x}. See: BDB—348a.

2701. חֲצַר סוּסָה {1x} **Chătsar Çûwçâh,** *khats-ar' soo-saw';* from 2691 and 5484; *village of cavalry; Chatsar-Susah,* a place in Pal.:—Hazar-susah {1x}. See: BDB—347c.

2702. חֲצַר סוּסִים {1x} **Chătsar Çûwçîym,** *khats-ar' soo-seem';* from 2691 and the plur. of 5483; *village of horses; Chatsar-Susim,* a place in Pal.:—Hazar-susim {1x}. See: BDB—347c.

2703. חֲצַר עֵינוֹן {1x} **Chătsar 'Êynôwn,** *khats-ar' ay-nône';* from 2691 and a der. of 5869; *village of springs; Chatsar-Enon,* a place in Pal.:—Hazar-enon {1x}. See: BDB—347c, 745d.

2704. חֲצַר עֵינָן {3x} **Chătsar 'Êynân,** *khats-ar' ay-nawn';* from 2691 and the same as 5881; *village of springs; Chatsar-Enan,* a place in Pal.:—Hazar-enan {3x}. See: BDB—347c, 745d.

2705. חֲצַר שׁוּעָל {4x} **Chătsar Shûw'âl,** *khats-ar' shoo-awl';* from 2691 and 7776; *village of* (the) *fox; Chatsar-Shual,* a

place in Pal.:—Hazar-shual {4x}. See: BDB—347c.

חֵק **chêq.** See 2436.

2706. חֹק {127x} **chôq,** *khoke;* from 2710; an *enactment;* hence, an *appointment* (of time, space, quantity, labor or usage):— statute {87x}, ordinance {9x}, decree {7x}, due {4x}, law {4x}, portion {3x}, bounds {2x}, custom {2x}, appointed {1x}, commandments {1x}, misc. {7x}: convenient, measure, X necessary, ordinary, set time, task.

Choq, as a noun, means "statute; prescription; rule; law; regulation." **(1)** This noun is derived from the verb *haqaq,* "to cut in, determine, decree." **(2)** The first usage of *choq* is in Gen 47:22: "Only the land of the priests bought he not; for the priests had a portion [*choq*] assigned them of Pharaoh." **(2a)** The meaning of *choq* in the first occurrence (Gen 47:22) differs from the basic meaning of "statute." **(2b)** It has the sense of something allotted or apportioned. **(2c)** A proverb speaks about "food convenient for me" (literally, "food of my prescription or portion"). **(2d)** Job recognized in his suffering that God does what is appointed for him: "For he performeth the thing that is appointed for me [literally, 'he will perform my Law']" (23:14). **(2e)** The "portion" may be something that is due to a person as an allowance or payment. The Egyptian priests received their income from Pharaoh (Gen 47:22), even as God permitted a part of the sacrifice to be enjoyed by the priests: "And it shall be Aaron's and his sons' [as their portion] for ever from the children of Israel: for it is a heave offering" (Ex 29:28).

(3) The word *choq* also signifies "law," or "statute." **(3a)** In a general sense it refers to the "laws" of nature like rain: "When he made a decree for the rain, and a way for the lightning of the thunder" (Job 28:26; cf. Jer 5:22); **(3b)** and the celestial bodies: "He hath also stablished them for ever and ever: he hath made a decree which shall not pass" (Ps 148:6) **(3c)** "Thus saith the LORD, which giveth the sun for a light by day, and the ordinances of the moon and of the stars for a light by night, which divideth the sea when the waves thereof roar; The LORD of hosts is his name: If those ordinances depart from before me, saith the LORD, then the seed of Israel also shall cease from being a nation before me for ever" (Jer 31:35–36). **(4)** Moreover, the word *choq* denotes a "law" promulgated in a country: "And Joseph made it a law over the land of Egypt unto this day, that Pharaoh should have the fifth part; except the land of the priests only, which became not Pharaoh's" (Gen 47:26). **(5)** Finally, and most important, the "law" given by God is

also referred to as a *choq:* "When they have a matter, they come unto me; and I judge between one and another, and I do make them know the statutes [*choq*] of God, and his laws [8451 - *torah*]" (Exod. 18:16). Syn: The word's synonyms are **(A)** mitswah (4687) "commandment"; **(B)** mishpat (4941) "judgment"; **(C)** berit (1285) "covenant"; **(D)** *torah* (8451) "law"; and **(E)** 'edut (5713) "testimony." **(D)** It is not easy to distinguish between these synonyms, as they are often found in conjunction with each other: "Ye shall diligently keep the commandments [*mitswah*] of the LORD your God, and his testimonies ['*edah*], and his statutes [*choq*], which he hath commanded thee" (Deut 6:17). See: TWOT—728a; BDB—348d, 349b, 350c.

2707. חָקָה {4x} **châqah**, *khaw-kaw';* a prim. root; to *carve;* by impl. to *delineate;* also to *intrench:*—portrayed {2x}, carved work {1x}, set a print {1x}. See: TWOT—727; BDB—348d.

2708. חֻקָּה {104x} **chuqqâh**, *khook-kaw';* fem. of 2706, and mean. substantially the same:—statute {77x}, ordinance {22x}, custom {2x}, appointed {1x}, manners {1x}, rites {1x}.

Chuqqah (2708), as a noun means, "statute; regulation; prescription; term." **(1)** *Chuqqah* is found for the first time in God's words of commendation about Abraham to Isaac: "Because that Abraham obeyed my voice, and kept my charge [4931 – mishmeret], my commandments [4687 - *mitswah*], my statutes [*chuqqah*], and my laws [8451 - *torah*]" (Gen 26:5). **(1a)** The primary use of *chuqqah* is in the Pentateuch, especially in Leviticus and Numbers. **(1b)** It is extremely rare in the poetical books and in the prophetic writings (except for Jeremiah and Ezekiel). **(2)** The meaning of "fixed" is similar to the usage of *choq,* in the sense of the laws of nature: **(2a)** "Thus saith the LORD; If my covenant be not with day and night, and if I have not appointed the ordinances of heaven and earth" (Jer 33:25; cf. Job 38:33). **(2b)** Even as the Israelites had a period of rainfall from October to April, there was a fixed period of harvest (from April to June): "Neither say they in their heart, Let us now fear the LORD our God, that giveth rain, both the former and the latter, in his season: he reserveth unto us the appointed weeks of the harvest" (Jer 5:24). **(3)** In addition to regularity of nature, the word *chuqqah* signifies regular payment to the priests: "Which the LORD commanded to be given them of the children of Israel, in the day that he anointed them, by a statute for ever throughout their generations" (Lev 7:36). **(4)** In non-religious usage, the word *chuqqah* refers to the customs of the nations: **(4a)**

"After the doings of the land of Egypt, wherein ye dwelt, shall ye not do: and after the doings of the land of Canaan, whither I bring you, shall ye not do: neither shall ye walk in their ordinances" (Lev 18:3; cf. 20:23). **(4b)** The reason for the requirement to abstain from the pagan practices is that they were considered to be degenerate (Lev 18:30). **(5)** The most significant usage of *chuqqah* is God's "law." It is more specific in meaning than *choq* (2706). **(5a)** Whereas *choq* is a general word for "law," *chuqqah* denotes the "law" of a particular festival or ritual. **(5b)** There is the "law" of the Passover (Ex 12:14), Unleavened Bread (Ex 12:17), Feast of Tabernacles (Lev 23:41), the Day of Atonement (Lev 16:29ff.), the priesthood (Ex 29:9), and the blood and fat (Lev 3:17). or **(6)** The "statutes" of people are to be understood as the practices contrary to God's expectations: "For the statutes of Omri are kept, and all the works of the home of Ahab, and ye walk in their counsels, that I should make thee a desolation, and the inhabitants thereof a hissing: therefore ye shall bear the reproach of my people" (Mic 6:16).

(7) The prophet Ezekiel condemned Judah for rejecting God's holy "statutes": **(7a)** "And she hath changed my judgments into wickedness more than the nations, and my statutes [*chuqqah*] more than the countries that are round about her: for they have refused my judgments and my statutes [*chuqqah*], they have not walked in them" (Eze 5:6). **(7b)** He also challenged God's people to repent and return to God's "statutes" that they might live: "If the wicked restore the pledge, give again that he had robbed, walk in the statutes of life, without committing iniquity; he shall surely live, he shall not die" (Eze 33:15). Syn: The word *chuqqah* has many synonyms. At times it forms a part of a series of three: "Beware that thou forget not the Lord thy God, in not keeping his **(1)** commandments [4687 - *mitswah*], and his **(2)** judgments [4941 - *mishpat*], and his statutes [*chuqqah*], which I command thee this day" (Deut 8:11), and at other times of a series of four: "Therefore thou shalt love the LORD thy God, and keep his charge **(3)** [4931 - *mishmeret*], and his statutes [*chuqqah*] and his judgments [4941 - *mishpat*], and his commandments [4687 - *mitswah*], always" (Deut 11:1; cf. Gen 26:5 with *torah* [8451] instead of *mishpat* [4941]). See: TWOT—728b; BDB—349a, 349d.

2709. חֲקוּפָא {2x} **Chăqûwphâ**, *khak-oo-faw';* from an unused root prob. mean. to *bend; crooked; Chakupha,* one of the Nethinim:—Hakupha {2x}. See: BDB—349a.

2710. חָקַק {19x} **châqaq**, *khaw-kak';* a prim. root; prop. to *hack,* i.e. *engrave*

(Judg. 5:14, to *be a scribe* simply); by impl. to *enact* (laws being *cut* in stone or metal tablets in primitive times) or (gen.) *prescribe:*—lawgiver {6x}, governor {2x}, decree {2x}, to grave {2x}, portray {2x}, law {1x}, printed {1x}, set {1x}, note {1x}, appoint {1x}.

Chaqaq, as a verb, means "to cut in, determine, decree." **(1)** *Chaqaq* is used in Is 22:16 with the meaning "to cut in": ". . . That graveth a habitation for himself in a rock." **(2)** In Is 10:1 the verb is used of "enacting a decree": "Woe unto them that decree unrighteous decrees, and that write grievousness which they have prescribed." See: TWOT—728; BDB—349a.

2711. חֵקֶק {2x} **chêqeq,** *khay'-kek;* from 2710; an *enactment,* a *resolution:*—decree {1x}, thought {1x}. See: TWOT—728a; BDB—349b.

2712. חֻקֹּק {2x} **Chuqqôq,** *Khook-koke';* or (fully)

חוּקֹק **Chûwqôq,** *khoo-koke';* from 2710; *appointed; Chukkok* or *Chukok,* a place in Pal.:—Hukkok {1x}, Hukok {1x}. See: BDB—301a, 350c.

2713. חָקַר {27x} **châqar,** *khaw-kar';* a prim. root; prop. to *penetrate;* hence, to *examine* intimately:—search {12x}, search out {9x}, found out {2x}, seek out {1x}, seek {1x}, sounded {1x}, try {1x}. See: TWOT—729; BDB—350c.

2714. חֵקֶר {12x} **chêqer,** *khay'-ker;* from 2713; *examination, enumeration, deliberation:*—search {6x}, unsearchable {2x}, unsearchable + 369 {1x}, finding out {1x}, without number {1x} search out {1x}. See: TWOT—729a; BDB—350d.

2715. חֹר {13x} **chôr,** *khore;* or (fully)

חוֹר **chôwr,** *khore;* from 2787; prop. *white* or *pure* (from the *cleansing* or *shining* power of fire [comp. 2751]; hence, (fig.) *noble* (in rank):—noble {13x}. See: TWOT—757a; BDB—301c, 351a, 359d.

חֻר **chûr.** See 2352.

2716. חֶרֶא {1x} **chere',** *kheh'-reh;* from an unused (and vulgar) root prob. mean. to *evacuate* the bowels: *excrement:*—dung {1x}. See: TWOT—730a; BDB—351a, 844b. Also

חֲרִי **chărîy,** *khar-ee'.*

2717. חָרַב {40x} **chârab,** *khaw-rab';* or

חָרֵב **chârêb,** *khaw-rabe';* a prim. root; to *parch* (through drought) i.e. (by anal.) to *desolate, destroy, kill:*—waste {16x}, dry {7x}, dry up {7x}, desolate {3x}, slay {2x}, decayeth {1x}, destroyed {1x}, destroyer {1x},

surely {1x}, utterly {1x}. See: TWOT—731, 732; BDB—351a, 351c, 352b, 1093d.

2718. חֲרַב {1x} **chărab** (Aram.), *khar-ab';* a root corresp. to 2717; to *demolish:*—destroy {1x}.

Charab means "to smite down, slaughter." The word appears in 2 Kin 3:23: "This is blood: the kings are surely slain." See: TWOT—2741; BDB—1093d.

2719. חֶרֶב {413x} **chereb,** *kheh'-reb;* from 2717; *drought;* also a *cutting* instrument (from its *destructive* effect), as a *knife, sword,* or other sharp implement:—sword {401x}, knife {5x}, dagger {3x}, axes {1x}, mattocks {1x}, tool {1x}, sword + 3027 {1x}.

Chereb, as a noun, means "sword; dagger; flint knife; chisel." **(1)** Usually *chereb* represents an implement that can be or is being used in war, such as a "sword." **(1a)** The exact shape of that implement, however, is not specified by this word. **(1b)** Present day archaeology has unearthed various sickle swords and daggers from the earliest periods. **(1b1)** Sickle swords are so named because they are shaped somewhat like a sickle with the outer edge of the arc being the cutting edge. **(1b2)** These were long one-edged "swords." This is what *chereb* refers to when one reads of someone's being slain with the edge of the "sword": "And they slew Hamor and Shechem his son with the edge of the sword, and took Dinah out of Shechem's house" (Gen 34:26). **(1c)** The first biblical occurrence of the word (Gen 3:24) probably also represents such an implement: "And he placed at the east of the garden of Eden cherubim, and a flaming sword which turned every way."

(2) The precise meaning of *chereb* is confused, however, by its application to what we know as a "dagger," a short two-edged sword: "But Ehud made him a dagger which had two edges, of a cubit [eighteen to twenty-four inches] length" (Judg 3:16). **(3)** The sickle sword was probably the implement used up to and during the conquest of Palestine. About the same time the Sea Peoples (among whom were the Philistines) were invading the ancient Near East. They brought with them a new weapon—the long two-edged "sword." **(3a)** The first clear mention of such a "sword" in the biblical record appears in 1 Sa 17:51: "Therefore David ran, and stood upon the Philistine [Goliath], and took his sword, and drew it out of the sheath thereof, and slew him." **(3b)** Perhaps Saul also used the highly superior Philistine armor and "sword" (1 Sa 17:39), but this is not clear. **(3c)** It is also possible that the angel who confronted Balaam with a drawn "sword" wielded a long two-edged "sword" (Num 22:23). Certainly this would have made him

(humanly speaking) a much more formidable sight. **(3d)** By the time of David, with his expertise and concern for warfare, the large two-edged "sword" was much more prominent if not the primary kind of "sword" used by Israel's heavy infantry.

(4) This two-edged "sword" can be compared **(4a)** to a tongue: ". . . Even the sons of men, whose teeth are spears and arrows, and their tongue a sharp sword" (Ps 57:4). This usage tells us not only about the shape of the "sword" but that such a tongue is a violent, merciless, attacking weapon. **(4b)** In Gen 27:40 "sword" is symbolic of violence: "And by thy sword shalt thou live." **(4c)** Prov 5:4 uses *chereb* (of a long twoedged "sword") to depict the grievous result of dealing with an adulteress; it is certain death: "But her end is bitter as wormwood, sharp as a two-edged sword." **(5)** The "sword" is frequently depicted as an agent of God. **(5a)** It is not only used to safeguard the garden of Eden, **(5b)** but figures in the judgment of God executed upon His enemies: "For my sword shall be bathed in heaven: behold, it shall come down upon Idumea" (Is 34:5; cf. Deut 28:22).

(6) *Chereb* may be used of various other cutting implements. **(6a)** In Josh 5:2 it means "knife": "Make thee sharp knives, and circumcise again the children of Israel the second time." **(6b)** Eze 5:1 uses *chereb* of a barber's "razor": "And thou, son of man, take thee a sharp knife, take thee a barber's razor, and cause it to pass upon thine head and upon thy beard." The exact size and shape of this tool cannot be determined, but it is clear that it was used as a razor. **(7)** This word can also be used of tools ("chisels") for hewing stone: "And if thou wilt make me an altar of stone, thou shalt not build it of hewn stone: for if thou lift up thy tool upon it, thou hast polluted it" (Ex 20:25). The fact that a "sword," an implement of death, would be used to cut the stone for an altar, the instrument of life, explains why this action would profane the altar. See: TWOT—732a; BDB—352b.

2720. חָרֵב {10x} **chârêb**, *khaw-rabe'*; from 2717; *parched* or *ruined:*—desolate {2x}, dry {2x}, waste {6x}. See: TWOT—731a; BDB—351b, 351d.

2721. חֹרֶב {16x} **chôreb**, *kho'-reb;* a collat. form of 2719; *drought* or *desolation:*—heat {6x}, dry {3x}, drought {3x}, waste {2x}, desolation {1x}, utterly {1x}. See: TWOT—731b; BDB—351b, 351c.

2722. חֹרֵב {17x} **Chôrêb**, *kho-rabe';* from 2717; *desolate; Choreb,* a (gen.) name for the Sinaitic mountains:—Horeb {17x}. See: TWOT—731c; BDB—352a.

2723. חָרְבָּה {42x} **chorbâh**, *khor-baw';* fem. of 2721; prop. *drought,* i.e. (by impl.) a *desolation:*—waste {18x}, desolation {8x}, desolate places {4x}, waste places {4x}, desert {3x}, desolate {3x}, decayed places {1x}, destructions {1x}. See: TWOT—731d; BDB—352a.

2724. חָרָבָה {8x} **chârâbâh**, *khaw-raw-baw';* fem. of 2720; a *desert:*—dry {1x}, dry ground {3x}, dry land {4x}. See: TWOT—731e; BDB—351c.

2725. חֲרָבוֹן {1x} **chărâbôwn**, *khar-aw-bone';* from 2717; *parching heat:*—drought {1x}. See: TWOT—731f; BDB—351c.

2726. חַרְבוֹנָא {2x} **Charbôwnâ³**, *khar-bo-naw';* or

חַרְבוֹנָה **Charbôwnâh**, *khar-bo-naw';* of Pers. or.; *Charbona* or *Charbonah,* a eunuch of Xerxes:—Harbona {1x}, Harbonah {1x}. See: BDB—353a.

2727. חָרַג {1x} **chârag**, *khaw-rag';* a prim. root; prop. to *leap* suddenly, i.e. (by impl.) to *be dismayed:*—be afraid {1x}. See: TWOT—733; BDB—353a.

2728. חַרְגֹּל {1x} **chargôl**, *khar-gole';* from 2727; the *leaping* insect, i.e. a *locust:*—beetle {1x}. See: TWOT—734a; BDB—353b.

2729. חָרַד {29x} **chârad**, *khaw-rad';* a prim. root; to *shudder* with terror; hence, to *fear;* also to *hasten* (with anxiety):—afraid {20x}, tremble {13x}, fray away {2x}, careful {1x}, discomfited {1x}, fray {1x}, quaked {1x}. See: TWOT—735; BDB—353b.

2730. חָרֵד {6x} **chârêd**, *khaw-rade';* from 2729; *fearful;* also *reverential:*—afraid {1x}, trembling {5x}. See: TWOT—735a; BDB—353d.

2731. חֲרָדָה {9x} **chărâdâh**, *khar-aw-daw';* fem. of 2730; *fear, anxiety:*—trembling {4x}, fear {2x}, exceedingly {1x}, care {1x}, quaking {1x}. See: TWOT—735b; BDB—353d.

2732. חֲרָדָה {2x} **Chărâdâh**, *khar-aw-daw';* the same as 2731; *Charadah,* a place in the Desert:—Haradah {2x}. See: BDB—354a.

2733. חֲרֹדִי {2x} **Chărôdîy**, *khar-o-dee';* patrial from a der. of 2729 [comp. 5878]; a *Charodite,* or inhab. of Charod:—Harodite {2x}. See: BDB—248b, 353d.

2734. חָרָה {90x} **chârâh**, *khaw-raw';* a prim. root [comp. 2787]; to *glow* or grow warm; fig. (usually) to *blaze* up, of anger, zeal, jealousy:—kindled {44x}, wroth {13x}, hot

{10x}, angry {9x}, displease {4x}, fret {4x}, incensed {2x}, burn {1x}, earnestly {1x}, grieved {1x}, very {1x}.

Charah means "to get angry, be angry." **(1)** In the basic stem, the word refers to the "burning of anger" as in Jonah 4:1. **(2)** In the causative stem, it means "to become heated with work" or "with zeal for work" (Neh 3:20). Syn.: See 8474. See: TWOT−736; BDB−354a.

2735. חֹר הַגִּדְגָּד {2x} **Chôr hag-Gidgâd**, *khore hag-ghid-gawd';* from 2356 and a collat. (masc.) form of 1412, with the art. interposed; *hole of the cleft; Chor-hag-Gidgad,* a place in the Desert:−Hor-hagidgad {2x}. See: BDB−151d, 301b, 351a.

2736. חַרְהֲיָה {1x} **Charhăyâh**, *khar-hah-yaw';* from 2734 and 3050; *fearing Jah; Charhajah,* an Isr.:−Harhaiah {1x}. See: BDB−354c, 354d.

2737. חָרוּז {1x} **chârûwz**, *khaw-rooz';* from an unused root mean. to *perforate;* prop. *pierced,* i.e. a *bead* of pearl, gems or jewels (as strung):−chain {1x}. See: TWOT−737a; BDB−354d.

2738. חָרוּל {3x} **chârûwl**, *khaw-rool';* or (short.)

חָרֻל **chârûl**, *khaw-rool';* appar. a pass. part. of an unused root prob. mean. to *be prickly;* prop. *pointed,* i.e. a *bramble* or other thorny weed:−nettle {3x}. See: TWOT−743a; BDB−355b.

חֹרוֹן **chôrôwn**. See 1032, 2772.

2739. חָרוּמַף {1x} **Chărûwmaph**, *khar-oo-maf';* from pass. part. of 2763 and 639; *snub-nosed; Charumaph,* an Isr.:−Harumaph {1x}. See: BDB−354d.

2740. חָרוֹן {41x} **chârôwn**, *khaw-rone';* or (short.)

חָרֹן **chârôn**, *khaw-rone';* from 2734; a *burning* of anger:−fierce {23x}, fierceness {9x}, wrath {6x}, fury {1x}, wrathful {1x}, displeasure {1x}.

Charon means "burning anger." This word refers exclusively to divine anger as that which is "burning." It first appears in Ex 32:12: "Turn from thy fierce wrath [charon], and repent of this evil against thy people." See: TWOT−736a; BDB−354c.

2741. חָרוּפִי {1x} **Chărûwphîy**, *khar-oo-fee';* a patrial from (prob.) a collat. form of 2756; a *Charuphite* or inhab. of Charuph (or Chariph):−Haruphite {1x}. See: BDB−358b.

2742. חָרוּץ {18x} **chârûwts**, *khaw-roots';* or

חָרֻץ **chârûts**, *khaw-roots';* pass. part. of 2782; prop. *incised* or (act.) *incisive;* hence, (as noun masc. or fem.) a *trench* (as dug), *gold* (as mined), a *threshing-sledge* (having sharp teeth); (fig.) *determination;* also *eager:*−gold {6x}, diligent {5x}, decision {2x}, threshing instrument {2x}, sharp {1x}, sharp things {1x}, wall {1x}. See: TWOT−752a,b, 753a; BDB−358c, 358d, 359a.

2743. חָרוּץ {1x} **Chârûwts**, *khaw-roots';* the same as 2742; *earnest; Charuts,* an Isr.:−Haruz {1x}. See: BDB−358d.

2744. חַרְחוּר {2x} **Charchûwr**, *khar-khoor';* a fuller form of 2746; *inflammation; Charchur,* one of the Nethinim:−Harhur {2x}. See: BDB−354d, 359c.

2745. חַרְחַס {1x} **Charchaç**, *khar-khas';* from the same as 2775; perh. *shining; Charchas,* an Isr.:−Harhas {1x}. See: BDB−354d.

2746. חַרְחֻר {1x} **charchûr**, *khar-khoor';* from 2787; *fever* (as *hot*):−extreme burning {1x}. See: TWOT−756b; BDB−354d, 359c.

2747. חֶרֶט {2x} **cheret**, *kheh'-ret;* from a prim. root mean. to *engrave;* a *chisel* or *graver;* also a *style* for writing:−graving tool {1x}, pen {1x}. See: TWOT−738a; BDB−354d.

חָרִט **chârît**. See 2754.

2748. חַרְטֹם {11x} **chartôm**, *khar-tome';* from the same as 2747; a *horoscopist* (as *drawing* magical lines or circles):−magician {11x}. See: TWOT−738b; BDB−355a, 1093d.

2749. חַרְטֹם {5x} **chartôm** (Aram.), *khar-tome';* the same as 2748:−magician {5x}. See: TWOT−2742; BDB−1093d.

2750. חֳרִי {6x} **chŏrîy**, *khor-ee';* from 2734; a *burning* (i.e. intense) anger:−fierce {3x}, great {2x}, heat {1x}. See: TWOT−736b; BDB−354c.

חֲרִי **chărîy**. See 2716.

2751. חֹרִי {1x} **chôrîy**, *kho-ree';* from the same as 2353; *white* bread:−white {1x}. Syn.: 3835, 3836, 7836. See: TWOT−740; BDB−301a, 355a.

2752. חֹרִי {6x} **Chôrîy**, *kho-ree';* from 2356; *cave-dweller* or troglodyte; a *Chorite* or aboriginal Idumæan:−Horims {2x}, Horites {4x}. See: BDB−355b, 360a.

2753. חֹרִי {4x} **Chôrîy,** *kho-ree';* or

חוֹרִי **Chôwrîy,** *kho-ree';* the same as 2752; *Chori,* the name of two men:—Hori {4x}. See: BDB—355b, 360a.

2754. חָרִיט {2x} **chârîyt,** *khaw-reet';* or

חָרִט **chârit,** *khaw-reet';* from the same as 2747; prop. *cut* out (or *hollow),* i.e. (by impl.) a *pocket:*—bag {1x}, crisping pin {1x}. See: TWOT—739a; BDB—355a.

2755. חֲרֵי־יֹונִים {2x} **chărêy-yôwnîym,** *khar-ay'-yo-neem';* from the plur. of 2716 and the plur. of 3123; *excrements of doves* [or perh. rather the plur. of a single word].

חֲרָאיֹון **chârâ'yôwn,** *khar-aw-yone';* of similar or uncert. der.], prob. a kind of vegetable:—doves' dung {2x}. See: TWOT—730a; BDB—351a, 355b.

2756. חָרִיף {2x} **Chârîyph,** *khaw-reef';* from 2778; *autumnal; Chariph,* the name of two Isr.:—Hariph {2x}. See: BDB—358b.

2757. חָרִיץ {2x} **chârîyts,** *khaw-reets';* or

חָרִץ **chârits,** *khaw-reets';* from 2782; prop. *incisure* or (pass.) *incised* [comp. 2742]; hence, a *threshing-sledge* (with *sharp* teeth): also a *slice* (as cut):—+ cheese {1x}, harrow {1x}. See: TWOT—752c; BDB—358d.

2758. חָרִישׁ {3x} **chârîysh,** *khaw-reesh';* from 2790; *plowing* or its season:—earing (time) {2x}, ground {1x}. See: TWOT—760c; BDB—361a.

2759. חֲרִישִׁי {1x} **chărîyshîy,** *khar-ee-shee';* from 2790 in the sense of *silence; quiet,* i.e. *sultry* (as fem. noun, the *sirocco* or hot east wind):—vehement {1x}. See: TWOT—760e; BDB—362a.

2760. חָרַךְ {1x} **chârak,** *khaw-rak';* a prim. root; to *braid* (i.e. to *entangle* or snare) or *catch* (game) in a net:—roast {1x}. See: TWOT—741, 742; BDB—355b.

2761. חֲרַךְ {1x} **chărak** (Aram.), *khar-ak';* a root prob. allied to the equiv. of 2787; to *scorch:*—singe {1x}. See: TWOT—2743; BDB—1093d.

2762. חֶרֶךְ {1x} **cherek,** *kheh'-rek;* from 2760; prop. a *net,* i.e. (by anal.) *lattice:*—lattice {1x}. See: TWOT—742a; BDB—355b.

חָרֻל **chârûl.** See 2738.

2763. חָרַם {52x} **charam,** *khaw-ram';* a prim. root; to *seclude;* spec. (by a ban) to *devote* to relig. uses (espec. destruction); phys. and refl. to *be blunt* as to the nose:—destroy

{34x}, utterly {10x}, devote {2x}, accursed {1x}, consecrate {1x}, forfeited {1x}, flat nose {1x}, utterly to make away {1x}, slay {1x}.

Charam is a religious word of great importance representing the devotion of some object to destruction or to a sacred use, not for the gratification of any selfish purpose. It is rendered **(1)** devote or dedicate **(1a)** a field (Lev 27:21), **(1b)** man (Lev 27:28), **(1c)** beast (Lev 27:28), and **(1d)** land (Lev 27:28–29) which rendered it priestly property (Num 18:14; Eze 44:29). **(2)** This word applied to the destruction of nations, **(2a)** because they were regarded as under the Divine doom, and **(2b)** because the destroyed nations' substance was dedicated to the LORD (Mic 4:13). **(3)** The word is used of the *accursed* (i.e., devoted) **(3a)** city and substance of Jericho (Josh 6:18), and **(3b)** Achan's conduct (Josh 22:20). Things which are cursed are **(3c)** the gold and silver from idols (Deut 7:26), **(3d)** the Edomites (Is 34:5), **(3e)** Jacob (Is 43:28). *Charam* is rendered **(4)** destroy with reference to **(4a)** the Canaanites by Israel, **(4b)** the nations by Nebuchadnezzar (2 Kin 19:11), **(4c)** Egypt by the Lord (Is 11:15), and **(4d)** Judah by Babylon (Jer 25:9).

With regard to exterminating the Canaanites, note: **First,** it was not to accomplish personal revenge, for Israel had no grudge against Canaan; the people had to be almost goaded into the land. **Second,** it was not for plunder for all plunder was devoted to God; hence, *Charam,* accursed. **Third,** it was not to gratify thirst for military glory for the Hebrews, the smallest of nations, and were told beforehand their success would be in God's strength, not theirs. **Fourth,** it was not as a reward for merit; they were a rebellious and stiffnecked people, and would have perished in the wilderness had not God remembered His holy covenant. **Fifth,** the extermination of the Canaanites was to be a security against idolatry and demoralization on the part of Israel. **Last,** these nations had filled up the measure of their iniquity and the Israelites in destroying them were acting magisterially as God's agents. See: TWOT—744, 745; BDB—355c, 356d.

2764. חֵרֶם {38x} **chêrem,** *khay'-rem;* or (Zec 14:11)

חֶרֶם **cherem,** *kheh'-rem;* from 2763; phys. (as *shutting in*) a *net* (either lit. or fig.); usually a *doomed* object; abstr. *extermination:*—net {9x}, accursed thing {9x}, accursed {4x}, curse {4x}, cursed thing {3x}, devoted {3x}, destruction {2x}, devoted thing {2x}, dedicated thing {1x}, destroyed {1x}. See: TWOT—744a, 745a; BDB—356a, 357a.

Hebrew

2765. חֹרֵם {1x} **Chŏrêm**, *khor-ame';* from 2763; *devoted; Chorem,* a place in Pal.:— Horem {1x}. See: BDB—356c.

2766. חָרִם {11x} **Chârîm**, *khaw-reem';* from 2763; *snub-nosed; Charim,* an Isr.:—Harim {11x}. See: BDB—356c.

2767. חָרְמָה {9x} **Chormâh**, *khor-maw';* from 2763; *devoted; Chormah,* a place in Pal.:—Hormah {9x}. See: BDB—356c.

2768. חֶרְמוֹן {13x} **Chermôwn**, *kher-mone';* from 2763; *abrupt; Chermon,* a mount of Pal.:—Hermon {13x}. See: TWOT—744b; BDB—356d.

2769. חֶרְמוֹנִים {1x} **Chermôwnîym**, *kher-mo-neem';* plur. of 2768; *Hermons,* i.e. its peaks:—the Hermonites {1x}. See: BDB—356d.

2770. חֶרְמֵשׁ {2x} **chermêsh**, *kher-mashe';* from 2763; a *sickle* (as *cutting*):— sickle {2x}. See: TWOT—746; BDB—357a.

2771. חָרָן {12x} **Chârân**, *kaw-rawn';* from 2787; *parched; Charan,* the name of a man and also of a place:—Haran {12x}. See: TWOT—747; BDB—357a, 357b.

חָרֹן **chârôn**. See 2740.

2772. חֹרֹנִי {3x} **Chôrônîy**, *kho-ro-nee';* patrial from 2773; a *Choronite* or inhab. of Choronaim:—Horonite {3x}. See: BDB—357b.

2773. חֹרֹנַיִם {4x} **Chôrônayim**, *kho-ro-nah'-yim;* dual of a der. from 2356; *double cave-town; Choronajim,* a place in Moab:—Horonaim {4x}. See: BDB—357b.

2774. חַרְנְפֶר {1x} **Charnepher**, *khar-neh'fer;* of uncert. der.; *Charnepher,* an Isr.:—Harnepher {1x}. See: BDB—357b.

2775. חֶרֶס {4x} **chereç**, *kheh'-res;* or (with a directive enclitic)

חַרְסָה **charçâh**, *khar'-saw;* from an unused root mean. to *scrape;* the *itch;* also [perh. from the mediating idea of 2777] the *sun:*—itch {1x}, sun {3x}. See: TWOT—759b, 748a; BDB—357b, 357c, 360b.

2776. חֶרֶס {1x} **Chereç**, *kheh'-res;* the same as 2775; *shining; Cheres,* a mountain in Pal.:—Heres {1x}. See: BDB—357c, 751c.

2777. חַרְסוּת {1x} **charçûwth**, *khar-sooth';* from 2775 (appar. in the sense of a red *tile* used for scraping); a *potsherd,* i.e. (by impl.) a *pottery;* the name of a gate at Jerusalem:—east {1x}. Syn.: 4217, 6921, 6924, 6926. See: TWOT—759c; BDB—357c, 360b.

2778. חָרַף {41x} **châraph**, *khaw-raf';* a prim. root; to *pull* off, i.e. (by impl.) to *expose* (as by *stripping*); spec. to *betroth* (as if a surrender); fig. to carp at, i.e. *defame;* denom. (from 2779) to spend the *winter:*—reproach {27x}, defy {8x}, betrothed {1x}, blasphemed {1x}, jeoparded {1x}, rail {1x}, upbraid {1x}, winter {1x}.

Charaph means "to say sharp things, reproach." **(1)** In Hebrew the verb refers to a manner of speech, i.e., to reproach someone. **(2)** Ps 42:10: "As with a sword in my bones, mine enemies reproach me; while they say daily unto me, Where is thy God?" See: TWOT—749, 750, 751; BDB—357c, 358b.

2779. חֹרֶף {7x} **chôreph**, *kho'-ref;* from 2778; prop. the *crop* gathered, i.e. (by impl.) the *autumn* (and winter) season; fig. *ripeness* of age:—winter {4x}, youth {1x}, cold {1x}, winterhouse + 1004 {1x}. See: TWOT—750a; BDB—358a.

2780. חָרֵף {1x} **Chârêph**, *khaw-rafe';* from 2778; *reproachful; Chareph,* an Isr.:—Hareph {1x}. See: BDB—358b.

2781. חֶרְפָּה {73x} **cherpâh**, *kher-paw';* from 2778; *contumely, disgrace,* the *pudenda:*—reproach {67x}, shame {3x}, rebuke {2x}, reproachfully {1x}.

Cherpah means "reproach." **(1)** It is rare in the Pentateuch and in the historical books. **(1a)** The noun appears most frequently in the Book of Psalms, in the major prophets, and in Daniel. **(1b)** The first occurrence is in Gen 30:23: "And she conceived, and bare a son; and said, God hath taken away my reproach." **(2)** "Reproach" denotes the state in which one finds himself. **(2a)** The unmarried woman (Is 4:1) or the woman without children (Gen 30:23) carried a sense of disgrace in a society where marriage and fertility were highly spoken of. **(2b)** The destruction of Jerusalem and the Exile brought Judah to the state of "reproach": "O Lord, according to all thy righteousness, I beseech thee, let thine anger and thy fury be turned away from thy city Jerusalem, thy holy mountain: because for our sins, and for the iniquities of our fathers, Jerusalem and thy people are become a reproach to all that are about us" (Dan 9:16).

(3) The disgrace found in a person or a nation became the occasion for taunting the oppressed. **(3a)** The disgraced received abuse by the words spoken against them and by the rumors which were spread about them. **(3b)** Whatever the occasion of the disgrace was whether defeat in battle, exile, or enmity, the psalmist prayed for deliverance from the "reproach": "Remove from me reproach and contempt; for I have kept thy testimonies" (Ps 119:22—see context; cf. Ps 109:25). **(3c)** The verbal abuse that could be heaped upon the unfortunate is

best evidenced by the synonyms found with *cherpah* (2781) in Jer 24:9: "And I will deliver them to be removed into all the kingdoms of the earth for their hurt, to be a reproach and a proverb, a taunt and a curse, in all places whither I shall drive them." **(3d)** Several prophets predicted that Israel's judgment was partly to be experienced by the humiliating "reproach" of the nations: "And I will persecute them with the sword, with the famine, and with the pestilence, and will deliver them to be removed to all the kingdoms of the earth, to be a curse, and an astonishment, and a hissing, and a reproach among all the nations whither I have driven them" (Jer 29:18; cf. Eze 5:14). **(4)** However, the Lord graciously promised to remove the "reproach" at the accomplishment of His purpose: "He will swallow up death in victory; and the Lord GOD will wipe away tears from off all faces; and the rebuke of his people shall he take away from off all the earth" (Is 25:8). See: TWOT—749a; BDB—357d.

2782. חָרַץ {12x} **chârats,** *khaw-rats';* a prim. root; prop. to *point* sharply, i.e. (lit.) to *wound;* fig. to *be alert,* to *decide:*—determined {6x}, move {2x}, decide {1x}, bestir {1x}, maim {1x}, decreed {1x}. See: TWOT—752; 358c.

2783. חֲרַץ {1x} **chărats** (Aram.), *khar-ats';* from a root corresp. to 2782 in the sense of *vigor;* the *loin* (as the seat of strength):—loin {1x}. See: TWOT—2744; BDB—1093d.

חָרֻץ **chârûts.** See 2742.

2784. חַרְצֻבָּה {2x} **chartsubbâh,** *khar-tsoob-baw';* of uncert. der.; a *fetter;* fig. a *pain:*—band {2x}. See: TWOT—754a; BDB—359a.

חָרִץ **chârîts.** See 2757.

2785. חַרְצָן {1x} **chartsan,** *khar-tsan';* from 2782; a *sour* grape (as *sharp* in taste):—kernel {1x}. See: TWOT—752d; BDB—359a, 359b.

2786. חָרַק {5x} **châraq,** *khaw-rak';* a prim. root; to *grate* the teeth:—gnash {5x}. See: TWOT—755; BDB—359b.

2787. חָרַר {11x} **chârar,** *khaw-rar';* a prim. root; to *glow,* i.e. lit. (to *melt, burn, dry* up) or fig. (to *show* or *incite passion):*—burn {8x}, dried {1x}, angry {1x}, kindle {1x}. See: TWOT—756; BDB—359b.

2788. חָרֵר {1x} **chârêr,** *khaw-rare';* from 2787; *arid:*—parched place {1x}. See: TWOT—756a; BDB—359c.

2789. חֶרֶשׂ {17x} **cheres,** *kheh'-res;* a collat. form mediating between 2775 and 2791; a piece of *pottery:*—earthen {8x}, pot-sherd {5x}, sherd {2x}, stone {1x}, earth {1x}. See: TWOT—759a; BDB—360a.

2790. חָרַשׁ {73x} **chârash,** *khaw-rash';* a prim. root; to *scratch,* i.e. (by impl.) to *engrave, plow;* hence, (from the use of tools) to *fabricate* (of any material); fig. to *devise* (in a bad sense); hence, (from the idea of secrecy) to *be silent,* to *let alone;* hence, (by impl.) to *be deaf* (as an accompaniment of dumbness):—peace {26x}, plow {13x}, devise {5x}, keep . . . silence {5x}, hold . . . tongue {4x}, altogether {3x}, plowman {2x}, cease {1x}, conceal {1x}, deaf {1x}, to ear {1x}, graven {1x}, imagine {1x}, leave off speaking {1x}, hold peace {1x}, be quiet {1x}, rest {1x}, practise secretly {1x}, be silent {1x}, speak not a word {1x}, be still {1x}, worker {1x}.

Charash, as a verb, means "to plow, engrave, work in metals." **(1)** A fitting word for the agricultural nature of Israelite culture, *charash* is frequently used of "plowing" a field, usually with animals such as oxen (1 Kin 19:19). **(2)** The imagery of cutting up or tearing up a field with a plow easily lent itself to the figurative use of the word to mean mistreatment by others: "The plowers plowed upon my back: they made long their furrows" (Ps 129:3). **(3)** The word is used to express the plotting of evil against a friend in Prov 3:29: "Devise not evil against thy neighbor, seeing he dwelleth securely by thee [literally, "do not plow evil"]."

(4) The use of *charash* in the sense of "working or engraving" metals is not used in the Old Testament as much as it might have been if Israel had been as given to such craftsmanship as her neighbors, or perhaps because of the commandment against images (Ex 20:4). **(4a)** The word is used in 1 Kin 7:14: "His father was a man of Tyre, a worker in brass [literally, 'a man who works in brass']." **(4b)** The first occurrence of *charash* is in Gen 4:22 where it is used of the "artificer in brass and iron." **(5)** The figurative use of "engraving" is vividly seen in the expression describing the extent of Israel's sin: "The sin of Judah is written with a pen of iron, and with the point of a diamond: it is graven upon the table of their heart" (Jer 17:1). See: TWOT—760, 761; BDB—360b, 361a.

2791. חֶרֶשׁ {4x} **cheresh,** *kheh'-resh;* from 2790; magical *craft;* also *silence:*—craftsmen {2x}, artificer {1x}, secretly {1x}. See: TWOT—761b, 763a; BDB—361c, 361d.

2792. חֶרֶשׁ {1x} **Cheresh,** *kheh'-resh;* the same as 2791; *Cheresh,* a Levite:—Heresh {1x}. See: BDB—361d.

2793. חֹרֶשׁ {7x} **chôresh,** *kho'-resh;* from 2790; a *forest* (perh. as furnishing the material for fabric):—wood {4x}, forest {1x},

bough {1x}, shroud {1x}. See: TWOT—762a; BDB—361c.

2794. חֹרֵשׁ {1x} **chôrêsh,** *kho-rashe';* act. part. of 2790; a *fabricator* or mechanic:—artificer {1x}. See: TWOT—763a; BDB—360c.

2795. חֵרֵשׁ {9x} **chêrêsh,** *khay-rashe';* from 2790; *deaf* (whether lit. or spir.):— deaf {9x}. See: TWOT—761a; BDB—361b.

2796. חָרָשׁ {33x} **chârâsh,** *khaw-rawsh';* from 2790; a *fabricator* or any material:—carpenter {11x}, workman {6x}, craftsman {4x}, engraver {3x}, artificers {2x}, smith {2x}, makers {1x}, skilful {1x}, smith + 1270 {1x}, workers {1x}, wrought {1x}.

Charash, as a noun, means "engraver; artificer." **(1)** The prophets denounced the craftsmanship of these workers in metals when they made images (Is 40:20; Hos 8:6). **(2)** A more positive approach to the word is conveyed in 1 Chr 29:5: "The gold for things of gold . . . and for all manner of work to be made by the hands of artificers. And who then is willing to consecrate his service this day unto the Lord?" See: TWOT—760a; BDB—360d, 361d.

2797. חַרְשָׁא {2x} **Charshâ',** *khar-shaw';* from 2792; *magician; Charsha,* one of the Nethinim:—Harsha {2x}. See: BDB—361d.

2798. חֲרָשִׁים {2x} **Chărâshîym,** *khar-aw-sheem';* plur. of 2796; *mechanics,* the name of a valley in Jerusalem:—Charashim {1x}, craftsmen {1x}. See: BDB—161b, 360d.

2799. חֲרֹשֶׁת {4x} **chărôsheth,** *khar-o'-sheth;* from 2790; mechanical *work:*— carving {2x}, cutting {2x}. See: TWOT—760b; BDB—360d.

2800. חֲרֹשֶׁת {3x} **Chărôsheth,** *khar-o'-sheth;* the same as 2799; *Charosheth,* a place in Pal.:—Harosheth {3x}. See: BDB—360d, 361d.

2801. חָרַת {1x} **chârath,** *khaw-rath';* a prim. root; to *engrave:*—graven {1x}. See: TWOT—764; BDB—362a.

2802. חֶרֶת {1x} **Chereth,** *kheh'-reth;* from 2801 [but equiv. to 2793]; *forest; Chereth,* a thicket in Pal.:—Hereth {1x}. See: BDB—362a.

2803. חָשַׁב {124x} **châshab,** *khaw-shab';* a prim. root; prop. to *plait* or interpenetrate, i.e. (lit.) to *weave* or (gen.) to *fabricate;* fig. to *plot* or contrive (usually in a malicious sense); hence, (from the ment. effort) to *think, regard, value, compute:*—count {23x}, devise {22x}, think {18x}, imagine {9x}, cunning {8x}, reckon {7x}, purpose {6x}, esteem {6x}, account {5x}, impute {4x}, forecast {2x}, regard

{2x}, workman {2x}, conceived {1x}, misc. {9x} = consider, find out, hold, invent, be like, mean.

(1) Generally, this root signifies a mental process whereby some course is planned or conceived. It means "to think, account, reckon, devise, plan." **(2)** The first time it is found is in Gen 15:6 "And he believed in the LORD; and he counted it to him for righteousness." Here the term has the meaning of "to be imputed." **(3)** Frequently used in the ordinary sense of "thinking," or the normal thought processes (Is 10:7; 53:4; Mal 3:16), it **(4)** also is used in the sense of "devising evil plans" (Gen 50:20; Jer 48:2). **(5)** The word refers to craftsmen "inventing" instruments of music, artistic objects, and weapons of war (Ex 31:4; 2 Chr 26:15; Amos 6:5). See: TWOT—767; BDB—362d, 1093d.

2804. חֲשַׁב {1x} **chăshab** (Aram.), *khash-ab';* corresp. to 2803; to *regard:*—repute {1x}. See: TWOT—2745; BDB—1093d.

2805. חֵשֶׁב {8x} **chêsheb,** *khay'-sheb;* from 2803; a *belt* or strap (as being interlaced):—curious girdle {8x}. See: TWOT—2745; BDB—363d.

2806. חַשְׁבַּדָּנָה {1x} **Chashbaddânâh,** *khash-bad-daw'-naw;* from 2803 and 1777; *considerate judge; Chasbaddanah,* an Isr.:—Hasbadana {1x}. See: TWOT—2745; BDB—364c.

2807. חֲשֻׁבָה {1x} **Chăshûbâh,** *khash-oo-baw';* from 2803; *estimation; Cashubah,* an Isr.:—Hashubah {1x}. See: BDB—363d.

2808. חֶשְׁבּוֹן {3x} **cheshbôwn,** *khesh-bone';* from 2803; prop. *contrivance;* by impl. *intelligence:*—account {1x}, device {1x}, reason {1x}. See: TWOT—767b; BDB—363d.

2809. חֶשְׁבּוֹן {38x} **Cheshbôwn,** *khesh-bone';* the same as 2808; *Cheshbon,* a place E. of the Jordan:—Heshbon {38x}. See: BDB—363d.

2810. חִשָּׁבוֹן {2x} **chishshâbôwn,** *khish-shaw-bone';* from 2803; a *contrivance,* i.e. actual (a warlike *machine*) or ment. (a *machination*):—engine {1x}, invention {1x}. See: TWOT—767c; BDB—364a.

2811. חֲשַׁבְיָה {15x} **Chăshabyâh,** *khash-ab-yaw';* or

חֲשַׁבְיָהוּ **Chăshabyâhûw,** *khash-ab-yaw'-hoo;* from 2803 and 3050; *Jah has regarded; Chashabjah,* the name of nine Isr.:—Hashabiah {15x}. See: BDB—364a.

2812. חֲשַׁבְנָה {1x} **Chăshabnâh,** *khash-ab-naw';* fem. of 2808; *inventiveness; Chashnah,* an Isr.:—Hashabnah {1x}. See: BDB—364b.

2813. חֲשַׁבְנְיָה {2x} Chăshabn°yâh, *khash-ab-neh-yaw'*; from 2808 and 3050; *thought of Jah; Chashabnejah,* the name of two Isr.:—Hashabniah {2x}. See: BDB—364b.

2814. חָשָׁה {16x} châshâh, *khaw-shaw';* a prim. root; to *hush* or keep quiet:—hold . . . peace {9x}, still {4x}, silence {2x}, silent {1x}. See: TWOT—768; BDB—364c.

2815. חָשׁוּב {5x} Chashshûwb, *khash-shoob';* from 2803; *intelligent; Chashshub,* the name of two or three Isr.:—Hashub {4x}, Hasshub {1x}. See: BDB—363d.

2816. חָשׁוֹךְ {1x} chăshôwk (Aram.), *khash-oke';* from a root corresp. to 2821; the *dark:*—darkness {1x}. See: TWOT—2747; BDB—1094a.

2817. חֲשׁוּפָא {2x} Chăsûwphâ', *khas-oo-faw';* or

חֲשֻׂפָא Chăsûphâ', *khas-oo-faw';* from 2834; *nakedness; Chasupha,* one of the Nethinim:—Hashupha {1x}, Hasupha {1x}. See: BDB—362d.

חָשׁוּק chăshûwq. See 2838.

2818. חֲשַׁח {2x} chăshach (Aram.), *khash-akh';* a collat. root to one corresp. to 2363 in the sense of *readiness;* to *be necessary* (from the idea of *convenience*) or (tran.) to *need:*—careful {1x}, have need of {1x}. See: TWOT—2746; BDB—1093d.

2819. חַשְׁחוּת {1x} chashchûwth (Aram.), *khash-khooth';* from a root corresp. to 2818; *necessity:*—be needful {1x}. See: TWOT—2746b; BDB—1093d.

חֲשֵׁיכָה chăshêykăh. See 2825.

חֻשִׁים Chûshîym. See 2366.

2820. חָשַׂךְ {26x} châsak, *khaw-sak';* a prim. root; to *restrain* or (reflex.) *refrain;* by impl. to *refuse, spare, preserve;* also (by interch. with 2821) to *observe:*—spare {8x}, keep back {3x}, withhold {3x}, refrain {3x}, asswage {1x}, reserved {2x}, hold back {1x}, variant {1x}, forbear {1x}, hindereth {1x}, kept {1x}, punished {1x}, withholdeth {1x}. See: TWOT—765; BDB—362a.

2821. חָשַׁךְ {19x} châshak, *khaw-shak';* a prim. root; to *be dark* (as *withholding* light); tran. to *darken:*—darken {9x}, dark {5x}, blacker {1x}, darkness {1x}, dim {1x}, hideth {1x}, variant {1x}. See: TWOT—769; BDB—364d.

2822. חֹשֶׁךְ {80x} chôshek, *kho-shek';* from 2821; the *dark;* hence, (lit.) *darkness;* fig. *misery, destruction, death, ignorance, sorrow, wickedness:*—darkness {70x}, dark {7x}, obscurity {2x}, night {1x}. See: TWOT—769a; BDB—365a, 1094a.

2823. חָשֹׁךְ {1x} châshôk, *khaw-shoke';* from 2821; *dark* (fig. i.e. *obscure):*—mean {1x}. See: TWOT—769b; BDB—365b.

2824. חֶשְׁכָה {1x} cheshkâh, *khesh-kaw';* from 2821; *darkness:*—dark {1x}. See: BDB—365b.

2825. חֲשֵׁכָה {5x} chăshêkâh, *khash-ay-kaw';* or

חֲשֵׁיכָה chăshêykâh, *khash-ay-kaw';* from 2821; *darkness;* fig. *misery:*—darkness {1x}. See: TWOT—769c; BDB—365b.

2826. חָשַׁל {1x} châshal, *khaw-shal';* a prim. root; to *make* (intrans. *be) unsteady,* i.e. *weak:*—feeble {1x}. See: TWOT—770; BDB—365b.

2827. חֲשַׁל {1x} chăshal (Aram.), *khash-al';* a root corresp. to 2826; to *weaken,* i.e. *crush:*—subdue {1x}. See: TWOT—2748; BDB—1094a.

2828. חָשֻׁם {5x} Châshûm, *khaw-shoom';* from the same as 2831; *enriched; Chashum,* the name of two or three Isr.:—Hashum {5x}. See: BDB—365c.

חֻשָׁם Chûshâm. See 2367.

חֻשִׁם Chûshîm. See 2366.

2829. חֶשְׁמוֹן {1x} Cheshmôwn, *khesh-mone';* the same as 2831; *opulent; Cheshmon,* a place in Pal.:—Heshmon {1x}. See: BDB—365c.

2830. חַשְׁמַל {3x} chashmal, *khash-mal';* of uncert. der.; prob. *bronze* or polished *spectrum metal:*—amber {3x}. See: TWOT—770.1; BDB—365c.

2831. חַשְׁמָן {1x} chashmân, *khash-man';* from an unused root (prob. mean. *firm* or *capacious* in resources); appar. *wealthy:*—princes {1x}. See: TWOT—771; BDB—365c.

2832. חַשְׁמֹנָה {2x} Chashmônâh, *khash-mo-naw';* fem. of 2831; *fertile; Chasmonah,* a place in the Desert:—Hashmonah {2x}. See: BDB—365c.

2833. חֹשֶׁן {25x} chôshen, *kho'-shen;* from an unused root prob. mean. to *contain* or *sparkle;* perh. a *pocket* (as holding the Urim and Thummim), or *rich* (as containing gems), used only of the *gorget* of the high priest:—breastplate {25x}. See: TWOT—772a; BDB—365d.

2834. חָשַׂף {1x} châsaph, *khaw-saf';* a prim. root; to *strip* off, i.e. gen. to *make naked* (for exertion or in disgrace), to *drain away* or *bail* up (a liquid):—make bare {4x}, discover {2x}, uncover {2x}, take {1x}, clean {1x}, draw out {1x}. See: TWOT—766; BDB—362c, 362d.

Hebrew

2835. חָשִׂף {1x} **châsîph**, *khaw-seef';* from 2834; prop. *drawn off,* i.e. separated; hence, a small *company* (as divided from the rest):—little flocks {1x}. See: TWOT—766a; BDB—362c.

2836. חָשַׁק {11x} **châshaq**, *khaw-shak';* a prim. root; to *cling,* i.e. *join,* (fig.) to *love, delight* in; ellip. (or by interch. for 2820) to *deliver:*—desire {3x}, set his love {2x}, filleted {3x}, log {1x}, delight {1x}, in love {1x}. See: TWOT—773; BDB—365d, 366b.

2837. חֵשֶׁק {4x} **chêsheq**, *khay'-shek;* from 2836; *delight:*—desire {1x}, that {1x}, pleasure {1x}, desire + 2836 {1x}. See: TWOT—773a; BDB—366a.

2838. חָשֻׁק {8x} **châshûq**, *khaw-shook';* or

חָשׁוּק **châshûwq**, *khaw-shook';* pass. part. of 2836; *attached,* i.e. a fence-*rail* or rod connecting the posts or pillars:—fillet {8x}. See: TWOT—773b; BDB—366a.

2839. חִשֻּׁק {1x} **chishshûq**, *khish-shook';* from 2836; *conjoined,* i.e. a wheel-*spoke* or rod connecting the hub with the rim:—felloes {1x}. See: TWOT—773d; BDB—366b.

2840. חִשֻּׁר {1x} **chishshûr**, *khish-shoor';* from an unused root mean. to *bind* together; *combined,* i.e. the *nave* or hub of a wheel (as holding the spokes together):—spoke {1x}. See: TWOT—774b; BDB—366b.

2841. חַשְׁרָה {1x} **chashrâh**, *khash-raw';* from the same as 2840; prop. a *combination* or gathering, i.e. of watery *clouds:*—dark {1x}. See: TWOT—774a; BDB—366b.

חֲשֻׁפָא **Chăsûphâ'**. See 2817.

2842. חָשַׁשׁ {2x} **châshash**, *khaw-shash';* by var. for 7179; dry *grass:*—chaff {2x}. See: TWOT—775a; BDB—366b.

2843. חֻשָׁתִי {5x} **Chûshâthîy**, *khoo-shaw-thee';* patron. from 2364; a *Chushathite* or desc. of Chushah:—Hushathite {5x}. See: TWOT—775a; 302a, 366c.

2844. חַת {4x} **chath**, *khath;* from 2865; concr. *crushed;* also *afraid;* abstr. *terror:*—broken {1x}, dismayed {1x}, dread {1x}, fear {1x}. See: TWOT—784a; BDB—366c, 369c.

2845. חֵת {14x} **Chêth**, *khayth;* from 2865; *terror; Cheth,* an aboriginal Canaanite:—Heth {14x}. See: TWOT—776; BDB—366c, 370c.

2846. חָתָה {4x} **châthâh**, *khaw-thaw';* a prim. root; to *lay hold* of; espec. to *pick* up fire:—heap {1x}, take {1x}, take away {1x}. See: TWOT—777; BDB—367a.

2847. חִתָּה {1x} **chittâh**, *khit-taw';* from 2865; *fear:*—terror {1x}. See: TWOT—784d; BDB—366c, 367b, 369d.

2848. חִתּוּל {1x} **chittûwl**, *khit-tool';* from 2853; *swathed,* i.e. a *bandage:*—roller {1x}. See: TWOT—779b; BDB—367c.

2849. חַתְחַת {1x} **chathchath**, *khath-khath';* from 2844; *terror:*—fear {1x}. See: TWOT—784e; BDB—369d.

2850. חִתִּי {48x} **Chittîy**, *khit-tee';* patron. from 2845; a *Chittite,* or desc. of Cheth:—Hittite {26x}, Hittities {22x}. See: TWOT—776a; BDB—366c, 370c.

2851. חִתִּית {8x} **chittîyth**, *khit-teeth';* from 2865; *fear:*—terror {8x}. See: TWOT—784f; BDB—369d.

2852. חָתַךְ {1x} **châthak**, *khaw-thak';* a prim. root; prop. to *cut off,* i.e. (fig.) to *decree:*—determine {1x}. See: TWOT—778; BDB—367b.

2853. חָתַל {2x} **châthal**, *khaw-thal';* a prim. root; to *swathe:*—✕ at all {1x}, swaddle {1x}. See: TWOT—779; BDB—367c.

2854. חֲתֻלָּה {1x} **chăthullâh**, *khath-ool-law';* from 2853; a *swathing* cloth (fig.):—swaddling band {1x}. See: TWOT—779a; BDB—367c.

2855. חֶתְלֹן {2x} **Chethlôn**, *kheth-lone';* from 2853; *enswathed; Chethlon,* a place in Pal.:—Hethlon {2x}. See: BDB—367c.

2856. חָתַם {27x} **châtham**, *khaw-tham';* a prim. root; to *close* up; espec. to *seal:*—seal {18x}, seal up {6x}, marked {1x}, stopped {1x}, variant {1x}. See: TWOT—780; BDB—367c, 1094a.

2857. חֲתַם {1x} **chătham** (Aram.), *khath-am';* a root corresp. to 2856; to *seal:*—seal {1x}. See: TWOT—2749; BDB—1094a.

חֹתָם **chôthâm**. See 2368.

2858. חֹתֶמֶת {1x} **chôthemeth**, *kho-the-meth';* fem. act. part. of 2856; a *seal:*—signet {1x}. See: TWOT—780b; BDB—368b.

2859. חָתַן {33x} **châthan**, *khaw-than';* a prim. root; to *give* (a daughter) *away* in marriage; hence, (gen.) to *contract affinity* by marriage:—join in affinity {3x}, father-in-law {21x}, make marriages {3x}, mother-in-law {1x}, son in law {5x}. See: TWOT—781b; BDB—368c, 368d.

2860. חָתָן {20x} **châthân**, *khaw-thawn';* from 2859; a *relative* by marriage (espec. through the bride); fig. a *circumcised* child (as a species of relig. espousal):—son-in-law {10x},

bridegroom {8x}, husband {2x}. See: TWOT—781c; BDB—368c.

2861. חֲתֻנָּה {1x} chăthunnâh, khath-oon-naw'; from 2859; a wedding:—espousal {1x}. See: TWOT—781d; BDB—368d.

2862. חָתַף {1x} châthaph, khaw-thaf'; a prim. root; to clutch:—take away {1x}. See: TWOT—782; BDB—368d.

2863. חֶתֶף {1x} chetheph, kheh'-thef; from 2862; prop. rapine; fig. robbery:—prey {1x}. See: TWOT—782a; BDB—369a.

2864. חָתַר châthar, khaw-thar'; a prim. root; to force a passage, as by burglary; fig. with oars:—dig {7x}, row {1x}. See: TWOT—783; BDB—369a.

2865. חָתַת {54x} châthath, khaw-thath'; a prim. root; prop. to prostrate; hence, to break down, either (lit.) by violence, or (fig.) by confusion and fear:—dismayed {27x}, afraid {6x}, break in pieces {6x}, broken {3x}, break down {2x}, abolished {1x}, affrighted {1x}, amazed {1x}, chapt {1x}, confound {1x}, discouraged {1x}, go down {1x}, beaten down {1x}, scarest {1x}, terrify {1x}.
   Chathath means "to be dismayed, shattered, broken, terrified." (1) It occurs for the first time in Deut. 1:21 as Moses challenged Israel: "Do not fear or be discouraged." (1a) As here, chathath is often used in parallelism with the Hebrew term for "fear" (cf. Deut 31:8; Josh 8:1; 1Sa 17:11). (1b) Similarly, chathath is frequently used in parallelism with "to be ashamed" (Is 20:5; Jer 8:9). (2) An interesting figurative use of the word is found in Jer 14:4, where the ground "is chapt", for there was no rain." (3) The meaning "to be shattered" is usually employed in a figurative sense, (3a) as with reference to the nations coming under God's judgment (Is 7:8; 30:31). (3b) The coming Messiah is to "shatter" or "break" the power of all His enemies (Is 9:4). See: TWOT—784; BDB—369a.

2866. חֲתַת {1x} chăthath, khath-ath'; from 2865; dismay:—casting down {1x}. See: TWOT—784c; 369c.

2867. חֲתַת {1x} Chăthath, khath-ath'; the same as 2866; Chathath, an Isr.:—Hathath {1x}. See: BDB—369d.

ט

2868. טְאֵב {1x} tᵉêb (Aram.), teh-abe'; a prim. root; to rejoice:—be glad {1x}. See: TWOT—2750; BDB—1094a.

2869. טָב {2x} tâb (Aram.), tawb; from 2868; the same as 2896; good:—fine {1x}, good {1x}. See: TWOT—2750a; BDB—1094b.

2870. טָבְאֵל {2x} Tâbᵉêl, taw-beh-ale'; from 2895 and 410; pleasing (to) God; Tabeël, the name of a Syrian and of a Persian:—Tabeal {1x}, Tabeel {1x}. See: TWOT—2750a; BDB—370b.

2871. טָבוּל {1x} tâbûwl, taw-bool'; pass. part. of 2881; prop. dyed, i.e. a turban (prob. as of colored stuff):—dyed attire {1x}. See: TWOT—788a; BDB—371b.

2872. טַבּוּר {2x} tabbûwr, tab-boor'; from an unused root mean. to pile up; prop. accumulated; i.e. (by impl.) a summit:—middle {1x}, midst {1x}. Syn.: 2677, 3820, 7130, 8432, 8484. See: TWOT—790a; BDB—371d.

2873. טָבַח {11x} tâbach, taw-bakh'; a prim. root; to slaughter (animals or men):—kill {1x}, killed {3x}, make slaughter {1x}, slaughter {3x}, slain {1x}, slay {2x}. Syn.: 2026, 2076, 2491, 4191, 5221, 7819. See: TWOT—786; BDB—370b.

2874. טֶבַח {12x} tebach, teh'-bakh; from 2873; prop. something slaughtered; hence, a beast (or meat, as butchered); abstr. butchery (or concr. a place of slaughter):—slaughter {9x}, slay {1x}, sore {1x}, beast {1x}. See: TWOT—786a; BDB—370d.

2875. טֶבַח {1x} Tebach, teh'-bakh; the same as 2874; massacre; Tebach, the name of a Mesopotamian and of an Isr.:—Tebah {1x}. See: BDB—370d.

2876. טַבָּח {32x} tabbâch, tab-bawkh'; from 2873; prop. a butcher; hence, a lifeguardsman (because acting as an executioner); also a cook (as usually slaughtering the animal for food):—cook {30x}, guard {2x}. See: TWOT—786c; BDB—371a, 1094b.

2877. טַבָּח {1x} tabbâch (Aram.), tab-bawkh'; the same as 2876; a lifeguardsman:—guard {1x}. See: TWOT—2751; BDB—1094b.

2878. טִבְחָה {3x} tibhâh, tib-khaw'; fem. of 2874 and mean. the same:—flesh {1x}, slaughter {2x}. See: TWOT—786b; BDB—370d.

2879. טַבָּחָה {1x} tabbâchâh, tab-baw-khaw'; fem. of 2876; a female cook:—cook {1x}. See: TWOT—786d; BDB—367b, 371a.

2880. טִבְחַת {1x} Tibchath, tib-khath'; from 2878; slaughter; Tibchath, a place in Syria:—Tibhath {1x}. See: BDB—371a.

2881. טָבַל {16x} tâbal, taw-bal'; a prim. root; to dip:—dip {15x}, plunge {1x}. This word means "dipped": (1) Joseph's coat (Gen 37:31), (2) the priest's finger (Lev 4:6),

(3) Ruth's morsel (Ruth 2:14), and **(4)** Hazael's cloth (2 Kin 8:15). See: TWOT—787, 788; BDB—371a.

2882. תְּבַלְיָהוּ {1x} **Tᵉbalyâhûw**, *teb-al-yaw'-hoo;* from 2881 and 3050; *Jah has dipped; Tebaljah,* an Isr.:—Tebaliah {1x}. See: BDB—371b.

2883. טָבַע {10x} **ṭâbaʿ**, *taw-bah';* a prim. root; to *sink:*—sink {7x}, drown {1x}, settle {1x}, fasten {1x}. See: TWOT—789; BDB—371c.

2884. טַבָּעוֹת {2x} **Ṭabbâʿôwth**, *tab-baw-othe';* plur. of 2885; *rings; Tabbaoth,* one of the Nethinim:—Tabbaoth {2x}. See: BDB—371d.

2885. טַבַּעַת {49x} **ṭabbaʿath**, *tab-bah'-ath;* from 2883; prop. a *seal* (as *sunk* into the wax), i.e. *signet* (for sealing); hence, (gen.) a *ring* of any kind:—ring {49x}. See: TWOT—789a; BDB—371c.

2886. טַבְרִמּוֹן {1x} **Ṭabrimmôwn**, *tab-rim-mone';* from 2895 and 7417; *pleasing* (to) *Rimmon; Tabrimmon,* a Syrian:—Tabrimmon {1x}. See: BDB—372a.

2887. טֵבֶת {1x} **Ṭêbeth**, *tay'-beth;* prob. of for. der.; *Tebeth,* the tenth Heb. month:—Tebeth {1x}. See: BDB—372a.

2888. טַבַּת {1x} **Ṭabbath**, *tab-bath';* of uncert. der.; *Tabbath,* a place E. of the Jordan:—Tabbath {1x}. See: BDB—372a.

2889. טָהוֹר {94x} **ṭâhôwr**, *taw-hore';* or

טָהֹר **ṭâhôr**, *taw-hore';* from 2891; *pure* (in a physical, chemical, ceremonial or moral sense):—clean {50x}, pure {40x}, fair {2x}, purer {1x}, variant {1x}.

Tahor, as an adjective, means "clean; pure." **(1)** The word denotes the absence of impurity, filthiness, defilement, or imperfection. **(2)** It is applied concretely to substances that are genuine or unadulterated as well as describing an unstained condition of a spiritual or ceremonial nature. **(3)** Gold is a material frequently said to be free of baser ingredients. **(3a)** Thus the ark of the covenant, the incense altar, and the porch of the temple were "overlaid with pure gold" (Ex 25:11; 37:11, 26; 2 Chr 3:4). **(3b)** Some of the furnishings and utensils in the temple—such as the mercy seat, the lampstand, the dishes, pans, bowls, jars, snuffers, trays— were of "pure gold" (Ex 37:6, 16–24). **(3c)** The high priest's vestment included "two chains of pure gold" and "a plate of pure gold" (Ex 28:14, 22, 36).

(4) God demands that His people have spiritual and moral purity, unsullied by sin. **(4a)** Anyone not clean of sin is subject to divine rejection and punishment. **(4b)** This contamination is never outgrown or overcome. **(4c)** Because sin pollutes one generation after another, Job asks: "Who can bring a clean thing out of an unclean?" (Job 14:4). **(4d)** All outward appearances to the contrary, it cannot be said that there is "one event . . . to the clean, and to the unclean" (Eccl 9:2). **(5)** Hope is available even to the chief of sinners, because any man can entreat the mercy of God and say: "Create in me a clean heart, O God; and renew a right spirit within me" (Ps 51:10). **(6)** In sharp contrast with mankind's polluted nature and actions, "the words of the LORD are pure words" (Ps 12:6). The Lord is "of purer eyes than to behold evil" (Hab 1:13). **(7)** "Clean" most frequently describes the purity maintained by avoiding contact with other human beings, abstaining from eating animals, and using things that are declared ceremonially clean. **(8)** Conversely, cleansing results if ritual procedures symbolizing the removal of contamination are observed.

(9) The people of the old covenant were told that "he that toucheth the dead body of any man shall be unclean seven days" (Num 19:11). **(9a)** A priest was not to defile himself "for the dead among his people" except "for his kin, that is near unto him" (Lev 21:1–2). **(9b)** This relaxation of the rule was even denied the high priest and a Nazarite during "all the days that he separateth himself unto the LORD" (Num 6:6ff.). **(10)** Cleansing rituals emphasized the fact that the people were conceived and born in sin. **(10a)** Though conception and birth were not branded immoral (just as dying itself was not sinful), a woman who had borne a child remained unclean until she submitted to the proper purification rites (Lev 12). **(10b)** Chapter 15 of Leviticus prescribes ceremonial cleansing for a woman having her menstrual flow, for a man having seminal emissions, and for "the woman also with whom man shall lie with seed of copulation" (Lev 15:18). **(11)** To be ceremonially "clean," **(11a)** the Israelite also had to abstain from eating certain animals and even from touching them (Lev 11; Deut 14:3–21). **(11b)** After the Israelites settled in the Promised Land, some modifications were made in the regulations (Deut 12:15, 22; 15:22).

(12) Purification rites frequently involved the use of water. **(12a)** The person to be cleansed was required to wash himself and his clothes (Lev 15:27). **(12b)** Water was sprinkled on the individual, on his tent, and on all its furnishings: "And a clean person shall take hyssop, and dip it in the water, and sprinkle it upon the tent, and upon all the vessels, and upon the persons that were there, and upon him that touched a bone, or the slain, or one

dead, or a grave" (Num 19:18). **(13)** Sometimes the person being cleansed also had to change garments (Lev 6:11). **(14)** However, the rites were not meritorious deeds, **(14a)** earning God's favor and forgiveness. **(14b)** Nor did the ceremonies serve their intended purpose if performed mechanically. **(14c)** Unless the rites expressed a person's contrite and sincere desire to be cleansed from the defilement of sin, they were an abomination to God and only aggravated a person's guilt. **(15)** Anyone who appeared before Him in ritual and ceremony with "hands . . . full of blood" (Is 1:15) and did not plead for cleansing of his crimes was judged to be as wicked as the people of Sodom and Gomorrah. **(16)** Zion's hope lay in this cleansing by means of an offering: "And they shall bring all your brethren for an offering unto the LORD out of all nations upon horses . . . as the children of Israel bring an offering in a clean vessel into the house of the LORD" (Is 66:20). See: TWOT−792d; BDB−373a.

2890. טָהוֹר {2x} ṭᵉhôwr, *teh-hore';* from 2891; *purity:*−pureness {2x}. See: TWOT−792b; BDB−373a, 779c.

2891. טָהֵר {94x} ṭâhêr, *taw-hare';* a prim. root; prop. *to be bright;* i.e. (by impl.) to *be pure* (phys. *sound, clear, unadulterated;* Levit. *uncontaminated;* mor. *innocent* or *holy*):−clean {80x}, purify {6x}, purge {5x}, pure {2x}, purifier {1x}.

Taher, means "to be clean, pure." **(1)** Since the fall of Adam and Eve, none of their offspring is clean in the sight of the holy God: **(1a)** "Who can say, I have made my heart clean, I am pure from my sin?" (Prov 20:9). **(1b)** Reminding Job that protestations of innocence are of no avail, Eliphaz asked: "Shall mortal man be more just than God? Shall a man be more pure than his Maker?" (Job 4:17). **(2)** There is hope, however, because God promised penitent Israel: **(2a)** "And I will cleanse them from all their iniquity, whereby they have sinned against me" (Jer 33:8). **(2b)** He said: "I will save them out of all their dwelling places, wherein they have sinned, and will cleanse them: so they shall be my people, and I will be their God" (Eze 37:23).

(3) The baleful effect of sin was recognized when a person contracted the dread disease of leprosy. After the priest diagnosed the disease, he could declare a person "clean" only after cleansing ceremonies had been performed: ". . . And he shall wash his clothes, also he shall wash his flesh in water, and he shall be clean" (Lev 14:9). **(4)** God required that His people observe purification rites when they came into His presence for worship. **(4a)** On the Day of Atonement, for example, prescribed

ceremonies were performed to "cleanse" the altar from "the uncleanness of the children of Israel" and to "hallow it" (Lev 16:17−19; cf. Ex 29:36ff.). **(4b)** The priests were to be purified before they performed their sacred tasks. Moses was directed to "take the Levites . . . and cleanse them" (Num 8:6; cf. Lev 8:5−13).

(5) After they had been held captive in the unclean land of Babylon, "the priests and the Levites purified themselves, and purified the people, and the gates, and the wall [of the rebuilt city of Jerusalem]" (Neh 12:30). **(6)** Cleansing might be achieved by physically removing the objects of defilement. During the reform of King Hezekiah, "the priests went into the inner part of the house of the LORD, to cleanse it, and brought out all the uncleanness that they found in the temple of the LORD" (2 Chr 29:16). **(7)** Some rites required blood as the purifying agent: "And he shall sprinkle of the blood upon it [the altar] with his finger seven times, and cleanse it, and hallow it from the uncleanness of the children of Israel" (Lev 16:19). **(8)** Sacrifices were offered to make atonement for a mother after childbirth: "she shall bring . . . the one for the burnt offering, and the other for a sin offering: and the priest shall make an atonement for her, and she shall be clean" (Lev 12:8). See: TWOT−792; BDB−372a.

2892. טֹהַר {4x} ṭôhar, *to'-har;* from 2891; lit. *brightness;* ceremonial *purification:*−clearness {1x}, glory {1x}, purifying {2x}. See: TWOT−792a; BDB−372d.

2893. טָהֳרָה {13x} ṭohŏrâh, *toh-or-aw';* fem. of 2892; ceremonial *purification;* moral *purity:*−✗ is cleansed {1x}, cleansing {7x}, purification {2x}, purifying {3x}. See: TWOT−792c; BDB−372d.

2894. טוּא {1x} ṭûwʾ, *too;* a prim. root; to *sweep away:*−sweep {1x}. See: TWOT−785; BDB−370a.

2895. טוֹב {33x} ṭowb, *tobe;* a prim. root, to *be* (tran. *do* or *make) good* (or *well*) in the widest sense:−well {10x}, good {9x}, please {6x}, goodly {2x}, better {2x}, cheer {1x}, comely {1x}, do {1x}, pleased + 5869 {1x}.

Towb means "to be joyful, glad, pleasant, lovely, appropriate, becoming, good, precious." Job 13:9 is one example of the word's meaning, "to be good": "Is it good that he should search you out?" See: TWOT−793; BDB−373b, 405c, 1094a.

2896. טוֹב {559x} ṭôwb, *tobe;* from 2895; *good* (as an adj.) in the widest sense; used likewise as a noun, both in the masc. and the fem., the sing. and the plur. (*good,* a *good* or *good* thing, a *good* man or woman; the *good, goods* or *good* things, *good* men or women),

also as an adv. (*well*):—good {361x}, better {72x}, well {20x}, goodness {16x}, goodly {9x}, best {8x}, merry {7x}, fair {7x}, prosperity {6x}, precious {4x}, fine {3x}, wealth {3x}, beautiful {2x}, fairer {2x}, favour {2x}, glad {2x}, misc. {35x} = bountiful, cheerful, at ease, graciously, joyful, kindly, kindness, liketh (best), loving, × most, pleasant, + pleaseth, pleasure, ready, sweet, welfare.

Towb (2896), means "good; favorable; festive; pleasing; pleasant; well; better; right; best." (**1**) This adjective denotes "good" in every sense of that word. (**1a**) For example, *towb* is used in the sense "pleasant" or "delightful": "And he saw that [a resting place] was good, and the land that it was pleasant; and bowed his shoulder to bear [burdens]" (Gen 49:15). (**1b**) An extension of this sense appears in Gen 40:16, where *towb* means "favorable" or "in one's favor": "When the chief baker saw that the interpretation was good, he said unto Joseph. . . ." (**1c**) In 1 Sa 25:8, the emphasis is on the nuance "delightful" or "festal": "Let the young men find favor in thine eyes: for we come in a good day." (**2**) God is described as One who is "good," or One who gives "delight" and "pleasure": "But it is good for me to draw near to God: I have put my trust in the Lord GOD, that I may declare all thy works" (Ps 73:28).

(**3**) In 1 Sa 29:6, this word describes human activities: "As the LORD liveth, thou hast been upright, and thy going out and thy coming in with me in the [army] is good in my sight." (**4**) *Towb* can be applied to scenic beauty, as in 2 Kin 2:19: "Behold, I pray thee, the situation of this city is pleasant, as my lord seeth: but the water is naught, and the ground barren." (**5**) Second Chr 12:12 employs a related nuance when it applies the word to the conditions in Judah under King Rehoboam, after he humbled himself before God: "Things went well." (**6**) *Towb* often qualifies a common object or activity. (**6a**) When the word is used in this sense, no ethical overtones are intended. (**6b**) In 1 Sa 19:4, *towb* describes the way Jonathan spoke about David: "And Jonathan spake good of David unto Saul his father, and said unto him, Let not the king sin against his servant, against David; because he hath not sinned against thee, and because his works have been [toward thee] very good."

(**7**) First Sa 25:15 characterizes a people as "friendly" or "useful": "But the men were very good unto us, and we were not hurt, neither missed we any thing, as long as we were conversant with them, when we were in the fields." (**8**) Often this word bears an even stronger emphasis, as in 1 Kin 12:7, where the "good word" is not only friendly but eases the life of one's servants. God's "good word" promises life in the face of oppression and uncertainty: "There hath not failed one word of all his good promise, which he promised by the hand of Moses his servant" (1 Kin 8:56). (**9**) *Towb* often characterizes a statement as an important assertion for salvation and prosperity (real or imagined): "Is not this the word that we did tell thee in Egypt, saying, Let us alone, that we may serve the Egyptians? For it had been better for us to serve the Egyptians, than that we should die in the wilderness" (Ex 14:12). (**10**) God judged that man's circumstance without a wife or helpmeet was not "good" (Gen 2:18).

(**11**) Elsewhere *towb* is applied to an evaluation of one's well-being or of the well-being of a situation or thing: "And God saw the light, that it was good: and God divided the light from the darkness" (Gen 1:4—the first occurrence). (**12**) *Towb* is used to describe land and agriculture: "And I am come down to deliver them out of the [power] of the Egyptians, and to bring them up out of that land unto a good [fertile] land and a large, unto a land flowing with milk and honey" (Ex 3:8). (**12a**) This suggests its potential of supporting life (Deut 11:17). (**12b**) Thus the expression "the good land" is a comment about not only its existing, but its potential, productivity. (**12c**) In such contexts the land is viewed as one aspect of the blessings of salvation promised by God; thus the Lord did not permit Moses to cross the Jordan and enter the land which His people were to inherit (Deut 3:26–28). (**12d**) This aspect of the "good land" includes overtones of its fruitfulness and "pleasantness": "And he will take your fields, and your vineyards, and your oliveyards, even the best of them" (1 Sa 8:14).

(**13**) *Towb* is used to describe men or women. (**13a**) Sometimes it is used of an "elite corps" of people: "And he will take your menservants, and your maidservants, and your goodliest young men, and your asses" (1 Sa 8:16). (**13b**) In 2 Sa 18:27, Ahimaaz is described as a "good" man because he comes with "good" military news. (**14**) In 1 Sa 15:28, the word has ethical overtones: "The LORD hath rent the kingdom of Israel from thee this day, and hath given it to a neighbor of thine, that is better than thou" (cf. 1 Kin 2:32). (**15**) In other passages, *towb* describes physical appearance: "And the damsel was very fair to look upon [literally, "good of appearance"]" (Gen 24:16). (**16**) When applied to one's heart, the word describes "well-being" rather than ethical status. Therefore, the parallel idea is "joyous and happy": ". . . And they . . . went unto their tents joyful and glad of heart for all the goodness that the LORD had done for David" (1 Kin 8:66). (**17**) Dying "at a

Hebrew

good old age" describes "advanced age," rather than moral accomplishment, but a time when due to divine blessings one is fulfilled and satisfied (Gen 15:15).

(18) *Towb* indicates that a given word, act, or circumstance contributes positively to the condition of a situation. **(18a)** Often this judgment does not mean that the thing is actually "good," only that it is so evaluated: "When the chief baker saw that the interpretation was good . . ." (Gen 40:16). **(18b)** The judgment may be ethical: "It is not good that ye do: ought ye not to walk in the fear of our God because of the reproach of the heathen?" (Neh 5:9). **(19)** The word may also represent "agreement" or "concurrence": "The thing proceedeth from the LORD: we cannot speak unto thee bad or good" (Gen 24:50). **(20)** *Towb* is often used in conjunction with the Hebrew word *ra'ah* (7451 - "bad; evil"). **(20a)** Sometimes this is intended as a contrast; **(20b)** but in other contexts it may mean "everything from good [friendly] to bad [unfriendly]," which is a way of saying "nothing at all." **(20c)** In other contexts, more contrast is suggested: "And what the land is that they dwell in, whether it be good or bad . . ." (Num 13:19). In this case, the evaluation would determine whether the land could support the people well or not.

(21) In Gen 2:9, *towb* contrasted with evil has moral overtones: ". . . the tree of life also in the midst of the garden, and the tree of knowledge of good and evil." The fruit of this tree, if consumed, would reveal the difference between moral evil and moral "good." This reference also suggests that, by eating this fruit, man attempted to determine for himself what "good" and evil are. *Towb,* as an adjective, means "good." **(22)** And God saw the light, that it was good: and God divided the light from the darkness. **(22a)** God appraises each day's creative work as being "good," climaxing it with a "very good" on the sixth day: "And God saw every thing that he had made, and, behold, it was very good" (Gen 1:31). **(23)** As a positive term, the word is used to express many nuances of that which is "good," such as **(23a)** a "glad" heart: "And the priest's heart was glad, and he took the ephod, and the teraphim, and the graven image, and went in the midst of the people" (Judg 18:20), **(23b)** "pleasing" words: "And their words pleased Hamor, and Shechem Hamor's son" (Gen 34:18), and **(23c)** a "cheerful" face: "A merry heart maketh a cheerful countenance: but by sorrow of the heart the spirit is broken" (Prov 15:13). See: TWOT— 793a; BDB—373c, 375a, 375c, 1094b.

2897. טוֹב {2x} **Tôwb,** *tobe;* the same as 2896; *good; Tob,* a region appar. E. of the Jordan:—Tob {2x}. See: BDB—376a.

2898. טוּב {32x} **tûwb,** *toob;* from 2895; *good* (as a noun), in the widest sense, espec. *goodness* (superl. concr. the *best*), *beauty, gladness, welfare:*—goodness {14x}, good {9x}, goods {3x}, good thing {2x}, fair {1x}, gladness {1x}, joy {1x}, well {1x}. See: TWOT—793b; BDB—375c.

2899. טוֹב אֲדֹנִיָּהוּ {1x} **Tôwb Ădônîyâhûw,** *tobe   ado-nee-yah'-hoo;* from 2896 and 138; *pleasing* (to) *Adonijah; Tob-Adonijah,* an Isr.:—Tob-adonijah {1x}. See: BDB—375b.

2900. טוֹבִיָּה {18x} **Tôwbîyâh,** *to-bee-yaw';* or

טוֹבִיָּהוּ **Tôwbîyâhûw,** *to-bee-yaw'-hoo;* from 2896 and 3050; *goodness of Jehovah; Tobijah,* the name of three Isr. and of one Samaritan:—Tobiah {15x}, Tobijah {1x}. See: BDB—375d.

2901. טָוָה {2x} **tâvâh,** *taw-vaw';* a prim. root; to *spin:*—spin {2x}. See: TWOT—794; BDB—376a.

2902. טוּחַ {12x} **tûwach,** *too'-akh;* a prim. root; to *smear,* espec. with lime:— daub {7x}, plaister {3x}, shut {1x}, overlay {1x}. Syn.: 2915, 7814. See: TWOT—795; BDB—376b, 377c.

2903. טוֹפָפָה {3x} **tôwphâphâh,** *to-faw-faw';* from an unused root mean. to *go around* or *bind;* a *fillet* for the forehead:— frontlet {3x}. See: TWOT—804a; BDB—376c, 377d.

2904. טוּל {1x} **tûwl,** *tool;* a prim. root; to *pitch over* or *reel;* hence, (tran.) to *cast down* or *out:*—cast {12x}, carry away {1x}, send out {1x}. See: TWOT—797; BDB—376c.

2905. טוּר {26x} **tûwr,** *toor;* from an unused root mean. to *range* in a reg. manner; a *row;* hence, a *wall:*—row {26x}. See: TWOT—798a; BDB—377a.

2906. טוּר {2x} **tûwr** (Aram.), *toor;* corresp. to 6697; a *rock* or hill:—mountain {2x}. See: TWOT—2752; BDB—1094b.

2907. טוּשׂ {1x} **tûws,** *toos;* a prim. root; to *pounce* as a bird of prey:—haste {1x}. See: TWOT—799; BDB—377b.

2908. טְוָת {1x} **tᵉvâth** (Aram.), *tev-awth';* from a root corresp. to 2901; *hunger* (as *twisting*):—fasting {1x}. See: TWOT— 2753; BDB—1094b.

2909. טָחָה {1x} **tâchâh,** *taw-khaw';* a prim. root; to *stretch* a bow, as an archer:—bowshot + 7198 {1x}. See: TWOT—800; BDB—377b.

2910. טֻחָה {2x} **tûwchâh,** *too-khaw';* from 2909 (or 2902) in the sense of over-

laying; (in the plur. only) the *kidneys* (as being *covered*); hence, (fig.) the inmost *thought:*—inward parts {2x}. See: TWOT—795b; BDB—376b.

2911. תְּחוֹן {1x} **tᵉchôwn,** *tekh-one';* from 2912; a hand *mill;* hence, a *millstone:*—to grind {1x}. See: TWOT—802a; BDB—377c.

2912. טָחַן **tâchan,** *taw-khan';* a prim. root; to *grind* meal; hence, to *be a concubine* (that being their employment):—grind {7x}, grinder {1x}. See: TWOT—802; BDB—377c.

2913. טַחֲנָה {1x} **tachănâh,** *takh-an-aw';* from 2912; a hand *mill;* hence, (fig.) *chewing:*—grinding {1x}. See: TWOT—802b; BDB—377d.

2914. טְחֹר {8x} **tᵉchôr,** *tekh-ore';* from an unused root mean. to *burn;* a *boil* or ulcer (from the inflammation), espec. a tumor in the anus or pudenda (the piles):—emerod {8x}. See: TWOT—803a; BDB—377d.

2915. טִיחַ {1x} **tîyach,** *tee'akh;* from (the equiv. of) 2902; mortar or *plaster:*—daubing {1x}. See: TWOT—795a; BDB—376b, 378a.

2916. טִיט {13x} **tîyṭ,** *teet;* from an unused root mean. appar. to *be sticky* [rather perh. a denom. from 2894, through the idea of dirt to *be swept* away]; *mud* or *clay;* fig. *calamity:*—clay {3x}, dirt {2x}, mire {8x}. Syn.: 2563, 4423, 4568. See: TWOT—796a; BDB—376c, 378a.

2917. טִין {2x} **tîyn** (Aram.), *teen;* perh. by interchange, for a word corresp. to 2916; *clay:*—miry {2x}. See: TWOT—2754; BDB—1094b.

2918. טִירָה {7x} **tîyrâh,** *tee-raw';* fem. of (an equiv. to) 2905; a *wall;* hence, a *fortress* or a *hamlet:*—(goodly) castle {3x}, habitation {1x}, palace {2x}, row {1x}. See: TWOT—798b; BDB—377a, 378a.

2919. טַל {31x} **tal,** *tal;* from 2926; *dew* (as *covering* vegetation):—dew {31x}. See: TWOT—807a; BDB—378a, 378b, 1094b.

2920. טַל {5x} **tal** (Aram.), *tal;* the same as 2919:—dew {5x}. See: TWOT—2755; BDB—1094b.

2921. טָלָא {8x} **tâlâʾ,** *taw-law';* a prim. root; prop. to *cover* with pieces; i.e. (by impl.) to *spot* or *variegate* (as tapestry):—clouted {1x}, with divers colours {1x}, spotted {6x}. Syn.: 7553. See: TWOT—805; BDB—378a.

2922. טְלָא {1x} **tᵉlâʾ,** *tel-aw';* appar. from 2921 in the (orig.) sense of *covering* (for protection); a *lamb* [comp. 2924]:—lamb {1x}.

Syn.: 3532, 3775. See: TWOT—806a; BDB—378b.

2923. טְלָאִים {1x} **Tᵉlâʾîym,** *tel-aw-eem';* from the plur. of 2922; *lambs; Telaim,* a place in Pal.:—Telaim {1x}. See: BDB—378a, 378b.

2924. טָלֶה {2x} **tâleh,** *taw-leh';* by var. for 2922; a *lamb:*—lamb {2x}. See: TWOT—806a; BDB—378b.

2925. טַלְטֵלָה {1x} **taltêlâh,** *tal-tay-law';* from 2904; *overthrow* or *rejection:*—captivity {1x}. See: TWOT—797a; BDB—376d.

2926. טָלַל {1x} **tâlal,** *taw-lal';* a prim. root; prop. to *strew* over, i.e. (by impl.) to *cover* in or *plate* (with beams):—cover {1x}. Syn.: 3680, 5526, 560, 6823. See: TWOT—808; BDB—378d, 1094b.

2927. טְלַל {1x} **tᵉlal** (Aram.), *tel-al';* corresp. to 2926; to *cover* with shade:—have a shadow {1x}. See: TWOT—2756; BDB—1094b.

2928. טֶלֶם {2x} **Telem,** *teh'-lem;* from an unused root mean. to *break* up or treat violently; *oppression; Telem,* the name of a place in Idumæa, also of a temple doorkeeper:—Telem {2x}. See: BDB—378d.

2929. טַלְמוֹן {5x} **Talmôwn,** *tal-mone';* from the same as 2728; *oppressive; Talmon,* a temple doorkeeper:—Talmon {5x}. See: BDB—379a.

2930. טָמֵא {161x} **tâmêʾ,** *taw-may';* a prim. root; to *be foul,* espec. in a cerem. or mor. sense (*contaminated*):—unclean {74x}, defile {71x}, pollute {14x}, uncleanness {1x}, utterly {1x}.

Tame', as a verb, means "to be unclean." **(1)** The verb occurs mainly in Leviticus, as in Lev 11:26: "The carcases of every beast which divideth the hoof, and is not clovenfooted, nor cheweth the cud, are unclean unto you: every one that toucheth them shall be unclean." **(2)** *Tame'* is the opposite of *taher* (2891), "to be pure." See: TWOT—809; BDB—379a, 380a.

2931. טָמֵא {87x} **tâmêʾ,** *taw-may';* from 2930; *foul* in a relig. sense:—unclean {79x}, defiled {5x}, infamous {1x}, polluted {1x}, pollution {1x}.

Tame', as an adjective, means "unclean." **(1)** The frequency of the word is high in Leviticus. **(2)** Its first occurrence is also in Leviticus: "Or if a soul touch any unclean thing, whether it be a carcase of an unclean beast, or a carcase of unclean cattle, or the carcase of unclean creeping things, and if it be hidden from him; he also shall be unclean, and guilty" (5:2). **(3)** The usage of *tame'* in the Old Testament

resembles that of *tahor* (2889), "pure."
(3a) First, uncleanness is a state of being. The
leper was compelled to announce his uncleanness wherever he went (Lev 13:45); however,
even here there is a religious overtone, in that
his uncleanness was ritual. Hence, it is more
appropriate to recognize that the second usage
is most basic. **(3b)** *Tame'* in the religio-cultic
sense is a technical term denoting a state of
being ceremonially unfit. **(3b1)** Animals, carcases, unclean people, and objects conveyed
the impurity to those who touched them: "And
whatsoever the unclean person toucheth shall
be unclean; and the soul that toucheth it shall
lie unclean until even" (Num 19:22). **(3b2)** The
impurity could also be brought about by a seminal issue (Lev 15:2) or a menstrual period (Lev
15:25), and whatever the unclean touched was
also rendered "unclean." Syn.: 2490, 2610,
2933. See: TWOT—809a; BDB—379d.

2932. טֻמְאָה {37x} **ṭum'âh**, *toom-aw';* from
2930; relig. *impurity:*—unclean-
ness {26x}, filthiness {7x}, unclean {4x}, unclean (-ness).

Tum'ah, as a noun, means "uncleanness."
(1) The word occurs in Num 5:19: "And the
priest shall charge her by an oath, and say unto
the woman, If no man have lain with thee, and
if thou hast not gone aside to uncleanliness
with another instead of thine husband, be thou
free from this bitter water that causeth the
curse." Here the word refers to sexual "uncleanness." **(2)** *Tum'ah* occurs twice in Lev
16:16 and refers to ethical and religious "uncleanness." See: TWOT—809b; BDB—380a.

2933. טָמָה {2x} **ṭâmâh**, *taw-maw';* a collat.
form of 2930; to *be impure* in a
relig. sense:—be defiled {1x}, be reputed vile
{1x}. See: TWOT—810; BDB—380b.

2934. טָמַן {32x} **ṭâman**, *taw-man';* a prim.
root; to *hide* (by *covering* over):—
hide {26x}, laid {2x}, lay privily {2x}, in secret
{1x}. Syn.: 2244, 2447, 3582, 5641, 6845. See:
TWOT—811; BDB—380b.

2935. טֶנֶא {4x} **ṭene'**, *teh'-neh;* from an unused root prob. mean. to *weave;* a
basket (of interlaced osiers):—basket {4x}.
Syn.: 1731, 3619, 5536. See: TWOT—812a;
BDB—380d.

2936. טָנַף {1x} **ṭânaph**, *taw-naf';* a prim. root;
to *soil:*—defile {1x}. Syn.: 1351,
2490, 2930. See: TWOT—813; BDB—380d.

2937. טָעָה {1x} **ṭâ'âh**, *taw-aw';* a prim. root;
to *wander;* caus. to *lead astray:*—
seduce {1x}. See: TWOT—814; BDB—380d.

2938. טָעַם {11x} **ṭâ'am**, *taw-am';* a prim. root;
to *taste;* fig. to *perceive:*—but

taste {2x}, perceiveth {1x}, taste {5x}, tasted
{2x}, tasteth {1x}. See: TWOT—815; BDB—
380d, 1094b.

2939. טְעַם {3x} **ṭ'ʿam** (Aram.), *teh-am';* corresp. to 2938; to *taste;* caus. to
feed:—make to eat {1x}, feed {2x}. See: TWOT—
2757; BDB—1094b.

2940. טַעַם {13x} **ṭa'am**, *tah'-am;* from 2938;
prop. a *taste,* i.e. (fig.) *perception;*
by impl. *intelligence;* tran. a *mandate:*—advice
{1x}, behaviour {2x}, decree {1x}, discretion
{1x}, judgment {1x}, reason {1x}, taste {5x}, understanding {1x}. See: TWOT—815a; BDB—
381a, 1094c.

2941. טַעַם {5x} **ṭa'am** (Aram.), *tah'-am;* from
2939; prop. a *taste,* i.e. (as in 2940)
a judicial *sentence:*—account {1x}, to be commanded {1x}, commandment {2x}, matter {1x}.
See: TWOT—2757a; 1094c.

2942. טְעֵם {25x} **ṭ'ʿêm** (Aram.), *teh-ame';*
from 2939, and equiv. to 2941;
prop. *flavor;* fig. *judgment* (both subj. and
obj.); hence, *account* (both subj. and obj.):—
decree {13x}, chancellor + 1169 {3x}, commanded + 7761 {3x}, regarded {1x}, commandment {2x}, regard + 7761 {1x}, tasted {1x},
wisdom {1x}. See: TWOT—2757a; BDB—
1094c, 1096a.

2943. טַעַן {1x} **ṭâ'an**, *taw-an';* a prim. root; to
load a beast:—lade {1x}. Syn.: 6006.
See: TWOT—816; BDB—381b.

2944. טָעַן {1x} **ṭâ'an**, *taw-an';* a prim. root; to
stab:—thrust through {1x}. Syn.:
1856. See: TWOT—817; BDB—381b.

2945. טַף {42x} **taph**, *taf;* from 2952 (perh. referring to the *tripping* gait of chil-
dren); a *family* (mostly used collect. in the
sing.):—little ones {49x}, children {12x}, families {1x}.

Taph means "weaker one; child; little one."
(1) Basically this word signifies those members
of a nomadic tribe who are not able to march
or who can only march to a limited extent.
(1a) The word implies the "weaker ones." Thus
we read of the men and the *taphim,* or the men
and those who were unable to move quickly
over long stretches: "And Judah said unto Israel, his father, Send the lad with me, and we
will arise and go; that we may live, and not die,
both we, and thou, and also our little ones"
(Gen 43:8). **(1b)** This nuance is clearer in Gen
50:7–8: "And Joseph went up to bury his father;
and with him went up all the servants of Pharaoh, the elders of his house, and all the elders
of the land of Egypt, and all the house of Joseph, and his brethren and his father's house:
only their little ones, and their flocks, and their

Hebrew

herds, they left in the land of Goshen." They left the women and the aged to take care of the beasts and babies. These verses certainly make it clear that only men went along. **(2)** In several passages *taph* represents only the children and old ones: "And all their wealth, and all their little ones, and their wives took they captive, and spoiled even all that was in the house" (Gen 34:29, first occurrence). All the able-bodied men of Shechem were killed (Gen 34:26). **(3)** Sometimes the word means "children": "But all the women children, that have not known a man by lying with him, keep alive for yourselves" (Num 31:18; cf. v. 17). See: TWOT—821a; BDB—381b, 381d.

2946. טָפַח {2x} **tâphach**, *taw-fakh';* a prim. root; to *flatten* out or *extend* (as a tent); fig. to *nurse* a child (as *promotive* of growth); or perh. a denom. from 2947, from *dandling* on the palms:—span {1x} swaddle {1x}. See: TWOT—821; BDB—381b.

2947. טֵפַח {4x} **têphach**, *tay'-fakh;* from 2946; a *spread* of the hand, i.e. a *palm-breadth* (not "span" of the fingers); arch. a *corbel* (as a supporting palm):—coping {1x}, hand-breadth {3x}. See: TWOT—818b; BDB—381c.

2948. טֹפַח {5x} **tôphach**, *to'-fakh;* from 2946 (the same as 2947):—hand-breadth {4x}, handbroad {1x}. See: TWOT—818c; BDB—381c.

182949. טִפֻּח {1x} **tippûch**, *tip-pookh';* from 2946; *nursing:*—span long {1x}. See: TWOT—818a; BDB—381c.

2950. טָפַל {3x} **tâphal**, *taw-fal';* a prim. root; prop. to *stick* on as a patch; fig. to *impute* falsely:—forge {1x}, forger {1x}, sew up {1x}. See: TWOT—819; BDB—381c.

2951. טִפְסַר {2x} **tiphçar**, *tif-sar';* of for. der.; a military *governor:*—captain {2x}. Syn.: 5057, 6346, 7218, 8269. See: TWOT—820; BDB—381d.

2952. טָפַף {1x} **tâphaph**, *taw-faf';* a prim. root; appar. to *trip* (with short steps) coquettishly:—mince {1x}. See: TWOT—821; BDB—381d.

2953. טְפַר {2x} **tᵉphar** (Aram.), *tef-ar';* from a root corresp. to 6852, and mean. the same as 6856; a finger-*nail;* also a *hoof* or *claw:*—nail {2x}. See: TWOT—2758; BDB—1094c.

2954. טָפַשׁ {1x} **tâphash**, *taw-fash';* a prim. root; prop. appar. to *be thick;* fig. to *be stupid:*—be fat {1x}. Syn.: 1277, 1878, 2459. See: TWOT—822; BDB—382a, 936a.

2955. טָפַת {1x} **Tâphath**, *taw-fath';* prob. from 5197; a *dropping* (of ointment); *Taphath,* an Israelitess:—Taphath {1x}. See: BDB—382a.

2956. טָרַד {2x} **târad**, *taw-rad';* a prim. root; to *drive* on; fig. to *follow* close:—continual {2x}. See: TWOT—823; BDB—382a, 1094c.

2957. טְרַד {4x} **tᵉrad** (Aram.), *ter-ad';* corresp. to 2956; to *expel:*—drive {4x}. See: TWOT—2759; BDB—1094c.

2958. טְרוֹם {1x} **tᵉrôwm**, *ter-ome';* a var. of 2962; *not yet:*—before {1x}. See: TWOT—826; BDB—382c.

2959. טָרַח {1x} **târach**, *taw-rakh';* a prim. root; to *overburden:*—weary {1x}. See: TWOT—825; BDB—382b.

2960. טֹרַח {2x} **tôrach**, *to'-rakh;* from 2959; a *burden:*—cumbrance {1x}, trouble {1x}. See: TWOT—825a; BDB—382b.

2961. טָרִי {2x} **târiy**, *taw-ree';* from an unused root appar. mean. to *be moist;* prop. *dripping;* hence, *fresh* (i.e. recently made such):—new {1x}, putrefying {1x}. See: TWOT—824a; BDB—382b.

2962. טֶרֶם {9x} **terem**, *teh'-rem;* from an unused root appar. mean. to *interrupt* or *suspend;* prop. *non-occurrence;* used adv. *not yet* or *before:*—before {5x}, ere {1x}, not yet {2x}, yet {1x}. See: TWOT—826; BDB—382c.

2963. טָרַף {25x} **târaph**, *taw-raf';* a prim. root; to *pluck off* or *pull* to pieces; caus. to *supply* with food (as in morsels):—tear {6x}, tear in pieces {6x}, ravening {3x}, catch {2x}, doubt {1x}, feed {1x}, rent in pieces {1x}, prey {1x}, ravin {1x}, surely {1x}, not translated {1x}, torn {1x}. See: TWOT—827; BDB—382d.

2964. טֶרֶף {23x} **tereph**, *teh'-ref;* from 2963; something *torn,* i.e. a *fragment,* e.g. a *fresh* leaf, *prey, food:*—leaves {1x}, meat {3x}, prey {18x}, spoil {1x}. See: TWOT—827b; BDB—383a.

2965. טָרָף {1x} **târâph**, *taw-rawf';* from 2963; recently *torn* off, i.e. *fresh:*—pluckt off {1x}. See: TWOT—827a; BDB—383a.

2966. טְרֵפָה {9x} **tᵉrêphâh**, *ter-ay-faw';* fem. (collect.) of 2964; *prey,* i.e. flocks devoured by animals:—ravin {1x}, (that which was) torn (of beasts, in pieces) {8x}. See: TWOT—827c; BDB—383c.

2967. טַרְפְּלָי {1x} **Tarpᵉlay** (Aram.), *tar-pel-ah'-ee;* from a name of for. der.; a *Tarpelite* (collect.) or inhab. of Tarpel, a place in Assyria:—Tarpelites {1x}. See: BDB—1094c.

2968. יָאַב {1x} **yâ°ab**, *yaw-ab'*; a prim. root; to *desire:*—long {1x}. See: TWOT—828; BDB—383b.

2969. יָאָה {1x} **yâ°âh**, *yaw-aw'*; a prim. root; to *be suitable:*—appertain {1x}. See: TWOT—829; BDB—383b.

יְאוֹר **y°ôwr**. See 2975.

2970. יַאֲזַנְיָה {4x} **Ya°ăzanyâh**, *yah-az-an-yaw'*; or

יַאֲזַנְיָהוּ **Ya°ăzanyâhûw**, *yah-az-an-yaw'-hoo*; from 238 and 3050; *heard of Jah; Jaazanjah*, the name of four Isr.:—Jaazaniah {4x}. Syn.: comp. 3153. See: BDB—24d, 383b.

2971. יָאִיר {9x} **Yâ°îyr**, *yaw-ere'*; from 215; *enlightener; Jaïr*, the name of four Isr.:—Jair {9x}. See: BDB—22c, 383b.

2972. יָאִרִי {1x} **Yâ°îrîy**, *yaw-ee-ree'*; patron. from 2971; a *Jaïrite* or desc. of Jair:—Jairite {1x}. See: BDB—22c, 383b.

2973. יָאַל {4x} **yâ°al**, *yaw-al'*; a prim. root; prop. to *be slack*, i.e. (fig.) to *be foolish:*—dote {1x}, be foolish {1x}, become foolish {1x}, do foolishly {1x}. See: TWOT—830; BDB—383b. Syn.: 191, 3684, 5034.

2974. יָאַל {19x} **yâ°al**, *yaw-al'*; a prim. root [prob. rather the same as 2973 through the idea of mental *weakness*]; prop. to *yield*, espec. *assent;* hence, (pos.) to *undertake* as an act of volition:—content {7x}, please {4x}, would {3x}, taken upon me {2x}, began {1x}, assayed {1x}, willingly {1x}.
This word represents the volitional element in an act rather than the feelings, dispositions, or motives that have prompted it. See: TWOT—831; BDB—383d.

2975. יְאֹר {64x} **y°ôr**, *yeh-ore'*; of Eg. or.; a *channel*, e.g. a fosse, canal, shaft; spec. the *Nile*, as the one river of Egypt, incl. its collat. trenches; also the *Tigris*, as the main river of Assyria:—brooks {5x}, flood {5x}, river {53x}, streams {1x}. Syn.: 5104. See: TWOT—832; BDB—383b, 384b, 456c.

2976. יָאַשׁ {6x} **yâ°ash**, *yaw-ash'*; a prim. root; to *desist*, i.e. (fig.) to *despond:*—(cause to) despair {2x}, one that is desperate {1x}, be no hope {3x}. See: TWOT—833; BDB—384c.

2977. יֹאשִׁיָה {53x} **Yô°shîyâh**, *yo-shee-yaw'*; or

יֹאשִׁיָהוּ **Yô°shîyâhûw**, *yo-she-yaw'-hoo*; from the same root as 803 and 3050; *founded of Jah; Joshijah*, the name of two Isr.:—Josiah {53x}. See: BDB—78c, 384c.

2978. יְאִתוֹן {1x} **y°îthôwn**, *yeh-ee-thone'*; from 857; an *entry:*—entrance {1x}. Syn.: 3996, 6607. See: TWOT—188a; BDB—36b, 87c.

2979. יְאָתְרַי {1x} **Y°âth°ray**, *yeh-aw-ther-ah'ee;* from the same as 871; *stepping; Jeätherai*, an Isr.:—Jeaterai {1x}. See: BDB—384d.

2980. יָבַב {1x} **yâbab**, *yaw-bab';* a prim. root; to *bawl:*—cry out {1x}. Syn.: 2199, 6817, 7121. See: TWOT—834; BDB—384d.

2981. יְבוּל {13x} **y°bûwl**, *yeb-ool';* from 2986; *produce*, i.e. a *crop* or (fig.) *wealth:*—fruit {1x}, increase {10x}. Syn.: 6521, 7235. See: TWOT—835c; BDB—385b.

2982. יְבוּס {4x} **Y°bûwç**, *yeb-oos';* from 947; *trodden*, i.e. threshing-place; *Jebus*, the aboriginal name of Jerusalem:—Jebus {4x}. See: BDB—101a, 384d.

2983. יְבוּסִי {41x} **Y°bûwçîy**, *yeb-oo-see';* patrial from 2982; a *Jebusite* or inhab. of Jebus:—Jebusite (-s) {41x}. See: BDB—101a, 384d.

2984. יִבְחַר {3x} **Yibchar**, *yib-khar';* from 977; *choice; Jibchar*, an Isr.:—Ibhar {3x}. See: BDB—104c, 384d.

2985. יָבִין {8x} **Yâbîyn**, *yaw-bene';* from 995; *intelligent; Jabin*, the name of two Canaanitish kings:—Jabin {8x}. See: BDB—108a, 384d.

יָבֵישׁ **Yâbêysh**. See 3003.

2986. יָבַל {18x} **yâbal**, *yaw-bal';* a prim. root; prop. to *flow;* caus. to *bring* (espec. with pomp):—bring {11x}, carry {4x}, bring forth {1x}, lead forth {1x}, lead {1x}. See: TWOT—835; BDB—384d, 1094d.

2987. יְבַל {3x} **y°bal** (Aram.), *yeb-al';* corresp. to 2986; to *bring:*—brought {2x}, carry {1x}. See: TWOT—2760; BDB—1094d.

יֹבֵל **yôbêl**. See 3104.

2988. יָבָל {2x} **yâbâl**, *yaw-bawl';* from 2986; a *stream:*—[water-] course {1x}, stream {1x}. See: TWOT—835a; BDB—385a.

2989. יָבָל {1x} **Yâbâl**, *yaw-bawl';* the same as 2988; *Jabal*, an antediluvian:—Jabal {1x}. See: BDB—385b.

יֹבֵל **yôbêl**. See 3104.

2990. יַבֵּל {1x} **yabbêl**, *yab-bale';* from 2986; having *running* sores:—wen {1x}. See: TWOT—835f; BDB—385c, 386a.

2991. יִבְלְעָם {3x} **Yibl⁽ᶜ⁾âm**, *yib-leh-awm';* from 1104 and 5971; *devouring people; Jibleam,* a place in Pal.:—Ibleam {3x}. See: BDB—385d.

2992. יָבָם {3x} **yâbam**, *yaw-bam';* a prim. root of doubtful mean.; used only as a denom. from 2993; to *marry* a (deceased) brother's widow:—perform the duty of a husband's brother {2x}, marry {1x}. See: TWOT—836; BDB—386a.

2993. יָבָם {2x} **yâbâm**, *yaw-bawm';* from (the orig. of) 2992; a *brother-in-law:*—husband's brother {2x}. See: TWOT—836a; BDB—386a.

2994. יְבֵמֶת {5x} **yᵉbêmeth**, *yeb-ay'-meth;* fem. part. of 2992; a *sister-in-law:*—brother's wife {3x}, sister-in-law {2x}. See: TWOT—836b; BDB—386a.

2995. יַבְנְאֵל {2x} **Yabnᵉêl**, *yab-neh-ale';* from 1129 and 410: *built of God; Jabneel,* the name of two places in Pal.:—Jabneel {2x}. See: BDB—125c, 386b.

2996. יַבְנֶה {1x} **Yabneh**, *yab-neh';* from 1129; a *building; Jabneh,* a place in Pal.:—Jabneh {1x}. See: BDB—125c, 386b.

2997. יִבְנְיָה {1x} **Yibnᵉyâh**, *yib-neh-yaw';* from 1129 and 3050; *built of Jah; Jibnejah,* an Isr.:—Ibneiah {1x}. See: BDB—125c, 386b.

2998. יִבְנִיָה {1x} **Yibnîyâh**, *yib-nee-yaw';* from 1129 and 3050; *building of Jah; Jibnijah,* an Isr.:—Ibnijah {1x}. See: BDB—125d, 386b.

2999. יַבֹּק {7x} **Yabbôq**, *yab-boke';* prob. from 1238; *pouring* forth; *Jabbok,* a river E. of the Jordan:—Jabbok {1x}. See: BDB—132d, 391d.

3000. יְבֶרֶכְיָהוּ {1x} **Yᵉberekyâhûw**, *yeb-eh-rek-yaw'-hoo;* from 1288 and 3050: *blessed of Jah; Jeberekjah,* an Isr.:—Jeberechiah {1x}. See: BDB—140a, 386b.

3001. יָבֵשׁ {78x} **yâbêsh**, *yaw-bashe';* a prim. root; to *be ashamed, confused* or *disappointed;* also (as failing) to *dry* up (as water) or *wither* (as herbage):—dry up {27x}, withered {22x}, confounded {9x}, ashamed {7x}, dry {7x}, wither away {2x}, clean {1x}, shamed {1x}, shamefully {1x}, utterly {1x}.

Yabesh means "to be dry, be dried up, be withered." **(1)** In its verbal form *yabesh* is found for the first time in Gen 8:7, when after the Flood, "the waters were dried up from the earth." However, the noun derivative, yabbashah, which means "dry ground," already occurs in Gen 1:9. **(2)** Physical "drying up" can involve **(2a)** bread (Josh 9:5), **(2b)** the ground in time

of drought (Jer 23:10; Amos 4:7), **(2c)** brooks and streams (1 Kin 17:7), and **(2c)** crops (Is 42:15). **(3)** The shortness of man's life is compared to the "drying up" of grass (Ps 90:6; 102:11; Is 40:7). **(4)** Because of affliction, the heart too "withers" like the grass (Ps 102:4). **(5)** In his parable of the vine, Ezekiel likens God's judgment on Judah to the "withering" of a vine that is pulled up (Eze 17:9–10). **(6)** Because of his disobedience, Jeroboam's hand "is dried up" as judgment from God (1 Kin 13:4). **(7)** Psychosomatic awareness is clearly demonstrated in Prov 17:22: "A broken spirit drieth the bones." Syn.: 5034, 6784, 7060. See: TWOT—837; BDB—386b.

3002. יָבֵשׁ {9x} **yâbêsh**, *yaw-bashe';* from 3001; *dry:*—dried {1x}, dried away {1x}, dry {7x}. See: TWOT—837a; BDB—386d.

3003. יָבֵשׁ {24x} **Yâbêsh**, *yaw-bashe';* the same as 3002 (also

יָבֵישׁ **Yâbêysh**, *yaw-bashe';* often with the addition of 1568, i.e. *Jabesh of Gilead*); *Jabesh,* the name of an Isr. and of a place in Pal.:—Jabesh {12x}, Jabeshgilead {12x}. See: BDB—386d.

3004. יַבָּשָׁה {14x} **yabbâshâh**, *yab-baw-shaw';* from 3001; *dry* ground:—dry {10x}, dry land {2x}, dry ground {1x}, land {1x}. See: TWOT—837b; BDB—387a.

3005. יִבְשָׂם {1x} **Yibsâm**, *yib-sawm';* from the same as 1314; *fragrant; Jibsam,* an Isr.:—Jibsam {1x}. See: BDB—142a.

3006. יַבֶּשֶׁת {2x} **yabbesheth**, *yab-beh'-sheth;* a var. of 3004; *dry* ground:—dry land {2x}. See: TWOT—837c; BDB—387a, 1094d.

3007. יַבֶּשֶׁת {1x} **yabbesheth** (Aram.), *yab-beh'-sheth;* corresp. to 3006; *dry* land:—earth {1x}. See: TWOT—2761; BDB—1094d.

3008. יִגְאָל {3x} **Yig'âl**, *yig-awl';* from 1350; *avenger; Jigal,* the name of three Isr.:—Igal {2x}, Igeal {1x}. See: BDB—145d, 387a.

3009. יָגַב {2x} **yâgab**, *yaw-gab';* a prim. root; to *dig* or plow:—husbandman {2x}. See: TWOT—838; BDB—387a.

3010. יָגֵב {1x} **yâgêb**, *yaw-gabe';* from 3009; a *plowed field:*—field {1x}. Syn.: 7704, 7709. See: TWOT—838a; BDB—387a.

3011. יָגְבְּהָה {2x} **Yogbᵉhâh**, *yog-beh-haw';* fem. from 1361; *hillock; Jogbehah,* a place E. of the Jordan:—Jogbehah {2x}. See: BDB—147b, 387a.

3012. יִגְדַּלְיָהוּ {1x} **Yigdalyâhûw**, *yig-dal-yaw'-hoo;* from 1431 and 3050; *magnified of Jah; Jigdaljah,* an Isr.:—Igdaliah {1x}. See: BDB—153d, 387a.

3013. יָגָה {8x} **yâgâh**, *yaw-gaw';* a prim. root; to *grieve:*—afflict {4x}, cause grief {1x}, grieve {1x}, sorrowful {1x}, vex {1x}. Syn.: 3015, 6031. See: TWOT—839; BDB—387a.

3014. יָגָה {1x} **yâgâh**, *yaw-gaw';* a prim. root [prob. rather the same as 3013 through the common idea of *dissatisfaction*]; to *push* away:—be removed {1x}. See: TWOT—840; BDB—387c.

3015. יָגוֹן {14x} **yâgôwn**, *yaw-gohn';* from 3013; *affliction:*—grief {2x}, sorrow {12x}. See: TWOT—839a; BDB—387b.

3016. יָגוֹר {2x} **yâgôwr**, *yaw-gore';* from 3025; *fearful:*—afraid {1x}, fearest {1x}. See: TWOT—843a; BDB—388d.

3017. יָגוּר {1x} **Yâgûwr**, *yaw-goor';* prob. from 1481; a *lodging; Jagur,* a place in Pal.:—Jagur {1x}. See: BDB—158c, 387c.

3018. יְגִיעַ {16x} **y°gîya°**, *yeg-ee'-ah;* from 3021; *toil;* hence, a *work, produce, property* (as the result of labor):—labour {15x}, work {1x}. Syn.: 3021, 5639, 6467. See: TWOT—842e; BDB—388c.

3019. יָגִיעַ {1x} **yâgîya°**, *yaw-ghee'-ah;* from 3021; *tired:*—weary {1x}. See: TWOT—842d; BDB—388c.

3020. יָגְלִי {1x} **Yoglîy**, *yog-lee';* from 1540; *exiled; Jogli,* an Isr.:—Jogli {1x}. See: BDB—163d, 387c.

3021. יָגַע {26x} **yâga°**, *yaw-gah';* a prim. root; prop. to *gasp;* hence, to *be exhausted,* to *tire,* to *toil:*—faint {1x}, (make to) labour {12x}, (be) weary {13x}. Syn.: 3023. See: TWOT—842; BDB—388a.

3022. יָגָע {1x} **yâgâ°**, *yaw-gaw';* from 3021; *earnings* (as the product of toil):—that which he laboured {1x} for. See: TWOT—842a; BDB—388b.

3023. יָגֵעַ {3x} **yâgêa°**, *yaw-gay'-ah;* from 3021; *tired;* hence, (tran.) *tiresome:*—full of labour {1x}, weary {2x}. See: TWOT—842b; BDB—388b.

3024. יְגֵעָה {1x} **y°gî°âh**, *yeg-ee-aw';* fem. of 3019; *fatigue:*—weariness {1x}. See: TWOT—842c; BDB—388b.

3025. יָגֹר {5x} **yâgôr**, *yaw-gore';* a prim. root; to *fear:*—be afraid {4x}, fear {1x}. Syn.: 3372, 6342. See: TWOT—843; BDB—388c.

3026. יְגַר שָׂהֲדוּתָא {1x} **Y°gar Sahădûwthâ³** (Aram.), *yegar' sah-had-oo-thaw';* from a word derived from an unused root (mean. to *gather*) and a der. of a root corresp. to 7717; *heap of the testimony; Jegar-Sahadutha,* a cairn E. of the Jordan:—Jegar-Sahadutha {1x}. See: BDB—1094d.

3027. יָד {1614x} **yâd**, *yawd;* a prim. word; a *hand* (the *open* one [indicating *power, means, direction,* etc.], in distinction from 3709, the *closed* one); used (as noun, adv., etc.) in a great variety of applications, both lit. and fig., both prox. and remote [as follows]:—hand {1359x}, by {44x}, consecrate + 4390 {14x}, him {14x}, power {12x}, them {11x}, places {8x}, tenons {6x}, thee {6x}, coast {6x}, side {5x}, misc. {129x} = (+ be) able, ✕ about, + armholes, at, axletree, because of, beside, border, ✕ bounty, + broad, [broken-] handed, charge, + creditor, custody, debt, dominion, ✕ enough, + fellowship, force, ✕ from, hand [-staves, -y work], ✕ he, ✕ in, labour, + large, ledge, [left-] handed, means, ✕ mine, ministry, near, ✕ of, ✕ order, ordinance, ✕ our, parts, pain, ✕ presumptuously, service, sore, state, stay, draw with strength, stroke, + swear, terror, ✕ thine own, ✕ thou, through, ✕ throwing, + thumb, times, ✕ to, ✕ under, ✕ us, ✕ wait on, [way-] side, where, + wide, ✕ with (him, me, you), work, + yield, ✕ yourselves.

Yad means "hand; side; border; alongside; hand-measure; portion; arm (rest); monument; manhood (male sex organ); power; rule." **(1)** The primary sense of this word is "hand": "And the Lord God said, Behold, the man is become as one of us, to know good and evil: and now, lest he put forth his hand, and take also of the tree of life . . ." (Gen 3:22—the first biblical occurrence). **(1a)** Sometimes the word is used in conjunction with an object that can be grasped by the "hand": "And if he smite him with throwing a stone [literally, "hand stone"] . . ." (Num 35:17). **(1b)** In a similar usage the word means "human": "He shall also stand up against the Prince of princes; but he shall be broken without hand [i.e., human agency]" (Dan 8:25; cf. Job 34:20). **(1c)** In Is 49:2, "hand" is used of God; God tells Moses that He will put His "hand" over the mouth of the cave and protect him. **(1c1)** This is a figure of speech, an anthropomorphism, by which God promises His protection. **(1c2)** God's "hand" is another term for God's "power" (cf. Jer 16:21). **(2)** *Yad* is employed in several other noteworthy phrases. **(2a)** The "lifting of the hand" may be involved in "taking an oath" (Gen 14:22). **(2b)** "Shaking" [literally, "giving one's hand"] is another oath-taking gesture (cf. Prov 11:21). **(2c)** For "one's hands to be on another" (Gen 37:27) or "laid upon another" (Ex 7:4) is to do harm to some-

one. **(2d)** "Placing one's hands with" signifies "making common cause with someone" (Ex 23:1). **(2e)** If one's hand does not "reach" something, he is "unable to pay" for it (Lev 5:7). **(2f)** When one's countryman is "unable to stretch out his hand to you," he is not able to support himself (Lev 25:35). **(2g)** "Putting one's hand on one's mouth" is a gesture of silence (Prov 30:32). **(2h)** "Placing one's hands under someone" means submitting to him (1 Chr 29:24). **(2i)** "Giving something into one's hand" is entrusting it to him (Gen 42:37). **(3)** A major group of passages uses *yad* to represent the location and uses of the hand. **(3a)** First, the word can mean "side," where the hand is located: "And Absalom rose up early, and stood beside the way of the gate" (2 Sa 15:2). **(3b)** In 2 Chr 21:16, the word means "border": "Moreover the Lord stirred up against Jehoram the spirit of the Philistines, and of the Arabians, that were near [literally, "by the hand of"] the Ethiopians." **(3c)** A similar use in Ex 25 applies this word to the "banks" of the Nile River: "And the daughter of Pharaoh came down to wash herself at the river, and her maidens walked along by the [Nile]." In this sense, *yad* can represent "length and breadth." **(3d)** In Gen 34:21 we read that the land was (literally) "broad of hands": "These men are peaceable with us; therefore let them dwell in the land, and trade therein; for the land, behold, it is large enough for them."

(4) Since the hand can receive only a part or fraction of something, the word can signify a "part" or "fraction": "And he took and sent [portions] unto them from before him: but Benjamin's [portion] was five times so much as any of theirs" (Gen 43:34). **(5)** *Yad* comes to mean that which upholds something, a "support" (1 Kin 7:35ff.) or an "arm rest" (1 Kin 10:19). **(6)** Since a hand may be held up as a "sign," *yad* can signify a "monument" or "stele": "Saul came to Carmel, and, behold, he set him up a place [monument], and is gone about, and passed on, and gone down to Gilgal" (1 Sa 15:12). **(7)** *Yad* sometimes represents the "male sex organ": ". . . And art gone up; thou hast enlarged thy bed, and made thee a covenant with them; thou lovedst their bed where thou sawest it [you have looked on their manhood]" (Is 57:8; cf. v. 10; 6:2; 7:20). **(8)** In several passages, *yad* is used in the sense of "power" or "rule": **(8a)** "And David smote Hadarezer king of Zobah unto Hamath, as he went to stablish his dominion by the river Euphrates" (1 Chr 18:3). **(8b)** "To be delivered into one's hands" means to be "given into one's power": "God hath delivered him into mine hand; for he is shut in, by entering into a town that hath gates and bars" (1 Sa 23:7; cf. Prov 18:21). **(8c)** "To fill

someone's hand" may be a technical term for "installing him" in office: "And thou shalt put them upon Aaron thy brother, and his sons with him; and shalt anoint them, and consecrate them [literally, "fill their hands"], and sanctify them, that they may minister unto me in the priest's office" (Ex 28:41). **(9)** *Yad* is frequently joined to the preposition be and other prepositions as an extension; there is no change in meaning, only a longer form: "For what have I done? or what evil is in mine hand?" (1 Sa 26:18). See: TWOT—844; BDB—388d, 406d, 1094d.

3028. יַד {17x} **yad** (Aram.), *yad;* corresp. to 3027:—hand {16x}, power {1x}. See: TWOT—2763; BDB—1094d.

3029. יְדָא {2x} **yᵉdâ** (Aram.), *yed-aw';* corresp. to 3034; to *praise:*—thank {1x}, give thanks {1x}. See: TWOT—2764; BDB—1095a.

3030. יִדְאֲלָה {1x} **Yidʾâlâh**, *yid-al-aw';* of uncert. der.; *Jidalah*, a place in Pal.:—Idalah {1x}. See: BDB—391d.

3031. יִדְבָּשׁ {1x} **Yidbâsh**, *yid-bawsh';* from the same as 1706; perh. *honeyed; Jidbash*, an Isr.:—Idbash {1x}. See: BDB—185c, 391d.

3032. יָדַד {3x} **yâdad**, *yaw-dad';* a prim. root; prop. to *handle* [comp. 3034], i.e. to *throw*, e.g. lots:—cast {3x}. See: TWOT—845, 846; BDB—391d.

3033. יְדִדוּת {1x} **yᵉdîdûwth**, *yed-ee-dooth';* from 3039; prop. *affection;* concr. a *darling* object:—dearly beloved {1x}. See: TWOT—846c; BDB—392a.

3034. יָדָה {114x} **yâdâh**, *yaw-daw';* a prim. root; used only as denom. from 3027; lit. to *use* (i.e. hold out) *the hand;* phys. to *throw* (a stone, an arrow) at or away; espec. to *revere* or *worship* (with extended hands); intens. to *bemoan* (by wringing the hands):—praise {53x}, give thanks {32x}, confess {16x}, thank {5x}, make confession {2x}, thanksgiving {2x}, cast {1x}, cast out {1x}, shoot {1x}, thankful {1x}.

Yadah means "to give thanks, laud, praise." **(1)** A common Hebrew word in all its periods, this verb is an important word in the language of worship. **(2)** *Yadah* is found 114 times in the Hebrew Bible, the first time being in the story of the birth of Judah, Jacob's son who was born to Leah: "And she conceived again, and bare a son: and she said, Now will I praise the LORD: therefore she called his name Judah; and left bearing (Gen 29:35). **(3)** The root, translated "confess" or "confession" about twenty times in the KJV, is also frequently rendered "praise"

or "give thanks." **(3a)** At first glance, the meanings may appear unrelated. But upon closer inspection, it becomes evident that each sense profoundly illumines and interprets the other. **(3)** As is to be expected, this word is found most frequently in the Book of Psalms (some 70 times). **(3a)** *Yadah* overlaps in meaning with a number of other Hebrew words implying "praise," such as *halal* (1984 - whence halleluyah). **(3b)** As an expression of thanks or praise, it is a natural part of ritual or public worship as well as personal praise to God (Ps 30:9, 12; 35:18).

(3c) Man is occasionally the object of *yadah;* but far more commonly, God is the object. **(3d)** The usual context seems to be public worship, where the worshipers affirm and renew their relationship with God. **(3e)** The subject is not primarily the isolated individual, but the congregation. **(3f)** Especially in the hymns and thanksgivings of the Psalter, it is evident that *yadah* is a recital of, and thanksgiving for, Yahweh's mighty acts of salvation. **(3g)** An affirmation or confession of God's undeserved kindness throws man's unworthiness into sharp relief. **(3h)** Hence, a confession of sin may be articulated in the same breath as a confession of faith or praise and thanksgiving. **(3i)** The confession is not a moralistic, autobiographical catalogue of sins—individual infractions of a legal code—but a confession of the underlying sinfulness that engulfs all mankind and separates us from the holy God. **(4)** God is even to be praised for His judgments, by which He awakens repentance (e.g., Ps 51:4). **(4a)** So one is not surprised to find praises in penitential contexts, and vice versa (1 Kin 8:33ff.; Neh 9:2ff.; Dan 9:4ff.). **(4b)** If praise inevitably entails confession of sin, the reverse is also true: The sure word of forgiveness elicits praise and thanksgiving on the confessor's part. **(4c)** This wells up almost automatically from the new being of the repentant person.

(5) The vista of *yadah* expands both vertically and horizontally—vertically to include all creation, and horizontally stretching forward to that day when praise and thanksgiving shall be eternal (e.g., Ps 29; 95:10; 96:7–9; 103:19–22). **(6)** Thanks often are directed to the name of the Lord (Ps 106:47; 122:4). **(7)** An affirmation or confession of God's undeserved kindness throws man's unworthiness into sharp relief. **(8)** Hence, a confession of sin may be articulated in the same breath as a confession of faith or praise and thanksgiving. **(9)** The confession is not a moralistic, autobiographical catalogue of sins—individual infractions of a legal code—**(10)** but a confession of the underlying sinfulness that engulfs all mankind and separates us from the holy God. **(11)** God

is even to be praised for His judgments, by which He awakens repentance (Ps 51:4). **(12)** So it is not surprising to find praises in penitential contexts, and vice versa (1 Kin 8:33; Neh 9:2; Dan 9:4).

(13) If praise inevitably entails confession of sin, the sure word of forgiveness elicits praise and thanksgiving on the confessor's part. This wells up almost automatically from the new being of the repentant person. **(14)** Often the direct object of *yadah* is the "name" of Yahweh (Ps 105:1; Is 12:4; 1 Chr 16:8). **(15)** This idiom is synonymous with praising Yahweh. **(16)** It introduces the entire dimension evoked by the "name" in biblical usage and reminds us that the holy God cannot be directly approached by fallen man, but only through His "name"—i.e., His Word and reputation, an anticipation of the incarnation. God reveals Himself only in His "name," especially in the sanctuary where He "causes His name to dwell." **(17)** *Yadah* expands vertically to include all creation, and horizontally stretching forward to that day when praise and thanksgiving shall be eternal (Ps 29; 95:10; 96:7–9; 103:19–22). See: TWOT—847; BDB—392a, 1095a.

3035. יִדּוֹ {2x} **Yiddôw**, *yid-do';* from 3034; *praised; Jiddo*, an Isr.:—Iddo {1x}, Jadua {1x}. See: BDB—392a.

3036. יָדוֹן {1x} **Yâdôwn**, *yaw-done';* from 3034; *thankful; Jadon*, an Isr.:—Jadon {1x}. See: BDB—193d.

3037. יַדּוּעַ {3x} **Yaddûwaʿ**, *yad-doo'-ah;* from 3045; *knowing; Jadduä*, the name of two Isr.:—Jaddua {3x}. See: BDB—396a.

3038. יְדוּתוּן {17x} **Yᵉdûwthûwn**, *yed-oo-thoon';* or

יְדֻתוּן **Yᵉdûthûwn**, *yed-oo-thoon';* or

יְדִיתוּן **Yᵉdîythûwn**, *yed-ee-thoon';* prob. from 3034; *laudatory; Jeduthun*, an Isr.:—Jeduthun {17x}. See: BDB—393a, 393b.

3039. יָדִיד {9x} **yᵉdîyd**, *yed-eed';* from the same as 1730; *loved:*—amiable {1x}, well-beloved {1x}, beloved {5x}, loves {1x}. See: TWOT—846a; BDB—391d.

3040. יְדִידָה {1x} **Yᵉdîydâh**, *yed-ee-daw';* fem. of 3039; *beloved; Jedidah*, an Israelitess:—Jedidah {1x}. See: BDB—392a.

3041. יְדִידְיָה {1x} **Yᵉdîydᵉyâh**, *yed-ee-deh-yaw';* from 3039 and 3050; *beloved of Jah; Jedidejah*, a name of Solomon:—Jedidiah {1x}. See: BDB—392a, 393a.

3042. יְדָיָה {2x} **Yᵉdâyâh**, *yed-aw-yaw';* from 3034 and 3050; *praised of Jah;*

Jedajah, the name of two Isr.:—Jedaiah {2x}. See: BDB—393a.

3043. יְדִיעֲאֵל {6x} Yᵉdîyᶜäᵉl, yed-ee-ah-ale'; from 3045 and 410; knowing God; Jediaël, the name of three Isr.:—Jediael {6x}. See: BDB—393a, 396a.

3044. יִדְלָף {1x} Yidlâph, yid-lawf'; from 1811; tearful; Jidlaph, a Mesopotamian:—Jidlaph {1x}. See: BDB—393b.

3045. יָדַע {947x} yâdaᶜ, yaw-dah'; a prim. root; to know (prop. to ascertain by seeing); used in a great variety of senses, fig., lit., euphem. and infer. (incl. observation, care, recognition; and caus. instruction, designation, punishment, etc.) [as follow]:—know {645x}, known {105x}, knowledge {19x}, perceive {18x}, shew {17x}, tell {8x}, wist {7x}, understand {7x}, certainly {7x}, acknowledge {6x}, acquaintance {6x}, consider {6x}, declare {6x}, teach {5x}, misc. {85x} = advise, answer, appoint, assuredly, be aware, [un-] awares, can [-not], for a certainty, comprehend, × could they, cunning, be diligent, (can, cause to) discern, discover, endued with, familiar friend, famous, feel, can have, be [ig-] norant, instruct, kinsfolk, kinsman, + be learned, + lie by man, mark, privy to, × prognosticator, regard, have respect, skillful, can (man of) skill, be sure, of a surety, have [understanding], × will be, wit, wot.

Yadaᶜ means "to know." (1) Essentially yadaᶜ means: (1a) to know by observing and reflecting (thinking), and (1b) to know by experiencing. (2) The first sense appears in Gen 8:11, where Noah "knew" the waters had abated as a result of seeing the freshly picked olive leaf in the dove's mouth; he "knew" it after observing and thinking about what he had seen. (2a) He did not actually see or experience the abatement himself. In contrast to this knowing through reflection is the knowing which comes through experience with the senses, by investigation and proving, by reflection and consideration (firsthand knowing). (2b) Consequently yada is used in synonymous parallelism with (2b1) "hear" (Ex 3:7), (2b2) "see" (Gen 18:21), and (2b3) "perceive, see" (Job 28:7). (2c) Joseph told his brothers that were they to leave one of their number with him in Egypt then he would "know," by experience, that they were honest men (Gen 42:33). (2d) In the Garden of Eden, Adam and Eve were forbidden to eat of the tree whose fruit if eaten would give them the experience of evil and, therefore, the knowledge of both good and evil. (2e) Somewhat characteristically the heart plays an important role in knowing. Because they experienced the sustaining presence of God during the wilderness wandering, the Israelites "knew" in their hearts that God was disciplining or caring for

them as a father cares for a son (Deut 8:5). Such knowing can be hindered by a wrongly disposed heart (Ps 95:10).

(3) Thirdly, this verb can represent that kind of knowing which one learns and can give back. (3a) So Cain said that he did not "know" he was Abel's keeper (Gen 4:9), and (3b) Abram told Sarai that he "knew" she was a beautiful woman (Gen 12:11). (3c) One can also "know" by being told—in Lev 5:1 a witness either sees or otherwise "knows" (by being told) pertinent information. (3d) In this sense "know" is paralleled (3d1) by "acknowledge" (Deut 33:9) and (3d2) "learn" (Deut 31:12-13). (3e) Thus, little children not yet able to speak do not "know" good and evil (Deut 1:39); (3e1) they have not learned it so as to tell another what it is. (3e2) In other words, their knowledge is not such that they can distinguish between good and evil.

(4) In addition to the essentially cognitive knowing already presented, this verb has a purely experiential side. (4a) The "knower" has actual involvement with or in the object of the knowing. (4a1) So Potiphar was unconcerned about (literally, "did not know about") what was in his house (Gen 39:6)—he had no actual contact with it. (4a2) In Gen 4:1 Adam's knowing Eve also refers to direct contact with her—in a sexual relationship. (4b) In Gen 18:19 God says He "knows" Abraham; He cared for him in the sense that He chose him from among other men and saw to it that certain things happened to him. The emphasis is on the fact that God "knew" him intimately and personally. (4b1) In fact, it is parallel in concept to "sanctified" (cf. Jer 1:5). (4b2) A similar use of this word relates to God's relationship to Israel as a chosen or elect nation (Amos 3:2).

(5) Yada in the intensive and causative stems is used to express a particular concept of revelation. (5a) God did not make Himself known by His name Jehovah to Abraham, Isaac, and Jacob. (5b) He did reveal that name to them, that He was the God of the covenant. (5c) Nevertheless, the covenant was not fulfilled (they did not possess the Promised Land) until the time of Moses. (5d) The statement in Ex 6:3 implies that now God was going to make Himself known "by His name"; He was going to lead them to possess the land. (5e) God makes Himself known through revelatory acts such as bringing judgment on the wicked (Ps 9:16) and deliverance to His people (Is 66:14). (5f) He also reveals Himself through the spoken word—for example, by the commands given through Moses (Eze 20:11), by promises like those given to David (2 Sa 7:21). (5g) Thus, God reveals Himself in law and promise. (6) "To know" God is to have an intimate experiential knowledge

of Him. **(6a)** So Pharaoh denies that he knows Jehovah (Ex 5:2) or that he recognizes His authority over him. **(6b)** Positively "to know" God is paralleled to fear Him (1 Kin 8:43), to serve (1 Chr 28:9), and to trust (Is 43:10). Syn: *Yada'* is related to **(7)** da'at (1847) which means "knowledge": Gen 2:9: ". . . and the tree of knowledge of good and evil." The word also appears in Ex 31:3. It is related **(7a)** to the particle, maddua' (4069) which is translated "why": Ex 1:18: "Why have ye done this thing, and have saved the men children alive?" See also: 5234. See: TWOT—848; BDB—393b, 1095a.

3046. יָדַע {47x} yᵉdaᶜ (Aram.), *yed-ah';* corresp. to 3045:—certify {4x}, know {18x}, make known {24x}, teach {1x}. See: TWOT—2765; BDB—1095a.

3047. יָדָע {2x} **Yâdâᶜ**, *yaw-daw';* from 3045; *knowing; Jada*, an Isr.:—Jada {2x}. See: BDB—395b.

3048. יְדַעְיָה {11x} **Yᵉdaʿyâh**, *yed-ah-yaw';* from 3045 and 3050; *Jah has known; Jedajah*, the name of two Isr.:—Jedaiah {11x}. See: BDB—396a.

3049. יִדְּעֹנִי {11x} **yiddᵉᶜônîy**, *yid-deh-o-nee';* from 3045; prop. a *knowing* one; spec. a *conjurer;* (by impl.) a *ghost:*—wizard {11x}.
   These "knowing ones" are always ranked with those who deal in 'owb (186 – necromancer) and are to be regarded with equal abhorrence. They were no doubt wise in their generation, prudent like the diviners, and skilled in the art of preying on the follies and superstitions of those who came in contact with them (Lev 19:31; 20:6; Deut 18:11; 1 Sa 28:8). See: TWOT—848d; BDB—396b.

3050. יָהּ {49x} **Yâhh**, *yaw;* contr. for 3068, and mean. the same; *Jah*, the sacred name:—JAH {1x}, the LORD {48x}, most vehement. comp. names in "-iah," "-jah." See: TWOT—484b; BDB—219c, 238a, 238b, 239c, 396c.

3051. יָהַב {34x} **yâhab**, *yaw-hab';* a prim. root; to *give* (whether lit. or fig.); gen. to *put;* imper. (refl.) *come:*—ascribe {1x}, bring {2x}, come on {1x}, give {23x}, go to {4x}, give out {1x}, set {1x}, take {1x}. See: TWOT—849; BDB—210c, 396c, 1095b.

3052. יְהַב {28x} **yᵉhab** (Aram.), *yeh-hab';* corresp. to 3051:—give {21x}, given + 1934 {2x}, delivered {1x}, laid {1x}, paid {1x}, prolonged {1x}, yielded {1x}. See: TWOT—2766; BDB—1095b.

3053. יְהָב {1x} **yᵉhâb**, *ye-hawb';* from 3051; prop. what is *given* (by Providence),

i.e. a *lot:*—burden {1x}. Syn.: 4853, 5448. See: TWOT—849a; BDB—396d.

3054. יָהַד {1x} **yâhad**, *yaw-had';* denom. from a form corresp. to 3061; to *Judaize*, i.e. become Jewish:—become Jews {1x}. See: TWOT—850; BDB—397a, 397c.

3055. יְהֻד {1x} **Yᵉhûd**, *yeh-hood';* a briefer form of one corresp. to 3061; *Jehud*, a place in Pal.:—Jehud {1x}. See: BDB—397a.

3056. יֶהְדַי {1x} **Yehday**, *yeh-dah'-ee;* perh. from a form corresp. to 3061; *Judaistic; Jehdai*, an Isr.:—Jehdai {1x}. See: BDB—213a, 397a.

3057. יְהֻדִיָּה {1x} **Yᵉhûdîyâh**, *yeh-hoo-dee-yaw';* fem. of 3064; *Jehudijah*, a Jewess:—Jehudijah {1x}. See: BDB—397c.

3058. יֵהוּא {58x} **Yêhûwʾ**, *yay-hoo';* from 3068 and 1931; *Jehovah (is) He; Jehu*, the name of five Isr.:—Jehu {58x}. See: BDB—219c, 397a.

3059. יְהוֹאָחָז {10x} **Yᵉhôwʾâchâz**, *yeh-ho-aw-khawz';* from 3068 and 270; *Jehovah-seized; Jehoächaz*, the name of three Isr.:—Jehoahaz {10x}. comp. 3099. See: BDB—219d.

3060. יְהוֹאָשׁ {17x} **Yᵉhôwʾâsh**, *yeh-ho-awsh';* from 3068 and (perh.) 784; *Jehovah-fired; Jehoäsh*, the name of two Isr. kings:—Jehoash {17x}. comp. 3101. See: BDB—219d.

3061. יְהוּד {7x} **Yᵉhûwd** (Aram.), *yeh-hood';* contr. from a form corresp. to 3063; prop. *Judah*, hence, *Judea:*—Jewry {1x}, Judah {5x}, Judea {1x}. See: BDB—1095c.

3062. יְהוּדָאִי {10x} **Yᵉhûwdâʾîy** (Aram.), *yeh-hoo-daw-ee';* patrial from 3061; a *Jehudâte* (or Judaite), i.e. Jew:—Jew {10x}. See: BDB—1095c.

3063. יְהוּדָה {818x} **Yᵉhûwdâh**, *yeh-hoo-daw';* from 3034; *celebrated; Jehudah* (or Judah), the name of five Isr.; also of the tribe descended from the first, and of its territory:—Judah {808x}, Bethlehem-judah + 1035 {10x}. See: TWOT—850c; BDB—397a, 1095c.

3064. יְהוּדִי {76x} **Yᵉhûwdîy**, *yeh-hoo-dee';* patron. from 3063; a *Jehudite* (i.e. Judaite or Jew), or desc. of Jehudah (i.e. Judah):—Jew {74x}, Jew + 376 {1x}, Judah {1x}. See: TWOT—850a; BDB—397c, 1095c.

3065. יְהוּדִי {4x} **Yᵉhûwdîy**, *yeh-hoo-dee';* the same as 3064; *Jehudi*, an Isr.:—Jehudi {4x}. See: BDB—397c.

3066. יְהוּדִית {6x} **Yᵉhûwdîyth**, *yeh-hoo-deeth';* fem. of 3064; the *Jewish* (used

adv.) language:—in the Jews' language {5x}, Jews' speech {1x}. See: BDB—397c.

3067. יְהוּדִית {1x} **Yᵉhûwdîyth**, *yeh-ho-deeth';* the same as 3066; *Jewess; Jehudith,* a Canaanitess:—Judith {1x}. See: BDB—397c.

3068. יְהֹוָה {6519x} **Yᵉhôvâh**, *yeh-ho-vaw';* from 1961; (the) self-*Existent* or *Eternal; Jehovah,* Jewish national name of God:—LORD {6510x}, GOD {4x}, JEHOVAH {4x}, variant {1x}. Yehwah (3068), "Lord."

(1) The Tetragrammaton YHWH appears without its own vowels, and its exact pronunciation is debated (Jehovah, *Yehovah,* Jahweh, Yahweh). **(2)** The Hebrew text does insert the vowels for adonay (136), and Jewish students and scholars read adonay whenever they see the Tetragrammaton. **(3)** The divine name YHWH appears only in the Bible. **(4)** Its precise meaning is much debated. God chose it as His personal name by which He related specifically to His chosen or covenant people. Its first appearance in the biblical record is Gen 2:4: "These are the generations of the heavens and of the earth when they were created, in the day that the Lord God made the earth and the heavens." Apparently Adam knew Him by this personal or covenantal name from the beginning, since Seth both called his son Enosh (i.e., man as a weak and dependent creature) and began (along with all other pious persons) to call upon (formally worship) the name of YHWH, "the Lord" (Gen 4:26). The covenant found a fuller expression and application when God revealed Himself to Abraham (Gen 12:8), promising redemption in the form of national existence.

This promise became reality through Moses, to whom God explained that He was not only the "God who exists" but the "God who effects His will": "Thus shalt thou say unto the children of Israel, The Lord [YHWH] God of your fathers, the God of Abraham, the God of Isaac, and the God of Jacob, hath sent me unto you: this is my name for ever, and this is my memorial unto all generations. Go, and gather the elders of Israel together, and say unto them, The Lord [YHWH] God of your fathers, the God of Abraham, of Isaac, and of Jacob, appeared unto me, saying, I have surely visited you, and seen that which is done to you in Egypt: And I have said, I will bring you up out of the affliction of Egypt unto the land of the Canaanites" (Ex 3:15–17). So God explained the meaning of "I am who I am" (Ex 3:14). He spoke to the fathers as YHWH, but the promised deliverance and, therefore, the fuller significance or experienced meaning of His name were unknown

to them (Ex 6:2–8). Syn.: 113, 3050, 3069. See: TWOT—484a; BDB—217d, 397a, 397d, 398a.

3069. יְהֹוִה {305x} **Yᵉhôvîh**, *yeh-ho-vee';* a var. of 3068 [used after 136, and pronounced by Jews as 430, in order to prevent the repetition of the same sound, since they elsewhere pronounce 3068 as 136]:—God {304x}, LORD {1x}. See: BDB—217d, 397d.

3070. יְהֹוָה יִרְאֶה {1x} **Yᵉhôvâh Yirʾeh**, *yeh-ho-vaw' yir-eh';* from 3068 and 7200; *Jehovah will see* (to it); *Jehovah-Jireh,* a symb. name for Mt. Moriah:—Jehovah-jireh {1x}. See: BDB—907d.

3071. יְהֹוָה נִסִּי {1x} **Yᵉhôvâh Niççîy**, *yeh-ho-vaw' nis-see';* from 3068 and 5251 with the pron. suff.; *Jehovah* (is) *my banner; Jehovah-Nissi,* a symb. name of an altar in the Desert:—Jehovah-nissi {1x}. See: BDB—651d.

3072. יְהֹוָה צִדְקֵנוּ {2x} **Yᵉhôvâh Tsidqênûw**, *ye-ho-vaw' tsid-kay'-noo;* from 3068 and 6664 with pron. suff.; *Jehovah* (is) *our right; Jehovah-Tsidkenu,* a symb. epithet of the Messiah and of Jerusalem:—the LORD our righteousness {2x}. See: BDB—842a.

3073. יְהֹוָה שָׁלוֹם {1x} **Yᵉhôvâh Shâlôwm**, *yeh-ho-vaw' shaw-lome';* from 3068 and 7965; *Jehovah* (is) *peace; Jehovah-Shalom,* a symb. name of an altar in Pal.:—Jehovah-shalom {1x}. See: BDB—1023a.

3074. יְהֹוָה שָׁמָּה {1x} **Yᵉhôvâh Shâmmâh**, *yeh-ho-vaw' shawm'-maw;* from 3068 and 8033 with directive enclitic; *Jehovah* (is) *thither; Jehovah-Shammah,* a symbol. title of Jerusalem:—Jehovah-shammah {1x}. See: BDB—1027c.

3075. יְהוֹזָבָד {4x} **Yᵉhôwzâbâd**, *yeh-ho-zaw-bawd';* from 3068 and 2064; *Jehovah-endowed; Jehozabad,* the name of three Isr.:—Jehozabad {4x}. Syn.: comp. 3107. See: BDB—220a.

3076. יְהוֹחָנָן {7x} **Yᵉhôwchânân**, *yeh-ho-khaw-nawn';* from 3068 and 2603; *Jehovah-favored; Jehochanan,* the name of eight Isr.:—Jehohanan {6x}, Johanan {1x}. See: BDB—220b. Syn.: comp. 3110.

3077. יְהוֹיָדָע {51x} **Yᵉhôwyâdâʿ**, *yeh-ho-yaw-daw';* from 3068 and 3045; *Jehovah-known; Jehojada,* the name of three Isr.:—Jehoiada {51x}. See: BDB—220b. Syn.: comp. 3111.

3078. יְהוֹיָכִין {10x} **Yᵉhôwyâkîyn**, *yeh-ho-yaw-keen';* from 3068 and 3559; *Jehovah will establish; Jehojakin,* a Jewish king:—Jehoiachin {10x}. See: BDB—220c, 408a, 487c. comp. 3112.

3079. יְהוֹיָקִים {37x} **Yᵉhôwyâqîym**, *yeh-ho-yaw-keem'*; from 3068 abb. and 6965; *Jehovah will raise; Jehojakim*, a Jewish king:—Jehoiakim {37x}. See: BDB—220c. comp. 3113.

3080. יְהוֹיָרִיב {2x} **Yᵉhôwyârîyb**, *yeh-ho-yaw-reeb'*; from 3068 and 7378; *Jehovah will contend; Jehojarib*, the name of two Isr.:—Jehoiarib {2x}. See: BDB—220d. comp. 3114.

3081. יְהוּכַל {1x} **Yᵉhûwkal**, *yeh-hoo-kal'*; from 3201; *potent; Jehukal*, an Isr.:—Jehucal {1x}. See: BDB—220d, 397d, 408a. comp. 3116.

3082. יְהוֹנָדָב {8x} **Yᵉhôwnâdâb**, *yeh-ho-naw-dawb'*; from 3068 and 5068; *Jehovah-largessed; Jehonadab*, the name of an Isr. and of an Arab:—Jehonadab {3x}, Jonadab {5x}. See: BDB—220d. comp. 3122.

3083. יְהוֹנָתָן {82x} **Yᵉhôwnâthân**, *yeh-ho-naw-thawn'*; from 3068 and 5414; *Jehovah-given; Jehonathan*, the name of four Isr.:—Jonathan or Jehonathan {82x}. See: BDB—220d. comp. 3129.

3084. יְהוֹסֵף {1x} **Yᵉhôwçêph**, *yeh-ho-safe'*; a fuller form of 3130; *Jehoseph* (i.e. Joseph), a son of Jacob:—Joseph {1x}. See: BDB—415c.

3085. יְהוֹעַדָּה {2x} **Yᵉhôwʿaddâh**, *yeh-ho-ad-daw'*; from 3068 and 5710; *Jehovah-adorned; Jehoäddah*, an Isr.:—Jehoada {2x}. See: BDB—221a.

3086. יְהוֹעַדִּין {2x} **Yᵉhôwʿaddîyn**, *yeh-ho-ad-deen'*; or

יְהוֹעַדָּן **Yᵉhôwʿaddân**, *yeh-ho-ad-dawn'*; from 3068 and 5727; *Jehovah-pleased; Jehoäddin* or *Jehoäddan*, an Israelitess:—Jehoaddan {2x}. See: BDB—221a.

3087. יְהוֹצָדָק {8x} **Yᵉhôwtsâdâq**, *yeh-ho-tsaw-dawk'*; from 3068 and 6663; *Jehovah-righted; Jehotsadak*, an Isr.:—Jehozadek {3x}, Josedech {6x}. See: BDB—221b. comp. 3136.

3088. יְהוֹרָם {29x} **Yᵉhôwrâm**, *yeh-ho-rawm'*; from 3068 and 7311; *Jehovah-raised; Jehoram*, the name of a Syrian and of three Isr.:—Jehoram {23x}, Joram {6x}. See: BDB—221b. comp. 3141.

3089. יְהוֹשֶׁבַע {1x} **Yᵉhôwshebaʿ**, *yeh-ho-sheh'-bah*; from 3068 and 7650; *Jehovah-sworn; Jehosheba*, an Israelitess:—Jehosheba {1x}. See: BDB—221b, 989d. comp. 3090.

3090. יְהוֹשַׁבְעַת {2x} **Yᵉhôwshabʿath**, *yeh-ho-shab-ath'*; a form of 3089; *Jehoshabath*, an Israelitess:—Jehoshabeath {2x}. See: BDB—221b, 221c.

3091. יְהוֹשׁוּעַ {218x} **Yᵉhôwshûwʿa**, *yeh-ho-shoo'-ah;* or

יְהוֹשֻׁעַ **Yᵉhôwshûʿa**, *yeh-ho-shoo'-ah;* from 3068 and 3467; *Jehovah-saved; Jehoshuä* (i.e. Joshua), the Jewish leader:—Jehoshua or Jehoshuah or Joshua {218x}. See: BDB—221c, 448a. comp. 1954, 3442.

3092. יְהוֹשָׁפָט {84x} **Yᵉhôwshâphât**, *yeh-ho-shaw-fawt'*; from 3068 and 8199; *Jehovah-judged; Jehoshaphat*, the name of six Isr.; also of a valley near Jerusalem:—Jehoshaphat {84x}. See: BDB—221d. comp. 3146.

3093. יָהִיר {2x} **yâhîyr**, *yaw-here'*; prob. from the same as 2022; *elated;* hence, *arrogant:*—haughty {1x}, proud {1x}. See: TWOT—851a; BDB—397d.

3094. יְהַלֶּלְאֵל {2x} **Yᵉhallelʾêl**, *yeh-hal-lel-ale';* from 1984 and 410; *praising God; Jehallelel*, the name of two Isr.:—Jehaleleel {1x}, Jehalelel {1x}. See: BDB—239c, 397d.

3095. יַהֲלֹם {3x} **yahǎlôm**, *yah-hal-ome';* from 1986 (in the sense of *hardness*); a precious stone, prob. *onyx:*—diamond {3x}. See: TWOT—502b; BDB—240d, 397d.

3096. יַהַץ {9x} **Yahats**, *yah'-hats;* or

יַהְצָה **Yahtsâh**, *yah'-tsaw;* or (fem.)

יַהְצָה **Yahtsâh**, *yah-tsaw';* from an unused root mean. to *stamp;* perh. *threshing*-floor; *Jahats* or *Jahtsah*, a place E. of the Jordan:—Jahaz {4x}, Jahazah {4x}, Jahzah {1x}. See: BDB—397d.

3097. יוֹאָב {145x} **Yôwʾâb**, *yo-awb';* from 3068 and 1; *Jehovah-fathered; Joâb*, the name of three Isr.:—Joab {145x}. See: BDB—222a, 398a.

3098. יוֹאָח {11x} **Yôwʾâch**, *yo-awkh';* from 3068 and 251; *Jehovah-brothered; Joach*, the name of four Isr.:—Joah {11x}. See: BDB—222a.

3099. יוֹאָחָז {4x} **Yôwʾâchâz**, *yo-aw-khawz';* a form of 3059; *Joächaz*, the name of two Isr.:—Jehoahaz {3x}, Joahaz {1x}. See: BDB—219d, 222a.

3100. יוֹאֵל {19x} **Yôwʾêl**, *yo-ale';* from 3068 and 410; *Jehovah* (is his) *God; Joël*, the name of twelve Isr.:—Joel {19x}. See: BDB—222a.

3101. יוֹאָשׁ {10x} **Yôwʾâsh**, *yo-awsh';* or

יֹאָשׁ **Yôʾâsh** (2 Chron. 24:1), *yo-awsh';* a form of 3060; *Joäsh*, the name of six Isr.:—Joash {47x}. See: BDB—219d, 222b.

3102. יוֹב {1x} **Yôwb,** *yobe;* perh. a form of 3103, but more prob. by err. transc. for 3437; *Job,* an Isr.:—Job {1x}. See: BDB—398a.

3103. יוֹבָב {9x} **Yôwbâb,** *yo-bawb';* from 2980; *howler; Jobab,* the name of two Isr. and of three foreigners:—Jobab {9x}. See: BDB—384d, 398a.

3104. יוֹבֵל {27x} **yôwbêl,** *yo-bale';* or

יֹבֵל **yôbêl,** *yob-ale';* appar. from 2986; the *blast* of a horn (from its *continuous* sound); spec. the *signal* of the silver trumpets; hence, the instrument itself and the festival thus introduced:—jubile {21x}, ram's horn {5x}, trumpet {1x}.

Yobel means "ram; ram's horn; jubilee year." **(1)** *Yobel* means ram's horn blown to assemble the people: "When the ram's horn [v, "trumpet"] sounds a long blast, they shall come up to the mountain" (Ex 19:13). **(2)** This word also signifies jubilee year (Lev 25:8–15; 27:16–25). **(2a)** In the fiftieth year on the Day of Atonement jubilee was to be declared. **(2b)** All land was returned to the individual or family to whom it had originally belonged by inheritance, even if he (or she) were in bondservice. **(2c)** When land was valued in anticipation of selling it or devoting it to God, it was to be valued in terms of anticipated productivity prior to the year of jubilee. **(2d)** Between jubilees land might be redeemed for its productivity value. **(2e)** City property, however, must be redeemed within a year of its sale or loss. **(2f)** Levitical property was not subject to these rules. **(2g)** Israelites who fell into bondage were to be released in the jubilee year, or redeemed in the interim period. See: TWOT—835e; BDB—385c, 398a.

3105. יוּבַל {1x} **yûwbal,** *yoo-bal';* from 2986; a *stream:*—river {1x}. Syn.: 180, 650, 2975. See: TWOT—835b; 385b, 398a.

3106. יוּבָל {1x} **Yûwbâl,** *yoo-bawl';* from 2986; *stream; Jubal,* an antediluvian:—Jubal {1x}. See: BDB—385b.

3107. יוֹזָבָד {10x} **Yôwzâbâd,** *yo-zaw-bawd';* a form of 3075; *Jozabad,* the name of ten Isr.:—Josabad {1x}, Jozabad {9x}. See: BDB—220a, 222b.

3108. יוֹזָכָר {1x} **Yôwzâkâr,** *yo-zaw-kawr';* from 3068 and 2142; *Jehovah-remembered; Jozacar,* an Isr.:—Jozachar {1x}. See: BDB—222b.

3109. יוֹחָא {2x} **Yôwchâʾ,** *yo-khaw';* prob. from 3068 and a var. of 2421; *Jehovah-revived; Jocha,* the name of two Isr.:—Joha {2x}. See: BDB—398a.

3110. יוֹחָנָן {24x} **Yôwchânân,** *yo-khaw-nawn';* a form of 3076; *Jochanan,* the name of nine Isr.:—Johanan {24x}. See: BDB—220b, 222b.

יוּטָה **Yûwṭâh**. See 3194.

3111. יוֹיָדָע {5x} **Yôwyâdâʿ,** *yo-yaw-daw';* a form of 3077; *Jojada,* the name of two Isr.:—Jehoiada {1x}, Joiada {4x}. See: BDB—220, 222b.

3112. יוֹיָכִין {1x} **Yôwyâkîyn,** *yo-yaw-keen';* a form of 3078; *Jojakin,* an Isr. king:—Jehoiachin {1x}. See: BDB—220c, 222c.

3113. יוֹיָקִים {4x} **Yôwyâqîym,** *yo-yaw-keem';* a form of 3079; *Jojakim,* an Isr.:—Joiakim {4x}. See: BDB—220c, 222c. comp. 3137.

3114. יוֹיָרִיב {5x} **Yôwyârîyb,** *yo-yaw-reeb';* a form of 3080; *Jojarib,* the name of four Isr.:—Joiarib {5x}. See: BDB—220d, 222c.

3115. יוֹכֶבֶד {2x} **Yôwkebed,** *yo-keh'-bed;* from 3068 contr. and 3513; *Jehovah-gloried; Jokebed,* the mother of Moses:—Jochebed {2x}. See: BDB—222c.

3116. יוּכַל {1x} **Yûwkal,** *yoo-kal';* a form of 3081; *Jukal,* an Isr.:—Jucal {1x}. See: BDB—220d, 222c, 398.

3117. יוֹם {2274x} **yôwm,** *yome;* from an unused root mean. to *be hot;* a *day* (as the *warm* hours), whether lit. (from sunrise to sunset, or from one sunset to the next), or fig. (a space of time defined by an associated term), [often used adv.]:—day {2008x}, time {64x}, chronicles + 1697 {37x}, daily {32x}, ever {17x}, year {14x}, continually {10x}, when {10x}, as {10x}, while {8x}, full {8x} always {4x}, whole {4x}, alway {4x}, misc. {44x} = age, + elder, X end, + evening, life, as (so) long as (. . . live), (even) now, + old, + outlived, + perpetually, presently, + remaineth, X required, season, X since, space, then, + in trouble, weather, + younger.

Yowm (3117) means "daylight; day; time; moment; year." **(1)** *Yowm* has several meanings. **(1a)** The word represents the period of "daylight" as contrasted with nighttime: "While the earth remaineth, seedtime and harvest, and cold and heat, and summer and winter, and day and night shall not cease" (Gen 8:22). **(1b)** The word denotes a period of twenty-four hours: "And it came to pass, as she spake to Joseph day by day . . ." (Gen 39:10). **(2)** *Yowm* can also signify a period of time of unspecified duration: "And God blessed the seventh day, and sanctified it: because that in it he had rested from all his work which God created and made" (Gen 2:3). **(2a)** In this verse, "day" refers to the entire period of God's resting from

creating this universe. **(2b)** This "day" began after He completed the creative acts of the seventh day and extends at least to the return of Christ. **(2c)** Compare Gen 2:4: "These are the generations of the heavens and of the earth when they were created, in the day [*beyom*] that the Lord God made the earth and the heavens." **(2d)** Here "day" refers to the entire period envisioned in the first six days of creation. **(3)** Another nuance appears in Gen 2:17, where the word represents a "point of time" or "a moment": "But of the tree of the knowledge of good and evil, thou shalt not eat of it: for in the day [beyom] that thou eatest thereof thou shalt surely die."

(4) When used in the plural, the word may represent "year": "Thou shalt therefore keep this ordinance in his season from year to year [yamim]" (Ex 13:10). **(5)** There are several other special nuances of *yowm* when it is used with various prepositions. **(5a)** First, when used with ke ("as," "like"), it can connote **(5a1)** "first": "And Jacob said, Sell me this day [first] thy birthright" (Gen 25:31). **(5a2)** It may also mean "one day," or "about this day": "And it came to pass about this time, that Joseph went into the house to do his business" (Gen 39:11). **(5a3)** On Joseph's lips, the phrase connotes "this present result" (literally, "as it is this day"): "But as for you, ye thought evil against me; but God meant it unto good, to bring to pass, as it is this day, to save much people alive" (Gen 50:20). **(5a4)** Adonijah used this same phrase to represent "today": "Let king Solomon swear unto me today that he will not slay his servant" (1 Kin 1:51). **(5a5)** Yet another nuance appears in 1 Sa 9:13: "Now therefore get you up; for about this time ye shall find him." **(5b)** When used with the definite article *ha*, the noun may mean **(5b1)** "today" (as it does in Gen 4:14) or refer **(5b2)** to some particular "day" (1 Sa 1:4) and the "daytime" (Neh 4:16).

(6) The first biblical occurrence of *yowm* is found in Gen 1:5: "And God called the light Day, and the darkness he called Night. And the evening and the morning were the first day." **(7)** The second use introduces one of the most debated occurrences of the word, which is the duration of the days of creation. **(7a)** Perhaps the most frequently heard explanations are that these "days" are **(7a1)** 24 hours long, **(7a2)** indefinitely long (i.e., eras of time), or **(7a3)** logical rather than temporal categories (i.e., they depict theological categories rather than periods of time). **(7b)** However, we know that these were literal 24 hour days. God based the Sabbath day's rest on His 7 days of creation. God did not work "7 long periods of time." Ex 20:9–11 "Six days shalt thou labour, and do all thy work: But the seventh day *is* the sabbath

of the LORD thy God: *in it* thou shalt not do any work, thou, nor thy son, nor thy daughter, thy manservant, nor thy maidservant, nor thy cattle, nor thy stranger that *is* within thy gates: For *in* six days the LORD made heaven and earth, the sea, and all that in them *is,* and rested the seventh day: wherefore the LORD blessed the sabbath day, and hallowed it."

(8) The "day of the Lord" is used to denote **(8a)** both the end of the age (eschatologically) or some occurrence during the present age (non-eschatologically). **(8b)** It may be a day of either judgment or blessing, or both (cf. Is 2). **(9)** It is noteworthy that Hebrew people did not divide the period of daylight into regular hourly periods, whereas nighttime was divided into three watches (Ex 14:24; Judg 7:19). **(10)** The beginning of a "day" is sometimes **(10)** said to be dusk (Est 4:16) and sometimes **(11)** dawn (Deut 28:66–67). See: TWOT–852; BDB–398a, 1095c.

3118. יוֹם {16x} **yôwm** (Aram.), *yome;* corresp. to 3117; a *day:*–day {14x}, time {2x}. See: TWOT–2767; BDB–1095c.

3119. יוֹמָם {52x} **yôwmâm**, *yo-mawm';* from 3117; *daily:*–daily {2x}, (by, in the) day {41x}, daytime {7x}, time {1x}. See: TWOT–852a; BDB–401b.

3120. יָוָן {11x} **Yâvân**, *yaw-vawn';* prob. from the same as 3196; *effervescing* (i.e. hot and active); *Javan,* the name of a son of Joktan, and of the race (*Ionians,* i.e. Greeks) descended from him, with their territory; also of a place in Arabia:–Javan {7x}, Grecia {3x}, Greece {1x}. See: TWOT–855; BDB–75a, 42a.

3121. יָוֵן {1x} **yâvên**, *yaw-ven';* from the same as 3196; prop. *dregs* (as *effervescing*); hence, *mud:*–mire {1x}, miry {1x}. See: TWOT–853a; BDB–401c.

3122. יוֹנָדָב {7x} **Yôwnâdâb**, *yo-naw-dawb';* a form of 3082; *Jonadab,* the name of an Isr. and of a Rechabite:–Jonadab {7x}. See: BDB–220d, 222c.

3123. יוֹנָה {32x} **yôwnâh**, *yo-naw';* prob. from the same as 3196; a *dove* (appar. from the *warmth* of their mating):–dove {21x}, pigeon {10x}, variant + 1686 {1x}. See: TWOT–854a; BDB–351a, 401d.

3124. יוֹנָה {19x} **Yôwnâh**, *yo-naw';* the same as 3123; *Jonah,* an Isr.:–Jonah {19x}. See: BDB–402a.

3125. יְוָנִי {1x} **Yᵉvânîy**, *yev-aw-nee';* patron. from 3121; a *Jevanite,* or desc. of Javan:–Grecian {1x}. See: BDB–402b.

3126. יוֹנֵק {1x} **yôwnêq**, *yo-nake';* act. part. of 3243; a *sucker;* hence, a *twig* (of a

tree felled and sprouting):—tender plant {1x}. See: TWOT—874a; BDB—413c.

3127. יוֹנֶקֶת {6x} yôwneqeth, yo-neh'-keth; fem. of 3126; a sprout:—tender branch {1x}, branch {4x}, young twigs {1x}. See: TWOT—874b; BDB—413c.

3128. יוֹנַת אֵלֶם רְחֹקִים {1x} Yôwnath 'êlem rᵉchôqîym, yo-nath' ay'-lem rekh-o-keem'; from 3123 and 482 and the plur. of 7350; dove of (the) silence (i.e. dumb Israel) of (i.e. among) distances (i.e. strangers); the title of a ditty (used for a name of its melody):—Jonath-elem-rechokim {1x}. See: BDB—401d.

3129. יוֹנָתָן {42x} Yôwnâthân, yo-naw-thawn'; a form of 3083; Jonathan, the name of ten Isr.:—Jonathan {42x}. See: BDB—220d, 222c.

3130. יוֹסֵף {213x} Yôwçêph, yo-safe'; future of 3254; let him add (or perh. simply act. part. adding); Joseph, the name of seven Isr.:—Joseph {213x}. See: BDB—402, 415c. comp. 3084.

3131. יוֹסִפְיָה {1x} Yôwçiphyâh, yo-sif-yaw'; from act. part. of 3254 and 3050; Jah (is) adding; Josiphjah, an Isr.:—Josiphiah {1x}. See: BDB—402b, 415d.

3132. יוֹעֵאלָה {1x} Yôw'ê'lâh, yo-ay-law'; perh. fem. act. part. of 3276; furthermore; Joelah, an Isr.:—Joelah {1x}. See: BDB—402b, 418d.

3133. יוֹעֵד {1x} Yôw'êd, yo-ade'; appar. the act. part. of 3259; appointer; Joed, an Isr.:—Joed {1x}. See: BDB—222c.

3134. יוֹעֶזֶר {1x} Yôw'ezer, yo-eh'-zer; from 3068 and 5828; Jehovah (is his) help; Joezer, an Isr.:—Joezer {1x}. See: BDB—222c.

3135. יוֹעָשׁ {2x} Yôw'âsh, yo-awsh'; from 3068 and 5789; Jehovah-hastened; Joash, the name of two Isr.:—Joash {2x}. See: BDB—222c.

3136. יוֹצָדָק {5x} Yôwtsâdâq, yo-tsaw-dawk'; a form of 3087; Jotsadak, an Isr.:—Jozadak {5x}. See: BDB—221b, 222c, 1095c.

3137. יוֹקִים {1x} Yôwqîym, yo-keem'; a form of 3113; Jokim, an Isr.:—Jokim {1x}. See: BDB—220c, 222d.

3138. יוֹרֶה {2x} yôwreh, yo-reh'; act. part. of 3384; sprinkling; hence, a sprinkling (or autumnal showers):—first rain {1x}, former [rain]{1x}. See: TWOT—910a; BDB—435c.

3139. יוֹרָה {1x} Yôwrâh, yo-raw'; from 3384; rainy; Jorah, an Isr.:—Jorah {1x}. See: BDB—402b, 435c.

3140. יוֹרַי {1x} Yôwray, yo-rah'-ee; from 3384; rainy; Jorai, an Isr.:—Jorai {1x}. See: BDB—436c.

3141. יוֹרָם {20x} Yôwrâm, yo-rawm'; a form of 3088; Joram, the name of three Isr. and one Syrian:—Joram {20x}. See: BDB—221b, 222d.

3142. יוֹשָׁב חֶסֶד {1x} Yûwshab Cheçed, yoo-shab' kheh'-sed; from 7725 and 2617; kindness will be returned; Jushab-Chesed, an Isr.:—Jushab-hesed {1x}. See: BDB—402b, 1000b.

3143. יוֹשִׁבְיָה {1x} Yôwshîbyâh, yo-shib-yaw'; from 3427 and 3050; Jehovah will cause to dwell; Josibjah, an Isr.:—Josibiah {1x}. See: BDB—444a.

3144. יוֹשָׁה {1x} Yôwshâh, yo-shaw'; prob. a form of 3145; Joshah, an Isr.:—Joshah {1x}. See: BDB—402b, 444b.

3145. יוֹשַׁוְיָה {1x} Yôwshavyâh, yo-shav-yaw'; from 3068 and 7737; Jehovah-set; Joshavjah, an Isr.:—Joshaviah {1x}. See: BDB—402b, 444b. comp. 3144.

3146. יוֹשָׁפָט {1x} Yôwshâphât, yo-shaw-fawt'; a form of 3092; Joshaphat, an Isr.:—Jehoshaphat {1x}, Joshaphat {1x}. See: BDB—221d, 222d.

3147. יוֹתָם {24x} Yôwthâm, yo-thawm'; from 3068 and 8535; Jehovah (is) perfect; Jotham, the name of three Isr.:—Jotham {24x}. See: BDB—222d.

3148. יוֹתֵר yôwthêr, yo-thare'; act. part. of 3498; prop. redundant; hence, over and above, as adj., noun, adv. or conjunc. [as follows]:—better {1x}, more {3x}, moreover {1x}, over {1x}, profit {1x}, further {1x}. See: TWOT—936d; BDB—452c.

3149. יְזַוְאֵל {1x} Yᵉzav'êl, yez-av-ale'; from an unused root (mean. to sprinkle) and 410; sprinkled of God; Jezavel, an Isr.:—Jeziel {1x}. See: BDB—402b.

3150. יִזִּיָּה {1x} Yizzîyâh, yiz-zee-yaw'; from the same as the first part of 3149 and 3050; sprinkled of Jah; Jizzijah, an Isr.:—Jeziah {1x}. See: BDB—402c, 633c.

3151. יָזִיז {1x} Yâzîyz, yaw-zeez'; from the same as 2123; he will make prominent; Jaziz, an Isr.:—Jaziz {1x}. See: BDB—265c, 402c.

3152. יִזְלִיאָה {1x} Yizlîy'ah, yiz-lee-aw'; perh. from an unused root (mean. to

draw up); he will draw out; Jizliah, an Isr.:—Jezliah {1x}. See: BDB—272c, 402c.

3153. יֶזַנְיָה {2x} **Yᵉzanyâh,** *yez-an-yaw';* or

יֶזַנְיָהוּ **Yᵉzanyâhûw,** *yez-an-yaw'-hoo;* prob. for 2970; *Jezanjah,* an Isr.:—Jezaniah {2x}. See: BDB—24d, 402c.

3154. יֶזַע {1x} **yeza',** *yeh'-zah;* from an unused root mean to *ooze; sweat,* i.e. (by impl.) a *sweating* dress:—any thing that causeth sweat {1x}. See: TWOT—857a; BDB—402c.

3155. יִזְרָח {1x} **Yizrâch,** *yiz-rawkh';* a var. for 250; a *Jizrach* (i.e. Ezrahite or Zarchite) or desc. of Zerach:—Izrahite {1x}. See: BDB—280d, 402c.

3156. יִזְרַחְיָה {3x} **Yizrachyâh,** *yiz-rakh-yaw';* from 2224 and 3050; *Jah will shine; Jizrachjah,* the name of two Isr.:—Izrahiah {1x}, Jezrahiah {1x}. See: BDB—280d, 402c.

3157. יִזְרְעֵאל {36x} **Yizrᵉʻêl,** *yiz-reh-ale';* from 2232 and 410; *God will sow; Jizreël,* the name of two places in Pal. and of two Isr.:—Jezreel {36x}. See: BDB—283b, 402c.

3158. יִזְרְעֵאלִי {8x} **Yizrᵉʻêlîy,** *yiz-reh-ay-lee';* patron. from 3157; a *Jizreëlite* or native of Jizreel:—Jezreelite {8x}. See: BDB—283c.

3159. יִזְרְעֵאלִית {5x} **Yizrᵉʻêlîyth,** *yiz-reh-ay-leeth';* fem. of 3158; a *Jezreëlitess:*—Jezreelitess {15x}. See: BDB—283c.

3160. יְחֻבָּה {1x} **Yᵉchubbâh,** *yekh-oob-baw';* from 2247; *hidden; Jechubbah,* an Isr.:—Jehubbah {1x}. See: BDB—285d, 286a, 402c.

3161. יָחַד {3x} **yâchad,** *yaw-khad';* a prim. root; *to be* (or *become*) *one:*—join {1x}, unite {2x}.

Yachad means "to be united, meet." Gen 49:6: "O my soul, come not thou into their secret; unto their assembly, mine honor, be not thou united." See: BDB—402d.

3162. יַחַד {142x} **yachad,** *yakh'-ad;* from 3161; prop. a *unit,* i.e. (adv.) *unitedly:*—together {120x}, altogether {5x}, alike {5x}, likewise {2x} withal {2x}, misc. {8x} = at all (once), both, only.

I. The adverbial form *yachad* means "together; alike; all at once; all together." **(1)** Used as an adverb, the word emphasizes a plurality in unity. **(2)** In some contexts the connotation is on community in action. Goliath challenged the Israelites, saying: "I defy the armies of Israel this day; give me a man, that we may fight together" (1 Sa 17:10). **(3)** Sometimes the emphasis is on commonality of place: "And it came to pass, that they which remained were scattered, so that two of them were not left together" (1 Sa 11:11). **(4)** The word can be used of being in the same place at the same time: "And he delivered them into the hands of the Gibeonites, and they hanged them in the hill before the Lord: and they fell all seven together" (2 Sa 21:9). **(5)** In other passages *yachad* means "at the same time": "O that my grief were thoroughly weighed, and my calamity laid in the balances together!" (Job 6:2). **(6)** In many poetic contexts *yachad* is a near synonym of *kullam* (3617), "altogether." **(6a)** *Yachad,* however, is more emphatic, meaning "all at once, all together." **(6b)** In Deut 33:5 (the first biblical occurrence) the word is used emphatically, meaning "all together," or "all of them together": "And he was king in Jeshurun, when the heads of the people and the tribes of Israel were gathered together." **(6c)** Cf.: "Surely men of low degree are vanity, and men of high degree are a lie: to be laid in the balance, they are altogether lighter than vanity" (Ps 62:9). **(6d)** In such contexts *yachad* emphasizes the totality of a given group (cf. Ps 33:15). **(7)** *Yachad* also sometimes emphasizes that things are "alike" or that the same thing will happen to all of them: "likewise the fool and brutish person perish" (Ps 49:10).

II. The form yachdaw, as an adverb, means "all alike; equally; all at once; all together." **(1)** It speaks of community **(1a)** in action (Deut 25:11), **(1b)** in place (Gen 13:6—the first biblical appearance of this form), and **(1c)** in time (Ps 4:8). **(2)** In other places it is synonymous with kullam (3617), "altogether." **(3)** In Is 10:8 yachdaw means "all alike," or "equally": "Are not my princes altogether kings?" **(4)** In Ex 19:8 this word implies "all at once" as well as "all together": "And all the people answered together, and said. . . ." **(5)** The sense "alike" appears in Deut 12:22: "Even as the roebuck and the hart is eaten, so thou shalt eat them: the unclean and the clean shall eat of them alike." See: TWOT—858b; BDB—403a, 403b.

3163. יַחְדּוֹ {1x} **Yachdôw,** *yakh-doe';* from 3162 with pron. suff.; *his unity,* i.e. (adv.) *together; Jachdo,* an Isr.:—Jahdo {1x}. See: BDB—403c.

3164. יַחְדִּיאֵל {1x} **Yachdîyʼêl,** *yakh-dee-ale';* from 3162 and 410; *unity of God; Jachdiël,* an Isr.:—Jahdiel {1x}. See: BDB—292d, 403d.

3165. יֶחְדִּיָהוּ {2x} **Yechdîyâhûw,** *yekh-dee-yaw'-hoo;* from 3162 and 3050;

unity of Jah; Jechdijah, the name of two Isr.:— Jehdeiah {2x}. See: BDB—292d.

יְחַוְאֵל   **Yᵉchavʼêl**. See 3171.

3166.   יַחֲזִיאֵל   {6x} **Yachăzîyʼêl**, *yakh-az-ee-ale'*; from 2372 and 410; *beheld of God; Jachaziël,* the name of five Isr.:—Jahaziel {6x}. See: BDB—303c, 403d.

3167.   יַחְזְיָה   {1x} **Yachzᵉyâh**, *yakh-zeh-yaw';* from 2372 and 3050; *Jah will behold; Jachzejah,* an Isr.:—Jahaziah {1x}. See: BDB—303c, 403d.

3168.   יְחֶזְקֵאל   {3x} **Yᵉchezqêʼl**, *yekh-ez-kale';* from 2388 and 410; *God will strengthen; Jechezkel,* the name of two Isr.:— Ezekiel {2x}, Jehezekel {1x}. See: BDB—306b, 403d.

3169.   יְחִזְקִיָּה   {44x} **Yᵉchizqîyâh**, *yekh-iz-kee-yaw';* or

יְחִזְקִיָּהוּ   **Yᵉchizqîyâhûw**, *yekh-iz-kee-yaw'-hoo;* from 3388 and 3050; *strengthened of Jah; Jechizkijah,* the name of five Isr.:—Hezekiah {43x}, Jehizkiah {1x}. See: BDB—306a, 306b, 403d. comp. 2396.

3170.   יַחְזֵרָה   {1x} **Yachzêrâh**, *yakh-zay-raw';* from the same as 2386; perh. *protection; Jachzerah,* an Isr.:—Jahzerah {1x}. See: BDB—306c, 403d.

3171.   יְחִיאֵל   {14x} **Yᵉchîyʼêl**, *yekh-ee-ale';* or (2 Chr 29:14)

יְחַוְאֵל   **Yᵉchavʼêl**, *yekh-av-ale';* from 2421 and 410; *God will live; Jechiel* (or *Jechavel),* the name of eight Isr.:—Jehiel {1x}. See: BDB—295d, 313c, 403d.

3172.   יְחִיאֵלִי   {2x} **Yᵉchîyʼêlîy**, *yekh-ee-ay-lee';* patron. from 3171; a *Jechiëlite* or desc. of Jechiel:—Jehieli {2x}. See: BDB—313d, 403d.

3173.   יָחִיד   {12x} **yâchîyd**, *yaw-kheed';* from 3161; prop. *united,* i.e. *sole;* by impl. *beloved;* also *lonely;* (fem.) the *life* (as not to be replaced):—only {6x}, darling {2x}, only child {1x}, only son {1x}, desolate {1x}, solitary {1x}.

Yachiyd means "very self, only; solitary; lonely." **(1)** The word can be used meaning "self, my soul": "Deliver my soul from the sword, my darling from the power of the dog" (Ps 22:20; cf. Ps 35:17). **(2)** Sometimes this word means "only": "Take now thy son, thine only son Isaac, whom thou lovest . . ." (Gen 22:2— the first biblical occurrence of the word). **(3)** In two passages this word means "solitary" or "lonely": "Turn thee unto me, and have mercy upon me; for I am desolate and afflicted" (Ps 25:16; cf. Ps 68:6). **(4)** The noun yachad occurs

only once to mean "unitedness." David said to the Benjaminites: "If ye be come peaceably unto me to help me, mine heart shall be knit unto you [I am ready to become one (or united) with you]" (1 Chr 12:17). This usage of the word as a substantive is unusual. See: TWOT—858a; BDB—402d.

3174.   יְחִיָּה   {1x} **Yᵉchîyâh**, *yekh-ee-yaw';* from 2421 and 3050; *Jah will live; Jechijah,* an Isr.:—Jehiah {1x}. See: BDB—313d, 403d.

3175.   יָחִיל   {1x} **yâchîyl**, *yaw-kheel';* from 3176; *expectant:*—should hope {1x}. This word signifies a long patient waiting. See: TWOT—859a; BDB—404a.

3176.   יָחַל   {42x} **yâchal**, *yaw-chal';* a prim. root; to *wait;* by impl. to *be patient, hope:*—(cause to, have, make to) hope {22x}, wait {12x}, tarry {3x}, trust {2x}, variant {2x}, stayed {1x}. See: TWOT—859; BDB—403d.

3177.   יַחְלְאֵל   {2x} **Yachlᵉʼêl**, *yakh-leh-ale';* from 3176 and 410; *expectant of God; Jachleël,* an Isr.:—Jahleel {2x}. See: BDB—404b.

3178.   יַחְלְאֵלִי   {1x} **Yachlᵉʼêlîy**, *yakh-leh-ay-lee';* patron. from 3177; a *Jach-leëlite* or desc. of Jachleel:—Jahleelites {1x}. See: BDB—404b.

3179.   יָחַם   {10x} **yâcham**, *yaw-kham';* a prim. root; prob. to *be hot;* fig. to *conceive:*—get heat {1x}, be hot {2x}, conceive {6x}, be warm {1x}.

Yacham means "to be fiery, be hot." In Deut 19:6 *yacham* means "to be hot": "Lest the avenger of the blood pursue the slayer while his heart is hot, and overtake him. . . ." Syn.: 2029, 2030. See: TWOT—860; BDB—404b, 1095c.

3180.   יַחְמוּר   {2x} **yachmûwr**, *yakh-moor';* from 2560; a kind of *deer* (from the color; comp. 2543):—fallow deer {1x}. See: TWOT—685b; BDB—331c, 405a.

3181.   יַחְמַי   {1x} **Yachmay**, *yakh-mah'-ee;* prob. from 3179; *hot; Jachmai,* an Isr.:— Jahmai {1x}. See: BDB—327d, 405a.

3182.   יָחֵף   {5x} **yâchêph**, *yaw-khafe';* from an unused root mean. to *take off the shoes; unsandalled:*—barefoot {4x}, being unshod {1x}. See: TWOT—861a; BDB—405a.

3183.   יַחְצְאֵל   {2x} **Yachtsᵉʼêl**, *yakh-tseh-ale';* from 2673 and 410; *God will allot; Jachtseël,* an Isr.:—Jahzeel {2x}. See: BDB—345d, 405a. comp. 3185.

3184.   יַחְצְאֵלִי   {1x} **Yachtsᵉʼêlîy**, *yakh-tseh-ay-lee';* patron. from 3183; a *Jach-*

tseëlite (collect.) or desc. of Jachtseel:—Jahze-elites {1x}. See: BDB—345d, 405a.

3185. יַחְצִיאֵל {1x} **Yachtsîy°êl**, *yakh-tsee-ale';* from 2673 and 410; *allotted of God; Jachtsiël,* an Isr.:—Jahziel {1x}. See: BDB—345d, 405a. Syn.: comp. 3183.

3186. יָחַר {1x} **yâchar**, *yaw-khar';* a prim. root; to *delay:*—tarry longer {1x}. See: TWOT—68; BDB—405b.

3187. יָחַשׂ **yâchas**, *yaw-khas';* a prim. root; to *sprout;* used only as denom. from 3188; to *enroll* by pedigree:—{12x}, genealogy {6x}, number . . . genealogy {2x}.

Yachas means "to reckon (according to race or family)." **(1)** In 1 Chr 5:17 *yachas* means "reckoned by genealogies": "All these were reckoned by genealogies in the days of Jothan King of Judah" (cf. 1 Chr 7:5). **(2)** A similar use is found in Ezr 2:62: "These sought their register among those that were reckoned by genealogy, but they were not found." See: TWOT—862; BDB—405b.

3188. יַחַשׂ {20x} **yachas**, *yakh'-as;* from 3187; a *pedigree* or family list (as *growing* spontaneously):—reckoned by genealogy {12x}, genealogy {6x}, number . . . genealogy {2x}.

Yachas means "genealogy." **(1)** This word appears in the infinitive form as a noun to indicate a register or table of genealogy: "And the number throughout the genealogy of them that were apt to the war, and to battle was twenty and six thousand men" (1 Chr 7:40; cf. 2 Chr 31:18). **(2)** Another rendering concerning the acts of Rehoboam, recorded in the histories of Shemaiah (2 Chr 12:15), meant that the particulars were related in a genealogical table. See: TWOT—862; BDB—405b.

3189. יַחַת {8x} **Yachath**, *yakh'-ath;* from 3161; *unity; Jachath,* the name of four Isr.:—Jahath {8x}. See: BDB—367a, 405c.

3190. יָטַב {107x} **yâtab**, *yaw-tab';* a prim. root; to *be* (caus.) *make well,* lit. (*sound, beautiful*) or fig. (*happy, successful, right*):—well {35x}, good {21x}, please {14x}, merry {5x}, amend {4x}, better {4x}, accepted {2x}, diligently {2x}, misc. {20x} = use aright, benefit, seem best, make cheerful, be comely, + be content, dress, earnestly, find favour, give, be glad, shew more [kindness], skilfully, × very small, surely, make sweet, thoroughly, tire, trim, very.

(1) *Yatab* does not mean amend nor improve your ways but to make one's course line up with that which is pleasing to God and that which is well-pleasing in His sight. **(2)** *Yatab,* as a verb, means "to be good, do well, be glad, please, do good to go well, be pleasing, be de-lighted, be happy." **(3)** The meaning of the word, as expressed in Neh 2:6, is "pleased." **(4)** This verbal form is found first in the story of Cain and Abel, where it is used twice in one verse: "if thou doest well, shalt thou not be accepted? and if thou doest not well, sin lieth at the door. And unto thee *shall be* his desire, and thou shalt rule over him" (Gen 4:7). **(5)** Among other nuances of the verb are **(5a)** "to deal well": "therefore God dealt well with the midwives: and the people multiplied, and waxed very mighty" (Ex 1:20); **(5b)** "to play [a musical instrument] well": "and Saul said unto his servants, Provide me now a man that can play well, and bring *him* to me" (1 Sa 16:17), **(5c)** "to adorn, make beautiful": "And when Jehu was come to Jezreel, Jezebel heard *of it;* and she painted [*yatab*] her face, and tired her head, and looked out at a window" (2 Kin 9:30), and **(5d)** "to inquire diligently": "and it be told thee, and thou hast heard *of it,* and enquired diligently, and, behold, *it be* true, *and* the thing certain, *that* such abomination is wrought in Israel" (Deut 17:4). See: TWOT—863; BDB—405c.

3191. יְטַב {1x} **y°tab** (Aram.), *yet-ab';* corresp. to 3190:—seem good {1x}. See: TWOT—2768; BDB—1095d.

3192. יָטְבָה {1x} **Yotbâh**, *yot-baw';* from 3190; *pleasantness; Jotbah,* a place in Pal.:—Jotbah {1x}. See: BDB—406a.

3193. יָטְבָתָה {2x} **Yotbâthâh**, *yot-baw'-thaw;* from 3192; *Jotbathah,* a place in the Desert:—Jotbath {1x}, Jotbathah {2x}. See: BDB—406a.

3194. יֻטָּה {2x} **Yuttâh**, *yoo-taw';* or

יוּטָה **Yûwtâh**, *yoo-taw';* from 5186; *extended; Juttah* (or *Jutah*), a place in Pal.:—Juttah {2x}. See: BDB—398a, 406b, 641a.

3195. יְטוּר {3x} **Y°tûwr**, *yet-oor';* prob. from the same as 2905; *encircled* (i.e. *inclosed*); *Jetur,* a son of Ishmael:—Jetur {3x}. See: BDB—377b, 406b, 452d.

3196. יַיִן {140x} **yayin**, *yah'-yin;* from an unused root mean. to *effervesce; wine* (as fermented); by impl. *intoxication:*—banqueting {1x}, wine {138x}, winebibbers + 5433 {1x}.

Yayin means "wine." **(1)** This is the usual Hebrew word for fermented grape. **(2)** It is usually rendered "wine." Such "wine" was commonly drunk for refreshment: "And Melchizedek king of Salem brought forth bread and wine . . ." (Gen 14:18; cf. 27:25). **(3)** Passages such as Eze 27:18 inform us that "wine" was an article of commerce: "Damascus

was thy merchant in the multitude of the wares of thy making, for the multitude of all riches; in the wine of Helbon, and white wool." **(4)** Strongholds were supplied with "wine" in case of siege: "and he fortified the strongholds, and put captains in them, and store of victual, and of oil and wine" (2 Chr 11:11). **(5)** Proverbs recommends that kings avoid "wine" and strong drink but that it be given to those troubled with problems that they might drink and forget their problems (Prov 31:4–7). **(6)** "Wine" was used to make merry, to make one feel good without being intoxicated: "Now Absalom had commanded his servants, saying, Mark ye now when Amnon's heart is merry with wine, and when I say unto you, Smite Amnon; then kill him, fear not: have not I commanded you? be courageous, and be valiant" (2 Sa 13:28).

(7) It was used in rejoicing before the Lord. **(7a)** Once a year all Israel is to gather in Jerusalem. **(7b)** The money realized from the sale of a tithe of all their harvest was to be spent "for whatsoever thy soul lusteth after, for oxen, or for sheep, or for wine, or for strong drink, or for whatsoever thy soul desireth: and thou shalt eat there before the Lord thy God, and thou shalt rejoice . . ." (Deut 14:26). **(8)** "Wine" was offered to God at His command as part of the prescribed ritual: "And with the one lamb a tenth deal of flour mingled with the fourth part of an hin of beaten oil; and the fourth part of an hin of wine for a drink offering" (Ex 29:40). **(9)** Thus it was part of the temple supplies available for purchase by pilgrims so that they could offer it to God: "Some of them also were appointed to oversee the vessels, and all the instruments of the sanctuary, and the fine flour, and the wine, and the oil, and the frankincense, and the spices" (1 Chr 9:29). **(10)** Pagans used "wine" in their worship, but "their wine is the poison of dragons, and the cruel venom of asps" (Deut 32:33).

(11) *Yayin* clearly represents an intoxicating beverage. **(11a)** This is evident in its first biblical appearance: "And Noah began to be a husbandman, and he planted a vineyard: and he drank of the wine, and was drunken" (Gen 9:20–21). **(11b)** In Gen 9:24 *yayin* means drunkenness: "And Noah awoke from his wine." **(12)** People in special states of holiness were forbidden to drink "wine," such as **(12a)** the Nazarites: "He shall separate himself from wine and strong drink, and shall drink no vinegar of wine, or vinegar of strong drink, neither shall he drink any liquor of grapes, nor eat moist grapes, or dried" (Num 6:3), **(12b)** Samson's mother: "Now therefore beware, I pray thee, and drink not wine nor strong drink, and eat not any unclean thing" (Judg 13:4), and **(12c)** priests approaching God: "Do not drink wine

nor strong drink, thou, nor thy sons with thee, when ye go into the tabernacle of the congregation, lest ye die: it shall be a statute for ever throughout your generations" (Lev 10:9).

(13) The word is used as a synonym of *tirosh* (8492), "new wine," in Hos 4:11, where it is evident that both can be intoxicating: "Whoredom and wine and new wine (*tirosh*) take away the heart." **(13a)** *Tirosh* is distinguished from *yayin* by referring only to new wine not fully fermented; *yayin* includes "wine" at any stage. **(13b)** In Gen 27:28 (the first biblical occurrence of the word) Jacob's blessing includes the divine bestowal of an abundance of new wine: "Therefore God give thee of the dew of heaven, and the fatness of the earth, and plenty of corn and wine." **(13c)** In 1 Sa 1:15 *yayin* parallels *shekar* (7941), "strong drink." **(13c1)** *Shekar* in early times included wine: "And the drink offering thereof shall be the fourth part of an hin for the one lamb: in the holy place shalt thou cause the strong wine to be poured unto the LORD for a drink offering" (Num 28:7); **(13c2)** but meant strong drink made from any fruit or grain: "He shall separate himself from wine and strong drink, and shall drink no vinegar of wine, or vinegar of strong drink, neither shall he drink any liquor of grapes, nor eat moist grapes, or dried" (Num 6:3). See: TWOT–864; BDB–406b.

3197. יָךְ {1x} **yak,** *yak;* by err. transc. for 3027; *a hand* or *side:*– [way-] side {1x}. See: TWOT–844; BDB–406d.

יָכֹל **yâkôwl.** See 3201.

יְכָוֹנְיָה **Yᵉkôwnᵉyâh.** See 3204.

3198. יָכַח {59x} **yâkach,** *yaw-kahh';* a prim. root; to *be right* (i.e. *correct*); recip. to *argue;* caus. to *decide, justify* or *convict:*– reprove {23x}, rebuke {12x}, correct {3x}, plead {3x}, reason {2x}, chasten {2x}, reprover + 376 {2x}, appointed {1x}, arguing {1x}, misc. {9x} = convince, daysman, dispute, judge, maintain, surely, in any wise.

Yakach (3198) means, "to decide, prove, convince, judge." **(1)** The first occurrence of the word is in Gen 20:16: "And unto Sarah he said, Behold, I have given thy brother a thousand *pieces* of silver: behold, he *is* to thee a covering of the eyes, unto all that *are* with thee, and with all other: thus she was reproved." Reprove in English means to "prove over again"; hence, Sarah was proven chaste, untouched by another man. **(2)** It is evident in most of the uses of *yakach* that there is a value judgment involved, as in Ps 50:21: "I will reprove thee, and [lay the charge before thee]." **(3)** Negative judgments may lead to reproof, especially by God (Job 5:17). **(3a)** Such divine reproof may

be physical: "I will chasten him with the rod of men" (2 Sa 7:14). **(3b)** But it is the conviction of the wise man that "For whom the LORD loveth he correcteth; even as a father the son in whom he delighteth" (Prov 3:12). See: TWOT—865; BDB—406d.

יְכִלְיָה Y^ekîyl^eyâh. See 3203.

3199. יָכִין {8x} Yâkîyn, *yaw-keen'*; from 3559; *he* (or *it*) *will establish; Jakin,* the name of three Isr. and of a temple pillar:—Jachin {8x}. See: BDB—467c, 937b.

3200. יָכִינִי {1x} Yâkîyniy, *yaw-kee-nee';* patron. from 3199; a *Jakinite* (collect.) or desc. of Jakin:—Jachinites {1x}. See: BDB—467c.

3201. יָכֹל {195x} yâkôl, *yaw-kole';* or (fuller)

יָכוֹל yâkôwl, *yaw-kole';* a prim. root; to *be able,* lit. (*can, could*) or mor. (*may, might*):—could {46x}, able {43x}, cannot {34x}, prevail {22x}, may {16x}, can {12x}, canst {5x}, endure {2x}, might {2x}, misc. {13x} = any at all (ways), attain, overcome, have power, still, suffer.

Yakowl means "can, may, to be able, prevail, endure." **(1)** As in English, the Hebrew word usually requires another verb to make the meaning complete. **(2)** *Yakowl* first occurs in Gen 13:6: "And the land was not able to bear them, that they might dwell together." **(3)** God promised Abraham: "And I will make thy seed as the dust of the earth: so that if a man can number the dust of the earth, then shall thy seed also be numbered" (Gen 13:16; cf. Gen 15:5). **(4)** The most frequent use of this verb is in the sense of "can" or "to be able." **(4a)** The word may refer specifically to "physical ability," as in 1 Sa 17:33: "And Saul said to David, Thou art not able to go against this Philistine to fight with him: for thou art but a youth, and he a man of war from his youth." **(4b)** *Yakowl* may express "moral inability," **(4b1)** as in Josh 7:13: "Thou canst not stand before thine enemies, until ye take away the accursed thing from among you." **(4b2)** For a similar sense, see Jer 6:10: "Behold, their ear is uncircumcised, and they cannot hearken."

(5) In the negative sense, it may be used to express "prohibition": "Thou mayest not eat within thy gates the tithe of thy corn, or of thy wine, or of thy oil, or the firstlings of thy herds or of thy flock, nor any of thy vows which thou vowest, nor thy freewill offerings, or heave offering of thine hand" (Deut 12:17). **(6)** Or the verb may indicate a "social barrier," as in Gen 43:32: "The Egyptians might not eat bread with the Hebrews; for that is an abomination unto the Egyptians." **(7)** *Yakowl* is also used of God, as when Moses pleaded with God not to de-

stroy Israel lest the nations say, "Because the LORD was not able to bring this people into the land which he sware unto them, therefore he hath slain them in the wilderness" (Num 14:16). **(8)** The word may indicate a positive sense: "If it be so, our God whom we serve is able to deliver us" (Dan 3:17). **(9)** The word *yakowl* appears when God limits His patience with the insincere: "So that the LORD could no longer bear, because of the evil of your doings, *and* because of the abominations which ye have committed; therefore is your land a desolation, and an astonishment, and a curse, without an inhabitant, as at this day" (Jer 44:22).

(10) When *yakowl* is used without another verb, the sense is "to prevail" or "to overcome," as in the words of the angel to Jacob: "And he said, Thy name shall be called no more Jacob, but Israel: for as a prince hast thou power with God and with men, and hast prevailed" (Gen 32:28). **(11)** With the word *yakowl,* God rebukes Israel's insincerity: **(11a)** "Bring no more vain oblations; incense is an abomination unto me; the new moons and sabbaths, the calling of assemblies, I cannot away with; *it is* iniquity, even the solemn meeting" (Is 1:13). **(11b)** "Thy calf, O Samaria, hath cast thee off; mine anger is kindled against them: how long will it be ere they attain to innocency?" (Hos 8:5). **(12)** There is no distinction in Hebrew between "can" and "may," **(12a)** since *yakowl* expresses both "ability" and "permission," or prohibition with the negative. **(12b)** Both God and man can act. **(12c)** There is no limit to God's ability apart from His own freely determined limits of patience with continued disobedience and insincerity (Is 59:1–2) and will (Dan 3:17–18). See: TWOT—866; BDB—407b, 1095d.

3202. יְכֵל {12x} y^ekêl (Aram.), *yek-ale';* or

יְכִיל y^ekîyl (Aram.), *yek-eel';* corresp. to 3201:—be able {4x}, can {6x}, couldest {1x}, prevail {1x}. See: TWOT—2769; BDB—1095d. 1096d.

3203. יְכָלְיָה {2x} Y^ekolyâh, *yek-ol-yaw';* and

יְכָלְיָהוּ Y^ekolyâhûw, *yek-ol-yaw'-hoo;* or (2 Chr 26:3)

יְכִילְיָה Y^ekîyl^eyâh, *yek-ee-leh-yaw';* from 3201 and 3050; *Jah will enable; Jekoljah* or *Jekiljah,* an Israelitess:—Jecholiah {1x}, Jecoliah {1x}. See: BDB—408a.

3204. יְכָנְיָה {7x} Y^ekonyâh, *yek-on-yaw';* and

יְכָנְיָהוּ Y^ekonyâhûw, *yek-on-yaw'-hoo;* or (Jer 27:20)

יוֹכָנְיָה Y^ekôwn^eyâh, *yek-o-neh-yaw';* from 3559 and 3050; *Jah will establish; Jekonjah,* a Jewish king:—Jeconiah

{7x}. See: BDB—220c, 408a, 467c, 487c. comp. 3659.

3205. יָלַד {498x} **yâlad**, *yaw-lad'*; a prim. root; to *bear* young; caus. to *beget;* medically, to *act as midwife;* spec. to *show lineage:*—beget {201x}, bare {110x}, born {79x}, bring forth {25x}, bear {23x}, travail {16x}, midwife {10x}, child {8x}, delivered {5x}, borne {3x}, birth {2x}, labour {2x}, brought up {2x}, misc. {12x} = calve, come, time of delivery, gender, hatch, declare pedigrees, be the son of.

Yalad means "to bear, bring forth, beget, be delivered." **(1)** Essentially, the word refers to the action of "giving birth" and its result, "bearing children." **(1a)** God cursed woman by multiplying her pain in "bringing forth" children (cf. Gen 3:16, the first occurrence of *yalad*). **(1b)** The second meaning is exemplified by Gen 4:18, which reports that Irad "begat" ("became the father of") Mehujael. **(1c)** This verb can also be used in reference to animals; in Gen 30:39, the strong among Laban's flocks "birthed" striped, speckled, and spotted offspring. **(2)** One recurring theme in biblical history is typified by Abram and Sarah. **(2a)** They had no heirs, but God made them a promise and gave them a son (Gen 16:1, 16). **(2a)** This demonstrates that God controls the opening of the womb (Gen 20:17–18) and bestows children as an indication of His blessing. **(3)** The prophets use the image of childbirth to illustrate the terror to overcome men in the day of the Lord: "And they shall be afraid: pangs and sorrows shall take hold of them; they shall be in pain as a woman that travaileth: they shall be amazed one at another; their faces shall be as flames" (Is 13:8).

(4) Hosea uses the image of marriage and childbearing to describe God's relationship to Israel (1:3, 6, 8). **(5)** Is 7:14, uses this verb to predict the "birth" of Immanuel: "Therefore the Lord himself shall give you a sign; Behold, a virgin shall conceive, and bear a son, and shall call his name Immanuel." **(6)** Finally, the prophets sometimes mourn the day of their "birth" (Jer 15:10). **(7)** *Yalad* describes the relationship between God and Israel at other places in the Bible as well. **(7a)** This relationship is especially relevant to the king who typifies the Messiah, the Son whom God "begot": "I will declare the decree: the LORD hath said unto me, Thou art my Son; this day have I begotten thee" (Ps 2:7). **(7b)** God also says He "begot" the nation of Israel as a whole: "Of the Rock that begat thee thou art unmindful, and hast forgotten God that formed thee" (Deut 32:18). **(7c)** This statement is in noticeable contrast to Moses' disclaimer that he did not "birth" them (Num 11:12) and, therefore, does not want to be responsible for them any longer.

(8) The motif that God "gave birth" to Israel is picked up by Jeremiah. In Jer 31:20, God states that His heart yearns for Ephraim His son (yeled). **(9)** Ezekiel develops this motif in the form of an allegory, giving the names Aholah and Aholibah to Samaria and Jerusalem respectively, to those whom He "bore" (Eze 23:4, 37). See: TWOT—867; BDB—408a, 529a.

3206. יֶלֶד {89x} **yeled**, *yeh'-led;* from 3205; something *born,* i.e. a *lad* or *offspring:*—child {72x}, young man {7x}, young ones {3x}, sons {3x}, boy {2x}, fruit {1x}, variant {1x}.

Yeled, as a noun, means "boy; child." **(1)** The noun *yeled* differs from *ben* (1121 - "son"), which more exactly specifies the parental relationship. **(2)** For example, the child that Naomi nursed was a "boy" (Ruth 4:16). Syn: *Yeled*, which appears 89 times in the Bible, has nouns built on it: **(2a)** *yaldah* (3207 - "girl"; 3 times), **(2b)** *yalid* (3211 - "son" or "slave"; 3 times), **(2c)** *yillod* (3209 - "newborn"; 5 times), **(2d)** walad (2056 - "child"; once), **(2e)** *ledah* (3205 - "bringing forth" or "birth"; 4 times), **(2f)** *moledet* (4138 - "offspring, kindred, parentage"; 22 times), and **(2g)** *toledot* (8435 - "descendants, contemporaries, generation, genealogy, record of the family"; 39 times), **(2h)** *yaldoth* (3208 - childhood, youth). See: TWOT—867b; BDB—409b.

3207. יַלְדָּה {3x} **yaldâh**, *yal-daw';* fem. of 3206; a *lass:*—damsel {1x}, girl {2x}. See: TWOT—867b; BDB—409c.

3208. יַלְדוּת {3x} **yaldûwth**, *yal-dooth';* abstr. from 3206; *boyhood* (or *girlhood*):—childhood {1x}, youth {2x}. See: TWOT—867c; BDB—409c.

3209. יִלּוֹד {5x} **yillôwd**, *yil-lode';* pass. from 3205; *born:*—born {5x}. See: TWOT—867d; BDB—409c.

3210. יָלוֹן {1x} **Yâlôwn**, *yaw-lone';* from 3885; *lodging; Jalon,* an Isr.:—Jalon {1x}. See: BDB—1124c.

3211. יָלִיד {13x} **yâlîyd**, *yaw-leed';* from 3205; *born:*—born {6x}, children {4x}, sons {2x}, homeborn + 1004 {1x}. See: TWOT—867e; BDB—409c.

3212. יָלַךְ {1043x} **yâlak**, *yaw-lak';* a prim. root [comp. 1980]; to *walk* (lit. or fig.); caus. to *carry* (in various senses):—go {628x}, walk {122x}, come {77x}, depart {66x}, . . . away {20x}, follow {20x}, get {14x}, lead {17x}, brought {8x}, carry {5x}, bring {4x}, misc. {62x} = X again, bear, flow, grow, let down, march, prosper, + pursue, cause to run, spread, take away ([-journey]), vanish, wax, X be weak. See: TWOT—498; BDB—229d.

3213. יָלַל {31x} **yâlal**, *yaw-lal';* a prim. root; to *howl* (with a wailing tone) or *yell* (with a boisterous one):—(make to) howl {29x}, be howling {2x}. See: TWOT—868; BDB—410a.

3214. יְלֵל {1x} **yᵉlêl**, *yel-ale';* from 3213; a *howl:*—howling {1x}. See: TWOT—868a; BDB—410b.

3215. יְלָלָה {5x} **yᵉlâlâh**, *yel-aw-law';* fem. of 3214; a *howling:*—howling {5x}. See: TWOT—868b; BDB—410b.

3216. יָלַע {1x} **yâlaᶜ**, *yaw-lah';* a prim. root; to *blurt* or utter inconsiderately:— devour {1x}. See: TWOT—1098; BDB—410c, 534b.

3217. יַלֶּפֶת {2x} **yallepheth**, *yal-leh'-feth;* from an unused root appar. mean. to *stick* or *scrape; scurf* or *tetter:*—scabbed {2x}. See: TWOT—869a; BDB—410c.

3218. יֶקֶק {9x} **yekeq**, *yeh'-lek;* from an unused root mean. to *lick* up; a *devourer;* spec. the young *locust:*—cankerworm {6x}, caterpillar {3x}. See: TWOT—870a; BDB—410c.

3219. יַלְקוּט {1x} **yalqûwṭ**, *yal-koot';* from 3950; a travelling *pouch* (as if for gleanings):—scrip {1x}. See: TWOT—1125b; BDB—410c, 545a.

3220. יָם {396x} **yâm**, *yawm;* from an unused root mean. to *roar; a sea* (as breaking in *noisy* surf) or large body of water; spec. (with the art.), the *Mediterranean;* sometimes a large *river,* or an artificial *basin;* locally, the *west,* or (rarely) the *south:*—sea {321x}, west {47x}, westward {21x}, west side {4x}, seafaring men {1x}, south {1x}, western {1x}.

Yam means "sea; ocean." **(1)** This word refers to the body of water as distinct from the land bodies (continents and islands) and the sky (heavens): "For in six days the Lord made heaven and earth, the sea and all that in them is" (Ex 20:11). **(1a)** Used in this sense *yam* means "ocean." **(1b)** This is its meaning in Gen 1:10, its first biblical appearance; unlike the use in the singular, where the word is a collective noun, it appears here in the plural: "And God called the dry land Earth; and the gathering together of the waters called he Seas. . . ." **(2)** *Yam* may be used of "seas," whether they are salty or fresh. **(2a)** The Great Sea is the Mediterranean: "From the wilderness and this Lebanon even unto the great river, the river Euphrates, all the land of the Hittites, and unto the Great Sea toward the going down of the sun, shall be your coast" (Josh 1:4). **(2b)** This sea is also called the sea of the Philistines (Ex 23:31) and **(2c)** the hinter or western sea (Deut 11:24 "uttermost sea"). **(3)** The Dead Sea is

called **(3a)** the Salt Sea (Gen 14:3), **(3b)** the Arabah (Deut 3:17; "plain"), and **(3c)** the east sea (Eze 47:18).

(4) Thus, *yam* can be used of **(4a)** an inland salty "sea." **(4b)** It can also be used of a fresh water "sea" such as the Sea of Galilee: "And the border shall descend, and shall reach unto the side of the Sea of Chinnereth eastward" (Num 34:11). **(5)** The word is sometimes used of the direction west or westward, in the sense of toward the (Great) Sea: "Lift up now thine eyes, and look from the place where thou art northward, and southward, and eastward, and westward" (Gen 13:14). **(5a)** In Gen 12:8 *yam* means "on the west side": "And he removed from thence unto a mountain on the east of Beth-el, and pitched his tent, having Beth-el on the west, and Hai on the east." **(5b)** This word can also refer to a side of something and not just a direction, but it is the side that faces westward: "He turned about to the west side . . ." (Eze 42:19). **(6)** Ex 10:19 uses *yam* as an adjective modifying "wind": "And the Lord turned a mighty strong west wind, which took away the locusts."

(7) *Yam* is used of the great basin immediately in front of the Holy Place: "And the pillars of brass that were in the house of the Lord, and the bases, and the brazen sea that was in the house of the Lord, did the Chaldees break in pieces, and carried the brass of them to Babylon" (2 Kin 25:13). This is also called **(7a)** the "molten sea" (of cast metal – 1 Kin 7:23) or simply **(7b)** the "sea" (Jer. 27:19). **(8)** *Yam* is used of mighty rivers such as the Nile: "And the waters shall fail from the sea, and the river shall be wasted and dried up" (Is 19:5). **(8a)** This statement occurs in the middle of a prophecy against Egypt. Therefore, "the river" is the Nile. **(8b)** But since the term "river" is in synonymous parallelism to "the sea," this latter term also refers to the Nile. **(8c)** Eze 32:2 uses *yam* of the branches of the Nile: "And thou art as a whale in the seas: and thou camest forth with thy rivers, and troubledst the waters with thy feet, and fouledst their rivers."

(9) This word can also be used of the Euphrates River (Jer 51:36). **(10)** Some scholars believe that in some instances the word *yam* may represent the Canaanite god Yamm, "which alone spreadeth out the heavens, and treadeth upon the waves of the sea" (Job 9:8). **(10a)** If understood as a statement about Yamm, this passage would read: "and tramples upon the back of Yamm." **(10b)** The parallelism between "heavens" and "seas," however, would lead us to conclude that the reference here is to the literal "sea." **(10c)** Ps. 89:9–10 is a more likely place to see a mention of Yamm, for there the word is identified as one of God's enemies

in immediate proximity to the goddess Rahab: "Thou rulest the raging of the sea [Yamm]: when the waves thereof arise, thou stillest them. Thou hast broken Rahab in pieces, as one that is slain; thou hast scattered thine enemies with thy strong arm." **(11)** Especially note Job 7:12: "Am I a sea [Yamm], or a whale, that thou settest a watch over me?" (cf. Job 26:12; Ps 74:13). See: TWOT—871a; BDB—410d, 1095d.

3221. יָם {2x} **yâm** (Aram.), *yawm;* corresp. to 3220:—sea {2x}. See: TWOT—2770; BDB—1095d.

3222. יֵם {1x} **yêm**, *yame;* from the same as 3117; a *warm* spring:—mule {1x}. Syn.: 6505. See: TWOT—871b; BDB—411b.

3223. יְמוּאֵל {2x} **Yᵉmûwʾêl**, *yem-oo-ale';* from 3117 and 410; *day of God; Je-muel*, an Isr.:—Jemuel {2x}. See: BDB—410c.

3224. יְמִימָה {1x} **Yᵉmîymâh**, *yem-ee-maw';* perh. from the same as 3117; prop. *warm*, i.e. *affectionate;* hence, *dove* [comp. 3123]; *Jemimah*, one of Job's daughters:—Jemimah {1x}. See: BDB—410d.

3225. יָמִין {139x} **yâmîyn**, *yaw-meen';* from 3231; the *right* hand or side (leg, eye) of a person or other object (as the *stronger* and more dexterous); locally, the *south:*—hand {105x}, right {24x}, side {5x}, south {3x}, left-handed + 334 {2x}.

Yamiyn means "right hand." **(1)** First, the word represents the bodily part called the "right hand": **(1a)** "And Joseph took them both, Ephraim in his right hand toward Israel's left hand, and Manasseh in his left hand toward Israel's right hand . . ." (Gen 48:13). **(1b)** Ehud was "bound as to his right hand"; he was left-handed: "But when the children of Israel cried unto the Lord, the Lord raised them up a deliverer, Ehud the son of Gera, a Benjamite, a man lefthanded" (Judg 3:15). **(2)** *Yamiyn* may be used in a figurative sense. God's taking one's "right hand" means that He strengthens him: "For I the Lord thy God will hold thy right hand, saying unto thee, Fear not: I will help thee" (Is 41:13). **(3)** The Bible speaks anthropomorphically, attributing to God human parts and, in particular, a "right hand" (Ex 15:6). **(3a)** The Bible teaches that God is a spirit and has no body or bodily parts (cf. Ex 20:4; Deut 4:15–19). **(3b)** This figure is used of God's effecting His will among men and of His working in their behalf (showing His favor): "And I said, This is my infirmity: but I will remember the years of the right hand of the Most High" (Ps 77:10).

(4) *Yamiyn* represents the direction, to the "right." In this use the word can specify the location of someone or something: "But the chil-dren of Israel walked upon dry land in the midst of the sea; and the waters were a wall unto them on their right hand, and on their left" (Ex 14:29). **(5)** In other contexts *yamiyn* signifies "direction toward": "Is not the whole land before thee? Separate thyself, I pray thee, from me: if thou wilt take the left hand, then I will go to the right; or if thou depart to the right hand, then I will go to the left" (Gen 13:9—the first biblical appearance). **(6)** *Yamiyn* can be used of bodily parts other than the right hand. In Judg 3:16 the word is used of one's thigh (literally, "thigh of the right hand"): "But Ehud made him a dagger which had two edges, of a cubit length; and he did gird it under his raiment upon his right thigh." **(6a)** The word is used in 1 Sa 11:2 in conjunction with one's eye and in **(6b)** Ex 29:22 with a thigh. **(7)** This word is used to mean "south," since the south is on one's "right" when he faces eastward: "Then came up the Ziphites to Saul to Gibeah, saying, Doth not David hide himself with us in strongholds in the wood, in the hill of Hachilah, which is on the south of Jeshimon?" (1 Sa 23:19). See: TWOT—872a; BDB—411c.

3226. יָמִין {6x} **Yâmîyn**, *yaw-meen';* the same as 3225; *Jamin*, the name of three Isr.:—Jamin {6x}. See: BDB—412c. See also: 1144.

3227. יְמִינִי {2x} **yᵉmîynîy**, *yem-ee-nee';* for 3225; *right:*—(on the) right (hand) {2x}. See: BDB—412a.

3228. יְמִינִי {1x} **Yᵉmîynîy**, *yem-ee-nee';* patron. from 3226; a *Jeminite* (collect.) or desc. of Jamin:—Jaminites {1x}. See: BDB—412b, 412c. See also 1145.

3229. יִמְלָא {4x} **Yimlâʾ**, *yeem-law';* or

יִמְלָה **Yimlâh**, *yim-law';* from 4390; *full; Jimla* or *Jimlah*, an Isr.:—Imla {2x}, Imlah {2x}. See: BDB—410d, 571c.

3230. יַמְלֵךְ {1x} **Yamlêk**, *yam-lake';* from 4427; *he will make king; Jamlek*, an Isr.:—Jamlech {1x}. See: BDB—576a.

3231. יָמַן {4x} **yâman**, *yaw-man';* a prim. root; *to be* (phys.) *right* (i.e. firm); but used only as denom. from 3225 and tran. *to be right-handed* or *take the right-hand* side:—go (turn) to (on, use) the right hand {4x}. See: TWOT—872c; BDB—412b.

3232. יִמְנָה {5x} **Yimnâh**, *yim-naw';* from 3231; *prosperity* (as betokened by the *right* hand); *Jimnah*, the name of two Isr.; also (with the art.) of the posterity of one of them:—Imna {1x}, Imnah {1x}, Jimnah {2x}, Jimnites {1x}. See: BDB—412c.

3233. יְמָנִי {33x} **yᵉmânîy**, *yem-aw-nee';* from 3231; *right* (i.e. at the right hand):— (on the) right (hand) {33x}.

Yemaniy, as a noun, means "right hand; on the right side; the right side (of one's body); southern." **(1)** *Yemaniy* means "right hand" in Ex 29:20: "Then shalt thou kill the ram, and take of his blood, and put *it* upon the tip of the right ear of Aaron, and upon the tip of the right ear of his sons, and upon the thumb of their right hand, and upon the great toe of their right foot, and sprinkle the blood upon the altar round about" (the first biblical occurrence). **(2)** In 1 Kin 7:21 the word refers to the "right side" in regard to a location: "And he set up the pillars in the porch of the temple: and he set up the right pillar, and called the name thereof Jachin: and he set up the left pillar, and called the name thereof Boaz." **(3)** *Yemaniy* appears in Eze 4:6 with the meaning of the "right side" of the body: "And when thou hast accomplished them, lie again on thy right side, and thou shalt bear the iniquity of the house of Judah forty days: I have appointed thee each day for a year." **(4)** The word implies "southern" in 1 Kin 6:8: "The door for the middle chamber was in the right side [southern side] of the house." See: TWOT—872d; BDB—412b. Syn.: 8486.

3234. יִמְנָע {1x} **Yimnâ⁽**, *yim-naw';* from 4513; *he will restrain; Jimna,* an Isr.:— Imna {1x}. See: BDB—413a, 586b.

3235. יָמַר {2x} **yâmar**, *yaw-mar';* a prim. root; to *exchange;* by impl. to *change places:*—boast selves {1x}, change {1x}. See: TWOT—118; BDB—413a.

3236. יִמְרָה {1x} **Yimrâh**, *yim-raw';* prob. from 3235; *interchange; Jimrah,* an Isr.:—Imrah {1x}. See: BDB—413a, 598c.

3237. יָמַשׁ {1x} **yâmash**, *yaw-mash';* a prim. root; to *touch:*—feel {1x}. See: BDB—413a.

3238. יָנָה {21x} **yânâh**, *yaw-naw';* a prim. root; to *rage* or *be violent;* by impl. to *suppress,* to *maltreat:*—oppress {11x}, vex {4x}, destroy {1x}, oppressor {1x}, proud {1x}, do wrong {1x}, oppression {1x}, thrust out {1x}. See: TWOT—873; BDB—402a, 413a.

3239. יָנוֹחַ {3x} **Yânôwach**, *yaw-no'-akh;* or (with enclitic)

יָנוֹחָה **Yânôwchâh**, *yaw-no'-khaw;* from 3240; *quiet; Janoäch* or *Janochah,* a place in Pal.:—Janoah {1x}, Janohah {2x}. See: BDB—413b, 629c.

יָנוּם **Yânûm.** See 3241.

3240. יָנַח {75x} **yânach**, *yaw-nakh';* a prim. root; to *deposit;* by impl. to *allow to stay:*—leave {24x}, up {10x}, lay {8x}, suffer {5x}, place {4x}, put {4x}, set {4x}, . . . down {4x}, let alone {4x}, . . . him {2x}, bestowed {1x}, leave off {1x}, pacifieth {1x}, still {1x}, withdraw {1x}, withhold {1x}. (The Hiphil forms with the *dagesh* are here referred to, in accordance with the older grammarians; but if any distinction of the kind is to be made, these should rather be referred to 5117, and the others here.) See: TWOT—1323; BDB—628d.

3241. יָנִים {1x} **Yânîym**, *yaw-neem';* from 5123; *asleep; Janim,* a place in Pal.:—Janum {1x}. See: BDB—413b, 630b.

3242. יְנִיקָה {1x} **yᵉnîqâh**, *yen-ee-kaw';* from 3243; a *sucker* or sapling:—young twigs {1x}. See: TWOT—874c; BDB—413c.

3243. יָנַק {32x} **yânaq**, *yaw-nak';* a prim. root; to *suck;* caus. to *give milk:*—suck {14x}, nurse {7x}, suckling {6x}, sucking child {3x}, milch {1x}, nursing mothers {1x}. See: TWOT—874; BDB—413b, 568c, 586b.

3244. יַנְשׁוּף {3x} **yanshûwph**, *yan-shoof';* or

יַנְשׁוֹף **yanshôwph**, *yan-shofe';* appar. from 5398; an unclean (aquatic) bird; prob. the *heron* (perh. from its *blowing* cry, or because the *night*-heron is meant [comp. 5399]):—great owl {2x}, owl {1x}. See: TWOT—1434b; BDB—413d, 676a.

3245. יָסַד {42x} **yâçad**, *yaw-sad';* a prim. root; to *set* (lit. or fig.); intens. to *found;* refl. to *sit* down together, i.e. *settle, consult:*—foundation {15x}, lay {8x}, founded {8x}, ordain {2x}, counsel {2x}, established {2x}, foundation + 3117 {1x}, appointed {1x}, instructed {1x}, set {1x}, sure {1x}. See: TWOT—875; BDB—413d.

3246. יְסֻד {1x} **yᵉçûd**, *yes-ood';* from 3245; a *foundation* (fig. i.e. *beginning*):—✗ began {1x}. See: TWOT—875a; BDB—414b.

3247. יְסוֹד {20x} **yᵉçôwd**, *yes-ode';* from 3245; a *foundation* (lit. or fig.):—bottom {9x}, foundation {10x}, repairing {1x}. See: TWOT—875b; BDB—414b.

3248. יְסוּדָה {1x} **yᵉçûwdâh**, *yes-oo-daw';* fem. of 3246; a *foundation:*—foundation {1x}. See: TWOT—875c; BDB—414b.

3249. יָסוּר {1x} **yâçûwr**, *yaw-soor';* from 5493; *departing:*—they that depart {1x}. See: TWOT—1480; BDB—693c.

3250. יִסּוֹר {1x} **yiççôwr**, *yis-sore';* from 3256; a *reprover:*—instruct {1x}. See: TWOT—877a; BDB—416b.

3251. יָסַךְ {1x} **yâçak**, *yaw-sak'*; a prim. root; to *pour* (intr.):—be poured {1x}. See: TWOT—1474; BDB—414c.

3252. יִסְכָּה {1x} **Yiçkâh**, *yis-kaw'*; from an unused root mean. to *watch; observant; Jiskah*, sister of Lot:—Iscah {1x}. See: BDB—414c.

3253. יִסְמַכְיָהוּ {1x} **Yiçmakyâhûw**, *yis-mak-yaw-hoo'*; from 5564 and 3050; *Jah will sustain; Jismakjah*, an Isr.:—Ismachiah {1x}. See: BDB—414d, 702b.

3254. יָסַף {213x} **yâçaph**, *yaw-saf'*; a prim. root; to *add* or *augment* (often adv. to *continue* to do a thing):—more {70}, again {54x}, add {28x}, increase {16x}, also {6x}, exceed {4x}, put {4x}, further {4x}, henceforth {4x}, can {2x}, continued {2x}, give {2x}, misc. {17x} = X cease, + conceive again, X gather together, join, X longer (bring, do, make, much, put), proceed (further), prolong, be [strong-] er, X yet, yield.

Yacaph means "to add, continue, do again, increase, surpass." **(1)** Basically, *yacaph* signifies increasing the number of something. **(2)** It may also be used to indicate adding one thing to another, e.g., "And if a man eat of the holy thing unwittingly, then he shall put the fifth part thereof unto it, and shall give it unto the priest" (Lev 22:14). **(3)** This verb may be used to signify the repetition of an act stipulated by another verb. For example, the dove that Noah sent out "returned not again" (Gen 8:12). **(4)** Usually the repeated action is indicated by an infinitive absolute, preceded by the preposition *le*—"And he did not have relations with her again." Literally, this reads "And he did not add again [5750 - *'od*] to knowing her [intimately]" (Gen 38:26). **(5)** In some contexts *yacaph* means "to heighten," but with no suggestion of numerical increase. **(5a)** God says, "The meek also shall increase [*yacaph*] their joy in the Lord . . ." (Is 29:19).

(5b) This same emphasis appears in Ps 71:14: ". . . and will yet praise thee more and more [*yacaph*]' or literally, "And I will add to all Thy praises." **(5c)** In such cases, more than an additional quantity of joy or praise is meant. The author is referring to a new quality of joy or praise—i.e., a heightening of them. **(6)** Another meaning of *yacaph* is "to surpass." The Queen of Sheba told Solomon, "Thy wisdom and prosperity exceedeth the fame which I heard," or literally, "You add [with respect to] wisdom and prosperity to the report which I heard" (1 Kin 10:7). **(7)** This verb may also be used in covenantal formulas, e.g., Ruth summoned God's curse upon herself by saying, "The Lord do so to me, and more also [*yacaph*], if ought but death part thee and me," or liter-

ally, "Thus may the Lord do to me, and thus may he add, if . . ." (Ruth 1:17; cf. Lev 26; Deut 27—28). See: TWOT—876; BDB—414d, 1095d.

3255. יְסַף {1x} **y⁰çaph** (Aram.), *yes-af'*; corresp. to 3254:—add {1x}. See: TWOT—2771; BDB—1095d.

3256. יָסַר {43x} **yâçar**, *yaw-sar'*; a prim. root; to *chastise*, lit. (with blows) or fig. (with words); hence, to *instruct:*—chastise {21x}, instruct {8x}, correct {7x}, taught {2x}, bound {1x}, punish {1x}, reformed {1x}, reproveth {1x}, sore {1x}.

Yacar means "to discipline." The verb appears 43 times in the Old Testament; cf. Prov 19:18: "Chasten thy son while there is hope, and let not thy soul spare for his crying." See: TWOT—877; BDB—415d, 978d, 979a.

3257. יָע {9x} **yâ'**, *yaw*; from 3261; a *shovel:*—shovel {9x}. See: TWOT—879a; BDB—416d, 418b.

3258. יַעְבֵּץ {4x} **Ya'bêts**, *yah-bates'*; from an unused root prob. mean. to *grieve; sorrowful; Jabets*, the name of an Isr., and also of a place in Pal.:—Jabez {4x}. See: BDB—416d, 716d.

3259. יָעַד {29x} **yâ'ad**, *yaw-ad'*; a prim. root; to *fix* upon (by agreement or appointment); by impl. to *meet* (at a stated time), to *summon* (to trial), to *direct* (in a certain quarter or position), to *engage* (for marriage):—meet {7x}, together {5x}, assemble {4x}, appointed {3x}, set {3x}, time {2x}, betrothed {2x}, agreed {1x}, appointment {1x}, gather {1x}. See: TWOT—878; BDB—416d.

יְעָדוּ **Y⁰dôw**. See 3260.

3260. יְעָדִי {1x} **Y⁰dîy**, *yed-ee'*; from 3259; *appointed; Jedi*, an Isr.:—Iddo {1x}. See: BDB—418a, 723b. Syn.: 3035.

3261. יָעָה {1x} **yâ'âh**, *yaw-aw'*; a prim. root; appar. to *brush* aside:—sweep away {1x}. See: TWOT—879; BDB—418a.

3262. יְעוּאֵל {1x} **Y⁰ûw'êl**, *yeh-oo-ale'*; from 3261 and 410; *carried away of God; Jeel*, the name of four Isr.:—Jeuel {1x}. See: BDB—418b. comp. 3273.

3263. יְעוּץ {1x} **Y⁰ûwts**, *yeh-oots'*; from 5779; *counsellor; Jets*, an Isr.:—Jeuz {1x}. See: BDB—418b, 734b.

3264. יָעוֹר {1x} **yâ'ôwr**, *yaw-ore'*; a var. of 3293; a *forest:*—wood {1x}. Syn.: 2793. See: TWOT—888a; BDB—418b, 420c.

3265. יָעוּר {1x} **Yâ'ûwr**, *yaw-oor'*; appar. pass. part. of the same as 3293; *wooded; Jar*, an Isr.:—Jair {1x}. See: BDB—418b, 418c, 753d.

3266. יְעוּשׁ {6x} Yᵉᶜûwsh, yeh-oosh'; from 5789; *hasty; Jesh,* the name of an Edomite and of four Isr.:—Jehush {1x}, Jeush {5x}. See: BDB—418b, 736b. comp. 3274.

3267. יָעַז {1x} yâ'az, yaw-az'; a prim. root; to *be bold* or *obstinate:*—fierce {1x}. See: TWOT—880; BDB—418b.

3268. יַעֲזִיאֵל {1x} Ya'ăzîy'êl, yah-az-ee-ale'; from 3267 and 410; *emboldened of God; Jaaziël,* an Isr.:—Jaaziel {1x}. See: BDB—418c, 739c, 739d.

3269. יַעֲזִיָּהוּ {2x} Ya'ăzîyâhûw, yah-az-ee-yaw'-hoo; from 3267 and 3050; *emboldened of Jah; Jaazijah,* an Isr.:—Jaaziah {2x}. See: BDB—418c, 739d.

3270. יַעְזֵיר {13x} Ya'ăzêyr, yah-az-ayr'; or

יַעְזֵר Ya'zêr, yah-zare'; from 5826; *helpful; Jaazer* or *Jazer,* a place E. of the Jordan:—Jaazer {2x}, Jazer {11x}. See: BDB—418c, 741b.

3271. יָעַט {1x} yâ'at, yaw-at'; a prim. root; to *clothe:*—cover {1x}. See: TWOT—881; BDB—418c.

3272. יְעַט {3x} yᵉᶜat (Aram.), yeh-at'; corresp. to 3289; to *counsel;* refl. to *consult:*—counsellor {2x}, consult together {1x}. See: TWOT—2772; BDB—1095d, 1096a.

3273. יְעִיאֵל {13x} Yᵉᶜîy'êl, yeh-ee-ale'; from 3261 and 410; *carried away of God; Jêel,* the name of six Isr.:—Jeiel {11x}, Jehiel {2x}. See: TWOT—2772; BDB—418b. comp. 3262.

יָעִיר Yâ'îyr. See 3265.

3274. יְעִישׁ {3x} Yᵉᶜîysh, yeh-eesh'; from 5789; *hasty; Jêsh,* the name of an Edomite and of an Isr.:—Jeush {3x}. See: BDB—418c, 736b. comp. 3266.

3275. יַעְכָּן {1x} Ya'kân, yah-kawn'; from the same as 5912; *troublesome; Jakan,* an Isr.:—Jachan {1x}. See: BDB—418c, 747c.

3276. יָעַל {23x} yâ'al, yaw-al'; a prim. root; prop. to *ascend;* fig. to *be valuable* (obj. *useful,* subj. *benefited*):—profit {19x}, at all {1x}, set forward {1x}, good {1x}, profitable {1x}.
See: TWOT—882; BDB—418c.

3277. יָעֵל {3x} yâ'êl, yaw-ale'; from 3276; an *ibex* (as *climbing*):—wild goat {3x}. See: TWOT—883a; BDB—418d.

3278. יָעֵל {6x} Yâ'êl, yaw-ale'; the same as 3277; *Jaël,* a Canaanite:—Jael {6x}. See: BDB—418d.

3279. יַעֲלָא {2x} Ya'ălâ', yah-al-aw'; or

יַעֲלָה Ya'ălâh, yah-al-aw'; the same as 3280 or direct from 3276; *Jaala* or *Jaalah,* one of the Nethinim:—Jaala {1x}, Jaalah {1x}. See: BDB—419a.

3280. יַעֲלָה {1x} ya'ălâh, yah-al-aw'; fem. of 3277:—roe {1x}. See: TWOT—883b; BDB—418d.

3281. יַעְלָם {4x} Ya'lâm, yah-lawm'; from 5956; *occult; Jalam,* an Edomite:—Jalam {4x}. See: BDB—419a, 761c.

3282. יַעַן {17x} ya'an, yah'-an; from an unused root mean. to *pay attention;* prop. *heed;* by impl. *purpose* (sake or account); used adv. to indicate the *reason* or cause:—because {7x}, because that {2x}, forasmuch {1x}, forasmuch as {4x}, seeing then that {1x}, whereas {1x}, + why {1x}. See: TWOT—1650e; BDB—419a, 774c.

3283. יָעֵן {1x} yâ'ên, yaw-ane'; from the same as 3282; the *ostrich* (prob. from its *answering* cry:—ostrich {1x}. See: TWOT—884a; BDB—419a, 943d.

3284. יַעֲנָה {8x} ya'ănâh, yah-an-aw'; fem. of 3283, and mean. the same:—+ owl {8x}. See: TWOT—884b; BDB—419a.

3285. יַעֲנַי {1x} Ya'ănay, yah-an-ah'ee; from the same as 3283; *responsive; Jaanai,* an Isr.:—Jaanai {1x}. See: BDB—419b.

3286. יָעַף {9x} yâ'aph, yaw-af'; a prim. root; to *tire* (as if from wearisome *flight*):—faint {4x}, cause to fly {1x}, (be) weary (self) {4x}. See: TWOT—885; BDB—419b.

3287. יָעֵף {4x} yâ'êph, yaw-afe'; from 3286; *fatigued;* fig. *exhausted:*—faint {2x}, wear {2x}. See: TWOT—885a; BDB—419b.

3288. יְעָף {1x} yᵉâph, yeh-awf'; from 3286; *fatigue* (adv. utterly *exhausted*):—swiftly {1x}. See: TWOT—885b; BDB—419b.

3289. יָעַץ {80x} yâ'ats, yaw-ats'; a prim. root; to *advise;* refl. to *deliberate* or *resolve:*—counsel {25x}, counsellor {22x}, consult {9x}, give {7x}, purposed {5x}, advice {2x}, determined {2x}, advise {2x}, deviseth {2x}, taken {2x}, advertise {1x}, guide {1x}.

Ya'ats means to advise, counsel, or consult. **I. Ya'ats, as a verb,** means "to advise, counsel, consult." **(1)** Ya'ats is found first in Ex 18:19, where Jethro says to his son-in-law Moses: "I will give thee counsel, and God shall be with thee." **(2)** The word is found only one other time in the Hexateuch, and that is in Num 24:14: "And now, behold, I go unto my people: come *therefore, and* I will advertise thee what this

people shall do to thy people in the latter days."
(3) While *ya'ats* most often describes the "giving of good advice," the opposite is sometimes true. A tragic example was the case of King Ahaziah of Judah, whose mother "was his counselor to do wickedly" (2 Chr 22:3). **(4)** The idea of "decision" is expressed in Is 23:9: "The Lord of hosts hath purposed it."

II. Yo'es, as a noun, means "counselor." Perhaps the most familiar use of this root is the noun form found in the messianic passage, Is 9:6. On the basis of the syntax involved, it is probably best to translate: "Wonderful, Counselor." **III. Ya'as, as a participal,** refers to "those who give counsel, especially in connection with political and military leaders: **(1)** "And Absalom sent for Ahithophel the Gilonite, David's counsellor, from his city, even from Giloh, while he offered sacrifices. And the conspiracy was strong; for the people increased continually with Absalom" (2 Sa 15:12); **(2)** "And David consulted with the captains of thousands and hundreds, *and* with every leader" (1 Chr 13:1). See: TWOT—887; BDB—419c, 1095d.

3290. יַעֲקֹב {349x} **Ya'āqôb,** *yah-ak-obe';* from 6117; *heel*-catcher (i.e. supplanter); *Jaakob,* the Isr. patriarch:—Jacob {349x}. See: BDB—420b, 784d.

3291. יַעֲקֹבָה {1x} **Ya'āqôbâh,** *yah-ak-o'-baw;* from 3290; *Jaakobah,* an Isr.:— Jaakobah {1x}. See: BDB—420b, 785b.

3292. יַעֲקָן {1x} **Ya'āqân,** *yah-ak-awn';* from the same as 6130; *Jaakan,* an Idumæan:—Jaakan {1x}. See: BDB—420c, 785c. comp. 1142.

3293. יַעַר {58x} **ya'ar,** *yah'-ar* from an unused root prob. mean. to *thicken* with verdure; a *copse* of bushes; hence, a *forest;* hence, *honey* in the *comb* (as hived in trees):— [honey-] comb {1x}, forest {37x}, forests {1x}, wood {19x}. See: TWOT—888, 889; BDB—420c, 421a.

3294. יַעֲרָה {2x} **Ya'râh,** *yah-raw';* a form of 3295; *Jarah,* an Isr.:—Jarah {2x}. See: BDB—421a.

3295. יַעֲרָה {2x} **ya'ărâh,** *yah-ar-aw';* fem. of 3293, and mean. the same:— honeycomb + 1706 {1x}, forest {2x}. See: TWOT—889b; BDB—421a.

3296. יַעֲרֵי אֹרְגִים {1x} **Ya'ărêy 'Or°gîym,** *yah-ar-ay' o-reg-eem';* from the plural of 3293 and the masc. plur. act. part. of 707; *woods of weavers; Jaare-Oregim,* an Isr.:—Jaare-oregim {1x}. See: BDB—421a.

3297. יְעָרִים {1x} **Y°ârîym,** *yeh-aw-reem';* plur. of 3293; *forests; Jeärim,* a

place in Pal.:—Jearim {1x}. See: BDB—421b. comp. 7157.

3298. יַעֲרֶשְׁיָה {1x} **Ya'ăreshyâh,** *yah-ar-esh-yaw';* from an unused root of uncert. signif. and 3050; *Jaareshjah,* an Isr.:— Jaresiah {1x}. See: BDB—421b, 793b.

3299. יַעֲשׂוּ {1x} **Ya'ăsûw,** *yah-as-oo';* from 6213; *they will do; Jaasu,* an Isr.:— Jaasau {1x}. See: BDB—421b, 795c.

3300. יַעֲשִׂיאֵל {2x} **Ya'ăsîy°êl,** *yah-as-ee-ale';* from 6213 and 410; *made of God; Jaasiel,* an Isr.:—Jaasiel {1x}, Jasiel {1x}. See: BDB—421b, 795c.

3301. יִפְדְיָה {1x} **Yiphd°yâh,** *yif-deh-yaw';* from 6299 and 3050; *Jah will liberate; Jiphdejah,* an Isr.:—Iphedeiah {1x}. See: BDB—421b.

3302. יָפָה {8x} **yâphâh,** *yaw-faw';* a prim. root; prop. to *be bright,* i.e. (by impl.) *beautiful:*—be beautiful {2x}, fair {3x}, make fair {1x}, fairer {1x}, deck {1x}. See: TWOT—890; BDB—421b.

3303. יָפֶה {41x} **yâpheh,** *yaw-feh';* from 3302; *beautiful* (lit. or fig.):—fair {21x}, beautiful {5x}, well {5x}, fairest {3x}, fair one {2x}, beauty {1x}, beautiful + 8389 {2x}, beauty {1x}, comely {1x}, pleasant {1x}. See: TWOT—890a; 421c.

3304. יְפֵה־פִיָּה {1x} **y°phêh-phîyâh,** *yef-eh' fee-yaw';* from 3302 by redupl.; *very beautiful:*—very fair {1x}. See: TWOT—890b; BDB—421d.

3305. יָפוֹ {4x} **Yâphôw,** *yaw-fo';* or

יָפוֹא **Yâphôw°** (Ezra 3:7), *yaw-fo';* from 3302; *beautiful; Japho,* a place in Pal.:—Japha {1x}, Joppa {3x}. See: BDB—421d.

3306. יָפַח {1x} **yâphach,** *yaw-fakh';* a prim. root; prop. to *breathe* hard, i.e. (by impl.) to *sigh:*—bewail {1x} self. See: TWOT—891; BDB—422a.

3307. יָפֵחַ {1x} **yâphêach,** *yaw-fay'-akh;* from 3306; prop. *puffing,* i.e. (fig.) *meditating:*—such as breathe out {1x}. See: TWOT—891a; BDB—422a.

3308. יְפִי {19x} **y°phîy,** *yof-ee';* from 3302; *beauty:*—beauty {19x}. See: TWOT—890c; BDB—421d.

3309. יָפִיעַ {5x} **Yâphîya°,** *yaw-fee'-ah;* from 3313; *bright; Japhia,* the name of a Canaanite, an Isr., and a place in Pal.:—Japhia {5x}. See: BDB—422b.

3310. יַפְלֵט {1x} **Yaphlêt,** *yaf-late';* from 6403; *he will deliver; Japhlet,* an Isr.:— Japhlet {1x}. See: BDB—422a, 812d.

3311. יַפְלֵטִי {1x} **Yaphlêtîy,** *yaf-lay-tee';* patron. from 3310; a *Japhletite* or desc. of Japhlet:—Japhleti {1x}. See: BDB—812d.

3312. יְפֻנֶּה {16x} **Yᵉphunneh,** *yef-oon-neh';* from 6437; *he will be prepared; Jephunneh,* the name of two Isr.:—Jephunneh {16x}. See: BDB—422a, 819c.

3313. יָפַע {8x} **yâphaʿ,** *yaw-fah';* a prim. root; to *shine:*—be light {1x}, shew self {1x}, shine {4x}, shine forth {2x}. See: TWOT—892; BDB—422a.

3314. יִפְעָה {1x} **yiphʿâh,** *yif-aw';* from 3313; *splendor* or (fig.) *beauty:*—brightness {1x}. See: TWOT—892a; BDB—422b.

3315. יֶפֶת {11x} **Yepheth,** *yeh'-feth;* from 6601; *expansion; Jepheth,* a son of Noah; also his posterity:—Japheth {11x}. See: BDB—422b, 834d.

3316. יִפְתָּח {30x} **Yiphtâch,** *yif-tawkh';* from 6605; *he will open; Jiphtach,* an Isr.; also a place in Pal.:—Jephthah {29x}, Jiphtah {1x}. See: BDB—422b, 836b.

3317. יִפְתַּח־אֵל {2x} **Yiphtach-ʾêl,** *yif-tach-ale';* from 6605 and 410; *God will open; Jiphtach-el,* a place in Pal.:—Jiphthah-el {2x}. See: BDB—422b, 836b.

3318. יָצָא { {1069x} **yâtsâ',** *yaw-tsaw';* a prim. root; to *go* (caus. *bring*) *out,* in a great variety of applications, lit. and fig., direct and proxim.:— . . . . out {518x}, ... forth {411x}, bring {24x}, come {24x}, proceed {16x}, go {13x}, depart {10x}, misc. {53x} = × after, appear, × assuredly, × begotten, + be condemned, in the end, escape, exact, fail, get away (hence,), grow, put away, be risen, × scarce, send with commandment, spread, × still, × surely, at any time, × to [and fro], utter.
  Yatsa' (3318), "to come forth, go out, proceed, go forth, bring out, come out." **(1)** Basically, this word means "movement away" from some point, even as bo' (935 - "come") means movement toward some point. **(2)** *Yatsa'* is the word used of "coming forth"—the observer is outside the point of departure but also speaks from the perspective of that departing point. **(2a)** For example, Gen 2:10 (the first occurrence of the word) reports that a river "came forth" or "flowed out" from the garden of Eden. **(2b)** In comparison to this continuing "going out," there is the one-time (punctiliar) "coming forth," as seen when all the animals "came out" of the ark (Gen 9:10). **(2c)** Thus, Goliath the champion of the Philistines "went forward" from the camp to challenge the Israelites to a duel: "And there went out a champion out of the camp of the Philistines, named Goliath, of

Gath, whose height was six cubits and a span" (1 Sa 17:4). In the art of ancient warfare, a battle was sometimes decided on the basis of two duelers.
  (3) This verb may be used with "come" (935 - bo') **(3a)** as an expression for "constant activity." **(3b)** The raven Noah sent out "went forth to and fro" (literally, "in and out") until the water had abated (Gen 8:7). **(4)** Various aspects of a man's personality may "go forth," indicating that they "leave" him. **(4a)** When one's soul "departs" the body, the person dies: "And it came to pass, as her soul was in departing, (for she died) that she called his name Benoni: but his father called him Benjamin" (Gen 35:18). **(4b)** When one's heart "departs," he loses all inner strength and confidence: "And he said unto his brethren, My money is restored; and, lo, it is even in my sack: and their heart failed them, and they were afraid, saying one to another, What is this that God hath done unto us?" (Gen 42:28).
  (5) *Yatsa'* has a number of special uses. **(5a)** It can be used of "giving birth": If men strive, and hurt a woman with child, so that her fruit depart from her" (Ex 21:22), or **(5b)** of "begetting" descendants: "And I will make thee exceeding fruitful, and I will make nations of thee, and kings shall come out of thee" (Gen 17:6). **(5c)** The "going forth" of a year is its close, as in the harvest season (Ex 23:16). **(5d)** Another special use of this verb has to do with "moving out" a camp for either a military campaign (1 Sa 8:20) or some other purpose (Deut 23:10). **(5e)** "Going and coming" may also be used of "fighting" in wars. **(5f)** Toward the end of his life Moses said he was unable to "come and go" (Deut 31:2; cf. Josh 14:11). He probably meant that he could not engage in war (Deut 31:3). **(5g)** On the other hand, this phrase can refer to the normal activities of life (1 Kin 3:7). **(6)** *Yatsa'* also has a cultic [religious] use, describing the "movement" of the priest in the tabernacle; bells were attached to the hem of the priest's robe so the people could follow his actions (Ex 28:35).
  (7) When applied to God, the action of "going out" only infrequently refers to His "abandoning" a certain location. **(7a)** In Eze 10:18, the glory of the Lord "left" the "threshhold of the [temple], and stood over the cherubim," and eventually departed the temple altogether (Eze 10:19). **(7b)** Often this verb pictures the Lord as "going forth" to aid His people, especially in texts suggesting or depicting His appearances among men (theophanies; cf. Judg 5:4). **(7c)** In Egypt, the Lord "went out" into the midst of the Egyptians to smite their first born (Ex 11:4). **(7d)** The Lord's departure point in such cases is variously represented as Seir

Hebrew

(Judg 5:4) and His heavenly dwelling place (Mic 1:3), although it is often unexpressed. **(8)** The messenger of God also "goes forth" to accomplish specific tasks (Num 22:32). **(9)** God's providential work in history is described by Laban and Bethuel as "the thing proceedeth from the Lord" (Gen 24:50). **(10)** Also, "going out" from the Lord are His hand (Ruth 1:13), His Word (Is 55:11), His salvation (Is 51:5), His justice (Is 45:23), and His wisdom (Is 51:4).

(11) *Yatsa*' is not used of God's initial creative act, but only of His using what already exists to accomplish His purposes, such as His causing water to "come out" of the rock (Deut 8:15). **(12)** Because *yatsa*' can mean "to bring forth," it is often used of "divine deliverance," as the One who "bringeth me forth from mine enemies" (2 Sa 22:49) "into a large place" (2 Sa 22:20). **(13)** One of the most important formulas in the Old Testament uses the verb *yatsa*': "the Lord [who] brought [Israel] out of [Egypt]"; He brought them from slavery into freedom (Ex 13:3). Syn: 4161, 8444. See: TWOT—893; BDB—422b, 1115a.

3319. **יְצָא** {1x} **yᵉtsâ᾽** (Aram.), *yets-aw';* corresp. to 3318:—finish {1x}. See: TWOT—3028; BDB—1096a, 1115a.

3320. **יָצַב** {48x} **yâtsab**, *yaw-tsab';* a prim. root; to *place* (anything so as to stay); refl. to *station, offer, continue:*—stand {24x}, present {9x}, set {6x}, stand still {2x}, stand up {2x}, withstand {1x}, stand fast {1x}, stand forth {1x}, remaining {1x}, resorted {1x}. See: TWOT—894; BDB—426a.

3321. **יְצַב** {1x} **yᵉtsêb** (Aram.), *yets-abe';* corresp. to 3320; to *be firm;* hence, to *speak surely:*—truth {1x}. See: TWOT—2773; BDB—1096a.

3322. **יָצַג** {16x} **yâtsag**, *yaw-tsag';* a prim. root; to *place* permanently:—establish {1x}, leave {1x}, made {2x}, present {1x}, put {2x}, set {8x}, stay {1x}. See: TWOT—895; BDB—426c.

3323. **יִצְהָר** {23x} **yitshâr**, *yits-hawr';* from 6671; *oil* (as producing *light*); fig. *anointing:*—oil {22x}, oil {1x}. Syn.: 8081. See: TWOT—1883c; BDB—426d, 844a.

3324. **יִצְהָר** {9x} **Yitshâr**, *yits-hawr';* the same as 3323; *Jitshar*, an Isr.:—Izhar {8x}, Izehar {1x}. See: BDB—844b.

3325. **יִצְהָרִי** {4x} **Yitshârîy**, *yits-haw-ree';* patron. from 3324; a *Jitsharite* or desc. of Jitshar:—Izeharites {1x}, Izharites {3x}. See: BDB—844b.

3326. **יָצוּעַ** {11x} **yâtsûwaᶜ**, *yaw-tsoo'-ah;* pass. part. of 3331; *spread,* i.e. a *bed;* (arch.) an *extension,* i.e. *wing* or *lean-to* (a sin-

gle story or collect.):—bed {4x}, chamber {6x}, couch {1x}. See: TWOT—896a; BDB—426d, 427a.

3327. **יִצְחָק** {108x} **Yitschâq**, *yits-khawk';* from 6711; *laughter* (i.e. *mockery*); *Jitschak* (or Isaac), son of Abraham:—Isaac {108x}. See: TWOT—1905b; BDB—426d, 850c. Syn.: comp. 3446.

3328. **יִצְחַר** {1x} **Yitschar**, *yits-khar';* from the same as 6713; *he will shine; Jitschar*, an Isr.:—and Zehoar {1x}. See: BDB—426d, 850d.

3329. **יָצִיא** {1x} **yâtsîy᾽**, *yaw-tsee';* from 3318; *issue*, i.e. offspring:—those that came forth {1x}. See: TWOT—893a; BDB—425c.

3330. **יַצִּיב** {5x} **yatstsîyb** (Aram.), *yats-tseeb';* from 3321; *fixed, sure;* concr. *certainty:*—certain {1x}, certainty {1x}, true {2x}, truth {1x}. See: TWOT—2773a; BDB—1096a.

יָצִיעַ **yâtsîyaᶜ**. See 3326.

3331. **יָצַע** {4x} **yâtsaᶜ**, *yaw-tsah';* a prim. root; to *strew* as a surface:—make [one's] bed {1x}, ✕ lie {1x}, spread {2x}. See: TWOT—896; BDB—426d.

3332. **יָצַק** {53x} **yâtsaq**, *yaw-tsak';* a prim. root; prop. to *pour* out (tran. or intr.); by impl. to *melt* or *cast* as metal; by extens. to *place* firmly, to *stiffen* or grow hard:—pour {21x}, cast {11x}, . . . out {7x}, molten {6x}, firm {1x}, set down {1x}, fast {1x}, groweth {1x}, hard {1x}, overflown {1x}, stedfast {1x}.

Yatsaq means "to pour, pour out, cast, flow." **(1)** The word is used first in **(1a)** Gen 28:18, where it is said that after Jacob had slept at Bethel with his head resting on a stone, he "poured oil upon the top of it." **(1b)** He again "poured" oil on a stone pillar at Bethel while on his return trip home twenty years later (Gen 35:14). **(1c)** The idea expressed in these two instances and others (Lev 8:12; 21:10) is that of anointing with oil; **(1c1)** it is not the ordinary term for "to anoint." **(1c2)** The regular term for "to anoint" is mashach (4886), which gives us the word "messiah." **(2)** Many things may "be poured out," such as **(2a)** oil in sacrifice: "And when any will offer a meat offering unto the LORD, his offering shall be of fine flour; and he shall pour oil upon it, and put frankincense thereon" (Lev 2:1), **(2b)** water for washing purposes: "But Jehoshaphat said, Is there not here a prophet of the LORD, that we may enquire of the LORD by him? And one of the king of Israel's servants answered and said, Here is Elisha the son of Shaphat, which poured water on the hands of Elijah" (2 Kin 3:11), and **(2c)** pottage for eating: "But he said, Then

bring meal. And he cast it into the pot; and he said, Pour out for the people, that they may eat. And there was no harm in the pot" (2 Kin 4:41). **(3)** This verb is used to express the idea of "pouring out" or "casting" molten metals (Ex 25:12; 26:37; 1 Kin 7:46). **(4)** The idea of "pouring upon or infusing" someone is found in Ps 41:8: "An evil disease, say they, cleaveth fast unto him: and *now* that he lieth he shall rise up no more." The context seems to imply the infusion of a sickness. Syn.: 8210. See: TWOT—897; BDB—427a.

3333. יְצֻקָה {1x} yᵉtsûqâh, *yets-oo-kaw′;* pass. part. fem. of 3332; *poured* out, i.e. *run* into a mould:—when it was cast {1x}. See: TWOT—897a; BDB—427c.

3334. יָצַר {9x} yâtsar, *yaw-tsar′;* a prim. root; to *press* (intr.), i.e. *be narrow;* fig. *be in distress:*—be distressed {4x}, be narrow {1x}, be straitened (in straits) {2x}, be vexed {1x}. See: TWOT—1973; BDB—864c.

3335. יָצַר {62x} yâtsar, *yaw-tsar′;* prob. ident. with 3334 (through the *squeezing* into shape); ([comp. 3331]); to *mould* into a form; espec. as a *potter;* fig. to *determine* (i.e. form a resolution):—form {26x}, potter {17x}, fashion {5x}, maker {4x}, frame {3x}, make {3x}, former {2x}, earthen {1x}, purposed {1x}.

Yatsar means "to form, mold, fashion." **(1)** The first occurrence in the Old Testament is in Gen 2:7: "God formed man of the dust of the ground," reflecting the basic meaning of "molding" something to a desired shape. **(2)** *Yatsar* is a technical potter's word, and it is often used in connection with the potter at work (Is 29:16; Jer 18:4, 6). **(3)** The word is sometimes used as a general term of "craftsmanship or handiwork," whether molding, carving, or casting (Is 44:9–10, 12). **(3)** The word may be used to express the "Shall the throne of iniquity have fellowship with thee, which frameth mischief by a law?" (Ps 94:20). **(4)** *Yatsar* is frequently used to describe God's creative activity, whether literally or figuratively. **(4a)** Thus, God "formed" not only man (Gen 2:7–8) but **(4b)** the animals (Gen 2:19). **(4c)** God also "formed" the nation of Israel (Is 27:11; 45:9, 11); **(4d)** Israel was "formed" as God's special servant even from the womb (Is 44:2, 24; 49:5). **(4e)** While yet in the womb, Jeremiah was "formed" to be a prophet: "Before I formed thee in the belly I knew thee; and before thou camest forth out of the womb I sanctified thee, and I ordained thee a prophet unto the nations" (Jer 1:5).

(5) God "formed" **(5a)** locusts as a special visual lesson for Amos (Amos 7:1); **(5b)** the great sea monster, Leviathan, was "formed" to play in the seas (Ps 104:26). **(6)** The concreteness of ancient Hebrew thinking is vividly seen in a statement such as this: "I form the light, and create darkness" (Is 45:7). **(7)** Similarly, the psalmist confessed to God: "Thou hast made summer and winter" (Ps 74:17). **(8)** God "formed" **(8a)** the spirit of man (Zec 12:1), as well as **(8b)** the heart or mind of man (Ps 33:15). **(9)** *Yatsar* is used to express God's "planning" or "preordaining" according to His divine purpose (Is 22:11; 46:11). **(10)** Almost one half of the uses of this word in the Old Testament are found in the Book of Isaiah, with God as the subject of most of them. See: TWOT—898; BDB—427c, 849b.

3336. יֵצֶר {9x} yêtser, *yay′-tser;* from 3335; a *form;* fig. *conception* (i.e. *purpose*):—frame {1x}, thing framed {1x}, imagination {5x}, mind {1x}, work {1x}. See: TWOT—898a; BDB—428a.

3337. יֵצֶר {3x} Yêtser, *yay-tser;* the same as 3336; *Jetser,* an Isr.:—Jezer {3x}. See: BDB—428a.

3338. יָצֻר {1x} yâtsûr, *yaw-tsoor′;* pass. part. of 3335; *structure,* i.e. limb or part:—member {1x}. See: TWOT—898b; BDB—428b.

3339. יִצְרִי {1x} Yitsrîy, *yits-ree′;* from 3335; *formative; Jitsri,* an Isr.:—Isri {1x}. See: BDB—428b.

3340. יִצְרִי {1x} Yitsrîy, *yits-ree′;* patron. from 3337; a *Jitsrite* (collect.) or desc. of Jetser:—Jezerites {1x}. See: BDB—428a.

3341. יָצַת {29x} yâtsath, *yaw-tsath′;* a prim. root; to *burn* or *set on fire;* fig. to *desolate:*—burned {7x}, burn up {2x}, be desolate {1x}, set on fire {7x}, kindle {12x}. See: TWOT—899; BDB—428b, 850a.

3342. יֶקֶב {16x} yeqeb, *yeh′-keb;* from an unused root mean. to *excavate;* a *trough* (as dug out); spec. a wine-*vat* (whether the lower one, into which the juice drains; or the upper, in which the grapes are crushed):—winepresses {10x}, press {2x}, fats {2x}, pressfat {1x}, wine {1x}. See: TWOT—900a; BDB—428c.

3343. יְקַבְצְאֵל {1x} Yᵉqabtsᵉêl, *yek-ab-tseh-ale′;* from 6908 and 410; *God will gather; Jekabtseël,* a place in Pal.:—Jekabzeel {1x}. See: BDB—428c, 868b. comp. 6909.

3344. יָקַד {9x} yâqad, *yaw-kad′;* a prim. root; to *burn:*—(be) burn (-ing) {7x}, ✕ from the hearth {1x}, kindle {1x}. See: TWOT—901; BDB—428d, 1096a.

3345. יְקַד {8x} yᵉqad (Aram.), *yek-ad′;* corresp. to 3344:—burning {8x}. See: TWOT—2774; BDB—1096a.

3346. קְדָא {1x} yᵉqêdâᵓ (Aram.), yek-ay-daw'; from 3345; a conflagration:—burning {1x}. See: TWOT—2774a; BDB—1096a.

3347. יָקְדְעָם {1x} Yoqdᵉᶜâm, yok-deh-awm'; from 3344 and 5971; burning of (the) people; Jokdeäm, a place in Pal.:—Jokdeam {1x}. See: BDB—429a.

3348. יָקֶה {1x} Yâqeh, yaw-keh'; from an unused root prob. mean. to obey; obedient; Jakeh, a symb. name (for Solomon):—Jakeh {1x}. See: BDB—429a.

3349. יִקָּהָה {2x} yiqqâhâh, yik-kaw-haw'; from the same as 3348; obedience:—gathering {1x}, to obey {1x}. Syn.: 8085. See: TWOT—902a; BDB—429b.

3350. יְקוֹד {1x} yᵉqôwd, yek-ode'; from 3344; a burning:—burning {1x}. See: TWOT—901a; BDB—428d.

3351. יְקוּם {3x} yᵉqûwm, yek-oom'; from 6965; prop. standing (extant), i.e. by impl. a living thing:—living substance {2x}, substance {1x}. See: TWOT—1999f; BDB—429b, 879c.

3352. יָקוֹשׁ {1x} yâqôwsh, yaw-koshe'; from 3369; prop. entangling; hence, a snarer:—fowler {1x}. See: TWOT—906a; BDB—430c.

3353. יָקוּשׁ {3x} yâqûwsh, yaw-koosh'; pass. part. of 3369; prop. entangled, i.e. by impl. (intr.) a snare, or (tran.) a snarer:—fowler {2x}, snare {1x}. See: TWOT—906b; BDB—430c.

3354. יְקוּתִיאֵל {1x} Yᵉqûwthîyᵓêl, yek-ooth-ee'-ale; from the same as 3348 and 410; obedience of God; Jekuthiël, an Isr.:—Jekuthiel {1x}. See: BDB—429a, 429b.

3355. יָקְטָן {6x} Yoqtân, yok-tawn'; from 6994; he will be made little; Joktan, an Arabian patriarch:—Joktan {6x}. See: BDB—429b.

3356. יָקִים {2x} Yâqîym, yaw-keem'; from 6965; he will raise; Jakim, the name of two Isr.:—Jakim {2x}. See: BDB—879c. Syn.: comp. 3079.

3357. יַקִּיר {1x} yaqqîyr, yak-keer'; from 3365; precious:—dear {1x}. See: TWOT—905c; BDB—430b.

3358. יַקִּיר {2x} yaqqîyr (Aram.), yak-keer'; corresp. to 3357:—noble {1x}, rare {1x}. See: TWOT—2775a; BDB—1096a.

3359. יְקַמְיָה {3x} Yᵉqamyâh, yek-am-yaw'; from 6965 and 3050; Jah will rise; Jekamjah, the name of two Isr.:—Jekamiah {2x}, Jecamiah {1x}. See: BDB—429b, 880c. comp. 3079.

3360. יְקָמְעָם {2x} Yᵉqamᶜâm, yek-am'-awm; from 6965 and 5971; (the) people will rise; Jekamam, an Isr.:—Jekameam {2x}. See: BDB—429b, 880c. comp. 3079, 3361.

3361. יָקְמְעָם {2x} Yoqmᵉᶜâm, yok-meh-awm'; from 6965 and 5971; (the) people will be raised; Jokmeäm, a place in Pal.:—Jokmeam {2x}. See: BDB—429b, 880c. comp. 3360, 3362.

3362. יָקְנְעָם {3x} Yoqnᵉᶜâm, yok-neh-awm'; from 6969 and 5971; (the) people will be lamented; Jokneäm, a place in Pal.:—Jokneam {3x}. See: BDB—429b.

3363. יָקַע {8x} yâqaᶜ, yaw-kah'; a prim. root; prop. to sever oneself, i.e. (by impl.) to be dislocated; fig. to abandon; caus. to impale (and thus allow to drop to pieces by rotting):—be alienated {2x}, depart {1x}, hang (up) {4x}, be out of joint {1x}. See: TWOT—903; BDB—429b.

3364. יָקַץ {11x} yâqats, yaw-kats'; a prim. root; to awake (intr.):—(be) awake (-d) {11x}. See: TWOT—904; BDB—429c.

יָקַף yâqaph. See 5362.

3365. יָקַר {11x} yâqar, yaw-kar'; a prim. root; prop. appar. to be heavy, i.e. (fig.) valuable; caus. to make rare (fig. to inhibit):—be (make) precious {8x}, be prized {1x}, be set by {1x}, withdraw {1x}.

Yaqar, as a verb, means "to be difficult, be valued from, be valued or honored, be precious." The word means "to be precious" in 1 Sa 26:21: "Then said Saul, I have sinned: return, my son David: for I will no more do thee harm, because my soul was precious in thine eyes this day." See: TWOT—905; BDB—429, 429c.

3366. יְקָר {17x} yᵉqâr, yek-awr'; from 3365; value, i.e. (concr.) wealth; abstr. costliness, dignity:—honour {12x}, precious {1x}, precious things {3x}, price {1x}.

Yeqar means precious thing; value; price; splendor; honor. Yeqar, as a noun, means "precious thing; value; price; splendor; honor." (1) The word signifies (1a) "value or price": "And the LORD said unto me, Cast it unto the potter: a goodly price that I was prised at of them. And I took the thirty pieces of silver, and cast them to the potter in the house of the LORD" (Zec 11:13), (1b) "splendor": "When he shewed the riches of his glorious kingdom and the honour of his excellent majesty many days, even an hundred and fourscore days" (Est 1:4), and (1c) "honor": "The Jews had light, and gladness, and joy, and honour" (Est 8:16). (2) In Jer 20:5 the word refers to "precious things": "Moreover I will deliver all the strength of this

city, and all the labors thereof, and all the precious things thereof." See: TWOT—905b; BDB—430b, 1096a.

3367. יְקָר {7x} yᵉqâr (Aram.), yek-awr'; corresp. to 3366:—glory {5x}, honour {2x}. See: TWOT—2775a; BDB—1096a.

3368. יְקָר {36x} yâqâr, yaw-kawr'; from 3365; valuable (obj. or subj.):—precious {25x}, costly {4x} excellent {2x}, brightness {1x}, clear {1x}, fat {1x}, reputation {1x}, honourable women {1x}.

Yaqar, as an adjective means "precious; rare; excellent; weighty; noble." (1) First, yaqar means "precious" in the sense of being rare and valuable: "And he took their king's crown from off his head, the weight whereof was a talent of gold with the precious stones: and it was set on David's head" (2 Sa 12:30). (2) The emphasis is on the nuance "rare" in 1 Sa 3:1: "And the word of the Lord was precious in those days; there was no open vision." (3) The word can focus on the value of a thing: "How excellent is thy loving-kindness, O God!" (Ps 36:7). (4) This word means "weighty" or "noble": "Dead flies cause the ointment of the apothecary to send forth a stinking savour: so doth a little folly him that is in reputation for wisdom and honour" (Eccl 10:1); like dead flies which make perfume stink, so a little foolishness spoils wisdom and honor—it is worth more in a negative sense (cf. Lam 4:2). See: TWOT—905a; BDB—429d, 891b, 903b.

3369. יָקֹשׁ {8x} yâqôsh, yaw-koshe'; a prim. root; to ensnare (lit. or fig.):—snare {5x}, lay a snare {1x}, laid {1x}, fowlers {1x}. See: TWOT—906; BDB—430b.

3370. יָקְשָׁן {4x} Yoqshân, yok-shawn'; from 3369; insidious; Jokshan, an Arabian patriarch:—Jokshan {4x}. See: BDB—430d.

3371. יָקְתְאֵל {2x} Yoqthᵉêl, yok-theh-ale'; prob. from the same as 3348 and 410; veneration of God [comp. 3354]; Joktheel, the name of a place in Pal., and of one in Idumæa:—Joktheel {2x}. See: BDB—430d.

יָרָא yârâ'. See 3384.

3372. יָרֵא {341x} yârê', yaw-ray'; a prim. root; to fear; mor. to revere; caus. to frighten:—fear {188x}, afraid {78x}, terrible {23x}, terrible thing {6x}, dreadful {5x}, reverence {3x}, fearful {2x}, terrible acts {1x}, misc. {8x}.

Yare' means "to be afraid, stand in awe, fear." (1) Basically, this verb connotes the psychological reaction of "fear." (1a) Yare' may indicate being afraid of something or someone. (1b) Jacob prayed: "Deliver me, I pray thee,

from the hand of my brother, from the hand of Esau: for I fear him, lest he will come and smite me, and the mother with the children" (Gen 32:11). (2) Used of a person in an exalted position, yare' connotes "standing in awe." (2a) This is not simple fear, but reverence, whereby an individual recognizes the power and position of the individual revered and renders him proper respect. (2b) In this sense, the word may imply submission to a proper ethical relationship to God; (2c) the angel of the Lord told Abraham: "I know that thou fearest God, seeing thou hast not withheld thy son, thine only son from me" (Gen 22:12). (3) The verb can be used absolutely to refer to the heavenly and holy attributes of something or someone. So Jacob said of Bethel: "How [awesome] is this place! this is none other but the house of God, and this is the gate of heaven" (Gen 28:17).

(4) The people who were delivered from Egypt saw God's great power, "feared the Lord, and believed the Lord, and his servant Moses" (Ex 14:31). (5) There is more involved here than mere psychological fear. (5a) The people also showed proper "honor" ("reverence") for God and "stood in awe of" Him and of His servant, as their song demonstrates (Ex 15). (5b) After experiencing the thunder, lightning flashes, sound of the trumpet, and smoking mountain, they were "afraid" and drew back; but Moses told them not to be afraid, "for God is come to prove you, and that his fear may be before your faces, that ye sin not" (Ex 20:20). (5c) In this passage, the word represents "fear" or "dread" of the Lord. (5d) This sense is also found when God says, "fear not" (Gen 15:1).

(6) Yare' can be used absolutely (with no direct object), meaning "to be afraid." Adam told God: "I was afraid, because I was naked; and I hid myself" (Gen 3:10—the first occurrence). (7) One may be "afraid" to do something, as when Lot "feared to dwell in Zoar" (Gen 19:30). See: TWOT—907, 908; BDB—431a, 1108c.

3373. יָרֵא {64x} yârê', yaw-ray'; from 3372; fearing; mor. reverent:—afraid {3x}, fear {59x}, fearful {2x}. See: TWOT—907a; BDB—431a, 531d.

3374. יִרְאָה {45x} yir'âh, yir-aw'; fem. of 3373; fear (also used as infin.); mor. reverence:—fear {41x}, exceedingly + 1419 {2x}, dreadful {1x}, fearfulness {1x}.

Yir'ah means "fear; reverence." (1) It may mean "fear" of men: "This day will I begin to put the dread of thee and the fear of thee upon the nations that are under the whole heaven, who shall hear report of thee, and shall tremble, and be in anguish because of thee" (Deut

Hebrew

2:25), **(2)** of things: "And on all hills that shall be digged with the mattock, there shall not come thither the fear of briers and thorns: but it shall be for the sending forth of oxen, and for the treading of lesser cattle" (Is 7:25), **(3)** of situations: "Then were the men exceedingly afraid, and said unto him, Why hast thou done this? For the men knew that he fled from the presence of the LORD, because he had told them" (Jonah 1:10), and **(4)** of God: "And he said unto them, Take me up, and cast me forth into the sea; so shall the sea be calm unto you: for I know that for my sake this great tempest *is* upon you" (Jonah 1:12); **(5)** it may also mean "reverence" of God: "And Abraham said, Because I thought, Surely the fear of God *is* not in this place; and they will slay me for my wife's sake" (Gen 20:11). See: TWOT—907b; BDB—432a.

3375. יִרְאוֹן {1x} **Yirʾôwn**, *yir-ohn'*; from 3372; *fearfulness; Jiron*, a place in Pal:— Iron {1x}. See: BDB—432a.

3376. יִרְאִיָּה {2x} **Yirʾîyâyh**, *yir-ee-yaw'*; from 3373 and 3050; *fearful of Jah; Jirijah*, an Isr.:—Irijah {2x}. See: BDB—432c, 909d.

3377. יָרֵב {1x} **Yârêb**, *yaw-rabe'*; from 7378; *he will contend; Jareb*, a symb. name for Assyria:—Jareb {1x} See: BDB—432c, 937a. comp. 3402.

3378. יְרֻבַּעַל {14x} **Yᵉrubbaʿal**, *yer-oob-bah'-al*; from 7378 and 1168; *Baal will contend; Jerubbaal*, a symbol. name of Gideon:—Jerubbaal {14x}. See: BDB—432c, 937c.

3379. יָרָבְעָם {104x} **Yârobʿâm**, *yaw-rob-awm'*; from 7378 and 5971; (the) *people will contend; Jarobam*, the name of two Isr. kings:—Jeroboam {104x}. See: BDB—432c, 914c, 937c.

3380. יְרֻבֶּשֶׁת {1x} **Yᵉrubbesheth**, *yer-oob-beh'-sheth;* from 7378 and 1322; *shame* (i.e. the idol) *will contend; Jerubbesheth*, a symbol. name for Gideon:—Jerubbesheth {1x}. See: BDB—432c, 937c.

3381. יָרַד {380x} **yârad**, *yaw-rad'*; a prim. root; to *descend* (lit. to *go downwards;* or conventionally to a lower region, as the shore, a boundary, the enemy, etc.; or fig. to *fall*); caus. to *bring down* (in all the above applications):—(come, go, etc) down {340x}, descend {18x}, variant {2x}, fell {2x}, let {1x}, abundantly {1x}, down by {1x}, indeed {1x}, put off {1x}, light off {1x}, out {1x}, sank {1x}, subdued {1x}, take {1x}.

Yarad means "to descend, go down, come down." **(1)** Basically, this verb connotes "move-

ment" from a higher to a lower location. **(1a)** In Gen 28:12, Jacob saw a "ladder set up on the earth, and the top of it reached to heaven: and behold the angels of God ascending and descending on it." **(1b)** In such a use, the speaker or observer speaks from the point of destination, and the movement is "downward" toward him. **(1c)** Thus one may "go down" below or under the ground's surface: "And the damsel *was* very fair to look upon, a virgin, neither had any man known her: and she went down to the well, and filled her pitcher, and came up" (Gen 24:16). **(1d)** The speaker may also speak as though he stands at the point of departure and the movement is away from him and "downward."

(1d1) Interestingly, one may "go down" to a lower spot in order to reach a city's gates (Judg 5:11) or **(1d2)** to get to a city located on a lower level than the access road (1 Sa 10:8)—**(1d3)** usually one goes up to a city and "goes down" to leave a city (1 Sa 9:27). **(1d4)** The journey from Palestine to Egypt is referred to as "going down" (Gen 12:10). This reference is not to a movement in space from a higher to a lower spot; it is a more technical use of the verb.

(2) *Yarad* is used frequently of "dying." **(2a)** One "goes down" to his grave. Here the idea of spatial movement is present, but in the background. **(2b)** This "going down" is much more of a removal from the world of conscious existence: For the grave cannot praise thee, death cannot celebrate thee: they that go down into the pit cannot hope for thy truth. The living, the living, he shall praise thee . . ." (Is 38:18–19). **(2c)** On the other hand, "going down to the dust" implies a return to the soil—i.e., a return of the body to the soil from which it came (Gen 3:19). "All they that go down to the dust shall bow before him" (Ps 22:29). **(2d)** There is also the idea of the "descent" of the human soul into the realm of the dead. When Jacob mourned over Joseph whom he thought to be dead, he said: "For I will go down into the grave unto my son mourning" (Gen 37:35). **(2e)** Since one can "descend" into Sheol alive as a form of punishment (Num 16:30), this phrase means more than the end of human life. **(2f)** This meaning is further established because Enoch was rewarded by being taken off the earth: "And Enoch walked with God: and he was not; for God took him" (Gen 5:24); he was rewarded by not having "to descend" into Sheol.

(3) *Yarad* may also be used of "coming down," when the emphasis is on "moving downward" toward the speaker: "And the Lord came down to see the city and the tower" of Babel (Gen 11:5—the first biblical occurrence). **(4)** This verb may also be used to express coming down

from the top of a mountain, as Moses did when he "descended" from Sinai (Ex 19:14). **(5)** The word may be used of "dismounting" from a donkey: "And when Abigail saw David, she hasted, and lighted off the ass" (1 Sa 25:23). Abigail's entire body was not necessarily lower than before, so movement from a higher to a lower location is not indicated. However, she was no longer on the animal's back. So the verb here indicates "getting off" rather than getting down or descending. **(6)** In a somewhat related nuance, one may "get out" of bed. Elijah told Ahaziah: "Thou shalt not come down from that bed on which thou art gone up . . ." (2 Kin 1:4). Again, the idea is not of descending from something. When one comes down from a bed, he stands up; he is higher than he was while yet in the bed. Therefore, the meaning here is "get out of" rather than "descend."

(7) This verb is used also to describe what a beard does—it "hangs down" (Ps 133:2). **(8)** *Yarad* is used to indicate "coming away from" the altar: "And Aaron lifted up his hand toward the people, and blessed them, and came down from offering of the sin offering" (Lev 9:22). This special use is best seen as the opposite of "ascending to" the altar, which is not just a physical movement from a lower to a higher plane but a spiritual ascent to a higher realm of reality. **(9)** For example, to "ascend" before a king is to go into the presence of someone who is on a higher social level. **(9a)** "To ascend" before God (represented by the altar) is to go before Someone on a higher spiritual plane. **(9b)** To stand before God is to stand in His presence before His throne, on a higher spiritual plane. **(10)** *Yarad* may thus be used of the humbled approach before God. God tells Moses that all the Egyptians shall "come down" to Him and bow themselves before Him (Ex 11:8). **(11)** Equally interesting is the occasional use of the verb to represent "descending" to a known sanctuary (cf. 2 Kings 2:2).

(12) Figuratively, the verb has many uses. **(12a)** The "going down" of a city is its destruction (Deut 20:20). **(12b)** When a day "descends," it comes to an end (Judg 19:11). **(12c)** The "descent" of a shadow is its lengthening (2 Kin 20:11). **(12d)** Tears "flow down" the cheeks when one weeps bitterly (Jer 13:17). **(13)** *Yarad* is also used figuratively of a "descent in social position": "The stranger that is within thee shall get up above thee very high; and thou shalt come down very low" (Deut 28:43). **(14)** At least once the word means "to go up." Jephthah's daughter said: "Let me alone two months, that I may go up and down upon the mountains, and bewail my virginity" (Judg 11:37). See: TWOT—909; BDB—432c.

3382. יֶרֶד {7x} **Yered,** *yeh'-red;* from 3381; a *descent; Jered,* the name of an antediluvian, and of an Isr.:—Jared {2x}, Jarad {5x}. See: BDB—434b.

3383. יַרְדֵּן {182x} **Yardên,** *yar-dane';* from 3381; a *descender; Jarden,* the principal river of Pal.:—Jordan {182x}. See: BDB—434c.

3384. יָרָה {84x} **yârâh,** *yaw-raw';* or (2 Chron. 26:15)

יָרָא {84x} **yârâ',** *yaw-raw';* a prim. root; prop. to *flow* as water (i.e. to *rain*); tran. to *lay* or *throw* (espec. an arrow, i.e. to *shoot*); fig. to *point* out (as if by *aiming* the finger), to *teach:*—teach {42x}, shoot {18x}, archers {5x}, cast {5x}, teacher {4x}, rain {2x}, laid {1x}, direct {1x}, inform {1x}, instructed {1x}, shewed {1x}, shooters {1x}, through {1x}, watered {1x}.

Yarah means to throw, cast (Gen 31:51), direct, teach (1 Sa 12:23), instruct, point out. *Yara'* means to cast, throw, teach, shoot, point out. **(1)** The basic meaning to cast is **(1a)** expressed in casting lots (Josh 18:6), by **(1b)** Pharaoh's army being cast into the sea (Ex 15:4), and **(1c)** a pillar cast: "And Laban said to Jacob, Behold this heap, and behold this pillar, which I have cast betwixt me and thee" (Gen 31:51). **(2)** The idea of "to throw" is easily extended to mean **(2a)** the shooting of arrows (1 Sa 20:36–37); and **(2b)** "to throw" seems to be further extended to mean "to point," by which fingers are thrown in a certain direction (Gen 46:28; Prov. 6:13). **(3)** From this it is easy to see the concept of teaching as the "pointing out" of fact and truth. **(3a)** Thus, Bezaleel was inspired by God "to teach" others his craftsmanship: "And he hath put in his heart that he may teach, both he, and Aholiab, the son of Ahisamach, of the tribe of Dan" (Ex 35:34); **(3b)** the false prophets "teach" lies: "The ancient and honourable, he *is* the head; and the prophet that teacheth lies, he is the tail" (Is 9:15); and **(3c)** the father "taught" his son (Prov 4:4). **(4)** *Yarah* means "to teach" in 1 Sa 12:23: ". . . but I will teach you the good and the right way." **(5)** It was the responsibility of the priests to interpret and "to teach" those things that had to do with ceremonial requirements and God's judgments: "They shall teach Jacob thy judgments, and Israel thy law" (Deut 33:10; cf. Deut 17:10–11). Interestingly, priests at a later time were said "to teach" for hire, presumably "to teach" what was wanted rather than true interpretation of God's word (Mic 3:11). **(6)** The noun torah (8451) is derived from this root. Syn: 8451. See: TWOT—910; BDB—432b, 434d.

Hebrew

3385. יְרוּאֵל {1x} **Yᵉrûwᵃêl**, *yer-oo-ale';* from 3384 and 410; *founded of God; Jeruel,* a place in Pal.:—Jeruel {1x}. See: BDB—436c.

3386. יְרוֹחַ {1x} **Yârôwach**, *yaw-ro'-akh;* perh. denom. from 3394; (born at the) new *moon; Jaroäch,* an Isr.:—Jaroah {1x}. See: BDB—437b.

3387. יָרוֹק {1x} **yârôwq**, *yaw-roke';* from 3417; *green,* i.e. an herb:—green thing {1x}. See: TWOT—918c; BDB—438d.

3388. יְרוּשָׁא {2x} **Yᵉrûwshâ'**, *yer-oo-shaw';* or

יְרוּשָׁה **Yᵉrûwshâh**, *yer-oo-shaw';* fem. pass. part. of 3423; *possessed; Jerusha* or *Jerushah,* an Israelitess:—Jerusha {1x}, Jerushah {1x}. See: BDB—440b.

3389. יְרוּשָׁלַםִ {643x} **Yᵉrûwshâlaim**, *yer-oo-shaw-lah'-im;* rarely

יְרוּשָׁלַיִם **Yᵉrûwshâlayim**, *yer-oo-shaw-lah'-yim;* a dual (in allusion to its two main hills [the true pointing, at least of the former reading, seems to be that of 3390]); prob. from (the pass. part. of) 3384 and 7999; *founded peaceful; Jerushalâm* or *Jerushalem,* the capital city of Pal.:—Jerusalem {643x}. See: BDB—436c, 1096b.

3390. יְרוּשְׁלֵם {26x} **Yᵉrûwshâlêm** (Aram.), *yer-oo-shaw-lame';* corresp. to 3389:—Jerusalem {26x}. See: BDB—1096b.

3391. יֶרַח {13x} **yerach**, *yeh'-rakh;* from an unused root of uncert. signif.; a *lunation,* i.e. *month:*—month {11x}, moon {2x}. See: TWOT—913b; BDB—437b, 1096b.

3392. יֶרַח {2x} **Yerach**, *yeh'-rakh;* the same as 3391; *Jerach,* an Arabian patriarch:—Jerah {2x}. See: BDB—437b.

3393. יְרַח {1x} **yᵉrach** (Aram.), *yeh-rakh';* corresp. to 3391; a *month:*—month {1x}. See: BDB—1096b.

3394. יָרֵחַ {26x} **yârêach**, *yaw-ray'-akh;* from the same as 3391; the *moon:*—moon {26x}. See: TWOT—913a; BDB—437a.

יְרֵחוֹ **Yᵉrêchôw**. See 3405.

3395. יְרֹחָם {10x} **Yᵉrôchâm**, *yer-o-khawm';* from 7355; *compassionate; Jerocham,* the name of seven or eight Isr.:—Jeroham {10x}. See: BDB—437b, 934a.

3396. יְרַחְמְאֵל {8x} **Yᵉrachmᵉ'êl**, *yer-akh-meh-ale';* from 7355 and 410; *God will compassionate; Jerachmeël,* the name of three Isr.:—Jerahmeel {8x}. See: BDB—437b, 934a.

3397. יְרַחְמְאֵלִי {2x} **Yᵉrachmᵉêlîy**, *yer-akh-meh-ay-lee';* patron. from

3396; a *Jerachmeëlite* or desc. of Jerachmeel:—Jerahmeelites {2x}. See: BDB—934a.

3398. יַרְחָע {2x} **Yarchâᶜ**, *yar-khaw';* prob. of Eg. or.; *Jarcha,* an Eg.:—Jarha {2x}. See: BDB—437c.

3399. יָרַט {2x} **yârat**, *yaw-rat';* a prim. root; to *precipitate* or *hurl* (*rush*) headlong; (intr.) to *be rash:*—be perverse {1x}, turn over {1x}. See: TWOT—914; BDB—437c, 936a.

3400. יְרִיאֵל {1x} **Yᵉrîyᵃêl**, *yer-ee-ale';* from 3384 and 410; *thrown of God; Jeriël,* an Isr.:—Jeriel {1x}. See: BDB—436c. comp. 3385.

3401. יָרִיב {3x} **yârîyb**, *yaw-rebe';* from 7378; lit. *he will contend;* prop. adj. *contentious;* used as noun, an *adversary:*—that content (-eth) {2x}, that strive {1x}. See: TWOT—2159b; BDB—937a.

3402. יָרִיב {3x} **Yârîyb**, *yaw-rebe';* the same as 3401; *Jarib,* the name of three Isr.:—Jarib {3x}. See: BDB—937b.

3403. יְרִיבַי {1x} **Yᵉrîybay**, *yer-eeb-ah'ee;* from 3401; *contentious; Jeribai,* an Isr.:—Jeribai {1x}. See: BDB—937a, 937b.

3404. יְרִיָּה {3x} **Yᵉrîyâh**, *yer-ee-yaw';* or

יְרִיָּהוּ **Yᵉrîyâhûw**, *yer-ee-yaw'-hoo;* from 3384 and 3050; *Jah will throw; Jerijah,* an Isr.:—Jeriah {1x}, Jerijah {2x}. See: BDB—436c.

3405. יְרִיחוֹ {57x} **Yᵉrîychôw**, *yer-ee-kho';* or

יְרֵחוֹ **Yᵉrêchôw**, *yer-ay-kho';* or var. (1 Kin 16:34)

יְרִיחֹה **Yᵉrîychôh**, *yer-ee-kho';* perh. from 3394; *its month;* or else from 7306; *fragrant; Jericho* or *Jerecho,* a place in Pal.:—Jericho {57x}. See: BDB—437b, 437c, 746d.

3406. יְרִימוֹת {13x} **Yᵉrîymôwth**, *yer-ee-mohth';* or

יְרֵימוֹת **Yᵉrêymôwth**, *yer-ay-mohth';* or

יְרֵמוֹת **Yᵉrêmôwth**, *yer-ay-mohth';* fem. plur. from 7311; *elevations; Jerimoth* or *Jeremoth,* the name of twelve Isr.:—Jeremoth {5x}, Jerimoth {8x}. See: BDB—438b, 928c.

3407. יְרִיעָה {1x} **yᵉrîyᶜâh**, *yer-ee-aw';* from 3415; a *hanging* (as *tremulous*):—curtain {1x}. See: TWOT—917a; BDB—438c.

3408. יְרִיעוֹת {1x} **Yᵉrîyᶜôwth**, *yer-ee-ohth';* plur. of 3407; *curtains; Jerioth,* an Israelitess:—Jerioth {1x}. See: BDB—438c.

3409. יָרֵךְ {34x} **yârêk**, *yaw-rake';* from an unused root mean. to *be soft;* the

thigh (from its fleshy *softness*); by euphem. the *generative parts;* fig. a *shank, flank, side:*—✕ body {1x}, loins {2x}, shaft {3x}, side {7x}, thigh {21x}. See: TWOT—916a; BDB—437d, 1096b.

3410. יַרְכָא {1x} **yarkâ᾽** (Aram.), *yar-kaw';* corresp. to 3411; a *thigh:*—thigh {1x}. See: TWOT—2777; BDB—1096b.

3411. יְרֵכָה {28x} **yᵉrêkâh**, *yer-ay-kaw';* fem. of 3409; prop. the *flank;* but used only fig., the *rear* or *recess:*—border {1x}, coasts {3x}, parts {2x}, quarter {1x}, side {21x}. See: TWOT—916b; BDB—438a.

3412. יַרְמוּת {7x} **Yarmûwth**, *yar-mooth';* from 7311; *elevation; Jarmuth,* the name of two places in Pal.:—Jarmuth {1x}. See: BDB—438b.

יְרֵמוֹת **Yᵉrêmôwth**. See 3406.

3413. יְרֵמַי {1x} **Yᵉrêmay**, *yer-ay-mah'-ee* from 7311; *elevated; Jeremai,* an Isr.:—Jeremai {1x}. See: BDB—438b.

3414. יִרְמְיָה {147x} **Yirmᵉyâh**, *yir-meh-yaw';* or

יִרְמְיָהוּ **Yirmᵉyâhûw**, *yir-meh-yaw'-hoo;* from 7311 and 3050; *Jah will rise; Jirmejah,* the name of eight or nine Isr.:—Jeremiah {147x}. See: BDB—438c, 941c.

3415. יָרַע {22x} **yâraʿ**, *yaw-rah';* a prim. root; prop. to *be broken* up (with any violent action) i.e. (fig.) to *fear:*—displease {9x}, grieved {4x}, grievous {3x}, evil {2x}, ill {2x}, harm {1x}, sad {1x}. See: TWOT—917; BDB—438c.

3416. יִרְפְּאֵל {1x} **Yirpᵉ᾽êl**, *yir-peh-ale';* from 7495 and 410; *God will heal; Jirpeël,* a place in Pal.:—Irpeel {1x}. See: BDB—438c, 951c.

3417. יָרַק {3x} **yâraq**, *yaw-rak';* a prim. root; to *spit:*—✕ but {1x}, spit {2x}. See: TWOT—918, 919; BDB—439a, 956d.

3418. יֶרֶק {6x} **yereq**, *yeh'-rek;* from 3417 (in the sense of *vacuity* of color); prop. *pallor,* i.e. hence, the yellowish *green* of young and sickly vegetation; concr. *verdure,* i.e. grass or vegetation:—grass {1x}, green {3x}, green thing {2x}. See: TWOT—918a; BDB—438d. Syn.: 1877, 2682, 3419, 6212.

3419. יָרָק {5x} **yârâq**, *yaw-rawk';* from the same as 3418; prop. *green;* concr. a *vegetable:*—green {2x}, herbs {3x}. See: TWOT—918b; BDB—438d.

יְרָקוֹן **Yarqôwn**. See 4313.

3420. יֵרָקוֹן {6x} **yêrâqôwn**, *yay-raw-kone';* from 3418; *paleness,* whether of persons (from fright), or of plants (from

drought):—mildew {5x}, paleness {1x}. See: TWOT—918d; BDB—439a.

3421. יָרְקְעָם {1x} **Yorqᵉʿâm**, *yor-keh-awm';* from 7324 and 5971; *people will be poured forth; Jorkeäm,* a place in Pal.:—Jorkeam {1x}. See: BDB—439a.

3422. יְרַקְרַק {3x} **yᵉraqraq**, *yer-ak-rak';* from the same as 3418; *yellowish-ness:*—greenish {2x}, yellow {1x}. See: TWOT—918e; BDB—439a.

3423. יָרַשׁ {232x} **yârash**, *yaw-rash';* or

יָרֵשׁ **yârêsh**, *yaw-raysh';* a prim. root; to *occupy* (by *driving* out previous tenants, and *possessing* in their place); by impl. to *seize,* to *rob,* to *inherit;* also to *expel,* to *impoverish,* to *ruin:*—possess {116x}, ... out {46x}, inherit {21x}, heir {10x}, possession {6x}, succeed {5x}, dispossess {4x}, poverty {3x}, drive {2x}, enjoy {2x}, poor {2x}, expelled {2x}, utterly {2x}, misc. {11x} = consume, destroy, disinherit, drive (-ing) out, ✕ without fail, seize upon.

Yarash, as a verb, means "to inherit, subdue, take possession, dispossess, impoverish." **(1)** Basically *yarash* means "to inherit." The verb can connote the state of being designated as an heir. Abram said to God: "Behold, to me thou hast given no [offspring]: and, lo, one born in my house is mine heir [literally, "is the one who is inheriting me"]" (Gen 15:3—the first biblical occurrence of the word). **(1a)** Whatever Abram had to be passed on to his legal descendants was destined to be given to his servant. **(1b)** Hence his servant was his legally designated heir. **(2)** This root can also represent the status of having something as one's permanent possession, as a possession which may be passed on to one's legal descendants. God told Abram: "I am the Lord that brought thee out of Ur of the Chaldees, to give thee this land to inherit it" (Gen 15:7). **(3)** *Yarash* can mean "to take over as a permanent possession": "And if his father have no brethren, then ye shall give his inheritance unto his kinsman that is next to him of his family, and he shall possess it" (Num 27:11). **(4)** The verb sometimes means to take something over (in the case of the Promised Land) by conquest as a permanent possession: "The Lord shall make the pestilence cleave unto thee, until he have consumed thee from off the land, whither thou goest to possess it" (Deut 28:21). **(5)** When people are the object, *yarash* sometimes means "to dispossess" in the sense of taking away their inheritable goods and putting them in such a social position that they cannot hold possessions or inherit permanent possessions: "The Horim also dwelt in Seir beforetime; but the children of Esau succeeded

them, when they had destroyed them from before them, and dwelt in their stead" (Deut 2:12). **(6)** To cause someone to be dispossessed is "to impoverish" him: "The Lord maketh poor, and maketh rich . . ." (1 Sa 2:7), the Lord makes one to be without permanent inheritable possessions. See: TWOT—920; BDB—439a.

3424. יְרֵשָׁה {2x} **yᵉrêshâh**, *yer-ay-shaw';* from 3423; *occupancy:*—possession {2x}. Yereshah, which appears twice, means "something given as a permanent possession; to be taken over by conquest": "And Edom shall be a possession, Seir also shall be a possession for his enemies; and Israel shall do valiantly" (Num 24:18). See: TWOT—920a; BDB—440b.

3425. יְרֻשָּׁה {14x} **yᵉrushshâh**, *yer-oosh-shaw';* from 3423; something *occupied;* a *conquest;* also a *patrimony:*—heritage {1x}, inheritance {1x}, possession {12x}.

Yerushshah occurs 14 times; it means **(1)** "to have as a possession": "Meddle not with them; for I will not give you of their land, no, not so much as a foot breadth; because I have given mount Seir unto Esau for a possession" (Deut 2:5), **(2)** "to be designated as a possession, to receive as a possession": "And the LORD said unto me, Distress not the Moabites, neither contend with them in battle: for I will not give thee of their land for a possession; because I have given Ar unto the children of Lot for a possession" (Deut 2:9). See: TWOT—920b; BDB—440b.

3426. יֵשׁ {133x} **yêsh**, *yaysh;* perh. from an unused root mean. to *stand* out, or *exist; entity;* used adv. or as a copula for the substantive verb (1961); there *is* or *are* (or any other form of the verb to *be,* as may suit the connection):—is {54x}, be {28x}, have {22x}, there {13x}, misc. {16x} = thou do, had, hast, (which) hath, substance, it was, ye will, thou wilt, wouldest.

Yesh means there is; substance; he/she/ it is/are. **(1)** This particle is used substantively only in Prov 8:21: ". . . That I may cause those that love me to inherit substance; and I will fill their treasures." **(2)** In all other appearances the word asserts existence with emphasis. **(2a)** Sometimes *yesh* appears with a predicate following, **(2b)** as it does in Gen 28:16: "And Jacob awaked out of his sleep, and he said, Surely the Lord is in this place; and I knew it not." **(3)** In a few passages the word is used as a response to an inquiry: "Is the seer here? And they [the young maidens] answered them, and said, He is; behold, he is before you" (1 Sa 9:11–12). **(4)** Used absolutely the word can mean "there is/are/was/were," as it does in Gen 18:24 (the first biblical appearance):

"Peradventure there be fifty righteous within the city . . ." **(5)** In many contexts *yesh* used in framing questions or protestations suggests doubt that the matter queried exists or is to be found: **(5a)** "As the Lord thy God liveth, there is no nation or kingdom, whither my lord hath not sent to seek thee: and when they said, He is not there; he took an oath of the kingdom and nation, that they found thee not" (1 Kin 18:10).

(5b) This is especially clear in Jer 5:1, where God commands the prophet to go and seek "if ye can find a man, if there be any that executeth judgment, that seeketh the truth." **(6)** There are several other special uses of *yesh.* **(6a)** Used with the particle *im* (518) and a participle, it emphasizes abiding intention: "And I came this day unto the well, and said, O Lord God of my master Abraham, if now thou do prosper my way which I go [literally, if there surely is a prospering of my way; or if it surely is that you intend to prosper]" (Gen 24:42). **(6b)** Possession is sometimes indicated by *yesh* plus the preposition le: "And Esau said, I have enough, my brother . . ." (Gen 33:9). **(6c)** Used with the infinitive and the preposition le, *yesh* signifies possibility—Elisha told the Shunammite woman: "Behold, thou hast been careful for us with all this care; what is to be done for thee? wouldest thou be spoken for to the king, or to the captain of the host [is it possible that you want me to speak a word in your behalf to]?" (2 Kin 4:13). See: TWOT—921; BDB—441b, 930d, 1080a.

3427. יָשַׁב {1088x} **yâshab**, *yaw-shab';* a prim. root; prop. to *sit* down (spec. as judgement in ambush, in quiet); by impl. to *dwell,* to *remain;* caus. to *settle,* to *marry:*—dwell {437x}, inhabitant {221x}, sit {172x}, abide {70x}, inhabit {39x}, down {26x}, remain {23x}, in {22x}, tarry {19x}, set {14x}, continue {5x}, place {7x}, still {5x}, taken {5x}, misc. {23x} = ease self, endure, establish, ✕ fail, habitation, haunt, make to keep [house], lurking, ✕ marry (-ing), return, seat.

I. *Yashab,* **as a verb,** means "to dwell, sit, abide, inhabit, remain." **(1)** *Yashab* is first used in Gen 4:16, in its most common connotation of **(1a)** "to dwell": "Cain went out . . . and dwelt in the land of Nod." **(1b)** The word appears again in Gen 18:1: "He [Abraham] sat in the tent door." **(1c)** In Gen 22:5, *yashab* is translated: "Abide ye here with the ass; and I and the lad will go yonder and worship." **(1d)** The word has the sense of "to remain": **(1d1)** "Remain a widow at thy father's house . . ." (Gen 38:11), and **(1d2)** it is used of God in a similar sense: "Thou, O Lord, remainest for ever; thy throne from generation to generation" (Lam 5:19). **(1e)** The promise of restoration from

captivity was: "And they shall build houses and inhabit them . . ." (Is 65:21). **(2)** *Yashab* is sometimes combined with other words to form expressions in common usage. **(2a)** For example, "When he sitteth upon the throne of his kingdom" (Deut 17:18; cf. 1 Kin 1:13, 17, 24) carries the meaning "begins to reign." **(2b)** "To sit in the gate" means "to hold court" or "to decide a case," as in Ruth 4:1–2 and 1 Kin 22:10. **(2c)** "Sit thou at my right hand" (Ps 110:1) means to assume a ruling position as deputy. **(2d)** "There will I sit to judge all the heathen" (Joel 3:12) was a promise of eschatological judgment. **(2e)** "To sit in the dust" or "to sit on the ground" (Is 47:1) was a sign of humiliation and grief.

(3) *Yashab* is often used figuratively of God. The sentences, "I saw the Lord sitting on his throne" (1 Kin 22:19); "He that sitteth in the heavens shall laugh" (Ps 2:4); and "God sitteth upon the throne of his holiness" (Ps 47:8) all describe God as the exalted Ruler over the universe. **(4)** The idea that God also "dwells" among men is expressed by this verb: "Shalt thou [David] build me a house for me to dwell in?" (2 Sa 7:5; cf. Ps 132:14). **(5)** The usage of *yashab* in such verses as 1 Sa 4:4: "The Lord of hosts, which dwelleth between the cherubim," describes His presence at the ark of the covenant in the tabernacle and the temple. **(6)** The word is also used to describe man's being in God's presence: **(6a)** "One thing have I desired of the Lord, . . . that I may dwell in the house of the Lord all the days of my life . . ." (Ps 27:4; cf. Ps 23:6). **(6b)** "Thou shalt bring them in, and plant them in the mountain of thine inheritance, in the place, O Lord, which thou hast made for thee to dwell in" (Ex 15:17).

II. *Yashab,* **as a participle,** means "remaining; inhabitant." **(1)** This participle is sometimes used as a simple adjective: "Jacob was a plain man, dwelling in tents" (Gen 25:27). **(2)** But the word is more often used as in Gen 19:25: ". . . All the inhabitants of the cities." Syn: 4908, 7931. See: TWOT—922; BDB—442a, 1096b.

3428. יְשֶׁבְאָב {1x} **Yesheb'âb**, *yeh-sheb-awb';* from 3427 and 1; *seat of* (his) *father; Jeshebab,* an Isr.:—Jeshebeab {1x}. See: BDB—444a.

3429. יֹשֵׁב בַּשֶּׁבֶת {1x} **Yôshêb bash-Shebeth**, *yo-shabe' bash-sheh'-beth;* from the act. part. of 3427 and 7674, with a prep. and the art. interposed; *sitting in the seat; Josheb-bash-Shebeth,* an Isr.:—that sat in the seat {1x}. See: BDB—444a.

3430. יָשְׁבוֹ בְּנֹב {1x} **Yishbôw be-Nôb**, *yish-bo' beh-nobe';* from 3427 and 5011, with a pron. suff. and a prep. interposed;

his dwelling (is) *in Nob; Jishbo-be-Nob,* a Philistine:—Ishbi-benob {1x}. See: BDB—444a.

3431. יִשְׁבַּח {1x} **Yishbach**, *yish-bakh';* from 7623; *he will praise; Jishbach,* an Isr.:—Ishbah {1x}. See: BDB—444c, 986d.

3432. יָשֻׁבִי {1x} **Yâshûbîy**, *yaw-shoo-bee';* patron. from 3437; a *Jashubite,* or desc. of Jashub:—Jashubites {1x}. See: BDB—444c, 1000b.

3433. יָשֻׁבִי לֶחֶם {1x} **Yâshûbîy Lechem**, *yaw-shoo-bee' leh'-khem;* from 7725 and 3899; *returner of bread; Jashubi-Lechem,* an Isr.:—Jashubi-lehem {1x}. See: BDB—1000b. or

יֹשְׁבֵי לֶחֶם **Yôshebêy Lechem**, *yo-sheh-bay' leh'-khem,* and rendered "(they were) inhab. of Lechem," i.e. of Bethlehem (by contr.). comp. 3902.

3434. יָשָׁבְעָם {3x} **Yâshob'âm**, *yaw-shob-awm';* from 7725 and 5971; *people will return; Jashobam,* the name of two or three Isr.:—Jashobeam {3x}. See: BDB—444c, 1000b.

3435. יִשְׁבָּק {2x} **Yishbâq**, *yish-bawk';* from an unused root corresp. to 7662; *he will leave; Jishbak,* a son of Abraham:—Ishbak {2x}. See: BDB—444c, 990b.

3436. יָשְׁבְּקָשָׁה {2x} **Yoshbeqâshâh**, *yosh-bek-aw-shaw';* from 3427 and 7186; a *hard seat; Joshbekashah,* an Isr.:—Joshbekashah {2x}. See: BDB—444a.

3437. יָשׁוּב {3x} **Yâshûwb**, *yaw-shoob';* or

יָשִׁיב **Yâshîyb**, *yaw-sheeb';* from 7725; *he will return; Jashub,* the name of two Isr.:—Jashub {3x}. See: BDB—445a, 445b, 1000a.

3438. יִשְׁוָה {2x} **Yishvâh**, *yish-vaw';* from 7737; *he will level; Jishvah,* an Isr.:—Ishvah {1x}, Isvah {1x}. See: BDB—445a, 1001a.

3439. יְשׁוֹחָיָה {1x} **Yeshôwchâyâh**, *yesh-o-khaw-yaw';* from the same as 3445 and 3050; *Jah will empty; Jeshochajah,* an Isr.:—Jeshoaiah {1x}. See: BDB—445a, 1001d, 1006a.

3440. יִשְׁוִי {4x} **Yishvîy**, *yish-vee';* from 7737; *level; Jishvi,* the name of two Isr.:—Ishuai {1x}, Ishvi {1x}, Isui {1x}, Jesui {1x}. See: BDB—445a, 1001a.

3441. יִשְׁוִי {1x} **Yishvîy**, *yish-vee';* patron. from 3440; a *Jishvite* (collect.) or desc. of Jishvi:—Jesuites {1x}. See: BDB—445a, 1001a.

3442. יֵשׁוּעַ {29x} **Yêshûwa'**, *yay-shoo'-ah;* for 3091; *he will save; Jeshua,* the name of ten Isr., also of a place in Pal.:—Jeshua {29x}. See: BDB—221c, 222d, 445a, 448a, 1096b.

3443. יְשׁוּעַ {1x} Yĕshûwaʿ (Aram.), yay-shoo'-ah; corresp. to 3442:—Jeshua {1x}. See: BDB—1096b.

3444. יְשׁוּעָה {78x} yᵉshûwʿâh, yesh-oo'-aw; fem. pass. part. of 3467; something saved, i.e. (abstr.) deliverance; hence, aid, victory, prosperity:—salvation {65x}, help {4x}, deliverance {3x}, health {3x}, save {1x}, saving {1x}, welfare {1x}.

Yeshuw'ah, as a noun, means "deliverance." (1) This noun appears 78 times in the Old Testament, predominantly in the Book of Psalms (45 times) and Isaiah (19 times). (2) The first occurrence is in Jacob's last words: "I have waited for thy salvation, O Lord" (Gen 49:18). (3) "Salvation" in the Old Testament is not understood as a salvation from sin, since the word denotes broadly anything from which "deliverance" must be sought: distress, war, servitude, or enemies. (3a) There are both human and divine deliverers, but the word yeshuw'ah rarely refers to human "deliverance." (3b) A couple of exceptions are when Jonathan brought respite to the Israelites from the Philistine pressure (1 Sa 14:45), and when Joab and his men were to help one another in battle (2 Sa 10:11). (4) "Deliverance" is generally used with God as the subject. (4a) He is known as the salvation of His people: "But Jeshurun waxed fat, and kicked: thou art waxen fat, thou art grown thick, thou art covered with fatness; then he forsook God which made him, and lightly esteemed the Rock of his salvation" (Deut 32:15; cf. Is 12:2).

(4b) He worked many wonders in behalf of His people: "O sing unto the Lord a new song; for he hath done marvelous things: his right hand, and his holy arm, hath [worked salvation for him]" (Ps 98:1). (5) Yeshuw'ah occurs either in the context of rejoicing (Ps 9:14) or in the context of a prayer for "deliverance": "But I am poor and sorrowful: let thy salvation, O God, set me up on high" (Ps 69:29). (6) Habakkuk portrays the Lord's riding on chariots of salvation (3:8) to deliver His people from their oppressors: "Was the LORD displeased against the rivers? was thine anger against the rivers? was thy wrath against the sea, that thou didst ride upon thine horses and thy chariots of salvation?" (7) The worst reproach that could be made against a person was that God did not come to his rescue: "Many there be which say of my soul, there is no help for him in God [literally, "he has no deliverance in God"]" (Ps 3:2). (9) Many personal names contain a form of the root, such as Joshua ("the Lord is help"), Isaiah ("the Lord is help"), and Jesus (a Greek form of yeshu'ah). Syn: 3467, 5414, 8668. See: TWOT—929b; BDB—447b.

3445. יְשַׁח {1x} yeshach, yeh'-shakh; from an unused root mean. to gape (as the empty stomach); hunger:—casting down {1x}. See: TWOT—924; BDB—445a.

3446. יִשְׂחָק {4x} Yischâq, yis-khawk'; from 7831; he will laugh; Jischak, the heir of Abraham:—Isaac {4x}. See: TWOT—1905b; BDB—850c, 966a. comp. 3327.

3447. יָשַׁט {3x} yâshat, yaw-shat'; a prim. root; to extend:—hold out {3x}. See: TWOT—925; BDB—445a.

3448. יִשַׁי {42x} Yîshay, yee-shah'-ee; by Aram.

אִישַׁי ʾÎyshay, ee-shah'-ee; from the same as 3426; extant; Jishai, David's father:—Jesse {42x}. See: TWOT—926; BDB—36b, 445a.

יָשִׁיב Yâshîyb. See 3437.

3449. יִשִּׁיָּה {7x} Yishshîyâh, yish-shee-yaw'; or

יִשִּׁיָּהוּ Yishshîyâhûw, yish-shee-yaw'-hoo; from 5383 and 3050; Jah will lend; Jishshijah, the name of five Isr.:—Ishiah {1x}, Isshiah {3x}, Ishijah {1x}, Jesiah {2x}. See: BDB—445b, 674d.

3450. יְשִׂימָאֵל {1x} Yᵉsîymâʾêl, yes-eem-aw-ale'; from 7760 and 410; God will place; Jesimaël, an Isr.:—Jesimael {1x}. See: BDB—964d.

3451. יְשִׂימָה {1x} yᵉshîymâh, yesh-ee-maw'; from 3456; desolation:—let death seize {1x}. See: TWOT—927a; BDB—445b.

3452. יְשִׁימוֹן {13x} yᵉshîymôwn, yesh-ee-mone'; from 3456; a desolation:—desert {4x}, Jeshimon {6x}, solitary {1x}, wilderness {2x}. See: TWOT—927b; BDB—445b.

יְשִׁימוֹת yᵉshîymôwth. See 1020, 3451.

3453. יָשִׁישׁ {4x} yâshîysh, yaw-sheesh'; from 3486; an old man:—aged {1x}, aged men {1x}, ancient {1x}, very old {1x}. Syn.: 2204, 2205, 2208, 2209, 3465, 5769, 7872. See: TWOT—931b; BDB—450a.

3454. יְשִׁישַׁי {1x} Yᵉshîyshay, yesh-ee-shah'-ee; from 3453; aged; Jeshishai, an Isr.:—Jeshishai {1x}. See: BDB—450b.

3455. יָשַׂם {2x} yâsam, yaw-sam'; a prim. root; to place; intr. to be placed:—be put {1x}, set {1x}. See: TWOT—2243; BDB—441a.

3456. יָשַׁם {4x} yâsham, yaw-sham'; a prim. root; to lie waste:—be desolate {4x}. Syn.: 1327, 2717, 2723, 8007. See: TWOT—927; BDB—445b.

3457. יִשְׁמָא {1x} **Yishmâ⁾**, *yish-maw'*; from 3456; *desolate; Jishma,* an Isr.:—Ishma {1x}. See: BDB—445c.

3458. יִשְׁמָעֵאל {48x} **Yishmâ⁽ê⁾l**, *yish-maw-ale';* from 8085 and 410; *God will hear; Jishmaël,* the name of Abraham's oldest son, and of five Isr.:—Ishmael {48x}. See: BDB—445c, 1035d.

3459. יִשְׁמָעֵאלִי {8x} **Yishmâ⁽ê⁾lîy**, *yish-maw-ay-lee';* patron. from 3458; a *Jishmaëlite* or desc. of Jishmael:—Ishmaelite {2x}, Ishmeelite {6x}. See: BDB—1035d.

3460. יִשְׁמַעְיָה {2x} **Yishma⁽yâh**, *yish-mah-yaw';* or

יִשְׁמַעְיָהוּ **Yishma⁽yâhûw**, *yish-mah-yaw'-hoo;* from 8085 and 3050; *Jah will hear; Jishmajah,* the name of two Isr.:—Ishmaiah {1x}, Ismaiah {1x}. See: BDB—1036a.

3461. יִשְׁמְרַי {1x} **Yishm⁽ray**, *yish-mer-ah'-ee;* from 8104; *preservative; Jishmerai,* an Isr.:—Ishmerai {1x}. See: BDB—445c, 1038b.

3462. יָשֵׁן {19x} **yâshên**, *yaw-shane';* a prim. root; prop. to *be slack* or *languid,* i.e. (by impl.) *sleep* (fig. to *die);* also to *grow old, stale* or *inveterate:*—old {1x}, old store {1x}, remain long {1x}, (make to) sleep {16x}. See: TWOT—928; BDB—445c, 1096b.

3463. יָשֵׁן {9x} **yâshên**, *yaw-shane';* from 3462; *sleepy:*—asleep {2x}, sleep {3x}, sleepeth {2x}, sleeping {1x}, slept {1x}. See: TWOT—928a; BDB—445d.

3464. יָשֵׁן {1x} **Yâshên**, *yaw-shane';* the same as 3463; *Jashen,* an Isr.:—Jashen {1x}. See: BDB—445d.

3465. יָשָׁן {7x} **yâshân**, *yaw-shawn';* from 3462; *old:*—old {7x}. See: TWOT—928b; BDB—445d.

3466. יְשָׁנָה {1x} **Y⁽shânâh**, *yesh-aw-naw';* fem. of 3465; *Jeshanah,* a place in Pal.:—Jeshanah {1x}. See: BDB—446a.

3467. יָשַׁע {205x} **yâsha⁽**, *yaw-shah';* a prim. root; prop. to *be open, wide* or *free,* i.e. (by impl.) to *be safe;* caus. to *free* or *succor:*—save {149x}, saviour {15x}, deliver {13x}, help {12x}, preserved {5x}, salvation {3x}, avenging {2x}, at all {1x}, avenged {1x}, defend {1x}, rescue {1x}, safe {1x}, victory {1x}.

Yasha⁽, means "to deliver, help." For example: "For thus saith the Lord God, the Holy One of Israel; In returning and rest shall ye be saved; in quietness and in confidence shall be your strength: and ye would not" (Is 30:15). See: TWOT—929; BDB—223c, 446b.

3468. יֶשַׁע {36x} **yesha⁽**, *yeh'-shah;* or

יֵשַׁע **yêsha⁽**, *yay'-shah;* from 3467; *liberty, deliverance, prosperity:*—safety {1x}, salvation {32x}, saving {3x}.

Yesha⁽, means "deliverance." This noun appears 36 times in the Old Testament. One appearance is in Ps 50:23: "Whoso offereth praise glorifieth me: and to him that ordereth his conversation aright will I show the salvation of God." See: TWOT—929a; BDB—447a.

3469. יִשְׁעִי {5x} **Yish⁽îy**, *yish-ee';* from 3467; *saving; Jishi,* the name of four Isr.:—Ishi {5x}. See: BDB—447d.

3470. יְשַׁעְיָה {39x} **Y⁽sha⁽yâh**, *yesh-ah-yaw';* or

יְשַׁעְיָהוּ **Y⁽sha⁽yâhûw**, *yesh-ah-yaw'-hoo;* from 3467 and 3050; *Jah has saved; Jeshajah,* the name of seven Isr.:—Isaiah {32x}, Jesaiah {2x}, Jeshaiah {5x}. See: BDB—447d.

3471. יָשְׁפֵה {3x} **yâsh⁽phêh**, *yaw-shef-ay';* from an unused root mean. to *polish;* a gem supposed to be *jasper* (from the resemblance in name):—jasper {3x}. See: TWOT—929.1; BDB—448C.

3472. יִשְׁפָּה {1x} **Yishpâh**, *yish-paw';* perh. from 8192; *he will scratch; Jishpah,* an Isr.:—Ispah {1x}. See: BDB—448c, 1046a.

3473. יִשְׁפָּן {1x} **Yishpân**, *yish-pawn';* prob. from the same as 8227; *he will hide; Jishpan,* an Isr.:—Ishpan {1x}. See: BDB—448c, 1051a.

3474. יָשַׁר {27x} **yâshar**, *yaw-shar';* a prim. root; to *be straight* or *even;* fig. to *be* (caus. to *make) right, pleasant, prosperous:*—please {6x}, straight {5x}, direct {4x}, right {3x}, well {2x}, fitted {1x}, good {1x}, make straight {1x}, meet {1x}, upright {1x}, uprightly {1x}.

Yashar, as a verb, means "to be straight, be smooth, be right." **(1)** This verb, which occurs rarely, has many derivatives in the Bible. **(2)** One occurrence of the verb is in 1 Chr 13:4: "And all the congregation said that they would do so: for the thing was right in the eyes of all the people." In this usage *yashar* has the sense of being pleasing or agreeable. **(3)** In Hab. 2:4 the word implies an ethical uprightness: "Behold, his soul which is lifted up is not upright in him: but the just shall live by his faith." See: TWOT—930; BDB—448c.

3475. יֶשֶׁר {1x} **Yêsher**, *yay'-sher;* from 3474; the *right; Jesher,* an Isr.:—Jesher {1x}. See: BDB—448c, 449c.

3476. יֹשֶׁר {14x} **yôsher**, *yo'-sher;* from 3474; the *right:*—equity {1x}, meet {1x}, right {2x}, upright {1x}, uprightness {9x}.

Yosher, as a noun, means "straightness." This noun occurs 14 times. One occurrence is in Prov 2:13: "Who leave the paths of uprightness, to walk in the ways of darkness." See: TWOT—930b; BDB—448c, 449c.

3477. יָשָׁר {119x} **yâshâr**, *yaw-shawr';* from 3474; *straight* (lit. or fig.):—right {53x}, upright {42x}, righteous {9x}, straight {3x}, convenient {2x}, Jasher {2x}, equity {1x}, just {1x}, meet {1x}, meetest {1x}, upright ones {1x}, uprightly {1x}, uprightness {1x}, well {1x}.

Yashar, as an adjective, means "upright; right; righteous; just." **(1)** This adjective occurs first in Exodus in the idiom "right in his eyes": "[He] said, If thou wilt diligently hearken to the voice of the Lord thy God, and wilt do that which is right in his sight, and wilt give ear to his commandments, and keep all his statutes, I will put none of these diseases upon thee, which I have brought upon the Egyptians: for I am the Lord that healeth thee" (Ex 15:26). **(2)** Its usage is infrequent in the Pentateuch and in the prophetical writings. Predominantly a poetic term, *yashar* also occurs idiomatically ("to do what is right") in the historical books; cf. 1 Kin 15:5: "Because David did that which was right in the eyes of the Lord, and turned not aside from any thing that he commanded him all the days of his life, save only in the matter of Uriah the Hittite." **(3)** The basic meaning is the root meaning "to be straight" in the sense of "to be level." **(3a)** The legs of the creatures in Ezekiel's vision were straight (Eze 1:7).

(3b) The Israelites designated an easy road for traveling as a "level road." It had few inclines and declines compared to the mountain roads (cf. Jer 31:9: "They shall come with weeping, and with supplications will I lead them: I will cause them to walk by the rivers of water in a straight way, wherein they shall not stumble: for I am a father to Israel, and Ephraim is my firstborn"). **(4)** *Yashar* with the meaning "right" pertains to things and to abstracts. **(4a)** Samuel promised himself to instruct God's people in "the good and the right way" (1 Sa 12:23). **(4b)** Nehemiah thanked God for having given just ordinances: "Thou camest down also upon mount Sinai, and spakest with them from heaven, and gavest them right judgments, and true laws, good statutes and commandments" (Neh 9:13). **(5)** Based on His revelation God expected His people to please Him in being obedient to Him: "And thou shalt do that which is right and good in the sight of the Lord: that it may be well with thee, and that thou mayest go in and possess the good

land which the Lord sware unto thy fathers" (Deut 6:18). **(6)** When *yashar* pertains to people, it is best translated "just" or "upright." God is the standard of uprightness for His people: "Good and upright is the Lord: therefore will he teach sinners in the way" (Ps 25:8): His word (Ps 33:4), His judgments (Ps 19:9), and His ways (Hos 14:9). He will reveal His uprightness as a blessing to His people. **(7)** The believer follows Him in being "upright" in heart: "Be glad in the Lord, and rejoice, ye righteous; and shout for joy, all ye that are upright in heart" (Ps 32:11; cf. 7:10; 11:2). **(7a)** In their daily walk they manifest that they are walking on the narrow road: "The wicked have drawn out the sword, and have bent their bow, to cast down the poor and needy, and to slay such as be of upright conversation" (Ps 37:14). **(7b)** The "just" are promised God's blessing upon their lives (Prov 11:10–11). **(8)** *Yashar* is also the abstract "rightness," especially when the Hebrew word has the definite article (hayyashar, "the right"): "Hear this, I pray you, ye heads of the house of Jacob, and princes of the house of Israel, that abhor judgment, and pervert all equity [all that is right]" (Mic 3:9). See: TWOT—930a; BDB—449a.

3478. יִשְׂרָאֵל {2505x} **Yisrâ'êl**, *yis-raw-ale';* from 8280 and 410; *he will rule (as) God; Jisraël,* a symb. name of Jacob; also (typ.) of his posterity:—Israel{2489x}, Israelites {16x}. See: BDB—441a, 975b, 1096b.

3479. יִשְׂרָאֵל {8x} **Yisrâ'êl** (Aram.), *yis-raw-ale';* corresp. to 3478:—Israel {8x}. See: BDB—1096.

3480. יְשַׂרְאֵלָה {1x} **Yᵉsar'êlâh**, *yes-ar-ale'-aw;* by var. from 3477 and 410 with directive enclitic; *right towards God; Jesarelah,* an Isr.:—Jesharelah {1x}. See: BDB—441a. Syn.: comp. 841.

3481. יִשְׂרְאֵלִי {1x} **Yisrᵉ'êlîy**, *yis-reh-ay-lee';* patron. from 3478; a *Jisreëlite* or desc. of Jisrael:—Israel + 3478 {1x}, Israelite {1x}. See: BDB—976a.

3482. יִשְׂרְאֵלִית {3x} **Yisrᵉ'êlîyth**, *yis-reh-ay-leeth';* fem. of 3481; a *Jisreëlitess* or female desc. of Jisrael:—Israelitiss {3x}. See: BDB—976a.

3483. יִשְׁרָה {1x} **yishrâh**, *yish-raw';* fem. or 3477; *rectitude:*—uprightness {1x}.

Yishrah means "uprightness" and occurs once: "And Solomon said, Thou hast shewed unto thy servant David my father great mercy, according as he walked before thee in truth, and in righteousness, and in uprightness of heart with thee; and thou hast kept for him

this great kindness, that thou hast given him a son to sit on his throne, as *it is* this day" (1Kin 3:6). See: TWOT—930c; BDB—449c.

3484. יְשֻׁרוּן {4x} **Yᵉshûrûwn**, *yesh-oo-roon'*; from 3474; *upright; Jeshurun,* a symbol. name for Israel:—Jeshurun {3x}, Jesurun {1x}.

The noun *Yeshuruwn* is an honorific title for Israel: "But Jeshurun waxed fat, and kicked: thou art waxen fat, thou art grown thick, thou art covered with fatness; then he forsook God which made him, and lightly esteemed the Rock of his salvation" (Deut 32:15; 33:5). See: BDB—449c.

3485. יִשָּׂשכָר {43x} **Yissâ°kâr**, *yis-saw-kawr'*; (strictly *yis-saws-kawr'*); from 5375 and 7939; *he will bring a reward; Jissaskar,* a son of Jacob:—Issachar {43x}. See: BDB—441a, 969b.

3486. יָשֵׁשׁ {1x} **yâshêsh**, *yaw-shaysh'*; from an unused root mean. to *blanch; gray-haired, i.e. an aged* man:—stoop for age {1x}. See: TWOT—931a; BDB—450a.

3487. יָת {1x} **yath** (Aram.), *yath;* corresp. to 853; a sign of the object of a verb:— + whom {1x}. See: TWOT—2779; BDB—1096b.

3488. יְתַב {5x} **yᵉthîb** (Aram.), *yeth-eeb';* corresp. to 3427; to *sit* or *dwell:*— dwell {1x}, (be) set {2x}, sit {2x}. See: TWOT—2780; BDB—1096b.

3489. יָתֵד {24x} **yâthêd**, *yaw-thade';* from an unused root mean. to *pin* through or fast; a *peg:*—nail {8x}, paddle {1x}, pin {13x}, stake {2x}. See: TWOT—932a; BDB—450b.

3490. יָתוֹם {42x} **yâthôwm**, *yaw-thome';* from an unused root mean. to *be lonely;* a *bereaved* person:—fatherles {38x}, fatherless child {3x}, orphan {1x}. See: TWOT—934a; BDB—450c.

3491. יָתוּר {1x} **yâthûwr**, *yaw-thoor';* pass. part. of 3498; prop. what is *left,* i.e. (by impl.) a *gleaning:*—range {1x}. See: TWOT—936; BDB—1064b, 1064d.

3492. יַתִּיר {4x} **Yattîyr**, *yat-teer';* from 3498; *redundant; Jattir,* a place in Pal.:— Jattir {4x}. See: BDB—452d.

3493. יַתִּיר {8x} **yattîyr** (Aram.), *yat-teer';* corresp. to 3492; *preeminent;* adv. *very:*—exceeding {2x}, exceedingly {1x}, excellent {5x}. See: TWOT—2781; BDB—1096c.

3494. יִתְלָה {1x} **Yithlâh**, *yith-law';* prob. from 8518; it *will hang,* i.e. *be high; Jithlah,* a place in Pal.:—Jethlah {1x}. See: BDB—450c, 1068b.

3495. יִתְמָה {1x} **Yithmâh**, *yith-maw';* from the same as 3490; *orphanage; Jithmah,* an Isr.:—Ithmah {1x}. See: BDB—450d.

3496. יַתְנִיאֵל {1x} **Yathnîy°êl**, *yath-nee-ale';* from an unused root mean. to *endure,* and 410; *continued of God; Jathniël,* an Isr.:—Jathniel {1x}. See: BDB—451a, 1072a.

3497. יִתְנָן {1x} **Yithnân**, *yith-nawn';* from the same as 8577; *extensive; Jithnan,* a place in Pal.:—Ithnan {1x}. See: BDB—451a.

3498. יָתַר {107x} **yâthar**, *yaw-thar';* a prim. root; to *jut* over or *exceed;* by impl. to *excel;* (intr.) to *remain* or *be left;* caus. to *leave, cause to abound, preserve:*—leave {52x}, remain {23x}, rest {12x}, remainder {4x}, remnant {4x}, reserved {3x}, residue {3x}, plenteous {2x}, behind {1x}, excel {1x}, much {1x}, preserve {1x}.

Yathar, as a verb, means "to be left; remain over; excel; show excess." (1) *Yathar* occurs for the first time in the biblical text in Gen 30:36, (1a) where it is stated that "Jacob fed the rest of Laban's flocks." (1b) This statement reflects the word's frequent use to show separation from a primary group. (1c) Thus, Jacob "was left alone" (Gen 32:24) when his family and flocks went on beyond the brook Jabbok. (2) Sometimes the word indicates survivors, as in 2 Sa 9:1: "Is there yet any that is left of the house of Saul . . ." (3) The remnant idea is reflected in Eze 6:8: "Yet will I leave a remnant, that ye may have some that shall escape the sword." See: TWOT—936; 451a, 1096c.

3499. יֶתֶר {101x} **yether**, *yeh'-ther;* from 3498; prop. an *overhanging,* i.e. (by impl.) an *excess, superiority, remainder;* also a small *rope* (as hanging free):—rest {63x}, remnant {14x}, residue {8x}, leave {4x}, excellency {3x}, withs {3x}, cord {1x}, exceeding {1x}, excellent {1x}, more {1x}, plentifully {1x}, string {1x}.

Yether, as a noun, means "remainder; excess." (1) As "remainder, excess," it is used especially in the sense of a lesser number or quality as compared to something of primary importance. (1a) So, *yether* is used to refer to "the residue of the vessels that remain in this city" left in Jerusalem by Nebuchadnezzar (Jer 27:19–20), and (1b) the men who were left after Joab had assigned his picked men in the battle lines: "And the rest of the people he delivered into the hand of Abishai his brother, that he might put them in array against the children of Ammon" (2 Sa 10:10). (2) Occasionally *yether* is used to indicate "excess" in a negative way, so the literal "lip of excess" has the meaning of "lying lips": "Excellent speech becometh

not a fool: much less do lying lips a prince" (Prov. 17:7). This is stressing that many times lying is adding to, instead of taking away from the truth. **(3)** A few times this noun implies "superiority" or "pre-eminence," as in Gen 49:3, where Jacob describes his son Reuben as being "Reuben, thou art my firstborn, my might, and the beginning of my strength, the excellency of dignity, and the excellency of power." **(4)** The name of Jethro (3503), Moses' father-in-law, is derived from this word. See: TWOT—936a; BDB—451d, 452a.

3500. יֶתֶר {9x} **Yether**, *yeh'-ther;* the same as 3499; *Jether,* the name of five or six Isr. and of one Midianite:—Jether {8x}, Jethro {1x}. See: BDB—452b. comp. 3503.

3501. יִתְרָא {1x} **Yithrâ**, *yith-raw';* by var. for 3502; *Jithra,* an Isr. (or Ishmaelite):—Ithra {1x}. See: BDB—452b.

3502. יִתְרָה {2x} **yithrâh**, *yith-raw';* fem. of 3499; prop. *excellence,* i.e. (by impl.) *wealth:*—abundance {1x}, riches {1x}. See: TWOT—936c; BDB—452b.

3503. יִתְרוֹ {9x} **Yithrôw**, *yith-ro';* from 3499 with pron. suff.; *his excellence; Jethro,* Moses' father-in-law:—Jethro {9x}. See: BDB—452b. comp. 3500.

3504. יִתְרוֹן {10x} **yithrôwn**, *yith-rone';* from 3498; *preeminence, gain:*—better {1x}, excellency {1x}, excelleth {2x}, profit {5x}, profitable {1x}. See: TWOT—936f; BDB—452c.

3505. יִתְרִי {1x} **Yithrîy**, *yith-ree';* patron. from 3500; a *Jithrite* or desc. of Jether:—Ithrite {1x}. See: BDB—452b.

3506. יִתְרָן {3x} **Yithrân**, *yith-rawn';* from 3498; *excellent; Jithran,* the name of an Edomite and of an Isr.:—Ithran {3x}. See: BDB—452d.

3507. יִתְרְעָם {2x} **Yithr**ᵉᶜ**âm**, *yith-reh-awm';* from 3499 and 5971; *excellence of people; Jithreäm,* a son of David:—Ithream {2x}. See: BDB—453c.

3508. יֹתֶרֶת {11x} **yôthereth**, *yo-theh'-reth;* fem. act. part. of 3498; the *lobe* or *flap* of the liver (as if redundant or outhanging):—caul {11x}. See: TWOT—936e; BDB—452c.

3509. יְתֵת {2x} **Y**ᵉ**thêyth**, *yeh-thayth';* of uncert. der.; *Jetheth,* an Edomite:—Jetheth {1x}. See: BDB—453c.

ד

3510. כָּאַב {22x} **kâ'ab**, *kaw-ab';* a prim. root; prop. to feel *pain;* by impl. to *grieve;* fig. to *spoil:*—... end {11x}, altogether {3x}, consume {3x}, consumption {2x}, consummation {1x}, determined {1x}, riddance {1x}. See: TWOT—982a; BDB—456a.

3511. כְּאֵב {6x} **k**ᵉ**'êb**, *keh-abe';* from 3510; *suffering* (phys. or ment.), *adversity:*—sorrow {3x}, grief {2x}, pain {1x}. See: TWOT—940a; BDB—456b.

3512. כָּאָה {3x} **kâ'âh**, *kaw-aw';* a prim. root; to *despond;* caus. to *deject:*—broken {1x}, be grieved {1x}, make sad {1x}. See: TWOT—941; BDB—456c.

3513. כָּבַד {116x} **kâbad**, *kaw-bad';* or

כָּבֵד **kâbêd**, *kaw-bade';* a prim. root; to *be heavy,* i.e. in a bad sense (*burdensome, severe, dull*) or in a good sense (*numerous, rich, honorable*); caus. to *make weighty* (in the same two senses):—honour {34x}, glorify {14x}, honourable {14x}, heavy {13x}, harden {7x}, glorious {5x}, sore {3x}, made heavy {3x}, chargeable {2x}, great {2x}, many {2x}, heavier {2x}, promote {2x}, misc. {10x} = abounding with, more grievously afflict, boast, X be dim, be grievous, lade, X more be laid, nobles, prevail, be rich, stop.

Kabed means "to honor." **(1)** One occurrence of *kabed* is in Deut 5:16: "Honor thy father and thy mother, as the Lord thy God hath commanded thee. . . ." Syn.: 2388, 7185, 7188, 8631. See: TWOT—943; BDB—457a.

3514. כֹּבֶד {4x} **kôbed**, *ko'-bed;* from 3513; *weight, multitude, vehemence:*—grievousness {1x}, heavy {2x}, great number {1x}. See: TWOT—943c; BDB—458c.

3515. כָּבֵד {38x} **kâbêd**, *kaw-bade';* from 3513; *heavy;* fig. in a good sense (*numerous*) or in a bad sense (*severe, difficult, stupid*):—great {8x}, grievous {8x}, heavy {8x}, sore {4x}, hard {2x}, much {2x}, slow {2x}, hardened {1x}, heavier {1x}, laden {1x}, thick {1x}.

Kabed means "heavy; numerous; severe; rich." **(1)** Basically this adjective connotes "heavy." In Ex 17:12 the word is used of physical weight: "But Moses' hands were heavy; and they took a stone, and put it under him, and he sat thereon; and Aaron and Hur stayed up his hands." **(2)** This adjective bears the connotation of heaviness as an enduring, ever-present quality, a lasting thing. **(3)** Used in a negative but extended sense, the word depicts sin as a yoke ever pressing down upon one: "For mine iniquities are gone over mine head: as a heavy burden they are too heavy for me" (Ps 38:4). **(4)** A task can be described as "heavy" (Ex 18:18). **(4a)** Moses argued his inability to lead God's people out of Egypt because he was "slow of speech, and of a slow tongue"; **(4b)** his

speech or tongue was not smooth-flowing but halting (heavy; Ex 4:10). **(4c)** This use of *kabed* appears with an explanation in Eze 3:6, where God is describing the people to whom Ezekiel is to minister: ". . . not to many people of a strange speech and of a hard language, whose words thou canst not understand."

(5) Another nuance of this word appears in Ex 7:14, where it is applied to Pharaoh's heart: "Pharaoh's heart is hardened, he refuseth to let the people go." **(6)** In all such contexts *kabed* depicts a burden which weighs down one's body (or some part of it) so that one is either disabled or unable to function successfully. **(7)** A second series of passages uses this word of something that falls upon or overcomes one. **(7a)** So God sent upon Egypt a "heavy" hail (Ex 9:18), a "great" swarm of insects (8:24), "numerous" locusts, and a "severe" pestilence (9:3). **(7b)** The first appearance of the word belongs to this category: "The famine was [severe] in the land" of Egypt (Gen 12:10). **(8)** Used with a positive connotation, *kabed* can describe the amount of "riches" one has: "And Abram was very rich in cattle, in silver, and in gold" (Gen 13:2). **(8a)** This usage vividly illustrates the basic implications of the word. **(8b)** Whenever *kabed* is used, it reflects the idea of "weightiness," or that which is added to something else. Thus, to be "very rich" means that Abram was heavily "weighted down" with wealth. **(8c)** This idea also explains how the word can be used to indicate the state of "being honored" or "glorious," for honor and glory are additional qualities that are added to a person or thing.

(9) In Gen 50:9 the word is used to modify a group of people, **(9a)** "a very great company." **(9b)** The next verse uses *kabed* in the sense of "imposing" or "ponderous": "They mourned with a great and very sore lamentation." **(10)** This adjective is never used of God. **(11)** "To be heavy" includes negative as well as positive aspects. **(11a)** Thus, calamity is "heavier than the sand of the sea" (Job 6:3), and the hand of God is "very heavy" in punishing the Philistines (1 Sa 5:11). **(11b)** Bondage and heavy work are "heavy" on the people (Ex 5:9; Neh 5:18). **(11c)** Eyes (Gen 48:10) and ears (Is 59:1) that have become insensitive, or "dull," have had debilitating conditions added to them, whether through age or other causes. **(11d)** The heart of a man may become excessively "weighted" with stubbornness and thus become "hardened" (Ex 9:7).

(12) "To honor" or "glorify" anything is to add something which it does not have in itself, or that which others can give. **(12a)** Children are commanded to "honor" their parents (Ex 20:12; Deut 5:16); **(12b)** Balak promised

"honor" to Balaam (Num 22:17); **(12c)** Jerusalem (Lam 1:8) and the Sabbath (Is 58:13) are "honored" or "made glorious." **(12d)** Above all, "honor" and "glory" are due to God, as repeatedly commanded in the biblical text: **(12d1)** "Honor the Lord with thy substance" (Prov 3:9); **(12d2)** "Let the Lord be glorified" (Is 66:5); **(12d3)** "Glorify ye the Lord" (Isa. 24:15). **(13)** *Kabed* is also the Hebrew word for "liver," apparently reflecting the sense that the liver is the heaviest of the organs of the body. See: TWOT—943a; BDB—458a, 1096b.

3516. כָּבֵד {1x} **kâbêd**, *kaw-bade';* the same as 3515; the *liver* (as the *heaviest* of the viscera):—liver {1x}. See: TWOT—943b; BDB—458b.

כָּבֹד **kâbôd**. See 3519.

3517. כְּבֵדָה {1x} **k⁰bêdûth**, *keb-ay-dooth';* fem. of 3515; *difficulty:*—× heavily {1x}. See: TWOT—943g; BDB—459c.

3518. כָּבָה {24x} **kâbâh**, *kaw-baw';* a prim. root; to *expire* or (caus.) to *extinguish* (fire, light, anger):—go (put) out {7x}, quench {8x}, quenched {9x}. See: TWOT—944; BDB—459c.

3519. כָּבוֹד {200x} **kâbôwd**, *kaw-bode';* rarely כָּבֹד **kâbôd**, *kaw-bode';* from 3513; prop. *weight,* but only fig. in a good sense, *splendor* or *copiousness:*—glory {156x}, honour {32x}, glorious {10x}, gloriously {1x}, honourable {1x}.

Kabod means "honor; glory; great quantity; multitude; wealth; reputation [majesty]; splendor."**(1)** *Kabod* refers to the great physical weight or "quantity" of a thing. **(2)** In Nah 2:9 one should read: "For there is no limit to the treasure—a great quantity of every kind of desirable object." **(3)** Is 22:24 likens Eliakim to a peg firmly anchored in a wall upon which is hung "all the [weighty things] of his father's house." **(4)** This meaning is required in Hos 9:11, where *kabod* represents a great crowd of people or "multitude": "As for Ephraim, their [multitude] shall fly away. . . ." **(5)** The word does not mean simply "heavy," but a heavy or imposing quantity of things. **(6)** *Kabod* often refers to both "wealth" and significant and positive "reputation" (in a concrete sense). **(6a)** Laban's sons complained that "Jacob hath taken away all that was our father's; and of that which was our father's hath he gotten all this [wealth]" (Gen 31:1—the first biblical occurrence). **(6b)** The second emphasis appears in Gen 45:13, where Joseph told his brothers to report to his "father . . . all my [majesty] in Egypt." Here this word includes a report of his position and the assurance that if the family

came to Egypt, Joseph would be able to provide for them.

(7) Trees, forests, and wooded hills have an imposing quality, a richness or "splendor." God will punish the king of Assyria by destroying most of the trees in his forests, "and shall consume the glory of his forest, . . . and the rest of the trees of his forest shall be few, that a child may write them" (Is 10:18–19). **(8)** In Ps 85:9 the idea of richness or abundance predominates: **(8a)** "Surely his salvation is nigh them that fear him; that glory [or abundance] may dwell in our land." **(8b)** This idea is repeated in Ps 85:12: "Yea, the Lord shall give that which is good; and our land shall yield her increase." **(9)** *Kabod* can also have an abstract emphasis of "glory," imposing presence or position. Phinehas' wife named their son Ichabod, "saying, The glory is departed from Israel: because the ark of God was taken, and because of her father-in-law and her husband" (they, the high priests, had died; 1 Sa 4:21). **(10)** In Is 17:3 *kabod* represents the more concrete idea of a fullness of things including fortified cities, sovereignty (self-rule), and people.

(11) Among such qualities is "honor," or respect and position. In Is 5:13 this idea of "honor" is represented by *kabod*: ". . . And their [my people's] honorable men are famished, and their multitude dried up with thirst." **(12)** Thus the word *kabod* and its parallel (the multitude) represent all the people of Israel: the upper classes and the common people. **(13)** In many passages the word represents a future rather than a present reality: "In that day shall the branch of the Lord be beautiful and glorious" (Is 4:2). **(14)** When used in the sense of "honor" or "importance" (cf. Gen 45:13) there are two nuances of the word. **(14a)** First, *kabod* can emphasize the position of an individual within the sphere in which he lives (Prov 11:16). **(14a1)** This "honor" can be lost through wrong actions or attitudes (Prov 26:1, 8) and evidenced in proper actions (Prov 20:3; 25:2). **(14a2)** This emphasis then is on a relationship between personalities. **(14b)** Second, there is a suggestion of nobility in many uses of the word, such as "honor" that belongs to a royal family (1 Kin 3:13). Thus, *kabod* can be used of the social distinction and position of respect enjoyed by nobility.

(15) When applied to God, the word represents a quality corresponding to Him and by which He is recognized. **(15a)** Joshua commanded Achan to give glory to God, to recognize His importance, worth, and significance (Josh 7:19). **(15b)** In this and similar instances "giving honor" refers to doing something; what Achan was to do was to tell the truth. **(16)** In other passages giving honor to God is a cultic

recognition and confession of God as God (Ps 29:1). **(16a)** Some have suggested that such passages celebrate the sovereignty of God over nature wherein the celebrant sees His "glory" and confesses it in worship. **(16b)** In other places the word is said to point to God's sovereignty over history and specifically to a future manifestation of that "glory" (Is 40:5). **(16c)** Still other passages relate the manifestation of divine "glory" to past demonstrations of His sovereignty over history and peoples (Ex 16:7; 24:16). Syn.: 1926. See: TWOT—943d, 943e; BDB—458c.

3520. כְּבוּדָה {3x} **k^ebûwddâh**, *keb-ood-daw';* irreg. fem. pass. part. of 3513; *weightiness*, i.e. *magnificence, wealth:*—carriage {1x}, all glorious {1x}, stately {1x}. See: TWOT—943f; BDB—458c, 459c.

3521. כָּבוּל {2x} **Kâbûwl**, *kaw-bool';* from the same as 3525 in the sense of *limitation; sterile; Cabul,* the name of two places in Pal.:—Cabul {2x}. See: BDB—459d.

3522. כַּבּוֹן {1x} **Kabbôwn**, *kab-bone';* from an unused root mean. to *heap* up; *hilly; Cabon,* a place in Pal.:—Cabbon {1x}. See: BDB—460a.

3523. כְּבִיר {2x} **k^ebîyr**, *keb-eer';* from 3527 in the orig. sense of *plaiting;* a *mattrass* (of intertwined materials):—pillow {2x}. Syn.: 3704, 4763. See: TWOT—948a; BDB—460d.

3524. כַּבִּיר {11x} **kabbîyr**, *kab-beer';* from 3527; *vast,* whether in extent (fig. of power, *mighty;* of time, *aged*), or in number, *many:*—mighty {4x}, much {2x}, strong {1x}, most {1x}, mighty men {1x}, valiant + 47 {1x}, feeble + 3808 {1x}. See: TWOT—947a; BDB—460b.

3525. כֶּבֶל {2x} **kebel**, *keh'-bel;* from an unused root mean. to *twine* or braid together; a *fetter:*—fetter {2x}. See: TWOT—945a; BDB—459d.

3526. כָּבַס {51x} **kâbaç**, *kaw-bas';* a prim. root; to *trample;* hence, to *wash* (prop. by stamping with the feet), whether lit. (incl. the *fulling* process) or fig.:—fuller {4x}, wash (-ing) {47x}.

Kabac means to wash [possibly by treading upon clothes in water]. **(1)** A common term throughout the history of Hebrew for the "washing" of clothes, this word is found also in ancient Ugaritic and Akkadian, reflecting the treading aspect. **(2)** It is found for the first time in the Old Testament in Gen 49:11 as part of Jacob's blessing on Judah: "He washed his garments in wine. . . ." **(3)** The word is used in the Old Testament primarily in the sense of

"washing" clothes, both **(3a)** for ordinary cleansing: "And Mephibosheth the son of Saul came down to meet the king, and had neither dressed his feet, nor trimmed his beard, nor washed his clothes, from the day the king departed until the day he came again in peace" (2 Sa 19:24), and **(3b)** for ritual cleansing: "And the LORD said unto Moses, Go unto the people, and sanctify them to day and tomorrow, and let them wash their clothes" (Ex 19:10; cf. Lev 11:25).

(4) It is often used in parallelism with the expression "to wash oneself," as in Lev 14:8–9 "And he that is to be cleansed shall wash his clothes, and shave off all his hair, and wash himself in water, that he may be clean: and after that he shall come into the camp, and shall tarry abroad out of his tent seven days. But it shall be on the seventh day, that he shall shave all his hair off his head and his beard and his eyebrows, even all his hair he shall shave off: and he shall wash his clothes, also he shall wash his flesh in water, and he shall be clean." **(5)** *Kabac* is used in the sense of "washing" or "bathing" oneself only in the figurative sense and in poetic usage, as in Jer 4:14: "O Jerusalem, wash thine heart from wickedness, that thou mayest be saved." Syn.: 7364. See: TWOT—946; BDB—460a.

3527. כָּבַר {1x} **kâbar**, *kaw-bar'*; a prim. root; prop. to *plait* together, i.e. (fig.) to *augment* (espec. in number or quantity, to *accumulate*):—in abundance, multiply {1x}. See: TWOT—947; BDB—460b.

3528. כְּבָר {9x} **keʰbâr**, *keb-awr'*; from 3527; prop. *extent* of time, i.e. a *great while;* hence, *long ago, formerly, hitherto:*—already {5x}, (seeing that which), now {4x}. See: TWOT—947c; BDB—460c.

3529. כְּבָר {8x} **Keʰbâr**, *keb-awr'*; the same as 3528; *length; Kebar*, a river of Mesopotamia:—Chebar {8x}. See: TWOT—947d; BDB—460c. comp. 2249.

3530. כִּבְרָה {3x} **kibrâh**, *kib-raw'*; fem. of 3528; prop. *length*, i.e. a *measure* (of uncert. dimension):—✕ little {3x}. See: TWOT—947b; BDB—460c.

3531. כְּבָרָה {1x} **keʰbârâh**, *keb-aw-raw'*; from 3527 in its orig. sense; a *sieve* (as netted):—sieve {1x}. See: TWOT—948b; BDB—460d.

3532. כֶּבֶשׂ {107x} **kebes**, *keh-bes'*; from an unused root mean. to *dominate;* a *ram* (just old enough to *butt*):—lamb {105x}, sheep {2x}.

Kebes means "lamb (male); kid." **(1)** The *kebes* is a "young lamb" which is nearly always used for sacrificial purposes. **(2)** The first usage in Exodus pertains to the Passover: "Your lamb shall be without blemish, a male of the first year: ye shall take it out from the sheep, or from the goats" (Ex 12:5). **(3)** The word *gedi* (1423), "kid," is a synonym for *kebes:* "The wolf also shall dwell with the lamb [*kebes*], and the leopard shall lie down with the kid [gedi]; and the calf and the young lion and the fatling together; and a little child shall lead them" (Is 11:6). **(4)** The traditional translation "lamb" leaves the gender uncertain. In Hebrew the word *kebes* is masculine, whereas the *kibshah* (3535), "young ewe lamb," is feminine; cf. "And Abraham set seven ewe lambs of the flock by themselves" (Gen 21:28). Syn.: 1423, 2924, 3535, 3775, 7716. See: TWOT—949; BDB—461a.

3533. כָּבַשׁ {15x} **kâbash**, *kaw-bash'*; a prim. root; to *tread* down; hence, neg. to *disregard;* pos. to *conquer, subjugate, violate:*—subdue {8x}, bring into subjection {3x}, bring into bondage {2x}, keep under {1x}, force {1x}. See: TWOT—951; BDB—461b.

3534. כֶּבֶשׁ {1x} **kebesh**, *keh'-besh;* from 3533; a *footstool* (as trodden upon):—footstool {1x}. See: TWOT—951a; BDB—461c.

3535. כִּבְשָׂה {8x} **kibsâh**, *kib-saw';* or

כַּבְשָׂה **kabsâh**, *kab-saw';* fem. of 3532; a *ewe:*—ewe lamb {6x}, lamb {2x}. See: TWOT—950; BDB—461a.

3536. כִּבְשָׁן {4x} **kibshân**, *kib-shawn';* from 3533; a smelting *furnace* (as *reducing* metals):—furnace {4x}. See: TWOT—952; BDB—461c.

3537. כַּד {18x} **kad**, *kad;* from an unused root mean. to *deepen;* prop. a *pail;* but gen. of earthenware; a *jar* for domestic purposes:—barrel {4x}, pitcher {14x}. See: TWOT—953a; BDB—461c.

3538. כְּדַב {1x} **keʰdab** (Aram.), *ked-ab';* from a root corresp. to 3576; *false:*—lying {1x}. See: TWOT—2783; BDB—1096c.

3539. כַּדְכֹּד {2x} **kadkôd**, *kad-kode';* from the same as 3537 in the sense of *striking fire* from a metal forged; a *sparkling* gem, prob. the ruby:—agate {2x}. See: TWOT—953c; BDB—461d.

3540. כְּדָרְלָעֹמֶר {5x} **Keʰdorlâʻômer**, *ked-or-law-o'-mer;* of for. or.; *Kedorlaomer*, an early Pers. king:—Chedorlaomer {5x}. See: BDB—462a.

3541. כֹּה {25x} **kôh**, *ko;* from the pref. *k* and 1931; prop. *like this*, i.e. by impl. (of manner) *thus* (or so); also (of place) *here* (or *hither*); or (of time) *now:*—{25x} = also, here, + hitherto, like, on the other side, so (and much), such, on that manner, (on) this (manner, side,

way, way and that way), + mean while, yonder. See: TWOT—955; BDB—462a, 1096d.

3542. כָּה {1x} **kâh** (Aram.), *kaw;* corresp. to 3541:—hitherto {1x}. See: TWOT—2784; BDB—1096d.

3543. כָּהָה {8x} **kâhâh**, *kaw-haw';* a prim. root; to *be weak,* i.e. (fig.) to *despond* (caus. *rebuke*), or (of light, the eye) to *grow dull:*—darkened {1x}, be dim {3x}, fail {1x}, faint {1x}, restrained {1x}, X utterly {1x}. See: TWOT—957; BDB—462c, 462d.

3544. כֵּהֶה {9x} **kêheh**, *kay-heh';* from 3543; *feeble, obscure:*—somewhat dark {5x}, darkish {1x}, wax dim {1x}, heaviness {1x}, smoking {1x}. See: TWOT—957a; BDB—462d.

3545. כֵּהָה {1x} **kêhâh**, *kay-haw';* fem. of 3544; prop a *weakening;* fig. *alleviation,* i.e. cure:—healing {1x}. See: TWOT—957b; BDB—462d.

3546. כְּהַל {4x} **kᵉhal** (Aram.), *keh-hal';* a root corresp. to 3201 and 3557; to *be able:*—be able {2x}, could {2x}. See: TWOT—2785; BDB—1096d.

3547. כָּהַן {23x} **kâhan**, *kaw-han';* a prim. root, appar. mean. to *mediate* in relig. services; but used only as denom. from 3548; to *officiate* as a priest; fig. to *put on regalia:*—priest's office {20x}, decketh {1x}, office of a priest {1x}, priest {1x}.

Kahan means "to act as a priest." **(1)** This verb, which appears 23 times in biblical Hebrew, is derived from the noun *kohen* (3548). **(2)** The verb appears only in the intensive stem. **(3)** One occurrence is in Ex 28:1: "And take thou unto thee Aaron thy brother, and his sons with him, from among the children of Israel, that he may minister unto me in the priest's office." See: TWOT—959; BDB—464c.

3548. כֹּהֵן {750x} **kôhên**, *ko-hane';* act. part. of 3547; lit. one *officiating,* a *priest;* also (by courtesy) an *acting priest* (although a layman):—priest {744x}, own {2x}, chief ruler {2x}, officer {1x}, princes {1x}.

Kohen means "priest." **(1)** This word is found 750 times in the Old Testament. **(1a)** More than one-third of the references to the "priests" are found in the Pentateuch. **(1b)** Leviticus, which has about 185 references, is called the "manual of the priests." **(2)** The term *kohen* was used to refer not only to the Hebrew priesthood but to Egyptian "priests" (Gen 41:50; 46:20; 47:26), the Philistine "priests" (1 Sa 6:2), the "priests" of Dagon (1 Sa 5:5), "priests" of Baal (2 Kin 10:19), "priests" of Chemosh (Jer 48:7), and "priests" of the Baalim and Asherim (2 Chr 34:5). **(2a)** Joseph married the daughter of the "priest" of On (Gen 41:45), and she bore him

two sons, Ephraim and Manasseh (Gen 46:20). **(2b)** Joseph did not purchase the land of the "priests" of Egypt, because the Egyptian "priests" received regular allotments from Pharaoh (Gen 47:22). **(3)** A "priest" is an authorized minister of deity who officiates at the altar and in other cultic rites. A "priest" performs sacrificial, ritualistic, and mediatorial duties; he represents the people before God. By contrast, a "prophet" is an intermediary between God and the people.

(4) The Jewish priestly office was established by the Lord in the days of Moses. **(4a)** But prior to the institution of the high priesthood and the priestly office, we read of the priesthood of Melchizedek (Gen 14:18) and of Midianite "priests" (Ex 2:16; 3:1; 18:1). **(4b)** In Ex 19:24, other "priests" are mentioned: these may have been either Midianite "priests" or "priests" in Israel prior to the official establishment of the Levitical priesthood. **(4c)** No doubt priestly functions were performed in pre-Mosaic times by the head of the family, such as Noah, Abraham, and Job. **(4c1)** After the Flood, for example, Noah built an altar to the Lord (Gen 8:20–21). **(4c2)** At Bethel, Mamre, and Moriah, Abraham built altars. In Gen 22:12–13, we read that Abraham was willing to offer his son as a sacrifice. **(4c3)** Job offered up sacrifices for his sinning children (Job 1:5). **(5)** The priesthood constituted one of the central characteristics of Old Testament religion. A passage showing the importance of the priesthood is Num 16:5–7: "And he spake unto Korah and unto all his company, saying, Even tomorrow the Lord will show who are his, and who is holy; and will cause him to come near unto him: even him whom he hath chosen will he cause to come near unto him. This do; Take you censers, Korah, and all his company; And put fire therein, and put incense in them before the Lord . . . the man whom the Lord doth choose, he shall be holy."

(6) God established Moses, Aaron, and Aaron's sons Nadab, Abihu, Eleazar, and Ithamar as "priests" in Israel (Ex 28:1, 41; 29:9, 29–30). **(6a)** Because Nadab and Abihu were killed when they "offered strange fire before the Lord," **(6b)** the priesthood was limited to the lines of Eleazar and Ithamar (Lev 10:1–2; Num 3:4; 1 Chr 24:2). **(6c)** However, not all individuals born in the family of Aaron could serve as "priest." **(6c1)** Certain physical deformities excluded a man from that perfection of holiness which a "priest" should manifest before Yahweh (Lev 21:17–23). **(6c2)** A "priest" who was ceremonially unclean was not permitted to perform his priestly duties. **(6c3)** Lev 21:1–15 gives a list of ceremonial prohibitions that forbade a "priest" from carrying out his duties.

(7) Ex 29:1–37 and Lev 8 describe the seven day consecration ceremony of Aaron and his sons. **(7a)** Both the high priest (*kohen hagga-dol*) and his sons were washed with water (Ex 29:4). **(7b)** Then Aaron the high priest dressed in holy garments with a breastplate over his heart, and there was placed on his head a holy crown—the mitre or turban (Ex 29:5–6). **(7c)** After that, Aaron was anointed with oil on his head (Ex 29:7; cf. Ps 133:2). **(7d)** Finally, the blood of a sacrificial offering was applied to Aaron and his sons (Ex 29:20–21). The consecrating bloodmark was placed upon the tip of the right ear, on the thumb of the right hand, and on the great toe of the right foot.

(8) The duties of the priesthood were very clearly defined by the Mosaic law. **(8a)** These duties were assumed on the eighth day of the service of consecration (Lev 9:1). **(8b)** The Lord told Aaron: "Therefore thou and thy sons with thee shall keep your priest's office for every thing of the altar, and within the veil; and ye shall serve . . ." (Num 18:7). **(9)** The "priests" were to act as teachers of the Law (Lev 10:10–11; Deut 33:10; 2 Chr 5:3; 17:7–9; Eze 44:23; Mal 2:6–9), a duty they did not always carry out (Mic 3:11; Mal 2:8). **(10)** In certain areas of health and jurisprudence, "priests" served as limited revelators of God's will. **(10a)** For example, it was the duty of the "priest" to discern the existence of leprosy and to perform the rites of cleansing (Lev 13—14). **(10b)** Priests determined punishments for murder and other civil matters (Deut 21:5; 2 Chr 19:8–11). See: TWOT—959a; BDB—463a, 1096d.

3549. כָּהֵן {8x} **kâhên** (Aram.), *kaw-hane'*; corresp. to 3548:—priest {8x}. See: TWOT—2786; BDB—1096d.

3550. כְּהֻנָּה {4x} **k⁰hunnâh**, *keh-hoon-naw'*; from 3547; *priesthood:*—priesthood {9x}, priest's office {5x}. See: TWOT—959b; BDB—464d.

3551. כַּו {1x} **kav** (Aram.), *kav;* from a root corresp. to 3854 in the sense of *piercing;* a *window* (as a perforation):—window {1x}. Syn.: 699, 2474, 8261. See: BDB—1096d.

3552. כּוּב {1x} **Kûwb**, *koob;* of for. der.; *Kub,* a country near Egypt:—Chub {1x}. See: BDB—464d.

3553. כּוֹבַע {6x} **kôwbaᶜ**, *ko'-bah;* from an unused root mean. to be *high* or *rounded;* a *helmet* (as *arched*):—helmet {6x}. See: TWOT—960; BDB—464d. comp. 6959.

3554. כָּוָה {2x} **kâvâh**, *kaw-vaw';* a prim. root; prop. to *prick* or *penetrate;* hence,

to *blister* (as smarting or eating into):—burned {2x}. See: TWOT—961; BDB—464d.

כּוֹחַ **kôwach**. See 3581.

3555. כְּוִיָה {1x} **k⁰vîyâh**, *kev-ee-yaw';* from 3554; a *branding:*—burning {1x}. See: TWOT—961b; BDB—465a.

3556. כּוֹכָב {37x} **kôwkâb**, *ko-kawb';* prob. from the same as 3522 (in the sense of *rolling*) or 3554 (in the sense of *blazing*); a *star* (as *round* or as *shining*); fig. a *prince:*—star {36x}, stargazers + 3674 {1x}. See: TWOT—942a; BDB—456d, 465a.

3557. כּוּל {37x} **kûwl**, *kool;* a prim. root; prop. to *keep in;* hence, to *measure;* fig. to *maintain* (in various senses):—contain {6x}, feed {6x}, sustain {4x}, abide {3x}, nourish {3x}, hold {2x}, receive {2x}, victual {2x}, bear {1x}, comprehended {1x}, misc. {7x} = forbearing, guide, be present, make provision, provide sustenance. See: TWOT—962; BDB—465a, 480d.

3558. כּוּמָז {2x} **kûwmâz**, *koo-mawz';* from an unused root mean. to *store away;* a *jewel* (prob. gold beads):—tablets {2x}. See: TWOT—990a; BDB—484d.

3559. כּוּן {219x} **kûwn**, *koon;* a prim. root; prop. to *be erect* (i.e. stand perpendicular); hence, (caus.) to *set up,* in a great variety of applications, whether lit. (*establish, fix, prepare, apply*), or fig. (*appoint, render sure, proper* or *prosperous*):—prepare {85x}, establish {58x}, ready {17x}, stablish {5x}, provide {5x}, right {5x}, fixed {4x}, set {4x}, direct {3x}, order {3x}, fashion {3x}, variant {2x}, certain {2x}, confirmed {2x}, firm {2x}, preparation {2x}, misc. {17x} = confirm, faithfulness, fasten, firm, be fitted, frame, be meet, ordain, perfect, (make) preparation, make provision, be stable, stand, tarry, × very deed.

Kuwn, as a verb, means "to be established, be readied, be prepared, be certain, be admissible." **(1)** This root used concretely connotes being firmly established, being firmly anchored and being firm. **(1a)** The first meaning is applied to a roof which is "firmly established" on pillars. So Samson said to the lad who was leading him: "Suffer me that I may feel the pillars whereupon the house standeth, that I may lean upon them" (Judg 16:26). **(1b)** In a similar sense the inhabited earth "is firmly established or anchored"; it is immovable: "The world also is established, that it cannot be moved" (Ps 93:1). **(1c)** In Ps 75:3 the image shifts to the earth "firmly established" upon pillars. **(1d)** In Ps 65:6 the divine establishing of the mountains is synonymous with divine creating. **(2)** The verb also means "to be firm": "I have caused thee to multiply as the bud of

the field, and thou hast increased and waxen great, and thou art come to excellent ornaments: thy breasts are fashioned [*kuwn*], and thine hair is grown, whereas thou wast naked and bare" (Eze 16:7).

(3) Used abstractly, *kuwn* can refer to a concept as "established," or "fixed" so as to be unchanging and unchangeable: "And for that the dream was doubled unto Pharaoh twice; it is because the thing is established by God, and God will shortly bring it to pass" (Gen 41:32 — the first occurrence of the word). **(3a)** In somewhat the same sense one can speak of the light of day "being firmly established," or having fully arrived: "But the path of the just is as the shining light, that shineth more and more unto the perfect day" (Prov 4:18). **(3b)** *Kuwn* can be used of the "establishing" of one's descendants, of seeing them prosperous (Job 21:8). **(4)** Something can be "fixed" in the sense of "being prepared or completed": "Now all the work of Solomon was prepared unto the day of the foundation of the house of the Lord" (2 Chr 8:16). **(5)** An "established" thing can be something that is enduring. **(5a)** In 1 Sa 20:31 Saul tells Jonathan: "For as long as the son of Jesse liveth upon the ground, thou shalt not be established, nor thy kingdom." **(5b)** Truthful lips (what they say) "shall be established," or will endure forever (Prov 12:19). **(5c)** One's plans "will endure" (be established) if he commits his works to the Lord (Prov 16:3).

(6) *Kuwn* can also mean "to be established" in the sense of "being ready." **(6a)** So Josiah told the people "to prepare" themselves for the Passover (2 Chr 35:4). **(6b)** This same sense appears in Ex 19:11 "And be ready against the third day: for the third day the Lord will come down in the sight of all the people upon mount Sinai." **(7)** A somewhat different nuance appears in Job 18:12; Bildad says that wherever godlessness breaks out, there is judgment: "Destruction shall be ready at his side." That is, calamity is "fixed or prepared" so that it exists potentially even before godlessness breaks out. **(8)** Something "fixed" or "established" can "be certain": "Then shalt thou inquire, and make search, and ask diligently; and, behold, if it be truth, and the thing certain . . ." (Deut 13:14). **(9)** In a somewhat different nuance the thing can be trustworthy or true. The psalmist says of the wicked that "there is no faithfulness in their mouth" (Ps 5:9). A further development of this emphasis is that a matter "may be admissible"—so Moses said to Pharaoh: "It is not meet so to do; for we shall sacrifice the abomination of the Egyptians to the Lord our God" (Ex 8:26). **(10)** When one "fixes" an arrow on the bow, he takes aim or "prepares" to shoot

his bow (cf. Ps 7:12). Syn.: 724, 3615, 3634. See: TWOT—964; BDB—465c.

3560. כּוּן {1x} **Kûwn**, *koon;* prob. from 3559; *established; Kun,* a place in Syria:—Chun {1x}. See: BDB—467b.

3561. כַּוָּן {2x} **kavvân**, *kav-vawn';* from 3559; something *prepared,* i.e. a sacrificial *wafer:*—cake {2x}. See: TWOT—964f; BDB—467d.

3562. כּוֹנַנְיָהוּ {3x} **Kôwnanyâhûw**, *ko-nan-yaw'-hoo;* from 3559 and 3050; *Jah has sustained; Conanjah,* the name of two Isr.:—Conaniah {1x}, Cononiah {2x}. See: BDB—467b, 487d. comp. 3663.

3563. כּוֹס {34x} **kôwç**, *koce;* from an unused root mean. to *hold* together; a *cup* (as a container), often fig. a *lot* (as if a potion); also some unclean bird, prob. an *owl* (perh. from the cup-like cavity of its eye):—cup {31x}, (small) owl {3x}. See: TWOT—965, 966; BDB—468a. comp. 3599.

3564. כּוּר {9x} **kûwr**, *koor;* from an unused root mean. prop. to *dig* through; a *pot* or *furnace* (as if excavated):—furnace {9x}. See: TWOT—967b, 968; BDB—468b. comp. 3600.

כּוּר **kôwr.** See 3733.

3565. כּוּר עָשָׁן {1x} **Kôwr ʿÂshân**, *kore aw-shawn';* from 3564 and 6227; *furnace of smoke; Cor-Ashan,* a place in Pal.:—Chor-ashan {1x}. See: BDB—468b.

3566. כּוֹרֶשׁ {15x} **Kôwresh**, *ko'-resh;* or (Ezra 1:1 [last time], 2)

כֹּרֶשׁ **Kôresh**, *ko'-resh;* from the Pers.; *Koresh* (or Cyrus), the Pers. king:—Cyrus {15x}. See: BDB—468d, 503c, 1096d.

3567. כּוֹרֶשׁ {8x} **Kôwresh** (Aram.), *ko'-resh;* corresp. to 3566:—Cyrus {8x}. See: BDB—1096d.

3568. כּוּשׁ **Kûwsh**, *koosh;* prob. of for. or.; *Cush* (or Ethiopia), the name of a son of Ham, and of his territory; also of an Isr.:—Ethiopians {3x}, Cush {8x}, Ethiopia {19x}. See: TWOT—969; BDB—468d, 469a.

3569. כּוּשִׁי {23x} **Kûwshîy**, *koo-shee';* patron. from 3568; a *Cushite,* or desc. of Cush:—Cushi {8x}, Ethiopians {9x}, Ethiopia {6x}. See: TWOT—969a; BDB—469a.

3570. כּוּשִׁי {2x} **Kûwshîy**, *koo-shee';* the same as 3569; *Cushi,* the name of two Isr.:—Cushi {2x}. See: BDB—469b, 505b.

3571. כּוּשִׁית {2x} **Kûwshîyth,** *koo-sheeth';*
fem. of 3569; a *Cushite wo-*
man:—Ethiopian {2x}. See: BDB—469a.

3572. כּוּשָׁן {1x} **Kûwshân,** *koo-shawn';* perh.
from 3568; *Cushan,* a region of
Arabia:—Cushan {1x}. See: BDB—469b.

3573. כּוּשַׁן רִשְׁעָתַיִם {4x} **Kûwshan Rishʿâ-**
thâyim, *koo-shan' rish-*
aw-thah'-yim; appar. from 3572 and the dual
of 7564; *Cushan of double wickedness; Cushan-*
Rishathajim, a Mesopotamian king:—Chus-
han-rishathayim {4x}. See: BDB—469b, 958a.

3574. כּוּשָׁרָה {1x} **kôwshârâh,** *ko-shaw-raw';*
from 3787; *prosperity;* in plur.
freedom:—× chain {1x}. See: TWOT—1052a;
BDB—469b, 507a.

3575. כּוּת {2x} **Kûwth,** *kooth;* or (fem.)

כּוּתָה **Kûwthâh,** *koo-thaw';* of for. or.;
Cuth or *Cuthah,* a province of Assyria:—Cuth {1x}, Cuthah {1x}. See: BDB—
469b.

3576. כָּזַב {16x} **kâzab,** *kaw-zab';* a prim.
root; to *lie* (i.e. *deceive*), lit. or
fig.:—fail {1x}, liar {2x}, liars {1x}, lie {7x}, lying
{1x}, lies {1x}, lied {2x}, be in vain {1x}. See:
TWOT—970; BDB—469b, 1096c.

3577. כָּזָב {31x} **kâzâb,** *kaw-zawb';* from
3576; *falsehood;* lit. (*untruth*) or
fig. (*idol*):—lie {23x}, lying {2x}, leasing {2x},
deceitful {1x}, false {1x}, liar {1x}, lies + 1697
{1x}. See: TWOT—970a; BDB—469c.

3578. כֹּזְבָא {1x} **Kôzʿbâʾ,** *ko-zeb-aw';* from
3576; *fallacious; Cozeba,* a place
in Pal.:—Choseba {1x}. See: BDB—469d.

3579. כָּזְבִּי {2x} **Kozbîy,** *koz-bee';* from 3576;
false; Cozbi, a Midianitess:—Cozbi
{2x}. See: BDB—469d.

3580. כְּזִיב {1x} **Kʿzîyb,** *kez-eeb';* from 3576;
falsified; Kezib, a place in Pal.:—
Chezib {1x}. See: BDB—469d.

3581. כֹּחַ {126x} **kôach,** *ko'-akh;* or (Dan. 11:6)

כּוֹחַ **kôwach,** *ko'-akh;* from an unused
root mean. to *be firm; vigor,* lit.
(*force,* in a good or a bad sense) or fig. (*capac-*
ity, means, produce); also (from its hardiness)
a large *lizard:*—strength {58x}, power {47x},
might {7x}, force {3x}, ability {2x}, able {2x}, able
+ 6113 {1x}, chameleon {1x}, fruits {1x}, powerful {1x}, substance {1x}, wealth {1x}, weary +
3019 {1x}.

Kowach (3581)means "strength; power;
force; ability." **(1)** *Kowach,* which occurs 126
times, is a poetic word as it is used most frequently in the poetic and prophetical literature. **(2)**

The basic meaning of *kowach* is an ability
to do something. **(1a)** Samson's "strength" lay
in his hair (Judg 16:5), and we must keep in mind
that his "strength" had been demonstrated
against the Philistines. **(1b)** Nations and kings
exert their "powers" (Josh 17:17; Dan 8:24).
(1c) It is even possible to say that a field has
kowach, as it does or does not have vital "powers" to produce and harvest: "When thou tillest
the ground, it shall not henceforth yield unto
thee her strength [i.e., crops]" (Gen 4:12—the
first occurrence). **(2)** In the Old Testament it is
recognized that by eating one gains "strength"
(1 Sa 28:22), whereas one loses one's "abilities"
in fasting (1Sa 28:20); "And he arose, and did
eat and drink, and went in the strength of that
meat forty days and forty nights unto Horeb
the mount of God" (1 Kin 19:8). **(3)** The above
definition of *kowach* fits well in the description of Daniel and his friends: **(3a)** "Children
in whom was no blemish, but well-favored, and
skillful in all wisdom, and cunning in knowledge, and understanding science, and such as
had ability [*kowach*] in them to stand in the
king's palace, and whom they might teach the
learning and the tongue of the Chaldeans"
(Dan 1:4).

(3b) The "ability" is here not physical but
mental. **(3c)** They were talented in having the
intellectual acumen of learning the skills of
the Babylonians and thus training for being
counselors to the king. **(4)** The internal fortitude was best demonstrated by the difficulties
and frustrations of life. A strong man withstood hard times. The proverb bears out this
important teaching: "If thou faint in the day
of adversity, thy strength is small" (Prov 24:10).
(5) A special sense of *kowach* is the meaning
"property." **(5a)** The results of native "abilities," the development of special gifts, and the
manifestation of one's "strength" led often to
prosperity and riches. **(5b)** Those who returned
from the Exile gave willingly out of their riches
(*kowach*) to the building fund of the temple
(Ezr 2:69). **(5c)** A proverb warns against adultery, because one's "strength," or one's wealth,
may be taken by others: "Lest strangers be
filled with thy wealth [*kowach*]; and thy labors
be in the house of a stranger" (Prov 5:10). **(6)** In
the Old Testament, God had demonstrated His
"strength" to Israel. **(6a)** The language of God's
"strength" is highly metaphorical. **(6a1)** God's
right hand gloriously manifests His "power"
(Ex 15:6). **(6a2)** His voice is loud: "The voice of
the Lord is powerful; the voice of the Lord is
full of majesty" (Ps 29:4).

(6b) In His "power," He delivered Israel from
Egypt (Ex 32:11) and brought them through
the Red Sea (Ex 15:6; cf. Num 14:13). **(6c)** Even
as He advances the rights of the poor and needy

(Is 50:2), He brought the Israelites as a needy people into the Promised Land with His "power": "He hath showed his people the power of his works, that he may give them the heritage of the heathen" (Ps 111:6). **(7)** He delights in helping His people; however, the Lord does not tolerate self-sufficiency on man's part. **(7a)** Isaiah rebuked the king of Assyria for his arrogance in claiming to have been successful in his conquests (10:12–14), and he remarked that the axe (Assyria) should not boast over the one who chops (God) with it (v. 15). **(7b)** Likewise God had warned His people against pride in taking the land of Canaan: "And thou say in thine heart, My power [*kowach*] and the might of mine hand hath gotten me this wealth. But thou shalt remember the Lord thy God: for it is he that giveth thee power [*kowach*] to get wealth, that he may establish his covenant which he sware unto thy fathers, as it is this day" (Deut 8:17–18). **(8)** The believer must learn to depend upon God and trust in Him: "This is the word of the Lord unto Zerubbabel, saying, Not by might, nor by power, but by my spirit, saith the Lord of hosts" (Zec 4:6). See: TWOT—973.1; BDB—470a, 470b, 470c.

3582. כָּחַד {32x} **kâchad**, *kaw-khad'*; a prim. root; to *secrete*, by act or word; hence, (intens.) to *destroy:*—hide {16x}, cut off {10x}, conceal {4x}, desolate {1x}, cut down {1x}. See: TWOT—972; BDB—470b.

3583. כָּחַל {1x} **kâchal** *kaw-khal'*; a prim. root; to *paint* (with stibium):—paint {1x}. See: TWOT—974; BDB—471a, 806d.

3584. כָּחַשׁ {22x} **kâchash**, *kaw-khash'*; a prim. root; to *be untrue*, in word (to *lie, feign, disown*) or deed (to *disappoint, fail, cringe*):—lie {5x}, submit {3x}, deny {3x}, fail {3x}, denied {2x}, belied {1x}, deceive {1x}, dissembled {1x}, deal falsely {1x}, liars {1x}, submitted {1x}. Syn.: 3576, 8266. See: TWOT—975; BDB—471a.

3585. כַּחַשׁ {6x} **kachash**, *kakh'-ash;* from 3584; lit. a *failure* of flesh, i.e. *emaciation;* fig. *hypocrisy:*—leanness {1x}, lies {4x}, lying {1x}. See: TWOT—975a; BDB—471c.

3586. כֶּחָשׁ {1x} **kechâsh**, *kekh-awsh';* from 3584; *faithless:*—lying {1x}. See: TWOT—975b; BDB—471c.

3587. כִּי {1x} **kîy**, *kee;* from 3554; a *brand* or *scar:*—burning {1x}. See: TWOT—961a; BDB—465a, 475d.

3588. כִּי {46x} **kîy**, *kee;* a prim. particle [the full form of the prepositional prefix] indicating *causal* relations of all kinds, antecedent or consequent; (by impl.) very widely used as a rel. conjunc. or adv. [as below]; often

largely modif. by other particles annexed:— {46x}= and, + (forasmuch, inasmuch, where-) as, assured [-ly], + but, certainly, doubtless, + else, even, + except, for, how, (because, in, so, than) that, + nevertheless, now, rightly, seeing, since, surely, then, therefore, + (al-) + though, + till, truly, + until, when, whether, while, whom, yea, yet. See: TWOT—976; BDB—210b, 465a, 471c, 474c, 475c, 758b, 774c, 774d, 1099a.

3589. כִּיד {1x} **kîyd**, *keed;* from a prim root mean. to *strike;* a *crushing;* fig. *calamity:*—destruction {1x}. Syn.: 3772, 5395, 7665. See: TWOT—977a; BDB—475d.

3590. כִּידוֹד {1x} **kîydôwd**, *kee-dode';* from the same as 3589 [comp. 3539]; prop. something *struck* off, i.e. a *spark* (as struck):—sparks {1x}. See: TWOT—953b; BDB—461d, 475d.

3591. כִּידוֹן {9x} **kîydôwn**, *kee-dohn';* from the same as 3589; prop. something to *strike* with, i.e. a *dart* (perh. smaller than 2595):—lance {1x}, shield {2x}, spear {5x}, target {1x}. See: TWOT—977b; BDB—475d.

3592. כִּידוֹן {1x} **Kîydôwn**, *kee-dohn';* the same as 3591; *Kidon*, a place in Pal.:—Chidon {1x}. See: BDB—475d, 647a.

3593. כִּידוֹר {1x} **kîydôwr**, *kee-dore';* of uncert. der.; perh. *tumult:*—battle {1x}. Syn.: 4421, 7128. See: TWOT—954a; BDB—461d, 475d.

3594. כִּיּוּן {1x} **Kîyûwn**, *kee-yoon';* from 3559; prop. a *statue*, i.e. idol; but used (by euphem.) for some heathen deity (perh. corresp. to Priapus or Baal-peor):—Chiun {1x}. See: BDB—475d.

3595. כִּיּוֹר {23x} **kîyôwr**, *kee-yore';* or

כִּיֹר **kîyôr**, *kee-yore';* from the same as 3564; prop. something *round* (as *excavated* or *bored*), i.e. a chafing-*dish* for coals or a *caldron* for cooking; hence, (from similarity of form) a *washbowl;* also (for the same reason) a *pulpit* or platform:—hearth {1x}, laver {20x}, pan {1x}, scaffold {1x}. See: TWOT—967d; BDB—468c, 476a.

3596. כִּילַי {2x} **kîylay**, *kee-lah'-ee;* or

כֵּלַי **kêlay**, *kay-lah'-ee;* from 3557 in the sense of *withholding; niggardly:*—churl {2x}. See: TWOT—1366b; BDB—476a, 67d.

3597. כֵּילַף {1x} **kêylaph**, *kay-laf';* from an unused root mean. to *clap* or strike with noise; a *club* or sledge-hammer:—hammer {1x}. Syn.: 1989, 4717. See: TWOT—978.1; BDB—476a.

3598. כִּימָה {3x} **Kîymâh**, *kee-maw';* from the same as 3558; a *cluster* of stars, i.e. the *Pleiades:*—Pleiades {2x}, seven stars {1x}. See: BDB—465b, 476a.

3599. כִּיס {6x} **kîyç**, *keece;* a form for 3563; a *cup;* also a *bag* for money or weights:—bag {4x}, cup {1x}, purse {1x}. See: TWOT—979; BDB—476a.

3600. כִּיר {1x} **kîyr**, *keer;* a form for 3564 (only in the dual); a cooking *range* (consisting of two parallel stones, across which the boiler is set):—ranges for pots {1x}. See: TWOT—967c; BDB—468c, 476a.

כִּיר **kîyôr**. See 3595.

3601. כִּישׁוֹר {1x} **kîyshôwr**, *kee-shore';* from 3787; lit. a *director,* i.e. the *spindle* or shank of a distaff (6418), by which it is twirled:—spindle {1x}. See: TWOT—1052c; BDB—476a, 507a.

3602. כָּכָה {9x} **kâkâh**, *kaw'-kaw;* from 3541; *just so,* referring to the previous or following context:—{9x}= after that (this) manner, this matter, (even) so, in such a case, thus. See: TWOT—956; BDB—462b, 476b.

3603. כִּכָּר {68x} **kikkâr**, *kik-kawr';* from 3769; a *circle,* i.e. (by impl.) a circumjacent *tract* or region, expec. the *Ghôr* or valley of the Jordan; also a (round) *loaf;* also a *talent* (or large [round] coin):—talent {48x}, plain {12x}, loaf {4x}, piece {2x}, country {1x}, morsel {1x}. See: TWOT 1046c; BDB—476b, 503a, 1098a.

3604. כִּכַּר {1x} **kikkêr** (C ald.), *kik-kare';* corresp. to 3603; a *talent:*—talent {1x}. See: TWOT—2804a; BDB—1096d, 1098a.

3605. כֹּל {25x} **kôl**, *kole;* or (Jer. 33:8)

כּוֹל **kôwl**, *kole;* from 3634; prop. the *whole;* hence, *all, any* or *every* (in the sing. only, but often in a plur. sense):—{25x} = (in) all (manner, [ye]), altogether, any (manner), enough, every (one, place, thing), howsoever, as many as, [no-] thing, ought, whatsoever, (the) whole, whoso (-ever).

Kowl, as a noun, means "all; the whole." **(1)** The word can be used alone, meaning "the entirety," "whole," or "all," as in: "And thou shalt put all [*kowl*] in the hands of Aaron, and in the hands of his sons" (Ex 29:24). **(2)** *Kowl* can signify everything in a given unit whose members have been selected from others of their kind: "That the sons of God saw the daughters of men that they were fair; and they took them wives of all which they chose" (Gen 6:2). See: TWOT—985a; BDB—481a, 1097a.

3606. כֹּל {95x} **kôl** (Aram.), *kole;* corresp. to 3605:—all {51x}, any {8x}, whole {6x}, as {4x}, every {4x}, because + 6903 {4x}, as + 6903 {2x}, no {2x}, whosoever + 606 {2x}, misc. {12x} = + there (where) -fore, + though, (what, where) -soever.

Kol, as an adjective, means "all; whole; entirety; every; each." **(1)** When *kol* precedes a noun, it expresses a unit and signifies the whole: "These are the three sons of Noah: and of them was the whole (*kol*) earth overspread" (Gen 9:19). **(2)** *Kol* may also signify the entirety of a noun that does not necessarily represent a unit: "All the people, both small and great" entered into the covenant (2 Kin 23:2). The use of the word in such instances tends to unify what is not otherwise a unit. **(3)** *Kol* can precede a word that is only part of a larger unit or not part of a given unit at all. **(3a)** In this case, the prominent idea is that of "plurality," a heterogeneous unit: "And it came to pass from the time that he had made him overseer in his house, and over all that he had, that the Lord blessed the Egyptian's house for Joseph's sake; and the blessing of the Lord was upon all that he had in the house, and in the field" (Gen 39:5). **(3b)** Related to the preceding nuance is the use of *kol* to express comprehensiveness. **(3b1)** Not only does it indicate that the noun modified is a plurality, but also that the unit formed by the addition of *kol* includes everything in the category indicated by the noun: "All the cities were ten with their suburbs for the families of the children of Kohath that remained" (Josh 21:26).

(3b2) In Gen 1:21 (its first occurrence), the word precedes a collective noun and may be translated "every": "And God created great whales, and every living creature that moveth,. . ." **(4)** When used to refer to the individual members of a group, *kol* means "every": **(4a)** "His hand will be against every man, and every man's hand against him" (Gen 16:12). **(4b)** Another example: "Thy princes are rebellious, and companions of thieves: every one loveth gifts, and followeth after rewards" (Is 1:23). **(4c)** Related to this use is the meaning "none but." **(5)** In Deut 19:15, *kol* means "every kind of" or "any"; the word focuses on each and every member of a given unit: **(5a)** "One witness shall not rise up against a man for any iniquity, or for any sin, in any sin that he sinneth." **(5b)** A related nuance appears in Gen 24:10, but here the emphasis is upon "all sorts": "And the servant took ten camels of the camels of his master, and departed; for all [i.e., a variety of] the goods of his master were in his hand." See: TWOT—2789; BDB—1096d, 1097a.

3607. כָּלָא {18x} **kâlâ³**, *kaw-law';* a prim. root; to *restrict,* by act (*hold* back or in) or word (*prohibit*):—shut up {4x}, stayed {3x}, refrained {2x}, restrained {2x}, withhold {2x},

keep back {1x}, finish {1x}, forbid {1x}, kept {1x}, retain {1x}. See: TWOT−980; BDB−476b, 478a.

3608. כְּלֶא {10x} kele³, keh'-leh; from 3607; a prison:−prison {10x}. See: TWOT−980a; BDB−476c. comp. 3610, 3628.

3609. כִּלְאָב {1x} Kil³âb, kil-awb'; appar. from 3607 and 1; restraint of (his) father; Kilab, an Isr.:−Chileab {1x}. See: BDB−476d.

3610. כִּלְאַיִם {4x} kil³ayim, kil-ah'-yim; dual of 3608 in the orig. sense of separation; two heterogeneities:−divers seeds {1x}, diverse kinds {1x}, mingled {1x}, mingled seed {1x}. See: TWOT−980d; BDB−476c.

3611. כֶּלֶב {32x} keleb, keh'-leb; from an unused root means. to yelp, or else to attack; a dog; hence, (by euphem.) a male prostitute:−dog {32x}. See: TWOT−981a; BDB−476d.

3612. כָּלֵב {35x} Kâlêb, kaw-labe'; perh. a form of 3611, or else from the same root in the sense of forcible; Caleb, the name of three Isr.:−Caleb {35x}. See: BDB−477a.

3613. כָּלֵב אֶפְרָתָה {1x} Kâlêb ³Ephrâthâh, kaw-labe' ef-raw'-thaw; from 3612 and 672; Caleb-Ephrathah, a place in Egypt (if the text is correct):−Caleb-ephrathah {1x}. See: BDB−68d.

3614. כָּלִבּוֹ {1x} Kâlibbôw, kaw-lib-bo'; prob. by err. transc. for

כָּלֵבִי Kâlêbîy, kaw-lay-bee'; patron. from 3612; a Calebite or desc. of Caleb:−of the house of Caleb {1x}. See: BDB−477a.

3615. כָּלָה {206x} kâlâh, kaw-law'; a prim. root; to end, whether intr. (to cease, be finished, perish) or tran. (to complete, prepare, consume):−consume {57x}, end {44x}, finish {20x}, fail {18x}, accomplish {12x}, done {9x}, spend {8x}, ended {7x}, determined {4x}, away {3x}, fulfil {3x}, fainteth {2x}, destroy {2x}, left {2x}, waste {2x}, misc. {13x} = cease, expire, × fully, × have, long, bring to pass, wholly reap, make clean riddance, quite take away.

Kalah (3615), as a noun, means "to cease, be finished, perish, be completed." (1) Basically, the word means "to cease or stop." (1a) Kalah may refer to the "end" of a process or action, such as the cessation of God's creating the universe: "And on the seventh day God ended his work which he had made . . ." (Gen 2:2−the first occurrence of the word). (1b) The word can also refer to the "disappearance" of something: "And the water was spent in the

bottle . . ." (Gen 21:15). (1c) Finally, kalah can be used of "coming to an end" or "the process of ending": "The barrel of meal shall not waste" (1 Kin 17:14). (2) Kalah can have the more positive connotation of "successfully completing" something. (2a) First Kings 6:38 says that the house of the Lord was "finished throughout all the parts thereof, and according to all [its plans]." (2b) In this same sense, the word of the Lord "is fulfilled": "Now in the first year of Cyrus king of Persia, that the word of the Lord by the mouth of Jeremiah might be fulfilled, the Lord stirred up the spirit of Cyrus king of Persia, that he made a proclamation" (Ezr 1:1). (3) Kalah sometimes means "making a firm decision." David tells Jonathan that if Saul is very angry, "be sure that evil is determined by him" (1 Sa 20:7).

(4) Negatively, "to complete" something may mean "to make it vanish" or "go away." (4a) Kalah is used in this sense in Deut 32:23, when God says: "I will heap mischiefs upon them; I will spend mine arrows upon them." In other words, His arrows will "vanish" from His possession. (4b) This nuance is used especially of clouds: "As the cloud is consumed and vanisheth away . . ." (Job 7:9). (4c) Another negative nuance is to "destroy" something or someone: "the famine shall consume the land" (Gen 41:30). (4d) Along this same line is the use of kalah in Is 1:28: "They that forsake the Lord shall be consumed"; here, however, the verb is a synonym for "dying" or "perishing." (4e) One's sight may also "vanish" and one may go blind: "But the eyes of the wicked shall fail, and they shall not escape" (Job 11:20). (5) An altogether different emphasis appears when one's heart comes "to an end" or "stops within": "My soul longeth, yea, even fainteth for the courts of the Lord" (Ps 84:2); the psalmist probably meant that his desire for God's presence was so intense that nothing else had any meaning for him—he "died" to be there. (6) It can mean successfully completing something: "And in the eleventh year, in the month Bul, which is the eighth month, was the house finished throughout all the parts thereof, and according to all the fashion of it. So was he seven years in building it" (1 Kin 6:38). (7) The word of the Lord "is fulfilled" (Ezr 1:1). (8) It can mean making a firm decision: "If he say thus, It is well; thy servant shall have peace: but if he be very wroth, then be sure that evil is determined by him" (1 Sa 20:7). (9) Negatively, to complete something may mean "to make it vanish" or "go away" (Deut 32:23; clouds – Job 7:9). See: TWOT−982, 983, 984; BDB−477b.

3616. כָּלֶה {1x} kâleh, kaw-leh'; from 3615; pining:−fail {1x}. See: TWOT−982b; BDB−479a.

Hebrew

3617. כָּלָה {22x} **kâlâh**, *kaw-law';* from 3615; a *completion;* adv. *completely;* also *destruction:—* . . . end {11x}, altogether {3x}, consume {3x}, consumption {2x}, consummation {1x}, determined {1x}, riddance {1x}.

Kalah, as a noun, means "consumption; complete annihilation." *Kalah* appears 22 times; one occurrence is Neh 9:31: "Nevertheless for thy great mercies' sake thou didst not utterly consume them, nor forsake them; . . . ." See: TWOT—982a; BDB—478d.

3618. כַּלָּה **kallâh**, *kal-law';* from 3634; a *bride* (as if *perfect*); hence, a *son's wife:—* bride {9x}, daughter-in-law {17x}, spouse {8x}. See: TWOT—986a; BDB—480c, 483c.

כְּלוּא **kᵉlûwᵓ** See 3628.

3619. כְּלוּב **kᵉlûwb**, *kel-oob';* from the same as 3611; a bird-*trap* (as furnished with a *clap*-stick or treadle to spring it); hence, a *basket* (as resembling a wicker cage):—basket {1x}, cage {2x}. See: TWOT—981b; BDB—477b.

3620. כְּלוּב **Kᵉlûwb**, *kel-oob';* the same as 3619; *Kelub,* the name of two Isr.:—Chelub {2x}. See: BDB—477b.

3621. כְּלוּבַי **Kᵉlûwbay**, *kel-oo-bay'-ee;* a form of 3612; *Kelubai,* an Isr.:—Chelubai {1x}. See: BDB—477b.

3622. כְּלוּהַי **Kᵉlûwhay**, *kel-oo-hah'-ee;* from 3615; *completed; Keluhai,* an Isr.:—Chelluh {1x}. See: BDB—479a.

3623. כְּלוּלָה **kᵉlûwlâh**, *kel-oo-law';* denom. pass. part. from 3618; *bridehood* (only in the plur.):—espousal {1x}. See: TWOT—986b; BDB—480c, 483c.

3624. כֶּלַח **kelach**, *keh'-lakh;* from an unused root mean. to *be complete; maturity:—*full age {1x}, old age {1x}. See: TWOT—984a; BDB—480c.

3625. כֶּלַח **Kelach**, *keh'-lakh;* the same as 3624; *Kelach,* a place in Assyria:—Calah {2x}. See: BDB—480d.

3626. כָּל־חֹזֶה **Kol-Chôzeh**, *kol-kho-zeh';* from 3605 and 2374; *every seer; Col-Chozeh,* an Isr.:—Col-hozeh {2x}. See: BDB—480d.

3627. כְּלִי **kᵉlîy**, *kel-ee';* from 3615; something *prepared,* i.e. any *apparatus* (as an implement, utensil, dress, vessel or weapon):—vessel {166x}, instrument {39x}, weapon {21x}, jewel {21x}, armourbearer + 5375 {18x}, stuff {14x}, thing {11x}, armour {10x}, furniture {7x}, carriage {3x}, bag {2x}, misc. {13x} = artillery, + furnish, that is made

of, × one from another, that which pertaineth, pot, + psaltery, sack, tool, ware, + whatsoever.

Keliy means "vessel; receptacle; stuff clothing; utensil; tool; instrument; ornament or jewelry; armor or weapon." **(1)** This word is used of "receptacles" of various kinds used for storing and transporting. Thus Jacob said to Laban: "Whereas thou hast searched through all my stuff [literally, receptacles], what hast thou found of all thy household stuff [literally, from all the receptacles of thy house]?" (Gen 31:37). **(1a)** Such "receptacles" may be made of wood (Lev 11:32) or potsherd or clay (Lev 6:28). **(1b)** They may be used to hold documents (Jer 32:14), wine, oil, fruits (Jer 40:10), food (Eze 4:9), beverage (Ruth 2:9), or bread (1 Sa 9:7). **(1c)** Even a shepherd's bag is a *keliy* (1 Sa 17:40). **(1d)** In 1 Sa 17:22 the word is used of baggage, or "receptacles" (his shepherd's bag?) and what is in them: "And David left his carriage in the hand of the [baggage keeper]. . . ." **(1e)** The sailors on the ship in which Jonah sailed "cast forth the wares [cargo] . . . into the sea, to lighten it of them" (Jonah 1:5). **(2)** Ships are called "receptacles," presumably because they can hold people: "That sendeth ambassadors by the sea, even in vessels of bulrushes upon the waters . . ." (Is 18:2). **(3)** *Keliy* can mean "clothing": "The woman shall not wear that which pertaineth unto a man, neither shall a man put on a woman's garment: for all that do so are abomination unto the Lord thy God" (Deut 22:5).

(4) The word may be used of various "vessels and utensils": "And the four tables were of hewn stone for the burnt offering . . . : whereupon also they laid the instruments wherewith they slew the burnt offering and the sacrifice" (Eze 40:42). **(5)** In Gen 45:20 this word refers to movable but large possessions: Pharaoh told Joseph to tell his brothers to take wagons and bring their family to Egypt, and "regard not your stuff; for the good of all the land of Egypt is yours." **(6)** Thus in Ex 27:19 the word represents all the furniture and utensils of the tabernacle (cf. Num 3:8). **(7)** Samuel warned Israel that the king on whom they insisted would organize them into levees (work crews) "to [plow] his ground, and to reap his harvest, and to make his instruments of war, and instruments of his chariots" (1 Sa 8:12). **(8)** More narrowly, *keliy* may be used of oxen harnesses: "Behold, here be oxen for burnt sacrifice, and threshing instruments and other instruments of the oxen for wood" (2 Sa 24:22). **(9)** This word may be used of various "implements or tools": "Simeon and Levi are brethren instruments of cruelty in their habitations" (Gen 49:5). **(10)** In Jer 22:7 the word represents "tools" with which trees may be cut down: "And I will prepare

Hebrew

destroyers against thee, every one with his weapons: and they shall cut down thy choice cedars, and cast them into the fire."

(11) Isaac told Esau to take his gear, his quiver, and his bow, "and go out to the field, and take me some venison" (Gen 27:3). **(12)** Weapons for war are called "implements": "And they [the Israelites] went after them unto Jordan: and, lo, all the way was full of garments and vessels, which the Syrians had cast away in their haste" (2 Kin 7:15). **(12a)** A bearer of implements is an armor-bearer (Judg 9:54). **(12b)** A house of arms or an armory is referred to in 2 Kin 20:13. **(13)** In Amos 6:5 and such passages (2 Chr 5:13; 7:6; 23:13; cf. Ps 71:22) "musical instruments" are called *kelim*: "That chant to the sound of the viol, and invent to themselves instruments of music." **(14)** *Keliy* stands for various kinds of "precious ornaments": **(14a)** "And the servant brought forth jewels of silver, and jewels of gold, and raiment, and gave them to Rebekah" (Gen 24:53 — the first biblical appearance of the word). **(14b)** Such "precious ornaments" adorned the typical bride: "I will greatly rejoice in the Lord, my soul shall be joyful in my God; for he hath clothed me with the garments of salvation, he hath covered me with the robe of righteousness, as a bridegroom decketh himself with ornaments and as a bride adorneth herself with her jewels" (Is 61:10). See: TWOT — 982g; BDB — 479b, 480d.

3628. כְּלִיא {2x} keˡîyʾ, *kel-ee';* or

כְּלוּא keˡûwʾ, *kel-oo';* from 3607 [comp. 3608]; a *prison:* — prison = 1004 {2x}. See: TWOT — 980b; BDB — 476c.

3629. כִּלְיָה {31x} kilyâh, *kil-yaw';* fem. of 3627 (only in the plur.); a *kidney* (as an essential *organ*); fig. the *mind* (as the interior self): — kidneys {18x}, reins {13x}. See: TWOT — 983a; BDB — 480b, 480d.

3630. כִּלְיוֹן {3x} Kilyôwn, *kil-yone';* a form of 3631; *Kiljon,* an Isr.: — Chilion {3x}. See: BDB — 479a.

3631. כִּלָּיוֹן {2x} killâyôwn, *kil-law-yone';* from 3615; *pining, destruction:* — consumption {1x}, failing {1x}. See: TWOT — 982c; BDB — 479a, 480d.

3632. כָּלִיל {15x} kâlîyl, *kaw-leel';* from 3634; *complete;* as noun, the *whole* (spec. a sacrifice *entirely consumed*); as adv. *fully:* — perfect {3x}, wholly {3x}, all {2x}, wholly burnt {1x}, flame {1x}, perfection {1x}, whole burnt sacrifice 1, utterly {1x}, every whit {1x}, whole {1x}.

Kaliyl means "the entire; whole, whole offering." **(1)** This word represents the "whole

offering" from which the worshiper does not partake: "It is a statute for ever unto the Lord; it shall be wholly burnt" (Lev 6:22). **(2)** In Num 4:6, *kaliyl* refers to the "cloth wholly of blue." In other words, it indicates "the entire" cloth. Syn.: 5930. See: TWOT — 985b; BDB — 483a.

3633. כַּלְכֹּל {2x} Kalkôl, *kal-kole';* from 3557; *sustenance; Calcol,* an Isr.: — Calcol {1x}, Chalcol {1x}. See: BDB — 465b, 480d.

3634. כָּלַל {2x} kâlal, *kaw-lal';* a prim. root; to *complete:* — made perfect {1x}, perfected {1x}.

Kalal, as a verb, means "to perfect." This common Semitic root appears in biblical Hebrew only 3 times. Eze 27:11 is a good example: "They have made thy beauty perfect [*kalal*]." Syn.: 8003, 8549. See: TWOT — 985, 986; BDB — 480d, 1007a.

3635. כְּלַל {8x} keˡlal (Aram.), *kel-al';* corresp. to 3634; to *complete:* — finished {2x}, make up {2x}, set up {4x}. See: TWOT — 2788; BDB — 1097a, 115b.

3636. כְּלָל {1x} Keˡlâl, *kel-awl';* from 3634; *complete; Kelal,* an Isr.: — Chelal {1x}. See: BDB — 483c.

3637. כָּלַם {38x} kâlam, *kaw-lawm';* a prim. root; prop. to *wound;* but only fig., to *taunt* or *insult:* — ashamed {12x}, confounded {11x}, shame {7x}, blush {3x}, hurt {2x}, reproach {2x}, confusion {1x}. See: TWOT — 987; BDB — 483c.

3638. כִּלְמָד {1x} Kilmâd, *kil-mawd';* of for. der.; *Kilmad,* a place appar. in the Ass. empire: — Chilmad {1x}. See: BDB — 484b.

3639. כְּלִמָּה {30x} keˡlimmâh, *kel-im-maw';* from 3637; *disgrace:* — confusion {6x}, dishonour {3x}, reproach {1x}, shame {20x}. See: TWOT — 987a; BDB — 484a.

3640. כְּלִמּוּת {1x} keˡlimmu wth, *kel-im-mooth';* from 3639; *disgrace:* — shame {1x}. Syn.: 954, 1322, 2659, 7036. See: TWOT — 987b; BDB — 484b.

3641. כַּלְנֶה {3x} Kalneh, *kal-neh';* or

כַּלְנֵה Kalnêh, *kal-nay';* also

כַּלְנוֹ Kalnôw, *kal-no';* of for. der.; *Calneh* or *Calno,* a place in the Ass. empire: — Calneh {2x}, Calno {1x}. See: BDB — 484c. comp. 3656.

3642. כָּמַהּ {1x} kâmahh, *kaw-mah';* a prim. root; to *pine* after: — long {1x}. Syn.: 183, 2968, 3700. See: TWOT — 988; BDB — 484c.

3643. כִּמְהָם {4x} Kimhâm, *kim-hawm';* from 3642; *pining; Kimham,* an Isr.: — Chimham {4x}. See: BDB — 158c, 484c, 484d.

3644. כְּמוֹ {20x} keˈmôw, *kem-o'*; or

כָּמוֹ kâmôw, *kaw-mo'*; a form of the
pref. *k*, but used separately [comp.
3651]; *as, thus, so:*—{20x} = according to, (such)
as (it were, well as), in comp. of, like (as, to,
unto), thus, when, worth. See: TWOT—938;
BDB—455d, 484d.

3645. כְּמוֹשׁ {8x} Keˈmôwsh, *kem-oshe'*; or
(Jer. 48:7)

כְּמִישׁ Keˈmîysh, *kem-eesh'*; from an unused root mean. to *subdue;* the
powerful; Kemosh, the god of the Moabites:—
Chemosh {8x}. See: BDB—484d.

3646. כַּמֹּן {3x} kammôn, *kam-mone';* from an
unused root mean. to *store* up or
preserve; "*cummin*" (from its use as a *condiment*):—cummin {3x}. See: TWOT—991, 991b;
BDB—485a.

3647. כָּמַס {1x} kâmaç, *kaw-mas';* a prim.
root; to *store* away, i.e. (fig.) in the
memory:—laid up in store {1x}. See: TWOT—
992; BDB—485a.

3648. כָּמַר {4x} kâmar, *kaw-mar';* a prim.
root; prop. to *intertwine* or *con-
tract,* i.e. (by impl.) to *shrivel* (as with heat);
fig. to be deeply *affected* with passion (love or
pity):—be black {1x}, be kindled {1x}, yearn
{2x}. See: TWOT—993, 994, 995; BDB—485a.

3649. כָּמָר {3x} kâmâr, *kaw-mawr';* from
3648; prop. an *ascetic* (as if *shrunk*
with self-maceration), i.e. an idolatrous *priest*
(only in plur.):—Chemarims {1x}, (idolatrous)
priests {2x}. Three out of the four places this
word is used it refers to idolatrous priests
(2 Kin 23:5; Hos 10:5; Zeph 1:4). See: TWOT—
996; BDB—485c.

3650. כִּמְרִיר {1x} kimrîyr, *kim-reer';* redupl.
from 3648; *obscuration* (as if
from *shrinkage* of light, i.e. an *eclipse* (only
in plur.):—blackness {1x}. See: TWOT—994a;
BDB—485b.

3651. כֵּן {42x} kên, *kane;* from 3559; prop. *set*
upright; hence, (fig. as adj.) *just;* but
usually (as adv. or conjunc.) *rightly* or *so* (in
various applications to manner, time and relation; often with other particles):—so, thus, like
manner, well, such thing, howbeit, state, after
that, following, after this, therefore, wherefore,
surely = {42x}.

Ken, as an adjective, means "right; veritable; honest." (1) The word implies "honest or
righteous" in Gen 42:11: "We are all one man's
sons; we are true men, thy servants are no
spies." (2) The word means not "right" in 2 Kin
17:9: "And the children of Israel did secretly
those things that were not right against the

LORD their God, and they built them high
places in all their cities, from the tower of the
watchmen to the fenced city." See: TWOT—
964a, 964b; BDB—467a, 467b, 475c, 485d,
487b, 540c, 1097b.

3652. כֵּן {8x} kên (Aram.), *kane;* corresp. to
3651; *so:*—thus {8x}. See: TWOT—
2790; BDB—1097b.

3653. כֵּן {17x} kên, *kane;* the same as 3651,
used as a noun; a *stand,* i.e. pedestal
or station:—foot {8x}, estate {4x}, base {2x}, office {1x}, place {1x}, well {1x}. See: TWOT—
998a; BDB—467b, 487b, 487c.

3654. כֵּן {7x} kên, *kane;* from 3661 in the
sense of *fastening;* a *gnat* (from in-
fixing its sting; used only in plur. [and irreg. in
Exod. 8:17, 18; 13:14]):—lice {6x}, × manner
{1x}. See: TWOT—999a; BDB—467b, 487b,
487c, 487d.

3655. כָּנָה {4x} kânâh, *kaw-naw';* a prim.
root; to *address* by an additional
name; hence, to *eulogize:*—give flattering titles
{2x}, surname (himself) {2x}. See: TWOT—997;
BDB—487b.

3656. כַּנֶּה {1x} Kanneh, *kan-neh';* for 3641;
Canneh, a place in Assyria:—Can-
neh {1x}. See: BDB—487c.

3657. כַּנָּה {1x} ka nâh, *kaw-naw';* from 3661;
a *plant* (as *set*):—× vineyard {1x}.
Syn.: 3754. See: TWOT—999b; BDB—487c,
488a.

3658. כִּנּוֹר {42x} kinnôwr, *kin-nore';* from a
unused root mean. to *twang;*
a *harp:*—harp {42x}. See: TWOT—1004a;
BDB—490a.

3659. כָּנְיָהוּ {3x} Konyâhûw, *kon-yaw'-hoo;*
for 3204; *Conjah,* an Isr. king:—
Coniah {3x}. See: BDB—220c.

3660. כְּנֵמָא {5x} keˈnêmâˈ (Aram.), *ken-ay-
maw';* corresp. to 3644; *so* or
thus:—so {1x}, (in) this manner {1x}, sort {1x},
thus {2x}. See: TWOT—2791; BDB—1097b.

3661. כָּנַן kânan, *kaw-nan';* a prim. root; to
set out, i.e. *plant:*—vineyard + 3657
{1x}. See: TWOT—999b; BDB—488a.

3662. כְּנָנִי {1x} Keˈnânîy, *ken-aw-nee';* from
3661; *planted; Kenani,* an Isr.:—
Chenani {1x}. See: BDB—487d.

3663. כְּנַנְיָה {3x} Keˈnanyâh, *ken-an-yaw';* or

כְּנַנְיָהוּ Keˈnanyâhûw, *ken-an-yaw'-hoo;*
from 3661 and 3050; *Jah has
planted; Kenanjah,* an Isr.:—Chenaniah {3x}.
See: BDB—487d.

Hebrew

3664. כָּנַס {11x} **kânaç,** *kaw-nas';* a prim. root; to *collect;* hence, to *enfold:*—gather {5x}, gather together {4x}, heap up {1x}, wrap {1x}.See: TWOT−1000; BDB−488a, 1097b.

3665. כָּנַע {36x} **kâna⁰,** *kaw-nah';* a prim. root; prop. to *bend* the knee; hence, to *humiliate, vanquish:*—humble {18x}, subdue {11x}, bring low {2x}, bring down {3x}, subjection {1x}, under {1x}.

Kana', means "to be humble, to humble, subdue." **(1)** The word can mean "to humble, to subdue," and it can have a passive or reflexive use, "to be humble" or "to humble oneself." **(1a)** While *kana'* occurs some 35 times in the Hebrew Old Testament, the word is not found until Deut 9:3: "The Lord thy God . . . shall destroy them, and he shall bring them down." **(1b)** *Kana'* is frequently used in this sense of "subduing, humbling," enemies: "And after this it came to pass, that David smote the Philistines, and subdued them: and David took Methegammah out of the hand of the Philistines" (2 Sa 8:1; cf. 1 Chr 17:10; Ps 81:14). **(1c)** "To humble oneself" before God in repentance is a common theme and need in the life of ancient Israel: "And *that* I also have walked contrary unto them, and have brought them into the land of their enemies; if then their uncircumcised hearts be humbled, and they then accept of the punishment of their iniquity" (Lev 26:41; cf. 2 Chr 7:14; 12:6–7, 12). Syn.: 8213. See: TWOT−1001; BDB−488b.

3666. כִּנְעָה {1x} **kin⁰âh,** *kin-aw';* from 365 in the sense of *folding* [comp. 3664]; a *package:*—wares {1x}. See: TWOT−1001a; BDB−488c.

3667. כְּנַעַן {94x} **K⁰na⁰an,** *ken-ah'-an;* from 3665; *humiliated; Kenaan,* a son of Ham; also the country inhabited by him:—Canaan {89x}, merchant {3x}, traffick {1x}, traffickers {1x}.

Kena'an means "Canaan" and *kena'ani* (3669) means "Canaanite; merchant." **(1)** "Canaan" is used 9 times as the name of a person and 80 times as a place name. **(1a)** "Canaanite" occurs 72 times of the descendants of "Canaan," the inhabitants of the land of Canaan. **(1b)** Most occurrences of these words are in Genesis through Judges, but they are scattered throughout the Old Testament. **(2)** "Canaan" is first used of a person in Gen 9:18: "and Ham is the father of Canaan" (cf. Gen 10:6). **(3)** After a listing of the nations descended from "Canaan," Gen 10:18–19 adds: "and afterward were the families of the Canaanites spread abroad. **(4)** And the border of the Canaanites was from Sidon, as thou comest to Gerar, unto Gaza; as thou goest, unto Sodom, and Gomorrah, ..."

(4a) "Canaan" is the land west of the Jordan, as in Num 33:51: "When ye are passed over Jordan into the land of Canaan" (cf. Josh 22:9–11). **(4b)** At the call of God, Abram ". . . went forth to go into the land of Canaan; and into the land of Canaan they came. . . . And the Canaanite was then in the land" (Gen 12:5–6). **(4c)** Later God promised Abram: "Unto thy seed have I given this land, . . . [the land of] the Canaanites" (Gen 15:18–20; cf. Ex 3:8, 17; Josh 3:10).

(5) "Canaanite" is a general term for all the descendants of "Canaan": **(5a)** "When the Lord thy God shall bring thee into the land whither thou goest to possess it, and hath cast out many nations before thee . . . the Canaanites . . ." (Deut 7:1). **(5b)** It is interchanged with Amorite in Gen 15:16: ". . . for the iniquity of the Amorites is not yet full" (cf. Josh 24:15, 18). **(6)** "Canaanite" is also used in the specific sense of one of the peoples of Canaan: **(6a)** ". . . and the Canaanites dwell by the sea, and by the coast of Jordan" (Num 13:29; cf. Josh 5:1; 2 Sa 24:7). **(6b)** As these peoples were traders, "Canaanite" is a symbol for "merchant" in Prov 31:24 and Job 41:6 and notably, in speaking of the sins of Israel, Hosea says, "He is a merchant, the balances of deceit are in his hand" (Hos 7:12; cf. Zeph 1:11). **(7)** Gen 9:25–27 stamps a theological significance on "Canaan" from the beginning: "Cursed be Canaan; a servant of servants shall he be unto his brethren. . . . Blessed be the Lord God of Shem; and Canaan shall be his servant. And God shall enlarge Japheth . . . and Canaan shall be his servant."

(8) Noah prophetically placed this curse on "Canaan" because his father had stared at Noah's nakedness and reported it grossly to his brothers. **(8a)** Ham's sin, deeply rooted in his youngest son, is observable in the Canaanites in the succeeding history. **(8b)** Leviticus 18 gives a long list of sexual perversions that were forbidden to Israel prefaced by the statement: ". . . and after the doings of the land of Canaan, whither I bring you, shall ye not do" (Lev 18:3). **(8c)** The list is followed by a warning: "Defile not ye yourselves in any of these things: for in all these the nations are defiled which I cast out before you" (Lev 18:24). **(9)** The command to destroy the "Canaanites" was very specific: **(9a)** "thou shalt smite them, and utterly destroy them. . . . ye shall destroy their altars, and break down their images. . . . For thou art a holy people unto the Lord thy God" (Deut 7:2–6). **(9b)** But too often the house of David and Judah "built them high places, and images, and groves, on every high hill, and under every green tree. And there were also sodomites in the land: and they did according to all the abominations of the nations which the Lord

cast out before the children of Israel" (1 Kin 14:23–24; cf. 2 Kin 16:3–4; 21:1–15).

(10) The nations were the "Canaanites"; thus "Canaanite" became synonymous with religious and moral perversions of every kind. **(11)** This fact is reflected in Zec 14:21: "and in that day there shall be no more the Canaanite in the house of the Lord of hosts." **(11a)** A "Canaanite" was not permitted to enter the tabernacle or temple; no longer would one of God's people who practiced the abominations of the "Canaanites" enter the house of the Lord. **(11b)** This prophecy speaks of the last days and will be fulfilled in the New Jerusalem, according to Rev 21:27: "And there shall in no wise enter into it any thing that defileth, neither whatsoever worketh abomination, or maketh a lie" (cf. Rev 22:15). See: TWOT—1002, 1002b; BDB—488c, 488d.

3668. כְּנַעֲנָה {5x} K°na'ănâh, ken-ah-an-aw′;
        fem. of 3667; Kenaanah, the name of two Isr.:—Chenaanah {5x}. See: BDB—489b.

3669. כְּנַעֲנִי {73x} K°na'ănîy, ken-ah-an-ee′;
        patrial from 3667; a Kenaanite or inhab. of Kenaan; by impl. a pedlar (the Canaanites standing for their neighbors the Ishmaelites, who conducted mercantile caravans):—Canaanite {67x}, merchant {2x}, Canaan {1x}, Canaanitess {1x}, Canaanitish woman {2x}.

Kena'aniy means Canaanite, merchant, inhabitants of the land of Canaan (Gen 10:18–19). **(1)** Canaan is the land west of the Jordan (Gen 12:5–6; Num 33:51) **(2)** promised to Abraham (Gen 15:18–20; Ex 3:8). **(3)** Canaanite is a general term for all the descendants of Canaan (Deut 7:1) and interchanged with Amorite in Gen 15:16. **(4)** Canaanite is also used in the specific sense of one people of Canaan (Num 13:29; Josh 5:1; 2 Sa 24:7). **(5)** Gen 9:25–27 stamps a theological significance on Canaan from the beginning; they are cursed (Lev 18:1–24). The nations were the Canaanites; thus Canaanite became synonymous with religious and moral perversions of every kind. **(6)** Israel was to utterly destroy them (Deut 7:2–6), **(7)** failed to do so (1 Kin 14:23–24; 2 Kin 16:3–4; 21:1–15). **(8)** They will be destroyed (Zec 14:21). See: TWOT—1002a, 1002b; BDB—489a, 489b.

3670. כָּנַף {1x} kânaph, kaw-naf′; a prim.
        root; prop. to project laterally, i.e. prob. (refl.) to withdraw:—be removed into a corner {1x}. See: TWOT—1003; BDB—489d.

3671. כָּנָף {108x} kânâph, kaw-nawf′; from
        3670; an edge or extremity; spec. (of a bird or army) a wing, (of a garment or bed-clothing) a flap, (of the earth) a quarter, (of a building) a pinnacle:—wing {74x}, skirt {14x}, borders {2x}, corners {2x}, ends {2x}, feathered {2x}, sort {2x}, winged {2x}, misc. {8x} = + bird, × flying, + (one an-) other, overspreading, × quarters, uttermost part.

Kanaph means "wing." **(1)** In the Old Testament kanaph occurs first in the Creation account: "And God created great whales, and every living creature that moveth which the waters brought forth abundantly, after their kind, and every winged fowl after his kind: and God saw that it was good" (Gen 1:21; cf. Ps 78:27). **(2)** In the biblical usage the idiom "any winged fowl" denotes the class of birds; cf. "They, and every beast after his kind, and all the cattle after their kind, and all the creeping thing that creepeth upon the earth after his kind, and every fowl after his kind, every bird of every sort" (Gen 7:14). **(3)** The word "wing" appears 109 times in the Hebrew Old Testament, **(3a)** with particular concentration in the description of the two cherubim of wood in Solomon's temple and in Ezekiel's vision of "creatures," or cherubim. **(3b)** Elsewhere the Bible speaks of "wings" of the cherubim (Ex 25:20; 37:9) and of the seraphim (Is 6:2). **(4)** As an extension of the usage "wing," kanaph signifies "extremity." **(4a)** The seam or lower part of a garment was known as the kanaph. **(4b)** In the "skirt" (kanaph) of the garment one could carry things (Hag 2:12). **(4c)** Saul tore the skirt ("edge" - kanaph) of Samuel's robe (1 Sa 15:27).

(5) The extremity of a land on the world was also known by the word kanaph and is translated by "corner" in English: "And he shall set up an ensign for the nations, and shall assemble the outcasts of Israel, and gather together the dispersed of Judah from the four corners of the earth" (Is 11:12; cf. Job 37:3; 38:13; Eze 7:2). **(6)** In the metaphorical use God is said to protect His people as a bird protects her young with her "wings" (Deut 32:11). **(6a)** The psalmist expressed God's care and protection as a "shadow" of the "wings" (Ps 17:8; cf. 36:7; 57:1; 61:4; 63:7; 91:4). This may be a reference to the care afforded "under the wings of the cherubim over the mercy seat." **(6b)** In keeping with this usage Malachi looked forward to a new age, when "the Sun of righteousness [will] arise with healing in his wings; and ye shall go forth, and grow up as calves of the stall" (4:2). **(7)** When the nations are compared to birds, the association is that of terror and conquest. This is best expressed in Ezekiel's parable of the two eagles and the vine: "And say, Thus saith the Lord God; A great eagle with great wings, longwinged, full of feathers, which had divers colors, came unto Lebanon, and took the highest branch of the cedar: he cropped off the top of his young twigs, and carried it into a land of traffic; he set it in a city of merchants" (Eze 17:3–4). **(8)** The

believer is enjoined to seek refuge with God when adversity strikes him or adversaries surround him: "He shall cover thee with his feathers, and under his wings shall thou trust: his truth shall be thy shield and buckler" (Ps 91:4). See: TWOT—1003a; BDB—489b.

3672. כִּנְּרוֹת {7x} **Kinnᵉrôwth**, *kin-ner-ōth'*; or

כִּנֶּרֶת **Kinnereth**, *kin-neh'-reth;* respectively plur. and sing. fem. from the same as 3658; perh. *harp*-shaped; *Kinneroth* or *Kinnereth,* a place in Pal.:—Chinnereth {4x}, Chinneroth {2x}, Cinneroth {1x}. See: BDB—490b.

3673. כְּנַשׁ {3x} **kânash** (Aram.), *kaw-nash';* corresp. to 3664; to *assemble:*—gather together {3x}. See: TWOT—2792; BDB—1097b.

3674. כְּנָת {1x} **kᵉnâth**, *ken-awth';* from 3655; a *colleague* (as having the same title):—companion {1x}. See: TWOT—1005; BDB—487c, 490c.

3675. כְּנָת {7x} **kᵉnâth** Aram.), *ken-awth';* corresp. to 3674:—companion {7x}. See: TWOT—2793; BDB—1097c.

3676. כֵּס {1x} **kêç**, *kace;* appar. a contr. for 3678, but prob. by err. transc. for 5251:—sworn {1x}. See: TWOT—1007; BDB—490c, 490d.

3677. כֶּסֶא {2x} **keçeʾ**, *keh'-seh;* or

כֶּסֶה **keçeh**, *keh'-seh;* appar. from 3680; prop. *fulness* or the *full moon,* i.e. its festival:—(time) appointed {1x}. See: TWOT—1006; BDB—490c, 492c.

3678. כִּסֵּא {135x} **kiççêʾ**, *kis-say';* or

כִּסֵּה **kiççêh**, *kis-say';* from 3680; prop. *covered,* i.e. a *throne* (as canopied):—seat {1x}, stool {7x}, throne {127x}.

Kicce' means "throne; seat." **(1)** *Kicce'* occurs 130 times in the Hebrew Old Testament and, as is to be expected, the frequency is greater in the historical books and the prophetical works. It is rare in the Pentateuch. **(2)** The first usage of *kicce'* is in Gen 41:40: "Thou shalt be over my house, and according unto thy word shall all my people be ruled: only in the throne will I be greater than thou." **(3)** In the Old Testament the basic meaning of *kicce'* is "seat" or "chair." **(3a)** Visitors were seated on a chair (1 Kin 2:19), as well as guests (2 Kin 4:10) and older men (1 Sa 1:9). **(3b)** When the king or elders assembled to administer justice, they sat on the throne of justice (Prov 20:8; cf. Ps 9:4). **(3c)** In these contexts kicce' is associated with honor. **(3d)** However, in the case of the prostitute (Prov 9:14) and soldiers who set up their chairs (Jer 1:15—*kicce'* may mean "throne"

here), *kicce'* signifies a place and nothing more. **(4)** The more frequent sense of *kicce'* is "throne" or "seat of honor," also known as the "royal seat": "And it shall be, when he sitteth upon the throne of his kingdom, that he shall write him a copy of this law in a book out of that which is before the priests the Levites" (Deut 17:18; cf. 1 Kin 1:46). **(5)** Since the Davidic dynasty received the blessing of God, the Old Testament has a number of references to "the throne of David" (2 Sa 3:10; Jer 22:2, 30; 36:30): "Of the increase of his government and peace there shall be no end, upon the throne of David, and upon his kingdom, to order it, and to establish it with judgment and with justice from henceforth even for ever" (Is 9:7). **(6)** The "throne of Israel" is a synonymous phrase for "throne of David" (1 Kin 2:4; cf. 8:20, 25; 9:5; 10:9; 2 Kin 10:30; 15:12, etc.). **(7)** The physical appearance of the "throne" manifested the glory of the king. Solomon's "throne" was an artistic product with ivory inlays, the wood covered with a layer of fine gold (1 Kin 10:18). **(8)** The word *kicce'* was also used to represent "kingship" and the succession to the throne. David had sworn that Solomon would sit on his "throne" (1 Kin 1:13; cf. 2 Kin 10:3). **(9)** Above all human kingship and "thrones" was the God of Israel: "God reigneth over the heathen: God sitteth upon the throne of his holiness" (Ps 47:8). **(10)** The Israelites viewed God as the ruler who was seated on a "throne." Micaiah said in the presence of Ahab and Jehoshaphat: "Hear thou therefore the word of the Lord: I saw the Lord sitting on his throne, and all the host of heaven standing by him on his right hand and on his left" (1 Kin 22:19). **(11)** Isaiah received a vision of God's glory revealed in the temple (Is 6:1). **(12)** The presence of the Lord in Jerusalem also gave rise to the conception that Jerusalem was the throne of God (Jer 3:17). See: TWOT—1007; BDB—490c, 492c, 1097c.

3679. כַּסְדַּי {1x} **Kaçday**, *kas-dah'-ee;* for 3778:—Chaldean {1x}. See: BDB—505a.

3680. כָּסָה {152x} **kâçâh**, *kaw-saw';* a prim. root; prop. to *plump,* i.e. *fill up* hollows; by impl. to *cover* (for clothing or secrecy):—cover {135x}, hide {6x}, conceal {4x}, covering {2x}, overwhelmed {2x}, clad {1x}, closed {1x}, clothed {1x}. See: TWOT—1008; BDB—491b. comp. 3780.

כֶּסֶה **keçeh**. See 3677.

כִּסֵּה **kiççêh**. See 3678.

3681. כָּסוּי {2x} **kâçûwy**, *kaw-soo'-ee;* pass. part. of 3680; prop. *covered,* i.e. (as noun) a *covering:*—covering {2x}. See: TWOT—1008a; BDB—492b, 492d.

3682. כְּסוּת {8x} k°çûwth, *kes-ooth';* from 3680; a *cover* (garment); fig. a *veiling:*—covering {6x}, raiment {1x}, vesture {1x}. See: TWOT—1008b; BDB—492b. 492d.

3683. כָּסַח {2x} kâçach, *kaw-sakh';* a prim. root; to *cut off:*—cut down {1x}, cut up {1x}. See: TWOT—1010; BDB—492d.

3684. כְּסִיל {70x} k°çîyl, *kes-eel';* from 3688; prop. *fat,* i.e. (fig.) stupid or *silly:*—fool {61x}, foolish {9x}.

Keçiyl means "stupid fellow; dull person; fool." **(1)** This word occurs in the Old Testament 70 times with all of its occurrences being in wisdom literature except 3 in the Psalms. **(2)** The *keçiyl* is "insolent" in religion and "stupid or dull" in wise living (living out a religion he professes). **(2a)** In Ps 92:6 the first emphasis is especially prominent: "A brutish man knoweth not; neither doth a fool understand this." **(2a1)** The psalmist is describing an enemy of God who knew God and His word but, seeing the wicked flourishing, reasoned that they have the right life-style: "When the wicked spring as the grass, and when all the workers of iniquity do flourish; it is that they shall be destroyed for ever" (Ps 92:7). **(2a2)** They have knowledge of God but do not properly evaluate or understand what they know. **(3)** The second emphasis is especially prominent in wisdom contexts: "How long, ye simple ones, will ye love simplicity? and the scorners delight in their scorning, and fools hate knowledge?" (Prov 1:22). **(3a)** In such contexts the person so described rejects the claims and teachings of wisdom. **(3b)** However, in the Bible wisdom is the practical outworking of one's religion. Therefore, even in these contexts there is a clear connotation of insolence in religion. Syn.: 191, 5036. See: TWOT—1011c; BDB—493a.

3685. כְּסִיל {4x} K°çîyl, *kes-eel';* the same as 3684; any notable *constellation;* spec. *Orion* (as if a *burly* one):—constellation {1x}, Orion{3}. See: TWOT—1011e; BDB—493a.

3686. כְּסִיל {1x} K°çîyl, *kes-eel';* the same as 3684; *Kesil,* a place in Pal.:—Chesil {1x}. See: BDB—493b.

3687. כְּסִילוּת {1} k°çîylûwth, *kes-eel-ooth';* from 3684; *silliness:*—foolish {1x}. See: TWOT—1011d; BDB—493a.

3688. כָּסַל {1x} kâçal, *kaw-sal';* a prim. root; prop. to *be fat,* i.e. (fig.) *silly:*—be foolish {1x}. See: TWOT—1011; BDB—492d.

3689. כֶּסֶל {13x} keçel, *keh'-sel;* from 3688; prop. *fatness,* i.e. by impl. (lit.) the *loin* (as the seat of the leaf *fat*) or (gen.) the *viscera;* also (fig.) *silliness* or (in a good sense)

trust:—flank {6x}, hope {3x}, folly {2x}, loins {1x}, confidence {1x}.

Keçel means "stupidity; imperturbability; confidence." **(1)** It means "stupidity": "I applied mine heart to know, and to search, and to seek out wisdom, and the reason of things, and to know the wickedness of folly, even of foolishness" (Eccl 7:25); and **(2)** "confidence": "For the LORD shall be thy confidence, and shall keep thy foot from being taken" (Prov 3:26). **(3)** The meaning of "confidence" also appears in Job 31:24: "If I have made gold my hope. . . ." See: TWOT—1011a; BDB—492d.

3690. כִּסְלָה {2x} kiçlâh, *kis-law';* fem. of 3689; in a good sense, *trust;* in a bad one, *silliness:*—confidence {1x}, folly {1x}. See: TWOT—1011b; BDB—493a.

3691. כִּסְלֵו {2x} Kîçlêv, *kis-lave';* prob. of for. or.; *Kisleu,* the 9th Heb. month:—Chisleu {2x}. See: TWOT—1012; BDB—493b.

3692. כִּסְלוֹן {1x} Kîçlôwn, *kis-lone';* from 3688; *hopeful; Kislon,* an Isr.:—Chislon {1x}. See: BDB—493b.

3693. כְּסָלוֹן {1x} K°çâlôwn, *kes-aw-lone';* from 3688; *fertile; Kesalon,* a place in Pal.:—Chesalon {1x}. See: BDB—493b.

3694. כְּסָלוֹת {1x} K°çullôwth, *kes-ool-lōth';* fem. plur. of pass. part. of 3688; *fattened; Kesulloth,* a place in Pal.:—Chesulloth {1x}. See: BDB—493b, 1061d.

3695. כַּסְלֻחִים {2x} Kaçlûchîym, *kas-loo'-kheem;* a plur. prob. of for. der.; *Casluchim,* a people cognate to the Eg.:—Casluhim {2x}. See: BDB—493b.

3696. כִּסְלֹת תָּבֹר {1x} Kiçlôth Tâbôr, *kis-lōth' taw-bore';* from the fem. plur. of 3689 and 8396; *flanks of Tabor; Kisloth-Tabor,* a place in Pal.:—Chisloth-tabor {1x}. See: BDB—493b, 493c.

3697. כָּסַם {2x} kâçam, *kaw-sam';* a prim. root; to *shear:*—× only {1x}, poll {1x}. See: TWOT—1013; BDB—493c. comp. 3765.

3698. כֻּסֶּמֶת {3x} kuççemeth, *koos-seh'-meth;* from 3697; *spelt* (from its bristliness as if just *shorn*):—fitches {1x}, rie {2x}. See: TWOT—1013a; BDB—493c.

3699. כָּסַס {1x} kâçaç, *kaw-sas';* a prim. root; to *estimate:*—make your count {1x}. See: TWOT—1014; BDB—493c.

3700. כָּסַף {6x} kâçaph, *kaw-saf';* a prim. root; prop. to *become pale,* i.e. (by impl.) to *pine* after; also to *fear:*—[have] desire {2x}, be greedy {1x}, long {2x}, sore {1x}.

Kaçaph means "to long for" in the sense of "to be pale by reason of longing": "And now,

though thou wouldest needs be gone, because thou sore longedst after thy father's house, yet wherefore hast thou stolen my gods?" (Gen 31:30). See: TWOT—1015; BDB—493d.

3701. כֶּסֶף {403x} **keçeph**, *keh'-sef;* from 3700; *silver* (from its *pale* color); by impl. *money:*—silver {287x}, money {112x}, price {1x}, silverlings {1x}. money, price, silver (-ling).

Keceph means "silver; money; price; property." **(1)** This word represents the "metal ore silver": "Take away the dross from the silver, and there shall come forth a vessel for the finer" (Prov 25:4; cf. Job 28:1). **(2)** *Keceph* may signify the "metal silver," or what has been refined from silver ore: "And the servant brought forth jewels of silver, and jewels of gold . . ." (Gen 24:53). **(3)** As a precious metal, "silver" was not as valuable as gold—probably because it is not so rare: "And all king Solomon's drinking vessels were of gold, and all the vessels of the house of the forest of Lebanon were of pure gold; none were of silver: it was nothing accounted of in the days of Solomon" (1 Kin 10:21). **(4)** "Silver" was often a form of wealth. This is the meaning of *keceph* in Gen 13:2 (the first biblical occurrence): "And Abram was very rich in cattle, in silver, and in gold." **(5)** Silver pieces (not coins) were used as money: "Then Joseph commanded to fill their sacks with corn, and to restore every man's money into his sack" (Gen 42:25).

(6) Frequently the word absolutely (by itself) and in the singular form means "pieces of silver": "Behold, I have given thy brother a thousand pieces of silver" (Gen 20:16). **(7)** In Lev 25:50 the word is used in the general sense of "money, value, price": "And he shall reckon with him that bought him from the year that he was sold to him unto the year of jubilee: and the price of his sale shall be according unto the number of years." **(8)** Since it was a form of wealth, "silver" often was one of the spoils of war: "The kings came and fought, then fought the kings of Canaan in Taanach by the waters of Megiddo; they took no gain of money" (Judg 5:19). **(9)** This word may be used in the sense of "valuable property": "Notwithstanding, if he [the slave who has been beaten] continue a day or two, he shall not be punished: for he is his money" (Ex 21:21). **(10)** *Keceph* sometimes represents the color "silver": "Though ye have lain among the pots, yet shall ye be as the wings of a dove covered with silver, and her feathers with yellow gold" (Ps 68:13). See: TWOT—1015a; BDB—494a.

3702. כְּסַף {13x} **k⁰çaph** (Aram.), *kes-af';* corresp. to 3701:—money {1x}, silver {12x}. See: TWOT—2794; BDB—1097c.

3703. כָּסְפְּיָא {2x} **Kâçiphyâ**, *kaw-sif-yaw';* perh. from 3701; *silvery; Casiphja*, a place in Bab.:—Casiphia {2x}. See: BDB—494d.

3704. כֶּסֶת {2x} **keçeth**, *keh'-seth;* from 3680; a *cushion* or pillow (as *covering* a seat or bed):—pillow {2x}. See: TWOT—1009a; BDB—492c, 492d.

3705. כְּעַן {13x} **k⁰an** (Aram.), *keh-an';* prob. from 3652; *now:*—now {12x}, now therefore {1x}. See: TWOT—2795; BDB—1097c, 1107b.

3706. כְּעֶנֶת {4x} **k⁰eneth** (Aram.), *keh-eh'-neth;* or

כְּעֶת **k⁰eth** (Aram.), *keh-eth';* fem. of 3705; *thus* (only in the formula "and *so forth*"):—at such a time {4x}. See: TWOT—2796; BDB—1097c, 1107b, 1107c, 1108a.

3707. כָּעַס **kâ⁰aç**, *kaw-as';* a prim. root; to *trouble;* by impl. to *grieve, rage, be indignant:*—anger {43x}, provoke {3x}, angry {2x}, grieved {1x}, indignation {1x}, sorrow {1x}, vex {1x}, wrath {1x}, wroth {1x}.

Ka'ac means "to provoke, vex, make angry." **(1)** A word that is characteristic of the Book of Deuteronomy, it seems fitting that *ka'ac* is found for the first time in the Old Testament in that book: ". . . To provoke him to anger" (Deut 4:25). **(2)** The word is characteristic also of the books of Jeremiah and Kings. **(3)** A review of the uses of this verb shows that around 80 percent of them involve Yahweh's "being provoked to anger" by Israel's sin, especially its worship of other gods. One such example is in 2 Kin 23:19: "And all the houses also of the high places that were in the cities of Samaria, which the kings of Israel had made to provoke the Lord to anger, Josiah took away." See: TWOT—1016; BDB—494d.

3708. כַּעַס {25x} **ka⁰aç**, *kah'-as;* or (in Job)

כַּעַשׂ **ka⁰as**, *kah'-as;* from 3707; *vexation:*—grief {7x}, provocation {4x}, wrath {4x}, sorrow {3x}, anger {2x}, angry {1x}, indignation {1x}, provoking {1x}, sore {1x}, spite {1x}. See: TWOT—1016a; BDB—495b.

כְּעֶת **k⁰eth**. See 3706.

3709. כַּף {191x} **kaph**, *kaf;* from 3721; the hollow *hand* or palm (so of the *paw* of an animal, of the *sole*, and even of the *bowl* of a dish or sling, the *handle* of a bolt, the *leaves* of a palm-tree); fig. *power:*—hand {127x}, spoon {24x}, sole {19x}, palm {5x}, hollow {3x}, handful {2x}, apiece {1x}, branches {1x}, breadth + 4096 {1x}, clouds {1x}, misc. {7x} = + foot, handle, [-led]), middle, paw, power.

Kaph means "palm (of hand)." (1) Basically, *kaph* represents the "palm," the hollow part of the hand as distinguished from its fingers, thumbs, and back. (1a) Thus we read that part of the ritual for cleansing a leper is that a "priest shall take some of the log of oil, and pour it into the palm of his own left hand" (Lev 14:15). (1b) The word represents the entire inside of the hand when it is cupped, or the "hollow of the hand." God told Moses: "While my glory passeth by, that I will put thee in a clift of the rock, and will cover thee with my hand while I pass by" (Ex 33:22; cf. Ps 139:5). (2) This word means fist, specifically the inside of a fist. The woman of Zarephath told Elijah: "I have not a cake, but a handful of meal in a barrel, and a little oil in a cruse . . ." (1 Kin 17:12). This was, indeed, a very small amount of flour—enough for only one little biscuit. (3) *Kaph* also refers to the flat of the hand, including the fingers and the thumb. These are what one claps together in joy and applause: "And he brought forth the king's son, and put the crown upon him, and gave him the testimony; and they made him king, and anointed him; and they clapped their hands, and said, God save the king" (2 Kin 11:12). (4) Clapping the hands may also be an expression of scorn and contempt (Num 24:10).

(5) The flat of the hands may be raised heavenward in prayer to symbolize one's longing to receive. Moses told Pharaoh: "As soon as I am gone out of the city, I will spread abroad my hands unto the Lord" (Ex 9:29). (6) This word can suggest the inside part of a hand grasp as distinguished from the hand as a whole: "And the Lord said unto Moses, Put forth thine hand, and take it by the tail. And he put forth his hand, and caught it, and it became a rod in his hand" (Ex 4:4). (7) A mutual hand grasp may signify entrance into a pledge (Prov 6:1). (8) To take one's life (5315 - nepesh) into one's own hands is to put oneself into danger (Judg 12:3). (9) In many passages *kaph* is synonymous with the entire hand. Jacob tells Laban that "God hath seen . . . the labor of my hands" (Gen 31:42). (10) Perhaps the same nuance occurs in passages such as Gen 20:5: "In the integrity of my heart and innocency of my hands have I done this." (10) The word may be used symbolically and figuratively meaning "power." (10a) Gideon complained to the Angel of the Lord that "now the Lord hath forsaken us, and delivered us into the hands [the power] of the Midianites" (Judg 6:13). (10b) Israel was not literally in the Midianites' hands but was dominated by them and under their control. (11) Once the word represents animal paws: "And whatsoever goeth upon his paws, among all manner

of beasts that go on all four, those are unclean unto you . . ." (Lev 11:27).

(12) In many passages *kaph* signifies the sole of the foot, the hollow part. This meaning appears in Gen 8:9 (first biblical appearance): "But the dove found no rest for the sole of her foot" (cf. Josh 3:13 where the word is used of the sole of a human foot). (13) Various hollow, bending, or beaten objects are represented by *kaph*. (13a) First, it is used of a thigh joint: "And when he [the Angel of the Lord] saw that he prevailed not against him [Jacob], he touched the hollow of his thigh; and the hollow of Jacob's thigh was out of joint, as he wrestled with him" (Gen 32:25). (13b) Second, a certain shaped pan or vessel is called a *kaph:* "And thou shalt make the dishes thereof, and spoons thereof, and covers thereof, and bowls thereof, to cover withal: of pure gold shalt thou make them" (Ex 25:29). (13c) Third, the word is used of the hollow of a sling: "And the souls of thine enemies, them shall he sling out, as out of the middle of a sling" (1Sa 25:29). (13d) Next, the huge hand-shaped branches of palm trees are represented by the word: "And ye shall take you on the first day the boughs of goodly trees, branches of palm trees, and the boughs of thick trees" (Lev 23:40). (13e) Finally, in Song 5:5 this word represents the bent piece of metal or wood which forms a door handle. See: TWOT—1022a; BDB—495b, 496a.

3710. כֵּף {2x} **kêph**, *kafe;* from 3721; a hollow *rock:*—rock {2x}. See: TWOT—1017; BDB—495b.

3711. כָּפָה {1x} **kâphâh**, *kaw-faw';* a p im. root; prop. to *bend,* i.e. (fig.) to *tame* or subdue:—pacify {1x}. See: TWOT—1018; BDB—495c.

3712. כִּפָּה {3x} **kippâh**, *k p-paw';* fem. of 3709; a *leaf* of a palm-tree:—branch {3x}. See: TWOT—1022b; BDB—495c, 497a.

3713. כְּפוֹר {9x} **kᵉphôwr**, *kef-ore';* from 3722; prop. a *cover,* i.e. (by impl.) a *tankard* (or *covered* goblet); also white *frost* (as *covering* the ground):—bason {6x}, hoar (-y) frost {3x}. See: TWOT—1026a, 1026b; BDB—499b.

3714. כָּפִיס {1x} **kâphîyç**, *kaw-fece;* from an unused root mean. to *connect;* a *girder:*—beam {1x}. See: TWOT—1021a; BDB—496a.

3715. כְּפִיר {32x} **kᵉphîyr**, *kef-eer';* from 3722; a *village* (as *covered* in by walls); also a young *lion* (perh. as *covered* with a mane):—young {1x}, lion {30x}, villages {1x}. See: TWOT—1025a, 1025d; BDB—498d. comp. 3723.

Hebrew

3716. כְּפִירָה {4x} **Kᵉphîyrâh**, *kef-ee-raw'*; fem. of 3715; the *village* (always with the art.); *Kephirah*, a place in Pal.:—Chephirah {4x}. See: BDB—499a.

3717. כָּפַל {5x} **kâphal**, *kaw-fal'*; a prim. root; to *fold* together; fig. to *repeat:*—double {5x}. See: TWOT—1019; BDB—495c.

3718. כֶּפֶל {3x} **kephel**, *keh'-fel;* from 3717; a *duplicate:*—double {3x}. See: TWOT—1019a; BDB—495c.

3719. כָּפַן {1x} **kâphan**, *kaw-fan'*; a prim. root; to *bend:*—bend {1x}. See: TWOT—1020; BDB—495d.

3720. כָּפָן {2x} **kâphân**, *kaw-fawn';* from 3719; *hunger* (as making to *stoop* with emptiness and pain):—famine {2x}. See: TWOT—1020a; BDB—495d.

3721. כָּפַף {5x} **kâphaph**, *kaw-faf';* a prim. root; to *curve:*—bow down (self) {4x}, bow {1x}.

Kaphaph means "to bend, bow down." **(1)** This word appears 5 times in biblical poetry. **(2)** The verb occurs in Is 58:5: ". . . is it to bow down his head as a bulrush, and to spread sackcloth and ashes under him?" See: TWOT—1022; BDB—496a.

3722. כָּפַר {102x} **kâphar**, *kaw-far';* a prim. root; to *cover* (spec. with bitumen); fig. to *expiate* or *condone*, to *placate* or *cancel:*—atonement {71x}, purge {7x}, reconciliation {4x}, reconcile {3x}, forgive {3x}, purge away {2x}, pacify {2x}, atonement . . . made {2x}, merciful {2x}, cleansed {1x}, disannulled {1x}, appease {1x}, put off {1x}, pardon {1x}, pitch {1x}.

Kaphar means to cover over, propitiate, ransom, atone, expiate." **(1)** *Kaphar* has an initial secular and non-theological range quite parallel to padah (6299). **(1a)** In addition, however, *kaphar* became a technical term in Israel's sacrificial rituals. **(1b)** On its most basic level of meaning, *kaphar* denotes a material transaction or "ransom." **(2)** Sometimes man is the subject of *kaphar*. **(2a)** In 2 Sa 21:3, David asks the Gibeonites, "And wherewith shall I make the atonement, that ye may bless the inheritance of the Lord?" He receives in answer the advice to hang seven of Saul's sons in compensation. **(2b)** In Ex 32:30, Moses ascends the mountain yet a third time in an effort to "make an atonement" for the people's sin (apparently merely by intercession, although this is not explicitly stated). **(2c)** Is 27:9 speaks of "purging" Israel's guilt by banishing idolatrous objects. **(2d)** In Num 25:13, Phinehas is said to have "made an atonement for the children of Israel"

by spearing a couple during orgiastic worship of Baal.

(3) God is often the subject of *kaphar* in this general sense, too. **(3a)** In 2 Chr 30:18, Hezekiah prays for God to "pardon" those who were not ritually prepared for the Passover. **(3b)** At the conclusion of the Song of Moses, Yahweh is praised because He "will be merciful (3722) unto his land, and to his people. **(3c)** Similar general uses of the word appear in Ps 65:3; 78:38; and Dan 9:24. **(4)** Jeremiah once uses *kaphar* to pray bitterly that Yahweh not "forgive" the iniquity of those plotting to slay him (Jer 18:23). **(5)** In Ps 79:9 the word means "to purge" sin. **(6)** Most often *kaphar* is used in connection with specific rites, and the immediate subject is a priest. All types of ritual sacrifice are explained in terms of *kaphar*. **(6a)** We find the priests' smearing of blood on the altar during the "sin offering" (2403 – chatta't) described as "atonement" (Ex 29: 36–37; Lev 4:20, 31; 10:17; Num 28:22; 29:5; Neh 10:33). **(6b)** The use of blood is not quite so prominent in sacrifices, but the relation to "atonement" still holds. It is clearly true of the "guilt offering" (Lev 5:16, 18; 6:7; 7:7; 14:21; 19:22; Num 5:8). **(6c)** The principle holds even when the poor cannot afford an animal or birds, and they sacrifice only a little flour—i.e., where obviously no blood is involved (Lev 5:11–13). **(7)** Making "atonement" (*kaphar*) is also part of the purpose of the "burnt offering" (Lev 1:4; Num 15:25).

(8) The only major type of sacrifice not classified an "atonement" in Leviticus is the "cereal offering" (4503 - *minchah*) of chapter 2; but Eze 45:15, 17 does include it under that heading. **(9)** First Chr 6:49 applies the concept to the priestly ministry in general. **(10)** The connection of all of the rituals with *kaphar* peaks in the complex ceremony of the annual Day of Atonement (Yom Kippur), as described in detail in Lev 16. **(11)** All the sacrifices in the world would not satisfy God's righteousness (e.g., Mic 6:7; Ps 50:7–15). **(11a)** Hence God alone can provide an atonement for sin, by which His wrath is assuaged. **(11b)** The righteous God is neither implacable nor capricious, but provides Himself the "ransom" or substitute sacrifice that would satisfy Him. **(11c)** The priest at the altar represents God Himself, bringing the requisite offering before God; sacrifice is not essentially man's action, but God's own act of pardoning mercy. **(12)** *Kaphar* is first found in Gen 6:14, where it is used in its primary sense of "to cover over." Here God gives Noah instructions concerning the ark, including, "Pitch it within and without with pitch." **(13)** Most uses of the word, however, involve the theological meaning of "covering over," often with the blood of a sacrifice, in

order to atone for some sin. This means that the "covering over" hides the sin from God's until the death of Christ takes away the sin of the world (cf. Jn 1:29; Heb 10:4).

(14) As might be expected, this word occurs more frequently in the Book of Leviticus than in any other book, since Leviticus deals with the ritual sacrifices that were made to atone for sin. **(14a)** For example, Lev 4:13–21 gives instructions for bringing a young bull to the tent of meeting for a sin offering. **(14b)** After the elders laid their hands on the bull (to transfer the people's sin to the bull), the bull was killed. **(14c)** The priest then brought some of the blood of the bull into the tent of meeting and sprinkled it seven times before the veil. **(14d)** Some of the blood was put on the horns of the altar and the rest of the blood was poured at the base of the altar of burnt offering. **(14e)** The fat of the bull was then burned on the altar. **(14f)** The bull itself was to be burned outside the camp. **(14g)** By means of this ritual, "the priest shall make an atonement [*kaphar*] for them, and it shall be forgiven them" (Lev 4:20).

(15) The term "atonement" is found at least 16 times in Lev 16, the great chapter concerning the Day of Atonement. **(15a)** Before anything else, the high priest had to "make atonement" for himself and his house by offering a bull as a sin offering. **(15b)** After lots were cast upon the two goats, one was sent away into the wilderness as an atonement (v. 10), while the other was sacrificed and its blood sprinkled on the mercy seat as an atonement for the people (vv. 15–20). **(15c)** The Day of Atonement was celebrated only once a year. **(15d)** Only on this day could the high priest enter the holy of holies of the tabernacle or temple on behalf of the people of Israel and make atonement for them. **(16)** Sometimes atonement for sin was made apart from or without blood offerings. **(16a)** During his vision-call experience, Isaiah's lips were touched with a coal of fire taken from the altar by one of the seraphim. With that, he was told, "Thy sin is purged [*kaphar*]" (Is 6:7). **(16b)** Isaiah's sin of unclean lips was purged (6:5); not sin purged unto salvation. See: TWOT–23, 1024, 1025, 1026; BDB–497b, 498b.

3723. כָּפָר {2x} **kâphâr**, *kaw-fawr';* from 3722; a *village* (as *protected* by walls):— village {2x}. See: TWOT–1025c; BDB–499a. comp. 3715.

3724. כֹּפֶר {17x} **kôpher**, *ko'-fer;* from 3722; prop. a *cover,* i.e. (lit.) a *village* (as *covered* in); (spec.) *bitumen* (as used for *coating*), and the *henna* plant (as used for *dyeing*); fig. a *redemption*-price:— ransom {8x}, satis-

faction {2x}, bribe {2x}, camphire {2x}, pitch {1x}, sum of money {1x}, village {1x}. See: TWOT–1025b; BDB–497a, 498d, 499a.

3725. כִּפֻּר {8x} **kippûr**, *kip-poor';* from 3722; *expiation* (only in plur.):—atonement {8x}. See: TWOT–1023b; BDB–498c.

3726. כְּפַר הָעַמֹּנִי {1x} **Kᵉphar hâ-ʿAmmôwnîy**, *kef-ar' haw-am-mo-nee';* from 3723 and 5984, with the art. interposed; *village of the Ammonite; Kefar-ha-Ammoni,* a place in Pal.:—Chefar-haamonai {1x}. See: BDB–499a.

3727. כַּפֹּרֶת {27x} **kappôreth**, *kap-po'-reth;* from 3722; a *lid* (used only of the *cover* of the sacred Ark):—mercy seat {26x}, mercy seatward {1x}.

Kapporeth, as a noun, means "mercy seat; throne of mercy." **(1)** It refers to a slab of gold that rested on top of the ark of the covenant. **(1a)** Images of two cherubims stood on this slab, facing each other. **(1b)** This slab of gold represented the throne of God and symbolized His real presence in the worship shrine. **(1c)** On the Day of Atonement, the high priest sprinkled the blood of the sin offering on it, apparently symbolizing the blood's reception by God. **(1d)** Thus the *kapporeth* was the central point at which Israel, through its high priest, could come into the presence of God. **(2)** This is further seen in the fact that the temple proper was distinguished from its porches and other accompanying structures by the name "place of the mercy seat (*kapporeth*)" (1Chr 28:11). See: TWOT–1023c; BDB–498c.

3728. כָּפַשׁ {1x} **kâphash**, *kaw-fash';* a prim. root; to *tread* down; fig. to *humiliate:*—cover {1x}. See: TWOT–1027; BDB–499b.

3729. כְּפַת {4x} **kᵉphath** (Aram.), *kef-ath';* a root of uncert. correspondence; to *fetter:*—bind {4x}. See: TWOT–2798; BDB–1097c.

3730. כַּפְתֹּר {18x} **kaphtôr**, *kaf-tore';* or (Amos 9:1)

כַּפְתּוֹר **kaphtôwr**, *kaf-tore';* prob. from an unused root mean. to *encircle;* a *chaplet;* but used only in an architectonic sense, i.e. the *capital* of a column, or a wreath-like *button* or *disk* on the candelabrum:—knop {16x}, (upper) lintel {2x}. See: TWOT–1029; BDB–499b.

3731. כַּפְתֹּר {3x} **Kaphtôr**, *kaf-tore';* or (Amos 9:7)

כַּפְתּוֹר **Kaphtôwr**, *kaf-tore';* appar. the same as 3730; *Caphtor* (i.e. a *wreath*-shaped island), the orig. seat of the

Philistines:—Caphtor {3x}. See: TWOT—1028; BDB—499c.

3732. כַּפְתֹּרִי {3x} **Kaphtôrîy**, *kaf-to-ree';* patrial from 3731; a *Caphtorite* (collect.) or native of Caphtor:—Caphthorim {1x}, Caphtorim (-s) {1x}. See: BDB—499c.

3733. כַּר {16x} **kar**, *kar;* from 3769 in the sense of *plumpness;* a *ram* (as *full-grown* and *fat*), incl. a *battering-ram* (as *butting*); hence, a *meadow* (as *for sheep*); also a *pad* or camel's saddle (as *puffed out*):—captain {1x}, furniture {1x}, lamb {10x}, (large) pasture {2x}, ram {2x}. Syn.: 352. See: TWOT—1046a; BDB—468b, 499c, 503a. See also 1033, 3746.

3734. כֹּר {9x} **kôr**, *kore;* from the same as 3564; prop. a deep round *vessel,* i.e. (spec.) a *cor* or measure for things dry:—cor {1x}, measure {8x}. See: TWOT—1031; BDB—499d, 1096d. Aram. the same.

3735. כָּרָא {1x} **kârâ**ʾ (Aram.), *kaw-raw';* prob. corresp. to 3738 in the sense of *piercing* (fig.); to *grieve:*—be grieved {1x}. See: TWOT—2799; BDB—1097d.

3736. כַּרְבֵּל {1x} **karbêl**, *kar-bale';* from the same as 3525; to *gird* or *clothe:*—clothed {1x}. See: TWOT—1032; BDB—499d, 1097d.

3737. כַּרְבְּלָא {1x} **karb**ᵉ**lâ**ʾ (Aram.), *kar-bel-aw';* from a verb corresp. to that of 3736; a *mantle:*—hat {1x}. See: TWOT—2800; BDB—1097d.

3738. כָּרָה {16x} **kârâh**, *kaw-raw';* a prim. root; prop. to *dig;* fig. to *plot;* gen. to *bore* or *open:*—dig {12x}, make (a banquet) {2x}, pierce {1x}, open {1x}. See: TWOT—1033, 1034, 1035; BDB—456c, 468c, 500a.

3739. כָּרָה {4x} **kârâh**, *kaw-raw';* usually assigned as a prim. root, but prob. only a special application of 3738 (through the common idea of *planning* impl. in a bargain); to *purchase:*—buy {2x}, prepared {1x}, banquet {1x}. See: TWOT—1034; BDB—500b.

3740. כֵּרָה {1x} **kêrâh**, *kay-raw';* from 3739; a *purchase:*—provision {1x}. See: TWOT—1035a; BDB—500c.

3741. כָּרָה {1x} **kârâh**, *kaw-raw';* fem. of 3733; a *meadow:*—cottage {1x}. See: TWOT—1033a; BDB—500b, 504d.

3742. כְּרוּב {91x} **k**ᵉ**rûwb**, *ker-oob';* of uncert. der.; a *cherub* or imaginary figure:—cherub {27x}, [*plur.*] cherubims {64x}. See: TWOT—1036; BDB—500c.

3743. כְּרוּב {2x} **K**ᵉ**rûwb**, *ker-oob';* the same as 3742; *Kerub,* a place in Bab.:—Cherub {2x}. See: BDB—500c.

3744. כָּרוֹז {1x} **kârôwz** (Aram.), *kaw-roze';* from 3745; a *herald:*—herald {1x}. See: TWOT—2802; BDB—1097d.

3745. כְּרַז {1x} **k**ᵉ**raz** (Aram.), *ker-az';* prob. of Gr. or. (κηρύσσω); to *proclaim:*—make a proclamation {1x}. See: TWOT—2801; BDB—1097d.

3746. כָּרִי {3x} **kârîy**, *kaw-ree';* perh. an abridged plur. of 3733 in the sense of *leader* (of the flock); a *life-guardsman:*—captains {2x}, Cherethites {1x}. See: BDB—501b.

3747. כְּרִית {2x} **K**ᵉ**rîyth**, *ker-eeth';* from 3772; a *cut; Kerith,* a brook of Pal.:—Cherith {2x}. See: BDB—501b, 504d.

3748. כְּרִיתוּת {4x} **k**ᵉ**rîythûwth**, *ker-ee-thooth';* from 3772; a *cutting* (of the matrimonial bond), i.e. *divorce:*—divorce {3x}, divorcement {1x}.

Keriythuwth, refers to a "bill of divorcement." **(1)** This word implies the cutting off of a marriage by means of a "bill of divorcement": "When a man hath taken a wife, and married her, and it come to pass that she find no favor in his eyes, because he hath found some uncleanness in her: then let him write her a bill of divorcement, and give it in her hand, and send her out of his house" (Deut 24:1). Syn.: 1644. See: TWOT—1048a; BDB—501b, 504d.

3749. כַּרְכֹּב {2x} **karkôb**, *kar-kobe';* expanded from the same as 3522; a *rim* or top margin:—compass {2x}. See: TWOT—1038a; BDB—501b.

3750. כַּרְכֹּם {1x} **ka kôm**, *kar-kome';* prob. of for. or.; the *crocus:*—saffron {1x}. See: TWOT—1039; BDB—501b.

3751. כַּרְכְּמִישׁ {3x} **Kark**ᵉ**mîysh**, *kar-kem-eesh';* of for. der.; *Karkemish,* a place in Syria:—Carchemish {3x}. See: BDB—501c.

3752. כַּרְכַּס {1x} **Karkaç**, *kar-kas';* of Pers. or.; *Karkas,* a eunuch of Xerxes:—Carcas {1x}. See: BDB—501c.

3753. כַּרְכָּרָה {1x} **karkârâh**, *kar-kaw-raw';* from 3769; a *dromedary* (from its *rapid* motion as if dancing):—swift beast {1x}. See: TWOT—1046b; BDB—501c, 503a.

3754. כֶּרֶם {93x} **kerem**, *keh'-rem;* from an unused root of uncert. mean.; a *garden* or *vineyard:*—vines {3x}, (increase of the) vineyard (-s) {89x}, vintage {1x}.

Kerem means "vineyard." **(1)** The first occurrence is in Gen 9:20: "And Noah began to be an husbandman, and he planted a vineyard:" **(2)** Isaiah gives a vivid description of the work involved in the preparation, planting, and cultivation of a "vineyard" (Is 5:1–7). **(2a)** The

"vineyard" was located on the slopes of a hill (Is 5:1). **(2b)** The soil was cleared of stones before the tender vines were planted (Is 5:2). **(2c)** A watchtower provided visibility over the "vineyard" (Is 5:2), and **(2d)** a winevat and place for crushing the grapes were hewn out of the rock (Is 5:2). **(2e)** When all the preparations were finished, the "vineyard" was ready and in a few years it was expected to produce crops. **(2f)** In the meantime the *kerem* required regular pruning (Lev 25:3–4). **(2g)** The time between planting and the first crop was of sufficient import as to free the owner from military duty: "And what man is he that hath planted a vineyard, and hath not yet eaten of it?" (Deut 20:6). **(3)** The harvest time was a period of hard work and great rejoicing. **(3a)** The enjoyment of the "vineyard" was a blessing of God: "And they shall build houses, and inhabit them; and they shall plant vineyards, and eat the fruit of them" (Is 65:21). **(3b)** The failure of the "vineyard" to produce or the transfer of ownership of one's "vineyard" was viewed as God's judgment: "Forasmuch therefore as your treading is upon the poor, and ye take from him burdens of wheat: ye have built houses of hewn stone, but ye shall not dwell in them; ye have planted pleasant vineyards, but ye shall not drink wine of them" (Amos 5:11; cf. Deut 28:30). **(4)** The words "vineyard" and "olive grove' (2132 - *zayit*) are often found together in the biblical text. **(4a)** These furnished the two major permanent agricultural activities in ancient Israel, as both required much work and time before the crops came in. **(4b)** God promised that the ownership of the "vineyards" and orchards of the Canaanites was to go to His people as a blessing from Him (Deut 6:11–12). **(5)** God's judgment to Israel extended to the "vineyards." **(5a)** The rejoicing in the "vineyard" would cease (Is 16:10) and **(5b)** the carefully cultivated "vineyard" would be turned into a thicket with thorns and briers (cf. Is 32:12–13). **(5c)** The "vineyard" would be reduced to a hiding place of wild animals and a grazing place for goats and wild donkeys (Is 32:14). **(6)** The postexilic hope lay in God's blessings on the agricultural activity of His people: "And I will bring again the captivity of my people of Israel, and they shall build the waste cities, and inhabit them; and they shall plant vineyards, and drink the wine thereof; they shall also make gardens, and eat the fruit of them" (Amos 9:14). **(7)** The "vineyards" were located mainly in the hill country and in the low-lying hill country. The Bible mentions the "vineyard" at Timnath (Judg 14:5), Jezreel (1 Kin 21:1), the hill country of Samaria (Jer 31:5), and even at Engedi (Song 1:14). **(8)** The metaphorical use of *kerem* **(8a)** allows the prophet Isaiah to draw

an analogy between the "vineyard" and Israel: "For the vineyard of the Lord of hosts is the house of Israel" (Is 5:7). See: TWOT−1040a; BDB−501c. See also 1021.

3755. כֹּרֵם {5x} **kôrêm**, *ko-rame'*; act. part. of an imaginary denom. from 3754; a *vinedresser:*—vine dresser [*as one or two words*] {5x}. See: TWOT−1040; BDB−501d.

3756. כַּרְמִי {8x} **Karmîy**, *kar-mee';* from 3754; *gardener; Karmi*, the name of three Isr.:—Carmi {8x}. See: BDB−501d.

3757. כַּרְמִי {1x} **Karmîy**, *kar-mee';* patron. from 3756; a *Karmite* or desc. of *Karmi:*—Carmites {1x}. See: BDB−502a.

3758. כַּרְמִיל {3x} **karmîyl** *kar-mele';* prob. of for. or.; *carmine*, a deep red:—crimson {3x}. See: TWOT−1043; BDB−502b.

3759. כַּרְמֶל {13x} **karmel**, *kar-mel';* from 3754; a planted *field* (garden, orchard, vineyard or park); by impl. garden *produce:*—fruitful field {7x}, plentiful field {2x}, full ear {1x}, green ear {1x}, full ears of corn {1x}, plentiful {1x}. See: TWOT−1041; BDB−502a.

3760. כַּרְמֶל {26x} **Karmel**, *kar-mel';* the same as 3759; *Karmel*, the name of a hill and of a town in Pal.:—Carmel {26x}. See: TWOT−1042; BDB−502a.

3761. כַּרְמְלִי {5x} **Karmᵉlîy**, *kar-mel-ee';* patron. from 3760; a *Karmelite* or inhab. of Karmel (the town):—Carmelite {5x}. See: BDB−502b.

3762. כַּרְמְלִית {2x} **Karmᵉlîyth**, *kar-mel-eeth';* fem. of 3761; a *Karmelitess* or female inhab. of Karmel:—Carmelitess {2x}. See: BDB−502b.

3763. כְּרָן {2x} **Kᵉrân**, *ker-awn';* of uncert. der.; *Keran*, an aboriginal Idumæan:—Cheran {2x}. See: TWOT−1042; BDB−502b.

3764. כָּרְסֵא {1x} **korçê** (Aram.), *kor-say';* corresp. to 3678; a *throne:*—throne {1x}. See: TWOT−2803; BDB−1097c, 1098a.

3765. כִּרְסֵם {1x} **kirçêm**, *kir-same';* from 3697; to *lay waste:*—waste {1x}. See: TWOT−1013b; BDB−493c, 502b.

3766. כָּרַע {36x} **kâraʿ**, *kaw-rah';* a prim. root; to *bend* the knee; by impl. to *sink*, to *prostrate:*—bow {14x}, . . . down {12x}, fell {2x}, subdued {2x}, brought low {1x}, couched {1x}, feeble {1x}, kneeling {1x}, very {1x}.

Kara' means "to bow, bow down, bend the knee." **(1)** *Karaʿ* appears for the first time in the deathbed blessing of Jacob as he describes Judah: "He stooped down, he couched as a lion" (Gen 49:9). **(2)** The implication of *kara'* seems to be the bending of one's legs or knees,

since a noun meaning "leg" is derived from it. **(3)** To "bow down" to drink was one of the tests for elimination from Gideon's army (Judg 7:5–6). **(4)** Kneeling" was a common attitude for the worship of God (1 Kin 8:54; Ezra 9:5; Is 45:23; cf. Phil. 2:10). **(5)** "Bowing down" before Haman was required by the Persian king's command (Est 3:2–5). **(6)** To "bow down upon" a woman was a euphemism for sexual intercourse (Job 31:10). **(7)** A woman in process of giving birth was said to "bow down": "And his daughter-in-law, Phinehas' wife, was with child, near to be delivered: and when she heard the tidings that the ark of God was taken, and that her father-in-law and her husband were dead, she bowed herself and travailed; for her pains came upon her" (1 Sa 4:19). **(8)** Tottering or feeble knees are those that "bend" from weakness or old age: "Thy words have upholden him that was falling, and thou hast strengthened the feeble knees" (Job 4:4). See: TWOT—1044; BDB—502c.

3767. כָּרָע {9x} **kârâ‘**, *kaw-raw'*; from 3766; the *leg* (from the knee to the ankle) of men or locusts (only in the dual):—leg {9x}. See: TWOT—1044a; BDB—502d.

3768. כַּרְפַּס {1x} **karpaç** *kar-pas';* of for. or.; *byssus* or fine vegetable wool:—green {1x}. See: TWOT—1045; BDB—502d.

3769. כָּרַר {2x} **kârar**, *kaw-rar';* a prim. root; to *dance* (i.e. *whirl*):—dance (-ing) {2x}. Syn.: 2342, 4234. See: TWOT—1046; BDB—502d, 1098a.

3770. כְּרֵשׁ {1x} **k‘rês**, *ker-ace';* by var. f om 7164; the *paunch* or belly (as *swelling* out):—belly {1x}. See: TWOT—1047a; BDB—503c.

כֹּרֶשׁ **Kôresh**. See 3567.

3771. כַּרְשְׁנָא {1x} **Karsh‘nâ’**, *kar-shen-aw';* of for. or.; *Karshena*, a courtier of Xerxes:—Carshena {1x}. See: BDB—503c.

3772. כָּרַת {288x} **kârath**, *kaw-rath';* a prim. root; to *cut* (off, down or asunder); by impl. to *destroy* or *consume; spec. to covenant* (i.e. make an alliance or bargain, orig. by cutting flesh and passing between the pieces):—cut off {145x}, make {85x}, cut down {23x}, cut {9x}, fail {6x}, destroy {4x}, want {3x}, covenanted {2x}, hew {2x}, misc. {9x}= be chewed, feller, be freed, × lose, perish, × utterly.

Karath means "to cut off, cut down, fell, cut or make (a covenant or agreement)." **(1)** Basically *karath* means "to sever" something from something else by cutting it with a blade. **(1a)** The nuance depends upon the thing being cut off. **(1a1)** In the case of a branch, one "cuts

it down" (Num 13:23), and one **(1a2)** "[swings] the axe to cut down the tree" (Deut 19:5). **(1b)** The word is also used of "chopping down" wooden idols (Ex 34:13). **(1c)** *Karath* can signify "chopping off" a man's head and feet (1 Sa 5:4). **(1d)** In Jer 34:18 this verb means "to cut into two pieces." **(1e)** "Cut off" may also imply cutting off in the sense of circumcision. In Ex 4:25 Zipporah took a flint knife and "cut off" her son's foreskin. **(1f)** In a related but different usage this word appears in Num. 11:33, where it means "to chew" meat. **(2)** "To cut off" can mean "to exterminate or destroy." God told Noah that "all flesh [shall never again] be cut off . . . by the waters of a flood" (Gen 9:11–the first occurrence of the word). **(3)** *Karath* can be used of spiritual and social extermination. A person "cut off" in this manner is not necessarily killed but may be driven out of the family and removed from the blessings of the covenant. God told Abraham that "the uncircumcised man child whose flesh of his foreskin is not circumcised, that soul shall be cut off from his people; he hath broken my covenant" (Gen 17:14). **(4)** One of the best known uses of this verb is "to make" a covenant. **(4a)** The process by which God made a covenant with Abraham is called "cutting": "In the same day the Lord made a covenant with Abram" (Gen 15:18). **(4b)** The word "covenant" appears nine times before this in Genesis, but it is not connected with *karath.* **(4c)** Furthermore, hereafter in Genesis and throughout the Bible *karath* is frequently associated with making a covenant. **(4d)** This verb, therefore, constitutes a rather technical term for making a covenant. **(4e)** In Genesis it often alludes to an act by which animals were cut in two and the party taking the oath passed between the pieces.

(5) Later, "cutting" a covenant did not necessarily include this act but seems to be an allusion to the Abrahamic covenantal process (cf. Jer 34:18). **(5a)** In such a covenant the one passing through the pieces pledged his faithfulness to the covenant. **(5b)** If that faithfulness was broken, he called death upon himself, or the same fate which befell the animals. **(6)** In some cases it is quite clear that no literal cutting took place and that *karath* is used in a technical sense of "making an agreement in writing": "And because of all this we make a sure covenant, and write it; and our princes, Levites, and priests, seal unto it" (Neh 9:38). See: TWOT—1048; BDB—503c.

3773. כָּרֻתָה {3x} **kârûthâh**, *kaw-rooth-aw';* pass. part. fem. of 3772; something *cut,* i.e. a hewn *timber:*—beam {3x}.

Karuthah means "beams." This noun, which occurs only 3 times, refers to "beams" in the sense of things "cut off" in 1 Kin 6:36: "And he

built the inner court with three rows of hewed stone, and a row of cedar beams." See: TWOT—1048b; BDB—503c.

3774. כְּרֵתִי {10x} **Kᵉrêthîy**, *ker-ay-thee';* prob. from 3772 in the sense of *executioner;* a *Kerethite* or *life-guardsman* [comp. 2876] (only collect. in the sing. as plur.):—Cherethites {10x}. See: BDB—504d.

3775. כֶּשֶׂב {13x} **keseb**, *keh'-seb;* appar. by transp. for 3532; a young *sheep:*—lamb {4x}, sheep {9x}. See: TWOT—949; BDB—461a, 505a.

3776. כִּשְׂבָּה {1x} **kisbâh**, *kis-baw';* fem. of 3775; a young *ewe:*—lamb {1x}. See: TWOT—949; BDB—461b, 505a.

3777. כֶּשֶׂד {1x} **Kesed**, *keh'-sed;* from an unused root of uncert. mean.; *Kesed,* a relative of Abraham:—Chesed {1x}. See: BDB—505a.

3778. כַּשְׂדִּי {80x} **Kasdîy**, *kas-dee';* (occasionally with enclitic)

כַּשְׂדִּימָה **Kasdîymâh**, *kas-dee'-maw; toward* (the) *Kasdites* (into Chaldea), patron. from 3777 (only in the plur.); a *Kasdite,* or desc. of Kesed; by impl. a *Chaldæan* (as if so descended); also an *astrologer* (as if proverbial of that people:—Chaldeans {59x}, Chaldees {14x}, Chaldea {7x}. See: BDB—505a, 1098a.

3779. כַּשְׂדַי {8x} **Kasday** (Aram.), *kas-dah'-ee;* corresp. to 3778; a *Chaldæan* or inhab. of Chaldæa; by impl. a *Magian* or professional astrologer:—Chaldean {8x}. See: BDB—1097c, 1098a.

3780. כָּשָׂה {1x} **kâsâh**, *kaw-saw';* a prim. root; to *grow fat* (i.e. *be covered* with flesh):—be covered {1x}. See: TWOT—1049; BDB—505b. comp. 3680.

3781. כַּשִּׂיל {1x} **kashshîyl** *kash-sheel';* from 3782; prop. a *feller,* i.e. an *axe:*—axes {1x}. See: TWOT—1050a; BDB—506a.

3782. כָּשַׁל {65x} **kâshal**, *kaw-shal';* a prim. root; to *totter* or *waver* (through weakness of the legs, espec. the ankle); by impl. to *falter, stumble,* faint or fall:—fall {27x}, stumble {19x}, cast down {4x}, feeble {4x}, overthrown {2x}, ruin {2x}, bereave + 7921 {1x}, decayed {1x}, faileth {1x}, utterly {1x}, weak {1x}, variant {2x}.

Kashal means "to stumble, stagger, totter, be thrown down." **(1)** It occurs the first time in Lev 26:37: "And they shall fall one upon another. . . ." **(1a)** This use illustrates the basic idea that one "stumbles" because of something or over something. **(1b)** Heavy physical burdens cause one "to stagger": "The children fell

under the [loads of] wood" (Lam 5:13). **(2)** This word is often used figuratively to describe the consequences of divine judgment on sin: "Behold, I will lay stumbling blocks before this people, and the fathers and the sons together shall fall upon them" (Jer 6:21). **(3)** Babylon, too, will know God's judgment: "And the most proud shall stumble and fall" (Jer 50:32). **(4)** When the psalmist says: "My knees totter from my fasting" (Ps 109:24 NAB), he means: "My knees are weak." See: TWOT—1050; BDB—505b.

3783. כִּשָּׁלוֹן {1x} **kishshâlôwn**, *kish-shaw-lone';* from 3782; prop. a *tottering,* i.e. *ruin:*—fall {1x}. See: TWOT—1050b; BDB—506a.

3784. כָּשַׁף {6x} **kâshaph**, *kaw-shaf';* a prim. root; prop. to *whisper* a spell, i.e. to *inchant* or *practise magic:*—sorcerer {3x}, witches {2x}, use witchcraft {1x}. See: TWOT—1051; BDB—506c.

3785. כֶּשֶׁף {6x} **kesheph**, *keh'-shef;* from 3784; *magic:*—sorcery {2x}, witchcraft {4x}. See: TWOT—1051a; BDB—506c.

3786. כַּשָּׁף {1x} **kashshâph**, *kash-shawf';* from 3784; a *magician:*—sorcerer {1x}. See: TWOT—1051b; BDB—506c.

3787. כָּשֵׁר {3x} **kâshêr**, *kaw-share';* a prim. root; prop. to *be straight* or *right;* by impl. to *be acceptable;* also to *succeed* or *prosper:*—direct {1x}, be right {1x}, prosper {1x}. See: TWOT—1052; BDB—506d.

3788. כִּשְׁרוֹן {3x} **kishrôwn**, *kish-rone';* from 3787; *success, advantage:*—equity {1x}, good {1x}, right {1x}. See: TWOT—1052b; BDB—507a.

3789. כָּתַב {223x} **kâthab**, *kaw-thab';* a prim. root; to *grave,* by impl. to *write* (describe, inscribe, prescribe, subscribe):—describe {7x}, recorded {1x}, prescribed {1x}, subscribe {4x}, write (-ing, -ten) {210x}.

Kathab means "to write, inscribe, describe, take dictation, engrave." **(1)** Basically, this verb represents writing down a message. **(2)** The judgment (ban) of God against the Amalekites was to be recorded in the book (scroll): "And the Lord said unto Moses, Write this for a memorial in a book, and rehearse it in the ears of Joshua: for I will utterly put out the remembrance of Amalek from under heaven" (Ex 17:14—the first biblical occurrence of the word). **(3)** One may "write" upon a stone or "write" a message upon it. Moses told Israel that after crossing the Jordan "thou shalt set thee up great stones, and plaster them with plaster: and thou shalt write upon them all the words of this law" (Deut 27:2–3). **(3a)** This use of the

word implies something more than keeping a record of something so that it will be remembered. **(3b)** This is obvious in the first passage because the memory of Amalek is "to be recorded" and also blotted out.

(3c) In such passages "to be recorded," therefore, refers to the unchangeableness and binding nature of the Word of God. **(3d)** God has said it, it is fixed, and it will occur. **(3e)** An extended implication in the case of divine commands is that man must obey what God "has recorded" (Deut 27:2–3). **(3f)** Thus, such uses of the word describe a fixed body of authoritative instruction, or a canon. **(3g)** These 2 passages also show that the word does not tell us anything specific about how the message was composed. **(3g1)** In the first instance Moses seems not to have merely "recorded" as a secretary but "to have written" creatively what he heard and saw. **(3g2)** Certainly in Ex 32:32 the word is used of creative writing by the author; God was not receiving dictation from anyone when He "inscribed" the Ten Commandments. **(3g3)** In Deut 27:2–3 the writers must reproduce exactly what was previously given (as mere secretaries).

(4) Sometimes *kathab* appears to mean "to inscribe" and "to cover with inscription." **(4a)** The two tablets of the testimony which were given to Moses by God were "tables of stone, written [fully inscribed] with the finger of God" (Ex 31:18). **(4b)** The verb means not only to write in a book but "to write a book," not just to record something in a few lines on a scroll but to complete the writing. **(4c)** Moses prays: "Yet now, if thou wilt forgive their sin—and if not, blot me, I pray thee, out of thy book which thou hast written" (Ex 32:32). **(4d)** Here "book" probably refers to a scroll rather than a book in the present-day sense. **(5)** Among the special uses of *kathab* is the meaning "to record a survey." **(5a)** At Shiloh, Joshua told Israel to choose three men from each tribe "and they shall arise, and go through the land, and describe it" (Josh 18:4). **(6)** An extended nuance of *kathab* is "to receive dictation": "And Baruch wrote from the mouth of Jeremiah" (Jer 36:4). **(7)** The word can also be used of signing one's signature: "And because of all this we make [are cutting] a sure covenant, and write it; and our princes, Levites, and priests, seal unto it" (Neh 9:38). **(7a)** Thus they "cut," or completed, the agreement by having the representatives sign it. **(7b)** The cutting was the signing. See: TWOT—1053; BDB—507a, 1098a.

3790. כְּתַב {8x} **kᵉthab** (Aram.), *keth-ab';* corresp. to 3789:—write (-ten) {8x}. See: TWOT—2805; BDB—1098a.

3791. כְּתָב {17x} **kâthâb**, *kaw-thawb';* from 3789; something *written*, i.e. a *writing, record* or *book*:—register {2x}, scripture {1x}, writing {14x}.

Kathab means "something written; register; scripture." **(1)** In 1 Chr 28:19 *kathab* is used to mean "something written," such as an edict: "All this, said David, the Lord made me understand in writing by his hand upon me, even all the works of this pattern." **(2)** The word also refers to a "register": "These sought their register among those that were reckoned by genealogy, but they were not found: therefore were they, as polluted, put from the priesthood" (Ezr 2:62), and **(3)** to "scripture": "But I will shew thee that which is noted in the scripture of truth: and there is none that holdeth with me in these things, but Michael your prince" (Dan 10:21). See: TWOT—1053a; BDB—508b.

3792. כְּתָב {12x} **kᵉthâb** (Aram.), *keth-awb';* corresp. to 3791:—prescribing {1x}, writing (-ten) {11x}. See: TWOT—2805a; 1098a.

3793. כְּתֹבֶת {1x} **kᵉthôbeth**, *keth-o'-beth;* from 3789; a *letter* or other *mark* branded on the skin:—✗ any [mark] {1x}.

Kethobeth occurs once to mean something inscribed, specifically a "tatooing": "Ye shall not make any cuttings (*kethobeth*) in your flesh for the dead, nor print any marks upon you: I am the LORD" (Lev 19:28). See: TWOT—1053b; BDB—508b.

3794. כִּתִּי {8x} **Kittîy**, *kit-tee'* or

כִּתִּיִּי **Kittîyîy**, *kit-tee-ee';* patrial from an unused name denoting Cyprus (only in the plur.); a *Kittite* or Cypriote; hence, an *islander* in gen., i.e. the Greeks or Romans on the shores opposite Pal.:—Chittim {6x}, Kittim {2x}. See: BDB—508c.

3795. כָּתִית {5x} **kâthîyth**, *kaw-theeth';* from 3807; *beaten*, i.e. *pure* (oil):—beaten {1x}, pure {4x}. See: TWOT—1062a; BDB—508c, 510c.

3796. כֹּתֶל {1x} **kôthel**, *ko'-thel;* from an unused root mean. to *compact;* a *wall* (as *gathering* inmates):—wall {1x}. Syn.: 1444, 1447, 2346, 7023. See: TWOT—1054a; BDB—508c, 1098b.

3797. כְּתַל {2x} **kᵉthal** (Aram.), *keth-al';* corresp. to 3796:—wall {2x}. See: TWOT—2806; BDB—1098b.

3798. כִּתְלִישׁ {1x} **Kithlîysh**, *kith-leesh';* from 3796 and 376; *wall of a man; Kithlish*, a place in Pal.:—Kithlish {1x}. See: BDB—508c.

3799. כָּתַם {1x} **kâtham**, *kaw-tham';* a prim. root; prop. to *carve* or *engrave*, i.e.

(by impl.) to *inscribe* indelibly:—marked {1x}. See: TWOT—1055; BDB—508d.

3800. כֶּתֶם {9x} **kethem,** *keh'-them;* from 3799; prop. something *carved* out, i.e. *ore;* hence, *gold* (pure as orig. mined):—fine gold {4x}, gold {2x}, most {1x}, golden wedge {1x}, pure gold {1x}. Syn.: 1220, 2091, 2742, 6337. See: TWOT—1057; BDB—508d.

3801. כְּתֹנֶת {23x} **kᵉthôneth,** *keth-o'-neth;* or

כֻּתֹּנֶת **kuttôneth,** *koot-to'-neth;* from an unused root mean. to *cover* [comp. 3802]; a *shirt:*—coat {23x}, garment {5x}, robe {1x}. See: TWOT—1058a; BDB—509a.

3802. כָּתֵף {67x} **kâthêph,** *kaw-thafe';* from an unused root mean. to *clothe;* the *shoulder* (proper, i.e. upper end of the arm; as being the spot where the garments hang); fig. *side-piece* or lateral projection of anything:—side {34x}, shoulders {22x}, shoulderpieces {4x}, undersetters {4x}, corner {2x}, arm {1x}. See: TWOT—1059; BDB—509b.

3803. כָּתַר {7x} **kâthar,** *kaw-thar';* a prim. root; to *enclose;* hence, (in a friendly sense) to *crown,* (in a hostile one) to *besiege;* also to *wait* (as restraining oneself):—compass (about) {3x}, inclosed {1x}, beset me round {1x}, suffer {1x}, crowned {1x}. See: TWOT—1060; BDB—509c.

3804. כֶּתֶר {1x} **kether,** *keh'-ther;* from 3803; prop. a *circlet,* i.e. a *diadem:*—crown {1x}. Syn.: 5850. See: TWOT—1060a; BDB—509d.

3805. כֹּתֶרֶת {1x} **kôthereth,** *ko-theh'-ret;* fem. act. part. of 3803; the *capital* of a column:—chapter {1x}. See: TWOT—1060c; BDB—509d.

3806. כָּתַשׁ {1x} **kâthash** *kaw-thash';* a prim. root; to *butt* or *pound:*—bray {1x}. See: TWOT—1061; BDB—509d.

3807. כָּתַת {17x} **kâthath,** *kaw-thath';* a prim. root; to *bruise* or violently *strike:*—beat {4x}, destroyed {3x}, beat down {2x}, break in pieces {2x}, smite {2x}, beat in pieces {1x}, discomfited {1x}, crushed {1x}, stamped {1x}. See: TWOT—1062; BDB—510a.

ל

3808. לֹא **lôʾ,** *lo;* or

לוֹא **lôwʾ,** *lo;* or

לֹה {76x} **lôh** (Deut. 3:11), *lo;* a prim. particle; *not* (the simple or abs. negation); by impl. *no;* often used with other particles (as follows):—{76x} = not, no, none, nay, never, neither, ere, otherwise, before. See: TWOT—1064; BDB—210b, 518b, 529a, 530a, 1098c, 1099a.

3809. לָא {82x} **lâʾ** (Aram.), *law;* or

לָה **lâh** (Aram.) (Dan. 4:32), *law;* corresp. to 3808:—not {49x}, no {9x}, nor {9x}, without {4x}, neither {3x}, none {3x}, cannot + 3202 {1x}, ever {1x}, never + 5957 {1x}, no + 3606 {1x}, nothing {1x}. See: TWOT—2808; BDB—1098c, 1098d, 1099a.

לָא **lûʾ.** See 3863.

3810. לֹא דְבַר {3x} **Lôʾ Dᵉbar,** *lo deb-ar';* or

לוֹ דְבַר **Lôw Dᵉbar** (2 Sa 9:4, 5), *lo deb-ar';* or

לִדְבִר **Lidbîr** (Josh. 13:26), *lid-beer';* [prob. rather

לֹדְבַר **Lôdᵉbar,** *lo-deb-ar'*]; from 3808 and 1699; *pastureless; Lo-Debar,* a place in Pal.:—Lo-debar {3x}. See: BDB—520d, 529a, 530d.

3811. לָאָה {19x} **lâʾâh,** *law-aw';* a prim. root; to *tire;* (fig.) to *be* (or *make*) *disgusted:*—weary {15x}, grieve {2x}, faint {1x}, loath {1x}. See: TWOT—1066; BDB—521a.

3812. לֵאָה {34x} **Lêʾâh,** *lay-aw';* from 3811; *weary; Leah,* a wife of Jacob:—Leah {34x}. See: BDB—521b.

לְאֹם **lᵉowm.** See 3816.

3813. לָאַט {1x} **lâʾat,** *law-at';* a prim. root; to *muffle:*—cover {1x}. See: TWOT—1067; BDB—521b.

3814. לָאט {1x} **lâʾt,** *lawt;* from 3813 (or perh. for act part. of 3874); prop. *muffled,* i.e. *silently:*—softly {1x}. See: TWOT—1092a; BDB—521b, 532a.

3815. לָאֵל {1x} **Lâʾêl,** *law-ale';* from the prep. pref. and 410; (belonging) *to God; Laël,* an Isr.:—Lael {1x}. See: BDB—522b.

3816. לְאֹם {35x} **lᵉôm,** *leh-ome'* or

לְאוֹם **lᵉôwm,** *leh-ome';* from an unused root mean. to *gather;* a *community:*—nation {10x}, people {24x}, folk {1x}. This word usually speaks of a race of people (Gen 25:23). See: TWOT—1069a; BDB—522c.

3817. לְאֻמִּים {1x} **Lᵉummîym,** *leh-oom-meem';* plur. of 3816; *communities; Leümmim,* an Arabian:—Leummim {1x}. See: BDB—522c.

3818. לֹא עַמִּי {2x} **Lôʾ ʿAmmîy,** *lo am-mee';* from 3808 and 5971 with pron. suff.; *not my people; Lo-Ammi,* the symbol. name of a son of Hosea:—Lo-ammi {2x}. See: BDB—520d.

3819. לֹא רֻחָמָה {2x} **Lô Rûchâmâh,** *lo roo-khaw-maw';* from 3808 and 7355; *not pitied; Lo-Ruchamah,* the symbol. name of a son of Hosea:—Lo-ruhamah {1x}. See: BDB—520d, 933d.

3820. לֵב {592x} **lêb,** *labe;* a form of 3824; the *heart;* also used (fig.) very widely for the feelings, the will and even the intellect; likewise for the *center* of anything:—heart {508x}, mind {12x}, midst {11x}, understanding {10x}, hearted {7x}, wisdom {6x}, comfortably {4x}, well {4x}, considered {2x}, friendly {2x}, kindly {2x}, stouthearted + 47 {2x}, care + 7760 {2x}, misc. {20x} = consent, courage, courageous, × heed, × I, × regard, regarded, × themselves, × unawares, willingly.

I. Leb as a noun: Summary: The heart includes not only the motives, feelings, affections, and desires, but also the will, the aims, the principles, the thoughts, and the intellect of man. In fact, it embraces the whole inner man, the head never being regarded as the seat of intelligence. While it is the source of all action and the center of all thought and feeling the heart is also described as receptive to the influences both from the outer world and from God Himself. *Leb* means heart; mind; midst. It is used of God (Gen 6:6; Jer 32:41) and man. **(1)** Heart may refer to the organ of the body (Ex 28:29; 2 Sa 18:14). **(2)** *Leb* may also refer to the inner part or middle of a thing (Ex 15:8; Deut 4:11). **(3)** *Leb* is used of the man himself or his personality (Gen 17:17); or **(4)** his seat of desire, inclination, or will (Ex 7:14; 35:5). **(5)** Two people are in agreement when their hearts are right with each other (2 Kin 10:15). **(6)** The heart is regarded as the seat of emotions (Deut 6:5; Ex 4:14); so there are **(6a)** merry hearts (Judg 16:25), **(6b)** fearful hearts (Is 35:4), and **(6c)** hearts that trembled (1 Sa 4:13). **(7)** The heart could be regarded as the seat of knowledge and wisdom and as a synonym of "mind" when "heart" appears with the verb "to know" (Deut 29:4; 1 Kin 3:9; cf. 4:29). **(8)** Memory is the activity of the heart (Job 22:22). **(10)** It may be the seat of conscience and moral character (Job 27:6; 2 Sa 24:10). **(11)** It is the fountain of man's deeds (Gen 20:5; 1 Kin 3:6; Is 38:3). **(12)** Rebellion and pride reside in the heart (Gen 8:21; Eze 28:2). **(13)** God controls the heart: He **(13a)** gives a new one (Eze 36:26); **(13b)** creates a clean one (Ps 51:10); **(13c)** unites the believer's heart to fear His name (Ps 86:11); and **(13d)** triest the heart (1 Chr 29:17). **(14)** Hence God's people seek His approval (Ps 26:2). **(15)** The heart stands for the inner being of man, the man himself, and is the fountain of all he does (Prov 4:4). All his thoughts, desires, words, and actions flow from deep within him.

Yet a man cannot understand his own heart (Jer 17:9).

II. Leb, as an adverb, means "tenderly; friendly; comfortably." **(1)** *Leb* is used as an adverb in Gen 34:3: "And his soul clave unto Dinah . . . and he loved the damsel, and spake kindly (*leb*) unto the damsel." **(2)** In Ruth 4:13, the word means "friendly": ". . . thou hast spoken friendly unto thine handmaid." **(3)** The word means "comfortably" **(3a)** in 2 Chr 30:22: "And Hezekiah spake comfortably unto all the Levites that taught the good knowledge of the LORD: and they did eat throughout the feast seven days, offering peace offerings, and making confession to the LORD God of their fathers" and in **(3b)** Is 40:2 "Speak ye comfortably to Jerusalem, and cry unto her, that her warfare is accomplished, that her iniquity is pardoned: for she hath received of the LORD's hand double for all her sins."Syn.: 4578, 5315, 7023, 7130. See: TWOT—1071a; BDB—522, 523a, 524b, 525d, 925c, 1098d.

3821. לֵב {1x} **lêb** (Aram.), *labe;* corresp. to 3820:—heart {1x}. See: TWOT—2809a; BDB—1098d.

3822. לְבָאוֹת {1x} **L°bâ²ôwth,** *leb-aw-ōth';* plur. of 3833; *lionesses; Lebaoth,* a place in Pal.:—Lebaoth {1x}. See: BDB—522d. See also 1034.

3823. לָבַב {5x} **lâbab,** *law-bab';* a prim. root; prop. to *be enclosed* (as if with *fat*); by impl. (as denom. from 3824) to *unheart,* i.e. (in a good sense) *transport* (with love), or (in a bad sense) *stultify;* also (as denom. from 3834) to *make cakes:*—ravished my heart {2x}, make {1x}, made cakes {1x}, be wise {1x}. See: TWOT—1071, 1071d; BDB—525d.

3824. לֵבָב {252x} **lêbâb,** *lay-bawb';* from 3823; the *heart* (as the most interior organ); used also like 3820:—heart {231x}, consider + 7760 {5x}, mind {4x}, understanding {3x}, misc. {9x} = + bethink themselves, breast, comfortably, courage, midst, × unawares.

Lebab, as a noun, means "heart; mind; midst." **(1)** "Heart" is used first of man in Gen 6:5: "And God saw that the wickedness of man was great in the earth, and that every imagination of the thoughts of his heart was only evil continually." **(2)** In Gen 6:6 it is used of God: "And it repented the Lord that he had made man on the earth, and it grieved him at his heart." **(3)** "Heart" may refer to the organ of the body: **(3a)** "And Aaron shall bear the names of the children of Israel in the breastplate of judgment upon his heart, when he goeth in unto the holy place" (Ex 28:29); **(3b)** "[Joab] took three darts in his hand, and thrust them through the heart of Absalom" (2 Sa 18:14);

(3c) "My heart panteth . . ." (Ps 38:10). **(4)** *Lebab* may also refer to the inner part or middle of a thing: **(4a)** "and the depths were congealed in the heart of the sea" (Ex 15:8); **(4b)** "and the mountain burned with fire in the midst [rsv, "to the heart"] of heaven" (Deut 4:11); **(4c)** "Yea, thou shalt be as he that lieth down in the midst of the sea" (Prov 23:34).

(5) *Lebab* can be used of the inner man, contrasted to the outer man, as **(5a)** in Deut 30:14: "But the word is very nigh unto thee, in thy mouth, and in thy heart, that thou mayest do it" (cf. Joel 2:13); **(5b)** "man looketh on the outward appearance, but the Lord looketh on the heart" (1 Sa 16:7). **(6)** *Lebab* is often compounded with "soul" for emphasis, as in 2 Chr 15:12; "And they entered into a covenant to seek the Lord God of their fathers with all their heart and with all their soul" (cf. 2 Chr 15:15). **(7)** *Nepesh* (5315 - "soul; life; self") is translated "heart" fifteen times in the KJV. **(7a)** Each time, it connotes the "inner man": **(7b)** "For as he thinketh in his heart [*nepesh*], so is he" (Prov 23:7). **(8)** *Lebab* can be used of the man himself or his personality: **(8a)** "Then Abraham fell upon his face and laughed, and said in his heart, . . ." (Gen 17:17); **(8b)** "my heart had great experience" (Eccl 1:16). **(8c)** *Lebab* is also used of God in this sense: "And I will give you pastors according to mine heart" (Jer 3:15).

(9) The seat of desire, inclination, or will can be indicated by "heart": **(9a)** "Pharaoh's heart is hardened . . ." (Ex 7:14); **(9b)** "whosoever is of a willing heart, let him bring it . . ." (Ex 35:5; cf. vv. 21, 29); **(9c)** "I will praise thee, O Lord my God, with all my heart" (Ps. 86:12). **(9d)** *Lebab* is also used of God in this sense: ". . . and I will plant them in this land assuredly with my whole heart and with my whole soul" (Jer 32:41). **(10)** Two people are said to be in agreement when their "hearts" are right with each other: "Is thine heart right, as my heart is with thy heart?" (2 Kin 10:15). **(11)** In 2 Chr 24:4, "Joash was minded to repair the house of the Lord" (Heb. "had in his heart"). **(12)** The "heart" is regarded as the seat of emotions: **(12a)** "And thou shalt love the Lord thy God with all thine heart, . . ." (Deut 6:5); **(12b)** "and when he [Aaron] seeth thee, he will be glad in his heart" (Ex 4:14; cf. 1 Sa 2:1). **(12b)** So there are **(12b1)** "merry" hearts (Judg 16:25), **(12b2)** "fearful" hearts (Is 35:4), and **(12b3)** hearts that "trembled" (1 Sa 4:13).

(13) The "heart" could be regarded as the seat of knowledge and wisdom and as a synonym of "mind." **(13a)** This meaning often occurs when "heart" appears with the verb "to know": **(13a1)** "Thou shalt also consider [know] in your heart . . ." (Deut 8:5); and **(13a2)** "Yet the Lord hath not given you an heart to perceive [know] . . ." (Deut 29:4). **(13a3)** Solomon prayed, "Give therefore thy servant an understanding heart to judge thy people, that I may discern between good and bad" (1 Kin 3:9; cf. 4:29). **(14)** Memory is the activity of the "heart," as in Job 22:22: ". . . lay up his [God's] words in thine heart." **(15)** The "heart" may be the seat of conscience and moral character. How does one respond to the revelation of God and of the world around him? **(15a)** Job answers: ". . . my heart shall not reproach me as long as I live" (27:6). **(15b)** On the contrary, "David's heart smote him . . ." (2 Sa 24:10). **(16)** The "heart" is the fountain of man's deeds: "in the integrity of my heart and innocency of my hands I have done this" (Gen 20:5; cf. v. 6). **(16a)** David walked "in uprightness of heart" (1 Kin 3:6) and **(16b)** Hezekiah walked "with a perfect heart" (Is 38:3) before God.

(17) Only the man with "clean hands, and a pure heart" (Ps 24:4) can stand in God's presence. **(18)** *Lebab* may refer to the seat of rebellion and pride. God said: "for the imagination of man's heart is evil from his youth" (Gen 8:21). **(18a)** Tyre is like all men: "Because thine heart is lifted up, and thou hast said, I am a God" (Eze 28:2). **(18b)** They all become like Judah, whose "sin . . . is graven upon the table of their heart" (Jer 17:1). **(19)** God controls the "heart." **(19a)** Because of his natural "heart," man's only hope is in the promise of God: "A new heart also will I give you, . . . and I will take away the stony heart out of your flesh, and I will give you a heart of flesh" (Eze 36:26). **(19b)** So the sinner prays: "Create in me a clean heart, O God" (Ps 51:10); **(19c)** and "unite my heart [give me an undivided heart] to fear thy name" (Ps 86:11). **(19d)** Also, as David says, "I know also, my God, that thou triest the heart, and hast pleasure in uprightness" (1 Chr 29:17). **(19e)** Hence God's people seek His approval: "try my reins and my heart" (Ps 26:2).

(20) The "heart" stands for the inner being of man, the man himself. As such, it is the fountain of all he does (Prov 4:4). **(20a)** All his thoughts, desires, words, and actions flow from deep within him. Yet a man cannot understand his own "heart" (Jer 17:9). **(20b)** As a man goes on in his own way, his "heart" becomes harder and harder. But God will circumcise (cut away the uncleanness of) the "heart" of His people, so that they will love and obey Him with their whole being (Deut 30:6). See: TWOT—1071a; BDB—523a, 925a, 1098d.

3825. לְבַב {1x} **l°bab** (Aram.), *leb-ab′*; corresp. to 3824:—heart {1x}. See: TWOT—2809b; BDB—1098d.

לְבִבָה **l°bîbâh**. See 3834.

3826. לִבָּה {1x} **libbâh**, *lib-baw';* fem. of 3820; the *heart:*—heart {1x}. See: TWOT—1071b; BDB—525d.

3827. לַבָּה {1x} **labbâh**, *lab-baw';* for 3852; *flame:*—flame {1x}. See: TWOT—1077b; BDB—529b.

3828. לְבוֹנָה {21x} **lebôwnâh**, *leb-o-naw';* or

לְבֹנָה **lebonâh**, *leb-o-naw';* from 3836; *frankincense* (from its *whiteness* or perh. that of its *smoke*):—frankincense {15x}, incense {1x}. Syn.: 6999, 7004. See: TWOT—1074d; BDB—526c.

3829. לְבוֹנָה {1x} **Lebôwnâh**, *leb-o- aw';* the same as 3828; *Lebonah,* a place in Pal.:—Lebonah {1x}. See: TWOT—1074d; BDB—526d.

3830. לְבוּשׁ {32x} **lebûwsh**, *leb-oosh';* or

לְבֻשׁ **lebûsh**, *leb-oosh';* from 3847; a *garment* (lit. or fig.); by impl. (euphem.) a *wife:*—clothing {9x}, garment {9x}, apparel {8x}, vesture {2x}, clothed {1x}, put on {1x}, raiment {1x}, vestments {1x}. See: TWOT—1075a; BDB—528c, 1098d.

3831. לְבוּשׁ {1x} **lebûwsh** (Aram.), *leb-oosh';* corresp. to 3830:—garment {2x}. See: TWOT—2810a; BDB—1098d.

3832. לָבַט {3x} **lâbaṭ**, *l w-bat';* a prim. root; to *overthrow;* intr. to *fall:*—fall {3x}. See: TWOT—1072; BDB—526a.

לֻבִּי **Lubbîy**. See 3864.

3833. לָבִיא {14x} **lâbîy**, *law-bee';* or (Eze 19:2)

לְבִיא **lebîyâ**, *leb-ee-yaw';* irreg. masc. plur.

לְבָאִים **lebâîym**, *leb-aw-eem';* irreg. fem. plur.

לְבָאוֹת **lebâôwth**, *leb-aw-ōth';* from an unused root mean. to *roar;* a *lion* (prop. a lioness as the fiercer [although not a *roarer;* comp. 738]):—lion {5x}, great lion {3x}, old lion {2x}, stout lion {1x}, lioness {2x}, young {1x}. Syn.: 738, 3918, 7826. See: TWOT—1070b, 1070c; BDB—522d, 526a.

3834. לְבִיבָה {3x} **lâbîybâh**, *law-bee-baw';* or rather

לְבִבָה **lebîbâh**, *leb-ee-baw';* from 3823 in its orig. sense of *fatness* (or perh. of *folding*); a *cake* (either as *fried* or *turned*):—cakes {3x}. See: TWOT—1071c; BDB—525d.

3835. לָבַן {8x} **lâban**, *law-ban';* a prim. root; to *be* (or *become*) *white;* also (as denom. from 3843) to *make bricks:*—make white {3x}, make {2x}, make brick {1x}, be white {1x}, be whiter {1x}. See: TWOT—1074b, 1074h; BDB—526a, 527c.

3836. לָבָן {29x} **lâbân**, *law-bawn';* or (Gen 49:12)

לָבֵן **lâbên**, *law-bane';* from 3835; *white:*—white {29x}. See: TWOT—1074a; BDB—526b.

3837. לָבָן {55x} **Lâbân**, *law-bawn';* the same as 3836; *Laban,* a Mesopotamian; also a place in the Desert:—Laban {55x}. See: BDB—526c.

לַבֵּן **Labbên**. See 4192.

3838. לְבָנָא {2x} **Lebânâ**, *leb-aw-naw';* or

לְבָנָה **Lebânâh**, *leb-aw-naw';* the same as 3842; *Lebana* or *Lebanah,* one of the Nethinim:—Lebana {1x}, Lebanah {1x}. See: BDB—526c.

3839. לִבְנֶה {2x} **libneh**, *lib-neh';* from 38 5; some sort of *whitish* tree, perh. the *storax:*—poplar {2x}. See: TWOT—1074f; BDB—527b.

3840. לִבְנָה {1x} **libnâh**, *lib-naw';* from 3 35; prop. *whiteness,* i.e. (by impl.) *transparency:*—paved {1x}. See: TWOT—1074g; BDB—527c.

3841. לִבְנָה {18x} **Libnâh**, *lib-naw';* the sa e as 3839; *Libnah,* a place in the Desert and one in Pal.:—Libnah {18x}. See: TWOT—1074g; BDB—526c.

3842. לְבָנָה {3x} **lebânâh**, *leb-aw-naw';* from 3835; prop. (the) *white,* i.e. the *moon:*—moon {3x}. See: TWOT—1074c; BDB—526b. See also 3838.

3843. לְבֵנָה {11x} **lebênâh**, *leb-ay-naw';* from 3835; a *brick* (from the *whiteness* of the clay):—(altar of) brick {10x}, tile {1x}. See: TWOT—1074g; BDB—527b.

לְבֹנָה **lebônâh**. See 3828.

3844. לְבָנוֹן {71x} **Lebânôwn**, *leb-aw-nohn';* from 3825; (the) *white* mountain (from its *snow*); *Lebanon,* a mountain range in Pal.:—Lebanon {71x}. See: TWOT—1074e; BDB—526d.

3845. לִבְנִי {5x} **Libnîy**, *lib-nee';* from 3835; *white; Libni,* an Isr.:—Libni {5x}. See: TWOT—1074e; BDB—526d.

3846. לִבְנִי {2x} **Libnîy**, *lib-nee';* patron. from 3845; a *Libnite* or desc. of Libni (collect.):—Libnites {2x}. See: TWOT—1074e; BDB—526d.

3847. לָבַשׁ {112x} **lâbash**, *law-bash';* or

לָבֵשׁ **lâbêsh**, *law-bashe';* a prim. root; prop. *wrap* around, i.e. (by impl.)

to *put on* a garment or *clothe* (oneself, or another), lit. or fig.:—clothe {51x}, put on {22x}, put {18x}, array {6x}, wear {4x}, armed {3x}, came {3x}, apparel {1x}, apparelled {1x}, clothed them {1x}, came upon {1x}, variant {1x}.

Labesh means "to put on (a garment), clothe, wear, be clothed." **(1)** *Labash* is found very early in the Old Testament, **(1a)** in Gen 3:21: "Unto Adam also and to his wife did the Lord God make coats of skin, and clothed them." **(1b)** As always, God provided something much better for man than man could do for himself—in this instance, coats of skins to replace fig-leaf garments (Gen 3:7). **(2)** *Labash* is regularly used for the "putting on" of ordinary clothing (Gen 38:19; Ex 29:30; 1 Sa 28:8). **(3)** The word also describes the "putting on" of armor (Jer 46:4). **(4)** Many times it is used in a figurative sense, as **(4a)** in Job 7:5: "My flesh is clothed [covered] with worms. . . ." **(4b)** Jerusalem is spoken of as "putting on" the Jews as they return after the Exile (Is 49:18). **(4c)** Often the figurative garment is an abstract quality: "For he put on righteousness as a breastplate, . . . he put on garments of vengeance for clothing" (Is 59:17).

(4d) God is spoken of as being "clothed with honor and majesty" (Ps 104:1). **(4e)** Job says, "I put on righteousness, and it clothed me" (Job 29:14). **(5)** These abstract qualities are sometimes negative: **(5a)** "The prince shall be clothed with desolation" (Eze 7:27). **(5b)** "They that hate thee shall be clothed with shame" (Job 8:22). **(5c)** "Let mine adversaries be clothed with shame" (Ps 109:29). **(6)** A very important figurative use of *labash* is found in Judg 6:34, where the stative form of the verb may be translated, **(6a)** "The spirit of the Lord clothed itself [was clothed] with Gideon." **(6b)** The idea seems to be that the Spirit of the Lord incarnated Himself in Gideon and thus empowered him from within. **(6c)** The KJV renders it "came upon": "But the Spirit of the LORD came upon Gideon, and he blew a trumpet; and Abiezer was gathered after him." See: TWOT—1075; BDB—527d, 1098d.

3848. לְבַשׁ {3x} l^ebash (Aram.), *leb-ash';* corresp. to 3847:—clothe {3x}. See: TWOT—2810; BDB—1098d.

לְבֻשׁ l^ebûsh. See 3830.

3849. לֹג {5x} lôg, *lohg;* from an unused root appar. mean. to *deepen* or *hollow* [like 3537]; a *log* or measure for liquids:—log [of oil] {5x}. See: TWOT—1076; BDB—528d.

3850. לֹד {4x} Lôd, *lode;* from an unused root of uncert. signif.; *Lod,* a place in Pal.:—Lod {4x}. See: BDB—528d.

לִדְבִר Lidbîr. See 3810.

3851. לַהַב {12x} lahab, *lah'-hab;* from an unused root mean. to *gleam;* a *flash;* fig. a sharply polished *blade* or *point* of a weapon:—blade {2x}, bright {1x}, flame {8x}, glittering {1x}. See: TWOT—1077, 1077a; BDB—529a.

3852. לֶהָבָה {19x} lehâbîym, *leh-aw-baw';* or

לַהֶבֶת lahebeth, *lah-eh'-beth;* fem. of 3851, and mean. the same:—flame {13x}, flaming {5x}, head [of a spear]{1x}. See: TWOT—1077b; BDB—529b.

3853. לְהָבִים {2x} L^ehâbîym, *leh-haw-beem';* plur. of 3851; *flames; Lehabim,* a son of Mizrain, and his desc.:—Lehabim {2x}. See: TWOT—1077b; BDB—529c.

3854. לַהַג {1x} lahag, *lah'-hag;* from an unused root mean. to *be eager;* intense mental *application:*—study {1x}. See: TWOT—1078a; BDB—529c.

3855. לַהַד {1x} Lahad, *lah'-had;* from an unused root mean. to *glow* [comp. 3851] or else to *be earnest* [comp. 3854]; *Lahad,* an Isr.:—Lahad {1x}. See: BDB—529c.

3856. לָהַהּ {2x} lâhahh, *law-hah';* a prim. root mean. prop. to *burn,* i.e. (by impl.) to *be rabid* (fig. *insane*); also (from the *exhaustion* of frenzy) to *languish:*—faint {1x}, mad {1x}. See: TWOT—1079; BDB—529c.

3857. לָהַט {11x} lâhat, *law-hat';* a prim. root; prop. to *lick,* i.e. (by impl.) to *blaze:*—set on fire {4x}, burn up {3x}, burn {2x}, kindle {1x}, flaming {1x}. See: TWOT—1081; BDB—529c.

3858. לַהַט {2x} lahat, *lah'-hat;* from 3857; a *blaze;* also (from the idea of *enwrapping*) *magic* (as *covert*):—flaming {1x}, enchantment {1x}. Those who practiced this did it in secrecy; compare "sleight of hand (Ex 7:11). See: TWOT—1081a; BDB—529d, 532a.

3859. לָהַם {2x} lâham, *law-ham'* a prim. root; prop. to *burn* in, i.e. (fig.) to *rankle:*—wound {1x}. See: TWOT—1082; BDB—529d.

3860. לָהֵן {2x} lâhên, *law-hane';* from the pref. prep. mean. *to* or *for* and 2005; prop. *for if;* hence, *therefore:*—for them {1x}. See: TWOT—1083; BDB—242a, 243b, 530a, 1099a.

3861. לָהֵן {10x} lâhên (Aram.), *law-hane';* corresp. to 3860; *therefore;* also *except:*—except {3x}, therefore {2x}, but {2x}, save {2x}, wherefore {1x}. See: TWOT—2811; BDB—242a, 539a, 1090d, 1099a.

3862. לָהֲקָה {1x} lahăqâh, *lah-hak-aw';* prob. from an unused root mean. to

gather; an *assembly:*—company {1x}. Syn.: 5712, 6915. See: TWOT—1084; BDB—530a.

לוֹא **lôw⁾.** See 3808.

3863. לוּא {22x} **lûw⁾,** *loo;* or

לֻא **lû⁾,** *loo;* or

לוּ **lûw,** *loo;* a conditional particle; *if;* by impl. (interj. as a wish) *would that!:*— if {6x}, would God {4x}, O that {3x}, Oh {2x}, would it might be {1x}, if haply {1x}, peradventure {1x}, Oh that {1x}, pray thee {1x}, Though {1x}, would {1x}. See: TWOT—1085; BDB— 520d, 530a.

3864. לוּבִי {4x} **Lûwbîy,** *loo-bee';* or

לֻבִּי **Lubbîy** (Dan. 11:43) *loob-bee';* patrial from a name prob. derived from an unused root mean. to *thirst,* i.e. a *dry* region; appar. a *Libyan* or inhab. of interior Africa (only in plur.):—Lubim (-s) {3x}, Libyans {1x}. See: BDB—526a, 530c.

3865. לוּד {5x} **Lûwd,** *lood;* prob. of for. der.; *Lud,* the name of two nations:— Lud {4x}, Lydia {1x}. See: BDB—530d.

3866. לוּדִי {3x} **Lûwdîy,** *loo-dee';* or

לוּדִיִי **Lûwdîyîy,** *loo-dee-ee';* patrial from 3865; a *Ludite* or inhab. of Lud (only in plural):—Ludim {2x}, Lydians {1x}. See: BDB—530d.

3867. לָוָה {26x} **lâvâh,** *law-vaw';* a prim. root; prop. to *twine,* i.e. (by impl.) to *unite,* to *remain;* also to *borrow* (as a form of *obligation*) or (caus.) to *lend:*—join {10x}, lend {7x}, borrow {3x}, borrower {2x}, abide {1x}, cleave {1x}, lender {1x}, lender + 376 {1x}. See: TWOT—1087, 1088; BDB—530d, 531a.

3868. לוּז {6x} **lûwz,** *looz;* a prim. root; to *turn* aside [comp. 3867, 3874 and 3885], i.e. (lit.) to *depart,* (fig.) be *perverse:*—froward {2x}, depart {2x}, perverse {1x}, perverseness {1x}. See: TWOT—1090; BDB—531b.

3869. לוּז {1x} **lûwz,** *looz;* prob. of for. or.; some kind of *nut*-tree, perh. the *almond:*—hazel {1x}. See: TWOT—1090b; BDB—531c.

3870. לוּז {8x} **Lûwz,** *looz;* prob. from 3869 (as growing there); *Luz,* the name of two places in Pal.:—Luz {8x}. See: BDB—531c.

3871. לוּחַ {43x} **lûwach,** *loo'-akh;* or

לֻחַ **luach,** *loo'-akh;* from a prim. root; prob. mean. to *glisten;* a *tablet* (as *polished*), of stone, wood or metal:—tables {38x}, boards {4x}, plates {1x}. See: TWOT—1091a; BDB—531d.

3872. לוּחִית {2x} **Lûwchîyth,** *loo-kheeth';* or

לֻחוֹת **Lûchôwth** (Jer. 48:5), *loo-khoth';* from the same as 3871; *floored; Luchith,* a place E. of the Jordan:—Luhith {2x}. See: BDB—229d, 532a, 751c.

3873. לוּחֵשׁ {2x} **Lôwchêsh,** *lo-khashe';* act. part. of 3907; (the) *enchanter; Lochesh,* an Isr.:—Hallohesh {1x}, Haloshesh [includ. the art.]{1x}. See: BDB—538a.

3874. לוּט {3x} **lûwt,** *loot;* a prim. root; to *wrap* up:—cast {1x}, wrapped {2x}. See: TWOT—1092; BDB—529d, 532a.

3875. לוֹט {1x} **lôwt,** *lote;* from 3874; a *veil:*— covering {1x}. Syn.: 3682, 4372, 4539. See: TWOT—1092b; BDB—532b.

3876. לוֹט {33x} **Lôwt,** *lote;* the same as 3875; *Lot,* Abraham's nephew:—Lot {33x}. See: BDB—532b.

3877. לוֹטָן {7x} **Lôwtân,** *lo-tawn';* from 3875; *covering; Lotan,* an Idumæan:— Lotan {7x}. See: BDB—532b.

3878. לֵוִי {64x} **Lêvîy,** *lay-vee';* from 3867; *attached; Levi,* a son of Jacob:—Levi {64x}. See: TWOT—1093; BDB—532b, 1099a. See also 3879, 3881.

3879. לֵוִי {4x} **Lêvîy** (Aram.), *lay-vee';* corresp. to 3880:—Levite {4x}. See: BDB— 1099a.

3880. לִוְיָה {2x} **livyâh,** *liv-yaw';* from 3867; something *attached,* i.e. a *wreath:*— ornament {2x}. See: TWOT—1089a; BDB— 531a.

3881. לֵוִיִי {286x} **Lêvîyîy,** *lay-vee-ee';* or

לֵוִי **Lêvîy,** *lay-vee';* patron. from 3878; a *Levite* or desc. of Levi:—Levite {286x}. See: BDB—532d.

3882. לִוְיָתָן {6x} **livyâthân,** *liv-yaw-thawn';* from 3867; a *wreathed* animal, i.e. a *serpent* (espec. the *crocodile* or some other large sea-monster); fig. the constellation of the *dragon;* also as a symbol of *Babylon:*— leviathan {5x}, mourning {1x}. See: TWOT— 1089b; BDB—531b.

3883. לוּל {1x} **lûwl,** *lool;* from an unused root mean. to *fold* back; a *spiral* step:— winding stair {1x}. See: TWOT—1094; BDB— 533b. comp. 3924.

3884. לוּלֵא {14x} **lûwlê⁾,** *loo-lay';* or

לוּלֵי **lûwlêy,** *loo lay';* from 3863 and 3808; *if not:*—except {4x}, unless {4x}, if {3x}, had not {1x}, were it not {1x}, were it not that {1x}. See: TWOT—1085a; BDB—530b, 533b, 533c.

3885. לוּן {87x} lûwn, loon; or

לִין lîyn, leen; a prim. root; to stop (usually over night); by impl. to stay
permanently; hence, (in a bad sense) to be obstinate (espec. in words, to complain):—lodge
{33x}, murmur {14x}, . . . the night {14x}, abide
{7x}, remain {6x}, tarry {2x}, lodge in {2x}, continue {1x}, dwell {1x}, endure {1x}, grudge {1x},
left {1x}, lie {1x}, variant {3x}.

Luwn means "to remain, lodge, spend the
night, abide." (1) Its first occurrence is in Gen
19:2, where it is used twice: "Behold now, my
lords, turn in, I pray you, into your servant's
house, and tarry all night (luwn). . . . And they
said, Nay; but we will abide (luwn) in the street
all night." (2) While it is usually used concerning human beings spending the night, luwn is
sometimes used of animals, such as (2a) the
unicorn (Job 39:9), (2b) the cormorant and the
bittern (Zeph 2:14). (3) The word does not necessarily mean sleeping through the night, but
may be used to indicate being located in one
place for the night: "Thou shalt not . . . [let]
the fat of my sacrifice remain until the morning
[literally, "pass the night until morning"] (Ex
23:18). (4) In a similar way, the figurative use of
the word often has the connotation of "abiding,
remaining": (4a) "Mine error remaineth with
myself" (Job 19:4); (4b) "Righteousness lodged
in it . . ." (Is 1:21); (4c) "His soul shall dwell
at ease . . ." (Ps 25:13); (4d) "[He] shall abide
satisfied . . ." (Prov 19:23). See: TWOT—1096,
1097; BDB—533c, 534a, 539b.

3886. לוּעַ {2x} lûwaʻ, loo'-ah; a prim. root; to
gulp; fig. to be rash:—swallow down
{1x}, swallowed up {1x}. See: TWOT—1098;
BDB—534b, 541d, 542a.

3887. לוּץ {27x} lûwts, loots; a prim. root; prop.
to make mouths at, i.e. to scoff;
hence, (from the effort to pronounce a foreign
language) to interpret, or (gen.) intercede:—
scorner {14x}, scorn {4x}, interpreter {2x},
mocker {2x}, ambassadors {1x}, derision {1x},
mock {1x}, scornful {1x}, teachers {1x}. See:
TWOT—1113; BDB—534c, 539b, 542c.

3888. לוּשׁ {5x} lûwsh, loosh; a prim. root; to
knead:—knead {5x}. See: TWOT—
1100; BDB—534c.

3889. לוּשׁ {1x} Lûwsh, loosh; from 3888; kneading; Lush, a place in Pal.:—Laish
{1x}. See: BDB—534c, 539d. comp. 3919.

3890. לְוָת {1x} lᵉvâth (Aram.), lev-awth'; from
a root corresp. to 3867; prop. adhe-

sion, i.e. (as prep.) with:—× thee {1x}. See:
TWOT—2813; BDB—1099a.

לָחוֹת Lûchôwth. See 3872.

לָז lâz and

לָזֶה lâzeh. See 1975 and 1976.

3891. לְזוּת {1x} lᵉzûwth, lez-ooth'; from 3868;
perverseness:—perverse {1x}. See:
TWOT—1090a; BDB—531c, 534c.

3892. לַח {6x} lach, lakh; from an unused root
mean. to be new; fresh, i.e. unused
or undried:—green {5x}, moist {1x}. See:
TWOT—1102a; BDB—534c, 535a.

3893. לֵחַ {1x} lêach, lay'-akh; fr m the same
as 3892; freshness, i.e. vigor:—natural force {1x}. See: TWOT—1102b; BDB—535a.

לַח lûach. See 3871.

3894. לָחוּם {2x} lâchûwm, law-khoom'; or

לָחֻם lâchûm, law-khoom'; pass. part. of
3898; prop. eaten, i.e. food; also
flesh, i.e. body:—while . . . is eating {1x}, flesh
{1x}. See: TWOT—1104b; BDB—535d.

3895. לְחִי {21x} lᵉchîy, lekh-ee'; from an unused root mean. to be soft; the
cheek (from its fleshiness); hence, the jaw-
bone:—cheek {10x}, bone {1x}, jaw {7x}, jaw-
bone {3x}. See: TWOT—1101a; BDB—534c,
535a.

3896. לֶחִי {3x} Lechîy, lekh'-ee; a form of
3895; Lechi, a place in Pal.:—Lehi
{3x}. See: BDB—534d, 535a. comp. also 7437.

3897. לָחַךְ {6x} lâchak, law-khak'; a prim.
root; to lick:—lick (up) {6x}. See:
TWOT—1103; BDB—535a.

3898. לָחַם {177x} lâcham, law-kham'; a prim.
root; to feed on; fig. to consume;
by impl. to battle (as destruction):—fight
{149x}, to war {10x}, make war {8x}, eat {5x},
overcome {2x}, devoured {1x}, ever {1x}, prevail {1x}.

Lacham means "to fight, do battle, engage
in combat." (1) Lacham appears first in Ex
1:10, where the Egyptian pharaoh expresses
his fears that the Israelite slaves will multiply
and join an enemy "to fight" against the Egyptians: "Come on, let us deal wisely with them;
lest they multiply, and it come to pass, that,
when there falleth out any war, they join also
unto our enemies, and fight against us, and so
get them up out of the land." (2) While the word
is commonly used in the context (2a) of "armies
engaged in pitched battle" against each other
(Num 21:23; Josh 10:5; Judg 11:5), (2b) it is also
used to describe "single, hand-to-hand combat": "And David said to Saul, Let no man's
heart fail because of him; thy servant will go

Hebrew

and fight with this Philistine. And Saul said to David, Thou art not able to go against this Philistine to fight with him: for thou *art but* a youth, and he a man of war from his youth" (1 Sa 17:32–33). **(3)** Frequently, God "fights" the battle for Israel (Deut 20:4). **(4)** Instead of swords, words spoken by a lying tongue are often used "to fight" against God's servants: "For the mouth of the wicked and the mouth of the deceitful are opened against me: they have spoken against me with a lying tongue" (Ps 109:2). See: TWOT—1104, 1105; BDB—535b, 536d.

3899. לֶחֶם {297x} **lechem,** *lekh'-em;* from 3898; *food* (for man or beast), espec. *bread,* or *grain* (for making it):—bread {237x}, food {21x}, meat {18x}, shewbread + 6440 {5x}, loaves {5x}, shewbread + 4635 {3x}, shewbread {2x}, victuals {2x}, eat {1x}, feast {1x}, fruit {1x}, provision {1x}.

Lechem means bread, meal, food, fruit. **(1)** This noun refers to "bread," as distinguished from meat. **(1a)** The diet of the early Hebrews ordinarily consisted of bread, meat, and liquids: "And he humbled thee, and suffered thee to hunger, and fed thee with manna, which thou knewest not, neither did thy fathers know; that he might make thee know that man doth not live by bread only, but by every word that proceedeth out of the mouth of the Lord" (Deut 8:3). **(1b)** "Bread" was baked in loaves: "And it shall come to pass, that every one that is left in thine house shall come and crouch to him for a piece of silver and a morsel of bread" (1 Sa 2:36). **(1c)** Even when used by itself, *lechem* can signify a "loaf of bread": **(1c1)** "They will salute thee, and give thee two loaves of bread . . ." (1 Sa 10:4). **(1c2)** In this usage, the word is always preceded by a number. **(1d)** "Bread" was also baked in cakes (2 Sa 6:19).

(2) A "bit of bread" is a term for a modest meal. So Abraham said to his three guests, "Let a little water, I pray you, be fetched . . . and I will fetch a morsel of bread, and comfort ye your hearts" (Gen 18:4–5). **(3)** In 1 Sa 20:27, *lechem* represents an entire meal: "Saul said unto Jonathan his son, Wherefore cometh not the son of Jesse to meat, neither yesterday, nor today?" **(4)** Thus, "to make bread" may actually mean "to prepare a meal": "A feast is made for laughter, and wine maketh merry" (Eccl 10:19). **(5)** The "staff of bread" is the "support of life": "And when I have broken the staff of your bread, ten women shall bake your bread in one oven, and they shall deliver you your bread again by weight: and ye shall eat, and not be satisfied" (Lev 26:26). **(6)** The Bible refers to the "bread of the face" or "the bread of the Presence," which was the bread constantly set before God in the holy place of the tabernacle

or temple: "And thou shalt set upon the table showbread before me always" (Ex 25:30).

(7) In several passages, *lechem* represents the grain from which "bread" is made: **(7a)** "And the seven years of dearth began to come, according as Joseph had said: and the dearth was in all the lands; but in all the land of Egypt there was bread" (Gen 41:54). **(7b)** The meaning "grain" is very clear in 2 Kin 18:32: "Until I come and take you away to a land like your own land, a land of corn and wine, a land of bread and vineyards." **(8)** *Lechem* can represent food in general. **(8a)** In Gen 3:19 (the first biblical occurrence), it signifies the entire diet: "In the sweat of thy face shalt thou eat bread." **(8b)** This nuance may include meat, as it does in Judg 13:15–16: "And Manoah said unto the angel of the Lord, I pray thee, let us detain thee, until we shall have made ready a kid for thee. And the angel of the Lord said unto Manoah, Though thou detain me, I will not eat of thy bread." **(8c)** In 1 Sa 14:24, 28, *lechem* includes honey, and in Prov 27:27 goat's milk.

(9) *Lechem* may also represent "food" for animals: "He giveth to the beast his food, and to the young ravens which cry" (Ps 147:9; cf. Prov 6:8). **(10)** Flesh and grain offered to God are called "the bread of God": "For the offerings of the Lord made by fire, and the bread of their God, they do offer . . ." (Lev 21:6; cf. 22:13). **(11)** There are several special or figurative uses of *lechem.* **(11a)** The "bread" of wickedness is "food" gained by wickedness: "For [evil men] eat the bread of wickedness, and drink the wine of violence" (Prov 4:17). **(11b)** Compare the "bread" or "food" gained by deceit (Prov 20:17) and lies (23:3). **(11c)** Thus, in Prov 31:27 the good wife "looketh well to the ways of her household, and eateth not the bread of idleness"—i.e., unearned food. **(11d)** The "bread of my portion" is the food that one earns (Prov 30:8). **(12)** Figuratively, men are the "food" or prey for their enemies: "Only rebel not ye against the Lord, neither fear ye the people of the land; for they are bread for us . . ." (Num 14:9).

(13) The psalmist in his grief says his tears are his "food" (Ps 42:3). **(14)** Evil deeds are likened to food: "[The evil man's] meat in his bowels is turned, it is the gall of asps within him" (Job 20:14). **(15)** In Jer. 11:19, *lechem* represents "fruit from a tree" and is a figure of a man and his offspring: "And I knew not that they had devised devices against me, saying, Let us destroy the tree with the fruit thereof, and let us cut him off from the land of the living, that his name may be no more remembered." Syn.: 1036. See: TWOT—1105a; BDB—536d, 1099a.

3900. לְחֵם {1x} l^echem (Aram.), *lekh-em'*; corresp. to 3899:—feast {1x}. See: TWOT—2814; BDB—1099a.

3901. לָחֶם {1x} lâchem, *law-khem'*; from 3898, *battle:*—war {1x}. Syn.: 3898, 4421. See: TWOT—1104a; BDB—535d.

לָחֻם lâchûm. See 3894.

3902. לַחְמִי {1x} Lachmîy, *lakh-mee'*; from 3899; *foodful; Lachmi*, a Philis.; or rather prob. a brief form (or perh. err. transc.) for 1022:—Lahmi {1x}. See: BDB—537c. See also 3433.

3903. לַחְמָס {1x} Lachmâç, *lakh-maws'*; prob. by err. transc. for

לַחְמָם Lachmâm, *lakh-mawm'*; from 3899; *food-like; Lachmam* or *Lachmas*, a place in Pal.:—Lahmam {1x}. See: BDB—537c.

3904. לְחֵנָה {3x} l^echênâh (Aram.), *lekh-ay-naw'*; from an unused root of uncert. mean.; a *concubine:*—concubine {3x}. See: TWOT—2815; BDB—1099b.

3905. לָחַץ {19x} lâchats, *law-khats'*; a prim. root; prop. to *press*, i.e. (fig.) to *distress:*—oppress {13x}, afflict {1x}, crushed {1x}, fast {1x}, forced {1x}, oppressors {1x}, thrust {1x}. See: TWOT—1106; BDB—537d.

3906. לַחַץ {12x} lachats, *lakh'-ats*; from 3905; *distress:*—affliction {5x}, oppression {7x}. See: TWOT—1106a; BDB—537d.

3907. לָחַשׁ {3x} lâchash, *law-khash'*; a prim. root; to *whisper*; by impl. to *mumble* a spell (as a magician):—charmer {1x}, whisper (together) {2x}. The secret and sorrowful sighing of the oppressed (Is 26:16). Enchantment? (Ps. 58:5). See: TWOT—1107; BDB—538a.

3908. לַחַשׁ {5x} lachash, *lakh'-ash;* from 3907; prop. a *whisper*, i.e. by impl. (in a good sense) a private *prayer*, (in a bad one) an *incantation;* concr. an *amulet:*—charmed {1x}, earring {1x}, enchantment {1x}, orator {1x}, prayer {1x}. See: TWOT—1107a; BDB—538a.

3909. לָט {6x} lât, *lawt;* a form of 3814 or else part. from 3874; prop. *covered*, i.e. *secret;* by impl. *incantation;* also *secrecy* or (adv.) *covertly:*—enchantment {3x}, privily {1x}, secretly {1x}, softly {1x}. Syn.: 328, 825, 826, 2267, 3858, 3907, 5172, 6049. See: TWOT—1092a; BDB—532a, 538b.

3910. לֹט {2x} lôt, *lote;* prob. from 3874; a gum (from its *sticky* nature), prob. *lada-num:*—myrrh {2x}. See: TWOT—1108; BDB—538b.

3911. לְטָאָה {1x} l^etâ'âh, *let-aw-aw';* from an unused root mean. to *hide;* a kind of *lizard* (from its *covert* habits):—lizard {1x}. See: TWOT—1109a; BDB—538b.

3912. לְטוּשִׁם {1x} L^etûwshîm, *let-oo-sheem';* masc. plur. of pass. part. of 3913; *hammered* (i.e. *oppressed*) ones; *Letushim*, an Arabian tribe:—Letushim {1x}. See: BDB—538c.

3913. לָטַשׁ {5x} lâtash, *law-tash';* a prim. root; prop. to *hammer* out (an edge), i.e. to *sharpen:*—instructer {1x}, sharp {1x}, sharpen {2x}, whet {1x}. See: TWOT—1110; BDB—538b.

3914. לֹיָה {3x} lôyâh, *lo-yaw';* a form of 3880; a *wreath:*—addition {3x}. See: TWOT—1089a; BDB—531b, 538c.

3915. לַיִל {233x} layil, *lah'-yil;* or (Isa. 21:11)

לֵיל lêyl, *lale;* also

לַיְלָה lay^elâh, *lah'-yel-aw;* from the same as 3883; prop. a *twist* (away of the light), i.e. *night;* fig. *adversity:*—night {205x}, nights {15x}, midnight + 2677 {4x}, season {3x}, midnight + 2676 {2x}, night + 1121 {2x}, midnight {1x}, midnight + 8432 {1x}.

Layelah means "night." **(1)** *Layelah* means "night," the period of time during which it is dark: "And God called the light Day, and the darkness he called Night" (Gen 1:5—the first biblical appearance). **(2)** In Ex 13:21 and similar passages the word means "by night," or "during the night": "And the Lord went before them by day in a pillar of cloud . . . and by night in a pillar of fire, to give them light; to go by day and night." **(3)** This word is used figuratively of protection: "Take counsel, execute judgment; make thy shadow as the night in the midst of the noonday; hide the outcasts; [betray] not him that wandereth" (Is 16:3). **(3)** *Layelah* also figures deep calamity without the comforting presence and guidance of God, and/or other kinds of distress: "Where is God my maker, who giveth songs in the night . . ." (Job 35:10). **(4)** During Old Testament times the "night" was divided into three watches: **(4a)** from sunset to 10 P.M., (Lam 2:19), **(4b)** from 10 P.M. to 2 A.M. (Judg 7:19), and **(4c)** from 2 A.M. to sunrise (Ex 14:24). See: TWOT—1111; BDB—538c, 1099b.

3916. לֵילְיָא {5x} leyl^eyâ' (Aram.), *lay-leh-yaw';* corresp. to 3915:—night {5x}. See: TWOT—2816; BDB—1099b.

3917. לִילִית {1x} lîylîyth, *lee-leeth';* from 3915; a *night* spectre:—screech owl {1x}. Syn.: 3563. See: TWOT—1112; BDB—539b.

Hebrew

3918. לַיִשׁ {3x} **layish**, *lah'-yish;* from 3888 in the sense of *crushing;* a lion (from his destructive *blows*):—old lion {2x}, lion {1x}. See: TWOT—1114a; BDB—539d.

3919. לַיִשׁ {7x} **Layish**, *lah'-yish;* the same as 3918; *Laïsh,* the name of two places in Pal.:—Laish {7x}. See: BDB—534c, 539d. comp. 3889.

3920. לָכַד {121x} **lâkad**, *law-kad';* a prim. root; to *catch* (in a net, trap or pit); gen. to *capture* or occupy; also to *choose* (by lot); fig. to *cohere:*—take {112x}, catch {5x}, at all {1x}, frozen {1x}, holden {1x}, stick together {1x}.

Lakad (3920) means "to capture; seize; take captive." **(1)** It is found for the first time in the text in Num 21:32, where the Israelites are said to have taken the villages of the Amorites. **(2)** The act of "capturing, seizing" is usually connected with fighting wars or battles, so a variety of objects may be taken. **(2a)** Cities are often "captured" in war (Josh 8:21; 10:1; Judg 1:8, 12). **(2b)** Land or territory also is taken as booty of war (Josh 10:42; Dan 11:18). **(2c)** Strategic geographic areas such as watercourses "are captured" (Judg 3:28). **(2d)** Sometimes kings and princes "are seized" in battle (Judg 7:25; 8:12, 14), **(2e)** as well as fighting men and horses (2 Sa 8:4). **(2f)** Saul is spoken of as actually taking the kingdom, apparently by force of arms (1 Sa 14:47). **(3)** In establishing the source of Israel's defeat by Ai, lots were used "to take or separate" the guilty party, Achan and his family (Josh 7:14). **(4)** Occasionally *lakad* is used in the figurative sense, especially in terms of men "being caught" in the trap of divine judgment (Ps 9:15; Is 8:15; 24:18). Syn: 3948, 4455, 4457, 4727, 4728. See: TWOT—1115; BDB—539d.

3921. לֶכֶד {1x} **leked**, *leh'ked;* from 392; something to *capture* with, i.e. a *noose:*—being taken {1x}. See: TWOT—1115a; BDB—540b.

3922. לֵכָה {1x} **Lêkâh**, *lay-kaw';* from 3212; a *journey; Lekah,* a place in Pal.:—Lecah {1x}. See: BDB—540b.

3923. לָחִישׁ {24x} **Lâchîysh**, *law-keesh';* from an unused root of uncert. mean.; *Lakish,* a place in Pal.:—Lachish {24x}. See: BDB—540b.

3924. לֻלָאָה {13x} **lûlâʾâh**, *loo-law-aw';* from the same as 3883; a *loop:*—loop {13x}. See: TWOT—1095a; BDB—533b, 540c.

3925. לָמַד {86x} **lâmad**, *law-mad';* a prim. root; prop. to *goad,* i.e. (by impl.) to *teach* (the rod being an Oriental *incentive*):—teach {56x}, learn {22x}, instruct {3x}, diligently {1x}, expert {1x}, skilful {1x}, teachers {1x}, unaccustomed + 3808 {1x}.

Lamad means "to teach, learn, cause to learn." **(1)** In its simple, active form, this verb has the meaning "to learn," but it is also found in a form giving the causative sense, "to teach." **(2)** This word is first used in the Hebrew Old Testament in Deut 4:1: "Hearken, O Israel, unto the statutes and unto the judgments, which I teach you." **(3)** In Deut 5:1 *lamad* is used of learning God's laws: **(3a)** "Hear, O Israel, the statutes and judgments which I speak in your ears this day, that ye may learn them, and keep, and do them." **(3b)** A similar meaning occurs in Ps 119:7: "I will praise thee with uprightness of heart, when I shall have learned thy righteous judgments." **(4)** The word may be used of learning other things: works of the heathen (Ps 106:35); wisdom (Prov 30:3); and war (Mic 4:3).

(5) About half the occurrences of *lamad* are found in the books of Deuteronomy and Psalms, underlining the teaching emphasis found in these books. **(5a)** Judaism's traditional emphasis on teaching and thus preserving its faith clearly has its basis in the stress on teaching the faith found in the Old Testament, specifically Deut. 6:4–9, better known as the "Shema". **(5b)** Following the Shemaʾ, the "watchword of Judaism" that declares that Yahweh is One (Deut 6:4), is the "first great commandment" (Deut 6:5; Mark 12:28–29). **(5c)** When Moses delivered the Law to his people, he said, "The Lord commanded me at that time to teach you statutes and judgments" (Deut 4:14). **(6)** The later Jewish term Talmud [not a biblical word], "instruction," is derived from this verb. Syn.: 502, 995, 1696, 2094, 2449, 3256, 7919, 8150. See: TWOT—1116; BDB—540c.

לֻמָּד **limmûd**. See 3928.

3926. לְמוֹ {4x} **lᵉmôw**, *lem-o';* a prol. and separable form of the pref. prep.; *to* or *for:*—at {1x}, for {1x}, to {1x}, upon {1x}. See: TWOT—1063; BDB—518b, 530c, 541a.

3927. לְמוּאֵל {2x} **Lᵉmûwʾêl**, *lem-oo-ale';* or

לְמוֹאֵל **Lᵉmôwʾêl**, *lem-o-ale';* from 3926 and 410; (belonging) *to God; Lemuël* or *Lemoël,* a symbol. name of Solomon:—Lemuel {2x}. See: BDB—541a.

3928. לִמּוּד {6x} **limmûwd**, *lim-mood';* or

לִמֻּד **limmûd**, *lim-mood';* from 3925; *instructed:*—accustomed {1x}, disciple {1x}, learned {2x}, taught {1x}, used {1x}.

Limmud means "taught." **(1)** This adjective forms an exact equivalent to the New Testament idea of "disciple, one who is taught." **(2)** This is well expressed in Is 8:16: "Seal the law among my disciples." **(3)** The word also occurs

in Is 54:13: "And all thy children shall be taught of the Lord." See: TWOT—1116a; BDB—541a.

3929. לֶמֶךְ {11x} **Lemek,** *leh'-mek;* from an unused root of uncert. mean.; *Lemek,* the name of two antediluvian patriarchs:—Lamech {11x}. See: BDB—541a.

3930. לֹעַ {1x} **lôaʻ,** *lo'ah;* from 3886; the *gullet:*—throat {1x}. Syn.: 1627. See: TWOT—1098a; BDB—534b, 541b.

3931. לָעַב {1x} **lâʻab,** *law-ab';* a prim. root; to *deride:*—mock {1x}. See: TWOT—1117; BDB—541b.

3932. לָעַג {18x} **lâʻag,** *law-ag';* a prim. root; to *deride;* by impl. (as if imitating a foreigner) to *speak unintelligibly:*—mock {8x}, scorn {3x}, laugh {3x}, have in derision {2x}, laugh to scorn {1x}, stammering {1x}. See: TWOT—1118; BDB—541b.

3933. לַעַג {7x} **laʻag,** *lah'-ag;* from 3932; *derision, scoffing:*—derision {3x}, scorn (-ing) {4x}. See: TWOT—1118a; BDB—541c.

3934. לָעֵג {2x} **lâʻêg,** *law-ayg';* from 3932; a *buffoon;* also a *foreigner:*—mocker {1x}, stammering {1x}. See: TWOT—1118b; BDB—541d.

3935. לַעְדָּה {1x} **Laʻdâh,** *lah-daw';* from an unused root of uncert. mean.; *Ladah,* an Isr.:—Laadah {1x}. See: BDB—541d.

3936. לַעְדָּן {7x} **Laʻdân,** *lah-dawn';* from the same as 3935; *Ladan,* the name of two Isr.:—Laadan {7x}. See: BDB—541d.

3937. לָעַז {1x} **lâʻaz,** *law-az';* a p im. root; to *speak in a foreign tongue:*—strange language {1x}. See: TWOT—1119; BDB—541d.

3938. לָעַט {1x} **lâʻat,** *la-at';* a prim. root; to *swallow* greedily; caus. to *feed:*—feed {1x}. See: TWOT—1120; BDB—542a.

3939. לַעֲנָה {8x} **laʻănâh,** *lah-an-aw';* from an unused root supposed to mean to *curse; wormwood* (regarded as *poisonous,* and therefore *accursed*):—hemlock {1x}, wormwood {7x}. See: TWOT—1121; BDB—542a.

3940. לַפִּיד {14x} **lappîyd,** *lap-peed';* or

לַפִּד **lappîd,** *lap-peed';* from an unused root prob. mean. to *shine;* a *flambeau, lamp* or *flame:*—lamp {7x}, firebrand {2x}, torch {2x}, brand {1x}, lightning {1x}, burning {1x}. See: TWOT—1122a; BDB—542a.

3941. לַפִּידוֹת {1x} **Lappîydôwth,** *lap-pee-dōth';* fem. plur. of 3940; *Lappidoth,* the husband of Deborah:—Lappidoth {1x}. See: BDB—542b.

3942. לִפְנַי {1x} **liphnay,** *lif-nah'ee;* from the pref. prep. (*to* or *for*) and 6440; *anterior:*—before {1x}. See: TWOT—1782b; BDB—542b, 816d, 819b.

3943. לָפַת {3x} **lâphath,** *law-fath';* a prim. root; prop. to *bend,* i.e. (by impl.) to *clasp;* also (refl.) to *turn* around or aside:—take hold {1x}, turn {1x}, turn aside (self) {1x}. See: TWOT—1123; BDB—542b.

3944. לָצוֹן {3x} **lâtsôwn,** *law-tsone';* from 3887; *derision:*—scornful {2x}, scorning {1x}. See: TWOT—1113a; BDB—539c.

3945. לָצַץ {1x} **lâtsats,** *law-tsats';* a prim. root; to *deride:*—scorn {1x}. See: TWOT—1113; BDB—539b, 539c.

3946. לַקּוּם {1x} **Laqqûwm,** *lak-koom';* from an unused root thought to mean to *stop* up by a barricade; perh. *fortification; Lakkum,* a place in Pal.:—Lakum {1x}. See: BDB—542c.

3947. לָקַח {965x} **lâqach,** *law-kakh';* a prim. root; to *take* (in the widest variety of applications):—take {747x}, receive {61x}, take away {51x}, fetch {31x}, bring {25x}, get {6x}, take out {6x}, carry away {5x}, married {4x}, buy {3x}, misc. {26x} = accept, drawn, infold, × many, mingle, place, reserve, seize, send for, use, win.

Laqach means "to take, receive, take away." **(1)** Primarily this word means "to take, grasp, take hold of," as when Noah reached out and "took hold of" the dove to bring it back into the ark (Gen 8:9). **(2)** A secondary meaning is "to take away, remove, take to oneself," as when the invading kings "took away" and "took to themselves" all the movable goods of the cities of the plain (Gen 14:11). **(3)** Sometimes this verb implies "to receive something from someone." So Abraham asks Ephron the Hittite to "receive from" his hand payment for the field which contained the sepulchre (Gen 23:13). **(4)** With the particle "for" *laqach* means "to take someone or something," as when Joseph's brothers remarked that they were afraid he was scheming "to take" them to be slaves, mentioned in Gen 43:18. **(5)** Another secondary use of this word is "to transfer" a thing, concept, or emotion, such as **(5a)** "take vengeance" (Is 47:3), **(5b)** "receive reproach" (Eze 36:30), and **(5c)** "receive a [whisper]" (Job 4:12). **(6)** In other passages this verb is virtually a helping verb serving to prepare for an action stipulated in a subsequent verb; God "took" Adam and put him into the garden of Eden (Gen 2:15—the first occurrence of the verb).

(7) This word can be used elliptically, suggesting the phrase "take and bring," but only "taken" is written. Noah is told to "take" (and

bring) clean animals by sevens into the ark (Gen 7:2). **(8)** This verb is used of God in several connections. **(8a)** Sometimes God is pictured as having bodily parts (anthropomorphically). **(8b)** This is the implication of Gen 2:15, where the Lord "took" Adam and put him into Eden. **(8b1)** God's taking sometimes connotes election, as when He "took" Abraham from his father's house (Gen 24:7). **(8b2)** He also "takes" in the sense of taking to Himself or accepting. Thus, He "accepts" offerings (Judg 13:23) and prayers (Ps 6:9). **(8c)** God "takes away" in judgment David's wives (2 Sa 12:11) and the kingdom (1 Kin 11:34). **(9)** Of special interest is the use of the verb in the absolute sense: God "took away" Enoch so that he was not found on earth (Gen 5:24). This meaning of receiving one into heaven to Himself seems to be the force of Ps 73:24 and perhaps of Ps 49:15. Syn: 3920, 4455, 4457, 4727, 4728. See: TWOT—1124; BDB—542c, 881c.

3948. לֶקַח **leqach**, *leh'-kakh;* from 3947; prop. something *received*, i.e. (ment.) *instruction* (whether on the part of the teacher or hearer); also (in an act. and sinister sense) *inveiglement:*—doctrine {4x}, learning {4x}, fair speech {1x}.

Leqach means teaching; instruction; persuasiveness; understanding, in the sense of something taken in. **(1)** The word is used in the sense of something taken in. **(2)** One occurrence is in Prov 1:5: "A wise man will hear, and will increase learning." **(3)** The word refers to "persuasiveness" in Prov 7:21. Syn: 3947, 4455, 4457, 4727, 4728. See: TWOT—1124a; BDB—544b.

3949. לִקְחִי **Liqchîy**, *lik-khee';* from 3947; *learned; Likchi*, an Isr.:—Likhi {1x}. See: BDB—544b.

3950. לָקַט **lâqat**, *law-kat';* a prim. root; prop. to *pick* up, i.e. (gen.) to *gather;* spec. to *glean:*—gather {23x}, gather up {2x}, glean {12x}. See: TWOT—1125; BDB—544c.

3951. לֶקֶט **leqet**, *leh'-ket;* from 3950; the *gleaning:*—gleaning {2x}. See: TWOT—1125a; BDB—545a.

3952. לָקַק **lâqaq**, *law-kak';* a prim. root; to *lick* or *lap:*—lap {4x}, lick {3x}. See: TWOT—1126; BDB—545a.

3953. לָקַשׁ **lâqash**, *l w-kash';* a prim. root; to *gather* the *after* crop:—gather {1x}. See: TWOT—1127c; BDB—545c.

3954. לֶקֶשׁ **leqesh**, *l h'-kesh;* from 3953; the *after crop:*—latter growth {2x}. See: TWOT—1127a; BDB—545b.

3955. לְשַׁד **lᵉshad**, *lesh-ad';* from an unused root of uncert. mean.; appar. *juice*, i.e. (fig.) *vigor;* also a sweet or fat *cake:*—fresh {1x}, moisture {1x}. See: TWOT—1128a; BDB—545c.

3956. לָשׁוֹן **lâshôwn**, *law-shone';* or

לָשֹׁן **lâshôn**, *law-shone';* also (in plur.) fem.

לְשֹׁנָה **lᵉshônâh**, *lesh-o-naw';* from 3960; the *tongue* (of man or animals), used lit. (as the instrument of licking, eating, or speech), and fig. (speech, an ingot, a fork of flame, a cove of water):—tongue {98x}, language {10x}, bay {3x}, wedge {2x}, babbler {1x}, flame {1x}, speaker + 376 {1x}, talkers {1x}.

Lashon means, "tongue; language; speech." **(1)** In the Hebrew Old Testament it appears 115 times, mainly in the poetic and, to a lesser extent, in the prophetical books. The first occurrence is in Gen 10:5: "By these were the isles of the Gentiles divided in their lands; every one after his tongue, after their families, in their nations." **(2)** The basic meaning of *lashon* is "tongue," which as an organ of the body refers **(2a)** to humans (Lam 4:4) and **(2b)** animals (Ex 11:7; Job 41:1). **(3)** The extended meaning of the word as an organ of speech occurs more frequently. **(3a)** A person may be "heavy" or "slow" of tongue (Ex 4:10); or **(3b)** he may be fluent and clear: "The heart also of the rash shall understand knowledge, and the tongue of the stammerers shall be ready to speak plainly" (Is 32:4). **(4)** And see the description of the "tongue" in Ps 45:1: "My heart is inditing a good matter: I speak of the things which I have made touching the King: my tongue is the pen of a ready writer."

(5) The word is often better translated as "speech," because of the negative and positive associations of *lashon.* **(5a)** Especially in the wisdom literature the manner of one's "speech" is considered to be the external expression of the character of the speaker. **(5b)** The fool's "speech" is unreliable (Ps 5:9), deceitful (Ps 109:2; 120:2–3; Prov 6:17), boastful (Ps 140:11), flattering (Prov 26:28), slanderous (Ps 15:3), and subversive (Prov 10:31). **(5c)** The "tongue" of the righteous man heals (Prov 15:4). **(5d)** While the "tongue" may be as sharp as a sword (Ps 57:4), it is a means of giving life to the righteous and death to the wicked: "Death and life are in the power of the tongue: and they that love it shall eat the fruit thereof" (Prov 18:21; cf. 21:23; 25:15). **(6)** The biblical authors speak of divine inspiration as the Lord's enabling them to speak: "The Spirit of the Lord spake by me, and his word was in my tongue" (2 Sa 23:2; cf. Prov 16:1). **(7)** "Tongue" with the meaning "speech" has as a synonym *peh* (6310),

"mouth" (Ps 66:17), and more rarely *sapah* (8222), "lip" (Job 27:4).

(8) A further extension of meaning is "language." In Hebrew both *sapah* (8222) and *lashon* denote a foreign "language": "For with stammering lips and another tongue will he speak to this people" (Is 28:11). The foreigners to the "language" are well described in these words: "Thou shalt not see a fierce people, a people of a deeper speech than thou canst perceive; of stammering tongue, that thou canst not understand" (Is 33:19). **(9)** *Lashon* also refers to objects that are shaped in the form of a tongue. Most important is the "tongue of fire," which even takes the character of "eating" or "devouring": "Therefore as the [tongues of fire] devoureth the stubble, and the flame consumeth the chaff . . ." (Is 5:24). **(10)** The association in Isaiah of God's appearance in judgment with smoke and fire gave rise to a fine literary description of the Lord's anger: "Behold, the name of the Lord cometh from far, burning with his anger, and the burden thereof is heavy: his lips are full of indignation, and his tongue as a devouring fire" (Is 30:27). Notice the words "lips" and "tongue" here with the meaning of "flames of fire," even though the language evokes the representation of a tongue (as an organ of the body) together with a tongue (of fire). **(11)** Also a bar of gold (Josh 7:21) and a bay of the sea (Is 11:15) shaped in the form of a tongue were called *lashon*. Syn.: 6310, 8193. See: TWOT—1131a; BDB—546a, 1099b.

3957. לִשְׁכָּה {47x} **lishkâh**, *lish-kaw′;* from an unused root of uncert. mean.; a *room* in a building (whether for storage, eating, or lodging):—chamber {46x}, parlour {1x}. See: TWOT—1129a; BDB—545c. comp. 5393.

3958. לֶשֶׁם {2x} **leshem**, *leh′-shem;* from an unused root of uncert. mean.; a *gem*, perh. the *jacinth:*—ligure {2x}. See: TWOT—1130; BDB—545d.

3959. לֶשֶׁם {2x} **Leshem**, *leh′-shem;* the same as 3958; *Leshem*, a place in Pal.:—Leshem {2x}. See: BDB—546a.

3960. לָשַׁן {3x} **lâshan**, *law-shan′;* a prim. root; prop. to *lick;* but used only as a denom. from 3956; to *wag the tongue*, i.e. to *calumniate:*—accuse {1x}, slander {2x}. See: TWOT—1131; BDB—546d.

3961. לִשָּׁן {7x} **lishshân** (Aram.), *lish-shawn′;* corresp. to 3956; *speech*, i.e. a *nation:*—language {7x}. See: TWOT—2817; BDB—1099b.

3962. לֶשַׁע {1x} **Lesha⁽**, *leh′-shah;* from an unused root thought to mean to *break* through; a boiling *spring; Lesha*, a place prob. E. of the Jordan:—Lasha {1x}. See: BDB—546d.

3963. לֶתֶךְ {1x} **lethek**, *leh′-thek;* from an unused root of uncert. mean.; a *measure* for things dry:—half homer {1x}. See: TWOT—1133a; BDB—547c.

מ

מַ־ **ma-**, or

מָ־ **mâ-**. See 4100.

3964. מָא {1x} **mâ°** (Aram.), *maw;* corresp. to 4100; (as indef.) *that:*—+ what {1x}. See: TWOT—2822; BDB—1099b, 1099c.

3965. מַאֲבוּס {1x} **ma°ăbûwç**, *mah-ab-ooce′;* from 75; a *granary:*—storehouse {1x}. Syn.: 618. See: TWOT—10b; BDB—7b, 547a.

3966. מְאֹד {299x} **m°ôd**, *meh-ode′;* from the same as 181; prop. *vehemence*, i.e. (with or without prep.) *vehemently;* by impl. *wholly, speedily*, etc. (often with other words as an intens. or superl.; espec. when repeated):—very {137x}, greatly {49x}, sore {23x}, exceeding {18x}, great {12x}, exceedingly {11x}, much {10x}, exceeding + 3966 {6x}, exceedingly + 3966 {5x}, diligently {4x}, good {3x}, might {2x}, mightily {2x}, misc. {17x} = especially, far, fast, X louder and louder, quickly, utterly, well.

I. Me°od, as an adverb, means "exceedingly; very; greatly; highly." **(1)** Me°od functions adverbially, meaning "very." **(2)** The more superlative emphasis appears in Gen 7:18, where the word is applied to the "amount (quantity)" of a thing: "And the waters prevailed, and were increased greatly upon the earth." **(3)** In Ps 47:9, *me°od* is used of "magnifying" and "exaltation": "For the shields of the earth belong unto God; he is greatly exalted." **(4)** The doubling of the word is a means of emphasizing its basic meaning, which is "very much": "And the waters prevailed exceedingly upon the earth" (Gen 7:19). **II. Me°od, as a noun**, means "might." This word is used substantively in the sequence "heart . . . soul . . . might": "And thou shalt love the Lord thy God with all thine heart, and with all thy soul, and with all thy might" (Deut 6:5). See: TWOT—1134; BDB—547a.

3967. מֵאָה {581x} **mê°âh**, *may-aw′;* or

מֵאיָה **mê°yâh**, *may-yaw′;* prob. a prim. numeral; a *hundred;* also as a multiplicative and a fraction:—hundred {571x}, eleven hundred + 505 {3x}, hundredth {3x}, hundredfold {2x}, sixscore + 6242 {1x}, hundred

times {1x}. See: TWOT—1135; BDB—547c, 549a, 1099b.

3968. מֵאָה {2x} **Mê'âh**, *may-aw';* the same as 3967; *Meäh*, a tower in Jerusalem:—Meah {2x}. See: BDB—548c.

3969. מְאָה {8x} **m°âh** (Aram.), *meh-aw';* corresp. to 3967:—hundred {8x}. See: TWOT—2818; BDB—1099b.

3970. מַאֲוַי {1x} **ma'ăvay**, *mah-av-ah'ee;* from 183; a *desire:*—desires {1x}. Syn.: 183, 2656. See: TWOT—40c; BDB—16c, 548c.

מוֹאֵל **môw'l**. See 4136.

3971. מְאוּם {22x} **m'ûwm**, *moom;* usually

מוּם **mûwm**, *moom;* as if pass. part. from an unused root prob. mean. to *stain;* a *blemish* (phys. or mor.):—blemish {16x}, blot {3x}, spot {3x}. See: TWOT—1137a; BDB—548c, 558a.

3972. מְאוּמָה {32x} **m°ûwmâh**, *meh-oo'-maw;* appar. a form of 3971; prop. a *speck* or *point,* i.e. (by impl.) *something;* with neg. *nothing:*—anything {12x}, nothing {9x}, ought {5x}, any {2x}, fault {1x}, harm {1x}, nought {1x}, somewhat {1x}. See: TWOT—1136; BDB—548d.

3973. מָאוֹס {1x} **mâ'ôwç**, *maw-oce';* from 3988; *refuse:*—refuse {1x}. Syn.: 3985, 3988. See: TWOT—1139a; BDB—549d.

3974. מָאוֹר {19x} **mâ'ôwr**, *maw-ore';* or

מָאֹר **mâ'ôr**, *maw-ore';* also (in plur.) fem.

מְאוֹרָה **m°ôwrâh**, *meh-o-raw';* or

מְאֹרָה **m°ôrâh**, *meh-o-raw';* from 215; prop. a *luminous* body or *luminary,* i.e. (abstr.) *light* (as an element); fig. *brightness,* i.e. *cheerfulness;* spec. a *chandelier:*—bright {1x}, light {18x}. See: TWOT—52f; BDB—22c, 549a.

3975. מְאוּרָה {1x} **m°ûwrâh**, *meh-oo-raw';* fem. pass. part. of 215; something *lighted,* i.e. an *aperture;* by impl. a *crevice* or *hole* (of a serpent):—den {1x}. See: TWOT—52g; BDB—22d.

3976. מֹאזֵן {15x} **mô'zên**, *mo-zane';* from 239; (only in the dual) a pair of *scales:*—balances {15x}. See: TWOT—58a; BDB—24d, 549a, 1079b.

3977. מֹאזֵן {1x} **mô'zên** (Aram.), *mo-zane';* corresp. to 3976:—balances {1x}. See: TWOT—2819; BDB—1079b, 1099b.

מֵאיָה **mê'yâh**. See 3967.

3978. מַאֲכָל {30x} **ma'ăkâl**, *mah-ak-awl';* from 398; an *eatable* (includ. proven-

der, flesh and fruit):—meat {22x}, food {5x}, fruit {1x}, manner {1x}, victual {1x}. See: TWOT—85d; BDB—38b, 549a.

3979. מַאֲכֶלֶת {4x} **ma'ăkeleth**, *mah-ak-eh'-leth;* from 398; something to *eat* with, i.e. a *knife:*—knife {4x}. See: TWOT—85e; BDB—38b, 549a.

3980. מַאֲכֹלֶת {2x} **ma'äkôleth**, *mah-ak-o'-leth;* from 398; something *eaten* (by fire), i.e. *fuel:*—fuel {2x}. See: TWOT—85f; BDB—38c, 549a.

3981. מַאֲמָץ {1x} **ma'ămâts**, *mah-am-awts';* from 553; *strength,* i.e. (plur.) *resources:*—force {1x}. See: TWOT—117e; BDB—55c, 549a.

3982. מַאֲמַר {3x} **ma'ămar**, *mah-am-ar';* from 559; something (authoritatively) *said,* i.e. an *edict:*—commandment {2x}, decree {1x}. See: TWOT—118e; BDB—57d, 549a.

3983. מֵאֲמַר {2x} **mê'mar** (Aram.), *may-mar';* corresp. to 3982:—appointment {1x}, word {1x}. See: TWOT—2585a; BDB—1081b, 1099b.

3984. מָאן {7x} **mâ'n** (Aram.), *mawn;* prob. from a root corresp. to 579 in the sense of an *inclosure* by sides; a *utensil:*—vessel {7x}. See: TWOT—2820; BDB—1099c.

3985. מָאֵן {41x} **mâ'ên**, *maw-ane';* a prim. root; to *refuse:*—refuse {40x}, × utterly {1x}. See: TWOT—1138; BDB—549a.

3986. מָאֵן {4x} **mâ'ên**, *maw-ane';* from 3985; *unwilling:*—refuse {4x}. See: TWOT—1138a; BDB—549b.

3987. מֵאֵן {1x} **mê'ên**, *may-ane';* from 3985; *refractory:*—refuse {1x}. See: TWOT—1138b; BDB—549b.

3988. מָאַס {76x} **mâ'aç**, *maw-as';* a prim. root; to *spurn;* also (intr.) to *disappear:*—despise {25x}, refuse {9x}, reject {19x}, abhor {4x}, become loathsome {1x}, melt away {1x}, misc. {17x} = cast away (off), contemn, disdain, reprobate, × utterly, vile person.

Ma'ac means "to reject, refuse, despise." **(1)** It is found for the first time in Lev 26:15: "If ye shall despise my statutes. . . ." **(2)** God will not force man to do His will, so He sometimes must "reject" him: "Because thou hast rejected knowledge, I will also reject thee, that thou shalt be no priest to me" (Hos 4:6). **(3)** Although God had chosen Saul to be king, Saul's response caused a change in God's plan for Saul: "Because thou hast rejected the word of the Lord, he hath also rejected thee from being king" (1 Sa 15:23). **(4)** As a creature of free choice, man may "reject" God: "Ye have despised the Lord which is among you" (Num

11:20). **(5)** At the same time, man may "reject" evil (Is 7:15–16). When the things that God requires are done with the wrong motives or attitudes, God "despised" his actions: "I hate, I despise your feast days" (Amos 5:21). **(6)** Purity of heart and attitude are more important to God than perfection and beauty of ritual. See: TWOT—1139, 1140; BDB—549b, 549d, 588a.

3989. מַאֲפֶה {1x} **mâ'ăpheh**, *mah-af-eh';* from 644; something *baked,* i.e. a *batch:*—baken {1x}. See: TWOT—143a; BDB—66b, 549d.

3990. מַאֲפֵל {1x} **ma'ăphêl**, *mah-af-ale';* from the same as 651; something *opaque:*—darkness {1x}. See: TWOT—145e; BDB—66d, 549d.

3991. מַאְפֵלְיָה {1x} **ma'ăphêl°yâh**, *mah-af-ay-leh-yaw';* prol. fem. of 3990; *opaqueness:*—darkness {1x}. See: TWOT—145f; BDB—66d.

3992. מָאַר {4x} **mâ'ar**, *maw-ar';* a prim. root; to *be bitter* or (caus.) to *embitter,* i.e. *be painful:*—fretting {3x}, picking {1x}. See: TWOT—1141; BDB—549d.

מָאֹר **mâ'ôr**. See 3974.

3993. מַאֲרָב {5x} **ma'ărâb**, *mah-ar-awb';* from 693; an *ambuscade:*—ambushment {2x}, lurking place {1x}, lying in wait {2x}. See: TWOT—156e; BDB—70d, 550a.

3994. מְאֵרָה {5x} **m°êrâh**, *meh-ay-raw';* from 779; an *execration:*—curse {4x}, cursing {1x}. See: TWOT—168a; BDB—76d, 550a.

מְאֹרָה **m°ôrâh**. See 3974.

3995. מִבְדָּלָה {1x} **mibdâlâh**, *mib-daw-law';* from 914; a *separation,* i.e. (concr.) a *separate* place:—separate cities {1x}. See: TWOT—203b; BDB—95d, 550a.

3996. מָבוֹא {24x} **mâbôw'**, *maw-bo';* from 935; an *entrance* (the place or the act); spec. (with or without 8121) *sunset* or the *west;* also (adv. with prep.) *towards:*—going down {6x}, entry {5x}, come {3x}, entrance {3x}, enter {2x}, in {2x}, west {1x}, westward {2x}. See: TWOT—212b; BDB—99d, 550a.

3997. מְבוֹאָה {1x} **m°bôw'âh**, *meb-o-aw';* fem. of 3996; a *haven:*—entry {1x}. See: TWOT—212b; BDB—99d.

3998. מְבוּכָה {2x} **m°bûwkâh**, *meb-oo-kaw';* from 943; *perplexity:*—perplexity {2x}. See: TWOT—214a; BDB—100c, 550a.

3999. מַבּוּל {13x} **mabbûwl**, *mab-bool';* from 2986 in the sense of *flowing;* a *deluge:*—flood {13x}. See: TWOT—1142; BDB—550a.

4000. מָבוֹן {1x} **mâbôwn**, *maw-bone';* from 995; *instructing:*—taught {1x}. See: TWOT—239; BDB—107a, 108a, 550a.

4001. מְבוּסָה {3x} **m°bûwçâh**, *meb-oo-saw';* from 947; a *trampling:*—treading (trodden) down (under foot) {3x}. See: TWOT—216b; BDB—101b, 550a.

4002. מַבּוּעַ {3x} **mabbûwa°**, *mab-boo-ah;* from 5042; a *fountain:*—fountain {2x}, spring {1x}. See: TWOT—1287a; BDB—550a, 616a.

4003. מְבוּקָה {1x} **m°bûwqâh**, *meb-oo-kah';* from the same as 950; *emptiness:*—void {1x}. See: TWOT—220b; BDB—101c.

4004. מִבְחוֹר {2x} **mibchôwr**, *mib-khore';* from 977; *select,* i.e. well fortified:—choice {2x}. See: TWOT—231e; BDB—104d, 550b.

4005. מִבְחָר {12x} **mibchâr**, *mib-khawr';* from 977; *select,* i.e. best:—choice {7x}, choicest {1x}, chosen {4x}. See: TWOT—231d; BDB—104d.

4006. מִבְחָר {1x} **Mibchâr**, *mib-khawr';* the same as 4005; *Mibchar,* an Isr.:—Mibhar {1x}. See: TWOT—231d; BDB—104d.

4007. מַבָּט {3x} **mabbât**, *mab-bawt';* or

מֶבָּט **mebbât**, *meb-bawt';* from 5027; something *expected,* i.e. (abstr.) *expectation:*—expectation {3x}. See: TWOT—1282a; BDB—550b, 613d.

4008. מִבְטָא {2x} **mibṭâ'**, *mib-taw';* from 981; a rash *utterance* (hasty vow):—(that which . . .) uttered (out of) {2x}. See: TWOT—232a; BDB—105a, 550b.

4009. מִבְטָח {15x} **mibṭâch**, *mib-tawkh';* from 982; prop. a *refuge,* i.e. (obj.) *security,* or (subj.) *assurance:*—confidence {9x}, trust {4x}, sure {1x}, hope {1x}.

Mibtach means "the act of confiding; the object of confidence; the state of confidence or security." **(1)** The word refers to "the act of confiding" in Prov 21:22: "A wise man scaleth the city of the mighty, and casteth down the strength of the confidence thereof." **(2)** *Mibtach* means the "object of confidence" in Job 8:14 and **(3)** the "state of confidence or security" in Prov 14:26. See: TWOT—233e; BDB—105c, 550b.

4010. מַבְלִיגִית {1x} **mablîygîyth**, *mab-leeg-eeth';* from 1082; *desistance* (or rather *desolation*):—comfort self {1x}. See: TWOT—245a; BDB—114d, 550b.

Hebrew

4011. מִבְנֶה {1x} **mibneh**, *mib-neh';* from 1129; a *building:*—frame {1x}. See: TWOT—255c; BDB—125d, 550b.

4012. מְבֻנַּי {1x} **Mᵉbunnay**, *meb-oon-hah'-ee;* from 1129; *built* up; *Mebunnai*, an Isr.:—Mebunnai {1x}. See: BDB—125d, 550b.

4013. מִבְצָר {37x} **mibtsâr**, *mib-tsawr';* also (in plur.) fem. (Dan 11:15)

מִבְצָרָה **mibtsârâh**, *mib-tsaw-raw';* from 1219; a *fortification, castle,* or *fortified* city; fig. a *defender:*—hold {13x}, fenced {12x}, fortress {6x}, defenced {4x}, strong {2x}. See: TWOT—270g; BDB—131b, 550b.

4014. מִבְצָר {2x} **Mibtsâr**, *mib-tsawr';* the same as 4013; *Mibtsar*, an Idumæan:—Mibzar {2x}. See: BDB—550b.

מִבְצָרָה **mibtsârâh.** See 4013.

4015. מִבְרָח {1x} **mibrâch**, *mib-rawkh';* from 1272; a *refugee:*—fugitive {1x}. See: TWOT—284c; BDB—138b, 550b.

4016. מָבֻשׁ {1x} **mâbûsh**, *maw-boosh';* from 954; (plur.) the (male) *pudenda:*—secrets {1x}. See: TWOT—222d; BDB—102b, 550b.

4017. מִבְשָׂם {3x} **Mibsâm**, *mib-sawm';* from the same as 1314; *fragrant; Mibsam*, the name of an Ishmaelite and of an Isr.:—Mibsam {3x}. See: BDB—142a, 550b.

4018. מְבַשְּׁלָה {1x} **mᵉbashshᵉlâh**, *meb-ash-shel-aw';* from 1310; a *cooking hearth:*—boiling-place {1x}. See: TWOT—292b; BDB—143b, 550b.

מָג **Mâg.** See 7248, 7249.

4019. מַגְבִּישׁ {1x} **Magbîysh**, *mag-beesh';* from the same as 1378; *stiffening; Magbish*, an Isr., or a place in Pal.:—Magbish {1x}. See: BDB—150d, 550d.

4020. מִגְבָּלָה {1x} **migbâlâh**, *mig-baw-law';* from 1379; a *border:*—end {1x}. See: TWOT—307d; BDB—148b, 550b.

4021. מִגְבָּעָה {4x} **migbâ‘âh**, *mig-baw-aw';* from the same as 1389; a *cap* (as *hemispherical*):—bonnet {4x}. See: TWOT—309c; BDB—149b, 550b.

4022. מֶגֶד {8x} **meged**, *meh'-ghed;* from an unused root prob. mean. to *be eminent;* prop. a *distinguished* thing; hence, something *valuable*, as a product or fruit:—pleasant {3x}, precious fruit {1x}, precious things {4x}. See: TWOT—1144a; BDB—550c.

4023. מְגִדּוֹן {12x} **Mᵉgiddôwn** (Zec 12:11), *meg-id-dône';* or

מְגִדּוֹ **Mᵉgiddôw**, *meg-id-do';* from 1413; *rendezvous; Megiddon* or *Megiddo*, a place in Pal.:—Megiddo {11x}, Megiddon {1x}. See: BDB—151d, 550c.

4024. מִגְדּוֹל {7x} **Migdôwl**, *mig-dole';* or

מִגְדָּל **Migdôl**, *mig-dole';* prob. of Eg. or.; *Migdol*, a place in Egypt:—Migdol {5x}, tower {2x}. See: BDB—154a.

4025. מַגְדִּיאֵל {2x} **Magdîy'êl**, *mag-dee-ale';* from 4022 and 410; *preciousness of God; Magdiel*, an Idumæan:—Magdiel {2x}. See: BDB—550c.

4026. מִגְדָּל {50x} **migdâl**, *mig-dawl';* also (in plur.) fem.

מִגְדָּלָה **migdâlâh**, *mig-daw-law';* from 1431; a *tower* (from its size or height); by anal. a *rostrum;* fig. a (pyramidal) *bed* of flowers:—castles {1x}, flowers {1x}, tower {47x}, pulpit {1x}.

Migdal means "strong place; wooden podium." This noun usually refers **(1)** to a tower or a "strong place" (Gen 11:4–5), but **(2)** it also occurs once to refer to a "wooden podium": "And Ezra the scribe stood upon a pulpit of wood" (Neh 8:4). See: BDB—153d, 550c, 955c. comp. the names following.

מִגְדָּל **Migdôl.** See 4024.

מִגְדָּלָה **migdâlâh.** See 4026.

4027. מִגְדַּל־אֵל {1x} **Migdal-'Êl**, *mig-dal-ale';* from 4026 and 410; *tower of God; Migdal-El*, a place in Pal.:—Migdal-el {1x}. See: BDB—154a.

4028. מִגְדַּל־גָּד {1x} **Migdal-Gâd**, *migdal-gawd';* from 4026 and 1408; *tower of Fortune; Migdal-Gad*, a place in Pal.:—Migdal-gad {1x}. See: BDB—154a.

4029. מִגְדַּל־אֵדֶר {1x} **Migdal-‘Êder**, *mig-dal'-ay'-der;* from 4026 and 5739; *tower of a flock; Migdal-Eder*, a place in Pal.:—Migdal-eder, tower of the flock {1x}. See: BDB—154a.

4030. מִגְדָּנָה {4x} **migdânâh**, *mig-daw-naw';* from the same as 4022; *preciousness,* i.e. a *gem:*—precious things {3x}, presents {1x}. See: TWOT—1144b; BDB—550c.

4031. מָגוֹג {4x} **Mâgôwg**, *maw-gogue';* from 1463; *Magog*, a son of Japheth; also a barbarous northern region:—Magog {4x}. See: TWOT 324a; BDB—156a, 550c, 550d.

4032. מָגוֹר {8x} **mâgôwr**, *maw-gore';* or (Lam. 2:22)

מָגוּר **mâgûwr**, *maw-goor';* from 1481 in the sense of *fearing;* a *fright* (obj. or subj.):—fear {6x}, terror {2x}. See: TWOT—332a; BDB—159a, 550d. comp. 4036.

4033. מָגוּר {11x} **mâgûwr**, *maw-goor';* or

מָגֻר **mâgûr**, *maw-goor';* from 1481 in the sense of *lodging;* a temporary *abode;* by extens. a permanent *residence:*—dwellings {2x}, pilgrimage {4x}, where sojourn {1x}, be a stranger {4x}. See: TWOT—330c; BDB—158c. comp. 4032.

4034. מְגוֹרָה {1x} **mᵉgôwrâh**, *meg-o-raw';* fem. of 4032; *affright:*—fear {1x}. See: TWOT—332b; BDB—159a, 550d.

4035. מְגוּרָה {3x} **mᵉgûwrâh**, *meg-oo-raw';* fem. of 4032 or of 4033; a *fright;* also a *granary:*—barn {1x}, fear {2x}. See: TWOT—330d; BDB—158c, 550d.

4036. מָגוֹר מִסָּבִיב {1x} **Mâgôwr miç-Çâbîyb**, *maw-gore' mis-saw-beeb';* from 4032 and 5439 with the prep. ins.; *affright from around; Magor-mis-Sabib,* a symbol; name of Pashur:—Magor-missabib {1x}. See: BDB—159a, 687a.

4037. מַגְזֵרָה {1x} **magzêrâh**, *mag-zay-raw';* from 1504; a *cutting* implement, i.e. a *blade:*—axe {1x}. See: TWOT—340d; BDB—160d, 550d.

4038. מַגָּל {2x} **maggâl**, *mag-gawl';* from an unused root mean. to *reap;* a *sickle:*—sickle {2x}. See: TWOT—1292a; BDB—409d, 550d, 618c.

4039. מְגִלָּה {21x} **mᵉgillâh**, *meg-il-law';* from 1556; a *roll:*—roll {20x}, volume {1x}. See: TWOT—353m; BDB—166b, 550d, 1086c.

4040. מְגִלָּה {1x} **mᵉgillâh** (Aram.), *meg-il-law';* corresp. to 4039:—roll {1x}. See: TWOT—2657c; BDB—1086c, 1099c.

4041. מְגַמָּה {1x} **mᵉgammâh**, *meg-am-maw';* from the same as 1571; prop. *accumulation,* i.e. *impulse* or *direction:*—sup up {1x}. See: TWOT—361b; BDB—169d.

4042. מָגַן {3x} **mâgan**, *maw-gan';* a denom. from 4043; prop. to *shield; encompass* with; fig. to *rescue,* to *hand* safely *over* (i.e. *surrender*):—deliver {3x}. See: TWOT—367e; BDB—171c, 689b, 698c.

4043. מָגֵן {63x} **mâgên**, *maw-gane';* also (in plur.) fem.

מְגִנָּה **mᵉginnâh**, *meg-in-naw';* from 1598; a *shield* (i.e. the small one or *buck-*

ler); fig. a *protector;* also the scaly *hide* of the crocodile:—shield {48x}, buckler {9x}, armed {2x}, defence {2x}, rulers {1x}, scales + 650 {1x}. See: TWOT—367c; BDB—171b, 550d.

4044. מְגִנָּה {1x} **mᵉginnâh**, *meg-in-naw';* from 4042; a *covering* (in a bad sense), i.e. *blindness* or *obduracy:*—sorrow {1x}. See: TWOT—367d; BDB—171c, 550d. Syn.: 4043.

4045. מִגְעֶרֶת {1x} **migʿereth**, *mig-eh'-reth;* from 1605; *reproof* (i.e. *curse*):—rebuke {1x}. See: TWOT—370b; BDB—172a, 550d.

4046. מַגֵּפָה {26x} **maggêphâh**, *mag-gay-faw';* from 5062; a *pestilence;* by anal. *defeat:*—plague {21x}; slaughter {3x}, plagued {1x}, stroke {1x}. See: TWOT—1294b; BDB—550d, 620a.

4047. מַגְפִּיעָשׁ {1x} **Magpîyʿâsh**, *mag-pee-awsh';* appar. from 1479 or 5062 and 6211; *exterminator of* (the) *moth; Magpiash,* an Isr.:—Magpiash {1x}. See: BDB—550d.

4048. מָגַר {2x} **mâgar**, *maw-gar';* a prim. root; to *yield up;* intens. to *precipitate:*—cast down {1x}, terrors {1x}. See: TWOT—1145; BDB—550d, 1099c.

4049. מְגַר {1x} **mᵉgar** (Aram.), *meg-ar';* corresp. to 4048; to *overthrow:*—destroy {1x}. See: TWOT—2821; BDB—1099c.

4050. מְגֵרָה {4x} **mᵉgêrâh**, *meg-ay-raw';* from 1641; a *saw:*—axe {1x}, saw {3x}. See: TWOT—386e; BDB—176b, 551a.

4051. מִגְרוֹן {2x} **Migrôwn**, *mig-rone';* from 4048; *precipice; Migron,* a place in Pal.:—Migron {2x}. See: TWOT—386e; BDB—550d.

4052. מִגְרָעָה {1x} **migrâʿâh**, *mig-raw-aw';* from 1639; a *ledge* or offset:—narrowed rests {1x}. See: TWOT—384a; BDB—175d, 551a.

4053. מִגְרָפָה {1x} **migrâphâh**, *mig-raw-faw';* from 1640; something *thrown off* (by the spade), i.e. a *clod:*—clod {1x}. See: TWOT—385b; BDB—175d, 551a.

4054. מִגְרָשׁ {110x} **migrâsh**, *mig-rawsh';* also (in plur.) fem. (Eze 27:28).

מִגְרָשָׁה **migrâshâh**, *mig-raw-shaw';* from 1644; a *suburb* (i.e. open country whither flocks are *driven* for pasture); hence, the *area* around a building, or the *margin* of the sea:—cast out {1x}, suburb {109x}.

Migrash means "suburbs; pasture land; open land." **(1)** It denotes the untilled ground outside a city or the "pasture land" belonging to the cities: "For the children of Joseph were two tribes, Manasseh and Ephraim: therefore they gave no part unto the Levites in the land,

save cities to dwell in, with their suburbs for their cattle and for their substance" (Josh 14:4). **(2)** Ezekiel describes a strip of land for the Levites around the city. Part of the land was to be used for houses and part to be left: "And the five thousand, that are left in the breadth over against the five and twenty thousand, shall be a profane place for the city, for dwelling, and for suburbs: and the city shall be in the midst thereof" (Eze 48:15). See: TWOT—388c; BDB—177b, 551a.

4055. מַד {12x} **mad**, *mad;* or

מֵד **mêd**, *made;* from 4058; prop. *extent,* i.e. *height;* also a *measure;* by impl. a *vesture* (as measured); also a *carpet:*—garment {4x}, armour {2x}, measure {2x}, raiment {1x}, judgement {1x}, variant {1x}, clothes {1x}, armour, clothes, garment, judgment, measure, raiment, stature. See: TWOT—1146a; BDB—551a, 551b.

4056. מַדְבַּח {1x} **madbach** (Aram.), *mad-bakh';* from 1684; a sacrificial *altar:*—altar {1x}. See: TWOT—2665b; BDB—1087a, 1099c.

4057. מִדְבָּר {271x} **midbâr**, *mid-bawr';* from 1696 in the sense of *driving;* a *pasture* (i.e. open field, whither cattle are driven); by impl. a *desert;* also *speech* (incl. its organs):—wilderness {255x}, desert {13x}, south {1x}, speech {1x}, wilderness + 776 {1x}. See: TWOT—399k, 399l; BDB—184c, 184d, 551a.

4058. מָדַד {51x} **mâdad**, *maw-dad';* a prim. root; prop. to *stretch;* by impl. to *measure* (as if by *stretching* a line); fig. to be *extended:*—measure {47x}, mete out {2x}, mete {1x}, stretched {1x}.

Madad, as a verb, means "to measure, measure off, extend." **(1)** This word has the nuance of "to survey." **(2)** The basic meaning of the verb is illustrated in its first occurrence in the Old Testament: ".they did mete it with an omer" (Ex 16:18). **(3)** *Madad* is used not only of "measuring" volume but also of "measuring" distance (Deut 21:2) and length (Num 35:5). **(4)** A rather gruesome use is found in 2 Sa 8:2, where, after defeating the Moabites, David "measured them with a line, casting them down to the ground; even with two lines measured he to put to death, and with one full line to keep alive." **(5)** The greatness of the creator God is expressed in the question, "Who hath measured the waters in the hollow of his hand . . ." (Is 40:12). **(6)** Also, God "stood, and measured the earth" (Hab 3:6). **(7)** *Madad* can express the idea of extending, stretching: "And he stretched himself upon the child three times" (1 Kin 17:21). See: TWOT—1146; BDB—551a.

4059. מָדַד {1x} **middad**, *mid-dad';* from 5074; *flight:*—be gone {1x}. See: TWOT—1146; BDB—551a.

4060. מִדָּה {55x} **middâh**, *mid-daw';* fem. of 4055; prop. *extension,* i.e. height or breadth; also a *measure* (incl. its standard); hence, a *portion* (as measured) or a *vestment;* spec. *tribute* (as measured):—measure {37x}, piece {7x}, stature {4x}, size {3x}, meteyard {1x}, garments {1x}, tribute {1x}, wide {1x}.

Middah means "measure; measurement; extent; size; stature; section; area." **(1)** Of the 53 times this noun appears, 25 appearances are in Ezekiel. **(2)** This noun refers to the act of "measurement": "Ye shall do no unrighteousness in judgment, in meteyard, in weight, or in measure" (Lev 19:35). **(3)** In Eze 41:17 this word is used of length "measurement," and in Job 28:25 of liquid "measurement." **(4)** *Middah* means the thing measured, or the "size." Ex 26:2 (the first occurrence) specifies: "Every one of the curtains shall have one measure [the same size]." **(5)** The word can also refer to the duration of one's life: "Lord, make me to know [realize] mine end, and the measure of my days [how short my life really is]" (Ps 39:4). **(6)** A "man of measure" is one of great "stature or size": "And he [Benaiah] slew an Egyptian, a man of great stature, five cubits [about 7½ feet] high" (1 Chr 11:23). **(7)** *Middah* sometimes represents a "measured portion" of a thing: "Malchijah the son of Harim, and Hashub the son of Pahath-moab, repaired the other piece, and the tower of the furnaces" (Neh 3:11). **(8)** In Eze 45:3 the word appears to represent a "measured area." See: TWOT—1146b; BDB—193c, 551c, 551d, 1101b.

4061. מִדָּה {4x} **middâh** (Aram.), *mid-daw'* or

מִנְדָה **mindâh** (Aram.), *min-daw';* corresp. to 4060; *tribute* in money:—toll {3x}, tribute {1x}. See: TWOT—1147; BDB—1099c, 1101b.

4062. מַדְהֵבָה {1x} **madhêbâh**, *mad-hay-baw';* perh. from the equiv. of 1722; *gold-making,* i.e. *exactress:*—golden city {1x}. See: TWOT—2125d; BDB—551d, 923c.

4063. מֶדֶו {2x} **medev**, *meh'-dev;* from an unused root mean. to *stretch;* prop. *extent,* i.e. *measure;* by impl. a *dress* (as measured):—garment {2x}. See: TWOT—1148a; BDB—551d.

4064. מַדְוֶה {1x} **madveh**, *mad-veh';* from 1738; *sickness:*—diseases {2x}. See: TWOT—411c; BDB—188c, 551d.

4065. מַדּוּחַ {1x} **maddûwach**, *mad-doo'-akh;* from 5080; *seduction:*—causes of

banishment {1x}. See: TWOT—1304a; BDB—551d, 623b.

4066. מָדוֹן {18x} **mâdôwn**, *maw-dohn';* from 1777; a *contest* or quarrel:—brawling {2x}, contention {3x}, contentions {2x}, contentious {3x}, discord {1x}, strife {7x}. See: TWOT—426c; BDB—193b, 551d, 552a. comp. 4079, 4090.

4067. מָדוֹן {1x} **mâdôwn**, *maw-dohn';* from the same as 4063; *extensiveness,* i.e. height:—stature {1x}. See: TWOT—1146d; BDB—193c, 551c, 551.

4068. מָדוֹן {1x} **Mâdôwn**, *maw-dohn';* the same as 4067; *Madon,* a place in Pal.:—Madon {1x}. See: BDB—193c.

4069. מַדּוּעַ {6x} **maddûwaᶜ**, *mad-doo'-ah;* or

מַדֻּעַ **maddûaᶜ**, *mad-doo'-ah;* from 4100 and the pass. part. of 3045; *what* (is) *known?;* i.e. (by impl.) (adv.) *why?:*—how {1x}, wherefore {2x}, why {3x}. This word is related to the verb *yadaᶜ* (3045) and is found in Ex 1:18: ". . . Why have ye done this thing, and have saved the men children alive?" See: TWOT—848h; BDB—396c, 551d.

4070. מָדוֹר {4x} **mᵉdôwr** (Aram.), *med-ore';* or

מְדֹר **mᵉdôr** (Aram.), *med-ore';* or

מְדָר **mᵉdâr** (Aram.), *med-awr';* from 1753; a *dwelling:*—dwelling {4x}. See: TWOT—2669b; BDB—1087b, 1099c.

4071. מְדוּרָה {2x} **mᵉdûwrâh**, *med-oo-raw';* or

מְדֻרָה **mᵉdûrâh**, *med-oo-raw';* from 1752 in the sense of *accumulation;* a *pile* of fuel:—pile thereof {1x}, pile for fire {1x}. See: TWOT—418c; BDB—190b, 551d, 552b.

4072. מִדְחֶה {1x} **midcheh**, *mid-kheh';* from 1760; *overthrow:*—ruin {1x}. See: TWOT—420b; BDB—191a, 551d.

4073. מְדַחְפָה {1x} **mᵉdachphâh**, *med-akh-faw';* from 1765; a *push,* i.e. ruin:—overthrow {1x}. See: TWOT—423a; BDB—191b, 551d.

4074. מָדַי {16x} **Mâday**, *maw-dah'-ee;* of for. der.; *Madai,* a country of central Asia:—Madai {2x}, Medes {8x}, Media {6x}. See: BDB—552a, 1099c.

4075. מָדַי {1x} **Mâday**, *maw-dah'-ee;* patrial from 4074; a *Madian* or native of Madai:—Mede {1x}. See: BDB—552a, 1099c.

4076. מָדַי {5x} **Mâday** (Aram.), *maw-dah'-ee;* corresp. to 4074:—Medes {5x}. See: BDB—1099c.

4077. מָדַי {1x} **Mâday** (Aram.), *maw-dah'-ee;* corresp. to 4075:—Median {1x}. See: BDB—1099c.

4078. מַדַי {1x} **madday**, *mad-dah'-ee;* from 4100 and 1767; *what* (is) *enough,* i.e. *sufficiently:*—sufficiently {1x}. See: TWOT—425; BDB—552a, 553b.

4079. מִדְיָן {9x} **midyân**, *mid-yawn';* a var. for 4066:—brawling {2x}, contention {4x}, contentous {3x}. See: TWOT—426c; BDB—193b, 552a.

4080. מִדְיָן {59x} **Midyân**, *mid-yawn';* the same as 4079; *Midjan,* a son of Abraham; also his country and (collect.) his desc.:—Midian {39x}, Midianite {20x}. See: BDB—193c, 552a.

4081. מִדִּין {1x} **Middîyn**, *mid-deen';* a var. for 4080:—Middin {1x}. See: TWOT—426c; BDB—551d.

4082. מְדִינָה {44x} **mᵉdîynâh**, *med-ee-naw';* from 1777; prop. a *judgeship,* i.e. *jurisdiction;* by impl. a *district* (as ruled by a judge); gen. a *region:*—(✕ every) province {44x}. See: TWOT—426d; BDB—193d, 552a, 1088c.

4083. מְדִינָה {11x} **mᵉdîynâh** (Aram.), *med-ee-naw';* corresp. to 4082:—province {11x}. See: TWOT—2674c; BDB—1088c.

4084. מִדְיָנִי {7x} **Midyânîy**, *mid-yaw-nee';* patron. or patrial from 4080; a *Midjanite* or descend. (native) of Midjan:—Midianite {4x}, Midianitish woman {2x}, Midianitish {1x}. See: BDB—193c, 552a. comp. 4092.

4085. מְדֹכָה {1x} **mᵉdôkâh**, *med-o-kaw';* from 1743; a *mortar:*—mortar {1x}. See: TWOT—413a; BDB—189a, 552a.

4086. מַדְמֵן {1x} **Madmên**, *mad-mane';* from the same as 1828; *dunghill; Madmen,* a place in Pal.:—Madmen {1x}. See: BDB—199b, 552a.

4087. מַדְמֵנָה {1x} **madmênâh**, *mad-may naw';* fem. from the same as 1828; *dunghill:*—dunghill {1x}. See: TWOT—441b; BDB—199b, 552a.

4088. מַדְמֵנָה {1x} **Madmênâh**, *mad-may-naw';* the same as 4087; *Madmenah,* a place in Pal.:—Madmenah {1x}. See: BDB—199b, 552a.

4089. מַדְמַנָּה {2x} **Madmannâh**, *mad-man-naw';* a var. for 4087; *Madmannah,* a place in Pal.:—Madmannah {2x}. See: BDB—199b, 552a.

4090. מְדָן {3x} **mᵉdân**, *med-awn';* a form of 4066:—discord {2x}, strifes {1x}. See: TWOT—426c; BDB—193b, 552a.

Hebrew

4091. מְדָן {2x} **Mᵉdân**, *med-awn;* the same as 4090; *Medan,* a son of Abraham:— Medan {2x}. See: TWOT—426c; BDB—193c, 552a.

4092. מְדָנִי {1x} **Mᵉdâniy**, *med-aw-nee';* a var. of 4084:—Midianite {1x}. See: BDB—193c.

4093. מַדָּע {6x} **maddâᶜ**, *mad-daw';* or

מַדָּע **maddaᶜ**, *mad-dah';* from 3045; *intel-ligence* or *consciousness:*—knowl-edge {4x}, science {1x}, thought {1x}. See: TWOT—848g; BDB—396b, 552a, 1095b.

מֹדָע **môdâᶜ**. See 4129.

מַדּוּעַ **maduaᶜ**. See 4069.

4094. מַדְקָרָה {1x} **madqârâh**, *mad-kaw-raw';* from 1856; a *wound:*—piercing {1x}. See: TWOT—449a; BDB—201b, 552a.

מְדֹר **mᵉdôr**. See 4070.

4095. מַדְרֵגָה {2x} **madrêgâh**, *mad-ray-gaw';* from an unused root mean. to *step;* prop. a *step;* by impl. a *steep* or inaccessi-ble place:—stair {1x}, steep place {1x}. See: TWOT—452a; BDB—201c, 552b.

מְדֻרָה **mᵉdûrâh**. See 4071.

4096. מִדְרָךְ {1x} **midrâk**, *mid-rawk';* from 1869; a *treading,* i.e. a place for step-ping on:—[foot-] breadth {1x}. See: TWOT—453b; BDB—204a, 258a, 552b.

4097. מִדְרָשׁ {2x} **midrâsh**, *mid-rawsh';* from 1875; prop. an *investigation,* i.e. (by impl.) a *treatise* or elaborate compila-tion:—story {2x}.

Midrash can mean "study; commentary; story." This noun occurs a few times in late biblical Hebrew (2 Chr 13:22); it is commonly used in post-biblical Judaism to refer to the various traditional commentaries by the Jew-ish sages. One occurrence of the word is in 2 Chr 24:27: "Now concerning his sons, and the greatness of the burdens laid upon him . . . they are written in the story [commentary] of the Book of the Kings." See: TWOT—455a; BDB—205d, 552b.

4098. מְדֻשָּׁה {1x} **mᵉdushshâh**, *med-oosh-shaw';* from 1758; a *threshing,* i.e. (concr. and fig.) *down-trodden* people:—threshing {1x}. See: TWOT—419b; BDB—190c, 552b.

4099. מְדָתָא {5x} **Mᵉdâthâ**, *med-aw-thaw';* of Pers. or.; *Medatha,* the father of Haman:—Hammedatha {5x} [*incl. the art.*]. See: BDB—241a.

4100. מָה {27x} **mâh**, *maw;* or

מַה **mah**, *mah;* or

מָ **mâ**, *maw;* or

מַ **ma**, *mah;* also

מֶה **meh**, *meh;* a prim. particle; prop. in-terrog. *what?* (incl. *how? why? when?*); but also exclamation, *what!* (incl. *how!*), or in-def. *what* (incl. *whatever,* and even rel. *that which*); often used with prefixes in various adv. or conjunc. senses:—what {8x}, how {3x}, why {3x}, whereby {1x}, wherein {1x}, how long {1x}, how oft {1x}, to what end {1x}; wherefore {3x}, wherewith {1x}, what good {1x}, howsoever {1x}, whereto {1x}, nothing {1x}. See: TWOT—1149; BDB—484d, 541a, 547a, 552a, 552b, 980a, 1099d.

4101. מָה {13x} **mâh** (Aram.), *maw;* corresp. to 4100:—how great {1x}, how mighty {1x}, that which {1x}, what {6x}, whatsoever {1x}, why {3x}. See: TWOT—2822; BDB—1099b, 1099c.

4102. מָהַהּ {9x} **mâhahh**, *maw-hah';* appar. a denom. from 4100; prop. to *ques-tion* or hesitate, i.e. (by impl.) to *be reluctant:*—delayed {1x}, linger {2x}, stay selves {1x}, tarry {5x}. See: TWOT—2822; BDB—554c.

4103. מְהוּמָה {12x} **mᵉhûwmâh**, *meh-hoo-maw';* from 1949; *confusion* or uproar:—destruction {3x}, discomfiture {1x}, trouble {3x}, tumult {2x}, vexation {2x}, vexed {1x}. See: TWOT—486a; BDB—223b.

4104. מְהוּמָן {1x} **Mᵉhûwmân**, *meh-hoo-mawn';* of Pers. or.; *Mehuman,* a eunuch of Xerxes:—Mehuman {1x}. See: BDB—54d, 554c.

4105. מְהֵיטַבְאֵל {3x} **Mᵉhêytabʾêl**, *meh-hay-tab-ale';* from 3190 (aug-mented) and 410; *bettered of God; Mehetabel,* the name of an Edomitish man and woman:—Mehetabeel {1x}, Mehetabel {2x}. See: BDB—406b, 554c.

4106. מָהִיר {4x} **mâhîyr**, *maw-here';* or

מָהִר **mâhir**, *maw-here';* from 4116; *quick;* hence, *skilful:*—diligent {1x}, hasty {1x}, ready {2x}. See: TWOT—1152c; BDB—554c, 555b.

4107. מָהַל {1x} **mâhal**, *maw-hal';* a prim. root; prop. to *cut down* or *reduce,* i.e. by impl. to *adulterate:*—mixed {1x}. See: TWOT—1151; BDB—554c.

4108. מַהְלֵךְ {1x} **mahlêk**, *mah-lake';* from 1980; a *walking* (plur. collect.), i.e. *ac-cess:*—place to walk {1x}. See: TWOT—498d; BDB—237b.

4109. מַהֲלָךְ {4x} **mahălâk**, *mah-hal-awk'*; from 1980; a *walk*, i.e. a *passage* or a *distance:*—journey {3x}, walk {1x}. *Mahalak*, which appears 4 times, means "passage" (Eze 42:4) and "journey" (Neh 2:6). See: TWOT—498d; BDB—237b, 554c.

4110. מַהֲלָל {1x} **mahălâl**, *mah-hal-awl'*; from 1984; *fame:*—praise {1x}. *Mahalal* occurs once (Prov 27:21) and denotes the degree of "praise" or its lack. See: TWOT—500b; BDB—239c, 554d.

4111. מַהֲלַלְאֵל {7x} **Mahălal'êl**, *mah-hal-al-ale'*; from 4110 and 410; *praise of God; Mahalalel*, the name of an antediluvian patriarch and of an Isr.:—Mahalaleel {7x}. See: BDB—239d, 554d.

4112. מַהֲלֻמָּה {2x} **mahălummâh**, *mah-hal-oom-maw'*; from 1986; a *blow:*—stripes {1x}, strokes {1x}. See: TWOT—502c; BDB—240d, 554d.

4113. מַהֲמֹרָה {1x} **mahămôrâh**, *mah-ham-o-raw'*; from an unused root of uncert. mean.; perh. an *abyss:*—deep pits {1x}. See: TWOT—509a; BDB—243b, 554d.

4114. מַהְפֵּכָה {6x} **mahpêkâh**, *mah-pay-kaw'*; from 2015; a *destruction:*—when . . . overthrew {3x}, overthrow {2x}, overthrown {1x}. See: TWOT—512d; BDB—245c, 246b, 554d.

4115. מַהְפֶּכֶת {4x} **mahpeketh**, *mah-peh'-keth*; from 2015; a *wrench,* i.e. the *stocks:*—prison {2x}, stocks {2x}. See: TWOT—512e; BDB—246b, 554d.

4116. מָהַר {64x} **mâhar**, *maw-har'*; a prim. root; prop. to *be liquid* or *flow* easily, i.e. (by impl.); to *hurry* (in a good or a bad sense); often used (with another verb) adv. *promptly:*—haste {42x}, swift {3x}, quickly {3x}, hastily {2x}, hasty {2x}, soon {2x}, speed {2x}, headlong {1x}, rash {1x}, fearful {1x}, ready {1x}, shortly {1x}, speedily {1x}, straightway {1x}, suddenly {1x}.

Mahar means "to hasten, make haste." This verb and various derivatives are common to both ancient and modern Hebrew. It occurs 64 times in the Hebrew Bible; it appears twice in the first verse in which it is found: "And Abraham hastened [*mahar*] into the tent unto Sarah, and said, Make ready quickly [*mahar*] three measures of fine meal" (Gen 18:6). It often has an adverbial use when it appears with another verb, such as in Gen 18:7: ". . . hasted to dress it" (or "quickly prepared it"). See: TWOT—1152; BDB—554d, 555a.

4117. מָהַר {2x} **mâhar**, *maw-har'*; a prim. root (perh. rather the same as 4116 through the idea of *readiness* in assent); to *bar-*

gain (for a wife), i.e. to *wed:*—endow {1x}, X surely {1x}. See: TWOT—1153; BDB—555c.

4118. מָהֵר {18x} **mahêr**, *mah-hare'*; from 4116; prop. *hurrying;* hence, (adv.) *in a hurry:*—hasteth {1x}, hastily {2x}, at once {1x}, quickly {8x}, soon {1x}, speedily {4x}, suddenly {1x}. See: TWOT—1152a, 1152b; BDB—555a.

מָהִיר **mâhîr**. See 4106.

4119. מֹהַר {3x} **môhar**, *mo'-har*; from 4117; a *price* (for a wife):—dowry {3x}. See: TWOT—1153a; BDB—555c.

4120. מְהֵרָה {20x} **m^ehêrâh**, *meh-hay-raw'*; fem. of 4118; prop. a *hurry;* hence, (adv.) *promptly:*—quickly {10x}, speedily {4x}, make speed {1x}, soon {1x}, swiftly {1x}, hastily {1x}, with speed {1x}, shortly {1x}. See: TWOT—1152d; BDB—555b.

4121. מַהֲרַי {3x} **Mahăray**, *mah-har-ah'-ee*; from 4116; *hasty; Maharai*, an Isr.:—Maharai {3x}. See: BDB—555b.

4122. מַהֵר שָׁלָל חָשׁ בַּז {2x} **Mahêr Shâlâl Châsh Baz**, *mah-hare' shaw-lawl' khawsh baz;* from 4118 and 7998 and 2363 and 957; *hasting (is he [the enemy] to the) booty, swift (to the) prey; Maher-Shalal-Chash-Baz;* the symb. name of the son of Isaiah:—Maher-shalal-hash-baz {2x}. See: BDB—555b.

4123. מַהֲתַלָּה {1x} **mahăthallâh**, *mah-hath-al-law';* from 2048; a *delusion:*—deceit {1x}. See: TWOT—2514a; BDB—555c.

4124. מוֹאָב {181x} **Mōw'âb**, *mo-awb;* from a prol. form of the prep. pref. *m-* and 1; *from* (her [the mother's]) *father; Moâb*, an incestuous son of Lot; also his territory and desc.:—Moab {166x}, Moabites {15x}. See: TWOT—1155; BDB—547a, 555d.

4125. מוֹאָבִי {16x} **Mōw'âbiy**, *mo-aw-bee';* fem.

מוֹאָבִיָּה **Mōw'âbîyah**, *mo-aw-bee-yaw';* or

מוֹאָבִית **Mōwâbîyth**, *mo-aw-beeth';* patron. from 4124; a *Moâbite* or *Moäbitess,* i.e. a desc. from Moab:—Moabite {7x}, Moabitess {6x}, Moab {2x}, Moabitish {1x}. See: TWOT—1155a; BDB—555d.

מוֹאָל **mōw'l**. See 4136.

4126. מוֹבָא {2x} **mōwbâ'**, *mo-baw';* by transp. for 3996; an *entrance:*—coming {2x}. See: TWOT—212b; BDB—100a, 556a.

4127. מוּג {17x} **mûwg**, *moog;* a prim. root; to *melt*, i.e. lit. (to *soften, flow down, disappear*), or fig. (to *fear, faint*):—melt {5x}, dissolve {4x}, faint {3x}, melt away {2x}, con-

sumed {1x}, fainthearted {1x}, soft {1x}. See: TWOT—1156; BDB—556a.

4128. מוּד {1x} **mûwd**, *mood;* a prim. root; to *shake:*—measure {1x}. See: TWOT—1157; BDB—551b, 556d.

4129. מוֹדַע {2x} **môwdaʿ**, *mo-dah´;* or rather מֹדָע **môdâʿ**, *mo-daw´;* from 3045; an *acquaintance:*—kinswoman {1x}, kinsman {1x}. See: TWOT—848e; BDB—396b, 552a, 556d, 568a.

4130. מוֹדַעַת {1x} **môwdaʿath**, *mo-dah´-ath;* from 3045; *acquaintance:*—kindred {1x}. See: TWOT—848f; BDB—396b, 552a.

4131. מוֹט {39x} **môwt**, *mote;* a prim. root; to *waver;* by impl. to *slip, shake, fall:*—moved {20x}, removed {5x}, slip {3x}, carried {1x}, cast {1x}, course {1x}, decay {1x}, falling down {1x}, exceedingly {1x}, fall {1x}, ready {1x}, shaketh {1x}, slide {1x}, variant {1x}. See: TWOT—1158; BDB—556d.

4132. מוֹט {6x} **môwt**, *mote;* from 4131; a *wavering,* i.e. *fall;* by impl. a *pole* (as shaking); hence, a *yoke* (as essentially a bent pole):—bar {3x}, be moved {1x}, staff {1x}, yoke {1x}. See: TWOT—1158a; BDB—557a.

4133. מוֹטָה {12x} **môwtâh**, *mo-taw´;* fem. of 4132; a *pole;* by impl. an ox-*bow;* hence, a *yoke* (either lit. or fig.):—bands {2x}, heavy {1x}, staves {1x}, yoke {8x}. See: TWOT—1158b; BDB—557b.

4134. מוּךְ {5x} **mûwk**, *mook;* a prim. root; to *become thin,* i.e. (fig.) *be impoverished:*—be (waxen) poor {1x}, poorer {1x}. See: TWOT—1159; BDB—557b.

4135. מוּל {36x} **mûwl**, *mool;* a prim. root; to *cut short,* i.e. *curtail* (spec. the prepuce, i.e. to *circumcise*); by impl. to *blunt;* fig. to *destroy:*—circumcise {30x}, destroy {3x}, cut down {1x}, needs {1x}, cut in pieces {1x}.

Muwl (4135) means "to circumcise, cut off." **(1)** Most of the occurrences in the Old Testament take place in the Pentateuch (20 times) and Joshua (8 times). *Muwl* occurs most frequently in Genesis (17 times, 11 of them in Genesis 17 alone) and Joshua (8 times). **(2)** The physical act of circumcision was introduced by God as a sign of the Abrahamic covenant: **(2a)** "This *is* my covenant, which ye shall keep, between me and you and thy seed after thee; Every man child among you shall be circumcised. And ye shall circumcise the flesh of your foreskin; and it shall be a token of the covenant betwixt me and you" (Gen 17:10–11). **(2b)** It was a permanent "cutting off" of the foreskin of the male organ, and as such was a reminder of the perpetuity of the covenantal relation-

ship. **(2c)** Israel was enjoined to be faithful in "circumcising" all males; each male baby was to be "circumcised" on the eighth day (Gen 17:12; Lev 12:3). **(2d)** Not only were the physical descendants of Abraham "circumcised," but also those who were servants, slaves, and foreigners in the covenant community (Gen 17:13–14).

(3) The special act of circumcision was a sign of God's gracious promise. With the promise and covenantal relations, God expected that His people would joyously and willingly live up to His expectations, and thus demonstrate His rule on earth. **(4)** To describe the "heart" attitude, several writers of Scripture use the verb "to circumcise." **(4a)** The "circumcision" of the flesh is a physical sign of commitment to God. **(4b)** Deuteronomy particularly is fond of the spiritual usage of the verb "to circumcise": "Circumcise therefore the foreskin of your heart, and be no more stiffnecked" (Deut 10:16; cf. 30:6). **(4c)** Jeremiah took over this usage: "Circumcise yourselves to the Lord, and take away the foreskins of your heart, ye men of Judah . . . , because of the evil of your doings" (Jer 4:4). **(5)** Few occurrences of the verb differ from the physical and the spiritual usage of "to circumcise." *Muwl* in the Book of Psalms has the meaning of "to cut off, destroy": "All nations compassed me about: but in the name of the LORD will I destroy them" (Ps 118:10; cf. vv. 11–12). See: TWOT—1161; BDB—557d.

4136. מוּל {36x} **mûwl**, *mool;* or מוֹל **môwl** (Deut 1:1), *mole;* or מוֹאל **môwˀl** (Neh 12:38), *mole;* or מֻל **mûl** (Num 22:5), *mool;* from 4135; prop. *abrupt,* i.e. a *precipice;* by impl. the *front;* used only adv. (with prep. pref.) *opposite:*—against {21x}, toward {3x}, forefront + 6440 {3x}, before {2x}, before it + 6440 {2x}, against + 6440 {1x}, forefront {1x}, from {1x}, Godward + 430 {1x}, with {1x}. See: TWOT—1160; BDB—541a, 556a, 557b.

4137. מוֹלָדָה {1x} **Môwlâdâh**, *mo-law-daw´;* from 3205; *birth; Moladah,* a place in Pal.:—Moladah {1x}. See: BDB—409d, 558a.

4138. מוֹלֶדֶת {22x} **môwledeth**, *mo-leh´-deth;* from 3205; *nativity* (plur. *birthplace*); by impl. *lineage, native country;* also *offspring, family:*—kindred {11x}, nativity {6x}, born {2x}, begotten {1x}, issue {1x}, native {1x}. See: TWOT—867f; BDB—558a.

4139. מוּלָה {1x} **mûwlâh**, *moo-law´;* from 4135; *circumcision:*—circumcision {1x}. *Muwlah* is found in Ex 4:26: "So he let him go: then she said, A bloody husband thou art,

because of the circumcision." See: TWOT—
1161a; BDB—558a.

4140. מוֹלִיד {1x} **Môwlîyd,** *mo-leed';* from 3205;
genitor; Molid, an Isr.:—Molid
{1x}. See: BDB—410a, 558a.

מוּם **muwm.** See 3971.

מוֹמְכָן **Môwmûkân.** See 4462.

4141. מוּסָב {1x} **mûwçâb,** *moo-sawb';* from
5437; a *turn,* i.e. *circuit* (of a
building):—winding about {1x}.

Muwcab occurs once with the meaning of
"circular passage": "For the winding about of
the house went still upward round about the
house" (Eze 41:7). See: TWOT—1456b; BDB—
558a, 687c.

4142. מוּסַבָּה {5x} **mûwçabbâh,** *moo-sab-baw';*
or

מֻסַבָּה **mûçabbâh,** *moo-sab-baw';* fem.
of 4141; a *reversal,* i.e. the *backside* (of a gem), *fold* (of a double-leaved door),
transmutation (of a name):—being changed
{1x}, inclosed {2x}, be set {1x}, turning {1x}. See:
TWOT—1456b; BDB—686d.

4143. מוּסָד {2x} **mûwçâd,** *moo-sawd';* from
3245; a *foundation:*—foundation
{2x}. See: TWOT—875d; BDB—414b, 558a.

4144. מוֹסָד {3x} **môwçâd,** *mo-sawd';* from 3245;
a *foundation:*—foundation {3x}.
See: TWOT—875f; BDB—414c, 558a.

4145. מוּסָדָה {1x} **mûwçâdâh,** *moo-saw-daw';*
fem. of 4143; a *foundation;* fig.
an *appointment:*—grounded {1x}. See: TWOT—
875e; BDB—414c, 558a. comp. 4328.

4146. מוֹסָדָה {10x} **môwçâdâh,** *mo-saw-daw';*
or

מֹסָדָה **môçâdâh,** *mo-saw-daw';* fem. of
4144; a *foundation:*—foundation
{10x}. See: TWOT—875f; BDB—414c.

4147. מוֹסֵר {11x} **môwçêr,** *mo-sare';* also (in
plur.) fem.

מוֹסֵרָה **môwçêrâh,** *mo-say-raw';* or

מֹסְרָה **môçᵉrâh,** *mo-ser-aw';* from 3256;
prop. *chastisement,* i.e. (by impl.)
a *halter;* fig. *restraint:*—bands {6x}, bond {5x}.
See: TWOT—141f; BDB—64c, 558a.

4148. מוּסָר {50x} **mûwçâr,** *moo-sawr';* from
3256; prop. *chastisement;* fig. *re-
proof, warning* or *instruction;* also *restraint:*—
instruction {30x}, correction {8x}, chasten {4x},
chastisement {3x}, check {1x}, bond {1x}, discipline {1x}, doctrine {1x}, rebuker {1x}.

Muwcar means "instruction; chastisement;
warning." **(1)** This noun occurs 50 times,
mainly in Proverbs. **(2)** The first occurrence is

in Deut 11:2: "I speak not with your children
which have not known, and which have not
seen the chastisement of the LORD your God,
his greatness, his mighty hand, and his
stretched out arm." **(3)** One of the major purposes of the wisdom literature was to teach
wisdom and *muwcar* (Prov 1:2). **(4)** *Muwcar*
is discipline, but more. **(4a)** As "discipline" it
teaches how to live correctly in the fear of the
Lord, so that the wise man learns his lesson
before temptation and testing: "Then I saw,
and considered it well: I looked upon it, and
received instruction" (Prov 24:32). **(4b)** This
"discipline" is training for life; hence, paying
attention to *muwcar* is important. **(4c)** Many
verbs bear out the need for a correct response:
"hear, obey, love, receive, obtain, take hold of,
guard, keep." **(4d)** Moreover, the rejection is
borne out by many verbs connected with *muwcar:* "reject, hate, ignore, not love, despise,
forsake."

(5) When *muwcar* as "instruction" has been
given, but was not observed, the *muwcar* as
"chastisement" or "discipline" may be the next
step: "Foolishness is bound in the heart of a
child; but the rod of correction shall drive it far
from him" (Prov 22:15). **(6)** Careful attention to
"instruction" brings honor (Prov 1:9), life (Prov
4:13), and wisdom (Prov 8:33), and above all it
pleases God: "For whoso findeth me findeth
life, and shall obtain favor of the Lord" (Prov
8:35). **(7)** The lack of observance of "instruction" brings its own results: death (Prov 5:23),
poverty, and shame (Prov 13:18), and is ultimately a sign that one has no regard for one's
own life (Prov 15:32). **(8)** The receptivity for
"instruction" from one's parents, teacher, the
wise, or the king is directly corollary to one's
subjugation to God's discipline. **(8a)** The prophets charged Israel with not receiving God's discipline: "O Lord, are not thine eyes upon the
truth? thou hast stricken them, but they have
not grieved; thou hast consumed them, but
they have refused to receive correction: they
have made their faces harder than a rock; they
have refused to return" (Jer 5:3).

(8b) Jeremiah asked the men of Judah and
the inhabitants in the besieged Jerusalem to
pay attention to what was happening around
them, that they still might subject themselves
to "instruction" (35:13). **(9)** Isaiah predicted
that God's chastisement on man was carried by
the Suffering Servant, bringing peace to those
who believe in Him: "But he was wounded for
our transgressions, he was bruised for our iniquities: the chastisement of our peace was upon
him; and with his stripes we are healed" (53:5).
See: TWOT—877b; BDB—416b, 558a.

4149. מוֹסֵרָה {3x} **Môwçêrâh**, *mo-say-raw';*
or (plur.)

מֹסְרוֹת **Môç'rôwth**, *mo-ser-othe'* fem. of
4147; *correction* or *corrections;*
Moserah or *Moseroth*, a place in the Desert:—
Mosera {1x}, Moseroth {2x}. See: BDB—64c, 588b.

4150. מוֹעֵד {223x} **môwʿêd**, *mo-ade';* or

מֹעֵד **môʿêd**, *mo-ade';* or (fem.)

מוֹעָדָה **môwʿâdâh** (2 Chr 8:13), *mo-aw-
daw';* from 3259; prop. an *appointment*, i.e. a fixed *time* or season; spec.
a *festival;* conventionally a *year;* by impl. an
assembly (as convened for a def. purpose); tech.
the *congregation;* by extens. The *place of meeting;* also a *signal* (as appointed beforehand):—
congregation {150x}, feast {23x}, season {13x},
appointed {12x}, time {12x}, assembly {4x}, solemnity {4x}, solemn {2x}, days {1x}, sign {1x},
synagogues {1x}.

Moʿed means "appointed place of meeting;
meeting." **(1)** The noun *moʿed* appears in the
Old Testament 223 times, of which 160 times
are in the Pentateuch. **(2)** The word *moʿed* keeps
its basic meaning of "appointed," **(2a)** but varies as to what is agreed upon or appointed according to the context: the time, the place, or
the meeting itself. **(2b)** The usage of the verb
in Amos 3:3 is illuminating: "Can two walk together, except they be agreed?" Whether they
have agreed on a time or a place of meeting,
or on the meeting itself, is ambiguous. **(3)** The
meaning of *moʿed* is fixed within the context
of Israel's religion. **(3a)** First, the festivals came
to be known as the "appointed times" or the
set feasts. These festivals were clearly prescribed in the Pentateuch.

(3b) The word refers to any "festival" or
"pilgrimage festival," such as Passover (Lev
23:15ff.), the feast of first fruits (Lev 23:15ff.),
the feast of tabernacles (Lev 23:33ff.), or the
Day of Atonement (Lev 23:27). **(3b)** God condemned the people for observing the *moʿed* rit-
ualistically: "Your new moons and your
appointed feasts my soul hateth" (Is 1:14).
(4) The word *moʿed* also signifies a "fixed
place." **(4a)** This usage is not frequent: "For
thou hast said in thine heart, I will ascend into
heaven, I will exalt my throne above the stars
of God: I will sit also upon the mount of the
congregation [*moʿed*], in the sides of the north"
(Is 14:13). **(4b)** "For I know that thou wilt bring
me to death, and to the house appointed for
all living" (Job 30:23). **(5)** In both meanings
of *moʿed*—"fixed time" and "fixed place"—a
common denominator is the "meeting" of two
or more parties at a certain place and time—
hence the usage of *moʿed* as "meeting." **(6)** The
phrase, "tabernacle of the congregation," is a

translation of the Hebrew *ʿohel moʿed* ("tent of
meeting"). **(6a)** The phrase occurs 139 times—
mainly in Exodus, Leviticus, and Numbers,
rarely in Deuteronomy.

(6b) It signifies that the Lord has an "appointed place" by which His presence is represented and through which Israel was assured
that their God was with them. **(6c)** The fact
that the tent was called the "tent of meeting"
signifies that Israel's God was among His people and that He was to be approached at a certain time and place that were "fixed" *(yaʿad)*
in the Pentateuch. **(6d)** In the KJV, this phrase
is translated as "tabernacle of the congregation" (Ex 28:43) because translators realized
that the noun *ʿedah* ("congregation") is derived
from the same root as *moʿed*. **(7)** Of the three
meanings, the appointed "time" is most basic.
The phrase "tent of meeting" lays stress on the
"place of meeting." The "meeting" itself is generally associated with "time" or "place." Syn.:
5172. See: TWOT—878b; BDB—417b, 558a,
588d.

4151. מוֹעָד {1x} **môwʿâd**, *mo-awd';* from 3259;
prop. an *assembly* [as in 4150]; fig.
a *troop:*—appointed time {1x}. See: TWOT—
878c; BDB—418a, 558a.

4152. מוּעָדָה {1x} **mûwʿâdâh**, *moo-aw-daw';*
from 3259; an *appointed* place,
i.e. *asylum:*—appointed {1x}. See: TWOT—
878d; BDB—418a, 558a.

4153. מוֹעַדְיָה {1x} **Môwʿadyâh**, *mo-ad-yaw';*
from 4151 and 3050; *assembly
of Jah; Moädjah*, an Isr.:—Moadiah {1x}. See:
BDB—558b, 588c. comp. 4573.

4154. מוּעֶדֶת {1x} **mûwʿedeth**, *moo-ay'-deth;*
fem. pass. part. of 4571; prop.
made to slip, i.e. *dislocated:*—out of joint {1x}.
See: TWOT—1226; BDB—588c.

4155. מוּעָף {1x} **mûwʿâph**, *moo-awf';* from
5774; prop. *covered*, i.e. *dark;*
abstr. *obscurity*, i.e. *distress:*—dimness {1x}.
See: TWOT—1583a; BDB—558b, 734a.

4156. מוֹעֵצָה {7x} **môwʿêtsâh**, *mo-ay-tsaw';*
from 3289; a *purpose:*—counsel
{6x}, device {1x}. See: TWOT—887b; BDB—
420b, 558b, 591d.

4157. מוּעָקָה {1x} **mûwʿâqâh**, *moo-aw-kaw';*
from 5781; *pressure*, i.e. (fig.)
distress:—affliction {1x}. See: TWOT—1585b;
BDB—558b, 734c.

4158. מוֹפַעַת {4x} **Môwphaʿath** (Jer 48:21),
mo-fah'-ath; or

מֵיפַעַת **Mêyphaʿath**, *may-fah'-ath;* or

מֵפַעַת **Mêphaʿath**, *may-fah'-ath;* from
3313; *illuminative; Mophaath* or

Mephaath, a place in Pal.:—Mephaath {4x}. See: BDB—422b, 558b, 568c, 592b.

4159. מוֹפֵת {36x} **môwphêth**, *mo-faith';* or

מֹפֵת **môphêth**, *mo-faith';* from 3302 in the sense of *conspicuousness;* a *miracle;* by impl. a *token* or *omen:*—wonder {25x}, sign {8x}, miracle {2x}, wondered at {1x}.

Mowpheth means "wonder; sign; portent." **(1)** First, this word signifies a divine act or a special display of divine power: "When thou goest to return into Egypt, see that thou do all those wonders before Pharaoh, which I have put in thine hand" (Ex 4:21—the first biblical occurrence of the word). **(2)** Acts effecting the divine curses are called "wonders." Thus the word does not necessarily refer to a miraculous act, if "miracle" means something outside the realm of ordinary providence. **(3)** The word can represent a "sign" from God or a token of a future event: "This is the sign which the LORD hath spoken: Behold, the altar shall be rent, and the ashes that are upon it shall be poured out" (1 Kin 13:3). **(3a)** This sense sometimes has the nuance "symbol": "Hear now, O Joshua the high priest, thou, and thy fellows that sit before thee: for they are men wondered at *(mowpheth):* for, behold, I will bring forth my servant the BRANCH" (Zec 3:8; cf. Ps 71:7). See: TWOT—152a; BDB—68d, 558b.

4160. מוּץ {1x} **mûwts**, *moots;* a prim. root; to *press,* i.e. (fig.) to *oppress:* extortioner {1x}. See: TWOT—1162; BDB—568c, 592b.

4161. מוֹצָא {27x} **môwtsâ'**, *mo-tsaw';* or

מֹצָא **môtsâ'**, *mo-tsaw';* from 3318; a *going forth,* i.e. (the act) an *egress,* or (the place) an *exit;* hence, a *source* or *product;* spec. *dawn,* the *rising* of the sun (the *East), exportation, utterance,* a *gate,* a *fountain,* a *mine,* a *meadow* (as producing grass):—go out {7x}, go forth {5x}, spring {3x}, brought {2x}, watersprings + 4325 {2x}, bud {1x}, east {1x}, outgoings {1x}, proceeded {1x}, proceedeth {1x}, vein {1x}, come out {1x}, watercourse {1x}.

Motsa' means place of going forth; that which comes forth; going forth. **(1)** *Motsa'* is a word for "east" (cf. Ps 19:6), where the sun rises ("goes forth"): "His going forth is from the end of the heaven, and his circuit unto the ends of it: and there is nothing hid from the heat thereof." **(2)** The word also represents the "place of departure" or "exit" from the temple in Ezekiel's vision (Eze 42:11): "And the way before them was like the appearance of the chambers which were toward the north, as long as they, and as broad as they: and all their goings out were both according to their fashions, and according to their doors." **(3)** *Motsa'*

also refers to the "starting point" of a journey (Num 33:2). **(4)** *Motsa'* may also refer to that which "comes forth," for example, **(4a)** an "utterance" (Num 30:13), and **(4b)** the "going forth" of the morning and evening, the dawn and dusk (Ps 65:8). **(5)** Finally, the word can represent the "actual going forth" itself. So Hosea says that the LORD's "going forth" to redeem His people is as certain as the sunrise (6:3). See: TWOT—893c; BDB—425c, 558b, 594b.

4162. מוֹצָא {5x} **Môwtsâ'**, *mo-tsaw';* the same as 4161; *Motsa,* the name of two Isr.:—Moza {5x}. See: BDB—426a, 558b, 594b.

4163. מוֹצָאָה {2x} **môwtsâ'âh**, *mo-tsaw-aw';* fem. of 4161; a family *descent;* also a *sewer* [marg.; comp. 6675]:—draught house {1x}; goings forth {1x}. See: TWOT—893d; BDB—426a, 558b.

4164. מוּצָק {3x} **mûwtsaq**, *moo-tsak';* or

מוּצָק **mûwtsâq**, *moo-tsawk';* from 3332; *narrowness;* fig. *distress:*—anguish {1x}, is straitened {1x}, straitness {1x}. See: TWOT—1895c; BDB—558b, 848a.

4165. מוּצָק {2x} **mûwtsâq**, *moo-tsawk';* from 5694; prop. *fusion,* i.e. lit. a *casting* (of metal); fig. a *mass* (of clay):—casting {1x}, hardness {1x}. See: TWOT—897b; BDB—427c, 558b, 848a.

4166. מוּצָקָה {2x} **mûwtsâqâh**, *moo-tsaw-kaw';* or

מֻצָקָה **mûtsâqâh**, *moo-tsaw-kaw';* from 3332; prop. something *poured out,* i.e. a *casting* (of metal); by impl. a *tube* (as cast):—when it was cast {1x}, pipe {1x}. See: TWOT—897c; BDB—427c, 558b, 595b.

4167. מוּק {1x} **mûwq**, *mook;* a prim. root; to *jeer,* i.e. (intens.) *blaspheme:*—be corrupt {1x}. See: TWOT—1163; BDB—558b.

4168. מוֹקֵד {2x} **môwqêd**, *mo-kade';* from 3344; a *fire* or *fuel;* abstr. a *conflagration:*—burning {1x}, hearth {1x}. See: TWOT—901b; BDB—428d, 558c.

4169. מוֹקְדָה {1x} **môwq'dâh**, *mo-ked-aw';* fem. of 4168; *fuel:*—burning {1x}. See: TWOT—901c; BDB—429a, 558c.

4170. מוֹקֵשׁ {27x} **môwqêsh**, *mo-kashe';* or

מֹקֵשׁ **môqêsh**, *mo-kashe';* from 3369; a *noose* (for catching animals) (lit. or fig.); by impl. a *hook* (for the nose):—snare {20x}, gin {3x}, trap {2x}, ensnared {1x}, snared {1x}. See: TWOT—906c; BDB—430c, 558c.

4171. מוּר {14x} **mûwr**, *moor;* a prim. root; to *alter;* by impl. to *barter,* to *dispose*

of:—change {10x}, at all {2x}, removed {1x}, exchange {1x}. See: TWOT—1164; BDB—558c.

4172. מוֹרָא {13x} **môwrâ**ʾ, *mo-raw'*; or

מֹרָא **môrâ**ʾ, *mo-raw'*; or

מוֹרָה **môrâh** (Ps 9:20), *mo-raw'*; from 3372; *fear;* by impl. a *fearful* thing or deed:—fear {8x}, terror {3x}, dread {1x}, terribleness {1x}.

Morah means "fear." **(1)** The noun *morah,* which appears 13 times, is used exclusively of the fear of being before a superior kind of being. **(2)** Usually it is used to describe the reaction evoked in men by God's mighty works of destruction and sovereignty: **(2a)** "For the LORD thy God is a consuming fire, even a jealous God" (Deut 4:24). **(2b)** Hence, the word represents a very strong "fear" or "terror." **(3)** In the singular, this word emphasizes the divine acts themselves. *Morah* may suggest the reaction **(3a)** of animals to men: "And the fear of you and the dread of you shall be upon every beast of the earth, and upon every fowl of the air, upon all that moveth upon the earth, and upon all the fishes of the sea; into your hand are they delivered" (Gen 9:2); and **(3b)** of the nations to conquering Israel: "There shall no man be able to stand before you: for the LORD your God shall lay the fear of you and the dread of you upon all the land that ye shall tread upon, as he hath said unto you" (Deut 11:25). See: TWOT—907c, 907d; BDB—432a, 432b, 558d, 559a, 597b.

4173. מוֹרַג {3x} **môwrag**, *mo-rag';* or

מֹרַג **môrag**, *mo-rag';* from an unused root mean. to *triturate;* a threshing *sledge:*—threshing instrument {3x}. See: TWOT—1165; BDB—558d.

4174. מוֹרָד {5x} **môwrâd**, *mo-rawd';* from 3381; a *descent;* arch. an ornamental *appendage,* perh. a *festoon:*—going down {3x}, steep place {1x}, thin work {1x}. See: TWOT—909a; BDB—434b, 559a.

4175. מוֹרֶה {3x} **môwreh**, *mo-reh';* from 3384; an *archer;* also *teacher* or *teaching;* also the *early rain* [see 3138]:—former rain {2x}, rain {1x}. See: TWOT—910b, 910c; BDB—435a, 435c, 598c.

4176. מוֹרֶה {3x} **Môwreh**, *mo-reh';* or

מֹרֶה **Môreh**, *mo-reh';* the same as 4175; *Moreh,* a Canaanite; also a hill (perh. named from him):—Moreh {3x}. See: BDB—435d, 598c.

4177. מוֹרָה {3x} **môwrâh**, *mo-raw;* from 4171 in the sense of *shearing;* a *razor:*—razor {3x}. See: TWOT—1166; BDB—559a.

4178. מוֹרָט {5x} **môwrât**, *mo-rawt';* from 3399; *obstinate,* i.e. independent:—peeled {2x}, furbished {2x}, bright {1x}. See: TWOT—1244; BDB—599a.

4179. מוֹרִיָּה {2x} **Môwrîyâh**, *mo-ree-yaw';* or

מֹרִיָּה **Môrîyâh**, *mo-ree-yaw';* from 7200 and 3050; *seen of Jah; Morijah,* a hill in Pal.:—Moriah {2x}. See: BDB—599a.

4180. מוֹרָשׁ {3x} **môwrâsh**, *mo-rawsh';* from 3423; a *possession;* fig. *delight:*—possession {2x}, thought {1x}.

The noun *mowrash* means "a place one has as a permanent possession": **(1)** "I will also make it a possession for the bittern" (Is 14:23); and **(2)** "But upon mount Zion shall be deliverance, and there shall be holiness; and the house of Jacob shall possess their possessions" (Obad 17). See: TWOT—920d; BDB—440c, 559a.

4181. מוֹרָשָׁה {9x} **môwrâshâh**, *mo-raw-shaw';* fem. of 4180; a *possession:*—heritage {1x}, inheritance {2x}, possession {6x}.

Mowrashah, which occurs 9 times, can refer to **(1)** "a place one has as a permanent possession": "And I will bring you in unto the land, concerning the which I did swear to give it to Abraham, to Isaac, and to Jacob; and I will give it you for an heritage: I am the LORD" (Ex 6:8); **(2)** "a thing one has as a permanent possession": "Moses commanded us a law, even the inheritance of the congregation of Jacob" (Deut 33:4); and **(3)** "people to be dispossessed": "Behold, therefore I will deliver thee to the men of the east for a possession, and they shall set their palaces in thee, and make their dwellings in thee: they shall eat thy fruit, and they shall drink thy milk" (Eze 25:4). See: TWOT—920e; BDB—440c, 559a.

4182. מוֹרֶשֶׁת גַּת {1x} **Môwresheth Gath**, *mo-reh'-sheth gath;* from 3423 and 1661; *possession of Gath; Moresheth-Gath,* a place in Pal.:—Moresheth-gath {1x}. See: BDB—440c, 559a.

4183. מוֹרַשְׁתִּי {2x} **Môwrashtîy**, *mo-rash-tee';* patrial from 4182; a *Morashtite* or inhab. of Moresheth-Gath:—Morashthite {2x}. See: BDB—440d, 559a, 601c.

4184. מוּשׁ {3x} **mûwsh**, *moosh;* a prim. root; to *touch:*—feel {2x}, handle {1x}. See: TWOT—1168; BDB—559b.

4185. מוּשׁ {21x} **mûwsh**, *moosh;* a prim. root [perh. rather the same as 4184 through the idea of *receding* by *contact*]; to *withdraw* (both lit. and fig., whether intr. or tran.):—depart {12x}, remove {6x}, take away {1x}, gone back {1x}, cease {1x}. See: TWOT—1167; BDB—559a, 568c.

4186. מוֹשָׁב {44x} **môwshâb,** *mo-shawb';* or

מֹשָׁב **môshâb,** *mo-shawb';* from 3427; a *seat;* fig. a *site;* abstr. a *session;* by extens. an *abode* (the place or the time); by impl. *population:*—habitation {12x}, dwellings {8x}, seat {7x}, dwelling {4x}, dwellingplace {3x}, dwell {3x}, places {2x}, sitting {2x}, assembly {1x}, situation {1x}, sojourning {1x}. See: TWOT—922c; BDB—444b, 559b.

4187. מוּשִׁי {8x} **Mûwshîy,** *moo-shee';* or

מֻשִׁי **Mushshîy,** *mush-shee';* from 4184; *sensitive; Mushi,* a Levite:—Mushi {8x}. See: BDB—559b, 603d.

4188. מוּשִׁי {2x} **Mûwshîy,** *moo-shee';* patron. from 4187; a *Mushite* (collect.) or desc. of Mushi:—Mushites {2x}. See: BDB—559b.

4189. מוֹשְׁכָה {1x} **môwshᵉkâh,** *mo-shek-aw';* act. part. fem. of 4900; something *drawing,* i.e. (fig.) a *cord:*—bands {1x}. See: TWOT—1257b; BDB—604d.

4190. מוֹשָׁעָה {1x} **môwshâᵃâh,** *mo-shaw-aw';* from 3467; *deliverance:*—salvation {1x}. See: TWOT—929d; BDB—448a, 559b.

4191. מוּת {835x} **mûwth,** *mooth;* a prim. root; to *die* (lit. or fig.); caus. to *kill:*—die {424x}, dead {130x}, slay {100x}, death {83x}, surely {50x}, kill {31x}, dead man {3x}, dead body {2x}, in no wise {2x}, misc. {10x} = X at all, X crying, destroy (-er), necro [-mancer], X must needs, X very suddenly.

Muwth means "to die, kill." **(1)** Essentially, *muwth* means "to lose one's life." **(1a)** The word is used of physical "death," with reference to both man and beast. **(1a1)** Gen 5:5 records that Adam lived "nine hundred and thirty years: and he died." **(1a2)** Jacob explains to Esau that, were his livestock to be driven too hard (fast), the young among them would "die" (Gen 33:13). **(1b)** At one point, this verb is also used to refer to the stump of a plant (Job 14:8). **(1c)** Occasionally, *muwth* is used figuratively of land (Gen 47:19) or wisdom (Job 12:2). **(1d)** Then, too, there is the unique hyperbolic expression that Nabal's heart had "died" within him, indicating that he was overcome with great fear (1 Sa 25:37). **(2)** In an intensive stem, this root is used of the last act inflicted upon one who is already near death. Thus Abimelech, his head having been cracked by a millstone, asked his armor-bearer to "kill" him (Judg 9:54). **(3)** In the usual causative stem, this verb can mean "to cause to die" or "to kill"; God is the one who "puts to death" and gives life (Deut 32:39). **(4)** Usually, both the subject and object of this usage are personal, although

there are exceptions—as when the Philistines personified the ark of the covenant, urging its removal so it would not "kill" them (1 Sa 5:11). **(5)** Death in this sense may also be inflicted by animals (Ex 21:29). **(6)** This word describes "putting to death" in the broadest sense, including war and judicial sentences of execution (Josh 10:26). **(7)** God is clearly the ultimate Ruler of life and death (cf. Deut 32:39). **(7a)** This idea is especially clear in the Creation account, in which God tells man that he will surely die if he eats of the forbidden fruit (Gen 2:17—the first occurrence of the verb). **(7b)** Apparently there was no death before this time. When the serpent questioned Eve, she associated disobedience with death (Gen 3:3). The serpent repeated God's words, but negated them (Gen 3:4). **(7c)** When Adam and Eve ate of the fruit, both spiritual and physical death came upon Adam and Eve and their descendants (cf. Rom 5:12). **(7d)** They experienced spiritual death immediately, resulting in their shame and their attempt to cover their nakedness (Gen 3:7). **(7e)** Sin and/or the presence of spiritual death required a covering, but man's provision was inadequate; so God made a perfect covering in the form of a promised redeemer (Gen 3:15) and a typological covering of animal skins (Gen 3:21). See: TWOT—1169; BDB—559b, 607a, 1099d.

4192. מוּת {2x} **Mûwth** (Ps 48:14), *mooth;* or

מוּת לַבֵּן **Mûwth lab-bên,** *mooth lab-bane';* from 4191 and 1121 with the prep. and art. interposed; *"To die for the son",* prob. the title of a popular song:—death {1x}, Muthlabben {1x}. See: BDB—527c, 761b, 761c, 763a.

4193. מוֹת {1x} **môwth** (Aram.), *mohth;* corresp. to 4194; *death:*—death {1x}. See: TWOT—2823; BDB—1099d.

4194. מָוֶת {160x} **mâveth,** *maw'-veth;* from 4191; *death* (nat. or violent); concr. the *dead,* their place or state (*hades*); fig. *pestilence, ruin:*—death {128x}, die {22x}, dead {8x}, deadly {1x}, slay {1x}.

Maveth means "death." **(1)** The word *maveth* occurs frequently as an antonym of *chayyim* (2416 - "life"): "I call heaven and earth to record this day against you, that I have set before you life and death, blessing and cursing: therefore choose life, that both thou and thy seed may live" (Deut 30:19). **(2)** In the poetic language, *maveth* is used more often than in the historical books: Job-Proverbs (about 60 times), Joshua-Esther (about 40 times); but in the major prophets only about 25 times. **(3)** "Death" is the natural end of human life on this earth; it is an aspect of God's judgment on

man: "But of the tree of the knowledge of good and evil, thou shalt not eat of it: for in the day that thou eatest thereof thou shalt surely die" (Gen 2:17). **(3a)** Hence all men die: "If these men die the common death of all men . . . then the LORD hath not sent me" (Num 16:29). **(3b)** The Old Testament uses "death" in phrases such as "the day of death" (Gen 27:2) and "the year of death" (Is 6:1), or to mark an event as occurring before (Gen 27:7, 10) or after (Gen 26:18) someone's passing away.

(4) "Death" may also come upon someone in a violent manner, as an execution of justice: "And if a man have committed a sin worthy of death and he be to be put to death, and thou hang him on a tree: his body shall not remain all night upon the tree" (Deut 21:22–23). **(4a)** Saul declared David to be a "son of death" because he intended to have David killed (1 Sa 20:31; cf. Prov 16:14). **(4b)** In one of his experiences, David composed a psalm expressing how close an encounter he had had with death: "When the waves of death compassed me, the floods of ungodly men made me afraid; the sorrows of hell compassed me about; the snares of death prevented me" (2 Sa 22:5–6; cf. Ps 18:5–6). **(5)** Isaiah predicted the Suffering Servant was to die a violent death: "And he made his grave with the wicked, and with the rich in his death; because he had done no violence, neither was any deceit in his mouth" (Is 53:9).

(6) Associated with the meaning of "death" is the meaning of "death by a plague." **(6a)** In a besieged city with unsanitary conditions, pestilence would quickly reduce the weakened population. **(6b)** Jeremiah alludes to this type of death as God's judgment on Egypt (43:11); note that "death" refers here to "death of famine and pestilence." **(6c)** Lamentations describes the situation of Jerusalem before its fall: "Abroad the sword bereaveth, at home there is as death" (Lam 1:20; cf. also Jer 21:8–9).

(7) The word *maveth* denotes the "realm of the dead" or *she'ol*. This place of death has gates (Ps 9:13; 107:18) and chambers (Prov 7:27); the path of the wicked leads to this abode (Prov 5:5). **(8)** Isaiah expected "death" to be ended when the Lord's full kingship would be established: "He will swallow up death in victory; and the Lord GOD will wipe away tears from off all faces; and the rebuke of his people shall he take away from off all the earth: for the LORD hath spoken it" (Is 25:8). See: TWOT—1169a; BDB—560c.

מוּת לָבֵן **Mûwth lab-bên.** See 4192.

4195. מוֹתָר {3x} **môwthâr**, *mo-thar'*; from 3498; lit. *gain*; fig. *superiority:*—plenteousness {1x}, preeminence {1x}, profit {1x}. See: TWOT—936g; BDB—560d.

4196. מִזְבֵּחַ {402x} **mizbêach**, *miz-bay'-akh;* from 2076; an *altar:*—altar {402x}.

Mizbeach means "altar." **(1)** This frequent use is obviously another direct evidence of the centrality of the sacrificial system in Israel. **(2)** This word signifies a raised place where a sacrifice was made, as in Gen 8:20 (its first biblical appearance): "And Noah builded an altar unto the Lord; and took of every clean beast, and of every clean fowl, and offered burnt offerings on the altar." The first appearance of *mizbeach* is in Gen 8:20, where Noah built an "altar" after the Flood. **(3)** Countless "altars" are referred to as the story of Israel progresses on the pages of the Old Testament: that **(3a)** of Noah (Gen 8:20); **(3b)** of Abram at Sichem (Gen 12:7), **(3c)** at Beth-el (Gen 12:8), and **(3d)** at Moriah (Gen 22:9); **(3e)** of Isaac at Beersheba (Gen 26:25); **(3f)** of Jacob at Shechem (Gen 33:20); **(3g)** of Moses at Horeb (Ex 24:4), **(3h)** of Samuel at Ramah (1 Sa 7:17); **(3i)** of the temple in Jerusalem (1 Kin 6:20; 8:64); and **(3j)** of the two "altars" planned by Ezekiel for the restored temple (Eze 41:22; 43:13–17). **(4)** In later references, this word may refer to a table upon which incense was burned: "And thou shalt make an altar to burn incense upon: of shittim wood shalt thou make it" (Ex 30:1). **(5)** From the dawn of human history, offerings were made on a raised table of stone or ground (Gen 4:3).

(5) At first, Israel's altars were to be made of earth—i.e., they were fashioned of material that was strictly the work of God's hands. **(5a)** If the Jews were to hew stone for altars in the wilderness, they would have been compelled to use war weapons to do the work. (Notice that in Ex 20:25 the word for "tool" is *chereb,* "sword.") **(5b)** At Sinai, God directed Israel to fashion altars of valuable woods and metals. This taught them that true worship required man's best and that it was to conform exactly to God's directives; God, not man, initiated and controlled worship. **(6)** The altar that stood before the holy place (Ex 27:1–8) and the altar of incense within the holy place (Ex 30:1–10) had "horns." **(6a)** These horns had a vital function in some offerings (Lev 4:30; 16:18). **(6b)** For example, the sacrificial animal may have been bound to these horns in order to allow its blood to drain away completely (Ps 118:27). **(7)** *Mizbeach* is also used of pagan altars: "But ye shall destroy their altars, break their images, and cut down their groves" (Ex 34:13). **(8)** This noun is derived from the Hebrew verb *zabach* (2076), **(8a)** which literally means "to slaughter for food" or "to slaughter for sacrifice." **(8b)** Another Old Testament noun derived from *zabach* is *zebach* (162 times), which usually refers to a sacrifice that

establishes communion between God and those who eat the thing offered. See: TWOT—525b; BDB—560d.

4197. מֶזֶג {1x} **mezeg**, *meh'-zeg;* from an unused root mean. to *mingle* (water with wine); *tempered* wine:—liquor {1x}. See: TWOT—1170a; BDB—561a.

4198. מָזֶה {1x} **mâzeh**, *maw-zeh';* from an unused root mean. to *suck* out; *exhausted:*—burnt {1x}. See: TWOT—1171a; BDB—561a.

4199. מִזָּה {3x} **Mizzâh**, *miz-zaw';* prob. from an unused root mean. to *faint* with fear; *terror; Mizzah,* an Edomite:—Mizzah {3x}. See: BDB—561a.

4200. מֶזֶו {1x} **mezev**, *meh'-zev;* prob. from an unused root mean. to *gather* in; a *granary:*—garner {1x}. See: TWOT—534b; BDB—265a, 561a.

4201. מְזוּזָה {1x} **mᵉzûwzâh**, *mez-oo-zaw';* or

מְזֻזָה **mᵉzûzâh**, *mez-oo-zaw';* from the same as 2123; a *door-post* (as prominent):—(door, side) post {19x}. See: TWOT—535b; BDB—265b, 561a.

4202. מָזוֹן {2x} **mâzôwn**, *maw-zone';* from 2109; *food:*—meat {1x}, victual {1x}. See: TWOT—539a; BDB—266a, 561a.

4203. מָזוֹן {2x} **mâzôwn** (Aram.), *maw-zone';* corresp. to 4202:—meat {2x}. See: TWOT—2705a; BDB—1091b, 1099d.

4204. מָזוֹר {1x} **mâzôwr**, *maw-zore';* from 2114 in the sense of *turning aside* from truth; *treachery,* i.e. a *plot:*—wound {1x}. See: TWOT—1175a; BDB—561a, 561c.

4205. מָזוֹר {3x} **mâzôwr**, *maw-zore';* or

מָזֹר **mâzôr**, *maw-zore';* from 2115 in the sense of *binding* up; a *bandage,* i.e. remedy; hence, a *sore* (as needing a compress):—bound up {1x}, wound {2x}. See: TWOT—543c; BDB—267a, 561a.

מְזֻזָה **mᵉzûzâh**. See 4201.

4206. מָזִיחַ {3x} **mâzîyach**, *maw-zee'-akh;* or

מֵזַח **mêzach**, *may-zakh';* from 2118; a *belt* (as movable):—girdle {1x}, strength {2x}. See: TWOT—1172a; BDB—561a, 561b.

4207. מַזְלֵג {7x} **mazlêg**, *maz-layg';* or (fem.)

מִזְלָגָה **mizlâgâh**, *miz-law-gaw';* from an unused root mean. to *draw* up; a *fork:*—fleshhook {7x}. See: TWOT—552a; BDB—272c, 561b.

4208. מַזָּלָה {1x} **mazzâlâh**, *maz-zaw-law';* appar. from 5140 in the sense of *raining;* a *constellation,* i.e. Zodiacal sign (perh.

as affecting the weather):—planet {1x}. See: TWOT—1173; BDB—561b. comp. 4216.

4209. מְזִמָּה {19x} **mᵉzimmâh**, *mez-im-maw';* from 2161; a *plan,* usually evil (*machination*), sometimes good (*sagacity*):—discretion {4x}, wicked device {3x}, device {3x}, thought {3x}, intents {1x}, mischievous device {1x}, wickedly {1x}, witty inventions {1x}, lewdness {1x}, mischievous {1x}.

Mezimmah means "purpose; evil device; evil thoughts; discretion." **(1)** This noun occurs 19 times. **(2)** The word means "purpose" in Job 42:2 and is translated "thought": I know that thou canst do every thing, and that no thought can be withholden from thee." This stresses that what ever God thinks to be, is purposed and will happen. **(3)** *Mezimmah* refers to "evil device (lewdness)" in Jer 11:15: "What hath my beloved to do in mine house, seeing she hath wrought lewdness with many." **(4)** In Job 21:27 the word is used to mean "evil thoughts," and **(5)** in Prov 1:4 the word is used for "discretion." Syn: 2154, 2161. See: TWOT—556c; BDB—273c, 561b.

4210. מִזְמוֹר {57x} **mizmôwr**, *miz-more';* from 2167; prop. instrumental *music;* by impl. a *poem* set to notes:—psalm {57x}. See: TWOT—558c; BDB—274c, 561b.

4211. מַזְמֵרָה {4x} **mazmêrâh**, *maz-may-raw';* from 2168; a *pruning-knife:*—pruning-hooks {4x}. See: TWOT—559c; BDB—275a, 561c.

4212. מְזַמְּרָה {5x} **mᵉzammᵉrâh**, *mez-am-mer-aw';* from 2168; a *tweezer* (only in the plur.):—snuffers {5x}. See: TWOT—559d; BDB—275a, 561c.

4213. מִזְעָר {4x} **mizʻâr**, *miz-awr';* from the same as 2191; *fewness;* by impl. as superl. *diminutiveness:*—few {3x}, X very {1x}. See: TWOT—571b; BDB—277d, 561c.

מָזֹר **mâzôr**. See 4205.

4214. מִזְרֶה {2x} **mizreh**, *miz-reh';* from 2219; a winnowing *shovel* (as scattering the chaff):—fan {2x}. See: TWOT—579a; BDB—280a, 561d.

4215. מְזָרֶה {1x} **mᵉzâreh**, *mez-aw-reh';* appar. from 2219; prop. a *scatterer,* i.e. the north *wind* (as dispersing clouds; only in plur.):—out of the north {1x}. See: TWOT—579; BDB—280a.

4216. מַזָּרָה {1x} **Mazzârâh**, *maz-zaw-raw';* appar. from 5144 in the sense of *distinction;* some noted *constellation* (only in the plur.), perh. collect. the *zodiac:*—Mazzaroth {1x}. See: TWOT—1176; BDB—561d. comp. 4208.

4217. מִזְרָח {74x} **mizrâch**, *miz-rawkh';* from 2224; *sunrise,* i.e. the *east:*—east {30x}, eastward {20x}, sunrising + 8121 {9x}, rising {8x}, east side {5x}, east end {1x}, sunrising {1x}. See: TWOT—580c; BDB—280d, 561d.

4218. מִזְרָע {1x} **mizrâ'**, *miz-raw';* from 2232; a planted *field:*—thing sown {1x}. See: TWOT—582f; BDB—283c, 561d.

4219. מִזְרָק {32x} **mîzrâq**, *miz-rawk';* from 2236; a *bowl* (as if for sprinkling):—basons {11x}, bowl {21x}. See: TWOT—585a; BDB—284c, 561d.

4220. מֵחַ {2x} **mêach**, *may'-akh;* from 4229 in the sense of *greasing; fat;* fig. *rich:*—fatling {1x}, fat one {1x}. See: TWOT—1181a; BDB—561d, 562d, 568a.

4221. מֹחַ {1x} **môach**, *mo'-akh;* from the same as 4220; *fat,* i.e. marrow:—marrow {1x}. See: TWOT—1181b; BDB—561d, 562d.

4222. מָחָא {3x} **mâchâ'**, *maw-khaw';* a prim. root; to *rub* or *strike* the hands together (in exultation):—clap {3x}. See: TWOT—1177; BDB—561d.

4223. מְחָא {4x} **mᵉchâ'** (Aram.), *mekh-aw';* corresp. to 4222; to *strike* in pieces; also to *arrest;* spec. to *impale:*—hanged {1x}, smote {3x}, stay {1x}. See: TWOT—2824; BDB—1099d.

4224. מַחֲבֵא {2x} **machâbê'**, *makh-ab-ay';* or

מַחֲבֹא **machâbô'**, *makh-ab-o';* from 2244; a *refuge:*—hiding place {1x}, lurking place {1x}. See: TWOT—588a, 589a; BDB—285c, 561d.

4225. מַחְבֶּרֶת {8x} **machbereth**, *makh-beh'-reth;* from 2266; a *junction,* i.e. seam or sewed piece:—coupling {8x}. See: TWOT—598j; BDB—289c, 561d.

4226. מְחַבְּרָה {2x} **mᵉchabbᵉrâh**, *mekh-ab-ber-aw';* from 2266; a *joiner,* i.e. brace or cramp:—coupling {1x}, joining {1x}. See: TWOT—598k; BDB—289c.

4227. מַחֲבַת {5x} **machâbath**, *makh-ab-ath';* from the same as 2281; a *pan* for baking in:—pan {5x}. See: TWOT—600b; BDB—290a, 561d.

4228. מַחֲגֹרֶת {1x} **machâgôreth**, *makh-ag-o'-reth;* from 2296; a *girdle:*—girding {1x}. See: TWOT—604d; BDB—292b, 561d.

4229. מָחָה {36x} **mâchâh**, *maw-khaw';* a prim. root; prop. to *stroke* or *rub;* by impl. to *erase;* also to *smooth* (as if with oil), i.e. *grease* or make fat; also to *touch,* i.e. reach to:—(blot, put, etc) . . . out {17x}, destroy {6x}, wipe {4x}, blot {3x}, wipe away {2x}, abolished {1x}, marrow {1x}, reach {1x}, utterly {1x}. See:

TWOT—1178, 1179, 1181c; BDB—562a, 562b, 562c, 562d, 1099d.

4230. מְחוּגָה {1x} **mᵉchûwgâh**, *mekh-oo-gaw';* from 2328; an instrument for marking a circle, i.e. *compasses:*—compass {1x}. See: TWOT—615b; BDB—295b, 562c.

4231. מָחוֹז {1x} **mâchôwz**, *maw-khoze';* from an unused root mean. to *enclose;* a *harbor* (as *shut* in by the shore):—haven {1x}. See: TWOT—1180; BDB—562c.

4232. מְחוּיָאֵל {2x} **Mᵉchûwyâ'êl**, *mekh-oo-yaw-ale';* or

מְחִיָּאֵל **Mᵉchîyyâ'êl**, *mekh-ee-yaw-ale';* from 4229 and 410; *smitten of God; Mechujael* or *Mechijael,* an antediluvian patriarch:—Mehujael {2x}. See: BDB—562c, 563a.

4233. מַחֲוִים {1x} **Machăvîym**, *makh-av-eem';* appar. a patrial, but from an unknown place (in the plur. only for a sing.); a *Machavite* or inhab. of some place named Machaveh:—Mahavite {1x}. See: BDB—296a, 562d.

4234. מָחוֹל {6x} **mâchôwl**, *maw-khole';* from 2342; a (round) *dance:*—dance {5x}, dancing {1x}. See: TWOT—623g; BDB—298b, 562d.

4235. מָחוֹל {1x} **Mâchôwl**, *maw-khole';* the same as 4234; *dancing; Machol,* an Isr.:—Mahol {1x}. See: BDB—562d.

מְחוֹלָה **mᵉchôwlâh**. See 65, 4246.

4236. מַחֲזֶה {4x} **machăzeh**, *makh-az-eh';* from 2372; a *vision:*—vision {4x}. See: TWOT—633f; BDB—303c, 562d.

4237. מֶחֱזָה {4x} **mechĕzâh**, *mekh-ez-aw';* from 2372; a *window:*—light {4x}. See: TWOT—633g; BDB—303d, 562d.

4238. מַחֲזִיאוֹת {2x} **Machăzîy'ôwth**, *makh-az-ee-oth';* fem. plur. from 2372; *visions; Machazioth,* an Isr.:—Mahazioth {2x}. See: BDB—303d, 562d.

4239. מְחִי {1x} **mᵉchîy**, *mekh-ee';* from 4229; a *stroke,* i.e. *battering-ram:*—engines {1x}. See: TWOT—1179a; BDB—562c, 562d.

4240. מְחִידָא {2x} **Mᵉchîydâ'**, *mekh-ee-daw';* from 2330; *junction; Mechida,* one of the Nethinim:—Mehida {2x}. See: BDB—563a.

4241. מִחְיָה {8x} **michyâh**, *mikh-yaw';* from 2421; *preservation of life;* hence, *sustenance;* also the live flesh, i.e. the *quick:*—reviving {2x}, quick {2x}, preserve life {1x},

sustenance {1x}, victuals {1x}, recover {1x}. See: TWOT—644h; BDB—313c, 563a.

מְחִיָּאֵל Mᵉchîyyâ'êl. See 4232.

4242. מְחִיר {15x} mᵉchîyr, mekh-eer'; from an unused root mean. to buy; price, payment, wages:—gain {1x}, hire {1x}, price {11x}, sold {1x}, worth {1x}. See: TWOT—1185c; BDB—564b.

4243. מְחִיר {1x} Mᵉchîyr, mekh-eer'; the same as 4242; price; Mechir, an Isr.:— Mehir {1x}. See: BDB—564b.

4244. מַחְלָה {5x} Machlâh, makh-law'; from 2470; sickness; Machlah, the name appar. of two Israelitesses:—Mahlah {4x}, Mahalah {1x}. See: BDB—563a.

4245. מַחֲלֶה {6x} machăleh, makh-al-eh'; or (fem.)

מַחֲלָה machălâh, makh-al-aw'; from 2470; sickness:—disease {2x}, infirmity {1x}, sickness {3x}. See: TWOT—655b, 655c; BDB—318b, 563a.

4246. מְחֹלָה {8x} mᵉchôwlâh, mekh-o-law'; fem. of 4284; a dance:—company {1x}, dances {5x}, dancing) {2x}. See: TWOT—623h; BDB—298b, 562d, 563a, 563b.

4247. מְחִלָּה {1x} mᵉchillâ, mekh-il-law'; from 2490; a cavern (as if excavated):—cave {1x}. See: TWOT—660f; BDB—320a, 563a.

4248. מַחְלוֹן {4x} Machlown, makh-lone'; from 2470; sick; Machlon, an Isr.:—Mahlon {4x}. See: TWOT—660f; BDB—563a.

4249. מַחְלִי {12x} Machlîy, makh-lee'; from 2470; sick; Machli, the name of two Isr.:—Mahli {11x}, Mahali {1x}. See: BDB—563a.

4250. מַחְלִי {2x} Machlîy, makh-lee'; patron. from 4249; a Machlite or (collect.) desc. of Machli:—Mahlites {2x}. See: BDB—563a.

4251. מַחְלִי {1x} machlûy, makh-loo'-ee; from 2470; a disease:—disease {1x}. See: TWOT—655d; BDB—318c, 563a.

4252. מַחֲלָף {1x} machălâph, makh-al-awf'; from 2498; a (sacrificial) knife (as gliding through the flesh):—knives {1x}. See: TWOT—666d; BDB—322c, 563b.

4253. מַחְלָפָה {2x} machlâphâh, makh-law-faw'; from 2498; a ringlet of hair (as gliding over each other):—lock {2x}. See: TWOT—666e; BDB—322c, 563b.

4254. מַחֲלָצָה {2x} machălâtsâh, makh-al-aw-tsaw'; from 2502; a mantle (as easily drawn off):—changeable suit of apparel {1x}, change of raiment {1x}. See: TWOT—667b; BDB—323a, 563b.

4255. מַחְלְקָה {1x} machlᵉqâh (Aram.), makh-lek-aw'; corresp. to 4256; a section (of the Levites):—courses {1x}. See: TWOT—2732b; BDB—1093b, 1099d.

4256. מַחֲלֹקֶת {43x} machălôqeth, makh-al-o'-keth; from 2505; a section (of Levites, people or soldiers):—company {1x}, course {33x}, division {8x}, portion {1x}. See: TWOT—669d; BDB—324d, 563b, 1093b. See also 5555.

4257. מַחֲלַת {2x} machălath, makh-al-ath'; from 2470; sickness; Machalath, prob. the title (initial word) of a popular song:—Mahalath {2x}. See: TWOT—623h or 655c; BDB—318d, 563b.

4258. מַחֲלַת {2x} Machălath, makh-al-ath'; the same as 4257; sickness; Machalath, the name of an Ishmaelitess and of an Israelitess:—Mahalath {2x}. See: BDB—563b.

4259. מְחֹלָתִי {2x} Mᵉchôlâthîy, mekh-o-law-thee'; patrial from 65; a Mecholathite or inhab. of Abel-Mecholah:—Mecholathite {2x}. See: BDB—563b.

4260. מַחֲמָאָה {1x} machămâ'âh, makh-am-aw-aw'; a denom. from 2529; something buttery (i.e. unctuous and pleasant), as (fig.) flattery:—✕ than butter {1x}. See: TWOT—1182; BDB—563b.

4261. מַחְמָד {13x} machmâd, makh-mawd'; from 2530; delightful; hence, a delight, i.e. object of affection or desire:—beloved {1x}, desire {3x}, goodly {1x}, lovely {1x}, pleasant {4x}, pleasant thing {3x}. See: TWOT—673d, 673e; BDB—326d, 563b.

4262. מַחְמֻד {2x} machmûd, makh-mood'; or

מַחְמוּד machmûwd, makh-mood'; from 2530; desired; hence, a valuable:—pleasant thing {2x}. See: TWOT—673; BDB—327a, 563b.

4263. מַחְמָל {1x} machmâl, makh-mawl'; from 2550; prop. sympathy; (by paronomasia with 4261) delight:—that which . . . pitieth {1x}. See: TWOT—676b; BDB—328c, 563c.

4264. מַחֲנֶה {216x} machăneh, makh-an-eh'; from 2583; an encampment (of travellers or troops); hence, an army, whether lit. (of soldiers) or fig. (of dancers, angels, cattle, locusts, stars; or even the sacred courts):—camp {136x}, host {61x}, company {6x}, tents {5x}, armies {4x}, bands {2x}, battle {1x}, drove {1x}.

Machaneh means "camp; encampment; host."
(1) Those who travel were called **(1a)** "camp-ers," or a "company" as in Gen 32:8: Naaman stood before Elisha "with all his company" (2 Kin 5:15). **(1b)** Travelers, tradesmen, and sol-diers spent much time on the road. They all set up "camp" for the night. Jacob "encamped" by the Jabbok with his retinue (Gen 32:10). **(2)** The name Mahanaim (Gen 32:2, "camps") owes its origin to Jacob's experience with the angels. **(2a)** He called the place Mahanaim in order to signify that it was God's "camp" (Gen 32:2), **(2b)** as he had spent the night "in the camp" (Gen 32:21) and wrestled with God (Gen 32:24). **(3)** Soldiers also established "camps" by the city to be conquered (Eze 4:2) **(4)** Usage of *machaneh* varies according to context. **(4a)** It signifies a nation set over against another (Ex 14:20). **(4b)** The word refers to a division con-cerning the Israelites; each of the tribes had a special "encampment" in relation to the tent of meeting (Num 1:52). **(4c)** The word "camp" is used to describe the whole people of Israel: "And it came to pass on the third day in the morning, that there were thunders and light-nings, and a thick cloud upon the mount, and the voice of the trumpet exceeding loud; so that all the people that was in the camp trembled" (Ex 19:16).
(5) God was present in the "camp" of Israel: "For the LORD thy God walketh in the midst of thy camp, to deliver thee, and to give up thine enemies before thee; therefore shall thy camp be holy: that he see no unclean thing in thee, and turn away from thee" (Deut 23:14). **(6)** As a result, sin could not be tolerated within the camp, and the sinner might have to be stoned outside the camp (Num 15:35). Syn.: 168, 4908. See: TWOT—690c; BDB—334a, 563c.

4265. מַחֲנֵה־דָן {1x} **Machănêh-Dân**, *makh-an-ay'-dawn;* from 4264 and 1835; *camp of Dan; Machaneh-Dan,* a place in Pal.:—Mahaneh-dan {1x}. See: BDB—334b, 563c.

4266. מַחֲנַיִם {3x} **Machănayim**, *makh-an-ah'-yim;* dual of 4264; *double camp; Machanajim,* a place in Pal.:—Mahanaim {13x}. See: BDB—334b, 563c.

4267. מַחֲנַק {1x} **machănaq**, *makh-an-ak';* from 2614; *choking:*—strangling {1x}. See: TWOT—697a; BDB—338b, 563c.

4268. מַחְסֶה {20x} **machăçeh**, *makh-as-eh';* or

מַחְסֶה **machçeh**, *makh-seh';* from 2620; a *shelter* (lit. or fig.):—hope {2x}, (place of) refuge {15x}, shelter {2x}, trust {1x}. See: TWOT—700b; BDB—340b, 563c.

4269. מַחְסוֹם {1x} **machçôwm**, *makh-sohm';* from 2629; a *muzzle:*—bridle {1x}. See: TWOT—702a; BDB—340d, 563c.

4270. מַחְסוֹר {13x} **machçôwr**, *makh-sore';* or

מַחְסֹר **machçôr**, *makh-sore';* from 2637; *deficiency;* hence, *impoverish-ment:*—lack {1x}, need {1x}, penury {1x}, poor {1x}, poverty {1x}, want {8x}. See: TWOT—705e; BDB—341d, 563c.

4271. מַחְסֵיָה {2x} **Machçêyâh**, *makh-say-yaw';* from 4268 and 3050; *ref-uge of* (i.e. *in*) *Jah; Machsejah,* an Isr.:—Maaseiah {2x}. See: BDB—340c, 563c.

4272. מָחַץ {14x} **mâchats**, *maw-khats';* a prim. root; to *dash* asunder; by impl. to *crush, smash* or violently *plunge;* fig. to *subdue* or *destroy:*—dipped {1x}, pierce {2x}, pierce through {1x}, smite (through) {2x}, strike through {1x}, wound {7x}. See: TWOT—1183; BDB—563c.

4273. מַחַץ {1x} **machats**, *makh'-ats;* from 4272; a *contusion:*—stroke {1x}. See: TWOT—1183a; BDB—563d.

4274. מַחְצֵב {3x} **machtsêb**, *makh-tsabe';* from 2672; prop. a *hewing;* concr. a *quarry:*—hewed {1x}, hewn {1x}. See: TWOT—718a; BDB—345b, 563d.

4275. מֶחֱצָה {2x} **mechĕtsâh**, *mekh-ets-aw';* from 2673; a *halving:*—half {2x}. See: TWOT—719d; BDB—345d, 563d.

4276. מַחֲצִית {17x} **machătsîyth**, *makh-ats-eeth';* from 2673; a *halving* or the *middle:*—half {15x}, much {1x}, midday + 3117 {1x}. See: TWOT—719e; BDB—345d, 563d.

4277. מָחַק {1x} **mâchaq**, *maw-khak';* a prim. root; to *crush:*—smote off {1x}. See: TWOT—1184; BDB—563d.

4278. מֶחְקָר {1x} **mechqâr**, *mekh-kawr';* from 2713; prop. *scrutinized,* i.e. (by impl.) a *recess:*—deep places {1x}. See: TWOT—729b; BDB—350d, 563d.

4279. מָחָר {52x} **mâchar**, *maw-khar';* prob. from 309; prop. *deferred,* i.e. the *morrow;* usually (adv.) *tomorrow;* indef. *here-after:*—time to come {8x}, tomorrow {44x}.

I. *Machar,* as a noun, means "tomorrow." **(1)** The word means the day following the present day: "Tomorrow is the rest of the holy sabbath unto the LORD: bake that which ye will bake today" (Ex 16:23). **(2)** *Machar* also occurs as a noun in Prov 27:1: "Boast not thy-self of tomorrow; for thou knowest not what a day may bring forth." **II.** *Machar,* as an adverb, means "tomorrow." **(1)** The basic meaning of

this word is clearly set forth in Ex 19:10: "And the LORD said unto Moses, Go unto the people, and sanctify them today and tomorrow, and let them wash their clothes." (2) In a few passages the phrase *yom machar* is used: "So shall my righteousness answer for me in time to come [later]" (Gen 30:33). (3) In most passages *machar* by itself (used absolutely) means "tomorrow": "Behold, I go out from thee, and I will entreat the LORD that the swarms of flies may depart from Pharaoh, from his servants, and from his people, tomorrow" (Ex 8:29). (4) Interestingly, in Ex 8:10 the phrase *lemachar* (which appears 5 times in the Bible) is used: "And he said, Tomorrow." (5) Used with the preposition *ke,* the word means "tomorrow about this time": "Behold, tomorrow about this time I will cause it to rain a very grievous hail" (Ex 9:18). Syn.: 4283. See: TWOT—1185a; BDB—563d.

4280. מַחֲרָאָה {1x} **machărâ'âh,** *makh-ar-aw-aw';* from the same as 2716; a *sink:*—draught house {1x}. See: TWOT—730b; BDB—351a, 564c.

4281. מַחֲרֵשָׁה {1x} **machărêshâh,** *makh-ar-ay-shaw';* from 2790; prob. a *pick*-axe:—mattock {1x}. See: TWOT—760d; BDB—361a, 564c.

4282. מַחֲרֵשָׁה {1x} **machăresheth,** *makh-ar-eh'-sheth;* from 2790; prob. a *hoe:*—share {1x}. See: TWOT—760d; BDB—361a, 564c.

4283. מָחֳרָת {32x} **machărâth,** *makh-ar-awth';* or

מָחֳרָתָם **machărâthâm** (1 Sa 30:17), *makh-ar-aw-thawm';* fem. from the same as 4279; the *morrow* or (adv.) *tomorrow:*—morrow {29x}, next day {2x}, next {1x}. *Macharath,* as an adverb, means "the next day." (1) Closely related to the noun *machar* (4279) is this adverb, which occurs about 32 times and in all periods of biblical Hebrew. (2) About 28 times *macharat* is joined to the preposition *min* to mean "on the next day." This is its form and meaning in its first biblical appearance: "And it came to pass on the morrow . . ." (Gen 19:34). (3) In 3 passages this adverb is preceded by the preposition *le,* but the meaning is the same: "And David smote them from the twilight even unto the evening of the next day" (1 Sa 30:17). (4) In Num 11:32 *macharath* appears after *yom,* "day," and is preceded by the definite article: "And the people stood up all that day, and all that night, and all the next day, and they gathered the quails." (5) First Chr 29:21 displays yet another construction, with the same meaning: "On the morrow after that day. . . ." Syn.: 4279. See: TWOT—1185b; BDB—564a, 564c.

4284. מַחֲשָׁבָה {56x} **machăshâbâh,** *makh-ash-aw-baw';* or

מַחֲשֶׁבֶת **machăshebeth,** *makh-ash-eh'-beth;* from 2803; a *contrivance,* i.e. (concr.) a *texture, machine,* or (abstr.) *intention, plan* (whether bad, a *plot;* or good, *advice*):—thought {28x}, device {12x}, purpose {6x}, work {3x}, imaginations {3x}, cunning {1x}, devised {1x}, invented {1x}, means {1x}. See: TWOT—767d; BDB—364b, 564c.

4285. מַחְשָׁךְ {7x} **machshâk,** *makh-shawk';* from 2821; *darkness;* concr. a *dark place:*—darkness {4x}, dark places {2x}, dark {1x}. See: TWOT—769d; BDB—365b, 564c.

4286. מַחְשׂף {1x} **machsôph,** *makh-sofe';* from 2834; a *peeling:*—made appear {1x}. See: TWOT—766b; BDB—362d, 564c.

4287. מָחַת {3x} **Machath,** *makh'-ath;* prob. from 4229; *erasure; Machath,* the name of two Isr.:—Mahath {3x}. See: BDB—367b, 564c.

4288. מְחִתָּה {11x} **mᵉchittâh,** *mekh-it-taw';* from 2846; prop. a *dissolution;* concr. a *ruin,* or (abstr.) *consternation:*—destruction {7x}, terror {2x}, ruin {1x}, dismaying {1x}. Syn.: 3238, 3772, 4135. See: TWOT—784g; BDB—369d, 564c.

4289. מַחְתָּה {22x} **machtâh,** *makh-taw';* the same as 4288 in the sense of *removal;* a *pan* for live coals:—censer {15x}, firepans {2x}, snuffdishes {3x}. See: TWOT—777a; BDB—367b, 564c.

4290. מַחְתֶּרֶת {2x} **machtereth,** *makh-teh'-reth;* from 2864; a *burglary;* fig. *unexpected examination:*—breaking up {1x}, secret search {1x}. See: TWOT—783a; BDB—369a, 564c.

4291. מְטָא {8x} **mᵉtâ'** (Aram.), *met-aw';* or

מְטָה **mᵉtâh** (Aram.) *met-aw';* appar. corresp. to 4672 in the intr. sense of being found *present;* to *arrive, extend* or *happen:*—come {5x}, reach {3x}. See: TWOT—783a; BDB—1100a.

4292. מַטְאֲטֵא {1x} **mat'ătê',** *mat-at-ay';* appar. a denom. from 2916; a *broom* (as removing *dirt* [comp. Engl. "to dust", i.e. remove dust]):—besom {1x}. See: TWOT—785a; BDB—370a, 564c,

4293. מַטְבֵּחַ {1x} **matbêach,** *mat-bay'-akh;* from 2873; *slaughter:*—slaughter {1x}. See: TWOT—786e; BDB—371a, 564c.

4294. מַטֶּה {251x} **matteh,** *mat-teh';* or (fem.)

מַטָּה **mattâh,** *mat-taw';* from 5186; a *branch* (as *extending*); fig. a *tribe;*

also a *rod,* whether for chastising (fig. *correction*), ruling (a *sceptre*), throwing (a *lance*), or walking (a *staff;* fig. a *support* of life, e.g. bread):—tribe {182x}, rod {52x}, staff {15x}, staves {1x}, tribe + 4294 {1x}.

Mattah means "rod; staff; tribe." **(1)** In Gen 38:18 the word refers to a shepherd's "staff": "And he said, What pledge shall I give thee? And she said, Thy signet, and thy bracelets, and thy staff that is in thine hand." **(2)** The word is used to refer to a number of kinds of "rods": **(2a)** A "rod" which symbolizes spiritual power, such as Moses' rod (Ex 4:2), **(2b)** Aaron's rod (Ex 7:9), **(2c)** the sorcerers' rods (Ex 7:12), and **(2d)** rods symbolizing authority (Num 17:7). **(3)** This noun is often used elliptically instead of "the rod of the tribe of"; the word signifies "tribe" (cf. Ex 31:2). **(4)** *Mattah* is also used in the phrase "the staff of bread,": "*And* when I have broken the staff of your bread, ten women shall bake your bread in one oven, and they shall deliver *you* your bread again by weight: and ye shall eat, and not be satisfied" (Lev 26:26). Syn.: 7626. See: TWOT—1352b; BDB—564c, 641c.

4295. מַטָּה {19x} **maṭṭâh**, *mat'-taw;* from 5786 with directive enclitic appended; *downward, below* or *beneath;* often adv. with or without prefixes:—beneath {7x}, downward {5x}, underneath {2x}, very {1x}, low {1x}, under {1x}, down {1x}, less {1x}.

Mattah, as an adverb, means "downwards; beneath." This word occurs 19 times. **(1)** It means "beneath": "And the LORD shall make thee the head, and not the tail; and thou shalt be above only, and thou shalt not be beneath; if that thou hearken unto the commandments of the LORD thy God, which I command thee this day, to observe and to do them" (Deut 28:13); **(2)** "downward": "And the remnant that is escaped of the house of Judah shall yet again take root downward, and bear fruit upward" (2 Kin 19:30); and **(3)** "underneath": "And two other rings of gold thou shalt make, and shalt put them on the two sides of the ephod underneath, toward the forepart thereof, over against the other coupling thereof, above the curious girdle of the ephod" (Ex 28:27). See: TWOT—1352a; BDB—564c, 641d.

4296. מִטָּה {29x} **miṭṭâh**, *mit-taw';* from 5186; a *bed* (as *extended*) for sleeping or eating; by anal. a *sofa, litter* or *bier:*—bed {26x}, bedchamber + 2315 {2x}, bier {1x}.

Mittah occurs about 29 times and means something which is stretched out. **(1)** *Mittah* is used of a couch: "Behold his bed, which *is* Solomon's; threescore valiant men are about it, of the valiant of Israel" (Song 3:7); **(2)** of a metal framework: "Where were white, green,

and blue, hangings, fastened with cords of fine linen and purple to silver rings and pillars of marble: the beds (*mittah*) were of gold and silver, upon a pavement of red, and blue, and white, and black, marble" (Est 1:6); and of **(3)** a room, a bedchamber: "But Jehosheba, the daughter of king Joram, sister of Ahaziah, took Joash the son of Ahaziah, and stole him from among the king's sons which were slain; and they hid him, *even* him and his nurse, in the bedchamber from Athaliah, so that he was not slain" (2 Kin 11:2). See: TWOT—1352c; BDB—564c, 641d.

4297. מֻטֶּה {1x} **mutteh**, *moot-teh';* from 5186; a *stretching,* i.e. *distortion* (fig. *iniquity*):—perverseness {1x}. See: TWOT—1352e; BDB—642a.

4298. מֻטָּה {1x} **muṭṭâh**, *moot-taw';* from 5186; *expansion:*—stretching out {1x}.

Muttot [plural] occurs once and refers to the "stretching out" of wings: "And he shall pass through Judah; he shall overflow and go over, he shall reach even to the neck; and the stretching out of his wings shall fill the breadth of thy land, O Immanuel" (Is 8:8). See: TWOT—1352d; BDB—564c, 642a.

4299. מַטְוֶה {1x} **matveh**, *mat-veh';* from 2901; something *spun:*—spun {1x}. See: TWOT—794a; BDB—376a, 564c.

4300. מְטִיל {1x} **mᵉtîyl**, *met-eel';* from 2904 in the sense of *hammering* out; an iron *bar* (as *forged*):—bar {1x}. See: TWOT—1186a; BDB—564c.

4301. מַטְמוֹן {5x} **matmôwn**, *mat-mone';* or

מַטְמֹן **matmôn**, *mat-mone';* or

מַטְמֻן **matmûn**, *mat-moon';* from 2934; a *secret* storehouse; hence, a *secreted* valuable (buried); gen. *money:*—hidden riches {1x}, (hid) treasure (-s) {5x}. See: TWOT—811a; BDB—380c, 564c.

4302. מַטָּע {6x} **matṭâ'**, *mat-taw';* from 5193; something *planted,* i.e. the place (a *garden* or vineyard), or the thing (a *plant,* fig. of men); by impl. the act, *planting:*—plant {2x}, plantation {1x}, planting {3x}. See: TWOT—1354c; BDB—564c, 642d.

4303. מַטְעַם {8x} **mat'am**, *mat-am';* or (fem.)

מַטְעַמָּה **mat'ammâh**, *mat-am-maw';* from 2938; a *delicacy:*—dainty (meat) {2x}, savoury meat {6x}. See: TWOT—815b; BDB—381b, 564d.

4304. מִטְפַּחַת {1x} **miṭpachath**, *mit-pakh'-ath;* from 2946; a wide *cloak* (for a woman):—vail {1x}, wimples {1x}. See: TWOT—818d; BDB—381c, 564d.

4305. מָטַר {17x} **mâtar**, *maw-tar';* a prim. root; to *rain:*—(cause to) rain (upon) {17x}. See: TWOT—1187; BDB—565a.

4306. מָטָר {38x} **mâtâr**, *maw-tawr';* from 4305; *rain:*—rain {36x}, great {1x}, small {1x}. See: TWOT—1187a; BDB—564d.

4307. מַטָּרָא {16x} **mattârâ**, *mat-taw-raw';* or

מַטָּרָה **mattârâh**, *mat-taw-raw';* from 5201; a *jail* (as a *guard*-house); also an *aim* (as being closely *watched*):—mark {3x}, prison {13x}. See: TWOT—1356a; BDB—565a, 643c.

4308. מַטְרֵד {2x} **Maṭrêd**, *mat-rade;* from 2956; *propulsive; Matred,* an Edomitess:—Matred {2x}. See: TWOT—1356a; BDB—382b.

4309. מַטְרִי {1x} **Matrîy**, *mat-ree';* from 4305; *rainy; Matri,* an Isr.:—Matri {1x}. See: TWOT—1356a; BDB—565a.

4310. מִי {12x} **mîy**, *me;* an interrog. pron. of persons, as 4100 is of things, *who?* (occasionally, by a peculiar idiom, of things); also (indef.) *whoever;* often used in oblique constr. with pref. or suff.:—any (man) {1x}, X he {1x}, for {1x}, + O that! {1x}, unto you {1x}, what {1x}, which {1x}, who {1x}, whom {1x}, whose {1x}, whosoever {1x}, + would to God {1x}. See: TWOT—1189; BDB—566a, 1100d.

4311. מֵידְבָא {5x} **Mêydᵉbâ**, *may-deb-aw';* from 4325 and 1679; *water of quiet; Medeba,* a place in Pal.:—Medeba {5x}. See: BDB—567d.

4312. מֵידָד {1x} **Mêydâd**, *may-dawd';* from 3032 in the sense of *loving; affectionate; Medad,* an Isr.:—Medad {1x}. See: BDB—392a, 568a.

4313. מֵי הַיַּרְקוֹן {1x} **Mêy hay-Yarqôwn**, *may hah'-ee-yar-kone';* from 4325 and 3420 with the art. interposed; *water of the yellowness; Me-haj-Jarkon,* a place in Pal.:—Me-jarkon {1x}. See: BDB—438d.

4314. מֵי זָהָב {2x} **Mêy Zâhâb**, *may zaw-hawb';* from 4325 and 2091, *water of gold; Me-Zahab,* an Edomite:—Mezahab {2x}. See: BDB—566a.

4315. מֵיטָב {6x} **mêyṭâb**, *may-tawb';* from 3190; the *best* part:—best {6x}. See: TWOT—863a; BDB—406b, 568a.

4316. מִיכָא {5x} **Mîykâ**, *mee-kaw';* a var. for 4318; *Mica,* the name of two Isr.:—Micha {1x}, Micah {1x}. See: BDB—567d, 568a.

4317. מִיכָאֵל {13x} **Mîykâ'êl**, *me-kaw-ale';* from 4310 and (the pref. der. from) 3588 and 410; *who (is) like God?; Mikael,* the name of an archangel and of nine Isr.:—Michael {13x}. See: BDB—567c, 568a.

4318. מִיכָה {31x} **Mîykâh**, *mee-kaw';* an abbrev. of 4320; *Micah,* the name of seven Isr.:—Micah {26x}, Micaiah {1x}, Michah {4x}. See: BDB—567d, 568a.

4319. מִיכָהוּ {1x} **Mîykâhûw**, *me-kaw'-hoo;* a contr. for 4321; *Mikehu,* an Isr. prophet:—Micaiah {1x} (2 Chr 18:8). See: BDB—567c.

4320. מִיכָיָה {4x} **Mîykâyâh**, *me-kaw-yaw';* from 4310 and (the pref. der. from) 3588 and 3050; *who (is) like Jah?; Micajah,* the name of two Isr.:—Micah {1x}, Michaiah {3x}. See: BDB—567c, 568a. comp. 4318.

4321. מִיכָיְהוּ {20x} **Mîykâyᵉhûw**, *me-kaw-yeh-hoo';* or

מִכָיְהוּ **Mîkâyᵉhûw** (Jer 36:11), *me-kaw-yeh-hoo';* abbrev. for 4322; *Mikajah,* the name of three Isr.:—Michah {2x}, Micaiah {16x}, Michaiah {2x}. See: BDB—567c, 568a.

4322. מִיכָיָהוּ {2x} **Mîykâyâhûw**, *me-kaw-yaw'-hoo;* for 4320; *Mikajah,* the name of an Isr. and an Israelitess:—Michaiah {2x}. See: TWOT—863a; BDB—567c.

4323. מִיכָל {1x} **mîykâl**, *me-kawl'* from 3201; prop. a *container,* i.e. a *streamlet:*—brook {1x}. See: TWOT—1190; BDB—568a.

4324. מִיכָל {18x} **Mîykâl**, *me-kawl';* appar. the same as 4323; *rivulet; Mikal,* Saul's daughter:—Michal {18x}. See: BDB—568a.

4325. מַיִם {582x} **mayim**, *mah'-yim;* dual of a prim. noun (but used in a sing. sense); *water;* fig. *juice;* by euphem. *urine, semen:*—water {571x}, piss {2x}, waters + 6440 {2x}, watersprings {2x}, washing {1x}, watercourse + 4161 {1x}, waterflood {1x}, watering {1x}, variant {1x}.

Mayim means "water; flood." **(1)** First, "water" is one of the original basic substances. **(1a)** This is its significance in Gen 1:2 (the first occurrence of the word): "And the Spirit of God moved upon the face of the waters." **(1b)** In Gen 1:7 God separated the "waters" above and the "waters" below (cf. Ex 20:4) the expanse of the heavens. **(2)** Second, the word represents that which is in a well, "water" to be drunk (Gen 21:19). **(2a)** "Living water" is "water" that flows: "And Isaac's servants digged in the valley, and found there a well of springing [living] water" (Gen 26:19). **(2b)** "Water" of oppression or affliction is so designated because it is drunk in prison: "Put this fellow in the prison, and feed him with bread of affliction and with water of affliction, until I come in peace"

(1 Kin 22:27). **(2c)** Job 9:30 speaks of slush or snow water: "If I wash myself with snow water, and make my hands never so clean. . . ."

(3) Third, *mayim* can represent liquid in general: "For the LORD our God hath put us to silence, and given us water of gall to drink, because we have sinned against the LORD" (Jer 8:14). **(3a)** The phrase, *me raglayim* ("water of one's feet") is urine: "Hath my master sent me to thy master, and to thee, to speak these words? hath he not sent me to the men which sit on the wall, that they may eat their own dung, and drink their own piss [water of their feet] with you?" (2 Kin 18:27; cf. Is 25:10). **(4)** Fourth, in Israel's cultus [rituals] "water" was poured or sprinkled (no one was ever immersed into water), symbolizing purification. **(4a)** So Aaron and his sons were to be washed with "water" as a part of the rite consecrating them to the priesthood: "And Aaron and his sons thou shalt bring unto the door of the tabernacle of the congregation, and shalt wash them with water" (Ex 29:4). **(4b)** Parts of the sacrificial animal were to be ritually cleansed with "water" during the sacrifice: "But his inwards and his legs shall he wash in water" (Lev 1:9).

(4c) Israel's rites sometimes include consecrated "water": "And the priest shall take holy water in an earthen vessel; and of the dust that is in the floor of the tabernacle the priest shall take, and put it into the water" (Num 5:17). **(4d)** "Bitter water" was used in Israel's rituals, too: "And the priest shall set the woman before the LORD, and uncover the woman's head, and put the offering of memorial in her hands, which is the jealousy offering: and the priest shall have in his hand the bitter water that causeth the curse" (Num 5:18). **(4e)** It was "water" which when drunk brought a curse and caused bitterness (Num 5:24). **(5)** Fifth, in proper names this word is used of springs, streams, or seas and/or the area in the immediate vicinity of such bodies of water: "Say unto Aaron, Take thy rod, and stretch out thine hand upon the waters of Egypt, upon their streams, upon their rivers, and upon their ponds, and upon all their pools of water, that they may become blood" (Ex 7:19).

(6) Sixth, this word is used figuratively in many senses. **(6a)** *Mayim* symbolizes danger or distress: "He sent from above, he took me; he drew me out of many waters" (2 Sa 22:17). **(6b)** Outbursting force is represented by *mayim* in 2 Sa 5:20: "The LORD hath broken forth upon mine enemies before me, as the [breakthrough] of waters." **(6c)** "Mighty waters" describes the onrush of the godless nations against God: "The nations shall rush like the rushing of many waters" (Is 17:13). **(6d)** Thus

the word is used to picture something impetuous, violent, and overwhelming: "Terrors take hold on him as waters, a tempest stealeth him away in the night" (Job 27:20). **(6e)** In other passages "water" is used to represent timidity: "Wherefore the hearts of the people melted, and became as water" (Josh 7:5). **(6f)** Related to this nuance is the connotation "transitory": "Because thou shalt forget thy misery, and remember it as waters that pass away" (Job 11:16).

(6g) In Is 32:2 "water" represents that which is refreshing: "And a man shall be as a hiding place from the wind, and a covert from the tempest; as rivers of water in a dry place, as the shadow of a great rock in a weary land." **(6h)** Rest and peace are figured by waters of rest, or quiet waters: "He leadeth me beside the still waters" (Ps 23:2). **(6i)** Similar ideas are involved when one's wife's charms are termed "water of life" or "water which enlivens": "Drink waters out of thine own cistern, and running waters out of thine own well" (Prov 5:15). **(6j)** Outpoured "water" represents bloodshed (Deut 12:16), wrath (Hos 5:10), judgment (Amos 5:24), and strong feelings (Job 3:24). See: TWOT—1188; BDB—555d, 565a, 568a.

4326. מִיָמָן {4x} **Mîyâmîn**, *me-yaw-meem'*; a form for 4509; *Mijamin*, the name of three Isr.:—Miamin {2x}, Mijamin {2x}. See: BDB—568a.

4327. מִין {31x} **mîyn**, *meen*; from an unused root mean. to *portion* out; a *sort*, i.e. *species:*—kind {31x}. See: TWOT—1191a; BDB—558a, 568b. comp. 4480.

4328. מִיסָדָה {1x} **meyuççâdâh**, *meh-yoos-saw-daw';* prop. fem. pass. part. of 3245; something *founded,* i.e. a *foundation:*—foundation {1x}. See: TWOT—875; BDB—414c.

4329. מִיסָךְ {1x} **meyçâk**, *may-sawk';* from 5526; a *portico* (as *covered*):—covert {1x}. See: TWOT—1492b; BDB—558a, 568c, 697b.

מֵיפַעַת **Mêypha'ath**. See 4158.

4330. מִיץ {3x} **mîyts**, *meets;* from 4160; *pressure:*—churning {1x}, forcing {1x}, wringing {1x}. See: TWOT—1192b; BDB—568c.

4331. מֵישָׁא {1x} **Mêyshâ'**, *may-shaw';* from 4185; *departure; Mesha,* a place in Arabia; also an Isr.:—Mesha {1x}. See: TWOT—1192b; BDB—568c.

4332. מִישָׁאֵל {7x} **Mîyshâ'êl**, *mee-shaw-ale';* from 4310 and 410 with the abbrev. insep. rel. [see 834] interposed; *who* (is) *what God* (is)*?*; *Mishaël,* the name of three Isr.:—Mishael {1x}. See: BDB—567d, 568c, 100a.

4333. מִישָׁאֵל {1x} **Mîyshâ'êl** (Aram.), *mee-shaw-ale';* corresp. to 4332; *Mishael,* an Isr.:—Mishael {1x}. See: BDB—1100a.

4334. מִישׁוֹר {23x} **mîyshôwr,** *mee-shore';* or

מִישֹׁר **mîyshôr,** *mee-shore';* from 3474; a *level,* i.e. a *plain* (often used [with the art. pref.] as a prop. name of certain districts); fig. *concord;* also *straightness,* i.e. (fig.) *justice* (sometimes adv. *justly):*—plain {15x}, equity {2x}, straight {2x}, even place {1x}, right {1x}, righteously {1x}, uprightness {1x}.

Miyshor means "level place, uprightness." **(1)** In 1 Kin 20:23 *miyshor* refers to "level country": "And the servants of the king of Syria said unto him, Their gods are gods of the hills; therefore they were stronger than we; but let us fight against them in the plain, and surely we shall be stronger than they"; and **(2)** in Is 11:4 the word refers to "uprightness": ". . . And reprove with equity for the meek of the earth." See: TWOT—930f; BDB—449d.

4335. מֵישַׁךְ {1x} **Mêyshak,** *may-shak';* borrowed from 4336; *Meshak,* an Isr.:—Meshak {1x}. See: BDB—568d, 1100a.

4336. מֵישַׁךְ {14x} **Mêyshak** (Aram.), *may-shak';* of for. or. and doubtful signif.; *Meshak,* the Bab. name of 4333:—Meshak {14x}. See: BDB—1100a.

4337. מֵישָׁע {1x} **Mêyshâ',** *may-shah';* from 3467; *safety; Mesha,* an Isr.:—Mesha {1x}. See: BDB—448a, 568d.

4338. מֵישַׁע {1x} **Mêysha',** *may-shaw';* a var. for 4337; *safety; Mesha,* a Moabite:—Mesha {1x}. See: BDB—448a, 568d.

4339. מֵישָׁר {19x} **mêyshâr,** *may-shawr';* from 3474; *evenness,* i.e. (fig.) *prosperity* or *concord;* also *straightness,* i.e. (fig.) *rectitude* (only in plur. with sing. sense; often adv.):—equity {4x}, uprightly {3x}, uprightness {3x}, right things {2x}, agreement {1x}, aright {1x}, equal {1x}, right {1x}, righteously {1x}, sweetly {1x}, upright {1x}. See: TWOT—930e; BDB—449d, 606d.

4340. מֵיתָר {9x} **mêythâr,** *may-thar';* from 3498; a *cord* (of a tent) [comp. 3499] or the *string* (of a bow):—cord {8x}, string {1x}. See: TWOT—936h; BDB—452d, 568d.

4341. מַכְאֹב {16x} **mak'ôb,** *mak-obe';* sometimes

מַכְאוֹב **mak'ôwb,** *mak-obe';* also (fem. Is 53:3)

מַכְאֹבָה **mak'ôbâh,** *mak-o-baw';* from 3510; *anguish* or (fig.) *affliction:*—grief {2x}, pain {2x}, sorrow {12x}. See: TWOT—940b; BDB—456b, 568d.

4342. מַכְבִּיר {1x} **makbîyr,** *mak-beer';* tran. part. of 3527; *plenty:*—abundance {1x}. See: TWOT—947; BDB—460b, 568d.

4343. מַכְבְּנָא {1x} **Makbênâ',** *mak-bay-naw';* from the same as 3522; *knoll; Macbena,* a place in Pal. settled by him:—Machbenah {1x}. See: BDB—460a, 568d.

4344. מַכְבַּנַּי {1x} **Makbannay,** *mak-ban-nah'-ee;* patrial from 4343; a *Macbannite* or native of Macbena:—Machbanai {1x}. See: BDB—460a.

4345. מַכְבֵּר {6x} **makbêr,** *mak-bare';* from 3527 in the sense of *covering* [comp. 3531]; a *grate:*—grate {6x}. See: TWOT—948d; BDB—460d, 568d.

4346. מַכְבָּר {1x} **makbâr,** *mak-bawr';* from 3527 in the sense of *covering;* a cloth (as *netted* [comp. 4345]):—thick cloth {1x}. See: TWOT—948c; BDB—460d, 568d.

4347. מַכָּה {48x} **makkâh,** *mak-kaw';* or (masc.)

מַכֶּה **makkeh,** *mak-keh';* (plur. only) from 5221; a *blow* (in 2 Chr 2:10, of the flail); by impl. a *wound;* fig. *carnage,* also *pestilence:*—wound {14x}, slaughter {14x}, plague {11x}, beaten {1x}, stripes {2x}, stroke {2x}, blow {1x}, smote {1x}, sores {1x}, wounded {1x}. See: TWOT—1364d; BDB—568d, 646d.

4348. מִכְוָה {5x} **mikvâh,** *mik-vaw';* from 3554; a *burn:*—that burneth {1x}, burning {4x}. See: TWOT—961c; BDB—465a, 568d.

4349. מָכוֹן {17x} **mâkôwn,** *maw-kone';* from 3559; prop. a *fixture,* i.e. a *basis;* gen. a *place,* espec. as an *abode:*—foundation {1x}, habitation {2x}, (dwelling-, settled) place {14x}.

Makown, which appears 17 times, means "an established place or site": "Thou shalt bring them in, and plant them in the mountain of thine inheritance, in the place, O LORD, which thou hast made for thee to dwell in, in the Sanctuary, O LORD, *which* thy hands have established" (Ex 15:17). See: TWOT—964c; BDB—467c, 467d, 568d.

4350. מְכוֹנָה {23x} **mᵉkôwnâh,** *mek-o-naw';* or

מְכֹנָה **mᵉkônâh,** *mek-o-naw';* fem. of 4349; a *pedestal,* also a *spot:*—base {23x}.

Mekonah, as a noun, means "proper place; base." **(1)** This noun occurs 25 times; it means "proper place" in Ezra 3:3: "And they set the altar upon his bases." **(2)** The word refers to "bases" in 1 Kin 7:27: "And he made ten bases of brass; four cubits was the length of one base, and four cubits the breadth thereof, and three cubits the height of it." See: TWOT—964d; BDB—467d, 568d, 569a.

4351. מְכוּרָה {3x} **meḳûwrâh**, *mek-oo-raw';* or

מְכֹרָה **meḳôrâh**, *mek-o-raw';* from the same as 3564 in the sense of *digging; origin* (as if a mine):—birth {1x}, habitation {1x}, nativity {1x}. See: TWOT—1033c; BDB—468d, 568d, 569d.

4352. מְכִי {1x} **Mâḳîy**, *maw-kee';* prob. from 4134; *pining; Maki,* an Isr.:—Machi {1x}. See: BDB—568d.

4353. מָכִיר {22x} **Mâḳîyr**, *maw-keer';* from 4376; *salesman; Makir,* an Isr.:—Machir {22x}. See: BDB—569c.

4354. מָכִירִי {1x} **Mâḳîyrîy**, *maw-kee-re';* patron. from 4353; a *Makirite* or descend. of Makir:—of Machir {1x}. See: TWOT—1033c; BDB—569c.

4355. מָכַךְ {3x} **mâḳak**, *maw-kak';* a prim. root; to *tumble* (in ruins); fig. to *perish:*—be brought low {2x}, decay {1x}. See: TWOT—1193; BDB—568d.

4356. מִכְלָאָה {3x} **miklâ'âh**, *mik-law-aw';* or

מִכְלָה **miklâh**, *mik-law';* from 3607; a *pen* (for flocks):—fold {2x}, sheepfold + 6629 {1x}. comp. 4357. See: TWOT—980c; BDB—476c, 479a, 569a.

4357. מִכְלָה {1x} **miklâh**, *mik-law';* from 3615; *completion* (in plur. concr. adv. *wholly*):—perfect {1x}. See: TWOT—982d; BDB—476c, 479a, 569a. comp. 4356.

4358. מִכְלוֹל {2x} **miklôwl**, *mik-lole';* from 3634; *perfection* (i.e. concr. adv. *splendidly*):—most gorgeously {1x}, all sorts {1x}. See: TWOT—985c; BDB—483b, 569a.

4359. מִכְלָל {1x} **miklâl**, *mik-lawl';* from 3634; *perfection* (of beauty):—perfection {1x}. See: TWOT—985e; BDB—483b, 569a.

4360. מִכְלֻל {1x} **miklûl**, *mik-lool';* from 3634; *something perfect,* i.e. a splendid *garment:*—all sorts {1x}. See: TWOT—985d; BDB—483b, 569a.

4361. מַכֹּלֶת {1x} **makkôleth**, *mak-ko'-leth;* from 398; *nourishment:*—food {1x}. See: TWOT—85g; BDB—38c, 569a.

4362. מִכְמָן {1x} **mikman**, *mik-man';* from the same as 3646 in the sense of *hiding; treasure* (as *hidden*):—treasure {1x}. See: TWOT—991a; BDB—485a, 569a.

4363. מִכְמָס {11x} **Mikmâç** (Ezr 2:27; Neh. 7:31), *mik-maws';* or

מִכְמָשׁ **Mikmâsh**, *mik-mawsh';* or

מִכְמָשׁ **Mikmash** (Neh 11:31), *mik-mash';* from 3647; *hidden; Mikmas* or

Mikmash, a place in Pal.:—Mikmas {2x}, Mikmash {9x}. See: BDB—485a, 569a.

4364. מַכְמָר {2x} **makmâr**, *mak-mawr';* or

מִכְמֹר **mikmôr**, *mik-more';* from 3648 in the sense of *blackening* by heat; a (hunter's) *net* (as *dark* from concealment):—net {2x}. See: TWOT—995b; BDB—485b, 485c, 569a.

4365. מִכְמֶרֶת {3x} **mikmereth**, *mik-meh'-reth;* or

מִכְמֹרֶת **mikmôreth**, *mik-mo'-reth;* fem. of 4364; a (fisher's) *net:*—drag {2x}, net {1x}. See: TWOT—995c; BDB—485c, 569a.

מִכְמָשׁ **Mikmâsh**. See 4363.

4366. מִכְמְתָה {2x} **Mikmethâth**, *mik-meth-awth';* appar. from an unused root mean. to *hide; concealment; Mikmethath,* a place in Pal.:—Michmethath {2x}. See: BDB—485c, 569a.

4367. מַכְנַדְבַי {1x} **Maknadbay**, *mak-nad-bah'-ee;* from 4100 and 5068 with a particle interposed; *what* (is) *like* (a) *liberal* (man)?; *Maknadbai,* an Isr.:—Machnadebai {1x}. See: BDB—569a.

מְכֹנָה **meḳônâh**. See 4350.

4368. מְכֹנָה {1x} **Meḳônâh**, *mek-o-naw';* the same as 4350; a *base; Mekonah,* a place in Pal.:—Mekonah {1x}. See: BDB—569a.

4369. מְכֻנָה {1x} **meḳûnâh**, *mek-oo-naw';* the same as 4350; a *spot:*—base {1x}. See: TWOT—964d; BDB—467d.

4370. מִכְנָס {5x} **miknâç**, *mik-nawce';* from 3647 in the sense of *hiding;* (only in dual) *drawers* (from *concealing* the private parts):—breeches {5x}. See: TWOT—1000a; BDB—488b, 569a.

4371. מֶכֶס {6x} **mekeç**, *meh'-kes;* prob. from an unused root mean. to *enumerate;* an *assessment* (as based upon a *census*):—tribute {6x}. See: TWOT—1014a; BDB—493d, 569a.

4372. מִכְסֶה {16x} **mikçeh**, *mik-seh';* from 3680; a *covering,* i.e. weather-*boarding:*—covering {16x}. See: TWOT—1008c; BDB—492c, 569a.

4373. מִכְסָה {2x} **mikçâh**, *mik-saw';* fem. of 4371; an *enumeration;* by impl. *valuation:*—according to the number {1x}, worth {1x}. See: TWOT—1014b; BDB—493d, 569a.

4374. מְכַסֶּה {4x} **meḳaççeh**, *mek-as-seh';* from 3680; a *covering,* i.e. *garment;* spec. a *coverlet* (for a bed), an *awning* (from the sun); also the *omentum* (as covering the

intestines):—clothing {1x}, to cover {1x}, that which covereth {2x}. See: TWOT—1008d; BDB—492c, 569a.

4375. מַכְפֵּלָה {6x} **Makpêlâh,** *mak-pay-law';* from 3717; a *fold; Makpelah,* a place in Pal.:—Machpelah {6x}. See: TWOT—1019b; BDB—495d, 569a.

4376. מָכַר {80x} **mâkar,** *maw-kar';* a prim. root; to *sell,* lit. (as merchandise, a daughter in marriage, into slavery), or fig. (to *surrender):*—✕ at all {1x}, sell (away, self) {75x}, seller {4x}.

Makar means "to sell." **(1)** It is found for the first time in the Old Testament in Gen 25:31: "And Jacob said, Sell me this day thy birthright." **(2)** Anything tangible may be "sold," such as land (Gen 47:20), houses (Lev 25:29), animals (Ex 21:35), and human beings as slaves (Gen 37:27–28). **(3)** Daughters were usually "sold" for an agreed bride price (Ex 21:7). **(4)** *Makar* is often used in the figurative sense to express various actions. **(4a)** Nineveh is accused of "selling" or "betraying" other nations (Nah 3:4). **(4b)** Frequently it is said that God "sold" Israel into the power of her enemies, meaning that He gave them over entirely into their hands (Judg 2:14). **(4c)** Similarly, it was said that "the LORD shall sell Sisera into the hand of a woman" (Judg 4:9). **(5)** "To be sold" sometimes means to be given over to death (Est 7:4). See: TWOT—1194; BDB—569a.

4377. מֶכֶר {3x} **meker,** *meh'-ker;* from 4376; *merchandise;* also *value:*—pay for it {1x}, price {1x}, ware {1x}. See: TWOT—1194a; BDB—569c.

4378. מַכָּר {1x} **makkâr,** *mak-kawr';* from 5234; an *acquaintance:*—acquaintance {2x}. See: TWOT—1368f; BDB—569d, 648c.

4379. מִכְרֶה {1x} **mikreh,** *mik-reh';* from 3738; a *pit* (for salt):—saltpit + 4417 {1x}. See: TWOT—1033b; BDB—500b, 569d.

4380. מְכֵרָה {1x} **mᵉkêrâh,** *mek-ay-raw';* prob. from the same as 3564 in the sense of *stabbing;* a *sword:*—habitation {1x}. See: TWOT—1194d; BDB—468d, 569d.

מְכֹרָה **mᵉkôrâh.** See 4351.

4381. מִכְרִי {1x} **Mikrîy,** *mik-ree';* from 4376; *salesman; Mikri,* an Isr.:—Michri {1x}. See: BDB—569d.

4382. מְכֵרָתִי {1x} **Mᵉkêrâthîy,** *mek-ay-raw-thee';* patrial from an unused name (the same as 4380) of a place in Pal.; a *Mekerathite,* or inhab. of Mekerah:—Mecherathite {1x}. See: BDB—569d.

4383. מִכְשׁוֹל {14x} **mikshôwl,** *mik-shole';* or

מִכְשֹׁל **mikshôl,** *mik-shole';* masc. from 3782; a *stumbling-block,* lit. or fig. (*obstacle, enticement* [spec. an idol], *scruple):*—stumblingblock {8x}, offence {2x}, ruins {2x}, offend {1x}, fall {1x}. See: TWOT—1050c; BDB—506a, 569d.

4384. מַכְשֵׁלָה {2x} **makshêlâh,** *mak-shay-law';* fem. from 3782; a *stumbling-block,* but only fig. (*fall, enticement* [idol]):—ruin {1x}, stumbling-block {1x}. See: TWOT—1050d; BDB—506b, 569d.

4385. מִכְתָּב {9x} **miktâb,** *mik-tawb';* from 3789; a thing *written,* the *characters,* or a *document* (letter, copy, edict, poem):—writing {9x}.

Miktab means "something written, a writing": "And the tables were the work of God, and the writing was the writing of God, graven upon the tables" (Ex 32:16; cf. Is 38:9). See: TWOT—1053c; BDB—508b, 569d.

4386. מְכִתָּה {1x} **mᵉkittâh,** *mek-it-taw';* from 3807; a *fracture:*—bursting {1x}. See: TWOT—1062b; BDB—510c, 569d.

4387. מִכְתָּם {6x} **Miktâm,** *mik-tawm';* from 3799; an *engraving,* i.e. (techn.) a *poem:*—Michtam {6x}. See: TWOT—1056a; BDB—508d, 569d.

4388. מַכְתֵּשׁ {2x} **maktêsh,** *mak-taysh';* from 3806; a *mortar;* by anal. a *socket* (of a tooth):—hollow places {1x}, mortar {1x}. See: TWOT—1061a; BDB—509d, 569d.

4389. מַכְתֵּשׁ {1x} **Maktêsh,** *mak-taysh';* the same as 4388; *dell;* the *Maktesh,* a place in Jerusalem:—Maktesh {1x}. See: BDB—509d, 569d.

מֻל **mûl.** See 4136.

4390. מָלֵא {249x} **mâlê²,** *maw-lay';* or

מָלָא **mâlâ²** (Est 7:5), *maw-law';* a prim. root, to *fill* or (intr.) *be full* of, in a wide application (lit. and fig.):—fill {107x}, full {48x}, fulfil {28x}, consecrate {15x}, accomplish {7x}, replenish {7x}, wholly {6x}, set {6x}, expired {3x}, fully {2x}, gather {2x}, overflow {2x}, satisfy {2x}, misc. {14x} = confirm, be at an end, be fenced, fulness, furnish, presume, space, take a [hand-] full.

I. *Male²*, as a verb, means "to fill, fulfill, overflow, ordain, endow." **(1)** Basically, *male²* means "to be full" in the sense of having something done to one. **(1a)** In 2 Kin 4:6, the word implies "to fill up": "And it came to pass, when the vessels were full, that she said. . . ." **(1b)** The verb is sometimes used figuratively as in Gen 6:13, when God noted that "the earth is filled with violence." **(2)** Used transitively, this verb

means the act or state of "filling something." **(2a)** In Gen 1:22 (the first occurrence of the word), God told the sea creatures to "penetrate" the waters thoroughly but not exhaustively: "Be fruitful, and multiply and fill the waters in the seas." **(2b)** *Male*ᵓ can also mean "to fill up" in an exhaustive sense: "And the glory of the Lord filled the tabernacle" (Ex 40:34). **(2c)** In this sense an appetite can be "filled up," "satiated," or "satisfied." **(3)** *Male*ᵓ is sometimes used in the sense "coming to an end" or "to be filled up," to the full extent of what is expected. **(3a)** For example, in 1 Kin 2:27 we read: "So Solomon thrust out Abiathar from being priest unto the Lord; that he might fulfill the word of the Lord, which he spake concerning the house of Eli in Shiloh." **(3b)** This constitutes a proof of the authority of the divine Word.

(4) In a different but related nuance, the verb signifies "to confirm" someone's word. Nathan told Bathsheba: "Behold, while thou yet talkest there with the king, I also will come in after thee, and confirm thy words" (1 Kin 1:14). **(5)** This verb is used to signify filling something to the full extent of what is necessary, in the sense of being "successfully completed": "When her days to be delivered were fulfilled . . ." (Gen 25:24). **(6)** This may also mean "to bring to an end"; so God tells Isaiah: "Speak ye comfortably to Jerusalem and cry unto her, that her warfare is accomplished" (Is 40:2). **(7)** *Male*ᵓ is used of "filling to overflowing"—not just filling up to the limits of something, but filling so as to go beyond its limits: "For Jordan overfloweth all his banks all the time of harvest" (Josh 3:15). **(8)** A special nuance appears when the verb is used with "heart"; in such cases, it means "to presume." King Ahasuerus asked Esther: "Who is he, and where is he, that durst presume [literally, "fill his heart"] to do so?" (Est 7:5). **(9)** To call out "fully" is to cry aloud, as in Jer 4:5.

(10) The word often has a special meaning in conjunction with "hand." **(10a)** *Male*ᵓ can connote "endow" ("fill one's hand"), as in Ex 28:3: "And thou shalt speak unto all that are wisehearted, whom I have [endowed] with the spirit of wisdom." **(10b)** In Judg 17:5, "to fill one's hand" is "to consecrate" someone to priestly service. **(10c)** A similar idea appears in Eze 43:26, where no literal hand is filled with anything, but the phrase is a technical term for "consecration": "Seven days shall they [make atonement for] the altar and purify it; and they shall consecrate themselves." **(10c1)** This phrase is used not only of setting someone or something aside for special religious or cultic use, but of formally installing someone with the authority and responsibility to fulfill a cultic [re-

ligious] function (i.e., to be a priest). **(10c2)** So God commands concerning Aaron and his sons: "And thou . . . shalt anoint them, and consecrate them, and sanctify them, that they may minister unto me in the priest's office" (Ex 28:41).

(11) In military contexts, "to fill one's hand" is to prepare for battle. **(11a)** This phrase may be used of "becoming armed," as in Jer 51:11: "Make bright the arrows; gather the shields." **(11b)** In a fuller sense, the phrase may signify the step immediately before shooting arrows: "And Jehu drew [literally, "filled his hand with"] a bow with his full strength" (2 Kin 9:24). **(11c)** It can also signify "being armed," or having weapons on one's person: "But the man that shall touch them must be [armed] with iron and the staff of a spear" (2 Sa 23:7).

II. *Male*ᵓ, as an adjective, means "full." The basic meaning of the word is "full" or "full of": "I went out full, and the LORD hath brought me home again empty: why then call ye me Naomi, seeing the LORD hath testified against me, and the Almighty hath afflicted me?" (Ruth 1:21; cf. Deut 6:11). See: TWOT—1195; BDB—569d, 1100a.

4391. מְלָא {2x} **mᵉlâᵓ** (Aram.), *mel-aw'*; corresp. to 4390; to *fill*:—fill {1x}, be full {1x}. See: TWOT—2826; BDB—1100a.

4392. מָלֵא {65x} **mâlê**, *maw-lay'*; from 4390; *full* (lit. or fig.) or *filling* (lit.); also (concr.) *fulness*; adv. *fully*:—full {57x}, fill {3x}, with child {1x}, fully {1x}, much {1x}, multitude {1x}, worth {1x}. See: TWOT—1195a; BDB—570d.

4393. מְלֹא {37x} **mᵉlô**, *mel-o'*; rarely

מְלוֹא **mᵉlôw**, *mel-o'*; or

מְלֹו **mᵉlôw** (Eze 41:8), *mel-o'*; from 4390; *fulness* (lit. or fig.):—full {12x}, fulness {8x}, all that is therein {7x}, all {2x}, fill {2x}, handful {2x}, multitude {2x}, handful + 7062 {1x}, handfuls + 2651 {1x}. See: TWOT—1195b; BDB—571a, 571d.

מְלֹא **Millô**. See 4407.

4394. מִלֻּא {15x} **millu**, *mil-loo'*; from 4390; a *fulfilling* (only in plur.), i.e. (lit.) a *setting* (of gems), or (tech.) *consecration* (also concr. a dedicatory *sacrifice*):—consecration {11x}, be set {4x}. See: TWOT—1195e; BDB—571b.

4395. מְלֵאָה {3x} **mᵉlêâh**, *mel-ay-aw'*; fem. of 4392; something *fulfilled*, i.e. *abundance* (of produce):—(first of ripe) fruit {1x}, fruit {1x}, fulness {1x}. See: TWOT—1195c; BDB—571b.

4396. מִלֻּאָה {3x} **millûᵓâh**, *mil-loo-aw'*; fem. of 4394; a *filling*, i.e. *setting* (of

gems):—inclosings {2x}, settings {1x}. See: TWOT—1195d; BDB—571b.

4397. מַלְאָךְ {214x} **mal'âk**, *mal-awk'*; from an unused root mean. to *despatch* as a deputy; a *messenger;* spec. of God, i.e. an *angel* (also a prophet, priest or teacher):—angel {111x}, messenger {98x}, ambassadors {4x}, variant {1x}.

Mal'ak means "messenger; angel." **(1)** The noun *mal'ak* appears 213 times in the Hebrew Old Testament. **(1a)** Its frequency is especially great in the historical books, where it usually means "messenger": Judg (31 times), 2 Kin (20 times), 1 Sa (19 times), and 2 Sa (18 times). **(1b)** The prophetical works are very moderate in their usage of *mal'ak*, **(1c)** with the outstanding exception of the Book of Zechariah, where the angel of the Lord communicates God's message to Zechariah. **(1d)** For example: "Then I answered and said unto the angel that talked to me, 'What are these, my lord?' And the angel answered and said unto me, 'These are the four spirits [pl. of *mal'ak*] of the heavens, which go forth from standing before the Lord of all the earth'" (Zec 6:4–5). **(2)** The word *mal'ak* denotes someone sent over a great distance by an individual (Gen 32:3) or by a community (Num 21:21), in order to communicate a message. Often several messengers are sent together: "And Ahaziah fell down through a lattice in his upper chamber that was in Samaria, and was sick: and he sent messengers [pl. of *mal'ak*] and said unto them, Go, inquire of Baal-zebub the god of Ekron whether I shall recover of this disease" (2 Kin 1:2).

(3) The introductory formula of the message borne by the *mal'ak* often contains the phrase "Thus says . . . ," or "This is what . . . says," signifying the authority of the messenger in giving the message of his master: "Thus saith Jephthah, Israel took not away the land of Moab, nor the land of the children of Ammon" (Judg 11:15). **(4)** As a representative of a king, the *mal'ak* might have performed the function of a diplomat. **(4a)** In 1 Kin 20:1ff., we read that Ben-hadad sent messengers with the terms of surrender: **(4b)** "He sent messengers to Ahab king of Israel into the city, and said unto him, Thus saith Benhadad . . ." (1 Kin 20:2). **(5)** These passages confirm the important place of the *mal'ak*. **(5a)** Honor to the messenger signified honor to the sender, and the opposite was also true. **(5b)** David took personally the insult of Nabal (1 Sa 25:14ff.); and when Hanun, king of Ammon, humiliated David's servants (2 Sa 10:4ff.), David was quick to dispatch his forces against the Ammonites.

(6) God also sent messengers. **(6a)** First, there are the prophetic messengers: "And the LORD God of their fathers sent to them by his messengers, rising up betimes, and sending; because he had compassion on his people, and on his dwelling place: But they mocked the messengers of God, and despised his words, and misused his prophets, until the wrath of the LORD arose against his people, till there was no remedy" (2 Chr 36:15–16). **(6b)** Haggai called himself "the messenger of the LORD," *mal'ak Yahweh*. **(7)** There were also angelic messengers. The English word angel is etymologically related to the Greek word *angelos,* whose translation is similar to the Hebrew: "messenger" or "angel." **(7a)** The angel is a supernatural messenger of the Lord sent with a particular message. **(7b)** Two angels came to Lot at Sodom: "And there came two angels to Sodom at even; and Lot sat in the gate of Sodom: and Lot seeing them rose up to meet them; and he bowed himself with his face toward the ground" (Gen 19:1). **(7c)** The angels were also commissioned to protect God's people: "For he shall give his angels charge over thee, to keep thee in all thy ways" (Ps 91:11).

(8) Most significant, are the phrases *mal'ak Yahweh,* "the angel of the LORD," and *mal'ak 'elohim,* "the angel of God." **(8a)** The phrase is always used in the singular. **(8b)** It denotes an angel who had mainly a saving and protective function: "For mine angel shall go before thee, and bring thee in unto the Amorites, and the Hittites, and the Perizzites, and the Canaanites, the Hivites, and the Jebusites: and I will cut them off" (Ex 23:23). **(8c)** He might also bring about destruction: "And David lifted up his eyes, and saw the angel of the LORD stand between the earth and the heaven, having a drawn sword in his hand stretched out over Jerusalem. Then David and the elders of Israel, who were clothed in sackcloth, fell upon their faces" (1 Chr 21:16). **(8d)** The relation between the Lord and the "angel of the LORD" is often so close that it is difficult to separate the two (Gen 16:7ff.; 21:17ff.; 22:11ff.; 31:11ff.; Ex 3:2ff.; Judg 6:11ff.; 13:21f.). **(8e)** This identification has led some interpreters to conclude that the "angel of the LORD" was the pre-incarnate Christ. See: TWOT—1068a; BDB—521c, 571c, 1098d.

4398. מַלְאַךְ {2x} **mal'ak** (Aram.), *mal-ak';* corresp. to 4397; an *angel:*—angel {2x}. See: TWOT—2827; BDB—1098d, 1100a.

4399. מְלָאכָה {167x} **me lâ'kâh**, *mel-aw-kaw';* from the same as 4397; prop. *deputyship,* i.e. ministry; gen. *employment* (never servile) or work (abstr. or concr.); also *property* (as the result of *labor*):—work {129x}, business {12x}, workmen + 6213 {7x}, workmanship {5x}, goods {2x}, cattle {1x}, stuff {1x}, thing {1x}, misc. {9x} = + industrious, occupa-

tion, (+ -pied), + officer, use. See: TWOT—
1068b; BDB—521d, 571c.

4400. מַלְאֲכוּת {1x} **malʾăkûwth**, *mal-ak-ooth'*; from the same as 4397;
a *message:*—message {1x}. See: TWOT—1068c;
BDB—522b, 571c.

4401. מַלְאָכִי {1x} **Malʾâkîy**, *mal-aw-kee'*;
from the same as 4397; *ministrative; Malaki*, a prophet:—Malachi {1x}. See:
BDB—522b, 571c.

4402. מִלֵּאת {1x} **millêʾth**, *mil-layth'*; from
4390; *fulness*, i.e. (concr.) a
plump socket (of the eye):—× fitly {1x}. See:
TWOT—1195f; BDB—571c.

4403. מַלְבּוּשׁ {8x} **malbûwsh**, *mal-boosh'*; or

מַלְבֻּשׁ **malbûsh**, *mal-boosh'*; from 3847;
a *garment*, or (collect.) *clothing:*—apparel {4x}, raiment {3x}, vestment {1x}.
See: TWOT—1075b; BDB—528c, 571c.

4404. מַלְבֵּן {1x} **malbên**, *mal-bane'*; from
3835 (denom.); a *brick-kiln:*—brickkiln {1x}. See: TWOT—1074i; BDB—527c,
571c, 576a.

4405. מִלָּה {38x} **millâh**, *mil-law'*; from 4448
(plur. masc. as if from

מִלָּה **milleh**, *mil-leh'*; a *word;* collect. a
discourse; fig. a *topic:*—word
{23x}, speech {6x}, say {2x}, speaking {2x}, answer + 7725 {1x}, byword {1x}, matter {1x},
speak {1x}, talking {1x}. Syn.: 559, 1696. See:
TWOT—1201a; BDB—571c, 576b.

4406. מִלָּה {24x} **millâh** (Aram.), *mil-law'*;
corresp. to 4405; a *word, command, discourse*, or *subject:*—commandment
{1x}, matter {5x}, thing {11x}, word {7x}. See:
TWOT—2831a; BDB—1100a, 1100c.

מְלוֹ **mᵉlôw**. See 4393.

מְלוֹא **mᵉlôwʾ**. See 4393.

4407. מִלּוֹא {10x} **millôwʾ**, *mil-lo';* or

מִלֹּא **millôʾ** (2 Kin 12:20) *mil-lo';* from
4390; a *rampart* (as *filled* in), i.e.
the *citadel:*—Millo {10x}. See: BDB—571c. See
also 1037.

4408. מַלּוּחַ {1x} **mallûwach**, *mal-loo'-akh;*
from 4414; *sea-purslain* (from its
saltness):—mallows {1x}. See: TWOT—1197c;
BDB—572a.

4409. מַלּוּךְ {7x} **Mallûwk**, *mal-luke';* or

מַלּוּכִי **Mallûwkîy** (Neh 12:14) *mal-loo-kee';* from 4427; *regnant; Malluk*, the name of five Isr.:—Malluch {6x},
Melichu {1x}. See: BDB—576a.

4410. מְלוּכָה {24x} **mᵉlûwkâh**, *mel-oo-kaw';*
fem. pass. part. of 4427; something *ruled*, i.e. a *realm:*—kingdom {18x},
king's {2x}, × royal {4x}. See: TWOT—1199d;
BDB—574c.

4411. מָלוֹן {8x} **mâlôwn**, *maw-lone';* from
3885; a *lodgment*, i.e. *caravanserai* or *encampment:*—inn {3x}, place where . . .
lodged {1x}, lodgings {2x}, lodging place {2x}.
See: TWOT—1096a; BDB—533d, 571d.

4412. מְלוּנָה {2x} **mᵉlûwnâh**, *mel-oo-naw';*
fem. from 3885; a *hut*, a *hammock:*—cottage {1x}, lodge {1x}. See: TWOT—
1096b; BDB—534a, 571d.

4413. מַלּוֹתִי {2x} **Mallôwthîy**, *mal-lo'-thee;*
appar. from 4448; *I have talked*
(i.e. *loquacious*); *Mallothi*, an Isr.:—Mallothi
{2x}. See: BDB—571d, 576c, 1100a.

4414. מָלַח {5x} **mâlach**, *maw-lakh';* a prim.
root; prop. to *rub* to pieces or pulverize; intr. to *disappear* as dust; also (as denom. from 4417) to *salt* whether intern. (to
season with salt) or extern. (to *rub* with salt):—
× at all {1x}, salt {1x}, season {1x}, temper together {1x}, vanish away {1x}. See: TWOT—
1196, 1197; BDB—571d, 572a, 1100b.

4415. מְלַח {1x} **mᵉlach** (Aram.), *mel-akh';*
corresp. to 4414; to *eat* salt, i.e.
(gen.) *subsist:*—+ have maintenance {1x}. See:
TWOT—2828; BDB—1090b, 1100b.

4416. מְלַח {3x} **mᵉlach** (Aram.), *mel-akh';*
from 4415; *salt:*—+ maintenance
{1x}, salt {2x}. See: TWOT—2828a; BDB—
1100a.

4417. מֶלַח {28x} **melach**, *meh'-lakh;* from
4414; prop. *powder*, i.e. (spec.) *salt*
(as easily pulverized and dissolved:—salt {27x},
saltpits + 4379 {1x}. See: TWOT—1197a;
BDB—571d, 1100a.

4418. מָלָח {2x} **mâlâch**, *maw-lawkh';* from
4414 in its orig. sense; a *rag* or old
garment:—rotten rags {2x}. See: TWOT—
1196a; BDB—571d.

4419. מַלָּח {4x} **mallâch**, *mal-lawkh';* from
4414 in its second. sense; a *sailor*
(as following "the salt"):—mariner {4x}. See:
TWOT—1197d; BDB—572a.

4420. מְלֵחָה {3x} **mᵉlêchâh**, *mel-ay-khaw';*
from 4414 (in its denom. sense);
prop. *salted* (i.e. land [776 being understood]),
i.e. a *desert:*—barren land {1x}, barreness {1x},
salt land {1x}. See: TWOT—1197b; BDB—572a.

4421. מִלְחָמָה {319x} **milchâmâh**, *mil-khaw-maw';* from 3898 (in the sense
of *fighting*); a *battle* (i.e. the *engagement*); gen.

war (i.e. *warfare*):—war {158x}, battle {151x}, fight {5x}, warriors + 6213 {2x}, fighting + 6213 {1x}, war + 376 {1x}, wars + 376 {1x}.

Milchamah means "battle; war." **(1)** This noun occurs more than 300 times in the Old Testament, indicating how large a part military experience and terminology played in the life of the ancient Israelites. **(2)** Gen 14:8 is an early occurrence of *milchamah:* "And there went out the king of Sodom, and the king of Gomorrah, . . . and they joined battle with them in the vale of Siddim." See: TWOT—1104c; BDB—536a, 572b.

4422. מָלַט {95x} **mâlaṭ,** *maw-lat';* a prim. root; prop. to *be smooth,* i.e. (by impl.) to *escape* (as if by *slipperiness);* caus. to *release* or *rescue;* spec. to *bring forth* young, *emit* sparks:—escape {47x}, deliver {33x}, save {5x}, . . . out {4x}, alone {1x}, get away {1x}, lay {1x}, preserve {1x}, speedily {1x}, surely {1x}.

Malat means to escape, slip away, deliver, give birth. **(1)** The word appears twice in the first verse in which it is found: "And it came to pass, when they had brought them forth abroad, that he said, Escape for thy life; look not behind thee, neither stay thou in all the plain; escape to the mountain, lest thou be consumed" (Gen 19:17). **(2)** Sometimes *malat* is used in parallelism **(2a)** with *nuç* (5127) "to flee": And Saul sought to smite David even to the wall with the javelin; but he slipped away out of Saul's presence, and he smote the javelin into the wall: and David fled *(nuç),* and escaped *(malat)* that night" (1 Sa 19:10), or **(2b)** with *barach* (1272) "to flee": "So Michal let David down through a window: and he went, and fled *(barach),* and escaped *(nuç)*" (1 Sa 19:12). **(3)** The most common use of this word is to express the "escaping" from any kind of danger such as an enemy (Is 20:6), a trap (2 Kin 10:24), or a temptress (Eccl 7:26). **(4)** When Josiah's reform called for burning the bones of false prophets, a special directive was issued to spare the bones of a true prophet buried at the same place: "So they let his bones alone . . ." (2 Kin 23:18; literally, "they let his bones escape"). **(5)** *Malat* is used once in the sense of "delivering a child" (Is 66:7). See: TWOT—1198; BDB—572b.

4423. מֶלֶט {1x} **melet,** *meh'-let;* from 4422, *cement* (from its plastic *smoothness):*—clay {1x}. See: TWOT—1198a; BDB—572d.

4424. מְלַטְיָה {1x} **Mᵉlaṭyâh,** *mel-at-yaw';* from 4423 and 3050; (whom) *Jah has delivered; Melatjah,* a Gibeonite:—Melatiah {1x}. See: TWOT—1198a; BDB—572d.

4425. מְלִילָה {1x} **mᵉlîylâh,** *mel-ee-law';* from 4449 (in the sense of *cropping* [comp. 4135]); a *head* of grain (as *cut* off):—ear {1x}. See: TWOT—1202a; BDB—576c.

4426. מְלִיצָה {2x} **mᵉlîytsâh,** *mel-ee-tsaw';* from 3887; an *aphorism;* also a *satire:*—interpretation {1x}, taunting {1x}. See: TWOT—1113b; BDB—539c, 572d.

4427. מָלַךְ {348x} **mâlak,** *maw-lak';* a prim. root; to *reign;* incept. to *ascend the throne;* caus. to *induct* into royalty; hence, (by impl.) to *take counsel:*—reign {289x}, king {46x}, made {4x}, queen {2x}, consulted {1x}, indeed {1x}, make {1x}, rule {1x}, set {1x}, surely {1x}, set up {1x}.

Malak means "to reign, be king (or queen)." **(1)** Basically the word means to fill the functions of ruler over someone. **(1a)** To hold such a position was to function as the commander-in-chief of the army, the chief executive of the group, and **(1b)** to be an important, if not central, religious figure. **(2)** The king was the head of his people and, therefore, in battle were the king to be killed, his army would disperse until a new king could be chosen. **(3)** The first appearance of *malak* is in Gen 36:31: "And these are the kings that reigned in the land of Edom, before there reigned any king over the children of Israel." **(4)** The king "reigned" as the earthly representative of the god (or God) who was recognized as the real king. **(4a)** Thus, he was considered to be god's (God's) son. **(4b)** This same idea recurs in Israel (Ps 2:6). In Israel, too, God was the King: "The Lord shall reign for ever and ever" (Ex 15:18). **(5)** That the word can also be used of what a queen does when she "reigns" proves that it refers to the function of anyone in the office of king: "And he was with her hid in the house of the Lord six years. And Athaliah did reign over the land" (2 Kin 11:3).

(6) *Malak* can also be used of the idea "to become king"—someone was made, or made himself, a king: "And Bela died, and Jobab the son of Zerah of Bozrah reigned in his stead" (Gen 36:33). **(7)** This verb can be used of the assumption of a kingly reign, or of "beginning to reign": "Saul reigned one year; and when he had reigned two years over Israel . . ." (1 Sa 13:1; cf. Prov 30:22). **(8)** Finally, the verb is used of receiving the title of queen (or king) whether or not one receives any political or military power. So it was said: "And let the maiden which pleaseth the king be queen instead of Vashti" (Est 2:4). See: TWOT—1199, 1200; BDB—573d, 576a, 1100b, 1100c.

4428. מֶלֶךְ {2523x} **melek,** *meh'-lek;* from 4427; a *king:*—king {2518x}, royal {2x}, Hammelech {1x}, Malcham {1x}, Moloch

{1x}. See: TWOT—1199a; BDB—572d, 574c, 575d.

4429. מֶלֶךְ {3x} **Melek**, *meh'-lek;* the same as 4428; *king; Melek,* the name of two Isr.:—Melech {2x}, Hammelech {1x} [by includ. the art.]. See: BDB—573a, 574b, 1100b.

4430. מֶלֶךְ {180x} **melek** (Aram.), *meh'-lek;* corresp. to 4428; a *king:*—king {179x}, royal {1x}. See: TWOT—2829a; BDB—1100b.

4431. מְלַךְ {1x} **melak** (Aram.), *mel-ak';* from a root corresp. to 4427 in the sense of *consultation; advice:*—counsel {1x}. See: TWOT—2830a; BDB—1100c.

4432. מֹלֶךְ {8x} **Môlek**, *mo'-lek;* from 4427; *Molek* (i.e. king), the chief deity of the Ammonites:—Molech {8x}. See: TWOT—1199h; BDB—574c. comp. 4445.

4433. מַלְכָּא {2x} **malkâ** (Aram.), *mal-kaw';* corresp. to 4436; a *queen:*—queen {2x}. See: TWOT—2829b; BDB—1100b.

4434. מַלְכֹּדֶת {1x} **malkôdeth**, *mal-ko'-deth;* from 3920; a *snare:*—trap {1x}. See: TWOT—1115b; BDB—540b, 576a.

4435. מִלְכָּה {11x} **Milkâh**, *mil-kaw';* a form of 4436; *queen; Milcah,* the name of a Hebrewess and of an Isr.:—Milcah {11x}. See: BDB—574c.

4436. מַלְכָּה {35x} **malkâh**, *mal-kaw';* fem. of 4428; a *queen:*—queen {35x}. See: TWOT—1199b; BDB—573c.

4437. מַלְכוּ {57x} **malkûw** (Aram.), *mal-koo';* corresp. to 4438; *dominion* (abstr. or concr.):—kingdom {49x}, kingly {1x}, realm {3x}, reign {4x}. See: TWOT—2829c; BDB—1100b.

4438. מַלְכוּת {91x} **malkûwth**, *mal-kooth';* or

מַלְכֻת **malkûth**, *mal-kooth';* or (in plur.)

מַלְכֻיָּה **malkûyâh**, *mal-koo-yâh';* from 4427; a *rule;* concr. a *dominion:*—kingdom {51x}, reign {21x}, royal {13x}, realm {4x}, empire {1x}, estate {1x}.
Malkuth means "kingdom; reign; rule." **(1)** The first occurrence is in Num 24:7: "He shall pour the water out of his buckets, and his seed shall be in many waters, and his king shall be higher than Agag, and his kingdom shall be exalted." **(2)** The word *malkuth* denotes: **(2a)** the territory of the kingdom: "When he showed the riches of his glorious kingdom and the honor of his excellent majesty many days, even a hundred and fourscore days" (Est 1:4); **(2b)** the accession to the throne: "For if thou altogether holdest thy peace at this time, then shall there enlargement and deliverance arise

to the Jews from another place; but thou and thy father's house shall be destroyed: and who knoweth whether thou art come to the kingdom for such a time as this?" (Est 4:14); **(2c)** the year of rule: "So Esther was taken unto king Ahasuerus into his house royal in the tenth month, which is the month Tebeth, in the seventh year of his reign" (Est 2:16); and **(2d)** anything "royal" or "kingly": throne (Est 1:2), wine (Est 1:7), crown (Est 1:11), word (Est 1:19), garment (Est 6:8), palace (Est 1:9), scepter (Ps 45:6), and glory (Ps 145:11–12). See: TWOT—1199e; BDB—574d.

4439. מַלְכִּיאֵל {3x} **Malkîyêl**, *mal-kee-ale';* from 4428 and 410; *king of* (i.e. appointed by) *God; Malkiël,* an Isr.:—Malchiel {3x}. See: BDB—575c.

4440. מַלְכִּיאֵלִי {1x} **Malkîyêlîy**, *mal-kee-ay-lee';* patron. from 4439; a *Malkiëlite* or desc. of Malkiel:—Malchielite {1x}. See: BDB—575c.

4441. מַלְכִּיָּה {16x} **Malkîyâh**, *mal-kee-yaw';* or

מַלְכִּיָּהוּ **Malkîyâhûw** (Jer 38:6), *mal-kee-yaw'-hoo;* from 4428 and 3050; *king of* (i.e. appointed by) *Jah; Malkijah,* the name of ten Isr.:—Malchiah {10x}, Malchijah {6x}. See: TWOT—1199g; BDB—575b.

4442. מַלְכִּי־צֶדֶק {2x} **Malkîy-Tsedeq**, *mal-kee-tseh'-dek;* from 4428 and 6664; *king of right; Malki-Tsedek,* an early king in Pal.:—Melchizedek {2x}. See: TWOT—1199i; BDB—575d.

4443. מַלְכִּירָם {1x} **Malkîyrâm**, *mal-kee-rawm';* from 4428 and 7311; *king of a high one* (i.e. of exaltation); *Malkiram,* an Isr.:—Malchiram {1x}. See: BDB—575d.

4444. מַלְכִּישׁוּעַ {5x} **Malkîyshûwa'**, *mal-kee-shoo'-ah;* from 4428 and 7769; *king of wealth; Malkishua,* an Isr.:—Malchishua {5x}. See: BDB—575d.

4445. מַלְכָּם {4x} **Malkâm**, *mal-kawm';* or

מִלְכּוֹם **Milkôwm**, *mil-kome';* from 4428 for 4432; *Malcam* or *Milcom,* the national idol of the Ammonites:—Malcham {1x}, Milcom {3x}. See: BDB—575d.

4446. מְלֶכֶת {5x} **meleketh**, *mel-eh'-keth;* from 4427; a *queen:*—queen {5x}. See: TWOT—1199c; BDB—573d.

4447. מֹלֶכֶת {1x} **Môleketh**, *mo-leh'-keth;* fem. act. part. of 4427; *queen; Moleketh,* an Israelitess:—Hammoleketh {1x} [incl. *the art.*]. See: BDB—574c.

4448. מָלַל {5x} **mâlal**, *maw-lal';* a prim. root; to *speak* (mostly poet.) or *say:*—

said {1x}, speak {2x}, utter {2x}. See: TWOT—1201; BDB—576a, 576c, 1100c.

4449. מְלַל {5x} **mᵉlal** (Aram.), *mel-al';* corresp. to 4448; to *speak:*—said {1x}, speak (-ing) {4x}. See: TWOT—2831; BDB—1100c.

4450. מְלָלַי {1x} **Mîlălay,** *mee-lal-ah'-ee;* from 4448; *talkative; Milalai,* an Isr.:—Milalai {1x}. See: BDB—576c.

4451. מַלְמָד {1x} **malmâd,** *mal-mawd';* from 3925; a *goad* for oxen:—goad {1x}. See: TWOT—1116b; BDB—541a, 576d.

4452. מָלַץ {1x} **mâlats,** *maw-lats;* a prim. root; to *be smooth,* i.e. (fig.) *pleasant:*—be sweet {1x}. See: TWOT—1205; BDB—576d.

4453. מֶלְצַר {2x} **Meltsâr,** *mel-tsawr';* of Pers. der.; the *butler* or other officer in the Bab. court:—Melzar {2x}. See: BDB—576d.

4454. מָלַק {2x} **mâlaq,** *maw-lak';* a prim. root; to *crack* a joint; by impl. to *wring* the neck of a fowl (without separating it):—wring off {2x}. See: TWOT—1207; BDB—577a.

4455. מַלְקוֹחַ {8x} **malqôwach,** *mal-ko'-akh;* from 3947; tran. (in dual) the *jaws* (as taking food); intr. *spoil* [and captives] (as taken):—booty {1x}, jaws {1x}, prey {6x}.
Malqowach refers (1) to "things taken in warfare,": "And the booty, being the rest of the prey which the men of war had caught, was six hundred thousand and seventy thousand and five thousand sheep" (Num 31:32). (2) *Malqowach* also means "jaws" once: "My strength is dried up like a potsherd; and my tongue cleaveth to my jaws; and thou hast brought me into the dust of death" (Ps 22:15). Syn: 3948, 4457, 4727, 4728. See: TWOT—1124b, 1124c; BDB—544b, 544c, 577a.

4456. מַלְקוֹשׁ {8x} **malqôwsh,** *mal-koshe';* from 3953; the spring *rain* (comp. 3954); fig. *eloquence:*—latter {2x}, latter rain {6x}. See: TWOT—1127b; BDB—545b, 577a.

4457. מֶלְקָח {6x} **melqâch,** *mel-kawkh';* or

מַלְקָח **malqâch,** *mal-kawkh';* from 3947; (only in dual) *tweezers:*—snuffers {1x}, tongs {5x}. *Melqachayim* [plural] refers to "snuffers" (Ex 37:23), and it is found 6 times. Syn: 3948, 4455, 4727, 4728. See: TWOT—1124d; BDB—544c, 577a.

4458. מֶלְתָּחָה {1x} **meltâchâh,** *mel-taw-khaw';* from an unused root mean. to *spread* out; a *wardrobe* (i.e. room where clothing is *spread*):—vestry {1x}. See: TWOT—1132a; BDB—547a, 577a.

4459. מַלְתָּעָה {1x} **maltâ‘âh,** *mal-taw-aw';* transp. for 4973; a *grinder,* i.e. back *tooth:*—great tooth {1x}. See: TWOT—2516d; BDB—577a, 1069a.

4460. מַמְּגֻרָה {1x} **mammᵉgûrâh,** *mam-meg-oo-raw';* from 4048 (in the sense of *depositing*); a *granary:*—barn {1x}. See: TWOT—330e; BDB—158c, 577a.

4461. מֵמַד {1x} **mêmad,** *may-mad';* from 4058; a *measure:*—measures {1x}. See: TWOT—1146c; BDB—551d, 577a.

4462. מְמוּכָן {3x} **Mᵉmûwkân,** *mem-oo-kawn';* or (transp.)

מוֹמֻכָן **Môwmûkân** (Est 1:16), *mo-moo-kawn';* of Pers. der.; *Memucan* or *Momucan,* a Pers. satrap:—Memucan {3x}. See: BDB—558a, 577a.

4463. מָמוֹת {2x} **mâmôwth,** *maw-mothe';* from 4191; a *mortal disease;* concr. a *corpse:*—death {2x}. *Mamowth* refers to "death." *Mamoth* appears in Jer 16:4: "They shall die of grievous deaths" (cf. Eze 28:8). See: TWOT—1169b; BDB—560d, 577a.

4464. מַמְזֵר {2x} **mamzêr,** *mam-zare';* from an unused root mean. to *alienate;* a *mongrel,* i.e. born of a Jewish father and a heathen mother:—bastard {2x}. See: TWOT—1174a; BDB—561c, 577a.

4465. מִמְכָּר {10x} **mimkâr,** *mim-kawr';* from 4376; *merchandise;* abstr. a *selling:*—that . . . sold {4x}, sale {2x}, that which cometh of the sale {1x}, ought {1x}, ware {1x}, sold {1x}. See: TWOT—1194b; BDB—569d, 577a.

4466. מִמְכֶּרֶת {1x} **mimkereth,** *mim-keh'-reth;* fem. of 4465; a *sale:*—+ sold as {1x}. See: TWOT—1194c; BDB—569d, 577a.

4467. מַמְלָכָה {117x} **mamlâkâh,** *mam-law-kaw';* from 4427; *dominion,* i.e. (abstr.) the *estate* (*rule*) or (concr.) the *country* (*realm*):—kingdom {110x}, royal {4x}, reign {2x}, king's {1x}.
Mamlakah means "kingdom; sovereignty; dominion; reign." (1) *Mamlakah* occurs first in Gen 10:10: "And the beginning of his kingdom was Babel, and Erech, and Accad, and Calneh, in the land of Shinar" in the sense of the "realm" of the kingdom. (2) The basic meaning of *mamlakah* is the area and people that constitute a "kingdom." (2a) The word refers to non-Israelite nations who are ruled by a *melek* (4428), "king": "And it shall come to pass after the end of seventy years, that the LORD will visit Tyre, and she shall turn to her hire, and shall commit fornication with all the kingdoms of the world upon the face of the earth" (Is

23:17). **(3)** *Mamlakah* is a synonym for ʿam (5971) "people," and *goy* (1471) "nation": "they went from one nation to another, from one kingdom to another people" (Ps 105:13). **(4)** *Mamlakah* also denotes Israel as God's "kingdom": "And ye shall be unto me a kingdom of priests, and a holy nation" (Ex 19:6). **(5)** The Davidic king was the theocratic agent by whom God ruled over and blessed His people: "And thine house and thy kingdom shall be established for ever before thee: thy throne shall be established for ever" (2 Sa 7:16).

(6) Nevertheless, the one *mamlakah* after Solomon was divided into two kingdoms which Ezekiel predicted would be reunited: "And I will make them one nation in the land upon the mountains of Israel; and one king shall be king to them all: and they shall be no more two nations, neither shall they be divided into two kingdoms" (Eze 37:22). **(7)** Close to the basic meaning is the usage of *mamlakah* to denote "king," **(7a)** as the king was considered to be the embodiment of the "kingdom." **(7b)** He was viewed as a symbol of the kingdom proper: "Thus saith the LORD God of Israel, I brought up Israel out of Egypt, and delivered you out of the hand of the Egyptians, and out of the hand of all kingdoms, and of them that oppressed you" (1 Sa 10:18); **(7c)** in Hebrew the noun "kingdoms" is feminine and the verb "oppress" has a masculine form, signifying that we must understand "kingdoms" as "kings". **(8)** The function and place of the king is important in the development of the concept "kingdom." **(8a)** "Kingdom" may signify the head of the kingdom.

(8b) The word further has the meaning of the royal "rule," the royal "sovereignty," and the "dominion." **(8b1)** The royal "sovereignty" was taken from Saul because of his disobedience (1 Sa 28:17). **(8b2)** "Royal sovereignty" is also the sense in Jer 27:1: "In the beginning of the reign of Jehoiakim. . . ." **(8c)** The Old Testament further defines as expressions of the royal "rule" all things associated with the king: **(8c1)** the throne: "And it shall be, when he sitteth upon the throne of his kingdom, that he shall write him a copy of this law in a book out of that which is before the priests the Levites" (Deut 17:18); **(8c2)** the pagan sanctuary supported by the throne: "But prophesy not again any more at Beth-el: for it is the king's chapel, and it is the king's court" (Amos 7:13); and **(8c3)** a royal city: "And David said unto Achish, If I have now found grace in thine eyes, let them give me a place in some town in the country, that I may dwell there: for why should thy servant dwell in the royal city with thee?" (1 Sa 27:5). **(9)** All human rule is under God's control.

Consequently the Old Testament fully recognizes the kingship of God.

(9a) The Lord ruled as king over His people Israel (1 Chr 29:11). **(9b)** He graciously ruled over His people through David and his followers until the Exile (2 Chr 13:5). **(10)** In the New Testament usage all the above meanings are to be associated with the Greek word *basileia* ("kingdom"). **(10a)** This is the major translation of *mamlakah* in the Septuagint, and as such it is small wonder that the New Testament authors used this word to refer to God's "kingdom": the realm, the king, the sovereignty, and the relationship to God Himself as *melek* (4428), "king." See: TWOT—1199f; BDB—575a, 577a.

4468. מַמְלָכוּת {9x} **mamlâkûwth**, *mam-law-kooth'*; a form of 4467 and equiv. to it:—kingdom {8x}, reign {1x}. See: TWOT—1199g; BDB—575c.

4469. מַמְסָךְ {2x} **mamçâk**, *mam-sawk'*; from 4537; *mixture*, i.e. (spec.) wine *mixed* (with water or spices):—drink-offering {1x}, mixed wine {1x}. See: TWOT—1220b; BDB—577a, 587c.

4470. מֶמֶר {1x} **memer**, *meh'-mer*; from an unused root mean. to *grieve*; *sorrow*:—bitterness {1x}. See: TWOT—1248j; BDB—577a, 601b.

4471. מַמְרֵא {10x} **Mamrêʾ**, *mam-ray'*; from 4754 (in the sense of *vigor*); *lusty*; *Mamre*, an Amorite:—Mamre {10x}. See: TWOT—1208; BDB—577b.

4472. מַמְרֹר {1x} **mamrôr**, *mam-ror '*; from 4843; a *bitterness*, i.e. (fig.) calamity:—bitterness {1x}. See: TWOT—1248k; BDB—577a, 601b.

4473. מִמְשַׁח {1x} **mimshach**, *mim-shakh'*; from 4886, in the sense of *expansion*; *outspread* (i.e. with outstretched wings):—anointed {1x}. See: TWOT—1255d; BDB—577b, 603d.

4474. מִמְשָׁל {3x} **mimshâl**, *mim-shawl'*; from 4910; a *ruler* or (abstr.) *rule*:—dominion {2x}, that ruled {1x}. See: TWOT—1259b; BDB—577b, 606a.

4475. מֶמְשָׁלָה {17x} **memshâlâh**, *mem-shaw-law'*; fem. of 4474; *rule*; also (concr. in plur.) a *realm* or a *ruler*:—dominion {10x}, rule {4x}, dominion + 3027 {1x}, government {1x}, power {1x}. See: TWOT—1259c; BDB—577b, 606a.

4476. מִמְשָׁק {1x} **mimshâq**, *mim-shawk'*; from the same as 4943; a *possession*:—breeding {1x}. See: TWOT—1261b; BDB—577b, 606c.

4477. מַמְתַּק {2x} **mamtaq**, *mam-tak'*; from 4985; something *sweet* (lit. or fig.):—(most) sweet {2x}. See: TWOT—1268d; BDB—577b, 609a.

4478. מָן {14x} **mân**, *mawn;* from 4100; lit. a *whatness* (so to speak), i.e. *manna* (so called from the question about it):—manna {14x}. See: TWOT—1208, 1209; BDB—577b, 577c.

4479. מָן {10x} **mân** (Aram.), *mawn;* from 4101; *who* or *what* (prop. interrog., hence, also indef. and rel.):—whomsoever {4x}, who {3x}, whoso {2x}, what {1x}. See: TWOT—2832; BDB—1100d.

4480. מִן {25x} **min**, *min;* or

מִנִּי **minnîy**, *min-nee';* or

מִנֵּי **minnêy** (constr. plur.) *min-nay';* (Is 30:11); for 4482; prop. a *part* of; hence, (prep.), *from* or *out of* in many senses (as follows):—{25x} = above, after, among, at, because of, by (reason of), from (among), in, × neither, × nor, (out) of, over, since, × then, through, × whether, with. See: TWOT—1212, 1213e; BDB—541b, 547a, 577a, 577c, 585d, 606b, 1100d.

4481. מִן {109x} **min** (Aram.), *min;* corresp. to 4480:—of {31x}, from {29x}, part {6x}, . . . I {4x}, . . . me {3x}, before {3x}, after {2x}, because {2x}, therefore {2x}, out {2x}, for {2x}, than {2x}, partly {2x}, misc. {19x} = according, by, × him, since, × these, to, upon, + when. See: TWOT—2833; BDB—1100d.

4482. מֵן {2x} **mên**, *mane;* from an unused root mean. to *apportion;* a *part;* hence, a musical *chord* (as parted into strings):— stringed instrument {1x}, whereby {1x}. See: TWOT—1211; BDB—577c, 585d.

4483. מְנָא {5x} **mᵉnâ** (Aram.), *men-aw';* or

מְנָה **mᵉnâh** (Aram.) *men-aw';* corresp. to 4487; to *count, appoint:*—number {1x}, ordain {1x}, set {3x}. See: TWOT—2835; BDB—1101b.

4484. מְנֵא {3x} **menê** (Aram.), *men-ay';* pass. part. of 4483; *numbered:*—Mene {3x}. See: TWOT—2835a; BDB—1101b, 1108b, 1118c.

4485. מַנְגִּינָה {1x} **mangîynâh**, *man-ghee-naw';* from 5059; a *satire:*—music {1x}. See: TWOT—1291; BDB—584a, 618d.

מִנְדָּה **mindâh**. See 4061.

4486. מַנְדַּע {4x} **mandaᶜ** (Aram.), *man-dah';* corresp. to 4093; *wisdom* or *intelligence:*—knowledge {2x}, reason {1x}, under-

standing {1x}. See: TWOT—2765a, 2834; BDB—1095b, 1101b.

מְנָה **mᵉnâh**. See 4483.

4487. מָנָה {28x} **mânâh**, *maw-naw';* a prim. root; prop. to *weigh* out; by impl. to *allot* or constitute officially; also to *enumerate* or enroll:—number {14x}, prepare {5x}, appointed {4x}, tell {3x}, count {1x}, set {1x}. See: TWOT—1213; BDB—584a, 1101b.

4488. מָנֶה {5x} **mâneh**, *maw-neh';* from 4487; prop. a fixed *weight* or measured amount, i.e. (techn.) a *maneh* or mina:—maneh {1x}, pound {4x}. See: TWOT—1213b; BDB—584b.

4489. מֹנֶה {2x} **môneh**, *mo-neh';* from 4487; prop. something *weighed* out, i.e. (fig.) a *portion* of time, i.e. an *instance:*—time {2x}. See: TWOT—1213c; BDB—584c.

4490. מָנָה {14x} **mânâh**, *maw-naw';* from 4487; prop. something *weighed* out, i.e. (gen.) a *division;* spec. (of food) a *ration;* also a *lot:*—such things as belonged {1x}, part {3x}, portion {10x}. See: TWOT—1213a; BDB—584b.

4491. מִנְהָג {2x} **minhâg**, *min-hawg';* from 5090; the *driving* (of a chariot):— driving {2x}. See: TWOT—1309a; BDB—584d, 624c.

4492. מִנְהָרָה {1x} **minhârâh**, *min-haw-raw';* from 5102; prop. a *channel* or fissure, i.e. (by impl.) a *cavern:*—den {1x}. See: TWOT—1316b; BDB—584d, 626a.

4493. מָנוֹד {1x} **mânôwd**, *maw-node';* from 5110 a *nodding* or *toss* (of the head in derision):—shaking {1x}. See: TWOT—1319c; BDB—584a, 627b.

4494. מָנוֹחַ {7x} **mânôwach**, *maw-no'-akh;* from 5117; *quiet,* i.e. (concr.) a *settled spot,* or (fig.) a *home:*—(place of) rest {7x}. See: TWOT—1323e; BDB—584d, 629c.

4495. מָנוֹחַ {18x} **Mânôwach**, *maw-no'-akh;* the same as 4494; *rest; Manoäch,* an Isr.:—Manoah {18x}. See: BDB—584d, 629d.

4496. מְנוּחָה {21x} **mᵉnûwchâh**, *men-oo-khaw';* or

מְנֻחָה **mᵉnuchâh**, *men-oo-khaw';* fem. of 4495; *repose* or (adv.) *peacefully;* fig. *consolation* (spec. *matrimony*); hence, (concr.) an *abode:*—rest {15x}, resting place {2x}, comfortable {1x}, ease {1x}, quiet {1x}, still {1x}. See: TWOT—1323f; BDB—584d, 629d.

4497. מָנוֹן {1x} **mânôwn** *maw-nohn';* from 5125; a *continuator,* i.e. *heir:*—son {1x}. See: TWOT—1213f; BDB—584d.

4498. מָנוֹס {8x} **mânôwç,** *maw-noce';* from 5127; a *retreat* (lit. or fig.); abstr. a *fleeing:*—× apace {1x}, escape {1x}, way to flee {1x}, flight {1x}, refuge {4x}. See: TWOT—1327a; BDB—651a.

4499. מְנוּסָה {2x} **mᵉnuwçâh,** *men-oo-saw';* or

מְנֻסָה **mᵉnûçâh,** *men-oo-saw';* fem. of 4498; *retreat:*—fleeing {1x}, flight {1x}. See: TWOT—1327b; BDB—586a, 631a.

4500. מָנוֹר {4x} **mânôwr,** *maw-nore';* from 5214; a *yoke* (prop. for *plowing*), i.e. the *frame* of a loom:—beam {4x}. See: TWOT—1361a; BDB—644d.

4501. מְנוֹרָה {40x} **mᵉnôwrâh,** *men-o-raw';* or

מְנֹרָה **mᵉnôrâh,** *men-o-raw';* fem. of 4500 (in the orig. sense of 5216); a *chandelier:*—candlestick {40x}. See: TWOT—1333c; BDB—586b, 633a.

4502. מִנְזָר {1x} **minnᵉzâr,** *min-ez-awr';* from 5144; a *prince:*—crowned {1x}. See: TWOT—1340d; BDB—634d.

4503. מִנְחָה {211x} **minchâh,** *min-khaw';* from an unused root mean. to *apportion,* i.e. *bestow;* a *donation;* euphem. *tribute;* spec. a sacrificial *offering* (usually bloodless and voluntary):—offering {164x}, present {28x}, gift {7x}, oblation {6x}, sacrifice {5x}, meat {1x}.

Minchah means meat [cereal] offering; offering; tribute; present; gift; sacrifice; oblation. **(1)** The *minchah* must be regarded as a token of love, gratitude, and thanksgiving to God, who is Himself the Giver of all good gifts. **(1a)** It was an acknowledgement on the part of man that "the earth is the LORD's and the fullness thereof." **(1b)** Part of it was called the *memorial* and was burned with fire, and the rest was eaten by the priest and his family, not by the offerer. **(1c)** The KJV translates the word as meat offering, which is solid food in contrast to drink [liquids] and flesh [of animals]. The word "meat" in this KJV use really means "solid food/grain offering." **(2)** *Minchah* occurs for the first time in Gen 4:3: "Cain brought of the fruit of the ground an offering unto the LORD." This use reflects the most common connotation of *minchah* as a "vegetable or cereal offering." **(3)** *Minchah* is used many times to designate a "gift" or "present" which is given by one person to another. **(3a)** For example, when Jacob was on his way back home after twenty years, his long-standing guilt and fear of Esau prompted him to send a rather large "present" (bribe) of goats, camels, and other animals (Gen 32:13–15).

(3b) Similarly, Jacob directed his sons to "carry down the man a present" (Gen 43:11) to appease the Egyptian ruler that later turned out to be his lost son Joseph. **(3c)** Those who came to hear Solomon's great wisdom all brought to him an appropriate "present" (1 Kin 10:25), doing so on a yearly basis. **(4)** Frequently *minchah* is used in the sense of "tribute" paid to a king or overlord. **(4a)** The delivering of the "tribute" of the people of Israel to the king of Moab by their judge-deliverer became the occasion for the deliverance of Israel from Moabite control as Ehud assassinated Eglon by a rather sly maneuver (Judg 3:15–23). **(4b)** Years later when David conquered the Moabites, they "became servants to David and brought gifts [tribute]" (2 Sa 8:2). **(4c)** Hosea proclaimed to Israel that its pagan bull-god would "be carried unto Assyria for a present [tribute]" (Hos 10:6). **(4d)** Other passages where *minchah* has the meaning of "tribute" are: Ps 72:10; 1 Kin 4:21; 2 Kin 17:3–4.

(5) *Minchah* is often used to refer to any "offering" or "gift" made to God, whether it was a "vegetable offering" or a "blood sacrifice." **(5a)** The story of Cain and Abel vividly illustrates this general usage: "Cain brought of the fruit of the ground an offering unto the LORD. And Abel, he also brought of the firstlings of his flock and of the fat thereof. And the LORD had respect unto Abel and to his offering: But unto Cain and to his offering he had not respect" (Gen 4:3–5). **(5b)** The animal sacrifices which were misappropriated by the wicked sons of Eli were simply designated as "the offering of the LORD" (1 Sa 2:17). In each case "offering" is the translation of *minchah.* **(6)** A common use of *minchah,* especially in later Old Testament texts, is to designate "meat [grain/cereal] offerings." **(6a)** Sometimes it referred to the "meat [cereal] offering" of first fruits, "green ears of corn, dried by the fire. . . ." (Lev 2:14). **(6b)** Such offerings included oil and frankincense which were burned with the grain.

(6c) Similarly, the "meat [grain] offering" could be in the form of finely ground flour upon which oil and frankincense had been poured also. Sometimes the oil was mixed with the "meat [cereal] offering" (Lev 14:10, 21; 23:13; Num 7:13), again in the form of fine flour. The priest would take a handful of this fine flour, burn it as a memorial portion, and the remainder would belong to the priest (Lev 2:9–10). **(6d)** The "meat [cereal] offering" frequently was in the form of fine flour which was mixed with oil and then formed into cakes and baked, either in a pan or on a griddle (Lev 2:4–5). **(6e)** Other descriptions of this type of baked "meat [cereal] offering" are found in Num 6:15 and Lev 7:9. **(7e)** These baked "meat [cereal] offerings" were always to be made without

leaven, but were to be mixed with salt and oil (Lev 2:11, 13). **(8)** The *minchah* was prescribed as a "meat offering" of flour kneaded with oil to be given along with the whole burnt offering. **(8a)** A libation of wine was to be given as well.

(9) This particular rule applied especially to the Feast of Weeks or Pentecost (Lev 23:18), to the daily "continual offering" (Ex 29:38–42), and to all the whole burnt offerings or general sacrifices (Num 15:1–16). **(9a)** The "meat [cereal] offering" was to be burned, **(9b)** while the wine seems to have been poured out at the foot of the altar like blood of the sacrificial animal. **(10)** The regular daily morning and evening sacrifices included the *minchah* and were specifically referred to as **(10a)** "the meat [cereal] offering of the morning" (Ex 29:41; cf. Num 28:8) and **(10b)** as "the evening meat [cereal] offering" (2 Kin 16:15; cf. Ezra 9:4–5 and Ps 141:2, "evening sacrifice"). **(11)** *Minchah* provides an interesting symbolism for the prophet when he refers to the restoration of the Jews: **(11a)** "And they shall bring all your brethren for an offering unto the LORD out of all nations upon horses, and in chariots . . . to my holy mountain Jerusalem, saith the LORD, as the children of Israel bring an offering in a clean vessel into the house of the LORD" (Is 66:20).

(11b) In his vision of the universal worship of God, even in Gentile lands, Malachi saw the *minchah* given as "a pure offering" to God by believers everywhere (Mal 1:11). Syn.: *ʾAsham* (817) means guilt offering, that which clears guilt away. *ʾIshsheh* (801) means those offerings made by fire. *ʾOlah* (5930) means whole burnt offering with nothing being shared or eaten. *Qorban* (7133) generally means offering, that which brings near to God. *Terumah* (8641) means that offering which was symbolically heaved/waved before God and then eaten by the priest and the one offering. See: TWOT—1214a; BDB—585a, 1101c.

4504. מִנְחָה {2x} **minchâh** (Aram.), *min-khaw';* corresp. to 4503; a sacrificial *offering:*—oblation {1x}, meat offering {1x}. See: TWOT—2836; BDB—1101c.

מְנֻחָה **mᵉnûchâh**. See 4496.

מְנֻחוֹת **Mᵉnûchôwth**. See 2679.

4505. מְנַחֵם {8x} **Mᵉnachêm**, *men-akh-ame';* from 5162; *comforter; Menachem,* an Isr.:—Menahem {8x}. See: BDB—637c.

4506. מָנַחַת {3x} **Mânachath**, *maw-nakh'-ath;* from 5117; *rest; Manachath,* the name of an Edomite and of a place in Moab:—Manahath {3x}. See: BDB—630a.

מְנַחְתִּי **Mᵉnachtîy**. See 2680.

4507. מְנִי {1x} **Mᵉnîy**, *men-ee';* from 4487; the *Apportioner,* i.e. Fate (as an idol):—number {1x}. See: BDB—584c.

מְנִי **mînnîy**. See 4480, 4482.

4508. מִנִּי {1x} **Minnîy**, *min-nee';* of for. der.; *Minni,* an Armenian province:—Minni {1x}. See: BDB—585d.

מְנָיוֹת **mᵉnâyôwth**. See 4521.

4509. מִנְיָמִין {3x} **Minyâmîyn**, *min-yaw-meen';* from 4480 and 3225; *from* (the) *right hand; Minjamin,* the name of two Isr.:—Miniamin {3x}. See: BDB—568a, 585d. comp. 4326.

4510. מִנְיָן {1x} **minyân** (Aram.), *min-yawn';* from 4483; *enumeration:*—number {1x}. See: TWOT—2835b; BDB—1101b, 1101c.

4511. מִנִּית {2x} **Minnîyth**, *min-neeth';* from the same as 4482; *enumeration; Minnith,* a place E. of the Jordan:—Minnith {2x}. See: TWOT—2835b; BDB—585d.

4512. מִנְלֶה {1x} **minleh**, *min-leh';* from 5239; *completion,* i.e. (in produce) *wealth:*—perfection {1x}. See: TWOT—1370a; BDB—585d, 649b.

מְנָסֶה **mᵉnûçâh**. See 4499.

4513. מָנַע {29x} **mânaʿ**, *maw-nah';* a prim. root; to *debar* (neg. or pos.) from benefit or injury:—withhold {18x}, keep back {4x}, refrain {2x}, denied {1x}, deny {1x}, hinder {1x}, keep {1x}, restrained {1x}. See: TWOT—1216; BDB—586a.

4514. מַנְעוּל {6x} **manʿûwl**, *man-ool';* or

מַנְעֻל **manʿûl**, *man-ool';* from 5274; a *bolt:*—lock {6x}. See: TWOT—1383c; BDB—586b, 653b.

4515. מִנְעָל {1x} **minʿâl**, *min-awl';* from 5274; a *bolt:*—shoe {1x}. See: TWOT—1383d; BDB—586b, 653b.

4516. מַנְעַם {1x} **manʿam**, *man-am';* from 5276; a *delicacy:*—dainty {1x}. See: TWOT—1384d; BDB—586b, 654b.

4517. מְנַעְנַע {1x} **mᵉnaʿnaʿ**, *men-ah-ah';* from 5128; a *sistrum* (so called from its *rattling* sound):—cornet {1x}. See: TWOT—1328a; BDB—586b, 631c.

4518. מְנַקִּית {4x} **mᵉnaqqîyth**, *men-ak-keeth';* from 5352; a *sacrificial basin* (for holding blood):—bowl {3x}, cup {1x}. See: TWOT—1412d; BDB—586b, 667d.

מְנֹרָה **mᵉnôrâh**. See 4501.

4519. מְנַשֶּׁה {146x} **Mᵉnashsheh**, *men-ash-sheh';* from 5382; *causing to forget; Menashsheh,* a grandson of Jacob, also the

tribe descended from him, and its territory:—Manasseh {146x}. See: TWOT—1217; BDB—586b.

4520. מְנַשִּׁי {4x} **M^enashshîy**, *men-ash-shee';* from 4519; a *Menashshite* or desc. of Menashsheh:—of Manasseh {2x}, Manassites {2x}. See: BDB—586d.

4521. מְנָת {7x} **m^enâth**, *men-awth';* from 4487; an *allotment* (by courtesy, law or providence):—portion {7x}. See: TWOT—1213d; BDB—584a, 584c, 585d, 586d.

4522. מַס {23x} **maç**, *mas;* or

מִס **miç**, *mees;* from 4549; prop. a *burden* (as causing to *faint*), i.e. a *tax* in the form of forced *labor:*—tribute {12x}, tributary {5x}, levy {4x}, discomfited {1x}, taskmasters {1x}. See: TWOT—1218; BDB—586d.

4523. מָס {1x} **mâç**, *mawce;* from 4549; *fainting*, i.e. (fig.) *disconsolate:*—is afflicted {1x}. See: TWOT—1223a; BDB—587a, 588a.

4524. מֵסַב {5x} **mêçab**, *may-sab';* plur. masc.

מְסִבִּים **m^eçibbîym**, *mes-ib-beem';* or fem.

מְסִבּוֹת **m^eçibbôwth**, *mes-ib-bohth';* from 5437; a *divan* (as *enclosing* the room); abstr. (adv.) *around:*—round about {3x}, compass me about {1x}, at his table {1x}.

Meçab occurs 5 times, and it refers to "that which surrounds or is round." **(1)** *Mecab* refers to a "round table" (Song 1:12) and **(2)** to "places round about" Jerusalem: "And he put down the idolatrous priests, whom the kings of Judah had ordained to burn incense in the high places in the cities of Judah, and in the places round about Jerusalem; them also that burned incense unto Baal, to the sun, and to the moon, and to the planets, and to all the host of heaven" (2 Kin 23:5). See: TWOT—1456c; BDB—587a, 686d, 687b.

מְסֻבָּה **mûçabbâh**. See 4142.

4525. מַסְגֵּר {7x} **maçgêr**, *mas-gare';* from 5462; a *fastener*, i.e. (of a person) a *smith*, (of a thing) a *prison:*—prison {3x}, smith {4x}. See: TWOT—1462c; BDB—587a, 689d.

4526. מִסְגֶּרֶת {17x} **miçgereth**, *mis-gheh'-reth;* from 5462; something *enclosing*, i.e. a *margin* (of a region, of a panel); concr. a *stronghold:*—border {14x}, close place {2x}, hole {1x}. See: TWOT—1462d; BDB—587a, 689d.

4527. מַסַּד {1x} **maççad**, *mas-sad';* from 3245; a *foundation:*—foundation {1x}. See: TWOT—875g; BDB—414c, 587b.

מֹסָדָה **môçâdâh**. See 4146.

4528. מִסְדְּרוֹן {1x} **miçd^erôwn**, *mis-der-ohn';* from the same as 5468; a *colonnade* or *internal portico* (from its *rows* of pillars):—porch {1x}. See: TWOT—1467c; BDB—587b, 690c.

4529. מָסָה {4x} **mâçâh**, *maw-saw';* a prim. root; to *dissolve:*—make to consume away {1x}, (make to) melt {2x}, water {1x}. See: TWOT—1219; BDB—587b.

4530. מִסָּה {1x} **miççâh**, *mis-saw';* from 4549 (in the sense of *flowing*); *abundance*, i.e. (adv.) *liberally:*—tribute {1x}. See: TWOT—1225; BDB—587b, 588b.

4531. מַסָּה {5x} **maççâh**, *mas-saw';* from 5254; a *testing*, of men (judicial) or of God (querulous):—temptation {4x}, trial {1x}. See: TWOT—1223b; BDB—587b, 588a, 650b.

4532. מַסָּה {4x} **Maççâh**, *mas-saw';* the same as 4531; *Massah*, a place in the desert:—Massah {4x}. See: BDB—587b, 650c.

4533. מַסְוֶה {3x} **maçveh**, *mas-veh';* appar. from an unused root mean. to *cover;* a *veil:*—vail {3x}. See: TWOT—1472b; BDB—587b, 691d.

4534. מְסוּכָה {1x} **m^eçûwkah**, *mes-oo-kaw';* for 4881; a *hedge:*—thorn hedge {1x}. See: TWOT—1475a; BDB—587b, 692b.

4535. מַסָּח {1x} **maççâch**, *mas-sawkh';* from 5255 in the sense of *staving* off; a *cordon*, (adv.) or (as a) military *barrier:*—broken down {1x}. See: TWOT—1374a; BDB—587b, 650c.

4536. מִסְחָר {1x} **miçchâr**, *mis-khawr';* from 5503; *trade:*—traffic {1x}. See: TWOT—1486d; BDB—587b, 695c.

4537. מָסַךְ {5x} **mâçak**, *maw-sak';* a prim. root; to *mix*, espec. wine (with spices):—mingle {5x}. See: TWOT—1220; BDB—587c.

4538. מֶסֶךְ {1x} **meçek**, *meh'-sek;* from 4537; a *mixture*, i.e. of wine with spices:—mixture {1x}. See: TWOT—1220a; BDB—587c.

4539. מָסָךְ {25x} **mâçâk**, *maw-sawk';* from 5526; a *cover*, i.e. *veil:*—covering {7x}, curtain {1x}, hanging {17x}. See: TWOT—1492a; BDB—587c, 697a.

4540. מְסֻכָּה {1x} **m^eçukkâh**, *mes-ook-kaw';* from 5526; a *covering*, i.e. garniture:—covering {1x}. See: TWOT—1492a; BDB—587c, 697b.

4541. מַסֵּכָה {28x} **maççêkâh**, *mas-say-kaw';* from 5258; prop. a *pouring* over, i.e. *fusion* of metal (espec. a *cast* image); by impl. a *libation*, i.e. league; concr. a *coverlet* (as if *poured* out):—covering {2x}, molten {7x},

image {18x}, vail {1x}. See: TWOT—1375c, 1376a; BDB—587c, 651a, 651b.

4542. מִסְכֵּן {4x} miçkên, *mis-kane';* from 5531; *indigent:*—poor {3x}, poor man {1x}. See: TWOT—1221; BDB—587c.

4543. מִסְכְּנָה {7x} miçkᵉnâh, *mis-ken-aw';* by transp. from 3664; a *magazine:*—store {5x}, storehouse {1x}, treasure {1x}. See: TWOT—1494a; BDB—587b, 698b.

4544. מִסְכֵּנֻת {1x} miçkênuth, *mis-kay-nooth';* from 4542; *indigence:*—scarceness {1x}. See: TWOT—1222; BDB—587d, 698c.

4545. מַסֶּכֶת {2x} maççeketh, *mas-seh'-keth;* from 5259 in the sense of *spreading* out; something *expanded,* i.e. the *warp* in a loom (as *stretched* out to receive the woof):—web {2x}. See: TWOT—1376b; BDB—587c, 651c.

4546. מְסִלָּה {27x} mᵉçillâh, *mes-il-law';* from 5549; a *thoroughfare* (as *turnpiked*), lit. or fig.; spec. a *viaduct,* a *staircase:*—highway {19x}, causeway {2x}, path {2x}, way {2x}, courses {1x}, terraces {1x}. See: TWOT—1506d; BDB—587d, 700c.

4547. מַסְלוּל {1x} maçlûwl, *mas-lool';* from 5549; a *thoroughfare* (as turnpiked):—highway {1x}. See: TWOT—1506d; BDB—587d, 700c.

4548. מַסְמֵר {4x} maçmêr, *mas-mare';* or

מִסְמֵר miçmêr, *mis-mare';* also (fem.)

מַסְמְרָה maçmᵉrâh, *mas-mer-aw';* or

מִסְמְרָה miçmᵉrâh, *mis-mer-aw';* or even

מַשְׂמְרָה masmᵉrâh (Eccl 12:11), *mas-mer-aw';* from 5568; a *peg* (as *bristling* from the surface):—nail {4x}. See: TWOT—1518b; BDB—587d, 601d, 702c, 971b.

4549. מָסַס {21x} mâçaç, *maw-sas';* a prim. root; to *liquefy;* fig. to *waste* (with disease), to *faint* (with fatigue, fear or grief):—melt {13x}, faint {2x}, melt away {1x}, discouraged {1x}, loosed {1x}, molten {1x}, refuse {1x}, utterly {1x}. See: TWOT—1223; BDB—549d, 587d.

4550. מַסַּע {12x} maççaʿ, *mas-sah';* from 5265; a *departure* (from *striking* the tents), i.e. march (not necessarily a single day's travel); by impl. a *station* (or point of *departure*):—journey {10x}, journeying {2x}. See: TWOT—1380a; BDB—588a, 652c.

4551. מַסָּע {2x} maççâʿ, *mas-saw';* from 5265 in the sense of *projecting;* a *missile* (spear or arrow); also a *quarry* (whence stones are, as it were, *ejected*):—before it was

brought {1x}, dart {1x}. See: TWOT—1380b, 1381a; BDB—588a, 652d.

4552. מִסְעָד {1x} miçʿâd, *mis-awd'* from 5582; a *balustrade* (for stairs):—pillar {1x}. See: TWOT—1525a; BDB—588a, 703c.

4553. מִסְפֵּד {16x} miçpêd, *mis-pade';* from 5594; a *lamentation:*—lamentation {3x}, one mourneth {1x}, mourning {6x}, wailing {6x}. See: TWOT—1530a; BDB—588a, 704d.

4554. מִסְפּוֹא {5x} miçpôwʾ, *mis-po';* from an unused root mean. to *collect; fodder:*—provender {5x}. See: TWOT—1529a; BDB—588a, 704d.

4555. מִסְפָּחָה {2x} miçpâchâh, *mis-paw-khaw';* from 5596; a *veil* (as *spread* out):—kerchief {2x}. See: TWOT—1534c; BDB—588a, 705d.

4556. מִסְפַּחַת {3x} miçpachath, *mis-pakh'-ath;* from 5596; *scurf* (as *spreading* over the surface):—scab {3x}. See: TWOT—1534b; BDB—588a, 705c.

4557. מִסְפָּר {134x} miçpâr, *mis-pawr';* from 5608; a *number,* def. (arithmetical) or indef. (large, *innumerable;* small, a *few*); also (abstr.) *narration:*—number {110x}, few {6x}, all {3x}, innumerable {3x}, sum {2x}, time {2x}, account {1x}, abundance + 369 {1x}, infinite {1x}, innumerable + 369 {1x}, numbered {1x}, tale {1x}, telling {1x}, finite {1x}.

Miçpar (4557) means "measure; (a certain) number; account." **(1)** *Miçpar* can mean "measure" (quantity) as in Gen 41:49: "And Joseph gathered corn as the sand of the sea, very much, until he left numbering; for it was without number." **(2)** In Gen 34:30, the first biblical occurrence, the word refers to "a certain number" in the sense of the sum total of individuals that are counted: ". . . and I being few in number, they shall gather themselves together against me, and slay me." **(3)** The word means "account" (what is set forth in a detailed report) as in Judg 7:15: "And it was so, when Gideon heard the telling of the dream, and the interpretation thereof, that he worshipped, and returned into the host of Israel, and said, Arise; for the LORD hath delivered into your hand the host of Midian." See: TWOT—1540e; BDB—588a, 708d.

4558. מִסְפָּר {1x} Miçpâr, *mis-pawr';* the same as 4457; *number; Mispar,* an Isr.:—Mizpar {1x}. See: BDB—588a, 709a. comp. 4559.

מִסְרוֹת Môçᵉrowth. See 4149.

4559. מִסְפֶּרֶת {1x} Miçpereth, *mis-peh'-reth;* fem. of 4457; *enumeration; Mis-*

pereth, an Isr.:—Mispereth {1x}. See: BDB—588a, 709a. comp. 4458.

4560. מָסַר {2x} **mâçar,** *maw-sar';* a prim. root; to *sunder,* i.e. (tran.) *set apart,* or (reflex.) *apostatize:*—commit {1x}, deliver {1x}. See: TWOT—1224; BDB—588a.

4561. מֹסָר {1x} **môçâr,** *mo-sawr';* from 3256; *admonition:*—instruction {1x}. See: TWOT—877b; BDB—416b, 416d, 558a, 588b.

4562. מֹסֶרֶת {1x} **mâçôreth,** *maw-so'-reth;* from 631; a *band:*—bond {1x}. See: TWOT—141e; BDB—64b, 588b.

4563. מִסְתּוֹר {1x} **miçtôwr,** *mis-tore';* from 5641; a *refuge:*—covert {1x}. See: TWOT—1551c; BDB—588b, 712c.

4564. מַסְתֵּר {1x} **maçtêr,** *mas-tare';* from 5641; prop. a *hider,* i.e. (abstr.) a hiding, i.e. *aversion:*—hid {1x}. See: TWOT—1551e; BDB—588b, 712c.

4565. מִסְתָּר {10x} **miçtâr,** *mis-tawr';* from 5641; prop. a *concealer,* i.e. a *covert:*—secret {1x}, secretly {2x}, places {7x}. See: TWOT—1551d; BDB—588b, 712c.

מְעָא **mᵉʿâ.** See 4577.

4566. מַעֲבָד {1x} **maʿbâd,** *mah-bawd';* from 5647; an *act:*—work {1x}. See: TWOT—1553f; BDB—588b, 716a, 1105a.

4567. מַעֲבָד {1x} **maʿbâd** (Aram.), *mah-bawd';* corresp. to 4566; an *act:*—work {1x}. See: TWOT—2896c; BDB—1101c, 1105a.

4568. מַעֲבֶה {1x} **maʿăbeh,** *mah-ab-eh';* from 5666; prop. *compact* (part of soil), i.e. *loam:*—clay {1x}. See: TWOT—1554b; BDB—588b, 716b.

4569. מַעֲבָר {11x} **maʿăbâr,** *mah-ab-awr';* or fem.

מַעֲבָרָה **maʿăbârâh,** *mah-ab-aw-raw';* from 5674; a *crossing*-place (of a river, a *ford;* of a mountain, a *pass*); abstr. a *transit,* i.e. (fig.) *overwhelming:*—ford {4x}, place where . . . pass {1x}, passage {6x}. *Maʿabar,* **the masculine form,** appears 3 times to mean: **(1)** "sweep" (of a staff): "And in every place where the grounded staff shall pass [*maʿabar*], which the LORD shall lay upon him, it shall be with tabrets and harps: and in battles of shaking will he fight with it" (Is 30:32); **(2)** "ford" (Gen 32:22); and **(3)** "ravine" or "passage" (1 Sa 13:23). **(4)** *Maʿbarah,* **the feminine form,** which appears 8 times, means **(4a)** "ford": "And the men pursued after them the way to Jordan unto the fords: and as soon as they which pursued after them were gone out, they shut the gate" (Josh 2:7); and **(4b)** "ravine" or "passage": "And between the passages [*maʿ-*

barah], by which Jonathan sought to go over unto the Philistines' garrison, there was a sharp rock on the one side, and a sharp rock on the other side: and the name of the one was Bozez, and the name of the other Seneh" (1 Sa 14:4). Syn.: 5674, 5676, 5680. See: TWOT—1556h; BDB—588c, 721b.

4570. מַעְגָּל {16x} **maʿgâl,** *mah-gawl';* or fem.

מַעְגָּלָה **maʿgâlâh,** *mah-gaw-law';* from the same as 5696; a *track* (lit. or fig.); also a *rampart* (as *circular*):—path {9x}, trench {3x}, goings {2x}, ways {1x}, wayside + 3027 {1x}. See: TWOT—1560f; BDB—588c, 722d.

4571. מָעַד {6x} **mâʿad,** *maw-ad';* a prim. root; to *waver:*—make to shake {1x}, slide {2x}, slip {3x}. See: TWOT—1226; BDB—588c.

מֹעֵד **môʿêd.** See 4150.

4572. מַעֲדַי {1x} **Maʿăday,** *mah-ad-ah'-ee;* from 5710; *ornamental; Maadai,* an Isr.:—Maadai {1x}. See: BDB—588c.

4573. מַעֲדְיָה {1x} **Maʿadyâh,** *mah-ad-yaw';* from 5710 and 3050; *ornament of Jah; Maadjah,* an Isr.:—Maadiah {1x}. See: BDB—588b, 588c. comp. 4153.

4574. מַעֲדָן {4x} **maʿădân,** *mah-ad-awn';* or (fem.)

מַעֲדַנָּה **maʿădannâh,** *mah-ad-an-naw';* from 5727; a *delicacy* or (abstr.) *pleasure* (adv. *cheerfully*):—dainty {1x}, delicately {2x}, delight {1x}. See: TWOT—1567d; BDB—588d, 726d.

4575. מַעֲדַנָּה {1x} **maʿădannâh,** *mah-ad-an-naw';* by tran. from 6029; a *bond,* i.e. *group:*—influence {1x}. See: TWOT—1649a; BDB—588d, 726d, 772c.

4576. מַעְדֵּר {1x} **maʿdêr,** *mah-dare';* from 5737; a (weeding) *hoe:*—mattock {1x}. See: TWOT—1571a; BDB—588d, 727c.

4577. מְעָה {1x} **mᵉʿâh** (Aram.), *meh-aw';* or

מְעָא **mᵉʿâ** (Aram.), *meh-aw';* corresp. to 4578; only in plur. the *bowels:*—belly {1x}. See: TWOT—2837; BDB—1101c.

4578. מֵעֶה {32x} **mêʿêh,** *may-eh';* from an unused root prob. mean. to *be soft;* used only in plur. the *intestines,* or (collect.) the *abdomen,* fig. *sympathy;* by impl. a *vest;* by extens. the *stomach,* the *uterus* (or of men, the seat of generation), the *heart* (fig.):—belly {3x}, bowels {27x}, X heart {1x}, womb {1x}. Syn.: 3820, 5315, 7023, 7130. See: TWOT—1227a; BDB—588d, 590c, 1101c.

4579. מֵעָה {1x} **mê'âh,** *may-aw';* fem. of 4578; the *belly,* i.e. (fig.) interior:— gravel {1x}. See: TWOT—1227b; BDB—589a.

4580. מָעוֹג {2x} **mâ'ôwg,** *maw-ogue';* from 5746; a *cake* of bread (with 3934 a *table-buffoon,* i.e. *parasite):*—cake {1x}, feast {1x}. See: TWOT—1575b; BDB—589b, 728b.

4581. מָעוֹז {37x} **mâ'ôwz,** *maw-oze'* (also

מָעוּז **mâ'ûwz,** *maw-ooz'*); or

מָעֹז **mâ'ôz,** *maw-oze'* (also

מָעֻז **mâ'uz,** *maw-ooz'*); from 5810; a *fortified* place; fig. a *defence:*— strength {24x}, strong {4x}, fortress {3x}, hold {2x}, forces {1x}, fort {1x}, rock {1x}, strengthen {1x}. See: TWOT—1578a; BDB—589b, 731d.

4582. מָעוֹךְ {1x} **Mâ'ôwk,** *maw-oke';* from 4600; *oppressed; Maok,* a Philistine:—Maoch {1x}. See: BDB—590d.

4583. מָעוֹן {19x} **mâ'ôwn,** *maw-ohn';* or

מָעִין **mâ'îyn** (1 Chr 4:41), *maw-een';* from the same as 5772; an *abode,* of God (the Tabernacle or the Temple), men (their home) or animals (their lair); hence, a *retreat* (asylum):—habitation {10x}, dwelling {4x}, den {2x}, dwelling place {2x}, dwellingplace {1x}. See: TWOT—1581a; BDB—589b, 732d.

4584. מָעוֹן {8x} **Mâ'ôwn,** *maw-ohn';* the same as 4583; a *residence; Maon,* the name of an Isr. and of a place in Pal.:—Maon {5x}, Maonites {3x}. See: BDB—589b, 733a. comp. 1010, 4586.

4585. מְעוֹנָה {9x} **me'ôwnâh,** *meh-o-naw';* or

מְעֹנָה **me'ônâh,** *meh-o-naw';* fem. of 4583, and mean. the same:—den {5x}, habitation {1x}, (dwelling) place {1x}, refuge {1x}. See: TWOT—1581b; BDB—589b, 591d, 733a.

4586. מְעוּנַי {3x} **Me'ûwnay,** *meh-oo-naw'-ee;* or

מְעִינִי **Me'îyniy,** *meh-ee-nee';* prob. patrial from 4584; a *Meünite,* or inhab. of Maon (only in plur.):—Mehunim {1x}, Mehunims {1x}, Meunim {1x}. See: BDB—589b, 590c.

4587. מְעוֹנֹתַי {1x} **Me'ôwnôthay,** *meh-o-no-thah'-ee;* plur. of 4585; *habitative; Meonothai,* an Isr.:—Meonothai {1x}. See: BDB—589b, 733b.

4588. מָעוּף {1x} **mâ'ûwph,** *maw-oof';* from 5774 in the sense of *covering* with shade [comp. 4155]; *darkness:*—dimness {1x}. See: TWOT—1583b; BDB—589b, 734a.

4589. מָעוֹר {1x} **mâ'ôwr,** *maw-ore';* from 5783; *nakedness,* i.e. (in plur.) the *pudenda:*—nakedness {1x}. See: TWOT—1588a; BDB—589b, 735d.

מָעֹז **mâ'ôz.** See 4581.

מָעֻז **mâ'uz.** See 4581.

4590. מַעַזְיָה {1x} **Ma'azyâh,** *mah-az-yaw';* or

מַעַזְיָהוּ **Ma'azyâhûw,** *mah-az-yaw'-hoo;* prob. from 5756 (in the sense of *protection*) and 3050; *rescue of Jah; Maazjah,* the name of two Isr.:— Maaziah {1x}. See: BDB—589b.

4591. מָעַט {22x} **mâ'at,** *maw-at';* a prim. root; prop. to *pare off,* i.e. *lessen;* intr. to *be* (or caus. to *make*) *small* or *few* (or fig. *ineffective*):—diminish {5x}, few {4x}, less {4x}, little {3x}, fewness {1x}, least {1x}, minished {1x}, decrease {1x}, nothing {1x}, few in number {1x}. See: TWOT—1228; BDB—589b.

4592. מְעַט {102x} **me'at,** *meh-at';* or

מְעָט **me'ât,** *meh-awt';* from 4591; a *little* or *few* (often adv. or compar.):— little {49x}, few {23x}, while {6x}, almost {5x}, small thing {4x}, small {3x}, some {2x}, matter {2x}, soon {2x}, fewer {1x}, fewest {1x}, lightly {1x}, very {1x}, little way {1x}, worth {1x}. See: TWOT—1228a; BDB—589d.

4593. מָעֹט {1x} **mâ'ôt,** *maw-ote';* pass. adj. of 4591; *thinned* (as to the edge), i.e. *sharp:*—wrapped up {1x}. See: TWOT—1602; BDB—599a.

4594. מַעֲטֶה {1x} **ma'ăteh,** *mah-at-eh';* from 5844; a *vestment:*—garment {1x}. See: TWOT—1601a; BDB—590c, 742a.

4595. מַעֲטָפָה {1x} **ma'ătâphâh,** *mah-at-aw-faw';* from 5848; a *cloak:*— mantle {1x}. See: TWOT—1606a; BDB—590c, 742c.

4596. מְעִי {1x} **me'îy,** *meh-ee';* from 5753; a *pile* of rubbish (as *contorted*), i.e. a *ruin* (comp. 5856):—heap {1x}. See: TWOT—1577e; BDB—590c, 730d.

4597. מָעַי {1x} **Mâ'ay,** *maw-ah'-ee;* prob. from 4578; *sympathetic; Maai,* an Isr.:— Maai {1x}. See: BDB—590c.

4598. מְעִיל {28x} **me'îyl,** *meh-eel';* from 4603 in the sense of *covering;* a *robe* (i.e. upper and outer *garment*):—cloke {1x}, coat {1x}, mantle {7x}, robe {19x}. See: TWOT—1230b; BDB—591c.

מֵעִים **mê'îym.** See 4578.

מְעִין **me'îyn** (Aram.). See 4577.

Hebrew

4599. מַעְיָן {23x} **maʿyân**, *mah-yawn'*; or

מַעְיְנוֹ **maʿyᵉnôw** (Ps 114:8) *mah-yen-o'*; or (fem.)

מַעְיָנָה **maʿyânâh**, *mah-yaw-naw'*; from 5869 (as a denom. in the sense of a *spring*); a *fountain* (also collect.), fig. a *source* (of satisfaction):—fountain {16x}, spring {2x}, well {5x}.

Maʿyan (4599) means "spring." **(1)** In Lev 11:36, *maʿyan* means "spring": "Nevertheless a fountain or pit, wherein there is plenty of water, shall be clean: but that which toucheth their carcase shall be unclean." **(2)** Another example is found in Gen 7:11: "In the six hundredth year of Noah's life, in the second month, . . . the same day were all the fountains of the great deep broken up, and the windows of heaven were opened." See: TWOT—1613a; BDB—590c, 745d.

מְעִינִי **Mᵉʿîyniy**. See 4586.

4600. מָעַךְ {3x} **mâʿak**, *maw-ak'*; a prim. root; to *press*, i.e. to *pierce, emasculate, handle*:—bruised {1x}, stuck {1x}, be pressed {1x}. See: TWOT—1229; BDB—590c.

4601. מַעֲכָה {23x} **Maʿăkâh**, *mah-ak-aw'*; or

מַעֲכָת **Maʿăkâth** (Josh 13:13), *mah-ak-awth'*; from 4600; *depression*; *Maakah* (or *Maakath*), the name of a place in Syria, also of a Mesopotamian, of three Isr., and of four Israelitesses and one Syrian woman:—Maachah {18x}, Maacah {3x}, Maachathites {1x}, Syriamaachah + 758 {1x}. See: BDB—590d, 591a. See also 1038.

4602. מַעֲכָתִי {8x} **Maʿăkâthiy**, *mah-ak-aw-thee'*; patrial from 4601; a *Maakathite*, or inhab. of Maakah:—Maachathite {7x}, Maachathi. See: BDB—591a.

4603. מָעַל {35x} **mâʿal**, *maw-al'*; a prim. root; prop. to *cover* up; used only fig. to *act covertly*, i.e. *treacherously*:—trespass {13x}, commit {11x}, transgress {10x}, done {1x}.

Maʿal means "to trespass, act unfaithfully." **(1)** Most of the time the noun *maʿal* will be combined with a verb into one phrase in which the verb takes the meaning of "to act" or "to commit"—e.g., Josh 7:1: "But the children of Israel committed [*maʿal*] a trespass [*maʿal*] in the accursed thing." **(2)** The first occurrence of the verb (together with the noun) is found in Lev 5:15: "If a soul commit a trespass, and sin through ignorance. . . ." **(2a)** The sense of the verb is similar to the verb "to sin." **(2b)** In fact, in the next chapter the verb for "to sin" and *maʿal* are used together: "If a soul sin, and commit a trespass against the LORD, and lie unto his neighbor . . ." (Lev 6:2). **(2c)** The combining of these two usages in Leviticus is significant.

(2c1) First, it shows that the verb may be a synonym for "to sin." *Maʿal* has basically this meaning in Lev 5:15, since the sin is here out of ignorance instead of a deliberate act of treachery. **(2c2)** Second, the meaning of *maʿal* is further expressed by a verb indicating the intent of being unfaithful to one's neighbor for personal profit ("commit a trespass against the LORD, and lie unto his neighbor . . .").

(3) The offense is against God, even when one acts unfaithfully against one's neighbor. **(3a)** In 2 Chr 29:6 we read: "For our fathers have trespassed, and done that which was evil in the eyes of the LORD our God, and have forsaken him"; and **(3b)** Daniel prayed: ". . . Because of their trespass that they have trespassed against thee" (Dan 9:7). **(4)** When God spoke to Ezekiel: "Son of man, when the land sinneth against me by trespassing grievously, then will I stretch out mine hand upon it, and . . . cut off man and beast from it" (Eze 14:13), He communicated also His displeasure with Israel's rebellious, treacherous attitude. **(5)** The verb *maʿal* generally expresses man's unfaithfulness to God (Lev 26:40; Deut 32:51; 2 Chr 12:2; Ezra 10:2; Eze 14:13). **(6)** The word further signifies man's unfaithfulness to his fellow man; particularly it is illustrative of unfaithfulness in marriage: "If any man's wife go aside, and commit a trespass against him, And a man lie with her carnally . . ." (Num 5:12–13). See: TWOT—1230; BDB—591a.

4604. מַעַל {29x} **maʿal**, *mah'-al*; from 4603; *treachery*, i.e. sin:—trespass {17x}, transgression {6x}, trespassed {2x}, falsehood {1x}, grievously {1x}, sore {1x}, very {1x}.

Maʿal means "trespass; unfaithful, treacherous act." **(1)** In addition to the primary sense of "trespass," **(1a)** there may be an indication of the motivation through which the sin was committed. **(1b)** Most of the usages support the idea of "faithlessness, treachery." **(1c)** It is an act committed by a person who knows better but who, for selfish motives, acts in bad faith. **(1d)** The story of Achan bears out the attitude of treachery (Josh 7:1). **(1e)** Joshua challenged Israel not to follow the example of Achan: "Did not Achan the son of Zerah commit [*maʿal*] a trespass [*maʿal*] in the accursed thing, and wrath fell on all the congregation of Israel?" (Josh 22:20). **(2)** In 2 Chr 29:19 the "faithlessness" was committed against God: "Moreover all the vessels which king Ahaz in his reign did cast away in his transgression." **(3)** *Maʿal* also appears in Ezra 9:2: "yea, the hand of the princes and rulers hath been chief in this trespass." See: TWOT—1230a; BDB—591b.

4605. מַעַל {138x} **maʿal**, *mah'-al*; from 5927; prop. the *upper* part, used only

adv. with pref. *upward, above, overhead, from the top,* etc.:—upward {59x}, above {53x}, high {6x}, exceedingly {4x}, upon {4x}, very {2x}, forward {2x}, exceeding {2x}, over {2x}, above only {1x}, overturned + 2015 {1x}, above them {1x}, up + 935 {1x}. See: TWOT—1624k; BDB—591d, 751c.

מֵעַל **mê°al**. See 5921.

4606. מֵעַל {1x} **mê°al** (Aram.), *may-awl';* from 5954; (only in plur. as sing.) the *setting* (of the sun):—going down {1x}. See: TWOT—2911a; BDB—1101c, 1106d.

4607. מֹעַל {1x} **mô°al,** *mo'-al;* from 5927; a *raising* (of the hands):—lifting up {1x}. See: TWOT—1624i; BDB—591d, 751b.

4608. מַעֲלֶה {18x} **ma°âleh,** *mah-al-eh';* from 5927; an *elevation,* i.e. (concr.) *acclivity* or *platform;* abstr. (the relation or state) a *rise* or (fig.) *priority:*—up {11x}, ascent {2x}, before {1x}, chiefest {1x}, cliff {1x}, hill {1x}, stairs {1x}. See: TWOT—1624j; BDB—591d, 751b.

4609. מַעֲלָה {47x} **ma°âlâh,** *mah-al-aw';* fem. of 4608; *elevation,* i.e. the act (lit. a *journey* to a higher place, fig. a *thought* arising), or (concr.) the condition (lit. a *step* or *grade*-mark, fig. a *superiority* of station); spec. a climactic *progression* (in certain Psalms):—degree {25x}, steps {11x}, stairs {5x}, dial {2x}, by {1x}, come {1x}, stories {1x}, go up {1x}.

Ma°alah means step; procession; pilgrimage. **(1)** It signifies a step or stair: "Neither shalt thou go up by steps unto mine altar, that thy nakedness be not discovered thereon" (Ex 20:26). **(2)** The word can mean procession: It is translated "degrees" in the titles of the Psalms sung by the men as they pilgrimed in procession to Jerusalem three times a year (Pss 120—134). See: TWOT—1624L, 1624m; BDB—591d, 752a.

4610. מַעֲלֵה עַקְרַבִּים {3x} **Ma°âleh °Aqrab-bîym,** *mah-al-ay' ak-rab-beem';* from 4608 and (the plur. of) 6137; *Steep of Scorpions,* a place in the Desert:—Maaleh-accrabim {2x}, the ascent (going up) of Akrabbim {1x}. See: BDB—751c, 785d.

4611. מַעֲלָל {41x} **ma°âlâl,** *mah-al-awl';* from 5953; an *act* (good or bad):—doings {35x}, endeavours {1x}, inventions {2x}, works {3x}. See: TWOT—1627e; BDB—591d, 760b.

4612. מַעֲמָד {5x} **ma°âmâd,** *mah-am-awd';* from 5975; (fig.) a *position:*—attendance {2x}, office {1x}, place {1x}, state {1x}.

Ma°amad, which occurs 5 times, refers **(1)** to "service or attendance upon": "And the meat of his table, and the sitting of his servants, and

the attendance [*ma°amad*] of his ministers, and their apparel; his cupbearers also, and their apparel; and his ascent by which he went up into the house of the LORD; there was no more spirit in her" (2 Chr 9:4) and to **(2)** "office or function" (in someone's service): "Because their office [*ma°amad*] was to wait on the sons of Aaron for the service of the house of the LORD, in the courts, and in the chambers, and in the purifying of all holy things, and the work of the service of the house of God;" (1 Chr 23:28). Syn.: 4613, 5977, 5979, 5982. See: TWOT—1637d; BDB—591d, 765b.

4613. מָעֳמָד {1x} **mâ°ŏmâd,** *maw-om-awd';* from 5975; lit. a *foothold:*—standing {1x}.

Ma°omad occurs once to mean "standing place" or "foothold": "I sink in deep mire, where there is no standing [*ma°omad*]: I am come into deep waters, where the floods overflow me" (Ps 69:2). Syn.: 4612, 5977, 5979, 5982. See: TWOT—1637e; BDB—591d, 765c.

4614. מַעֲמָסָה {1x} **ma°âmâçâh,** *mah-am-aw-saw';* from 6006; *burdensomeness:*—burdensome {1x}. See: TWOT—1643a; BDB—591d, 770c.

4615. מַעֲמָק {5x} **ma°âmâq,** *mah-am-awk';* from 6009; a *deep:*—deep {2x}, depths {3x}. See: TWOT—1644e; BDB—591d, 771b.

4616. מַעַן {10x} **ma°an,** *mah'-an;* from 6030; prop. *heed,* i.e. *purpose;* used only adv., *on account of* (as a motive or an aim), teleologically *in order that:*—{10x} = because of, to the end (intent) that, for (to, . . . 's sake), + lest, that, to. See: TWOT—1650g; BDB—541b, 591d, 775a.

4617. מַעֲנֶה {8x} **ma°ăneh,** *mah-an-eh';* from 6030; a *reply* (favorable or contradictory):—answer {7x}, ✗ himself {1x}. See: TWOT—1650f; BDB—591d, 775a, 775d.

4618. מַעֲנָה {2x} **ma°ânâh,** *mah-an-aw';* from 6031, in the sense of *depression* or *tilling;* a *furrow:*—+ acre {1x}, furrows {1x}. See: TWOT—1651b; BDB—591d, 776a.

מְעֹנָה **me°ônâh.** See 4585.

4619. מַעַץ {1x} **Ma°ats,** *mah'-ats;* from 6095; *closure; Maats,* an Isr.:—Maaz {1x}. See: BDB—591d.

4620. מַעֲצֵבָה {1x} **ma°âtsêbâh,** *mah-ats-ay-baw';* from 6087; *anguish:*—sorrow {1x}. See: TWOT—1666f; BDB—591d, 781a.

4621. מַעֲצָד {2x} **ma°âtsâd,** *mah-ats-awd';* from an unused root mean. to *hew;* an *axe:*—ax {1x}, tongs {1x}. See: TWOT—1668a; BDB—591d, 781b.

4622. מָעְצוֹר {1x} **ma‘tsôwr,** *mah-tsore';* from 6113; obj. a *hindrance:*—restraint {1x}. See: TWOT—1675d; BDB—591d, 784a.

4623. מַעְצָר {1x} **ma‘tsâr,** *mah-tsawr';* from 6113; subj. *control:*—rule {1x}. Prov 25:28 stresses self-restraint. See: TWOT—1675e; BDB—591d, 784a.

4624. מַעֲקֶה {1x} **ma‘ǎqeh,** *mah-ak-eh';* from an unused root mean. to *repress;* a *parapet:*—battlement {1x}. See: TWOT—1679a; BDB—591d, 785b.

4625. מַעֲקָשׁ {1x} **ma‘ǎqâsh,** *mah-ak-awsh';* from 6140; a *crook* (in a road):—crooked things {1x}. See: TWOT—1684c; BDB—591d, 786a.

4626. מַעַר {1x} **ma‘ar,** *mah'-ar;* from 6168; a *nude* place, i.e. (lit.) the *pudenda,* or (fig.) a vacant *space:*—nakedness {1x}, proportion {1x}. See: TWOT—1692d; BDB—591d, 789a.

4627. מַעֲרָב {9x} **ma‘ǎrâb,** *mah-ar-awb';* from 6148, in the sense of *trading; traffic;* by impl. mercantile *goods:*—market {4x}, merchandise {5x}. See: TWOT—1686c; BDB—591d.

4628. מַעֲרָב {14x} **ma‘ǎrâb,** *mah-ar-awb';* or (fem.)

מַעֲרָבָה **ma‘ǎrâbâh,** *mah-ar-aw-baw';* from 6150, in the sense of *shading;* the *west* (as a region of the *evening* sun):—west {10x}, westward {4x}. See: TWOT—1689b; BDB—591d, 788a.

4629. מַעֲרֶה {1x} **ma‘ǎreh,** *mah-ar-eh';* from 6168; a *nude* place, i.e. a *common:*—meadows {1x}. See: TWOT—1692d; BDB—591d, 788b, 789a.

4630. מַעֲרָה {1x} **ma‘ǎrâh,** *mah-ar-aw';* fem. of 4629; an *open* spot:—armies {1x}. See: TWOT—1692d; BDB—592a, 790b.

4631. מְעָרָה {39x} **mᵉ‘ârâh,** *meh-aw-raw';* from 5783; a *cavern* (as dark):—cave {36x}, den {2x}, hole {1x}. See: TWOT—1704a; BDB—592a, 792c.

4632. מְעָרָה {1x} **Mᵉ‘ârâh,** *meh-aw-raw';* the same as 4631; *cave; Meärah,* a place in Pal.:—Mearah {1x}. See: BDB—792c.

4633. מַעֲרָךְ {1x} **ma‘ǎrâk,** *mah-ar-awk';* from 6186; an *arrangement,* i.e. (fig.) mental *disposition:*—preparation {1x}. See: TWOT—1694c; BDB—592a, 790a.

4634. מַעֲרָכָה {20x} **ma‘ǎrâkâh,** *mah-ar-aw-kaw';* fem. of 4633; an *arrangement;* concr. a *pile;* spec. a military *array:*—army {15x}, fight {1x}, be set in order {1x}, or-

dered place {1x}, rank {1x}, row {1x}. See: TWOT—1694d; BDB—592a, 790a.

4635. מַעֲרֶכֶת {9x} **ma‘ǎreketh,** *mah-ar-eh'-keth;* from 6186; an *arrangement,* i.e. (concr.) a *pile* (of loaves):—shewbread + 3899 {5x}, shewbread {2x}, row {2x}. See: TWOT—1694e; BDB—592a, 790b.

4636. מַעֲרֹם {1x} **ma‘ǎrôm,** *mah-ar-ome';* from 6191, in the sense of *stripping; bare:*—naked {1x}. See: TWOT—1588d; BDB—592a, 736a, 791a.

4637. מַעֲרָצָה {1x} **ma‘ǎrâtsâh,** *mah-ar-aw-tsaw';* from 6206; *violence:*—terror {1x}. See: TWOT—1702c; BDB—592a, 792b.

4638. מַעֲרָת {1x} **Ma‘ǎrâth,** *mah-ar-awth';* a form of 4630; *waste; Maarath,* a place in Pal.:—Maarath {1x}. See: BDB—592a, 789b.

4639. מַעֲשֶׂה {235x} **ma‘ǎseh,** *mah-as-eh';* from 6213; an *action* (good or bad); gen. a *transaction;* abstr. *activity;* by impl. a *product* (spec. a *poem*) or (gen.) *property:*—work {189x}, needlework + 7551 {5x}, acts {4x}, labour {4x}, doing {4x}, art {3x}, deed {3x}, misc. {23x} = + bakemeat, business, thing made, ware of making, occupation, thing offered, operation, possession, × well, wrought.

Ma‘aseh means "work; deed; labor; behavior." **(1)** Lamech, Noah's father, in expressing his hope for a new world, used the noun for the first time in the Old Testament: "And he called his name Noah, saying, This same shall comfort us concerning our work and toil of our hands, because of the ground which the LORD hath cursed" (Gen 5:29). **(2)** The basic meaning of *ma‘aseh* is "work." **(2a)** Lamech used the word to signify agricultural labor (Gen 5:29). **(2b)** The Israelites were commanded to celebrate the Festival of the Firstfruits, as it signified the blessing of God upon their "labors" (Ex 23:16). **(2c)** It is not to be limited to this. **(3)** As the word is the most general word for "work," it may be used to refer to the "work" of **(3a)** a skillful craftsman (Ex 26:1), **(3b)** a weaver (26:36), **(3c)** a jeweler (28:11), and **(3d)** a perfumer (30:25). **(4)** The finished product of the worker is also known as *ma‘aseh:* **(4a)** "And in the uppermost basket there was of all manner of bakemeats [literally, "work of a baker"] for Pharaoh" (Gen 40:17); **(4b)** "And Moses and Eleazar the priest took the gold of them, even all wrought jewels" [literally, "articles of work"] (Num 31:51).

(5) The artisan plied his craft during the work week, known in Hebrew as "the days of work," and rested on the Sabbath: "Thus saith the Lord GOD; The gate of the inner court that

looketh toward the east shall be shut the six working days; but on the sabbath it shall be opened, and in the day of the new moon it shall be opened" (Eze 46:1; cf. Ex 23:12). **(6)** The phrase "work of one's hands" signifies the worthlessness of the idols fashioned by human hands: "Asshur shall not save us; we will not ride upon horses: neither will we say any more to the work of our hands, Ye are our gods: for in thee the fatherless findeth mercy" (Hos 14:3). **(7)** However, the prayer of the psalmist includes the request that the "works" of God's people might be established: "And let the beauty of the LORD our God be upon us: and establish thou the work of our hands upon us; yea, the work of our hands establish thou it" (Ps 90:17). **(8)** Since the righteous work out God's work and are a cause of God's rejoicing, "the glory of the LORD shall endure for ever: the LORD shall rejoice in his works" (Ps 104:31).

(9) In addition to "work," ma‛aseh also denotes "deed," "practice," or "behavior." Joseph asked his brothers, accused of having taken his cup of divination: "What deed is this that ye have done? wot ye not that such a man as I can certainly divine?" (Gen 44:15). **(10)** The Israelites were strongly commanded not to imitate the grossly immoral behavior of the Canaanites and the surrounding nations: "After the doings of the land of Egypt, wherein ye dwelt, shall ye not do: and after the doings of the land of Canaan, whither I bring you, shall ye not do: neither shall ye walk in their ordinances" (Lev 18:3; cf. Ex 23:24). **(11)** However, the Israelites did not listen to the warning, and they "were mingled among the heathen, and learned their works. . . . Thus were they defiled with their own works, and went a whoring with their own inventions" (Ps 106:35, 39). **(12)** Thus far, we have dealt with ma‛aseh from man's perspective. **(12a)** The word may have a positive connotation ("work, deed") as **(12b)** well as a negative ("corrupt practice").

(13) The Old Testament also calls us to celebrate the "work" of God. The psalmist was overwhelmed with the majesty of the Lord, as he looked at God's "work" of creation: "When I consider thy heavens, the work of thy fingers, the moon and the stars, which thou hast ordained" (Ps 8:3; cf. 19:1; 102:25). **(14)** The God of Israel demonstrated His love by His mighty acts of deliverance on behalf of Israel: "And Israel served the LORD all the days of Joshua, and all the days of the elders that [out] lived Joshua, and which had known all the works of the LORD, that he had done for Israel" (Josh 24:31). **(15)** All of God's "works" are characterized by faithfulness to His promises and covenant: "For the word of the LORD is right; and

all his works are done in truth" (Ps 33:4). See: TWOT—1708a; BDB—592a, 795c.

4640. מַעֲשַׂי {1x} **Ma‛ăsay,** *mah-as-ah'ee;* from 6213; *operative; Maasai,* an Isr.:— Maasiai {1x}. See: BDB—592a, 796b.

4641. מַעֲשֵׂיָה {23x} **Ma‛ăsêyâh,** *mah-as-ay-yaw';* or

מַעֲשֵׂיָהוּ **Ma‛ăsêyâhûw,** *mah-as-ay-yaw'-hoo;* from 4639 and 3050; *work of Jah; Maasejah,* the name of sixteen Isr.:— Maaseiah {23x}. See: BDB—592a, 796b.

4642. מַעֲשַׁקָּה {2x} **ma‛ăshaqqâh,** *mah-ash-ak-kaw';* from 6231; *oppression:*—oppression {1x}, × oppressor {1x}. See: TWOT—1713e; BDB—592a, 799a.

4643. מַעֲשֵׂר {32x} **ma‛ăsêr,** *mah-as-ayr';* or

מַעֲשַׂר **ma‛ăsar,** *mah-as-ar';* and (in plur.) fem.

מַעֲשְׂרָה **ma‛asrâh,** *mah-as-raw';* from 6240; a *tenth;* espec. a *tithe:*— tithe {27x}, tenth part {2x}, tenth {2x}, tithing {1x}. See: TWOT—1711h; BDB—592a, 798b.

4644. מֹף {1x} **Môph,** *mofe;* of Eg. or.; *Moph,* the capital of Lower Egypt:—Memphis {1x}. See: BDB—592a. comp. 5297.

מְפִבֹשֶׁת **Mᵉphîbôsheth.** See 4648.

4645. מִפְגָּע {1x} **miphgâ‛,** *mif-gaw';* from 6293; an *object of attack:*—mark {1x}. See: TWOT—1731b; BDB—592a, 803c.

4646. מַפָּח {1x} **mappâch,** *map-pawkh';* from 5301; a *breathing out* (of life), i.e. expiring:—giving up {1x}. See: BDB—592a, 656a.

4647. מַפֻּחַ {1x} **mappûach,** *map-poo'-akh;* from 5301; the *bellows* (i.e. *blower*) of a forge:—bellows {1x}. See: TWOT—1390b; BDB—592a, 656b.

4648. מְפִיבֹשֶׁת {15x} **Mᵉphîybôsheth,** *mef-ee-bo'-sheth;* or

מְפִבֹשֶׁת **Mᵉphîbôsheth,** *mef-ee-bo'-sheth;* prob. from 6284 and 1322; *dispeller of shame* (i.e. of Baal); *Mephibosheth,* the name of two Isr.:—Mephibosheth {15x}. See: BDB—592b, 937c.

4649. מֻפִּים {1x} **Muppîym,** *moop-peem';* a plur. appar. from 5130; *wavings; Muppim,* an Isr.:—Muppim {1x}. See: BDB—592b. comp. 8206.

4650. מֵפִיץ {1x} **mêphîyts,** *may-feets';* from 6327; a *breaker,* i.e. mallet:— maul {1x}. See: TWOT—1745a; BDB—592b, 807b.

4651. מַפָּל {1x} **mappâl**, *map-pawl';* from 5307; a *falling* off, i.e. chaff; also something *pendulous,* i.e. a flap:—flakes {1x}, refuse {1x}. See: TWOT—1392b; BDB—592b, 658c.

4652. מִפְלָאָה {1x} **miphlâ᾽âh**, *mif-law-aw';* from 6381; a *miracle:*—wondrous work {1x}. See: TWOT—1768c; BDB—592b, 811a.

4653. מִפְלַגָּה {1x} **miphlaggâh**, *mif-lag-gaw';* from 6385; a *classification:*—division {1x}. See: TWOT—1769d; BDB—592b, 811b.

4654. מַפָּלָה {3x} **mappâlâh**, *map-paw-law';* or

מַפֵּלָה **mappêlâh**, *map-pay-law';* from 5307; something *fallen,* i.e. a *ruin:*—ruin {1x}, ruinous {1x}. See: TWOT—1392d; BDB—592b, 658c.

4655. מִפְלָט {1x} **miphlât**, *mif-lawt';* from 6403; an *escape:*—escape {1x}. See: TWOT—1774e; BDB—592b, 812d.

4656. מִפְלֶצֶת {4x} **miphletseth**, *mif-leh'-tseth;* from 6426; a *terror,* i.e. an *idol:*—idol {4x}. See: TWOT—1778b; BDB—592b, 814a.

4657. מִפְלָשׂ {1x} **miphlâs**, *mif-lawce';* from an unused root mean. to *balance;* a *poising:*—balancings {1x}. See: TWOT—1777b; BDB—592b, 814a.

4658. מַפֶּלֶת {8x} **mappeleth**, *map-peh'-leth;* from 5307; *fall,* i.e. *decadence;* concr. a *ruin;* spec. a *carcase:*—carcase {1x}, fall {5x}, ruin {2x}. See: TWOT—1392e; BDB—592b, 658c.

4659. מִפְעָל {3x} **miph‘âl**, *mif-awl';* or (fem.)

מִפְעָלָה **miph‘âlâh**, *mif-aw-law';* from 6466; a *performance:*—work {3x}. See: TWOT—1792c; BDB—592b. 821d.

4660. מַפָּץ {1x} **mappâts**, *map-pawts';* from 5310; a *smiting* to pieces:—slaughter {1x}. See: TWOT—1394b; BDB—592b, 658d.

4661. מַפֵּץ {1x} **mappêts**, *map-pates';* from 5310; a *smiter,* i.e. a war *club:*—battle ax {1x}. See: TWOT—1394c; BDB—592b, 659a.

4662. מִפְקָד {4x} **miphqâd**, *mif-kawd';* from 6485; an *appointment,* i.e. *mandate;* concr. a designated *spot;* spec. a *census:*—appointed place {1x}, commandment {1x}, number {2x}. See: TWOT—1802g; BDB—592b, 824c.

4663. מִפְקָד {1x} **Miphqâd**, *mif-kawd';* the same as 4662; *assignment; Miphkad,* the name of a gate in Jerusalem:—Miphkad {1x}. See: BDB—592b, 824c.

4664. מִפְרָץ {1x} **miphrâts**, *mif-rawts';* from 6555; a *break* (in the shore), i.e. a *haven:*—breaches {1x}. See: TWOT—1827a; BDB—592b, 830a.

4665. מִפְרֶקֶת {1x} **miphreketh**, *mif-reh'-keth;* from 6561; prop. a *fracture,* i.e. *joint* (*vertebra*) of the neck:—neck {1x}. See: TWOT—1828c; BDB—592b, 830b.

4666. מִפְרָשׂ {12x} **miphrâs**, *mif-rawce';* from 6566; an *expansion:*—that which … spreadest forth {1x}, spreadings {1x}. See: TWOT—1832a; BDB—592b, 831c.

4667. מִפְשָׂעָה {1x} **miphsâ᾽âh**, *mif-saw-aw';* from 6585; a *stride,* i.e. (by euphem.) the *crotch:*—buttocks {1x}. See: TWOT—1841b; BDB—592b, 832c.

מֹפֵת **môphêth**. See 4159.

4668. מַפְתֵּחַ {3x} **maphtêach**, *maf-tay'-akh;* from 6605; an *opener,* i.e. a *key:*—key {2x}, opening {1x}. See: TWOT—1854f; BDB—592b, 836b.

4669. מִפְתָּח {1x} **miphtâch**, *mif-tawkh';* from 6605; an *aperture,* i.e. (fig.) *utterance:*—opening {1x}. See: TWOT—1854e; BDB—592b, 836b.

4670. מִפְתָּן {8x} **miphtân**, *mif-tawn';* from the same as 6620; a *stretcher,* i.e. a *sill:*—threshold {8x}. See: TWOT—1858b; BDB—592, 837b.

4671. מֹץ {8x} **môts**, *motes;* or

מוֹץ **môwts** (Zeph 2:2), *motes;* from 4160; *chaff* (as *pressed* out, i.e. *winnowed* or [rather] threshed loose):—chaff {8x}. See: TWOT—1162a; BDB—558b, 592b.

4672. מָצָא {456x} **mâtsâ᾽**, *maw-tsaw';* a prim. root; prop. to *come forth* to, i.e. *appear* or *exist;* tran. to *attain,* i.e. *find* or *acquire;* fig. to *occur, meet* or *be present:*—find {359x}, present {20x}, find out {20x}, come {8x}, meet {5x}, befall {5x}, get {4x}, suffice {3x}, deliver {2x}, hit {2x}, left {2x}, hold {2x}, misc. {24x}= + be able, being, catch, × certainly, × have (here), be here, light (up-) on, × occasion serve, ready, speed.

Matsa᾽ means "to find, meet, get." **(1)** *Matsa᾽* refers to "finding" someone or something that is lost or misplaced, or "finding" where it is. **(1a)** The thing may be found as the result of a purposeful search, as when the Sodomites were temporarily blinded by Lot's visitors and were not able to "find" the door to his house (Gen 19:11). **(1b)** In a very similar usage, the dove sent forth by Noah searched for a spot to land and was unable to "find" it (Gen 8:9). **(1c)** On other occasions, the location of something or someone may be found without an intentional

search, as when Cain said: "[Whoever] findeth me shall slay me" (Gen 4:14). **(2)** *Matsa'* may connote not only "finding" a subject in a location, but "finding something" in an abstract sense. **(2a)** This idea is demonstrated clearly by Gen 6:8: "But Noah found grace in the eyes of the LORD." **(2b)** He found—"received"—something he did not seek.

(3) This sense also includes "finding" something one has sought in a spiritual or mental sense: **(3a)** "Mine hand had gotten much" (Job 31:25). **(3b)** Laban tells Jacob: "If I have found favor in thine eyes, [stay with me]" (Gen 30:27). Laban is asking Jacob for a favor that he is seeking in an abstract sense. **(4)** *Matsa'* can also mean "to discover." **(4a)** God told Abraham: "If I find in Sodom fifty righteous within the city, then I will spare all the place for their sakes" (Gen 18:26). **(4b)** This same emphasis appears in the first biblical occurrence of the word: "But for Adam there was not found a help meet for him" (Gen 2:20). **(5)** As noted earlier, there can be a connotation of the unintentional here, as when the Israelites "found" a man gathering wood on the Sabbath (Num 15:32). **(6)** Another special nuance is "to find out," in the sense of "gaining knowledge about." For example, Joseph's brothers said: "God hath found out the iniquity of thy servants" (Gen 44:16).

(7) *Matsa'* sometimes suggests "being under the power" of something, in a concrete sense. David told Abishai: "Take thou thy lord's servants, and pursue after him, lest he get him fenced cities, and escape us" (2 Sa 20:6). The idea is that Sheba would "find," enter, and defend himself in fortified cities. So to "find" them could be to "take them over." **(8)** This usage appears also in an abstract sense. Judah told Joseph: "For how shall I go up to my father, and the lad be not with me? lest peradventure I see the evil that shall come on my father" (Gen 44:34). **(9)** The word *matsa'*, therefore, can mean not only to "find" something, but to "obtain" it as one's own: "Then Isaac sowed in that land and received in the same year" (Gen 26:12). **(10)** Infrequently, the word implies movement in a direction until one arrives at a destination. This sense is found in Job 11:7: "Canst thou by searching find out God?" (cf. 1 Sa 23:17). **(11)** In a somewhat different nuance, this meaning appears in Num 11:22: "Shall the flocks and the herds be slain for them, to suffice them?" See: TWOT—1231; BDB—592c.

מֹצָא **môtsâ'**. See 4161.

4673. מַצָּב {10x} **matstsâb**, *mats-tsawb';* from 5324; a fixed *spot;* fig. an *office,* a military *post:*—garrison {7x}, station {1x},

place where . . . stood {2x}. See: TWOT—1398c; BDB—594b, 662d.

4674. מֻצָּב {1x} **mutstsâb**, *moots-tsawb';* from 5324; a *station,* i.e. military *post:*—mount {1x}. See: TWOT—1398d; BDB—594b, 663a.

4675. מַצָּבָה {2x} **matstsâbâh**, *mats-tsaw-baw';* or

מִצָּבָה **mitstsâbâh**, *mits-tsaw-baw';* fem. of 4673; a military *guard:*—army {1x}, garrison {1x}. See: TWOT—1398f; BDB—594b, 663a.

4676. מַצֵּבָה {32x} **matstsêbâh**, *mats-tsay-baw';* fem. (caus.) part. of 5324; something *stationed,* i.e. a *column* or (memorial *stone*); by anal. an *idol:*—garrison {1x}, (standing) image {19x}, pillar {12x}.

Matstsebah means "pillar; monument; sacred stone." **(1)** This word refers to a "pillar" as a personal memorial in 2 Sa 18:18: "Now Absalom in his lifetime had taken and reared up for himself a pillar . . . and he called the pillar after his own name: and it is called unto this day, Absalom's place." **(2)** In Gen 28:18 the "monument" is a memorial of the Lord's appearance: "And Jacob rose up early in the morning, and took the stone that he had put for his pillows, and set it up for a pillar, and poured oil upon the top of it." **(3)** *Matstsebah* is used in connection with the altar built by Moses in Ex 24:4: "And Moses wrote all the words of the LORD, and rose up early in the morning, and builded an altar under the hill, and twelve pillars, according to the twelve tribes of Israel." Syn.: 352. See: TWOT—1398g; BDB—594b, 663a.

4677. מְצֹבָיָה {1x} **Mᵉtsôbâyâh**, *mets-o-baw-yaw';* appar. from 4672 and 3050; *found of Jah; Metsobajah,* a place in Pal.:—Mesobaite {1x}. See: BDB—594b.

4678. מַצֶּבֶת {6x} **matstsebeth**, *mats-tseh'-beth;* from 5324; something *stationary,* i.e. a monumental *stone;* also the *stock* of a tree:—pillar {2x}, substance {4x}. See: TWOT—1398g; BDB—594b, 663a.

4679. מְצַד {11x} **mᵉtsad**, *mets-ad';* or

מְצָד **mᵉtsâd**, *mets-awd';* or (fem.)

מְצָדָה **mᵉtsâdâh**, *mets-aw-daw';* from 6679; a *fastness* (as a *covert* of ambush):—castle {1x}, fort {1x}, strongholds {5x}, holds {3x} munition {1x}. See: TWOT—1885c; BDB—594c, 844d, 845a.

מְצֻדָה **mᵉtsûdâh**. See 4686.

4680. מָצָה {7x} **mâtsâh**, *maw-tsaw';* a prim. root; to *suck* out; by impl. to *drain,*

to *squeeze* out:—suck {1x}, wring (out) {6x}. See: TWOT—1232; BDB—594c.

4681. מֹצָה {1x} **Môtsâh**, *mo-tsaw';* act. part. fem. of 4680; *drained; Motsah,* a place in Pal.:—Mozah {1x}. See: BDB—594c.

4682. מַצָּה {53x} **matstsâh**, *mats-tsaw';* from 4711 in the sense of *greedily* devouring for sweetness; prop. *sweetness;* concr. *sweet* (i.e. not soured or bittered with yeast); spec. an *unfermented cake* or loaf, or (ellip.) the festival of *Passover* (because no leaven was then used):—unleavened bread {33x}, unleavened {14x}, cakes {5x}, without leaven {1x}.

Matstsah means "unleavened bread." **(1)** This noun occurs 53 times, **(1a)** all but 14 of them in the Pentateuch. **(1b)** The rest of the occurrences are in prose narratives or in Ezekiel's discussion of the new temple: "In the first month, in the fourteenth day of the month, ye shall have the passover, a feast of seven days; unleavened bread shall be eaten" (Eze 45:21). **(2)** In the ancient Orient, household bread was prepared **(2a)** by adding fermented dough to the kneading trough and working it through the fresh dough. **(2b)** Hastily made bread omitted the fermented (leavened) dough: Lot "made them a feast, and did bake unleavened bread, and they did eat" (Gen 19:3). In this case, the word represents bread hastily prepared for unexpected guests. **(3)** The feasts of Israel often involved the use of unleavened bread, perhaps because of the relationship between fermentation, rotting, and death (Lev 2:4ff.), or because unleavened bread reminded Jews of the hasty departure from Egypt and the rigors of the wilderness march. Syn.: 3899. See: TWOT—1105a; BDB—594c, 595a.

4683. מַצָּה {3x} **matstsâh**, *mats-tsaw';* from 5327; a *quarrel:*—contention {1x}, debate {1x}, strife {1x}. See: TWOT—1400a; BDB—594c, 663c.

4684. מַצְהָלָה {2x} **matshâlâh**, *mats-haw-law';* from 6670; a *whinnying* (through impatience for battle or lust):—neighing {1x}. See: TWOT—1881a; BDB—843d.

4685. מָצוֹד {6x} **mâtsôwd**, *maw-tsode';* or (fem.)

מְצוֹדָה **mᵉtsôwdâh**, *mets-o-daw';* or

מְצֹדָה **mᵉtsôdâh**, *mets-o-daw';* from 6679; a *net* (for *capturing* animals or fishes); also (by interch. for 4679) a *fastness* or (besieging) *tower:*—bulwark {1x}, hold {1x}, munition {1x}, net {2x}, snare {1x}. See: TWOT—1885d, 1885e; BDB—594c, 594d, 844d, 845a.

4686. מָצוּד {22x} **mâtsûwd**, *maw-tsood';* or (fem.)

מְצוּדָה **mᵉtsûwdâh**, *mets-oo-daw';* or

מְצֻדָה **mᵉtsûdâh**, *mets-oo-daw';* for 4685; a *net,* or (abstr.) *capture;* also a *fastness:*—fortress {6x}, hold {6x}, snare {2x}, strong hold {1x}, castle {1x}, net {1x}, strong place {1x}, hunted {1x}, strong hold {1x}, fort {1x}, defence {1x}. See: TWOT—1885g, 1885i; BDB—594c, 594d, 845a.

4687. מִצְוָה {181x} **mitsvâh**, *mits-vaw';* from 6680; a *command,* whether human or divine (collect. the *Law):*—commandments {177x}, precept {4x}, commanded {2x}, law {1x}, ordinances {1x}.

Mitsvah means "commandment." **(1)** Its first occurrence is in Gen 26:5, where *mitsvah* is synonymous with *choq* ("statute", 2706) and *torah* ("law", 8451): "Because that Abraham obeyed my voice, and kept my charge (4931 – *mishmeret*), my commandments (*mitsvah*), my statutes (2708 – *chuqqah* – plural), and my laws (8451 – *torah*)." **(2)** In the Pentateuch, God is always the Giver of the *mitsvah.* "All the commandments which I command thee this day shall ye observe to do, that ye may live, and multiply, and go in and possess the land which the Lord sware unto your fathers. And thou shalt remember all the way which the LORD thy God led thee these forty years in the wilderness, to humble thee, and to prove thee, to know what was in thine heart, whether thou wouldest keep his commandments, or no" (Deut 8:1–2). **(3)** The "commandment" may be a prescription ("thou shalt do . . .") or a proscription ("thou shalt not do . . .").

(4) The commandments were **(4a)** given in the hearing of the Israelites (Ex 15:26; Deut 11:13), **(4b)** who were to "do" (Lev 4:2ff.) and "keep" (Deut 4:2; Ps 78:7) them. **(4c)** Any failure to do so signified a covenantal breach (Num 15:31), transgression (2 Chr 24:20), and apostasy (1 Kin 18:18). **(5)** The plural of *mitsvah* often denotes a "body of laws" given by divine revelation. **(5a)** They are God's "word": "Wherewithal shall a young man cleanse his way? By taking heed thereto according to thy word" (Ps 119:9). **(5b)** They are also known as "the commandments of God." **(6)** Outside the Pentateuch, "commandments" are given by kings (1 Kin 2:43), fathers (Jer 35:14), people (Is 29:13), and teachers of wisdom (Prov 6:20; cf. 5:13). Only about ten percent of all occurrences in the Old Testament fit this category. See: TWOT—1887b; BDB—594d, 846b.

4688. מְצוֹלָה {11x} m^etsôwlâh, *mets-o-law';*
or

מְצֹלָה m^etsôlâh, *mets-o-law';* also

מְצוּלָה m^etsûwlâh, *mets-oo-law';* or

מְצֻלָה m^etsûlâh, *mets-oo-law';* from the
same as 6683; a *deep* place (of
water or mud):—deep {5x}, deeps {3x}, depths
{2x}, bottom {1x}. See: TWOT—1889b; BDB—
594a, 595a, 846d.

4689. מָצוֹק {6x} mâtsôwq, *maw-tsoke';* from
6693; a *narrow* place, i.e. (abstr.
and fig.) *confinement* or *disability:*—anguish
{1x}, distress {1x}, straitness {4x}. See: TWOT—
1895d; BDB—594d, 848a.

4690. מָצוּק {2x} mâtsûwq, *maw-tsook';* or

מָצֻק mâtsûq, *maw-tsook';* from 6693;
something *narrow,* i.e. a *column* or
*hill*top:—pillar {1x}, situate {1x}. See: TWOT—
1896a; BDB—594d, 595b, 848b.

4691. מְצוּקָה {7x} m^etsûwqâh, *mets-oo-kaw';*
or

מְצֻקָה m^etsûqâh, *mets-oo-kaw';* fem. of
4690; *narrowness,* i.e. (fig.) *trou-
ble:*—anguish {1x}, distress {6x}. See: TWOT—
1895e; BDB—594d, 595b, 848a.

4692. מָצוֹר {25x} mâtsôwr, *maw-tsore';* or

מָצוּר mâtsûwr, *maw-tsoor';* from 6696;
something *hemming* in, i.e. (obj.)
a *mound* (of besiegers), (abstr.) a *siege,* (fig.)
distress; or (subj.) a *fastness:*—siege {13x}, besieged {2x}, strong {2x}, besieged + 935 {2x},
bulwarks {1x}, defence {1x}, fenced {1x}, fortress {1x}, hold {1x}, tower {1x}. See: TWOT—
1898a; BDB—594d, 848d.

4693. מָצוֹר {5x} mâtsôwr, *maw-tsore';* the
same as 4692 in the sense of a
limit; Egypt (as the *border* of Pal.):—besieged
places {2x}, defence {1x}, fortress {1x}, fortified
{1x}. See: TWOT—1898a; BDB—594d, 596a,
849a.

4694. מְצוּרָה {8x} m^etsûwrâh, *mets-oo-raw';*
or

מְצֻרָה m^etsûrâh, *mets-oo-raw';* fem. of
4692; a *hemming* in, i.e. (obj.) a
mound (of siege), or (subj.) a *rampart* (of protection), (abstr.) *fortification:*—fenced (city)
{5x}, fort {1x}, munition {1x}, strong hold {1x}.
See: TWOT—1898b; BDB—596a, 849a.

4695. מַצּוּת {1x} matstsûwth, *mats-tsooth';*
from 5327; a *quarrel:*—that contended {1x}. See: TWOT—1400b; BDB—594d,
596b, 663c.

4696. מֵצַח {11x} mêtsach, *may'-tsakh;* from
an unused root mean. to *be clear,*

i.e. *conspicuous;* the *forehead* (as *open* and
prominent):—brow {1x}, forehead {11x}, + impudent {1x}. See: TWOT—1233a; BDB—594d.

4697. מִצְחָה {1x} mitschâh, *mits-khaw';* from
the same as 4696; a *shin-piece* of
armor (as *prominent*), only plur.:—greaves {1x}.
See: TWOT—1233b; BDB—595a.

מְצֹלָה m^etsôlâh. See 4688.

מְצֻלָה m^etsûlâh. See 4688.

4698. מְצִלָּה {1x} m^etsillâh *mets-il-law';* from
6750; a *tinkler,* i.e. a *bell:*—bell
{1x}. See: TWOT—1919e; BDB—595a, 853a.

4699. מְצֻלָּה {1x} m^etsullâh, *mets-ool-law';*
from 6751; *shade:*—bottom {1x}.
See: TWOT—1889c; BDB—847a.

4700. מְצֵלֶת {13x} m^etsêleth, *mets-ay'-leth;*
from 6750; (only dual) double
tinklers, i.e. cymbals:—cymbals {13x}. See:
TWOT—1919f; BDB—595a, 853a.

4701. מִצְנֶפֶת {12x} mitsnepheth, *mits-neh'-
feth;* from 6801; a *tiara,* i.e. official *turban* (of a king or high priest):—diadem
{1x}, mitre {11x}. See: TWOT—1940c; BDB—
595a, 857b.

4702. מַצָּע {1x} matstsâ^c, *mats-tsaw';* from
3331; a *couch:*—bed {1x}. See:
TWOT—896c; BDB—427a, 595a.

4703. מִצְעָד {3x} mits^câd, *mits-awd';* from
6805; a *step;* fig. *companion-
ship:*—goings {1x}, steps {2x}. See: TWOT—
1943d; BDB—595a, 857d.

4704. מִצְעִירָה {1x} mitsts^eîyrâh, *mits-tseh-
ee-raw';* fem. of 4705; prop.
littleness; concr. *diminutive:*—little {1x}. See:
TWOT—1948c; BDB—859a.

4705. מִצְעָר {5x} mits^câr, *mits-awr';* from
6819; *petty* (in size or number);
adv. a *short* (time):—little one {1x}, little while
{1x}, small {2x}. See: TWOT—1948c; BDB—
595a, 859b.

4706. מִצְעָר {1x} Mits^câr, *mits-awr';* the same
as 4705; *Mitsar,* a peak of Leba-
non:—Mizar {1x}. See: BDB—595a, 859b.

4707. מִצְפֶּה {2x} mitspeh, *mits-peh';* from
6822; an *observatory,* espec. for
military purposes:—watch tower {2x}. See:
TWOT—1950b; BDB—859d.

4708. מִצְפֶּה {15x} Mitspeh, *mits-peh';* the
same as 4707; *Mitspeh,* the name
of five places in Pal.:—Mizpeh {9x}, Mizpah
{5x}, watch tower {1x}. See: BDB—595a, 859d.
comp. 4709.

4709. מִצְפָּה {32x} Mitspah, *mits-paw';* fem.
of 4708; *Mitspah,* the name of

two places in Pal.:—Mitspah {18x}, Mitspeh {14x}. [This seems rather to be only an orth. var. of 4708 when "in pause".] See: BDB—595a, 859d.

4710. מִצְפֻּן {1x} **mitspûn**, *mits-poon'*; from 6845; a *secret* (place or thing, perh. *treasure*):—hidden thing {1x}. See: TWOT—1953d; BDB—595a, 861b.

4711. מָצַץ {1x} **mâtsats**, *maw-tsats'*; a prim. root; to *suck*:—milk {1x}. See: TWOT—1234; BDB—595a.

מְצֻקָה **mûtsâqâh**. See 4166.

4712. מֵצַר {3x} **mêtsar**, *may-tsar'*; from 6896; something *tight*, i.e. (fig.) *trouble*:—distress {1x}, pain {1x}, strait {1x}. See: TWOT—1973f; BDB—595b, 865c.

מָצָק **mâtsûq**. See 4690.

מְצֻקָה **m°tsûqâh**. See 4691.

מְצֻרָה **m°tsûrâh**. See 4694.

4713. מִצְרִי {30x} **Mitsrîy**, *mits-ree'*; from 4714; a *Mitsrite*, or inhab. of Mitsrajim:—Egyptian {25x}, Egyptian + 376 {3x}, Egypt {1x}, Egyptian women {1x}. See: BDB—596a.

4714. מִצְרַיִם {681x} **Mitsrayim**, *mits-rah'-yim*; dual of 4693; *Mitsrajim*, i.e. Upper and Lower Egypt:—Egypt {586x}, Egyptian {90x}, Mizraim {4x}, Egyptians + 1121 {1x}. See: TWOT—1235; BDB—595c.

4715. מִצְרֵף {2x} **mitsrêph**, *mits-rafe'*; from 6884; a *crucible*:—fining pot {2x}. See: TWOT—1972b; BDB—596b, 864c.

4716. מַק {2x} **maq**, *mak*; from 4743; prop. a *melting*, i.e. *putridity*:—rottenness {1x}, stink {1x}. See: TWOT—1237a; BDB—596b, 597a.

4717. מַקָּבָה {3x} **maqqâbâh**, *mak-kaw-baw'*; from 5344; prop. a *perforatrix*, i.e. a *hammer* (as *piercing*):—hammer {3x}. See: TWOT—1409c; BDB—666a.

4718. מַקֶּבֶת {2x} **maqqebeth**, *mak-keh'-beth*; from 5344; prop. a *perforator*, i.e. a *hammer* (as *piercing*); also (intr.) a *perforation*, i.e. a *quarry*:—hammer {1x}, hole {1x}. See: TWOT—1409d; BDB—596b, 666c.

4719. מַקֵּדָה {9x} **Maqqêdâh**, *mak-kay-daw'*; from the same as 5348 in the denom. sense of *herding* (comp. 5349); *fold; Makkedah*, a place in Pal.:—Makkedah {9x}. See: BDB—596b.

4720. מִקְדָּשׁ {74x} **miqdâsh**, *mik-dawsh'*; or

מִקְּדָשׁ **miqq°dâsh** (Ex 15:17), *mik-ked-awsh'*; from 6942; a *consecrated* thing or place, espec. a *palace, sanctuary* (whether of Jehovah or of idols) or *asylum*:—sanctuary {69x}, holy place {3x}, chapel {1x}, hallowed part {1x}. See: TWOT—1990f; BDB—596b, 874a.

4721. מַקְהֵל {2x} **maqhêl**, *mak-hale'*; or (fem.)

מַקְהֵלָה **maqhêlâh**, *mak-hay-law'*; from 6950; an *assembly*:—congregation {2x}. See: TWOT—1991d; BDB—596b, 875b.

4722. מַקְהֵלֹת {2x} **Maqhêlôth**, *mak-hay-loth'*; plur. of 4721 (fem.); *assemblies; Makheloth*, a place in the desert:—Makheloth {2x}. See: BDB—596b, 875b.

4723. מִקְוֶה {12x} **miqveh**, *mik-veh'*; or

מִקְוֵה **miqvêh** (1 Kin 10:28) *mik-vay'*; or

מִקְוֵא **miqvê°** (2 Chr 1:16), *mik-vay'*; from 6960; something *waited* for, i.e. *confidence* (obj. or subj.); also a *collection*, i.e. (of water) a *pond*, or (of men and horses) a *caravan* or *drove*:—abiding {1x}, gathering together {1x}, hope {4x}, linen yarn {4x}, plenty [of water] {1x}, pool {1x}. See: TWOT—1994c, 1995a; BDB—596b, 875c, 876a, 876c.

4724. מִקְוָה {1x} **miqvâh**, *mik-vaw'*; fem. of 4723; a *collection*, i.e. (of water) a *reservoir*:—ditch {1x}. See: TWOT—1995a; BDB—596b, 876c.

4725. מָקוֹם {402x} **mâqôwm**, *maw-kome'*; or

מָקֹם **mâqôm**, *maw-kome'*; also (fem.)

מְקוֹמָה **m°qôwmâh**, *mek-o-mah'*; or

מְקֹמָה **m°qômâh**, *mek-o-mah'*; from 6965; prop. a *standing*, i.e. a *spot*; but used widely of a *locality* (gen. or spec.); also (fig.) of a *condition* (of body or mind):—place {391x}, home {3x}, room {3x}, whithersoever {2x}, open {1x}, space {1x}, country {1x}.

Maqowm means "place; height; stature; standing." **(1)** It refers to the place where something **(1a)** stands: "And when they of Ashdod arose early on the morrow, behold, Dagon was fallen upon his face to the earth before the ark of the LORD. And they took Dagon, and set him in his place [*maqowm*] again" (1 Sa 5:3), **(1b)** sits: "The throne had six steps, and the top of the throne was round behind: and there were stays on either side on the place [*maqom*] of the seat, and two lions stood beside the stays."(1 Kin 10:19), **(1c)** dwells: "And I have set there a place [*maqom*] for the ark, wherein is the covenant of the LORD, which he made with our fathers, when he brought them out of the land of Egypt" (1 Kin 8:21), or **(1d)** is: "And God said, Let the waters under the heaven be gathered together unto one place [*maqom*], and

let the dry land appear: and it was so" (Gen 1:9). **(2)** It may also refer to a larger location, such as a country (Ex 3:8) or to an undetermined "space between": "Then David went over to the other side and stood on the top of an hill afar off; a great space [*maqown*] being between them:" (1 Sa 26:13). **(3)** A "place" is sometimes a task or office: "If the spirit of the ruler rise up against thee, leave not thy place [*maqown*]; for yielding pacifieth great offences" (Eccl 10:4). **(4)** This noun is used to signify a sanctuary—i.e., a "place" of worship (Gen 22:3). See: TWOT—1999h; BDB—596b, 596c, 879d.

4726. מָקוֹר {18x} **mâqôwr**, *maw-kore';* or

מָקֹר **mâqôr**, *maw-kore';* from 6979; prop. something *dug,* i.e. a (gen.) *source* (of water, even when naturally flowing; also of tears, blood [by euphem. of the female *pudenda*]; fig. of happiness, wisdom, progeny):—fountain {11x}, issue {1x}, spring {3x}, wellspring {2x}, well {1x}. See: TWOT—2004a; BDB—596b, 881b.

4727. מְקַח {1x} **miqqâch**, *mik-kawkh';* from 3947; *reception:*—taking {1x}.
   Miqqach occurs once to mean "taking": "Wherefore now let the fear of the LORD be upon you; take heed and do it: for there is no iniquity with the LORD our God, nor respect of persons, nor taking of gifts" (2 Chr 19:7). Syn: 3948, 4455, 4457, 4728. See: TWOT—1124e; BDB—544c.

4728. מַקָּחָה {1x} **maqqâchâh**, *mak-kaw-khaw';* from 3947; something *received,* i.e. *merchandise* (purchased):—ware {1x}.
   Maqqachot [plural] means "wares" once (Neh. 10:31). Syn: 3948, 4455, 4457, 4727. See: TWOT—1124f; BDB—544c.

4729. מִקְטָר {1x} **miqtâr**, *mik-tawr';* from 6999; something to *fume* (incense) on, i.e. a *hearth* place:—to burn . . . upon {1x}.
   Miqtar means a "place of sacrificial smoke; altar." The word appears once (Ex 30:1). Syn.: 4730, 6988, 6999, 7002, 7008. See: TWOT—2011d, 2011e; BDB—596b, 883b.

מִקְטְרָה **mᵉqattᵉrâh**. See 6999.

4730. מִקְטֶרֶת {2x} **miqtereth**, *mik-teh'-reth;* fem. of 4729; something to *fume* (incense) in, i.e. a *coal-pan:*—censer {2x}.
   Miqtereth means "censer; incense." **(1)** *Miqtereth* represents a "censer"—a utensil in which coals are carried—in 2 Chr 26:19. **(2)** The word refers to "incense" in Eze 8:11. Syn.: 6988, 6999, 7002, 7004, 7008. See: TWOT—2011f; BDB—596b, 883b.

4731. מַקֵּל {18x} **maqqêl**, *mak-kale';* or (fem.)

מַקְּלָה **maqqᵉlâh**, *mak-kel-aw';* from an unused root mean. appar. to *germinate;* a *shoot,* i.e. *stick* (with leaves on, or for walking, striking, guiding, divining):—rod {8x}, staff {7x}, stave {2x}, handstave + 3027 {1x}. See: TWOT—1236; BDB—596b.

4732. מִקְלוֹת {4x} **Miqlôwth**, *mik-lohth';* (or perh. *mik-kel-ohth';*) plur. of (fem.) 4731; *rods; Mikloth,* a place in the Desert:—Mikloth {4x}. See: BDB—596c.

4733. מִקְלָט {20x} **miqlât**, *mik-lawt';* from 7038 in the sense of *taking* in; an *asylum* (as a *receptacle*):—refuge {20x}. See: TWOT—2026a; BDB—596c, 886a.

4734. מִקְלַעַת {4x} **miqlaʿath**, *mik-lah'-ath;* from 7049; a *sculpture* (prob. in bas-relief):—carved {1x}, carved figure {1x}, carving {1x}, graving {1x}. See: TWOT—2031a; BDB—596c, 887c.

מָקֹם **mâqôm**. See 4725.

מְקֹמָה **mᵉqômâh**. See 4725.

4735. מִקְנֶה {75x} **miqneh**, *mik-neh';* from 7069; something *bought,* i.e. *property,* but only live *stock;* abstr. *acquisition:*—cattle {63x}, possession {5x}, flocks {3x}, substance {2x}, herds {1x}, purchase {1x}. See: TWOT—2039b; BDB—596d, 889b.

4736. מִקְנָה {15x} **miqnâh**, *mik-naw';* fem. of 4735; prop. a *buying,* i.e. *acquisition;* concr. a piece of *property* (land or living); also the *sum* paid:—bought {7x}, purchase {5x}, price {2x}, possession {1x}. See: TWOT—2039c; BDB—596d, 889b.

4737. מִקְנֵיָהוּ {2x} **Miqnêyâhûw**, *mik-nay-yaw'-hoo;* from 4735 and 3050; *possession of Jah; Miknejah,* an Isr.:—Mikneiah {2x}. See: BDB—596d, 889c.

4738. מִקְסָם {2x} **miqçâm**, *mik-sawm';* from 7080; an *augury:*—divination {2x}. See: TWOT—2044b; BDB—596d, 890d.

4739. מָקָץ {1x} **Mâqats**, *maw-kats';* from 7112; *end; Makats,* a place in Pal.:—Makaz {1x}. See: BDB—596d.

4740. מַקְצוֹעַ {12x} **maqtsôwaʿ**, *mak-tso'-ah;* or

מַקְצֹעַ **maqtsôaʿ**, *mak-tso'-ah;* or (fem.)

מַקְצֹעָה **maqtsôʿâh**, *mak-tso-aw';* from 7106 in the denom. sense of *bending;* an *angle* or recess:—corner {7x}, turning {12x}. See: TWOT—2057a; BDB—596d, 893a.

4741. מַקְצֻעָה {1x} **maqtsûʿâh**, *mak-tsoo-aw';* from 7106; a *scraper,* i.e. a carv-

ing *chisel:*—plane {1x}. See: TWOT—2056b; BDB—596d, 893a.

4742. מְקֻצְעָה {2x} **mᵉqutsᶜâh**, *mek-oots-aw';* from 7106 in the denom. sense of *bending;* an *angle:*—corner {2x}. See: TWOT—2057a; BDB—596d, 893b.

4743. מְקַק {10x} **mâqaq**, *maw-kak';* a prim. root; to *melt;* fig. to *flow, dwindle, vanish:*—consume away {4x}, be corrupt {1x}, dissolve {1x}, pine away {4x}. See: TWOT—1237; BDB—596d.

מָקֹר **mâqôr**. See 4726.

4744. מִקְרָא {23x} **miqrâ'**, *mik-raw';* from 7121; something *called* out, i.e. a public *meeting* (the act, the persons, or the place); also a *rehearsal:*—assemblies {2x}, calling {1x}, convocation {1x}, reading {1x}.

Miqra' means public worship service; convocation. **(1)** The word implies the product of an official summons to worship ("convocation") for the reading and exposition of the Law. The day was to be kept free from secular work and to be regarded as sacred by Divine command. **(2)** In Lev 23:2 it refers to Sabbaths as "convocation days": "Speak unto the children of Israel, and say unto them, Concerning the feasts of the LORD, which ye shall proclaim to be holy convocations, even these are my feasts." See: TWOT—2063d; BDB—597a, 896d.

4745. מִקְרֶה {10x} **miqreh**, *mik-reh';* from 7136; something *met* with, i.e. an *accident* or *fortune:*—befall {4x}, event {3x}, hap {1x}, chance {1x}, happeneth {1x}. See: TWOT—2068c; BDB—597a, 899d.

4746. מְקָרֶה {1x} **mᵉqâreh**, *mek-aw-reh';* from 7136; prop. something *meeting,* i.e. a *frame* (of timbers):—building {1x}. See: TWOT—2068f; BDB—597a, 900a.

4747. מְקֵרָה {2x} **mᵉqêrâh**, *mek-ay-raw';* from the same as 7119; a *cooling* off:—✕ summer {2x}. See: TWOT—2077d; BDB—597a, 903b.

מֹקֵשׁ **môqêsh**. See 4170.

4748. מִקְשֶׁה {1x} **miqsheh**, *mik-sheh';* from 7185 in the sense of *knotting* up round and hard; something *turned* (rounded), i.e. a *curl* (of tresses):—✕ well [set] hair {1x}. See: TWOT—2086a; BDB—597a, 904d.

4749. מִקְשָׁה {10x} **miqshâh**, *mik-shaw';* fem. of 4748; *rounded* work, i.e. moulded by *hammering* (repoussé):—beaten work {6x}, beaten out of one piece {1x}, beaten {1x}, whole piece {1x}, upright {1x}. See: TWOT—2086b; BDB—597a, 904d.

4750. מִקְשָׁה {1x} **miqshâh**, *mik-shaw';* denom. from 7180; lit. a *cucumbered* field, i.e. a *cucumber* patch:—garden of cucumbers {1x}. See: TWOT—2083b; BDB—597a, 903d, 904d.

4751. מַר {38x} **mar**, *mar;* or (fem.)

מָרָה **mârâh**, *maw-raw';* from 4843; *bitter* (lit. or fig.); also (as noun) *bitterness,* or (adv.) *bitterly:*—bitter {20x}, bitterness {10x}, bitterly {3x}, chafed {1x}, angry {1x}, discontented {1x}, heavy {1x}, bitter thing {1x}. See: TWOT—1248a, 1248c; BDB—597a, 600c.

4752. מַר {1x} **mar**, *mar;* from 4843 in its orig. sense of *distillation;* a *drop:*—drop {1x}. See: TWOT—1249a; BDB—597a, 601c.

4753. מֹר {12x} **môr**, *more;* or

מוֹר **môwr**, *more;* from 4843; *myrrh* (as *distilling* in drops, and also as *bitter*):—myrrh {12x}. See: TWOT—1248b; BDB—558d, 597a, 600d.

4754. מָרָא {2x} **mârâ'**, *maw-raw';* a prim. root; to *rebel;* hence, (through the idea of *maltreating*) to *whip,* i.e. *lash* (self with wings, as the ostrich in running):—be filthy {1x}, lift up self {1x}. See: TWOT—1238; BDB—597a, 598a.

4755. מָרָא {1x} **Mârâ'**, *maw-raw';* for 4751 fem.; *bitter; Mara,* a symbol. name of Naomi:—Mara {1x}. See: BDB—597a, 600c.

4756. מָרֵא {4x} **mârê'** (Aram.), *maw-ray';* from a root corresp. to 4754 in the sense of *domineering;* a *master:*—lord {2x}, Lord {2x}. See: TWOT—2839; BDB—1101c, 1101d.

מֹרָא **môrâ'**. See 4172.

4757. מְרֹאדַךְ בַּלְאָדָן {1x} **Mᵉrô'dak Balᵃdân**, *mer-o-dak' bal-aw-dawn';* of for. der.; *Merodak-Baladan,* a Bab. king:—Merodach-baladan {1x}. See: BDB—596b, 597b, 597d. comp. 4781.

4758. מַרְאֶה {1x} **marᵉeh**, *mar-eh';* from 7200; a *view* (the act of seeing); also an *appearance* (the thing seen), whether (real) a *shape* (espec. if handsome, *comeliness;* often plur. the *looks*), or (mental) a *vision:*—appearance {35x}, sight {18x}, countenance {11x}, vision {11x}, favoured {7x}, look upon {4x}, fair + 2896 {2x}, misc. {15x} = ✕ apparently, ✕ as soon as beautiful (-ly), form, goodly, look [-eth], pattern, to see, seem, visage.

(1) *Marᵉeh* and *to'ar* (8389) are descriptive of blessing in Gen 39:6: "And Joseph was *a* goodly [*to'ar*] person, and well favoured [*marᵉeh*]."

(2) *Mar°eh* refers more to external "appearance" (Gen 2:9). **(3)** The word can also connote "sight" as in a range of vision (Lev 13:3) and **(4)** "sight" in the sense of a supernatural "sight" or manifestation (Ex 3:3). Syn.: 4759, 7207, 7209, 7210, 8389. See: TWOT—2095i; BDB—596b, 597b, 909c.

4759. מַרְאָה {12x} **mar°âh,** *mar-aw';* fem. of 4758; a *vision;* also (caus.) a *mirror:*—looking glasses {1x}, vision {11x}.

Mar°âh means "visionary appearance" or "(prophetic) vision" (Gen 46:2) and "looking glasses" (Ex 38:8). Syn.: 4758, 7207, 7209, 7210, 8389. See: TWOT—2095g, 2095h; BDB—597b, 909b, 909c.

4760. מֻרְאָה {1x} **mur°âh,** *moor-aw';* appar. fem. pass. caus. part. of 7200; something *conspicuous,* i.e. the *craw* of a bird (from its *prominence):*—crop {1x}. See: TWOT—1239b; BDB—597b.

מְרָאוֹן **M°rôwn.** See 8112.

4761. מַרְאָשָׁה {1x} **mar°âshâh,** *mar-aw-shaw';* denom. from 7218; prop. *headship,* i.e. (plur. for collect.) *dominion:*—principality {1x}. See: TWOT—2097f; BDB—912b.

4762. מַרְאֵשָׁה {8x} **Mar°êshâh,** *mar-ay-shaw';* or

מַרֵשָׁה **Marêshâh,** *mar-ay-shaw';* formed like 4761; *summit; Mareshah,* the name of two Isr. and of a place in Pal.:—Mareshah {8x}. See: BDB—597b, 601c, 912b.

4763. מְרַאֲשָׁה {8x} **m°ra°ăshâh,** *mer-ah-ash-aw';* formed like 4761; prop. a *headpiece,* i.e. (plur. for adv.) *at* (or *as*) the *head-rest* (or pillow):—bolster {5x}, head {1x}, pillow {2x}. See: TWOT—2097f; BDB—597b, 910c, 912a, 912b. comp. 4772.

4764. מֵרָב {3x} **Mêrâb,** *may-rawb';* from 7231; *increase; Merab,* a daughter of Saul:—Merab {3x}. See: BDB—597b.

4765. מַרְבַד {1x} **marbad,** *mar-bad';* from 7234; a *coverlet:*—covering of tapestry {1x}. See: TWOT—2102a; BDB—597b, 915a.

4766. מַרְבֶה {2x} **marbeh,** *mar-beh';* from 7235; prop. *increasing;* as noun, *greatness,* or (adv.) *greatly:*—great {1x}, increase {1x}. See: TWOT—2103b; BDB—597c, 916a.

4767. מִרְבָּה {1x} **mirbâh,** *meer-baw';* from 7235; *abundance,* i.e. a great quantity:—much {1x}. See: TWOT—2103c; BDB—597c, 916b.

4768. מַרְבִּית {5x} **marbîyth,** *mar-beeth';* from 7235; a *multitude;* also *offspring;* spec. *interest* (on capital):—greatest part {1x}, greatness {1x}, increase {2x}, multi-

tude {1x}. See: TWOT—2103d; BDB—597c, 916b.

4769. מַרְבֵּץ {2x} **marbêts,** *mar-bates';* from 7257; a *reclining* place, i.e. *fold* (for flocks):—couching place {1x}, place to lie down {1x}. See: TWOT—2109b; BDB—597c, 918c.

4770. מַרְבֵּק {4x} **marbêq,** *mar-bake';* from an unused root mean. to *tie* up; a *stall* (for cattle):—✕ fat {1x}, fatted {1x}, stall {2x}. See: TWOT—2110a; BDB—597c, 918d.

מֹרַג **môrag.** See 4173.

4771. מַרְגּוֹעַ {1x} **margôwa°,** *mar-go'-ah;* from 7280; a *resting* place:—rest {1x}. See: TWOT—2117b; BDB—597c, 921b.

4772. מַרְגְּלָה {5x} **marg°lâh,** *mar-ghel-aw';* denom. from 7272; (plur. for collect.) a *footpiece,* i.e. (adv.) *at the foot,* or (direct.) the *foot* itself:—feet {5x}. See: TWOT—2113c; BDB—597c, 920b. comp. 4763.

4773. מַרְגֵּמָה {1x} **margêmah,** *mar-gay-maw';* from 7275; a *stone*-heap:—sling {1x}. See: TWOT—2114b; BDB—597c, 920c.

4774. מַרְגֵּעָה {1x} **margê°âh,** *mar-gay-aw';* from 7280; *rest:*—refreshing {1x}. See: TWOT—2117c; BDB—597c, 921c.

4775. מָרַד {25x} **mârad,** *maw-rad';* a prim. root; to *rebel:*—rebel {23x}, rebels {1x}, rebellious {1x}. See: TWOT—1240; BDB—597c.

4776. מְרַד {1x} **m°rad** (Aram.), *mer-ad';* from a root corresp. to 4775; *rebellion:*—rebellion {1x}. See: TWOT—2840a; BDB—597c, 1101c.

4777. מֶרֶד {1x} **mered,** *meh'-red;* from 4775; *rebellion:*—rebellion {1x}. See: TWOT—1240a; BDB—597c, 597d, 1101c.

4778. מֶרֶד {2x} **Mered,** *meh'-red;* the same as 4777; *Mered,* an Isr.:—Mered {2x}. See: BDB—597d.

4779. מָרָד {1x} **mârâd** (Aram.), *maw-rawd';* from the same as 4776; *rebellious:*—rebellious {1x}. See: TWOT—2840b; BDB—1101c.

4780. מַרְדּוּת {1x} **mardûwth,** *mar-dooth';* from 4775; *rebelliousness:*—✕ rebellious {1x}. See: TWOT—1240b; BDB—597d.

4781. מְרֹדָךְ {1x} **M°rôdâk,** *mer-o-dawk';* of for. der.; *Merodak,* a Bab. idol:—Merodach {1x}. comp. 4757. See: TWOT—1241; BDB—597d.

4782. מָרְדְּכַי {60x} **Mord°kay,** *mor-dek-ah'-ee;* of for. der.; *Mordecai,* an Isr.:—Mordecai {60x}. See: BDB—598a.

Hebrew

4783. מִרְדָּךְ {1x} **murdâph**, *moor-dawf';* from
7291; *persecuted:*—persecuted
{1x}. See: TWOT—2124a; BDB—598a, 022a,
923a.

4784. מָרָה {44x} **mârâh**, *maw-raw';* a prim.
root; to *be* (caus. *make*) *bitter* (or
unpleasant); (fig.) to *rebel* (or resist; caus. to
provoke):—rebel {19x}, rebellious {9x}, provoke
{7x}, disobedient {2x}, against {1x}, bitter {1x},
changed {1x}, disobeyed {1x}, grievously {1x},
provocation {1x}, rebels {1x}.

Marah means "to rebel, be contentious." **(1)**
Marah signifies an opposition to someone mo-
tivated by pride: **(1a)** "If a man have a stubborn
[5637 - *carar*] and rebellious [*marah*] son,
which will not obey the voice of his father . . ."
(Deut 21:18). **(1b)** The sense comes out more
clearly in Is 3:8: "For Jerusalem is ruined, and
Judah is fallen: because their tongue and their
doings are against the LORD, to provoke the
eyes of his glory." **(2)** More particularly, the
word generally connotes a rebellious attitude
against God. Several prepositions are used to
indicate the object of rebellion (ʿim, et, generally translated as "against"): **(2a)** "Ye have been
rebellious against [ʿim] the LORD" (Deut 9:7);
(2b) "She hath been rebellious against [et] me"
(Jer 4:17). **(3)** The primary meaning of *marah*
is "to disobey." Several passages attest to this:
(3a) "Forasmuch as thou hast disobeyed the
mouth of the LORD, and hast not kept the commandment which the LORD thy God commanded thee" (1 Kin 13:21); **(3b)** 1 Kin 13:26:
"It is the man of God, who was disobedient
unto the word of the LORD."

(4) The Old Testament sometimes specifically states that someone "rebelled" **(4a)** against
the Lord; at other times it may refer to **(4b)** a
rebelling against the word of the Lord (Ps
105:28; 107:11), or **(4c)** against the word of God
(cf. Num 20:24; Deut 1:26, 43; 9:23; 1 Sa 12:14–
15). **(4d)** The intent of the Hebrew is to signify
the act of defying the command of God: "The
LORD is righteous; for I have rebelled against
his commandment" (Lam 1:18). **(5)** The verb
marah is at times strengthened by a form of
the verb *carar* (5637 - "to be stubborn"):
"[They] might not be as their fathers, a stubborn [*carar*] and rebellious [*marah*] generation;
a generation that set not their heart aright"
(Ps 78:8; cf. Deut 21:18, 20; Jer 5:23). **(6)** An
individual (Deut 21:18, 20), a nation (Num
20:24), and a city (Zeph 3:1) may be described
as "being rebellious." **(7)** Zephaniah gave a
vivid image of the nature of the rebellious
spirit: "Woe to her that is filthy and polluted,
to the oppressing city! She obeyed not the
voice; she received not correction; she trusted
not in the LORD; she drew not near to her God"

(Zeph 3:1–2). See: TWOT—1242; BDB—597b,
598a, 598c.

4785. מָרָה {5x} **Mârâh**, *maw-raw';* the same
as 4751 fem.; *bitter; Marah*, a place
in the desert:—*Marah* {5x}. See: BDB—598c,
600d.

מֹרֶה **Môreh**. See 4175.

4786. מֹרָה {1x} **môrâh**, *mo-raw';* from 4843;
bitterness, i.e. (fig.) *trouble:*—grief
{1x}. See: TWOT—1248d; BDB—598c, 601a.

4787. מָרָה {1x} **mârrâh**, *mawr-raw';* a form of
4786; *trouble:*—bitterness {1x}.
See: TWOT—1248c; BDB—598c, 601a.

4788. מָרוּד {3x} **mârûwd**, *maw-rood';* from
7300 in the sense of *maltreat-
ment;* an *outcast;* (abstr.) *destitution:*—cast out
{1x}, misery {2x}. See: TWOT—2129a; BDB—
598c, 924a.

4789. מֵרוֹז {1x} **Mêrôwz**, *may-roze';* of uncert.
der.; *Meroz*, a place in Pal.:—Me-
roz {1x}. See: BDB—72d, 598c.

4790. מָרוֹחַ {1x} **mᵉrôwach**, *mer-o-akh';* from
4799; *bruised*, i.e. *emasculated:*—
broken {1x}. See: BDB—598c.

4791. מָרוֹם {54x} **mârôwm**, *maw-rome';* from
7311; *altitude*, i.e. concr. (an *ele-
vated place*), abstr. (*elevation*), fig. (*elation*),
or adv. (*aloft*):—high {29x}, height {10x}, above
{5x}, high places {4x}, highest places {1x}, dignity {1x}, haughty {1x}, loftily {1x}, high ones
{1x}, upward {1x}.

Marowm means "higher plane; height, high
social position." **(1)** In its first biblical occurrence (Judg 5:18), *marowm* means "a higher
plane on the surface of the earth." **(2)** Job 16:19
and Is 33:5 contain the word with the meaning
of "the height" as the abode of God. **(3)** Job
5:11 uses the word to refer to "a high social
position." **(4)** *Marowm* can also signify "self-
exaltation" (2 Kin 19:22; Ps 73:8). See: TWOT—
2133h; BDB—598c, 928d.

4792. מֵרוֹם {2x} **Mêrôwm**, *may-rome';* formed
like 4791; *height; Merom*, a lake
in Pal.:—Merom {2x}. See: BDB—598c.

4793. מֵרוֹץ {1x} **mêrôwts**, *may-rotes';* from
7323; a *run* (the trial of speed):—
race {1x}. See: TWOT—2137a; BDB—598c,
930c.

4794. מְרוּצָה {4x} **mᵉrûwtsâh**, *mer-oo-tsaw';*
        or

מְרֻצָה **mᵉrûtsâh**, *mer-oo-tsaw';* fem. of
4793; a *race* (the act), whether
the manner or the progress:—course {2x}, running {2x}. See: TWOT—2137a; BDB—598c,
599d, 930c, 954d. comp. 4835.

4795. מָרוּק {1x} **marûwq**, *maw-rook';* from 4838; prop. *rubbed;* but used abstr. a *rubbing* (with perfumery):—purification {1x}. See: TWOT—1246a; BDB—598c, 599d.

מְרוֹר **mᵉrôwr**. See 4844.

מְרוֹרָה **mᵉrôwrâh**. See 4846.

4796. מָרוֹת {1x} **Mârôwth**, *maw-rohth';* plur. of 4751 fem.; *bitter* springs; *Maroth,* a place in Pal.:—Maroth {1x}. See: BDB—598c.

4797. מִרְזַח {1x} **mirzach**, *meer-zakh';* from an unused root mean. to *scream;* a *cry,* i.e. (of joy), a *revel:*—banquet {1x}. See: TWOT—2140a; BDB—931a.

4798. מַרְזֵחַ {1x} **marzêach**, *mar-zay'-akh;* formed like 4797; a *cry,* i.e. (of grief) a *lamentation:*—mourning {1x}. See: TWOT—2140a; BDB—598d, 931a.

4799. מָרַח {1x} **mârach**, *maw-rakh';* a prim. root; prop. to *soften* by rubbing or pressure; hence, (medicinally) to *apply* as an emollient:—lay for a plaister {1x}. See: TWOT—1243; BDB—598d.

4800. מֶרְחָב {6x} **merchâb**, *mer-khawb';* from 7337; *enlargement,* either lit. (an *open space,* usually in a good sense), or fig. (*liberty*):—breadth {1x}, large place (room) {5x}. See: TWOT—2143c; BDB—598d, 932c.

4801. מֶרְחָק {18x} **merchâq**, *mer-khawk';* from 7368; *remoteness,* i.e. (concr.) a *distant* place; often (adv.) *from afar:*—far {12x}, far off {4x}, afar off {1x}, far countries {1x}. See: TWOT—2151c; BDB—598d, 935d. See also 1023.

4802. מַרְחֶשֶׁת {2x} **marchesheth**, *mar-kheh'-sheth;* from 7370; a *stew*-pan:—frying pan {2x}. See: TWOT—2152a; BDB—598d, 935d.

4803. מָרַט {9x} **mârat**, *maw-rat';* a prim. root; to *polish;* by impl. to *make bald* (the head), to *gall* (the shoulder); also, to *sharpen:*—furbished {3x}, fallen {2x}, plucked off {2x}, peeled {1x}, plucked off their hair {1x}. See: TWOT—1244; BDB—590c, 598d, 1101d.

4804. מְרַט {1x} **mᵉrat** (Aram.), *mer-at';* corresp. to 4803; to *pull* off:—be plucked {1x}. See: TWOT—2841; BDB—1101d.

4805. מְרִי {23x} **mᵉrîy**, *mer-ee';* from 4784; *bitterness,* i.e. (fig.) *rebellion;* concr. *bitter,* or *rebellious:*—rebellious {17x}, rebellion {4x}, bitter {1x}, rebels {1x}.

I. *Meriy,* as a noun, means "rebellion." This word occurs infrequently: "For I know thy rebellion, and thy stiff neck . . ." (Deut 31:27; cf. Prov 17:11). II. *Meriy,* as an adjective, means

"rebellious." (1) This word occurs 23 times, mainly in Ezekiel. (2) The word modifies "house" (referring to Israel) in Eze 2:8: "Be not thou rebellious like that rebellious house." See: TWOT—1242a; BDB—598b, 599a.

4806. מְרִיא {8x} **mᵉrîyʾ**, *mer-ee';* from 4754 in the sense of *grossness,* through the idea of *domineering* (comp. 4756); *stall-fed;* often (as noun) a *beeve:*—fatling {3x}, fat cattle {3x}, fed beast {1x}, fat beast {1x}. See: TWOT—1239a; BDB—597a.

4807. מְרִיב בַּעַל {3x} **Mᵉrîyb Baʿal**, *mer-eeb' bah'-al;* from 7378 and 1168; *quarreller of Baal; Merib-Baal,* an epithet of Gideon:—Merib-baal {3x}. See: BDB—565a, 599a, 937c. comp. 4810.

4808. מְרִיבָה {7x} **mᵉrîybâh**, *mer-ee-baw';* from 7378; *quarrel:*—strife {5x}, Meribah-kadesh + 6946 {1x}, provocation {1x}. See: TWOT—2159c; BDB—599a, 937b.

4809. מְרִיבָה {9x} **Mᵉrîybâh**, *mer-ee-baw';* the same as 4808; *Meribah,* the name of two places in the Desert:—Meribah {6x}, strife {3x}. See: BDB—599a, 937b.

4810. מְרִי בַעַל {1x} **Mᵉrîy Baʿal**, *mer-ee' bah'-al;* from 4805 and 1168; *rebellion of* (i.e. *against*) *Baal; Meri-Baal,* an epithet of Gideon:—Meri-baal {1x}. See: BDB—599a, 937c. comp. 4807.

4811. מְרָיָה {1x} **Mᵉrâyâh**, *mer-aw-yaw';* from 4784; *rebellion; Merajah,* an Isr.:—Meraiah {1x}. See: BDB—599a. comp. 3236.

מֹרִיָּה **Môrîyâh**. See 4179.

4812. מְרָיוֹת {7x} **Mᵉrâyôwth**, *mer-aw-yohth';* plur. of 4811; *rebellious; Merajoth,* the name of two Isr.:—Meraioth {7x}. See: BDB—599a.

4813. מִרְיָם {15x} **Miryâm**, *meer-yawm';* from 4805; *rebelliously; Mirjam,* the name of two Israelitesses:—Miriam {15x}. See: BDB—599b.

4814. מְרִירוּת {1x} **mᵉrîyrûwth**, *mer-ee-rooth';* from 4843; *bitterness,* i.e. (fig.) *grief:*—bitterness {1x}. See: TWOT—1248i; BDB—599b, 601b.

4815. מְרִירִי {1x} **mᵉrîyrîy**, *mer-ee-ree';* from 4843; *bitter,* i.e. *poisonous:*—bitter {1x}. See: TWOT—1248h; BDB—599b, 601b.

4816. מֹרֶךְ {1x} **môrek**, *mo'-rek;* perh. from 7401; *softness,* i.e. (fig.) *fear:*—faintness {1x}. See: TWOT—2164c; BDB—599b, 940b.

4817. מֶרְכָּב {3x} **merkâb**, *mer-kawb';* from 7392; a *chariot;* also a *seat* (in a vehicle):—chariot {1x}, covering {1x}, saddle {1x}. See: TWOT—2163e; BDB—599b, 939c.

4818. מֶרְכָּבָה {44x} **merkâbâh**, *mer-kaw-baw';* fem. of 4817; a *chariot:*—chariot {44x}.

Merkabah represents a war-chariot (Ex 14:25), which may have been used as a chariot of honor (Gen 41:43) and may also be translated traveling coach or cart (2 Kin 5:21). Syn.: 7393. See: TWOT—2163f; BDB—599b, 939c. See also 1024.

4819. מַרְכֹּלֶת {1x} **markôleth**, *mar-ko'-leth;* from 7402; a *mart:*—merchandise {1x}. See: TWOT—2165c; BDB—940c.

4820. מִרְמָה {39x} **mirmâh**, *meer-maw';* from 7411 in the sense of *deceiving; fraud:*—deceit {20x}, deceitful {8x}, deceitfully {3x}, false {2x}, guile {2x}, feigned {1x}, craft {1x}, subtilty {1x}, treachery {1x}. See: TWOT—2169b; BDB—599b, 941b.

4821. מִרְמָה {1x} **Mirmâh**, *meer-maw';* the same as 4820; *Mirmah*, an Isr.:—Mirma {1x}. See: BDB—599b, 941b.

4822. מְרֵמוֹת {6x} **Mᵉrêmôwth**, *mer-ay-mohth';* plur. from 7311; *heights; Meremoth*, the name of two Isr.:—Meremoth {6x}. See: BDB—599b.

4823. מִרְמָס {7x} **mirmâç**, *meer-mawce';* from 7429; *abasement* (the act or the thing):—tread down {4x}, tread {2x}, trodden under foot {1x}. See: TWOT—2176a; BDB—599b, 942d.

4824. מֵרֹנֹתִי {2x} **Mêrônôthîy**, *may-ro-no-thee';* patrial from an unused noun; a *Meronothite*, or inhab. of some (otherwise unknown) Meronoth.:—Meronothite {2x}. See: BDB—599c.

4825. מֶרֶס {1x} **Mereç**, *meh'-res;* of for. der.; *Meres*, a Pers.:—Meres {1x}. See: BDB—599c.

4826. מַרְסְנָא {1x} **Marçᵉnâʾ**, *mar-sen-aw';* of for. der.; *Marsena*, a Pers.:—Marsena {1x}. See: BDB—599c.

4827. מֵרַע {1x} **mêraʿ**, *may-rah';* from 7489; used as (abstr.) noun, *wickedness:*—do mischief {1x}. See: TWOT—2186f; BDB—949c, 949d.

4828. מֵרֵעַ {7x} **mêrêaʿ**, *may-ray'-ah;* from 7462 in the sense of *companionship;* a *friend:*—companion {4x}, friend {3x}. See: TWOT—2186f; BDB—599c, 946c.

4829. מִרְעֶה {13x} **mirʿeh**, *meer-eh';* from 7462 in the sense of *feeding; pasture* (the place or the act); also the *haunt* of wild animals:—feeding place {1x}, pasture {12x}. See: TWOT—2185b; BDB—599c, 945c.

4830. מְרְעִית {10x} **mirʿîyth**, *meer-eeth';* from 7462 in the sense of *feeding; pasturage;* concr. a *flock:*—flock {1x}, pasture {9x}. See: TWOT—2185c; BDB—945c.

4831. מַרְעָלָה {1x} **Marʿâlâh**, *mar-al-aw';* from 7477; perh. *earthquake; Maralah*, a place in Pal.:—Maralah {1x}. See: BDB—599c, 947a.

4832. מַרְפֵּא {16x} **marpê**, *mar-pay';* from 7495; prop. *curative*, i.e. lit. (concr.) a *medicine*, or (abstr.) a *cure;* fig. (concr.) *deliverance*, or (abstr.) *placidity:*—health {5x}, healing {3x}, remedy {3x}, incurable + 369 {1x}, cure {1x}, sound {1x}, wholesome {1x}, yielding {1x}. See: TWOT—2196c; BDB—599c, 951b.

4833. מִרְפָּשׂ {1x} **mirpâs**, *meer-paws';* from 7515; *muddled* water:—that which ... have fouled {1x}. See: TWOT—2199a; BDB—590c, 952c.

4834. מָרַץ {4x} **mârats**, *maw-rats';* a prim. root; prop. to *press*, i.e. (fig.) to be *pungent* or vehement; to *irritate:*—embolden {1x}, be forcible {1x}, grievous {1x}, sore {1x}. See: TWOT—1245; BDB—599c.

4835. מְרֻצָה {1x} **mᵉrûtsâh**, *mer-oo-tsaw';* from 7533; *oppression:*—violence {1x}. See: TWOT—2212b; BDB—598c, 599d, 930d, 954d. See also 4794.

4836. מַרְצֵעַ {2x} **martsêaʿ**, *mar-tsay'-ah;* from 7527; an *awl:*—aul {2x}. See: TWOT—2209a; BDB—599d, 954b.

4837. מַרְצֶפֶת {1x} **martsepheth**, *mar-tseh'-feth;* from 7528; a *pavement:*—pavement {1x}. See: TWOT—2210b; BDB—599d, 954b.

4838. מָרַק {3x} **mâraq**, *maw-rak';* a prim. root; to *polish;* by impl. to *sharpen;* also to *rinse:*—bright {1x}, furbish {1x}, scour {1x}. See: TWOT—1246; BDB—599d.

4839. מָרָק {3x} **mârâq**, *maw-rawk';* from 4838; *soup* (as if a *rinsing*):—broth {3x}. See: TWOT—1247a; BDB—600a, 601d. See also 6564.

4840. מֶרְקָח {1x} **merqâch**, *mer-kawkh';* from 7543; a *spicy* herb:—× sweet {1x}. See: TWOT—2215f; BDB—600a, 955c.

4841. מֶרְקָחָה {2x} **merqâchâh**, *mer-kaw-khaw';* fem. of 4840; abstr. a *seasoning* (with spicery); concr. an *unguent-kettle* (for preparing spiced oil):—pot of ointment {1x}, × well {1x}. See: TWOT—2215g; BDB—600a, 955c.

4842. מִרְקַחַת {3x} **mirqachath**, *meer-kakh'-ath;* from 7543; an *aromatic unguent;* also an *unguent-pot:*—prepared by the apothecaries' art {1x}, compound {1x},

ointment {1x}. See: TWOT—2215h; BDB—600a, 955c.

4843. מָרַר {16x} **mârar**, *maw-rar'*; a prim. root; prop. to *trickle* [see 4752]; but used only as a denom. from 4751; to *be* (caus. *make*) *bitter* (lit. or fig.):—bitterness {3x}, bitter {2x}, bitterly {2x}, choler {2x}, grieved {2x}, vexed {2x}, bitterness + 4751 {1x}, grieved him {1x}, provoke {1x}. See: TWOT—1248; BDB—600a.

4844. מְרֹר {3x} **m°rôr**, *mer-ore'*; or

מָרוֹר   **m°rôwr**, *mer-ore'*; from 4843; a *bitter* herb:—bitter {2x}, bitterness {1x}. See: TWOT—1248e; BDB—601a.

4845. מְרֵרָה {1x} **m°rêrâh**, *mer-ay-raw'*; from 4843; *bile* (from its bitterness):—gall {1x}. See: TWOT—1248g; BDB—601a.

4846. מְרֹרָה {4x} **m°rôrâh**, *mer-o-raw'*; or

מְרוֹרָה   **m°rôwrâh**, *mer-o-raw'*; from 4843; prop. *bitterness;* concr. a *bitter thing;* spec. *bile;* also *venom* (of a serpent):—bitter {1x}, bitter thing {1x}, gall {2x}. See: TWOT—1248f; BDB—601a.

4847. מְרָרִי {39x} **M°râriy**, *mer-aw-ree';* from 4843; *bitter; Merari*, an Isr.:—Merari {39x}. See: BDB—601b. See also 4848.

4848. מְרָרִי {1x} **M°râriy**, *mer-aw-ree';* from 4847; a *Merarite* (collect.), or desc. of Merari:—Merarites {1x}. See: BDB—601b.

מָרֵשָׁה   **Mârêshâh.** See 4762.

4849. מִרְשַׁעַת {1x} **mirsha'ath**, *meer-shah'-ath;* from 7561; a female *wicked doer:*—wicked woman {1x}. See: TWOT—2222d; BDB—601c, 958a.

4850. מְרָתַיִם {1x} **M°râthayim**, *mer-aw-thah'-yim;* dual of 4751 fem.; *double bitterness; Merathajim*, an epithet of Bab.:—Merathaim {1x}.

The noun *merathayim* means "double rebellion." This reference to Babylon (Jer 50:21) is translated "Merathaim". See: BDB—601c.

4851. מַשׁ {1x} **Mash**, *mash;* of for. der.; *Mash*, a son of Aram, and the people desc. from him:—Mash {1x}. See: BDB—602a.

4852. מֵשָׁא {1x} **Mêshâ**, *may-shaw';* of for. der.; *Mesha*, a place in Arabia:—Mesha {1x}. See: BDB—602a,.

4853. מַשָּׂא {66x} **massâ**, *mas-saw';* from 5375; a *burden;* spec. *tribute*, or (abstr.) *porterage;* fig. an *utterance*, chiefly a *doom*, espec. *singing;* ment. *desire:*—burden {57x}, song {3x}, prophecy {2x}, set {1x}, exaction {1x}, carry away {1x}, tribute {1x}.

Massa' means "load; burden; tribute; delight." (1) The word means that which is borne by a man, an ass, a mule, or a camel: "If thou see the ass of him that hateth thee lying under his burden, and wouldest forbear to help him ..." (Ex 23:5—the first occurrence). (2) A "load" may be hung on a peg (Is 22:25). (3) This word is used figuratively of spiritual "loads" one is carrying: "For mine iniquities are gone over mine head: as a heavy burden they are too heavy for me" (Ps 38:4). (4) *Massa'* means "burden" in the sense of something burdensome, a hardship. Moses asked God: "Wherefore have I not found favor in thy sight, that thou layest the burden of all this people upon me?" (Num 11:11). (5) Once the word represents that which is borne to a lord, a "tribute": "Also some of the Philistines brought Jehoshaphat presents, and tribute silver" (2 Chr 17:11). (6) In Eze 24:25 *massa'* bears a unique meaning: "Also, thou son of man, hall it not be in the day when I take from them their strength, the joy of their glory, the desire of their eyes, and that whereupon they set [*massa'*] their minds, their sons and their daughters."

(7) *Massa'* means "utterance" or "oracle," a "weighty message": "Then said Jehu to Bidkar his captain, Take up, and cast him in the portion of the field of Naboth the Jezreelite: for remember how that, when I and thou rode together after Ahab his father, the LORD laid this burden [*massa'*] upon him" (2 Kin 9:25). (8) In Jer 23:33–38 the word appears to connote both a burden and an oracle. (9) By a burden we are to understand the message laid on the mind of the prophet, and by him pressed on the attention of the people. The message of the Lord ought not to have been regarded as a burden by the people; but it could not fail to be realized as such by the prophets, who at times felt heavily laden with the weight of their message (Jer 20:9; Nah 1:1, Hab 1:1). See: TWOT—1421d, 1421e; BDB—601d, 672c, 672d.

4854. מַשָּׂא {2x} **Massâ**, *mas-saw';* the same as 4853; *burden; Massa*, a son of Ishmael:—Massa {2x}. See: BDB—601d, 672d.

4855. מַשָּׁא {2x} **mashshâ**, *mash-shaw';* from 5383; a *loan;* by impl. *interest* on a debt:—exaction {1x}, usury {1x}. See: TWOT—1424a; BDB—600d, 601d, 602a, 673d.

4856. מַשֹּׂא {1x} **massô**, *mas-so';* from 5375; *partiality* (as a *lifting* up):—respect {1x}. See: TWOT—1421f; BDB—601d, 673a.

4857. מַשְׁאָב {1x} **mash'âb**, *mash-awb';* from 7579; a *trough* for cattle to drink from:—place of drawing water {1x}. See: TWOT—2299.1a; BDB—602b, 980c.

מְשֹׁאָה   **m°shô'âh.** See 4875.

4858. מַשָּׂאָה {1x} **massâʾâh**, *mas-saw-aw′;* from 5375; a *conflagration* (from the *rising* of smoke):—burden {1x}. See: TWOT—1421g; BDB—601d, 673a.

4859. מַשָּׁאָה {2x} **mashshâʾâh**, *mash-shaw-aw′;* fem. of 4855; a *loan:*—anything {1x}, debt {1x}. See: TWOT—1424b; BDB—602a, 673d.

מַשֻּׁאָה **mashshûʾâh.** See 4876.

4860. מַשָּׁאוֹן {1x} **mashshâʾôwn**, *mash-shaw-ohn′;* from 5377; *dissimulation:*—deceit {1x}. See: TWOT—1425a; BDB—602b, 674b.

4861. מִשְׁאָל {2x} **Mishʾâl**, *mish-awl′;* from 7592; *request; Mishal,* a place in Pal.:—Mishal {1x}, Misheal {1x}. See: TWOT—1425a; BDB—602b. comp. 4913.

4862. מִשְׁאָלָה {2x} **mishʾâlâh**, *mish-aw-law′;* from 7592; a *request:*—desire {1x}, petition {1x}. See: TWOT—2303b; BDB—602b, 982c.

4863. מִשְׁאֶרֶת {4x} **mishʾereth**, *mish-eh′-reth;* from 7604 in the orig. sense of *swelling;* a *kneading-trough* (in which the dough *rises*):—kneading trough {2x}, store {2x}. See: TWOT—1252; BDB—602b, 985a.

4864. מַשְׂאֵת {15x} **masʾêth**, *mas-ayth′;* from 5375; prop. (abstr.) a *raising* (as of the hands in prayer), or *rising* (of flame); fig. an *utterance;* concr. a *beacon* (as *raised*); a *present* (as taken), *mess,* or *tribute;* fig. a *reproach* (as a burden):—burden {3x}, mess {3x}, collection {2x}, flame {2x}, gifts {1x}, oblations {1x}, reward {1x}, sign {1x}, lifting up {1x}. See: TWOT—1421h; BDB—601d, 673a.

מֹשָׁב **môshâb.** See 4186.

מְשֻׁבָה **mᵉshûbâh.** See 4878.

4865. מִשְׁבְּצָה {9x} **mishbᵉtsâh**, *mish-bets-aw′;* from 7660; a *brocade;* by anal. a (reticulated) *setting* of a gem:—ouches {8x}, wrought {1x}. See: TWOT—2320b; BDB—602b, 990b.

4866. מִשְׁבֵּר {3x} **mishbêr**, *mish-bare′;* from 7665; the *orifice* of the womb (from which the fetus *breaks* forth):—birth {2x}, breaking forth {1x}. See: TWOT—2321c; BDB—602b, 991b.

4867. מִשְׁבָּר {5x} **mishbâr**, *mish-bawr′;* from 7665; a *breaker* (of the sea):—billows {1x}, waves {4x}. See: TWOT—2321d; BDB—602b, 991c.

4868. מִשְׁבָּת {1x} **mishbâth**, *mish-bawth′;* from 7673; *cessation,* i.e. destruction:—sabbaths {1x}. See: TWOT—2323e; BDB—602b, 992d.

4869. מִשְׂגָּב {16x} **misgâb**, *mis-gawb′;* from 7682; prop. a *cliff* (or other *lofty* or *inaccessible* place); abstr. *altitude;* fig. a *refuge:*—defence {7x}, refuge {5x}, high tower {3x}, high fort {1x}, *Misgab* {1x}. See: TWOT—2234a; BDB—601d, 960d.

4869. מִשְׂגָּב {1x} **misgâb**, *mis-gawb′; Misgab,* a place in Moab:—*Misgab* {1x}.

4870. מִשְׁגֶּה {1x} **mishgeh**, *mish-gay′;* from 7686; an *error:*—oversight {1x}. See: TWOT—2325b; BDB—602b, 993b.

4871. מָשָׁה {3x} **mâshâh**, *maw-shaw′;* a prim. root; to *pull* out (lit. or fig.):—draw (out) {3x}. See: TWOT—1253; BDB—602b.

4872. מֹשֶׁה {766x} **Môsheh**, *mo-sheh′;* from 4871; *drawing* out (of the water), i.e. *rescued; Mosheh,* the Isr. lawgiver:—Moses {766x}. See: TWOT—1254; BDB—602c, 1101d.

4873. מֹשֶׁה {1x} **Môsheh** (Aram.), *mo-sheh′;* corresp. to 4872:—Moses {1x}. See: BDB—1101d.

4874. מַשֶּׁה {1x} **mashsheh**, *mash-sheh′;* from 5383; a *debt:*—creditor + 1167 {1x}. See: TWOT—1427b; BDB—602d, 674c.

4875. מְשׁוֹאָה {3x} **mᵉshôwʾâh**, *mesh-o-aw′;* or מְשֹׁאָה **mᵉshôʾâh**, *mesh-o-aw′;* from the same as 7722; (a) *ruin,* abstr. (the act) or concr. (the wreck):—desolation {1x}, waste {2x}. See: TWOT—2339b; BDB—602b, 602d, 674b, 996c.

4876. מַשּׁוּאָה {2x} **mashshûwʾâh**, *mash-shoo-aw′;* or מַשֻּׁאָה **mashshûʾâh**, *mash-shoo-aw′;* for 4875; *ruin:*—desolation {1x}, destruction {1x}. See: TWOT—2339b; BDB—601d, 602b, 602f, 674b.

4877. מְשׁוֹבָב {1x} **Mᵉshôwbâb**, *mesh-o-bawb′;* from 7725; *returned; Meshobab,* an Isr.:—Meshobab {1x}. See: BDB—1000c.

4878. מְשׁוּבָה {12x} **mᵉshûwbâh**, *mesh-oo-baw′;* or מְשֻׁבָה **mᵉshûbâh**, *mesh-oo-baw′;* from 7725; *apostasy:*—backsliding {11x}, turning away {1x}.

Meshubah means "backturning; apostasy." This noun occurs 12 times, and it refers to "backsliding" in Hos 14:4: "I will heal their backsliding, I will love them freely: for mine anger is turned away from him." See: TWOT—2340c; BDB—602b, 602d, 1000b.

4879. מְשׁוּגָה {1x} **mᵉshûwgâh**, *mesh-oo-gaw′;* from an unused root mean. to

stray; mistake:—error {1x}. See: BDB—602d, 1000c.

4880. מָשׁוֹט {2x} **mâshôwṭ**, *maw-shote';* or

מִשּׁוֹט **mishshôwṭ**, *mish-shote';* from 7751; an *oar:*—oar {2x}. See: TWOT—2344e; BDB—602d, 1002b.

4881. מְשׂוּכָה {2x} **mᵉsûwkâh**, *mes-oo-kaw';* or

מְשֻׂכָה **mᵉsukâh**, *mes-oo-kaw';* from 7753; a *hedge:*—hedge {2x}. See: TWOT—2241a; BDB—601d, 962b, 968a.

4882. מְשׁוּסָה {1x} **mᵉshûwçâh**, *mesh-oo-saw';* from an unused root mean. to *plunder; spoilation:*—spoil {1x}. See: TWOT—2426a; BDB—602d, 1042c, 1042d.

4883. מָשׂוֹר {1x} **massôwr**, *mas-sore';* from an unused root mean. to *rasp;* a *saw:*—saw {1x}. See: TWOT—1423a; BDB—601d, 673d, 965a.

4884. מְשׂוּרָה {4x} **mᵉsûwrâh**, *mes-oo-raw';* from an unused root mean. appar. to *divide;* a *measure* (for liquids):—measure {4x}. See: TWOT—1250; BDB—601d.

4885. מָשׂוֹשׂ {17x} **mâsôws**, *maw-soce';* from 7797; *delight,* concr. (the cause or object) or abstr. (the feeling):—joy {12x}, mirth {3x}, rejoice {2x}. See: TWOT—2246b; BDB—601d, 965c.

4886. מָשַׁח {69x} **mâshach**, *maw-shakh';* a prim. root; to *rub* with oil, i.e. to *anoint;* by impl. to *consecrate;* also to *paint:*—anoint {68x}, painted {1x}.

Mashach means "to anoint, smear, consecrate." (1) The word is found for the first time in the Old Testament in Gen 31:13: ". . . where thou anointedst the pillar, and . . . vowedst a vow unto me." (1a) This use illustrates the idea of anointing something or someone as an act of consecration. (1b) The basic meaning of the word, however, is simply to "smear" something on an object. (1c) Usually oil is involved, but it could be other substances, such as paint or dye (cf. Jer 22:14). (2) The expression "anoint the shield" in Is 21:5 probably has more to do with lubrication than consecration in that context. (3) When unleavened bread is "tempered with oil" in Ex 29:2, it is basically equivalent to our act of buttering bread. (4) The Old Testament most commonly uses *mashach* to indicate "anointing" in the sense of a special setting apart for an office or function. (4a) Thus, Elisha was "anointed" to be a prophet (1 Kin 19:16). (4b) More typically, kings were "anointed" for their office (1 Sa 16:12; 1 Kin 1:39). (5) Vessels used in the worship at the sacred shrine (both tabernacle and temple) were consecrated for use by "anointing" them (Ex 29:36; 30:26; 40:9–10).

(6) In fact, the recipe for the formulation of this "holy anointing oil" is given in detail in Ex 30:22–25. See: TWOT—1255; BDB—602d, 1101d.

4887. מְשַׁח {2x} **mᵉshach** (Aram.), *mesh-akh';* from a root corresp. to 4886; *oil:*—oil {2x}. See: TWOT—2842; BDB—1101d.

4888. מִשְׁחָה {26x} **mishchâh**, *meesh-khaw';* or

מָשְׁחָה **moshchâh**, *mosh-khaw';* from 4886; *unction* (the act); by impl. a consecratory *gift:*—anointing {24x}, anointed {1x}, ointment {1x}.

This noun occurs 26 times and only in Exodus, Leviticus, and Numbers. It always follows the Hebrew word for oil. The first occurrence is Ex 25:6: "Oil for the light, spices for anointing oil, and for sweet incense." See: TWOT—1255a, 1255b; BDB—603b, 603c.

4889. מַשְׁחִית {11x} **mashchîyth**, *mash-kheeth';* from 7843; *destructive,* i.e. (as noun) *destruction,* lit. (spec. a *snare*) or fig. (*corruption*):—destroy {4x}, corruption {2x}, destruction {2x}, set a trap {1x}, destroying {1x}, utterly {1x}. See: TWOT—2370a; BDB—603d, 1008c.

4890. מִשְׁחָק {1x} **mischâq** *mis-khawk';* from 7831; a *laughing-stock:*—scorn {1x}. See: TWOT—1905f; BDB—601d, 966a.

4891. מִשְׁחָר {1x} **mishchâr**, *mish-khawr';* from 7836 in the sense of day *breaking; dawn:*—morning {1x}. See: TWOT—2369b; BDB—603d, 1007d.

4892. מַשְׁחֵת {1x} **mashchêth**, *mash-khayth';* for 4889; *destruction:*—destroying {1x}. See: TWOT—2370b; BDB—603d, 1008c.

4893. מִשְׁחָת {2x} **mishchâth**, *mish-khawth';* or

מָשְׁחָת **mâshchâth**, *mosh-khawth';* from 7843; *disfigurement:*—corruption {1x}, marred {1x}. See: TWOT—2370c; BDB—603d, 1008c.

4894. מִשְׁטוֹחַ {3x} **mishṭôwach**, *mish-to'-akh;* or

מִשְׁטַח **mishṭach**, *mish-takh';* from 7849; a *spreading*-place:—spread forth {1x}, spread upon {1x}, spreading {1x}. See: TWOT—2372b; BDB—603d, 1009a.

4895. מַשְׂטֵמָה {2x} **masṭêmâh**, *mas-tay-maw';* from the same as 7850; *enmity:*—hatred {2x}. See: TWOT—2251a; BDB—601d, 966b.

4896. מִשְׁטָר {1x} **mishṭâr**, *mish-tawr';* from 7860; *jurisdiction:*—dominion {1x}. See: TWOT—2374b; BDB—603d, 1009c.

4897. מֶשִׁי {2x} **meshîy**, *meh'-shee;* from 4871; *silk* (as *drawn* from the cocoon):— silk {2x}. See: TWOT—1256; BDB—603d.

מֹשִׁי **Mushîy.** See 4187.

4898. מְשֵׁיזַבְאֵל {3x} **Mᵉshêyzabʾêl**, *mesh-ay-zab-ale';* from an equiv. to 7804 and 410; *delivered of God; Meshezabel,* an Isr.:—Meshezabeel {3x}. See: TWOT—1256; BDB—604a, 1115a.

4899. מָשִׁיחַ {39x} **mâshîyach**, *maw-shee'-akh;* from 4886; *anointed;* usually a *consecrated* person (as a king, priest, or saint); spec. the *Messiah:*—anointed {37x}, Messiah {2x}.

Mashiyach means "anointed one." **(1)** A word that is important both to Old Testament and New Testament understandings is the noun *mashiyach,* which gives us the term messiah. **(2)** As is true of the verb, *mashiyach* implies an anointing for a special office or function. **(2a)** Thus, David refused to harm Saul because Saul was "the Lord's anointed" (1 Sa 24:6). **(2b)** The Psalms often express the messianic ideals attached to the Davidic line by using the phrase "the Lord's anointed" (Ps 2:2; 18:50; 89:38, 51). **(3)** Interestingly enough, the only person named "messiah" in the Old Testament was Cyrus, the pagan king of Persia, **(3a)** who was commissioned by God to restore Judah to her homeland after the Exile (Is 45:1). **(3b)** The anointing in this instance was more figurative than literal, since Cyrus was not aware that he was being set apart for such a divine purpose. **(4)** The New Testament title of Christ is derived from the Greek *Christos* which is exactly equivalent to the Hebrew *mashiyach,* for it is also rooted in the idea of "to smear with oil." So the term Christ emphasizes the special anointing of Jesus of Nazareth for His role as God's chosen one. See: TWOT—1255c; BDB—603c.

4900. מָשַׁךְ {36x} **mâshak**, *maw-shak';* a prim. root; to *draw,* used in a great variety of applications (incl. to *sow,* to *sound,* to *prolong,* to *develop,* to *march,* to *remove,* to *delay,* to *be tall,* etc.):—draw {15x}, draw out {3x}, prolonged {3x}, scattered {2x}, draw along {1x}, draw away {1x}, continue {1x}, deferred {1x}, misc. {9x} = extend, forbear, × give, handle, make (sound) long, × sow, stretch out. See: TWOT—1257; BDB—604a.

4901. מֶשֶׁךְ {2x} **meshek**, *meh'shek;* from 4900; a *sowing;* also a *possession:*—precious {1x}, price {1x}. See: TWOT—1257a; BDB—604d.

4902. מֶשֶׁךְ {2x} **Meshek**, *meh'-shek;* the same in form as 4901, but prob. of for.

der.; *Meshek,* a son of Japheth, and the people desc. from him:—Mesech {1x}, Meshech {1x}. See: BDB—604d.

4903. מִשְׁכַּב {6x} **mishkab** (Aram.), *mish-kab';* corresp. to 4904; a *bed:*—bed {6x}. See: TWOT—3029a; BDB—1101d, 1115b.

4904. מִשְׁכָּב {46x} **mishkâb**, *mish-kawb';* from 7901; a *bed* (fig. a *bier);* abstr. *sleep;* by euphem. carnal *intercourse:*—bed {34x}, bedchamber + 2315 {4x}, couch {1x}, misc. {7x} = lieth (lying) with.

Mishkab means a "place to lie; couch; bed; act of lying." **(1)** In Gen 49:4 *mishkab* is used to mean a "place to lie" or "bed": ". . . because thou wentest up to thy father's bed." **(2)** The word refers to the "act of lying" in Num 31:17: ". . . kill every woman that hath known man by lying with him." See: TWOT—2381c; BDB—605a, 1012d, 1115b.

מְשֻׁכָה **mᵉsûkâh.** See 4881.

4905. מַשְׂכִּיל {13x} **maskîyl**, *mas-keel';* from 7919; *instructive,* i.e. a *didactic* poem:—Maschil {13x}.

Maskiyl means a "didactic psalm(?)." **(1)** This noun form, derived from *sakal* (7919), is found in the title of 13 psalms and also in Ps 47:7. **(2)** Scholars are not agreed on the significance of this term, but on the basis of the general meaning of *sakal,* such psalms must have been considered didactic or teaching psalms. See: TWOT—2263b; BDB—601d, 968d.

מַשְׂכִּים **mashkîym.** See 7925.

4906. מַשְׂכִּית {6x} **maskîyth**, *mas-keeth';* from the same as 7906; a *figure* (carved on stone, the wall, or any object); fig. *imagination:*—conceit {1x}, image {1x}, imagery {1x}, picture {2x}, × wish {1x}. See: TWOT—2257c; BDB—601d, 967c.

4907. מִשְׁכַּן {1x} **mishkan** (Aram.), *mish-kan';* corresp. to 4908; *residence:*—habitation {1x}. See: TWOT—3031a; BDB—1101d.

4908. מִשְׁכָּן {139x} **mishkân**, *mish-kawn';* from 7931; a *residence* (incl. a shepherd's *hut,* the *lair* of animals, fig. the *grave;* also the *temple);* spec. the *tabernacle* (prop. its wooden walls):—tabernacle {119x}, dwelling {9x}, habitation {5x}, dwellingplaces {3x}, place {1x}, dwelleth {1x}, tents {1x}.

Mishkan, "dwelling place; tent." **(1)** This word occurs nearly 140 times, and often refers to the wilderness "tabernacle" (Ex 25:9). **(2)** *Mishkan* was also used later to refer to the "temple" (4908). This usage probably prepared the way for the familiar term *shekinah,* which was widely used in later Judaism to refer to the "presence" of God. Syn: 3427, 7931. See: TWOT—2387c; BDB—605a, 1015c, 1115b.

4909. מַשְׂכֹּרֶת {4x} **maskôreth**, *mas-koh'-reth;* from 7936; *wages* or a *reward:*—reward {1x}, wages {3x}. See: TWOT—2264.1d; BDB—601d, 969b.

4910. מָשַׁל {81x} **mâshal**, *maw-shal';* a prim. root; to *rule:*—rule {38x}, ruler {19x}, reign {8x}, dominion {7x}, governor {4x}, ruled over {2x}, power {2x}, indeed {1x}.

Mashal means "to rule, reign, have dominion." **(1)** The word is used for the first time in the Old Testament in Gen 1:18, where the sun, moon, and stars are designated "to rule over the day and over the night." **(2)** *Mashal* is used most frequently in the text to express the "ruling or dominion" of one person over another (Gen 3:16; 24:2). **(2a)** Cain is advised "to rule over" or "master" sin (Gen 4:7). **(2b)** Joseph's brothers respond to his dreams with the angry question: "Shalt thou indeed reign over us?" (Gen 37:8; the Hebrew verb here is literally "ruling will you rule," the repetition of the same root giving the needed emphasis). **(3)** As Creator and Sovereign over His world, God "ruleth by his power for ever" (Ps 66:7). **(4)** When God allowed Israel to have a king, it was with the condition that God was still the ultimate King and that first loyalty belonged to Him (Deut 17:14–20). **(4a)** This theocratic ideal is perhaps best expressed by Gideon: "I will not rule over you, neither shall my son rule over you: the LORD shall rule over you" (Judg 8:23). **(4b)** With the possible exception of David, no king of Israel fully lived up to the theocratic ideal, and David himself had some problems with it. See: TWOT—1259; BDB—605c.

4911. מָשַׁל {16x} **mâshal**, *maw-shal';* denom. from 4912; to *liken*, i.e. (tran.) to use fig. language (an allegory, adage, song or the like); intr. to *resemble:*—like {5x}, proverb {4x}, speak {2x}, use {2x}, become {1x}, compare {1x}, utter {1x}. See: TWOT—1258, 1258b; BDB—605a, 605b.

4912. מָשָׁל {39x} **mâshâl**, *maw-shawl';* appar. from 4910 in some orig. sense of *superiority* in mental action; prop. a pithy *maxim*, usually of metaph. nature; hence, a *simile* (as an adage, poem, discourse):—proverb {19x}, parable {18x}, byword {1x}, like {1x}. See: TWOT—1258a; BDB—605a.

4913. מָשָׁל {1x} **Mâshâl**, *maw-shawl';* for 4861; *Mashal*, a place in Pal.:—Mashal {1x}. See: BDB—602b, 605a.

4914. מְשׁל {1x} **mᵉshôl**, *mesh-ol';* from 4911; a *satire:*—byword {1x}. See: TWOT—1258d; BDB—605c.

4915. מֹשֶׁל {3x} **môshel**, *mo'-shel;* (1) from 4910; *empire;* (2) from 4911; a *parallel:*—dominion {2x}, like {1x}. See: TWOT—1259a, 1258c; BDB—605c, 606a.

מִשְׁלוֹשׁ **mishlôwsh**. See 7969.

4916. מִשְׁלוֹחַ {10x} **mishlôwach**, *mish-lo'-akh;* or

מִשְׁלֹחַ **mishlôach**, *mish-lo'-akh;* also

מִשְׁלָח **mishlâch**, *mish-lawkh';* from 7971; a *sending* out, i.e. (abstr.) *presentation* (favorable), or *seizure* (unfavorable); also (concr.) a place of *dismissal*, or a *business* to be discharged:—to lay {1x}, to put {1x}, put-test {2x}, settest {3x}, sending {2x}, sending forth {1x}. See: TWOT—2394d, 2394e; BDB—606b, 1043c.

4917. מִשְׁלַחַת {2x} **mishlachath**, *mish-lakh'-ath;* fem. of 4916; a *mission*, i.e. (abstr.) and favorable) *release*, or (concr. and unfavorable) an *army:*—discharge {1x}, sending {1x}. See: TWOT—2394f; BDB—606b, 1020a.

4918. מְשֻׁלָּם {25x} **Mᵉshullâm**, *mesh-ool-lawm';* from 7999; *allied; Meshullam*, the name of seventeen Isr.:—*Meshullam* {25x}. See: BDB—606b, 1024b, 1024c.

4919. מְשֵׁלֵמוֹת {2x} **Mᵉshillêmôwth**, *mesh-il-lay-mohth';* plur. from 7999; *reconciliations; Meshillemoth*, an Isr.:—*Meshillemoth* {2x}. See: BDB—606b, 1024c. comp. 4921.

4920. מְשֶׁלֶמְיָה {4x} **Mᵉshelemyâh**, *mesh-eh-lem-yaw';* or

מְשֶׁלֶמְיָהוּ **Mᵉshelemyâhûw**, *mesh-eh-lem-yaw'-hoo;* from 7999 and 3050; *ally of Jah; Meshelemjah*, an Isr.:—*Meshelemiah* {4x}. See: BDB—606b, 1024b, 1024c.

4921. מְשִׁלֵמִית {1x} **Mᵉshillêmîyth**, *mesh-il-lay-meeth';* from 7999; *reconciliation; Meshillemith*, an Isr.:—*Meshillemith* {1x}. See: BDB—606b, 1024c. comp. 4919.

4922. מְשֻׁלֶּמֶת {1x} **Mᵉshullemeth**, *mesh-ool-leh'-meth;* fem. of 4918; *Meshullemeth*, an Israelitess:—*Meshullemeth* {1x}. See: BDB—606b, 1024c.

4923. מְשַׁמָּה {7x} **mᵉshammâh**, *mesh-am-maw';* from 8074; a *waste* or *amazement:*—astonishment {1x}, desolate {6x}. See: TWOT—2409f; BDB—606b, 1031d.

4924. מַשְׁמָן {7x} **mashmân**, *mash-mawn';* from 8080; *fat*, i.e. (lit. and abstr.) *fatness;* but usually (fig. and concr.) a *rich dish*, a *fertile* field, a *robust* man:—fat {1x}, fat ones {1x}, fatness {4x}, fattest places {1x}. See: TWOT—2410e, 2410f; BDB—606b, 1032a, 1032c, 1032d, 1033b.

4925. מִשְׁמַנָּה {1x} **Mishmannâh**, *mish-man-naw'*; from 8080; *fatness; Mash-mannah*, an Isr.:—*Mishmannah* {1x}. See: BDB—606b, 1032d.

4926. מִשְׁמָע {1x} **mishmâ**ᶜ, *mish-maw'*; from 8085; a *report:*—hearing {1x}. See: TWOT—2412f; BDB—606b, 1036a.

4927. מִשְׁמָע {4x} **Mishmâ**ᶜ, *mish-maw'*; the same as 4926; *Mishma*, the name of a son of Ishmael, and of an Isr.:—*Mishma* {4x}. See: TWOT—2412f; BDB—606b, 1036a.

4928. מִשְׁמַעַת {4x} **mishma**ᶜ**ath**, *mish-mah'-ath;* fem. of 4926; *audience,* i.e. the royal *court;* also *obedience,* i.e. (concr.) a *subject:*—bidding {1x}, guard {2x}, obey {1x}. See: TWOT—2412g; BDB—606b, 1036a.

4929. מִשְׁמָר {22x} **mishmâr**, *mish-mawr'*; from 8104; a *guard* (the man, the post, or the *prison*); fig. a *deposit;* also (as observed) a *usage* (abstr.), or an *example* (concr.):—ward {12x}, watch {4x}, guard {3x}, diligence {1x}, offices {1x}, prison {1x}.

Mishmar, as a noun, means "guard; guard-post." **(1)** In the first of its 22 occurrences *mishmar* means "guard": "And he put them in ward [*mishmar*] in the house of the captain of the guard, into the prison" (Gen 40:3). **(2)** The word implies "guardpost" in Neh 7:3. **(3)** The word also refers to men on "guard" (Neh 4:23) and **(4)** to groups of attendants (Neh 12:24). Syn.: 5341, 8104. See: TWOT—2414f; BDB—606b, 1038b.

4930. מַשְׂמְרָה {1x} **masm**ᵉ**râh**, *mas-mer-aw'*; for 4548 fem.; a *peg:*—nail {1x}. See: TWOT—1518b; BDB—702d.

4931. מִשְׁמֶרֶת {78x} **mishmereth**, *mish-meh'-reth;* fem. of 4929; *watch,* i.e. the act (*custody*) or (concr.) the *sentry*, the *post;* obj. *preservation*, or (concr.) *safe;* fig. *observance,* i.e. (abstr.) *duty,* or (obj.) a *usage* or *party:*—charge {50x}, ward {9x}, watch {7x}, keep {7x}, ordinance {3x}, offices {1x}, safeguard {1x}.

Mishmereth means "those who guard; obligation." **(1)** The word refers to "those who guard" in 2 Kin 11:5: "A third part of you that enter in on the sabbath shall even be keepers of the watch of the king's house." **(2)** In Gen 26:5 the word refers to an "obligation": "Because that Abraham obeyed my voice, and kept my charge, my commandments, my statutes, and my laws." See: TWOT—2414g; BDB—606b, 1038b.

4932. מִשְׁנֶה {35x} **mishneh**, *mish-neh'*; from 8138; prop. a *repetition,* i.e. a *duplicate* (*copy* of a document), or a *double* (in amount); by impl. a *second* (in order, rank, age,

quality or location):—second {11x}, double {8x}, next {7x}, college {2x}, copy {2x}, twice {2x}, fatlings {1x}, much {1x}, second order {1x}. See: TWOT—2421c; BDB—606b, 1032d, 1041c.

4933. מְשִׁסָּה {6x} **m**ᵉ**shiççâh**, *mesh-is-saw';* from 8155; *plunder:*—booty {2x}, spoil {4x}. See: TWOT—2426a; BDB—606b, 1042d.

4934. מִשְׁעוֹל {1x} **mish**ᶜ**ôwl**, *mish-ole';* from the same as 8168; a *hollow,* i.e. a narrow passage:—path {1x}. See: TWOT—2432b; BDB—606c, 1043c.

4935. מִשְׁעִי {1x} **mish**ᶜ**îy**, *mish-ee';* prob. from 8159; *inspection:*—to supple {1x}. See: TWOT—1260a; BDB—606b.

4936. מִשְׁעָם {1x} **Mish**ᶜ**âm**, *mish-awm';* appar. from 8159; *inspection; Misham,* an Isr.:—Misham {1x}. See: BDB—606c.

4937. מִשְׁעֵן {5x} **mish**ᶜ**ên**, *mish-ane';* or

מִשְׁעָן **mish**ᶜ**ân**, *mish-awn';* from 8172; a *support* (concr.), i.e. (fig.) a *protector* or *sustenance:*—stay {5x}. See: TWOT—2434a, 2434b; BDB—606c, 1044a.

4938. מִשְׁעֵנָה {12x} **mish**ᶜ**ênâh**, *mish-ay-naw';* or

מִשְׁעֶנֶת **mish**ᶜ**eneth**, *mish-eh'-neth;* fem. of 4937; *support* (abstr.), i.e. (fig.) *sustenance* or (concr.) a *walking-stick:*—staff {11x}, stave {1x}. See: TWOT—2434c, 2434d; BDB—606c, 1044a.

4939. מִשְׂפָּח {1x} **mispâch**, *mis-pawkh';* from 5596; *slaughter:*—oppression {1x}. See: TWOT—1534d; BDB—705c, 974a.

4940. מִשְׁפָּחָה {300x} **mishpâchâh**, *mish-paw-khaw';* from 8192 [comp. 8198]; a *family,* i.e. circle of relatives; fig. a *class* (of persons), a *species* (of animals) or *sort* (of things); by extens. a *tribe* or *people:*—families {289x}, kinds {1x}, kindred {9x}.

Mishpachah means "family; clan." **(1)** The word is first used in Gen 8:19: "Every beast, every creeping thing, and every fowl, and whatsoever creepeth upon the earth, after their kinds, went forth out of the ark." **(2)** The noun *mishpachah* is used predominantly in the Pentateuch (as many as 154 times in Numbers) and in the historical books, but rarely in the poetical literature (5 times) and the prophetical writings. **(3)** All members of a group who were related by blood and who still felt a sense of consanguinity belonged to the "clan" or "the extended family." **(3a)** Saul argued that since he belonged to the least of the "clans," he had no right to the kingship (1 Sa 9:21). **(3b)** This meaning determined the extent of Rahab's family that was spared from Jericho: "And they brought out all her kindred, and left them

without the camp of Israel" (Josh 6:23). **(3c)** So the "clan" was an important division within the "tribe." **(3d)** The Book of Numbers gives a census of the leaders and the numbers of the tribes according to the "families" (Num 1—4; 26). **(3e)** In capital cases, where revenge was desired, the entire clan might be taken: "And, behold, the whole family is risen against thine handmaid, and they said, Deliver him that smote his brother, that we may kill him, for the life of his brother whom he slew; and we will destroy the heir also: and so they shall quench my coal which is left, and shall not leave to my husband neither name nor remainder upon the earth" (2 Sa 14:7). **(4)** A further extension of the meaning "division" or "clan" is the idiomatic usage of "class" or "group," such as "the families" of the animals that left the ark (Gen 8:19) or the "families" of the nations (Ps 22:28; 96:7; cf. Gen 10:5). **(5)** Even God's promise to Abraham had reference to all the nations: "And I will bless them that bless thee, and curse him that curseth thee: and in thee shall all families of the earth be blessed" (Gen 12:3). **(6)** The narrow meaning of *mishpachah* is similar to our usage of "family" and similar to the meaning of the word in modern Hebrew. Abraham sent his servant to his relatives in Padanaram to seek a wife for Isaac (Gen 24:38). **(7)** The law of redemption applied to the "close relatives in a family": "After that he is sold he may be redeemed again; one of his brethren may redeem him: Either his uncle, or his uncle's son, may redeem him, or any that is nigh of kin unto him of his family may redeem him; or if he be able, he may redeem himself" (Lev 25:48–49). See: TWOT—2442b; BDB—606c, 1046.

4941. מִשְׁפָּט {421x} **mishpât**, *mish-pawt';* from 8199; prop. a *verdict* (favorable or unfavorable) pronounced judicially, espec. a *sentence* or formal decree (human or [participant's] divine *law*, indiv. or collect.), incl. the act, the place, the suit, the crime, and the penalty; abstr. *justice*, incl. a participant's *right* or *privilege* (statutory or customary), or even a *style:*—judgment {296x}, manner {38x}, right {18x}, cause {12x}, ordinance {11x}, lawful {7x}, order {5x}, worthy {3x}, fashion {3x}, custom {2x}, discretion {2x}, law {2x}, measure {2x}, sentence {2x}, misc. {18x} = + adversary, ceremony, charge, × crime, desert, determination, disposing, due, form, to be judged, just (-ice, -ly), usest, + wrong.

Mishpat means "judgment; rights." **(1)** This word has two main senses; the first deals with the act of sitting as a judge, hearing a case, and rendering a proper verdict. Eccl 12:14 is one such occurrence: "For God shall bring every work into judgment, with every secret thing, whether it be good, or whether it be

evil." **(2)** *Mishpat* can also refer to the "rights" belonging to someone: "Thou shalt not wrest the judgment of thy poor in his cause" (Ex 23:6). This second sense carries several nuances: **(2a)** the sphere in which things are in proper relationship to one's claims: "For I know him, that he will command his children and his household after him, and they shall keep the way of the LORD, to do justice and judgment; that the LORD may bring upon Abraham that which he hath spoken of him" (Gen 18:19—the first occurrence); **(2b)** a judicial verdict: "And thou shalt come unto the priests the Levites, and unto the judge that shall be in those days, and enquire; and they shall shew thee the sentence of judgment" (Deut 17:9); **(2c)** the statement of the case for the accused: "And Moses brought their cause before the LORD" (Num 27:5); and an established ordinance: "Now these are the judgments which thou shalt set before them" (Ex 21:1). See: TWOT—2443c; BDB—606c, 1048b.

4942. מִשְׁפָּת {2x} **mishpâth**, *mish-pawth';* from 8192; a *stall* for cattle (only dual):—burden {1x}, sheepfold {1x}. See: TWOT—2441c; BDB—606c, 1046b, 1052a.

4943. מֶשֶׁק {1x} **mesheq**, *meh'-shek;* from an unused root mean. to *hold; possession:*—+ steward {1x}. See: TWOT—1261a; BDB—606c.

4944. מַשָּׁק {1x} **mashshâq**, *mash-shawk';* from 8264; a *traversing*, i.e. rapid *motion:*—running to and fro {1x}. See: TWOT—2460a; BDB—606d, 1055b.

4945. מַשְׁקֶה {7x} **mashqeh**, *mash-keh';* from 8248; prop. *causing to drink*, i.e. a *butler;* by impl. (intr.), *drink* (itself); fig. a *well-watered* region:—drink {2x}, drinking {2x}, watered {1x}, butlership {1x}, fat pastures {1x}. See: TWOT—2452c; BDB—606d, 1052d.

4946. מִשְׁקוֹל {1x} **mishqôwl**, *mish-kole';* from 8254; *weight:*—weight {1x}. See: TWOT—2454b; BDB—606d, 1054a.

4947. מַשְׁקוֹף {3x} **mashqôwph**, *mash-kofe';* from 8259 in its orig. sense of *overhanging;* a *lintel:*—lintel {2x}, upper door post {1x}. See: TWOT—2458c; BDB—606d, 1054d.

4948. מִשְׁקָל {49x} **mishqâl**, *mish-kawl';* from 8254; *weight* (numerically estimated); hence, *weighing* (the act):—(full) weight {47x}, weigh {2x}. See: TWOT—2454c; BDB—606d, 1054a.

Hebrew

4949. מִשְׁקֶלֶת {2x} **mishqeleth**, *mish-keh'-leth;*
or

מִשְׁקֹלֶת **mishqôleth**, *mish-ko'-leth;* fem.
of 4948 or 4947; a *weight,* i.e. a
plummet (with line attached):—plummet {1x}.
See: TWOT—2454d; BDB—606d, 1054a.

4950. מִשְׁקָע {1x} **mishqâʻ**, *mish-kaw';* from
8257; a *settling* place (of water),
i.e. a pond:—deep {1x}. See: TWOT—2456a;
BDB—606d, 1054b.

4951. מִשְׂרָה {2x} **misrâh**, *mis-raw';* from 8280;
empire:—government {1x}. See:
TWOT—2288a; BDB—601d, 976a.

4952. מִשְׁרָה {1x} **mishrâh**, *mish-raw';* from
8281 in the sense of *loosening;*
maceration, i.e. steeped *juice:*—liquor {1x}.
See: TWOT—2464a; BDB—606d, 1056a.

4953. מַשְׁרוֹקִי {4x} **mashrôwqîy** (Aram.), *mash-
ro-kee';* from a root corresp. to
8319; a (musical) *pipe* (from its *whistling*
sound):—flute {4x}. See: TWOT—3049a; BDB—
1101d, 1117b.

4954. מִשְׁרָעִי {1x} **Mishrâʻîy**, *mish-raw-ee';*
patrial from an unused noun
from an unused root; prob. mean. to *stretch
out; extension;* a *Mishraite,* or inhab. (collect.) of Mishra:—Mishraites {1x}. See: BDB—
606d.

4955. מִשְׂרָפָה {2x} **misrâphâh**, *mis-raw-faw';*
from 8313; *combustion,* i.e. cre-
mation (of a corpse), or *calcination* (of lime):—
burnings {2x}. See: TWOT—2292d; BDB—
602a, 977c.

4956. מִשְׂרְפוֹת מַיִם {2x} **Misrᵉphôwth Mayim**,
mis-ref-ohth' mah'-yim;
from the plur. of 4955 and 4325; *burnings of
water; Misrephoth-Majim,* a place in Pal.:—
Misrephoth-mayim {2x}. See: BDB—602a,
977c.

4957. מַשְׂרֵקָה {2x} **Masrêqâh**, *mas-ray-kaw';*
a form for 7796 used denom.;
vineyard; Masrekah, a place in Idumæa:—
Masrekah {2x}. See: BDB—602a, 977d.

4958. מַשְׂרֵת {1x} **masrêth**, *mas-rayth';* appar.
from an unused root mean. to
perforate, i.e. hollow out; a *pan:*—pan {1x}.
See: TWOT—1251; BDB—602a.

4959. מָשַׁשׁ {9x} **mâshash**, *maw-shash';* a prim.
root; to *feel* of; by impl. to *grope:*—
feel {3x}, grope {4x}, search {2x}. See: TWOT—
1262; BDB—606d.

4960. מִשְׁתֶּה {46x} **mishteh**, *mish-teh';* from
8354; *drink,* by impl. *drinking*
(the act); also (by impl.) a *banquet* or (gen.)
feast:—banquet {10x}, drink {5x}, feast ([-ed],

-ing {31x}). See: TWOT—2477c; BDB—607a,
1059c, 1117c.

4961. מִשְׁתֶּה {1x} **mishteh** (Aram.), *mish-teh';*
corresp. to 4960; a *banquet:*—
banquet {1x}. See: TWOT—3051a; BDB—1101d,
1117c.

4962. מַת {22x} **math**, *math;* from the same as
4970; prop. an *adult* (as of full
length); by impl. a *man* (only in the plur.):—
men {14x}, few {2x}, few + 4557 {1x}, friends
{1x}, number {1x}, persons {1x}, small {1x}, with
{1x}. See: TWOT—1263; BDB—607a, 607d,
608a, 1071b.

4963. מַתְבֵּן {1x} **mathbên**, *math-bane';* denom.
from 8401; *straw* in the heap:—
straw {1x}. See: TWOT—2493a; BDB—607b,
1062a.

4964. מֶתֶג {4x} **metheg**, *meh-theg;* from an
unused root mean. to *curb;* a *bit:*—
bit {1x}, bridle {3x}. See: TWOT—1264a; BDB—
607c.

4965. מֶתֶג הָאַמָּה {1x} **Metheg hâ-ʼAmmâh**,
meh'-theg haw-am-maw';
from 4964 and 520 with the art. interposed;
bit of the metropolis; Metheg-ha-Ammah, an
epithet of Gath:—Metheg-ammah {1x}. See:
BDB—52a, 607c.

4966. מָתוֹק {12x} **mâthôwq**, *maw-thoke';* or

מָתוּק **mâthûwq**, *maw-thook';* from 4985;
sweet:—sweet {8x}, sweetner {2x},
sweetness {2x}. See: TWOT—1268c; BDB—
608b.

4967. מְתוּשָׁאֵל {2x} **Mᵉthûwshâʼêl**, *meth-oo-
shaw-ale';* from 4962 and 410,
with the rel. interposed; *man who* (is) *of God;
Methushaël,* an antediluvian patriarch:—
Methusael {2x}. See: BDB—607b, 607c.

4968. מְתוּשֶׁלַח {6x} **Mᵉthûwshelach**, *meth-oo-
sheh'-lakh;* from 4962 and
7973; *man of a dart; Methushelach,* an antediluvian patriarch:—Methuselah {6x}. See: BDB—
607b, 607c.

4969. מָתַח {1x} **mâthach**, *maw-thakh';* a prim.
root; to *stretch* out:—spreadest
them out {1x}. See: TWOT—1265; BDB—607c.

4970. מָתַי {3x} **mâthay**, *maw-thah'ee;* from an
unused root mean. to *extend;* prop.
extent (of time); but used only adv. (espec. with
other particles pref.), *when* (either rel. or interrog.):—long {1x}, when {2x}. See: TWOT—
1266; BDB—607d.

מְתִים **mᵉthîwm**. See 4962.

4971. מַתְכֹּנֶת {5x} **mathkôneth**, *math-ko'-neth;*
or

מַתְכֻּנֶת **mathkûneth**, *math-koo'-neth;*
        from 8505 in the transferred
sense of *measuring; proportion* (in size, number or ingredients):—composition {2x}, measure {1x}, state {1x}, tale {1x}. See: TWOT—
2511c; BDB—607d, 1067c.

4972. מַתְלָאָה {1x} **mattᵉlâ⁾âh**, *mat-tel-aw-aw';*
        from 4100 and 8513; *what a
trouble!:*—what a weariness {1x}. See: TWOT—
1066a; BDB—608a, 1067d.

4973. מְתַלְּעָה {3x} **mᵉthallᵉ⁽âh**, *meth-al-leh-aw';*
        contr. from 3216; prop. a *biter,*
i.e. a *tooth:*—cheek (jaw) {1x}, tooth {1x}, jaw
{1x}. See: TWOT—1066a; BDB—577a, 608a,
1069a.

4974. מְתֹם {4x} **mᵉthôm**, *meth-ohm';* from 8552;
        wholesomeness; also (adv.) *completely:*—men [by reading 4962]{1x}, soundness
{3x}. See: TWOT—2522e; BDB—607a, 608a,
1071b.

מֶתֶן **Methen**. See 4981.

4975. מֹתֶן {47x} **môthen**, *mo'-then;* from an
        unused root mean. to *be slender;*
prop. the *waist* or small of the back; only in
plur. the *loins:*—+ greyhound {1x}, loins {42x},
side {4x}. See: TWOT—1267a; BDB—608a.

4976. מַתָּן {5x} **mattân**, *mat-tawn';* from 5414;
        a *present:*—gift {4x}, gifts {1x}. See:
TWOT—1443b; BDB—608c, 682b.

4977. מַתָּן {3x} **Mattân**, *mat-tawn';* the same
        as 4976; *Mattan,* the name of a
priest of Baal, and of an Isr.:—*Mattan* {3x}. See:
BDB—608c, 682b.

4978. מַתְּנָא {3x} **mattᵉnâ⁾** (Aram.), *mat-ten-
        aw';* corresp. to 4979:—gift {3x}.
See: TWOT—2880a; BDB—1101d, 1103d.

4979. מַתָּנָה {17x} **mâttânâh**, *mat-taw-naw';*
        fem. of 4976; a *present;* spec. (in
a good sense), a sacrificial *offering,* (in a bad
sense) a *bribe:*—gift {16x}, as he is able {1x}.
See: TWOT—1443c; BDB—608c, 682b.

4980. מַתָּנָה {1x} **Mattânâh**, *mat-taw-naw';*
        the same as 4979; *Mattanah,* a
place in the desert:—*Mattanah* {1x}. See:
BDB—608c, 682c.

4981. מִתְנִי {1x} **Mithnîy**, *mith-nee';* prob. patrial from an unused noun mean.
slenderness; a *Mithnite,* or inhab. of Methen:—
Mithnite {1x}. See: BDB—608c.

4982. מַתְּנַי {3x} **Mattᵉnay**, *mat-ten-ah'ee;*
        from 4976; *liberal; Mattenai,* the
name of three Isr.:—*Mattenai* {3x}. See: BDB—
608c, 682c, 682d.

4983. מַתַּנְיָה {16x} **Mattanyâh**, *mat-tan-yaw';*
or

מַתַּנְיָהוּ **Mattanyâhûw**, *mat-tan-yaw'-
        hoo;* from 4976 and 3050; *gift of
Jah; Mattanjah,* the name of ten Isr.:—Mattaniah {16x}. See: BDB—608c, 682c.

מָתְנַיִם **mâthnayim**. See 4975.

4984. מִתְנַשֵּׂא {2x} **mithnassê⁾**, *mith-nas-say';*
        from 5375; (used as abstr.) supreme *exaltation:*—exalted {2x}. See: TWOT—
1421; BDB—669d.

4985. מָתַק {5x} **mâthaq**, *maw-thak';* a prim.
        root; to *suck,* by impl. to *relish,* or
(intr.) *be sweet:*—be (made, X take) sweet {5x}.
See: TWOT—1268; BDB—608c.

4986. מֶתֶק {2x} **metheq**, *meh'-thek;* from 4985;
        fig. *pleasantness* (of discourse):—
sweetness {2x}. See: TWOT—1268a; BDB—
608d.

4987. מֹתֶק {1x} **môtheq**, *mo'-thek;* from 4985;
        sweetness:—sweetness {1x}. See:
TWOT—1268b; BDB—608d.

4988. מָתָק {1x} **mâthâq**, *maw-thawk';* from
        4985; a *dainty,* i.e. (gen.) *food:*—
feed sweetly {1x}. See: TWOT—1268c?; BDB—
608c.

4989. מִתְקָה {1x} **Mithqâh**, *mith-kaw';* fem. of
        4987; *sweetness; Mithkah,* a
place in the desert:—Mithcah {1x}. See: BDB—
609a.

4990. מִתְרְדָת {2x} **Mithrᵉdâth**, *mith-red-awth';*
        of Pers. or.; *Mithredath,* the
name of two Pers.:—*Mithredath* {2x}. See:
BDB—609c.

4991. מַתָּת {6x} **mattâth**, *mat-tawth';* fem. of
        4976 abb.; a *present:*—gift {3x},
give {2x}, reward {1x}. See: TWOT—1443d;
BDB—609c, 682c.

4992. מַתַּתָּה {1x} **Mattattâh**, *mat-tat-taw';* for
        4993; *gift of Jah; Mattattah,* an
Isr.:—Mattathah {1x}. See: BDB—609c, 683a.

4993. מַתִּתְיָה {8x} **Mattithyâh**, *mat-tith-yaw';*
or

מַתִּתְיָהוּ **Mattithyâhûw**, *mat-tith-yaw'-
        hoo;* from 4991 and 3050; *gift
of Jah; Mattithjah,* the name of four Isr.:—Mattithiah {8x}. See: BDB—609c, 682d.

נ

4994. נָא {1x} **nâ⁾**, *naw;* a prim. particle of incitement and entreaty, which may
usually be rendered *I pray, now* or *then;* added
mostly to verbs (in the imperative or future), or

to interj., occasionally to an adv. or conjunc.:—{9x} = I beseech (pray) thee (you), go to, now, oh. Syn.: 577, 2603, 6279, 6419, 6739, 7592. See: TWOT—1269; BDB—609a, 644b.

4995. נָא {1x} nâ, naw; appar. from 5106 in the sense of *harshness* from refusal; prop. *tough*, i.e. *uncooked* (flesh):—raw {1x}. See: TWOT—1358a; BDB—609d, 644b.

4996. נֹא {5x} Nô, no; of Eg. or.; *No* (i.e. *Thebes*), the capital of Upper Egypt:—No {5x}. comp. 528. See: BDB—609d.

4997. נֹאד {6x} nô'd, node; or

נֹאוד nô'wd, node; also (fem.)

נֹאדָה nô'dâh, no-daw'; from an unused root of uncert. signif.; a (skin or leather) *bag* (for fluids):—bottle {6x}. See: TWOT—1270; BDB—609d.

נְאֹדְרִי ne'dârîy. See 142.

4998. נָאָה {3x} nâ'âh, naw-aw'; a prim. root; prop. *to be at home*, i.e. (by impl.) to be *pleasant* (or *suitable*), i.e. *beautiful*:—be beautiful {1x}, become {1x}, be comely {1x}. See: TWOT—1271; BDB—610a.

4999. נָאָה {12x} nâ'âh, naw-aw'; from 4998; a *home*; fig. a *pasture*:—habitations {5x}, houses {1x}, pastures {5x}, pleasant places {1x}. See: TWOT—1322a; BDB—627d.

5000. נָאוֶה {9x} nâ'veh, naw-veh'; from 4998 or 5116; *suitable*, or *beautiful*:—becometh {1x}, comely {6x}, seemly {2x}. See: TWOT—1271a; BDB—610a.

5001. נָאַם {1x} nâ'am, naw-am'; a prim. root; prop. *to whisper*, i.e. (by impl.) to *utter* as an oracle:—say {1x}.

Na'am occurs only once in the entire Old Testament: "Behold, I am against the prophets, saith [5002 - ne'um] the Lord, that use their tongues, and say [na'am], He saith [5002 - ne'um]" (Jer 23:31). See: TWOT—1272; BDB—610c.

5002. נְאֻם {376x} n°ûm, neh-oom'; from 5001; an *oracle*:—saith {366x}, said {9x}, spake {1x}.

I. Ne'um, as a verb, means, "to say, utter an affirmation, speak." **(1)** The word is a verbal form of the verb na'am, which occurs only once in the entire Old Testament: "Behold, I am against the prophets, saith [ne'um] the Lord, that use their tongues, and say [5001 - na'am], He saith [ne'um]" (Jer 23:31). **(2)** The word ne'um appears as many as 361 times and, because of the frequency in the prophetical books, it is characteristic of prophetic speech. **(3)** Ne'um is an indicator which generally appears at the end of the quotation: "What

mean ye that ye beat my people to pieces, and grind the faces of the poor? saith [ne'um] the Lord God of hosts" (Is 3:15). **(4)** The word may also be found in the middle of an argument: "And I raised up of your sons for prophets, and of your young men for Nazarites. Is it not even thus, O ye children of Israel? saith [ne'um] the Lord. But ye gave the Nazarites wine to drink; and commanded the prophets, saying, Prophesy not" (Amos 2:11–12). **II. Ne'um, as a noun,** means "utterance; saying." **(1)** The use of ne'um is rare at the beginning of a statement: "The Lord said unto my Lord [literally, 'a statement of Jehovah to my Lord']. Sit thou at my right hand, until I make thine enemies thy footstool" (Ps 110:1).

(2) With one exception (Prov 30:1) in the sayings of Agur, the usage throughout the Old Testament is virtually limited to a word from God. **(3)** In Numbers the utterances of Balaam are introduced with the formula "and he uttered his oracle": "And he took up his parable, and said, Balaam the son of Beor hath said, and the man whose eyes are open hath said" (Num 24:3; cf. v. 15). **(4)** David's concluding words begin with these words: "Now these be the last words of David. David the son of Jesse said, and the man who was raised up on high, the anointed of the God of Jacob, and the sweet psalmist of Israel, said" (2 Sa 23:1). **(5)** Apart from these instances there are a few more examples, but as a rule ne'um is a prophetic term, which even beyond the prophetical literature is associated with a word from God. See: TWOT—1272a; BDB—610b.

5003. נָאַף {13x} nâ'aph, naw-af'; a prim. root; to *commit adultery*; fig. to *apostatize*:—adultery {17x}, adulterer {8x}, adulteress {4x}, adulterous {1x}, women that break wedlock {1x}. See: TWOT—1273; BDB—610c.

5004. נִאֻף {2x} nî'ûph, nee-oof'; from 5003; *adultery*:—adulteries {2x}. See: TWOT—1273a; BDB—610d.

5005. נַאֲפוּף {1x} na'ăphûwph, nah-af-oof'; from 5003; *adultery*:—adulteries {1x}. See: TWOT—1273b; BDB—610d.

5006. נָאַץ {25x} nâ'ats, naw-ats'; a prim. root; to *scorn*; or (Eccl 12:5) by interchange for 5132, to *bloom*:—despise {8x}, provoke {5x}, abhor {4x}, blaspheme {4x}, contemn {2x}, flourish {1x}, great occasion to blaspheme {1x}. See: TWOT—1274; BDB—610d, 665b.

5007. נָאָצָה {5x} n°âtsâh, neh-aw-tsaw'; or

נֶאָצָה ne'âtsâh, neh-aw-tsaw'; from 5006; *scorn*:—blasphemy {3x}, provocation {2x}. See: TWOT—1274a, 1274b; BDB—611a.

5008. נָאַק {2x} **nâ'aq**, *naw-ak';* a prim. root; to *groan:*—groan {2x}. See: TWOT— 1275; BDB—611a.

5009. נְאָקָה {4x} **nᵉ'âqâh**, *neh-aw-kaw';* from 5008; a *groan:*—groaning {4x}. See: TWOT—1275a; BDB—611a.

5010. נָאַר {2x} **nâ'ar**, *naw-ar';* a prim. root; to *reject:*—abhorred {1x}, make void {1x}. See: TWOT—1276; BDB—611b.

5011. נֹב {6x} **Nôb**, *nobe;* the same as 5108; *fruit; Nob,* a place in Pal.:—*Nob* {6x}. See: BDB—611b, 612c.

5012. נָבָא {115x} **nâbâ'**, *naw-baw';* a prim. root; to *prophesy,* i.e. speak (or sing) by inspiration (in prediction or simple discourse):—prophesy {111x}, prophesying {2x}, prophet {2x}.

Naba' means "to prophesy." **(1)** Its first appearance is in 1 Sa 10:6, where Saul is told by Samuel that when he meets a certain band of ecstatic prophets, he too will "prophesy with them, and . . . be turned into another man." **(2)** Most frequently *naba'* is used to describe the function of the true prophet as he speaks God's message to the people, under the influence of the divine spirit (1 Kin 22:8; Jer 29:27; Eze 37:10). **(2a)** "To prophesy" was a task that the prophet could not avoid: "The Lord GOD hath spoken, who can but prophesy?" (Amos 3:8; cf. Jer 20:7, where Jeremiah says that he was both attracted to and forced into being a prophet). **(2b)** While the formula "The word of the LORD came [to the prophet]" is used literally hundreds of times in the Old Testament, **(2b1)** there is no real indication as to the manner in which it came—whether it came through the thought-processes, through a vision, or in some other way. **(2b2)** Sometimes, especially in the earlier prophets, it seems that some kind of ecstatic experience may have been involved, as in 1 Sa 10:6, 11; 19:20. **(2b3)** Music is sometimes spoken of as a means of prophesying, as in 1 Chr 25:1–3.

(3) The false prophets, although not empowered by the divine spirit, are spoken of as prophesying also: "I have not spoken to them, yet they prophesied" (Jer 23:21). **(3a)** The false prophet is roundly condemned because he speaks a non-authentic word: "Prophesy against the prophets of Israel that prophesy, and say thou unto them that prophesy out of their own hearts, Hear ye the word of the LORD; . . . Woe unto the foolish prophets, that follow their own spirit, and have seen nothing!" (Eze 13:2–3). **(3b)** The false prophet especially is subject to frenzied states of mind which give rise to his prophesying, although the content of such activity is not clearly

spelled out (1 Kin 22:10). **(3c)** The point is that in the biblical context "to prophesy" can refer to anything from the frenzied ecstaticism of a false prophet to the cold sober proclamation of God's judgment by an Amos or an Isaiah. **(4)** "To prophesy" is much more than the prediction of future events. **(4a)** Indeed, the first concern of the prophet is to speak God's word to the people of his own time, calling them to covenant faithfulness.

(4b) The prophet's message is conditional, dependent upon the response of the people. Thus, by their response to this word, the people determine in large part what the future holds, as is well illustrated by the response of the Ninevites to Jonah's preaching. **(4c)** Of course, prediction does enter the picture at times, such as in Nahum's prediction of the fall of Nineveh (Nah 2:13) and in the various messianic passages (Is 9:1–6; 11:1–9; 52:13–53:12). See: TWOT—1277; BDB—612a, 1101d.

5013. נְבָא {1x} **nᵉbâ'** (Aram.), *neb-aw';* corresp. to 5012:—prophesy {1x}. See: TWOT—2843a; BDB—1101d.

5014. נָבַב {4x} **nâbab**, *naw-bab';* a prim. root; to *pierce;* to *be hollow,* or (fig.) *foolish:*—hollow {3x}, vain {1x}. See: TWOT—1278; BDB—612c.

5015. נְבוֹ {13x} **Nᵉbôw**, *neb-o';* prob. of for. der.; *Nebo,* the name of a Bab. deity, also of a mountain in Moab, and of a place in Pal.:—Nebo {13x}. See: BDB—612d.

5016. נְבוּאָה {3x} **nᵉbûw'âh**, *neb-oo-aw';* from 5012; a *prediction* (spoken or written):—prophecy {3x}. See: TWOT—1277b; BDB—612c.

5017. נְבוּאָה {1x} **nᵉbûw'âh** (Aram.), *neb-oo-aw';* corresp. to 5016; *inspired teaching:*—prophesying {1x}. TWOT—2843b; See: BDB—1102a.

5018. נְבוּזַרְאֲדָן {15x} **Nᵉbûwzarʾădân**, *neb-oo-zar-ad-awn';* of for. or.; *Nebuzaradan,* a Bab. general:—Nebuzaradan {15x}. See: BDB—613a.

5019. נְבוּכַדְנֶאצַּר {60x} **Nᵉbûwkadneʾtstsar**, *neb-oo-kad-nets-tsar';* or

נְבֻכַדְנֶאצַּר **Nᵉbûkadneʾtstsar** (2 Kin 24:1, 10), *neb-oo-kad-nets-tsar';* or

נְבוּכַדְנֶצַּר **Nᵉbûwkadnetstsar** (Est 2:6; Dan. 1:18), *neb-oo-kad-nets-tsar';* or

נְבוּכַדְרֶאצַּר **Nᵉbûwkadreʾtstsar**, *neb-oo-kad-rets-tsar';* or

נְבוּכַדְרֶאצּוֹר **Nᵉbûwkadreʾtstsôwr** (Ezr 2:1; Jer 49:28), *neb-oo-*

kad-rets-tsore'; or for. der.; *Nebukadnetstsar* (or *-retstsar,* or *-retstsor*), king of Bab.:—Nebuchadnezzar {31x}, Nebuchadrezzar {29x}. See: BDB—613a, 1102a.

5020. נְבוּכַדְנֶצַּר {31x} **Nᵉbûwkadnetstsar** (Aram.), *neb-oo-kad-nets-tsar';* corresp. to 5019:—Nebuchadnezzar {31x}. See: BDB—1102a.

5021. נְבוּשַׁזְבָּן {1x} **Nᵉbûwshazbân,** *neb-oo-shaz-bawn';* of for. der.; *Nebushazban,* Nebuchadnezzar's chief eunuch:—Nebushazban {1x}. See: BDB—613b.

5022. נָבוֹת {22x} **Nâbôwth,** *naw-both';* fem. plur. from the same as 5011; *fruits; Naboth,* an Isr.:—Naboth {22x}. See: BDB—613b.

5023. נְבִזְבָּה {2x} **nᵉbizbâh** (Aram.), *neb-iz-baw';* of uncert. der.; a *largess:*—reward {2x}. See: TWOT—2844; BDB—1102a.

5024. נָבַח {1x} **nâbach,** *naw-bakh';* a prim. root; to *bark* (as a dog):—bark {1x}. See: TWOT—1281; BDB—613b.

5025. נֹבַח {3x} **Nôbach,** *no'-bach;* from 5024; a *bark; Nobach,* the name of an Isr., and of a place E. of the Jordan:—Nobah {3x}. See: BDB—613b.

5026. נִבְחַז {1x} **Nibchaz,** *nib-khaz';* of for. or.; *Nibchaz,* a deity of the Avites:—Nibhaz {1x}. See: BDB—613b.

5027. נָבַט {69x} **nâbat,** *naw-bat';* a prim. root; to *scan,* i.e. look intently at; by impl. to *regard* with pleasure, favor or care:—look {36x}, behold {13x}, consider {5x}, regard {4x}, see {4x}, respect {3x}, look down {2x}, look about {1x}, look back {1x}.

Nabat means "to look, regard, behold." **(1)** The first use of this term is in Gen 15:5, where it is used in the sense of "take a good look," as God commands Abraham: "Look now toward heaven, and [number] the stars." **(2)** While *nabat* is commonly used of physical "looking" (Ex 3:6), the word is frequently used in a figurative sense to mean a spiritual and inner apprehension. Thus, Samuel is told by God: "Look not on his countenance" (1 Sa 16:7) as he searched for a king among Jesse's sons. **(3)** The sense of "consider" (with insight) is expressed in Is 51:1–2: "Look unto the rock whence ye are hewn. . . . Look unto Abraham your father." **(4)** "Pay attention to" seems to be the meaning in Is 5:12: ". . . they regard not the work of the Lord." See: TWOT—1282; BDB—613c.

5028. נְבָט {25x} **Nᵉbât,** *neb-awt';* from 5027; *regard; Nebat,* the father of Jeroboam I:—Nebat {25x}. See: BDB—614a.

5029. נְבִיא {4x} **nᵉbîy⁾** (Aram.), *neb-ee';* corresp. to 5030; a *prophet:*—prophet {4x}. See: TWOT—2843a; BDB—1101d.

5030. נָבִיא {316x} **nâbîy⁾,** *naw-bee';* from 5012; a *prophet* or (gen.) *inspired* man:—prophet {312x}, prophecy {1x}, them that prophesy {1x}, prophet + 376 {1x}, variant {1x}.

Nabiy⁾ means "prophet." **(1)** *Nabiy⁾* represents "prophet," whether a true or false prophet (cf. Deut 13:1–5). **(2)** True prophets were mouthpieces of the true God. **(3)** In 1 Chr 29:29 three words are used for "prophet": "Now the acts of David the king, first and last, behold, they are written in the Book of Samuel the Seer [7203 - *ro⁾eh*] and in the Book of Nathan the Prophet [*nabiy⁾*], and in the Book of Gad the Seer [2374 - *chozeh*]." **(4)** The words translated "seer" emphasize the means by which the "prophet" communicated with God but do not identify the men as anything different from prophets (cf. 1 Sa 9:9). **(5)** The first occurrence of *nabiy⁾* does not help to clearly define it either: "Now therefore restore the man [Abraham] his wife; for he is a prophet, and he shall pray for thee, and thou shalt live" (Gen 20:7). **(6)** The second occurrence of *nabiy⁾* establishes its meaning: "And the LORD said unto Moses, See, I have made thee a god to Pharaoh: and Aaron thy brother shall be thy prophet" (Ex 7:1). The background of this statement is Ex 4:10–16, where Moses argued his inability to speak clearly. God promised to appoint Aaron (Moses' brother) to be the speaker: "And he shall be thy spokesman unto the people: and he shall be, even he shall be to thee instead of a mouth, and thou shalt be to him instead of God" (Ex 4:16).

(7) Ex 7:1 expresses the same idea in different words. It is clear that the word "prophet" is equal to one who speaks for another, or his mouth. **(8)** This basic meaning of *nabiy⁾* is supported by other passages. In the classical passage Deut 18:14–22, God promised to raise up another "prophet" like Moses who would be God's spokesman (v. 18). They were held responsible for what he told them and were admonished to obey him (Deut 18:19). However, if what the "prophet" said proved to be wrong, he was to be killed (Deut 18:20). Immediately, this constitutes a promise and definition of the long succession of Israel's prophets. Ultimately, it is a promise of the Great Prophet, Jesus Christ (cf. Acts 3:22–23). **(9)** The "prophet" or dreamer of dreams might perform miracles to demonstrate that he was God's man, but the people were to look to the message rather than the miracle before they heeded his message (Deut 13:1–5).

(10) In the plural *nabiy⁾* is used of some who

do not function as God's mouthpieces. **(10a)** In the time of Samuel there were men who followed him. They went about praising God (frequently with song) and trying to stir the people to return to God (1 Sa 10:5, 10; 19:20). **(10b)** Followers of Elijah and Elisha formed into groups to assist and/or to learn from these masters. They were called sons of the prophets (1 Kin 20:35). **(10c)** Used in this sense, the word *nabiy°* means a companion and/or follower of a prophet. **(11)** The word is also used of "heathen prophets": "Now therefore send, and gather to me all Israel unto mount Carmel, and the prophets of Baal four hundred and fifty, and the prophets of the groves four hundred, which eat at Jezebel's table" (1 Kin 18:19). Syn.: 2374, 4853. See: TWOT—1277a; BDB—611c, 1101d.

5031. נְבִיאָה {6x} **nebîy°âh**, *neb-ee-yaw'*; fem. of 5030; a *prophetess* or (gen.) *inspired* woman; by impl. a *poetess*; by association a *prophet's wife:*—prophetess {6x}.

　(1) In Ex 15:20 Miriam is called a "prophetess." **(2)** Isaiah's wife, too, is called a "prophetess" (Is 8:3). This usage may be related to the meaning "a companion and/or follower of a prophet." See: TWOT—1277c; BDB—612c.

5032. נְבָיוֹת {5x} **Nebâyôwth**, *neb-aw-yoth'*; or

　　　נְבָיֹת **Nebâyôth**, *neb-aw-yoth'*; fem. plur. from 5107; *fruitfulnesses; Nebajoth,* a son of Ismael, and the country settled by him:—Nebaioth {2x}, Nebajoth {3x}. See: BDB—614a.

5033. נֶבֶךְ {1x} **nêbek**, *nay'-bek;* from an unused root mean. to *burst* forth; a *fountain:*—spring {1x}. Syn.: 1543, 4002, 4599. See: TWOT—1283; See: BDB—614a.

5034. נָבֵל {25x} **nâbêl**, *naw-bale'*; a prim. root; to *wilt;* gen. to *fall away, fail, faint;* fig. to *be foolish* or (mor.) *wicked;* caus. to *despise, disgrace:*—fade {8x}, fade away {3x}, wear away {2x}, wither {2x}, disgrace {1x}, surely {1x}, dishonoureth {1x}, fall down {1x}, esteemed {1x}, falling {1x}, foolishly {1x}, come to nought {1x}, fall off {1x}, surely {1x}, make vile {1x}. See: TWOT—1286; BDB—614c, 615b.

5035. נֶבֶל {3x} **nebel**, *neh'-bel;* or

　　　נֵבֶל **nêbel**, *nay'-bel;* from 5034; a *skin-bag* for liquids (from *collapsing* when empty); hence, a *vase* (as similar in shape when full); also a *lyre* (as having a body of like form):—psalteries {23}, bottle {8x}, viol {4x}, flagons {1x}, pitchers {1x}, vessel {1x}. See: TWOT—1284a, 1284b; BDB—614b.

5036. נָבָל {18x} **nâbâl**, *naw-bawl';* from 5034; *stupid; wicked* (espec. *impious*):—fool {9x}, foolish {5x}, vile person {2x}, foolish

man {1x}, foolish women {1x}. Syn.: 191, 3684. See: TWOT—1285a; BDB—614d.

5037. נָבָל {22x} **Nâbâl**, *naw-bawl';* the same as 5036; *dolt; Nabal,* an Isr.:—Nabal {18x}, Nabhal {4x}. See: BDB—615a.

5038. נְבֵלָה {48x} **nebêlâh**, *neb-ay-law';* from 5034; a *flabby* thing, i.e. a *carcase* or *carrion* (human or bestial, often collect.); fig. an *idol:*—carcase {36x}, dead body {5x}, dieth of itself {4x}, dead of itself {1x}, died {1x}, body {1x}. See: TWOT—1286a; BDB—615c.

5039. נְבָלָה {13x} **nebâlâh**, *neb-aw-law';* fem. of 5036; *foolishness,* i.e. (mor.) *wickedness;* concr. a *crime;* by extens. *punishment:*—folly {10x}, vile {1x}, villany {2x}.

　Nebalah means "foolishness; senselessness; impropriety; stupidity." **(1)** It signifies "disregarding God's will": "Let not my lord, I pray thee, regard this man of Belial, even Nabal: for as his name is, so is he; Nabal is his name, and folly is with him: but I thine handmaid saw not the young men of my lord, whom thou didst send" (1 Sa 25:25). **(2)** *Nebalah* is most often used as a word for a serious sin: "And the sons of Jacob came out of the field when they heard it: and the men were grieved, and they were very wroth, because he had wrought folly [*nebalah*] in Israel in lying with Jacob's daughter; which thing ought not to be done" (Gen 34:7 — the first occurrence). Syn.: 200. See: TWOT—1285b; BDB—615a.

5040. נַבְלוּת {1x} **nablûwth**, *nab-looth';* from 5036; prop. *disgrace,* i.e. the (female) *pudenda:*—lewdness {1x}. See: TWOT—1285c; BDB—615b.

5041. נְבַלָּט {1x} **Neballât**, *neb-al-lawt';* appar. from 5036 and 3909; *foolish secrecy; Neballat,* a place in Pal.:—Neballat {1x}. See: BDB—615d.

5042. נָבַע {11x} **nâbaʿ**, *naw-bah';* a prim. root; to *gush* forth; fig. to *utter* (good or bad words); spec. to *emit* (a foul odor):—belch out {1x}, flowing, {1x} pour out {3x}, send forth {1x}, utter (abundantly) {5x}. See: TWOT—1287; BDB—615d.

5043. נֶבְרְשָׁא {1x} **nebreshâ°** (Aram.), *neb-reh-shaw';* from an unused root mean. to *shine;* a *light;* plur. (collect.) a *chandelier:*—candlestick {1x}. Syn.: 4501. See: TWOT—2845; BDB—1102a.

5044. נִבְשָׁן {1x} **Nibshân**, *nib-shawn';* of uncert. der.; *Nibshan,* a place in Pal.:—Nibshan {1x}. See: BDB—143c, 616a.

5045. נֶגֶב {112x} **negeb**, *neh'-gheb;* from an unused root mean. to *be parched;* the *south* (from its drought); spec. the *Negeb*

or southern district of Judah, occasionally, *Egypt* (as south to Pal.):—south {89x}, southward {16x}, south side {5x}, south country {2x}. See: TWOT—1288a; BDB—616a, 918b.

5046. נָגַד {370x} **nâgad**, *naw-gad';* a prim. root; prop. to *front,* i.e. stand boldly out opposite; by impl. (caus.), to *manifest;* fig. to *announce* (always by word of mouth to one present); spec. to *expose, predict, explain, praise:*—tell {222x}, declare {63x}, shew {59x}, utter {5x}, shew forth {3x}, expound {2x}, messenger {2x}, report {2x}, misc. {13x} = bewray, × certainly, certify, denounce, × fully, plainly, profess, rehearse, speak, × surely.

Nagad means "to tell, explain, inform." **(1)** The first emphasis of the word is "to tell." This especially means that A (frequently a messenger or some other person who has witnessed something) "tells" B (the one to whom the report is made) C (the report). In such instances B (the one told) is spatially separated from the original source of the information. So, in Gen 9:22, Ham (A) saw his father naked and went outside the tent and "told" his brothers (B) what he had seen (C). **(2)** In another group of passages *nagad* represents the reporting of a messenger about a matter of life-or-death importance for the recipient. **(2a)** So a fugitive "came . . . and told Abram" that Lot had been captured and led away captive (Gen 14:13). **(2b)** A note of this emotionally charged situation is seen in Jacob's message to Esau: "I have sent to tell my lord, that I may find grace in thy sight" (Gen 32:5). **(2c)** Although not a report from a messenger from afar, Gen 12:18 uses the verb of a report that is of crucial importance to the one addressed. Pharaoh asked Abram: "Why didst thou not tell me that she was thy wife?" **(2d)** Gen 12:17 reports that because Pharaoh had taken Sarai into his harem to become his wife, God had smitten his household with great plagues.

(3) *Nagad* means "to explain or reveal" something one does not otherwise know. **(3a)** In Gen 3:11 (the first biblical occurrence of the word) God asked Adam: "Who told thee that thou wast naked?" This was information immediately before them but not previously grasped by them. **(3b)** This usage appears in Gen 41:24, where Pharaoh said of his dream: "I told this unto the magicians; but there was none that could declare it to me." **(3c)** Similarly, David made certain there were no survivors from the Philistine cities he looted so no one would "tell" it to Achish (1 Sa 27:11). **(4)** This word sometimes has a more forceful significance—God told the prophet to "show my people their transgression" (Is 58:1). See: TWOT—1289; BDB—616c.

5047. נְגַד {1x} **n°gad** (Aram.), *neg-ad';* corresp. to 5046; to *flow* (through the idea of *clearing* the way):—issue {1x}. See: TWOT—2846; BDB—1102a.

5048. נֶגֶד {23x} **neged**, *neh'-ghed;* from 5046; a *front,* i.e. part opposite; spec. a *counterpart,* or mate; usually (adv., espec. with prep.) *over against* or *before:*—{23x} = about, (over) against, × aloof, × far (off), × from, over, presence, × other side, sight, × to view.

Neged means "before; in the presence of; in the sight of; in front of; in one's estimation; straight ahead." **(1)** Basically the word indicates that its object is immediately "before" something or someone. **(1a)** It is used in Gen 2:18, where God said He would make Adam "a help meet for him," or someone to correspond to him, just as the males and females of the animals corresponded to (matched) one another. **(1b)** To be immediately "before" the sun is to be fully in the sunlight (Num 25:4). **(2)** In Ex 10:10 Pharaoh told Moses that evil was immediately "before" his face, or was in his mind. **(3)** *Neged* signifies "in front of" (Ex 19:2), **(4)** "before" in the sense of "in one's estimation" (Is 40:17), and **(5)** "straight ahead (before)" (Josh 6:5). **(6)** In combination with other particles *neged* means "contrary to" (Num 22:32). **(7)** The word indicates that its object is immediately "before" something or someone. As an adverb it means opposite, over against: "And she went, and sat her down over against him a good way off" (Gen 21:16). See: TWOT—1289a; BDB—617a, 1102a.

5049. נֶגֶד {1x} **neged** (Aram.), *neh'-ghed;* corresp. to 5048; *opposite:*—toward {1x}. See: TWOT—2846a; BDB—1102a.

5050. נָגַהּ {6x} **nâgahh**, *naw-gah';* a prim. root; to *glitter;* caus. to *illuminate:*—(en-) lighten {2x}, (cause to) shine {4x}. See: TWOT—1290; BDB—618b.

5051. נֹגַהּ {19x} **nôgahh**, *no'-gah;* from 5050; *brilliancy* (lit. or fig.):—brightness {11x}, light {1x}, bright {1x}, (clear) shining {6x}. See: TWOT—1290a; BDB—618b, 1102a.

5052. נֹגַהּ {2x} **Nôgahh**, *no'-gah;* the same as 5051; *Nogah,* a son of David:—Nogah {2x}. See: BDB—618b.

5053. נֹגַהּ {1x} **nogahh** (Aram.), *no'-gah;* corresp. to 5051; *dawn:*—morning {1x}. See: TWOT—2847; BDB—1102a.

5054. נְגֹהָה {1x} **n°gôhâh**, *neg-o-haw';* fem. of 5051; *splendor:*—brightness {1x}. See: TWOT—1290b; BDB—618c.

5055. נָגַח {11x} **nâgach**, *naw-gakh';* a prim. root; to *butt* with the horns; fig. to

Hebrew

war against:—gore {3x}, push (down, -ing) {8x}. See: TWOT—1291; BDB—618c.

5056. נַגָּח {2x} **naggâch**, *nag-gawkh';* from 5055; *butting,* i.e. *vicious:*—used (wont) to push {2x}. See: TWOT—1291a; BDB—618c.

5057. נָגִיד {44x} **nâgîyd**, *naw-gheed';* or

נָגִד **nâgîd**, *naw-gheed';* from 5046; a *commander* (as occupying the *front*), civil, military or religious; gen. (abstr. plur.), *honorable* themes:—ruler {20x}, prince {9x}, captain {6x}, leader {4x}, governor {3x}, nobles {1x}, excellent things {1x}.

Nagiyd means "chief leader." **(1)** In 1 Sa 9:16 the word is used as a "chief leader" that is equivalent to a king: "Tomorrow about this time I will send thee a man out of the land of Benjamin, and thou shalt anoint him to be captain over my people Israel." **(2)** *Nagiyd* appears in 1 Chr 9:11 to refer to a "chief leader" (ruler) of a smaller region: "And Azariah the son of Hilkiah, the son of Meshullam, the son of Zadok, the son of Meraioth, the son of Ahitub, the ruler of the house of God." **(3)** The word may also be used of a head of a family: "And Phinehas the son of Eleazar was the ruler over them in time past, and the LORD was with him" (1Chr 9:20). See: TWOT—1289b; BDB—618d.

5058. נְגִינָה {14x} **nᵉgîynâh**, *neg-ee-naw';* or

נְגִינַת **nᵉgîynath** (Ps 61:title), *neg-ee-nath';* from 5059; prop. instrumental *music;* by impl. a stringed *instrument;* by extens. a *poem* set to music; spec. an *epigram:*—stringed instruments {1x}, music {1x}, Neginoth [*plur.*] {6x}, song {5x}, Neginah {1x}. See: TWOT—1292.1a; BDB—618d.

5059. נָגַן {15x} **nâgan**, *naw-gan';* a prim. root; prop. to *thrum,* i.e. *beat* a tune with the fingers; espec. to *play* on a stringed instrument; hence, (gen.), to *make music:*—play {8x}, instrument {3x}, minstrel {2x}, melody {1x}, player {1x}. See: TWOT—1292.1; BDB—618d.

5060. נָגַע {150x} **nâgaᶜ**, *naw-gah';* a prim. root; prop. to *touch,* i.e. *lay the hand upon* (for any purpose; euphem. to *lie with* a woman); by impl. to *reach* (fig. to *arrive, acquire*); violently, to *strike* (punish, defeat, destroy, etc.):—touch {92x}, came {18x}, reach {11x}, bring {4x}, near {4x}, smite {4x}, nigh {3x}, plagued {3x}, happeneth {2x}, strike {2x}, beaten {1x}, cast {1x}, reach up {1x}, brought down {1x}, join {1x}, laid {1x}, get up {1x}.

Nagaᶜ means "to touch, strike, reach, smite." **(1)** *Nagaᶜ* first occurs in Gen 3:3 in the Garden of Eden story, where the woman reminds the serpent that God had said: "Ye shall not eat of

[the fruit of the tree which is in the midst of the garden], neither shall ye touch it." **(2)** This illustrates the common meaning of physical touch involving various kinds of objects: **(2a)** Jacob's thigh was "touched" by the man at Jabbok (Gen 32:25, 32); **(2b)** the Israelites were commanded not "to touch" Mount Horeb under pain of death (Ex 19:12); and **(2c)** unclean things were not "to be touched" (Lev 5:2–3). **(3)** Sometimes *nagaᶜ* is used figuratively in the sense of emotional involvement: "And Saul also went home to Gibeah; and there went with him a band of men, whose hearts God had touched" (1 Sa 10:26). **(4)** The word is used to refer to sexual contact with another person, such as in Gen 20:6, where God tells Abimelech that He did not allow him "to touch" Sarah, Abraham's wife (cf. Prov 6:29). **(5)** To refer to the touch of God's hand means that divine chastisement has been received: "Have pity upon me, O ye my friends; for the hand of God hath touched me" (Job 19:21). **(6)** The word is commonly used also to describe "being stricken" with a disease: King Uzziah "was smitten" with leprosy (2 Chr 26:20). See: TWOT—1293; BDB—619a.

5061. נֶגַע {78x} **negaᶜ**, *neh'-gah;* from 5060; a *blow* (fig. *infliction*); also (by impl.) a *spot* (concr. a *leprous* person or dress):—plague {65x}, sore {5x}, stroke {4x}, stripes {2x}, stricken {1x}, wound {1x}.

Negaᶜ means "plague: stroke; wound." **(1)** The word refers to a "plague" most frequently: "And the LORD plagued Pharaoh and his house with great plagues because of Sarai Abram's wife" (Gen 12:17; cf. Ex 11:1). **(2)** *Negaᶜ* can also mean "stroke": "If there arise a matter too hard for thee in judgment, between blood and blood, between plea and plea, and between stroke and stroke, *being* matters of controversy within thy gates: then shalt thou arise, and get thee up into the place which the LORD thy God shall choose" (Deut 17:8; cf. 21:5) or **(3)** "wound": "A wound and dishonour shall he get; and his reproach shall not be wiped away" (Prov 6:33). **(4)** Each meaning carries with it the sense of a person "being stricken or smitten in some way." See: TWOT—1293a; BDB—619c.

5062. נָגַף {49x} **nâgaph**, *naw-gaf';* a prim. root; to *push, gore, defeat, stub* (the toe), *inflict* (a disease):—smite {27x}, put to the worse {5x}, smitten down {3x}, plague {3x}, hurt {2x}, slain {2x}, struck {2x}, stumble {2x}, beaten {1x}, dash {1x}, surely {1x}. Syn.: 4046, 5061. See: TWOT—1294; BDB—619d.

5063. נֶגֶף {7x} **negeph**, *neh'-ghef;* from 5062; a *trip* (of the foot); fig. an *infliction* (of disease):—plague {6x}, stumbling {1x}. See: TWOT—1294a; BDB—620a.

5064. נָגַר {10x} **nâgar**, *naw-gar'*; a prim. root; to *flow;* fig. to *stretch* out; caus. to *pour* out or down; fig. to *deliver* over:—fall {1x}, flow away {1x}, pour down {1x}, pour out {2x}, run {1x}, shed {1x}, spilt {1x}, trickle down {1x}. See: TWOT—1295; BDB—620b.

5065. נָגַשׂ {23x} **nâgas**, *naw-gas'*; a prim. root; to *drive* (an animal, a workman, a debtor, an army); by impl. to *tax, harass, tyrannize:*—oppressor {7x}, taskmasters {5x}, exact {4x}, distressed {2x}, oppressed {2x}, driver {1x}, exactors {1x}, taxes {1x}. See: TWOT—1296; BDB—620b.

5066. נָגַשׁ {125x} **nâgash**, *naw-gash';* a prim. root; to *be* or *come* (caus. *bring*) *near* (for any purpose); euphem. to *lie with* a woman; as an enemy, to *attack;* relig. to *worship;* caus. to *present;* fig. to *adduce* an argument; by reversal, to *stand back:*—(come, draw, etc) . . . near {55x}, come {14x}, (come, draw, etc) . . . nigh {12x}, bring {13x}, . . . hither {7x}, offer {7x}, approach {5x}, forth {3x}, misc. {9x} = give place, go hard (up), overtake, present, put, stand.

Nagash means "to approach, draw near, bring." **(1)** *Nagash* is used for the first time in the biblical text in Gen 18:23, where Abraham is said to "draw near" to God to plead that Sodom be spared. **(2)** The word is often used to describe ordinary "contact" of one person with another: "And Jacob went near unto Isaac his father; and he felt him, and said, The voice *is* Jacob's voice, but the hands *are* the hands of Esau" (Gen 27:22; cf. 43:19). **(3)** Sometimes *nagash* describes "contact" for the purpose of sexual intercourse: "And he said unto the people, Be ready against the third day: come not at your wives" (Ex 19:15). **(4)** More frequently, it is used to speak of the priests "coming into the presence of" God (Eze 44:13) or of the priests' "approach" to the altar (Ex 30:20). **(5)** Opposing armies are said "to go up" to battle each other (Judg 20:23). **(6)** Inanimate objects, such as the close-fitting scales of the crocodile, are said to be so "near" to each other that no air can come between them (Job 41:16). **(7)** Sometimes the word is used to speak of "bringing" an offering to the altar (Mal 1:7). See: TWOT—1297; BDB—620c.

5067. נֵד {6x} **nêd**, *nade;* from 5110 in the sense of *piling* up; a *mound,* i.e. *wave:*—heap {6x}. See: TWOT—1301a; BDB—621b, 622d.

5068. נָדַב {1x} **nâdab**, *naw-dab';* a prim. root; to *impel;* hence, to *volunteer* (as a soldier), to *present* spontaneously:—offered willingly {6x}, willingly offered {5x}, willing {2x}, offered {1x}, willing {1x}, offered freely {1x}, give willingly {1x}. See: TWOT—1299; BDB—621c, 1102b.

5069. נְדַב {4x} **neदab** (Aram.), *ned-ab';* corresp. to 5068; *be* (or *give*) *liberal (-ly):*—freely offered {1x}, freewill offering {1x}, offering willingly {1x}, minded of their own freewill {1x}. See: TWOT—2848; BDB—1102b.

5070. נָדָב {20x} **Nâdâb**, *naw-dawb';* from 5068; *liberal; Nadab,* the name of four Isr.:—*Nadab* {20x}. See: BDB—621c.

5071. נְדָבָה {26x} **nedâbâh**, *ned-aw-baw';* from 5068; prop. (abstr.) *spontaneity,* or (adj.) *spontaneous;* also (concr.) a *spontaneous* or (by infer., in plur.) *abundant* gift:—freewill offering {15x}, offerings {9x}, free offering {2x}, freely {2x}, willing offering {1x}, voluntary offering {1x}, plentiful {1x}, voluntarily {1x}, voluntary {1x}, willing {1x}, willingly {1x}.

This offering is always given willingly, bountifully, liberally, or as a prince would offer. It refers not to the nature of the offering or the external mode in which it is offered, but to the motive and spirit of the offerer. See: TWOT—1299a; BDB—621d.

5072. נְדַבְיָה {1x} **Neदabyâh**, *ned-ab-yaw';* from 5068 and 3050; *largess of Jah; Nedabjah,* an Isr.:—Nedabiah {1x}. See: BDB—622a.

5073. נִדְבָּךְ {2x} **nidbâk** (Aram.), *nid-bawk';* from a root mean. to *stick;* a *layer* (of building materials):—row {2x}. Syn.: 2905. See: TWOT—2849; BDB—1102b.

5074. נָדַד {28x} **nâdad**, *naw-dad';* a prim. root; prop. to *wave* to and fro (rarely to *flap* up and down); fig. to *rove, flee,* or (caus.) to *drive* away:—flee {9x}, wander {6x}, . . . away {4x}, wandereth abroad {1x}, flee apace {1x}, chased {1x}, misc. {6x} = × could not, depart, (re-) move, thrust away. See: TWOT—1300; BDB—622b, 1102b.

5075. נְדַד {1x} **neदad** (Aram.), *ned-ad';* corresp. to 5074; to *depart:*—go from {1x}. See: TWOT—2850; BDB—1102b, 1102c.

5076. נָדֻד {1x} **nâdûd**, *naw-dood';* pass. part. of 5074; prop. *tossed;* abstr. a *rolling* (on the bed):—tossing to and fro {1x}. See: TWOT—1300a; BDB—622c.

5077. נָדָה {3x} **nâdâh**, *naw-daw';* or

נָדָא **nâdâ'** (2 Kin 17:21), *naw-daw';* a prim. root; prop. to *toss;* fig. to *exclude,* i.e. *banish, postpone, prohibit:*—cast out {1x}, drive {1x}, put far away {1x}. See: TWOT—1302; BDB—621b, 622d.

5078. נֵדֶה {1x} **nêdeh,** *nay'-deh;* from 5077 in the sense of freely *flinging* money; a *bounty* (for prostitution):—gifts {1x}. See: TWOT—1303a; BDB—622d.

5079. נִדָּה {29x} **niddâh,** *nid-daw';* from 5074; prop. *rejection;* by impl. *impurity,* espec. Pers. (menstruation) or mor. (idolatry, incest):—separation {14x}, put apart {2x}, filthiness {2x}, flowers {2x}, far {1x}, set apart {1x}, menstruous {1x}, removed {1x}, unclean thing {1x}, unclean {1x}, uncleanness {1x}, menstruous woman {1x}, removed woman {1x}. See: TWOT—1302a; BDB—622c, 622d.

5080. נָדַח {52x} **nâdach,** *naw-dakh';* a prim. root; to *push* off; used in a great variety of applications, lit. and fig. (to expel, mislead, strike, inflict, etc.):—drive {18x}, drive out {6x}, . . . away {6x}, outcasts {5x}, cast out {3x}, banished {2x}, bring {1x}, go astray {1x}, chased {1x}, compelled {1x}, down {1x}, expelled {1x}, misc. {6x}= fetch a stroke, force, thrust away (out), withdraw.

Nadach means "to drive out, banish, thrust, move." **(1)** *Nadach* occurs approximately 50 times in the Hebrew Old Testament, and **(1a)** its first use is in the passive form: "And lest thou . . . shouldest be driven to worship them . . ." (Deut 4:19). **(1b)** The implication seems to be that an inner "drivenness" or "drawing away," as well as an external force, was involved in Israel's potential turning toward idolatry. **(2)** *Nadach* expresses the idea of "being scattered" in exile, as in Jer 40:12: "Even all the Jews returned out of all places whither they were driven." **(3)** Job complained that any resource he once possessed no longer existed, for it "is . . . driven quite from me" (Job 6:13). **(4)** Evil "shepherds" or leaders did not lead but rather "drove away" and scattered Israel (Jer 23:2). **(5)** The enemies of a good man plot against him "They only consult to cast him down from his excellency: they delight in lies: they bless with their mouth, but they curse inwardly" (Ps 62:4). See: TWOT—1304; BDB—623a.

5081. נָדִיב {28x} **nâdîyb,** *naw-deeb';* from 5068; prop. *voluntary,* i.e. generous; hence, *magnanimous;* as noun, a *grandee* (sometimes a *tyrant*):—prince {15x}, nobles {4x}, willing {3x}, free {2x}, liberal {2x}, liberal things {2x}. See: TWOT—1299b; BDB—622a.

5082. נְדִיבָה {1x} **nᵉdîybâh,** *ned-ee-baw';* fem. of 5081; prop. *nobility,* i.e. reputation:—soul {1x}. See: TWOT—1299c; BDB—622a.

5083. נָדָן {1x} **nâdân,** *naw-dawn';* prob. from an unused root mean. to *give;* a

present (for prostitution):—gift {1x}. Syn.: 5078. See: TWOT—1305; BDB—623c.

5084. נָדָן {1x} **nâdân,** *naw-dawn';* of uncert. der.; a *sheath* (of a sword):—sheath {1x}. See: TWOT—1306; BDB—623c, 1102b.

5085. נִדְנֶה {1x} **nidneh** (Aram.), *nid-neh';* from the same as 5084; a *sheath;* fig. the *body* (as the receptacle of the soul):—body {1x}. See: TWOT—2851; BDB—1086, 1102b.

5086. נָדַף {9x} **nâdaph,** *naw-daf';* a prim. root; to *shove* asunder, i.e. *disperse:*—drive away {4x}, drive {1x}, thrust him down {1x}, shaken {1x}, driven to and fro {1x}, tossed to and fro {1x}. See: TWOT—1307; BDB—623c.

5087. נָדַר {31x} **nâdar,** *naw-dar';* a prim. root; to *promise* (pos., to do or give something to God):—make a vow {1x}, vow {30x}.

Nadar, as a verb, means "to vow." **(1)** Both men and women could "vow" a vow. **(2)** Numbers 30 deals with the law concerning vows; cf. **(2a)** Num 30:2: "If a man vow a vow unto the LORD, or swear an oath to bind his soul with a bond . . ."; and **(2b)** Num. 30:3: "If a woman also vow a vow unto the LORD, and bind herself by a bond. . . ." Syn.: 5088. See: TWOT—1308; BDB—623d.

5088. נֶדֶר {60x} **neder,** *neh'-der;* or

נֵדֶר **nêder,** *nay'-der;* from 5087; a *promise* (to God); also (concr.) a thing *promised:*—vow {58x}, vowed {2x}.

Neder, as a noun, means "vow; votive offering." **(1)** This noun occurs 60 times in biblical Hebrew and is often used in conjunction with the verb (19 times): "Any of thy vows which thou vowest . . ." (Deut 12:17). **(2)** The vow has two basic forms, the unconditional and the conditional. **(2a)** The unconditional is an "oath" where someone binds himself without expecting anything in return: "I will pay my vows unto the LORD now in the presence of all his people" (Ps 116:14). The obligation is binding upon the person who has made a "vow." The word spoken has the force of an oath which generally could not be broken: "If a man vow a vow unto the Lord, or swear an oath to bind his soul with a bond; he shall not break his word, he shall do [everything he said]" (Num 30:2). **(2b)** The conditional "vow" generally had a preceding clause before the oath giving the conditions which had to come to pass before the "vow" became valid: "And Jacob vowed a vow, saying, If God will be with me, and will [watch over me] . . . , so that I come again to my father's house in peace; then

shall the LORD be my God . . . and of all that thou shalt give me I will surely give the tenth unto thee" (Gen 28:20–22).

(3) "Vows" usually occurred in serious situations. **(3a)** Jacob needed the assurance of God's presence before setting out for Padan-aram (Gen 28:20–22); **(3b)** Jephthah made a rash "vow" before battle (Judg 11:30; cf. Num 21:1–3); **(3c)** Hannah greatly desired a child (1 Sa 1:11), when she made a "vow." **(3d)** Though conditional "vows" were often made out of desperation, there is no question of the binding force of the "vow." **(4)** Ecclesiastes amplifies the Old Testament teaching on "vowing": "When thou vowest a vow unto God, defer not to pay it. . . . Better is it that thou shouldest not vow, than that thou shouldest vow and not pay. . . . Neither say thou before the angel, that it was an error" (5:4–6). **(4a)** First, "vow" is always made to God. Even non-Israelites made "vows" to Him (Jonah 1:16). **(4b)** Second, a "vow" is made voluntarily. It is never associated with a life of piety or given the status of religious requirement in the Old Testament. **(4c)** Third, a "vow" once made must be kept. One cannot annul the "vow." **(4c1)** However, the Old Testament allows for "redeeming" the "vow"; by payment of an equal amount in silver, a person, a field, or a house dedicated by "vow" to the Lord could be redeemed (Lev 27:1–25). **(4c2)** This practice, however, declined in Jesus' time, and therefore the Talmud frowns upon the practice of "vowing" and refers to those who vow as "sinners."

(5) *Neder* signifies a kind of offering: "And thither ye shall bring your burnt offerings, and your sacrifices, and your tithes, and [contributions] of your hand, and your vows, and your freewill offerings" (Deut 12:6). **(5a)** In particular the word represents a kind of peace or "votive offering" (Ezr 7:16). **(5b)** It also is a kind of thank offering: "Behold upon the mountains the feet of him that bringeth good tidings, that publisheth peace! . . . Perform thy vows . . ." (Nah 1:15). **(5c)** Here even Gentiles expressed their thanks to God presumably with a gift promised upon condition of deliverance (cf. Num 21:1–3). **(5d)** Such offerings may also be expressions of zeal for God (Ps 22:25). **(5e)** One can give to God anything not abominable to Him (Lev 27:9ff.; Deut 23:18), including one's services (Lev 27:2). **(6)** Pagans were thought to feed and/or tend their gods, while God denied that "vows" paid to Him were to be so conceived (Ps 50:9–13). **(6a)** In paganism the god rewarded the devotee because of and in proportion to his offering. **(6b)** It was a contractual relationship whereby the god was obligated to pay a debt thus incurred. In Israel no such contractual relationship was in view.

(7) The Israelites' unique and concrete demonstrations of love for God show that under Moses love (Deut 6:4) was more than pure legalism; it was spiritual devotion. **(8)** God's Messiah was pledged to offer Himself as a sacrifice for sin (Ps 22:25; cf. Lev 27:2ff.). This was the only sacrifice absolutely and unconditionally acceptable to God. **(9)** Every man is obliged to pay the "vow" before God: "Praise waiteth for thee, O God in Zion: and unto thee shall the vow be performed. . . . Unto thee shall all flesh come" (Ps 65:1–2). See: TWOT–1308a; BDB–623d.

5089. נֹהַ {1x} **nôahh,** *no'-ăh;* from an unused root mean. to *lament; lamentation:*–wailing {1x}. Syn.: 4533, 5091, 5204. See: TWOT–1320a; BDB–624a, 627b.

5090. נָהַג {31x} **nâhag,** *naw-hag';* a prim. root; to *drive* forth (a person, an animal or chariot), i.e. *lead, carry away;* refl. to *proceed* (i.e. impel or guide oneself); also (from the *panting* induced by effort), to *sigh:*–lead {10x}, (carry, lead) . . . away {7x}, drive {6x}, forth {2x}, guide {2x}, brought {2x}, acquainting {1x}, brought in {1x}. See: TWOT–1309, 1310; BDB–624a, 624c.

5091. נָהָה {3x} **nâhâh,** *naw-haw';* a prim. root; to *groan,* i.e. *bewail;* hence, (through the idea of *crying* aloud), to *assemble* (as if on proclamation):–lament {2x}, wail {1x}. Syn.: 4533, 5089, 5204. See: TWOT–1311; BDB–624c.

5092. נְהִי {7x} **nᵉhîy,** *neh-hee';* from 5091; an *elegy:*–lamentation {3x}, wailing {4x}. See: TWOT–1311a; BDB–624c.

5093. נִהְיָה {1x} **nihyâh,** *nih-yaw';* fem. of 5092; *lamentation:*–doleful {1x}. See: TWOT–1311b; BDB–624d.

5094. נְהִיר {3x} **nᵉhîyr** (Aram.), *neh-heere';* or

נְהִירוּ **nâhîyrûw** (Aram.), *nâh-hee-roo';* from the same as 5105; *illumination,* i.e. (fig.) *wisdom:*–light {3x}. See: TWOT–2853a, 2853b; BDB–1102c.

5095. נָהַל {10x} **nâhal,** *naw-hal';* a prim. root; prop. to *run* with a *sparkle,* i.e. *flow;* hence, (tran.), to *conduct,* and (by infer.) to *protect, sustain:*–carry {1x}, feed {1x}, guide {5x}, lead (gently, on) {3x}. See: TWOT–1312; BDB–624d.

5096. נַהֲלָל {3x} **Nahălâl,** *năh-hal-awl';* or

נַהֲלֹל **Nahălôl,** *năh-hal-ole';* the same as 5097; *Nahalal* or *Nahalol,* a place in Pal.:–Nahalal {1x}, Nahallal {1x}, *Nahalol* {1x}. See: TWOT–1312; BDB–625b.

5097. נַהֲלֹל {1x} **nahălôl**, *năh-hal-ole';* from 5095; *pasture:*—bushes {1x}. See: TWOT—1312a; BDB—625b.

5098. נָהַם {5x} **nâham**, *naw-ham';* a prim. root; to *growl:*—mourn {2x}, roar {2x}, roaring {1x}. See: TWOT—1313; BDB—625b.

5099. נַהַם {2x} **naham**, *năh'-ham;* from 5098; a *snarl:*—roaring {2x}. See: TWOT—1313a; BDB—625b.

5100. נְהָמָה {2x} **nᵉhâmâh**, *neh-haw-maw';* fem. of 5099; *snarling:*—disquietness {1x}, roaring {1x}. See: TWOT—1313b; BDB—625b.

5101. נָהַק {2x} **nâhaq**, *naw-hak';* a prim. root; to *bray* (as an ass), *scream* (from hunger):—bray {2x}. See: TWOT—1314; BDB—625c.

5102. נָהַר {6x} **nâhar**, *naw-har';* a prim. root; to *sparkle*, i.e. (fig.) *be cheerful;* hence, (from the *sheen* of a running stream) to *flow*, i.e. (fig.) *assemble:*—flow {2x}, flow together {3x}, be lightened {1x}.

Nahar means "to flow." This verb occurs in Is 2:2: "And it shall come to pass in the last days that the mountain of the LORD's house shall be established in the top of the mountains, and shall be exalted above the hills; and all nations shall flow unto it." See: TWOT—1316, 1315; BDB—625c, 626a, 1102c.

5103. נְהַר {15x} **nᵉhar** (Aram.), *neh-har';* from a root corresp. to 5102; a *river*, espec. the Euphrates:—river {14x}, stream {1x}. See: TWOT—2852; BDB—1102c.

5104. נָהָר {120x} **nâhâr**, *naw-hawr';* from 5102; a *stream* (incl. the *sea;* espec. the Nile, Euphrates, etc.); fig. *prosperity:*—river {98x}, flood {18x}, streams {2x}, Aramnaharaim + 763 {1x}, river side {1x}.

Nahar (5104) means "river; stream; canal; current." **(1)** First, this word usually refers to permanent natural watercourses. **(1a)** In its first biblical appearance *nahar* represents the primeval "rivers" of Eden: "And a river went out of Eden to water the garden; and from thence it was parted, and became into four heads" (Gen 2:10). **(2)** In some passages *nahar* may represent a "canal(s)": "Say unto Aaron, Take thy rod, and stretch out thine hand upon the waters of Egypt, upon their streams [the branches of the Nile], upon their rivers [canals], and upon their ponds" (Ex 7:19; cf. Eze 1:1). **(3)** Third, this word is used of "ocean currents": "For thou hadst cast me into the deep, in the midst of the seas; and the floods compassed me about: all thy billows and thy waves passed over me" (Jonah 2:3). **(4)** Fourth, *nahar* is used of underground streams: "For he hath founded it [the earth] upon the seas, and established it upon the floods" (Ps 24:2). This passage appears to be a literary allusion to the pagan concept of the creation and structure of the world—the next verse is "Who shall ascend into the hill of the LORD?" (Ps 24:3). **(5)** This word plays a prominent role in the figure of divine blessing set forth in Ps 46:4: "There is a river, the streams whereof shall make glad the city of God." This may be an allusion to the primeval "river" in Eden whose water gave life to the garden. **(6)** In Is 33:21 the same Jerusalem is depicted as having "rivers" of blessing: "A place of broad rivers and streams; wherein shall go no galley with oars, neither shall gallant ship pass thereby" (cf. Is 48:18). **(7)** In other passages a "river" is a figure of trouble and difficulty: "When thou passest through the waters, I will be with thee; and through the rivers, they shall not overflow thee" (Is 43:2). **(8)** This is in marked contrast to the use of the same idea in Is 66:12, where an "overflowing stream" depicts respectively the onrush of God's glory and divine peace. Syn.: 5158. See: TWOT—1315a; BDB—625c.

5105. נְהָרָה {1x} **nᵉhârâh**, *neh-haw-raw';* from 5102 in its orig. sense; *daylight:*—light {1x}. See: TWOT—1316a; BDB—626a.

5106. נוּא {9x} **nûw'**, *noo;* a prim. root; to *refuse, forbid, dissuade*, or *neutralize:*—disallow {1x}, disallowed {3x}, discourage {2x}, discouraged {1x}, make to no effect {1x}, break {1x}. See: TWOT—1317; BDB—626b.

5107. נוּב {4x} **nûwb**, *noob;* a prim. root; to *germinate*, i.e. (fig.) to (caus. *make*) *flourish;* also (of words), to *utter:*—bring forth (fruit) {2x}, make cheerful {1x}, increase {1x}. See: TWOT—1318; BDB—626b.

5108. נוֹב {2x} **nôwb**, *nobe;* or

נֵיב **nêyb**, *nabe;* from 5107; *produce*, lit. or fig.:—fruit {2x}. Syn.: 6529. See: TWOT—1318a, 1318b; BDB—626c, 644b.

5109. נוֹבַי {1x} **Nôwbay**, *no-bah'ee;* from 5108; *fruitful; Nobai*, an Isr.:—Nebai {1x}. See: BDB—626c, 644b.

5110. נוּד {24x} **nûwd**, *nood;* a prim. root; to *nod*, i.e. waver; fig. to *wander, flee, disappear;* also (from *shaking* the head in sympathy), to *console, deplore*, or (from *tossing* the head in scorn) *taunt:*—bemoan {7x}, remove {5x}, vagabond {2x}, flee {1x}, get {1x}, mourn {1x}, move {1x}, pity {1x}, shaken {1x}, skippedst {1x}, sorry {1x}, wag {1x}, wandering {1x}. See: TWOT—1319; BDB—626c, 1102c.

5111. נוּד {1x} **nûwd** (Aram.), *nood;* corresp. to 5116; to *flee:*—get away {1x}. See: TWOT—2854; BDB—1102c.

5112. נוֹד {1x} **nôwd**, *node* [only defect.

נֹד *nôd*, *node*]; from 5110; *exile:*—wandering {1x}. See: TWOT—1319a; BDB—621b, 627a.

5113. נוֹד {1x} **Nôwd**, *node;* the same as 5112; *vagrancy; Nod,* the land of Cain:— Nod {1x}. See: BDB—627a.

5114. נוֹדָב {1x} **Nôwdâb**, *no-dawb';* from 5068; *noble; Nodab,* an Arab tribe:—Nodab {1x}. See: BDB—622a.

5115. נָוָה {2x} **nâvâh**, *naw-vaw';* a prim. root; to *rest* (as at home); caus. (through the impl. idea of *beauty* [comp. 5116]), to *celebrate* (with praises):—keep at home {1x}, prepare an habitation {1x}. See: TWOT—1321, 1322; BDB—627b, 627d.

5116. נָוֶה {36x} **nâveh**, *naw-veh';* or (fem.)

נָוָה *nâvâh*, *naw-vaw';* from 5115; (adj.) *at home;* hence, (by impl. of satisfaction) *lovely;* also (noun) a *home,* of God (temple), men (residence), flocks (pasture), or wild animals (*den*):—habitation {22x}, fold {4x}, dwelling {3x}, sheepcote {2x}, comely {1x}, stable {1x}, dwelling place {1x}, pleasant place {1x}, tarried {1x}. See: TWOT—1322a, 1322b, 1322c; BDB—610a, 627c, 627d.

5117. נוּחַ {64x} **nûwach**, *noo'-akh;* a prim. root; to *rest*, i.e. *settle* down; used in a great variety of applications, lit. and fig., intr., tran. and caus. (to *dwell, stay, let fall, place, let alone, withdraw, give comfort,* etc.):—rest {55x}, ceased {1x}, confederate {1x}, let down {1x}, set down {1x}, lay {1x}, quiet {2x}, remain {1x}, set {1x}.
Nuwach means "to rest, remain, be quiet." **(1)** The first occurrence is in Gen 8:4: "And the ark [came to rest] . . . upon the mountains of Ararat." **(1a)** This illustrates the frequent use of this word to show a physical settling down of something at some particular place. **(1b)** Other examples are birds (2 Sa 21:10), insects (Ex 10:14), and soles of feet in the waters of the Jordan (Josh 3:13). **(2)** "To rest" sometimes indicates a complete envelopment and thus permeation, as **(2a)** in the spirit of Elijah "resting" on Elisha (2 Kin 2:15), **(2b)** the hand of God "resting" on the mountain (Is 25:10), and **(2c)** when Wisdom "resteth in the heart of him that hath understanding" (Prov 14:33). **(3)** Frequently *nuwach* means "to be quiet" or "to rest" **(3a)** after hard work (Ex 20:11), **(3b)** from onslaught of one's enemies (Est 9:16), **(3c)** from trouble (Job 3:26), and **(3d)** in death (Job 3:17).

(4) The word may mean "to set one's mind at rest," as when a child receives the discipline of his parent (Prov 29:17). **(5)** Sometimes *nuwach* means "to leave at rest" or "to allow to remain." Thus, God "allowed" the pagan nations "to remain" in Canaan during Joshua's lifetime (Judg 2:23). **(6)** God threatened to abandon the Israelites in the wilderness (Num 32:15). **(7)** It should be noted that while *nuwach* is used sometimes as a synonym for *shabath* (7673), "to cease, to rest" (Ex 20:11), *shabath* really is basically "to cease" from work which may imply rest, but not necessarily so. The writer of Gen 2:3 is not stressing rest from work but rather God's ceasing from His creative work since it was complete. Syn.: 7673. See: TWOT—1323; BDB—628a. comp. 3241.

5118. נוּחַ {4x} **nûwach**, *noo'-akh;* or

נוֹחַ **nôwach**, *no'-akh;* from 5117; *quiet:*—rest {1x}, rested {2x}, resting place {1x}. See: TWOT—1323?; BDB—628a, 629a, 629b.

5119. נוֹחָה {1x} **Nôwchâh**, *no-chaw';* fem. of 5118; *quietude; Nochah,* an Isr.:— Nohah {1x}. See: BDB—629a.

5120. נוּט {1x} **nûwṭ**, *noot;* to *quake:*—be moved {1x}. See: TWOT—1324; BDB—630a.

5121. נָוִית {6x} **Nâvîyth**, *naw-veeth';* from 5115; *residence; Navith,* a place in Pal.:—Naioth {6x}. See: BDB—627d, 630b, 644b.

5122. נְוָלוּ {3x} **nᵉvâlûw** (Aram.), *nev-aw-loo';* or

נְוָלִי **nᵉvâlîy** (Aram.), *nev-aw-lee';* from an unused root prob. mean. to *be foul;* a *sink:*—dunghill {3x}. See: TWOT—2855; BDB—1102c.

5123. נוּם {6x} **nûwm**, *noom;* a prim. root; to *slumber* (from drowsiness):—slept {1x}, slumber {5x}. See: TWOT—1325; BDB—630b.

5124. נוּמָה {1x} **nûwmâh**, *noo-maw';* from 5123; *sleepiness:*—drowsiness {1x}. See: TWOT—1325a; BDB—630b.

5125. נוּן {2x} **nûwn**, *noon;* a prim. root; to *re-sprout,* i.e. propagate by shoots; fig. to *be perpetual:*—be continued {2x}. See: TWOT—1326; BDB—630c.

5126. נוּן {30x} **Nûwn**, *noon;* or

נוֹן **Nôwn** (1 Chron. 7:27), *nohn;* from 5125; *perpetuity, Nun* or *Non,* the father of Joshua:—Non {1x}, Nun {29x}. See: BDB—630c.

5127. נוּס {161x} **nûwç,** *noos;* a prim. root; to *flit,* i.e. *vanish* away (subside, escape; caus. chase, impel, deliver):—flee {142x}, flee away {12x}, abated {1x}, displayed {1x}, flight {1x}, hide {1x}, flee out {1x}, lift up a standard {1x}, variant {1x}.

Nuwc means to flee, escape, take flight, depart. **(1)** *Nuwc* occurs for the first time in Gen 14:10, where it is used twice to describe the "fleeing" of the kings of Sodom and Gomorrah. **(2)** *Nuwc* is the common word for "fleeing" from an enemy or danger (Gen 39:12; Num 16:34; Josh 10:6). **(3)** The word is also used to describe "escape,": "Let not the swift flee away, nor the mighty man escape; they shall stumble, and fall toward the north by the river Euphrates" (Jer 46:6; cf. Amos 9:1). **(4)** In a figurative use, the word describes **(4a)** the "disappearance" of physical strength: "And Moses was an hundred and twenty years old when he died: his eye was not dim, nor his natural force abated" (Deut 34:7), **(4b)** the "fleeing" of evening shadows: "Until the day break, and the shadows flee away, turn, my beloved, and be thou like a roe or a young hart upon the mountains of Bether" (Song 2:17), and **(4c)** the "fleeing away" of sorrow: "And the ransomed of the LORD shall return, and come to Zion with songs and everlasting joy upon their heads: they shall obtain joy and gladness, and sorrow and sighing shall flee away" (Is 35:10). Syn.: 1272. See: TWOT—1327; BDB—630c.

5128. נוּעַ {42x} **nûwaʻ,** *noo'-ah;* a prim. root; to *waver,* in a great variety of applications, lit. and fig. (as subjoined):—shake {6x}, wander {6x}, move {6x}, promoted {3x}, fugitive {2x}, sift {2x}, stagger {2x}, wag {2x}, misc. {13x} = continually, ✕ make, to [go] up and down, be gone away, reel, remove, scatter, set, to and fro, be vagabond. See: TWOT—1328; BDB—631a.

5129. נוֹעַדְיָה {2x} **Nôwʻadyâh,** *no-ad-yaw';* from 3259 and 3050; *convened of Jah; Noadjah,* the name of an Isr., and a false prophetess:—Noadiah {2x}. See: BDB—418a, 631d.

5130. נוּף {37x} **nûwph,** *noof;* a prim. root; to *quiver* (i.e. *vibrate* up and down, or *rock* to and fro); used in a great variety of applications (incl. *sprinkling, beckoning, rubbing, bastinadoing, sawing, waving,* etc.):—wave {16x}, shake {7x}, offer {5x}, lift up {4x}, move {1x}, perfumed {1x}, send {1x}, sift {1x}, strike {1x}. See: TWOT—1329, 1330; BDB—245a, 631d.

5131. נוֹף {1x} **nôwph,** *nofe;* from 5130; *elevation:*—situation {1x}. See: TWOT—1331a; BDB—632c. comp. 5297.

5132. נוּץ {3x} **nûwts,** *noots;* a prim. root; prop. to *flash;* hence, to *blossom* (from the brilliancy of color); also, to *fly* away (from the quickness of motion):—flee away {1x}, bud {1x}, bud forth {1x}. See: TWOT—1399; BDB—663b, 665b.

5133. נוֹצָה {4x} **nôwtsâh,** *no-tsaw';* or

נֹצָה **nôtsâh,** *no-tsaw';* fem. act. part. of 5327 in the sense of *flying;* a *pinion* (or wing feather); often (collect.) *plumage:*—feathers {3x}, ostrich {1x}. Syn.: 3283. See: TWOT—1399a; BDB—632c, 663b, 663d.

5134. נוּק {1x} **nûwq,** *nook;* a prim. root; to *suckle:*—nurse {1x}. Syn.: 3243. See: TWOT—1332; BDB—632d.

5135. נוּר {17x} **nûwr** (Aram.), *noor;* from an unused root (corresp. to that of 5216) mean. to *shine; fire:*—fiery {10x}, fire {7x}. See: TWOT—2856; BDB—1102c.

5136. נוּשׁ {1x} **nûwsh,** *noosh;* a prim. root; to *be sick,* i.e. (fig.) *distressed:*—be full of heaviness {1x}. See: TWOT—1334; BDB—633b.

5137. נָזָה {24x} **nâzâh,** *naw-zaw';* a prim. root; to *spirt,* i.e. *besprinkle* (espec. in expiation):—sprinkle {24x}. See: TWOT—1335, 1336; BDB—633b, 633c.

5138. נָזִיד {6x} **nâzîyd,** *naw-zeed';* from 2102; something *boiled,* i.e. *soup:*—pottage {6x}. See: TWOT—547d; BDB—268a, 633c.

5139. נָזִיר {16x} **nâzîyr,** *naw-zeer';* or

נָזִר **nâzîr,** *naw-zeer';* from 5144; *separate,* i.e. *consecrated* (as *prince,* a Nazirite); hence, (fig. from the latter) an *unpruned* vine (like an unshorn Nazirite):—Nazarite {12x}, separate {1x}, separated {1x}, vine undressed {2x}.

Nazir means "one who is separated; Nazarite." **(1)** There are 16 occurrences of the word in the Old Testament. **(1a)** The earliest use of *nazir* is found in Gen 49:26: "The blessings of thy father . . . shall be on the head of Joseph . . . that was separate from his brethren" (cf. Deut 33:16). **(1b)** Joseph was separated from his brethren to become the savior of his father, his brethren, and their families. **(2)** Most frequently in Old Testament usage, *nazir* is an appellation for one who vowed to refrain from certain things for a period of time: "And this is the law of the Nazarite, when the days of his separation are fulfilled: he shall be brought unto the door of the tabernacle of the congregation" (Num 6:13). **(2a)** According to Num 6, a lay person of either sex could take a special vow of consecration to God's service for a cer-

tain period of time. **(2b)** A "Nazarite" usually made a vow voluntarily; however, in the case of Samson, (Judg 13:5, 7) his parents dedicated him for life. **(3)** Num 6:1– 23 laid down regulatory laws pertaining to Nazaritism. **(4)** There were two kinds of "Nazarites": the temporary and the perpetual. **(4a)** The temporary was much more common than the perpetual/lifelong. **(4b)** From the Bible we have knowledge only of Samson, Samuel, and John the Baptist as persons who were lifelong "Nazarites." **(5)** The Bible does not specify the length of a Nazarite's separation. **(5a)** According to the Mishna, the normal time for keeping a Nazarite vow was thirty days; but sometimes a double vow was taken, lasting sixty days. **(5b)** In fact, a vow was sometimes undertaken for a hundred days. **(6)** During the time of his vow, **(6a)** a "Nazarite" was required to abstain from wine and every kind of intoxicating drink. **(6b)** He was also forbidden to cut the hair of his head or to approach a dead body, even that of his nearest relative. **(6c)** If a "Nazarite" accidently defiled himself, he had to undergo certain rites of purification and then had to begin the full period of consecration over again. **(7)** There is but one reference in the prophetic literature to "Nazarites": The prophet Amos complained that the Lord had given the Israelites, Nazarites and prophets as spiritual leaders, but that the people "gave the Nazarites wine to drink; and commanded the prophets, saying, Prophesy not" (Amos 2:11–12). **(8)** The New Testament occasionally refers to what appear to have been Nazarite vows. For example, Acts 18:18 says that Paul sailed with Priscilla and Aquila, "having shorn his head . . . for he had a vow" (cf. Acts 21:23–24). Syn.: 6504. See: TWOT—1340b; BDB—634c.

5140. נָזַל {16x} **nâzal**, *naw-zal';* a prim. root; to *drip*, or *shed* by trickling:—flood {3x}, flow {3x}, stream {2x}, pour out {1x}, distil {1x}, melted {1x}, drop {1x}, running waters {1x}, flow out {1x}, pour down {1x}, gush out {1x}. See: TWOT—1337; BDB—633c.

5141. נֶזֶם {17x} **nezem**, *neh'-zem;* from an unused root of uncert. mean.; a nose-*ring:*—earring {14x}, jewel {3x}. See: TWOT—1338a; BDB—633d.

5142. נְזַק {4x} **nᵉzaq** (Aram.), *nez-ak';* corresp. to the root of 5143; to *suffer* (caus. *inflict*) *loss:*—have endamage {1x}, damage {1x}, hurt {1x}, hurtful {1x}. See: TWOT—2857; BDB—1102c.

5143. נֶזֶק {1x} **nêzeq**, *nay'zek;* from an unused root mean. to *injure; loss:*—damage {1x}. See: TWOT—1339; BDB—413b, 634a.

5144. נָזַר {10x} **nâzar**, *naw-zar';* a prim. root; to *hold aloof*, i.e. (intr.) *abstain* (from food and drink, from impurity, and even from divine worship [i.e. *apostatize*]); spec. to *set apart* (to sacred purposes), i.e. *devote:*— consecrate {1x}, separate (-ing, self) {9x}.

Nazar, "to separate, be separated." **(1)** "To separate" and "to consecrate" are not distinguished from one another in the early Old Testament books. **(1a)** For example, the earliest use of *nazar* in the Pentateuch is in Lev 15:31: "Thus shall ye separate the children of Israel from their uncleanness; that they die not in their uncleanness, when they defile my tabernacle that is among them." **(1b)** Here Moses uses the word in a cultic [religious] sense, meaning a kind of "consecration." **(2)** In the days of the prophet Zechariah, Jews asked the Lord whether certain fasts which they had voluntarily adopted were to be continued and observed. **(2a)** "When they had sent unto the home of God Sherezer and Regemmelech, and their men, to pray before the Lord, and to speak unto the priests which were in the house of the Lord of hosts, and to the prophets, saying, Should I weep in the fifth month, separating myself, as I have done these so many years?" (Zec 7:2–3). **(2b)** The Lord's response stated that it was no longer necessary and therefore needed not to be continued.

(3) In prophetic literature, the verb *nazar* indicates Israel's deliberate separation **(3a)** from Jehovah to dedication of foreign gods or idols. **(3b)** Hos 9:10: "I found Israel like grapes in the wilderness; I saw your fathers as the firstripe in the fig tree at her first time: but they went to Baalpeor, and separated themselves unto that shame; and their abominations were according as they loved." **(4)** The prophet Ezekiel employed *nazar:* "For every one of the house of Israel, or of the stranger that sojourneth in Israel, which separateth himself from me, and setteth up his idols in his heart, and putteth the stumbling block of his iniquity before his face, and cometh to a prophet to inquire of him concerning me; I the Lord will answer him by myself" (Eze 14:7). See: TWOT—1340; BDB—634a, 634c.

5145. נֵזֶר {25x} **nezer**, *neh'-zer;* or

נֶזֶר **nêzer**, *nay'-zer;* from 5144; prop. something *set apart*, i.e. (abstr.) *dedication* (of a priest or Nazirite); hence, (concr.) unshorn *locks;* also (by impl.) a *chaplet* (espec. of royalty):—consecration {2x}, crown {11x}, hair {1x}, separation {11x}. See: TWOT—1340a; BDB—634b.

5146. נֹחַ {46x} **Nôach**, *no'-akh;* the same as 5118; *rest; Noach*, the patriarch of

the flood:—Noah {46x}. See: TWOT—1323b; BDB—629b, 634d.

5147. נַחְבִּי {1x} **Nachbîy,** *nakh-bee';* from 2247; *occult; Nachbi,* an Isr.:— Nakbi {1x}. See: BDB—286a, 634d.

5148. נָחָה {39x} **nâchâh,** *naw-khaw';* a prim. root; to *guide;* by impl. to *transport* (into exile, or as colonists):—lead {24x}, guide {6x}, bring {4x}, bestowed {1x}, lead forth {1x}, govern {1x}, put {1x}, straiteneth {1x}. See: TWOT—1341; BDB—634d.

5149. נְחוּם {1x} **Neᵉchûwm,** *neh-khoom';* from 5162; *comforted; Nechum,* an Isr.:—Nehum {1x}. See: BDB—637b.

5150. נָחוּם {3x} **nichûwm,** *nee-khoom';* or

נָחֻם **nichûm,** *nee-khoom';* from 5162; prop. *consoled;* abstr. *solace:*— comfort {1x}, comfortable {1x}, repentings {1x}. See: TWOT—1344b; BDB—637b.

5151. נַחוּם {1x} **Nachûwm,** *nakh-oom';* from 5162; *comfortable; Nachum,* an Isr. prophet:—Nahum {1x}. See: BDB—637b.

5152. נָחוֹר {18x} **Nâchôwr,** *naw-khore';* from the same as 5170; *snorer; Nachor,* the name of the grandfather and a brother of Abraham:—Nahor {8x}. See: BDB—637d.

5153. נָחוּשׁ {1x} **nâchûwsh,** *naw-khoosh';* ap- par. pass. part. of 5172 (perh. in the sense of *ringing,* i.e. bell-metal; or from the *red* color of the throat of a serpent 5175, as denom. when hissing); *coppery,* i.e. (fig.) hard:—of brass {1x}. See: TWOT—1349b; BDB—639a.

5154. נְחוּשָׁה {10x} **nᵉchûwshâh,** *nekh-oo- shaw';* or

נְחֻשָׁה **nᵉchûshâh,** *nekh-oo-shaw';* fem. of 5153; *copper:*—brass {7x}, steel {3x}. See: TWOT—1349b; BDB—639a, 1102d. comp. 5176.

5155. נְחִילָה {1x} **Nᵉchîylâh,** *nekh-ee-law';* prob. denom. from 2485; a *flute:*—[plur.] Nehiloth {1x}. See: TWOT— 1342b; BDB—636a.

5156. נְחִיר {1x} **nᵉchîyr,** *nekh-eer';* from the same as 5170; a *nostril:*—[dual] nostrils {1x}. See: TWOT—1346c; BDB—638a.

5157. נָחַל {62x} **nâchal,** *naw-khal';* a prim. root; to *inherit* (as a [fig.] mode of descent), or (gen.) to *occupy;* caus. to *bequeath,* or (gen.) *distribute, instate:*—inherit {30x}, in- heritance {20x}, possess {5x}, have {2x}, had {1x}, divide {1x}, heritage {1x}, possession {1x}, defiled {1x}.

Nachal means to inherit, get possession of, take as a possession. **(1)** The first time *nachal*

is used in the Old Testament text is in Ex 23:30: "inherit the land." **(2)** To inherit **(2a)** does not always require a "last will and testament." **(2b)** The basic meaning of *nachal* is to receive with the ability to control, possess, and direct. **(3)** One of the few instances of "to inherit" by last will and testament is in Deut 21:16: ". . . when he maketh his sons to inherit that which he hath." This clause is more literally translated "in the day he causes his sons to inherit that which is his." **(4)** When Moses prayed: "O Lord, . . . take us for thine inheri- tance" (Ex 34:9), he did not mean that God should "inherit" through a will, but that He should "take possession of" Israel. **(5)** The meaning "to get as a possession" is seen in its figurative use. Thus, **(5a)** "the wise shall inherit [possess as their due] glory" (Prov 3:35); **(5b)** "the upright shall have good things in posses- sion" (Prov 28:10); **(5c)** "our fathers have inher- ited lies" (Jer 16:19); **(5d)** "he that troubleth his own house shall inherit the wind" (Prov 11:29). See: TWOT—1342; BDB—635c.

5158. נַחַל {141x} **nachal,** *nakh'-al;* or (fem.)

נַחְלָה **nachlâh** (Ps 124:4), *nakh'-law;* or

נַחֲלָה **nachălâh** (Eze 47:19; 48:28), *nakh-al-aw';* from 5157 in its orig. sense; a *stream,* espec. a winter *torrent;* (by impl.) a (narrow) *valley* (in which a brook runs); also a *shaft* (of a mine):—brook {46x}, flood {5x}, river {56x}, stream {11x}, valley {23x}.

Nachalah means "wadi (or wady); torrent valley; torrent; river; shaft." **(1)** This noun rep- resents a dry valley in which water runs during the rainy season: "And Isaac departed thence, and pitched his tent in the valley of Gerar, and dwelt there" (Gen 26:17—the first biblical ap- pearance). **(2)** The word can signify the "wady" when it is full of rushing water. Indeed, it ap- pears to describe the rushing water itself: "And he took them, and sent them over the brook" (Gen 32:23). **(3)** Sometimes *nachalah* means a permanent stream or "river": "These shall ye eat of all that are in the waters: whatsoever hath fins and scales in the waters, in the seas, and in the rivers, them shall ye eat" (Lev 11:9). **(4)** The Pentateuch consistently distinguishes between extra-Egyptian waterways; calling them *nachalah,* 13 times, and *nahar* (5104), 13 times, and inter-Egyptian waterways (calling them ye'or). This distinction demonstrates the kind of firsthand knowledge and historical concern expected from a mature eyewitness. **(5)** *Nachalah* is used figuratively of many things that emerge and disappear suddenly or that have extreme on-rushing power such as the pride of nations (Is 66:12), the strength of the invader (Jer 47:2), and the power of the foe

Hebrew

(Ps 18:4). **(6)** Torrents of oil do not please God if the offerer's heart is wrongly disposed (Mic 6:7). **(7)** God overfloods the godly with torrents of His good pleasure (Ps 36:8). **(8)** The eschaton is typified by streams, or torrents, in the desert (Eze 47:5–19; cf. Ex 17:3ff.). See: TWOT—1343a, 1343b; BDB—636a, 636d.

5159. נַחֲלָה {222x} **nachălâh**, *nakh-al-aw'*; from 5157 (in its usual sense); prop. something *inherited*, i.e. (abstr.) *occupancy*, or (concr.) an *heirloom;* gen. an *estate, patrimony* or *portion:*—heritage {27x}, to inherit {2x}, inheritance {192x}, possession {1x}.

Nachalah means "possession; property; inheritance." **(1)** The first occurrence of the word is in Gen 31:14: "And Rachel and Leah answered and said unto him, Is there yet any portion or inheritance for us in our father's house?" **(2)** The basic translation of *nachalah* is "inheritance": "And Naboth said to Ahab, The Lord forbid it me, that I should give the inheritance of my fathers unto thee" (1 Kin 21:3). **(3)** The word stresses a "possession" to which one has received the legal claim. **(3a)** Technically, the 12 tribes were inheriting the land given to Abraham, Isaac, and Jacob. **(3b)** The usage of *nachalah* in the Pentateuch and Joshua indicates that the word often denotes that "possession" which all of Israel or a tribe or a clan received as their share in the Promised Land. **(3c)** The share was determined by lot (Num 26:56) shortly before Moses' death, and it fell upon Joshua to execute the division of the "possession": "So Joshua took the whole land, according to all that the Lord said unto Moses; and Joshua gave it for an inheritance unto Israel according to their divisions by their tribes" (Josh 11:23). **(3d)** After the Conquest the term "inheritance" is no longer used to refer to newly gained territory by warfare. **(3e)** Once "possession" had been taken of the land, the legal process came into operation by which the hereditary property was supposed to stay within the family. **(3f)** For this reason Naboth could not give his rights over to Ahab (1 Kin 21:3–4). **(4)** One could redeem the property, whenever it had come into other hands, as did Boaz, in order to maintain the name of the deceased: "Moreover Ruth the Moabitess, the wife of Mahlon, have I purchased to be my wife, to raise up the name of the dead upon his inheritance, that the name of the dead be not cut off from among his brethren, and from the gate of his place" (Ruth 4:10). **(5)** Metaphorically, Israel is said to be God's "possession": "But the Lord hath taken you, and brought you forth out of the iron furnace, even out of Egypt, to be unto him a people of inheritance, as ye are this day" (Deut 4:20).

(6) Within the special covenantal status Israel experienced the blessing that its children were a special gift from the Lord (Ps 127:3). **(6a)** However, the Lord abandoned Israel as His "possession" to the nations (cf. Is 47:6), and **(6b)** permitted a remnant of the "possession" to return: "Who is a God like unto thee, that pardoneth iniquity, and passeth by the transgression of the remnant of his heritage? he retaineth not his anger for ever, because he delighteth in mercy" (Mic 7:18). **(7)** On the other hand, it can even be said that the Lord is the "possession" of His people. The priests and the Levites, whose earthly "possessions" were limited, were assured that their "possession" is the Lord: "Wherefore Levi hath no part nor inheritance with his brethren; the Lord is his inheritance, according as the Lord thy God promised him" (Deut 10:9; cf. 12:22; Num 18:23). See: TWOT—1342a; BDB—635a. comp. 5158.

5160. נַחֲלִיאֵל {2x} **Nachălîyʾêl**, *nakh-al-ee-ale';* from 5158 and 410; *valley of God; Nachaliël,* a place in the desert:—Nahaliel {2x}. See: BDB—636d.

5161. נֶחְלָמִי {3x} **Nechĕlâmîy**, *nekh-el-aw-mee';* appar. a patron. from an unused name (appar. pass. part. of 2492); *dreamed;* a *Nechelamite,* or desc. of Nechlam:—Nehelamite {3x}. See: BDB—636d.

5162. נָחַם {108x} **nâcham**, *naw-kham';* a prim. root; prop. to *sigh*, i.e. *breathe* strongly; by impl. to *be sorry*, i.e. (in a favorable sense) to *pity, console* or (refl.) *rue;* or (unfavorably) to *avenge* (oneself):—comfort {57x}, repent {41x}, comforter {9x}, ease {1x}.

Nacham means "to repent, comfort." **(1)** *Nacham* is translated "to repent" 41 times and "to comfort" 57 times in the Old Testament. **(1a)** To repent means to make a strong turning to a new course of action. **(1a1)** The emphasis is on *turning to* a positive course of action, not **(1a2)** *turning from* a less desirable course. **(1a3)** Comfort is derived from "com" (with) and "fort" (strength). **(1b)** Hence, when one repents, he exerts strength to change, to re-grasp the situation, and exert effort for the situation to take a different course of purpose and action. **(1c)** The stress is not upon new information or new facts which cause the change as it is upon the visible action taken. **(2)** Most uses of the term in the Old Testament are connected with God's repentance: **(2a)** "It repented the Lord that he had made man" (Gen 6:6); **(2b)** "And the Lord repented of the evil which he thought to do unto his people" (Ex 32:14). **(2c)** Sometimes the Lord "repented" of the discipline He had planned to carry out concerning His people: "If that nation, against whom I have

pronounced, turn from their evil, I will repent of the evil that I thought to do unto them" (Jer 18:8); **(2d)** "If it do evil in my sight, that it obey not my voice, then I will repent of the good" (Jer 18:10); **(2e)** "And rend your heart, and not your garments, and turn unto the Lord your God: for he is gracious and merciful, slow to anger . . . and repenteth him of evil" (Joel 2:13). **(3)** In other instances, the Lord exhibited new actions when man changed to make the right choices, **(3a)** but He could not change His attitude toward evil when man continued on the wrong course. **(3b)** As God demonstrated His actions, He always remained faithful to His own righteousness. **(4)** In some situations, God was weary of "repenting" (Jer 15:6), **(4a)** suggesting that He has grown weary with Israel's constant insincere repentance. **(4b)** An instance of this action was in Samuel's word to Saul, that God took the kingdom from Israel's first king and intended to give it to another; Samuel declared, "And also the Strength of Israel will not lie nor repent: for he is not a man, that he should repent" (1 Sa 15:29). **(5)** God usually "repented" of His actions because of man's intercession and repentance of his evil deeds. **(5a)** Moses pleaded with God as the intercessor for Israel: "Turn from thy fierce wrath, and repent of this evil against thy people" (Ex 32:12). **(5b)** The Lord did that when He "repented of the evil which he thought to do unto his people" (Ex 32:14). **(5c)** As God's prophet preached to Nineveh, "God saw their works, that they turned from their evil way; and God repented of the evil, that he had said that he would do unto them" (Jonah 3:10). **(5d)** In such instances, God "repented," to bring about a change of plan than previously proclaimed by the prophet. Again, however, God remained faithful to His absolutes of righteousness in His relation to and with man. **(6)** Other passages refer to a change (or lack of it) in man's attitude. When man did not "repent" of his wickedness, he chose rebellion (Jer 8:6). **(7)** In the eschatological sense, when Ephraim (as a representative of the northern branch of Israel) will "repent" (Jer 31:19), God then will have mercy (Jer 31:20). **(8)** Man also expressed repentance to other men. Benjamin suffered greatly from the crime of immorality (Judg 19—20): "And the children of Israel [eleven tribes] repented them from Benjamin their brother, and said, There is one tribe cut off from Israel this day" (Judg 21:6; cf. v. 15). **(9)** *Nacham* may also mean "to comfort." **(9a)** The refugees in Babylon would be "comforted" when survivors arrived from Jerusalem (Eze 14:23); the connection between "comfort" and "repent" here resulted from the calamity

God brought upon Jerusalem as a testimony to the truth of His Word. **(9b)** David "comforted" Bathsheba after the death of her child born in sin (2 Sa 12:24); this probably indicates his repentance of what had happened in their indiscretion. **(10)** On the other hand, the word was used in the human sense of "comfort." Job asked his three companions, "How then comfort ye me in vain seeing in your answers there remaineth falsehood?" (Job 21:34; he meant that their attitude seemed cruel and unfeeling). **(11)** The psalmist looked to God for "comfort": "Thou shalt increase my greatness, and comfort me on every side" (Ps 71:21). **(12)** In an eschatological sense God indicated that He would "comfort" Jerusalem with the restoration of Israel, as a mother comforts her offspring (Is 66:13). See: TWOT—1344; BDB—636d.

5163. נַחַם {1x} **Nacham**, *nakh'-am;* from 5162; *consolation; Nacham,* an Isr.:—Naham {1x}. See: BDB—637b.

5164. נֹחַם {1x} **nôcham**, *no'-kham;* from 5162; *ruefulness,* i.e. *desistance:*—repentance {1x}. See: TWOT—1344a; BDB—637b.

5165. נֶחָמָה {2x} **nechâmâh**, *nekh-aw-maw';* from 5162; *consolation:*—comfort {2x}. See: TWOT—1344c; BDB—637c.

5166. נְחֶמְיָה {8x} **N°chemyâh**, *nekh-em-yaw';* from 5162 and 3050; *consolation of Jah; Nechemjah,* the name of three Isr.:—Nehemiah {8x}. See: BDB—637c.

5167. נַחֲמָנִי {1x} **Nachămânîy**, *nakh-am-aw-nee';* from 5162; *consolatory; Nachamani,* an Isr.:—Nahamani {1x}. See: BDB—637c.

5168. נַחְנוּ {6x} **nachnûw**, *nakh-noo';* for 587; *we:*—we {6x}. See: TWOT—128a; BDB—59d, 637d.

5169. נָחַץ {1x} **nâchats**, *naw-khats';* a prim. root; to *be urgent:*—require hasted {1x}. See: TWOT—1345; BDB—637d.

5170. נַחַר **nachar**, *nakh'-ar;* and (fem.)

נַחֲרָה **nachărâh**, *nakh-ar-aw';* from an unused root mean. to *snort* or *snore;* a *snorting:*—nostrils {1x}, snorting {1x}. See: TWOT—1346, 1346a, 1346b; BDB—637d.

5171. נַחֲרַי {2x} **Nachăray**, *nakh-ar-ah'-ee;* or

נַחְרַי **Nachray**, *nakh-rah'-ee;* from the same as 5170; *snorer; Nacharai* or *Nachrai,* an Isr.:—Naharai {1x}, Nahari {1x}. See: BDB—638a.

5172. נָחַשׁ {11x} **nâchash**, *naw-khash';* a prim. root; prop. to *hiss,* i.e. *whisper* a (magic) spell; gen. to *prognosticate:*—enchant-

ment {4x}, divine {2x}, enchanter {1x}, indeed {1x}, certainly {1x}, learn by experience {1x}, diligently observe {1x}. See: TWOT—1348; BDB—638c.

5173. נַחַשׁ {2x} **nachash,** *nakh′-ash;* from 5172; an *incantation* or *augury:*—enchantment {2x}. See: TWOT—1348a; BDB—638d.

5174. נְחָשׁ {9x} **nᵉchâsh** (Aram.), *nekh-awsh′;* corresp. to 5154; *copper:*—brass {9x}. See: TWOT—2858; BDB—1102d.

5175. נָחָשׁ {31x} **nâchâsh,** *naw-khawsh′;* from 5172; a *snake* (from its *hiss*):—serpent {31x}. See: TWOT—1347a; BDB—638a.

5176. נָחָשׁ {9x} **Nâchâsh,** *naw-khawsh′;* the same as 5175; *Nachash,* the name of two persons appar. non-Isr.:—Nahash {9x}. See: BDB—638b.

נְחֻשָׁה **nᵉchûshâh.** See 5154.

5177. נַחְשׁוֹן {10x} **Nachshôwn,** *nakh-shone′;* from 5172; *enchanter; Nachshon,* an Isr.:—Naashon {1x}, Nahshon {9x}. See: BDB—638b.

5178. נְחֹשֶׁת {141x} **nᵉchôsheth,** *nekh-o′-sheth;* for 5154; *copper,* hence, something made of that metal, i.e. *coin,* a *fetter;* fig. *base* (as compared with gold or silver):—brass {103x}, brasen {28x}, fetters {4x}, chain {3x}, copper {1x}, filthiness {1x}, steel {1x}.

Nechosheth means "brass, bronze; bronze chains, copper." **(1)** This word refers to the metal ore usually translated brass: "A land wherein thou shalt eat bread without scarceness, thou shalt not lack any thing in it; a land whose stones are iron, and out of whose hills thou mayest dig brass" (Deut 8:9). **(1b)** The word can also represent the refined ore: "And Zillah, she also bare Tubal-cain, an instructor of every artificer in brass and iron" (Gen 4:22). **(1c)** Copper ore rarely occurs in the earth in its pure state, hence, copper is a mixture in the earth of other metals; usually zinc, which is why the translation "brass" [a combination of zinc and copper]. **(2)** Inasmuch as it was a semiprecious metal, *nechosheth* is sometimes listed as a spoil of war (2 Sa 8:8). **(2a)** In such passages, it is difficult to know whether the reference is to copper or to copper mixed with tin (i.e., bronze). **(2b)** Certainly, "bronze" is intended in 1 Sa 17:5, where *nechosheth* refers to the material from which armor is made. **(2c)** Bronze is the material from which utensils (Lev 6:21), altars (Ex 38:30), and other objects were fashioned. **(2d)** This material could be polished (1 Kin 7:45) or shined (Ezra 8:27). **(2e)** This metal was less valuable than gold and more valuable than wood (Is 60:17).

(3) Still another meaning of *nechosheth* appears in Judg 16:21: "But the Philistines took [Samson], and put out his eyes, and brought him down to Gaza, and bound him with fetters of [bronze]; and he did grind in the prison house." Usually, when the word has this meaning it appears in the dual form (in the singular form only in Lam 3:7). **(4)** Deut 28:23 uses *nechosheth* to symbolize the cessation of life-giving rain and sunshine: "And thy heaven that is over thy head shall be [bronze], and the earth that is under thee shall be iron." See: TWOT—1349a, 1350a; BDB—638b, 639b, 1102d.

5179. נְחֻשְׁתָּא {1x} **Nᵉchushtâʾ,** *nekh-oosh-taw′;* from 5178; *copper; Nechushta,* an Israelitess:—Nehushta {1x}. See: BDB—639a.

5180. נְחֻשְׁתָּן {1x} **Nᵉchushtân,** *nekh-oosh-tawn′;* from 5178; something made of *copper,* i.e. the copper *serpent* of the desert:—Nehushtan {1x}. See: TWOT—1347b; BDB—639b.

5181. נָחַת {9x} **nâchath,** *naw-khath′;* a prim. root; to *sink,* i.e. *descend;* caus., to *press* or *lead* down:—broken {2x}, come down {2x}, enter {1x}, stick fast {1x}, settle {1x}, press sore {1x}, go down {1x. See: TWOT—1351; BDB—639b, 1102d.

5182. נְחַת {6x} **nᵉchâth** (Aram.), *nekh-ath′;* corresp. to 5181; to *descend;* caus., to *bring away, deposit, depose:*—come down {2x}, carry {1x}, place {1x}, laid up {1x}, deposed {1x}. See: TWOT—2859; BDB—1102d.

5183. נַחַת {8x} **nachath,** *nakh′-ath;* from 5182; a *descent,* i.e. imposition, unfavorable (*punishment*) or favorable (*food*); also (intr.; perh. from 5117), *restfulness:*—lighting down {1x}, quiet {1x}, quietness {1x}, to rest {4x}, be set on {1x}. See: TWOT—1323a, 1351a; BDB—629b, 639c.

5184. נַחַת {5x} **Nachath,** *nakh′-ath;* the same as 5183; *quiet; Nachath,* the name of an Edomite and of two Isr.:—Nahath {5x}. See: BDB—629b, 639c.

5185. נָחֵת {1x} **nâchêth,** *naw-khayth′;* from 5181; *descending:*—come down {1x}. See: TWOT—1351b; BDB—639c.

5186. נָטָה {215x} **nâṭâh,** *naw-taw′;* a prim. root; to *stretch* or spread out; by impl. to *bend* away (incl. mor. deflection); used in a great variety of application (as follows):—stretch out {60x}, incline {28x}, turn {16x}, stretch forth {15x}, turn aside {13x}, bow {8x}, decline {8x}, pitched {8x}, bow down {5x}, turn away {5x}, spread {5x}, stretched out still {4x}, pervert {4x}, stretch {4x}, extend {3x}, wrest {3x}, outstretched {3x}, carried aside {2x}, misc.

{20x} = + afternoon, apply, deliver, go down, be gone, intend, lay, let down, offer, overthrown, prolong, put away, shew, take (aside), cause to yield.

Natah means "to stretch forth, spread out, stretch down, turn aside." (1) *Natah* connotes "extending something outward and toward" something or someone. So God told Moses: "I will redeem you with a stretched out arm, and with great judgments" (Ex 6:6). (1a) This is a figure of God's active, sovereign, and mighty involvement in the affairs of men. (1b) So this phrase means "to stretch out" something until it reaches a goal. (2) The verb can also mean "to stretch out toward" but not to touch or reach anything. (2a) God told Moses to tell Aaron to take his staff in hand (cf. Ex 9:23) and "stretch it out." (2b) This act was to be done as a sign. (2c) The pointed staff was a visible sign that God's power was directly related to God's messengers: "Take thy rod, and stretch out thine hand upon the waters of Egypt, upon their streams, upon their rivers, and upon their ponds . . . ," over all the water in Egypt (Ex 7:19). (3) God "stretched out" (offered) 3 things to David (1 Chr 21:10); this is a related sense with the absence of anything physical being "stretched out."

(4) This verb may connote "stretch out" but not toward anything. When a shadow "stretches out," it lengthens. Hezekiah remarked: "It is a light thing for the shadow to go down ten degrees . . ." (2 Kin 20:10), to grow longer. (5) *Natah* may be used in this sense without an object and referring to a day. The Levite was asked to "comfort thine heart, I pray thee. And they tarried until afternoon [literally, the "stretching" (of the day, or of the shadows)]" (Judg 19:8). (6) "To stretch out" one's limbs full length is to recline: "And they lay themselves down upon clothes laid to pledge by every altar" (Amos 2:8). This is a figure of temple prostitution. (7) This verb may also mean "to extend" in every direction. (7a) It represents what one does in pitching a tent by unrolling the canvas (or skins sewn together) and "stretching it out." (7b) The end product is that the canvas is properly "spread out." Abram "pitched his tent, having Beth-el on the west, and Hai on the east" (Gen 12:8—the first appearance of the word). (8) This act and its result is used as a figure of God's creating the heavens: ". . . Which alone spreadeth out the heavens" (Job 9:8). (9) This verb also implies "stretching down toward" so as to reach something. Earlier in the Bible Rebekah was asked to "let down thy pitcher, . . . that I may drink" (Gen 24:14); she was asked to "stretch it down" into the water.

(10) This is the nuance when God is said to

have "inclined [stretched down] unto me, and heard my cry" (Ps 40:1). (11) Issachar is described as a donkey which "bowed his shoulder to bear [burdens]" (Gen 49:15). (12) In somewhat the same sense the heavens are bowed; the heavens are made to come closer to the earth. (12a) This is a figure of the presence of thick clouds: "He bowed the heavens also, and came down: and darkness was under his feet" (Ps 18:9). (12b) The somewhat new element here is that the heavens do not touch the speaker but only "stretch downward" toward him. (13) This verb may mean "to turn aside" in the sense of "to visit": "Judah went down from his brethren, and turned in to [visited] a certain Adullamite" (Gen 38:1). (14) Another special nuance appears in Num 22:23, where it means "to go off the way": "And the ass saw the angel of the Lord standing in the way . . . , and the ass turned aside out of the way." (15) Applied to human relationships, this may connote seduction: "With her much fair speech she caused him to yield" (Prov 7:21). See: TWOT—1352; BDB—639d. Syn.: 4294, 4295.

5187. נְטִיל {1x} n^etîyl, *net-eel';* from 5190; *laden:*—that bear {1x}. See: TWOT—1353b; BDB—642b.

5188. נְטִיפָה {2x} n^etîyphâh, *net-ee-faw';* from 5197; a *pendant* for the ears (espec. of pearls):—chain {1x}, collar {1x}. See: TWOT—1355c; BDB—643b.

5189. נְטִישָׁה {3x} n^etîyshâh, *net-ee-shaw';* from 5203; a *tendril* (as an offshoot):—battlements {1x}, branches {1x}, plant {1x}. See: TWOT—1357a; BDB—644a.

5190. נָטַל {4x} nâtal, *naw-tal';* a prim. root; to *lift;* by impl. to *impose:*—bare {1x}, hath borne {1x}, offer {1x}, taketh up {1x}. See: TWOT—1353; BDB—642a, 1102d.

5191. נְטַל {2x} n^etal (Aram.), *net-al';* corresp. to 5190; to *raise:*—lifted up {2x}. See: TWOT—2860; BDB—1102d.

5192. נֵטֶל {1x} nêtel, *nay'-tel;* from 5190; a *burden:*—weighty {1x}. See: TWOT—1353a; BDB—642b.

5193. נָטַע {58x} nâta^c, *naw-tah';* a prim. root; prop. to *strike* in, i.e. *fix;* spec. to *plant* (lit. or fig.):—fastened {1x}, plant {56x}, planters {1x}.

Nata^c means "to plant." (1) The word is used for the first time in the text in Gen 2:8: "And the Lord God planted a garden eastward in Eden." (2) The regular word for planting trees and vineyards, *nata^c* is used figuratively of planting people: "Yet I had planted thee [Judah] a noble vine . . ." (Jer 2:21). (3) This use is a close parallel to the famous "Song of the

Vineyard" (Is 5:1–10) where Israel and Judah are called God's "pleasant plant" (Is 5:7). **(4)** *Nata⁽* is used in Is 17:10 in an unusual description of idolatry: "Therefore shalt thou plant pleasant plants, and shalt set it with strange slips." **(5)** "To plant" sometimes has the meaning of "to establish." Thus, God promises in the latter days, "I will plant them upon their land" (Amos 9:15). See: TWOT—1354; BDB— 642b, 785c.

5194. נֶטַע {4x} **neta⁽**, *neh'-tah;* from 5193; a *plant;* collect. a *plantation;* abstr. a *planting:*—plant {4x}. See: TWOT—1354a; BDB—642c.

5195. נָטִיעַ {1x} **nâṭîyaʿ**, *naw-tee'-ah;* from 5193; a *plant:*—plants {1x}. See: TWOT—1354b; BDB—642d.

5196. נְטָעִים {1x} **Nᵉṭâʿîym**, *net-aw-eem';* plur. of 5194; *Netaim,* a place in Pal.:—among plants {1x}. See: BDB—642d.

5197. נָטַף {18x} **nâṭaph**, *naw-taf';* a prim. root; to *ooze,* i.e. *distil* gradually; by impl. to *fall in drops;* fig. to *speak* by inspiration:—drop {12x}, down {1x}, prophesy {4x}, prophet {1x}. See: TWOT—1355; BDB—642d.

5198. נָטָף {2x} **nâṭâph**, *naw-tawf';* from 5197; a *drop;* spec., an aromatic *gum* (prob. *stacte*):—drops {1x}, stacte {1x}. See: TWOT—1355a, 1355b; BDB—643a, 643b.

5199. נְטֹפָה {2x} **Nᵉṭôphâh**, *net-o-faw';* from 5197; *distillation; Netophah,* a place in Pal.:—Netophah {2x}. See: BDB—643b.

5200. נְטֹפָתִי {11x} **Nᵉṭôphâthîy**, *net-o-faw-thee';* patron. from 5199; a *Netophathite,* or inhab. of Netophah:—Netophathite {10x}, Netophathi {1x}. See: BDB—643b.

5201. נָטַר {9x} **nâṭar**, *naw-tar';* a prim. root; to *guard;* fig., to *cherish* (anger):— bear grudge {1x}, keep {4x}, keeper {2x}, reserve {2x}. See: TWOT—1356; BDB—643b, 1102d.

5202. נְטַר {1x} **nᵉṭar** (Aram.), *net-ar';* corresp. to 5201; to *retain:*—keep {1x}. See: TWOT—2861; BDB—1102d.

5203. נָטַשׁ {40x} **nâṭash**, *naw-tash';* a prim. root; prop. to *pound,* i.e. *smite;* by impl. (as if beating out, and thus expanding) to *disperse;* also, to *thrust* off, down, out or upon (incl. *reject, let alone, permit, remit,* etc.):—forsake {15x}, leave {12x}, spread {3x}, spread abroad {1x}, drawn {1x}, fall {1x}, joined {1x}, lie {1x}, loosed {1x}, cast off {1x}, misc. {3x} = stretch out, suffer. See: TWOT—1357; BDB—643c.

5204. נִי {1x} **nîy**, *nee;* doubtful word; appar. from 5091; *lamentation:*—wailing {1x}. See: TWOT—1311c; BDB—624d, 644b.

5205. נִיד {1x} **nîyd**, *need;* from 5110; *motion* (of the lips in speech):—moving {1x}. See: TWOT—1319b; BDB—627a, 644b.

5206. נִידָה {1x} **nîydâh**, *nee-daw';* fem. of 5205; *removal,* i.e. *exile:*—removed {1x}. See: TWOT—1302b; BDB—622c, 627b, 644b.

5207. נִיחוֹחַ {43x} **nîchôwach**, *nee-kho'-akh;* or

נִיחֹחַ **nîychôach**, *nee-kho'-akh;* from 5117; prop. *restful,* i.e. *pleasant;* abstr. *delight:*—sweet {42x}, sweet odours {1x}. See: TWOT—1323c; BDB—629b, 644b, 1102d.

5208. נִיחוֹחַ {2x} **nîychôwach** (Aram.), *nee-kho'-akh;* or (short.)

נִיחֹחַ **nîychôach** (Aram.), *nee-kho'-akh;* corresp. to 5207; *pleasure:*—sweet odours {1x}, sweet odours {1x}. See: TWOT—2862; BDB—1102d.

5209. נִין {3x} **nîyn**, *neen;* from 5125; *progeny:*—son {3x}. See: TWOT—1326a; BDB—630c, 644b.

5210. נִינְוֵה {17x} **Nîynᵉvêh**, *nee-nev-ay';* of for. or.; *Nineveh,* the capital of Assyria:—Nineveh {17x}. See: BDB—644b.

5211. נִיס {1x} **nîyç**, *neece;* from 5127; *fugitive:*—that fleeth {1x}. See: TWOT—1327; BDB—630d.

5212. נִיסָן {2x} **Nîyçân**, *nee-sawn';* prob. of for. or.; *Nisan,* the first month of the Jewish sacred year:—Nisan {2x}. See: TWOT—1359; BDB—644c.

5213. נִיצוֹץ {1x} **nîytsôwts**, *nee-tsotes';* from 5340; a *spark:*—spark {1x}. See: TWOT—1405a; BDB—665b.

5214. נִיר {2x} **nîyr**, *neer;* a root prob. ident. with that of 5216, through the idea of the *gleam* of a fresh furrow; to *till* the soil:— break up {2x}. See: TWOT—1360; BDB—644c.

5215. נִיר {4x} **nîyr**, *neer;* or

נִר **nîr**, *neer;* from 5214; prop. *plowing,* i.e. (concr.) freshly *plowed* land:— fallow ground {2x}, ploughing {1x}, tillage {1x}. See: TWOT—1360a; BDB—644c, 669c.

5216. נִיר {48x} **nîyr**, *neer* or

נִר **nîr**, *neer;* also

נֵיר **nêyr**, *nare;* or

נֵר **nêr**, *nare;* or (fem.)

נֵרָה **nêrâh**, *nay-raw';* from a prim. root [see 5214; 5135] prop. mean. to

glisten; a *lamp* (i.e. the burner) or *light* (lit. or fig.):—candle {9x}, lamp {35x}, light {4x}. See: TWOT—1333b; BDB—632d, 633a, 644c, 669c, 1102c.

5217. **נָבָא** {1x} **nâkâ**, *naw-kaw';* a prim. root; to *smite,* i.e. *drive* away:—be viler {1x}. See: TWOT—1362; BDB—644d.

5218. **נָכֵא** {4x} **nâkê**, *naw-kay';* or

נָכָא **nâkâ**, *naw-kaw';* from 5217; *smitten,* i.e. (fig.) *afflicted:*—broken {2x}, stricken {1x}, wounded {1x}. See: TWOT—1362a, 1362b; BDB—644d.

5219. **נְכֹאת** {2x} **n°kô'th**, *nek-ohth';* from 5218; prop. a *smiting,* i.e. (concr.) an aromatic *gum* [perh. *styrax*] (as *powdered*):—spicery {1x}, spices {1x}. See: TWOT—1362c; BDB—644d.

5220. **נֶכֶד** {3x} **neked**, *neh'-ked;* from an unused root mean. to *propagate; offspring:*—nephew {2x}, son's son {1x}. See: TWOT—1363a; BDB—645a.

5221. **נָכָה** {500x} **nâkâh**, *naw-kaw';* a prim. root; to *strike* (lightly or severely, lit. or fig.):—smite {348x}, slay {92x}, kill {20x}, beat {9x}, slaughter {5x}, stricken {3x}, given {3x}, wounded {3x}, strike {2x}, stripes {2x}, misc. {13x} = cast forth, clap, × go forward, × indeed, murderer, punish, × surely. See: TWOT—1364; BDB—645a.

5222. **נָכֶה** {1x} **nêkeh**, *nay-keh';* from 5221; a *smiter,* i.e. (fig.) *traducer:*—abjects {1x}. See: TWOT—1364b; BDB—646d.

5223. **נָכֶה** {3x} **nâkeh**, *naw-keh'; smitten,* i.e. (lit.) *maimed,* or (fig.) *dejected:*—contrite {1x}, lame {2x}. See: TWOT—1364a; BDB—646d.

5224. **נְכוֹ** {3x} **N°kôw**, *nek-o';* prob. of Eg. or.; *Neko,* an Eg. king:—Necho {3x}. See: BDB—647a. comp. 6549.

5225. **נָכוֹן** {1x} **Nâkôwn**, *naw-kone';* from 3559; *prepared; Nakon,* prob. an Isr.:—Nachon {1x}. See: BDB—467d, 647a.

5226. **נֵכַח** {2x} **nêkach**, *nay'-kakh;* from an unused root mean. to *be straightforward;* prop. the *fore* part; used adv., *opposite:*—before {1x}, over against {1x}. See: TWOT—1365a; BDB—647b.

5227. **נֹכַח** {23x} **nôkach**, *no'-kakh;* from the same as 5226; prop., the *front* part; used adv. (espec. with prep.), *opposite, in front of, forward, in behalf of:*—against {10x}, before {9x}, directly {1x}, for {1x}, on {1x}, over {1x}. See: TWOT—1365a; BDB—647b.

5228. **נָכֹחַ** {4x} **nâkôach**, *naw-ko'-akh;* from the same as 5226; *straightforward,*

i.e. (fig.), *equitable, correct,* or (abstr.), *integrity:*—plain {1x}, right {2x}, uprightness {1x}. See: TWOT—1365a; BDB—647c.

5229. **נְכֹחָה** {4x} **n°kôchâh**, *nek-o-khaw';* fem. of 5228; prop. *straightforwardness,* i.e. (fig.) *integrity,* or (concr.) a *truth:*—equity {1x}, right {1x}, right things {1x}, uprightness {1x}. See: TWOT—1365a; BDB—647c.

5230. **נָכַל** {4x} **nâkal**, *naw-kal';* a prim. root; to *defraud,* i.e. *act treacherously:*—beguile {1x}, conspire {1x}, deceiver {1x}, deal subtilly {1x}. See: TWOT—1366; BDB—647c.

5231. **נֵכֶל** {1x} **nêkel**, *nay'-kel;* from 5230; *deceit:*—wiles {1x}. See: TWOT—1366a; BDB—647d.

5232. **נְכַס** {2x} **n°kaç** (Aram.), *nek-as';* corresp. to 5233:—goods {2x}. See: TWOT—2863; BDB—1103a.

5233. **נֶכֶס** {5x} **nekeç**, *neh'-kes;* from an unused root mean. to *accumulate; treasure:*—riches {1x}, wealth {4x}. See: TWOT—1367; BDB—647d, 1103a.

5234. **נָכַר** {50x} **nâkar**, *naw-kar';* a prim. root; prop. to *scrutinize,* i.e. look intently at; hence (with *recognition* impl.), to *acknowledge, be acquainted with, care for, respect, revere,* or (with *suspicion* impl.), to *disregard, ignore, be strange* toward, *reject, resign, dissimulate* (as if ignorant or disowning):—know {16x}, acknowledge {7x}, discern {6x}, respect {4x}, knowledge {2x}, known {2x}, feign to another {2x}, misc. {11x} = × could, deliver, dissemble, estrange, perceive, regard, behave (make) self strange (-ly).

Nakar means "to know, regard, recognize, pay attention to, be acquainted with." **(1)** The first time is in Gen 27:23: ". . . he discerned him not." **(2)** The basic meaning of the term is a physical apprehension, whether through sight, touch, or hearing. **(2a)** Darkness sometimes makes recognition impossible (Ruth 3:14). **(2b)** People are often "recognized" by their voices (Judg 18:3). **(3)** *Nakar* sometimes has the meaning "pay attention to," a special kind of recognition: "Blessed be the man who took knowledge of you" (Ruth 2:19). **(4)** This verb can mean "to be acquainted with," a kind of intellectual awareness: ". . . neither shall his place know him any more" (Job 7:10; cf. Ps 103:16). **(5)** The sense of "to distinguish" is seen in Ezra 3:13: "The people could not discern the noise of the shout of joy from the noise of the weeping of the people." Syn: 1847, 3045, 4069. See: TWOT—1368; BDB—647d, 649a.

5235. נֶכֶר {2x} **neker**, *neh'-ker;* or

נֹכֶר **nôker**, *no'-ker;* from 5234; something *strange*, i.e. unexpected *calamity:*—strange {1x}, stranger {1x}. See: TWOT—1368a; BDB—648c.

5236. נֵכָר {35x} **nêkâr**, *nay-kawr';* from 5234; *foreign*, or (concr.) a *foreigner*, or (abstr.) *heathendom:*—strange {17x}, stranger + 1121 {10x}, stranger {7x}, alien {1x}. See: TWOT—1368b; BDB—648c.

5237. נָכְרִי {45x} **nokrîy**, *nok-ree';* from 5235 (second form); *strange*, in a variety of degrees and applications (*foreign, non-relative, adulterous, different, wonderful*):—stranger {18x}, strange {17x}, alien {4x}, strange woman {3x}, foreigner {2x}, outlandish {1x}, stranger + 376 {1x}. See: TWOT—1368c; BDB—648d.

5238. נְכֹת {2x} **nᵉkôth**, *nek-ōth';* prob. for 5219; *spicery*, i.e. (gen.) *valuables:*—precious things {2x}. See: TWOT—1369; BDB—649b.

5239. נָלָה {1x} **nâlâh**, *naw-law';* appar. a prim. root; to *complete:*—make an end {1x}. See: TWOT—1370; BDB—649b.

5240. נִמְבְזֶה {1x} **nᵉmibzeh**, *nem-ib-zeh';* from 959, *despised:*—vile {1x}. See: TWOT—224; BDB—102c, 649c.

5241. נְמוּאֵל {3x} **Nᵉmûw'êl**, *nem-oo-ale';* appar. for 3223; *Nemuel*, the name of two Isr.:—Nemuel {3x}. See: BDB—649c.

5242. נְמוּאֵלִי {1x} **Nᵉmûw'êlîy**, *nem-oo-ay-lee';* from 5241; a *Nemuelite*, or desc. of Nemuel:—Nemuelite {1x}. See: BDB—649c, 974b.

5243. נָמֵל {5x} **nâmal**, *naw-mal';* a prim. root; to *become clipped* or (spec.) *circumcised:*—(branch to) be cut down {1x}, cut off {2x}, circumcised {1x}. See: TWOT—1161; BDB—576c, 576d.

5244. נְמָלָה {2x} **nᵉmâlâh**, *nem-aw-law';* fem. from 5243; an *ant* (prob. from its almost *bisected* form):—ant {2x}. See: TWOT—1371a; BDB—649c.

5245. נְמַר {1x} **nᵉmar** (Aram.), *nem-ar';* corresp. to 5246:—leopard {1x}. See: TWOT—2864; BDB—1103a.

5246. נָמֵר {6x} **nâmêr**, *naw-mare';* from an unused root mean. prop. to *filtrate*, i.e. *be limpid* [comp 5247 and 5249]; and thus to *spot* or *stain* as if by dripping; a *leopard* (from its stripes):—leopard {6x}. See: TWOT—1372a; BDB—649d, 1103a.

נִמְרֹד **Nimrôd**. See 5248.

5247. נִמְרָה {1x} **Nimrâh**, *nim-raw';* from the same as 5246; *clear* water; *Nimrah*, a place E. of the Jordan:—Nimrah {1x}. See: BDB—649d. See also 1039, 5249.

5248. נִמְרוֹד {4x} **Nimrôwd**, *nim-rode';* or

נִמְרֹד **Nimrôd**, *nim-rode';* prob. of for. or.; *Nimrod*, a son of Cush:—Nimrod {4x}. See: BDB—650a.

5249. נִמְרִים {2x} **Nimrîym**, *nim-reem';* plur. of a masc. corresp. to 5247; *clear* waters; *Nimrim*, a place E. of the Jordan:—Nimrim {2x}. See: BDB—649d. comp. 1039.

5250. נִמְשִׁי {5x} **Nimshîy**, *nim-shee';* prob. from 4871; *extricated; Nimshi*, the (grand-) father of Jehu:—Nimshi {5x}. See: BDB—650a.

5251. נֵס {20x} **nêç**, *nace;* from 5264; a *flag;* also a *sail;* by impl. a *flagstaff;* gen. a *signal;* fig. a *token:*—banner {2x}, sign {1x}, pole {2x}, sail {2x}, ensign {6x}, standard {7x}. See: TWOT—1379a; BDB—650a, 651d.

5252. נְסִבָּה {1x} **nᵉçibbâh**, *nes-ib-baw';* fem. pass. part. of 5437; prop. an *environment*, i.e. *circumstance* or *turn* of affairs:—cause {1x}.

Necibbah is found in 2 Chr 10:15 and is translated "cause" and means "turn of events: "So the king hearkened not unto the people: for the cause [*necibbah*] was of God, that the LORD might perform his word, which he spake by the hand of Ahijah the Shilonite to Jeroboam the son of Nebat." See: TWOT—1456a; BDB—650a, 687c.

5253. נָסַג {9x} **nâçag**, *naw-sag';* a prim. root; to *retreat:*—departing away {1x}, remove {5x}, take {1x}, take hold {1x}, turn away {1x}. See: TWOT—1469; BDB—690d.

נָסָה **nᵉçâh**. See 5375.

5254. נָסָה {36x} **nâçâh**, *naw-saw';* a prim. root; to *test;* by impl. to *attempt:*—adventure {1x}, assay {2x}, prove {20x}, tempt {12x}, try {1x}. See: TWOT—1373; BDB—650a.

5255. נָסַח {4x} **nâçach**, *naw-sakh';* a prim. root; to *tear* away:—destroy {1x}, pluck {2x}, root {1x}. See: TWOT—1373; BDB—650c, 1103a.

5256. נְסַח {1x} **nᵉçach** (Aram.), *nes-akh';* corresp. to 5255:—pulled down {1x}. See: TWOT—2865; BDB—1103a.

5257. נְסִיךְ {6x} **nᵉçîyk**, *nes-eek';* from 5258; prop. something *poured* out, i.e. a *libation;* also a molten *image;* by impl. a *prince* (as *anointed*):—drink offering {1x}, duke {1x}, prince {3x}, principal {1x}. See: TWOT—1375b, 1377a; BDB—651a, 651c.

5258. נָסַךְ {25x} **nâçak**, *naw-sak';* a prim. root; to *pour* out, espec. a libation, or to *cast* (metal); by anal. to *anoint* a king:— cover {3x}, melteth {1x}, molten {1x}, offer {2x}, pour {4x}, cause to pour out {12x}, set {1x}, set up {1x}. See: TWOT—1375, 1377; BDB—650c, 651c, 1103a.

5259. נָסַךְ {1x} **nâçak**, *naw-sak';* a prim. root [prob. ident. with 5258 through the idea of fusion]; to *interweave,* i.e. (fig.) to *overspread:*—that is spread {1x}. See: TWOT—1376; BDB—651b.

5260. נְסַךְ {1x} **n°çak** (Aram.), *nes-ak';* corresp. to 5258; to *pour* out a libation:—offer {1x}. See: TWOT—2866; BDB—1103a.

5261. נְסַךְ {1x} **n°çak** (Aram.), *nes-ak';* corresp. to 5262; a *libation:*—drink offering {1x}. See: TWOT—2866a; BDB—1103a.

5262. נֶסֶךְ {64x} **neçek**, *neh'-sek;* or

נֵסֶךְ **nêçek**, *nay'-sek;* from 5258; a *libation;* also a *cast idol:*—cover {1x}, drink offering {59x}, molten image {4x}. See: TWOT—1375a; BDB—651a, 1103a.

נִסְמָן **niçmân**. See 5567.

5263. נָסַס {1x} **nâçaç**, *naw-sas';* a prim. root; to *wane,* i.e. *be sick:*—standardbearer {1x}. See: TWOT—1378; BDB—651c.

5264. נָסַס {1x} **nâçaç**, *naw-sas';* a prim. root; to *gleam* from afar, i.e. to *be conspicuous* as a signal; or rather perh. a denom. from 5251 [and ident. with 5263, through the idea of a flag as *fluttering* in the wind]; to *raise a beacon:*—lift up as an ensign {1x}. See: TWOT—1379; BDB—651c.

5265. נָסַע {146x} **nâça'**, *naw-sah';* a prim. root; prop. to *pull* up, espec. the tent-pins, i.e. *start* on a journey:—journey {41x}, departed {30x}, remove {28x}, forward {18x}, went {8x}, go away {3x}, brought {3x}, set forth {2x}, go forth {3x}, get {1x}, set aside {1x}, misc. {8x} = cause to blow, march, × still, be on his (go their) way.

Naca' means to journey, depart, set out, march. **(1)** It is probably the most common term in the Old Testament referring to the movement of clans and tribes. Indeed, the word is used almost 90 times in the Book of Numbers alone, since this book records the "journeying" of the people of Israel from Sinai to Canaan. **(2)** It occurs for the first time in Gen 11:2, where *naca'* refers to the "migration" of people to the area of Babylon: "And it came to pass, as they journeyed from the east, that they found a plain in the land of Shinar; and they dwelt

there." **(3)** This word has the basic meaning of "pulling up" tent pegs (Is 33:20) in preparation for "moving" one's tent and property to another place; thus it lends itself naturally to the general term of "traveling" or "journeying": "Look upon Zion, the city of our solemnities: thine eyes shall see Jerusalem a quiet habitation, a tabernacle that shall not be taken down; not one of the stakes thereof shall ever be removed, neither shall any of the cords thereof be broken."

(4) Samson is said to have "pulled up" **(4a)** the city gate and posts (Judg 16:3), as well as **(4b)** the pin on the weaver's loom: "And she fastened it with the pin, and said unto him, The Philistines be upon thee, Samson. And he awaked out of his sleep, and went away with the pin of the beam, and with the web" (Judg 16:14). **(4)** *Naca'* describes the movement of the angel of God and the pillar of cloud as they came between Israel and the pursuing Egyptians at the Red Sea (Ex 14:19). **(5)** *Naca'* lends itself to a wide range of renderings, depending upon the context. See: TWOT—1380; BDB—652a.

5266. נָסַק {1x} **nâçaq**, *naw-sak';* a prim. root; to *go* up:—ascend {1x}. See: TWOT—1511; BDB—652d, 701c.

5267. נְסַק {3x} **n°çaq** (Aram.), *nes-ak';* corresp. to 5266:—take up {3x}. See: TWOT—2889; BDB—1103a, 1104b.

5268. נִסְרֹךְ {2x} **Niçrôk**, *nis-roke';* of for. or.; *Nisrok,* a Bab. idol:—Nisroch {2x}. See: TWOT—1382; BDB—652d.

5269. נֵעָה {1x} **Nê'âh**, *nay-aw';* from 5128; *motion; Neäh,* a place in Pal.:—Neah {1x}. See: TWOT—1382; BDB—631c, 652d.

5270. נֹעָה {4x} **Nô'âh**, *no-aw';* from 5128; *movement; Noah,* an Israelitess:—Noah {4x}. See: TWOT—1382; BDB—631c, 652d.

5271. נָעוּר {47x} **nâ'ûwr**, *naw-oor';* or

נָעֻר **nâ'ûr**, *naw-oor';* and (fem.)

נְעֻרָה **n°'ûrâh**, *neh-oo-raw';* prop. pass. part. from 5288 as denom.; (only in plur. collect. or emphat.) *youth,* the state (*juvenility*) or the persons (*young* people):—childhood {1x}, youth {46x}. See: TWOT—1389d, 1389e; BDB—655b, 655c.

5272. נְעִיאֵל {1x} **N°'îy°êl**, *neh-ee-ale';* from 5128 and 410; *moved of God; Neiel,* a place in Pal.:—Neiel {1x}. See: BDB—653a.

5273. נָעִים {13x} **nâ'îym**, *naw-eem';* from 5276; *delightful* (obj. or subj., lit.

Hebrew

or fig.):—pleasant {8x}, pleasures {2x}, sweet {2x}, sweet thing {1x}. See: TWOT—1384b, 1385a; BDB—653d, 654b.

5274. נָעַל {8x} **nâ‘al**, *naw-al'*; a prim. root; prop. to *fasten* up, i.e. with a bar or cord; hence, (denom. from 5275), to *sandal*, i.e. furnish with slippers:—bolt {2x}, inclosed {1x}, lock {2x}, shoe {2x}, shut up {1x}. See: TWOT—1383, 1383b; BDB—653a, 653b.

5275. נַעַל {22x} **na‘al**, *nah'-al;* or (fem.)

נַעֲלָה **na‘ălâh**, *nah-al-aw';* from 5274; prop. a sandal *tongue;* by extens. a *sandal* or slipper (sometimes as a symbol of occupancy, a refusal to marry, or of something valueless):—shoe {20x}, dryshod {1x}, shoelatchet + 8288 {1x}. See: TWOT—1383a; BDB—653a.

5276. נָעֵם {8x} **nâ‘êm**, *naw-ame';* a prim. root; to *be agreeable* (lit. or fig.):—pass in beauty {1x}, be delight {1x}, be pleasant {5x}, be sweet {1x}. See: TWOT—1384; BDB—653c.

5277. נַעַם {1x} **Na‘am**, *nah'-am;* from 5276; *pleasure; Naam*, an Isr.:—Naam {1x}. See: BDB—653d.

5278. נֹעַם {7x} **no‘am**, *no'-am;* from 5276; *agreeableness*, i.e. *delight, suitableness, splendor* or *grace:*—beauty {4x}, pleasant {2x}, pleasantness {1x}. See: TWOT—1384a; BDB—653c.

5279. נַעֲמָה {5x} **Na‘ămâh**, *nah-am-aw';* fem. of 5277; *pleasantness; Naamah*, the name of an antediluvian woman, of an Ammonitess, and of a place in Pal.:—Naamah {5x}. See: BDB—653d, 654a.

5280. נַעֲמִי {1x} **Na‘âmîy**, *nah-am-ee';* patron. from 5283; a *Naamanite*, or desc. of Naaman (collect.):—Naamites {1x}. See: BDB—654a, 654b.

5281. נָעֳמִי {21x} **No‘ŏmîy**, *no-ŏm-ee';* from 5278; *pleasant; Noomi*, an Israelitess:—Naomi {21x}. See: BDB—654a.

5282. נַעֲמָן {1x} **na‘ămân**, *nah-am-awn';* from 5276; *pleasantness* (plur. as concr.):—pleasant {1x}. See: TWOT—1384c; BDB—654a.

5283. נַעֲמָן {16x} **Na‘ămân**, *nah-am-awn';* the same as 5282; *Naaman*, the name of an Isr. and of a Damascene:—Naaman {16x}. See: BDB—654a.

5284. נַעֲמָתִי {4x} **Na‘ămâthîy**, *nah-am-aw-thee';* patrial from a place corresp. in name (but not ident.) with 5279; a *Naamathite*, or inhab. of Naamah:—Naamathite {4x}. See: BDB—654b.

5285. נַעֲצוּץ {2x} **na‘ătsûwts**, *nah-ats-oots';* from an unused root mean. to *prick;* prob. a *brier;* by impl. a *thicket* of thorny bushes:—thorn {2x}. See: TWOT—1386a; BDB—654c.

5286. נָעַר {1x} **nâ‘ar**, *naw-ar';* a prim. root; to *growl:*—yell {1x}. See: TWOT—1387; BDB—654c.

5287. נָעַר {4x} **nâ‘ar**, *naw-ar';* a prim. root [prob. ident. with 5286, through the idea of the *rustling* of mane, which usually accompanies the lion's roar]; to *tumble* about:—shake {4x}, shake out {3x}, overthrow {2x}, toss to and fro {1x}, shake off {1x}. See: TWOT—1388; BDB—654c.

5288. נַעַר {238x} **na‘ar**, *nah'-ar;* from 5287; (concr.) a *boy* (as act.), from the age of infancy to adolescence; by impl. a *servant;* also (by interch. of sex), a *girl* (of similar latitude in age):—young man {76x}, servant {54x}, child {44x}, lad {33x}, young {15x}, children {7x}, youth {6x}, babe {1x}, boys {1x}, young {1x}.

Na‘ar means "youth; lad; young man." **(1)** The root with the meaning of "youth" occurs only as a noun and occurs in Hebrew in the feminine (5291 - *na'arah*, "young girl") as well as the masculine form (e.g., Gen 24:14). **(1a)** *Na‘ar* occurs 235 times in the Hebrew Old Testament. **(1b)** The first occurrence is in Gen 14:23–24: "I will not take any thing . . . save only that which the young men have eaten, and the portion of the men which went with me, Aner, Eshcol, and Mamre; let them take their portion." **(3)** The basic meaning of *na‘ar* is "youth," over against an older man. **(3a)** At times it may signify a very young child: "For before the child shall know to refuse the evil, and choose the good, the land that thou abhorrest shall be forsaken of both her kings" (Is 7:16). **(4)** Generally *na‘ar* denotes a "young man" who is of marriageable age but is still a bachelor. **(4a)** When Jeremiah said: "Ah, Lord God! behold, I cannot speak: for I am a child" (Jer 1:6), he was not referring to his chronological age, but his inexperience as a spokesman for God. **(4b)** Absalom was considered a *na'ar,* even though he was old enough to lead the troups in rebellion against David: "And the king commanded Joab and Abishai and Ittai, saying, Deal gently for my sake with the young man, even with Absalom" (2 Sa 18:5).

(4c) A derived meaning of *na‘ar* is "servant." Jonathan used a "servant" as armorbearer: "Now it came to pass upon a day, that Jonathan the son of Saul said unto the young man that bare his armor, Come, and let us go over to the Philistines' garrison, that is on the other side" (1 Sa 14:1). **(4c)** The *na‘ar* ("servant") addressed

his employer as "master": "And when they were by Jebus, the day was far spent; and the servant said unto his master, Come, I pray thee, and let us turn into this city of the Jebusites, and lodge in it" (Judg 19:11). **(4d)** Kings and officials had "servants" who were referred to by the title *na'ar.* In this context the word is better translated as "attendant," as in the case of the attendants of King Ahasuerus, who gave counsel to the king: "Then said the king's servants that ministered unto him, Let there be fair young virgins sought for the king" (Est 2:2). **(4e)** When a *na'ar* is commissioned to carry messages, he is a "messenger." **(4f)** Thus, we see that the meaning of the word *na'ar* as "servant" does not denote a "slave" or a performer of low duties. **(4g)** He carried important documents, was trained in the art of warfare, and even gave counsel to the king. See: TWOT—1389a; BDB—654d.

5289. נַעַר {1x} **na'ar,** *nah'-ar;* from 5287 in its der. sense of *tossing* about; a *wanderer:*—young one {1x}. See: TWOT—1388a; BDB—654d.

5290. נֹעַר {4x} **nô'ar,** *no'-ar;* from 5287; (abstr.) *boyhood* [comp. 5288]:—child {2x}, youth {2x}.

Another noun *no'ar* means "youth." This noun appears only 4 times in the Bible, once in Ps 88:15: "I am afflicted and ready to die from my youth up: while I suffer thy terrors I am distracted" (cf. Job 36:14). See: TWOT—1389b; BDB—655a.

נָעוּר **nâ'ûr.** See 5271.

5291. נַעֲרָה {62x} **na'ărâh,** *nah-ar-aw';* fem. of 5288; a *girl* (from infancy to adolescence):—damsel {34x}, maid {7x}, maiden {16x}, young {4x}, young woman {1x}. See: TWOT—1389c; BDB—655a.

5292. נַעֲרָה {4x} **Na'ărâh,** *nah-ar-aw';* the same as 5291; *Naarah,* the name of an Israelitess, and of a place in Pal.:—Naarah {3x}, Naarath {1x}. See: BDB—655c.

נְעֻרָה **n°'ûrâh.** See 5271.

5293. נַעֲרַי {1x} **Na'ăray,** *nah-ar-ah'-ee;* from 5288; *youthful; Naarai,* an Isr.:—Naarai {1x}. See: BDB—655c.

5294. נְעַרְיָה {3x} **N°'aryâh,** *neh-ar-yaw';* from 5288 and 3050; *servant of Jah; Nearjah,* the name of two Isr.:—Neariah {3x}. See: BDB—655d.

5295. נַעֲרָן {1x} **Na'ărân,** *nah-ar-awn';* from 5288; *juvenile; Naaran,* a place in Pal.:—Naaran {1x}. See: BDB—655d.

5296. נְעֹרֶת {2x} **n°'ôreth,** *neh-o'-reth;* from 5287; something *shaken* out, i.e.

tow (as the refuse of flax):—tow {2x}. See: TWOT—1388b; BDB—654d.

נַעֲרָתָה **Na'ărâthâh.** See 5292.

5297. נֹף {7x} **Nôph,** *nofe;* a var. of 4644; *Noph,* the capital of Upper Egypt:—Noph {7x}. See: BDB—592a, 655d.

5298. נֶפֶג {4x} **Nepheg,** *neh'-feg;* from an unused root prob. mean. to *spring* forth; a *sprout; Nepheg,* the name of two Isr.:—Nepheg {4x}. See: BDB—655d.

5299. נָפָה {4x} **nâphâh,** *naw-faw';* from 5130 in the sense of *lifting;* a *height;* also a *sieve:*—border {1x}, coast {1x}, region {1x}, sieve {1x}. See: TWOT—1331b, 1330a; BDB—190b, 632b, 632c, 655d.

5300. נְפוּשְׁסִים {2x} **N°phûwsh°çîym,** *nef-oo-shes-eem';* for 5304; *Nephushesim,* a temple-servant:—Nephisesim {1x}, Nephusim {1x}. See: BDB—655d, 656b, 656c.

5301. נָפַח {12x} **nâphach,** *naw-fakh';* a prim. root; to *puff,* in various applications (lit., to *inflate, blow hard, scatter, kindle, expire;* fig., to *disesteem*):—blow {4x}, blown {1x}, breathe {2x}, give up {1x}, cause to lose [life]{1x}, seething {2x}, snuff {1x}. See: TWOT—1390; BDB—655d.

5302. נֹפַח {1x} **Nôphach,** *no'-fakh;* from 5301; a *gust; Nophach,* a place in Moab:—Nophah {1x}. See: BDB—656a.

5303. נְפִיל {3x} **n°phîyl,** *nef-eel';* or

נְפִל **n°phil,** *nef-eel';* from 5307; prop., a *feller,* i.e. a *bully* or *tyrant:*—giant {3x}. See: TWOT—1393a; BDB—658c.

5304. נְפִיסִים {2x} **N°phîyçîym,** *nef-ee-seem';* plur. from an unused root mean. See 5300. to *scatter; expansions; Nephisim,* a temple-servant:—Nephusim {2x}. See: BDB—656b.

5305. נָפִישׁ {3x} **Nâphîysh,** *naw-feesh';* from 5314; *refreshed; Naphish,* a son of Ishmael, and his posterity:—Naphish {3x}. See: BDB—661c.

5306. נֹפֶךְ {4x} **nôphek,** *no'-fek;* from an unused root mean. to *glisten; shining;* a gem, prob. the *garnet:*—emerald {4x}. See: TWOT—1391; BDB—656c.

5307. נָפַל {434x} **nâphal,** *naw-fal';* a prim. root; to *fall,* in a great variety of applications (intr. or caus., lit. or fig.):—fall {318x}, fall down {25x}, cast {18x}, cast down {9x}, fall away {5x}, divide {5x}, overthrow {5x}, present {5x}, lay {3x}, rot {3x}, accepted {2x}, lie down {2x}, inferior {2x}, lighted {2x}, lost {2x}, misc. {22x} = cease, die, (let) fail, fell (-ing), fugitive, have [inheritance], be judged,

lying, overwhelm, perish, slay, smite out, ✕ surely, throw down. See: TWOT—1392; BDB—656c, 1103a.

5308. נְפַל {11x} n°phal (Aram.), nef-al'; corresp. to 5307:—fall down {7x}, fall {3x}, have occasion {1x}. See: TWOT—2867; BDB—1103a.

5309. נֶפֶל {3x} nephel, neh'-fel; or

נֵפֶל nêphel, nay'-fel; from 5307; something fallen, i.e. an abortion:—untimely birth {3x}. See: TWOT—1392a; BDB—658b.

נְפִל n°phîl. See 5303.

5310. נָפַץ {22x} nâphats, naw-fats'; a prim. root; to dash to pieces, or scatter:—break in pieces {9x}, scatter {3x}, break {3x}, dash {2x}, discharged {1x}, dispersed {1x}, overspread {1x}, dash in pieces {1x}, sunder {1x}. See: TWOT—1394; BDB—658c, 659a.

5311. נֶפֶץ {1x} nephets, neh'-fets; from 5310; a storm (as dispersing):—scattering {1x}. See: TWOT—1394a; BDB—658d.

5312. נְפַק {11x} n°phaq (Aram.), nef-ak'; a prim. root; to issue; caus. to bring out:—take out {4x}, come forth {4x}, go forth {2x}, take forth {1x}. See: TWOT—2868; BDB—1103b.

5313. נִפְקָא {2x} niphqâ' (Aram.), nif-kaw'; from 5312; an outgo, i.e. expense:—expense {2x}. See: TWOT—2868a; BDB—1103b.

5314. נָפַשׁ {3x} nâphash, naw-fash'; a prim. root; to breathe; pass., to be breathed upon, i.e. (fig.) refreshed (as if by a current of air):—refreshed {2x}, refreshed themselves {1x}.

Napash means "to breathe; respire; be refreshed." This verb appears 3 times in the Old Testament (Ex 23:12; 31:17). The other appearance is in 2 Sa 16:14: "And the king, and all the people that were with him, came weary and refreshed themselves there." See: TWOT—1395; BDB—661c.

5315. נֶפֶשׁ {753x} nephesh, neh'-fesh; from 5314; prop. a breathing creature, i.e. animal of (abstr.) vitality; used very widely in a lit., accommodated or fig. sense (bodily or ment.):—soul {475x}, life {117x}, person {29x}, mind {15x}, heart {15x}, creature {9x}, body {8x}, himself {8x}, yourselves {6x}, dead {5x}, will {4x}, desire {4x}, man {3x}, themselves {3x}, any {3x}, appetite {2x}, misc. {47x} = beast, breath, ✕ [dis-] contented, ✕ fish, ghost, + greedy, he, lust, me, mortally, one, own, pleasure, + slay, + tablet, they, thing, ✕ would have it.

Nephesh means soul; self; life; person; heart. (1) The basic meaning comes from its verbal form, naphash (5314), which refers to the essence of life, the act of breathing, taking breath (Gen 2:7). From this many abstract meanings were developed. (1a) In its primary sense the noun appears in its first occurrence in Gen 1:20: "the moving creature that hath life," and (1b) in its second occurrence in Gen 2:7: "living soul." (1c) The best biblical definition is found in Ps 103:1 where nephesh is defined as "all that is within" a person: "Bless the LORD, O my soul: and all that is within me, bless his holy name." (2) It is translated "soul" which makes sense in most passages. All other English translations, in the particular context, are stressing some aspect of the soul. (3) The Hebrew system of thought does not include the opposition of the terms "body" and "soul," which are really Greek and Latin in origin. (3a) The Hebrew compares/contrasts "the inner self" and "the outer appearance" or, as viewed in a different context, "what one is to oneself" as opposed to "what one appears to be to one's observers."

(3b) The goal of the Scriptures is to make the inner and the outer consistent. (3c) The inner person is nephesh, while the outer person, or reputation, is shem (8034), most commonly translated "name." (4) In narrative or historical passages of the Old Testament, nephesh is translated as "soul." as (4a) in Lev 17:11: "For the life of the flesh is in the blood: and I have given it to you upon the altar to make an atonement for your souls: for it is the blood that maketh an atonement for the soul." (4b) The soul of man, that immaterial part, which moves into the after life [the body is buried and decomposes] needs atonement to enter into God's presence upon death. (5) Hebrew parallelism brings out the various aspects contained in one's soul. (5a) Soul parallels the whole individual "him": Many there be which say of my soul, There is no help for him in God" (Ps 3:2); (5b) The Lord has a soul [stressing His inward attributes which are demonstrated in action]: "The LORD trieth the righteous: but the wicked and him that loveth violence His soul hateth" (Ps 11:5); (5c) Soul is parallel to the whole person "I": "My soul is continually in my hand: yet do I not forget thy law" (Ps 119:109). See: TWOT—1395a; BDB—659b, 925a, 925b, 925c.

5316. נֶפֶת {1x} nepheth, neh'-feth; for 5299; a height:—country {1x}. See: TWOT—1331c; BDB—190b, 632c, 661d.

5317. נֹפֶת {5x} nôpheth, no'-feth; from 5130 in the sense of shaking to pieces; a dripping, i.e. of honey (from the comb):—

honeycomb {5x}. See: TWOT—1396; BDB—661d.

5318. נְפתּוֹחַ {2x} **Nephtôwach**, *nef-to'-akh;* from 6605; *opened,* i.e. a *spring; Nephtoach,* a place in Pal.:—Neptoah {2x}. See: BDB—661d, 836b.

5319. נִפתּוּל {1x} **naphtûwl,** *naf-tool';* from 6617; prop. *wrestled;* but used (in the plur.) tran., a *struggle:*—wrestling {1x}. See: TWOT—1857c; BDB—661d, 836d.

5320. נַפתֻּחִים {2x} **Naphtûchîym,** *naf-too-kheem';* plur. of for. or., *Naphtuchim,* an Eg. tribe:—Naptuhim {2x}. See: BDB—661d.

5321. נַפתָּלִי {50x} **Naphtâlîy,** *naf-taw-lee';* from 6617; *my wrestling; Naphtali,* a son of Jacob, with the tribe desc. from him, and its territory:—Naphtali {50x}. See: BDB—661d, 836d.

5322. נֵץ {4x} **nêts,** *nayts;* from 5340; a *flower* (from its *brilliancy*); also a *hawk* (from it *flashing* speed):—blossom {1x}, hawk {3x}. See: TWOT—1405b, 1406a; BDB—661d, 665b, 665c.

5323. נָצָא {1x} **nâtsâ',** *naw-tsaw';* a prim. root; to *go away:*—flee {1x}. See: TWOT—1397; BDB—661d.

5324. נָצַב {75x} **nâtsab,** *naw-tsab';* a prim. root; to *station,* in various applications (lit. or fig.):—stand {34x}, set {12x}, officers {6x}, set up {7x}, upright {2x}, appointed {1x}, deputy {1x}, erected {1x}, establish {1x}, Huzzab 1, misc. {9x} = lay, pillar, present, rear up, settle, sharpen, stablish, best state.

Natsab means "to stand, station, set up, erect." **(1)** Its first occurrence in the Old Testament is in Gen 18:2: "Three men stood by him. . . ." **(2)** There are various ways of standing. One may "stand" for a definite purpose at a particular spot: "Get thee unto Pharaoh in the morning; lo, he goeth out unto the water; and thou shalt stand by the river's brink against he come; and the rod which was turned to a serpent shalt thou take in thine hand" (Ex 7:15). **(3)** One often stands upright: **(3a)** "And stood every man at his tent door . . ." (Ex 33:8); **(3b)** "my sheaf arose, and also stood upright . . ." (Gen 37:7). **(4)** One who is "stationed" in a position is usually over someone else: "And Azariah the son of Nathan was over the officers [literally, "those standing over" (1 Kin 4:5). **(5)** "To stand" something may be "to erect" something: "And Jacob set up a pillar . . ." (Gen 35:14). **(6)** The waters of the Sea of Reeds were said to "stand as a heap" (Ps 78:13). **(7)** To fix a boundary is "to establish or erect" a boundary marker (Deut 32:8). Syn.:

5975. See: TWOT—1398; BDB—246c, 662a, 663b, 1103b.

נְצִב **n⁰tsîb.** See 5333.

5325. נִצָּב {1x} **nitstsâb,** *nits-tsawb';* pass. part. of 5324; *fixed,* i.e. a *handle:*—haft {1x}. See: TWOT—1398a; BDB—662c.

5326. נִצְבָּה {1x} **nitsbâh** (Aram.), *nits-baw';* from a root coresp. to 5324; *fixedness,* i.e. *firmness:*—strength {1x}. TWOT—2869; See: BDB—1103b.

5327. נָצָה {11x} **nâtsâh,** *naw-tsaw';* a prim. root; prop. to *go forth,* i.e. (by impl.) to *be expelled,* and (consequently) *desolate;* caus. to *lay waste;* also (spec.), to *quarrel:*—be laid waste {1x}, ruinous {2x}, strive {2x}, strove together {3x}, strove against {2x}, strove {1x}. See: TWOT—1399, 1400, 1401; BDB—663c, 663d.

נֹצָה **nôtsâh.** See 5133.

5328. נִצָּה {2x} **nitstsâh,** *nits-tsaw';* fem. of 5322; a *blossom:*—flower {2x}. See: TWOT—1405c; BDB—663d, 665b.

נְצוּרָה **n⁰tsûwrâh.** See 5341.

5329. נָצַח {65x} **nâtsach,** *naw-tsakh';* a prim. root; prop. to *glitter* from afar, i.e. to *be eminent* (as a superintendent, espec. of the temple services and its music); also (as denom. from 5331), to *be permanent:*—Musician {55x}, set forward {3x}, overseers {3x}, excel {1x}, oversee {1x}, perpetual {1x}, chief singer {1x}.

I. *Natsach,* **as a verb,** means (5329) "to keep, oversee, have charge over." **(1)** The word appears as "to set forward" in the sense of "to oversee or to lead": "Then stood Jeshua with his sons and his brethren, Kadmiel and his sons, the sons of Judah, together, to set forward the workmen in the house of God" (Ezra 3:9; cf. 1 Chr 23:4; 2 Chr 34:12). **(2)** The word appears as "to oversee" in 2 Chr 2:2: "And Solomon told out threescore and ten thousand men to bear burdens . . . and three thousand and six hundred to oversee them."

II. Natstseach, as a masculine participle, means "overseer; director." **(1)** While this word is used approximately 65 times in the Hebrew Old Testament, almost all of them (except for 5 or 6) are participles, used as verbal-nouns. **(1a)** The participial form has the meaning of "overseer, director," reflecting the idea that one who is pre-eminent or conspicuous is an "overseer." **(1b)** Thus, *natstseach* is found in the Book of Psalms a total of 55 times in the titles of various psalms (Ps 5, 6, 9, et al.) with the meaning, "To the chief musician." **(1c)** Of the 55 psalms involved, 39 are connected with the name of David, 9 with Korah, and 5 with

Hebrew

Asaph, leaving only two anonymous psalms. **(1d)** The Hebrew preposition, *le,* used with this participle is a *lamed* of authorship. **(1e)** This title refers to the One who can bring harmony to all, the Coming One, the Messiah, the Chief Musician unto Whom all tune their songs and instruments. **(2)** This title is found also at the end of Hab 3, showing that this psalm was in the theme: "the just One shall live by faith." **(3)** The word refers to "overseers" in 2 Chr 2:18: ". . . and three thousand and six hundred overseers to set the people a work." **(4)** The feminine participle *natsach* is used only in Jer 8:5 in the sense of "enduring": "Why then is this people of Jerusalem slidden back by a perpetual [*natsach*] backsliding? they hold fast deceit, they refuse to return." See: TWOT—1402; BDB—663d, 1103b.

5330. נְצַח {1x} **nᵉtsach** (Aram.), *nets-akh';* corresp. to 5329; to *become chief:*—be preferred {1x}. See: TWOT—2870; BDB—1103b.

5331. נֶצַח {43x} **netsach**, *neh'-tsakh;* or

נֵצַח **nêtsach**, *nay'-tsakh;* from 5329; prop. a *goal,* i.e. the bright object at a distance travelled toward; hence, (fig.) *splendor,* or (subj.) *truthfulness,* or (obj.) *confidence;* but usually (adv.), *continually* (i.e. to the most distant point of view):—ever {24x}, never {4x}, perpetual {3x}, always {2x}, end {2x}, victory {2x}, strength {2x}, alway {1x}, constantly {1x}, evermore {1x}, never + 3808 {1x}. See: TWOT—1402a; BDB—664b.

5332. נֶצַח {2x} **nêtsach**, *nay'-tsakh;* prob. ident. with 5331, through the idea of *brilliancy* of color; *juice* of the grape (as blood red):—blood {1x}, strength {1x}. See: TWOT—1403a; BDB—664c.

5333. נְצִיב {12x} **nᵉtsîyb**, *nets-eeb';* or

נְצִב **nᵉtsîb**, *nets-eeb';* from 5324; something *stationary,* i.e. a *prefect,* a military *post,* a *statue:*—garrison {9x}, officer {2x}, pillar {1x}. See: TWOT—1398b; BDB—662c.

5334. נְצִיב {1x} **Nᵉtsîyb**, *nets-eeb';* the same as 5333; *station; Netsib,* a place in Pal.:—Nezib {1x}. See: BDB—662d.

5335. נְצִיחַ {2x} **Nᵉtsîyach**, *nets-ee'-akh;* from 5329; *conspicuous; Netsiach,* a temple-servant:—Neziah {2x}. See: BDB—664c.

5336. נָצִיר {1x} **nâtsîyr**, *naw-tsere';* from 5341; prop. *conservative;* but used pass., *delivered:*—preserved {1x}. See: TWOT—1407a; BDB—666a.

5337. נָצַל {213x} **nâtsal**, *naw-tsal';* a prim. root; to *snatch* away, whether in a good or a bad sense:—deliver {179x}, recover {5x}, rid {3x}, escape {2x}, rescue {2x}, spoil {2x}, at all {2x}, take out {2x}, misc. {16x} = defend, × without fail, part, pluck, preserve, save, strip, × surely. See: TWOT—1404; BDB—664c, 1103b.

5338. נְצַל {3x} **nᵉtsal** (Aram.), *nets-al';* corresp. to 5337; to *extricate:*—deliver {2x}, rescue {1x}. See: TWOT—2871; BDB—1103b.

5339. נִצָּן {1x} **nitstsân**, *nits-tsawn';* from 5322; a *blossom:*—flower {1x}. See: TWOT—1405d; BDB—665a, 665b.

5340. נָצַץ {1x} **nâtsats**, *naw-tsats';* a prim. root; to *glare,* i.e. *be bright*-colored:—sparkle {1x}. See: TWOT—1405; BDB—665a.

5341. נָצַר {63x} **nâtsar**, *naw-tsar';* a prim. root; to *guard,* in a good sense (to *protect, maintain, obey,* etc.) or a bad one (to *conceal,* etc.):—keep {38x}, preserve {13x}, watchmen {3x}, besieged {2x}, keeper {1x}, monuments {1x}, observe + 7521 {1x}, preserver {1x}, subtil {1x}, hidden things {1x}, watchers {1x}.

Natsar means "to watch, to guard, to keep." **(1)** *Natsar* is found for the first time in the biblical text in Ex 34:7 where it has the sense of **(1a)** "keeping with faithfulness": "Keeping [*natsar*] mercy for thousands, forgiving iniquity and transgression and sin, and that will by no means clear the guilty; visiting the iniquity of the fathers upon the children, and upon the children's children, unto the third and to the fourth generation." **(1b)** This meaning is usually found when man is the subject: **(1b1)** "keeping" the covenant (Deut 33:9); **(1b2)** "keeping" the law (Ps 105:45 and 10 times in Ps 119); **(1b3)** "keeping" the rules of parents (Prov 6:20). **(2)** *Natsar* is frequently used to express the idea of "guarding" something, such as a vineyard (Is 27:3) or a fortification (Nah 2:1).

(3) "To watch" one's speech is a frequent concern, so advice is given **(3a)** "to watch" one's mouth (Prov 13:3), **(3b)** the tongue (Ps 34:13), and **(3c)** the lips (Ps. 141:3). **(4)** Many references are made to God as the one who "preserves" His people from dangers of all kinds: "He found him in a desert land, and in the waste howling wilderness; he led him about, he instructed him, he kept him as the apple of his eye" (Deut 32:10; cf. Ps 31:23). **(5)** Generally, *natsar* is a close synonym to the much more common verb, *shamar* (8104), "to keep, tend." **(6)** sometimes "to keep" has the meaning of "to besiege," as in Is 1:8, ". . . as a besieged city."

Syn: 8104, 8105, 8107, 8108. See: TWOT—1407; BDB—665c, 666a, 1102d.

5342. נֵצֶר {4x} **nêtser,** *nay'-tser;* from 5341 in the sense of *greenness* as a striking color; a *shoot;* fig. a *descendant:*—branch {4x}. See: TWOT—1408a; BDB—666a.

5343. נְקֵא {1x} **nᵉqê** (Aram.), *nek-ay';* from a root corresp. to 5352; *clean:*—pure {1x}. See: TWOT—2872; BDB—1103c.

5344. נָקַב {25x} **nâqab,** *naw-kab';* a prim. root; to *puncture,* lit. (to *perforate,* with more or less violence) or fig. (to *specify, designate, libel*):—curse {6x}, expressed {6x}, blaspheme {3x}, bore {2x}, name {2x}, pierce {2x}, appoint {1x}, holes {1x}, pierce through {1x}, strike through {1x}. See: TWOT—1409; BDB—666a, 666d.

5345. נֶקֶב {1x} **neqeb,** *neh'keb;* a *bezel* (for a gem):—pipe {1x}. See: TWOT—1409a; BDB—666b.

5346. נֶקֶב {1x} **Neqeb,** *neh'-keb;* the same as 5345; *dell; Nekeb,* a place in Pal.:—Nekeb {1x}. See: BDB—10a, 666c.

5347. נְקֵבָה {22x} **nᵉqêbâh,** *nek-ay-baw';* from 5344; *female* (from the sexual form):—female {18x}, woman {3x}, maid {1x}. See: BDB—666c.

5348. נָקֹד {9x} **nâqôd,** *naw-kode';* from an unused root mean. to *mark* (by *puncturing* or *branding*); *spotted:*—speckled {9x}. See: TWOT—1410a; BDB—666d.

5349. נֹקֵד {2x} **nôqêd,** *no-kade';* act. part. from the same as 5348; a *spotter* (of sheep or cattle), i.e. the owner or tender (who thus marks them):—herdman {1x}, sheepmaster {1x}. See: TWOT—1411a; BDB—667a.

5350. נִקֻּד {3x} **niqqud,** *nik-kood';* from the same as 5348; a *crumb* (as *broken* to spots); also a *biscuit* (as *pricked*):—cracknels {1x}, mouldy {2x}. See: TWOT—1410b; BDB—666d.

5351. נְקֻדָּה {1x} **nᵉquddâh,** *nek-ood-daw';* fem. of 5348; a *boss:*—studs {1x}. See: TWOT—1410c; BDB—667a.

5352. נָקָה {44x} **nâqâh,** *naw-kaw';* a prim. root; to *be* (or *make*) *clean* (lit. or fig.); by impl. (in an adverse sense) to *be bare,* i.e. *extirpated:*—unpunished {11x}, guiltless {5x}, innocent {5x}, clear {4x}, cleanse {3x}, free {2x}, by no means {2x}, acquit {2x}, altogether {2x}, cut off {2x}, at all {1x}, blameless {1x}, desolate {1x}, quit {1x}, utterly {1x}, wholly {1x}.

Naqah, as a verb, means "to be pure, innocent." **(1)** Isaiah described the future of Jerusa-

lem as an empty ("desolate") city: "And her gates shall lament and mourn; and she being desolate shall sit upon the ground" (Is 3:26). **(2)** On the more positive side, a land may also be "cleansed" of robbers: "Then said he unto me, This *is* the curse that goeth forth over the face of the whole earth: for every one that stealeth shall be cut off [*naqah*] as on this side according to it; and every one that sweareth shall be cut off [*naqah*] as on that side according to it" (Zec 5:3). **(3)** The verb is more often used to mean being "free" (with the preposition min). **(3a)** The first occurrence in the Old Testament is in Gen 24:8, and is illustrative of this usage. **(3b)** Abraham ordered his servant to find a wife for Isaac. The servant pledged that he would fulfill his commission; however, if he did not succeed—that is, in case the woman was unwilling to make the long journey with him—Abraham would free him: ". . . Then thou shalt be clear from this my oath."

(4) The freedom may be **(4a)** from wrongdoing: "Then shall the man be guiltless from iniquity, and this woman shall bear her iniquity" (Num 5:31), or **(4b)** from punishment: "If he rise again, and walk abroad upon his staff, then shall he that smote him be quit [*naqah*]: only he shall pay for the loss of his time, and shall cause him to be thoroughly healed" (Ex 21:19; cf. Num 5:28). **(5)** The verb *naqah* also appears with the legal connotation of "innocence." **(5a)** First, a person may be declared "innocent," or "acquitted." David prayed: "Keep back thy servant also from presumptuous *sins;* let them not have dominion over me: then shall I be upright, and I shall be innocent from the great transgression" (Ps 19:13). **(5b)** On the other hand, the sinner is not "acquitted" by God: "I am afraid of all my sorrows, I know that thou wilt not hold me innocent" (Job 9:28). **(5c)** The punishment of the person who is not "acquitted" is also expressed by a negation of the verb *naqah:* "Thou shalt not take the name of the LORD thy God in vain; for the LORD will not hold him guiltless that taketh his name in vain" (Ex 20:7).

(5d) "For I am with thee, saith the LORD, to save thee: though I make a full end of all nations whither I have scattered thee, yet will I not make a full end of thee: but I will correct thee in measure, and will not leave thee altogether unpunished" (Jer 30:11). **(5e)** The fate of the wicked is the judgment of God: "the wicked shall not be unpunished: but the seed of the righteous shall be delivered" (Prov 11:21). See: TWOT—1412; BDB—667a, 1103c.

5353. נְקוֹדָא {4x} **Nᵉqôwdâ**, *nek-o-daw';* fem. of 5348 (in the fig. sense of *marked*); *distinction; Nekoda,* a temple-servant:—Nekoda {4x}. See: BDB—667a.

5354. נָקַט {1x} **nâqaṭ,** *naw-kat';* a prim. root; to *loathe:*—weary {1x}. See: TWOT—1996; BDB—667d, 876c.

5355. נָקִיּ {44x} **nâqîy,** *naw-kee';* or

נָקִיא **nâqîy⁾** (Joel 4:19; Jonah 1:14), *naw-kee';* from 5352; *innocent:*—innocent {31x}, guiltless {4x}, quit {2x}, blameless {2x}, clean {1x}, clear {1x}, exempted {1x}, free {1x}, variant {1x}.

Naqiy, as an adjective, means "innocent." This adjective appears 43 times in the Old Testament. One occurrence is in Ps 15:5, which says of the righteous man, "He that putteth not out his money to usury, nor taketh reward against the innocent [*naqiy*]. He that doeth these things shall never be moved." See: TWOT—1412a, 1412b; BDB—667c, 667d.

5356. נִקָּיוֹן {5x} **niqqâyôwn,** *nik-kaw-yone';* or

נִקָּיֹן **niqqâyôn,** *nik-kaw-yone';* from 5352; *clearness* (lit. or fig.):—cleanness {1x}, innocency {4x}. See: TWOT—1412c; BDB—667d, 874c.

5357. נָקִיק {3x} **nâqîyq,** *naw-keek';* from an unused root mean. to *bore;* a *cleft:*—hole {3x}. See: TWOT—1417a; BDB—669b.

5358. נָקַם {35x} **nâqam,** *naw-kam';* a prim. root; to *grudge,* i.e. *avenge* or *punish:*—avenge {18x}, vengeance {4x}, revenge {4x}, take {4x}, avenger {2x}, punished {2x}, surely {1x}.

Naqam means "to avenge, take vengeance, punish." **(1)** Lamech's sword song is a scornful challenge to his fellows and a blatant attack on the justice of God: ". . . for I have slain a man to my wounding, and a young man to my hurt. If Cain shall be avenged sevenfold, truly Lamech seventy and sevenfold" (Gen 4:23–24). **(2)** The Lord reserves vengeance as the sphere of His own action: "To me belongeth vengeance, and recompense . . . for he will avenge the blood of his servants, and will render vengeance to his adversaries" (Deut 32:35, 43). **(3)** The law therefore forbade personal vengeance: "Thou shalt not avenge, nor bear any grudge against the children of thy people, but thou shalt love thy neighbor as thyself: I am the Lord" (Lev 19:18). **(4)** Hence the Lord's people commit their case to Him, as David: "The Lord judge between me and thee [Saul], and the Lord avenge me of thee: but mine hand shall not be upon thee" (1 Sa 24:12). **(5)** The Lord uses men to take vengeance, as He said to Moses: "Avenge the children of Israel of the Midianites. . . . And Moses spake unto the people, saying, Arm some of yourselves unto the war, and let them go against the Midianites, and avenge the Lord of Midian" (Num 31:2– 3).

(6) Vengeance for Israel is the Lord's vengeance. **(7)** The law stated, "And if a man smite his servant, or his maid, with a rod, and he die under his hand; he shall be surely punished" (Ex 21:20). **(7a)** In Israel, this responsibility was given to the "avenger of blood" (Deut 19:6). **(7b)** He was responsible to preserve the life and personal integrity of his nearest relative. **(8)** When a man was attacked because he was God's servant, he could rightly call for vengeance on his enemies, as Samson prayed for strength, ". . . that I may be at once avenged of the Philistines for my two eyes" (Judg 16:28). **(9)** In the covenant, God warned that His vengeance may fall on His own people: "And I will bring a sword upon you, that shall avenge the quarrel of my covenant" (Lev 26:25). **(10)** Isaiah thus says of Judah: "Therefore saith the Lord, the Lord of hosts . . . Ah, I will ease me of mine adversaries, and avenge me of my enemies" (1:24). See: TWOT—1413; BDB—667d.

5359. נָקָם {17x} **nâqâm,** *naw-kawm';* from 5358; *revenge:*—+ avenged {1x}, quarrel {1x}, vengeance {15x}.

Naqam means "vengeance." **(1)** The noun is first used in the Lord's promise to Cain: "Therefore whosoever slayeth Cain, vengeance shall be taken on him sevenfold" (Gen 4:15). **(2)** In some instances a man may call for "vengeance" on his enemies, such as when another man has committed adultery with his wife: "For jealousy is the rage of a man: therefore he will not spare in the day of vengeance" (Prov 6:34). **(3)** The prophets frequently speak of God's "vengeance" on His enemies: Is 59:17; Mic 5:15; Nah 1:2. **(4)** It will come at a set time: "For it is the day of the Lord's vengeance, and the year of recompenses for the controversy of Zion" (Is 34:8). **(5)** Isaiah brings God's "vengeance" and redemption together in the promise of messianic salvation: **(5a)** "The Spirit of the Lord God is upon me; . . . he hath sent me . . . to proclaim the acceptable year of the Lord, and the day of vengeance of our God" (61:1–2). **(5b)** When Jesus announced that this was fulfilled in Himself, He stopped short of reading the last clause; but His sermon clearly anticipated that "vengeance" that would come on Israel for rejecting Him. Isaiah also said: "For the day of vengeance is in mine heart, and the year of my redeemed is come" (63:4). See: TWOT—1413a; BDB—668b.

5360. נְקָמָה {27x} **n⁰qâmâh,** *nek-aw-maw';* fem. of 5359; *avengement,* whether the act or the passion:—vengeance {18x}, avenge + 5414 {3x}, revenge {3x}, avenge + 5358 {1x},

avenged {1x}, take vengeance for thee + 5358 {1x}. See: TWOT—1413b; BDB—668c.

5361. נָקַע {3x} **nâqaᶜ**, *naw-kah'*; a prim. root; to *feel aversion:*—be alienated {3x}. See: TWOT—1414; BDB—668c.

5362. נָקַף {19x} **nâqaph**, *naw-kaf'*; a prim. root; to *strike* with more or less violence (*beat, fell, corrode*); by impl. (of attack) to *knock together*, i.e. *surround* or *circulate:*—compass {7x}, go round about {3x}, go about {2x}, compass about {2x}, destroy {1x}, down {1x}, inclosed {1x}, kill {1x}, round {1x}. See: TWOT—1415, 1416; BDB—596d, 668c, 668d, 880d.

5363. נֹקֶף {2x} **nôqeph**, *no'-kef*; from 5362; a *threshing* (of olives):—shaking {2x}. See: TWOT—1415a; BDB—668d.

5364. נִקְפָּה {1x} **niqpâh**, *nik-paw'*; from 5362; prob. a *rope* (as *encircling*):—rent {1x}. See: TWOT—1416a; BDB—669a.

5365. נָקַר {6x} **nâqar**, *naw-kar'*; a prim. root; to *bore* (*penetrate, quarry*):—dig {1x}, pick out {1x}, pierce {1x}, put thrust out {1x}, put out {2x}. See: TWOT—1418; BDB—669b.

5366. נְקָרָה {2x} **nᵉqârâh**, *nek-aw-raw'*; from 5365, a *fissure:*—cleft {1x}, clift {1x}. See: TWOT—1418a; BDB—669b.

5367. נָקַשׁ {5x} **nâqash**, *naw-kash'*; a prim. root; to *entrap* (with a noose), lit. or fig.:—catch {1x}, lay a snare {2x}, snare {2x}. See: TWOT—1419; BDB—669b, 1103c.

5368. נְקַשׁ {1x} **nᵉqash** (Aram.), *nek-ash'*; corresp. to 5367; but used in the sense of 5362; to *knock:*—smote {1x}. See: TWOT—2873; BDB—1103c.

נֵר **nêr**,

נִר **nîr**. See 5215, 5216.

5369. נֵר {16x} **Nêr**, *nare*; the same as 5216; *lamp*; *Ner*, an Isr.:—*Ner* {6x}. See: TWOT—1333a; BDB—633a.

5370. נֵרְגַּל {1x} **Nêrgal**, *nare-gal'*; of for. or.; *Nergal*, a Cuthite deity:—*Nergal* {1x}. See: BDB—669c.

5371. נֵרְגַּל שַׂרְאֶצֶר {3x} **Nêrgal Shar°etser**, *nare-gal' shar-eh'-tser*; from 5370 and 8272; *Nergal-Sharetser*, the name of two Bab.:—Nergal-sharezer {3x}. See: BDB—669c.

5372. נִרְגָּן {4x} **nirgân**, *neer-gawn'*; from an unused root mean. to *roll* to pieces; a *slanderer:*—talebearer {3x}, whisperer {1x}. See: TWOT—2115; BDB—669d, 920d.

5373. נֵרְדְּ {3x} **nêrd**, *nayrd;* of for. or.; *nard*, an aromatic:—spikenard {3x}. See: TWOT—1420; BDB—669d.

נֵרָה **nêrâh**. See 5216.

5374. נֵרִיָּה {10x} **Nêrîyâh**, *nay-ree-yaw';* or

נֵרִיָּהוּ **Nêrîyâhûw**, *nay-ree-yaw'-hoo;* from 5216 and 3050; *light of Jah; Nerijah*, an Isr.:—Neriah {10x}. See: BDB—633a, 669d.

5375. נָשָׂא {654x} **nâsâ°**, *naw-saw';* or

נָסָה **nâçâh** (Ps 4:6 7]) *naw-saw'*; a prim. root; to *lift*, in a great variety of applications, lit. and fig., absol. and rel. (as follows):—(bare, lift, etc . . .) up {219x}, bear {115x}, take {58x}, bare {34x}, carry {30x}, (take, carry) . . . away {22x}, borne {22x}, armourbearer {18x}, forgive {16x}, accept {12x}, exalt {8x}, regard {5x}, obtained {4x}, respect {3x}, misc. {74x} = advance, arise, bring (forth), burn, cast, contain, desire, ease, exact, extol, fetch, furnish, further, give, go on, help, high, hold up, honorable (+ man), lade, lay, lift (self) up, lofty, marry, magnify, × needs, pardon, receive, spare, stir up, + swear, × utterly, wear, yield.

Nacah is used of the undertaking of the responsibilities for sins of others by substitution or representation (Ex 28:12; Lev 16:22; Is 53:12; cf. 1 Pe 2:24). *Nashsha'* means "to lift up, carry." This verb appears 654 times in the Old Testament; once in Gen 44:1: "Fill the men's sacks with food, as much as they can carry." See: TWOT—1421; BDB—650a, 669d, 959a, 962b, 1103c.

5376. נְשָׂא {3x} **nᵉsâ°** (Aram.), *nes-aw';* corresp. to 5375:—carry away, make insurrection, take {3x}. See: TWOT—2874; BDB—1103c.

5377. נָשָׁא {12x} **nâshâ°**, *naw-shaw';* a prim. root; to *lead astray*, i.e. (ment.) to *delude*, or (mor.) to *seduce:*—deceive {12x}, greatly {1x}, beguiled me {1x}, seize {1x}, utterly {1x}. See: TWOT—1425; BDB—674a.

5378. נָשָׁא {4x} **nâshâ°**, *naw-shaw';* a prim. root [perh. ident. with 5377, through the idea of *imposition*]; to *lend* on interest; by impl. to *dun* for debt:—× debt {1x}, exact {2x}, giver of usury {1x}. See: TWOT—1424; BDB—673d, 674b.

נָשִׂא **nâsî°**. See 5387.

נְשֻׂאָה **nᵉsû°âh**. See 5385.

5379. נִשֵּׂאת {1x} **nissê°th**, *nis-sayth';* pass. part. fem. of 5375; *something taken*, i.e. a *present:*—gift {1x}. See: TWOT—1421; BDB—671c, 672a.

5380. נָשַׁב {3x} **nâshab**, *naw-shab';* a prim. root; to *blow;* by impl. to *disperse:*—(cause to) blow {2x}, drive away {1x}. See: TWOT—1426; BDB—674b.

5381. נָשַׂג {50x} **nâsag**, *naw-sag';* a prim. root; to *reach* (lit. or fig.):—overtake {23x}, hold {5x}, get {3x}, get + 3027 {3x}, attain {2x}, obtain {2x}, reach {2x}, ability + 3027 {1x}, able {1x}, able + 1767 {1x}, bring {1x}, layeth {1x}, put {1x}, remove {1x}, wax rich {1x}, surely {1x}, take {1x}.

Nasag means "to reach, overtake, attain." **(1)** It is used in the text of the Hebrew Old Testament approximately 50 times, the first time being Gen 31:25: "Then Laban overtook Jacob."**(2)** Often it is used in connection with the verb, "to pursue, follow," as in Gen 44:4: "... follow after the men; and when thou dost overtake them...." **(3)** *Nasag* is sometimes used in the figurative sense to describe "being overtaken" by something undesirable or unwanted, such as **(3a)** war (Hos 10:9), **(3b)** the sword (Jer 42:16), or **(3c)** curses (Deut 28:15, 45). **(4)** Fortunately, blessings may "overtake" those who are obedient (Deut 28:2). **(5)** *Nasag* may mean "to attain to" something, "to come into contact" with it: "The sword of him that layeth at him [Leviathan] . . ." (Job 41:26). **(6)** Used figuratively, "The ransomed of the Lord . . . shall obtain joy and gladness" (Is 35:10). **(7)** Jacob complained: ". . . the days of the years of my pilgrimage . . . have not attained unto the days of the years of the life of my fathers" (Gen 47:9). See: TWOT—1422; BDB—673b.

5382. נָשָׁה {6x} **nâshâh**, *naw-shaw';* a prim. root; to *forget;* fig. to *neglect;* caus. to *remit, remove:*—forget {4x}, deprive {1x}, exact {1x}. See: TWOT—1428; BDB—674b, 674c.

5383. נָשָׁה {13x} **nâshâh**, *naw-shaw';* a prim. root [rather ident. with 5382, in the sense of 5378]; to *lend* or (by reciprocity) *borrow* on security or interest:—See: exact {3x}, lend {3x}, lend on usury {2x}, creditor {2x}, extortioner {1x}, taker of usury {1x}, usurer {1x}. See: TWOT—1427; BDB—673d.

5384. נָשֶׁה {2x} **nâsheh**, *naw-sheh';* from 5382, in the sense of *failure; rheumatic* or *crippled* (from the incident to Jacob):—which shrank {2x}. See: TWOT—1429; BDB—674d.

5385. נְשׂוּאָה {1x} **nᵉsûw'âh**, *nes-oo-aw';* or rather,

נְשֻׂאָה **nᵉsu'âh**, *nes-oo-aw';* fem. pass. part. of 5375; something *borne,* i.e. a *load:*—carriage {1x}. See: TWOT—1421a; BDB—672b.

5386. נְשִׁי {1x} **nᵉshîy**, *nesh-ee';* from 5383; a *debt:*—debt {1x}. See: TWOT—1427a; BDB—674c.

5387. נָשִׂיא {132x} **nâsîy'**, *naw-see';* or

נָשִׂא **nâsî'**, *naw-see';* from 5375; prop. an *exalted* one, i.e. a *king* or *sheik;* also a rising *mist:*—prince {96x}, captain 12, chief {10x}, ruler {6x}, vapours {3x}, governor {1x}, chief + 5387 {1x}, clouds {1x}, part {1x}, prince + 5387 {1x}.

Nasi' means prince; chief; leader. **(1)** Literally translated, it means one who bears responsibility, or who holds aloft an ensign. **(1a)** An early occurrence of *nasi'* is in Gen 23:6: "Hear us, my lord: thou art a mighty prince among us." **(1b)** The books of Numbers and Ezekiel use the word most frequently; elsewhere it rarely occurs. **(2)** Though the origin and meaning of *nasi'* are controversial, it is clearly associated with leadership, both Israelite and non-Israelite. **(2a)** Ishmael was promised to give rise to twelve "princes" (Gen 17:20; cf. 25:16); **(2b)** the Midianites had "princes" (Num 25:18), **(2c)** as well as the Amorites (Josh 13:21), **(2d)** the peoples of the sea (Eze 26:16), **(2e)** Kedar (Eze 27:21), **(2f)** Egypt (Eze 30:13), and **(2g)** Edom (Eze 32:29).

(3) Also Israel had her "princes" ("rulers"): "On the sixth day they gathered twice as much bread, two omers for one man: and all the rulers of the congregation came and told Moses" (Ex 16:22). **(3a)** The "princes" ("leaders") of Israel did not only participate in the civil leadership; **(3b)** they were also regarded as pillars in Israelite religious life, the upholders of the covenantal way of life: "And Moses called unto them; and Aaron and all the rulers of the congregation returned unto him: and Moses talked with them" (Ex 34:31; cf. Josh 22:30). **(3c)** Hence, Israel was to obey her "leaders": "Thou shalt not revile the gods, nor curse the ruler of thy people" (Ex 22:28). **(4)** The masculine plural noun, which is found 4 times, means "vapors, clouds": "Whoso boasteth himself of a false gift is like clouds and wind without rain" (Prov 25:14; cf. Ps 135:7; Jer 10:13; 51:16). See: TWOT—1421b, 1421c; BDB—672b, 672c.

5388. נְשִׁיָּה {1x} **nᵉshîyâh**, *nesh-ee-yaw';* from 5382; *oblivion:*—forgetfulness {1x}. See: TWOT—1428a; BDB—674d.

נָשִׁים **nâshîym**. See 802.

5389. נָשִׁין **nâshîyn** (Aram.), *naw-sheen';* irreg. plur. fem. of 606:—women {1x}. See: TWOT—2875; BDB—1081d, 1103c.

5390. נְשִׁיקָה {2x} **nᵉshîyqâh**, *nesh-ee-kaw';* from 5401; a *kiss:*—kisses {2x}. See: TWOT—1435a; BDB—676c.

5391. נָשַׁךְ {14x} **nâshak**, *naw-shak';* a prim. root; to *strike* with a sting (as a serpent); fig. to *oppress* with interest on a loan:—bite {12x}, lend upon usury {2x}. See: TWOT—1430, 1430b; BDB—675a, 675b.

5392. נֶשֶׁךְ {12x} **neshek**, *neh'-shek;* from 5391; *interest* on a debt:—usury {12x}. See: TWOT—1430a; BDB—675b.

5393. נִשְׁכָּה {3x} **nishkâh**, *nish-kaw';* for 3957; a *cell:*—chamber {3x}. See: TWOT—1431; BDB—675b.

5394. נָשַׁל {7x} **nâshal**, *naw-shal';* a prim. root; to *pluck* off, i.e. *divest, eject,* or *drop:*—cast {1x}, cast out {1x}, drive {1x}, loose {1x}, put off {1x}, put out {1x}, slip {1x}. See: TWOT—1432; BDB—675b.

5395. נָשַׁם {1x} **nâsham**, *naw-sham';* a prim. root; prop. to *blow* away, i.e. *destroy:*—destroy {1x}. See: TWOT—1433; BDB—675c, 1103c.

5396. נִשְׁמָא {1x} **nishmâ'** (Aram.), *nish-maw';* corresp. to 5397; vital *breath:*—breath {1x}. See: TWOT—2876; BDB—1103c.

5397. נְשָׁמָה {24x} **nᵉshâmâh**, *nesh-aw-maw';* from 5395; a *puff,* i.e. *wind,* angry or vital *breath,* divine *inspiration, intellect,* or (concr.) an *animal:*—breath {17x}, blast {3x}, spirit {2x}, inspiration {1x}, souls {1x}.

A *neshamah* is literally a "breathing being": "But of the cities of these people, which the LORD thy God doth give thee for an inheritance, thou shalt save alive nothing that breatheth:" (Deut 20:16). See: TWOT—1433a; BDB—675c, 1103c.

5398. נָשַׁף {2x} **nâshaph**, *naw-shaf';* a prim. root; to *breeze,* i.e. *blow* up fresh (as the wind):—blow {2x}. See: TWOT—1434; BDB—676a.

5399. נֶשֶׁף {12x} **nesheph**, *neh'-shef;* from 5398; prop. a *breeze,* i.e. (by impl.) *dusk* (when the evening breeze prevails):—twilight {6x}, night {3x}, dark {1x}, dawning of the morning {1x}, dawning of the day {1x}. See: TWOT—1434a; BDB—676a.

5400. נָשַׂק {3x} **nâsaq**, *naw-sak';* a prim. root; to *catch* fire:—burn {1x}, kindle {2x}. See: TWOT—2266; BDB—673d, 969c.

5401. נָשַׁק {35x} **nâshaq**, *naw-shak';* a prim. root [ident. with 5400, through the idea of *fastening* up; comp. 2388, 2836]; to *kiss,* lit. or fig. (*touch*); also (as a mode of *attachment*), to *equip* with weapons:—armed {2x}, armed men {1x}, ruled {1x}, kiss {29x}, that touched {1x}.

Nashaq means to kiss, whether as **(1)** a mark of respect: "Kiss the Son, lest he be angry, and ye perish from the way, when his wrath is kindled but a little. Blessed are all they that put their trust in him" (Ps 2:12) or otherwise is rendered **(2)** "rule": "Thou shalt be over my house, and according unto thy word shall all my people be ruled: only in the throne will I be greater than thou" (Gen 41:40). **(3)** It is applied to armor because it fits closely and is folded together: "The children of Ephraim, being armed, and carrying bows, turned back in the day of battle" (Ps 78:9). It is also applied to the wings of the living creatures that touched one another (Eze 3:13). See: TWOT—1435, 1436; BDB—676b, 676c.

5402. נֶשֶׁק {10x} **nesheq**, *neh'-shek;* or נֵשֶׁק **nêsheq**, *nay'-shek;* from 5401; military *equipment,* i.e. (collect.) *arms* (offensive or defensive), or (concr.) an *arsenal:*—armed men {1x}, armour {3x}, armoury {1x}, battle {1x}, harness {1x}, weapon {3x}. See: TWOT—1436a; BDB—676d.

5403. נְשַׁר {2x} **nᵉshar** (Aram.), *nesh-ar';* corresp. to 5404; an *eagle:*—eagle {2x}. See: TWOT—2877; BDB—1103c.

5404. נֶשֶׁר {26x} **nesher**, *neh'-sher;* from an unused root mean. to *lacerate;* the *eagle* (or other large bird of prey):—eagle {26x}. See: TWOT—1437; BDB—676d, 1103c.

5405. נָשַׁת {3x} **nâshath**, *naw-shath';* a prim. root; prop. to *eliminate,* i.e. (intr.) to *dry* up:—fail {3x}. See: TWOT—1438; BDB—677a.

נְתִבָה **nᵉthîbâh**. See 5410.

5406. נִשְׁתְּוָן {2x} **nishtᵉvân**, *nish-tev-awn';* prob. of Pers. or.; an *epistle:*—letter {2x}. See: TWOT—1439; BDB—677a, 1103c.

5407. נִשְׁתְּוָן {3x} **nishtᵉvân** (Aram.), *nish-tev-awn';* corresp. to 5406:—letter {3x}. See: TWOT—2878; BDB—1103c.

נָתוּן **Nathûwn**. See 5411.

5408. נָתַח {9x} **nâthach**, *naw-thakh';* a prim. root; to *dismember:*—cut {5x}, cut into pieces {2x}, divided {1x}, hewed them in pieces {1x}. See: TWOT—1441; BDB—677c.

5409. נֵתַח {13x} **nêthach**, *nay'-thakh;* from 5408; a *fragment:*—parts {1x}, pieces {12x}. See: TWOT—1441a; BDB—677c.

5410. נָתִיב {26x} **nâthîyb**, *naw-theeb';* or (fem.) נְתִיבָה **nᵉthîybâh**, *neth-ee-baw';* or נְתִבָה **nᵉthîbâh** (Jer. 6:16), *neth-ee-baw';* from an unused root mean. to *tramp;* a (beaten) *track:*—path {22x}, way {2x},

pathway {1x}, byways + 6128 {1x}. See: TWOT−1440a, 1440b; BDB−677a, 677b.

5411. נָתִין {18x} **Nâthîyn**, *naw-theen'*; or

נָתוּן **Nâthûwn** (Ezra 8:17), *naw-thoon'* (the proper form, as pass. part.), from 5414; one *given*, i.e. (in the plur. only) the *Nethinim*, or temple-servants (as *given* to that duty):−Nethinims {18x}. See: TWOT−1443a; BDB−682a, 1103c.

5412. נְתִין {1x} **Neᵗhîyn** (Aram.), *netheen'*; corresp. to 5411:−Nethinims {1x}. See: TWOT−2879; BDB−1103c.

5413. נָתַך {21x} **nâthak**, *naw-thak'*; a prim. root; to *flow* forth (lit. or fig.); by impl. to *liquefy*:−pour out {7x}, melt {4x}, poured {3x}, poured forth {3x}, gathered {1x}, molten {1x}, dropped {1x}, gathered together {1x}. See: TWOT−1442; BDB−677c.

5414. נָתַן {2008x} **nâthan**, *naw-than'*; a prim. root; to *give*, used with greatest latitude of application (*put, make*, etc.):−give {1078x}, put {191x}, deliver {174x}, made {107x}, set {99x}, up {26x}, lay {22x}, grant {21x}, suffer {18x}, yield {15x}, bring {15x}, cause {13x}, utter {12x}, laid {11x}, send {11x}, recompense {11x}, appoint {10x}, shew {7x}, misc. {167x} = add, apply, ascribe, assign, X avenge, X be ([healed]), bestow, cast, charge, come, commit, consider, count, + cry, direct, distribute, do, X doubtless, X without fail, fasten, frame, X get, hang (up), X have, X indeed, (give) leave, lend, let (out), lift up, + O that, occupy, offer, ordain, pay, perform, place, pour, print, X pull, render, requite, restore, shoot forth (up), + sing, + slander, strike, [sub-] mit, X surely, X take, thrust, trade, turn, + weep, X willingly, + withdraw, + would (to) God.

Nathan means "to deliver, give, place, set up, lay, make, do." **(1)** First, *nathan* represents the action by which something is set going or actuated. Achsah asked her father Caleb to "give" her a blessing, such as a tract of land with abundant water, as her dowry; she wanted him to "transfer" it from his possession to hers: "Who answered, Give me a blessing; for thou hast given me a south land; give me also springs of water. And he gave her the upper springs, and the nether springs" (Josh 15:19). **(2)** There is a technical use of this verb without an object: Moses instructs Israel to "give" generously to the man in desperate need: "Thou shalt surely give him, and thine heart shall not be grieved when thou givest unto him: because that for this thing the LORD thy God shall bless thee in all thy works, and in all that thou puttest thine hand unto" (Deut 15:10). **(3)** In some instances, *nathan* can mean to "send forth," as in "sending forth" a fragrance: "While the king sitteth

at his table, my spikenard sendeth forth the smell thereof" (Song 1:12). **(4)** When used of a liquid, the word means to "send forth" in the sense of "spilling," for example, to spill blood: "Be merciful, O LORD, unto thy people Israel, whom thou hast redeemed, and lay not innocent blood unto thy people of Israel's charge. And the blood shall be forgiven them" (Deut 21:8).

(5) *Nathan* also has a technical meaning in the area of jurisprudence, meaning to hand something over to someone−for example: **(5a1)** "to pay": "That he may give me the cave of Machpelah, which he hath, which *is* in the end of his field; for as much money as it is worth he shall give it me for a possession of a burying place amongst you" (Gen 23:9); or **(5a2)** "to loan": "Thou shalt surely give him, and thine heart shall not be grieved when thou givest unto him: because that for this thing the LORD thy God shall bless thee in all thy works, and in all that thou puttest thine hand unto" (Deut 15:10). **(5b)** A girl's parent or someone else in a responsible position may "give" her to a man to be his wife (Gen 16:3), as well as presenting a bride price (Gen 34:12) and dowry (1 Kin 9:16). **(5c)** The verb also is used of "giving" or "granting" a request (Gen 15:2). **(6)** Sometimes, *nathan* can be used to signify "putting" ("placing") someone into custody (2 Sa 14:7) or into prison (Jer 37:4), or even of "destroying" something (Judg 6:30). **(7)** This same basic sense may be applied to "dedicating" ("handing over") something or someone to God, such as the first-born son (Ex 22:29). Levites are those who have been "handed over" in this way (Num 3:9).

(8) This word is used of "bringing reprisal" upon someone or of "giving" him what he deserves; in some cases, the stress is on the act of reprisal (1 Kin 8:32), or bringing his punishment on his head. **(9)** *Nathan* can be used of "giving" or "ascribing" something to someone, such as "giving" glory and praise to God (Josh 7:19). Obviously, nothing is passed from men to God; nothing is added to God, since He is perfect. This means, therefore, that a worshiper recognizes and confesses what is already His. **(10)** Another major emphasis of *nathan* is the action of "giving" or "effecting" a result. For example, the land will "give" ("yield") its fruit (Deut 25:19). **(11)** In some passages, this verb means "to procure" ("to set up"), as when God "gave" ("procured, set up") favor for Joseph (Gen 39:21). **(12)** The word can be used of sexual activity, too, emphasizing the act of intercourse or "one's lying down" with an animal (Lev 18:23). **(13)** God "placed" (literally, "gave") the heavenly lights into the expanse of the heavens (Gen 1:17−the first

occurrence of the verb). **(14)** A garland is "placed" (literally, "given") upon one's head (Prov 4:9).

(15) The children of Israel are commanded not to "set up" idols in their land. **(16)** Another meaning of *nathan* is seen in Gen 17:5: "For a father of many nations have I made [literally, "given"] thee." There are several instances where the verb bears this significance. **(17)** *Nathan* has a number of special implications when used with bodily parts—for example, **(17a)** "to give" or "turn" a stubborn shoulder (Neh 9:29). Similarly, compare expressions such as **(17b)** "turning [giving] one's face" (2 Chr 29:6). **(17c)** To "turn [give] one's back" is to flee (Ex 23:27). **(17d)** "Giving one's hand" may be no more than "putting it forth," as in the case of the unborn Zarah (Gen 38:28). **(18)** This word can also signify **(18a)** an act of friendship as when Jehonadab "gave his hand" (instead of a sword) to Jehu to help him into the chariot (2 Kin 10:15); **(18b)** an act of oath-taking, as when the priests "pledged" ("gave their hands") to put away their foreign wives (Ezra 10:19); and **(18c)** "making" or "renewing" a covenant, as when the leaders of Israel "pledged" themselves ("gave their hands") to follow Solomon (1 Chr 29:24).

(19) "To give something into someone's hand" is to "commit" it to his care. **(19a)** So after the Flood, God "gave" the earth into Noah's hand (Gen 9:2). **(19b)** This phrase is used to express the "transfer of political power," such as the divine right to rule (2 Sa 16:8). **(20)** *Nathan* is used especially in a military and judicial sense, meaning "to give over one's power or control," or to grant victory to someone; so Moses said God would "give" the kings of Canaan into Israel's hands (Deut 7:24). **(21)** "To give one's heart" to something or someone is "to be concerned about it"; Pharaoh was not "concerned" about ("did not set his heart to") Moses' message from God (Ex 7:23). **(22)** "To put [give] something into one's heart" is to give one ability and concern to do something; thus God "put" it in the heart of the Hebrew craftsmen to teach others (Ex 36:2). **(23)** "To give one's face to" is to focus one's attention on something, as when Jehoshaphat was afraid of the alliance of the Transjordanian kings and "set [his face] to seek the Lord" (2 Chr 20:3). **(23b)** This same phrase can merely mean "to be facing someone or something" (cf. Gen 30:40).

(24) "To give one's face against" is a hostile action (Lev 17:10). **(25)** Used with *lipne* (*lamed* + 6440 - literally, "before the face of"), this verb may mean **(25a)** "to place an object before" or **(25b)** to "set it down before" (Ex 30:6). **(25c)** It may also mean **(25c1)** "to put before" (Deut

11:26), **(25c2)** "to smite" (cf. Deut 2:33), or **(25c3)** "to give as one's possession" (Deut 1:8). Syn.: 3467. See: TWOT—1443; BDB—678a, 1103c.

5415. נְתַן {7x} **nᵉthan** (Aram.), *neth-an′;* corresp. to 5414; *give:*—bestow {2x}, give {4x}, pay {1x}. See: TWOT—2880; BDB—1103c.

5416. נָתָן {42x} **Nâthân**, *naw-thawn′;* from 5414; *given; Nathan,* the name of five Isr.:—*Nathan* {42x}. See: BDB—681d.

5417. נְתַנְאֵל {14x} **Nᵉthan'êl**, *neth-an-ale′;* from 5414 and 410; *given of God; Nethanel,* the name of ten Isr.:—Nethaneel {14x}. See: BDB—682a.

5418. נְתַנְיָה {20x} **Nᵉthanyâh**, *neth-an-yaw′;* or

נְתַנְיָהוּ **Nᵉthanyâhûw**, *neth-an-yaw′- hoo;* from 5414 and 3050; *given of Jah; Nethanjah,* the name of four Isr.:—Nethaniah {20x}. See: BDB—682b.

5419. נְתַן־מֶלֶךְ {1x} **Nᵉthan-Melek**, *neth-an′ meh′-lek;* from 5414 and 4428; *given of* (the) *king; Nethan-Melek,* an Isr.:—Nathan-melech {1x}. See: BDB—682a.

5420. נָתַס {1x} **nâthaç**, *naw-thas′;* a prim. root; *to tear* up:—mar {1x}. See: TWOT—1444; BDB—683a.

5421. נָתַע {1x} **nâthaʿ**, *naw-thah′;* for 5422; *to tear* out:—break {1x}. See: TWOT—1445; BDB—683a.

5422. נָתַץ {42x} **nâthats**, *naw-thats′;* a prim. root; *to tear* down:—break down {22x}, throw down {5x}, destroy {5x}, cast down {3x}, beat down {3x}, pull down {2x}, break out {1x}, overthrow {1x}. See: TWOT—1446; 683a.

5423. נָתַק {27x} **nâthaq**, *naw-thak′;* a prim. root; *to tear* off:—break {12x}, drawn away {2x}, lifted up {2x}, plucked away {1x}, draw {1x}, drawn {1x}, break off {1x}, pluck off {1x}, root out {1x}, pull out {1x}, pluck {1x}, burst in sunder {1x}, break in sunder {2x}. See: TWOT—1447; BDB—683c.

5424. נֶתֶק {14x} **netheq**, *neh′-thek;* from 5423; *scurf:*—(dry) scall {14x}. See: TWOT—1447a; BDB—683d.

5425. נָתַר {8x} **nâthar**, *naw-thar′;* a prim. root; *to jump,* i.e. *be* violently *agitated;* caus., to *terrify, shake* off, *untie:*—drive asunder {1x}, leap {1x}, let loose {2x}, loose {1x}, × make {1x}, move {1x}, undo {1x}. See: TWOT—1448, 1449; BDB—684a.

5426. נְתַר {1x} **nᵉthar** (Aram.), *neth-ar′;* corresp. to 5425:—shake off {1x}. See: TWOT—2881; BDB—1083d, 1103d.

5427. נֶתֶר {2x} **nether**, *neh'-ther;* from 5425; mineral *potash* (so called from *effervescing* with acid):—nitre {2x}. See: TWOT—1450a; BDB—684a.

5428. נָתַשׁ {21x} **nâthash**, *naw-thash';* a prim. root; to *tear* away:—pluck up {10x}, pluck out {3x}, destroyed {1x}, forsaken {1x}, root out {1x}, rooted {1x}, roots {1x}, root up {1x}, pull up {1x}, utterly {1x}. See: TWOT—1451; BDB—684c.

ס

5429. סְאָה {9x} **ç°âh**, *seh-aw';* from an unused root mean. to *define; a seah,* or certain measure (as *determinative*) for grain:—measure {9x}. See: TWOT—1452; BDB—684b.

5430. סְאוֹן {1x} **ç°ôwn**, *seh-own';* from 5431; perh. a military *boot* (as a protection from *mud:*—battle {1x}. See: TWOT—1453a; BDB—684b.

5431. סָאַן {1x} **çâ°an**, *saw-an';* a prim. root; to *be miry;* used only as denom. from 5430; to *shoe,* i.e. (act. part.) a *soldier* shod:—warrior {1x}. See: TWOT—1453; BDB—684b.

5432. סַאסְּאָה {1x} **ça°ç°âh**, *sah-seh-aw';* for 5429; *measurement,* i.e. *moderation:*—measure {1x}. See: TWOT—1452; BDB—684b, 684d.

5433. סָבָא {6x} **çâbâ°**, *saw-baw';* a prim. root; to *quaff* to satiety, i.e. *become tipsy:*—See: drunkard {2x}, winebibbers {1x}, fill {1x}, drunken {1x}, variant {1x}. See: TWOT—1455; BDB—684b, 685a.

5434. סְבָא {4x} **Ç°bâ°**, *seb-aw';* of for. or.; *Seba,* a son of Cush, and the country settled by him:—Seba {4x}. See: BDB—685b.

5435. סֹבֶא {3x} **çôbe°**, *so'-beh;* from 5433; *potation,* concr. (*wine*), or abstr. (*carousal*):—drink {1x}, drunken {1x}, wine {1x}. See: TWOT—1455a; BDB—685a.

5436. סְבָאִי {2x} **Ç°bâ°îy**, *seb-aw-ee';* patrial from 5434; a *Sebaite,* or inhab. of Seba:—Sabean {2x}. See: BDB—685b.

5437. סָבַב {154x} **çâbab**, *saw-bab';* a prim. root; to *revolve, surround,* or *border;* used in various applications, lit. and fig. (as follows):—(stood, turned, etc.) about {54x}, compass {41x}, turn {34x}, turn away {4x}, remove {3x}, returned {2x}, round {2x}, side {2x}, turn aside {2x}, turn back {2x}, beset {2x}, driven {2x}, compass in {2x}, misc. {8x}.

Cabab means "to turn, go around, turn around (change direction)." **(1)** Basically this verb represents a circular movement—"to take a turning." It refers to such movement in general. **(2)** The first occurrence of *cabab* having this emphasis is in **(2a)** Gen 42:24, where Joseph "turned himself about" from his brothers and wept. Here the verb does not tell the precise direction of his departure, only that he left their presence. **(2b)** Similarly, when Samuel was told that Saul went to Carmel and "is gone about, and passed on, and gone down to Gilgal" (1 Sa 15:12), we are not told that he reversed direction in order to get from his origin to Carmel and Gilgal. **(3)** God led Israel out of the way (by an out-of-the-way route) when He took them into the Promised Land. **(3a)** He wanted to avoid having them face war with the Philistines, an event that was unavoidable if they proceeded directly north from Egypt to Palestine. **(3b)** Therefore, He led them through the wilderness—a back route into the land: "But God led the people about, through the way of the wilderness of the Red Sea" (Ex 13:18).

(4) Perhaps one of the passages where this meaning is clearest is Prov 26:14, which speaks of the "turning" of a door on its hinges. **(4a)** An extension of this meaning occurs in 1 Sa 5:8–9, "to remove, to take away": "And they answered, Let the ark of the God of Israel be carried about [taken away] unto Gath. And they carried the ark of the God of Israel about thither" (cf. 2 Kin 16:18). **(5)** *Cabab* is "to go around," in the sense of to proceed or be arranged in a circle. **(5a)** Joseph tells his family: "Lo, my sheaf arose, and also stood upright; and, behold, your sheaves stood round about, and made obeisance to my sheaf" (Gen 37:7). They moved so as to surround his sheaf. **(5b)** This is the action pictured when Israel besieged Jericho, except with the further nuance of encircling in a processional and religious march: "And ye shall compass the city, all ye men of war, and go round about the city once" (Josh 6:3). **(6)** "To travel" and "to return" are used together to represent traveling a circuit. It is said of Samuel that he used to go annually "in circuit" (1 Sa 7:16).

(7) Another variation of this emphasis is "to go around" a territory in order to avoid crossing through it: "And they journeyed from mount Hor by the way of the Red Sea, to compass [go around] the land of Edom: and the soul of the people was much discouraged because of the way" (Num 21:4). **(8)** *Cabab* is also used of the completion of this movement, the state of literally or figuratively surrounding something or someone. **(8a)** The very first biblical occurrence of the word carries this force (according to many scholars): "The name of the first is Pison: that is it which compasseth [flows around] the whole land of Havilah" (Gen 2:11).

(8b) Judg 16:2, where the Gazites "compassed [Samson] in, and laid wait for him all night in the gate of the city," represents another occurrence of this nuance. **(9)** When David spoke of the cords (as a trap) of Sheol "surrounding" him (2 Sa 22:6), he meant that they actually touched him and held him fast.

(10) *Cabab* can be used of sitting down around a table. So Samuel told Jesse to fetch David, "for we will not sit down till he come hither" (1 Sa 16:11). **(10)** This verb can mean "to change direction." **(10a)** This can be a change of direction toward:"Neither shall the inheritance remove from one tribe to another tribe . . ." (Num 36:9); **(10b)** the usual direction of passing on an inheritance is down family lines, and God's commandment that the daughters of Zelophehad marry within their father's families would make certain that this movement of things not be interrupted. **(10c)** This emphasis appears more clearly in 1 Sa 18:11: "And David [escaped] out of his presence twice"; it is certain that David is putting as much space between himself and Saul as possible. He is "running away or turning away" (cf. 1 Sa 22:17). **(11)** *Cabab* may also refer to a change of direction, as in Num 34:4: "And your border shall turn."

(12) There are three special nuances under this emphasis. **(12a)** First, the verb may mean "to roam through" as a scout looking for water: "And they fetched a compass [made a circuit] of seven days' journey: and there was no water for the host, and for the cattle that followed them" (2 Kin 3:9). Some scholars suggest that this is the idea expressed in Gen 2:11 that the Pison meandered through Havilah rather than flowed around it. **(12b)** Second, *cabab* may be used of "turning something over" to someone. So Adonijah said of Solomon: "The kingdom was mine, . . . howbeit the kingdom is turned about, and is become my brother's" (1 Kin 2:15). **(12c)** Third, *cabab* may be used of "changing or turning one thing into another": "And the land shall be turned as a plain from Geba to Rimmon south of Jerusalem" (Zec 14:10). Syn.: 2015. See: TWOT—1456; BDB—685b, 687a, 687b, 687c.

5438. סִבָּה {1x} **çibbâh**, *sib-baw';* from 5437; a (providential) *turn* (of affairs):—cause {1x}.

Cibbah is found in 1 Kin 12:15 and is translated "cause" and means "turn of events." See: TWOT—1456a; BDB—686d.

5439. סָבִיב {308x} **çâbîyb**, *saw-beeb';* or (fem.)

סְבִיבָה **çᵉbîybâh**, *seb-ee-baw';* from 5437; (as noun) a *circle, neighbour,* or *environs;* but chiefly (as adv., with or without prep.) *around:*—round about {25x}2,

on every side {26x}, about {24x} compass {2x}, about us {2x}, circuits {1x}, about them {1x}.

Cebiybah, as a noun, means "area round about; circuit." **(1)** The word can be used as a noun, but it usually occurs as an adverb or preposition. **(2)** In 1 Chr 11:8 it refers to the "parts round about": "And he built the city round about, even from Millo round about." **(3)** The word may also be used for "circuits": "And the wind returneth again according to his circuits" (Eccl 1:6). **(4)** The first biblical appearance of the word is in Gen 23:17, and it refers to "within the circuit of": "And the field of Ephron, which was in Machpelah, which was before Mamre, the field, and the cave which was therein, and all the trees that were in the field, that were in all the borders round about, were made sure." See: TWOT—1456b; BDB—686d.

5440. סָבַךְ {2x} **çâbak**, *saw-bak';* a prim. root; to *entwine:*—fold together, wrap {2x}. See: TWOT—1457; BDB—687c.

5441. סֹבֶךְ {1x} **çôbek**, *so'-bek;* from 5440; a *copse:*—thicket {1x}. See: TWOT—1457b; BDB—687c.

5442. סְבָךְ {4x} **çᵉbâk**, *seb-awk';* from 5440, a *copse:*—thick {1x}, thicket {3x}. See: TWOT—1457a; BDB—687c.

5443. סַבְּכָא {4x} **çabbᵉkâ**ʾ (Aram.), *sab-bek-aw';* or

שַׂבְּכָא **sabbᵉkâ**ʾ (Aram.), *sab-bek-aw';* from a root corresp. to 5440; a *lyre:*—sackbut {4x}. See: TWOT—3003; BDB—1103d, 1113c.

5444. סִבְּכַי {4x} **Çibbᵉkay**, *sib-bek-ah'-ee;* from 5440; *copse-like; Sibbecai,* an Isr.:—Sibbecai {2x}, Sibbechai {2x}. See: BDB—687c.

5445. סָבַל {9x} **çâbal**, *saw-bal';* a prim. root; to *carry* (lit. or fig.), or (refl.) *be burdensome;* spec. to *be gravid:*—bear {1x}, be a burden {1x}, carry {4x}, strong to labour {1x}. Syn.: 5375. See: TWOT—1458; BDB—687d, 1103d.

5446. סְבַל {1x} **çᵉbal** (Aram.), *seb-al';* corresp. to 5445; to *erect:*—strongly laid {1x}. See: TWOT—2882; BDB—1103d.

5447. סֵבֶל {3x} **çêbel**, *say'-bel;* from 5445; a *load* (lit. or fig.):—burden {2x}, charge {1x}. See: TWOT—1458a; BDB—687d.

5448. סֹבֶל {3x} **çôbel**, *so'-bel;* [only in the form

סֻבָּל **çubbâl**, *soob-bawl'*]; from 5445; a *load* (fig.):—burden {3x}. See: TWOT—1458a; BDB—687d.

5449. סַבָּל {5x} çabbâl, sab-bawl'; from 5445; a *porter*:—bearer of burden {3x}, . . . bear burden {1x}, burden {1x}. See: TWOT—1458b; BDB—687d, 688a.

5450. סְבָלָה {6x} çᵉbâlâh, seb-aw-law'; from 5447; *porterage*:—burden {6x}. See: TWOT—1458c; BDB—688a.

5451. סִבֹּלֶת {1x} Çibbôleth, sib-bo'-leth; for 7641; an *ear* of grain:—Sibboleth {1x}. See: TWOT—1458d; BDB—688a.

5452. סְבַר {1x} çᵉbar (Aram.), seb-ar'; a prim. root; to *bear in mind*, i.e. *hope*:—think {1x}. See: TWOT—2883; BDB—1104a.

5453. סִבְרַיִם {1x} Çibrayim, sib-rah'-yim; dual from a root corresp. to 5452; *double hope; Sibrajim*, a place in Syria:—Sibraim {1x}. See: BDB—688a.

5454. סַבְתָּא {2x} Çabtâ', sab-taw'; or

סַבְתָּה Çabtâh, sab-taw'; prob. of for. der.; *Sabta* or *Sabtah*, the name of a son of Cush, and the country occupied by his posterity:—Sabta {1x}, Sabtah {1x}. See: BDB—688b.

5455. סַבְתְּכָא {2x} Çabtᵉkâ', sab-tek-aw'; prob. of for. der.; *Sabteca*, the name of a son of Cush, and the region settled by him:—Sabtecha {1x}, Sabtechah {1x}. See: BDB—688b.

5456. סָגַד {4x} çâgad, saw-gad'; a prim. root; to *prostrate* oneself (in homage):—fall down {4x}. See: TWOT—1459; BDB—688b, 1104a.

5457. סְגִד {12x} çᵉgîd (Aram.), seg-eed'; corresp. to 5456:—worship {2x}. See: TWOT—2884; BDB—1104a.

5458. סְגוֹר {2x} çᵉgôwr, seg-ore'; from 5462; prop. *shut up*, i.e. the *breast* (as inclosing the heart); also *gold* (as gen. *shut* up safely):—caul {1x}, gold {1x}. See: TWOT—1462a; BDB—689c.

5459. סְגֻלָּה {8x} çᵉgullâh, seg-ool-law'; fem. pass. part. of an unused root mean. to *shut* up; *wealth* (as closely *shut* up):—peculiar treasure {3x}, peculiar {2x}, special {1x}, jewel {1x}, particular treasure {1x}.

(1) *Cegullah* means "possession." (2) *Cegullah* signifies "property" in the special sense of a private possession one personally acquired and carefully preserves. Six times this word is used of Israel as God's personally acquired (elected, delivered from Egyptian bondage, and formed into what He wanted them to be), carefully preserved, and privately possessed people: "Now therefore, if ye will obey my voice indeed, and keep my covenant, then ye shall be a peculiar treasure unto me above all people: for all the earth is mine" (Ex 19:5—first occurrence). See: TWOT—1460a; BDB—688c.

5460. סְגַן {5x} çᵉgan (Aram.), seg-an'; corresp. to 5461:—governor {5x}. See: TWOT—2885; BDB—1104a.

5461. סָגָן {17x} çâgân, saw-gawn'; from an unused root mean. to *superintend; a praefect* of a province:—prince {1x}, ruler {16x}. See: TWOT—1461; BDB—688c, 1104a.

5462. סָגַר {91x} çâgar, saw-gar'; a prim. root; to *shut* up; fig. to *surrender*:—shut {40x}, shut up {12x}, deliver {9x}, pure {8x}, deliver up {7x}, shut in {3x}, give up {2x}, gave over {2x}, inclosed {1x}, repaired {1x}, closed {1x}, shutting {1x}, stop {1x}, straitly {1x}, together {1x}, close up {1x}.

Cagar means "to shut, close, shut up or imprison." (1) *Cagar* is used for the first time in the Old Testament in the story of the creation of the woman from the rib of the man: "And the Lord God . . . closed up the flesh instead thereof" (Gen 2:21). (2) The obvious use of this verb is to express the "shutting" of doors and gates, and it is used in this way many times in the text (Gen 19:10; Josh 2:7). (3) More specialized uses are: fat closing over the blade of a sword (Judg 3:22) and closing up a breach in city walls (1 Kin 11:27). (4) Figuratively, men may "close their hearts to pity" (Ps 17:10; KJV, "They are inclosed in their own fat," with "fat" symbolizing an unresponsive heart). (5) In the books of Samuel, *cagar* is used in the special sense of "to deliver up," implying that all avenues of escape "are closed": "This day will the Lord deliver thee into mine hand . . ." (1 Sa 17:46; cf. 1 Sa 24:18; 26:8; 2 Sa 18:28). (6) In Lev 13—14, in which the priest functions as a medical inspector of contagious diseases, *cagar* is used a number of times in the sense of "to isolate, to shut up" a sick person away from other people (see Lev 13:5, 11, 21, 26). (7) The more extreme sense of "to imprison" is found in Job 11:10: "If he cut off, and shut up, or gather together, then who can hinder him?" See: TWOT—1462; BDB—688d, 689b, 698c, 1104a.

5463. סְגַר {1x} çᵉgar (Aram.), seg-ar'; corresp. to 5462:—shut up {1x}. See: TWOT—2886; BDB—1104a.

5464. סַגְרִיד {1x} çagrîyd, sag-reed'; prob. from 5462 in the sense of *sweeping* away; a *pouring rain*:—very rainy {1x}. See: TWOT—1463a; BDB—690a.

5465. סַד {2x} çad, sad; from an unused root mean. to *estop*; the *stocks*:—stocks {2x}. See: TWOT—1464; BDB—690a.

5466. סְדִין {4x} çâdîyn, *saw-deen';* from an unused root mean. to *envelop;* a *wrapper,* i.e. *shirt:*—fine linen {2x}, sheet {2x}. See: TWOT—1466; BDB—690b.

5467. סְדֹם {39x} Çᵉdôm, *sed-ome';* from an unused root mean. to *scorch; burnt* (i.e. *volcanic* or *bituminous*) district; *Sedom,* a place near the Dead Sea:—Sodom {39x}. See: TWOT—1465; BDB—690a.

5468. סֶדֶר {1x} çeder, *seh'-der;* from an unused root mean. to *arrange; order:*—order {1x}. See: TWOT—1467a; BDB—690b.

5469. סָהַר {1x} çahar, *sah'-har;* from an unused root mean. to *be round; roundness:*—round {1x}. See: TWOT—1468a; BDB—690c.

5470. סֹהַר {8x} çôhar, *so'-har;* from the same as 5469; a *dungeon* (as *surrounded* by walls):—prison {8x}. See: TWOT—1468b; BDB—690c.

5471. סוֹא {1x} Çôwʾ, *so;* of for. der.; *So,* an Eg. king:—So {1x}. See: BDB—690c.

5472. סוּג {14x} çûwg, *soog;* a prim. root; prop. to *flinch,* i.e. (by impl.) to *go back,* lit. (to *retreat*) or fig. (to *apostatize*):—turned {6x}, turn away {2x}, go back {2x}, turn back {2x}, backslider {1x}, driven {1x}. See: TWOT—1469; BDB—690d.

5473. סוּג {1x} çûwg, *soog;* a prim. root [prob. rather ident. with 5472 through the idea of *shrinking* from a hedge; comp. 7735]; to *hem* in, i.e. *bind:*—set about {1x}. See: TWOT—1470; BDB—691b, 960d.

סוּג çûwg. See 5509.

5474. סוּגַר {1x} çûwgar, *soo-gar';* from 5462; an *inclosure,* i.e. *cage* (for an animal):—ward {1x}. See: TWOT—1462b; BDB—689c.

5475. סוֹד {21x} çôwd, *sode;* from 3245; a *session,* i.e. *company* of persons (in close deliberation); by impl. *intimacy, consultation,* a *secret:*—assembly {5x}, counsel {6x}, inward, {1x} secret (counsel) {9x}.

Cowd means "secret or confidential plan(s); secret or confidential talk; secret; council; gathering; circle." **(1)** *Cowd* means, first, "confidential talk": "Hide me from the secret counsel of the wicked" (Ps 64:2). **(2)** In Prov 15:22: "Without counsel [sel-made] purposes are disappointed: but in the multitude of counselors they are established." **(3)** Sometimes the word signifies simply a talk about something that should be kept confidential: "Debate thy cause with thy neighbor himself; and discover not a secret to another" (Prov 25:9). **(4)** The word

represents a group of intimates with whom one shares confidential matters: "O my soul, come not thou into their [Simeon's and Levi's] secret; unto their assembly, mine honor, be not thou united" (Gen 49:6—the first occurrence of the word). **(5)** Jer 6:11 speaks of the "assembly [informal but still sharing confidential matters] of young men together." **(6)** To "have sweet counsel" is to be in a group where everyone both shares and rejoices in what is being discussed and/or done (Ps 55:14). See: TWOT—1471a; BDB—691c.

5476. סוֹדִי {1x} Çôwdîy, *so-dee';* from 5475; a *confidant; Sodi,* an Isr.:—Sodi {1x}. See: BDB—691d.

5477. סוּחַ {1x} Çûwach, *soo'-akh;* from an unused root mean. to *wipe* away; *sweeping; Suach,* an Isr.:—Suah {1x}. See: BDB—691d.

5478. סוּחָה {1x} çûwchâh, *soo-khaw';* from the same as 5477; something *swept* away, i.e. *filth:*—torn {1x}. See: TWOT—1473a; BDB—492c.

סוּט çûwt. See 7750.

5479. סוֹטַי {2x} Çôwtay, *so-tah'-ee;* from 7750; *roving; Sotai,* one of the Nethinim:—Sotai {2x}. See: BDB—691d.

5480. סוּךְ {9x} çûwk, *sook;* a prim. root; prop. to *smear* over (with oil), i.e. *anoint:*—anoint (self) {8x}, ✕ at all {1x}. See: TWOT—1474; BDB—414c, 691d.

סוֹלְלָה çôwlᵉlâh. See 5550.

5481. סוּמְפּוֹנְיָה {4x} çûwmpôwnᵉyâh (Aram.), *soom-po-neh-yaw';* or

סוּמְפֹּנְיָה çûwmpônᵉyâh (Aram.), *soom-po-neh-yaw';* or

סִיפֹנְיָא çîyphônᵉyâʾ (Dan. 3:10) (Aram.), *see-fo-neh-yaw';* of Gr. or. (sumfwniva); a *bagpipe* (with a double pipe):—dulcimer {4x}. See: BDB—1104a, 1104b.

5482. סְוֵנֵה {2x} Çᵉvênêh, *sev-ay-nay'* [rather to be written

סְוֵנָה Çᵉvênâh, *sev-ay'-naw;* for

סְוֵן Çᵉvên, *sev-ane';* i.e. *to Seven*]; of Eg. der.; *Seven,* a place in Upper Egypt:—Syene {2x}. See: BDB—692b.

5483. סוּס {140x} çûwç, *soos;* or

סֻס çûç, *soos;* from an unused root mean. to *skip* (prop. for joy); a *horse* (as *leaping*); also a *swallow* (from its rapid *flight*):—horse {133x}, crane {2x}, horseback {2x}, horseback + 7392 {2x}, horsehoofs + 6119 {1x}.

Cuc means "horse." **(1)** The first biblical ap-

pearance of *cuc* is in Gen 47:17: "And they brought their cattle unto Joseph: and Joseph gave them bread in exchange for horses, and for the flocks, and for the cattle of the herds, and for the asses." **(2)** In the second quarter of the second millennium the chariot became a major military weapon and "horses" a very desirable commodity. This was the time of Joseph. It was not until the end of the second millennium that a rudimentary cavalry appeared on the battlefield. **(3)** In the period of the eighth-century prophets and following, **(3a)** "horses" became a sign of luxury and apostasy: "Their land also is full of silver and gold, neither is there any end of their treasures; their land is also full of horses, neither is there any end of their chariots:" (Is 2:7; cf. Amos 4:10) **(3b)** inasmuch as Israel's hope for freedom and security was to be the Lord: "But he [the king] shall not multiply horses to himself, nor cause the people to return to Egypt, to . . . multiply horses" (Deut 17:16). **(4)** The "horses" of God are the storm clouds with which he treads upon the sea: "Thou didst walk through the sea with thine horses, through the heap of great waters" (Hab 3:15). See: TWOT—1476, 1477; BDB—692b. comp. 6571.

5484. סוּסָה {1x} **çûwçâh,** *soo-saw';* fem. of 5483; a *mare:*—company of horses {1x}. See: TWOT—1477; BDB—692d.

5485. סוּסִי {1x} **Çûwçiy,** *soo-see';* from 5483; *horse-like; Susi,* an Isr.:—Susi {1x}. See: BDB—692d.

5486. סוּף {8x} **çûwph,** *soof;* a prim. root; to *snatch* away, i.e. *terminate:*—consume {5x}, have an end {1x}, perish {1x}, X be utterly {1x}. See: TWOT—1478; BDB—692d, 1104b.

5487. סוּף {2x} **çûwph** (Aram.), *soof;* corresp. to 5486; to *come to an end:*—consume {1x}, fulfill {1x}. See: TWOT—2888; BDB—1104b.

5488. סוּף {28x} **çûwph,** *soof;* prob. of Eg. or.; a *reed,* espec. the *papyrus:*—flag {3x}, Red [sea] {23x}, weeds {1x}. comp. 5489. See: TWOT—1479; BDB—693a.

5489. סוּף {1x} **Çûwph,** *soof;* for 5488 (by ellip. of 3220); the *Reed* (Sea):—Red Sea {1x}. See: TWOT—1479; BDB—693b.

5490. סוֹף {5x} **çôwph,** *sofe;* from 5486; a *termination:*—conclusion {1x}, end {3x}, hinder part {1x}. See: TWOT—1478a; BDB—693a.

5491. סוֹף {5x} **çôwph** (Aram.), *sofe;* corresp. to 5490:—end {5x}. See: TWOT—2888a; BDB—1104b.

5492. סוּפָה {16x} **çûwphâh,** *soo-faw';* from 5486; a *hurricane:*—storm {3x}, tempest {1x}, whirlwind {11x}, Red sea {1x}. See: TWOT—1478b; BDB—693a, 693b.

5493. סוּר {301x} **çûwr,** *soor;* or

שׂוּר **sûwr** (Hosea 9:12), *soor;* a prim. root; to *turn* off (lit. or fig.):—(put, take, . . .) away {97x}, depart {76x}, remove {35x}, aside {29x}, take {14x}, turn {12x}, turn in {9x}, take off {6x}, go {3x}, put {3x}, eschewed {3x}, misc. {14x} = be [-head], bring, call back, decline, get [you], X grievous, leave undone, be past, rebel, revolt, X be sour, withdraw, be without. See: TWOT—1480; BDB—693b, 694c, 963a, 965a.

5494. סוּר {1x} **çûwr,** *soor;* prob. pass. part. of 5493; *turned* off, i.e. *deteriorated:*—degenerate {1x}. See: TWOT—1480; BDB—693b, 694c.

5495. סוּר {1x} **Çûwr,** *soor;* the same as 5494; *Sur,* a gate of the temple:—Sur {1x}. See: BDB—694c.

5496. סוּת {18x} **çûwth,** *sooth;* perh. denom. from 7898; prop. to *prick,* i.e. (fig.) stimulate; by impl. to *seduce:*—entice {1x}, move {5x}, persuade {5x}, provoke {1x}, remove {1x}, set on {2x}, stir up {2x}, take away {1x}. See: TWOT—1481; BDB—694c.

5497. סוּת {1x} **çûwth,** *sooth;* prob. from the same root as 4533; *covering,* i.e. *clothing:*—clothes {1x}. See: TWOT—1472a; BDB—691d, 694d.

5498. סָחַב {5x} **çâchab,** *saw-khab';* a prim. root; to *trail* along:—draw {2x}, draw out {2x}, tear {1x}. See: TWOT—1482; BDB—694d.

5499. סְחָבָה {2x} **çechâbâh,** *seh-khaw-baw';* from 5498; a *rag:*—cast clout {2x}. See: TWOT—1482a; BDB—695a.

5500. סָחָה {1x} **çâchâh,** *saw-khaw';* a prim. root; to *sweep* away:—scrape {1x}. See: TWOT—1483; BDB—691d, 695a.

5501. סְחִי {1x} **çechiy,** *seh-khee';* from 5500; *refuse* (as *swept* off):—offscouring {1x}. See: TWOT—1483a; BDB—695a.

סָחִישׁ **çâchiysh.** See 7823.

5502. סָחַף {2x} **çâchaph,** *saw-khaf';* a prim. root; to *scrape* off:—sweep away {1x}, sweeping away {1x}. See: TWOT—1485; BDB—695a.

5503. סָחַר {20x} **çâchar,** *saw-khar';* a prim. root; to *travel* round (spec. as a *pedlar*); intens. to *palpitate:*—merchant {14x}, trade {2x}, about {1x}, merchantmen + 582 {1x},

panteth {1x}, traffick {1x}. See: TWOT—1486; BDB—695b.

5504. סָחַר {4x} çachar, sakh'-ar; from 5503; profit (from trade):—merchandise {4x}. See: TWOT—1486a; BDB—695c.

5505. סָחַר {3x} çâchar, saw-khar'; from 5503; an emporium; abstr. profit (from trade):—mart {1x}, merchandise {2x}. See: TWOT—1486a; BDB—695c.

5506. סְחֹרָה {1x} çᵉc ôrâh, sekh-o-raw'; from 5503; traffic:—merchandise {1x}. See: TWOT—1486b; BDB—695c.

5507. סֹחֵרָה {1x} çôchêrâh, so-khay-raw'; prop. act. part. fem. of 5503; something surrounding the person, i.e. a shield:—buckler {1x}. See: TWOT—1486c; BDB—695c.

5508. סֹחֶרֶת {1x} çôchereth, so-kheh'-reth; similar to 5507; prob. a (black) tile (or tessara) for laying borders with:—black marble {1x}. See: TWOT—1486e; BDB—695c.

סֵט çêt. See 7750.

5509. סִיג {8x} çîyg, seeg; or

סוּג çûwg (Eze 22:18), soog; from 5472 in the sense of refuse; scoria:—dross {8x}. See: TWOT—1469a; BDB—688c, 691a.

5510. סִיוָן {1x} Çîyvân, see-vawn'; prob. of Pers. or.; Sivan, the third Heb. month:—Sivan {1x}. See: TWOT—1487; BDB—695d.

5511. סִיחוֹן {37x} Çîychôwn, see-khone'; or

סִיחֹן Çîychôn, see-khone'; from the same as 5477; tempestuous; Sichon, an Amoritish king:—Sihon {37x}. See: BDB—695d.

5512. סִין {6x} Çîyn, seen; of uncert. der.; Sin, the name of an Eg. town and (prob.) desert adjoining:—Sin {6x}. See: BDB—695d.

5513. סִינִי {2x} Çîynîy, see-nee'; from an otherwise unknown name of a man; a Sinite, or desc. of one of the sons of Canaan:—Sinite {2x}. See: BDB—696b.

5514. סִינַי {35x} Çîynay, see-nah'-ee; of uncert. der.; Sinai, a mountain of Arabia:—Sinai {35x}. See: BDB—696a.

5515. סִינִים {1x} Çîynîym, see-neem'; plur. of an otherwise unknown name; Sinim, a distant Oriental region:—Sinim {1x}. See: BDB—692b, 696b.

5516. סִיסְרָא {21x} Çîyçᵉrâ, see-ser-aw'; of uncert. der.; Sisera, the name of a Canaanitish king and of one of the Nethinim:—Sisera {21x}. See: BDB—696b.

5517. סִיעָא {2x} Çîyʿâ, see-ah'; or

סִיעֲהָא Çîyʿăhâ, see-ah-haw'; from an unused root mean. to converse; congregation; Sia, or Siaha, one of the Nethinim:—Sia {1x}, Siaha {1x}.

סִיפְנְיָא çîyphônᵉyâ. See 5481.

5518. סִיר {34x} çîyr, seer; or (fem.)

סִירָה çîyrâh, see-raw'; or

סִרָה çîrâh (Jer. 52:18), see-raw'; from a prim. root mean. to boil up; a pot; also a thorn (as springing up rapidly); by impl. a hook:—pot {21x}, caldron {5x}, thorns {4x}, washpot + 7366 {2x}, pans {1x}, fishhooks + 1729 {1x}. See: TWOT—1489, 1490; BDB—696c.

5519. סָךְ {1x} çâk, sawk; from 5526; prop. a thicket of men, i.e. a crowd:—multitude {1x}. See: TWOT—1492c; BDB—697c.

5520. סֹךְ {4x} çôk, soke; from 5526; a hut (as of entwined boughs); also a lair:—covert {1x}, den {1x}, pavilion {1x}, tabernacle {1x}. See: TWOT—1492d; BDB—697c.

5521. סֻכָּה {31x} çukkâh, sook-kaw'; fem. of 5520; a hut or lair:—booth {11x}, cottage {1x}, covert {1x}, pavilion {5x}, tabernacle {12x}, tent {1x}. Syn.: 168, 4908, 6898. See: TWOT—1492d; BDB—697c.

5522. סִכּוּת {1x} çikkûwth, sik-kooth'; fem. of 5519; an (idolatrous) booth:—tabernacle {1x}. See: TWOT—1491; BDB—696d.

5523. סֻכּוֹת {18x} Çukkôwth, sook-kohth'; or

סֻכֹּת Çukkôth, sook-kohth'; plur. of 5521; booths; Succoth, the name of a place in Egypt and of three in Pal.:—Succoth {18x}. See: TWOT—1492e; BDB—697d.

5524. סֻכּוֹת בְּנוֹת {1x} Çukkôwth Bᵉnôwth, sook-kohth' ben-ohth'; from 5523 and the (irreg.) plur. of 1323; booths of (the) daughters; brothels, i.e. idolatrous tents for impure purposes:—Succoth-benoth {1x}. See: BDB—696d.

5525. סֻכִּי {1x} Çukkîy, sook-kee'; patrial from an unknown name (perh. 5520); a Sukkite, or inhab. of some place near Egypt (i.e. hut-dwellers):—Sukkiims {1x}. See: BDB—696d.

5526. סָכַךְ {23x} çâkak, saw-kak'; or

שָׂכַךְ sâkak (Exod. 33:22), saw-kak'; a prim. root; prop. to entwine as a screen; by impl. to fence in, cover over, (fig.) protect:—cover {15x}, covering {2x}, defence {1x}, defendest {1x}, hedge in {1x}, join together {1x}, set {1x}, shut up {1x}. See: TWOT—1475,

1492, 2259, 2260; BDB—692a, 696d, 697b, 697d, 698c, 962b, 967d, 968a.

5527. סְכָכָה {1x} **Çᵉkâkâh,** *sek-aw-kaw';* from 5526; *inclosure; Secacah,* a place in Pal.:—Secacah {1x}. See: BDB—698a.

5528. סָכַל {8x} **çâkal,** *saw-kal';* for 3688; to *be silly:*—done foolishly {5x}, turn into foolishness {1x}, make foolish {1x}, play the fool {1x}. See: TWOT—1493; BDB—698a.

5529. סֶכֶל {1x} **çekel,** *seh'-kel;* from 5528; *silliness;* concr. and collect. *dolts:*—folly {1x}. See: TWOT—1493b; BDB—698a.

5530. סָכָל {7x} **çâkâl,** *saw-kawl';* from 5528; *silly:*—fool {4x}, foolish {2x}, sottish {1x}. See: TWOT—1493a; BDB—698a.

5531. סִכְלוּת {7x} **çiklûwth,** *sik-looth';* or

סִׂכְלוּת **siklûwth** (Eccl. 1:17) *sik-looth';* from 5528; *silliness:*—folly {5x}, foolishness {2x}. Syn.: 191, 200, 3689, 5036, 5528. See: TWOT—1493c, 1493d; BDB—698a, 968d.

5532. סָכַן {12x} **çâkan,** *saw-kan';* a prim. root; to *be familiar* with; by impl. to *minister* to, *be serviceable* to, *be customary:*—acquaint {2x}, profitable {2x}, cherish {2x}, advantage {1x}, ever {1x}, profiteth {1x}, treasurer {1x}, unprofitable {1x}, wont {1x}. See: TWOT—1494; BDB—698b.

5533. סָכַן {2x} **çâkan,** *saw-kan';* prob. a denom. from 7915; prop. to *cut,* i.e. *damage;* also to *grow* (caus. *make*) *poor:*—endangered {1x}, impoverished {1x}. See: TWOT—1495, 1496; BDB—698b, 698c.

5534. סָכַר {4x} **çâkar,** *saw-kar';* a prim. root; to *shut* up; by impl. to *surrender:*—stopped {2x}, give over {1x}, impoverished {1x}. See: TWOT—1497, 1498; BDB—698c. See also 5462, 7936.

5535. סָכַת {1x} **çâkath,** *saw-kath';* a prim. root; to *be silent;* by impl. to *observe* quietly:—take heed {1x}. See: TWOT—1499; BDB—698d.

סֻכֹּת **Çukkôth.** See 5523.

5536. סַל {15x} **çal,** *sal;* from 5549; prop. a *willow twig* (as *pendulous*), i.e. an *osier;* but only as woven into a *basket:*—basket {15x}. See: TWOT—1507a; BDB—698d, 700d.

5537. סָלָא {1x} **çâlâ,** *saw-law';* a prim. root; to *suspend* in a balance, i.e. *weigh:*—compare {1x}. See: TWOT—1500; BDB—698d.

5538. סִלָּא {1x} **Çillâ,** *sil-law';* from 5549; an *embankment; Silla,* a place in Jerusalem:—Silla {1x}. See: BDB—698d.

5539. סָלַד {1x} **çâlad,** *saw-lad';* a prim. root; prob. to *leap* (with joy), i.e. *exult:*—harden self {1x}. See: TWOT—1501; BDB—698d.

5540. סֶלֶד {2x} **Çeled,** *seh'-led;* from 5539; *exultation; Seled,* an Isr.:—Seled {2x}. See: BDB—699a.

5541. סָלָה {4x} **çâlâh,** *saw-law';* a prim. root; to *hang* up, i.e. *weigh,* or (fig.) *contemn:*—trodden down {1x}, trodden down under foot {1x}, valued {2x}. See: TWOT—1502, 1503; BDB—699a.

5542. סֶלָה {74x} **Çelâh,** *seh'-law;* from 5541; *suspension* (of music), i.e. *pause:*—Selah {74x}. See: TWOT—1506a; BDB—699a, 699d.

5543. סַלּוּ {6x} **Çallûw,** *sal-loo';* or

סַלּוּא **Çallûw,** *sal-loo';* or

סָלוּא **Çâlûw,** *sal-loo';* or

סַלַּי **Çallay,** *sal-lah'-ee;* from 5541; *weighed; Sallu* or *Sallai,* the name of two Isr.:—Sallai {2x}, Sallu {3x}, Salu {1x}. See: BDB—699a, 699b.

5544. סִלּוֹן {2x} **çillôwn,** *sil-lone';* or

סַלּוֹן **çallôwn,** *sal-lone';* from 5541; a *prickle* (as if *pendulous*):—brier {1x}, thorn {1x}. See: TWOT—1504; BDB—699b.

5545. סָלַח {46x} **çâlach,** *saw-lakh';* a prim. root; to *forgive:*—forgive {19x}, forgiven {13x}, pardon {13x}, spare {1x}.

Calach is reserved especially to mark the pardon extended to the sinner by God. **(1)** It is never used to denote that inferior kind and measure of forgiveness that is exercised by one man toward another. **(2)** It is the Divine restoration of an offender into favor, whether through his own repentance or the intercession of another. **(3)** Though not identical with atonement, the two are closely related. In fact, the covering of the sin and the forgiveness of the sinner can only be understood as two aspects of one truth; for both found their fullness in God's provision of mercy through Christ (cf. Heb 9:22). **(4)** God is always the subject of forgiveness. **(5)** No other Old Testament verb means "to forgive," although several verbs include "forgiveness" in the range of meanings given a particular context [e.g., (maca' – 4229 in Ex 32:32; and kapar - 3722 in Eze 16:63]. **(6)** The first biblical occurrence is in Moses' prayer of intercession on behalf of the Israelites: "It is a stiffnecked people; and [forgive] our iniquity and our sin, and take us for thine inheritance" (Ex 34:9).

(7) Most occurrences of *calach* are in the

sacrificial laws of Leviticus and Numbers. **(8)** In the typology of the Old Testament, sacrifices foreshadowed the accomplished work of Jesus Christ, and the Old Testament believer was assured of "forgiveness" based on sacrifice: "And the priest shall make an atonement [for him in regard to his sin]" (Num 15:25, 28), **(8a)** "And it shall be forgiven him" (Lev 4:26; cf. vv. 20, 31, 35; 5:10, 13, 16, 18). **(8b)** The mediators of the atonement were the priests who offered the sacrifice. **(8c)** The sacrifice was ordained by God to promise ultimate "forgiveness" in God's sacrifice of His own Son. **(8d)** Moreover, sacrifice was appropriately connected to atonement, as there is no forgiveness without the shedding of blood (Lev 4:20; cf. Heb 9:22). **(9)** Out of His grace, God alone "forgives" sin. **(9a)** The Israelites experienced God's "forgiveness" in the wilderness and in the Promised Land. **(9b)** As long as the temple stood, sacrificial atonement continued and the Israelites were assured of God's "forgiveness."

(10) When the temple was destroyed and sacrifices ceased, God sent the prophetic word that He graciously would restore Israel out of exile and "forgive" its sins: "And they shall teach no more every man his neighbour, and every man his brother, saying, Know the LORD: for they shall all know me, from the least of them unto the greatest of them, saith the LORD: for I will forgive their iniquity, and I will remember their sin no more" (Jer 31:34). **(11)** The psalmist appealed to God's great name in his request for "forgiveness": "For thy name's sake, O Lord, pardon mine iniquity; for it is great" (Ps 25:11). **(12)** David praised God for the assurance of "forgiveness" of sins: "Bless the Lord, O my soul . . . , who forgiveth all thine iniquities" (Ps 103:2–3). **(13)** The Old Testament saints, while involved in sacrificial rites, put their faith in God. It was their faith in God that saved, not the sacrifices. See: TWOT—1505; BDB—699b.

5546. סָלַח {1x} **çallâch,** *saw-lawkh';* from 5545; *placable:*—ready to forgive {1x}. See: TWOT—1505a; BDB—699c.

סַלַי **Çallay.** See 5543.

5547. סְלִיחָה {3x} **çᵉlîychâh,** *sel-ee-khaw';* from 5545; *pardon:*—forgiveness {2x}, pardon {1x}. See: TWOT—1505b; BDB—699c.

5548. סַלְכָה {4x} **Çalkâh,** *sal-kaw';* from an unused root. mean. to *walk; walking; Salcah,* a place E. of the Jordan:—Salcah {2x}, Salchah {2x}. See: TWOT—1505b; BDB—699c.

5549. סָלַל {12x} **çâlal,** *saw-lal';* a prim. root; to *mound* up (espec. a turnpike);

fig. to *exalt;* refl. to *oppose* (as by a dam):—cast up {6x}, raise up {2x}, exalt {2x}, extol {1x}, made plain {1x}. See: TWOT—1506; BDB—699c.

5550. סֹלְלָה {11x} **çôlᵉlâh,** *so-lel-aw';* or

סוֹלְלָה **çôwlᵉlâh,** *so-lel-aw';* act. part. fem. of 5549, but used pass.; a military *mound,* i.e. *rampart* of besiegers:—bank {3x}, mount {8x}. See: TWOT—1506b; BDB—700c.

5551. סֻלָּם {1x} **çullâm,** *sool-lawm';* from 5549; a *stair-case:*—ladder {1x}. See: TWOT—1506c; BDB—700c.

5552. סַלְסִלָּה {1x} **çalçillâh,** *sal-sil-law';* from 5541; a *twig* (as *pendulous*):—baskets {1x}. See: TWOT—1507b; BDB—700d.

5553. סֶלַע {60x} **çela',** *seh'-lah;* from an unused root mean. to be *lofty;* a craggy *rock,* lit. or fig. (a *fortress*):—rock {57x}, strong hold {1x}, stones {1x}, stony {11x}. See: TWOT—1508a; BDB—700d.

5554. סֶלַע {2x} **Çela',** *seh'-lah;* the same as 5553; *Sela,* the rock-city of Idumaea:—Sela {1x}, Selah {1x}. See: BDB—701a.

5555. סֶלַע הַמַּחְלְקוֹת {1x} **Çela' ham-machlᵉqôwth,** *seh'-lah ham-makh-lek-ōth';* from 5553 and the plur. of 4256 with the art. interposed; *rock of the divisions; Sela-ham-Machlekoth,* a place in Pal.:—Sela-hammalekoth {1x}. See: BDB—325d, 563b.

5556. סָלְעָם {1x} **çol'âm,** *sol-awm';* appar. from the same as 5553 in the sense of *crushing* as with a rock, i.e. consuming; a kind of *locust* (from its *destructiveness*):—bald locust {1x}. See: TWOT—1509; BDB—701b.

5557. סָלַף {7x} **çâlaph,** *saw-laf';* a prim. root; prop. to *wrench,* i.e. (fig.) to *subvert:*—overthrow {4x}, pervert {3x}. See: TWOT—1510; BDB—701b.

5558. סֶלֶף {2x} **çeleph,** *seh'-lef;* from 5557; *distortion,* i.e. (fig.) *viciousness:*—perverseness {2x}. See: TWOT—1510a; BDB—701b.

5559. סְלִק {5x} **çᵉlîq** (Aram.), *sel-eek';* a prim. root; to *ascend:*—came up {4x}, came {1x}. See: TWOT—2889; BDB—1104b.

5560. סֹלֶת {53x} **çôleth,** *so'-leth;* from an unused root mean. to *strip; flour* (as *chipped* off):—fine {1x}, flour {52x}. See: TWOT—1512; BDB—701c.

5561. סַם {17x} **çam,** *sam;* from an unused root mean. to *smell sweet;* an *aroma:*—sweet {14x}, sweet spices {3x}. See: TWOT—1516a; BDB—701c, 702c.

5562. סַמְגַּר נְבוֹ {1x} **Çamgar Nᵉbôw**, *sam-gar' neb-o';* of for. or.; *Sam-gar-Nebo*, a Bab. general:—Samgar-nebo {1x}. See: BDB—701c.

5563. סְמָדַר {3x} **çᵉmâdar**, *sem-aw-dar';* of uncert. der.; a vine *blossom;* used also adv. *abloom:*—tender grape {3x}. Syn.: 1154, 6025. See: TWOT—1513; BDB—701d.

5564. סָמַךְ {48x} **çâmak**, *saw-mak';* a prim. root; to *prop* (lit. or fig.); refl. to *lean* upon or *take hold* of (in a favorable or unfavorable sense):—lay {18x}, uphold {9x}, put {5x}, lean {3x}, stay {3x}, sustained {3x}, holden up {1x}, borne up {1x}, established {1x}, stand fast {1x}, lieth hard {1x}, rested {1x}, set {1x}. See: TWOT—1514; BDB—701d.

5565. סְמַכְיָהוּ {1x} **Çᵉmakyâhûw**, *sem-ak-yaw'-hoo;* from 5564 and 3050; *supported of Jah; Semakjah*, an Isr.:—Semachiah {1x}. See: BDB—702b.

5566. סֶמֶל {5x} **çemel**, *seh'-mel;* or

סֵמֶל **çêmel**, *say'-mel;* from an unused root mean. to *resemble;* a *likeness:*—figure {1x}, idol {2x}, image {2x}.
   Cemel means an image, figure, or likeness; to be construed as a standardized likeness of a false deity in which it is imagined by its worshipers. Syn.: 2796, 4906, 6459, 6736, 6754, 8544. See: TWOT—1515; BDB—702b.

5567. סָמַן {1x} **çâman**, *saw-man';* a prim. root; to *designate:*—appointed {1x}. See: TWOT—1517; BDB—651c, 702c.

5568. סָמַר {2x} **çâmar**, *saw-mar';* a prim. root; to *be erect,* i.e. *bristle* as hair:—stood up {1x}, tremble {1x}. See: TWOT—1518; BDB—702c.

5569. סָמָר {1x} **çâmâr**, *saw-mar';* from 5568; *bristling,* i.e. *shaggy:*—rough {1x}. See: TWOT—1518a; BDB—702c.

5570. סְנָאָה {3x} **Çᵉnâʼâh**, *sen-aw-aw';* from an unused root mean. to *prick; thorny; Senaah*, a place in Pal.:—Senaah {2x}, Hassenaah [*with the art.*]{1x}. See: BDB—702d, 703a.

סְנָאָה **çᵉnûʼâh**. See 5574.

5571. סַנְבַלַּט {10x} **Çanballat**, *san-bal-lat';* of for. or.; *Sanballat*, a Pers. satrap of Samaria:—Sanballat {10x}. See: BDB—702d.

5572. סְנֶה {6x} **çᵉneh**, *sen-eh';* from an unused root mean. to *prick;* a *bramble:*—bush {6x}. See: TWOT—1520; BDB—702d.

5573. סֶנֶה {1x} **Çeneh**, *seh-neh';* the same as 5572; *thorn; Seneh*, a crag in Pal.:—Seneh {1x}. See: BDB—702d.

סַנָּה **Çannâh**. See 7158.

5574. סְנוּאָה {2x} **Çᵉnûwʼâh**, *sen-oo-aw';* or

סְנָאָה **Çᵉnûʼâh**, *sen-oo-aw'* from the same as 5570; *pointed;* (used with the art. as a proper name) *Senuah*, the name of two Isr.:—Hasenuah [*incl. the art.*] {1x}, Senuah {1x}. See: BDB—703a.

5575. סַנְוֵר {3x} **çanvêr**, *san-vare';* of uncert. der.; (in plur.) *blindness:*—blindness {3x}. See: TWOT—1520; BDB—703a.

5576. סַנְחֵרִיב {13x} **Çanchêrîyb**, *san-khay-reeb';* of for. or.; *Sancherib*, an Ass. king:—Sennacherib {13x}. See: BDB—703a.

5577. סַנְסִן {1x} **çançin**, *san-seen';* from an unused root mean. to *be pointed;* a *twig* (as *tapering*):—boughs {1x}. See: TWOT—1522; BDB—703b.

5578. סַנְסַנָּה {1x} **Çançannâh**, *san-san-naw';* fem. of a form of 5577; a *bough; Sansannah*, a place in Pal.:—Sansannah {1x}. See: BDB—703a.

5579. סְנַפִּיר {1x} **çᵉnappîyr**, *sen-ap-peer';* of uncert. der.; a *fin* (collect.):—fins {1x}. See: TWOT—1523; BDB—703b.

5580. סָס {1x} **çâç**, *sawce;* from the same as 5483; a *moth* (from the *agility* of the fly):—moth {1x}. See: TWOT—1524; BDB—703b.

סָס **çûç**. See 5483.

5581. סִסְמַי {2x} **Çiçmay**, *sis-mah'-ee;* of uncert. der.; *Sismai*, an Isr.:—Sisamai {2x}. See: BDB—703b.

5582. סָעַד {12x} **çâʻad**, *saw-ad';* a prim. root; to *support* (mostly fig.):—comfort {3x}, strengthen {3x}, hold me up {3x}, upholden {1x}, establish {1x}, refresh {1x}. See: TWOT—1525; BDB—703c, 1104a.

5583. סְעַד {1x} **çᵉʻad** (Aram.), *seh-ad';* corresp. to 5582; to *aid:*—helping {1x}. See: TWOT—2890; BDB—1104b.

5584. סָעָה {1x} **çâʻâh**, *saw-aw';* a prim. root; to *rush:*—storm {1x}. See: TWOT—1526; BDB—703c.

5585. סָעִיף {6x} **çâʻîyph**, *saw-eef';* from 5586; a *fissure* (of rocks); also a *bough* (as *subdivided*):—(outmost) branches {2x}, clifts, top {3x}. See: TWOT—1527a; BDB—703d.

5586. סָעַף {1x} çâʿaph, *saw-af'*; a prim. root; prop. to *divide* up; but used only as denom. from 5585, to *disbranch* (a tree):— top {1x}. See: TWOT—1527c; BDB—703d.

5587. סָעִף {3x} çâʿîph, *saw-eef'* or

סָעִיף sâʿîph, *saw-eef'*; from 5586; *divided* (in mind), i.e. (abstr.) a *sentiment:*—opinion {1x}, thoughts {2x}. See: TWOT—1527f; BDB—704a, 972a.

5588. סֵעֵף {1x} çêʿêph, *say-afe'*; from 5586; *divided* (in mind), i.e. (concr.) a *skeptic:*—thoughts {1x}. See: TWOT—1527e; BDB—704a.

5589. סְעַפָּה {2x} çᵉʿappâh, *seh-ap-paw'*; fem. of 5585; a *twig:*—bough {1x}, branch {1x}. See: TWOT—1527b; BDB—703d. comp. 5634.

5590. סָעַר {7x} çâʿar, *saw-ar'*; a prim. root; to *rush* upon; by impl. to *toss* (tran. or intr., lit. or fig.):—whirlwind {3x}, tempestuous {2x}, troubled {1x}, tossed with tempest {1x}. See: TWOT—1528b; BDB—704a.

5591. סַעַר {24x} çaʿar, *sah'-ar;* or (fem.)

סְעָרָה çᵉʿârâh, *seh-aw-raw'*; from 5590; a *hurricane:*—whirlwind {12x}, tempest {6x}, stormy {4x}, storm {1x}, whirlwind + 7307 {1x}. Syn.: 5036, 5492, 8183. See: TWOT—1528; BDB—704b, 973b.

5592. סַף {32x} çaph, *saf;* from 5605, in its orig. sense of *containing;* a *vestibule* (as a *limit);* also a *dish* (for holding blood or wine):—door {12x}, threshold {8x}, bason {4x}, posts {3x}, bowls {2x}, gates {2x}, cup {1x}. See: TWOT—1528b; BDB—704c, 706b.

5593. סַף {1x} Çaph, *saf;* the same as 5592; *Saph,* a Philistine:—Saph {1x}. See: BDB—704c, 706c. comp. 5598.

5594. סָפַד {30x} çâphad, *saw-fad'*; a prim. root; prop. to *tear* the hair and *beat* the breasts (as Orientals do in grief); gen. to *lament;* by impl. to *wail:*—lament {13x}, mourn {15x}, mourners {1x}, wail {1x}. Syn.: 56, 6969. See: TWOT—1530; BDB—704c, 973c.

5595. סָפָה {20x} çâphâh, *saw-faw'*; a prim. root; prop. to *scrape* (lit. to *shave;* but usually fig.) together (i.e. to *accumulate* or *increase*) or away (i.e. to *scatter, remove,* or *ruin;* intr. to *perish*):—add {3x}, augment {1x}, consume {6x}, destroy {5x}, heap {1x}, join {1x}, perish {2x}, put {1x}. See: TWOT—1531; BDB—705a.

5596. סָפַח {6x} çâphach, *saw-fakh'*; or

שָׂפַח sâphach (Isa. 3:17) *saw-fakh'*; a prim. root; prop. to *scrape* out, but in certain peculiar senses (of *removal* or *associ-*

ation):—put {2x}, abiding {1x}, gather together {1x}, cleave {1x}, smite with the scab {1x}. See: TWOT—1532, 1534; BDB—705b, 705c, 974a.

5597. סַפַּחַת {2x} çappachath, *sap-pakh'-ath;* from 5596; the *mange* (as making the hair fall off):—scab {2x}. See: TWOT—1534a; BDB—705c.

5598. סִפַּי {1x} Çippay, *sip-pah'-ee;* from 5592; *bason-like; Sippai,* a Philistine:— Sippai {1x}. See: BDB—705d, 706c. comp. 5593.

5599. סָפִיחַ {5x} çâphîyach, *saw-fee'-akh;* from 5596; something (spontaneously) *falling* off, i.e. a *self-sown* crop; fig. a *freshet:*— grow of itself {2x}, things which grow {2x}, that which groweth {1x}. See: TWOT—1533a, 1533b; BDB—705b, 705c.

5600. סְפִינָה {1x} çᵉphîynâh, *sef-ee-naw'*; from 5603; a (sea-going) *vessel* (as *ceiled* with a deck):—ship {1x}. Syn.: 591, 6716. See: TWOT—1537b; BDB—706b.

5601. סַפִּיר {11x} çappîyr, *sap-peer'*; from 5608; a *gem* (perh. as used for *scratching* other substances), prob. the *sapphire:*—sapphire {10x}, sapphire stone {1x}. See: TWOT—1535; BDB—705d.

5602. סֵפֶל {2x} çêphel, *say'-fel;* from an unused root mean. to *depress;* a *basin* (as *deepened* out):—bowl {1x}, dish {1x}. See: TWOT—1536; BDB—705d.

5603. סָפַן {6x} çâphan, *saw-fan'*; a prim. root; to *hide* by covering; spec. to *roof* (pass. part. as noun, a *roof*) or *paneling;* fig. to *reserve:*—cieled {2x}, covered {3x}, seated {1x}. See: TWOT—1537; BDB—706a, 974a.

5604. סִפֻּן {1x} çippûn, *sip-poon'*; from 5603; a *wainscot:*—cieling {1x}. See: TWOT—1537a; BDB—706a.

5605. סָפַף {1x} çâphaph, *saw-faf'*; a prim. root; prop. to *snatch* away, i.e. to *terminate;* but used only as denom. from 5592 (in the sense of a *vestibule*), to *wait at* (the) *threshold:*—be a doorkeeper {1x}. See: TWOT—1538c; BDB—706c.

5606. סָפַק {10x} çâphaq, *saw-fak';* or

שָׂפַק sâphaq (1 Kings 20:10; Job 27:23; Isa. 2:6), *saw-fak'*; a prim. root; to *clap* the hands (in token of compact, derision, grief, indignation, or punishment); by impl. of satisfaction, to *be enough;* by impl. of excess, to *vomit:*—clap {2x}, smite {1x}, striketh {1x}, suffice {1x}, wallow {1x}, smote {1x}, smote together {1x}, clappeth {1x}, please {1x}. See: TWOT—1539; BDB—706c, 974a.

5607. סֶפֶק {2x} **çêpheq,** *say'-fek;* or

שֶׂפֶק **sepheq** (Job 20:22; 36:18) *seh'-fek;* from 5606; *chastisement;* also *satiety:*—stroke {1x}, sufficiency {1x}. See: TWOT—1539a; BDB—706d, 974a, 974b.

5608. סָפַר {161x} **çâphar,** *saw-far';* a prim. root; prop. to *score* with a mark as a tally or record, i.e. (by impl.) to *inscribe,* and also to *enumerate;* intens. to *recount,* i.e. *celebrate:*—scribe {50x}, tell {40x}, declare {24x}, number {23x}, count {6x}, shew forth {5x}, writer {4x}, speak {2x}, accounted {1x}, commune {1x}, told out {1x}, reckon {1x}, penknife + 8593 {1x}, shewing {1x}, talk {1x}.

Caphar means "to number, count, proclaim, declare." **(1)** In the basic verbal form this verb signifies "to number or count." **(1a)** This meaning is in its first biblical appearance, Gen 15:5: "Look now toward heaven, and tell the stars, if thou be able to number them." **(1b)** Here the counting is a process which has no completion in view. **(1c)** In Lev 15:13 the emphasis is on a completed task: "And when [the man with the discharge becomes cleansed]; then he shall number to himself seven days for his cleansing, and wash his clothes, and bathe his flesh." **(1d)** Another nuance of this usage is "to count up" or "to take a census": "And David's heart smote him after that he had numbered the people" (2 Sa 24:10). **(2)** The verb is also used of assigning persons to particular jobs: "And Solomon told out threescore and ten thousand men to bear burdens" (2 Chr 2:2). **(3)** Another special use appears in Ezra 1:8, where *caphar* means "to count out according to a list" as the recipient listens: "Even those [the temple furnishings] did Cyrus king of Persia bring forth by the hand of Mithredath the treasurer, and numbered them unto Sheshbazzar, the prince of Judah." **(4)** In Ps 56:8 the word signifies "taking account of," or being aware and concerned about each detail of: "Thou tellest my wanderings. . . ."
(5) This verb can also mean "to measure," in the sense of what one does with grain: "And Joseph gathered corn as the sand of the sea, very much, until he left numbering; for it was without number" (Gen 41:49). **(6)** The verb *caphar* can represent recording something in writing, or enumerating. So, "the Lord shall count, when he writeth up the people, that this man was born there" (Ps 87:6). **(7)** In about 90 instances this verb appears in an intensive form. **(7a)** For the most part the verb in this form means "to recount," to orally list in detail. **(7b)** The one exception to this significance is Job 38:37: "Who can number the clouds in wisdom? Or who can stay the bottles of heaven?" **(7c)** In every other instance the verb signifies a vocal statement (listing or enumeration) of a series of given facts. **(7c1)** In Gen 24:66 Eliezer, Abraham's servant, "told Isaac all things that he had done"; he gave him a summarized but complete account of his activities. Thus Isaac knew who Rebekah was, and why she was there, so he took her to be his wife. **(7c2)** In a similar but somewhat different sense Jacob "told Laban" who he was, that he was from the same family (Gen 29:13). In this case the word represents something other than a report; it represents an account of Jacob's genealogy and perhaps of the events of his parents' lives.
(8) This emphasis on accurate recounting is especially prominent in Num 13:27, where the spies report back to Moses concerning what they saw in Palestine. **(9)** Even more emphatic is Ex 24:3, where one word represents a detailed repetition of what Moses heard from God: "And Moses came and told the people all the words of the Lord, and all the judgments." **(10)** Again, in Is 43:26 a detailed and accurate recounting is clearly in view. In this case the prophet has in mind the presentation of a law case: "Put me in remembrance: let us plead together: declare thou, that thou mayest be justified." **(11)** Because of the predominant meaning presented above, Ps 40:5 could be translated: "If I would declare and speak of them, they would be too numerous to recount" (instead of "to count"). **(12)** In at least one case the verb in the intensive stem means "to exhibit," "to recount or list in detail by being a living example." This meaning first appears in Ex 9:16, where God tells Moses to say to Pharaoh: "And in very deed for this cause have I raised thee up, for to show in thee my power; and that my name may be declared throughout all the earth." See: TWOT—1540, 1540c; BDB—707d, 708b, 1104c.

5609. סְפַר {5x} **çᵉphar** (Aram.), *sef-ar';* from a root corresp. to 5608; a *book:*—book {4x}, roll {1x}. See: TWOT—2891a; BDB—1104c.

5610. סְפָר {1x} **çᵉphâr,** *sef-awr';* from 5608; a *census:*—numbering {1x}.

Cephar means a "numbering or census": "And Solomon numbered all the strangers that were in the land of Israel, after the numbering wherewith David his father had numbered them; and they were found an hundred and fifty thousand and three thousand and six hundred" (2 Chr 2:17). Syn: 5608, 5612, 5615. See: TWOT—1540d; BDB—708c.

5611. סְפָר {1x} **Çᵉphâr,** *sef-awr';* the same as 5610; *Sephar,* a place in Arabia:—Sephar {1x}. See: BDB—708c.

5612. סֵפֶר {184x} çêpher, *say'-fer;* or (fem.)

סִפְרָה çiphrâh (Psa. 56:8 [9]), *sif-raw';* from 5608; prop. *writing* (the art or a document); by impl. a *book:*—book {138x}, letter {29x}, evidence {8x}, bill {4x}, learning {2x}, register {1x}, learned + 3045 {1x}, scroll {1x}.

Cepher means book; tablet. **(1)** Basically this word represents something one writes upon. **(1a)** So in Ex 17:14 "the Lord said unto Moses, Write this for a memorial in a book." **(1b)** In Is 30:8 *cepher* represents a tablet: "Now go, write it before them in a table (3871 – *luwach*), and note it in a book (*cepher*), that it may be for the time to come for ever and ever." **(2)** In Gen 5:1 (the first biblical occurrence of this word) it signifies something that has been written upon, or a written record: "This is the book of the generations of Adam." **(3)** Such a written document may be a summary of God's law (Ex 24:7). **(4)** During the monarchy *cepher* came to represent a letter (2 Sa 11:14). **(5)** Even later it means a king's written decree sent throughout his empire (Est 1:22). **(6)** Usually the word means "book": **(6a)** "Yet now, if thou wilt forgive their sin—; and if not, blot me, I pray thee, out of thy book which thou hast written" (Ex 32:32)—a complete record of whatever one wants to preserve accurately. **(6b)** "Thou tellest my wanderings: put thou my tears into thy bottle: are they not in thy book?" (Ps 56:8). **(7)** Often this word can signify the way a people writes, the written language or script (Is 29:11).

(8) A manuscript **(8a)** was written (Ex 32:32; Deut 17:18) and **(8b)** sealed (Is 29:11), and **(8c)** to be read by the addressee (2 Kin 22:16). **(9)** In Is 30:8 *cepher* represents a tablet. **(9a)** *Cepher,* in Jer 36:6, is similar to scroll (4309 - *megillah*) and **(9b)** book (5612 – *cipra* - Ps 56:8). **(9c)** In Gen 5:1 it signifies something that has been written down, or a written record. **(10)** Many books are named: the book of **(10a)** remembrance (Mal 3:16), **(10b)** life (Ps 69:28), **(10c)** Jasher (Josh 10:13), **(10d)** the generations (Gen 5:1), **(10e)** the Lord, **(10f)** the chronicles of the kings of Israel and of Judah (2 Chr 24:27). **(11)** Usually the word means "book" (Ex 32:32)—a complete record of whatever one wants to preserve accurately. **(12)** *Cepher* can represent a letter (2 Sa 11:14), **(13)** a king's written decree (Est 1:22). **(14)** Prophets wrote books: Nah 1:1; Jer 36. **(15)** Symbolically, Ezekiel ate a book (Eze 2:8–3:1). **(16)** In divorcing his wife, a man gave her a legal document known as the *cepher* of divorce (Deut 24:1). Syn.: 5608, 5610, 5615. See: TWOT—1540a, 1540b; BDB—706d, 707c, 708d, 1104c.

5613. סְפַר {6x} çâphêr (Aram.), *saw-fare';* from the same as 5609; a *scribe* (secular or sacred):—scribe {6x}.

Capher means "scribe." **(1)** In the early monarchy the chief "scribe" was the highest court official next to the king (2 Sa 8:17). **(1a)** His job was to receive and evaluate all royal correspondence—to answer the unimportant and give the rest to the proper officer or to the king himself. **(1b)** He also wrote and/or composed royal communications to those within the kingdom. **(1c)** There was probably an entire corps of lesser scribes under his direction. **(1d)** As a highly trusted official he was sometimes involved in counting and managing great influxes of royal revenue (2 Kin 12:10) and in certain diplomatic jobs (2 Kin 19:2). **(2)** Later *coper* represented the Jewish official in the Persian court who was responsible for Jewish belongings (Ezra 7:11). **(3)** In the post-exilic community this word came to mean someone who was learned in the Old Testament Scripture and especially the Mosaic Law (the Pentateuch; Ezra 7:6). **(4)** The word first occurs in Judg 5:14: "they that handle the pen of the writer"). Syn.: 5610, 5612, 5615. See: TWOT—2891b; BDB—1104c.

5614. סְפָרָד {1x} Çᵉphârâd, *sef-aw-rawd';* of for. der.; *Sepharad,* a region of Assyria:—Sepharad {1x}. See: BDB—709b.

סִפְרָה çiphrâh. See 5612.

5615. סְפֹרָה {1x} çᵉp ôrâh, *sef-o-raw';* from 5608; a *numeration:*—number {1x}.

Ceporah, means a "number or sum": "My mouth shall shew forth thy righteousness and thy salvation all the day; for I know not the numbers thereof" (Ps 71:15). Syn.: 5608, 5610, 5612. See: TWOT—1540e; BDB—707d, 708d.

5616. סְפַרְוִי {1x} Çᵉpharvîy, *sef-ar-vee';* patrial from 5617; a *Sepharvite* or inhab. of Sepharvain:—Sepharvite {1x}. See: BDB—709c.

5617. סְפַרְוַיִם {6x} Çᵉpharvayim (dual), *sef-ar-vah'-yim;* or

סְפָרִים Çᵉphârîym (plur.), *sef-aw-reem';* of for. der.; *Sepharvajim* or *Sepharim,* a place in Assyria:—Sepharvaim {6x}. See: BDB—709b.

5618. סֹפֶרֶת {2x} Çôphereth, *so-feh'-reth;* fem. act. part. of 5608; a *scribe* (prop. female); *Sophereth,* a temple servant:—Sophereth {2x}. See: BDB—709b.

5619. סָקַל {22x} çâqal, *saw-kal';* a prim. root; prop. to *be weighty;* but used only in the sense of *lapidation* or its contrary (as if a delapidation):—stone {15x}, surely {2x}, cast

{1x}, gather out {1x}, gather out stones {1x}, stoning {1x}, threw {1x}. See: TWOT—1541; BDB—709c, 920c.

5620. סַר {3x} **çar,** *sar;* from 5637 contr.; *peevish:*—heavy {2x}, sad {1x}. See: TWOT—1549a; BDB—709d.

5621. סָרַב {1x} **çârâb,** *saw-rawb';* from an unused root mean. to *sting;* a thistle:—brier {1x}. See: TWOT—1542; BDB—709d.

5622. סָרְבַּל {2x} **çarbal** (Aram.), *sar-bal';* of uncert. der.; a *cloak:*—coat {2x}. See: TWOT—2892; BDB—1104c.

5623. סַרְגּוֹן {1x} **Çargôwn,** *sar-gōne';* of for. der.; *Sargon,* an Assy. king:—Sargon {1x}. See: BDB—709d.

5624. סֶרֶד {2x} **Çered,** *seh'-red;* from a prim. root mean. to *tremble; trembling; Sered,* an Isr.:—Sered {2x}. See: BDB—710a.

5625. סַרְדִּי {1x} **Çardiy,** *sar-dee';* patron. from 5624; a *Seredite* (collect.) or desc. of Sered:—Sardites {1x}. See: BDB—710a.

5626. סִרָה {1x} **Çîrâh,** *see-raw';* from 5493; *departure; Sirah,* a cistern so-called:—Sirah {1x}. See: BDB—92d, 694c, 710a. See also 5518.

5627. סָרָה {8x} **çârâh,** *saw-raw';* from 5493; *apostasy, crime;* fig. *remission:*—X continual, rebellion {2x}, revolt {3x}, turn away {1x}, wrong {1x}. See: TWOT—1480a; BDB—694c, 710a.

5628. סָרַח {7x} **çârach,** *saw-rakh';* a prim. root; to *extend* (even to *excess*):—exceeding {1x}, hang {2x}, spread {1x}, stretch self {2x}, banish {1x}. See: TWOT—1543; BDB—710a.

5629. סֶרַח {1x} **çerach,** *seh'-rakh;* from 5628; a *redundancy:*—remnant {1x}. See: TWOT—1543a; BDB—710b.

5630. סִרְיֹן {2x} **çiyrôn,** *sir-yone';* for 8302; a coat of *mail:*—brigandine {2x}. See: TWOT—1544; BDB—710b.

5631. סָרִיס {42x} **çârîyç,** *saw-reece';* or

סָרִס **çârîç,** *saw-reece';* from an unused root mean. to *castrate;* a *eunuch;* by impl. *valet* (espec. of the female apartments), and thus, a *minister* of state:—chamberlain {13x}, eunuch {17x}, officer {12x}. See: TWOT—1545; BDB—710b. comp. 7249.

5632. סָרֵךְ {5x} **çârêk** (Aram.), *saw-rake';* of for. or.; an *emir:*—president {5x}. See: TWOT—2893; BDB—1104c.

5633. סֶרֶן {22x} **çeren,** *seh'-ren;* from an unused root of uncert. mean.; an *axle;* fig. a *peer:*—lord {22x}, plate {1x}. See: TWOT—1546, 1547; BDB—710c, 710d.

5634. סַרְעַפָּה {1x} **çar'appâh,** *sar-ap-paw';* for 5589; a *twig:*—bough {1x}. See: TWOT—1527d; BDB—703d, 710d.

5635. סָרַף {1x} **çâraph,** *saw-raf';* a prim. root; to *cremate,* i.e. to *be* (near) *of kin* (such being privileged to kindle the pyre):—burn {1x}. See: TWOT—2292; BDB—710d, 977a.

5636. סַרְפָּד {1x} **çarpâd,** *sar-pawd';* from 5635; a *nettle* (as stinging like a burn):—brier {1x}. See: TWOT—1548; BDB—710d.

5637. סָרַר {17x} **çârar,** *saw-rar';* a prim. root; to *turn* away, i.e. (mor.) be *refractory:*—rebellious {6x}, stubborn {4x}, revolters {2x}, revolting {1x}, slide back {1x}, backslide {1x}, away {1x}, withdrew {1x}. See: TWOT—1549; BDB—693c, 710d.

5638. סְתָו {1x} **çᵉthâv,** *seth-awv';* from an unused root mean. to *hide; winter* (as the dark season):—winter {1x}. See: TWOT—1549.1; BDB—711a.

5639. סְתוּר {1x} **Çᵉthûwr,** *seth-oor';* from 5641; *hidden; Sethur,* an Isr.:—Sethur {1x}. See: BDB—712c.

5640. סָתַם {14x} **çâtham,** *saw-tham';* or

שָׂתַם **sâtham** (Num. 24:15), *saw-tham';* a prim. root; to *stop* up; by impl. to *repair;* fig. to *keep secret:*—stop {8x}, shut up {2x}, hidden {1x}, shut out {1x}, secret {1x}, close up {1x}. See: TWOT—1550; BDB—711a, 979c.

5641. סָתַר {82x} **çâthar,** *saw-thar';* a prim. root; to *hide* (by covering), lit. or fig.:—hide {72x}, secret {4x}, close {2x}, absent {1x}, conceal {1x}, surely {1x}, variant {1x}.

Cathar means "to conceal, hide, shelter." **(1)** The word is found for the first time in Gen 4:14 as Cain discovers that because of his sin, he will be "hidden" from the presence of God, which implies a separation: "Behold, thou hast driven me out this day from the face of the earth; and from thy face shall I be hid; and I shall be a fugitive and a vagabond in the earth; and it shall come to pass, that every one that findeth me shall slay me."**(2)** In the so-called Mizpah Benediction (which is really a warning), *cathar* again has the sense of "separation": "The Lord watch between me and thee, when we are absent one from another" (Gen 31:49). **(3)** To "hide oneself" is to take refuge: "Doth not David hide himself with us?" (1 Sa

23:19). **(4)** Similarly, to "hide" someone is to "shelter" him from his enemy: "The Lord hid them" (Jer 36:26). **(5)** To pray, "Hide thy face from my sins" (Ps 51:9), is to ask God to ignore them. **(6)** But when the prophet says, "And I will wait upon the Lord, that hideth his face from the house of Jacob" (Is 8:17), he means that God's favor has been withdrawn. **(7)** Similarly, Judah's sins have "hidden" God's face from her: "But your iniquities have separated between you and your God, and your sins have hid his face from you, that he will not hear" (Is 59:2). See: TWOT—1551; BDB—711b, 1104c.

5642. סְתַר {2x} **çᵉthar** (Aram.), *seth-ar';* corresp. to 5641; to *conceal;* fig. to *demolish:*—destroy {1x}, secret thing {1x}. See: TWOT—2894; BDB—1104c, 1104d.

5643. סֵתֶר {36x} **çêther,** *say'-ther;* or (fem.)

סִתְרָה **çithrâh** (Deut 32:38), *sith-raw';* from 5641; a *cover* (in a good or a bad, a lit. or a fig. sense):—secret {12x}, secretly {9x}, covert {5x}, secret place {3x}, hiding place {2x}, backbiting {1x}, covering {1x}, disguiseth {1x}, privily {1x}, protection {1x}. See: TWOT—1551a, 1551b; BDB—712a, 712c.

5644. סִתְרִי {1x} **Çithrîy,** *sith-ree';* from 5643; *protective; Sithri,* an Isr.:—Zithri {1x}. See: BDB—712c.

ע

5645. עָב {32x} **ʿâb,** *awb* (masc. and fem.); from 5743; prop. an *envelope,* i.e. *darkness* (or *density,* 2 Chr 4:17); spec. a (scud) *cloud;* also a *copse:*—clay {1x}, (thick) cloud {29x}, × thick {1x}, thicket {1x}. See: TWOT—1574a; BDB—712b, 716a, 728a. comp. 5672.

5646. עָב {3x} **ʿâb,** *awb;* or

עֹב **ʿôb,** *obe;* from an unused root mean. to *cover;* prop. equiv. to 5645; but used only as an arch. term, an *architrave* (as *shading* the pillars):—thick beam {2x}, plank {1x}. See: TWOT—1552a; BDB—712b, 728a.

5647. עָבַד {290x} **ʿâbad,** *aw-bad';* a prim. root; to *work* (in any sense); by impl. to *serve, till,* (caus.) *enslave,* etc.:—serve {227x}, do {15x}, till {9x}, servant {5x}, work {5x}, worshippers {5x}, service {4x}, dress {2x}, labour {2x}, ear {2x}, misc. {14x} = × be, keep in bondage, be bondmen, bond-service, compel, execute, + husbandman, keep, be wrought.

ʿAbad, as a verb, means "to serve, cultivate, enslave, work." **(1)** The verb is first used in **(1a)** Gen 2:5: "And there was not a man to till the ground." **(1b)** God gave to man the task "to

dress [the ground]" (Gen 2:15; 3:23). **(2)** In Gen 14:4 "they served Chedorlaomer . . ." means that they were his vassals. **(3)** God told Abraham that his descendants would "serve" the people of a strange land 400 years: "And he said unto Abram, Know of a surety that thy seed shall be a stranger in a land that is not theirs, and shall serve them; and they shall afflict them four hundred years" (Gen 15:13). **(4)** ʿAbad is often used toward God: "Ye shall serve God upon this mountain" (Ex 3:12), meaning "to worship." **(5)** The word is frequently used with another verb: **(5a)** "Thou shalt fear the Lord thy God, and serve him" (Deut 6:13), or **(5b)** "hearken diligently unto my commandments which I command you this day, to love the Lord your God, and to serve him" (Deut 11:13). **(6)** All nations are commanded: **(6a)** "Serve the Lord with gladness" (Ps 100:2). **(6b)** In the reign of Messiah, "all nations shall serve him" (Ps 72:11). **(7)** The verb and the noun may be used together as in Num 8:11 "And Aaron shall offer the Levites before the Lord . . . that they may execute the service of the Lord." Syn.: 5650, 5656, 8334. See: TWOT—1553; BDB—712b, 1104d.

5648. עֲבַד {28x} **ʿăbad** (Aram.), *ab-bad';* corresp. to 5647; to *do, make, prepare, keep,* etc.:—do {10x}, made {7x}, cut {2x}, do + 1934 {2x}, do + 5922 {1x}, worketh {1x}, executed + 1934 {1x}, goeth {1x}, kept {1x}, moved {1x}, wrought {1x}. See: TWOT—2896; BDB—1104d.

5649. עֲבַד {7x} **ʿăbad** (Aram.), *ab-bad';* from 5648; a *servant:*—servant {7x}. See: TWOT—2896a; BDB—1105a.

5650. עֶבֶד {800x} **ʿebed,** *eh'-bed;* from 5647; a *servant:*—servant {744x}, manservant {23x}, bondman {21x}, bondage {10x}, bondservant {1x}, on all sides {1x}.

ʿEbed means "servant." **(1)** ʿEbed first appears in Gen 9:25: "And he said, Cursed be Canaan; a servant of servants shall he be unto his brethren." **(2)** A "servant" may be bought with money (Ex 12:44) or hired (1 Kin 5:6). **(3)** The often repeated statement of God's redemption of Israel is: "I brought you out of the house of bondage" (Ex 13:3). **(4)** ʿEbed was used as a mark of humility and courtesy, as in Gen 18:3: "Pass not away, I pray thee, from thy servant" (cf. Gen 42:10). **(5)** Moses addressed God: "O my Lord, I am not eloquent, neither heretofore, nor since thou hast spoken unto thy servant" (Ex 4:10). **(6)** It is the mark of those called by God, as in Ex 14:31: "[They] believed the Lord, and his servant Moses." **(6b)** God claimed: "For unto me the children of Israel are servants" (Lev 25:55; cf. Is 49:3). **(6c)** "And the Lord spake by his servants the prophets . . ." (2 Kin

21:10). **(6d)** The psalmist said: "I am thy servant" (116:16 indicating the appropriateness of the title to all believers).

(7) Of prime significance is the use of "my servant" for the Messiah in Isaiah (42:1–7; 49:1–7; 50:4–10; 52:13–53:12). **(7a)** Israel was a blind and deaf "servant" (Is 42:18–22). **(7b)** So the Lord called "my righteous servant" (Is 53:11; cf. 42:6) **(7b1)** "[to bear] the sin of many" (Is 53:12), **(7b2)** "that thou mayest be my salvation unto the end of the earth" (Is 49:6). **(8)** The "servant" was not a free man. **(8a)** He was subject to the will and command of his master. **(8b)** But one might willingly and lovingly submit to his master (Ex 21:5), remaining in his service when he was not obliged to do so: "And if the servant shall plainly say, I love my master, my wife, and my children; I will not go out free:" **(8c)** Hence it is a very fitting description of the relationship of man to God. Syn.: 5647, 5656, 8334. See: TWOT—1553a; BDB—713d, 1105a.

5651. עֶבֶד {6x} **ʿEbed,** *eh'-bed;* the same as 5650; *Ebed,* the name of two Isr.:—*Ebed* {6x}. See: BDB—714c.

5652. עֲבָד {1x} **ʿăbâd,** *ab-awd';* from 5647; a *deed:*—work {1x}. See: TWOT—1553b; BDB—715a.

5653. עַבְדָא {2x} **ʿAbdâʾ,** *ab-daw';* from 5647; *work; Abda,* the name of two Isr.:—*Abda* {2x}. See: BDB—715a.

5654. עֹבֵד אֱדוֹם {20x} **ʿObêd ʾĔdôwm,** *o-bade' ed-ome';* from the act. part. of 5647 and 123; *worker of Edom; Obed-Edom,* the name of five Isr.:—Obed-edom {20x}. See: BDB—714d.

5655. עַבְדְאֵל {1x} **ʿAbdᵉʾêl,** *ab-deh-ale';* from 5647 and 410; *serving God; Abdeel,* an Isr.:—*Abdeel* {1x}. See: BDB—715a. comp. 5661.

5656. עֲבֹדָה {141x} **ʿăbôdâh,** *ab-o-daw';* or

עֲבוֹדָה **ʿăbôwdâh,** *ab-o-daw';* from 5647; *work* of any kind:—service {96x}, servile {12x}, work {10x}, bondage {8x}, act {2x}, serve {2x}, servitude {2x}, tillage {2x}, effect {1x}, labour {1x}, misc. {5x} = + bondservant, ministering (-try), office, use, × wrought. *'Abodah,* as a noun, means "work; labors; service." **(1)** This noun appears 141 times in the Hebrew Old Testament, and **(1a)** the occurrences are concentrated in Numbers and Chronicles. **(1b)** '*Abodah* is first used in Gen 29:27: "We will give thee this also for the service which thou shalt serve with me." **(2)** The more general meaning of '*abodah* is close to our English word for "work.": **(2a)** "Labor" in the field: "And over them that did the work of

the field for tillage of the ground *was* Ezri the son of Chelub:" (1 Chr 27:26), **(2b)** daily "work" from morning till evening: "Man goeth forth unto his work and to his labour until the evening" (Ps 104:23), and **(2c)** "work" in the linen industry: "The sons of Shelah the son of Judah were, Er the father of Lecah, and Laadah the father of Mareshah, and the families of the house of them that wrought fine linen, of the house of Ashbea" (1 Chr 4:21) indicate a use with which we are familiar.

(3) To this, it must be added that '*abodah* may also be "hard labor," **(3a)** such as that of a slave: "And if thy brother that dwelleth by thee be waxen poor, and be sold unto thee; thou shalt not compel him to serve as a bondservant:" (Lev 25:39) or **(3b)** of Israel while in Egypt: "Go ye, get you straw where ye can find it: yet not aught of your work shall be diminished" (Ex 5:11). **(4)** The more limited meaning of the word is "service." Israel was in the "service" of the Lord: "But that it may be a witness between us, and you, and our generations after us, that we might do the service of the Lord before him with our burnt offerings, and with our sacrifices, and with our peace offerings; that your children may not say to our children in time to come, Ye have no part in the Lord" (Josh 22:27). **(5)** Whenever God's people were not fully dependent on Him, they had to choose to serve the Lord God or human kings with their requirements of forced "labor" and tribute: "Nevertheless they shall be his servants; that they may know my service, and the service of the kingdoms of the countries" (2 Chr 12:8).

(6) Further specialization of the usage is in association with the tabernacle and the temple. **(6a)** The priests were chosen for the "service" of the Lord: "And they shall keep his charge, and the charge of the whole congregation before the tabernacle of the congregation, to do the service of the tabernacle" (Num 3:7). **(6b)** The Levites also had many important functions in and around the temple; they sang, played musical instruments, and were secretaries, scribes, and doorkeepers (2 Chr 34:13; cf. 8:14). **(7)** Thus anything, people and objects (1 Chr 28:13), associated with the temple was considered to be in the "service" of the Lord. **(8)** Our understanding of "worship," with all its components, comes close to the Hebrew meaning of '*abodah* as "service"; cf. "So all the service of the Lord was prepared the same day, to keep the passover, and to offer burnt offerings upon the altar of the Lord, according to the commandment of King Josiah" (2 Chr 35:16). Syn.: 5647, 5650, 8334. See: TWOT—1553c; BDB—715a, 1105a.

5657. עֲבֻדָּה {2x} **'ăbuddâh**, *ab-ood-daw'*; pass. part. of 5647; something *wrought*, i.e. (concr.) *service*:—household {1x}, store of servants {1x}. See: TWOT—1553d; BDB—715c.

5658. עַבְדּוֹן {8x} **'Abdôwn**, *ab-dohn'*; from 5647; *servitude; Abdon*, the name of a place in Pal. and of four Isr.:—Abdon {8x}. See: BDB—715c, 716c, 720d. comp. 5683.

5659. עַבְדוּת {3x} **'abdûwth**, *ab-dooth'*; from 5647; *servitude*:—bondage {3x}. See: TWOT—1553e; BDB—715c.

5660. עַבְדִּי {3x} **'Abdîy**, *ab-dee'*; from 5647; *serviceable; Abdi*, the name of two Isr.:—Abdi {3x}. See: BDB—715d.

5661. עַבְדִּיאֵל {1x} **'Abdîy'êl**, *ab-dee-ale'*; from 5650 and 410; *servant of God; Abdiel*, an Isr.:—Abdiel {1x}. See: BDB—715d. comp. 5655.

5662. עֹבַדְיָה {20x} **'Ôbadyâh**, *o-bad-yaw'*; or

עֹבַדְיָהוּ **'Ôbadyâhûw**, *o-bad-yaw'-hoo*; act. part. of 5647 and 3050; *serving Jah; Obadjah*, the name of thirteen Isr.:—Obadiah {20x}. See: BDB—715d.

5663. עֶבֶד מֶלֶךְ {6x} **'Ebed Melek**, *eh'-bed meh'-lek*; from 5650 and 4428; *servant of a king; Ebed-Melek*, a eunuch of Zezekiah:—Ebed-melech {6x}. See: BDB—715a.

5664. עֲבֵד נְגוֹ {1x} **'Ăbêd N°gôw**, *ab-ade' neg-o'*; the same as 5665; *Abed-Nego*, the Bab. name of one of Daniel's companions:—Abed-nego {1x}. See: BDB—715a, 1105a.

5665. עֲבֵד נְגוֹא {4x} **'Ăbêd N°gôw'** (Aram.), *ab-ade' neg-o'*; of for. or.; *Abed-Nego*, the name of Azariah:—Abed-nego {4x}. See: BDB—1105a.

5666. עָבָה {3x} **'âbâh**, *aw-baw'*; a prim. root; to *be dense*:—thicker {2x}, thick {1x}. See: TWOT—1554; BDB—716a.

5667. עֲבוֹט {4x} **'ăbôwt**, *ab-ote'*; or

עֲבֹט **'ăbôt**, *ab-ote'*; from 5670; a *pawn*:—pledge {4x}. See: TWOT—1555a; BDB—716b.

5668. עָבוּר {8x} **'âbûwr**, *aw-boor'*; or

עָבֻר **'âbûr**, *aw-boor'*; pass. part. of 5674; prop. *crossed*, i.e. (abstr.) *transit*; used only adv. on *account* of, in *order that*:—sake {1x}, that {1x}, because of {1x}, to {3x}, to the intent that {1x}. See: TWOT—1556g; BDB—721a.

5669. עָבוּר {2x} **'âbûwr**, *aw-boor'*; the same as 5668; *passed*, i.e. *kept* over;

used only of *stored* grain:—old corn {2x}. See: TWOT—1556f; BDB—721a.

5670. עָבַט {6x} **'âbat**, *aw-bat'*; a prim. root; to *pawn*; caus. to *lend* (on security); fig. to *entangle*:—lend {2x}, fetch {1x}, borrow {1x}, surely {1x}, break {1x}. See: TWOT—1555; BDB—716b.

5671. עַבְטִיט {1x} **'abtîyt**, *ab-teet'*; from 5670; something *pledged*, i.e. (collect.) *pawned* goods:—thick clay {1x}. See: TWOT—1555b; BDB—716b.

5672. עֳבִי {4x} **'ăbîy**, *ab-ee'*; or

עֹבִי **'ŏbîy**, *ob-ee'*; from 5666; *density*, i.e. *depth* or *width*:—thickness {2x}, thick {2x}. See: TWOT—1554a; BDB—716a, 728a. comp. 5645.

5673. עֲבִידָה {6x} **'ăbîydâh** (Aram.), *ab-ee-daw'*; from 5648; *labor* or *business*:—work {3x}, affairs {2x}, service {1x}. See: TWOT—2896b; BDB—1105a.

5674. עָבַר {559x} **'âbar**, *aw-bar'*; a prim. root; to *cross*; used very widely of any *transition* (lit. or fig.; tran., intr., intens., or caus.); spec. to *cover* (in copulation):—(pass, went, . . .) over {174x}, pass {108x}, (pass, etc . . .) through {58x}, pass by {27x}, go {26x}, (put, pass, etc . . .) away {24x}, pass on {19x}, misc. {123x} = alienate, alter, ✕ at all, beyond, bring (over, through), carry over, (over-) come (on, over), conduct (over), convey over, current, deliver, enter, escape, fail, gender, get over, lay, meddle, overrun, make partition, (cause to, make) + proclaim (-amation), perish, provoke to anger, rage, + raiser of taxes, remove, send over, set apart, + shave, cause to (make) sound, ✕ speedily, ✕ sweet smelling, (make to) transgress (-or), translate, [way-] faring man, be wrath.

This word communicates the idea of transgression, or crossing over the boundary of right and entering the forbidden land of wrong. '*Abar*, **the masculine form,** means "to pass away, pass over." **(1)** The verb refers primarily to spatial movement, to "moving over, through, or away from." **(1a)** This basic meaning can be used of "going over or through" a particular location to get to the other side, as when Jacob "crossed over" the Euphrates to escape Laban (Gen 31:21). **(1b)** Another specific use of this general meaning is to pass through something; Ps. 8:8 speaks of whatever "passes through" the sea as being under Adam's control. **(1c)** '*Abar* can also merely mean "to go as far as"—Amos tells his audience not to "cross over" to Beer-sheba (Amos 5:5). **(2)** "To go as far as" an individual is to overtake him: "But howsoever, said he, let me run. And he said

unto him, Run. Then Ahimaaz ran by the way of the plain, and overran [ʿabar] Cushi" (2 Sa 18:23). **(3)** Abram "passed through" Canaan as far as Mamre; he did not go out of the land (cf. Gen 12:6). **(4)** The word can also be used of "passing by" something; Abraham begged the three men not "to pass by" him but to stop and refresh themselves: "And said, My Lord, if now I have found favour in thy sight, pass not away, I pray thee, from thy servant" (Gen 18:3).

(5) ʿAbar is sometimes used of "passing over" a law, order, or covenant as if it were not binding. When the people decided to enter Palestine against the command of God, Moses said, "Wherefore now do ye transgress the commandment of the Lord?" (Num 14:41). **(6)** This verb first occurs in Gen 8:1 where it means "pass over on top of.": "And God remembered Noah, and every living thing, and all the cattle that was with him in the ark: and God made a wind to pass over the earth, and the waters assuaged;" God caused the wind "to pass over" the flood waters and to carry them away. **(7)** The word can also mean "to pass away," to cease to be, as in Gen 50:4 where the days of mourning over Jacob "were past." **(8)** A number of technical phrases where this root has a regular and specialized meaning appear. **(8a)** For example, one who "passes over" the sea is a seafarer or sailor (Is 23:2). **(8b)** ʿAbar is used in business affairs with silver or money in the sense of reckoning money according to the "going" (passing) rate (Gen 23:16ff.). **(9)** In Song 5:5 the verb is used to mean "flow" as what a liquid does ("flowing" or "liquid" myrrh): "I rose up to open to my beloved; and my hands dropped [ʿabar] with myrrh, and my fingers with sweet smelling myrrh, upon the handles of the lock."

(10) The phrase "pass over to be numbered" is a phrase meaning to move from one status to another (to move into the ranks of the militia) in Ex 30:13–14: "This they shall give, every one that passeth among them that are numbered, half a shekel after the shekel of the sanctuary: (a shekel is twenty gerahs:) an half shekel shall be the offering of the LORD. Every one that passeth among them that are numbered, from twenty years old and above, shall give an offering unto the LORD." **(11)** The intensive stem of ʿabar is used in two special senses: **(11a)** of "overlaying" with precious metals: "So Solomon overlaid the house within with pure gold: and he made a partition by the chains of gold before the oracle; and he overlaid it with gold" (1 Kin 6:21), and **(11b)** of the ox's act of making a cow pregnant: "Their bull gendereth [ʿabar], and faileth not; their cow calveth, and casteth not her calf" (Job 21:10).

(12) The verb also has special meanings in the causative stem: **(12a)** "to devote" the firstborn to the Lord: "That thou shalt set apart [ʿabar] unto the LORD all that openeth the matrix, and every firstling that cometh of a beast which thou hast; the males shall be the LORD'S" (Ex 13:12); **(12b)** "to offer" a child by burning him in fire: "There shall not be found among you any one that maketh his son or his daughter to pass through [ʿabar] the fire, or that useth divination, or an observer of times, or an enchanter, or a witch," (Deut 18:10); **(12c)** "to make" a sound "come forth": "Then shalt thou cause the trumpet of the jubile to sound [ʿabar] on the tenth day of the seventh month, in the day of atonement shall ye make the trumpet sound throughout all your land." (Lev 25:9); **(12c)** "to sovereignly transfer" a kingdom or cause it to pass over to another's leadership: "To translate [ʿabar] the kingdom from the house of Saul, and to set up the throne of David over Israel and over Judah, from Dan even to Beersheba" (2 Sa 3:10); **(12d)** "to put away or cause to cease": "And he took away [ʿabar] the sodomites out of the land, and removed all the idols that his fathers had made" (1 Kin 15:12); **(12e)** and "to turn" something "away": "Turn away [ʿabar] mine eyes from beholding vanity; and quicken thou me in thy way" (Ps 119:37).

(13) ʿAbarah, **the feminine noun form** which occurs twice, means "crossing or ford": "And there went over a ferry boat to carry over [ʿabarah] the king's household, and to do what he thought good. And Shimei the son of Gera fell down before the king, as he was come over [ʿabarah] Jordan" (2 Sa 19:18). **(14)** ʿAbar, **as a verb,** occurs only when it refers to sin. **(15)** ʿAbar often carries the sense of "transgressing" a covenant or commandment—i.e., the offender "passes beyond" the limits set by God's law and falls into transgression and guilt. **(15a)** This meaning appears in Num 14:41: "And Moses said, wherefore now do ye transgress the commandment of the Lord? but it shall not prosper." **(15b)** Another example is in Judg 2:20: "And the anger of the Lord was hot against Israel; and he said, Because that this people hath transgressed my covenant which I commanded their fathers, and have not hearkened unto my voice" (cf. 1 Sa 15:24; Hos 8:1).

(16) Most frequently, ʿabar illustrates the motion of "crossing over" or "passing over." **(16a)** This word refers to crossing a stream or boundage ("pass through," Num 21:22), **(16b)** invading a country ("passed over," Judg 11:32), **(11c)** crossing a boundary against a hostile army ("go over," 1 Sa 14:4), **(16d)** marching over ("go over," Is 51:23), **(16e)** overflowing the banks of a river or other natural barriers ("pass through," Is 23:10), **(16f)** passing a razor over

one's head ("come upon," Num 6:5), and **(16g)** the passing of time ("went over," 1 Chr 29:30). See: TWOT—1556; BDB—716d, 720d, 1105b.

5675. עֲבַר {14x} **ʿăbar** (Aram.), *ab-ar′;* corresp. to 5676:—beyond {7x}, side {7x}. See: TWOT—2897; BDB—1105a.

5676. עֵבֶר {91x} **ʿêber,** *ay′-ber;* from 5674; prop. a region *across;* but used only adv. (with or without a prep.) on the *opposite* side (espec. of the Jordan; usually mean. the *east*):—side {58x}, beyond {21x}, straight {3x}, passage {2x}, by {1x}, from {1x}, other {1x}, against {1x}, over {1x}, quarter {1x}, Strong's synonym {1x}.

'*Eber,* which occurs 91 times, refers to the **(1)** "side": "Now it came to pass upon a day, that Jonathan the son of Saul said unto the young man that bare his armour, Come, and let us go over to the Philistines' garrison, that is on the other side. But he told not his father" (1 Sa 14:1) or **(2)** "edge" of something: "And thou shalt make two rings of gold, and thou shalt put them upon the two ends of the breastplate in the border thereof, which is in the side of the ephod inward" (Ex 28:26). **(3)** When speaking of rivers or seas, '*eber* means the "edge or side opposite the speaker" or "the other side": "For we have heard how the LORD dried up the water of the Red sea for you, when ye came out of Egypt; and what ye did unto the two kings of the Amorites, that were on the other side Jordan, Sihon and Og, whom ye utterly destroyed" (Josh 2:10). Syn.: 4569, 5676, 5680. See: TWOT—1556a; BDB—719b, 1105a.

5677. עֵבֶר {15x} **ʿÊber,** *ay′-ber;* the same as 5676; *Eber,* the name of two patriarchs and four Isr.:—Eber {13x}, Heber {2x}. See: BDB—720a

5678. עֶבְרָה {34x} **ʿebrâh,** *eb-raw′;* fem. of 5676; an *outburst* of passion:—wrath {31x}, rage {2x}, anger {1x}. See: TWOT—1556d; BDB—720c.

5679. עֲבָרָה {3x} **ʿăbârâh,** *ab-aw-raw′;* from 5674; a *crossing*-place:—ferry boat {1x}, variant {2x}. See: TWOT—1556c; BDB—720b.

5680. עִבְרִי {34x} **ʿIbrîy,** *ib-ree′;* patron. from 5677; an *Eberite* (i.e. Hebrew) or desc. of Eber:—Hebrew {29x}, Hebrew woman {2x}, Hebrew + 376 {1x}, Hebrewess {1x}, Hebrew man {1x}.

'*Ibriy* means "Hebrew." **(1)** The origin and meaning of this word, which appears 34 times, is much debated. **(2)** The word is an early generic term for a variety of Semitic peoples and is somewhat akin to our word barbarian. **(3)** So

Abram is identified as a "Hebrew" (Gen 14:13). **(4)** This ethnic term indicates family origin whereas the term "sons of Israel" is a political and religious term. **(5)** Unquestionably in the ancient Near East "Hebrew" was applied to a far larger group than the Israelites. **(6)** The word occurs in Ugaritic, Egyptian, and Babylonian writings describing a diverse mixture of nomadic wanderers or at least those who appear to have at one time been nomadic. **(7)** Sometimes the word seems to be a term of derision. Such usage recalls 1 Sa 29:3, where the Philistine leaders asked Achish, "What do these Hebrews here?" **(8)** There is considerable debate about identifying Hebrew with the well-known Habiru (Semitic warlords) who occupied Egypt in the first half of the second millennium B.C. Syn.: 4569, 5674, 5676. See: BDB—720a.

5681. עִבְרִי {1x} **ʿIbrîy,** *ib-ree′;* the same as 5680; *Ibri,* an Isr.:—Ibri {1x}. See: BDB—720b.

5682. עֲבָרִים {4x} **ʿĂbârîym,** *ab-aw-reem′;* plur. of 5676; regions *beyond; Abarim,* a place in Pal.:—Abarim {4x}. See: BDB—720d.

5683. עֶבְרֹן {1x} **ʿEbrôn,** *eb-rone′;* from 5676; *transitional; Ebron,* a place in Pal.:—Hebron {1x}. See: BDB—715c, 720d.

5684. עֶבְרֹנָה {2x} **ʿEbrônâh,** *eb-raw-naw′;* fem. of 5683; *Ebronah,* a place in the desert:—Ebronah {2x}. See: BDB—720d.

5685. עָבַשׁ {1x} **ʿâbash,** *aw-bash′;* a prim. root; to *dry* up:—rotten {1x}. See: TWOT—1557; BDB—721b.

5686. עָבַת {1x} **ʿâbath,** *aw-bath′;* a prim. root; to *interlace,* i.e. (fig.) to *pervert:*—wrap it up {1x}. See: TWOT—1558; BDB—721c.

5687. עָבֹת {4x} **ʿâbôth,** *aw-both′;* or

עָבוֹת **ʿâbôwth,** *aw-both′;* from 5686; *intwined,* i.e. *dense:*—thick {4x}. See: TWOT—1558a; BDB—721c.

5688. עֲבֹת {25x} **ʿăbôth,** *ab-oth′;* or

עֲבוֹת **ʿăbôwth,** *ab-oth′;* or (fem.)

עֲבֹתָה **ʿăbôthâh,** *ab-oth-aw′;* the same as 5687; something *intwined,* i.e. a *string, wreath* or *foliage:*—wreathen {7x}, cords {5x}, ban {4x}, boughs {3x}, rope {3x}, chains {2x}, branches {1x}. See: TWOT—1558b; BDB—716b, 721c.

5689. עָגַב {7x} **ʿâgab,** *aw-gab′;* a prim. root; to *breathe* after, i.e. to *love* (sensually):—doted {6x}, lovers {1x}. This word is used

of impure love. Syn.: 157, 1730, 2617, 2836, 3039, 7453. See: TWOT—1558b; BDB—721d.

5690. עֶגֶב {2x} **‘egeb**, *eh'-gheb;* from 5689; *love* (concr.), i.e. *amative* words:— much love {1x}, very lovely {1x}. See: TWOT— 1559a; BDB—721d.

5691. עֲגָבָה {1x} **‘ăgâbâh**, *ag-aw-baw';* from 5689; *love* (abstr.), i.e. *amorousness:*—inordinate love {1x}. See: TWOT— 1559b; BDB—721d.

5692. עֻגָּה {7x} **‘uggâh**, *oog-gaw';* from 5746; an *ash-cake* (as *round*):—cake (upon the hearth) {7x}. See: TWOT—1575a; BDB—722a, 728a.

עָגוֹל **‘ăgôwl**. See 5696.

5693. עָגוּר {2x} **‘âgûwr**, *aw-goor';* pass. part. [but with act. sense] of an unused root mean. to *twitter;* prob. the *swallow:*— swallow {2x}. See: TWOT—1563a; BDB—723a.

5694. עָגִיל {2x} **‘âgîyl**, *aw-gheel';* from the same as 5696; something *round,* i.e. a *ring* (for the ears):—earring {2x}. See: TWOT—1560e; BDB—722d.

5695. עֵגֶל {35x} **‘êgel**, *ay-ghel;* from the same as 5696; a (male) *calf* (as *frisking* round), espec. one nearly grown (i.e. a *steer*):— bullock {2x}, calf {33x}. See: TWOT—1560a; BDB—722a.

5696. עָגֹל {6x} **‘âgôl**, *aw-gole';* or

עָגוֹל **‘âgôwl**, *aw-gole';* from an unused root mean. to *revolve, circular:*— round {6x}. See: TWOT—1560c; BDB—722c.

5697. עֶגְלָה {14x} **‘eglâh**, *eg-law';* fem. of 5695; a (female) *calf,* espec. one nearly grown (i.e. a *heifer*):—calf {1x}, cow {1x}, heifer {12x}. See: TWOT—1560b; BDB—722b, 722c, 1026b.

5698. עֶגְלָה {2x} **‘Eglâh**, *eg-law';* the same as 5697; *Eglah,* a wife of David:— Eglah {2x}. See: BDB—722c.

5699. עֲגָלָה {25x} **‘ăgâlâh**, *ag-aw-law';* from the same as 5696; something *revolving,* i.e. a wheeled *vehicle:*—cart {15x}, chariot {1x}, wagon {9x}. See: TWOT—1560d; BDB—722c.

5700. עֶגְלוֹן {13x} **‘Eglôwn**, *eg-lawn';* from 5695; *vituline; Eglon,* the name of a place in Pal. and of a Moabitish king:— Eglon {13x}. See: BDB—722d.

5701. עָגַם {1x} **‘âgam**, *aw-gam';* a prim. root; to *be sad:*—grieve {1x}. See: TWOT— 1561; BDB—723a.

5702. עָגַן {1x} **‘âgan**, *a -gan';* a prim. root; to *debar,* i.e. from marriage:—stay {1x}. See: TWOT—1562; BDB—723a.

5703. עַד {49x} **‘ad**, *ad;* from 5710; prop. a (peremptory) *terminus,* i.e. (by impl.) *duration,* in the sense of *advance* or *perpetuity* (substantially as a noun, either with or without a prep.):—ever {41x}, everlasting {2x}, end {1x}, eternity {1x}, ever + 5769 {1x}, evermore {1x}, old {1x}, perpetually {1x}. Syn.: 753, 1755, 5331, 6256, 6783, 6924. See: TWOT—1565a; BDB— 723b, 723c.

5704. עַד {99x} **‘ad**, *ad;* prop. the same as 5703 (used as a prep., adv. or conjunc.; espec. with a prep.); *as far* (or *long,* or *much*) *as,* whether of space (*even unto*) or time (*during, while, until*) or degree (*equally with*):—{99x} = against, and, as, at, before, by (that), even (to), for (-asmuch as), [hither-] to, + how long, into, as long (much) as, (so) that, till, toward, until, when, while, (+ as) yet. See: TWOT—1565c; BDB—723b, 723d, 774b, 1105b.

5705. עַד {32x} **‘ad** (Aram.), *ad;* corresp. to 5704:—till {11x}, until {5x}, unto {4x}, ever {2x}, for {2x}, to {2x}, but at {1x}, even {1x}, hitherto + 3542 {1x}, mastery + 7981 {1x}, on {1x}, within {1x}. See: TWOT—2899; BDB—1105b.

5706. עַד {3x} **‘ad**, *ad;* the same as 5703 in the sense of the *aim* of an attack; *booty:*—prey {3x}. See: TWOT—1565b; BDB— 723b, 723d.

5707. עֵד {69x} **‘ēd**, *ayd;* contr. from 5749; concr. a *witness;* abstr. *testimony;* spec. a *recorder,* i.e. *prince:*—witness {69x}.

'*Ed* means a "witness." **(1)** This word has to do with the legal or judicial sphere. **(1a)** First, in the area of civil affairs the word can mean someone who is present at a legal transaction and can confirm it if necessary. **(1b)** Such people worked as notaries, e.g., for an oral transfer of property: "Now this was the manner in former time in Israel concerning redeeming and concerning changing, for to confirrn all things. . . . And Boaz said unto the elders, and unto all the people, Ye are witnesses this day, that I have bought all that was Elimelech's, and all that was Chilion's and Mahlon's, of the hand of Naomi" (Ruth 4:7, 9). **(2)** At a later time the "witnesses" not only acted to attest the transaction and to confirm it orally, but they signed a document or deed of purchase. **(2a)** Thus "witness" takes on the new nuance of those able and willing to affirm the truth of a transaction by affixing their signatures: **(2b)** "And I gave the evidence of the purchase unto Baruch the son of Neriah . . . in the sight

of Hanameel mine uncle's son, and in the presence of the witnesses that subscribed the book of the purchase" (Jer 32:12).

(3) An object or animal(s) can signify the truthfulness of an act or agreement. **(3a)** Its very existence or the acceptance of it by both parties (in the case of the animals given to Abimelech in Gen 21:30) bears witness: "Now therefore come thou, let us make a covenant, I and thou; and let it be for a witness between me and thee [let it attest to our mutual relationship]" (Gen 31:44 — the first biblical occurrence of the word). **(3b)** Jacob then set up a stone pillar or heap as a further "witness" (Gen 31:48) calling upon God to effect judgment if the covenant were broken. **(4)** In Mosaic criminal law the accused has the right to be faced by his/her accuser and to give evidence of his/her innocence. **(4a)** In the case of a newly married woman charged by her own husband, his testimony is sufficient to prove her guilty of adultery unless her parents have clear evidence proving her virginity before her marriage (Deut 22:14ff.). **(4b)** Usually the accused is faced with someone who either saw or heard of his guilt: "And if a soul sin, and hear the voice of swearing, and is a witness, whether he hath seen or known of it . . ." (Lev 5:1).

(5) Heavy penalties fell on anyone who lied to a court. **(5a)** The ninth commandment may well have immediate reference to such a concrete court situation (Ex 20:16). **(5b)** If so, it serves to sanction proper judicial procedure, to safeguard individuals from secret accusation and condemnation and giving them the right and privilege of self-defense. **(6)** In the exchange between Jacob and Laban mentioned above, Jacob also cites God as a "witness" (Gen 31:50) between them, the one who will see violations; God, however, is also the Judge: "If thou shalt afflict my daughters, or if thou shalt take other wives beside my daughters, no man is with us; see, God is witness betwixt me and thee." **(7)** Although human courts are (as a rule) to keep judge and "witness" separate, the "witnesses" do participate in executing the penalty upon the guilty party (Deut 17:7), even as God does: "The hands of the witnesses shall be first upon him to put him to death, and afterward the hands of all the people. So thou shalt put the evil away from among you." Syn.: 5749. See: TWOT—1576b; BDB—723b, 729c, 1113d.

5708. עֵד {1x} ʿêd, *ayd;* from an unused root mean. to *set* a period [comp. 5710, 5749]; the *menstrual* flux (as periodical); by impl. (in plur.) *soiling:*—filthy {1x}. See: TWOT—1564a; BDB—723b, 726b.

עֹד ʿôd. See 5750.

5709. עֲדָא {9x} ʿădâʾ (Aram.), *ad-aw';* or

עֲדָה ʿădâh (Aram.), *ad-aw';* corresp. to 5710:—take away {3x}, passed {1x}, departed {1x}, altereth {1x}, took {1x}, pass away {1x}, removeth {1x}. See: TWOT—2898; BDB—1105b.

עֹדֵד ʿÔdêd. See 5752.

5710. עָדָה {10x} ʿâdâh, *aw-daw';* a prim. root; to *advance,* i.e. *pass* on or *continue;* caus. to *remove;* spec. to *bedeck* (i.e. bring an ornament upon):—deck . . . {6x}, adorn {2x}, passed {1x}, take away {1x}. See: TWOT—1565; BDB—723c, 725c, 1105b.

5711. עָדָה {8x} ʿÂdâh, *aw-daw';* from 5710; *ornament; Adah,* the name of two women:—*Adah* {8x}. See: BDB—725b.

5712. עֵדָה {149x} ʿêdâh, *ay-daw';* fem. of 5707 in the orig. sense of *fixture;* a stated *assemblage* (spec. a *concourse,* or gen. a *family* or *crowd*):—congregation {124x}, company {13x}, assembly {9x}, multitude {1x}, people {1x}, swarm {1x}.

ʿEdah means "congregation." **(1)** In ordinary usage, *ʿedah* refers to a "group of people." **(1a)** It occurs 149 times in the Old Testament, most frequently in the Book of Numbers. **(1b)** The first occurrence is in Ex 12:3, where the word is a synonym for *qahal* (6951), "assembly": "Speak ye unto all the congregation of Israel, saying, In the tenth day of this month they shall take to them every man a lamb, according to the house of their fathers, a lamb for an house:" **(2)** The most general meaning of *ʿedah* is "group," whether of animals—such as a swarm of bees (Judg 14:8), a herd of bulls (Ps 68:30), and the flocking together of birds (Hos 7:12)—or of people, such as the righteous (Ps 1:5), the evildoers (Ps 22:16), and the nations (Ps 7:7). **(3)** The most frequent reference is to the "congregation of Israel" (9 times), "the congregation of the sons of Israel" (26 times), "the congregation" (24 times), or "all of the congregation" (30 times). **(4)** Elders (Lev 4:15), family heads (Num 31:26), and princes (Num 16:2; 31:13; 32:2) were placed in charge of the "congregation" in order to assist Moses in a just rule. Syn.: 4150, 6951. See: TWOT—878a; BDB—417a, 726b, 729d. comp. 5713.

5713. עֵדָה {22x} ʿêdâh, *ay-daw';* fem. of 5707 in its techn. sense; *testimony:*—testimonies {22x}, witness {4x}. See: TWOT—1576c, 1576e; BDB—726b, 729d, 730a. comp. 5712.

5714. עִדּוֹ {10x} ʿIddôw, id-do'; or

עִדּוֹא ʿIddôwʾ, id-do'; or

עִדִּיא ʿIddîyʾ, id-dee'; from 5710; timely; Iddo (or Iddi), the name of five Isr.:—Iddo {10x}. See: BDB—418a, 723b, 726b. comp. 3035, 3260.

5715. עֵדוּת {59x} ʿêdûwth, ay-dooth'; fem. of 5707; testimony:—testimony {55x}, witness {4x}.

'Eduwth means "testimony; ordinance." **(1)** This word refers to the Ten Commandments as a solemn divine charge or duty. **(1a)** In particular, it represents those commandments as written on the tablets and existing as a reminder and "testimony" of Israel's relationship and responsibility to God: "And he gave unto Moses, when he had made an end of communing with him upon Mount Sinai, two tables of testimony, tables of stone, written with the finger of God" (Ex 31:18). **(1c)** Elsewhere these tablets are called simply "the testimony": "And thou shalt put into the ark the testimony which I shall give thee" (Ex 25:16). **(1d)** Since they were kept in the ark, it became known as the "ark of the testimony" (Ex 25:22) or simply "the testimony": "As the Lord commanded Moses, so Aaron laid it up before the Testimony, to be kept" (Ex 16:34—the first biblical occurrence of the word). **(1e)** The tabernacle as the housing for the ark containing these tablets was sometimes called the "tabernacle of testimony" (Ex 38:21) or the "tent of the testimony" (Num 9:15).

(2) The word sometimes refers to the entire law of God: "The law of the Lord is perfect, converting the soul: the testimony of the Lord is sure, making wise the simple" (Ps 19:7). Here 'eduwth is synonymously parallel to "law," making it a synonym to that larger concept. **(3)** Special or particular laws are sometimes called "testimonies": "And keep the charge of the Lord thy God, to walk in his ways, to keep his statutes, and his commandments, and his judgments, and his testimonies, as it is written in the law of Moses, that thou mayest prosper in all that thou doest, and whithersoever thou turnest thyself:" (1 Kin 2:3). **(4)** In Ps 122:4 the annual pilgrimage feasts are called "the testimony of Israel": "Whither the tribes go up, the tribes of the LORD, unto the testimony of Israel, to give thanks unto the name of the LORD." See: TWOT—1576f; BDB—726b, 730b.

5716. עֲדִי {13x} ʿădîy, ad-ee'; from 5710 in the sense of trappings; finery; gen. an outfit; spec. a headstall:—mouth {2x}, ornament {11x}. See: TWOT—1566a; BDB—725d, 726b.

5717. עֲדִיאֵל {3x} ʿĂdîyʾêl, ad-ee-ale'; from 5716 and 410; ornament of God; Adiel, the name of three Isr.:—Adiel {3x}. See: BDB—726a, 726b.

5718. עֲדָיָה {9x} ʿĂdâyâh, ad-aw-yaw'; or

עֲדָיָהוּ ʿĂdâyâhûw, ad-aw-yaw'-hoo; from 5710 and 3050; Jah has adorned; Adajah, the name of eight Isr.:—Adaiah {9x}. See: BDB—726a, 726b.

5719. עָדִין {1x} ʿâdîyn, aw-deen'; from 5727; voluptuous:—given to pleasures {1x}. See: TWOT—1567c; BDB—726d, 783b.

5720. עָדִין {4x} ʿĂdîyn, aw-deen'; the same as 5719; Adin, the name of two Isr.:—Adin {4x}. See: BDB—726d.

5721. עֲדִינָא {1x} ʿĂdîynâʾ, ad-ee-naw'; from 5719; effeminacy; Adina, an Isr.:—Adina {1x}. See: BDB—726d.

5722. עֲדִינוֹ {1x} ʿădîynôw, ad-ee-no'; prob. from 5719 in the orig. sense of slender (i.e. a spear); his spear:—Adino {1x}. See: BDB—726d.

5723. עֲדִיתַיִם {1x} ʿĂdîythayim, ad-ee-thah'-yim; dual of a fem. of 5706; double prey; Adithajim, a place in Pal.:—Adithaim {1x}. See: BDB—726b.

5724. עַדְלַי {1x} ʿAdlay, ad-lah'-ee; prob. from an unused root of uncert. mean.; Adlai, an Isr.:—Adlai {1x}. See: BDB—726b.

5725. עֲדֻלָּם {8x} ʿĂdullâm, ad-ool-lawm'; prob. from the pass. part. of the same as 5724; Adullam, a place in Pal.:—Adullam {8x}. See: BDB—726b.

5726. עֲדֻלָּמִי {3x} ʿĂdullâmîy, ad-ool-law-mee'; patrial from 5725; an Adullamite or native of Adullam:—Adullamite {3x}. See: BDB—726c.

5727. עָדַן {1x} ʿâdan, aw-dan'; a prim. root; to be soft or pleasant; fig. and refl. to live voluptuously:—delighted themselves {1x}. See: TWOT—1567; BDB—726c.

5728. עֶדֶן {2x} ʿăden, ad-en'; or

עֶדֶנָה ʿădennâh, ad-en'-naw; from 5704 and 2004; till now:—yet {2x}. See: TWOT—1565c?; BDB—725c, 727a.

5729. עֶדֶן {3x} ʿEden, eh'-den; from 5727; pleasure; Eden, a place in Mesopotamia:—Eden {3x}. See: BDB—726c, 727a.

5730. עֵדֶן {4x} ʿêden, ay'-den; or (fem.)

עֶדְנָה ʿednâh, ed-naw'; from 5727; pleasure:—delicates {1x}, delights {1x}, pleasure {2x}. See: TWOT—1567a; BDB—726c, 726d. See also 1040.

5731. עֵדֶן {17x} **ʻÉden**, *ay'-den;* the same as 5730 (masc.); *Eden,* the region of Adam's home:—Eden {17x}. See: TWOT—1568; BDB—727a.

5732. עִדָּן {13x} **ʻiddân** (Aram.), *id-dawn';* from a root corresp. to that of 5708; a set *time;* tech. a *year:*—time {13x}. See: TWOT—2900; BDB—1105c.

5733. עַדְנָא {2x} **ʻAdnâ**, *ad-naw'* from 5727; *pleasure; Adna,* the name of two Isr.:—Adna {2x}. See: BDB—726c, 726d.

5734. עַדְנָה {2x} **ʻAdnâh**, *ad-naw';* from 5727; *pleasure; Adnah,* the name of two Isr.:—Adnah {2x}. See: BDB—726c, 726d, 727a.

5735. עֲדְעָדָה {1x} **ʻĂdʻâdâh**, *ad-aw-daw';* from 5712; *festival; Adadah,* a place in Pal.:—Adadah {1x}. See: BDB—727a, 793a.

5736. עָדַף {9x} **ʻâdaph**, *aw-daf';* a prim. root; to *be* (caus. *have*) *redundant:*—remains {4x}, overplus {1x}, more {1x}, odd number {1x}, over and above {1x}, over {1x}. See: TWOT—1569; BDB—727a.

5737. עָדַר {11x} **ʻâdar**, *aw-dar';* a prim. root; to *arrange,* as a battle, a vineyard (to *hoe*); hence, to *muster* and so to *miss* (or find *wanting*):—dig {2x}, fail {4x}, keep {1x}, keep rank {1x}, lack {3x}. See: TWOT—1570, 1571, 1572; BDB—727b, 727c.

5738. עֶדֶר {1x} **ʻEder**, *eh'-der;* from 5737; an *arrangement* (i.e. drove); *Eder,* an Isr.:—Ader {1x}. See: BDB—727d.

5739. עֵדֶר {38x} **ʻêder**, *ay'-der;* from 5737; an *arrangement,* i.e. *muster* (of animals):—drove {4x}, flock {32x}, herds {2x}. See: TWOT—1572a; BDB—727c.

5740. עֵדֶר {3x} **ʻÉder**, *ay'-der;* the same as 5739; *Eder,* the name of an Isr. and of two places in Pal.:—Eder {3x}. See: BDB—727d.

5741. עַדְרִיאֵל {2x} **ʻAdrîyʼêl**, *ad-ree-ale';* from 5739 and 410; *flock of God; Adriel,* an Isr.:—Adriel {2x}. See: BDB—727b.

5742. עָדָשׁ {4x} **ʻâdâsh**, *aw-dawsh';* from an unused root of uncert. mean.; a *lentil:*—lentiles {4x}. See: TWOT—1573; BDB—727d.

עַוָּא **ʻAvvâ**. See 5755.

5743. עוּב {1x} **ʻûwb**, *oob;* a prim. root; to *be dense* or *dark,* i.e. to *becloud:*—cover with a cloud {1x}. See: TWOT—1574; BDB—728a, 743b, 726b.

5744. עוֹבֵד {10x} **ʻÔwbêd**, *o-bade';* act. part. of 5647; *serving; Obed,* the name of five Isr.:—Obed {10x}. See: BDB—714d.

5745. עוֹבָל {1x} **ʻÔwbâl**, *o-bawl';* of for. der.; *Obal,* a son of Joktan:—Obal {1x}. See: BDB—716c.

5746. עוּג {1x} **ʻûwg**, *oog;* a prim. root; prop. to *gyrate;* but used only as a denom. from 5692, to *bake* (round cakes on the hearth):—bake {1x}. See: TWOT—1575; BDB—728b.

5747. עוֹג {22x} **ʻÔwg**, *ogue;* prob. from 5746; *round; Og,* a king of Bashan:—Og {22x}. See: BDB—721d, 728b.

5748. עוּגָב {4x} **ʻûwgâb**, *oo-gawb';* or

עֻגָּב **ʻuggâb**, *oog-gawb';* from 5689 in the orig. sense of *breathing;* a *reed-instrument* of music:—organ {2x}, flute {1x}. pipe {1x}. See: TWOT—1559c; BDB—721d, 728b.

5749. עוּד **ʻûwd**, *ood;* a prim. root; to *duplicate* or *repeat;* by impl. to *protest, testify* (as by reiteration); intens. to *encompass, restore* (as a sort of redupl.):—testify {15x}, protest {6x}, witness {6x}, record {3x}, charge {2x}, solemnly {2x}, take {3x}, admonished {1x}, misc. {7x} = earnestly, lift up, relieve, rob, stand upright, give warning.

ʻUwd means "to take as witness, bear witness, repeat, admonish, warn, assure protection, relieve." **(1)** In 1 Kin 21:10 *ʻuwd* means "to bear witness": "And set two men, sons of Belial, before him, to bear witness against him." **(2)** The word means "to warn" in Jer 6:10: "To whom shall I speak, and give warning, that they may hear?" **(3)** The Law of God is His testimony, because it is His own affirmation concerning His nature, attributes, and consequent demands. See: TWOT—1576, 1576d; BDB—728c, 729d.

5750. עוֹד {30x} **ʻôwd**, *ode;* or

עֹד **ʻôd**, *ode;* from 5749; prop. *iteration* or *continuance;* used only adv. (with or without prep.), *again, repeatedly, still, more:*—{30x} = again, × all life long, at all, besides, but, else, further (-more), henceforth, (any) longer, (any) more (-over), × once, since, (be) still, when, (good, the) while (having being), (as, because, whether, while) yet (within). See: TWOT—1576a; BDB—723b, 728c, 1105c.

5751. עוֹד {1x} **ʻôwd** (Aram.), *ode;* corresp. to 5750:—while {1x}. See: TWOT—2901; BDB—1105c.

5752. עוֹדֵד {3x} **ʻÔwdêd**, *o-dade';* or

עֹדֵד **ʻÔdêd**, *o-dade';* from 5749; *reiteration; Oded,* the name of two Isr.:—Oded {3x}. See: BDB—723b, 729c.

Hebrew

5753. עָוָה {17x} **'âvâh**, *aw-vaw'*; a prim. root; to *crook*, lit. or fig. (as follows):— iniquity {4x}, perverse {2x}, perversely {2x}, perverted {2x}, amiss {1x}, turn {1x}, crooked {1x}, bowed down {1x}, troubled {1x}, wickedly {1x}, wrong {1x}.

(1) The perversion or distortion of nature that is caused by evildoing is represented by this word. *'Avah* means "to do iniquity." **(2)** *'Avah* is often used as a synonym of *chata'* (2398), "to sin," as in Ps 106:6: "We have sinned [*chata'*] with our fathers, we have committed iniquity [*'avah*], we have done wickedly [7561 – *rasha'*]." See: TWOT—1577; BDB—730c, 731c, 1105c.

5754. עֻוָּה {3x} **'avvâh**, *av-vaw'*; intens. from 5753 abb.; *overthrow*:—overturn {3x}. See: TWOT—1577b; BDB—730c, 731d.

5755. עִוָּה {4x} **'Ivvâh**, *iv-vaw'*; or

עַוָּא **'Avvâ** (2 Kin 17: 24) *av-vaw'*; for 5754; *Ivvah* or *Avva*, a region of Assyria:—Ava {1x}, Ivah {3x}. See: BDB—727d, 731d.

עָוֹן **'âvôwn**. See 5771.

5756. עוּז {4x} **'ûwz**, *ooz*; a prim. root; to *be strong*; caus. to *strengthen*, i.e. (fig.) to *save* (by flight):—gather . . . {2x}, gather {1x}, retire {1x}. See: TWOT—1578; BDB—731d.

5757. עַוִּי {1x} **'Avvîy**, *av-vee'*; patrial from 5755; an *Avvite* or native of *Avvah* (only plur.):—Avites {1x}. See: BDB—731d, 732a.

5758. עִוְיָא {1x} **'ivyâ** (Aram.), *iv-yaw'*; from a root corresp. to 5753; *perverseness*:—iniquities {1x}. See: TWOT—2902; BDB—1105c.

5759. עֲוִיל {2x} **'ăvîyl**, *av-eel'*; from 5764; a *babe*:—young children {1x}, little ones {1x}. See: TWOT—1579b; BDB—732a, 732b.

5760. עֲוִיל {1x} **'ăvîyl**, *av-eel'*; from 5765; *perverse* (morally):—ungodly {1x}. See: TWOT—1580d; BDB—732b, 732d.

5761. עַוִּים {3x} **'Avvîym**, *av-veem'*; plur. of 5757; *Avvim* (as inhabited by Avvites), a place in Pal. (with the art. pref.):—Avim {2x}, Avites {1x}. See: BDB—731d, 732a.

5762. עֲוִית {2x} **'Ăvîyth**, *av-veeth'*; or [perh.

עַיּוֹת **'Ayôwth**, *ah-yōth'*, as if plur. of 5857]

עַיּוּת **'Ayûwth**, *ah-yōth'*; from 5753; *ruin*; *Avvith* (or *Avvoth*), a place in Pal.:— Avith {2x}. See: BDB—732a, 743b.

5763. עוּל {5x} **'ûwl**, *ool*; a prim. root; to *suckle*, i.e. *give milk*:—milch {2x}, young {1x}, ewes great with young {1x}, those that are young {1x}. See: TWOT—1579; BDB—732b.

5764. עוּל {2x} **'ûwl**, *ool*; from 5763; a *babe*:— sucking child {1x}, infant {1x}. See: TWOT—1579a; BDB—732b.

5765. עָוַל {2x} **'âval**, *aw-val'*; a prim. root; to *distort* (morally):—deal unjustly {1x}, unrighteous {1x}.

This word is thought to designate the want of integrity and rectitude that is the accompaniment, if not the essential part, of wrongdoing. This word is taken in its original sense as a departure from that which equal and right. See: TWOT—1580; BDB—732c.

עוּל **'ôwl**. See 5923.

5766. עֶוֶל {55x} **'evel**, *eh'-vel*; or

עָוֶל **'âvel**, *aw'-vel*; and (fem.)

עַוְלָה **'avlâh**, *av-law'*; or

עוֹלָה **'ôwlâh**, *o-law'*; or

עֹלָה **'ôlâh**, *o-law'*; from 5765; (moral) *evil*:—iniquity {36x}, wickedness {7x}, unrighteousness {3x}, unjust {2x}, perverseness {1x}, unjustly {1x}, unrighteously {1x}, wicked {1x}, wickedly {1x}, variant {2x}. See: TWOT—1580a, 1580b; BDB—732b, 732c, 732d, 759b, 763c.

5767. עַוָּל {5x} **'avvâl**, *av-vawl'*; intens. from 5765; *evil* (morally):—wicked {3x}, unjust {1x}, unrighteous {1x}. See: TWOT—1580c; BDB—732d.

עוֹלָה **'ôwlâh**. See 5930.

5768. עוֹלֵל {20x} **'ôwlêl**, *o-lale'*; or

עֹלָל **'ôlâl**, *o-lawl'*; from 5763; a *suckling*:—children {13x}, infant {3x}, babes {2x}, child {1x}, little ones {1x}. See: TWOT—1579c; BDB—732d, 760c.

5769. עוֹלָם {439x} **'ôwlâm**, *o-lawm'*; or

עֹלָם **'ôlâm**, *o-lawm'*; from 5956; prop. *concealed*, i.e. the *vanishing* point; gen. time *out of mind* (past or future), i.e. (practically) *eternity*; freq. adv. (espec. with prep. pref.) *always*:—ever {272x}, everlasting {63x}, old {22x}, perpetual {22x}, evermore {15x}, never {13x}, time {6x}, ancient {5x}, world {4x}, always {3x}, alway {2x}, long {2x}, more {2x}, never + 408 {2x}, misc. {6x}.

'Olam means "eternity; remotest time; perpetuity." **(1)** First, in a few passages the word means "eternity" in the sense of not being limited to the present. Thus, in Eccl. 3:11 we read that God had bound man to time and given

him the capacity to live "above time" (i.e., to remember yesterday, plan for tomorrow, and consider abstract principles); yet He has not given him divine knowledge: "He hath made every thing beautiful in his time: also he hath set the world in their heart, so that no man can find out the work that God maketh from the beginning to the end."

(2) Second, the word signifies "remotest time" or "remote time." **(2a)** In 1 Chr 16:36, God is described as blessed "for ever and ever," or from the most distant past time to the most distant future time: "Blessed be the LORD God of Israel for ever and ever. And all the people said, Amen, and praised the LORD." **(2b)** In passages where God is viewed as the One who existed before the creation was brought into existence, ʿolam means: **(2b1)** "at the very beginning": "Remember the former things [the beginning things at the very beginning] of old: for I am God, and there is none else" (Is 46:9); or **(2b2)** "from eternity, from the pre-creation, till now": "Remember, O Lord, thy tender mercies and thy lovingkindnesses; for they have been ever of old [from eternity]" (Ps 25:6). **(3)** In other passages, the word means "from (in) olden times": "Mighty men which were of old, men of renown" (Gen 6:4).

(4) In Is 42:14, the word is used hyperbolically meaning "for a long time": "I have long time holden my peace; I have been still, and refrained myself." **(5)** This word may include all the time between the ancient beginning and the present: "The prophets that have been before me and before thee of old prophesied" (Jer 28:8). **(6)** The word can mean "long ago" (from long ago): "For [long ago] I have broken thy yoke, and burst thy bands" (Jer 2:20). **(7)** In Josh 24:2, the word means "formerly; in ancient times." **(8)** The word is used in Jer 5:15, where it means "ancient": "Lo, I will bring a nation upon you from far, O house of Israel, saith the Lord: it is a mighty nation, it is an ancient nation. . . ." **(9)** When used with the negative, ʿolam can mean "never": "We are thine: thou never barest rule [literally, "not ruled from the most distant past"] over them" (Is 63:19). **(10)** Similar meanings emerge when the word is used without a preposition and in a genitive relationship to some other noun.

(11) With the preposition ʿad, the word can mean **(11a)** "into the indefinite future": "An Ammonite or Moabite shall not enter into the congregation of the Lord; even to their tenth generation shall they not enter into the congregation of the Lord for ever" (Deut 23:3). **(11b)** The same construction can signify "as long as one lives": "I will not go up until the child be weaned, and then I will bring him, that he may appear before the Lord, and there

abide for ever" (1 Sa 1:22). **(11c)** This construction then sets forth an extension into the indefinite future, beginning from the time of the speaker. **(12)** In the largest number of its occurrences, ʿolam appears with the preposition le. **(12a)** This construction is weaker and less dynamic in emphasis than the previous phrase, insofar as it envisions a "simple duration." **(12b)** This difference emerges in 1 Kin 2:33, where both phrases occur: "Their blood shall therefore return upon the head of Joab, and upon the head of his seed for ever (le ʿolam): but upon David, and upon his seed, and upon his house, and upon his throne, shall there be peace for ever (ʿad ʿolam) from the LORD." **(12b1)** Le ʿolam is applied to the curse set upon the dead Joab and his descendants. The other more dynamic phrase (ʿad ʿolam), applied to David and his descendants, emphasizes the ever-continued, ever-acting presence of the blessing extended into the "indefinite future."

(13) In Ex 21:6 the phrase le ʿolam means "as long as one lives": "And his master shall bore his ear through with an awl; and he shall serve him for ever." **(13a)** This phrase emphasizes "continuity," "definiteness," and "unchangeability." **(13b)** This is its emphasis in Gen 3:22, the first biblical occurrence of ʿolam: "And now, lest he put forth his hand, and take also of the tree of life, and eat, and live for ever." **(14)** The same emphasis on "simple duration" pertains when ʿolam is used in passages such as **(14a)** Ps 61:8, where it appears by itself: "So will I sing praise unto thy name for ever, that I may daily perform my vows." **(14b)** The parallelism demonstrates that ʿolam means "day by day," or "continually." **(15)** In Gen 9:16, the word (used absolutely) means the "most distant future": "And the bow shall be in the cloud; and I will look upon it, that I may remember the everlasting covenant between God and every living creature." **(16)** In other places, the word means "without beginning, without end, and ever-continuing": "Trust ye in the Lord for ever: for in the Lord Jehovah is everlasting strength" (Is 26:4). **(17)** The plural of this word is an intensive form. Syn.: 5331, 5703. See: TWOT—1631a; BDB—732d, 761d, 1106d.

5770. עָוַן {1x} ʿâvan, aw-van'; denom. from 5869; to watch (with jealousy):— eyed {1x}. See: TWOT—1612; BDB—745a.

5771. עָוֹן {230x} ʿâvôn, aw-vone'; or

עָווֹן ʿâvôwn (2 Kin 7:9; Ps 51:5 [7]), aw-vone'; from 5753; perversity, i.e. (moral) evil:—iniquity {220x}, punishment {5x}, fault {2x}, Iniquities + 1697 {1x}, mischief {1x}, sin {1x}.

ʿAvown means "iniquity; guilt; punishment." **(1)** This word is derived from the root

ʿavah (5753), which means "to be bent, bowed down, twisted, perverted" or "to twist, pervert." (2) ʿAvown portrays sin as (2a) a perversion of life (a twisting out of the right way), (2b) a perversion of truth (a twisting into error), or (2c) a perversion of intent (a bending of rectitude into willful disobedience). (3) The word "iniquity" is the best single-word equivalent. (4) The first use of ʿavown comes from Cain's lips, where the word takes the special meaning of "punishment": "And Cain said unto the Lord, My punishment is greater than I can bear" (Gen 4:13). (2) The word signifies (2a) an offense, intentional or not, against God's law. (2b) This meaning is also most basic to the word chatta't (2403), "sin," in the Old Testament, and for this reason the words chatta't and ʿavown are virtually synonymous; "Lo, this [the live coal] hath touched thy [Isaiah's] lips; and thine iniquity [ʿavown] is taken away, and thy sin [chatta't] purged" (Is 6:7). (3) "Iniquity" as an offense to God's holiness is punishable. The individual is warned that the Lord punishes man's transgression: "But every one shall die for his own iniquity: every man that eateth the sour grape, his teeth shall be set on edge" (Jer 31:30).

(4) There is also a collective sense in that the one is responsible for the many: "Thou shalt not bow down thyself to them, nor serve them: for I the Lord thy God am a jealous God, visiting the iniquity of the fathers upon the children unto the third and fourth generation of them that hate me" (Ex 20:5). (5) No generation, however, was to think that it bore God's judgment for the "iniquity" of another generation: "Yet say ye, Why? doth not the son bear the iniquity of the father? When the son hath done that which is lawful and right, and hath kept all my statutes, and hath done them, he shall surely live. The soul that sinneth, it shall die. The son shall not bear the iniquity of the father, neither shall the father bear the iniquity of the son: the righteousness of the righteous shall be upon him, and the wickedness of the wicked shall be upon him" (Eze 18:19–20). (6) Israel went into captivity for the sin of their fathers and for their own sins: "And the heathen shall know that the house of Israel went into captivity for their iniquity; because they trespassed against me, therefore hid I my face from them, and gave them into the hand of their enemies: so fell they all by the sword" (Eze 39:23).

(7) Serious as "iniquity" is in the covenantal relationship between the Lord and His people, the people are reminded that He is a living God who willingly forgives "iniquity": "Keeping mercy for thousands, forgiving iniquity and transgression and sin, and that will by no means clear the guilty; visiting the iniquity of the fathers upon the children, and upon the children's children, unto the third and to the fourth generation" (Ex 34:7). (8) God expects (8a) confession of sin: "I acknowledged my sin unto thee, and mine iniquity have I not hid. I said, I will confess my transgressions unto the Lord; and thou forgavest the iniquity of my sin" (Ps 32:5), and (8b) a trusting, believing heart which expresses the humble prayer: "Wash me thoroughly from mine iniquity, and cleanse me from my sin" (Ps 51:2). (9) Isaiah 53 teaches that God put upon Jesus Christ our "iniquities" (v. 6), that He having been bruised for our "iniquities" (v. 5) might justify those who believe on Him: "He shall see of the travail of his soul, and shall be satisfied: by his knowledge shall my righteous servant justify many; for he shall bear their iniquities" (Is 53:11).

(10) The usage of ʿavown includes the whole area of sin, judgment, and "punishment" for sin. The Old Testament teaches that God's forgiveness of "iniquity" extends to the actual sin, the guilt of sin, God's judgment upon that sin, and God's punishment of the sin. "Blessed is the man unto whom the Lord imputeth not iniquity, and in whose spirit there is no guile" (Ps 32:2). (11a) The penitent wrongdoer recognized his "iniquity" in Is 59:12: "For our transgressions are multiplied before thee, and our sins testify against us: for our transgressions are with us; and as for our iniquities, we know them" (cf. 1 Sa 3:13). (11b) "Iniquity" is something to be confessed: (11b1) "And Aaron shall lay both his hands upon the head of the live goat, and confess over him all the iniquities of the children of Israel" (Lev 16:21). (11b2) "And the seed of Israel . . . confessed their sins, and the iniquities of their fathers" (Neh 9:2; cf. Ps 38:18). (12) The grace of God may (12a) remove or forgive "iniquity": "And unto him he said, Behold, I have caused thine iniquity to pass from thee" (Zec 3:4; cf. 2 Sa 24:10). (12b) His atonement may cover over "iniquity": "By mercy and truth iniquity is purged; and by the fear of the Lord men depart from evil" (Prov 16:6; cf. Ps 78:38).

(13) ʿAvown may refer to "the guilt of iniquity," as in Eze 36:31: "Then shall ye remember your own evil ways . . . and shall loathe yourselves in your own sight for your iniquities and for your abominations" (cf. Eze 9:9). (14) The word may also refer to "punishment for iniquity": "And Saul sware to her by the Lord, saying, As the Lord liveth, there shall no punishment happen to thee for this thing" (1 Sa 28:10). (15) In Ex 28:38, ʿavown is used as the object of natsa' (5375 - "to bear, carry away, forgive"): "And it shall be upon Aaron's forehead, that Aaron may bear (natsa') the

iniquity ('avown) of the holy things, which the children of Israel shall hallow in all their holy gifts; and it shall be always upon his forehead, that they may be accepted before the LORD." **(15a)** to suggest bearing the punishment for the "iniquity" of others. **(15b)** In Is 53:11, we are told that the servant of Yahweh bears the consequences of the "iniquities" of sinful mankind, including Israel. Syn: 'Avown occurs frequently throughout the Old Testament in parallelism with other words related to sin, such as **(A)** chatta't (2403 - "sin") and **(B)** pesha' (6588 - "transgression"). **(B1)** Some examples are 1 Sa 20:1: "And David . . . said before Jonathan, what have I done? what is mine iniquity [5771 - 'avown]? and what is my sin [2403 - chatta't] before thy father, that he seeketh my life?" (cf. Is 43:24; Jer 5:25). **(B2)** Also note Job 14:17: "My transgression [6588 – pesha'] is sealed up in a bag, and thou sewest up mine iniquity [5771 - 'avown]" (cf. Ps 107:17; Is 50:1). See: TWOT—1577a; BDB—730d, 733b, 773b, 1105c.

5772. עוֹנָה {1x} 'ôwnâh, o-naw'; from an unused root appar. mean. to dwell together; sexual (cohabitation):—duty of marriage {1x}. See: TWOT—1650a; BDB—733b, 773b.

5773. עֲוֵה {1x} 'av'eh, av-eh'; from 5753; perversity:—perverse {1x}. See: TWOT—1577c; BDB—730c, 733b.

5774. עוּף {32x} 'ûwph, oof; a prim. root; to cover (with wings or obscurity); hence, (as denom. from 5775) to fly; also (by impl. of dimness) to faint (from the darkness of swooning):—fly {17x}, (fly, flee . . .) away {6x}, faint {3x}, brandish {1x}, shine forth {1x}, set {1x}, weary {1x}, variant {2x}. See: TWOT—1582, 1583, 1583c; BDB—733b, 734a, 746a, 1074a, 1105c.

5775. עוֹף {71x} 'ôwph, ofe; from 5774; a bird (as covered with feathers, or rather as covering with wings), often collect.:—fowl {59x}, bird {9x}, flying {2x}, flieth {1x}. See: TWOT—1582a; BDB—733d.

5776. עוֹף {2x} 'ôwph (Aram.), ofe; corresp. to 5775:—fowl {2x}. See: TWOT—2903; BDB—1105c.

5777. עוֹפֶרֶת {9x} 'ôwphereth, o-feh'-reth; or

עֹפֶרֶת 'ôphereth, o-feh'-reth; fem. part. act. of 6080; lead (from its dusty color):—lead {9x}. See: TWOT—1665b; BDB—780b.

5778. עוֹפַי {1x} 'Ôwphay, o-fah'-ee; from 5775; birdlike; Ephai, an Isr.:—Ephai {1x}. See: BDB—734a, 746a.

5779. עוּץ {2x} 'ûwts, oots; a prim. root; to consult:—take advice {1x}, take . . . together {1x}. See: TWOT—1584; BDB—734a.

5780. עוּץ {8x} 'Ûwts, oots; appar. from 5779; consultation; Uts, a son of Aram, also a Seirite, and the regions settled by them.:—Uz {8x}. See: BDB—734b.

5781. עוּק {2x} 'ûwq, ook; a prim. root; to pack:—be pressed {2x}. See: TWOT—1585; BDB—734b.

5782. עוּר {81x} 'ûwr, oor; a prim. root [rather ident. with 5783 through the idea of opening the eyes]; to wake (lit. or fig.):—(stir, lift . . . .) up {40x}, awake {25x}, wake {6x}, raise {6x}, arise {1x}, master {1x}, raised out {1x}, variant {1x}.

'Uwr means "to awake, stir up, rouse oneself, rouse." **(1)** Its first use in the Old Testament has the sense **(1a)** of "rousing" someone to action: "Awake, awake, Deborah" (Judg 5:12). **(1b)** This same meaning is reflected in Ps 7:6, where it is used in parallelism with "arise": "Arise, O Lord, in thine anger, . . . awake for me to the judgment that thou hast commanded." **(2)** 'Uwr commonly signifies awakening out of ordinary sleep: "And the angel that talked with me came again, and waked me, as a man that is wakened out of his sleep" (Zec 4:1), or **(3)** out of the sleep of death: "So man lieth down, and riseth not: till the heavens be no more, they shall not awake, nor be raised out of their sleep" (Job 14:12). **(4)** In Job 31:29, it expresses the idea of "being excited" or "stirred up": "If I . . . lifted up myself when evil found him. . . ." **(5)** This verb is found several times in the Song of Solomon, for instance, **(5a)** in contrast with sleep: "I sleep, but my heart waketh . . ." (5:2). **(5b)** It is found three times in an identical phrase: ". . . that you stir not up, nor awake my love, till he please" (Song 2:7; 3:5; 8:4). See: TWOT—1587; BDB—BDB—734d.

5783. עוּר {1x} 'ûwr, oor; a prim. root; to (be) bare:—naked {1x}. See: TWOT—1588; BDB—735d.

5784. עוּר {1x} 'ûwr (Aram.), oor; chaff (as the naked husk):—chaff {1x}. See: TWOT—2904; BDB—1105c.

5785. עוֹר {99x} 'ôwr, ore; from 5783; skin (as naked); by impl. hide, leather:—skin {96x}, hide {2x}, leather {1x}. See: TWOT—1589a; BDB—736a.

5786. עוּר· {5x} 'âvar, aw-var'; a prim. root [rather denom. from 5785 through the idea of a film over the eyes]; to blind:—put out {3x}, blind {2x}. See: TWOT—1586; BDB—734c. See also 5895.

5787. עִוֵּר {26x} **‘ivvêr**, *iv-vare′;* intens. from 5786; *blind* (lit. or fig.):—blind {25x}, blind men {1x}. See: TWOT—1586a; BDB—734c.

עוֹרֵב **‘ôwrêb.** See 6159.

5788. עִוָּרוֹן {3x} **‘ivvârôwn**, *iv-vaw-rone′;* and (fem.)

עַוֶּרֶת **‘avvereth**, *av-veh′-reth;* from 5787; *blindness:*—blindness {2x}, blind {1x}. See: TWOT—1586b, 1586c; BDB—734d.

5789. עוּשׁ {1x} **‘ûwsh**, *oosh;* a prim. root; to *hasten:*—assemble yourselves {1x}. See: TWOT—1590; BDB—736b.

5790. עוּת {1x} **‘ûwth**, *ooth;* for 5789; to *hasten,* i.e. *succor:*—speak {1x}. See: TWOT—1592; BDB—736c.

5791. עָוַת {11x} **‘âvath**, *aw-vath′;* a prim. root; to *wrest:*—pervert {3x}, crooked {2x}, bow {1x}, bow down {1x}, falsifying {1x}, overthrown {1x}, perversely {1x}, subvert {1x}. See: TWOT—1591; BDB—736c.

5792. עַוָּתָה {1x} **‘avvâthâh**, *av-vaw-thaw′;* from 5791; *oppression:*—my wrong {1x}. See: TWOT—1591a; BDB—736c.

5793. עוּתַי {2x} **‘Ûwthay**, *oo-thah′-ee;* from 5790; *succoring; Uthai,* the name of two Isr.:—Uthai {2x}. See: BDB—736d, 800d.

5794. עַז {23x} **‘az**, *az;* from 5810; *strong, vehement, harsh:*—strong {12x}, fierce {4x}, mighty {3x}, power {1x}, greedy {1x}, roughly {1x}, stronger {1x}. See: TWOT—1596a; BDB—736d, 738c.

5795. עֵז {74x} **‘êz**, *aze;* from 5810; a she-*goat* (as *strong*), but masc. in plur. (which also is used ellipt. for *goat′s hair*):—goat {63x}, kid + 1423 {5x}, kid {4x}, he {1x}, kids + 1121 {1x}. See: TWOT—1654a; BDB—736d, 777c, 1107c.

5796. עֵז {1x} **‘êz** (Aram.), *aze;* corresp. to 5795:—goats {1x}. See: TWOT—2920a; BDB—1105d, 1107c.

5797. עֹז {93x} **‘ôz**, *oze;* or (fully)

עוֹז **‘ôwz**, *oze;* from 5810; *strength* in various applications (*force, security, majesty, praise*):—strength {60x}, strong {17x}, power {11x}, might {2x}, boldness {1x}, loud {1x}, mighty {1x}. See: TWOT—1596b; BDB—731d, 736d, 738d.

5798. עֻזָּא {14x} **‘Uzzâ′**, *ooz-zaw′;* or

עֻזָּה **‘Uzzâh**, *ooz-zaw′;* fem. of 5797; *strength; Uzza* or *Uzzah,* the name of five Isr.:—Uzza {10x}, Uzzah {4x}. See: BDB—736d, 738a, 739b, 739c.

5799. עֲזָאזֵל {4x} **‘azâ′zêl**, *az-aw-zale′;* from 5795 and 235; *goat of departure;* the *scapegoat:*—scapegoat {4x}. See: TWOT—1593; BDB—736d.

5800. עָזַב {215x} **‘âzab**, *aw-zab′;* a prim. root; to *loosen,* i.e. *relinquish, permit,* etc.:—forsake {129x}, leave {72x}, leave off {4x}, faileth {2x}, fortify {2x}, help {2x}, committeth {1x}, destitute {1x}, refuseth {1x}, surely {1x}.

‘Azab means "to leave, forsake, abandon, leave behind, be left over, let go." **(1)** Basically *‘azab* means "to depart from something," or "to leave." **(1a)** This is the meaning of the word in its first biblical appearance: "[For this cause] shall a man leave his father and his mother, and shall cleave unto his wife" (Gen 2:24). **(1b)** A special nuance of the word is "to leave in the lurch," or to leave someone who is depending upon one's services. So Moses said to Hobab the Midianite (Kenite): "Leave us not [in the lurch] I pray thee; forasmuch as thou knowest how we are to encamp in the wilderness, and thou mayest be to us instead of eyes" (Num 10:31). **(2)** The word also carries the meaning "forsake," or "leave entirely." Such passages convey a note of finality or completeness. So Isaiah is to preach that ". . . the land that thou abhorrest shall be forsaken of both her kings" (Is 7:16). **(3)** In other places, the abandonment is complete but not necessarily permanent. God says that Israel is "as a woman forsaken and grieved in spirit. . . . For a small moment have I forsaken thee; but with great mercies will I gather thee" (Is 54:6–7).

(4) This word carries a technical sense of "completely and permanently abandoned" or "divorced." Isaiah employs this sense in 62:4: "Thou shalt no more be termed Forsaken; . . . but thou shalt be called [My delight is in her], and thy land [Married]." **(5)** Another special use of the word is "to disregard advice": "But he forsook the counsel of the old men which they had given him" (1 Kin 12:8). **(6)** A second emphasis of *‘azab* is "to leave behind," meaning to allow something to remain while one leaves the scene. In Gen 39:12, Joseph "left" his garment in the hand of Potiphar's wife and fled. **(7)** The word may also refer to an intentional "turning over one's possessions to another's trust," or "leaving something in one's control." Potiphar "left all that he had in Joseph's hand" (Gen 39:6). **(8)** In a somewhat different nuance, the word means to "let someone or something alone with a problem": "If thou see the ass of him that hateth thee lying under his burden, and wouldest forbear to help him . . ." (Ex 23:5). **(9)** Used figuratively, *‘azab* means to "put distance between" in a spiritual or intellectual sense: "Cease from anger, and forsake wrath" (Ps 37:8).

(10) The emphasis of the word is "to be left over," or "to take most of something and leave the rest behind": "And thou shalt not glean thy vineyard, neither shalt thou gather every grape of thy vineyard; thou shalt leave them [over] for the poor and stranger: I am the Lord your God" (Lev 19:10). **(11)** Finally, ʿazab can mean "to let go" or "allow to leave." The "stupid and senseless men" are those who make no provision for the future; they die leaving ("allowing it to go") their wealth to others (Ps 49:10). **(12)** A different nuance occurs in Ruth 2:16, where the verb means "to let something lie" on the ground. **(13)** ʿAzab can also mean "to give up": "He that covereth his sins shall not prosper: but whoso confesseth and forsaketh them [gives them up] shall have mercy" (Prov 28:13), and **(14)** the word can mean "to set free," as in 2 Chr 28:14: "So the armed men left the captives and the spoil before the princes and all the congregation." **(15)** ʿAzab can signify "let go," or "make it leave." Concerning evil, Zophar remarks, "[The wicked] forsake it not, but keep it still within his mouth" (Job 20:13).

(16) ʿAzab can mean to "allow someone to do something," as in 2 Chr 32:31, where "God left [Hezekiah], to try him, that he might know all that was in his heart"; God "let" Hezekiah do whatever he wanted. **(17)** "Letting an activity go" may also signify its discontinuance: "I pray you, let us leave off this usury" (Neh 5:10). **(18)** ʿAzab is sometimes used in a judicial technical sense of "being free," which is the opposite of being in bondage. The Lord will vindicate His people, and will have compassion on His servants "when he seeth that their power is gone, and there is none shut up, or left" (Deut 32:36). See: TWOT—1594, 1595; BDB—736d, 738a, 1115a.

5801. עִזָּבוֹן {7x} ʿizzâbôwn, iz-zaw-bone'; from 5800 in the sense of letting go (for a price, i.e. selling); trade, i.e. the place (mart) or the payment (revenue):—fair {6x}, wares {1x}. See: TWOT—1594b; BDB—738a.

5802. עַזְבּוּק {1x} ʿAzbûwq, az-book'; from 5794 and the root of 950; stern depopulator; Azbuk, an Isr.:—Azbuk {1x}. See: BDB—738a, 739d.

5803. עַזְגָּד {4x} ʿAzgâd, az-gawd'; from 5794 and 1409; stern troop; Azgad, an Isr.:—Azgad {4x}. See: BDB—738a, 739d.

5804. עַזָּה {2x} ʿAzzâh, az-zaw'; fem. of 5794; strong; Azzah, a place in Pal.:—Azzah {18x}, Gaza {3x}. See: BDB—738a.

5805. עֲזוּבָה {1x} ʿăzûwbâh, az-oo-baw'; fem. pass. part. of 5800; desertion (of inhabitants):—forsaking {1x}. See: BDB—737d.

5806. עֲזוּבָה {4x} ʿĂzûwbâh, az-oo-baw'; the same as 5805; Azubah, the name of two Israelitesses:—Azubah {4x}. See: BDB—738a.

5807. עֱזוּז {3x} ʿĕzûwz, ez-ooz'; from 5810; forcibleness:—might {2x}, strength {1x}. See: TWOT—1596c; BDB—739b.

5808. עִזּוּז {2x} ʿizzûwz, iz-zooz'; from 5810; forcible; collect. and concr. an army:—strong {1x}, power {1x}. See: TWOT—1596d; BDB—739b.

5809. עַזּוּר {3x} ʿAzzûwr, az-zoor'; or

עַזֻּר ʿAzzûr, az-zoor'; from 5826; helpful; Azzur, the name of three Isr.:—Azur {2x}, Azzur {1x}. See: BDB—741a.

5810. עָזַז {12x} ʿâzaz, aw-zaz'; a prim. root; to be stout (lit. or fig.):—strengthen {6x}, prevail {3x}, strong {1x}, impudent {1x}, hardeneth {1x}. See: TWOT—1596; BDB—738b.

5811. עָזָז {1x} ʿÂzâz, aw-zawz'; from 5810; strong; Azaz, an Isr.:—Azaz {1x}. See: BDB—739b.

5812. עֲזַזְיָהוּ {3x} ʿĂzazyâhûw, az-az-yaw'-hoo; from 5810 and 3050; Jah has strengthened; Azazjah, the name of three Isr.:—Azaziah {3x}. See: BDB—739c.

5813. עֻזִּי {11x} ʿUzzîy, ooz-zee'; from 5810; forceful; Uzzi, the name of six Isr.:—Uzzi {11x}. See: BDB—739d.

5814. עֻזִּיָּא {1x} ʿUzzîyâʾ, ooz-zee-yaw'; perh. for 5818; Uzzija, an Isr.:—Uzzia {1x}. See: BDB—739d.

5815. עֲזִיאֵל {1x} ʿĂzîyʾêl, az-ee-ale'; from 5756 and 410; strengthened of God; Aziël, an Isr.:—Aziel {1x}. See: BDB—739d. comp. 3268.

5816. עֻזִּיאֵל {16x} ʿUzzîyʾêl, ooz-zee-ale'; from 5797 and 410; strength of God; Uzziël, the name of six Isr.:—Uzziel {16x}. See: BDB—739c.

5817. עָזִּיאֵלִי {2x} ʿOzzîyʾêlîy, oz-zee-ay-lee'; patron. from 5816; an Uzziëlite (collect.) or desc. of Uzziel:—Uzzielites {2x}. See: BDB—739c.

5818. עֻזִּיָּה {27x} ʿUzzîyâh, ooz-zee-yaw'; or

עֻזִּיָּהוּ ʿUzzîyâhûw, ooz-zee-yaw'-hoo; from 5797 and 3050; strength of Jah; Uzzijah, the name of five Isr.:—Uzziah {27x}. See: BDB—739c.

5819. עֲזִיזָא {1x} ʿĂzîyzâʾ, az-ee-zaw'; from 5756; strengthfulness; Aziza, an Isr.:—Aziza {1x}. See: BDB—739c.

5820. עַזְמָוֶת {8x} **ʿAzmâveth**, *az-maw′-veth;* from 5794 and 4194; *strong* (one) *of death;* Azmaveth, the name of three Isr. and of a place in Pal.:—Azmaveth {8x}. See: BDB—730a. See also 1041.

5821. עַזָּן {1x} **ʿAzzân**, *az-zawn′;* from 5794; *strong* one; Azzan, an Isr.:—Azzan {1x}. See: BDB—740a.

5822. עָזְנִיָּה {2x} **ʿoznîyâh**, *oz-nee-yaw′;* prob. fem. of 5797; prob. the *sea-eagle* (from its *strength*):—osprey {2x}. See: TWOT—1596e; BDB—740a.

5823. עָזַק {1x} **ʿâzaq**, *aw-zak′;* a prim. root; to *grub* over:—fenced {1x}. See: TWOT—1597; BDB—740a, 1105d.

5824. עִזְקָא {2x} **ʿizqâʾ** (Aram.), *iz-kaw′;* from a root corresp. to 5823; a *signet-ring* (as engraved):—signet {2x}. See: TWOT—2905; BDB—1105d.

5825. עֲזֵקָה {7x} **ʿĂzêqâh**, *az-ay-kaw′;* from 5823; *tilled;* Azekah, a place in Pal.:—Azekah {7x}. See: BDB—740a.

5826. עָזַר {82x} **ʿâzar**, *aw-zar′;* a prim. root; to *surround,* i.e. *protect* or *aid:*—help {64x}, helper {11x}, holpen {3x}, succour {3x}, variant {1x}.

ʿAzar means "to help, assist, aid." **(1)** *ʿAzar* is first found in the Old Testament in Jacob's deathbed blessing of Joseph: "The God of thy father, who shall help thee . . ." (Gen 49:25). **(2)** Help or aid comes from a variety of sources: Thirty-two kings "helped" Ben-hadad (1 Kin 20:6); one city "helps" another (Josh 10:33); even false gods are believed to be of "help" (2 Chr. 28:23). **(3)** Of course, the greatest source of help is God Himself; **(3a)** He is "the helper of the fatherless" (Ps 10:14). **(3b)** God promises: "I will help thee" (Is 41:10); "and the Lord shall help them, and deliver them" (Ps 37:40). See: TWOT—1598; BDB—740a.

5827. עֵזֶר {1x} **ʿEzer**, *eh′-zer;* from 5826; *help;* Ezer, the name of two Isr.:—Ezer {1x}. See: BDB—740d. comp. 5829.

5828. עֵזֶר {21x} **ʿêzer**, *ay′-zer;* from 5826; *aid:*—help {19x}, help meet {2x}. See: TWOT—1598a; BDB—740c.

5829. עֵזֶר {4x} **ʿÊzer**, *ay′-zer;* the same as 5828; *Ezer,* the name of four Isr.:—Ezer {4x}. See: BDB—740d. comp. 5827.

עַזּוּר **ʿAzzûr.** See 5809.

5830. עֶזְרָא {22x} **ʿEzrâʾ**, *ez-raw′;* a var. of 5833; *Ezra,* an Isr.:—Ezra {22x}. See: BDB—740d, 1105d.

5831. עֶזְרָא {3x} **ʿEzrâ** (Aram.), *ez-raw′;* corresp. to 5830; *Ezra,* an Isr.:—Ezra {3x}. See: BDB—1105d.

5832. עֲזַרְאֵל {6x} **ʿĂzarʾêl**, *az-ar-ale′;* from 5826 and 410; *God has helped; Azarel,* the name of five Isr.:—Azareel {5x}, Azarael {1x}. See: BDB—741a.

5833. עֶזְרָה {26x} **ʿezrâh**, *ez-raw′;* or

עֶזְרָת **ʿezrâth** (Ps 60:11 [13]; 108:12 [13]), *ez-rawth′;* fem. of 5828; *aid:*—help {25x}, helpers {1x}. See: TWOT—1598b; BDB—740d.

5834. עֶזְרָה {1x} **ʿEzrâh**, *ez-raw′;* the same as 5833; *Ezrah,* an Isr.:—Ezrah {1x}. See: BDB—741a.

5835. עֲזָרָה {9x} **ʿăzârâh**, *az-aw-raw′;* from 5826 in its orig. mean. of *surrounding;* an *inclosure;* also a *border:*—settle {6x}, court {3x}. See: TWOT—1599a; BDB—741c.

5836. עֶזְרִי {1x} **ʿEzrîy**, *ez-ree′;* from 5828; *helpful; Ezri,* an Isr.:—Ezri {1x}. See: BDB—741b.

5837. עַזְרִיאֵל {3x} **ʿAzrîyʾêl**, *az-ree-ale′;* from 5828 and 410; *help of God; Azriël,* the name of three Isr.:—Azriel {3x}. See: BDB—741a.

5838. עֲזַרְיָה {48x} **ʿĂzaryâh**, *az-ar-yaw′;* or

עֲזַרְיָהוּ **ʿĂzaryâhûw**, *az-ar-yaw′-hoo;* from 5826 and 3050; *Jah has helped; Azarjah,* the name of nineteen Isr.:—Azariah {48x}. See: BDB—741a, 1105d.

5839. עֲזַרְיָה {1x} **ʿĂzaryâh** (Aram.), *az-ar-yaw′;* corresp. to 5838; *Azarjah,* one of Daniel's companions:—Azariah {1x}. See: BDB—1105d.

5840. עַזְרִיקָם {6x} **ʿAzrîyqâm**, *az-ree-kawm′;* from 5828 and act. part. of 6965; *help of an enemy; Azrikam,* the name of four Isr.:—Azrikam {6x}. See: BDB—741b.

5841. עַזָּתִי {2x} **ʿAzzâthîy**, *az-zaw-thee′;* patrial from 5804; an *Azzathite* or inhab. of Azzah:—Gazites {1x}, Gazathites {1x}. See: BDB—738b, 741c.

5842. עֵט {4x} **ʿêṭ**, *ate;* from 5860 (contr.) in the sense of *swooping,* i.e. *side-long stroke;* a *stylus* or *marking stick:*—pen {4x}. See: TWOT—1600; BDB—741c.

5843. עֵטָא {1x} **ʿêṭâ** (Aram.), *ay-taw′;* from 3272; *prudence:*—counsel {1x}. See: TWOT—2772b; BDB—1096a, 1105d.

5844. עָטָה {17x} **ʿâtâh**, *aw-taw′;* a prim. root; to *wrap,* i.e. *cover, veil, clothe,* or *roll:*—cover {10x}, array {1x}, turn aside {1x},

clad {1x}, covering {1x}, filleth {1x}, put on {1x}, surely {1x}. See: TWOT—1601, 1602; BDB—741d, 742a.

5845. עָטִין {1x} ʿătîyn, *at-een';* from an unused root mean. appar. to *contain;* a *receptacle* (for milk, i.e. *pail; fig. breast):—* breasts {1x}. See: TWOT—1604a; BDB—742b.

5846. עֲטִישָׁה {1x} ʿătîyshâh, *at-ee-shaw';* from an unused root mean. to *sneeze; sneezing:—*sneezings {1x}. See: TWOT—1609a; BDB—743a.

5847. עֲטַלֵּף {3x} ʿătallêph, *at-al-lafe';* of uncert. der.; a *bat:—*bat {3x}. See: TWOT—1603; BDB—742a.

5848. עָטַף {16x} ʿâtaph, *aw-taf';* a prim. root; to *shroud,* i.e. *clothe* (whether tran. or reflex.); hence, (from the idea of *darkness*) to *languish:—*overwhelmed {5x}, faint {3x}, swoon {2x}, covereth {1x}, fail {1x}, feeble {1x}, feebler {1x}, hideth {1x}, covered over {1x}. See: TWOT—1605, 1606, 1607; BDB—742b, 742c.

5849. עָטַר {7x} ʿâtar, *aw-tar';* a prim. root; to *encircle* (for attack or protection); espec. to *crown* (lit. or fig.):—crown {4x}, compass {2x}, crowning {1x}. See: TWOT—1608, 1608b; BDB—742c, 742d.

5850. עֲטָרָה {23x} ʿătârâh, *at-aw-raw';* from 5849; a *crown:—*crown {23x}. See: TWOT—1608a; BDB—742d.

5851. עֲטָרָה {1x} ʿĂtârâh, *at-aw-raw';* the same as 5850; *Atarah,* an Israelitess:—*Atarah* {1x}. See: BDB—742d.

5852. עֲטָרוֹת {5x} ʿĂtârôwth, *at-aw-rōth';* or

עֲטָרֹת ʿĂtârôth, *at-aw-rōth';* plur. of 5850; *Ataroth,* the name (thus simply) of two places in Pal.:—*Ataroth* {5x}. See: BDB—743a.

5853. עֲטָרוֹת אַדָּר {2x} ʿAtrôwth ʾAddâr, *at-rōth' ad-dawr';* from the same as 5852 and 146; *crowns of Addar; Atroth-Addar,* a place in Pal.:—Atarothadar {1x}, Atarothaddar {1x}. See: BDB—743a.

5854. עֲטָרוֹת בֵּית יוֹאָב {1x} ʿAtrôwth Bêyth Yôwʾâb, *at-rōth' bayth yo-awb';* from the same as 5852 and 1004 and 3097; *crowns of* (the) *house of Joab; Atroth-beth-Joab,* a place in Pal.:—the house of Joab {1x}. See: BDB—743a.

5855. עֲטָרוֹת שׁוֹפָן {1x} ʿAtrôwth Shôwphân, *at-rōth' sho-fawn';* from the same as 5852 and a name otherwise unused [being from the same as 8226] mean. *hidden; crowns of Shophan; Atroth-Shophan,* a place

in Pal.:—Atroth Shophan {1x}. See: BDB—743a, 1051a.

5856. עִי {4x} ʿîy, *ee;* from 5753; a *ruin* (as if overturned):—heap {4x}. See: TWOT—1577d; BDB—730c, 743b.

5857. עַי {41x} ʿAy, *ah'ee;* or (fem.)

עַיָּא ʿAyâ (Neh. 11:31), *ah-yaw';* or

עַיָּת ʿAyâth (Isa. 10:28), *ah-yawth';* for 5856; *Ai, Aja* or *Ajath,* a place in Pal.:—Ai {36x}, Hai {2x}, Aiath {1x}, city {1x}. See: BDB—743b, 747b.

5858. עֵיבָל {8x} ʿÊybâl, *ay-bawl';* perh. from an unused root prob. mean. to *be bald; bare; Ebal,* a mountain of Pal.:—Ebal {8x}. See: BDB—743b.

עַיָּה ʿAyâh. See 5857.

5859. עִיּוֹן {3x} ʿIyôwn, *ee-yone';* from 5856; *ruin; Ijon,* a place in Pal.:—Ijon {3x}. See: BDB—743b.

5860. עִיט {3x} ʿîyt, *eet;* a prim. root; to *swoop down upon* (lit. or fig.):—fly {2x}, rail {1x}. See: TWOT—1610, 1610b; BDB—743b, 743c.

5861. עַיִט {8x} ʿayit, *ah'-yit;* from 5860; a *hawk* or other bird of prey:—fowl {4x}, bird {2x}, ravenous bird {2x}. See: TWOT—1610a; BDB—743c.

5862. עֵיטָם {5x} ʿÊytâm, *ay-tawm';* from 5861; *hawk-ground; Etam,* a place in Pal.:—Etam {5x}. See: BDB—743c.

5863. עִיֵּי הָעֲבָרִים {2x} ʿIyêy hâ-ʿĂbârîym, *ee-yay' haw-ab-aw-reem';* from the plur. of 5856 and the plur. of the act. part. of 5674 with the art. interposed; *ruins of the passers; Ije-ha-Abarim,* a place near Pal.:—Ijeabarim {2x}. See: BDB—743d.

5864. עִיִּים {2x} ʿIyîym, *ee-yeem';* plur. of 5856; *ruins; Ijim,* a place in the desert:—Iim {2x}. See: BDB—743d.

5865. עֵילוֹם {1x} ʿêylôwm, *ay-lome';* for 5769:—for ever {1x}. See: TWOT—1631a; BDB—743d, 761d, 763a.

5866. עִילַי {1x} ʿÎylay, *ee-lah'-ee;* from 5927; *elevated; Ilai,* an Isr.:—Ilai {1x}. See: BDB—743d.

5867. עֵילָם {28x} ʿÊylâm, *ay-lawm';* or

עוֹלָם ʿÔwlâm (Ezra 10:2; Jer. 49:36), *o-lawm';* prob. from 5956; *hidden,* i.e. *distant; Elam,* a son of Shem, and his desc., with their country; also of six Isr.:—Elam {28x}. See: BDB—743d, 1106d.

5868. עֲיָם {1x} ʿăyâm, *ah-yawm';* of doubtful or. and authenticity; prob. mean.

strength:—mighty {1x}. See: TWOT—1611; BDB—744a.

5869. עַיִן {887x} **'ayin,** *ah'-yin;* prob. a prim. word; an *eye* (lit. or fig.); by anal. a *fountain* (as the *eye* of the landscape):—eye {495x}, sight {216x}, seem {19x}, colour {12x}, fountain {11x}, well {11x}, face {10x}, pleased + 3190 {10x}, presence {8x}, displeased + 3415 {8x}, before {8x}, pleased + 3474 {4x}, conceit {4x}, think {4x}, misc. {66x} = affliction, outward appearance, + think best, + be content, countenance, + favour, furrow, × him, + humble, knowledge, look, (+ well), × me, open (-ly), + regard, resemblance, × thee, × them, × us, × you (-rselves).

'Ayin means "eye; well; surface; appearance; spring." **(1)** First, the word represents the bodily part, "eye." **(1a)** In Gen 13:10, *'ayin* is used of the "human eye": "And Lot lifted up his eyes, and beheld all the plain of Jordan." **(1b)** It is also used of the "eyes" of animals (Gen 30:41), idols (Ps 115:5), and God (Deut 11:12—anthropomorphism). **(2)** The expression "between the eyes" means "on the forehead": "And it shall be for a sign unto thee upon thine hand, and for a memorial between thine eyes, that the Lord's law may be in thy mouth" (Ex 13:9). **(3)** "Eyes" are used as typical of one's "weakness" or "hurt": "And it came to pass, that when Isaac was old, and his eyes were dim, so that he could not see, he called Esau his eldest son, and said . . ." (Gen 27:1). **(4)** The "apple of the eye" is the central component, the iris: "Keep me as the apple of the eye" (Ps 17:8). **(5)** "Eyes" might be a special feature of "beauty": "Now he was ruddy, and withal [fair of eyes], and goodly to look to" (1 Sa 16:12). **(6)** *'Ayin* is often used in connection with expressions of "seeing": "And, behold, your eyes see, and the eyes of my brother Benjamin, that it is my mouth that speaketh unto you" (Gen 45:12). **(7)** The expression "to lift up one's eyes" is explained by a verb following it: one lifts up his eyes to do something—whatever the verb stipulates (cf. Gen 13:10).

(8) "Lifting up one's eyes" may also be an act expressing "desire," "longing," "devotion": "And it came to pass after these things, that his master's wife [looked with desire at] Joseph" (Gen 39:7). **(9)** The "eyes" may be used in gaining or seeking a judgment, in the sense of "seeing intellectually," "making an evaluation," or "seeking an evaluation or proof of faithfulness": "And thou saidst unto thy servants, Bring him down unto me, that I may set mine eyes upon him" (Gen 44:21). **(10)** "Eyes" sometimes show mental qualities, such as regret: "Also regard not [literally, "do not let your eye look with regret upon"] your stuff; for the good of all the land of Egypt is yours" (Gen

45:20). **(11)** "Eyes" are used figuratively of mental and spiritual abilities, acts and states. So the "opening of the eyes" in Gen 3:5 (the first occurrence) means to become autonomous by setting standards of good and evil for oneself. **(12)** In passages such as Prov 4:25, "eye" represents a moral faculty: "Let thine eyes look right on, and let thine eyelids look straight before thee." **(13)** Prov 23:6 uses the word of a moral state (literally"evil eye"): "Eat thou not the bread of [a selfish man], neither desire thou his dainty meats."

(14) An individual may serve as a guide, or one's "eyes": "And he said, Leave us not, I pray thee; forasmuch as thou knowest how we are to encamp in the wilderness, and thou mayest be to us instead of eyes" (Num 10:31). **(15)** The phrase, "in the eye of," means "in one's view or opinion": "And he went in unto Hagar, and she conceived: and when she saw that she had conceived, her mistress was despised in her eyes" (Gen 16:4). **(16)** Another phrase, "from the eyes of," may signify that a thing or matter is "hidden" from one's knowledge: "And a man lie with her carnally, and it be hid from the eyes of her husband, and [she be undetected] . . ." (Num 5:13). **(17)** In Ex 10:5, the word represents the "visible surface of the earth": "And they shall cover the face of the earth, that one cannot be able to see the earth." **(18)** Lev 13:5 uses *'ayin* to represent "one's appearance": "And the priest shall look on him the seventh day: and behold, if the plague in his sight be at a stay . . ." **(19)** A "gleam or sparkle" is described in the phrase, "to give its eyes," in passages such as Prov 23:31: "Look not thou upon the wine when it is red, when it giveth his color [gives its eyes] in the cup. . . ." **(20)** *'Ayin* also represents a "spring" (literally, an "eye of the water"): "And the angel of the Lord found her by a fountain of water in the wilderness, by the fountain on the way to Shur" (Gen 16:7). See: TWOT—1612a, 1613; BDB—733b, 744a, 745a, 1044d, 1105d.

5870. עַיִן {5x} **'ayin** (Aram.), *ah'-yin;* corresp. to 5869; an *eye:*—eye {5x}. See: TWOT—2906; BDB—1105d.

5871. עַיִן {5x} **'Ayin,** *ah'-yin;* the same as 5869; *fountain; Ajin,* the name (thus simply) of two places in Pal.:—Ain {5x}. See: BDB—745a, 745b, 745c, 942a.

5872. עֵין גֶּדִי {6x} **'Êyn Gedîy,** *ane geh'-dee;* from 5869 and 1423; *fountain of a kid; En-Gedi,* a place in Pal.:—Engedi {6x}. See: BDB—745b.

5873. עֵין גַּנִּים {3x} **'Êyn Gannîym,** *ane ganneem';* from 5869 and the plur. of 1588; *fountain of gardens; En-Gannim,* a

place in Pal.:—Engannim {3x}. See: BDB—745c.

5874. עֵין־דֹּאר {3x} **Êyn-Dôʾr**, *ane-dore'*; or

עֵין דּוֹר **Êyn Dôwr**, *ane dore*; or

עֵין־דֹּר **Êyn-Dôr**, *ane-dore'*; from 5869 and 1755; *fountain of dwelling; En-Dor*, a place in Pal.:—Endor {3x}. See: BDB—745c.

5875. עֵין הַקּוֹרֵא {1x} **Êyn haq-Qôwrêê**, a place near Pal.:—Enhakkore {1x}. See: BDB—745b.

עֵינוֹן **Êynôwn**. See 2703.

5876. עֵין חַדָּה {1x} **Êyn Chaddâh**, *ane khaddaw'*; from 5869 and the fem. of a der. from 2300; *fountain of sharpness; En-Chaddah*, a place in Pal.:—Enhaddah {1x}. See: BDB—292c, 745c.

5877. עֵין חָצוֹר {1x} **Êyn Châtsôwr**, *ane khaw-tsore'*; from 5869 and the same as 2674; *fountain of a village; En-Chatsor*, a place in Pal.:—Enhazor {1x}. See: BDB—745c.

5878. עֵין חֲרֹד {1x} **Êyn Chărôd**, *ane kharode'*; from 5869 and a der. of 2729; *fountain of trembling; En-Charod*, a place in Pal.:—well of Harod {1x}. See: BDB—353d, 745b, 745c.

5879. עֵינַיִם {1x} **Êynayim**, *ay-nah'-yim*; or

עֵינָם **Êynâm**, *ay-nawm'*; dual of 5869; *double fountain; Enajim* or *Enam*, a place in Pal.:—Enam {1x}. See: BDB—745d.

5880. עֵין מִשְׁפָּט {1x} **Êyn Mishpât**, *ane mish-pawt'*; from 5869 and 4941; *fountain of judgment; En-Mishpat*, a place near Pal.:—En-mishpat {1x}. See: BDB—745c, 874a.

5881. עֵינָן {5x} **Êynân**, *ay-nawn'*; from 5869; *having eyes; Enan*, an Isr.:—Enan {5x}. See: BDB—745d. comp. 2704.

5882. עֵין עֶגְלַיִם {1x} **Êyn ʿEglayim**, *ane eg-lah'-yim*; from 5869 and the dual of 5695; *fountain of two calves; En-Eglajim*, a place in Pal.:—Eneglaim {1x}. See: BDB—722d, 745c.

5883. עֵין רֹגֵל {4x} **Êyn Rôgêl**, *ane ro-gale'*; from 5869 and the act. part. of 7270; *fountain of a traveller; En-Rogel*, a place near Jerusalem:—Enrogel {4x}. See: BDB—745b, 920b.

5884. עֵין רִמּוֹן {1x} **Êyn Rimmôwn**, *ane rim-mone'*; from 5869 and 7416; *fountain of a pomegranate; En-Rimmon*, a place in Pal.:—Enrimmon {1x}. See: BDB—745b, 745c, 942a.

5885. עֵין שֶׁמֶשׁ {2x} **Êyn Shemesh**, *ane sheh'-mesh*; from 5869 and 8121; *fountain of* (the) *sun; En-Shemesh*, a place in Pal.:—Enshemesh {2x}. See: BDB—745d.

5886. עֵין תַּנִּים {1x} **Êyn Tannîym**, *ane tan-neem'*; from 5869 and the plur. of 8565; *fountain of jackals; En-Tannim*, a pool near Jerusalem:—Strong's synonym {1x}.

5887. עֵין תַּפּוּחַ {1x} **Êyn Tappûwach**, *ane tap-poo'-akh*; from 5869 and 8598; *fountain of an apple tree; En-Tappuäch*, a place in Pal.:—Entappuah {1x}. See: BDB—745d.

5888. עָיֵף {1x} **ʿâyêph**, *aw-yafe'*; a prim. root; to *languish*:—wearied {1x}. See: TWOT—1614a; BDB—746a.

5889. עָיֵף {17x} **ʿâyêph**, *aw-yafe'*; from 5888; *languid*:—weary {8x}, faint {6x}, thirsty {3x}. See: TWOT—1614a; BDB—746a.

5890. עֵיפָה {2x} **ʿêyphâh**, *ay-faw'*; fem. from 5774; *obscurity* (as if from *covering*):—darkness {2x}. See: TWOT—1583d; BDB—734a, 746a, 780c.

5891. עֵיפָה {5x} **ʿÊyphâh**, *ay-faw'*; the same as 5890; *Ephah*, the name of a son of Midian, and of the region settled by him; also of an Isr. and of an Israelitess:—Ephah {5x}. See: BDB—734a, 746a.

5892. עִיר {1089x} **ʿîyr**, *eer*; or (in the plur.)

עָר **ʿâr**, *awr*; or

עָיַר **ʿâyar** (Judg 10:4), *aw-yar'*; from 5782 a *city* (a place guarded by *waking* or a watch) in the widest sense (even of a mere *encampment* or *post*):—city {1074x}, town {7x}, every one {2x}, variant {6x}.

'Iyr means city; town; village; quarter [of a city]. **(1)** This word suggests a village, maybe with or without walls: "All these cities were fenced with high walls, gates, and bars; beside unwalled towns ['*iyr*] a great many" (Deut 3:5); an unwalled village being Hebrew word *chatser* (2968). **(2)** '*Iyr* can signify a village in a permanent place, even though the dwellings are tents: "And Saul came to a city ['*iyr*] of Amalek, and laid wait in the valley" (1 Sa 15:5). **(3)** In Gen 4:17 '*iyr* means a permanent dwelling center consisting of residences of stone and clay: "And Cain knew his wife; and she conceived, and bare Enoch: and he builded a city, and called the name of the city, after the name of his son, Enoch." **(4)** As a rule, there are usually no political overtones to the word; **(4a)** '*iyr* simply represents the place where people dwell on a permanent basis. **(4b)** '*Iyr*, however, can represent a political entity: "And to them which were in Rachal, and to them which were

in the cities of the Jerahmeelites, and to them which were in the cities of the Kenites," (1 Sa 30:29). **(5)** This word can represent those who live in a given town: "And when he came, lo, Eli sat upon a seat by the wayside watching: for his heart trembled for the ark of God. And when the man came into the city, and told it, all the city cried out" (1 Sa 4:13). **(6)** ʿIyr can signify only a part of a city, such as a part that is surrounded by a wall: "Nevertheless David took the strong hold of Zion: the same is the city of David" (2 Sa 5:7). See: TWOT—1587a, 1615; BDB—735c, 746b, 746d.

5893. עִיר {1x} **ʿÎyr**, *eer;* the same as 5892; *Ir,* an Isr.:—Ir {1x}. See: BDB—746d.

5894. עִיר {3x} **ʿÎyr** (Aram.), *eer;* from a root corresp. to 5782; a *watcher,* i.e. an *angel* (as guardian):—watcher {3x}. See: TWOT—2907; BDB—1105d.

5895. עַיִר {8x} **ʿayîr**, *ah′-yeer;* from 5782 in the sense of *raising* (i.e. *bearing* a burden); prop. a *young ass* (as just broken to a load); hence, an *ass-colt:*—colt {4x}, foal {2x}, young ass {2x}. See: TWOT—1616a; BDB—736b, 747a.

5896. עִירָא {6x} **ʿÎyrâʾ**, *ee-raw′;* from 5782; *wakefulness; Ira,* the name of three Isr.:—Ira {6x}. See: BDB—747a.

5897. עִירָד {2x} **ʿÎyrâd**, *ee-rawd′;* from the same as 6166; *fugitive; Irad,* an antediluvian:—Irad {2x}. See: BDB—747a.

5898. עִיר הַמֶּלַח {1x} **ʿÎyr ham-Melach**, *eer ham-meh′-lakh;* from 5892 and 4417 with the art. of substance interp.; *city of* (the) *salt; Ir-ham-Melach,* a place near Pal.:—city of salt {1x}. See: BDB—746d.

5899. עִיר הַתְּמָרִים {4x} **ʿÎyr hat-Tᵉmârîym**, *eer hat-tem-aw-reem′;* from 5892 and the plur. of 8558 with the art. interpolated; *city of the palmtrees; Ir-hat-Temarim,* a place in Pal.:—variant {2x}, (city of) palm) trees {2x}. See: BDB—746d.

5900. עִירוּ {1x} **ʿÎyrûw**, *ee-roo′;* from 5892; a *citizen; Iru,* an Isr.:—Iru {1x}. See: BDB—747a.

5901. עִירִי {1x} **ʿÎyrîy**, *ee-ree′;* from 5892; *ur-bane; Iri,* an Isr.:—Iri {1x}. See: BDB—747a.

5902. עִירָם {2x} **ʿÎyrâm**, *ee-rawm′;* from 5892; *city-wise; Iram,* an Idumæan:—Iram {2x}. See: BDB—747a.

5903. עֵירֹם {10x} **ʿêyrôm**, *ay-rome′;* or

עֵרֹם **ʿêrôm**, *ay-rome′;* from 6181; *nu-dity:*—naked {9x}, nakedness {1x}. See: TWOT—1588b; BDB—735d, 747a, 790d.

5904. עִיר נָחָשׁ {1x} **ʿÎyr Nâchâsh**, *eer naw-khawsh′;* from 5892 and 5175; *city of a serpent; Ir-Nachash,* a place in Pal.:—Irnahash {1x}. See: BDB—638b, 746d.

5905. עִיר שֶׁמֶשׁ {1x} **ʿÎyr Shemesh**, *eer sheh′-mesh;* from 5892 and 8121; *city of* (the) *sun; Ir-Shemesh,* a place in Pal.:—Irshemesh {1x}. See: BDB—747b.

5906. עַיִשׁ {2x} **ʿAyish**, *ah′-yish;* or

עָשׁ **Âsh**, *awsh;* from 5789; the constel-lation of the Great *Bear* (perh. from its *migration* through the heavens):—Arcturus {2x}. See: TWOT—1617; BDB—747a, 798b.

עָיַת **ʿAyâth.** See 5857.

5907. עַכְבּוֹר {7x} **ʿAkbôwr**, *ak-bore′;* prob. for 5909; *Akbor,* the name of an Idumæan and two Isr.:—Achbor {7x}. See: BDB—747b.

5908. עַכָּבִישׁ {2x} **ʿakkâbîysh**, *ak-kaw-beesh′;* prob. from an unused root in the lit. sense of *entangling;* a *spider* (as *weav-ing* a network):—spider {2x}. See: TWOT—1619; BDB—747B.

5909. עַכְבָּר {6x} **ʿakbâr**, *ak-bawr′;* prob. from the same as 5908 in the second. sense of *attacking;* a *mouse* (as *nibbling*):—mouse {6x}. See: TWOT—1618; BDB—747b.

5910. עַכּוֹ {1x} **ʿAkkôw**, *ak-ko′;* appar. from an unused root mean. to *hem* in; *Akko* (from its situation on a *bay*):—Accho {1x}. See: BDB—747b.

5911. עָכוֹר {5x} **ʿÂkôwr**, *aw-kore′;* from 5916; *troubled; Akor,* the name of a place in Pal.:—Achor {5x}. See: TWOT—1621a; BDB—747d.

5912. עָכָן {6x} **ʿÂkân**, *aw-kawn′;* from an un-used root mean. to *trouble; trouble-some; Akan,* an Isr.:—Achan {6x}. See: BDB—747c. comp. 5917.

5913. עָכַס {1x} **ʿâkaç**, *aw-kas′;* a prim. root; prop. to *tie,* spec. with fetters; but used only as denom. from 5914; to *put on anklets:*—tinkling {1x}. See: TWOT—1620; BDB—747c.

5914. עֶכֶס {2x} **ʿekeç**, *eh′-kes;* from 5913; a *fetter;* hence, an *anklet:*—stocks {1x}, tinkling ornament {1x}. See: TWOT—1620a; BDB—747c.

5915. עַכְסָה {5x} **ʿAkçâh**, *ak-saw′;* fem. of 5914; *anklet; Aksah,* an Israel-itess:—Achsah {5x}. See: BDB—747c.

5916. עָכַר {14x} **ʿâkar**, *aw-kar′;* a prim. root; prop. to *roil* water; fig. to *disturb*

or *afflict:*—trouble {12x}, stirred {1x}, troubler {1x}. See: TWOT—1621; BDB—747c.

5917. עָכָר {1x} ʿÂkâr, *aw-kawr'*; from 5916; *troublesome; Akar,* an Isr.:—Achar {1x}. See: BDB—747c, 747d. comp. 5912.

5918. עָכְרָן {5x} ʿOkrân, *ok-rawn'*; from 5916; *muddler; Okran,* an Isr.:—Ocran {5x}. See: BDB—747d.

5919. עַכְשׁוּב {1x} ʿakshûwb, *ak-shoob';* prob. from an unused root mean. to *coil;* an asp (from lurking *coiled* up):—adder {1x}. See: TWOT—1622; BDB—747d.

5920. עַל {6x} ʿal, *al;* from 5927; prop. the *top;* spec. the *Highest* (i.e. *God*); also (adv.) *aloft, to Jehovah:*—above {3x}, most High {2x}, on high {1x}. See: TWOT—1624p; BDB—748a, 752b.

5921. עַל {48x} ʿal, *al;* prop. the same as 5920 used as a prep. (in the sing. or plur. often with pref., or as conjunc. with a particle following); *above, over, upon,* or *against* (yet always in this last relation with a downward aspect) in a great variety of applications (as follow):—{48x} = upon, in, on, over, by, for, both, beyond, through, throughout, against, beside, forth, off, from off. See: TWOT—1624p; BDB—475c, 591d, 748a, 752b, 752c, 759d, 761b, 763a, 1106a.

5922. עַל {99x} ʿal (Aram.), *al;* corresp. to 5921:—upon {19x}, over {13x}, unto {9x}, against {7x}, concerning {6x}, in {6x}, for {4x}, unto me {4x}, about {3x}, in him {3x}, misc. 25. See: TWOT—2908; BDB—1105d, 1106a.

5923. עֹל {40x} ʿôl, *ole;* or

עוֹל ʿôwl, *ole;* from 5953; a *yoke* (as *imposed* on the neck), lit. or fig.:—yoke {40x}. See: TWOT—1628a; BDB—748a, 760d.

5924. עֵלָּא {1x} ʿêllâ (Aram.), *ale-law';* from 5922; *above:*—over {1x}. See: TWOT—2909a; BDB—1105d, 1106a.

5925. עֻלָּא {1x} ʿUllâ, *ool-law';* fem. of 5923; *burden; Ulla,* an Isr.:—Ulla {1x}. See: BDB—748a.

5926. עִלֵּג {1x} ʿillêg, *il-layg';* from an unused root mean. to *stutter; stuttering:*—stammerers {1x}. See: TWOT—1623a; BDB—748a.

5927. עָלָה {889x} ʿâlâh, *aw-law';* a prim. root; to *ascend,* intr. (*be high*) or act. (*mount*); used in a great variety of senses, primary and second., lit. and fig. (as follow):—(come, etc . . .) up {676x}, offer {67x}, come {22x}, bring {18x}, ascend {15x}, go {12x}, chew {9x}, offering {8x}, light {6x}, increase {4x},

burn {3x}, depart {3x}, put {3x}, spring {2x}, raised {2x}, arose {2x}, break {2x}, exalted {2x}, misc. {33}.

ʿAlah means "to go up, ascend, offer up." (1) Basically, ʿalah suggests movement from a lower to a higher place. (1a) That is the emphasis in Gen 2:6 (the first occurrence of the word), which reports that Eden was watered by a mist or stream that "went up" over the ground. (1b) ʿAlah may also mean "to rise up" or "ascend." The king of Babylon [satan] said in his heart, "I will ascend into heaven" (Is 14:13). (2) This word may mean "to take a journey," as in traveling from Egypt (Gen 13:1) toward Palestine or other points northward. (3) The verb may be used in a special sense meaning "to extend, reach"—for example, the border of Benjamin "went up ["extended, reached"] through the mountains westward" (Josh 18:12). (4) The use of ʿalah to describe the journey from Egypt to Palestine is such a standard phrase that it often appears without the geographical reference points. Joseph told his brothers to "go up" to their father in peace (Gen 44:17). (5) Even the return from the Exile, which was a journey from north to south (Palestine), is described as a "going up" (Ezra 2:1). (6) Thus, the reference may be not so much to physically "going up," but to a figurative or spiritual "going up." This usage appears long before Ezra's time, when it is said that one "goes up" to the place where the sanctuary is located (cf. Deut 17:8).

(7) The verb became a technical term for "making a pilgrimage" (Ex 34:24) or "going up" before the Lord; in a secular context, compare Joseph's "going up" before Pharaoh (Gen 46:31). (8) In instances where an enemy located himself in a superior position (frequently a higher place), one "goes up" to battle (Josh 22:12). (9) The verb can also refer merely to "going out" to make war against someone, even though there is no movement from a lower to a higher plane. So Israel "went up" to make war against the Moabites, who heard of the Israelites' approach while still dwelling in their cities (2 Kin 3:21). (10) Even when ʿalah is used by itself, it can mean "to go to war"; the Lord told Phinehas, "Go up; for tomorrow I will deliver them into thine hand" (Judg 20:28). (11) On the other hand, if the enemy is recognized to be on a lower plane, one can "go down" (3381 - yarad) to fight (Judg 1:9). (12) The opposite of "going up" to war is not descending to battle, but "leaving off" (ʿalah meʿal), literally, "going up from against." (12) Another special use of ʿalah is "to overpower" (literally, "to go up from"). For example, the Pharaoh feared the Israelites lest in a

war they join the enemy, fight against Egypt, and "overpower" the land (Ex 1:10). **(13)** "To go up" may also be used of "increasing in strength," as the lion that becomes strong from his prey: The lion "goes up from his prey" (Gen 49:9; cf. Deut 28:43). **(14)** Not only physical things can "go up." *'Alah* can be used also of the "increasing" of wrath (2 Sa 11:20), the "ascent" of an outcry before God (Ex 2:23), and the "continual" sound of battle (although "sound of" is omitted; cf. 1 Kin 22:35). **(15)** The word can also be used passively to denote mixing two kinds of garments together, causing one "to lie upon" or "be placed upon" the other (Lev 19:19). **(16)** Sometimes "go up" means "placed," even when the direction is downward, as when placing a yoke upon an ox (Num 19:2) or going to one's grave (Job 5:26). This may be an illustration of how Hebrew verbs can sometimes mean their opposite. **(17)** The verb is also used of "recording" a census (1 Chr 27:24). **(18)** The verb *'alah* is used in a causative stem to signify "presenting an offering" to God. In 63 cases, the word is associated with the presentation of the whole burnt offering ('olah). **(19)** *'Alah* is used of the general act of "presenting offerings" when the various offerings are mentioned in the same context (Lev 14:20), or when the purpose of the offering is not specifically in mind (Is 57:6). **(20)** Sometimes this verb means merely "to offer" (e.g., Num 23:2). See: TWOT—1624; BDB—748a, 1105d.

5928. עָלָה {1x} ʿ**älâh** (Aram.), *al-aw'*; corresp. to 5930; a *holocaust:*—burnt offerings {1x}. See: TWOT—2909e; BDB—1106a, 1106d.

5929. עָלֶה {18x} ʿ**âleh**, *aw-leh'*; from 5927; a *leaf* (as *coming up* on a tree); collect. *foliage:*—leaf {12x}, branch {5x}, branches + 6086 {1x}. See: TWOT—1624a; BDB—750a.

5930. עֹלָה {289x} ʿ**ôlâh**, *o-law'*; or

עוֹלָה ʿ**ôwlâh**, *o-law'*; fem. act. part. of 5927; a *step* or (collect. *stairs,* as *ascending*); usually a *holocaust* (as *going up* in smoke):—burnt offering {264x}, burnt sacrifice {21x}, ascent {1x}, go up {1x}.

'*Olah* means "whole burnt offering." **(1)** In its first biblical occurrence *olah* identifies a kind of "offering" presented to God: "And Noah builded an altar unto the Lord; and took of every clean beast, and of every clean fowl, and offered burnt offerings on the altar" (Gen 8:20). **(2)** Its second nuance appears in Lev 1:4, where it represents the "thing being offered":"And he shall put his hand upon the head of the burnt offering; and it shall be accepted for him to make atonement for him."

(3) This kind of "offering" could be made **(3a)** with a bull (Lev 1:3–5), a sheep, a goat (Lev 1:10), or a bird (Lev 1:14). **(3b)** The offerer laid his hands on the sacrificial victim, symbolically transferring his sin and guilt to it. **(3c)** After he slew the animal (on the north side of the altar), the priest took its blood, which was presented before the Lord prior to being sprinkled around the altar. **(3d)** A bird was simply given to the priest, but he wrung its neck and allowed its blood to drain beside the altar (Lev 1:15). **(3e)** This sacrifice effected an atonement, a covering for sin necessary before the essence of the sacrifice could be presented to God. **(3f)** Next, the "offering" was divided into sections. They were carefully purified (except those parts which could not be purified) and arranged on the altar (Lev 1:6–9, 12–13). **(3g)** The entire sacrifice was then consumed by the fire and its essence sent up to God as a placating (pleasing) odor. **(3h)** The animal skin was given to the priest as his portion (Lev 7:8).

(4) The word *olah* was listed first in Old Testament administrative prescriptions and descriptions as the most frequent offering. **(4a)** Every day required the presentation of a male lamb morning and evening—the continual "whole burnt offering" (Ex 29:38–42). **(4b)** Each month was consecrated by a "whole burnt offering," of two young bulls, one ram, and seven male lambs (Num 28:11–14). **(4c)** The same sacrifice was mandated, for each day of the Passover-Unleavened Bread feast (Num 28:19–24), and the Feast of Weeks (Num 28:26–29). **(5)** Other stated feasts required "burnt offerings" as well. **(6)** The various purification rites mandated both "burnt" and sin "offerings." **(7)** The central significance of *'olah* as the "whole burnt offering" was the total surrender of the heart and life of the offerer to God. **(7a)** Sin offerings could accompany them when the offerer was especially concerned with a covering or expiation for sin (2 Chr 29:27). **(7b)** When peace offerings accompanied "burnt offerings," the offerer's concern focused on fellowship with God (2 Chr 29:31–35). **(7c)** Before the Mosaic legislation, it appears, the "whole burnt offering" served the full range of meanings expressed in all the various Mosaic sacrifices. Syn.: 2077. See: TWOT—1624c, 1624d; BDB—732d, 750b, 751a. See also 5766.

5931. עָלָה {3x} ʿ**illâh** (Aram.), *il-law'*; fem. from a root corresp. to 5927; a *pretext* (as *arising* artificially):—occasion {3x}. See: TWOT—2910; BDB—1105d, 1106c.

5932. עַלְוָה {1x} ʿ**alvâh**, *al-vaw'*; for 5766; *moral perverseness:*—iniquity {1x}. See: TWOT—1580b; BDB—759b.

5933. עֲלְוָה {2x} ʿAlvâh, *al-vaw';* or

עֲלְיָה ʿAlyâh, *al-yaw';* the same as 5932; *Alvah* or *Aljah,* an Idumæan:— Aliah {1x}, Alvah {1x}. See: BDB—759b, 759d.

5934. עֲלוּם {4x} ʿâlûwm, *aw-loom';* pass. part. of 5956 in the denom. sense of 5958; (only in plur. as abstr.) *adolescence;* fig. *vigor:*—youth {4x}. See: TWOT—1630c; BDB—761c.

5935. עֲלְוָן {2x} ʿAlvân, *al-vawn';* or

עֲלְיָן ʿAlyân, *al-yawn';* from 5927; *lofty; Alvan* or *Aljan,* an Idumæan:— Alian {1x}, Alvan {1x}. See: BDB—759b, 759d.

5936. עֲלוּקָה {1x} ʿâlûwqâh, *al-oo-kaw';* fem. pass. part. of an unused root mean. *to suck;* the *leech:*—horseleach {1x}. See: TWOT—1636a; BDB—763c.

5937. עֲלַז {16x} ʿâlaz, *aw-laz';* a prim. root; to *jump* for joy, i.e. *exult:*—rejoice {12x}, triumph {2x}, joyful {2x}. See: TWOT—1625; BDB—759c.

5938. עֲלֵז {1x} ʿâlêz, *aw-laze';* from 5937; *exultant:*—rejoice {1x}. See: TWOT—1625a; BDB—759c.

5939. עֲלָטָה {4x} ʿălâṭâh, *al-aw-taw';* fem. from an unused root mean. to *cover; dusk:*—twilight {3x}, dark {1x}. See: TWOT—1626; BDB—759c.

5940. עֲלִי {1x} ʿĕlîy, *el-ee';* from 5927; a *pestle* (as *lifted*):—pestle {1x}. See: TWOT—1624b; BDB—750a, 759c.

5941. עֵלִי {33x} ʿÊlîy, *ay-lee';* from 5927; *lofty; Eli,* an Isr. high-priest:—Eli {33x}. See: BDB—750a, 759c.

5942. עִלִּי {2x} ʿillîy, *il-lee';* from 5927; *high;* i.e. comparative:—upper {2x}. See: TWOT—1624e; BDB—751a, 759c.

5943. עִלִּי {10x} ʿillay (Aram.), *il-lah'-ee;* corresp. to 5942; *supreme* (i.e. *God*):— the most High {5x}, most high {4x}, high {1x}. See: TWOT—2909d; BDB—1106a.

עֲלְיָה ʿAlyâh. See 5933.

5944. עֲלִיָּה {20x} ʿălîyâh, *al-ee-yaw';* fem. from 5927; something *lofty,* i.e. a *stair-way;* also a *second-story* room (or even one on the roof); fig. the *sky:*—chamber {12x}, parlour {4x}, going up {2x}, ascent {1x}, loft {1x}. See: TWOT—1624f; BDB—751a, 759c, 1106a.

5945. עֶלְיוֹן {53x} ʿelyôwn, *el-yone';* from 5927; an *elevation,* i.e. (adj.) *lofty* (comp.); as title, the *Supreme:*—High {18x}, most high {9x}, high {9x}, upper {8x}, higher {4x}, highest {2x}, above {1x}, Highest {1x}, uppermost {1x}.

ʿElyown means "the upper; the highest."
(1) The use of ʿelyown in Gen 40:17 means "the upper" as opposed to "the lower": "And in the uppermost basket there was of all manner of bakemeats for Pharaoh; and the birds did eat them out of the basket upon my head."
(2) Where referring to or naming God, ʿelyown means "the highest": "And Melchizedek king of Salem brought forth bread and wine: and he was the priest of the most high God" (Gen 14:18). See: TWOT—1624g; BDB—751b, 759c, 1106a.

5946. עֶלְיוֹן {4x} ʿelyôwn (Aram.), *el-yone';* corresp. to 5945; the *Supreme:*— the most high {4x}. See: TWOT—2909c; BDB—1106a.

5947. עַלִּיז {7x} ʿallîyz, *al-leez';* from 5937; *exultant:*—rejoice {4x}, joyous {3x}. See: TWOT—1625b; BDB—759c.

5948. עֲלִיל {1x} ʿălîyl, *al-eel';* from 5953 in the sense of *completing;* prob. a *crucible* (as *working* over the metal):—furnace {1x}. See: TWOT—1628b; BDB—760d.

5949. עֲלִילָה {24x} ʿălîylâh, *al-ee-law';* or

עֲלִלָה ʿălîlâh, *al-ee-law';* from 5953 in the sense of *effecting;* an *exploit* (of God), or a *performance* (of man, often in a bad sense); by impl. an *opportunity:*—doing {14x}, works {3x}, deeds {2x}, occasions {2x}, actions {1x}, acts {1x}, inventions {1x}. See: TWOT—1627c; BDB—760a.

5950. עֲלִילִיָה {1x} ʿălîylîyâh, *al-ee-lee-yaw';* for 5949; (miraculous) *execution:*—work {1x}. See: TWOT—1627d; BDB—760b.

עֲלְיָן ʿAlyân. See 5935.

5951. עֲלִיצוּת {1x} ʿălîytsûwth, *al-ee-tsooth';* from 5970; *exultation:*—rejoicing {1x}. See: TWOT—1635a; BDB—763c.

5952. עֲלִית {1x} ʿallîyth (Aram.), *al-leeth';* from 5927; a *second-story* room:—chamber {1x}. See: BDB—1106a. comp. 5944.

5953. עֲלַל {20x} ʿâlal, *aw-lal';* a prim. root; to *effect* thoroughly; spec. to *glean* (also fig.); by impl. (in a bad sense) to *overdo,* i.e. maltreat, be saucy to, pain, impose (also lit.):—glean {4x}, done {3x}, abuse {3x}, mock {2x}, affecteth {1x}, children {1x}, do {1x}, defiled {1x}, practise {1x}, throughly {1x}, wrought wonderfully {1x}, wrought {1x}. See: TWOT—1627, 1627b, 1628; BDB—759d, 760a, 760c, 1106c.

5954. עֲלַל {13x} ʿălal (Aram.), *al-al'*; corresp. to 5953 (in the sense of *thrusting* oneself in), to *enter; caus.* to *introduce:*—bring in {6x}, come in {2x}, went in {2x}, bring {1x}, went {1x}, come {1x}. See: TWOT—2911; BDB—1106c.

עֲלַל ʿôlâl. See 5768.

עֲלִילָה ʿălîlâh. See 5949.

5955. עֹלֵלָה {6x} ʿôlêlâh, *o-lay-law'*; fem. act. part. of 5953; only in plur. *gleanings;* by extens. *gleaning-time:*—gleaning grapes {3x}, grapegleanings {1x}, gleaning of the grape {1x}, grapes {1x}. See: TWOT—1627a; BDB—760a.

5956. עָלַם {28x} ʿâlam, *aw-lam'*; a prim. root; to *veil* from sight, i.e. *conceal* (lit. or fig.):—hide {22x}, blind {1x}, dissemblers {1x}, hidden {1x}, secret {1x}, secret thing {1x}, any ways {1x}. See: TWOT—1629; BDB—761a.

5957. עָלַם {20x} ʿâlam (Aram.), *aw-lam'*; corresp. to 5769; *remote* time, i.e. the *future* or *past* indefinitely; often adv. *forever:*—ever {12x}, everlasting {4x}, old {2x}, ever + 5705 {1x}, never {1x}. See: TWOT—2912; BDB—1106d.

5958. עֶלֶם {2x} ʿelem, *eh'-lem;* from 5956; *prop.* something *kept out of sight* [comp. 5959], i.e. a *lad:*—young man {1x}, stripling {1x}.

The only 2 appearances of the masculine form (5958 - ʿelem) are in First Samuel: "And the king said, Enquire thou whose son the stripling [ʿelem] is" (17:56); and "But if I say thus unto the young man [ʿelem], Behold, the arrows are beyond thee; go thy way: for the LORD hath sent thee away" (20:22). See: TWOT—1630a; BDB—761c.

עֹלָם ʿôlâm. See 5769.

5959. עַלְמָה {7x} ʿalmâh, *al-maw'*; fem. of 5958; a *lass* (as *veiled* or private):—virgin {4x}, maid {2x}, damsels {1x}.

ʿAlmah means virgin; maiden. **(1)** That ʿalmah means virgin is quite clear in **(1a1)** Gen 24:43 the word describes Rebekah, "Behold, I stand by the well of water; and it shall come to pass, that when the virgin cometh forth to draw water, and I say to her, Give me, I pray thee, a little water of thy pitcher to drink;" **(1a2)** and that she was a "maiden" with whom no man had had relations: "And the damsel was very fair to look upon, a virgin, neither had any man known her: and she went down to the well, and filled her pitcher, and came up" (Gen 24:16). Then again in **(1b)** Song 6:8: "There are threescore queens, and fourscore concubines, and virgins without number." **(1b1)** Thus all the women in the court are described. **(1b2)**

The word ʿalmah represents those who are eligible for marriage but are neither wives (queens) nor concubines. **(1b3)** These "virgins" all loved the king and longed to be chosen to be with him (to be his bride), **(1b4)** even as did the Shulamite who became his bride (1:3–4). **(2)** It is used more of the concept "virgin" than that of "maiden," **(3)** yet always of a woman who had not borne a child. **(4)** Solomon wrote that the process of wooing a woman was mysterious to him (Prov 30:19). **(4a)** Certainly in that day a man ordinarily wooed one whom he considered to be a "virgin." **(4b)** There are several contexts, therefore, in which a young girl's virginity is expressly in view.

(5) All virgins are maidens, but not all maidens are necessarily a virgin. **(6)** This makes it the ideal word to be used in Is 7:14, since the word betulah emphasizes virility more than virginity (although it is used with both emphases, too). **(6a)** The reader of Is 7:14 in the days preceding the birth of Jesus would read that a "virgin who is a maiden" would conceive a child. **(6b)** This was a possible, but irregular, use of the word since the word can refer merely to the unmarried status of the one so described. **(6c)** The child immediately in view was the son of the prophet and his wife (cf. Is 8:3) who served as a sign to Ahaz that his enemies would be defeated by God. **(6c)** On the other hand, the reader of that day must have been extremely uncomfortable with this use of the word, since its primary connotation is "virgin" rather than "maiden." **(6d)** Thus the clear translation of the Greek in Mt 1:23 whereby this word is rendered "virgin" satisfies its fullest implication. **(6e)** Therefore, there was no embarrassment to Isaiah when his wife conceived a son by him, since the word ʿalmah allowed for this. Neither is there any embarrassment in Matthew's understanding of the word. See: TWOT—1630b; BDB—761c.

5960. עַלְמוֹן {1x} ʿAlmôwn, *al-mone'*; from 5956; *hidden; Almon,* a place in Pal.:—Almon {1x}. See: BDB—761b. See also 5963.

5961. עֲלָמוֹת {2x} ʿĂlâmôwth, *al-aw-mōth'*; plur. of 5959; *prop. girls,* i.e. the *soprano* or female voice, perh. *falsetto:*—Alamoth {2x}. See: BDB—761b, 761c, 763a.

עֲלָמוֹת ʿalmûwth. See 4192.

5962. עַלְמִי {1x} ʿAlmîy (Aram.), *al-mee';* patrial from a name corresp. to 5867 contr.; an *Elamite* or inhab. of Elam:—Elamites {1x}. See: BDB—1106d.

5963. עַלְמֹן דִּבְלָתָיְמָה {2x} ʿAlmôn Diblâthây͏ᵉmâh, *al-mone' dib-law-thaw'-yem-aw;* from the same as 5960 and the

dual of 1690 [comp. 1015] with enclitic of direction; *Almon toward Diblathajim; Almon-Diblathajemah,* a place in Moab:—Almond-iblathaim {2x}. See: BDB—761b.

5964. עַלֶמֶת {4x} ʿÂlemeth, *aw-leh'-meth;* from 5956; a *covering; Alemeth,* the name of a place in Pal. and of two Isr.:— Alemeth {3x}, Alameth {1x}. See: BDB—761b.

5965. עָלַס {3x} ʿâlaç, *aw-las';* a prim. root; to *leap* for joy, i.e. *exult, wave* joyously:—rejoice {1x}, peacock {1x}, solace {1x}. See: TWOT—1632; BDB—763a.

5966. עָלַע {1x} ʿâlaʿ, *aw-lah';* a prim root; to *sip* up:—suck up {1x}. See: TWOT—1633; BDB—763a.

5967. עֲלַע {1x} ʿălaʿ (Aram.), *al-ah';* corresp. to 6763; a *rib:*—ribs {1x}. See: TWOT—2913; BDB—1106d.

5968. עָלַף {5x} ʿâlaph, *aw-laf';* a prim. root; to *veil* or *cover;* fig. to *be languid:*—faint {3x}, overlaid {1x}, wrapped {1x}. TWOT—1634; BDB—763a.

5969. עֻלְפֶּה {1x} ʿulpeh, *ool-peh';* from 5968; an *envelope,* i.e. (fig.) *mourning:*—fainted {1x}. See: TWOT—1634; BDB—763b.

5970. עָלַץ {8x} ʿâlats, *aw-lats';* a prim. root; to *jump* for joy, i.e. *exult:*—rejoice {6x}, joyful {1x}, triumph {1x}. See: TWOT—1635; BDB—763b.

5971. עַם {1861x} ʿam, *am;* from 6004; a *people* (as a congregated *unit*); spec. a *tribe* (as those of Israel); hence, (collect.) *troops* or *attendants;* fig. a *flock:*—people {1836x}, nation {17x}, people + 1121 {4x}, folk {2x}, Ammi {1x}, men {1x}.

ʿAm means "people; relative." **(1)** The word bears subjective and personal overtones. **(1a)** *ʿAm* represents a familial relationship. **(1b)** In Ruth 3:11 the word means "male kinsmen" with special emphasis on the paternal relationship: **(1b1)** "And now, my daughter, fear not; I will do to thee all that thou requirest: for all the city of my people doth know that thou art a virtuous woman." **(1b2)** Here the word is a collective noun insofar as it occurs in the singular; indeed, it is almost an abstract noun. **(2)** In the plural the word refers to all the individuals who are related to a person through his father: "But he shall not defile himself, being a chief man among his people, to profane himself" (Lev 21:4). **(3)** The word is quite often combined with divine names and titles in people's names (theophoric names) where God is set forth as the God of a particular tribe, clan, or family—for example, **(3a)** Jekameam (God has raised up a clan or

family, 1 Chr 23:19) and **(3b)** Jokneam (God has created a clan or family, Josh 12:22). **(4)** *ʿAm* may signify those relatives (including women and children) who are grouped together locally whether or not they permanently inhabit a given location: "Then Jacob was greatly afraid and distressed: and he divided the people that was with him, and the flocks, and herds, and the camels, into two bands" (Gen 32:7).

(5) This word may refer to the whole of a nation formed and united primarily by their descent from a common ancestor. Such a group has strong blood ties and social interrelationships and interactions. **(5a)** Often they live and work together in a society in a common location. **(5b)** This is the significance of the word in its first biblical appearance: "And the Lord said, Behold, the people is one, and they have all one language" (Gen 11:6). **(5c)** Hence, in this usage *ʿam* refers not simply to male relatives but to men, women, and children. **(5d)** *ʿAm* may also include those who enter by religious adoption and marriage. **(6)** The people of Israel initially were the descendants of Jacob (Israel) and their families: "And he said unto his people [Egyptians], Behold, the people of the children of Israel are more and mightier than we" (Ex 1:9).

(7) Later the basic unity in a common covenant relationship with God becomes the unifying factor underlying *ʿam.* **(7a)** When they left Egypt, the people of Israel were joined by many others: "And a mixed multitude went up also with them; and flocks, and herds, even very much cattle" (Ex 12:38). **(7b)** Such individuals and their families were taken into Israel before they observed the Passover: "And when a stranger shall sojourn with thee, and will keep the passover to the LORD, let all his males be circumcised, and then let him come near and keep it; and he shall be as one that is born in the land" (Ex 12:48). **(7c)** There is another mention of this group (perhaps) in Num 11:4: "And the mixed multitude that was among them fell a lusting: and the children of Israel also wept again, and said. . . ." **(7d)** After that, however, we read of them no more. By the time of the conquest we read only of the "people" (*ʿam*) of Israel entering the land of Canaan and inheriting it (Judg 5:11). **(7e)** Passages such as Deut 32:9 clearly focus on this covenantal relationship as the basis of unity: "For the Lord's portion is his people; Jacob is the lot of his inheritance." **(7f)** This sense certainly emerges in the concept "to be cut off from one's people": "And the uncircumcised man child whose flesh of his foreskin is not circumcised, that soul shall be cut off from his people; he hath broken my covenant" (Gen 17:14).

(8) '*Am* can mean all those physical ancestors who lived previously and are now dead. **(8a)** So Abraham was gathered to his people: "Then Abraham gave up the ghost, and died in a good old age, an old man, and full of years; and was gathered to his people" (Gen 25:8). **(8b)** There might be covenantal overtones here in the sense that Abraham was gathered to all those who were true believers. Jesus argued that such texts taught the reality of life after death (cf. Mt 22:32). **(9)** '*Am* can represent the individuals who together form a familial (and covenantal) group within a larger group: "Zebulun and Naphtali were a people that jeoparded their lives unto the death in the high places of the field [on the battlefield]" (Judg 5:18). **(9a)** Some scholars have suggested that the reference here is to a fighting unit with the idea of blood relationship in the background. **(9b)** One must never forget, however, that among nomadic and semi-nomadic tribes there is no distinction between the concepts "militia" and "kinsmen": "And the Lord said unto Joshua, Fear not, neither be thou dismayed: take all the people of war with thee, and arise " (Josh 8:1). **(9c)** Compare Josh 8:5 where '*am* by itself means fighting unit: "And I, and all the people that are with me, will approach unto the city" (cf. Gen 32:7). **(10)** '*Am* may signify the inhabitants of a city regardless of their familial or covenantal relationship; it is a territorial or political term: "And Boaz said unto the elders, and unto all the people, Ye are witnesses . . ." (Ruth 4:9). **(11)** This noun can be used of those who are privileged. In the phrase "people of the land" '*am* may signify those who have feudal rights, or those who may own land and are especially protected under the law: "And Abraham stood up, and bowed himself to the people of the land, even to the children of Heth" (Gen 23:7). **(12)** This sense of a full citizen appears when the phrase is used of Israel, too (cf. 2 Kin 11:14ff.). **(12a)** In some contexts this phrase excludes those of high office such as the king, his ministers, and priests; "For, behold, I have made thee this day a defenced city, and an iron pillar, and brazen walls against the whole land, against the kings of Judah, against the princes thereof, against the priests thereof, and against the people of the land" (Jer 1:18). **(12b)** In Lev 4:27 this same phrase signifies the entire worshiping community of Israel: "And if any one of the common people [people of the land] sin through ignorance. . . ." **(12c)** The sense of privileged people with a proper relationship to and unique knowledge of God appears in Job 12:2: "No doubt but ye are the people, and wisdom shall die with you." **(12d)** Could it be that in Is 42:5 all mankind are conceived to be the

privileged recipients of divine revelation and blessing: "Thus saith God the Lord, he that created the heavens, and stretched them out; he that spread forth the earth, and that which cometh out of it; he that giveth breath unto the people upon it, and spirit to them that walk therein."

(13) Finally, sometimes '*am* used of an entire nation has political and territorial overtones. As such it may be paralleled to the Hebrew word with such overtones (1471 - *goy*): "For thou art a holy people unto the Lord thy God, and the Lord hath chosen thee to be a peculiar people unto himself, above all the nations that are upon the earth" (Deut 14:2; cf. Ex 19:5–6). Syn.: 523, 1471. See: TWOT—1640a, 1640e; BDB—763c, 766b, 769b, 770c, 1107a.

5972. עַם {15x} '**am** (Aram.), *am;* corresp. to 5971:—people {15x}. See: TWOT—2914; BDB—1107a.

5973. עִם {26x} '**im**, *eem;* from 6004; adv. or prep., *with* (i.e. in *conjunction* with), in varied applications; spec. *equally with;* often with prep. pref. (and then usually unrepresented in English):—{26x} = with, unto, by, as long, neither, from between, from among, to, unto. See: TWOT—1640b; BDB—763c, 765c, 767a, 769b, 1107a.

5974. עִם {20x} '**im** (Aram.), *eem;* corresp. to 5973:—with {9x}, with . . . {3x}, to {2x}, from {2x}, toward {1x}, like {1x}, unto {1x}, by {1x}. See: TWOT—2915; BDB—1107a.

5975. עָמַד {521x} '**âmad**, *aw-mad´;* a prim. root; to *stand,* in various relations (lit. and fig., intr. and tran.):—stood {171x}, stand {137x}, (raise, stand . . .) up {42x}, set {32x}, stay {17x}, still {15x}, appointed {10x}, standing {10x}, endure {8x}, remain {8x}, present {7x}, continue {6x}, withstand {6x}, waited {5x}, establish {5x}, misc. {42x} = abide (behind), arise, cease, confirm, dwell, be employed, leave, make, ordain, be [over], place, raise up, repair, + serve, tarry.

'*Amad* means "to take one's stand; stand here or be there; stand still." **(1)** The basic meaning of this verb is "to stand upright." **(1a)** This is its meaning in Gen 18:8, its first biblical occurrence: "And he took butter, and milk, and the calf which he had dressed, and set it before them; and he stood by them under the tree, and they did eat." **(1b)** It is what a soldier does while on watch: "And the king said unto him, Turn aside, and stand here. And he turned aside, and stood still" (2 Sa 18:30). **(2)** From this basic meaning comes the meaning "to be established, immovable, and standing upright" on a single spot; **(2a)** the soles of the priests' feet "rested" (stood still, unmoving) in

the waters of the Jordan (Josh 3:13). **(2b)** Also, the sun and the moon "stood still" at Joshua's command (Josh 10:13). **(3)** Idols "stand upright" in one spot, never moving. The suggestion here is that they never do anything that is expected of living things (Is 46:7).

(4) *ʿAmad* may be used of the existence of a particular experience. **(4a)** In 2 Sa 21:18 there "was" (1961 - *hayah*) war again, **(4b)** while in 1 Chr 20:4 war "existed" or "arose" (*ʿamad*) again. **(5)** Cultically (with reference to the formal worship activities) this verb is used of approaching the altar to make a sacrifice. **(5a)** It describes the last stage of this approaching, "to stand finally and officially" before the altar (before God; cf. Deut 4:11). **(5b)** Such standing is not just a standing still doing nothing but includes all that one does in ministering before God (Num 16:9). **(6)** In other contexts *ʿamad* is used as the opposite of verbs indicating various kinds of movement. **(6a)** The psalmist praises the man who does not walk (behave according to) in the counsel of the ungodly or "stand" (serve) in the path of the sinful (Ps 1:1). **(6b)** Laban told Abraham not "to stand" (remain stationary, not entering) outside his dwelling but to come in (Gen 24:31).

(7) The verb can suggest "immovable," or not being able to be moved. So the "house of the righteous shall stand" (Prov 12:7). **(8)** Yet another nuance appears in Ps 102:26, which teaches the indestructibility and/or eternity of God—the creation perishes but He "shalt endure [will ever stand]." **(8a)** This is not the changelessness of doing nothing or standing physically upright, **(8b)** but the changelessness of ever-existing being, a quality that only God has in Himself. **(8c)** All other existing depends upon Him; the creation and all creatures are perishable. **(9)** In a more limited sense the man who does not die as the result of a blow "stands," or remains alive (Ex 21:21). **(10)** In a military context "to stand" refers to gaining a victory: "Behold, two kings stood not before him: how then shall we stand?" (2 Kin 10:4; cf. Judg 2:14). **(11)** *ʿAmad* can be used of the ever unchanged content and/or existence of **(11a)** a document (Jer 32:14), **(11b)** a city (1 Kin 15:4), **(11c)** a people (Is 66:22), and **(11d)** a divine worship (Ps. 19:9).

(12) Using the causative aspect of the Hebrew verb, Jeroboam "ordained" (made to stand, to minister) priests in Bethel (1 Kin 12:32). **(13)** Certain prepositions sometimes give this verb special meanings. **(13a)** With "to" the verb can signify being in a certain place to accomplish a pre-designated task—**(13a1)** so Moses said that certain tribes should "stand upon mount Gerizim to bless the people" (Deut 27:12). **(13a2)** With this same preposition this verb can be used **(13a2i)** judicially of the act of being in court, or standing before a judge (1 Kin 3:16), and **(13a2ii)** the position (whether literal or figurative) assumed by a judge when pronouncing the sentence (Eze 44:24) or **(13a2iii)** delivering judgment (Is 3:13; cf. Ex 17:6). **(13a3)** With the preposition "before" *ʿamad* is used to describe the service of a servant before a master—so Joshua "stood" before Moses (Deut 1:38). This is not inactivity but activity. **(14)** In Neh 8:5 the verb means "to stand up or rise up"; when Ezra opened the book, all the people "stood up" (cf. Dan 12:13). Syn.: 4612, 4613, 5977, 5979, 5982. See: TWOT—1637; BDB—763c.

5976. עָמַד {1x} **ʿâmad,** *aw-mad';* for 4571; to *shake:*—to be at a stand {1x}. See: TWOT—1637; BDB—588c.

5977. עֹמֶד {10x} **ʿômed,** *o'-med;* from 5975; a *spot* (as being *fixed*):—place {6x}, upright {2x}, where I stood {1x}, I stood {1x}.

ʿOmed occurs 10 times and refers to "standing places": "And they stood in their place after their manner, according to the law of Moses the man of God:" (2 Chr 30:16). Syn.: 4612, 4613, 5979, 5982. See: TWOT—1637a; BDB—765a.

5978. עִמָּד {12x} **ʿimmâd,** *im-mawd';* prol. for 5973; along *with:*—with me {1x}, within me {1x}, by me {1x}, upon me {1x}, mine {1x}, against me {1x}, unto me {1x}, me {1x}, from me {1x}, of me {1x}, that I take {1x}, in me {1x}. See: TWOT—1640b; BDB—767a.

עַמֻּד **ʿammûd.** See 5982.

5979. עֶמְדָּה {1x} **ʿemdâh,** *em-daw';* from 5975; a *station,* i.e. domicile:—standing {1x}.

ʿEmdah means "standing ground" once: "Pass ye away, thou inhabitant of Saphir, having thy shame naked: the inhabitant of Zaanan came not forth in the mourning of Bethezel; he shall receive of you his standing" (Mic 1:11). Syn.: 4612, 4613, 5977, 5982.See: TWOT—1637b; BDB—765a.

5980. עֻמָּה {32x} **ʿummâh,** *oom-maw';* from 6004; *conjunction,* i.e. *society;* mostly adv. or prep. (with prep. pref.), *near, beside, along with:*—against {26x}, beside {2x}, answerable {1x}, at {1x}, hard {1x}, points {1x}. See: TWOT—1640f; BDB—769c.

5981. עֻמָּה {1x} **ʿUmmâh,** *oom-maw';* the same as 5980; *association; Ummah,* a place in Pal.:—Ummah {1x}. See: BDB—769d.

Hebrew

5982. עַמּוּד {110x} ʿ**ammûwd,** *am-mood';* or

עַמֻּד ʿ**ammûd,** *am-mood';* from 5975; a *column* (as *standing*); also a *stand,* i.e. platform:—pillar {109x}, apiece + 259 {1x}.
'*Ammud* means "pillar; standing place."
(1) The noun '*ammud* occurs 110 times and usually signifies something that stands upright like a "pillar": "And thou shalt hang it upon four pillars of shittim wood overlaid with gold: their hooks shall be of gold, upon the four sockets of silver" (Ex 26:32; cf. Judg 16:25). (2) It may occasionally refer to a "standing place": "And when she looked, behold, the king stood by a pillar, as the manner was, and the princes and the trumpeters by the king, and all the people of the land rejoiced," (2 Kin 11:14). Syn.: 4612, 4613, 5977, 5979. See: TWOT—1637c; BDB—765a.

5983. עַמּוֹן {105x} ʿ**Ammôwn,** *am-mone';* from 5971; *tribal,* i.e. *inbred; Ammon,* a son of Lot; also his posterity and their country:—Ammon {90x}, Ammonites + 1121 {13x}, Ammonites {2x}. See: TWOT—1642; BDB—769d.

5984. עַמּוֹנִי {18x} ʿ**Ammôwnîy,** *am-mo-nee';* patron. from 5983; an *Ammonite* or (adj.) *Ammonitish:*—Ammonite {17x}, Ammon {1x}. See: TWOT—1642a; BDB—770a.

5985. עַמּוֹנִית {4x} ʿ**Ammôwnîyth,** *am-mo-neeth';* fem. of 5984; an *Ammonitess:*—Ammonitess {4x}. See: BDB—770a.

5986. עָמוֹס {7x} ʿ**Âmôwç,** *aw-moce';* from 6006; *burdensome; Amos,* an Isr. prophet:—Amos {7x}. See: BDB—770c.

5987. עָמוֹק {2x} ʿ**Âmôwq,** *aw-moke';* from 6009; *deep; Amok,* an Isr.:—Amok {2x}. See: BDB—771b.

5988. עַמִּיאֵל {6x} ʿ**Ammîyʾêl,** *am-mee-ale';* from 5971 and 410; *people of God; Ammiël,* the name of three or four Isr.:—Ammiel {6x}. See: BDB—765c, 770a.

5989. עַמִּיהוּד {10x} ʿ**Ammîyhûwd,** *am-mee-hood';* from 5971 and 1935; *people of splendor; Ammihud,* the name of three Isr.:—Ammihud {10x}. See: BDB—770a.

5990. עַמִּיזָבָד {1x} ʿ**Ammîyzâbâd,** *am-mee-zaw-bawd';* from 5971 and 2064; *people of endowment; Ammizabad,* an Isr.:—Ammizabad {1x}. See: BDB—770b.

5991. עַמִּיחוּר {1x} ʿ**Ammîychûwr,** *am-mee-khoor';* from 5971 and 2353; *people of nobility; Ammichur,* a Syrian prince:—Ammihud {1x}. See: BDB—770a, 770b.

5992. עַמִּינָדָב {13x} ʿ**Ammîynâdâb,** *am-mee-naw-dawb';* from 5971 and 5068; *people of liberality; Amminadab,* the name of four Isr.:—Amminadab {13x}. See: BDB—770b.

5993. עַמִּי נָדִיב {1x} ʿ**Ammîy Nâdîyb,** *am-mee' naw-deeb';* from 5971 and 5081; *my people* (is) *liberal; Ammi-Nadib,* prob. an Isr.:—Amminadib {1x}. See: BDB—766c.

5994. עֲמִיק {1x} ʿ**ămîyq** (Aram.), *am-eek';* corresp. to 6012; *profound,* i.e. unsearchable:—deep {1x}. See: TWOT—2916; BDB—1107a.

5995. עָמִיר {4x} ʿ**âmîyr,** *aw-meer';* from 6014; a *bunch* of grain:—sheaf {3x}, handful {1x}. See: TWOT—1645c; BDB—771c.

5996. עַמִּישַׁדַּי {5x} ʿ**Ammîyshadday,** *am-mee-shad-dah'ee;* from 5971 and 7706; *people of* (the) *Almighty; Ammishaddai,* an Isr.:—Ammishaddai {5x}. See: BDB—770b.

5997. עָמִית {12x} ʿ**âmîyth,** *aw-meeth';* from a prim. root mean. to *associate; companionship;* hence, (concr.) a *comrade* or kindred man:—neighbour {9x}, another {2x}, fellow {1x}. See: TWOT—1638a; BDB—765c.

5998. עָמַל {11x} ʿ**âmal,** *aw-mal';* a prim. root; to *toil,* i.e. *work severely* and with irksomeness:—labour {8x}, take {3x}.
'*Amal* means to labor: "Then I looked on all the works that my hands had wrought, and on the labour that I had laboured to do: and, behold, all was vanity and vexation of spirit, and there was no profit under the sun" (Eccl 2:11, cf. 11:19, 21; 5:16; Ps 127:1). See: TWOT—1639; BDB—765c, 766a.

5999. עָמָל {55x} ʿ**âmâl,** *aw-mawl';* from 5998; *toil,* i.e. *wearing effort;* hence, *worry,* wheth. of body or mind:—labour {25x}, mischief {9x}, misery {3x}, travail {3x}, trouble {3x}, sorrow {2x}, grievance {1x}, grievousness {1x}, iniquity {1x}, miserable {1x}, pain {1x}, painful {1x}, perverseness {1x}, toil {1x}, wearisome {1x}, wickedness {1x}.
'*Amal* means labor; toil; anguish; troublesome work; trouble; misery; evil; trouble; misfortune; mischief; grievance; wickedness. (1) The Book of Ecclesiastes clearly represents this use: (1a) "Yea, I hated all my labor which I had taken under the sun" (Eccl 2:18). (1b) "And also that every man should eat and drink, and enjoy the good of all his labor" (Eccl 3:13). (1c) A related example appears in Ps 107:12: "Therefore he brought down their heart with labor; they fell down and there was none to help." (2) In general, '*amal* refers either to the

trouble and suffering which sin causes the sinner or to the trouble that he inflicts upon others. **(2a)** Jer 20:18 depicts self-inflicted sorrow: "Wherefore came I forth out of the womb to see labor ['*amal*] and sorrow [3015 - *yagon*], that my days should be consumed with shame?" **(2b)** Another instance is found in Deut 26:7: "And when we cried unto the Lord God of our fathers, the Lord heard our voice, and looked on our affliction [6040 – '*oni*], and our labor ['*amal*], and our oppression [3906 - *lachats*]."

(3) Job 4:8 illustrates the sense of trouble as mischief inflicted on others: "They that plow iniquity [205 - '*awen*], and sow wickedness ['*amal*] reap the same." **(3a)** The word appears in Ps 140:9: "As for the head of those that compass me about, let the mischief of their own lips cover them." **(3b)** Hab 1:3 also refers to the trouble inflicted on others: "Why dost thou show me iniquity [205 - '*awen*], and cause me to behold grievance ['*amal*]? For spoiling and violence are before me; and there are that raise up strife and contention." **(4)** The word means labor in the sense of toil or oppression, **(4a)** generally (Deut 26:7) or **(4b)** of Messiah (Is 53:11). **(5)** Something gained by toil or labor is '*amal* (Ps 105:44). **(6)** '*Amal* means troublesome work, emphasizing the difficulty involved in a task or work as troublesome and burdensome (Eccl 1:3). **(7)** It can ethically connote sin (Ps 7:14; cf. Job 4:8). See: TWOT—1639a; BDB—765d.

6000. עָמָל {1x} **'Âmâl**, *aw-mawl';* the same as 5999; *Amal,* an Isr.:—Amal {1x}. See: BDB—765d.

6001. עָמֵל {9x} **'âmêl**, *aw-male';* from 5998; *toiling;* concr. a *laborer;* fig. *sorrowful:*—labour {4x}, take {2x}, workman {1x}, misery {1x}, wicked {1x}. See: TWOT—1639b, 1639c; BDB—766a.

6002. עֲמָלֵק {39x} **'Ămâlêq**, *am-aw-lake';* prob. of for. or.; *Amalek,* a desc. of Esau; also his posterity and their country:—Amalek {24x}, Amalekites {15x}. See: BDB—766a.

6003. עֲמָלֵקִי {12x} **'Ămâlêqîy**, *am-aw-lay-kee';* patron. from 6002; an *Amalekite* (or collect. the *Amalekites*) or desc. of Amalek:—Amalekite {11x}, Amalekite + 376 {1x}. See: BDB—766a.

6004. עָמַם {3x} **'âmam**, *aw-mam';* a prim. root; to *associate;* by impl. to *overshadow* (by *huddling* together):—hide {2x}, dim {1x}. See: TWOT—1641; BDB—770b.

6005. עִמָּנוּאֵל {2x} **'Immânûw'êl**, *im-maw-noo-ale';* from 5973 and 410 with a pron. suff. ins.; *with us* (is) *God; Immanuel,* a

typical name of Isaiah's son:—Immanuel + 410 {2x}. See: TWOT—1640d; BDB—769b, 770c.

6006. עָמַס {9x} **'âmaç**, *aw-mas';* or

עָמַשׂ **'âmas**, *aw-mas';* a prim. root; to *load,* i.e. *impose* a burden (or fig. *infliction*):—lade {4x}, load {2x}, put {1x}, borne {1x}, burden {1x}. See: TWOT—1643; BDB—770c, 771d.

6007. עֲמַסְיָה {1x} **'Ămaçyâh**, *am-as-yaw';* from 6006 and 3050; *Jah has loaded; Amasjah,* an Isr.:—Amasiah {1x}. See: BDB—770c.

6008. עַמְעָד {1x} **'Am'âd**, *am-awd';* from 5971 and 5703; *people of time; Amad,* a place in Pal.:—Amad {1x}. See: BDB—770c.

6009. עָמַק {9x} **'âmaq**, *aw-mak';* a prim. root; to *be* (caus. *make) deep* (lit. or fig.):—deep {5x}, deeply {2x}, depth {1x}, profound {1x}. See: TWOT—1644; BDB—770d.

6010. עֵמֶק {69x} **'êmeq**, *ay'-mek;* from 6009; a *vale* (i.e. broad *depression*):—valley {63x}, vale {4x}, dale {2x}. See: TWOT—1644a; BDB—770d. See also 1025.

6011. עֹמֶק {1x} **'ômeq**, *o'-mek;* from 6009; *depth:*—depth {1x}. See: TWOT—1644b; BDB—771b.

6012. עָמֵק {4x} **'âmêq**, *aw-make';* from 6009; *deep* (lit. or fig.):—strange {2x}, depths {1x}, deeper {1x}. See: TWOT—1644c; BDB—771b, 1107a.

6013. עָמֹק {16x} **'âmôq**, *aw-moke';* from 6009; *deep* (lit. or fig.):—deeper {8x}, deep {7x}, deep things {1x}. See: TWOT—1644d; BDB—771b, 1008a.

6014. עָמַר {3x} **'âmar**, *aw-mar';* a prim. root; prop. appar. to *heap;* fig. to *chastise* (as if *piling* blows); spec. (as denom. from 6016) to *gather* grain:—merchandise {2x}, sheaves {1x}. See: TWOT—1645, 1646; BDB—771c.

6015. עֲמַר {1x} **'ămar** (Aram.), *am-ar';* corresp. to 6785; *wool:*—wool {1x}. See: TWOT—2917; BDB—1107a.

6016. עֹמֶר {14x} **'ômer**, *o'-mer;* from 6014; prop. a *heap,* i.e. a *sheaf;* also an *omer,* as a dry measure:—sheaf {8x}, omer {6x}. See: TWOT—1645b, 1645a; BDB—771b, 771c.

6017. עֲמֹרָה {16x} **'Ămôrâh**, *am-o-raw';* from 6014; a (ruined) *heap; Amorah,* a place in Pal.:—Gomorrah {16x}. See: BDB—771c.

6018. עָמְרִי {18x} **'Omrîy**, *om-ree';* from 6014; *heaping; Omri,* an Isr.:—Omri {18x}. See: BDB—771d.

Hebrew

6019. עַמְרָם {14x} ʿAmrâm, *am-rawm'*; prob. from 5971 and 7311; *high people*; *Amram*, the name of two Isr.:—*Amram* {14x}. See: BDB—771d.

6020. עַמְרָמִי {2x} ʿAmrâmîy, *am-raw-mee'*; patron. from 6019; an *Amramite* or desc. of Amram:—*Amramites* {2x}.See: BDB—771d.

עָמַשׂ ʿâmas. See 6006.

6021. עֲמָשָׂא {16x} ʿĂmâsâʾ, *am-aw-saw'*; from 6006; *burden*; *Amasa*, the name of two Isr.:—*Amasa* {16x}. See: BDB—771d.

6022. עֲמָשַׂי {5x} ʿĂmâsay, *am-aw-sah'-ee*; from 6006; *burdensome*; *Amasai*, the name of three Isr.:—*Amasai* {5x}. See: BDB—772a.

6023. עֲמָשְׁסַי {1x} ʿĂmashçay, *am-ash-sah'-ee*; prob. from 6006; *burdensome*; *Amashsay*, an Isr.:—*Amashai* {1x}. See: BDB—772a.

6024. עֲנָב {2x} ʿĂnâb, *an-awb'*; from the same as 6025; *fruit*; *Anab*, a place in Pal.:—*Anab* {2x}. See: BDB—772b.

6025. עֵנָב {19x} ʿênâb, *ay-nawb'*; from an unused root prob. mean. to *bear* fruit; a *grape*:—grape {18x}, wine {1x}. See: TWOT—1647a; BDB—772a.

6026. עָנַג {10x} ʿânag, *aw-nag'*; a prim. root; to *be soft* or *pliable*, i.e. (fig.) *effeminate* or luxurious:—delight {7x}, delicate {1x}, delicateness {1x}, sport {1x}. See: TWOT—1648; BDB—772b.

6027. עֹנֶג {2x} ʿôneg, *o'-neg*; from 6026; *luxury*:—pleasant {1x}, delight {1x}. See: TWOT—1648a; BDB—772b.

6028. עָנֹג {3x} ʿânôg, *aw-nogue'*; from 6026; *luxurious*:—delicate {2x}, delicate woman {1x}. See: TWOT—1648b; BDB—772b.

6029. עָנַד {2x} ʿânad, *aw-nad'*; a prim. root; to *lace* fast:—tie {1x}, bind {1x}. See: TWOT—1649; BDB—772c.

6030. עָנָה {329x} ʿânâh, *aw-naw'*; a prim. root; prop. to *eye* or (gen.) to *heed*, i.e. *pay attention*; by impl. to *respond*; by extens. to *begin* to speak; spec. to *sing, shout, testify, announce*:—answer {242x}, hear {42x}, testify {12x}, speak {8x}, sing {4x}, bear {3x}, cry {2x}, witness {2x}, give {1x}, misc. {13x}.

ʿAnah means "to respond, answer, reply." **(1)** *ʿAnah* means "to respond," but not necessarily with a verbal response. **(1a)** For example, in Gen 35:3 Jacob tells his household, "And let us arise, and go up to Bethel; and I will make there an altar unto God, who answered [ʿanah] me in the day of my distress." **(1a1)** In Gen 28:10ff., where this "answering" is recorded, it is quite clear that God initiated the encounter and that, although He spoke with Jacob, **(1a2)** the emphasis is on the vision of the ladder and the relationship with God that it represented. **(1b)** This meaning is even clearer in Ex 19:18, where we read that God reacted to the situation at Sinai with a sound (of thunder). **(1c)** A nonverbal reaction is also indicated in Deut 20:11. God tells Israel that before they besiege a city they should demand its surrender. Its inhabitants are to live as Israel's slaves "if it [the city] make thee answer of peace [literally, "responds peaceably"], and open unto thee." **(1d)** In Job 30:20, Job says he cried out to God, who did not "respond" to him (i.e., did not pay any attention to him). **(1e)** In Is 49:8 the Lord tells the Messiah, "In an acceptable time have I heard thee, and in a day of salvation have I helped thee." Here responding ("hearing") is synonymously parallel to helping—i.e., it is an action (cf. Ps 69:17; Is 41:17).

(2) A second major meaning of *ʿanah* is "to respond with words," as when one engages in dialogue. **(2a)** In Gen 18:27 (the first occurrence of *ʿanah*), we read: "Abraham answered and said" to the Lord, who had just spoken. **(2a1)** In this formula, the two verbs represent one idea (i.e., they form an hendiadys). **(2a2)** A simpler translation might be "respond," since God had asked no question and required no reply. **(2b)** On the other hand, when the sons of Heth "answer and say" (Gen 23:5), they are responding verbally to the implied inquiry made by Abraham (v. 4). Therefore, they really do answer. **(3)** *ʿAnah* may mean "respond" in the special sense of verbally reacting to a truth discovered: **(3a)** "Then answered the five men that went to spy out the country of Laish, and said . . ." (Judg 18:14). Since no inquiry was addressed to them, this word implies that they gave a report; they responded to what they had discovered. **(3b)** In Deut 21:7, the children of Israel are told how to respond to the rite of the heifer—viz., "They shall answer and say, Our hands have not shed this blood, neither have our eyes seen it."

(4) *ʿAnah* can also be used in the legal sense of "testify": "Thou shalt not bear false witness against thy neighbor" (Ex 20:16). **(4a)** Or we read in Ex 23:2: "Thou shalt not follow a multitude to do evil." **(4b)** In a similar sense, Jacob proposed that Laban give him all the spotted and speckled sheep of the flock, so that "my righteousness [will] answer [i.e., testify] for me in time to come, when it shall come [to make an investigation] for my hire before thy face" (Gen 30:33). See: TWOT—1650, 1653; BDB—732d, 772c, 777a, 1107a. See also 1042, 1043.

6031. עָנָה {84x} ʿânâh, *aw-naw'*; a prim. root [possibly rather ident. with 6030 through the idea of *looking* down or *browbeating*]; to *depress* lit. or fig., tran. or intr. (in various applications, as follows):—afflict {50x}, humble {11x}, force {5x}, exercised {2x}, sing {2x}, Leannoth {1x}, troubled {1x}, weakened {1x}, misc. {11}.

ʿAnah, as a verb, means "to be afflicted, be bowed down, be humbled, be meek." **(1)** This word, common to both ancient and modern Hebrew, is the source of several important words in the history and experience of Judaism: "humble, meek, poor, and affliction." **(2)** It is found for the first time in Gen 15:13: "they shall afflict them four hundred years." **(3)** *ʿAnah* often expresses harsh and painful treatment. **(3a)** Sarai "dealt hardly" with Hagar (Gen 16:6). **(3b)** When Joseph was sold as a slave, his feet were hurt with fetters (Ps 105:18). **(4)** Frequently the verb expresses the idea that God sends affliction for disciplinary purposes: "the Lord thy God led thee these forty years in the wilderness, to humble thee, and to prove thee, to know what was in thine heart" (Deut 8:2; see also 1 Kin 11:39; Ps 90:15). **(5)** To take a woman sexually by force may be "to humble" her (Gen 34:2). **(6)** In the Day of Atonement observance, "to humble oneself" is probably connected with the requirement for fasting on that day (Lev 23:28–29). **(7)** *ʿAnah* means "to be exercised": "And I gave my heart to seek and search out by wisdom concerning all things that are done under heaven: this sore travail hath God given to the sons of man to be exercised therewith" (Eccl 1:13). See: TWOT— 1651, 1652; BDB—775d, 776a, 1107c.

6032. עֲנָה {30x} ʿănâh (Aram.), *an-aw'*; corresp. to 6030:—answered {16x}, spake {14x}. See: TWOT—2918; BDB—1107a.

6033. עֲנָה {1x} ʿănâh (Aram.), *an-aw'*; corresp. to 6031:—poor {1x}. See: TWOT—2919a; BDB—1107c.

6034. עֲנָה {12x} ʿĂnâh, *an-aw'*; prob. from 6030; an *answer*; *Anah*, the name of two Edomites and one Edomitess:—Anah {12x}. See: BDB—777b.

6035. עָנָו {26x} ʿânâv, *aw-nawv'*; or [by intermixture with 6041]

עָנָיו ʿânâyv, *aw-nawv'*; from 6031; *depressed* (fig.), in mind (*gentle*) or circumstances (*needy,* espec. *saintly*):—meek {13x}, humble {5x}, poor {5x}, lowly {2x}, very meek {1x}.

ʿAnayv, as an adjective, means "humble; poor; meek." **(1)** This adjective, which appears about 21 times in biblical Hebrew, is closely related to *ʿani* (6041) and derived from the same verb. **(1a)** Sometimes this word is synonymous with *ʿani.* Perhaps this is due to the well-known *waw-yodh* interchange. **(1b)** *ʿAnayv* appears almost exclusively in poetical passages and describes the intended outcome of affliction from God, namely "humility." **(2)** In its first appearance the word depicts the objective condition as well as the subjective stance of Moses. He was entirely dependent on God and saw that he was: "Now the man Moses was very meek, above all the men which were upon the face of the earth" (Num 12:3). See: TWOT— 1652a; BDB—776c, 1107c. comp. 6041.

6036. עָנוּב {1x} ʿĂnûwb, *aw-noob'*; pass. part. from the same as 6025; *borne* (as fruit); *Anub,* an Isr.:—Anub {1x}. See: BDB— 772b.

6037. עַנְוָה {2x} ʿanvâh, *an-vaw'*; fem. of 6035; *mildness* (royal); also (concr.) *oppressed:*—gentleness {1x}, meekness {1x}.

This word occurs only 5 times, setting forth the two characteristics gained from affliction: "humility and gentleness." Applied to God, it represents His submission to His own nature: "And in thy majesty ride prosperously because of truth and meekness and righteousness; and thy right hand shall teach thee terrible things" (Ps 45:4). See: TWOT—1652b; BDB—776c.

6038. עֲנָוָה {5x} ʿănâvâh, *an-aw-vaw'*; from 6035; *condescension,* human and subj. (*modesty*), or divine and obj. (*clemency*):—humility {3x}, gentleness {1x}, meekness {1x}. See: TWOT—1652b; BDB—776c.

6039. עֱנוּת {1x} ʿênûwth, *en-ooth'*; from 6031; *affliction:*—affliction {1x}. See: TWOT—1652c; BDB—776d.

6040. עֳנִי {37x} ʿŏnîy, *on-ee'*; from 6031; *depression,* i.e. *misery:*—affliction {32x}, trouble {3x}, afflicted + 1121 {1x}, variant {1x}.

The noun *ʿoniy,* means "affliction." **(1)** *ʿOniy* represents the state of pain and/or punishment resulting from affliction. **(2)** In Deut 16:3 the shewbread is termed the bread of "affliction" because it is a physical reminder of **(2a)** sin, the cause of "affliction": "Look upon mine affliction and my pain; and forgive all my sins" (Ps 25:18), **(2b)** the hardship involved in sin (especially the Egyptian bondage), and **(2c)** divine deliverance from sin: "This is my comfort in my affliction: for thy word hath quickened me" (Ps 119:50). See: TWOT— 1652e; BDB—777a.

6041. עָנִי {80x} ʿânîy, *aw-nee'*; from 6031; *depressed,* in mind or circumstances [practically the same as 6035, although the marg. constantly disputes this, making 6035

subj. and 6041 obj.]:—poor {58x}, afflicted {15x}, lowly {1x}, man {1x}, variant {3x}.

'Aniy, as a noun, means "poor; weak; afflicted; humble." **(1)** This noun is frequently used in synonymous parallelism with ʿebyon (34 - "needy") and/or dal (1802 - "poor"). **(1a)** It differs from both in emphasizing some kind of disability or distress. **(1b)** A hired servant as one who is in a lower (oppressive) social and material condition is described both as an ʿebyon and ʿaniy: "Thou shalt not oppress a hired servant that is poor and needy, whether he be of thy brethren, or of thy strangers that are in thy land within thy gates: At his day thou shalt give him his hire, neither shall the sun go down upon it; for he is poor, and setteth his heart upon it: lest he cry against thee unto the Lord, and it be sin unto thee" (Deut 24:14–15). **(1c)** If wrongly oppressed, he can call on God for defense.

(2) Financially, the ʿaniy lives from day to day and is socially defenseless, being subject to oppression. **(2a)** In its first biblical occurrence the ʿaniy is guaranteed (if men obey God's law) his outer garment for warmth at night even though that garment might be held as collateral during the day: "If thou lend money to any of my people that is poor by thee, thou shall not be to him as a usurer, neither shalt thou lay upon him usury" (Ex 22:25). **(2b)** The godly protect and deliver the "afflicted" (Is 10:2; Eze 18:17), while the ungodly take advantage of them, increasing their oppressed condition: "Is it not to deal thy bread to the hungry, and that thou bring the poor that are cast out to thy house? when thou seest the naked, that thou cover him; and that thou hide not thyself from thine own flesh?" (Is 58:7). **(2c)** The king is especially charged to protect the ʿaniy: "Open thy mouth, judge righteously, and plead the cause of the poor and needy" (Prov 31:9.)

(3) 'Aniy can refer to one who is physically oppressed: "Therefore hear now this, thou afflicted, and drunken, but not with wine" (Is 51:21). **(4)** Physical oppression is sometimes related to spiritual oppression as in Ps 22:24: "For he hath not despised nor abhorred the affliction of the afflicted; neither hath he hid his face from him." Outward affliction frequently leads to inner spiritual affliction and results in an outcry to God: "Turn thee unto me, and have mercy upon me; for I am desolate and afflicted" (Ps 25:16). **(5)** Even apart from outward affliction, the pious are frequently described as the "afflicted" or "poor" for whom God provides: "Thy congregation hath dwelt therein: thou, O God, hast prepared of thy goodness for the poor" (Ps 68:10). In such cases spiritual poverty and want are clearly in view.

(6) Sometimes the word means "humble" or "lowly," as it does in Zec 9:9, where it describes the Messiah: "Behold, thy King cometh unto thee: he is just, and having salvation; lowly, and riding upon an ass" (cf. Ps 18:27; Prov 3:34; Is 66:2). See: TWOT—1652d; BDB—776c, 776d, 1107c.

6042. עֻנִּי {3x} **Unnîy,** oon-nee'; from 6031; afflicted; Unni, the name of two Isr.:— Unni {3x}. See: BDB—777b, 777d.

6043. עֲנָיָה {2x} **'Ănâyâh,** an-aw-yaw'; from 6030; Jah has answered; Anajah, the name of two Isr.:—Anaiah {2x}. See: BDB—777d.

עָנָיו **ʿânâyv** See 6035.

6044. עָנִים {1x} **'Ănîym,** aw-neem'; for plur. of 5869; fountains; Anim, a place in Pal.:—Anim {1x}. See: BDB—745d.

6045. עִנְיָן {8x} **ʿinyân,** in-yawn'; from 6031; ado, i.e. (gen.) employment or (spec.) an affair:—travail {6x}, business {2x}. See: TWOT—1651a; BDB—775d.

6046. עֲנֵם {1x} **'Ănêm,** aw-name'; from the dual of 5869; two fountains; Anem, a place in Pal.:—Anem {1x}. See: BDB—745c.

6047. עֲנָמִם {2x} **'Ănâmîm,** an-aw-meem'; as if plur. of some Eg. word; Anamim, a son of Mizraim and his desc., with their country:—Anamim {2x}. See: BDB—777d.

6048. עֲנַמֶּלֶךְ {1x} **'Ănammelek,** an-am-meh'-lek; of for. or.; Anammelek, an Ass. deity:—Anammelech {1x}. See: BDB—777d.

6049. עָנַן {11x} **ʿânan,** aw-nan'; a prim. root; to cover; used only as a denom. from 6051, to cloud over; fig. to act covertly, i.e. practise magic:—observer of times {5x}, soothsayer {2x}, bring {1x}, sorceress {1x}, enchanter {1x}, Meonenim.

(1) A mode of attempting to obtain information was by the examination of the clouds. **(2)** These observers are ranked with all the other intruders into unlawful pursuits in Deut 18:10, under the title of soothsayers. **(3)** They are called "sons of the sorceress" (Is 57:3) and are classed with the vile, the impure, and the idolater. **(4)** They are called enchanters (Jer 27:9). **(5)** They are also called "observers of times," persons who by examining the clouds profess to be able to tell at what exact crisis any event is to be expected to take place, and when a good opportunity arrives for doing a certain work (Lev 1:26; 2 Kin 21:6; 2 Chr 33:6). Syn.: 825, 826, 1505, 2267, 3858, 3907, 5172. See: TWOT—1655, 1656; BDB—778a, 1107c.

6050. עֲנַן {1x} 'ănan (Aram.), an-an'; corresp. to 6051:–cloud {1x}. See: TWOT– 2921; BDB–1107c.

6051. עָנָן {81x} 'ânân, aw-nawn'; from 6049; a cloud (as covering the sky), i.e. the nimbus or thunder-cloud:–cloud {81x}, cloudy {6x}.

'Anan, means "cloud; fog; storm cloud; smoke." (1) The word commonly means "cloud mass." (1a) 'Anan is used especially of the "cloud mass" that evidenced the special presence of God: "And the Lord went before them by day in a pillar of a cloud, to lead them the way" (Ex 13:21). (1b) In Ex 34:5, this presence is represented by 'anan only: "And the Lord descended in the cloud, and stood with him [Moses] there, and proclaimed the name of the Lord." (2) When the ark of the covenant was brought into the holy place, "The cloud filled the house of the Lord, so that the priests could not stand to minister because of the cloud: for the glory of the Lord had filled the house of the Lord" (1 Kin 8:10–11). (2a) Thus the "cloud" evidenced the presence of God's glory. (2b) So the psalmist wrote that God was surrounded by "clouds and darkness" (Ps 97:2); hence, (2b) God appears as the controller and sovereign of nature. (3) The "cloud" is a sign and figure of "divine protection": "And the LORD will create upon every dwelling place of mount Zion, and upon her assemblies, a cloud and smoke by day, and the shining of a flaming fire by night: for upon all the glory shall be a defence" (Is 4:5), and (4) serves as a barrier hiding the fullness of divine holiness and glory, as well as barring sinful man's approach to God: "Thou hast covered thyself with a cloud, that our prayer should not pass through" (Lam 3:44). Man's relationship to God, therefore, is God-initiated and God-sustained, not humanly initiated or humanly sustained.

(5) In its first biblical occurrence, 'anan is used in conjunction with God's sign that He would never again destroy the earth by a flood: "I do set my bow in the cloud, and it shall be for a token of a covenant between me and the earth" (Gen 9:13). (6) Elsewhere, the transitory quality of a cloud is used to symbolize (6a) the loyalty: "O Ephraim, what shall I do unto thee? O Judah, what shall I do unto thee? for your goodness is as a morning cloud, and as the early dew it goeth away" (Hos 6:4) and (6b) existence of Israel: "Therefore they shall be as the morning cloud, and as the early dew that passeth away, as the chaff that is driven with the whirlwind out of the floor, and as the smoke out of the chimney" (Hos 13:3).

(7) In Is 44:22, God says that after proper punishment He will wipe out, "as a thick cloud, thy transgressions, and, as a cloud, thy sins."

(8) 'Anan can mean "storm cloud" and is used (8a) to symbolize "an invading force": "Thou shalt ascend and come like a storm, thou shalt be like a cloud to cover the land, thou, and all thy bands, and many people with thee" (Eze 38:9; cf. Jer 4:13). (8b) In Job 26:8, the storm cloud is said to be God's: "He bindeth up the waters in his thick clouds; and the cloud is not rent under them." (8c) In several passages, the thick storm cloud and the darkness accompanying it are symbols of "gloom" (Eze 30:18) and/or "divine judgment" (Eze 30:3). (9) 'Anan can represent the "smoke" arising from burning incense: "And he shall put the incense upon the fire before the Lord, that the cloud of the incense may cover the mercy seat that is upon the testimony, that he die not" (Lev 16:13). (9a) This "cloud of smoke" may represent the covering between God's presence (above the mercy seat) and sinful man. (9b) If so, it probably also symbolizes the "divine glory." (9c) On the other hand, many scholars feel it represents the human prayers offered up to God. See: TWOT–1655a; BDB–777d, 1107c.

6052. עָנָן {1x} 'Ânân, aw-nawn'; the same as 6051; cloud; Anan, an Isr.:–Anan {1x}. See: BDB–778b.

6053. עֲנָנָה {1x} 'ănânâh, an-aw-naw'; fem. of 6051; cloudiness:–cloud {1x}. See: TWOT–1655a; BDB–778a.

6054. עֲנָנִי {1x} 'Ânânîy, an-aw-nee'; from 6051; cloudy; Anani, an Isr.:– Anani {1x}. See: BDB–778b.

6055. עֲנַנְיָה {2x} 'Ănanyâh, an-an-yaw'; from 6049 and 3050; Jah has covered; Ananjah, the name of an Isr. and of a place in Pal.:–Ananiah {2x}. See: BDB–778b.

6056. עֲנַף {4x} 'ănaph (Aram.), an-af'; or

עֶנֶף 'eneph (Aram.), eh'-nef; corresp. to 6057:–branches {3x}, boughs {1x}. See: TWOT–2922; BDB–1107c.

6057. עָנָף {7x} 'ânâph, aw-nawf'; from an unused root mean. to cover; a twig (as covering the limbs):–branch {4x}, boughs {3x}. See: TWOT–1657a; BDB–778c, 1107c.

6058. עָנֵף {1x} 'ânêph, aw-nafe'; from the same as 6057; branching:– branches {1x}. See: TWOT–1657b; BDB– 778c.

6059. עָנַק {3x} 'ânaq, aw-nak'; a prim. root; prop. to choke; used only as denom. from 6060, to collar, i.e. adorn with a necklace; fig. to fit out with supplies:–compass {1x}, furnish {1x}, liberally {1x}. See: TWOT–1658c; BDB–778d.

6060. עֲנָק {3x} 'ânâq, *aw-nawk'*; from 6059; a *necklace* (as if *strangling*):—chain {3x}. See: TWOT—1658b, 1658a; BDB—778d.

6061. עֲנָק {9x} 'Ânâq, *aw-nawk'*; the same as 6060; *Anak*, a Canaanite:—Anak {9x}. See: BDB—778c.

6062. עֲנָקִי {9x} 'Ănâqîy, *an-aw-kee'*; patron. from 6061; an *Anakite* or desc. of Anak:—Anakim {9x}. See: BDB—778c.

6063. עָנֵר {3x} 'Ânêr, *aw-nare'*; prob. for 5288; *Aner*, a Amorite, also a place in Pal.:—Aner {3x}. See: BDB—778d.

6064. עָנַשׁ {9x} 'ânash, *aw-nash'*; a prim. root; prop. to *urge*; by impl. to *inflict* a penalty, spec. to *fine*:—punish {5x}, condemned {2x}, amerce {1x}, surely {1x}. See: TWOT—1659; BDB—778d.

6065. עֲנַשׁ {1x} 'ănash (Aram.), *an-ash'*; corresp. to 6066; a *mulct*:—confiscation {1x}. See: TWOT—2923; BDB—1107c.

6066. עֹנֶשׁ {2x} 'ônesh, *o'-nesh*; from 6064; a *fine*:—tribute {1x}, punishment {1x}. See: TWOT—1659a; BDB—778d, 1107c.

עֲנָת 'eneth See 3706.

6067. עֲנָת {2x} 'Ănâth, *an-awth'*; from 6030; *answer; Anath*, an Isr.:—Anath {2x}. See: BDB—779a.

6068. עֲנָתוֹת {15x} 'Ănâthôwth, *an-aw-thōth'*; plur. of 6067; *Anathoth*, the name of two Isr., also of a place in Pal:—Anathoth {15x}. See: BDB—779a.

6069. עַנְתֹתִי {5x} 'Anthôthîy, *an-tho-thee'*; or

עַנְּתוֹתִי 'Ann°thôwthîy, *an-ne-tho-thee'*; patrial from 6068; a *Antothite* or inhab. of Anathoth:—Anethothite {2x}, Antothite {2x}, Anathoth {1x}. See: BDB—779a.

6070. עֲנְתֹתִיָּה {1x} 'Anthôthîyâh, *an-tho-thee-yaw'*; from the same as 6068 and 3050; *answers of Jah; Anthothijah*, an Isr.:—Antothijah {1x}. See: BDB—779a.

6071. עָסִיס {5x} 'âçîyç, *aw-sees'*; from 6072; *must* or fresh grape-juice (as just *trodden* out):—new wine {2x}, sweet wine {2x}, juice {1x}. See: TWOT—1660a; BDB—779b.

6072. עָסַס {1x} 'âçaç, *aw-sas'*; a prim. root; to *squeeze* out juice; fig. to *trample*:—tread down {1x}. See: TWOT—1660; BDB—779a.

6073. עֳפֶא {1x} 'ôphe›, *of-eh'*; from an unused root mean. to *cover*; a *bough* (as covering the tree):—branches {1x}. See: TWOT—1661; BDB—779b, 1107c.

6074. עֳפִי {3x} 'ŏphîy (Aram.), *of-ee'*; corresp. to 6073; a *twig*; bough, i.e. (collect.) *foliage*:—leaves {3x}. See: TWOT—2924; BDB—1107c.

6075. עָפַל {2x} 'âphal, *aw-fal'*; a prim. root; to *swell*; fig. *be elated*:—lifted up {1x}, presume {1x}. See: TWOT—1662, 1663; BDB—779b, 779c.

6076. עֹפֶל {9x} 'ôphel, *o'-fel*; from 6075; a *tumor*; also a *mound*, i.e. *fortress*:—forts {1x}, strong hold {1x}, tower {1x}, variant for emerods {6x}. See: TWOT—1662a, 1662b; BDB—779b.

6077. עֹפֶל {5x} 'Ôphel, *o'-fel*; the same as 6076; *Ophel*, a ridge in Jerusalem:—Ophel {5x}. See: TWOT—1662a; BDB—779b.

6078. עָפְנִי {1x} 'Ophnîy, *of-nee'*; from an unused noun [denoting a place in Pal.; from an unused root of uncert. mean.]; an *Ophnite* (collect.) or inhab. of Ophen:—Ophni {1x}. See: BDB—779c.

6079. עַפְעַף {10x} 'aph'aph, *af-af'*; from 5774; an *eyelash* (as *fluttering*); fig. morning *ray*:—eyelid {9x}, dawning {1x}. See: TWOT—1582b; BDB—733d, 779c.

6080. עָפַר {1x} 'âphar, *aw-far'*; a prim. root: mean. either to *be gray* or perh. rather to *pulverize*; used only as denom. from 6083, to *be dust*:—cast {1x}. See: TWOT—1664; BDB—780a.

6081. עֵפֶר {4x} 'Êpher, *ay'-fer*; prob. a var. of 6082; *gazelle; Epher*, the name of an Arabian and of two Isr.:—Epher {4x}. See: BDB—780b.

6082. עֹפֶר {5x} 'ôpher, *o'-fer*; from 6080; a *fawn* (from the *dusty* color):—young {5x}. See: TWOT—1665a; BDB—780a.

6083. עָפָר {110x} 'âphâr, *aw-fawr'*; from 6080; *dust* (as *powdered* or *gray*); hence, *clay, earth, mud*:—dust {93x}, earth {7x}, powder {3x}, rubbish {2x}, ashes {2x}, morter {2x}, ground {1x}.

'Apar means "dust; clods; plaster; ashes." **(1)** This noun represents the "porous loose earth on the ground," or "dust." **(2)** In its first biblical occurrence, *'apar* appears to mean this porous loose earth: "And the Lord God formed man of the dust of the ground, and breathed into his nostrils the breath of life" (Gen 2:7). **(3)** In Gen 13:16, the word means the "fine particles of the soil": "And I will make thy [descendants] as the dust of the earth." **(4)** In the plural, the noun can mean "dust masses" or "clods" of earth: ". . . While as yet he had not made the earth, nor the fields, nor the highest

part of the dust of the world" (Prov 8:26). **(5)** '*Apar* can signify "dry crumbled mortar or plaster": "And he shall cause the house to be scraped within round about, and they shall pour out the dust that they scrape off without the city into an unclean place" (Lev 14:41). **(6)** In Lev 14:42, the word means "wet plaster": "And they shall take other stones, and put them in the place of those stones; and he shall take other mortar, and shall plaster the house." **(7)** '*Apar* represents "finely ground material" in Deut 9:21: "And I took your sin, the calf which ye had made, and burnt it with fire, and stamped it, and ground it very small, even until it was as small as dust: and I cast the dust thereof into the brook that descended out of the mount."

(8) '*Apar* can represent the "ashes" of something that has been burned: **(8a)** "And the king commanded Hilkiah the high priest, and the priests of the second order, and the keepers of the door, to bring forth out of the temple of the Lord all the vessels that were made for Baal, and for the grove, and for all the host of heaven: and he burned them [outside] Jerusalem . . . and carried the ashes of them unto Bethel" (2 Kin 23:4). **(8a)** In a similar use, the word represents the "ashes" of a burnt offering (Num 19:17). **(9)** The "rubble" of a destroyed city sometimes is called "dust": "And Ben-hadad sent unto him, and said, The gods do so unto me, and more also, if the dust of Samaria shall suffice for handfuls for all the people that follow me" (1 Kin 20:10). **(10)** In Gen 3:14 the serpent was cursed with "dust" as his perpetual food (cf. Is 65:25; Mic 7:17). **(11)** Another nuance arising from the characteristics of dust appears in Job 28:6, where the word parallels "stones." Here the word seems to represent "the ground": "The stones of it are the place of sapphires: and it hath dust of gold."

(12) '*Apar* may be used as a symbol of a "large mass" or "superabundance" of something. This use, already cited (Gen 13:16), appears again in its fulfillment in Num 23:10: "Who can count the dust of Jacob, and the number of the fourth part of Israel?" **(13)** "Complete destruction" is represented by '*apar* in 2 Sa 22:43: "Then did I beat them as small as the dust of the earth: I did stamp them as the mire of the street." **(14)** In Ps 7:5, the word is used of "valuelessness" and "futility": "Let the enemy persecute my soul, and take it; yea, let him tread down my life upon the earth, and lay mine honor in the dust." **(15)** To experience defeat is "to lick the dust" (Ps 72:9), and **(16)** to be restored from defeat is "to shake oneself from the dust" (Is 52:2). **(17)** To throw "dust" ("dirt") at someone is a sign of shame and humiliation (2 Sa 16:13), **(18)** while

mourning is expressed by various acts of self-abasement, which may include throwing "dust" or "dirt" on one's own head (Josh 7:6). **(19)** Abraham says he is but "dust and ashes," not really important (Gen 18:27). **(20)** In Job 7:21 and similar passages, '*apar* represents "the earth" of the grave: "For now shall I sleep in the dust; and thou shalt seek me in the morning, but I shall not be." **(21)** This word is also used as a simile for a "widely scattered army": "For the king of Syria had destroyed them, and had made them like the dust by threshing" (2 Kin 13:7). See: TWOT—1664a; BDB—779c.

עֶפְרָה '**Aphrâh**. See 1036.

6084. עָפְרָה {8x} '**Ophrâh**, *of-raw'*; fem. of 6082; *female fawn; Ophrah,* the name of an Isr. and of two places in Pal.:— *Ophrah* {8x}. See: BDB—780b.

6085. עֶפְרוֹן {14x} '**Ephrôwn**, *ef-rone'*; from the same as 6081; *fawn-like; Ephron,* the name of a Canaanite and of two places in Pal.:—Ephron {13x}, Ephrain {1x}. See: BDB—780b.

עֹפֶרֶת '**ôphereth**. See 5777.

6086. עֵץ {328x} '**êts**, *ates;* from 6095; a *tree* (from its *firmness*); hence, *wood* (plur. *sticks*):—tree {162x}, wood {107x}, timber {23x}, stick {14x}, gallows {8x}, staff {4x}, stock {4x}, carpenter + 2796 {2x}, branches {1x}, helve {1x}, planks {1x}, stalks {1x}.

'*Ets* means "tree; wood; timber; stick; stalk." **(1)** In its first biblical appearance '*ets* is used as a collective noun representing all trees bearing fruit (Gen 1:11). **(2)** In Ex 9:25 the word means "tree" indiscriminately: ". . . And the hail smote every herb of the field, and brake every tree of the field." **(3)** God forbids Israel to destroy the orchards around besieged cities: "When thou shalt besiege a city a long time, in making war against it to take it, thou shalt not destroy the trees . . . : for thou mayest eat of them [literally, ". . . its tree or orchard . . . for you may eat from it . . ."]" (Deut 20:19). **(4)** This word may signify a single "tree," as it does in Gen 2:9: "The tree of life also in the midst of the garden, and the tree of knowledge of good and evil." **(5)** This word may be used of the genus "tree." So Is 41:19 lists the olive "tree" and the box "tree" in the midst of a long list of various species of trees. **(6)** '*Ets* can mean "wood." Thus, Deut 16:21: "Thou shalt not plant thee a grove of any trees near unto the altar of the LORD thy God, which thou shalt make thee."

(7) This word can represent "wood" as a material from which things are constructed, as a raw material to be carved: "And in carving of

timber, to work in all manner of workmanship"
(Ex 31:5). **(7a)** Large unprocessed pieces of
"wood or timber" are also signified by *ʿets:* "Go
up to the mountain, and bring wood [timber],
and build the house" (Hag 1:8). **(7b)** The end
product of wood already processed and fashioned into something may be indicated by *ʿets:*
"And upon whatsoever any of them, when they
are dead, doth fall, it shall be unclean; whether
it be any vessel of wood . . ." (Lev 11:32).
(8) This word means "stick" or "piece of wood"
in Eze 37:16: "Thou son of man, take thee one
stick, and write upon it." **(9)** This may also refer
to a "pole" or "gallows": "Within three days
shall Pharaoh lift up thy head from off thee,
and shall hang thee on a tree [gallows or pole]"
(Gen 40:19).

   (10) *ʿEts* once means "stalk": "But she had
brought them up to the roof of the house, and
hid them with the stalks of flax, which she had
laid in order upon the roof" (Josh 2:6). Syn.:
(A) *ʿAyil* (352) means "large, mighty tree." This
word occurs 4 times and only in poetical passages. This does not mean a particular genus
or species of tree but merely a large, mighty
tree: "For they shall be ashamed of the oaks
which ye have desired" (Is 1:29—the first biblical occurrence). **(B)** *ʿElon* (436) means "large
tree." **(B1)** This noun is probably related to *ʿayil*
(352), "large tree." *ʿElon* occurs 10 times and
only in relation to places of worship. It may
well be that these were all ancient cultic sites.
(B2) The word does not represent a particular
genus or species of tree but, like the noun to
which it is related, simply a "big tree": "And
Gaal spake again and said, See there come people down by the middle of the land, and another company come along by the plain of
Meonenim" (Judg 9:37). **(B3)** Judg 9:6 speaks
of the "plain (*ʿelon*) of the pillar" in Shechem
where the men of Shechem and Beth-millo
made Abimelech king." This is probably
stressing a lone tree on a plain. See: TWOT—
1670a; BDB—780c, 781c, 1082b.

6087. עָצַב **{17x}** ʿâtsab, *aw-tsab';* a prim.
          root; prop. to *carve,* i.e. *fabricate*
or *fashion;* hence, (in a bad sense) to *worry,*
pain or *anger:*—grieve {10x}, displeased {1x},
hurt {1x}, made {1x}, sorry {1x}, vexed {1x},
worship {1x}, wrest {1x}.

   In Jer 44:19 this word signifies the fashioning of cakes as images of the "the queen of
heaven." See: TWOT—1666, 1667; BDB—780c,
781a, 1107d.

6088. עֲצַב **{1x}** ʿătsab (Aram.), *ats-ab';* cor-
          resp. to 6087; to *afflict:*—lamenta-
ble {1x}. See: TWOT—2925; BDB—1107d.

6089. עֶצֶב **{7x}** ʿetseb, *eh'-tseb;* from 6087; an
          earthen *vessel;* usually (painful)

toil; also a *pang* (whether of body or mind):—
sorrow {3x}, labour {2x}, grievous {1x}, idol
{1x}. See: TWOT—1666a, 1667a; BDB—780d,
781a.

6090. עֹצֶב **{4x}** ʿôtseb, *o'-tseb;* a var. of 6089;
          an *idol* (as fashioned); also *pain*
(bodily or mental):—sorrow {2x}, wicked {1x},
idol {1x}. See: TWOT—1666b, 1667b; BDB—
780d, 781b.

6091. עָצָב **{17x}** ʿâtsâb, *aw-tsawb';* from
          6087; an (idolatrous) *image:*—idol
{16x}, image {1x}.

   The stress of this word is labor [see 6090,
6092]. Does this mean that worship is laborious? Scripture always teaches that true worship is not wearisome to the child of God
whereas the worship of idols is hard labor
without profit. Syn.: 205, 367, 457, 1534, 4656,
6089, 8251. See: TWOT—1667c; BDB—781b.

6092. עָצֵב **{1x}** ʿâtsêb, *aw-tsabe';* from 6087;
          a (hired) *workman:*—labours {1x}.
See: TWOT—1666c; BDB—780d.

6093. עִצָּבוֹן **{3x}** ʿitstsâbôwn, *its-tsaw-bone';*
          from 6087; *worrisomeness,* i.e.
labor or *pain:*—sorrow {2x}, toil {1x}. See:
TWOT—1666e; BDB—781a.

6094. עַצֶּבֶת **{5x}** ʿatstsebeth, *ats-tseh'-beth;*
          from 6087; an *idol;* also a *pain* or
wound:—sorrow {4x}, wounds {1x}. See:
TWOT—1666d; BDB—781a.

6095. עָצָה **{1x}** ʿâtsâh, *aw-tsaw';* a prim. root;
          prop. to *fasten* (or *make firm*), i.e.
to *close* (the eyes):—shut {1x}. See: TWOT—
1669; BDB—781b, 783b.

6096. עָצֶה **{1x}** ʿâtseh, *aw-tseh';* from 6095;
          the *spine* (as giving *firmness* to
the body):—backbone {1x}. See: TWOT—
1671a; BDB—782b.

6097. עֵצָה **{1x}** ʿêtsâh, *ay-tsaw';* fem. of 6086;
          timber:—tree {1x}. See: TWOT—
1670b; BDB—782a.

6098. עֵצָה **{88x}** ʿêtsâh, *ay-tsaw';* from 3289;
          advice; by impl. *plan;* also *pru-*
dence:—counsel {79x}, counsels {2x}, purpose
{2x}, advice {1x}, counsellors + 582 {1x}, advisement {1x}, counsel + 3289 + 8799 {1x}, counsellor + 376 {1x}. See: TWOT—887a; BDB—420a.

6099. עָצוּם **{31x}** ʿâtsûwm, *aw-tsoom';* or

          עָצֻם ʿâtsûm, *aw-tsoom';* pass. part. of
          6105; *powerful* (spec. a *paw*); by
impl. *numerous:*—strong {13x}, mighty {8x},
mightier {7x}, feeble {1x}, great {1x}, much {1x}.
See: TWOT—1673d; BDB—783a, 783b.

6100. עֶצְיוֹן גֶּבֶר {7x} ʿEtsyôwn (short.

עֶצְיוֹן ʿEtsyôn) Geber, ets-yone' gheh'-ber; from 6096 and 1397; back-bone-like of a man; Etsjon-Geber, a place on the Red Sea:—Eziongeber {4x}, Eziongaber {3x}. See: BDB—782b.

6101. עָצַל {1x} ʿâtsal, aw-tsal'; a prim. root; to lean idly, i.e. to be indolent or slack:—slothful {1x}. See: TWOT—1672; BDB—782b.

6102. עָצֵל {14x} ʿâtsêl, aw-tsale'; from 6101; indolent:—slothful {8x}, sluggard {6x}. See: TWOT—1672a; BDB—782b.

6103. עַצְלָה {2x} ʿatslâh, ats-law'; fem. of 6102; (as abstr.) indolence:—slothfulness {2x}. See: TWOT—1672b; BDB—782b.

6104. עַצְלוּת {1x} ʿatslûwth, ats-looth'; from 6101; indolence:—idleness {1x}. See: TWOT—1672c; BDB—782c.

6105. עָצַם {20x} ʿâtsam, aw-tsam'; a prim. root; to bind fast, i.e. close (the eyes); intr. to be (caus. make) powerful or numerous; denom. (from 6106) to crunch the bones:—increased {4x}, mighty {4x}, ... strong {4x}, more {2x}, broken his bones {1x}, closed {1x}, great {1x}, mightier {1x}, shutteth {1x}, stronger {1x}. See: TWOT—1673, 1674; BDB—782c, 783b.

6106. עֶצֶם {126x} ʿetsem, eh'tsem; from 6105; a bone (as strong); by extens. the body; fig. the substance, i.e. (as pron.) selfsame:—bone {104x}, selfsame {11x}, same {5x}, body {2x}, very {2x}, life {1x}, strength {1x}.

(1) This word commonly represents a human bone as one of the constituent parts of the human body: "Thou hast clothed me with skin and flesh, and hast fenced me with bones and sinews" (Job 10:11). (2) ʿEtsem used with flesh (1320) can indicate a blood relationship: "And Laban said to him, Surely thou art my bone and my flesh. And he abode with him the space of a month" (Gen 29:14). (3) In Job 2:5, used with flesh (1320), ʿetsem represents one's body: "But put forth thine hand now, and touch his bone and his flesh, and he will curse thee to thy face." (4) The plural form represents (4a) the seat of vigor or sensation: "His bones are full of the sin of his youth, which shall lie down with him in the dust" (Job 20:11; cf. 4:14), or (4b) one's whole being: "Have mercy upon me, O LORD; for I am weak: O LORD, heal me; for my bones are vexed" (Ps 6:2). (5) This word is frequently used for the bones of the dead (Num 19:16) or (6) human remains, including a mummified corpse (Gen 50:25). (7) ʿEtsem

sometimes represents animal bones (Ex 12:46). See: TWOT—1673c; BDB—782c.

6107. עֶצֶם {3x} ʿEtsem, eh'-tsem; the same as 6106; bone; Etsem, a place in Pal.:—Azem {2x}, Ezem {1x}. See: BDB—783a.

6108. עֹצֶם {3x} ʿôtsem, o'-tsem; from 6105; power; hence, body:—might {1x}, strong {1x}, substance {1x}. See: TWOT—1673a; BDB—782c.

עָצֻם ʿâtsûm. See 6099.

6109. עָצְמָה {3x} ʿotsmâh, ots-maw'; fem. of 6108; powerfulness; by extens. numerousness:—strength {2x}, abundance {1x}. See: TWOT—1673b; BDB—782c.

6110. עַצֻמָה {1x} ʿatstsûmâh, ats-tsoo-maw'; fem. of 6099; a bulwark, i.e. (fig.) argument:—strong {1x}. See: TWOT—1674b; BDB—783a, 783b.

6111. עַצְמוֹן {3x} ʿAtsmôwn, ats-mone'; or

עַצְמֹן ʿAtsmôn, ats-mone'; from 6107; bone-like; Atsmon, a place near Pal.:—Azmon {3x}. See: BDB—783b.

6112. עֵצֶן {1x} ʿÊtsen, ay'-tsen; from an unused root mean. to be sharp or strong; a spear:—Eznite {1x}. See: BDB—783b.

6113. עָצַר {46x} ʿâtsar, aw-tsar'; a prim. root; to inclose; by anal. to hold back; also to maintain, rule, assemble:—shut up {15x}, stayed {7x}, retain {3x}, detain {3x}, able {2x}, withhold {2x}, keep {2x}, prevail {1x}, recover {1x}, refrained {1x}, reign {1x}, misc. {8x}. See: TWOT—1675; BDB—783c.

6114. עֶצֶר {1x} ʿetser, eh'-tser; from 6113; restraint:—magistrate {1x}. See: TWOT—1675a; BDB—783d.

6115. עֹצֶר {3x} ʿôtser, o'-tser; from 6113; closure; also constraint:—oppression {1x}, barren {1x}, prison {1x}. See: TWOT—1675b; BDB—783d.

6116. עֲצָרָה {11x} ʿătsârâh, ats-aw-raw'; or

עֲצֶרֶת ʿătsereth, ats-eh'-reth; from 6113; an assembly, espec. on a festival or holiday:—solemn assembly {9x}, solemn meeting {1x}, assembly {1x}. See: TWOT—1675c; BDB—783d.

6117. עָקַב {5x} ʿâqab, aw-kab'; a prim. root; prop. to swell out or up; used only as denom. from 6119, to seize by the heel; fig. to circumvent (as if tripping up the heels); also to restrain (as if holding by the heel):—supplant {2x}, take by the heel {1x}, stay {1x}, utterly {1x}. See: TWOT—1676; BDB—784b.

6118. עֵקֶב {15x} ʿêqeb, ay'-keb; from 6117 in the sense of 6119; a heel, i.e. (fig.)

the *last* of anything (used adv. *for ever*); also *result,* i.e. *compensation;* and so (adv. with prep. or rel.) on *account* of:—× because {6x}, reward {3x}, end {2x}, because + 834 {1x}, by {1x}, for {1x}, if {1x}. See: TWOT—1676e; BDB—784c.

6119. עָקֵב {13x} ʿâqêb, *aw-kabe';* or (fem.)

עִקְבָה ʿiqqᵉbâh, *ik-keb-aw';* from 6117; a *heel* (as *protuberant*); hence, a *track;* fig. the *rear* (of an army):—heel {6x}, footsteps {3x}, horsehoofs {1x}, at the last {1x}, steps {1x}, liers in wait {1x}. See: TWOT—1676a; BDB—784a.

6120. עָקֵב {1x} ʿâqêb, *aw-kabe';* from 6117 in its denom. sense; a *lier in wait:*—heels {1x}. See: TWOT—1676b; BDB—784c.

6121. עָקֹב {3x} ʿâqôb, *aw-kobe';* from 6117; in the orig. sense, a *knoll* (as *swelling* up); in the denom. sense (tran.) *fraudulent* or (intr.) *tracked:*—crooked {1x}, deceitful {1x}, polluted {1x}. See: TWOT—1676c; BDB—784c.

6122. עָקְבָה {1x} ʿoqbâh, *ok-baw';* fem. of an unused form from 6117 mean. a *trick; trickery:*—subtilty {1x}. See: TWOT—1676d; BDB—784c.

6123. עָקַד {1x} ʿâqad, *aw-kad';* a prim. root; to *tie* with thongs:—bound {1x}. See: TWOT—1677; BDB—785b.

עֵקֶד ʿÊqed. See 1044.

6124. עָקֹד {7x} ʿâqôd, *aw-kode';* from 6123; *striped* (with *bands*):—ringstraked {7x}. See: TWOT—1678a; BDB—785b.

6125. עָקָה {1x} ʿâqâh, *aw-kaw';* from 5781; *constraint:*—oppression {1x}. See: TWOT—1585a; BDB—734b, 785b.

6126. עַקּוּב {8x} ʿAqqûwb, *ak-koob';* from 6117; *insidious; Akkub,* the name of five Isr.:—Akkub {8x}. See: BDB—784d.

6127. עָקַל {1x} ʿâqal, *aw-kal';* a prim. root; to *wrest:*—wrong {1x}. See: TWOT—1680; BDB—785b.

6128. עֲקַלְקַל {2x} ʿăqalqal, *ak-al-kal';* from 6127; *winding:*—byways + 5410 {1x}, crooked ways {1x}. See: TWOT—1680a; BDB—785c.

6129. עֲקַלָּתוֹן {1x} ʿăqallâthôwn, *ak-al-law-thone';* from 6127; *tortuous:*—crooked {1x}. See: TWOT—1680b; BDB—785c.

6130. עָקָן {1x} ʿÂqân, *aw-kawn';* from an unused root mean. to *twist; tortuous;* *Akan,* an Idumæan:—Akan {1x}. See: BDB—785c. comp. 3292.

6131. עָקַר {7x} ʿâqar, *aw-kar';* a prim. root; to *pluck* up (espec. by the roots);

spec. to *hamstring;* fig. to *exterminate:*—hough {4x}, pluck up {1x}, rooted up {1x}, digged down {1x}. See: TWOT—1681, 1682; BDB—785c.

6132. עֲקַר {1x} ʿăqar (Aram.), *ak-ar';* corresp. to 6131:—plucked up by the roots {1x}. See: TWOT—2926; BDB—1107d.

6133. עֵקֶר {1x} ʿêqer, *ay'-ker;* from 6131; fig. a *transplanted* person, i.e. naturalized citizen:—stock {1x}. See: TWOT—1681a; BDB—785c.

6134. עֵקֶר {1x} ʿÊqer, *ay'-ker;* the same as 6133; *Eker,* an Isr.:—Eker {1x}. See: BDB—785d.

6135. עָקָר {12x} ʿâqâr, *aw-kawr';* from 6131; *sterile* (as if *extirpated* in the generative organs):—barren {12x}. See: TWOT—1682a; BDB—785d.

6136. עִקַּר {3x} ʿiqqar (Aram.), *ik-kar';* from 6132; a *stock:*—stump {3x}. See: TWOT—2926a; BDB—1107d.

6137. עַקְרָב {6x} ʿaqrâb, *ak-rawb';* of uncert. der.; a *scorpion;* fig. a *scourge* or knotted whip:—scorpion {6x}. See: TWOT—1683; BDB—785d.

6138. עֶקְרוֹן {22x} ʿEqrôwn, *ek-rone';* from 6131; *eradication; Ekron,* a place in Pal.:—Ekron {22x}. See: BDB—785d.

6139. עֶקְרוֹנִי {2x} ʿEqrôwniy, *ek-ro-nee';* or

עֶקְרֹנִי ʿEqrôniy, *ek-ro-nee';* patrial from 6138; an *Ekronite* or inhab. of Ekron:—Ekronites {2x}. See: BDB—785d.

6140. עָקַשׁ {5x} ʿâqash, *aw-kash';* a prim. root; to *knot* or *distort;* fig. to *pervert* (act or declare perverse):—perverse {2x}, pervert {2x}, crooked {1x}. See: TWOT—1684; BDB—786a.

6141. עִקֵּשׁ {11x} ʿiqqêsh, *ik-kashe';* from 6140; *distorted;* hence, *false:*—froward {6x}, perverse {4x}, crooked {1x}. See: TWOT—1684a; BDB—786a.

6142. עִקֵּשׁ {3x} ʿÎqqêsh, *ik-kashe';* the same as 6141; *perverse; Ikkesh,* an Isr.:—Ikkesh {2x}. See: BDB—786a.

6143. עִקְּשׁוּת {2x} ʿiqqᵉshûwth, *ik-kesh-ooth';* from 6141; *perversity:*—froward {2x}. See: TWOT—1684b; BDB—786A.

עַר ʿâr. See 5892.

6144. עָר {6x} ʿÂr, *awr;* the same as 5892; a *city; Ar,* a place in Moab:—Ar {6x}. See: BDB—786a.

6145. עָר {6x} ʿâr, *awr;* from 5782; a *foe* (as *watchful* for mischief):—city {3x},

enemy {2x}, Strong's synonym {1x}. See: TWOT−1684+; BDB−786b, 1108a.

6146. עָר {1x} **'âr** (Aram.), *awr;* corresp. to 6145:−enemies {1x}. See: TWOT−2930a; BDB−1107d, 1108a.

6147. עֵר {10x} **'Êr**, *ayr;* from 5782; *watchful; Er,* the name of two Isr.:−Er {10x}. See: BDB−735c, 786b.

6148. עָרַב {22x} **'ârab**, *aw-rab';* a prim. root; to *braid,* i.e. *intermix;* tech. to *traffic* (as if by barter); also to *give* or *be security* (as a kind of exchange):−surety {9x}, meddle {2x}, mingled {2x}, pledges {2x}, becometh {1x}, engaged {1x}, intermeddle {1x}, mortgaged {1x}, occupiers {1x}, occupy {1x}, undertake {1x}. See: TWOT−1686; BDB−786c, 1107d.

6149. עָרֵב {8x} **'ârêb**, *aw-rabe'* a prim. root [rather ident. with 6148 through the idea of close *association*]; to *be agreeable:*−sweet {5x}, pleasure {1x}, pleasing {1x}, pleasant {1x}. See: TWOT−1687a; BDB−787a, 1107d.

6150. עָרַב {3x} **'ârab**, *aw-rab';* a prim. root [rather ident. with 6148 through the idea of *covering* with a texture]; to *grow dusky* at sundown:−evening {2x}, darkened {1x}. See: TWOT−1689; BDB−788a.

6151. עֲרַב {4x} **'ărab** (Aram.), *ar-ab';* corresp. to 6148; to *commingle:*−mix {3x}, mingle {1x}. See: TWOT−2927; BDB−1107d.

6152. עֲרָב {5x} **'Ărâb**, *ar-awb'* or

עֲרָב **'Ărab**, *ar-ab';* from 6150 in the fig. sense of *sterility; Arab* (i.e. *Arabia*), a country E. of Pal.:−Arabia {5x}. See: TWOT−1688a, 1688c; BDB−787a, 787b.

6153. עֶרֶב {137x} **'ereb**, *eh'-reb;* from 6150; *dusk:*−even {72x}, evening {47x}, night {4x}, mingled {2x}, people {2x}, eventide {2x}, eveningtide + 6256 {2x}, Arabia {1x}, days {1x}, even + 996 {1x}, evening + 3117 {1x}, evening + 6256 {1x}, eventide + 6256 {1x}.

'*Ereb* means "evening, night." **(1)** This word represents the time of the day immediately preceding and following the setting of the sun. **(1a)** During this period, the dove returned to Noah's ark (Gen 8:11). **(1b)** Since it was cool, women went to the wells for water in the "evening" (Gen 24:11). **(1c)** It was at "evening" that David walked around on top of his roof to refresh himself and cool off, and observed Bathsheba taking a bath (2 Sa 11:2). In its first biblical appearance, '*ereb* marks the "opening of a day": "And the evening and the morning were the first day" (Gen 1:5). **(1d)** The phrase "in the evening" [literally, "between the eve-

nings"] means the period between sunset and darkness, "twilight" (Ex 12:6; KJV, "in the evening"). **(2)** Second, in poetic use, the word can mean "night": "When I lie down, I say, When shall I arise, and the night be gone? And I am full of tossings to and fro unto the dawning of the day" (Job 7:4). See: TWOT−1689a; BDB−787d.

6154. עֵרֶב {11x} **'êreb**, *ay'-reb;* or

עֶרֶב **'ereb** (1 Kin 10:15), (with the art. pref.), *eh'-reb;* from 6148; the *web* (or transverse threads of cloth); also a *mixture,* (or *mongrel* race):−woof {9x}, mixed multitude {2x}. See: TWOT−1685a, 1685b; BDB−786b, 786c.

6155. עָרָב {5x} **'ârâb**, *aw-rawb';* from 6148; a *willow* (from the use of osiers as wattles):−willow {5x}. See: TWOT−1690b; BDB−788b.

6156. עָרֵב {2x} **'ârêb**, *aw-rabe';* from 6149; *pleasant:*−sweet {2x}. See: TWOT−1687a; BDB−787a.

6157. עָרֹב {9x} **'ârôb**, *aw-robe';* from 6148; a *mosquito* (from its *swarming*):−swarm {7x}, divers sorts of flies {2x}. See: TWOT−1685c; BDB−786c.

6158. עֹרֵב {10x} **'ôrêb**, *o-rabe';* or

עוֹרֵב **'ôwrêb**, *o-rabe';* from 6150; a *raven* (from its *dusky* hue):−raven {10x}. See: TWOT−1690a; BDB−788b.

6159. עֹרֵב {7x} **'Ôrêb**, *o-rabe';* or

עוֹרֵב **'Ôwrêb**, *o-rabe';* the same as 6158; *Oreb,* the name of a Midianite and of a cliff near the Jordan:−Oreb {7x}.

6160. עֲרָבָה {61x} **'ărâbâh**, *ar-aw-baw';* from 6150 (in the sense of *sterility*); a *desert;* espec. (with the art. pref.) the (gen.) sterile valley of the Jordan and its continuation to the Red Sea:−plain {42x}, desert {9x}, wilderness {5x}, Arabah {2x}, champaign {1x}, evenings {1x}, heavens {1x}. See: TWOT−1688d; BDB−787b. See also 1026.

6161. עֲרֻבָּה {2x} **'ărubbâh**, *ar-oob-baw';* fem. pass. part. of 6148 in the sense of a *bargain* or *exchange;* something given as *security,* i.e. (lit.) a *token* (of safety) or (met-aph.) a *bondsman:*−pledge {1x}, surety {1x}. See: TWOT−1686a; BDB−786d.

6162. עֵרָבוֹן {3x} **'ărâbôwn**, *ar-aw-bone';* from 6148 (in the sense of *exchange*); a *pawn* (given as security):−pledge {3x}. See: TWOT−1686b; BDB−786d.

6163. עַרְבִי {9x} **ʿĂrâbîy,** *ar-aw-bee';* or

עַרְבִי **ʿArbîy,** *ar-bee';* patrial from 6152; an *Arabian* or inhab. of Arab (i.e. Arabia):—Arabian {9x}. See: BDB—787b.

6164. עַרְבָתִי {2x} **ʿArbâthîy,** *ar-baw-thee';* patrial from 1026; an *Arbathite* or inhab. of (Beth-) Arabah:—Arbathite {2x}. See: BDB—112c, 787c.

6165. עָרַג {3x} **ʿârag,** *aw-rag';* a prim. root; to *long* for:—pant {2x}, cry {1x}. See: TWOT—1691; BDB—788b.

6166. עֲרָד {5x} **ʿĂrâd,** *ar-awd';* from an unused root mean. to *sequester* itself; *fugitive; Arad,* the name of a place near Pal., also of a Canaanite and an Isr.:—Arad {5x}. See: BDB—788c.

6167. עֲרָד {1x} **ʿărâd** (Aram.), *ar-awd';* corresp. to 6171; an *onager:*—wild ass {1x}. See: TWOT—2928; BDB—1107d.

6168. עָרָה {15x} **ʿârâh,** *aw-raw';* a prim. root; to *be* (caus. *make*) *bare;* hence, to *empty, pour* out, *demolish:*—uncover {3x}, discover {3x}, emptied {2x}, rase {2x}, leave destitute {1x}, make naked {1x}, poured out {1x}, poured {1x}, spreading {1x}.

ʿArah, as a verb, means "to pour out, make bare, destroy, spread oneself out." **(1)** The word means "to pour out" in Is 32:15: " Until the spirit be poured upon us from on high. . . ." **(2)** The verb implies "to make bare" in Lev 20:19: "And thou shalt not uncover the nakedness of thy mother's sister, nor of thy father's sister: for he uncovereth his near kin: they shall bear their iniquity." **(3)** ʿArah is used in the sense of "to destroy" in Is 3:17: "Therefore the Lord will smite with a scab the crown of the head of the daughters of Zion, and the Lord will discover their secret parts." **(4)** In Ps 37:35 the word means "to spread oneself out": "I have seen the wicked in great power, and spreading himself like a green bay tree." See: TWOT—1692; BDB—788c, 1107d.

6169. עָרָה {1x} **ʿârâh,** *aw-raw';* fem. from 6168; a *naked* (i.e. level) plot:—paper reeds {1x}. See: TWOT—1692a; BDB—788d.

6170. עֲרוּגָה {4x} **ʿărûwgâh,** *ar-oo-gaw';* or

עֲרֻגָה **ʿărûgâh,** *ar-oo-gaw';* fem. pass. part. of 6165; something *piled* up (as if [fig.] *raised* by mental aspiration), i.e. a *parterre:*—bed {2x}, furrow {2x}. See: TWOT—1691a; BDB—788c.

6171. עָרוֹד {1x} **ʿârôwd,** *aw-rode';* from the same as 6166; an *onager* (from his *lonesome* habits):—wild ass {1x}. See: TWOT—1693; BDB—789b, 1107d.

6172. עֶרְוָה {54x} **ʿervâh,** *er-vaw';* from 6168; *nudity,* lit. (espec. the *pudenda*) or fig. (*disgrace, blemish*):—nakedness {50x}, nakedness + 1320 {1x}, shame {1x}, unclean {1x}, uncleanness {1x}.

'Ervah, as a noun, means "nakedness; indecent thing." **(1)** Thirty-two of the 54 occurrences of this noun are in the social laws of Lev 18, 20. **(2)** This word represents the male sexual organ. In its first biblical appearance 'ervah implies shameful exposure: "And Ham, the father of Canaan, saw the nakedness of his father. . . . And Shem and Japheth took a garment, and laid it upon both their shoulders, and went backward, and covered the nakedness of their father; and their faces were backward, and they saw not their father's nakedness" (Gen 9:22–23). **(3)** This word is often used of female nakedness (the uncovered sex organs) and **(3a)** is symbolical of shame. **(3b)** In Lam 1:8 plundered, devastated Jerusalem is pictured as a woman whose nakedness is exposed. **(4)** To uncover one's nakedness is a frequent euphemism for cohabitation: "None of you shall approach to any that is near of kin to him, to uncover their nakedness: I am the Lord" (Lev 18:6).

(5) The phrase "indecent thing" represents any uncleanness in a military camp or any violation of the laws of sexual abstinence—nocturnal emission not properly cleansed, sexual cohabitation and other laws of purity (for example, excrement buried in the camp): "For the Lord thy God walketh in the midst of thy camp, to deliver thee, and to give up thine enemies before thee; therefore shall thy camp be holy: that he see no unclean thing [literally, "a matter of an indecent thing"] in thee, and turn away from thee" (Deut 23:14). **(6)** In Deut 24:1 'ervah appears to bear this emphasis on any violation of the laws of purity—if a groom is dissatisfied with his bride "because he hath found some uncleanness in her," he may divorce her. Obviously this evidence is not of previous cohabitation, since such a sin merits death (Deut 22:13ff.).

(7) The "undefended parts" or "nakedness" of a land is represented by 'ervah in Gen 42:9: "Ye are spies; to see the nakedness of the land ye are come." Syn.: Other nouns related to this word appear less often. **(A)** Ma'ar (4626), which refers to "sexual nakedness," appears in a figurative sense in Nah 3:5: "Behold, I am against thee, saith the Lord of hosts; and I will discover thy skirts upon thy face, and I will shew the nations thy nakedness, and the kingdoms thy shame." **(B)** 'Erom (6174) appears as a noun abstract in several instances. This word represents the more general idea of being without clothes, with no necessary suggestion of

shamefulness; it means the "state of being un-clothed." In Eze 16:7, 39 the word *'erom* ap-pears as "naked," but it can literally be translated as "nakedness" or one being in his "nakedness." **(C)** *Ta'ar* (8593), which occurs 13 times, means "razor" (Num 6:5), a "knife" to sharpen scribal pens (Jer 36:23), or "sword sheath" (1 Sa 17:51). **(D)** *Morah* (4177) also means "razor" (1 Sa 1:11). See also: 4626, 5903. See: TWOT—1692b; BDB—788d.

6173. עֶרְוָה {1x} **'arvâh** (Aram.), *ar-vaw';* cor-resp. to 6172; *nakedness,* i.e. (fig.) *impoverishment:*—dishonour {1x}. See: TWOT—2929; BDB—1107d.

6174. עָרוֹם {16x} **'ârôwm**, *aw-rome';* or

עָרֹם **'ârôm**, *aw-rome';* from 6191 (in its orig. sense); *nude,* either partially or totally:—naked {16x}.

'Arowm, as an adjective, means "naked." The first occurrence is in Gen 2:25: "And they were both naked, the man and his wife, and were not ashamed." Syn.: 5903. See: TWOT—1588c; BDB—736a, 790d.

6175. עָרוּם {11x} **'ârûwm**, *aw-room';* pass. part. of 6191; *cunning* (usually in a bad sense):—prudent {8x}, crafty {2x}, subtil {1x}. See: TWOT—1698c; BDB—791a.

6176. עֲרוֹעֵר {1x} **'ârôw'êr**, *ar-o-ayr';* or

עַרְעָר **'ar'âr**, *ar-awr';* from 6209 re-dupl.; a *juniper* (from its *nudity* of situation):—heath {1x}. See: TWOT—1705b, 1705c; BDB—791b, 792d.

6177. עֲרוֹעֵר {16x} **'Ârôw'êr**, *ar-o-ayr';* or

עֲרֹעֵר **'Ârô'êr**, *ar-o-ayr';* or

עַרְעוֹר **'Ar'ôwr**, *ar-ore';* the same as 6176; *nudity* of situation; *Aroër,* the name of three places in or near Pal.:—Aroer {16x}. See: BDB—791b, 792d.

6178. עָרוּץ {1x} **'ârûwts**, *aw-roots';* pass. part. of 6206; *feared,* i.e. (concr.) a *horrible* place or *chasm:*—cliff {1x}. See: TWOT—1702a; BDB—792a.

6179. עֵרִי {2x} **'Êrîy**, *ay-ree';* from 5782; *watchful; Eri,* an Isr.:—Eri {2x}. See: BDB—735c.

6180. עֵרִי {1x} **'Êrîy**, *ay-ree';* patron. of 6179; a *Erite* (collect.) or desc. of Eri:—Erites {1x}. See: BDB—735c.

6181. עֶרְיָה {6x} **'eryâh**, *er-yaw';* for 6172; *nu-dity:*—bare {4x}, naked {1x}, quite {1x}.

Another adjective, found 6 times, is *'eryah.* One appearance is in Eze 16:22: "When thou wast naked and bare. . . ." See: TWOT—1692c; BDB—789a.

6182. עֲרִיסָה {4x} **'ărîyçâh**, *ar-ee-saw';* from an unused root mean. to *commi-nute; meal:*—dough {4x}. See: TWOT—1699a; BDB—791b.

6183. עָרִיף {1x} **'ârîyph**, *aw-reef';* from 6201; the *sky* (as *drooping* at the ho-rizon):—heavens {1x}. See: TWOT—1701a; BDB—791d.

6184. עָרִיץ {20x} **'ârîyts**, *aw-reets';* from 6206; *fearful,* i.e. *powerful* or *ty-rannical:*—terrible {8x}, terrible one {5x}, op-pressor {3x}, mighty {1x}, power {1x}, strong {1x}, violent {1x}. See: TWOT—1702b; BDB—792a.

6185. עֲרִירִי {4x} **'ărîyrîy**, *ar-e-ree';* from 6209; *bare,* i.e. destitute (of chil-dren):—childless {4x}. See: TWOT—1705a; BDB—792d.

6186. עָרַךְ {75x} **'ârak**, *aw-rak';* a prim. root; to set in a *row,* i.e. *arrange,* put in *order* (in a very wide variety of applications):—array {26x}, order {21x}, prepare {5x}, expert {3x}, value {3x}, compare {2x}, direct {2x}, equal {2x}, estimate {2x}, furnish {2x}, ordained {2x}, misc. {4x}.

'Arak means "to arrange, set in order, com-pare." **(1)** The word is first found in the Old Testament in Gen 14:8: "They joined battle [lit-erally, "they arranged," referring to opposing battle lines]. . . ." It is used in this way many times in the record of the battles of Israel. **(2)** A common word in everyday life, *'arak* often re-fers to "arranging" a table: "Prepare the table, watch in the watchtower, eat, drink: arise, ye princes, and anoint the shield" (Is 21:5; cf. Eze 23:41). **(3)** The word is used several times in the Book of Job with reference to "arranging" or "setting" words "in order," **(3a)** as in an ar-gument or rebuttal (Job 32:14; 33:5; 37:19). **(3b)** In Job 13:18, Job declares: "Behold now, I have ordered my cause [literally, "I have set my judgment in order"]." **(3c)** "To arrange in order" makes it possible "to compare" one thing with another. **(4)** So, to show the superi-ority of God over the idols, the prophet asks: "To whom then will ye liken God? or what like-ness will ye compare unto him?" (Is 40:18). See: TWOT—1694; BDB—789b, 790a.

6187. עֵרֶךְ {33x} **'êrek**, *eh'rek;* from 6186; a *pile, equipment, estimate:*—esti-mation {24x}, set at {1x}, equal {1x}, set in order {1x}, price {1x}, proportion {1x}, set {1x}, suit {1x}, taxation {1x}, valuest {1x}. See: TWOT—1694a; BDB—789d.

6188. עָרֵל {2x} **'ârêl**, *aw-rale';* a prim. root; prop. to *strip;* but used only as de-nom. from 6189; to *expose* or *remove* the *pre-*

puce, whether lit. (to *go naked*) or fig. (to *refrain* from using):—count as uncircumcised {1x}, foreskin be uncovered {1x}. See: TWOT—1695; BDB—790c, 947a.

6189. עָרֵל {35x} **ʿârêl**, *aw-rale'*; from 6188; prop. *exposed*, i.e. projecting loose (as to the prepuce); used only tech. *uncircumcised* (i.e. still having the prepuce uncurtailed):—uncircumcised {34x}, uncircumcised person {1x}. See: TWOT—1695b; BDB—790c.

6190. עָרְלָה {16x} **ʿorlâh**, *or-law';* fem. of 6189; the *prepuce:*—foreskin {13x}, uncircumcised {3x}. See: TWOT—1695a; BDB—790b.

6191. עָרַם {5x} **ʿâram**, *aw-ram';* a prim. root; prop. to *be* (or *make*) *bare;* but used only in the der. sense (through the idea perh. of *smoothness*) to *be cunning* (usually in a bad sense):—subtilty {1x}, crafty {1x}, prudent {1x}, beware {1x}, very {1x}. TWOT—1698; BDB—791a.

6192. עָרַם {1x} **ʿâram**, *aw-ram'* a prim. root; to *pile* up:—gathered together {1x}. See: TWOT—1696; BDB—790d.

6193. עֹרֶם {1x} **ʿôrem**, *o'-rem;* from 6191; a *stratagem:*—craftiness {1x}. See: TWOT—1698a; BDB—791a.

עָרֹם **ʿÊrôm**. See 5903.

עָרֹם **ʿârôm**. See 6174.

6194. עָרֵם {10x} **ʿârêm** (Jer 50:26), *aw-rame';* or (fem.)

עֲרֵמָה **ʿărêmâh**, *ar-ay-maw';* from 6192; a *heap;* spec. a *sheaf:*—heap {8x}, heap of corn {1x}, sheaves {1x}. See: TWOT—1696a; BDB—790d.

6195. עָרְמָה {5x} **ʿormâh**, *or-maw';* fem. of 6193; *trickery;* or (in a good sense) *discretion:*—guile {1x}, wilily {1x}, subtilty {1x}, wisdom {1x}, prudence {1x}. See: TWOT—1698b; BDB—791a.

עֲרֵמָה **ʿârêmâh**. See 6194.

6196. עַרְמוֹן {2x} **ʿarmôwn**, *ar-mone';* prob. from 6191; the *plane* tree (from its *smooth* and shed bark):—chestnut tree {2x}. See: TWOT—1697a; BDB—790d.

6197. עֵרָן {1x} **ʿÊrân**, *ay-rawn';* prob. from 5782; *watchful; Eran*, an Isr.:—Eran {1x}. See: BDB—735d, 791b.

6198. עֵרָנִי {1x} **ʿÊrâniy**, *ay-raw-nee';* patron. from 6197; an *Eranite* or desc. (collect.) of Eran:—Eranites {1x}. See: BDB—735d, 791b.

עַרְעוֹר **ʿArʿôwr**. See 6177.

6199. עַרְעָר {2x} **ʿarʿâr**, *ar-awr';* from 6209; *naked,* i.e. (fig.) *poor:*—destitute {1x}, health {1x}. See: TWOT—1705b; BDB—791b, 792d. See also 6176.

עַרְעֵר **ʿArôʿêr**. See 6177.

6200. עֲרֹעֵרִי {1x} **ʿĂrôʿêriy**, *ar-o-ay-ree';* patron. from 6177; an *Aroërite* or inhab. of Aroër:—Aroerite {1x}. See: BDB—793a.

6201. עָרַף {2x} **ʿâraph**, *aw-raf';* a prim. root; to *droop;* hence, to *drip:*—drop {1x}, drop down {1x}. See: TWOT—1701; BDB—791c.

6202. עָרַף {6x} **ʿâraph**, *aw-raf';* a prim. root [rather ident. with 6201 through the idea of *sloping*]; prop. to *bend* downward; but used only as a denom. from 6203, to *break the neck;* hence, (fig.) to *destroy:*—break . . . neck {2x}, strike off {1x}, break down {1x}, cut off . . . neck {1x}, behead {1x}. See: TWOT—1700; BDB—791c.

6203. עֹרֶף {33x} **ʿôreph**, *o-ref';* from 6202; the *nape* or back of the neck (as *declining*); hence, the *back* generally (whether lit. or fig.):—neck {17x}, back {7x}, stiffnecked + 7186 {4x}, stiffnecked {3x}, backs + 310 {1x}, stiffnecked + 7185 {1x}. See: TWOT—1700a; BDB—791b.

6204. עָרְפָּה {2x} **ʿOrpâh**, *or-paw';* fem. of 6203; *mane; Orpah,* a Moabitess:—Orpah {2x}. See: BDB—791c.

6205. עֲרָפֶל {15x} **ʿărâphel**, *ar-aw-fel';* prob. from 6201; *gloom* (as of a *lowering* sky):—thick darkness {8x}, darkness {3x}, gross darkness {2x}, dark cloud {1x}, dark {1x}. See: TWOT—1701b; BDB—791d.

6206. עָרַץ {15x} **ʿârats**, *aw-rats';* a prim. root; to *awe* or (intr.) to *dread;* hence, to *harass:*—afraid {3x}, fear {3x}, dread {2x}, terribly {2x}, break {1x}, affrighted {1x}, oppress {1x}, prevail {1x}, terrified {1x}. See: TWOT—1702; BDB—592a, 791d.

6207. עָרַק {2x} **ʿâraq**, *aw-rak';* a prim. root; to *gnaw,* i.e. (fig.) *eat* (by hyperbole); also (part.) a *pain:*—fleeing {1x}, sinew {1x}. See: TWOT—1703; BDB—792b.

6208. עַרְקִי {2x} **ʿArqiy**, *ar-kee';* patrial from an unused name mean. a *tush;* an *Arkite* or inhab. of Erek:—Arkite {2x}. See: BDB—792b.

6209. עָרַר {4x} **ʿârar**, *aw-rar';* a prim. root; to *bare;* fig. to *demolish:*—make bare {1x}, raise up {1x}, utterly {1x}, broken {1x}. See: TWOT—1705; BDB—792c.

6210. עֶרֶשׂ {10x} ʿeres, *eh'res;* from an unused root mean. perh. to *arch;* a *couch* (prop. with a *canopy*):—bed {5x}, couch {3x}, bedstead {2x}. See: TWOT—1706a; BDB—793a.

6211. עָשׁ {12x} ʿâsh, *awsh;* from 6244; a *moth:*—moth {7x}, grass {5x}. See: TWOT—1715a, 1617, 2931; BDB—747b, 798b, 799c. See also 5906.

6211'. עֲשַׁב {33x} ʿăsab (Aram.), *as-ab';* 6212:—herb {17x}, grass {16x}. See: TWOT—1707a.

6212. עֶשֶׂב {33x} ʿeseb, *eh'seb;* from an unused root mean. to *glisten* (or *be green*); *grass* (or any tender shoot):—herb {17x}, grass {16x}. See: TWOT—1707a; BDB—793b, 1108a.

6213. עָשָׂה {2633x} ʿâsâh, *aw-saw';* a prim. root; to *do* or *make,* in the broadest sense and widest application (as follows):—do {1333x}, make {653x}, wrought {52x}, deal {52x}, commit {49x}, offer {49x}, execute {48x}, keep {48x}, shew {43x}, prepare {37x}, work {29x}, do so {21x}, perform {18x}, get {14x}, dress {13x}, maker {13x}, maintain {7x}, misc. {154x} = accomplish, advance, appoint, apt, be at, become, bear, bestow, bring forth, bruise, be busy, × certainly, have the charge of, deck, + displease, exercise, fashion, + feast, [fight-]ing man, + finish, fit, fly, follow, fulfill, furnish, gather, go about, govern, grant, great, + hinder, hold ([a feast]), × indeed, + be industrious, + journey, labour, be meet, observe, be occupied, + officer, pare, bring (come) to pass, practise, procure, provide, put, requite, × sacrifice, serve, set, × sin, spend, × surely, take, × throughly, trim, × very, + vex, be [warr-] ior, yield, use.

'Asah means "to create, do, make." I. CRE-ATION: (1) This verb, which occurs over 2,600 times in the Old Testament, is used as a synonym for "create" only about 60 times. (1a) There is nothing inherent in the word to indicate the nature of the creation involved; (1b) it is only when ʿasah is parallel to bara' that we can be sure that it implies creation. (1c) Because ʿasah describes the most common of human (and divine) activities, it is ill-suited to communicate theological meaning—except where it is used with bara' or other terms whose technical meanings are clearly established. (1d) The most instructive occurrences of ʿasah are in the early chapters of Genesis. (1d1) Gen 1:1 uses the verb bara' to introduce the Creation account, and Gen 1:7 speaks of its detailed execution: "And God made [ʿasah] the firmament. . . ." (1d2) Whether or not the firmament was made of existing material cannot be determined, since the passage uses only

ʿasah. (1d3) But it is clear that the verb expresses creation, since it is used in that context and follows the technical word bara'. The same can be said of other verses in Genesis: 1:16 (the lights of heaven); 1:25, 3:1 (the animals); 1:31; 2:2 (all his work); and 6:6 (man). (1d4) In Gen 1:26–27, however, ʿasah must mean creation from nothing, since it is used as a synonym for bara'. The text reads, "Let us make [ʿasah] man in our image, after our likeness. . . . So God created [bara'] man in his own image." (1d5) Similarly, Gen 2:4 states: "These are the generations of the heavens and of the earth when they were created [bara'], in the day that the Lord God made [ʿasah] the earth and the heavens." (1d6) Finally, Gen 5:1 equates the two as follows: "In the day that God created [bara'] man, in the likeness of God made [ʿasah] him." (1d7) The unusual juxtaposition of bara' and ʿasah in Gen 2:3 refers to the totality of creation, which God had "created" by "making." (2) It is unwarranted to overly refine the meaning of ʿasah to suggest that it means creation from something, as opposed to creation from nothing. (3) Only context can determine its special nuance. It can mean either, depending upon the situation.

II. GENERAL: ʿAshah means "to make, do, create." (1) In its primary sense this verb represents the production of various objects. (1a) This includes making images and idols: "Thou shalt not make unto thee any graven image" (Ex 20:4). (1b) The verb can mean to make something into something: "And the residue thereof he maketh a god, even his graven image" (Is 44:17). (2) In an extended use this verb means to prepare a meal, a banquet, or even an offering: "And he [Abraham] took butter, and milk, and the calf which he had dressed, and set it before them [his three guests]" (Gen 18:8). (3) In Gen 12:5 ʿashah means "to acquire" (as it often does): "And Abram took Sarai his wife, and Lot his brother's son, and all their substance that they had gathered, and the souls that they had gotten in Haran. . . ." The "souls that they had gotten" probably were slaves. (4) Used in association with "Sabbath" or the name of other holy days, this word signifies "keeping" or "celebrating": "All the congregation of Israel shall keep it [the Passover]" (Ex 12:47).

(5) In a related sense the word means "to spend" a day: "For who knoweth what is good for man in this life, all the days of his vain life which he spendeth as a shadow?" (Eccl 6:12). (6) Depending upon its object, ʿashah has several other nuances within the general concept of producing some product. (6a) For example, with the object "book" the verb means "to write": "Of making many books there is no

end" (Eccl 12:12). **(6b)** The Bible also uses this word of the process of war: "These made war with Bera king of Sodom" (Gen 14:2). **(6c)** Sometimes the word represents an action: "And Joshua made peace with them, and made a league with them . . ." (Josh 9:15). **(6d)** "To make a mourning" is to observe it: "And he [Joseph] made a mourning for his father seven days" (Gen 50:10). **(6d)** With "name" the verb means "to gain prominence and fame": "Go to, let us build us a city and a tower, whose top may reach unto heaven; and let us make us a name" (Gen 11:4). **(6e)** With the word "workmanship" the word signifies "to work": "And I have filled him with the spirit of God . . . , and in all manner of workmanship, . . . to work in gold, and in silver, and in brass" (Ex 31:3–4). **(7)** ʿAshah may represent the relationship of an individual to another in his action or behavior, in the sense of what one does. So Pharaoh asks Abram: "What is this that thou hast done unto me?" (Gen 12:18).

(8) Israel pledged: "All that the Lord hath said will we do, and be obedient" (Ex 24:7). **(9)** With the particle le the verb signifies inflicting upon another some act or behavior: "Then Abimelech called Abraham, and said unto him, What hast thou done unto us?" (Gen 20:9). **(10)** With the particle ʿim the word may mean "to show," or "to practice" something toward someone. The emphasis here is on an ongoing mutual relationship between two parties obligating them to a reciprocal act: "O Lord God of my master Abraham, I pray thee, send me good speed this day, and show kindness unto my master Abraham" (Gen 24:12). **(11)** In Gen 26:29 ʿashah appears twice in the sense "to practice toward": "That thou wilt do us no harm, as we have not touched thee, and as we have done unto thee nothing but good. . . ." **(12)** Used absolutely this verb sometimes means "to take action": "Let Pharaoh do this, and let him appoint officers over the land" (Gen 41:34). **(12a)** In the Hebrew ʿashah has no object in this passage—it is used absolutely. **(12b)** Used in this manner it may also signify "to be active": "She seeketh wool, and flax, and worketh willingly with her hands" (Prov 31:13). **(13)** In 1 Chr 28:10 the verb (used absolutely) means "to go to work," to go about doing a task: "Take heed now; for the Lord hath chosen thee to build a house for the sanctuary: be strong, and do it."

(14) This verb used of plants signifies "bringing forth." In Gen 1:11 it means "to bear" fruit: "And the fruit tree [bearing] fruit after his kind. . . ." **(15)** In another nuance this verb represents what a plant does in producing grain: "It hath no stalk: the bud shall yield no meal" (Hos 8:7). **(16)** The word signifies the production of branches, too: "It was planted in a good soil by great waters, that it might bring forth branches, and that it might bear fruit, that it might be a goodly vine" (Eze 17:8). **(17)** ʿAshah is used theologically of man's response to divine commands. **(17a)** God commanded Noah: "Make thee an ark of gopher wood" (Gen 6:14). **(17b)** Similarly Israel was commanded "to construct" a sanctuary for God (Ex 25:8). **(18)** The manipulation of the blood of the sacrifice is what the priest is to do (Lev 4:20). **(19)** The entire cultic [religious] activity is described by ʿashah: "As he hath done this day, so the Lord hath commanded to do" (Lev 8:34). **(20)** Thus in his acts a man demonstrates his inward commitment and, therefore, his relationship to God (Deut 4:13). **(21)** Doing God's commands brings life upon a man (Lev 18:5).

(22) This verb is also applied specifically to all aspects of divine acts and actions. **(22a)** In the general sense of His actions toward His people Israel, the word first occurs in Gen 12:2, where God promises "to make" Abram a great nation. **(22b)** ʿAshah is also the most general Old Testament expression for divine creating. Every aspect of this activity is described by this word: "For in six days the Lord made heaven and earth . . ." (Ex 20:11). This is its meaning in its first biblical occurrence: "And God made the firmament, and divided the waters which were under the firmament from the waters which were above the firmament . . ." (Gen 1:7). **(23)** This word is used of God's acts effecting the entire created world and individual men (Ex 20:6). **(24)** God's acts and words perfectly correspond, so that what He says He does, and what He does is what He has said (Gen 21:1; Ps 115:3). Syn.: 1254, 3335, 3559, 6466, 7069. See: TWOT—1708, 1709; BDB—793c, 796b.

6214. עֲשָׂהאֵל {18x} **ʿĂsâhʾêl**, as-aw-ale'; from 6213 and 410; God has made; Asahel, the name of four Isr.:—Asahel {18x}. See: BDB—795c.

6215. עֵשָׂו {97x} **ʿÊsâv**, ay-sawv'; appar. a form of the pass. part. of 6213 in the orig. sense of handling; rough (i.e. sensibly felt); Esau, a son of Isaac, incl. his posterity:—Esau {97x}. See: BDB—796c.

6216. עָשׁוֹק {1x} **ʿâshôwq**, aw-shoke'; from 6231; oppressive (as noun, a tyrant):—oppressor {1x}. See: TWOT—1713c; BDB—799a.

6217. עָשׁוּק {3x} **ʿâshûwq**, aw-shook'; or

עָשֻׁק **ʿâshûq**, aw-shook'; pass. part. of 6231; used in plur. masc. as abstr. tyranny:—oppression {2x}, oppressed {1x}. See: TWOT—1713d; BDB—799a.

6218. עָשׂוֹר {16x} 'âsôwr, aw-sore'; or

עָשֹׂר 'âsôr, aw-sore'; from 6235; ten; by abbrev. ten strings, and so a deca-chord:—tenth {12x}, instrument of ten strings {3x}, ten {1x}. See: TWOT—1711d; BDB—797c.

6219. עָשׂוֹת {1x} 'âshôwth, aw-shôth'; from 6245; shining, i.e. polished:—bright {1x}. See: TWOT—1716b; BDB—799d.

6220. עַשְׂוָת {1x} 'Ashvâth, ash-vawth'; for 6219; bright; Ashvath, an Isr.:—Ashvath {1x}. See: BDB—798b.

6221. עֲשִׂיאֵל {1x} 'Ăsîy'êl, as-ee-ale'; from 6213 and 410; made of God; Asiël, an Isr.:—Asiel {1x}. See: BDB—795c.

6222. עֲשָׂיָה {8x} 'Ăsâyâh, aw-saw-yaw'; from 6213 and 3050; Jah has made; Asajah, the name of three or four Isr.:—Asaiah {8x}. See: BDB—795c.

6223. עָשִׁיר {23x} 'âshîyr, aw-sheer'; from 6238; rich, whether lit. or fig. (noble):—rich {20x}, rich man {3x}. See: TWOT—1714b; BDB—799b.

6224. עֲשִׂירִי {29x} 'ăsîyrîy, as-ee-ree'; from 6235; tenth; by abb. tenth month or (fem.) part:—tenth {27x}, tenth part {2x}. See: TWOT—1711f; BDB—798a.

6225. עָשַׁן {6x} 'âshan, aw-shan'; a prim. root; to smoke, whether lit. or fig.:—smoke {5x}, angry {1x}. See: TWOT—1712; BDB—798c.

6226. עָשֵׁן {2x} 'âshên, aw-shane'; from 6225; smoky:—smoking {2x}. See: TWOT—1712b; BDB—798c.

6227. עָשָׁן {25x} 'âshân, aw-shawn'; from 6225; smoke, lit. or fig. (vapor, dust, anger):—smoke {24x}, smoking {1x}. See: TWOT—1712a; BDB—798c.

6228. עָשָׁן {4x} 'Âshân, aw-shawn'; the same as 6227; Ashan, a place in Pal.:—Ashan {4x}. See: BDB—92d, 798c.

6229. עָשַׂק {1x} 'âsaq, aw-sak'; a prim. root (ident. with 6231); to press upon, i.e. quarrel:—strove {1x}. See: TWOT—1710; BDB—796c.

6230. עֵשֶׂק {1x} 'Êseq, ay'sek; from 6229; strife:—Esek {1x}. See: BDB—796c.

6231. עָשַׁק {37x} 'âshaq, aw-shak'; a prim. root (comp. 6229); to press upon, i.e. oppress, defraud, violate, overflow:—oppress {23x}, oppressor {4x}, defraud {3x}, wrong {2x}, deceived {1x}, deceitfully gotten {1x}, oppression {1x}, drink up {1x}, violence {1x}. See: TWOT—1713; BDB—798d.

6232. עֵשֶׁק {1x} 'Êsheq, ay-shek'; from 6231; oppression; Eshek, an Isr.:—Eshek {1x}. See: BDB—799a.

6233. עֹשֶׁק {15x} 'ôsheq, o'-shek; from 6231; injury, fraud, (subj.) distress, (concr.) unjust gain:—oppression {11x}, cruelly {1x}, extortion {1x}, oppression + 6231 {1x}, thing {1x}. See: TWOT—1713a; BDB—799a.

עָשׁוּק 'âshûq. See 6217.

6234. עָשְׁקָה {1x} 'oshqâh, osh-kaw'; fem. of 6233; anguish:—oppressed {1x}. See: TWOT—1713b; BDB—799a.

6235. עֶשֶׂר {175x} 'eser, eh'ser; masc.

עֲשָׂרָה 'ăsârâh, as-aw-raw'; from 6237; ten (as an accumulation to the extent of the digits):—ten {172x}, fifteen + 2568 {1x}, seventeen + 7651 {1x}, ten times {1x}. See: TWOT—1711a; BDB—796c, 797d, 1108a.

6236. עֲשַׂר {6x} 'ăsar (Aram.), as-ar'; masc.

עֶשְׂרָה 'ăsrâh (Aram.), as-raw'; corresp. to 6235; ten:—ten {4x}, twelve + 8648 {2x}. See: TWOT—2932; BDB—1108a.

6237. עָשַׂר {9x} 'âsar, aw-sar'; a prim. root (ident. with 6238); to accumulate; but used only as denom. from 6235; to tithe, i.e. take or give a tenth:—tithe {4x}, take . . . tenth {2x}, give tenth {1x}, surely {1x}, truly {1x}. See: TWOT—1711c; BDB—797c.

6238. עָשַׁר {17x} 'âshar, aw-shar'; a prim. root; prop. to accumulate; chiefly (spec.) to grow (caus. make) rich:—be (-come, make, make self, wax) rich {13x}, enrich {3x}, richer {1x}. See: TWOT—1714; BDB—799a. See 6240.

6239. עֹשֶׁר {37x} 'ôsher, o'-sher; from 6238; wealth:—× far [richer]{1x}, riches {36x}. See: TWOT—1714a; BDB—799b.

6240. עָשָׂר {335x} 'âsâr, aw-sawr'; for 6235; ten (only in combination), i.e. teen; also (ord.) -teenth:—eleven + 259 {9x}, eleven + 6249 {6x}, eleventh + 6249 {13x}, eleventh + 259 {4x}, twelve + 8147 {106x}, twelfth + 8147 {21x}, thirteen + 7969 {13x}, thirteenth + 7969 {11x} to nineteen {152x}. See: TWOT—1711b; BDB—797a.

עָשֹׂר 'âsôr. See 6218.

6241. עִשָּׂרוֹן {28x} 'issârôwn, is-saw-rone'; or

עִשָּׂרֹן 'issârôn, is-saw-rone'; from 6235; (fractional) a tenth part:—tenth {3x}, tenth deal {25x}. See: TWOT—1711h; BDB—798a.

6242. עֶשְׂרִים {315x} 'esrîym, es-reem'; from 6235; twenty; also (ord.) twentieth:—twenty {278x}, twentieth {36x}, sixscore

+ 3967 {1x}. See: TWOT—1711e; BDB—796d, 797d.

6243. עֶשְׂרִין {1x} ʿesrîyn (Aram.), es-reen'; corresp. to 6242:—twenty {1x}. See: TWOT—2932a; BDB—1108a.

6244. עָשֵׁשׁ {3x} ʿâshêsh, aw-shaysh'; a prim. root; prob. to shrink, i.e. fail:—be consumed {3x}. See: TWOT—1715; BDB—799c.

6245. עָשַׁת {2x} ʿâshath, aw-shath'; a prim. root; prob. to be sleek, i.e. glossy; hence, (through the idea of polishing) to excogitate (as if forming in the mind):—shine {1x}, think {1x}. See: TWOT—1716, 1717; BDB—799c, 799d, 1108a.

6246. עֲשִׁת {1x} ʿǎshîth (Aram.), ash-eeth'; corresp. to 6245; to purpose:—think {1x}. See: TWOT—2933; BDB—1108a.

6247. עֶשֶׁת {1x} ʿesheth, eh'-sheth; from 6245; a fabric:—bright {1x}. See: TWOT—1716a; BDB—799d.

6248. עַשְׁתּוּת {1x} ʿashtûwth, ash-tooth'; from 6245; cogitation:—thought {1x}. See: TWOT—1717a; BDB—799d.

6249. עַשְׁתֵּי {19x} ʿashtêy, ash-tay'; appar. masc. plur. constr. of 6247 in the sense of an afterthought (used only in connection with 6240 in lieu of 259) eleven or (ord.) eleventh:—eleven + 6240 {19x}. See: TWOT—1717c; BDB—799d.

6250. עֶשְׁתֹּנָה {1x} ʿeshtônâh, esh-to-naw'; from 6245; thinking:—thought {1x}. See: TWOT—1717b; BDB—799d.

6251. עַשְׁתְּרָה {4x} ʿashtʿrâh, ash-ter-aw'; prob. from 6238; increase:—flock {4x}. See: TWOT—1718a; BDB—800b.

6252. עַשְׁתָּרוֹת {12x} ʿAshtârôwth, ash-taw-rôth'; or

עַשְׁתָּרֹת ʿAshtârôth, ash-taw-rôth'; plur. of 6251; Ashtaroth, the name of a Sidonian deity, and of a place E. of the Jordan:—Ashtaroth {11x}, Astaroth {1x}. See: BDB—800b, 902b. See also 1045, 6253, 6255.

6253. עַשְׁתֹּרֶת {3x} ʿAshtôreth, ash-to'reth; prob. for 6251; Ashtoreth, the Phœnician goddess of love (and increase):—Ashtoreth {3x}. See: TWOT—1718; BDB—800a.

6254. עַשְׁתְּרָתִי {1x} ʿAshtʿrâthîy, ash-ter-aw-thee'; patrial from 6252; an Ashterathite or inhab. of Ashtaroth:—Ashterathite {1x}. See: BDB—800c.

6255. עַשְׁתְּרֹת קַרְנַיִם {1x} ʿAshtʿrôth Qarnayim, ash-ter-ōth' kar-nah'-yim;

from 6252 and the dual of 7161; Ashtaroth of (the) double horns (a symbol of the deity); Ash-teroth-Karnâm, a place E. of the Jordan:—Ashtoreth Karnaim {1x}. See: BDB—800b.

6256. עֵת {296x} ʿêth, ayth; from 5703; time, espec. (adv. with prep.) now, when, etc.:—time {257x}, season {16x}, when {7x}, always {4x}, eveningtide + 6153 {2x}, misc. {10x} = + after, × certain, + continually, + evening, long, so [long] as.

ʿEth means "time; period of time; appointed time; proper time; season." (1) Basically this noun connotes "time" conceived as an opportunity or season. (1a) First, the word signifies an appointed, fixed, and set time or period. This is what astrologers claimed to discern: "Then the king said to the wise men, which knew the times" (Est 1:13). (1b) God alone, however, knows and reveals such "appointed times": "In the time of their visitation they shall be cast down, saith the Lord" (Jer 8:12). (2) This noun also is used of the concept "proper or appropriate time." This nuance is applied to the "time" God has appointed for one to die: "Be not over much wicked, neither be thou foolish: why shouldest thou die before thy time?" (Eccl 7:17). (2a) It is used of the "appropriate or suitable time" for a given activity in life: "He hath made every thing beautiful in his time" (Eccl 3:11; cf. Ps 104:27). (2b) Finally, the "appropriate time" for divine judgment is represented by ʿeth: "It is time for thee, Lord, to work: for they have made void thy law" (Ps 119:126).

(3) A third use connotes "season," or a regular fixed period of time such as springtime: "And he said, I will certainly return unto thee according to the time of life; and, lo, Sarah thy wife shall have a son" (Gen 18:10). (3a) Similarly, the word is used of the rainy "season" (Ezra 10:13), (3b) the harvest "time" (Jer 50:16), (3c) the migratory "period" (Jer 8:7), and (3d) the mating "season" (Gen 31:10). (4) This noun also is applied to differing "extensions of time." In its first biblical appearance, for example, ʿeth represents the "time" (period of the day) when the sun is setting: "And the dove came in to him in the evening [literally, time of the evening]" (Gen 8:11). (5) The word is used of special occasions such as the birth of a child: "Therefore will he give them up, until the time that she which travaileth hath brought forth: then the remnant of his brethren shall return unto the children of Israel" (Mic 5:3) and (6) of periods during which certain conditions persist: "And let them judge the people at all seasons: and it shall be, that every great matter they shall bring unto thee, but every small matter they shall judge: so shall it be easier for thyself, and they shall bear the

burden with thee" (Ex 18:22; cf. Dan 12:11). See: TWOT—1650b; BDB—773b, 800c.

6257. עָתַד {2x} ʿâthad, *aw-thad'*; a prim. root; to *prepare:*—make fit {1x}, be ready to become heaps {1x}. See: TWOT—1719; BDB—800c, 1108a.

עָתֻד ʿattûd. See 6260.

6258. עַתָּה {9x} ʿattâh, *at-taw'*; from 6256; at *this time*, whether adv., conjunc. or expletive:—{9x} = henceforth, now, straightway, this time, whereas. See: TWOT—1650c; BDB—773d, 800d, 1107b.

6259. עָתוּד {2x} ʿâthûwd, *aw-thood'*; pass. part. of 6257; *prepared:*—ready {1x}, treasures {1x}. See: TWOT—1719a; BDB—800c.

6260. עַתּוּד {29x} ʿattûwd, *at-tood'*; or

עַתֻּד ʿattûd, *at-tood'*; from 6257; *prepared*, i.e. *full grown*; spoken only (in plur.) of *he-goats*, or (fig.) *leaders* of the people:—chief one {1x}, (he) goat {2x}, ram {26x}. See: TWOT—1719b; BDB—800c.

6261. עִתִּי {1x} ʿittîy, *it-tee'*; from 6256; *timely:*—fit {1x}. See: TWOT—1650d; BDB—774c, 800d.

6262. עַתַּי {4x} ʿAttay, *at-tah'ee*; for 6261; *Attai*, the name of three Isr.:—Attai {4x}. See: BDB—774c, 800d.

6263. עֲתִיד {1x} ʿăthîyd (Aram.), *ath-eed'*; corresp. to 6264; *prepared:*—ready {1x}. See: TWOT—2934; BDB—1108a.

6264. עָתִיד {6x} ʿâthîyd, *aw-theed'*; from 6257; *prepared;* by impl. *skilful;* fem. plur. the *future;* also *treasure:*—things that shall come {1x}, ready {4x}, treasures {1x}. See: TWOT—1719a; BDB—800c, 1108a.

6265. עֲתָיָה {1x} ʿĂthâyâh, *ath-aw-yaw'*; from 5790 and 3050; *Jah has helped; Athajah*, an Isr.:—Athaiah {1x}. See: BDB—800d.

6266. עָתִיק {1x} ʿâthîyq, *aw-theek'*; from 6275; prop. *antique*, i.e. *venerable* or *splendid:*—durable {1x}. See: TWOT—1721c; BDB—801b.

6267. עַתִּיק {2x} ʿattîyq, *at-teek'*; from 6275; *removed*, i.e. *weaned;* also *antique:*—ancient {1x}, drawn {1x}. See: TWOT—1721d; BDB—801c, 1108a.

6268. עַתִּיק {3x} ʿattîyq (Aram.), *at-teek'*; corresp. to 6267; *venerable:*—ancient {3x}. See: TWOT—2935; BDB—810a, 1108a.

6269. עֲתָךְ {1x} ʿĂthâk, *ath-awk'*; from an unused root mean. to *sojourn; lodg-*

ing; Athak, a place in Pal.:—Athach {1x}. See: BDB—800d, 801d.

6270. עַתְלַי {1x} ʿAthlay, *ath-lah'ee*; from an unused root mean. to *compress; constringent; Athlai*, an Isr.:—Athlai {1x}. See: BDB—800d.

6271. עֲתַלְיָה {17x} ʿĂthalyâh, *ath-al-yaw'*; or

עֲתַלְיָהוּ ʿĂthalyâhûw, *ath-al-yaw'-hoo;* from the same as 6270 and 3050; *Jah has constrained; Athaljah*, the name of an Israelitess and two Isr.:—Athaliah {17x}. See: BDB—800d.

6272. עָתַם {1x} ʿâtham, *aw-tham'*; a prim. root; prob. to *glow*, i.e. (fig.) *be desolated:*—be darkened {1x}. See: TWOT—1720; BDB—801a.

6273. עָתְנִי {1x} ʿOtnîy, *oth-nee'*; from an unused root mean. to *force; forcible; Othni*, an Isr.:—Othni {1x}. See: BDB—801a.

6274. עָתְנִיאֵל {7x} ʿOthnîyʾêl, *oth-nee-ale'*; from the same as 6273 and 410; *force of God; Othniël*, an Isr.:—Othniel {7x}. See: BDB—801a.

6275. עָתַק {9x} ʿâthaq, *aw-thak'*; a prim. Root; to *remove* (intr. or tran.) fig. to *grow old;* spec. to *transcribe:*—copy out {1x}, leave off {1x}, become old {1x}, wax old {1x}, removed {5x}. See: TWOT—1721; BDB—801a, 1108a.

6276. עָתֵק {1x} ʿatheq, *aw-thake'*; from 6275; *antique*, i.e. *valued:*—durable {1x}. See: TWOT—1721b; BDB—801b.

6277. עָתָק {4x} ʿâthâq, *aw-thawk'*; from 6275 in the sense of *license; impudent:*—arrogancy {1x}, grievous things {1x}, hard things {1x}, stiff {1x}. See: TWOT—1721a; BDB—801b.

6278. עֵת קָצִין {1x} ʿÊth Qâtsîyn, *ayth kaw-tseen'*; from 6256 and 7011; *time of a judge; Eth-Katsin*, a place in Pal.:—Ittah-kazin {1x}. See: BDB—773d.

6279. עָתַר {20x} ʿâthar, *aw-thar'*; a prim. root [rather denom. from 6281]; to *burn incense* in worship, i.e. *intercede* (recip. *listen* to prayer):—intreat {18x}, pray {1x}, prayer {1x}. See: TWOT—1722; BDB—801c.

6280. עָתַר {2x} ʿâthar, *aw-thar'*; a prim. root; to *be* (caus. *make*) *abundant:*—deceitful {1x}, multiply {1x}. See: TWOT—1723; BDB—801d.

6281. עֶתֶר {2x} ʿEther, *eh'ther;* from 6280; *abundance; Ether*, a place in Pal.:—Ether {2x}. See: BDB—800d, 801d.

Hebrew

6282. עָתָר {2x} ʿâthâr, *aw-thawr'*; from 6280; *incense* (as increasing to a *volume* of smoke); hence, (from 6279) a *worshipper:*—suppliant {1x}, thick {1x}. See: TWOT—1722a, 1724a; BDB—801c, 801d.

6283. עֲתֶרֶת {1x} ʿâthereth, *ath-eh'-reth;* from 6280; *copiousness:*—abundance {1x}. See: TWOT—1723a; BDB—801d.

פ

פֹּא pôʾ. See 6311.

6284. פָּאָה {1x} pâʾâh, *paw-aw';* a prim. root; to *puff,* i.e. *blow* away:—scatter into corners {1x}. See: TWOT—1725; BDB—802a.

6285. פֵּאָה {86x} pêʾâh, *pay-aw';* fem. of 6311; prop. *mouth* in a fig. sense, i.e. *direction, region, extremity:*—corner {16x}, end {1x}, part {1x}, quarter {4x}, side {64x}. See: TWOT—1725a; BDB—802a.

6286. פָּאַר {14x} pâʾar, *paw-ar';* a prim. root; to *gleam,* i.e. (caus.) *embellish;* fig. to *boast;* also to *explain* (i.e. make clear) oneself; denom. from 6288, to *shake* a tree:—beautify {3x}, boast self {1x}, go over the boughs {1x}, glorify self {7x}, glory {1x}, vaunt self {1x}.

Pa'ar means "to glorify." One appearance of this verb is in Is 60:9: "And to the Holy One of Israel, because he hath gloried thee." See: TWOT—1726, 1727; BDB—802b, 802d.

6287. פְּאֵר {7x} pᵉʾêr, *peh-ayr';* from 6286; an *embellishment,* i.e. fancy *head-dress:*—beauty {1x}, bonnets {2x}, goodly {1x}, ornament {1x}, tire of thine head {1x}, tires {1x}. See: TWOT—1726a; BDB—802c.

6288. פְּאֹרָה {7x} pᵉʾôrâh, *peh-o-raw';* or

פֹּרָאה pôrâʾh, *po-raw';* or

פֻּרָה puʾrâh, *poo-raw';* from 6286; prop. *ornamentation,* i.e. (plur.) *foliage* (incl. the limbs) as *bright* green:—bough {2x}, branch {4x}, sprig {1x}. See: TWOT—1727a; BDB—802d, 825b.

6289. פָּארוּר {2x} pâʾrûwr, *paw-roor';* from 6286; prop. *illuminated,* i.e. a *glow;* as noun, a *flush* (of anxiety):—blackness {2x}. See: TWOT—1727b; BDB—802d.

6290. פָּארָן {11x} Pâʾrân, *paw-rawn';* from 6286; *ornamental; Paran,* a desert of Arabia:—Paran {11x}. See: TWOT—1728; BDB—803a.

6291. פַּג {1x} pag, *pag;* from an unused root mean. to *be torpid,* i.e. *crude;* an *unripe* fig:—green figs {1x}. See: TWOT—1729a; BDB—803a.

6292. פִּגּוּל {4x} piggûwl, *pig-gool';* or

פִּגֻּל piggûl, *pig-gool';* from an unused root mean. to *stink;* prop. *fetid,* i.e. (fig.) *unclean* (ceremonially):—abominable {2x}, abominable things {1x}, abomination {1x}. See: TWOT—1730a; BDB—803b.

6293. פָּגַע {46x} pâgaʿ, *paw-gah';* a prim. root; to *impinge,* by accident or violence, or (fig.) by importunity:—fall {12x}, meet {11x}, reach {7x}, intercession {4x}, intreat {2x}, entreat {1x}, misc. {9x} = come (betwixt), lay, light [upon], pray, run. See: TWOT—1731; BDB—803b.

6294. פֶּגַע {2x} pegaʿ, *peh'-gah;* from 6293; *impact* (casual):—chance {1x}, occurrent {1x}. See: TWOT—1731a; BDB—803c.

6295. פַּגְעִיאֵל {5x} Pagʿîyʾêl, *pag-ee-ale';* from 6294 and 410; *accident of God; Pagiël,* an Isr.:—Pagiel {5x}. See: BDB—803c.

6296. פָּגַר {2x} pâgar, *paw-gar';* a prim. root; to *relax,* i.e. *become exhausted:*—be faint {2x}. See: TWOT—1732; BDB—803c.

6297. פֶּגֶר {22x} peger, *peh'gher;* from 6296; a *carcase* (as *limp*), whether of man or beast; fig. an idolatrous *image:*—carcase (carcass) {14x}, corpse {2x}, dead body {6x}. Syn.: 5038. See: TWOT—1732a; BDB—803d.

6298. פָּגַשׁ {14x} pâgash, *paw-gash';* a prim. root; to *come in contact with,* whether by accident or violence; fig. to *concur:*—meet (with, together) {14x}. See: TWOT—1732a; BDB—803d.

6299. פָּדָה {59x} pâdâh, *paw-daw';* a prim. root; to *sever,* i.e. *ransom;* gen. to *release, preserve:*—redeem {48x}, deliver {5x}, ransom {2x}, rescued {1x}, misc. {3x} = ✕ at all, ✕ by any means, ✕ surely.

Padah means "to redeem, ransom." (1) *Padah* indicates that some intervening or substitutionary action effects a release from an undesirable condition. (1a) In more secular contexts, it implies a payment of some sort. (1b) But 1 Sa 14:45 indicates that money is not intrinsic in the word; Saul is determined to execute Jonathan for his involuntary transgression, but ". . . the people rescued Jonathan, that he died not." (1c) Slavery appears as a condition from which one may be "ransomed" (Ex 21:8; Lev 19:20). (2) The word is connected with the laws of the firstborn. As a reminder of slaying all the Egyptian firstborn but sparing the Israelites, God retained an eternal claim on the life of all Israelite firstborn males, both of men and of cattle. The latter were often sacrificed, "but all the firstborn of my children I redeem" (Ex 13:15). (3) God accepted the separation of the

tribe of Levi for liturgical service in lieu of all Israelite firstborn (Num 3:40ff.). However, the Israelite males still had to be "redeemed" (padah) from this service by payment of specified "redemption money" (Num 3:44–51).

(4) When God is the subject of padah, the word emphasizes His complete, sovereign freedom to liberate human beings. **(5)** Sometimes God is said to "redeem" **(5a)** individuals (Abraham, Is 29:22; David, 1 Kin 1:29; Ps 26:11; 21:5; 71:23); **(5b)** but usually Israel, the elect people, is the beneficiary. **(5c)** Sometimes the redemption or deliverance is proclaimed absolutely (2 Sa 7:23; Ps 44:26; Hos 7:13); but the subject is said to be "ransomed" from a specific oppression. **(5d)** At other times, the reference is less explicit—e.g., from "troubles" (Ps 25:22) and from "wicked" men (Jer 15:21). **(6)** Only once is padah used to describe liberation from sin or iniquity: "And he shall redeem Israel from all his iniquity" (Ps 130:8). Syn.: 1350, 1353, 3722, 6304. Syn.: 1350, 3724. See: TWOT—1734; BDB—804a, 804b.

6300. פְּדַהְאֵל {1x} Pᵉdahʾêl, ped-ah-ale'; from 6299 and 410; God has ransomed; Pedahel, an Isr.:—Pedahel {1x}. See: BDB—804b.

6301. פְּדָהצוּר {5x} Pᵉdâhtsûwr, ped-awtsoor'; from 6299 and 6697; a rock (i.e. God) has ransomed; Pedahtsur, an Isr.:—Pedahzur {5x}. See: BDB—804c.

6302. פָּדוּי {4x} pâdûwy, paw-doo'-ee; pass. part. of 6299; ransomed (and so occurring under 6299); as abstr. (in plur. masc.) a ransom:—(that are) to be (that were) redeemed {4x}. See: TWOT—1734a; BDB—804a, 804b.

6303. פָּדוֹן {2x} Pâdôwn, paw-done'; from 6299; ransom; Padon, one of the Nethinim:—Padon {2x}. See: BDB—804b.

6304. פְּדוּת {4x} pᵉdûwth, ped-ooth'; or

פְּדֻת pᵉdûth, ped-ooth'; from 6299; distinction; also deliverance:—division {1x}, redeem {1x}, redemption {2x}.

The noun related to padah (6299) is peduth. It occurs about 5 times and means "ransom or redemption": "He sent redemption unto his people: he hath commanded his covenant for ever" (Ps 111:9). See: TWOT—1734b; BDB—804b.

6305. פְּדָיָה {8x} Pᵉdâyâh, ped-aw-yaw'; or

פְּדָיָהוּ Pᵉdâyâhûw, ped-aw-yaw'-hoo; from 6299 and 3050; Jah has ransomed; Pedajah, the name of six Isr.:—Pedaiah {8x}. See: BDB—804c.

6306. פִּדְיוֹם {4x} pidyôwm, pid-yome'; or

פִּדְיֹם pidyôm, pid-yome'; also

פִּדְיוֹן pidyôwn, pid-yone'; or

פִּדְיֹן pidyôn, pid-yone'; from 6299; a ransom:—ransom {1x}, that were redeemed {1x}, redemption {2x}.

6307. פַּדָּן {11x} Paddân, pad-dawn'; from an unused root mean. to extend; a plateau; or

פַּדַּן אֲרָם Paddan ʾĂrâm, pad-dan' arawm'; from the same and 758; the table-land of Aram; Paddan or Paddan-Aram, a region of Syria:—Padan {1x}, Padan-aram {11x}. See: TWOT—1735; BDB—804c.

6308. פָּדַע {1x} pâdaʿ, paw-dah'; a prim. root; to retrieve:—deliver {1x}. See: TWOT—1736; BDB—804c.

6309. פֶּדֶר {3x} peder, peh'der; from an unused root mean. to be greasy; suet:—fat {3x}. See: TWOT—1737; BDB—804d.

פְּדָת pᵉdûth. See 6304.

6310. פֶּה {498x} peh, peh; from 6284; the mouth (as the means of blowing), whether lit. or fig. (particularly speech); spec. edge, portion or side; adv. (with prep.) according to:—mouth {340x}, commandment {37x}, edge {35x}, according {22x}, word {15x}, hole {6x}, end {3x}, appointment {2x}, portion {2x}, tenor {2x}, sentence {2x}, misc. {32x} = after, assent, collar, × eat, entry, + file, × in, mind, part, × (should) say (-ing), skirt, sound, speech, × spoken, talk, × to, + two-edged, wish.

Peh means mouth; edge; opening; entrance; collar; utterance; order; command; evidence. **(1)** The word means mouth of **(1a)** a human (Ex 4:16), **(1b)** an animal (Num 22:28), **(1c)** a bird's beak (Gen 8:11). **(2)** Figuratively, it speaks of the mouth of **(2a)** the ground (Gen 4:11), **(2b)** the grave (Ps 141:7), **(2c)** a well (Gen 29:2), **(2d)** brooks (Is 19:7), **(2e)** a sack (Gen 42:27), **(2f)** a cave (Josh 10:18), **(2g)** a city gate (Prov 8:3), **(2h)** a tunic's collar (Ex 28:32). **(3)** Peh represents the edge of a sword, perhaps in the sense of the part that consumes and/or bites (Gen 34:26). **(4)** Several noteworthy idioms employ peh: **(4a)** In Josh 9:2 "with one mouth" means "with one accord;" **(4b1)** "mouth to mouth" means person to person (Num 12:8; Jer 32:3, 4), or **(4b2)** "from end to end" (2 Kin 10:21); **(4c)** "with open mouth" emphasizes greedy consumption (Is 9:12); **(4d)** placing one's hands on one's mouth is a gesture of silence (Job 29:9); **(4e)** "to ask someone's mouth" is to ask him personally (Gen 24:57); **(4f)** "the mouth of two witnesses" means their testimony (Num

35:30); **(4g)** in Jer. 36:4 "from the mouth of Jeremiah" means "by dictation."

(5) This word can also stand for utterance or order (Gen 41:40). **(6)** *Peh* used with various prepositions has special meanings. **(6a)** Used with *ke*, it means **(6a1)** "according to" (Num 7:5), or **(6a2)** "in proportion to" (Lev 25:52), or **(6a3)** "as much as" (Ex 16:21). **(7)** When the word is preceded by *le*, it means **(7a)** "in proportion to" (Lev 25:51), **(7b)** "according to" (Jer 29:10). **(8)** With *'al* the word also means "according to" or "in proportion to" (cf. Lev 27:18). **(9)** The phrase *pi shenayim* (literally, "two mouths") has two different meanings. **(9a)** In Deut 21:17 it means "double portion" (two parts); and **(9b)** in Zec 13:8 it means "two thirds." Syn.: 6680. See: TWOT—1738; BDB—804d, 809d, 810a, 1108c.

6311. פֹּה {8x} **pôh,** *po;* or

פֹּא **pô** (Job 38:11), *po;* or

פֹּו **pow,** *po;* prob. from a prim. inseparable particle פ **p** (of demonstr. force) and 1931; *this place* (French *içi*), i.e. *here* or *hence:*—here {2x}, hither {1x}, hitherto {1x}, on this side {1x}, on that side {1x}, on the one side {1x}, on the other side {1x}. See: TWOT—1739; BDB—802a, 805d.

פֹּוא **pow.** See 375.

6312. פּוּאָה {4x} **Pûw'âh,** *poo-aw'* or

פֻּוָּה **Puvvâh,** *poov-vaw';* from 6284; a *blast;* Puäh or Puvvah, the name of two Isr.:—Puah {2x}, Pua {1x}, Phuvah {1x}. See: BDB—806a, 806d.

6313. פּוּג {4x} **pûwg,** *poog;* a prim. root; to *be sluggish:*—cease {1x}, be feeble {1x}, faint {1x}, be slacked {1x}. See: TWOT—1740; BDB—806a.

6314. פּוּגָה {1x} **pûwgâh,** *poo-gaw';* from 6313; *intermission:*—rest {1x}. See: TWOT—1740b; BDB—806b.

פֻּוָּה **Puvvâh.** See 6312.

6315. פּוּחַ {14x} **pûwach,** *poo'akh;* a prim. root; to *puff,* i.e. blow with the breath or air; hence, to *fan* (as a breeze), to *utter,* to *kindle* (a fire), to *scoff:*—blow (upon) {2x}, break {2x}, puff {2x}, bring into a snare {1x}, speak {6x}, utter {1x}. See: TWOT—1741; BDB—806b.

6316. פּוּט {7x} **Pûwt,** *poot;* of for. or.; *Put,* a son of Ham, also the name of his desc. or their region, and of a Pers. tribe:—Put {2x}, Phut {2x}, Libyan {2x}, Libya {1x}. See: BDB—806c.

6317. פּוּטִיאֵל {1x} **Pûwṭîy'êl,** *poo-tee-ale';* from an unused root (prob. mean. to

disparage) and 410; *contempt of God; Putiël,* an Isr.:—Putiel {1x}. See: BDB—806c.

6318. פּוֹטִיפַר {2x} **Pôwṭîyphar,** *po-tee-far';* of Eg. der.; *Potiphar,* an Eg.:—Potiphar {2x}. See: BDB—806c.

6319. פּוֹטִי פֶרַע {3x} **Pôwṭîy Pheraʿ,** *po-tee feh'-rah;* of Eg. der.; *Poti-Phera,* an Eg.:—Poti-pherah {3x}. See: BDB—806c.

6320. פּוּךְ {4x} **pûwk,** *pook;* from an unused root mean. to *paint; dye* (spec. *stibium* for the eyes):—fair colours {1x}, glistering {1x}, painted {1x}, painting {1x}. See: TWOT—1742; BDB—806c.

6321. פּוֹל {2x} **pôwl,** *pole;* from an unused root mean. to *be thick;* a bean (as *plump*):—beans {2x}. See: TWOT—1743; BDB—806d.

6322. פּוּל {4x} **Pûwl,** *pool;* of for. or.; *Pul,* the name of an Ass. king and of an Ethiopian tribe:—Pul {4x}. See: BDB—806d.

6323. פּוּן {1x} **pûwn,** *poon;* a prim. root mean. to *turn,* i.e. *be perplexed:*—be distracted {1x}. See: TWOT—1744; BDB—67a, 806d.

6324. פּוּנִי {1x} **Pûwnîy,** *poo-nee';* patron. from an unused name mean. a *turn;* a *Punite* (collect.) or desc. of an unknown Pun:—Punites {1x}. See: BDB—806a, 806d.

6325. פּוּנֹן {2x} **Pûwnôn,** *poo-none';* from 6323; *perplexity; Punon,* a place in the desert:—Punon {2x}. See: BDB—806d.

6326. פּוּעָה {1x} **Pûwʿâh,** *poo-aw';* from an unused root mean. to *glitter; brilliancy; Puäh,* an Israelitess:—Puah {1x}. See: BDB—806d.

6327. פּוּץ **pûwts,** *poots;* a prim. root; to *dash in pieces,* lit. or fig. (espec. to *disperse*):—scatter {48x}, scatter abroad {6x}, disperse {3x}, spread abroad {2x}, cast abroad {2x}, drive {1x}, break to pieces {1x}, shake to pieces {1x}, dash to pieces {1x}, retired {1x}.

Puwts means "to scatter, disperse, be scattered." **(1)** The word is found for the first time in Gen 10:18: "The families of the Canaanites spread abroad." **(2)** The word is used 3 times in the story of the tower of Babel (Gen 11:4, 8–9), apparently to emphasize how men and their languages "were spread" throughout the world. **(3)** *Puwts,* in the sense of "scattering," often has an almost violent connotation to it. **(3a)** Thus, when Saul defeated the Ammonites, "they which remained were scattered, so that two of them were not left together" (1 Sa 11:11). **(3b)** Such "scattering" of forces seems to have been a common thing after defeats in

battle (1 Kin 22:17; 2 Kin 25:5). **(4)** Many references are made to Israel as a people and nation "being scattered" among the nations, especially in the imagery of a scattered flock of sheep (Eze 34:5–6; Zec 13:7). **(5)** Ezekiel also promises the gathering together of this scattered flock: "I will even gather you from the people, . . . where ye have been scattered" (Eze 11:17; 20:34, 41). **(6)** In a figurative sense, this word is used to refer to lightning as arrows which God "scatters" (2 Sa 22:15). **(7)** No harvest is possible unless first the seeds "are scattered" in rows (Is 28:25). See: TWOT—1745, 1746, 1800; BDB—806d, 807b, 822d.

6328. פּוּק {2x} **pûwq,** *pook;* a prim. root; to *waver:*—stumble {1x}, move {1x}. See: TWOT—1747; BDB—807b.

6329. פּוּק {7x} **pûwq,** *pook;* a prim. root [rather ident. with 6328 through the idea of *dropping* out; comp. 5312]; to *issue,* i.e. *furnish;* caus. to *secure;* fig. to *succeed:*—afford {1x}, draw out {1x}, further {1x}, get {1x}, obtain {3x}. See: TWOT—1748; BDB—807c.

6330. פּוּקָה {1x} **pûwqâh,** *poo-kaw';* from 6328; a *stumbling-block:*—grief {1x}. See: TWOT—1747a; BDB—807c.

6331. פּוּר {3x} **pûwr,** *poor;* a prim. root; to *crush:*—break {1x}, bring to nought {1x}, ✕ utterly take {1x}. See: TWOT—1750; BDB—830b, 830c.

6332. פּוּר {8x} **Pûwr,** *poor;* also (plur.)

פּוּרִים **Pûwrîym,** *poo-reem';* or

פֻּרִים **Purîym,** *poo-reem';* from 6331; a *lot* (as by means of a *broken* piece):—Pur {3x}, Purim {5x}. See: TWOT—1749; BDB—807c.

6333. פּוּרָה {2x} **pûwrâh,** *poo-raw';* from 6331; a *wine-press* (as *crushing* the grapes):—winepress {1x}, press {1x}. See: TWOT—1750a; BDB—802d, 807d.

פּוּרִים **Pûwrîym.** See 6332.

6334. פּוֹרָתָא {1x} **Pôwrâthâʾ,** *po-raw-thaw';* of Pers. or.; *Poratha,* a son of Haman:—Poratha {1x}. See: BDB—807d.

6335. פּוּשׁ {4x} **pûwsh,** *poosh;* a prim. root; to *spread;* fig. *act proudly:*—spread {1x}, grow up {1x}, grown fat {1x}, scattered {1x}. See: TWOT—1751, 1752; BDB—807d.

6336. פּוּתִי {1x} **Pûwthîy,** *poo-thee';* patron. from an unused name mean. a *hinge;* a *Puthite* (collect.) or desc. of an unknown Puth:—Puhites {1x}. See: BDB—807d.

6337. פָּז {9x} **pâz,** *pawz;* from 6338; *pure* (gold); hence, *gold* itself (as refined):—fine {8x}, pure {1x}. See: TWOT—1753a; BDB—808a.

6338. פָּזַז {1x} **pâzaz,** *paw-zaz';* a prim. root; to *refine* (gold):—best {1x}. See: TWOT—1753; BDB—558b, 808a.

6339. פָּזַז {2x} **pâzaz,** *paw-zaz';* a prim. root [rather ident. with 6338]; to *solidify* (as if by *refining*); also to *spring* (as if *separating* the limbs):—made strong {1x}, leaping {1x}. See: TWOT—1754; BDB—808a.

6340. פָּזַר {10x} **pâzar,** *paw-zar';* a prim. root; to *scatter,* whether in enmity or bounty:—scattered {9x}, dispersed {1x}. See: TWOT—1755; BDB—808a.

6341. פַּח {27x} **pach,** *pakh;* from 6351; a (metallic) *sheet* (as *pounded* thin); also a spring *net* (as spread out like a *lamina*):—snare {22x}, gin {2x}, plate {2x}, snares + 3027 {1x}. See: TWOT—1759a, 1759b; BDB—808b, 809a.

6342. פָּחַד {25x} **pâchad,** *paw-khad';* a prim. root; to *be startled* (by a sudden alarm); hence, to *fear* in general:—fear {14x}, afraid {9x}, awe {1x}, shake {1x}. See: TWOT—1756; BDB—808b, 1108c.

6343. פַּחַד {49x} **pachad,** *pakh'-ad;* from 6342; a (sudden) *alarm* (prop. the object feared, by impl. the feeling):—fear {40x}, dread {3x}, great {2x}, terror {2x}, dreadful {1x}, greatly {1x}. See: TWOT—1756a; BDB—808b.

6344. פַּחַד {1x} **pachad,** *pakh'-ad;* the same as 6343; a *testicle* (as a cause of *shame* akin to fear):—stones {1x}. See: TWOT—1756c; BDB—808c.

6345. פַּחְדָּה {1x} **pachdâh,** *pakh-daw';* fem. of 6343; *alarm* (i.e. *awe*):—fear {1x}. See: TWOT—1756b; BDB—808c.

6346. פֶּחָה {28x} **pechâh,** *peh-khaw';* of for. or.; a *prefect* (of a city or small district):—governor {17x}, captain {9x}, deputies {2x}. Syn.: 1166, 3027, 4427, 4910, 5057, 5401, 7980, 7985, 8269. See: TWOT—1757; BDB—808d, 1108b.

6347. פֶּחָה {10x} **pechâh** (Aram.), *peh-khaw';* corresp. to 6346:—governor {6x}, captain {4x}. See: TWOT—2936; BDB—1108b.

6348. פָּחַז {2x} **pâchaz,** *paw-khaz';* a prim. root; to *bubble* up or *froth* (as boiling water), i.e. (fig.) to *be unimportant:*—light {2x}. See: TWOT—1758; BDB—808d.

6349. פַּחַז {1x} **pachaz,** *pakh'-az;* from 6348; *ebullition,* i.e. froth (fig. lust):—unstable {1x}. See: TWOT—1758a; BDB—808d.

6350. פַּחֲזוּת {1x} **pachăzûwth**, *pakh-az-ooth'*; from 6348; *frivolity:*—lightness {1x}. See: TWOT—1758b; BDB—808d.

6351. פָּחַח {1x} **pâchach**, *paw-khakh'*; a prim. root; to *batter* out; but used only as denom. from 6341, to *spread a net:*—snared {1x}. See: TWOT—1759; BDB—809a.

6352. פֶּחָם {3x} **pechâm**, *peh-khawm'*; perh. from an unused root prob. mean. to *be black;* a *coal,* whether charred or live:—coals {3x}. See: TWOT—1760a; BDB—809a, 809b.

6353. פֶּחָר {1x} **pechâr** (Aram.), *peh-khawr'*; from an unused root prob. mean. to *fashion;* a *potter:*—potter {1x}. See: TWOT—2937; BDB—1108b.

6354. פַּחַת {10x} **pachath**, *pakh'-ath;* prob. from an unused root appar. mean. to *dig;* a *pit,* espec. for catching animals:—pit {8x}, hole {1x}, snare {1x}. See: TWOT—1761a; BDB—809b.

6355. פַּחַת מוֹאָב {6x} **Pachath Môwʾâb**, *pakh'-ath mo-awb'*; from 6354 and 4124; *pit of Moäb; Pachath-Moäb,* an Isr.:—Pahathmoab {6x}. See: BDB—809b.

6356. פְּחֶתֶת {1x} **pᵉchetheth**, *pekh-eh'-theth;* from the same as 6354; a *hole* (by mildew in a garment):—fret inward {1x}. See: TWOT—1761b; BDB—809b.

6357. פִּטְדָה {4x} **pitdâh**, *pit-daw';* of for. der.; a *gem,* prob. the *topaz:*—topaz {4x}. See: TWOT—1762; BDB—809b.

6358. פָּטוּר {2x} **pâṭûwr**, *paw-toor';* pass. part. of 6362; *opened,* i.e. (as noun) a *bud:*—dismissed {1x}, shoot out {1x}. See: TWOT—1764; BDB—809c.

6359. פָּטִיר {1x} **pâṭîyr**, *paw-teer';* from 6362; *open,* i.e. *unoccupied:*—free {1x}. See: TWOT—1764; BDB—809c.

6360. פַּטִּישׁ {3x} **pattîysh**, *pat-teesh';* intens. from an unused root mean. to *pound;* a *hammer:*—hammer {3x}. See: TWOT—1763; BDB—809c.

6361. פַּטִּישׁ {2x} **pattîysh** (Aram.), *pat-teesh';* from a root corresp. to that of 6360; a *gown* (as if *hammered* out wide):—hosen {2x}. See: TWOT—2938; BDB—1108b.

6362. פָּטַר {7x} **pâṭar**, *paw-tar';* a prim. root; to *cleave* or burst through, i.e. (caus.) to *emit,* whether lit. or fig. (*gape*):—open {4x}, slip away {1x}, free {1x}, let out {1x}. See: TWOT—1764; BDB—809c, 809d.

6363. פֶּטֶר {12x} **peter**, *peh'-ter;* or

פִּטְרָה **pitrâh**, *pit-raw';* from 6362; a *fissure,* i.e. (concr.) *firstling* (as *opening* the matrix):—firstling {4x}, openeth {6x}, such as open {1x}. See: TWOT—1764a, 1764b; BDB—809d.

6364. פִּי־בֶסֶת {1x} **Pîy-Beçeth**, *pee beh'-seth;* of Eg. or.; *Pi-Beseth,* a place in Egypt:—Pi-beseth {1x}. See: BDB—809d.

6365. פִּיד {3x} **pîyd**, *peed;* from an unused root prob. mean. to *pierce;* (fig.) *misfortune:*—destruction {2x}, ruin {1x}. See: TWOT—1765a; BDB—810a.

6366. פֵּיָה {1x} **pêyâh**, *pay-aw';* or

פִּיָה **pîyâh**, *pee-yaw';* fem. of 6310; an *edge:*—two edged {1x}. See: TWOT—1738; BDB—804d.

6367. פִּי הַחִירֹת {4x} **Piy ha-Chîrôth**, *pee hah-khee-rōth';* from 6310 and the fem. plur. of a noun (from the same root as 2356), with the art. interpolated; *mouth of the gorges; Pi-ha-Chiroth,* a place in Egypt:—Pihahiroth {4x}. See: BDB—809d.

6368. פִּיחַ {2x} **pîyach**, *pee'-akh;* from 6315; a *powder* (as easily *puffed* away), i.e. *ashes* or *dust:*—ashes {2x}. See: TWOT—1741a; BDB—806b.

6369. פִּיכֹל {3x} **Pîykôl**, *pee-kole';* appar. from 6310 and 3605; *mouth of all; Picol,* a Philistine:—Phichol {3x}. See: BDB—810a.

6370. פִּילֶגֶשׁ {37x} **pîylegesh**, *pee-leh'-ghesh;* or

פִּלֶגֶשׁ **pîlegesh**, *pee-leh'-ghesh;* of uncert. der.; a *concubine;* also (masc.) a *paramour:*—concubine {35x}, concubine + 802 {1x}, paramour]. See: TWOT—1770; BDB—810a, 811b.

6371. פִּימָה {1x} **pîymâh**, *pee-maw';* prob. from an unused root mean. to *be plump; obesity:*—collops of fat {1x}. See: TWOT—1766a; BDB—802b, 810a.

6372. פִּינְחָס {25x} **Pîynᵉchâç**, *pee-nekh-aws';* appar. from 6310 and a var. of 5175; *mouth of a serpent; Pinechas,* the name of three Isr.:—Phinehas {25x}. See: BDB—810a, 819c.

6373. פִּינֹן {2x} **Pîynôn**, *pee-none';* prob. the same as 6325; *Pinon,* an Idumæan:—Pinon {2x}. See: BDB—810a.

6374. פִּיפִיָה {2x} **pîyphîyâh**, *pee-fee-yaw';* for 6366; an *edge* or *tooth:*—teeth {1x}, × two-edged {1x}. See: TWOT—1738; BDB—804d, 810a.

6375. פִּיק {1x} **pîyq**, *peek;* from 6329; a *tottering:*—smite together {1x}. See: TWOT—1747b; BDB—807c, 810a, 823a.

6376. פִּישׁוֹן {1x} **Pîyshôwn**, *pee-shone';* from 6335; *dispersive; Pishon,* a river of Eden:—Pison {1x}. See: BDB—810b.

6377. פִּיתוֹן {2x} **Pîythôwn**, *pee-thone';* prob. from the same as 6596; *expansive; Pithon,* an Isr.:—Pithon {2x}. See: BDB—810b.

6378. פַּךְ {3x} **pak**, *pak;* from 6379; a *flask* (from which a liquid may *flow*):—box {2x}, vial {1x}. See: TWOT—1767a; BDB—810b.

6379. פָּכָה {1x} **pâkâh**, *paw-kaw';* a prim. root; to *pour:*—ran out {1x}. See: TWOT—1767b; BDB—810b.

6380. פֹּכֶרֶת צְבָיִים {2x} **Pôkereth Tsᵉbâyîym**, *po-keh'-reth tseb-aw-yeem';* from the act. part. (of the same form as the first word) fem. of an unused root (mean. to *entrap*) and plur. of 6643; *trap of gazelles; Pokereth-Tsebajim,* one of the "servants of Solomon":—Pochereth of Zebaim {2x}. See: BDB—810b.

6381. פָּלָא {71x} **pâlâ**, *paw-law';* a prim. root; prop. perh. to *separate,* i.e. *distinguish* (lit. or fig.); by impl. to *be* (caus. *make) great, difficult, wonderful:*—(wondrous, marvellous . . .) work {18x}, wonders {9x}, marvellous {8x}, wonderful {8x}, . . . things {6x}, hard {5x}, wondrous {3x}, wondrously {2x}, marvellously {2x}, performing {2x}, misc. {8x} = accomplish, hidden, things too high, miracles, perform, separate, make singular.

Pala', as a verb, means "to be marvelous, be extraordinary, be beyond one's power to do, do wonderful acts." **(1)** As a denominative verb, it is based on the noun for "wonder, marvel," so it expresses the idea of doing or making a wondrous thing. **(2)** The verb is found for the first time in Gen 18:14: "Is any thing too hard for the Lord?" **(3)** *Pala'* is used primarily with God as its subject, expressing actions that are beyond the bounds of human powers or expectations. This idea is well expressed by the psalmist: "This is the Lord's doing; it is marvelous in our eyes" (Ps 118:23). **(4)** Deliverance from Egypt was the result of God's wondrous acts: "And I will stretch out my hand, and smite Egypt with all my wonders which I will do in [it]" (Ex 3:20). **(5)** Praise is constantly due God for all His wonderful deeds (Ps 9:1). **(6)** At the same time, God does not require anything of His people that is too hard for them (Deut 30:11). **(7)** Although something may appear impossible to man, it still is within God's power: "If it be marvelous in the eyes of the remnant

of this people in these days, should it also be marvelous in mine eyes? saith the Lord of hosts" (Zec 8:6). See: TWOT—1768; BDB—810c.

6382. פֶּלֶא {13x} **pele**, *peh'-leh;* from 6381; a *miracle:*—marvellous thing {1x}, wonder {8x}, wonderful {3x}, wonderfully {1x}.

Pele', as a noun, means "wonder; marvel." **(1)** This noun frequently expresses the "wonder," the extraordinary aspects, of God's dealings with His people: "Who is like unto thee, O LORD, among the gods? who is like thee, glorious in holiness, fearful in praises, doing wonders?" (Ex 15:11; cf. Ps 77:11; Is 29:14). **(2)** The messianic title, "wonderful counselor" (Is 9:6) points toward God's Anointed continuing the marvelous acts of God. See: TWOT—1768a; BDB—810b.

6383. פִּלְאִי {4x} **pilʾîy**, *pil-ee';* or

פָּלִיא **pâlîy**, *paw-lee';* from 6381; *remarkable:*—secret {1x}, wonderful {1x}, variant {2x}. See: TWOT—1768b; BDB—811a, 813a.

6384. פַּלֻּאִי {1x} **Pallûʾîy**, *pal-loo-ee';* patron. from 6396; a *Palluite* (collect.) or desc. of Pallu:—Palluites {1x}. See: BDB—811a.

פְּלָאיָה **Pᵉlâyâh**. See 6411.

פְּלָאֶסֶר **Pilʾeçer**. See 8407.

6385. פָּלַג {4x} **pâlag**, *paw-lag';* a prim. root; to *split* (lit. or fig.):—divide {4x}. See: TWOT—1769; BDB—811a, 1108b.

6386. פְּלַג {1x} **pᵉlag** (Aram.), *pel-ag';* corresp. to 6385:—divided {1x}. See: TWOT—2939; BDB—1108b.

6387. פְּלַג {1x} **pᵉlag** (Aram.), *pel-ag';* from 6386; a *half:*—dividing {1x}. See: TWOT—2939a; BDB—1108b.

6388. פֶּלֶג {10x} **peleg**, *peh'-leg;* from 6385; a *rill* (i.e. small *channel* of water, as in irrigation):—river {9x}, stream {1x}. See: TWOT—1769a; BDB—811b.

6389. פֶּלֶג {7x} **Peleg**, *peh'-leg;* the same as 6388; *earthquake; Peleg,* a son of Shem:—Peleg {7x}. See: BDB—811b.

6390. פְּלַגָּה {3x} **pᵉlaggâh**, *pel-ag-gaw';* from 6385; a *runlet,* i.e. *gully:*—division {2x}, river {1x}. See: TWOT—1769b; BDB—811b

6391. פְּלֻגָּה {1x} **pᵉluggâh**, *pel-oog-gaw';* from 6385; a *section:*—divisions {1x}. See: TWOT—1769c; BDB—811b.

Hebrew

6392. פְּלֻגָּה {1x} **peluggâh** (Aram.), *pel-oog-gaw';* corresp. to 6391:—divisions {1x}. See: TWOT—2939b; BDB—1108c.

פִּלֶגֶשׁ **pîlegesh**. See 6370.

6393. פְּלָדָה {1x} **pelâdâh**, *pel-aw-daw';* from an unused root mean. to *divide;* a *cleaver,* i.e. iron *armature* (of a chariot):—torches {1x}. See: TWOT—1771; BDB—811c.

6394. פִּלְדָּשׁ {1x} **Pildâsh**, *pil-dawsh';* of uncert. der.; *Pildash,* a relative of Abraham:—*Pildash* {1x}. See: BDB—811c.

6395. פָּלָה {7x} **pâlâh**, *paw-law';* a prim. root; to *distinguish* (lit. or fig.):—sever {2x}, separated {1x}, wonderfully {1x}, set apart {1x}, marvellous {1x}, put a difference {1x}. See: TWOT—1772; BDB—811c.

6396. פַּלּוּא {5x} **Pallûw'**, *pal-loo';* from 6395; *distinguished; Pallu,* an Isr.:—Pallu {4x}, Phallu {1x}. See: BDB—811a.

6397. פְּלוֹנִי {3x} **Pelôwnîy**, *pel-o-nee';* patron. from an unused name (from 6395) mean. *separate;* a *Pelonite* or inhab. of an unknown Palon:—Pelonite {3x}. See: BDB—812a, 813d.

6398. פָּלַח {5x} **pâlach**, *paw-lakh';* a prim. root; to *slice,* i.e. *break* open or *pierce:*—cut {1x}, shred {1x}, cleave {1x}, bring forth {1x}, strike through {1x}. See: TWOT—1773; BDB—812a.

6399. פְּלַח {10x} **pelach** (Aram.), *pel-akh';* corresp. to 6398; to *serve* or worship:—serve {9x}, ministers {1x}. See: TWOT—2940; BDB—1108c.

6400. פֶּלַח {6x} **pelach**, *peh'-lakh;* from 6398; a *slice:*—piece {6x}. See: TWOT—1773a; BDB—812a.

6401. פִּלְחָא {1x} **Pilchâ'**, *pil-khaw';* from 6400; *slicing; Pilcha,* an Isr.:—Pilcha {1x}. See: BDB—812a.

6402. פָּלְחָן {1x} **polchân** (Aram.), *pol-khawn';* from 6399; *worship:*—service {1x}. See: TWOT—2940a; BDB—1108c.

6403. פָּלַט {25x} **pâlat**, *paw-lat';* a prim. root; to *slip* out, i.e. *escape;* caus. to *deliver:*—deliver {16x}, deliverer {5x}, calveth {1x}, escape {2x}, safe {1x}. See: TWOT—1774; BDB—812b.

6404. פֶּלֶט {2x} **Pelet**, *peh'-let;* from 6403; *escape; Pelet,* the name of two Isr.:—Pelet {2x}. See: BDB—812b. See also 1046.

פָּלֵט **pâlêt**. See 6412.

6405. פַּלֵּט {5x} **pallêt**, *pal-late';* from 6403; *escape:*—deliverance {1x}, escape {4x}. See: TWOT—1774a; BDB—812c.

פְּלֵטָה **pelêtâh**. See 6413.

6406. פַּלְטִי {2x} **Paltîy**, *pal-tee';* from 6403; *delivered; Palti,* the name of two Isr.:—Palti {1x}, Phalti {1x}. See: BDB—812d.

6407. פַּלְטִי {1x} **Paltîy**, *pal-tee';* patron. from 6406; a *Paltite* or desc. of Palti:—Paltite {1x}. See: BDB—112c.

6408. פִּלְטַי {1x} **Piltay**, *pil-tah'-ee;* for 6407; *Piltai,* an Isr.:—Piltai {1x}. See: BDB—812d.

6409. פַּלְטִיאֵל {2x} **Paltîy'êl**, *pal-tee-ale';* from the same as 6404 and 410; *deliverance of God; Paltiël,* the name of two Isr.:—Paltiel {1x}, Phaltiel {1x}. See: BDB—812d.

6410. פְּלַטְיָה {5x} **Pelatyâh**, *pel-at-yaw';* or

פְּלַטְיָהוּ **Pelatyâhûw**, *pel-at-yaw'-hoo;* from 6403 and 3050; *Jah has delivered; Pelatjah,* the name of four Isr.:—Pelatiah {5x}. See: BDB—812d.

פָּלִיא **pâlîy'**. See 6383.

6411. פְּלָיָה {3x} **Pelâyâh**, *pel-aw-yaw';* or

פְּלָאיָה **Pelâ'yâh**, *pel-aw-yaw';* from 6381 and 3050; *Jah has distinguished; Pelajah,* the name of three Isr.:—Pelaiah {3x}. See: BDB—811a, 813a.

6412. פָּלִיט {21x} **pâlîyt**, *paw-leet';* or

פָּלֵיט **pâleyt**, *paw-late';* or

פָּלֵט **pâlêt**, *paw-late';* from 6403; a *refugee:*—escape {20x}, fugitive {1x}. See: TWOT—1774b, 1774c; BDB—812c.

6413. פְּלֵיטָה {28x} **peleytâh**, *pel-ay-taw';* or

פְּלֵטָה **peletâh**, *pel-ay-taw';* fem. of 6412; *deliverance;* concr. an *escaped* portion:—deliverance {5x}, escape {22x}, remnant {1x}. See: TWOT—1774d; BDB—812c.

6414. פָּלִיל {3x} **pâlîyl**, *paw-leel';* from 6419; a *magistrate:*—judge {3x} See: TWOT—1776b; BDB—813c.

6415. פְּלִילָה {1x} **pelîylâh**, *pel-ee-law';* fem. of 6414; *justice:*—judgment {1x}. See: TWOT—1776c; BDB—813d.

6416. פְּלִילִי {1x} **pelîylîy**, *pel-ee-lee';* from 6414; *judicial:*—judge {1x}. See: TWOT—1776d; BDB—813d.

6417. פְּלִילִיָה {1x} **pelîylîyâh** *pel-ee-lee-yaw';* fem. of 6416; *judicature:*—judgment {1x}. See: TWOT—1776e; BDB—813d.

6418. פֶּלֶךְ {10x} **pelek**, *peh'-lek;* from an unused root mean. to *be round;* a *circuit* (i.e. *district*); also a *spindle* (as *whirled*); hence, a *crutch:* — distaff {1x}, staff {1x}, part {8x}. See: TWOT — 1775a; BDB — 813a.

6419. פָּלַל {84x} **pâlal**, *paw-lal';* a prim. root; to *judge* (officially or mentally); by extens. to *intercede, pray:* — pray {74x}, made {3x}, judge {2x}, intreat {1x}, judgment {1x}, prayer {1x}, supplication {1x}, thought {1x}.

Palal, as a verb, means "to pray, intervene, mediate, judge." **(1)** The word is used 4 times in the intensive verbal form; the remaining 80 times are found in the reflexive or reciprocal form, in which the action generally points back to the subject. **(1a)** In the intensive form *palal* expresses the idea of "to mediate, to come between two parties," always between human beings. **(1b)** Thus, "If one man sins against another, the judge shall judge him: but if a man sins against the LORD, who shall intreat for him?" (1 Sa 2:25). **(1c)** "To mediate" requires "making a judgment," as in Eze 16:52: "Thou also, which hast judged thy sisters. . . ." **(1d)** In the remaining 2 references in which the intensive form is used, *palal* expresses **(1d1)** "having thought" in Gen 48:11: "And Israel said unto Joseph, I had not thought [*palal*] to see thy face: and, lo, God hath shewed me also thy seed." and **(1d2)** "coming between/executing judgment for another" in Ps 106:30: "Then stood up Phinehas, and executed judgment [*palal*]: and so the plague was stayed."

(2) The reflexive/reciprocal form: The first occurrence of *palal* in the Old Testament is in Gen 20:7, where the reflexive or reciprocal form of the verb expresses the idea of "interceding for, prayer in behalf of": "He shall pray for thee. . . ." Such intercessory praying is frequent in the Old Testament: **(2a)** Moses "prays" for the people's deliverance from the fiery serpents (Num 21:7); **(2b)** he "prays" for Aaron (Deut 9:20); and **(2c)** Samuel "intercedes" continually for Israel (1 Sa 12:23). **(3)** Prayer is directed not only toward Yahweh but toward pagan idols as well (Is 44:17). **(4)** Sometimes prayer is made to Yahweh that He would act against an enemy: "That which thou hast prayed to me against Sennacherib king of Assyria I have heard" (2 Kin 19:20). **(5)** Just why this verb form is used to express the act of praying is not completely clear. **(5a)** Since this verb form points back to the subject, in a reflexive sense, perhaps it emphasizes the part which the person praying has in his prayers. **(5b)** Also, since the verb form can have a reciprocal meaning between subject and object, it may emphasize the fact that prayer is basically communication, which always has to be two-way in order to be real. **(6)** Prayer is directed also toward pagan idols (Is 44:17). Syn.: 1777, 6279, 6739, 7592, 8199, 8605. See: TWOT — 1776; BDB — 813a.

6420. פָּלָל {1x} **Pâlâl**, *paw-lawl';* from 6419; *judge; Palal,* an Isr.: — *Palal* {1x}. See: BDB — 813c.

6421. פְּלַלְיָה {1x} **Pᵉlalyâh**, *pel-al-yaw';* from 6419 and 3050; *Jah has judged; Pelaljah,* an Isr.: — *Pelaliah* {1x}. See: BDB — 813d.

6422. פַּלְמוֹנִי {1x} **palmôwnîy**, *pal-mo-nee';* prob. for 6423; a *certain* one, i.e. *so-and-so:* — certain {1x}. See: TWOT — 1772a; BDB — 812a, 813d.

פִּלְנְאֶסֶר **Pilnᵉᵉçer**. See 8407.

6423. פְּלֹנִי {3x} **pᵉlônîy**, *pel-o-nee';* from 6395; *such* a one, i.e. a specified *person:* — such {3x}. See: TWOT — 1772a; BDB — 811d.

פִּלְנֶסֶר **Pilneçer**. See 8407.

6424. פָּלַס **pâlaç**, *paw-las';* a prim. root; prop. to *roll* flat, i.e. *prepare* (a road); also to *revolve,* i.e. *weigh* (mentally): — made {1x}, ponder {3x}, weigh {2x}. See: TWOT — 1777; BDB — 814a, 814b.

6425. פֶּלֶס {2x} **peleç**, *peh'-les;* from 6424; a *balance:* — scales {1x}, weight {1x}. See: TWOT — 1777a; BDB — 813d.

פִּלֶסֶר **Pᵉleçer**. See 8407.

6426. פָּלַץ {1x} **pâlats**, *paw-lats';* a prim. root; prop. perh. to *rend,* i.e. (by impl.) to *quiver:* — tremble {1x}. See: TWOT — 1778; BDB — 814a.

6427. פַּלָּצוּת {4x} **pallâtsûwth**, *pal-law-tsooth';* from 6426; *affright:* — fearfulness {1x}, horror {2x}, trembling {1x}. See: TWOT — 1778a; BDB — 814a.

6428. פָּלַשׁ {5x} **pâlash**, *paw-lash';* a prim. root; to *roll* (in dust): — roll {2x}, wallow {3x}. See: TWOT — 1779; BDB — 814b.

6429. פְּלֶשֶׁת {8x} **Pᵉlesheth**, *pel-eh'-sheth;* from 6428; *rolling,* i.e. *migratory; Pelesheth,* a region of Syria: — Palestina {3x}, Palestine {1x}, Philistia {3x}, Philistines {1x}. See: BDB — 814b.

6430. פְּלִשְׁתִּי {288x} **Pᵉlishtîy**, *pel-ish-tee';* patrial from 6429; a *Pelishtite* or inhab. of Pelesheth: — Philistine {287x}, Philistim {1x}. See: BDB — 814b.

6431. פֶּלֶת {2x} **Peleth**, *peh'-leth;* from an unused root mean. to *flee; swiftness; Peleth,* the name of two Isr.: — *Peleth* {2x}. See: BDB — 814c.

6432. פְּלֵתִי {7x} **Pᵉlêthîy**, *pel-ay-thee';* from the same form as 6431; a *courier* (collect.) or official *messenger:*—Pelethites {7x}. See: BDB—814c.

6433. פֻּם {6x} **pûm** (Aram.), *poom;* prob. for 6310; the *mouth* (lit. or fig.):—mouth {6x}. See: TWOT—2941; BDB—1108c.

6434. פֵּן {2x} **pên**, *pane;* from an unused root mean. to *turn;* an *angle* (of a street or wall):—corner {2x}. See: TWOT—1783a; BDB—819c.

6435. פֵּן {4x} **pên**, *pane;* from 6437; prop. *removal;* used only (in the constr.) adv. as conjunc. *lest:*—(lest) (peradventure), that . . . not {4x}. See: TWOT—1780; BDB—814c.

6436. פַּנַּג {1x} **Pannag**, *pan-nag';* of uncert. der.; prob. *pastry:*—Pannag {1x}. See: TWOT—1781;BDB—815a.

6437. פָּנָה {135x} **pânâh**, *paw-naw';* a prim. root; to *turn;* by impl. to *face,* i.e. *appear, look,* etc.:—turn {53x}, look {42x}, prepare {6x}, regard {4x}, respect {4x}, look back {4x}, turn away {2x}, turn back {2x}, misc. {16x} = appear, at [even-] tide, behold, cast out, come on, × corner, dawning, empty, go away, lie, mark, pass away, × right [early].

Panah, as a verb, means "to turn towards, turn back, turn around, attach to, pass away, make clear." **(1)** Most occurrences of this verb carry the sense "to turn in another direction"; this is a verb of either physical or mental motion. **(1a)** Used of physical motion, the word signifies turning so as to move in another direction: "Ye have compassed this mountain long enough: turn you northward" (Deut 2:3). **(1b)** *Panah* can also mean to turn so as to face or look at something or someone: "And it came to pass, as Aaron spake unto the whole congregation of the children of Israel, that they looked toward the wilderness" (Ex 16:10). **(2)** "Turning toward" something may also signify looking at, or seeing it: "Remember thy servants, Abraham, Isaac, and Jacob; look not unto [do not see] the stubbornness of this people, nor to their wickedness, nor to their sin" (Deut 9:27). **(3)** A further extension in meaning is seen in Hag 1:9, where *panah* means "to look for," or to expect: "Ye looked for much, and, lo, it came to little." **(4)** Another focus of meaning is "to turn back" so as to see. This is found in Josh 8:20: "And when the men of Ai looked behind them, they saw, and, behold, the smoke of the city ascended up to heaven, and they had no power to flee this way or that way: and the people that fled to the wilderness turned back upon the pursuers." **(5)** In other passages the verb means "to turn around," in the sense of to look in every

direction. So Moses "looked this way and that way, and when he saw there was no man, he slew the Egyptian, and hid him in the sand" (Ex 2:12). **(6)** In the sense of "to turn around" *panah* is used of changing one's direction so as to leave the scene. So "the men turned their faces from thence, and went toward Sodom" (Gen 18:22—the first biblical occurrence of the verb). **(7)** Used of intellectual and spiritual turning, this verb signifies attaching oneself to something. God commanded Israel: "Turn ye not unto idols, nor make to yourselves molten gods" (Lev 19:4); they should not shift their attention to and attach themselves to idols. In an even stronger use this verb represents dependence on someone: "Which bringeth their iniquity to remembrance, when they shall look after [depend on] them . . ." (Eze 29:16). **(8)** "To turn towards" sometimes means to pay attention to someone. Job tells his friends: "Now . . . look upon me; for it is evident unto you if I lie" (Job 6:28).

(9) In a still different emphasis the word connotes the "passing away" of something, such as the turning away of a day: "And Isaac went out to meditate in the field at the eventide"—he went out "at the turning of the evening" (Gen 24:63). **(9a)** Similarly the Bible speaks of the dawn as the "turning of the morning" (Ex 14:27). **(9b)** The "turning of the day" is the end of the day (Jer 6:4). **(10)** Used in a military context, *panah* can signify giving up fighting or fleeing before one's enemies. Because of Achan's sin the Lord was not with Israel at the battle of Ai: "Therefore the children of Israel could not stand before their enemies, but turned their backs before their enemies, because they were accursed" (Josh 7:12). **(11)** In the intensive stem the verb means "to remove," to take away: "The Lord hath taken away thy judgments, he hath cast out thine enemy" (Zeph 3:15). **(12)** "To clear a house" (to set things in order) is often the means by which conditions are prepared for guests: "Come in, thou blessed of the Lord; wherefore standest thou without? for I have prepared the house" (Gen 24:31). **(13)** Another nuance is "to prepare" a road for a victory march; Isaiah says: "Prepare ye the way of the Lord, make straight in the desert a highway for our God" (Is 40:3; cf. Mt 3:3). See: TWOT—1782; BDB—806d, 815a.

פָּנֶה **pâneh**. See 6440.

6438. פִּנָּה {28x} **pinnâh**, *pin-naw';* fem. of 6434; an *angle;* by impl. a *pinnacle;* fig. a *chieftain:*—bulwarks {1x}, chief {2x}, corner {22x}, stay {1x}, towers {2x}.

Pinnah, as a noun, means "corner." **(1)** The word refers to "corners" in Ex 27:2: "And thou

shalt make the horns of it upon the four corners thereof." (2) In 2 Kin 14:13 the word refers to a corner-tower, and (3) in Judg 20:2 *pinnah* is used figuratively of a "chief" as the "corner" or defense of the people. See: TWOT—1783a; BDB—806d, 819c.

6439. פְּנוּאֵל {9x} **Pᵉnûwʾêl**, *pen-oo-ale';* or (more prop.)

פְּנִיאֵל **Pᵉnîyʾêl**, *pen-ee-ale';* from 6437 and 410; *face of God; Penuël* or *Peniël,* a place E. of Jordan; also (as Penuel) the name of two Isr.:—Peniel {1x}, Penuel {8x}. See: BDB—819c.

פְּנִי **pânîy**. See 6443.

6440. פָּנִים {2109x} **pânîym**, *paw-neem';* plur. (but always as sing.) of an un-used noun.

פָּנֶה **pâneh**, *paw-neh';* from 6437]; the *face* (as the part that *turns*); used in a great variety of applications (lit. and fig.); also (with prep. pref.) as a prep. (*before,* etc.):—before {1137x}, face {390x}, presence {76}, because {67x}, sight {40x}, countenance {30x}, from {27x}, person {21x}, upon {20x}, of {20x}, . . . me {18x}, against {17x}, . . . him {16x}, open {13x}, for {13x}, toward {9x}, misc. {195x} = + accept, a- fore (-time), anger, × as (long as), at, + battle, + beseech, edge, + employ, endure, + enquire, favour, fear of, forefront (-part), form (-er time, -ward), front, heaviness, + honourable, + impudent, + in, it, look [-eth] (-s), + meet, × more than, mouth, off, (of) old (time), × on, + out of, over against, the partial, + please, propect, was purposed, by reason, of, + regard, right forth, + serve, × shewbread, state, straight, + street, × thee, × them (-selves), through (+ -out), till, time (-s) past, unto, upside (+ down), with (-in, + -stand), × ye, × you. *Paniym* means "face." (1) This noun appears in biblical Hebrew about 2,100 times and in all periods, except when it occurs with the names of persons and places, it always appears in the plural. (2) In its most basic meaning, this noun refers to the "face" of something. (2a) First, it refers to the "face" of a human being: "And Abram fell on his face: and God talked with him" (Gen 17:3). (2b) In a more specific application, the word represents the look on one's face, or one's "countenance": "And Cain was very [angry], and his countenance fell" (Gen 4:5). (3) To pay something to someone's "face" is to pay it to him personally (Deut 7:10); in such contexts, the word connotes the person himself. (4) *Paniym* can also be used of the surface or visible side of a thing, as in Gen 1:2: "The Spirit of God moved upon the face of the waters." (5) In other contexts, the word represents the "front side" of some-

thing: "And thou shalt couple five curtains by themselves, and six curtains by themselves and shalt double the sixth curtain in the forefront of the tabernacle" (Ex 26:9). (6) When applied to time, the word (preceded by the preposition *le*) means "formerly": "The Horim also dwelt in Seir [formerly] . . . (Deut 2:12). (7) This noun is sometimes used anthropomorphically of God; the Bible speaks of God as though He had a "face": "For therefore I have seen thy face, as though I had seen the face of God" (Gen 33:10). (7a) The Bible clearly teaches that God is a spiritual being and ought not to be depicted by an image or any likeness whatever (Ex 20:4). (7b) Therefore, there was no image or likeness of God in the innermost sanctuary—only the ark of the covenant was there, and God spoke from above it (Ex 25:22). (8) The word *paniym,* then, is used to identify the bread that was kept in the holy place, "the shewbread" (Num 4:7). This bread was always kept in the presence of God. Syn.: 977, 5375, 7521. See: TWOT—1782a; BDB—542b, 815d, 819d, 819c.

6441. פְּנִימָה {14x} **pᵉnîymâh**, *pen-ee'-maw;* from 6440 with directive enclitic; *faceward,* i.e. *indoors:*—within {10x}, inward {2x}, in {1x}, inner part {1x}.

Peniymah, as an adverb, means "within." One appearance is in 1 Kin 6:18: "And the cedar of the house within was carved with knobs and open flowers." Here the word refers to the inside of the house. See: TWOT—1782c; BDB—542b, 819b.

6442. פְּנִימִי {32x} **pᵉnîymîy**, *pen-ee-mee';* from 6440; *interior:*—inner {30x}, inward {1x}, within {1x}.

Peniymiy, as an adjective, means "inner." This adjective occurs 32 times and it refers to a part of a building, usually a temple. One occurrence is in 1 Kin 6:27: "And he set the cherubim within the inner house." See: TWOT—1782d; BDB—819b.

6443. פָּנִין {6x} **pânîyn**, *paw-neen';* or

פְּנִי **pânîy**, *paw-nee';* from the same as 6434; prob. a *pearl* (as *round*):—rubies {6x}. See: TWOT—1783b; BDB—819c.

6444. פְּנִנָּה {3x} **Pᵉninnâh**, *pen-in-naw';* prob. fem. from 6443 contr.; *Peninnah,* an Israelitess:—Peninnah {3x}. See: BDB—819d.

6445. פָּנַק {1x} **pânaq**, *paw-nak';* a prim. root; to *enervate:*—delicately bring up {1x}. See: TWOT—1784; BDB—819d.

6446. פַּס {5x} **paç**, *pas;* from 6461; prop. the *palm* (of the hand) or *sole* (of the foot) [comp. 6447]; by impl. (plur.) a *long and*

sleeved tunic (perh. simply a *wide* one; from the orig. sense of the root, i.e. of *many breadths*):—colours {5x}. See: TWOT—1789a; BDB—819d, 821a, 1108d.

6447. פַּס {2x} **paç** (Aram.), *pas;* from a root corresp. to 6461; the *palm* (of the hand, as being *spread* out):—part {2x}. See: TWOT—2942; BDB—1108c, 1108d.

6448. פָּסַג {1x} **pâçag**, *paw-sag';* a prim. root; to *cut up*, i.e. (fig.) *contemplate:*—consider {1x}. See: TWOT—1785; BDB—819d.

6449. פִּסְגָּה {5x} **Piçgâh**, *pis-gaw';* from 6448; a *cleft; Pisgah*, a mountain E. of Jordan:—Pisgah {5x}. See: BDB—820a.

6450. פַּס דַּמִּים {1x} **Paç Dammîym**, *pas dam-meem';* from 6446 and the plur. of 1818; *palm* (i.e. *dell*) *of bloodshed; Pas-Dammim*, a place in Pal.:—Pasdammim {1x}. See: BDB—67c. comp. 658.

6451. פִּסָּה {1x} **piççâh**, *pis-saw';* from 6461; *expansion*, i.e. *abundance:*—handful {1x}. See: TWOT—1789b; BDB—820a, 821a.

6452. פָּסַח {7x} **pâcach**, *paw-sakh';* a prim. root; to *hop*, i.e. (fig.) *skip* over (or *spare*); by impl. to *hesitate;* also (lit.) to *limp*, to *dance:*—pass over {4x}, halt {1x}, become lame {1x}, leap {1x}. See: TWOT—1786, 1787; BDB—820a, 820c.

6453. פֶּסַח {49x} **Peçach**, *peh'-sakh;* from 6452; a *pretermission*, i.e. *exemption;* used only tech. of the Jewish *Passover* (the festival or the victim):—Passover {46x}, passover offerings {3x}. See: TWOT—1786a; BDB—820a.

6454. פָּסֵחַ {4x} **Pâçêach**, *paw-say'-akh;* from 6452; *limping; Paseäch*, the name of two Isr.:—Paseah {3x}, Phaseah {1x}. See: BDB—820c.

6455. פִּסֵּחַ {14x} **piççêach**, *pis-say'-akh;* from 6452; *lame:*—lame {14x}. See: TWOT—1787a; BDB—820c.

6456. פְּסִיל {23x} **pᵉçîyl**, *pes-eel';* from 6458; an *idol:*—graven images {18x}, carved images {3x}, quarries {2x}. See: TWOT—1788b; BDB—820d.

6457. פָּסַךְ {1x} **Pâçak**, *paw-sak';* from an unused root mean. to *divide; divider; Pasak*, an Isr.:—Pasach {1x}. See: BDB—820d.

6458. פָּסַל {6x} **pâçal**, *paw-sal';* a prim. root; to *carve*, whether wood or stone:—hew {5x}, graven {1x}. See: TWOT—1788; BDB—820d.

6459. פֶּסֶל {31x} **peçel**, *peh'-sel;* from 6458; an *idol:*—graven image {28x}, carved image {2x}, graven {1x}. Syn.: 2796, 4906, 5566, 6754. See: TWOT—1788a; BDB—820d.

6460. פְּסַנְטְרִין {4x} **pᵉçantêrîyn** (Aram.), *pes-an-tay-reen';* or

פְּסַנְתֵּרִין **pᵉçantêrîyn**, *pes-an-tay-reen';* a transliteration of the Gr. ψαλτήριον *psaltériŏn; a lyre:*—psaltery {4x}. See: TWOT—2943; BDB—1108c.

6461. פָּסַס {1x} **paçaç**, *paw-sas';* a prim. root; prob. to *disperse*, i.e. (intr.) *disappear:*—fail {1x}. See: TWOT—1790; BDB—821a.

6462. פִּסְפָּה {1x} **Piçpâh**, *pis-paw';* perh. from 6461; *dispersion; Pispah*, an Isr.:—Pispah {1x}. See: BDB—821a.

6463. פָּעָה {1x} **pâꜥâh**, *paw-aw';* a prim. root; to *scream:*—cry {1x}. See: TWOT—1791; BDB—821a.

6464. פָּעוּ {2x} **Pâꜥûw**, *paw-oo';* or

פָּעִי **Pâꜥîy**, *paw-ee';* from 6463; *screaming; Paü* or *Paï*, a place in Edom:—Pai {1x}, Pau {1x}. See: BDB—821b.

פָּעִי **Pâꜥîy**. See 6464.

6466. פָּעַל {56x} **pâꜥal**, *paw-al';* a prim. root; to *do* or *make* (systematically and habitually), espec. to *practise:*—work {19x}, workers {19x}, do {10x}, make {4x}, commit {1x}, doers {1x}, Maker {1x}, ordaineth {1x}.

Pa'al means "to do, work." **(1)** Found only 56 times in the Hebrew Old Testament, **(1a)** it is used primarily as a poetic synonym for the much more common verb *'ashah* (6213), "to do, to make." **(1b)** Thus, almost half the occurrences of this verb are in the Book of Psalms. **(2)** *Pa'al* is used for the first time in the Old Testament in the Song of Moses: "The place, O Lord, which thou hast made for thee to dwell in . . ." (Ex 15:17). **(3)** There is no distinction in the use of this verb, whether God or man is its subject. In Ps 15:2 man is the subject: "He that walketh uprightly and worketh righteousness, and speaketh the truth in his heart." Syn.: 6213. See: TWOT—1792; BDB—821b.

6467. פֹּעַל {38x} **pôꜥal**, *po'-al;* from 6466; an *act* or *work* (concr.):—work {30x}, act {3x}, deeds {2x}, do {1x}, getting {1x}, maker {1x}. See: TWOT—1792a; BDB—821c.

6468. פְּעֻלָּה {14x} **pᵉꜥullâh**, *peh-ool-law';* fem. pass. part. of 6466; (abstr.) *work:*—work {10x}, labour {2x}, reward {1x}, wages {1x}. See: TWOT—1792b; BDB—821c.

6469. פְּעֻלְּתָי {1x} **Peullcthay**, *peh-ool-leh-thah'-ee;* from 6468; *laborious; Peüllethai,* an Isr.:—Peulthai {1x}. See: BDB—821d.

6470. פָּעַם {5x} **pâʻam**, *paw-am';* a prim. root; to *tap,* i.e. *beat regularly;* hence, (gen.) to *impel* or *agitate:*—troubled {4x}, move {1x}. See: TWOT—1793; BDB—821d.

6471. פַּעַם {112x} **paʻam**, *pah'-am;* or (fem.)

פַּעֲמָה **paʻămâh**, *pah-am-aw';* from 6470; a *stroke,* lit. or fig. (in various applications, as follow):— . . . time {58x}, once {14x}, now {7x}, feet {6x}, twice {5x}, thrice + 7969 {4x}, steps {4x}, corners {3x}, ranks {2x}, oftentimes {2x}, misc. {7x}= hoofbeats, pedestal, stroke, anvil.

I. Pa'am, as a noun, means "step; foot; hoofbeats; pedestal; stroke; anvil." **(1)** The nuances of this word are related to the basic meaning "a human foot." The psalmist uses this meaning in Ps 58:10: "The righteous shall rejoice when he seeth the vengeance: he shall wash his feet in the blood of the wicked." **(2)** In Ex 25:12 the word is applied to the "pedestals or feet" of the ark of the covenant: "And thou shalt cast four rings of gold for it, and put them in the four [feet] thereof; and two rings shall be in the one side of it, and two rings in the other side of it." **(3)** Elsewhere the word signifies the "steps" one takes, or "footsteps": "Hold up my goings in thy paths, that my footsteps slip not" (Ps 17:5). **(4)** Judg 5:28 applies the word to the "steps" of a galloping horse, or its hoofbeats. **(5)** This focus on the falling of a foot once is extended to the "stroke" of a spear: "Then said Abishai to David, God hath delivered thine enemy into thine hand this day: now therefore let me smite him, I pray thee, with the spear even to the earth at once, and I will not smite him the second time" (1 Sa 26:8). **(6)** Finally, *pa'am* represents a foot-shaped object, an "anvil" (Is 41:7).

II. Pa'am as an adverb, means "once; now; anymore." **(1)** This word functions as an adverb with the focus on an occurrence or time. **(2)** In Ex 10:17 the word bears this emphasis: "Now therefore forgive, I pray thee, my sin only this once, and entreat the Lord your God. . . ." **(3)** The first biblical appearance of the word focuses on the finality, the absoluteness, of an event: "This is now bone of my bones" (Gen 2:23). **(4)** The thrust of this meaning appears clearly in the translation of Gen 18:32—Abraham said to God: "Oh, let not the Lord be angry, and I will speak yet but this once [only one more time]." See: TWOT—1793a; BDB—821d.

6472. פַּעֲמֹן {7x} **paʻămôn**, *pah-am-one';* from 6471; a *bell* (as *struck*):—bell {7x}. See: TWOT—1793b; BDB—822b.

6473. פָּעַר {4x} **pâʻar**, *paw-ar';* a prim. root; to *yawn,* i.e. *open* wide (lit. or fig.):—open {3x}, gaped {1x}. See: TWOT—1794; BDB—822b.

6474. פַּעֲרַי {1x} **Paʻăray**, *pah-ar-ah'-ee;* from 6473; *yawning; Paarai,* an Isr.:—Paarai {1x}. See: BDB—822b

6475. פָּצָה {15x} **pâtsâh**, *paw-tsaw';* a prim. root; to *rend,* i.e. *open* (espec. the mouth):—open {10x}, rid {2x}, gaped {1x}, utter {1x}, deliver {1x}. See: TWOT—1795; BDB—822c.

6476. פָּצַח {8x} **pâtsach**, *paw-tsakh';* a prim. root; to *break* out (in joyful sound):—break forth {6x}, break {1x}, make a loud noise {1x}. See: TWOT—1796; BDB—822c.

6477. פְּצִירָה {1x} **petsîyrâh**, *pets-ee-raw';* from 6484; *bluntness:*—file {1x}. See: TWOT—1801a; BDB—823a.

6478. פָּצַל {2x} **pâtsal**, *paw-tsal';* a prim. root; to *peel:*—pilled {2x}. See: TWOT—1797; BDB—822d.

6479. פְּצָלָה {1x} **petsâlâh**, *pets-aw-law';* from 6478; a *peeling:*—strake {1x}. See: TWOT—1797a; BDB—822d.

6480. פָּצַם {1x} **pâtsam**, *paw-tsam';* a prim. root; to *rend* (by earthquake):—broken {1x}. See: TWOT—1798; BDB—822d.

6481. פָּצַע {3x} **pâtsaʻ**, *paw-tsah';* a prim. root; to *split,* i.e. *wound:*—wounded {3x}. See: TWOT—1799; BDB—822d.

6482. פֶּצַע {8x} **petsaʻ**, *peh'-tsah;* from 6481; a *wound:*—wound {7x}, wounding {1x}. See: TWOT—1799a; BDB—822d.

פָּצֵץ **Patstsets**. See 1048.

6483. פִּצֵּץ {1x} **Pitstsêts**, *pits-tsates';* from an unused root mean. to *dissever; dispersive; Pitstsets,* a priest:—Aphses {1x}. See: BDB—823a.

6484. פָּצַר {7x} **pâtsar**, *paw-tsar';* a prim. root; to *peck* at, i.e. (fig.) *stun* or *dull:*—urge {4x}, press {2x}, stubbornness {1x}. See: TWOT—1801; BDB—823a.

6485. פָּקַד {305x} **pâqad**, *paw-kad';* a prim. root; to *visit* (with friendly or hostile intent); by anal. to *oversee, muster, charge, care for, miss, deposit,* etc.:—number {119x}, visit {59x}, punish {31x}, appoint {14x}, commit {6x}, miss {6x}, set {6x}, charge {5x}, governor {5x}, lack {4x}, oversight {4x}, officers {4x},

counted {3x}, empty {3x}, ruler {3x}, overseer {3x}, judgment {2x}, misc. {28x}. ✕ at all, avenge, bestow, deliver to keep, enjoin, go see, hurt, do judgment, lay up, look, make, ✕ by any means, reckon, (call to) remember (-brance), sum, ✕ surely, want.

Paqad means to number, visit, be concerned with, look after, make a search for, punish. **(1)** The first occurrence is in Gen 21:1 **(1a)** ("The Lord visited Sarah") in the special sense of "to intervene on behalf of," so as to demonstrate the divine intervention in the normal course of events to bring about or fulfill a divine intent. **(1b)** Often this intervention is by miraculous means. **(2)** The verb is used in an expression which is unique to Hebrew and which shows great intensity of meaning. **(2a)** Such an occurrence appears in Ex 3:16ff. **(2b)** in which it is used twice in two different grammatical forms to portray the intensity of the action; the text reads (literally): "Looking after, I have surely visited". **(2c)** The usage refers to God's intervention in His saving the children of Israel from their bondage in Egypt.

(3) The same verb in a similar expression can also be used for divine intervention for punishment: "Shall I not visit them for these things?" (Jer 9:9), which means literally: "Shall I not punish them for these things?" **(4)** Hebrew usage also allows a use which applies to the speaker in a nearly passive sense. **(4a)** This is termed the reflexive, since it turns back upon the speaker. **(4b)** *Paqad* is used in such a sense meaning "be missed, be lacking," as in 1 Sa 25:7: "Neither was there aught missing." **(5)** However, the most common usage of the verb in the whole of the Old Testament is in the sense of "drawing up, mustering, or numbering," as of troops for marching or battle (Ex 30:12 and very frequently in Num; less so in 1 and 2 Samuel). Syn.: 502, 7101, 7218, 7336. See: TWOT—1802; BDB—823a, 824b.

פָּקֻד **piqqûd**. See 6490.

6486. פְּקֻדָּה {32x} **pᵉquddâh**, *pek-ood-daw'*; fem. pass. part. of 6485; *visitation* (in many senses, chiefly official):—visitation {13x}, office {5x}, charge {2x}, oversight {2x}, officers {2x}, orderings {1x}, account {1x}, custody {1x}, numbers {1x}, misc. {4x}. See: TWOT—1802a; BDB—824a.

6487. פִּקָּדוֹן {3x} **piqqâdôwn**, *pik-kaw-done'*; from 6485; a *deposit:*—that which was delivered {2x}, store {1x}. See: TWOT—1802f; BDB—824c.

6488. פְּקִדֻת {1x} **pᵉqîdûth**, *pek-ee-dooth'*; from 6496; *supervision:*—ward {1x}. See: TWOT—1802d; BDB—824b.

6489. פְּקוֹד {2x} **pᵉqôwd**, *pek-ode'*; from 6485; *punishment; Pekod,* a symbol. name for Bab.:—Pekod {2x}. See: BDB—824c.

6490. פִּקּוּד {24x} **piqqûwd**, *pik-kood';* or פִּקֻּד **piqqûd**, *pik-kood';* from 6485; prop. *appointed,* i.e. a *mandate* (of God; plur. only, collect. for the *Law*):—precept {21x}, commandment {2x}, statute {1x}. See: TWOT—1802e; BDB—824b.

6491. פָּקַח {20x} **pâqach**, *paw-kakh';* a prim. root; to *open* (the senses, espec. the eyes); fig. to *be observant:*—open {20x}. See: TWOT—1803; BDB—824c.

6492. פֶּקַח {11x} **Peqach**, *peh'-kakh;* from 6491; *watch; Pekach,* an Isr. king:—Pekah {11x}. See: BDB—842d.

6493. פִּקֵּחַ {2x} **piqqêach**, *pik-kay'-akh;* from 6491; *clear-sighted;* fig. *intelligent:*—seeing {1x}, wise {1x}. See: TWOT—1803a; BDB—824d.

6494. פְּקַחְיָה {3x} **Pᵉqachyâh**, *pek-akh-yaw';* from 6491 and 3050; *Jah has observed; Pekachjah,* an Isr. king:—Pekahiah {3x}. See: BDB—824d.

6495. פְּקַח־קוֹחַ {1x} **pᵉqach-qôwach**, *pek-akh-ko'-akh;* from 6491 redoubled; *opening* (of a dungeon), i.e. *jail-delivery* (fig. *salvation* from sin):—opening of the prison {1x}. See: TWOT—1803b; BDB—824d, 876c.

6496. פָּקִיד {13x} **pâqîyd**, *paw-keed';* from 6485; a *superintendent* (civil, military, or religious):—officer {6x}, overseer {5x}, governor {1x}, which had the charge {1x}.

Paqiyd, as a noun, means "one who looks after." **(1)** This noun, derived from *paqad* (6485) in the sense "to number, muster, draw up (troops)," possibly means "one who draws up troops," hence "officer" (2 Chr 24:11). **(2)** Another example of this meaning occurs in Jer 20:1: "Now Pashur the son of Immer the priest, who was also chief governor in the house of the Lord. . . ." See: TWOT—1802c; BDB—824b.

6497. פֶּקַע {3x} **peqaʿ**, *peh'-kah;* from an unused root mean. to *burst;* only used as an arch. term of an ornament similar to 6498, a *semi-globe:*—knops {3x}. See: TWOT—1804a; BDB—825a.

6498. פַּקֻּעָה {1x} **paqquʿâh**, *pak-koo-aw';* from the same as 6497; the *wild cucumber* (from *splitting* open to shed its seeds):—gourd {1x}. See: TWOT—1804b; BDB—825a.

6499. פַּר {133x} **par**, *par;* or פָּר **pâr**, *pawr;* from 6565; a *bullock* (appar. as *breaking* forth in wild

strength, or perh. as *dividing* the hoof):—bullock {127x}, bulls {2x}, oxen {2x}, calves {1x}, young {1x}.

Par, the masculine noun, means "bullock." **(1)** *Par* means "young bull," which is the significance in its first biblical appearance (Gen 32:15), which tells us that among the gifts Jacob sent to placate Esau were "ten bulls." **(2)** In Ps 22:12, the word is used to describe "fierce, strong enemies": "Many bulls have compassed me: strong bulls of Bashan have beset me round." **(3)** When God threatens the nations with judgment in Is 34:7, He describes their princes and warriors as "young bulls," which He will slaughter (cf. Jer 50:27; Eze 39:18). **(4)** *Parah,* **the feminine form of** *par,* is used disdainfully of women in Amos 4:1: "Hear this word, you kine of Bashan. . . ." See: TWOT—1831a; BDB—825a, 830d.

6500. פָּרָא {1x} **pârâ²,** *paw-raw';* a prim. root; to *bear fruit:*—fruitful {1x}. See: TWOT—1805; BDB—825a, 826b.

6501. פֶּרֶא {10x} **pere²,** *peh'-reh;* or

פֶּרֶה **pereh** (Jer. 2:24), *peh'-reh;* from 6500 in the second. sense of *running* wild; the *onager:*—wild ass {9x}, wild {1x}. See: TWOT—1805a; BDB—825b, 826c.

פֹּרָאה **pôrâ²h.** See 6288.

6502. פִּרְאָם {1x} **Pir²âm,** *pir-awm';* from 6501; *wildly; Piram,* a Canaanite:—*Piram* {1x}. See: BDB—825b.

6503. פַּרְבָּר {3x} **Parbâr,** *par-bawr';* or

פַּרְוָר **Parvâr,** *par-vawr';* of for. or.; *Parbar* or *Parvar,* a quarter of Jerusalem:—Parbar {2x}, suburb {1x}. See: BDB—825b, 826c.

6504. פָּרַד {26x} **pârad,** *paw-rad';* a prim. root; to *break* through, i.e. *spread* or *separate* (oneself):—separate {12x}, part {4x}, divided {3x}, scattered abroad {1x}, dispersed {1x}, joint {1x}, scattered {1x}, severed {1x}, stretched {1x}, sundered {1x}.

Parad (6504) means "to divide, separate." **(1)** *Parad* occurs for the first time in the text in Gen 2:10: "And a river went out of Eden . . . and from thence it was parted, and became into four heads." The meaning here must be "dividing into four branches." **(2)** This word often expresses separation of people from each other, sometimes with hostility: "Separate thyself . . . from me . . ." (Gen 13:9). **(3)** A reciprocal separation seems to be implied in the birth of Jacob and Esau: "Two nations are in thy womb, and two manner of people shall be separated from thy bowels" (Gen 25:23). **(4)** Sometimes economic status brings about separation: "The poor is separated from his neighbor" (Prov

19:4). **(5)** Generally speaking, *parad* has more negative than positive connotations. Syn.: 5139, 5144. See: TWOT—1806; BDB—825b.

6505. פֶּרֶד {15x} **pered,** *peh'-red;* from 6504; a *mule* (perh. from his *lonely* habits):—mule {15x}. See: TWOT—1807a; BDB—825d.

6506. פִּרְדָּה {3x} **pirdâh,** *pir-daw';* fem. of 6505; a *she-mule:*—mule {3x}. See: TWOT—1807b; BDB—825d.

6507. פְּרֻדָה {1x} **p°rûdâh,** *per-oo-daw';* fem. pass. part. of 6504; something *separated,* i.e. a *kernel:*—seed {1x}. See: TWOT—1806a; BDB—825c.

6508. פַּרְדֵּס {3x} **pardês,** *par-dace';* of for. or.; a *park:*—orchard {2x}, forest {1x}. See: TWOT—1808; BDB—825d.

6509. פָּרָה {29x} **pârâh,** *paw-raw';* a prim. root; to *bear fruit* (lit. or fig.):—fruitful {19x}, increased {3x}, grow {2x}, beareth {1x}, forth {1x}, bring fruit {1x}, make fruitful {1x}.

Parah, the verb, means "to be fruitful, bear fruit." Its first occurrence is in Gen 1:22: "And God blessed them, saying, Be fruitful, and multiply, . . ." See: TWOT—1809; BDB—825a, 826a, 832c.

6510. פָּרָה {26x} **pârâh,** *paw-raw';* fem. of 6499; a *heifer:*—kine {18x}, heifer {6x}, cow {2x}. See: TWOT—1831b; BDB—826c, 831a.

6511. פָּרָה {1x} **Pârâh,** *paw-raw';* the same as 6510; *Parah,* a place in Pal.:—Parah {1x}. See: BDB—826c, 831a.

פֶּרֶה **pereh.** See 6501.

6512. פֵּרָה {1x} **pêrâh,** *pay-raw';* from 6331; a *hole* (as *broken,* i.e. *dug*):—moles {1x}. See: TWOT—714a; BDB—344a, 826c. comp. 2661.

6513. פֻּרָה {2x} **Pûrâh,** *poo-raw';* for 6288; *foliage; Purah,* an Isr.:—Phurah {2x}. See: BDB—826c.

6514. פְּרוּדָא {2x} **P°rûdâ²,** *per-oo-daw';* or

פְּרִידָא **P°rîydâ²,** *per-ee-daw';* from 6504; *dispersion; Peruda* or *Perida,* one of "Solomon's servants":—Peruda {1x}, Perida {1x}. See: BDB—825c.

פְּרוֹזִי **p°rôwzîy.** See 6521.

6515. פָּרוּחַ {1x} **Pârûwach,** *paw-roo'-akh;* pass. part. of 6524; *blossomed; Paruäch,* an Isr.:—Paruah {1x}. See: BDB—827c.

Hebrew

6516. פַּרְוָיִם {1x} **Parvayim,** *par-vah'-yim;* of for. or.; *Parvajim,* an Oriental region:—Parvaim {1x}. See: BDB—826c.

6517. פָּרוּר {3x} **pârûwr,** *paw-roor';* pass. part. of 6565 in the sense of *spreading* out [comp. 6524]; a *skillet* (as *flat* or *deep*):—pot {2x}, pan {1x}. See: TWOT—1750b, 1810; BDB—807d.

פַּרְוָר **Parvâr.** See 6503.

6518. פָּרָז {1x} **pârâz,** *paw-rawz';* from an unused root mean. to *separate,* i.e. *decide;* a *chieftain:*—villages {1x}. See: TWOT—1812?; BDB—826d.

6519. פְּרָזָה {3x} **p⁰râzâh,** *per-aw-zaw';* from the same as 6518; an *open* country:—unwalled town {1x}, unwalled village {1x}, town without walls {1x}. See: TWOT—1812a; BDB—826d.

6520. פְּרָזוֹן {2x} **p⁰râzôwn,** *per-aw-zone';* from the same as 6518; *magistracy,* i.e. *leadership* (also concr. *chieftains*):—village {2x}. See: TWOT—1812b; BDB—826d.

6521. פְּרָזִי {3x} **p⁰râzîy,** *per-aw-zee';* or

פְּרוֹזִי **p⁰rôwzîy,** *per-o-zee';* from 6519; a *rustic:*—village {1x}, country {1x}, unwalled {1x}. See: TWOT—1812c; BDB—826d.

6522. פְּרִזִּי {23x} **P⁰rîzzîy,** *per-iz-zee';* for 6521; inhab. *of the open country;* a *Perizzite,* one of the Canaanitish tribes:—Perizzite {23x}. See: BDB—827a.

6523. פַּרְזֶל {20x} **parzel** (Aram.), *par-zel';* corresp. to 1270; *iron:*—iron {20x}. See: TWOT—2944; BDB—1108d.

6524. פָּרַח {36x} **pârach,** *paw-rakh';* a prim. root; to *break* forth as a bud, i.e. *bloom;* gen. to *spread;* spec. to *fly* (as extending the wings); fig. to *flourish:*—flourish {10x}, bud {5x}, blossom {4x}, grow {3x}, break {3x}, fly {2x}, spring {2x}, break forth {2x}, abroad {1x}, abundantly {1x}, break out {1x}, spreading {1x}, spring up {1x}. See: TWOT—1813, 1814, 1815; BDB—827a, 827b, 827c.

6525. פֶּרַח {17x} **perach,** *peh'-rakh;* from 6524; a *calyx* (nat. or artif.); gen. *bloom:*—flower {14x}, bud {2x}, blossom {1x}. See: TWOT—1813a; BDB—827b.

6526. פִּרְחָח {1x} **pirchach,** *pir-khakh';* from 6524; *progeny,* i.e. a *brood:*—youth {1x}. See: TWOT—1813b; BDB—827b, 1107b.

6527. פָּרַט {1x} **pârat,** *paw-rat';* a prim. root; to *scatter* words, i.e. *prate* (or *hum*):—chant {1x}. See: TWOT—1816; BDB—827c.

6528. פֶּרֶט {1x} **peret,** *peh'-ret;* from 6527; a *stray* or *single* berry:—grape {1x}. See: TWOT—1816a; BDB—827c, 1107b.

6529. פְּרִי {119x} **p⁰rîy,** *per-ee';* from 6509; *fruit* (lit. or fig.):—fruit {113x}, fruitful {2x}, boughs {1x}, firstfruits + 7225 {1x}, reward {1x}, fruit thereof {1x}.

Periy, as a noun, means "fruit; reward; price; earnings; product; result." **(1)** First, *periy* represents the mature edible product of a plant, which is its "fruit." **(1a)** This broad meaning is evident in Deut 7:13: "He will also bless the fruit of thy womb, and the fruit of thy land, thy corn, and thy wine, and thine oil, the increase of thy kine and the flocks of thy sheep." **(1b)** In its first biblical appearance, the word is used to signify both "trees" and the "fruit" of trees: "And God said, Let the earth bring forth grass, the herb yielding seed, and the fruit tree yielding fruit after his kind" (Gen 1:11). **(1c)** In Ps 107:34, the word is used as a modifier of land. The resulting term is "a fruitful land" in the sense of a "land of fruit." **(2)** Second, *periy* means "offspring," or the "fruit of a womb." **(2a)** In Deut 7:13, the word represents "human offspring," but it can also be used **(2b)** of animal "offspring" (Gen 1:22).

(3) Third, the "product" or "result" of an action is, in poetry, sometimes called its "fruit": **(3a)** "A man shall say, Verily there is a reward [*periy*] for the righteous: verily he is a God that judgeth in the earth" (Ps 58:11). **(3b)** Is 27:9 speaks of "all the fruit to take away his sin"), i.e., the result of God's purifying acts toward Israel. **(3c)** The wise woman buys and plants a field with her earnings or the "fruit of her hands" (Prov 31:16). In other words, she is to be rewarded by receiving the "product" of her hands (Prov 31:31). **(3d)** The righteous will be rewarded "I the LORD search the heart, I try the reins, even to give every man according to his ways, and according to the fruit of his doings" (Jer 17:10; cf. 21:14). See: TWOT—1809a; BDB—826b.

פְּרִידָא **P⁰rîydâ.** See 6514.

פֻּרִים **Pûrîym.** See 6332.

6530. פְּרִיץ {6x} **p⁰rîyts,** *per-eets';* from 6555; *violent,* i.e. a *tyrant:*—robber {4x}, destroyer {1x}, ravenous {1x}. See: TWOT—1826b; BDB—829b.

6531. פֶּרֶךְ {6x} **perek,** *peh'-rek;* from an unused root mean. to *break* apart; *fracture,* i.e. *severity:*—rigour {5x}, cruelty {1x}. See: TWOT—1817a; BDB—827d.

6532. פֹּרֶכֶת {25x} **pôreketh,** *po-reh'-keth;* fem. act. part. of the same as 6531; a

separatrix, i.e. (the sacred) *screen:*—vail {25x}. See: TWOT—1817a; BDB—827d.

6533. פָּרַם {3x} **páram,** *paw-ram';* a prim. root; to *tear:*—rend {3x}. See: TWOT—1819; BDB—827d.

6534. פַּרְמַשְׁתָּא {1x} **Parmashtâ',** *par-mash-taw';* of Pers. or.; *Parmashta,* a son of Haman:—*Parmashta* {1x}. See: BDB—828a.

6535. פַּרְנָךְ {1x} **Parnak,** *par-nak';* of uncert. der.; *Parnak,* an Isr.:—Parnach {1x}. See: BDB—828a.

6536. פָּרַס {14x} **páraç,** *paw-ras';* a prim. root; to *break* in pieces, i.e. (usually without violence) to *split, distribute:*—divide {9x}, parteth {2x}, deal {1x}, hoofs {1x}, tear {1x}. See: TWOT—1821; BDB—828a, 1108d.

6537. פְּרַס {3x} **p°raç** (Aram.), *per-as';* corresp. to 6536; to *split* up:—UPHARSIN {1x}, PERES {1x}, divided {1x}. See: TWOT—2945; BDB—1101b, 1108d.

6538. פֶּרֶס {2x} **pereç,** *peh'-res;* from 6536; a *claw;* also a kind of *eagle:*—ossifrage {2x}. See: TWOT—1821a; BDB—828b.

6539. פָּרַס {28x} **Pâraç,** *paw-ras';* of for. or.; *Paras* (i.e. *Persia*), an E. country, incl. its inhab.:—Persia {27x}, Persian {1x}. See: TWOT—1820; BDB—828a, 1108d.

6540. פָּרַס {6x} **Pâraç** (Aram.), *paw-ras';* corresp. to 6539:—Persians {4x}, Persia {2x}. See: BDB—1108d.

6541. פַּרְסָה {19x} **parçâh,** *par-saw';* fem. of 6538; a *claw* or split *hoof:*—hoof {17x}, claws {2x}. See: TWOT—1821b; BDB—828b.

6542. פַּרְסִי {1x} **Parçîy,** *par-see';* patrial from 6539; a *Parsite* (i.e. *Persian*), or inhab. of Peres:—Persian {1x}. See: BDB—828a.

6543. פַּרְסִי {1x} **Parçîy** (Aram.), *par-see';* corresp. to 6542:—Persian {1x}. See: BDB—1108d.

6544. פָּרַע {16x} **pâra',** *paw-rah';* a prim. root; to *loosen;* by impl. to *expose, dismiss;* fig. *absolve, begin:*—refuse {3x}, uncover {3x}, naked {2x}, avenging {1x}, avoid {1x}, go back {1x}, bare {1x}, let {1x}, made naked {1x}, set at nought {1x}, perish {1x}. See: TWOT—1822, 1823, 1824; BDB—828c, 828d.

6545. פֶּרַע {2x} **pera',** *peh'-rah;* from 6544; the *hair* (as *dishevelled*):—locks {2x}. See: TWOT—1823a, 1822a; BDB—828c, 828d.

6546. פִּרְעָה {2x} **par'âh,** *par-aw';* fem. of 6545 (in the sense of *beginning*); *leadership* (plur. concr. *leaders*):—revenge {1x}, avenge {1x}. See: TWOT—1822a; BDB—828d.

6547. פַּרְעֹה {268x} **Par'ôh,** *par-o';* of Eg. der.; *Paroh,* a gen. title of Eg. kings:—Pharaoh {268x}. See: TWOT—1825; BDB—829a.

6548. פַּרְעֹה חָפְרַע {1x} **Par'ôh Chophra',** *par-o' khof-rah';* of Eg. der.; *Paroh-Chophra,* an Eg. king:—Pharaohhophra {1x}. See: BDB—344b.

6549. פַּרְעֹה נְכֹה {5x} **Par'ôh N°kôh,** *par-o' nek-o';* or

פַּרְעֹה נְכוֹ **Par'ôh N°kôw,** *par-o' nek-o';* of Eg. der.; *Paroh-Nekoh* (or *-Neko*), an Eg. king:—Pharaoh-necho {5x}. See: BDB—647a.

6550. פַּרְעֹשׁ {2x} **par'ôsh,** *par-oshe';* prob. from 6544 and 6211; a *flea* (as the *isolated insect*):—flea {2x}. See: TWOT—1825.1; BDB—829a.

6551. פַּרְעֹשׁ {6x} **Par'ôsh,** *par-oshe';* the same as 6550; *Parosh,* the name of four Isr.:—Parosh {5x}, Pharosh {1x}. See: BDB—829b.

6552. פִּרְעָתוֹן {1x} **Pir'âthôwn,** *pir-aw-thone';* from 6546; *chieftaincy; Pirathon,* a place in Pal.:—Pirathon {1x}. See: BDB—828c.

6553. פִּרְעָתוֹנִי {5x} **Pir'âthôwnîy,** *pir-aw-tho-nee';* or

פִּרְעָתֹנִי **Pir'âthônîy,** *pir-aw-tho-nee';* patrial from 6552; a *Pirathonite* or inhab. of Pirathon:—Pirathonite {5x}. See: BDB—828d.

6554. פַּרְפַּר {1x} **Parpar,** *par-par';* prob. from 6565 in the sense of *rushing; rapid; Parpar,* a river of Syria:—Pharpar {1x}. See: BDB—829b.

6555. פָּרַץ {49x} **pârats,** *paw-rats';* a prim. root; to *break* out (in many applications, dir. and indirect, lit. and fig.):—break down {11x}, break forth {5x}, increase {5x}, break {4x}, abroad {3x}, breach {2x}, break in {2x}, made {2x}, break out {2x}, pressed {2x}, break up {2x}, break away {1x}, breaker {1x}, compelled {1x}, misc. {6x}. See: TWOT—1826; BDB—829b.

6556. פֶּרֶץ {19x} **perets,** *peh'-rets;* from 6555; a *break* (lit. or fig.):—breach {14x}, gap {2x}, breaking {1x}, breaking forth {1x}, breaking in {1x}. See: TWOT—1826a; BDB—829c.

6557. פֶּרֶץ {15x} **Perets,** *peh'-rets;* the same as 6556; *Perets,* the name of two Isr.:—Pharez {12x}, Perez {3x}. See: BDB—829d.

6558. פַּרְצִי {1x} **Partsiy,** *par-tsee';* patron. from 6557; a *Partsite* (collect.) or desc. of Perets:—Pharzites {1x}. See: BDB—829d.

6559. פְּרָצִים {1x} **Pᵉrâtsîym,** *per-aw-tseem';* plur. of 6556; *breaks; Peratsim,* a mountain in Pal.:—Perazim {1x}. See: BDB—829c.

6560. פֶּרֶץ עֻזָּא {2x} **Perets 'Uzzâ',** *peh'-rets ooz-zaw';* from 6556 and 5798; *break of Uzza; Perets-Uzza,* a place in Pal.:—Perezuzza {2x}. See: BDB—829d.

6561. פָּרַק {10x} **pâraq,** *paw-rak';* a prim. root; to *break* off or *crunch;* fig. to *deliver:*—break off {3x}, break {2x}, rent {1x}, rend in pieces {1x}, redeem {1x}, deliver {1x}, tear in pieces {1x}. See: TWOT—1828; BDB—830a, 1108d.

6562. פְּרַק {1x} **pᵉraq** (Aram.), *per-ak';* corresp. to 6561; to *discontinue:*—break off {1x}. See: TWOT—2946; BDB—1108d.

6563. פֶּרֶק {2x} **pereq,** *peh'-rek;* from 6561; *rapine;* also a *fork* (in roads):—crossway {1x}, robbery {1x}. See: TWOT—1828a; BDB—830a.

6564. פָּרָק {1x} **pârâq,** *paw-rawk';* from 6561; *soup* (as full of *crumbed* meat):—broth {1x}. See also 4832.

6565. פָּרַר {50x} **parar,** *paw-rar';* a prim. root; to *break* up (usually fig., i.e. to *violate, frustrate:*—break {25x}, make void {5x}, defeat {2x}, disannul {2x}, disappoint {2x}, frustrate {2x}, come to nought {2x}, break asunder {1x}, cause to cease {1x}, clean {1x}, dissolved {1x}, divide {1x}, misc. {5x}. See: TWOT—1829, 1830, 1831; BDB—830b, 830c.

6566. פָּרַשׂ {67x} **pâras,** *paw-ras';* a prim. root; to *break* apart, *disperse,* etc.:—spread {31x}, spread forth {12x}, spread out {6x}, spread abroad {5x}, stretch {3x}, stretch forth {2x}, stretch out {2x}, scattered {2x}, breaketh {1x}, lay open {1x}, chop in pieces {1x}, spread up {1x}.

Paras, as a verb, means "to spread out, scatter, display." **(1)** It is found for the first time in Ex 9:29: "I will spread abroad my hands unto the Lord." Such stretching of the hands probably reflected the characteristic posture of prayer in the Bible (cf. Ps 143:6; Is 1:15). **(2)** *Paras* sometimes expresses the "spreading out" of a garment to its widest extent (Judg

8:25). **(3)** It is commonly used of wings' "being spread," opened fully (Deut 32:11; 1 Kin 6:27). **(4)** "To spread out" a net is to set a snare or trap (Hos 7:12). **(5)** Sometimes "to spread out" is "to display": "A fool layeth open his folly" (Prov 13:16). **(6)** "To spread" may mean "to cover over" and thus to hide from vision: "And the woman took and spread a covering over the well's mouth, and spread ground corn thereon; and the thing was not known" (2 Sa 17:19). **(7)** In some instances, "to spread" may have a more violent meaning of "to scatter": "They that remain shall be scattered toward all winds" (Eze 17:21). See: TWOT—1832; BDB—831A.

6567. פָּרַשׁ {5x} **pârash,** *paw-rash';* a prim. root; to *separate,* lit. (to *disperse*) or fig. (to *specify*); also (by impl.) to *wound:*—shew {1x}, scatter {1x}, declare {1x}, distinctly {1x}, sting {1x}. See: TWOT—1833, 1834; BDB—831c, 831d, 1109a.

6568. פְּרַשׁ {1x} **pᵉrash** (Aram.), *per-ash';* corresp. to 6567; to *specify:*—plainly {1x}. See: TWOT—2947; BDB—1109a.

6569. פֶּרֶשׁ {7x} **peresh,** *peh'-resh;* from 6567; *excrement* (as *eliminated*):—dung {7x}. See: TWOT—1835a; BDB—831d.

6570. פֶּרֶשׁ {1x} **Peresh,** *peh'-resh;* the same as 6569; *Peresh,* an Isr.:—Peresh {1x}. See: BDB—831d.

6571. פָּרָשׁ {57x} **pârâsh,** *paw-rawsh';* from 6567; a *steed* (as *stretched* out to a vehicle, not single nor for mounting [comp. 5483]); also (by impl.) a *driver* (in a chariot), i.e. (collect.) cavalry:—horsemen {56x}, horsemen + 1167 {1x}. See: TWOT—1836a; BDB—832a.

6572. פַּרְשֶׁגֶן {4x} **parshegen,** *par-sheh'-ghen;* or

פַּתְשֶׁגֶן **pathshegen,** *path-sheh'-gen;* of for. or.; a *transcript:*—copy {4x}. See: TWOT—1837; BDB—832b, 837d, 1109a.

6573. פַּרְשֶׁגֶן {3x} **parshegen** (Aram.), *par-sheh'-ghen;* corresp. to 6572:—copy {3x}. See: TWOT—2948; BDB—1109a.

6574. פַּרְשְׁדֹן {1x} **parshᵉdôn,** *par-shed-one';* perh. by compounding 6567 and 6504 (in the sense of *straddling*) [comp. 6576]; the *crotch* (or *anus*):—dirt {1x}. See: TWOT—1838; BDB—832b.

6575. פָּרָשָׁה {2x} **pârâshâh,** *paw-raw-shaw';* from 6567; *exposition:*—sum {1x}, declaration {1x}. See: TWOT—1833a; BDB—831d.

6576. פַּרְשֵׁז {1x} **parshêz**, *par-shaze';* a root appar. formed by compounding 6567 and that of 6518 [comp. 6574]; to *expand:*—spread {1x}. See: TWOT—1832; BDB—831c, 832b.

6577. פַּרְשַׁנְדָּתָא {1x} **Parshandâthâ**, *par-shan-daw-thaw';* of Pers. or.; *Par-shandatha*, a son of Haman:—*Parshandatha* {1x}. See: BDB—832b.

6578. פְּרָת {19x} **Pᵉrâth**, *per-awth';* from an unused root mean. to *break* forth; *rushing; Perath* (i.e. *Euphrates*), a river of the East:—Euphrates {19x}. See: BDB—832b.

פֹּרָת **pôrâth**. See 6509.

6579. פַּרְתָּם {3x} **partam**, *par-tam';* of Pers. or.; a *grandee:*—noble {2x}, prince {1x}. See: TWOT—1839; BDB—832c.

6580. פַּשׁ {1x} **pash**, *pash;* prob. from an unused root mean. to *disintegrate; stupidity* (as a result of *grossness* or of *degeneracy*):—extremity {1x}. See: TWOT—1843; BDB—832d.

6581. פָּשָׂה {22x} **pâsâh**, *paw-saw';* a prim. root; to *spread:*—spread {15x}, spread much {4x}, abroad {3x}. See: TWOT—1840; BDB—832c.

6582. פָּשַׁח {1x} **pâshach**, *paw-shakh';* a prim. root; to *tear* in pieces:—pulled in pieces {1x}. See: TWOT—1844; BDB—832d.

6583. פַּשְׁחוּר {14x} **Pashchûwr**, *pash-khoor';* prob. from 6582; *liberation; Pashchur*, the name of four Isr.:—Pashur {14x}. See: BDB—832d.

6584. פָּשַׁט {43x} **pâshat**, *paw-shat';* a prim. root; to *spread* out (i.e. *deploy* in hostile array); by anal. to *strip* (i.e. *unclothe, plunder, flay,* etc.):—strip {13x}, put off {6x}, flay {4x}, invaded {4x}, spoil {3x}, strip off {2x}, fell {2x}, spread abroad {1x}, forward {1x}, invasion {1x}, pull off {1x}, made a road {1x}, rushed {1x}, set {1x}, spread {1x}, ran upon {1x}. See: TWOT—1845; BDB—832d.

6585. פָּשַׂע {1x} **pâsa‘**, *paw-sah';* a prim. root; to *stride* (from *spreading* the legs), i.e. *rush* upon:—go {1x}. See: TWOT—1841; BDB—832c.

6586. פָּשַׁע {41x} **pâsha‘**, *paw-shah';* a prim. root [rather ident. with 6585 through the idea of *expansion*]; to *break* away (from just authority), i.e. *trespass, apostatize, quarrel:*—transgress {17x}, transgressor {9x}, rebelled {6x}, revolt {6x}, offended {1x}, transgression {1x}, trespassed {1x}.

Pasha' means to transgress, rebel. **(1)** The basic sense of *pasha'* is to rebel with one of two rebellion's stages in focus: **(1a)** a goal of independence (2 Kin 1:1), and **(1b)** the state of independence itself (2 Kin 8:20). **(2)** A more radical meaning is the state of rebellion in which there is no end of the rebellion in view; it is no longer goal-oriented (1 Kin 12:19). **(3)** When the act is committed against the Lord it is usually translated "transgress" (Hos 7:13; Is 66:24) and is an expression of an apostate way of life (Is 59:13). See: TWOT—1846; BDB—833b.

6587. פֶּשַׂע {1x} **pesa‘**, *peh'-sah;* from 6585; a *stride:*—step {1x}. See: TWOT—1841a; BDB—832c.

6588. פֶּשַׁע {93x} **pesha‘**, *peh'-shah;* from 6586; a *revolt* (national, moral, or religious):—transgression {84x}, trespass {5x}, sin {3x}, rebellion {1x}.

Pesha', as a noun, means "transgression; guilt; punishment; offering." **(1)** Basically, this noun signifies willful deviation from, and therefore rebellion against, the path of godly living. **(2)** This emphasis is especially prominent in Amos 2:4: "For three transgressions of Judah, and for four, I will not turn away the punishment thereof; because they have despised the law of the Lord, and have not kept his commandments, and their lies caused them to err, after the which their fathers have walked." Such a willful rebellion from a prescribed or agreed-upon path may be perpetrated against another man: **(3)** "Jacob answered and said to Laban, What is my trespass? what is my sin, that thou hast so hotly pursued after me?" (Gen 31:36—the first occurrence of the word). Jacob is asking what he has done by way of violating or not keeping his responsibility (contract) with Laban.

(4) A nation can sin in this sense against another nation: "For three transgressions of Damascus, and for four . . . because they have threshed Gilead with threshing instruments of iron" (Amos 1:3). **(5)** Usually, however, *pesha'* has immediate reference to one's relationship to God. **(6)** This word sometimes represents the guilt of such a transgression: "I am clean, without [guilt of] transgression, I am innocent; neither is there iniquity in me" (Job 33:9). **(7)** *Pesha'* can signify the punishment for transgression: **(7a)** "And a host was given him against the daily sacrifice by reason of transgression" (Dan 8:12); **(7b)** "How long shall be the vision concerning the daily sacrifice, and [punishment for] the transgression of desolation, to give both the sanctuary and the host to be trodden under foot?" (Dan 8:13). **(8)** Finally, in Mic 6:7 *pesha'* signifies an offering for "transgression": "Shall I give my first-born for my transgression?"

See: TWOT—1846a; BDB—833b. Syn.: 2398, 5771, 7686.

6589. פָּסַק {2x} **pâsaq**, *paw-sak';* a prim. root; to *dispart* (the feet or lips), i.e. *become licentious:*—open {1x}, open wide {1x}. See: TWOT—1842; BDB—832d.

6590. פְּשַׁר {2x} **pᵉshar** (Aram.), *pesh-ar';* corresp. to 6622; to *interpret:*—make {1x}, interpreting {1x}. See: TWOT—2949; BDB—1109a.

6591. פְּשַׁר {31x} **pᵉshar** (Aram.), *pesh-ar';* from 6590; an *interpretation:*—interpretation {31x}. See: TWOT—2949a; BDB—1109a.

6592. פֵּשֶׁר {1x} **pêsher**, *pay'-sher;* corresp. to 6591:—interpretation {1x}. See: TWOT—1847; BDB—833d, 1109a.

6593. פִּשְׁתֶּה {16x} **pishteh**, *pish-teh';* from the same as 6580 as in the sense of *comminuting; linen* (i.e. the thread, as *carded*):—linen {9x}, flax {7x}. See: TWOT—1848; BDB—833d.

6594. פִּשְׁתָּה {4x} **pishtâh**, *pish-taw';* fem. of 6593; *flax;* by impl. a *wick:*—flax {3x}, tow {1x}. See: TWOT—1849; BDB—834a.

6595. פַּת {15x} **path**, *path;* from 6626; a *bit:*—morsel {9x}, piece {5x}, meat {1x}. See: TWOT—1862a; BDB—834a, 837d.

6596. פֹּת {2x} **pôth**, *pohth;* or

פֹּתָה **pothâh** (Eze 13:19), *po-thaw';* from an unused root mean. to *open;* a *hole,* i.e. *hinge* or the female *pudenda:*—hinge {1x}, secret parts {1x}. See: TWOT—1850; BDB—834a.

פְּתָאֵי **pᵉthâ'îy.** See 6612.

6597. פִּתְאֹם {25x} **pith'ôwm**, *pith-ome';* or

פִּתְאֹם **pith'ôm**, *pith-ome';* from 6621; *instantly:*—suddenly {22x}, sudden {2x}, straightway {1x}. See: TWOT—1859a; BDB—834a, 837b.

6598. פַּתְבַּג {6x} **pathbag**, *pathbag';* of Pers. or.; a *dainty:*—portion of meat {4x}, meat {2x}. See: TWOT—1851; BDB—834a.

6599. פִּתְגָּם {2x} **pithgâm**, *pith-gawm';* of Pers. or.; a (judicial) *sentence:*—decree {1x}, sentence {1x}. See: TWOT—1852; BDB—834a, 1109b.

6600. פִּתְגָּם {6x} **pithgâm** (Aram.), *pith-gawm';* corresp. to 6599; a *word, answer, letter* or *decree:*—answer {2x}, matter {2x}, word {1x}, letter {1x}. See: TWOT—2950; BDB—1109b.

6601. פָּתָה **pâthâh**, *paw-thaw';* a prim. root; to *open,* i.e. *be* (caus. *make*) *roomy;* usually fig. (in a mental or moral sense) to *be* (caus. *make*) *simple* or (in a sinister way) *delude:*—entice {10x}, deceive {8x}, persuade {4x}, flatter {2x}, allure {1x}, enlarge {1x}, silly one {1x}, silly {1x}. See: TWOT—1853; BDB—834b, 834c, 1109b.

6602. פְּתוּאֵל {1x} **Pᵉthûw'êl**, *peth-oo-ale';* from 6601 and 410; *enlarged of God; Pethuël,* an Isr.:—Pethuel {1x}. See: BDB—834b.

6603. פִּתּוּחַ {11x} **pittûwach**, *pit-too'-akh;* or

פִּתֻּחַ **pittûach**, *pit-too'-akh;* pass. part. of 6605; *sculpture* (in low or high relief or even intaglio):—engravings {5x}, graving {2x}, carved {1x}, grave + 6605 {1x}, graven {1x}, carved work {1x}. See: TWOT—1855a; BDB—836c.

6604. פְּתוֹר {2x} **Pᵉthôwr**, *peth-ore';* of for. or.; *Pethor,* a place in Mesopotamia:—Pethor {2x} See: BDB—834b.

6605. פָּתַח {144x} **pâthach**, *paw-thakh';* a prim. root; to *open* wide (lit. or fig.); spec. to *loosen, begin, plow, carve:*—open {107x}, loose {13x}, grave {7x}, wide {3x}, engrave {2x}, put off {2x}, out {2x}, appear {1x}, drawn {1x}, break forth {1x}, set forth {1x}, let go free {1x}, ungird {1x}, unstop {1x}, have vent {1x}.

Pathach, as a verb, means "to open." **(1)** The first occurrence is in Gen 7:11: "In the six hundredth year of Noah's life, in the second month, the seventeenth day of the month, the same day were all the fountains of the great deep broken up, and the windows of heaven were opened." **(2)** Although the basic meaning of *pathach* is "to open," the word is extended to mean "to cause to flow," "to offer for sale," "to conquer," "to surrender," "to draw a sword," "to solve [a riddle]," "to free." **(3)** In association with *min,* the word becomes "to deprive of." See: TWOT—1854, 1855; BDB—834d, 836b, 1109b.

6606. פְּתַח {2x} **pᵉthach** (Aram.), *peth-akh';* corresp. to 6605; to *open:*—open {2x}. See: TWOT—2951; BDB—1109b.

6607. פֶּתַח {163x} **pethach**, *peh'-thakh;* from 6605; an *opening* (lit.), i.e. *door* (*gate*) or *entrance* way:—door {126x}, entering {10x}, entry {8x}, gate {7x}, in {7x}, entrance {3x}, openings {1x}, place {1x}.

Pethach, as a noun, means "doorway; opening; entrance; gate." **(1)** *Pethach* basically represents the "opening through which one enters a building, tent, tower (fortress), or city." **(1a)** Abraham was sitting at the "doorway" of his tent in the heat of the day when his three

heavenly visitors appeared (Gen 18:1). **(1b)** Lot met the men of Sodom at the "doorway" of his home, having shut the door behind him (Gen 19:6). **(2)** Larger buildings had larger entryways, so in Gen 43:19 *pethach* may be rendered by the more general word, "entrance." **(3)** In Gen 38:14, *pethach* may be translated "gateway": Tamar "sat in the open place." **(4)** Thus a *pethach* was both a place to sit (a location) and an opening for entry (a passageway): "And the incense altar, and his staves, and the anointing oil, and the sweet incense, and the hanging for the door at the entering in of the tabernacle . . ." (Ex 35:15). **(5)** There are a few notable special uses of *pethach*. **(5a)** The word normally refers to a part of the intended construction plans of a dwelling, housing, or building; **(5a)** but in Eze 8:8 it represents an "entrance" not included in the original design of the building: "When I had digged in the wall, behold a door." **(5b)** This is clearly not a doorway.

(6) This word may be used of a cave's "opening," as when Elijah heard the gentle blowing that signified the end of a violent natural phenomenon: "He wrapped his face in his mantle, and went out, and stood in the entering in of the cave" (1 Kin 19:13). **(7)** In the plural form, *pethach* sometimes **(7a)** represents the "city gates" themselves: "And her [Zion's] gates shall lament and mourn" (Is 3:26). **(7b)** This form of the word is used as a figure for one's lips; in Mic 7:5, for example, the prophet mourns the low morality of his people and advises his hearers to trust no one, telling them to guard their lips (literally, the "openings" of their mouths). **(8)** In its first biblical occurrence, *pethach* is used figuratively. The heart of men is depicted as a house or building with the devil crouching at the "entrance," ready to subdue it utterly and destroy its occupant (Gen 4:7). See: TWOT—1854a; BDB—835d.

6608. פֶּתַח {1x} **pêthach**, *pay'-thakh;* from 6605; *opening* (fig.) i.e. *disclosure:*—entrance {1x}. See: TWOT—1854b; BDB—836a.

פָּתֻחַ **pâthûach**. See 6603.

6609. פְּתִחָה {1x} **pᵉthîchâh**, *peth-ee-khaw';* from 6605; something *opened,* i.e. a *drawn* sword:—drawn sword {1x}. See: TWOT—1854d; BDB—836a.

6610. פִּתְחוֹן {2x} **pithchôwn**, *pith-khone';* from 6605; *opening* (the act):—open {1x}, opening {1x}. See: TWOT—1854c; BDB—836a.

6611. פְּתַחְיָה {4x} **Pᵉthachyâh**, *peth-akh-yaw';* from 6605 and 3050; *Jah has opened; Pethachjah,* the name of four Isr.:—Pethakiah {4x}. See: BDB—836a.

6612. פְּתִי {19x} **pᵉthîy**, *peth-ee';* or

פֶּתִי **pethîy**, *peh'-thee;* or

פְּתָאִי **pᵉthâ'îy**, *peth-aw-ee';* from 6601; *silly* (i.e. *seducible*):—foolish {2x}, simple {15x}, simplicity {1x}, simple ones {1x}. See: TWOT—1853a; BDB—834a, 834b, 834c, 836a.

6613. פְּתַי {2x} **pᵉthay** (Aram.), *peth-ah'-ee;* from a root corresp. to 6601; *open,* i.e. (as noun) *width:*—breadth {2x}. See: TWOT—2952; BDB—1109b.

6614. פְּתִיגִיל {1x} **pᵉthîygîyl**, *peth-eeg-eel';* of uncert. der.; prob. a figured *mantle* for holidays:—stomacher {1x}. See: TWOT—1856; BDB—836c.

6615. פְּתִיוּת {1x} **pᵉthayûwth**, *peth-ah-yooth';* from 6612; *silliness* (i.e. *seducibility*):—simple {1x}. See: TWOT—1853a; BDB—834c, 836b.

6616. פָּתִיל {11x} **pâthîyl**, *paw-theel';* from 6617; *twine:*—bound {1x}, bracelet {2x}, lace {4x}, line {1x}, ribband {1x}, thread {1x}, wire {1x}. See: TWOT—1857a; BDB—836d.

6617. פָּתַל {5x} **pâthal**, *paw-thal';* a prim. root; to *twine,* i.e. (lit.) to *struggle* or (fig.) *be* (morally) *tortuous:*—shew self froward {1x}, forward {2x}, shew self unsavoury {1x}, wrestle {1x}. See: TWOT—1857; BDB—836c.

6618. פְּתַלְתֹּל {1x} **pᵉthaltôl**, *peth-al-tole';* from 6617; *tortuous* (i.e. *crafty*):—crooked {1x}. See: TWOT—1857b; BDB—836d.

6619. פִּתֹם {1x} **Pîthôm**, *p e-thome';* of Eg. der.; *Pithom,* a place in Egypt:—Pithom {1x}. See: TWOT—1857b; BDB—837a.

6620. פֶּתֶן {6x} **pethen**, *peh'-then;* from an unused root mean. to *twist;* an *asp* (from its *contortions*):—adder {2x}, asp {4x}. See: TWOT—1858a; BDB—837a.

6621. פֶּתַע {7x} **petha'**, *peh'-thah;* from an unused root mean. to *open* (the eyes); a *wink,* i.e. *moment* [comp. 6597] (used only [with or without prep.] adv. *quickly* or *unexpectedly*):—at an instant {1x}, suddenly {4x}, × very {1x}. See: TWOT—1859; BDB—837b.

6622. פָּתַר {9x} **pâthar**, *paw-thar';* a prim. root; to *open* up, i.e. (fig.) *interpret* (a dream):—interpret {4x}, interpreted {3x}, interpreter {1x}, interpretation {1x}. See: TWOT—1860; BDB—837a.

6623. פִּתְרוֹן {5x} **pithrôwn,** *pith-rone';* or

פִּתְרֹן **pithrôn,** *pith-rone';* from 6622; *interpretation* (of a dream):—interpretation {5x}. See: TWOT—1860a; BDB—837a.

6624. פַּתְרוֹס {5x} **Pathrôwç,** *path-roce';* of Eg. der.; *Pathros,* a part of Egypt:—Pathros {5x}. See: BDB—837d.

6625. פַּתְרֻסִי {2x} **Pathrûçîy,** *path-roo-see';* patrial from 6624; a *Pathrusite,* or inhab. of Pathros:—Pathrusim {2x}. See: BDB—837d.

פַּתְשֶׁגֶן **pathshegen.** See 6572.

6626. פָּתַח {1x} **pathath,** *paw-thath';* a prim. root; to *open,* i.e. *break:*—part {1x}. See: TWOT—1862; BDB—834b, 837d.

צ

6627. צֵאָה **tsâ'âh,** *tsaw-aw';* from 3318; *issue,* i.e. (human) *excrement:*—that which cometh from thee {1x}, that cometh out of; {2x}. See: TWOT—1884a; BDB—838a, 844b.

צֹאָה **tsô'âh.** See 6675.

צֹאוֹן **tsᵉ'ôwn.** See 6629.

6628. צֶאֱל {2x} **tse'el,** *tseh'-el;* from an unused root mean. to *be slender;* the *lotus* tree:—shady trees {2x}. See: TWOT—1863; BDB—838a.

6629. צֹאן {274x} **tsô'n,** *tsone;* or

צֹאוֹן **tsᵉ'ôwn** (Psa. 144:13) *tseh-one';* from an unused root mean. to *migrate;* a collect. name for a *flock* (of sheep or goats); also fig. (of men):—flock {138x}, sheep {110x}, cattle {15x}, shepherd + 7462 {2x}, lamb + 1121 {2x}, lamb {1x}, sheep + 4480 {1x}, sheepcotes + 1448 {1x}, sheepfold + 1448 {1x}, sheepfold + 4356 {1x}, sheepshearers + 1494 {1x}, shepherd + 7462 {1x}.

Ts'own means flock; small cattle; sheep; goats. **(1)** The primary meaning of *ts'own* is small cattle, to be distinguished from baqar (1241 - herd). **(2)** The word may refer to **(2a)** sheep only (1 Sa 25:2), or **(2b)** to both sheep and goats (Gen 30:33). **(3)** The flock was important economically with the animals being **(3a)** eaten (1 Sa 14:32; Ps 44:11), **(3b)** shorn for their wool (Gen 31:19), **(3c)** milked (Deut 32:14), and offered as a sacrifice (Gen 4:4). **(4)** Metaphorically, it applies to people (Eze 36:38) with God viewed as the shepherd (Ps 100:3; Ps 23; 79:13; Mic 7:14). **(5)** God's people are considered as **(5a)** sheep for the slaughter (Ps 44:22); **(5b)** a flock without a shepherd (1 Kin 22:17; Zec 10:2; 13:7); **(5c)** guided astray

by their shepherds, or leaders (Jer 50:6); **(5d)** individually going astray (Is 53:6); and **(5e)** prophetically promised to be regathered **(5e1)** under Messiah (Jer 23:3) **(5e2)** as Israel's Shepherd (Eze 34:23–24). See: 1864a; BDB—838a.

6630. צַאֲנָן {1x} **Tsa'ănân,** *tsah-an-awn';* from the same as 6629 used denom.; *sheep* pasture; *Zaanan,* a place in Pal.:—Zaanan {1x}. See: BDB—838c.

6631. צֶאֱצָא {11x} **tse'ĕtsâ',** *tseh-ets-aw';* from 3318; *issue,* i.e. *produce, children:*—that which cometh forth {1x}, which cometh out {1x}, offspring {1x}. See: TWOT—893b; BDB—425c, 838c.

6632. צָב {3x} **tsâb,** *tsawb;* from an unused root mean. to *establish;* a *palanquin* or *canopy* (as a *fixture*); also a species of *lizard* (prob. as clinging *fast*):—covered wagon {1x}, litter {1x}, tortoise {1x}. See: TWOT—1866a, 1867a; BDB—838c, 839d.

6633. צָבָא {13x} **tsâbâ',** *tsaw-baw';* a prim. root; to *mass* (an army or servants):—fight {4x}, assemble {3x}, mustered {2x}, warred {2x}, perform {1x}, wait {1x}.

Tsaba', as a verb, means "to wage war, to muster an army, to serve in worship." **(1)** *Tsaba'* means "to wage war" in Num 31:7: "And they warred against the Midianites, as the Lord commanded Moses." **(2)** The word is used in 2 Kin 25:19 to refer to "mustering an army." **(3)** Another sense of *tsaba'* appears in Num. 4:23 with the meaning of "serving in worship": ". . . all that enter in to perform the service, to do the work in the tabernacle of the congregation." See: TWOT—1865; BDB—838c, 1109b.

6634. צְבָא {10x} **tsᵉbâ'** (Aram.), *tseb-aw';* corresp. to 6633 in the fig. sense of *summoning* one's wishes; to *please:*—will {9x}, his will {1x}. See: TWOT—2953; BDB—1109b.

6635. צָבָא {485x} **tsâbâ',** *tsaw-baw';* or (fem.)

צְבָאָה **tsᵉbâ'âh,** *tseb-aw-aw';* from 6633; a *mass* of persons (or fig. things), espec. reg. organized for war (an *army*); by impl. a *campaign,* lit. or fig. (spec. *hardship, worship*):—host {393x}, war {41x}, army {29x}, battle {5x}, service {5x}, appointed time {3x}, warfare {2x}, soldiers {1x}, company {1x}, misc. {5x}.

Tsaba', as a noun, means "host; military service; war; army; service; labor; forced labor; conflict." **(1)** This word involves several interrelated ideas: a group; impetus; difficulty; and force. **(1a)** These ideas undergird the general concept of "service" which one does for or under a superior rather than for himself. **(1b)** *Tsaba'* is usually applied to "military ser-

vice" but is sometimes used of "work" in general (under or for a superior). **(1c)** In Num 1:2–3 the word means "military service": "Take ye the sum of all the congregation of the children of Israel ... from twenty years old and upward, all that are able to go forth to war in Israel." **(1d)** The idea is more concrete in Josh 22:12, where the word represents serving in a military campaign: "And when the children of Israel heard of it, the whole congregation of the children of Israel gathered themselves together at Shiloh, to go to war against them." **(1e)** Num 31:14 uses *tsaba'* of the actual battling itself: "And Moses was wroth with the officers of the host [army], ... which came from the battle."

(2) The word can also represent an "army host": **(2a)** "And Eleazer the priest said unto the men of war which went to the battle . . ." (Num 31:21). **(2b)** Even clearer is Num 31:48: "And the officers which were over thousands of the host, the captains of thousands, and captains of hundreds, came near unto Moses." **(2c)** This meaning first appears in Gen 21:22, which mentions Phichol, the captain of Abimelech's "army." **(3)** At several points this is the meaning of the feminine plural: "And it shall be, when the officers have made an end of speaking unto the people, that they shall make captains of the armies to lead the people" (Deut 20:9). **(4)** In Num 1, 2, and 10, where *tsaba'* occurs with regard to a census of Israel, it is suggested that this was a military census by which God organized His "army" to march through the wilderness. **(4a)** Some scholars have noted that the plan of the march, or the positioning of the tribes, recalls the way ancient armies were positioned during military campaigns. **(4b)** On the other hand, groupings of people might be indicated regardless of military implications, as seems to be the case in passages such as Ex 6:26: "These are that Aaron and Moses, to whom the Lord said, Bring out the children of Israel from the land of Egypt according to their armies."

(5) That *tsaba'* can refer to a "nonmilitary host" is especially clear in Ps 68:11: "The Lord gave the word: great was the company of those that published it." **(6)** The phrase "hosts of heaven" signifies the stars as visual indications of the gods of the heathen: **(6a)** "And them that worship the host of heaven upon the housetops; and them that worship and that swear by the Lord, and that swear by Malcham . . ." (Zeph 1:5). **(6b)** This meaning first appears in Deut 4:19: "And lest thou lift up thine eyes unto heaven, and when thou seest the sun, and the moon, and the stars, even all the host of heaven, shouldest be driven to worship them, and serve them, which the LORD thy God hath divided unto all nations under the whole heaven."

(7) Sometimes this phrase refers to the "host of heaven," or the angels: "And [Micaiah] said, Hear thou therefore the word of the Lord: I saw the Lord sitting on his throne, and all the host of heaven [the angels] standing by him on his right hand and on his left" (1 Kin 22:19). **(7a)** God Himself is the commander of this "host" (Dan 8:10–11). **(7b)** In Josh 6:14 the commander of the "host" of God confronted Joshua. **(7c)** This heavenly "host" not only worships God but serves to do all His will: "Bless ye the Lord, all ye his hosts; ye ministers of his, that do his pleasure" (Ps 103:21). **(7d)** Another meaning of the phrase "the host(s) of heaven" is simply "the numberless stars": "As the host of heaven cannot be numbered, neither the sand of the sea measured: so will I multiply the seed of David my servant, and the Levites that minister unto me" (Jer 33:22). **(7e)** This phrase can include all the heavenly bodies, as it does in Ps 33:6: "By the word of the Lord were the heavens made; and all the host of them by the breath of his mouth." **(8)** In Gen 2:1 *tsaba'* includes the heavens, the earth, and everything in the creation: "Thus the heavens and the earth were finished, and all the host of them."

(9) The meaning "nonmilitary service in behalf of a superior" emerges in Num 4:2–3: "Take the sum of the sons of Kohath . . . from thirty years old and upward even until fifty years old, all that enter [the service], to do the work in the tabernacle of the congregation." **(10)** In Job 7:1 the word represents the burdensome everyday "toil" of mankind: "Is there not an appointed time to man upon earth? Are not his days also like the days of a hireling?" **(11)** In Job 14:14 *tsaba'* seems to represent "forced labor." **(12)** In Dan 10:1 the word is used for "conflict": "In the third year of Cyrus king of Persia a thing was revealed unto Daniel, whose name was called Belteshazzar; and the thing was true, but the time appointed was long: and he understood the thing, and had understanding of the vision." See: TWOT—1865a, 1865b; BDB—219b, 838d.

6636. צְבֹאִים {5x} **Tsᵉbôʾiym**, *tseb-o-eem'*; or (more correctly)

צְבִיִּים **Tsᵉbîyîym**, *tseb-ee-yeem'*; or

צְבֹיִם **Tsᵉbîyim**, *tseb-ee-yeem'*; plur. of 6643; *gazelles; Tseboïm or Tsebijim*, a place in Pal.:—Zeboim {3x}, Zeboiim {2x}. See: BDB—839c, 840d.

6637. צֹבֵבָה {1x} **Tsôbêbâh**, *tso-bay-baw'*; fem. act. part. of the same as 6632; the *canopier* (with the art.); *Tsobebah*, an Israelitess:—Zobebah {1x}. See: BDB—839d.

6638. צָבָה {3x} **tsâbâh**, *tsaw-baw';* a prim. root; to *amass*, i.e. *grow turgid;* spec. to *array* an army against:—swell {2x}, fight {1x}. See: TWOT—1868; BDB—839d.

6639. צָבֶה {1x} **tsâbeh**, *tsaw-beh';* from 6638; *turgid:*—swell {1x}. See: TWOT—1868a; BDB—839d.

צֹבָה **Tsôbâh.** See 6678.

6640. צְבוּ {1x} **tsᵉbûw** (Aram.), *tseb-oo';* from 6634; prop. *will;* concr. an *affair* (as a matter of *determination*):—purpose {1x}. See: TWOT—2953a; BDB—1109c.

6641. צָבוּעַ {1x} **tsâbûwaʿ**, *tsaw-boo'-ah;* pass. part. of the same as 6648; *dyed* (in stripes), i.e. the *hyena:*—speckled {1x}. See: TWOT—1872b; BDB—840c.

6642. צָבַט {1x} **tsâbat**, *tsaw-bat';* a prim. root; to *grasp*, i.e. *hand* out:—reached {1x}. See: TWOT—1871; BDB—840b.

6643. צְבִי {32x} **tsᵉbîy**, *tseb-ee';* from 6638 in the sense of *prominence; splendor* (as *conspicuous*); also a *gazelle* (as *beautiful*):—roe {9x}, roebuck {5x}, glory {8x}, glorious {6x}, beautiful {1x}, beauty {1x}, goodly {1x}, pleasant {1x}. See: TWOT—1869a, 1870a; BDB—839c, 840a.

6644. צִבְיָא {1x} **Tsibyâ**, *tsib-yaw';* for 6645; *Tsibja*, an Isr.:—Zibia {1x}. See: BDB—840b.

6645. צִבְיָה {2x} **Tsibyâh**, *tsib-yaw';* for 6646; *Tsibjah*, an Israelitess:—Zibiah {2x}. See: BDB—840b.

6646. צְבִיָּה {2x} **tsᵉbîyâh**, *tseb-ee-yaw';* fem. of 6643; a *female* gazelle:—roe {2x}. See: TWOT—1870b; BDB—840b.

צְבִיִּים **Tsᵉbîyîym.** See 6636.

צְבָיִם **Tsᵉbâyîm.** See 6380.

6647. צְבַע {5x} **tsᵉbaʿ** (Aram.), *tseb-ah';* a root corresp. to that of 6648; to *dip:*—wet {5x}. See: TWOT—2954; BDB—1109c.

6648. צֶבַע {3x} **tsebaʿ**, *tseh'-bah;* from an unused root mean. to *dip* (into coloring fluid); a *dye:*—diverse colours {3x}. See: TWOT—1872a; BDB—840c, 1109c.

6649. צִבְעוֹן {8x} **Tsibʿôwn**, *tsib-one';* from the same as 6648; *variegated; Tsibon*, an Idumæan:—Zibeon {8x}. See: BDB—840d.

6650. צְבֹעִים {2x} **Tsᵉbôʿîym**, *tseb-o-eem';* plur. of 6641; *hyenas; Tseboïm*, a place in Pal.:—Zeboim {2x}. See: BDB—840d.

6651. צָבַר {7x} **tsâbar**, *tsaw-bar';* a prim. root; to *aggregate:*—heap up {3x}, heap {1x}, gather {2x}, lay {1x}. See: TWOT—1874; BDB—840d.

6652. צִבֻּר {1x} **tsibbûr**, *tsib-boor';* from 6551; a *pile:*—heap {1x}. See: TWOT—1874a; BDB—840d.

6653. צֶבֶת {1x} **tsebeth**, *tseh'-beth;* from an unused root appar. mean. to *grip;* a *lock* of stalks:—handful {1x}. See: TWOT—1875a; BDB—841a.

6654. צַד {33} **tsad**, *tsad;* contr. from an unused root mean. to *sidle* off; a *side;* fig. an *adversary:*—side {9x}beside {3x}, another {1x}. See: TWOT—1876a; BDB—841a, 1109c.

6655. צַד {2x} **tsad** (Aram.), *tsad;* corresp. to 6654; used adv. (with prep.) *at* or *upon* the *side* of:—concerning {1x}, against {1x}. See: TWOT—2955; BDB—1109c.

6656. צְדָא {1x} **tsᵉdâ** (Aram.), *tsed-aw';* from an unused root corresp. to 6658 in the sense of *intentness;* a (sinister) *design:*—true {1x}. Syn.: 539, 543, 571, 3330. See: TWOT—2956; BDB—1109c.

6657. צְדָד {2x} **Tsᵉdâd**, *tsed-awd';* from the same as 6654; a *siding; Tsedad*, a place near Pal.:—Zedad {2x}. See: BDB—841a.

6658. צָדָה {3x} **tsâdâh**, *tsaw-daw';* a prim. root; to *chase;* by impl. to *desolate:*—wait {1x}, hunt {1x}, destroyed {1x}. Syn.: 5362, 5422, 5595. See: TWOT—1877, 1878; BDB—841b, 1109c.

צֵדָה **tsêdâh.** See 6720.

6659. צָדוֹק {53x} **Tsâdôwq**, *tsaw-doke';* from 6663; *just; Tsadok*, the name of eight or nine Isr.:—Zadok {53x}. See: BDB—843b.

6660. צְדִיָּה {2x} **tsᵉdîyâh**, *tsed-ee-yaw';* from 6658; *design* [comp. 6656]:—laying of wait {2x}. See: TWOT—1877a; BDB—841b, 1109c.

6661. צִדִּים {1x} **Tsiddîym**, *tsid-deem';* plur. of 6654; *sides; Tsiddim* (with the art.), a place in Pal.:—Ziddim {1x}. See: BDB—841b.

6662. צַדִּיק {206x} **tsaddîyq**, *tsad-deek';* from 6663; *just:*—righteous {162x}, just {42x}, righteous man {1x}, lawful {1x}.

Tsaddîyq, as an adjective, means "righteous; just." **(1)** The word is used of God in Ex 9:27: "I have sinned this time: the Lord is righteous, and I and my people are wicked." **(2)** *Tsaddîyq* is used of a nation in Gen 20:4: "And he said, Lord, wilt thou slay also a righteous nation?" See: TWOT—1879c; BDB—843a.

צִדֹנִי **Tsîdônîy.** See 6722.

6663. צָדַק {41x} **tsâdaq**, *tsaw-dak'*; a prim. root; to *be* (caus. *make*) *right* (in a moral or forensic sense):—justify {23x}, righteous {10x}, just {3x}, justice {2x}, cleansed {1x}, clear ourselves {1x}, righteousness {1x}.

The basic meaning of *tsadaq* is to be righteous, be in the right, be justified, be just. **(1)** Originally this word meant to be stiff or straight. **(1a)** This word is used of a man regarded as having obtained deliverance from condemnation, and as being thus entitled to a certain inheritance. **(1b)** Thus a man is accounted or dealt with as righteous. It is really the reception and exercise of *tsedeq* (6664). **(1c)** Nowhere is the issue of righteousness more appropriate than in the problem of the suffering of the righteous presented to us in Job, **(1c1)** where the verb occurs 17 times. **(1c2)** Apart from the Book of Job the frequency of *tsadaq* in the various books is small. **(1d)** The first occurrence of the verb is in Gen 38:26, where Judah admits that Tamar was just in her demands: "She hath been more righteous than I; because that I gave her not to Shelah my son."

(2) The basic meaning of *tsadaq* is "to be righteous." **(2a)** It is a legal term which involves the whole process of justice. **(2b)** God "is righteous" in all of His relations, and **(2c)** in comparison with Him man is not righteous: "Shall mortal man be more just [righteous] than God?" (Job 4:17). **(3)** In a derived sense, the case presented may be characterized as a just cause in that all facts indicate that the person is to be cleared of all charges. **(3a)** Isaiah called upon the nations to produce witnesses who might testify that their case was right: "Let them bring forth their witnesses that they may be justified: or let them hear, and say, It is truth" (43:9). **(3b)** Job was concerned about his case and defended it before his friends: "Though I were righteous, yet would I not answer, but I would make supplication to my judge" (9:15). **(4)** *Tsadaq* may also be used to signify the outcome of the verdict, when a man is pronounced "just" and is judicially cleared of all charges. Job believed that the Lord would ultimately vindicate him against his opponents (Job 13:18).

(5) In its causative pattern, the meaning of the verb brings out more clearly the sense of a judicial pronouncement of innocence: "If there be a controversy between men, and they come unto judgment, that the judges may judge them; then they shall justify [tsadaq] the righteous [tsaddiq], and condemn the wicked" (Deut 25:1). **(6)** The Israelites were charged with upholding righteousness in all areas of life. **(6a)** When the court system failed because of corruption, the wicked were falsely "justified" and the poor were robbed of justice because of trumped-up charges. **(6b)** Absalom, thus, gained a large following by promising justice to the landowner (2 Sa 15:4). **(7)** God, however, assured Israel that justice would be done in the end: "Thou shalt not wrest the judgment of thy poor in his cause. Keep thee far from a false matter; and the innocent and righteous slay thou not: for I will not justify the wicked" (Ex 23:6–7). The righteous person followed God's example. **(8)** The psalmist exhorts his people to change their judicial system: "Defend the poor and fatherless: do justice to the afflicted and needy" (Ps 82:3). **(9)** Job's ultimate hope was in God's declaration of justification. The Old Testament is in agreement with this hope. When injustice prevails, God is the One who "justifies." See: TWOT—1879; BDB—842c, 1109d.

6664. צֶדֶק {116x} **tsedeq**, *tseh'-dek;* from 6663; the *right* (nat., mor. or legal); also (abstr.) *equity* or (fig.) *prosperity:*—righteousness {77x}, just {11x}, justice {10x}, righteous {8x}, righteously {3x}, right {3x}, righteous cause {1x}, unrighteousness {1x}, misc. {2x}.

Tsedeq, the masculine noun form, and *tsedaqah* (6666), the feminine form of the noun, **(1)** mean "righteousness." **(1a)** The feminine form of the word *tsedaqah*, which occurs 157 times, is found throughout the Old Testament (except for Ex, Lev, 2 Kin, Eccl, Lam, Hab, and Zeph). **(1b)** *Tsedeq*, which occurs 119 times, is found mainly in poetic literature. **(1b1)** The first usage of *tsedeq* is: "Ye shall do no unrighteousness in judgment: thou shalt not respect the person of the poor, nor honor the person of the mighty: but in righteousness shalt thou judge thy neighbor" (Lev 19:15); and **(1b2)** of *tsedaqah* is: "[Abram] believed in the Lord; and he counted it to him for righteousness" (Gen 15:6).

(2) Exegetes have spilled much ink in an attempt to understand contextually the words *tsedeq* and *tsedaqah*. **(2a)** The conclusions of the researchers indicate a two-fold significance: relational and legal. **(2a1)** On the one hand, the relationships among people and of a man to his God can be described as *tsedeq*, supposing the parties are faithful to each other's expectations. It is a **relational word. (2a2)** In Jacob's proposal to Laban, Jacob used the word *tsedaqah* to indicate the relationship. The KJV gives the following translation of *tsedaqah:* "So shall my righteousness answer for me in time to come, when it shall come for my hire before thy face" (Gen 30:33). **(2b)** On the other hand "righteousness" as an abstract or as the **legal status** of a relationship is also present in the Old Testament. The *locus classicus* is Gen 15:6: "And he [the Lord] counted it to him

[Abraham] for righteousness." **(2c)** Regrettably, in a discussion of the dynamic versus the static sense of the word, one or the other wins out, though both elements are present. **(2c1)** The books of Psalms and of the prophets particularly use the sense of **"righteousness" as a state;** cf. "Hearken to me, ye that follow after righteousness, ye that seek the Lord: look unto the rock whence ye are hewn, and to the hole of the pit whence ye are digged" (Is 51:1); and **(2c2)** "My righteousness is near; my salvation is gone forth, and mine arms shall judge the people; the isles shall wait upon me, and on mine arm shall they trust" (Is 51:5). **(2d)** Thus, in the discussion of the two nouns below the meanings lie between the dynamic and the static.

(3) *Tsedeq* and *tsedaqah* are legal terms signifying justice in conformity **(3a)** with the legal corpus (the Law; Deut 16:20), **(3b)** the judicial process (Jer 22:3), **(3c)** the justice of the king as judge (1 Kin 10:9; Ps 119:121; Prov 8:15), and also **(3d)** the source of justice, God Himself: "Judge me, O Lord my God, according to thy righteousness; and let them not rejoice over me.... And my tongue shall speak of thy righteousness and of thy praise all the day long" (Ps 35:24, 28). **(4)** The word "righteousness" also embodies all that God expects of His people. **(4a)** The verbs associated with "righteousness" indicate the practicality of this concept. One judges, deals, sacrifices, and speaks righteously; and one learns, teaches, and pursues after righteousness. **(4b)** Based upon a special relationship with God, the Old Testament saint asked God to deal righteously with him: "Give the king thy judgments, O God, and thy righteousness unto the king's son" (Ps 72:1). See: TWOT—1879a; BDB—575d, 841c.

6665. צִדְקָה {1x} **tsidqâh** (Aram.), *tsid-kaw'*; corresp. to 6666; *beneficence:*—righteousness {1x}. See: TWOT—2957; BDB—1109d.

6666. צְדָקָה {157x} **ts⁰dâqâh**, *tsed-aw-kaw'*; from 6663; *rightness* (abstr.), subj. (*rectitude*), obj. (*justice*), mor. (*virtue*) or fig. (*prosperity*):—righteousness {128x}, justice {15x}, right {9x}, righteous acts {3x}, moderately {1x}, righteously {1x}. For a complete discussion, see 6664. See: TWOT—1879b; BDB—842a, 1109d.

6667. צִדְקִיָה {63x} **Tsidqîyâh**, *tsid-kee-yaw'*; or

צִדְקִיָהוּ **Tsidqîyâhûw**, *tsid-kee-yaw'-hoo;* from 6664 and 3050; *right of Jah; Tsidkijah,* the name of six Isr.:—Zedekiah {62x}, Zidkijah {1x}. See: BDB—843b.

6668. צָהַב {1x} **tsâhab**, *tsaw-hab';* a prim. root; to *glitter,* i.e. *be golden* in color:—fine {1x}. See: TWOT—1880; BDB—843c.

6669. צָהֹב {3x} **tsâhôb**, *tsaw-obe';* from 6668; *golden* in color:—yellow {3x}. See: TWOT—1880a; BDB—843c.

6670. צָהַל {9x} **tsâhal**, *tsaw-hal';* a prim. root; to *gleam,* i.e. (fig.) *be cheerful;* by transf. to *sound* clear (of various animal or human expressions):—cry aloud {2x}, bellow {1x}, neighed {1x}, cry out {1x}, rejoiced {1x}, shine {1x}, shout {1x}, lift up {1x}. See: TWOT—1881, 1882; BDB—843c, 843d.

6671. צָהַר {1x} **tsâhar**, *tsaw-har';* a prim. root; to *glisten;* used only as denom. from 3323, to *press* out *oil:*—make oil {1x}. See: TWOT—1883d; BDB—844a.

6672. צֹהַר {24x} **tsôhar**, *tso'-har;* from 6671; *a light* (i.e. *window*): dual *double light,* i.e. *noon:*—noon {11x}, noonday {9x}, day {1x}, midday {1x}, noontide + 6256 {1x}, window {1x}. See: TWOT—1883a, 1883b; BDB—843d, 844a.

6673. צַו {9x} **tsav**, *tsav;* or

צָו **tsâv;**, *tsawv;* from 6680; an *injunction:*—precept {8x}, commandment {1x}. See: TWOT—1887c; BDB—844b, 846c.

6674. צוֹא {2x} **tsôw'**, *tso;* or

צֹא **tsô'**, *tso;* from an unused root mean. to *issue; soiled* (as if *excrementitious*):—filthy {2x}. See: TWOT—1884; BDB—838a, 844b.

6675. צוֹאָה {5x} **tsôw'âh**, *tso-aw';* or

צֹאָה **tsô'âh**, *tso-aw':* fem. of 6674; *excrement;* gen. *dirt;* fig. *pollution:*—dung {2x}, filthiness {2x}, filth {1x}. See: TWOT—1884b; BDB—838a, 844b. [*marg. for* 2716.]

6676. צַוָּאר **tsavvᵃ'r** (Aram.), *tsav-var';* corresp. to 6677:—neck {3x}. See: TWOT—2958; BDB—1109d.

6677. צַוָּאר {42x} **tsavvâ'r**, *tsav-vawr';* or

צַוָּר **tsavvâr** (Neh. 3:5), *tsav-vawr';* or

צַוָּרֹן **tsavvârôn** (Cant. 4:9), *tsav-vaw-rone';* or (fem.)

צַוָּארָה **tsavvâ'râh** (Mic. 2:3) *tsav-vaw-raw';* intens. from 6696 in the sense of *binding;* the *back of the neck* (as that on which burdens are *bound*):—neck {42x}. See: TWOT—1897a; BDB—844b, 848b, 848c, 850a, 1109d.

6678. צוֹבָא {12x} **Tsôwbâ᾽**, *tso-baw'*; or

צוֹבָה **Tsôwbâh**, *tso-baw'*; or

צֹבָה **Tsôbâh**, *tso-baw'*; from an unused root mean. to *station; a station; Zoba* or *Zobah*, a region of Syria:—Zobah {10x}, Zoba {2x}. See: BDB—844b.

6679. צוּד {18x} **tsûwd**, *tsood;* a prim. root; to *lie* alongside (i.e. in wait); by impl. to *catch* an animal (fig. men); (denom. from 6718) to *victual* (for a journey):—hunt {13x}, take {2x}, chased {1x}, provision {1x}, sore {1x}. See: TWOT—1885; BDB—844c, 845b.

6680. צָוָה {494x} **tsâvâh**, *tsaw-vaw';* a prim. root; (intens.) to *constitute, enjoin:*—command {514x}, charge {39x}, commandment {9x}, appoint {5x}, bade {3x}, order {3x}, commander {1x}, misc. {4x}.

This word signifies to set up or appoint. *Tsavah*, as a verb, means "to command." **(1)** Essentially, this verb refers to verbal communication by which a superior "orders" or "commands" a subordinate. **(1a)** The word implies the content of what was said. **(1b)** Pharaoh "ordered" ("commanded") his men concerning Abraham, and they escorted Abraham and his party out of Egypt (Gen 12:20). **(1c)** This "order" defines an action relevant to a specific situation. **(2)** *Tsavah* can also connote "command" in the sense of the establishment of a rule by which a subordinate is to act in every recurring similar situation. **(2a)** In the Garden of Eden (the first appearance of this word in the Bible), God "commanded" ("set down the rule"): "Of every tree of the garden thou mayest freely eat: . . ." (Gen 2:16). **(2b)** In this case, the word does not contain the content of the action but focuses on the action itself. **(2c)** One of the recurring formulas in the Bible is "X did all that Y commanded him"—e.g., Ruth "did according to all that her mother-in-law bade her" (Ruth 3:6). This means that she carried out Naomi's "orders." **(2d)** A similar formula, "X did just as Y commanded," is first found in Num 32:25, where the sons of Reuben and Gad say to Moses that they "will do as my lord commandeth." **(2e)** These formulas indicate the accomplishment of, or the intention to accomplish, the "orders" of a superior.

(3) The verb *tsavah* can be used of a commission or charge, such as the act of "commanding," "telling," or "sending" someone to do a particular task. **(3a)** In Gen 32:4, Jacob "commissioned" his servants to deliver a particular message to his brother Esau. They acted as his emissaries. **(3b)** Jacob commissioned (literally, "commanded") his sons to bury him in the cave of Machpelah (Gen 49:30), and then he died. This "command" constituted a last will and testament—an obligation or duty. The verb again indicates, therefore, appointing someone to be one's emissary. **(4)** The most frequent subject of this verb is God. **(4a)** However, He is not to be questioned or "commanded" to explain the work of His hands (Is 45:11). **(4b)** He tells Israel that His "commands" are unique, requiring an inner commitment and not just external obedience, as the commands of men do (Gen 29:13). **(4c)** His "ordering" is given to Moses from above the mercy seat (Ex 25:22) and from His "commands" at Sinai (Lev 7:38; cf. 17:1ff.). **(4d)** At other times when He "commands," the thing simply occurs; His word is active and powerful (Ps 33:9). **(4e)** He also issues "orders" through and to the prophets (Jer 27:4) who explain, apply, and speak His "commands" (Jer 1:17). See: TWOT—1887; BDB—845b.

6681. צָוַח {1x} **tsâvach**, *tsaw-vakh';* a prim. root; to *screech* (exultingly):—shout {1x}. See: TWOT—1888; BDB—846d.

6682. צְוָחָה {4x} **tsᵉvâchâh**, *tsev-aw-khaw';* from 6681; a *screech* (of anguish):—cry {2x}, crying {1x}, complaining {1x}. See: TWOT—1888a; BDB—846d.

6683. צוּלָה {1x} **tsûwlâh**, *tsoo-law';* from an unused root mean. to *sink;* an *abyss* (of the sea):—deep {1x}. See: TWOT—1889a; BDB—846d.

6684. צוּם {21x} **tsûwm**, *tsoom;* a prim. root; to *cover* over (the mouth), i.e. to *fast:*—fast {20x}, at all {1x}. See: TWOT—1890; BDB—847a.

6685. צוֹם {26x} **tsôwm**, *tsome;* or

צֹם **tsôm**, *tsome;* from 6684; a *fast:*—fast {16x}, fasting {9x}, fasted + 6684 {1x}. See: TWOT—1890a; BDB—847b.

6686. צוּעָר {5x} **Tsûwʿâr**, *tsoo-awr';* from 6819; *small; Tsuär*, an Isr.:—Zuar {5x}. See: BDB—859b.

6687. צוּף {3x} **tsûwph**, *tsoof;* a prim. root; to *overflow:*—flow {1x}, overflow {1x}, swim {1x}. See: TWOT—1892; BDB—847b.

6688. צוּף {2x} **tsûwph**, *tsoof;* from 6687; *comb* of honey (from *dripping*):—honeycomb {2x}. See: TWOT—1892a; BDB—847b.

6689. צוּף {4x} **Tsûwph**, *tsoof;* or

צוֹפַי **Tsôwphay**, *tso-fah'-ee;* or

צִיף **Tsîyph**, *tseef;* from 6688; *honeycomb; Tsuph* or *Tsophai* or *Tsiph*, the name of an Isr. and of a place in Pal.:—Zuph {4x}. See: BDB—847c, 851c.

6690. צוֹפַח {2x} **Tsôwphach**, *tso-fakh';* from an unused root mean. to *expand, breadth; Tsophach*, an Isr.:—Zophah {2x}. See: BDB—860c.

צוֹפִי **Tsôwphay.** See 6689.

6691. צוֹפַר {4x} **Tsôwphar**, *tso-far';* from 6852; *departing; Tsophar*, a friend of Job:—Zophar {4x}. See: BDB—862b.

6692. צוּץ {9x} **tsûwts**, *tsoots;* a prim. root; to *twinkle*, i.e. *glance;* by anal. to *blossom* (fig. *flourish*):—flourish {5x}, blossom {2x}, bloomed {1x}, shewing {1x}. See: TWOT—1893, 1894; BDB—847c, 847d.

6693. צוּק {11x} **tsûwq**, *tsook;* a prim. root; to *compress*, i.e. (fig.) *oppress, distress:*—distress {5x}, oppressor {2x}, sore {1x}, press {1x}, straiten {1x}. See: TWOT—1895; BDB—847d.

6694. צוּק {3x} **tsûwq**, *tsook;* a prim. root [rather ident. with 6693 through the idea of *narrowness* (of orifice)]; to *pour out*, i.e. (fig.) *smelt, utter:*—pour {2x}, molten {1x}. See: TWOT—1896; BDB—848b, 862c.

6695. צוֹק {4x} **tsôwq**, *tsoke;* or (fem.)

צוּקָה **tsûwqâh**, *tsoo-kaw';* from 6693; a *strait*, i.e. (fig.) *distress:*—anguish {4x}. See: TWOT—1895a, 1895b; BDB—848a.

6696. צוּר {38x} **tsûwr**, *tsoor;* a prim. root; to *cramp*, i.e. *confine* (in many applications, lit. and fig., formative or hostile):—besiege {21x}, lay siege {3x}, distress {3x}, bind {2x}, adversaries {1x}, assault {1x}, bags {1x}, beset {1x}, cast {1x}, fashioned {1x}, fortify {1x}, inclose {1x}, bind up {1x}. See: TWOT—1898, 1899, 1900; BDB—848d, 849a, 849b, 1109d.

6697. צוּר {78x} **tsûwr**, *tsoor;* or

צֻר **tsur**, *tsoor;* from 6696; prop. a *cliff* (or sharp rock, as *compressed*); gen. a *rock* or *boulder;* fig. a *refuge;* also an *edge* (as *precipitous*):—rock {64x}, strength {5x}, sharp {2x}, God {2x}, beauty {1x}, edge {1x}, stones {1x}, mighty One {1x}, strong {1x}.
(1) *Tsur* means rocky wall or cliff (Ex 17:6; 33:21–22). **(2)** It frequently means rocky hill or mountains (Is 2:10, 19). **(3)** Figuratively, **(3a)** the rock flowing with honey and oil pictures the abundant overflowing blessing of God (Deut 32:13); **(3b)** The rock (or mountain) serves as a figure of security (Ps 61:2), firmness (Job 14:18), and something that endures (Job 19:24). **(4)** *Tsur* can mean rocky ground or perhaps a large flat rock (2 Sa 21:10; Prov 30:19). **(5)** The word means boulder in the sense of a rock large enough to serve as an altar (Judg 6:21). **(6)** Rock frequently pictures God's support and defense of His people (Deut 32:15). **(7)** It can be a name **(7a)** of God (Deut 32:4), or **(7b)** of heathen gods (Deut 32:31). **(8)** Abraham is the source (rock) from which Israel was hewn (Is 51:1). See: TWOT—1901a; BDB—849c, 866a. See also 1049.

6698. צוּר {5x} **Tsûwr**, *tsoor;* the same as 6697; *rock; Tsur*, the name of a Midianite and of an Isr.:—Zur {5x}. See: BDB—849d.

צוֹר **Tsôwr.** See 6865.

צַוָּר **tsavvâr.** See 6677.

6699. צוּרָה {4x} **tsûwrâh**, *tsoo-raw';* fem. of 6697; a *rock* (Job 28:10); also a *form* (as if *pressed* out):—form {4x}. See: TWOT—1900a; BDB—849b, 849c, 849d.

צַוָּרֹן **tsavvârôn.** See 6677.

6700. צוּרִיאֵל {1x} **Tsûwrîy'êl**, *tsoo-ree-ale';* from 6697 and 410; *rock of God; Tsuriël*, an Isr.:—Zuriel {1x}. See: BDB—849d.

6701. צוּרִישַׁדָּי {5x} **Tsûwrîyshadday**, *tsoo-ree-shad-dah'-ee;* from 6697 and 7706; *rock of* (the) *Almighty; Tsurishaddai*, an Isr.:—Zurishaddai {5x}. See: BDB—849d.

6702. צוּת {1x} **tsûwth**, *tsooth;* a prim. root; to *blaze:*—burn {1x}. See: TWOT—899; BDB—850a.

6703. צַח {4x} **tsach**, *tsakh;* from 6705; *dazzling*, i.e. *sunny, bright*, (fig.) *evident:*—white {1x}, clear {1x}, plainly {1x}, dry {1x}. See: TWOT—1903a; BDB—850a.

צְחָא **Tsîchâ'.** See 6727.

6704. צְחֶה {1x} **tsîcheh**, *tsee-kheh';* from an unused root mean. to *glow; parched:*—dried up {1x}. See: TWOT—1902a; BDB—850a.

6705. צָחַח {1x} **tsâchach**, *tsaw-khakh';* a prim. root; to *glare*, i.e. *be dazzling white:*—whiter {1x}. See: TWOT—1903; BDB—850a.

6706. צְחִיחַ {5x} **tsᵉchîyach**, *tsekh-ee'-akh;* from 6705; *glaring*, i.e. *exposed* to the bright sun:—top {4x}, higher places {1x}. See: TWOT—1903b; BDB—850a.

6707. צְחִיחָה {1x} **tsᵉchîychâh**, *tsekh-ee-khaw';* fem. of 6706; a *parched* region, i.e. the *desert:*—dry land {1x}. See: TWOT—1903c; BDB—850b.

6708. צְחִיחִי {1x} **tsᵉchîychîy**, *tsekh-ee-khee';* from 6706; *bare* spot, i.e. in the *glaring* sun:—higher place {1x}. See: TWOT—1903b; BDB—850a.

6709. צַחֲנָה {1x} **tsachănâh**, *tsakh-an-aw';* from an unused root mean. to

putrefy; stench:—ill savour {1x}. See: TWOT—1904a; BDB—850b.

6710. צַחְצָחָה {1x} **tsachtsâchâh**, *tsakh-tsaw-khaw';* from 6705; a *dry* place, i.e. *desert:*—drought {1x}. See: TWOT—1903d; BDB—850b.

6711. צָחַק {13x} **tsâchaq**, *tsaw-khak';* a prim. root; to *laugh* outright (in merriment or scorn); by impl. to *sport:*—laugh {6x}, mock {4x}, sport {2x}, play {1x}. See: TWOT—1905; BDB—850b.

6712. צְחֹק {2x} **ts°chôq**, *tsekh-oke';* from 6711; *laughter* (in pleasure or derision):—laugh {2x}. See: TWOT—1905a; BDB—850b.

6713. צָחַר **tsachar**, *tsakh'-ar;* from an unused root mean. to *dazzle; sheen,* i.e. *whiteness:*—white {1x}. See: TWOT—1906a; BDB—850c.

6714. צֹחַר {5x} **Tsôchar**, *tso'-khar;* from the same as 6713; *whiteness; Tsochar,* the name of a Hittite and of an Isr.:—Zoar {4x}, Jezoar {1x}. See: BDB—850c. comp. 3328.

6715. צָחֹר {1x} **tsâchôr**, *tsaw-khore';* from the same as 6713; *white:*—white {1x}. See: TWOT—1906b; BDB—850c.

6716. צִי {4x} **tsîy**, *tsee;* from 6680; a *ship* (as a *fixture*):—ship {4x}. See: TWOT—1907; BDB—850d, 851c.

6717. צִיבָא {16x} **Tsîybâ'**, *tsee-baw';* from the same as 6678; *station; Tsiba,* an Isr.:—Ziba {16x}. See: BDB—850d.

6718. צַיִד {19x} **tsayid**, *tsah'-yid;* from a form of 6679 and mean. the same; the *chase;* also *game* (thus taken); (gen.) *lunch* (espec. for a journey):—venison {8x}, hunter {3x}, victuals {2x}, provision {2x}, hunting {1x}, catch {1x}, food {1x}, hunting {1x}. See: TWOT—1885a, 1886a; BDB—844d, 845b.

6719. צַיָּד {1x} **tsayâd**, *tsah'-yawd;* from the same as 6718; a *huntsman:*—hunter {1x}. See: TWOT—1885b; BDB—844d.

6720. צֵידָה {10x} **tsêydâh**, *tsay-daw';* or

צֵדָה **tsêdâh**, *tsay-daw';* fem. of 6718; *food:*—victuals {6x}, provision {2x}, meat {1x}, venison {1x}. See: TWOT—1886b; BDB—841b, 845b.

6721. צִידוֹן {22x} **Tsîydôwn**, *tsee-done';* or

צִידֹן **Tsîydôn**, *tsee-done';* from 6679 in the sense of *catching* fish; *fishery; Tsidon,* the name of a son of Canaan, and of a place in Pal.:—Zidon {20x}, Sidon {2x}. See: BDB—850d.

6722. צִידֹנִי {16x} **Tsîydôniy**, *tsee-do-nee';* patrial from 6721; a *Tsidonian* or inhab. of Tsidon:—Zidonians {10x}, Sidonians {5x}, them of Zidon {1x}. See: BDB—841b, 851a.

6723. צִיָּה {16x} **tsîyâh**, *tsee-yaw';* from an unused root mean. to *parch; aridity;* concr. a *desert:*—dry {7x}, dry land {2x}, wilderness {2x}, drought {2x}, dry places {1x}, solitary place {1x}, barren {1x}. See: TWOT—1909a; BDB—851a.

6724. צִיוֹן {2x} **tsîyôwn**, *tsee-yone';* from the same as 6723; a *desert:*—dry place {2x}. See: TWOT—1909b; BDB—851b, 851c.

6725. צִיּוּן {3x} **tsîyûwn**, *tsee-yoon';* from the same as 6723 in the sense of *conspicuousness* [comp. 5329]; a *monumental* or guiding *pillar:*—title {1x}, waymark {1x}, sign {1x}. See: TWOT—1887a; BDB—846b, 851c.

6726. צִיּוֹן {154x} **Tsîyôwn**, *tsee-yone';* the same (reg.) as 6725; *Tsijon* (as a permanent *capital*), a mountain of Jerusalem:—Zion {153x}, Sion {1x}. See: TWOT—1910; BDB—851b.

6727. צִיחָא {3x} **Tsîychâ'**, *tsee-khaw';* or

צִחָא **Tsîchâ'**, *tsee-khaw';* as if fem. of 6704; *drought; Tsicha,* the name of two Nethinim:—Ziha {3x}. See: BDB—850a, 851c.

6728. צִיִּי {6x} **tsîyîy**, *tsee-ee';* from the same as 6723; a *desert-dweller,* i.e. *nomad* or wild *beast:*—desert {3x}, wilderness {3x}. See: TWOT—1908; BDB—850d, 851c.

6729. צִינֹק {1x} **tsîynôq**, *tsee-noke';* from an unused root mean. to *confine;* the *pillory:*—stocks {1x}. See: TWOT—1941a; BDB—851c, 857b.

6730. צִיעֹר {1x} **Tsîy‘ôr**, *tsee-ore';* from 6819; *small; Tsior,* a place in Pal.:—Zior {1x}. See: BDB—851c, 859b.

צִיף **Tsîyph**. See 6689.

6731. צִיץ {15x} **tsîyts**, *tseets;* or

צִץ **tsîts**, *tseets;* from 6692; prop. *glistening,* i.e. a burnished *plate;* also a *flower* (as *bright* colored); a *wing* (as *gleaming* in the air):—flower {10x}, plate {3x}, blossom {1x}, wings {1x}. See: TWOT—1911; BDB—751c, 847c, 847d, 851c, 862c.

6732. צִיץ {1x} **Tsîyts**, *tseets;* the same as 6731; *bloom; Tsits,* a place in Pal.:—Ziz {1x}. See: BDB—847d, 851d.

6733. צִיצָה {1x} **tsîytsâh**, *tsee-tsaw';* fem. of 6731; a *flower:*—flower {1x}. See: BDB—847d, 851c.

6734. צִיצִת {4x} **tsîytsîth**, *tsee-tseeth'*; fem. of 6731; a *floral* or *wing*-like projection, i.e. a *fore-lock* of hair, a *tassel*:—fringe {3x}, lock {1x}. See: TWOT—1912; BDB—851d.

צִיקְלַג **Tsîyqᵉlag**. See 6860.

6735. צִיר {12x} **tsîyr**, *tseer;* from 6696; a *hinge* (as *pressed* in turning); also a *throe* (as a physical or mental *pressure*); also a *herald* or errand-doer (as *constrained* by the principal):—ambassador {4x}, pang {3x}, messenger {2x}, pains {1x}, hinge {1x}, sorrow {1x}. See: TWOT—1913a, 1914a, 1914b; BDB—851d, 852a. comp. 6736.

6736. צִיר {2x} **tsîyr**, *tseer;* the same as 6735; a *form* (of beauty; as if *pressed* out, i.e. *carved*); hence, an (idolatrous) *image*:—idol {1x}, variant {1x}. Syn.: 5566, 6754, 8544. See: TWOT—1900b; BDB—849c, 851d.

6737. צָיַר {1x} **tsâyar**, *tsaw-yar'*; a denom. from 6735 in the sense of *ambassador;* to *make an errand,* i.e. *betake* oneself:—ambassador {1x}. See: BDB—851d.

6738. צֵל {49x} **tsêl**, *tsale;* from 6751; *shade,* whether lit. or fig.:—shadow {45x}, defence {3x}, shade {1x}. See: TWOT—1921a; BDB—852a, 853b, 853c.

6739. צְלָא {2x} **tsᵉlâ³** (Aram.), *tsel-aw';* prob. corresp. to 6760 in the sense of *bowing; pray:*—pray {2x}. Syn.: 577, 1156, 4994, 6279, 6419, 7592. See: TWOT—2959; BDB—1109d.

6740. צָלָה {3x} **tsâlâh**, *tsaw-law';* a prim. root; to *roast:*—roast {3x}. See: TWOT—1915; BDB—852a.

6741. צִלָּה {3x} **Tsillâh**, *tsil-law';* fem. of 6738; *Tsillah,* an antediluvian woman:—Zillah {3x}. See: BDB—852a, 853c.

6742. צְלוּל {2x} **tsᵉlûwl**, *tsel-ool';* from 6749 in the sense of *rolling;* a (round or flattened) *cake:*—cake {1x}, variant {1x}. See: TWOT—1922a; BDB—853d.

6743. צָלַח {65x} **tsâlach**, *tsaw-lakh';* or

צָלֵחַ **tsâlêach**, *tsaw-lay'-akh;* a prim. root; to *push* forward, in various senses (lit. or fig., tran. or intr.):—prosper {44x}, come {6x}, prosperous {5x}, come mightily {2x}, effected {1x}, good {1x}, meet {1x}, break out {1x}, went over {1x}, misc. {3x}.

Tsaleach means "to succeed, prosper." **(1)** The word is first found in Gen 24:21: ". . . whether the Lord had made his journey prosperous [literally, "to prosper"] or not." **(2)** This word generally expresses the idea of a successful venture, as contrasted with failure. The source of such success is God: "as long as

he sought the Lord, God made him to prosper" (2 Chr 26:5). **(3)** In spite of that, the circumstances of life often raise the question, "Wherefore doth the way of the wicked prosper?" (Jer 12:1). **(4)** It is sometimes used in such a way as to indicate "victory": "In your majesty ride prosperously" (Ps 45:4). See: TWOT—1916, 1917; BDB—852a, 852b, 1109d.

6744. צְלַח {4x} **tsᵉlach** (Aram.), *tsel-akh';* corresp. to 6743; to *advance* (tran. or intr.):—prosper {3x}, promote {1x}. See: TWOT—2960; BDB—1109d.

6745. צֵלָחָה {1x} **tsêlâchâh**, *tsay-law-khaw';* from 6743; something *protracted* or flattened out, i.e. a *platter:*—pan {1x}. See: TWOT—1918a; BDB—852c.

6746. צְלֹחִית {1x} **tsᵉlôchîyth**, *tsel-o-kheeth';* from 6743; something *prolonged* or tall, i.e. a *vial* or salt-*cellar:*—cruse {1x}. See: TWOT—1918c; BDB—852d.

6747. צַלַּחַת {3x} **tsallachath**, *tsal-lakh'-ath;* from 6743; something *advanced* or deep, i.e. a *bowl;* fig. the *bosom:*—bosom {2x}, dish {1x}. See: TWOT—1918b; BDB—852c.

6748. צָלִי {3x} **tsâlîy**, *tsaw-lee';* pass. part. of 6740; *roasted:*—roast {3x}. See: TWOT—1915a; BDB—852a, 852d.

6749. צָלַל {1x} **tsâlal**, *tsaw-lal';* a prim. root; prop. to *tumble* down, i.e. *settle* by a waving motion:—sink {1x}. See: TWOT—1920; BDB—853a. comp. 6750, 6751.

6750. צָלַל {4x} **tsâlal**, *tsaw-lal';* a prim. root [rather ident. with 6749 through the idea of *vibration*]; to *tinkle,* i.e. *rattle* together (as the ears in *reddening* with shame, or the teeth in *chattering* with fear):—tingle {3x}, quiver {1x}. See: TWOT—1919; BDB—852d.

6751. צָלַל {2x} **tsâlal**, *tsaw-lal';* a prim. root [rather ident. with 6749 through the idea of *hovering* over (comp. 6754)]; to *shade,* as twilight or an opaque object:—begin to be dark {1x}, shadowing {1x}. See: TWOT—1921; BDB—853a, 1094b.

6752. צֵלֶל {4x} **tsêlel**, *tsay'-lel;* from 6751; *shade:*—shadow {4x}. See: TWOT—1921a; BDB—853b.

6753. צְלֶלְפּוֹנִי {1x} **Tsᵉlelpôwnîy**, *tsel-el-po-nee';* from 6752 and the act. part. of 6437; *shade-facing; Tseleleponi,* an Israelitess:—Hazelelponi {1x}. See: BDB—853c.

6754. צֶלֶם {17x} **tselem**, *tseh'-lem;* from an unused root mean. to *shade;* a *phantom,* i.e. (fig.) *illusion, resemblance;*

hence, a representative *figure*, espec. an *idol*:—image {16x}, vain shew {1x}. **(1)** This word means statue (2 Kin 11:18; Num 33:52). **(2)** It signifies a replica (1 Sa 6:5). **(3)** In Eze 23:14 *tselem* represents a wall painting of some Chaldeans. **(4)** The word means image in the sense of essential nature: **(4a)** human nature in its internal and external characteristics rather than an exact duplicate: "And Adam lived an hundred and thirty years, and begat a son in his own likeness, after his image; and called his name Seth:" (Gen 5:3); or **(4b)** God made man in His own image, **(4b1)** reflecting some of His own perfections: perfect in knowledge, righteousness, and holiness, and with dominion over the creatures (Gen 1:26). **(4b2)** Being created in God's image meant being created male and female, in a loving unity of more than one person (Gen 1:27). **(5)** In Ps 39:6 *tselem* means shadow of a thing which represents the original very imprecisely, or it means merely a phantom, a thing which represents the original more closely but lacks its essential characteristic [reality]: "Surely every man walketh in a vain shew: surely they are disquieted in vain: he heapeth up riches, and knoweth not who shall gather them." **(6)** In Ps 73:20 the word represents a dream image: "As a dream when one awaketh; so, O Lord, when thou awakest, thou shalt despise their image." See: TWOT—1923a; BDB—853d, 1109d.

6755. צֶלֶם {17x} **tselem** (Aram.), *tseh'-lem;* or

צְלֵם **tsᵉlem** (Aram.), *tsel-em';* corresp. to 6754; an idolatrous *figure*:—form {16x}, image {1x}. See: TWOT—2961; BDB—1109d.

6756. צַלְמוֹן {3x} **Tsalmôwn**, *tsal-mone';* from 6754; *shady; Tsalmon,* the name of a place in Pal. and of an Isr.:—Zalmon {2x}, Salmon {1x}. See: BDB—854a.

6757. צַלְמָוֶת {18x} **tsalmâveth**, *tsal-maw'-veth;* from 6738 and 4194; *shade of death,* i.e. the *grave* (fig. *calamity*):—shadow of death {18x}. See: TWOT—1921b; BDB—853c, 854a.

6758. צַלְמֹנָה {2x} **Tsalmônâh**, *tsal-mo-naw';* fem. of 6757; *shadiness; Tsalmonah,* a place in the desert:—Zalmonah {2x}. See: BDB—854a.

6759. צַלְמֻנָּע {12x} **Tsalmunnâʿ**, *tsal-moon-naw';* from 6738 and 4513; *shade has been denied; Tsalmunna,* a Midianite:—Zalmunna {12x}. See: BDB—854a.

6760. צָלַע {4x} **tsâlaʿ**, *tsaw-lah';* a prim. root: prob. to *curve;* used only as denom. from 6763, to *limp* (as if *one-sided*):—halt {4x}. See: TWOT—1925; BDB—854b.

6761. צֶלַע {3x} **tselaʿ**, *tseh'-lah;* from 6760; a *limping* or *full* (fig.):—halt {1x}, adversity {1x}, variant {1x}. See: TWOT—1925a; BDB—854c.

6762. צֶלַע {2x} **Tselaʿ**, *tseh'-lah;* the same as 6761; *Tsela,* a place in Pal.:—Zelah {2x}. See: BDB—854b.

6763. צֵלָע {41x} **tsêlâʿ**, *tsay-law';* or (fem.)

צַלְעָה **tsalʿâh**, *tsal-aw';* from 6760; a *rib* (as *curved*), lit. (of the body) or fig. (of a door, i.e. *leaf*); hence, a *side*, lit. (of a person) or fig. (of an object or the sky, i.e. *quarter*); arch. a (espec. floor or ceiling) *timber* or *plank* (single or collect., i.e. a *flooring*):—side {19x}, chamber {11x}, boards {2x}, corners {2x}, rib {2x}, another {1x}, beams {1x}, halting {1x}, leaves {1x}, planks {1x}. See: TWOT—1924a; BDB—854b, 1106d.

6764. צָלָף {1x} **Tsâlâph**, *tsaw-lawf';* from an unused root of unknown mean.; *Tsalaph,* an Isr.:—Zalaph {1x}. See: BDB—854c.

6765. צְלָפְחָד {11x} **Tsᵉlophchâd**, *tsel-of-chawd';* from the same as 6764 and 259; *Tselophchad,* an Isr.:—Zelophehad {11x}. See: BDB—854c.

6766. צֶלְצַח {1x} **Tseltsach**, *tsel-tsakh';* from 6738 and 6703; *clear shade; Tseltsach,* a place in Pal.:—Zelzah {1x}. See: BDB—854c.

6767. צְלָצַל {6x} **tsᵉlâtsal**, *tsel-aw-tsal';* from 6750 redupl.; a *clatter,* i.e. (abstr.) *whirring* (of wings); (concr.) a *cricket;* also a *harpoon* (as *rattling*), a *cymbal* (as *clanging*):—cymbal {3x}, locust {1x}, spear {1x}, shadowing {1x}. See: TWOT—1919a, 1919b, 1919c; BDB—852d, 854c.

6768. צֶלֶק {2x} **Tseleq**, *tseh'-lek;* from an unused root mean. to *split; fissure; Tselek,* an Isr.:—Zelek {2x}. See: BDB—854c.

6769. צִלְּתַי {2x} **Tsillᵉthay**, *tsil-leth-ah'-ee;* from the fem. of 6738; *shady; Tsillethai,* the name of two Isr.:—Zilthai {2x}. See: BDB—853c, 854c.

צֹם **tsôm**. See 6685.

6770. צָמֵא {10x} **tsâmêʾ**, *tsaw-may';* a prim. root; to *thirst* (lit. or fig.):—thirst {5x}, athirst {2x}, thirsty {1x}, suffer thirst {1x}, suffer thirst {1x}. See: TWOT—1926; BDB—854c.

6771. צָמֵא {9x} **tsâmêʾ**, *tsaw-may';* from 6770; *thirsty* (lit. or fig.):—thirsty {7x}, thirst {2x}. See: TWOT—1926b; BDB—854d.

6772. צָמָא **tsâmâ⁾,** *tsaw-maw';* from 6770; *thirst* (lit. or fig.):—thirst {16x}, thirsty {1x}. See: TWOT—1926a; BDB—854d.

6773. צִמְאָה {1x} **tsim⁾âh,** *tsim-aw';* fem. of 6772; *thirst* (fig. of *libidinousness*):—thirst {1x}. See: TWOT—1926c; BDB—854d.

6774. צִמָּאוֹן {3x} **tsimmâ⁾ôwn,** *tsim-maw-one';* from 6771; *a thirsty* place, i.e. *desert:*—drought {1x}, dry ground {1x}, thirsty land {1x}. See: TWOT—1926d; BDB—855a.

6775. צָמַד {5x} **tsâmad,** *tsaw-mad';* a prim. root; to *link,* i.e. *gird;* fig. to *serve,* (mentally) *contrive:*—join {3x}, fasten {1x}, frame {1x}. See: TWOT—1927; BDB—855a.

6776. צֶמֶד {15x} **tsemed,** *tseh'-med;* a *yoke* or *team* (i.e. *pair*); hence, an *acre* (i.e. day's task for a yoke of cattle to plow):—yoke {7x}, couple {4x}, two {2x}, together {1x}, acres {1x}. See: TWOT—1927a; BDB—855a.

6777. צַמָּה {4x} **tsammâh,** *tsam-maw';* from an unused root mean. to *fasten on;* a *veil:*—locks {4x}. See: TWOT—1929a; BDB—855b, 855d.

6778. צַמּוּק {4x} **tsammûwq,** *tsam-mook';* from 6784; a cake of *dried* grapes:—cluster of raisins {2x}, bunch of raisins {2x}. See: TWOT—1930a; BDB—856a.

6779. צָמַח {33x} **tsâmach,** *tsaw-makh';* a prim. root; to *sprout* (tran. or intr., lit. or fig.):—grow {13x}, spring forth {6x}, spring up {4x}, grow up {2x}, bring forth {2x}, bud {2x}, spring out {2x}, beareth {1x}, bud forth {1x}. See: TWOT—1928; BDB—855b.

6780. צֶמַח {12x} **tsemach,** *tseh'-makh;* from 6779; a *sprout* (usually concr.), lit. or fig.:—Branch {4x}, bud {3x}, branch {1x}, that which grew {1x}, spring {1x}, springing {1x}, grew {1x}. See: TWOT—1928a; BDB—855c.

6781. צָמִיד {7x} **tsâmîyd,** *tsaw-meed';* or

צָמִד **tsâmid,** *tsaw-meed';* from 6775; a *bracelet* or *arm-clasp;* gen. a *lid:*—bracelet {6x}, covering {1x}. See: TWOT—1927b, 1927c; BDB—855b.

6782. צַמִּים {2x} **tsammîym,** *tsam-meem';* from the same as 6777; a *noose* (as *fastening*); fig. *destruction:*—robber {2x}. See: TWOT—1929b; BDB—855d.

6783. צְמִיתֻת {2x} **tsᵉmîythuth,** *tsem-ee-thooth';* or

צְמִתֻת **tsᵉmîthuth,** *tsem-ee-thooth';* from 6789; *excision,* i.e. *destruction;* used only (adv.) with prep. pref. to *extinction,*

i.e. *perpetually:*—for ever {2x}. Syn.: 753, 5331, 5703, 8548. See: TWOT—1932a; BDB—855d, 856c.

6784. צָמַק {1x} **tsâmaq,** *tsaw-mak';* a prim. root; to *dry* up:—dry {1x}. See: TWOT—1930; BDB—855d.

6785. צֶמֶר {16x} **tsemer,** *tseh'-mer;* from an unused root prob. mean. to *be shaggy; wool:*—woollen {5x}, wool {11x}. See: TWOT—1931a; BDB—856a, 1107a.

6786. צְמָרִי {2x} **Tsᵉmârîy,** *tsem-aw-ree';* patrial from an unused name of a place in Pal.; a *Tsemarite* or branch of the Canaanites:—Zemarite {2x}. See: BDB—856a.

6787. צְמָרַיִם {2x} **Tsᵉmârayim,** *tsem-aw-rah'-yim;* dual of 6785; *double fleece; Tsemarajim,* a place in Pal.:—Zemaraim {2x}. See: BDB—856b.

6788. צַמֶּרֶת {5x} **tsammereth,** *tsam-meh'-reth;* from the same as 6785; *fleeciness,* i.e. *foliage:*—top {3x}, highest branch {2x}. See: TWOT—1931b; BDB—856a.

6789. צָמַת {15x} **tsâmath,** *tsaw-math';* a prim. root; to *extirpate* (lit. or fig.):—cut off {8x}, destroy {5x}, vanish {1x}, consume {1x}. See: TWOT—1932; BDB—856b.

צְמִתֻת **tsᵉmîthuth.** See 6783.

6790. צִן {10x} **Tsîn,** *tseen;* from an unused root mean. to *prick;* a *crag; Tsin,* a part of the desert:—Zin {10x}. See: BDB—851c, 856c.

6791. צֵן {2x} **tsên,** *tsane;* from an unused root mean. to *be prickly;* a *thorn;* hence, a cactus-*hedge:*—thorn {2x}. See: TWOT—1936a; BDB—856c, 856d.

6792. צֹנֵא {2x} **tsônê⁾,** *tso-nay';* or

צֹנֶה **tsôneh,** *tso-neh';* for 6629; a *flock:*—sheep {2x}. See: TWOT—1864a, 1933; BDB—856c.

6793. צִנָּה {22x} **tsinnâh,** *tsin-naw';* fem. of 6791; a *hook* (as *pointed*); also a (large) *shield* (as if guarding by *prickliness*); also *cold* (as *piercing*):—shield {10x}, buckler {5x}, target {5x}, hook {1x}, cold {1x}. See: TWOT—1936b, 1937a, 1938a; BDB—856c, 856d, 857a.

6794. צִנּוּר {2x} **tsinnûwr,** *tsin-noor';* from an unused root perh. mean. to *be hollow;* a *culvert:*—gutter {1x}, waterspout {1x}. See: TWOT—1942a; BDB—857c.

6795. צָנַח {3x} **tsânach,** *tsaw-nakh';* a prim. root; to *alight;* (tran.) to *cause to descend,* i.e. *drive* down:—lighted {2x}, fasten {1x}. See: TWOT—1934; BDB—856c.

6796. צָנִין {2x} **tsânîyn**, *tsaw-neen';* or

צְנִן **tsânin**, *tsaw-neen';* from the same as 6791; a *thorn:*—thorn {2x}. See: TWOT—1936c; BDB—856d.

6797. צָנִיף {6x} **tsânîyph**, *tsaw-neef';* or

צָנֹוף **tsânôwph**, *tsaw-nofe';* or (fem.)

צָנִיפָה **tsânîyphâh**, *tsaw-nee-faw';* from 6801; a *head-dress* (i.e. piece of cloth *wrapped* around):—diadem {2x}, mitre {2x}, hood {1x}, variant {1x}. See: TWOT—1940a; BDB—857b.

6798. צָנַם {1x} **tsânam**, *tsaw-nam';* a prim. root; to *blast* or *shrink:*—withered {1x}. See: TWOT—1935; BDB—856d.

6799. צְנָן {1x} **Ts⁽e⁾nân**, *tsen-awn';* prob. for 6630; *Tsenan,* a place near Pal.:— Zenan {1x}. See: BDB—838c, 857a.

צְנִן **tsânin.** See 6796.

6800. צָנַע {2x} **tsâna⁽c⁾**, *tsaw-nah';* a prim. root; to *humiliate:*—lowly {1x}, humbly {1x}. See: TWOT—1939; BDB—857a.

6801. צָנַף {3x} **tsânaph**, *tsaw-naf';* a prim. root; to *wrap,* i.e. *roll* or *dress:*— attired {1x}, violently turn {1x}, surely {1x}. See: TWOT—1940; BDB—857a.

6802. צְנֵפָה {1x} **ts⁽e⁾nêphâh**, *tsen-ay-faw';* from 6801; a *ball:*—toss {1x}. See: TWOT—1940b; BDB—857b.

6803. צִנְצֶנֶת {1x} **tsintseneth**, *tsin-tseh'-neth;* from the same as 6791; a *vase* (prob. a vial *tapering* at the top):—pot {1x}. See: TWOT—1938b; BDB—857a.

6804. צִנְתָּרָה {1x} **tsantârâh**, *tsan-taw-raw';* prob. from the same as 6794; a *tube:*—pipe {1x}. See: TWOT—1942b; BDB—857c.

6805. צָעַד {8x} **tsâ⁽c⁾ad**, *tsaw-ad';* a prim. root; to *pace,* i.e. *step* regularly; (up-ward) to *mount;* (along) to *march;* (down and caus.) to *hurl:*—go {3x}, march {3x}, run over {1x}, bring {1x}. See: TWOT—1943; BDB—857c.

6806. צַעַד {14x} **tsa⁽c⁾ad**, *tsah'-ad;* from 6804; a *pace* or regular *step:*—step {11x}, pace {1x}, goings {1x}, go {1x}. See: TWOT—1943a; BDB—857d.

6807. צְעָדָה {3x} **ts⁽e⁾‘âdâh**, *tseh-aw-daw';* fem. of 6806; a *march;* (concr.) an (or-namental) *ankle-chain:*—going {2x}, orna-ments of the legs {1x}. See: TWOT—1943b, 1943c; BDB—857d.

6808. צָעָה {5x} **tsâ⁽c⁾âh**, *tsaw-aw';* a prim. root; to *tip* over (for the purpose of

spilling or *pouring* out), i.e. (fig.) *depopulate;* by impl. to *imprison* or *conquer;* (refl.) to *lie down* (for coitus, sexual intercourse):—wander {2x}, captive exile {1x}, travelling {1x}, wan-derer {1x}. See: TWOT—1944; BDB—858a.

צָעֹור **tsâ⁽c⁾ôwr.** See 6810.

6809. צָעִיף {3x} **tsâ⁽c⁾îyph**, *tsaw-eef';* from an unused root mean. to *wrap* over; a *veil:*—vail {3x}. See: TWOT—1946a; BDB—858b.

6810. צָעִיר {22x} **tsâ⁽c⁾îyr**, *tsaw-eer';* or

צָעֹור **tsâ⁽c⁾ôwr**, *tsaw-ore';* from 6819; *lit-tle;* (in number) *few;* (in age) *young,* (in value) *ignoble:*—younger {8x}, least {4x}, youngest {3x}, little {2x}, little ones {2x}, small one {1x}, small {1x}, young + 3117 {1x}. See: TWOT—1948a; BDB—859a.

6811. צָעִיר {1x} **Tsâ⁽c⁾îyr**, *tsaw-eer';* the same as 6810; *Tsaïr,* a place in Idumaea:—Zair {1x}. See: BDB—859a.

6812. צְעִירָה {1x} **ts⁽e⁾‘îyrâh**, *tseh-ee-raw';* fem. of 6810; *smallness* (of age), i.e. *juvenility:*—youth {1x}. See: TWOT—1948b; BDB—859a.

6813. צָעַן {1x} **tsâ⁽c⁾an**, *tsaw-an';* a prim. root; to *load* up (beasts), i.e. to *mi-grate:*—taken down {1x}. See: TWOT—1945; BDB—858a.

6814. צֹעַן {7x} **Tsô⁽c⁾an**, *tso'-an;* of Eg. der.; *Tsoän,* a place in Egypt:—Zoan {7x}. See: BDB—130c, 858a.

6815. צַעֲנַנִּים {2x} **Tsa⁽c⁾ănannîym**, *tsah-an-an-neem';* or (dual)

צַעֲנַיִם **Tsa⁽c⁾ănayim**, *tsah-an-ah'-yim;* plur. from 6813; *removals; Tsaa-nannim* or *Tsaanajim,* a place in Pal.:—Zaan-nannim {1x}, Zaanaim {1x}. See: BDB—858b.

6816. צַעְצֻעַ {1x} **tsa⁽c⁾tsûa⁽c⁾**, *tsah-tsoo'-ah;* from an unused root mean. to *be-strew* with carvings; *sculpture:*—image {1x}. See: TWOT—1891a; BDB—847b, 858b.

6817. צָעַק {55x} **tsâ⁽c⁾aq**, *tsaw-ak';* a prim. root; to *shriek;* (by impl.) to *pro-claim* (an assembly):—cry {44x}, gather to-gether {4x}, cry out {3x}, at all {1x}, called {1x}, gathered {1x}, call together {1x}.

Tsa'aq means "to cry, cry out, call." **(1)** Its first occurrence is in the record of the suffering of the Israelite bondage in Egypt: "And the children of Israel sighed by reason of the bond-age, and they cried [for help]" (Ex 2:23). **(2)** *Tsa'aq* is perhaps most frequently used to indi-cate the "crying out" for aid in time of emer-gency, **(2a)** especially "crying out" for divine aid. **(2b)** God often heard this "cry" for help in

the time of the judges, as Israel found itself in trouble because of its backsliding (Judg 3:9, 15; 6:7; 10:10). **(3)** The word is used also in appeals to pagan gods (Judg 10:14; Jer 11:12; Jonah 1:5). **(4)** That *tsa'aq* means more than a normal speaking volume is indicated in appeals to the king: "For all of my father's house were but dead men before my lord the king: yet didst thou set thy servant among them that did eat at thine own table. What right therefore have I yet to cry any more unto the king?" (2 Sa 19:28). **(5)** The word may imply **(5a)** a "crying out" in distress (1 Sa 4:13), **(5b)** a "cry" of horror (1 Sa 5:10), or **(5c)** a "cry" of sorrow (2 Sa 13:19). **(6)** Used figuratively, it is said that "the stone shall cry out of the wall" (Hab 2:11) of a house that is built by means of evil gain. Syn.: 2199. See: TWOT—1947; BDB—858b.

6818. צְעָקָה {21x} **tsaⁿqâh**, *tsah-ak-aw'*; from 6817; a *shriek:*—cry {19x}, crying {2x}. See: TWOT—1947a; BDB—858c.

6819. צָעַר {3x} **tsaⁿar**, *tsaw-ar'*; a prim. root; to *be small*, i.e. (fig.) *ignoble:*—brought low {1x}, shall be small {1x}, little ones {1x}. See: TWOT—1948; BDB—858d.

6820. צֹעַר {10x} **Tsôⁿar**, *tso'ar*; from 6819; *little; Tsoär*, a place E. of the Jordan:—Zoar {10x}. See: BDB—118d, 858d.

6821. צָפַד {1x} **tsâphad**, *tsaw-fad'*; a prim. root; to *adhere:*—cleaveth {1x}. See: TWOT—1949; BDB—859b.

6822. צָפָה {37x} **tsâphâh**, *tsaw-faw'*; a prim. root; prop. to *lean* forward, i.e. to *peer* into the distance; by impl. to *observe, await:*—watchman {20x}, watch {8x}, behold {2x}, look {2x}, espy {1x}, look up {1x}, waited {1x}, look well {1x}, variant for Zophim {1x}.
I. Tsapah, as a verb, means "to overlay, spy, keep watch." **(1)** It occurs for the first time in the Old Testament in the so-called Mizpah Benediction: "The Lord watch between me and thee . . ." (Gen 31:49). **(1a)** The meaning in this context is "to watch" with a purpose, that of seeing that the covenant between Laban and Jacob was kept. **(1b)** Thus, the statement by Laban is more of a threat than a benediction. **(2)** Similarly, when God's "eyes behold the nations" (Ps 66:7), it is much more than a casual look. Perhaps in most uses, the connotation of "to spy" would be the most accurate.
II. As a participle, *tsaphah* is often used as a noun, *tsopeh*, meaning "watchman," or one whose task it is "to keep close watch": "But Absalom fled. And the young man that kept the watch lifted up his eyes, and looked, and, behold, there came much people by the way of the hill side behind him" (2 Sa 13:34). See: TWOT—1950; BDB—859b.

6823. צָפָה {46x} **tsâphâh**, *tsaw-faw'*; a prim. root [prob. rather ident. with 6822 through the idea of *expansion* in outlook, transferring to act]; to *sheet* over (espec. with metal):—overlay {40x}, covered {5x}, garnished {1x}. See: TWOT—1951; BDB—860a.

6824. צָפָה {1x} **tsâphâh**, *tsaw-faw'*; from 6823; an *inundation* (as *covering*):—swim {1x}. See: TWOT—1892b; BDB—847c, 859b.

6825. צְפוֹ {3x} **Tsᵉphôw**, *tsef-o'*; or

צְפִי **Tsᵉphîy**, *tsef-ee'*; from 6822; *observant; Tsepho* or *Tsephi*, an Idumæan:—Zepho {2x}, Zephi {1x}. See: BDB—859d, 860c.

6826. צִפּוּי {5x} **tsippûwy**, *tsip-poo'-ee;* from 6823; *encasement* (with metal):—covering {3x}, overlay {2x}. See: TWOT—1951a; BDB—860b.

6827. צְפוֹן {1x} **Tsᵉphôwn**, *tsef-one';* prob. for 6837; *Tsephon*, an Isr.:—Zephon {1x}. See: BDB—859d.

6828. צָפוֹן {153x} **tsâphôwn**, *tsaw-fone';* or

צָפֹן **tsâphôn**, *tsaw-fone';* from 6845; prop. *hidden,* i.e. *dark;* used only of the *north* as a quarter (*gloomy* and *unknown*):—north {116x}, northward {24x}, north side {11x}, northern {1x}, north wind {1x}. See: TWOT—1953b; BDB—859d, 860d, 861b.

6829. צָפוֹן {1x} **Tsâphôwn**, *tsaw-fone';* the same as 6828; *boreal; Tsaphon*, a place in Pal.:—Zaphon {1x}. See: BDB—861b.

6830. צְפוֹנִי {1x} **tsᵉphôwnîy**, *tsef-o-nee';* from 6828; *northern:*—northern {1x}. See: TWOT—1953c; BDB—859d, 861a.

6831. צְפוֹנִי {1x} **Tsᵉphôwnîy**, *tsef-o-nee';* patron. from 6827; a *Tsephonite*, or (collect.) desc. of Tsephon:—Zephonites {1x}. See: BDB—859d, 861b.

6832. צְפוּעַ {1x} **tsᵉphûwaⁿ**, *tsef-oo'-ah;* from the same as 6848; *excrement* (as *protruded*):—dung {1x}. See: TWOT—1955a; BDB—861c.

6833. צִפּוֹר {40x} **tsippôwr**, *tsip-pore';* or

צִפֹּר **tsippôr**, *tsip-pore';* from 6852; a little *bird* (as *hopping*):—bird {32x}, fowl {6x}, sparrow {2x}. See: TWOT—1959a; BDB—861d, 1110a.

6834. צִפּוֹר {7x} **Tsippôwr**, *tsip-pore';* the same as 6833; *Tsippor*, a Moabite:—Zippor {7x}. See: BDB—862a.

6835. צַפַּחַת {7x} **tsappachath**, *tsap-pakh'-ath;* from an unused root mean.

to *expand;* a *saucer* (as *flat*):—cruse {7x}. See: TWOT—1952a; BDB—860b.

6836. צְפִיָּה {1x} ts°phîyâh, *tsef-ee-yaw';* from 6822; *watchfulness:*—watching {1x}. See: TWOT—1950a; BDB—859d, 860c, 871a.

6837. צָפְיוֹן {1x} Tsiphyôwn, *tsif-yone';* from 6822; *watch*-tower; *Tsiphjon,* an Isr.:—Ziphion {1x}. See: BDB—859d, 860c. comp. 6827.

6838. צַפִּיחִת {1x} tsappîychîth, *tsap-pee-kheeth';* from the same as 6835; a flat thin *cake:*—wafers {1x}. See: TWOT—1952b; BDB—860c.

6839. צֹפִים {1x} Tsôphîym, *tso-feem';* plur. of act. part. of 6822; *watchers; Tso-phim,* a place E. of the Jordan:—Zophim {1x}. See: BDB—859c.

6840. צָפִין {1x} tsâphîyn, *tsaw-feen';* from 6845; a *treasure* (as *hidden*):—thy hid (treasure) {1x}. See: TWOT—1953a; BDB—860d.

6841. צְפִיר {1x} ts°phîyr (Aram.), *tsef-eer';* corresp. to 6842; a he-*goat:*—he {1x}. See: TWOT—2963; BDB—1110a.

6842. צָפִיר {6x} tsâphîyr, *tsaw-feer';* from 6852; a male *goat* (as *prancing*):—he {3x}, goat {2x}, he goat {1x}. See: TWOT—1962a; BDB—862b, 1110a.

6843. צְפִירָה {3x} ts°phîyrâh, *tsef-ee-raw';* fem. formed like 6842; a *crown* (as *encircling* the head); also a *turn* of affairs (i.e. *mishap*):—morning {2x}, diadem {1x}. See: TWOT—1960a; BDB—862a.

6844. צָפִית {1x} tsâphîyth, *tsaw-feeth';* from 6822; a *sentry:*—watchtower {1x}. See: TWOT—1951b; BDB—860b, 860c.

6845. צָפַן {33x} tsâphan, *tsaw-fan';* a prim. root; to *hide* (by *covering* over); by impl. to *hoard* or *reserve;* fig. to *deny;* spec. (favorably) to *protect,* (unfavorably) to *lurk:*—hide {16x}, lay up {7x}, esteemed {1x}, lurk {1x}, hidden ones {1x}, privily {1x}, secret places {1x}, secret {1x}, misc. {4x}. See: TWOT—1953; BDB—860c, 860d.

צָפֹן tsâphôn. See 6828.

6846. צְפַנְיָה {10x} Ts°phanyâh, *tsef-an-yaw';* or

צְפַנְיָהוּ Ts°phanyâhûw, *tsef-an-yaw'-hoo;* from 6845 and 3050; *Jah has secreted; Tsephanjah,* the name of four Isr.:—Zephaniah {10x}. See: BDB—861b.

6847. צָפְנַת פַּעְנֵחַ {1x} Tsophnath Pa°nêach, *tsof-nath' pah-nay'-akh;* of

Eg. der.; *Tsophnath-Paneäch,* Joseph's Eg. name:—Zaphnathpaaneah {1x}. See: BDB—861b.

6848. צֶפַע {5x} tsepha°, *tseh'-fah;* or

צִפְעֹנִי tsiph°ônîy, *tsif-o-nee';* from an unused root mean. to *extrude;* a *viper* (as *thrusting* out the tongue, i.e. *hissing*):—cockatrice {4x}, adder {1x}. See: TWOT—1954a, 1954b; BDB—861c.

6849. צְפִעָה {1x} ts°phi°âh, *tsef-ee-aw';* fem. from the same as 6848; an *outcast* thing:—issue {1x}. See: TWOT—1953a; BDB—861c.

צִפְעֹנִי tsiph°ônîy. See 6848.

6850. צָפַף {4x} tsâphaph, *tsaw-faf';* a prim. root; to *coo* or *chirp* (as a bird):—peep {2x}, chatter {1x}, whisper {1x}. See: TWOT—1957; BDB—861c.

6851. צַפְצָפָה {1x} tsaphtsâphâh, *tsaf-tsaw-faw';* from 6687; a *willow* (as growing in *overflowed* places):—willow tree {1x}. See: TWOT—1957a; BDB—861d.

6852. צָפַר {1x} tsâphar, *tsaw-far';* a prim. root; to *skip* about, i.e. *return:*—depart early {1x}. See: TWOT—1958; BDB—861d.

6853. צְפַר {4x} ts°phar (Aram.), *tsef-ar';* corresp. to 6833; a *bird:*—fowl {3x}, like birds {1x}. See: TWOT—2962; BDB—1110a.

צִפֹּר tsippôr. See 6833.

6854. צְפַרְדֵּעַ {13x} ts°phardêa°, *tsef-ar-day'-ah;* from 6852 and a word elsewhere unused mean. a *swamp;* a *marsh-leaper,* i.e. *frog:*—frog {13x}. See: TWOT—1963; BDB—862c.

6855. צִפֹּרָה {3x} Tsippôrâh, *tsip-po-raw';* fem. of 6833; *bird; Tsipporah,* Moses' wife:—Zipporah {3x}. See: BDB—862a.

6856. צִפֹּרֶן {2x} tsippôren, *tsip-po'-ren;* from 6852 (in the denom. sense [from 6833] of *scratching*); prop. a *claw,* i.e. (human) *nail;* also the *point* of a style (or pen, tipped with adamant):—nail {1x}, point {1x}. See: TWOT—1961a; BDB—862b, 1094c.

6857. צְפַת {1x} Ts°phath, *tsef-ath';* from 6822; *watch*-tower; *Tsephath,* a place in Pal.:—Zephath {1x}. See: BDB—862c.

6858. צֶפֶת {1x} tsepheth, *tseh'-feth;* from an unused root mean. to *encircle;* a *capital* of a column:—chapiter {1x}. See: TWOT—1951c; BDB—860b, 862c.

6859. צְפָתָה {1x} Ts°phâthâh, *tsef-aw'-thaw;* the same as 6857; *Tsephathah,* a

place in Pal.:—Zephathah {1x}. See: BDB—862c.

צִץ **tsîts.** See 6732.

6860. צִקְלַג {15x} **Tsiqlâg,** *tsik-lag';* or

צִיקְלַג **Tsîyqᵉlag** (1 Chron. 12:1, 20), *tsee-kel-ag';* of uncert. der.: Tsiklag or Tsikelag, a place in Pal.:—Ziklag {15x}. See: BDB—851d, 862c.

6861. צִקְלֹן {1x} **tsiqlôn,** *tsik-lone';* from an unused root mean. to *wind;* a *sack* (as *tied* at the mouth):—husk {1x}. See: TWOT—1964; BDB—862d.

6862. צַר {105x} **tsar,** *tsar;* or

צָר **tsâr,** *tsawr;* from 6887; *narrow;* (as a noun) a *tight* place (usually fig., i.e. *trouble*); also a *pebble* (as in 6864); (tran.) an *opponent* (as *crowding*):—enemy {37x}, adversary {26x}, trouble {17x}, distress {5x}, affliction {3x}, foes {2x}, narrow {2x}, strait {2x}, flint {1x}, sorrow {1x}, misc. {9x} = afflicted, anguish, close, small, tribulation.

Tsar, **as a noun,** means "adversary; enemy; foe; distress; affliction." **(1)** This word also occurs mostly in poetry. **(1a)** In Prov 24:10, *tsar* means "scarcity" or the "distress" caused by scarcity: "If thou faint in the day of adversity, thy strength is small." **(1b)** The emphasis of the noun is sometimes on the feeling of "dismay" arising from a distressful situation (Job 7:11). In this usage the word *tsar* represents a psychological or spiritual status. **(1c)** In Is 5:30, the word describes conditions that cause distress: "If one look unto the land, behold darkness and sorrow . . ." (cf. Is 30:20). This nuance appears to be the most frequent use represented by *tsar.* **(1d)** The first use of the noun is in Gen 14:20: "And blessed be the most high God, which hath delivered thine enemies into thy hand." **(2)** *Tsar* is a general designation for "enemy." **(2a)** The "enemy" may be a nation (2 Sa 24:13) or, **(2b)** more rarely, the "opponent" of an individual (cf. Gen 14:20; Ps 3:1).

(3) The Lord may also be the "enemy" of His sinful people as His judgment comes upon them (cf. Deut 32:41–43). Hence, the Book of Lamentations describes God as an "adversary" of His people: "He hath bent his bow like an enemy [341 - *oyeb*]: he stood with his right hand as an adversary [*tsar*], and slew all that were pleasant to the eye in the tabernacle of the daughter of Zion: he poured out his fury like fire" (Lam 2:4). **(4)** *Tsar* means scarcity or the distress caused by scarcity with the emphasis on the psychological or spiritual feeling of dismay arising from that distressful situation (Job 7:11). **(5)** In Is 5:30, the word describes conditions that cause distress (cf. Is 30:20).

This nuance appears to be the most frequent use represented by *tsar.* **(6)** *Tsar,* **as an adjective,** describes a space as narrow and easily blocked by a single person (Num 22:26). Syn: The word *tsar* has several synonyms: **(A)** *oyeb* (341), "enemy" (cf. Lam 2:5); **(B)** *sone* (8130), "hater" (Ps 44:7); **(C)** *rodep* (7291), "persecutor" (Ps 119:157); **(D)** *arits* (6184), "tyrant; oppressor" (Job 6:23). See: TWOT—1973a, 1973b, 1974a, 1975a; BDB—862d, 865a, 865d, 866a, 1108a.

6863. צֵר {1x} **Tsêr,** *tsare;* from 6887; *rock;* Tser, a place in Pal.:—Zer {1x}. See: BDB—862d.

6864. צֹר {2x} **tsôr,** *tsore;* from 6696; a *stone* (as if *pressed* hard or to a point); (by impl. of use) a *knife:*—sharp stone {1x}, flint {1x}. See: TWOT—1975b; BDB—862d, 863a, 866a.

6865. צֹר {42x} **Tsôr,** *tsore;* or

צוֹר **Tsôwr,** *tsore;* the same as 6864; a *rock; Tsor,* a place in Pal.:—Tyrus {22x}, Tyre {20x}. See: TWOT—1965; BDB—850a, 862d, 863c, 866a.

צֻר **tsûr.** See 6697.

6866. צָרַב {1x} **tsârab,** *tsaw-rab';* a prim. root; to *burn:*—burned {1x}. See: TWOT—1966; BDB—863a.

6867. צָרֶבֶת {3x} **tsârebeth,** *tsaw-reh'-beth;* from 6686; *conflagration* (of fire or disease):—burning {2x}, inflammation {1x}. See: TWOT—1966a, 1966b; BDB—863a.

6868. צְרֵדָה {2x} **Tsᵉrêdâh,** *tser-ay-daw';* or

צְרֵדָתָה **Tsᵉrêdâthâh,** *tser-ay-daw'-thaw;* appar. from an unused root mean. to *pierce; puncture; Tseredah,* a place in Pal.:—Zereda {1x}, Zeredathah {1x}. See: BDB—863a, 866c.

6869. צָרָה {73x} **tsârâh,** *tsaw-raw';* fem. of 6862; *tightness* (i.e. fig. *trouble*); tran. a female *rival:*—trouble {44x}, distress {8x}, affliction {7x}, adversity {5x}, anguish {5x}, tribulation {3x}, adversary {1x}.

Tsarah, **as a noun,** means "distress; straits." **(1)** The 73 appearances of *tsarah* occur in all periods of biblical literature, although most occurrences are in poetry (poetical, prophetical, and wisdom literature). **(2)** *Tsarah* means "straits" or "distress" in a psychological or spiritual sense, which is its meaning in Gen 42:21 (the first occurrence): "We are verily guilty concerning our brother, in that we saw the anguish of his soul, when he besought us, and we would not hear." See: TWOT—1973c, 1974b; BDB—863a, 865b, 865d.

6870. צְרוּיָה {26x} Ts⁰rûwyâh, tser-oo-yaw'; fem. pass. part. from the same as 6875; wounded; Tserujah, an Israelitess:— Zeruiah {26x}. See: BDB—863b, 863c.

6871. צְרוּעָה {1x} Ts⁰rûw⁰âh, tser-oo-aw'; fem. pass. part. of 6879; leprous; Tseruäh, an Israelitess:—Zeruah {1x}. See: BDB—864a.

6872. צְרוֹר {11x} ts⁰rôwr, tser-ore'; or (short.)

צְרֹר ts⁰rôr, tser-ore'; from 6887; a parcel (as packed up); also a kernel or particle (as if a package):—bundle {4x}, bag {3x}, bindeth {1x}, grain {1x}, stone {1x}, Zeror {1x}. See: TWOT—1973e, 1975c; BDB—865c, 866a, 866c.

6873. צָרַח {2x} tsârach, tsaw-rakh'; a prim. root; to be clear (in tone, i.e. shrill), i.e. to whoop:—cry {1x}, roar {1x}. See: TWOT—1968; BDB—863c.

6874. צְרִי {1x} Ts⁰rîy, tser-ee'; the same as 6875; Tseri, an Isr.:—Zeri {1x}. See: BDB—863b. comp. 3340.

6875. צְרִי {6x} ts⁰rîy, tser-ee'; or

צֳרִי tsŏrîy, tsor-ee'; from an unused root mean. to crack [as by pressure], hence, to leak; distillation, i.e. balsam:— balm {6x}. See: TWOT—1967a; BDB—863b, 863c.

6876. צֹרִי Tsôrîy, tso-ree'; {5x} patrial from 6865; a Tsorite or inhab. of Tsor (i.e. Syrian):— ...of Tyre {5x}. See: BDB—863a.

6877. צְרִיחַ {4x} ts⁰rîyach, tser-ee'-akh; from 6873 in the sense of clearness of vision; a citadel:—hold {3x}, high places {1x}. See: TWOT—1969a; BDB—863c.

6878. צֹרֶךְ {1x} tsôrek, tso'-rek; from an unused root mean. to need; need:— need {1x}. See: TWOT—1970a; BDB—863d.

6879. צָרַע {20x} tsâra⁰, tsaw-rah'; a prim. root; to scourge, i.e. (intr. and fig.) to be stricken with leprosy:—leper {14x}, leprous {6x}. See: TWOT—1971; BDB—863d.

6880. צִרְעָה {3x} tsir⁰âh, tsir-aw'; from 6879; a wasp (as stinging):—hornet {3x}. See: TWOT—1971b; BDB—864a.

6881. צָרְעָה {10x} Tsor⁰âh, tsor-aw'; appar. another form for 6880; Tsorah, a place in Pal.:—Zorah {8x}, Zoreah {1x}, Zareah {1x}. See: BDB—864a.

6882. צָרְעִי {3x} Tsor⁰îy, tsor-ee'; or

צָרְעָתִי Tsor⁰âthîy, tsor-aw-thee'; patrial from 6881; a Tsorite or Tsorathite, i.e. inhab. of Tsorah:—Zorites {1x},

Zorathites {1x}, Zareathites {1x}. See: BDB— 864a.

6883. צָרַעַת {35x} tsâra⁰ath, tsaw-rah'-ath; from 6879; leprosy:—leprosy {35x}. See: TWOT—1971a; BDB—863d.

6884. צָרַף {33x} tsâraph, tsaw-raf'; a prim. root; to fuse (metal), i.e. refine (lit. or fig.):—try {11x}, founder {5x}, goldsmith {5x}, refine {3x}, refiner {2x}, melt {2x}, pure {2x}, purge away {1x}, casteth {1x}, finer {1x}.

(1) Tsaraph means to refine, try, smelt, test. (2) It means to test, to find out who is qualified for battle: "And the LORD said unto Gideon, The people are yet too many; bring them down unto the water, and I will try them for thee there: and it shall be, that of whom I say unto thee, This shall go with thee, the same shall go with thee; and of whomsoever I say unto thee, This shall not go with thee, the same shall not go" (Judg 7:4). (3) The word is equivalent to the English "smith" (Jer 17:4 - a silversmith). (3a) Jeremiah describes the process of smelting, refining, and also its failures (Jer 6:29–30). (3b) Isaiah details the work of the smith as involving smelting, refining, and particularly the use of the refined metals in making the final product (Is 40:19; 41:7). (4) Metaphorically, it is used with the sense "to refine by means of suffering" (Ps 66:10-12). (5) God's judgment is also described as a process of refining: "And I will turn my hand upon thee, and purely purge away thy dross, and take away all thy tin:" (Is 1:25).

(6) Those purified call on the name of the Lord and receive the gracious benefits of the covenant: "And I will bring the third part through the fire, and will refine them as silver is refined, and will try them as gold is tried: they shall call on my name, and I will hear them: I will say, It is my people: and they shall say, The LORD is my God." (Zec 13:9). (8) The coming of the messenger of the covenant (Jesus Christ) is compared to the work of a smith: "But who may abide the day of his coming? and who shall stand when he appeareth? for he is like a refiner's fire, and like fullers' soap: And he shall sit as a refiner and purifier of silver: and he shall purify the sons of Levi, and purge them as gold and silver, that they may offer unto the LORD an offering in righteousness" (Mal 3:2–3). (9) The believer can take comfort in the Word of God which alone on earth is tried and purified and by which we can be purified (Ps 119:140; Ps 18:30; Prov 30:5). See: TWOT—1972; BDB—864a.

6885. צֹרְפִי {1x} Tsôr⁰phîy, tso-ref-ee'; from 6884; refiner; Tsorephi (with the

art.), an Isr.:—goldsmith {1x}. See: TWOT—1972a; BDB—864c.

6886. צָרְפַת {3x} **Tsârᵉphath**, tsaq-ref-ath'; from 6884; refinement; Tsarephath, a place in Pal.:—Zarephath {3x}. See: BDB—864c.

6887. צָרַר {58x} **tsârar**, tsaw-rar'; a prim. root; to cramp, lit. or fig., tran. or intr. (as follows):—enemy {14x}, distress {7x}, bind up {6x}, vex {6x}, afflict {4x}, besiege {4x}, adversary {3x}, strait {3x}, trouble {2x}, bound {2x}, pangs {2x}, misc. {5x} = be in affliction, narrower, oppress, shut up.

Tsarar means to wrap, tie up, be narrow, be in pangs of birth, be distressed: "And Jephthah said unto the elders of Gilead, Did not ye hate me, and expel me out of my father's house? and why are ye come unto me now when ye are in distress?" (Judg 11:7). See: TWOT—1973, 1974; BDB—864c, 865b, 865c, 865d.

6888. צְרֵרָה {1x} **Tsᵉrêrâh**, tser-ay-raw'; appar. by err. transc. for 6868; Tsererah for Tseredah:—Zererath {1x}. See: BDB—866c.

6889. צֶרֶת {1x} **Tsereth**, tseh'-reth; perh. from 6671; splendor; Tsereth, an Isr.:—Zereth {1x}. See: BDB—866c.

6890. צֶרֶת הַשַּׁחַר {1x} **Tsereth hash-Shachar**, tseh'-reth hash-shakh'-ar; from the same as 6889 and 7837 with the art. interposed; splendor of the dawn; Tsereth-hash-Shachar, a place in Pal.:—Zarethshahar {1x}. See: BDB—866c.

6891. צָרְתָן {3x} **Tsârᵉthân**, tsaw-reth-awn'; perh. for 6868; Tsarethan, a place in Pal.:—Zarthan {1x}, Zaretan {1x}, Zartanah {1x}. See: BDB—863a, 866c.

ק

6892. קֵא {1x} **qê**, kay; or

קִיא qîy', kee; from 6958; vomit:—vomit {1x}. See: TWOT—2013a, 2013b; BDB—866b, 883c.

6893. קָאַת {5x} **qâ'ath**, kaw-ath'; from 6958; prob. the pelican (from vomiting):—cormorant {3x}, pelican {2x}. See: TWOT—1976; BDB—866b.

6894. קַב {1x} **qab**, kab; from 6895; a hollow, i.e. vessel used as a (dry) measure:—cab {1x}. See: TWOT—1977a; BDB—866b.

6895. קָבַב {8x} **qâbab**, kaw-bab'; a prim. root; to scoop out, i.e. (fig.) to malign or execrate (i.e. stab with words):—✕ at all {1x}, curse {7x}. See: TWOT—1978; BDB—866d.

6896. קֵבָה {1x} **qêbâh**, kay-baw'; from 6895; the paunch (as a cavity) or first stomach of ruminants:—maw {1x}. See: TWOT—1979a; BDB—867a, 869a.

6897. קֹבָה {1x} **qôbâh**, ko'-baw; from 6895; the abdomen (as a cavity):—belly {1x}. See: TWOT—1979a; BDB—867a, 869a.

6898. קֻבָּה {1x} **qubbâh**, koob-baw'; from 6895; a pavilion (as a domed cavity):—tent {1x}. Syn.: 168, 4264, 4908. 5521. See: TWOT—1977b; BDB—866d.

6899. קִבּוּץ {1x} **qibbûwts**, kib-boots'; from 6908; a throng:—company {1x}. See: TWOT—1983a; BDB—868b.

6900. קְבוּרָה {14x} **qᵉbûwrâh**, keb-oo-raw'; or

קְבֻרָה qᵉbûrâh, keb-oo-raw'; fem. pass. part. of 6912; sepulture; (concr.) a sepulchre:—burial {4x}, burying place {1x}, grave {4x}, sepulchre {5x}. See: TWOT—1984b; BDB—869a.

6901. קָבַל {13x} **qâbal**, kaw-bal'; a prim. root; to admit, i.e. take (lit. or fig.):—receive {6x}, took {3x}, choose {1x}, held {1x}, take hold {1x}, undertook {1x}. See: TWOT—1980; BDB—867a, 1110b.

6902. קְבַל {3x} **qᵉbal** (Aram.), keb-al'; corresp. to 6901; to acquire:—receive {1x}, take {2x}. See: TWOT—2964; BDB—1110b.

6903. קְבֵל {29x} **qᵉbêl** (Aram.), keb-ale'; or

קֳבֵל qŏbêl (Aram.), kob-ale'; (corresp. to 6905; (adv.) in front of; usually (with other particles) on account of, so as, since, hence:—as + 3606 {5x}, because + 3606 {4x}, therefore + 3606 {3x}, before {3x}, as {2x}, wherefore + 3606 {2x}, according {1x}, against {1x}, misc. {8x} = + for this cause, + by this means, by reason of, + that, + though. See: TWOT—2965; BDB—1097b, 1110a.

6904. קֹבֵל {1x} **qôbel**, ko'-bel; from 6901 in the sense of confronting (as standing opposite in order to receive); a battering-ram:—war {1x}. See: TWOT—1980a; BDB—867b.

6905. קָבָל {1x} **qâbâl**, kaw-bawl'; from 6901 in the sense of opposite [see 6904]; the presence, i.e. (adv.) in front of:—before {1x}. See: TWOT—1980a; BDB—867b.

6906. קָבַע {6x} **qâbaᶜ**, kaw-bah'; a prim. root; to cover, i.e. (fig.) defraud:—rob {4x}, spoil {2x}. See: TWOT—1981; BDB—867b.

6907. קֻבַּעַת {2x} **qubbaᶜath**, koob-bah'-ath; from 6906; a goblet (as deep like a cover):—dregs {2x}. See: TWOT—1982; BDB—867c.

Hebrew

6908. קָבַץ {127x} **qâbats,** *kaw-bats';* a prim. root; to *grasp,* i.e. *collect:*—gather {70x}, gather together {42x}, assemble {6x}, gather up {3x}, heap {1x}, gather out {1x}, resort {1x}, surely {1x}, take up {2x}.

(1) *Qabats* means "to collect, gather, assemble." **(2)** *Qabats* means "to gather" things together into a single location. **(2a)** The word may focus on the process of "gathering," as in Gen 41:35 (the first occurrence): Joseph advised Pharaoh to appoint overseers to "gather all the food of those good years that come, and lay up corn under the hand of Pharaoh." **(2b)** The verb may also focus on the result of the process, as in Gen 41:48: "And he gathered up all the food of the seven years, which were in the land of Egypt." **(3)** Only in one passage does *qabats* mean "to harvest" (Is 62:9): "But they that have gathered [harvested] it [grain] shall eat it, and praise the Lord;" **(4)** This verb is used metaphorically of things that can be "gathered" only in a figurative sense. So in Ps 41:6, the enemy's "heart gathereth iniquity to itself"— i.e., the enemy considers how he can use everything he hears and sees against his host.

(5) It is often used of "gathering" people or "assembling" them. This "gathering" is usually a response to a summons, but not always. In 1 Kin 11:24, David "gathered men unto him, and became captain over a [marauding] band." This action was not the result of a summons David issued, but resulted from reports that circulated about him. The entire story makes it quite clear that David was not seeking to set up a force rivaling Saul's. But when men came to him, he marshalled them. **(6)** Quite often this verb is used of "summoning" people to a central location. When Jacob blessed his sons, for example, he "summoned" them to him and then told them to gather around closer (Gen 49:2). **(7)** This same word is used of "summoning" the militia. All able-bodied men in Israel between the ages of 20 and 40 were members of the militia. In times of peace they were farmers and tradesmen; but when danger threatened, a leader would "assemble" them or "summon" them to a common location and organize them into an army (cf. Judg 12:4). **(8)** All Israel could be "summoned" or "gathered" for battle (as a militia); thus "Saul gathered all Israel together, and they pitched in Gilboa" (1 Sa 28:4). **(9)** This military use may also signify "marshalling" a standing army in the sense of "setting them up" for battle. The men of Gibeon said: "All the kings of the Amorites that dwell in the mountains are gathered together against us" (Josh 10:6). **(10)** In 1 Kin 20:1, *qabats* carries this sense in addition to overtones of "concentrating" an entire army against a particular point: "And Ben-hadad the king of Syria gathered all his host together: and there were thirty and two kings with him, and horses, and chariots: and he went up and besieged Samaria, and warred against it." **(11)** Ordered assemblies may include assemblies for covenant-making: "And Abner said unto David, I will arise and go, and will gather all Israel unto my lord the king, that they may make a league with thee" (2 Sa 3:21). **(12)** In several instances, assemblies are "convened" for public worship activities: "Samuel said, Gather all Israel to Mizpeh. . . . And they gathered together to Mizpeh, and drew water, and poured it out before the Lord, and fasted on that day" (1 Sa 7:5–6; cf. Joel 2:16).

(13) When *qabats* appears in the intensive stem, God is often the subject. This usage connotes that something will result that would not result if things were left to themselves. The verb is used in this sense to refer to "divine judgment": "As they gathered silver, and brass . . . into the midst of the furnace, to blow the fire upon it, to melt it; so will I gather you in mine anger and in my fury (Eze 22:20). **(14)** *Qabats* is also applied to "divine deliverance": "The Lord thy God will turn thy captivity, and have compassion upon thee, and will return and gather thee from all the nations, whither the Lord thy God hath scattered thee" (Deut 30:3). **(15)** A special use of the verb *qabats* appears in Joel 2:6, namely "to glow" or "glow with excitement" or "become pale [white]": "Before their face the people shall be much pained: all faces shall gather blackness." Syn: The verb *'acaph* (622) is a near synonym to *qabats,* differing from it only by having a more extensive range of meanings and duplicating all the meanings of *qabats.* See: TWOT—1983; BDB—867c.

6909. קַבְצְאֵל {3x} **Qabtse'êl,** *kab-tseh-ale';* from 6908 and 410; *God has gathered; Kabtseël,* a place in Pal.:—Kabzeel {3x}. See: BDB—868b. comp. 3343.

6910. קְבֻצָה {1x} **qᵉbûtsâh,** *keb-oo-tsaw';* fem. pass. part. of 6908; a *hoard:*—✗ gather {1x}. See: BDB—868b.

6911. קִבְצַיִם {1x} **Qibtsayim,** *kib-tsah'-yim;* dual from 6908; a *double heap; Kibtsajim,* a place in Pal.:—Kibzaim {1x}. See: BDB—868b.

6912. קָבַר **qâbar,** *kaw-bar';* a prim. root; to *inter:*—bury {131x}, buriers {1x}, in any wise {1x}.

Qabar, as a verb, means "to bury." **(1)** This root is used almost exclusively of burying human beings, the act of placing a dead body into a grave or tomb. **(1a)** In its first biblical appearance, *qabar* bears this meaning. God

told Abraham, "And thou shalt go to thy fathers in peace; thou shalt be buried in a good old age" (Gen 15:15). **(1b)** A proper burial was a sign of special kindness and divine blessing. As such, it was an obligation of the responsible survivors. Abraham bought the cave of Machpelah so that he might bury his dead. **(1c)** David thanked the men of Jabesh-gilead for their daring reclamation of the bodies of Saul and Jonathan (1 Sa 31:11–13), and for properly "burying" them. He said, "Blessed be ye of the Lord, that ye have showed this kindness unto your lord, even unto Saul, and have buried him" (2 Sa 2:5). **(1d)** Later, David took the bones of Saul and Jonathan and buried them in their family tomb (2 Sa. 21:14); here the verb means both "bury" and "rebury." **(1e)** A proper burial was not only a kindness; it was a necessity. If the land were to be clean before God, all bodies had to be "buried" before nightfall: "His body shall not remain all night upon the tree, but thou shalt in any wise bury him that day; (for he that is hanged is accursed of God;) that thy land be not defiled, which the Lord thy God giveth thee for an inheritance" (Deut 21:23). **(1f)** Thus, if a body was not buried, divine approval was withdrawn.

(2) Not to be "buried" was a sign of divine disapproval, both on the surviving kinsmen and on the nation. **(2a)** Ahijah the prophet told Jeroboam's wife, "And all Israel shall mourn for him [Jeroboam's son], and bury him: for he only of Jeroboam shall come to the grave" (1 Kin 14:13). **(2b)** As for the rest of his family, they would be eaten by dogs and birds of prey (v. 11; cf. Jer 8:2). Jeremiah prophesied that Jehoiakim would "be buried with the burial of an ass, drawn and cast forth beyond the gates of Jerusalem" (Jer 22:19). **(3)** Bodies may be "buried" in caves (Gen 25:9), sepulchers (Judg 8:32), and graves (Gen 50:5). **(4)** In a few places, *qabar* is used elliptically of the entire act of dying. So in Job 27:15 we read: "Those that remain of him [his survivors] shall be buried in death: and his widows shall not weep." Syn.: 6913. See: TWOT−1984; BDB−868b.

6913. קֶבֶר {67x} **qeber,** *keh'-ber;* or (fem.)

קִבְרָה **qibrâh,** *kib-raw';* from 6912; a *sepulchre:*—burying place {6x}, grave {35x}, sepulchre {25x}.

(1) The state that we call death, i.e., the condition consequent on the act of dying, is to be viewed in three aspects: **(1a)** first, there is the tomb or sepulcher; the location of the physical frame called *qeber* (6913 – Gen 50:5); **(1b)** secondly, there is the corruption whereby the body itself is dissolved, which is represented by *sha-chath* (7843); and **(1c)** thirdly, there is *sheowl* (7585) which represents the locality or condi-

tion of the departed. **(2)** *Qeber* refers to a **(2a)** a tomb-grave/sepulcher (Gen 23:4), **(2b)** grave (Jer 5:16), and **(2c)** in Ps 88:11, it is used of a grave that is the equivalent of the underworld. **(3)** In Judg 8:32, the word signifies a family sepulcher. **(4)** Jer 26:23 uses the word for a burial place, an open pit. See: TWOT−1984a; BDB−868d.

קְבֻרָה **qᵉbûrâh.** See 6900.

6914. קִבְרוֹת הַתַּאֲוָה {5x} **Qibrôwth hat-Taʾă-vâh,** *kib-rōth' hat-tah-av-aw';* from the fem. plur. of 6913 and 8378 with the art. interposed; *graves of the longing; Kibroth-hat-Taavh,* a place in the desert:—Kibroth-hattaavah {5x}. See: BDB−869a.

6915. קָדַד {15x} **qâdad,** *kaw-dad';* a prim. root; to *shrivel* up, i.e. *contract* or *bend* the body (or neck) in deference:—bow {2x}, bow down the head {11x}, stoop {2x}. See: TWOT−1985; BDB−869a.

6916. קִדָּה {2x} **qiddâh,** *kid-daw';* from 6915; *cassia* bark (as in *shrivelled* rolls):—cassia {2x}. See: TWOT−1986b; BDB−869b.

6917. קָדוּם {1x} **qâdûwm,** *kaw-doom';* pass. part. of 6923; a *pristine* hero:—ancient {1x}. See: TWOT−1988g; BDB−870c.

6918. קָדוֹשׁ {116x} **qâdôwsh,** *kaw-doshe';* or

קָדֹשׁ **qâdôsh,** *kaw-doshe';* from 6942; *sacred* (cerem. or mor.); (as noun) *God* (by eminence), an *angel,* a *saint,* a *sanctuary:*—holy {65x}, Holy One {39x}, saint {12x}. **(1)** *Qadosh,* as an adjective, means "holy." **(1)** The word describes something or someone. **(1a)** In Hebrew the verb *qadash* and the word *qadesh* combine both elements: the descriptive and the static. **(1b)** The traditional understanding of "separated" is only a derived meaning, and not the primary. **(1c)** The first of its 116 occurrences is in Ex 19:16: "And ye shall be unto me a kingdom of priests, and a holy nation. These are the words which thou shalt speak unto the children of Israel." **(2)** In the Old Testament *qadosh* has a strongly religious connotation. **(2a)** In one sense the word describes an object or place or day to be "holy" with the meaning of "devoted" or "dedicated" to a particular purpose: "And the priest shall take holy water in an earthen vessel . . ." (Num 5:17). **(2b)** Particularly the Sabbath day is "devoted" as a day of rest: "If thou turn away thy foot from the sabbath, from doing thy pleasure on my holy day; and call the sabbath a delight, the holy of the Lord, honorable; and shalt honor him, not doing thine own ways, nor finding thine own pleasure, nor speaking thine own words: Then shalt thou delight thyself in the Lord" (Is 58:13–14). **(2c)** The prescription is

based on Gen 2:3 where the Lord "sanctified," or "dedicated," the Sabbath.

(3) God has dedicated Israel as His people. **(3a)** They are "holy" by their relationship to the "holy" God. **(3b)** All of the people are in a sense "holy," as members of the covenant community, irrespective of their faith and obedience: "And they gathered themselves together against Moses and against Aaron, and said unto them, Ye take too much upon you, seeing all the congregation are holy, every one of them, and the Lord is among them: wherefore then lift ye up yourselves above the congregation of the Lord?" (Num 16:3). **(4)** God's intent was to use this "holy" nation as a "holy," royal priesthood amongst the nations (Ex 19:6). **(5)** Based on the intimate nature of the relationship, God expected His people to live up to His "holy" expectations and, thus, to demonstrate that they were a "holy nation": "And ye shall be holy unto me: for I the Lord am holy, and have severed you from other people, that ye should be mine" (Lev 20:26).

(5) The priests were chosen to officiate at the Holy Place of the tabernacle/temple. Because of their function as intermediaries between God and Israel and because of their proximity to the temple, they were dedicated by God to the office of priest: "They shall be holy unto their God, and not profane the name of their God: for the offerings of the Lord made by fire, and the bread of their God, they do offer: therefore they shall be holy. They shall not take a wife that is a whore, or profane; neither shall they take a woman put away from her husband: for he is holy unto his God. Thou shalt sanctify him therefore; for he offereth the bread of thy God: he shall be holy unto thee: for I the Lord, which sanctify you, am holy" (Lev 21:6-8). **(6)** Aaron as the high priest was "They envied Moses also in the camp, and Aaron the saint of the LORD" (Ps 106:16).

(7) The Old Testament clearly and emphatically teaches that God is "holy." **(7a)** He is "the Holy One of Israel" (Is 1:4), the "holy God" (Is 5:16), and "the Holy One" (Is 40:25). **(7b)** His name is "Holy": "For thus saith the high and lofty One that inhabiteth eternity, whose name is Holy; I dwell in the high and holy place, with him also that is of a contrite and humble spirit, to revive the spirit of the humble, and to revive the heart of the contrite ones" (Is 57:15). **(7c)** The negative statement, "There is none holy as the Lord: for there is none besides thee: neither is there any rock like our God" (1 Sa 2:2), explains that He is most "holy" and that no one is as "holy" as He is. **(8)** Also the angels in the heavenly entourage are "holy": "And ye shall flee to the valley of the mountains; for the valley of the mountains shall reach unto

Azal: yea, ye shall flee, like as ye fled from before the earthquake in the days of Uzziah king of Judah: and the LORD my God shall come, and all the saints with thee" (Zec 14:5). **(9)** The seraphim proclaimed to each other the holiness of God: "And one cried unto another, and said, "Holy, holy, holy, is the Lord of hosts: the whole earth is full of his glory" (Is 6:3). See: TWOT—1990b; BDB—872c, 1110d.

6919. קָדַח {5x} **qâdach**, *kaw-dakh'*; a prim. root; to *inflame:*—burn {1x}, kindle {4x}. See: TWOT—1987; BDB—869b.

6920. קַדַּחַת {2x} **qaddachath**, *kad-dakh'-ath;* from 6919; *inflammation,* i.e. febrile disease:—burning ague {1x}, fever {1x}. See: TWOT—1987a; BDB—869b.

6921. קָדִים {69x} **qâdîym**, *kaw-deem';* or

קָדִם **qâdîm**, *kaw-deem';* from 6923; the *fore* or front part; hence, (by orientation) the *East* (often adv. *eastward,* for brevity the *east wind*):—east {50x}, east wind {10x}, eastward {7x}, eastward + 1870 {1x}, east side {1x}. See: TWOT—1988d; BDB—870b.

6922. קַדִּישׁ {13x} **qaddîysh** (Aram.), *kaddeesh';* corresp. to 6918:—holy {4x}, holy One {3x}, saint {6x}. See: TWOT—2967; BDB—872d.

6923. קָדַם {26x} **qâdam**, *kaw-dam';* a prim. root; to *project* (one self), i.e. *precede;* hence, to *anticipate, hasten, meet* (usually for help):—prevent {15x}, before {6x}, met {2x}, come {1x}, disappoint {1x}, go {1x}.

Most often, this verb is used in a martial context. Such confrontations may be peaceful, as in the meeting of allies: "For thou [dost meet] him with the blessings of goodness . . ." (Ps 21:3). They may also be hostile: "The sorrows of hell compassed me about; the snares of death confronted (KJV, "prevented") me" (2 Sa 22:6). See: TWOT—1988; BDB—869d, 870c.

6924. קֶדֶם {87x} **qedem**, *keh'-dem;* or

קֵדְמָה **qêdmâh**, *kayd'-maw;* from 6923; the *front,* of place (absolutely, the *fore part,* rel. the *East*) or time (*antiquity*); often used adv. (*before, anciently, eastward*):—east {32x}, old {17x}, eastward {11x}, ancient {6x}, east side {5x}, before {3x}, east part {2x}, ancient time {2x}, aforetime {1x}, eternal {1x}, misc. {7x} = ✕ ever (-lasting), forward, past. See: TWOT—1988a; BDB—869c, 870a, 870b, 1110c. comp. 6783, 6926.

6925. קֳדָם {42x} **qŏdâm** (Aram.), *kod-awm';* or

קְדָם **qᵉdâm** (Aram.) (Dan. 7:13), *kedawm';* corresp. to 6924; *before:*—before {29x}, before + 4481 {2x}, of + 4481 {2x}, him {2x}, misc. {7x} = ✕ from, ✕ I (thought), ✕

me, + of, X it pleased, presence. See: TWOT—2966a; BDB—1110b.

קָדִם **qâdîm**. See 6921.

6926. קִדְמָה {4x} **qidmâh**, *kid-maw'*; fem. of 6924; the *forward* part (or rel.) *East* (often adv. *on* (the) *east* or *in front*):—east {3x}, eastward {1x}. See: TWOT—1988a; BDB—870b.

6927. קִדְמָה {6x} **qadmâh**, *kad-maw'*; from 6923; *priority* (in time); also used adv. (*before*):—former estate {3x}, old estate {1x}, afore {1x}, antiquity {1x}. See: TWOT—1988c; BDB—870b, 1110c.

6928. קַדְמָה {2x} **qadmâh** (Aram.), *kad-maw'*; corresp. to 6927; *former* time:—ago {1x}, aforetime + 4481 + 1836 {1x}. See: TWOT—2966b; BDB—1110c.

קֵדְמָה **qêdmâh**. See 6924.

6929. קֵדְמָה {2x} **Qêdᵉmâh**, *kayd'-maw*; from 6923; *precedence; Kedemah*, a son of Ishmael:—Kedemah {2x}. See: BDB—870b.

6930. קַדְמוֹן {1x} **qadmôwn**, *kad-mone'*; from 6923; *eastern*:—east {1x}. See: TWOT—1988e; BDB—870c.

6931. קַדְמוֹנִי {10x} **qadmôwnîy**, *kad-mo-nee'*; or

קַדְמֹנִי **qadmônîy**, *kad-mo-nee'*; from 6930; (of time) *anterior* or (of place) *oriental*:—east {4x}, former {2x}, ancients {1x}, that went before {1x}, things of old {1x}, old {1x}. See: TWOT—1988f; BDB—870c.

6932. קְדֵמוֹת {4x} **Qᵉdêmôwth**, *ked-ay-mothe'*; from 6923; *beginnings; Kedemoth*, a place in eastern Pal.:—Kedemoth {4x}. See: BDB—870d.

6933. קְדָמַי {3x} **qadmay** (Aram.), *kad-mah'-ee*; from a root corresp. to 6923; *first*:—first {3x}. See: TWOT—2966c; BDB—1110c.

6934. קַדְמִיאֵל {8x} **Qadmîyᵓêl**, *kad-mee-ale'*; from 6924 and 410; *presence of God; Kadmiël*, the name of three Isr.:—Kadmiel {8x}. See: BDB—870d.

קַדְמֹנִי **qadmônîy**. See 6931.

6935. קַדְמֹנִי {1x} **Qadmônîy**, *kad-mo-nee'*; the same as 6931; *ancient*, i.e. aboriginal; *Kadmonite* (collect.), the name of a tribe in Pal.:—Kadmonites {1x}. See: BDB—870d.

6936. קָדְקֹד {11x} **qodqôd**, *kod-kode'*; from 6915; the *crown* of the head (as the part most *bowed*):—crown of the head {6x},

top of the head {2x}, crown {1x}, pate {1x}, scalp {1x}. See: TWOT—1986a; BDB—869a, 903a.

6937. קָדַר {17x} **qâdar**, *kaw-dar'*; a prim. root; to *be ashy*, i.e. *dark*-colored; by impl. to *mourn* (in sackcloth or sordid garments):—mourn {6x}, black {4x}, dark {4x}, blackish {1x}, darkened {1x}, heavily {1x}. See: TWOT—1989; BDB—871a.

6938. קֵדָר {12x} **Qêdâr**, *kay-dawr'*; from 6937; *dusky* (of the skin or the tent); *Kedar*, a son of Ishmael; also (collect.) *bedawin* (as his desc. or representatives):—Kedar {12x}. See: BDB—871a.

6939. קִדְרוֹן {11x} **Qidrôwn**, *kid-rone'*; from 6937; *dusky* place; *Kidron*, a brook near Jerusalem:—Kidron {11x}. See: BDB—871b.

6940. קַדְרוּת {1x} **qadrûwth**, *kad-rooth'*; from 6937; *duskiness*:—blackness {1x}. See: TWOT—1989a; BDB—871a.

6941. קְדֹרַנִּית {1x} **qᵉdôrannîyth**, *ked-o-ran-neeth'*; adv. from 6937; *blackish ones* (i.e. *in sackcloth*); used adv. in *mourning* weeds:—mournfully {1x}. See: TWOT—1989b; BDB—871a.

6942. קָדַשׁ {172x} **qâdâsh**, *kaw-dash'*; a prim. root; to *be* (caus. *make, pronounce* or *observe* as) *clean* (cerem. or mor.):—sanctify {108x}, hallow {25x}, dedicate {10x}, holy {7x}, prepare {7x}, consecrate {5x}, appointed {1x}, bid {1x}, purified {1x}, misc. {7x} = defile, keep, proclaim, X wholly.

(1) This word is used in some form or another to represent being set apart for the work of God. *Qadesh*, or *qadash*, as verbs, mean "to be holy; to sanctify." This verb, which occurs 172 times, can mean **(2)** "to be holy": "Seven days thou shalt make an atonement for the altar, and sanctify it; and it shall be an altar most holy: whatsoever toucheth the altar shall be holy" (Ex 29:37; cf. Lev 6:18) or **(3)** "to sanctify": "Hear me, ye Levites, sanctify now yourselves, and sanctify the house of the Lord God of your fathers, and carry forth the filthiness out of the holy place" (2 Chr 29:5). See: TWOT—1990; BDB—872d.

6943. קֶדֶשׁ {12x} **Qedesh**, *keh'-desh;* from 6942; a *sanctum; Kedesh*, the name of four places in Pal.:—Kedesh {11x}, Kedesh-naphtali {1x}. See: TWOT—1990d; BDB—873d, 904d.

6944. קֹדֶשׁ {468x} **qôdesh**, *ko'-desh;* from 6942; a *sacred* place or thing; rarely abstr. *sanctity*:—holy {262x}, sanctuary {68x}, (holy, hallowed, . . .) things {52x}, most {44x}, holiness {30x}, dedicated {5x}, hallowed {3x}, consecrated {1x}, misc. {3x}.

Qodesh, as a noun, means "holiness; holy thing; sanctuary." This noun occurs 469 times with the meanings: **(1)** "holiness": "Who is like unto thee, O LORD, among the gods? who is like thee, glorious in holiness, fearful in praises, doing wonders?" (Ex 15:11); **(2)** "holy thing": "And when Aaron and his sons have made an end of covering the sanctuary, and all the vessels of the sanctuary, as the camp is to set forward; after that, the sons of Kohath shall come to bear it: but they shall not touch any holy thing, lest they die" (Num 4:15); and **(3)** "sanctuary": "And all the wise men, that wrought all the work of the sanctuary, came every man from his work which they made;" (Ex 36:4). See: TWOT—1990a; BDB—871c, 873d, 874a, 874b.

6945. קָדֵשׁ {6x} **qâdêsh**, *kaw-dashe'*; from 6942; a (quasi) *sacred* person, i.e. (tech.) a (male) *devotee* (by prostitution) to licentious idolatry:—sodomite {5x}, unclean {1x}.

Another noun, *qadesh*, means "temple-prostitute" or "sodomite": "There shall be no whore of the daughters of Israel, nor a sodomite of the sons of Israel" (Deut 23:17). Syn.: 6948. See: TWOT—1990c; BDB—873c.

6946. קָדֵשׁ {18x} **Qâdêsh**, *kaw-dashe'*; the same as 6945; *sanctuary; Kadesh,* a place in the desert:—Kadesh {17x}, Meribahkadesh + 4808 {1x}. See: TWOT—1990e; BDB—872c, 873d, 937b. comp. 6947.

קָדֹשׁ **qâdôsh**. See 6918.

6947. קָדֵשׁ בַּרְנֵעַ {10x} **Qâdêsh Barnêaᶜ**, *kaw-dashe' bar-nay'-ah;* from the same as 6946 and an otherwise unused word (appar. compounded of a correspondent to 1251 and a der. of 5128) mean. *desert of a fugitive; Kadesh of* (the) *Wilderness of Wandering; Kadesh-Barneä,* a place in the desert:—Kadeshbarnea {10x}. See: BDB—140b, 745c, 873d, 874a.

6948. קְדֵשָׁה {5x} **qᵉdêshâh**, *ked-ay-shaw'*; fem. of 6945; a female *devotee* (i.e. *prostitute*):—harlot {4x}, whore {1x}.

Qadesh means temple-prostitute or sodomite (Deut 23:17). This word stresses the separation aspect of the word. These two individuals are totally separate to the extreme from God, instead of to Him alone. See: TWOT 1990c; BDB—873d.

6949. קָהָה {4x} **qâhâh**, *kaw-haw'*; a prim. root; to *be dull:*—set on edge {3x}, blunt {1x}. See: TWOT—1990.1; BDB—874b.

6950. קָהַל {39x} **qâhal**, *kaw-hal'*; a prim. root; to *convoke:*—(gather, assemble) together {14x}, gather {16x}, assembled {9x}.

Qahal means to gather for conflict or war,

for religious purposes, and for judgment (1 Kin 8:1). See: TWOT—1991; BDB—874d.

6951. קָהָל {123x} **qâhâl**, *kaw-hawl';* from 6950; *assemblage* (usually concr.):—congregation {86x}, assembly {17x}, company {17x}, multitude {3x}.

(1) *Qahal* can mean an assembly gathered to plan or execute war (Gen 49:6; 1 Kin 12:3; Eze 17:17). **(2)** It can denote a gathering to judge or deliberate (Eze 23:45–47). **(3)** It may signify an assembly representing a larger group (1 Chr 13:1–2; 2 Chr 1:2; Lev 4:13). **(4)** Sometimes *qahal* represents all the males of Israel who were eligible to bring sacrifices to the Lord (Deut 23:1). **(5)** In Num 16:3 and 33, it is clear that the "assembly" was the worshiping, voting community (cf. 18:4). **(6)** The word *qahal* also signifies all the people of Israel (Ex 16:31; Gen 28:3). See: TWOT—1991a; BDB—874c.

6952. קְהִלָּה {2x} **qᵉhillâh**, *keh-hil-law';* from 6950; an *assemblage:*—congregation {1x}, assembly {1x}. See: TWOT—1991b; BDB—875a.

6953. קֹהֶלֶת {7x} **qôheleth**, *ko-heh'-leth;* fem. of act. part. from 6950; a (female) *assembler* (i.e. *lecturer*): abstr. *preaching* (used as a "nom de plume", *Koheleth*):—preacher {7x}. See: TWOT—1991c; BDB—875a.

6954. קְהֵלָתָה {2x} **Qᵉhêlâthâh**, *keh-hay-law'-thaw;* from 6950; *convocation; Kehelathah,* a place in the desert:—Kehelathah {2x}. See: BDB—875b.

6955. קְהָת {32x} **Qᵉhâth**, *keh-hawth';* from an unused root mean. to *ally* oneself; *allied; Kehath,* an Isr.:—Kohath {32x}. See: BDB—875b.

6956. קְהָתִי {15x} **Qᵉhâthîy**, *ko-haw-thee';* patron. from 6955; a *Kohathite* (collect.) or desc. of Kehath:—Kohathite {15x}. See: BDB—875c.

6957. קַו {21x} **qav**, *kav;* or

קָו **qâv**, *kawv;* from 6960 [comp. 6961]; a *cord* (as *connecting*), espec. for measuring; fig. a *rule;* also a *rim,* a musical *string* or *accord:*—line {20x}, rule {1x}. See: TWOT—1992, 1994a; BDB—875c, 876a, 876a. comp. 6978.

6958. קוֹא {8x} **qôw**, *ko;* or

קָיָה **qâyâh** (Jer. 25:27), *kaw-yaw';* a prim. root; to *vomit:*—vomit {5x}, spue {3x}. See: TWOT—2014; BDB—883c, 883d.

6959. קוֹבַע {2x} **qôwbaᶜ**, *ko'-bah or ko-bah';* a form collat. to 3553; a *helmet:*—helmet {2x}. See: TWOT—1993; BDB—875c.

6960. קָוָה {49x} **qâvâh**, *kaw-vaw';* a prim. root; to *bind* together (perh. by *twisting*), i.e. *collect;* (fig.) to *expect:*—wait {29x}, look {13x}, wait for {1x}, look for {1x}, gathered {1x}, misc. {4x}.

This word stresses the straining of the mind in a certain direction with an expectant attitude . . . a forward look with assurance. See: TWOT—1994, 1995; BDB—875c, 876b.

6961. קָוֶה {3x} **qâveh**, *kaw-veh';* from 6960; a (measuring) *cord* (as if for *binding*):—line. See: TWOT—1994a; BDB—876a.

קוֹחַ **qôwach**. See 6495.

6962. קוּט {7x} **qûwt**, *koot;* a prim. root; prop. to *cut off,* i.e. (fig.) *detest:*—grieve {3x}, lothe {3x}, very {1x}. See: TWOT—1996; BDB—876c, 878c.

6963. קוֹל {506x} **qôwl**, *kole;* or

קֹל **qôl**, *kole;* from an unused root mean. to *call* aloud; a *voice* or *sound:*—voice {383x}, noise {49x}, sound {39x}, thunder {10x}, proclamation + 5674 {4x}, send out + 5414 {2x}, thunderings {2x}, fame {1x}, misc. {16x} = + aloud, bleating, crackling, cry (+ out), fame, lightness, lowing, + hold peace, proclaim, + sing, + spark, + yell.

(1) It denotes a sound produced by vocal cords including **(1a)** the human voice (Josh 10:14), **(1b)** the vocal sounds produced by animals (1 Sa 15:14), and **(1c)** the voice of personified inanimate objects or things: "And he said, What hast thou done? the voice of thy brother's blood crieth unto me from the ground" (Gen 4:10). **(2)** This word also covers a great variety of noises and sounds, such as **(2a)** the noise or sound of battle (Ex 32:17), **(2b)** the sound of words (Deut 1:34), **(2c)** water (Eze 1:24), **(2d)** weeping (Is 65:19), and **(2e)** thunder (Ex 9:23). **(3)** The word can represent the thing that is spoken (Gen 3:17) even if written down (2 Kin 10:6). **(4)** There are several special phrases related to *qol:* **(4a)** "To lift up one's voice and weep" signifies **(4a1)** crying out for help (Gen 39:14), **(4a2)** mourning for present or anticipated tragedy (Gen 21:16), **(4a3)** the sound of disaster (Num 16:34), **(4a4)** or joy (Gen 29:11). **(4b)** "To hearken to one's voice" means **(4b1)** taking note of something and believing it (Gen 4:23), **(4b2)** following another's suggestions (Gen 3:17), **(4b3)** complying with another's request (Gen 21:12), **(4b4)** obeying another's command (Gen 22:18), and **(4b5)** answering a prayer (2 Sa 22:7).

(5) Theologically the word is crucial in prophecy. **(5a)** The prophet's voice is God's voice (Ex 3:18; 7:1; Deut 18:18–19). **(5b)** God's voice is sometimes **(5b1)** the roar of thunder, demonstrating His tremendous power which evokes fear and submission (Ex 9:23, 29); or **(5b2)** a "still small voice" (1 Kin 19:12). **(5c)** In covenantal contexts God stipulates that His voice, heard in both the roar of thunder and the prophetic message, is authoritative and when obeyed brings reward (Ex 19:5; 1 Sa 12:14–18). See: TWOT—1998a, 2028b; BDB—876d, 877b, 885c, 887a, 1110d.

6964. קוֹלָיָה {2x} **Qôwlâyâh**, *ko-law-yaw';* from 6963 and 3050; *voice of Jah; Kolajah,* the name of two Isr.:—Kolaiah {2x}. See: BDB—877b.

6965. קוּם {628x} **qûwm**, *koom;* a prim. root; to *rise* (in various applications, lit., fig., intens. and caus.):—(stood, rise, etc.) up {240x}, arise {211x}, raise {47x}, establish {27x}, stand {27x}, perform {25x}, confirm {9x}, again {5x}, set {5x}, stablish {3x}, surely {3x}, continue {3x}, sure {2x}, abide {1x}, accomplish {1x}, misc. {19x} = × be clearer, decree, × be dim, endure, × enemy, enjoin, make good, help, hold, make, × but newly, ordain, pitch, remain, strengthen, succeed.

Quwm means "to arise, stand up, come about." **(1)** It may denote any movement to an erect position, **(1a)** such as getting up out of a bed (Gen 19:33), or **(1b)** it can be used as the opposite of sitting or kneeling, as when Abraham "stood up from before his dead" (Gen 23:3). **(1c)** It can also refer to the result of arising, as when Joseph saw his sheaf arise and remain erect (Gen 37:7). **(2)** *Quwm* may be used by itself, with no direct object to refer to the origin of something, as when Isaiah says, "It shall not stand . . ." (Is 7:7). **(3)** Sometimes *quwm* is used in an intensive mood to signify empowering or strengthening: "Strengthen thou me according unto thy word" (Ps 119:28). **(4)** It is also used to denote the inevitable occurrence of something predicted or prearranged: "They have seen vanity and lying divination, saying, The LORD saith: and the LORD hath not sent them: and they have made others to hope that they would confirm [*quwm*] the word" (Eze 13:6). **(5)** In a military context, *quwm* may mean "to engage in battle." In Ps 18:38, for instance, God says, "I have wounded them that were not able to rise" (cf. 2 Sa 23:10).

(6) *Quwm* may also be used very much like *'amad* (5975) to indicate the continuation of something—e.g., "Thy kingdom shall not continue" (1 Sa 13:14). **(7)** Sometimes it indicates validity, as when a woman's vow shall not "stand" (be valid) if her father forbids it (Num 30:5). **(8)** Also see Deut 19:15, which states that a matter may be "confirmed" only by the testimony of two or more witnesses. **(9)** In some passages, *quwm* means "immovable"; so Eli's eyes were "set" (1 Sa 4:15). **(10)** Another special

use of *quwm* is "rise up again," as when a child-less widow complains to the elders, "My husband's brother refuseth to raise up unto his brother a name in Israel" (Deut 25:7). In other words, the brother refuses to continue that name or "raise it up again." **(11)** When used with another verb, *quwm* may suggest simply the beginning of an action. When Scripture says that "[Jacob] rose up, and passed over the [Euphrates] river" (Gen 31:21), it does not mean that he literally stood up—merely that he began to cross the river.

(12) Sometimes *quwm* is part of a compound verb and carries no special meaning of its own. This is especially true in commands. Thus Gen 28:2 could simply be rendered, "Go to Padanaram," rather than, "Arise, go . . ." (KJV). **(13)** Other special meanings emerge when *quwm* is used with certain particles. **(13a)** With *'al*, "against," it often means "to fight against or attack": "A man riseth against his neighbor, and slayeth him" (Deut 22:26). This is its meaning in Gen 4:8, the first biblical occurrence. **(13b)** With the particle *be* ("against"), *quwm* means "make a formal charge against": "One witness shall not rise up against a man . . ." (Deut 19:15). **(13c)** With *le* ("for"), *quwm* means "to testify in behalf of": "Who will rise up for me against the evildoers?" (Ps 94:16). **(13c)** The same construction can mean "to deed over," as when Ephron's field was made sure"—Gen 23:17). Syn.: 4725. See: TWOT—1999; BDB—525d, 877c, 879d, 1110d.

6966. קוּם {35x} **qûwm** (Aram.), *koom;* corresp. to 6965:—set up {11x}, arise {5x}, stand {5x}, set {4x}, establish {3x}, rise up {3x}, appointeth {1x}, stood by {1x}, made {1x}, rise {1x}. See: TWOT—2968; BDB—1110d.

6967. קוֹמָה {45x} **qôwmâh**, *ko-maw';* from 6965; *height:*—height {30x}, stature {7x}, high {5x}, tall {2x}, along {1x}. See: TWOT—1999a; BDB—879b.

6968. קוֹמְמִיּוּת {1x} **qôwm°mîyûwth**, *ko-mem-ee-yooth';* from 6965; *elevation,* i.e. (adv.) *erectly* (fig.):—upright {1x}. See: TWOT—1999e; BDB—879c.

6969. קוּן {8x} **qûwn**, *koon;* a prim. root; to *strike* a musical note, i.e. *chant* or *wail* (at a funeral):—lament {7x}, mourning women {1x}. See: TWOT—2018; BDB—880c, 884b.

6970. קוֹעַ {1x} **Qôwa°**, *ko'-ah;* prob. from 6972 in the orig. sense of *cutting* off; *curtailment; Koä,* a region of Bab.:—Koa {1x}. See: BDB—880c.

6971. קוֹף {2x} **qôwph**, *kofe;* or

קֹף **qôph**, *kofe;* prob. of for. or.; a *monkey:*—apes {2x}. See: TWOT—2000; BDB—880d.

6972. קוּץ {1x} **qûwts**, *koots;* a prim. root; to *clip* off; used only as denom. from 7019; to *spend the harvest* season:—summer {1x}. See: BDB—884d.

6973. קוּץ {9x} **qûwts**, *koots;* a prim. root [rather ident. with 6972 through the idea of *severing* oneself from (comp. 6962)]; to *be* (caus. *make*) *disgusted* or *anxious:*—abhor {3x}, weary {2x}, loath {1x}, distressed {1x}, vex {1x}, grieved {1x}. See: TWOT—2002; BDB—880d.

6974. קוּץ {22x} **qûwts**, *koots;* a prim. root [rather ident. with 6972 through the idea of *abruptness* in starting up from sleep (comp. 3364)]; to *awake* (lit. or fig.):—awake {18x}, wake {2x}, arise {1x}, watch {1x}. See: TWOT—904a, 2019; BDB—884c.

6975. קוֹץ {12x} **qôwts**, *kotse;* or

קֹץ **qôts**, *kotse;* from 6972 (in the sense of *pricking*); a *thorn:*—thorn {12x}. See: TWOT—2003a; BDB—881a.

6976. קוֹץ {6x} **Qôwts**, *kotse;* the same as 6975; *Kots,* the name of two Isr.:—Koz {4x}, Coz {1x}, Hakkoz {1x}. See: BDB—881a.

6977. קְוֻצָּה {2x} **q°vutstsâh**, *kev-oots-tsaw';* fem. pass. part. of 6972 in its orig. sense; a *forelock* (as *shorn*):—lock {2x}. See: TWOT—2003b; BDB—881b.

6978. קַו־קָו {2x} **qav-qav**, *kav-kav';* from 6957 (in the sense of a *fastening*); *stalwart:*—meted out {2x}. See: TWOT—1994b; BDB—876a.

6979. קוּר {6x} **qûwr**, *koor;* a prim. root; to *trench;* by impl. to *throw forth;* also (denom. from 7023) to *wall up,* whether lit. (to *build* a wall) or fig. (to *estop*):—dig {2x}, cast out {2x}, destroy {1x}, break down {1x}. See: TWOT—2004, 2077; BDB—876a, 881b, 903b.

6980. קוּר {2x} **qûwr**, *koor;* from 6979; (only plur.) *trenches,* i.e. a *web* (as if so formed):—web {2x}. See: TWOT—2005a; BDB—881c.

6981. קוֹרֵא {3x} **Qôwrê**, *ko-ray';* or, the name of two Isr.:—Kore {3x}. See: BDB—881c, 896c.

6982. קוֹרָה {5x} **qôwrâh**, *ko-raw';* or

קֹרָה **qôrâh**, *ko-raw';* from 6979; a *rafter* (forming *trenches* as it were); by

impl. a *roof:*—beam {4x}, roof {1x}. See: TWOT—2068d; BDB—881c, 900a.

6983. קוֹשׁ {1x} **qôwsh,** *koshe;* a prim. root; to *bend;* used only as denom. for 3369, to *set a trap:*—snare {1x}. See: TWOT—2006; BDB—881c.

6984. קוּשָׁיָהוּ {1x} **Qûwshâyâhûw,** *koo-shaw-yaw'-hoo;* from the pass. part. of 6983 and 3050; *entrapped of Jah; Kushajah,* an Isr.:—Kushaiah {1x}. See: BDB—881c, 885c.

6985. קָט {1x} **qat,** *kat;* from 6990 in the sense of *abbreviation; a little,* i.e. (adv.) *merely:*—very {1x}. See: TWOT—2006.1; BDB—876c, 881c.

6986. קֶטֶב {3x} **qeteb,** *keh'-teb;* from an unused root mean. to *cut off; ruin:*—destruction {2x}, destroying {1x}. See: TWOT—2007a; BDB—881c.

6987. קֹטֶב {1x} **qôteb,** *ko'-teb;* from the same as 6986; *extermination:*—destruction {1x}. See: TWOT—2007a; BDB—881c.

6988. קְטוֹרָה {1x} **qᵉtôwrâh,** *ket-o-raw';* from 6999; *perfume:*—incense {1x}.
  Qetowrah, means "incense." This word's only appearance is in Deut 33:10. Syn.: 4730, 6999, 7002, 7004, 7008. See: TWOT—2011a; BDB—882c.

6989. קְטוּרָה {4x} **Qᵉtûwrâh,** *ket-oo-raw';* fem. pass. part. of 6999; *perfumed; Keturah,* a wife of Abraham:—Keturah {4x}. See: BDB—882c.

6990. קָטַט {1x} **qâtat,** *kaw-tat';* a prim. root; to *clip* off, i.e. (fig.) *destroy:*—shall be cut off {1x}. See: TWOT—1997; BDB—876c.

6991. קָטַל {3x} **qâtal,** *kaw-tal';* a prim. root; prop. to *cut off,* i.e. (fig.) *put to death:*—slay {2x}, kill {1x}. See: TWOT—2008; BDB—881d, 1111a.

6992. קְטַל {7x} **qᵉtal** (Aram.), *ket-al';* corresp. to 6991; to *kill:*—slay {7x}. See: TWOT—2969; BDB—1111a.

6993. קֶטֶל {1x} **qetel,** *keh'-tel;* from 6991; a violent *death:*—slaughter {1x}. See: TWOT—2008a; BDB—881d.

6994. קָטֹן {4x} **qâtôn,** *kaw-tone';* a prim. root [rather denom. from 6996]; to *diminish,* i.e. *be* (caus. *make*) *diminutive* or (fig.) *of no account:*—was a small thing {2x}, make small {1x}, am not worthy {1x}.
  Qaton (6994) and *qatan* (6996) are synonomous adjectives meaning small; youngest, insignificant: "I am not worthy of the least of all the mercies, and of all the truth, which thou hast shewed unto thy servant;" (Gen 32:10). **(1)** They bear the sense **(1a)** younger: "And

Noah awoke from his wine, and knew what his younger son had done unto him" (Gen 9:24), **(1b)** smaller and less significant: "And God made two great lights; the greater light to rule the day, and the lesser light to rule the night:" (Gen 1:16), **(1c)** small, with reference to **(1c1)** the size of a set of weights (Deut 25:13), **(1c2)** the size of the smallest finger of one's hand (1 Kin 12:10), and **(1c3)** to the degree of seriousness of a given sin: "And Balaam answered and said unto the servants of Balak, If Balak would give me his house full of silver and gold, I cannot go beyond the word of the LORD my God, to do less or more" (Num 22:18).
  (2) In the sense of young these words refer to the relative age of an individual: "And the Syrians had gone out by companies, and had brought away captive out of the land of Israel a little [*qaton*] maid; and she waited on Naaman's wife" (2 Kin 5:2, 14; Gen 42:15). **(3)** These adjectives can represent the idea of **(3a)** insignificant, small in importance or strength: (Deut 1:17); **(3b)** low in social standing: "And Samuel said, When thou wast little in thine own sight, wast thou not made the head of the tribes of Israel, and the LORD anointed thee king over Israel?" (1 Sa 15:17), or **(3c)** triviality: "And let them judge the people at all seasons: and it shall be, that every great matter they shall bring unto thee, but every small matter they shall judge:" (Ex 18:22). See: TWOT—2009; BDB—881d.

6995. קֹטֶן {2x} **qôten,** *ko'-ten;* from 6994; a *pettiness,* i.e. the *little finger:*—finger {2x}. See: TWOT—2009c; BDB—882b.

6996. קָטָן {101x} **qâtân,** *kaw-tawn';* or
  קָטֹן **qâtôn,** *kaw-tone';* from 6962; *abbreviated,* i.e. *diminutive,* lit. (in quantity, size or number) or fig. (in age or importance):—small {33x}, little {19x}, youngest {15x}, younger {14x}, least {10x}, less {3x}, lesser {2x}, little one {2x}, smallest {1x}, small things {1x}, young {1x}. See 6994 for discussion. See: TWOT—2009a, 2009b; BDB—881d, 882b.

6997. קָטָן {1x} **Qâtân,** *kaw-tawn';* the same as 6996; *small; Katan,* an Isr.:—Hakkatan {1x}. See: BDB—882a.

6998. קָטַף {5x} **qâtaph,** *kaw-taf';* a prim. root; to *strip* off:—crop off {2x}, pluck {1x}, cut up {1x}, cut down {1x}. See: TWOT—2010; BDB—882b.

6999. קָטַר {117x} **qâtar,** *kaw-tar';* a prim. root [rather ident. with 7000 through the idea of fumigation in a *close* place and perh. thus *driving* out the occupants]; to *smoke,* i.e. turn into fragrance by fire (espec. as

an act of worship):—incense {59x}, burn {49x}, offer {3x}, kindle {1x}, offering {1x}, misc. {4x}.

This word stresses the turning of a substance into a vapor. **(1)** Technically this verb means offering true offerings every time it appears in the causative stem (Hos 4:13; 11:2), although it may refer only to the burning of incense (2 Chr 13:11). **(2)** Offerings are burned to change the offering into smoke (the ethereal essence of the offering), which would ascend to God as a pleasing savor. **(3)** The things sacrificed were mostly common foods, and in this way Israel offered up to God life itself, their labors, and the fruit of their labors. **(4)** Such offerings represent both the giving of the thing offered and a vicarious substitution of the offering for the offerer. **(5)** Because of man's sinfulness (Gen 8:21), he was unable to initiate a relationship with God. **(6)** Therefore, God Himself told man what was necessary in order to worship and serve Him. **(7)** God specified that only the choicest of one's possessions could be offered, and the best of the offering belonged to Him (Lev 4:10). **(8)** Only His priests were to offer sacrifices (2 Kin 16:13). **(9)** All offerings were to be made at the designated place; after the conquest, this was the central sanctuary (Lev 17:6).

(10) Some of Israel's kings tried to legitimatize their idolatrous offerings, although they were in open violation of God's directives. Thus the causative stem is used to describe, for example, Jeroboam's idolatrous worship: "So he offered upon the altar which he had made in Beth-el the fifteenth day of the eighth month, even in the month which he had devised of his own heart; and ordained a feast unto the children of Israel: and he offered upon the altar, and burnt incense" (1 Kin 12:33; cf. 2 Kin 16:13; 2 Chr 28:4). **(11)** The intensive stem (occurring only after the Pentateuch) always represents "false worship." **(11a)** This form of *qatar* may represent the "total act of ritual" (2 Chr. 25:14). **(11b)** Such an act was usually a conscious act of idolatry, imitative of Canaanite worship (Is 65:7). **(11c)** Such worship was blasphemous and shameful (Jer 11:17). **(11d)** Those who performed this "incense-burning" were guilty of forgetting God (Jer 19:4), **(11e)** while the practice itself held no hope for those who were involved in it (Jer 11:12). **(11f)** Amos ironically told Israelites to come to Gilgal and Bethel (idolatrous altars) and "offer" a thank offering. This irony is even clearer in the Hebrew, for Amos uses *qatar* in the intensive stem. Syn.: 5930. See: TWOT—2011, 2011e, 2011g; BDB—882b, 883b.

7000. קָטַר {1x} **qâtar**, *kaw-tar';* a prim. root; to *inclose:*—joined {1x}. See: TWOT—2012; BDB—883b, 1111b.

7001. קְטַר {3x} **qᵉtar** (Aram.), *ket-ar';* from a root corresp. to 7000; a *knot* (as *tied* up), i.e. (fig.) a *riddle;* also a *vertebra* (as if a knot):—doubts {2x}, joints {1x}. See: TWOT—2970; BDB—1111b.

7002. קִטֵּר {1x} **qittêr**, *kit-tare';* from 6999; *perfume:*—incense {1x}.

Qitter means "incense." This word appears once in Jer 44:21. Syn.: 4730, 6988, 6999, 7004, 7008. See: TWOT—2011c; BDB—883b.

7003. קִטְרוֹן {1x} **Qitrôwn**, *kit-rone';* from 6999; *fumigative; Kitron,* a place in Pal.:—Kitron {1x}. See: BDB—883c.

7004. קְטֹרֶת {60x} **qᵉtôreth**, *ket-o'-reth;* from 6999; a *fumigation:*—incense {57x}, perfume {3x}.

Qetoreth, as a noun, means "incense." **(1)** The first biblical occurrence of *qetoreth* is in Ex 25:6: "Oil for the light, spices for anointing oil, and for sweet incense." **(2)** The word represents "perfume" in Prov 27:9. Syn.: 4730. See: TWOT—2011a; BDB—882c.

7005. קַטָּת {1x} **Qattâth**, *kat-tawth';* from 6996; *littleness; Kattath,* a place in Pal.:—Kattath {1x}. See: BDB—883c.

7006. קָיָה {1x} **qâyâh**, *kaw-yaw';* a prim. root; to *vomit:*—spue {1x}. See: TWOT—2013, 2013b; BDB—883d.

7007. קַיִט {1x} **qâyit** (Aram.), *kah'-yit;* corresp. to 7019; *harvest:*—summer {1x}. See: TWOT—2971; BDB—1111b.

7008. קִיטוֹר {4x} **qîytôwr**, *kee-tore';* or

קִיטֹר **qîytôr**, *kee-tore';* from 6999; a *fume,* i.e. *cloud:*—smoke {3x}, vapour {1x}.

Qiytowr refers to "smoke; vapor." This word does not refer to the smoke of an offering, but to other kinds of smoke or vapor. The reference in Ps 148:8 ("vapor") is one of its four biblical occurrences. Syn.: **(A)** *Muqtar* means "the kindling of incense." The word is used only once, and that is in Mal 1:11: "And in every place incense shall be offered unto my name. . . ." **(B)** *Meqatterah* refers to "incense altar." The word occurs once (2 Chr 26:19). See also: 4730, 6988, 7002, 7004, 7008. See: TWOT—2011b; BDB—882c, 883d.

7009. קִים {1x} **qîym**, *keem;* from 6965; an *opponent* (as *rising* against one), i.e. (collect.) enemies:—substance {1x}. See: TWOT—1999c; BDB—879c, 883d.

7010. קְיָם {2x} **qᵉyâm** (Aram.), *keh-yawm';* from 6966; an *edict* (as *arising* in law):—decree {1x}, statute {1x}. See: TWOT—2968a; BDB—1111a, 1111b.

Hebrew

7011. קָיָם {2x} **qayâm** (Aram.), *kah-yawm';* from 6966; *permanent* (as *rising firmly*):—sure {1x}, steadfast {1x}. See: TWOT—2968b; BDB—1111a, 1111b.

7012. קִימָה {1x} **qîymâh**, *kee-maw';* from 6965; an *arising:*—rising up {1x}. See: TWOT—1999d; BDB—879c, 883d.

קִימוֹשׁ **Qîymôwsh**. See 7057.

7013. קָיִן {1x} **qayin**, *kah'-yin;* from 6969 in the orig. sense of *fixity;* a *lance* (as *striking fast*):—spear {1x}. See: TWOT—2015a; BDB—883d.

7014. קַיִן {18x} **Qayin**, *kah'-yin;* the same as 7013 (with a play upon the affinity to 7069); *Kajin,* the name of the first child, also of a place in Pal., and of an Oriental tribe:—Cain {17x}, Kenite {1x}. See: TWOT—2017, 2016; BDB—883d, 884a.

7015. קִינָה {18x} **qîynâh**, *kee-naw';* from 6969; a *dirge* (as accompanied by *beating* the breasts or on instruments):—lamentation {18x}. See: TWOT—2018a; BDB—884b.

7016. קִינָה {1x} **Qîynâh**, *kee-naw';* the same as 7015; *Kinah,* a place in Pal.:—Kinah {1x}. See: BDB—884a.

7017. קֵינִי {13x} **Qêyniy**, *kay-nee';* or

קֵינִי **Qîyniy** (1 Chron. 2:55) *kee-nee';* patron. from 7014; a *Kenite* or member of the tribe of Kajin:—Kenite {13x}. See: TWOT—2016; BDB—884a, 889d.

7018. קֵינָן {6x} **Qêynân**, *kay-nawn';* from the same as 7064; *fixed; Kenan,* an antediluvian:—Cainan {5x}, Kenan {1x}. See: BDB—884b.

7019. קַיִץ {20x} **qayits**, *kah'-yits;* from 6972; *harvest* (as the *crop*), whether the product (grain or fruit) or the (dry) season:—summer {11x}, summer fruit {9x}. See: TWOT—2020a; BDB—884d, 1111b.

7020. קִיצוֹן {4x} **qîytsôwn**, *kee-tsone';* from 6972; *terminal:*—uttermost {3x}, outmost {1x}. See: TWOT—2060b; BDB—884d, 894a.

7021. קִיקָיוֹן {5x} **qîyqâyôwn**, *kee-kaw-yone';* perh. from 7006; the *gourd* (as *nauseous*):—gourd {5x}. See: TWOT—2021; BDB—884d.

7022. קִיקָלוֹן {1x} **qîyqâlôwn**, *kee-kaw-lone';* from 7036; intense *disgrace:*—shameful spewing {1x}. See: TWOT—2028f; BDB—884d, 887b.

7023. קִיר {74x} **qîyr**, *keer;* or

קִר **qir** (Isa. 22:5), *keer;* or (fem.)

קִירָה **qîyrâh**, *kee-raw';* from 6979; a *wall* (as built in a *trench*):—wall {66x}, side {4x}, masons {2x}, town {1x}, very {1x}. Syn.: 3820, 5315, 4578, 7130. See: TWOT—2022; BDB—885a, 885b, 894d.

7024. קִיר {5x} **Qîyr**, *keer;* the same as 7023; *fortress; Kir,* a place in Ass.; also one in Moab:—Kir {5x}. See: BDB—885b. comp. 7025.

7025. קִיר חֶרֶשׂ {5x} **Qîyr Cheres**, *keer kheh'-res;* or (fem. of the latter word)

קִיר חֲרֶשֶׂת **Qîyr Chăreseth**, *keer khar-eh'-seth;* from 7023 and 2789; *fortress of earthenware; Kir-Cheres* or *Kir-Chareseth,* a place in Moab:—Kirheres {2x}, Kirharaseth {1x}, Kirhareseth {1x}, Kirharesh {1x}. See: BDB—885b.

7026. קִירֹס {2x} **Qêyrôç**, *kay-roce';* or

קֵרֹס **Qêrôç**, *kay-roce';* from the same as 7166; *ankled; Keros,* one of the Nethinim:—Keros {2x}. See: BDB—885b, 902b.

7027. קִישׁ {21x} **Qîysh**, *keesh;* from 6983; a *bow; Kish,* the name of five Isr.:—Kish {21x}. See: BDB—885c.

7028. קִישׁוֹן {6x} **Qîyshôwn**, *kee-shone';* from 6983; *winding; Kishon,* a river of Pal.:—Kishon {6x}. See: BDB—885c.

7029. קִישִׁי {1x} **Qîyshiy**, *kee-shee';* from 6983; *bowed; Kishi,* an Isr.:—Kishi {1x}. See: BDB—881c, 885c.

7030. קִיתָרֹס {8x} **qîythârôç** (Aram.), *kee-thaw-roce';* of Gr. or. (kitharis); a *lyre:*—harp {4x}, variant spelling {4x}. See: TWOT—2972; BDB—1111b, 1112a.

7031. קַל {13x} **qal**, *kal;* contr. from 7043; *light;* (by impl.) *rapid* (also adv.):—swift {9x}, swiftly {2x}, swifter {1x}, light {1x}. See: TWOT—2028a; BDB—885c, 886d.

7032. קָל {7x} **qâl** (Aram.), *kawl;* corresp. to 6963:—sound {4x}, voice {3x}. See: TWOT—2973; BDB—1110b, 1111b.

קֹל **qôl**. See 6963.

7033. קָלָה {4x} **qâlâh**, *kaw-law';* a prim. root [rather ident. with 7034 through the idea of *shrinkage* by heat]; to *toast,* i.e. *scorch* partially or slowly:—roasted {1x}, dried {1x}, parched {1x}, loathsome {1x}. See: TWOT—2023; BDB—885c.

7034. קָלָה {6x} **qâlâh**, *kaw-law';* a prim. root; to *be light* (as impl. in *rapid*

motion), but fig. only (*be* [caus. *hold*] *in con-tempt*):—seem vile {1x}, shall be condemned {1x}, lightly esteemed {1x}, despised {1x}, base {1x}, settest light {1x}. See: TWOT—2024; BDB—885d.

7035. קָלָה {1x} **qâlahh,** *kaw-lah';* for 6950; to *assemble:*—gather together {1x}. See: TWOT—1991; BDB—874d, 885c.

7036. קָלוֹן {17x} **qâlôwn,** *kaw-lone';* from 7034; *disgrace;* (by impl.) the *pu-denda:*—shame {13x}, confusion {1x}, dishon-our {1x}, ignominy {1x}, reproach {1x}. See: TWOT—2024a; BDB—885d.

7037. קַלַּחַת {2x} **qallachath,** *kal-lakh'-ath;* appar. but a form for 6747; a *ket-tle:*—caldron {2x}. See: TWOT—2025; BDB—886a.

7038. קָלַט {1x} **qâlat,** *kaw-lat';* a prim. root; to *maim:*—lacking in his parts {1x}. See: TWOT—2027; BDB—886a.

7039. קָלִי {6x} **qâlîy,** *kaw-lee';* or

קָלִיא **qâlîy',** *kaw-lee';* from 7033; *roasted* ears of grain:—parched corn {5x}, parched {1x}. See: TWOT—2023a; BDB—885d, 886b.

7040. קַלָּי {1x} **Qallay,** *kal-lah'-ee;* from 7043; *frivolous; Kallai,* an Isr.:—Kallai {1x}. See: BDB—886b, 887a.

7041. קֵלָיָה {1x} **Qêlâyâh,** *kay-law-yaw';* from 7034; *insignificance; Kelajah,* an Isr.:—Kelaiah {1x}. See: BDB—886b.

7042. קְלִיטָא {3x} **Qᵉlîytâ',** *kel-ee-taw';* from 7038; *maiming; Kelita,* the name of three Isr.:—Kelita {3x}. See: BDB—886b.

7043. קָלַל {82x} **qâlal,** *kaw-lal';* a prim. root; to *be* (caus. *make*) *light,* lit. (*swift, small, sharp,* etc.) or fig. (*easy, trifling, vile,* etc.):—curse {39x}, swifter {5x}, light thing {5x}, vile {4x}, lighter {4x}, despise {3x}, abated {2x}, ease {2x}, light {2x}, lighten {2x}, slightly {2x}, misc. {12x} = make bright, bring into con-tempt, accurse, eas (-y, -ier), ✕ slight, be swift, revile, whet.

Qalal means "to be trifling, light, swift; to curse." **(1)** As will be seen, its various nuances grow out of the basic idea of being "trifling" or "light," with somewhat negative connotations involved. **(2)** Qalal is found for the first time in Gen 8:8: ". . . to see if the waters had abated;" indicating a lessening of what had existed. **(2)** The idea of "to be swift" is expressed in the Hebrew comparative form. So, Saul and Jonathan "were swifter than eagles" (2 Sa 1:23—literally, "more than eagles they were light"). **(3)** A similar idea is expressed in 1 Sa

18:23: "And David said, Seemeth it to you a light thing to a king's son-in-law?" **(4)** Qalal frequently includes the idea of "cursing" or "making little or contemptible": "And he that curseth [belittles] his father, or his mother, shall surely be put to death" (Ex 21:17). **(5)** "To curse" had the meaning of an "oath" when related to one's gods: "And the Philistine cursed David by his gods" (1 Sa 17:43). **(6)** The negative aspect of "non-blessing" was ex-pressed by the passive form: "The sinner being a hundred years old shall be accursed [by death]" (Is 65:20). Similar usage is reflected in: "Their portion is cursed in the earth . . ." (Job 24:18). **(7)** The causative form of the verb some-times expressed the idea of "lightening, lifting a weight": "Peradventure he will lighten his hand from off you . . ." (1 Sa 6:5); ". . . so shall it be easier for thyself" (Ex 18:22). Syn.: 423, 779. See: TWOT—2028; BDB—886b.

7044. קָלָל {2x} **qâlâl,** *kaw-lawl';* from 7043; *brightened* (as if *sharpened*):—burnished {1x}, polished {1x}. See: TWOT—2028c; BDB—887a.

7045. קְלָלָה {33x} **qᵉlâlâh,** *kel-aw-law';* from 7043; *vilification:*—curse {27x}, cursing {5x}, accursed {1x}. See: TWOT—2028d; BDB—887a.

7046. קָלַס {4x} **qâlaç,** *kaw-las';* a prim. root; to *disparage,* i.e. ridicule:—mock {2x}, scorn {1x}, scoff {1x}. See: TWOT—2029; BDB—887b.

7047. קֶלֶס {3x} **qeleç,** *keh'-les;* from 7046; a *laughing-stock:*—derision {3x}. See: TWOT—2029a; BDB—887b.

7048. קַלָּסָה {1x} **qallâçâh,** *kal-law-saw';* in-tens. from 7046; *ridicule:*—mocking {1x}. See: TWOT—2029b; BDB—887b.

7049. קָלַע {7x} **qâlaʿ,** *kaw-lah';* a prim. root; to *sling;* also to *carve* (as if a *circu-lar* motion, or into *light* forms):—sling {4x}, carve {3x}. See: TWOT—2030, 2031; BDB—887b, 887c.

7050. קֶלַע {22x} **qelaʿ,** *keh'-lah;* from 7049; a *sling;* also a (door) *screen* (as if *slung* across), or the *valve* (of the door) itself:—hangings {15x}, sling {4x}, sling + 3709 {1x}, slingstones + 68 {1x}, leaves {1x}. See: TWOT—2030a, 2030c; BDB—887c.

7051. קַלָּע {1x} **qallâʿ,** *kal-law';* intens. from 7049; a *slinger:*—slinger {1x}. See: TWOT—2030b; BDB—887c.

7052. קְלֹקֵל {1x} **qᵉlôqêl,** *kel-o-kale';* from 7043; *insubstantial:*—light {1x}. See: TWOT—2028e; BDB—887b, 887d.

7053. קִלְּשׁוֹן {1x} qillᵉshôwn, *kil-lesh-one';* from an unused root mean. to *prick;* a *prong,* i.e. hay-fork:—fork {1x}. See: TWOT—2032; BDB—887d.

7054. קָמָה {10x} qâmâh, *kaw-maw';* fem. of act. part. of 6965; something that *rises,* i.e. a *stalk* of grain:—standing corn {5x}, corn {2x}, grown up {2x}, stalk {1x}. See: TWOT—1999b; BDB—879b, 887d.

7055. קְמוּאֵל {3x} Qᵉmûw⁾êl, *kem-oo-ale';* from 6965 and 410; *raised of God; Kemuël,* the name of a rel. of Abraham, and of two Isr.:—Kemuel {3x}. See: BDB—887d.

7056. קָמוֹן {1x} Qâmôwn, *kaw-mone';* from 6965; an *elevation; Kamon,* a place E. of the Jordan:—Camon {1x}. See: BDB—879c, 887d.

7057. קִמּוֹשׁ {2x} qimmôwsh, *kim-moshe';* or

קִימוֹשׁ qîymôwsh, *kee-moshe';* from an unused root mean. to *sting;* a *prickly* plant:—nettles {2x}. See: TWOT—2037a; BDB—883d, 888b. comp. 7063.

7058. קֶמַח {14x} qemach, *keh'-makh;* from an unused root prob. mean. to *grind; flour:*—meal {10x}, flour {4x}. See: TWOT—2033a; BDB—887d.

7059. קָמַט {2x} qâmaṭ, *kaw-mat';* a prim. root; to *pluck,* i.e. *destroy:*—cut down {1x}, filled me with wrinkles {1x}. See: TWOT—2034; BDB—888a.

7060. קָמַל {2x} qâmal, *kaw-mal';* a prim. root; to *wither:*—wither {1x}, hewn down {1x}. See: TWOT—2035; BDB—888a.

7061. קָמַץ {3x} qâmats, *kaw-mats';* a prim. root; to *grasp* with the hand:—take {2x}, take a handful {1x}. See: TWOT—2036; BDB—888a.

7062. קֹמֶץ {4x} qômets, *ko'mets;* from 7061; a *grasp,* i.e. *handful:*—handful {2x}, handful + 4393 {2x}. See: TWOT—2036a; BDB—888a.

7063. קִמָּשׁוֹן {1x} qimmâshôwn, *kim-maw-shone';* from the same as 7057; a *prickly* plant:—thorn {1x}. See: TWOT—2037a; BDB—888b.

7064. קֵן {13x} qên, *kane;* contr. from 7077; a *nest* (as *fixed*), sometimes incl. the *nestlings;* fig. a *chamber* or *dwelling:*—nest {12x}, room {1x}. See: TWOT—2042a; BDB—888b, 890a.

7065. קָנָא {33} qânâ⁾, *kaw-naw';* a prim. root; to *be* (caus. *make*) *zealous,* i.e. (in a bad sense) *jealous* or *envious:*—jealous {10x},

envy {9x}, jealousy {5x}, envious {4x}, zealous {2x}, very {2x}, zeal {1x}.

Qana' means "to be jealous; to be zealous." **(1)** At the interhuman level *qana'* has a strongly competitive sense. **(1a)** In its most positive sense the word means "to be filled with righteous zeal or jealousy." **(1b)** The law provides that a husband who suspects his wife of adultery can bring her to a priest, who will administer a test of adultery. **(1c)** Whether his accusation turns out to be grounded or not, the suspicious man has a legitimate means of ascertaining the truth. **(1d)** In his case a spirit of jealousy has come over him, as he "is jealous" of his wife (Num 5:30). **(1e)** However, even in this context (Num 5:12–31), the jealousy has arisen out of a spirit of rivalry which cannot be tolerated in a marriage relationship. **(1f)** The jealousy must be cleared by a means ordained by the law and administered by the priests. **(1g)** *Qana',* then, in its most basic sense is the act of advancing one's rights to the exclusion of the rights of others: **(1g1)** "Ephraim shall not envy Judah, and Judah shall not vex Ephraim" (Is 11:13). **(1g2)** Saul sought to murder the Gibeonite enclave "in his zeal to the children of Israel and Judah" (2 Sa 21:2).

(2) Next, the word signifies the attitude of envy toward an opponent. **(2a)** Rachel in her barren state "envied her sister" (Gen 30:1) and in the state of envy approached Jacob: "Give me children, or else I die." **(2b)** The Philistines envied Isaac because of the multitude of his flocks and herds (Gen 26:14). **(3)** The Bible contains a strong warning against being envious of sinners, who might prosper and be powerful today, but will be no more tomorrow: "Envy thou not the oppressor, and choose none of his ways" (Prov 3:31; cf. Ps 37:1). **(4)** In man's relation to God, the act of zeal is more positively viewed as the act of the advancement of God and His glory over against substitutes. **(4a)** The tribe of Levi received the right to service because "he was zealous for his God" (Num 25:13). **(4b)** Elijah viewed himself as the only faithful servant left in Israel: "I have been very jealous for the Lord God of hosts: for the children of Israel have forsaken thy covenant . . . And I, even I only, am left" (1 Kin 19:10).

(5) However, the sense of *qana'* is "to make jealous," that is, "to provoke to anger": "They provoked him to jealousy with strange gods, with abominations provoked they him to anger" (Deut 32:16). **(6)** God is not tainted with the negative connotation of the verb. **(6a)** His holiness does not tolerate competitors or those who sin against Him. **(6b)** In no single passage in the whole Old Testament is God described as envious. **(6c)** When God is the subject of the verb *qana',* the meaning is "be zealous," and

the preposition *le* ("to, for") is used before the object: His holy name (Eze 39:25); His land (Joel 2:18); and His inheritance (Zec 1:14). Cf. Zec 8:2: "Thus saith the LORD of hosts; I was jealous for Zion with great jealousy, and I was jealous for her with great fury." See: TWOT—2038; BDB—888c.

7066. אָנְקָ {1x} qᵉnâ² (Aram.), *ken-aw'*; corresp. to 7069; to *purchase:*—buy {1x}. See: TWOT—2974; BDB—1111b.

7067. אָנַּקָ {6x} qannâ², *kan-naw'*; from 7065; *jealous:*—jealous {6x}.
Qanna', as an adjective, means "jealous." **(1)** The word refers directly to the attributes of God's justice and holiness, as He is the sole object of human worship and does not tolerate man's sin. **(2)** One appearance is in Ex 20:5: "For I the Lord thy God am a jealous God, visiting the iniquity of the fathers upon the children unto the third and fourth generation of them that hate me." See: TWOT—2038b; BDB—888d. comp. 7072.

7068. קִנְאָה {43x} qin'âh, *kin-aw'*; from 7065; *jealousy or envy:*—jealousy {25x}, zeal {9x}, envy {8x}, for my sake {1x}.
Qin'ah means "ardor; zeal; jealousy." This noun occurs 43 times in biblical Hebrew. One occurrence is in Deut 29:20: "The Lord will not spare him, but then the anger of the Lord and his jealousy shall smoke against that man." See: TWOT—2038a; BDB—888b.

7069. קָנָה qânâh, *kaw-naw'*; a prim. root; to *erect,* i.e. *create;* by extens. to *procure,* espec. by purchase (caus. *sell);* by impl. to *own:*—buy {46x}, get {15x}, purchased {5x}, buyer {3x}, possessor {3x}, possessed {2x}, owner {1x}, recover {1x}, redeemed {1x}, misc. {7x} = attain, teach to keep cattle, provoke to jealousy, × surely, × verily.
(1) In Gen 4:1 Eve says "I have gotten a man from the Lord" expressing God's creating or bringing into being; thus Eve said "I have created a man-child with the help of the Lord" (cf. Gen 14:19, 22). **(2)** In Deut 32:6, God is called the father who created Israel; a father begets or creates, rather than acquires children. **(3)** *Qanah* expresses one person making a purchase agreement with another; buying a slave (Ex 21:2) or land (Gen 47:20). **(4)** Some have related *qanah* to creation: *Qanah* means "to get, acquire, earn" and these basic meanings are dominant in the Old Testament, but certain poetic passages have long suggested that this verb means "create." **(4a)** In Gen 14:19, Melchizedek blessed Abram and said: "Blessed be Abram by God Most High, possessor of heaven and earth." **(4b)** Gen 14:22 repeats this divine epithet. **(4c)** Deut 32:6 makes

this meaning certain in that *qanah* is parallel to (6213 – *'asah,* "to make"): "is not he thy father that hath bought (7069 – *qanah*) thee? hath he not made (6213 – *'asah*) thee, and established (3559 - *kun*) thee? **(4d)** Ps 78:54; 139:13; and Prov 8:22–23 also suggest the idea of creation. See: TWOT—2039; BDB—888d, 1111b.

7070. קָנֶה {62x} qâneh, *kaw-neh'*; from 7069; *a reed* (as *erect);* by resemblance a *rod* (espec. for measuring), *shaft, tube, stem,* the *radius* (of the arm), *beam* (of a steelyard):—reed {28x}, branch {24x}, calamus {3x}, cane {2x}, stalk {2x}, balance {1x}, bone {1x}, spearmen {1x}. See: TWOT—2040a; BDB—889c.

7071. קָנָה {3x} Qânâh, *kaw-naw'*; fem. of 7070; *reediness; Kanah,* the name of a stream and of a place in Pal.:—Kanah {3x}. See: BDB—889d.

7072. קַנּוֹא {2x} qannôw², *kan-no'*; for 7067; *jealous or angry:*—jealous {2x}.
The adjective *qannow'* means "jealous." **(1)** Josh 24:19 is one example: "And Joshua said unto the people, Ye cannot serve the Lord: for he is a holy God; for he is a jealous God; he will not forgive your transgressions nor your sins." **(2)** Nah. 1:2 contains the other occurrence of *qannow':* "God is jealous, and the LORD revengeth; the LORD revengeth, and is furious; the LORD will take vengeance on his adversaries, and he reserveth wrath for his enemies." See: TWOT—2038c; BDB—888d.

7073. קְנַז {11x} Qᵉnaz, *ken-az'*; prob. from an unused root mean. to *hunt; hunter; Kenaz,* the name of an Edomite and of two Isr.:—Kenaz {11x}. See: BDB—889d.

7074. קְנִזִּי {4x} Qᵉnizzîy, *ken-iz-zee'*; patron. from 7073, a *Kenizzite* or desc. of Kenaz:—Kenezite {3x}, Kenizzites {1x}. See: BDB—889d.

7075. קִנְיָן {10x} qinyân, *kin-yawn'*; from 7069; *creation,* i.e. (concr.) *creatures;* also *acquisition, purchase, wealth:*—substance {4x}, of . . . getting {2x}, goods {2x}, riches {1x}, with {1x}. See: TWOT—2039a; BDB—889a.

7076. קִנָּמוֹן {3x} qinnâmôwn, *kin-naw-mone'*; from an unused root (mean. to *erect);* cinnamon bark (as in *upright* rolls):—cinnamon {3x}. See: TWOT—2041; BDB—890a.

7077. קָנַן {5x} qânan, *kaw-nan'*; a prim. root; to *erect;* but used only as denom. from 7064; to *nestle,* i.e. *build* or *occupy* as a nest:—make . . . nest {5x}. See: TWOT—2042; BDB—890a.

7078. קֶנֶץ {1x} **qênets**, *kay'-nets;* from an unused root prob. mean. to *wrench; perversion:*—end {1x}. See: TWOT—2043a; BDB—890b.

7079. קְנָת {2x} **Q°nâth**, *ken-awth';* from 7069; *possession; Kenath,* a place E. of the Jordan:—Kenath {2x}. See: BDB—890b.

7080. קָסַם {20x} **qâçam**, *kaw-sam';* a prim. root; prop. to *distribute,* i.e. *determine* by lot or magical scroll; by impl. to *divine:*—divine {7x}, diviners {7x}, use {3x}, divination {1x}, prudent {1x}, soothsayer {1x}.

(1) Divination was a pagan parallel to prophesying (Deut 18:10, 14–15). (2) Qacam is a seeking after the will of the gods, in an effort to learn their future action or divine blessing on some proposed future action (Josh 13:22). (3) It seems probable that the diviners conversed with demons (cf. 1 Cor 10:20). (4) The practice of divination might involve (4a) offering sacrifices to the deity on an altar (Num 23:1ff.), (4b) the use of a hole (?) in the ground, through which the diviner spoke to the spirits of the dead: "And Saul disguised himself, and put on other raiment, and he went, and two men with him, and they came to the woman by night: and he said, I pray thee, divine unto me by the familiar spirit, and bring me him up, whom I shall name unto thee" (1 Sa 28:8), (4c) the shaking of arrows, (4d) consulting with household idols, or (4e) studying the livers of dead animals (Eze 21:21). (5) Divination was one of man's attempts to know and control the world and the future, apart from the true God. (6) It was the opposite of true prophecy, the submission to God's sovereignty (Deut 18:14). See: TWOT—2044; BDB—890c.

7081. קֶסֶם {11x} **qeçem**, *keh'-sem;* from 7080; a *lot;* also *divination* (incl. its *fee*), *oracle:*—divination {9x}, witchcraft {1x}, divine sentence {1x}. See: TWOT—2044a; BDB—890c.

7082. קָסַס {1x} **qâçaç**, *kaw-sas';* a prim. root; to *lop* off:—cut off {1x}. See: TWOT—2045; BDB—890d.

7083. קֶסֶת {3x} **qeçeth**, *keh'-seth;* from the same as 3563 (or as 7185); prop. a *cup,* i.e. an *ink-stand:*—inkhorn {3x}. See: TWOT—2080b; BDB—890d, 1099c.

7084. קְעִילָה {18x} **Q°îylâh**, *keh-ee-law';* perh. from 7049 in the sense of *inclosing; citadel; Keïlah,* a place in Pal.:—Keilah {18x}. See: BDB—890d.

7085. קַעֲקַע {1x} **qa'ăqa'**, *kah-ak-ah';* from the same as 6970; an *incision* or gash:—mark {1x}. See: TWOT—2046a; BDB—891a.

7086. קְעָרָה {17x} **q°'ârâh**, *keh-aw-raw';* prob. from 7167; a *bowl* (as *cut* out hollow):—charger {14x}, dish {3x}. See: TWOT—2047a; BDB—891a.

קוף **qôph**. See 6971.

7087. קָפָא {5x} **qâphâ'**, *kaw-faw';* a prim. root; to *shrink,* i.e. *thicken* (as unracked wine, curdled milk, clouded sky, frozen water):—congeal {1x}, settled {1x}, curdle {1x}, variant {1x}, dark {1x}. See: TWOT—2048, 2048a; BDB—891a, 891b.

7088. קָפַד {1x} **qâphad**, *kaw-fad';* a prim. root; to *contract,* i.e. *roll together:*—cut off {1x}. See: TWOT—2049; BDB—891b.

7089. קְפָדָה {1x} **q°phâdâh**, *kef-aw-daw';* from 7088; *shrinking,* i.e. *terror:*—destruction {1x}. See: TWOT—2049b; BDB—891c.

7090. קִפּוֹד {3x} **qippôwd**, *kip-pode';* or

קִפֹּד **qippôd**, *kip-pode';* from 7088; a *species of bird,* perh. the *bittern* (from its *contracted* form):—bittern {3x}. See: TWOT—2049a; BDB—891b.

7091. קִפּוֹז {1x} **qippôwz**, *kip-poze';* from an unused root mean. to *contract,* i.e. *spring* forward; an *arrow-snake* (as *darting* on its prey):—great owl {1x}. See: TWOT—2050a; BDB—891c.

7092. קָפַץ {7x} **qâphats**, *kaw-fats';* a prim. root; to *draw together,* i.e. *close;* by impl. to *leap* (by *contracting* the limbs); spec. to *die* (from *gathering* up the feet):—shut {2x}, stop {2x}, shut up {1x}, take out of the way {1x}, skip {1x}. See: TWOT—2051; BDB—891c.

7093. קֵץ {67x} **qêts**, *kates;* contr. from 7112: an *extremity;* adv. (with prep. pref.) *after:*—end {52x}, after {10x}, border {3x}, infinite {1x}, process {1x}.

Qets means "end." (1) First, the word is used to denote the "end of a person" or "death": (1a) "And God said unto Noah, The end of all flesh is come before me" (Gen 6:13). (1b) In Ps 39:4, qets speaks of the "farthest extremity of human life," in the sense of how short it is: "Lord, make me to know mine end, and the measure of my days, what it is; that I may know how frail I am." (2) Second, qets means "end" as the state of "being annihilated": "He setteth an end to darkness, and searcheth out all perfection" (Job 28:3). (3) Third, related to the previous meaning but quite distinct, is the connotation "farthest extremity of," such as the "end of a given period of time": "And after certain years [literally, "at the end of years"] he went down to Ahab to

Samaria" (2 Chr 18:2; cf. Gen 4:3—the first biblical appearance). **(4)** A fourth nuance emphasizes a "designated goal," not simply the extremity but a conclusion toward which something proceeds: "For the vision is yet for an appointed time, but at the end it shall speak, and not lie" (Hab 2:3). **(5)** In another emphasis, *qets* represents the "boundary" or "limit" of something: "I have seen an end of all perfection" (Ps 119:96). **(6)** In 2 Kin 19:23, the word (with the preposition *le*) means "farthest": "And I will enter into the lodgings of his borders, and into the forest of his Carmel." See: TWOT—2060a; BDB—891d, 893d.

קֵץ **qôts.** See 6975.

7094. קָצַב {2x} **qâtsab,** *kaw-tsab';* a prim. root; to *clip,* or (gen.) *chop:*—cut down {1x}, shorn {1x}. See: TWOT—2052; BDB—891d.

7095. קֶצֶב {3x} **qetseb,** *keh'-tseb;* from 7094; *shape* (as if *cut* out); *base* (as if there *cut* off):—size {2x}, bottom {1x}. See: TWOT—2052a; BDB—891d.

7096. קָצָה {5x} **qâtsâh,** *kaw-tsaw';* a prim. root; to *cut* off; (fig.) to *destroy;* (partially) to *scrape* off:—cut off {2x}, cut short {1x}, scrape {1x}, scrape off {1x}. See: TWOT—2053; BDB—891d.

7097. קָצֶה {96x} **qâtseh,** *kaw-tseh';* or (neg. only)

קֵצֶה **qêtseh,** *kay'-tseh;* from 7096: an *extremity* (used in a great variety of applications and idioms; comp. 7093):—end {56x}, . . . part {7x}, edge {6x}, border {3x}, outside {3x}, utmost {3x}, uttermost {3x}, coast {2x}, quarter {2x}, misc. {11x} = × after, brim, brink, [in-] finite, frontier, shore, side, × some.
Qatseh means "end; border; extremity." **(1)** In Gen 23:9, *qatseh* means "end" in **(1a)** the sense of "extremity": "That he may give me the cave of Machpelah, which he hath, which is in the end of his field." **(1b)** The word means "[nearest] edge or border" in Ex 13:20: "And they took their journey from Succoth, and encamped in the Etham, in the edge of the wilderness." **(1c)** At other points, the word clearly indicates the "farthest extremity": "If any of thine be driven out unto the outmost parts of heaven, from thence will the Lord thy God gather thee, and from thence will he fetch thee" (Deut 30:4). **(2)** Second, *qatseh* can signify a "temporal end," such as the "end of a period of time"; that is the use in Gen 8:3, the first biblical occurrence of the word: "After the end of the hundred and fifty days the waters were abated."
(3) One special use of *qatseh* occurs in Gen

47:2, where **(3a)** the word is used with the preposition *min* ("from"): "And from among his brothers he took five men and presented them to Pharaoh" (cf. Eze 33:2). **(3b)** In Gen 19:4, the same construction means "from every quarter (or "part") of a city": "The men of the city, even the men of Sodom, compassed the house round, both old and young, all the people from every quarter." **(3c)** A similar usage occurs in Gen 47:21, except that the phrase is repeated twice and is rendered "from one end of the borders of Egypt to the other." **(3d)** In Jer 51:31, the phrase means "in every quarter" or completely." See: TWOT—2053a, 2053c; BDB—892a, 892c, 1111b.

7098. קָצָה {35x} **qâtsâh,** *kaw-tsaw';* fem. of 7097; a *termination* (used like 7097):—end {22x}, lowest {3x}, uttermost part {2x}, edges {2x}, selvedge {2x}, misc. {4x} = coast, corner.
Qatsah means "end; border; edge; extremity." This word refers primarily to concrete objects. In a few instances, however, *qatsah* is used of abstract objects; one example is of God's way (Job 26:14). See: TWOT—2053b; BDB—892b.

7099. קֶצֶו {7x} **qetsev,** *keh'-tsev;* and (fem.)

קִצְוָה **qitsvâh,** *kits-vaw';* from 7096; a *limit* (used like 7097, but with less variety):—end {4x}, uttermost {1x}, variant {2x}. See: TWOT—2053d; BDB—892c.

7100. קֶצַח {3x} **qetsach,** *keh'-tsakh;* from an unused root appar. mean. to *incise; fennel-flower* (from its *pungency*):—fitches {3x}. See: TWOT—2055a; BDB—892d.

7101. קָצִין {12x} **qâtsîyn,** *kaw-tseen';* from 7096 in the sense of *determining;* a *magistrate* (as *deciding*) or other *leader:*—ruler {4x}, prince {4x}, captain {3x}, guide {1x}. See: TWOT—2054a; BDB—892d. comp. 6278.

7102. קְצִיעָה {1x} **qᵉtsîyʻâh,** *kets-ee-aw';* from 7106; *cassia* (as *peeled;* plur. the *bark*):—cassia {1x}. See: TWOT—2056a; BDB—893a, 893b.

7103. קְצִיעָה {1x} **Qᵉtsîyʻâh,** *kets-ee-aw';* the same as 7102; *Ketsiah,* a daughter of Job:—Kezia {1x}. See: BDB—893a.

7104. קְצִיץ {1x} **Qᵉtsîyts,** *kets-eets';* from 7112; *abrupt; Keziz,* a valley in Pal.:—Keziz {1x}. See: BDB—894a.

7105. קָצִיר {54x} **qâtsîyr,** *kaw-tseer';* from 7114; *severed,* i.e. *harvest* (as *reaped*), the crop, the time, the reaper, or fig.; also a *limb* (of a tree, or simply *foliage*):—harvest {47x}, boughs {3x}, branch {2x}, harvest-

man {1x}, harvest time {1x}. See: TWOT—2062a, 2062b; BDB—894c, 894d.

7106. קָצַע {2x} **qâtsaᶜ**, *kaw-tsah';* a prim. root; to *strip* off, i.e. (partially) *scrape;* by impl. to *segregate* (as an angle):—cause to scrape {1x}, corner {1x}. See: TWOT—2056, 2057; BDB—892d.

7107. קָצַף {34x} **qâtsaph**, *kaw-tsaf';* a prim. root; to *crack* off, i.e. (fig.) *burst* out in rage:—wroth {22x}, wrath {5x}, displeased {3x}, angry {2x}, angered {1x}, fret {1x}.

Qatsaph, as a verb, means "to be wroth, angry." **(1)** The general meaning of *qatsaph* is a strong emotional outburst of anger, especially when man is the subject of the reaction. **(1a)** The first usage of the word brings this out: "And Pharaoh was wroth against two of his officers . . . and he put them in [custody]" (Gen 40:2–3; cf. 41:10). **(1b)** Moses became bitterly angry with the disobedient Israelites (Ex 16:20). **(1c)** The leaders of the Philistines "were wroth" with Achish (1 Sa 29:4), and **(1d)** Naaman was strongly irritated by Elisha's lack of a sense of protocol (2 Kin 5:11). **(1e)** Elisha expressed his anger with Joash, king of Israel (2 Kin 13:19). **(1f)** King Ahasuerus deposed Vashti in his anger (Est 1:12). **(1g)** In these examples an exalted person (generally a king) demonstrated his royal anger in radical measures against his subjects. He was in a position "to be angered" by the response of his subjects. **(2)** It is rarer for a person "to become angry" with an equal. **(3)** It is even rarer for a subject "to be angry" with his superior: "Two of the king's chamberlains . . . were wroth, and sought to lay hand on the king Ahasuerus" (Est 2:21).

(4) The verb *qatsaph* is used 11 times to describe man's anger and 18 times to refer to God's anger. This fact, coupled with the observation that the verb generally is an expression of a superior against a subject, explains why the biblical text more frequently uses *qatsaph* to describe God's anger. **(5)** The object of the anger is often indicated by the preposition 'al ("against"). "For I was afraid of the anger [639 - 'ap] and hot displeasure [2534 - chemah], wherewith the Lord was wroth [qatsaph] against ['al] you to destroy you" (Deut 9:19). **(6)** The Lord's anger expresses itself against disobedience (Lev 10:6) and sin (Eccl 5:5ff.). **(6a)** However, people themselves can be the cause for God's anger (Ps 106:32). **(6b)** In the wilderness the Israelites provoked God to wrath by their disobedience and lack of faith: "Remember, and forget not, how thou provokedst the Lord thy God to wrath in the wilderness: from the day that thou didst depart out of the land of Egypt, until ye came unto this place, ye have been rebellious against the Lord" (Deut 9:7; cf.

vv. 8, 22). **(6c)** Moses spoke about God's wrath against Israel's disobedience which would in time be the occasion for the Exile (Deut 29:27), and the prophets amplify Moses' warning of God's coming "wrath" (Jer 21:5). **(7)** After the Exile, God had compassion on Israel and turned His anger against Israel's enemies (Is 34:2). See: TWOT—2058; BDB—893b.

7108. קְצַף {1x} **qᵉtsaph** (Aram.), *kets-af';* corresp. to 7107; to *become enraged:*—be furious {1x}. See: TWOT—2975; BDB—1111c.

7109. קְצַף {1x} **qᵉtsaph** (Aram.), *kets-af';* from 7108; *rage:*—wrath {1x}. See: TWOT—2975a; BDB—1111c.

7110. קֶצֶף {29x} **qetseph**, *keh'-tsef;* from 7107; a *splinter* (as *chipped* off); fig. *rage* or *strife:*—wrath {23x}, indignation {3x}, sore {2x}, foam {1x}.

Qetseph (7110), as a noun, means "wrath." **(1)** This noun occurs 28 times in biblical Hebrew and **(1a)** generally with reference to God. **(1b)** One occurrence of God's "wrath" is in 2 Chr 29:8: "Wherefore the wrath of the Lord was upon Judah and Jerusalem. . . ." **(2)** An example of man's "wrath" appears in Est 1:18: "Likewise shall the ladies of Persia and Media say this day unto all the king's princes, which have heard of the deed of the queen. Thus shall there arise too much contempt and wrath" (cf. Eccl 5:17). See: TWOT—2058a, 2059b; BDB—893c.

7111. קְצָפָה {1x} **qᵉtsâphâh**, *kets-aw-faw';* from 7107; a *fragment:*—barked {1x}. See: TWOT—2059a; BDB—893c.

7112. קָצַץ {14x} **qâtsats**, *kaw-tsats';* a prim. root; to *chop* off (lit. or fig.):—cut off {6x}, utmost {3x}, cut in pieces {2x}, cut {1x}, cut asunder {1x}, cut in sunder {1x}. See: TWOT—2060; BDB—893c.

7113. קְצַץ {1x} **qᵉtsats** (Aram.), *kets-ats';* corresp. to 7112:—cut off {1x}. See: BDB—893c.

7114. קָצַר {49x} **qâtsar**, *kaw-tsar';* a prim. root; to *dock* off, i.e. *curtail* (tran. or intr., lit. or fig.); espec. to *harvest* (grass or grain):—reap {22x}, reaper {8x}, shortened {5x}, shorter {2x}, discouraged {1x}, lothed {1x}, straitened {1x}, misc. {9x} = ✕ at all, cut down, much, grieve, harvestman, mourn, trouble, vex. See: TWOT—2061, 2062; BDB—894a, 894b, 894d.

7115. קֹצֶר {1x} **qôtser**, *ko'-tser;* from 7114; *shortness* (of spirit), i.e. *impatience:*—anguish {1x}. See: TWOT—2061b; BDB—894b.

7116. קָצֵר {5x} **qâtsêr**, *kaw-tsare';* from 7114; *short* (whether in size, number, life, strength or temper):—small {2x}, few {1x}, soon {1x}, hasty {1x}. See: TWOT—2061a; BDB—894b.

7117. קְצָת {5x} **qᵉtsâth**, *kets-awth';* from 7096; a *termination* (lit. or fig.); also (by impl.) a *portion;* adv. (with prep. pref.) *after:*—end {3x}, part {1x}, some {1x}. See: TWOT—2053e; BDB—596d, 892c, 892d, 894d, 1111c.

7118. קְצָת {4x} **qᵉtsâth** (Aram.), *kets-awth';* corresp. to 7117:—end {2x}, partly {2x}. See: TWOT—2976; BDB—1111c.

7119. קַר {3x} **qar**, *kar;* contr. from an unused root mean. to *chill; cool;* fig. *quiet:*—cold {2x}, variant {1x}. See: TWOT—2077a; BDB—894d.

      קִר **qîr**. See 7023.

7120. קֹר {1x} **qôr**, *kore;* from the same as 7119; *cold:*—cold {1x}. See: TWOT—2077b; BDB—894d, 903b.

7121. קָרָא {735x} **qârâ'**, *kaw-raw';* a prim. root [rather ident. with 7122 through the idea of *accosting* a person met]; to *call* out to (i.e. prop. *address* by name, but used in a wide variety of applications):—call {528x}, cried {98x}, read {38x}, proclaim {36x}, named {7x}, guests {4x}, invited {3x}, gave {3x}, renowned {3x}, bidden {2x}, preach {2x}, misc. {11x} = bewray [self], (be) famous, mention, (make) proclamation, pronounce, publish, say. *Qara'* means "to call, call out, recite." **(1)** *Qara'* may signify the "specification of a name." **(1a)** Naming a thing is frequently an assertion of sovereignty over it, which is the case in the first use of *qara':* "And God called the light Day, and the darkness he called Night" (Gen 1:5). **(1b)** God's act of creating, "naming," and numbering includes the stars (Ps 147:4) and all other things (Is 40:26). **(2)** He allowed Adam to "name" the animals as a concrete demonstration of man's relative sovereignty over them (Gen 2:19). **(3)** Divine sovereignty and election are extended over all generations, for God "called" them all from the beginning (Is 41:4; cf. Amos 5:8). **(4)** "Calling" or "naming" an individual **(4a)** may specify the individual's primary characteristic: "And he said, Is not he rightly named Jacob? for he hath supplanted me these two times: he took away my birthright; and, behold, now he hath taken away my blessing" (Gen 27:36); **(4b)** it may consist of a confession or evaluation (Is 58:13; 60:14); and **(4c)** it may recognize an eternal truth: "Therefore the Lord himself shall give you a sign; Behold, a virgin shall conceive, and bear a son, and shall call his name Immanuel" (Is 7:14).

(5) This verb also is used to indicate "calling to a specific task." **(5a)** In Ex 2:7, Moses' sister Miriam asked Pharaoh's daughter if she should go and "call" (summon) a nurse. **(5b)** Israel was "called" (elected) by God to be His people (Is 65:12), as were the Gentiles in the messianic age (Is 55:5). **(6)** To "call" on God's name is to summon His aid. **(6a)** This emphasis appears in Gen 4:26, where men began to "call" on the name of the Lord. **(6b)** Such a "calling" on God's name occurs against the background of the Fall and the murder of Abel. **(6c)** The "calling" on God's name is clearly not the beginning of prayer, since communication between God and man existed since the Garden of Eden; nor is it an indication of the beginning of formal worship, since formal worship began at least as early as the offerings of Cain and Abel (Gen 4:7ff.). **(7)** The sense of "summoning" God to one's aid was surely in Abraham's mind when he "called upon" God's name (Gen 12:8). **(7a)** "Calling" in this sense constitutes a prayer prompted by recognized need and **(7b)** directed to One who is able and willing to respond (Ps 145:18; Is 55:6).

(8) Basically, *qara'* means "to call out loudly" in order to get someone's attention so that contact can be initiated. So Job is told: "Call now, if there be any that will answer thee; and to which of the saints wilt thou turn?" (Job 5:11). **(9)** Often this verb represents sustained communication, paralleling "to say" (559 - '*amar*), as in Gen 3:9: "And the Lord God called unto Adam, and said unto him. . . ." **(10)** *Qara'* can also mean "to call out a warning," so that direct contact may be avoided: "And the leper in whom the plague is, his clothes shall be rent, and his head bare, and he shall put a covering upon his upper lip, and shall cry, Unclean, unclean" (Lev 13:45). **(11)** *Qara'* may mean "to shout" or "to call out loudly." **(11a)** Goliath "shouted" toward the ranks of Israel (1 Sa 17:8) and challenged them to individual combat (duel). **(11b)** Sometimes ancient peoples settled battles through such combatants. **(11c)** Before battling an enemy, Israel was directed to offer them peace: "When thou comest nigh unto a city to fight against it, then proclaim peace unto it [call out to it in terms of peace]" (Deut 20:10).

(12) *Qara'* may also mean "to proclaim" or "to announce," as when Israel proclaimed peace to the sons of Benjamin (Judg 21:13). **(12a)** This sense first occurs in Gen 41:43, where we are told that Joseph rode in the second chariot; "and they cried before him, Bow the knee." **(12b)** Haman recommended to King Ahasuerus that he adorn the one to be honored and "proclaim" ("announce") before him, "Thus shall it be done to the man whom the

king delighteth to honor" (Est 6:9). This proclamation would tell everyone that the man so announced was honored by the king. **(13)** The two emphases, "proclamation" and "announce," occur in Ex 32:5: "Aaron made proclamation, and said, Tomorrow is a feast to the Lord." This instance implies "summoning" an official assemblage of the people. **(14)** In prophetic literature, *qara'* is a technical term for "declaring" a prophetic message: "For the saying which he cried by the word of the Lord . . . shall surely come to pass" (1 Kin 13:32).

(15) Another major emphasis of *qara'* is "to summon." **(15a)** When Pharaoh discovered Abram's deceit concerning Sarai, he "summoned" ("called") Abram so that he might correct the situation (Gen 12:18). **(15b)** Often the summons is in the form of a friendly invitation, as when Reuel (or Jethro) told his daughters to "invite him [Moses] that he may eat bread," (Ex 2:20). **(16)** The participial form of *qara'* is used to denote "invited guests": "As soon as ye be come into the city, ye shall straightway find him, before he go up to the high place to eat: for the people will not eat until he come, because he doth bless the sacrifice; and afterwards they eat that be bidden. Now therefore get you up; for about this time ye shall find him" (1 Sa 9:13). **(17)** This verb is also used in judicial contexts, to mean being "summoned to court" if a man is accused of not fulfilling his levirate responsibility, "then the elders of his city shall call him, and speak unto him . . ." (Deut 25:8). **(18)** *Qara'* is used of "summoning" someone and/or "mustering" an army: "Why hast thou served us thus, that thou calledst us not, when thou wentest to fight with the Midianites?" (Judg 8:1).

(19) The meaning "to read" apparently arose from the meaning "to announce" and "to declare," inasmuch as reading was done out loud so that others could hear. This sense appears in Ex 24:7: "And he took the book of the covenant, and read in the audience of the people: and they said, All that the LORD hath said will we do, and be obedient." **(20)** *Qara'* means "to read to oneself" only in a few passages. **(21)** At least once, the verb *qara'* means "to dictate": "Then Baruch answered them, He [dictated] all these words unto me . . . and I wrote them with ink in the book" (Jer. 36:18). Syn.: 1319, 4744. See: TWOT—2063; BDB—894d, 1111c.

7122. קָרָא {16x} **qârâ᾽**, *kaw-raw'*; a prim. root: to *encounter*, whether accidentally or in a hostile manner:—befall {5x}, come {4x}, chance {2x}, happened {2x}, met {2x}, fall out {1x}.

(1) *Qara'* represents an intentional confrontation, whereby one person is immediately before another person. This may be **(1a)** friendly (Gen 14:17; Josh 9:11) or **(1b)** hostile (Josh 8:5; Amos 4:12). **(2)** Religiously, one meets God or is met by God (Ex 5:3). **(3)** This verb infrequently represents an accidental meeting, so it is translated "befall" (Gen 42:4). See: TWOT—2064; BDB—896d, 897a.

7123. קְרָא {11x} **qᵉrâ᾽** (Aram.), *ker-aw'*; corresp. to 7121:—read {7x}, cry {3x}, called {1x}. See: TWOT—2977; BDB—1111c.

7124. קֹרֵא {2x} **qôrê**, *ko-ray'*; prop. act. part. of 7121; a *caller*, i.e. *partridge* (from its *cry*):—partridge {2x}. See: TWOT—2063a; BDB—896c. See also 6981.

7125. קִרְאָה {121x} **qîr᾽âh**, *keer-aw'*; from 7122; an *encountering*, accidental, friendly or hostile (also adv. *opposite*):—meet {76x}, against {40x}, come {2x}, help {1x}, seek {1x}, way {1x}. See: TWOT—2064; BDB—896d, 897a.

7126. קָרַב {280x} **qârab**, *kaw-rab'*; a prim. root; to *approach* (caus. *bring near*) for whatever purpose:—offer {95x}, (come, draw, . . .) near {58x}, bring {58x}, (come, draw, . . .) nigh {18x}, come {12x}, approach {10x}, at hand {4x}, presented {2x}, misc. {13x} = join, produce, make ready, stand, take.

(1) This word stresses to approach or draw near and is often used of man's entrance into the presence of the living God; a nearness of the closest and most intimate kind (Num 16:9; Ps 65:4). **(1a)** In general *qarab* signifies approach or coming near someone or something apart from any sense of intimacy. *Qarab* (7126), as a verb, means "to offer, come near, approach." **(1b)** In general *qarab* signifies "approach or coming near someone or something" apart from any sense of intimacy. **(1c)** In Gen 12:11 (the first biblical occurrence) the word is used of spatial proximity, of being spatially close to something: "And it came to pass, when he was come near to enter into Egypt, that he said unto Sarai his wife. . . ." **(1d)** Usually the word represents being so close to something (or someone) that the subject can see (Ex 32:19), speak to (Num 9:6), or even touch (Ex 36:2) the object or person in question. **(2)** This verb also is used of temporal nearness, in the sense that something is about to occur. **(2a)** *Qarab* can be used of the imminence of joyous occasions, such as religious feasts: "Beware that there be not a thought in thy wicked heart, saying, The seventh year, the year of release, is at hand" (Deut 15:9). **(2b)** The word is also used of the imminence of foreboding events: "Esau said in his heart, The days of mourning for my father are at hand [literally, "my father will soon die"]" (Gen 27:41).

(3) *Qarab* is used in a number of technical

senses. In all these instances personal involvement is suggested; the idea is not simply being close to something (someone) but being actively and personally involved with it (him). **(3a)** In military contexts the word signifies armed conflict. **(3a1)** In Deut 2:37 the Lord commended Israel because "unto the land of the children of Ammon thou camest not." **(3a2)** Yet in Deut. 2:19 He allowed them to "come nigh" that land: "And when thou comest nigh over against the children of Ammon, distress them not, nor meddle with them." **(3a3)** The later passage (Deut 2:37) uses the word technically, to close in battle. Therefore, Israel did not come close to the land of Ammon; they did not close in battle with them (cf. Josh 8:5). **(3b)** In some passages this martial coloring is not immediately obvious to the casual reader but is nonetheless present: "When the wicked . . . came upon me to eat up my flesh . . ." (Ps 27:2). Ps 27:3 ("though a host should encamp against me") substantiates that this use of the verb is "to close in battle" (cf. Ps 91:10; 119:150).

(4) Qarab is used technically of having sexual relations. In Gen 20:4 before Abimelech states his innocence with regard to Sarah we read he "had not come near her" (cf. Deut 22:14; Is 8:3). **(5)** In another technical use the word represents every step one performs in presenting his offering and worship to God. **(5a)** This idea first appears in Ex 3:5 where God tells Moses not to "draw near" before removing his sandals. **(5b)** Later Israel's meeting with God's representative was a drawing near to God (Ex 16:9). **(5c)** At Sinai they drew near to receive God's law (Deut 5:23, 27). **(6)** In the causative stem the verb often represents the sacrificial presentation of offerings (Lev 1:14) through the priests (Lev 1:5) to the Lord (Lev 1:13). **(7)** Israel also came near the Lord's representative in serious legal cases so that God the great King and Judge could render a decision (Josh 7:14). **(8)** In the eschaton all peoples are to gather before God; they are "to come near" Him to hear and receive His judgment (Is 41:1; 48:16). See: TWOT—2065; BDB—897b, 1111c.

7127. קְרֵב {9x} q°rêb (Aram.), ker-abe'; corresp. to 7126:—come near {4x}, offer {2x}, come {1x}, bring near {1x}, offer {1x}. See: TWOT—2978; BDB—1111c.

7128. קְרָב {9x} q°râb, ker-awb'; from 7126: hostile encounter:—battle {5x}, war {4x}.

(1) The word qerab, means "war, battle," or the actual engaging in battle (Ps 55:18). **(2)** It is used of hand to hand combat. Syn.: 7131, 7132, 7138. See: TWOT—2063b; BDB—898b, 1111d.

7129. קְרָב {1x} q°râb (Aram.), ker-awb'; corresp. to 7128:—war {1x}. See: TWOT—2978a; BDB—1111d.

7130. קֶרֶב {227x} qereb, keh'-reb; from 7126; prop. the nearest part, i.e. the center, whether lit., fig. or adv. (espec. with prep.):—among {76x}, midst {73x}, within {24x}, inwards {22x}, in {6x}, misc. {26x} = ✕ before, bowels, ✕ unto charge, + eat (up), ✕ heart, ✕ him, + out of, purtenance, ✕ therein, ✕ through.

I. Qereb (7130), as a preposition, means "among." The first usage of this preposition is in Genesis: "Abram dwelled in the land of Canaan, and Lot dwelled in [among] the cities of the plain, and pitched his tent toward Sodom" (13:12). **II. Qereb, as a noun,** means "inward part; midst." **(1)** One idiomatic usage of qereb denotes an inward part of the body that is the seat of laughter (Gen 18:12) and of thoughts (Jer 4:14). **(2)** The Bible limits another idiomatic usage, meaning "inner parts," to animals: "Eat not of it raw, nor sodden at all with water, but roast with fire—his head with his legs, and with the purtenance thereof" (Ex 12:9). **(3)** The noun approximates the prepositional use with the meaning of "midst" or "in." **(3a)** Something may be "in the midst of" a place: "Peradventure there be fifty righteous within [qereb] the city: wilt thou also destroy and not spare the place for the fifty righteous that are therein?" (Gen 18:24). **(3b)** It may be in the midst of people: "Then Samuel took the horn of oil, and anointed him in the midst [qereb] of his brethren: and the Spirit of the Lord came upon David from that day forward" (1 Sa 16:13).

(4) God is said to be in the midst of the land (Ex 8:22), the city of God (Ps 46:4), and Israel (Num 11:20). **(4a)** Even when He is close to His people, God is nevertheless holy: **(4b)** "Cry out and shout, thou inhabitant of Zion: for great is the Holy One of Israel in the midst [qereb] of thee" (Is 12:6; cf. Hos 11:9). **(5)** The idiomatic use of qereb in Psalm 103:—"Bless the Lord, O my soul: and all that is within me, bless his holy name"—has the noun in the plural. **(5a)** It seems best to take "all that is within me" as a reference to the psalmist's whole being, **(5b)** rather than to a distinct part of the body that is within him. See: TWOT—2066a; BDB—899a.

7131. קָרֵב {11x} qârêb, kaw-rabe'; from 7126; near:—come nigh {4x}, come near {3x}, draw near {2x}, approach {1x}, came {1x}.

Qareb, which occurs 11 times, means "near"; it represents intimate proximity (usually in a cultic context referring to cultic activity). One appearance is in Eze 45:4: "The holy portion of the land shall be for the priests the ministers of the sanctuary, which shall come near to min-

ister unto the Lord." Syn.: 7128, 7132, 7138. See: TWOT−2065a; BDB−898a.

קְרָב **qârôb**. See 7138.

7132. קְרָבָה {2x} **qᵉrâbâh**, *ker-aw-baw'*; from 7126; *approach:*—draw near {1x}, approach {1x}.

Qerabah occurs twice with the meaning of drawing near to worship God and offer sacrifice (Ps 73:28; Is 58:2). Syn.: 7128, 7131, 7138. See: TWOT−2065c; BDB−898b.

7133. קָרְבָּן {82x} **qorbân**, *kor-bawn'*; or

קֻרְבָּן **qurbân**, *koor-bawn'*; from 7126; something *brought near* the altar, i.e. a sacrificial *present:*—offering {68x}, oblation {12x}, offered {1x}, sacrifice {1x}.

Qorban means "offering; oblation; sacrifice." **(1)** While the root, "to come/bring near," is found literally hundreds of times in the Old Testament, the derived noun *qorban* occurs 82 times. All but two of the occurrences in the Old Testament are found in the books of Numbers and Leviticus. The two exceptions are in Ezekiel (20:28; 40:43), a book which has a great concern for ritual. The word occurs for the first time in Lev. 1:2. **(2)** *Qorban* may be translated as "that which one brings near to God or the altar." It is not surprising, then, that the word is used as a general term for all sacrifices, whether animal or vegetable. The very first reference to "sacrifice" in Leviticus is to the *qorban* as a burnt "offering": "If any man of you bring an offering unto the Lord, ye shall bring your offering of the cattle, even of the herd, and of the flock. If his offering be a burnt sacrifice . . ." (Lev 1:2–3; cf. Lev 1:10; 3:2, 6; 4:23). **(3)** The first reference to *qorban* as a "meat [cereal] offering" is in Lev. 2:1: "And when any will offer a meat offering unto the Lord, his offering shall be of fine flour."

(4) What is perhaps the best concentration of examples of the use of *qorban* is Numbers 7. In this one chapter, the word is used some 28 times, referring to all kinds of animal and meat [cereal] offerings, but with special attention to the various silver and gold vessels which were offered to the sanctuary. For example, Eliab's "offering was one silver charger, the weight whereof was a hundred and thirty shekels, one silver bowl of seventy shekels, . . . both of them full of fine flour mingled with oil for a meat offering; one golden spoon of ten shekels, full of incense; one young bullock, one ram, one lamb of the first year, for a burnt offering" (Num 7:25–27). **(5)** In the two uses found in Ezekiel, both are in the general sense of "offering." **(5a)** In Eze 20:28 the word refers to the pagan "provocation of their offering" which apostate Israel gave to other gods, while **(5b)** in

Eze 40:43, *qorban* refers to regular animal sacrifices. **(6)** *Qurban* means "wood offering." *Qurban* is closely related to *qorban*, and it is found in Neh 10:34; 13:31. Here it refers to the "wood offering" which was to be provided for the burning of the sacrifices in the second temple. Lots were to be cast among the people, priests, and Levites to determine who would bring in the "wood offering" or fuel at the scheduled times throughout the year. Syn.: 801, 2077, 2282. See: TWOT−2065e; BDB−898d.

7134. קַרְדֹּם {5x} **qardôm**, *kar-dome'*; perh. from 6923 in the sense of *striking* upon; an *axe:*—ax {5x}. See: TWOT−2067; BDB−899c.

7135. קָרָה {5x} **qârâh**, *kaw-raw'*; fem. of 7119; *coolness:*—cold {5x}. See: TWOT− 2067; BDB−899c, 903b.

7136. קָרָה {27x} **qârâh**, *kaw-raw'*; a prim. root; to *light upon* (chiefly by accident); caus. to *bring about;* spec. to *impose* timbers (for roof or floor):—happen {7x}, meet {5x}, beams {4x}, befall {3x}, brought {1x}, misc. {7x} = appoint, come (to pass unto), floor, [hap] was, send good speed. See: TWOT−2068, 2068e; BDB−899c, 900a.

7137. קָרֶה {1x} **qâreh**, *kaw-reh'*; from 7136; an (unfortunate) *occurrence*, i.e. some accidental (ceremonial) *disqualification:*—uncleanness that chanceth {1x}. See: TWOT−2068a; BDB−899d.

קֹרָה **qôrâh**. See 6982.

7138. קָרוֹב {78x} **qârôwb**, *kaw-robe'*; or

קָרֹב **qârôb**, *kaw-robe'*; from 7126; *near* (in place, kindred or time):—near {35x}, nigh {13x}, at hand {6x}, neighbour {5x}, next {5x}, kin {3x}, approach {2x}, short {2x}, kinsfolk {1x}, kinsmen {1x}, misc. {5x} = allied, approach, more ready, short (-ly).

This word stresses kinsman or near neighbor. *Qarob,* as an adjective, means "near." **(1)** *Qarob* can represent nearness in space: "Behold now, this city is near to flee unto, and it is a little one" (Gen 19:20—the first biblical occurrence) and **(2)** an epistemological nearness: "But the word is very nigh unto thee, in thy mouth, and in thy heart, that thou mayest do it" (Deut 30:14). **(3)** The adjective also appears in Eze 6:12: "He that is far off shall die of the pestilence; and he that is near shall fall by the sword." **(4)** It means neighbor in Ex 32:27. Syn.: 7128, 7131, 7132. See: TWOT−2065d; BDB−898b.

7139. קָרַח {5x} **qârach**, *kaw-rakh'*; a prim. root; to *depilate:*—make bald {4x}, make {1x}. TWOT−2069; BDB−901a.

7140. קֶרַח {7x} **qerach**, *keh'-rakh;* or

קֹרַח **qôrach**, *ko'-rakh;* from 7139; *ice* (as if bald, i.e. *smooth*); hence, *hail;* by resemblance, rock *crystal:*—frost {3x}, ice {3x}, crystal {1x}. See: TWOT—2070a; BDB—901c.

7141. קֹרַח {37x} **Qôrach**, *ko'rakh;* from 7139; *ice; Korach,* the name of two Edomites and three Isr.:—Korah {37x}. See: BDB—901b.

7142. קֵרֵחַ {3x} **qêrêach**, *kay-ray'-akh;* from 7139; *bald* (on the back of the head):—bald {3x}. See: TWOT—2069a; BDB—901b.

7143. קָרֵחַ {14x} **Qârêach**, *kaw-ray'-akh;* from 7139; *bald; Kareäch,* an Isr.:—Kareah {13x}, Careah {1x}. See: BDB—901b.

7144. קָרְחָה {11x} **qorchâh**, *kor-khaw';* or

קָרְחָא **qorchâ'** (Eze 27:31), *kor-khaw';* from 7139; *baldness:*—baldness {9x}, bald {1x}, utterly {1x}. See: TWOT—2069b; BDB—901b.

7145. קָרְחִי {8x} **Qorchîy**, *kor-khee';* patron. from 7141; a *Korchite* (collect.) or desc. of Korach:—Korhites {4x}, Korahite {3x}, Kore {1x}. See: BDB—687c, 901c.

7146. קָרַחַת {4x} **qârachath**, *kaw-rakh'-ath;* from 7139; a *bald* spot (on the back of the head); fig. a *threadbare* spot (on the back side of the cloth):—bald head {3x}, bare within {1x}. See: TWOT—2069c; BDB—901b.

7147. קְרִי {7x} **qᵉrîy**, *ker-ee';* from 7136; *hostile encounter:*—contrary {7x}. See: TWOT—2068b; BDB—899d, 901c.

7148. קָרִיא {3x} **qârîy'**, *kaw-ree';* from 7121; *called,* i.e. *select:*—famous {2x}, variant {1x}. See: TWOT—2063b; BDB—896c.

7149. קִרְיָא **qiryâ'** (Aram.), *keer-yaw';* or

קִרְיָה **qiryâh** (Aram.), *keer-yaw';* corresp. to 7151:—city {9x}. See: TWOT—2979; BDB—1111d.

7150. קְרִיאָה {1x} **qᵉrîy'âh**, *ker-ee-aw';* from 7121; a *proclamation:*—preaching {1x}. See: TWOT—2063c; BDB—896d.

7151. קִרְיָה {31x} **qiryâh**, *kir-yaw';* from 7136 in the sense of *flooring,* i.e. *building;* a *city:*—city {31x}. See: TWOT—2068g; BDB—900a, 901c, 1111d.

7152. קְרִיּוֹת {4x} **Qᵉrîyôwth**, *ker-ee-yōth';* plur. of 7151; *buildings; Kerioth,* the name of two places in Pal.:—Kerioth {4x}. See: BDB—901a, 901c.

7153. קִרְיַת עַרְבַּע {9x} **Qiryath 'Arbaʿ**, *keer-yath' ar-bah';* or (with the art. interposed)

קִרְיַת הָאַרְבַּע **Qiryath hâ-'Arbaʿ** (Neh. 11:25), *keer-yath' haw-ar-bah';* from 7151 and 704 or 702; *city of Arba,* or *city of the four* (giants); *Kirjath-Arba* or *Kirjath-ha-Arba,* a place in Pal.:—Kirjatharba {6x}, city of Arba {1x}, synonym {2x}. See: BDB—900b, 917b.

7154. קִרְיַת בַּעַל {2x} **Qiryath Baʿal**, *keer-yath' bah'-al;* from 7151 and 1168; *city of Baal; Kirjath-Baal,* a place in Pal.:—Kirjathbaal {2x}. See: BDB—900c.

7155. קִרְיַת חֻצוֹת {1x} **Qiryath Chûtsôwth**, *keer-yath' khoo-tsōth';* from 7151 and the fem. plur. of 2351; *city of streets; Kirjath-Chutsoth,* a place in Moab:—Kirjathhuzoth {1x}. See: BDB—900c.

7156. קִרְיָתַיִם {6x} **Qiryâthayim**, *keer-yaw-thah'-yim;* dual of 7151; *double city; Kirjathaïm,* the name of two places in Pal.:—Kirjathaim {3x}, Kiriathaim {3x}. See: BDB—900b, 1001a.

7157. קִרְיַת יְעָרִים **Qiryath Yᵉârîym**, *keer-yath' yeh-aw-reem';* or (Jer. 26:20) with the art. interposed; or (Josh. 18:28) simply the former part of the word; or

קִרְיַת עָרִים **Qiryath 'Ârîym**, *keer-yath' aw-reem';* from 7151 and the plur. of 3293 or 5892; *city of forests,* or *city of towns; Kirjath-Jeärim* or *Kirjath-Arim,* a place in Pal.:—Kirjathjearim {19x}, Kirjath {1x}. See: BDB—900b, 900c, 900d, 901c.

7158. קִרְיַת סַנָּה **Qiryath Çannâh**, *keer-yath' san-naw';* or

קִרְיַת סֵפֶר **Qiryath Çêpher**, *keer-yath' say-fer;* from 7151 and a simpler fem. from the same as 5577, or (for the latter name) 5612; *city of branches,* or *of a book; Kirjath-Sannah* or *Kirjath-Sepher,* a place in Pal.:—Kirjathsepher {4x}, Kirjathsannah {1x}. See: BDB—703a, 707c, 900d.

7159. קָרַם {2x} **qâram**, *kaw-ram';* a prim. root; to *cover:*—cover {2x}. See: TWOT—2071; BDB—901c.

7160. קָרַן {4x} **qâran**, *kaw-ran';* a prim. root; to *push* or gore; used only as denom. from 7161, to *shoot out horns;* fig. *rays:*—shine {3x}, has horns {1x}. See: TWOT—2072; BDB—902a.

7161. קֶרֶן {76x} **qeren**, *keh'-ren;* from 7160; a *horn* (as *projecting*); by impl. a *flask, cornet;* by resembl. an elephant's *tooth* (i.e. *ivory*), a *corner* (of the altar), a *peak* (of a

mountain), a *ray* (of light); fig. *power:*—horn {75x}, hill {1x}. See: TWOT—2072a; BDB—901d, 902b, 1111d.

7162. קֶרֶן {14x} **qeren** (Aram.), *keh'-ren;* corresp. to 7161; a *horn* (lit. or for sound):—horn {10x}, cornet {4x}. See: TWOT—2980; BDB—1111d.

7163. קֶרֶן הַפּוּךְ {1x} **Qeren Hap-pûwk**, *keh'-ren hap-pook';* from 7161 and 6320; *horn of cosmetic; Keren-hap-Puk,* one of Job's daughters:—Keren-happuch {1x}. See: BDB—806c, 902a.

7164. קָרַס {2x} **qâraç**, *kaw-ras';* a prim. root; prop. to *protrude;* used only as denom. from 7165 (for alliteration with 7167), to *hunch,* i.e. be hump-backed:—stoop {2x}. See: TWOT—2073; BDB—902b.

7165. קֶרֶס {10x} **qereç**, *keh'-res;* from 7164; a *knob* or belaying-pin (from its swelling form):—tache {10x}. See: TWOT—2073a; BDB—902b.

קֶרֶס **Qêrôç**. See 7026.

7166. קַרְסֹל {2x} **qarçôl**, *kar-sole';* from 7164; an *ankle* (as a *protuberance* or joint):—feet {2x}. See: TWOT—2073b; BDB—902b.

7167. קָרַע {62x} **qâra**ᶜ, *kaw-rah';* a prim. root; to *rend,* lit. or fig. (*revile, paint* the eyes, as if enlarging them):—rent {54x}, tear {4x}, rend away {2x}, cut {1x}, cut out {1x}, surely {1x}. "to rend, tear, tear away." **(1)** It is found for the first time in Gen 37:29: "He rent his clothes." **(2)** In the expression, "to tear one's clothes," *qara'* is used 39 times. Usually such "rending" of clothes is an expression of grief (Gen 37:34; 44:13; 2 Sa 13:19). **(3)** Sometimes the word is used in a symbolic act, such as Ahijah's "tearing" a new garment into twelve pieces and sending them to the twelve tribes as a symbol of coming division (1 Kin 11:30). **(4)** Samuel used *qara'* figuratively when he said to Saul: "The Lord hath rent the kingdom of Israel from thee this day" (1 Sa 15:28). **(5)** Wild animals "rend" or "tear" their prey (Hos 13:8). See: TWOT—2074; BDB—902b.

7168. קֶרַע {4x} **qera**ᶜ, *keh'-rah;* from 7167; a *rag:*—piece {3x}, rags {1x}. See: TWOT—2074; BDB—902d.

7169. קָרַץ {5x} **qârats**, *kaw-rats';* a prim. root; to *pinch,* i.e. (partially) to *bite* the lips, *blink* the eyes (as a gesture of malice), or (fully) to *squeeze* off (a piece of clay in order to mould a vessel from it):—winketh {3x}, moving {1x}, formed {1x}. See: TWOT—2075; BDB—902d.

7170. קְרָץ {2x} **q**ᵉ**rats** (Aram.), *ker-ats';* corresp. to 7171 in the sense of a *bit* (to "eat the *morsels* of" any one, i.e. *chew* him up [fig.] by *slander*):—accused {2x}. See: TWOT—2981; BDB—1111d.

7171. קֶרֶץ {1x} **qerets**, *keh'-rets;* from 7169; *extirpation* (as if by *constriction*):—destruction {1x}. See: TWOT—2075a; BDB—903a, 1111d.

7172. קַרְקַע {8x} **qarqa**ᶜ, *kar-kah';* from 7167; *floor* (as if a pavement of pieces or *tesseræ*), of a building or the sea:—floor {6x}, other {1x}, bottom {1x}. See: TWOT—2076; BDB—903a.

7173. קַרְקַע {1x} **Qarqa**ᶜ, *kar-kah';* the same as 7172; *ground-floor; Karka* (with the art. pref.), a place in Pal.:—Karkaa {1x}. See: BDB—903a.

7174. קַרְקֹר {1x} **Qarqôr**, *kar-kore';* from 6979; *foundation; Karkor,* a place E. of the Jordan:—Karkor {1x}. See: BDB—903a.

7175. קֶרֶשׁ {51x} **qeresh**, *keh'-resh;* from an unused root mean. to *split* off; a *slab* or plank; by impl. a *deck* of a ship:—board {50x}, benches {1x}. See: TWOT—2079a; BDB—903c.

7176. קֶרֶת {5x} **qereth**, *keh'-reth;* from 7136 in the sense of building; a *city:*—city {5x}. See: TWOT—2068h; BDB—900d, 903c.

7177. קַרְתָּה {1x} **Qartâh**, *kar-taw';* from 7176; *city; Kartah,* a place in Pal.:—Kartah {1x}. See: BDB—900d.

7178. קַרְתָּן {1x} **Qartân**, *kar-tawn';* from 7176; *city-plot; Kartan,* a place in Pal.:—Kartan {1x}. See: BDB—900b, 900d.

7179. קַשׁ {16x} **qash**, *kash;* from 7197; *straw* (as *dry*):—stubble {16x}. See: TWOT—2091a; BDB—903b.

7180. קִשֻּׁא {1x} **qishshû**ʾ, *kish-shoo';* from an unused root (mean. to *be hard*); a *cucumber* (from the difficulty of *digestion*):—cucumbers {1x}. See: TWOT—2083a; BDB—903d.

7181. קָשַׁב {46x} **qâshab**, *kaw-shab';* a prim. root; to *prick up* the ears, i.e. *hearken:*—hearken {27x}, attend {10x}, heed {3x}, hear {2x}, incline {1x}, marked {1x}, regarded {1x}, mark well {1x}. See: TWOT—2084; BDB—904a.

7182. קֶשֶׁב {4x} **qesheb**, *keh'-sheb;* from 7181; a *hearkening:*—record {1x}, hearing {1x}, diligently {1x}, heed {1x}. See: TWOT—2084a; BDB—904a.

7183. קַשָּׁב {5x} qashshâb, kash-shawb'; or

קַשֻּׁב qashshûb, kash-shoob'; from 7181; *hearkening:*—attentive {3x}, attent {2x}. See: TWOT—2084b, 2084c; BDB—903c, 904a, 904b.

7184. קֻשָּׂה {4x} qâsâh, kaw-saw'; or

קַשְׂוָה qasvâh, kas-vaw'; from an unused root mean. to *be round;* a *jug* (from its shape):—cover {3x}, cup {1x}. See: TWOT—2080, 2080a; BDB—903c.

7185. קָשָׁה {28x} qâshâh, kaw-shaw'; a prim. root; prop. to *be dense,* i.e. *tough* or *severe* (in various applications):—harden {12x}, hard {4x}, stiffnecked + 6203 {2x}, grievous {2x}, misc. {8x} = be cruel, be fiercer, be sore, (be, make) stiff (-en).

This word marks the restlessness, impatience, petulance, and irritability with which Pharaoh's course of action was characterized while he was resisting the urgent appeals of both Moses and his own people. Syn.: 7188, 8631. See: TWOT—2085; BDB—904b.

7186. קָשֶׁה {36x} qâsheh, kaw-sheh'; from 7185; *severe* (in various applications):—stiffnecked + 6203 {6x}, hard {5x}, roughly {5x}, cruel {3x}, grievous {3x}, sore {2x}, churlish {1x}, hardhearted {1x}, heavy {1x}, misc. {9x} = + impudent, obstinate, prevailed, sorrowful, stubborn, + in trouble. See: TWOT—2085a; BDB—904c.

7187. קְשׁוֹט {2x} qᵉshôwṭ (Aram.), kesh-ote'; or

קְשֹׁט qᵉshôṭ (Aram.), kesh-ote'; corresp. to 7189; *fidelity:*—truth {2x}. See: TWOT—2982; BDB—1112a.

7188. קָשַׁח {2x} qâshach, kaw-shakh'; a prim. root; to *be* (caus. *make*) *unfeeling:*—harden {2x}. See: TWOT—2087; BDB—905a.

7189. קֹשֶׁט {2x} qôshet, ko'-shet; or

קֹשְׁט qôsht, kōsht; from an unused root mean. to *balance; equity* (as evenly weighed), i.e. *reality:*—certainty {1x}, truth {1x}. See: TWOT—2088, 2089a; BDB—905a, 1112a.

קֹשׁוֹט qôshôt. See 7187.

7190. קְשִׁי {1x} qᵉshîy, kesh-ee'; from 7185; *obstinacy:*—stubbornness {1x}. See: TWOT—2085b; BDB—904d, 905a.

7191. קִשְׁיוֹן {2x} Qishyôwn, kish-yone'; from 7190; *hard ground; Kishjon,* a place in Pal.:—Kishion {1x}, Kishon {1x}. See: BDB—904d, 905a.

7192. קְשִׂיטָה {3x} qᵉsîyṭah, kes-ee-taw'; from an unused root (prob. mean. to *weigh* out); an *ingot* (as def. *estimated* and stamped for a coin):—piece of money {2x}, piece of silver {1x}. See: TWOT—2081a; BDB—903d.

7193. קַשְׂקֶשֶׂת {8x} qasqeseth, kas-keh'-seth; by redupl. from an unused root mean. to *shale* off as bark; a *scale* (of a fish); hence, a coat of *mail* (as composed of or covered with jointed *plates* of metal):—scale {7x}, mail {1x}. See: TWOT—2082a; BDB—903d.

7194. קָשַׁר {44x} qâshar, kaw-shar'; a prim. root: to *tie,* phys. (*gird, confine, compact*) or ment. (in *love, league*):—conspired {18x}, bind {14x}, made {5x}, stronger {2x}, misc. {5x} = conspiracy, conspirator, join together, knit, work [treason]. See: TWOT—2090; BDB—905a.

7195. קֶשֶׁר {16x} qesher, keh'-sher; from 7194; an (unlawful) *alliance:*—conspiracy {9x}, treason {5x}, confederacy {2x}. See: TWOT—2090a; BDB—905c.

7196. קִשֻּׁר {2x} qishshûr, kish-shoor'; from 7194; an (ornamental) *girdle* (for women):—headband {1x}, attire {1x}. See: TWOT—2090b; BDB—905c.

7197. קָשַׁשׁ {8x} qâshash, kaw-shash'; a prim. root; to *become sapless* through drought; used only as denom. from 7179; to *forage* for straw, stubble or wood; fig. to *assemble:*—gather {6x}, gather together {2x}. See: TWOT—2091, 2092; BDB—905d.

7198. קֶשֶׁת {77x} qesheth, keh'-sheth; from 7185 in the orig. sense (of 6983) of *bending;* a *bow,* for *shooting* (hence, fig. *strength*) or the *iris:*—bow {68x}, archers + 3384 {3x}, archers {2x}, archers + 1869 {1x}, misc. {3x}. See: TWOT—2093; BDB—905d.

7199. קַשָּׁת {1x} qashshâth, kash-shawth'; intens. (as denom.) from 7198; a *bowman:*—archer {1x}. See: TWOT—2094; BDB—906c.

ר

7200. רָאָה {1313x} râʾâh, raw-aw'; a prim. root; to *see,* lit. or fig. (in numerous applications, dir. and impl., tran., intr. and caus.):—see {879x}, look {104x}, behold {83x}, shew {68x}, appear {66x}, consider {22x}, seer {12x}, spy {6x}, respect {5x}, perceive {5x}, provide {4x}, regard {4x}, enjoy {4x}, lo {3x}, foreseeth {2x}, heed {2x}, misc. {74x} = advise self, approve, × certainly, discern, have experience, gaze, × indeed, × joyfully, mark, meet, × be

near, present, seem, × sight of others, espy, stare, × surely, × think, view, visions.

Ra'ah, as a verb, means "to see, observe, perceive, get acquainted with, gain understanding, examine, look after (see to), choose, discover." **(1)** Basically *ra'ah* connotes seeing with one's eyes: **(1a)** Isaac's "eyes were dim, so that he could not see" (Gen 27:1). **(1b)** This is its meaning in Gen 1:4, its first biblical appearance. **(1c)** The word can be used in the sense of seeing only what is obvious: "For the Lord seeth not as man seeth . . ." (1 Sa 16:7). **(1d)** This verb can also mean "to observe": "And there were upon the roof about three thousand men and women, that beheld while Samson made sport" (Judg 16:27). **(2)** The second primary meaning is "to perceive," or to be consciously aware of—so idols "neither see, nor hear" (Deut 4:28). **(3)** Third, *ra'ah* can represent perception in the sense of hearing something— God brought the animals before Adam "to see what he would call them" (Gen 2:19).

(4) In Is 44:16 the verb means "to enjoy": "I am warm, I have seen the fire." **(5)** It can also mean "to realize" or "to get acquainted with": "When I applied mine heart to know wisdom, and to see the business that is done upon the earth . . ." (Eccl 8:16). **(6)** The rebellious men of Jerusalem tell God they will not "see sword nor famine"; they will not experience it (Jer 5:12). **(7)** This verb has several further extended meanings. For example, *ra'ah* can refer to "perceiving or ascertaining" something apart from seeing it with one's eyes, as when Hagar saw that she had conceived (Gen 16:4). **(8)** It can represent mentally recognizing that something is true: "We saw certainly that the Lord was with thee" (Gen 26:28). **(9)** Seeing and hearing together can mean "to gain understanding": "Kings shall shut their mouths at him: for that which had not been told them shall they see; and that which they had not heard shall they consider" (Is 52:15). **(10)** In Mal 3:18 the verb means "to distinguish": "Then shall ye return, and discern between the righteous and the wicked."

(11) The word can mean to consider the fact that Israel is God's people (Ex 33:13). **(12)** In addition to these uses of *ra'ah* referring to intellectual seeing, there is seeing used in the sense of living. **(12a)** "To see the light" is to live life (Job 3:16; cf. 33:28). **(12b)** It can mean "experience" in the sense of what one is aware of as he lives: "Even as I have seen, they that plow iniquity . . . reap the same" (Job 4:8). **(12c)** In 2 Kin 25:19 the verb is used in the unique sense of "having trusted concourse with" when it speaks of the five advisors of the king. **(13)** Another idea of seeing is "to examine": "And the Lord came down to see the city

and the tower" (Gen 11:5). **(13a)** This examining can have to do with more than looking something over; it can refer to looking after or supervising something (Gen 39:23). **(13b)** Used in this sense *ra'ah* can imply looking upon with joy or pain. Hagar asked that she not be allowed to look on the death of Ishmael (Gen 21:16).

(14) This verb may be used of attending to or visiting—so Jonadab said to Amnon: "When thy father cometh to see thee, say unto him . . ." (2 Sa 13:5). **(15)** When Joseph advised Pharaoh "to look out a man discreet and wise," he was telling him to choose or select such a man (Gen 41:33). **(16)** "To examine" may also be "to observe" someone **(16a)** in order to imitate what he does (Judg 7:17), or **(16b)** "to discover" something (find it out; Judg 16:5). See: TWOT—2095; BDB—906b, 909b, 1112a.

7201. רָאָה {1x} **râ'âh,** raw-aw'; from 7200; a *bird* of prey (prob. the *vulture,* from its sharp *sight*):—glede {1x}. See: TWOT— 394a; BDB—906b. comp. 1676.

7202. רָאֶה {1x} **râ'eh,** raw-eh'; from 7200; *seeing,* i.e. experiencing:—see {1x}. See: TWOT—2095a; BDB—909a.

7203. רֹאֶה {1x} **rô'eh,** ro-eh'; act. part. of 7200; a *seer* (as often rendered); but also (abstr.) a *vision:*—vision {1x}.

Ro'eh, as a noun, means "vision": "But they also have erred through wine, and through strong drink are out of the way; the priest and the prophet have erred through strong drink, they are swallowed up of wine, they are out of the way through strong drink; they err in vision, they stumble in judgment" (Is 28:7). See: TWOT—2095b, 2095c; BDB—906d, 909a, 909b.

7204. רֹאֵה {1x} **Rô'êh,** ro-ay'; for 7203; *prophet; Roëh,* an Isr.:—Haroeh {1x}. See: BDB—909b.

7205. רְאוּבֵן {72x} **R°ûwbên,** reh-oo-bane'; from the imper. of 7200 and 1121; *see ye a son; Reben,* a son of Jacob:— Reuben {72x}. See: BDB—910a.

7206. רְאוּבֵנִי {18x} **R°ûwbênîy,** reh-oob-ay-nee'; patron. from 7205; a *Reübenite* or desc. of Reüben:—Reubenite {17x}, Reuben {1x}. See: BDB—910a.

7207. רַאֲוָה {1x} **ra'ăvâh,** rah-av-aw'; from 7200; *sight,* i.e. *satisfaction:*—beholding + 7212 {1x}.

Re'ut [from *ra'avah*] occurs once, and it means "look" (Eccl 5:11). Syn.: 4758, 4759, 7209, 7210, 8389. See: TWOT—2095; BDB— 906d, 908a, 909b.

7208. רְאוּמָה {1x} **R°ûwmâh,** reh-oo-maw'; fem. pass. part. of 7213; *raised;*

Remah, a Syrian woman:—Reumah {1x}. See: BDB—910b.

7209. **רְאִי** {1x} **r°îy**, *reh-ee'*; from 7200; a *mirror* (as *seen*):—looking glass {1x}.

Re'iy appears once to mean "looking-glass" (Job 37:18). Syn.: 4758, 4759, 7207, 7210, 8389. See: TWOT—2095e; BDB—909b, 910b.

7210. **רְאִי** {6x} **rô'îy**, *ro-ee'*; from 7200; *sight*, whether abstr. (*vision*) or concr. (a *spectacle*):—see {4x}, look {1x}, gazingstock {1x}.

Ro'iy, which occurs 6 times, means "looking, appearance": "Now he was ruddy, and withal of a beautiful countenance, and goodly to look to [*ro'iy*]" (1 Sa 16:12). Syn.: 4758, 4759, 7207, 7209, 8389. See: TWOT—2095f; BDB—909b, 910b.

7211. **רְאָיָה** {4x} **R°âyâh**, *reh-aw-yaw'*; from 7200 and 3050; *Jah has seen; Reäjah*, the name of three Isr.:—Reaiah {3x}, Reaia {1x}. See: BDB—909b, 909d, 910b.

7212. **רְאִית** {1x} **r°îyth**, *reh-eeth'*; from 7200; *sight:*—beholding {1x}. See: TWOT—2095d; BDB—909b, 910b.

7213. **רָאַם** {1x} **râ'am**, *raw-am'*; a prim. root; to *rise:*—lifted up {1x}. See: TWOT—2096; BDB—910b, 910c, 926c.

7214. **רְאֵם** {9x} **r°êm**, *reh-ame';* or

רְאֵים **r°êym**, *reh-ame';* or

רֵים **rêym**, *rame;* or

רֵם **rêm**, *rame;* from 7213; a wild *bull* (from its *conspicuousness*):—unicorn {9x}. See: TWOT—2096a; BDB—910b, 937c, 941a.

7215. **רָאמָה** {2x} **râ'mâh**, *raw-maw';* from 7213; something *high* in value, i.e. perh. *coral:*—coral {2x}. See: TWOT—2096b; BDB—910c.

7216. **רָאמוֹת** {4x} **Râ'môwth**, *raw-môth';* or

רָאמֹת **Râmôth**, *raw-môth';* plur. of 7215; *heights; Ramoth*, the name of two places in Pal.:—Ramoth {4x}. See: BDB—910c.

7217. **רֵאשׁ** {14x} **rê'sh** (Aram.), *raysh;* corresp. to 7218; the *head;* fig. the *sum:*—head {12x}, sum {1x}, chief {1x}. See: TWOT—2983; BDB—1112a.

7218. **רֹאשׁ** {598x} **rô'sh**, *roshe;* from an unused root appar. mean. to *shake;* the *head* (as most easily *shaken*), whether lit. or fig. (in many applications, of place, time, rank, etc.):—head {349x}, chief {91x}, top {73x}, beginning {14x}, company {12x}, captain {10x}, sum {9x}, first {6x}, principal {5x}, chapters

{4x}, rulers {2x}, misc. {23x} = band, end, × every [man], excellent, forefront, height, (on) high (-est part, [priest]), × lead, × poor.

Ro'sh, means "head; top; first; sum." **(1)** This word often represents a "head," **(1a)** a bodily part (Gen 40:20). **(1b)** *Rosh* is also used of a decapitated "head" (2 Sa 4:8), **(1c)** an animal "head" (Gen 3:15), and **(1d)** a statue "head" (Dan 2:32). **(1e)** In Dan 7:9, where God is pictured in human form, His "head" is crowned with hair like pure wool (i.e., white).

(2) To "lift up one's own head" may be **(2a)** a sign of declaring one's innocence: "If I be wicked, woe unto me; and if I be righteous, yet will I not lift up my head. I am full of confusion; therefore see thou mine affliction" (Job 10:15). **(2b)** This same figure of speech may indicate an intention to begin a war, the most violent form of self-assertion: "For, lo, thine enemies make a tumult: and they that hate thee have lifted up the head" (Ps 83:2). **(2c)** With a negation, this phrase may symbolize submission to another power: "Thus was Midian subdued before the children of Israel, so that they lifted up their heads no more" (Judg 8:28). **(2d)** Used transitively (i.e., to lift up someone else's "head"), this word may connote restoring someone to a previous position: "Yet within three days shall Pharaoh lift up thine head, and restore thee unto thy place" (Gen 40:13). **(2e)** It can also denote the release of someone from prison: "Evil-Merodach king of Babylon in the year that he began to reign did lift up the head of Jehoiachin king of Judah out of prison" (2 Kin 25:27). **(3)** With the verb *rum* (7311 - "to raise"), **(3a)** *ro'sh* can signify the victory and power of an enthroned king—God will "lift up [His] head," or exert His rule (Ps 110:7). **(3b)** When God lifts up (*rum*) one's "head," He fills one with hope and confidence: "But thou, O Lord, art a shield for me; my glory, and the lifter up of mine head" (Ps 3:3).

(4) There are many secondary nuances of *ro'sh*. **(4a)** First, the word can represent the "hair on one's head": "But it shall be on the seventh day, that he shall shave all his hair off his head and his beard and his eyebrows, even all his hair he shall shave off:" (Lev 14:9). **(4b)** The word can connote unity, representing every individual in a given group: "Have they not sped? have they not divided the prey; to every man a damsel or two . . ." (Judg 5:30). **(4c)** This word may be used numerically, meaning the total number of persons or individuals in a group: "Take ye the sum (*ro'sh*) of all the congregation of the children of Israel, after their families, by the house of their fathers, with the number of their names, every male by their polls" (Num 1:2). **(4d)** *Ro'sh* can also emphasize the individual: "And there was a

great famine in Samaria: and, behold, they besieged it, until an ass's head [i.e., an individual donkey] was sold for fourscore pieces of silver" (2 Kin 6:25). **(4e)** It is upon the "head" (upon the person himself) that curses and blessings fall: "The blessings of thy father have prevailed above the blessings of my progenitors . . . : they shall be on the head of Joseph" (Gen 49:26). **(4f)** *Ro'sh* sometimes means "leader," whether appointed, elected, or self-appointed. The word can be used of the tribal fathers, who are the leaders of a group of people: "And Moses chose able men out of all Israel, and made them heads over the people" (Ex 18:25). **(4g)** Military leaders are also called "heads": "These be the names of the mighty men whom David had: The Tachmonite that sat in the seat, chief among the captains" (2 Sa 23:8). **(4h)** In Num 1:16, the princes are called "heads" (cf. Judg 10:18). **(4i)** This word is used of those who represent or lead the people in worship (2 Kin 25:18—the chief priest).

(5) When used of things, *ro'sh* means "point" or "beginning." **(5a)** With a local emphasis, the word refers to the "top" or summit of a mountain or hill: "Tomorrow I will stand on the top of the hill with the rod of God in mine hand" (Ex 17:9). **(5b)** Elsewhere the word represents the topmost end of a natural or constructed object: "Go to, let us build us a city and a tower, whose top may reach unto heaven" (Gen 11:4). **(5c)** In Gen 47:31, the word denotes the "head" of a bed, or where one lays his "head." **(5d)** In 1 Kin 8:8, *ro'sh* refers to the ends of poles. **(5e)** The word may be used of the place where a journey begins: "Thou hast built thy high place at every head of the way" (Eze 16:25; cf. Dan 7:1: "the sum of the matters. . . ."). **(5f)** This sense of the place of beginning appears in Gen 2:10 (the first occurrence): "And a river went out of Eden to water the garden; and from thence it was parted, and became [the source of four rivers]." **(5g)** This nuance identifies a thing as being placed spatially in front of a group; it stands in front or at the "head" (Deut 20:9; cf. 1 Kin 21:9). **(5h)** The "head" of the stars is a star located at the zenith of the sky (Job 22:12). **(5i)** The "head" cornerstone occupies a place of primary importance. It is the stone by which all the other stones are measured; it is the chief cornerstone (Ps 118:22).

(6) This word may have a temporal significance meaning "beginning" or "first." **(6a)** The second sense is seen in Ex 12:2: "This month shall be unto you the beginning of months." **(6b)** In 1 Chr 16:7 the word describes the "first" in a whole series of acts: "Then on that day David delivered first this psalm to thank the Lord into the hand of Asaph and his brethren." **(7)** *Ro'sh* may also have an estimative connota-

tion: "Take thou also unto thee [the finest of] spices . . ." (Ex 30:23). Syn.: 7101, 7336. See: TWOT—2097; BDB—910c, 1112a.

7219. רֹאשׁ {12x} **rôʾsh**, *roshe;* or

רוֹשׁ **rôwsh** (Deut. 32:32), *roshe;* appar. the same as 7218; a poisonous *plant*, prob. the *poppy* (from its conspicuous *head*); gen. *poison* (even of serpents):—gall {9x}, venom {1x}, poison {1x}, hemlock {1x}. See: TWOT—2098; BDB—911b, 912c, 930d.

7220. רֹאשׁ {1x} **Rôʾsh**, *roshe;* prob. the same as 7218; *Rosh,* the name of an Isr. and of a for. nation:—*Rosh* {1x}. See: BDB—911b, 912c.

רֵאשׁ **rêʾsh**. See 7389.

7221. רֵאשָׁה {1x} **rîʾshâh**, *ree-shaw';* from the same as 7218; a *beginning:*—beginnings {1x}. See: TWOT—2097a; BDB—911c.

7222. רֹאשָׁה {1x} **rôʾshâh**, *ro-shaw';* fem. of 7218; the *head:*—headstone + 68 {1x}. See: TWOT—2097b; BDB—911c.

7223. רִאשׁוֹן {185x} **rîʾshôwn**, *ree-shone';* or

רִאשֹׁן **rîʾshôn**, *ree-shone';* from 7221; *first,* in place, time or rank (as adj. or noun):—first {129x}, former {26x}, former things {6x}, beginning {4x}, chief {3x}, before {3x}, old time {2x}, foremost {3x}, aforetime {1x}, misc. {8x} = ancestor, eldest, forefather, past.

Ri'shon (7223), as an adjective, means "first; foremost; preceding; former." **(1)** It denotes the "first" in a temporal sequence: "And it came to pass in the six hundredth and first year, in the first month, the first day of the month . . ." (Gen 8:13). **(2)** In Ezra 9:2, *ri'shon* is used both of precedence in time and of leadership: "The holy seed have mingled themselves with the people of those lands: yea, the hand of the princes and rulers hath been chief (*ri'shon*) in this trespass." **(3)** Another meaning of this adjective is "preceding" or "former": ". . . unto the place of the altar, which he had made there at the first" (Gen 13:4). **(4)** Gen 33:2 uses this word locally: "And he put the handmaids and their children foremost (*ri'shon*), and Leah and her children after, and Rachel and Joseph hindermost." **(5)** The "former ones" are "ancestors": "But I will for their sakes remember the covenant of their ancestors, whom I brought forth out of the land of Egypt in the sight of the heathen" (Lev 26:45). **(6)** But in most cases, this adjective has a temporal emphasis. See: TWOT—2097c; BDB—910b, 911c, 938c.

7224. רִאשֹׁנִי {1x} **rîʾshônîy**, *ree-sho-nee';* from 7223; *first:*—first {1x}. See: TWOT—2097d; BDB—912a.

7225. רֵאשִׁית {51x} rê·shîyth, *ray-sheeth'*; from the same as 7218; the *first*, in place, time, order or rank (spec. a *first-fruit*):—beginning {18x}, firstfruits {11x}, first {9x}, chief {8x}, misc. {5x}.

Re'shiyth (7225), means "beginning; first; choicest." **(1)** The abstract word *re'shiyth* corresponds to the temporal and estimative sense of *ro'sh* (7218). **(1a)** *Re'shiyth* connotes the "beginning" of a fixed period of time: "The eyes of the Lord thy God are always upon it, from the beginning of the year even unto the end of the year" (Deut 11:12). **(1b)** The "beginning" of one's period of life is intended in Job 42:12: "So the Lord blessed the latter end of Job more than his beginning." **(2)** This word can represent a point of departure, as it does in Gen 1:1 (the first occurrence): "In the beginning God created the heaven and the earth." **(3)** Estimatively, this word can mean the "first" or "choicest": "The first of the first fruits of thy land thou shalt bring into the house of the Lord thy God" (Ex 23:19). **(4)** This nuance of *re'shiyth* may appear in the comparative sense, meaning "choicest" or "best." Dan 11:41 exhibits the nuance of "some": "But these shall escape out of his hand, even Edom, and Moab, and the chief of the children of Ammon" (Dan 11:41). **(5)** Used substantively, the word can mean "first fruits": **(5a)** "As for the oblation of the first fruits, ye shall offer them unto the Lord: but they shall not be burnt on the altar for a sweet savor" (Lev 2:12). **(5b)** "The first fruits of them which they shall offer unto the Lord, them have I given thee" (Num 18:12). **(6)** Sometimes this word represents the "first part" of an offering: "Ye shall offer up a cake of the first of your dough for a heave offering" (Num 15:20). See: TWOT—2097e; BDB—912a, 957a.

7226. רַאֲשׁוֹת {1x} ra·'ăshôth, *rah-ash-ōth'*; from 7218; a *pillow* (being for the *head*):—bolster {1x}. See: TWOT—2097f; BDB—910c, 912a.

7227. רַב {458x} rab, *rab*; by contr. from 7231; *abundant* (in quantity, size, age, number, rank, quality):—many {190x}, great {118x}, much {36x}, captain {24x}, more {12x}, long {10x}, enough {9x}, multitude {7x}, mighty {5x}, greater {4x}, greatly {3x}, misc. {40x} = (in) abound (-undance, -ant, -antly), elder, exceedingly, full, increase, manifold, things, a time), ([ship-]) master, multiply, officer, often [-times], plenteous, populous, prince, process [of time], suffice (-ient).

I. *Rab,* as a noun, means "chief." **(1)** The first appearance: "And it came to pass, that at midnight [literally, "the middle of the officers of his house]. . . ." **(2)** *Rab,* designating chief, is **(2a)** an indication of military rank similar to our word general (Jer 39:3). **(2b)** One should especially note the titles in Jeremiah: "And all the princes [officials] of the king of Babylon came in, and sat in the middle gate, even Nergal-shar-ezer, Samgar-nebo, Sarsechim, Rab-saris, Nergal-sharezer, Rab-mag, with all the residue of the princes of the king of Babylon" (39:3). Verses 9, 10, 11, and 13 of Jeremiah 39 mention Nebuzaradan as the "captain" of the bodyguard.

II. *Rab,* as an adjective, means "many; great; large; prestigious; powerful." **(1)** First, this word represents plurality in number or amount, whether applied to people or to things. **(1a)** *Rab* is applied to people in Gen 26:14: "For he [Isaac] had possession of flocks, and possession of herds, and great store of servants." **(1b)** In Gen 13:6, the word is applied to things: "And the land was not able to bear them, that they might dwell together: for their substance was great, so that they could not dwell together." This word is sometimes used of "large groups of people" (Ex 5:5).

(2) This basic idea of "numerical multiplicity" is also applied to amounts of liquids or masses of non-liquids: **(2a)** "And Moses lifted up his hand, and with his rod he smote the rock twice: and the water came out abundantly" (Num 20:11); a "great" amount of water came forth. **(2b)** Rebekah told Abraham's servant that her father had "straw and provender enough, and room to lodge in" (Gen 24:25). **(3)** The phrase "many waters" is a fixed phrase meaning the "sea": **(3a)** "Thou whom the merchants of Zidon, that pass over the sea, have replenished. And by great waters the seed of Sihor, the harvest of the river, is her revenue" (Is 23:2–3). **(3b)** "And the channels of the sea appeared, the foundations of the world were discovered, at the rebuking of the Lord, at the blast of the breath of his nostrils. He sent from above, he took me; he drew me out of many waters" (2 Sa 22:16–17). **(3c)** This imagery is used in several Old Testament poetical passages; it would be wrong to conclude that this view of the world was true or actual. **(3d)** On the other hand, Gen 7:11 uses a related phrase as a figure of the "sources of all water": "The same day were all the fountains of the great deep broken up." **(4)** Used in conjunction with "days" or "years," *rab* means "long," and the resulting phrase means "a long time": "And Abraham sojourned in the Philistines' land many days" (Gen 21:34). **(5)** The word can be used metaphorically, describing an abstract concept: "And God saw that the wickedness of man was great in the earth, and that every imagination of the thoughts of his heart was only evil continually" (Gen 6:5—the first biblical occur-

rence). **(5a)** This use of *rab* does not describe the relative value of the thing modified, but its numerical recurrence. **(5b)** The statement implies, however, that man's constant sinning was more reprehensible than the more occasional sinning previously committed. **(6)** When *rab* is applied to land areas, it means "large" (1 Sa 26:13). This usage is related to the usual meaning of the Semitic cognates, which represent "size" rather than numerical multiplicity (also cf. *gadal* - 1431): "And the Lord delivered them into the hand of Israel, who smote them, and chased them unto great Zidon" (Josh 11:8).

(7) When God is called the "great King" (Ps 48:2), the adjective refers to His superior power and sovereignty over all kings (vv. 4ff.). **(7a)** This meaning emerges in Job 32:9: "The great may not be wise, nor may elders understand justice" (cf. Job 35:9). **(7b)** Uses such as these in Job emphasize "greatness in prestige," whereas passages such as 2 Chr 14:11 emphasize "strength and might": "And Asa cried unto the LORD his God, and said, LORD, it is nothing with thee to help, whether with many, or with them that have no power: help us, O LORD our God; for we rest on thee, and in thy name we go against this multitude. O LORD, thou art our God; let not man prevail against thee." See: TWOT—2099a, 2099b; BDB—912c, 912d, 913c, 914d, 918d, 1112a.

7228. רַב ‏{2x} **rab**, *rab;* by contr. from 7232; an *archer* [or perh. the same as 7227]:—archer {2x}. See: TWOT—2100a; BDB—912c, 914d.

7229. רַב ‏{15x} **rab** (Aram.), *rab;* corresp. to 7227:—great {9x}, master {2x}, stout {1x}, chief {1x}, captain {1x}, lord {1x}. See: TWOT—2984a; BDB—1112a, 1112c.

רִב **rîb.** See 7378.

7230. רֹב ‏{155x} **rôb**, *robe;* from 7231; *abundance* (in any respect):—multitude {70x}, abundance {35x}, great {9x}, greatness {8x}, much {8x}, abundantly {4x}, plenty {3x}, many {3x}, long {2x}, excellent {1x}, misc. {12x} = all, × common [sort], greatly, huge, be increased, more in number, most, plentifully, × very [age].

Rob, as a noun, means "multitude; abundance." **(1)** The word basically means "multitude" or "abundance"; it has numerical implications apparent in its first biblical appearance: "I will multiply thy seed exceedingly, that it shall not be numbered for multitude" (Gen 16:10). **(2)** When applied to time or distance, *rob* indicates a "large amount" or "long": "And these bottles of wine, which we filled, were new; and, behold, they be rent; and these our garments and our shoes are become

old by reason of the very long journey" (Josh 9:13). **(3)** In several passages, the word is applied to abstract ideas or qualities. In such cases, *rob* means "great" or "greatness": ". . . This that is glorious in his apparel, traveling in the greatness of his strength" (Is 63:1).

(4) The preposition *le* when prefixed to the noun *rob* sometimes forms an adverbial phrase **(4a)** meaning "abundantly": "For it was little which thou hadst before I came, and it is now increased unto a multitude" (Gen 30:30). **(4b)** The same phrase bears a different sense in 1 Kin 10:10, where it seems to be almost a substantive: "There came no more such abundance of spices as these which the queen of Sheba gave to king Solomon." **(4c)** The phrase literally appears to mean "great" with respect to "multitude." **(4d)** This phrase is applied to Uzziah's building activities: ". . . And on the wall of Ophel he built much" (2 Chr 27:3), where it means "much." **(4e)** This phrase is extended by the addition of *'ad* (5704). Thus we have *'ad lerob,* meaning "exceeding much": "Since the people began to bring the offerings into the house of the Lord, we have had enough to eat, and have left plenty [literally, "the remainder is exceeding much"]" (2 Chr 31:10). See: TWOT—2099c; BDB—912c, 913d, 923d.

7231. רָבַב ‏{17x} **râbab**, *raw-bab';* a prim. root; prop. to *cast* together [comp. 7241], i.e. *increase*, espec. in number; also (as denom. from 7233) to *multiply by the myriad:*—are many {6x}, are multiplied {3x}, increased {3x}, are more {2x}, manifold {1x}, ten thousands {1x}, multiply {1x}.

Rabab, as a verb, means "to be numerous, great, large, powerful." **(1)** The first occurrence means "to be (or become) numerous": "And it came to pass, when men began to multiply on the face of the earth, and daughters were born unto them," (Gen 6:1). **(2)** *Rabab* can also mean "to be great" in size, prestige, or power: "And the LORD said, Because the cry of Sodom and Gomorrah is great, and because their sin is very grievous . . ." (Gen 18:20; cf. Job 33:12; Ps 49:16). **(3)** With a subject indicating time, this verb **(3a)** implies "lengthening": "And in process of time the daughter of Shuah Judah's wife died;" (Gen 38:12), and **(3b)** with special subjects the word may imply "extension of space": "And if the way be too long for thee, so that thou art not able to carry it; or if the place be too far from thee, which the LORD thy God shall choose to set his name there, when the LORD thy God hath blessed thee:" (Deut 14:24). Syn.: 3515. See: TWOT—2099; BDB—912c, 912d, 914b, 914c, 1112a.

7232. רָבַב ‏{2x} **râbab**, *raw-bab';* a prim. root [rather ident. with 7231 through

the idea of *projection*]; to *shoot* an arrow:— shot {1x}, shot out {1x}. See: TWOT—2100; BDB—914d.

7233. רְבָבָה {16x} **rᵉbâbâh**, *reb-aw-baw'*; from 7231; *abundance* (in number), i.e. (spec.) a *myriad* (whether def. or indef.):—ten thousand {13x}, million {1x}, many {1x}, multiply {1x}. See: TWOT—2099d; BDB—914b.

7234. רְבַד {1x} **râbad**, *raw-bad'*; a prim. root; to *spread:*—deck {1x}. See: TWOT—2102; BDB—914d.

7235. רָבָה **râbâh**, *raw-baw'*; a prim. root; to *increase* (in whatever respect):— multiply {74x}, increase {40x}, much {29x}, many {28x}, more {12x}, great {8x}, long {3x}, store {2x}, exceedingly {2x}, greater {2x}, abundance {2x}, misc. {24x} = [bring in] abundance (✕ -antly), + archer [*by mistake for* 7232], be in authority, bring up, ✕ continue, enlarge, excel, exceeding (-ly), be full of, grow up, heap, nourish, plenty (-eous), ✕ process [of time], sore, store, thoroughly, very.

Rabah, as a verb, means "to multiply, become numerous, become great." **(1)** Basically this word connotes numerical increase. **(1a)** It can refer to the process of increasing numerically: God told the sea and air creatures to "be fruitful, and multiply" (Gen 1:22—the first occurrence). **(1b)** In Gen 38:12 the word refers to the end result in the sense that a great many of something existed: "And in process of time the daughter of Shuah Judah's wife died [literally, "and the days became multiplied"]." **(1c)** When used with "days," the word may also signify "long life": "I shall multiply my days as the sand" (Job 29:18: cf. Prov 4:10). **(2)** *Rabah* sometimes refers to increasing in wealth, although in such cases the material is clearly specified (cf. Deut 8:13: "... and thy silver and thy gold is multiplied"). **(3)** This verb can be used of being quantitatively large. In Gen 7:17 the waters are said to have "increased, and bare up the ark, and it was lifted up above the earth." **(3a)** So here the verb means "to increase in quantity." **(3b)** A similar use occurs in Gen 15:1, where God tells Abram: "I am ... thy exceeding great reward." **(3c)** The first instance speaks of the process of increasing and the latter of the end product (something that is larger).

(4) In a special nuance this verb signifies the process of growing up: "Their young ones are in good liking, they grow up [in the open field]" (Job 39:4). **(5)** *Rabah* can also be used of the end product: "I have caused thee to multiply as the bud of the field, and thou hast increased and waxen great, and thou art come to excellent ornaments: thy breasts are fashioned,

and thine hair is grown" (Eze 16:7). **(6)** A somewhat different nuance occurs in Eze 19:2, where the verb speaks of a parent's care for an offspring: "She nourished her whelps." **(7)** *Rabah* is sometimes used with another verb to signify its increase in occurrence or frequency. **(7a)** In some passages it signifies that a process is continuing: "The people bring much more than enough for the service of the work" (Ex 36:5), literally, "the people continue to bring." **(7b)** It can also signify a great number of times with the sense of "repeatedly." **(8)** The sinner is urged to return to God, **(8a)** "for he will abundantly pardon" (Is 55:7). **(8b)** This sense appears clearly in Amos 4:4: "Come to Beth-el and transgress; at Gilgal multiply transgression...." Syn.: 697, 4766, 4768, 8635, 8636. See: TWOT—2103, 2104; BDB—915a, 916c, 1112b.

7236. רְבָה {6x} **rᵉbâh** (Aram.), *reb-aw'*; corresp. to 7235:—grow {5x}, great {1x}. Syn.: 7101, 7218, 7336. See: TWOT—2985; BDB—1112b.

7237. רַבָּה {15x} **Rabbâh**, *rab-baw'*; fem. of 7227; *great; Rabbah,* the name of two places in Pal., East and West:—*Rabbah*{13x}, Rabbath {2x}. See: BDB—851a, 913d, 916c.

7238. רְבוּ **rᵉbûw** (Aram.), *reb-oo'*; from a root corresp. to 7235; *increase* (of dignity):—majesty {4x}, greatness {1x}. See: TWOT—2985a; BDB—1112c.

7239. רִבּוֹ {11x} **ribbôw**, *rib-bo'*; from 7231; or

רִבּוֹא **ribbôwʾ**, *rib-bo'*; from 7231; a *myriad*, i.e. indef. *large number:*— .... thousand {4x}, forty, etc ... (thousand) {4x}, ten thousand {2x}, variant {1x}. See: TWOT—2099e; BDB—914b, 916c, 1112a.

7240. רִבּוֹ {2x} **ribbôw** (Aram.), *rib-bo'*; corresp. to 7239:—ten thousand {2x}. See: TWOT—2984b; BDB—1112b.

7241. רָבִיב {6x} **râbîyb**, *raw-beeb'*; from 7231; a *rain* (as an *accumulation* of drops):—shower {6x}. See: TWOT—2099f; BDB—914c.

7242. רָבִיד {2x} **râbîyd**, *raw-beed'*; from 7234; a *collar* (as *spread* around the neck):—chain {2x}. See: TWOT—2101a; BDB—914d.

7243. רְבִיעִי {56x} **rᵉbîyʿîy**, *reb-ee-ee'*; or

רְבִעִי **rᵉbîʿîy**, *reb-ee-ee'*; from 7251; *fourth;* also (fractionally) a *fourth:*—fourth {51x}, fourth part {4x}, foursquare {1x}. See: TWOT—2107c; BDB—917d, 1112c.

7244. רְבִיעִי {6x} **rᵉbîyʿay** (Aram.), *reb-ee-ah'-ee;* corresp. to 7243:—fourth {6x}. See: TWOT—2986b; BDB—1112c.

7245. רַבִּית {1x} **Rabbîyth**, *rab-beeth';* from 7231; *multitude; Rabbith,* a place in Pal.:—Rabbith {1x}. See: BDB—914c, 916c.

7246. רָבַךְ {3x} **râbak**, *raw-bak';* a prim. root; to *soak* (bread in oil):—fried {2x}, baken {1x}. See: TWOT—2105; BDB—916c.

7247. רִבְלָה {11x} **Riblâh**, *rib-law';* from an unused root mean. to *be fruitful; fertile; Riblah,* a place in Syria:—Riblah {11x}. See: BDB—916c.

7248. רַב־מָג {2x} **Rab-Mâg**, *rab-mawg';* from 7227 and a for. word for a Magian; *chief Magian; Rab-Mag,* a Bab. official:—Rabmag {2x}. See: TWOT—1143; BDB—550b, 913c, 916c.

7249. רַב־סָרִיס {3x} **Rab-Çârîyç**, *rab-saw-reece';* from 7227 and a for. word for a eunuch; *chief chamberlain; Rab-Saris,* a Bab. official:—Rabsaris {3x}. See: BDB—913c, 916c.

7250. רָבַע {3x} **râbaʿ**, *raw-bah';* a prim. root; to *squat* or *lie* out flat, i.e. (spec.) in copulation:—lie down {2x}, gender {1x}. See: TWOT—2108; BDB—918a.

7251. רָבַע {12x} **râbaʿ**, *raw-bah';* a prim. root [rather ident. with 7250 through the idea of *sprawling* "at all fours" (or possibly the reverse is the order of der.); comp. 702]; prop. to *be four* (sided); used only as denom. of 7253; to *be quadrate:*—foursquare {8x}, square {4x}. See: TWOT—2107; BDB—917c.

7252. רֶבַע {1x} **rebaʿ**, *reh'-bah;* from 7250; *prostration* (for sleep):—lying down {1x}. See: TWOT—2108; BDB—918a.

7253. רֶבַע {7x} **rebaʿ**, *reh'-bah;* from 7251; a *fourth* (part or side):—sides {3x}, fourth part {2x}, squares {2x}. See: TWOT—2107a; BDB—917d.

7254. רֶבַע {2x} **Rebaʿ**, *reh'-bah;* the same as 7253; *Reba,* a Midianite:—Reba {2x}. See: BDB—918b.

7255. רֹבַע {2x} **rôbaʿ**, *ro'-bah;* from 7251; a *quarter:*—fourth part {2x}. See: TWOT—2107b; BDB—917d.

7256. רִבֵּעַ {4x} **ribbêaʿ**, *rib-bay'-ah;* from 7251; a desc. of the *fourth* generation, i.e. *great great grandchild:*—fourth {4x}. See: TWOT—2107d; BDB—918a.

רְבִיעִי **rᵉbîyʿîy**. See 7243.

7257. רָבַץ {30x} **râbats**, *raw-bats';* a prim. root; to *crouch* (on all four legs folded, like a recumbent animal); by impl. to *recline, repose, brood, lurk, imbed:*—lay down {15x}, lay {9x}, couch beneath {1x}, couched {1x}, misc. {4x} = crouch (down), fall down, make a fold, lay, (cause to, make to) lie (down), make to rest, sit. See: TWOT—2109; BDB—918b.

7258. רֶבֶץ {4x} **rêbets**, *raÿ'-bets;* from 7257; a *couch* or place of repose:—resting place {2x}, where each lay {1x}, to lie down in {1x}. See: TWOT—2109a; BDB—918c.

7259. רִבְקָה {30x} **Ribqâh**, *rib-kaw';* from an unused root prob. mean. to *clog* by tying up the fetlock; *fettering* (by beauty); *Ribkah,* the wife of Isaac:—Rebekah {30x}. See: BDB—918d.

7260. רַבְרַב {8x} **rabrab** (Aram.), *rab-rab';* from 7229; *huge* (in size); *domineering* (in character):—great {6x}, great things {2x}. See: TWOT—2984a; BDB—1112b, 1112c.

7261. רַבְרְבָן {8x} **rabrᵉbân** (Aram.), *rab-reb-awn';* from 7260; a *magnate:*—lord {6x}, prince {2x}. See: TWOT—2984c; BDB—1112b, 1112c.

7262. רַבְשָׁקֵה {16x} **Rabshâqêh**, *rab-shaw-kay';* from 7227 and 8248; *chief butler; Rabshakeh,* a Bab. official:—Rabshakeh {15x}, Rabshakeh + 5631 + 7227 {1x}. See: BDB—913d, 918d.

7263. רֶגֶב {2x} **regeb**, *reh'-gheb;* from an unused root mean. to *pile* together; a *lump* of clay:—clod {2x}. See: TWOT—2111a; BDB—918d.

7264. רָגַז {41x} **râgaz**, *raw-gaz';* a prim. root; to *quiver* (with any violent emotion, espec. anger or fear):—tremble {12x}, move {7x}, rage {5x}, shake {3x}, disquiet {3x}, troubled {3x}, quake {2x}, afraid {1x}, misc. {5x} = stand in awe, fall out, fret, provoke, be wroth. See: TWOT—2112; BDB—919a, 1112c.

7265. רְגַז {1x} **rᵉgaz** (Aram.), *reg-az';* corresp. to 7264:—provoke unto wrath {1x}. See: TWOT—2987; BDB—1112c.

7266. רְגַז {1x} **rᵉgaz** (Aram.), *reg-az';* from 7265; *violent anger:*—rage {1x}. See: TWOT—2987a; BDB—1112c.

7267. רֹגֶז {7x} **rôgez**, *ro'-ghez;* from 7264; *commotion, restlessness* (of a horse), *crash* (of thunder), *disquiet, anger:*—trouble {2x}, troubling {1x}, noise {1x}, rage {1x}, fear {1x}, wrath {1x}. See: TWOT—2112a; BDB—919c.

7268. רַגָּז {1x} **raggâz**, *rag-gawz';* intens. from 7264; *timid:*—trembling {1x}. See: TWOT—2112c; BDB—919c.

7269. רָגְזָה {1x} **rogzâh**, *rog-zaw';* fem. of 7267; *trepidation:*—trembling {1x}. See: TWOT—2112b; BDB—919c.

7270. רָגַל {25x} **râgal**, *raw-gal';* a prim. root; to *walk* along; but only in spec. applications, to *reconnoiter,* to *be a tale-bearer* (i.e. *slander*); also (as denom. from 7272) to *lead about:*—spy {12x}, spy out {8x}, view {2x}, backbiteth {1x}, espy out {1x}, slandered {1x}. See: TWOT—2113; BDB—920a, 1076a.

7271. רְגַל {7x} **rᵉgal** (Aram.), *reg-al';* corresp. to 7272:—feet {7x}. See: TWOT—2988; BDB—1112c.

7272. רֶגֶל {247x} **regel**, *reh'-gel;* from 7270; a *foot* (as used in *walking*); by impl. a *step;* by euphem. the *pudenda:*—feet {216x}, footstool + 1916 {6x}, after {4x}, times {4x}, follow {4x}, piss + 4325 {2x}, toes {2x}, journey {1x}, legs {1x}, misc. {7x} = × be able to endure, × according as, × coming, × follow, × haunt, + possession.

Regel, means "foot; leg." **(1)** Its first occurrence is in Gen 8:9: "But the dove found no rest for the sole of her foot, and she returned unto him into the ark." **(2)** *Regel* may refer to the "foot" of a human (Gen 18:4), an animal (Eze 29:11), a bird (Gen 8:9), or even a table (a rare usage; Ex. 25:26). **(3)** The word's usage is also extended to signify the "leg": "And he had greaves of brass upon his legs, and a target of brass between his shoulders" (1 Sa 17:6). **(4)** *Regel* is used euphemistically for urine; the "water of the legs" (2 Kin 18:27). **(5)** The foot's low place gave rise to an idiom: "From the sole of the foot to the crown of the head" (cf. Deut 28:35), signifying the "total extent of the body." **(6)** "Foot" may be a metaphor of "arrogance": "Let not the foot of pride come against me, and let not the hand of the wicked remove me" (Ps 36:11). **(7)** It is used to represent Israel: "Neither will I make the feet of Israel move any more out of the land which I gave their fathers; only if they will observe to do according to all that I have commanded them, and according to all the law that my servant Moses commanded them" (2 Kin 21:8).

(8) In anthropomorphic expressions, God has "feet." **(8a)** Thus God revealed Himself with a pavement of sapphire as clear as the sky under His "feet" (Ex 24:10). **(8b)** The authors of Scripture portray God as having darkness (Ps 18:9) and clouds of dust beneath His "feet" (Nah 1:3), and sending a plague out from His "feet" (Hab 3:5). **(8c)** His "feet" are said to rest on the earth (Is 66:1); the temple is also the resting place of His "feet": "And I will make the place of my feet glorious" (Is 60:13). **(9)** Similarly, **(9a)** the seraphim had "feet," which they covered with a pair of wings as they

stood in the presence of God (Is 6:2); **(9b)** the cherubim had "feet" that Ezekiel described (Eze 1:7). See: TWOT—2113a; BDB—919c, 1112c.

7273. רַגְלִי {12x} **raglîy**, *rag-lee';* from 7272; a *footman* (soldier):—footman {7x}, footman + 376 {4x}, foot {1x}. See: TWOT—2113b; BDB—920b.

7274. רֹגְלִים {2x} **Rôgᵉlîym**, *ro-gel-eem';* plur. of act. part. of 7270; *fullers* (as *tramping* the cloth in washing); *Rogelim,* a place E. of the Jordan:—Rogelim {2x}. See: BDB—920c.

7275. רָגַם {16x} **râgam**, *raw-gam';* a prim. root [comp. 7263, 7321, 7551]; to *cast* together (stones), i.e. to *lapidate:*—stone {15x}, certainly {1x}. See: TWOT—2114; BDB—920c.

7276. רֶגֶם {1x} **Regem**, *reh'-gem;* from 7275; *stone-heap; Regem,* an Isr.:—Regem {1x}. See: BDB—920d.

7277. רִגְמָה {1x} **rigmâh**, *rig-maw';* fem. of the same as 7276; a *pile* (of stones), i.e. (fig.) a *throng:*—council {1x}. See: TWOT—2114a; BDB—920c.

7278. רֶגֶם מֶלֶךְ {1x} **Regem Melek**, *reh'-gem meh'-lek;* from 7276 and 4428; *king's heap; Regem-Melek,* an Isr.:—Regemmelech {1x}. See: BDB—920d.

7279. רָגַן {3x} **râgan**, *raw-gan';* a prim. root; to *grumble,* i.e. *rebel:*—murmur {3x}. See: TWOT—2115; BDB—920d.

7280. רָגַע {13x} **râgaʿ**, *raw-gah';* a prim. root; prop. to *toss* violently and suddenly (the sea with waves, the skin with boils); fig. (in a favorable manner) to *settle,* i.e. *quiet;* spec. to *wink* (from the motion of the eyelids):—break {1x}, divide {2x}, find ease {1x}, be a moment {1x}, (cause, give, make to) rest {5x}, make suddenly {2x}. See: TWOT—2116, 2117, 2118; BDB—920d, 921b, 921c.

7281. רֶגַע {22x} **regaʿ**, *reh'-gah;* from 7280. a *wink* (of the eyes), i.e. a very *short space* of time:—instant {2x}, moment {18x}, space {1x}, suddenly {1x}. See: TWOT—2116a; BDB—921a.

7282. רָגֵעַ {1x} **râgêaʿ**, *raw-gay'-ah;* from 7280; *restful,* i.e. *peaceable:*—that are quiet {1x}. See: TWOT—2117a; BDB—921b.

7283. רָגַשׁ {1x} **râgash**, *raw-gash';* a prim. root; to *be tumultuous:*—rage {1x}. See: TWOT—2119; BDB—921c, 1112c.

7284. רְגַשׁ {3x} **rᵉgash** (Aram.), *reg-ash';* corresp. to 7283; to *gather* tumultu-

ously:—assembled {2x}, assembled together {1x}. See: TWOT—2989; BDB—1112c.

7285. רֶגֶשׁ {2x} **regesh**, *reh'-ghesh;* or (fem.)

רִגְשָׁה **rigshâh**, *rig-shaw';* from 7283; a tumultuous *crowd:*—company {1x}, insurrection {1x}. See: TWOT—2119a, 2119b; BDB—920c, 921c.

7286. רָדַד {4x} **râdad**, *raw-dad';* a prim. root; to *tread* in pieces, i.e. (fig.) to *conquer,* or (spec.) to *overlay:*—spend {1x}, spread {1x}, subdue {2x}. See: TWOT—2120; BDB—921c.

7287. רָדָה {27x} **râdâh**, *raw-daw';* a prim. root; to *tread down,* i.e. *subjugate;* spec. to *crumble* off:—rule {13x}, dominion {1x}9, take {1x}2, prevaileth {1x}1, reign {1x}1, ruler {1x}. See: TWOT—2121, 2122; BDB—921d, 922a.

7288. רַדַּי {1x} **Radday**, *rad-dah'-ee;* intens. from 7287; *domineering; Raddai,* an Isr.:—Raddai {1x}. See: BDB—921d, 922b.

7289. רָדִיד {2x} **râdîyd**, *raw-deed';* from 7286 in the sense of *spreading;* a *veil* (as expanded):—vails {2x}, veil {1x}. See: TWOT—2120a; BDB—921d.

7290. רָדַם {7x} **râdam**, *raw-dam';* a prim. root; to *stun,* i.e. *stupefy* (with sleep or death):— . . . deep sleep {3x}, was fast asleep {2x}, sleep {1x}, sleeper {1x}. See: TWOT—2123; BDB—922b.

7291. רָדַף **râdaph**, *raw-daf';* a prim. root; to *run after* (usually with hostile intent; fig. [of time] *gone by*):—pursue {74x}, persecute {20x}, follow {18x}, chase {13x}, persecutors {7x}, pursuer {6x}, follow after {1x}, flight {1x}, misc. {3x}.

Radaph, means "to pursue, follow after, pass away, persecute." **(1)** The basic meaning of this verb is "to pursue after" an enemy with the intent of overtaking and defeating him. **(1a)** In most of its occurrences *radaph* is a military term. **(1b)** It first occurs in Gen 14:14, where it is reported that Abram mustered his 318 men and "pursued them [men who took his nephew, Lot] unto Dan." **(1c)** A nuance of this verb is "to pursue" a defeated enemy with the intent of killing him: "And he divided himself against them, he and his servants, by night, and smote them, and pursued them unto Hobah, which is on the left hand of Damascus" (Gen 14:15). **(2)** The one pursued is not always a hostile force—so Laban "took his brethren [army] with him, and pursued after him [Jacob] seven days' journey; and they overtook him in the mount Gilead" (Gen 31:23).

(3) At times *radaph* signifies pursuing without having a specific location or direction in mind, as in hunting for someone. This meaning is in 1 Sa 26:20—David asked Saul why he was exerting so much effort on such an unimportant task (namely, pursuing him), "as when one doth hunt a partridge in the mountains." **(4)** The word occurs in Josh 2:5, where Rahab tells the soldiers of Jericho: "Whither the men [Israelite spies] went I wot not: pursue after them quickly; for ye shall overtake them." **(4a)** This verse embodies the meaning first mentioned, but by **(4b)** Josh 2:22 the emphasis has shifted to hunting, not intentional pursuit after an enemy whose location is known but a searching for an enemy in order to kill him: "And they went, and came unto the mountain, and abode there three days, until the pursuers were returned: and the pursuers sought them throughout all the way, but found them not." **(5)** In another nuance *radaph* can signify "to put to flight" or "to confront and cause to flee." **(5a)** Moses reminded the Israelites that "the Amorites . . . came out against you, and chased you, as bees do, and destroyed you in Seir, even unto Hormah" (Deut 1:44). **(5b)** Bees do not pursue their victims, but they certainly do put them to flight, or cause them to flee. **(5c)** In Josh 23:10 Israel is reminded: "One man of you shall chase a thousand: for the Lord your God he it is that fighteth for you, as he hath promised you" (cf. Lev 26:8). **(6)** Used in another sense, *radaph* signifies the successful accomplishment of a pursuit; the pursuer overtakes the pursued but does not utterly destroy him (in the case of an army) and, therefore, continues the pursuit until the enemy is utterly destroyed. **(6a)** So Israel is warned of the penalty of disobedience to God: "The Lord shall smite thee with a consumption, and with a fever . . . ; and they shall pursue thee until thou perish" (Deut 28:22; cf. v. 45). **(6b)** This is the emphasis when God admonishes Israel: "That which is altogether just shalt thou follow, that thou mayest live, and inherit the land" (Deut 16:20). **(7)** Israel is "to pursue" justice and only justice, as a goal always achieved but never perfected. **(7a)** They are to always have justice in their midst, and always "to pursue" it. This same sense appears in other figurative uses of the word: "Surely goodness and mercy shall follow me all the days of my life" (Ps 23:6; cf. Is 1:23; 5:11; Hos 6:3). **(8)** In a related meaning *radaph* can signify "follow after." **(8a)** This is not with any intention to do harm to the one pursued but merely "to overtake" him. **(8b)** So Gehazi "pursued" (followed after) Naaman, overtook him, and asked him for a talent of silver and two changes of clothes (2 Kin 5:21–22). **(9)** The word also means "to follow after" in the sense of "practicing," or following a leader: "They

also that render evil for good are mine adversaries; because I follow the thing that good is" (Ps 38:20; cf. 119:150; Prov 21:21). **(10)** Another meaning of *radaph,* "to persecute," represents the constant infliction of pain or trouble upon one's enemies. This meaning is seen in Deut 30:7: "And the Lord thy God will put all these curses upon thine enemies, and on them that hate thee, which persecuted thee" (cf. Job 19:22, 28). **(11)** A special use of *radaph* appears in Eccl 3:15: "God requireth [holds men accountable for] that which is past." Men should serve God (literally, "fear him") because God controls all things. Men should be on His side, since He is totally sovereign. **(12)** The intensive stem sometimes means to pursue relentlessly and passionately as a harlot "pursues" her lovers (Prov 11:19). See: TWOT—2124; BDB—922c, 923b.

7292. רָהַב {4x} **râhab,** *raw-hab';* a prim. root; to *urge* severely, i.e. (fig.) *importune, embolden, capture, act insolently:*—overcome {1x}, behave self proudly {1x}, make sure {1x}, strengthen {1x}. See: TWOT—2125; BDB—923b.

7293. רַהַב {3x} **rahab,** *rah'-hab;* from 7292, *bluster (-er):*—proud {2x}, strength {1x}. See: TWOT—2125c; BDB—923c.

7294. רַהַב {3x} **Rahab,** *rah'-hab;* the same as 7293; *Rahab* (i.e. *boaster*), an epithet of Egypt:—*Rahab* {3x}. See: BDB—923c.

7295. רָהָב {1x} **râhâb,** *raw-hawb';* from 7292; *insolent:*—proud {1x}. See: TWOT—2125a; BDB—923b.

7296. רֹהַב {1x} **rôhab,** *ro'-hab;* from 7292; *pride:*—strength {1x}. See: TWOT—2125b; BDB—923b.

7297. רָהָה {1x} **râhâh,** *raw-haw';* a prim. root; to *fear:*—be afraid {1x}. See: TWOT—2126; BDB—436c, 923c.

7298. רַהַט {4x} **rahat,** *rah'-hat;* from an unused root appar. mean. to *hollow out;* a *channel* or watering-box; by resemblance a *ringlet* of hair (as forming parallel lines):—gallery {1x}, gutter {2x}, trough {1x}. See: TWOT—2127a, 2128a; BDB—923d.

7299. רֵו {2x} **rêv** (Aram.), *rave;* from a root corresp. to 7200; *aspect:*—form {2x}. See: TWOT—2990; BDB—1112a, 1112b.

רוּב **rûwb.** See 7378.

7300. רוּד {4x} **rûwd,** *rood;* a prim. root; to *tramp* about, i.e. *ramble* (free or disconsolate):—have the dominion {1x}, be lord {1x}, mourn {1x}, rule {1x}. See: TWOT—2129; BDB—923d.

7301. רָוָה {14x} **râvâh,** *raw-vaw';* a prim. root; to *slake* the thirst (occasionally of other appetites):—water {4x}, make drunk {2x}, fill {2x}, satiate {2x}, bathed {1x}, satisfied {1x}, abundantly satisfy {1x}, soaked {1x}. See: TWOT—2130; BDB—924a.

7302. רָוֶה {3x} **râveh,** *raw-veh';* from 7301; *sated* (with drink):—drunkenness {1x}, watered {2x}. See: TWOT—2130b; BDB—924b.

7303. רוֹהֲגָה {1x} **Rôwhăgâh,** *ro-hag-aw';* from an unused root prob. mean. to *cry* out; *outcry; Rohagah,* an Isr.:—Rohgah {1x}. See: BDB—923c, 924b.

7304. רָוַח {3x} **râvach,** *raw-vakh';* a prim. root [rather ident. with 7306]; prop. to *breathe* freely, i.e. *revive;* by impl. to *have ample room:*—be refreshed {2x}, large {1x}. See: TWOT—2132; BDB—926b. This word connotes being refreshed (1 Sa 16:23; Job 32:20).

7305. רֶוַח {2x} **revach,** *reh'-vakh;* from 7304; *room,* lit. (an *interval*) or fig. (*deliverance*):—enlargement {1x}, space {1x}. See: TWOT—2132a; BDB—926c.

7306. רוּחַ {11x} **rûwach,** *roo'-akh;* a prim. root; prop. to *blow,* i.e. *breathe;* only (lit.) to *smell* or (by impl.) *perceive* (fig. to *anticipate, enjoy*):—accept {1x}, smell {8x}, ✕ touch {1x}, make of quick understanding {1x}.

(1) This word means to smell; hence, to be keen or quick of understanding: "And shall make him of quick understanding (*ruwach*) in the fear of the LORD: and he shall not judge after the sight of his eyes, neither reprove after the hearing of his ears:" (Is 11:3). **(2)** *Ruwach* means to perceive, enjoy, smell: "And the Lord smelled a sweet savor." (Gen 8:21). See: TWOT—2131; BDB—926b.

7307. רוּחַ {378x} **rûwach,** *roo'-akh;* from 7306; *wind;* by resemblance *breath,* i.e. a sensible (or even violent) *exhalation;* fig. *life, anger, unsubstantiality;* by extens. a *region* of the sky; by resemblance *spirit,* but only of a rational being (incl. its expression and functions):—Spirit or spirit {232x}, wind {92x}, breath {27x}, side {6x}, mind {5x}, blast {4x}, vain {2x}, air {1x}, anger {1x}, cool {1x}, courage {1x}, misc. {6x} = ✕ cool, ✕ quarter, spiritual, tempest, whirlwind, windy.

Introduction: It is clear that the wind is regarded in Scripture as a fitting emblem of the mighty penetrating power of the invisible God. Moreover, the breath is supposed to symbolize not only the deep feelings that are generated within man, such as sorrow and anger; but also kindred feelings in the Divine nature. It is re-

vealed that God and God alone has the faculty of communicating His Spirit or life to His creatures, who are thus enabled to feel, think, speak, and act in accordance with the Divine will. *Ruwach* (7307), means "breath; air; strength; wind; breeze; spirit; courage; temper; Spirit." **(1)** First, this word means "breath," air for breathing, air that is being breathed. **(1a)** This meaning is especially evident in Jer 14:6: "And the wild asses did stand in the high places, they snuffed up the wind like dragons." **(1b)** When one's "breath" returns, he is revived: "When he [Samson] had drunk [the water], his spirit [literally, "breath"] came again, and he revived" (Judg 15:19). **(1c)** Astonishment may take away one's "breath": "And when the queen of Sheba had seen all Solomon's wisdom, and the home that he had built, And the meat of his table, . . . there was no more spirit in her [she was overwhelmed and breathless]" (1 Kin 10:4–5). **(1d)** *Ruwach* may also represent speaking, or the breath of one's mouth: "By the word of the Lord were the heavens made; and all the host of them by the breath of his mouth" (Ps 33:6; cf. Ex 15:8; Job 4:9; 19:17). **(2)** Second, this word can be used with emphasis on the invisible, intangible, fleeting quality of "air": "O remember that my life is wind: mine eyes shall no more see good" (Job 7:7). **(2a)** There may be a suggestion of purposelessness, uselessness, or even vanity (emptiness) when *ruwach* is used with this significance: "And the prophets shall become wind, and the word is not in them" (Jer 5:13). **(2b)** "Windy words" are really "empty words" (Job 16:3), just as "windy knowledge" is "empty knowledge" (Job 15:2; cf. Eccl 1:14, 17 – "meaningless striving"). **(2c)** In Prov 11:29 *ruwach* means "nothing": "He that troubleth his own house shall inherit the wind." This nuance is especially prominent in Eccl 5:15–16: "And he came forth of his mother's womb, naked shall he return to go as he came, and shall take nothing of his labor, which he may carry away in his hand. And this also is a sore evil, that in all points as he came, so shall he go: and what profit hath he that hath labored for the wind?" **(3)** Third, *ruwach* can mean "wind." **(3a)** In Gen 3:8 it seems to mean the gentle, refreshing evening breeze so well known in the Near East: "And they heard the voice of the Lord God walking in the garden in the cool [literally, "breeze"] of the day." **(3b)** It can mean a strong, constant wind: ". . . And the Lord brought an east wind upon the land all that day, and all that night" (Ex 10:13). **(3c)** It can also signify an extremely strong wind: "And the Lord turned a mighty strong west wind . . ." (Ex 10:19). **(3d)** In Jer 4:11 the word appears to represent a gale or tornado (cf. Hos 8:7). **(3e)** God is the Creator (Amos 4:13) and sover-

eign Controller of the winds (Gen 8:1; Num 11:31; Jer 10:13). **(4)** Fourth, the wind represents direction. **(4a)** In Jer 49:36 the four winds represent the four ends of the earth, which in turn represent every quarter: "And upon Elam will I bring the four winds [peoples from every quarter of the earth] from the four quarters of heaven, and will scatter them toward all those winds; and there shall be no nation whither the outcasts of Elam shall not come." **(5)** Fifth, *ruwach* frequently represents the element of life in a man, his natural "spirit": "And all flesh died that moved upon the earth, . . . All in whose nostrils was the breath of life" (Gen 7:21–22). **(5a)** In these verses the animals have a "spirit" (cf Ps. 104:29). **(5b)** On the other hand, in Prov 16:2 the word appears to mean more than just the element of life; it seems to mean "soul": "All the ways of a man are clean in his own eyes; but the Lord weigheth the spirits." **(5c)** Thus, Isaiah can put *nepesh* (5315), "soul," and *ruwach* in synonymous parallelism: "With my soul have I desired thee in the night; yea, with my spirit within me will I seek thee early" (26:9). **(5d)** It is the "spirit" of a man that returns to God (Eccl 12:7). **(6)** Sixth, *ruwach* is often used of a man's mind-set, disposition, or "temper": "Blessed is the man unto whom the Lord imputeth not iniquity, and in whose spirit there is no guile" (Ps 32:2). **(6a)** In Eze 13:3 the word is used of one's mind or thinking: "Woe unto the foolish prophets, that follow their own spirits, and have seen nothing" (cf. Prov 29:11). **(6b)** *Ruwach* can represent particular dispositions, as it does in Josh 2:11: "And as soon as we had heard these things, our hearts did melt, neither did there remain any more courage in any man, because of you" (cf. Josh 5:1; Job 15:13). **(6c)** Another disposition represented by this word is "temper": "If the spirit [temper] of the ruler rise up against thee, leave not thy place" (Eccl 10:4). **(6d)** David prayed that God would "restore unto me the joy of thy salvation; and uphold me with thy free Spirit" (Ps 51:12). In this verse "joy of salvation" and "free Spirit" are parallel and, therefore, synonymous terms. Therefore, "Spirit" refers to the One who restores that "joy." **(7)** Seventh, the Bible often speaks of God's "Spirit," the third person of the Trinity. **(7a)** This is the use of the word in its first biblical occurrence: "And the earth was without form, and void; and darkness was upon the face of the deep. And the Spirit of God moved upon the face of the waters" (Gen 1:2). **(7b)** Is 63:10–11 and Ps 51:12 specifically speak of the "holy or free Spirit." **(8)** Eighth, the non-material beings (angels) in heaven are sometimes called "spirits": "And there came forth a spirit, and stood before the Lord, and said, I will persuade

him" (1 Kin 22:21; cf. 1 Sa 16:14). **(9)** Ninth, the "spirit" may also be used of that which enables a man to do a particular job or that which represents the essence of a quality of man: **(9a)** "And Joshua the son of Nun was full of the spirit of wisdom; for Moses had laid his hands upon him" (Deut 34:9). **(9b)** Elisha asked Elijah for a double portion of his "spirit" (2 Kin 2:9) and received it. Syn.: 5397. See: TWOT—2131a; BDB—924c, 1112d.

7308. רוּחַ {11x} **rûwach** (Aram.), *roo'-akh;* corresp. to 7307:—mind {1x}, spirit {8x}, wind {2x}. See: TWOT—2991a; BDB—1112d.

7309. רְוָחָה {2x} **rᵉvâchâh,** *rev-aw-khaw';* fem. of 7305; *relief:*—breathing {1x}, respite {1x}. See: TWOT—2132b; BDB—926c.

7310. רְוָיָה {2x} **rᵉvâyâh,** *rev-aw-yaw';* from 7301; *satisfaction:*—runneth over {1x}, wealthy {1x}. See: TWOT—2130c; BDB—924b, 926c.

7311. רוּם {194x} **rûwm,** *room;* a prim. root; to *be high;* act. to *rise* or *raise* (in various applications, lit. or fig.):—(lift, hold, etc . . .) up {63x}, exalt {47x}, high {25x}, offer {13x}, give {5x}, heave {3x}, extol {3x}, lofty {3x}, take {3x}, tall {3x}, higher {2x}, misc. {24x} = haughty, levy, (✕ a-) loud, + presumptuously, (be) promote (-ion), proud, taller, breed worms.
Ruwm means "to be high, exalted." **(1)** Basically, *ruwm* represents either the "state of being on a higher plane" or "movement in an upward direction." **(1a)** The former meaning appears in the first biblical occurrence of the word: "And the flood was forty days upon the earth; and the waters increased, and bare up the ark, and it was lifted [rose] up above the earth" (Gen 7:17). **(1b)** Used of men, this verb may refer to their "physical stature"; for example, the spies sent into Canaan reported that "the people is greater and taller than we; the cities are great and walled up to heaven" (Deut 1:28). **(1c)** The other emphasis, representing what is done to the subject or what it does to itself, appears in Ps 12:8: "The wicked walk on every side, when the vilest men are exalted." **(1d)** The psalmist confesses that the Lord will "set me up upon a rock" so as to be out of all danger (Ps 27:5). **(1e)** A stormy wind (Ps 107:25) "lifts up" the waves of the sea. **(2)** *Ruwm* is used of the building of an edifice. Ezra confessed that God had renewed the people of Israel, allowing them "to set up the house of our God, and to repair the desolations thereof, and to give us a wall in Judah and Jerusalem" (Ezra 9:9; cf. Gen 31:45). **(3)** In Eze 31:4, this verb is used of "making

a plant grow larger": "The waters made him [the cedar in Lebanon] great, the deep set him up on high." **(4)** Since in Deut. 1:28 *gadal* (1419 - "larger") and *ruwm* ("taller") are used in close connection, Eze 31:4 could be translated: "The waters made it grow bigger, the deep made it grow taller." **(5)** Closely related to this nuance is the use of *ruwm* to represent the process of child-rearing. God says through Isaiah: "I have nourished [1419 - *gadal*] and brought up children, and they have rebelled against me" (Is 1:2). **(6)** *Ruwm* sometimes means "to take up away from," as in Is 57:14: "Cast ye up, cast ye up, prepare the way, take up the stumbling block out of the way of my people." **(7)** When used in reference to offerings, the word **(7a)** signifies the "removal of a certain portion" (Lev 2:9). **(7b)** The presentation of the entire offering is also referred to as an "offering up" (Num 15:19).
(8) In extended applications, *ruwm* has both negative and positive uses. **(8a)** Positively, this word can signify "to bring to a position of honor." **(8a1)** So God says: "Behold, my servant shall deal prudently, he shall be exalted and extolled, and be very high" (Is 52:13). **(8a2)** This same meaning occurs in 1 Sa 2:7, where Hannah confessed: "The Lord maketh poor, and maketh rich: he bringeth low, and lifteth up." **(8b)** Used in a negative sense, *ruwm* means "to be haughty": "And the afflicted people thou wilt save: but thine eyes are upon the haughty, that thou mayest bring them down" (2 Sa 22:28). **(9)** *Ruwm* is often used with other words in special senses. **(9a)** For example, to lift one's voice is "to cry aloud." Potiphar's wife reported that when Joseph attacked her, she "raised" her voice screaming. These two words (*ruwm* and "voice") are used together to mean "with a loud voice" (Deut 27:14). **(10)** The raising of the hand **(10a)** serves as a symbol of power and strength and signifies being "mighty" or "triumphant": "Were it not that I feared the wrath of the enemy, lest their adversaries should behave themselves strangely, and lest they should say, Our hand is high [literally, "is raised"]" (Deut 32:27). **(10b)** To raise one's hand against someone is to rebel against him. Thus, "Jeroboam . . . lifted up his hand against the king" (1 Kin 11:26).
(11) The raising of one's horn suggests the picture of a wild ox standing in all its strength. **(11a)** This is a picture of "triumph" over one's enemies: "My heart rejoiceth in the Lord, mine horn is exalted in the Lord; my mouth is enlarged over mine enemies" (1 Sa 2:1). **(11b)** Moreover, horns symbolized the focus of one's power. Thus, when one's horn is "exalted," one's power is exalted. When one exalts another's horn, he gives him "strength": "He

[the Lord] shall give strength unto his king, and exalt the horn of his anointed" (1 Sa 2:10). **(12)** Raising one's head may be a public gesture of "triumph and supremacy," as in Ps 110:7, where it is said that after defeating all His enemies the Lord will "lift up the head." **(12a)** This nuance is sometimes used transitively, as when someone else lifts a person's head. Some scholars suggest that in such cases the verb signifies the action of a judge who has pronounced an accused person innocent by raising the accused's head. **(12b)** This phrase also came to signify "to mark with distinction," "to give honor to," or "to place in a position of strength": "But thou, O Lord, art a shield for me, my glory, and the lifter up of mine head" (Ps 3:3). **(13)** To raise one's eyes or heart is to be "proud" and "arrogant": "Then thine heart be lifted up, and thou forget the Lord thy God, which brought thee forth out of the land of Egypt" (Deut 8:14). See: TWOT—2133; BDB—575d, 910b, 926c, 941a, 942c, 1112d.

7312. רוּם {6x} **rûwm**, *room;* or

רֻם **rûm**, *room;* from 7311; (lit.) *elevation* or (fig.) *elation:*—haughtiness {3x}, height {1x}, × high {2x}.

Ruwm, as a noun, means "height; haughtiness." **(1)** This word occurs 6 times, and it means "height" in Prov 25:3. **(2)** *Rum* signifies "haughtiness" in Is 2:11. Syn.: 4791. See: TWOT—2133a; BDB—927d, 941a.

7313. רוּם {4x} **rûwm** (Aram.), *room;* corresp. to 7311; (fig. only):—extol {1x}, lift up (self) {2x}, set up {1x}. See: TWOT—2992; BDB—1112d.

7314. רוּם {5x} **rûwm** (Aram.), *room;* from 7313; (lit.) *altitude:*—height {5x}. See: TWOT—2992a; BDB—1112d.

7315. רוֹם {1x} **rôwm**, *rome;* from 7311; *elevation,* i.e. (adv.) *aloft:*—on high {1x}. See: TWOT—2133b; BDB—927d.

7316. רוּמָה {1x} **Rûwmâh**, *roo-maw';* from 7311; *height; Rumah,* a place in Pal.:—Rumah {1x}. See: BDB—928a.

7317. רוֹמָה {1x} **rôwmâh**, *ro-maw';* fem. of 7315; *elation,* i.e. (adv.) *proudly:*—haughtily {1x}. See: BDB—928a.

7318. רוֹמָם {1x} **rôwmâm**, *ro-mawm';* from 7426; *exaltation,* i.e. (fig. and spec.) *praise:*—be extolled {1x}. See: TWOT—2133f; BDB—928c.

7319. רוֹמְמָה {1x} **rôwmᵉmâh**, *ro-mem-aw';* fem. act. part. of 7426; *exaltation,* i.e. *praise:*—high {1x}. See: TWOT—2133f?;BDB—927a, 928c.

7320. רוֹמַמְתִּי עֶזֶר {2x} **Rôwmamtîy ʿEzer** (or

לַמְתִּי **Rômamtîy**), *ro-mam'-tee eh'-zer;* from 7311 and 5828; *I have raised* up a *help; Romamti-Ezer,* an Isr.:—Romamti-ezer {2x}. See: BDB—928d, 942c.

7321. רוּעַ {46x} **rûwaʿ**, *roo-ah';* a prim. root; to *mar* (espec. by breaking); fig. to *split* the ears (with sound), i.e. *shout* (for alarm or joy):—shout {23x}, noise {7x}, . . . alarm {4x}, cry {4x}, triumph {3x}, smart {1x}, misc. {4x} = destroy, smart, sound an alarm. See: TWOT—2135; BDB—929c, 937c.

7322. רוּף {1x} **rûwph**, *roof;* a prim. root; prop. to *triturate* (in a mortar), i.e. (fig.) to *agitate* (by concussion):—tremble {1x}. See: TWOT—2201; BDB—952c.

7323. רוּץ {104x} **rûwts**, *roots;* a prim. root; to *run* (for whatever reason, espec. to *rush*):—run {72x}, guard {14x}, post {8x}, run away {2x}, speedily {1x}, misc. {7x} = break down, footman, bring hastily, stretch out.

(1) *Ruwts* signifies moving very quickly or hastening rather than running (Gen 18:2, 7; 41:14; Ps 68:31). **(2)** It can mean to run (Josh 8:19). **(3)** In a military sense, the charging into battle, **(3a)** metaphorically describes the lifestyle of the wicked—they rush headlong at God (Job 15:26). **(3b)** This emphasis explains 2 Sa 22:30 which means to charge at the enemy. **(4)** *Ruwts* also means running away from something or someone (Judg 7:21). **(5)** *Ruwts* can signify running into somewhere not only in a hostile sense but in order to be united with or hidden by it: "The name of the Lord is a strong tower: the righteous runneth (7323) into it, and is safe" (Prov 18:10). **(6)** Runners **(6a)** preceded kings and pretenders to the throne (2 Sa 15:1) and **(6a)** served as official messengers (2 Sa 18:19). See: TWOT—2137; BDB—929c, 930a, 943b, 952d.

7324. רוּק {19x} **rûwq**, *rook;* a prim. root; to *pour* out (lit. or fig.), i.e. *empty:*—(pour, draw . . .) out {7x}, empty {7x}, draw {3x}, armed {1x}, pour forth {1x}. See: TWOT—2161; BDB—937d.

7325. רוּר {1x} **rûwr**, *roor;* a prim. root; to *slaver* (with spittle), i.e. (by anal.) to *emit* a fluid (ulcerous or natural):—run {1x}. See: TWOT—2162; BDB—938b.

7326. רוּשׁ {24x} **rûwsh**, *roosh;* a prim. root; to *be destitute:*—poor {19x}, poor man {3x}, lack {1x}, needy {1x}. See: TWOT—2138; BDB—910c, 930d, 957a.

רוֹשׁ **rôwsh**. See 7219.

7327. רוּת {12x} **Rûwth**, *rooth;* prob. for 7468; *friend; Ruth,* a Moabitess:—Ruth {12x}. See: BDB—930d, 946c.

7328. רָז {9x} **râz** (Aram.), *rawz;* from an unused root prob. mean. to *attenuate,* i.e. (fig.) *hide; a mystery:*—secret {9x}. See: TWOT—2993; BDB—1112d.

7329. רָזָה {2x} **râzâh**, *raw-zaw';* a prim. root; to *emaciate,* i.e. *make* (*become*) *thin* (lit. or fig.):—famish {1x}, wax lean {1x}. See: TWOT—2139; BDB—930d.

7330. רָזֶה {2x} **râzeh**, *raw-zeh';* from 7329; *thin:*—lean {2x}. See: TWOT—2139a; BDB—931a.

7331. רְזוֹן {1x} **Rᵉzôwn**, *rez-one';* from 7336; *prince; Rezon,* a Syrian:—Rezon {1x}. See: BDB—931b.

7332. רָזוֹן {3x} **râzôwn**, *raw-zone';* from 7329; *thinness:*—leanness {2x}, ✕ scant {1x}. See: TWOT—2139c; BDB—931a, 931b.

7333. רָזוֹן {1x} **râzôwn**, *raw-zone';* from 7336; a *dignitary:*—prince {1x}. See: TWOT—2142a; BDB—931a, 931b.

7334. רְזִי {2x} **râziy**, *raw-zee';* from 7329; *thinness:*—leanness {2x}. See: TWOT—2139b; BDB—931a.

7335. רָזַם {1x} **râzam**, *raw-zam';* a prim. root; to *twinkle* the eye (in mockery):—wink {1x}. See: TWOT—2141; BDB—931b.

7336. רָזַן {6x} **râzan**, *raw-zan';* a prim. root; prob. to *be heavy,* i.e. (fig.) *honorable:*—prince {5x}, ruler {1x}. See: TWOT—2142; BDB—931b.

7337. רָחַב {25x} **râchab**, *raw-khab';* a prim. root; to *broaden* (intr. or tran., lit. or fig.):—enlarge {18x}, wide {3x}, large {2x}, make room {2x}. See: TWOT—2143; BDB—931b.

7338. רַחַב {2x} **rachab**, *rakh'-ab;* from 7337; a *width:*—breadth {1x}, broad place {1x}. See: TWOT—2143a; BDB—931d.

7339. רְחֹב {43x} **rᵉchôb**, *rekh-obe';* or

רְחוֹב **rᵉchôwb**, *rekh-obe';* from 7337; a *width,* i.e. (concr.) *avenue* or *area:*—broad places {1x}, broad ways {2x}, street {40x}.

Rechowb represents the town square immediately near the gate(s) which often served for social functions such as assemblies, courts, and official proclamations (Gen 19:2). See: TWOT—2143d; BDB—932a. See also 1050.

7340. רְחֹב {10x} **Rᵉchôb**, *rekh-obe';* or

רְחוֹב **Rᵉchôwb**, *rekh-obe';* the same as 7339; *Rechob,* the name of a place

in Syria, also of a Syrian and an Isr.:—Rehob {10x}. See: BDB—932b.

7341. רֹחַב {101x} **rôchab**, *ro'-khab;* from 7337; *width* (lit. or fig.):—breadth {74x}, broad {21x}, thickness {2x}, largeness {1x}, thick {1x}, as broad as + 3651 {1x}, wideness {1x}.

Rochab, means "breadth; width; expanse." **(1)** First, the word refers to how broad a flat expanse is. In Gen 13:17, we read: "Arise, walk through the land in the length of it and in the breadth of it; for I will give it unto thee." **(1a)** *Rochab* itself sometimes represents the concept of length, breadth, or the total territory: "And the stretching out of his wings shall fill the breadth of thy land, O Immanuel" (Is 8:8; cf. Job 37:10). **(1b)** This idea is used figuratively in 1 Kin 4:29, describing the dimensions of Solomon's discernment: "And God gave Solomon wisdom and understanding exceeding much, and largeness [*rochab*] of heart, even as the sand that is on the seashore." **(2)** Second, *rochab* is used to indicate the "thickness" or "width" of an object. **(2a)** In its first biblical occurrence the word is used of Noah's ark: "The length of the ark shall be three hundred cubits, the breadth of it fifty cubits, and the height of it thirty cubits" (Gen 6:15). **(2b)** In Eze 42:10, the word represents the "thickness" of a building's wall in which there were chambers (cf. Eze 41:9). See: TWOT—2143b; BDB—931d.

7342. רָחָב {21x} **râchâb**, *raw-khawb';* from 7337; *roomy,* in any (or every) direction, lit. or fig.:—broad {5x}, broader {1x}, large {8x}, at liberty {1x}, proud {3x}, wide {3x}. See: TWOT—2143c; BDB—932a.

7343. רָחָב {5x} **Râchâb**, *raw-khawb';* the same as 7342; *proud; Rachab,* a Canaanitess:—Rahab {5x}. See: BDB—932a.

7344. רְחֹבוֹת {4x} **Rᵉchôbôwth**, *rekh-o-bōth';* or

רְחֹבֹת **Rᵉchôbôth**, *rekh-o-bōth';* plur. of 7339; *streets; Rechoboth,* a place in Assyria and one in Pal.:—Rehoboth {4x}. See: BDB—932c.

7345. רְחַבְיָה {5x} **Rᵉchabyâh**, *rekh-ab-yaw';* or

רְחַבְיָהוּ **Rᵉchabyâhûw**, *rek-ab-yaw'-hoo;* from 7337 and 3050; *Jah has enlarged; Rechabjah,* an Isr.:—Rehabiah {5x}. See: BDB—932c.

7346. רְחַבְעָם {50x} **Rᵉchabᶜâm**, *rekh-ab-awm';* from 7337 and 5971; a

people has enlarged; Rechabam, an Isr. king:—
Rehoboam {50x}. See: BDB—932c.

רְחֹבֹת **R^echôbôth**. See 7344.

7347. רֶחֶה {5x} **rêcheh,** *ray-kheh′;* from an
unused root mean. to *pulverize;* a
mill-stone:—mill {2x}, millstone {2x}, nether
{1x}. See: TWOT—2144a; BDB—932d.

רְחוֹב **R^echôwb**. See 7339, 7340.

7348. רְחוּם {8x} **R^echûwm,** *rekh-oom′;* a form
of 7349; *Rechum,* the name of a
Pers. and of three Isr.:—Rehum {8x}. See:
BDB—933d, 1113a.

7349. רַחוּם {13x} **rachûwm,** *rakh-oom′;* from
7355; *compassionate:*—merciful
{8x}, compassion {5x}.

The adjective is used in that important
proclamation of God's name to Moses: "The
Lord, The Lord God, merciful and gracious . . ."
(Ex 34:6). See: TWOT—2146c; BDB—933d.

7350. רָחוֹק {84x} **râchôwq,** *raw-khoke′;* or

רָחֹק **râchôq,** *raw-khoke′;* from 7368;
remote, lit. or fig., of place or time;
spec. *precious;* often used adv. (with prep.):—
(far, afar . . .) off {39x}, far {30x}, long ago {3x},
far from {3x}, come {2x}, afar {2x}, old {2x}, far
abroad {1x}, long {1x}, space {1x}. See: TWOT—
2151b; BDB—935b, 1113a.

7351. רְחִים {2x} **r^echîyt,** *rekh-eet′;* from the
same as 7298; a *panel* (as resem-
bling a *trough*):—rafter {1x}, variant {1x}. See:
TWOT—2128b; BDB—923d, 932d.

7352. רְחִיק {1x} **rachîyq** (Aram.), *rakh-eek′;*
corresp. to 7350:—far {1x}. See:
TWOT—2994; BDB—1113a.

7353. רָחֵל {4x} **râchêl,** *raw-kale′;* from an unused root mean. to *journey;* a *ewe*
[the *females* being the predominant element of
a flock] (as a good *traveller*):—ewe {2x}, sheep
{2x}. See: TWOT—2145a; BDB—932d.

7354. רָחֵל {47x} **Râchêl,** *raw-khale′;* the same
as 7353; *Rachel,* a wife of Jacob:—
Rachel {46x}, Rahel {1x}. See: BDB—932d.

7355. רָחַם {47x} **râcham,** *raw-kham′;* a prim.
root; to *fondle;* by impl. to *love,*
espec. to *compassionate:*— . . . mercy {32x}, . . .
compassion {8x}, pity {3x}, love {1x}, merciful
{1x}, Ruhamah {1x}, surely {1x}.

Racham, the verb, means "to have compassion, be merciful, pity." **(1)** The verb is translated "love" once: "I will love thee, O Lord . . ."
(Ps 18:1). **(2)** *Racham* is also used in God's
promise to declare His name to Moses: "I will
make all my goodness pass before thee, and I
will proclaim the name of the Lord before thee;
and will be gracious to whom I will be gra-

cious, and will show mercy on whom I will
show mercy" (Ex 33:19). **(3)** So men pray: "Remember, O Lord, thy tender mercies and thy
loving-kindnesses" (Ps 25:6); and **(4)** Isaiah
prophesies messianic restoration: "With great
mercies will I gather thee. . . . But with everlasting kindness will I have mercy on thee,
saith the Lord thy Redeemer" (Is 54:7–8). This
is the heart of salvation by the suffering Ser-
vant-Messiah. See: TWOT—2146; BDB—933c.

7356. רַחַם {44x} **racham,** *rakh′-am;* from
7355; *compassion* (in the plur.); by
extens. the *womb* (as *cherishing* the fetus); by
impl. a *maiden:*—mercy {30x}, compassion
{4x}, womb {4x}, bowels {2x}, pity {2x}, damsel
{1x}, tender love {1x}.

(1) *Racham* expresses a deep and tender
feeling of compassion, such as is aroused by
the sight of weakness or suffering in those who
are dear to us or need our help. Rachamim, as
a plural noun, means "bowels; mercies; compassion." **(2)** This noun, always used in the plural intensive, occurs in Gen 43:14: "And God
Almighty give you mercy." **(3)** In Gen 43:30, it
is used of Joseph's feelings toward Benjamin:
"His bowels did yearn upon his brother."
(4) Rachamim is most often used of God, as by
David in 2 Sa 24:14: "Let us fall now into the
hand of the Lord; for his mercies are great."
(5) We have the equivalent Aramaic word in
Daniel's request to his friends: "That they
would desire mercies of the God of heaven concerning this secret . . ." (Dan 2:18). Syn.: 2896.
See: TWOT—2146a; BDB—933a, 933b, 1113a.

7357. רַחַם {1x} **Racham,** *rakh′-am;* the same
as 7356; *pity; Racham,* an Isr.:—
Raham {1x}. See: BDB—933d.

7358. רֶחֶם {26x} **rechem,** *rekh′-em;* from
7355; the *womb* [comp. 7356]:—
womb {21x}, matrix {5x}.

Rechem, as a noun, means "bowels; womb;
mercy." **(1)** The first use of *rechem* is in its primary meaning of "womb": "The Lord had fast
closed up all the wombs of the house of Abimelech" (Gen 20:18). **(2)** The word is personified
in Judg 5:30: "Have they not divided the prey;
to every man a damsel or two?" **(3)** In another
figurative sense, in 1 Kin 3:26: "Her bowels
yearned upon her son." See: TWOT—2146a;
BDB—933a.

7359. רְחֵם {1x} **r^echêm** (Aram.), *rekh-ame′;*
corresp. to 7356; (plur.) *pity:*—
mercies {1x}. See: TWOT—2995; BDB—1113a.

7360. רָחָם {2x} **râchâm,** *raw-khawm′;* or
(fem.)

רָחָמָה **râchâmâh,** *raw-khaw-maw′;*
from 7355; a kind of *vulture*

(supposed to be *tender* toward its young):—gier eagle. See: TWOT—2147a; BDB—934b.

7361. רְחֵמָה {1x} **rachămâh**, *rakh-am-aw'*; fem. of 7356; a *maiden:*—two {1x}. See: TWOT—2146a; BDB—933a.

7362. רַחְמָנִי {1x} **rachmâniy**, *rakh-maw-nee'*; from 7355; *compassionate:*—pitiful {1x}. See: TWOT—2146d; BDB—933d.

7363. רָחַף {3x} **râchaph**, *raw-khaf'*; a prim. root; to *brood;* by impl. to *be relaxed:*—shake {1x}, move {1x}, flutter {1x}. See: TWOT—2148, 2149; BDB—934b.

7364. רָחַץ {72x} **râchats**, *raw-khats';* a prim. root; to *lave* (the whole or a part of a thing):—wash {53x}, bathe {18x}, wash away {1x}.
    Rachats means "to wash, bathe." **(1)** The first occurrence of the word in the text illustrates one of its most common uses: "Let a little water . . . be fetched, and wash your feet" (Gen 18:4). **(2)** When the word is used figuratively to express vengeance, the imagery is a bit more gruesome: "He shall wash his feet in the blood of the wicked" (Ps 58:10). **(3)** Pilate's action in Mt 27:24 is reminiscent of the psalmist's statement "I will wash mine hands in innocency" (Ps 26:6). **(4)** The parts of a sacrificial animal usually "were washed" before they were burned on the altar (Ex 29:17). **(5)** *Rachats* is frequently used in the sense of "bathing" or "washing" oneself (Ex 2:5; 2 Sa 11:2). **(6)** Beautiful eyes are figuratively described as "washed with milk" (Song 5:12). Syn.: 1740, 3526, 7857. See: TWOT—2150; BDB—934b.

7365. רְחַץ {1x} **rᵉchats** (Aram.), *rekh-ats';* corresp. to 7364 [prob. through the accessory idea of *ministering* as a servant at the bath]; to *attend* upon:—trust {1x}. See: TWOT—2996; BDB—1113a.

7366. רַחַץ {2x} **rachats**, *rakh'-ats;* from 7364; a *bath:*—washpot {2x}. See: TWOT—2150a; BDB—934d.

7367. רַחְצָה {2x} **rachtsâh**, *rakh-tsaw';* fem. of 7366; a *bathing* place:—washing {2x}. See: TWOT—2150b; BDB—934d.

7368. רָחַק {58x} **râchaq**, *raw-khak';* a prim. root; to *widen* (in any direction), i.e. (intr.) *recede* or (tran.) *remove* (lit. or fig., of place or relation):— . . . far {36x}, . . . off {9x}, . . . away {7x}, remove {5x}, good way {1x}.
    Rachaq, means "far." **(1)** The word is used about 55 times in the Hebrew Old Testament and it occurs for the first time in Gen 21:16: "And she went, and sat her down over against him a good way off (*rachaq*), as it were a bowshot:" **(2)** *Rachaq* is used to express "distance" of various types. It may be "distance" from a

place (Deut. 12:21), as when Job felt that his friends kept themselves "aloof" from him (Job 30:10). **(3)** Sometimes the word expresses "absence" altogether: "The comforter that should relieve my soul is far from me" (Lam 1:16). **(4)** "To be distant" was also "to abstain": "Keep thee far from a false matter" (Ex 23:7). **(5)** Sometimes *rachaq* implies the idea of "exile": "The Lord [removes] men far away" (Is 6:12). **(6)** "To make the ends of the land distant" is "to extend the boundaries": "thou hast increased the [borders of the land]" (Is 26:15). See: TWOT—2151; BDB—934d, 1113a.

7369. רָחֵק {1x} **râchêq**, *raw-khake';* from 7368; *remote:*—far from thee {1x}. See: TWOT—2151a, 2151b; BDB—935b.

רָחֹק **râchôq**. See 7350.

7370. רָחַשׁ {1x} **râchash**, *raw-khash';* a prim. root; to *gush:*—inditing {1x}. See: TWOT—2152; BDB—935d.

7371. רַחַת {1x} **rachath**, *rakh'-ath;* from 7306; a *winnowing*-fork (as *blowing* the chaff away):—shovel {1x}. See: TWOT—2153; BDB—935d.

7372. רָטַב {1x} **râtab**, *raw-tab';* a prim. root; to *be moist:*—wet {1x}. See: TWOT—2154; BDB—936a.

7373. רָטֹב {1x} **râtôb**, *raw-tobe';* from 7372; *moist* (with sap):—green {1x}. See: TWOT—2154a; BDB—936a.

7374. רֶטֶט {1x} **retet**, *reh'-tet;* from an unused root mean. to *tremble; terror:*—fear {1x}. See: TWOT—2156a; BDB—936a.

7375. רֻטֲפַשׁ {1x} **rûwtăphash**, *roo-taf-ash';* a root compounded from 7373 and 2954; to *be rejuvenated:*—fresher {1x}. See: TWOT—2157; BDB—936a.

7376. רָטַשׁ {6x} **râtash**, *raw-tash';* a prim. root; to *dash* down:—dash . . . pieces {5x}, dash {1x}. See: TWOT—2158; BDB—936b.

7377. רִי {1x} **rîy**, *ree;* from 7301; *irrigation,* i.e. a *shower:*—watering {1x}. See: TWOT—2130a; BDB—138c, 924b, 936b.

7378. רִיב {67x} **rîyb**, *reeb;* or
    רוּב **rûwb**, *roob;* a prim. root; prop. to *toss,* i.e. *grapple;* mostly fig. to *wrangle,* i.e. *hold a controversy;* (by impl.) to *defend:*—plead {27x}, strive {13x}, contend {12x}, chide {6x}, debate {2x}, misc. {7x} = adversary, complain, × ever, × lay wait, rebuke, × thoroughly.
    Riyb, as a verb, means "to plead, strive, conduct a legal case, make a charge." **(1)** It appears in the text for the first time in Gen 26:20: "And

the herdmen of Gerar did strive with Isaac's herdmen." **(2)** Such "striving" with words is found frequently in the biblical text (Gen 31:36; Ex 17:2). **(3)** Sometimes contentious words lead to bodily struggle and injury: "And if men strive together, and one smite another . . ." (Ex 21:18). **(4)** The prophets use *riyb* frequently to indicate that God has an indictment, a legal case, against Israel: "The Lord standeth up to plead (*riyb*), and standeth to judge the people" (Is 3:13). **(5)** In one of his visions, Amos noted: "the Lord God called to contend by fire . . ." (Amos 7:4). **(6)** Micah 6 is a classic example of such a legal case against Judah, calling on the people "to plead" their case (6:1) and progressively showing how only God has a valid case (6:8). See: TWOT–2159; BDB–912c, 923d, 936b.

7379. רִיב {62x} **rîyb**, *reeb;* or

רִב **rîb**, *reeb;* from 7378; a *contest* (personal or legal):—cause {24x}, strife {16x}, controversy {13x}, contention {2x}, misc. {7x} = + adversary, chiding, contend, multitude, pleading, strive (-ing), suit.

Riyb, as a noun, means "strife; dispute." The word appears twice in Mic 6:2: "Hear ye, O mountains, the Lord's controversy, and ye strong foundations of the earth: for the Lord hath a controversy with his people, and he will plead with Israel." See: TWOT–2159a; BDB–936d.

7380. רִיבַי {2x} **Rîybay**, *ree-bah'-ee;* from 7378; *contentious; Ribai*, an Isr.:—Ribai {2x}. See: BDB–937a.

7381. רֵיחַ {58x} **rêyach**, *ray'-akh;* from 7306; *odor* (as if *blown*):—savour {45x}, smell {11x}, scent {2x}.

Reyach, as a noun, means "savor; smell; fragrance; aroma." **(1)** Of the 61 appearances of this word, 43 refer specifically to sacrifices made to God and appear in Genesis–Numbers and Ezekiel. **(2)** This word refers to the "scent or smell" of a person or thing: "And he [Jacob] came near, . . . and he [Isaac] smelled the smell of his raiment" (Gen 27:27). **(3)** In Song 1:12 *reyach* signifies the "fragrance" of perfume and in Song 2:3 the "fragrance" of a flower. **(4)** This word is used of a bad "smell" in Ex 5:21: ". . . Because ye have made our savor to be abhorred [have made us odious] in the eyes of Pharaoh." **(5)** Most frequently *reyach* is used of the "odor" of a sacrifice being offered up to God. The sacrifice, or the essence of the thing it represents, ascends to God as a placating "odor": "And the Lord smelled a sweet savor . . ." (Gen 8:21—the first occurrence of the word). See: TWOT–2131b; BDB–926b, 937c, 1112d.

7382. רֵיחַ {1x} **rêyach** (Aram.), *ray'-akh;* corresp. to 7381:—smell {1x}. See: TWOT–2991b; BDB–1112d, 1113a.

רֵים **rêym**. See 7214.

רֵיעַ **rêya⁶**. See 7453.

7383. רִיפָה {2x} **rîyphâh**, *ree-faw';* or

רִפָה **riphâh**, *ree-faw';* from 7322; (only plur.), *grits* (as *pounded*):—ground corn {1x}, wheat {1x}. See: TWOT–2160a; BDB–937d, 952b.

7384. רִיפַת {2x} **Rîyphath**, *ree-fath';* or (prob. by orth. err.)

דִּיפַת **Dîyphath**, *dee-fath';* of for. or.; *Riphath*, a grandson of Japheth and his desc.:—Riphath {2x}. See: BDB–193d, 937d.

7385. רִיק {12x} **rîyq**, *reek;* from 7324; *emptiness;* fig. a *worthless* thing; adv. *in vain:*—vain {7x}, vanity {2x}, no purpose {1x}, empty {1x}, vain thing {1x}. See: TWOT–2161b; BDB–938a, 938b.

7386. רֵיק {14x} **rêyq**, *rake;* or (short.)

רֵק **rêq**, *rake;* from 7324; *empty;* fig. *worthless:*—empty {6x}, vain {5x}, emptied {1x}, vain men {1x}, vain fellows {1x}. See: TWOT–2161a; BDB–938a, 938b, 954d.

7387. רֵיקָם {16x} **rêyqâm**, *ray-kawm';* from 7386; *emptily;* fig. (obj.) *ineffectually,* (subj.) *undeservedly:*—empty {12x}, without cause {2x}, void {1x}, vain {1x}. See: TWOT–2161c; BDB–938b.

7388. רִיר {2x} **rîyr**, *reer;* from 7325; *saliva;* by resemblance *broth:*—spittle {1x}, white [of an egg] {1x}. See: TWOT–2162a; BDB–938c.

7389. רֵישׁ {7x} **rêysh**, *raysh;* or

רֵאשׁ **rê³sh**, *raysh;* or

רִישׁ **rîysh**, *reesh;* from 7326; *poverty:*—poverty {7x}. See: TWOT–2138a, 2138b; BDB–910c, 930d, 938c.

7390. רַךְ {16x} **rak**, *rak;* from 7401; *tender* (lit. or fig.); by impl. *weak:*—tender {9x}, soft {3x}, fainthearted + 3824 {1x}, one {1x}, weak {1x}, tenderhearted + 3824 {1x}. See: TWOT–2164a; BDB–938c, 940a.

7391. רֹךְ {1x} **rôk**, *roke;* from 7401; *softness* (fig.):—tenderness {1x}. See: TWOT–2164b; BDB–938c, 940a.

7392. רָכַב {78x} **rầkab**, *raw-kab';* a prim. root; to *ride* (on an animal or in a vehicle); caus. to *place upon* (for riding or gen.), to *despatch:*—ride {50x}, rider {12x},

Hebrew

horseback {3x}, put {3x}, set {2x}, carried {2x}, misc. {6x} = get [oneself] up, on horse.

Rakab means "to ride upon, drive, mount (an animal)." The first occurrence is in Gen 24:61: "And Rebekah arose, and her damsels, and they rode upon the camels." See: TWOT—2163; BDB—938c.

7393. רֶכֶב {120x} **rekeb**, *reh'-keb;* from 7392; a *vehicle;* by impl. a *team;* by extens. *cavalry;* by anal. a *rider,* i.e. the upper millstone:—chariot {115x}, millstone {3x}, wagons {1x}, variant {1x}.

Rekeb means "chariotry; chariot units; chariot horse; chariot; train; upper millstone." **(1)** The word is used collectively of an entire force of "military chariotry": "And he took six hundred chosen chariots, and all the chariots (Ex 14:7). **(1a)** This use of *rekeb* might well be rendered "chariot-units" (the chariot, a driver, an offensive and a defensive man). **(1b)** The immediately preceding verse uses *rekeb* of a single "war-chariot" (or perhaps "chariot unit"). **(1c)** The following translation distinguishes the separate units in Ex 14:6–7: "So he made his chariot ready and took his courtiers with him, and he took six hundred select chariot units, and all the chariotry of Egypt with defensive men." **(2)** In its first biblical appearance, *rekeb* means "chariotry": "And there went up with him both chariots and horsemen . . ." (Gen 50:9). **(3)** In 2 Sa 8:4, the word represents "chariot-horse": ". . . And David hocked all the chariot horses."

(4) *Rekeb* also is used of the "chariot" itself: "And the king was stayed up in his chariot against the Syrians" (1 Kin 22:35). **(5)** Next, *rekeb* refers to a "column" or "train of donkeys and camels": "And he saw a chariot with a couple of horsemen, a chariot of asses, and a chariot of camels" (Is 21:7). **(6)** Finally, *rekeb* sometimes signifies an "upper millstone": "No man shall take the nether or the upper millstone to pledge" (Deut 24:6; cf. Judg 9:53; 2 Sa 11:21). Syn.: 4818. See: TWOT—2163a; BDB—939a.

7394. רֵכָב {13x} **Rêkâb**, *ray-kawb';* from 7392; *rider; Rekab,* the name of two Arabs and of two Isr.:—Rechab {13x}. See: BDB—939c.

7395. רַכָּב {3x} **rakkâb**, *rak-kawb';* from 7392; a *charioteer:*—driver of his chariot {1x}, horseman {1x}, chariot man {1x}. See: TWOT—2163c; BDB—939b.

7396. רִכְבָּה {1x} **rikbâh**, *rik-baw';* fem. of 7393; a *chariot* (collect.):—chariot {1x}. See: TWOT—2163b; BDB—939b.

7397. רֵכָה {5x} **Rêkâh**, *ray-kaw';* prob. fem. from 7401; *softness; Rekah,* a

place in Pal.:—Rechabites {4x}, Rechah {1x}. See: BDB—939d.

7398. רְכוּב {1x} **rekûwb**, *rek-oob';* from pass. part. of 7392; a *vehicle* (as *ridden* on):—chariot {1x}. See: TWOT—2163d; BDB—939c.

7399. רְכוּשׁ {28x} **rekûwsh**, *rek-oosh';* or

רְכֻשׁ **rekûsh**, *rek-oosh';* from pass. part. of 7408; *property* (as *gathered*):—goods {12x}, substance {11x}, riches {5x}. See: TWOT—2167b; BDB—940d.

7400. רָכִיל {6x} **râkîyl**, *raw-keel';* from 7402 a *scandal-monger* (as *travelling* about):—slander {2x}, talebearer {2x}, talebearer + 1980 {1x}, carry tales {1x}. See: TWOT—2165b; BDB—940c.

7401. רָכַךְ {8x} **râkak**, *raw-kak';* a prim. root; to *soften* (intr. or tran.), used fig.:—tender {2x}, faint {2x}, fainthearted + 3824 {1x}, mollified {1x}, soft {1x}, softer {1x}. See: TWOT—2164; BDB—939d.

7402. רָכַל {17x} **râkal**, *raw-kal';* a prim. root; to *travel* for trading:—merchant {17x}. See: TWOT—2165; BDB—940b.

7403. רָכָל {1x} **Râkâl**, *raw-kawl';* from 7402; *merchant; Rakal,* a place in Pal.:—Rachal {1x}. See: BDB—940b.

7404. רְכֻלָּה {4x} **rekullâh**, *rek-ool-law';* fem. pass. part. of 7402; *trade* (as *peddled*):—merchandise {2x}, traffick {2x}. See: TWOT—2165a; BDB—940b.

7405. רָכַס {2x} **râkaç**, *raw-kas';* a prim. root; to *tie:*—bind {2x}. See: TWOT—2166; BDB—940c.

7406. רֶכֶס {1x} **rekeç**, *reh'-kes;* from 7405; a mountain *ridge* (as of *tied* summits):—rough places {1x}. See: TWOT—2166a; BDB—940c.

7407. רֹכֶס {1x} **rôkeç**, *ro'-kes;* from 7405; a *snare* (as of *tied* meshes):—pride {1x}. See: TWOT—2166b; BDB—940c.

7408. רָכַשׁ {5x} **râkash**, *raw-kash';* a prim. root; to *lay up,* i.e. *collect:*—got {4x}, gather {1x}. See: TWOT—2167; BDB—940d.

7409. רֶכֶשׁ {4x} **rekesh**, *reh'-kesh;* from 7408; a *relay* of animals on a post-route (as *stored* up for that purpose); by impl. a *courser:*—mule {2x}, dromedaries {1x}, swift beast {1x}. See: TWOT—2167a; BDB—940d.

רְכֻשׁ **rekûsh**. See 7399.

רֵם **rêm**. See 7214.

7410. רָם {7x} **Râm**, *rawm;* act. part. of 7311; *high; Ram,* the name of an Arabian and of an Isr.:—*Ram* {7x}. See: BDB—928a. See also 1027.

רָם **rûm**. See 7311.

7411. רָמָה {12x} **râmâh**, *raw-maw';* a prim. root; to *hurl;* spec. to *shoot;* fig. to *delude* or *betray* (as if causing to fall):—deceived {4x}, beguiled {2x}, thrown {2x}, betray {1x}, bowmen + 7198 {1x}, carrying {1x}, deceived so {1x}. See: TWOT—2168, 2169; BDB—941a, 1113a.

7412. רְמָה {12x} **rᵉmâh** (Aram.), *rem-aw';* corresp. to 7411; to *throw, set,* (fig.) *assess:*—cast {10x}, impose {1x}, cast down {1x}. See: TWOT—2997; BDB—1113a.

7413. רָמָה {4x} **râmâh**, *raw-maw';* fem. act. part. of 7311; a *height* (as a seat of idolatry):—high place {4x}. See: TWOT—2133d; BDB—928a, 941d.

7414. רָמָה {37x} **Râmâh**, *raw-maw';* the same as 7413; *Ramah,* the name of four places in Pal.:—*Ramah* {37x}. See: BDB—910b, 910c, 928a, 928c, 941d.

7415. רִמָּה {7x} **rimmâh**, *rim-maw';* from 7426 in the sense of *breeding* [comp. 7311]; a *maggot* (as rapidly *bred*), lit. or fig.:—worm {7x}. See: TWOT—2175a; BDB—941d, 942c.

7416. רִמּוֹן {32x} **rimmôwn**, *rim-mone';* or

רִמֹּן **rimmôn**, *rim-mone';* from 7426; a *pomegranate,* the tree (from its *upright* growth) or the fruit (also an artificial ornament):—pomegranate {31x}, pomegranate tree {1x}. See: TWOT—2170; BDB—745c, 941d.

7417. רִמּוֹן {16x} **Rimmôwn**, *rim-mone';* or (short.)

רִמֹּן **Rimmôn**, *rim-mone';* or

רִמּוֹנוֹ **Rimmôwnôw** (1 Chron. 6:62 [77]), *rim-mo-no';* the same as 7416; *Rimmon,* the name of a Syrian deity, also of five places in Pal.:—*Rimmon* {16x}. See: TWOT—2171; BDB—942a, 942b. The addition "-methoar" (Josh. 19:13) is

הַמְּתֹאָר **ham-mᵉthôʼâr**, *ham-meth-o-awr';* pass. part. of 8388 with the art.; *the* (one) *marked off,* i.e. *which pertains;* mistaken for part of the name.

רָמוֹת **Râmôwth**. See 7418, 7433.

7418. רָמוֹת־נֶגֶב {1x} **Râmôwth-Negeb**, *raw-môth-neh'-gheb;* or

רָמַת נֶגֶב **Râmath Negeb**, *raw'-math neh'-gheb;* from the plur. or constr. form of 7413 and 5045; *heights* (or

height) of (the) *South; Ramoth-Negeb* or *Ramath-Negeb,* a place in Pal.:—Ramoth {1x}. See: BDB—910c, 928b, 928c.

7419. רָמוּת {1x} **râmûwth**, *raw-mooth';* from 7311; a *heap* (of carcases):—height {1x}. See: TWOT—2133e; BDB—928c, 942b.

7420. רֹמַח {15x} **rômach**, *ro'-makh;* from an unused root mean. to *hurl;* a *lance* (as *thrown*); espec. the iron *point:*—spear {12x}, javelin {1x}, lancet {1x}, buckler {1x}. See: TWOT—2172; BDB—942b.

7421. רַמִּי {1x} **rammiy**, *ram-mee';* for 761; a *Ramite,* i.e. Aramæan:—Syrian {1x}. See: BDB—74c.

7422. רַמְיָה {1x} **Ramyâh**, *ram-yaw';* from 7311 and 3050; *Jah has raised; Ramjah,* an Isr.:—Ramiah {1x}. See: BDB—941d, 942b.

7423. רְמִיָּה {15x} **rᵉmîyâh**, *rem-ee-yaw';* from 7411; *remissness, treachery:*—deceitful {4x}, deceitfully {3x}, deceit {2x}, slothful {2x}, false {1x}, guile {1x}, idle {1x}, slack {1x}. See: TWOT—2169a; BDB—941a, 941c, 942b, 945a.

7424. רַמָּךְ {1x} **rammâk**, *ram-mawk';* of for. or.; a *brood mare:*—dromedaries {1x}. See: TWOT—2173; BDB—942b.

7425. רְמַלְיָהוּ {13x} **Rᵉmalyâhûw**, *rem-al-yaw'-hoo;* from an unused root and 3050 (perh. mean. to *deck*); *Jah has bedecked; Remaljah,* an Isr.:—Remaliah {13x}. See: BDB—942b.

7426. רָמַם {7x} **râmam**, *raw-mam';* a prim. root; to *rise* (lit. or fig.):—exalted {3x}, get [oneself] up {1x}, lifted up (self) {2x}, mount up {1x}. See: TWOT—2174; BDB—942c.

7427. רֹמֵמֻת {1x} **rômᵉmûth**, *ro-may-mooth';* from the act. part. of 7426; *exaltation:*—lifting up of self {1x}. See: TWOT—2133g; BDB—928c.

רִמֹּן **rimmôn**. See 7416.

7428. רִמֹּן פֶּרֶץ {2x} **Rimmôn Perets**, *rim-mone' peh'-rets;* from 7416 and 6556; *pomegranate of* (the) *breach; Rimmon-Perets,* a place in the desert:—Rimmonparez {2x}. See: BDB—829d, 942a.

7429. רָמַס {19x} **râmaç**, *raw-mas';* a prim. root; to *tread* upon (as a potter, in walking or abusively):—tread down {7x}, trea {5x}, stamped {2x}, trample . . . feet {1x}, oppressors {1x}, tread under foot {1x}, trample {1x}, trodden {1x}. See: TWOT—2176; BDB—942c.

7430. רָמַשׂ {17x} **râmas,** *raw-mas';* a prim. root; prop. to *glide* swiftly, i.e. to *crawl* or *move* with short steps; by anal. to *swarm:*—creep {11x}, move {6x}. See: TWOT—2177; BDB—942d.

7431. רֶמֶשׂ {17x} **remes,** *reh'-mes;* from 7430; a *reptile* or any other rapidly moving animal:—that creepeth {1x}, creeping thing {15x}, moving thing {1x}. See: TWOT—2177a; BDB—943a.

7432. רֶמֶת {1x} **Remeth,** *reh'-meth;* from 7411; *height; Remeth,* a place in Pal.:—*Remeth* {1x}. See: BDB—928c, 928d, 943a.

7433. רָמֹת {22x} (or רָמוֹת **Râmôwth**) גִּלְעָד **Râmôth Gilʿâd** (2 Chron. 22:5), *raw-moth' gil-awd';* from the plur. of 7413 and 1568; *heights of Gilad; Ramoth-Gilad,* a place E. of the Jordan:—Ramoth-gilead + 1568 {19x}, Ramoth {3x}. See: BDB—928b. See also 7216.

7434. רָמַת הַמִּצְפֶּה {1x} **Râmath ham-Mitspeh,** *raw-math' ham-mits-peh';* from 7413 and 4707 with the art. interpolated; *height of the watch-*tower; *Ramath-ham-Mitspeh,* a place in Pal.:—Ramath-mizpeh {1x}. See: BDB—859d, 928b.

7435. רָמָתִי {1x} **Râmâthiy,** *raw-maw-thee';* patron. of 7414; a *Ramathite* or inhab. of Ramah:—Ramathite {1x}. See: BDB—928b, 943a.

7436. רָמָתַיִם צוֹפִים {1x} **Râmâthayim Tsôwphîym,** *raw-maw-thah'-yim tso-feem';* from the dual of 7413 and the plur. of the act. part. of 6822; *double height of watchers; Ramathajim-Tsophim,* a place in Pal.:—Ramathaim-zophim {1x}. See: BDB—847c, 928a, 928c, 943a.

7437. רָמַת לֶחִי {1x} **Râmath Lechîy,** *raw'-math lekh'-ee;* from 7413 and 3895; *height of* (a) *jaw-bone; Ramath-Lechi,* a place in Pal.:—Ramath-lehi {1x}. See: BDB—928b.

רָן **Rân.** See 1028.

7438. רֹן {1x} **rôn,** *rone;* from 7442; a *shout* (of deliverance):—song {1x}. See: TWOT—2179a; BDB—943a, 943c.

7439. רָנָה {1x} **rânâh,** *raw-naw';* a prim. root; to *whiz:*—rattle {1x}. See: TWOT—2178; BDB—943a.

7440. רִנָּה {33x} **rinnâh,** *rin-naw';* from 7442; prop. a *creaking* (or shrill sound), i.e. *shout* (of joy or grief):—cry {12x}, singing {9x}, rejoicing {3x}, joy {3x}, gladness {1x}, proclamation {1x}, shouting {1x}, sing {1x}, songs {1x}, triumph {1x}. See: TWOT—2179c; BDB—943a, 943c.

7441. רִנָּה {1x} **Rinnâh,** *rin-naw';* the same as 7440; *Rinnah,* an Isr.:—*Rinnah* {1x}. See: BDB—943a, 943d.

7442. רָנַן {52x} **rânan,** *raw-nan';* a prim. root; prop. to *creak* (or emit a stridulous sound), i.e. to *shout* (usually for joy):—sing {20x}, rejoice {11x}, sing aloud {4x}, shout {4x}, shout for joy {3x}, sing for joy {2x}, crieth {2x}, cry out {2x}, shout aloud {1x}, misc. {3x}.

Ranan, as a verb, means "to sing, shout, cry out." **(1)** It occurs approximately 50 times in the Hebrew Old Testament, with about half of these uses being in the Book of Psalms, where there is special emphasis on "singing" and "shouting" praises to God. **(2)** *Ranan* is found for the first time in Lev 9:24 at the conclusion of the consecration of Aaron and his sons to the priesthood. When the fire fell and consumed the sacrifice, the people "shouted, and fell on their faces." **(3)** *Ranan* is often used to express joy, exultation, which seems to demand loud singing, especially when it is praise to God: "Cry out and shout, thou inhabitant of Zion: for great is the Holy One of Israel in the midst of thee" (Is 12:6). **(4)** When Wisdom calls, she cries aloud to all who will hear (Prov 8:3). **(5)** To shout for joy (Ps 32:11) is to let joy ring out! Syn.: 7891. See: TWOT—2134, 2179; BDB—929c, 930c, 943b, 943c.

7443. רֶנֶן {1x} **renen,** *reh'-nen;* from 7442; an *ostrich* (from its *wail*):—✕ goodly {1x}. See: TWOT—2179d; BDB—943d.

7444. רַנֵּן {2x} **rannên,** *ran-nane';* intens. from 7442; *shouting* (for joy):—singing {1x}, joy {1x}. See: TWOT—2179; BDB—943b.

7445. רְנָנָה {4x} **rᵉnânâh,** *ren-aw-naw';* from 7442; a *shout* (for joy):—joyful {1x}, joyful voice {1x}, singing {1x}, triumphing {1x}. See: TWOT—2179b; BDB—943c.

7446. רִסָּה {2x} **Riççâh,** *ris-saw';* from 7450; a *ruin* (as *dripping* to pieces); *Rissah,* a place in the desert:—Rissah {2x}. See: BDB—943d.

7447. רָסִיס {2x} **râçîyç,** *raw-sees';* from 7450; prop. *dripping* to pieces, i.e. a *ruin;* also a dew-*drop:*—breach {1x}, drop {1x}. See: TWOT—2181a, 2182a; BDB—944a.

7448. רֶסֶן {4x} **reçen,** *reh'-sen;* from an unused root mean. to *curb;* a *halter* (as *restraining*); by impl. the *jaw:*—bridle {4x}. See: TWOT—2180a; BDB—943d.

7449. רֶסֶן {1x} **Reçen,** *reh'-sen;* the same as 7448; *Resen,* a place in Ass.:—Resen {1x}. See: BDB—944a.

7450. רָסַס {1x} **rāçaç**, *raw-sas';* a prim. root; to *comminute;* used only as denom. from 7447, to *moisten* (with drops):— temper {1x}. See: TWOT—2181; BDB—944a.

7451. רַע {663x} **raᶜ**, *rah;* from 7489; *bad* or (as noun) *evil* (nat. or mor.):—evil {442x}, wickedness {59x}, wicked {25x}, mischief {21x}, hurt {20x}, bad {13x}, trouble {10x}, sore {9x}, affliction {6x}, ill {5x}, adversity {4x}, favoured {3x}, harm {3x}, naught {3x}, noisome {2x}, grievous {2x}, sad {2x}, misc. {34x} = calamity, + displease (-ure), distress, + exceedingly, × great, grief, heavy, hurtful, + mark, misery, + not please, sorrow, vex, worse (-st), wretchedness, wrong.

Introduction: This word combines together in one the wicked deed and its consequences. It generally indicates the rough exterior of wrongdoing as a breach of harmony, and as breaking up of what is good and desirable in man and in society. While the prominent characteristic of the godly is lovingkindness (2617), one of the most marked features of the ungodly man is that his course is an injury both to himself and to everyone around him. **(1)** *Ra'* refers to that which is "bad" or "evil," in a wide variety of applications. A greater number of the word's occurrences signify something morally evil or hurtful, often referring to man or men: **(1a)** "Then answered all the wicked men and men of Belial, of those that went with David . . ." (1 Sa 30:22). **(1b)** "And Esther said, The adversary and enemy is this wicked Haman" (Est 7:6). **(1c)** "There they cry, but none giveth answer, because of the pride of evil men" (Job 35:12; cf. Ps 10:15).

(2) *Ra'* is also used to denote **(2a)** evil words (Prov 15:26), **(2b)** evil thoughts (Gen 6:5), or **(2c)** evil actions (Deut 17:5, Neh 13:17). **(3)** Eze 6:11 depicts grim consequences for Israel as a result of its actions: "Thus saith the Lord God; smite with thine hand, and stamp with thy foot, and say, Alas for all the evil abominations of the house of Israel! For they shall fall by the sword, by the famine, and by the pestilence." **(4)** *Ra'* may mean "bad" or unpleasant in the sense of giving pain or calming unhappiness: **(4a)** "And Jacob said unto Pharaoh, . . . Few and evil have the days of the years of my life been" (Gen 47:9). **(4b)** "And when the people heard these evil tidings, they mourned" (Ex 33:4; cf. Gen 37:2). **(4c)** "Correction is grievous [ra'] unto him that forsaketh the way: and he that hateth reproof shall die" (Prov 15:10). **(5)** *Ra'* may also connote a fierceness or wildness: **(5a)** "He cast upon them the fierceness of his anger, wrath, and indignation, and trouble, by sending evil [ra'] angels among them" (Ps 78:49). **(5b)** "Some evil beast hath devoured him" (Gen 37:20; cf. Gen 37:33; Lev

26:6). **(6)** In less frequent uses, *ra'* implies **(6a)** severity: "For thus saith the Lord God; How much more when I send my four sore [ra'] judgments upon Israel . . ." (Eze 14:21; cf. Deut 6:22); **(6b)** unpleasantness: "And the Lord will take away from thee all sickness, and will put more of the evil diseases of Egypt . . . upon thee" (Deut 7:15; cf. Deut 28:59); **(6c)** deadliness: "When I shall send upon them the evil arrows of famine, which shall be for their destruction" (Eze 5:16; cf. "hurtful sword," Ps 144:10); **(6d)** or sadness: "Wherefore the king said unto me, why is thy countenance sad . . ." (Neh 2:2).

(7) The word may also refer to something of poor or inferior quality, such as **(7a)** "bad" land (Num 13:19), **(7b)** "naughty" figs (Jer 24:2), **(7c)** "ill-favored" cattle (Gen 41:3, 19), or **(7d)** a "bad" sacrificial animal (Lev 27:10, 12, 14). **(8)** In Is 45:7 Yahweh describes His actions by saying, "I make peace, and create evil [ra']"; **(8a)** moral "evil" is not intended in this context, but rather the antithesis of *shalom* ("peace; welfare; well-being"). **(8b)** The whole verse affirms that as absolute Sovereign, the Lord creates a universe governed by a moral order. Calamity and misfortune will surely ensue from the wickedness of ungodly men. **(8c)** When He purposely withdraws His powerful hand, resorting to providence and sovereignty, and leaves the situation to ungodly men, He has created a situation wherein peace and wholesomeness will not stand. **(8d)** The ungodly men will wreck the peace and establish that which is poor, less than His reflection, and hurtful to all considered. Syn.: 205, 817, 2403, 5674, 5771, 5999. See: TWOT—2191a, 2191c; BDB—944a, 948a, 948c, 949a. [incl. Fem.

רָעָה **râᶜâh**; *as adj. or noun.*]

7452. רֵעַ {3x} **rêaᶜ**, *ray'-ah;* from 7321; a *crash* (of thunder), *noise* (of war), *shout* (of joy):—× aloud {1x}, noise {1x}, shouted {1x}. See: TWOT—2135a; BDB—929d, 944a, 946b.

7453. רֵעַ {188x} **rêaᶜ**, *ray'-ah;* or

רֵיעַ **rêyaᶜ**, *ray'-ah;* from 7462; an *associate* (more or less close):—neighbour {102x}, friend {42x}, another {23x}, fellow {10x}, companion {5x}, other {2x}, brother {1x}, husband {1x}, lovers {1x}, neighbour + 1121 {1x}.

Rea', as a noun, means "friend; companion." **(1)** The basic meaning of *rea'* is in the narrow usage of the word. A *rea'* is a "personal friend" with whom one shares confidences and to whom one feels very close: "And the Lord spake unto Moses face to face, as a man speaketh unto his friend" (Ex 33:11). **(1a)** The closeness

of relationship is best expressed by those texts where the *rea'* is like a brother or son, a part of the family: "For my brethren and companions' sakes . . . ." (Ps 122:8, cf. Deut 13:6). For this reason, when Zimri became king over Israel he killed not only all relatives of Baasha, but also his "friends" (1 Kin 16:11). **(1b)** In this sense, the word is a synonym of *'ah* (251 - "brother") and of *qarob* (7138 - "kin"): "Go in and out from gate to gate throughout the camp, and slay every man his brother (*'ah*), and every man his companion (*rea'*), and every man his neighbor (*qarob*)" (Ex 32:27). **(2)** Similar to the above is the sense of "marriage partner": "His mouth is most sweet: yea, he is altogether lovely. This is my beloved, and this is my friend, O daughters of Jerusalem" (Song 5:16).

(6) However, *rea'* may also signify "illegitimate partners": "If a man put away his wife, and she go from him, and become another man's, shall he return unto her again? shall not that land be greatly polluted? but thou has played the harlot with many lovers (*rea'*); yet return again to me, saith the Lord" (Jer 3:1). **(7)** The wider usage of *rea'* resembles the English word neighbor, the person with whom one associates regularly or casually without establishing close relations. **(7a)** One may borrow from his "neighbor" (Ex 22:14), but not bear false witness (Ex 20:16) nor covet his neighbor's possessions (Ex 20:17–18). The laws regulate how one must not take advantage of one's "neighbors." **(7b)** The second greatest commandment, which Jesus reiterated—"Love thy neighbor as thyself" (Lev 19:18)—receives reinforcement in the laws of the Pentateuch. **(7c)** The prophets charged Israel with breaking the commandment: They oppressed each other (Is 3:5) and desired their neighbors' wives (Jer 5:8); they committed adultery with these women (Eze 18:6); they did not pay wages to the worker (Jer 22:13); and they improperly took advantage of their "neighbors" (Eze 22:12).

(8) According to Proverbs, not loving one's neighbor is a sign of foolishness: "He that is void of wisdom despiseth his neighbour: but a man of understanding holdeth his peace" (Prov 11:12). **(9)** The wider meaning comes to expression in the proverb of the rich man and his "friends": "Wealth maketh many friends; but the poor is separated from his neighbor" (Prov 19:4). Here the "friend" is a person whose association is not long-lasting, whose friendship is superficial. Syn.: 1730, 2617, 2836, 3039, 5689, 7463, 7464, 7468, 7474. See: TWOT—2186a; BDB—929d, 937c, 944a, 945d, 946c.

7454. רֵעַ {2x} **rêaᶜ**, *ray'-ah;* from 7462; a *thought* (as *association* of ideas):—thought

{2x}. See: TWOT—2187a;BDB—929d, 944a, 946b, 946d.

7455. רֹעַ {19x} **rôaᶜ**, *ro'-ah;* from 7489; *badness* (as *marring*), phys. or mor.:—evil {11x}, wickedness {3x}, bad {1x}, badness {1x}, naughtiness {1x}, sorrow {1x}, sadness {1x}. See: TWOT—2191b; BDB—944a, 947d.

7456. רָעֵב {11x} **râᶜêb**, *raw-abe';* a prim. root: to *hunger:*— . . . hunger {5x}, hungry {4x}, suffer famish {1x}, famished {1x}.
Ra'eb, as a verb, means to be hungry, suffer hunger: "And when all the land of Egypt was famished. . . ." (Gen 41:55). See: TWOT—2183; BDB—944a.

7457. רָעֵב {21x} **râᶜêb**, *raw-abe';* from 7456; *hungry* (more or less intensely):—hunger bitten {1x}, hungry {20x}.
The first biblical occurrence is in 1 Sa 2:5: "And they that were hungry ceased: . . ." See: TWOT—2183b; BDB—944c.

7458. רָעָב {101x} **râᶜâb**, *raw-awb';* from 7456; *hunger* (more or less extensive):—dearth {5x}, famine {87x}, + famished {1x}, hunger {8x}.
Ra'ab, as a noun, means "famine; hunger." **(1)** *Ra'ab* means "hunger" as opposed to "thirst": "Therefore shalt thou serve thine enemies which the Lord shall send against thee, in hunger, and in thirst, and in nakedness, and in want of all things" (Deut 28:48). **(2)** Another meaning of the word is "famine," or the lack of food in an entire geographical area: "And there was a famine in the land: and Abram went down into Egypt" (Gen 12:10—the first occurrence). **(2a)** God used a "famine" as a means of judgment (Jer 5:12), **(2b)** of warning (1 Kin 17:1), **(2c)** of correction (2 Sa 21:1), or **(2d)** of punishment (Jer 14:12). **(2d)** The "famine" was always under divine control, being planned and used by Him. **(3)** *Ra'ab* was also used to picture the "lack of God's word" (Amos 8:11; cf. Deut 8:3). See: TWOT—2183a; BDB—944b.

7459. רְעָבוֹן {3x} **rᵉâbôwn**, *reh-aw-bone';* from 7456; *famine:*—famine {3x}. See: TWOT—2183c; BDB—944c.

7460. רָעַד {3x} **râᶜad**, *raw-ad';* a prim. root: to *shudder* (more or less violently):—tremble {3x}. See: TWOT—2184; BDB—944c.

7461. רַעַד {6x} **raᶜad**, *rah'-ad;* or (fem.)

רְעָדָה **rᵉâdâh**, *reh-aw-daw';* from 7460; a *shudder:*—trembling {4x}, fearful {1x}, fearfulness {1x}. See: TWOT—2184a, 2184b; BDB—944c, 944d.

7462. רָעָה {173x} **râᶜâh**, *raw-aw';* a prim. root; to *tend* a flock; i.e. *pasture*

it; intr. to *graze* (lit. or fig.); gen. to *rule;* by extens. to *associate* with (as a friend):—feed {75x}, shepherd {63x}, pastor {8x}, herdmen {7x}, keep {3x}, companion {2x}, broken {1x}, company {1x}, devour {1x}, eat {1x}, entreateth {1x}, misc. {10x} = use as a friend, make friendship with, + shearing house, wander, waste.

Ra'ah, as a verb, means "to associate with." This word appears in Prov 22:24: "Make no friendship with an angry man; and with a furious man thou shalt not go." See: TWOT—2185, 2186; BDB—944d, 945c, 946b, 950a, 1113b.

7463. רֵעֶה {3x} **rê'eh**, *ray-eh';* from 7462; a (male) *companion:*—friend {3x}.

Re'eh also means "friend." This noun appears in 1 Kin 4:5: "Zabud the son of Nathan was principal officer, and the king's friend." Syn.: 7453, 7464, 7468, 7474. See: TWOT—2186b; BDB—946b.

7464. רֵעָה {3x} **rê'âh**, *ray'-aw;* fem. of 7453; a female *associate:*—companion {2x}, fellows {1x}.

Re'ah refers to a "female friend." See Judg 11:37 for this usage: "And she said unto her father . . . let me alone two months, that I may go up and down upon the mountains, and bewail my virginity, I and my fellows" (cf. Judg 11:38; Ps 45:14). Syn.: 7453, 7463, 7468, 7474. See: TWOT—2186c; BDB—946b.

7465. רֹעָה {1x} **rô'âh**, *ro-aw';* for 7455; *breakage:*—broken {1x}. See: TWOT—2192; BDB—949d.

7466. רְעוּ {5x} **R⁰'ûw**, *reh-oo';* for 7471 in the sense of 7453; *friend; Re*, a postdiluvian patriarch:—Reu {5x}. See: BDB—946c.

7467. רְעוּאֵל {11x} **R⁰'ûw'êl**, *reh-oo-ale';* from the same as 7466 and 410; *friend of God; Reuel*, the name of Moses' father-inlaw, also of an Edomite and an Isr.:—Raguel {1x}, Reuel {10x}. See: BDB—946c.

7468. רְעוּת {6x} **r⁰'ûwth**, *reh-ooth';* from 7462 in the sense of 7453; a female *associate;* gen. an *additional* one:—neighbour {2x}, another {2x}, mate {2x}.

Re'uwth refers to a "fellow woman." This word is usually translated idiomatically in a reciprocal phrase of "one another," as in Zec 11:9: "Then said I, I will not feed you: that that dieth, let it die; and that that is to be cut off, let it be cut off; and let the rest eat every one the flesh of another (*re'uwth*)." Syn.: 7453, 7463, 7464, 7468, 7474. See: TWOT—2186e; BDB—946b.

7469. רְעוּת {7x} **r⁰'ûwth**, *reh-ooth';* prob. from 7462; a *feeding* upon, i.e. *grasping* after:—vexation {7x}. See: TWOT—2187b; BDB—946d.

7470. רְעוּת {2x} **r⁰'ûwth** (Aram.), *reh-ooth';* corresp. to 7469; *desire:*—pleasure {1x}, will {1x}. See: TWOT—2998a; BDB—1113b.

7471. רְעִי {1x} **r⁰'îy**, *reh-ee';* from 7462; *pasture:*—pasture {1x}. See: TWOT—2185a; BDB—945c.

7472. רֵעִי {1x} **Rê'îy**, *ray-ee';* from 7453; *social; Rê*, an Isr.:—Rei {1x}. See: BDB—946c.

7473. רֹעִי {2x} **rô'îy**, *ro-ee';* from act. part. of 7462; *pastoral;* as noun, a *shepherd:*—shepherd {2x}. See: BDB—944d, 945a, 945c.

7474. רַעְיָה {10x} **ra'yâh**, *rah-yaw';* fem. of 7453; a female *associate:*—love {9x}, variant {1x}.

The noun *ra'yah* means "beloved companion; bride." *Ra'yah* occurs many times in the Song of Solomon: 1:9, 15; 2:2, 10, 13; 4:1, 7; 5:2; 6:4. Syn.: 7453, 7463, 7464, 7468. See: TWOT—2186d; BDB—946b.

7475. רַעְיוֹן {3x} **ra'yôwn**, *rah-yone';* from 7462 in the sense of 7469; *desire:*—vexation {3x}. See: TWOT—2187c; BDB—946d.

7476. רַעְיוֹן {6x} **ra'yôwn** (Aram.), *rah-yone';* corresp. to 7475; a *grasp,* i.e. (fig.) mental *conception:*—thought {5x}, cogitation {1x}. See: TWOT—2998b; BDB—1113b.

7477. רָעַל {1x} **râ'al**, *raw-al';* a prim. root; to *reel,* i.e. (fig.) to *brandish:*—terribly shaken {1x}. See: TWOT—2188; BDB—947a.

7478. רַעַל {1x} **ra'al**, *rah'-al;* from 7477; a *reeling* (from intoxication):—trembling {1x}. See: TWOT—2188a; BDB—947a.

7479. רַעֲלָה {1x} **ra'ălâh**, *rah-al-aw';* fem. of 7478; a long *veil* (as *fluttering*):—muffler {1x}. See: TWOT—2188b; BDB—947a.

7480. רְעֵלָיָה {1x} **R⁰'êlâyâh**, *reh-ay-law-yaw';* from 7477 and 3050; *made to tremble* (i.e. *fearful*) *of Jah; Reëlajah*, an Isr.:—Reeliah {1x}. See: BDB—947a, 947c.

7481. רָעַם {13x} **râ'am**, *raw-am';* a prim. root; to *tumble,* i.e. *be* violently *agitated;* spec. to *crash* (of thunder); fig. to *irritate* (with anger):—thunder {8x}, roar {3x}, trouble {1x}, fret {1x}. See: TWOT—2189; BDB—947b.

7482. רַעַם {6x} **ra'am**, *rah'am;* from 7481; a *peal* of thunder:—thunder {6x}. See: TWOT—2189a; BDB—947b.

7483. רַעְמָה {1x} **ra'mâh**, *rah-maw';* fem. of 7482; the *mane* of a horse (as

quivering in the wind):—thunder {1x}. See: TWOT—2189b; BDB—947c.

7484. רַעְמָה {5x} **Ra‘mâh**, *rah-maw';* the same as 7483; *Ramah,* the name of a grandson of Ham, and of a place (perh. founded by him):—Raamah {5x}. See: BDB—947c.

7485. רַעְמְיָה {1x} **Ra‘amyâh**, *rah-am-yaw';* from 7481 and 3050; *Jah has shaken; Raamjah,* an Isr.:—Raamiah {1x}. See: BDB—947a, 947c.

7486. רַעְמְסֵס {5x} **Ra‘m°çêç**, *rah-mes-ace';* or

רַעַמְסֵס **Ra‘amçêç**, *rah-am-sace';* of Eg. or.; *Rameses* or *Raamses,* a place in Egypt:—Rameses {5x}, Raamses {1x}. See: BDB—947c.

7487. רַעֲנַן {1x} **ra‘ănan** (Aram.), *rah-aw-nan';* corresp. to 7488; *green,* i.e. (fig.) *prosperous:*—flourishing {1x}. See: TWOT—2999; BDB—1113b.

7488. רַעֲנָן {20x} **ra‘ănân**, *rah-an-awn';* from an unused root mean. to *be green; verdant;* by anal. *new;* fig. *prosperous:*—green {18x}, fresh {1x}, flourishing {1x}. See: TWOT—2190a; BDB—947d, 1113b.

7489. רָעַע {83x} **râ‘a‘**, *raw-ah';* a prim. root; prop. to *spoil* (lit. by *breaking* to pieces); fig. to *make* (or *be*) *good for nothing,* i.e. *bad* (physically, socially or morally):—evil {20x}, evildoer {10x}, hurt {7x}, wickedly {5x}, worse {5x}, afflict {5x}, wicked {4x}, break {3x}, doer {3x}, ill {3x}, harm {3x}, displease {2x}, misc. {13x} = associate selves, show self friendly, X indeed, do mischief, punish, still, vex. Syn.: 2398, 3256, 5358, 5771, 6064. See: TWOT—2191, 2192; BDB—945b, 948a, 949b, 949d, 1084a.

7490. רְעַע {2x} **r°a‘** (Aram.), *reh-ah';* corresp. to 7489:—bruise {1x}, break {1x}. See: TWOT—3000; BDB—1113b.

7491. רָעַף {5x} **râ‘aph**, *raw-af';* a prim. root; to *drip:*—drop {3x}, drop down {1x}, distil {1x}. See: TWOT—2193; BDB—950a.

7492. רָעַץ {2x} **râ‘ats**, *raw-ats';* a prim. root; to *break* in pieces; fig. *harass:*—dash in pieces {1x}, vex {1x}. See: TWOT—2194; BDB—950a.

7493. רָעַשׁ {30x} **râ‘ash**, *raw-ash;* a prim. root; to *undulate* (as the earth, the sky, etc.; also a field of grain), partic. through fear; spec. to *spring* (as a locust):—shake {16x}, tremble {9x}, moved {2x}, afraid {1x}, quake {1x}, remove {1x}. See: TWOT—2195; BDB—950a.

7494. רַעַשׁ {17x} **ra‘ash**, *rah'-ash;* from 7493; *vibration, bounding, uproar:*—earthquake {6x}, rushing {3x}, shake {3x}, fierceness {1x}, confused noise {1x}, commotion {1x}, rattling {1x}, quaking {1x}. See: TWOT—2195a; BDB—950b.

7495. רָפָא {67x} **râphâ’**, *raw-faw';* or

רָפָה **râphâh**, *raw-faw';* a prim. root; prop. to *mend* (by stitching), i.e. (fig.) to *cure:*—heal {57x}, physician {5x}, cure {1x}, repaired {1x}, misc. {3x} = X thoroughly, make whole.

(1) *Raphah* means to heal, a restoring to normal, an act which God typically performs (Gen 20:17). **(2)** Thus, appeals to God for healing are common (Jer 17:14). **(3)** Not only are human diseases healed, but **(3a)** bad water is restored to normal or healed (2 Kin 2:22); **(3b)** salt water is healed or made fresh (Eze 47:8); even **(3c)** pottery is healed or restored (Jer 19:11). **(4)** Nations are healed—such healing not only involves God's grace and forgiveness, but also the nation's repentance. Divine discipline leads to repentance and healing (Hos 6:1; Jer 30:17). **(5)** Foreign cities and powers can know God's healing if they repent (Jer 51:8–9). **(6)** False prophets are condemned because they deal only with the symptoms and not with the deep spiritual hurts of the people: "They have healed also the hurt of the daughter of my people slightly, saying, Peace, peace; when there is no peace" (Jer 6:14; also 8:11). Syn.: 7503. See: TWOT—2196; BDB—950c.

7496. רָפָא {8x} **râphâ’**, *raw-faw';* from 7495 in the sense of 7503; prop. *lax,* i.e. (fig.) a *ghost* (as *dead;* in plur. only):—dead {7x}, deceased {1x}. See: TWOT—2198c; BDB—951a, 952b.

7497. רָפָא {25x} **râphâ’**, *raw-faw';* or

רָפָה **râphâh**, *raw-faw';* from 7495 in the sense of *invigorating;* a *giant:*—giant {17x}, Rephaim {8x}. Syn.: 1368, 5307. See: TWOT—2198d; BDB—951a, 952b. See also 1051.

7498. רָפָא {2x} **Râphâ’**, *raw-faw';* or

רָפָה **Râphâh**, *raw-faw';* prob. the same as 7497; *giant; Rapha* or *Raphah,* the name of two Isr.:—Rapha {2x}. See: BDB—951a, 951b, 952a, 952b.

7499. רְפֻאָה {3x} **r°phu’âh**, *ref-oo-aw';* fem. pass. part. of 7495; a *medicament:*—medicine {2x}, healed {1x}. See: TWOT—2196a; BDB—951b.

7500. רִפְאוּת {1x} **riph’ûwth**, *rif-ooth';* from 7495; a *cure:*—health {1x}. See: TWOT—2196b; BDB—951b.

7501. רְפָאֵל {1x} **Rᵉphâʾêl**, *ref-aw-ale';* from 7495 and 410; *God has cured; Rephaël*, an Isr.:—*Rephael* {1x}. See: BDB—951b.

7502. רָפַד {3x} **râphad**, *raw-fad';* a prim. root; to *spread* (a bed); by impl. to *refresh:*—spread {1x}, made {1x}, comfort {1x}. See: TWOT—2197; BDB—951c.

7503. רָפָה {46x} **râphâh**, *raw-faw';* a prim. root; to *slacken* (in many applications, lit. or fig.):—feeble {6x}, fail {4x}, weaken {4x}, go {4x}, alone {4x}, idle {3x}, stay {3x}, slack {3x}, faint {2x}, forsake {2x}, abated {1x}, cease {1x}, misc. {9x} = consume, draw [toward evening], leave, be still, be slothful. See: TWOT—2198; BDB—951c, 952a. See 7495.

7504. רָפֶה {4x} **râpheh**, *raw-feh';* from 7503; *slack* (in body or mind):—weak {4x}. See: TWOT—2198a; BDB—952a.

רָפָה **râphâh, Râphâh.** See 7497, 7498.

רִפָה **riphâh.** See 7383.

7505. רָפוּא {1x} **Râphûʾ**, *raw-foo';* pass. part. of 7495; *cured; Raphu*, an Isr.:—Raphu {1x}. See: BDB—951b.

7506. רֶפַח {1x} **Rephach**, *reh'-fakh;* from an unused root appar. mean. to *sustain; support; Rephach*, an Isr.:—Rephah {1x}. See: BDB—952c.

7507. רְפִידָה {1x} **rᵉphîydâh**, *ref-ee-daw';* from 7502; a *railing* (as spread along):—bottom {1x}. See: TWOT—2197a;BDB—951c.

7508. רְפִידִים {5x} **Rᵉphîydîym**, *ref-ee-deem';* plur. of the masc. of the same as 7507; *ballusters; Rephidim*, a place in the Desert:—Rephidim {5x}. See: BDB—951c.

7509. רְפָיָה {5x} **Rᵉphâyâh**, *ref-aw-yaw';* from 7495 and 3050; *Jah has cured; Rephajah*, the name of five Isr.:—Rephaiah {5x}. See: BDB—951b, 952c.

7510. רִפְיוֹן {1x} **riphyôwn**, *rif-yone';* from 7503; *slackness:*—feebleness {1x}. See: TWOT—2198b; BDB—952a, 952c.

7511. רָפַס {2x} **râphaç**, *raw-fas';* a prim. root; to *trample*, i.e. *prostrate:*—humble thyself {1x}, submit thyself {1x}. See: TWOT—2199; BDB—952c, 952d, 1113b.

7512. רְפַס {2x} **rᵉphaç** (Aram.), *ref-as';* corresp. to 7511:—stamp {2x}. See: TWOT—3001; BDB—1113b.

7513. רַפְסֹדָה {1x} **raphçôdâh**, *raf-so-daw';* from 7511; a *raft* (as *flat* on the water):—flote {1x}. See: TWOT—2200; BDB—952c.

7514. רָפַק {1x} **râphaq**, *raw-fak';* a prim. root; to *recline:*—lean {1x}. See: TWOT—2202; BDB—952d.

7515. רָפַשׂ {3x} **râphas**, *raw-fas';* a prim. root; to *trample*, i.e. *roil* water:—foul {2x}, trouble {1x}. See: TWOT—2199; BDB—952c, 952d.

7516. רֶפֶשׁ {1x} **rephesh**, *reh'-fesh;* from 7515; *mud* (as *roiled*):—mire {1x}. See: TWOT—2203a; BDB—952d.

7517. רֶפֶת {1x} **repheth**, *reh'-feth;* prob. from 7503; a *stall* for cattle (from their *resting* there):—stall {1x}. See: TWOT—2204; BDB—952d.

7518. רָץ {1x} **rats**, *rats;* contr. from 7533; a *fragment:*—piece {1x}. See: TWOT—2212a; BDB—952d, 954d.

7519. רָצָא {1x} **râtsâʾ**, *raw-tsaw';* a prim. root; to *run;* also to *delight* in:—run {1x}. See: TWOT—2205; BDB—952d.

7520. רָצַד {1x} **râtsad**, *raw-tsad';* a prim. root; prob. to *look askant*, i.e. (fig.) be *jealous:*—leap {1x}. See: TWOT—2206; BDB—952d.

7521. רָצָה {57x} **râtsâh**, *raw-tsaw';* a prim. root; to *be pleased with;* spec. to *satisfy* a debt:—accept {22x}, please {6x}, pleasure {6x}, delight {5x}, enjoy {4x}, favourable {3x}, acceptable {1x}, accomplish {1x}, affection {1x}, approve {1x}, misc. {7x} = consent with, like, observe, pardon, reconcile self.

Ratsah, the verb, means to be pleased with or favorable to (Gen 33:10), be delighted with, be pleased to make friends with; be graciously received; make oneself favored. **(1)** It is evident that by the Divine acceptance is to be understood the pleasure with which God welcomes into personal contact with Himself those who approach Him in His own appointed way, and in a spirit cognate to His own. **(2)** An evildoer, as such, is not acceptable to God even though he offers sacrifices. He must be sheltered by atonement, and must have the germ at least of a Divine life working in him if he would be regarded by God with pleasure. **(3)** When God is pleased with someone, it is translated "to be delighted," which seems to reflect a sense of greater pleasure (Is 42:1). **(4)** When one must merit *ratsah*, it is translated with "to please" or "to accept" (Mic 6:7; Amos 5:22). **(4)** *Ratsah* can be used in the sense of "to pay for" or "to satisfy a debt," especially as it relates to land lying fallow in the sabbath years (Lev 26:34). Syn.: 977, 2656, 5375, 7613. See: TWOT—2207; BDB—952d, 953a.

7522. רָצוֹן {56x} **râtsôwn**, *raw-tsone'*; or

רָצֹן **râtsôn**, *raw-tsone'*; from 7521; *delight* (espec. as shown):—favour {15x}, will {14x}, acceptable {8x}, delight {5x}, pleasure {5x}, accepted {4x}, desire {3x}, acceptance {1x}, selfwill {1x}.

Ratson means "favor; goodwill; acceptance; will; desire; pleasure." **(1)** *Ratson* represents a concrete reaction of the superior to an inferior. **(1a)** When used of God, *ratson* may represent that which is shown in His blessings: "And for the precious things of the earth and fullness thereof, and for the good will of him that dwelt in the bush" (Deut 33:16). **(1b)** Thus Isaiah speaks of the day, year, or time of divine "favor"—in other words, the day of the Lord when all the blessings of the covenant shall be heaped upon God's people (Is 49:8; 58:5; 61:2). **(2)** In wisdom literature, this word is used in the sense of "what men can bestow": **(2a)** "He that diligently seeketh good procureth favor: but he that seeketh mischief, it shall come unto him" (Prov 11:27). **(2b)** In Prov 14:35, *ratson* refers to what a king can or will do for someone he likes. **(3)** This word represents the position one enjoys before a superior who is favorably disposed toward him. **(3a)** This nuance is used only of God and frequently in a cultic [religious worship] context: "And it [the plate engraved with "holy to the Lord"] shall be always upon his [the high priest's] forehead, that they may be accepted before the Lord" (Ex 28:38). **(3b)** Being "accepted" means that God subjectively feels well disposed toward the petitioner. **(4)** *Ratson* also signifies a voluntary or arbitrary decision. **(4a)** Ezra told the people of Israel to do the "will" of God, to repent and observe the law of Moses (Ezra 10:11). **(4b)** This law was dictated by God's own nature; His nature led Him to be concerned for the physical well-being of His people. **(4c)** Ultimately, His laws were highly personal; they were simply what God wanted His people to be and do. Thus the psalmist confessed his delight in doing God's "will," or His law (Ps 40:8). **(5)** When a man does according to his own "will," he does "what he desires": "I saw the ram pushing westward, and northward, and southward; so that no beasts might stand before him, neither was there any that could deliver out of his hand; but he did according to his will and became great" (Dan 8:4). **(6)** In Ps 145:16, the word *ratson* means "one's desire" or "what one wants" (cf. Est 1:8). **(7)** This emphasis is found in Gen 49:6 (the first occurrence): "And in their self-will they [brought disaster upon themselves]." See: TWOT—2207a; BDB—953c.

7523. רָצַח {47x} **râtsach**, *raw-tsakh'*; a prim. root; prop. to *dash* in pieces, i.e.

kill (a human being), espec. to *murder*:—slayer {16x}, murderer {14x}, kill {5x}, murder {3x}, slain {3x}, manslayer {2x}, killing {1x}, slayer + 310 {1x}, slayeth {1x}, death {1x}.

Ratsach means "to kill, murder, slay." **(1)** This verb occurs 47 times in the Old Testament, and its concentration is in the Pentateuch. **(2)** *Ratsach* occurs primarily in the legal material of the Old Testament. **(2a)** This is not a surprise, as God's law included regulations on life and provisions for dealing with the murderer. **(2b)** The Decalogue gives the general principle in a simple statement, which contains the first occurrence of the verb: "Thou shalt not kill [murder]" (Ex 20:13). **(3)** Another provision pertains to the penalty: "Whoso killeth any person, the murderer shall be put to death by the mouth of witnesses" (Num 35:30). However, before a person is put to death, he is assured of a trial.

(4) The Old Testament recognizes the distinction between premeditated murder and unintentional killing. **(4a)** In order to assure the rights of the manslayer, who unintentionally killed someone, the law provided for three cities of refuge (Num 35; Deut 19; Josh 20; 21) on either side of the Jordan, to which a manslayer might flee and seek asylum: ". . . that the slayer may flee thither, which killeth any person at unawares" (Num 35:11). **(4b)** The provision gave the manslayer access to the court system, for he might be "killed" by the blood avenger if he stayed within his own community (Num 35:21). **(4c)** He is to be tried (Num 35:12), and **(4d)** if he is found to be guilty of unintentional manslaughter, he is required to stay in the city of refuge until the death of the high priest (Num 35:28). **(4e)** The severity of the act of murder is stressed in the requirement of exile even in the case of unintentional murder. **(4f)** The man guilty of manslaughter is to be turned over to the avenger of blood, who keeps the right of killing the manslayer if the manslayer goes outside the territory of the city of refuge before the death of the high priest. **(4g)** On the other hand, if the manslayer is chargeable with premeditated murder (examples of which are given in Num 35:16–21), the blood avenger may execute the murderer without a trial. **(4h)** In this way the Old Testament underscores the principles of the sanctity of life and of retribution; only in the cities of refuge is the principle of retribution suspended.

(5) The prophets use *ratsach* to describe the effect of injustice and lawlessness in Israel: ". . . because there is no truth, nor mercy, nor knowledge of God in the land. By swearing, and lying, and killing, and stealing, and committing adultery . . ." (Hos 4:1–2; cf. Is 1:21; Jer 7:9). **(6)** The psalmist, too, metaphorically

expresses the deprivation of the rights of help-less murder victims: "They slay the widow and the stranger, and murder the fatherless" (Ps 94:6). **(7)** The KJV gives these senses: "kill; murder; be put to death; be slain." Syn.: 2026, 7819. See: TWOT—2208; BDB—953d.

7524. רֶצַח {2x} **retsach**, *reh-tsakh;* from 7523; a *crushing;* spec. a *murder*-cry:—slaughter {1x}, sword {1x}. See: TWOT—2208a; BDB—954a.

7525. רִצְיָא {1x} **Ritsyâ**, *rits-yaw';* from 7521; *delight; Ritsjah,* an Isr.:—Rezia {1x}. See: BDB—954a.

7526. רְצִין {11x} **Rᵉtsîyn**, *rets-een';* prob. for 7522; *Retsin,* the name of a Syrian and of an Isr.:—Rezin {11x}. See: BDB—954a.

7527. רָצַע {1x} **râtsaʿ**, *raw-tsah';* a prim. root; to *pierce:*—bore {1x}. See: TWOT—2209; BDB—954a.

7528. רָצַף {1x} **râtsaph**, *raw-tsaf';* a denom. from 7529; to *tessellate,* i.e. embroider (as if with bright stones):—pave {1x}. See: TWOT—2210; BDB—954b.

7529. רֶצֶף {1x} **retseph**, *reh'-tsef;* for 7565; a red-hot *stone* (for baking):—coals {1x}. See: TWOT—2223a; BDB—954b, 954c.

7530. רֶצֶף {2x} **Retseph**, *reh'-tsef;* the same as 7529; *Retseph,* a place in Ass.:—Rezeph {2x}. See: BDB—954b.

7531. רִצְפָּה {8x} **ritspâh**, *rits-paw';* fem. of 7529; a hot *stone;* also a tessellated *pavement:*—live coal {1x}, pavement {1x}. See: TWOT—2210a, 2211a; BDB—954b, 954c.

7532. רִצְפָּה {4x} **Ritspâh**, *rits-paw';* the same as 7531; *Ritspah,* an Israelitess:—Rizpah {4x}. See: BDB—954c.

7533. רָצַץ **râtsats**, *raw-tsats';* a prim. root; to *crack* in pieces, lit. or fig.:—oppressed {6x}, broken {4x}, break {3x}, bruised {2x}, crush {2x}, discouraged {1x}, struggle together {1x}. See: TWOT—2212; BDB—930d, 954c, 1113b.

7534. רַק {3x} **raq**, *rak;* from 7556 in its orig. sense; *emaciated* (as if *flattened* out):—lean {1x}, thin {1x}, leanfleshed + 1320 {1x}. See: TWOT—2218a; BDB—954d, 956b.

7535. רַק **raq**, *rak;* the same as 7534 as a noun; prop. *leanness,* i.e. (fig.) *limitation;* only adv. *merely,* or conjunc. *although:*—but {1x}, even {1x}, except {1x}, howbeit {1x}, howsoever {1x}, nevertheless {1x}, nothing but {1x}, notwithstanding {1x}, only {1x}, save {1x}, so {1x}, so that {1x}, surely {1x}, yet {1x}, yet so {1x}, in any wise {1x}. See: TWOT—2218a; BDB—954d, 956b.

7536. רֹק {3x} **rôq**, *roke;* from 7556; *spittle:*—spit {1x}, spitting {1x}, spittle {1x}. See: TWOT—2219a; BDB—954d, 956d.

7537. רָקַב {2x} **râqab**, *raw-kab';* a prim. root; to *decay* (as by worm-eating):—rot {2x}. See: TWOT—2213; BDB—955a.

7538. רָקָב {5x} **râqâb**, *raw-kawb';* from 7537; *decay* (by *caries):*—rottenness {4x}, rotten thing {1x}. See: TWOT—2213a; BDB—955a.

7539. רִקָּבוֹן {1x} **riqqâbôwn**, *rik-kaw-bone';* from 7538; *decay* (by *caries):*—rotten {1x}. See: TWOT—2213b; BDB—955a.

7540. רָקַד {9x} **râqad**, *raw-kad';* a prim. root; prop. to *stamp,* i.e. to *spring* about (wildly or for joy):—dance {4x}, skip {3x}, leap {1x}, jump {1x}. See: TWOT—2214; BDB—955a.

7541. רַקָּה {5x} **raqqâh**, *rak-kaw';* fem. of 7534; prop. *thinness,* i.e. the *side* of the head:—temple {5x}. See: TWOT—2218c; BDB—955b, 956d.

7542. רַקּוֹן {1x} **Raqqôwn**, *rak-kone';* from 7534; *thinness; Rakkon,* a place in Pal.:—Rakkon {1x}. See: BDB—955b, 956d.

7543. רָקַח {8x} **râqach**, *raw-kakh';* a prim. root; to *perfume:*—apothecary {4x}, compound {1x}, make ointment {1x}, prepare {1x}, spice {1x}. See: TWOT—2215; BDB—955b.

7544. רֶקַח {1x} **reqach**, *reh'-kakh;* from 7543; prop. *perfumery,* i.e. (by impl.) *spicery* (for flavor):—spiced {1x}. See: TWOT—2215a; BDB—955b.

7545. רֹקַח {2x} **rôqach**, *ro'-kakh;* from 7542; an *aromatic:*—confection {1x}, ointment {1x}. See: TWOT—2215b; BDB—955b.

7546. רַקָּח {1x} **raqqâch**, *rak-kawkh';* from 7543; a male *perfumer:*—apothecaries {1x}. See: TWOT—2215c; BDB—955c.

7547. רַקֻּחַ {1x} **raqqûach**, *rak-koo'-akh;* from 7543; a *scented* substance:—perfume {1x}. See: TWOT—2215e; BDB—955c.

7548. רַקָּחָה {1x} **raqqâchâh**, *rak-kaw-khaw';* fem. of 7547; a female *perfumer:*—confectionaries {1x}. See: TWOT—2215d; BDB—955c.

7549. רָקִיעַ {17x} **râqîyaʿ**, *raw-kee'-ah;* from 7554; prop. an *expanse,* i.e. the *firmament* or (appar.) visible arch of the sky:—firmament {17x}.

(1) *Raqiya* means that which is fixed and steadfast, rather than that which is solid. **(1a)** The application to the heavenly bodies is

simple and beautiful: **(1b)** they are not fickle and uncertain in their movements, but are regulated by a law that they cannot pass over. **(2)** It comes from *raqa* (7554) which means spread out. The firmament, then, is that which is spread or stretched out—hence an expanse. Thus it is extended and fixed, or fixed space. **(3)** The interplanetary spaces are measured out by God, and though the stars are ever moving, they generally preserve fixed relative positions; their movements are not erratic, not in straight lines, but in orbits, and thus, though ever changing, they are always the same. See: TWOT—2217a; BDB—956a.

7550. רָקִיק {8x} **râqîyq,** *raw-keek';* from 7556 in its orig. sense; a thin *cake:*—cake {1x}, wafer {7x}. See: TWOT—2218b; BDB—956d.

7551. רָקַם {9x} **râqam,** *raw-kam';* a prim. root; to *variegate* color, i.e. *embroider;* by impl. to *fabricate:*—needlework + 4639 {4x}, needlework {2x}, embroiderer {2x}, curiously wrought {1x}.

7552. רֶקֶם {6x} **Reqem,** *reh'-kem;* from 7551; *versi-color; Rekem,* the name of a place in Pal., also of a Midianite and an Isr.:—Rekem {6x}. See: BDB—955d.

7553. רִקְמָה {12x} **riqmâh,** *rik-maw';* from 7551; *variegation* of color; spec. *embroidery:*—broidered work {5x}, needlework {3x}, divers colours {2x}, broidered {2x}. See: TWOT—2216a; BDB—955d.

7554. רָקַע {11x} **râqa⁽,** *raw-kah';* a prim. root; to *pound* the earth (as a sign of passion); by anal. to *expand* (by hammering); by impl. to *overlay* (with thin sheets of metal):—spread . . . {6x}, stamp {2x}, stretch {1x}, beat {1x}, made broad {1x}. See: TWOT—2217; BDB—955d. See 7549 for discussion of the firmament.

7555. רִקֻּעַ {1x} **riqqûa⁽,** *rik-koo'-ah;* from 7554; *beaten* out, i.e. a (metallic) *plate:*—broad {1x}. See: TWOT—2217b; BDB—956b.

7556. רָקַק {1x} **râqaq,** *raw-kak';* a prim. root; to *spit:*—spit {1x}. See: TWOT—2219; BDB—956d.

7557. רַקַּת {1x} **Raqqath,** *rak-kath';* from 7556 in its orig. sense of *diffusing;* a *beach* (as *expanded* shingle); *Rakkath,* a place in Pal.:—Rakkath {1x}. See: BDB—957a.

7558. רִשְׁיוֹן {1x} **rîshyôwn,** *rish-yone';* from an unused root mean. to *have leave;* a *permit:*—grant {1x}. See: TWOT—2220a; BDB—957a.

7559. רָשַׁם {1x} **râsham,** *raw-sham';* a prim. root; to *record:*—note {1x}. See: TWOT—2221; BDB—957a, 1113b.

7560. רְשַׁם {7x} **r⁽sham** (Aram.), *resh-am';* corresp. to 7559:—sign {5x}, write {2x}. See: TWOT—3002; BDB—1113b.

7561. רָשַׁע {34x} **râsha⁽,** *raw-shah';* a prim. root; to *be* (caus. *do* or *declare*) *wrong;* by impl. to *disturb, violate:*—condemn {15x}, wickedly {10x}, wicked {4x}, departed {2x}, trouble {1x}, vexed {1x}, wickedness {1x}.

(1) This verb appears in 2 Chr 6:37: "Yet if they bethink themselves in the land whither they are carried captive, and turn and pray unto thee in the land of their captivity, saying, We have sinned, we have done amiss, and have dealt wickedly." **(2)** This word means to deal with or account as wicked. Syn.: 8199. See: TWOT—2222; BDB—957d.

7562. רֶשַׁע {30x} **resha⁽,** *reh'-shah;* from 7561; a *wrong* (espec. moral):—iniquity {1x}, wicked {4x}, wickedness {25x}.

Resha', found 30 times, usually means "wickedness": "Remember thy servants, Abraham, Isaac, and Jacob; look not unto the stubborness of this people, nor to their wickedness (*resha'*), nor to their sin" (Deut 9:27). See: TWOT—2222a; BDB—957c.

7563. רָשָׁע {263x} **râshâ⁽,** *raw-shaw';* from 7561; morally *wrong;* concr. an (actively) *bad* person:—wicked {249x}, ungodly {8x}, wicked man {3x}, misc. {3x} = + condemned, guilty, that did wrong.

I. *Rasha'*, as a noun, means "wicked; ungodly; guilty." **(1)** The narrow meaning of *rasha'* lies in the concept of "wrongdoing" or "being in the wrong." **(1a)** It is a legal term. **(1b)** *Rasha'* means wicked; guilty enough to deserve punishment (Deut 25:2), and maybe even death (2 Sa 4:11; cf. Eze 3:18–19). **(1c)** *Rasha'* generally connotes a turbulence and restlessness (cf. Is 57:21) or something disjointed or ill-regulated; thus suggesting that it refers to the tossing and confusion in which the wicked live, and to the perpetual agitation they cause to others. **(2)** In some instances, *rasha'* carries the sense of being "guilty of crime": **(2a)** "Thou shalt not raise a false report: put not thine hand with the wicked to be an unrighteous witness" (Ex 23:1). **(2b)** "Take away the wicked from before the king, and his throne shall be established in righteousness" (Prov 25:5). **(2c)** "An ungodly witness scorneth judgment: and the mouth of the wicked [plural form] devoureth iniquity" (Prov 19:28; cf. Prov 20:26). **(3)** Justifying the "wicked" is classed as a heinous crime: "He that justifieth the wicked, and he that condemneth the just, even they both

Hebrew

are abomination to the Lord" (Prov 17:15; cf. Ex 23:7).

(4) The *rasha'* is guilty of hostility to God and His people: **(4a)** "Arise, O Lord, disappoint him, cast him down: deliver my soul from the wicked, which is thy sword" (Ps 17:13); "**(4b)** Oh let the wickedness of the wicked [plural form] come to an end; but establish the just" (Ps 7:9). **(5)** The word is applied to the people **(5a)** of Babylon in Is 13:11 and **(5b)** to the Chaldeans in Hab 1:13. **(6)** The *rasha'* is guilty of hostility to God and His people (Ex 9:27; Ps 17:13). **(7)** Its narrow meaning—a legal term asserting one has sinned against the law—lies in the concept of wrongdoing or being in the wrong (Prov 28:4). **(8)** When in Israel's history justice did not prevail, the guilty were acquitted (Prov 29:2; cf. 2 Chr 6:23). **(9)** Its more general meaning denotes the category of people who have done wrong, are still living in sin, and are intent on continuing with wrongdoing (Ps 10:4). **(9a)** He challenges God (Ps 10:13), **(9b)** loves violence (Ps 11:5), **(9c)** oppresses the righteous (Ps 17:9), **(9d)** does not repay his debts (Ps 37:21), and **(9e)** lays a snare to trap the righteous (Ps 119:110). **(9f)** Ps 37 gives a vivid description of the acts of the wicked and also of God's judgment upon them.

(10) Facing the terrible force of the wicked, the righteous prayed for God's deliverance and for His judgment upon them (Ps 1:6). **(10a)** The expectation of the righteous includes God's judgment on the wicked in this life that they might **(10a1)** be ashamed (Ps 31:17), **(10a2)** be overcome by sorrows (Ps 32:10), **(10a3)** fall by their devices (Ps 141:10), **(10a4)** die a premature death (Prov 10:27), and **(10a5)** that their remembrance will be no more (Prov 10:7). **(10b)** It is expected that at the time of their death there will be great shouting (Prov 11:10). **(11)** In the typical example of Deut 25:2, this word refers to a person "guilty of a crime": **(11a)** "And it shall be, if the wicked man be worthy to be beaten, that the judge shall cause him . . . to be beaten." **(11b)** A similar reference appears in Jer 5:26: "For among my people are found wicked [plural form] men: they lay wait, as he that setteth snares; they set a trap, they catch men." **(12)** *Rasha'* is used specifically of murderers in 2 Sa 4:11: **(12a)** "How much more, when wicked men have slain a righteous person in his own house upon his bed?" **(12b)** The expression "guilty of death" (*rasha' lamut*) occurs in Num 35:31 and is applied to a murderer.

(13) Pharaoh and his people are portrayed as "wicked" people guilty of hostility to God and His people (Ex 9:27). **(14)** The person who has sinned against the law is guilty: "They that forsake the law praise the wicked: but such as keep the law contend with them" (Prov 28:4).

(15) The judgment upon the "wicked" is particularly strong in Proverbs, where the author contrasts the advantages of wisdom and righteousness and the disadvantages of the "wicked" (cf. 2:22: "But the wicked shall be cut off from the earth, and the transgressors shall be rooted out of it"). **(16)** In Job another theme finds expression: why are the "wicked" not cut off? "Wherefore do the wicked live, become old, yea, are mighty in power?" (21:7). There is no clear answer to this question in the Old Testament. **(17)** Malachi predicts a new age in which the distinction of the righteous and the "wicked" will be clear and where the righteous will triumph: "Then shall ye return, and discern between the righteous and the wicked, between him that serveth God and him that seeth him not" (Mal 3:18).

II. Rasha', as an adjective, means "wicked; guilty." **(1)** In some cases a person is so guilty that he deserves death: "If the wicked man worthy to be beaten, that the judge shall cause him to lie down, and to be beaten before his face . . . by a certain number" (Deut 25:2). **(2)** The characteristics of a "wicked" person qualify him as a godless, impious man: "How much more, when wicked men have slain a righteous person in his own house upon his bed? shall I not therefore now require his blood of your hand, and take you away from the earth?" (2 Sa 4:11; cf. Eze 3:18–19). Syn.: 7562, 7564. See: TWOT—2222b; BDB—957b.

7564. רִשְׁעָה {15x} **rish‘âh**, *rish-aw'*; fem. of 7562; *wrong* (espec. moral):— fault {1x}, wickedly {1x}, wickedness {13x}.

Rish'ah, which appears 15 times, refers to "wickedness" or "guilt": "For my righteousness the Lord hath brought me in to possess this land: but for the wickedness of these nations the Lord doth drive them out from before thee" (Deut 9:4). See: TWOT—2222c; BDB—957d, 958a.

7565. רֶשֶׁף {7x} **resheph**, *reh'-shef;* from 8313; a live *coal;* by anal. *lightning;* fig. an *arrow,* (as *flashing* through the air); spec. *fever:*—coals {2x}, burning coals {1x}, burning heat {1x}, spark {1x}, arrow {1x}, hot thunderbolt {1x}. See: TWOT—2223a; BDB—958b.

7566. רֶשֶׁף {1x} **Resheph**, *reh'-shef;* the same as 7565; *Resheph,* an Isr.:—Resheph {1x}. See: BDB—958b.

7567. רָשַׁשׁ {2x} **râshash**, *raw-shash';* a prim. root; to *demolish:*—impoverish {2x}. See: TWOT—2224; BDB—930d, 958b.

7568. רֶשֶׁת {20x} **resheth**, *reh'-sheth;* from 3423; a *net* (as *catching* animals):—net {20x}, network + 4639 {1x}. See: TWOT—920c; BDB—440b, 958b.

7569. רַתּוֹק {1x} **rattôwq**, *rat-toke'*; from 7576; a *chain*:—chain {1x}. See: TWOT—2227b; BDB—958d.

7570. רָתַח {3x} **râthach**, *raw-thakh'*; a prim. root; to *boil*:—boil {3x}. See: TWOT—2225; BDB—958b.

7571. רֶתַח {1x} **rethach**, *reh'-thakh*; from 7570; a *boiling*:—✕ [boil] well {1x}. See: TWOT—2225a; BDB—958c.

7572. רַתִּיקָה {2x} **rattîyqâh**, *rat-tee-kaw'*; from 7576; a *chain*:—chain {2x}. See: TWOT—2227b; BDB—958d.

7573. רָתַם {1x} **râtham**, *raw-tham'*; a prim. root; to *yoke* up (to the pole of a vehicle):—bind {1x}. See: TWOT—2226; BDB—958c.

7574. רֶתֶם {4x} **rethem**, *reh'-them*; or

רֹתֶם **rôthem**, *ro'-them*; from 7573; the Spanish *broom* (from its pole-like stems):—juniper {2x}, juniper tree {2x}. See: TWOT—2226a; BDB—958c.

7575. רִתְמָה {2x} **Rithmâh**, *rith-maw'*; fem. of 7574; *Rithmah*, a place in the desert:—*Rithmah* {2x}. See: BDB—958c.

7576. רָתַק {2x} **râthaq**, *raw-thak'*; a prim. root; to *fasten*:—loose {1x}, bound {1x}. See: TWOT—2227; BDB—958d.

7577. רְתוּקָה {1x} **rᵉthûqâh**, *reth-oo-kaw'*; fem. pass. part. of 7576; something *fastened*, i.e. a *chain*:—chain {1x}. See: TWOT—2227a; BDB—958d.

7578. רְתֵת {1x} **rᵉthêth**, *reth-ayth'*; for 7374; *terror*:—trembling {1x}. See: TWOT—2228a; BDB—958d.

ש

7579. שָׁאַב {19x} **shâ'ab**, *sahw-ab'*; a prim. root; to *bale* up water:—draw {15x}, drawer {4x}. See: TWOT—2299.1; BDB—980b.

7580. שָׁאַג {21x} **shâ'ag**, *shaw-ag'*; a prim. root; to *rumble* or *moan*:—roar {20x}, mightily {1x}. See: TWOT—2300; BDB—980c.

7581. שְׁאָגָה {7x} **shᵉâgâh**, *sheh-aw-gaw'*; from 7580; a *rumbling* or *moan*:—roaring {7x}. See: TWOT—2300a; BDB—980d.

7582. שָׁאָה {6x} **shâ'âh**, *shaw-aw'*; a prim. root; to *rush*; by impl. to *desolate*:—lay waste {2x}, rushing {2x}, waste {1x}, desolate {1x}. See: TWOT—2301; BDB—980d.

7583. שָׁאָה {1x} **shâ'âh**, *shaw-aw'*; a prim. root [rather ident. with 7582 through the idea of *whirling* to giddiness]; to *stun*, i.e. (intr.) be *astonished*:—wondering + 8693 {1x}. See: TWOT—2302; BDB—981b.

7584. שַׁאֲוָה {1x} **sha'ăvâh**, *shah-av-aw'*; from 7582; a *tempest* (as *rushing*):—desolation {1x}. See: TWOT—2301a; BDB—981a.

7585. שְׁאוֹל {65x} **shᵉôwl**, *sheh-ole'*; or

שְׁאֹל **shᵉôl**, *sheh-ole'*; from 7592; *hades* or the *world of the dead* (as if a subterranean *retreat*), incl. its accessories and inmates:—grave {31x}, hell {31x}, pit {3x}.

Sheol is the abode of the dead, a place of degradation, the locality or condition of those who have died or have been destroyed. It is implied that although, so far as the world is concerned, they have perished, yet they are still in a state of existence and are within God's cognizance. **(1)** *She'ol* is the place of the dead. It refers to the underground cavern to which all buried dead go. **(2)** It was not understood to be a place of punishment, but simply the ultimate resting place of all mankind (Gen 37:35). **(3)** Thus, it was thought to be the land of no return (Job 16:22; 17:14–16). **(4)** It was a place to be dreaded, not only because it meant the end of physical life on earth, but also because there was no praise of God there (Ps 6:5). **(5)** Deliverance from going there was a blessing (Ps 30:3). **(6)** Everything about *she'ol* was negative. **(6a)** First, there is the tomb or sepulcher; the local habitation of the physical frame called *qeber* (6913). **(6b)** Secondly, there is the corruption whereby the body itself is dissolved, which is represented by the word *shachath* (7843); and **(6b)** thirdly, there is *sheol*, the locality or condition of the departed.

(7) *Sheol* is the netherworld. **(8)** It is not used in one single passage for punishment after the resurrection. **(9)** It is contrasted, in regards to locality, with heaven, the one being regarded as down and the other up. **(10)** It is spoken of as an abode for those who have departed from the way of life and have chosen the path of evil. **(11)** It involves deprivation of the only kind of existence about which we have any definite knowledge, but some passages where it occurs imply a certain companionship. **(12)** Though man knows so little about it, *sheol* is naked and open before God. He can find men there; He can hide them there; He can redeem them thence. Syn.: 6, 2011 + 1516. See: TWOT—2303c; BDB—982c, 982d.

7586. שָׁאוּל {406x} **Shâ'ûwl**, *shaw-ool'*; pass. part. of 7592; *asked*; *Shaül*, the

name of an Edomite and two Isr.:—Saul {399x}, Shaul {7x}. See: BDB—982b.

7587. שָׁאוּלִי {1x} **Shâʾûwlîy**, shaw-oo-lee'; patron. from 7856; a Shaülite or desc. of Shaul:—Shaulites {1x}. See: BDB—982c.

7588. שָׁאוֹן {17x} **shâʾôwn**, shaw-one'; from 7582; uproar (as of rushing); by impl. destruction:—noise {8x}, tumult {3x}, tumultuous {2x}, rushing {2x}, horrible {1x}, pomp {1x}. See: TWOT—2301c; BDB—981a.

7589. שְׁאָט {3x} **sheʾât**, sheh-awt'; from an unused root mean. to push aside; contempt:—despiteful {2x}, despite {1x}. See: TWOT—2345a; BDB—981b, 1002b.

7590. שָׁאט {3x} **shâʾt**, shawt; for act. part of 7750 [comp. 7589]; one contemning:—despise {3x}. See: TWOT—2345; BDB—1002b.

7591. שְׁאִיָּה {1x} **sheʾîyâh**, sheh-ee-yaw'; from 7582; desolation:—destruction {1x}. See: TWOT—2301b; BDB—981a, 981b.

7592. שָׁאל {173x} **shâʾal**, shaw-al'; or

שָׁאֵל **shâʾêl**, shaw-ale'; a prim. root; to inquire; by impl. to request; by extens. to demand:—ask {94x}, enquire {22x}, desire {9x}, require {7x}, borrow {6x}, salute {4x}, demand {4x}, lent {4x}, request {3x}, earnestly {2x}, beg {2x}, misc. {16x} = lay to charge, consult, + greet, obtain leave, pray, X straitly, X surely, wish.

Sha'el means to ask, inquire, consult. **(1)** It is commonly used for simple requests (Judg 5:25). **(2)** Sha'el is sometimes used in the sense of praying for something (Ps 122:6). **(3)** "To ask another of his welfare" carries the sense of a greeting (Ex 18:7; Judg 18:15; 1 Sa 10:4). **(4)** Frequently, it is used to indicate someone's asking for God's direction or counsel (Josh 9:14; Is 30:2). **(5)** In Ps 109:10 it is used to indicate begging. Syn.: 577, 6279, 6419, 6739. See: TWOT—2303; BDB—981b, 1114a.

7593. שְׁאֵל {6x} **sheʾêl** (Aram.), sheh-ale'; corresp. to 7592:—ask {3x}, require {2x}, demand {1x}. See: TWOT—3012; BDB—1114a.

7594. שְׁאָל {1x} **Sheʾâl**, sheh-awl'; from 7592; request; Sheal, an Isr.:—Sheal {1x}. See: BDB—982b.

שְׁאֹל **sheʾôl**. See 7585.

7595. שְׁאֵלָא {1x} **sheʾêlâ** (Aram.), sheh-ay-law'; from 7593; prop. a question (at law), i.e. judicial decision or mandate:—demand {1x}. See: TWOT—3012a; BDB—1114a.

7596. שְׁאֵלָה {14x} **sheʾêlâh**, sheh-ay-law'; or

שֵׁלָה **shêlâh** (1 Sa 1:17), shay-law'; from 7592; a petition; by impl. a loan:—petition {10x}, request {3x}, loan {1x}. See: TWOT—2303a; BDB—982c, 1017c, 1115c.

7597. שְׁאַלְתִּיאֵל {9x} **Sheʾaltîyʾêl**, sheh-al-tee-ale'; or

שַׁלְתִּיאֵל **Shaltîyʾêl**, shal-tee-ale'; from 7592 and 410; I have asked God; Sheältiël, an Isr.:—Shealtiel {8x}, Salathiel {1x}. See: BDB—982c, 1027a.

7598. שְׁאַלְתִּיאֵל {1x} **Sheʾaltîyʾêl** (Aram.), sheh-al-tee-ale'; corresp. to 7597:—Shealtiel {1x}. See: BDB—982d.

7599. שָׁאן {5x} **shâʾan**, shaw-an'; a prim. root; to loll, i.e. be peaceful:—at ease {2x}, quiet {2x}, rest {1x}. See: TWOT—2304; BDB—983b. See also 1052.

7600. שַׁאֲנָן {10x} **shaʾănân**, shah-an-awn'; from 7599; secure; in a bad sense, haughty:—ease {6x}, quiet {2x}, tumult {2x}. See: TWOT—2304a; BDB—983b. comp. 7946.

7601. שָׁאַס {1x} **shâʾaç**, shaw-as'; a prim. root; to plunder:—spoil {1x}. See: TWOT—2426; BDB—983c.

7602. שָׁאַף {14x} **shâʾaph**, shaw-af'; a prim. root; to inhale eagerly; fig. to covet; by impl. to be angry; also to hasten:—swallow up {6x}, snuff up {2x}, pant {2x}, earnestly desire {1x}, desire {1x}, devour {1x}, hast {1x}. See: TWOT—2305, 2306; BDB—983c.

7603. שְׂאֹר {5x} **seʾôr**, seh-ore'; from 7604; barm or yeast-cake (as swelling by fermentation):—leaven {5x}. See: TWOT—2229a; BDB—959a.

7604. שָׁאַר {133x} **shâʾar**, shaw-ar'; a prim. root; prop. to swell up, i.e. be (caus. make) redundant:—leave {75x}, remain {46x}, remnant {4x}, let {3x}, rest {2x}, misc. {3x} = (be) left, reserve.

(1) Noah and his family were a remnant delivered through the Flood (Gen 7:23). **(2)** Seven thousand remained true to God during the days of Elijah (1 Kin 19:18). **(3)** Remants were considered holy (Is 4:3). **(4)** The doctrine of the remnant was revealed early in Israel's history by Moses (Deut 4:27; 28:62). **(5)** Conditions for the remnant were not always ideal (Neh 1:2–3). See: TWOT—2307, 2308; BDB—983d.

7605. שְׁאָר {26x} **sheʾâr**, sheh-awr'; from 7604; a remainder:—remnant {11x}, rest {10x}, residue {4x}, other {1x}.

(1) Isaiah characterizes the remnant of Israel (Is 10:20). **(2)** He also describes the twofold theme which emerges from most prophetic

passages concerning the remnant: **(2a)** A remnant will survive when the people are subjected to punishment, and **(2b)** the fact that a remnant does survive and does remain contains a note of hope for the future (Is 10:20–21; 11:11). See: TWOT—2307a; BDB—984b, 1114b.

7606. שְׁאָר {12x} **shᵉâr** (Aram.), *sheh-awr';* corresp. to 7605:—rest {9x}, residue {2x}, rest {1x}. See: TWOT—3013; BDB—1114b.

7607. שְׁאֵר {16x} **shᵉêr**, *sheh-ayr';* from 7604; *flesh* (as *swelling* out), as living or for food; gen. *food* of any kind; fig. *kindred* by blood:—flesh {7x}, near kinswoman {2x}, food {1x}, near {1x}, nigh {1x}, near kin {1x}, kin {1x}, body {1x}, kinsman {1x}. See: TWOT—2308a; BDB—984d, 985a.

7608. שַׁאֲרָה {1x} **shaʾărâh**, *shah-ar-aw';* fem. of 7607; *female kindred* by blood:—near kinswomen {1x}. See: TWOT—2308a; BDB—985a.

7609. שֶׁאֱרָה {1x} **Shᵉʾĕrâh**, *sheh-er-aw';* the same as 7608; *Sheërah*, an Israelitess:—Sherah {1x}. See: BDB—985a.

7610. שְׁאָר יָשׁוּב {1x} **Shᵉâr Yâshûwb**, *sheh-awr' yaw-shoob';* from 7605 and 7725; *a remnant will return; Shear-Jashub*, the symbol. name of one of Isaiah's sons:—Shearjashub {1x}. See: BDB—984c, 1000b.

7611. שְׁאֵרִית {1x} **shᵉêrîyth**, *sheh-ay-reeth';* from 7604; a *remainder* or residual (surviving, final) portion:—remnant {44x}, residue {13x}, rest {3x}, remainder {2x}, escaped {1x}, misc. {3x} = that had escaped, be left, posterity.

(1) The idea of the remnant plays a prominent part in the divine economy of salvation throughout the Old Testament. **(1a)** The remnant concept is applied especially to the Israelites who survived such calamities as war, pestilence, and famine—**(1b)** people whom the Lord in His mercy spared to be His chosen people (2 Kin 19:31; cf. Ezra 9:14). **(2)** The Israelites repeatedly suffered major catastrophes **(2a)** that brought them to the brink of extinction. **(2b)** So they often prayed as in Jer 42:2. **(3)** Isaiah prayed for the remnant which would be left after the Assyrian invasions (Is 37:32). **(4)** Micah announced the regathering of the Jewish people after the Exile in Babylon (2:12; 4:7; 5:7–8). **(5)** Jeremiah discussed the plight of the Jews who fled to Egypt after Jerusalem's capture by Nebuchadnezzar (Jer 40:11, 15). **(6)** Zephaniah identified the remnant with the poor and humble (2:3, 7; 3:12–13). **(7)** Zechariah announced that a remnant would be

present at the time of the coming of the Messiah's kingdom (12:10–13:1; 13:8–9). See: TWOT—2307b; BDB—984c, 1056c.

7612. שֵׁאת {1x} **shêʾth**, *shayth;* from 7582: *devastation:*—desolation {1x}. See: TWOT—2301d; BDB—981b, 985a, 1059a.

7613. שְׂאֵת {14x} **sᵉêth**, *seh-ayth';* from 5375; an *elevation* or leprous scab; fig. *elation* or cheerfulness; *exaltation* in rank or character:—rising {7x}, dignity {2x}, excellency {2x}, accepted {1x}, highness {1x}, raise up {1x}. See: TWOT—1421j; BDB—673b, 979c.

7614. שְׁבָא {23x} **Shᵉbâ**, *sheb-aw';* of for. or.; *Sheba*, the name of three early progenitors of tribes and of an Ethiopian district:—Sheba {23x}. See: BDB—985a.

7615. שְׁבָאִי {1x} **Shᵉbâʾîy**, *sheb-aw-ee';* patron. from 7614; a *Shebaïte* or desc. of Sheba:—Sabeans {1x}. See: BDB—985b.

7616. שָׁבָב {1x} **shâbâb**, *shaw-bawb';* from an unused root mean. to *break* up; a *fragment,* i.e. *ruin:*—broken in pieces {1x}. See: TWOT—2309a; BDB—985b.

7617. שָׁבָה {47x} **shâbâh**, *shaw-baw';* a prim. root; to *transport* into captivity:—(carry, take away, . . .) captive {37x}, (take, drive, . . .) away {8x}, take {2x}. See: TWOT—2311; BDB—985c.

7618. שְׁבוּ {2x} **shᵉbûw**, *sheb-oo';* from an unused root (prob. ident. with that of 7617 through the idea of *subdivision* into flashes or streamers [comp. 7632] mean. to *flame;* a *gem* (from its sparkle), prob. the *agate:*—agate {2x}. See: TWOT—2311e; BDB—986b.

7619. שְׁבוּאֵל {6x} **Shᵉbûwʾêl**, *sheb-oo-ale';* or

שׁוּבָאֵל **Shûwbâʾêl**, *shoo-baw-ale';* from 7617 (abbrev.) or 7725 and 410; *captive* (or *returned*) *of God; Shebuël* or *Shubaël*, the name of two Isr.:—Shebuel {3x}, Shubael {3x}. See: BDB—986c.

7620. שָׁבוּעַ {20x} **shâbûwaᶜ**, *shaw-boo'-ah;* or

שָׁבֻעַ **shâbûaᶜ**, *shaw-boo'-ah;* also (fem.)

שְׁבֻעָה **shᵉbûᶜâh**, *sheb-oo-aw';* prop. pass. part. of 7650 as a denom. of 7651; lit. *sevened,* i.e. a *week* (spec. of years):—week {19x}, seven {1x}.

(1) In Gen 29:27 it refers to an entire week of feasting. **(2)** Ex 34:22 speaks of a special feast in Israel's religious calendar. **(3)** In Lev 12:5 the word appears with the dual suffix and signifies a period of two weeks. See: TWOT—2318d; BDB—988d.

7621. שְׁבוּעָה {30x} **shᵉbûwᶜâh**, *sheb-oo-aw'*; fem. pass. part. of 7650; prop. something *sworn*, i.e. an *oath*:—oath {28x}, sworn + 1167 {1x}, curse {1x}. See: TWOT—2319a; BDB—989d.

7622. שְׁבוּת {44x} **shᵉbûwth**, *sheb-ooth'*; or

שְׁבִית **shᵉbîyth**, *sheb-eeth'*; from 7617; *exile*, concr. *prisoners*; fig. a *former state* of prosperity:—captivity {31x}, captives {1x}. See: TWOT—2311d; BDB—986a, 987b, 1000a.

7623. שָׁבַח {11x} **shâbach**, *shaw-bakh'*; a prim. root; prop. to *address* in a loud tone, i.e. (spec.) *loud;* fig. to *pacify* (as if by words):—praise {5x}, still {2x}, keep it in {1x}, glory {1x}, triumph {1x}, commend {1x}. Syn.: 1288, 1984, 2167, 3034. See: TWOT—2312, 2313; BDB—986c, 1114b.

7624. שְׁבַח {5x} **shᵉbach** (Aram.), *sheb-akh'*; corresp. to 7623; to *adulate*, i.e. *adore*:—praise {5x}. See: TWOT—3014; BDB—1114b.

7625. שְׁבַט {1x} **shᵉbat** (Aram.), *sheb-at'*; corresp. to 7626; a *clan*:—tribe {1x}. See: TWOT—3015; BDB—1114b.

7626. שֵׁבֶט {190x} **shêbet**, *shay'-bet*; from an unused root prob. mean. to *branch* off; a *scion*, i.e. (lit.) a *stick* (for punishing, writing, fighting, ruling, walking, etc.) or (fig.) a *clan*:—tribe {140x}, rod {34x}, scepter {10x}, staff {2x}, misc. {4x} = × correction, dart.

Shebet, means a "tribe; rod." **(1)** The "rod" as a tool is used by the shepherd (Lev 27:32) and the teacher (2 Sa 7:14). **(2)** It is a symbol of authority in the hands of a ruler, whether it is the scepter (Amos 1:5, 8) or an instrument of warfare and oppression: "Thou shalt break them with a rod of iron; thou shalt dash them in pieces like a potter's vessel" (Ps 2:9; cf. Zec 10:11). **(3)** The symbolic element comes to expression in a description of the messianic rule: "But with righteousness shall he judge the poor, and reprove with equity for the meek of the earth: and he shall smite the earth with the rod of his mouth" (Is 11:4). **(4)** The word *shebet* is most frequently used (143 times) to denote a "tribe," a division in a nation. It is the preferred term for the twelve "tribes" of Israel (Gen 49:16; Ex 28:21). **(5)** Jeremiah referred to all of Israel as the "tribe": "The portion of Jacob is not like them; for he is the former of all things: and Israel is the rod of his inheritance: the Lord of hosts is his name" (51:19). Syn.: 2945, 4294, 4940. See: TWOT—2314a; BDB—986d, 1114b.

7627. שְׁבָט {1x} **Shᵉbât**, *sheb-awt'*; of for. or.; *Shebat*, a Jewish month:—Sebat {1x}. See: BDB—987b.

7628. שְׁבִי {49x} **shᵉbîy**, *sheb-ee'*; from 7618; *exiled; captured;* as noun, *exile* (abstr. or concr. and collect.); by extens. *booty*:—captivity {35x}, captive {10x}, prisoners {2x}, taken away {1x}, taken {1x}. See: TWOT—2311a; BDB—985d, 987b.

7629. שֹׁבִי {1x} **Shôbîy**, *sho-bee'*; from 7617; *captor; Shobi*, an Ammonite:—Shobi {1x}. See: BDB—986b.

7630. שֹׁבָי {2x} **Shôbay**, *sho-bah'-ee*; for 7629; *Shobai*, an Isr.:—Shobai {2x}. See: BDB—986b.

7631. שְׁבִיב {2x} **sᵉbîyb** (Aram.), *seb-eeb'*; corresp. to 7632:—flame {2x}. See: TWOT—3016; BDB—1114b.

7632. שָׁבִיב {1x} **shâbîyb**, *shaw-beeb'*; from the same as 7616; *flame* (as *split* into tongues):—spark {1x}. See: TWOT—2310a; BDB—985b.

7633. שִׁבְיָה {9x} **shibyâh**, *shib-yaw'*; fem. of 7628; *exile* (abstr. or concr. and collect.):—captive {8x}, captivity {1x}. See: TWOT—2311c; BDB—986a, 987b.

7634. שָׁבְיָה {1x} **Shobyâh**, *shob-yaw'*; fem. of the same as 7629; *captivation; Shobjah*, an Isr.:—Shachia {1x}. See: BDB—967d.

7635. שָׁבִיל {3x} **shâbîyl**, *shaw-beel'*; from the same as 7640; a *track* or *passageway* (as if *flowing* along):—path {3x}. See: TWOT—2316d; BDB—987c.

7636. שָׁבִיס {1x} **shâbîyç**, *shaw-beece'*; from an unused root mean. to *interweave;* a *netting* for the hair:—caul {1x}. See: TWOT—2317a; BDB—987d.

7637. שְׁבִיעִי {98x} **shᵉbîyᶜîy**, *sheb-ee-ee'*; or

שְׁבִעִי **shᵉbîᶜîy**, *sheb-ee-ee'*; ord. from 7657; *seventh*:—seventh {96x}, seventh time {1x}, seven {1x}. See: TWOT—2318b; BDB—988c.

שְׁבִית **shᵉbîyth**. See 7622.

7638. שָׂבָךְ {1x} **sâbâk**, *saw-bawk'*; from an unused root mean. to *intwine;* a *netting* (ornament to the capital of a column):—net {1x}. See: TWOT—2230; BDB—959a, 959b.

שַׂבְּכָא **sabbᵉkâʾ**. See 5443.

7639. שְׂבָכָה {15x} **sᵉbâkâh**, *seb-aw-kaw'*; fem. of 7638; a *net-work*, i.e (in hunting) a *snare*, (in arch.) a *ballustrade*; also a *reticulated* ornament to a pillar:—network {7x},

wreath {3x}, wreathen work {2x}, checker {1x}, lattice {1x}, snare {1x}. See: TWOT—2230b; BDB—959a, 959b, 1113c.

7640. שֹׁבֶל {1x} **shôbel**, *show'-bel;* from an unused root mean. to *flow;* a lady's *train* (as *trailing* after her):—leg {1x}. See: TWOT—2316a; BDB—987c.

7641. שִׁבֹּל {19x} **shibbôl**, *shib-bole';* or (fem.)

שִׁבֹּלֶת **shibbôleth**, *shib-bo'-leth;* from the same as 7640; a *stream* (as *flowing*); also an *ear* of grain (as *growing* out); by anal. a *branch*:—ears {11x}, ears of corn {3x}, branches {1x}, channel {1x}, floods {1x}, *Shibboleth* {1x}, waterflood + 4325 {1x}. comp. 5451. See: TWOT—2316b, 2316c; BDB—987c.

7642. שַׁבְלוּל {1x} **shablûwl**, *shab-lool';* from the same as 7640; a *snail* (as if *floating* in its own slime):—snail {1x}. See: TWOT—248c; BDB—117d, 987c.

שִׁבֹּלֶת **shibbôleth**. See 7641.

7643. שְׂבָם {6x} **Sᵉbâm**, *seb-awm';* or (fem.)

שְׂבָמָה **Sibmâh**, *sib-maw';* prob. from 1313; *spice; Sebam* or *Sibmah,* a place in Moab:—Shebam {1x}, Shibmah {1x}, Sibmah {4x}. See: BDB—959b.

7644. שֶׁבְנָא {9x} **Shebnâ**, *sheb-naw';* or

שֶׁבְנָה **Shebnâh**, *sheb-naw';* from an unused root mean. to *grow; growth; Shebna* or *Shebnah,* an Isr.:—Shebna {9x}. See: BDB—987d.

7645. שְׁבַנְיָה {7x} **Shᵉbanyâh**, *sheb-an-yaw';* or

שְׁבַנְיָהוּ **Shᵉbanyâhûw**, *sheb-an-yaw'-hoo;* from the same as 7644 and 3050; *Jah has grown* (i.e. *prospered*); *Shebanjah,* the name of three or four Isr.:—Shebaniah {7x}. See: BDB—987d.

7646. שָׂבַע {95x} **sâbaᶜ**, *saw-bah';* or

שָׂבֵעַ **sâbêaᶜ**, *saw-bay'-ah;* a prim. root; to *sate,* i.e. *fill* to satisfaction (lit. or fig.):—satisfy {47x}, fill {25x}, full {15x}, plenty {2x}, enough {2x}, satiate {1x}, sufficed {1x}, unsatiable {1x}, weary {1x}.
(1) *Sabea'* expresses the idea of being filled, sated (Ex 16:8). **(2)** Figuratively, Israel is compared to sated cattle or sheep (Jer 50:19). **(3)** The earth too can be sated, have its fill, of rain (Job 38:27). **(4)** *Sabea'* sometimes expresses over-indulgence (Prov 25:16). **(5)** God too can become surfeited, especially when men offer sacrifices with the wrong motives (Is 1:11). **(6)** The lazy man shall have poverty enough (Prov 28:19). **(7)** *Sabea'* often expresses God's satisfying, supplying man with his ma-

terial needs (Ps 103:5). See: TWOT—2231; BDB—959b.

7647. שָׂבָע {8x} **sâbâ**ᶜ, *saw-baw';* from 7646; *copiousness:*—abundance {1x}, plenty {4x}, plenteous {3x}. See: TWOT—2231c; BDB—960a.

7648. שֹׂבַע {8x} **sôbaᶜ**, *so'-bah;* from 7646; *satisfaction* (of food or [fig.] joy):—full {5x}, fulness {1x}, satisfying {1x}, sufficed {1x}. See: TWOT—2231a; BDB—959d.

7649. שָׂבֵעַ {10x} **sâbêaᶜ**, *saw-bay'-ah;* from 7646; *satiated* (in a pleasant or disagreeable sense):—full (of) {8x}, satisfied (with) {2x}. See: TWOT—2231d; BDB—960a.

7650. שָׁבַע **shâba**ᶜ, *shaw-bah';* a prim. root; prop. to *be complete,* but used only as a denom. from 7651; to *seven* oneself, i.e. *swear* (as if by repeating a declaration seven times):—sware {167x}, charge {8x}, oath {7x}, adjure {3x}, straitly {2x}.
(1) Often to swear or to take an oath is to strongly affirm a promise (Gen 21:23–24; Josh 6:22; 1 Sa 20:17). **(2)** Allegiance to God is pledged by an oath (Is 19:18). **(3)** Zephaniah condemns the idolatrous priests that swear by the Lord and by Malcham [the Ammonite god] (Zeph 1:5). **(4)** In making and upholding His promises to men, God often swears by Himself (Gen 22:16–17; cf. Isa 45:23; Jer 22:5). **(5)** God also swears by His holiness (Amos 4:2). **(5)** The root for "to swear" and the root for "seven" are the same in Hebrew, and since the number seven is the "perfect number," some have conjectured that "to swear" is to somehow "seven oneself," thus to bind oneself with seven things. Perhaps this is paralleled by the use of "seven" in Samson's allowing himself to be bound by seven fresh bowstrings (Judg 16:7) and weaving the seven locks of his head (Judg. 16:13). The relationship between "to swear" and "seven" is inconclusive. See: TWOT—2318; BDB—989a.

7651. שֶׁבַע {394x} **shebaᶜ**, *sheh'-bah;* or (masc.)

שִׁבְעָה **shib**ᶜ**âh**, *shib-aw';* from 7650; a prim. cardinal number; *seven* (as the sacred *full* one); also (adv.) *seven times;* by impl. a *week;* by extens. an *indefinite* number:—seven 355, seventh {13x}, seventeen + 6240 {8x}, seven times {6x}, seventeenth + 6240 {6x}, seventeenth {5x}, sevens + 7657 {2x}, seven men {1x}, sevenfold {1x}, seventeen + 6235 {1x}, seventeen + 7657 {1x}. See: TWOT—2318; BDB—987d, 988d, 1114b. comp. 7658.

7652. שֶׁבַע {10x} **Sheba**ᶜ, *sheh'-bah;* the same as 7651; *seven; Sheba,* the name of

a place in Pal., and of two Isr.:—*Sheba* {10x}. See: BDB—989d.

שְׁבֻעַ **shâbûa'.** See 7620.

7653. שִׁבְעָה {1x} **sib'âh,** *sib-aw';* fem. of 7647; *satiety:*—fulness {1x}. See: TWOT—2231b; BDB—960a.

7654. שָׂבְעָה {6x} **sob'âh,** *sob-aw';* fem. of 7648; *satiety:*—satisfy {2x}, enough {2x}, full {1x}, sufficiently {1x}. See: TWOT—2231b; BDB—960a.

שִׁבְעָה **shib'âh.** See 7651.

7655. שִׁבְעָה {6x} **shib'âh** (Aram.), *shib-aw';* corresp. to 7651:—seven {5x}, seven times {1x}. See: TWOT—3017; BDB—1114b.

7656. שֶׁבַע {1x} **Shib'âh,** *shib-aw';* masc. of 7651; *seven (-th); Shebah,* a well in Pal.:—*Shebah* {1x}. See: BDB—988b.

שְׁבֻעָה **sh⁽e⁾bû'âh.** See 7620.

שְׁבִיעִי **sh⁽e⁾bîy'îy.** See 7637.

7657. שִׁבְעִים {91x} **shib'îym,** *shib-eem';* multiple of 7651; *seventy:*—seventy {58x}, three score and (ten, twelve, etc . . .) {33x}. See: TWOT—2318b; BDB—988c.

7658. שִׁבְעָנָה {1x} **shib'ânâh,** *shib-aw-naw';* prol. for the masc. of 7651; *seven:*—seven {1x}. See: TWOT—2318; BDB—988d.

7659. שִׁבְעָתַיִם {7x} **shib'âthayim,** *shib-aw-thah'-yim;* dual (adv.) of 7651; *seven-times:*—sevenfold {6x}, seven times {1x}. See: TWOT—2318c; BDB—988d.

7660. שָׁבַץ {2x} **shâbats,** *shaw-bats';* a prim. root; to *interweave* (colored) threads in squares; by impl. (*of reticulation*) to *inchase* gems in gold:—embroider {1x}, set {1x}. See: TWOT—2320; BDB—990a.

7661. שָׁבָץ {1x} **shâbâts,** *shaw-bawts';* from 7660; *intanglement,* i.e. (fig.) *perplexity:*—anguish {1x}. See: TWOT—2320a; BDB—990b.

7662. שְׁבַק {5x} **sh⁽e⁾baq** (Aram.), *sheb-ak';* corresp. to the root of 7733; to *quit,* i.e. *allow to remain:*—leave {4x}, let alone {1x}. See: TWOT—3018; BDB—1114c.

7663. שָׂבַר {8x} **sâbar,** *saw-bar';* err.

שָׁבַר **shâbar** (Neh. 2:13, 15), *shaw-bar';* a prim. root; to *scrutinize;* by impl. (of *watching*) to *expect* (with hope and patience):—hope {3x}, tarry {1x}, view {2x}, wait {2x}. See: TWOT—2232; BDB—960b, 1104a.

7664. שֵׂבֶר {2x} **sêber,** *say'-ber;* from 7663; *expectation:*—hope {2x}. See: TWOT—2232a; BDB—960b.

7665. שָׁבַר {2x} **shâbar,** *shaw-bar';* a prim. root; to *burst* (lit. or fig.):—break {115x}, destroy {9x}, break in pieces {8x}, break down {4x}, hurt {3x}, torn {2x}, give birth {1x}, crush {1x}, quench {1x}, misc. {6x} = broken ([-hearted]), × quite, view [*by mistake for* 7663].

(1) The common word for breaking things, *shabar* describes the breaking of **(1a)** earthen vessels (Judg 7:20; Jer 19:10), **(1b)** bows (Hos 1:5), **(1c)** doors (Gen 19:9), **(1d)** swords (Hos 2:18), **(1e)** bones (Ex 12:46), and **(1f)** yokes or bonds (Jer 28:10, 12–13). **(2)** Figuratively, it describes a shattered heart or emotion (Ps 69:20; Eze 6:9). **(3)** Intensively, *shabar* connotes shattering something, such as **(3a)** the tablets of the Law (Ex 32:19), **(3b)** idol images (2 Kin 11:18), or **(3c)** trees by hail (Ex 9:25). Syn.: 7591, 7703, 8074, 8154. See: TWOT—2321; BDB—990c, 991b, 1117c.

7666. שָׁבַר {21x} **shâbar,** *shaw-bar';* denom. from 7668; to *deal* in grain:—buy {15x}, sell {6x}. See: TWOT—2322; BDB—991c.

7667. שֶׁבֶר {44x} **sheber,** *sheh'-ber;* or

שֵׁבֶר **shêber,** *shay'-ber;* from 7665; a *fracture,* fig. *ruin;* spec. a *solution* (of a dream):—destruction {21x}, breach {7x}, hurt {4x}, breaking {3x}, affliction {2x}, bruise {2x}, crashing {1x}, interpretation {1x}, vexation {1x}, broken footed {1x}, broken handed {1x}. See: TWOT—2321a; BDB—991a, 991c.

7668. שֶׁבֶר {9x} **sheber,** *sheh'-ber;* the same as 7667; *grain* (as if *broken* into kernels):—corn {8x}, victuals {1x}. See: TWOT—2322a; BDB—991c.

7669. שֶׁבֶר {1x} **Sheber,** *sheh'-ber;* the same as 7667; *Sheber,* an Isr.:—*Sheber* {1x}. See: BDB—991b.

7670. שִׁבָּרוֹן {2x} **shibrôwn,** *shib-rone';* from 7665; *rupture,* i.e. a *pang;* fig. *ruin:*—breaking {1x}, destruction {1x}. See: TWOT—2321b; BDB—991b.

7671. שְׁבָרִים {1x} **Sh⁽e⁾bârîym,** *sheb-aw-reem';* plur. of 7667; *ruins; Shebarim,* a place in Pal.:—*Shebarim* {1x}. See: BDB—991b.

7672. שְׁבַשׁ {1x} **sh⁽e⁾bash** (Aram.), *sheb-ash';* corresp. to 7660; to *intangle,* i.e. *perplex:*—be astonied {1x}. See: TWOT—3019; BDB—1114c.

7673. שָׁבַת {71x} **shâbath,** *shaw-bath';* a prim. root; to *repose,* i.e. *desist* from exertion; used in many impl. relations (caus., fig.

or spec.):—cease {47x}, rest {11x}, away {3x}, fail {2x}, celebrate {1x}, misc. {7x} = keep (sabbath), suffer to be lacking, leave, rid, still.

Shabath means "to rest, cease." **(1)** The verb first occurs in Gen 2:2–3: "And on the seventh day God ended his work which he had made; and he rested on the seventh day from all his work which he had made. And God blessed the seventh day, and sanctified it: because that in it he had rested from all his work which God created and made." **(2)** The basic and most frequent meaning of *shabath* is shown in Gen 8:22: "While the earth remaineth, seedtime and harvest, and cold and heat, and summer and winter, and day and night shall not cease." **(3)** This promise became a prophetic sign of God's faithfulness: "If those ordinances depart from before me, saith the Lord, then the seed of Israel also shall cease from being a nation before me for ever" (Jer 31:36). **(4)** We find a variety of senses: **(4a)** "Even the first day ye shall put away (*shabath*) leaven out of your houses" (Ex 12:15). **(4b)** "Neither shalt thou suffer the salt of the covenant of thy God to be lacking from thy meat offering" (Lev 2:13). **(4c)** Josiah "put down (*shabath*) the idolatrous priests" (2 Kin 23:5). **(4d)** "I will also rid (*shabath*) beasts out of the land" (Lev 26:6). Syn: 2308, 7676. See: TWOT—2323, 2323c; BDB—991d, 992c.

7674. שֶׁבֶת {3x} **shebeth,** *sheh'-beth;* from 7673; *rest, interruption, cessation:*—cease {1x}, sit still {1x}, loss of time {1x}. See: TWOT—2323a; BDB—444a, 992a.

7675. שֶׁבֶת {4x} **shebeth,** *sheh'-beth;* infin. of 3427; prop. *session;* but used also concr. an *abode* or *locality:*—place {1x}, seat {3x}. See: TWOT—922a; BDB—443d. comp. 3429.

7676. שַׁבָּת {107x} **shabbâth,** *shab-bawth';* intens. from 7673; *intermission,* i.e (spec.) the *Sabbath:*—(+ every) sabbath {107x}, another {1x}.

Shabbath, as a noun, means "the sabbath." **(1)** The verb *shabath* (7673) is the root of *shabbat:* "Six days you are to do your work, but on the seventh day you shall rest" (Ex 23:12). **(2)** In Ex 31:15, the seventh day is called the "sabbath rest." **(3)** A man's "rest" was to include his animals and servants (Ex 23:12): even "in earing time and in harvest thou shalt rest" (Ex 34:21). **(4)** "It is a sign between me and the children of Israel for ever: for in six days the Lord made heaven and earth, and on the seventh day he rested, and was refreshed" (Ex 31:17). **(5)** "Then shall the land keep a sabbath unto the Lord" (Lev 25:2). Six years crops will be sown and harvested, but the seventh year "shall be a sabbath of rest unto the land, a sabbath for

the Lord" (Lev 25:4). **(6)** The feast of trumpets, the Day of Atonement, and the first and eighth days of the Feast of Tabernacles are also called "a sabbath observance" or "a sabbath of complete rest" (Lev 23:24, 32, 39). **(7)** The "sabbath" was a "day of worship" (Lev 23:3) as well as a "day of rest and refreshment" for man (Ex 23:12). **(8)** God "rested and was refreshed" (Ex 31:17).

(9) The "sabbath" was the covenant sign of God's lordship over the creation. **(9a)** By observing the "sabbath," Israel confessed that they were God's redeemed people, subject to His lordship to obey the whole of His law. **(9b)** They were His stewards to show mercy with kindness and liberality to all (Ex 23:12; Lev 25). **(10)** By "resting," man witnessed his trust in God to give fruit to his labor; he entered into God's "rest." Thus "rest" and the "sabbath" were eschatological in perspective, looking to the accomplishment of God's ultimate purpose through the redemption of His people, to whom the "sabbath" was a covenant sign. **(11)** The prophets rebuked Israel for their neglect of the sabbath (Is 1:13; Jer 17:21–27; Eze 20:12–24; Amos 8:5). **(12)** They also proclaimed "sabbath" observance as a blessing in the messianic age and a sign of its fullness (Is 56:2–4; 58:13; 66:23; Eze 44:24; 45:17; 46:1, 3–4, 12). **(13)** The length of the Babylonian captivity was determined by the extent of Israel's abuse of the sabbatical year (2 Chr 36:21; cf. Lev 26:34–35). Syn: 2308, 7673. See: TWOT—2323b; BDB—992a.

7677. שַׁבָּתוֹן {11x} **shabbâthôwn,** *shab-baw-thone';* from 7676; a *sabbatism* or special holiday:—rest {8x}, sabbath {3x}. See: TWOT—2323d; BDB—992d.

7678. שַׁבְּתַי {3x} **Shabbᵉthay,** *shab-beth-ah'-ee;* from 7676; *restful; Shabbethai,* the name of three Isr.:—Shabbethai {3x}. See: BDB—992d.

7679. שָׂגָא {2x} **sâgâ',** *saw-gaw';* a prim. root; to *grow,* i.e. (caus.) to *enlarge,* (fig.) *laud:*—increase {1x}, magnify {1x}. See: TWOT—2233; BDB—960b, 1113c.

7680. שְׂגָא {3x} **sᵉgâ'** (Aram.), *seg-aw';* corresp. to 7679; to *increase:*—grow {1x}, be multiplied {2x}. See: TWOT—3004; BDB—1113c.

7681. שָׁגֵא {1x} **age,** an Isr.:—Shage {1x}. See: BDB—992d, 993b.

7682. שָׂגַב **sâgab,** *saw-gab';* a prim. root; to *be* (caus. *make*) *lofty,* espec. *inaccessible;* by impl. *safe, strong;* used lit. and fig.—high {6x}, exalted {6x}, defend {2x}, safe {2x},

excellent {1x}, misc. {3x} = lofty, be too strong. See: TWOT—2234; BDB—960c.

7683. שָׁגַג {5x} **shâgag**, *shaw-gag'*; a prim. root; to *stray*, i.e. (fig.) *sin* (with more or less apology):—X also for that {1x}, deceived {1x}, err {1x}, go astray {1x}, sin ignorantly {1x}. See: TWOT—2324; BDB—992d.

7684. שְׁגָגָה {19x} **sh⁰gâgâh**, *sheg-aw-gaw'*; from 7683; a *mistake* or inadvertent *transgression*:—error {2x}, through ignorance {6x}, by ignorance {2x}, in ignorance {1x}, ignorance {3x}, at unawares {4x}, unwittingly {1x}. See: TWOT—2324a; BDB—993a.

7685. שָׂגָה {4x} **sâgâh**, *saw-gaw'*; a prim. root; to *enlarge* (espec. upward, also fig.):—grow (up) {2x}, increase {2x}. See: TWOT—2233b; BDB—960d.

7686. שָׁגָה {21x} **shâgâh**, *shaw-gaw'*; a prim. root; to *stray* (caus. *mislead*), usually (fig.) to *mistake*, espec. (mor.) to *transgress*; by extens. (through the idea of intoxication) to *reel*, (fig.) *be enraptured*:—err {11x}, ravished {2x}, wander {3x}, deceiver {1x}, cause to go astray {1x}, sin through ignorance {1x}, go astray {1x}, deceived {1x}. Syn.: 2398, 5771, 6588. See: TWOT—2325; BDB—993a.

7687. שְׂגוּב {3x} **S⁰gûwb**, *seg-oob'*; from 7682; *aloft*; *Segub*, the name of two Isr.:—Segub {3x}. See: BDB—960d.

7688. שָׁגַח {3x} **shâgach**, *shaw-gakh'*; a prim. root; to *peep*, i.e. *glance* sharply at:—look (narrowly) {3x}. See: TWOT—2326; BDB—993b.

7689. שַׂגִּיא {2x} **saggîy'**, *sag-ghee'*; from 7679; (superl.) *mighty*:—excellent {1x}, great {1x}. See: TWOT—2233a; BDB—960c.

7690. שַׂגִּיא {13x} **saggîy'** (Aram.), *sag-ghee'*; corresp. to 7689; *large* (in size, quantity or number, also adv.):—exceeding {1x}, great {3x}, greatly {1x}; many {2x}, much {4x}, sore {1x}, very {1x}. See: TWOT—3004a; BDB—1113c.

7691. שְׂגִיאָה {1x} **sh⁰gîy'âh**, *sheg-ee-aw'*; from 7686; a moral *mistake*:—error {1x}. See: TWOT—2325a; BDB—993b.

7692. שִׁגָּיוֹן {2x} **Shiggâyôwn**, *shig-gaw-yone'*; or

שִׁגָּיֹנָה **Shiggâyônâh**, *shig-gaw-yo-naw'*; from 7686; prop. *aberration*, i.e. (tech.) a *dithyramb* or rambling poem:—Shiggaion {1x}, Shigionoth {1x}. See: BDB—993a, 993c.

7693. שָׁגַל {4x} **shâgal**, *shaw-gal'*; a prim. root; to *copulate* with:—lie with {1x}, ravish {3x}. See: TWOT—2327; BDB—993c.

7694. שֵׁגָל {2x} **shêgâl**, *shay-gawl'*; from 7693; a *queen* (from cohabitation):—queen {2x}. See: TWOT—2327a; BDB—993c, 1114c.

7695. שֵׁגָל {3x} **shêgâl** (Aram.), *shay-gawl'*; corresp. to 7694; a (legitimate) *queen*:—wife {3x}. See: TWOT—3020; BDB—1114c.

7696. שָׁגַע {7x} **shâga'**, *shaw-gah'*; a prim. root; to *rave* through insanity:—mad {5x}, mad man {2x}. See: TWOT—2328; BDB—993c.

7697. שִׁגָּעוֹן {3x} **shiggâ'ôwn**, *shig-gaw-yone'*; from 7696; *craziness*:—furiously {1x}, madness {2x}. See: TWOT—2328a; BDB—993d.

7698. שֶׁגֶר {5x} **sheger**, *sheh'-ger*; from an unused root prob. mean. to *eject*; the *fetus* (as finally *expelled*):—that cometh of {1x}, increase {4x}. See: TWOT—2329a; BDB—993d.

7699. שַׁד {24x} **shad**, *shad*; or

שֹׁד **shôd**, *shode*; prob. from 7736 (in its orig. sense) contr.; the *breast* of a woman or animal (as *bulging*):—breast {22x}, pap {1x}, teat {1x}. See: TWOT—2332a; BDB—993d, 994c, 994d.

7700. שֵׁד {2x} **shêd**, *shade*; from 7736; a *demon* (as *malignant*):—devil {2x}. Syn.: 7854, 8163. See: TWOT—2330; BDB—993d.

7701. שֹׁד {25x} **shôd**, *shode*; or

שׁוֹד **shôwd** (Job 5:21), *shode*; from 7736; *violence, ravage*:—spoil {10x}, destruction {7x}, desolation {2x}, robbery {2x}, wasting {2x}, oppression {1x}, spoiler {1x}. See: TWOT—2331a; BDB—994a, 994c, 1000c.

7702. שָׂדַד {3x} **sâdad**, *saw-dad'*; a prim. root; to *abrade*, i.e. *harrow* a field:—break clods {2x}, harrow {1x}. See: TWOT—2235; BDB—961a.

7703. שָׁדַד {58x} **shâdad**, *shaw-dad'*; a prim. root; prop. to *be burly*, i.e. (fig.) *powerful* (pass. *impregnable*); by impl. to *ravage*:—spoil {30x}, spoiler {11x}, waste {8x}, destroy {2x}, robbers {2x}, misc. {5x} = dead, destroyer, oppress, X utterly. Syn.: 5302, 7591, 7665, 7722, 8074. See: TWOT—2331; BDB—994a, 1000d.

7704. שָׂדֶה {333x} **sâdeh**, *saw-deh'*; or

שָׂדַי **sâday**, *saw-dah'-ee*; from an unused root mean. to *spread* out; a

field (as *flat*):—field {292x}, country {17x}, land {11x}, wild {8x}, ground {4x}, soil {1x}.

The form, *sadeh*, means "field; country; domain [of a town]." **(1)** This word often represents the "open field" where the animals roam wild. **(1a)** That is its meaning in its first biblical appearance: "And every plant of the field before it was in the earth, and every herb of the field before it grew: for the Lord God had not caused it to rain upon the earth" (Gen 2:5). **(1b)** Thus, "Esau was a cunning hunter, a man of the field; and Jacob was a plain man, dwelling in tents" (Gen 25:27). **(1c)** A city in the "open field" was unfortified; David wisely asked Achish for such a city, showing that he did not intend to be hostile (1 Sa 27:5). Dwelling in an unfortified city meant exposure to attack. **(2)** *Sadeh* represents the "fields surrounding a town" (Josh 21:12; cf. Neh 11:25). **(3)** "Arable land," land that is either cultivated or to be cultivated, is also signified by *sadeh*: "If it be your mind that I should bury my dead out of my sight; hear me, and entreat for me to Ephron the son of Zohar, that he may give me the cave of Machpelah, which he hath, which is in the end of his field" (Gen 23:8–9). **(4)** The entirety of one's cultivated or pasture land is called his "field": "And the king [David] said unto him [Mephibosheth], Why speakest thou any more of thy matters? I have said, Thou and Ziba divide the land [previously owned by Saul]" (2 Sa 19:29). **(5)** Sometimes particular sections of land are identified by name: "And after this, Abraham buried Sarah his wife in the cave of the field of Machpelah before Mamre" (Gen 23:19). **(6)** The form, *saday*, also means "open field." *Saday* occurs 12 times, only in poetical passages. Deut 32:13 is the first biblical appearance: "He made him ride on the high places of the earth, that he might eat the increase of the fields." Syn.: 127, 776. See: TWOT—2236a, 2236b; BDB—961a, 961b.

7705. שִׁדָּה {2x} **shiddâh**, *shid-dah'*; from 7703; a *wife* (as *mistress* of the house):—✕ all sorts, musical instrument {2x}. See: TWOT—2332b; BDB—994d.

7706. שַׁדַּי {48x} **Shadday**, *shad-dah'-ee*; from 7703; the *Almighty*:—Almighty {48x}.

(1) The title *Shadday* really indicates the fullness and riches of God's grace, and would remind the Hebrew reader that from God comes every good and perfect gift—that He is never weary of pouring forth His mercies on His people, and that He is more ready to give than they are to receive. **(2)** Bountiful expresses the sense most exactly. **(3)** *El* (410) sets forth the might of God and the title *Shadday* points

to the inexhaustible stores of His bounty. See: TWOT—2333; BDB—994c, 994d.

7707. שְׁדֵיאוּר {5x} **Sh⁰dêy'ûwr**, *shed-ay-oor'*; from the same as 7704 and 217; *spreader of light; Shedejur*, an Isr.:—Shedeur {5x}. See: BDB—994d.

7708. שִׂדִּים {3x} **Siddîym**, *sid-deem'*; plur. from the same as 7704; *flats; Siddim*, a valley in Pal.:—Siddim {3x}. See: BDB—961a, 961d.

7709. שְׁדֵמָה {6x} **sh⁰dêmâh**, *shed-ay-maw'*; appar. from 7704; a *cultivated field*:—blasted {1x}, field {5x}. See: TWOT—2334a; BDB—995a, 1056c.

7710. שָׁדַף {3x} **shâdaph**, *shaw-daf'*; a prim. root; to *scorch*:—blast {3x}. See: TWOT—2335; BDB—995b.

7711. שְׁדֵפָה {6x} **sh⁰dêphâh**, *shed-ay-faw'*; or

שִׁדָּפוֹן **shiddâphôwn**, *shid-daw-fone'*; from 7710; *blight*:—blasted {1x}, blasting {5x}. See: TWOT—2335a, 2335b; BDB—995b

7712. שְׁדַר {1x} **sh⁰dar** (Aram.), *shed-ar'*; a prim. root; to *endeavor*:—laboured {1x}. See: TWOT—3021; BDB—1114c.

7713. שְׂדֵרָה {4x} **s⁰dêrâh**, *sed-ay-raw'*; from an unused root mean. to *regulate*; a *row*, i.e. *rank* (of soldiers), *story* (of rooms):—board {1x}, range {3x}. See: TWOT—1467b; BDB—690b, 961d.

7714. שַׁדְרַךְ {1x} **Shadrak**, *shad-rak'*; prob. of for. or.; *Shadrak*, the Bab. name of one of Daniel's companions:—Shadrach {1x}. See: BDB—995b, 1114c.

7715. שַׁדְרַךְ {14x} **Shadrak** (Aram.), *shad-rak'*; the same as 7714:—Shadrach {14x}. See: BDB—1114c.

7716. שֶׂה {46x} **seh**, *seh*; or

שֵׂי **sêy**, *say*; prob. from 7582 through the idea of *pushing* out to graze; a member of a flock, i.e. a *sheep* or *goat*:—sheep {18x}, cattle {10x}, lamb {16x}, ewe {1x}, lamb + 3532 {1x}. See: TWOT—2237; BDB—961d, 966d. comp. 2089.

7717. שָׂהֵד {1x} **sâhêd**, *saw-hade'*; from an unused root mean. to *testify*; a *witness*:—record {1x}. See: TWOT—2238; BDB—962a, 1113c.

7718. שֹׁהַם {11x} **shôham**, *sho'-ham*; from an unused root prob. mean to *blanch*; a *gem*, prob. the *beryl* (from its *pale* green color):—onyx {11x}. See: TWOT—2337; BDB—965d.

7719. שֹׁהַם {1x} **Shôham,** *sho'-ham;* the same as 7718; *Shoham,* an Isr.:—*Shoham* {1x}. See: BDB—996a.

7720. שַׂהֲרֹן {3x} **sahărôn,** *sah-har-one';* from the same as 5469; a round *pendant* for the neck:—ornament {2x}, round tires like the moon {1x}. See: TWOT—2239a; BDB—962a.

שֵׁ **shav.** See 7723.

7721. שֹׁוא {1x} **sôw°,** *so;* from an unused root (akin to 5375 and 7722) mean. to *rise;* a *rising:*—arise {1x}. See: TWOT—1421; BDB—962b.

7722. שֹׁוא {13x} **shôw°,** *sho;* or (fem.)

שֹׁואָה **shôw°âh,** *sho-aw';* or

שֹׁאָה **shô°âh,** *sho-aw';* from an unused root mean. to *rush* over; a *tempest;* by impl. *devastation:*—desolation {5x}, destruction {3x}, desolate {2x}, destroy {1x}, storm {1x}, wasteness {1x}. Syn.: 7591, 8074, 8154. See: TWOT—2339, 2339a; BDB—980b, 980d, 996b.

7723. שָׁוא {53x} **shâv°,** *shawv;* or

שָׁו **shav,** *shav;* from the same as 7722 in the sense of *desolating; evil* (as *destructive*), lit. (*ruin*) or mor. (espec. *guile*); fig. *idolatry* (as false, subj.), *uselessness* (as deceptive, obj.; also adv. in *vain*):—vain {22x}, vanity {22x}, false {5x}, lying {2x}, falsely {1x}, lies {1x}.

Shav° means "deceit; deception; malice; falsity; vanity; emptiness." **(1)** The 53 occurrences of *shav°* are primarily in poetry. **(2)** The basic meaning of this word is "deceit" or "deception," "malice," and "falsehood." **(2a)** This meaning emerges when it is used in a legal context: "Put not thine hand with the wicked to be an unrighteous witness" (Ex 23:1). **(2b)** Used in cultic [religious worship] contexts, the word bears these same overtones but may be rendered variously. For example, in Ps 31:6 the word may be rendered "lying", in the sense of "deceitful" (cf. Eze 12:24). Eliphaz described the ungodly as those who trust in "emptiness" or "deception," though they gain nothing but emptiness as a reward for that trust (Job 15:31). See: TWOT—2338a; BDB—981a, 996a.

7724. שָׁוא {1x} **Shᵉvâ°,** *shev-aw';* from the same as 7723; *false; Sheva,* an Isr.:—*Sheva* {1x}. See: BDB—976a, 996a, 1009d.

7725. שׁוּב {1066x} **shûwb,** *shoob;* a prim. root; to *turn* back (hence, *away*) tran. or intr., lit. or fig. (not necessarily with the idea of *return* to the starting point); gen. to *retreat;*

often adv. *again:*—return {391x}, . . . again {248x}, turn {123x}, . . . back {65x}, . . . away {56x}, restore {39x}, bring {34x}, render {19x}, answer {18x}, recompense {8x}, recover {6x}, deliver {5x}, put {5x}, withdraw {5x}, requite {4x}, misc. {40x} = × in any case (wise), × at all, averse, call [to mind], cease, × certainly, × consider, + continually, convert, + deny, × fro, [go] out, hinder, let, [see] more, × needs, be past, × pay, pervert, recall, refresh, relieve, rescue, retrieve, reverse, reward, + say nay, still, × surely.

Shuwb means "to return or go back, bring back." **(1)** The basic meaning of the verb is movement back to the point of departure (unless there is evidence to the contrary). **(1a)** In the first occurrence of this verb God told Adam that he and Eve would "eat bread, till thou return unto the ground;" (Gen 3:19). **(1b)** Used in this emphasis, *shuwb* can be applied specifically of returning along a path already traversed: "So Esau returned that day on his way unto Seir" (Gen 33:16). **(2)** The word can mean "turn away from," as **(2a)** in Ps 9:3: "When mine enemies are turned back . . . ," or **(2b)** "reverse a direction," as in 2 Kin 20:10: "Let the shadow return backward ten degrees." **(3)** It can mean the opposite of going out, as when the raven Noah sent forth was constantly going "to and fro" (Gen 8:7)—this phrase, however, may also mean merely constant movement; the raven went about constantly "here and there." **(4)** In Gen 8:3 the word is used of the receding of the flood water: "And the waters returned (*shuwb*) from off the earth continually (1980 – *halak*): and after the end of the hundred and fifty days the waters were abated." **(5)** The verb can also mean "to follow after": "Behold, thy sister-in-law is gone back unto her people, and unto her gods: return thou after thy sister-in-law" (Ruth 1:15).

(6) *Shuwb* can imply the cessation of something. In this sense, the word can imply "to go away or disappear": "And tarry with him a few days, until thy brother's fury turn away" (Gen 27:44). **(7)** It can refer to the initiation of the cessation of something. In some cases violence is the means of bringing something to cease: "How then wilt thou turn away the face of one captain of the least of my master's servants . . ." (2 Kin 18:24). **(8)** In Is 47:10 the verb implies both turning away and destroying: "Thy wisdom and thy knowledge, it hath perverted thee." **(9)** In the case of spiritually returning (metaphorically) to the Lord, *shuwb* can mean **(9a)** "turning away from" following Him (Num 14:43), **(9b)** "turning from" pursuing evil (1 Kin 8:35), and **(9c)** "to return" to Him and obey Him (Deut 30:2). **(10)** The verb can also be used in close relation to another verb to indicate the

repetition of an action presented by the other verb: "I will again feed and keep thy flock" (Gen 30:31). (11) The process called conversion or turning to God is in reality a re-turning or a turning back again to Him from whom sin has separated us, but whose we are by virtue of creation, preservation and redemption. Syn.: 2105, 4878, 5162, 8666. See: TWOT—2340; BDB—996d, 1000a, 1117d.

שׁוּבָאֵל   **Shûwbâ'êl**. See 7619.

7726. שׁוֹבָב   {4x} **shôwbâb**, *sho-bawb'*; from 7725; *apostate*, i.e. *idolatrous*:—backsliding {2x}, frowardly {1x}, turn away [*from marg.*] {1x}. See: TWOT—2340c; BDB—1000a.

7727. שׁוֹבָב   {4x} **Shôwbâb**, *sho-bawb'*; the same as 7726; *rebellious*; Shobab, the name of two Isr.:—Shobab {4x}. See: BDB—1000a.

7728. שׁוֹבֵב   {2x} **shôwbêb**, *sho-babe'*; from 7725; *apostate*, i.e. *heathenish* or (actually) *heathen*:—backsliding {2x}. See: TWOT—2340d; BDB—1000a.

7729. שׁוּבָה   {1x} **shûwbâh**, *shoo-baw'*; from 7725; a *return*:—returning {1x}. 7729 *Shuwbah* occurs once to mean "coming back" or "turning back": "For thus saith the Lord God, the Holy One of Israel; In returning (*shuwbah*) and rest shall ye be saved; in quietness and in confidence shall be your strength: and ye would not" (Is 30:15). See: TWOT—2340a; BDB—1000a.

7730. שׁוֹבֶךְ   {1x} **sôwbek**, *so'-bek*; for 5441; a *thicket*, i.e. interlaced branches:—thick boughs {1x}. See: TWOT—2230a; BDB—959a.

7731. שׁוֹבָךְ   {2x} **Shôwbâk**, *sho-bawk'*; perh. for 7730; *Shobak*, a Syrian:—Shobach {2x}. See: BDB—1000c.

7732. שׁוֹבָל   {9x} **Shôwbâl**, *sho-bawl'*; from the same as 7640; *overflowing*; Shobal, the name of an Edomite and two Isr.:—Shobal {9x}. See: BDB—987c, 1000c.

7733. שׁוֹבֵק   {1x} **Shôwbêq**, *sho-bake'*; act. part. from a prim. root mean. to *leave* (comp. 7662); *forsaking*; Shobek, an Isr.:—Shobek {1x}. See: BDB—990b, 1000c, 1114c.

7734. שׂוּג   {1x} **sûwg**, *soog*; a prim. root; to *retreat*:—turned back {1x}. See: TWOT—1469; BDB—690d.

7735. שׂוּג   {1x} **sûwg**, *soog*; a prim. root; to *hedge* in:—make to grow {1x}. See: TWOT—1470; BDB—691b.

7736. שׁוּד   {1x} **shûwd**, *shood*; a prim. root; prop. to *swell* up, i.e. fig. (by impl. of *insolence*) to *devastate*:—waste {1x}. See: TWOT—2331; BDB—994a, 1000d.

שׁוֹד   **shôwd**. See 7699, 7701.

7737. שָׁוָה   {21x} **shâvâh**, *shaw-vaw'*; a prim. root; prop. to *level*, i.e. *equalize*; fig. to *resemble*; by impl. to *adjust* (i.e. *counterbalance, be suitable, compose, place, yield,* etc.):—laid {3x}, equal {3x}, like {2x}, compared {2x}, profit {2x}, set {1x}, misc. {8x} = avail, behave, bring forth, countervail, make plain, reckon. See: TWOT—2342, 2343; BDB—1000d, 1001a, 1114d.

7738. שָׁוָה   {1x} **shâvâh**, *shaw-vaw'*; a prim. root; to *destroy*:—× substance {1x} [*from the marg.*]. See: TWOT—2343; BDB—996c.

7739. שְׁוָה   {2x} **shᵉvâh** (Aram.), *shev-aw'*; corresp. to 7737; to *resemble*:—made {2x}. See: TWOT—3023, 3024; BDB—1114d.

7740. שָׁוֵה   {1x} **Shâvêh**, *shaw-vay'*; from 7737; *plain*; Shaveh, a place in Pal.:—Shaveh {1x}. See: TWOT—2342a; BDB—1001a.

7741. שָׁוֵה קִרְיָתַיִם   {1x} **Shâvêh Qiryâthayim**, *shaw-vay' kir-yaw-thah'-yim*; from the same as 7740 and the dual of 7151; *plain of a double city*; Shaveh-Kirjathajim, a place E. of the Jordan:—Shaveh Kiriathaim {1x}. See: BDB—1001a.

7742. שׂוּחַ   {1x} **sûwach**, *soo'-akh*; a prim. root; to *muse* pensively:—meditate {1x}. See: TWOT—2255; BDB—962b, 1002a.

7743. שׁוּחַ   {3x} **shûwach**, *shoo'-akh*; a prim. root; to *sink*, lit. or fig.:—bow down {1x}, incline {1x}, humble {1x}. See: TWOT—2343.1; BDB—1001b, 1008a, 1009d, 1060c.

7744. שׁוּחַ   {2x} **Shûwach**, *shoo'-akh*; from 7743; *dell*; Shuach, a son of Abraham:—Shuah {2x}. See: BDB—1001d.

7745. שׁוּחָה   {5x} **shûwchâh**, *shoo-khaw'*; from 7743; a *chasm*:—ditch {4x}, pit {1x}. See: TWOT—2343.1a; BDB—1001c.

7746. שׁוּחָה   {1x} **Shûwchâh**, *shoo-khaw'*; the same as 7745; *Shuchah*, an Isr.:—Shuah {1x}. See: BDB—1001d.

7747. שׁוּחִי   {5x} **Shuchîy**, *shoo-khee'*; patron. from 7744; a *Shuchite* or desc. of Shuach:—Shuhite {5x}. See: BDB—1001d.

7748. שׁוּחָם   {1x} **Shûwchâm**, *shoo-khawm'*; from 7743; *humbly*; Shucham, an Isr.:—Shuham {1x}. See: BDB—1001d.

7749. שׂוּחָמִי {2x} **Shûwchâmîy,** *shoo-khaw-mee';* patron. from 7748; a *Shuchamite* (collect.):—Shuhamites {2x}. See: BDB—1001d.

7750. שׂוּט {2x} **sûwt,** *soot;* or (by perm.)

סוּט **çûwt,** *soot;* a prim. root; to *detrude,* i.e. (intr. and fig.) *become derelict* (wrongly practise; namely, idolatry):—turn aside to {2x}. See: TWOT—2240; BDB—962b.

7751. שׂוּט {13x} **shûwt,** *shoot;* a prim. root; prop. to *push* forth; (but used only fig.) to *lash,* i.e. (the sea with oars) to *row;* by impl. to *travel:*—run to and fro {6x}, go to and fro {2x}, go about {1x}, gone {1x}, mariners {1x}, rowers {1x}, go through {1x}. See: TWOT—2344, 2344d; BDB—967b, 1001d, 1002b.

7752. שׂוֹט {11x} **shôwt,** *shote;* from 7751; a *lash* (lit. or fig.):—scourge {5x}, whip {6x}. See: TWOT—2344a; BDB—1002a, 1002b.

7753. שׂוּךְ {3x} **sûwk,** *sook;* a prim. root; to *entwine,* i.e. *shut* in (for formation, protection or restraint):—fence {1x}, make an hedge {1x}, hedge up {1x}. See: TWOT—2241; BDB—962b, 968a.

7754. שׂוֹךְ {2x} **sôwk,** *soke;* or (fem.)

שׂוֹכָה **sôwkâh,** *so-kaw';* from 7753; a *branch* (as *interleaved*):—bough {2x}. See: TWOT—2242a, 2242b; BDB—962c.

7755. שׂוֹכֹה {8x} **Sôwkôh,** *so-ko';* or

שׂכֹה **Sôkôh,** *so-ko';* or

שׂוֹכוֹ **Sôwkôw,** *so-ko';* from 7753; *Sokoh* or *Soko,* the name of two places in Pal.:—Socoh {2x}, Shochoh {2x}, Sochoh {1x}, Shoco {1x}, Socho {1x}, Shocho {1x}. See: BDB—962c.

7756. שׂוּכָתִי {1x} **Sûwkâthîy,** *soo-kaw-thee';* prob. patron. from a name corresp. to 7754 (fem.); a *Sukathite* or desc. of an unknown Isr. named Sukah:—Suchathite {1x}. See: BDB—962c.

7757. שׂוּל {11x} **shûwl,** *shool;* from an unused root mean. to *hang* down; a *skirt;* by impl. a bottom *edge:*—hem {6x}, skirt {4x}, train {1x}. See: TWOT—2346a; BDB—1002c.

7758. שׂוֹלָל {4x} **shôwlâl,** *sho-lawl';* or

שׂילָל **shêylâl** (Mic. 1:8), *shay-lawl';* from 7997; *nude* (espec. bare-foot); by impl. *captive:*—spoiled {2x}, stripped {2x}. See: TWOT—2399a; BDB—1002c, 1010a, 1021d.

7759. שׂוּלַמִּית {2x} **Shûwlammîyth,** *shoo-lam-meeth';* from 7999; *peaceful* (with the art. always pref., making it a pet name); the *Shulammith,* an epithet of Solomon's queen:—Shulamite {2x}. See: BDB—1002c, 1025a.

7760. שׂוּם {586x} **sûwm,** *soom;* or

שׂים **sîym,** *seem;* a prim. root; to *put* (used in a great variety of applications, lit., fig., infer. and ellip.):—put {155x}, make {123x}, set {119x}, lay {64x}, appoint {19x}, give {11x}, set up {10x}, consider {8x}, turn {5x}, brought {4x}, ordain {3x}, place {3x}, take {3x}, shew {2x}, regard {2x}, mark {2x}, disposed {2x}, care {2x}, misc. {49x} = × any wise, call [a name], cast in, change, charge, commit, convey, determine, + disguise, do, get, heap up, hold, impute, leave, look, + name, × on, order, + paint, preserve, purpose, rehearse, reward, + stedfastly, × tell, + tread down, × wholly, work.

Siym means **(1)** to put or place someone somewhere (Gen 2:8). **(2)** In Ex 40:8 it means to set up, putting something so that it is perpendicular or vertical. **(3)** Figuratively, **(3a)** a "wall" is erected before someone (Mic 5:1; 1 Kin 20:12; 1 Sa 15:2); or **(3b)** something is set or put before one's mind (Ps 54:3; cf. Eze 14:4). **(4)** *Siym* denotes to set over, impose on negatively (Ex 1:11). **(5)** A more positive use of the word is to appoint (1 Sa 8:5). **(6)** *Siym* also means to put down in the sense of literally setting something on the ground, on a chair, or a flat surface (Gen 22:9). **(7)** In a related sense one puts down a distance or space between himself and someone else (Gen 30:36). **(8)** In Job 4:18 the word means to charge someone with an error, or to put it down against him. **(9)** It means to impute, lay to one's charge (1 Sa 22:15) or **(10)** to bring guilt upon one's self (Deut 22:8). **(11)** This verb is used of putting clothing on, setting it down upon one's body (Ruth 3:3).

(12) One may obligate someone with a task, impose/set it upon him (Ex 5:8). **(13)** When used **(13a)** with hand, it signifies **(13a1)** putting (Ex 4:21) or **(13b1)** taking something (Judg 4:21) into one's grasp, or **(13b)** putting hands on to arrest (2 Kin 11:16). **(14)** This verb may be used in giving in behalf of (Job 17:3) as the Servant of the Lord would "make his soul an offering for sin" (Is 53:10). **(15)** In Dan 1:7 *siym* signifies to assign something to, or give to as new names. **(16)** To place or put something on one's heart means **(16a)** to consider it (Is 47:7) or **(16b)** to pay heed to it (1 Sa 21:12). **(17)** The meaning to fix, as to fix something in a particular place, appears in Gen 24:47. **(18)** The word signifies the creation of the thing [fixing its nature] and its use [its disposition] in Ex 4:11 (cf. Gen 13:16). **(19)** It means to state, to appoint, or to assign (Ex 21:13). **(20)** It can mean

to assign to continue, or to preserve (Gen 45:7; Ex 8:12). Syn.: 2803, 8667. See: TWOT—2243; BDB—962c, 965a, 967c, 1113d.

7761. שׂוּם {26x} **sûwm** (Aram.), *soom;* corresp. to 7760:—made {15x}, commanded {3x}, give {2x}, laid {2x}, have {1x}, named {1x}, misc. {2x} = + regard, set. See: TWOT—3006; BDB—1113d.

7762. שׁוּם {1x} **shûwm**, *shoom;* from an unused root mean. to *exhale; garlic* (from its rank *odor*):—garlic {1x}. See: TWOT—2347; BDB—1002c.

7763. שׁוֹמֵר {2x} **Shôwmêr**, *sho-mare';* or

שֹׁמֵר **Shômêr**, *sho-mare';* act. part. of 8104; *keeper; Shomer,* the name of two Isr.:—Shomer {2x}. See: BDB—1037c.

7764. שׁוּנִי {2x} **Shûwnîy**, *shoo-nee';* from an unused root mean. to *rest; quiet; Shuni,* an Isr.:—Shuni {2x}. See: BDB—1002c.

7765. שׁוּנִי {1x} **Shûwnîy**, *shoo-nee';* patron. from 7764; a *Shunite* (collect.) or desc. of Shuni:—Shunites {1x}. See: BDB—1002c.

7766. שׁוּנֵם {3x} **Shûwnêm**, *shoo-name';* prob. from the same as 7764; *quietly; Shunem,* a place in Pal:—Shunem {3x}. See: BDB—1002d.

7767. שׁוּנַמִּית {8x} **Shûwnammîyth**, *shoo-nam-meeth';* patrial from 7766; a *Shunammitess,* or female inhab. of Shunem:—Shunamite {8x}. See: BDB—1002d.

7768. שָׁוַע {21x} **shâva**ᶜ, *shaw-vah';* a prim. root; prop. to *be free;* but used only caus. and refl. to *halloo* (for help, i.e. *freedom* from some trouble):—cried {17x}, cry out {2x}, aloud {1x}, shout {1x}. See: TWOT—2348; BDB—1002d.

7769. שׁוּעַ {2x} **shûwa**ᶜ, *shoo'-ah;* from 7768; a *halloo:*—cry {1x}, riches {1x}. See: TWOT—2348a; BDB—447d, 575d, 1002d, 1003a.

7770. שׁוּעַ {2x} **Shûwa**ᶜ, *shoo'-ah;* the same as 7769; *Shua,* a Canaanite:—Shuah {2x}. See: BDB—447c.

7771. שׁוֹעַ {3x} **shôwa**ᶜ, *sho'-ah;* from 7768 in the orig. sense of *freedom;* a *noble,* i.e. *liberal, opulent;* also (as noun in the der. sense) a *halloo:*—bountiful {1x}, crying {1x}, rich {1x}. See: TWOT—929c, 2348b; BDB—447c, 1003a.

7772. שׁוֹעַ {1x} **Shôwa**ᶜ, *sho'-ah;* the same as 7771; *rich; Shoä,* an Oriental people:—Shoa {1x}. See: BDB—447c, 1003a.

7773. שֶׁוַע {1x} **sheva**ᶜ, *sheh'-vah;* from 7768; a *halloo:*—cry {1x}. See: TWOT—2348a; BDB—1002d.

7774. שׁוּעָא {2x} **Shûw**ᶜâ**ʾ**, *shoo-aw';* from 7768; *wealth; Shua,* an Israelitess:—Shua {2x}. See: BDB—447d, 1003a.

7775. שַׁוְעָה {11x} **shav**ᶜâh, *shav-aw';* fem. of 7773; a *hallooing:*—cry {11x}. See: TWOT—2348c; BDB—1003a.

7776. שׁוּעָל {7x} **shûw**ᶜâl, *shoo-awl';* or

שֻׁעָל **shu**ᶜâl, *shoo-awl';* from the same as 8168; a *jackal* (as a *burrower*):—fox {7x}. See: TWOT—2433a; BDB—1043c.

7777. שׁוּעָל {2x} **Shûw**ᶜâl, *shoo-awl';* the same as 7776; *Shual,* the name of an Isr. and of a place in Pal.:—Shual {2x}. See: BDB—1043c.

7778. שׁוֹעֵר {37x} **shôw**ᶜêr, *sho-are';* or

שֹׁעֵר **sho**ᶜêr, *sho-are';* act. part. of 8176 (as denom. from 8179); a *janitor:*—doorkeepers {2x}, porter {35x}. See: TWOT—2437b; BDB—1045b.

7779. שׁוּף {4x} **shûwph**, *shoof;* a prim. root; prop. to *gape,* i.e. *snap* at; fig. to *overwhelm:*—break {1x}, bruise {2x}, cover {1x}. See: TWOT—2349; BDB—1003a.

7780. שׁוֹפָךְ {2x} **Shôwphâk**, *sho-fawk';* from 8210; *poured; Shophak,* a Syrian:—Shophach {2x}. See: BDB—1000c, 1003a.

7781. שׁוּפָמִי {1x} **Shûwphâmîy**, *shoo-faw-mee';* patron. from 8197; a *Shuphamite* (collect.) or desc. of Shephupham:—Shuphamites {1x}. See: BDB—1003a, 1050d, 1051b.

שׁוֹפָן **Shôwphân**. See 5855.

7782. שׁוֹפָר {72x} **shôwphâr**, *sho-far';* or

שֹׁפָר **shôphâr**, *sho-far';* from 8231 in the orig. sense of *incising;* a *cornet* (as giving a *clear* sound) or curved horn:—trumpet {68x}, cornet {4x}. See: TWOT—2449c; BDB—1051c.

7783. שׁוּק {3x} **shûwq**, *shook;* a prim. root; to *run* after or over, i.e. *overflow:*—overflow {2x}, water {1x}. See: TWOT—2351; BDB—1003b.

7784. שׁוּק {4x} **shûwq**, *shook;* from 7783; a *street* (as *run* over):—street {4x}. See: TWOT—2350b; BDB—1003b.

7785. שׁוֹק {19x} **shôwq**, *shoke;* from 7783; the (lower) *leg* (as a *runner*):—shoulder {13x}, legs {4x}, hip {1x}, thigh {1x}. See: TWOT—2350a; BDB—1003b, 1114d.

7786. שׁוּר {3x} **sûwr,** *soor;* a prim. root; prop. to *vanquish;* by impl. to *rule* (caus. *crown*):—reign {1x}, have power {1x}, made prince {1x}. See: TWOT—2287; BDB—975b, 979a. See 5493.

7787. שׁוּר {1x} **sûwr,** *soor;* a prim. root [rather ident. with 7786 through the idea of *reducing* to pieces; comp. 4883]; to *saw:*—cut {1x}. See: TWOT—2245; BDB—963a, 965a, 975b.

7788. שׁוּר {2x} **shûwr,** *shoor;* a prim. root; prop. to *turn,* i.e. *travel* about (as a harlot or a merchant):—went {1x}, sing {1x}. See: TWOT—2353; BDB—1003c. See also 7891.

7789. שׁוּר {16x} **shûwr,** *shoor;* a prim. root [rather ident. with 7788 through the idea of *going round* for inspection]; to *spy* out, i.e. (gen.) *survey,* (for evil) *lurk for,* (for good) *care for:*—behold {5x}, see {4x}, look {2x}, observe {2x}, lay wait {1x}, regard {1x}, perceive {1x}. See: TWOT—2354; BDB—1003d.

7790. שׁוּר {1x} **shûwr,** *shoor;* from 7889; a *foe* (as *lying in wait*):—enemy {1x}. See: TWOT—2354a; BDB—1004a.

7791. שׁוּר {4x} **shûwr,** *shoor;* from 7788; a *wall* (as *going about*):—wall {4x}. See: TWOT—2355b; BDB—1004b, 1004c, 1114d.

7792. שׁוּר {3x} **shûwr** (Aram.), *shoor;* corresp. to 7791:—wall {3x}. See: TWOT—3025; BDB—1114d.

7793. שׁוּר {6x} **Shûwr,** *shoor;* the same as 7791; *Shur,* a region of the desert:—Shur {6x}. See: BDB—1004b.

7794. שׁוֹר {78x} **shôwr,** *shore;* from 7788; a *bullock* (as a *traveller*):—ox {62x}, bullock {12x}, cow {2x}, bull {1x}, wall {1x}. See: TWOT—2355a; BDB—1004a, 1117d.

7795. שׁוֹרָה {1x} **sôwrâh,** *so-raw′;* from 7786 in the prim. sense of 5493; prop. a *ring,* i.e. (by anal.) a *row* (adv.):—principal {1x}. See: TWOT—2245a; BDB—965a, 975b.

שׁוֹרֵק **sôwrêq.** See 8321.

7796. שׁוֹרֵק {1x} **Sôwrêq,** *so-rake′;* the same as 8321; a *vine; Sorek,* a valley in Pal.:—Sorek {1x}. See: BDB—977d.

7797. שׂוּשׂ {27x} **sûws,** *soos;* or

שׂישׂ **sîys,** *sece;* a prim. root; to *be bright,* i.e. *cheerful:*—rejoice {20x}, glad {4x}, greatly {1x}, joy {1x}, mirth {1x}. See: TWOT—2246; BDB—965a.

7798. שַׁוְשָׁא {1x} **Shavshâ′,** *shav-shaw′;* from 7797; *joyful; Shavsha,* an Isr.:—Shavsha {1x}. See: BDB—1004c.

7799. שׁוּשַׁן {15x} **shûwshan,** *shoo-shan′;* or

שׁוֹשָׁן **shôwshân,** *sho-shawn′;* or

שֹׁשָׁן **shôshân,** *sho-shawn′;* and (fem.)

שׁוֹשַׁנָּה **shôwshannâh,** *sho-shan-naw′;* from 7797; a *lily* (from its *whiteness*), as a flower or arch. ornament; also a (straight) *trumpet* (from the *tubular* shape):—lily {13x}, Shoshannim {2x}. See: TWOT—2356; BDB—1004c.

7800. שׁוּשַׁן {21x} **Shûwshan,** *shoo-shan′;* the same as 7799; *Shushan,* a place in Pers.:—Shushan {21x}. See: BDB—1004d.

7801. שׁוּשַׁנְכִי {1x} **Shûwshankîy** (Aram.), *shoo-shan-kee′;* of for. or.; a *Shushankite* (collect.) or inhab. of some unknown place in Ass.:—Susanchites {1x}. See: BDB—1114d.

7802. שׁוּשַׁן עֵדוּת {2x} **Shûwshan ʻÊdûwth,** *shoo-shan′ ay-dooth′;* or (plur. of former)

שׁוֹשַׁנִּים עֵדוּת **Shôwshannîym ʻÊdûwth,** *sho-shan-neem′ ay-dooth′;* from 7799 and 5715; *lily* (or *trumpet*) *of assemblage; Shushan-Eduth* or *Shoshannim-Eduth,* the title of a popular song:—Shoshannimeduth {1x}, Shushaneduth {1x}. See: BDB—1004c.

שׁוּשַׁק **Shûwshaq.** See 7895.

7803. שׁוּתֶלַח {4x} **Shûwthelach,** *shoo-theh′-lakh;* prob. from 7582 and the same as 8520; *crash of breakage; Shuthelach,* the name of two Isr.:—Shuthelah {4x}. See: BDB—1004d.

7804. שְׁזַב {9x} **shᵉzab** (Aram.), *shez-ab′;* corresp. to 5800; to *leave,* i.e. (caus.) *free:*—deliver {9x}. See: TWOT—3027; BDB—1095c, 1115a.

7805. שָׁזַף {3x} **shâzaph,** *shaw-zaf′;* a prim. root; to *tan* (by sun-burning); fig. (as if by a piercing ray) to *scan:*—see {2x}, look {1x}. See: TWOT—2357; BDB—1004d.

7806. שָׁזַר {21x} **shâzar,** *shaw-zar′;* a prim. root; to *twist* (a thread of straw):—twine {21x}. See: TWOT—2358; BDB—1004d.

7807. שַׁח {1x} **shach,** *shakh;* from 7817; *sunk,* i.e. *downcast:*—+ humble {1x}. See: TWOT—2361a; BDB—1005a, 1006a.

7808. שֵׂחַ {1x} **sêach,** *say′-akh;* for 7879; *communion,* i.e. (refl.) *meditation:*—thought {1x}. See: TWOT—2255c; BDB—965c, 967b.

7809. שָׁחַד {2x} **shâchad,** *shaw-khad′;* a prim. root; to *donate,* i.e. *bribe:*—reward

{1x}, hire {1x}. See: TWOT–2359; BDB–
1005a, 1007c.

7810. שָׁחַד {23x} **shachad**, *shakh'-ad;* from
7809; a *donation* (venal or re-
demptive):—gift {10x}, reward {7x}, bribes {3x},
present {2x}, bribery {1x}. See: TWOT–2359a;
BDB–1005a.

7811. שָׂחָה {3x} **sâchâh**, *saw-khaw';* a prim.
root; to *swim;* caus. to *inundate:*—
swim {3x}. See: TWOT–2247; BDB–965c.

7812. שָׁחָה {172x} **shâchâh**, *shaw-khaw';* a
prim. root; to *depress,* i.e. *prostrate* (espec. refl. in homage to royalty or
God):—worship {99x}, bow {31x}, bow down
{18x}, obeisance {9x}, reverence {5x}, fall down
{3x}, themselves {2x}, stoop {1x}, crouch {1x},
misc. {3x}.
    Shachah portrays (1) the act of bowing
down in homage by an inferior (1a) before a
superior ruler (1 Sa 24:8), and (1b) before a
social or economic superior to whom one bows
(Ruth 2:10). (2) It is the common term for coming before God in worship (1 Sa 15:25; Jer 7:2).
(3) Other gods and idols are also the object
of such worship by one's prostrating oneself
before them (Is 2:20; 44:15, 17). Syn.: 5457. See:
TWOT–2360; BDB–1005b.

7813. שָׂחוּ {1x} **sâchûw**, *saw'-khoo;* from 7811;
a *pond* (for *swimming*):—swim
{1x}. See: TWOT–2247a; BDB–965c.

7814. שְׂחוֹק {15x} **s°chôwq**, *sekh-oke';* or
שְׂחֹק **s°chôq**, *sekh-oke';* from 7832;
laughter (in merriment or defiance):—laughter {6x}, derision {5x}, laughing
{1x}, mock {1x}, laugh to scorn {1x}, sport {1x}.
See: TWOT–1905d; BDB–966a.

7815. שְׁחוֹר {1x} **sh°chôwr**, *shekh-ore';* from
7835; *dinginess,* i.e. perh. *soot:*—
coal {1x}. See: TWOT–2368a; BDB–1005d,
1007a.

שִׁחוֹר **shîchôwr**. See 7883.

שָׁחוֹר **shâchôwr**. See 7838.

7816. שְׁחוּת {1x} **sh°chûwth**, *shekh-ooth';*
from 7812; *pit:*—pit {1x}. See:
TWOT–2360a; BDB–1005c.

7817. שָׁחַח {21x} **shâchach**, *shaw-khakh';* a
prim. root; to *sink* or *depress* (refl.
or caus.):—bow down {5x}, cast down {4x},
bring down {3x}, brought low {2x}, bow {2x},
bending {1x}, couch {1x}, humbleth {1x}, low
{1x}, stoop {1x}. See: TWOT–2361; BDB–
1001c, 1005d.

7818. שָׂחַט {1x} **sâchat**, *saw-khat';* a prim.
root; to *tread* out, i.e. *squeeze*

(grapes):—press {1x}. See: TWOT–2248;
BDB–965c.

7819. שָׁחַט {81x} **shâchat**, *shaw-khat';* a prim.
root; to *slaughter* (in sacrifice or
massacre):—kill 42, slay 36, offer {1x}, shot out
{1x}, slaughter {1x}.
    Shachat means "to slaughter, kill." (1) It
first appears in Gen 22:10: "And Abraham . . .
took the knife to slay his son." (2) Expressing
"slaying" for sacrifice is the most frequent use
of *shachat* (51 times); and as might be expected, the word is found some 30 times in the
Book of Leviticus alone. (3) *Shachat* sometimes
implies the "slaughtering" of animals for food
(1 Sa 14:32, 34; Is 22:13). (4) The word is used
of the "killing" of people a number of times
(Judg 12:6; 1 Kin 18:40; 2 Kin 10:7, 14).
(5) Sometimes God is said "to slay" people
(Num 14:16). (6) Backslidden Judah went so
far as "to slaughter" children as sacrifices to
false gods (Eze 16:21; 23:39; Is 57:5). Syn.: 2026,
7523. See: TWOT–2362; BDB–1006a, 1006b.

7820. שָׁחַט {5x} **shâchat**, *shaw-khat';* a prim.
root [rather ident. with 7819
through the idea of *striking*]; to *hammer* out:—
beaten {5x}. See: TWOT–2362; BDB–1006a.

7821. שְׁחִיטָה {1x} **sh°chîytâh**, *shekh-ee-taw';*
from 7819; *slaughter:*—killing
{1x}. See: TWOT–2362a; BDB–1006b.

7822. שְׁחִין {13x} **sh°chîyn**, *shekh-een';* from
an unused root prob. mean. to
burn; inflammation, i.e. an *ulcer;*—boil {11x},
botch {2x}. See: TWOT–2364a; BDB–1006b,
1006c.

7823. שָׁחִיס {2x} **shâchîyç**, *shaw-khece';* or
סָחִישׁ **çâchîysh**, *saw-kheesh';* from an
unused root appar. mean. to
sprout; after-growth:—that which springeth of
the same {2x}. See: TWOT–1484; BDB–
695a, 1006b.

7824. שָׁחִיף {1x} **shâchîyph**, *shaw-kheef';*
from the same as 7828; a *board*
(as *chipped* thin):—cieled {1x}. See: TWOT–
2249; BDB–965d, 1006b.

7825. שְׁחִית {2x} **sh°chîyth**, *shekh-eeth';* from
7812; a *pit*-fall (lit. or fig.):—destruction {1x}, pit {1x}. See: TWOT–2360b;
BDB–1005d.

7826. שַׁחַל {7x} **shachal**, *shakh'-al;* from an
unused root prob. mean. to *roar;* a
lion (from his characteristic *roar*):—lion {4x},
fierce lion {3x}. See: TWOT–2363a; BDB–
1006c.

7827. שְׁחֵלֶת {1x} **sh°chêleth**, *shekh-ay'-leth;*
appar. from the same as 7826
through some obscure idea, perh. that of *peel-*

ing off by concussion of sound; a *scale* or shell, i.e. the aromatic *mussel:*—onycha {1x}. See: TWOT—2363b; BDB—1006c.

7828. שַׁחַף {2x} **shachaph**, *shakh'-af;* from an unused root mean. to *peel,* i.e. *emaciate;* the *gull* (as *thin):*—cuckow {2x}. See: TWOT—2365a; BDB—1006d.

7829. שַׁחֶפֶת {2x} **shachepheth**, *shakh-eh'-feth;* from the same as 7828; *emaciation:*—consumption {2x}. See: TWOT—2365b; BDB—1006d.

7830. שַׁחַץ {2x} **shachats**, *shakh'-ats;* from an unused root appar. mean. to *strut; haughtiness* (as evinced by the attitude):—lion {1x}, pride {1x}. See: TWOT—2366a; BDB—1006d.

7831. שַׁחֲצוֹם {1x} **Shachatsôwm**, *shakh-ats-ome';* from the same as 7830; *proudly; Shachatsom,* a place in Pal.:—Shahazimah {1x}. See: BDB—1006d.

7832. שָׂחַק {36x} **sâchaq**, *saw-khak';* a prim. root; to *laugh* (in pleasure or detraction); by impl. to *play:*—play {10x}, laugh {10x}, rejoice {3x}, scorn {3x}, sport {3x}, merry {2x}, mock {2x}, deride {1x}, derision {1x}, mockers {1x}. See: TWOT—1905c; BDB—965d.

7833. שָׁחַק {4x} **shâchaq**, *shaw-khak';* a prim. root; to *comminate* (by trituration or attrition):—beat {3x}, wear {1x}. See: TWOT—2367; BDB—1006d.

7834. שַׁחַק {21x} **shachaq**, *shakh'-ak;* from 7833; a *powder* (as *beaten* small): by anal. a thin *vapor;* by extens. the *firmament:*—cloud {11x}, sky {7x}, heaven {2x}, small dust {1x}. Syn.: 1534, 6160, 8064. See: TWOT—2367a; BDB—1007a.

שְׂחֹק s*e*chôq. See 7814.

7835. שָׁחַר {1x} **shâchar**, *shaw-khar';* a prim. root [rather ident. with 7836 through the idea of the *duskiness* of early dawn]; to *be dim* or dark (in color):—black {1x}. See: TWOT—2368; BDB—1007a, 1009d.

7836. שָׁחַר {12x} **shâchar**, *shaw-khar';* a prim. root; prop. to *dawn,* i.e. (fig.) *be* (up) *early* at any task (with the impl. of earnestness); by extens. to *search* for (with painstaking):—seek early {4x}, seek {2x}, diligently seek {2x}, betimes {1x}, misc. {3x} = [do something] betimes, enquire early, rise (seek) betimes, seek (diligently) early, in the morning. See: TWOT—2369; BDB—1007c.

7837. שַׁחַר {24x} **shachar**, *shakh'-ar;* from 7836; *dawn* (lit., fig. or adv.):—morning {12x}, day {6x}, early {2x}, dayspring

{1x}, light {1x}, riseth {1x}, Shahar {1x}. See: TWOT—2369a; BDB—1007b.

שִׁחֹר **Shîchôr.** See 7883.

7838. שָׁחֹר {6x} **shâchôr**, *shaw-khore';* or

שָׁחוֹר **shâchôwr**, *shaw-khore';* from 7835; prop. *dusky,* but also (absol.) *jetty:*—black {6x}. See: TWOT—2368b; BDB—1007b.

7839. שַׁחֲרוּת {1x} **shachărûwth**, *shakh-ar-ooth';* from 7836; a *dawning,* i.e. (fig.) *juvenescence:*—youth {1x}. See: TWOT—2368c; BDB—1007b, 1007d.

7840. שְׁחַרְחֹרֶת {1x} **sh*e*charchôreth**, *shekh-ar-kho'-reth;* from 7835; *swarthy:*—black {1x}. See: TWOT—2368d; BDB—1007b.

7841. שְׁחַרְיָה {1x} **Sh*e*charyâh**, *shekh-ar-yaw';* from 7836 and 3050; *Jah has sought; Shecharjah,* an Isr.:—Shehariah {1x}. See: BDB—1007d.

7842. שַׁחֲרַיִם {1x} **Shachărayim**, *shakh-ar-ah'-yim;* dual of 7837; *double dawn; Shacharajim,* an Isr.:—Shaharaim {1x}. See: BDB—1007d.

7843. שָׁחַת {147x} **shâchath**, *shaw-khath';* a prim. root; to *decay,* i.e. (caus.) *ruin* (lit. or fig.):—destroy {96x}, corrupt {22x}, mar {7x}, destroyer {3x}, corrupters {2x}, waster {2x}, spoilers {2x}, battered {1x}, corruptly {1x}, misc. {11x} = cast off, destruction, lose, perish, spill, X utterly, waste.

This word especially marks dissolution or corruption and also to the physical destruction of all that was living on the earth and of the earth itself. **(1)** Anything that is good can be corrupted or spoiled: **(1a)** all on the earth (Gen 6:11–12, 17); **(1b)** Jeremiah's loincloth (Jer 13:7), **(1c)** a vineyard (Jer 12:10), **(1d)** cities (Gen 13:10), and **(1e)** a temple (Lam 2:6). **(2)** *Shachath* has the meaning of "to waste" when words are inappropriately spoken (Prov 23:8). **(3)** In its participial form, it describes **(3a)** a destroying lion (Jer 2:30 RSV) and **(3b)** the destroying angel (1 Chr 21:15). **(4)** The word symbolizes a trap in Jer 5:26. **(5)** *Shachath* is used frequently by the prophets in the sense of "to corrupt morally" (Is 1:4; Eze 23:11; Zeph 3:7). Syn.: 7585. See: TWOT—2370; BDB—1007d, 1115a.

7844. שְׁחַת {3x} **sh*e*chath** (Aram.), *shekh-ath';* corresp. to 7843:—fault {2x}, corrupt {1x}. See: TWOT—3026; BDB—1115a.

7845. שַׁחַת {23x} **shachath**, *shakh'-ath;* from 7743; a *pit* (espec. as a trap); fig. *destruction:*—corruption {4x}, pit {14x}, destruction {2x}, ditch {2x}, grave {1x}. See:

TWOT—2343.1c, 2370d; BDB—1001c, 1008b, 1008d.

7846. שֵׂט {1x} sêṭ, *sayte;* or

שֵׂט çêṭ, *sayt;* from 7750; a *departure* from right, i.e. *sin:*—revolters {1x}. See: TWOT—2240a; BDB—962b, 966a.

7847. שָׂטָה {6x} sâṭâh, *saw-taw';* a prim. root; to *deviate* from duty:—go aside {4x}, turn {1x}, decline {1x}. See: TWOT—2250; BDB—966a.

7848. שִׂטָּה {28x} shiṭṭâh, *shit-taw';* fem. of a der. [only in the plur.

שִׂטִּים shiṭṭîym, *shit-teem';* mean. the *sticks* of wood] from the same as 7850; the *acacia* (from its *scourging* thorns):— shittim {27x}, shittah tree {1x}. See: TWOT—2371; BDB—1008d. See also 1029.

7849. שָׂטַח {6x} shâṭach, *shaw-takh';* a prim. root; to *expand:*—spread {3x}, enlarge {1x}, stretch out {1x}, all abroad {1x}. See: TWOT—2372; BDB—1008d.

7850. שֹׁטֵט {1x} shôṭêṭ, *sho-tate';* act. part. of an otherwise unused root mean. (prop. to *pierce;* but only as a denom. from 7752) to *flog;* a *goad:*—scourge {1x}. See: TWOT—2344b; BDB—1002b, 1009a.

7851. שִׁטִּים {5x} Shiṭṭîym, *shit-teem';* the same as the plur. of 7848; *acacia* trees; *Shittim,* a place E. of the Jordan:— Shittim {5x}. See: BDB—1008d.

7852. שָׂטַם {6x} sâṭam, *saw-tam';* a prim. root; prop. to *lurk* for, i.e. *persecute:*— hate {5x}, oppose {1x}. See: TWOT—2251; BDB—966b.

7853. שָׂטַן {6x} sâṭan, *saw-tan';* a prim. root; to *attack,* (fig.) *accuse:*—adversary {5x}, resist {1x}. See: TWOT—2252; BDB—966c.

7854. שָׂטָן {27x} sâṭân, *saw-tawn';* from 7853; an *opponent;* espec. (with the art. pref.) *Satan,* the arch-enemy of good:—Satan {19x}, adversary {7x}, withstand {1x}.

Satan is an adversary or plotter, one who devises means for opposition. *Satan* means "adversary; *Satan."* **(1)** In Ps 38:20, David cried out because he was the target of attack by his "adversaries": "They also that render evil for good are mine adversaries; because I follow *the thing that* good *is."* **(2)** In another psalm of distress by an individual, a godly man expressed his deep faith in the Lord. The writer prayed concerning those who were "adversaries" to his soul: "Let them be confounded and consumed that are adversaries to my soul; let them be covered with reproach and dishonor

that seek my hurt" (Ps 71:13). He expressed the reality of the powers of darkness against an individual who sought to live for God.

(3) Imprecatory psalms call for judgment upon one's enemies. **(3a)** David's enemies became his "adversaries," but he continued to pray for them (Ps 109:4). **(3b)** Because those enemies repaid him evil for good and hatred for his love, the king prayed: "Set thou a wicked man over him: and let *Satan* stand at his right hand" (Ps 109:6). **(3c)** When they spoke evil against his soul, David called for the Lord's reward against his "adversaries" (Ps 109:20), and finally, **(3d)** because David's accusers had intended him so much harm, he asked that his accusers be clothed with shame and dishonor (Ps 109:29). **(3e)** In all of these passages, God worked indirectly by permitting individuals to act as "adversaries" of His people. **(4)** In another instance, David was merciful with members of Saul's family who cursed him and wished him harm when he fled from Absalom (2 Sa 16:5ff.). **(4a)** David restrained his army commanders from killing Saul's family who had repented of their misdeeds. **(4b)** The king did not want his officers to be his "adversaries" on the day of victory and joy (2 Sa 19:22).

(5) God can also be the "adversary." When Balaam went to curse the sons of Israel, God warned him not to do so. **(5a)** When the prophet persisted, God disciplined him: "And God's anger was kindled because he went: and the angel of the Lord stood in the way for an adversary against him" (Num 22:22). **(5b)** God stood as an "adversary" because no curse could undo the covenants and agreements already made with Israel. **(6)** God took up a controversy with Solomon. **(6a)** When Solomon added more and more pagan wives to his harem, God was greatly displeased (Deut 17:17). **(6b)** But when the king built pagan shrines for his wives, God raised up "adversaries" against him (1 Kin 11:14), a direct action which caused the Edomites and Syrians to revolt against Israel. **(7)** Another special instance of intervention was the occasion when "*Satan* [literally, "an adversary"] stood up against Israel, and provoked David to number Israel" (1 Chr 21:1). (No definite article is here in Hebrew and, therefore, "an adversary" is in mind.)

(8) In a parallel passage the Lord moved David to number Israel and Judah (2 Sa 24:1). Even as the Lord stirred up an "adversary" against Solomon, so here God took a direct action to test David to help him learn a vital lesson. God tests believers to help them make the right choices and not depend upon their own human strength. **(9)** In the Book of Job, the word *Satan* always has the definite article

preceding it (Job 1:6–12; 2:1–7), so the term emphasizes *Satan's* role as "the adversary." **(9a)** God permitted *Satan* to test Job's faith, and the adversary inflicted the patriarch with many evils and sorrows. **(9b)** *Satan* was not all-powerful because he indicated that he could not get beyond God's protection of Job (Job 1:10). **(9c)** He penetrated the "hedge" only with God's permission and only for specific instances that would demonstrate God's righteousness.

(10) Zechariah recorded a vision of "Joshua the high priest standing before the angel of the Lord, and *Satan* standing at his right hand to resist him" (literally, "be his adversary"; Zec 3:1). **(10a)** The Lord rebuked "the adversary" (Zec 3:2). **(10b)** *Satan* was once again in conflict with God's purposes and the angels of God, but "the adversary" was not all-powerful and was subject to rebuke by God Himself **(11)** A general usage of *satan* ("adversary") appears in 1 Kin 5:4: "But now the Lord my God hath given me rest on every side, so that there is neither adversary or evil occurrent." **(12)** In another instance, David went over to the side of the Philistines; in attempting to fight with them against Israel, some of the Philistine leaders doubted David's sincerity and felt that he would be "an adversary" in any battle between the two armies (1 Sa 29:4). Syn.: 7700, 8163. See: TWOT—2252a; BDB—966b.

7855. שִׂטְנָה {1x} **siṭnâh**, *sit-naw';* from 7853; *opposition* (by letter):—accusation {1x}. See: TWOT—2252b; BDB—966c.

7856. שִׂטְנָה {1x} **Siṭnâh**, *sit-naw';* the same as 7855; *Sitnah*, the name of a well in Pal.:—Sitnah {1x}. See: BDB—966c.

7857. שָׁטַף {13x} **shâṭaph**, *shaw-taf';* a prim. root; to *gush;* by impl. to *inundate, cleanse;* by anal. to *gallop, conquer:*—overflow {20x}, rinsed {3x}, wash away {2x}, drown {1x}, flowing {1x}, misc. {4x} = overwhelm, run, rush. Syn.: 1740, 3526, 7364. See: TWOT—2373; BDB—1009a.

7858. שֶׁטֶף {6x} **sheṭeph**, *sheh'-tef;* or

שֵׁטֶף **shêṭeph**, *shay'-tef;* from 7857; a *deluge* (lit. or fig.):—flood {4x}, overflowing of waters {1x}, outrageous {1x}. See: TWOT—2373a; BDB—1009b.

7859. שְׁטַר {1x} **sᵉṭar** (Aram.), *set-ar';* of uncert. der.; a *side:*—one side {1x}. See: TWOT—3007; BDB—1113d.

7860. שֹׁטֵר {25x} **shôṭêr**, *sho-tare';* act. part. of an otherwise unused root prob. mean. to *write;* prop. a *scribe,* i.e. (by anal. or impl.) an official *superintendent* or *magis-*

trate:—officers {23x}, ruler {1x}, overseer {1x}. See: TWOT—2374a; BDB—1009c, 1104c.

7861. שִׁטְרַי {1x} **Shiṭray**, *shit-rah'-ee;* from the same as 7860; *magisterial; Shitrai,* an Isr.:—Shitrai {1x}. See: BDB—1009c, 1056c.

7862. שַׁי {3x} **shay**, *shah'-ee;* prob. from 7737; a *gift* (as *available*):—present {3x}. See: TWOT—2375; BDB—1009c.

7863. שִׂיא {1x} **sîyʾ**, *see;* from the same as 7721 by perm.; *elevation:*—excellency {1x}. See: TWOT—1421i; BDB—673b, 966c.

7864. שְׁיָא {1x} **Shᵉyâʾ**, *sheh-yaw';* for 7724; *Sheja,* an Isr.:—Sheva {1x}. See: BDB—1009d.

7865. שִׂיאֹן {1x} **Sîyʾôn**, *see-ohn';* from 7863; *peak; Sion,* the summit of Mt. Hermon:—Sion {1x}. See: BDB—673b, 966c.

7866. שִׁאיֹן {1x} **Shiʾyôwn**, *shee-ohn';* from the same as 7722; *ruin; Shijon,* a place in Pal.:—Shion {1x}. See: BDB—1009d.

7867. שִׂיב {2x} **sîyb**, *seeb;* a prim. root; prop. to *become aged,* i.e. (by impl.) to *grow gray:*—grayheaded {2x}. See: TWOT—2253; BDB—959a, 966c.

7868. שִׂיב {5x} **sîyb** (Aram.), *seeb;* corresp. to 7867:—elder {5x}. See: TWOT—3008; BDB—1114a.

7869. שֵׂיב {1x} **sêyb**, *sabe;* from 7867; old *age:*—age {1x}. See: TWOT—2253a; BDB—966c, 1114a.

7870. שִׁיבָה {1x} **shîybâh**, *shee-baw';* by perm. from 7725; a *return* (of property):—captivity {1x}. See: TWOT—2340b; BDB—1000a, 1009d.

7871. שִׁיבָה {1x} **shîybâh**, *shee-baw';* from 3427; *residence:*—lay {1x}. See: TWOT—922b; BDB—444a, 1000a, 1009d.

7872. שֵׂיבָה {19x} **sêybâh**, *say-baw';* fem. of 7869; old *age:*—old age {6x}, gray hairs {6x}, hoar head {3x}, hoary head {2x}, grayheaded {1x}, hoary {1x}. See: TWOT—2253b; BDB—966c.

7873. שִׂיג {1x} **sîyg**, *seeg;* from 7734; a *withdrawal* (into a private place):—pursuing {1x}. See: TWOT—1469a; BDB—691a, 966d.

7874. שִׂיד {2x} **sîyd**, *seed;* a prim. root prob. mean. to *boil* up (comp. 7736); used only as denom. from 7875; to *plaster:*—plaister {2x}. See: TWOT—2254; BDB—966d.

7875. שִׂיד {4x} **sîyd**, *seed;* from 7874; *lime* (as *boiling* when slacked):—plaister

{2x}, lime {2x}. See: TWOT—2254a; BDB—966d.

7876. שָׁיָה {1x} **shâyâh**, *shaw-yaw'*; a prim. root; to *keep* in memory:—be unmindful {1x}. See: TWOT—1428; BDB—1009d. [Render Deut 32:18, "A Rock bore thee, thou must recollect; and (yet) thou hast forgotten," etc.]

7877. שִׁיזָא {1x} **Shîyzâ'**, *shee-zaw'*; of unknown der.; *Shiza*, an Isr.:—Shiza {1x}. See: BDB—1009d.

7878. שִׂיחַ {20x} **sîyach**, *see'-akh;* a prim. root; to *ponder*, i.e. (by impl.) *converse* (with oneself, and hence, aloud) or (tran.) *utter:*—talk {5x}, meditate {5x}, speak {4x}, complain {2x}, pray {1x}, commune {1x}, muse {1x}, declare {1x}. See: TWOT—2255; BDB—967a, 1002a.

7879. שִׂיחַ {14x} **sîyach**, *see'-akh;* from 7878; a *contemplation;* by impl. an *utterance:*—complaint {9x}, meditation {1x}, prayer {1x}, talking {1x}, communication {1x}, babbling {1x}. See: TWOT—2255a; BDB—967a.

7880. שִׂיחַ {4x} **sîyach**, *see'-akh;* from 7878; a *shoot* (as if *uttered* or put forth), i.e. (gen.) *shrubbery:*—bush {2x}, plant {1x}, shrub {1x}. See: TWOT—2256a; BDB—967b.

7881. שִׂיחָה {3x} **sîychâh**, *see-khaw';* fem. of 7879; *reflection;* by extens. *devotion:*—meditation {2x}, prayer {1x}. Syn.: 577, 4994, 6279, 6419, 6739, 7592. See: TWOT—2255b; BDB—967a.

7882. שִׁיחָה {3x} **shîychâh**, *shee-khaw';* for 7745; a *pit*-fall:—pit {3x}. See: TWOT—2343.1b; BDB—1001c, 1009d.

7883. שִׁיחוֹר {4x} **Shîychôwr**, *shee-khore';* or

שִׁחוֹר **Shîchôwr**, *shee-khore';* or

שִׁחֹר **Shîchôr**, *shee-khore';* prob. from 7835; *dark*, i.e. *turbid; Shichor*, a stream of Egypt:—Shihor {1x}, Sihor {3x}. See: BDB—1005d, 1007a, 1009d.

7884. שִׁיחוֹר לִבְנָת {1x} **Shîychôwr Libnâth**, *shee-khore' lib-nawth';* from the same as 7883 and 3835; *darkish whiteness; Shichor-Libnath*, a stream of Pal.:—Shihor-libnath {1x}. See: BDB—527d, 1009d.

7885. שַׁיִט {2x} **shayiṭ**, *shay'-yit;* from 7751; an *oar;* also (comp. 7752) a *scourge* (fig.):—oar {2x}. See: TWOT—2344c; BDB—1002a, 1002b, 1009d.

7886. שִׁילֹה {1x} **Shîylôh**, *shee-lo';* from 7951; *tranquil; Shiloh*, an epithet of the Messiah:—Shiloh {1x}. See: BDB—1010a.

7887. שִׁילֹה {32x} **Shîylôh**, *shee-lo';* or

שִׁלֹה **Shîlôh**, *shee-lo';* or

שִׁילוֹ **Shîylôw**, *shee-lo';* or

שִׁלוֹ **Shîlôw**, *shee-lo';* from the same as 7886; *Shiloh*, a place in Pal.:—Shiloh {32x}. See: BDB—1009d, 1017d.

7888. שִׁילוֹנִי {6x} **Shiylôwnîy**, *shee-lo-nee';* or

שִׁילֹנִי **Shîylônîy**, *shee-lo-nee';* or

שִׁלֹנִי **Shîlônîy**, *shee-lo-nee';* from 7887; a *Shilonite* or inhab. of Shiloh:—Shilonite {6x}. See: BDB—1009d, 1017c, 1018a, 1025b.

שֵׁילָל **shêylâl**. See 7758.

7889. שִׁימוֹן {1x} **Shîymôwn**, *shee-mone';* appar. for 3452; *desert; Shimon*, an Isr.:—Shimon {1x}. See: BDB—1010a.

7890. שַׁיִן {2x} **shayin**, *shah'-yin;* from an unused root mean. to *urinate; urine:*—piss {2x}. See: TWOT—2377a; BDB—1010a.

7891. שִׁיר {87x} **shîyr**, *sheer;* or (the orig. form)

שׁוּר **shûwr** (1 Sa 18:6), *shoor;* a prim. root [rather ident. with 7788 through the idea of *strolling* minstrelsy]; to *sing:*—sing {41x}, singer {37x}, singing men {4x}, singing women {4x}, behold {1x}.

I. Shiyr (7891), as a verb, means "to sing." **(1)** While it occurs 87 times in the Hebrew Old Testament, it is not used until Ex 15:1: "Then sang Moses and the children of Israel this song unto the Lord. . . ." One might wonder if it took the miracle of the Exodus from Egypt to give the Israelites something "to sing" about! **(2)** Over one quarter of the instances of *shiyr* are found in the Book of Psalms, often in the imperative form, calling the people to express their praise to God in singing. One such example is found in Ps 96:1: "O sing unto the Lord a new song: sing unto the Lord, all the earth." **(3)** Frequently *shiyr* is found in parallelism with *zamar* (2167), "to sing" (Ps 68:4, 32). **II. Shiyr, as a participle,** means "singers." **(1)** In the Books of Chronicles, *shiyr* is used in the participial form some 33 times to designate the Levitical "singers" (1 Chr 15:16). **(2)** "Female singers" are referred to occasionally (2 Sa 19:35; 2 Chr 35:25; Eccl 2:8). See: TWOT—2378; BDB—1010c.

7892. שִׁיר {90x} **shîyr**, *sheer;* or fem.

שִׁירָה **shîyrâh**, *shee-raw';* from 7891; a *song;* abstr. *singing:*—song {74x}, musick {7x}, singing {4x}, musical {2x}, sing {1x}, singers {1x}, song + 1697 {1x}.

Shiyr, as a noun, means "song." **(1)** This noun is found about 30 times in the titles of various psalms as well as elsewhere in the Old

Testament. **(2)** *Shiyr* is used of a joyous "song" in Gen 31:27: "And didst not tell me, that I might have sent thee away with mirth, and with songs, with tabret, and with harp?" **(3)** In Judg 5:12 the word refers to a triumphal "song," and **(4)** in Neh 12:46 the word is used of a religious "song" for worship. **(5)** The book that is commonly designated "The Song of Solomon" actually has the title "The Song of Songs" in Hebrew, a love "song," pure and simple, and that love has its rightful place in the divine plan for mature men and women. See: TWOT−2378a, 2378b; BDB−1010b, 1010c.

שִׁישׁ **sîys.** See 7797.

7893. שַׁישׁ {1x} **shayish,** *shah'-yish;* from an unused root mean. to *bleach,* i.e. *whiten; white,* i.e. *marble:*−marble {1x}. See: TWOT−2379; BDB−1010d. See 8336.

7894. שִׁישָׁא {1x} **Shîyshâ',** *shee-shaw';* from the same as 7893; *whiteness; Shisha,* an Isr.:−Shisha {1x}. See: BDB−1010d.

7895. שִׁישַׁק {7x} **Shîyshaq,** *shee-shak';* or

שׁוּשַׁק **Shûwshaq,** *shoo-shak';* of Eg. der.; *Shishak,* an Eg. king:−Shishak {7x}. See: BDB−1004d, 1011a.

7896. שִׁית {85x} **shîyth,** *sheeth;* a prim. root; to *place* (in a very wide application):−set {23x}, made {19x}, lay {13x}, put {11x}, appoint {3x}, regard {2x}, misc. {14x} = apply, array, bring, consider, let alone, × look, mark, shew, be stayed, × take.

Shiyth, as a verb, means "to put, place, set, station, fix." **(1)** It occurs 85 times in the Hebrew Old Testament, for the first time in Gen 3:15: "And I will put enmity between thee and the woman." **(2)** Generally speaking, this word is a term of physical action, typically expressing movement from one place to another. **(3)** Often it expresses "putting" hands on someone or something: "Joseph shall put his hand upon thine eyes [close your eyes]" (Gen 46:4). **(3a)** One may "put on" ornaments (Ex 33:4); **(3b)** Naomi laid her "grandchild" Obed in her bosom (Ruth 4:16); **(3c)** a fine may be "laid" on someone for injury (Ex 21:22); **(3d)** Sheep may be "set" or stationed, at a particular place (Gen 30:40). **(4)** "To set" one's heart to something is **(4a)** to give heed to, to pay attention (Ex 7:23). **(4b)** To set one's heart may also be to reflect: "Then I saw, and considered it [set my heart to it]" (Prov 24:32).

(5) "To set" boundaries is "to set," or "fix," limits: "And I will set thy bounds from the Red Sea even unto the sea of the Philistines" (Ex 23:31). **(6)** When Job cries: "Oh . . . that thou wouldest appoint me a set time, and remember me!" (Job 14:13), he wants limits "set" for him.

(7) *Shiyth* is sometimes used to express the making of something: **(7a)** "I will make him prince . . ." (1 Kin 11:34); **(7b)** "And I will lay it waste" (Is 5:6); **(7c)** "I will make thee a wilderness . . ." (Jer 22:6). See: TWOT−2380; BDB−1004d, 1011a, 1011d.

7897. שִׁית {1x} **shîyth,** *sheeth;* from 7896; a *dress* (as *put* on):−attire {1x}. See: TWOT−2380a; BDB−1011c.

7898. שַׁיִת {7x} **shayith,** *shah'-yith;* from 7896; *scrub* or *trash,* i.e. wild *growth* of weeds or briers (as if *put* on the field):−thorns {7x}. See: TWOT−2380c; BDB−1011d.

7899. שֵׂךְ {1x} **sêk,** *sake;* from 5526 in the sense of 7753; a *brier* (as of a hedge):−prick {1x}. See: TWOT−2262a; BDB−967c, 968a.

7900. שֹׂךְ {1x} **sôk,** *soke;* from 5526 in the sense of 7753; a *booth* (as *interlaced*):−tabernacle {1x}. Syn.: 168, 4264, 4908, 5521. See: TWOT−2260a; BDB−967c, 968a.

7901. שָׁכַב {212x} **shâkab,** *shaw-kab';* a prim. root; to *lie* down (for rest, sexual connection, decease or any other purpose):−lie {106x}, sleep {48x}, lie down {43x}, rest {3x}, lien {2x}, misc. {10x} = × at all, cast down, lodge, ravish, stay.

Shakab means "to lie down, lie, have sexual intercourse with." **(1)** Basically this verb signifies a person's lying down−**(1a)** though in Job 30:17 and Eccl 2:23 it refers to something other than a human being. **(1b)** *Shakab* is used of the state of reclining as opposed to sitting: "And every thing that she lieth upon in her [menstruation] shall be unclean: every thing also that she sitteth upon" (Lev 15:20). **(2)** This general sense appears in several nuances. **(2a)** There is the meaning "to lie down to rest." **(2a1)** Elisha "came thither, and he turned into the chamber [which the Shunammite had prepared for his use], and lay there" (2 Kin 4:11). **(2a2)** Job remarks that his gnawing pains "take no rest" (Job 30:17; cf. Eccl 2:23). **(3)** *Shakab* can also be used of lying down on a bed, for example, when one is sick. Jonadab told Amnon: "Lay thee down on thy bed, and make thyself [pretend to be] sick" (2 Sa 13:5). **(4)** The word can be used as an equivalent of the phrase "to go to bed": "But before they [Lot's visitors] lay down, the men of the city, even the men of Sodom, compassed the house round" (Gen 19:4−the first occurrence of the verb).

(5) *Shakab* also signifies "lying down asleep." The Lord told Jacob: "The land whereon thou liest, to thee will I give it, and to thy seed" (Gen 28:13). **(6)** In Ex 22:26−27 the verb denotes the act of sleeping more than the lying down: "If thou at all take thy neighbor's raiment to

pledge, thou shalt deliver it unto him by that the sun goeth down . . . [In what else] shall he sleep?" **(7)** *Shakab* can also be used to mean "lodge" and thus refers to sleeping and eating. Israel's spies lodged with Rahab: "And they went, and came into a harlot's house, named Rahab, and lodged there" (Josh 2:1; cf. 2 Kin 4:11). **(8)** This verb can mean "to lie down" in a figurative sense of to be humbled or to be robbed of power. The trees of Lebanon are personified and say concerning the king of Babylon: "Since thou art laid down, no feller [tree cutter] is come up against us" (Is 14:8). **(9)** Used reflexively, *shakab* means "to humble oneself, to submit oneself": "We lie down in our shame" (Jer 3:25). **(10)** Another special nuance is "to put something on its side": "Who can number the clouds in wisdom? Or who can [tip] the bottles of heaven, when the dust groweth into hardness, and the clods cleave fast together?" (Job 38:37–38).

(11) An emphasis of *shakab* is "to die," to lie down in death. Jacob instructed his sons as follows: "But I will lie with my fathers, and thou shalt carry me out of Egypt, and bury me in their burying place" (Gen 47:30). **(12)** This phrase ("lie down with one's fathers") does not necessarily refer to being buried or to dying an honorable death (cf. 1 Kin 22:40) but is a synonym for a human's dying. (It is never used of animals or inanimate things.) **(13)** The idea is that when one dies he no longer stands upright. Therefore, to "lie with one's fathers" parallels the concept of "lying down" in death. **(14)** *Shakab*, as 1 Kin 22:40 suggests, can refer to the state of being dead ("so Ahab slept with his fathers"), since v. 37 already reports that he had died and was buried in Samaria. **(15)** The verb used by itself may mean "to die," or "to lie dead"; cf. "At her feet he bowed, he fell, he lay [dead]: at her feet he bowed, he fell: where he bowed, there he fell down dead" (Judg 5:27). **(16)** Another major use of *shakab* is "to have sexual relations with." The first occurrence of this use is in Gen 19:32, where Lot's daughters say: "Come, let us make our father drink wine, and we will lie with him, that we may preserve seed of our father."

(17) Even when a physical "lying down" is not necessarily in view, the word is used of having sexual relations: "Whosoever lieth with a beast shall surely be put to death" (Ex 22:19). **(18)** The word is also used of homosexual activities (Lev 18:22). See: TWOT—2381; BDB—1011d, 1014d, 1115b.

7902. שְׁכָבָה {9x} shekâbâh, *shek-aw-baw'*; from 7901; a *lying* down (of dew, or for the sexual act):—copulation {3x}, lie {2x}, carnally {2x}, from him {1x}, not translated {1x}.

Shekabah means "layer of dew." In one of its 9 appearances, *shekabah* refers to a "layer of dew": ". . . and in the morning the dew lay round about the host" (Ex 16:13). See: TWOT—2381a; BDB—1012c.

7903. שְׁכֹבֶת {4x} shekôbeth, *shek-o'-beth;* from 7901; a (sexual) *lying* with:—✗ lie {4x}.

Shekobeth refers to "copulation." This noun occurs rarely (4 times), as in Lev 18:20: "Moreover thou shalt not lie carnally with thy neighbor's wife, to defile thyself with her." See: TWOT—2381b; BDB—1012d.

7904. שָׁכָה {1x} shâkâh, *shaw-kaw';* a prim. root; to *roam* (through lust):—in the morning {1x}. See: TWOT—2382; BDB—1013a.

7905. שֻׂכָּה {1x} sukkâh, *sook-kaw';* fem. of 7900 in the sense of 7899; a *dart* (as pointed like a *thorn*):—barbed irons {1x}. See: TWOT—2262b; BDB—967c, 968a.

7906. שֵׂכוּ {1x} Sêkûw, *say'-koo;* from an unused root appar. mean. to *surmount;* an *observatory* (with the art.); *Seku,* a place in Pal.:—Sechu {1x}. See: BDB—967d.

7907. שֶׂכְוִי {1x} sekvîy, *sek-vee';* from the same as 7906; *observant,* i.e. (concr.) the *mind:*—heart {1x}. See: TWOT—2257a; BDB—967c.

7908. שְׁכוֹל {3x} shekôwl, *shek-ole';* infin. of 7921; *bereavement:*—loss of children {2x}, spoiling {1x}. See: TWOT—2385a; BDB—1013d.

7909. שַׁכּוּל {6x} shakkuwl, *shak-kool';* or

שַׁכֻּל shakkul, *shak-kool';* from 7921; *bereaved:*—barren {2x}, robbed of whelps {2x}, bereaved of children {1x}, bereaved of whelps {1x}. See: TWOT—2385b, 2385c; BDB—1014a.

7910. שִׁכּוֹר {13x} shikkôwr, *shik-kore';* or

שִׁכֹּר shikkôr, *shik-kore';* from 7937; *intoxicated,* as a state or a habit:—drunken {5x}, drunkard {5x}, drunk {2x}, drunken man {1x}. See: TWOT—2388b; BDB—1016c.

7911. שָׁכַח {102x} shâkach, *shaw-kakh';* or

שָׁכֵחַ shâkêach, *shaw-kay'-akh;* a prim. root; to *mislay,* i.e. to be *oblivious of,* from want of memory or attention:—forget {61x}, forgotten {40x}, at all {1x}.

Shakeach, means "to forget." **(1)** *Shakeach* is found for the first time in the Old Testament in Gen 27:45, when Rebekah urges Jacob to flee his home until Esau "forget that which thou hast done to him." **(2)** As the people wor-

shiped strange gods, Jeremiah reminded Judah that "all thy lovers have forgotten thee; they seek thee not" (Jer 30:14). **(3)** But God does not "forget" His people: "Can a woman forget her suckling child, that she should not have compassion on the son of her womb? yea, they may forget, yet will I not forget thee" (Is 49:15). **(4)** In spite of this, when destruction came, Judah complained: "Wherefore dost thou forget us for ever?" (Lam 5:20). **(5)** Israel would often "forget" God's law (Hos 4:6) and God's name (Jer 23:27). See: TWOT—2383; BDB—1013a.

7912. שְׁכַח {18x} **shᵉkach** (Aram.), *shek-akh';* corresp. to 7911 through the idea of disclosure of a *covered* or *forgotten* thing; to *discover* (lit. or fig.):—find {18x}. See: BDB—1115b.

7913. שָׁכֵחַ {2x} **shâkêach**, *shaw-kay'-akh;* from 7911; *oblivious:*—forget {2x}. See: TWOT—2383a; BDB—1013c.

7914. שְׂכִיָּה {1x} **sᵉkîyâh**, *sek-ee-yaw';* fem. from the same as 7906; a *conspicuous* object:—picture {1x}. See: TWOT—2257b; BDB—967c.

7915. שַׂכִּין {1x} **sakkîyn**, *sak-keen';* intens. perh. from the same as 7906 in the sense of 7753; a *knife* (as *pointed* or edged):—knife {1x}. See: TWOT—2258; BDB—967d.

7916. שָׂכִיר {17x} **sâkîyr**, *saw-keer';* from 7936; a man *at wages* by the day or year:—hired servant {8x}, hireling {6x}, hired {2x}, hired man {1x}. See: TWOT—2264.1c; BDB—969b.

7917. שְׂכִירָה {1x} **sᵉkîyrâh**, *sek-ee-raw';* fem. of 7916; a *hiring:*—hired {1x}. See: TWOT—2264.1c; BDB—969b.

7918. שָׁכַךְ {5x} **shâkak**, *shaw-kak';* a prim. root; to *weave* (i.e. *lay*) a trap; fig. (through the idea of *secreting*) to *allay* (passions; phys. *abate* a flood):—pacified {1x}, appeased {1x}, set {1x}, asswage {1x}, cease {1x}. See: TWOT—2384; BDB—968a, 1013c.

7919. שָׂכַל {63x} **sâkal**, *saw-kal';* a prim. root; to *be* (caus. *make* or *act*) *circumspect* and hence, *intelligent:*—understand {12x}, wise {12x}, prosper {8x}, wisely {6x}, understanding {5x}, consider {4x}, instruct {3x}, prudent {2x}, skill {2x}, teach {2x}, misc. {7x} = expert, prosper, have good success, wisdom, guide wittingly.

Sakal means "to be prudent, act wisely, give attention to, ponder, prosper." **(1)** Its first use in the text, in Gen 3:6, contributes to an interesting paradox, for while the forbidden fruit was "to be desired to make one wise," it was a very unwise thing to take it! **(2)** The basic meaning of *sakal* seems to be "to look at, to

give attention to," as illustrated in this parallelism: "That they may see, and know, and consider, and understand" (Is 41:20). **(3)** From this develops the connotation of insight, intellectual comprehension: "Let not the wise man glory in his wisdom . . . But let him that glorieth glory in this, that he understandeth and knoweth me" (Jer 9:23–24). **(4)** As here, it is frequently used along with and in parallelism to the Hebrew *yada* (3045), "to know" (primarily experientially). **(5)** As is true of *chakam* (2450), "to be wise," *sakal* never concerns abstract prudence, but acting prudently: "Therefore the prudent shall keep silence" (Amos 5:13); "He hath left off to be wise . . ." (Ps 36:3). Syn.: 502, 995, 998, 2094, 2449, 3256, 4905, 8150, 8394. See: TWOT—2263, 2264; BDB—968a, 968d, 1114a.

7920. שְׂכַל {1x} **sᵉkal** (Aram.), *sek-al';* corresp. to 7919:—consider {1x}. See: TWOT—3009; BDB—1114a.

7921. שָׁכֹל {25x} **shâkôl**, *shaw-kole';* a prim. root; prop. to *miscarry*, i.e. *suffer abortion;* by anal. to *bereave* (lit. or fig.):—bereave {10x}, barren {2x}, childless {2x}, cast young {2x}, cast a calf {1x}, lost children {1x}, rob of children {1x}, deprived {1x}, misc. {5x} = destroy, ✕ expect, miscarry, spoil. See: TWOT—2385; BDB—1013c, 1014a.

7922. שֶׂכֶל {16x} **sekel**, *seh'-kel;* or

שֵׂכֶל **sêkel**, *say'-kel;* from 7919; *intelligence;* by impl. *success:*—understanding {7x}, wisdom {3x}, wise {1x}, prudence {1x}, knowledge {1x}, sense {1x}, discretion {1x}, policy {1x}. See: TWOT—2263a; BDB—968c.

שַׂכֻּל **shakkûl**. See 7909.

שִׂכְלוּת **siklûwth**. See 5531.

7923. שִׁכֻּלִים {1x} **shikkûlîym**, *shik-koo-leem';* plur. from 7921; *childlessness* (by continued bereavements):—have, after you have lost the other {1x}. See: TWOT—2385d; BDB—1014a.

7924. שָׂכְלְתָנוּ **sokᵉthânûw** (Aram.), *sok-leth-aw-noo';* from 7920; *intelligence:*—understanding {3x}. See: TWOT—3009a; BDB—1114a.

7925. שָׁכַם {65x} **shâkam**, *shaw-kam';* a prim. root; prop. to *incline* (the shoulder to a *burden*); but used only as denom. from 7926; lit. to *load up* (on the back of man or beast), i.e. to *start early* in the morning:—(rise up, get you, . . .) early {61x}, betimes {2x}, morning {2x}.

Shakam means "to rise early, start early." **(1)** It is found for the first time in Gen 19:2:

"And ye shall rise up early, and go on your ways." **(2)** As in this instance, many of the instances of the use of *shakam* are in connection with traveling. **(2a)** Thus, it may be used with verbs of going (as above) or **(2b)** encamping (Judg 7:1). **(3)** The word is used some 30 times in reference to rising early in the morning, as in 1 Sa 29:10, in which this phrase appears twice: "Wherefore now rise up early in the morning with thy master's servants that are come with thee: and as soon as ye be up early in the morning, and have light, depart." **(4)** A number of times in the Book of Jeremiah, "rising up early" is used with "speaking" (7:13; 25:3; 35:14), "sending" (7:25; 25:4; 29:19; 35:15; 44:4), "protesting" (11:7), or "teaching" (32:33). **(5)** Ps 127:2 gives some interesting advice while using this word: "It is vain for you to rise up early, to sit up late, to eat the bread of sorrows: for so he giveth his beloved sleep." See: TWOT—2386; BDB—1014c.

7926. שְׁכֶם {22x} **sh⁰kem**, *shek-em';* from 7925; the *neck* (between the shoulders) as the place of burdens; fig. the *spur* of a hill:—shoulder {17x}, back {2x}, consent {2x}, portion {1x}. See: TWOT—2386a; BDB—1014a.

7927. שְׁכֶם {63x} **Sh⁰kem**, *shek-em';* the same as 7926; *ridge; Shekem*, a place in Pal.:—Shechem {61x}, Sichem {1x}, consent {1x}. See: TWOT—2386b; BDB—1014b.

7928. שֶׁכֶם {3x} **Shekem**, *sheh'-kem;* for 7926; *Shekem*, the name of a Hivite and two Isr.:—Shechem {3x}. See: BDB—1014c.

7929. שִׁכְמָה {1x} **shikmâh**, *shik-maw';* fem. of 7926; the *shoulder*-bone:—shoulder blade {1x}. See: TWOT—2386a; BDB—1014a, 1014b.

7930. שִׁכְמִי {1x} **Shikmîy**, *shik-mee';* patron. from 7928; a *Shikmite* (collect.), or desc. of Shekem:—Shechemites {1x}. See: BDB—1014c.

7931. שָׁכַן {129x} **shâkan**, *shaw-kan';* a prim. root [appar. akin (by transm.) to 7901 through the idea of *lodging;* comp. 5531, 7925]; to *reside* or permanently stay (lit. or fig.):—dwell {92x}, abide {8x}, place {7x}, remain {5x}, inhabit {4x}, rest {3x}, set {2x}, continue {1x}, dwellers {1x}, dwelling {1x}, misc. {5x} = continue, have habitation, lay.

Shakan means "to dwell, inhabit, settle down, abide." **(1)** *Shakan* is first used in the sense of "to dwell" in **(1a)** Gen 9:27: "And he shall dwell in the tents of Shem." **(1b)** Moses was commanded: "And let them make me a sanctuary, that I may dwell among them" (Ex 25:8). **(2)** *Shakan* is a word from nomadic life,

meaning "to live in a tent." Thus, Balaam "saw Israel abiding in his tents according to their tribes" (Num 24:2). **(2a)** In that verse, *shakan* refers to temporary "camping," **(2b)** but it can also refer to being permanently "settled": "But thou art the same, and thy years shall have no end" (Ps 102:28). **(3)** God promised to give Israel security, "that they may dwell in a place of their own, and move no more" (2 Sa 7:10). Syn: 3427, 4908. See: TWOT—2387; BDB—1014d, 1015c, 1115b.

7932. שְׁכַן {2x} **sh⁰kan** (Aram.), *shek-an';* corresp. to 7931:—habitation {1x}, dwell {1x}. See: TWOT—3031; BDB—1115b.

7933. שֶׁכֶן {1x} **sheken**, *sheh'-ken;* from 7931; a *residence:*—habitation {1x}. See: TWOT—387a; BDB—1015c.

7934. שָׁכֵן {20x} **shâkên**, *shaw-kane';* from 7931; a *resident;* by extens. a fellow-*citizen:*—neighbour {17x}, inhabitant {2x}, nigh thereunto {1x}. See: TWOT—2387b; BDB—1015c.

7935. שְׁכַנְיָה {10x} **Sh⁰kanyâh**, *shek-an-yaw';* or (prol.)

שְׁכַנְיָהוּ **Sh⁰kanyâhûw**, *shek-an-yaw'-hoo;* from 7931 and 3050; *Jah has dwelt; Shekanjah*, the name of nine Isr.:—Shechaniah {8x}, Shecaniah {2x}. See: BDB—1016a.

7936. שָׂכַר {21x} **sâkar**, *saw-kar';* or (by perm.)

סָכַר **çâkar** (Ezra 4:5), *saw-kar';* a prim. root [appar. akin (by prosthesis) to 3739 through the idea of temporary *purchase;* comp. 7937]; to *hire:*—hire {15x}, rewardeth {2x}, wages {2x}, surely {1x}, hire out {1x}. See: TWOT—2264.1; BDB—698d, 968d.

7937. שָׁכַר {19x} **shâkar**, *shaw-kar';* a prim. root; to *become tipsy;* in a qualified sense, to *satiate* with a stimulating drink or (fig.) influence:—drunken {12x}, drunk {4x}, filled with drink {1x}, abundantly {1x}, were merry {1x}. See: TWOT—2388; BDB—1016a. [Superlative of 8248.]

7938. שֶׁכֶר {2x} **seker**, *seh'-ker;* from 7936; *wages:*—reward {1x}, sluices {1x}. See: TWOT—2264.1a; BDB—969a.

7939. שָׂכָר {28x} **sâkâr**, *saw-kawr';* from 7936; *payment* of contract; concr. *salary, fare, maintenance;* by impl. *compensation, benefit:*—hire {9x}, reward {9x}, wages {6x}, price {2x}, fare {1x}, worth {1x}. See: TWOT—2264.1b; BDB—969a.

7940. שָׂכָר {2x} **Sâkar**, *saw-kar';* the same as 7939; *recompense; Sakar*, the name of two Isr.:—Sacar {2x}. See: BDB—969b.

7941. שֵׁכָר {23x} **shêkâr**, *shay-kawr'*; from 7937; an *intoxicant*, i.e. intensely alcoholic *liquor:*—strong drink {21x}, strong wine {1x}, drunkard {1x}. See: TWOT—2388a; BDB—1016b.

שִׁכּוֹר **shikkôr**. See 7910.

7942. שִׁכְּרוֹן {1x} **Shikkᵉrôwn**, *shik-ker-one';* for 7943; *drunkenness, Shik-keron,* a place in Pal.:—Shicron {1x}. See: BDB—1016c.

7943. שִׁכָּרוֹן {3x} **shikkârôwn**, *shik-kaw-rone';* from 7937; *intoxication:*—drunkenness {2x}, drunken {1x}. See: TWOT—2388c; BDB—1016c.

7944. שַׁל {1x} **shal**, *shal;* from 7952 abbrev.; a *fault:*—error {1x}. See: TWOT—2389.1; BDB—1016d.

7945. שֶׁל {3x} **shel**, *shel;* for the rel. 834; used with prep. pref., and often followed by some pron. aff.; on *account* of, *what*soever, *which*soever:—though {1x}, for whose cause {1x}, for my sake {1x}. See: TWOT—184; BDB—979b, 980a, 1016d.

7946. שַׁלְאֲנָן {1x} **shaľănân**, *shal-an-awn';* for 7600; *tranquil:*—ease {1x}. See: TWOT—2304a; BDB—1016d.

7947. שָׁלַב {2x} **shâlab**, *shaw-lab';* a prim. root; to *space* off; intens. *(evenly)* to *make equidistant:*—set in order {1x}, equally distant {1x}. See: TWOT—2390; BDB—1016d.

7948. שָׁלָב {3x} **shâlâb**, *shaw-lawb';* from 7947; a *spacer* or raised *interval,* i.e. the *stile* in a frame or panel:—ledge {3x}. See: TWOT—2390a; BDB—1016d.

7949. שָׁלַג {1x} **shâlag**, *shaw-lag';* a prim. root; prop. mean. to *be white;* used only as denom. from 7950; to *be snow-white* (with the linen clothing of the slain):—snow {1x}. See: TWOT—2391; BDB—1017a.

7950. שֶׁלֶג {20x} **sheleg**, *sheh'-leg;* from 7949; *snow* (prob. from its *whiteness*):—snow {19x}, snowy {1x}. See: TWOT—2391a; BDB—1017a, 1117d.

7951. שָׁלָה {5x} **shâlâh**, *shaw-law';* or

שָׁלַו **shâlav** (Job 3:26), *shaw-lav';* a prim. root; to *be tranquil,* i.e. *se-cure* or *successful:*—prosper {3x}, safety {1x}, happy {1x}. See: TWOT—2392; BDB—1017a, 1115c.

7952. שָׁלָה {2x} **shâlâh**, *shaw-law';* a prim. root [prob. rather ident. with 7953 through the idea of *educing*]; to *mislead:*—negligent {1x}, deceive {1x}. See: BDB—1017b, 1017d.

7953. שָׁלָה {1x} **shâlâh**, *shaw-law';* a prim. root [rather cognate (by contr.) to the base of 5394, 7997 and their congeners through the idea of *extracting*]; to *draw* out or off, i.e. *remove* (the soul by death):—take away {1x}. See: TWOT—2393; BDB—1017b, 1017d.

7954. שָׁלָה {1x} **shᵉlâh** (Aram.), *shel-aw';* corresp. to 7951; to *be secure:*—at rest {1x}. See: TWOT—3032; BDB—1115c.

שִׁלֹה **Shîlôh**. See 7887.

7955. שָׁלָה {1x} **shâlâh** (Aram.), *shaw-law';* from a root corresp. to 7952; a *wrong:*—anything amiss {1x}. See: BDB—1115c.

שֵׁלָה **shêlâh**. See 7596.

7956. שֵׁלָה {8x} **Shêlâh**, *shay-law';* the same as 7596 (short.); *request; Shelah,* the name of a postdiluvian patriarch and of an Isr.:—Shelah {8x}. See: BDB—982c, 1017c, 1018a.

7957. שַׁלְהֶבֶת {3x} **shalhebeth**, *shal-heh'-beth;* from the same as 3851 with sibilant pref.; a *flare* of fire:—(flaming) flame {3x}. See: TWOT—1077c; BDB—529b, 1018a.

שָׁלַו **shâlav**. See 7951.

7958. שְׂלָו {4x} **sᵉlâv**, *sel-awv';* or

שְׂלָיו **sᵉlâyv**, *sel-awv';* by orth. var. from 7951 through the idea of *sluggish-ness;* the *quail* collect. (as *slow* in flight from its weight):—quails {4x}. See: TWOT—2265; BDB—969b.

7959. שֶׁלֶו {1x} **shelev**, *sheh'-lev;* from 7951; *security:*—prosperity {1x}. See: TWOT—2392a; BDB—1017b, 1017d.

שִׁלֹו **Shîlôw**. See 7887.

7960. שָׁלוּ {4x} **shâlûw** (Aram.), *shaw-loo';* or

שָׁלוּת **shâlûwth** (Aram.), *shaw-looth';* from the same as 7955; a *fault:*—error {1x}, × fail {2x}, thing amiss {1x}. See: BDB—1115c.

7961. שָׁלֵו {8x} **shâlêv**, *shaw-lave';* or

שָׁלֵיו **shâlêyv**, *shaw-lave';* fem.

שְׁלֵוָה **shᵉlêvâh**, *shel-ay-vaw';* from 7951; *tranquil;* (in a bad sense) *careless;* abstr. *security:*—at ease {2x}, peaceable {1x}, quietness {1x}, prosperity {1x}, quiet {1x}, prosper {1x}, wealthy {1x}. See: TWOT—2392c; BDB—1017c.

7962. שַׁלְוָה {8x} **shalvâh**, *shal-vaw';* from 7951; *security* (genuine or false):—prosperity {3x}, peaceably {2x}, quietness {1x},

abundance {1x}, peace {1x}. See: TWOT—2392d; BDB—1017b, 1017c.

7963. שְׁלֵוָה {1x} **sheʾlêvâh** (Aram.), *shel-ay-vaw';* corresp. to 7962; *safety:*—tranquillity {1x}. See: TWOT—3032b; BDB—1115c. See also 7961.

7964. שִׁלּוּחַ {3x} **shillûwach,** *shil-loo'-akh;* or

שִׁלֻּחַ **shillûach,** *shil-loo'-akh;* from 7971; (only in plur.) a *dismissal,* i.e. (of a wife) *divorce* (espec. the document); also (of a daughter) *dower:*—presents {2x}, have sent back {1x}.

Shilluachim [plural] occurs 3 times and means "presents" in the sense of something sent out to or with someone (1 Kin 9:16). Syn.: 7971, 7973, 7975, 7999, 8002, 8003. See: TWOT—2394b; BDB—1019d.

7965. שָׁלוֹם {236x} **shâlôwm,** *shaw-lome';* or

שָׁלֹם **shâlôm,** *shaw-lome';* from 7999; *safe,* i.e. (fig.) *well, happy, friendly;* also (abstr.) *welfare,* i.e. *health, prosperity, peace:*—peace {175x}, well {14x}, peaceably {9x}, welfare {5x}, salute + 7592 {4x}, prosperity {4x}, did {3x}, safe {3x}, health {2x}, peaceable {2x}, misc. {15x} = familiar, × fare, favour, + friend, × great, prosperous, rest, safety, × wholly.

Shalom, as a noun, means "peace; completeness; welfare; health." **(1)** The first two occurrences in Genesis already indicate the changes in meaning: **(1a)** "And thou shalt go to thy fathers in peace [*shalom* in the sense of "in tranquility," "at ease," "unconcerned"]; thou shalt be buried in a good old age" (Gen 15:15); and **(1b)** "that thou wilt do us no hurt, as we have not touched thee, and as we have done unto thee nothing but good, and have sent thee away in peace [*shalom* with the meaning of "unharmed" and "unhurt"]" (Gen 26:29). **(1c)** Yet, both uses are essentially the same, as they express the root meaning of "to be whole." **(2)** The phrase *ish shelomi* ("friend of my peace") in Ps 41:9, "Yea, mine own familiar friend [literally, "friend of my peace"], in whom I trusted, which did eat of my bread, hath lifted up his heel against me" (cf. Jer 20:10), **(2a)** signifies a state in which one can feel at ease, comfortable with someone. **(2b)** The relationship is one of harmony and wholeness, which is the opposite of the state of strife and war: "I am for peace: but when I speak, they are for war" (Ps 120:7).

(3) *Shalom* as a harmonious state of the soul and mind encourages the development of the faculties and powers. **(3a)** The state of being at ease is experienced both externally and internally. **(3a)** In Hebrew it finds expression in the phrase *beshalom* ("in peace"): **(3b)** "I will

both lay me down in peace [*beshalom*], and sleep: for thou, Lord, only makest me dwell in safety" (Ps 4:8). **(4)** Closely associated to the above is the meaning "welfare," specifically personal "welfare" or "health." **(4a)** This meaning is found in questions: "And Joab said to Amasa, Art thou in health, my brother? And Joab took Amasa by the beard with the right hand to kiss him" (2 Sa 20:9), or **(4b)** in the prepositional phrase *leshalom* with the verb "to ask": "And he asked them of their welfare, and said, Is your father well, the old man of whom ye spake? Is he yet alive?" (Gen 43:27).

(5) *Shalom* also signifies "peace," indicative of a prosperous relationship between two or more parties. **(5a)** *Shalom* in this sense finds expression in speech: "Their tongue is as an arrow shot out; it speaketh deceit: one speaketh peaceably [literally, "in peace"] to his neighbor with his mouth, but in heart he layeth his wait" (Jer 9:8); **(5b)** in diplomacy: "Howbeit Sisera fled away on his feet to the tent of Jael the wife of Heber the Kenite: for there was peace between Jabin the king of Hazor and the house of Heber the Kenite" (Judg 4:17); **(5c)** and in warfare: ". . . If it make thee answer of peace, and open unto thee, then it shall be, that all the people that is found therein shall be tributaries unto thee, and they shall serve thee" (Deut 20:11). **(6)** Isaiah prophesied concerning the "prince of peace" (Is 9:6), whose kingdom was to introduce a government of "peace" (Is 9:7). **(7)** Ezekiel spoke about the new covenant as one of "peace": "Moreover I will make a covenant of peace with them; it shall be an everlasting covenant with them: and I will place them, and multiply them, and will set my sanctuary in the midst of them for evermore" (Eze 37:26). **(8)** Psalm 122 is one of those great psalms in celebration of and in prayer for the "peace of Jerusalem": "Pray for the peace of Jerusalem: they shall prosper that love thee" (Ps 122:6). **(9)** In benedictions God's peace was granted to His people: ". . . Peace shall be upon Israel" (Ps 125:5). Syn.: 7999, 8002, 8003. See: TWOT—2401a; BDB—1022d.

7966. שִׁלּוּם {3x} **shillûwm,** *shil-loom';* or

שִׁלֻּם **shillûm,** *shil-loom';* from 7999; a *requital,* i.e. (secure) *retribution,* (venal) a *fee:*—recompense {2x}, reward {1x}. See: TWOT—2401h; BDB—1024b.

7967. שַׁלּוּם {27x} **Shallûwm,** *shal-loom';* or (short.)

שַׁלֻּם **Shallûm,** *shal-loom';* the same as 7966; *Shallum,* the name of fourteen Isr.:—*Shallum* {27x}. See: BDB—1024b, 1024c, 1025a.

שְׁלוֹמִית **Sheʾlôwmîyth.** See 8019.

7968. שַׁלּוּן {1x} **Shallûwn**, *shal-loon';* prob. for 7967; *Shallun*, an Isr.:—Shallum {1x}. See: BDB—1024c.

7969. שָׁלוֹשׁ {430x} **shâlôwsh**, *shaw-loshe';* or

שָׁלֹשׁ **shâlôsh**, *shaw-loshe';* masc.

שְׁלוֹשָׁה **sheʰlôwshâh**, *shel-o-shaw';* or

שְׁלֹשָׁה **sheʰlôshâh**, *shel-o-shaw';* a prim. number; *three;* occasionally (ord.) *third,* or (multipl.) *thrice:*—three {388x}, thirteen + 6240 {13x}, thirteenth + 6240 {11x}, third {9x}, thrice + 6471 {4x}, threescore and thirteen + 7657 {2x}, stories {1x}, forks + 7053 {1x}, oftentimes + 6471 {1x}. See: TWOT—2403a; BDB—606b, 1025c, 1118a. comp. 7991.

7970. שְׁלוֹשִׁים {175x} **sheʰlôwshîym**, *shel-o-sheem';* or

שְׁלֹשִׁים **sheʰlôshîym**, *shel-o-sheem';* multiple of 7969; *thirty;* or (ord.) *thirtieth:*—thirty {163x}, thirtieth {9x}, captains {1x}, variant {2x}. See: TWOT—2403d; BDB—1026c. comp. 7991.

שָׁלוּת **shâlûwth**. See 7960.

7971. שָׁלַח {847x} **shâlach**, *shaw-lakh';* a prim. root; to *send* away, for, or out (in a great variety of applications):—send {566x}, go {73x}, (send, put, . . .) forth {54x}, send away {48x}, lay {14x}, send out {12x}, put {10x}, put away {7x}, cast out {7x}, stretch out {5x}, cast {5x}, set {5x}, put out {4x}, depart {4x}, soweth {3x}, loose {3x}, misc. {22x} = ✕ any wise, appoint, bring (on the way), conduct, ✕ earnestly, forsake, give (up), grow long, lay, leave, let depart (down, go), push away, reach forth, spread.
Shalach, as a verb, means "to send, stretch forth, get rid of." **(1)** Basically this verb means "to send," in the sense of **(1a)** to initiate and to see that such movement occurs: "Judah sent the kid by the hand of his friend . . . , he found her not"; it never reached its goal (Gen 38:20), or **(1b)** to successfully conclude such an action: ". . . these animals are a present sent unto my lord Esau." (Gen 32:18). **(1c)** In 1 Sa 15:20 Saul told Samuel about the "way which the lord sent" him; here, too, the emphasis is on the initiation of the action. **(2)** The most frequent use of *shalach* suggests the sending of someone or something as a messenger to a particular place: **(2a)** "He shall send his angel before thee, and thou shalt take a wife unto my son from thence" (Gen 24:7); **(2b)** God's angel (messenger) will be sent to Nahor to prepare things for the successful accomplishment of the servant's task. **(2c)** One may also "send a word" by the hand of a messenger (fool), **(2c1)** one may send a message (Prov 26:6), **(2c2)** send a letter (2 Sa 11:14), and **(2c3)** send instructions (Gen 20:2).

(3) *Shalach* can refer to shooting arrows by sending them to hit a particular target: "And he sent out arrows, and scattered them . . ." (2 Sa 22:15). **(4)** In Ex 9:14 God "sends" His plague into the midst of the Egyptians; He "sends" them forth and turns them loose among them. **(5)** Other special meanings of this verb include letting something go freely or without control: "Thou givest thy mouth to evil" (Ps 50:19). **(6)** Quite often this verb means "to stretch out." God was concerned lest after the Fall Adam "put forth his hand, and take also of the tree of life" (Gen 3:22). **(7)** One may stretch forth a staff (1 Sa 14:27) or a sickle (Joel 3:13). **(8)** For the most part **the intensive stems** merely intensify the meanings already set forth, but the meaning "to send away" is especially frequent: "And, behold, the servants of David and Joab came from pursuing a troop, and brought in a great spoil with them: but Abner was not with David in Hebron; for he had sent him away, and he was gone in peace" (2 Sa 3:22). **(9)** God sent man out of the garden of Eden; **(9a)** He made man leave (Gen 3:23—the first occurrence of the verb). **(9b)** Noah sent forth a raven (Gen 8:7). **(10)** *Shalach* can also mean to give someone a send off, or "to send" someone on his way in a friendly manner: "And Abraham went with them to bring them on the way [send them off]" (Gen 18:16). **(11)** In Deut 22:19 the word is used of divorcing a wife, or sending her away. **(12)** This verb can signify "to get rid of" something: "They bow themselves, they bring forth their young ones, they cast out their [labor pains]" (Job 39:3). **(13)** It can also be used of setting a bondservant free: "And when thou sendest him out free from thee, thou shalt not let him go away empty" (Deut 15:13). **(14)** In a less technical sense *shalach* can mean to release someone held by force. The angel with whom Jacob wrestled said: "Let me go, for the day breaketh" (Gen 32:26). **(15)** Yet another nuance is "to hand someone over," as in Ps 81:12: "So I gave them up unto their own hearts' lust." **(16)** *Shalach* can also mean to set something afire, as in "set the city on fire" (Judg 1:8). **(17)** In the **passive sense** the verb has some additional special meanings; in Prov 29:15 it means "to be left to oneself": "But a child left to himself [who gets his own way] bringeth his mother to shame." Syn.: 7964, 7973, 7975, 7999, 8002, 8003.See: TWOT—2394; BDB—1018a, 1115c.

7972. שְׁלַח {14x} **sheʰlach** (Aram.), *shel-akh';* corresp. to 7971:—put {1x}, send {13x}. See: TWOT—3033; BDB—1115c.

7973. שֶׁלַח {8x} **shelach**, *sheh'-lakh;* from 7971; a *missile* of attack, i.e. *spear;* also (fig.) a *shoot* of growth; i.e. *branch:*—sword

{3x}, weapon {2x}, dart {1x}, plant {1x}, put them off {1x}.

(1) *Shelach* means " something sent forth as a missile," and it can refer to a sword or a weapon. **(2)** *Shelach* occurs 8 times (2 Chr 32:5; Job 33:18; Neh 4:17). Syn.: 7964, 7971, 7975, 7999, 8002, 8003. See: TWOT—2394a; BDB—1019c.

7974. שֶׁלַח {9x} **Shelach**, *sheh'-lakh;* the same as 7973; *Shelach,* a postdiluvian patriarch:—Salah {6x}, Shelah {3x}. See: BDB—1019d. comp. 7975.

7975. שִׁלֹחַ {2x} **Shilôach**, *shee-lo'-akh;* or (in imitation of 7974)

שֶׁלַח **Shelach** (Neh. 3:15), *sheh'-lakh;* from 7971; *rill; Shiloäch,* a fountain of Jerusalem:—Siloah {2x}. Shiloah appears in Is 8:6 and refers to a channel through which water is sent forth. Syn.: 7964, 7971, 7973, 7999, 8002, 8003. See: BDB—1019d.

שִׁלֻּחַ **shillûach**. See 7964.

7976. שִׁלְחָה {1x} **shilluchâh**, *shil-loo-khaw';* fem. of 7964; a *shoot:*—branch {1x}. See: TWOT—2394c; BDB—1020a.

7977. שִׁלְחִי {2x} **Shilchîy**, *shil-khee';* from 7973; *missive,* i.e. *armed; Shilchi,* an Isr.:—Shilhi {2x}. See: BDB—1019d.

7978. שִׁלְחִים {1x} **Shilchîym**, *shil-kheem';* plur. of 7973; *javelins* or *sprouts; Shilchim,* a place in Pal.:—Shilhim {1x}. See: BDB—1019d.

7979. שֻׁלְחָן {70x} **shulchân**, *shool-khawn';* from 7971; a *table* (as *spread* out); by impl. a *meal:*—table {70x}. See: TWOT—2395a; BDB—1020b.

7980. שָׁלַט {8x} **shâlat**, *shaw-lat';* a prim. root; to *dominate,* i.e. *govern;* by impl. to *permit:*—(bear, have) rule {4x}, have dominion {1x}, give (have) power {3x}. Syn.: 4427, 4910, 7985. See: TWOT—2396; BDB—1020c, 1115c.

7981. שְׁלֵט {7x} **shᵉlêt** (Aram.), *shel-ate';* corresp. to 7980:—have the mastery {1x}, have power {1x}, bear rule {1x}, be (make) ruler {4x}. See: TWOT—3034; BDB—1115c.

7982. שֶׁלֶט {7x} **shelet**, *sheh'-let;* from 7980; prob. a *shield* (as *controlling,* i.e. *protecting* the person):—shield {7x}. See: TWOT—2397a; BDB—1020d.

7983. שִׁלְטוֹן {2x} **shiltôwn**, *shil-tone';* from 7980; a *potentate:*—power {2x}. See: TWOT—2396b; BDB—1020d.

7984. שִׁלְטוֹן {2x} **shiltôwn** (Aram.), *shil-tone';* or

שִׁלְטֹן **shiltôn**, *shil-tone';* corresp. to 7983:—ruler {2x}. See: TWOT—3034c; BDB—[does not appear in BDB]

7985. שָׁלְטָן {14x} **sholtân** (Aram.), *shol-tawn';* from 7981; *empire* (abstr. or concr.):—dominion {14x}. See: TWOT—3034a; BDB—1115d.

7986. שַׁלֶּטֶת {1x} **shalleteth**, *shal-leh'-teth;* fem. from 7980; a *vixen:*—imperious {1x}. See: TWOT—2396c; BDB—1020d.

7987. שְׁלִי {1x} **shᵉlîy**, *shel-ee';* from 7951; *privacy:*—+ quietly {1x}. See: TWOT—2392b; BDB—1017b.

7988. שִׁלְיָה {1x} **shilyâh**, *shil-yaw';* fem. from 7953; a *fetus* or *babe* (as *extruded* in birth):—young one {1x}. See: TWOT—2393a; BDB—1017d.

שְׁלָיו **sᵉlâyv**. See 7958.

שָׁלֵיו **shalêyv**. See 7961.

7989. שַׁלִּיט {4x} **shallîyt**, *shal-leet';* from 7980; *potent;* concr. a *prince* or *warrior:*—governor {1x}, mighty {1x}, that hath power {1x}, ruler {1x}. See: TWOT—2396a; BDB—1020c, 1020d.

7990. שַׁלִּיט {10x} **shallîyt** (Aram.), *shal-leet';* corresp. to 7989; *mighty;* abstr. *permission;* concr. a *premier:*—captain {1x}, be lawful {1x}, rule {6x}, ruler {2x}. See: TWOT—3034b; BDB—1115d.

7991. שָׁלִישׁ {20x} **shâlîysh**, *shaw-leesh';* or

שָׁלוֹשׁ **shâlôwsh** (1 Chr 11:11; 12:18), *shaw-loshe';* or

שָׁלֹשׁ **shâlôsh** (2 Sa 23:13), *shaw-loshe';* from 7969; a *triple,* i.e. (as a musical instrument) a *triangle* (or perh. rather *three*-stringed lute); also (as an indef. great quantity) a *three*-fold measure (perh. a *treble* ephah; also (as an officer) a *general* of the *third* rank (upward, i.e. the highest):—captain {11x}, lord {4x}, instrument of musick {1x}, great measure {1x}, excellent thing {1x}, measure {1x}, prince {1x}. See: TWOT—2403e, 2403f, 2403g; BDB—1026b, 1026c, 1026d.

7992. שְׁלִישִׁי {108x} **shᵉlîyshîy**, *shel-ee-shee';* ord. from 7969; *third;* fem. a *third* (part); by extens. a *third* (day, year or time); spec. a *third*-story cell):—third {84x}, third part {18x}, three years old {2x}, three {2x}, third rank {1x}, third time {1x}. See: TWOT—2403b; BDB—722c, 1026a.

7993. שָׁלַךְ {125x} **shâlak**, *shaw-lak;* a prim. root; to *throw* out, down or away

(lit. or fig.):—cast {77x}, cast out {15x}, cast away {11x}, cast down {11x}, cast forth {4x}, cast off {2x}, adventured {1x}, hurl {1x}, misc. {3x} = cast out, pluck, throw.

Shalak means to throw, fling, cast, overthrow. **(1)** Its first use is in Gen 21:15, where Hagar cast Ishmael under one of the shrubs. **(2)** It describe the throwing or casting of anything tangible: **(2a)** Moses threw a tree into water to sweeten it (Ex 15:25); **(2b)** Aaron claimed he threw gold into the fire and a golden calf walked out (Ex 32:24). **(2c)** Trees shed or cast off wilted blossoms (Job 15:33). **(3)** *Shalak* indicates rejection in Lam 2:1. **(4)** The word is used figuratively in Ps 55:22. See: TWOT—2398; BDB—1020d.

7994. שָׁלָךְ {2x} **shâlâk**, *shaw-lawk';* from 7993; *bird of prey,* usually thought to be the *pelican* (from *casting* itself into the sea):—cormorant {2x}. See: TWOT - 2398a; BDB—1021c.

7995. שַׁלֶּכֶת {1x} **shalleketh**, *shal-leh'-keth;* from 7993; a *felling* (of trees):—when cast {1x}. See: TWOT—2398b; BDB—1021c.

7996. שַׁלֶּכֶת {1x} **Shalleketh**, *shal-leh'-keth;* the same as 7995; *Shalleketh,* a gate in Jerusalem:—Shalleketh {1x}. See: BDB—1021c.

7997. שָׁלַל {16x} **shâlal**, *shaw-lal';* a prim. root; to *drop* or *strip;* by impl. to *plunder:*—spoil {8x}, take {5x}, fall {1x}, prey {1x}, purpose {1x}. See: TWOT—2399, 2400; BDB—1021c, 1021d.

7998. שָׁלָל {73x} **shâlâl**, *shaw-lawl';* from 7997; *booty:*—prey {10x}, spoil {63x}.

Shalal **(1)** literally means prey which an animal tracks down, kills, and eats (Gen 49:27). **(2)** The word may mean booty or spoil of war, which includes **(2a)** anything and everything a soldier or army captures from an enemy and carries off (Deut 20:14) up to **(2b)** an entire nation as plunder or a spoil of war (Jer 50:10). **(3)** To "save one's own life as booty" is to have one's life spared (cf. Jer 21:9). **(4)** *Shalal* is used a few times for private plunder (Is 10:1–2). **(5)** This word may also represent private gain (Prov 31:11). See: TWOT—2400a; BDB—1021d.

7999. שָׁלַם {116x} **shâlam**, *shaw-lam';* a prim. root; to *be safe* (in mind, body or estate); fig. to *be* (caus. *make*) *completed;* by impl. to *be friendly;* by extens. to *reciprocate* (in various applications):—pay {19x}, peace {11x}, recompense {11x}, reward {10x}, render {9x}, restore {8x}, repay {7x}, perform {7x}, good {6x}, end {4x}, requite {4x}, restitution {4x}, fin-

ished {3x}, again {3x}, amends {1x}, full {1x}, misc. {8x} = full, peaceable, that is perfect, (make) prosper (-ous), requite, X surely.

Shalam means to finish, complete, repay, reward. **(1)** The Hebrew root denotes perfection in the sense that a condition or action is complete. When sufficient building materials were at hand and workmen had enough time to apply them, the wall of Jerusalem was finished (Neh 6:15). **(2)** Perfection and completeness is primarily attributed to God. He is deficient in nothing; His attributes are not marred by any shortcomings; His power is not limited by weakness. God reminded Job of His uninhibited independence and absolute self-sufficiency (Job 41:11). **(3)** Israel's social law required one to meet his obligations in full; either by **(3a)** equal replacement (Ex 22:14; Lev 24:18), **(3b)** double (Ex 22:9), or **(3c)** fourfold (2 Sa 12:6). **(4)** Debts were not to be left unpaid (2 Kin 4:7; Ps 37:21). **(5)** National relationships were established on the basis of complete negotiations, making peace (Josh 10:1; 1 Kin 22:44). **(6)** *Shalam,* as a verb, means "to be complete, be sound." **(6a)** The word signifies "to be complete" in 1 Kin 9:25: "So he finished the house." **(6b)** Another form of the verb, *shalam,* means "to make peace": "When a man's ways please the Lord, he maketh even his enemies to be at peace with him" (Prov 16:7). Syn.: 7964, 7971, 7973, 7975, 8002, 8003. See: TWOT—2401c; BDB—1022b, 1023d, 1115d.

8000. שְׁלַם {3x} **shᵉlam** (Aram.), *shel-am';* corresp. to 7999; to *complete,* to *restore:*—deliver {1x}, finish {2x}. See: TWOT—3035; BDB—1115d.

8001. שְׁלָם {4x} **shᵉlâm** (Aram.), *shel-awm';* corresp. to 7965; *prosperity:*—peace {4x}. See: TWOT—3035a; BDB—1116a.

8002. שֶׁלֶם {87x} **shelem**, *sheh'-lem;* from 7999; prop. *requital,* i.e. a (voluntary) *sacrifice* in *thanks:*—peace offering {81x}, peace {6x}.

(1) *Shelem* conveys the idea of completeness or perfection, and also of compensation, as well as that of peace. **(2)** It was a special kind of *zebach* (2077) or sacrificial feast, occasioned by some particular event in family life that called for a thankful acknowledgement of God's goodness, and a rendering to Him of what return was due and possible. **(3)** *Shelem* means "peace offering": "And he sent young men of the children of Israel, which offered burnt offerings, and sacrificed peace offerings of oxen unto the Lord" (Ex 24:5). Syn.: 7964, 7971, 7973, 7975, 7999, 8003. See: TWOT—2401b; BDB—1023b.

8003. שָׁלֵם {27x} shâlêm, *shaw-lame';* from
7999; *complete* (lit. or fig.); espec.
friendly:—perfect {16x}, whole {4x}, full {2x},
just {1x}, peaceable {1x}, misc. {3x} = made
ready, quiet, *Shalem.*

Shalem, as an adjective, means "complete;
perfect." **(1)** This word is found in Gen 15:16
with the meaning of not quite "complete": "But
in the fourth generation they shall come hither
again: for the iniquity of the Amorites is not
yet full." **(2)** The word means "perfect" in Deut
25:15. **(3)** God demanded total obedience from
His people: "Let [their] heart therefore be perfect with the Lord our God, to walk in his statutes, and to keep his commandments" (1 Kin
8:61). **(4)** Solomon failed to meet this requirement because "his heart was not perfect with
the Lord his God" (1 Kin 11:4). **(5)** Hezekiah,
on the other hand, protested: "I have walked
before thee in truth and with a perfect heart"
(2 Kin 20:3). **(6)** In business transactions, the
Israelites were required to "have a perfect and
just weight, a perfect and just measure" (Deut
25:15). Syn.: 7964, 7971, 7973, 7975, 7999, 8002.
See: TWOT—2401d; BDB—1023d.

8004. שָׁלֵם {3x} Shâlêm, *shaw-lame';* the same
as 8003; *peaceful; Shalem,* an early
name of Jerusalem:—Salem {2x}, Shalem {1x}.
See: BDB—1024a.

שָׁלֹם   shâlôm. See 7965.

8005. שִׁלֵּם {1x} shillêm, *shil-lame';* from 7999;
requital:—recompense {1x}. See:
TWOT—2401e; BDB—1024a.

8006. שִׁלֵּם {2x} Shillêm, *shil-lame';* the same
as 8005; *Shillem,* an Isr.:—Shillem
{2x}. See: BDB—1024a.

שִׁלֻּם   shillûm. See 7966.

שַׁלֻּם   Shallûm. See 7967.

8007. שַׁלְמָא {4x} Salmâ', *sal-maw';* prob. for
8008; *clothing; Salma,* the name
of two Isr.:—Salma {4x}. See: BDB—969c.

8008. שַׂלְמָה {16x} salmâh, *sal-maw';* transp.
for 8071; a *dress:*—clothes {3x},
garment {8x}, raiment {5x}. See: TWOT—
2270b; BDB—969c, 971a, 1070b.

8009. שַׂלְמָה {1x} Salmâh, *sal-maw';* the same
as 8008; *clothing; Salmah,* an
Isr.:—Salmon {1x}. See: BDB—969c, 971b.
comp. 8012.

8010. שְׁלֹמֹה {293x} Shᵉlômôh, *shel-o-mo';*
from 7965; *peaceful; Shelomah,*
David's successor:—Solomon {293x}. See:
BDB—1024c.

8011. שִׁלֻּמָה {1x} shillumâh, *shil-loo-maw';*
fem. of 7966; *retribution:*—re-
ward {1x}. See: TWOT—2401h; BDB—1024b.

8012. שַׁלְמוֹן {1x} Salmôwn, *sal-mone';* from
8008; *investiture; Salmon,* an
Isr.:—Salmon {1x}. See: BDB—969c. comp.
8009.

8013. שְׁלֹמוֹת {5x} Shᵉlômôwth, *shel-o-moth';*
fem. plur. of 7965; *pacifications;*
Shelomoth, the name of two Isr.:—Shelomith
{3x}, Shelomoth {2x}. See: BDB—1024d. comp.
8019.

8014. שַׁלְמָי {1x} Salmay, *sal-mah'-ee;* from
8008; *clothed; Salmai,* an Isr.:—
Shalmai {1x}. See: BDB—969c, 971b, 1030c.

8015. שְׁלֹמִי {1x} Shᵉlômîy, *shel-o-mee';* from
7965; *peaceable; Shelomi,* an
Isr.:—Shelomi {1x}. See: BDB—1025a.

8016. שִׁלֵּמִי {1x} Shillêmîy, *shil-lay-mee';* patron. from 8006; a *Shilemite* (col-
lect.) or desc. of Shillem:—Shillemites {1x}.
See: BDB—1024b.

8017. שְׁלֻמִיאֵל {5x} Shᵉlûmîy'êl, *shel-oo-mee-*
ale'; from 7965 and 410; *peace*
of God; Shelumiel, an Isr.:—Shelumiel {5x}.
See: BDB—1025a.

8018. שֶׁלֶמְיָה {10x} Shelemyâh, *shel-em-yaw';*
or

שֶׁלֶמְיָהוּ   Shelemyâhuw, *shel-em-yaw'-*
hoo; from 8002 and 3050;
thank-offering of Jah; Shelemjah, the name of
nine Isr.:—Shelemiah {10x}. See: BDB—1024b,
1024c, 1025a.

8019. שְׁלֹמִית {8x} Shᵉlômîyth, *shel-o-meeth';* or

שְׁלוֹמִית   Shᵉlôwmiyth (Ezra 8:10), *shel-*
o-meeth'; from 7965; *peace-*
ableness; Shelomith, the name of five Isr. and
three Israelitesses:—Shelomith {8x}. See: BDB—
1024d, 1025a.

8020. שַׁלְמָן {1x} Shalman, *shal-man';* of for.
der.; *Shalman,* a king appar. of
Assyria:—Shalman {1x}. See: BDB—1025a.
comp. 8022.

8021. שַׁלְמֹן {1x} shalmôn, *shal-mone';* from
7999; a *bribe:*—reward {1x}. See:
TWOT—2401f; BDB—1024b.

8022. שַׁלְמַנְאֶסֶר {2x} Shalman'eçer, *shal-man-*
eh'-ser; of for. der.; *Shalman-*
eser, an Ass. king:—Shalmaneser {2x}. See:
BDB—1025b. Comp 8020.

8023. שִׁלֹנִי {1x} Shîlônîy, *shee-lo-nee';* the
same as 7888; *Shiloni,* an Isr.:—
Shiloni {1x}. See: BDB—1017c, 1018a, 1025b.

8024. שֶׁלָנִי {1x} **Shêlânîy**, *shay-law-nee';* from 7956; a *Shelanite* (collect.), or desc. of Shelah:—Shelanites {1x}. See: BDB—1017c, 1025b.

8025. שָׁלַף {25x} **shâlaph**, *saw-laf';* a prim. root; to *pull* out, up or off:—draw {22x}, pluck off {2x}, grow up {1x}. See: TWOT—2402; BDB—1025b.

8026. שֶׁלֶף {2x} **Sheleph**, *sheh'-lef;* from 8025; *extract; Sheleph,* a son of Jokthan:—Sheleph {2x}. See: BDB—1025c.

8027. שָׁלַשׁ {9x} **shâlash**, *shaw-lash';* a prim. root perh. orig. to *intensify,* i.e. *treble;* but appar. used only as denom. from 7969, to *be* (caus. *make*) *triplicate* (by restoration, in portions, strands, days or years):— three years old {3x}, third time {2x}, threefold {1x}, three {1x}, three parts {1x}, three days {1x}. See: TWOT—2403; BDB—1026a.

8028. שֶׁלֶשׁ {1x} **Shelesh**, *sheh'-lesh;* from 8027; *triplet; Shelesh,* an Isr.:—Shelesh {1x}. See: BDB—1026d.

שָׁלֹשׁ **shâlôsh**. See 7969.

8029. שִׁלֵּשׁ {5x} **shillêsh**, *shil-laysh';* from 8027; a desc. of the *third* degree, i.e. *great grandchild:*—third {5x}. See: TWOT—2403h; BDB—1026d.

8030. שִׁלְשָׁה {1x} **Shilshâh**, *shil-shaw';* fem. from the same as 8028; *triplication; Shilshah,* an Isr.:—Shilshah {1x}. See: BDB—1027a.

8031. שָׁלִשָׁה {1x} **Shâlîshâh**, *shaw-lee-shaw';* fem. from 8027; *trebled* land; *Shalishah,* a place in Pal.:—Shalisha {1x}. See: BDB—1027a.

שָׁלֹשָׁה **shâlôshâh**. See 7969.

8032. שִׁלְשׁוֹם {25x} **shilshôwm**, *shil-shome';* or

שִׁלְשֹׁם **shilshôm**, *shil-shome';* from the same as 8028; *trebly,* i.e. (in time) *day before yesterday:*—times past + 8543 {7x}, heretofore + 8543 {6x}, before {3x}, past + 0865 {2x}, beforetime + 8543 {2x}, beforetime + 865 {1x}, misc. {4x} = excellent things, three days. See: TWOT—2403c; BDB—1026b, 1026d, 1070a.

שְׁלֹשִׁים **shᵉlôshîym**. See 7970.

שַׁלְתִּיאֵל **Shaltîyᵉêl**. See 7597.

8033. שָׁם {10x} **shâm**, *shawm;* a prim. particle [rather from the rel. 834]; *there* (transferring to time) *then;* often *thither,* or *thence:*—{10x} = there, therein, thither, whither, in it, thence, thereout. See: TWOT—2404; BDB—1027a, 1030b, 1031d, 1118b.

8034. שֵׁם {864x} **shêm**, *shame;* a prim. word [perh. rather from 7760 through the idea of def. and conspicuous *position;* comp. 8064]; an *appellation,* as a mark or memorial of individuality; by impl. *honor, authority, character:*—name {832x}, renown {7x}, fame {4x}, famous {3x}, named {3x}, named + 7121 {2x}, famous + 7121 {1x}, infamous + 2931 {1x}, report {1x}, misc. {10x} = + base, report.

Shem means name; reputation; memory; renown. (1) Names were not always indicative of the persons who bore them such as "dog" (Caleb) and "bee" (Deborah). (2) Perhaps some names indicated a single decisive characteristic of their bearer. (3) In other cases, a name recalls an event or mood which the parent(s) experienced at or shortly before the child's birth and/or naming. (4) Other names make a statement about an individual. (5) The sense of a name as an identification appears in Gen 2:19: "And out of the ground the LORD God formed every beast of the field, and every fowl of the air; and brought them unto Adam to see what he would call them: and whatsoever Adam called every living creature, that was the name thereof." (6) The names by which God revealed Himself do reflect something of His person and work.

(7) *Shem* can be a synonym for reputation or fame: "And they said, Go to, let us build us a city and a tower, whose top may reach unto heaven; and let us make us a name, lest we be scattered abroad upon the face of the whole earth." (Gen 11:4). (8) To "give a name for one" is to make him famous (2 Sa 7:23). (9) This word is sometimes a synonym for memory or reputation (2 Sa 14:7). In this respect name may include property, or an inheritance (Num 27:4). (10) *Shem* can connote (10a) renown (Num 16:2) and (10b) continuance (Ruth 4:5; Deut 9:14). See: TWOT—2405; BDB—1027d, 1116a.

8035. שֵׁם {17x} **Shêm**, *shame;* the same as 8034; *name; Shem,* a son of Noah (often includ. his posterity):—Shem {17x}. See: BDB—1028d.

8036. שֻׁם {12x} **shum** (Aram.), *shoom;* corresp. to 8034:—name {11x}, named + 7761 {1x}. See: TWOT—3036; BDB—1116a.

8037. שַׁמָּא {1x} **Shammâ**, *sham-maw';* from 8074; *desolation; Shamma,* an Isr.:—Shamma {1x}. See: BDB—1031c.

8038. שְׁמְאֵבֶר {1x} **Shemᵉêber**, *shem-ay'-ber;* appar. from 8034 and 83; *name of pinion,* i.e. *illustrious; Shemeber,* a king of Zeboim:—Shemeber {1x}. See: BDB—1028d.

8039. שִׁמְאָה {1x} **Shim'âh**, *shim-aw'*; perh. for 8093; *Shimah*, an Isr.:— Shimeah {1x}. See: BDB—1029a. comp. 8043.

8040. שְׂמֹאול {54x} **s°mô'wl**, *sem-ole'*; or

שְׂמֹאל **s°mô'l**, *sem-ole'*; a prim. word [rather perh. from the same as 8071 (by insertion of א) through the idea of *wrapping* up]; prop. *dark* (as *enveloped*), i.e. the *north*; hence (by orientation), the *left* hand:—left {36x}, left hand {17x}, left side {1x}. See: TWOT—2267a; BDB—541a, 965a, 969d.

8041. שָׂמַאל {5x} **sâma'l**, *saw-mal'*; a prim. root [rather denom. from 8040]; to use the *left* hand or pass in that direction):— left {5x}. See: TWOT—2267; BDB—970a, 971b.

8042. שְׂמָאלִי {9x} **s°mâ'lîy**, *sem-aw-lee'*; from 8040; situated on the *left* side:— left {7x}, left hand {2x}. See: TWOT—2267b; BDB—970a.

8043. שְׁמְאָם {1x} **Shim'âm**, *shim-awm'*; for 8039 [comp. 38]; *Shimam*, an Isr.:—Shimeam {1x}. See: BDB—1029a.

8044. שַׁמְגַּר {2x} **Shamgar**, *sham-gar'*; of uncert. der.; *Shamgar*, an Isr. judge:—Shamgar {2x}. See: BDB—1029a.

8045. שָׁמַד {90x} **shâmad**, *shaw-mad'*; a prim. root; to *desolate*:—destroy {83x}, destruction {1x}, overthrown {1x}, perished {1x}, misc. {4x} = bring to nought, pluck down, × utterly.
Shamad means to destroy, annihilate, exterminate. **(1)** This word always expresses complete destruction or annihilation: **(1a)** of people (Deut 2:12; Judg 21:16), **(1b)** of the pagan high places (Hos 10:8), and **(1c)** of Baal and his images (2 Kin 10:28). **(2)** When God wants to completely destroy, He will sweep with the [broom] of destruction (Is 14:23). Syn.: 6, 343, 7665, 7843. See: TWOT—2406; BDB—1029a, 1116a.

8046. שְׁמַד {1x} **sh°mad** (Aram.), *shem-ad'*; corresp. to 8045:—consume {1x}. TWOT—3037; BDB—1116a.

שָׁמֶה **shâmeh**. See 8064.

8047. שַׁמָּה {39x} **shammâh**, *sham-maw'*; from 8074; *ruin*; by impl. *consternation*:—astonishment {13x}, desolation {12x}, desolate {10x}, waste {3x}, wonderful {1x}. See: TWOT—2409d; BDB—1030b, 1031c.

8048. שַׁמָּה {8x} **Shammâh**, *sham-maw'*; the same as 8047; *Shammah*, the name of an Edomite and four Isr.:—Shammah {8x}. See: BDB—1030b, 1031c, 1035a.

8049. שַׁמְהוּת {1x} **Shamhûwth**, *sham-hooth'*; for 8048; *desolation; Sham-*

huth, an Isr.:—Shamhuth {1x}. See: BDB—1030b, 1031c.

8050. שְׁמוּאֵל {140x} **Sh°mûw'êl**, *sehm-oo-ale'*; from the pass. part. of 8085 and 410; *heard of God; Shemuel*, the name of three Isr.:—Samuel {137x}, Shemuel {3x}. See: BDB—1028d, 1030b.

שְׁמוֹנֶה **sh°môwneh**. See 8083.

שְׁמוֹנָה **sh°môwnâh**. See 8083.

שְׁמוֹנִים **sh°môwnîym**. See 8084.

8051. שַׁמּוּעַ {5x} **Shammûwa°**, *sham-moo'-ah*; from 8074; *renowned; Shammua*, the name of four Isr.:—Shammua {5x}. See: BDB—1035a, 1035b.

8052. שְׁמוּעָה {27x} **sh°mûw°âh**, *sehm-oo-aw'*; fem. pass. part. of 8074; something *heard*, i.e. an *announcement*:—rumour {9x}, tidings {8x}, report {4x}, fame {2x}, bruit {1x}, doctrine {1x}, mentioned {1x}, news {1x}. Syn.:
Shemuw'ah means revelation; something heard, doctrine (Is 28:9). *Shoma* (8089) means things heard by accident; hearsay (Josh 6:27). *Shema* (8088) is something heard by design; report (Gen 29:13). See: TWOT—2412d; BDB—1035b.

8053. שָׁמוּר {1x} **Shâmûwr**, *shaw-moor'*; pass. part. of 8103; *observed; Shamur*, an Isr.:—Shamir {1x}. See: BDB—1038d, 1039a.

8054. שַׁמּוֹת {1x} **Shammôwth**, *sham-môth'*; plur. of 8047; *ruins; Shammoth*, an Isr.:—Shammoth {1x}. See: BDB—1030b, 1031c.

8055. שָׂמַח {152x} **sâmach**, *saw-makh'*; a prim. root; prob. to *brighten* up, i.e. (fig.) *be* (caus. *make*) *blithe* or *gleesome*:— rejoice {95x}, glad {45x}, joy {5x}, joyful {2x}, merry {2x}, misc. {3x} = cheer up, × very.
(1) *Samach* usually refers to a spontaneous emotion or extreme happiness which is expressed in some visible and/or external manner. **(1a)** It does not normally represent an abiding state of well-being or feeling. **(1b)** This emotion arises at festivals, circumcision feasts, wedding feasts, harvest feasts, the overthrow of one's enemies (1 Sa 11:9), and other such events. **(2)** The emotion expressed in the verb *samach* usually finds a visible expression. **(2a)** In Jer 50:11 the Babylonians are denounced as being glad and jubilant over the pillage of Israel. **(2b)** Their emotion is expressed externally by their skipping about like a threshing heifer and neighing like stallions. **(2c)** The emotion represented in the verb (and concretized in the noun *simchah*—8057) is sometimes accompanied by dancing, singing,

and playing musical instruments (1 Sa 18:6). **(2d)** This emotion is usually described as the product of some external situation, circumstance, or experience (Ex 4:14). **(2d1)** This passage speaks of inner feeling which **(2d2)** is visibly expressed as Aaron was overcome with joy and kissed him (4:27).

(3) The verb *samach* suggests three elements: **(3a)** a spontaneous, unsustained feeling of jubilance, **(3b)** a feeling so strong that it finds expression in some external act, and **(3c)** a feeling prompted by some external and unsustained stimulus. **(4)** This verb intransitively signifies that the action is focused on the subject (1 Sa 11:9). **(4a)** God is sometimes the subject, the one who rejoices and is jubilant (Ps 104:31). **(4b)** The godly are to be glad in the Lord, rejoice, and shout for joy (Ps 32:11). **(5)** *Samach* can also mean to be joyful or glad (Deut 12:7) describing a state into which one places himself. **(6)** It describes all that one does in making a feast before God (Lev 23:40). **(7)** In a few cases the verb describes an on-going state (1 Kin 4:20). See: TWOT—2268; BDB—970a.

8056. שָׂמֵחַ {23x} **sâmeach**, *saw-may'-akh;* from 8055; *blithe* or *gleeful:*—rejoice {11x}, glad {4x}, joyful {3x}, merry {3x}, merrily {1x}, merryhearted {1x}.

The first biblical occurrence is in Deut 16:15: "Seven days shalt thou keep a solemn feast unto the Lord thy God in the place which the Lord shall choose: because the Lord thy God shall bless thee . . . therefore thou shalt surely rejoice." See: TWOT—2268a; BDB—970c.

8057. שִׂמְחָה {94x} **simchâh**, *sim-khaw';* from 8056; *blithesomeness* or *glee,* (relig. or festival):—joy {44x}, gladness {31x}, mirth {8x}, rejoice {3x}, rejoicing {2x}, misc. {6x} = ✕ exceeding (-ly), joyfulness, pleasure.

This noun is both **(1)** a technical term for the external expression of "joy" (Gen 31:27—the first biblical occurrence; cf. 1 Sa 18:6; Jer 50:11) and **(2)** (usually) a representation of the abstract feeling or concept "joy" (Deut 28:47). **(3)** In another technical use this noun signifies the entire activity of making a feast before God: "And all the people went their way to eat, and to drink, and to send portions, and to make great mirth [literally, "to make a great rejoicing"]" (Neh 8:12). **(4)** The noun catches the concrete coloring of the verb, as in Is 55:12: "For ye shall go out with joy . . . : the mountains and the hills shall break forth before you into singing, and all the trees of the field shall clap their hands." See: TWOT—2268b; BDB—965a, 970d.

8058. שָׁמַט {9x} **shâmat**, *shaw-mat';* a prim. root; to *fling* down; incipiently to

jostle; fig. to *let alone, desist, remit:*—release {2x}, throw down {2x}, shake {1x}, stumble {1x}, discontinue {1x}, overthrown {1x}, let rest {1x}. See: TWOT—2408; BDB—1030c.

8059. שְׁמִטָּה {5x} **sh⁰mittâh**, *shem-it-taw';* from 8058; *remission* (of debt) or *suspension* of labor):—release {5x}. See: TWOT—2408a; BDB—1030d.

8060. שַׁמַּי {6x} **Shammay**, *sham-mah'-ee;* from 8073; *destructive; Shammai,* the name of three Isr.:—Shammai {6x}. See: BDB—1030c, 1031d.

8061. שְׁמִידָע {3x} **Sh⁰mîydâ⁰**, *shem-ee-daw';* appar. from 8034 and 3045; *name of knowing; Shemida,* an Isr.:—Shemida {3x}. See: BDB—1029a, 1030c.

8062. שְׁמִידָעִי {1x} **Sh⁰mîydâ⁰îy**, *shem-ee-daw-ee';* patron. from 8061; a *Shemidaite* (collect.) or desc. of Shemida:—Shemidaites {1x}. See: BDB—1029a, 1030c.

8063. שְׂמִיכָה {1x} **s⁰mîykâh**, *sem-ee-kaw';* from 5564; a *rug* (as *sustaining* the Oriental sitter):—mantle {1x}. See: TWOT—2269a; BDB—970d.

8064. שָׁמַיִם {420x} **shâmayim**, *shaw-mah'-yim;* dual of an unused sing.

שָׁמֶה **shâmeh**, *shaw-meh';* from an unused root mean. to *be lofty;* the *sky* (as *aloft;* the dual perh. alluding to the visible arch in which the clouds move, as well as to the higher ether where the celestial bodies revolve):—heaven {398x}, air {21x}, astrologers + 1895 {1x}.

Introduction: Sometimes it signifies the atmosphere immediately surrounding the earth, in which the fowls of the air fly. Sometimes it is used of the space in which the clouds are floating. In other places it refers to the vast expanse through which the stars are moving in their courses. It is opposed to *sheowl* (7585), the one being regarded as a place of exaltation, the other of degradation; the one being represented as the dwelling place of the Most High and the angels of God, the other as the abode of the dead. It includes all space that is not occupied by the terrestrial globe, and extends from the air we breathe and the winds we feel around us to the firmament or expanse that contains the innumerable stars. This it includes and exceeds, for where our intellect ceases to operate, and fails to find a limit to the extension of space, there faith comes in. And while before the eye of the body there is spread out an infinity of space, the possession of a super-material nature brings us into communion with a Being whose nature and condition cannot adequately be described by terms

of locality or extension. The heavens and the heaven of heavens cannot contain Him. The countless stars are not only known and numbered by Him, but are called into existence and fixed in their courses by His will and wisdom. Where He is, there the true heaven is; and the glories of the firmament faintly shadow forth the ineffable bliss that those must realize who are brought into relationship with Him.

(1) *Shamayim* is the usual for the sky and the realm of the sky **(1a)** birds fly (Deut 4:17). **(1b)** This area, high above the ground but below the stars and heavenly bodies, is often the locus of visions (1 Chr 21:16). **(2)** This word represents an area farther removed from the earth's surface **(2a)** from which come such things as **(2a1)** frost (Job 38:29), **(2a2)** snow (Is 55:10), **(2a3)** fire (Gen 19:24), **(2a4)** dust (Deut 28:24), **(2a5)** hail (Josh 10:11), and **(2a6)** rain (Gen 8:2). **(2b)** This realm is God's storehouse; God is **(3a)** the dispenser of the stores and Lord of the realm (Deut 28:12). **(2c)** This meaning of *shamayim* occurs in Gen 1:7–8. **(3)** *Shamayim* also represents the realm in which the sun, moon, and stars are located (Gen 1:14). **(4)** The phrase "heaven and earth" may denote the entire creation (Gen 1:1). **(5)** Heaven is the dwelling place of God (Ps 2:4; Deut 4:39; 26:15). **(5a)** Another expression representing the dwelling place of God is "the highest heaven [literally, the heaven of heavens] (Deut 10:14). **(5b)** This does not indicate height, but an absolute—i.e., God's abode is a unique realm not to be identified with the physical creation. Syn.: 7834. See: TWOT—2407a; BDB—1029c, 1116a.

8065. שָׁמַיִן {38x} **shâmayin** (Aram.), *shaw-mah'-yin;* corresp. to 8064:—heaven {38x}. See: TWOT—3038; BDB—1116a.

8066. שְׁמִינִי {28x} **sh°mîynîy,** *shem-ee-nee';* from 8083; *eight:*—eight {28x}. See: TWOT—2411c; BDB—1033b.

8067. שְׁמִינִית {3x} **sh°mîynîyth,** *shem-ee-neeth';* fem. of 8066; prob. an *eight*-stringed lyre:—Sheminith {3x}. See: TWOT—2411c; BDB—1033b.

8068. שָׁמִיר {11x} **shâmîyr,** *shaw-meer';* from 8104 in the orig. sense of *pricking;* a *thorn;* also (from its *keenness* for scratching) a gem, prob. the *diamond:*—brier {8x}, adamant {1x}, adamant stone {1x}, diamond {1x}. See: TWOT—2416a; BDB—1038d, 1039a.

8069. שָׁמִיר {3x} **Shâmîyr,** *shaw-meer';* the same as 8068; *Shamir,* the name of two places in Pal.:—Shamir {3x}. See: BDB—1039a. comp. 8053.

8070. שְׁמִירָמוֹת {4x} **Sh°mîyrâmôwth,** *shem-ee-raw-môth';* or

שְׁמָרִימוֹת **Sh°mârîymôwth,** *shem-aw-ree-môth';* prob. from 8034 and plur. of 7413; *name of heights; Shemiramoth,* the name of two Isr.:—Shemiramoth {4x}. See: BDB—1029a, 1030d.

8071. שִׂמְלָה {29x} **simlâh,** *sim-law';* perh. by perm. for the fem. of 5566 (through the idea of a *cover* assuming the shape of the object beneath); a *dress,* espec. a *mantle:*—raiment {11x}, clothes {6x}, garment {6x}, apparel {2x}, cloth {2x}, clothing {2x}. See: TWOT—2270a; BDB—969c, 971a. comp. 8008.

8072. שַׂמְלָה {4x} **Samlâh,** *sam-law';* prob. for the same as 8071; *Samlah,* an Edomite:—Samlah {4x}. See: BDB—971a.

8073. שַׂמְלַי {1x} **Shamlay,** *sham-lah'-ee;* for 8014; *Shamlai,* one of the Nethinim:—Shalmai {1x}. See: BDB—969c, 1030c.

8074. שָׁמֵם {92x} **shâmêm,** *shaw-mame';* a prim. root; to *stun* (or intr. *grow numb*), i.e. *devastate* or (fig.) *stupefy* (both usually in a pass. sense):—desolate {49x}, astonished {20x}, desolation {7x}, waste {5x}, destroy {3x}, wondered {2x}, amazed {1x}, astonishment {1x}, misc. {4x} = be astonied, be destitute.

(1) *Shamem* means to be desolate (2 Sa 13:20), astonished (Job 21:5), appalled, devastated (Hos 2:12), ravaged. **(2)** What one sees sometimes is so horrible that it "horrifies" or "appalls": "Mark me, and be astonished, and lay your hand upon your mouth [i.e., be speechless]" (Job 21:5). Syn.: 7591, 7665, 7703, 7722. See: TWOT—2409; BDB—1030d, 1031c, 1116b.

8075. שְׁמַם {1x} **sh°mam** (Aram.), *shem-am';* corresp. to 8074:—be astonied {1x}. See: TWOT—3039; BDB—1116b.

8076. שָׁמֵם {2x} **shâmêm,** *shaw-mame';* from 8074; *ruined:*—desolate {2x}. See: TWOT—2409a; BDB—1031b.

8077. שְׁמָמָה {58x} **sh°mâmâh,** *shem-aw-maw';* or

שִׁמָמָה **shîmâmâh,** *shee-mam-aw';* fem. of 8076; *devastation;* fig. *astonishment:*—desolate {40x}, desolation {14x}, waste {1x}, misc. {3x} = (laid, × most) desolate (-ion), waste. See: TWOT—2409b, 2409c; BDB—1031b, 1031c.

8078. שִׁמָּמוֹן {2x} **shimmâmôwn,** *shim-maw-mone';* from 8074; *stupefaction:*—astonishment {2x}. See: TWOT—2409e; BDB—1031d.

8079. שְׁמָמִית {1x} sᵉmâmîyth, *sem-aw-meeth';* prob. from 8074 (in the sense of *poisoning*); a *lizard* (from the superstition of its *noxiousness*):—spider {1x}. See: TWOT—2271; BDB—971b, 1031d.

8080. שָׁמַן {5x} shâman, *shaw-man';* a prim. root; to *shine*, i.e. (by anal.) *be* (caus. *make*) *oily* or *gross:*—wax fat {3x}, make fat {1x}, became fat {1x}.

   Shaman, the verb, means to grow or be fat (Neh 9:25; Jer 5:28). See: TWOT—2410; BDB—1031d.

8081. שֶׁמֶן {193x} shemen, *sheh'-men;* from 8080; *grease*, espec. liquid (as from the olive, often perfumed); fig. *richness:*—oil {165x}, ointment {14x}, olive {4x}, oiled {2x}, fat {2x}, things {2x}, misc. {4x} = anointing, X fruitful, + pine.

   Shemen means **(1)** (olive) oil used to anoint **(1a)** a memorial (Gen 28:18), **(1b)** a future office bearer (Ex 25:6; 2 Kin 9:6); **(1c)** one's head as a sign of mourning (2 Sa 14:2); **(1d)** one's head as a sign of rejoicing (Ps 23:5); and **(1e)** one's ear lobe, thumb, and toe as signs of dedication: to hear only God [the ear], to do only God's will [right thumb = power], and to go only where He leads [right big toe] (Lev 14:17). **(2)** *Shemen* is used **(2a)** as a preservative on shield-leather (2 Sa 1:21); **(2b)** in baking (Ex 29:2); and **(2c)** as a medication (Eze 16:9). **(3)** This oil is burned for light (Ex 25:6). **(4)** Its many uses made olive oil a valuable trade item (Eze 27:17). **(5)** *Shemen* perhaps means the olive itself (Jer 40:10). **(6)** *Shemen* is a kind of perfume or mixed with certain odors to make a perfume (Song 1:3). **(7)** *Shemen* sometimes modifies wood (1 Kin 6:23). See: TWOT—2410c; BDB—1032a.

8082. שָׁמֵן {10x} shâmên, *shaw-mane';* from 8080; *greasy*, i.e. *gross;* fig. *rich:*—fat {8x}, plenteous {1x}, lusty {1x}.

   The adjective *shamen* means **(1)** fat (Eze 34:16); **(2)** rich in the sense of fattening (Gen 49:20); **(3)** fertile (Num 13:20); **(4)** robust or muscular (Judg 3:29); and **(5)** large (Hab 1:16). See: TWOT—2410a; BDB—1032a.

8083. שְׁמֹנֶה {109x} shᵉmôneh, *shem-o-neh';* or

שְׁמוֹנֶה shᵉmôwneh, *shem-o-neh';* fem.

שְׁמֹנָה shᵉmônâh, *shem-o-naw';* or

שְׁמוֹנָה shᵉmôwnâh, *shem-o-naw';* appar. from 8082 through the idea of *plumpness;* a cardinal number, *eight* (as if a *surplus* above the "perfect" seven); also (as ord.) *eighth:*—eight {74x}, eighteen + 6240 {18x}, eighteenth + 6240 {11x}, eighth {5x}, eighteen thousand + 7239 {1x}. See: TWOT—2411a; BDB—1032d.

8084. שְׁמֹנִים {38x} shᵉmônîym, *shem-o-neem';* or

שְׁמוֹנִים shᵉmôwnîym, *shem-o-neem';* mult. from 8083; *eighty*, also *eightieth:*—four fourscore {34x}, eighty {3x}, eightieth {1x}. See: TWOT—2411b; BDB—1033b.

8085. שָׁמַע {1159x} shâmaᶜ, *shaw-mah';* a prim. root; to *hear* intelligently (often with impl. of attention, obedience, etc.; caus. to *tell*, etc.):—hear {785x}, hearken {196x}, obey {81x}, publish {17x}, understand {9x}, obedient {8x}, diligently {8x}, shew {6x}, sound {3x}, declare {3x}, discern {2x}, noise {2x}, perceive {2x}, tell {2x}, reported {2x}, misc. {33x} = X attentively, call (gather) together, X carefully, X certainly, consent, consider, be content, give ear, X indeed, listen, (make a) proclaim (-ation), regard, X surely, whosoever [heareth], witness.

   (1) Basically, this verb means to hear something with one's ears, but there are several other nuances. **(1a)** In Gen 37:17, a man unintentionally overheard. **(1b)** *Shama* can also be used of eavesdropping, or intentionally listening in on a conversation (Gen 18:10). **(1c)** *Shama* means to give undivided attention (Gen 37:6; 1 Chr 28:2). **(2)** To hear something may imply to have knowledge (Gen 21:26). **(3)** *Shama* may also imply to gain or get knowledge (Jer 37:5). **(4)** It may mean to come into knowledge about something (Num 9:8). **(5)** The verb can represent the mere hearing of something (Gen 3:8). **(6)** To make someone hear something (without any specification of what was heard) suggests summoning the person (1 Kin 15:22). **(7)** Hearing can be both intellectual and spiritual. **(7a)** Spiritually, one may hear God's Word (Num 24:4). Gen 17:20). **(8)** To hear means not only to hear what is said, but to agree with its intention or petition (Gen 16:11; 17:20). **(9)** In the case of hearing and hearkening to a higher authority, *shama* can mean to obey (Gen 22:18). **(10)** To have a hearing heart is to have discernment or understanding (1 Kin 3:9). **(11)** Certainly when Moses told Israel's judges to "hear" cases, he meant more than listening with one's ear. He meant for them to examine the merits of a case, so as to render a just decision (Deut 1:16). See: TWOT—2412, 2412a; BDB—1033b, 1116b.

8086. שְׁמַע {9x} shᵉmaᶜ (Aram.), *shem-ah';* corresp. to 8085:—hear {8x}, obey {1x}. See: TWOT—3040; BDB—1116b.

8087. שֶׁמַע {5x} Shemaᶜ, *sheh'-mah;* for the same as 8088; *Shema*, the name of a place in Pal. and of four Isr.:—*Shema* {5x}. See: BDB—1034d, 1035c.

8088. שֵׁמַע {18x} shêmaᶜ, *shay'-mah;* from 8085; something *heard*, i.e. a *sound, rumor, announcement;* abstr. *audience:*—fame

{5x}, report {5x}, hear {3x}, tidings {2x}, bruit {1x}, loud {1x}, speech {1x}. Syn.:

(1) *Shema* is something heard by design; report (Gen 29:13). **(2)** *Shoma* (8089) means things heard by accident; hearsay (Josh 6:27). **(3)** *Shemuw'ah* (8052) means revelation; something heard, doctrine (Is 28:9). See: TWOT—2412b; BDB—1034d.

8089. שֵׁמַע {4x} **shôma**, *sho'-mah;* from 8085; a *report:*—fame {4x}. Syn.:
(A) *Shoma* means things heard by accident; hearsay (Josh 6:27). **(B)** *Shema* (8088) is something heard by design; report (Gen 29:13). **(C)** *Shemuw'ah* (8052) means revelation; something heard, doctrine (Is 28:9). See: TWOT—2412c; BDB—1035a.

8090. שֶׁמַע {1x} **Shᵉmâ**, *shem-aw';* for 8087; *Shema,* a place in Pal.:—*Shema* {1x}. See: BDB—1035a.

8091. שָׁמָע {1x} **Shâmâ**, *shaw-maw';* from 8085; *obedient; Shama,* an Isr.:—*Shama* {1x}. See: BDB—1035a.

8092. שִׁמְעָא {6x} **Shim̀â**, *shim-aw';* for 8093; *Shima,* the name of four Isr.:—*Shimea* {6x}. See: BDB—1031c, 1035a, 1035b, 1035c.

8093. שִׁמְעָה {2x} **Shim̀âh**, *shim-aw';* fem. of 8088; *annunciation; Shimah,* an Isr.:—*Shimeah* {2x}. See: BDB—1031c, 1035a.

8094. שְׁמָעָה {1x} **Shᵉmầâh**, *shem-aw-aw';* for 8093; *Shemaah,* an Isr.:—*Shemaah* {1x}. See: BDB—1035a.

8095. שִׁמְעוֹן {44x} **Shim̀ôwn**, *shim-ōne';* from 8085; *hearing; Shimon,* one of Jacob's sons, also the tribe desc. from him:—Simeon {43x}, Shimeon {1x}. See: BDB—1035b.

8096. שִׁמְעִי {43x} **Shim̀iy**, *shim-ee';* from 8088; *famous; Shimi,* the name of twenty Isr.:—Shimei {41x}, Shimhi {1x}, Shimi {1x}. See: BDB—1031c, 1034d, 1035c.

8097. שִׁמְעִי {2x} **Shim̀iy**, *shim-ee';* patron. from 8096; a *Shimite* (collect.) or desc. of Shimi:—Shimites {1x}, Shimei {1x}. See: BDB—1035c.

8098. שְׁמַעְיָה {41x} **Shᵉmàyâh**, *shem-aw-yaw';* or

שְׁמַעְיָהוּ **Shᵉmàyâhûw**, *shem-aw-yaw'-hoo;* from 8085 and 3050; *Jah has heard; Shemajah,* the name of twenty-five Isr.:—Shemaiah {41x}. See: BDB—1035c.

8099. שִׁמְעֹנִי {4x} **Shim̀ôniy**, *shim-o-nee';* patron. from 8095; a *Shimonite* (collect.) or desc. of Shimon:—Simeonite {3x}, Simeon {1x}. See: BDB—1035c.

8100. שִׁמְעַת {2x} **Shim̀âth**, *shim-awth';* fem. of 8088; *annunciation; Shimath,* an Ammonitess:—*Shimeath* {2x}. See: BDB—1035a.

8101. שִׁמְעָתִי {1x} **Shim̀âthiy**, *shim-aw-thee';* patron. from 8093; a *Shimathite* (collect.) or desc. of Shimah:—Shimeathites {1x}. See: BDB—1035a.

8102. שֶׁמֶץ {2x} **shemets**, *sheh'-mets;* from an unused root mean. to *emit* a sound; an *inkling:*—little {2x}. See: TWOT—2413a; BDB—1036b.

8103. שִׁמְצָה {1x} **shimtsâh**, *shim-tsaw';* fem. of 8102; *scornful whispering* (of hostile spectators):—shame {1x}. See: TWOT—2413b; BDB—1036b.

8104. שָׁמַר {468x} **shâmar**, *shaw-mar';* a prim. root; prop. to *hedge* about (as with thorns), i.e. *guard;* gen. to *protect, attend to,* etc.:—keep {283x}, observe {46x}, heed {35x}, keeper {28x}, preserve {21x}, beware {9x}, mark {8x}, watchman {8x}, wait {7x}, watch {7x}, regard {5x}, save {2x}, misc. {9x} = be circumspect, look narrowly, reserve, sure.

Shamar means "to keep, tend, watch over, retain." **(1)** *Shamar* means "to keep" in the sense of "tending" and taking care of. **(1a)** So God put Adam "into the garden of Eden to dress it and to keep it" (Gen 2:15—the first occurrence). **(1b)** In 2 Kin 22:14 Harhas is called "keeper of the wardrobe" (the priest's garments). **(1c)** Satan was directed "to keep," or "to tend" (so as not to allow it to be destroyed) Job's life: "Behold, he is in thine hand; but save his life" (Job 2:6). **(1d)** In this same sense God is described as the keeper of Israel (Ps 121:4). **(2)** The word also means "to keep" in the sense of "watching over" or giving attention to. David, ironically chiding Abner for not protecting Saul, says: "Art not thou a valiant man? and who is like to thee in Israel? wherefore then hast thou not kept thy lord the king?" (1 Sa 26:15). **(3)** In extended application this emphasis comes to mean "to watch, observe": "And it came to pass, as she continued praying before the Lord, that Eli [was watching] her mouth" (1 Sa 1:12). **(4)** Another extended use of the verb related to this emphasis appears in covenantal contexts. **(4a)** In such cases "keep" means "to watch over" in the sense of seeing that one observes the covenant, keeping one to a covenant. **(4b)** God says of Abraham: "For I know him, that he will command his children and his household after him, and they shall keep the way of the Lord, to do justice and judgment" (Gen 18:19). **(4c)** As God had said earlier, "Thou shalt keep my covenant therefore, thou, and thy seed after thee in their gen-

erations" (Gen 17:9). **(5)** When used in close connection with another verb, *shamar* can signify carefully or watchfully doing that action: "And he answered and said, Must I not take heed to speak that which the Lord hath put in my mouth?" (Num 23:12). **(6)** Not only does *shamar* signify watching, but it signifies doing it as a watchman in the sense of fulfilling a responsibility: "And the spies saw a man come forth out of the city . . ." (Judg 1:24). **(7)** This verb means "to keep" in the sense of saving or "retaining." **(7a)** When Jacob told his family about his dream, "his brethren envied him; but his father observed the saying" (Gen 37:11); he "retained" it mentally. **(7b)** Joseph tells Pharaoh to appoint overseers to gather food: "And let them . . . lay up corn under the hand of Pharaoh, and let them keep food in the cities" (Gen 41:35); let them not give it out but see that it is "retained" in storage. **(8)** *Shamar* seems to mean, "to revere." So the psalmist says: "I have hated them that regard [revere] lying vanities: but I trust in the Lord" (Ps 31:6). Syn.: 821, 4929, 4931, 5341, 8105, 8107, 8108. See: TWOT—2414; BDB—1036b.

8105. שָׁמֶר {5x} **shemer**, *sheh'-mer;* from 8104; something *preserved*, i.e. the *settlings* (plur. only) of wine:—lees {4x}, dregs {1x}. *Shemerim* [plural] refers to "dregs of wine, lees." One of the 4 appearances of this word is in Is 25:6: ". . . shall the Lord of hosts make unto all people a feast of fat things, a feast of wines on the lees (*shemarim*), of fat things full of marrow, of wines on the lees (*shemarim*) well refined." See: TWOT—2415a; BDB—1038d.

8106. שֶׁמֶר {5x} **Shemer**, *sheh'-mer;* the same as 8105; *Shemer*, the name of three Isr.:—*Shemer* {2x}, Shamer {2x}, Shamed {1x}. See: BDB—1029c, 1037c, 1038d.

8107. שִׁמֻּר {2x} **shimmûr**, *shim-moor';* from 8104; an *observance:*—observed {2x}. *Shimmurim* [plural] means a "night vigil." In Ex 12:42 this word carries the meaning of "night vigil" in the sense of "night of watching": "It is a night to be much observed (*shimmurim*) unto the Lord for bringing them out from the land of Egypt: this is that night of the Lord to be observed (*shimmurim*) of all the children of Israel in their generations." This noun occurs twice in this entry and in no other verse. Syn.: 821, 4929, 4931, 5341, 8108. See: TWOT—2414c; BDB—1037d.

שֹׁמֵר **Shômêr.** See 7763.

8108. שָׁמְרָה {1x} **shomrâh**, *shom-raw';* fem. of an unused noun from 8104 mean. a *guard; watchfulness:*—watch {1x}.

The noun *shomrah* means "guard, watch." The single appearance of this word is in Ps

141:3: "Set a watch (*shomrah*), O LORD, before my mouth; keep the door of my lips." Syn.: 821, 4929, 4931, 5341, 8107. See: TWOT—2414a; BDB—1037c.

8109. שְׁמֻרָה {1x} **sh͎mûrâh**, *shem-oo-raw';* fem. of pass. part. of 8104; something *guarded*, i.e. an *eye-lid:*—waking {1x}. See: TWOT—2414b; BDB—1037d.

8110. שִׁמְרוֹן {5x} **Shimrôwn**, *shim-rone';* from 8105 in its orig. sense; *guardianship; Shimron*, the name of an Isr. and of a place in Pal.:—Shimron {5x}. See: BDB—1038a.

8111. שֹׁמְרוֹן {109x} **Shôm͎rown**, *sho-mer-ōne';* from the act. part. of 8104; *watch-station; Shomeron*, a place in Pal.:—Samaria {109x}. See: TWOT—2414d; BDB—1037d, 1116b.

8112. שִׁמְרוֹן מְראוֹן {1x} **Shimrôwn M͎rôwn**, *shim-rone' mer-one';* from 8110 and a der. of 4754; *guard of lashing; Shimron-Meron*, a place in Pal.:—Shimronmeron {1x}. See: BDB—597b, 598c, 1038a.

8113. שִׁמְרִי {4x} **Shimriy**, *shim-ree';* from 8105 in its orig. sense; *watchful; Shimri*, the name of four Isr.:—Shimri {4x}. See: BDB—1037c.

8114. שְׁמַרְיָה {4x} **Sh͎maryâh**, *shem-ar-yaw';* or שְׁמַרְיָהוּ **Sh͎maryâhûw**, *shem-ar-yaw'-hoo;* from 8104 and 3050; *Jah has guarded; Shemarjah*, the name of four Isr.:—Shemariah {4x}. See: BDB—1037d.

שְׁמָרִימוֹת **Sh͎mârîymôwth.** See 8070.

8115. שָׁמְרַיִן {2x} **Shomrayin** (Aram.), *shom-rah'-yin;* corresp. to 8111; *Shomrain*, a place in Pal.:—Samaria {2x}. See: BDB—1116b.

8116. שִׁמְרִית {1x} **Shimrîyth**, *shim-reeth';* fem. of 8113; *female guard; Shimrith*, a Moabitess:—Shimrith {1x}. See: BDB—1037d.

8117. שִׁמְרֹנִי {1x} **Shimrôniy**, *shim-ro-nee';* patron. from 8110; a *Shimronite* (collect.) or desc. of Shimron:—Shimronites {1x}. See: BDB—1038a.

8118. שֹׁמְרֹנִי {1x} **Shôm͎rôniy**, *sho-mer-o-nee';* patrial from 8111; a *Shomeronite* (collect.) or inhab. of Shomeron:—Samaritans {1x}. See: BDB—1038a.

8119. שִׁמְרָת {1x} **Shimrâth**, *shim-rawth';* from 8104; *guardship; Shimrath*, an Isr.:—Shimrath {1x}. See: BDB—1037d.

8120. שְׁמַשׁ {1x} **sh͎mash** (Aram.), *shem-ash';* corresp. to the root of 8121

through the idea of *activity* impl. in day-light; to *serve:*—ministered {1x}. See: TWOT—3042; BDB—1116b.

8121. שֶׁמֶשׁ **shemesh**, *sheh'-mesh;* from an unused root mean. to *be brilliant;* the *sun;* by impl. the *east;* fig. a *ray,* i.e. (arch.) a notched *battlement:*—sun {119x}, sunrising + 4217 {9x}, east side + 4217 {2x}, windows {1x}, eastward + 4217 {1x}, west + 3996 {1x}, westward + 3996 {1x}.

(1) This word means sun (Gen 15:12). **(2)** The "wings of the sun" are probably its rays (Mal 4:2). **(3)** The sun's regularity **(3a)** is supported by divine sovereignty (Gen 8:22) and **(3b)** figures the security of God's allies (Judg 5:31). **(4)** God can **(4a)** make the sun stand still when He wishes (Josh 10:12–13) or **(4b)** darken **(4b1)** as an indication of His judgment upon His enemies and **(4b2)** salvation for His people (Joel 2:31–32). **(5)** The sun and all the heavenly bodies were created by God (Gen 1:16) and **(6)** are summoned to praise Him (Ps 148:3). **(7)** The Canaanites and other people worshiped the sun as a god, and this paganism appeared among Israelites in times of spiritual decline (Deut 4:19). **(8)** The east is "the rising of the sun" (Num 21:11). **(9)** The west is "the setting of the sun" (Deut 11:30). **(10)** To be "before the sun" or "before the eyes of the sun" is to be openly exposed (Num 25:4). **(11)** To "see the sun" is "to live" (Ps 58:8). **(12)** Something "under the sun" is life lived on the earth apart from God in contrast to life lived on earth with a proper relationship with God (Eccl 1:3). See: TWOT—2417a; BDB—1039a, 1116b. See also 1053.

8122. שְׁמַשׁ {1x} **shemesh** (Aram.), *sheh'-mesh;* corresp. to 8121; the *sun:*—sun {1x}. See: TWOT—3041; BDB—1116b.

8123. שִׁמְשׁוֹן {38x} **Shimshôwn**, *shim-shone';* from 8121; *sunlight; Shimshon,* an Isr.:—Samson {38x}. See: BDB—1039c.

שִׁמְשִׁי **Shimshîy**. See 1030.

8124. שִׁמְשַׁי {4x} **Shimshay** (Aram.), *shim-shah'-ee;* from 8122; *sunny; Shimshai,* a Samaritan:—Shimshai {4x}. See: BDB—1116c.

8125. שַׁמְשְׁרַי {1x} **Shamshᵉray**, *sham-sher-ah'-ee;* appar. from 8121; *sun-like; Shamsherai,* an Isr.:—Shamsherai {1x}. See: BDB—1039c.

8126. שֻׁמָתִי {1x} **Shûmâthîy**, *shoo-maw-thee';* patron. from an unused name from 7762 prob. mean. *garlic*-smell; a *Shu-mathite* (collect.) or desc. of Shumah:—Shumathites {1x}. See: BDB—1002c, 1029c, 1039c.

8127. שֵׁן {55x} **shên**, *shane;* from 8150; a *tooth* (as *sharp*); spec. (for 8143) *ivory;* fig. a *cliff:*—teeth {31x}, tooth {10x}, ivory {10x}, sharp {2x}, crag {1x}, forefront {1x}. See: TWOT—2422a; BDB—1039c, 1042a, 1116d.

8128. שֵׁן {3x} **shên** (Aram.), *shane;* corresp. to 8127; a *tooth:*—teeth {3x}. See: TWOT—3043; BDB—1116c, 1116d.

8129. שֵׁן {1x} **Shên**, *shane;* the same as 8127; *crag; Shen,* a place in Pal.:—Shen {1x}. See: BDB—1039c, 1042b.

8130. שָׂנֵא {146x} **sânê'**, *saw-nay';* a prim. root; to *hate* (personally):—hate {136x}, enemies {3x}, enemy {2x}, foes {1x}, hateful {1x}, misc. {3x} = hater, odious, ✕ utterly.

(1) *Sane'* represents an emotion ranging from intense hatred to the much weaker "set against" and is used of persons and things (including ideas, words, inanimate objects). **(2)** The strong sense of the word typifies the emotion of jealousy (Gen 37:4; cf. v. 11). The word covers emotion ranging from bitter disdain to outright hatred (Gen 37:18ff). **(3)** This emphasis can be further heightened by a double use of the root [literally, "hating, you hated her"] (Judg 15:2). **(4)** One special use of *sane'* is ingressive, indicating the initiation of the emotion (2 Sa 13:15; Hos 9:15; Jer 12:8). **(5)** In a weaker sense, *sane'* signifies being set against something (Ex 18:21). **(6)** It means to be unloved (Deut 22:16; Eze 23:28). See: TWOT—2272; BDB—971b, 1114a.

8131. שְׂנֵא {1x} **sᵉnê'** (Aram.), *sen-ay';* corresp. to 8130:—them that hate thee {1x}. See: TWOT—3010; BDB—1114a.

8132. שָׁנָא {3x} **shânâ'**, *shaw-naw';* a prim. root; to *alter:*—change {3x}. See: TWOT—2419; BDB—1039c, 1039d, 1040a.

8133. שְׁנָא {21x} **shᵉnâ'** (Aram.), *shen-aw';* corresp. to 8132:—change {14x}, diverse {5x}, alter {2x}. See: BDB—1039d.

שֵׁנָא **shênâ'**. See 8142.

8134. שִׁנְאָב {1x} **Shin'âb**, *shin-awb';* prob. from 8132 and 1; a *father has turned; Shinab,* a Canaanite:—Shinab {1x}. See: BDB—1039c.

8135. שִׂנְאָה {16x} **sin'âh**, *sin-aw';* from 8130; *hate:*—hatred {13x}, hated {2x}, hatefully {1x}. See: TWOT—2272b; BDB—971d.

8136. שִׁנְאָן {1x} **shin'ân**, *shin-awn';* from 8132; *change,* i.e. *repetition:*—angels {1x}. See: TWOT—2421d; BDB—1039c, 1041d.

8137. שְׁנְאַצַּר {1x} **Shen'atstsar**, *shen-ats-tsar'*; appar. of Bab. or.; *Shenatstsar*, an Isr.:—Shenazar {1x}. See: BDB—1039c.

8138. שָׁנָה {22x} **shânâh**, *shaw-naw'*; a prim. root; to *fold,* i.e. *duplicate* (lit. or fig.); by impl. to *transmute* (tran. or intr.):—change {7x}, second time {3x}, again {3x}, diverse {2x}, alter {1x}, disguise {1x}, doubled {1x}, pervert {1x}, preferred {1x}, repeateth {1x}, misc. {1x} = disguise, return. See: TWOT—2421; BDB—1039c, 1039d, 1040d.

8139. שְׁנָה {1x} **sh'nâh** (Aram.), *shen-aw'*; corresp. to 8142:—sleep {1x}. See: TWOT—2778a; BDB—1096b, 1116d.

8140. שְׁנָה {7x} **sh'nâh** (Aram.), *shen-aw'*; corresp. to 8141:—year {7x}. See: BDB—1096b, 1116d.

8141. שָׁנֶה {875x} **shâneh** (in plur. only), *shaw-neh'*; or (fem.)

שָׁנָה **shânâh**, *shaw-naw'*; from 8138; a *year* (as a *revolution* of time):—year {797x}, not translated {55x}, yearly {3x}, yearly + 8141 {2x}, year + 1121 {1x}, live + 2416 {1x}, old + 2416 + 3117 {1x}, misc. {4x}.

Shanah means year (Gen 1:14). **(1)** The year may be based on the relationship between the seasons and the sun, the solar year or agricultural year (Ex 23:16; Deut 16:9–12). **(2)** It can be based on a correlation of the seasons and the moon (lunar year) (Num 28:11–15). **(3)** These systems appear side by side at least from the time of Moses. An exact picture of the Old Testament year is difficult to obtain. See: TWOT—2419a; BDB—1040a.

8142. שֵׁנָה {23x} **shênâh**, *shay-naw'*; or

שֵׁנָא **shênâ'** (Ps 127:2), *shay-naw'*; from 3462; *sleep*:—sleep {23x}. See: TWOT—928c; BDB—446a, 1039c, 1041d, 1042b, 1096b.

8143. שֶׁנְהַבִּים {2x} **shenhabbîym**, *shen-habbeem'*; from 8127 and the plur. appar. of a for. word; prob. *tooth of elephants,* i.e. *ivory tusk*:—ivory {2x}. See: TWOT—2422c; BDB—1041d, 1042b.

8144. שָׁנִי {42x} **shânîy**, *shaw-nee'*; of uncert. der.; *crimson,* prop. the insect or its color, also stuff dyed with it:—scarlet {34x}, scarlet + 8438 {5x}, scarlet thread {2x}, crimson {1x}. See: TWOT—2420a; BDB—1040c.

8145. שֵׁנִי {156x} **shênîy**, *shay-nee'*; from 8138; prop. *double,* i.e. *second;* also adv. *again*:—second {87x}, other {37x}, time {13x}, again {7x}, another {7x}, more {3x}, either {1x}, second rank {1x}. See: TWOT—2421b; BDB—1041b, 1118b.

8146. שָׂנִיא {1x} **sânîy'**, *saw-nee'*; from 8130; *hated*:—hated {1x}. See: TWOT—2272a; BDB—971d.

8147. שְׁנַיִם {768x} **sh'nayim**, *shen-ah'-yim;* dual of 8145; fem.

שְׁתַּיִם **sh'ttayim**, *shet-tah'-yim; two;* also (as ord.) *twofold*:—two {533x}, twelve + 6240 {105x}, both {69x}, twelfth + 6240 {21x}, second {10x}, twain {7x}, both of them {5x}, twice {5x}, double {5x}, misc. {8x} = couple, twain, + twenty (sixscore) thousand. See: TWOT—2421a; BDB—1040d, 1060a, 1118b.

8148. שְׁנִינָה {4x} **sh'nîynâh**, *shen-ee-naw'*; from 8150; something *pointed,* i.e. a *gibe*:—byword {3x}, taunt {1x}. See: TWOT—2422b; BDB—1042b.

8149. שְׁנִיר {4x} **Sh'nîyr**, *shen-eer'*; or

שְׂנִיר **S'nîyr**, *sen-eer'*; from an unused root mean. to *be pointed; peak; Shenir* or *Senir,* a summit of Lebanon:—Senir {2x}, Shenir {2x}. See: BDB—972a.

8150. שָׁנַן {9x} **shânan**, *shaw-nan'*; a prim. root; to *point* (tran. or intr.); intens. to *pierce;* fig. to *inculcate*:—sharp {4x}, whet {2x}, sharpen {1x}, prick {1x}, teach diligently {1x}. Syn.: 502, 2094, 3384, 3925, 7919. See: TWOT—2422; BDB—1041d, 1116d.

8151. שָׁנַס {1x} **shânaç**, *shaw-nas'*; a prim. root; to *compress* (with a belt):—gird up {1x}. See: TWOT—2423; BDB—1042b.

8152. שִׁנְעָר {8x} **Shin'âr**, *shin-awr'*; prob. of for. der.; *Shinar,* a plain in Bab.:—Shinar {7x}, Babylonish {1x}. See: TWOT—2424; BDB—1042b.

8153. שְׁנָת {1x} **sh'nâth**, *shen-awth'*; from 3462; *sleep*:—sleep {1x}. See: TWOT—928c; BDB—445c, 446a, 1042b, 1042c.

8154. שָׁסָה {12x} **shâçâh**, *shaw-saw'*; or

שָׁשָׂה **shâsâh** (Isa. 10:13), *shaw-saw'*; a prim. root; to *plunder*:—destroyer {1x}, rob {2x}, spoil {7x}, spoiler {2x}. Syn.: 7591, 7665, 7722, 7703. See: TWOT—2425; BDB—983c, 1042c, 1042d, 1058b.

8155. שָׁסַס {5x} **shâçaç**, *shaw-sas'*; a prim. root; to *plunder*:—rifle {1x}, spoil {4x}. See: TWOT—2426; BDB—983c, 1042c.

8156. שָׁסַע {9x} **shâça'**, *shaw-sah'*; a prim. root; to *split* or *tear;* fig. to *upbraid*:—clovenfooted {3x}, cleave {2x}, rent {2x}, cleft {1x}, stayed {1x}. See: TWOT—2427; BDB—1042d, 1043c.

8157. שֶׁסַע {4x} **sheça'**, *sheh'-sah;* from 8156; a *fissure*:—clovenfooted + 8156

{3x}, cleave {1x}. See: TWOT–2427a; BDB–1043a.

8158. שָׂסַף {1x} shâçaph, shaw-saf'; a prim. root; to *cut in pieces*, i.e. *slaughter*:—hew in pieces {1x}. See: TWOT–2428; BDB–1043a.

8159. שָׁעָה {15x} shâʿâh, shaw-aw'; a prim. root; to *gaze* at or about (prop. for help); by impl. to *inspect, consider, compassionate, be nonplussed* (as looking around in amazement) or *bewildered*:—look {5x}, respect {3x}, dismay {2x}, turn {1x}, regard {1x}, spare {1x}, be dim {1x}, depart {1x}. See: TWOT–2429; BDB–1043a, 1044b.

8160. שָׁעָה {5x} shâʿâh (Aram.), shaw-aw'; from a root corresp. to 8159; prop. a *look*, i.e. a *moment*:—hour {5x}. See: TWOT–3044; BDB–1116d.

שְׁעוֹר sᵉʿôwr. See 8184.

שְׁעוֹרָה sᵉʿôwrâh. See 8184.

8161. שַׁעֲטָה {1x} shaʿăṭâh, shah'-at-aw; fem. from an unused root mean. to *stamp*; a *clatter* (of hoofs):—stamping {1x}. See: TWOT–2430a; BDB–1043b.

8162. שַׁעַטְנֵז {2x} shaʿaṭnêz, shah-at-naze'; prob. of for. der.; *linsey-woolsey*, i.e. cloth of linen and wool carded and spun together:—garment of divers sorts {1x}, linen and woollen {1x}. See: TWOT–2431; BDB–1043b.

8163. שָׂעִיר {59x} sâʿîyr, saw-eer'; or

שָׂעִר sâʿir, saw-eer'; from 8175; *shaggy*; as noun, a *he-goat*; by anal. a *faun*:—kid {28x}, goat {24x}, devil {2x}, satyr {2x}, hairy {2x}, rough {1x}.
   Saʿir is translated "devils" (Lev 17:7). This passage demonstrates that the word represents beings that were objects of pagan worship, appearing under Jeroboam I [929–909 B.C.] (2 Chr 11:15). Josiah's revival probably involved the breaking down of the high places of these devils (2 Kin 23:8). Some translate them as "goat-demons; goat-idols." Syn.: 7700, 7854. See: TWOT–2274c, 2274e; BDB–972c, 972d.

8164. שָׂעִיר {1x} sâʿîyr, saw-eer'; formed the same as 8163; a *shower* (as *tempestuous*):—small rain {1x}. See: TWOT–2277a; BDB–973c.

8165. שֵׂעִיר {39x} Sêʿîyr, say-eer'; formed like 8163; *rough*; *Seir*, a mountain of Idumaea and its aboriginal occupants, also one in Pal.:—Seir {39x}. See: TWOT–2274h, 2274g; BDB–973a, 1043b.

8166. שְׂעִירָה {2x} sᵉʿîyrâh, seh-ee-raw'; fem. of 8163; a *she-goat*:—kid {2x}. See: BDB–972c.

8167. שְׂעִירָה {1x} Sᵉʿîyrâh, seh-ee-raw'; formed as 8166; *roughness*; *Seirah*, a place in Pal.:—Seirath {1x}. See: BDB–972c.

8168. שֹׁעַל {3x} shôʿal, sho'-al; from an unused root mean. to *hollow out*; the *palm*; by extens. a *handful*:—handful {2x}, hollow of his hand {1x}. See: TWOT–2432a; BDB–1043b.

שֻׁעָל shûʿâl. See 7776.

8169. שַׁעַלְבִים {3x} Shaʿalbîym, shah-al-beem'; or

שַׁעֲלַבִּין Shaʿălabbîyn, shah-al-ab-been'; plur. from 7776; *fox-holes*; *Shaalbim* or *Shaalabbin*, a place in Pal.:—Shaalbim {2x}, Shaalabbin {1x}. See: BDB–1043c.

8170. שַׁעַלְבֹנִי {2x} Shaʿalbônîy, shah-al-bo-nee'; patrial from 8169; a *Shaalbonite* or inhab. of Shaalbin:—Shaalbonite {2x}. See: BDB–1043d.

8171. שַׁעֲלִים {1x} Shaʿălîym, shah-al-eem'; plur. of 7776; *foxes*; *Shaalim*, a place in Pal.:—Shalim {1x}. See: BDB–1043d.

8172. שָׁעַן {22x} shâʿan, shaw-an'; a prim. root; to *support* one's self:—lean {9x}, stay {5x}, rely {4x}, rest {3x}, lieth {1x}. See: TWOT–2434; BDB–1043d.

8173. שָׁעַע {9x} shâʿaʿ, shaw-ah'; a prim. root; (in a good acceptation) to *look* upon (with complacency), i.e. *fondle, please* or *amuse* (self); (in a bad one) to *look* about (in dismay), i.e. *stare*:—delight {4x}, cry {1x}, cry out {1x}, play {1x}, dandle {1x}, shut {1x}. See: TWOT–2435, 2436; BDB–1043a, 1044a, 1044b.

שָׂעִף sâʿiph. See 5587.

8174. שַׁעַף {2x} Shaʿaph, shah'-af; from 5586; *fluctuation*; *Shaaph*, the name of two Isr.:—Shaaph {2x}. See: BDB–1044c.

8175. שָׂעַר {8x} sâʿar, saw-ar'; a prim. root; to *storm*; by impl. to *shiver*, i.e. *fear*:—be (horrible) afraid {4x}, come like (to take away as with) a whirlwind {2x}, be tempestuous {1x}, hurl as a storm {1x}. See: TWOT–2274d, 2275, 2276; BDB–972b, 972c, 973b.

8176. שָׁעַר {1x} shâʿar, shaw-ar'; a prim. root; to *split* or *open*, i.e. (lit., but only as denom. from 8179) to *act as gate-keeper* (see 7778): (fig.) to *estimate*:—think {1x}. See: TWOT–2438; BDB–1045c.

8177. שְׂעַר {3x} **sᵉʿar** (Aram.), *seh-ar';* corresp. to 8181; *hair:*—hair {3x}. See: TWOT—3011; BDB—1114a.

8178. שַׂעַר {4x} **saʿar**, *sah'-ar;* from 8175; a *tempest;* also a *terror:*—storm {1x}, affrighted + 270 {1x}, sore {1x}, horribly {1x}. See: TWOT—2275a; BDB—972c, 973b. See 8181.

8179. שַׁעַר {371x} **shaʿar**, *shah'-ar;* from 8176 in its orig. sense; an *opening*, i.e. *door* or *gate:*—gate {364x}, city {3x}, door {2x}, port {1x}, porters {1x}.

(1) Basically, this word represents a structure closing and enclosing a large opening through a wall, or a barrier through which people and things pass to an enclosed area. (2) The gate of a city often was a fortified structure deeper than the wall. This is especially true of strong, well-fortified cities (Gen 19:1). (3) Within major cities there were usually strongly fortified citadels with gates (Neh 2:8). (4) Certain gates were only the thickness of a curtain (Ex 27:16). (5) The temple had large openings between its various courts (Jer 7:2). (5) Both the (5a) underworld (Job 38:17) and (5b) heaven, the domain of God (Gen 28:17), are pictured as cities with gates. (6) The gates of ancient cities sometimes enclosed city squares or were immediately in front of squares (2 Chr 32:6). (6a) The entry way (2 Chr 23:15) could be secured with heavy doors that were attached to firmly embedded pillars and reinforced by bars (Judg 16:3; cf. Ps 147:13; Neh 3:3). (6b) Palaces could be citadels with strongly fortified gates large enough to have rooms over them (2 Sa 18:33). (6c) Gates had rooms to house guards (Eze 40:7). (6d) The rooms bordering the gates could also be used to store siege supplies (Neh 12:25). (7) The gates were the place where local courts convened (Deut 25:7). (7a) The sentence sometimes was executed at the city gates (Jer 15:7). See: TWOT—2437a; BDB—745b, 1044c, 1118d.

8180. שַׁעַר {1x} **shaʿar**, *shah'-ar;* from 8176; a *measure* (as a *section*):—hundredfold + 3967 {1x}. See: TWOT—2438a; BDB—1045c.

שָׂעִר **sâʿîr**. See 8163.

8181. שֵׂעָר {28x} **sêʿâr**, *say-awr';* or

שַׂעַר **saʿar** (Is 7:20), *sah'-ar;* from 8175 in the sense of *dishevelling; hair* (as if *tossed* or *bristling*):—hair {24x}. hairy {3x}, × rough {1x} See: TWOT—2274a; BDB—972b, 1114a.

שֹׂעֵר **shôʿêr**. See 7778.

8182. שֹׂעָר {1x} **shôʿâr**, *sho-aw';* from 8176; *harsh* or *horrid*, i.e. *offensive:*—vile {1x}. See: TWOT—2439a; BDB—1045d.

8183. שְׂעָרָה {2x} **sᵉʿârâh**, *seh-aw-raw';* fem. of 8178; a *hurricane:*—storm {1x}, tempest {1x}. See: TWOT—2275b; BDB—973b.

8184. שְׂעֹרָה {34x} **sᵉʿôrâh**, *seh-o-raw';* or

שְׂעוֹרָה **sᵉʿôwrâh**, *seh-o-raw'* (fem. mean. the *plant*); and (masc. mean. the *grain*); also

שְׂעֹר **sᵉʿôr**, *seh-ore';* or

שְׂעוֹר **sᵉʿôwr**, *seh-ore';* from 8175 in the sense of *roughness; barley* (as *villose*):—barley {34x}. See: TWOT—2274f; BDB—972d.

8185. שַׂעֲרָה {1x} **saʿãrâh**, *sah-ar-aw';* fem. of 8181; *hairiness:*—hair {1x}. See: TWOT—2274b; BDB—972b.

8186. שַׁעֲרוּרָה {4x} **shaʿãrûwrâh**, *shah-ar-oo-raw';* or

שַׁעֲרִירִיָּה **shaʿãrîyrîyâh**, *shah-ar-ee-ree-yaw';* or

שַׁעֲרֻרִת **shaʿãrûrîth**, *shah-ar-oo-reeth';* fem. from 8176 in the sense of 8175; something *fearful:*—horrible thing {4x}. See: TWOT—2439b; BDB—1045d.

8187. שְׁעַרְיָה {2x} **Shᵉʿaryâh**, *sheh-ar-yaw';* from 8176 and 3050; *Jah has stormed; Shearjah*, an Isr.:—Sheariah {2x}. See: BDB—1045c.

8188. שְׂעֹרִים {1x} **Sᵉʿôrîym**, *seh-o-reem';* masc. plur. of 8184; *barley grains; Seorim*, an Isr.:—Seorim {1x}. See: BDB—972d.

8189. שַׁעֲרַיִם {3x} **Shaʿãrayim**, *shah-ar-ah'-yim;* dual of 8179; *double gates; Shaarajim*, a place in Pal.:—Sharaim {1x}, Shaarim {2x}. See: BDB—1045c.

שַׁעֲרִירִיָה **shaʿãrîyrîyâh**. See 8186.

שַׁעֲרֻרִת **shaʿãrûrîth**. See 8186.

8190. שַׁעַשְׁגַּז {1x} **Shaʿashgaz**, *shah-ash-gaz';* of Pers. der.; *Shaashgaz*, a eunuch of Xerxes:—Shaashgaz {1x}. See: BDB—1045d.

8191. שַׁעֲשֻׁעַ {9x} **shaʿshûaʿ**, *shah-shoo'-ah;* from 8173; *enjoyment:*—delight {7x}, pleasure {2x}. See: TWOT—2436a; BDB—1044b.

8192. שָׁפָה {2x} **shâphâh**, *shaw-faw';* a prim. root; to *abrade*, i.e. *bare:*—high {1x}, stick out {1x}. See: TWOT—2440; BDB—1045d, 1046a.

8193. שָׂפָה {176x} **sâphâh**, *saw-faw';* or (in dual and plur.)

שֶׂפֶת **sepheth**, *sef-eth';* prob. from 5595 or 8192 through the idea of *termination* (comp. 5490); the *lip* (as a nat. boundary); by impl. *language;* by anal. a *margin* (of a vessel, water, cloth, etc.):—lip {112x}, bank {10x}, brim {8x}, edge {8x}, language {7x}, speech {6x}, shore {6x}, brink {5x}, border {3x}, side {3x}, prating {2x}, vain {2x}, misc. {4x} = band, binding, talk.

(1) Lip is a part of the body (Is 6:7). **(2)** With the lips, or human speech, **(2a)** one may flatter (Ps 12:3), **(2b)** lie (Ps 31:18), **(2c)** speak mischief (Ps 140:9), and **(2d)** speak perversity (Prov 4:24). **(3)** The lip (speech) of the people of God is described as **(3a)** not sinful (Job 2:10), **(3b)** rejoicing (Job 8:21), **(3c)** prayerful (Ps 17:1), **(3d)** speaking God's word (Ps 119:13), **(3e)** truthful (Prov 12:19), **(3f)** wise (Prov 14:7; 15:7), **(3g)** righteous (Prov 16:13), and **(3h)** excellent (Prov 17:7). **(4)** Metaphorically, *saphah* (edge) denotes **(4a1)** the shore of a sea (Gen 22:17), the edge **(4a2)** of a river (Gen 41:3), **(4b)** the edge of material (Ex 26:4), or **(4c)** the brim of a vessel (1 Kin 7:23). See: TWOT—2278a; BDB—973c.

8194. שָׂפָה {1x} **shâphâh**, *shaw-faw';* from 8192 in the sense of *clarifying; a cheese* (as *strained* from the whey):—cheese {1x}. See: TWOT—2440a; BDB—1045d.

8195. שְׂפוֹ {2x} **Sheᵉphôw**, *shef-o';* or

שְׂפִי **Sheᵉphîy**, *shef-ee';* from 8192; *baldness* [comp. 8205]; *Shepho or Shephi*, an Idumaean:—Shephi {1x}, Shepho {1x}. See: BDB—1046a.

8196. שְׂפוֹט {2x} **sheᵉphôwṭ**, *shef-ote';* or

שְׂפוּט **sheᵉphûwṭ**, *shef-oot';* from 8199; a judicial *sentence,* i.e. *punishment:*—judgment {2x}. See: TWOT—2443b; BDB—1048a.

8197. שְׂפוּפָם {2x} **Sheᵉphûwphâm**, *shef-oo-fawm';* or

שְׂפוּפָן **Sheᵉphûwphân**, *shef-oo-fawn';* from the same as 8207; *serpentlike; Shephupham or Shephuphan*, an Isr.:—Shupham {1x}, Shephuphan {1x}. See: BDB—1051b.

8198. שִׁפְחָה {63x} **shiphchâh**, *shif-khaw';* fem. from an unused root mean. to *spread* out (as a *family;* see 4940); a *female slave* (as a member of the *household*):—handmaid {29x}, maid {12x}, maidservant {8x}, bondwomen {3x}, maiden {3x}, womenservants {3x}, handmaidens {2x}, bondmaid {1x}, servant {1x}, wench {1x}. See: TWOT—2442a; BDB—1046c.

8199. שָׁפַט {203x} **shâphaṭ**, *shaw-faṭ';* a prim. root; to *judge*, i.e. pronounce *sentence* (for or against); by impl. to *vindicate* or *punish;* by extens. to *govern;* pass. to *litigate* (lit. or fig.):—judge (v) {119x}, judge (n) {60x}, plead {11x}, avenged {2x}, condemn {2x}, execute {2x}, judgment {2x}, defend {1x}, deliver {1x}, misc. {3x} = X needs, reason, rule.

Shaphat means "to judge, deliver, rule." **(1)** In many contexts this root has a judicial sense. **(1a)** *Shaphat* refers to the activity of a third party who sits over two parties at odds with one another. **(1b)** This third party hears their cases against one another and decides where the right is and what to do about it (he functions as both judge and jury). **(1c)** So Sarai said to Abram: "My wrong [outrage done me] be upon thee [in your lap]: I have given my maid into thy bosom; and when she saw that she had conceived, I was despised in her eyes: the Lord judge between me and thee" (Gen 16:5—the first occurrence of the word). **(1d)** Sarai had given Hagar to Abram in her stead. This act was in keeping with ancient Nuzu law, which Abram apparently knew and followed. The legal rights to the child would be Sarai's. This would mean that Hagar "did all the work" and received none of the privileges. Consequently she made things miserable for Sarai. As the tribal and family head Abram's responsibility was to keep things in order. This he did not do. Thus Sarai declares that she is innocent of wrongdoing; she has done nothing to earn Hagar's mistreatment, and Abram is at fault in not getting the household in order. Her appeal is: since Abram has not done his duty (normally he would be the judge of tribal matters), "the Lord decide" between us, that is, in a judicial sense, as to who is in the right. Abram granted the legitimacy of her case and handed Hagar over to her to be brought into line (Gen 16:6).

(2) *Shaphat* also speaks of the accomplishing of a sentence. Both this concept and those of hearing the case and rendering a decision are seen in **(2a)** Gen 18:25, where Abraham speaks of "the Judge [literally, "One who judges"] of all the earth." **(2b)** In 1 Sa 3:13 the emphasis is solely on "delivering" the sentence: "For I have told him that I will judge his house for ever for the iniquity which he knoweth." **(3)** In some cases "judging" really means delivering from injustice or oppression. David says to Saul: "The Lord therefore be judge and judge between me and thee, and see, and plead my cause, and deliver me out of thine hand" (1 Sa 24:15). **(4)** This sense (in addition to the judicial sense), "to deliver," is to be understood

when one speaks of the judges of Israel (Judg 2:16): "Nevertheless the Lord raised up judges, which delivered them out of the hand of those that [plundered] them." **(5)** *Shaphat* can be used not only of an act of deliverance, but of a process whereby order and law are maintained within a group. This idea also is included in the concept of the judges of Israel: "And Deborah, a prophetess, the wife of Lapidoth, she judged Israel at that time" (Judg 4:4). The judge had two roles: to discern the will of God and then to lead an army to overthrow the oppressors. Deborah could discern the will of God, but she could not lead men into battle. Barak did that. (Judg 4:4–9).

(6) Certainly ruling is in mind in Num 25:5: "And Moses said unto the judges of Israel, 'Slay ye every one his men that were joined unto Baal-Peor'" (cf. 1 Sa 8:1). **(7)** The military deliverer was the head over a volunteer army summoned when danger threatened (militia). In the time of Samuel this procedure proved inadequate for Israel. They wanted a leader who would organize and lead a standing army. They asked Samuel, therefore, for a king such as the other nations had, one who was apt and trained in warfare, and whose successor (son) would be carefully trained, too. There would be more continuity in leadership as a result. Included in this idea of a king who would "judge" them like the other nations was the idea of a ruler; in order to sustain a permanent army and its training, the people had to be organized for taxation and conscription. This is what is in view in 1 Sa 8:6–18 as Samuel explains. These men were raised up from time to time to be rulers over the land, to defend the people from enemies, to save them from their oppressors, to teach them the truth, and to uphold them in the right course. Syn.: 1777, 2940, 3198, 6419, 7561. See: TWOT–2443; BDB–251c, 1047a, 1117a.

8200. שְׁפַט {1x} **sh°phaṭ** (Aram.), *shef-aṭ';* corresp. to 8199; to *judge:*—magistrates {1x}. See: TWOT–2045; BDB–1117a.

8201. שֶׁפֶט {16x} **shephet,** *sheh'-fet;* from 8199; a *sentence,* i.e. *infliction:*—judgment {16x}.

The noun *shephet* [plural – *shepatim*] refers to "acts of judgment." One of the 16 occurrences is in Num 33:4: "For the Egyptians buried all their firstborn, which the Lord had smitten among them: upon their gods also the Lord executed judgments." See: TWOT–2443a; BDB–1048a.

8202. שָׁפָט {8x} **Shâphâṭ,** *shaw-fawt';* from 8199; *judge; Shaphat,* the name of four Isr.:—*Shaphat* {8x}. See: BDB–1048b.

8203. שְׁפַטְיָה {13x} **Sh°phaṭyâh,** *shef-at-yaw';* or

שְׁפַטְיָהוּ **Sh°phaṭyâhûw,** *shef-at-yaw'-hoo;* from 8199 and 3050; *Jah has judged; Shephatjah,* the name of ten Isr.:—Shephatiah {13x}. See: BDB–1049b.

8204. שִׁפְטָן {1x} **Shiphṭân,** *shif-tawn';* from 8199; *judge-like; Shiphtan,* an Isr.:—*Shiphtan* {1x}. See: BDB–1049b.

8205. שְׁפִי {10x} **sh°phîy,** *shef-ee';* from 8192; *bareness;* concr. a *bare* hill or plain:—high place {9x}, variant {1x}. See: TWOT–2440b; BDB–1045d, 1046a.

8206. שֻׁפִּים {3x} **Shuppîym,** *shoop-peem';* plur. of an unused noun from the same as 8207 and mean. the same; *serpents; Shuppim,* an Isr.:—Shuppim {3x}. See: BDB–1047a, 1049b, 1050d, 1051b.

8207. שְׁפִיפֹן {1x} **sh°phîyphôn,** *shef-ee-fone';* from an unused root mean. the same as 7779; a kind of *serpent* (as *snapping*), prob. the *cerastes* or horned adder:—adder {1x}. See: TWOT–2448a; BDB–1051b.

8208. שָׁפִיר {1x} **Shâphîyr,** *shaf-eer';* from 8231; *beautiful; Shaphir,* a place in Pal.:—Saphir {1x}. See: BDB–1051c.

8209. שַׁפִּיר {2x} **shappîyr** (Aram.), *shap-peer';* intens. of a form corresp. to 8208; *beautiful:*—fair {2x}. See: TWOT–3046a; BDB–1117a.

8210. שָׁפַךְ {115x} **shâphak,** *shaw-fak';* a prim. root; to *spill* forth (blood, a libation, liquid metal; or even a solid, i.e. to *mound* up); also (fig.) to *expend* (life, soul, complaint, money, etc.); intens. to *sprawl* out:—pour out {46x}, shed {36x}, pour {20x}, cast {6x}, gush out {1x}, misc. {6x} = shedder, slip.

Shaphak means "to pour out, pour, shed." **(1)** In its first use in the Old Testament, the word is part of the general principle concerning the taking of human life: "Whoso sheddeth man's blood, by man shall his blood be shed" (Gen 9:6). **(2)** While it is frequently used in this sense of "shedding" or "pouring out" blood, **(3)** the word is commonly used of the "pouring out" of the contents of a vessel, such as water (Ex 4:9; 1 Sa 7:6), plaster or dust (Lev 14:41), and drink offerings to false gods (Is 57:6). **(4)** In its figurative use, *shaphak* indicates the "pouring out" **(4a)** of God's wrath (Hos 5:10), **(4b)** of contempt (Job 12:21), **(4c)** of wickedness (Jer 14:16), and **(4d)** of the Spirit of God (Eze 39:29). **(5)** The psalmist describes his helpless condition in this picturesque phrase: "I am poured out like water" (Ps 22:14). See: TWOT–2444; BDB–706c, 1049b.

8211. שֶׁפֶךְ {2x} **shephek**, *sheh'-fek;* from
8210; an *emptying* place, e.g. an
ash-*heap:*—poured out {2x}. See: TWOT—
2444a; BDB—1050a.

8212. שְׁפְכָה {1x} **shophkâh**, *shof-kaw';* fem.
of a der. from 8210; a *pipe* (for
pouring forth, e.g. wine), i.e. the *penis:*—privy
member {1x}. See: TWOT—2444b; BDB—1050a.

8213. שָׁפֵל {29x} **shâphêl**, *shaw-fale';* a prim.
root; to *depress* or *sink* (expec. fig.
to *humiliate*, intr. or tran.):— . . . low {10x}, . . .
down {8x}, humble {7x}, abase {2x}, debase {1x},
put lower {1x}.

Shaphel means "to be low, become low; sink
down; be humiliated; be abased." **(1)** *Shaphel*
occurs about 29 times in the Old Testament. It
is a poetic term. **(2)** The verb, as can be expected in poetic usage, is generally used in a
figurative sense. **(3)** *Shaphel* rarely denotes a
literal lowness. Even in passages where the
meaning may be taken literally, the prophet
communicates a spiritual truth: "The high
[trees] of stature shall be hewn down, and the
haughty shall be humbled" (Is 10:33), or "Every
valley shall be exalted, and every mountain
and hill shall be made low" (Is 40:4).

(4) Isaiah particularly presented Judah's sin
as one of rebellion, self-exaltation, and pride:
"And the loftiness of man shall be bowed down,
and the haughtiness of men shall be made low:
and the LORD alone shall be exalted in that
day. (2:17; cf. 3:16–17). **(4a)** In the second chapter he repeated God's indictment on human
pride. When the Lord comes in judgment, He
will not tolerate pride: "The Lord alone shall
be exalted in that day" (Is 2:11); then "the Lord
of hosts shall be upon every one that is proud
and lofty, and upon every one that is lifted up;
and he shall be brought low" (Is 2:12).
(4b) Isaiah applied to Judah the principle
found in Proverbs: "A man's pride shall bring
him low: but honor shall uphold the humble in
spirit" (Prov 29:23). **(4c)** Pride and self-
exaltation have no place in the life of the godly,
as the Lord "brings low" a person, a city, and
a nation: "The Lord maketh poor, and maketh
rich: he bringeth low, and lifteth up" (1 Sa 2:7).

(5) The prophets called the people to repent
and to demonstrate their return to God by lowliness. Their call was generally unheeded. Ultimately the Exile came, and the people were
humbled by the Babylonians. Nevertheless, the
promise came that, regardless of the obstacles,
God would initiate the redemption of His people. Isaiah expressed the greatness of the redemption in this way: "Prepare ye the way of
the Lord. . . . Every valley shall be exalted, and
every mountain and hill shall be made low. . . .
And the glory of the Lord shall be revealed"

(Is 40:3–5). **(6)** It is translated as "to be low";
"to bring low"; "to be humble." See: TWOT—
2445; BDB—1050a, 1117a.

8214. שְׁפַל {4x} **sh⁰phal** (Aram.), *shef-al';* corresp. to 8213:—humble {1x}, abase
{1x}, subdue {1x}, put down {1x}. See: BDB—
1117a.

8215. שְׁפַל {1x} **sh⁰phal** (Aram.), *shef-al';* from
8214; *low:*—basest {1x}. See:
BDB—1117a.

8216. שֶׁפֶל {2x} **shêphel**, *shay'-fel;* from 8213;
an *humble* rank:—low estate {1x},
low place {1x}. *Shephel*, as a noun, refers to a
"low condition, low estate" and appears twice
(Ps 136:23; Eccl 10:6). See: TWOT—2445a;
BDB—1050c.

8217. שָׁפָל {19x} **shâphâl**, *shaw-fawl';* from
8213; *depressed*, lit. or fig.:—low
{5x}, lower {4x}, base {4x}, humble {4x}, basest
{1x}, lowly {1x}. *Shaphal* as an adjective means
"low; humble." **(1)** This word means "low" in
Eze 17:24: "And all the trees of the field shall
know that I the Lord have brought down the
high tree, have exalted the low tree." **(2)** In Is
57:15 *shaphal* refers to "humble": "I dwell in
the high and holy place, with him also that is
of a contrite and humble spirit, to revive the
spirit of the humble, and to revive the heart of
the contrite ones." See: TWOT—2445c; BDB—
1050c.

8218. שְׁפְלָה {1x} **shiphlâh**, *shif-law';* fem. of
8216; *depression:*—low place {1x}.

The noun *shiphlah* means a "humiliated
state" and occurs once: "When it shall hail,
coming down on the forest; and the city shall
be low in a low place" (Is 32:19); the city is
leveled completely. See: TWOT—2445b;
BDB—1050c.

8219. שְׁפֵלָה {20x} **sh⁰phêlâh**, *shef-ay-law';*
from 8213; *Lowland*, i.e. (with
the art.) the maritime slope of Pal.:—valley
{8x}, vale {5x}, plain {3x}, low country {2x}, low
plain {2x}.

Shephelah means "lowland" and is used
most often as a technical designation for the
low-lying hills of the Judean hill country (cf.
Deut 1:7; Josh 9:1). See: TWOT—2445d;
BDB—1050c.

8220. שְׁפְלוּת {1x} **shiphlûwth**, *shif-looth';*
from 8213; *remissness:*—idle-
ness {1x}.

Shiphluwth refers to a "sinking" and it's
single appearance is in Eccl 10:18: "By much
slothfulness the building decayeth; and
through idleness [*shiphluwth*] of the hands the
house droppeth through." The word implies a

negligence or "sinking" of the hands. See: TWOT—2445e; BDB—1050d.

8221. שְׁפָם {2x} **Sh°phâm,** *shef-awm';* prob. from 8192; *bare spot; Shepham,* a place in or near Pal.:—Shepham {2x}. See: BDB—1050d.

8222. שָׂפָם {5x} **sâphâm,** *saw-fawm';* from 8193; the *beard* (as a *lip-piece*):—lip {3x}, upper lip {1x}, beard {1x}. See: TWOT—2279; BDB—974a.

8223. שָׁפָם {1x} **Shâphâm,** *shaw-fawm';* formed like 8221; *baldly; Shapham,* an Isr.:—Shapham {1x}. See: BDB—1050d.

8224. שִׁפְמוֹת {1x} **Siphmôwth,** *sif-môth';* fem. plur. of 8221; *Siphmoth,* a place in Pal.:—Siphmoth {1x}. See: BDB—974a, 1050d.

8225. שִׁפְמִי {1x} **Shiphmîy,** *shif-mee';* patrial from 8221; a *Shiphmite* or inhab. of Shepham:—Shiphmite {1x}. See: BDB—1050d.

8226. שָׁפַן {1x} **sâphan,** *saw-fan';* a prim. root; to *conceal* (as a valuable):—treasure {1x}. See: TWOT—1537; BDB—706a.

8227. שָׁפָן {34x} **shâphân,** *shaw-fawn';* from 8226; a species of *rock-rabbit* (from its *hiding*), i.e. prob. the *hyrax:*—Shaphan {30x}, coney {4x}. See: TWOT—2446a; BDB—1050d.

8228. שֶׁפַע {1x} **shephac,** *sheh'-fah;* from an unused root mean. to *abound; resources:*—abundance {1x}. See: TWOT—2447a; BDB—1051a.

8229. שִׁפְעָה {6x} **shiphcâh,** *shif-aw';* fem. of 8228; *copiousness:*—abundance {3x}, company {2x}, multitude {1x}. See: TWOT—2447b; BDB—1051a.

8230. שִׁפְעִי {1x} **Shiphciy,** *shif-ee';* from 8228; *copious; Shiphi,* an Isr.:—Shiphi {1x}. See: BDB—1051b.

שָׁפַק **sâphaq.** See 5606.

8231. שָׁפַר {1x} **shâphar,** *shaw-far';* a prim. root; to *glisten,* i.e. (fig.) be (caus. make) *fair:*—goodly {1x}. See: TWOT—2449; BDB—1051c.

8232. שְׁפַר {3x} **sh°phar** (Aram.), *shef-ar';* corresp. to 8231; to *be beautiful:*—think it good {1x}, please {1x}, acceptable {1x}. See: TWOT—3046; BDB—1117a.

8233. שֶׁפֶר {1x} **shepher,** *sheh'-fer;* from 8231; *beauty:*—goodly {1x}. See: TWOT—2449a; BDB—1051c.

8234. שֶׁפֶר {2x} **Shepher,** *sheh'-fer;* the same as 8233; *Shepher,* a place in the desert:—Shapher {2x}. See: BDB—1051c.

שׁוֹפָר **shôphâr.** See 7782.

8235. שִׁפְרָה {1x} **shiphrâh,** *shif-raw';* from 8231; *brightness:*—garnished {1x}. See: TWOT—2449b; BDB—1051c.

8236. שִׁפְרָה {1x} **Shiphrâh,** *shif-raw';* the same as 8235; *Shiphrah,* an Israelitess:—Shiphrah {1x}. See: BDB—1051c.

8237. שַׁפְרוּר {1x} **shaphrûwr,** *shaf-roor';* from 8231; *splendid,* i.e. a *tapestry* or *canopy:*—royal pavilion {1x}. See: TWOT—2449d; BDB—1051d.

8238. שְׁפַרְפַר {1x} **sh°pharphar** (Aram.), *shef-ar-far';* from 8231; the *dawn* (as *brilliant* with aurora):—early in the morning. See: TWOT—3046b; BDB—1117a.

8239. שָׁפַת {5x} **shâphath,** *shaw-fath';* a prim. root; to *locate,* i.e. (gen.) *hang on* or (fig.) *establish, reduce:*—set on {3x}, brought {1x}, ordain {1x}. See: TWOT—2441a; BDB—1046a, 1052a.

8240. שְׁפָת {2x} **shâphâth,** *shaw-fawth';* from 8239; a (double) *stall* (for cattle); also a (two-pronged) *hook* (for flaying animals on):—pot {1x}, hook {1x}. See: TWOT—2450; BDB—1046b, 1052a.

8241. שֶׁצֶף {1x} **shetseph,** *sheh'-tsef;* from 7857 (for alliteration with 7110); an *outburst* (of anger):—little {1x}. See: TWOT—2373a; BDB—1009b, 1052a.

8242. שַׂק {48x} **saq,** *sak;* from 8264; prop. a *mesh* (as allowing a liquid to *run* through), i.e. coarse loose cloth or *sacking* (used in mourning and for bagging); hence, a *bag* (for grain, etc.):—sackcloth {41x}, sack {6x}, sackclothes {1x}. See: TWOT—2282a; BDB—974b.

8243. שָׁק {1x} **shâq** (Aram.), *shawk;* corresp. to 7785; the *leg:*—legs {1x}. See: TWOT—3047; BDB—1114d, 1117b.

8244. שָׂקַד {1x} **sâqad,** *saw-kad';* a prim. root; to *fasten:*—bound {1x}. See: TWOT—2281; BDB—974b.

8245. שָׁקַד {12x} **shâqad,** *shaw-kad';* a prim. root; to *be alert,* i.e. *sleepless;* hence, to *be on the lookout* (whether for good or ill):—watch {9x}, wake {1x}, remain {1x}, hasten {1x}. See: TWOT—2451; BDB—1052a.

8246. שָׁקַד {6x} **shâqad,** *shaw-kad';* a denom. from 8247; to *be* (intens. *make*) *almond-shaped:*—almonds {6x}. See: TWOT—2451b; BDB—1052b.

8247. שָׁקֵד {4x} **shâqêd,** *shaw-kade';* from 8245; the *almond* (tree or nut; as being the *earliest* in bloom):—almond {2x}, almond tree {2x}. See: TWOT—2451a; BDB—1052b.

8248. שָׁקָה {74x} **shâqâh,** *shaw-kaw';* a prim. root; to *quaff,* i.e. (caus.) to *irrigate* or *furnish a potion* to:—drink {43x}, water {17x}, butler {9x}, cupbearer {3x}, misc. {1x}.

Shaqah, as a verb, means "to give drink, water." **(1)** The word usually occurs in the causative sense, while its much more common counterpart, *shatah* (8354), is used primarily in the simple active form, "to drink." **(1a)** In its first occurrence in the biblical text, *shaqah* expresses the idea of "to water": **(1b)** "But there went up a mist from the earth, and watered the whole face of the ground" (Gen 2:6). **(2)** The dry climate of the Middle East makes *shaqah* a most important word, since it expresses the act of "irrigating" or "watering" crops ["waterest with thy foot" means directing the water into the irrigation canals with the foot serving as a deflector/director for the water] (Deut 11:10). **(3)** God "waters" the earth and causes plants to grow (Ps 104:13–14). **(4)** Figuratively, He "irrigates" His vineyard, Israel (Is 27:3). **(5)** A frequent use of *shaqah* is to express the "giving of water to drink" to animals (Gen 24:14, 46; 29:2–3, 7–8, 10). **(6)** Men are given a variety of things to drink, such as water (Gen 24:43), wine (Gen 19:32; Amos 2:12), milk (Judg 4:19), and vinegar (Ps 69:21). **(7)** In a symbol of divine judgment, God is said to give "water of gall to drink" to Israel (Jer 8:14; 9:15; 23:15). **(8)** In this time of judgment and mourning, Israel was not to be given "the cup of consolation to drink" (Jer 16:7). **(9)** A healthy person is one whose bones "are moistened" with marrow (Job 21:24; literally, whose bones "are watered" or "irrigated" with marrow). See: TWOT—2452; BDB—913d, 1052b, 1054b. See 7937, 8354.

8249. שִׁקּוּי {1x} **shiqqûv,** *shik-koov';* from 8248; (plur. collect.) a *draught:*—drink {1x}. See: TWOT—2452a; BDB—1052d.

8250. שִׁקּוּי {2x} **shiqqûwy,** *shik-koo'-ee;* from 8248; a *beverage; moisture,* i.e. (fig.) *refreshment:*—marrow {1x}, drink {1x}. See: TWOT—2452a; BDB—1052c.

8251. שִׁקּוּץ {28x} **shiqqûwts,** *shik-koots';* or

שִׁקֻּץ **shiqqûts,** *shik-koots';* from 8262; *disgusting,* i.e. *filthy;* espec. *idolatrous* or (concr.) an *idol:*—abomination {20x}, detestable things {5x}, detestable {1x}, abominable filth {1x}, abominable idols {1x}.

This word is often used to testify to God's

hatred of the whole system of idolatry. Syn.: 205, 367. See: TWOT—2459b; BDB—1055a.

8252. שָׁקַט {41x} **shâqat,** *shaw-kat';* a prim. root; to *repose* (usually fig.):—rest {16x}, quiet {16x}, quietness {4x}, still {2x}, appeaseth {1x}, idleness {1x}, settled {1x}. See: TWOT—2453; BDB—1052d.

8253. שֶׁקֶט {1x} **sheqet,** *sheh'-ket;* from 8252; *tranquillity:*—quietness {1x}. See: TWOT—2453a; BDB—1053b.

8254. שָׁקַל **shâqal,** *shaw-kal';* a prim. root; to *suspend* or *poise* (espec. in trade):—weigh {14x}, pay {4x}, throughly {1x}, receive {1x}, receiver {1x}, spend {1x}. See: TWOT—2454a; BDB—1053b, 1118c.

8255. שֶׁקֶל {88x} **sheqel,** *sheh'-kel;* from 8254; prob. a *weight;* used as a commercial standard:—shekel {88x}. See: TWOT—2454a; BDB—1053c, 1118c.

8256. שָׁקָם {7x} **shâqâm,** *shaw-kawm';* or (fem.)

שִׁקְמָה **shiqmâh,** *shik-maw';* of uncert. der.; a *sycamore* (usually the tree):—sycamore {1x}, sycamore fruit {1x}, sycamore tree {5x}. See: TWOT—2455; BDB—1054a.

8257. שָׁקַע {6x} **shâqaʻ,** *shaw-kah';* (abb. Am. 8:8); a prim. root; to *subside;* by impl. to *be overflowed, cease;* caus. to *abate, subdue:*—make deep {1x}, let down {1x}, drown {2x}, quench {1x}, sink {1x}. See: TWOT—2456; BDB—1052c, 1054b.

8258. שְׁקַעֲרוּרָה {1x} **sheʻqaʻrûwrâh,** *shek-ah-roo-raw';* from 8257; a *depression:*—hollow strakes {1x}. See: TWOT—2047b; BDB—891a, 1054c.

8259. שָׁקַף {22x} **shâqaph,** *shaw-kaf';* a prim. root; prop. to *lean out* (of a window), i.e. (by impl.) *peep* or *gaze* (pass. *be a spectacle*):—look {11x}, look down {6x}, look out {3x}, look forth {1x}, appear {1x}. See: TWOT—2457; BDB—1054c.

8260. שֶׁקֶף {1x} **sheqeph,** *sheh'-kef;* from 8259; a *loophole* (for *looking out*), to admit light and air:—window {1x}. See: TWOT—2458a; BDB—1054d.

8261. שָׁקֻף {2x} **shâqûph,** *shaw-koof';* pass. part. of 8259; an *embrasure* or opening [comp. 8260] with bevelled jam:—light {1x}, window {1x}. See: TWOT—2458b; BDB—1054d.

8262. שָׁקַץ {7x} **shâqats,** *shaw-kats';* a prim. root; to *be filthy,* i.e. (intens.) to *loathe, pollute:*—abhor {1x}, make abominable

{2x}, have in abomination {2x}, detest {1x}, ✕ utterly {1x}. See: TWOT—2459; BDB—1055a.

8263. שֶׁקֶץ {11x} **sheqets,** *sheh'-kets;* from 8262; *filth,* i.e. (fig. and spec.) an *idolatrous* object:—abominable {2x}, abomination {9x}. See: TWOT—2459a, 2459b; BDB—1054d.

     שִׁקּוּץ **shiqqûts.** See 8251.

8264. שָׁקַק {6x} **shâqaq,** *shaw-kak';* a prim. root; to *course* (like a beast of prey); by impl. to *seek* greedily:—have appetite {1x}, justle one against another {1x}, long {1x}, range {1x}, run {1x}, run to and fro {1x}. See: TWOT—2460; BDB—1055b.

8265. שָׁקַר {1x} **sâqar,** *saw-kar';* a prim. root; to *ogle,* i.e. *blink* coquettishly:—wanton {1x}. See: TWOT—2283; BDB—974c.

8266. שָׁקַר {6x} **shâqar,** *shaw-kar';* a prim. root; to *cheat,* i.e. *be untrue* (usually in words):—fail {1x}, deal falsely {2x}, lie {3x}. See: TWOT—2461; BDB—1055d.

8267. שֶׁקֶר {113x} **sheqer,** *sheh'-ker;* from 8266; an *untruth;* by impl. a *sham* (often adv.):—lie {28x}, lying {21x}, false {20x}, falsehood {13x}, falsely {13x}, vain {5x}, wrongfully {4x}, deceitful {2x}, deceit {1x}, liar {1x}, misc. {5x} = without a cause, feignedly, vain thing.

Sheqer, as a noun, means "falsehood; lie." **(1)** It is rare in all but the poetic and prophetic books, and even in these books its usage is concentrated in Psalms (24 times) Proverbs (20 times), and Jeremiah (37 times). **(2)** The first occurrence is in Ex 5:9: "Let there more work be laid upon the men, that they may labor therein: and let them not regard vain words [lies]." **(3)** In about 35 passages, *sheqer* describes the nature of "deceptive speech": "to speak" (Is 59:3), "to teach" (Is 9:15), "to prophesy" (Jer 14:14), and "to lie" (Mic 2:11). **(4)** It may also indicate a "deceptive character," as expressed in one's acts: "to deal treacherously" (2 Sa 18:13) and "to deal falsely" (Hos 7:1).

(5) Thus *sheqer* defines a way of life that goes contrary to the law of God. **(5a)** The psalmist, desirous of following God, prayed: "Remove from me the way of lying: and grant me thy law graciously. I have chosen the way of truth: thy judgments have I laid before me" (Ps 119:29–30; cf. vv. 104, 118, 128). **(5b)** Here we see the opposites: "falsehood" and "faithfulness." **(5c)** As "faithfulness" is a relational term, "falsehood" denotes "one's inability to keep faith" with what one has said or to respond positively to the faithfulness of another being. **(6)** The Old Testament saint was instructed to avoid "deception" and the liar: "Keep thee far

from a false matter; and the innocent and righteous slay thou not: for I will not justify the wicked" (Ex 23:7; cf. Prov 13:5). See: TWOT—2461a; BDB—1055b.

8268. שֹׁקֶת {2x} **shôqeth,** *sho'-keth;* from 8248; a *trough* (for *watering*):—trough {2x}. See: TWOT—2452b; BDB—1052d, 1055d.

8269. שַׂר {421x} **sar,** *sar;* from 8323; a *head person* (of any rank or class):—prince {208x}, captain {130x}, chief {33x}, ruler {33x}, governor {6x}, keeper {3x}, principal {2x}, general {1x}, lords {1x}, misc. {4x} = task master, master, steward.

Sar, means "official; leader; commander; captain; chief; prince; ruler." **(1)** The word is often applied to certain non-Israelite "officials or representatives of the king." **(1a)** This meaning appears in Gen 12:15, its first biblical appearance: "The princes also of Pharaoh saw her [Sarah], and commended her before Pharaoh." **(1b)** In other contexts *sar* represents "men who clearly have responsibility over others"; they are "rulers or chieftains." **(2)** *Sar* may mean simply a "leader" of a profession, a group, or a district, **(2a)** as Phichol was the "commander" of Abimelech's army (Gen 21:22) and **(2b)** Potiphar was "an officer of Pharaoh's and captain of the [body]guard" (Gen 37:36). **(2c)** In such usage, "chief" means "head official" (cf. Gen 40:2). **(2d)** *Sarim* (plural) were "honored men" (Is 23:8).

(3) *Sar* is used of certain "notable men" within Israel. **(3a)** When Abner was killed by Joab, David said to his servants (palace officials), "Know ye not that there is a prince and a great man fallen this day in Israel?" (2 Sa 3:38; cf. Num 21:18). **(3b)** Joab, Abishai, and Ittai were "commanders" in David's army (cf. 2 Sa 23:19). **(3c)** "Local leaders in Israel" are also called *sarim:* "And the princes of Succoth said . . ." (Judg 8:6). **(4)** In several passages, *sar* refers to the task of "ruling." **(4a)** Moses tried to break up a fight between two Hebrews and one of them asked him, "Who made thee a prince and a judge over us?" (Ex 2:14). **(4b)** In such a context, *sar* means "leader," "ruler," and "judge": "Moreover thou shalt provide out of all the people able men, such as fear God, men of truth, hating covetousness; and place such over them, to be rulers of thousands, and rulers of hundreds, rulers of fifties, and rulers of tens" (Ex 18:21).

(5) The "commander" of Israel's army was called a *sar* (1 Sa 17:55). **(6)** In Judg 9:30, *sar* represents a "ruler" of a city. **(7)** Any government official might be called a *sar* (Neh 3:14). **(8)** "Religious officiants" who served in the temple of God were also called *sarim* (Jer 35:4). **(9)** The "leaders" or "chiefs" of the Levites

(1 Chr 15:16) or priests (Ezra 8:24) are *sarim*.
(10) In 1 Chr 24:5, the word appears to be a
title: "Thus were they divided by lot, one sort
with another; for the governors of the sanctuary [*sarim qodes*] and governors of the house
of God [*sarim ha'elohim*], were of the sons of
Eleazar and of the sons of Ithamar." **(11)** In the
Book of Daniel, *sar* is used of "superhuman
beings" or "patron angels." Thus, Michael is
the "prince" of Judah (Dan 10:21; cf. Josh 5:14).
Daniel 8:25 speaks of a king who will arise and
"stand up against the Prince of princes" (i.e.,
the Messiah). See: TWOT—2295a; BDB—694a,
974c, 978a, 979.

8270. שֹׁר   {2x} **shôr**, *shore;* from 8324; a *string*
(as *twisted* [comp. 8306]), i.e. (spec.)
the umbilical cord (also fig. as the centre of
strength):—navel {2x}. See: TWOT—2469a;
BDB—1055d, 1057a.

8271. שְׁרֵא   {6x} **shᵉrê** (Aram.), *sher-ay';* a root
corresp. to that of 8293; to *free,
separate;* fig. to *unravel, commence;* by impl.
(of unloading beasts) to *reside:*—begin {1x},
dissolve {2x}, dwell {1x}, loose {2x}. See:
TWOT—3048; BDB—1117b.

8272. שַׁרְאֶצֶר   {3x} **Sharᵉetser**, *shar-eh'-tser;*
of for. der.; *Sharetser*, the name
of an Ass. and an Isr.:—Sharezer {2x}, Sherezer
{1x}. See: TWOT—3048; BDB—974c, 1055d.

8273. שָׁרָב   {2x} **shârâb**, *shaw-rawb';* from an
unused root mean. to *glare;* quiv-
ering *glow* (of the air), expec. the *mirage:*—
heat {1x}, parched ground {1x}. See: TWOT—
2462a; BDB—1055d.

8274. שֵׁרֵבְיָה   {8x} **Shêrêbyâh**, *shay-rayb-
yaw';* from 8273 and 3050; *Jah
has brought heat; Sherebjah*, the name of two
Isr.:—Sherebiah {8x}. See: BDB—1055d.

8275. שַׁרְבִיט   {4x} **sharbîyṭ**, *shar-beet';* for
7626; a *rod* of empire:—sceptre
{4x}. See: TWOT—2314b; BDB—987b, 1056a.

8276. שָׂרַג   {2x} **sârag**, *saw-rag';* a prim. root;
to *intwine:*—wrap together {1x},
wreath {1x}. See: TWOT—2284; BDB—974d.

8277. שָׂרַד   {1x} **sârad**, *saw-rad';* a prim. root;
prop. to *puncture* [comp. 8279],
i.e. (fig. through the idea of *slipping* out) to
escape or survive:—remained {1x}. See:
TWOT—2285; BDB—974d.

8278. שְׂרָד   {4x} **sᵉrâd**, *ser-awd';* from 8277;
stitching (as *pierced* with a nee-
dle):—service {4x}. See: TWOT—2286a; BDB—
975a.

8279. שֶׂרֶד   {1x} **sered**, *seh'-red;* from 8277; a
(carpenter's) *scribing-awl* (for

pricking or scratching measurements):—line
{1x}. See: TWOT—2286b; BDB—975b.

8280. שָׂרָה   {2x} **sârâh**, *saw-raw';* a prim. root;
to *prevail:*—power {2x}. See:
TWOT—2287; BDB—975b.

8281. שָׁרָה   {2x} **shârâh**, *shaw-raw';* a prim.
root; to *free:*—remnant {1x}, it
{1x}. See: TWOT—2463; BDB—1056a, 1056c,
1117b.

8282. שָׂרָה   {5x} **sârâh**, *saw-raw';* fem. of 8269;
a *mistress*, i.e. *female noble:*—lady
{2x}, princess {2x}, queen {1x}. See: TWOT—
2295b; BDB—979a, 994d.

8283. שָׂרָה   {38x} **Sârâh**, *saw-raw';* the same
as 8282; *Sarah*, Abraham's wife:—
Sarah {38x}. See: BDB—979a.

8284. שָׁרָה   {1x} **shârâh**, *shaw-raw';* prob. fem.
of 7791; a *fortification* (lit. or
fig.):—wall {1x}. See: TWOT—2355b; BDB—
1004b, 1056c.

8285. שֵׁרָה   {1x} **shêrâh**, *shay-raw';* from 8324
in its orig. sense of *pressing;* a
wrist-*band* (as *compact* or *clasping*):—bracelet
{1x}. See: TWOT—2469b; BDB—1056b, 1057b.

8286. שְׂרוּג   {5x} **Sᵉrûwg**, *ser-oog';* from 8276;
tendril; Serug, a postdiluvian pa-
triarch:—Serug {5x}. See: BDB—974d.

8287. שָׁרוּחֶן   {1x} **Shârûwchen**, *shaw-roo-
khen';* prob. from 8281 (in the
sense of *dwelling* [comp. 8271] and 2580; *abode
of pleasure; Sharuchen*, a place in Pal.:—Sharuhen {1x}. See: BDB—1056b.

8288. שְׂרוֹךְ   {2x} **sᵉrôwk**, *ser-oke';* from 8308; a
thong (as *laced* or *tied*):—latchet
{1x}, shoelatchet + 5275 {1x}. See: TWOT—
2290a; BDB—976c.

8289. שָׁרוֹן   {7x} **Shârôwn**, *shaw-rone';* prob.
abridged from 3474; *plain,
Sharon*, the name of a place in Pal.:—Sharon
{6x}, Lasharon {1x}. See: BDB—450a, 546d,
1056c.

8290. שָׁרוֹנִי   {1x} **Shârôwnîy**, *shaw-ro-nee';*
patrial from 8289; a *Sharonite* or
inhab. of Sharon:—Sharonite {1x}. See: BDB—
1056c.

8291. שָׂרוּק   {1x} **sarûwq**, *sar-ook';* pass. part.
from the same as 8321; a *grape-
vine:*—principal plant {1x}. See: TWOT—
2294b; BDB—977d. See 8320, 8321.

8292. שְׁרוּקָה   {3x} **shᵉrûwqâh**, *sher-oo-kaw';*
or (by perm.)

שְׁרִיקָה   **shᵉrîyqâh**, *sher-ee-kaw';* fem.
pass. part. of 8319; a *whistling*
(in scorn); by anal. a *piping:*—hissing {2x},

bleating {1x}. See: TWOT—2468b; BDB—1057a.

8293. שֵׁרוּת {1x} **shêrûwth**, *shay-rooth';* from 8281 abb.; *freedom:*—variant {1x}. See: TWOT—2463; BDB—1056a.

8294. שֶׂרַח {3x} **Serach**, *seh'-rakh;* by perm. for 5629; *superfluity; Serach*, an Israelitess:—Serah {2x}, Sarah {1x}. See: BDB—976a.

8295. שָׂרַט {3x} **sârat**, *saw-rat';* a prim. root; to *gash:*—cut in pieces {1x}, in pieces {1x}, make {1x}. See: TWOT—2289; BDB—976b.

8296. שֶׂרֶט {2x} **seret**, *seh'-ret;* and

שָׂרֶטֶת **sâreteth**, *saw-reh'-teth;* from 8295; an *incision:*—cuttings {2x}. See: TWOT—2289a; BDB—976b.

8297. שָׂרַי {17x} **Sâray**, *saw-rah'-ee;* from 8269; *dominative; Sarai*, the wife of Abraham:—Sarai {17x}. See: BDB—976b, 979c.

8298. שָׂרַי {1x} **Shâray**, *shaw-rah'-ee;* prob. from 8324; *hostile; Sharay*, an Isr.:—Sharai {1x}. See: BDB—1056c.

8299. שָׂרִיג {3x} **sârîyg**, *saw-reeg';* from 8276; a *tendril* (as *intwining*):—branch {3x}. See: TWOT—2284a; BDB—974d.

8300. שָׂרִיד {28x} **sârîyd**, *saw-reed';* from 8277; a *survivor:*—remain {12x}, remaining {9x}, left {3x}, remnant {2x}, alive {1x}, rest {1x}. See: TWOT—2285a; BDB—975a.

8301. שָׂרִיד {2x} **Sârîyd**, *saw-reed';* the same as 8300; *Sarid*, a place in Pal.:—Sarid {2x}. See: BDB—975a.

8302. שִׁרְיוֹן {9x} **shiryôwn**, *shir-yone';* or

שִׁרְיֹן **shiryôn**, *shir-yone';* and

שִׁרְיָן **shiryân**, *shir-yawn';* also (fem.)

שִׁרְיָה **shiryâh**, *shir-yaw';* and

שִׁרְיֹנָה **shiryônâh**, *shir-yo-naw';* from 8281 in the orig. sense of *turning;* a *corslet* (as if *twisted*):—habergeon {3x}, coat {2x}, harness {2x}, coat of mail {1x}, breastplate {1x}. See: TWOT—2466a, 2465a; BDB—1056b, 1056c. See 5630.

8303. שִׁרְיוֹן {2x} **Shiryôwn**, *shir-yone';* and

שִׁרְיֹן **Siryôn**, *sir-yone';* the same as 8304 (i.e. *sheeted* with snow); *Shirjon* or *Sirjon*, a peak of the Lebanon:—Sirion {2x}. See: BDB—976b.

8304. שְׂרָיָה {20x} **Seʾrâyâh**, *ser-aw-yaw';* or

שְׂרָיָהוּ **Seʾrâyâhûw**, *ser-aw-yaw'-hoo;* from 8280 and 3050; *Jah has pre-*

vailed; Serajah, the name of nine Isr.:—Seraiah {20x}. See: BDB—976a, 976b, 996a.

8305. שְׂרִיקָה {1x} **seʾrîyqâh**, *ser-ee-kaw';* from the same as 8321 in the orig. sense of *piercing; hetchelling* (or combing flax), i.e. (concr.) *tow* (by extens. *linen* cloth):—fine {1x}. See: TWOT—2293a; BDB—977c.

8306. שָׂרִיר {1x} **shârîyr**, *shaw-reer';* from 8324 in the orig. sense as in 8270 (comp. 8326); a *cord*, i.e. (by anal.) *sinew:*—navel {1x}. See: TWOT—2469c; BDB—1057b.

8307. שְׂרִירוּת {10x} **sheʾrîyrûwth**, *sher-ee-rooth';* from 8324 in the sense of *twisted*, i.e. *firm; obstinacy:*—imagination {9x}, lust {1x}. See: TWOT—2469d; BDB—1057b.

8308. שָׂרַךְ {1x} **sârak**, *saw-rak';* a prim. root; to *interlace:*—traversing {1x}. See: TWOT—2290; BDB—976c.

8309. שְׂרֵמָה {1x} **sheʾrêmâh**, *sher-ay-maw';* prob. by an orth. err. for 7709; a *common:*—field {1x}. See: TWOT—2334a; BDB—995a, 1056c.

8310. שַׂרְסְכִים {1x} **Sarçekîym**, *sar-seh-keem';* of for. der.; *Sarsekim*, a Bab. general:—Sarsechim {1x}. See: BDB—976c.

8311. שָׂרַע {3x} **sâraʿ**, *saw-rah';* a prim. root; to *prolong*, i.e. (reflex.) *be deformed* by excess of members:—superfluous {2x}, stretch out {1x}. See: TWOT—2291; BDB—976c.

8312. שַׂרְעַף {2x} **sarʿaph**, *sar-af';* for 5587; *cogitation:*—thought {2x}. See: TWOT—2273b; BDB—972a, 976d.

8313. שָׂרַף {117x} **sâraph**, *saw-raf';* a prim. root; to *be* (caus. *set*) *on fire:*—burn {112x}, burn up {2x}, kindled {1x}, made {1x}, utterly {1x}.

(1) Since burning is the main characteristic of fire, the term *saraph* is used to describe the destroying of objects of all kinds: **(1a)** the door of a city tower (Judg 9:52), **(1b)** various cities (Josh 6:24; 1 Sa 30:1), **(1c)** chariots (Josh 11:6, 9), **(1d)** idols (Ex 32:20; Deut 9:21), and **(1e)** the scroll that Jeremiah had dictated to Baruch (Jer 36:25, 27–28). **(2)** Some burnings were abominable: **(2a)** the Moabites' burning of the bones of the king of Edom (Amos 2:1) and **(2b)** burning of men's bodies on the sacred altar was a great act of desecration (1 Kin 13:2). **(3)** Ezekiel burned a third of his hair as a symbol that part of the people of Judah would be destroyed (Eze 5:4).

(4) The burning of a red heifer produced ashes for purification (Lev 19:5, 8). Syn.: It is important to notice that throughout the Levitical ritual two distinct words are used to

represent burning. *Qatar* (6999) which properly means to turn into smoke or vapor, is used of the burning of the *Olah* (5930), of the memorial portion of the *minchah* (4503), and of the fat of the *zebach* (2077), all of which were intended as offerings for God's good pleasure and not for sin. This burning took place on the altar at the door of the tabernacle. *Saraph* means to consume or burn up, and is used of the burning of the bodies of certain sin-offerings. Nothing is said of their smoke ascending as a sweet savor to God, because they represent "the body of sin, "an object that is by no means pleasing in His sight. This is the aspect of the matter presented by the sin-offering that the priest offered for himself, and still more emphatically by the offering of the goat for the sins for the people on the great Day of Atonement. Ordinary sin-offerings were eaten by the priest. See: TWOT—2292; BDB—976d.

8314. שָׂרָף {7x} **sârâph**, *saw-rawf'*; from 8313; *burning*, i.e. (fig.) *poisonous* (serpent); spec. a *saraph* or symb. creature (from their copper color):—fiery serpent {3x}, fiery {2x}, seraphim {2x}.
   (1) *Saraph*, in the singular, means burning one; fiery being (Num 21:6, 8; cf. Is 14:29; 30:6). (2) *Seraphim*, the plural form, means burning, noble. Seraphim refers to the ministering beings in Is 6:2, 6, and may imply either a serpentine form (albeit with wings, human hands, and voices) or beings that have a glowing quality about them. See: TWOT—2292a, 2292b; BDB—977b.

8315. שָׂרָף {1x} **Sâraph**, *saw-raf'*; the same as 8314; *Saraph*, an Isr.:—Saraph {1x}. See: BDB—977b.

8316. שְׂרֵפָה {13x} **seʰrêphâh**, *ser-ay-faw'*; from 8313; *cremation:*—burning {9x}, burn {3x}, throughly {1x}. See: TWOT—2292c; BDB—977b.

8317. שָׁרַץ {14x} **shârats**, *shaw-rats'*; a prim. root; to *wriggle*, i.e. (by impl.) *swarm* or *abound:*—creep {6x}, bring forth abundantly {5x}, move {1x}, breed abundantly {1x}, increase abundantly {1x}. See: TWOT—2467; BDB—1056c.

8318. שֶׁרֶץ {15x} **sherets**, *sheh'-rets*; from 8317; a *swarm*, i.e. active mass of minute animals:—creeping thing {11x}, creep {2x}, creature {1x}, move {1x}. See: TWOT—2467a; BDB—1056d.

8319. שָׁרַק {12x} **shâraq**, *shaw-rak'*; a prim. root; prop. to *be shrill*, i.e. to whistle or *hiss* (as a call or in scorn):—hiss {12x}. See: TWOT—2468; BDB—1056d, 1117b.

8320. שָׂרֻק {1x} **sâruq**, *saw-rook'*; from 8319; *bright red* (as *piercing* to the sight), i.e. *bay:*—speckled {1x}. See: TWOT—2294a; BDB—977d. See 8291.

8321. שֹׂרֵק {3x} **sôrêq**, *so-rake'*; or

   שׂוֹרֵק **sôwrêq**, *so-rake'*; and (fem.)

   שֹׂרֵקָה **sôrêqâh**, *so-ray-kaw'*; from 8319 in the sense of *redness* (comp. 8320); a *vine* stock (prop. one yielding *purple* grapes, the richest variety):—choice wine {2x}, noble wine {1x}. See: TWOT—2294c; BDB—977d. comp. 8291.

8322. שְׂרֵקָה {7x} **sheʰrêqâh**, *sher-ay-kaw'*; from 8319; a *derision:*—hissing {7x}. See: TWOT—2468a; BDB—1056d.

8323. שָׂרַר {5x} **sârar**, *saw-rar'*; a prim. root; to *have* (tran. *exercise;* refl. *get*) *dominion:*—rule {3x}, make prince {1x}, altogether {1x}. See: TWOT—2295; BDB—965a, 979a.

8324. שָׂרַר {5x} **shârar**, *shaw-rar'*; a prim. root; to *be hostile* (only act. part. an *opponent*):—enemies {5x}. See: TWOT—2469; BDB—1004a.

8325. שָׁרָר {1x} **Shârâr**, *shaw-rawr'*; from 8324; *hostile; Sharar*, an Isr.:—Sharar {1x}. See: BDB—1057a.

8326. שֹׁרֶר {1x} **shôrer**, *sho'-rer;* from 8324 in the sense of *twisting* (comp. 8270); the umbilical *cord*, i.e. (by extens.) a *bodice:*—navel {1x}. See: TWOT—2469a; BDB—1057a.

8327. שָׁרַשׁ {8x} **shârash**, *shaw-rash'*; a prim. root; to *root*, i.e. strike into the soil, or (by impl.) to pluck from it:—. . . root {7x}, root out {1x}. See: TWOT—2471; BDB—1057d.

8328. שֶׁרֶשׁ {33x} **sheresh**, *sheh'-resh;* from 8327; a *root* (lit. or fig.):—root {30x}, bottom {1x}, deep {1x}, heels {1x}. See: TWOT—2471a; BDB—1057c, 1117b.

8329. שֶׁרֶשׁ {1x} **Sheresh**, *sheh'-resh;* the same as 8328; *Sheresh*, an Isr.:—Sheresh {1x}. See: BDB—1058a, 1058c.

8330. שֹׁרֶשׁ {3x} **shôresh** (Aram.), *sho'-resh;* corresp. to 8328:—root {3x}. See: TWOT—3050a; BDB—1117b.

8331. שַׁרְשָׁה {1x} **sharshâh**, *shar-shaw'*; from 8327; a *chain* (as *rooted*, i.e. *linked*):—chain {1x}. See: TWOT—2470; BDB—1057b, 1058a. comp. 8333.

8332. שְׁרֹשׁוּ {1x} **sheʰrôshûw** (Aram.), *sher-o-shoo'*; from a root corresp. to 8327; *eradication*, i.e. (fig.) *exile:*—banishment {1x}. See: TWOT—3050b; BDB—1117b.

8333. שַׁרְשְׁרָה {7x} **sharsh°râh**, *shar-sher-aw'*; from 8327 [comp. 8331]; a *chain;* (arch.) prob. a *garland:*—chain {7x}. See: TWOT—2470; BDB—1057b, 1058a.

8334. שָׁרַת {97x} **shârath**, *shaw-rath'*; a prim. root; to *attend* as a menial or worshipper; fig. to *contribute* to:—minister (v) {62x}, minister (n) {17x}, serve {8x}, servant {5x}, service {3x}, servitor {1x}, waited {1x}.

I. Sharath, as a noun, means "to serve, minister." **(1a)** This word occurs less than 100 times in the Old Testament. **(1b)** In the vast majority of instances, *sharath* appears in the form of an infinitive or participle. **(1c)** When the participle is translated as a verbal noun, such as "servant" or "minister," it loses the connotation of duration or repetition. [see below] **(1d)** Another grammatical feature of *sharath* is its usage exclusively in the intensive form. **(2)** *Sharath* often denotes "service" rendered in connection with Israel's worship; about 60 of its 97 occurrences have this meaning. **(2a)** When Samuel was still a boy, he ". . . did minister unto the Lord before Eli the priest" (1 Sa 2:11), and **(2b)** the Lord called to him while he "ministered unto the Lord before Eli" (1 Sa 3:1). **(2c)** This kind of "service" was to honor only the Lord, for Israel was not to be "as the heathen, as the families of the countries; to serve wood and stone" (Eze 20:32).

(3) In the temple of Ezekiel's vision, those Levites who had "ministered unto them [the people] before their idols" were forbidden by the Lord to serve as priests (Eze 44:12). **(4)** Furthermore, "the Lord separated the tribe of Levi . . . to minister unto him, and to bless in his name" (Deut 10:8). **(5)** From the tribe of Levi, Moses was to anoint Aaron and his sons and consecrate them, that they might "minister" as priests (Ex 29:30). **(6)** Those not of the family of Aaron, though chosen "to minister unto him forever," acted as assistants to the priests, performing such physical tasks as keeping the gates, slaughtering the burnt offering, caring for the altars and the utensils of the sanctuary: "Then David said, None ought to carry the ark of God but the Levites: for them hath the LORD chosen to carry the ark of God, and to minister unto him for ever" (1 Chr 15:2; cf. Eze 44:11). **(7)** But Isaiah foresees the time when "the sons of strangers . . . shall minister unto thee" (Is 60:10).

(8) In a number of situations, the word is used to denote "service" rendered to a fellow human being. **(8a)** Though the person "served" usually is of a higher rank or station in life, this word never describes a slave's servitude to his master. **(8b)** Moses was instructed: "Bring the tribe of Levi near, and present them before Aaron, the priest, that they may minister unto

him" (Num 3:6; cf. 8:26). **(8c)** Elisha "ministered" to Elijah: "And he returned back from him, and took a yoke of oxen, and slew them, and boiled their flesh with the instruments of the oxen, and gave unto the people, and they did eat. Then he arose, and went after Elijah, and ministered unto him." (1 Kin 19:21). **(8d)** Abishag is said to have "ministered" unto David: "And Bathsheba went in unto the king into the chamber: and the king was very old; and Abishag the Shunammite ministered unto the king" (1 Kin 1:15). **(8e)** Various kinds of officials "ministered" to David: "And David assembled all the princes of Israel, the princes of the tribes, and the captains of the companies that ministered to the king by course, and the captains over the thousands, and captains over the hundreds, and the stewards over all the substance and possession of the king, and of his sons, with the officers, and with the mighty men, and with all the valiant men, unto Jerusalem" (1 Chr 28:1). **(8f)** David's son Amnon had a "servant that ministered unto him" (2 Sa 13:17). **(9)** There were seven eunuchs that "served in the presence of Ahasuerus the king" (Est 1:10). He also had "servants that ministered unto him" (Esth 2:2).

II. Sharath, as a participle, means "servant; minister." **(1)** This word is most regularly translated "minister." Josh 1:1 is one example: "Now after the death of Moses the servant ['*ebed*] of the Lord it came to pass, that the Lord spake unto Joshua, the son of Nun, Moses' minister [*sharath*]." **(2)** Eze 46:24 refers to a place in the temple complex which is reserved for "the ministers of the house.": "Then said he unto me, These are the places of them that boil, where the ministers of the house shall boil the sacrifice of the people." **(3)** The privilege of serving the Lord is not restricted to human beings: **(3a)** "Bless ye the Lord, all ye his hosts [angels]; ye ministers of his, that do his pleasure" (Ps 103:21). **(3b)** Fire and wind, conceived poetically as persons, are also God's "ministers": "Who layeth the beams of his chambers in the waters: who maketh the clouds his chariot: who walketh upon the wings of the wind: Who maketh his angels spirits; his ministers a flaming fire:" (Ps 104:3–4).

(4) Joshua was the "minister" of Moses (Ex 24:13), and **(5)** Elisha had a "servitor": "And his servitor said, What, should I set this before an hundred men? He said again, Give the people, that they may eat: for thus saith the LORD, They shall eat, and shall leave thereof" (2 Kin 4:43). Syn.: 5647, 5650, 5656. See: TWOT—2472; BDB—1058a.

8335. שָׁרֵת {2x} **shârêth**, *shaw-rayth'*; infin. of 8334; *service* (in the Temple):—

ministry {1x}, minister {1x}. See: TWOT—2472a; BDB—1058b.

8336. שֵׁשׁ {42x} **shêsh**, *shaysh;* or (for alliteration with 4897)

שְׁשִׁי **shᵉshiy**, *shesh-ee';* for 7893; *bleached* stuff, i.e. *white* linen or (by anal.) marble:—linen {20x}, fine linen {17x}, marble {3x}, silk {1x}, variant {1x}. See: TWOT—2473, 2379a; BDB—1010d, 1058b, 1058c.

8337. שֵׁשׁ {215x} **shêsh**, *shaysh;* masc.

שִׁשָּׁה **shishshâh**, *shish-shaw';* a prim. number; *six* (as an overplus [see 7797] beyond five or the fingers of the hand); as ord. *sixth:*—six {187x}, sixteen + 6240 {21x}, sixteenth + 6240 {3x}, sixth {2x}, sixteen + 7657 {1x}, threescore + 7239 {1x}. See: 995c, 1010d, 1058b, 1114d.

8338. שָׁשָׁו {1x} **shâwshâw**, *shaw-shaw';* a prim. root; appar. to *annihilate:*—leave the sixth part of thee {1x}. See: TWOT—2474; BDB—995d.

8339. שֵׁשְׁבַּצַּר {2x} **Shêshbatstsar**, *shaysh-bats-tsar';* of for. der.; *Sheshbatstsar,* Zerubbabel's Pers. name:—Sheshbazzar {2x}. See: BDB—1058c.

8340. שֵׁשְׁבַּצַּר {2x} **Shêshbatstsar** (Aram.), *shaysh-bats-tsar';* corresp. to 8339:—Sheshbazzar {2x}. See: BDB—1058c.

שָׁשָׂה **shâsâh**. See 8154.

8341. שָׁשָׁה {1x} **shâshâh**, *shaw-shaw';* a denom. from 8337; to *sixth* or divide into sixths:—sixth part {1x}. See: TWOT—2336d; BDB—995d.

8342. שָׂשׂוֹן {22x} **sâsôwn**, *saw-sone';* or

שָׂשֹׂן **sâsôn**, *saw-sone';* from 7797; *cheerfulness;* spec. *welcome:*—joy {15x}, gladness {3x}, mirth {3x}, rejoicing {1x}. See: TWOT—2246a; BDB—965b, 979c.

8343. שָׁשַׁי {1x} **Shâshay**, *shaw-shah'-ee;* perh. from 8336; *whitish; Shashai,* an Isr.:—Shashai {1x}. See: BDB—1058d.

8344. שֵׁשַׁי {3x} **Shêshay**, *shay-shah'-ee;* prob. for 8343; *Sheshai,* a Canaanite:—Sheshai {3x}. See: BDB—1058d.

8345. שִׁשִּׁי {28x} **shishshiy**, *shish-shee';* from 8337; *sixth,* ord. or (fem.) fractional:—sixth {25x}, sixth part {3x}. See: TWOT—2336b; BDB—995d, 1058d.

8346. שִׁשִּׁים {59x} **shishshîym**, *shish-sheem';* multiple of 8337; *sixty:*—threescore {47x}, sixty {12x}. See: TWOT—2336c; BDB—995d, 1058d.

8347. שֵׁשַׁךְ {2x} **Shêshak**, *shay-shak';* of for. der.; *Sheshak,* a symbol. name of Bab.:—Sheshach {2x}. See: TWOT—2475; BDB—525d, 1058d.

8348. שֵׁשָׁן {5x} **Shêshân**, *shay-shawn';* perh. for 7799; *lily; Sheshan,* an Isr.:—Sheshan {5x}. See: BDB—1058d.

שׁוֹשָׁן **Shôshân**. See 7799.

8349. שָׁשַׁק {2x} **Shâshaq**, *shaw-shak';* prob. from the base of 7785; *pedestrian; Shashak,* an Isr.:—Shashak {2x}. See: BDB—1059a.

8350. שָׁשָׁר {2x} **shâshar**, *shaw-shar';* perh. from the base of 8324 in the sense of that of 8320; *red* ochre (from its *piercing* color):—vermilion {2x}. See: TWOT—2476; BDB—1059a.

8351. שֵׁת {1x} **shêth** (Num. 24:17), *shayth;* from 7582; *tumult:*—Sheth {1x}. TWOT—2301d, 2478a; BDB—981b, 1059a.

8352. שֵׁת {9x} **Shêth**, *shayth;* from 7896; *put,* i.e. *substituted; Sheth,* third son of Adam:—Seth {7x}, Sheth {2x}. See: BDB—1011c, 1059a.

8353. שֵׁת {2x} **shêth** (Aram.), *shayth;* or

שִׁת **shîth** (Aram.), *sheeth;* corresp. to 8337:—sixth {1x}, six {1x}. See: TWOT—3022a; BDB—1114d, 1117b.

8354. שָׁתָה {217x} **shâthâh**, *shaw-thaw';* a prim. root; to *imbibe* (lit. or fig.):—drink {208x}, drinkers {1x}, drunkards {1x}, banquet {1x}, misc. {6x} = × assuredly, × certainly, drinking, surely. See: TWOT—2477; BDB—1059a, 1117c. [*prop. intens. of 8248.*]

8355. שְׁתָה {5x} **shᵉthâh** (Aram.), *sheth-aw';* corresp. to 8354:—to drink {5x}.

(1) This verb primarily means to drink or to consume a liquid, and is used of inanimate subjects (land – Deut 11:1), as well as of persons (Gen 9:21), or animals (Gen 24:19). **(2)** "To drink a cup" is a metaphor for consuming all that a cup may contain (Is 51:17). **(3)** Not only liquids may be drunk (Job 15:16). **(4)** This word may be used of a communal activity (Judg 9:27). **(5)** The phrase "eat and drink" may mean **(5a)** to eat a meal (Gen 24:54); or **(5b)** to banquet, which included many activities in addition to just eating and drinking, or participating in a feast (1 Kin 1:25). **(6)** The phrase, "eating and drinking," may signify a religious meal—i.e., a communion meal with God (Ex 24:11), sacramentally uniting with God (cf. 1 Cor. 10:19). **(7)** The phrase, "eating and drinking," may also signify life in general (1 Kin 4:20; cf. Eccl 2:24; 5:18; Jer 22:15). See: TWOT—3051; BDB—1083b, 1117c.

8356. שָׁתָה {2x} **shâthâh**, *shaw-thaw'*; from 7896; a *basis*, i.e. (fig.) political or moral *support*:—foundations {1x}, purposes {1x}. See: TWOT—2380b; BDB—1011d, 1059a, 1059d, 1060a.

8357. שֵׁתָה {2x} **shêthâh**, *shay-thaw'*; from 7896; the *seat* (of the person):—buttocks {2x}. See: TWOT—2478a; BDB—1011d, 1059a, 1059d.

8358. שְׁתִי {1x} **shᵉthîy**, *sheth-ee'*; from 8354; *intoxication*:—drunkenness {1x}. See: TWOT—2477a; BDB—1059c.

8359. שְׁתִי {9x} **shᵉthîy**, *sheth-ee'*; from 7896; a *fixture*, i.e. the *warp* in weaving:—warp {9x}. See: TWOT—2479a; BDB—1059d.

8360. שְׁתִיָּה {1x} **shᵉthîyâh**, *sheth-ee-yaw'*; fem. of 8358; *potation*:—drinking {1x}. See: TWOT—2477b; BDB—1059c.

שְׁתַּיִם **shᵉttayim**. See 8147.

8361. שִׁתִּין {4x} **shittîyn** (Aram.), *shit-teen'*; corresp. to 8346 [comp. 8353]; *sixty*:—threescore {4x}. See: TWOT—3022b; BDB—1114d, 1117c.

8362. שָׁתַל {10x} **shâthal**, *shaw-thal'*; a prim. root; to *transplant*:—plant {10x}. See: TWOT—2480; BDB—1060a.

8363. שְׁתִיל {1x} **shᵉthîyl**, *sheth-eel'*; from 8362; a *sprig* (as if *transplanted*), i.e. *sucker*:—plant {1x}. See: TWOT—2480a; BDB—1060a.

8364. שֻׁתַלְחִי {1x} **Shûthalchîy**, *shoo-thal-kee'*; patron. from 7803; a *Shuthalchite* (collect.) or desc. of Shuthelach:—Shuthalhites {1x}. See: BDB—1004d.

שָׁתָם **sâtham**. See 5640.

8365. שָׁתַם {2x} **shâtham**, *shaw-tham'*; a prim. root; to *unveil* (fig.):—open {2x}. See: TWOT—2481; BDB—1060c.

8366. שָׁתַן {6x} **shâthan**, *shaw-than'*; a prim. root; (caus.) to *make water*, i.e. *urinate*:—pisseth {6x}. See: TWOT—2377; BDB—1010b, 1060c.

8367. שָׁתַק {4x} **shâthaq**, *shaw-thak'*; a prim. root; to *subside*:—calm {2x}, quiet {1x}, cease {1x}. See: TWOT—2482; BDB—1060c.

8368. שָׁתַר {1x} **sâthar**, *saw-thar'*; a prim. root; to *break* out (as an eruption):—secret parts {1x}. See: TWOT—2297; BDB—979c, 1104d.

8369. שֵׁתָר {1x} **Shêthâr**, *shay-thawr'*; of for. der.; *Shethar*, a Pers. satrap:—Shethar {1x}. See: BDB—1060c.

8370. שְׁתַר בּוֹזְנַי {4x} **Shᵉthar Bôwzᵉnay**, *sheth-ar' bo-zen-ah'-ee;* of for. der.; *Shethar-Bozenai*, a Pers. officer:—Shethar-boznai {4x}. See: BDB—1117c.

8371. שָׁתַת {2x} **shâthath**, *shaw-thath'*; a prim. root; to *place*, i.e. *array;* reflex. to *lie*:—laid {1x}, set {1x}. See: TWOT—2483; BDB—1001c, 1060c.

ת

8372. תָּא {13x} **tâʾ**, *taw;* and (fem.)

תָּאָה **tâʾâh** (Eze 40:12), *taw-aw'*; from (the base of) 8376; a *room* (as circumscribed):—little chamber {11x}, chamber {2x}. See: TWOT—2484; BDB—1060b.

8373. תָּאַב {2x} **tâʾab**, *taw-ab';* a prim. root; to *desire*:—long {2x}. See: TWOT—2485; BDB—1060b.

8374. תָּאַב {1x} **tâʾab**, *taw-ab';* a prim. root [prob. rather ident. with 8373 through the idea of *puffing* disdainfully at; comp. 340]; to *loathe* (mor.):—abhor {1x}. See: TWOT—2486; BDB—1060b.

8375. תַּאֲבָה {1x} **taʾăbâh**, *tah-ab-aw';* from 8374 [comp. 15]; *desire*:—longing {1x}. See: TWOT—2485a; BDB—1060b.

8376. תָּאָה {2x} **tâʾâh**, *taw-aw';* a prim. root; to *mark* off, i.e. (intens.) *designate*:—point out {2x}. See: TWOT—2487; BDB—1060d, 1061c, 1063b.

8377. תְּאוֹ {2x} **tᵉʾôw**, *teh-o';* and

תּוֹא **tôwʾ** (the orig. form), *toh;* from 8376; a species of *antelope* (prob. from the white *stripe* on the cheek):—wild ox {1x}, wild bull {1x}. See: TWOT—2488; BDB—1060d, 1063a.

8378. תַּאֲוָה {20x} **taʾăvâh**, *tah-av-aw';* from 183 (abb.); a *longing;* by impl. a *delight* (subj. *satisfaction*, obj. a *charm*):—desire {13x}, lust {1x}, greedily {1x}, pleasent {1x}, misc. {4x} = dainty, × exceedingly, lusting. See: TWOT—40d; BDB—16c. See also 6914.

8379. תַּאֲוָה {1x} **taʾăvâh**, *tah-av-aw';* from 8376; a *limit*, i.e. *full extent*:—utmost bound {1x}. See: TWOT—2496b; BDB—1060d, 1063b.

8380. תְּאוֹם {4x} **tâʾôwm**, *taw-ome';* or

תְּאֹם **tâʾôm**, *taw-ome';* from 8382; a *twin* (in plur. only), lit. or fig.:—twin {4x}. See: TWOT—2489a; BDB—1060d, 1063a, 1064a.

8381. תַּאֲלָה {1x} ta'ălâh, tah-al-aw'; from 422; an imprecation:—curse {1x}. See: TWOT—94b; BDB—46d, 1060d.

8382. תָּאַם {6x} tâ'am, taw-am'; a prim. root; to be complete; but used only as denom. from 8380, to be (caus. make) twinned, i.e. (fig.) duplicate or (arch.) jointed:—coupled together {3x}, bear twins {2x}, coupled {1x}. See: TWOT—2489; BDB—1060d, 1069c, 1071a.

תָּאֹם tâ'ôm. See 8380.

8383. תְּאֻן {1x} t°ûn, teh-oon'; from 205; naughtiness, i.e. toil:—lies {1x}. See: TWOT—48b; BDB—20b, 1061b.

8384. תְּאֵן {39x} t°ên, teh-ane'; or (in the sing., fem.)

תְּאֵנָה t°ênâh, teh-ay-naw'; perh. of for. der.; the fig (tree or fruit):—fig tree {23x}, fig {16x}. See: TWOT—2490; BDB—1061a.

8385. תַּאֲנָה {2x} ta'ănâh, tah-an-aw'; or

תֹּאֲנָה tô'ănâh, to-an-aw'; from 579; an opportunity or (subj.) purpose:—occasion {2x}. See: TWOT—126a, 126b; BDB—58c, 1061a.

8386. תַּאֲנִיָּה {2x} ta'ănîyâh, tah-an-ee-yaw'; from 578; lamentation:—heaviness {1x}, mourning {1x}. See: TWOT—124b; BDB—1061b.

8387. תַּאֲנַת שִׁלֹה {1x} Ta'ănath Shîlôh, tah-an-ath' shee-lo'; from 8385 and 7887; approach of Shiloh; Taanath-Shiloh, a place in Pal.:—Taanathshiloh {1x}. See: BDB—1061b.

8388. תָּאַר {7x} tâ'ar, taw-ar'; a prim. root; to delineate; reflex. to extend:—draw {5x}, mark out {2x}. See: TWOT—2491, 2491b; BDB—1060d, 1061b, 1061c.

8389. תֹּאַר {15x} tô'ar, to'-ar; from 8388; outline, i.e. figure or appearance:—form {3x}, goodly {2x}, beautiful + 3303 {2x}, favoured {2x}, comely {1x}, countenance {1x}, fair + 3303 {1x}, goodly + 2896 {1x}, resembled {1x}, visage {1x}.

The noun to'ar means (1) "form, shape" in 1 Sa 28:14 and (2) "stately appearance" in 1 Sa 25:3. Syn.: 4758, 4759, 7207, 7209, 7210.See: TWOT—2491a; BDB—1061b, 1064c.

8390. תַּאֲרֵעַ {1x} Ta'ărêa‛, tah-ar-ay'-ah; perh. from 772; Taarea, an Isr.:—Tarea {1x}. See: BDB—357c, 1061c. See 8475.

8391. תְּאַשּׁוּר {2x} t°ashshûwr, teh-ash-shoor'; from 833; a species of cedar (from its erectness):—box tree {1x}, box {1x}. See: TWOT—183g; BDB—81b, 1061c.

8392. תֵּבָה {28x} têbâh, tay-baw'; perh. of for. der.; a box:—ark {28x}. See: TWOT—2492; BDB—1061c.

8393. תְּבוּאָה {42x} t°bûw'âh, teb-oo-aw'; from 935; income, i.e. produce (lit. or fig.):—increase {23x}, fruit {13x}, revenue {5x}, gain {1x}. See: TWOT—212c; BDB—100a, 1061d.

8394. תָּבוּן {43x} tâbûwn, taw-boon'; and (fem.)

תְּבוּנָה t°bûwnâh, teb-oo-naw'; or

תּוֹבֻנָה tôwbûnâh, to-boo-naw'; from 995; intelligence; by impl. an argument; by extens. caprice:—understanding {38x}, discretion {1x}, reasons {1x}, misc. {3x} = skilfulness, wisdom.

Towbunah means "understanding." (1) This word is a wisdom term. (2) Like binah (995), it represents the act of wisdom: "He divideth the sea with his power, and by his understanding he smiteth through the proud" (Job 26:12), (3) the faculty of wisdom: "And I have filled him with the spirit of God, in wisdom, and in understanding, and in knowledge, and in all manner of workmanship," (Ex 31:3), (4) the object of wisdom: "Yea, if thou criest after knowledge, and liftest up thy voice for understanding;" (Prov 2:3), and (5) the personification of wisdom (Prov 8:1). Syn.: 995, 998, 4905, 7919, 8394. See: TWOT—239c; BDB—108a, 108b, 1061d, 1063b.

8395. תְּבוּסָה {1x} t°bûwçâh, teb-oo-saw'; from 947; a treading down, i.e. ruin:—destruction {1x}. See: TWOT—216c; BDB—101b, 1061d.

8396. תָּבוֹר {10x} Tâbôwr, taw-bore'; from a root corresp. to 8406; broken region; Tabor, a mountain in Pal., also a city adjacent:—Tabor {10x}. See: BDB—58b, 493b, 1061d.

8397. תֶּבֶל {2x} tebel, teh'-bel; appar. from 1101; mixture, i.e. unnatural bestiality:—confusion {2x}. See: TWOT—248d; BDB—117d, 1061d.

8398. תֵּבֵל {36x} têbêl, tay-bale'; from 2986; the earth (as moist and therefore inhabited); by extens. the globe; by impl. its inhabitants; spec. a partic. land, as Babylonia, Pal.:—world {35x}, habitable part {1x}.

This word signified, first, the solid material on which man dwells, and that was formed, founded, established, and disposed by God; and secondly, the inhabitants thereof. See: TWOT—835h; BDB—385c, 1061d.

תֻּבַל Tûbal. See 8422.

8399. תַּבְלִית {1x} **tablîyth**, *tab-leeth';* from 1086; *consumption:* — destruction {1x}. See: TWOT—246c; BDB—115b, 1061d.

8400. תְּבַלֻּל {1x} **tᵉballûl**, *teb-al-lool';* from 1101 in the orig. sense of *flowing:* — a *cataract* (in the eye): — blemish {1x}. See: TWOT—248e; BDB—117d, 1061d.

8401. תֶּבֶן {17x} **teben**, *teh'-ben;* prob. from 1129; prop. *material,* i.e. (spec.) refuse *haum* or stalks of grain (as *chopped* in threshing and used for fodder): — straw {15x}, stubble {1x}, chaff {1x}. See: TWOT—2493; BDB—1061d.

8402. תִּבְנִי {3x} **Tibnîy**, *tib-nee';* from 8401; *strawy; Tibni,* an Isr.: — Tibni {3x}. See: BDB—1062a.

8403. תַּבְנִית {20x} **tabnîyth**, *tab-neeth';* from 1129; *structure;* by impl. a *model, resemblance:* — pattern {9x}, likeness {5x}, form {3x}, similitude {2x}, figure {1x}. See: TWOT—255d; BDB—125d, 1062a.

8404. תַּבְעֵרָה {2x} **Tab'êrâh**, *tab-ay-raw';* from 1197; *burning; Taberah,* a place in the desert: — Taberah {2x}. See: BDB—1062a.

8405. תֵּבֵץ {3x} **Têbêts**, *tay-bates';* from the same as 948; *whiteness; Tebets,* a place in Pal.: — Thebez {3x}. See: BDB—1062a.

8406. תְּבַר {1x} **tᵉbar** (Aram.), *teb-ar';* corresp. to 7665; to *be fragile* (fig.): — break {1x}. See: TWOT—3052; BDB—1117c.

8407. תִּגְלַת פִּלְאֶסֶר {6x} **Tiglath Pil'eçer**, *tig-lath' pil-eh'-ser;* or

תִּגְלַת פְּלֶסֶר **Tiglath Pᵉleçer**, *tig-lath pel-eh-ser;* or

תִּלְגַּת פִּלְנְאֶסֶר **Tilgath Pilnᵉ'eçer**, *til-gath' pil-neh-eh'-ser;* or

תִּלְגַּת פִּלְנֶסֶר **Tilgath Pilneçer**, *til-gath' pil-neh'-ser;* of for. der.; *Tiglath-Pileser* or *Tilgath-pilneser,* an Assy. king: — Tiglath-pileser {3x}, Tilgath-pilneser {3x}. See: BDB—129c, 1062a, 1067d.

8408. תַּגְמוּל {1x} **tagmûwl**, *tag-mool';* from 1580; a *bestowment:* — benefit {1x}. See: TWOT—360c; BDB—1062b.

8409. תִּגְרָה {1x} **tigrâh**, *tig-raw';* from 1624; *strife,* i.e. *infliction:* — blow {1x}. See: TWOT—378b; BDB—173d, 1062b.

תֹּגַרְמָה **Tôgarmâh**. See 8425.

8410. תִּדְהָר {2x} **tidhâr**, *tid-hawr';* appar. from 1725; *enduring;* a species of hard-wood or *lasting* tree (perh. *oak*): — pine {1x}, pine tree {1x}. See: TWOT—408b; BDB—187b, 1062b.

8411. תְּדִירָא {2x} **tᵉdîyrâ** (Aram.), *ted-ee-raw';* from 1753 in the orig. sense of *enduring; permanence,* i.e. (adv.) *constantly:* — continually {2x}. See: TWOT—2669d; BDB—1087b, 1117c.

8412. תַּדְמֹר {2x} **Tadmôr**, *tad-more';* or

תַּמֹּר **Tammôr** (1 Kings 9:18), *tam-more';* appar. from 8558; *palm-city; Tadmor,* a place near Pal.: — Tadmor {2x}. See: BDB—1062b.

8413. תִּדְעָל {2x} **Tid'âl**, *tid-awl';* perh. from 1763; *fearfulness; Tidal,* a Canaanite: — Tidal {2x}. See: BDB—1062b.

8414. תֹּהוּ {20x} **tôhûw**, *to'-hoo;* from an unused root mean. to lie *waste;* a *desolation* (of surface), i.e. *desert;* fig. a *worthless* thing; adv. in *vain:* — vain {4x}, vanity {4x}, confusion {3x}, without form {2x}, wilderness {2x}, nought {2x}, nothing {1x}, empty place {1x}, waste {1x}. See: TWOT—2494a; BDB—1062c.

8415. תְּהוֹם {36x} **tᵉhôwm**, *teh-home';* or

תְּהֹם **tᵉhôm**, *teh-home';* (usually fem.) from 1949; an *abyss* (as a *surging* mass of water), espec. the *deep* (the *main* sea or the subterranean *water-supply*): — deep {20x}, depth {15x}, deep places {1x}.

Tehom means "deep water; ocean; water table; waters; flood of waters." **(1)** The word represents the "deep water" whose surface freezes when cold: "The waters are hid as with a stone, and the face of the deep is frozen" (Job 38:30). **(2)** In Ps 135:6 *tehom* is used of the "ocean" in contrast to the seas: "Whatsoever the Lord pleased, that did he in heaven, and in earth, in the seas, and all deep places [in the entire ocean]" (cf. Ps 148:7 et al.). **(3)** The word has special reference to the deep floods or sources of water. **(3a)** Sailors in the midst of a violent storm "mount up to the heaven, they go down again to the depths" (Ps 107:26). **(3b)** This is hyperbolic or exaggerated poetical talk, but it presents the "depths" as the opposite of the heavens or skies. **(3c)** This emphasis is especially prominent in the Song of Moses, where the word represents the ever-existing (but not eternal), ever-threatening, and perilous "deep," not simply an element of nature but a dangerous element: "The depths have covered them: they sank into the bottom as a stone" (Ex 15:5). **(3d)** On the other hand, in such contexts *tehom* may mean no more than "deep water" into which heavy objects quickly sink.

(4) *Tehom* can represent an inexhaustible source of water or, by way of poetic comparison, of blessing: "With blessings of heaven above, blessings of the deep that lieth under . . ." (Gen 49:25). **(4a)** In such contexts the

word represents the "water table" always available below the surface of the earth—what was tapped by digging wells, out of which flowed springs, and what was one with the waters beneath the surface of oceans, lakes, seas, and rivers. **(4b)** This was what God opened together with the waters above the expanse (Gen 7:11; cf. 1:7) and what later was closed to cause and terminate the great Flood (Gen 8:2; cf. Ps 33:6; 104:6; Eze 26:19). **(4c)** In such contexts the word represents a "flood of waters" (Ps 33:6). **(5)** In Gen 1:2 (the first occurrence of the word) *tehom* is used of "all waters" which initially covered the surface of the entire earth: "And darkness was upon the face of the deep" (cf. Prov 3:20; 8:24, 27–28). Syn.: 4325. See: TWOT—2495a; BDB—1062d.

8416. תְּהִלָּה {57x} t**ᵉhillâh,** *teh-hil-law';* from 1984; *laudation;* spec. (concr.) a *hymn:*—praise {57x}.

Tehillah means "glory; praise; song of praise; praiseworthy deeds." **(1)** This word denotes a quality or attribute of some person or thing, "glory or praiseworthiness": "He is thy praise, and he is thy God, that hath done for thee these great and terrible things, which thine eyes have seen" (Deut 10:21). **(2)** Israel is God's "glory" when she exists in a divinely exalted and blessed state: "And give him no rest, till he establish, and till he make Jerusalem a praise in the earth" (Is 62:7; cf. Jer 13:11). **(3)** In some cases *tehillah* represents the words or song by which God is publicly lauded, or by which His "glory" is publicly declared: **(3a)** "My praise [the Messiah is speaking here] shall be of thee in the great congregation" (Ps 22:25). **(3b)** Ps 22:22 is even clearer: "I will declare thy name unto my brethren: in the midst of the congregation will I praise thee."

(4) *Tehillah* is a technical-musical term for a song (7892 - *shir*) which exalts or praises God: "David's psalm of praise" (heading for Ps 145; v. 1 in the Hebrew). **(5)** Perhaps Neh 11:17 refers to a choirmaster or one who conducts such singing of "praises": "And Mattaniah . . . , the son of Asaph, was the principal to begin the thanksgiving in prayer [who at the beginning was the leader of praise at prayer]." **(6)** Finally, *tehillah* may represent deeds which are worthy of "praise," or deeds for which the doer deserves "praise and glory." This meaning is in the word's first biblical appearance: "Who is like unto thee, O Lord, among the gods? Who is like thee, glorious in holiness, fearful in praises [in praiseworthy deeds], doing wonders [miracles]?" (Ex 15:11). See: TWOT—500c; BDB—239d, 1062d.

8417. תְּהֻלָּה {1x} **tohŏlâh,** *to-hol-aw';* fem. of an unused noun (appar. from

1984) mean. *bluster; braggadocio,* i.e. (by impl.) *fatuity:*—folly {1x}. See: TWOT—2494b; BDB—1062d.

8418. תַּהֲלֻכָה {1x} **tahălûkâh,** *tah-hal-oo-kaw';* from 1980; a *procession:*—X went {1x}.

Tahalukot [plural of *tahalukah*] occurs once to mean "procession," specifically a thanksgiving procession (Neh 12:31). See: TWOT—498e; BDB—237c, 1062d.

תְּהֹם **t**ᵉ**hôm.** See 8415.

8419. תַּהְפֻּכָה {10x} **tahpûkâh,** *tah-poo-kaw';* from 2015; a *perversity* or *fraud:*—froward {4x}, frowardness {3x}, froward things {2x}, perverse things {1x}. See: TWOT—512f; BDB—246c, 1063a.

8420. תָּו {3x} **tâv,** *tawv;* from 8427; a *mark;* by impl. a *signature:*—desire {1x}, mark {2x}. See: TWOT—2496a; BDB—1063a, 1063b.

8421. תּוּב {8x} **tûwb** (Aram.), *toob;* corresp. to 7725, to *come back;* spec. (tran. and ellip.) to *reply:*—answer {2x}, restore {1x}, return {4x}, return an answer {1x}. See: TWOT—3053; BDB—1117d.

8422. תּוּבַל {8x} **Tûwbal,** *too-bal';* or

תֻּבַל **Tûbal,** *too-bal';* prob. of for. der.; *Tubal,* a postdiluvian patriarch and his posterity:—*Tubal* {8x}. See: BDB—1061d, 1063a.

8423. תּוּבַל קַיִן {2x} **Tûwbal Qayin,** *too-bal' kah'-yin;* appar. from 2986 (comp. 2981) and 7014; *offspring of Cain; Tubal-Kajin,* an antediluvian patriarch:—*Tubalcain* {2x}. See: BDB—1063b.

תּוּבְנָה **tôwbûnâh.** See 8394.

8424. תּוּגָה {4x} **tûwgâh,** *too-gaw';* from 3013; *depression* (of spirits); concr. a *grief:*—heaviness {3x}, sorrow {1x}. See: TWOT—839b; BDB—387b.

8425. תּוֹגַרְמָה {4x} **Tôwgarmâh,** *to-gar-maw';* or

תֹּגַרְמָה **Tôgarmâh,** *to-gar-maw';* prob. of for. der.; *Togarmah,* a son of Gomer and his posterity:—*Togarmah* {4x}. See: BDB—1062b.

8426. תּוֹדָה {32x} **tôwdâh,** *to-daw';* from 3034; prop. an *extension* of the hand, i.e. (by impl.) *avowal,* or (usually) *adoration;* spec. a *choir* of worshipers:—thanksgiving {18x}, praise {6x}, thanks {3x}, thank offerings {3x}, confession {2x}.

(1) *Towdah* means "thanksgiving." **(2)** In the Hebrew text *towdah* is used to indicate "thanksgiving" in songs of worship (Ps 26:7; 42:4). **(3)** Sometimes the word is used to refer

Hebrew

to the thanksgiving choir or procession (Neh 12:31, 38). **(4)** One of the peace offerings, or "sacrings," was designated the thanksgiving offering (Lev 7:12). Syn.: 1984, 2026, 2077, 3034, 4503, 5930, 7133, 8416. See: TWOT— 847b; BDB—392d, 1063b.

8427. תָּוָה {2x} **tâvâh**, *taw-vaw';* a prim. root; to *mark* out, i.e. (prim.) *scratch* or (def.) *imprint:*—scrabble {1x}, set [a mark] {1x}. See: TWOT—2496; BDB—1061c, 1063b.

8428. תָּוָה {1x} **tâvâh**, *taw-vaw';* a prim. root [or perh. ident. with 8427 through a similar idea from *scraping* to pieces]; to *grieve:*—limit {1x}. See: TWOT—2497; BDB— 1063b.

8429. תְּוַהּ {1x} **tᵉvahh** (Aram.), *tev-ah';* corresp. to 8539 or perh. to 7582 through the idea of *sweeping* to ruin [comp. 8428]; to *amaze,* i.e. (reflex. by impl.) *take alarm:*—be astonied {1x}. See: TWOT—3054; BDB—1117d.

8430. תּוֹחַ {1x} **Tôwach**, *to'-akh;* from an unused root mean. to *depress; humble; Toach,* an Isr.:—Toah {1x}. See: BDB— 1063c.

8431. תּוֹחֶלֶת {6x} **tôwcheleth**, *to-kheh'-leth;* from 3176; *expectation:*—hope {6x}. See: TWOT—859b; BDB—404b, 1063c, 1064a.

תּוּך **tôwk**. See 8496.

8432. תָּוֶךְ {415x} **tâvek**, *taw'-vek;* from an unused root mean. to *sever;* a bisection, i.e. (by impl.) the *centre:*—midst {209x}, among {140x}, within {20x}, middle {7x}, in {6x}, between {3x}, therein {3x}, through {2x}, into {2x}, misc. {23x} = amongst, half, ✗ wherein, mid [-night], ✗ out (of).

(1) *Tavek* indicates the part of a space, place, number of people, things, or line which is not on the end or outside edge (Gen 9:21). **(2)** The word means among, not necessarily in the middle (Gen 40:20). **(3)** Ex 14:29 uses *tavek* as an extension of the word through. **(4)** This word also sometimes means simply "in" in the sense of "mixed into something" (Ex 39:3). **(5)** *Tavek* can mean middle when applied to an object or person between two others (Ex 39:25). **(6)** In Num 35:5 the word means "in the center." **(7)** This word signifies the hypothetical center line dividing something into two equal parts (Gen 15:10; Eze 15:4). **(8)** *Tavek* is used substantively, meaning the middle or the center part of a thing (Josh 12:2). See: TWOT—2498; BDB—1063c.

8433. תּוֹכֵחָה {28x} **tôwkêchâh**, *to-kay-khaw';* and

תּוֹכַחַת **tôwkachath**, *to-kakh'-ath;* from 3198; *chastisement;* fig. (by words) *correction, refutation, proof* (even in defence):—reproof {14x}, rebuke {7x}, reproved {2x}, arguments {1x}, misc. {4x} = ✗ chastened, correction, reasoning. See: TWOT—865a, 865b; BDB—407b, 1064a.

תּוּכִּי **tûwkkîy**. See 8500.

8434. תּוֹלָד {1x} **Tôwlâd**, *to-lawd';* from 3205; *posterity; Tolad,* a place in Pal.:— Tolad {1x}. See: BDB—410a, 1064a. comp. 513.

8435. תּוֹלְדָה {39x} **tôwlᵉdâh**, *to-led-aw';* or

תֹּלְדָה **tôlᵉdâh**, *to-led-aw';* from 3205; (plur. only) *descent,* i.e. *family;* (fig.) *history:*—generations {38x}, birth {1x}. See: TWOT—867g; BDB—410a, 1064a.

8436. תּוֹלוֹן {1x} **Tûwlôn**, *too-lone';* from 8524; *suspension; Tulon,* an Isr.:—Tilon {1x}. See: BDB—1064a, 1066c, 1066d.

8437. תּוֹלָל {1x} **tôwlâl**, *to-lawl';* from 3213; *causing to howl,* i.e. an *oppressor:*—they that wasted us {1x}. See: TWOT— 868c; BDB—1064a.

8438. תּוֹלָע {43x} **tôwlâ**, *to-law';* and (fem.)

תּוֹלֵעָה **tôwlêʿâh**, *to-lay-aw';* or

תּוֹלַעַת **tôwlaʿath**, *to-lah'-ath;* or

תֹּלַעַת **tôlaʿath**, *to-lah'-ath;* from 3216; a *maggot* (as *voracious*); spec. (often with ellip. of 8144) the crimson-*grub,* but used only (in this connection) of the color from it, and cloths dyed therewith:—scarlet {34x}, worm {8x}, crimson {1x}. See: TWOT— 2516b; BDB—1068d, 1069a.

8439. תּוֹלָע {6x} **Tôwlâ**, *to-law';* the same as 8438; *worm; Tola,* the name of two Isr.:—Tola {6x}. See: BDB—1064d, 1069a.

8440. תּוֹלָעִי {1x} **Tôwlâʿiy**, *to-law-ee';* patron. from 8439; a *Tolaite* (collect.) or desc. of Tola:—Tolaites {1x}. See: BDB— 1046b, 1069a.

8441. תּוֹעֵבָה {117x} **tôwʿêbâh**, *to-ay-baw';* or

תֹּעֵבָה **tôʿêbâh**, *to-ay-baw';* fem. act. part. of 8581; prop. something *disgusting* (mor.), i.e. (as noun) an *abhorrence;* espec. *idolatry* or (concr.) an *idol:*—abomination {113x}, abominable thing {2x}, abominable {2x}.

To'ebah means abomination; loathsome, detestable thing. **(1)** *To'ebah* defines something or someone as essentially unique in the sense of being dangerous, sinister, and repulsive to

another individual (Gen 43:32; 46:34; Prov 29:27). **(2)** When used with reference to God, this word describes people, things, acts, relationships, and characteristics that are detestable to Him because they are contrary to His nature; such as **(2a)** things related to death and idolatry (Deut 14:3); **(2b)** people with loathsome habits are themselves detestable to Him (Deut 22:5). **(3)** It is used in some contexts to describe pagan practices and objects (Deut 7:25–26). **(4)** It describes the repeated failures to observe divine regulations (Eze 5:7, 9). **(5)** To'ebah may represent **(5a)** the pagan cultic practices themselves (Deut 12:31), or **(5b)** the people who perpetrate such practices (Deut 18:12). **(6)** It is used in the sphere of jurisprudence and of family or tribal relationships; certain acts or characteristics are destructive of societal and familial harmony; both such things and the people who do them are described by to'ebah (Prov 6:16–19). See: TWOT—2530a; BDB—1072d.

8442. תּוֹעָה {2x} **tôw'âh**, *to-aw';* fem. act. part. of 8582; *mistake,* i.e. (mor.) *impiety,* or (political) *injury:*—hinder {1x}, error {1x}. See: TWOT—2531a; BDB—1064a, 1073c.

8443. תּוֹעָפָה {4x} **tôw'âphâh**, *to-aw-faw';* from 3286; (only in plur. collect.) *weariness,* i.e. (by impl.) *toil (treasure* so obtained) or *speed:*—strength {3x}, plenty {1x}. See: TWOT—886a; BDB—419b, 1064a.

8444. תּוֹצָאָה {23x} **tôwtsâ'âh**, *to-tsaw-aw';* or

תֹּצָאָה **tôtsâ'âh**, *to-tsaw-aw';* from 3318; (only in plur. collect.) *exit,* i.e. (geographical) *boundary,* or (fig.) *deliverance,* (act.) *source:*—goings out {11x}, outgoings {7x}, going forth {2x}, issues {2x}, borders {1x}.

Totsa'ah means "departure; place of departure." The word *totsa'ah* can connote both **(1)** the source of "departure": "Keep thy heart with all diligence; for out of it are the issues of life" (Prov 4:23) and **(2)** the actual "departure" itself: "He that is our God *is* the God of salvation; and unto GOD the Lord belong the issues from death" ("escape," Ps 68:20). **(3)** However, the word may also represent the extremity of a territory or its "border"—the place where one departs a given territory: "And the border went up toward Debir from the valley of Achor, . . .and the goings out thereof were at Enrogel:" (Josh 15:7). Syn.: 3318, 4161. See: TWOT—893e; BDB—426a, 1064a.

8445. תּוֹקָהַת {1x} **Tôwqahath**, *to-kah'-ath;* from the same as 3349; *obedience; Tokahath,* an Isr.:—Tikvath {1x}. See: BDB—876b, 1064b, 1075b.

8446. תּוּר {23x} **tûwr**, *toor;* a prim. root; to *meander* (caus. *guide*) about, espec. for trade or reconnoitring:—search {11x}, search out {3x}, spy out {2x}, seek {2x}, chapmen + 582 {1x}, descry {1x}, espied {1x}, excellent {1x}, merchantmen + 582 {1x}. See: TWOT—2500; BDB—451d, 1064b, 1064d.

8447. תּוֹר {4x} **tôwr**, *tore;* or

תֹּר **tôr**, *tore;* from 8446; a *succession,* i.e. a *string* or (abstr.) *order:*—turn {2x}, row {1x}, border {1x}. See: TWOT—2500a; BDB—1061b, 1064c, 1076a.

8448. תּוֹר {1x} **tôwr**, *tore;* prob. the same as 8447; a *manner* (as a sort of *turn):*—estate {1x}. See: TWOT—2500a; BDB—1061b, 1064c, 1076a.

8449. תּוֹר {14x} **tôwr**, *tore;* or

תֹּר **tôr**, *tore;* prob. the same as 8447; a *ring*-dove, often (fig.) as a term of endearment:—turtledove {9x}, turtle {5x}. See: TWOT—2500c; BDB—1064d, 1076a.

8450. תּוֹר {7x} **tôwr** (Aram.), *tore;* corresp. (by perm.) to 7794; a *bull:*—oxen {4x}, bullock {3x}. See: TWOT—3055; BDB—1117d.

8451. תּוֹרָה {219x} **tôwrâh**, *to-raw';* or

תֹּרָה **tôrâh**, *to-raw';* from 3384; a *precept* or *statute,* espec. the *Decalogue* or *Pentateuch:*—law {219x}.

Summary: *Torah* signifies primarily direction, teaching, instruction (Prov 13:14). It is derived from the verb, *yarah* "to project, point out" (3384) and hence to point out or teach. The law of God is that which points out or indicates His will to man. It is not an arbitrary rule, still less is it a subjective impulse; it is rather to be regarded as a course of guidance from above. Seen against the background of the verb *yarah,* it becomes clear that *torah* is much more than law or a set of rules. *Torah* is not restriction or hindrance, but instead the means whereby one can reach a goal or ideal. In the truest sense, *torah* was given to Israel to enable her to truly become and remain God's special people. One might say that in keeping *torah,* Israel was kept. Unfortunately, Israel fell into the trap of keeping *torah* as something imposed, and for itself, rather than as a means of becoming what God intended for her. The means became the end. Instead of seeing *torah* as a guideline, it became an external body of rules, and thus a weight rather than a freeing and guiding power. This burden, plus the legalism of Roman law, forms the background of the New Testament tradition of law, especially as Paul struggles with it in his letter to the church at Rome.

(1) In the wisdom literature, where the noun

does not appear with a definite article, **(1a)** *torah* signifies primarily "direction, teaching, instruction": **(1a1)** "The law of the wise is a fountain of life, to depart from the snares of death" (Prov 13:14), and **(1a2)** "Receive, I pray thee, the law from his mouth, and lay up his words in thine heart" (Job 22:22). **(2)** The "instruction" of the sages of Israel, who were charged with the education of the young, was intended to cultivate in the young a fear of the Lord so that they might live in accordance with God's expectations. **(2a)** The sage was a father to his pupils: "Whoso keepeth the law is a wise son: but he that is a companion of riotous men shameth his father" (Prov 28:7; cf. 3:1; 4:2; 7:2). **(2b)** The natural father might also instruct his son in wise living, even as a God-fearing woman was an example of kind "instruction": "She openeth her mouth with wisdom; and in her tongue is the law of kindness" (Prov 31:26).

(3) The "instruction" given by God to Moses and the Israelites became **(3a)** known as "the law" or **(3b)** "the direction" (*ha-torah*), and quite frequently **(3c)** as "the Law of the Lord": "Blessed are the undefiled in the way, who walk in the law of the Lord" (Ps 119:1), or **(3d)** "the Law of God": "Also day by day, from the first day unto the last day, [Ezra] read in the book of the law of God" (Neh 8:18), and also **(3e)** as "the Law of [given through] Moses": "Remember ye the law of Moses my servant, which I commanded unto him in Horeb for all Israel . . ." (Mal 4:4). **(4)** The word can refer to **(4a)** the whole of the "law": "For he established a testimony in Jacob, and appointed a law in Israel, which he commanded our fathers, that they should make them known to their children" (Ps 78:5), or **(4b)** or particulars: "And this is the law which Moses set before the children of Israel" (Deut 4:44). **(5)** God had communicated the "law" that Israel might observe and live: "And what nation is there so great, that hath statutes and judgments so righteous as all this law, which I set before you this day?" (Deut 4:8). **(6)** The king was instructed to have a copy of the "law" prepared for him at his coronation (Deut 17:18).

(7) The priests were charged with the study and teaching of, as well as the jurisprudence based upon, the "law" (Jer 18:18). **(7a)** Because of rampant apostasy the last days of Judah were times when there were no teaching priests (2 Chr 15:3); in fact, **(7b)** in Josiah's days the "law" (whether the whole *Torah*, or a book or a part) was recovered: "And Hilkiah . . . said to Shaphan the scribe, I have found the book of the law in the house of the Lord" (2 Chr 34:15). **(8)** The prophets called Israel to repent by returning to the *torah* ("instruction") of God (Is 1:10). **(8a)** Jeremiah prophesied concerning

God's new dealing with His people in terms of the New Covenant, in which God's law is to be internalized, God's people would willingly obey Him: "But this shall be the covenant that I will make with the house of Israel; After those days, saith the Lord, I will put my law in their inward parts, and write it in their hearts; and will be their God, and they shall be my people" (Jer 31:33). **(8b)** The last prophet of the Old Testament reminded the priests of their obligations (Mal 2) and challenged God's people to remember the "law" of Moses in preparation for the coming Messiah (Mal 4:4). Syn.: 3384. See: TWOT—910d; BDB—435d, 1064c, 1064d.

8452. תּוֹרָה {1x} **tôwrâh**, *to-raw'*; prob. fem. of 8448; a *custom:*—manner {1x}. See: TWOT—910d; BDB—435d, 1064c, 1064d.

8453. תּוֹשָׁב {14x} **tôwshâb**, *to-shawb'*; or

תֹּשָׁב **tôshâb** (1 Kings 17:1), *to-shawb'*; from 3427; a *dweller* (but not outlandish [5237]); espec. (as distinguished from a native citizen [act. part. of 3427] and a temporary inmate [1616] or mere lodger [3885]) resident *alien:*—sojourner {9x}, stranger {3x}, foreigner {2x}. See: TWOT—922d; BDB—444c, 1064d, 1077b.

8454. תּוּשִׁיָּה {12x} **tûwshîyâh**, *too-shee-yaw'*; or

תֻּשִׁיָּה **tûshîyâh**, *too-shee-yaw'*; from an unused root prob. mean. to *substantiate; support* or (by impl.) *ability*, i.e. (direct) *help*, (in purpose) an *undertaking*, (intellectual) *understanding:*—wisdom {7x}, enterprise {1x}, thing as it is {1x}, that which is {1x}, substance {1x}, working {1x}. Syn.: 995, 2450, 7919. See: TWOT—923a; BDB—444d, 1064d, 1077b.

8455. תּוֹתָח {1x} **tôwthâch**, *to-thawkh'*; from an unused root mean. to *smite;* a *club:*—darts {1x}. Syn.: 2671. See: TWOT—933a; BDB—450c, 1064d.

8456. תָּזַז {1x} **tâzaz**, *taw-zaz'*; a prim. root; to *lop* off:—cut down {1x}. See: TWOT—2501; BDB—1064d.

8457. תַּזְנוּת {20x} **taznûwth**, *taz-nooth'*; or

תַּזְנֻת **taznûth**, *taz-nooth'*; from 2181; *harlotry*, i.e. (fig.) *idolatry:*—fornication {2x}, whoredom {18x}. See: TWOT—563c; BDB—276b, 1064d.

8458. תַּחְבֻּלָה {6x} **tachbûlâh**, *takh-boo-law'*; or

תַּחְבּוּלָה **tachbûwlâh**, *takh-boo-law'*; from 2254 as denom. from 2256; (only in plur.) prop. *steerage* (as a management of *ropes*), i.e. (fig.) *guidance* or (by

impl.) a *plan:*—good advice {1x}, (wise) counsels {5x}. See: TWOT—596a; BDB—287a,
1064d.

8459. תֹחוּ {1x} **Tôchûw**, *to'-khoo;* from an unused root mean. to *depress; abase-
ment; Tochu,* an Isr.:—Tohu {1x}. See: BDB—
1063c, 1064d.

8460. תְּחוֹת {4x} **t°chôwth** (Aram.), *tekh-
??th';* or

תְּחֹת **t°chôth** (Aram.), *tekh-ōth';* corresp. to 8478; *beneath:*—under
{4x}. Syn.: 8478. See: TWOT—3056; BDB—
1117d.

8461. תַּחְכְּמֹנִי {1x} **Tachk°mônîy**, *takh-kem-o-
nee';* prob. for 2453; *sagacious;
Tachkemoni,* an Isr.:—Tachmonite {1x}. See:
BDB—315d, 1064d.

8462. תְּחִלָּה {22x} **t°chillâh**, *tekh-il-law';*
from 2490 in the sense of *open-
ing;* a *commencement;* rel. *original* (adv. *-ly*):—
beginning {14x}, first {5x}, first time {2x}, begin
{1x}. See: TWOT—661d; BDB—321a, 1064d.

8463. תַּחֲלוּא {5x} **tachălûw²**, *takh-al-oo';* or

תַּחֲלֻא **tachălu̇**, *takh-al-oo';* from 2456;
a *malady:*—disease {2x}, ✕ griev-
ous {1x}, (that are) sick {1x}, sickness {1x}. See:
TWOT—648a; BDB—316a, 1066d.

8464. תַּחְמָס {2x} **tachmâç**, *takh-mawce';*
from 2554; a species of unclean
bird (from its *violence*), perh. an *owl:*—night
hawk {2x}. See: TWOT—678b; BDB—329d,
1064d.

8465. תַּחַן {2x} **Tachan**, *takh'-an;* prob. from
2583; *station; Tachan,* the name of
two Isr.:—Tahan {2x}. See: BDB—334c, 1064d.

8466. תַּחֲנָה {1x} **tachănâh**, *takh-an-aw';* from
2583; (only plur. collect.) an *en-
campment:*—camp {1x}. Syn.: 2583, 4264. See:
TWOT—690d; BDB—334c, 1064d.

8467. תְּחִנָּה {25x} **t°chinnâh**, *tekh-in-naw';*
from 2603; *graciousness;* caus.
entreaty:—supplication {23x}, favour {1x},
grace {1x}. See: TWOT—694f; BDB—337c,
1064d.

8468. תְּחִנָּה {1x} **T°chinnâh**, *tekh-in-naw';* the
same as 8467; *Techinnah,* an
Isr.:—Tehinnah {1x}. See: BDB—337c.

8469. תַּחֲנוּן {18x} **tachănûwn**, *takh-an-oon';*
or (fem.)

תַּחֲנוּנָה **tachănûwnâh**,
takh-an-oo-naw'; from 2603;
earnest *prayer:*—supplications {17x}, intreaties {1x}. See: TWOT—694g; BDB—337c, 1064d.

8470. תַּחֲנִי {1x} **Tachănîy**, *takh-an-ee';* patron. from 8465; a *Tachanite* (col-
lect.) or desc. of Tachan:—Tahanites {1x}. See:
BDB—334c, 1064d, 1071d.

8471. תַּחְפַּנְחֵס {7x} **Tachpanchêç**, *takh-pan-
khace';* or

תְּחַפְנְחֵס **T°chaphn°chêç** (Eze 30:18),
tekh-af-nekh-ace'; or

תַּחְפְּנֵס **Tachp°nêç** (Jer 2:16), *takh-pen-
ace';* of Eg. der.; *Tachpanches,
Techaphneches* or *Tachpenes,* a place in
Egypt:—Tahpanhes {5x}, Tahapanes {1x},
Tehaphnehes {1x}. See: BDB—1064d.

8472. תַּחְפְּנֵיס {3x} **Tachp°nêyç**, *takh-pen-
ace';* of Eg. der.; *Tachpenes,* an
Eg. woman:—Tahpenes {3x}. See: BDB—
1065a.

8473. תַּחְרָא {2x} **tachără²**, *takh-ar-aw';* from
2734 in the orig. sense of 2352 or
2353; a linen *corslet* (as *white* or *hollow*):—
habergeon {2x}. See: TWOT—2502; BDB—
1065a.

8474. תַּחְרָה {2x} **tachârâh**, *takh-aw-raw';*
a factitious root from 2734
through the idea of the *heat* of jealousy; to *vie*
with a rival:—closest {1x}, contend {1x}. See:
TWOT—736; BDB—354a.

8475. תַּחְרֵעַ {1x} **Tachrêaʿ**, *takh-ray'-ah;* for
8390; *Tachrea,* an Isr.:—Tahrea
{1x}. See: BDB—357c, 1065a.

8476. תַּחַשׁ {14x} **tachash**, *takh'-ash;* prob. of
for. der.; a (clean) animal with fur,
prob. a species of *antelope:*—badger {14x}. See:
TWOT—2503; BDB—1065a.

8477. תַּחַשׁ {1x} **Tachash**, *takh'-ash;* the same
as 8476; *Tachash,* a rel. of Abra-
ham:—Thahash {1x}. See: BDB—1065a.

8478. תַּחַת {24x} **tachath**, *takh'-ath;* from the
same as 8430; the *bottom* (as *de-
pressed*); only adv. *below* (often with prep. pref.
underneath), in *lieu of,* etc.:—{24x} = instead,
under, for, as, with, from, flat, in the same
place. See: TWOT—2504; BDB—1065a, 1117d.

8479. תְּחַת {1x} **tachath** (Aram.), *takh'-ath;*
corresp. to 8478:—under {1x}. See:
TWOT—3056; BDB—1117d.

8480. תַּחַת {6x} **Tachath**, *takh'-ath;* the same
as 8478; *Tachath,* the name of a
place in the desert, also of three Isr.:—Tahath
{6x}. See: BDB—1066c.

תְּחֹת **t°chôth**. See 8460.

8481. תַּחְתּוֹן {13x} **tachtôwn**, *takh-tone';* or

תַּחְתֹּן **tachtôn**, *takh-tone';* from 8478;
bottommost:—lower {5x}, lowest

{2x}, nether {5x}, nethermost {1x}. See: TWOT—2504a; BDB—1066b.

8482. תַּחְתִּי {19x} **tachtîy**, *takh-tee'*; from 8478; *lowermost;* as noun (fem. plur.) the *depths* (fig. a *pit,* the *womb*):—nether parts {5x}, nether {4x}, lowest {3x}, lower {2x}, lower parts {2x}, misc. {3x}. See: TWOT—2504b; BDB—1066d.

8483. תַּחְתִּים חָדְשִׁי {1x} **Tachtîym Chodshîy**, *takh-teem' khod-shee';* appar. from the plur. masc. of 8482 or 8478 and 2320; *lower* (ones) *monthly; Tachtim-Chodshi,* a place in Pal.:—Tahtim-hodshi {1x}. See: BDB—295a, 874a, 1066c.

8484. תִּיכוֹן {11x} **tîykôwn**, *tee-kone';* or

תִּיכֹן **tîykôn**, *tee-kone';* from 8432; *cen-tral:*—middle {8x}, middlemost {2x}, midst {1x}. See: TWOT—2498a; BDB—1064a, 1066c.

8485. תֵּימָא {5x} **Têymâʾ**, *tay-maw';* or

תֵּמָא **Têmâʾ**, *tay-maw';* prob. of for. der.; *Tema,* a son of Ishmael, and the region settled by him:—*Tema* {5x}. See: BDB—1066d, 1069b.

8486. תֵּימָן {23x} **têymân**, *tay-mawn';* or

תֵּמָן **têmân**, *tay-mawn';* denom. from 3225; the *south* (as being on the *right* hand of a person facing the east):—south {11x}, southward {8x}, south side {2x}, south coast {1x}, south wind {1x}.

(1) *Teman* means "south; southern quarter; southwards." **(2)** In its first biblical occurrence (Ex 26:18), the word refers to the direction "southward." **(3)** *Teman* can mean "south" or "southern quarter" as in Josh 15:1: "This then was the lot of the tribe of the children of Judah by their families; even to the border of Edom the wilderness of Zin southward was the utter-most part of the south coast." Syn.: 3233. See: TWOT—872e; BDB—412c, 1066d, 1071b.

8487. תֵּימָן {11x} **Têymân**, *tay-mawn';* or

תֵּמָן **Têmân**, *tay-mawn';* the same as 8486; *Teman,* the name of two Edom-ites, and of the region and desc. of one of them:—*Teman* {11x}. See: BDB—412d, 1064a, 1071b.

8488. תֵּימְנִי {1x} **Têymʿnîy**, *tay-men-ee';* prob. for 8489; *Temeni,* an Isr.:—Tem-eni {1x}. See: BDB—412d, 1066d.

8489. תֵּימָנִי {8x} **Têymânîy**, *tay-maw-nee';* pa-tron. from 8487; a *Temanite* or desc. of Teman:—Temani {1x}, Temanite {7x}. See: BDB—412d, 1066d, 1071b.

8490. תִּימָרָה {2x} **tîymârâh**, *tee-maw-raw';* or

תִּמָרָה **tîmârâh**, *tee-maw-raw';* from the same as 8558; a *column,* i.e. *cloud:*—pillar {2x}. Syn.: 4676, 5982. See: TWOT—2523d; BDB—1066d.

8491. תִּיצִי {1x} **Tîytsîy**, *tee-tsee';* patrial or patron. from an unused noun of uncert. mean.; a *Titsite* or desc. or inhab. of an unknown Tits:—Tizite {1x}. See: BDB—1066d.

8492. תִּירוֹשׁ {38x} **tîyrôwsh**, *tee-roshe';* or

תִּירֹשׁ **tîyrôsh**, *tee-roshe';* from 3423 in the sense of *expulsion; must* or fresh grape-juice (as just *squeezed* out); by impl. (rarely) fermented *wine:*—(new, sweet) wine {38x}. Syn.: 3196, 4469, 6071. See: TWOT—2505; BDB—440d, 1066d.

8493. תִּירְיָא {1x} **Tîyrʿyâʾ**, *tee-reh-yaw';* prob. from 3372; *fearful, Tirja,* an Isr.:—Tiria {1x}. See: BDB—432b, 1066d.

8494. תִּירָס {2x} **Tîyrâç**, *tee-rawce';* prob. of for. der.; *Tiras,* a son of Japheth:—Tiras {2x}. See: BDB—1066d.

תִּירֹשׁ **tîyrôsh**. See 8492.

8495. תַּיִשׁ {4x} **tayish**, *tah'-yeesh;* from an un-used root mean. to *butt;* a *buck* or he-goat (as given to *butting*):—he goat {4x}. Syn.: 5795, 6842, 8163. See: TWOT—2506; BDB—1066d.

8496. תֹּךְ {3x} **tôk**, *toke;* or

תּוֹךְ **tôwk** (Psa. 72:14), *toke;* from the same base as 8432 (in the sense of *cutting* to pieces); *oppression:*—deceit {2x}, fraud {1x}. See: TWOT—2509a; BDB—1063c, 1067a.

8497. תָּכָה {1x} **tâkâh**, *taw-kaw';* a prim. root; to *strew,* i.e. *encamp:*—sat down {1x}. See: TWOT—2507; BDB—1067a.

8498. תְּכוּנָה {2x} **t⁰kûwnâh**, *tek-oo-naw';* fem. pass. part. of 8505; *adjustment,* i.e. *structure;* by impl. *equipage:*—fashion {1x}, store {1x}.

Tekuwnah means "fixed matter" as in Eze 43:11: "Show them the form of the house, and the fashion [*tekuwnah*] thereof . . ." See: 8499. See: TWOT—964e; BDB—467d, 1067a.

8499. תְּכוּנָה {1x} **t⁰kûwnâh**, *tek-oo-naw';* from 3559; or prob. ident. with 8498; *something arranged* or *fixed,* i.e. a *place:*—seat {1x}.

Tekuwnah means "fixed place" as in Job 23:3: "Oh that I knew where I might find him! that I might come even to his seat!" See: TWOT—964e; BDB—467d, 1067a.

8500. תֻּכִּי {2x} **tukkîy**, *took-kee';* or

תּוּכִּי **tûwkkîy**, *took-kee';* prob. of for.
der.; some imported creature,
prob. a *peacock:*—peacock {2x}. See: TWOT—
2508; BDB—1064a, 1067a.

8501. תָּכָךְ {1x} **tâkâk**, *taw-kawk';* from an
unused root mean. to *dissever,* i.e.
crush:—deceitful {1x}. See: TWOT—2509?;
BDB—1067a.

8502. תִּכְלָה {1x} **tiklâh**, *tik-law';* from 3615;
completeness:—perfection {1x}.
See: TWOT—982e; BDB—479a, 1067a.

8503. תַּכְלִית {5x} **taklîyth**, *tak-leeth';* from
3615; *completion;* by impl. an
extremity:—end {2x}, perfect {1x}, perfection
{2x}. See: TWOT—982f; BDB—479b, 1067a.

8504. תְּכֵלֶת {50x} **tᵉkêleth**, *tek-ay'-leth;* prob.
for 7827; the cerulean *mussel,*
i.e. the color (*violet*) obtained therefrom or
stuff dyed therewith:—blue {50x}. See:
TWOT—2510; BDB—1067a.

8505. תָּכַן {18x} **tâkan**, *taw-kan';* a prim. root;
to *balance,* i.e. *measure* out (by
weight or dimension); fig. to *arrange, equalize,*
through the idea of *levelling* (ment. *estimate,*
test):—equal {7x}, weigh {3x}, pondereth {2x},
unequal {2x}, directed {1x}, misc. {3x} = bear
up, mete, tell. See: TWOT—2511; BDB—1067b.

8506. תֹּכֶן {2x} **tôken**, *to'-ken;* from 8505; a
fixed *quantity:*—measure {1x}, tale
{1x}. See: TWOT—2511a; BDB—1067c.

8507. תֹּכֶן {1x} **Tôken**, *to'-ken;* the same as
8506; *Token,* a place in Pal.:—To-
chen {1x}. See: BDB—1067c.

8508. תָּכְנִית {2x} **toknîyth**, *tok-neeth';* from
8506; *admeasurement,* i.e. *con-*
summation:—pattern {1x}, sum {1x}. See:
TWOT—2511b; BDB—1067c.

8509. תַּכְרִיךְ {1x} **takrîyk**, *tak-reek';* appar.
from an unused root mean. to
encompass; a *wrapper* or robe:—garment {1x}.
See: TWOT—1037a; BDB—501b, 1067c.

8510. תֵּל {5x} **têl**, *tale;* by contr. from 8524; a
mound:—heap {4x}, × strength {1x}.
See: TWOT—2513a; BDB—1067c, 1068b,
1068d.

8511. תָּלָא {3x} **tâlâʾ**, *taw-law';* a prim. root;
to *suspend;* fig. (through *hesita-*
tion) to *be uncertain;* by impl. (of mental *de-*
pendence) to *habituate:*—be bent {1x}, hang (in
doubt) {2x}. See: BDB—1067d.

8512. תֵּל אָבִיב {1x} **Têl ʾÂbîyb**, *tale aw-beeb';*
from 8510 and 24; *mound* of
green growth; *Tel-Abib,* a place in Chaldaea:—
Tel-abib {1x}. See: BDB—1068b.

8513. תְּלָאָה {4x} **tᵉlâʾâh**, *tel-aw-aw';* from
3811; *distress:*—travail {2x},
travel {1x}, trouble {1x}. See: TWOT—1066a;
BDB—521b.

8514. תַּלְאוּבָה {1x} **talʾûwbâh**, *tal-oo-baw';*
from 3851; *desiccation:*—
great drought {1x}. See: TWOT—1065a;BDB—
520d, 1067d.

8515. תְּלַאשָּׂר {2x} **Tᵉlaʾssar**, *tel-as-sar';* or

תְּלַשָּׂר **Tᵉlassar**, *tel-as-sar';* of for. der.;
Telassar, a region of Assyria:—
Telassar {1x}, Thelasar {1x}. See: BDB—1067d.

8516. תַּלְבֹּשֶׁת {1x} **talbôsheth**, *tal-bo'-sheth;*
from 3847; a *garment:*—cloth-
ing {1x}. Syn.: 3830. See: TWOT—1075c;
BDB—528d, 1067d.

8517. תְּלַג {1x} **tᵉlag** (Aram.), *tel-ag';* corresp.
to 7950; *snow:*—snow {1x}. See:
TWOT—3057; BDB—1117d.

תִּלְגַת **Tilgath**. See 8407.

תֹּלְדָה **tôlᵉdâh**. See 8435.

8518. תָּלָה {28x} **tâlâh**, *taw-law';* a prim. root;
to *suspend* (espec. to *gibbet*):—
hang {25x}, hang up {3x}. See: TWOT—2512;
BDB—1067d.

8519. תְּלוּנָה {8x} **tᵉlûwnâh**, *tel-oo-naw';* or

תְּלֻנָּה **tᵉlunnâh**, *tel-oon-naw';* from
3885 in the sense of *obstinacy;* a
grumbling:—murmuring {8x}. See: TWOT—
1097a; BDB—534b, 1068d.

8520. תֶּלַח {1x} **Telach**, *teh'-lakh;* prob. from
an unused root mean. to *dissever;*
breach; Telach, an Isr.:—Telah {1x}. See:
BDB—1068b.

8521. תֵּל חַרְשָׁא {2x} **Têl Charshâʾ**, *tale khar-*
shaw'; from 8510 and the
fem. of 2798; *mound of workmanship; Tel-*
Charsha, a place in Bab.:—Tel-haresha {1x},
Tel-harsa {1x}. See: BDB—1068b.

8522. תְּלִי {1x} **tᵉlîy**, *tel-ee';* prob. from 8518;
a *quiver* (as *slung*):—quiver {1x}.
See: TWOT—2512a; BDB—1068a.

8523. תְּלִיתַי {2x} **tᵉlîythay** (Aram.), *tel-ee-*
thah'-ee; or

תַּלְתִּי **taltîy** (Aram.), *tal-tee';* ord. from
8532; *third:*—third {2x}. See:
TWOT—3058c; BDB—1118a.

8524. תָּלַל {1x} **tâlal**, *taw-lal';* a prim. root; to
pile up, i.e. *elevate:*—eminent {1x}.
See: TWOT—2513; BDB—1068c. comp. 2048.

8525. תֶּלֶם {5x} **telem**, *teh'-lem;* from an unused root mean. to *accumulate;* a

bank or *terrace:*—furrow {4x}, ridge {1x}. See: TWOT—2515a; BDB—1068d.

8526. תַּלְמַי {6x} **Talmay**, *tal-mah'-ee;* from 8525; *ridged; Talmai*, the name of a Canaanite and a Syrian:—Talmai {6x}. See: BDB—1068d.

8527. תַּלְמִיד {1x} **talmîyd**, *tal-meed';* from 3925; a *pupil:*—scholar {1x}. See: TWOT—1116c; BDB—541a, 1068d.

8528. תֵּל מֶלַח {2x} **Têl Melach**, *tale meh'-lakh;* from 8510 and 4417; *mound of salt; Tel-Melach*, a place in Bab.:—Tel-melah {2x}. See: BDB—1068b.

תְּלֻנָּה **tᵉlunnâh**. See 8519.

8529. תָּלַע {1x} **tâlaʻ**, *taw-law';* a denom. from 8438; to *crimson*, i.e. dye that color:—scarlet {1x}. See: TWOT—2516c; BDB—1069a.

תִּלְעַת **tôlaʻath**. See 8438.

8530. תַּלְפִּיָּה {1x} **talpîyâh**, *tal-pee-yaw';* fem. from an unused root mean. to *tower;* something *tall*, i.e. (plur. collect.) *slenderness:*—armoury {1x}. See: TWOT—2517; BDB—1069b.

תְּלַשָּׂר **Tᵉlassar**. See 8515.

8531. תְּלַת {2x} **tᵉlath** (Aram.), *tel-ath';* from 8532; a *tertiary* rank:—third {2x}. See: TWOT—3058b; BDB—1118a.

8532. תְּלָת {11x} **tᵉlâth** (Aram.), *tel-awth';* masc.

תְּלָתָה **tᵉlâthâh** (Aram.), *tel-aw-thaw';* or

תְּלָתָא **tᵉlâthâ** (Aram.), *tel-aw-thaw';* corresp. to 7969; *three* or *third:*—three {10x}, third {1x}. See: TWOT—3058a; BDB—1118a.

תַּלְתִּי **taltiy**. See 8523.

8533. תְּלָתִין {2x} **tᵉlâthîyn** (Aram.), *tel-aw-theen';* mult. of 8532; *ten times three:*—thirty {2x}. See: TWOT—3058d; BDB—1118a.

8534. תַּלְתַּל {1x} **taltal**, *tal-tal';* by redupl. from 8524 through the idea of *vibration;* a trailing *bough* (as *pendulous*):—bushy {1x}. See: TWOT—2513c; BDB—1068c, 1069b.

8535. תָּם {13x} **tâm**, *tawm;* from 8552; *complete;* usually (mor.) *pious;* spec. *gentle, dear:*—perfect {9x}, undefiled {2x}, plain {1x}, upright {1x}.

Tam means perfect and stresses integrity (Job 1:1). See: TWOT—2522c; BDB—1069b, 1070d.

8536. תָּם {4x} **tâm** (Aram.), *tawm;* corresp. to 8033; *there:*—there {2x}, where {1x}, thence {1x}. See: TWOT—3059; BDB—1118a.

8537. תֹּם {23x} **tôm**, *tome;* from 8552; *completeness;* fig. *prosperity;* usually (mor.) *innocence:*—integrity {11x}, upright {2x}, uprightly {2x}, uprightness {2x},venture {2x}, full {1x}, perfect {1x}, perfection {1x}, simplicity {1x}.

Tom signifies completeness in the following senses: **(1)** fullness (Job 21:23), **(2)** innocency or simplicity (2 Sa 15:11), **(3)** integrity (Gen 20:5). See: TWOT—2522a; BDB—1069b, 1070d, 1071b. See 8550.

תֵּמָא **Têmâ**. See 8485.

8538. תֻּמָּה {5x} **tummâh**, *toom-maw';* fem. of 8537; *innocence:*—integrity {5x}. See: TWOT—2522b; BDB—1069b, 1070d.

8539. תָּמַהּ {9x} **tâmahh**, *taw-mah';* a prim. root; to *be in consternation:*—marvel {3x}, wonder {2x}, marvellously {1x}, astonied {1x}, astonished {1x}, amazed {1x}. See: TWOT—2518; BDB—1069b.

8540. תְּמַהּ {3x} **tᵉmahh** (Aram.), *tem-ah';* from a root corresp. to 8539; a *miracle:*—wonder {3x}. See: TWOT—3060; BDB—1118b.

8541. תִּמָּהוֹן {2x} **timmâhôwn**, *tim-maw-hone';* from 8539; *consternation:*—astonishment {2x}. See: TWOT—2518a; BDB—1069b.

8542. תַּמּוּז {1x} **Tammûwz**, *tam-mooz';* of uncert. der.; *Tammuz*, a Phoenician deity:—Tammuz {1x}. See: TWOT—2519; BDB—1069c.

8543. תְּמוֹל {23x} **tᵉmôwl**, *tem-ole';* or

תְּמֹל **tᵉmôl**, *tem-ole';* prob. for 865; prop. *ago*, i.e. a (short or long) *time since;* espec. *yesterday*, or (with 8032) *day before yesterday:*—times past + 8032 {7x}, heretofore + 8032 {6x}, yesterday {4x}, as {3x}, beforetime + 8032 {2x}, about these days {1x}. See: TWOT—2521; BDB—1069d.

8544. תְּמוּנָה {10x} **tᵉmûwnâh**, *tem-oo-naw';* or

תְּמֻנָה **tᵉmûnâh**, *tem-oo-naw';* from 4327; *something portioned* (i.e. *fashioned*) out, as a *shape*, i.e. (indef.) *phantom*, or (spec.) *embodiment*, or (fig.) *manifestation* (of favor):—likeness {5x}, similitude {4x}, image {1x}.

This word does not refer to an idol, but to some form or outline that presented itself in vision; a likeness (see Ps 17:15). Syn.: 5566. See: TWOT—1191b; BDB—568b, 1069c.

8545. תְּמוּרָה {6x} te̱mûwrâh, *tem-oo-raw'*; from 4171; *barter, compensation:*—exchange {2x}, change {1x}, changing {1x}, recompense {1x}, restitution {1x}. See: TWOT—1164a; BDB—558c, 1069c.

8546. תְּמוּתָה {2x} te̱mûwthâh, *tem-oo-thaw'*; from 4191; *execution* (as a doom):—die {1x}, death {1x}.

Temuwthah means "death." One occurrence is in Ps 79:11: "Let the sighing of the prisoner come before thee; according to the greatness of thy power preserve thou those that are appointed to die [literally, sons of death]" (cf. Ps 102:20). See: TWOT—1169c; BDB—560d, 1069c.

8547. תֶּמַח {2x} Temach, *teh'-makh;* of uncert. der.; *Temach,* one of the Nethinim:—Thamah {1x}, Tamah {1x}. See: BDB—1069c.

8548. תָּמִיד {104x} tâmîyd, *taw-meed';* from an unused root mean. to *stretch;* prop. *continuance* (as indef. *extension*); but used only (attributively as adj.) *constant* (or adv. *constantly*); ellipt. the *regular* (daily) sacrifice:—continually {53x}, continual {26x}, daily {7x}, always {6x}, alway {4x}, ever {3x}, perpetual {2x}, continual employment {1x}, evermore {1x}, never {1x}.

Tamiyd means always; continually: regularly. (1) Tamiyd expresses continually, with continuity (Ex 25:30; Is 21:8; 2 Sa 9:7). (2) Tamiyd occurs most frequently of the daily rituals in the tabernacle and temple (Ex 29:38). (2a) Both ideas—regularity and continuousness—are present in the word. (2b) These rituals were to be performed regularly and without interruption for the duration of the old covenant. (3) The word is also used of God describing (3a) His visible presence at the tabernacle (Num 9:16), and (3b) His care for His people (Ps 40:11). (4) Tamiyd is also used of Jerusalem (Is 49:16). (5) The word describes man's response to God (Ps. 16:8; 34:1;119:44). (6) it is said of Zion eschatologically: "Therefore thy gates shall be open continually; they shall not be shut day nor night" (Is 60:11). (7) Tamiyd, the adjective, means continual (Ex 30:7–8; Num 28:6; Eze 46:15). Syn.: 753, 5331, 5703. See: TWOT—1157a; BDB—556b, 1069c.

8549. תָּמִים {91x} tâmîym, *taw-meem';* from 8552; *entire* (lit., fig. or mor.); also (as noun) *integrity, truth:*—without blemish {44x}, perfect {18x}, upright {8x}, without spot {6x}, uprightly {4x}, whole {4x}, sincerely {2x}, complete {1x}, full {1x}, sincerity {1x}, sound {1x}, undefiled {1x}.

Tamiym means perfect; blameless; sincerity; entire; whole; complete; full. (1) Tamiym means complete, in the sense of the entire or whole thing: (1a) the whole day (Josh 10:13), (1b) seven complete sabbaths (Lev 23:15), (1c) a full year (Lev 25:30). (2) This word may mean intact, not cut up into pieces (Eze 15:5). (3) *Tamiym* may mean incontestable or free from objection: (3a) God's work (Deut 32:4), (3b) an unblemished sacrifice (Lev 22:18–21). (4) When one is described by *tamiym,* there is nothing in his outward activities or internal disposition that is odious to God (Gen 6:9). This word describes his entire relationship to God. (5) Another adjective, *tam,* means (5a) complete or perfect (Song 5:2), (5b) sound or wholesome (Gen 25:27), and (5c) complete, morally innocent, having integrity (Job 1:8). See: TWOT—2522d; BDB—1070d.

8550. תֻּמִּים {5x} Tummîym, *toom-meem';* plur. of 8537; *perfections,* i.e. (tech.) one of the epithets of the objects in the high-priest's breastplate as an emblem of *complete* Truth:—Thummim {5x}. See: BDB—1070d.

8551. תָּמַךְ {21x} tâmak, *taw-mak';* a prim. root; to *sustain;* by impl. to *obtain, keep fast;* fig. to *help, follow close:*—hold {7x}, uphold {5x}, retain {4x}, hold up {2x}, misc. {3x} = maintain {1x}, stay {1x}, stay up {1x}. See: TWOT—2520; BDB—1064a, 1069c.

תְּמֹל te̱môl. See 8543.

8552. תָּמַם {64x} tâmam, *taw-mam';* a prim. root; to *complete,* in a good or a bad sense, lit. or fig., tran. or intr. (as follows):—consume {26x}, end {9x}, finished {4x}, clean {3x}, upright {3x}, spent {3x}, perfect {2x}, done {2x}, failed {2x}, accomplish {2x}, misc. {8x} = cease, come to the full, be all gone, × be all here, sum, be wasted, whole.

Tamam means to be complete, finished, perfect, spent, sound, used up, have integrity. (1) The basic meaning of this word is that of being complete or finished, with nothing else expected or intended. (2) The temple was finished or complete (1 Kin 6:22). (3) Tamam is sometimes used to express the fact that something is completed or finished with regard to its supply: (3a) money (Gen 47:15, 18); (3b) bread (Jer 37:21); and (3c) a people (Num 14:35). (4) Tamam expresses moral and ethical soundness (Ps 19:13). See: TWOT—2522; BDB—1064a, 1070b.

תֵּמָן têmân, Têmân. See 8486, 8487.

8553. תִּמְנָה {12x} Timnâh, *tim-naw';* from 4487; a *portion* assigned; *Timnah,* the name of two places in Pal.:—Timnath {8x},

Timnah {3x}, Thimnathah {1x}. See: BDB— 584c, 1071b.

תְּמֻנָה **t⁰mûnâh**. See 8544.

8554. תִּמְנִי {1x} **Timnîy**, *tim-nee'*; patrial from 8553; a *Timnite* or inhab. of Tim- nah:—Timnite {1x}. See: BDB—584d, 1071b.

8555. תִּמְנָע {6x} **Timnâ͑**, *tim-naw'*; from 4513; *restraint*; *Timna*, the name of two Edomites:—*Timna* {4x}, Timnah {2x}. See: BDB—586b, 1071b.

8556. תִּמְנַת חֶרֶס {3x} **Timnath Chereç**, *tim- nath kheh'-res*; or

תִּמְנַת סֶרַח **Timnath Çerach**, *tim-nath seh'-rakh*; from 8553 and 2775; *portion of* (the) *sun*; *Timnath-Cheres*, a place in Pal.:—Timnathserah {2x}, Timnathhe- res {1x}. See: BDB—584b, 1071b.

8557. תֶּמֶס {1x} **temeç**, *teh'-mes*; from 4529; *liquefaction*, i.e. *disappearance*:— melt {1x}. See: TWOT—1223c; BDB—588a, 1071b.

8558. תָּמָר {12x} **tâmâr**, *taw-mawr'*; from an unused root mean. to *be erect*; a *palm* tree:—palm tree {12x}. See: TWOT— 2523; BDB—1071c.

8559. תָּמָר {24x} **Tâmâr**, *taw-mawr'*; the same as 8558; *Tamar*, the name of three women and a place:—Tamar {24x}. See: BDB— 1062b, 1071c.

8560. תֹּמֶר {2x} **tômer**, *to'-mer*; from the same root as 8558; a *palm* trunk:—palm tree {2x}. See: TWOT—2523a; BDB—1071c.

8561. תִּמֹּר {19x} **timmôr** (plur. only), *tim- more'*; or (fem.)

תִּמֹּרָה **timmôrâh** (sing. and plur.), *tim- mo-raw'*; from the same root as 8558; (arch.) a *palm*-like pilaster (i.e. *umbel- late*):—palm tree {19x}. See: TWOT—2523c; BDB—1071c.

תַּמֹּר **Tammôr**. See 8412.

תִּמְרָה **timârâh**. See 8490.

8562. תַּמְרוּק {4x} **tamrûwq**, *tam-rook'*; or

תַּמְרֻק **tamrûq**, *tam-rook'*; or

תַּמְרִיק **tamrîyq**, *tam-reek'*; from 4838; prop. a *scouring*, i.e. *soap* or *perfumery* for the bath; fig. a *detergent*:— things for purification {2x}, purifying {1x}, cleanse {1x}. See: TWOT—1246b; BDB—600a, 1071d.

8563. תַּמְרוּר {3x} **tamrûwr**, *tam-roor'*; from 4843; *bitterness* (plur. as col-

lect.):—bitter {2x}, bitterly {1x}. See: TWOT— 1248L; BDB—601b, 1071d.

תַּמְרֻק **tamrûq** and

תַּמְרִיק **tamrîyq**. See 8562.

8564. תַּמְרוּר {1x} **tamrûwr**, *tam-roor'*; from the same root as 8558; an *erec- tion*, i.e. *pillar* (prob. for a guide-board):—high heaps {1x}. See: TWOT—2523e; BDB—1071d.

8565. תַּן {1x} **tan**, *tan*; from an unused root prob. mean. to *elongate*; a *monster* (as preternaturally formed), i.e. a *sea-serpent* (or other huge marine animal); also a *jackal* (or other hideous land animal):—whale {1x}. See: TWOT—2528a; BDB—1071d, 1072b. comp. 8577.

8566. תָּנָה {2x} **tânâh**, *taw-naw'*; a prim. root; to *present* (a mercenary induce- ment), i.e. *bargain* with (a harlot):—hired {2x}. See: TWOT—2524; BDB—1071d.

8567. תָּנָה {2x} **tânâh**, *taw-naw'*; a prim. root [rather ident. with 8566 through the idea of *attributing* honor]; to *ascribe* (praise), i.e. *celebrate, commemorate*:—lament {1x}, rehearse {1x}. See: TWOT—2525; BDB— 1072a.

8568. תַּנָּה {1x} **tannâh**, *tan-naw'*; prob. fem. of 8565; a female *jackal*:—dragon {1x}. See: TWOT—2528b; BDB—1072b.

8569. תְּנֻאָה {2x} **t⁰nûw᾽âh**, *ten-oo-aw'*; from 5106; *alienation*; by impl. en- *mity*:—occasion {1x}, breach of promise {1x}. See: TWOT—1317a; BDB—626b, 1072a.

8570. תְּנוּבָה {5x} **t⁰nûwbâh**, *ten-oo-baw'*; from 5107; *produce*:—fruit {3x}, increase {2x}. See: TWOT—1318c; BDB— 626c, 1072a.

8571. תְּנוּךְ {8x} **t⁰nûwk**, *ten-ook'*; perh. from the same as 594 through the idea of *protraction*; a *pinnacle*, i.e. *extremity*:—tip {8x}. See: TWOT—2527a; BDB—1072a.

8572. תְּנוּמָה {5x} **t⁰nûwmâh**, *ten-oo-maw'*; from 5123; *drowsiness*, i.e. *sleep*:—slumber {4x}, slumbering {1x}. See: TWOT—1325b; BDB—630b, 1072a.

8573. תְּנוּפָה {30x} **t⁰nûwphâh**, *ten-oo-faw'*; from 5130; a *brandishing* (in threat); by impl. *tumult*; spec. the official un- *dulation* of sacrificial offerings:—wave offer- ing {14x}, wave {8x}, offering {6x}, shaking {2x}. See: TWOT—1330b; BDB—632b, 1072a.

8574. תַּנּוּר {15x} **tannûwr**, *tan-noor'*; from 5216; a *fire-pot*:—oven {11x}, fur- nace {4x}. See: TWOT—2526; BDB—1072a.

8575. תַּנְחוּם {5x} **tanchûwm**, *tan-khoom';* or

תַּנְחֻם **tanchûm**, *tan-khoom';* and (fem.)

תַּנְחוּמָה **tanchûwmâh**, *tan-khoo-maw';* from 5162; *compassion, solace:* — consolation {4x}, comfort {1x}. See: TWOT — 1344d; BDB — 637c, 1072b.

8576. תַּנְחֻמֶת {2x} **Tanchûmeth**, *tan-khoo'-meth;* for 8575 (fem.); *Tanchumeth,* an Isr.: — Tanhumeth {2x}. See: BDB — 637c, 1072b.

8577. תַּנִּין {28x} **tannîyn**, *tan-neen';* or

תַּנִּים **tannîym** (Eze 29:3), *tan-neem';* intens. from the same as 8565; a marine or land *monster,* i.e. *sea-serpent* or *jackal:* — dragon {21x}, serpent {3x}, whale {3x}, sea monster {1x}. See: TWOT — 2528b; BDB — 1072c.

8578. תִּנְיָן {1x} **tinyân** (Aram.), *tin-yawn';* corresp. to 8147; *second:* — second {1x}. See: TWOT — 3061a; BDB — 1118b.

8579. תִּנְיָנוּת {1x} **tinyânûwth** (Aram.), *tin-yaw-nooth';* from 8578; a *second time:* — again {1x}. See: TWOT — 3061b; BDB — 1118b.

8580. תַּנְשֶׁמֶת {3x} **tanshemeth**, *tan-sheh'-meth;* from 5395; prop. a hard *breather,* i.e. the name of two unclean creatures, a lizard and a bird (both perh. from changing color through their *irascibility*), prob. the *tree-toad* and the *water-hen:* — swan {2x}, mole {1x}. See: TWOT — 1433b; BDB — 675d, 1072d.

8581. תָּעַב {22x} **tâʿab**, *taw-ab';* a prim. root; to *loathe,* i.e. (mor.) *detest:* — abhor {14x}, abominable {6x}, abominably {1x}, utterly {1x}.

Ta'ab means to abhor, treat as abhorrent, cause to be an abomination, act abominably: Deut 7:26: "Neither shalt thou bring an abomination into thine house." See: TWOT — 2530; BDB — 1073a.

תּוֹעֵבָה **tôʿêbâh**. See 8441.

8582. תָּעָה {50x} **tâʿâh**, *taw-aw';* a prim. root; to *vacillate,* i.e. *reel* or *stray* (lit. or fig.); also caus. of both: — err {17x}, astray {12x}, wander {10x}, seduced {3x}, stagger {2x}, out of the way {2x}, away {1x}, deceived {1x}, dissemble {1x}, pant {1x}. See: TWOT — 2531; BDB — 1073b.

8583. תֹּעוּ {5x} **Tôʿûw**, *to'-oo;* or

תֹּעִי **Tôʿîy**, *to'-ee;* from 8582; *error, Tou* or *Toi,* a Syrian king: — Toi {3x}, Tou {2x}. See: BDB — 1073d.

8584. תְּעוּדָה {3x} **tᵉʿûwdâh**, *teh-oo-daw';* from 5749; *attestation,* i.e. a *precept, usage:* — testimony {3x}. See: TWOT — 1576g; BDB — 730c, 1073d.

8585. תְּעָלָה {11x} **tᵉʿâlâh**, *teh-aw-law';* from 5927; a *channel* (into which water is *raised* for irrigation); also a *bandage* or *plaster* (as placed *upon* a wound): — conduit {4x}, trench {3x}, watercourse {1x}, healing {1x}, cured {1x}, little rivers {1x}. See: TWOT — 1624n, 1624o; BDB — 752b, 1073d.

8586. תַּעֲלוּל {2x} **taʿălûwl**, *tah-al-ool';* from 5953; *caprice* (as a fit *coming on*), i.e. *vexation;* concr. a *tyrant:* — babe {1x}, delusion {1x}. See: TWOT — 1627f; BDB — 760c, 1073d.

8587. תַּעֲלֻמָה {3x} **taʿălummâh**, *tah-al-oom-maw';* from 5956; a *secret:* — secret {2x}, thing that is hid {1x}. See: TWOT — 1629a; BDB — 761b, 1073d.

8588. תַּעֲנוּג {5x} **taʿănûwg**, *tah-an-oog';* or

תַּעֲנֻג **taʿănûg**, *tah-an-oog';* and (fem.)

תַּעֲנֻגָה **taʿănûgâh**, *tah-ah-oog-aw';* from 6026; *luxury:* — delight {3x}, delicate {1x}, pleasant {1x}. See: TWOT — 1648c; BDB — 772c, 1073b.

8589. תַּעֲנִית {1x} **taʿănîyth**, *tah-an-eeth';* from 6031; *affliction* (of self), i.e. *fasting:* — heaviness {1x}. See: TWOT — 1652f; BDB — 777a, 1073d.

8590. תַּעֲנָךְ {7x} **Taʿănâk**, *tah-an-awk';* or

תַּעְנָךְ **Taʿnâk**, *tah-nawk';* of uncert. der.; *Taanak* or *Tanak,* a place in Pal.: — Taanach {6x}, Tanach {1x}. See: BDB — 1073d.

8591. תָּעַע {2x} **tâʿaʿ**, *taw-ah';* a prim. root; to *cheat;* by anal. to *maltreat:* — deceiver {1x}, misused {1x}. See: TWOT — 2532; BDB — 1073d.

8592. תַּעֲצֻמָה {1x} **taʿătsûmâh**, *tah-ats-oo-maw';* from 6105; *might* (plur. collect.): — power {1x}. See: TWOT — 1673e; BDB — 783b, 1074a.

8593. תַּעַר {13x} **taʿar**, *tah'-ar;* from 6168; a *knife* or *razor* (as *making* bare): also a *scabbard* (as *being* bare, i.e. *empty*): — sheath {6x}, razor {4x}, penknife {1x}, scabbard {1x}, shave {1x}.

Ta'ar means "razor" (Num 6:5), a "knife" to sharpen scribal pens (Jer 36:23), or "sword sheath" (1 Sa 17:51). Syn.: Morah (4177) also means "razor"(1 Sa 1:11). See: TWOT — 1692e; BDB — 789b, 1074a.

8594. תַּעֲרֻבָה {2x} **taʿărûbâh**, *tah-ar-oo-baw';* from 6148; *suretyship,* i.e. (concr.)

a *pledge:*—hostage {2x}. See: TWOT—1686d; BDB—787a, 1074a.

8595. תַּעְתֻּעַ {2x} **ta‘tûa‘**, *tah-too’-ah;* from 8591; a *fraud:*—error {2x}. See: TWOT—2532a; BDB—1074a.

8596. תֹּף {17x} **tôph**, *tofe;* from 8608 contr.; a *tambourine:*—timbrel {9x}, tabret {8x}. See: TWOT—2536a; BDB—1074a, 1074b.

8597. תִּפְאָרָה {51x} **tiph’ârâh**, *tif-aw-raw’;* or

תִּפְאֶרֶת **tiph’ereth**, *tif-eh’-reth;* from 6286; *ornament* (abstr. or concr., lit. or fig.):—glory {22x}, beauty {10x}, beautiful {6x}, honour {4x}, fair {3x}, glorious {3x}, bravery {1x}, comely {1x}, excellent {1x}.

Tiph’ereth means "glory; beauty; ornament; distinction; pride." **(1)** The word represents "beauty," in the sense of the characteristic enhancing one's appearance: "And thou shalt make holy garments for Aaron thy brother for glory and for beauty" (Ex 28:2—the first occurrence). **(2)** In Is 4:2, the word identifies the fruit of the earth as the "beauty" or "adornment" of the survivors of Israel. **(3)** *Tip’ereth* (or the feminine form, *tip’arah*) means "glory" in several instances. **(3a)** The word is used of one's rank. A crown of "glory" is a crown which, by its richness, indicates high rank—Wisdom will "[present you with] a crown of glory" (Prov 4:9). **(3b)** "The hoary head is a crown of glory" (Prov 16:31), **(3c)** a reward for righteous living. **(3c)** In Is 62:3, the phrase "crown of glory" is paralleled by "royal diadem." **(4)** This word also modifies **(4a)** the greatness of a king (Est 1:4) and **(4b)** the greatness of the inhabitants of Jerusalem (Zec 12:7). **(4c)** In each of these instances, this word emphasizes the rank of the persons or things so modified. **(5)** The word is used of one's renown: "And to make thee high above all nations which he hath made, in praise, and in name, and in honor [distinction]" (Deut 26:19). **(6)** In another related nuance, *tip’eret* (or *tip’arah*) is used of God, to emphasize His rank, renown, and inherent "beauty": "Thine, O Lord, is the greatness, and the power, and the glory, and the victory, and the majesty" (1 Chr 29:11). **(7)** This word represents the "honor" of a nation, in the sense of its position before God: **(7a)** "[He has] cast down from heaven unto the earth the beauty [honor or pride] of Israel" (Lam 2:1). **(7b)** This nuance is especially clear in passages such as Judg 4:9: "I will surely go with thee: notwithstanding the journey that thou takest shall not be for thine honor [i.e., distinction]; for the Lord shall sell Sisera into the hand of a woman." **(8)** In Is 10:12, *tip’eret* (or *tip’arah*) represents a raising of oneself to a high rank in one's own eyes: "I will punish the fruit of the stout heart of the king of Assyria, and the glory of his high looks." Syn.: 6286. See: TWOT—1726b; BDB—802c, 1074a.

8598. תַּפּוּחַ {6x} **tappûwach**, *tap-poo’-akh;* from 5301; an *apple* (from its *fragrance*), i.e. the fruit or the tree (prob. includ. others of the *pome* order, as the quince, the orange, etc.):—apple tree {3x}, apple {3x}. See: TWOT—1390c; BDB—656b, 745d, 1074a. See also 1054.

8599. תַּפּוּחַ {6x} **Tappûwach**, *tap-poo’-akh;* the same as 8598; *Tappuach,* the name of two places in Pal., also of an Isr.:—Tappuah {6x}. See: BDB—656b, 1074a.

8600. תְּפוֹצָה {1x} **t⁰phôwtsâh**, *tef-o-tsaw’;* from 6327; a *dispersal:*—dispersion {1x}. See: TWOT—1745b; BDB—807b, 1074a.

8601. תֻּפִין {1x} **tûphîyn**, *too-feen’;* from 644; *cookery,* i.e. (concr.) a *cake:*—baken {1x}. See: TWOT—2533; BDB—1074a.

8602. תָּפֵל {7x} **tâphêl**, *taw-fale’;* from an unused root mean. to *smear; plaster* (as *gummy*) or *slime;* (fig.) *frivolity:*—untempered {5x}, foolish {1x}, unsavoury {1x}. See: TWOT—2534a, 2535a; BDB—1074a, 1074b.

8603. תֹּפֶל {1x} **Tôphel**, *to’-fel;* from the same as 8602; *quagmire; Tophel,* a place near the desert:—Tophel {1x}. See: BDB—1074b.

8604. תִּפְלָה {3x} **tiphlâh**, *tif-law’;* from the same as 8602; *frivolity:*—folly {2x}, foolishly {1x}. See: TWOT—2534b; BDB—1074a.

8605. תְּפִלָּה {77x} **t⁰phillâh**, *tef-il-law’;* from 6419; *intercession, supplication;* by impl. a *hymn:*—prayer {77x}.

Tephillah means "prayer." **(1)** This word is the most general Hebrew word for "prayer." **(1a)** It first appears in 1 Kin 8:28: "Yet have thou respect unto the prayer of thy servant, and to his supplication." **(1b)** In the eschaton God's house will be a house of "prayer" for all peoples (Is 56:7); **(1c)** it will be in this house that all nations will come to worship God. **(2)** The word can mean both a non-liturgical, non-poetical "prayer" and a liturgical, poetical "prayer." **(2a)** In the latter special meaning *tephillah* is used as a psalm title in 5 psalms and as the title of Habakkuk's prayer (Hab 3:1). **(2c)** In these uses *tephillah* means a prayer set to music and sung in the formal worship service. **(3)** In Ps 72:20 the word describes all the psalms or "prayers" of Psalms 1—72, only one of which is specifically called a "prayer" (17:1). Syn.: 6419. See: TWOT—1776a; BDB—813c, 1074b.

8606. תִּפְלֶצֶת {1x} **tiphletseth**, *tif-leh'-tseth;* from 6426; *fearfulness:*—terribleness {1x}. See: TWOT—1778c; BDB—814a, 1074b.

8607. תִּפְסַח {2x} **Tiphçach**, *tif-sakh';* from 6452; *ford; Tiphsach,* a place in Mesopotamia:—Tiphsah {2x}. See: BDB—820b, 1074b.

8608. תָּפַף {2x} **tâphaph**, *taw-faf';* a prim. root; *to drum,* i.e. play (as) on the tambourine:—playing with timbrels {1x}, tabering {1x}. See: TWOT—2536; BDB—1074c.

8609. תָּפַר {4x} **tâphar**, *taw-far';* a prim. root; *to sew:*—sew {4x}. See: TWOT—2537; BDB—1074c.

8610. תָּפַשׂ {65x} **tâphas**, *taw-fas';* a prim. root; *to manipulate,* i.e. *seize;* chiefly to *capture, wield;* spec. to *overlay;* fig. to *use* unwarrantably:—take {27x}, taken {12x}, handle {8x}, hold {8x}, catch {4x}, surprised {2x}, misc. {4x} = stop, X surely.

Taphas means to catch, seize, lay hold of, grasp, play. **(1)** This verb expresses the idea of grasping something in one's hand in order to use it (Gen 4:21). **(2)** Other things that are seized with the hand are: **(2a)** swords (Eze 21:11), **(2b)** shields (Jer 46:9), **(2c)** bows (Amos 2:15), and **(2d)** sickles (Jer 50:16). **(3)** To seize someone may be to arrest him (Jer 37:14). **(4)** Frequently, *taphas* is used in the sense of to capture (Josh 8:23). Syn.: 270. See: TWOT—2538; BDB—1074c.

8611. תֹּפֶת {1x} **tôpheth**, *to'-feth;* from the base of 8608; a *smiting,* i.e. (fig.) *contempt:*—spit {1x}. See: TWOT—2499a; BDB—1064b, 1075a.

8612. תֹּפֶת {9x} **Tôpheth**, *to'-feth;* the same as 8611; *Topheth,* a place near Jerusalem:—Tophet {8x}, *Topheth* {1x}. See: TWOT—2539; BDB—1064b, 1075a, 1075b.

8613. תָּפְתֶּה {1x} **Tophteh**, *tof-teh';* prob. a form of 8612; *Tophteh,* a place of cremation:—Tophet {1x}. See: BDB—1075a.

8614. תִּפְתָּי {2x} **tiphtay** (Aram.), *tif-tah'-ee;* perh. from 8199; *judicial,* i.e. a *lawyer:*—sheriffs {2x}. See: TWOT—3062; BDB—1118b.

תֹּצָאָה **tôtsâʾâh.** See 8444.

8615. תִּקְוָה {34x} **tiqvâh**, *tik-vaw';* from 6960; lit. a *cord* (as an *attachment* [comp. 6961]); fig. *expectancy:*—hope {23x}, expectation {7x}, line {2x}, the thing that I long for {1x}, expected {1x}. See: TWOT—1994d, 1994e; BDB—876c, 1075b.

8616. תִּקְוָה {3x} **Tiqvâh**, *tik-vaw';* the same as 8615; *Tikvah,* the name of two Isr.:—Tikvah {2x}, Tikvath {1x}. See: BDB—876b, 1075b.

8617. תְּקוּמָה {1x} **teqûwmâh**, *tek-oo-maw';* from 6965; *resistfulness:*—power to stand {1x}. See: TWOT—1999g; BDB—879c, 1075b.

8618. תְּקוֹמֵם {1x} **teqôwmêm**, *tek-o-mame';* from 6965; an *opponent:*—that rise up against thee {1x}. See: TWOT—1999; BDB—878c, 879d, 1075b.

8619. תָּקוֹעַ {1x} **tâqôwaʿ**, *taw-ko'-ah;* from 8628 (in the musical sense); a *trumpet:*—trumpet {1x}. See: TWOT—2541b; BDB—1075d.

8620. תְּקוֹעַ {7x} **Teqôwaʿ**, *tek-o'-ah;* a form of 8619; *Tekoa,* a place in Pal.:—Tekoa {6x}, Tekoah {1x}. See: BDB—1075d.

8621. תְּקוֹעִי {17x} **Teqôwʿîy**, *tek-o-ee';* or

תְּקֹעִי **Teqôʿîy**, *tek-o-ee';* patron. from 8620; a *Tekoite* or inhab. of Tekoah:—Tekoite {5x}, Tekoah {2x}. See: BDB—1075d.

8622. תְּקוּפָה {4x} **teqûwphâh**, *tek-oo-faw';* or

תְּקֻפָה **teqûphâh**, *tek-oo-faw';* from 5362; a *revolution,* i.e. (of the sun) *course,* (of time) *lapse:*—end {2x}, circuit {1x}, come about {1x}. See: TWOT—2001a; BDB—880d, 1075b.

8623. תַּקִּיף {1x} **taqqîyph**, *tak-keef';* from 8630; *powerful:*—mightier {1x}. See: TWOT—2542b; BDB—1076a.

8624. תַּקִּיף {5x} **taqqîyph** (Aram.), *tak-keef';* corresp. to 8623:—strong {3x}, mighty {2x}. See: TWOT—3065c; BDB—1118c.

8625. תְּקַל {3x} **teqal** (Aram.), *tek-al';* corresp. to 8254; *to balance:*—Tekel {2x}, weighed {1x}. See: TWOT—3063, 3063a; BDB—1101b, 1118c.

8626. תָּקַן {3x} **tâqan**, *taw-kan';* a prim. root; *to equalize,* i.e. *straighten* (intr. or tran.); fig. *to compose:*—make straight {2x}, set in order {1x}. See: TWOT—2540; BDB—1075b, 1118c.

8627. תְּקַן {1x} **teqan** (Aram.), *tek-an';* corresp. to 8626; *to straighten* up, i.e. *confirm:*—established {1x}. See: TWOT—3064; BDB—1118c.

8628. תָּקַע {69x} **tâqaʿ**, *taw-kah';* a prim. root; *to clatter,* i.e. *slap* (the hands together), *clang* (an instrument); by anal. *to drive* (a nail or tent-pin, a dart, etc.); by impl. *become bondsman* (by handclasping):—blow

{46x}, fasten {5x}, strike {4x}, pitch {3x}, thrust {2x}, clap {2x}, sounded {2x}, cast {1x}, misc. {4x} = smite, × suretiship.

Taqa' means to strike, give a blast, clap, blow, drive. **(1)** Striking or driving a tent peg means **(1a)** pitching a tent (Gen 31:25); and **(1b)** was used of Jael's driving the peg into Sisera's temple (Judg 4:21). **(2)** *Taqa'* describes **(2a)** the strong west wind that drove the locusts into the Red Sea (Ex 10:19), **(2b)** striking one's hands in praise or triumph (Ps 47:1), or **(2c)** to shake hands was a surety or guarantor of the agreement. (Prov 6:1; 17:18; 22:26). **(3)** *Taqa'* expresses giving a blast on a trumpet (Josh 6:4, 8–9, 13, 16, 20). See: TWOT—2541; BDB—1075b.

8629. תְּקַע {1x} **têqaᶜ**, *tay-kah';* from 8628; a blast of a trumpet:—sound {1x}. See: TWOT—2541a; BDB—1075d.

    תְּקֹעִי **Tᵉqôᶜîy**. See 8621.

8630. תָּקַף {3x} **tâqaph**, *taw-kaf';* a prim. root; to *overpower:*—prevail {3x}. See: TWOT—2542; BDB—1075d, 1118c.

8631. תְּקַף {5x} **tᵉqêph** (Aram.), *tek-afe';* corresp. to 8630; to *become* (caus. *make*) *mighty* or (fig.) *obstinate:*— . . . strong {3x}, harden {1x}, make firm {1x}. Syn.: 2388, 3513, 7188. See: TWOT—3065; BDB—1118c.

8632. תְּקֹף {2x} **tᵉqôph** (Aram.), *tek-ofe';* corresp. to 8633; *power:*—strength {1x}, might {1x}. See: TWOT—3065b; BDB—1118c.

8633. תֹּקֶף {3x} **tôqeph**, *to'-kef;* from 8630; *might* or (fig.) *positiveness:*—power {1x}, strength {1x}, authority {1x}. See: TWOT—2542a; BDB—1076a.

    תְּקֻפָה **tᵉqûphâh**. See 8622.

    תֹּר **tôr**. See 8447, 8449.

8634. תַּרְאֵלָה {1x} **Tarʾălâh**, *tar-al-aw';* prob. for 8653; a *reeling; Taralah,* a place in Pal.:—*Taralah* {1x}. See: BDB—1076a.

8635. תַּרְבּוּת {1x} **tarbûwth**, *tar-booth';* from 7235; *multiplication,* i.e. *progeny:*—increase {1x}.

Tarbuwth has a single appearance to mean "increase": "And, behold, ye are risen up in your fathers' stead, an increase (*tarbuwth*) of sinful men, to augment yet the fierce anger of the LORD toward Israel" (Num 32:14). See: TWOT—2103e; BDB—916b, 1076a.

8636. תַּרְבִּית {6x} **tarbîyth**, *tar-beeth';* from 7235; *multiplication,* i.e. *percentage* or *bonus* in addition to principal:—increase {5x}, unjust gain {1x}.

Tarbiyth can mean "interest, increment, us-

ury": "Take thou no usury of him, or increase: but fear thy God; that thy brother may live with thee" (Lev 25:36). See: TWOT—2103f; BDB—916b.

8637. תִּרְגַּל {1x} **tirgal**, *teer-gal';* a denom. from 7270; to *cause to walk:*—to go {1x}. See: TWOT—2113; BDB—920b, 1076a.

8638. תִּרְגַּם {1x} **tirgam**, *teer-gam';* a denom. from 7275 in the sense of *throwing* over; to *transfer,* i.e. *translate:*—interpreted {1x}. See: TWOT—2543; BDB—1076a.

    תֹּרָה **tôrâh**. See 8451.

8639. תַּרְדֵּמָה {7x} **tardêmâh**, *tar-day-maw';* from 7290; a *lethargy* or (by impl.) *trance:*—deep sleep {7x}. See: TWOT—2123a; BDB—922b, 1076b.

8640. תִּרְהָקָה {2x} **Tirhâqâh**, *teer-haw'-kaw;* of for. der.; *Tirhakah,* a king of Kush:—*Tirhakah* {2x}. See: BDB—1076b.

8641. תְּרוּמָה {76x} **tᵉrûwmâh**, *ter-oo-maw';* or

    תְּרֻמָה **tᵉrûmâh** (Deut 12:11), *ter-oo-maw';* from 7311; a *present* (as offered *up*), espec. in *sacrifice* or as *tribute:*—offering {51x}, oblation {19x}, heave {4x}, gifts {1x}, offered {1x}.

Terumah means "heave offering; offering; oblation." **(1)** *Terumah* is used for the first time in Ex 25:2: "Speak unto the children of Israel, that they bring me an offering: of every man that giveth it willingly with the heart ye shall take my offering." **(2)** In more than a third of its occurrences in the text, the KJV translates *terumah* as "heave offering," all of these instances being found in Exodus, Leviticus, Numbers (where the majority are found), and Deuteronomy. **(2a)** This translation apparently is derived from the fact that the word is based on the common Semitic root, "to be high, exalted." **(2b)** The inference seems to be that such "offerings" were raised high by the priest in some sort of motion as it was placed on the altar. **(2c)** This is clearly illustrated in Num 15:20: "Ye shall offer up a cake of the first of your dough for a heave offering: as ye do the heave offering of the threshing floor, so shall ye heave it." **(2d)** From texts like this, it appears that *terumah* was used in the early period to refer to "contributions" or "gifts" which consisted of the produce of the ground, reflecting the agricultural character of early Israel. See Deut 12:6, 11, 17 for other examples. **(3)** *Terumah* often is used to designate those gifts or contributions to God, but which were set apart specifically for the priests: "And every offering of all the holy things of the children of Israel, which they bring unto the priest,

shall be his" (Num 5:9). **(3a)** Such "offerings" were to go to the priests because of a special covenant God had made: "All the holy offerings which the people of Israel present to the Lord I give to you [Aaron], and to your sons and daughters with you, as a perpetual due; it is a covenant of salt for ever before the Lord for you and for your offspring with you" (Num 18:19). **(3b)** Such offerings, or contributions, sometimes were of grain or grain products: "Besides the cakes, he shall offer for his offering leavened bread with the sacrifice of thanksgiving of his peace offerings. And of it he shall offer one out of the whole oblation for a heave offering unto the Lord, and it shall be the priest's that sprinkleth the blood of the peace offerings" (Lev 7:13–14).

(4) Part of the animal sacrifices was also designated as a *terumah* for the priests: "And the right shoulder shall ye give unto the priest for a heave offering of the sacrifices of your peace offerings" (Lev 7:32; cf. Lev 10:14–15; Num 6:20). Such contributions to the priests obviously were given to provide the needed foodstuffs for the priests and their families since their tribe, Levi, was given no land on which to raise their own food. **(5)** While all the priests had to be from the tribe of Levi, inheriting their office through their fathers, not all Levites could function as priests. For one thing, there were too many of them. Also, some were needed to work in the tabernacle, and later the temple, as maintenance and cleanup people, something that is readily understandable when one thinks of all that was involved in the sacrificial system. The Levites actually lived in various parts of Israel, and they were the welfare responsibility of the Israelites among whom they lived. They, like the widow, the orphan, and the resident alien, were to be given the tithe of all farm produce every third year (Deut 14:28–29). The Levites, then, were to tithe the tithe they received, giving their own tithe from what they received from the people to the Lord. Part of that tithe was to be a *terumah* or "heave offering" to the priests, the descendants of Aaron (see Num 18:25–32).

(6) In order to provide for the materials necessary for the construction of the wilderness tabernacle, Moses was instructed to receive an "offering" or *terumah*. **(6a)** The "offering" was to consist of all kinds of precious metals and stones, as well as the usual building materials such as wood and skins (Ex 25:3–9). **(6b)** When Moses announced this to the people of Israel, he said: "Take ye from among you an offering unto the Lord; whosoever is of a willing heart, let him bring it, an offering of the Lord" (Ex 35:5), following this with a list of the needed

materials (Ex 35:6–8). **(6)** The implication here is twofold: the *terumah* is really the Lord's, and it is best given freely, willingly, from a generous heart. **(7)** In the Second Temple Period, following the Exile, the silver and gold and the vessels for the temple are called "the offering for the house of our God" (Ezra 8:25), also signifying a contribution.

(8) The *terumah* sometimes was an "offering" which had the meaning of a tax, an obligatory assessment which was made against every Israelite male who was twenty years old or older, to be paid for the support of the tabernacle and later, the temple (Ex 30:11–16). **(8a)** This tax was levied on all males without any allowance for their financial situation: "The rich shall not give more, and the poor shall not give less than half a shekel, when they give an offering unto the Lord, to make an atonement for your souls" (Ex 30:15). **(8c)** This tax actually had its basis in the census or count of the male population, the tax then being required as a ransom or atonement from the wrath of God because such a census was taken (2 Sa 24:1). **(8d)** The practical aspect of it was that it provided needed financial support for the sanctuary. **(9)** Another example of *terumah* in the sense of taxes may be seen in Prov 29:4: "The king by judgment establisheth the land; but he that receiveth gifts overthroweth it." Solomon's heavy taxation which led to the split of the kingdom may be a case in point (1 Kin 12).

(10) A very different use of *terumah* is found in Eze 45:1; 48:9, 29–21, where it refers to an "oblation" which was that portion of land on which the post-exilic temple was to be built, as well as accommodations for the priests and Levites. **(10a)** This tract of land is referred to as "the holy oblation" (Eze 48:20), **(10b)** since it belongs to God just as much as the *terumah* which was given to Him as a sacrifice. Syn.: 801, 817, 4503, 5930, 7133. See: TWOT—2133i; BDB—929a, 1076b.

8642. תְּרוּמִיָּה {1x} **t^erûwmîyâh**, *ter-oo-mee-yaw'*; formed as 8641; a sacrificial *offering:*—oblation {1x}. See: TWOT—2133j; BDB—929b, 1076b.

8643. תְּרוּעָה {36x} **t^erûw^câh**, *ter-oo-aw'*; from 7321; *clamor,* i.e. *acclamation* of joy or a *battle-cry;* espec. *clangor* of trumpets, as an *alarum:*—shout {11x}, shouting {8x}, alarm {6x}, sound {3x}, blowing {2x}, joy {2x}, jubile {1x}, loud noise {1x}, rejoicing {1x}, sounding {1x}. See: TWOT—2135b; BDB—929d, 1076b.

8644. תְּרוּפָה {1x} **t^erûwphâh**, *ter-oo-faw'*; from 7322 in the sense of its congener

7495; a *remedy:*—medicine {1x}. See: TWOT—2136a; BDB—930a, 1076b.

8645. תִּרְזָה {1x} **tirzâh**, *teer-zaw';* prob. from 7329; a species of tree (appar. from its *slenderness*), perh. the *cypress:*—cypress {1x}. See: TWOT—2543.1; BDB—1076b.

8646. תֶּרַח {13x} **Terach**, *teh'-rakh;* of uncert. der.; *Terach,* the father of Abraham; also a place in the desert:—Terah {11x}, Tarah {1x}, Tahath {1x}. See: BDB—1076b.

8647. תִּרְחֲנָה {1x} **Tirchănâh**, *teer-khan-aw';* of uncert. der.; *Tirchanah,* an Isr.:—Tirhanah {1x}. See: BDB—934b, 1076c.

8648. תְּרֵין {4x} **tʾrêyn** (Aram.), *ter-ane';* fem.

תַּרְתֵּין **tartêyn**, *tar-tane';* corresp. to 8147; *two:*—twelve + 6236 {2x}, two {1x}, second {1x}. See: TWOT—3061c; BDB—1118b, 1118d.

8649. תָּרְמָה {6x} **tormâh**, *tor-maw';* and

תַּרְמוּת **tarmûwth**, *tar-mooth';* or

תַּרְמִית **tarmîyth**, *tar-meeth';* from 7411; *fraud:*—deceit {4x}, deceitful {1x}, privily {1x}. See: TWOT—2169c; BDB—941b, 941c, 1076c.

תְּרָמָה **tʾrûmâh**. See 8641.

8650. תֹּרֶן {3x} **tôren**, *to'-ren;* prob. for 766; a *pole* (as a mast or flag-staff):—mast {2x}, beacon {1x}. See: TWOT—2544; BDB—1076c.

8651. תְּרַע {2x} **tʾra**ᶜ (Aram.), *ter-ah';* corresp. to 8179; a *door;* by impl. a *palace:*—gate {1x}, mouth {1x}. See: TWOT—3066; BDB—1118d.

8652. תָּרָע {1x} **târâ**ᶜ (Aram.), *taw-raw';* from 8651; a *doorkeeper:*—porters {1x}. See: TWOT—3067; BDB—1118d.

8653. תַּרְעֵלָה {3x} **tarʿêlâh**, *tar-ay-law';* from 7477; *reeling:*—trembling {2x}, astonishment {1x}. See: TWOT—2188c; BDB—947a, 1076c.

8654. תִּרְעָתִי {1x} **Tirʿâthîy**, *teer-aw-thee';* patrial from an unused name mean. *gate;* a *Tirathite* or inhab. of an unknown Tirah:—Tirathites {1x}. See: BDB—1076c.

8655. תְּרָפִים {15x} **tʾrâphîym**, *ter-aw-feme';* plur. perh. from 7495; a *healer;* *Teraphim* (sing. or plur.) a family idol:—image {7x}, teraphim {6x}, idol {1x}, idolatry {1x}.

Teraphiym means "idol; household idol; divine symbol." **(1)** Its basic meaning is "spirit" or "demon." **(2)** *Teraphiym* first appears in Gen 31:19: "And Laban went to shear his sheep: and Rachel had stolen the [household gods] that

were her father's." Hurrian law of this period recognized "household idols" as deeds to the family's succession and goods. This makes these *teraphim* (possibly a plural of majesty as is *elohim* when used of false gods; cf. 1 Kin 11:5, 33) extremely important to Laban in every way. **(3)** In 1 Sa 19:13 we read that "Michal took the *teraphim* [here a plural of "majesty"] and laid it on the bed, and put a quilt of goat's hair at its head, and covered it with blankets" (author's translation). In view of 1 Sa 19:11, where it is said that they were in David's private quarters, supposing that this *teraphim* was a "household idol" is difficult, although not impossible. This was probably a statue instead of an idol.

(4) In Judg 17:5: "Micah had a house of gods, and made an ephod, and *teraphim,* and consecrated one of his sons, who became his priest." In Judg 18:14 *teraphim* appears to be distinguished from idols: ". . . there is in these houses an ephod, and *teraphim,* and a graven image, and a molten image?" The verses that follow suggest that the graven image and the molten image may have been the same thing: Judg 18:17 uses all four words in describing what the Danites stole; Judg 18:20 omits "molten image" from the list; and Judg 18:31 reports that only the graven image was set up for worship. We know that the *ephod* was a special priestly garment. Syn.: 457. See: TWOT—2545; BDB—1076c.

8656. תִּרְצָה {18x} **Tirtsâh**, *teer-tsaw';* from 7521; *delightsomeness; Tirtsah,* a place in Pal.; also an Israelitess:—Tirzah {18x}. See: BDB—953c, 1076d.

8657. תֶּרֶשׁ {2x} **Teresh**, *teh'-resh;* of for. der.; *Teresh,* a eunuch of Xerxes:—Teresh {2x}. See: BDB—1076d.

8658. תַּרְשִׁישׁ {7x} **tarshîysh**, *tar-sheesh';* prob. of for. der. [comp. 8659]; a *gem,* perh. the *topaz:*—beryl {7x}. See: TWOT—2546; BDB—1076d.

8659. תַּרְשִׁישׁ {28x} **Tarshîysh**, *tar-sheesh';* prob. the same as 8658 (as the region of the stone, or the reverse); *Tarshish,* a place on the Mediterranean, hence, the epithet of a *merchant* vessel (as if for or from that port); also the name of a Pers. and of an Isr.:—Tarshish {24x}, Tharshish {4x}. See: TWOT—2547; BDB—1076d.

8660. תִּרְשָׁתָא {5x} **Tirshâthâ**, *teer-shaw-thaw';* of for. der.; the title of a Pers. deputy or *governor:*—Tirshatha {5x}. See: TWOT—2548; BDB—1077a.

תַּרְתֵּין **tartêyn**. See 8648.

8661. תַּרְתָּן {2x} **Tartân**, *tar-tawn';* of for. der.; *Tartan*, an Ass.:—*Tartan* {2x}. See: TWOT—2549; BDB—1077a.

8662. תַּרְתָּק {1x} **Tartâq**, *tar-tawk';* of for. der.; *Tartak*, a deity of the Avvites:—Tartak {1x}. See: BDB—1077b.

8663. תְּשָׁאָה {4x} **t^{e}shu'âh**, *tesh-oo-aw';* from 7722; a *crashing* or loud *clamor:*—noise {1x}, crying {1x}, stirs {1x}, shouting {1x}. See: TWOT—2339c; BDB—996c, 1077b.

תֹּשָׁב **tôshâb**. See 8453.

8664. תִּשְׁבִּי {6x} **Tishbîy**, *tish-bee';* patrial from an unused name mean. *recourse;* a *Tishbite* or inhab. of Tishbeh (in Gilead):—Tishbite {6x}. See: BDB—986c, 1077b.

8665. תַּשְׁבֵּץ {1x} **tashbêts**, *tash-bates';* from 7660; *checkered* stuff (as *reticulated*):—broidered {1x}. See: TWOT—2320c; BDB—990b, 1077b.

8666. תְּשׁוּבָה {8x} **t^{e}shûwbâh**, *tesh-oo-baw';* or

תְּשֻׁבָה **t^{e}shûbâh**, *tesh-oo-baw';* from 7725; a *recurrence* (of time or place); a *reply* (as *returned*):—return {3x}, expired {3x}, answers {2x}.

Teshubah may mean (1) "return" or "beginning": "And his return was to Ramah; for there was his house; and there he judged Israel; and there he built an altar unto the LORD" (1 Sa 7:17); and (2) "answer": "How then comfort ye me in vain, seeing in your answers (*teshubah*) there remaineth falsehood?" (Job 21:34). See: TWOT—2340f; BDB—1000c, 1077b.

8667. תְּשׁוּמֶת {1x} **t^{e}sûwmeth**, *tes-oo-meth';* from 7760; a *deposit,* i.e. *pledging:*—fellowship {1x}. Syn.: 7760. See: TWOT—2243a; BDB—965a, 1077b.

8668. תְּשׁוּעָה {34x} **t^{e}shûw'âh**, *tesh-oo-aw';* or

תְּשֻׁעָה **t^{e}shu'âh**, *tesh-oo-aw';* from 7768 in the sense of 3467; *rescue* (lit. or fig., Pers., national or spir.):—salvation {17x}, deliverance {5x}, help {5x}, safety {4x}, victory {3x}.

Teshu'ah means "deliverance." One example is Is 45:17: "But Israel shall be saved in the Lord with an everlasting salvation: ye shall not be ashamed nor confounded world without end." Syn.: 3444, 3467, 3468, 5414. See: TWOT—929e; BDB—448b, 1077b.

8669. תְּשׁוּקָה {3x} **t^{e}shûwqâh**, *tesh-oo-kaw';* from 7783 in the orig. sense of *stretching* out after; a *longing:*—desire {3x}. See: TWOT—2352a; BDB—1003c, 1077b.

8670. תְּשׁוּרָה {1x} **t^{e}shûwrâh**, *tesh-oo-raw';* from 7788 in the sense of *arrival;* a *gift:*—present {1x}. See: TWOT—2353a; BDB—1003d, 1077b.

תַּשְׁחֵת **tashchêth**. See 516.

תֻּשִׁיָּה **tûshîyâh**. See 8454.

8671. תְּשִׁיעִי {18x} **t^{e}shîy'îy**, *tesh-ee-ee';* ord. from 8672; *ninth:*—ninth {18x}. See: TWOT—2551; BDB—1077d.

תְּשֻׁעָה **t^{e}shu'âh**. See 8668.

8672. תֵּשַׁע {58x} **têsha'**, *tay'-shah;* or (masc.)

תִּשְׁעָה **tish'âh**, *tish-aw';* perh. from 8159 through the idea of a *turn* to the next or full number ten; *nine* or (ord.) *ninth:*—nine {45x}, ninth {6x}, nineteenth + 6240 {4x}, nineteen + 6240 {3x}. See: TWOT—2550; BDB—1077c.

8673. תִּשְׁעִים {20x} **tish'îym**, *tish-eem';* multiple from 8672; *ninety:*—ninety {20x}. See: TWOT—2552; BDB—1077d.

8674. תַּתְּנַי {4x} **Tatt^{e}nay**, *tat-ten-ah'-ee;* of for. der.; *Tattenai*, a Pers.:—Tatnai {4x}. See: BDB—1118d.

The New Strong's® Expanded Dictionary

of the Words in the

Greek New Testament

---

with their Renderings in the King James Version

and with Additional Definitions Adapted from W. E. Vine and Cross-references to Other Word Study Resources

Note regarding the Greek Dictionary: The numbering of Greek words skips *2717* and from *3202* to *3303*. This error in numbering is part of the original edition of the dictionary. Because the original numbering system (with these errors) has been used by so many Bible students and other Bible reference works, it has been left unchanged to avoid the confusion that would result from having an old and a new Strong's numbering system. The only error is the skipping of *numbers, not* the omission of Greek words. No Greek words that Strong listed in the original are missing from this dictionary.

Read this first!

How to Use the Greek Dictionary

For many people Strong's unique system of numbers continues to be *the* bridge between the original languages of the Bible and the English of the *King James Version* (AV). *Strong's Greek Dictionary* is a fully integrated companion to *Strong's Concordance,* and its entries contain a wealth of information about the words of the Bible in their original language. In order to enhance the strategic importance of the dictionary for Bible students, significant features have been added in this new, expanded edition.

New Features

The dictionary is designed to provide maximum information so that your word studies are enriching and satisfying. The most significant enhancement is the expanded definitions, which come from the best of standard word study resources such as *Vine's Complete Expository Dictionary of Old and New Testament Words* and *Thayer's Greek-English Lexicon of the New Testament.* The expanded definitions reveal the entire range of meanings so that the user can conduct more precise and accurate word studies. In addition, they help to convey the depth and richness of Greek words.

The second item that has been added is the frequency word counts, which appear in curly brackets {}. Frequency counts are provided for both the Greek and English words used in the King James Bible. For example, the Greek word *agathos* (entry #18) has {102x} following it. This means that this Greek word occurs 102 times in the Greek text. Then after the :— symbol, a list of English translations along with the number of times this English word is used in the AV is given. For example, the Greek word *agathos* is translated 77 times as "good," 14 times as "good thing," etc.

For those wanting to conduct more advanced word studies, a cross-reference to other lexicons is given at the end of the definition. These lexicons are *A Greek-English Lexicon of the New Testament and Other Christian Literature,* 2d ed., edited by Walter Bauer, William F. Arndt, F. Wilbur Gingrich, and Frederick Danker (University of Chicago, 1979); *Theological Dictionary of the New Testament,* edited by Gerhard Kittel and Gerhard Friedrich (Eerdmans, 1964–1974 [9-volume edition]; 1985 [1-volume edition]); and *Thayer's Greek-English Lexicon of the New Testament* (Baker, 1977). These first two lexicons are abbreviated as BAGD and TDNT. Thayer's lexicon is not abbreviated.

Using the Dictionary to Do Word Studies

Careful Bible students do word studies, and *The New Strong's® Expanded Dictionary of Bible Words* with enhanced *Greek Dictionary* offers unique assistance. Consider the word "love" as found in the AV. By skimming the main concordance, you find these numbers for Greek words that the King James Bible translates with the English word "love": *25, 5368, 26, 2309, 5360, 5365, 5362, 5388, 5363,* and *5361.* Now for any one Bible reference in this entry there is only one Greek word cited and you may be interested only in establishing the precise meaning for just that word in that occurrence. If so, it will be very helpful for you to observe that same Greek word in *each* of its occurrences in the Bible. In that way, you develop an idea of its possible range of meanings, and you can help clarify what is most likely the precise meaning in the specific Bible reference you are studying.

Now see the dictionary entry *25* itself, and notice that after the symbol :— all the words and word prefixes and suffixes are listed. These show you that this one Greek word, *agapao,* is translated into several different but related words in the King James Bible: beloved, love, loved. This list tells you the range of uses of the one Greek word in the AV. This information can help you distinguish between the nuances of the meaning found where this and the other Greek words are translated by these same words and similar ones in the King James Bible.

These three ways of using the dictionary in conjunction with *Strong's Concordance* show you only a sampling of the many ways *The New Strong's® Expanded Dictionary of Bible Words* can enrich your study of the Bible. (See also *Getting the Most from Your New Strong's® Exhaustive Bible Concordance,* Nelson, 2000.) The examples given above also show why it is important that you take the time to become familiar with each feature in the dictionary as illustrated on the following page.

An Example
from the
Greek New Testament Dictionary

Strong's number in *italics*, corresponding to the numbers at the ends of the context lines in the English Index.

An unnumbered cross-reference entry.

The word as it appears in the original Greek spelling.

Where appropriate, important discussion of multiple uses and functions of the word.

The Greek word represented in English letters in **bold** type (the transliteration).

Strong's syllable-by-syllable pronunciation in *italics*, with the emphasized syllable marked by the accent.

When the Greek word relates to a Hebrew or Aramaic word from the Old Testament, the Strong's numbers is encased in square brackets [...].

Brief English definitions (shown by *italics*).

ἀπέπω **apépō**. See 550.

728. ἀρραβών **arrhabōn**, *ar-hrab-ohn´;* of Heb. or. [6162]; a *pledge,* i.e. part of the purchase-money or property given in advance as *security* for the rest:— earnest.

3360. μέχρι **mĕchri** *mekh´-ree;* or

μεχρίς **mĕchris** *mekh-ris´;* from 3372; *as far as,* i.e. *up to* a certain point (as a prep. of extent [denoting the *terminus,* whereas *891* refers espec. to the *space* of time or place intervening] or a conjunc.):— till, (un-) to, until.

3361. μή **mē** *may;* a primary particle of qualified *negation* (whereas *3756* expresses an absolute denial); (adv.) *not,* (conjunc.) *lest;* also (as an interrog. implying a *neg.* answer [whereas *3756* expects an *affirmative* one]) *whether:*— any, but (that), × forbear, + God forbid, + lack, lest, neither, never, no (× wise in), none, nor, [can-] not, nothing, that not, un [-taken], without. Often used in compounds in substantially the same relations. See also *3362, 3363, 3364, 3372, 3373, 3375, 3378.*

See "Special Symbols."

Italic Strong's numbers refer to related Greek words in this Dictionary.

After the long dash (—), there is a complete, alphabetical listing of all ways this Greek word is translated in the KJV. (See also "Special Symbols").

Improved, consistent abbreviations. All abbreviations occur with their full spelling in the list of abbreviations.

Note that Greek spelling variations are conveniently indented for easy comparison.

Plan of the Greek Dictionary

1. All the original words are presented in their alphabetical order (according to Greek). They are numbered for easy matching between this dictionary and *Strong's Concordance*. Many reference books also use these same numbers created by Dr. Strong.

2. The number of times the Greek word occurs in the Greek New Testament is given in curly brackets {} with an "x" inside of it.

3. After each word, the exact equivalent of each sound (phoneme) is given in English characters, according to the transliteration system given below.

4. Next follows the precise pronunciation, with the proper stress mark.

5. Then comes the etymology, root meaning, and common uses of the word, along with other important related details. In the case of proper nouns, the normal English spelling is given.

6. After the colon and dash (:—), all the different ways that the word appears in the King James Bible are listed in alphabetical order. The number surrounded by curly brackets {} refers to the number of times this word is translated in the AV. When the Greek word appears in English as a phrase, the main word of the phrase is used to alphabetize it.

7. The main new feature of the dictionary is the expanded word studies. These provide the full range of meaning, and they give the student of the Bible all the various nuances of the word.

8. The information following "See" at the end of each entry provides cross-references to three other word study dictionaries. The first is the *Theological Dictionary of the Old Testament* (abbreviated TDNT). Following the TDNT abbreviation is the volume and page number for the 9-volume edition (e.g., 1:1 refers to volume 1, page 1). This is followed by a slash (/) and a number, which refers to the page number for the 1-volume edition. The second word study dictionary is *A Greek-English Lexicon of the New Testament and Other Christian Literature*, 2d ed. (abbreviated as BAGD). The third word study dictionary is *Thayer's Greek-English Lexicon of the New Testament*. The numbers for the final two resources refer to the page number and quadrant (e.g., 2d means page 2, quadrant d). The schema for quadrants is as follows: A   C
                                                                                                                    B   D

Transliteration and Pronunciation of the Greek

The following shows how the Greek words are transliterated into English in this Dictionary.

1. The *Alphabet* is as follows:

No.	Form upper	Name lower	Transliteration and Pronunciation	
1.	A	α	Alpha (*al´-fah*)	**a**, as in *Arm* or *mAn* [1]
2.	B	β	Bēta (*bay´-tah*)	**b**
3.	Γ	γ	Gamma (*gam´-mah*)	**g**, as in *Guard* [2]
4.	Δ	δ	Dĕlta (*del´-tah*)	**d**
5.	E	ε	Ĕpsilŏn (*ep´-see-lon*)	**ĕ**, as in *mEt*
6.	Z	ζ	Zēta (*dzay´-tah*)	**z**, as in *aDZe* [3]
7.	H	η	Ēta (*ay´-tah*)	**ē**, as in *thEy*
8.	Θ	θ	Thēta (*thay´-tah*)	**th**, as in *THin* [4]
9.	I	ι	Iota (*ee-o´-tah*)	**i**, as in *machIne* [5]
10.	K	κ	Kappa (*kap´-pah*)	**k**
11.	Λ	λ	Lambda (*lamb´-dah*)	**l**
12.	M	μ	Mu (*moo*)	**m**
13.	N	ν	Nu (*noo*)	**n**
14.	Ξ	ξ	Xi (*ksee*)	**x** = ks
15.	O	ο	Omikrŏn (*om´-e-cron*)	**ŏ**, as in *not*
16.	Π	π	Pi (*pee or pai*)	**p**
17.	P	ρ	Rhō (*hro*)	**r**
18.	Σ	σ, final ς	Sigma (*sig´-mah*)	**s** sharp
19.	T	τ	Tau (*tŏw*)	**t**, as in *Tree* [6]
20.	Υ	υ	Upsilŏn (*u´-pse-lon*)	**u**, as in *fUll*
21.	Φ	φ	Phi (*fee or fai*)	**ph** = f
22.	X	χ	Chi (*khee or khai*)	German **ch** [7]
23.	Ψ	ψ	Psi (*psee or psai*)	**ps**
24.	Ω	ω	Omĕga (*o´-meg-ah*)	**ō**, as in *no*

---

[1] *a*, when *final*, or before a final ρ or followed by any *other* consonant, is sounded like *a* in *Arm*; elsewhere like *a* in *mAn*.

[2] γ, when followed by γ, **k**, **c**, or ξ is sounded like *ng* in *kiNG*.

[3] ζ is always sounded like *dz*.

[4] θ never has the guttural sound, like *th* in *THis*.

[5] ι has the sound of *ee* when it *ends* an *accented* syllable; in other situations a more obscure sound, like *i* in *amIable* or *Imbecile*.

[6] τ never has an s-sound, like *t* in *naTion*.

[7] From the difficulty of producing the true sound of χ, it is generally sounded like *k*.

2. The mark ', placed over the *initial* vowel of a word, is called the *Rough Breathing*, and is equivalent to the English *h*, by which we have accordingly represented it. Its *absence* over an initial vowel is indicated by the mark ', called the *Smooth Breathing*, which is silent, and is therefore not represented in our method of transliteration. [8]

3. The following are the Greek *diphthongs*, properly so called: [9]

Form	Transliteration and Pronunciation
αι	**ai** (*ah'ee*) [ă + ē]
ει	**ei**, as in h*EI*ght
οι	**oi**, as in *OI*l
υι	**we**, as in s*WE*et
αυ	**ow**, as in n*OW*
ευ	**eu**, as in f*EU*d
ου	**ou**, as in thr*OU*gh

4. The *accent* (stress of voice) falls on the syllable where it is written. [10] It occurs in three forms: the *acute* ('), which is the only true accent; the *grave* (`) which is its substitute; and the *circumflex* (ˆ), which is the union of the two. The acute may stand on any one of the last *three* syllables, and in case it occurs on the final syllable, before another word in the same sentence, it is written as a grave. The grave is understood (but never written as such) on every other syllable. The circumflex is written on any syllable (necessarily the last syllable or next to the last syllable of a word) formed by the contraction of two syllables, of which the *first* would properly have the acute accent.

5. The following *punctuation* marks are used: the comma (,), the semicolon (·), the colon or period (.), the question mark (;), and by some editors, also the exclamation mark, parentheses, and quotation marks.

Special Symbols

+ (*addition*) denotes a rendering in the A.V. of one or more Greek words in connection with the one under consideration. For example, in Rev. 17:17, No. 1106, γνώμη (**gnōmē**) is translated as a verb ("to agree"), when it is actually a noun and part of a Greek idiom that is literally translated "to do one mind."

× (*multiplication*) denotes a rendering in the A.V. that results from an idiom peculiar to the Greek. For example, in Heb. 12:21, the whole Greek phrase in which ἔντρομος, **ĕntrŏmŏs** (1790) appears is a way of expressing great anxiety. The same idiom is used about Moses in Acts 7:32.

( ) (*parentheses*), in the renderings from the A.V., denote a word or syllable which is sometimes given in connection with the principal word to which it is attached. In Mark 15:39 there are two Greek prepositions (1537 and 1727) which are used together ("over against"). One English preposition, "opposite," communicates the same idea.

[ ] (*brackets*), in the rendering from the A.V., denote the inclusion of an additional word in the Greek. For example, No. 2596 κατά (**kata**) is translated "daily" in Luke 19:47, along with No. 2250 ἡμέρα (**hēmĕra**). So, two Greek words were translated by one English word.

Italics, at the end of a rendering from the A.V., denote an explanation of the variations from the usual form.

Note

Because of some changes in the numbering system (while the original work was in progress) no Greek words are cited for 2717 or 3203-3302. These numbers were dropped altogether. This will not cause any problems in *Strong's* numbering system. **No Greek words have been left out.** Because so many other reference works use this numbering system, it has **not** been revised. If it were revised, much confusion would certainly result.

---

[8] These signs are placed over the *second* vowel of a diphthong. The same is true of the accents.

The *Rough* Breathing always belongs to an initial υ.

The *Rough* Breathing is always used with ρ, that it begins a word. If this letter is doubled in the middle of a word, the first ρ takes the Smooth Breathing mark and the second ρ takes the Rough Breathing mark.

Since these signs cannot conveniently be written above the first letter of a word, when it is a *capital*, they are placed *before* it in such cases. This observation applies also to the *accents*. The aspiration *always* begins the syllable.

Occasionally, in consequence of a contraction (*crasis*), the Smooth Breathing is made to stand in the middle of a word, and is then called *Coro'nis*.

[9] The above are combinations of two *short* vowels, and are pronounced like their respective elements, but in more rapid succession than otherwise. Thus, αι is midway between *i* in h*I*gh, and *ay* in s*AY*.

Besides these, there are what are called *improper* diphthongs, in which the former is a *long* vowel. In these,

ᾳ	sounds like	α
ῃ	"	η
ῳ	"	ω
ηυ	"	η + υ
ωυ	"	ω + υ

the second vowel, when it is ι, is written *under* the first vowel (unless it is a capital), and is *silent*; when it is υ, it is sounded separately. When the initial vowel is a capital, the ι is placed after it, but it does not take a breathing mark or any accent.

The sign is called *diær;esis*. It is placed over the *second* of two vowels, indicating that they do *not* form a diphthong.

[10] Every word (except a few monosyllables, called *Aton'ics*) must have one accent; several small words (called *Enclit'ics*) put their accent (always as an acute) on the last syllable of the preceding word (in addition to its own accent, which still has the principal stress), where this is possible.

abb. = abbreviated / abbreviation
abstr. = abstract / abstractly
act. = active (voice) / actively
acc. = accusative (case) [1]
adj. = adjective / adjectivally
adv. = adverb / adverbial / adverbially
aff. = affix [2] / affixed
affin. = affinity
alt. = alternate / alternately
anal. = analogy
appar. = apparent / apparently
arch. = architecture / architectural / architecturally
art. = article [3]
artif. = artificial / artificially
Ass. = Assyrian
A.V. = Authorized Version (King James Version)
Bab. = Babylon / Babylonia / Babylonian
caus. = causative [4] / causatively
cerem. = ceremony / ceremonial / ceremonially
Chald. = Chaldee (Aramaic) / Chaldaism (Aramaism)
Chr. = Christian
collat. = collateral / collaterally
collect. = collective / collectively
comp. = compare [5] / comparison / comparative / comparatively
concr. = concrete / concretely
conjec. = conjecture / conjectural / conjecturally
conjug. = conjugation [6] / conjugational / conjugationally
conjunc. = conjunction / conjunctional / conjunctionally
constr. = construct [7] / construction / constructive / constructively

contr. = contracted [8] / contraction
correl. = correlated / correlation / correlative / correlatively
corresp. = corresponding / correspondingly
dat. = dative (case) [9]
def. = definite [10] / definitely
demonstr. = demonstrative [11]
denom. = denominative [12] / denominatively
der. = derived / derivation / derivative / derivatively
desc. = descended / descendant / descendants
dimin. = diminutive [13]
dir. = direct / directly
E. = East / Eastern
eccl. = ecclesiastical / ecclesiastically
e.g. = for example
Eg. = Egypt / Egyptian / Egyptians
ellip. = ellipsis [14] / elliptical / elliptically
emphat. = emphatic / emphatically
equiv. = equivalent / equivalently
err. = error / erroneous / erroneously
espec. = especially
etym. = etymology [15] / etymological / etymologically
euphem. = euphemism [16] / euphemistic / euphemistically
euphon. = euphonious [17] / euphonically
extens. = extension [18] / extensive
extern. = external / externally
fem. = feminine (gender)
fig. = figurative / figuratively
for. = foreign / foreigner
freq. = frequentative / frequentatively
fut. = future

gen. = general / generally / generic / generical / generically
Gr. = Greek / Graecism
gut. = guttural [19]
Heb. = Hebrew / Hebraism
i.e. = that is
ident. = identical / identically
immed. = immediate / immediately
imper. = imperative [20] / imperatively
imperf. = imperfect [21]
impers. = impersonal / impersonally
impl. = implied / impliedly / implication
incept. = inceptive [22] / inceptively
incl. = including / inclusive / inclusively
indef. = indefinite / indefinitely
ind. = indicative [23] / indicatively
indiv. = individual / individually
infer. = inference / inferential / inferentially
infin. = infinitive
inhab. = inhabitant / inhabitants
ins. = inserted
intens. = intensive / intensively
interch. = interchangeable
intern. = internal / internally
interj. = interjection [24] / interjectional / interjectionally
interrog. = interrogative [25] / interrogatively
intr. = intransitive [26] / intransitively
invol. = involuntary / involuntarily
irreg. = irregular / irregularly
Isr. = Israelite / Israelites / Israelitish
Lat. = Latin
Levit. = Levitical / Levitically

lit. = literal / literally
marg. = margin / marginal reading
masc. = masculine (gender)
mean. = meaning
ment. = mental / mentally
metaph. = metaphorical / metaphorically
mid. = middle (voice) [27]
modif. = modified / modification
mor. = moral / morally
mult. = multiplicative [28]
nat. = natural / naturally
neg. = negative / negatively
neut. = neuter (gender)
obj. = object / objective / objectively
obs. = obsolete
ord. = ordinal [29]
or. = origin
orig. = original / originally
orth. = orthography [30] / orthographical / orthographically
Pal. = Palestine
part. = participle
pass. = passive (voice) / passively
patron. = patronymic [31] / patronymical / patronymically
perh. = perhaps
perm. = permutation [32] (of adjacent letters)
pers. = person / personal / personally
Pers. = Persia / Persian / Persians
phys. = physical / physically
plur. = plural
poet. = poetry / poetical / poetically
pos. = positive / positively
pref. = prefix / prefixed
prep. = preposition / prepositional / prepositionally
prim. = primitive
prob. = probable / probably

prol. = prolonged [33] / prolongation
pron. = pronoun / pronominal / pronominally
prop. = properly
prox. = proximate / proximately
recip. = reciprocal / reciprocally
redupl. = reduplicated [34] / reduplication
refl. = reflexive [35] / reflexively
reg. = regular
rel. = relative / relatively
relig. = religion / religious / religiously
Rom. = Roman
second. = secondary / secondarily
signif. = signification / signifying
short. = shorter / shortened
sing. = singular
spec. = specific / specifically
streng. = strengthening
subdiv. = subdivision / subdivisional / subdivisionally
subj. = subjectively / subjective / subject
substit. = substituted
suff. = suffix
superl. = superlative [36] / superlatively
symb. = symbolic / symbolical / symbolically
tech. = technical / technically
term. = termination
tran. = transitive [37] / transitively
transc. = transcription
transm. = transmutation [38]
transp. = transposed [39] / transposition
typ. = typical / typically
uncert. = uncertain / uncertainly
var. = various / variation
voc. = vocative (case) [40]
vol. = voluntary / voluntarily

---

[1] often indicating the direct object of an action verb

[2] part of a word which, when attached to the beginning of the word is called a prefix; if attaching within a word, an infix; and if at the end, a suffix

[3] "the" is the definite article; "a" and "an" are indefinite articles

[4] expressing or denoting causation

[5] the comparative of an adjective or adverb expresses a greater degree of an attribute, e.g. "higher"; "more slowly"

[6] a systematic array of various verbal forms

[7] the condition in Hebrew and Aramaic when two adjacent nouns are combined semantically as follows, e.g. "sword" + "king" = "(the) sword of (the) king" or "(the) king's sword". These languages tend to throw the stress of the entire noun phrase toward the end of the whole expression.

[8] a shortened form of a word. It is made by omitting or combining some elements or by reducing vowels or syllables, e.g. "is not" becomes "isn't".

[9] often the indirect object of an action verb

[10] the definite article ("the")

[11] demonstrative pronouns which point (show), e.g. "this," "that"

[12] derived from a noun

[13] a grammatical form which expresses smallness and/or endearment

[14] a construction which leaves out understood words

[15] the historical origin of a word

[16] the use of a pleasant, polite, or harmless-sounding word or phrase to hide harsh, rude, or infamous truths, e.g. "to pass away" = "to die"

[17] a linguistic mechanism to make pronunciation easier, e.g. "an" before "hour" instead of "a"

[18] when a general term can denote an entire class of things

[19] speech sounds which are produced deep in the throat

[20] the mood which expresses a command

[21] used of a tense which expresses a continuous but unfinished action or state

[22] used of a verbal aspect which denotes the beginning of an action

[23] used of the mood which expresses a verbal action as actually occurring (not hypothetical)

[24] an exclamation which expresses emotion

[25] indicating a question

[26] referring to verbs which do not govern direct objects

[27] reflexive

[28] capable of multiplying or tending to multiply

[29] This shows the position or the order within a series, e.g. "second"; the corresponding cardinal number is "two".

[30] the written system of spelling in a given language

[31] a name derived from that of a paternal ancestor, often created by an affix in various languages

[32] a rearrangement

[33] lengthening a pronunciation

[34] the repetition of a letter or syllable to form a new, inflected word

[35] denoting an action by the subject upon itself

[36] expressing the highest degree of comparison of the quality indicated by an adjective or an adverb, e.g. "highest"; "most timely"

[37] expressing an action directed toward a person or a thing (the direct object)

[38] the change of one grammatical element to another

[39] switching word order

[40] an inflection which is used when one is addressing a person or a thing directly, e.g. "John, come here!"

GREEK DICTIONARY
OF THE NEW TESTAMENT

A

1. **A** {4x} **A**, *al'-fah;* of Heb. or.; the first letter of the alphabet; fig. only (from its use as a numeral) the *first.* Often used (usually ἄν **an**, before a vowel) also in composition (as a contr. from *427*) in the sense of *privation;* so in many words beginning with this letter; occasionally in the sense of *union* (as a contr. of *260*).:— Alpha {4x}. See: TDNT—1:1,*; BAGD—1a; THAYER—1a.

2. **Ἀαρών** {5x} **Aarōn**, *ah-ar-ōhn';* of Heb. or. [175]; *Aaron*, the brother of Moses:—*Aaron* {5x}. See: TDNT—1:3, 1; BAGD—1a; THAYER—1b.

3. **ἀβαδδών** {1x} **Abaddōn**, *ab-ad-dōhn';* of Heb. or. [11]; a destroying *angel:—Abaddon* {1x}. See: TDNT—1:4, 1; BAGD—1a; THAYER—1b.

4. **ἀβαρής** {1x} **abarēs**, *ab-ar-ace';* from *1* (as a neg. particle) and *922; weightless,* i.e. (fig.) *not burdensome:*—from being burdensome {1x}.

Abares means without weight "without weight" lit. "I kept myself burdensomeless" (2 Cor 11:9). See: BAGD—1b; THAYER—1c.

5. **Ἀββᾶ** {3x} **Abba**, *ab-bah';* of Chald. or. *father* (as a voc.):—*Abba* {3x}.

Father, customary title used of God in prayer. *Abba,* approximating a personal name, framed by the lips of infants betokens unreasoning trust. Father expresses an intelligent apprehension of the relationship by the child. The two together express the love and intelligent confidence of the child (Mk 14:36; Rom 8:15; Gal 4:6). See: TDNT—1:5, 1; BAGD—1b; THAYER—1c.

6. **Ἄβελ** {4x} **Abĕl**, *ab'-el;* of Heb. or. [1893]; *Abel,* "vanity/transitory," the second son of Adam:—*Abel* {4x}. See: TDNT—*, 2; BAGD—1c; THAYER—1d.

7. **Ἀβιά** {3x} **Abia**, *ab-ee-ah';* of Heb. or. [29]; *Abijah,* "my father is Jehovah," the name of two Isr.:—*Abia* {3x}. See: BAGD—1c; THAYER—1d.

8. **Ἀβιάθαρ** {1x} **Abiathar**, *ab-ee-ath'-ar;* of Heb. or. [54]; *Abiathar,* "father of abundance," an Isr.:—*Abiathar* {1x}. See: BAGD—1c; THAYER—1d.

9. **Ἀβιληνή** {1x} **Abilēnē**, *ab-ee-lay-nay';* of for. or. [comp. 58]; *Abilene,* "grassy meadow," a region of Syria:—*Abilene* {1x}. See: BAGD—1d; THAYER—2a.

10. **Ἀβιούδ** {2x} **Abiŏud**, *ab-ee-ood';* of Heb. or. [31]; *Abihud,* "my father is majesty," an Isr.:—Abiud {2x}. See: BAGD—1d; THAYER—2a.

11. **Ἀβραάμ** {73x} **Abraam**, *ab-rah-am';* of Heb. or. [85]; *Abraham,* "father of a multitude," the Heb. patriarch:—Abraham {73x}. See: TDNT—1:8, 2; BAGD—1d; THAYER—2a.

12. **ἄβυσσος** {9x} **abussŏs**, *ab'-us-sos;* from *1* (as a neg. particle) and a var. of *1037; depthless,* i.e. (spec.) (infernal) "*abyss*":— deep {2x}, bottomless {2x}, bottomless pit {5x}.

Abussos means bottomless. It describes an immeasurable depth, the underworld, the lower regions, the abyss of Sheol, the lower region, the abode of demons (Rev 11:7; 17:8). See: TDNT—1:9, 2; BAGD—2a; THAYER—2a.

13. **Ἄγαβος** {2x} **Agabŏs**, *Ag'-ab-os;* of Heb. or. [comp. 2285]; *Agabus,* "locust," an Isr.:—Agabus {2x}. See: BAGD—2b; THAYER—2b.

14. **ἀγαθοεργέω** {1x} **agathŏĕrgĕō**, *ag-ath-o-er-gheh'-o;* from *18* and *2041;* to *work good:*—do good {1x}.

In 1 Ti 6:18 the rich are enjoined to do good: "That they do good, that they be rich in good works, ready to distribute, willing to communicate." Syn.: 14, 18, 19, 2095, 2109, 2140, 2570, 2573, 5544. See: TDNT—1:17, 3; BAGD—2b; THAYER—2b.

15. **ἀγαθοποιέω** {11x} **agathŏpŏiĕō**, *ag-ath-op-oy-eh'-o;* from *17;* to *be a well-doer* (as a favor or a duty):—do good {7x}, well doing {2x}, do well {2x}.

This word is used **(1)** in a general way, "to do well": "For so is the will of God, that with well doing ye may put to silence the ignorance of foolish men" (1 Pet 2:15; cf, vv. 20; 3:6, 17; 3 Jn 11); and **(2)** with pointed reference "to the benefit of another": "Then said Jesus unto them, I will ask you one thing; Is it lawful on the sabbath days to do good, or to do evil? to save life, or to destroy it?" (Lk 6:9; cf. 33, 35). Syn.: 16, 17, 2569. See: TDNT—1:17, 3; BAGD—2c; THAYER—2b.

16. **ἀγαθοποιΐα** {1x} **agathŏpŏiïa**, *ag-ath-op-oy-ee'-ah;* from *17; well-doing,* i.e. *virtue:*—well-doing {1x}.

This word occurs in occurs in 1 Pt 4:19 – "Wherefore let them that suffer according to

the will of God commit the keeping of their souls to him in well-doing, as unto a faithful Creator." Syn.: 15, 17, 2569. See: TDNT—1:17, 3; BAGD—2c; THAYER—2b.

17. ἀγαθοποιός {1x} **agathŏpŏiŏs,** *ag-ath-op-oy-os'*; from *18* and *4160*; a *well-doer,* i.e. *virtuous:*—them that do well {1x}.

This word means "doing good, beneficent," and is translated "them that do well" in 1 Pt 2:14 [lit., "well-doing (ones)."]. See: TDNT—1:17, 3; BAGD—2c.; THAYER—2c.

18. ἀγαθός {102x} **agathŏs,** *ag-ath-os';* a prim. word; *"good"* (in any sense, often as noun):—good {77x}, good thing {14x}, that which is good + 3588 {8x}, the thing which is good + 3588 {1x}, well {1x}, benefit {1x}.

Agathos, as an adjective, describes that which, being "good" in its character or constitution, is beneficial in its effect. **(1)** It is used **(1a)** of things physical, **(1a1)** e.g., a tree: "Even so every good tree bringeth forth good fruit; but a corrupt tree bringeth forth evil fruit" (Mt 7:17); **(1a2)** ground: "And other fell on good ground, and sprang up, and bare fruit an hundredfold" (Lk 8:8); **(1b)** in a moral sense, frequently of persons and things. **(1b1)** God is essentially, absolutely and consummately "good": "And he said unto him, Why callest thou me good? there is none good but one, that is, God" (Mt 19:17; cf. Mk 10:18; Lk 18:19). **(1b2)** To certain persons the word is applied: "Is it not lawful for me to do what I will with mine own? Is thine eye evil, because I am good?" (Mt 20:15; cf. 25:21, 23; Lk 19:17; 23:50; Jn 7:12; Acts 11:24; Titus 2:5); and **(1c)** in a general application: "That ye may be the children of your Father which is in heaven: for He maketh His sun to rise on the evil and on the good, and sendeth rain on the just and on the unjust" (Mt 5:45; cf. 12:35; Lk 6:45; Rom 5:7; 1 Pet 2:18).

(2) The neuter of the adjective with the definite article signifies that which is "good," lit., "the good," as being morally honorable, pleasing to God, and therefore beneficial. **(2a)** Christians are to prove it (Rom 12:2); **(2b)** to cleave to it (Rom 12:9); **(2c)** to do it (Rom 13:3; cf. Gal 6:10); **(2d)** to work it (Rom 2:10; Eph 4:28; 6:8); **(2e)** to follow after it (1 Th 5:15); **(2f)** to be zealous of it (1 Pt 3:13); **(2g)** to imitate it (3 Jn 11); **(2h)** to overcome evil with it (Rom 12:21). **(3)** Governmental authorities are ministers of "good," i.e., that which is salutary, suited to the course of human affairs: "For he is the minister of God to thee for good. But if thou do that which is evil, be afraid" (Rom 13:4). **(4)** The neuter plural is also used of material "goods," riches, etc.: "He hath filled the hungry with good things; and the rich he hath sent empty away" (Lk 1:53; cf. 12:18, 19; 16:25; Gal 6:6 (of temporal supplies).

(5) In Rom 10:15, the "good" things are the benefits provided through the sacrifice of Christ, in regard both to those conferred through the gospel and to those of the coming messianic kingdom: "And how shall they preach, except they be sent? as it is written, How beautiful are the feet of them that preach the gospel of peace, and bring glad tidings of good things!" (cf. Heb 9:11; 10:1). Syn.: **(A)** *Kalos* (*2570*) and *agathos* occur together in Lk 8:15: "But that on the good (*kalos*) ground are they, which in an honest (*kalos*) and good (*agathos*) heart, having heard the word, keep *it,* and bring forth fruit with patience." An "honest" (*kalos*) heart is the attitude which is right towards God and a "good" (*agathos*) heart is one that, instead of working ill to a neighbor, acts beneficially towards him. **(B)** In Rom 7:18, "in me . . . dwelleth no good thing" (*agathos*) signifies that in him is nothing capable of doing "good," and hence he lacks the power "to do that which is good" (*kalos*). **(C)** In 1 Th 5:15, "follow after that which is good" (*agathos*), the "good" is that which is beneficial; in v. 21, "hold fast that which is good (*kalos*)," the "good" describes the intrinsic value of the teaching. See also: 2108, 2110, 2570, 5543, 5485. See: TDNT—1:10, 3; BAGD—2d; THAYER—2c.

19. ἀγαθωσύνη {4x} **agathōsunē,** *ag-ath-o-soo'-nay;* from *18; goodness,* i.e. *virtue* or *beneficence:*—goodness {4x}.

(1) *Agathosune,* as a noun, means "goodness," and **(1a)** signifies that moral quality which is described by the adjective *agathos* (*18*): being "good" in its character or constitution, is beneficial in its effect. **(1b)** This word means a zeal for goodness and truth. **(2)** It is used, in the NT, of regenerate persons (Rom 15:14; Gal 5:22; Eph 5:9; 2 Th 1:11). Syn.: **(A)** *Chrestotes* (*5544*) describes the kindlier aspects of "goodness," a kindly disposition towards others. Christ illustrates this quality in His dealings with the penitent woman (Lk 7:37–50). **(B)** *Agathosune* includes the sterner qualities by which doing "good" to others is not necessarily by gentle means; yet the sterner element in the ideal character which acts in a manner for the benefit of others. Christ illustrates this quality in cleansing the temple (Mt 21:12, 13) and in denouncing the scribes and Pharisees (Mt 23:13–29). Syn.: 5544. See: TDNT—1:18, 3; BAGD—3d; THAYER—3b.

20. ἀγαλλίασις {5x} **agalliasis,** *ag-al-lee'-as-is;* from *21; exultation;* spec. *welcome:*—gladness {3x}, exceeding joy {1x}, joy {1x}.

This word means "exultation, exuberant joy" and is translated **(1)** "gladness": "And thou [Elisabeth] shalt have joy and gladness; and many shall rejoice at his birth" (Lk 1:14; cf. Acts 2:6; Heb 1:9); **(2)** "joy": "For, lo, as soon as the voice of thy salutation sounded in mine ears, the babe leaped in my womb for joy" (Lk 1:44); and **(3)** "exceeding joy": "Now unto him that is able to keep you from falling, and to present you faultless before the presence of his glory with exceeding joy" (Jude 24). Syn.: It indicates a more exultant "joy" than *chara* (5479). See: TDNT—1:19, 4; BAGD—3d; THAYER—3b.

21. ἀγαλλιάω {11x} **agalliaō,** *ag-al-lee-ah'-o;* from ἄγαν **agan** (*much*) and *242;* prop. to *jump for joy,* i.e. *exult:*—rejoice {7x}, be exceeding glad {1x}, be glad {1x}, greatly rejoice {1x}, with exceeding joy {1x}.

Agalliao, as a verb, means "to exult, rejoice greatly," is chiefly used in the middle voice. It conveys the idea of jubilant exultation, spiritual "gladness": **(1)** "Rejoice, and be exceeding glad: for great is your reward in heaven: for so persecuted they the prophets which were before you" (Mt 5:12 - the Lord's command to His disciples); **(2)** Lk 1:47 - in Mary's song; **(3)** Lk 10:21 - of Christ's exultation ("rejoiced"); **(4)** Jn 8:56 - of Abraham; **(5)** Acts 16:34 - of the Philippian jailor; **(6)** 1 Pt 1:6, 8; 4:13 - "with exceeding joy", of believers in general. Syn.: 2165, 5463. See: TDNT—1:19, *; BAGD—3d; THAYER—3c.

22. ἄγαμος {4x} **agamŏs,** *ag'-am-os;* from *1* (as a neg. particle) and *1062; unmarried:*—unmarried {4x}.

This word is translated "unmarried" and occurs in 1 Cor 7:8, 11, 32, 34. See: BAGD—4b; THAYER—3c.

23. ἀγανακτέω {7x} **aganaktĕō,** *ag-an-ak-teh'-o;* from ἄγαν **agan** (*much*) and ἄχθος **achthŏs** (*grief;* akin to the base of *43*); to *be greatly afflicted,* i.e. (fig.) *indignant:*—have indignation {2x}, be much displeased {2x}, with indignation {2x}, be sore displeased {1x}.

Aganakteo means to be indignant, feel a violent irritation, to be moved with indignation and is translated **(1)** "were moved with indignation" of the ten disciples against James and John (Mt 20:24); **(2)** "they were sore displeased" of the chief priests and scribes against Christ and the children (Mt 21:15); **(3)** "they had indignation" of the disciples against the woman

who anointed Christ's feet (Mt 26:8); **(4)** "he was much displeased" of Christ against the disciples for rebuking the children (Mk 10:14); and **(5)** "(answered) with indignation" of the ruler of the synagogue against Christ for healing on the Sabbath (Lk 13:14). Syn.: 2371, 4360. See: BAGD—4b; THAYER—3d.

24. ἀγανάκτησις {1x} **aganaktēsis,** *ag-an-ak'-tay-sis;* from *23; indignation:*—indignation {1x}. See: BAGD—4b; THAYER—3d.

25. ἀγαπάω {142x} **agapaō,** *ag-ap-ah'-o;* perh. from ἄγαν **agan** (*much*) [or comp. *5689*]; to *love* (in a social or moral sense):—love {135x}, beloved {7x}.

Agapao, **in its perfect participle passive form,** is translated "beloved" in Rom 9:25; Eph 1:6; Col 3:12; 1 Th 1:4; 2 Th 2:13. Syn.: 5368. See: TDNT—1:21, 5; BAGD—4d; THAYER—3d. comp. *5368.*

26. ἀγάπη {116x} **agapē,** *ag-ah'-pay;* from *25; love,* i.e. *affection* or *benevolence;* spec. (plur.) a *love-feast:*—love {86x}, charity {27}, dear {1x}, charitably + *2596* {1x}, feast of charity {1x}.

(1) The attitude of God toward His Son (Jn 17:26), the human race (Jn 3:16; Rom 5:8); and to believers on the Lord Jesus Christ particularly (Jn 14:2). **(2)** It is His will to His children concerning their attitude **(2a)** one toward another (Jn 13:34), and **(2b)** toward all men (1 Th 3:12; 1 Cor 16:14; 2 Pet 1:7). **(3)** He desires for them to express His essential nature (1 Jn 4:8). **(4)** Love can be known only from the actions it prompts as God's love is seen in the gift of His Son (1 Jn 4:9, 10). **(5)** This is not the love drawn out by any excellency in its objects (Rom 5:8). **(6)** It was an exercise of the divine will in deliberate choice, made without assignable cause save that which lies in the nature of God Himself (cf. Deut 7:7, 8). **(7)** Love had its perfect expression among men in the Lord Jesus Christ (2 Cor 5:14; Eph 2:4; 3:19; 5:2). **(8)** Christian love is the fruit of His Spirit in the Christian (Gal 5:22).

(9) Christian love has God for its primary object, and expresses itself first of all in implicit obedience to His commandments (Jn 14:15, 21, 23; 15:10; 1 Jn 2:5; 5:3; 2 Jn 6). **(10)** Self-will, that is, self-pleasing, is the negation of love to God. **(11)** Christian love, whether exercised toward the brethren, or toward men generally, is not an impulse from the feelings, it does not always run with the natural inclinations, nor does it spend itself only upon those for whom some affinity is discovered. **(11a)** Love seeks the welfare of all (Rom 15:2), and **(11b)** works no ill to any (Rom 13:8–10); **(11c)**

seeks opportunity to do good to "all men, and especially toward them that are of the household of the faith" (Gal 6:10). **(12)** See further 1 Cor 13 and Col 3:11–14. **(13)** In respect of *agapao* as used of God, **(13a)** it expresses the deep and constant love and interest of a perfect Being towards entirely unworthy objects, **(13b)** producing and fostering a reverential love in them towards the Giver, **(13c)** a practical love towards those who are partakers of the same, and **(13d)** a desire to help others to seek the Giver.

(14) *Agape* is used in the plural in Jude 12, signifying "feasts of charity." Syn.: *Agape* expresses a more reasoning attachment, of choice and selection, from a seeing in the object upon whom it is bestowed that which is worthy of regard; or else from a sense that such is due toward the person so regarded, as being a benefactor or the like. *Phileo* (*5368*), without being necessarily an unreasoning attachment, does yet give less account of itself to itself; is more instinctive, is more of the feelings or natural affections, implies more passion. In the NT *agapao* is purged of all coldness, and is deeper than *phileo* . . . . *phileo* implies an instinctive, affectionate attachment; but *agapao* of a sentiment based on judgment and adulation, which selects its object for a reason. See also: 1062, 1173, 1403, 1859. See: TDNT—1:21, 5; BAGD—5b; THAYER—4b.

27. ἀγαπητός {62x} **agapētŏs,** *ag-ap-ay-tos';* from *25; beloved:*—beloved {47x}, dearly beloved {9x}, well beloved {3x}, dear {3x}.

Agapetos, as an adjective, from *agapao* (*25*), means "loved," is used of **(1)** Christ as loved by God: "And lo a voice from heaven, saying, This is my beloved Son, in whom I am well pleased" (Mt 3:17); **(2)** of believers: "To all that be in Rome, beloved of God, called to be saints" (Rom 1:7); **(3)** of believers, one of another: "I write not these things to shame you, but as my beloved sons I warn you" (1 Cor 4:14); **(4)** often, as a form of address: "Wherefore, my dearly beloved, flee from idolatry" (e.g. 1 Cor 10:14). See: TDNT—1:21, 5; BAGD—6b; THAYER—4d.

28. Ἄγαρ {2x} **Agar,** *ag'-ar;* of Heb. or. [1904]; *Hagar,* the concubine of Abraham:— Hagar {2x}. See: TDNT—1:55, 10; BAGD—6d; THAYER—5a.

29. ἀγγαρεύω {3x} **aggarĕuō,** *ang-ar-yew'-o;* of for. or. [comp. 104]; prop. to *be a courier,* i.e. (by impl.) to *press* into public service:—compel (to go) {3x}.

Aggareuo means to impress into service and is used of compelling a person to go a mile (Mt

5:41) or impressing of Simon to bear Christ's cross (Mt 27:32; Mk 15:21). Syn.: 315. See: BAGD—6d; THAYER—5b.

30. ἀγγεῖον {2x} **aggĕiŏn,** *ang-eye'-on;* from ἄγγος **aggŏs** (a *pail,* perh. as *bent;* comp. the base of *43*); a *receptacle:*—vessel {2x}. See: BAGD—6d; THAYER—5b.

31. ἀγγελία {1x} **aggĕlia,** *ang-el-ee'-ah;* from *32;* an *announcement,* i.e. (by impl.) *precept:*—message {1x}.

Aggelia means to bring a message, to proclaim, denoting a message, a proclamation, news (1 Jn 1:5). Syn.: 189, 2782. See: TDNT— 1:56, 10; BAGD—7a; THAYER—5c.

32. ἄγγελος {186x} **aggĕlŏs,** *ang'-el-os;* from ἀγγέλλω **aggĕllō** [prob. der. from *71;* comp. *34*] (to *bring tidings*); a *messenger;* esp. an "*angel*"; by impl. a *pastor:*—angel {179x}, messenger {7x}.

(1) *Angelos* is a messenger sent by God or by man or by Satan. **(2)** It is also used of a guardian or representative in Rev 1:20. **(3)** The word most frequently refers to an order of created beings **(3a)** superior to man (Heb 2:7; Ps 8:5), **(3b)** belonging to heaven (Mt 24:36), **(3c)** belonging to God (Lk 12:8), and **(3d)** engaged in His service (Ps 103:20). **(4)** Angels are **(4a)** spirits, **(4b)** not having material bodies as men (Heb 1:14), **(4c1)** are either human in form, or **(4c2)** can assume the human form when necessary (cf. Lk 24:4 with v. 23, Acts 10:3 with v. 30), and **(4d)** they are called holy (Mk 8:38) and elect (1 Ti 5:21). See: TDNT—1:74, 12; BAGD—7; THAYER—5c.

33. ἄγε {2x} **agĕ,** *ag'-eh;* imper. of *71;* prop. *lead,* i.e. *come* on:—go to {2x}. See: BAGD—8b; THAYER—6a.

34. ἀγέλη {8x} **agĕlē,** *ag-el'-ay;* from *71* [comp. *32*]; a *drove:*—herd {8x}.

It is used in the NT only of swine (Mt 8:30– 32; Mk 5:11, 13; Lk 8:32, 33). See: BAGD—8b; THAYER—6a.

35. ἀγενεαλόγητος {1x} **agĕnĕalŏgētŏs,** *ag-en-eh-al-og'-ay-tos;* from *1* (as neg. particle) and *1075; unregistered as to birth:*—without descent {1x}.

This word is rendered "without genealogy" in Heb 7:3. See: TDNT—1:665, 114; BAGD—8c; THAYER—6a.

36. ἀγενής {1x} **agĕnēs,** *ag-en-ace';* from *1* (as neg. particle) and *1085;* prop. *without kin,* i.e. (of unknown descent, and by impl.) *ignoble:*—base things {1x}.

Agenes means of low birth; hence, denoting that which is of no reputation, of no account. It is translated "the base things of the world,"

i.e., those which are of no account or fame in the world's esteem and being in the neuter plural of the adjective bears reference to persons (1 Cor 1:28; note esp. vs. 26). Syn.: 60, 5011. See: BAGD—8c; THAYER—6b.

37. **ἁγιάζω** {29x} **hagiazō**, *hag-ee-ad'-zo;* from *40;* to *make holy,* i.e. (cer.) *purify* or *consecrate;* (mentally) to *venerate:*—sanctify {26x}, hallow {2x}, be holy {1x}.

(1) *Hagiazo* means to make holy and signifies to set apart for God, to sanctify, to make a person or thing the opposite of *koinos* (2839 – common). (2) It is translated "Hallowed," with reference to the name of God, the Father, in the Lord's Prayer (Mt 6:9; Lk 11:2). (3) In the passive voice, it means "to be made holy, be sanctified," and (3a) is translated "let him be made holy" (Rev 22:11), (3b) the tense expressing the definiteness and completeness of the divine act; (3c) elsewhere it is rendered by the verb "to sanctify." See: TDNT—1:111, 14; BAGD—8c; THAYER—6b.

38. **ἁγιασμός** {10x} **hagiasmŏs**, *hag-ee-as-mos';* from *37;* prop. *purification,* i.e. (the state) *purity;* concr. (by Heb.) a *purifier:*—holiness {5x}, sanctification {5x}.

Hagiasmos signifies (1) separation to God (1 Cor 1:30; 2 Th 2:13; 1 Pet 1:2) and (2) the resultant state, the conduct befitting those so separated (1 Th 4:3, 4, 7). (3) It is translated "holiness" in Rom 6:19, 22; 1 Th 4:7; 1 Ti 2:15; Heb 12:14. (4) Sanctification is thus the state predetermined by God for believers, into which in grace He calls them, and in which they begin their Christian course and so pursue it. (5) Hence they are called "saints" (40 - *hagioi*). Syn.: 40, 41, 42, 3741, 3743. See: TDNT—1:113, 14; BAGD—9a; THAYER—6d.

39. **ἅγιον** {11x} **hagiŏn**, *hag'-ee-on;* neut. of *40;* a *sacred* thing (i.e. spot):—sanctuary {4x}, holy place {3x}, holiest of all {3x}, holiness {1x}.

Hagion, the neuter of the adjective *hagios* (*40*), means holy and is used (1) of those structures which are set apart to God: (1a) of the tabernacle in the wilderness (Heb 9:1), and (1b) in 9:2 the outer part is called the Holy place (KJV, "the sanctuary"). (2) It is used of heaven itself, i.e., the immediate presence of God and His throne (Heb 8:2, "the sanctuary). Syn.: 3485. See: BAGD—9b; THAYER—6d.

40. **ἅγιος** {229x} **hagiŏs**, *hag'-ee-os;* from ἅγος **hagŏs** (an *awful* thing) [comp. *53,* 2282]; *sacred* (phys. *pure,* mor. *blameless* or *religious,* cer. *consecrated*):—holy {161x}, saints {61x}, Holy One {4x}, misc. {3x} = holy one, holy thing.

Hagios fundamentally signifies separated,

and hence, in Scripture in its moral and spiritual significance, separated from sin and therefore consecrated to God, sacred. (1) It is predicated of God (as the absolutely "Holy" One, in His purity, majesty and glory): (1a) of the Father (Lk 1:49; Jn 17:11; 1 Pet 1:15), (1b) of the Son (Lk 1:35; Acts 3:14; 4:27), and (1c) of the Spirit (Mt 1:18; 2 Ti 1:14). (2) It is used of men and things in so far as they are devoted to God. (2a) Indeed the quality, as attributed to God, is often presented in a way which involves divine demands upon the conduct of believers who are called *hagioi*, "saints," "sanctified," or "holy" ones. (3) This sainthood is not an attainment, (3a) it is a state into which God in grace calls men; yet (3b) believers are called to sanctify themselves (3b1) consistently with their calling (2 Ti 1:9), (3b2) cleansing themselves from all defilement, (3b3) forsaking sin, (3b4) living a holy manner of life (1 Pet 1:15; 2 Pet 3:11), and (3b5) experiencing fellowship with God in His holiness.

(4) The saints are thus figuratively spoken of as a holy temple (4a) (1 Cor 3:17—a local church); (4b) (Eph 2:21—the whole Church). (5) *Hagios* expresses something more and higher than sacred, outwardly associated with God; something more than worthy, honorable; something more than pure, free from defilement. *Hagios* is more comprehensive. It is characteristically godlikeness. (6) The **adjective** is used (6a) of the outer part of the tabernacle (Heb 9:2 "sanctuary" = "the holy place"); (6b) of the inner sanctuary (Heb 9:3 "holiest of all" = "the Holy of Holies"; (6c) of the city of Jerusalem (Rev 11:2); (6d) its temple (Acts 6:13); (6e) of the faith (Jude 20); (6f) of the greetings of saints (1 Cor 16:20); (6g) of angels (Mk 8:38); (6h) of apostles and prophets (Eph 3:5); (6i) of the future heavenly Jerusalem (Rev 21:2, 10; 22:19). Syn.: 38, 41, 42, 3741, 3742, 3743. See: TDNT—1:88, 14; BAGD—9b; THAYER—6d.

41. **ἁγιότης** {1x} **hagiŏtēs**, *hag-ee-ot'-ace;* from *40;* *sanctity* (i.e. prop. the state):—holiness {1x}.

Hagiotes means sanctity, the abstract quality of holiness, and is used of God: "For they verily for a few days chastened us after their own pleasure; but he for our profit, that we might be partakers of his holiness" (Heb 12:10). Syn.: 38, 40, 42, 3741, 3742, 3743. See: TDNT—1:114, 14; BAGD—10b; THAYER—7c.

42. **ἁγιωσύνη** {3x} **hagiōsunē**, *hag-ee-o-soo'-nay;* from *40;* *sacredness* (i.e. prop. the quality):—holiness {3x}.

Hagiosune denotes the manifestation of the quality of holiness in personal conduct and is used (1) in Rom 1:4 of the absolute holiness

of Christ in the days of His flesh, **(1a)** which distinguished Him from all merely human beings; this (which is indicated in the phrase "the spirit of holiness") and **(1b)** (in vindication of it) His resurrection from the dead, marked Him out as (He was "declared to be") the Son of God.

(2) Believers are to be "perfecting holiness in the fear of God," (2 Cor 7:1, **(2a)** i.e., bringing "holiness" to its predestined end), whereby **(2b)** they may be found "unblameable in holiness" in the Parousia of Christ (1 Th 3:13). **(2c)** In each place character is in view, **(2c1)** perfect in the case of the Lord Jesus, and **(2c2)** growing toward perfection in the case of the Christian. **(2d)** Here the exercise of love is declared to be the means God uses to develop likeness to Christ in His children. **(2e)** The sentence may be paraphrased thus:—The Lord enable you more and more to spend your lives in the interests of others, in order that He may so establish you in Christian character now, that you may be vindicated from every charge that might possibly be brought against you at the Judgment-seat of Christ (cf. 1 Jn 4:16, 17). Syn.: 38, 40, 41, 3741, 3743. See: TDNT—1:114, 14; BAGD—10b; THAYER—7c.

43. **ἀγκάλη** {1x} **agkalē**, *ang-kal'-ay;* from ἄγκος **agkŏs** (a *bend,* "ache"); an *arm* (as *curved*):—arm {1x}.

Ankale, used in the plural in Lk 2:28, originally denoted the curve, or the inner angle, of the arm. Syn.: *Brachion* (*1023*), "the shorter part of the arm, from the shoulder to the elbow," is used metaphorically to denote strength, power, and always in the NT of the power of God (Lk 1:51; Jn 12:38; Acts 13:17). Syn.: 1023. See: BAGD—10c; THAYER—7c.

44. **ἄγκιστρον** {1x} **agkistrŏn**, *ang'-kis-tron;* from the same as *43;* a *hook* (as *bent*):—hook {1x}.

Agkistron is a fish-hook and is used in Mt 17:27. See: BAGD—10c; THAYER—7d.

45. **ἄγκυρα** {4x} **agkura**, *ang'-koo-rah;* from the same as *43;* an *"anchor"* (as *crooked*):—anchor {4x}.

Agkura was so called because of its curved form [*ankos,* "a curve"] (Acts 27:29–30, 40; Heb 6:19). See: BAGD—10c; THAYER—7d.

46. **ἄγναφος** {2x} **agnaphŏs**, *ag'-naf-os;* from *1* (as a neg. particle) and the same as *1102;* prop. *unfulled,* i.e. (by impl.) *new* (cloth):—new {2x}.

Agnaphos literally means "uncarded" (*a,* negative, *knapto,* "to card wool"), is rendered "undressed/new," of cloth, in Mt 9:16 and Mk 2:21. See: BAGD—10d; THAYER—7d.

47. **ἀγνεία** {2x} **hagnĕia**, *hag-ni'-ah;* from *53; cleanliness* (the quality), i.e. (spec.) *chastity:*—purity {2x}.

Hagneia occurs in 1 Ti 4:12; 5:2, where it denotes the chastity which excludes all impurity of spirit, manner, or act. Syn.: 54. See: TDNT—1:123, 19; BAGD—10d; THAYER—7d.

48. **ἀγνίζω** {7x} **hagnizō**, *hag-nid'-zo;* from *53;* to *make clean,* i.e. (fig.) *sanctify* (cer. or mor.):—purify {5x}, purify self {2x}.

Hagnizo is used of purifying **(1)** ceremonially (Jn 11:55; Acts 21:24, 26), **(2a)** morally, the heart (Jas 4:8), **(2b)** the soul (1 Pet 1:22), or **(2c)** oneself (1 Jn 3:3). Syn.: 2511. See: TDNT—1:123, 19; BAGD—11a; THAYER—7d.

49. **ἀγνισμός** {1x} **hagnismŏs**, *hag-nis-mos';* from *48;* a *cleansing* (the act), i.e. (cer.) *lustration:*—purification {1x}.

Hagnismos denotes a ceremonial purification (Acts 21:26; cf. Num. 6:9–13). Syn.: 2512, 2514. See: TDNT—1:124, 19; BAGD—11a; THAYER—ba.

50. **ἀγνοέω** {22x} **agnŏĕō**, *ag-no-eh'-o;* from *1* (as a neg. particle) and *3539; not to know* (through lack of information or intelligence); by impl. to *ignore* (through disinclination):—be ignorant {7x}, ignorant {4x}, know not {4x}, understand not {3x}, ignorantly {2x}, unknown {2x}.

Agnoeo, as a verb, signifies **(1)** "to be ignorant, not to know," either **(1a)** intransitively **(1a1)** 1 Cor 14:38: "But if any man be ignorant, let him be ignorant," **(1a2)** 1 Ti 1:13: "Who was before a blasphemer, and a persecutor, and injurious: but I obtained mercy, because I did it ignorantly in unbelief" [lit., "being ignorant (I did it)"]; or **(1a3)** Heb 5:2: "Who can have compassion on the ignorant, and on them that are out of the way; for that he himself also is compassed with infirmity"; or **(2)** transitively, **(2a)** 2 Pet 2:12: "But these, as natural brute beasts, made to be taken and destroyed, speak evil of the things that they understand not [*agnoeo*]; and shall utterly perish in their own corruption;" **(2a1)** Acts 13:27: "For they that dwell at Jerusalem, and their rulers, because they knew him not [*agnoeo*]," **(2a2)** Acts 17:23: "For as I passed by, and beheld your devotions, I found an altar with this inscription, TO THE UNKNOWN GOD. Whom therefore ye ignorantly [*agnoeo*] worship, him declare I unto you" (lit., "what not knowing ye worship").

(3) This word is also rendered by the verb **(3a)** "to be ignorant that," or "to be ignorant of" (Rom 1:13; 10:3; 11:25; 1 Cor 10:1; 12:1; 2 Cor 1:8; 2:11; 1 Th 4:13); **(3b)** to know not (Rom 2:4; 6:3; 7:1); **(3c)** to be unknown [passive voice] (2 Cor 6:9; Gal 1:22); **(3d)** "not to understand" (Mk

9:32; Lk 9:45). Syn.: 51, 52, 56, 2399, 2990. See: TDNT—1:115, 18; BAGD—11b; THAYER—8a. Syn.: 2990.

51. ἀγνόημα {1x} **agnŏēma,** *ag-no'-ay-mah;* from *50;* a thing *ignored,* i.e. *shortcoming:*—error {1x}.

Agnoema, as a noun, means **(1)** "a sin of ignorance" and **(2)** occurs in Heb 9:7: "But into the second went the high priest alone once every year, not without blood, which he offered for himself, and for the errors of the people." **(3)** What is especially in view in these passages is unwitting error. **(3a)** For Israel a sacrifice was appointed, greater in proportion to the culpability of the guilty, greater, for instance, for a priest or ruler than for a private person. **(3b)** Sins of "ignorance," being sins, must be expiated. **(3c)** A believer guilty of a sin of "ignorance" needs the efficacy of the expiatory sacrifice of Christ, and finds "grace to help." **(3d)** Yet, as the conscience of the believer receives enlightenment, what formerly may have been done in "ignorance" becomes a sin against the light and demands a special confession, to receive forgiveness (1 Jn 1:8, 9). **(4)** It is a sin that resulted from a weakness of the flesh—not a highhanded sin—from an imperfect insight into God's law, and from a lack of due circumspection that afterwards was viewed with shame and regret. Syn.: 50, 52, 56, 2399, 2990. See: TDNT—1:115, 18; BAGD—11c; THAYER—8b.

52. ἄγνοια {4x} **agnŏia,** *ag'-noy-ah;* from *50;* *ignorance* (prop. the quality):—ignorance {4x}.

Agnoia, as a noun, literally means "want of knowledge or perception" and denotes "ignorance" **(1)** on the part of the Jews regarding Christ (Acts 3:17); **(2)** of Gentiles in regard to God (Acts 17:30; cf. Eph 4:18 which includes the idea of willful blindness: see Rom 1:28, not the "ignorance" which mitigates guilt); **(3)** of the former unregenerate condition of those who became believers (1 Pet 1:14). Syn.: 50, 51, 56, 2399, 2990. See: TDNT—1:116, 18; BAGD—11d; THAYER—8b.

53. ἀγνός {8x} **hagnŏs,** *hag-nos';* from the same as *40;* prop. *clean,* i.e. (fig.) *innocent, modest, perfect:*—chaste {3x}, clean {1x}, pure {4x}.

Hagnos signifies **(1)** pure from every fault, immaculate, clear (2 Cor 7:11; Phil 4:8; 1 Ti 5:22); or **(2)** pure from carnality, modest (2 Cor 11:2; Titus 2:5). Syn.: **(A)** *Hagios* (*40*), holy, as being free from admixture of evil; **(B)** *hosios* (*3741*), holy, as being free from defilement; **(C)** *eilikrines* (*1506*), pure, as being tested, lit., judged by the sunlight, and **(D)** *katharos* (*2513*),

pure, as being cleansed. See: TDNT—1:122, 19; BAGD—11d; THAYER—8b.

54. ἀγνότης {1x} **hagnŏtēs,** *hag-not'-ace;* from *53; cleanness* (the state), i.e. (fig.) *blamelessness:*—pureness {1x}.

Hagnotes occurs in 2 Cor 6:6 and means "pureness." Syn.: 47. See: TDNT—1:124, 19; BAGD—12a; THAYER—8b.

55. ἀγνῶς {1x} **hagnŏs,** *hag-noce';* adv. from *53; purely,* i.e. *honestly:*—sincerely {1x}.

Hagnos denotes "with pure motives" and is rendered "sincerely" in Phil 1:16: "The one preach Christ of contention, not sincerely, supposing to add affliction to my bonds:" See: BAGD—12a; THAYER—8b.

56. ἀγνωσία {2x} **agnōsia,** *ag-no-see'-ah;* from *1* (as neg. particle) and *1108; ignorance* (prop. the state):—ignorance {1x}, not the knowledge {1x}.

Agnosia as a noun, denotes **(1)** "ignorance" as directly opposed to *gnosis* [1108 - which signifies "knowledge" as a result of observation and experience (*a,* negative, *ginosko,* "to know"; cf. Eng., "agnostic")]. **(2)** It is used in 1 Cor 15:34 ("no knowledge"), and 1 Pet 2:15. **(3)** In both these passages reprehensible "ignorance" is suggested. Syn.: 50, 51, 52, 2399, 2990. See: TDNT—1:116, 18; BAGD—12b; THAYER—8b.

57. ἄγνωστος {1x} **agnōstŏs,** *ag'-noce-tos';* from *1* (as neg. particle) and *1110; unknown:*—unknown {1x}.

This word is found only in Acts 17:23: "For as I passed by, and beheld your devotions, I found an altar with this inscription, TO THE UNKNOWN GOD." See: TDNT—1:119, 18; BAGD—12b; THAYER—8c.

58. ἀγορά {11x} **agŏra,** *ag-or-ah';* from ἀγ-είρω **agĕirō** (to *gather;* prob. akin to *1453*); prop. the *town-square* (as a place of public resort); by impl. a *market* or *thoroughfare:*—market {6x}, marketplace {4x}, street {1x}.

Agora denotes a place of assembly, a public place or forum, a marketplace. **(1)** A variety of events occurred there: **(1a)** business dealings such as the hiring of laborers (Mt 20:3); **(1b)** the buying and selling of goods (Mk 7:4); **(1c)** the games of children (Mt 11:16; Lk 7:32); **(1d)** exchange of greetings (Mt 23:7; Mk 12:38; Lk 11:43; 20:46); **(1e)** the holding of trials (Acts 16:19); or **(1f)** public discussions (Acts 17:17). **(2)** Mk 6:56 records the bringing of the sick there. **(3)** The word always carries with it the idea of publicity, in contrast to private circumstances. See: BAGD—12c; THAYER—8c.

59. **ἀγοράζω** {31x} **agŏrazō**, *ag-or-ad'-zo;* from *58;* prop. to *go to market,* i.e. (by impl.) to *purchase;* spec. to *redeem:*—buy {28x}, redeem {3x}.

Agorazo means primarily, "to frequent the marketplace," the *agora;* hence to do business there, to buy or sell. **(1)** It is used literally in Mt 14:15: "And when it was evening, his disciples came to him, saying, This is a desert place, and the time is now past; send the multitude away, that they may go into the villages, and buy themselves victuals." **(2)** Figuratively, Christ is spoken of as having bought His redeemed, making them His property at the price of His blood (1 Cor 6:20; 7:23; 2 Pet 2:1; Rev 5:9; 14:3–4). Syn.: 5608. See: TDNT—1:124, 19; BAGD—12d; THAYER—8c.

60. **ἀγοραῖος** {2x} **agŏraiŏs**, *ag-or-ah'-yos;* from *58; relating to the market-place,* i.e. *forensic* (times); by impl. *vulgar:*—baser sort {1x}, low {1x}.

Agoraios literally signifies relating to the marketplace; hence, **(1)** frequenting markets, and so sauntering about idly. **(2)** It is also used of affairs usually transacted in the marketplace, such as judicial assemblies (Acts 19:38 - law). Syn.: 36, 5011. See: BAGD—13a; THAYER—8d.

61. **ἄγρα** {2x} **agra**, *ag'-rah;* from *71;* (abstr.) a *catching* (of fish); also (concr.) a *haul* (of fish):—draught {2x}.

(1) *Agra* means to go hunting or catching and is used only **(2)** in connection with fishing. **(2a)** In Lk 5:4 it signifies the act of catching fish and **(2b)** in Lk 5:9 it stands for the catch itself. Syn.: 856. See: BAGD—13a; THAYER—8d.

62. **ἀγράμματος** {1x} **agrammatŏs**, *ag-ram-mat-os;* from *1* (as neg. particle) and *1121; unlettered,* i.e. *illiterate:*—unlearned {1x}.

In its only occurrence, Acts 4:13, the disciples are accused of being unversed in the learning of the Jewish schools. Syn.: 261, 521, 2399. See: BAGD—13b; THAYER—8d.

63. **ἀγραυλέω** {1x} **agraulĕō**, *ag-row-leh'-o;* from *68* and *832* (in the sense of *833*); to *camp out:*—abide in the field {1x}.

Agrauleo means to lodge in a fold in a field (Lk 2:8). Syn.: 390, 835, 1304, 1961, 2476, 2650, 3306, 3887, 4160, 4357, 5278. See: BAGD—13b; THAYER—8d.

64. **ἀγρεύω** {1x} **agrĕuō**, *ag-rew'-o;* from *61;* to *hunt,* i.e. (fig.) to *entrap:*—catch {1x}. See: BAGD—13b; THAYER—9a.

65. **ἀγριέλαιος** {2x} **agriĕlaiŏs**, *ag-ree-el'-ah-yos;* from *66* and *1636;* an *oleaster:*—wild olive tree {1x}, olive tree which is wild {1x}.

Agrielaios is an adjective used as a noun in Rom 11:17, 24 —a wild olive tree. Syn.: 1636, 1638, 2565. See: BAGD—13b; THAYER—9a.

66. **ἄγριος** {3x} **agriŏs**, *ag'-ree-os;* from *68; wild* (as pertaining to the country), lit. (*natural*) or fig. (*fierce*):—wild {2x}, raging {1x}.

Agrios denotes **(1)** of or in fields; hence, not domestic, said of honey (Mt 3:4; Mk 1:6); or **(2)** savage, fierce, used metaphorically in Jude 13, raging waves. See: BAGD—13c; THAYER—9a.

67. **Ἀγρίππας** {12x} **Agrippas**, *ag-rip'-pas;* appar. from *66* and *2462; wild-horse* tamer; *Agrippas,* one of the Herods:—Agrippa {12x}. See: BAGD—13d; THAYER—9b.

68. **ἀγρός** {36x} **agrŏs**, *ag-ros';* from *71;* a *field* (as a *drive* for cattle); gen. the *country;* spec. a *farm,* i.e. *hamlet:*—field {22x}, country {8x}, land {4x}, farm {1x}, piece of ground {1x}.

Agros denotes a field, especially a cultivated field; hence, the country in contrast to the town (Mk 5:14; 6:36; 15:21; 16:12; Lk 8:34; 9:12). Syn.: 3313, 3968, 4066, 5561. See: BAGD—13d; THAYER—9b.

69. **ἀγρυπνέω** {4x} **agrupnĕō**, *ag-roop-neh'-o;* ultimately from *1* (as neg. particle) and *5258;* to *be sleepless,* i.e. *keep awake:*—watch {4x}.

Agrupneo means to be sleepless and is used metaphorically to be watchful (Mk 13:33; Lk 21:36; Eph 6:18; Heb 13:17). The word expresses not mere wakefulness, but the watchfulness of those who are intent upon a thing. Syn.: 1127, 3525, 3906. See: TDNT—2:338, 195; BAGD—14a; THAYER—9b.

70. **ἀγρυπνία** {2x} **agrupnia**, *ag-roop-nee'-ah;* from *69; sleeplessness,* i.e. *keeping awake:*—watching {2x}.

Agrupnia means sleeplessness and is rendered "watchings" (2 Cor 6:5; 11:27). Syn.: 2892, 5438. See: BAGD—14a; THAYER—9c.

71. **ἄγω** {72x} **agō**, *ag'-o;* a prim. verb; prop. to *lead;* by impl. to *bring, drive,* (refl.) *go,* (spec.) *pass* (time), or (fig.) *induce:*—bring {45x}, lead {12x}, go {7x}, bring forth {2x}, bring {1x}, misc. {5x} = be, carry, keep, be open.

Ago means to lead, to lead along, to bring, and connotes to bring: "For if we believe that Jesus died and rose again, even so them also which sleep in Jesus will God bring (*ago*) with Him" (1 Th 4:14; cf. 2 Ti 4:11; Heb 2:10). Syn.:

321, 520, 1521, 3919, 4254, 4311, 5342. See: BAGD—14b; THAYER—9c.

72. ἀγωγή {1x} **agōgē**, *ag-o-gay'*; redupl. from *71*; a *bringing* up, i.e. *mode of living:*—manner of life {1x}.

Agoge properly denotes **(1)** a teaching; figuratively, **(2)** a training, discipline, and so, **(3)** the life led, a way or course of life, conduct (2 Ti 3:10 – manner of life). See: TDNT—1:128, 20; BAGD—14d; THAYER—10a.

73. ἀγών {6x} **agōn**, *ag-one'*; from *71*; prop. a place of *assembly* (as if *led*), i.e. (by impl.) a *contest* (held there); fig. an *effort* or *anxiety:*—conflict {2x}, fight {2x}, contention {1x}, race {1x}.

Agon means to lead and signifies **(1)** a place of assembly, especially the place where the Greeks assembled for the Olympic and Pythian games; **(2)** a contest of athletes, metaphorically, and translated **(2a1)** "fight" (1 Ti 6:12; 2 Ti 4:7), or **(2a2)** "race" (Heb 12:1). Hence, **(3)** the inward conflict of the soul is often the result, or the accompaniment, of outward conflict (Phil 1:30; 1 Th 2:2). It implies a contest against spiritual foes as well as human adversaries (Col 2:1 — conflict). Syn.: 119. See: TDNT—1:135, 20; BAGD—15a; THAYER—10a.

74. ἀγωνία {1x} **agōnia**, *ag-o-nee'-ah;* from *73;* a *struggle* (prop. the state), i.e. (fig.) *anguish:*—agony {1x}.

Agonia [cf. Eng., "agony"] was used among the Greeks **(1)** as an alternative to *agon* (73), "a place of assembly"; **(2)** then for the contests or games which took place there, and then **(3)** to denote intense emotion. **(3a)** It was more frequently used eventually in this last respect, to denote severe emotional strain and anguish. **(3b)** So in Lk 22:44, of the Lord's "agony" in Gethsemane (Lk 22:44). See: TDNT—1:140, 20; BAGD—15a; THAYER—10b.

75. ἀγωνίζομαι {7x} **agōnizomai**, *ag-o-nid'-zom-ahee;* from *73;* to *struggle*, lit. (to *compete* for a prize), fig. (to *contend* with an adversary), or gen. (to *endeavor* to accomplish something):—strive {3x}, fight {3x}, labour fervently {1x}.

Agonizomai denotes **(1)** to contend in the public games (1 Cor 9:25); **(2)** to fight, engage in conflict: "Jesus answered, My kingdom is not of this world: if my kingdom were of this world, then would my servants fight, that I should not be delivered to the Jews: but now is my kingdom not from hence" (Jn 18:36); **(3)** metaphorically, **(3a)** to contend perseveringly against opposition and temptation: "Fight [*aganizomai*] the good fight [73 – *agon*] of faith, lay hold on eternal life, whereunto thou art also called, and hast professed a good profes-

sion before many witnesses" (1 Ti 6:12; cf. 2 Ti 4:7); **(3b)** to strive as in a contest for a prize, straining every nerve to attain to the object: "Strive [*aganizomai*] to enter in at the strait gate: for many, I say unto you, will seek to enter in, and shall not be able" (Lk 13:24); **(3c)** to put forth every effort, involving toil (Col 1:29; 1 Ti 4:10); **(3d)** to wrestle earnestly in prayer: "Epaphras, who is one of you, a servant of Christ, saluteth you, always labouring fervently [*aganizomai*] for you in prayers, that ye may stand perfect and complete in all the will of God" (Col 4:12). Syn.: 2341, 3164, 4438. See: TDNT—1:135, 20; BAGD—15b; THAYER—10b.

76. Ἀδάμ {9x} **Adam**, *ad-am';* of Heb. or. [121]; *Adam*, the first man; typ. (of Jesus) *man* (as his representative):—Adam {9x}. See: TDNT—1:141, 21; BAGD—15c; THAYER—10c.

77. ἀδάπανος {1x} **adapanŏs**, *ad-ap'-an-os;* from *1* (as neg. particle); and *1160; costless*, i.e. *gratuitous:*—without charge {1x}.

Adapanos literally means "without expense" and is used in 1 Cor 9:18 as without charge of service in the gospel. See: BAGD—15d; THAYER—10c.

78. Ἀδδί {1x} **Addi**, *ad-dee';* prob. of Heb. or. [comp. 5716]; *Addi*, an Isr.:—Addi {1x}. See: BAGD—15d; THAYER—10c.

79. ἀδελφή {24x} **adĕlphē**, *ad-el-fay';* fem of *80;* a *sister* (nat. or eccl.):—sister {24x}.

Adelphe is used **(1)** of natural relationship (e.g., Mt 19:29; of the "sisters" of Christ, the children of Joseph and Mary after the virgin birth of Christ (cf. Mt 13:56); **(2)** of "spiritual kinship" with Christ, an affinity marked by the fulfillment of the will of the Father: "For whosoever shall do the will of my Father which is in heaven, the same is my brother, and sister, and mother" (Mt 12:50; Mk 3:35); **(3)** of spiritual relationship based upon faith in Christ: "I commend unto you Phebe our sister, which is a servant of the church which is at Cenchrea:"(Rom 16:1; cf. 1 Cor 7:15; 9:5). See: TDNT—1:144, 22; BAGD—15d; THAYER—10c.

80. ἀδελφός {346x} **adĕlphŏs**, *ad-el-fos';* from *1* (as a connective particle) and δελφύς **dĕlphus** (the *womb*); a *brother* (lit. or fig.) near or remote [much like 1]:—brother {346x}.

Adelphos denotes a brother, or near kinsman; in the plural, a community based on identity of origin or life. It is used of: **(1)** male children of the same parents: "Abraham begat Isaac; and Isaac begat Jacob; and Jacob begat

Judas and his brethren;" (Mt 1:2; cf. 14:3); **(2)** male descendants of the same parents: "And when he was full forty years old, it came into his heart to visit his brethren the children of Israel" (Acts 7:23; cf. 7:26; Heb 7:5); **(3)** male children of the same mother: "Is not this the carpenter's son? is not his mother called Mary? and his brethren, James, and Joses, and Simon, and Judas?" (Mt 13:55; cf. 1 Cor 9:5; Gal 1:19); **(4)** people of the same nationality: "And now, brethren, I wot that through ignorance ye did it, as did also your rulers" (Acts 3:17; cf. 3:22; Rom 9:3); **(5)** any man, a neighbor: "But I say unto you, That whosoever is angry with his brother (*adelphos*) without a cause shall be in danger of the judgment: and whosoever shall say to his brother (*adelphos*), Raca, shall be in danger of the council: but whosoever shall say, Thou fool, shall be in danger of hell fire" (Mt 5:22; cf. 7:3);

(6) persons united by a common interest: "And if ye salute your brethren only, what do ye more than others? do not even the publicans so?" (Mt 5:47; **(7)** persons united by a common calling: "Then saith he unto me, See thou do it not: for I am thy fellowservant, and of thy brethren the prophets, and of them which keep the sayings of this book: worship God" (Rev 22:9); **(8)** mankind: "Wherefore in all things it behoved him to be made like unto his brethren, that he might be a merciful and faithful high priest in things pertaining to God, to make reconciliation for the sins of the people" (Heb 2:17; **(9)** the disciples, and so, by implication, all believers: "Then said Jesus unto them, Be not afraid: go tell my brethren that they go into Galilee, and there shall they see me" (Mt 28:10; cf. Jn 20:17); **(10)** believers, apart from sex (Mt 23:8; Acts 1:15; Rom 1:13; 1 Th 1:4; Rev 19:10 [the word "sisters" is used of believers, only in 1 Ti 5:2). Syn.: **A.** *adelphotes* (*81*), primarily, a brotherly relation; the community possessed of this relation, a brotherhood (1 Pet 2:17); **B.** *philadelphos* (*5361*), fond of one's brethren (1 Pet 3:8); **C.** *philadelphia* (*5359*), brotherly love (Rom 12:10; 1 Th 4:9); **D.** *pseudadelphos* (*5569*) false brethren (2 Cor 11:26; Gal 2:4). See: TDNT—1:144, 22; BAGD—15d; THAYER—10d.

81. ἀδελφότης {2x} **adĕlphŏtēs**, *ad-el-fot'-ace;* from *80; brotherhood* (prop. the feeling of *brotherliness*), i.e. the (Chr.) *fraternity:*—brotherhood {1x}, brethren {1x}. See: TDNT—1:144, 22; BAGD—16c; THAYER—11b.

82. ἄδηλος {2x} **adēlŏs**, *ad'-ay-los;* from *1* (as a neg. particle) and *1212; hidden,* fig. *indistinct:*—appear not {1x}, uncertain {1x}. *Adelos* denotes **(1)** unseen; with the article,

translated "which appear not": "Woe unto you, scribes and Pharisees, hypocrites! for ye are as graves which appear not (*adelos*), and the men that walk over them are not aware of them" (Lk 11:44); and **(2)** uncertain, indistinct: "For if the trumpet give an uncertain sound, who shall prepare himself to the battle?" (1 Cor 14:8). See: BAGD—16d; THAYER—11b.

83. ἀδηλότης {1x} **adēlŏtēs**, *ad-ay-lot'-ace;* from *82; uncertainty:*—uncertain {1x}. *Adelotes* means uncertainty [of riches] and occurs in 1 Tim 6:17. See: BAGD—16d; THAYER—11b.

84. ἀδήλως {1x} **adēlōs**, *ad-ay'-loce;* adv. from *82; uncertainly:*—uncertainly {1x}. *Adelos* is translated as "uncertainly" in 1 Cor 9:26: "I therefore so run, not as uncertainly; so fight I, not as one that beateth the air." See: BAGD—16d; THAYER—11b.

85. ἀδημονέω {3x} **adēmŏnĕō**, *ad-ay-mon-eh'-o;* from a der. of ἀδέω **adeo** (to be *sated* to loathing); to *be in distress* (of mind):—be very heavy {2x}, be full of heaviness {1x}.

Ademoneo means to be troubled, much distressed and is used of **(1)** the Lord's sorrow in Gethsemane: "And he took with him Peter and the two sons of Zebedee, and began to be sorrowful and very heavy (*ademoneo*)" (Mt 26:37; cf. Mk 14:33); and **(2)** of Epaphroditus: "For he longed after you all, and was full of heaviness, because that ye had heard that he had been sick" (Phil 2:26). Syn.: 916, 3076. See: BAGD—16d; THAYER—11b.

86. ᾅδης {11x} **ha͵dēs**, *hah'-dace;* from *1* (as neg. particle) and *1492;* prop. *unseen,* i.e. "*Hades*" or the place (state) of departed souls:—hell {10x}, grave {1x}.

Hades is **(1)** the region of departed spirits of the lost (but including the blessed dead in periods preceding the ascension of Christ). **(2)** It corresponds to Sheol in the OT. **(3)** For the condition of the inhabitants see Lk 16:23-31. **(4)** The word is used always by the Lord (Mt 11:23; 16:18; Lk 10:15; 16:23). **(5)** It is used with reference to the soul of Christ (Acts 2:27, 31). **(6)** Christ declares that He has the keys of it (Rev 1:18). **(7)** In Rev 6:8 it is personified, **(7a)** with the signification of the temporary destiny of the doomed; **(7b)** it is to give up those who are therein (Rev 20:13), and **(7c)** it is to be cast into the lake of fire (Rev 20:14). See: TDNT—1:146, 22; BAGD—16d; THAYER—11c.

87. ἀδιάκριτος {1x} **adiakritŏs**, *ad-ee-ak'-ree-tos;* from *1* (as a neg. parti-

cle) and a der. of *1252;* prop. *undistinguished,* i.e. (act.) *impartial:*—without partiality {1x}.

Adiakritos primarily signifies not to be parted; hence, without uncertainty, or indecision, without partiality: "But the wisdom that is from above is first pure, then peaceable, gentle, and easy to be intreated, full of mercy and good fruits, without partiality (*adiakritos*), and without hypocrisy" (Jas 3:17). See: TDNT—3:950, 469; BAGD—17a; THAYER—11d.

88. **ἀδιάλειπτος** {2x} **adialĕiptŏs,** *ad-ee-al'-ipe-tos;* from *1* (as a neg. particle) and a der. of a compound of *1223* and *3007; unintermitted,* i.e. *permanent:*—continual {1x}, without ceasing {1x}.

Adialeiptos means unceasing and is used **(1)** of incessant, continual heart pain: KJV "That I have great heaviness and continual sorrow in my heart" (Rom 9:2); and **(2)** in 2 Ti 1:3 of remembrance in prayer: "I thank God, whom I serve from my forefathers with pure conscience, that without ceasing I have remembrance of thee in my prayers night and day." **(3)** The meaning in each place is not that of unbroken continuity, but without the omission of any occasion. See: BAGD—17b; THAYER—11d.

89. **ἀδιαλείπτως** {4x} **adialĕiptŏs,** *ad-ee-al-ipe'-toce;* adv. from *88; uninterruptedly,* i.e. *without omission* (on an appropriate occasion):—without ceasing {4x}.

Adialeiptos means unceasingly, without ceasing and is used with the same significance as the adjective (*88*); not of what is not interrupted, but of that which is constantly recurring: **(1)** prayer: "For God is my witness, whom I serve with my spirit in the gospel of his Son, that without ceasing I make mention of you always in my prayers" (Rom 1:9; cf. 1 Th 5:17); **(2)** in 1 Th 1:3 of the remembrance of the work, labor and patience of saints: "Remembering without ceasing your work of faith, and labour of love, and patience of hope in our Lord Jesus Christ, in the sight of God and our Father" and **(3)** in 1 Th 2:13 of thanksgiving: "For this cause also thank we God without ceasing." See: BAGD—17b; THAYER—11d.

90. **ἀδιαφθορία** {1x} **adiaphthŏria,** *ad-ee-af-thor-ee'-ah;* from a der. of a compound of *1* (as a neg. particle) and a der. of *1311; incorruptibleness,* i.e. (fig.) *purity* (of doctrine):—uncorruptness {1x}. See: BAGD—17b; THAYER—11d.

91. **ἀδικέω** {28x} **adikĕō,** *ad-ee-keh'-o;* from *94;* to *be unjust,* i.e. (act.) *do wrong* (mor., socially or phys.):—hurt {10x}, do wrong {8x}, wrong {2x}, suffer wrong {2x}, be unjust {2x}, take wrong {1x}, injure {1x}, be an offender {1x}, hope {1x}.

Adikeo signifies, **(1)** intransitively, to do wrong, do hurt, act unjustly: "For their power is in their mouth, and in their tails: for their tails were like unto serpents, and had heads, and with them they do hurt" (Rev 9:19); and **(2)** transitively to wrong, hurt or injure a person: "Behold, I give unto you power to tread on serpents and scorpions, and over all the power of the enemy: and nothing shall by any means hurt you" (Lk 10:19; cf. Rev 6:6; 7:2). Syn.: 984, 2559. See: TDNT—1:157, 22; BAGD—17c; THAYER—11d.

92. **ἀδίκημα** {3x} **adikēma,** *ad-eek'-ay-mah;* from *91;* a *wrong* done:—matter of wrong {1x}, evil doing {1x}, iniquity {1x}.

Adikema denotes a wrong, injury, misdeed and is translated **(1)** a matter of wrong: "And when Paul was now about to open his mouth, Gallio said unto the Jews, If it were a matter of wrong or wicked lewdness, O ye Jews, reason would that I should bear with you" (Acts 18:14); **(2)** evildoing: "Or else let these same here say, if they have found any evil doing in me, while I stood before the council" (Acts 24:20); **(3)** iniquities: "For her sins have reached unto heaven, and God hath remembered her iniquities" (Rev 18:5). Syn.: 93, 458, 3892, 4189. See: TDNT—1:161, 22; BAGD—17d; THAYER—12a.

93. **ἀδικία** {25x} **adikia,** *ad-ee-kee'-ah;* from *94;* (legal) *injustice* (prop. the quality, by impl. the act); mor. *wrongfulness* (of character, life or act):—unrighteousness {16x}, iniquity {6x}, unjust {2x}, wrong {1x}.

Adikia denotes **(1)** unrighteousness, literally, unrightness, a condition of not being right, whether with God, according to the standard of His holiness and righteousness, or with man, according to the standard of what man knows to be right by his conscience. **(2)** The word is usually translated "unrighteousness," but is rendered "iniquity" in Lk 13:27; Acts 1:18; 8:23; 1 Cor 13:6. **(3)** In Lk 16:8 and 18:6, the phrases lit. are, "the steward of unrighteousness" and "the judge of injustice," the subjective genitive describing their character; in 18:6 the meaning is "injustice" and so perhaps in Rom 9:14. Syn.: 92, 458, 3892, 4189. See: TDNT—1:153, 22; BAGD—17d; THAYER—12a.

94. **ἄδικος** {12x} **adikŏs,** *ad'-ee-kos;* from *1* (as a neg. particle) and *1349; unjust;* by extens. *wicked;* by impl. *treacherous;* spec. *heathen:*—unjust {8x}, unrighteous {4x}.

Adikos means "not in conformity with *dike* (1349 - 'right,')" and is rendered "unjust": "That ye may be the children of your Father which is in heaven: for he maketh his sun to

rise on the evil and on the good, and sendeth rain on the just and on the unjust" (Mt 5:45; cf. Lk 18:11; Acts 24:15). See: TDNT—1:149, 22; BAGD—18b; THAYER—12b.

95. ἀδίκως {1x} **adikōs**, *ad-ee'-koce;* adv. from *94; unjustly:*—wrongfully {1x}.

This word occurs only in 1 Pet 2:19: "For this is thankworthy, if a man for conscience toward God endure grief, suffering wrongfully." See: BAGD—18b; THAYER—12c.

96. ἀδόκιμος {8x} **adŏkimŏs**, *ad-ok'-ee-mos;* from *1* (as a neg. particle) and *1384; unapproved,* i.e. *rejected;* by impl. *worthless* (lit. or mor.):—reprobate {6x}, castaway {1x}, rejected {1x}.

Adokimos signifies not standing the test, rejected. It is said of things **(1)** the land as rejected (Heb 6:8); and **(2)** of persons as **(2a)** reprobate in mind (Rom 1:28); **(2b)** reprobate concerning the faith (Titus 1:16); and **(2c)** castaway (1 Cor 9:27). See: TDNT—2:255, 181; BAGD—18c; THAYER—12c.

97. ἄδολος {1x} **adŏlŏs**, *ad'-ol-os;* from *1* (as a neg. particle) and *1388; undeceitful,* i.e. (fig.) *unadulterated:*—sincere {1x}.

Adolos, as a noun, means "without guile," "pure, unadulterated," and is used metaphorically of the teaching of the Word of God: "As newborn babes, desire the sincere milk of the word, that ye may grow thereby" (1 Pet 2:2). Syn.: As the *akakos* (*172*) has no harmfulness in him, and the *adolos* (*97*) no guile, so the *akeraios* (*185*) no foreign mixture, and the *haplous* (*573*) no folds or wrinkles. See also: 185. See: BAGD—18d; THAYER—12c.

98. Ἀδραμυττηνός {1x} **Adramuttēnŏs**, *ad-ram-oot-tay-nos';* from Ἀδραμύττειον **Adramuttĕiŏn** (a place in Asia Minor); *Adramyttene* or belonging to Adramyttium:—Adramyttium {1x}. See: BAGD—18d; THAYER—12c.

99. Ἀδρίας {1x} **Adrias**, *ad-ree'-as;* from Ἀδρία **Adria** (a place near its shore); the *Adriatic* sea (incl. the Ionian):—Adria {1x}. See: BAGD—18d; THAYER—12d.

100. ἀδρότης {1x} **hadrŏtēs**, *had-rot'-ace;* from ἁδρός **hadrŏs** (stout); *plumpness,* i.e. (fig.) *liberality:*—abundance {1x}.

Hadrotes means thick, fat, full-grown, rich; so regarding the offering in 2 Cor 8:20 the thought is that of bountiful giving, a fat offering, not mere abundance. Syn.: 4050. See: BAGD—18d; THAYER—12d.

101. ἀδυνατέω {2x} **adunatĕō**, *ad-oo-nat-eh'-o;* from *102;* to *be unable,* i.e. (pass.) *impossible:*—be impossible {2x}.

Adunateo signifies to be impossible, unable, and in the NT it is used only of things: **(1)** nothing to a believer: "And Jesus said unto them, Because of your unbelief: for verily I say unto you, If ye have faith as a grain of mustard seed, ye shall say unto this mountain, Remove hence to yonder place; and it shall remove; and nothing shall be impossible unto you" (Mt 17:20); **(2)** nothing with God: "For with God nothing shall be impossible" (Lk 1:37). See: TDNT—2:284, 186; BAGD—19a; THAYER—12d.

102. ἀδύνατος {10x} **adunatŏs**, *ad-oo'-nat-os;* from *1* (as a neg. particle) and *1415; unable,* i.e. *weak* (lit. or fig.); pass. *impossible:*—impossible {6x}, impotent {1x}, could not do {1x}, weak {1x}, not possible {1x}. See: TDNT—2:284, 186; BAGD—19a; THAYER—12d.

103. ᾄδω {5x} **a₁dō**, *ad'-o* a prim. verb; to *sing:*—sing {5x}.

Ado is used always of "praise to God," **(1)** intransitively: "Speaking to yourselves in psalms and hymns and spiritual songs, singing and making melody in your heart to the Lord" (Eph 5:19; cf. Col 3:16); **(2)** transitively: "And they sung a new song, saying, Thou art worthy to take the book, and to open the seals thereof" (Rev 5:9; cf. 14:3; 15:3). Syn.: 5214, 5567. See: TDNT—1:163, 24; BAGD—19b; THAYER—13a.

104. ἀεί {8x} **aĕi**, *ah-eye';* from an obs. prim. noun (appar. mean. continued *duration*); *"ever,"* by qualification *regularly;* by impl. *earnestly:*—always {4x}, always {3x}, ever {1x}.

Aei has two meanings: **(1)** "perpetually, incessantly": "Ye stiffnecked and uncircumcised in heart and ears, ye do always (*aei*) resist the Holy Ghost: as your fathers did, so do ye" (Acts 7:51; cf. 2 Cor 4:11; 6:10; Titus 1:12; Heb 3:10; **(2)** "invariably, at any and every time," of successive occurrences, when some thing is to be repeated, according to the circumstances: "But sanctify the Lord God in your hearts: and be ready always to give an answer to every man that asketh you a reason of the hope that is in you with meekness and fear" (1 Pet 3:15; cf. 2 Pet 1:12). See: BAGD—19c; THAYER—13a.

105. ἀετός {4x} **aĕtŏs**, *ah-et-os';* from the same as *109;* an *eagle* (from its *wind*-like flight):—eagle {4x}. See: BAGD—19d; THAYER—13a.

106. ἄζυμος {9x} **azumŏs**, *ad'-zoo-mos;* from *1* (as a neg. particle) and *2219; unleavened,* i.e. (fig.) *uncorrupted;* (in the neut.

plur.) spec. (by impl.) the *Passover* week:—unleavened bread {8x}, unleavened {1x}.

Azumos denotes "unleavened bread," i.e., without any process of fermentation; hence, **(1)** metaphorically, **(1a)** "of a holy, spiritual condition": "Purge out therefore the old leaven (*azumos*), that ye may be a new lump, as ye are unleavened. For even Christ our passover is sacrificed for us" (1 Cor 5:7), and **(1b)** of "sincerity and truth": "Therefore let us keep the feast, not with old leaven (*azumos*), neither with the leaven of malice and wickedness; but with the unleavened bread of sincerity and truth" (1 Cor 5: 8). **(2)** With the article it signifies the feast of unleavened bread: "Now the first day of the feast of unleavened bread the disciples came to Jesus, saying unto him, Where wilt thou that we prepare for thee to eat the passover?" (Mt 26:17; cf. Mk 14:1, 12; Lk 22:1, 7; Acts 12:3; 20:6). See: TDNT—2:902, 302; BAGD—19d; THAYER—13b.

107. Ἀζώρ {2x} **Azōr**, *ad-zore'*; of Heb. or. [comp. 5809]; *Azor*, an Isr.:—*Azor* {2x}. See: BAGD—20a; THAYER—13b.

108. Ἄζωτος {1x} **Azōtŏs**, *ad'-zo-tos*; of Heb. or. [795]; *Azotus* (i.e. Ashdod), a place in Pal.:—*Azotus* {1x}. See: BAGD—20a; THAYER—13b.

109. ἀήρ {7x} **aēr**, *ah-ayr'*; from ἄημι **aēmi** (to *breathe* unconsciously, i.e. *respire;* by anal. to *blow*); "*air*" (as naturally *circumambient*):—air {7x}.

This word signifies "the atmosphere" **(1)** certainly in five of the seven occurrences (Acts 22:23; 1 Cor 9:26; 14:9; Rev 9:2; 16:11), and **(2)** almost certainly in the other two (Eph 2:2 and 1 Th 4:17). See: TDNT—1:165, 25; BAGD—20b; THAYER—13c. Syn.: 3772, 5594.

     ἀθά atha. See *3134*.

110. ἀθανασία {3x} **athanasia**, *ath-an-as-ee'-ah;* from a compound of *1* (as a neg. particle) and *2288; deathlessness:*—immortality {3x}.

Athanasia literally means deathlessness and is rendered **(1)** "immortality" **(1a)** of the glorified body of the believer (1 Cor 15:53, 54); and **(1b)** of the nature of God (1 Ti 6:16). **(2)** In the NT *athanasia* expresses more than deathlessness, it suggests the quality of the life enjoyed because for the believer what is mortal is to be "swallowed up of life": "For we that are in this tabernacle do groan, being burdened: not for that we would be unclothed, but clothed upon, that mortality might be swallowed up of life" (2 Cor 5:4). See: TDNT—3:22, 312; BAGD—20c; THAYER—13c.

111. ἀθέμιτος {2x} **athĕmitŏs**, *ath-em'-ee-tos;* from *1* (as a neg. particle) and a der. of θέμις **thĕmis** (*statute;* from the base of *5087*); *illegal;* by impl. *flagitious:*—unlawful thing {1x}, abominable {1x}.

Athemitos occurs in Acts 10:28, "unlawful," and 1 Pet 4:3, "abominable." Syn.: 947. See: TDNT—1:166, 25; BAGD—20d; THAYER—13d.

112. ἄθεος {1x} **athĕŏs**, *ath'-eh-os;* from *1* (as a neg. particle) and *2316; godless:*—without God {1x}.

Atheos (*112*), means "atheist," primarily signifying godless, destitute of God. In Eph 2:12 the phrase indicates, not only that the Gentiles were void of any true recognition of God, and hence became morally godless (Rom 1:19–32); but, being given up by God, they were excluded from communion with God and from the privileges granted to Israel (cf. Gal 4:8). See: TDNT—3:120, 322; BAGD—20d; THAYER—13d.

113. ἄθεσμος {2x} **athĕsmŏs**, *ath'-es-mos;* from *1* (as a neg. particle) and a der. of *5087* (in the sense of *enacting*); *lawless,* i.e. (by impl.) *criminal:*—wicked {2x}.

Athesmos means lawless, wicked: "And delivered just Lot, vexed with the filthy conversation of the wicked" (2 Pet 2:7; cf. 3:17). Syn.: 4190. See: TDNT—1:167, 25; BAGD—21a; THAYER—13d.

114. ἀθετέω {16x} **athĕtĕō**, *ath-et-eh'-o;* from a compound of *1* (as a neg. particle) and a der. of *5087; to set aside,* i.e. (by impl.) to *disesteem, neutralize* or *violate:*—despise {8x}, reject {4x}, bring to nothing {1x}, frustrate {1x}, disannul {1x}, cast off {1x}.

Atheteo signifies to put as of no value; hence, **(1)** to act towards anything as though it were annulled; to deprive a law of its force by opinions or acts contrary to it: "Brethren, I speak after the manner of men; Though it be but a man's covenant, yet if it be confirmed, no man disannulleth (*atheteo*), or addeth thereto" (Gal 3:15); or **(2)** to thwart the efficacy of anything, to nullify, to frustrate it, reject it: "But the Pharisees and lawyers rejected (*atheteo*) the counsel of God against themselves, being not baptized of him" (Lk 7:30); **(2a)** "will I reject": "For it is written, I will destroy the wisdom of the wise, and will bring to nothing (*atheteo*) the understanding of the prudent" (1 Cor 1:19), **(2b)** make void/frustrate: "I do not frustrate (*atheteo*) the grace of God: for if righteousness come by the law, then Christ is dead in vain" (Gal 2:21); **(2c)** set at nought/despise: "Likewise also these filthy dreamers defile the flesh, despise dominion, and speak evil of dignities"

(Jude 8). Syn.: 208. See: TDNT—8:158, 1176; BAGD—21a; THAYER—13d.

115. ἀθέτησις {2x} **athĕtēsis,** *ath-et'-ay-sis;* from *114; cancellation* (lit. or fig.):—disannulling {1x}, to put away + 1519 {1x}.

Athetesis means a setting aside, abolition, and is translated **(1)** disannulling (Heb 7:18) with reference to a commandment; and **(2)** to put away (lit. "for a putting away") with reference to sin (Heb 9:26). See: TDNT—8:158, 1176; BAGD—21b; THAYER—14a.

116. Ἀθῆναι {6x} **Athēnai,** *ath-ay-nahee;* plur. of Ἀθήνη **Athēnē** (the goddess of wisdom, who was reputed to have founded the city); *Athenæ,* the capitol of Greece:—Athens {6x}. See: BAGD—21b; THAYER—14a.

117. Ἀθηναῖος {2x} **Athēnaiŏs,** *ath-ay-nah'-yos;* from *116;* an *Athenæan* or inhab. of Athenæ:—Athenians {1x}, of Athens {1x}. See: BAGD—21b; THAYER—14b.

118. ἀθλέω {2x} **athlĕō,** *ath-leh'-o;* from ἆθλος **athlŏs** (a *contest* in the public lists); to *contend* in the competitive games:—strive {2x}.

Athleo means to engage in a contest (cf. Eng., "athlete"), to contend in public games, is used both times in 2 Ti 2:5: "And if a man also strive for masteries (*athleo*), yet is he not crowned, except he strive (*athleo*) lawfully." Syn.: 1252, 1864. See: TDNT—1:167, 25; BAGD—21b; THAYER—14b.

119. ἄθλησις {1x} **athlēsis,** *ath'-lay-sis;* from *118;* a *struggle* (fig.):—fight {1x}.

Athlesis denotes a combat, contest of athletes; hence, a struggle, fight, affliction: "But call to remembrance the former days, in which, after ye were illuminated, ye endured a great fight of afflictions" (Heb 10:32). Syn.: 73. See: TDNT—1:167, 25; BAGD—21c; THAYER—14b.

120. ἀθυμέω {1x} **athumĕō,** *ath-oo-meh'-o;* from a comp. of *1* (as a neg. particle) and *2372;* to *be spiritless,* i.e. *disheartened:*—be discouraged {1x}.

Athumeo means "to be disheartened, dispirited, discouraged" (*a,* negative, *thumos,* "spirit, courage," from the root *thu,* found in *thuo,* "to rush," denoting "feeling, passion"; hence Eng., "fume"), and is found in Col 3:21: "Fathers, provoke not your children to anger, lest they be discouraged (*athumeo*)." See: BAGD—21c; THAYER—14b.

121. ἄθωος {2x} **athōŏs,** *ath'-o-os;* from *1* (as a neg. particle) and prob. a der. of *5087* (mean. a *penalty*); *not guilty:*—innocent {2x}.

Athoos primarily denotes "unpunished" (*a,*

negative, *thoe,* "a penalty"); then, "innocent": **(1)** "[Judas] Saying, I have sinned in that I have betrayed the innocent blood. And they said, What is that to us? see thou to that" (Mt 27:4), **(1a)** "innocent blood," i.e., the blood of an "innocent" person, the word "blood" being used both by synecdoche (a part standing for the whole), and **(1b)** by metonymy (one thing standing for another), i.e., for death by execution; **(2)** In Mt 27: 24 Pilate speaks of himself as "innocent": **(2a)** "When Pilate saw that he could prevail nothing, but that rather a tumult was made, he took water, and washed his hands before the multitude, saying, I am innocent of the blood of this just person: see ye to it." **(2b)** Pilate is declaring his innocence; and hence, he asserts he should go unpunished for his part in the crucifixion. Syn.: 172. See: BAGD—21d; THAYER—14b.

122. αἴγειος {1x} **aigĕiŏs,** *ah'-ee-ghi-os;* from αἴξ **aix** (a *goat*); belonging to a *goat:*—goatskin + 1192 {1x}. See: BAGD—21d; THAYER—14c.

123. αἰγιαλός {6x} **aigialŏs,** *ahee-ghee-al-os';* from ἀίσσω **aïssō** (to *rush*) and *251* (in the sense of the *sea;* a *beach* (on which the *waves dash*):—shore {6x}. See: BAGD—21d; THAYER—14c.

124. Αἰγύπτιος {5x} **Aiguptiŏs,** *ahee-goop'-tee-os;* from *125; Ægyptian* or inhab. of Aegyptus:—Egyptian {3x}, Egyptians {2x}. See: BAGD—21d; THAYER—14c.

125. Αἴγυπτος {24x} **Aiguptŏs,** *ah'-ee-goop-tos;* of uncert. der.; *Ægyptus,* the land of the Nile:—Egypt {24x}. See: BAGD—22a; THAYER—14c.

126. ἀίδιος {2x} **aïdiŏs,** *ah-id'-ee-os;* from *104; everduring* (forward and backward, or forward only):—eternal {1x}, everlasting {1x}.

Aidios denotes "everlasting" (from *aei,* "ever"): "And the angels which kept not their first estate, but left their own habitation, he hath reserved in everlasting chains under darkness unto the judgment of the great day" (Jude 6). Syn.: *Aionios (166)* should always be translated "eternal" and *aidios,* "everlasting." *Aionios* **stresses time** and negates the end either of a space of time or of unmeasured time, and is used chiefly where something future is spoken of, *aidios* **stresses quality,** excluding interruption and lays stress upon permanence and unchangeableness. See: TDNT—1:168, 25; BAGD—22a; THAYER—14d.

127. αἰδώς {2x} **aidōs,** *ahee-doce';* perh. from *1* (as a neg. particle) and *1492* (through the idea of *downcast* eyes); *bashful-*

ness, i.e. (toward men), *modesty* or (toward God) *awe:*—shamefacedness {1x}, reverence {1x}.

(1) This word stresses an innate moral response to the performing of dishonorable acts. **(2)** It is self-motivated and implies a reverence for the good as good, not merely as that to which honor and reputation are attached. **(3)** *Aidos* is "a sense of shame, modesty" and is used regarding the demeanor of women in the church: "In like manner also, that women adorn themselves in modest apparel, with shamefacedness (*aidos*) and sobriety; not with braided hair, or gold, or pearls, or costly array" (1 Ti 2:9). **(3a)** Shamefacedness is that which is fast or rooted [shamefastness – 1611 KJV] in the character . . . **(3b)** which is reflected in the face. **(4)** It is translated "reverence" in Heb 12:28 "Wherefore we receiving a kingdom which cannot be moved, let us have grace, whereby we may serve God acceptably with reverence and godly fear." Syn.: As to *aidos* and *aischune* (*152*), *aidos* is more objective, having regard to others; it is the stronger word. *Aidos* would always restrain a good man from an unworthy act, *aischune* would sometimes restrain a bad one. Syn.: 152, 1791, 4997. See: TDNT—1:169, 26; BAGD—22b; THAYER—14d.

128. Αἰθίοψ {2x} **Aithiŏps,** *ahee-thee'-ops;* from αἴθω **aithō** (to *scorch*) and ὤψ **ōps** (the *face,* from *3700;* an *Æthiopian* (as a *blackamoor*):—Ethiopian {2x}. See: BAGD—22b; THAYER—14d.

129. αἷμα {99x} **haima,** *hah'-ee-mah;* of uncert. der.; *blood,* lit. (of men or animals), fig. (the *juice* of grapes) or spec. (the atoning *blood* of Christ); by impl. *bloodshed,* also *kindred:*—blood {99x}.

Haima, (Eng., prefix haem—), besides its natural meaning of blood, stands **(1)** in conjunction with *sarx* (4651 flesh) as "flesh and blood," and signifies man, human beings: "And Jesus answered and said unto him, Blessed art thou, Simon Barjona: for flesh and blood hath not revealed it unto thee, but my Father which is in heaven" (Mt 16:17; cf. 1 Cor 15:50); **(2)** for human generation: "Which were born, not of blood, nor of the will of the flesh, nor of the will of man, but of God" (Jn 1:13); **(3)** for blood shed by violence: "That upon you may come all the righteous blood shed upon the earth, from the blood of righteous Abel unto the blood of Zacharias son of Barachias, whom ye slew between the temple and the altar" (Mt 23:35; cf. Rev 17:6); **(4)** for the blood of sacrificial victims (Heb 9:7); **(5)** for the blood of Christ, which betokens **(5a)** His death by the shedding of His blood in propiatory sacrifice; and **(5b)** to drink His blood is to appropriate the saving effects of His pro-

piatory death: "Then Jesus said unto them, Verily, verily, I say unto you, Except ye eat the flesh of the Son of man, and drink his blood, ye have no life in you" (Jn 6:53). Syn.: 130. See: TDNT—1:172, 26; BAGD—22c; THAYER—15a.

130. αἱματεκχυσία {1x} **haimatĕkchusia,** *hahee-mat-ek-khoo-see'-ah;* from *129* and a der. of *1632;* an *effusion of blood:*—shedding of blood {1x}.

Haimatekchusia denotes "shedding of blood": KJV "And almost all things are by the law purged with blood; and without shedding of blood is no remission" (Heb 9:22). Syn.: 129. See: TDNT—1:176, 26; BAGD—23b; THAYER—15d.

131. αἱμορρέω {1x} **haimŏrrhĕō,** *hahee-mor-rheh'-o;* from *129* and *4482;* to *flow blood,* i.e. *have a hemorrhage:*—diseased with an issue of blood {1x}.

Haimorrheo means to flow (Eng., hemorrhage), and signifies to suffer from a flow of blood: "And, behold, a woman, which was diseased with an issue of blood twelve years, came behind him, and touched the hem of his garment" (Mt 9:20). See: BAGD—23c; THAYER—15d.

132. Αἰνέας {2x} **Ainĕas,** *ahee-neh'-as;* of uncert. der.; *Ænèas,* an Isr.:—Aeneas {2x}. See: BAGD—23c; THAYER—16a.

133. αἴνεσις {1x} **ainĕsis,** *ah'-ee-nes-is;* from *134;* a *praising* (the act), i.e. (spec.) a *thank* (-offering):—praise {1x}.

Ainesis means praise and is found in Heb 13:15 where it is metaphorically represented as a sacrificial offering: "By him therefore let us offer the sacrifice of praise to God continually, that is, the fruit of our lips giving thanks to His name." Syn.: 136, 1868. See: BAGD—23c; THAYER—16a.

134. αἰνέω {9x} **ainĕō,** *ahee-neh'-o;* from *136;* to *praise* (God):—praise {9x}.

Aineo means to speak in praise of, to praise and is always used of praise to God: **(1)** by angels: "And it came to pass, as the angels were gone away from them into heaven, the shepherds said one to another, Let us now go even unto Bethlehem, and see this thing which is come to pass, which the Lord hath made known unto us" (Lk 2:13); **(2)** by men: "And when he was come nigh, even now at the descent of the mount of Olives, the whole multitude of the disciples began to rejoice and praise God with a loud voice for all the mighty works that they had seen" (Lk 19:37; cf. 24:53; Acts 2:20; Rom 15:11). Syn.: 1843, 1867, 5214, 5567. See: TDNT—1:177, 27; BAGD—23c; THAYER—16a.

135. **αἴνιγμα** {1x} **ainigma,** *ah'-ee-nig-ma;* from a der. of *136* (in its prim. sense); an *obscure* saying ("enigma"), i.e. (abstr.) *obscureness:*—darkly + 1722 {1x}. See: TDNT—1:178, 27; BAGD—23c; THAYER—16a.

136. **αἶ-νος** {2x} **ainŏs,** *ah'-ee-nos;* appar. a prim. word; prop. a *story,* but used in the sense of *1868; praise* (of God):—praise {2x}.

Ainos primarily means a tale, narration, and came to denote detailed praise in the NT only of praise to God (Mt 21:16; Lk 18:43). Syn.: 133, 1868. See: TDNT—1:177, 27; BAGD—23d; THAYER—16b.

137. **Αἰνών** {1x} **Ainōn,** *ahee-nohn';* of Heb. or. [a der. of 5869, *place of springs*]; *Ænon,* a place in Pal.:—Aenon {1x}. See: BAGD—23d; THAYER—16b.

138. **αἱρέομαι** {3x} **hairĕŏmai,** *hahee-reh'-om-ahee;* prob. akin to *142;* to *take for oneself,* i.e. to *prefer:*—choose {3x}.

Haireomai means to take, and is used in the middle voice only, in the sense of taking for oneself, choosing **(1)** by God: "But we are bound to give thanks alway to God for you, brethren beloved of the Lord, because God hath from the beginning chosen you to salvation through sanctification of the Spirit and belief of the truth" (2 Th 2:13); or **(2)** by man: "But if I live in the flesh, this is the fruit of my labour: yet what I shall choose I wot not" (Phil 1:22; cf. Heb 11:25). **(3)** Its special significance is to select rather by the act of taking, than by showing preference or favor. Syn.: 140, 1586, 1951, 4401, 5500. See: TDNT—1:180, 27; BAGD—24a; THAYER—16c.

139. **αἵρεσις** {9x} **hairĕsis,** *hah'-ee-res-is;* from *138;* prop. a *choice,* i.e. (spec.) a *party* or (abstr.) *disunion:*—sect {5x}, heresy {4x}.

Hairesis denotes **(1)** a choosing, choice; then **(2)** that which is chosen, and hence, **(3)** an opinion, **(3a)** especially a self-willed opinion, **(3b)** which is substituted for submission to the power of truth, and **(3c)** leads to division and the formation of sects: "Idolatry, witchcraft, hatred, variance, emulations, wrath, strife, seditions, heresies" (Gal 5:20). **(4)** Such erroneous opinions are **(4a)** frequently the outcome of personal preference or the prospect of advantage: "But there were false prophets also among the people, even as there shall be false teachers among you, who privily shall bring in damnable heresies, even denying the Lord that bought them, and bring upon themselves swift destruction" (2 Pet 2:1—damnable signifies leading to ruin) and create **(4b)** sects: "Then the high priest rose up, and all they that were with

him, (which is the sect [*hairesis*] of the Sadducees,) and were filled with indignation" (Acts 5:17; cf. 15:5; 24:5, 14) and **(4c)** "heresies": "For there must be also heresies among you, that they which are approved may be made manifest among you" (1 Cor 11:19). See: TDNT—1:180, 27; BAGD—23d; THAYER—16b.

140. **αἱρετίζω** {1x} **hairĕtizō,** *hahee-ret-id'-zo;* from a der. of *138;* to *make a choice:*—choose {1x}.

Hairetizo means that which may be taken and signifies to take. It implies that what is taken is eligible or suitable; hence, to choose by reason of suitability: "Behold my servant, whom I have chosen; my beloved, in whom my soul is well pleased: I will put my spirit upon him, and He shall shew judgment to the Gentiles" (Mt 12:18—of God's delight in Christ as His chosen). Syn.: 138, 1586, 1951, 4401, 5500. See: TDNT—1:184, 27; BAGD—24a; THAYER—16c.

141. **αἱρετικός** {1x} **hairĕtikŏs,** *hahee-ret-ee-kos';* from the same as *140;* a *schismatic:*—that is a heretick {1x}.

This word primarily denotes capable of choosing; hence, causing division by a party spirit, factious: "A man that is an heretick after the first and second admonition reject" (Titus 3:10). [Heretick is now spelled heretic.] See: TDNT—1:184, 27; BAGD—24a; THAYER—16c.

142. **αἴρω** {102x} **airō,** *ah'-ee-ro;* a prim. verb; to *lift;* by impl. to *take up* or *away;* fig. to *raise* (the voice), *keep in suspense* (the mind), spec. to *sail* away (i.e. *weigh anchor*); by Heb. [comp. 5375] to *expiate* sin:—take up {32x}, take away {25x}, take {25x}, away with {5x}, lift up {4x}, bear {3x}, misc. {8x} = carry, loose, make to doubt, put away, remove.

Airo signifies **(1)** to raise up, to lift, to take upon oneself and carry what has been raised, physically: "Every branch in me that beareth not fruit He [God] taketh away: and every branch that beareth fruit, he purgeth it, that it may bring forth more fruit" (Jn 15:2) [*Airo* here indicates those branches which are on the ground, hence unable to bear fruit, God raises up so the branch can be fruitful.], or **(2)** as applied to the mind, to suspend, to keep in suspense: "Then came the Jews round about him, and said unto him, How long dost thou make us to doubt? If thou be the Christ, tell us plainly" (Jn 10:24, lit., "How long doth thou suspend our souls?"); **(3)** to take away what is attached to anything, to remove, as of Christ, in taking away the sin of the world (Jn 1:29); **(4)** Christ was manifested to take away sins: "And ye know that He was manifested to take away our sins; and in Him is no sin" (1 Jn 3:5),

where, not the nature of the Atonement is in view, but its effect in the believer's life. Syn.: 399, 430, 941, 1627, 3114, 3356, 4064, 4160, 4722, 5159, 5297, 5342, 5409. See: TDNT— 1:185, 28; BAGD—24b; THAYER—16c.

143. αἰσθάνομαι {1x} **aisthanŏmai,** *ahee-sthan'-om-ahee;* of uncert. der.; to *apprehend* (prop. by the senses):—perceive {1x}.

Aisthenomai means "to perceive, to notice, understand," and is used in Lk 9:45: "But they understood not this saying, and it was hid from them, that they perceived it not: and they feared to ask him of that saying." See: TDNT— 1:187, 29; BAGD—24d; THAYER—17b.

144. αἴσθησις {1x} **aisthēsis,** *ah'-ee-sthay-sis;* from *143; perception,* i.e. (fig.) *discernment:*—judgment {1x}. See: TDNT— 1:187, 29; BAGD—25a; THAYER—17b.

145. αἰσθητήριον {1x} **aisthētēriŏn,** *ahee-sthay-tay'-ree-on;* from a der. of *143;* prop. an *organ of perception,* i.e. (fig.) *judgment:*—senses {1x}.

Aistheterion is the faculty of perception, the organ of sense, the senses, the capacities for spiritual apprehension: "But strong meat belongeth to them that are of full age, even those who by reason of use have their senses (*aistheterion*) exercised to discern both good and evil" (Heb 5:14). See: TDNT—1:187, 29; BAGD— 25a; THAYER—17b.

146. αἰσχροκερδής {3x} **aischrŏkĕrdēs,** *ahee-skhrok-er-dace';* from *150* and κέρδος **kerdos** (*gain*); *sordid:*—greedy of filthy lucre {2x}, given to filthy lucre {1x}.

This word means "greedy of base gain" and is used in 1 Ti 3:3, 8 and Titus 1:7: "greedy of filthy lucre." Syn.: 150, 4508. See: BAGD—25a; THAYER—17b.

147. αἰσχροκερδῶς {1x} **aischrŏkĕrdōs,** *ahee-skhrok-er-doce';* adv. from *146; sordidly:*—for filthy lucre {1x}.

Aischrokerdos means an "eagerness for base gain": "Feed the flock of God which is among you, taking the oversight thereof, not by constraint, but willingly; not for filthy lucre, but of a ready mind" (1 Pet 5:2). See: BAGD—25b; THAYER—17b.

148. αἰσχρολογία {1x} **aischrŏlŏgia,** *ahee-skhrol-og-ee'-ah;* from *150* and *3056; vile conversation:*—filthy communication {1x}.

This word indicates every kind of foul-mouthed abusiveness, not just the most obvious and offensive kind; an outbreak of a loveless spirit toward our neighbor: "But now ye also put off all these; anger, wrath, malice,

blasphemy, filthy communication out of your mouth" (Col 3:8). Syn.: *Morologia* (*3473*) refers to foolishness, *aischrologia* to foulness, and *eutrapelia* (*2160*) to false refinement, to discourse that is not reasoned with the salt of grace. All three of these are sins of speech and are noted and condemned. See: BAGD—25b; THAYER—17b.

149. αἰσχρόν {3x} **aischrŏn,** *ahee-skhron';* neut. of *150;* a *shameful* thing, i.e. *indecorum:*—shame {3x}. See: BAGD—25b; THAYER—17c.

150. αἰσχρός {1x} **aischrŏs,** *ahee-skhros';* from the same as *153; shameful,* i.e. *base* (spec. *venal*):—filthy {1x}.

Aischros means "a shameful thing": "For if the woman be not covered, let her also be shorn: but if it be a shame for a woman to be shorn or shaven, let her be covered" (1 Cor 11:6; cf. 14:35; Eph 5:12). Syn.: 150, 152, 422, 808, 818, 819, 1788, 1791, 2617. See: TDNT—1:189, 29; BAGD—25b; THAYER—17c.

151. αἰσχρότης {1x} **aischrŏtēs,** *ahee-skhrot'-ace;* from *150; shamefulness,* i.e. *obscenity:*—filthiness {1x}.

This word represents all that is contrary to purity (Eph 5:4). Syn.: 766, 3436, 4507. See: TDNT—1:189, 29; BAGD—25b; THAYER— 17c.

152. αἰσχύνη {6x} **aischunē,** *ahee-skhoo'-nay;* from *153; shame* or *disgrace* (abstr. or concr.):—shame {5x}, dishonesty {1x}.

This word refers to the feeling that leads one to shun what is unworthy out of anticipation of dishonor; a fear of anticipated ill-repute. *Aischune* means shame and signifies **(1)** subjectively, **(1a)** the confusion of one who is ashamed of anything, a sense of shame (Lk 14:9); **(1b)** those things which shame conceals (2 Cor 4:2); and **(2)** objectively, **(2a)** ignominy, that which is visited on a person by the wicked (Heb 12:2); and **(2b)** that which should arise from guilt (Phil 3:19); **(3)** concretely, a thing to be ashamed of (Rev 3:18; Jude 13). Syn.: 127, 1791. See: TDNT—1:189, 29; BAGD—25b; THAYER—17c.

153. αἰσχύνομαι {5x} **aischunŏmai,** *ahee-skhoo'-nom-ahee;* from αισχος **aischŏs** (*disfigurement,* i.e. *disgrace*); to *feel shame* (for oneself):—be ashamed {5x}.

Aischuno means shame and always being in the passive voice, signifies **(1)** to have a feeling of fear or shame which prevents a person from doing a thing (Lk 16:3); and **(2)** the feeling of shame arising from something that has been done (2 Cor 10:8; Phil 1:20), or **(3)** of the possibility of being ashamed before the Lord Jesus in His Parousia with His saints (1 Jn 2:28); and

(4) in 1 Pet 4:16 of being ashamed of suffering as a Christian. Syn.: 1788, 1870, 2617. See: TDNT—1:189, 29; BAGD—25c; THAYER—17c.

154. αἰτέω {71x} **aitĕō,** *ahee-teh'-o;* of uncert. der.; to *ask* (in gen.):—ask {48x}, desire {17x}, beg {2x}, require {2x}, crave {1x}, call for {1x}.

Aiteo, as a verb, means "to ask." **(1)** *Aiteo* more frequently suggests the attitude of a suppliant, the petition of one who is lesser in position than he to whom the petition is made; **(1a)** in the case of men in asking something from God: "Ask (*aiteo*), and it shall be given you; seek, and ye shall find; knock, and it shall be opened unto you" (Mt 7:7); **(1b)** a child from a parent (Mt 7:9–10); **(1c)** a subject from a king: (Acts 12:20); **(1d)** priests and people from Pilate: "And they were instant with loud voices, requiring (*aiteo*) that he might be crucified" (Lk 23:23); **(1e)** a beggar from a passerby (Acts 3:2). **(2)** With reference to petitioning God, this verb is found in Paul's epistles in Eph 3:20 and Col 1:9; in Jas four times, 1:5–6; 4:1–3; in 1 Jn, five times, 3:22; 5:14, 15 (twice), 16. Syn.: *Aiteo* is the more submissive and suppliant term; *erotao* (*2065*) implies an equality between the one who asks and the one who is asked—a king of another king (Lk 14:32); or if not equality, then a familiarity that lends authority to the request. See also: 155, 350, 1833, 1905, 2065, 3004, 4441. See: TDNT—1:191, 30; BAGD—25d; THAYER—17d.

155. αἴτημα {3x} **aitēma,** *ah'-ee-tay-mah;* from *154;* a *thing asked* or (abstr.) an *asking:*—require {1x}, request {1x}, petition {1x}.

Aitema means lit., "that which has been asked for" is used of: **(1)** "as what is required": "And Pilate gave sentence that it should be as they required" (Lk 23:24); **(2)** "requests": "Be careful for nothing; but in every thing by prayer and supplication with thanksgiving let your requests be made known unto God" (Phil 4:6); and **(3)** "petitions": "And if we know that he hear us, whatsoever we ask, we know that we have the petitions that we desired of him" (1 Jn 5:15). Syn.: Several *aitemata* (155 pl.) make up one *proseuche* (*4335*). See also: 154, 155, 1833, 1905, 2065, 3004, 4441. See: TDNT—1:193, 30; BAGD—26b; THAYER—18a.

156. αἰτία {20x} **aitia,** *ahee-tee'-a;* from the same as *154;* a *cause* (as if *asked* for), i.e. (logical) *reason* (motive, matter), (legal) *crime* (alleged or proved):—cause {9x}, wherefore + 1223 & 3739 {3x}, accusation {3x}, fault {3x}, case {1x}, crime {1x}.

(1) *Aitia,* as a noun, has the primary meaning of "a cause, especially an occasion of some-

thing evil, hence a charge, an accusation." **(2)** It is used in a forensic sense, of **(2a)** an accusation: "Against whom when the accusers stood up, they brought none accusation of such things as I supposed" (Acts 25:18); or **(2b)** a crime: "And set up over his head his accusation written, THIS IS JESUS THE KING OF THE JEWS" (Mt 27:37; cf. Jn 18:38; 19:4, 6; Acts 13:28; 23:28; 28:18). Syn.: *Aitia* refers to an accusation that may be true or false. It is a term that was used in an accusation made against the Lord (Mk 15:26). *Elenchos* (*1650*) refers to an accusation that is true, and often implies an inward or outward acknowledgment of that truthfulness on the part of the accused. See also: 157, 1225, 1458, 1462, 1908, 2723, 2724, 4811. See: BAGD—26b; THAYER—18b.

157. αἰτίαμα {1x} **aitiama,** *ahee-tee'-am-ah;* from a der. of *156;* a *thing charged:*—complaint {1x}.

Aitiama, as a noun, means "an accusation," expressing *aitia* (*156*) more concretely, and is found in Acts 25:7: "And when he was come, the Jews which came down from Jerusalem stood round about, and laid many and grievous complaints (*aitiama*) against Paul, which they could not prove." Syn.: 156, 1225, 1458, 1462, 1908, 2723, 2724, 4811. See: BAGD—26c; THAYER—18b, 18c.

158. αἴτιον {4x} **aitiŏn,** *ah'-ee-tee-on;* neut. of *159;* a *reason* or *crime* [like *156*]:—fault {2x}, cause {2x}.

Aition means a fault, synonymous with *156* but more limited in scope, and is translated **(1)** "cause (of death)" in Lk 23:22; **(2)** "cause" (of a riot) in Acts 19:40; and **(3)** "fault" in Luke 23:4, 14. Syn.: 156, 3056. See: BAGD—26d; THAYER—18b.

159. αἴτιος {1x} **aitiŏs,** *ah'-ee-tee-os;* from the same as *154;* *causative,* i.e. (concr.) a *causer:*—author {1x}.

Aitios, as an adjective (cf. 156 - *aitia,* a cause), denotes "that which causes something;" literally, one who causes an event to happen. **(1)** This and *archegos* (*747*) are both translated "author" in Hebrews. **(2)** *Aitios,* in Heb 5:9, describes Christ as the "Author of eternal salvation unto all them that obey Him," **(2a)** signifying that Christ, exalted and glorified as our High Priest, on the ground of His finished work on earth, has become the personal mediating cause of eternal salvation. **(2b)** Christ is not the merely formal cause of our salvation. He is the concrete and active cause of it. **(2c)** He has not merely caused or effected it, He is, as His name, "Jesus," implies, our salvation itself (Lk 2:30; 3:6). Syn.: 747. See: BAGD—26d; THAYER—18b.

160. **αἰφνίδιος** {2x} **aiphnidiŏs**, *aheef-nid'-ee-os;* from a comp. of *1* (as a neg. particle) and *5316* [comp. *1810*] (mean. *non-apparent*); *unexpected*, i.e. (adv.) *suddenly:*—unawares {1x}, sudden {1x}.

Aiphnidios, as an adjective, means **(1)** "sudden": "For when they shall say, Peace and safety; then sudden (*aiphnidios*) destruction cometh upon them, as travail upon a woman with child; and they shall not escape" (1 Th 5:3); or **(2)** "unawares": "And take heed to yourselves, lest at any time your hearts be overcharged with surfeiting, and drunkenness, and cares of this life, and so that day come upon you unawares (*aiphnidios*)." Syn.: 869, 1810, 1819. See: BAGD—26d; THAYER—18c.

161. **αἰχμαλωσία** {3x} **aichmalōsia**, *aheekh-mal-o-see'-ah;* from *164; captivity:*—captivity {3x}.

Aichmalosia, as a noun, means **(1)** "captivity," is found in Rev 13:10: "He that leadeth into captivity shall go into captivity: he that killeth with the sword must be killed with the sword." **(2)** Eph 4:8 reads "He led captivity captive" **(2a)** which seems to be an allusion to the triumphal procession by which a victory was celebrated, the "captives" taken forming part of the procession. **(2b)** The quotation is from Ps 68:18, and probably is a forceful expression for Christ's victory, through His death, and that at His ascension Christ transferred the redeemed Old Testament saints from Sheol to His own presence in glory. Syn.: 162, 163, 164, 2221. See: TDNT—1:195, 31; BAGD—26d; THAYER—18c.

162. **αἰχμαλωτεύω** {2x} **aichmalōtĕuō**, *aheekh-mal-o-tew'-o;* from *164;* to *capture* [like *163*]:—lead captive {2x}.

Aichmaloteuo, as a verb, signifies "to make a prisoner of war": "Wherefore he saith, When he ascended up on high, he led captivity captive, and gave gifts unto men" (Eph 4:8). Syn.: 161, 163, 164, 2221. See: TDNT—1:195, 31; BAGD—26d; THAYER—18c.

163. **αἰχμαλωτίζω** {3x} **aichmalōtizō**, *aheekh-mal-o-tid'-zo;* from *164;* to *make captive:*—bring into captivity {2x}, lead away captive {1x}.

Aichmalotizo, practically synonymous with *aichmaloteuo* (*162*), denotes **(1)** "to lead away captive": "And they shall fall by the edge of the sword, and shall be led away captive into all nations" (Lk 21:24), or **(2)** "to subjugate, to bring under control": "But I see another law in my members, warring against the law of my mind, and bringing me into captivity to the law of sin which is in my members" [said of the effect of the Law in one's members in bringing

the person into captivity under the law of sin] (Rom 7:23); or **(3)** of subjugating the thoughts to the obedience of Christ: "Casting down imaginations, and every high thing that exalteth itself against the knowledge of God, and bringing into captivity every thought to the obedience of Christ" (2 Cor 10:5); or **(4)** of those who took captive "silly women laden with sins" (2 Ti 3:6). Syn.: 161, 162, 164, 2221. See: TDNT—1:195, 31; BAGD—27a; THAYER—18c.

164. **αἰχμαλωτός** {1x} **aichmalōtŏs**, *aheekh-mal-o-tos';* from αἰχμή **aichmē** (a *spear*) and a der. of the same as *259;* prop. a *prisoner of war,* i.e. (gen.) a *captive:*—captive {1x}.

Aichmalotos, as a noun, literally means "one taken by the spear" (from *aichme*, "a spear," and *halotos*, a verbal adjective, from *halonai*, "to be captured"); hence denotes "a captive": "The Spirit of the Lord is upon me, because he hath anointed me to preach the gospel to the poor; he hath sent me to heal the brokenhearted, to preach deliverance to the captives, and recovering of sight to the blind, to set at liberty them that are bruised." Syn.: 161, 162, 163, 2221. See: TDNT—1:195, 31; BAGD—27a; THAYER—18d.

165. **αἰών** {128x} **aiōn**, *ahee-ohn';* from the same as *104;* prop. an *age;* by extens. *perpetuity* (also past); by impl. the *world;* spec. (Jewish) a Messianic period (present or future):—ever {71x}, world {38x}, never + 3364 + 1519 + 3588 {6x}, evermore {4x}, age {2x}, eternal {2x}, misc. {5x} = course, forever.

The primary stress of this word is time in its unbroken duration. *Aion*, as a noun, means **(1)** "an age, era" and **(1a)** signifies a period of indefinite duration, or **(1b)** time viewed in relation to what takes place in the period. **(1c)** The force attaching to the word is not so much that of the actual length of a period, but that of a period marked by spiritual or moral characteristics. **(1d)** This is illustrated in the use of the adjective in the phrase "life eternal," in Jn 17:3, in respect of the increasing knowledge of God. **(1e)** Eternal life stresses the quality of life; everlasting life stresses its length. **(2)** The phrases containing this word should not be rendered literally, but consistently with its sense of indefinite duration. **(2a)** Thus *"eis ton aiona"* does not mean "unto the age" but "for ever": "As he saith also in another place, Thou art a priest for ever after the order of Melchisedec" (Heb 5:6). **(2b)** The Greeks contrasted that which came to an end with that which was expressed by this phrase, which shows that they conceived of it as expressing interminable duration. **(3)** The word occurs most

frequently in the Gospel of John, the Hebrews and Revelation. Syn.: 166, 1074, 2244, 2250, 5046, 5230. See: TDNT—1:197, 31; BAGD—27b; THAYER—18d. comp. *5550*.

166. **αἰώνιος** {71x} **aiōniŏs**, *ahee-o'-nee-os;* from *165; perpetual* (also used of past time, or past and future as well):—eternal {42x}, everlasting {25x}, the world began + 5550 {2x}, since the world began + 5550 {1x}, for ever {1x}.

Aionios, the adjective, describes **(1)** duration, **(1a)** either undefined but not endless: "Now to him that is of power to stablish you according to my gospel, and the preaching of Jesus Christ, according to the revelation of the mystery, which was kept secret since the world began (*aionios*)" (Rom 16:25; cf. 2 Ti 1:9; Titus 1:2); or **(1b)** undefined because endless: "But now is made manifest, and by the scriptures of the prophets, according to the commandment of the everlasting (*aionios*) God, made known to all nations for the obedience of faith" (Rom 16:26). **(1c)** *Aionios,* denoting "eternal," is set in contrast with *proskairos* (*4340*), lit., "for a season": "While we look not at the things which are seen, but at the things which are not seen: for the things which are seen are temporal (*proskairos*); but the things which are not seen are eternal (*aionios*)" (2 Cor 4:18).

(2) It is used of that which in nature is endless, as, e.g., **(2a)** of God (Rom 16:26), **(2b)** His power (1 Ti 6:16), **(2c)** His glory (1 Pet 5:10), **(2d)** the Holy Spirit (Heb 9:14), **(2e)** redemption (Heb 9:12), **(2f)** salvation (Heb 5:9), **(2g)** life in Christ (Jn 3:16), **(2h)** the resurrection body (2 Cor 5:1), **(2i)** the future rule of Christ (2 Pet 1:11), which is declared to be without end (Lk 1:33), **(2j)** of sin that never has forgiveness (Mk 3:29), **(2k)** the judgment of God (Heb 6:2), and **(2l)** of fire, one of judgment's instruments (Mt 18:8; 25:41; Jude 7). **(2m)** The punishment referred to in 2 Th 1:9, is not temporary, but final, and, accordingly, the phraseology shows that its purpose is not remedial but retributive. Syn.: 126, 165, 1074, 2244, 2250, 5046, 5230. See: TDNT—1:208, 31; BAGD—28b; THAYER—20c.

167. **ἀκαθαρσία** {10x} **akatharsia**, *ak-ath-ar-see'-ah;* from *169; impurity* (the quality), phys. or mor.:—uncleanness {10x}.

Akatharsia, as a noun, denotes "uncleanness": **(1)** physical: "Woe unto you, scribes and Pharisees, hypocrites! for ye are like unto whited sepulchres, which indeed appear beautiful outward, but are within full of dead men's bones, and of all uncleanness" (Mt 23:27; **(2)** moral: "Wherefore God also gave them up to unclean-

ness through the lusts of their own hearts, to dishonour their own bodies between themselves" (Rom 1:24; cf. 6:19; 2 Cor 12:21; Gal 5:19; Eph 4:19; 5:3; Col 3:5; 1 Th 2:3—suggestive of the fact that sensuality and evil doctrine are frequently associated; 4:7). Syn.: 169, 2839, 2840, 3394. See: TDNT—3:427, 381; BAGD—28d; THAYER—21a.

168. **ἀκαθάρτης** {1x} **akathartēs**, *ak-ath-ar'-tace;* from *169; impurity* (the state), mor.:—filthiness {1x}. See: BAGD—29a; THAYER—21a.

169. **ἀκάθαρτος** {30x} **akathartŏs**, *ak-ath'-ar-tos;* from *1* (as a neg. particle) and a presumed der. of *2508* (mean. *cleansed*); *impure* (cer., mor. [*lewd*] or spec. [*demonic*]):—unclean {28x}, foul {2x}.

Akathartos, as an adjective, means "unclean, impure" [*a,* negative, *kathairo* (*2508*), "to purify"], and is used **(1)** of "unclean" spirits: "There came also a multitude out of the cities round about unto Jerusalem, bringing sick folks, and them which were vexed with unclean spirits: and they were healed every one" (Acts 5:16); **(1a)** frequently in the Synoptics, **(1b)** not in John's Gospel; **(2)** ceremonially unclean: "But Peter said, Not so, Lord; for I have never eaten any thing that is common or unclean" (Acts 10:14, cf. 10:28; 11:8; 1 Cor 7:14);

(3) morally unclean: "Wherefore come out from among them, and be ye separate, saith the Lord, and touch not the unclean thing; and I will receive you" (2 Cor 6:17), including **(3a)** an "unclean person": "For this ye know, that no whoremonger, nor unclean person, nor covetous man, who is an idolater, hath any inheritance in the kingdom of Christ and of God" (Eph 5:5); **(3b)** "the filthiness/unclean things": "And the woman was arrayed in purple and scarlet colour, and decked with gold and precious stones and pearls, having a golden cup in her hand full of abominations and filthiness (168/169) of her fornication" (Rev 17:4); **(3c)** always, in the Gospels, of unclean spirits; **(3d)** it is translated "foul": "When Jesus saw that the people came running together, he rebuked the foul spirit, saying unto him, Thou dumb and deaf spirit, I charge thee, come out of him, and enter no more into him" (Mk 9:25; c. Rev 18:2). **(3e)** Since the word primarily had a ceremonial significance, the moral significance is less prominent as applied to a spirit, than when *poneros* (*4190*), "wicked," is so applied. Syn.: 167, 2839, 2840, 3394. See: TDNT—3:427, 381; BAGD—29a; THAYER—21b.

170. **ἀκαιρέομαι** {1x} **akaireŏmai**, *ak-ahee-reh'-om-ahee;* from a comp. of *1* (as a neg. particle) and *2540* (mean. *unsea-*

sonable); to be inopportune (for one-self), i.e. to fail of a proper occasion:—lack of opportunity {1x}.

Akaireomai, as a verb, means "to have no opportunity": "But I rejoiced in the Lord greatly, that now at the last your care of me hath flourished again; wherein ye were also careful, but ye lacked opportunity" (Phil 4:10) [a, negative, and kairos (2540), "season"]. Syn.: 2119, 2120, 2540, 5117. See: TDNT—3:462,*; BAGD—29b; THAYER—21b.

171. ἀκαίρως {1x} akairōs, ak-ah'-ee-roce; adv. from the same as 170; inopportunely:—out of season {1x}.

Akairos, as an adverb, denotes "out of season, unseasonably": "Preach the word; be instant in season, out of season (akairos); reprove, rebuke, exhort with all longsuffering and doctrine" (2 Ti 4:2). Syn.: 2111, 2122, 2540, 3641, 4340, 5550, 5610. See: TDNT—3:462, 389; BAGD—29b; THAYER—21b.

172. ἄκακος {2x} akakŏs, ak'-ak-os; from 1 (as a neg. particle) and 2556; not bad, i.e. (obj.) innocent or (subj.) unsuspecting:—simple {1x}, harmless {1x}.

(1) Akakos lit. means without evil, free from evil and signifies simple, guileless, unsuspecting, innocent, free from admixture of evil: (1a) of believers: "For they that are such serve not our Lord Jesus Christ, but their own belly; and by good words and fair speeches deceive the hearts of the simple (akakos)" (Rom 16:18); (1b) of the character of Christ: "For such an high priest became us, who is holy, harmless, undefiled, separate from sinners, and made higher than the heavens" (Heb 7:26). (2) The absence of all evil implies the presence of all good. Syn.: Akakos contains no harmfulness, so the adolos (97) has no guile, the akeraios (185) contains no foreign mixture, and the haplous (573) has no folds or wrinkles. See also: 185. See: TDNT—3:482, 391; BAGD—29b; THAYER—21b.

173. ἄκανθα {14x} akantha, ak'-an-thah; prob. from the same as 188; a thorn:—thorns {14x}.

Akantha, as a noun, means (1) "a brier, a thorn" is always used in the plural in the NT (Mt 7:16; Lk 6:44; Mt 13:7 (twice); Mt 13:22); (2) in Mt 27:29 and Jn 19:2, of the crown of "thorns" placed on Christ's head in mock imitation of the garlands worn by emperors. Syn.: 174, 4647. See: BAGD—29c; THAYER—21c.

174. ἀκάνθινος {2x} akanthinŏs, ak-an'-thee-nos; from 173; thorny:—of thorns {2x}.

Akanthinos, as an adjective, means "of thorns": "And they clothed him with purple,

and platted a crown of thorns, and put it about his head" (Mk 15:17; cf. Jn 19:5). Syn.: 173, 4647. See: BAGD—29c; THAYER—21c.

175. ἄκαρπος {7x} akarpŏs, ak'-ar-pos; from 1 (as a neg. particle) and 2590; barren (lit. or fig.):—unfruitful {6x}, without fruit {1x}.

Akarpos, as an adjective, means "unfruitful" and is used figuratively (1) of "the word of the Kingdom," rendered "unfruitful" in the case of those influenced by the cares of the world and the deceitfulness of riches (Mt 13:22; Mk 4:19); (2) of the understanding of one praying with a "tongue," which effected no profit to the church without an interpretation of it (1 Cor 14:14); (3) of the works of darkness (Eph 5:11); (4) of believers who fail "to maintain good works," indicating the earning of one's living so as to do good works to others (Titus 3:14); (5) of the effects of failing to supply in one's faith the qualities of virtue, knowledge, temperance, patience, godliness, love of the brethren, and love (2 Pet 1:8). (6) In Jude 12 it is rendered "without fruit," of ungodly men, who oppose the gospel while pretending to uphold it, depicted as "autumn trees." Syn.: 2590, 2592, 2593, 3703, 5352. See: TDNT—3:616, 416; BAGD—29d; THAYER—21c.

176. ἀκατάγνωστος {1x} akatagnōstŏs, ak-at-ag'-noce-tos; from 1 (as a neg. particle) and a der. of 2607; unblamable:—that cannot be condemned {1x}.

Akatagnostos, as an adjective, means, with negative prefix, a, "not to be condemned" and is said of sound speech: "Sound speech, that cannot be condemned; that he that is of the contrary part may be ashamed, having no evil thing to say of you" (Titus 2:8). Syn.: 843, 2607, 2613, 2631, 2632, 2633, 2917, 2919, 2920. See: TDNT—1:714, 119; BAGD—29d; THAYER—21c.

177. ἀκατακάλυπτος {2x} akatakaluptŏs, ak-at-ak-al'-oop-tos; from 1 (as a neg. particle) and a der. of a comp. of 2596 and 2572; unveiled:—uncovered {2x}.

Akatakaluptos means "uncovered" and is used in 1 Cor 11:5 with reference to the injunction forbidding women to be "unveiled" in a church gathering: "But every woman that prayeth or prophesieth with her head uncovered dishonoureth her head: for that is even all one as if she were shaven" (cf. 1 Cor 11:13). See: BAGD—29d; THAYER—21d.

178. ἀκατάκριτος {2x} akatakritŏs, ak-at-ak'-ree-tos; from 1 (as a neg. particle) and a der. of 2632; without (legal) trial:—uncondemned {2x}.

Akatakritos is rendered "uncondemned" in

Acts 16:37 and properly means "without trial, not yet tried": "But Paul said unto them, They have beaten us openly uncondemned (akatakritos), being Romans, and have cast us into prison; and now do they thrust us out privily? nay verily; but let them come themselves and fetch us out" (cf. Acts 22:25). See: TDNT—3:952, 469; BAGD—29d; THAYER—21d.

179. ἀκατάλυτος {2x} **akatalutŏs,** *ak-at-al'-oo-tos;* from *1* (as a neg. particle) and a der. of *2647; indissoluble,* i.e. (fig.) *permanent:*—endless {2x}.

Akatalutos denotes indissoluble, Heb 7:16, "endless": "Who is made, not after the law of a carnal commandment, but after the power of an endless life" i.e., a life which makes its possessor the holder of His priestly office for evermore. Syn.: 562. See: TDNT—3:952, 469; BAGD—30a; THAYER—21d.

180. ἀκατάπαυστος {1x} **akatapaustŏs,** *ak-at-ap'-ow-stos;* from *1* (as a neg. particle) and a der. of *2664; unrefraining:*—that cannot cease {1x}. See: BAGD—30a; THAYER—21d.

181. ἀκαταστασία {5x} **akatastasia,** *ak-at-as-tah-see'-ah;* from *182; instability,* i.e. *disorder:*—commotion {1x}, confusion {2x}, tumult {2x}.

Akatastasia, as a noun, means "instability" and denotes **(1)** "a state of disorder, disturbance, confusion, tumult": "For God is not the author of confusion, but of peace, as in all churches of the saints" (1 Cor 14:33); **(2)** "revolution or anarchy": "For where envying and strife is, there is confusion (akatasia) and every evil work" (Jas 3:16); **(3)** "commotions": "But when ye shall hear of wars and commotions, be not terrified: for these things must first come to pass; but the end is not by and by" (Lk 21:9); **(4)** "tumults" 2 Cor 6:5; 12:20). Syn.: 2617, 4797, 4799. See: TDNT—3:446, 387; BAGD—30a; THAYER—21d.

182. ἀκατάστατος {1x} **akatastatŏs,** *ak-at-as'-tat-os;* from *1* (as a neg. particle) and a der. of *2525; inconstant:*—unstable {1x}.

Akatastatos means "unsettled, unstable, disorderly," is translated "unstable" in Jas 1:8. See: TDNT—3:447, 387; BAGD—30b; THAYER—22a.

183. ἀκατάσχετος {1x} **akataschĕtŏs,** *ak-at-as'-khet-os;* from *1* (as a neg. particle) and a der. of *2722; unrestrainable:*—unruly {1x}.

Akataschetos is translated "unruly" in Jas 3:8. See: BAGD—30b.; THAYER—22a.

184. Ἀκελδαμά {1x} **Akeldama,** *ak-el-dam-ah';* of Chald. or. [mean. *field of blood;* corresp. to 2506 and 1818]; *Akeldama,* a place near Jerusalem:—Aceldama {1x}. See: BAGD—30b; THAYER—22a.

185. ἀκέραιος {3x} **akĕraiŏs,** *ak-er'-ah-yos;* from *1* (as a neg. particle) and a presumed der. of *2767; unmixed,* i.e. (fig.) *innocent:*—harmless {2x}, simple {1x}.

Akeraios, literally means "unmixed, with absence of foreign mixture, pure" and is used **(1)** metaphorically of what is guileless, sincere, harmless: "Behold, I send you forth as sheep in the midst of wolves: be ye therefore wise as serpents, and harmless as doves" (Mt 10:16), i.e., with the simplicity of a single eye, discerning what is evil, and choosing only what glorifies God (cf. Phil 2:15); **(2)** "simple": "For your obedience is come abroad unto all men. I am glad therefore on your behalf: but yet I would have you wise unto that which is good, and simple concerning evil" (Rom 16:19). Syn.: As the *akakos* (172) has no harmfulness in him, and the *adolos* (97) no guile, so the *akeraios* no foreign mixture, and the *haplous* (573) no folds. See: TDNT—1:209, 33; BAGD—30b; THAYER—22a.

186. ἀκλινής {1x} **aklinēs,** *ak-lee-nace';* from *1* (as a neg. particle) and *2827; not leaning,* i.e. (fig.) *firm:*—without wavering {1x}.

Aklines means "without bending/without wavering" and occurs in Heb 10:23: "Let us hold fast the profession of our faith without wavering; (for he is faithful that promised)." See: BAGD—30c; THAYER—22a.

187. ἀκμάζω {1x} **akmazō,** *ak-mad'-zo;* from the same as *188;* to *make a point,* i.e. (fig.) *mature:*—be fully ripe {1x}.

Akmazo, means "to be at the prime, to be ripe" and is translated "are fully ripe": "And another angel came out from the altar, which had power over fire; and cried with a loud cry to him that had the sharp sickle, saying, Thrust in thy sharp sickle, and gather the clusters of the vine of the earth; for her grapes are fully ripe" (Rev 14:18). Syn.: 3583, 3860. See: BAGD—30d; THAYER—22a.

188. ἀκμήν {1x} **akmēn,** *ak-mane';* acc. of a noun ("*acme*") akin to ἀκή **akē** (a *point*) and mean. the same; adv. *just* now, i.e. *still:*—yet {1x}. See: BAGD—30d; THAYER—22a.

189. ἀκοή {24x} **akŏē,** *ak-o-ay';* from *191; hearing* (the act, the sense or the thing heard):—hearing {10x}, ears {4x}, fame {3x}, rumour {2x}, report {2x}, audience {1x}, which ye heard {1x}, preached {1x}.

Akoe means "hearing" denotes **(1)** the sense of "hearing" (1 Cor 12:17; 2 Pet 2:8); **(2)** that which is "heard," a report (Mt 4:24); **(3)** the physical organ (Mk 7:35), standing for the sense of "hearing"; **(4)** so in Lk 7:1 for "audience"; **(5)** Acts 17:20; 2 Tim 4:3–4 ("being tickled as to the ears"); **(6)** a message or teaching (Jn 12:38; Rom 10:16–17; Gal 3:2, 5; 1 Th 2:13; Heb 4:2 - "(the word) preached." **(7)** A combination of verb and noun is used in phrases which have been termed Hebraic as they express somewhat literally an OT phraseology **(7a)** "by hearing ye shall hear" (Mt 13:14; Acts 28:26 a mode of expression conveying emphasis); **(7b)** "the receiving of a message" Rom 10:17, something more than the mere sense of "hearing"; an interaction with the Word and a decision is always made [compare a courtroom hearing]. Syn.: 191, 1251, 1522, 1873, 1874, 3775, 3878, 4257, 5621. See: TDNT—1:221, 34; BAGD—30d; THAYER—22b.

190. **ἀκολουθέω** {92x} **akŏlŏuthĕō,** *ak-ol-oo-theh'-o;* from *1* (as a particle of union) and κέλευθος **kĕlĕuthŏs** (a *road*); prop. to *be in the same way with,* i.e. to *accompany* (spec. as a disciple):—follow {91x}, reach {1x}.

Akoloutheo, as a verb, gives rise to be an *akolouthos,* "a follower," or "companion" (from the prefix *a,* here expressing "union, likeness," and *keleuthos,* "a way"; hence, "one going in the same way") and is used **(1)** frequently in the literal sense (Mt 4:25); **(2)** metaphorically, of "discipleship" (Mk 8:34; 9:38; 10:21). **(3)** It is used 77 times in the Gospels, of "following" Christ, and only once otherwise: "And he sendeth forth two of his disciples, and saith unto them, Go ye into the city, and there shall meet you a man bearing a pitcher of water: follow him" (Mk 14:13). Syn.: 1096, 1377, 1811, 1872, 2614, 2628, 3877, 4870. See: TDNT—1:210, 33; BAGD—31a; THAYER—22b.

191. **ἀκούω** {437x} **akŏuō,** *ak-oo'-o;* a prim. verb; to *hear* (in various senses):—hear {418x}, hearken {6x}, give audience {3x}, hearer {2x}, misc. {8x} = come (to the ears), be noised, be reported, understand.

Akouo, as a verb, is the usual word denoting "to hear" is used **(1)** intransitively: "He that hath ears to hear, let him hear" (Mt 11:15; cf. Mk 4:23); **(2)** transitively when the object is expressed, sometimes in the accusative case, sometimes in the genitive. **(2a)** Thus in Acts 9:7, "hearing the voice," the noun "voice" is in the partitive genitive case [i.e., hearing (something) of], whereas in 22:9, "they heard not the voice," the construction is with the accusative. **(2b)** This removes the idea of any contradiction. The former indicates a "hearing" of the sound, the latter indicates the meaning or message of the voice (this they did not hear). **(2c)** The former denotes the sensational perception, the latter (the accusative case) the thing perceived. **(3)** In Jn 5:25, 28, **(3a)** the genitive case is used, indicating a "sensational perception" that the Lord's voice is sounding; **(3b)** in 3:8, of "hearing" the wind, the accusative is used, stressing "the thing perceived."

(4) That God "hears" prayer signifies that He answers prayer (Jn 9:31; 1 Jn 5:14, 15). **(5)** Sometimes the verb is used with *para* ("from beside"), **(5a)** e.g., Jn 1:40, "one of the two which heard John speak," lit., "heard from beside John," suggesting that he stood beside him; **(5b)** in Jn 8:26, 40, indicating the intimate fellowship of the Son with the Father; **(5c)** the same construction is used in Acts 10:22 and 2 Ti 2:2, in the latter case, of the intimacy between Paul and Timothy. Syn.: 189, 1251, 1522, 1873, 1874, 3878, 4257. See: TDNT—1:216, 34; BAGD—31d; THAYER—22c.

192. **ἀκρασία** {2x} **akrasia,** *ak-ras-ee'-a;* from *193; want of self-restraint:*—excess {1x}, incontinency {1x}.

Akrasia literally denotes "want of strength," hence, "want of self-control, incontinence, excess": **(1)** "Woe unto you, scribes and Pharisees, hypocrites! for ye make clean the outside of the cup and of the platter, but within they are full of extortion and excess (*akrasia*)" (Mt 23:25); **(2)** "Defraud ye not one the other, except it be with consent for a time, that ye may give yourselves to fasting and prayer; and come together again, that Satan tempt you not for your incontinency" (1 Cor 7:5). Syn.: 193, 401. See: TDNT—2:339, 196; BAGD—33a; THAYER—23d.

193. **ἀκράτης** {1x} **akratēs,** *ak-rat'-ace;* from *1* (as a neg. particle) and *2904; powerless,* i.e. *without self-control:*—incontinent {1x}.

Akrates, "powerless, incontinent": "Without natural affection, truce breakers, false accusers, incontinent, fierce, despisers of those that are good" (2 Ti 3:3 - "without self-control"). Syn.: 192, 401. See: TDNT—2:339, 196; BAGD—33a; THAYER—23d.

194. **ἄκρατος** {1x} **akratŏs,** *ak'-rat-os;* from *1* (as a neg. particle) and a presumed der. of *2767; undiluted:*—without mixture {1x}. See: BAGD—33a; THAYER—23d.

195. **ἀκρίβεια** {1x} **akribĕia,** *ak-ree'-bi-ah;* from the same as *196; exactness:*—perfect manner {1x}.

Akribeia, as a noun, means "exactness, precision": "I am verily a man which am a Jew,

born in Tarsus, a city in Cilicia, yet brought up in this city at the feet of Gamaliel, and taught according to the perfect manner of the law of the fathers, and was zealous toward God, as ye all are this day" (Acts 22:3). Syn.: 1485, 2239, 3634, 3668, 3697, 3779, 4169, 4187, 4217, 4459, 5158, 5159, 5179, 5615. See: BAGD—33a; THAYER—23d.

196. ἀκριβέστατος {1x} **akribĕstatŏs**, *ak-ree-bes'-ta-tos;* superlative of ἀκρίβης **akribēs** (a der. of the same as *206*); *most exact:*—most straitest {1x}.

This word means "accurate, exact" and occurs in Acts 26:5 "the most straitest (sect)." See: BAGD—33b; THAYER—23d.

197. ἀκριβέστερον {4x} **akribĕstĕrŏn**, *ak-ree-bes'-ter-on;* neut. of the comparative of the same as *196;* (adv.) *more exactly:*—more perfectly {3x}, more perfect {1x}.

This word means "accurately, carefully" is translated (1) "more perfectly" (Acts 18:26; 23:15); (2) "more perfect" (Acts 23: 20; 24:22, lit., "knowing more exactly"). See: BAGD—33b; THAYER—23d.

198. ἀκριβόω {2x} **akribŏō**, *ak-ree-bŏ'-o;* from the same as *196;* to *be exact,* i.e. *ascertain:*—enquire diligently {2x}.

Akriboo, as a verb, means "to learn carefully" is translated "diligently enquired" (Mt 2:7, 16). Syn.: 1097, 3129, 3453. See: BAGD—33b; THAYER—24a.

199. ἀκριβῶς {5x} **akribōs**, *ak-ree-boce';* adv. from the same as *196; exactly:*—diligently {2x}, perfect {1x}, perfectly {1x}, circumspectly {1x}.

The word expresses that "accuracy" which is the outcome of carefulness. *Akribos* is translated (1) "having had perfect understanding" (Lk 1:3 "having traced the course of all things accurately"). (2) It is used in Mt 2:8 of Herod's command to the wise men as to searching for the young Child "diligently"; (3) in Acts 18:25 of Apollos' teaching of "the things concerning Jesus" ("carefully/diligently"); (4) in Eph 5:15 of the way in which believers are to walk ("circumspectly"); (5) in 1 Th 5:2 of the knowledge gained by the saints through the apostle's teaching concerning the Day of the Lord ("perfectly"). See: BAGD—33b; THAYER—24a.

200. ἀκρίς {4x} **akris**, *ak-rece';* appar. from the same as *206;* a *locust* (as *pointed,* or as *lightning* on the *top* of vegetation):—locust {4x}.

Akris occurs (1) in Mt 3:4 and Mk 1:6 (1a) of the insects themselves, (1b) as forming part of the diet of John the Baptist; (1c) they are used

as food; (1d) the Arabs stew them with butter, after removing the head, legs and wings. (2) In Rev 9:3, 7, they appear as monsters representing satanic agencies, let loose by divine judgments inflicted upon men for five months, the time of the natural life of the "locust." See: BAGD—33c; THAYER—24a.

201. ἀκροατήριον {1x} **akrŏatērion**, *ak-rŏ-at-ay'-ree-on;* from *202;* an *audience-room:*—place of hearing {1x}.

Akroaterion, as a noun, denotes "a place of audience" [cf. *akroaomai* - 202 "to listen"], "a place of hearing": "And on the morrow, when Agrippa was come, and Bernice, with great pomp, and was entered into the place of hearing (*akroaterion*), with the chief captains, and principal men of the city, at Festus' commandment Paul was brought forth" (Acts 25:23). Syn.: 402, 1096, 1502, 3837, 4042, 5117, 5247, 5564, 5602. See: BAGD—33c; THAYER—24b.

202. ἀκροατής {4x} **akrŏatēs**, *ak-rŏ-at-ace';* from ἀκροάομαι **akrŏaŏmai** (to *listen;* appar. an intens. of *191);* a *hearer* (merely):—hearer {4x}.

This word means "to listen" and is used of being a hearer (1) "of the Law": "For not the hearers of the law are just before God, but the doers of the law shall be justified" (Rom 2:13); (2) "of the word" (Jas 1:22, 23); and (3) in Jas 1: 25 one should not be "a [forgetful] hearer [of the word]." See: BAGD—33c; THAYER—24b.

203. ἀκροβυστία {20x} **akrŏbustia**, *ak-rob-oos-tee'-ah;* from *206* and prob. a modified form of πόσθη **pŏsthē** (the *penis* or male sexual organ); the *prepuce;* by impl. an *uncircumcised* (i.e. *gentile,* fig. *unregenerate*) state or person:—uncircumcision {16x}, being circumcised {2x}, uncircumcised + *2192* {1x}, though not circumcised {1x}.

Akrobustia, as a noun, means "uncircumcision" and is used (1) of the physical state, in contrast to the act of "circumcision": (1a) "having uncircumcision (Acts 11:3); (1b) "though they be in uncircumcision" (Rom 2:25–26; 4:10–11, 12; 1 Cor 7:18–19; Gal 5:6; 6:15; Col 3:11); (2) by metonymy, for Gentiles (e.g., Rom 2:26–27; 3:30; 4:9; Gal 2:7; Eph 2:11); (3) in a metaphorical or transferred sense, of the moral condition in which the corrupt desires of the flesh still operate (Col 2:13). Syn.: 564, 1986, 4059, 4061. See: TDNT—1:225, 36; BAGD—33d; THAYER—24b.

204. ἀκρογωνιαῖος {2x} **akrŏgōniaiŏs**, *ak-rog-o-nee-ah'-yos;* from *206* and *1137;* belonging to the extreme *corner:*—chief corner {2x}.

This words denotes "a chief corner-stone" [from *akros,* "highest, extreme," *gonia,* "a cor-

ner, angle"] (Eph 2:20; 1 Pet 2:6). See: TDNT—1:792, 137; BAGD—33d; THAYER—24c.

205. ἀκροθίνιον {1x} **akrŏthiniŏn,** *ak-roth-in'-ee-on;* from *206* and θίς **this** (a *heap*); prop. (in the plur.) the *top of the heap,* i.e. (by impl.) *best of the booty:*—spoils {1x}.

Akrothinion, primarily means the top of a heap; hence firstfruit offerings, and in war the choicest spoils: "Now consider how great this man was, unto whom even the patriarch Abraham gave the tenth of the spoils" (Heb 7:4). Syn.: 724, 4661. See: BAGD—33d; THAYER—24c.

206. ἄκρον {6x} **akrŏn,** *ak'-ron;* neut. of an adj. prob. akin to the base of *188;* the *extremity:*—uttermost part {2x}, one end {1x}, other + 846 {1x}, tip {1x}, top {1x}.

This word means "the top, an extremity," is translated "tip" in Luke 16:24. See: BAGD—34a; THAYER—24d.

207. Ἀκύλας {6x} **Akulas,** *ak-oo'-las;* prob. for Lat. *aquila* (an *eagle*); *Akulas,* an Isr.:—Aquila {6x}. See: BAGD—34b; THAYER—24d.

208. ἀκυρόω {3x} **akurŏō,** *ak-oo-rŏ'-o;* from *1* (as a neg. particle) and *2964;* to *invalidate:*—make of none effect {2x}, disannul {1x}.

This word means **(1)** "to deprive of authority"; hence, "to make of none effect": "And honour not his father or his mother, he shall be free. Thus have ye made the commandment of God of none effect by your tradition" (Mt 15:6; cf. Mk 7:13, with reference to the commandment or word of God); and **(2)** "to disannul": "And this I say, that the covenant, that was confirmed before of God in Christ, the law, which was four hundred and thirty years after, cannot disannul, that it should make the promise of none effect" (Gal 3:17 of the inability of the Law to deprive of force God's covenant with Abraham). **(3)** This verb stresses the effect of the act, while *atheteo* (*114*) stresses the attitude of the rejector. Syn.: 114, 115. See: TDNT—3:1099, 494; BAGD—34b; THAYER—24d.

209. ἀκωλύτως {1x} **akŏlutōs,** *ak-o-loo'-toce;* adv. from a compound of *1* (as a neg. particle) and a der. of *2967;* in an *unhindered manner,* i.e. *freely:*—no man forbidding him {1x}.

This word means "without hindrance" and is translated "none forbidding him" (Acts 28:31). It is interesting to read the triumphant note on which the word brings the Acts to a close. See: BAGD—34b; THAYER—24d.

210. ἄκων {1x} **akōn,** *ak'-ohn;* from *1* (as a neg. particle) and *1635; unwilling:*—against (one's) will {1x}.

This word means "unwillingly," occurs in 1 Cor 9:17, and is translated "against my will." Syn.: 1635. See: TDNT—2:469, 221; BAGD—34b; THAYER—24d.

211. ἀλάβαστρον {4x} **alabastrŏn,** *al-ab'-as-tron;* neut. of ἀλάβασ-τρος **alabastrŏs** (of uncert. der.), the name of a stone; prop. an "*alabaster*" box, i.e. (by extens.) a perfume *vase* (of any material):—alabaster box {3x}, box {1x}.

This word means "an alabaster vessel" and is translated "box" (Mt 26:7; Mk 14:3; Lk 7:37). The breaking refers to the seal, not to the box or cruse. See: BAGD—34c; THAYER—24d.

212. ἀλαζονεία {2x} **alazŏnĕia,** *al-ad-zon-i'-a;* from *213; braggadocio,* i.e. (by impl.) *self-confidence:*—boasting {1x}, pride {1x}.

Alazoneia is **(1)** the practice of an *alazon* (*213*) and denotes **(2)** quackery; hence, arrogant display, or boastings: "But now ye rejoice in your boastings: all such rejoicing is evil" (Jas 4:16); and **(3)** pride: "For all that is in the world, the lust of the flesh, and the lust of the eyes, and the pride of life, is not of the Father, but is of the world" (1 Jn 2:16). Syn.: 2744, 3166. See: TDNT—1:226, 36; BAGD—34c; THAYER—25a.

213. ἀλαζών {2x} **alazōn,** *al-ad-zone';* from ἄλη **alē** (*vagrancy*); *braggart:*—boaster {2x}.

Alazon means a boaster and primarily signifies "a wanderer about the country, a vagabond; hence, an impostor; one who is full of empty and boastful professions and only while in the company of others": "For men shall be lovers of their own selves, covetous, boasters, proud, blasphemers, disobedient to parents, unthankful, unholy" (2 Ti 3:2; Rom 1:30). Syn.: *Alazon, hyperephanos* (*5244*) and *hybristes* (*5197*) portray an ascending scale of guilt, respectively designating those who are boastful in words (*213*), those who are proud and overbearing in thoughts (*5244*), and those who are insolent and injurious in deeds (*5197*). See also: 2744, 3166, 5197, 5244. See: TDNT—1:226, 36; BAGD—34d; THAYER—25a.

214. ἀλαλάζω {2x} **alalazō,** *al-al-ad'-zo;* from ἀλαλή **alalē** (a *shout,* "*halloo*"); to *vociferate,* i.e. (by impl.) to *wail;* fig. to *clang:*—wail {1x}, tinkle {1x}.

This word is derived from the battle-cry, *alala,* is used of "raising the shout of battle" (cf. Josh 6:20); hence, **(1)** "to make a loud cry or shout": "And He cometh to the house of the

ruler of the synagogue, and seeth the tumult, and them that wept and wailed (*alalazo*) greatly" (cf. Ps 47:1; Jer 29:2; of wailing mourners); and **(2)** in 1 Cor 13:1 of the "tinkling" of cymbals. See: TDNT—1:227, 36; BAGD—34d; THAYER—25b.

215. ἀλάλητος {1x} **alalētŏs,** *al-al'-ay-tos;* from *1* (as a neg. particle) and a der. of *2980; unspeakable:*—which cannot be uttered {1x}. See: BAGD—34d; THAYER—25b.

216. ἄλαλος {3x} **alalŏs,** *al'-al-os;* from *1* (as a neg. particle) and *2980; mute:*—dumb {3x}.

Alalos, as an adjective, literally means "speechless" (*a*, negative, and *laleo*, "to speak"), and is found in Mk 7:37: "And were beyond measure astonished, saying, He hath done all things well: He maketh both the deaf to hear, and the dumb to speak" (cf. 9:17, 25). Syn.: *Aphonos* (*880*), lit., "voiceless, or soundless" has reference to voice, while *alalos* (*216*) has reference to words. See also: 880, 2974, 4623. See: BAGD—34d; THAYER—25b.

217. ἅλας {8x} **halas,** *hal'-as;* from *251; salt;* fig. *prudence:*—salt {8x}. See: TDNT—1:228, 36; BAGD—35a; THAYER—25b.

218. ἀλείφω {9x} **alĕiphō,** *al-i'-fo;* from *1* (as particle of union) and the base of *3045;* to *oil* (with perfume):—anoint {9x}.

Aleipho, as a verb, is a general term used for "an anointing" of any kind, whether **(1)** of physical refreshment after washing: "But thou, when thou fastest, anoint thine head, and wash thy face" (Mt 6:17; cf. Lk 7:38, 46; Jn 11:2; 12:3); or **(2)** of the sick: "And they cast out many devils, and anointed with oil many that were sick, and healed them" (Mk 6:13; cf. Jas 5:14); or **(3)** a dead body: "And when the sabbath was past, Mary Magdalene, and Mary the mother of James, and Salome, had bought sweet spices, that they might come and anoint Him"(Mk 16:1).

(4) The material used was either oil, or ointment: "And stood at His feet behind him weeping, and began to wash His feet with tears, and did wipe them with the hairs of her head, and kissed His feet, and anointed them with the ointment" (Lk 7:38; cf. vs 46). Syn.: *Aleiphein* and *chriein* (*5548*) are clearly distinguished. *Chriein* is absolutely restricted to the Father's anointing of the Son with the Holy Spirit for the accomplishment of the Son's greater office. *Chriein* has no profane or common uses. *Aleiphein* is used as the mundane and profane term, and is used indiscriminately of all actual anointings whether with oil or with ointment. See also: 1472, 1637, 2025, 3462, 3464, 5545,

5548. See: TDNT—1:229, 37; BAGD—35b; THAYER—25d.

219. ἀλεκτοροφωνία {1x} **alektŏrŏphōnia,** *al-ek-tor-of-o-nee'-ah;* from *220* and *5456; cock-crow,* i.e. the third night-watch:—cockcrowing {1x}.

This word denotes "cock-crowing." **(1)** There were two "cock-crowings," one after midnight, the other before dawn. **(2)** In these watches the Jews followed the Roman method of dividing the night. **(2a)** The first "cock-crowing" was at the third watch of the night. **(2b)** That is the one mentioned in Mk 13:35. **(2c)** Mark mentions both; see 14:30. **(3)** The latter, the second, is that referred to in the other Gospels and is mentioned especially as "the cock-crowing." See: BAGD—35b; THAYER—25d.

220. ἀλέκτωρ {12x} **alĕktōr,** *al-ek'-tore;* from ἀλέκω **(to ward off)**; a *cock* or male fowl:—cock {12x}. See: BAGD—35c; THAYER—26a.

221. Ἀλεξανδρεύς {2x} **Alĕxandrĕus,** *al-ex-and-reuce';* from Ἀλεξάνδρεια (the city so called); an *Alexandreian* or inhab. of Alexandria:—Alexandrian {1x}, born at Alexander + 1085 {1x}. See: BAGD—35c; THAYER—26a.

222. Ἀλεξανδρῖνος {2x} **Alĕxandrinŏs,** *al-ex-an-dree'-nos;* from the same as *221; Alexandrine,* or belonging to Alexandria:—of Alexandria {2x}. See: BAGD—35c; THAYER—26a.

223. Ἀλέξανδρος {6x} **Alĕxandrŏs,** *al-ex'-an-dros;* from the same as (the first part of) *220* and *435; man-defender; Alexander,* the name of three Isr. and one other man:—Alexander {6x}. See: BAGD—35c; THAYER—26a.

224. ἄλευρον {2x} **alĕurŏn,** *al'-yoo-ron;* from ἀλέω **alĕō** (to *grind*); *flour:*—meal {2x}.

This verb for this word means "to grind," and therefore, literally, "what is ground": "Another parable spake he unto them; The kingdom of heaven is like unto leaven, which a woman took, and hid in three measures of meal, till the whole was leavened" (Mt. 13:33; cf. Lk 13:21). See: BAGD—35d; THAYER—26a.

225. ἀλήθεια {110x} **alēthĕia,** *al-ay'-thi-a;* from *227; truth:*—truth {107x}, truly + 1909 {1x}, true {1x}, verity {1x}.

Aletheia, as a noun, means "truth" and is used **(1)** objectively, **(1a)** signifying the reality lying at the basis of an appearance; the manifested, veritable essence of a matter: "I say the

truth in Christ, I lie not, my conscience also bearing me witness in the Holy Ghost" (Rom 9:1; cf. 2 Cor 11:10); **(1b)** especially of Christian doctrine: "To whom we gave place by subjection, no, not for an hour; that the truth of the gospel might continue with you" (Gal 2:5, where "the truth of the Gospel" denotes the "true" teaching of the Gospel, in contrast to perversions of it); **(1c)** Rom 1:25 where "the truth of God" may be "the truth concerning God" or "God whose existence is a verity"; **(1d)** but in Rom 15:8 **(1d1)** "the truth of God" is indicative of His faithfulness in the fulfillment of His promises as exhibited in Christ; **(1d2)** the word has an absolute force in Jn 14:6; 17:17; 18:37, 38; **(1d3)** in Eph 4:21 "as the truth is in Jesus", the meaning is not merely ethical "truth," but "truth" in all its fullness and scope, as embodied in Him; **(1e)** He was the perfect expression of the truth; this is virtually equivalent to His statement in Jn 14:6;

(2) subjectively, "truthfulness/truth," not merely verbal, but sincerity and integrity of character: "Ye are of your father the devil, and the lusts of your father ye will do. He was a murderer from the beginning, and abode not in the truth, because there is no truth in him" (Jn 8:44; cf. 3 Jn 3). Syn.: 226, 227, 228, 230, 1103, 1104. See: TDNT—1:232, 37; BAGD—35d; THAYER—26a.

226. **ἀληθεύω** {2x} **alēthĕuō**, al-ayth-yoo'-o; from 227; to be true (in doctrine and profession):—tell the truth {1x}, speak the truth {1x}.

Aletheuo, as a verb, signifies "to deal faithfully or truly with anyone." **(1)** "speaking the truth": "But speaking the truth in love, may grow up into him in all things, which is the head, even Christ" (Eph 4:15); **(2)** "I tell [you] the truth": "Am I therefore become your enemy, because I tell you the truth?" (Gal 4:16 - where probably the apostle is referring to the contents of his epistle). Syn.: 225, 227, 228, 230, 1103, 1104. See: TDNT—1:251, 37; BAGD—36c; THAYER—26d.

227. **ἀληθής** {25x} **alēthēs**, al-ay-thace'; from 1 (as a neg. particle) and 2990; true (as not concealing):—true {23x}, truly {1x}, truth {1x}.

Alethes, as an adjective, means primarily "unconcealed, manifest"; hence, actual, "true to fact" and is used **(1)** of "truthful" persons: "And they sent out unto him their disciples with the Herodians, saying, Master, we know that thou art true, and teachest the way of God in truth, neither carest thou for any man: for thou regardest not the person of men"(Mt 22:16; cf. Mk 12:14; Jn 3:33; 7:18; 8:26; Rom

3:4; 2 Cor 6:8); **(2)** of "true" things, conforming to reality: "For thou hast had five husbands; and he whom thou now hast is not thy husband: in that saidst thou truly" (Jn 4:18; cf. 10:41; 19:35; 21:24; Acts 12:9; Phil 4:8; Titus 1:13; 1 Pet 5:12; 2 Pet 2:22; 1 Jn 2:8, 27; 3 Jn 2). Syn.: *Alethinos* (228) is related to *alethes* as form to contents or substances; *alethes* denotes the reality of the thing, *alethinos* defines the relation of the conception to the thing to which it corresponds = genuine. Syn.: 225, 226, 228, 230, 1103, 1104. See: TDNT—1:247, 37; BAGD—36d; THAYER—27a.

228. **ἀληθινός** {27x} **alēthĭnŏs**, al-ay-thee-nos'; from 227; truthful:—true {27x}.

Alethinos, as an adjective, denotes "true" in the sense of real, ideal, genuine. It is used **(1)** of God: "Then cried Jesus in the temple as he taught, saying, Ye both know me, and ye know whence I am: and I am not come of myself, but He that sent me is true, whom ye know not" (Jn 7:28; cf. 17:3; 1 Th 1:9; Rev 6:10). These declare that God fulfills the meaning of His Name; He is "very God," in distinction from all other gods, false gods; it signifies that He is veracious, "true" to His utterances, He cannot lie; **(2)** of Christ: "And we know that the Son of God is come, and hath given us an understanding, that we may know him that is true, and we are in him that is true, even in his Son Jesus Christ. This is the true God, and eternal life" (1 Jn 5:20; cf. Rev 3:7, 14; 19:11); **(3)** Christ's judgment: "And yet if I judge, my judgment is true: for I am not alone, but I and the Father that sent me" (Jn 8:16);

(4) God's words: "And herein is that saying true, One soweth, and another reapeth" (Jn 4:37; cf. Rev 19:9, 21:5; 22:6); **(5)** His ways: "And they sing the song of Moses the servant of God, and the song of the Lamb, saying, Great and marvellous are thy works, Lord God Almighty; just and true are thy ways, thou King of saints" (Rev 15:3); **(6)** His judgments: "And I heard another out of the altar say, Even so, Lord God Almighty, true and righteous are thy judgments" (Rev 16:7; cf. 19:2); **(7)** His worshipers: "But the hour cometh, and now is, when the true worshippers shall worship the Father in spirit and in truth: for the Father seeketh such to worship Him" (Jn 4:23); **(8)** believers' hearts: "Let us draw near with a true heart in full assurance of faith, having our hearts sprinkled from an evil conscience, and our bodies washed with pure water" (Heb 10:22);

(9) the witness of the apostle John: "And he that saw it bare record, and his record is true: and he knoweth that he saith true, that ye might believe" (Jn 19:35); **(10)** the spiritual,

Greek

antitypical tabernacle: "A minister of the sanctuary, and of the true tabernacle, which the Lord pitched, and not man" (Heb 8:2; cf. 9:24, not that the wilderness tabernacle was false, but that it was a weak and earthly copy of the heavenly). Syn.: *Alethinos* is related to *alethes* (227) as form to contents or substances; *alethes* denotes the reality of the thing, *alethinos* defines the relation of the conception to the thing to which it corresponds = genuine. See also: 225, 226, 227, 230, 1103, 1104. See: TDNT—1:249, 37; BAGD—37a; THAYER—27a.

229. ἀλήθω {2x} **alēthō**, *al-ay'-tho;* from the same as *224;* to *grind at the mill:*—grinding {2x}.

Aletho, as a verb, signifies "to grind at the mill" (Mt 24:41; Lk 17:35). See: BAGD—37b; THAYER—27b.

230. ἀληθῶς {21x} **alēthōs**, *al-ay-thoce';* adv. from *227; truly:*—of a truth {6x}, indeed {6x}, surely {3x}, truly {2x}, very {1x}, misc. {3x} = of a surety, verily.

Alethos, as an adverb, means "truly, surely" and is rendered **(1)** "of a truth": "Then they that were in the ship came and worshipped him, saying, Of a truth thou art the Son of God" (Mt 14:33; cf. 26:73); **(2)** "surely": "And he denied it again. And a little after, they that stood by said again to Peter, Surely thou art one of them: for thou art a Galilaean, and thy speech agreeth thereto" (Mk 14:70; cf. Lk 9:27; 12:44; 21:3; Jn 6:14; 7:40; 17:8; **(3)** "of a surety": "And when Peter was come to himself, he said, Now I know of a surety, that the Lord hath sent his angel, and hath delivered me out of the hand of Herod, and from all the expectation of the people of the Jews" (Acts 12:11); **(4)** "in truth": "For this cause also thank we God without ceasing, because, when ye received the word of God which ye heard of us, ye received it not as the word of men, but as it is in truth, the word of God, which effectually worketh also in you that believe" (1 Th 2:13); **(5)** "truly": "Now when the centurion, and they that were with him, watching Jesus, saw the earthquake, and those things that were done, they feared greatly, saying, Truly this was the Son of God" (Mt 27:54; cf. Mk 15:39). Syn.: 225, 226, 227, 228, 1103, 1104. Syn.: 1104. See: BAGD—37b; THAYER—27b.

231. ἀλιεύς {5x} **haliĕus**, *hal-ee-yoos';* from *251;* a *sailor* (as engaged on the *salt* water), i.e. (by impl.) a *fisher:*—fishers {4x}, fishermen {1x}.

This word means "a fisherman, fisher" and occurs in Mt 4:18, 19; Mk 1:16, 17; Lk 5:2). See: BAGD—37c; THAYER—27c.

232. ἀλιεύω {1x} **haliĕuō**, *hal-ee-yoo'-o;* from *231;* to *be a fisher,* i.e. (by impl.) to *fish:*—a fishing {1x}.

Halieuo means "to fish" and occurs in Jn 2:3. See: BAGD—37d; THAYER—27c.

233. ἀλίζω {3x} **halizō**, *hal-id'-zo;* from *251;* to *salt:*—to salt {3x}.

Halizo, as a verb, signifies "to sprinkle" or "to season with salt" (Mt 5:13; Mk 9:49). Syn.: 251, 252, 358. See: BAGD—37d; THAYER—27c.

234. ἀλίσγεμα {1x} **alisgĕma**, *al-is'-ghem-ah;* from ἀλισγέω **alisgĕō** (to *soil*); (cer.) *defilement:*—pollution {1x}.

This word denotes a pollution, contamination (Acts 15:20—"pollutions of idols," i.e., all the contaminating associations connected with idolatry including meats from sacrifices offered to idols. See: BAGD—37d; THAYER—27d.

235. ἀλλά {637x} **alla**, *al-lah';* neut. plur. of *243;* prop. *other* things, i.e. (adv.) *contrariwise* (in many relations):—but {573x}, yea {15x}, yet {11x}, nevertheless {10x}, howbeit {9x}, nay {4x}, therefore {3x}, save {2x}, not tr {2x}, misc. {8x} = and, indeed, no, notwithstanding. Syn.: 3304, 3756, 3780. See: BAGD—38a; THAYER—27d.

236. ἀλλάσσω {6x} **allassō**, *al-las'-so;* from *243;* to *make different:*—change {6x}.

Allasso means **(1)** to make other than it is, to transform, change, and is used **(1a)** of the effect of the gospel upon the precepts of the Law (Acts 6:14); **(1b)** of the effect, on the body of a believer, of Christ's return (1 Cor 15:51–52); **(1c)** of the final renewal of the material creation (Heb 1:12); **(1d)** of a change in the apostle's mode of speaking or dealing (Gal 4:20). **(2)** In Rom 1:23 it means to exchange. Syn.: 3328, 3337, 3346. See: TDNT—1:251, 40; BAGD—39a; THAYER—28c.

237. ἀλλαχόθεν {1x} **allachŏthĕn**, *al-lakh-oth'-en;* from *243; from elsewhere:*—some other way {1x}. See: BAGD—39b; THAYER—28d.

238. ἀλληγορέω {1x} **allēgŏrĕō**, *al-lay-gor-eh'-o;* from *243* and ἀγορ-έω **agŏrĕō** (to *harangue* [comp. *58*]); to *allegorize:*—be an allegory {1x}.

Allegoreo is translated in Gal 4:24 "are an allegory" and came to signify to speak, not according to the primary sense of the word, but so that the facts stated are applied to illustrate principles. Using a text in an allegorical way does not do away with the literal historical narrative from which the allegory is taken. See:

TDNT—1:260, 42; BAGD—39b; THAYER—28d.

239. ἀλληλουϊα {4x} **allēlŏuïa,** *al-lay-loo'-ee-ah;* of Heb. or. [imper. of 1984 and 3050]; *praise ye Jah!,* an adoring exclamation:—alleluia {4x}. See: TDNT—1:264, 43; BAGD—39c; THAYER—28d.

240. ἀλλήλων {100x} **allēlōn,** *al-lay'-lone;* a reciprocal pronoun; gen. plur. from 243 redupl.; *one another:*—one another {76x}, themselves {12x}, yourselves {3x}, misc. {9x} = each other, mutual, the other. [*sometimes with 3326 or 4314*]. See: BAGD—39c; THAYER—28d.

241. ἀλλογενής {1x} **allŏgĕnēs,** *al-log-en-ace';* from 243 and 1085; *foreign,* i.e. not a Jew:—stranger {1x}.

Allogenes (241) (allos, "another," genos, "a race") occurs in Lk 17:18 of a Samaritan. Syn.: 245, 3580, 3581. See: TDNT—1:266, 43; BAGD—39c; THAYER—28d.

242. ἅλλομαι {3x} **hallŏmai,** *hal'-lom-ahee;* mid. voice of appar. a prim. verb; to *jump;* fig. to *gush:*—leap {2x}, spring up {1x}.

Hallomai means to leap **(1)** metaphorically, of the springing up of water (Jn 4:14); **(2)** literally, of the leaping of healed cripples (Acts 3:8; 14:10). Syn.: 1814, 2177, 4640. See: BAGD—39d; THAYER—28d.

243. ἄλλος {160x} **allŏs,** *al'-los;* a prim. word; *"else,"* i.e. *different* (in many applications):—other(s) {81x}, another {62x}, some {11x}, one {4x}, misc. {2x} = more, one.

Allos (243) and *heteros* (2087) **(1)** have a difference in meaning, which despite a tendency to be lost, is to be observed in numerous passages. **(1a)** *Allos* expresses a numerical difference and denotes "another of the same sort"; **(1b)** *heteros* expresses a qualitative difference and denotes "another of a different sort." **(2)** Examples are: **(2a)** Christ promised to send "another Comforter" (*allos,* "another like Himself," not *heteros*), John 14:16. **(2b)** Paul says "I see another law," *heteros,* a law different from that of the spirit of life (not *allos,* "a law of the same sort"), Rom 7:23. **(2c)** After Joseph's death "another king arose," *heteros,* one of quite a different character, Acts 7:18. **(2d)** Paul speaks of "a different gospel (*heteros*), which is not another" (*allos,* another like the one he preached), Gal 1:6–7. **(3)** They are not interchangeable. See: TDNT—1:264, 43; BAGD—39d; THAYER—29a.

244. ἀλλοτριεπίσκοπος {1x} **allotriĕpiskŏpŏs,** *al-lot-ree-ep-is'-kop-os;* from 245 and 1985; *overseeing others'* affairs, i.e. a *meddler* (spec. in Gentile customs):—a busybody in other men's matters {1x}.

Allotrioepiskopos, [from *allotrios,* "belonging to another person," and *episkopos,* "an overseer,"] is translated "busybody" (1 Pet 4:15). It was a legal term for a charge brought against Christians as being hostile to civilized society, their purpose being to make Gentiles conform to Christian standards. Syn.: 4020, 4021. See: TDNT—2:620, 244; BAGD—40c; THAYER—29a.

245. ἀλλότριος {14x} **allŏtriŏs,** *al-lot'-ree-os;* from 243; *another's,* i.e. not one's own family/country; by extens. *foreign, not akin, hostile:*—stranger {4x}, another man's {4x}, strange {2x}, other men's {2x}, other {1x}, alien {1x}. See: TDNT—1:265, 43; BAGD—40c; THAYER—29b.

246. ἀλλόφυλος {1x} **allŏphulŏs,** *al-lof'-oo-los;* from 243 and 5443; *for.,* i.e. (spec.) *Gentile:*—one of another nation {1x}. Syn.: 1085, 1484. See: TDNT—1:267, 43; BAGD—41a; THAYER—29b.

247. ἄλλως {1x} **allōs,** *al'-loce;* adv. from 243; *differently:*—otherwise {1x}. Syn.: 243, 1893, 2088. See: BAGD—41a; THAYER—29b.

248. ἀλοάω {3x} **alŏaō,** *al-o-ah'-o;* from the same as 257; to *tread* out grain:—tread out the corn {2x}, thresh {1x}. See: BAGD—41a; THAYER—29b.

249. ἄλογος {3x} **alŏgŏs,** *al'-og-os;* from 1 (as a neg. particle) and 3056; *irrational:*—brute {2x}, unreasonable {1x}.

The stress in this word is on being without the possession of reason. See: TDNT—4:141, 505; BAGD—41a; THAYER—29b.

250. ἀλόη {1x} **alŏē,** *al-o-ay';* of for. or. [comp. 174]; *aloes* (the gum):—aloes {1x}. See: BAGD—41b; THAYER—29c.

251. ἅλς {1x} **hals,** *halce;* a prim. word; *"salt"*:—salt {1x}.

Hals, as a noun, is used **(1)** literally (Mt 5:13; Mk 9:50; Lk 14:34); **(2)** metaphorically, **(2a)** of "believers" (Mt 5:13); **(2b)** of their "character and condition": "Salt is good: but if the salt have lost his saltness, wherewith will ye season it? Have salt in yourselves, and have peace one with another" (Mk 9:50); **(2c)** of "wisdom" exhibited in their speech (Col 4:6). **(3)** Being possessed of purifying, perpetuating and antiseptic qualities, "salt" became emblematic of fidelity and friendship. **(3a)** In Scripture, it is an emblem of the covenant between God and His people (cf. Num 18:19; 2 Chr

13:5); **(3b)** so again when the Lord says "Have salt in yourselves, and be at peace one with another" (Mk 9:50). **(3c)** In the Lord's teaching it is also symbolic of that spiritual health and vigor essential to Christian virtue and counteractive of the corruption that is in the world (e.g. Mt 5:13, see (2a) above. **(3d)** Food is seasoned with "salt." **(3e)** Every meal offering was to contain it, and it was to be offered with all offerings presented by Israelites, as emblematic of the holiness of Christ, and as betokening the reconciliation provided for man by God on the ground of the death of Christ (cf. Lev 2:13). **(3f)** To refuse God's provision in Christ and the efficacy of His expiatory sacrifice is to expose oneself to the doom of being "salted with fire" (Mk 9:49). Syn.: 233, 252, 358. See: BAGD— 41b; THAYER—29c.

252. **ἁλυκός** {1x} **halukŏs**, *hal-oo-kos';* from *251; briny:*—salt {1x}.

   Halukos occurs in Jas 3:12 and means "salt (water)." Syn.: 233, 251, 358. See: BAGD—41c; THAYER—29c.

253. **ἀλυπότερος** {1x} **alupŏtĕrŏs**, *al-oo-pot'-er-os;* comparative of a comp. of *1* (as a neg. particle) and *3077; more without grief:*—less sorrowful {1x}.

   Alupos, as an adjective, denotes "free from grief, less sorrowful": "I sent him therefore the more carefully, that, when ye see him again, ye may rejoice, and that I may be the less sorrowful" (Phil 2:28, their joy would mean the removal of a burden from his heart). Syn.: 3076, 3077, 3600, 3601, 3997, 4036, 5604. See: TDNT— 4:323,*; BAGD—41c; THAYER—29c.

254. **ἅλυσις** {11x} **halusis**, *hal'-oo-sis;* of uncert. der.; a *fetter* or *manacle:*— chain {10x}, bonds {1x}.

   Halusis, as a noun, denotes "bonds/chains": "For which I am an ambassador in bonds: that therein I may speak boldly, as I ought to speak" (Eph 6:20). Syn.: 1198, 1199, 4886. See: BAGD— 41c; THAYER—29c.

255. **ἀλυσιτελής** {1x} **alusitĕlēs**, *al-oo-sit-el-ace';* from *1* (as a neg. particle) and the base of *3081; gainless,* i.e. (by impl.) *pernicious:*—unprofitable {1x}.

   Alusiteles, as an adjective, means "not advantageous, not making good the expense involved": "Obey them that have the rule over you, and submit yourselves: for they watch for your souls, as they that must give account, that they may do it with joy, and not with grief: for that is unprofitable (*alusiteles*) for you" (Heb 13:17). Syn.: 512, 888, 889, 890. See: BAGD— 41c; THAYER—29d.

256. **Ἀλφαῖος** {5x} **Alphaiŏs**, *al-fah'-yos;* of Heb. or. [comp. 2501]; *Alphæus,* an Isr.:—Alphaeus (father of James) {4x}, Alphaeus (father of Levi) {1x}. See: BAGD— 41c; THAYER—29d.

257. **ἅλων** {2x} **halōn**, *hal'-ohn;* prob. from the base of *1507;* a threshing-*floor* (as *rolled* hard), i.e. (fig.) the *grain* (and chaff, as just threshed):—floor {2x}.

   Halon is "a threshing floor," is so translated "floor" in Mt 3:12, and Lk 3:17, perhaps by metonymy for the grain. See: BAGD—41d; THAYER—29d.

258. **ἀλώπηξ** {3x} **alōpēx**, *al-o'-pakes;* of uncert. der.; a *fox,* i.e. (fig.) a *cunning* person:—fox {3x}.

   Alopex is **(1)** literal in Mt 8:20; Lk 9:58; and **(2)** metaphorically, of Herod, in Lk 13:32. See: BAGD—41d; THAYER—29d.

259. **ἅλωσις** {1x} **halōsis**, *hal'-o-sis;* from a collat. form of *138; capture:*—to be taken + 1519 {1x}. See: BAGD—42a; THAYER— 30a.

260. **ἅμα** {10x} **hama**, *ham'-ah;* a prim. particle; prop. *at the* "*same*" *time,* but freely used as a prep. or adv. denoting close association:—together {3x}, withal {3x}, with {1x}, and {1x}, also {2x}.

   Hama (*260*), "at once," is translated "together" and stresses the temporal "together at the same time": "Then we which are alive and remain shall be caught up together with them in the clouds, to meet the Lord in the air: and so shall we ever be with the Lord" (1 Th 4:17; cf. 1 Th 5:10; Rom 3:12). Syn.: *Homou* (*3674*) stresses together at the same place. See: BAGD— 42a; THAYER—30a.

261. **ἀμαθής** {1x} **amathēs**, *am-ath-ace';* from *1* (as a neg. particle) and *3129; ignorant:*—unlearned {1x}.

   Amathes, as an adjective, means "unlearned" (*3129 - manthano,* "to learn"), is translated "unlearned": "As also in all his epistles, speaking in them of these things; in which are some things hard to be understood, which they that are unlearned and unstable wrest, as they do also the other scriptures, unto their own destruction" (2 Pet 3:16). Syn.: 62, 521. See: BAGD—42b; THAYER—30a.

262. **ἀμαράντινος** {1x} **amarantinŏs**, *am-ar-an'-tee-nos;* from *263;* "*amaranthine*", i.e. (by impl.) *fadeless:*—that fadeth not away {1x}.

   Amarantinos, as an adjective, primarily signifies "composed of amaranth"; hence, "unfading," 1 Pet 5:4, of the crown of glory promised to faithful elders. Syn.: This word stresses that

the inheritance is intrinsically strong; whereas *amarantos* (*263*) focuses on forces which can attempt to affect its worth. See also: 862, 3133. See: BAGD—42b; THAYER—30a.

263. ἀμάραντος {1x} **amarantŏs**, *am-ar'-antos;* from *1* (as a neg. particle) and a presumed der. of *3133; unfading,* i.e. (by impl.) *perpetual:*—that fadeth not away {1x}.

Amarantos, as an adjective, means "unfading" whence the "amaranth," an unfading flower, a symbol of perpetuity is used in 1 Pet 1:4 of the believer's inheritance, "that fadeth not away." Syn.: 262, 3133.

Our inheritance is without corruption from within itself (*862*), without defilement from outside itself (*283*), and will not wither or fade away (*263*). See also: 262, 862, 3133. See: BAGD—42b; THAYER—30b.

264. ἀμαρτάνω {43x} **hamartanō**, *ham-ar-tan'-o;* perh. from *1* (as a neg. particle) and the base of *3313;* prop. to *miss* the mark (and so *not share* in the prize), i.e. (fig.) to *err,* esp. (mor.) to *sin:*—sin {38x}, trespass {3x}, offend {1x}, for your faults {1x}.

Hamartano, as a verb, means literally "to miss the mark" and is used **(1)** of "sinning" against God **(1a)** by angels (2 Pet 2:4); **(1b)** by man (Mt 27:4; Lk 15:18, 21 [heaven standing, by metonymy, for God]; Jn 5:14; 8:11; 9:2, 3; Rom 2:12 [twice]; 3:23; 5:12, 14, 16; 6:15; 1 Cor 7:28 [twice], 36; 15:34; Eph 4:26; 1 Ti 5:20; Titus 3:11; Heb 3:17; 10:26; 1 Jn 1:10; in 2:1 [twice]), the aorist tense in each place, referring to an act of "sin"; on the contrary, in 3:6 [twice], 8, 9, the present tense indicates, not the committal of an act, but the continuous practice of "sin"; in 5:16 [twice] the present tense indicates the condition resulting from an act, "unto death" signifying "tending towards death"; **(2)** against Christ (1 Cor 8:12); **(3)** against man, **(3a)** a brother (Mt 18:15 - "trespass"; v. 21; Lk 17:3, 4 - "trespass"; 1 Cor 8:12; **(3b)** in Lk 15:18, 21, against the father by the Prodigal Son, "in thy sight" being suggestive of befitting reverence; **(3c)** against Jewish law, the temple, and Caesar (Acts 25:8, - "offended"); **(4)** against one's own body, by fornication (1 Cor 6:18); **(5)** against earthly masters by servants (1 Pet 2:20) - "(when ye be buffeted) for your faults," lit., "having sinned". Syn.: 265, 266, 361, 4258. See: TDNT—1:267, 44; BAGD—42b; THAYER—30b.

265. ἀμάρτημα {4x} **hamartēma**, *ham-ar'-tay-mah;* from *264; a sin* (prop. concr.):—sin {4x}.

Hamartema, as a noun, denotes "an act of disobedience to divine law" (plural in Mk 3:28; Rom 3:25; 1 Cor 6:18). Syn.: 264, 266, 361, 4258.

See: TDNT—1:267, 44; BAGD—42c; THAYER—30c.

266. ἀμαρτία {174x} **hamartia**, *ham-ar-tee'-ah;* from *264; sin* (prop. abstr.):—sin {172x}, sinful {1x}, offense {1x}.

Hamartia, as a verb, is literally **(1)** "a missing of the mark" but this etymological meaning is largely lost sight of in the NT. **(1a)** It is the most comprehensive term for moral deviations. **(1b)** It is used of "sin" as **(1b1)** a principle or source of action, or an inward element producing acts: "What then? are we better than they? No, in no wise: for we have before proved both Jews and Gentiles, that they are all under sin" (Rom 3:9; cf. 5:12, 13, 20; 6:1, 2; 7:7 [abstract for concrete]; 7:8 [twice], 9, 11, 13, "sin, that it might be shown to be sin," i.e., "sin became death to me, that it might be exposed in its heinous character": in the last clause, "sin might become exceeding sinful," i.e., through the holiness of the Law, the true nature of sin was designed to be manifested to the conscience; **(1b2)** a governing principle or power: "Knowing this, that our old man is crucified with him, that the body of sin might be destroyed, that henceforth we should not serve sin" (Rom 6:6, "[the body] of sin," here "sin" is spoken of as an organized power, acting through the members of the body, though the seat of "sin" is in the will [the body is the organic instrument]; in the next clause, and in other passages, as follows, this governing principle is personified (e.g., Rom 5:21; 6:12, 14, 17; 7:11, 14, 17, 20, 23, 25; 8:2; 1 Cor 15:56; Heb 3:13; 11:25; 12:4; Jas 1:15).

(2) This word is also **(2a)** a generic term [distinct from specific terms such as *hamartema* (*265*) yet sometimes inclusive of concrete wrong doing (e.g., Jn 8:21, 34, 46; 9:41; 15:22, 24; 19:11)]; **(2b)** in Rom 8:3, "God, sending His own Son in the likeness of sinful flesh," **(2b1)** means Christ had a human nature, but He did not have a sinful human nature (2 Cor 5:21; 1 Jn 3:5; Jn 14:30; Jn 8:46; Heb 4:15; 1 Pet 2:22). **(2b2)** Christ, pre-existently the Son of God, assumed human flesh; **(2b3)** the reality of incarnation was His, without taint of sin (3667 - *homoioma,* "likeness"], and **(2b4)** as an offering for sin," i.e., "a sin offering" (Heb 9:28; cf. Lev 4:32; 5:6, 7, 8, 9), **(2b5)** "condemned sin in the flesh," i.e., Christ, having taken human nature, "sin" apart (Heb 4:15), and having lived a sinless life, died under the condemnation and judgment due to our "sin." **(2b6)** In 2 Cor 5:21, "Him . . . He made to be sin" indicates that God dealt with Him as He must deal with "sin," and that Christ fulfilled what was typified in the guilt offering. Syn.: 264, 265, 361, 4258. See:

TDNT—1:267, 44; BAGD—43a; THAYER— 30d.

267. ἀμάρτυρος {1x} **amarturŏs**, *am-ar'-too-ros;* from *1* (as a neg. particle) and a form of *3144; unattested:*—without witness {1x}.

Amarturos, as an adjective, denotes "without witness": "Nevertheless He left not himself without witness, in that He did good, and gave us rain from heaven, and fruitful seasons, filling our hearts with food and gladness" (Acts 14:17). Syn.: 2649, 3140, 3141, 3142, 3143, 3144, 4828, 4901, 5571, 5576, 5577. See: BAGD—44a; THAYER—31c.

268. ἀμαρτωλός {47x} **hamartōlŏs**, *ham-ar-to-los';* from *264; sinful,* i.e. a *sinner:*—sinner {43x}, sinful {4x}.

Hamartolos is used as an adjective "sinful": "Whosoever therefore shall be ashamed of me and of my words in this adulterous and sinful generation; of him also shall the Son of man be ashamed, when He cometh in the glory of His Father with the holy angels" (Mk 8:38; cf. Lk 5:8; 19:7 [lit., "a sinful man"]; 24:7; Jn 9:16, and 24 [lit., "a man sinful"]; Rom 7:13). See: TDNT—1:317, 51; BAGD—44a; THAYER—31c.

269. ἄμαχος {2x} **amachŏs**, *am'-akh-os;* from *1* (as a neg. particle) and *3163; peaceable:*—not a brawler {1x}, no brawler {1x}.

Amachos (*a*, negative, *mache*, a fight), an adjective, literally means "not fighting" and came to denote, metaphorically, "not contentious, not a brawler" (1 Ti 3:3; Titus 3:2). Syn.: 3943. See: TDNT—4:527, 573; BAGD—44c; THAYER—31d.

270. ἀμάω {1x} **amaō**, *am-ah'-o;* from *260;* prop. to *collect,* i.e. (by impl.) *reap:*—reap down {1x}.

Amao is translated "have reaped down " (Jas 5:4) with the sense that cutting down is primary and that of gathering-in secondary. See: BAGD—44c; THAYER—31d.

271. ἀμέθυστος {1x} **amĕthustŏs**, *am-eth'-oos-tos;* from *1* (as a neg. particle) and a der. of *3184;* the *"amethyst"* (supposed to *prevent intoxication*):—amethyst {1x}.

Some feel this jewel gets its name from its reddish purple, almost wine, color. See: BAGD—44d; THAYER—31d.

272. ἀμελέω {5x} **amĕlĕō**, *am-el-eh'-o;* from *1* (as a neg. particle) and *3199;* to *be careless* of; not to care:—neglect {2x}, make light of {1x}, regard not {1x}, be negligent {1x}.

Ameleo denotes "to be careless, not to care"

(Mt 22:5 - "they made light of (it)," lit. "making light of it);" an aorist participle, indicating the definiteness of their decision. See: BAGD— 44d; THAYER—31d.

273. ἄμεμπτος {5x} **amĕmptŏs**, *am'-emp-tos;* from *1* (as a neg. particle) and a der. of *3201; irreproachable:*—blameless {3x}, unblameable {1x}, faultless {1x}.

Amemptos, as an adjective, related to *memphomai* (*3201*), is translated **(1)** "unblameable" (1 Th 3:13); **(2)** "blameless" (Lk 1:6; Phil 2:15; 3:6); and **(3)** "faultless" (Heb 8:7). Syn.: If *amomos* (*299*) is the "unblemished," *amemptos* (*273*) is the "unblamed." Christ was *amomos* in that there was in Him no spot or blemish, and He could say, "Which of you convinceth Me of sin? (Jn 8:46);" but in strictness of speech He was not *amemptos* (unblamed), nor is this epithet ever given to Him in the NT, seeing that He endured the contradiction of sinners against Himself, who slandered His footsteps and laid to His charge 'things that He knew not' (i.e., of which He was guiltless). Syn.: 274, 298, 299, 338, 410, 423, 2607, 3201, 3469. See: TDNT— 4:571, 580; BAGD—45a; THAYER—31d.

274. ἀμέμπτως {2x} **amĕmptōs**, *am-emp'-toce;* adv. from *273; faultlessly:*—unblameably {1x}, blameless {1x}.

Amemptos, as an adverb, is translated **(1)** "unblameably": "Ye *are* witnesses, and God *also*, how holily and justly and unblameably we behaved ourselves among you that believe" (1 Th 2:10); **(2)** "blameless": "And the very God of peace sanctify you wholly; and I pray God your whole spirit and soul and body be preserved blameless unto the coming of our Lord Jesus Christ" (1 Th 5:23) which is said of believers at the judgment-seat of Christ in His Parousia [His presence after His coming], as the outcome of present witness and steadfastness. Syn.: 273, 298, 299, 338, 410, 423, 2607, 3201, 3469. See: BAGD—45a; THAYER—32a.

275. ἀμέριμνος {2x} **amĕrimnŏs**, *am-er'-im-nos;* from *1* (as a neg. particle) and *3308; not anxious:*—secure + 4060 {1x}, without carefulness {1x}. See: TDNT—4:593, 584; BAGD—45b; THAYER—32a.

276. ἀμετάθετος {2x} **amĕtathĕtŏs**, *am-et-ath'-et-os;* from *1* (as a neg. particle) and a der. of *3346; unchangeable,* or (neut. as abstr.) *unchangeability:*—immutability {1x}, immutable {1x}.

Ametathetos is an adjective signifying "immutable" (*a*, negative, *metatithemi*, "to change") and is used in Heb 6:18, where the "two immutable things" are the promise and the oath. In v. 17 the word is used in the neuter with the

article, as a noun, denoting "the immutability," with reference to God's counsel. See: BAGD—45b; THAYER—32a.

277. ἀμετακίνητος {1x} **amĕtakinĕtŏs**, *am-et-ak-in'-ay-tos;* from *1* (as a neg. particle) and a der. of *3334; firm, immovable:*—unmoveable {1x}.

Ametakinetos, as an adjective, means "firm, immoveable": "Therefore, my beloved brethren, be ye stedfast, unmoveable, always abounding in the work of the Lord, forasmuch as ye know that your labour is not in vain in the Lord" (1 Cor 15:58). Syn.: 383, 761, 2795, 2796, 3334, 4525, 4531, 4579, 4787, 5342. See: BAGD—45c; THAYER—32a.

278. ἀμεταμέλητος {2x} **amĕtamĕlētŏs**, *am-et-am-el'-ay-tos;* from *1* (as a neg. particle) and a presumed der. of *3338; irrevocable:*—without repentance {1x}, not to be repented of {1x}.

Ametameletos, as an adjective, means "not repented of" and is translated **(1)** "not to be repented of": "For godly sorrow worketh repentance to salvation not to be repented of: but the sorrow of the world worketh death" (2 Cor 7:10); and **(2)** "without repentance": "For the gifts and calling of God are without repentance" (Rom 11:29). Syn.: 3338. See: TDNT—4:626, 589; BAGD—45c; THAYER—32a.

279. ἀμετανόητος {1x} **amĕtanŏētŏs**, *am-et-an-o'-ay-tos;* from *1* (as a neg. particle) and a presumed der. of *3340; unrepentant:*—impenitent {1x}. See: TDNT—4:1009, 636; BAGD—45c; THAYER—32a.

280. ἄμετρος {2x} **amĕtrŏs**, *am'-et-ros;* from *1* (as a neg. particle) and *3358; immoderate:*—things without measure {2x}.

Ametros, as an adjective, means **(1)** "without measure" and **(2)** is used in the neuter plural in an adverbial phrase in 2 Cor. 10:13, 15, *eis ta ametra*, "(we will not boast) of things without measure," [lit., "unto the (things) without measure"] **(3)** referring to the sphere divinely appointed for the apostle as to his gospel ministry; **(4)** this had reached to Corinth, and by the increase of the faith of the church there, would extend to regions beyond. **(5)** His opponents had no scruples about intruding into the spheres of other men's work. Syn.: 488, 943, 2884, 3313, 3354, 3358, 4057, 4568, 5234, 5249, 5518. See: TDNT—4:632, 590; BAGD—45d; THAYER—32b.

281. ἀμήν {152x} **amēn**, *am-ane';* of Heb. or. [543]; prop. *firm*, i.e. (fig.) *trustworthy;* adv. *surely* (often as interj. *so be it*):—verily {101x}, amen {51x}.

Amen is **(1)** transliterated from Hebrew into

both Greek and English. **(2)** Its meanings may be seen in such passages as **(2a)** Deut 7:9, "the faithful (the *Amen*) God" **(2b)** Is 49:7, "Jehovah that is faithful." **(2c)** Is 65:16, "the God of truth," **(2d)** And if God is faithful His testimonies and precepts are "sure (*amen*)," Ps 19:7; 111:7, as **(2e)** are also His warnings, Hos 5:9, and **(2f)** promises, Is 33:16; 55:3. **(3)** *Amen* is used of men also, e.g., Prov 25:13. **(4)** There are cases where the people used it to express their assent to a law and their willingness to submit to the penalty attached to the breach of it, Deut 27:15, cf. Neh 5:13. **(5)** It is also used to express acquiescence in another's prayer, 1 Kin 1:36, where it is defined as "(let) God say so too," or **(6)** in another's thanksgiving, 1 Chr 16:36, whether **(6a)** by an individual, Jer 11:5, or by **(6b)** the congregation, Ps 106:48. **(7)** Thus "*Amen*" said by God "it is and shall be so," and by men, "so let it be." **(8)** Once in the NT *Amen* is a title of Christ, Rev 3:14, because through Him the purposes of God are established, 2 Cor 1:20. **(9)** The early Christian churches followed the example of Israel in associating themselves audibly with the prayers and thanksgivings offered on their behalf, 1 Cor 14:16, where the article "the" points to a common practice. **(10)** Moreover this custom conforms to the pattern of things in the Heavens, see Rev 5:14. **(11)** The individual also said *Amen* to express his "let it be so" in response to the Divine "thus it shall be,'" Rev 22:20. **(12)** Frequently the speaker adds *Amen* to his own prayers and doxologies, as is the case at Eph 3:21. **(13)** The Lord Jesus often used *Amen*, translated "verily," to introduce new revelations of the mind of God. **(14)** In John's Gospel it is always repeated, "*Amen, Amen*," but not elsewhere. Luke does not use it at all, but where Matthew, 16:28, and Mark, 9:1, have *Amen*, Luke has "of a truth"; thus by varying the translation of what the Lord said, Luke throws light on His meaning. See: TDNT—1:335, 53; BAGD—45d; THAYER—32b.

282. ἀμήτωρ {1x} **amētōr**, *am-ay'-tore;* from *1* (as a neg. particle) and *3384; motherless*, i.e. *of unknown maternity:*—without mother {1x}.

Ametor, "without a mother," is used in Heb 7:3 of the Genesis record of Melchizedek, certain details concerning him being purposely omitted, in order to conform the description to facts about Christ as the Son of God. Syn.: 3384, 3389. See: BAGD—46a; THAYER—32b.

283. ἀμίαντος {4x} **amiantŏs**, *am-ee'-an-tos;* from *1* (as a neg. particle) and a der. of *3392; unsoiled*, i.e. (fig.) *pure; free from contamination:*—undefiled {4x}.

Amiantos means "undefiled, free from contamination" and is used **(1)** of Christ: "For such an high priest became us, who is holy, harmless, undefiled, separate from sinners, and made higher than the heavens" (Heb 7:26); **(2)** of pure religion (Jas 1:27); **(3)** of the eternal inheritance of believers (1 Pet 1:4); and **(4)** of the marriage bed as requiring to be free from unlawful sexual intercourse (Heb 13:4). See: TDNT—4:647, 593; BAGD—46b; THAYER—32c.

284. Ἀμιναδάβ {3x} **Aminadab,** *am-ee-nad-ab';* of Heb. or. [5992]; *Aminadab,* an Isr.:—*Aminadab* {3x}. See: BAGD—46b; THAYER—32c.

285. ἄμμος {5x} **ammŏs,** *am'-mos;* perh. from *260; sand* (as *heaped* on the beach):—sand {5x}.

Ammos means "sand" or "sandy ground" and describes **(1)** an insecure foundation (Mt 7:26); **(2)** numberlessness, vastness: "Esaias also crieth concerning Israel, Though the number of the children of Israel be as the sand of the sea, a remnant shall be saved" (Rom 9:27; cf. Heb 11:12; Rev 20:8); and **(3)** symbolically in Rev 13:1: "And I stood upon the sand of the sea, and saw a beast rise up out of the sea, having seven heads and ten horns, and upon his horns ten crowns, and upon his heads the name of blasphemy"—the position taken up by John, to view the rising of the Beast out of the sea (emblematic of the restless condition of nations). See: BAGD—46b; THAYER—32c.

286. ἀμνός {4x} **amnŏs,** *am-nos';* appar a prim. word; a *lamb:*—lamb {4x}. Syn.: 704, 721.

Amnos, "a lamb," is used figuratively of Christ: **(1)** Jn 1:29, 36, with the article, pointing Him out as the expected One, the One to be well known as the personal fulfillment and embodiment of all that had been indicated in the OT, the One by whose sacrifice deliverance from divine judgment was to be obtained; **(2)** in Acts 8:32 and 1 Pet 1:19, the absence of the article stresses the nature and character of His sacrifice as set forth in the symbolism. **(3)** The reference in each case is to the lamb of God's providing, Gen 22:8, and the Paschal lamb of God's appointment for sacrifice in Israel (e.g. cf. Ex 12:5, 14, 27; and cf. 1 Cor 5:7). Syn.: See discussion under 721. See: TDNT—1:338, 54; BAGD—46c; THAYER—32d.

287. ἀμοιβή {1x} **amŏibē,** *am-oy-bay';* from ἀμείβω **amĕibō** (to *exchange*); *requital:*—requite + 591 {1x}.

Amoibe means "a requital, recompence," is used with the verb *apodidomi* (591 - "to render") in 1 Ti 5:4, and is translated "to requite": "But if any widow have children or nephews, let them learn first to shew piety at home, and to requite their parents: for that is good and acceptable before God." See: BAGD—46c; THAYER—32d.

288. ἄμπελος {8x} **ampělŏs,** *am'-pel-os;* prob. from the base of *297* and that of *257;* a *vine* (as *coiling about* a support):—vine {8x}.

This word is used **(1)** of a literal vine (Mt 26:29; Jas 3:12); **(2)** figuratively, **(2a)** of Christ (Jn 15:1, 4, 5); **(2b)** of His enemies (Rev 14:18, 19 - "the vine of the earth"). TDNT—1:342, 54; BAGD—46d; THAYER—32d.

289. ἀμπελουργός {1x} **ampělŏurgŏs,** *am-pel-oor-gos';* from *288* and *2041;* a *vine-worker,* i.e. *pruner:*—dresser of vineyard {1x}.

This word means "a worker in a vineyard" and is rendered "vinedresser" in Lk 13:7. See: BAGD—47a; THAYER—32d.

290. ἀμπελών {23x} **ampělōn,** *am-pel-ohn';* from *288;* a *vineyard:*—vineyard {23x}.

Ampelon is used 22 times in the Synoptic Gospels; elsewhere in 1 Cor 9:7: ". . . who planteth a vineyard, and eateth not of the fruit thereof?" See: BAGD—47a; THAYER—32d.

291. Ἀμπλίας {1x} **Amplias,** *am-plee'-as;* contr. for Lat. *ampliatus* [*enlarged*]; *Amplias,* a Rom. Chr.:—Amplias {1x}. See: BAGD—47a; THAYER—32d.

292. ἀμύνομαι {1x} **amunŏmai,** *am-oo'-nom-ahee;* mid. voice of a prim. verb; to *ward off* (for oneself), i.e. *protect:*—defend {1x}.

Amunomai means "to ward off," is used in the middle voice in Acts 7:24, of the assistance given by Moses to his fellow Israelite against an Egyptian (translated, "defended"). The middle voice indicates the special personal interest Moses had in the act. See: BAGD—47a; THAYER—33a.

293. ἀμφίβληστρον {2x} **amphiblēstrŏn,** *am-feeb'-lace-tron;* from a comp. of the base of *297* and *906;* a (fishing) *net* (as *thrown about* the fish):—net {2x}.

Amphiblestron literally means "something thrown around" and denotes a casting net, a somewhat small net, cast over the shoulder, spreading out in a circle and made to sink by weights (Mt 4:18). Syn.: *Diktyon (1350)* is the more general term for nets, including the hunting net and the fishing nets. *Amphiblestron (293)* and *sagene (4522)* are types of fishing nets. See also: 1350, 4522. See: BAGD—47b; THAYER—33b.

294. ἀμφιέννυμι {4x} **amphiĕnnumi**, *am-fee-en'-noo-mee;* from the base of *297* and ἕννυμι **hĕnnumi** (to *invest*); to *enrobe:*—clothes {4x}.

Amphiennumi, as a verb, means "to put clothes round" signifies, in the middle voice, to put clothing on oneself (Mt 6:30; 11:8; Lk 7:25; 12:28). Syn.: 1463, 1737, 1746, 1902, 2439, 4016. See: BAGD—47c; THAYER—33a.

295. Ἀμφίπολις {1x} **Amphipŏlis**, *am-fip'-ol-is;* from the base of *297* and *4172;* a *city surrounded* by a river; *Amphipolis,* a place in Macedonia:—*Amphipolis* {1x}. See: BAGD—47c; THAYER—33b.

296. ἄμφοδον {1x} **amphŏdŏn**, *am'-fod-on;* from the base of *297* and *3598;* a *fork* in the road:—place where two ways meet {1x}.

Amphodon, as a noun, properly means "a way around, where two ways meet": "And they went their way, and found the colt tied by the door without in a place where two ways met; and they loose him" (Mk 11:4). Syn.: 4113, 4505. See: BAGD—47c; THAYER—33b.

297. ἀμφότερος {14x} **amphŏtĕrŏs**, *am-fot'-er-os;* comp. of ἀμφί **amphi** (*around*); (in plur.) *both:*—both {14x}. See: BAGD—47c; THAYER—33b.

298. ἀμώμητος {2x} **amōmētŏs**, *am-o'-may-tos;* from *1* (as a neg. particle) and a der. of *3469; unblameable:*—without rebuke {1x}, blameless {1x}.

Amometos, as an adjective, is translated **(1)** "without rebuke": "That ye may be blameless and harmless, the sons of God, without rebuke (*amometos*), in the midst of a crooked and perverse nation, among whom ye shine as lights in the world" (Phil 2:15), **(2)** and is rendered "blameless": "Wherefore, beloved, seeing that ye look for such things, be diligent that ye may be found of him in peace, without spot, and blameless" (2 Pet 3:14). Syn.: 273, 274, 299, 338, 410, 423, 2607, 3201, 3469. See: TDNT—4:831, 619; BAGD—47d; THAYER—33c.

299. ἄμωμος {7x} **amōmŏs**, *am'-o-mos;* from *1* (as a neg. particle) and *3470; unblemished* (lit. or fig.):—without rebuke {2x}, without blame {1x}, unblameable {1x}, without spot {1x}, faultless {1x}, without fault {1x}.

Amomos, as an adjective, means "without blame": "According as He hath chosen us in Him before the foundation of the world, that we should be holy and without blame before Him in love" (Eph 1:4). Syn.: If *amomos* (299) is the "unblemished," *amemptos* (273) is the "unblamed." Christ was *amomos* in that there was

in Him no spot or blemish, and He could say, "Which of you convinceth Me of sin? (Jn 8:46);" but in strictness of speech He was not *amemptos* (unblamed), nor is this epithet ever given to Him in the NT, seeing that He endured the contradiction of sinners against Himself, who slandered His footsteps and laid to His charge "things that He knew not" (i.e., of which He was guiltless). Syn.: 273, 274, 298, 338, 410, 423, 2607, 3201, 3469. See: TDNT—4:830, 619; BAGD—47d; THAYER—33c.

300. Ἀμών {2x} **Amōn**, *am-one';* of Heb. or. [526]; *Amon,* an Isr.:—*Amon* {2x}. See: BAGD—48a; THAYER—33c.

301. Ἀμώς {1x} **Amōs**, *am-oce';* of Heb. or. [531]; *Amos,* an Isr.:—*Amos* {1x}. See: BAGD—48a; THAYER—33c.

302. ἄν {191x} **an**, *an;* a prim. particle, denoting a *supposition, wish, possibility* or *uncertainty:*—whosoever {35x}, whatsoever {7x}, whomsoever {5x}, whereinsoever {1x}, what things soever {1x}, whatsoever + 3745 {7x}, an many as + 3745 {4x}, whosoever + 3745 {2x}, what things so ever + 3745 {1x}, wherewith soever + 3745 {1x}, whithersoever + 3699 {4x}, wheresoever + 3699 {2x}, whatsoever + 3748 {5x}, whosoever + 3748 {3x}, whose soever + 5100 {2x}, not tr {111x}. See: BAGD—48a; THAYER—33c. Also contr. for *1437.*

303. ἀνά {15x} **ana**, *an-ah';* a prim. prep. and adv.; prop. *up;* but (by extens.) used (distributively) *severally,* or (locally) *at* (etc.):—by {3x}, apiece {2x}, every man {2x}, each {1x}, several {1x}, two and two + 1417 {1x}, among {1x}, through {1x}, between {1x}, by {1x}, in {1x}. In compounds (as a prefix) it often means (by impl.) *repetition, intensity, reversal,* etc.

Ana is used with numerals or measures of quantity with a distributive force, is translated **(1)** "apiece" **(1a)** in Lk 9:3, "two coats apiece"; **(1b)** in Jn 2:6, "two or three firkins apiece." **(2)** In Mt 20:9–10, "every man a penny," is a free rendering for "a penny apiece"; **(3)** in Lk 10:1, *ana duo* is "two by two"; and **(4)** Rev 4:8, "each."

304. ἀναβαθμός {2x} **anabathmŏs**, *an-ab-ath-mos';* from *305* [comp. *898*]; a *stairway:*—stairs {2x}.

Anabathmos is "an ascent" and denotes "a flight of stairs" (Acts 21:35, 40). These were probably the steps leading down from the castle of Antonia to the temple. See: BAGD—50a; THAYER—35a.

305. ἀναβαίνω {82x} **anabainō**, *an-ab-ah'-ee-no;* from *303* and the base of *939;* to *go up* (lit. or fig.):—go up {37x}, come up {10x}, ascend {10x}, ascend up {8x}, climb up {2x}, spring up {2x}, grow up {2x}, come {2x},

enter {2x}, arise {2x}, rise up {2x}, misc. {2x}, vr ascend {1x}. Syn.: 450, 1096, 1326, 1453, 1525, 1817, 4911.

Anabaino, as a verb, means "to go up, to ascend," is rendered **(1)** "arise"- of thoughts/reasonings: "And He said unto them, Why are ye troubled? and why do thoughts arise in your hearts?" (Lk 24:38); **(2)** "rise up" - of the beast: "And I stood upon the sand of the sea, and saw a beast rise up out of the sea" (Rev 13:1); **(3)** "ascend" – of the beast: "The beast that thou sawest was, and is not; and shall ascend out of the bottomless pit" (Rev 17:8); **(4)** "rose up" – of the smoke of burning Babylon: "And again they said, Alleluia. And her smoke rose up for ever and ever" (Rev 19:3). Syn.: 393, 450, 1096, 1326, 1453, 1525, 1817, 4911. See: TDNT – 1:519, 90; BAGD – 50a; THAYER – 35a.

306. **ἀναβάλλομαι** {1x} **anaballōmai**, *an-ab-al'-lom-ahee;* mid. voice from *303* and *906;* to *put off* (for oneself); to postpone:—defer {1x}.

This word literally means "to throw up"; hence; "to postpone," and is used in the middle voice in Acts 24:22, in the forensic sense of "deferring" the hearing of a case. See: BAGD – 50c; THAYER – 35c.

307. **ἀναβιβάζω** {1x} **anabibazō**, *an-ab-ee-bad'-zo;* from *303* and a der. of the base of *939;* to *cause to go up,* i.e. *haul* (a net):—draw {1x}.

Anabibazo, as a verb, a causal form of *anabaino* (305 - "to go up") denotes, lit., "to make go up, cause to ascend"; hence, "to draw a boat up on land" (Mt 13:48). Syn.: 385, 392, 501, 502, 645, 868, 1096, 1670, 1448, 1828, 2020, 2464, 4317, 4334, 4358, 4685, 4951, 5288, 5289. See: BAGD – 50d; THAYER – 35c.

308. **ἀναβλέπω** {26x} **anablĕpō**, *an-ab-lep'-o;* from *303* and *991;* to *look up;* by impl. to *recover sight:*—receive sight {15x}, look up {9x}, look {1x}, see {1x}.

Anablepo, as a verb, denotes **(1)** "looking up": "And He commanded the multitude to sit down on the grass, and took the five loaves, and the two fishes, and looking up to heaven, he blessed" (Mt 14:19; Mk 8:24, 25; **(2)** "to recover sight": "The blind receive their sight, and the lame walk" (Mt 11:5; 20:34; Jn 9:11). Syn.: 352, 578, 816, 872, 991, 1689, 1896, 1914, 1980, 1983, 2300, 2334, 3706, 3708, 3879, 4017, 4648. See: BAGD – 50d; THAYER – 35c.

309. **ἀνάβλεψις** {1x} **anablĕpsis**, *an-ab'-lep-sis;* from *308; restoration of sight:*—recovering of sight {1x}.

Anablepsis, as a verb, denotes "recovering of sight": "The Spirit of the Lord is upon Me, because He hath anointed me to preach the

gospel . . . and recovering of sight to the blind" (Lk 4:18). See: BAGD – 51a; THAYER – 35d.

310. **ἀναβοάω** {3x} **anabŏaō**, *an-ab-o-ah'-o;* from *303* and *994;* to *halloo:*—cry 1, cry aloud {1x}, cry out {1x}.

Anaboao, as a verb, [*ana* makes it intesive] means "to lift up the voice, cry out" and is said **(1)** of Christ at the moment of His death, a testimony to His supernatural power in giving up His life: "And about the ninth hour Jesus cried with a loud voice, saying, Eli, Eli, lama sabachthani? that is to say, My God, my God, why hast thou forsaken me?" (Mt 27:46); **(2)** of the multitude: "And the multitude crying aloud began to desire him to do as he [Pilate] had ever done unto them" (Mk 15:8); **(3)** of a man out of a company (Lk 9:38). Syn.: 349, 994, 995, 1916, 2019, 2896, 2905, 2906, 5455. See: BAGD – 51a; THAYER – 35d.

311. **ἀναβολή** {1x} **anabŏlē**, *an-ab-ol-ay';* from *306;* a *putting off:*—delay + *4160* {1x}.

Anabole, as a noun, literally signifies "that which is thrown up"; hence "a delay": "Therefore, when they were come hither, without any delay on the morrow I sat on the judgment seat, and commanded the man to be brought forth" (Acts 25:17). Syn.: 3635, 5549. Syn.: 3635, 5549. See: BAGD – 51a; THAYER – 35d.

312. **ἀναγγέλλω** {18x} **anaggĕllō**, *an-ang-el'-lo;* from *303* and the base of *32;* to *announce* (in detail):—tell {6x}, show {6x}, declare {3x}, rehearse {1x}, speak {1x}, report {1x}.

Anaggello, as a verb, means "to declare, announce," is used especially of heavenly messages, and is translated **(1)** "reported" in 1 Pet 1:12: "Unto whom it was revealed, that not unto themselves, but unto us they did minister the things, which are now reported unto you", or **(2)** "declare": "This then is the message which we have heard of Him, and declare unto you" (1 Jn 1:5). See: TDNT – 1:61, 10; BAGD – 51b; THAYER – 36a.

313. **ἀναγεννάω** {2x} **anagĕnnaō**, *an-ag-en-nah'-o;* from *303* and *1080;* to *beget* or (by extens.) *bear* (again):—begat again {1x}, be born again {1x}.

Anagennao, as a verb, means "begotten": "Blessed be the God and Father of our Lord Jesus Christ, which according to His abundant mercy hath begotten us again" (1 Pet 1:3; cf. 1:23). Syn.: 616, 738, 1080, 1084, 1085, 1626, 5088. Syn.: 1080. See: TDNT – 1:673, 114; BAGD – 51c; THAYER – 36a.

314. **ἀναγινώσκω** {33x} **anaginōskō**, *an-ag-in-oce'-ko;* from *303* and

1097; to *know again,* i.e. (by extens.) to *read:*— read {33x}.

Anaginosko, as a verb, means primarily "to know certainly, to know again, recognize" and is used of **(1)** "reading" written characters: "But He said unto them, Have ye not read what David did, when he was an hungered, and they that were with him?" (Mt 12:3; cf. 12:5; 21:16; 24:15); **(1a)** of the private "reading" of Scripture (Acts 8:28, 30, 32); **(1b)** of the public "reading" of Scripture (Lk 4:16; Acts 13:27; 15:21; 2 Cor 3:15; Col 4:16 [thrice]; 1 Th 5:27; Rev 1:3). **(2)** In 2 Cor 1:13 there is a purposive play upon words; firstly, "we write none other things unto you, than what ye read (*anaginosko*)" signifies that there is no hidden or mysterious meaning in his epistles; whatever doubts may have arisen and been expressed in this respect, he means what he says; then follows the similar verb *epiginosko* (*1921*), "to acknowledge," "or even acknowledge, and I hope ye will acknowledge unto the end." **(3)** Similarly, in 2 Cor 3:2 the verb *ginosko* (*1097*), "to know," and *anaginosko,* "to read," are put in that order, and metaphorically applied to the church at Corinth as being an epistle, a message to the world, written by the apostle and his fellow missionaries, through their ministry of the gospel and the consequent change in the lives of the converts, an epistle "known and read of all men." Syn.: 320. See: TDNT—1:343, 55; BAGD—51c; THAYER—36b.

315. ἀναγκάζω {9x} **anagkazō,** *an-ang-kad'-zo;* from *318;* to *necessitate:*—compel {5x}, constrain {4x}.

Anankazo denotes "to put constraint upon, to constrain, to compel, whether by threat, entreaty, force or persuasion." **(1)** Christ "constrained" the disciples to get into a boat (Mt 14:22; Mk 6:45); **(2)** the servants of the man who made a great supper were to compel people to come in (Lk 14:23); **(3)** Saul of Tarsus "compelled" saints to blaspheme (Acts 26:11); **(4)** Titus, though a Greek, was not "compelled" to be circumcised (Gal 2:3), as Galatian converts were "constrained" (6:12); **(5)** Peter was "compelling" Gentiles to live as Jews (Gal 2:14); **(6)** Paul was "constrained" to appeal to Caesar (Acts 28:19), and **(7)** was "compelled" by the church at Corinth to become foolish in speaking of himself (2 Cor 12:11). Syn.: 29. See: TDNT—1:344, 55; BAGD—52a; THAYER—36b.

316. ἀναγκαῖος {8x} **anagkaiŏs,** *an-ang-kah'-yos;* from *318; necessary;* by impl. *close* (of kin):—necessary {5x}, near {1x}, more needful {1x}, of necessity {1x}.

Anankaios, as an adjective means "necessary"

and is used in a secondary sense of persons connected by bonds of nature or friendship, with the meaning "intimate": "And the morrow after they entered into Caesarea. And Cornelius waited for them, and had called together his kinsmen and near (*anankaios*) friends" (Acts 10:24 "(his) near friends)." Syn.: 1448, 1451, 1452, 4139, 4317, 4334. See: TDNT—1:344, 55; BAGD—52b; THAYER—36b.

317. ἀναγκαστῶς {1x} **anagkastōs,** *an-ang-kas-toce';* adv. from a der. of *315; by force, unwillingly, compulsorily:*—by constraint {1x}.

Anankastos, as an adverb, means "by force, unwillingly, by constraint": "Feed the flock of God which is among you, taking the oversight thereof, not by constraint, but willingly; not for filthy lucre, but of a ready mind" (1 Pet 5:2). Syn.: 315, 3849, 4912. See: BAGD—52b; THAYER—36c.

318. ἀναγκή {18x} **anagkē,** *an-ang-kay';* from *303* and the base of *43; constraint* (lit. or fig.); by impl. *distress:*—necessity {7x}, must needs {3x}, distress {3x}, must of necessity {2x}, need + *2192* {1x}, necessary {1x}, needful {1x}.

Ananke denotes **(1)** a necessity imposed whether **(1a)** by external circumstances: "For of necessity (*ananke*) he [Pilate] must release one unto them at the feast" (Lk 23:17) or **(1b)** inward pressure: "For though I preach the gospel, I have nothing to glory of: for necessity (*anagke*) is laid upon me; yea, woe is unto me, if I preach not the gospel!" (1 Cor 9:16); **(2)** straits, distress: "But woe unto them that are with child, and to them that give suck, in those days! for there shall be great distress (*ananke*) in the land, and wrath upon this people" (Lk 21:23; cf. 1 Cor 7:26; 1 Th 3:7). Syn.: 928, 2347, 2669, 4660, 4729, 4730, 4928. See: TDNT—1:344, 55; BAGD—52b; THAYER—36c.

319. ἀναγνωρίζομαι {1x} **anagnōrizŏmai,** *an-ag-no-rid'-zom-ahee;* mid. voice from *303* and *1107;* to *make* (oneself) *known:*—be made known {1x}. See: BAGD—52d; THAYER—36c.

320. ἀνάγνωσις {3x} **anagnōsis,** *an-ag'-no-sis;* from *314;* (the act of) *reading:*—reading {3x}.

Anagnosis, as a noun, means "reading"; the public "reading" of Scripture: "And after the reading of the law and the prophets the rulers of the synagogue sent unto them . . ." (Acts 13:15; cf. 2 Cor 3:14; 1 Ti 4:13 where the context makes clear that the reference is to the care required in reading the Scriptures to a company, a duty ever requiring the exhortation

"take heed"). Syn.: 314. See: TDNT—1:343, 55; BAGD—52d; THAYER—36d.

321. ἀνάγω {24x} **anagō**, *an-ag'-o;* from *303* and *71;* to *lead up;* by extens. to *bring out;* spec. to *sail* away:—bring {3x}, loose {3x}, sail {3x}, launch {3x}, depart {3x}, misc. {9x} = lead (up), loose, offer, set forth, take up.

Anago, as a verb, means **(1)** "to lead or bring up to": "And when the days of her purification according to the law of Moses were accomplished, they brought Him to (*anago*) Jerusalem, to present him to the Lord" (Lk 2:22; cf. Acts 9:39); **(2)** "to bring forth": "And when he [Herod] had apprehended him [Peter], he put him in prison, and delivered him to four quaternions of soldiers to keep him; intending after Easter to bring him forth (*anago*) to the people" (Acts 12:4); **(3)** "to bring again": "Now the God of peace, that brought again (*anago*) from the dead our Lord Jesus, that great shepherd of the sheep, through the blood of the everlasting covenant" (Heb 13:20); **(4)** "to bring up again": "Or, Who shall descend into the deep? (that is, to bring up Christ again (*anago*) from the dead)" (Rom 10:7). See: BAGD—53a; THAYER—36d.

322. ἀναδείκνυμι {2x} **anadĕiknumi**, *an-ad-ike'-noo-mee;* from *303* and *1166;* to *exhibit,* i.e. (by impl.) to *indicate, appoint:*—appoint {1x}, show {1x}.

Anadeiknumi, as a verb, means literally "to show up, to show clearly" and signifies "to appoint to a position or a service." It is used in this sense of the 70 disciples: "After these things the Lord appointed other seventy also, and sent them two and two before His face into every city and place, whither He himself would come" (Lk 10:1). Syn.: 1299, 1303, 2476, 2525, 4929, 5021, 5087. See: TDNT—2:30, 141; BAGD—53b; THAYER—36d.

323. ἀνάδειξις {1x} **anadĕixis**, *an-ad'-ike-sis;* from *322;* (the act of) *exhibition:*—showing {1x}.

Anadeixis means "a shewing forth" [*ana,* "up or forth," and *deiknumi* "to show") and is translated "showing" in Lk 1:80: "And the child grew, and waxed strong in spirit, and was in the deserts till the day of His shewing unto Israel." See: TDNT—2:31, 141; BAGD—53c; THAYER—37a.

324. ἀναδέχομαι {2x} **anadĕchŏmai**, *an-ad-ekh'-om-ahee;* from *303* and *1209;* to *entertain* (as a guest); to *receive* gladly:—receive {2x}.

Anadechomai, as a verb, means "to receive gladly" is used **(1)** in Acts 28:7 of the reception by Publius of the shipwrecked company in Melita; **(2)** in Heb 11:17, of Abraham's recep-

tion of God's promises, "gladly received". **(3)** This means that Abraham was taking the responsibility of something, becoming security for, undertaking. **(3a)** The predominance of this meaning suggests its application in Heb 11:17. **(3b)** The statement that Abraham had "undertaken," "assumed the responsibility of," the promises, means that the responsibility would surely be that of his faith in "receiving" the promises. **(3c)** It is a little difficult to attach any other sense to the circumstances, save perhaps that Abraham's faith undertook to exercise the assurance of the fulfillment of the promises. Syn.: 353, 354, 568, 588, 618, 1209, 1523, 1926, 2210, 2865, 2975, 2983, 3028, 3335, 3336, 3858, 3880, 3970, 4327, 4355, 4356, 4380, 4381, 4382, 5562, 5264, 5274. See: BAGD—53c; THAYER—37a.

325. ἀναδίδωμι {1x} **anadidōmi**, *an-ad-eed'-om-ee;* from *303* and *1325;* to *hand over:*—deliver {1x}.

Anadidomi, as a verb, means "to deliver over, give up" and is used of "delivering" the letter mentioned in Acts 23:33: "Who, when they came to Caesarea, and delivered the epistle to the governor, presented Paul also before him." Syn.: 525, 629, 591, 859, 1325, 1560, 1659, 1807, 1929, 3086, 3860, 4506, 5483. See: BAGD—53c; THAYER—37a.

326. ἀναζάω {5x} **anazaō**, *an-ad-zah'-o* from *303* and *2198;* to *recover life* (lit. or fig.):—be alive again {2x}, revive {2x}, live again {1x}.

Anazao, as a verb, denotes "to live again, to revive": "For this my son was dead, and is alive again; he was lost, and is found. And they began to be merry" (Lk 15:24); and "to manifest activity again": "For I was alive without the law once: but when the commandment came, sin revived, and I died" (Rom 7:9). Syn.: 390, 980, 1236, 2198, 2225, 4176, 4800, 5225. See: TDNT—2:872, 290; BAGD—53d; THAYER—37a.

327. ἀναζητέω {2x} **anazētĕō**, *an-ad-zay-teh'-o;* from *303* and *2212;* to *search* out:—seek {2x}.

Anazeteo, as a verb, means "to seek carefully" (*ana,* "up," used intensively), and is used of searching for human beings, difficulty in the effort being implied: "But they, supposing Him to have been in the company, went a day's journey; and they sought Him among their kinsfolk and acquaintance" (Lk 2:44; Acts 11:25). Syn.: 1567, 1934, 2206, 2212, 3713. Syn.: 1567, 1934, 2212, 3713. See: BAGD—53d; THAYER—37b.

328. ἀναζώννυμι {1x} **anazōnnumi**, *an-ad-zone'-noo-mee;* from *303* and *2224;* to *gird afresh:*—gird up {1x}.

Anazonnumi, as a verb, means "to gird up" and is used **(1)** metaphorically of the loins of the mind: "Wherefore gird up (*anazonnumi*) the loins of your mind, be sober, and hope to the end for the grace that is to be brought unto you at the revelation of Jesus Christ" (1 Pet 1:13; cf. Lk 12:35). **(2)** The figure is taken from the circumstances of the Israelites as they ate the Passover in readiness for their journey (cf. Ex 12:11); **(3)** the Christian is to have his mental powers alert in expectation of Christ's coming. **(4)** The verb is in the middle voice, indicating the special interest the believer is to take in so doing. Syn.: 1241, 2224, 4024. Syn.: 1241, 2224, 4024. See: BAGD—53d; THAYER—37b.

329. ἀναζωπυρέω {1x} **anazōpureō,** *an-ad-zo-poor-eh'-o;* from *303* and a comp. of the base of *2226* and *4442;* to *re-enkindle:*—stir up {1x}.

Anazopureo, as a verb, denotes "to kindle afresh" or "keep in full flame" [*ana,* "up," or "again," *zoos,* "alive," *pur,* "fire"], and is used metaphorically: "Wherefore I put thee in remembrance that thou stir up the gift of God, which is in thee by the putting on of my hands" (2 Ti 1:6, where "the gift of God" is regarded as a fire capable of dying out through neglect). Syn.: 383, 387, 1326, 1892, 2042, 3947, 3951, 4531, 4579, 4787, 4797, 5017. See: BAGD—54a; THAYER—37b.

330. ἀναθάλλω {1x} **anathallō,** *an-ath-al'-lo;* from *303* and θάλλω **thallō** (to *flourish*); to *revive:*—flourish {1x}.

Anathallo means "to flourish anew" [*ana,* "again, anew," *thallo,* "to flourish or blossom"], hence, "to revive," is used metaphorically in Phil 4:10: "But I rejoiced in the Lord greatly, that now at the last your care of me hath flourished again; wherein ye were also careful, but ye lacked opportunity." See: BAGD—54a; THAYER—37c.

331. ἀνάθεμα {6x} **anathĕma,** *an-ath'-em-ah;* from *394;* a (religious) *ban* or (concr.) *excommunicated* (thing or person):—accursed {4x}, anathema {1x}, bind under a great curse + 332 {1x}.

Anathema, as a noun, is transliterated from the Greek, is **(1)** "a thing devoted to God," whether **(1a)** for His service, as the sacrifices (cf. Lev 27:28), or **(1b)** for its destruction, as **(1b1)** an idol (cf. Deut 7:26), or **(1b2)** a city (Josh 6:17). **(1c)** Later it acquired the more general meaning of "the disfavor of Jehovah" (e.g., Zech 14:11). **(2)** This is the meaning in the NT. It is used **(2a)** of the sentence pronounced: "And they came to the chief priests and elders, and said, We have bound ourselves under a great curse that we will eat nothing until we have

slain Paul" [lit., "cursed themselves with a curse"; see *anathematizo* – 332]. **(2b)** of the object on which the "curse" is laid, "accursed": "For I could wish that myself were accursed from Christ for my brethren, my kinsmen according to the flesh:" (Rom 9:3; cf. 1 Cor 12:3; 16:22; Gal 1:8–9, all of which the KJV renders by "accursed" except 1 Cor 16:22, where it has "Anathema").

(3) In Gal 1:8–9, the apostle declares in the strongest manner that the gospel he preached was the one and only way of salvation, and that to preach another was to nullify the death of Christ: "But though we, or an angel from heaven, preach any other gospel unto you than that which we have preached unto you, let him be accursed. As we said before, so say I now again, If any man preach any other gospel unto you than that ye have received, let him be accursed." **(4)** This word stresses that which is dedicated to God's honor but to its own destruction. Syn.: 332, 334, 685, 1944, 2552, 2652, 2653, 2671, 2672. See: TDNT—1:354, 57; BAGD—54b; THAYER—37c.

332. ἀναθεματίζω {4x} **anathĕmatizō,** *an-ath-em-at-id'-zo;* from *331;* to *declare* or *vow* under penalty of execration:—curse {1x}, bind under a curse {1x}, bind with an oath {1x}, bind under a great curse + 331 {1x}.

Anathematizo, as a verb, signifies **(1)** "to declare anathema," i.e., "devoted to destruction, accursed, to curse": "But he began to curse and to swear, saying, I know not this man of whom ye speak" (Mk 14:71), or **(2)** "to bind by a curse": "And when it was day, certain of the Jews banded together, and bound themselves under a curse, saying that they would neither eat nor drink till they had killed Paul" (Acts 23:12; cf. vss. 14, 21). Syn.: 331, 685, 1944, 2551, 2652, 2653, 2671, 2672. See: TDNT—1:355, 57; BAGD—54a; THAYER—37d.

333. ἀναθεωρέω {2x} **anathĕōreō,** *an-ath-eh-o-reh'-o;* from *303* and *2334;* to *look again* (i.e. *attentively*) at (lit. or fig.):—behold {1x}, consider {1x}.

Anatheoreo, [*ana,* "up" (intensive)], as a verb, means "to view with interest, consider contemplatively," is translated **(1)** "beheld": "For as I passed by, and beheld (*anatheoreo*) your devotions, I found an altar with this inscription, TO THE UNKNOWN GOD. Whom therefore ye ignorantly worship, him declare I unto you" (Acts 17:23); **(2)** "considering": "Remember them which have the rule over you, who have spoken unto you the word of God: whose faith follow, considering (*anatheoreo*) the end of their conversation" (Heb 13:7). Syn.: 816,

Greek

991, 1689, 1896, 2029, 2300, 2334, 2657, 2734, 3708. See: BAGD—54c; THAYER—38a.

334. ἀνάθημα {1x} **anathēma**, *an-ath'-ay-mah;* from *394* [like *331*, but in a good sense]; a *votive* offering:—gift {1x}.

Anathema denotes a gift set up in a temple, a votive offering (Lk 21:5). Syn.: 331, 3646, 4376, 4689. This word stresses that which was dedicated to God for its own honor as well as for God's glory. See: TDNT—1:354, 57; BAGD—54c; THAYER—38a.

335. ἀναίδεια {1x} **anaidĕia**, *an-ah'-ee-die-ah';* from a comp. of *1* (as a neg. particle [comp. *427*]) and *127; impudence,* i.e. (by impl.) *importunity:*—importunity {1x}.

Anaideia denotes shamelessness, importunity and is used in the Lord's illustration concerning the need of earnestness and perseverance in prayer (Lk 11:8). If shameless persistence can obtain a boon from a neighbor, then certainly earnest prayer will receive our Father's answer. See: BAGD—54c; THAYER—38a.

336. ἀναίρεσις {2x} **anairĕsis**, *an-ah'-ee-res-is;* from *337;* (the act of) *killing:*—death {2x}.

Anairesis, another word for "death" literally signifies "a taking up or off" as of the taking of a life, or "putting to death." It is found in Acts 8:1, of the murder of Stephen (cf. Acts 22:20). Syn.: 520, 615, 1935, 2288, 2289, 5054. See: BAGD—54d; THAYER—38b.

337. ἀναιρέω {23x} **anairĕō**, *an-ahee-reh'-o;* from *303* and (the act. of) *138;* to *take up,* i.e. *adopt;* by impl. to *take away* (violently), i.e. *abolish, murder:*—kill {10x}, slay {8x}, put to death {2x}, take up {1x}, do {1x}, take away {1x}.

Anaireo literally means to take or lift up or away; hence, to put to death and is usually translated "to kill, slay, put to death" (Lk 23:32; Acts 26:10). It is used 17 times, with this meaning, in Acts. Syn.: 520, 615, 1935, 2288, 2289, 5054. See: BAGD—54d; THAYER—38b.

338. ἀναίτιος {2x} **anaitiŏs**, *an-ah'-ee-tee-os;* from *1* (as a neg. particle) and *159* (in the sense of *156*); *innocent:*—blameless {1x}, guiltless {1x}.

Anaitios, as an adjective, means "guiltless" and is translated (1) "blameless": "Or have ye not read in the law, how that on the sabbath days the priests in the temple profane the sabbath, and are blameless?" (Mt 12:5) and (2) "guiltless": "But if ye had known what this meaneth, I will have mercy, and not sacrifice, ye would not have condemned the guiltless" (Mt 12:7). Syn.: 273, 274, 298, 299, 410, 423,

2607, 3201, 3469. See: BAGD—55b; THAYER—38b.

339. ἀνακαθίζω {2x} **anakathizō**, *an-ak-ath-id'-zo;* from *303* and *2523;* prop. to *set up,* i.e. (refl.) to *sit up:*—sit up {2x}.

Anakathizo, as a verb, means "to set up" and is used intransitively, "to sit up," of two who were raised from the dead: "And he that was dead sat up, and began to speak. And He delivered him to his mother" (Lk 7:15; and Acts 9:40). Syn.: 345, 347, 377, 1910, 2516, 2521, 2621, 2523, 2625, 4775, 4776, 4873. See: BAGD—55b; THAYER—38b.

340. ἀνακαινίζω {1x} **anakainizō**, *an-ak-ahee-nid'-zo;* from *303* and a der. of *2537;* to *restore:*—renew {1x}. See: TDNT—3:451, 388; BAGD—55b; THAYER—38c.

341. ἀνακαινόω {2x} **anakainŏō**, *an-ak-ahee-nŏ'-o;* from *303* and a der. of *2537;* to *renovate:*—renew {2x}.

Anakainoo means to make new, not recent but different, to renew and is (1) used in the passive voice in 2 Cor 4:16 of the daily renewal of the inward man (in contrast to the physical frame), i.e., of the renewal of spiritual power; and (2) in Col 3:10, of the new man (in contrast to the old unregenerate nature), which is being renewed unto the true knowledge in Christ, as opposed to heretical teachings. Syn.: *Anakainoo* means substantially different but not recently new; whereas, *anaeoo* (*365*) means recently new but not substantially different. See: TDNT—3:452, 388; BAGD—55c; THAYER—38c.

342. ἀνακαίνωσις {2x} **anakainōsis**, *an-ak-ah'-ee-no-sis;* from *341; renovation:*—renewing {2x}.

Anakainosis means "a renewal" and is used (1) in Rom 12:2 "the renewing (of your mind)," i.e., the adjustment of the moral and spiritual vision and thinking to the mind of God, which is designed to have a transforming effect upon the life; and (1a) stresses the willing response on the part of the believer. (2) In Titus 3:5, "the renewing of the Holy Spirit" is (2a) not a fresh bestowment of the Spirit, but (2b) a revival of His power, (2b1) developing the Christian life, (2b2) stressing the continual operation of the indwelling Spirit of God. Syn.: 3824. *Palingenesis* (*3824*) stresses the new birth; whereas, *anakainosis* stresses the process of sanctification. See: TDNT—3:453, 388; BAGD—55c; THAYER—38c.

343. ἀνακαλύπτω {2x} **anakaluptō**, *an-ak-al-oop'-to;* from *303* (in the sense of *reversal*) and *2572;* to *unveil:*—untaken away + 3361 {1x}, open {1x}.

Anakalupto means "to uncover, unveil," and

is used in **(1)** 2 Cor 3:14 with the negative *me,* "not," is rendered "untaken away." The best rendering seems to be, "the veil remains unlifted (for it is in Christ that it is done away)." Judaism does not recognize the vanishing of the glory of the Law as a means of life, under God's grace in Christ. **(2)** In 2 Cor 3:18 "open" continues the metaphor of the veil (vv. 13–17), referring to hindrances to the perception of spiritual realities, hindrances removed in the unveiling. See: TDNT–3:560, 405; BAGD–55c; THAYER–38c.

344. **ἀνακάμπτω** {4x} **anakamptō,** *an-ak-amp'-to;* from *303* and *2578;* to *turn back:*—return {3x}, turn again {1x}.

Anakampto, as a verb, means "to turn or bend back": "And being warned of God in a dream that they [the magi] should not return to Herod, they departed into their own country another way" (Mt 2:12; cf. Lk 10:6; Acts 18:21; Heb 11:15). Syn.: 360, 390, 1880, 1877, 1994, 5290. See: BAGD–55c; THAYER–38d.

345. **ἀνακεῖμαι** {14x} **anakĕimai,** *an-ak-i'-mahee;* from *303* and *2749;* to *recline* (as a corpse or at a meal):—sit at meat {5x}, guests {2x}, sit {2x}, sit down {1x}, be set down {1x}, lie {1x}, lean {1x}, at the table {1x}.

Anakeimai, as a verb, means "to recline at table" and is rendered **(1)** "to sit at meat" (Mt 9:10; 26:7); **(2)** Mt 26:20, "He sat down" (cf. Mk 16:14; Lk 7:37; 22:27 [twice]); **(3)** in Mk 14:18, "sat"; **(4)** in Jn 6:11 "were set down." Syn.: 339, 347, 377, 1910, 2516, 2521, 2621, 2523, 2625, 4775, 4776, 4873. See: TDNT–3:654, 425; BAGD–55d; THAYER–38d.

346. **ἀνακεφαλαίομαι** {2x} **anakĕphalaiŏmai,** *an-ak-ef-al-ah'-ee-om-ahee;* from *303* and *2775* (in its or. sense); to *sum up:*—briefly comprehend {1x}, gather together in one {1x}.

Anakephalaiomai means to sum up, gather up, to present as a whole and is used **(1)** in the passive voice in Rom 13:9: "For this, Thou shalt not commit adultery, Thou shalt not kill, Thou shalt not steal, Thou shalt not bear false witness, Thou shalt not covet; and if there be any other commandment, it is briefly comprehended (*anakephalaiomai*) in this saying, namely, Thou shalt love thy neighbour as thyself"; i.e., the one commandment expresses all that the Law enjoins, and to obey this one is to fulfil the Law (cf. Gal 5:14); and **(2)** in the middle voice in Eph 1:10: "That in the dispensation of the fulness of times He might gather together (*anakephalaiomai*) in one all things in Christ, both which are in heaven, and which are on earth; even in Him", of God's purpose to "sum up" all things in the heavens and on the earth in Christ, a consummation extending beyond the limits of the church, though the latter is to be a factor in its realization. See: TDNT–3:681, 429; BAGD–55d; THAYER–38d.

347. **ἀνακλίνω** {8x} **anaklinō,** *an-ak-lee'-no;* from *303* and *2827;* to *lean back:*—sit down {3x}, make sit down {2x}, sit down to meat {1x}, make sit down to meat {1x}, lay {1x}.

Anaklino, as a verb, means "to cause to recline, make to sit down," and is used **(1)** in the active voice: "Blessed are those servants, whom the lord when he cometh shall find watching: verily I say unto you, that he shall gird himself, and make them to sit down (*anaklino*) to meat, and will come forth and serve them" (Lk 12:37; cf. Lk 2:7 of "laying" the infant Christ in the manger); and **(2)** in the passive: "And I say unto you, That many shall come from the east and west, and shall sit down with Abraham, and Isaac, and Jacob, in the kingdom of heaven" (Mt 8:11; 14:19; Mk 6:39; Lk 7:36; 9:15; 13:29). Syn.: 339, 345, 377, 1910, 2516, 2521, 2621, 2523, 2625, 4775, 4776, 4873. See: BAGD–56a; THAYER–39a.

348. **ἀνακόπτω** {1x} **anakŏptō,** *an-ak-op'-to;* from *303* and *2875;* to *beat back,* i.e. *check:*—hinder {1x}. See: BAGD–56b; THAYER–39a.

349. **ἀνακράζω** {5x} **anakrazō,** *an-ak-rad'-zo;* from *303* and *2896;* to *scream up* (aloud):—cry out {5x}.

Anakrazo, as a verb, [*ana,* "up," intensive], signifies "to cry out loudly": "And there was in their synagogue a man with an unclean spirit; and he cried out" (Mk 1:23; 6:49; Lk 4:33; 8:28; 23:18). Syn.: 310, 994, 995, 1916, 2019, 2896, 2905, 2906, 5455. See: TDNT–3:898, 465; BAGD–56b; THAYER–39a.

350. **ἀνακρίνω** {16x} **anakrinō,** *an-ak-ree'-no;* from *303* and *2919;* prop. to *scrutinize,* i.e. (by impl.) *investigate, interrogate, determine:*—examine {6x}, judge {6x}, ask question {2x}, search {1x}, discern {1x}.

Anakrino, as a verb, means "to judge," and sometimes has the meaning to ask a question: "Whatsoever is sold in the shambles, that eat, asking no question for conscience sake" (1 Cor 10:25; cf. 10:27). Syn.: 154, 155, 1833, 1905, 2065, 3004, 4441. See: TDNT–3:943, 469; BAGD–56b; THAYER–39b.

351. **ἀνάκρισις** {1x} **anakrisis,** *an-ak'-ree-sis;* from *350;* a (judicial) *investigation:*—examination {1x}.

This word means to distinguish and was a

legal term denoting the preliminary investigation for gathering evidence for the information of the judges: "Of whom I have no certain thing to write unto my lord. Wherefore I have brought him forth before you, and specially before thee, O king Agrippa, that, after examination (*anakrisis*) had, I might have somewhat to write" (Acts 25:26). See: TDNT—3:943, 469; BAGD—56c; THAYER—39b.

352. **ἀνακύπτω** {4x} **anakuptō**, *an-ak-oop'-to;* from *303* (in the sense of *reversal*) and *2955;* to *unbend*, i.e. *rise;* fig. *be elated:*—lift up (one's) self {3x}, look up {1x}.

Anakupto, as a verb, means "to lift oneself up" and is translated "look up": "And when these things begin to come to pass, then look up (*anakupto*), and lift up your heads; for your redemption draweth nigh" (Lk 21:28 of being elated in joyous expectation). Syn.: 308, 578, 816, 872, 991, 1689, 1896, 1914, 1980, 1983, 2300, 2334, 3706, 3708, 3879, 4017, 4648. See: BAGD—56c; THAYER—39c.

353. **ἀναλαμβάνω** {13x} **analambanō**, *an-al-am-ban'-o;* from *303* and *2983;* to *take up:*—take up {4x}, receive up {3x}, take {3x}, take in {2x}, take into {1x}.

Analambano, as a verb, means "to take up, to take to oneself, receive" and is rendered "to receive": "So then after the Lord had spoken unto them, He was received up into heaven, and sat on the right hand of God" (Mk 16:19; cf. Acts 1:2, 11, 22; 10:16; 1 Ti 3:16). Syn.: 324, 354, 568, 588, 618, 1209, 1523, 1926, 2210, 2865, 2975, 2983, 3028, 3335, 3336, 3858, 3880, 3970, 4327, 4355, 4356, 4380, 4381, 4382, 5562, 5264, 5274. See: TDNT—4:7, 495; BAGD—56d; THAYER—39c.

354. **ἀνάληψις** {1x} **analēpsis**, *an-al'-aip-sis;* from *353; ascension:*—receive up {1x}.

Analepsis, as a noun, means "a taking up" and is used in Lk 9:51 with reference to Christ's ascension; "that He should be received up" is, lit., "of the receiving up (of Him): "And it came to pass, when the time was come that He should be received up (*analepsis*), He stedfastly set His face to go to Jerusalem." Syn.: 324, 353, 568, 588, 618, 1209, 1523, 1926, 2210, 2865, 2975, 2983, 3028, 3335, 3336, 3858, 3880, 3970, 4327, 4355, 4356, 4380, 4381, 4382, 5562, 5264, 5274. See: TDNT—4:7, 495; BAGD—57a; THAYER—39c.

355. **ἀναλίσκω** {3x} **analiskō**, *an-al-is'-ko;* from *303* and a form of the alt. of *138;* prop. to *use up*, i.e. *destroy:*—consume {3x}.

Analisko means to use up, spend up, especially in a bad sense, to destroy and is said of the destruction of persons **(1)** literally: "And when His disciples James and John saw this, they said, Lord, wilt thou that we command fire to come down from heaven, and consume them, even as Elias did?" (Lk 9:54); and **(2)** metaphorically: "But if ye bite and devour one another, take heed that ye be not consumed one of another" (Gal 5:15; 2 Th 2:8). Syn: 2654, 853. See: BAGD—57a; THAYER—39c.

356. **ἀναλογία** {1x} **analŏgia**, *an-al-og-ee'-ah;* from a comp. of *303* and *3056; proportion:*—proportion {1x}.

Analogia [cf. Eng., "analogy"] signified the right relation, the coincidence or agreement existing or demanded according to the standard of the several relations, not agreement as equality. **(1)** It is used in Rom 12:6: "Having then gifts differing according to the grace that is given to us, whether prophecy, let us prophesy according to the proportion (*analogia*) of faith" where "let us prophesy according to the proportion of faith." **(2)** It recalls 12: 3: "For I say, through the grace given unto me, to every man that is among you, not to think of himself more highly than he ought to think; but to think soberly, according as God hath dealt to every man the measure of faith." **(3)** It is a warning against going beyond what God has given and faith receives. **(4)** "Proportion" here represents its true meaning. **(5)** The fact that there is a definite article before "faith" in the original does not necessarily afford an intimation that the faith, the body of Christian doctrine, is here in view. **(5a)** The presence of the definite article is due to the fact that faith is an abstract noun. **(5b)** The meaning "the faith" is not relevant to the context. See: TDNT—1:347, 56; BAGD—57b; THAYER—39d.

357. **ἀναλογίζομαι** {1x} **analŏgizŏmai**, *an-al-og-id'-zom-ahee;* mid. voice from *356;* to *estimate*, i.e. (fig.) *contemplate:*—consider {1x}.

Analogizomai means "to consider": "For consider Him that endured such contradiction of sinners against Himself, lest ye be wearied and faint in your minds" (Heb 12:3). See: BAGD—57b; THAYER—39d.

358. **ἄναλος** {1x} **analŏs**, *an'-al-os;* from *1* (as a neg. particle) and *251; saltless*, i.e. *insipid:*—lose saltness + 1096 {1x}.

Analos denotes "saltless, insipid, have lost its saltness" lit., "have become (ginomai) saltless (*analos*)" (Mk 9:50). Salt looses its saltness when it clumps together and becomes useless. Syn.: 233, 251, 252. See: BAGD—57b; THAYER—39d.

Greek

359. ἀνάλυσις {1x} **analusis**, *an-al'-oo-sis;* from *360; departure:*—departure {1x}.

Analusis, as a noun, means "an unloosing" [as of things woven], "a dissolving into separate parts" [Eng., "analysis"], and is once used of "departure from life": "For I am now ready to be offered, and the time of my departure is at hand" (2 Ti 4:6), where the metaphor is either nautical, from loosing from moorings [thus used in Greek poetry], or military, from breaking up an encampment. Syn.: 867, 1841. See: TDNT—4:337, 543; BAGD—57b; THAYER—39d.

360. ἀναλύω {2x} **analuō**, *an-al-oo'-o;* from *303* and *3089; to break up,* i.e. *depart* (lit. or fig.):—return {1x}, depart {1x}.

(1) *Analuo* literally means to unloose, undo, and signifies to depart in the sense of departing from life; a metaphor drawn from loosing moorings preparatory to setting sail. **(2)** *Analuo,* as a verb, means "to depart [die]" in Phil 1:23: "For I am in a strait betwixt two, having a desire to depart, and to be with Christ; which is far better" and **(3)** signifies "to return" in Lk 12:36, used in a simile of the "return" of a lord for his servants after a marriage feast. Syn.: 344, 390, 630, 868, 1880, 1877, 1994, 3327, 3332, 5290. See: TDNT—4:337, 543; BAGD—57c; THAYER—40a.

361. ἀναμάρτητος {1x} **anamartētŏs**, *an-am-ar'-tay-tos;* from *1* (as a neg. particle) and a presumed der. of *264; sinless:*—without sin {1x}.

Anamartetos, as an adjective, means "without sin": "So when they continued asking Him, He lifted up himself, and said unto them, He that is without sin among you, let him first cast a stone at her" (Jn 8:7). Syn.: 264, 265, 266, 4258. See: TDNT—1:333, 51; BAGD—57c; THAYER—40a.

362. ἀναμένω {1x} **anamĕnō**, *an-am-en'-o;* from *303* and *3306; to await:*—wait for {1x}.

Anameno, as a verb, means "to wait for" [*ana,* "up," used intensively, and *meno,* "to abide"], and is used in 1 Th 1:10 of "waiting" for the Son of God from heaven: "And to wait for His Son from heaven, whom He raised from the dead, even Jesus, which delivered us from the wrath to come." The word carries with it the suggestion of "waiting" with patience and confident expectancy. See: BAGD—57d; THAYER—40a.

363. ἀναμιμνήσκω {6x} **anamimnēskō**, *an-am-im-nace'-ko;* from *303* and *3403; to remind;* (refl.) to *recollect:*—call to remembrance {2x}, call to mind {1x},

bring to remembrance {1x}, remember {1x}, put to remembrance {1x}.

Anamimnesko, as a verb, means "to remind, call to remembrance" [*ana,* "up," *mimnesko,* "to remind"], and is translated "called to mind": "And the second time the cock crew. And Peter called to mind the word that Jesus said unto him, Before the cock crow twice, thou shalt deny me thrice. And when he thought thereon, he wept" in Mk 14:72 (passive voice). See: BAGD—57d; THAYER—40b.

364. ἀνάμνησις {4x} **anamnēsis**, *an-am'-nay-sis;* from *363; recollection:*—remembrance {3x}, remembrance again {1x}.

Anamnesis means a remembrance and is used **(1)** in Christ's command in the institution of the Lord's Supper: "And He took bread, and gave thanks, and brake it, and gave unto them, saying, This is My body which is given for you: this do in remembrance of Me" (Lk 22:19; cf. 1 Cor 11:24, 25); not in memory of as in remembering a deceased loved one, but in an affectionate calling of the Person Himself to mind; **(2)** of the remembrance of sins: "But in those sacrifices there is a remembrance again made of sins every year" (Heb 10:3). This is not just an external bringing to remembrance but an awakening of mind; a heart-felt conviction. Syn.: 3403, 3420, 3421, 5279, 5280. See: TDNT—1:348, 56; BAGD—58a; THAYER—40b.

365. ἀνανεόω {1x} **ananĕŏō**, *an-an-eh-o'-o;* from *303* and a der. of *3501; to renovate,* i.e. *reform:*—renew {1x}.

Ananeoo means to renew, make young and is used in Eph 4:23 "be renewed (in the spirit of your mind)." The renewal here mentioned is not that of the mind itself in its natural powers of memory, judgment and perception, but "the spirit of the mind"; which, under the controlling power of the indwelling Holy Spirit, directs its bent and energies God-ward in the enjoyment of fellowship with the Father and with His Son, Jesus Christ, and of the fulfillment of the will of God. Syn.: 340, 341, 342. See: TDNT—4:899, 628; BAGD—58a; THAYER—40b.

366. ἀνανήφω {1x} **ananēphō**, *an-an-ay'-fo;* from *303* and *3525; to become sober again,* i.e. (fig.) *regain* (one's) *senses:*—recover (one's) self {1x}.

Ananepho means to return to soberness as from a state of delirium or drunkenness and is used in 2 Ti 2:26: "And that they may recover themselves out of the snare of the devil, who are taken captive by him at his will"; said of those who, opposing the truth through accepting perversions of it, fall into the snare of the

devil, become intoxicated with error. Syn.:
4982. See: BAGD—58b; THAYER—40c.

367. **Ἀνανίας** {11x} **Ananias,** *an-an-ee'-as;*
of Heb. or. [2608]; *Ananias,*
the name of three Isr.:—*Ananias* (of Damascus) {6x}, *Ananias* (of Jerusalem) {3x}, *Ananias* (high priest) {2x}. See: BAGD—58b;
THAYER—40c.

368. **ἀναντίρρητος** {1x} **anantirrhētŏs,** *an-
an-tir'-hray-tos;* from *1*
(as a neg. particle) and a presumed der. of a
comp. of *473* and *4483; indisputable:*—cannot
be spoken against + 5607 {1x}.

Anantirrhetos literally means "not to be
spoken against" [*a,* negative, *n,* euphonic, *anti,*
"against," *rhetos,* "spoken"], and is rendered
"cannot be gainsaid, spoken against": "Seeing
then that these things cannot be spoken against,
ye ought to be quiet, and to do nothing rashly"
(Acts 19:36). Syn.: 369, 483, 485. See: BAGD—
58c; THAYER—40c.

369. **ἀναντιρρήτως** {1x} **anantirrhētōs,** *an-
an-tir-hray'-toce;* adv.
from *368; promptly:*—without gainsaying {1x}.

Anantirrhetos, corresponds to 368 and is
translated "without gainsaying": "Therefore
came I unto you without gainsaying, as soon
as I was sent for: I ask therefore for what intent
ye have sent for me?" (Acts 10:29 it might be
rendered "unquestioningly"). See: BAGD—58c;
THAYER—40c.

370. **ἀνάξιος** {1x} **anaxiŏs,** *an-ax'-ee-os;* from
1 (as a neg. particle) and *514;*
unfit:—unworthy {1x}.

Anaxios [*a,* negative, *n,* euphonic, *axios,*
"worthy"] means "unworthy" and is used in
1 Cor 6:2: "Do ye not know that the saints shall
judge the world? and if the world shall be
judged by you, are ye unworthy to judge the
smallest matters?" See: TDNT—1:379, 63;
BAGD—58c; THAYER—40d.

371. **ἀναξίως** {2x} **anaxiōs,** *an-ax-ee'-oce;*
adv. from *370; irreverently:*—
unworthily {2x}.

Anaxios is used in 1 Cor 11:27 of partaking
of the Lord's Supper "unworthily," i.e., treating
it as a common meal, the bread and cup as
common things, not apprehending their solemn symbolic import: "Wherefore whosoever
shall eat this bread, and drink this cup of the
Lord, unworthily, shall be guilty of the body
and blood of the Lord (cf. 11:19)." Syn.: 370.
See: BAGD—58d; THAYER—40d.

372. **ἀνάπαυσις** {5x} **anapausis,** *an-ap'-ŏw-
sis;* from *373; intermission;*
by impl. *recreation:*—rest {4x}, rest + 2192 {1x}.

Anapausis means cessation, refreshment,

rest, and is used in Mt 11:29: "Take My yoke
upon you, and learn of Me; for I am meek and
lowly in heart: and ye shall find rest unto your
souls"; where the contrast is with the burdens
imposed by the Pharisees. Christ's rest is not a
rest from work, but in work; not the rest of
inactivity but of the harmonious working of
all the faculties and affections—of will, heart,
imagination, conscience—because each has
found in God the ideal sphere for its satisfaction and development. Syn.: 373, 425, 1879,
1981, 2270, 2663, 2664, 2681, 2838, 4520. See:
TDNT—1:350, 56; BAGD—58d; THAYER—
40d.

373. **ἀναπαύω** {12x} **anapauō,** *an-ap-ow'-o;*
from *303* and *3973;* (refl.) to
repose (lit. or fig. [*be exempt*], *remain*); by impl.
to *refresh:*—rest {4x}, refresh {4x}, take rest
{2x}, give rest {1x}, take ease {1x}.

(1) *Anapauo* signifies to give intermission
from labor, to give rest, to refresh so to recover
strength. **(2)** It signifies "to cause or permit one
to cease from any labor or movement" so as to
recover strength. **(2a)** It implies previous toil
and care. **(2b)** Its chief significance is that of
taking, or causing to take, rest. **(2c)** It is used
in the middle voice in Lk 12:19: "And I will say
to my soul, Soul, thou hast much goods laid up
for many years; take thine ease, eat, drink, and
be merry," **(3)** "take (thine) ease" is indicative
of unnecessary, self-indulgent relaxation. (cf.
Mt 11:28; Lk 12:19; 1 Cor 16:18). Syn.: 372, 425,
1879, 1981, 2270, 2663, 2664, 2681, 2838, 4520.
See: TDNT—1:350, 56; BAGD—58d; THAYER—
40d.

374. **ἀναπείθω** {1x} **anapĕithō,** *an-ap-i'-tho;*
from *303* and *3982;* to *incite:*—
persuade {1x}.

Anapeitho means "to persuade, induce," in
an evil sense and is used in Acts 18:13: "Saying,
This fellow persuadeth men to worship God contrary to the law." See: BAGD—59b; THAYER—
41a.

375. **ἀναπέμπω** {4x} **anapĕmpō,** *an-ap-em'-
po;* from *303* and *3992;* to
send up or *back:*—send {2x}, send again {2x}.

Anapempo denotes **(1)** to send up to a higher
authority: "And as soon as he [Pilate] knew
that He belonged unto Herod's jurisdiction, he
sent Him to Herod, who himself also was at
Jerusalem at that time" (Lk 23:7; cf; 23:15; Acts
25:21); and **(2)** to send back: "And Herod with
his men of war set Him at nought, and mocked
Him, and arrayed Him in a gorgeous robe, and
sent Him again to Pilate" (Lk 23:11; cf. Philem
12). Syn.: 649, 1599, 1821, 3343, 3992, 4842,
4882. See: BAGD—59b; THAYER—41a.

376. ἀνάπηρος {2x} anapērŏs, *an-ap'-ay-ros*); from *303* (in the sense of *intensity*) and πῆρος pērŏs (*maimed*); *crippled:*—maimed {2x}.

Anaperos means "crippled, maimed" [from *ana*, "up," and *peros*, "disabled in a limb"], and is found in Lk 14:13: "But when thou makest a feast, call the poor, the maimed (*anaperos*), the lame, the blind" (cf. Lk 14: 21). Syn.: 2948. See: BAGD—59c; THAYER—41b.

377. ἀναπίπτω {11x} anapiptō, *an-ap-ip'-to;* from *303* and *4098;* to *fall back,* i.e. *lie down, lean back:*—sit down {7x}, sit down to meat {2x}, be set down {1x}, lean {1x}.

Anapipto, as a verb, means literally "to fall back" [*ana*, "back," *pipto*, "to fall"], and is used of reclining at a repast and translated **(1)** "leaning back, [as he was, on Jesus' breast]": "He [the apostle John] then lying on Jesus' breast saith unto Him, Lord, who is it?" (Jn 13:25); **(2)** "leaned back": "Then Peter, turning about, seeth the disciple whom Jesus loved following; which also leaned on His breast at supper, and said, Lord, which is he that betrayeth thee?" (Jn 21:20 the apostle's reminder of the same event in his experience). **(3)** *Anapipto* also means "to fall back" and denotes "to recline for a repast [meal]": "And He commanded the multitude to sit down (*anapipto*) on the ground" (Mt 15:35; cf. Mk 6:40; 8:6; Lk 11:37; 14:10; 17:7; 22:14; Jn 6:10 [twice]; 13:12). Syn.: 339, 345, 347, 1910, 2516, 2521, 2621, 2523, 2625, 4775, 4776, 4873. See: BAGD—59c; THAYER—41b.

378. ἀναπληρόω {6x} anaplērŏō, *an-ap-lay-rŏ'-o;* from *303* and *4137;* to *complete;* by impl. to *occupy, supply;* fig. to *accomplish* (by coincidence or obedience):—fulfil {2x}, supply {2x}, occupy {1x}, fill up {1x}.

Anapleroo means "to fill up adequately, completely" and is translated **(1)** by the verb "occupieth": "Else when thou shalt bless with the spirit, how shall he that occupieth (*anapleroo*) the room of the unlearned say Amen at thy giving of thanks, seeing he understandeth not what thou sayest?" (1 Cor 14:16 of a believer as a member of an assembly, who "fills" the position or condition [not one who "fills" it by assuming it] of being unable to understand the language of him who had the gift of tongues; and **(2)** "to fill up their sins" of the Jews who persisted in their course of antagonism and unbelief: "Forbidding us to speak to the Gentiles that they might be saved, to fill up their sins alway: for the wrath is come upon them to the uttermost" (1 Th 2:16). Syn.: 466, 1072, 1705, 2880, 3325, 4130, 4137, 4845. See:

379. ἀναπολόγητος {2x} anapŏlŏgētŏs, *an-ap-ol-og'-ay-tos;* from *1* (as a neg. particle) and a presumed der. of *626; indefensible:*—without excuse {1x}, inexcuseable {1x}.

Anapologetos means **(1)** "without excuse, inexcusable": "For the invisible things of Him from the creation of the world are clearly seen, being understood by the things that are made, *even* His eternal power and Godhead; so that they are without excuse", (Rom 1:20 "without excuse," of those who reject the revelation of God in creation); or **(2)** "inexcusable": "Therefore thou art inexcusable, O man, whosoever thou art that judgest: for wherein thou judgest another, thou condemnest thyself; for thou that judgest doest the same things" (Rom 2:1 of the Jew who judges the Gentile). See: BAGD—60a; THAYER—41c.

380. ἀναπτύσσω {1x} anaptussō, *an-ap-toos'-so;* from *303* (in the sense of *reversal*) and *4428;* to *unroll* (a scroll or volume):—open {1x}.

Anaptusso literally means "to unroll" [*ana*, "back," *ptusso*, "to roll"], and is found in Lk 4:17 (of the roll of Isaiah): "And there was delivered unto Him the book of the prophet Esaias. And when He had opened (*anaptusso*) the book, He found the place where it was written . . ." See: BAGD—60a; THAYER—41c.

381. ἀνάπτω {3x} anaptō, *an-ap'-to;* from *303* and *681;* to *enkindle:*—kindle {3x}.

Anapto means "to light up" and is used **(1)** literally, translated "kindleth" in Jas 3:5: "Even so the tongue is a little member, and boasteth great things. Behold, how great a matter a little fire kindleth!" (cf. Acts 28:2). **(2)** Metaphorically, in the passive voice, in Lk 12:49, of the "kindling" of the fire of hostility: "I am come to send fire on the earth; and what will I, if it be already kindled?" Syn.: 681, 4012. See: BAGD—60a; THAYER—41d.

382. ἀναρίθμητος {1x} anarithmētŏs, *an-ar-ith'-may-tos;* from *1* (as a neg. particle) and a der. of *705; unnumbered,* i.e. *without number:*—innumerable {1x}.

Anarithmetos, as a verb, [*a*, negative, *n*, euphonic, *arithmeo* "to number"] means a number too large to count: "Therefore sprang there even of one, and him [Abraham] as good as dead, so many as the stars of the sky in multitude, and as the sand which is by the sea shore innumerable" (Heb 11:12). Syn.: 3461. See: BAGD—60a; THAYER—41d.

TDNT—6:305, 867; BAGD—59d; THAYER—41b.

Greek

383. **ἀνασείω** {2x} **anasĕiō,** *an-as-i'-o;* from *303* and *4579;* fig. to *excite:—* move {1x}, stir up {1x}.

Anaseio, as a verb, primarily denotes "to shake back or out, move to and fro"; then, "to stir up," used metaphorically in Mk 15:11: "But the chief priests moved the people, that he [Pilate] should rather release Barabbas unto them" (cf. Lk 23:5). Syn.: 329, 387, 1326, 1892, 2042, 3947, 3951, 4531, 4579, 4787, 4797, 5017. See: BAGD—60a; THAYER—41d.

384. **ἀνασκευάζω** {1x} **anaskĕuazō,** *an-ask-yoo-ad'-zo;* from *303* (in the sense of *reversal*) and a der. of *4632;* prop. to *pack up* (baggage), i.e. (by impl. and fig.) to *upset:*—subvert {1x}.

Anaskeuazo primarily means "to pack up baggage"; hence, from a military point of view, to dismantle a town, to plunder and is used metaphorically in Acts 15:24, of unsettling or subverting the souls of believers: "Forasmuch as we have heard, that certain which went out from us have troubled you with words, subverting (*anaskeuazo*) your souls, saying, *Ye* must be circumcised, and keep the law: to whom we gave no *such* commandment." See: BAGD—60b; THAYER—41d.

385. **ἀνασπάω** {2x} **anaspaō,** *an-as-pah'-o;* from *303* and *4685;* to *take up* or *extricate:*—pull out {1x}, draw out {1x}.

Anaspao, as a verb, means "to draw up" and is used **(1)** of "drawing up, pulling out" an animal out of a pit: "And answered them, saying, Which of you shall have an ass or an ox fallen into a pit, and will not straightway pull him out on the sabbath day?" (Lk 14:5), and **(2)** of the "drawing" up of the sheet into heaven, in the vision in Acts 11:10: "And this was done three times: and all were drawn up again into heaven." Syn.: 307, 392, 501, 502, 645, 868, 1096, 1670, 1448, 1828, 2020, 2464, 4317, 4334, 4358, 4685, 4951, 5288, 5289. See: BAGD—60b; THAYER—41d.

386. **ἀνάστασις** {42x} **anastasis,** *an-as'-tas-is;* from *450;* a *standing up* again, i.e. (lit.) a *resurrection* from death (individual, gen. or by impl. [its author]), or (fig.) a (moral) *recovery* (of spiritual truth):—resurrection {39x}, rising again {1x}, that should rise {1x}, raised to life again + 1537 {1x}.

Anastasis denotes **(1)** a raising up, or rising; literally, "to cause to stand up on one's feet again": "And Simeon blessed them, and said unto Mary his mother, Behold, this child is set for the fall and rising again of many in Israel; and for a sign which shall be spoken against" (Lk 2:34—the Child would be like a stone over which many in Israel would stumble; while

many others would find in its strength and firmness a means of their salvation and spiritual life. They would be caused to rise up and once again to lean upon the Creator they had been rejecting. Jesus, the stone, the corner stone would be the One against Whom they would return and lean against (cf. Mt 21:24; Acts 4:11; 26:26; Eph 2:20; 1 Pet 2:6–7);

(2) of resurrection from the dead, **(2a)** of Christ: "Beginning from the baptism of John, unto that same day that He was taken up from us, must one be ordained to be a witness with us of His resurrection" (Acts 1:22; cf. 2:31; 4:33; Rom 1:4; 6:5; Phil 3:10); **(2b)** of those who are Christ's at His Parousia: "And thou shalt be blessed; for they cannot recompense thee: for thou shalt be recompensed at the resurrection of the just" (Lk 14:14); **(2c)** of the rest of the dead, after the millennium: "But the rest of the dead lived not again until the thousand years were finished. This *is* the first resurrection" (Rev 20:5); **(2d)** of those who were raised in more immediate connection with Christ's resurrection: "That Christ should suffer, and that He should be the first that should rise from the dead, and should shew light unto the people, and to the Gentiles" (Acts 26:23); **(2e)** of the resurrection spoken of in general terms: "The same day came to Him the Sadducees, which say that there is no resurrection, and asked Him" (Mt 22:23; Mk 12:18); **(2f)** of those who were raised in OT times, to die again: "Women received their dead raised to life again: and others were tortured, not accepting deliverance; that they might obtain a better resurrection" (Heb 11:35). Syn.: *Anastasis* stresses the final state of the one raised [upon his own feet]; whereas, *exanastasis* (*1815*) stresses the state from which the one was raised; and *egersis* (*1454*) stresses the invigoration which raises the one up. See: TDNT—1:371, 60; BAGD—60b; THAYER—41d.

387. **ἀναστατόω** {3x} **anastatŏō,** *an-as-tat-ŏ'-o;* from a der. of *450* (in the sense of *removal*); prop. to *drive out* of home, i.e. (by impl.) to *disturb* (lit. or fig.):— turn upside down {1x}, make an uproar {1x}, trouble {1x}.

Anastatoo, as a verb, means "to excite, unsettle" and is used **(1)** of "stirring up, turned . . . upside down" to sedition, and tumult: "And when they found them not, they drew Jason and certain brethren unto the rulers of the city, crying, These that have turned the world upside down are come hither also" (Acts 17:6; cf. 21:38); **(2)** "to upset, trouble" by false teaching: "I would they were even cut off which trouble you" (Gal 5:12). Syn.: 329, 383, 1326, 1892,

2042, 3947, 3951, 4531, 4579, 4787, 4797, 5017. See: BAGD—61a; THAYER—42b.

388. ἀνασταυρόω {1x} **anastauróō**, *an-as-tŏw-rŏ'-o;* from *303* and *4717;* to *recrucify* (fig.):—crucify afresh {1x}.

Anastauroo is used in Heb 6:6 of Hebrew apostates, who as merely nominal Christians, in turning back to Judaism, were thereby virtually guilty of "crucifying" Christ again: "If they shall fall away, to renew them again unto repentance; seeing they crucify to themselves the Son of God afresh, and put Him to an open shame." See: TDNT—7:583, 1071; BAGD—61a; THAYER—42b.

389. ἀναστενάζω {1x} **anastĕnazo**, *an-as-ten-ad'-zo;* from *303* and *4727;* to *sigh deeply:*—sigh deeply {1x}.

Anastenazo means "to sigh deeply" [*ana*, "up," suggesting "deep drawn," and *stenazo* (4727), "to groan,"], and occurs in Mk 8:12: "And He sighed deeply in His spirit, and saith, Why doth this generation seek after a sign? verily I say unto you, There shall no sign be given unto this generation" See: BAGD—61b; THAYER—42b.

390. ἀναστρέφω {11x} **anastrĕphō**, *an-as-tref'-o;* from *303* and *4762;* to *overturn;* also to *return;* by impl. to *busy* oneself, i.e. *remain, live:*—return {2x}, have conversation {2x}, live {2x}, abide {1x}, overthrow {1x}, behave (one's) self {1x}, be used {1x}, pass {1x}.

Anastrepho, as a verb, used metaphorically, in the middle voice, "to conduct oneself, behave, live," is translated "to live": **(1)** "honestly": "Pray for us: for we trust we have a good conscience, in all things willing to live honestly" (Heb 13:18); and **(2)** "in error": "For when they speak great swelling words of vanity, they allure through the lusts of the flesh, through much wantonness, those that were clean escaped from them who live in error" (2 Pet 2:18). Syn.: 326, 980, 1236, 2198, 2225, 4176, 4800, 5225. See: TDNT—7:715, 1093; BAGD—61b; THAYER—42b.

391. ἀναστροφή {13x} **anastrŏphē**, *an-as-trof-ay';* from *390; behavior:*—conversation {13x}.

Anastrophe, as a noun, means literally "a turning back" and is translated "manner of life, living, conversation": "For ye have heard of my conversation in time past in the Jews' religion, how that beyond measure I persecuted the church of God, and wasted it" (Gal 1:13; Eph 4:22; 1 Ti 4:12; Heb 13:7; Jas 3:13; 1 Pet 1:15, 18; 2:1 "behavior"; 3:1, 2, 16; 2 Pet 2:7; 3:11). "Conversation" in English primarily means "give and take, back and forth" and pictures a life style of going and coming in every

day events. Syn.: 2688. See: TDNT—7:715, 1093; BAGD—61c; THAYER—42c.

392. ἀνατάσσομαι {1x} **anatassŏmai**, *an-at-as'-som-ahee;* from *303* and the mid. voice of *5021;* to *arrange:*—set forth in order {1x}.

Anatassomai, as a verb, means "to arrange in order": "Forasmuch as many have taken in hand to set forth in order (*anatassomai*) a declaration of those things which are most surely believed among us" (Lk 1:1 - some interpret the word to mean to "bring together" from memory assisted by the Holy Spirit). Syn.: 307, 385, 501, 502, 645, 868, 1096, 1670, 1448, 1828, 2020, 2464, 4317, 4334, 4358, 4685, 4951, 5288, 5289. See: TDNT—8:32,*; BAGD—61d; THAYER—42d.

393. ἀνατέλλω {9x} **anatĕllō**, *an-at-el'-lo;* from *303* and the base of *5056;* to (*cause* to) *arise:*—be up {2x}, rise {2x}, spring up {1x}, make rise {1x}, at the rising of {1x}, spring {1x}, arise {1x}.

Anatello, as a verb, means "to arise" and is used especially of things in the natural creation: **(1)** metaphorically, of light: "The people which sat in darkness saw great light; and to them which sat in the region and shadow of death light is sprung up" (Mt 4:16); **(2)** of the sun: "That ye may be the children of your Father which is in heaven: for He maketh His sun to rise on the evil and on the good" (Mt 5:45; Mk 4:6; Jas 1:11); **(3)** of a cloud: "And He said also to the people, When ye see a cloud rise out of the west, straightway ye say, There cometh a shower; and so it is" (Lk 12:54); **(4)** of the day-star: "We have also a more sure word of prophecy; whereunto ye do well that ye take heed, as unto a light that shineth in a dark place, until the day dawn, and the day star arise in your hearts" (2 Pet 1:19); **(5)** metaphorically, of the Incarnation of Christ: "Our Lord hath sprung out of Judah" (Heb 7:14 - more lit., "Our Lord hath arisen out of Judah," as of the rising of the light of the sun). Syn.: 305, 450, 1096, 1326, 1453, 1525, 1817, 4911. See: TDNT—1:351, 57; BAGD—62a; THAYER—42d.

394. ἀνατίθεμαι {2x} **anatithĕmai**, *an-at-ith'-em-ahee;* from *303* and the mid. voice of *5087;* to *set forth* (for oneself), i.e. *propound:*—declare {1x}, communicate {1x}.

Anatithemai means to put up or before and is used of laying a case, declaring/detailing its parts, before an authority: "And when they had been there many days, Festus declared (*anath-themai*) Paul's cause unto the king, saying, There is a certain man left in bonds by Felix"

(Acts 25:14; cf. Gal 2:2). See: TDNT—1:353, 57; BAGD—62a; THAYER—42d.

395. **ἀνατολή** {10x} **anatŏlē**, *an-at-ol-ay′;* from *393;* a *rising* of light, i.e. *dawn* (fig.); by impl. the *east* (also in plur.):—east {9x}, dayspring {1x}.

Anatole literally means "a rising up" and is used of the rising of the sun; **(1)** it chiefly means the east: "Now when Jesus was born in Bethlehem of Judaea in the days of Herod the king, behold, there came wise men from the east to Jerusalem" (Mt 2:1; cf. 2:2, 9; 8:11; 24:27; Lk 13:29; Rev 7:2; 16:12; 21:13); and it is also rendered **(2)** "dayspring": "Through the tender mercy of our God; whereby the dayspring from on high hath visited us" (Lk 1:78). See: TDNT—1:352, 57; BAGD—62b; THAYER—43a.

396. **ἀνατρέπω** {2x} **anatrĕpō**, *an-at-rep′-o;* from *303* and the base of *5157;* to *overturn* (fig.):—overthrow {1x}, subvert {1x}.

Anatrepo literally means "to turn up or over" [*ana*, "up," *trepo*, "to turn"] "to upset, overthrow" and is used metaphorically **(1)** in 2 Ti 2:18: "Who concerning the truth have erred, saying that the resurrection is past already; and overthrow the faith of some"; and **(2)** "subvert" in Titus 1:11: "Whose mouths must be stopped, who subvert whole houses, teaching things which they ought not, for filthy lucre's sake." See: BAGD—62c; THAYER—43a.

397. **ἀνατρέφω** {3x} **anatrĕphō**, *an-at-ref′-o;* from *303* and *5142;* to *rear* (phys. or ment.):—nourish {1x}, nourish up {1x}, bring up {1x}.

Anatrepho, as a verb, means **(1)** "to nourish": "In which time Moses was born, and was exceeding fair, and nourished up (*anatrepho*) in his father's house three months" (Acts 7:20; cf. 7:21); **(2)** "brought up": "I am verily a man which am a Jew, born in Tarsus, a city in Cilicia, yet brought up (*anatrepho*) in this city at the feet of Gamaliel" (Acts 22:3). See: BAGD—62d; THAYER—43a.

398. **ἀναφαίνω** {2x} **anaphainō**, *an-af-ah′-ee-no;* from *303* and *5316;* to *show*, i.e. (refl.) *appear*, or (pass.) to *have pointed* out:—appear {1x}, discover {1x}.

This word means to bring to light, hold up to view, to show, to appear, be made apparent. *Anaphaino* means "forth, or up," perhaps originally a nautical term, "to come up into view," hence, in general, "to appear suddenly," and is used **(1)** in the passive voice, in Lk 19:11, of the kingdom of God: "And as they heard these things, He added and spake a parable, because He was nigh to Jerusalem, and because they thought that the kingdom of God should im-

mediately appear (*anaphaino*)"; **(2)** active voice, in Acts 21:3 "to come in sight of": "Now when we had discovered (*anaphaino*) Cyprus, we left it on the left hand, and sailed into Syria, and landed at Tyre: for there the ship was to unlade her burden." See: BAGD—63a; THAYER—43b.

399. **ἀναφέρω** {10x} **anaphĕrō**, *an-af-er′-o;* from *303* and *5342;* to *take up* (lit. or fig.):—offer up {3x}, bear {2x}, offer {2x}, bring up {1x}, lead up {1x}, carry up {1x}.

Anaphero means up and is used of leading persons up to a higher place: **(1)** of the Lord's ascension: "And it came to pass, while He blessed them, He was parted from them, and carried up (*anaphero*) into heaven" (Lk 24:51); or **(2)** of the Lord's propitiatory sacrifice, in His bearing sins on the cross: "So Christ was once offered to bear the sins of many; and unto them that look for him shall he appear the second time without sin unto salvation" (Heb 9:28; cf. 1 Pet 2:24). **(3)** *Anaphero* also denotes "to bring up": "And after six days Jesus taketh Peter, James, and John his brother, and bringeth them up (*anaphero*) into an high mountain apart" (Mt 17:1). Syn.: 941, 5342. See: TDNT—9:60, 1252; BAGD—63a; THAYER—43b.

400. **ἀναφωνέω** {1x} **anaphōnĕō**, *an-af-o-neh′-o;* from *303* and *5455;* to *exclaim:*—speak out {1x}.

In Lk 1:42 *anaphoneo* means "to lift up one's voice," and is rendered "spake out": "And she spake out with a loud voice, and said, Blessed art thou among women, and blessed is the fruit of thy womb." See: BAGD—63b; THAYER—43c.

401. **ἀνάχυσις** {1x} **anachusis**, *an-akh′-oo-sis;* from a comp. of *303* and χέω **chĕō** (to *pour*); prop. *effusion*, i.e. (fig.) *license:*—excess {1x}.

Anachusis, literally means "a pouring out, overflowing" and is used metaphorically in 1 Pet 4:4: "Wherein they think it strange that ye run not with them to the same excess of riot, speaking evil of you" said of the riotous conduct described in v. 3. Syn.: 192, 193. See: BAGD—63c; THAYER—43c.

402. **ἀναχωρέω** {14x} **anachōrĕō**, *an-akh-o-reh′-o;* from *303* and *5562;* to *retire:*—depart {8x}, withdraw (one's) self {2x}, go aside {2x}, turn aside {1x}, give place {1x}.

Anachoreo, as a verb, means "to withdraw, to go back, recede, retire" [*ana*, "back or up," *choreo*, "to make room for, betake oneself," *choros*, "a place"], and is translated **(1)** "departed": "When Jesus therefore perceived that they would come and take Him by force, to make Him a king, He departed again into a mountain

Himself alone" (Jn 6:15; cf. Mt 2:12–14; 4:12; 14:13; 15:21; 27:5); and **(2)** "turned aside": "But when he [Joseph] heard that Archelaus did reign in Judaea in the room of his father Herod, he was afraid to go thither: notwithstanding, being warned of God in a dream, he turned aside into the parts of Galilee" (Mt 2:22); and **(3)** "give place": "He said unto them, Give place: for the maid is not dead, but sleepeth. And they laughed him to scorn" (Mt 9:24). Syn.: 201, 1096, 1502, 3837, 4042, 5117, 5247, 5564, 5602. See: BAGD – 63c; THAYER – 43c.

403. ἀνάψυξις {1x} **anapsuxis,** *an-aps'-ook-sis;* from *404;* prop. a *recovery of breath,* i.e. (fig.) *revival:*—refeshing {1x}.

Anapsuxis means "a refreshing" and occurs in Acts 3:19: "Repent ye therefore, and be converted, that your sins may be blotted out, when the times of refreshing shall come from the presence of the Lord." See: TDNT – 9:664, 1342; BAGD – 63c; THAYER – 43c.

404. ἀναψύχω {1x} **anapsuchō,** *an-aps-oo'-kho;* from *303* and *5594;* prop. to *cool off,* i.e. (fig.) *relieve:*—refresh {1x}.

This word means to cool again, to cool off, recover from the effects of heat; to refresh one's spirit [*ana,* "back," *psucho,* "to cool"] and is used in 2 Ti 1:16: "The Lord give mercy unto the house of Onesiphorus; for he oft refreshed me, and was not ashamed of my chain." See: TDNT – 9:663, 1342; BAGD – 63d; THAYER – 43d.

405. ἀνδραποδιστής {1x} **andrapŏdistēs,** *an-drap-od-is-tace';* from a der. of a comp. of *435* and *4228;* an *enslaver* (as bringing *men* to his *feet*):—menstealer {1x}.

This word means "a slave dealer, kidnapper," from *andrapodon,* "a slave captured in war" a word found in the plural in the papyri, e.g., in a catalogue of property and in combination with *tetrapoda,* "four-footed things" (*andrapodon, aner,* "a man," *pous,* "a foot"); *andrapodon* "was never an ordinary word for slave; it was too brutally obvious a reminder of the principle which made quadruped and human chattels differ only in the number of their legs. The verb *andrapodizo* supplied the noun "with the like odious meaning": "For whoremongers, for them that defile themselves with mankind, for menstealers, for liars, for perjured persons, and if there be any other thing that is contrary to sound doctrine" (1 Ti 1:10). See: BAGD – 63d; THAYER – 43d.

406. Ἀνδρέας {13x} **Andrĕas,** *an-dreh'-as;* from *435; manly; Andreas,* an Isr.:—Andrew {13x}. See: BAGD – 63d; THAYER – 43d.

407. ἀνδρίζομαι {1x} **andrizŏmai,** *an-drid'-zom-ahee;* mid. voice from *435;* to *act manly:*—quit you like men {1x}.

This word means to quit something that will free you to be a man; thus "quit you like men" means "stop present activities which frees you to be the man God calls you to be;" to make a man of or make brave; to show one's self a man: "Watch ye, stand fast in the faith, quit you like men, be strong." See: TDNT – 1:360, 59; BAGD – 64a; THAYER – 43d.

408. Ἀνδρόνικος {1x} **Andrŏnikŏs,** *an-dron'-ee-kos;* from *435* and *3534; man of victory; Andronicos,* an Isr.:—Adronicus {1x}. See: BAGD – 64a; THAYER – 43d.

409. ἀνδροφόνος {1x} **andrŏphŏnŏs,** *an-drof-on'-os;* from *435* and *5408;* a *murderer:*—manslayer {1x}.

This word comes from *aner,* "a man," and *phoneus,* "a murderer," and occurs in the plural in 1 Ti 1:9: "Knowing this, that the law is not made for a righteous man, but for the lawless and disobedient, for the ungodly and for sinners, for unholy and profane, for murderers of fathers and murderers of mothers, for manslayers (*androphonos*)." See: BAGD – 64a; THAYER – 44a.

410. ἀνέγκλητος {5x} **anĕgklētŏs,** *an-eng'-klay-tos;* from *1* (as a neg. particle) and a der. of *1458; unaccused,* i.e. (by impl.) *irreproachable:*—blameless {4x}, unreproveable {1x}.

Anenkletos, as an adjective, signifies "that which cannot be called to account" [from *a,* negative, *n,* euphonic, and *enkaleo,* "to call in"], i.e., with nothing laid to one's charge, as the result of public investigation, and is translated **(1)** "blameless": "Who shall also confirm you unto the end, that ye may be blameless in the day of our Lord Jesus Christ" (1 Cor 1:8; cf. 1 Ti 3:10; Titus 1:6–7); and **(2)** "unreproveable": "In the body of His flesh through death, to present you holy and unblameable and unreproveable in His sight" (Col 1:22). **(3)** It implies not merely acquittal, but the absence of even a charge or accusation against a person. This is to be the case with elders: "And let these also first be proved; then let them use the office of a deacon, being found blameless" (1 Ti 3:10; cf. Titus 1:6–7). Syn.: 273, 274, 298, 299, 338, 423, 2607, 3201, 3469. See: TDNT – 1:356, 58; BAGD – 64b; THAYER – 44a.

411. ἀνεκδιήγητος {1x} **anĕkdiēgētŏs,** *an-ek-dee-ay'-gay-tos;* from *1* (as a neg. particle) and a presumed der. of *1555; not expounded* in full, i.e. *indescribable:*—unspeakable {1x}.

The stress of this word is that the object is inexpressible; i.e. adequate words cannot be

found to correctly describe the object, which is in 2 Cor 9:15 the unspeakable of the gift of God—His Son, Jesus: "Thanks be unto God for His unspeakable gift." Some scholars feel this "gift" may be the Holy Spirit. Syn.: 412, 731. See: BAGD—64b; THAYER—44a.

412. ἀνεκλάλητος {1x} **anĕklalētŏs,** *an-ek-lal'-ay-tos;* from *1* (as a neg. particle) and a presumed der. of *1583; not spoken out,* i.e. (by impl.) *unutterable:—*unspeakable {1x}.

With this word, the words can be found, but due to joy, they are overwhelmed and not spoken: "Whom having not seen, ye love; in whom, though now ye see Him not, yet believing, ye rejoice with joy unspeakable and full of glory" (1 Pet 1:8). Syn.: 411, 731. See: BAGD—64b; THAYER—44a.

413. ἀνέκλειπτος {1x} **anĕklĕiptŏs,** *an-ek'-lipe-tos;* from *1* (as a neg. particle) and a presumed der. of *1587; not left out,* i.e. (by impl.) *inexhaustible:—*not to fail {1x}.

This word means "unfailing" and is rendered "that faileth not": "Sell that ye have, and give alms; provide yourselves bags which wax not old, a treasure in the heavens that faileth not (*anekleiptos*), where no thief approacheth, neither moth corrupteth" (Lk 12:33). See: BAGD—64b; THAYER—44a.

414. ἀνεκτότερος {6x} **anĕktŏtĕrŏs,** *an-ek-tot'-er-os;* comp. of a der. of *430; more endurable:—*more tolerable {6x}.

This word is used in its comparative form, *anektoteros:* KJV Matthew 10:15 "Verily I say unto you, It shall be more tolerable for the land of Sodom and Gomorrha in the day of judgment, than for that city" (Mt 10:15; cf 11:22, 24; Mk 6:11; Lk 10:12, 14). See: TDNT—1:359,*; BAGD—64c; THAYER—44a.

415. ἀνελεήμων {1x} **anĕlĕēmōn,** *an-eleh-ay'-mone;* from *1* (as a neg. particle) and *1655; merciless:—*unmerciful {1x}.

This word means "without mercy" [*a*, negative, *n*, euphonic, *eleemon*, "merciful"] and occurs in Rom 1:31: "Without understanding, covenantbreakers, without natural affection, implacable, unmerciful (*aneleemon*) . . ." See: TDNT—2:487, 222; BAGD—64c; THAYER—44a.

416. ἀνεμίζω {1x} **anemizō,** *an-em-id'-zo;* from *417;* to *toss with the wind:—*drive with the wind {1x}.

Anemizo means "to drive by the wind" [*anemos*, "wind"] and is used in Jas 1:6: "But let him ask in faith, nothing wavering. For he that wavereth is like a wave of the sea driven with

the wind and tossed." See: BAGD—64c; THAYER—44b.

417. ἄνεμος {31x} **anĕmŏs,** *an'-em-os;* from the base of *109; wind;* (plur.) by impl. (the four) *quarters* (of the earth):—wind {31x}.

Anemos, **(1)** besides its literal meaning of a strong often tempestuous wind: "And the rain descended, and the floods came, and the winds (*anemos*) blew, and beat upon that house; and it fell not: for it was founded upon a rock" (Mt 7:25; cf. Jn 6:18; Acts 27:14; Jas 3:4), is used **(2)** metaphorically of variable teaching: "That we henceforth be no more children, tossed to and fro, and carried about with every wind of doctrine, by the sleight of men, and cunning craftiness, whereby they lie in wait to deceive" (Eph 4:14 – No one ever sees the wind; only its devastating after effects. God's gifted men are to be pro-active, preventing the winds from inflicting damage). **(3)** The four winds stand for the four cardinal points of the compass: "And He shall send His angels with a great sound of a trumpet, and they shall gather together His elect from the four winds, from one end of heaven to the other" (Mt 24:31; cf. Mk 13:27; Rev 7:1). **(4)** The contexts indicate that these are connected with the execution of divine judgments. Syn.: 2366, 2978, 4151, 4157. See: BAGD—64c; THAYER—44b.

418. ἀνένδεκτος {1x} **anĕndĕktŏs,** *an-en'-dek-tos;* from *1* (as a neg. particle) and a der. of the same as *1735; unadmitted,* i.e. (by impl.) *not supposable:—*impossible {1x}.

Anendektos signifies "inadmissible" [*a*, negative, *n*, euphonic, and *endechomai*, "to admit, allow"], of occasions of stumbling, where the meaning is "it cannot be but that they will come": "Then said He unto the disciples, It is impossible but that offences will come; but woe unto him, through whom they come!" (Lk 17:1). Syn.: 101, 102. See: BAGD—65a; THAYER—44b.

419. ἀνεξερεύνητος {1x} **anĕxĕrĕunētŏs,** *an-ex-er-yoo'-nay-tos;* from *1* (as a neg. particle) and a presumed der. of *1830; not searched out,* i.e. (by impl.) *inscrutable:—*unsearchable {1x}.

Anexereunetos, as an adjective [*a*, negative, *n*, euphonic, *ex* (*ek*), "out," *eraunao*, "to search, examine,"] is used in Rom 11:33, of the judgments of God: "O the depth of the riches both of the wisdom and knowledge of God! how unsearchable are His judgments, and His ways past finding out!" Syn.: 421. See: TDNT—1:357, 58; BAGD—65a; THAYER—44c.

420. ἀνεξίκακος {1x} **anĕxikakŏs,** *an-ex-ik'-ak-os;* from *430* and *2556;* *enduring of ill,* i.e. *forbearing:*—patient {1x}.

Anexikakos denotes "patiently forbearing evil," literally "patient of wrong," [from *anecho* and *kakos,* "evil"], "enduring"; it is rendered "forbearing": "And the servant of the Lord must not strive; but be gentle unto all men, apt to teach, patient (*anexikakos*)" (2 Ti 2:24). Syn.: 420, 430, 447, 463, 1933, 4722, 5339. See: TDNT—3:486, 391; BAGD—65a; THAYER—44c.

421. ἀνεξιχνίαστος {2x} **anĕxichniastŏs,** *an-ex-ikh-nee'-as-tos;* from *1* (as a neg. particle) and a presumed der. of a comp. of *1537* and a der. of *2487; not tracked out,* i.e. (by impl.) *untraceable:*—past finding out {1x}, unsearchable {1x}.

This word is rendered **(1)** "past finding out": "O the depth of the riches both of the wisdom and knowledge of God! how unsearchable are His judgments, and His ways past finding out!" (Rom 11:33) and **(2)** "unsearchable": "Unto me, who am less than the least of all saints, is this grace given, that I should preach among the Gentiles the unsearchable riches of Christ" (Eph 3:8). **(3)** The stress is on the fact that God's ways are not ways that leave a trail behind; they are unique for each situation. See: TDNT—1:358, 58; BAGD—65a; THAYER—44c.

422. ἀνεπαίσχυντος {1x} **anĕpaischuntŏs,** *an-ep-ah'-ee-skhoon-tos;* from *1* (as a neg. particle) and a presumed der. of a comp. of *1909* and *153; not ashamed,* i.e. (by impl.) *irreprehensible:*—that needeth not to be ashamed {1x}. See: BAGD—65a; THAYER—44c.

423. ἀνεπίληπτος {3x} **anĕpilēptŏs,** *an-ep-eel'-ape-tos;* from *1* (as a neg. particle) and a der. of *1949; not arrested,* i.e. (by impl.) *inculpable:*—blameless {2x}, unrebukeable {1x}.

Anepileptos, as an adjective, literally means "that cannot be laid hold of"; hence, "not open to censure, irreproachable" and is translated **(1)** "blameless": "A bishop then must be blameless, the husband of one wife, vigilant, sober, of good behaviour, given to hospitality, apt to teach" (1 Ti 3:2; cf. 5:7) and **(2)** "unrebukeable": "That thou keep this commandment without spot, unrebukeable, until the appearing of our Lord Jesus Christ" (1 Ti 6:14). Syn.: 273, 274, 298, 299, 338, 410, 2607, 3201, 3469. See: TDNT—4:9, 495; BAGD—65b; THAYER—44c.

424. ἀνέρχομαι {3x} **anĕrchŏmai,** *an-erkh'-om-ahee;* from *303* and *2064;* to *ascend:*—go up {3x}.

Anerchomai means "to go up" and occurs in Jn 6:3: "And Jesus went up (*anerchomai*) into a mountain, and there He sat with his disciples" (cf. Gal 1:17, 18). See: BAGD—65b; THAYER—44c.

425. ἄνεσις {5x} **anĕsis,** *an'-es-is;* from *447; relaxation* or (fig.) *relief:*—eased {1x}, liberty {1x}, rest {3x}.

Anesis denotes a letting loose, relaxation, easing and signifies rest, not from toil, but from endurance and suffering. Thus it is said **(1)** of a less vigorous condition in imprisonment: "And he commanded a centurion to keep Paul, and to let him have liberty (*anesis*), and that he should forbid none of his acquaintance to minister or come unto him" (Acts 24:23), **(2)** relief from anxiety: "I had no rest (*anesis*) in my spirit, because I found not Titus my brother: but taking my leave of them, I went from thence into Macedonia" (2 Cor 2:13; cf. 7:5), **(3)** relief from persecutions: "And to you who are troubled rest (*anesis*) with us, when the Lord Jesus shall be revealed from heaven with His mighty angels" (2 Th 1:7), **(4)** of relief from the sufferings of poverty": "For I mean not that other men be eased (*anesis*), and ye burdened" (2 Cor 8:13). Syn.: 373; see esp. 372. See: TDNT—1:367, 60; BAGD—65b; THAYER—44d.

426. ἀνετάζω {2x} **anĕtazō,** *an-et-ad'-zo;* from *303* and ἐτάζω **ĕtazō** (to *test*); to *investigate* (judicially):—(should have) examine (-d) {2x}.

Anetazo means "to examine judicially" [*ana,* "up," *etazo,* "to test"], and is used in Acts 22:24: "The chief captain commanded him to be brought into the castle, and bade that he should be examined (*anetazo*) by scourging; that he might know wherefore they cried so against him" (cf. Acts 22:29). Syn.: 1833. See: TDNT—1:367, 60; BAGD—65c; THAYER—44d.

427. ἄνευ {3x} **anĕu,** *an'-yoo;* a prim. particle; *without:*—without {3x}.

This word stresses without one's will or intervention: "Are not two sparrows sold for a farthing? and one of them shall not fall on the ground without (*aneu*) your Father" (Mt 10:19; cf. 1 Pe 3:1; 4:9). See: BAGD—65c; THAYER—44d. comp. *1.*

428. ἀνεύθετος {1x} **anĕuthĕtŏs,** *an-yoo'-the-tos;* from *1* (as a neg. particle) and *2111; not well set,* i.e. *inconvenient:*—not commodious {1x}.

Aneuthetos means "not commodious," literally "not-well-placed" [from *a,* "not," *n,* euphonic, *eu,* "well," *thetos,* "from" *tithemi* "to put, place"] and is found in Acts 27:12, where it is said of the haven at the place called Fair Havens: "And because the haven was not commodious (*aneuthetos*) to winter in, the more

part advised to depart thence also, if by any means they might attain to Phenice, and there to winter; which is an haven of Crete, and lieth toward the south west and north west." See: BAGD—65c; THAYER—44d.

429. ἀνευρίσκω {2x} **anĕuriskō**, *an-yoo-ris'-ko;* from *303* and *2147;* to *find out:*—find {2x}.

Aneurisko means "to find out" (by search), "discover" implying diligent searching and is used **(1)** in Lk 2:16, of the shepherds in searching for and "finding" Mary and Joseph and the Child: "And they came with haste, and found Mary, and Joseph, and the babe lying in a manger"; and **(2)** in Acts 21:4, of Paul and his companions, in searching for and "finding" "the disciples" at Tyre: "And finding (*aneurisko*) disciples, we tarried there seven days: who said to Paul through the Spirit, that he should not go up to Jerusalem." See: BAGD—65c; THAYER—44d.

430. ἀνέχομαι {15x} **anĕchŏmai**, *an-ekh'-om-ahee;* mid. voice from *303* and *2192;* to *hold oneself up* against, i.e. (fig.) *put up* with:—bear with {4x}, endure {2x}, forbear {2x}, suffer {7x}.

This word signifies "to hold up against a thing and so to bear with" [*ana*, "up," and *echomai*, the middle voice of *echo*, "to have, to hold"]: "Then Jesus answered and said, O faithless and perverse generation, how long shall I be with you? how long shall I suffer you? bring him hither to Me" (Mt 17:17; cf. 1 Cor 4:12; 2 Cor 11:1, 4, 19–20; Heb 13:22). See: TDNT—1:359,* BAGD—65d; THAYER—44d.

431. ἀνέψιος {1x} **anĕpsiŏs**, *an-eps'-ee-os;* from *1* (as a particle of union) and an obs. νέπος **nĕpŏs** (a *brood*); prop. *akin,* i.e. (spec.) a *cousin:*—sister's son {1x}.

This word denotes a nephew; hence we are to understand, therefore, that Mark was the cousin of Barnabas. See: BAGD—66a; THAYER—45a.

432. ἄνηθον {1x} **anēthŏn**, *an'-ay-thon;* prob. of for. or.; *dill:*—anise {1x}.

This word means "dill, anise" and was used for food and for pickling: "Woe unto you, scribes and Pharisees, hypocrites! for ye pay tithe of mint and anise and cummin, and have omitted the weightier matters of the law, judgment, mercy, and faith: these ought ye to have done, and not to leave the other undone" (Mt 23:23). See: BAGD—66a; THAYER—45a.

433. ἀνήκω {3x} **anēkō**, *an-ay'-ko;* from *303* and *2240;* to *attain to,* i.e. (fig.) *be proper:*—convenient {2x}, be fit {1x}.

Aneko means **(1)** primarily "to have arrived at, reached to, pertained to," came to denote "what is due to a person, one's duty, what is

befitting." **(2)** It is used ethically in the NT: **(2a)** Eph 5:4: "Neither filthiness, nor foolish talking, nor jesting, which are not convenient (*aneko*): but rather giving of thanks"; **(2b)** "Wives, submit yourselves unto your own husbands, as it is fit (*aneko*) in the Lord" (Col 3:18 concerning the duty of wives towards husbands). **(2c)** In Philem 8, the participle is used with the article, signifying "that which is convenient": "Wherefore, though I might be much bold in Christ to enjoin thee that which is convenient (*aneko*)." See: TDNT—1:359,* BAGD—66b; THAYER—45b.

434. ἀνήμερος {1x} **anēmĕrŏs**, *an-ay'-mer-os;* from *1* (as a neg. particle) and ἥμερος **hēmĕrŏs** (*lame, gentle*); *not tame, savage:*—fierce {1x}.

This word signifies "not tame, savage" [from *a* negative, and *hemeros,* "gentle"]: "Without natural affection, trucebreakers, false accusers, incontinent, fierce (*anemeros*), despisers of those that are good" (2 Ti 3:3). See: BAGD—66c; THAYER—45b.

435. ἀνήρ {215x} **anēr**, *an-ayr';* a prim. word [comp. *444*]; a *man* (prop. as an indiv. male):—fellow {1x}, husband {50x}, man {156x}, sir {6x}, not trans. {2x}.

Aner is never used of the female sex; it stands **(1)** in distinction from a woman: "But when they believed Philip preaching the things concerning the kingdom of God, and the name of Jesus Christ, they were baptized, both men and women" (Acts 8:12; cf. 1 Ti 2:12); **(2)** as a husband: "And Jacob begat Joseph the husband of Mary, of whom was born Jesus, who is called Christ" (Mt 1:16; cf. Jn 4:16; Rm 7:2); **(3)** as distinct from a boy or infant: "When I was a child, I spake as a child, I understood as a child, I thought as a child: but when I became a man, I put away childish things" (1 Cor 13:11); **(4)** metaphorically: "Till we all come in the unity of the faith, and of the knowledge of the Son of God, unto a perfect man, unto the measure of the stature of the fulness of Christ" (Eph 4:13); **(5)** denotes "a man," in relation to his sex or age; in Acts 17:5 (plural) it is rendered "fellows," as more appropriate to the accompanying description of them: "But the Jews which believed not, moved with envy, took unto them certain lewd fellows of the baser sort, and gathered a company, and set all the city on an uproar, and assaulted the house of Jason, and sought to bring them out to the people." Syn.: 444, 730, 5046. See: TDNT—1:360, 59; BAGD—66c; THAYER—45b.

436. ἀνθίστημι {14x} **anthistēmi**, *anth-is'-tay-mee;* from *473* and *2476;*

to *stand against,* i.e. *oppose:*—resist {9x}, withstand {5x}.

Anthistemi, as a verb, means "to set against" [*anti,* "against," *histemi,* "to cause to stand"], and is used in the middle (or passive) voice and in the intransitive 2nd aorist and perfect active, signifying "to withstand, oppose, resist." It is translated **(1)** "to resist": "But I say unto you, That ye resist not evil: but whosoever shall smite thee on thy right cheek, turn to him the other also" (Mt 5:39; cf. Lk 21:15; Acts 6:10; Rom 9:19; 13:2 [twice]; **(2)** "withstand, withstood": "But Elymas the sorcerer (for so is his name by interpretation) withstood them, seeking to turn away the deputy from the faith" (Acts 13:8; cf. Gal 2:11; Eph 6:13; 2 Ti 4:15; Jas 4:7; 1 Pet 5:9); **(3)** both "to withstood" and "resist" in 2 Ti 3:8: "Now as Jannes and Jambres withstood (*anthistemi*) Moses, so do these also resist (*anthistemi*) the truth: men of corrupt minds, reprobate concerning the faith." Syn.: 478, 498. See: BAGD—67b; THAYER—45c.

437. ἀνθομολογέομαι {1x} **anthŏmŏlŏgĕŏ-mai,** *anth-om-ol-og-eh'-om-ahee;* from *473* and the mid. voice of *3670;* to *confess in turn,* i.e. *respond* in praise:—give thanks {1x}.

Anthomologeomai means "to acknowledge fully, to celebrate fully in praise with thanksgiving," and is used of Anna in Lk 2:35: "And she [Anna] coming in that instant gave thanks (*anthomologeomai*) likewise unto the Lord, and spake of Him to all them that looked for redemption in Jerusalem." Syn.: 1843, 2168. See: TDNT—5:199, 687; BAGD—67b; THAYER—45d.

438. ἄνθος {4x} **anthŏs,** *anth'-os;* a prim. word; a *blossom:*—flower {4x}.

Anthos is "a blossom, flower": "For all flesh is as grass, and all the glory of man as the flower of grass. The grass withereth, and the flower thereof falleth away" (1 Pe 1:24; cf. Jas 1:10). See: BAGD—67c; THAYER—45d.

439. ἀνθρακιά {2x} **anthrakia,** *anth-rak-ee-ah';* from *440;* a bed of burning *coals:*—fire of coals {2x}.

Anthrakia is "a heap of burning coals, or a charcoal fire": "And the servants and officers stood there, who had made a fire of coals; for it was cold: and they warmed themselves: and Peter stood with them, and warmed himself" (Jn 18:18; cf. 21:9). Syn.: 440. See: BAGD—67c; THAYER—45d.

440. ἄνθραξ {1x} **anthrax,** *anth'-rax;* of uncert. der.; a live *coal:*—coals of fire {1x}.

Anthrax, "a burning coal" [cf. Eng., "anthracite,"] is used in the plural in Rom 12:20, meta-

phorically in a proverbial expression, "thou shalt heap coals of fire on his head" [from Prov 25:22], signifying retribution by kindness, i.e., that, by conferring a favor on your enemy, you recall the wrong he has done to you, so that he repents, with pain of heart. Syn.: 439. See: BAGD—67c; THAYER—45d.

441. ἀνθρωπάρεσκος {2x} **anthrōparĕskŏs,** *anth-ro-par'-es-kos;* from *444* and *700; man-courting,* i.e. *fawning:*—men-pleaser {2x}.

Anthropareskos, an adjective signifying "studying to please men" [*anthropos,* "man," *aresko,* "to please"], designates, not simply one who is pleasing to men . . . , but one who endeavors to please men and not God. It is used in Eph 6:6: "Not with eyeservice, as menpleasers; but as the servants of Christ, doing the will of God from the heart" (cf. Col 3:22). See: TDNT—1:465, 77; BAGD—67d; THAYER—46a.

442. ἀνθρώπινος {7x} **anthrōpinŏs,** *anth-ro'-pee-nos;* from *444; human:*—man's {3x}, after the manner of man {1x}, of man {1x}, common to man {1x}, mankind + 5449 {1x}.

Anthropinos means "human, belonging to man" [from *anthropos*), and is used **(1)** of man's wisdom: "Which things also we speak, not in the words which man's wisdom teacheth, but which the Holy Ghost teacheth; comparing spiritual things with spiritual" (1 Cor 2:13); **(2)** of "man's judgment: "But with me it is a very small thing that I should be judged of you, or of man's judgment: yea, I judge not mine own self" (1 Cor 4:3); **(3)** of "mankind": "For every kind of beasts, and of birds, and of serpents, and of things in the sea, is tamed, and hath been tamed of mankind" (Jas 3:7 lit., "nature of man");

(4) of human ordinance: "Submit yourselves to every ordinance of man for the Lord's sake: whether it be to the king, as supreme" (1 Pet 2:13); **(5)** of temptation: "There hath no temptation taken you but such as is common to man: but God is faithful, who will not suffer you to be tempted above that ye are able; but will with the temptation also make a way to escape, that ye may be able to bear it" (1 Cor 10:13 "such as is common to man," i.e., such as must and does come to "men"); **(6)** of "men's" hands: "Neither is worshipped with men's hands, as though He needed any thing, seeing He giveth to all life, and breath, and all things" (Acts 17:25); **(7)** in the phrase "after the manner of men": "I speak after the manner of men because of the infirmity of your flesh" (Rom 6:19). See:

Greek

TDNT—1:366, 59; BAGD—67d; THAYER—46a.

443. ἀνθρωποκτόνος {3x} **anthrōpŏktŏnŏs**, *anth-ro-pok-ton'-os;* from *444* and κτείνω **ktĕinō** (to *kill*); a *manslayer:*—murderer {3x}.

Anthropoktonos, an adjective, lit., "manslaying," used as a noun, "a manslayer, murderer" [*anthropos*, "a man," *kteino*, "to slay"], is used **(1)** of Satan: "Ye are of your father the devil, and the lusts of your father ye will do. He was a murderer from the beginning, and abode not in the truth" (Jn 8:44); **(2)** of one who hates his brother, and who, being a "murderer," has not eternal life: "Whosoever hateth his brother is a murderer: and ye know that no murderer hath eternal life abiding in him" (1 Jn 3:15). *Anthropoktonos* corresponds exactly to the English manslayer and homicide. Syn.: 4607, 5406. *Phoneus* (*5406*) refers to any murderer. *Sikarious* (*4607*) is an assassin using a particular knife (*sicarii*). *Anthropoktonos* refers to the murder of men/males only. See: TDNT—1:366, 59; BAGD—68a; THAYER—46b.

444. ἄνθρωπος {559x} **anthrōpŏs**, *anth'-ro-pos;* from *435* and ὤψ **ōps** (the *countenance;* from *3700*); *man-faced*, i.e. a *human* being:—man {552x}, not tr {4x}, misc. {3x}.

Anthropos is used **(1)** generally, of a human being, male or female, without reference to sex or nationality: "But He answered and said, It is written, Man shall not live by bread alone, but by every word that proceedeth out of the mouth of God" (Mt 4:4; cf. 12:35; Jn 2:25); **(2)** in distinction from God: "Wherefore they are no more twain, but one flesh. What therefore God hath joined together, let not man put asunder" (Mt 19:6; cf. Jn 10:33); **(3)** in distinction from animals: "And so was also James, and John, the sons of Zebedee, which were partners with Simon. And Jesus said unto Simon, Fear not; from henceforth thou shalt catch men" (Lk 5:10); **(4)** sometimes, in the plural, of men and women, people: "Ye are the salt of the earth: but if the salt have lost his savour, wherewith shall it be salted? it is thenceforth good for nothing, but to be cast out, and to be trodden under foot of men" (Mt 5:13; cf. 5:16); **(5)** in some instances with a suggestion of human frailty and imperfection: "That your faith should not stand in the wisdom of men, but in the power of God" (1 Cor 2:5);

(6) in the phrases translated "after man," "after the manner of men," "as a man" means **(6a)** the practices of fallen humanity: "For ye are yet carnal: for whereas there is among you envying, and strife, and divisions, are ye not carnal, and walk as men?" (1 Cor 3:3); **(6b)** any-thing of human origin: "But I certify you, brethren, that the gospel which was preached of me is not after man" (Gal 1:11); **(6c)** the standard generally accepted among men: "Brethren, I speak after the manner of men; Though it be but a man's covenant, yet if it be confirmed, no man disannulleth, or addeth thereto" (Gal 3:15); **(6d)** an illustration not drawn from Scripture: "Say I these things as a man? or saith not the law the same also?" (1 Cor 9:8); **(6e)** in the phrase the inward man means **(6e1)** the regenerate person's spiritual nature personified, the inner self of the believer: "For I delight in the law of God after the inward man" (Rom 7:22), **(6e2)** as the sphere of the renewing power of the Holy Spirit: "That He would grant you, according to the riches of His glory, to be strengthened with might by His Spirit in the inner man" (Eph 3:16); **(6e3)** in contrast to the outward man, the physical frame, the man as cognizable by the senses: "For which cause we faint not; but though our outward man perish, yet the inward man is renewed day by day" (2 Cor 4:16); **(6e4)** the inward man is identical with the hidden man of the heart: "But let it be the hidden man of the heart, in that which is not corruptible, even the ornament of a meek and quiet spirit, which is in the sight of God of great price" (1 Pet 3:4);

(7) in the expression "the old man," it stands for the unregenerate nature personified as the former self of a believer: "Knowing this, that our old man is crucified with Him, that the body of sin might be destroyed, that henceforth we should not serve sin" (Rom 6:6; cf. Eph 4:22; Col 3:9); **(8)** "the new man" standing for the new nature personified as the believer's regenerate self, **(8a)** a nature created in righteousness and holiness of truth: "And that ye put on the new man, which after God is created in righteousness and true holiness" (Eph 4:24), and **(8b)** having been put on at regeneration: "And have put on the new man, which is renewed in knowledge after the image of Him that created him" (Col 3:10); and it is to be put on in practical apprehension of these facts. **(9)** The phrase "the man of God" (2 Ti 3:17) is not used as an official designation, nor denoting a special class of believers, but specifies what every believer should be, namely, a person whose life and conduct represent the mind of God and fulfill His will: "But thou, O man of God, flee these things; and follow after righteousness, godliness, faith, love, patience, meekness" (1 Ti 6:11). Syn.: 435, 730, 5046. See: TDNT—1:364, 59; BAGD—68a; THAYER—46b.

445. ἀνθυπατεύω {1x} **anthupatĕuō**, *anth-oo-pat-yoo'-o;* from *446;* to *act as a proconsul:*—be the deputy {1x}.

Anthupateuo means to act as a pro-consul. Syn.: 446. See: BAGD—69c; THAYER—47a.

446. ἀνθύπατος {4x} **anthupatŏs**, *anth-oo'-pat-os;* from *473* and a superl. of *5228; instead of* the *highest* officer, i.e. (spec.) a Roman *proconsul:*—deputy {4x}.

Anthupatos comes from *anti,* "instead of," and *hupatos,* "supreme," and **(1)** denotes "a consul, one acting in place of a consul, a proconsul, the governor of a senatorial province" [i.e., one which had no standing army]. **(2)** The "proconsuls" were of two classes, **(2a)** exconsuls, the rulers of the provinces of Asia and Africa, who were therefore "proconsuls." These are the "proconsuls" at Ephesus, Acts 19:38 ("deputies"); **(2b)** those who were ex-pretors or "proconsuls" of other senatorial provinces [a pretor being virtually the same as a consul]. These were men like Sergius Paulus in Cyprus, Acts 13:7, 8, 12, and Gallio at Corinth, 18:12. **(3)** In the NT times Egypt was governed by a prefect. Provinces in which a standing army was kept were governed by an imperial legate [e.g., Quirinius in Syria, Luke 2:2]. Syn.: 755, 1481, 2232, 3623. See: BAGD—69c; THAYER—47a.

447. ἀνίημι {4x} **aniĕmi**, *an-ee'-ay-mee;* from *303* and ἵημι **hiēmi** (to *send);* to *let up,* i.e. (lit.) *slacken* or (fig.) *desert, desist* from:—forbear {1x}, leave {1x}, loose {2x}.

Aniemi literally means to send up or back; hence, to relax, loosen or metaphorically to desist from and is translated forbearing: "And, ye masters, do the same things unto them, forbearing threatening: knowing that your Master also is in heaven; neither is there respect of persons with him" (Eph 6:9—giving up your threatening). Syn.: 420, 430, 463, 5339. See: TDNT—1:367, 60; BAGD—69d; THAYER—47b.

448. ἀνίλεως {1x} **anilĕōs**, *an-ee'-leh-oce;* from *1* (as a neg. particle) and *2436; inexorable:*—without mercy {1x}.

Anileos "unmerciful, merciless" [*a,* negative, *n,* euphonic, and *eleos,* "mercy"], occurs in Jas 2:13, said of judgment on him who shows no mercy: "For he shall have judgment without mercy, that hath shewed no mercy; and mercy rejoiceth against judgment." See: TDNT—2:487,*; BAGD—69d; THAYER—47b.

449. ἄνιπτος {3x} **aniptŏs**, *an'-ip-tos;* from *1* (as a neg. particle) and a presumed der. of *3538; without ablution:*—unwashen {3x}.

Aniptos means "unwashed" [*a,* negative, *nipto,* "to wash"] and occurs in Mt 15:20: "These are the things which defile a man: but to eat with

unwashen hands defileth not a man" (cf. Mk 7:2, 5). See: TDNT—4:947, 635; BAGD—69d; THAYER—47b.

450. ἀνίστημι {112x} **anistēmi**, *an-is'-tay-mee;* from *303* and *2476;* to *stand up* (lit. or fig., trans. or intr.):—arise {38x}, rise {19x}, rise up {16x}, rise again {13x}, raise up {11x}, stand up {8x}, raise up again {2x}, misc. {5x} = lift up, stand upright.

Anistemi, as a verb, means "to stand up or to make to stand up," according as its use is intransitive or transitive and is used **(1)** of a physical change of position **(1a)** of "rising" from sleep (Mk 1:35); **(1b)** rising from a meeting in a synagogue (Lk 4:29); **(1c)** of the illegal "rising" of the high priest in the tribunal in Mt 26:62; **(1d)** of an invalid "rising" from his couch (Lk 5:25); **(1e)** the "rising" up of a disciple from his vocation to follow Christ (Lk 5:28; cf. Jn 11:31); **(1f)** "rising" up from prayer (Lk 22:45); **(1g)** of a whole company (Acts 26:30; 1 Cor 10:7); **(2)** metaphorically, of "rising" up antagonistically against persons: **(2a)** of officials against people (Acts 5:17); **(2b)** of a seditious leader (Acts 5:36); **(2c)** of the "rising" up of Satan (Mk 3:26); **(2d)** of false teachers (Acts 20:30); **(3)** of "rising" to a position of preeminence or power: **(3a)** of Christ as a prophet (Acts 3:22; 7:37); **(3b)** as God's servant in the midst of the nation of Israel (Acts 3:26); **(3c)** as the Son of God in the midst of the nation (Acts 13:33); **(3d)** as a priest (Heb 7:11, 15); **(3e)** as king over the nations (Rom 15:12);

(4) of a spiritual awakening from lethargy (Eph 5:14); **(5)** of resurrection from the dead: **(5a)** of the resurrection of Christ (Mt 17:9; 20:19; Mk 8:31; 9:9–10, 31; 10:34; Lk 18:33; 24:7, 46; Jn 20:9; Acts 2:24, 32; 10:41; 13:34; 17:3, 31; 1 Th 4:14); **(5b)** of believers (Jn 6:39–40, 44, 54; 11:24; 1 Th 4:16); **(5c)** of unbelievers (Mt 12:41). Syn.: *Egeiro* (*1453*) stands in contrast to *anistemi* (450 - when used with reference to resurrection) in this respect, that *egeiro* is frequently used both in the transitive sense of "raising up" and the intransitive of "rising," whereas *anistemi* is comparatively infrequent in the transitive use. See also: 305, 393, 1096, 1326, 1453, 1525, 1817, 4911. See: TDNT—1:368, 60; BAGD—70a; THAYER—47b.

451. Ἄννα {1x} **Anna**, *an'-nah;* of Heb. or. [2584]; *Anna,* an Israelitess:—Anna {1x}. See: BAGD—70c; THAYER—47d.

452. Ἄννας {4x} **Annas**, *an'-nas;* of Heb. or. [2608]; *Annas* (i.e. *367*), an Isr.:—Annas {4x}. See: BAGD—70c; THAYER—47d.

453. ἀνόητος {6x} **anŏĕtŏs**, *an-o'-ay-tos;* from *1* (as a neg. particle) and a der.

of *3539; unintelligent;* by impl. *sensual:*—fool
{1x}, foolish {4x}, unwise {1x}.

Anoetos means not understanding, not applying the mind; it signifies **(1)** senseless, an
unworthy lack of understanding: "Then He
said unto them, O fools (*anoetos*), and slow of
heart to believe all that the prophets have spoken" (Lk 24:25; cf. Rom 1:14; Gal 3:1, 3); or
(2) sometimes it carries a moral reproach and
describes one who does not govern his lusts:
"For we ourselves also were sometimes foolish
(*anoetos*), disobedient, deceived, serving divers
lusts and pleasures, living in malice and envy,
hateful, and hating one another" (Titus 3:3; cf.
1 Ti 6:9). Syn.: 801, 877, 878, 3471, 3472, 3474,
3912. See: TDNT—4:961, 636; BAGD—70d;
THAYER—48a.

454. ἄνοια {2x} **anŏia,** *an'-oy-ah;* from a comp.
of *1* (as a neg. particle) and *3563*
stupidity; by impl. *rage:*—folly {1x}, madness
{1x}.

Anoia literally signifies "without understanding" [*a,* negative, *nous,* "mind"]; hence,
"folly," or, rather, **(1)** "senselessness": "But they
shall proceed no further: for their folly (*anoia*)
shall be manifest unto all men, as theirs also
was" (2 Ti 3:9); and **(2)** in Lk 6:11 it denotes violent or mad rage, "madness": "And they were
filled with madness; and communed one with
another what they might do to Jesus." See:
TDNT—4:962, 636; BAGD—70d; THAYER—
48a.

455. ἀνοίγω {77x} **anŏigō,** *an-oy'-go;* from *303*
and οἴγω **ŏigō** (to *open*); to *open
up* (lit. or fig., in various applications):—open
{77x}.

Anoigo is used **(1)** transitively, **(1a)** literally,
(1a1) of a door or gate (Acts 5:19); **(1a2)** graves
(Mt 27:52); **(1a3)** a sepulcher (Rom 3:13); **(1a4)**
a book (Lk 4:17; Rev. 5:2–5); **(1a5)** the seals of
a roll (Rev. 5:9; 6:1); **(1a6)** the eyes (Acts 9:40);
(1a7) the mouth of a fish (Mt 17:27); **(1a8)** the
pit of the abyss (Rev 9:2); **(1a9)** heaven and
the heavens (Mt 3:16; Lk 3:21; Acts 10:11); **(1b)**
metaphorically,: "Ask, and it shall be given you;
seek, and ye shall find; knock, and it shall be
opened unto you: For every one that asketh
receiveth; and he that seeketh findeth; and to
him that knocketh it shall be opened" (Mt
7:7–8; cf. 25:11; Rev 3:7); **(2)** intransitively
(2a) literally, of the heaven: "And He saith unto
him [Nathanael], Verily, verily, I say unto you,
Hereafter ye shall see heaven open, and the
angels of God ascending and descending upon
the Son of man" (Jn 1:51); **(2b)** metaphorically,
of speaking freely: "O ye Corinthians, our
mouth is open unto you, our heart is enlarged"

(2 Cor 6:11). Syn.: 457, 1272, 3692. See: BAGD—
70d; THAYER—48a.

456. ἀνοικοδομέω {2x} **anŏikŏdŏmĕō,** *an-oy-
kod-om-eh'-o;* from *303* and
3618; to *rebuild:*—build again {2x}.

Anoikodomeo signifies "to build again":
"After this I will return, and will build again
(*anoikodomeo*) the tabernacle of David, which
is fallen down; and I will build again (*anoikodomeo*) the ruins thereof, and I will set it up"
(Acts 15:16). Syn.: 2026, 4925. See: BAGD—
71c; THAYER—48c.

457. ἄνοιξις {1x} **anŏixis,** *an'-oix-is;* from
455; opening (throat):—that (one)
may open + 1722 {1x}.

Anoixis is "an opening" and is used in Eph
6:19, metaphorically, of the "opening" of the
mouth: "And for me [Paul], that utterance may
be given unto me, that I may open my mouth
boldly, to make known the mystery of the gospel." Syn.: 455, 1272, 3692. See: BAGD—71c;
THAYER—48c.

458. ἀνομία {15x} **anŏmia,** *an-om-ee'-ah;* from
459; illegality, i.e. *violation of
law* or (gen.) *wickedness:*—iniquity {12x}, unrighteousness {1x}, transgress the law + 4160
{1x}, transgression of the law {1x}.

Anomia **(1)** refers **(1a)** not to one living
without law, **(1b)** but to one who acts contrary
to law; **(1c)** where there is no law given there
can be *hamartia* (*266*) but not *anomia;* an error
against adopted law. **(2)** Its usual rendering is
iniquity, which lit. means unrighteousness and
it is used **(2a)** of iniquity in general: "And then
will I profess unto them, I never knew you:
depart from Me, ye that work iniquity" (Mt
7:23; cf. 13:41; Rom 6:19); and **(2b)** in the plural, of acts or manifestations of lawlessness:
"Saying, Blessed are they whose iniquities are
forgiven, and whose sins are covered" (Rom 4:7;
cf. Heb 10:17). Syn.: 51, 92, 93, 265, 266, 2275,
3847, 3876, 3892, 3900, 4189. See: TDNT—
4:1085, 646; BAGD—71d; THAYER—48c.

459. ἄνομος {10 x} **anŏmŏs,** *an'-om-os;* from
1 (as a neg. particle) and *3551;
lawless,* i.e. (neg.) *not subject to* (the Jewish) *law;*
(by impl. a *Gentile*), or (pos.) *wicked:*—without
law {4x}, transgressor {2x}, wicked {2x}, lawless
{1x}, unlawful {1x}.

Anomos signifies "without law, having no
existing law" and has this meaning in 1 Cor
9:21: "To them that are without law (*anomos*),
as without law (*anomos*), [being not without
law (*anomos*), to God, but under the law to
Christ,] that I might gain them that are without law (*anomos*)." See: TDNT—4:1086, 646;
BAGD—72a; THAYER—48d.

460. ἀνόμως {2x} **anŏmōs,** *an-om'-oce;* adv. from *459; lawlessly,* i.e. (spec.) *not amenable to* (the Jewish) *law:*—without law {2x}.

Anomos, as an adverb, means without law and is used **(1)** in Rom 2:12: "For as many as have sinned without law (*anomos*) shall also perish without law (*anomos*): and as many as have sinned in the law shall be judged by the law"; **(2)** where "have sinned without law" means in the absence of some specifically revealed law, like the law of Sinai; and **(3)** "shall perish without law" predicates that the absence of such a law will not prevent their doom. Syn.: *459.* See: BAGD—72b; THAYER—48d.

461. ἀνορθόω {3x} **anŏrthŏō,** *an-orth-ŏ'-o;* from *303* and a der. of the base of *3717;* to *straighten up; to set upright:*—lift up {1x}, set up {1x}, make straight {1x}.

Anorthoo, as a verb, means "to set upright" [*ana,* "up," *orthos,* "straight"] and is used **(1)** metaphorically, **(1a)** of "lifting" up "hands that hang down": "Wherefore lift up the hands which hang down, and the feeble knees" (Heb 12:12); **(1b)** of setting up a building, restoring ruins: "After this I [God] will return, and will build again the tabernacle of David, which is fallen down; and I will build again the ruins thereof, and I will set it up" (Acts 15:16); **(2)** literally, of the healing of the woman with a spirit of infirmity: "And He laid His hands on her: and immediately she was made straight, and glorified God" (Lk 13:13 "was made straight"). See: BAGD—72c; THAYER—49a.

462. ἀνόσιος {2x} **anŏsiŏs,** *an-os'-ee-os;* from *1* (as a neg. particle) and *3741; wicked:*—unholy {2x}.

Anosios, as an adjective [*a,* negative, *n,* euphonic, *hosios,* "holy"] means "unholy, profane": "Knowing this, that the law is not made for a righteous man, but for the lawless and disobedient, for the ungodly and for sinners, for unholy (*anosios*) and profane, for murderers of fathers and murderers of mothers, for manslayers" (1 Ti 1:9; cf. 2 Ti 3:2). Syn.: *2839.* See: TDNT—5:492, 734; BAGD—72c; THAYER—49a.

463. ἀνοχή {2x} **anŏchē,** *an-okh-ay';* from *430; self-restraint,* i.e. *tolerance:*—forbearance {2x}.

Anoche means a holding back and denotes forbearance, a delay of punishment, a demonstration of God's forbearance with men used **(1)** in Rom 2:4 where it represents a suspension of wrath which must eventually be exercised unless the sinner accepts God's conditions: "Or despisest thou the riches of his goodness and forbearance and longsuffering; not knowing that the goodness of God leadeth thee to repen-

tance?"; and **(2)** in Rom 3:25 it is connected with the passing over of sins in times past, previous to the atoning work of Christ: "Whom God hath set forth to be a propitiation through faith in His blood, to declare His righteousness for the remission of sins that are past, through the forbearance of God." His forbearance is the ground, not of His forgiveness, but of His pretermission of sins, His withholding punishment. Syn.: *420, 1933, 3115, 5281.* See: TDNT—1:359, 58; BAGD—72c; THAYER—49a.

464. ἀνταγωνίζομαι {1x} **antagōnizŏmai,** *an-tag-o-nid'-zom-ahee;* from *473* and *75;* to *struggle against* (fig.) ["antagonize"]:—strive against {1x}.

Antagonizomai means "to struggle against": "Ye have not yet resisted unto blood, striving against sin" (Heb 12:4 "striving against"). Syn.: *4865, 4866.* See: TDNT—1:134, 20; BAGD—72d; THAYER—49a.

465. ἀντάλλαγμα {2x} **antallagma,** *an-tal'-lag-mah;* from a comp. of *473* and *236;* an *equivalent* or *ransom:*—in exchange {2x}.

Antallagma is the price received as an equivalent of, or in exchange for, an article, an exchange; hence, it denotes the price at which the exchange is effected: "For what is a man profited, if he shall gain the whole world, and lose his own soul? or what shall a man give in exchange (*antallagma*) for his soul?" (Mt 16:26; cf. Mk 8:37). Syn.: *3337.* See: TDNT—1:252, 40; BAGD—72d; THAYER—49a.

466. ἀνταναπληρόω {1x} **antanaplērŏō,** *an-tan-ap-lay-rŏ'-o;* from *473* and *378;* to *supplement:*—fill up {1x}.

Antanapleroo means to fill up in turn and is used in Col 1:24, of the apostle's responsive devotion to Christ in "filling" up, or undertaking on his part a full share of, the sufferings which follow after the sufferings of Christ, and are experienced by the members of His Body, the church: "Who now rejoice in my sufferings for you, and fill up that which is behind of the afflictions of Christ in my flesh for His body's sake, which is the church." The point of the apostle's boast is that Christ, the sinless Master, should have left something for Paul, the unworthy servant, to suffer. Syn.: *4845.* See: TDNT—1:252, 40; BAGD—72d; THAYER—49b.

467. ἀνταποδίδωμι {7x} **antapŏdidōmi,** *an-tap-od-ee'-do-mee;* from *473* and *591;* to *requite* (good or evil):—recompense {3x}, recompense again {1x}, render {1x}, repay {1x}.

Antapodidomi means "to give back as an equivalent, to requite, recompense" [the *anti* expressing the idea of a complete return] and

is translated **(1)** "render": "For what thanks can we render to God again for you, for all the joy wherewith we joy for your sakes before our God" (1 Th 3:9 here only in the NT of thanksgiving to God); elsewhere it is used of **(2)** "recompense" **(2a)** whether between men: "See that none render (apodidomi) evil for evil unto any man; but ever follow that which is good, both among yourselves, and to all men" (1 Th 5:15; cf. Lk 14:14 see the corresponding noun in v. 12); or **(2b)** between God and evil-doers: "Dearly beloved, avenge not yourselves, but rather give place unto wrath: for it is written, Vengeance is mine; I will repay (apodidomi), saith the Lord" (Rom 12:19; cf. Heb 10:30); or **(2c)** between God and those who do well: "And thou shalt be blessed; for they cannot recompense (apodidomi) thee: for thou shalt be recompensed (apodidomi) at the resurrection of the just" (Lk 14:14; cf. Rom 11:35); **(2d)** in 2 Th 1:6 retribution are in view: "Seeing *it is* a righteous thing with God to recompense (apodidomi) tribulation to them that trouble you." Syn.: 469, 591. See: TDNT—2:169, 166; BAGD—73a; THAYER—49b.

468. **ἀνταπόδομα** {2x} **antapŏdŏma**, *an-tap-od'-om-ah;* from *467;* a *requital* (prop. the thing):—recompense {2x}.

Antapodoma means "a recompense," lit., "a giving back in return," a requital, recompence, and is used **(1)** in a favorable sense: "Then said He also to him that bade Him, When thou makest a dinner or a supper, call not thy friends, nor thy brethren, neither thy kinsmen, nor thy rich neighbours; lest they also bid thee again, and a recompence (antapodoma) be made thee" (Lk 14:12); **(2)** in an unfavorable sense: "And David saith, Let their table be made a snare, and a trap, and a stumblingblock, and a recompence (antapodoma) unto them" (Rom 11:9) indicating that the present condition of the Jewish nation is the retributive effect of their transgressions, on account of which that which was designed as a blessing ("their table") has become a means of judgment. Syn.: 459, 489. See: TDNT—2:169, 166; BAGD—73a; THAYER—49b.

469. **ἀνταπόδοσις** {1x} **antapŏdŏsis**, *an-tap-od'-os-is;* from *467; requital* (prop. the act):—reward {1x}.

Antapodosis is rendered "reward" in Col 3:24: "Knowing that of the Lord ye shall receive the reward of the inheritance: for ye serve the Lord Christ." Syn.: 468, 489. See: TDNT—2:169, 166 BAGD—73a; THAYER—49b.

470. **ἀνταποκρίνομαι** {2x} **antapŏkrinŏmai**, *an-tap-ok-ree'-nom-*

ahee; from *473* and *611;* to *contradict* or *dispute:*—answer again {1x}, reply against {1x}.

This word is a strengthened form and means "to answer by contradiction, to reply against": "And they could not answer (antapokrinomai) Him again to these things" (Lk 14:6; cf. Rom 9:20). See: TDNT—3:944, 469; BAGD—73b; THAYER—49c.

471. **ἀντέπω** {2x} **antĕpō**, *an-tep'-o;* from *473* and *2036;* to *refute* or *deny:*—gainsay {1x}, say against {1x}.

(1) This word means to say against, to weigh in [gain] against; to declare weighty matters against someone to gain advantage. **(2)** *Antepo,* as a verb, means serves as an aorist tense of *antilego* (*483*) and is rendered **(2a)** "gainsay": "For I will give you a mouth and wisdom, which all your adversaries shall not be able to gainsay nor resist" (Lk 21:15); and **(2b)** "say against": "And beholding the man which was healed standing with them, they could say nothing against it" (Acts 4:14). Syn.: 368, 369, 483, 485. See: BAGD—73b; THAYER—49c.

472. **ἀντέχομαι** {4x} **antĕchŏmai**, *an-tekh'-om-ahee;* from *473* and the mid. voice of *2192;* to *hold* oneself *opposite* to, i.e. (by impl.) *adhere to;* by extens. to *care for:*—hold fast {1x}, hold to {2x}, support {1x}.

This word signifies in **(1)** the middle voice, **(1a)** "to hold firmly to, cleave to," of "holding" or cleaving to a person: "No man can serve two masters: for either he will hate the one, and love the other; or else he will hold to the one, and despise the other" (Mt 6:24; cf. Lk 16:13); **(1b)** of "holding fast" to the faithful word: "Holding fast the faithful word as he hath been taught, that he may be able by sound doctrine both to exhort and to convince the gainsayers" (Titus 1:9); **(2)** "to support": "Now we exhort you, brethren, warn them that are unruly, comfort the feebleminded, support the weak, be patient toward all men" (1 Th 5:14 the weak). Syn.: See: TDNT—2:827, 286; BAGD—73b; THAYER—49c.

473. **ἀντί** {22x} **anti**, *an-tee';* a prim. particle; *opposite,* i.e. *instead* or *because* of (rarely *in addition* to):—for {15x}, because + 3639 {4x}, for . . . cause {1x}, therefore + 3639 {1x}, in the room of {1x}.

This preposition is first of equivalence and then of exchange, stressing being in the place where another should be; total replacement. Syn.: 528. See: TDNT—1:372, 61; BAGD—73c; THAYER—49d.

474. **ἀντιβάλλω** {1x} **antiballō**, *an-tee-bal'-lo;* from *473* and *906;* to *bandy:*—have {1x}.

Antiballo, as a verb, means literally "to throw

in turn, exchange, to cast back and forth from one to another; one has and gives to another"; hence, metaphorically, "to exchange thoughts": "And He said unto them, What manner of communications are these that ye have (*antiballo*) one to another, as ye walk, and are sad?" (Lk 24:17). See: BAGD—74a; THAYER—50a.

475. ἀντιδιατίθεμαι {1x} **antidiatithĕmai**, *an-tee-dee-at-eeth'-em-ahee;* from *473* and *1303;* to *set oneself opposite,* i.e. *be disputatious:*—that oppose themselves {1x}.

This word signifies "to place oneself in opposition, oppose": "In meekness instructing those that oppose themselves; if God peradventure will give them repentance to the acknowledging of the truth" (2 Ti 2:25). See: BAGD—74a; THAYER—50a.

476. ἀντίδικος {5x} **antidikŏs**, *an-tid'-ee-kos;* from *473* and *1349;* an *opponent* (in a lawsuit); spec. *Satan* (as the archenemy):—adversary {5x}.

Antidikos, firstly means **(1)** "an opponent in a lawsuit": "Agree with thine adversary (*antidikos*) quickly, whiles thou art in the way with him; lest at any time the adversary (*antidikos*) deliver thee to the judge, and the judge deliver thee to the officer, and thou be cast into prison" (Mt 5:25; cf. Lk 12:58; 18:3), and is also used **(2)** to denote "an adversary or an enemy," without reference to legal affairs, and this is perhaps its meaning in 1 Pet 5:8 where it is used of the devil. Some would regard the word as there used in a legal sense, since the devil accuses men before God. See: TDNT—1:373, 62; BAGD—74a; THAYER—50a.

477. ἀντίθεσις {1x} **antithĕsis**, *an-tith'-es-is;* from a comp. of *473* and *5087;* *opposition,* i.e. a *conflict* (of theories):—opposition {1x}.

This word means "a contrary position" [*anti,* "against," *tithemi,* "to place"; Eng., "*antithesis*"]: "O Timothy, keep that which is committed to thy trust, avoiding profane *and* vain babblings, and oppositions (*antithesis*) of science falsely so called" (1 Ti 6:20). See: TDNT—1:373,*; BAGD—74b; THAYER—50a.

478. ἀντικαθίστημι {1x} **antikathistēmi**, *an-tee-kath-is'-tay-mee;* from *473* and *2525;* to *set down* (troops) *against,* i.e. *withstand:*—resist {1x}.

This word stresses taking a stand firm against [*anti,* "against," *kathistemi,* "to set down," *kata*] and is translated "ye have (not) resisted": "Ye have not yet resisted unto blood, striving against sin" (Heb 12:4). Syn.: *496, 498.* See: BAGD—74b; THAYER—50b.

479. ἀντικαλέω {1x} **antikalĕō**, *an-tee-kal-eh'-o;* from *473* and *2564;* to *invite in return:*—bid again {1x}.

Antikaleo means "to bid again, invite in turn": "Then said He also to him that bade Him, When thou makest a dinner or a supper, call not thy friends, nor thy brethren, neither thy kinsmen, nor thy rich neighbours; lest they also bid thee again, and a recompence be made thee" (Lk 14:12). See: TDNT—3:496, 394; BAGD—74b; THAYER—50b.

480. ἀντίκειμαι {8x} **antikĕimai**, *an-tik'-i-mahee;* from *473* and *2749;* to *lie opposite,* i.e. *be adverse* (fig. *repugnant*) to:—adversary {5x}, be contrary {2x}, oppose {1x}.

(1) This word literally means "to lie opposite to, to be set over against." **(2)** In addition to its legal sense it signifies "to withstand"; the present participle of the verb with the article, which is equivalent to a noun, signifies "an adversary": "And when He had said these things, all His adversaries (*antikeimai*) were ashamed: and all the people rejoiced for all the glorious things that were done by Him" (Lk 13:17; cf. 21:15; 1 Cor 16:9; Phil 1:28; 1 Ti 5:14). **(3)** This construction is used of the Man of Sin, in 2 Th. 2:4, and is translated "He that opposeth," where, adopting the noun form, we might render by "the opponent and self-exalter against. . . ." **(4)** In Gal 5:17 it is used of the antagonism between ["contrary to"] the Holy Spirit and the flesh in the believer; **(5)** in 1 Ti 1:10, of anything, in addition to persons, that is opposed to the doctrine of Christ: "For whoremongers, for them that defile themselves with mankind, for menstealers, for liars, for perjured persons, and if there be any other thing that is contrary to (*antikeimai*) sound doctrine." See: TDNT—3:655, 425; BAGD—74b; THAYER—50b.

481. ἀντικρύ {1x} **antikru**, *an-tee-kroo';* prol. from *473;* *opposite:*—over against {1x}. See: BAGD—74c; THAYER—50b.

482. ἀντιλαμβάνομαι {3x} **antilambanŏmai**, *an-tee-lam-ban'-om-ahee;* from *473* and the mid. voice of *2983;* to *take hold of in turn,* i.e. *succor;* also to *participate:*—help {1x}, partaker {1x}, support {1x}.

This word literally means "to take instead of, or in turn" and is used in the middle voice, and rendered **(1)** "He hath holpen": "He hath holpen His servant Israel, in remembrance of His mercy" (Lk 1:54; "holpen" is an aorist participle stressing that God characteristically always helped His servant Israel); **(2)** "to support": "I have shewed you all things, how that so labouring ye ought to support (*antilambanomai*) the weak" (Acts 20:35); and **(3)** "partakers of": "And they that have believing masters, let them not despise

them, because they are brethren; but rather do them service, because they are faithful and beloved, partakers of the benefit" (1 Ti 6:2). See: TDNT—1:375, 62; BAGD—74c; THAYER—50b.

483. ἀντίλεγω {10x} **antilĕgō,** *an-til'-eg-o;* from *473* and *3004;* to *dispute, refuse:*—speak against {5x}, deny {1x}, contradict {1x}, gainsay {1x}, gainsayer {1x}, answer again {1x}.

This word means "to speak against" and is rendered "answering again": "Exhort servants to be obedient unto their own masters, and to please them well in all *things;* not answering again" (Titus 2:9). See: BAGD—74d; THAYER—50c.

484. ἀντίληψις {1x} **antilēpsis,** *an-til'-ape-sis;* from *482; relief:*—help {1x}.

Antilepsis properly signifies "a laying hold of, an exchange." It is mentioned in 1 Cor 12:28, as one of the ministrations in the local church, by way of rendering assistance, perhaps especially of "help" ministered to the weak and needy. These are not official functionaries are in view in the term "helps," but rather the functioning of those who, like the household of Stephanas, devote themselves to minister to the saints; anything that would be done for poor or weak or outcast brethren. See: TDNT— 1:375, 62; BAGD—75a; THAYER—50c.

485. ἀντιλογία {4x} **antilŏgia,** *an-tee-log-ee'-ah;* from a der. of *483; dispute, disobedience:*—contradiction {2x}, gainsaying {1x}, strife {1x}.

(1) This word literally means to speak against in order to gain advantage for one's self and is translated "contradiction" (Heb 7:7; 12:3), **(2)** "strife" (Heb 6:16), and **(3)** "gainsaying" (Jude 11). See: BAGD—75a; THAYER—50c.

486. ἀντιλοιδορέω {1x} **antilŏidŏrĕō,** *an-tee-loy-dor-eh'-o;* from *473* and *3058;* to *rail in reply:*—revile again {1x}.

Antiloidoreo means "to revile back or again" and is found in 1 Pet 2:23: "Who, when He was reviled, reviled not again; when He suffered, He threatened not; but committed Himself to Him that judgeth righteously." See: TDNT— 4:293, 538; BAGD—75a; THAYER—50d.

487. ἀντίλυτρον {1x} **antilutrŏn,** *an-til'-oo-tron;* from *473* and *3083;* a *redemption-price:*—ransom {1x}.

This word stresses what is given in exchange for another as the price of his redemption, ransom: "Who gave Himself a ransom (*antilutron*) for (*huper* – 5228) all, to be testified in due time." The preposition, *anti,* stresses a substitutionary "ransom." The prep-

osition is *huper,* "on behalf of," and the statement is made that He "gave Himself a ransom for all," indicating that the "ransom" was provisionally universal, while being of a vicarious character. See: TDNT—4:349, 543; BAGD— 75b; THAYER—50d.

488. ἀντιμετρέω {2x} **antimĕtrĕō,** *an-tee-met-reh'-o;* from *473* and *3354;* to *mete in return:*—measure again {2x}.

Antimetreo, as a verb, means "to measure in return," is used in the passive voice, and found in Mt 7:2: "For with what judgment ye judge, ye shall be judged: and with what measure ye mete, it shall be measured to you again (*antimetreo*)" (cf. Lk 6:38). Syn.: 280, 943, 2884, 3313, 3354, 3358, 4057, 4568, 5234, 5249, 5518. See: BAGD—75b; THAYER—50d.

489. ἀντιμισθία {2x} **antimisthia,** *an-tee-mis-thee'-ah;* from a comp. of *473* and *3408; requital, correspondence:*—recompense {2x}.

Antimisthia means "a reward, requital" [*anti,* "in return," *misthos,* "wages, hire"] and is used **(1)** in a good sense: "Now for a recompence in the same, (I speak as unto my children,) be ye also enlarged" (2 Cor 6:13); **(2)** in a bad sense: "And likewise also the men, leaving the natural use of the woman, burned in their lust one toward another; men with men working that which is unseemly, and receiving in themselves that recompence of their error which was meet" (Rom 1:27). See: TDNT—4:695, 599; BAGD—75b; THAYER—50d.

490. Ἀντιόχεια {18x} **Antiŏchĕia,** *an-tee-okh'-i-ah;* from Ἀντίοχυς **Antiŏchus** (a Syrian king); *Antiochia,* a place in Syria:—Antioch {18x}. See: BAGD—75b; THAYER—50d.

491. Ἀντιοχεύς {1x} **Antiŏchĕus,** *an-tee-okh-yoos';* from *490;* an *Antiochian* or inhab. of Antiochia:—of Antioch {1x}. See: BAGD—75c; THAYER—51a.

492. ἀντιπαρέρχομαι {2x} **antiparĕrchŏmai,** *an-tee-par-er'-khom-ahee;* from *473* and *3928;* to *go along opposite:*—pass by on the other side {2x}.

This word denotes "to pass by opposite to": "And by chance there came down a certain priest that way: and when he saw him, he passed by on the other side (*antiparerchomai*). And likewise a Levite, when he was at the place, came and looked on him, and passed by on the other side (*antiparerchomai*)" (Lk 10:31, 32). See: BAGD—75c; THAYER—51a.

493. Ἀντίπας {1x} **Antipas,** *an-tee'-pas;* contr. for a comp. of *473* and a der.

of 3962; Antipas, a Chr.:—Antipas {1x}. See: BAGD—75d; THAYER—51b.

494. Ἀντιπατρίς {1x} **Antipatris**, an-tip-at-rece'; from the same as 493; Antipatris, a place in Pal.:—Antipatris {1x}. See: BAGD—75d; THAYER—51b.

495. ἀντιπέραν {1x} **antipĕran**, an-tee-per'-an; from 473 and 4008; on the opposite side:—over against {1x}.

This word occurs only in Lk 8:26: "And they arrived at the country of the Gadarenes, which is over against Galilee." See: BAGD—75d; THAYER—51b.

496. ἀντιπίπτω {1x} **antipiptō**, an-tee-pip'-to; from 473 and 4098 (incl. its alt.); to oppose:—resist {1x}.

This word literally and primarily means "to fall against or upon" [anti, "against," pipto, "to fall"], then by extension, "to strive against, resist" and is used in Acts 7:51 of "resisting" the Holy Spirit. See: BAGD—75d; THAYER—51b.

497. ἀντιστρατεύομαι {1x} **antistratĕuŏmai**, an-tee-strat-yoo'-om-ahee; from 473 and 4754; (fig.) to attack, i.e. (by impl.) destroy:—war against {1x}.

This word means to make a military expedition, or take the field, against anyone, to oppose, war against (Rom 7:23). See: BAGD—75d; THAYER—51b.

498. ἀντιτάσσομαι {5x} **antitassŏmai**, an-tee-tas'-som-ahee; from 473 and the mid. voice of 5021; to range oneself against, i.e. oppose:—oppose themselves {1x}, resist {4x}.

This word is used in the middle voice in the sense of setting oneself against [anti, "against," tasso, "to order, set"], and denotes **(1)** "opposing oneself to": "And when they opposed themselves, and blasphemed, he (Paul) shook his raiment, and said unto them, Your blood be upon your own heads; I am clean: from henceforth I will go unto the Gentiles" (Acts 18:6); and **(2)** elsewhere rendered by the verb "to resist": (Rom 13:2; Jas 4:6; 5:6; 1 Pet 5:5). Syn.: 475, 480. See: BAGD—76a; THAYER—51b.

499. ἀντίτυπον {2x} **antitupŏn**, an-teet'-oo-pon; neut. of a comp. of 473 and 5179; corresponding ["antitype"], i.e. a representative, counterpart:—figure {1x}, like figure whereunto {1x}.

Antitupos, an adjective, used as a noun, denotes, lit., "a striking back"; metaphorically, "resisting, adverse"; then, in a passive sense, "struck back"; in the NT metaphorically, "corresponding to," **(1)** a copy of an archetype, i.e., the event or person or circumstance corresponding to the type, Heb 9:24, "the figure of", of the tabernacle, which, with its structure and appurtenances, was a pattern of that "holy place," "Heaven itself," "the true," into which Christ entered, "to appear before the face of God for us." The earthly tabernacle anticipatively represented what is now made good in Christ; it was a "figure" or "parable" (9:9), "for the time now present"; **(2)** "a corresponding type," 1 Pet 3:21, said of baptism; the circumstances of the flood, the ark and its occupants, formed a type, and baptism forms "a corresponding type," each setting forth the spiritual realities of the death, burial, and resurrection of believers in their identification with Christ. It is not a case of type and antitype, but of two types, that in Genesis, the type, and baptism, the corresponding type. Syn.: 3850, 5179. See: TDNT—8:246, 1193; BAGD—76a; THAYER—51c.

500. ἀντίχριστος {5x} **antichristŏs**, an-tee'-khris-tos; from 473 and 5547; an opponent of, an imposter for the Messiah:—antichrist {5x}.

Antichristos can mean either "against Christ" or "instead of Christ," or perhaps, combining the two, "one who, assuming the guise of Christ, opposes Christ and takes His place. Syn.: 5580. The antichristos denies Jesus in the flesh is the Christ (2 Jn 2:7); the pseudochristos (5580) affirms himself to be the Christ. See: TDNT—9:493, 1322; BAGD—76b; THAYER—51c.

501. ἀντλέω {4x} **antlĕō**, ant-leh-o; from ἄντλος **antlŏs** (the hold of a ship); to bale up (prop. bilge water), i.e. dip water (with a bucket, pitcher, etc.):—draw {3x}, draw out {1x}.

Antleo, as a verb, signified primarily, "to draw out a ship's bilgewater, to bale or pump out"; hence, "to draw water" in any way: "And He saith unto them, Draw out (antleo) now, and bear unto the governor of the feast. And they bare it. When the ruler of the feast had tasted the water that was made wine, and knew not whence it was: but the servants which drew (antleo) the water knew . . ." (Jn 2:8–9; cf. 4:7, 15). Syn.: 307, 385, 392, 502, 645, 868, 1096, 1670, 1448, 1828, 2020, 2464, 4317, 4334, 4358, 4685, 4951, 5288, 5289. See: TDNT—9:493, 1322; BAGD—76b; THAYER—51d.

502. ἄντλημα {1x} **antlēma**, ant'-lay-mah; from 501; a baling-vessel:—nothing to draw with + 3777 {1x}.

In Jn 4:11, "to draw with" translates the corresponding noun antlema, "a bucket for drawing water by a rope." Syn.: 307, 385, 392, 501, 645, 868, 1096, 1670, 1448, 1828, 2020, 2464, 4317, 4334, 4358, 4685, 4951, 5288, 5289. See: TDNT—9:493, 1322; BAGD—76c; THAYER—52a.

503. **ἀντοφθαλμέω** {1x} **antŏphthalmĕō**, *ant-of-thal-meh'-o;* from a compound of *473* and *3788;* to *face:*—bear up into {1x}.

This word literally means to look against or straight at; and hence, metaphorically, to bear up against, withstand, "to face": "And when the ship was caught, and could not bear up into (*antophthalmeo*) the wind, we let her drive" (Acts 27:15. See: BAGD—76c; THAYER—52a.

504. **ἄνυδρος** {4x} **anudrŏs**, *an'-oo-dros;* from *1* (as a neg. particle) and *5204; waterless,* i.e. *dry:*—dry {2x}, without water {2x}.

Anudros literally means "waterless" and is rendered **(1)** "dry" in Mt 12:43 and Lk 11:24, and **(2)** "without water" in 2 Pet 2:17 and Jude 12. See: BAGD—76c; THAYER—52a.

505. **ἀνυπόκριτος** {6x} **anupŏkritŏs**, *an-oo-pok'-ree-tos;* from *1* (as a neg. particle) and a presumed der. of *5271; undissembled,* i.e. *sincere:*—without dissimulation {1x}, without hypocrisy {1x}, unfeigned {4x}.

This word signifies "true, unfeigned, without hypocrisy": **(1)** of love (2 Cor 6:6; 1 Pet 1:22; Rom 12:9 "without dissimulation); **(2)** of faith (1 Ti 1:5; 2 Tim 1:5); **(3)** of the wisdom that is from above (Jas 3:17 "without hypocrisy"). See: TDNT—8:570, 1235; BAGD—76d; THAYER—52a.

506. **ἀνυπότακτος** {4x} **anupŏtaktŏs**, *an-oo-pot'-ak-tos;* from *1* (as a neg. particle) and a presumed der. of *5293; unsubdued,* i.e. *insubordinate* (in fact or temper):—disobedient {1x}, that is not put under {1x}, unruly {2x}.

This word stresses "not subject to rule" and is used **(1)** of things: "Thou hast put all things in subjection under His feet. For in that He put all in subjection under Him, He left nothing that is not put under (*anupotaktos*) Him. But now we see not yet all things put under Him" (Heb 2:8 "not put under"); **(2)** of persons: "Knowing this, that the law is not made for a righteous man, but for the lawless and disobedient (*anupotaktos*), for the ungodly and for sinners..." (1 Ti 1:9; cf. Titus 1:6, 10). Syn.: 814. See: TDNT—8:47, 1156; BAGD—76d; THAYER—52b.

507. **ἄνω** {9x} **anō**, *an'-o;* adv. from *473; upward* or *on the top; in a higher place:*—above {5x}, brim {1x}, high {1x}, up {2x}.

This word denotes **(1)** "above, in a higher place"(Acts 2:19). **(2)** With the article it means "that which is above" (Gal 4:26; Phil 3:14 "the high calling"); **(3)** with the plural article, "the things above" (Jn 8:23, lit., "from the things above"; Col 3:1–2). **(4)** With *heos,* "as far as," it is translated "up to the brim" (Jn 2:7). **(5)** It

has the meaning "upwards" (Jn 11:41; Heb 12:15). See: TDNT—1:376, 63; BAGD—76d; THAYER—52b.

508. **ἀνώγεον** {2x} **anōgĕŏn**, *an-ogue'-eh-on* (or, ἀνάγαιον *an-ag-ahee'-on;* from *507* and *1093; above* the *ground,* i.e. (prop.) the *second floor* of a building; used for a *dome* or a *balcony* on the upper story:—upper room {2x}.

Anogeon is "an upper room" and occurs in Mk 14:15; Lk 22:12, "a chamber," often over a porch, or connected with the roof, where meals were taken and privacy obtained. See: BAGD—77a; THAYER—52b.

509. **ἄνωθεν** {13x} **anōthĕn**, *an'-o-then;* from *507; from above;* by anal. *from the first;* by impl. *anew:*—from above {5x}, top {3x}, again {2x}, from the first {1x}, from the beginning {1x}, not tr {1x}.

This word literally means "from above" and is used **(1)** of place **(1a)** with the meaning "from the top" (Mt 27:51; Mk 15:38 of the temple veil); **(1b)** in Jn 19:23 of the garment of Christ, lit., "from the upper parts" (plural); **(2)** of things which come from heaven, or from God in Heaven (Jn 3:31; 19:11; Jas 1:17; 3:15, 17). It is also used in the sense of "again" (Jn 3:3). See: TDNT—1:378, 63; BAGD—77a; THAYER—52b.

510. **ἀνωτερικός** {1x} **anōtĕrikŏs**, *an-o-ter-ee-kos';* from *511; superior,* i.e. (locally) *more remote:*—upper {1x}.

Anoterikos means "upper" and is used in the plural in Acts 19:1 to denote "upper regions, coast"; i.e., the high central plateau, in contrast to the roundabout way by the river through the valley. See: BAGD—77c; THAYER—52c.

511. **ἀνώτερος** {2x} **anōtĕrŏs**, *an-o'-ter-os;* comparative degree of *507; upper,* i.e. (neut. as adv.) to a *more conspicuous* place, in a *former* part of the book:—above {1x}, higher {1x}.

It is used **(1)** of motion to a higher place, "higher," Lk 14:10; **(2)** of location in a higher place, i.e., in the preceding part of a passage, "above" Heb 10:8. See: TDNT—1:376,*; BAGD—77c; THAYER—52c.

512. **ἀνωφέλες** {2x} **anōphĕlĕs**, *an-o-fel'-ace;* from *1* (as a neg. particle) and the base of *5624; useless* or (neut.) *inutility:*—unprofitable {1x}, unprofitableness {1x}.

Anopheles, as an adjective, means "not beneficial or serviceable" and is rendered **(1)** "unprofitable": "But avoid foolish questions, and genealogies, and contentions, and strivings about the law; for they are unprofitable and vain" (Titus 3:9); **(2)** "unprofitableness": "For there is verily a disannulling of the commandment

going before for the weakness and unprofitableness thereof" (Heb 7:18 in the neuter, used as a noun) said of the Law as not accomplishing that which the "better hope" could alone bring. Syn.: 255, 888, 889, 890. See: BAGD—77c; THAYER—52d.

513. ἀξίνη {2x} **axinē**, *ax-ee'-nay;* prob. from ἄγνυμι **agnumi** (to *break;* comp. *4486);* an *axe:*—axe {2x}.

This word is found in Mt 3:10, and Lk 3:9. See: BAGD—77d; THAYER—52d.

514. ἄξιος {41x} **axiŏs**, *ax'-ee-os;* prob. from *71; deserving, being of worth, comparable* or *suitable* (as if *drawing* praise):—worthy {35x}, meet {4x}, due reward {1x}, unworthy + 3756 {1x}.

Axios has the meaning of being of "weight, value, worth"; also "befitting, becoming, right on the ground of fitness" (Mt 3:8 "meet"; Acts 26:20; Lk 3:8 "worthy"; 23:41 "due reward"). See: TDNT—1:379, 63; BAGD—78a; THAYER—52d.

515. ἀξιόω {7x} **axiŏō**, *ax-ee-ŏ'-o;* from *514;* to *deem entitled* or *fit:*—count worthy {3x}, think worthy {2x}, think good {1x}, desire {1x}.

This word means **(1)** "to think meet, fit, right (Acts 15:38; 28:22); or **(2)** to judge worthy, deem, deserving (Lk 7:7; 2 Th 1:11; 1 Ti 5:17; Heb 3:3; 10:29). See: TDNT—1:380, 63; BAGD—78c; THAYER—53a.

516. ἀξίως {6x} **axiōs**, *ax-ee'-oce;* adv. from *514; appropriately:*—worthy {3x}, as becometh {2x}, after a godly sort + 2316 {1x}.

This word means **(1)** "worthily" and is translated in **(1a)** "worthily of God" (1 Th 2:12 of the Christian walk as it should be; 3 John 6 of assisting servants of God in a way which reflects God's character and thoughts); **(1b)** "worthily of the Lord" (Col. 1:10); **(2)** of the calling of believers (Eph 4:1 in regard to their "walk" or manner of life); **(3)** "worthy of the gospel of Christ" (Phil 1:27 of a manner of life in accordance with what the gospel declares); **(4)** "worthily of the saints" (Rom 16:2 of receiving a fellow believer in such a manner as befits those who bear the name of "saints"). See: BAGD—78d; THAYER—53a.

517. ἀόρατος {5x} **aŏratŏs**, *ah-or'-at-os;* from *1* (as a neg. particle) and *3707; invisible:*—invisible {4x}, invisible things {1x}.

This word literally means "unseen" and is translated "invisible" **(1)** in Rom 1:20 of the power and divinity of God; **(2)** of God Himself (Col 1:15; 1 Ti 1:17; Heb 11:27); **(3)** of things unseen (Col 1:16). See: TDNT—5:368, 706; BAGD—79a; THAYER—53b.

518. ἀπαγγέλλω {45x} **apaggĕllō**, *ap-ang-el'-lo;* from *575* and the base of *32;* to *announce:*—tell {26x}, show {10x}, declare {3x}, report {2x}, bring word {1x}, bring word again {1x}, show again {1x}, vr show {1x}.

Apangello, as a verb, means "to announce" and is translated "bring word" in Mt 2:8: "And he [Herod] sent them [the magi] to Bethlehem, and said, Go and search diligently for the young child; and when ye have found him, bring me word again [apangello], that I may come and worship him also" (cf. Mt 28:8). See: TDNT—1:64, 10; BAGD—79b; THAYER—53b.

519. ἀπάγχομαι {1x} **apagchŏmai**, *ap-ang'-khom-ahee* from *575* and ἄγχω **agchō** (to *choke;* akin to the base of *43);* to *strangle oneself off* (i.e. to death):—hang himself {1x}.

Apagchomai signifies "to strangle" and in the middle voice means to "hang" one's self (Mt 27:5). See: BAGD—79c; THAYER—53c.

520. ἀπάγω {16x} **apagō**, *ap-ag'-o;* from *575* and *71;* to *take off* (in various senses):—lead away {10x}, lead {2x}, put to death {1x}, bring {1x}, take away {1x}, carry away {1x}.

(1) *Apago,* as a verb, means "to lead away, bring forth, bring unto": "Then Paul called one of the centurions unto *him,* and said, Bring this young man unto (*apago*) the chief captain: for he hath a certain thing to tell him" (Acts 23:17). **(2)** *Apago* is used especially in a judicial sense, "to put to death," e.g., Acts 12:19. Syn.: 336, 337, 520, 1935, 2288, 2289, 5054. See: BAGD—79c; THAYER—53c.

521. ἀπαίδευτος {1x} **apaidĕutŏs**, *ap-ah'-ee-dyoo-tos;* from *1* (as a neg. particle) and a der. of *3811; uninstructed,* i.e. (fig.) *stupid:*—unlearned {1x}.

Apaideutos, as an adjective, means "uninstructed" (3811 - *paideuo,* "to train, teach") and is translated "unlearned": "But foolish and unlearned questions avoid, knowing that they do gender strifes" (2 Ti 2:23). Syn.: 62, 261. See: TDNT—5:596, 753; BAGD—79d; THAYER—53c.

522. ἀπαίρω {3x} **apairō**, *ap-ah'-ee-ro;* from *575* and *142;* to *lift off,* i.e. *remove:*—take {1x}, take away {2x}.

Apairo means "to lift off" and is used, in the passive voice, of Christ, metaphorically as the Bridegroom taken from His followers (Mt 9:15; Mk 2:20; Lk 5:35). See: BAGD—79d; THAYER—53d.

523. ἀπαιτέω {2x} **apaitĕō**, *ap-ah'-ee-teh-o;* from *575* and *154;* to *demand back:*—ask again {1x}, require {1x}.

Apaiteo means "to ask back, demand back" and is translated **(1)** "shall be required" in Lk 12:20, lit. "do they require," in the impersonal sense; and **(2)** "to ask again" in Lk 6:30: "Give to every man that asketh of thee; and of him that taketh away thy goods ask them not again." It is used in the papyri frequently in the sense of "demanding, making demands." See: TDNT—1:193, 30; BAGD—80a; THAYER—53d.

524. **ἀπαλγέω** {1x} **apalgĕō**, *ap-alg-eh'-o;* from *575* and ἀλγέω **algĕō** (to *smart*); to *grieve out,* i.e. *become apathetic:*—be past feeling {1x}.

Apalgeo signifies to cease to feel pain for [*apo* "from," *algeo,* "to feel pain"; cf. Eng., "neuralgia"]; hence, to be callous, "past feeling," insensible to honor and shame: "Who being past feeling have given themselves over unto lasciviousness, to work all uncleanness with greediness" (Eph 4:19). See: BAGD—80a; THAYER—53d.

525. **ἀπαλλάσσω** {3x} **apallassō**, *ap-al-las'-so;* from *575* and *236;* to *change away,* i.e. *release,* (refl.) *remove:*—deliver {2x}, depart {1x}.

Apallasso, as a verb, means literally "to change from" [*apo,* "from," *allasso,* "to change"], "to free from, release" and is **(1)** translated "deliver": "And deliver them who through fear of death were all their lifetime subject to bondage" (Heb 2:15); **(2)** in Lk 12:58, it is used in a legal sense of being quit of a person, i.e., the opponent being appeased and withdrawing his suit: "When thou goest with thine adversary to the magistrate, as thou art in the way, give diligence that thou mayest be delivered (*apallasso*) from him; lest he hale thee to the judge, and the judge deliver thee to the officer, and the officer cast thee into prison." Syn.: 325, 629, 591, 859, 1325, 1560, 1659, 1807, 1929, 3086, 3860, 4506, 5483. See: TDNT—1:252, 40; BAGD—80a; THAYER—53d.

526. **ἀπαλλοτριόω** {3x} **apallŏtriŏō**, *ap-al-lot-ree-ŏ'-o;* from *575* and a der. of *245;* to *estrange away,* i.e. (pass. and fig.) to *be non-participant:*—be alienated with + *5607* {2x}, be alien {1x}.

This word signifies "to be rendered an alien, to be alienated." **(1)** In Eph 2:12: "That at that time ye were without Christ, being aliens (*apallotrioo*) from the commonwealth of Israel, and strangers from the covenants of promise"; **(2)** elsewhere in Eph 4:18 and Col 1:21 the condition of the unbeliever is presented in a threefold state of "alienation," **(2a)** from the commonwealth of Israel, **(2b)** from the life of God, **(2c)** from God Himself. See: TDNT—1:265, 43; BAGD—80b; THAYER—54a.

527. **ἀπαλός** {2x} **hapalŏs**, *hap-al-os';* of uncert. der.; *soft:*—tender {2x}.

This word means "soft, tender" and is used of the branch of a tree which is full of sap (Mt 24:32; Mk 13:28). See: BAGD—80b; THAYER—54a.

528. **ἀπαντάω** {7x} **apantaō**, *ap-an-tah'-o;* from *575* and a der. of *473;* to *meet away,* i.e. *encounter:*—meet {7x}.

Apantao means to go to meet, to meet with a purpose, to meet with, come face to face with and is used in Mk 14:13; Lk 17:12; Mt 28:9; Mk 5:2; Lk 14:31; Jn 4:51; Acts 16:16. See: BAGD—80c; THAYER—54a.

529. **ἀπάντησις** {4x} **apantēsis**, *ap-an'-tay-sis;* from *528;* a (friendly) *encounter:*—to meet + *1519* {4x}.

This word means "a meeting" and occurs in Mt 25:1, 6; Acts 28:15; 1 Th 4:17. It is used in the papyri of a newly arriving magistrate. It seems that the special idea of the word was the official welcome of a newly arrived dignitary. See: TDNT—1:380, 64; BAGD—80c; THAYER—54a.

530. **ἄπαξ** {15x} **hapax**, *hap'-ax;* prob. from *537; one* (or a *single) time* (numerically or conclusively):—once {15x}.

This word denotes **(1)** "once, one time" (2 Cor 11:25; Heb 9:7, 26–27; 12:26–27; in the phrase "once and again," lit., "once and twice" Phil 4:16; 1 Th 2:18); **(2)** "once, once for all" of what is of perpetual validity, not requiring repetition (Heb 6:4; 9:28; 10:2; 1 Pet 3:18; Jude 3 & 5 "once"; 1 Pet 3:20). See: TDNT—1:381, 64; BAGD—80c; THAYER—54a.

531. **ἀπαράβατος** {1x} **aparabatŏs**, *ap-ar-ab'-at-os;* from *1* (as a neg. particle) and a der. of *3845; not passing away,* i.e. *untransferable* (perpetual):—unchangeable {1x}.

This word means unviolated, not to be violated, inviolable, unchangeable and therefore not liable to pass to a successor and is used of the priesthood of Christ in Heb 7:24. See: TDNT—5:742, 772; BAGD—80d; THAYER—54b.

532. **ἀπαρασκεύαστος** {1x} **aparaskĕuastŏs**, *ap-ar-ask-yoo'-as-tos;* from *1* (as a neg. particle) and a der. of *3903; unready:*—unprepared {1x}.

This word means unprepared and occurs in 2 Cor 9:4: "Lest haply if they of Macedonia come with me, and find you unprepared, we (that we say not, ye) should be ashamed in this same confident boasting." See: BAGD—80d; THAYER—54b.

533. **ἀπαρνέομαι** {13x} **aparnĕŏmai,** *ap-ar-neh'-om-ahee;* from *575* and *720;* to *deny utterly,* i.e. *disown, abstain:*—deny {13x}.

This word means **(1)** "to deny utterly," to abjure, to affirm that one has no connection with a person, **(1a)** as in Peter's denial of Christ (Mt 26:34–35, 75; Mk 14:30–31, 72; Lk 22:34, 61; Jn 13:38). **(1a1)** This stronger form is used in the Lord's statements foretelling Peter's "denial," and in Peter's assurance of fidelity; **(1a2)** the simple verb (*arneomai* - 720) is used in all the records of his actual denial. **(1b)** The strengthened form is the verb used in the Lord's warning as to being "denied" in the presence of the angels (Lk 12:9); **(1b1)** in the preceding clause, "he that denieth Me," the simple verb *arneomai* is used; **(1b2)** the rendering therefore should be understood as "he that denieth Me in the presence of men, shall be utterly denied in the presence of the angels of God"; **(2)** "to deny oneself" as a follower of Christ (Mt 16:24; Mk 8:34; Lk 9:23). See: TDNT—1:471,*; BAGD—81a; THAYER—54b.

534. **ἀπάρτι** {1x} **aparti,** *ap-ar'-tee;* from *575* and *737; from now,* i.e. *henceforth* (*already*):—from henceforth {1x}.

This word means from this point in time and forward without end. See: BAGD—81a; THAYER—54c.

535. **ἀπαρτισμός** {1x} **apartismŏs,** *ap-ar-tis-mos';* from a der. of *534; completion:*—finish {1x}. See: BAGD—81b; THAYER—54c.

536. **ἀπαρχή** {8x} **aparchē,** *ap-ar-khay';* from a compound of *575* and *756;* a *beginning* of sacrifice, i.e. the (Jewish) *firstfruit* (fig.):—firstfruits {8x}.

Aparche denotes, primarily, "an offering of firstfruits." **(1)** Though the English word is plural in each of its occurrences save Rom. 11:16, **(1a)** the Greek word is always singular. **(1b)** Two Hebrew words are thus translated, **(1b1)** one meaning the "chief" or "principal part," e.g., Num 18:12; Prov 3:9; **(1b2)** the other, "the earliest ripe of the crop or of the tree," e.g., Ex 23:16; Neh 10:35; **(1b3)** they are found together, e.g., in Ex 23:19, "the first of the firstfruits." **(2)** The term is applied in things spiritual, **(2a)** to the presence of the Holy Spirit with the believer as the firstfruits of the full harvest of the Cross, Rom 8:23; **(2b)** to Christ Himself in resurrection in relation to all believers who have fallen asleep, 1 Cor 15:20, 23; **(2c)** to the earliest believers in a country in relation to those of their countrymen subsequently converted, Rom 16:5; 1 Cor 16:15; **(2d)** to the believers of this age in relation to the whole of the redeemed, 2 Th 2:13; Jas 1:18; Rev 14:4. See: TDNT—1:484, 81; BAGD—81b; THAYER—54c.

537. **ἄπας** {44x} **hapas,** *hap'-as;* from *1* (as a particle of union) and *3956;* absolutely *all* or (sing.) *every* one:—all {34x}, all things {5x}, whole {3x}, every one {1x}, every {1x}.

This is a strengthened form of *pas (3956)* and signifies "quite all, the whole," and, in the plural, "all, all things." Preceded by an article and followed by a noun it means "the whole of." In 1 Ti 1:16 the significance is "the whole of His longsuffering," or "the fulness of His longsuffering." See: TDNT—5:886, 795; BAGD—81d; THAYER—54d, 55a.

538. **ἀπατάω** {4x} **apataō,** *ap-at-ah'-o;* of uncert. der.; to *cheat,* i.e. *delude:*—deceive {4x}. Syn.: 1185, 1818. See: TDNT—1:384, 65; BAGD—81d; THAYER—55a.

539. **ἀπάτη** {7x} **apatē,** *ap-at'-ay;* from *538; delusion:*—deceitfulness {3x}, deceitful {1x}, deceit {1x}, deceivableness {1x}, deceivings {1x}.

Apate means **(1)** "deceit or deceitfulness, that which gives a false impression, whether by appearance, statement or influence" and is said **(1a)** of riches (Mt 13:22; Mk 4:19); **(1b)** of sin (Heb 3:13). **(2)** The phrase in Eph 4:22 "deceitful lusts" signifies lusts excited by "deceit," of which "deceit" is the source of strength, not lusts "deceitful" in themselves. **(3)** In 2 Th 2:10 "all deceivableness of unrighteousness" signifies all manner of unscrupulous words and deeds designed to "deceive" (see Rev 13:13–15). **(4)** In Col 2:8, "vain deceit" suggests that "deceit" is void of anything profitable. Syn.: 538, 1386, 1388, 1818, 5422. See: TDNT—1:385, 65; BAGD—82a; THAYER—55a.

540. **ἀπάτωρ** {1x} **apatōr,** *ap-at'-ore;* from *1* (as a neg. particle) and *3962; fatherless,* i.e. *of unrecorded paternity:*—without father {1x}.

Apator signifies in Heb 7:3 with no recorded genealogy. See: TDNT—5:1019, 805; BAGD—82b; THAYER—55b.

541. **ἀπαύγασμα** {1x} **apaugasma,** *ap-ŏw'-gas-mah;* from a compound of *575* and *826;* an *off-flash,* i.e. *effulgence:*—brightness {1x}.

This word means "a shining forth" [*apo,* "from," *auge,* "brightness"], of a light coming from a luminous body, is said of Christ in Heb 1:3, i.e., shining forth (not a reflected brightness). See: TDNT—1:508, 87; BAGD—82b; THAYER—55b.

542. ἀπείδω {1x} **apĕidō**, *ap-i'-do;* from *575* and the same as *1492;* to *see* fully:—see {1x}.

This word is used in Phil 2:23 and means to wait and perceive how things unfold before making a decision: "Him [Timotheus] therefore I hope to send presently, so soon as I shall see how it will go with me." See: BAGD—82c; THAYER—55b.

543. ἀπείθεια {7x} **apĕithĕia**, *ap-i'-thi-ah;* from *545; disbelief* (obstinate and rebellious):—disobedience {3x}, unbelief {4x}.

This word literally means "the condition of being unpersuadable" and denotes "obstinacy, obstinate rejection of the will of God"; hence, "disobedience, unbelief" (Eph 2:2; 5:6; Col 3:6; Rom 11:30, 32; Heb 4:6, 11). See: TDNT—6:11, 818; BAGD—82c; THAYER—55c.

544. ἀπειθέω {16x} **apĕithĕō**, *ap-i-theh'-o;* from *545;* to *disbelieve* (wilfully and perversely):—believe not {8x}, disobedient {4x}, obey not {3x}, unbelieving {1x}.

This word means "to refuse to be persuaded, to refuse belief, to be disobedient" and is translated **(1)** "believeth not" (Jn 3:36); **(2)** "unbelieving" (Acts 14:2); **(3)** "believed not" (Acts 17:5; 19:9; Heb 3:18; 11:31), **(4)** "do not obey" (Rom 2:8), **(5)** "disobedient" (Rom 10:21), **(6)** "have not believed" (Rom 11:3, 31), **(7)** "do not believe" (Rom 15:31), **(8)** "disobedient" (1 Pet 2:7, 8; 3:20), **(9)** "obey not" (1 Pet 3:1; 4:17). See: TDNT—6:10, 818; BAGD—82c; THAYER—55c.

545. ἀπειθής {6x} **apĕithēs**, *ap-i-thace';* from *1* (as a neg. particle) and *3982; unpersuadable,* i.e. *contumacious:*—disobedient {6x}.

This word signifies "unwilling to be persuaded, spurning belief, disobedient" (Lk 1:17; Acts 26:19; Rom 1:30; 2 Ti 3:2; Titus 1:16; 3:3). See: TDNT—6:10, 818; BAGD—82d; THAYER—55c.

546. ἀπειλέω {2x} **apĕilĕō**, *ap-i-leh'-o;* of uncert. der.; to *menace;* by impl. to *forbid:*—threaten {2x}.

Apeileo is **(1)** used of Christ, negatively, in 1 Pet 2:23: "Who, when He was reviled, reviled not again; when He suffered, He threatened not; but committed Himself to Him that judgeth righteously"; and **(2)** in the middle voice, "But that it spread no further among the people, let us straitly threaten (*apeilo*) them, that they speak henceforth to no man in this name" (Acts 4:17 lit., "let us threaten . . . with threatening). See: BAGD—82d; THAYER—55d.

547. ἀπειλή {4x} **apĕilē**, *ap-i-lay';* from *546;* a *menace:*—✕ straitly {1x}, threatening {3x}.

This word means a strong threatening (Acts 4:17, 29; 9:1; Eph 6:9). See: BAGD—83a; THAYER—55d.

548. ἄπειμι {7x} **apĕimi**, *ap'-i-mee;* from *575* and *1510;* to *be away:*—be absent {1x}, absent {6x}.

This word means to go away, depart, and hence to be absent (1 Cor 5:3; 2 Cor 10:1, 11; 13:2, 10; Phil 1:27; Col 2:5). See: BAGD—83a; THAYER—55d. comp. *549.*

549. ἄπειμι {1x} **apĕimi**, *ap'-i-mee;* from *575* and εἶμι **ĕimi** (to *go*); to *go away:*—go {1x}.

This word means "to go away, depart" (Acts 17:10). See: BAGD—83a; THAYER—55d. comp. *548.*

550. ἀπειπόμην {1x} **apĕipŏmēn**, *ap-i-pom'-ane;* refl. past of a compound of *575* and *2036;* to *say off* for oneself, i.e. *disown:*—renounce {1x}.

This word literally means "to tell from" and signifies "to renounce" (2 Cor 4:2 middle voice, of disowning "the hidden things of shame"). In the Sept. of 1 Kin 11:2 it signifies "to forbid," a meaning found in the papyri. The meaning "to renounce" may therefore carry with it the thought of forbidding the approach of the things disowned. See: BAGD—83b; THAYER—55d.

551. ἀπείραστος {1x} **apĕirastŏs**, *ap-i'-ras-tos;* from *1* (as a neg. particle) and a presumed der. of *3987; untried,* i.e. *not temptable:*—not to be tempted + 2076.

This word means "untempted, untried" and occurs in Jas 1:13: "Let no man say when he is tempted, I am tempted of God: for God cannot be tempted (*apeirastos*) with evil, neither tempteth He any man" [with *eimi-* 2076, "to be," "cannot be tempted," "untemptable"]. See: TDNT—6:23, 822; BAGD—83b; THAYER—55d.

552. ἄπειρος {1x} **apĕirŏs**, *ap'-i-ros;* from *1* (as a neg. particle) and *3984; inexperienced,* i.e. *ignorant:*—unskillful {1x}.

This word means "without experience, inexperienced" [*a*, negative, *peira*, "a trial, experiment"]: "For every one that useth milk is unskilful in the word of righteousness: for he is a babe" (Heb 5:13). See: BAGD—83b; THAYER—56a.

553. ἀπεκδέχομαι {7x} **apĕkdĕchŏmai**, *ap-ek-dekh'-om-ahee;* from *575* and *1551;* to *expect fully:*—look for {2x}, wait for {5x}.

This word means "to await or expect ea-

gerly" and is rendered "to wait for" (Rom 8:19, 23, 25; 1 Cor 1:7; Gal 5:5; Phil. 3:20 "look for"; Heb 9:28 "look for"; 1 Pet 3:20). See: TDNT— 2:56, 146; BAGD—83c; THAYER—56a.

554. ἀπεκδύομαι {2x} apĕkduŏmai, *ap-ek-doo'-om-ahee;* mid. voice from *575* and *1562;* to *divest wholly* oneself, or (for oneself) *despoil:*—put off {1x}, spoil {1x}.

This word means "to strip off clothes or armaments" and is used in the middle voice: **(1)** Col 2:15: "And having spoiled (*apekduomai*) principalities and powers, He made a shew of them openly, triumphing over them in it"; and **(2)** Col 3:9: "ye have put off" of "the old man." See: TDNT—2:318,*; BAGD—83c; THAYER—56a.

555. ἀπέκδυσις {1x} apĕkdusis, *ap-ek'-doo-sis;* from *554; divestment:*— putting off {1x}.

This word means "a putting off, a stripping off, a laying aside" and is used in Col 2:11 of "the body of the flesh." See: TDNT—2:321, 192; BAGD—83c; THAYER—56a.

556. ἀπελαύνω {1x} apĕlaunō, *ap-el-ŏw'-no;* from *575* and *1643;* to *dismiss:*—drive {1x}.

This word means "to drive from, to drive off" and is used in Acts 18:16: "And he drave them from the judgment seat." See: BAGD— 83c; THAYER—56a.

557. ἀπελεγμός {1x} apĕlĕgmŏs, *ap-el-eg-mos';* from a compound of *575* and *1651; refutation,* i.e. (by impl.) *contempt:*—nought {1x}.

Apelegmos denotes "censure, repudiation" [of something shown to be worthless], hence, "contempt, disrepute": "So that not only this our craft is in danger to be set at nought (*apelegmos*); but also that the temple of the great goddess Diana should be despised, and her magnificence should be destroyed, whom all Asia and the world worshippeth" (Acts 19:27). See: BAGD—83d; THAYER—56a.

558. ἀπελεύθερος {1x} apĕlĕuthĕrŏs, *ap-el-yoo'-ther-os;* from *575* and *1658;* one *freed away from slavery,* i.e. a *freedman:*—freeman {1x}.

An *apeleutheros* is a slave that has been released from servitude, a "freeman, a freed man" and is used in 1 Cor 7:22: "For he that is called in the Lord, being a servant, is the Lord's freeman: likewise also he that is called, being free, is Christ's servant." Here the fuller word brings out the spiritual emancipation in contrast to the natural "freedman." See: TDNT— 2:487, 224; BAGD—83d; THAYER—56b.

559. Ἀπελλῆς {1x} Apĕllēs, *ap-el-lace';* of Lat. or.; *Apelles,* a Chr.:— *Apelles* {1x}. See: BAGD—83d; THAYER—56b.

560. ἀπελπίζω {1x} apĕlpizō, *ap-el-pid'-zo;* from *575* and *1679;* to *hope out,* i.e. *fully expect:*—hope for again {1x}.

This word means literally "to give up in despair, to despair" and is used in Lk 6:35: "But love ye your enemies, and do good, and lend, hoping for nothing again (*apelpizo*); and your reward shall be great, and ye shall be the children of the Highest: for He is kind unto the unthankful and to the evil." "Hoping for nothing again" is a wonderful phrase which stresses that a believer, when anticipating the future, rests without anxiety as to the result, or not "despairing" of the recompense from God. See: TDNT—2:533, 229; BAGD—83d; THAYER—56b.

561. ἀπέναντι {6x} apĕnanti, *ap-en'-an-tee;* from *575* and *1725; from in front,* i.e. *opposite, before* or *against:*—before {2x}, contrary {1x}, over against {2x}, in the presence of {1x}.

This word denotes **(1)** "opposite": "And there was Mary Magdalene, and the other Mary, sitting over against the sepulchre" (Mt 27:61); **(2)** "in the sight of, before": "When Pilate saw that he could prevail nothing, but that rather a tumult was made, he took water, and washed his hands before (*apenanti*) the multitude, saying, I am innocent of the blood of this just person: see ye to it" (Mt 27:24; Acts 3:16; Rom 3:18); **(3)** "contrary, against": "Whom Jason hath received: and these all do contrary (*apenanti*) to the decrees of Caesar, saying that there is another king, one Jesus" (Acts 17:7). See: BAGD— 84a; THAYER—56b.

ἀπέπω apĕpō. See *550.*

562. ἀπέραντος {1x} apĕrantŏs, *ap-er'-an-tos;* from *1* (as a neg. particle) and a second. der. of *4008; unfinished,* i.e. (by impl.) *interminable:*—endless {1x}.

Aperantos means "to complete, finish" and signifies "interminable, endless"; it is said of genealogies: "Neither give heed to fables and endless genealogies, which minister questions, rather than godly edifying which is in faith: so do" (1 Ti 1:4). Syn.: *179.* See: BAGD—84a; THAYER—56b.

563. ἀπερισπάστως {1x} apĕrispastōs, *ap-er-is-pas-toce';* adv. from a compound of *1* (as a neg. particle) and a presumed der. of *4049; undistractedly,* i.e. *free from* (domestic) *solicitude:*—without distraction {1x}.

This word means without distraction, without solicitude or anxiety or care: "And this I

Greek

speak for your own profit; . . . that ye may attend upon the Lord without distraction." See: BAGD—84b; THAYER—56c.

564. ἀπερίτμητος {1x} **apĕritmētŏs,** *ap-er-eet'-may-tos;* from *1* (as a neg. particle) and a presumed der. of *4059; uncircumcised* (fig.):—uncircumcised {1x}.

Aperitmetos, as an adjective, means "uncircumcised" is used in Acts 7:51, metaphorically, of "heart and ears." Syn.: 203, 1986, 4059, 4061. See: TDNT—6:72, 831; BAGD—84b; THAYER—56c.

565. ἀπέρχομαι {120x} **apĕrchŏmai,** *ap-erkh'-om-ahee;* from *575* and *2064; to go off* (i.e. *depart), aside* (i.e. *apart)* or *behind* (i.e. *follow),* lit. or fig.:—go {53x}, depart {27x}, go (one's) way {16x}, go away {14x}, come {4x}, misc. {6x} = pass away, be past. See: TDNT—2:675, 257; BAGD—84c; THAYER—56c.

566. ἀπέχει {1x} **apĕchĕi,** *ap-ekh'-i;* third pers. sing. pres. ind. act. of *568* used impers.; *it is sufficient:*—it is enough {1x}. See: BAGD—84d; THAYER—57a.

567. ἀπέχομαι {6x} **apĕchŏmai,** *ap-ekh'-om-ahee;* mid. voice (refl.) of *568; to hold oneself off,* i.e. *refrain:*—abstain {6x}.

This word invariably refers to abstaining from evil practices, moral and ceremonial: "But that we write unto them, that they abstain (*apechomai*) from pollutions of idols, and *from* fornication, and from things strangled, and from blood" (Acts 15:20, 29; 1 Th 4:3; 5:22; 1 Ti 4:3; 1 Pet 2:11). See: BAGD—84d; THAYER—57a.

568. ἀπέχω {11x} **apĕchō,** *ap-ekh'-o;* from *575* and *2192;* (act.) to *have out,* i.e. *receive in full;* (intr.) to *keep* (oneself) *away,* i.e. *be distant* (lit. or fig.):—be {5x}, have {4x}, receive {2x}.

Apecho, as a verb, denotes **(1)** transitively, **(1a)** "to have in full, to have received": "Therefore when thou doest thine alms, do not sound a trumpet before thee, as the hypocrites do in the synagogues and in the streets, that they may have glory of men. Verily I say unto you, They (*apecho*) have their reward" (Mt 6:2; cf. 6:5, 16; Lk 6:24). **(1b)** In all these instances the present tense has a perfective force, consequent upon the combination with the prefix *apo* ["from"], not that it stands for the perfect tense, but that it views the action in its accomplished result; **(1c)** so in Phil 4:18: "But I have all, and abound: I am full, having received of Epaphroditus the things which were sent from you, an odour of a sweet smell, a sacrifice acceptable, well-pleasing to God"; **(1d)** in Philem 15, "(that) thou shouldest receive (have him for

ever)" **(2)** intransitively, **(2a)** "to be away, distant"; "This people draweth nigh unto me with their mouth, and honoureth me with their lips; but their heart is far from me" (Mt 15:8; cf. Mk 7:6); **(2b)** "far off, afar": "Then Jesus went with them. And when He was now not far from the house, the centurion sent friends to Him, saying unto Him, Lord, trouble not thyself: for I am not worthy that thou shouldest enter under my roof" (Lk 7:6; 15:20); **(2c)** without an accompanying adverb, "which was from": "And, behold, two of them went that same day to a village called Emmaus, which was from Jerusalem about threescore furlongs" (Lk 24:13). Syn.: 324, 353, 354, 588, 618, 1209, 1523, 1926, 2210, 2865, 2975, 2983, 3028, 3335, 3336, 3858, 3880, 3970, 4327, 4355, 4356, 4380, 4381, 4382, 5562, 5264, 5274. See: TDNT—2:828, 286; BAGD—84d; THAYER—57a.

569. ἀπιστέω {7x} **apistĕō,** *ap-is-teh'-o;* from *571;* to *be unbelieving,* i.e. (trans.) *disbelieve,* or (by impl.) *disobey:*—believe not {7x}.

This word is used in Mk 16:11, 16; Lk 24:11, 41; Acts 28:24; Rom 3:3; 2 Ti 2:13 and is translated disbelieve, implying that the unbeliever has had a full opportunity of believing and has rejected it. See: TDNT—6:174, 849; BAGD—85b; THAYER—57b.

570. ἀπιστία {12x} **apistia,** *ap-is-tee'-ah;* from *571; faithlessness,* i.e. (neg.) *disbelief* (*want* of Chr. *faith),* or (pos.) *unfaithfulness* (*disobedience*):—unbelief {12x}. See: TDNT—6:174, 849; BAGD—85c; THAYER—57b.

571. ἄπιστος {23x} **apistŏs,** *ap'-is-tos;* from *1* (as a neg. particle) and *4103;* (act.) *disbelieving,* i.e. *without* Chr. *faith* (spec. a *heathen*); (pass.) *untrustworthy* (person), or *incredible* (thing):—that believe not {6x}, unbelieving {5x}, faithless {4x}, unbeliever {4x}, infidel {2x}, thing incredible {1x}, which believe not {1x}.

Apistos is used with meanings somewhat parallel to *apistia* (*570*): **(1)** "untrustworthy, not worthy of confidence or belief, is said of things "incredible": "Why should it be thought a thing incredible (*apistos*) with you, that God should raise the dead?" (Acts 26:8); **(2)** "unbelieving, distrustful" used as a noun, "unbeliever" (Lk 12:46; 1 Ti 5:8 "infidel"; in Titus 1:15 and Rev 21:8 "unbelieving"); **(3)** "faithless" (Mt 17:17; Mk 9:19; Lk 9:41; Jn 20:27). **(4)** The word is most frequent in 1 and 2 Corinthians. See: TDNT—6:174, 849; BAGD—85d; THAYER—57b.

572. ἁπλότης {8x} **haplŏtēs,** *hap-lot'-ace;* from *573; singleness,* i.e. (subj.) *sin-*

cerity (without dissimulation or self-seeking), or (obj.) generosity (copious bestowal):—bountifulness {1x}, liberal {1x}, liberalty {1x}, simplicity {3x}, singleness {2x}.

This word means "simple, single" and is **(1)** translated "bountifulness" (2 Cor 9:11; cf. 8:2; 9:13); from sincerity of mind springs "liberality." **(2)** The thought of sincerity is present in (Rom 12:8; 2 Cor 11:3; Eph 6:5; Col 3:22). See: TDNT—1:386, 65; BAGD—85d; THAYER—57c.

573. ἁπλοῦς {2x} **haplŏus**, hap-looce'; prob. from 1 (as a particle of union) and the base of 4120; prop. folded together, i.e. single (fig. clear):—single {2x}.

This word means "simple, single" and is used in a moral sense in Mt 6:22 and Lk 11:34, said of the eye; "singleness" of purpose keeps us from the snare of having a double treasure and consequently a divided heart. Syn.: As the akakos (172) has no harmfulness in him, and the adolos (97) no guile, so the akeraios (185) no foreign mixture, and the haplous (573) no folds within which to hide something. See: TDNT—1:386, 65; BAGD—86a; THAYER—57c.

574. ἁπλῶς {1x} **haplōs**, hap-loce'; adv. from 573 (in the obj. sense of 572); bountifully:—liberally {1x}.

This word means "liberally, with singleness of heart" and is used in Jas 1:5 of God as the gracious and "liberal" giver. The word may be taken either (a) in a logical sense, signifying unconditionally, simply, or (b) in a moral sense, generously. See: BAGD—86b; THAYER—57d.

575. ἀπό {669x} **apŏ**, apo'; a primary particle; "off," i.e. away (from something near), in various senses (of place, time, or relation; lit. or fig.):—from {392x}, of {129x}, out of {48x}, for {10x}, off {10x}, by {9x}, at {9x}, in {6x}, since + 3739 {5x}, on {5x}, not tr. {15x}, misc. {31x} = (✕ here-) after, ago, because of, before, by the space of, forth, upon, once, with. See: BAGD—86c; THAYER—57d. In composition (as a prefix) it usually denotes separation, departure, cessation, completion, reversal, etc.

576. ἀποβαίνω {4x} **apŏbainō**, ap-ob-ah'-ee-no; from 575 and the base of 939; lit. to disembark; fig. to eventuate:—become {1x}, go out {1x}, turn {2x}.

This word **(1)** literally means to come down from, i.e. a ship (Lk 5:2; Jn 21:9); or **(2)** to turn out, result, to be the outcome (Lk 21:13; Phil 1:19). See: BAGD—88c; THAYER—59d.

577. ἀποβάλλω {2x} **apŏballō**, ap-ob-al'-lo; from 575 and 906; to throw off; fig. to lose:—cast away {2x}.

Apoballo means "to throw off from, to lay aside, to cast away" **(1)** a garment (Mk 10:50

twice); or **(2)** "confidence" (Heb 10:35). See: BAGD—88D; THAYER—60a.

578. ἀποβλέπω {1x} **apŏblĕpō**, ap-ob-lep'-o; from 575 and 991; to look away from everything else, i.e. (fig.) intently regard:—have respect {1x}.

Apoblepo, as a verb, signifies "to look away from" all else at one object; hence, "to look steadfastly": "Esteeming the reproach of Christ greater riches than the treasures in Egypt: for he [Moses] had respect (apoblepo) unto the recompence of the reward" (Heb 11:26). Syn.: 308, 352, 816, 872, 991, 1689, 1896, 1914, 1980, 1983, 2300, 2334, 3706, 3708, 3879, 4017, 4648. See: BAGD—89a; THAYER—60a.

579. ἀπόβλητος {1x} **apŏblētŏs**, ap-ob'-lay-tos; from 577; cast off, i.e. (fig.) such as to be rejected:—be refused {1x}.

This word means to be thrown away, rejected, despised, abominated as unclean: "For every creature of God is good, and nothing to be refused, if it be received with thanksgiving" (1 Ti 4:4). See: BAGD—89a; THAYER—60a.

580. ἀποβολή {2x} **apŏbŏlē**, ap-ob-ol-ay'; from 577; rejection; fig. loss:—casting away {1x}, loss {1x}.

This word literally means "casting away" and is translated **(1)** "loss" in Acts 27:22; and **(2)** in Rom 11:15 "casting away" of the temporary exclusion of the nation of Israel from its position of divine favor involving the reconciling of the world (i.e., the provision made through the gospel, which brings the world within the scope of reconciliation). See: BAGD—89a; THAYER—60a.

581. ἀπογενόμενος {1x} **apŏgĕnŏmĕnŏs**, ap-og-en-om'-en-os; past part. of a compound of 575 and 1096; absent, i.e. deceased (fig. renounced):—being dead {1x}.

This word literally means "to be away from" [apo here signifies "separation"] and is used in 1 Pet 2:24 of the believer's attitude towards sin as the result of Christ's having borne our sins in His body on the tree. BAGD—89b; THAYER—60a.

582. ἀπογραφή {2x} **apŏgraphē**, ap-og-raf-ay'; from 583; an enrollment; by impl. an assessment:—taxing {2x}.

This word means primarily a written copy (Luke 2:2; Acts 5:37). Taxing means an enrollment or registration in the public records of persons together with their income and property, as the basis of a census or valuation, i.e. that it might appear how much tax should be levied upon each one. See: BAGD—89b; THAYER—60a.

Greek

583. **ἀπογράφω** {4x} **apŏgraphō**, *ap-og-raf'-o;* from *575* and *1125;* to *write off* (a copy or list), i.e. *enroll:*—tax {3x}, write {1x}.

This is the verb for 582 and means to enter in a register or records, specifically to enter in public records the names of men, their property and income. See: BAGD—89c; THAYER—60b.

584. **ἀποδείκνυμι** {4x} **apŏdĕiknumi**, *ap-od-ike'-noo-mee;* from *575* and *1166;* to *show off,* i.e. *exhibit;* fig. to *demonstrate,* i.e. *accredit:*—approve {1x}, prove {1x}, set forth {1x}, shew {1x}.

This word means to point away from one's self, to point out, show forth, to expose to view, exhibit, to declare, to show, to prove what kind of person anyone is, to prove by arguments, and is used once in the sense of proving by demonstration, and so bringing about an "approval." The Lord Jesus was "a Man approved of God by mighty works and wonders and signs" (Acts 2:22). See: BAGD—89c; THAYER—60b.

585. **ἀπόδειξις** {1x} **apŏdĕixis**, *ap-od'-ike-sis;* from *584; manifestation:*—demonstration {1x}.

This word literally means "a pointing out, a showing" or demonstrating by argument and is found in 1 Cor 2:4, where the apostle speaks of a proof, a "showing" forth or display, by the operation of the Spirit of God in him, as affecting the hearts and lives of his hearers, in contrast to the attempted methods of proof by rhetorical arts and philosophic arguments. See: BAGD—89d; THAYER—60b.

586. **ἀποδεκατόω** {4x} **apŏdĕkatŏō**, *ap-od-ek-at-ŏ'-o;* from *575* and *1183;* to *tithe* (as debtor or creditor):—give tithe {1x}, pay tithe {1x}, take tithe {1x}, tithe {1x}.

This word means one-tenth and denotes **(1)** "to pay tithe of" (Mt 23:23; Lk 11:42; Lk 18:12); or **(2)** "to exact tithes" (Heb 7:5). See: BAGD—89d; THAYER—60c.

587. **ἀπόδεκτος** {2x} **apŏdĕktŏs**, *ap-od'-ek-tos;* from *588; accepted,* i.e. *agreeable:*—acceptable {2x}.

This word denotes that which is pleasing and welcome (1 Ti 2:3; 5:4). See: TDNT—2:58, 146; BAGD—90a; THAYER—60c.

588. **ἀποδέχομαι** {6x} **apŏdĕchŏmai**, *ap-od-ekh'-om-ahee;* from *575* and *1209;* to *take fully,* i.e. *welcome* (persons), *approve* (things):—accept {1x}, receive {3x}, receive gladly {2x}.

Apodechomai, as a verb, means "to welcome, to accept gladly, to receive without reserve" and is used **(1)** literally: "And it came to

pass, that, when Jesus was returned, the people gladly received Him: for they were all waiting for Him" (Lk 8:40; cf. Acts 18:27; 28:30); and **(2)** metaphorically: "Then they that gladly received his [Peter's] word were baptized: and the same day there were added unto them about three thousand souls" (Acts 2:41; cf. 24:3, "we accept," in the sense of acknowledging, the term being used in a tone of respect). Syn.: 324, 353, 354, 568, 618, 1209, 1523, 1926, 2210, 2865, 2975, 2983, 3028, 3335, 3336, 3858, 3880, 3970, 4327, 4355, 4356, 4380, 4381, 4382, 5562, 5264, 5274. See: TDNT—2:55, 146; BAGD—90a; THAYER—60c.

589. **ἀποδημέω** {6x} **apŏdēmĕō**, *ap-od-ay-meh'-o;* from *590;* to *go abroad,* i.e. *visit a foreign land:*—go into a far country {3x}, take (one's) journey {2x}, travel into a far country {1x}.

This word signifies "to go or travel into a far country," literally "to be away from one's people" (Mt 21:33; 25:14; in v. 15 the verb is translated "took his journey"; Mk 12:1; Lk 15:13 "took his journey" "into a far country"; 20:9). See: BAGD—90a; THAYER—60d.

590. **ἀπόδημος** {1x} **apŏdēmŏs**, *ap-od'-ay-mos;* from *575* and *1218;* *absent from* one's own *people,* i.e. a *foreign traveller:*—taking a far journey {1x}.

This word means "gone abroad" and signifies "taking a far journey " (Mk 13:34). Syn.: 3927, 3941. See: BAGD—90b; THAYER—60d.

591. **ἀποδίδωμι** {48x} **apŏdidōmi**, *ap-od-eed'-o-mee;* from *575* and *1325;* to *give away,* i.e. *up, over, back,* etc. (in various applications):—pay {9x}, give {9x}, render {9x}, reward {7x}, sell {3x}, yield {2x}, misc. {9x} = deliver, deliver again, repay, payment be made, perform, recompense, requite, restore.

Apodidomi, as a verb, means literally "to give away"; hence, "to give back or up" is used **(1)** in Pilate's command for the Lord's body to be "given up": "He went to Pilate, and begged the body of Jesus. Then Pilate commanded the body to be delivered" (Mt 27:58); **(2)** in the sense of "giving back": "And as he was yet a coming, the devil threw him down, and tare him. And Jesus rebuked the unclean spirit, and healed the child, and delivered him again to his father" (Lk 9:42 of the Lord's act in giving a healed boy back to his father). Syn.: 325, 525, 629, 859, 1325, 1560, 1659, 1807, 1929, 3086, 3860, 4506, 5483. See: TDNT—2:167, 166; BAGD—90b; THAYER—60d.

592. **ἀποδιορίζω** {1x} **apŏdiŏrizō**, *ap-od-ee-or-id'-zo;* from *575* and a compound of *1223* and *3724;* to *disjoin, to make*

Greek

separations (by a boundary, fig. a party):—separate {1x}.

This word means "to mark off", hence denotes metaphorically to make "separations": "These be they who separate themselves, sensual, having not the Spirit" (Jude 19); of persons who make divisions (in contrast with v. 20); there is no pronoun in the original representing "themselves." See: TDNT—5:455, 728; BAGD—90d; THAYER—61b.

593. ἀποδοκιμάζω {9x} **apŏdŏkimazō**, *ap-od-ok-ee-mad'-zo;* from 575 and 1381; to *disapprove,* i.e. (by impl.) to *repudiate:*—disallow {2x}, reject {7x}.

This word means "to reject as the result of disapproval" is **(1)** always translated "to reject" (Mt 21:42; Mk 8:31; 12:10; Lk 9:22; 17:25; 20:17; Heb 12:17); except in **(2)** 1 Pet 2:4 and 7. See: TDNT—2:255, 181; BAGD—90d; THAYER—61b.

594. ἀποδοχή {2x} **apŏdŏchē**, *ap-od-okh-ay';* from 588; *acceptance:*—acceptation {2x}.

This word denotes worthy to be received (1 Tim 1:15; 4:9). See: TDNT—2:55, 146; BAGD—91a; THAYER—61b.

595. ἀπόθεσις {2x} **apŏthĕsis**, *ap-oth'-es-is;* from 659; a *laying aside* (lit. or fig.):—putting away {1x}, must put off + 2076 {1x}.

This word denotes a "putting off or away" and is used metaphorically **(1)** in 1 Pet 3:21 of the "putting" away of the filth of the flesh; and **(2)** in 2 Pet 1:14 of "the putting off" of the body (as a tabernacle) at death. See: BAGD—91a; THAYER—61b.

596. ἀποθήκη {6x} **apŏthēkē**, *ap-oth-ay'-kay;* from 659; a *repository,* i.e. *granary:*—barn {4x}, garner {2x}.

This word designates a place where anything is stored [Eng., "apothecary"] hence denoting a garner, granary, barn (Mt 3:12; 6:26; 13:30; Lk 3:17; 12:18, 24). Syn.: 597. See: BAGD—91a; THAYER—61b.

597. ἀποθησαυρίζω {1x} **apŏthēsaurizō**, *ap-oth-ay-sŏw-rid'-zo;* from 575 and 2343; to *treasure away:*—lay up in store {1x}.

This word means "to treasure up, store away" and is used in 1 Ti 6:19 of "laying up in store" a good foundation for the hereafter by being rich in good works. Syn.: 596. See: BAGD—91b; THAYER—61b.

598. ἀποθλίβω {1x} **apŏthlibō**, *ap-oth-lee'-bo;* from 575 and 2346; to *crowd* (from every side):—press {1x}.

This is a strengthened form of *thlibo,* ["to

throng" *apo,* intensive] and is used in Lk 8:45 "press" of the multitude who were pressing around Christ. See: BAGD—91b; THAYER—61c.

599. ἀποθνήσκω {112x} **apŏthnēskō**, *ap-oth-nace'-ko;* from 575 and 2348; to *die* off (lit. or fig.):—die {98x}, be dead {29x}, be at the point of death + 3195 {1x}, perish {1x}, lie a dying {1x}, be slain + 5408 {1x}, vr dead {1x}.

Apothnesko, as a verb, means lit., "to die off or out" and is used **(1)** of the separation of the soul from the body, i.e., the natural "death" of human beings (e.g., Mt 9:24; Rom 7:2); **(1a)** by reason of descent from Adam (1 Cor 15:22); or **(1b)** of violent "death" whether of men or animals; with regard to the latter it is once translated "perished," Mt 8:32; of vegetation, Jude 12; of seeds, Jn 12:24; 1 Cor 15:36; **(1c)** it is used of "death" as a punishment in Israel under the Law, in Heb 10:28; **(2)** of the separation of man from God, **(2a)** all who are descended from Adam not only "die" physically, owing to sin, see **(1a)** above, but **(2b)** are naturally in the state of separation from God, 2 Cor 5:14. **(2c)** From this believers are freed both now and eternally, Jn 6:50; 11:26, through the "death" of Christ, Rom 5:8, e.g.; **(2d)** unbelievers, who "die" physically as such, remain in eternal separation from God, Jn 8:24. **(3)** Believers have spiritually "died" **(3a)** to the Law as a means of life, Gal 2:19; Col 2:20; **(3b)** to sin, Rom 6:2, and in general **(3c)** to all spiritual association with the world and with that which pertained to their unregenerate state, Col 3:3, because of their identification with the "death" of Christ, Rom 6:8. **(4)** As life never means mere existence, so "death," the opposite of life, never means nonexistence; but separation always. Syn.: 2348, 2837, 4880, 5053. See: TDNT—3:7, 312; BAGD—91b; THAYER—61c.

600. ἀποκαθίστημι {8x} **apŏkathistēmi**, *ap-ok-ath-is'-tay-mee;* from 575 and 2525; to *reconstitute* (in health, home or organization):—restore {7x}, restore again {1x}.

This word is used **(1)** of "restoration" to a former condition of health (Mt 12:13; Mk 3:5; 8:25; Lk 6:10); **(2)** of the divine "restoration" of Israel and conditions affected by it, including the renewal of the covenant broken by them (Mt 17:11; Mk 9:12; Acts 1:6); **(3)** of "giving" or "bringing" a person back: "But I beseech you the rather to do this, that I may be restored to you the sooner" (Heb 13:19). See: TDNT—1:387, 65; BAGD—91d; THAYER—62a.

601. ἀποκαλύπτω {26x} **apŏkaluptō**, *ap-ok-al-oop'-to;* from 575 and

2572; to take *off the cover,* i.e. *disclose:*—reveal {26x}.

Apokalupto, as a verb, signifies "to uncover, unveil." **(1)** The subjective use of *apokalupto* is that in which something is presented to the mind directly, as, **(1a)** the meaning of the acts of God (Mt 11:25; Lk 10:21); **(1b)** the secret of the Person of the Lord Jesus (Mt 16:17; Jn 12:38); **(1c)** the character of God as Father (Mt 11:27; Lk 10:22); **(1d)** the will of God for the conduct of His children (Phil 3:15); **(1e)** the mind of God to the prophets of Israel (1 Pet 1:12), and of the church (1 Cor 14:30; Eph 3:5). **(2)** The objective use is that in which something is presented to the senses, sight or hearing, as, referring to the past **(2a)** the truth declared to men in the gospel (Rom 1:17; 1 Cor 2:10; Gal 3:23); **(2b)** the Person of Christ to Paul on the way to Damascus (Gal 1:16); **(2c)** thoughts before hidden in the heart (Lk 2:35); **(2d)** referring to the future, **(2d1)** the coming in glory of the Lord Jesus (Lk 17:30); **(2d2)** the salvation and glory that await the believer (Rom 8:18; 1 Pet 1:5; 5:1); **(2d3)** the true value of service (1 Cor 3:13); **(2d4)** the wrath of God [at the Cross, against sin, and, at the revelation of the Lord Jesus, against the sinner] (Rom 1:18); **(2d5)** the Lawless One (2 Th 2:3, 6, 8). Syn.: 5537. See: TDNT—3:563, 405; BAGD—92a; THAYER—62a.

602. ἀποκάλυψις {18x} **apŏkalupsis,** *ap-ok-al'-oop-sis;* from *601; disclosure:*—revelation {12x}, be revealed {2x}, to lighten + 1519 {1x}, manifestation {1x}, coming {1x}, appearing {1x}.

This word is more comprehensive than *epiphaneia* (*2015*) and depicts the progressive and immediate unveiling of the otherwise unknown and unknowable God to His church. Syn.: 2015, 5321. See: TDNT—3:563, 405; BAGD—92b; THAYER—62c.

603. ἀποκαραδοκία {2x} **apŏkaradŏkia,** *ap-ok-ar-ad-ok-ee'-ah;* from a compound of *575* and a comp. of κάρα **kara** (the *head*) and *1380* (in the sense of *watching*); *intense anticipation:*—earnest expectation {2x}.

This word primarily means "a watching with outstretched head" and signifies "strained expectancy, eager longing," the stretching forth of the head indicating an "expectation" of something from a certain place, Rom 8:19 and Phil 1:20. The prefix *apo* suggests "abstraction and absorption" i.e., abstraction from anything else that might engage the attention, and absorption in the object expected till the fulfillment is realized. The intensive character of the noun is clear from the contexts: in Rom

8:19 it is said figuratively of the creation as waiting for the revealing of the sons of God. In Phil 1:20 the apostle states it as his "earnest expectation" and hope, that, instead of being put to shame, Christ shall be magnified in his body, "whether by life, or by death," suggesting absorption in the person of Christ, abstraction from aught that hinders. See: BAGD—92c; THAYER—62d.

604. ἀποκαταλλάσσω {3x} **apŏkatallassō,** *ap-ok-at-al-las'-so;* from *575* and *2644;* to *reconcile fully:*—reconcile {3x}.

This word means to change from one condition to another so as to remove all enmity and leave no impediment to unity and peace and is used in Eph 2:16, of the "reconciliation" of believing Jew and Gentile in one body unto God through the Cross. In Col 1:21 not the union of Jew and Gentile is in view, but the change wrought in the individual believer from alienation and enmity, on account of evil works, to "reconciliation" with God; in v. 20 the word is used of the divine purpose to "reconcile" through Christ "all things unto Himself . . . whether things upon the earth, or things in the heavens," the basis of the change being the peace effected "through the blood of His Cross." It is the divine purpose, on the ground of the work of Christ accomplished on the Cross, to bring the whole universe, except rebellious angels and unbelieving man, into full accord with the mind of God, Eph 1:10. Things "under the earth," Phil 2:10, are subdued, not reconciled. See: TDNT—1:258, 40; BAGD—92c; THAYER—63a.

605. ἀποκατάστασις {1x} **apŏkatastasis,** *ap-ok-at-as'-tas-is;* from *600; reconstitution:*—restitution {1x}.

This word means "to set in order" and is used in Acts 3:21: "Whom the heaven must receive until the times of restitution of all things, which God hath spoken by the mouth of all his holy prophets since the world began." See: TDNT—1:258, 40; BAGD—92d; THAYER—63a.

606. ἀπόκειμαι {4x} **apŏkĕimai,** *ap-ok'-i-mahee;* from *575* and *2749;* to *be reserved;* fig. to *await:*—be appointed {1x}, (be) laid up {3x}.

Apokeimai, as a verb, signifies **(1)** "to be laid, reserved": "And another came, saying, Lord, behold, here is thy pound, which I have kept laid (*apokeimai*) up in a napkin" (Lk 19:20; cf. Col 1:5; 2 Ti 4:8); **(2)** to be "appointed": "And as it is appointed unto men once to die, but after this the judgment" (Heb 9:27 where it is said of death and the judgment

following). See: TDNT−3:655, 425; BAGD−92d; THAYER−63a.

607. ἀποκεφαλίζω {4x} **apŏkĕphalizō**, *ap-ok-ef-al-id'-zo;* from *575* and *2776;* to *decapitate:*—beheaded {4x}.

This word means to cut off the head (Mt 14:10; Mk 6:16, 27; Lk 9:9). See: BAGD−93a; THAYER−63b.

608. ἀποκλείω {1x} **apŏklĕiō**, *ap-ok-li'-o;* from *575* and *2808;* to *close fully:*—shut up {1x}.

This word is used in Lk 13:25 and expresses the impossibility of entrance after the closing. See: BAGD−93a; THAYER−63b.

609. ἀποκόπτω {6x} **apŏkŏptō**, *ap-ok-op'-to;* from *575* and *2875;* to *amputate;* refl. (by irony) to *mutilate* (the privy parts):—cut off {6x}.

This word means "to cut off, or cut away" and is used **(1)** literally, **(1a)** of members of the body: "And if thy hand offend thee, cut it off: it is better for thee to enter into life maimed, than having two hands to go into hell, into the fire that never shall be quenched" (Mk 9:43; cf. 9:45; Jn 18:10, 26); **(1b)** of ropes (Acts 27:32); **(2)** metaphorically, in the middle voice, of "cutting off oneself," to excommunicate, Gal 5:12, of the Judaizing teachers, with a sarcastic reference, no doubt, to the "cutting away" of the Juadaizers themselves. See: TDNT−3:852, 453; BAGD−93a; THAYER−63b. comp. *2699.*

610. ἀπόκριμα {1x} **apŏkrima**, *ap-ok'-ree-mah;* from *611* (in its orig. sense of *judging*); a judicial *decision:*—sentence {1x}.

Apokrima denotes a judicial "sentence" and in 2 Cor 1:9 it is the answer of God to the apostle's appeal, giving him strong confidence: "But we had the sentence of death in ourselves, that we should not trust in ourselves, but in God which raiseth the dead." See: TDNT−3:945, 469; BAGD−93b; THAYER−63b.

611. ἀποκρίνομαι {250x} **apŏkrinŏmai**, *ap-ok-ree'-nom-ahee;* from *575* and κρίνω **krinō**; to *conclude for oneself,* i.e. (by impl.) to *respond;* by Heb. [comp. 6030] to *begin to speak* (where an address is expected):—answer {250x}.

Apokrinomai signifies either **(1)** "to give an answer to a question" (its more frequent use) or **(2)** "to begin to speak," but always where something has preceded, either statement or act to which the remarks refer (Mt 11:25; Lk 14:3; Jn 2:18). It is translated by "answered" (Mt 28:5; Mk 12:35; Lk 3:16 where some have suggested "began to say" or "uttered solemnly," whereas the speaker is replying to the unut-

tered thought or feeling of those addressed by him). See: TDNT−3:944,*; BAGD−93b; THAYER−63b.

612. ἀπόκρισις {4x} **apŏkrisis**, *ap-ok'-ree-sis;* from *611;* a *response:*—answer {4x}.

This word literally means "a separation or distinction" and is the regular word for "answer" (Lk 2:47; 20:26; Jn 1:22; 19:9). See: TDNT−3:946, 469; BAGD−93c; THAYER−63d.

613. ἀποκρύπτω {6x} **apŏkruptō**, *ap-ok-roop'-to;* from *575* and *2928;* to *conceal away* (i.e. *fully*); fig. to *keep secret:*—hide {6x}.

This word means "to conceal from, to keep secret" and is used metaphorically **(1)** in Lk 10:21 of truths "hidden" from the wise and prudent and revealed to babes (cf. Mt 11:25); **(1a)** in 1 Cor 2:7 of God's wisdom; **(1b)** in Eph 3:9 of the mystery of the unsearchable riches of Christ, revealed through the gospel; Col 1:26, of the mystery associated with the preceding. **(2)** It is used literally of hiding an object (Mt 25:18). See: TDNT−3:957, 476; BAGD−93d; THAYER−63d.

614. ἀπόκρυφος {3x} **apŏkruphŏs**, *ap-ok'-roo-fos;* from *613;* secret; by impl. *treasured:*—hid, kept secret {3x}.

This word means "hidden away from" and is translated **(1)** "kept secret" (Mk 4:22; Lk 8:17 "hid"; Col 2:3 "hid"). See: TDNT−3:957, 476; BAGD−93d; THAYER−64a.

615. ἀποκτείνω {75x} **apŏktĕinō**, *ap-ok-ti'-no;* from *575* and κτείνω **ktĕinō** (to *slay*); to *kill* outright; fig. to *destroy:*—put to death {6x}, kill {55x}, slay {14x}.

Apokteino, as a verb, means "to kill, put to death" and is so translated in Mk 14:1; Lk 18:33; Jn 11:53; 12:10; 18:31. Syn.: 336, 337, 520, 1935, 2288, 2289, 5054. See: BAGD−93d; THAYER−64a.

616. ἀποκυέω {2x} **apŏkuĕō**, *ap-ok-oo-eh'-o;* from *575* and the base of *2949;* to *breed forth, to give birth to,* i.e. (by transf.) to *generate* (fig.):—beget {1x}, bring forth {1x}.

Apokueo, as a verb, means "to give birth to, to bring forth, to begat" and is used metaphorically **(1)** of spiritual birth by means of the Word of God: "Of His own will begat (*apokueo*) He us with the word of truth" (Jas 1:18), and **(2)** of death as the offspring of sin: "Then when lust hath conceived, it bringeth forth (*tikto* – 5088) sin: and sin, when it is finished, bringeth forth (*apokueo*) death" (Jas 1:15). Syn.: 313, 738, 1080, 1084, 1085, 1626, 5088. See: BAGD−94a; THAYER−64b.

617. **ἀποκυλίω** {4x} **apŏkuliō**, *ap-ok-oo-lee'-o;* from *575* and *2947;* to *roll away:*—roll away {3x}, roll back {1x}.

This word means "to roll away" and is used of the sepulchre stone (Mt 28:2; Mk 16:3, 4; Lk 24:2). See: BAGD—94b; THAYER—64b.

618. **ἀπολαμβάνω** {12x} **apŏlambanō**, *ap-ol-am-ban'-o;* from *575* and *2983;* to *receive* (spec. in *full,* or as a host); also to *take aside:*—receive {10x}, take aside {1x}, receive again {1x}.

Apolambano, as a verb, signifies "to receive from another," (1) to "receive" as one's due: "And we indeed justly; for we receive (*apolambano*) the due reward of our deeds: but this Man hath done nothing amiss" (Lk 23:41; cf. Rom 1:27; Col 3:24; 2 Jn 8); (2) without the indication of what is due: "But Abraham said, Son, remember that thou in thy lifetime receivedst (*apolambano*) thy good things, and likewise Lazarus evil things: but now he is comforted, and thou art tormented" (Lk 16:25; cf. Gal 4:5); (3) to receive back: "And if ye lend to them of whom ye hope to receive (*apolambano*), what thank have ye? for sinners also lend to sinners, to receive (*apolambano*) as much again" (Lk 6:34; cf. 15:27). (4) It also means "to take apart": "And He took him aside from the multitude, and put His fingers into his ears, and He spit, and touched his tongue" (Mk 7:33). Syn.: 324, 353, 354, 568, 588, 1209, 1523, 1926, 2210, 2865, 2975, 2983, 3028, 3335, 3336, 3858, 3880, 3970, 4327, 4355, 4356, 4380, 4381, 4382, 5562, 5264, 5274. See: BAGD—94b; THAYER—64b.

619. **ἀπόλαυσις** {2x} **apŏlausis**, *ap-ol'-ow-sis;* from a compound of *575* and λαύω **lauō** (to *enjoy*); full *enjoyment:*—to enjoy + 1519 {1x}, enjoy the pleasures + 2192 {1x}.

This word means "enjoyment" and suggests the advantage or pleasure to be obtained from a thing. (1) It is used with the preposition *eis,* in 1 Ti 6:17: "Charge them that are rich in this world, that they be not highminded, nor trust in uncertain riches, but in the living God, who giveth us richly all things to enjoy", lit., "unto enjoyment" rendered "to enjoy"; (2) with *echo,* "to have" in Heb 11:25 lit., means "to have pleasure (of sin)" and is translated "to enjoy the pleasures." See: BAGD—94d; THAYER—64c.

620. **ἀπολείπω** {6x} **apŏlĕipō**, *ap-ol-ipe'-o;* from *575* and *3007;* to *leave* behind (pass. *remain*); by impl. to *forsake:*—leave {3x}, remain {3x}.

This word means "to leave behind" and is used (1) in the active voice, of (1a) "leaving"

behind a cloak (2 Ti 4:3); (1b) a person (2 Ti 4:20); (1c) of "abandoning" a principality [by angels] (Jude 6); and (2) in the passive voice, "to be reserved, to remain" (Heb 4:6, 9; 10:26). See: BAGD—94d; THAYER—64c.

621. **ἀπολείχω** {1x} **apŏlĕichō**, *ap-ol-i'-kho;* from *575* and λείχω **lĕichō** (to "*lick*"); to *lick* clean:—lick {1x}.

This word is used only in Lk 16:21 of the dogs licking Lazarus' wounds. See: BAGD—95a; THAYER—64c.

622. **ἀπόλλυμι** {92x} **apŏllumi**, *ap-ol'-loo-mee;* from *575* and the base of *3639;* to *destroy* fully (refl. to *perish,* or *lose*), lit. or fig.:—perish {33x}, destroy {26x}, lose {22x}, be lost {5x}, lost {4x}, misc. {2x} = die, mar.

Apollumi signifies (1) "to destroy utterly"; (1a) in middle voice, "to perish." (1b) The idea is not extinction but ruin, loss, not of being, but of well-being. (2) This is clear from its use, as, e.g., (2a) of the marring of wine skins (Lk 5:37); (2b) of lost sheep, i.e., lost to the shepherd, metaphorical of spiritual destitution (Lk 15:4, 6); (2c) the lost son (Lk 15:24); (2d) of the perishing of food (Jn 6:27); (2e) of gold (1 Pet 1:7). (3) So of persons: (3a) Mt 2:13 "destroy"; (3b) Mt 8:25 "perish" (cf. 22:7; 27:20); (3c) of the loss of well-being in the case of the unsaved hereafter (Mt 10:28; Lk 13:3, 5; Jn 3:15, 16; 10:28; 17:12; Rom 2:12; 1 Cor 15:18; 2 Cor 2:15 "are perishing"; 4:3; 2 Th 2:10; Jas 4:12; 2 Pet 3:9). See: TDNT—1:394, 67; BAGD—95a; THAYER—64c.

623. **Ἀπολλύων** {1x} **Apŏlluōn**, *ap-ol-loo'-ohn;* act. part. of *622;* a *destroyer* (i.e. *Satan*):—Apollyon {1x}. See: TDNT—1:397, 67; BAGD—95c; THAYER—65a.

624. **Ἀπολλωνία** {1x} **Apŏllōnia**, *ap-ol-lo-nee'-ah;* from the pagan deity Ἀπόλλων **Apŏllōn** (i.e. the *sun;* from *622*); *Apollonia,* a place in Macedonia:—Apollonia {1x}. See: BAGD—95c; THAYER—65a.

625. **Ἀπολλώς** {10x} **Apŏllōs**, *ap-ol-loce';* prob. from the same as *624; Apollos,* an Isr.:—Apollos {10x}. See: BAGD—95c; THAYER—65b.

626. **ἀπολογέομαι** {10x} **apŏlŏgĕŏmai**, *ap-ol-og-eh'-om-ahee;* mid. voice from a compound of *575* and *3056;* to give an *account* (legal *plea*) of oneself, i.e. *exculpate* (self):—answer {3x}, answer for (one's) self {3x}, make defense {1x}, excuse {1x}, excuse (one's) self {1x}, speak for (one's) self {1x}.

The English word "excuse" means to give cogent reasons why one acts with the goal of

clearing charges. Syn.: See 627 for an explanation. See: BAGD—95d; THAYER—65b.

627. ἀπολογία {8x} **apŏlŏgia,** *ap-ol-og-ee′-ah;* from the same as *626;* a *plea* ("apology"):—defence {3x}, answer {3x}, answer for (one's) self {1x}, clearing of (one's) self {1x}.

(1) This does not mean saying "I'm sorry. I apologize." **(2)** The root means to give a cogent explanation for one's beliefs. **(3)** The word means "to talk one's self off from" i.e. to explain one's basis for operation, explain the basis upon which and from which one makes his decisions. **(4)** Making a defense is not to escape punishment nor trial but to explain forcefully and completely why one does what he does. **(5)** It is translated: **(5a)** "to answer, give an answer" (Acts 25:16; 1 Cor 9:3; 2 Ti 4:16; 1 Pet 3:15), **(5b)** "defense" (Acts 22:1; Phil 1:7, 17), and **(5c)** "clearing of [yourselves]" (2 Cor 7:11). See: BAGD—96a; THAYER—65c.

628. ἀπολούω {2x} **apŏlŏuō,** *ap-ol-oo′-o;* from *575* and *3068;* to *wash* fully, i.e. (fig.) *have remitted* (refl.):—wash {1x}, wash away {1x}.

Apolouo means "to wash off or away," is used **(1)** in the middle voice, metaphorically, "to wash oneself," in Acts 22:16, where the command to Saul of Tarsus to "wash away" his sins indicates that by his public confession, he would testify to the removal of his sins, and to the complete change from his past life; this "washing away" was not in itself the actual remission of his sins, which had taken place at his conversion; the middle voice implies his own particular interest in the act (as with the preceding verb "baptize," lit., "baptize thyself," i.e., "get thyself baptized"); the aorist tenses mark the decisiveness of the acts; **(2)** in 1 Cor. 6:11, lit., "ye washed yourselves clean"; here the middle voice (rendered in the passive) again indicates that the converts at Corinth, by their obedience to the faith, voluntarily gave testimony to the complete spiritual change divinely wrought in them. See: TDNT—4:295, 538; BAGD—96a; THAYER—65c.

629. ἀπολύτρωσις {10x} **apŏlutrōsis,** *ap-ol-oo′-tro-sis;* from a compound of *575* and *3083;* (the act) *ransom* in full, i.e. (fig.) *riddance,* or (spec.) Chr. *salvation:*—deliverance {1x}, redemption {9x}.

Summary: This word means to be purchased from the slave market of sin, totally set free, never to be sold again. *Apolutrosis,* as a noun, is a strengthened form of *lutrosis (3085),* and means lit., "a releasing, for (i.e., on payment of) a ransom." It is used of **(1)** "deliverance" from physical torture (Heb 11:35); and **(2)** the deliverance of the tribulation saints at the coming of Christ with His glorified saints, **(2a)** "in a cloud with power and great glory," (Lk 21:28), a "redemption" to be accomplished at the "outshining of His Parousia" (2 Th 2:8), **(2b)** i.e., at His second advent; **(3)** It is used of forgiveness and justification, **(3a)** "redemption" as the result of propitiation and expiation, **(3b)** deliverance from the guilt of sins (Rom 3:24), **(3c)** "through the redemption that is in Christ Jesus" (Eph 1:7), **(3d)** defined as "the forgiveness of sins" (cf. Col 1:14), **(3e)** indicating both the liberation from the guilt and doom of sin and the introduction into a life of liberty, "newness of life" (Rom 6:4); and **(3f)** "for the redemption of the transgressions that were under the first testament," (Heb 9:15 - here "redemption of" is equivalent to "redemption from," the genitive case being used of the object from which the "redemption" is effected, not from the consequence of the transgressions, but from the transgressions themselves); **(4)** It is used of the deliverance of the believer from the presence and power of sin, and of his body from bondage to corruption, at the coming (the Parousia in its inception) of the Lord Jesus (Rom 8:23; cf. 1 Cor 1:30; Eph 1:4; 4:30). Syn.: 2434, 2643. See: TDNT—4:351,*; BAGD—96b; THAYER—65c.

630. ἀπολύω {69x} **apŏluō,** *ap-ol-oo′-o;* from *575* and *3089;* to *free* fully, i.e. (lit.) *relieve, release, dismiss* (refl. *depart*), or (fig.) *let die, pardon* or (spec.) *divorce:*—release {17x}, put away {14x}, send away {13x}, let go {13x}, set at liberty {2x}, let depart {2x}, dismiss {2x}, misc. 6x} = divorce, forgive, loose.

This word means **(1)** to set free; **(2)** to let go, dismiss, (to detain no longer): **(2a)** a petitioner to whom liberty to depart is given by a decisive answer (Mt 15:25; Lk 2:29), **(2b)** to bid depart, send away (Mt 14:15; Mk 6:36); **(3)** to let go free, release: **(3a)** a captive i.e. to loose his bonds and bid him depart, to give him liberty to depart (Lk 22:68; 23:22), **(3b)** to acquit one accused of a crime and set him at liberty (Jn 19:12; Acts 3:13), **(3c)** indulgently to grant a prisoner leave to depart (Acts 4:21, 23), **(3d)** to release a debtor, i.e. not to press one's claim against him, to remit his debt (Mt 18:27); **(4)** used of divorce, to dismiss from the house, to repudiate (Mt 1:19); and **(5)** to send one's self away, to depart (Acts 28:25). See: BAGD—96c; THAYER—65d.

631. ἀπομάσσομαι {1x} **apŏmassŏmai,** *ap-om-as′-som-ahee;* mid. voice from *575* and

     μάσσω massō (to *squeeze, knead, smear);* to *scrape away:*—wipe off {1x}.
This word means "to wipe off, wipe clean"

and is used in the middle voice, of "wiping" dust from the feet (Lk 10:11). Syn.: 1591, 1813. See: BAGD—96d; THAYER—66b.

632. ἀπονέμω {1x} **apŏnĕmō**, *ap-on-em'-o;* from 575 and the base of 3551; to *apportion,* i.e. *bestow:*—give {1x}.

This word means "to assign, apportion" and is rendered "giving" in 1 Pet 3:7 of giving honor to the wife. See: BAGD—97a; THAYER—66b.

633. ἀπονίπτω {1x} **apŏniptō**, *ap-on-ip'-to;* from 575 and 3538; to *wash off* (refl. one's own hands symb.):—wash {1x}.

This word means "to wash off" and is used in the middle voice in Mt 27:24. See: BAGD—97a; THAYER—66c.

634. ἀποπίπτω {1x} **apŏpiptō**, *ap-op-ip'-to;* from 575 and 4098; to *fall off:*—fall {1x}.

This word means "to fall from, to slip down from" and is used in Acts 9:18 of the scales which "fell" from the eyes of Saul of Tarsus. Syn.: 1601. See: BAGD—97b; THAYER—66c.

635. ἀποπλανάω {2x} **apŏplanaō**, *ap-op-lan-ah'-o;* from 575 and 4105; to *lead astray* (fig.); pass. to *stray* (from truth):—err {1x}, seduce {1x}.

This word means "to cause to wander away from the truth, to lead astray from the truth" and is used **(1)** metaphorically of leading into error (Mk 13:22 "seduce"); and **(2)** in 1 Ti 6:10, in the passive voice, "have erred" [by being led astray]. See: TDNT—6:228, 857; BAGD—97b; THAYER—66c.

636. ἀποπλέω {4x} **apŏplĕō**, *ap-op-leh'-o;* from 575 and 4126; to *set sail:*—sail away {4x}.

This word means "to sail away from, depart by ship" and occurs in Acts 13:4; 14:26; 20:15; 27:1. See: BAGD—97c; THAYER—66c.

637. ἀποπλύνω {1x} **apŏplunō**, *ap-op-loo'-no;* from 575 and 4150; to *rinse off:*—wash {1x}.

This word means to wash off and is used of nets in Lk 5:2. See: BAGD—97c; THAYER—66c.

638. ἀποπνίγω {3x} **apŏpnigō**, *ap-op-nee'-go;* from 575 and 4155; to *stifle* (by drowning or overgrowth):—choke {3x}.

This word is used **(1)** metaphorically, of "thorns crowding out seed sown and preventing its growth" (Mt 13:7; Lk 8:7). **(2)** It is Luke's word for "suffocation by drowning": "Then went the devils out of the man, and entered into the swine: and the herd ran violently down a steep place into the lake, and were choked [*apopnigo*]" (Lk 8:33). See: TDNT—6:455, 895 BAGD—97c; THAYER—66d.

639. ἀπορέω {4x} **apŏrĕō**, *ap-or-eh'-o;* from a compound of 1 (as a neg. particle) and the base of 4198; to *have no way* out, i.e. *be at a loss* (mentally):—stand in doubt {1x}, doubt {2x}, be perplexed {1x}.

(1) This word is always used in the middle voice, lit. means "to be without a way, to be without resources, embarrassed, in doubt, perplexity, at a loss" **(1a)** as was Herod regarding John the Baptist (Mk 6:20); **(1b)** as the disciples were, **(1b1)** regarding the Lord's betrayal, (Jn 13:22 "doubting"); and **(1b2)** regarding the absence of His body from the tomb (Lk 24:4 "were perplexed"); **(1c)** as was Festus, about the nature of the accusations brought against Paul (Acts 25:20 "doubted"); **(1d)** as Paul was, in his experiences of trial (2 Cor 4:8 "perplexed"); and, **(1d1)** as to his attitude towards the believers of the churches in Galatia concerning Judaistic errors (Gal 4:20 "I stand in doubt"). **(2)** Perplexity is the main idea. See: BAGD—97c; THAYER—66d.

640. ἀπορία {1x} **apŏria**, *ap-or-ee'-a;* from the same as 639; a (state of) *quandary; at a loss for a way:*—perplexity {1x}.

This word is translated "perplexity" in Lk 21:25 (lit., "at a loss for a way,"), of the distress of nations, finding no solution to their embarrassments; papyri illustrations are in the sense of being at one's wit's end, at a loss how to proceed, without resources. See: BAGD—97d; THAYER—66d.

641. ἀπορρίπτω {1x} **apŏrrhiptō**, *ap-or-hrip'-to;* from 575 and 4496; to *hurl off,* i.e. *precipitate* (oneself):—cast one's self {1x}.

This word means "to cast off," Acts 27:43, of shipwrecked people in throwing themselves into the water. See: TDNT—6:991,*; BAGD—97d; THAYER—66d.

642. ἀπορφανίζω {1x} **apŏrphanizō**, *ap-or-fan-id'-zo;* from 575 and a der. of 3737; to *bereave wholly,* i.e. (fig.) *separate* (from intercourse):—taken {1x}.

This word means taken from, literally, to be rendered an orphan" and is used metaphorically in 1 Th. 2:17 ("taken from"), in the sense of being "bereft" of the company of the saints through being compelled to leave them (cf. the similes in 7 and 11). The word has a wider meaning than that of being an orphan. See: BAGD—98a; THAYER—67a.

643. ἀποσκευάζω {1x} **apŏskĕuazō**, *ap-osk-yoo-ad'-zo;* from 575 and

a der. of *4632;* to *pack up* (one's) *baggage:*—take up (one's) carriages {1x}.

This word means "to furnish with things necessary"; in the middle voice, "to furnish for oneself"; it was used of equipping baggage animals for a journey; in Acts 21:15, it is translated "we took up our carriages." The form is the 1st aorist participle, and lit. means "having made ready (the things that were necessary for the journey)." Bags are containers in which things are carried; hence, "carriages." See: BAGD—98a; THAYER—67a.

644. ἀποσκίασμα {1x} **apŏskiasma,** *ap-os-kee'-as-mah;* from a compound of *575* and a der. of *4639;* a *shading off,* i.e. *obscuration:*—shadow {1x}.

This word means "a shadow," and denotes a "shadow that is cast" in Jas 1:17. The probable significance of this word is "overshadowing" or "shadowing-over" (which *apo* may indicate), and this with the genitive case of *trope,* "turning," yields the meaning "shadowing-over of mutability" implying an alternation of "shadow" and light; of this there are two alternative explanations, namely, "overshadowing" (a) not caused by mutability in God, or (b) caused by change in others, i.e., no changes in this lower world can cast a shadow on the unchanging Fount of light. The meaning of the passage will then be, God is alike incapable of change and incapable of being changed by the action of others. See: TDNT—7:399, 1044; BAGD—98a; THAYER—67a.

645. ἀποσπάω {4x} **apŏspaō,** *ap-os-pah'-o;* from *575* and *4685;* to *drag forth,* i.e. (lit.) *unsheathe* (a sword), or rel. (with a degree of force impl.) *retire* (pers. or factiously):—draw {1x}, withdraw {1x}, draw away {1x}, be gotten {1x}.

Apospao, as a verb, means "to draw away," lit., "to wrench away from" and is used (1) of a sword: "And, behold, one of them which were with Jesus stretched out his hand, and drew his sword" (Mt 26:51); (2) of "drawing" away disciples into error: "Also of your own selves shall men arise, speaking perverse things, to draw away disciples after them" (Acts 20:30); (3) of Christ's "withdrawal" from the disciples in Gethsemane (Lk 22:41); (4) of "parting" from a company: "And it came to pass, that after we were gotten (*apospao*) from them, and had launched, we came with a straight course unto Coos" (Acts 21:1). Syn.: 307, 385, 392, 501, 502, 868, 1096, 1670, 1448, 1828, 2020, 2464, 4317, 4334, 4358, 4685, 4951, 5288, 5289. See: BAGD—98a; THAYER—67a.

646. ἀποστασία {2x} **apŏstasia,** *ap-os-tas-ee'-ah;* fem. of the same as

647; *defection* from truth (prop. the state) ["apostasy"]:—to forsake + 575 {1x}, falling away {1x}.

This word means "a defection, revolt, apostasy" and is used in the NT of religious apostasy; (1) in Acts 21:21, it is translated "to forsake," lit., "thou teachest apostasy from Moses." (2) In 2 Th 2:3 "the falling away" signifies apostasy from the faith. (3) In papyri documents it is used politically of rebels. See: TDNT—1:513, 88; BAGD—98b; THAYER—67b.

647. ἀποστάσιον {3x} **apŏstasiŏn,** *ap-os-tas'-ee-on;* neut. of a (presumed) adj. from a der. of *868;* prop. something *separative,* i.e. (spec.) *divorce:*—divorcement {2x}, writing of divorcement {1x}.

This word primarily means "a defection," lit., "a standing off" and denotes, in the NT, "a writing or bill of divorcement" (Mt 5:31; 19:7; Mk 10:4). See: BAGD—98b; THAYER—67b.

648. ἀποστεγάζω {1x} **apŏstĕgazō,** *ap-os-teg-ad'-zo;* from *575* and a der. of *4721;* to *unroof:*—uncover {1x}.

This word signifies "to unroof" [*apo,* from, *stege,* "a roof"] (Mk 2:4). See: BAGD—98c; THAYER—67b.

649. ἀποστέλλω {133x} **apŏstĕllō,** *ap-os-tel'-lo;* from *575* and *4724; set apart,* i.e. (by impl.) to *send out* (prop. on a mission) lit. or fig.:—send {110x}, send forth {15x}, send away {4x}, send out {2x}, misc. {2x} = put in, set [at liberty].

This word means (1) to order (one) to go to a place appointed: (1a) Jesus sent by the Father (Mt 10:40), (1b) the apostles sent by Jesus (Mk 6:7), (1c) messengers are sent (Lk 7:3), (1d) servants are sent (Mk 6:27), (1e) angels (Mk 12:27), (1f) things are sent (Mt 21:3); (2) to send away, dismiss: (2a) to allow one to depart, that he may be in a state of liberty (Lk 4:18), (2b) to order one to depart, send off (Mk 8:26), (2c) to drive away (Mk 5:10). See: TDNT—1:398, 67; BAGD—98c; THAYER—67b.

650. ἀποστερέω {6x} **apŏstĕrĕō,** *ap-os-ter-eh'-o;* from *575* and στερέω **stĕrĕō** (to *deprive*); to *despoil:*—defraud {4x}, destitute {1x}, keep back by fraud {1x}.

This word means "to rob, defraud, deprive" and is used in 1 Ti 6:5, in the passive voice, of being deprived or "bereft, destitute" (of the truth), with reference to false teachers (cf. Mk 10:19; 1 Cor 6:7, 8; 7:5; Jas 5:4). See: BAGD—99a; THAYER—68a.

651. ἀποστολή {4x} **apŏstŏlē,** *ap-os-tol-ay';* from *649; commission,* i.e. (spec.) *apostolate:*—apostleship {4x}.

Greek

This word signifies "a sending, a mission, a commission," an apostleship (Acts 1:25; Rom 1:5; 1 Cor 9:2; Gal 2:8). See: TDNT—1:446, 67; BAGD—99b; THAYER—68a.

652. ἀπόστολος {81x} **apŏstŏlŏs,** *ap-os'-tol-os;* from *649;* a *delegate;* spec. an *ambassador* of the Gospel; officially a *commissioner* of Christ ["*apostle*"] (with miraculous powers):—apostle {78x}, messenger {2x}, he that is sent {1x}.

Apostolos is, lit., "one sent forth" [*apo,* "from," *stello,* "to send"]. (1) The word is used of the Lord Jesus to describe His relation to God (Heb 3:1; see Jn 17:3). (2) The twelve disciples chosen by the Lord for special training were so called (Lk 6:13; 9:10). (3) Paul, though he had seen the Lord Jesus, 1 Cor 9:1; 15:8, had not "companied with" the Twelve "all the time" of His earthly ministry, and hence was not eligible for a place among them, according to Peter's description of the necessary qualifications, Acts 1:22. Paul was commissioned directly, by the Lord Himself, after His Ascension, to carry the gospel to the Gentiles. (4) The word has also a wider reference. (4a) In Acts 14:4, 14, it is used of Barnabas as well as of Paul; (4b) in Rom 16:7 of Andronicus and Junias. (4c) In 2 Cor 8:23 two unnamed brethren are called "messengers [apostles – sent ones] of the churches"; (4d) in Phil 2:25 Epaphroditus is referred to as "your messenger [apostle – sent one]." (4e) It is used in 1 Th 2:6 of Paul, Silas and Timothy, to define their relation to Christ. See: TDNT—1:407, 67; BAGD—99c; THAYER—68b.

653. ἀποστοματίζω {1x} **apŏstŏmatizō,** *ap-os-tom-at-id'-zo;* from *575* and a (presumed) der. of *4750;* to *speak off-hand* (prop. *dictate*), i.e. to *catechize* (in an invidious manner):—provoke to speak {1x}.

This word in (1) classical Greek meant "to speak from memory, to dictate to a pupil"; in (2) later Greek, "to catechize"; and in (3) Lk 11:53 "to provoke (Him) to speak." Jesus's enemies were tempting Him to speak systematically concerning the doctrine of God in order to trap Him into blasphemy; a false charge that eventually accomplished its purpose. See: BAGD—100b; THAYER—68c.

654. ἀποστρέφω {10x} **apŏstrĕphō,** *ap-os-tref'-o;* from *575* and *4762;* to *turn away* or *back* (lit. or fig.):—turn away {4x}, turn away from {2x}, put up again {1x}, turn from {1x}, bring again {1x}, pervert {1x}.

This word means (1) to turn away (2 Ti 4:4): (1a) to remove anything from anyone (Rom 11:26), (1b) to turn him away from allegiance to any one, tempt to defect (Lk 23:14); (2) to turn back, return, bring back: (2a) of putting a sword back in its sheath (Mt 26:52), (2b) of Judas returning money to temple (Mt 27:3); (3) to turn one's self away, turn back, return (Acts 3:26); (4) to turn one's self away from, deserting (2 Ti 1:15). See: TDNT—7:719, 1093; BAGD—100b; THAYER—68c.

655. ἀποστυγέω {1x} **apŏstugĕō,** *ap-os-toog-eh'-o;* from *575* and the base of *4767;* to *detest* utterly:—abhor {1x}.

This word means "to shudder" [*apo,* "from," *stugeo,* "to hate"]; here used intensively, hence, "to abhor, dislike intensely" (Rom. 12:9). See: BAGD—100c; THAYER—68d.

656. ἀποσυνάγωγος {3x} **apŏsunagōgŏs,** *ap-os-oon-ag'-o-gos;* from *575* and *4864; excommunicated:*—be put out of the synagogue + *1096* {2x}, put out of the synagogue + *4160* {1x}.

This word is an adjective denoting "expelled from the congregation, excommunicated," is used (1) with *ginomai,* "to become, be made [out of the synagogue]" (Jn 9:22; 12:42); and (2) with *poieo,* "to make [one go from the synagogue]" (Jn 16:2). (3) This excommunication involved prohibition not only from attendance at the "synagogue," but from all fellowship with Israelites. See: TDNT—7:848, 1107; BAGD—100d; THAYER—68d.

657. ἀποτάσσομαι {6x} **apŏtassŏmai,** *ap-ot-as'-som-ahee;* mid. voice from *575* and *5021;* lit. to *say adieu* (by departing or dismissing); fig. to *renounce:*—bid farewell {2x}, take leave {2x}, send away {1x}, forsake {1x}.

This word is (1) used in the middle voice to signify "to bid adieu to a person." (2) It primarily means (2a) "to set apart, separate"; then, (2b) "to take leave of, to bid farewell to" (Mk 6:46; Lk 9:61), (2c) "to give parting instructions to" (Acts 18:18, 21; 2 Cor 2:13); (2d) "to forsake, renounce" (Lk 14:33). See: TDNT—8:33,*; BAGD—100d; THAYER—69a.

658. ἀποτελέω {1x} **apŏtĕlĕō,** *ap-ot-el-eh'-o;* from *575* and *5055;* to *complete entirely,* i.e. *consummate:*—finish {1x}.

This word means "to bring to an end, accomplish, to perfect" and is translated "I do" in Lk 13:32. See: BAGD—100d; THAYER—69a.

659. ἀποτίθημι {8x} **apŏtithēmi,** *ap-ot-eeth'-ay-mee;* from *575* and *5087;* to *put away* (lit. or fig.):—put off {2x}, lay aside {2x}, lay down {1x}, cast off {1x}, put away {1x}, lay apart {1x}.

This word means "to put off, lay aside," denotes, in the middle voice, "to put off from oneself, cast off" and is used figuratively of works

of darkness (Rom 13:12 "let us cast off" cf. Acts 7:58; Eph 4:22; 4:25; Col 3:8; Heb 12:1; Jas 1:21; 1 Pet 2:1). See: BAGD—101a; THAYER—69a.

660. ἀποτινάσσω {2x} **apŏtinassō**, *ap-ot-in-as'-so;* from *575* and τινάσσω **tinassō** (to *jostle*); to *brush off:*—shake off {2x}.

This word means "to shake off" and is used (1) in Lk 9:5, of dust from the feet; and (2) Acts 28:5 of a viper from the hand. See: BAGD—101b; THAYER—69b.

661. ἀποτίνω {1x} **apŏtinō**, *ap-ot-ee'-no;* from *575* and *5099;* to *pay in full:*—repay {1x}.

This word signifies "to pay off" and is used in Philem 19 of Paul's promise to "repay" whatever Onesimus owed Philemon, or to whatever extent the runaway slave had wronged his master. See: BAGD—101b; THAYER—69b.

662. ἀποτολμάω {1x} **apŏtŏlmaō**, *ap-ot-ol-mah'-o;* from *575* and *5111;* to *venture* plainly:—be very bold {1x}.

This word means "to be very bold, to speak out boldly" and is used in Rom 10:20. See: TDNT—8:181, 1183; BAGD—101b; THAYER—69b.

663. ἀποτομία {2x} **apŏtŏmia**, *ap-ot-om-ee'-ah;* from the base of *664;* (fig.) *decisiveness,* i.e. *rigor:*—severity {2x}.

This word means "steepness, sharpness" and is used metaphorically in Rom 11:22 (twice) of "the severity of God," which lies in His temporary retributive dealings with Israel. In the papyri it is used of exacting to the full the provisions of a statute. See: TDNT—8:106, 1169; BAGD—101c; THAYER—69b.

664. ἀποτόμως {2x} **apŏtŏmōs**, *ap-ot-om'-oce;* adv. from a der. of a compound of *575* and τέμνω **tĕmnō** (to *cut*); *abruptly,* i.e. *peremptorily:*—sharpness {1x}, sharply {1x}.

This word signifies "abruptly, curtly," lit., "in a manner that cuts"; hence "sharply, severely": (1) 2 Cor 13:10: ""Therefore I write these things being absent, lest being present I should use sharpness, according to the power which the Lord hath given me to edification, and not to destruction"; the pronoun "you" is to be understood, i.e., "that I may not use (or deal with) . . . sharply *with you*"; (2) Titus 1:13 of rebuking: "This witness is true. Wherefore rebuke them sharply, that they may be sound in the faith." See: TDNT—8:106, 1169; BAGD—101c; THAYER—69b.

665. ἀποτρέπω {1x} **apŏtrĕpō**, *ap-ot-rep'-o;* from *575* and the base of

5157; to *deflect,* i.e. (refl.) *avoid:*—turn away {1x}.

This word means "to cause to turn away" (*apo*), is used in the middle voice in 2 Tim. 3:5: "Having a form of godliness, but denying the power thereof: from such turn away." See: BAGD—101c; THAYER—69c.

666. ἀπουσία {1x} **apŏusia**, *ap-oo-see'-ah;* from the part. of *548;* a *being away:*—absence {1x}.

This word means lit., "a being away from," is used in Phil 2:12, of the apostle's absence from Philippi, in contrast to his parousia, his presence with the saints there ("parousia" does not signify merely "a coming," it includes or suggests "the presence" which follows the arrival). See: BAGD—101d; THAYER—69c.

667. ἀποφέρω {5x} **apŏphĕrō**, *ap-of-er'-o;* from *575* and *5342;* to *bear off* (lit. or rel.):—carry away {3x}, carry {1x}, bring {1x}.

Apophero, as a verb, means "to carry forth" and is rendered "bring": "And when I come, whomsoever ye shall approve by your letters, them will I send to bring your liberality unto Jerusalem" (1 Cor 16:3; cf. Acts 19:12). Syn.: 399, 1533. See: BAGD—101d; THAYER—69c.

668. ἀποφεύγω {3x} **apŏphĕugō**, *ap-of-yoo'-go;* from *575* and *5343;* (fig.) to *escape:*—escape {2x}, escape from {1x}.

This word means "to flee away from, escape from" and is used in 2 Pet 1:4: "Whereby are given unto us exceeding great and precious promises: that by these ye might be partakers of the divine nature, having escaped the corruption that is in the world through lust" (cf. 2:18, 20). Syn.: 1628. See: BAGD—101d; THAYER—69c.

669. ἀποφθέγγομαι {3x} **apŏphthĕggŏmai**, *ap-of-theng'-om-ahee;* from *575* and *5350;* to *enunciate* plainly, i.e. *declare:*—utterance {1x}, speak forth {1x}, say {1x}.

This word means (1) "to speak forth, said" (Acts 2:14; 26:25). (2) In Acts 2:4 it denotes to give utterance: "And they were all filled with the Holy Ghost, and began to speak with other tongues, as the Spirit gave them utterance." (3) This is not a word of everyday speech but one "belonging to dignified and elevated discourse. See: TDNT—1:447, 75; BAGD—102a; THAYER—69c.

670. ἀποφορτίζομαι {1x} **apŏphŏrtizŏmai**, *ap-of-or-tid'-zom-ahee;* from *575* and the mid. voice of *5412;* to *unload:*—unlade {1x}.

This word means "to discharge a cargo" and

is used in Acts 21:3. See: BAGD—102a; THAYER—69d.

671. ἀπόχρησις {1x} **apŏchrēsis**, *ap-okh'-ray-sis;* from a compound of *575* and *5530;* the act of *using up,* i.e. *consumption:*—using {1x}.

This word is a strengthened form of *chresis* (*5540*), "a using," signifies "a misuse" and is translated "using" in Col 2:22; the clause may be rendered "by their using up." The unusual word was chosen for its expressiveness; the *chresis* here was an *apochresis;* the things could not be used without rendering them unfit for further use. See: BAGD—102a; THAYER—69d.

672. ἀποχωρέω {3x} **apŏchōrĕō**, *ap-okh-o-reh'-o;* from *575* and *5562;* to *go away:*—depart {3x}.

This word means "to depart from" and is so translated in Mt 7:23; Lk 9:39; Acts 13:13. Syn.: 1633. See: BAGD—102a; THAYER—70a.

673. ἀποχωρίζω {2x} **apŏchōrizō**, *ap-okh-o-rid'-zo;* from *575* and *5563;* to *rend apart;* refl. to *separate:*—depart asunder {1x}, depart {1x}.

This word signifies "to separate off" and **(1)** in the middle voice means "to depart from, depart asunder" (Acts 15:39); and **(2)** in Rev 6:14 it is translated "departed." See: BAGD—102b; THAYER—70a.

674. ἀποψύχω {1x} **apŏpsuchō**, *ap-ops-oo'-kho;* from *575* and *5594;* to *breathe out,* i.e. *faint:*—heart failing {1x}.

This word means to breathe out life, expire, to faint or swoon away (Lk 21:26). See: BAGD—102b; THAYER—70a.

675. Ἄππιος {1x} **'Appiŏs**, *ap'-pee-os;* of Lat. or.; (in the gen., i.e. possessive case) of *Appius,* the name of a Rom.:—Appii {1x}. See: BAGD—102b; THAYER—70a.

676. ἀπρόσιτος {1x} **aprŏsitŏs**, *ap-ros'-ee-tos;* from *1* (as a neg. particle) and a der. of a compound of *4314* and εἰμι **ĕimi** (to *go*); *inaccessible:*—which no man can approach unto {1x}.

This word means "unapproachable, inaccessible" and is used in 1 Ti 6:16 of the light in which God dwells. See: BAGD—102c; THAYER—70a.

677. ἀπρόσκοπος {3x} **aprŏskŏpŏs**, *ap-ros'-kop-os;* from *1* (as a neg. particle) and a presumed der. of *4350;* act. *inoffensive,* i.e. *not leading into sin;* pass. *faultless,* i.e. *not led into sin:*—void of offense {1x}, none offence {1x}, without offence {1x}.

This word is used **(1)** in the active sense, "not causing to stumble, none offence" (1 Cor 10:32 metaphorically of "refraining from doing anything to lead astray" either Jews or Greeks or the church of God i.e., the local church); **(2)** in the passive sense, "blameless, without stumbling, void of offense" (Acts 24:16 "a conscience void of offense"; Phil 1:10 "without offense"). See: TDNT—6:745, 946; BAGD—102c; THAYER—70b.

678. ἀπροσωπολήπτως {1x} **aprŏsōpŏlēptōs**, *ap-ros-o-pol-ape'-toce;* adv. from a compound of *1* (as a neg. particle) and a presumed der. of a presumed comp. of *4383* and *2983* [comp. *4381*]; in a way *not accepting* the *person,* i.e. *impartially:*—without respect of persons {1x}.

This word only occurs in 1 Pet 1:17. See: TDNT—6:779, 950; BAGD—102c; THAYER—70b.

679. ἄπταιστος {1x} **aptaistŏs**, *ap-tah'-ee-stos;* from *1* (as a neg. particle) and a der. of *4417; not stumbling,* i.e. (fig.) *without sin:*—keep from falling + *5442* {1x}.

This word means not stumbling, standing firm, and is used in Jude 1:24. See: BAGD—102c; THAYER—70b.

680. ἅπτομαι {36x} **haptŏmai**, *hap'-tom-ahee;* refl. of *681;* prop. to *attach* oneself to, i.e. to *touch* (in many impl. relations):—touch {36x}. See: BAGD—102d; THAYER—70b.

681. ἅπτω {4x} **haptō**, *hap'-to;* a primary verb; prop. to *fasten* to, i.e. (spec.) to *set* on fire:—light {3x}, kindle {1x}.

This word means primarily "to fasten to," hence, of fire, "to kindle," denotes, in the middle voice **(1)** "to touch" (Mt 8:3, 15; 9:20, 21, 29); **(2)** "to cling to, lay hold of" (Jn 20:17; here the Lord's prohibition as to clinging to Him was indicative of the fact that communion with Him would, after His ascension, be by faith, through the Spirit; **(3)** "to have carnal intercourse with a woman" (1 Cor 7:1); **(4)** "to have fellowship and association with unbelievers" (2 Cor 6:17); **(5)** (negatively) "to adhere to certain Levitical and ceremonial ordinances," in order to avoid contracting external defilement, or to practice rigorous asceticism, all such abstentions being of "no value against the indulgence of the flesh" (Col 2:21); **(6)** "to assault," in order to sever the vital union between Christ and the believer, said of the attack of the Evil One (1 Jn 5:18). See: BAGD—102d; THAYER—70b.

682. Ἀπφία {1x} **Apphia**, *ap-fee'-a;* prob. of for. or.; *Apphia,* a woman of Collossæ:—*Apphia* {1x}. See: BAGD—103b; THAYER—70d.

683. **ἀπωθέομαι** {6x} **apōthĕŏmai**, *ap-o-theh'-om-ahee;* or ἀπώθομαι **apōthŏmai**, *ap-o'-thom-ahee;* from *575* and the mid. voice of ὠθέω **ōthĕō** or ὤθω **ōthō** (to *shove*); to *push off*, fig. to *reject*:—cast away {2x}, thrust away {1x}, put from {1x}, thrust from {1x}, put away {1x}.

This word means "to thrust away" and in the NT used in the middle voice, signifying "to thrust from oneself, to cast off, by way of rejection" (Acts 7:27, 39; 13:46; Rom 11:1–2; 1 Ti 1:19). See: TDNT—1:448,*; BAGD—103b; THAYER—70d.

684. **ἀπώλεια** {20x} **apōlĕia**, *ap-o'-li-a;* from a presumed der. of *622; ruin* or *loss* (phys. spiritual or eternal):—perdition {8x}, destruction {5x}, waste {2x}, damnable {1x}, to die + *1519* {1x}, perish + *1498* + *1519* {1x}, pernicious {1x}.

Apoleia means "loss of well-being, not of being" and is used (1) of things, signifying their waste, or ruin; (1a) of ointment (Mt 26:8; Mk 14:4); (1b) of money (Acts 8:20 "perish"); (2) of persons, signifying their spiritual and eternal perdition (Mt 7:13; Jn 17:12); 2 Th 2:3 where "son of perdition" signifies the proper destiny of the person mentioned; metaphorically of men persistent in evil; Rom 9:22, where "fitted" is in the middle voice, indicating that the vessels of wrath fitted themselves for "destruction", (2a) of the adversaries of the Lord's people (Phil 1:28 "perdition"); (2b) of professing Christians, really enemies of the cross of Christ (Phil 3:19); (2c) of those who are subjects of foolish and hurtful lusts (1 Ti. 6:9); (2d) of professing Hebrew adherents who shrink back into unbelief (Heb 10:39); (2e) of false teachers (2 Pet 2:1, 3); (2f) of ungodly men (2 Pet 3:7); (2g) of those who wrest the Scriptures (2 Pet 3:16); (2h) of the Beast, the final head of the revived Roman Empire (Rev 17:8, 11); (3) of impersonal subjects, as heresies (2 Pet 2:1, where "damnable heresies" is lit., "heresies of destruction"). See: TDNT—1:396, 67; BAGD—103b; THAYER—70d.

685. **ἀρά** {1x} **ara**, *ar-ah';* prob. from *142; prop. prayer* (as *lifted* to Heaven), i.e. (by impl.) *imprecation*:—curse {1x}.

Ara, as a noun, in its most usual meaning, "a malediction, cursing" is used in Rom 3:14: "Whose mouth is full of cursing and bitterness." Syn.: 331, 332, 944, 2552, 2652, 2653, 2671, 2672. See: TDNT—1:448, 75; BAGD—103d; THAYER—71d.

686. **ἄρα** {51x} **ara**, *ar'-ah;* prob. from *142* (through the idea of *drawing* a conclusion); a particle denoting an *inference* more or less decisive (as follows):—therefore + *3767*

{7x}, so then + *3767* {4x}, now therefore + *3767* {1x}, then + *1065* {2x}, wherefore + *1065* {1x}, haply + *1065* {1x}, not tr {7x}, misc. {7x} = (what) manner (of man), no doubt, perhaps, truly. Often used in connection with other particles, esp. *1065* or *3767* (after) or *1487* (before). See: BAGD—103d; THAYER—71a. comp. also *687*.

687. **ἄρα** {3x} **ara**, *ar'-ah;* a form of *686*, denoting an *interrogation* to which a negative answer is presumed:—therefore {1x}, not tr {2x}. See: BAGD—104a; THAYER—71c.

688. **Ἀραβία** {2x} **Arabia**, *ar-ab-ee'-ah;* of Heb. or. [6152]; *Arabia*, a region of Asia:—*Arabia* {2x}. See: BAGD—104a; THAYER—71d.

ἄραγε **aragĕ**. See *686* and *1065*.

689. **Ἀράμ** {3x} **Aram**, *ar-am';* of Heb. or. [7410]; *Aram* (i.e. *Ram*), an Isr.:—*Aram* {3x}. See: BAGD—104b; THAYER—71d.

690. **Ἄραψ** {1x}} ᾽**Araps**, *ar'-aps;* from *688;* an *Arab* or native of Arabia:—Arabians {1x}. See: BAGD—104c; THAYER—72a.

691. **ἀργέω** {1x} **argĕō**, *arg-eh'-o;* from *692;* to *be idle*, i.e. (fig.) to *delay*:—linger {1x}.

This word means "to be idle, inactive, to linger, delay" and is used in 2 Pet 2:3: "And through covetousness shall they with feigned words make merchandise of you: whose judgment now of a long time lingereth not, and their damnation slumbereth not." See: BAGD—104c; THAYER—72a.

692. **ἀργός** {8x} **argŏs**, *ar-gos';* from *1* (as a neg. particle) and *2041; inactive*, i.e. *unemployed;* (by impl.) *lazy, useless*:—barren {1x}, idle {6x}, slow {1x}.

This word denotes "idle, barren, yielding no return, because of inactivity" is rendered (1) "barren" (2 Pet 1:8); (2) "idle" (Mt 12:36 the "idle word" means the word that is thoughtless or profitless; cf. 20:3, 6 [twice]; 1 Ti 5:13 [twice]); and (3) "slow" (Titus 1:12). Syn.: 1021, 3576. See: TDNT—1:452, 76; BAGD—104c; THAYER—72a.

693. **ἀργύρεος** {3x} **argurĕŏs**, *ar-goo'-reh-os;* from *696;* made *of silver*:—of silver {1x}, silver {2x}.

This word signifies "silver, made of silver," (Acts 19:24; 2 Ti 2:20; Rev 9:20). See: BAGD—104d; THAYER—72b.

694. **ἀργύριον** {20x} **arguriŏn**, *ar-goo'-ree-on;* neut. of a presumed der. of

696; silvery, i.e. (by impl.) *cash;* spec. a *silverling* (i.e. *drachma* or *shekel*):—money {11x}, piece of silver {5x}, silver {3x}, silver piece {1x}.

This word means properly "a piece of silver" and denotes **(1)** "silver," e.g., Acts 3:6; **(2)** a "silver coin," often in the plural, "pieces of silver," e.g., Mt 26:15; so 28:12, where the meaning is "many pieces of silver"; **(3)** "money"; it has this meaning in Mt 25:18, 27; 28:15; Mk 14:11; Lk 9:3; 19:15, 23; 22:5; Acts 8:20. See: BAGD—104d; THAYER—72b.

695. ἀργυροκόπος {1x} **argurŏkŏpŏs,** *ar-goo-rok-op'-os;* from *696* and *2875;* a *beater* (i.e. *worker*) *of silver:*—silversmith {1x}.

This word means "to beat" occurs in Acts 19:24 of the one who smoothes the silver through tapping. See: BAGD—105a; THAYER—72b.

696. ἄργυρος {5x} **argurŏs,** *ar'-goo-ros;* from ἀργός **argŏs** (*shining*); *silver* (the metal, in the articles or coin):—silver {5x}.

This word denotes "silver" and in each occurrence in the NT it follows the mention of gold, Mt 10:9; Acts 17:29; Jas 5:3; Rev 18:12. See: BAGD—105a; THAYER—72b.

697. Ἄρειος Πάγος {2x} **Arĕiŏs Pagŏs,** *ar'-i-os pag'-os;* from Ἄρης **Arēs** (the name of the Greek deity of war) and a der. of *4078; rock of Ares,* a place in Athens:—Areopagus {1x}, Mars' Hill {1x}. See: BAGD—105b; THAYER—72c.

698. Ἀρεοπαγίτης {1x} **Arĕŏpagitēs,** *ar-eh-op-ag-ee'-tace;* from *697;* an *Areopagite* or member of the court held on Mars' Hill:—Areopagite {1x}. See: BAGD—105b; THAYER—72c.

699. ἀρέσκεια {1x} **arĕskĕia,** *ar-es'-ki-ah;* from a der. of *700; complaisance:*—pleasing {1x}.

This word means a "pleasing," a giving pleasure, Col 1:10, of the purpose Godward of a walk worthy of the Lord (cf. 1 Th 4:1). See: TDNT—1:456, 77; BAGD—105c; THAYER—72c.

700. ἀρέσκω {17x} **arĕskō,** *ar-es'-ko;* prob. from *142* (through the idea of *exciting* emotion); to *be agreeable* (or by impl. to seek to be so):—please {17x}.

This word signifies **(1)** "to be pleasing to, be acceptable to," Mt 14:6; Mk 6:22; Acts 6:5; Rom 8:8; 15:2; 1 Cor 7:32–34; Gal 1:10; 1 Th 2:15; 4:1 where the preceding *kai,* "and," is epexegetical, "even," explaining the "walking," i.e., Christian manner of life as "pleasing" God; 2 Tim. 2:4; **(2)** "to endeavor to please," and so, "to render service," **(2a)** doing so evilly in one's own interests, Rom 15:1, which Christ did not, v. 3; or

(2b) unselfishly, 1 Cor 10:33; 1 Th 2:4. See: TDNT—1:455, 77; BAGD—105c; THAYER—72d.

701. ἀρεστός {4x} **arĕstŏs,** *ar-es-tos';* from *700; agreeable;* by impl. *fit:*—those things that please {1x}, reason {1x}, please + *2076* {1x}, those things that are pleasing {1x}. See: TDNT—1:456, 77; BAGD—105d; THAYER—72d.

702. Ἀρέτας {1x} **Arĕtas,** *ar-et'-as;* of for. or.; *Aretas,* an Arabian:—Aretas {1x}. See: BAGD—105d; THAYER—72d.

703. ἀρέτη {5x} **arĕtē,** *ar-et'-ay;* from the same as *730;* prop. *manliness* (*valor*), i.e. *excellence* (intrinsic or attributed):—praise {1x}, virtue {4x}.

This word properly denotes whatever procures preeminent estimation for a person or thing; hence, "intrinsic eminence, moral goodness, virtue," **(1)** of God, **(1a)** 1 Pet 2:9 "praises"; here the original and general sense seems to be blended with the impression made on others, i.e., renown, excellence or praise; **(1b)** in 2 Pet 1:3, "by His own glory and virtue" i.e., the manifestation of His divine power; **(2)** of any particular moral excellence, Phil 4:8; 2 Pet 1:5 [twice] where virtue is enjoined as an essential quality in the exercise of faith. See: TDNT—1:457, 77; BAGD—105d; THAYER—73a.

704. ἀρήν {1x} **arēn,** *ar-ane';* perh. the same as *730;* a *lamb* (as a *male*):—lamb {1x}.

Aren, a noun, the nominative case of which is found only in early times occurs in Lk 10:3. Syn.: The *aren* is a little older than the *arnion* (*721*). See discussion under 721. See: TDNT—1:340, 54; BAGD—106a; THAYER—73b.

705. ἀριθμέω {3x} **arithmĕō,** *ar-ith-meh'-o;* from *706;* to *enumerate* or *count:*—number {3x}.

This word means "to number" and is found in Mt 10:30; Lk 12:7; Rev 7:9. See: TDNT—1:461, 78; BAGD—106b; THAYER—73b.

706. ἀριθμός {18x} **arithmŏs,** *ar-ith-mos';* from *142;* a *number* (as reckoned up):—number {18x}.

This word means "a number" [Eng., "arithmetic"] and occurs in Lk 22:3; Jn 6:10; Rom 9:27; elsewhere five times in Acts, ten times in the Apocalypse. See: TDNT—1:461, 78; BAGD—106b; THAYER—73b.

707. Ἀριμαθαία {4x} **Arimathaia,** *ar-ee-math-ah'-ee-ah;* of Heb. or. [7414]; *Arimathæa* (or *Ramah*), a place in Pal.:—Arimathæa {4x}. See: BAGD—106c; THAYER—73b.

708. Ἀρίσταρχος {5x} **Aristarchŏs,** *ar-is'-tar-khos;* from the same as *712* and *757; best ruling; Aristarchus,* a Macedonian:—Aristarchus {5x}. See: BAGD—106c; THAYER—73c.

709. ἀριστάω {3x} **aristaō,** *ar-is-tah'-o;* from *712;* to *take the principle meal:*—dine {3x}.

This word means primarily, "to breakfast" was later used also with the meaning "to dine," e.g., Lk 11:37; in Jn 21:12, 15; obviously there it was the first meal in the day. See: BAGD—106c; THAYER—73c.

710. ἀριστερός {3x} **aristĕrŏs,** *ar-is-ter-os';* appar. a comparative of the same as *712;* the *left* hand (as *second-best*):—left hand {1x}, left {1x}, on the left {1x}.

This word is used **(1)** of the "left" hand **(1a)** in Mt 6:3, the word "hand" being understood; **(1b)** in connection with the armor of righteousness, in 2 Cor 6:7, "(on the right hand and) on the left," lit., "(of the weapons . . . the right and) the left"; **(2)** in the phrase "on the left," formed by *ex* (for *ek*), "from," and the genitive plural of this adjective, Mk 10:37. See: BAGD—106c; THAYER—73c.

711. Ἀριστόβουλος {1x} **Aristŏbŏulŏs,** *ar-is-tob'-oo-los;* from the same as *712* and *1012; best counselling; Aristoboulus,* a Chr.:—Aristobulus {1x}. See: BAGD—106d; THAYER—73c.

712. ἄριστον {3x} **aristŏn,** *ar'-is-ton;* appar. neut. of a superl. from the same as *730;* the *best* meal [or *breakfast;* perh. from ἦρι **ēri** (*"early"*)], i.e. *luncheon:*—dinner {3x}.

This word means primarily, "the first food," taken early in the morning before work; the meal in the Pharisee's house, in Lk 11:37, was a breakfast or early meal. It also became known as any meal during the day. See: BAGD—106d; THAYER—73c.

713. ἀρκετός {3x} **arkĕtŏs,** *ar-ket-os';* from *714; satisfactory:*—enough {1x}, suffice {1x}, sufficient {1x}.

This word means "sufficient" and is rendered **(1)** "enough" in Mt 10:25; **(2)** "sufficient" in Mt 6:34; and **(3)** "suffice" in 1 Pet 4:3 lit. "(is) sufficient." See: TDNT—1:464, 78; BAGD—107a; THAYER—73d.

714. ἀρκέω {8x} **arkĕō,** *ar-keh'-o;* appar. a primary verb [but prob. akin to *142* through the idea of *raising* a barrier]; prop. to *ward off,* i.e. (by impl.) to *avail* (fig. *be satisfactory*):—be content {3x}, be sufficient {2x}, enough {1x}, suffice {1x}, content {1x}.

Arkeo, as a verb, primarily signifies "to be sufficient, to be possessed of sufficient strength, to be strong, to be enough for a thing"; hence, "to defend, ward off"; in the middle voice, "to be satisfied, contented with": **(1)** Lk 3:14 with wages; **(2)** 1 Ti 6:8 with food and raiment; **(3)** Heb 13:5 with "such things as ye have"; **(4)** negatively of Diotrephes in 3 Jn 10, "not content therewith." Syn.: 841, 842, 2425, 4909. See: TDNT—1:464, 78; BAGD—107a; THAYER—73d.

715. ἄρκτος {1x} **arktŏs,** *ark'-tos;* prob. from *714;* a *bear* (as *obstructing* by ferocity):—bear {1x}.

This word denotes the animal and is found only in Rev 13:2. See: BAGD—107b; THAYER—73d.

716. ἅρμα {4x} **harma,** *har'-mah;* prob. from *142* [perh. with *1* (as a particle of union) prefixed]; a *chariot* (as *raised* or fitted *together* [comp. *719*]):—chariot {4x}.

This word denotes "a war chariot with two wheels," Acts 8:28, 29, 38; Rev 9:9. Syn.: 4480. See: BAGD—107b; THAYER—73d.

717. Ἁρμαγεδδών {1x} **Armagĕddōn,** *ar-mag-ed-dohn';* of Heb. or. [2022 and 4023]; *Armageddon* (or *Har-Meggiddon*), a symbol. name:—Armageddon {1x}. See: TDNT—1:468, 79; BAGD—107c; THAYER—73d.

718. ἁρμόζω {1x} **harmŏzō,** *har-mod'-zo;* from *719;* to *joint,* i.e. (fig.) to *woo* (refl. to *betroth*):—espouse {1x}.

This word is used in the middle voice, of marrying or giving in marriage; in 2 Cor 11:2 and is rendered "espoused," metaphorically of the relationship established between Christ and the local church, through the apostle's instrumentality. The thought may be that of "fitting" or "joining" to one husband, the middle voice expressing the apostle's interest or desire in doing so. Syn.: 3423. See: BAGD—107c; THAYER—74a.

719. ἁρμός {1x} **harmŏs,** *har-mos';* from the same as *716;* an *articulation* (of the body):—joint {1x}.

This word means "a joining, joint" and is found in Heb 4:12, figuratively (with the word "marrow") of the inward moral and spiritual being of man, as just previously expressed literally in the phrase "soul and spirit." Syn.: 860. See: BAGD—107d; THAYER—74b.

720. ἀρνέομαι {29x} **arnĕŏmai,** *ar-neh'-om-ahee;* perh. from *1* (as a neg. particle) and the mid. voice of *4483;* to *contradict,* i.e. *disavow, reject, abnegate:*—deny {29x}, refuse {2x}.

This word signifies **(1)** "to say . . . not, to contradict," e.g., Mk 14:70; Jn 1:20; 18:25, 27; 1 Jn 2:22; **(2)** "to deny" by way of disowning a

person, as, **(2a)** e.g., the Lord Jesus as master, e.g., Mt 10:33; Lk 12:9; 2 Ti 2:12; or, on the other hand, **(2b)** of Christ Himself, "denying" that a person is His follower, Mt 10:33; 2 Ti 2:12; or **(2c)** to "deny" the Father and the Son, by apostatizing and by disseminating pernicious teachings, **(2d)** to "deny" Jesus Christ as master and Lord by immorality under a cloak of religion, 2 Pet 2:1; Jude 4; **(3)** "to deny oneself," either **(3a)** in a good sense, by disregarding one's own interests, Lk 9:23, or **(3b)** in a bad sense, to prove false to oneself, to act quite unlike oneself, 2 Ti 2:13; **(4)** to "abrogate, forsake, or renounce a thing," **(4a)** whether evil, Titus 2:12, or **(4b)** good, 1 Ti 5:8; 2 Ti 3:5; Rev 2:13; 3:8; **(5)** "not to accept, to reject" something offered, Acts 3:14; 7:35, "refused"; Heb 11:24, "refused." See: TDNT—1:469, 79; BAGD—107d; THAYER—74b.

721. ἀρνίον {30x} **arniŏn,** *ar-nee'-on;* dimin. from *704;* a *lambkin:*—lamb {2x}, Lamb, i.e. Christ {28x}.

Arnion is a diminutive in form of *aren* (*704*). **(1)** It is used only by the apostle John, **(1a)** in the plural, in the Lord's command to Peter: "He saith unto him, Feed my lambs" (Jn 21:15, with symbolic reference to young converts); **(1b)** in the singular, in the Apocalypse, some 28 times, of Christ as the "Lamb" of God, the symbolism having reference to His character and His vicarious sacrifice, as the basis both of redemption and of divine vengeance. **(1c)** He is seen in the position of sovereign glory and honor, (e.g., Rev 7:17, which He shares equally with the Father, 22:1, 3), **(1d)** the center of angelic beings and of the redeemed and the object of their veneration (e.g. 5:6, 8, 12, 13; 15:3), **(1e)** the Leader and Shepherd of His saints (e.g., 7:17; 14:4), **(1f)** the Head of His spiritual bride (e.g., 21:9), **(1g)** the luminary of the heavenly and eternal city (21:23), **(1h)** the One to whom all judgment is committed (e.g., 6:1, 16; 13:8), **(1i)** the Conqueror of the foes of God and His people (17:14); **(1j)** the song that celebrates the triumph of those who "gain the victory over the Beast," is the song of Moses . . . and the song of the Lamb (15:3).

(2) His sacrifice, the efficacy of which avails for those who accept the salvation thereby provided, forms the ground of the execution of divine wrath for the rejector, and the defier of God (14:10); **(3)** in the description of the second "Beast" (Rev 13:11), seen in the vision "like a lamb," suggestive of his acting in the capacity of a false messiah, a travesty of the true. Syn.: The contrast between *arnion* and *amnos* (*286*) does not lie in the diminutive character of the former as compared with the latter. The contrast lies in the manner in which Christ is pre-

sented in the two respects. The use of *amnos* points directly to the fact, the nature and character of His sacrifice; *arnion* (only in the Apocalypse) presents Him, on the ground, indeed, of His sacrifice, but in His acquired majesty, dignity, honor, authority and power. See: TDNT—1:340,*; BAGD—108b; THAYER—74c.

722. ἀροτριόω {3x} **arŏtriŏō,** *ar-ot-ree-o'-o;* from *723;* to *plough:*—plow {3x}.

This verb means "to plow" and occurs in Lk 17:7 and 1 Cor 9:10 [twice]. See: BAGD—108b; THAYER—74c.

723. ἄροτρον {1x} **arŏtrŏn,** *ar'-ot-ron;* from ἀρόω **arŏō** (to *till*); a *plow:*—plow {1x}.

This noun means "a plough" and occurs in Lk 9:62. See: BAGD—108b; THAYER—74c.

724. ἁρπαγή {3x} **harpagē,** *har-pag-ay';* from *726;* *pillage* (prop. abstr.):—extortion {1x}, ravening {1x}, spoiling {1x}.

This word denotes "pillage, plundering, robbery, extortion" [akin to *harpazo,* "to seize, carry off by force," and *harpagmos,* "a thing seized, or the act of seizing"; from the root *arp,* seen in Eng., "rapacious"; an associated noun, with the same spelling, denoted a rake, or hook for drawing up a bucket] and is translated **(1)** "extortion" in Mt 23:25; **(2)** "ravening" in Lk 11:39; and **(3)** "spoiling" in Heb 10:34. See: BAGD—108b; THAYER—74d.

725. ἁρπαγμός {1x} **harpagmŏs,** *har-pag-mos';* from *726;* *plunder* (prop. concr.):—robbery {1x}.

Harpagmos, as a verb, means "to seize, carry off by force" and is **(1)** found in Phil 2:6, "thought it not robbery" to be equal with God. **(2)** Christ possessed equality with God prior to His Incarnation, and then for a time veiled that glory, being always God in all of the co-equal attributes, but in the Incarnation never using His Godly powers to better Himself. **(3)** He was fully God, fully man, God taking on the likeness of sinful flesh (Rom 8:3), not a man adding Godliness. **(4)** His glory was all that was veiled, present but veiled (cf. His transfiguration – Mt 17:2). **(4a)** He prayed for its restoration (Jn 17:5). **(4b)** It was restored after His ascension (cf. His appearing to Saul on the Damascus road, Act 9:3; and John's vision of Him in the midst of the candlesticks, Rev 1:13f). **(5)** The middle/passive sense gives meaning to the passage as the purpose of the passage is to set forth Christ as the supreme example to the Philippians (and us) of humility and self-renunciation: "Who though He was subsisting in the essential form of God, yet did not regard His being on an equality of glory and majesty with God as a

prize and a treasure to be held fast. He would not feel as if He had been robbed to give up His shared glory." See: TDNT—1:473, 80; BAGD—108c; THAYER—74d.

726. **ἁρπάζω** {13x} **harpazō**, *har-pad'-zo;* from a der. of *138;* to *seize* (in various applications):—catch up {4x}, take by force {3x}, catch away {2x}, pluck {2x}, catch {1x}, pull {1x}.

Harpazo means (1) to snatch or catch away and is said of (1a) the act of the Spirit of the Lord in regard to Philip (Acts 8:39); (1b) of Paul caught up to paradise (2 Cor 12:2, 4); (1c) of the rapture of the saints to meet the Lord (1 Th 4:17); (1d) of the rapture of the man child in the vision of Rev 12:5. (2) This verb conveys the idea of force suddenly exercised (Mt 11:12; 12:29; Jn 6:15). Syn.: 4815, 4884. See: TDNT—1:472, 80; BAGD—109a; THAYER—74d.

727. **ἅρπαξ** {5x} **harpax**, *har'-pax;* from *726; rapacious:*—extortioner {4x}, ravening {1x}.

This word means "rapacious" and is translated as (1) a noun, "extortioners," in Lk 18:11; 1 Cor 5:10–11; 6:10; and (2) in Mt 7:15 "ravening" (of wolves). See: BAGD—109b; THAYER—75a.

728. **ἀρραβών** {3x} **arrhabōn**, *ar-hrab-ohn';* of Heb. or. [6162]; a *pledge*, i.e. part of the purchase-money or property given in advance as *security* for the rest:—earnest {3x}.

(1) This word meant originally, "earnest-money" deposited by the purchaser and forfeited if the purchase was not completed. (2) In general usage it came to denote "a pledge" or "earnest" of any sort; in the NT it is used only of that which is assured by God to believers; it is said (2a) of the Holy Spirit as the divine "pledge" of all their future blessedness, 2 Cor 1:22; 5:5; and (2b) in Eph 1:14, particularly of their eternal inheritance. See: TDNT—1:472, 80; BAGD—109b; THAYER—75a.

729. **ἄρραφος** {1x} **arrhaphŏs**, *ar'-hraf-os;* from *1* (as a neg. particle) and a presumed der. of the same as *4476; unsewed,* i.e. of a single piece:—without seam {1x}.

Arrhaphos denotes "without seam" [*a*, negative, and *rhapto,* "to sew"] in Jn 19:23. See: BAGD—109c; THAYER—75a.

730. **ἄρρην** {9x} **arrhēn**, *ar'-hrane;* or

ἄρσην **arsēn**, *ar'-sane;* prob. from *142; male* (as stronger for *lifting*):—male {4x}, man {3x}, man child {1x}, man child + 5207 {1x}.

Arsen is translated (1) "men" in Rom 1:27 [three times]; (2) "man child" in Rev 12:5, 13;

and (3) "male" in Mt 19:4; Mk 10:6; Lk 2:23; Gal 3:28 "there is neither male nor female," i.e. sex distinction does not obtain benefits in Christ; nor is sex a barrier either to salvation or the development of Christian graces. See: BAGD—109c; THAYER—75b.

731. **ἄρρητος** {1x} **arrhētŏs**, *ar'-hray-tos;* from *1* (as a neg. particle) and the same as *4490; unsaid,* i.e. (by impl.) *inexpressible:*—unspeakable {1x}.

Unspeakable due to their sacredness or that which is observed cannot be adequately described by presently known human words (2 Cor 12:4). See: BAGD—109c; THAYER—75b.

732. **ἄρρωστος** {5x} **arrhōstŏs**, *ar'-hroce-tos;* from *1* (as a neg. particle) and a presumed der. of *4517; infirm:*—sick {2x}, sick folk {1x}, be sick {1x}, sickly {1x}.

This word means "feeble, sickly" [*a*, negative, *rhonnumi,* "to be strong"], is translated (1) "sick" in Mt 14:14; Mk 16:18; (2) "sick folk" in Mk 6:5; (3) "that were sick" in Mk 6:13; and (4) "sickly" in 1 Cor 11:30, here also of the physical state. See: BAGD—109d; THAYER—75b.

733. **ἀρσενοκοίτης** {2x} **arsĕnŏkŏitēs**, *ar-sen-ok-oy'-tace;* from *730* and *2845;* a *sodomite:*—abuser of (one's) self with mankind {1x}, defile (one's) self with mankind {1x}.

This word means one who lies with a male as with a female; he is a sodomite, a homosexual (1 Cor 6:9; 1 Ti 1:10). See: BAGD—109d; THAYER—75b.

734. **Ἀρτεμάς** {1x} **Artĕmas**, *ar-tem-as';* contr. from a compound of *735* and *1435; gift of Artemis; Artemas* (or *Artemidorus*), a Chr.:—*Artemas* {1x}. See: BAGD—110a; THAYER—75b.

735. **Ἄρτεμις** {5x} **Artĕmis**, *ar'-tem-is;* prob. from the same as *736; prompt; Artemis,* the name of a Grecian goddess borrowed by the Asiatics for one of their deities:—Diana {5x}. See: BAGD—110a; THAYER—75b.

736. **ἀρτέμων** {1x} **artĕmōn**, *ar-tem'-ohn;* from a der. of *737;* prop. something *ready* [or else more remotely from *142* (comp. *740*); something *hung* up], i.e. (spec.) the *topsail* (rather *foresail* or *jib*) of a vessel:—mainsail {1x}.

Artemon is rendered "mainsail" in Acts 27:40. As to the particular kind of sail there mentioned, Sir William Ramsay, quoting from Juvenal concerning the entrance of a disabled ship into harbor by means of a prow-sail, indicates that

the *artemon* would be a sail set on the bow. See: BAGD—110a; THAYER—75c.

737. ἄρτι {36x} **arti**, *ar'-tee;* adv. from a der. of *142* (comp. *740*) through the idea of *suspension;* just *now:*—now {24x}, henceforth + 575 {2x}, hereafter + 575 {2x}, this present {2x}, hitherto + 2193 {2x}, misc. {4x} = this day (hour), hither, (even) now.

(1) *Arti* expresses "coincidence," and denotes "strictly present time." **(2)** It signifies "just now, this moment," in contrast **(2a)** to the past, e.g., Mt 11:12; Jn 2:10; 9:19, 25; 13:33; Gal 1:9–10; **(2b)** to the future, e.g., Jn 13:37; 16:12, 31; 1 Cor 13:12; 2 Th 2:7; 1 Pet 1:6, 8; **(2c)** sometimes without necessary reference to either, e.g., Mt 3:15; 9:18; 26:53; Gal 4:20; Rev 12:10. See: TDNT—4:1106, 658; BAGD—110b; THAYER—75c.

738. ἀρτιγέννητος {1x} **artigĕnnētŏs**, *ar-teeg-en'-nay-tos;* from *737* and *1084; just born,* i.e. (fig.) a *young convert:*—newborn {1x}.

Artigennetos, as an adjective, [*arti*, "newly, recently"] is translated "newborn": "As newborn babes, desire the sincere milk of the word, that ye may grow thereby" (1 Pet 2:2). Syn.: 313, 616, 1080, 1084, 1085, 1626, 5088. See: TDNT—1:672, 114; BAGD—110c; THAYER—75d.

739. ἄρτιος {1x} **artiŏs**, *ar'-tee-os;* from *737; fresh,* i.e. (by impl.) *complete:*—perfect {1x}. Syn.: 3648, 5046.

This word stresses that in which nothing is maimed. It refers not only to the presence of all the parts that are necessary for completeness but also to the further adaptation and aptitude of these parts for their designed purpose (2 Ti 3:17). See: TDNT—1:475, 80; BAGD—110c; THAYER—75d.

740. ἄρτος {99x} **artos**, *ar'-tos;* from *142; bread* (as *raised*) or a *loaf:*—bread {72x}, loaf {23x}, shewbread + 4286 + 3588 {4x}.

Artos, as a noun, means "bread" and signifies **(1)** "a small loaf or cake" **(1a)** composed of flour and water, and baked, **(1b)** as thick as the thumb; **(1c)** these were not cut, but broken and were consecrated to the Lord every Sabbath and called the "shewbread" [loaves of presentation], Mt 12:4; **(1d)** when the "shewbread" was reinstituted by Nehemiah (Neh 10:32) a poll-tax of ⅓ shekel was laid on the Jews, Mt 17:24; **(2)** "the bread at the Lord's Supper," e.g., Mt 26:26; **(2a)** the breaking of "bread" became the name for this institution, Acts 2:42; 20:7; 1 Cor 10:16; 11:23; **(3)** "bread of any kind," Mt 16:11; **(4)** metaphorically, "of Christ as the Bread of God, and of Life," John 6:33, 35; **(5)** "food in

general," the necessities for the sustenance of life, Mt 6:11; 2 Cor. 9:10. Syn.: 106. See: TDNT—1:477, 80; BAGD—110c; THAYER—75d.

741. ἀρτύω {3x} **artuō**, *ar-too'-o;* from a presumed der. of *142;* to *prepare,* i.e. *spice* (with *stimulating* condiments):—to season {3x}.

This word is used of "seasoning" Mk 9:50; Lk 14:34; Col 4:6. See: BAGD—111a; THAYER—76a.

742. Ἀρφαξάδ {1x} **Arphaxad**, *ar-fax-ad';* of Heb. or. [*775*]; *Arphaxad,* a post-diluvian patriarch:—*Arphaxad* {1x}. See: BAGD—111a; THAYER—76b.

743. ἀρχάγγελος {2x} **archaggĕlŏs**, *ar-khang'-el-os;* from *757* and *32; a chief angel:*—archangel {2x}.

Archaggelos is **(1)** not found in the OT, and in the NT only in 1 Th 4:16 and Jude 9, where it is used of Michael, who in Daniel is called "one of the chief princes," and "the great prince", 10:13, 21; 12:1. Cf. also Rev 12:7. **(2)** Whether there are other beings of this exalted rank in the heavenly hosts, Scripture does not say, though the description "one of the chief princes" suggests that this may be the case. **(3)** In 1 Th 4:16 the meaning seems to be that the voice of the Lord Jesus will be of the character of an "archangelic" shout. See: TDNT—1:87, 12; BAGD—111a; THAYER—76b.

744. ἀρχαῖος {12x} **archaiŏs**, *ar-khah'-yos;* from *746; original* or *primeval:*—old {8x}, of old time {3x}, a good while ago + 575 + 2250 {1x}.

Archaios means "original, ancient" and is used **(1)** of persons belonging to a former age, "(to) them of old time," Mt 5:21, 27, 33; **(1a)** of prophets, Lk 9:8, 19; **(1b)** of time long gone by, Acts 15:21; **(2)** of days gone by in a person's experience, Acts 15:7, "a good while ago," lit., "from old (days)," i.e., from the first days onward in the sense of originality, not age; **(3)** of Mnason, "an old disciple," Acts 21:16, not referring to age, but to his being one of the first who had accepted the gospel from the beginning of its proclamation; **(4)** of things which are "old" in relation to the new, earlier things in contrast to things present, 2 Cor 5:17, i.e., of what characterized and conditioned the time previous to conversion in a believer's experience, i.e., they have taken on a new complexion and are viewed in an entirely different way; **(5)** of the world (i.e., the inhabitants of the world) just previous to the Flood, 2 Pet 2:5; **(6)** of the devil, as "that old serpent," Rev 12:9; 20:2, "old," not in age, but as characterized for a long period by the evils indicated. Syn.: 1088,

4246. Syn.: *Archaios* designates something that is both ancient and venerable and stresses going back to the beginning. *Palaios* (*3820*) stresses old and worn out; it has existed a long time and has suffered from the wrongs and injuries of time. See: TDNT—1:486, 81; BAGD—111b; THAYER—76b.

745. Ἀρχέλαος {1x} **Archĕlaŏs**, *ar-khel'-ah-os;* from *757* and *2994; people-ruling; Archelaus*, a Jewish king:—Archelaus {1x}. See: BAGD—111a; THAYER—76a.

746. ἀρχή {58x} **archē**, *ar-khay';* from *756;* (prop. abstr.) a *commencement*, or (concr.) *chief* (in various applications of order, time, place, or rank):—beginning {40x}, principality {8x}, corner {2x}, first {2x}, misc. {6x} = first estate, magistrate, power, principle, rule.

Arche, as a noun, means "a beginning." **(1)** The root *arch* primarily indicated what was of worth. Hence the verb **(1a)** *archo* meant "to be first," and *archon* denoted "a ruler." **(1b)** So also arose the idea of "a beginning," the origin, the active cause, whether a person or thing, e.g., Col 1:18. **(2)** In Heb 2:3 the phrase "having at the first been spoken" is, lit., "having received a beginning to be spoken." **(3)** In Heb 6:1, where the word is rendered "first principles," the original has "let us leave the word of the beginning of Christ," i.e., the doctrine of the elementary principles relating to Christ. **(4)** In Jn 8:25, Christ's reply to the question "Who art Thou?" "Even that which I have spoken unto you from the beginning," does not mean that He had told them before; He declares that He is consistently the unchanging expression of His own teaching and testimony from the first, the immutable embodiment of His doctrine. Syn.: 756, 4412. See: TDNT—1:479, 81; BAGD—111d; THAYER—76a, 77b.

747. ἀρχηγός {4x} **archēgŏs**, *ar-khay-gos';* from *746* and *71;* a *chief leader:*—prince {2x}, captain {1x}, author {1x}.

Archegos **(1)** primarily signifies one who takes a lead in, or provides the first occasion of anything. **(1a)** It is translated "Prince" (Acts 3:15; 5:31), but **(1b)** "Author" (Heb 2:10; 12:2), **(1c)** primarily signifies "one who takes a lead in, or provides the first occasion of, anything." **(1d)** In Heb 2:10, the word suggests a combination of the meaning of leader with that of source from whence a thing proceeds. **(1e)** That Christ is the Prince of life signifies the life He had was not from another; the Prince or Author of life must be He who has life from Himself. **(2)** But the word does not necessarily combine the idea of the source or originating cause with that of leader. **(2a)** In Heb 12:2 where Christ is called the "Author and Perfecter of faith," He

is represented as the one who takes precedence in faith and is thus the perfect exemplar of it. **(2b)** Christ in the days of His flesh trod undeviatingly the path of faith, and as the Perfecter has brought it to a perfect end in His own person. **(2c)** Thus He is the leader of all others who tread that path. **(3)** Jesus, being the Author of faith wrote the first and last chapters in the life of faith. Syn.: 159. See: TDNT—1:487, 81; BAGD—112c; THAYER—77b.

748. ἀρχιερατικός {1x} **archiĕratikŏs**, *ar-khee-er-at-ee-kos';* from *746* and a der. of *2413; high-priestly:*—of the high priest {1x}. See: BAGD—112d; THAYER—77c.

749. ἀρχιερεύς {123x} **archiĕrĕus**, *ar-khee-er-yuce';* from *746* and *2409;* the *high-priest* (lit. of the Jews, typ. Christ); by extens. a *chief priest:*—chief priest {64x}, high priest {58x}, chief of the priest {1x}.

This word means **(1)** "a chief priest, high priest" and is **(2)** frequent in the Gospels, Acts and Hebrews, but there only in the NT. **(3)** It is used of Christ, e.g., in Heb 2:17; 3:1; **(4)** of "chief" priests, including ex-high priests and members of their families, e.g., Mt 2:4; Mk 8:31. See: TDNT—3:265, 349; BAGD—112d; THAYER—77c.

750. ἀρχιποίμην {1x} **archipŏimēn**, *ar-khee-poy'-mane;* from *746* and *4166;* a *head shepherd:*—chief shepherd {1x}.

This word means "a chief shepherd" and is said of Christ only, 1 Pet 5:4. See: TDNT—6:485, 901; BAGD—113a; THAYER—78a.

751. Ἄρχιππος {2x} **Archippŏs**, *ar'-khip-pos;* from *746* and *2462; horse-ruler; Archippus*, a Chr.:—Archippus {2x}. See: BAGD—113a; THAYER—78b.

752. ἀρχισυνάγωγος {9x} **archisunagōgŏs**, *ar-khee-soon-ag'-o-gos;* from *746* and *4864; director of* the *synagogue* services:—ruler of the synagogue {7x}, chief ruler of the synagogue {2x}.

This word means "a ruler of a synagogue," translated "chief ruler of the synagogue," in Acts 18:8, 17. He was the administrative officer supervising the worship. See: TDNT—6:844, 1107; BAGD—113b; THAYER—78b.

753. ἀρχιτέκτων {1x} **architĕktōn**, *ar-khee-tek'-tone;* from *746* and *5045;* a *chief constructor*, i.e. "*architect*":—masterbuilder {1x}.

This word means "a principal artificer" and is used figuratively by the apostle in 1 Cor 3:10, of his work in laying the foundation of the local church in Corinth, inasmuch as the inception of the spiritual work there devolved upon him.

The examples from the papyri and from inscriptions show that the word had a wider application than our "architect," and confirm the rendering "masterbuilder" in this passage, which is of course borne out by the context. See: BAGD—113b; THAYER—78b.

754. **ἀρχιτελώνης** {1x} **architĕlōnēs,** *ar-khee-tel-o'-nace;* from *746* and *5057;* a *principle tax-gatherer:*—chief among the publicans {1x}.

This word denotes "a chief tax-collector, or publican," Lk 19:2. See: BAGD—113b; THAYER—78b.

755. **ἀρχιτρίκλινος** {3x} **architriklinŏs,** *ar-khee-tree'-klee-nos;* from *746* and a compound of *5140* and *2827* (a *dinner-bed,* because composed of three couches); *director of* the *entertainment:*—governor of the feast {2x}, ruler of the feast {1x}.

This word means literally "a room with three couches" and denotes "the governor of a feast," Jn 2:8, a man appointed to see that the table and couches were duly placed and the courses arranged, and to taste the food and wine. The center couch was most prominent, with the adjoining side couches bearing significance; hence, the desire of the two apostles (Mk 10:37). See: BAGD—113b; THAYER—78c.

756. **ἄρχομαι** {84x} **archŏmai,** *ar'-khom-ahee;* mid. voice of *757* (through the impl. of *precedence*); to *commence* (in order of time):—begin {83x}, rehearse from the beginning {1x}.

Archomai, as a verb, denotes "to begin." (1) In Lk 3:23 the present participle is used in a condensed expression, lit., "And Jesus Himself was beginning about thirty years." (2) Some verb is to be supplied in English. (3) The meaning seems to be that He was about thirty years when He "began" His public career (cf. Acts 1:1). See: TDNT—1:478,*; BAGD—113c; THAYER—77b.

757. **ἄρχω** {2x} **archō,** *ar'-kho;* a primary verb; to be *first* (in political rank or power):—rule over {1x}, reign over {1x}. See: TDNT—1:478, 81; BAGD—113c; THAYER—78c.

758. **ἄρχων** {37x} **archōn,** *ar'-khone;* pres. part. of *757;* a *first* (in rank or power):—ruler {22x}, prince {11x}, chief {2x}, magistrate {1x}, chief ruler {1x}. See: TDNT—1:488, 81; BAGD—113d; THAYER—79a.

759. **ἄρωμα** {4x} **"arōma,"** *ar'-o-mah;* from *142* (in the sense of *sending* off scent); an *aromatic:*—spices {3x}, sweet spices {1x}.

This word means "sweet spice" and occurs in Mk 16:1; Lk 23:56; 24:1; Jn 19:40. See: BAGD—114b; THAYER—79b.

760. **Ἀσά** {2x} **Asa,** *as-ah';* of Heb. or. [609]; *Asa,* an Isr.:—*Asa* {2x}. See: BAGD—114b; THAYER—79b.

761. **ἀσάλευτος** {2x} **asalĕutŏs,** *as-al'-yoo-tos;* from *1* (as a neg. particle) and a der. of *4531; unshaken,* i.e. (by impl.) *immovable* (fig.):—unmoveable {1x}, which cannot be moved {1x}.

Asaleutos, as an adjective, means "unmoved, immoveable" and is translated (1) "unmoveable": "And falling into a place where two seas met, they ran the ship aground; and the forepart stuck fast, and remained unmoveable, but the hinder part was broken with the violence of the waves" (Acts 27:41); and (2) "which cannot be moved": "Wherefore we receiving a kingdom which cannot be moved, let us have grace, whereby we may serve God acceptably with reverence and godly fear" (Heb 12:28). Syn.: 277, 383, 2795, 2796, 3334, 4525, 4531, 4579, 4787, 5342. See: BAGD—114b; THAYER—79c.

762. **ἄσβεστος** {4x} **asbĕstŏs,** *as'-bes-tos;* from *1* (as a neg. particle) and a der. of *4570; not extinguished,* i.e. (by impl.) *perpetual:*—unquenchable {2x}, never shall be quenched {2x}.

This word means "not quenched" and is used of the doom (1) of persons described figuratively as "chaff" into "unquenchable" fire, Mt 3:12 and Luke 3:17; (2) of the fire of Gehenna, Mk 9:43, 45. See: BAGD—114b; THAYER—79c.

763. **ἀσέβεια** {6x} **asĕbĕia,** *as-eb'-i-ah;* from *765; impiety,* i.e. (by impl.) *wickedness:*—ungodliness {4x}, ungodly {2x}.

Asebeia means impiety, ungodliness and is used of (1) general impiety (Rom 1:18; 11:26; 2 Ti 2:16; Titus 2:12); (2) ungodly deeds (Jude 15); (3) of lusts or desires after evil things (Jude 18). (4) It is the opposite of *eusebeia* (2150 – godliness). Syn.: *Anomia* (*458*) is disregard for, or defiance of, God's laws; *asebeia* is the same attitude towards God's Person. See: TDNT—7:185, 1010; BAGD—114c; THAYER—79c.

764. **ἀσεβέω** {2x} **asĕbĕō,** *as-eb-eh'-o;* from *765;* to *be* (by impl. *act*) *impious* or *wicked:*—live ungodly {1x}, commit ungodly {1x}.

Asebeo signifies (1) "to be or live ungodly," 2 Pet 2:6; (2) "to commit ungodly deeds," Jude 15. See: TDNT—7:185, 1010; BAGD—114c; THAYER—79d.

765. **ἀσεβής** {9x} **asĕbēs,** *as-eb-ace';* from *1* (as a neg. particle) and a presumed der. of *4576; irreverent,* i.e. (by extens.) *impious* or *wicked:*—ungodly {8x}, ungodly men {1x}.

This word means "impious, ungodly, with-

out reverence for God," not merely irreligious, but acting in contravention of God's demands, Rom 4:5; 5:6; 1 Ti 1:9; 1 Pet 4:18; 2 Pet 2:5; 3:7; Jude 4, 15 [twice]. See: TDNT—7:185, 1010; BAGD—114c; THAYER—79d.

766. ἀσέλγεια {9x} **asĕlgĕia**, *as-elg'-i-a;* from a compound of *1* (as a neg. particle) and a presumed σελγής **sĕlgēs** (of uncert. der., but appar. mean. *continent*); *licentiousness* (sometimes incl. other vices):— lasciviousness {6x}, wantonness {2x}, filthy {1x}.

Aselgeia is best described as wanton, lawless insolence; a disposition of the soul not having or bearing a struggle with remorse; no restraints and is translated "filthy (conversation)," in 2 Pet. 2:7. Syn.: 810. See: TDNT— 1:490, 83; BAGD—114d; THAYER—79d.

767. ἄσημος {1x} **asēmŏs**, *as'-ay-mos;* from *1* (as a neg. particle) and the base of *4591; unmarked,* i.e. (fig.) *ignoble:*—mean {1x}.

This word stresses that someone or something is not made special by any distinguishing marks; lit., "without mark", i.e., "undistinguished, obscure," was applied by the apostle Paul negatively, to his native city, Tarsus, Acts 21:39. See: TDNT—7:267, 1015; BAGD—115a; THAYER—80a.

768. Ἀσήρ {2x} **Asēr**, *as-ayr';* of Heb. or. [836]; *Aser* (i.e. *Asher*), an Isr. tribe:— Aser {2x}. See: BAGD—115a; THAYER—80a.

769. ἀσθένεια {24x} **asthĕnĕia**, *as-then'-i-ah;* from *772; feebleness* (of body or mind); by impl. *malady;* mor. *frailty:*— infirmity {17x}, weakness {5x}, diseases {1x}, sickness {1x}.

This word means lit., "lacking strength, weakness, infirmity" and is translated **(1)** "infirmities" in Mt 8:17; its most used rendering; **(2)** "diseases" in Acts 28:9; **(3)** "sickness" in Jn 11:4; and **(4)** "weakness" in 1 Cor 2:3; 15:43; 2 Cor 12:9 [first mention]; 13:4; Heb 11:34. See: TDNT—1:490, 83; BAGD—115a; THAYER— 80a.

770. ἀσθενέω {36x} **asthĕnĕō**, *as-then-eh'-o;* from *772;* to *be feeble* (in any sense):—be weak {12x}, be sick {10x}, sick {7x}, weak {3x}, impotent man {1x}, be diseased {1x}, be made weak {1x}.

This word means to be weak, feeble, to be without strength, powerless. See: TDNT— 1:490, 83; BAGD—115b; THAYER—80b.

771. ἀσθένημα {1x} **asthĕnēma**, *as-then'-ay-mah;* from *770;* a *scruple* of conscience:—infirmity {1x}.

This word is found in the plural in Rom 15:1, "infirmities," i.e., those scruples which arise through weakness of faith. The strong must support the infirmities of the weak (*adunatos*) by submitting to self-restraint. See: TDNT—1:490, 83; BAGD—115c; THAYER— 80c.

772. ἀσθενής {25x} **asthĕnēs**, *as-then-ace';* from *1* (as a neg. particle) and the base of *4599; strengthless* (in various applications, lit., fig. and mor.):—weak {12x}, sick {6x}, weakness {2x}, weaker {1x}, weak things {1x}, impotent {1x}, more feeble {1x}, without strength {1x}. See: TDNT—1:490, 83; BAGD— 115c; THAYER—80c.

773. Ἀσία {19x} **Asia**, *as-ee'-ah;* of uncert. der.; *Asia,* i.e. *Asia Minor,* or (usually) only its western shore:—Asia {19x}. See: BAGD—116a; THAYER—80c.

774. Ἀσιανός {1x} **Asianŏs**, *as-ee-an-os';* from *773;* an *Asian* (i.e. *Asiatic*) or an inhabitant of Asia:—of Asia {1x}. See: BAGD—116a; THAYER—80d.

775. Ἀσιάρχης {1x} **Asiarchēs**, *as-ee-ar'-khace;* from *773* and *746;* an *Asiarch* or president of the public festivities in a city of Asia Minor:—chief of Asia {1x}.

An "Asiarch" was one of certain officers elected by various cities in the province of Asia, whose function consisted in celebrating, partly at their own expense, the public games and festivals; in Acts 19:31, "chief of Asia". It seems probable that they were "the high priests of the temples of the Imperial worship in various cities of Asia"; further, that "the Council of the Asiarchs sat at stated periods in the great cities alternately . . . and were probably assembled at Ephesus for such a purpose when they sent advice to St. Paul to consult his safety." A festival would have brought great crowds to the city. See: BAGD—116a; THAYER—80d.

776. ἀσιτία {1x} **asitia**, *as-ee-tee'-ah;* from *777; fasting* (the state):—abstinence {1x}.

Asitia stresses abstinence from food whether voluntary or inforced, Acts 27:21. See: BAGD— 116a; THAYER—81a.

777. ἄσιτος {1x} **asitŏs**, *as'-ee-tos;* from *1* (as a neg. particle) and *4621; without* (taking) *food:*—fasting {1x}.

This word means fasting, without having eaten, Acts 27:33. Syn.: 3521. See: BAGD— 116b; THAYER—81a.

778. ἀσκέω {1x} **askĕō**, *as-keh'-o;* prob. from the same as *4632;* to *elaborate,* i.e. (fig.) *train* (by impl. *strive*):—exercise {1x}.

Askeo signifies to form by art, to adorn, to

work up raw material with skill; hence, in general, to take pains, endeavor, exercise by training or discipline with a view to a conscience void of offense (Acts 24:16). See: TDNT—1:494, 84; BAGD—116b; THAYER—81a.

779. **ἀσκός** {12x} **askŏs**, *as-kos';* from the same as *778;* a leathern (or skin) *bag* used as a bottle:—bottle {12x}.

This word means **(1)** "a leather bottle, wineskin," occurs in Mt 9:17 [four times]; Mk 2:22 [four times]; Lk 5:37 [three times], 38. **(2)** A whole goatskin, for example, would be used with the apertures bound up, and when filled, tied at the neck. **(3)** They were tanned with acacia bark and left hairy on the outside. New wines, by fermenting, would rend old skins (cf. Josh 9:13; Job 32:19). **(4)** Hung in the smoke to dry, the skin-bottles become shriveled (see Ps 119:83). **(5)** The English word "bottle" has a root which signifies "a container for liquids" usually with a somewhat long, narrow neck for pouring. See: BAGD—116c; THAYER—81a.

780. **ἀσμένως** {2x} **asmĕnōs**, *as-men'-oce;* adv. from a der. of the base of *2237; with pleasure:*—gladly {2x}.

Asmenos, as an adverb, means "with delight, delightedly, gladly," and is found in 21:17: "And when we were come to Jerusalem, the brethren received us gladly" (cf. Acts 2:41). Syn.: 2234, 2236. See: BAGD—116c; THAYER—81a.

781. **ἄσοφος** {1x} **asŏphŏs**, *as'-of-os;* from *1* (as a neg. particle) and *4680; unwise:*—fool {1x}.

This word means "unwise, foolish," Eph 5:15. Syn.: 3471. See: BAGD—116c; THAYER—81a.

782. **ἀσπάζομαι** {60x} **aspazŏmai**, *as-pad'-zom-ahee;* from *1* (as a particle of union) and a presumed form of *4685;* to *enfold* in the arms, i.e. (by impl.) to *salute,* (fig.) to *welcome:*—embrace {2x}, greet {15x}, salute {42x}, take leave {1x}.

This word lit. **(1)** signifies "to draw to oneself"; hence, **(1a)** "to greet, salute, welcome," the ordinary meaning, **(1b)** e.g., in Rom16, where it is used 21 times. **(2)** It also signifies "embraced to bid farewell," e.g., Acts 20:1. A "salutation or farewell" was generally made by embracing and kissing (see Lk 10:4, which indicates the possibility of delay on the journey by frequent salutation). **(3)** In Heb 11:13 it is said of those who greeted/embraced the promises from afar. See: TDNT—1:496, 84; BAGD—116c; THAYER—81a.

783. **ἀσπασμός** {10x} **aspasmŏs**, *as-pas-mos';* from *782;* a *greeting* (in person or by letter):—greeting {3x}, salutation {7x}.

This word means a salutation, is rendered "greetings" in Mt 23:7; Lk 11:43; 20:46, and is used **(1)** orally in those instances and in Mk 12:38; Lk 1:29, 41, 44; and **(2)** in written salutations, 1 Cor 16:21; Col 4:18; 2 Th 3:17. See: TDNT—1:496, 84; BAGD—117a; THAYER—81b.

784. **ἄσπιλος** {4x} **aspilŏs**, *as'-pee-los;* from *1* (as a neg. particle) and *4695; unblemished* (phys. or mor.):—without spot {3x}, unspotted {1x}.

This word means "unspotted, unstained" and is used **(1)** of a lamb, 1 Pet 1:19; **(2)** metaphorically, of keeping a commandment without alteration and in the fulfillment of it, 1 Ti 6:14; **(3)** of the believer **(3a)** in regard to the world, Jas 1:27, and **(3b)** free from all defilement in the sight of God, 2 Pet 3:14. See: TDNT—1:502, 85; BAGD—117a; THAYER—81b.

785. **ἀσπίς** {1x} **aspis**, *as-pece';* of uncert. der.; a *buckler* (or *round* shield); used of a serpent (as *coiling* itself), prob. the "*asp*":—asp {1x}.

A small and very venomous serpent, the bite of which is fatal, unless the part affected is at once cut away. In Rom 3:13 is said, metaphorically, of the conversation of the ungodly. See: BAGD—117b; THAYER—81c.

786. **ἄσπονδος** {2x} **aspŏndŏs**, *as'-pon-dos;* from *1* (as a neg. particle) and a der. of *4689;* lit. *without libation* (which usually accompanied a treaty), i.e. (by impl.) *truceless:*—implacable {1x}, truce-breaker {1x}.

This word denotes **(1)** "without a libation," i.e., **(2)** "without a truce," as a libation accompanied the making of treaties and compacts; then, **(3)** "one who cannot be persuaded to enter into a covenant," "implacable, trucebreakers" 2 Ti 3:3 and Rom. 1:31. Syn.: *Asunthetos* (*802*) presumes a state of peace interrupted by the unrighteous, *aspondos* (*786*) a state of war, which the implacable refuse to terminate equitably. The words are clearly not synonymous. See: BAGD—117b; THAYER—81c.

787. **ἀσσάριον** {2x} **assariŏn**, *as-sar'-ee-on;* of Lat. or.; an *assarius* or *as,* a Roman coin:—farthing {2x}.

An *assarion* was one-tenth of a *drachma,* or one-sixteenth of a Roman *denarius,* i.e., about three farthings, Mt 10:29; Lk 12:6. Syn.: 2835. See: BAGD—117b; THAYER—81c.

788. **ἆσσον** {1x} **assŏn**, *as'-son;* neut. comparative of the base of *1451; more nearly,* i.e. *very near:*—close {1x}.

This word is found in Acts 27:13, of sailing "close" by a place. See: BAGD—117b; THAYER—81d.

789. Ἄσσος {2x} **Assŏs**, *as'-sos;* prob. of for. or.; *Assus,* a city of Asia Minor:— *Assos* {2x}. See: BAGD—117b; THAYER—81d.

790. ἀστατέω {1x} **astatĕō**, *as-tat-eh'-o;* from *1* (as a neg. particle) and a der. of *2476;* to *be non-stationary,* i.e. (fig.) *homeless:*—have no certain dwelling-place {1x}.

This word means "to wander about," "to have no fixed dwelling-place" and is used in 1 Cor 4:11. See: TDNT—1:503, 86; BAGD—117b; THAYER—81d.

791. ἀστεῖος {2x} **astĕiŏs**, *as-ti'-os;* from ἄστυ **astu** (a *city*); *urbane,* i.e. (by impl.) *handsome:*—fair {1x}, proper {1x}.

This word stresses (1) "city-bred," polished (cf. πόλις, Eng. polite). (2) It is found in the NT only of Moses, (2a) Acts 7:20, "(exceeding) fair," lit., "fair (to God)," and (2b) Heb 11:23, "proper". (3) Fair in the English means all things treated equally; hence, Moses' parents saw him as a normal child, yet one who if dedicated to God by them would fulfill God's particular calling for him. (4) They were probably unaware of the specifics. (5) He was also considered proper which means fitted for a particular service. (6) Moses' mother, Jochabed, much like Mary, the mother of Jesus, pondered God's consecration of her son and released his care unto Him. Syn.: 2570, 5611. See: BAGD—117c; THAYER—81d.

792. ἀστήρ {24x} **astēr**, *as-tare';* prob. from the base of *4766;* a *star* (as *strown* over the sky), lit. or fig.:—star {24x}.

Aster is (1) a literal heavenly body, a star (Mt 2:2-10; 24:29; 1 Cor 15:41) and is used (2) metaphorically, (2a) of Christ as the morning star, figurative of the approach of the day when He will appear as the sun of righteousness to govern the earth in peace; an event to be preceded by the rapture of the church (Rev 2:28; 22:16); (2b) of the angels of the seven churches (Rev 1:16, 20); and (2c) of certain false teachers, described as wandering stars (Jude 13), as if the stars intended for light and guidance, became the means of deceit by irregular movements. Syn.: 798. See: TDNT—1:503, 86; BAGD—117c; THAYER—81d.

793. ἀστήρικτος {2x} **astēriktŏs**, *as-tay'-rik-tos;* from *1* (as a neg. particle) and a presumed der. of *4741; unfixed,* i.e. (fig.) *vacillating:*—unstable {2x}.

This word means not fixed, not fastened and is used in 2 Pet. 2:14; 3:16, "unstable." See:

TDNT—7:653, 1085; BAGD—118a; THAYER—82a.

794. ἄστοργος {2x} **astŏrgŏs**, *as'-tor-gos;* from *1* (as a neg. particle) and a presumed der. of στέργω **stĕrgō** (to *cherish* affectionately); *hard-hearted* toward kindred:— without natural affection {2x}.

This word means without natural affection [*a*, negative, and *storge*, "love of kindred,"] especially of parents for children and children for parents, Rom 1:31; 2 Tim 3:3. See: BAGD—118a; THAYER—82a.

795. ἀστοχέω {3x} **astŏchĕō**, *as-tokh-eh'-o;* from a compound of *1* (as a neg. particle) and στόιχος **stŏichŏs** (an *aim*); to *miss* the mark, i.e. (fig.) *deviate* from truth:—err {2x}, swerve {1x}.

This word means "to miss the mark, fail" and is used only in the Pastoral Epistles, 1 Ti 1:6, "having swerved"; 6:21 and 2 Ti 2:18, "have erred." See: BAGD—118a; THAYER—82a.

796. ἀστραπή {9x} **astrapē**, *as-trap-ay';* from *797; lightning;* by anal. *glare:*— lightning {8x}, bright shining {1x}.

Astrape denotes (1) "lightning", Mt 24:27; 28:3; Lk 10:18; 17:24; in the plural, Rev 4:5; 8:5; 11:19; 16:18; (2) "bright shining," or "shining brightness," Lk 11:36. See: TDNT—1:505, 86; BAGD—118a; THAYER—82b.

797. ἀστράπτω {2x} **astraptō**, *as-trap'-to;* prob. from *792;* to *flash* as lightning:—lighten {1x}, shine {1x}.

This word means "to flash forth, lighten," is said (1) of lightning, Lk 17:24, and (2) "shining" of the apparel of the two men by the Lord's sepulchre, 24:4. Syn.: 1823. See: BAGD—118b; THAYER—82b.

798. ἄστρον {4x} **astrŏn**, *as'-tron;* neut. from *792;* prop. a *constellation;* put for a single *star* (nat. or artif.):—star {4x}.

This word means "star" and is used (1) in the sing. in Acts 7:43, "the star of the god Remphan," probably of Saturn, worshiped as a god, apparently the same as Chiun in Amos 5:26. Remphan being the Egyptian deity corresponding to Saturn, Chiun the Assyrian; (2) in the plur., of literal stars, Lk 21:25; Acts 27:20; Heb 11:12. See: TDNT—1:503, 86; BAGD—118b; THAYER—82b.

799. Ἀσύγκριτος {1x} **Asugkritŏs**, *as-oong'-kree-tos;* from *1* (as a neg. particle) and a der. of *4793; incomparable; Asyncritus,* a Chr.:—Asyncritus {1x}. See: BAGD—118b; THAYER—82b.

800. ἀσύμφωνος {1x} **asumphōnŏs**, *as-oom'-fo-nos;* from *1* (as a neg.

particle) and *4859; inharmonious* (fig.):—agree
not + 5607 {1x}.

This word means not agreeing in sound, dissonant, inharmonious, at variance and is used
in Acts 28:25, "they agreed not." See: BAGD—
118c; THAYER—82b.

801. ἀσύνετος {5x} **asunĕtŏs**, *as-oon'-ay-
                    tos;* from *1* (as a neg. parti-
cle) and *4908; unintelligent;* by impl. *wicked:*—
foolish {2x}, without understanding {3x}.

This word denotes "without discernment,
unintelligent, stupid" or **(1)** "without understanding" Mt 15:16; Mk 7:8; Rom 1:31; and **(2)**
"senseless/foolish," Rom 1:21 of the heart;
10:19. See: TDNT—7:888, 1119; BAGD—118c;
THAYER—82b.

802. ἀσύνθετος {1x} **asunthĕtŏs**, *as-oon'-thet-
                    os;* from *1* (as a neg. particle)
and a der. of *4934;* prop. *not agreed,* i.e. *treacherous* to compacts:—covenant-breaker {1x}.

This word stresses one who is in a covenant/
treaty and refuses to abide by the terms stipulated, Rom 1:31. Syn.: *Asunthetos* (*802*) presumes a state of peace interrupted by the
unrighteous, *aspondos* (*786*) a state of war,
which the implacable refuse to terminate equitably. The words are clearly not synonymous.
See: BAGD—118d; THAYER—82c.

803. ἀσφάλεια {3x} **asphalĕia**, *as-fal'-i-ah;*
                    from *804; security* (lit. or
fig.):—certainty {1x}, safety {2x}.

Asphaleia primarily means not liable to fall,
steadfast, firm; hence, denoting safety (Acts
5:23; 1 Th 5:3) and has the further meaning
of certainty (Lk 1:4). See: TDNT—1:506, 87;
BAGD—118d; THAYER—82c.

804. ἀσφαλής {5x} **asphalēs**, *as-fal-ace';* from
                    1 (as a neg. particle) and
σφάλλω **sphallō** (to "*fail*"); *secure* (lit. or
fig.):—certain {1x}, certainty {2x}, safe {1x},
sure {1x}.

This word means safe and is translated **(1)**
"certainty" Acts 21:34; 22:30; **(2)** "certain,"
Acts 25:26; **(3)** "safe," Phil 3:1; **(4)** "sure," Heb
6:19. See: TDNT—1:506, 87; BAGD—119a;
THAYER—82c.

805. ἀσφαλίζω {4x} **asphalizō**, *as-fal-id'-zo;*
                    from *804;* to *render secure:*—
make fast {1x}, make sure {3x}.

This word means "to make secure, safe,
firm" is translated **(1)** "make . . . fast," in Acts
16:24, of prisoners' feet in the stocks. **(2)** In
Matt. 27:64, 65, 66, it is rendered "to make
sure." See: TDNT—1:506, 87; BAGD—119a;
THAYER—82c.

806. ἀσφαλῶς {3x} **asphalōs**, *as-fal-oce';* adv.
                    from *804; securely* (lit. or
fig.):—assuredly {1x}, safely {2x}.

This adverb means **(1)** "safely," Mk 14:44;
Acts 16:23; and **(2)** "assuredly," Acts 2:36; the
knowledge there enjoined involves freedom
from fear of contradiction, with an intimation of the impossibility of escape from the effects. See: TDNT—1:506, 87; BAGD—119a;
THAYER—82d.

807. ἀσχημονέω {2x} **aschēmŏnĕō**, *as-kay-
                    mon-eh'-o;* from *809;* to *be*
(i.e. *act*) *unbecoming:*—behave (one's) self uncomely {1x}, behave (one's) self unseemly {1x}.

This word means "to be unseemly" and is
used **(1)** in 1 Cor 7:36, "behave (himself) unseemly," i.e., so as to run the risk of bringing
the virgin daughter into danger or disgrace,
and **(2)** in 1 Cor 13:5, "doth (not) behave itself
unseemly." See: BAGD—119b; THAYER—82d.

808. ἀσχημοσύνη {2x} **aschēmŏsunē**, *as-kay-
                    mos-oo'-nay;* from *809;* an
indecency; by impl. the *pudenda:*—shame {1x},
that which is unseemly {1x}.

Aschemosune, as a noun, denotes **(1)** "unseemliness": "And likewise also the men, leaving the natural use of the woman, burned in
their lust one toward another; men with men
working that which is unseemly (*aschemo-
sune*), and receiving in themselves that recompence of their error which was meet" (Rom
1:27); **(2)** "shame, nakedness": "Behold, I come
as a thief. Blessed is he that watcheth, and
keepeth his garments, lest he walk naked, and
they see his shame (*aschemosune*)" (Rev 16:15).
Syn.: 150, 152, 818, 819, 1788, 1791, 2617, 3856.
See: BAGD—119b; THAYER—82d.

809. ἀσχήμων {1x} **aschēmōn**, *as-kay'-mone;*
                    from *1* (as a neg. particle) and
a presumed der. of *2192* (in the sense of its
congener *4976*); prop. *shapeless,* i.e. (fig.) *inelegant:*—uncomely {1x}.

This word means does not seem to fit, to not
correspond to the rest of the form and is used
in 1 Cor 12:23. See: BAGD—119b; THAYER—
82d.

810. ἀσωτία {3x} **asōtia**, *as-o-tee'-ah;* from a
                    compound of *1* (as a neg. particle) and a presumed der. of *4982;* prop. *un-
savedness,* i.e. (by impl.) *profligacy:*—excess
{1x}, riot {2x}.

Asotia denotes "prodigality, profligacy,
riot" and is translated **(1)** "excess" in Eph 5:18
and **(2)** "riot" in Titus 1:6 and 1 Pet 4:4. Syn.:
see discussion under 766. See: TDNT—1:506,
87; BAGD—119c; THAYER—82d.

811. **ἀσώτως** {1x} **asōtōs**, *as-o'-toce;* adv. from the same as *810; wastefully, dissolutely:*—riotous {1x}.

Asotos, as an adverb, means "wastefully," "in riotous living" (Lk 15:13). A synonymous noun is *aselgeia* (766) "lasciviousness, outrageous conduct, wanton violence." See: TDNT— 1:506, 87 BAGD—119c; THAYER—83a.

812. **ἀτακτέω** {1x} **ataktĕō**, *at-ak-teh'-o;* from *813;* to *be* (i.e. *act*) *irregular:*— behave (one's) self disorderly {1x}. See: TDNT— 8:47, 1156; BAGD—119c; THAYER—83a.

813. **ἄτακτος** {1x} **ataktŏs**, *at'-ak-tos;* from *1* (as a neg. particle) and a der. of *5021; unarranged, not keeping order,* i.e. (by impl.) *insubordinate* (religiously):—unruly {1x}.

Ataktos signifies "not keeping order"; it was especially a military term, denoting "not keeping rank, insubordinate" and is used in 1 Th 5:14, describing certain church members who manifested an insubordinate spirit, whether by excitability or officiousness or idleness. See: TDNT—8:47, 1156; BAGD— 119c; THAYER—83a.

814. **ἀτάκτως** {2x} **ataktōs**, *at-ak'-toce;* adv. from *813; irregularly* (mor.):— disorderly {2x}.

Ataktos signifies disorderly, with slackness, like soldiers not keeping rank (2 Th 3:6, 11). See: TDNT—8:47, 1156; BAGD—119d; THAYER—83a.

815. **ἄτεκνος** {3x} **atĕknŏs**, *at'-ek-nos;* from *1* (as a neg. particle) and *5043; childless:*—childless {1x}, without children {2x}. See: BAGD—119d; THAYER—83a.

816. **ἀτενίζω** {14x} **atĕnizō**, *at-en-id'-zo;* from a compound of *1* (as a particle of union) and τείνω **tĕinō** (to *stretch*); to *gaze* intently:—look steadfastly {2x}, behold steadfastly {2x}, fasten (one's) eyes {2x}, look earnestly on {1x}, look earnestly upon {1x}, look up steadfastly {1x}, behold earnestly {1x}, misc. {4x} = look earnestly, set eyes.

Atenizo, as a verb, means "to look fixedly, gaze," is translated (1) "earnestly looked": "But a certain maid beheld him [Peter] as he sat by the fire, and earnestly looked upon him, and said, This man was also with him" (Lk 22:56; cf. Acts 3:12); (2) "looked steadfastly": "And while they looked stedfastly toward heaven as He went up, behold, two men stood by them in white apparel" (Acts 1:10); (3) "fasten . . . eyes": "And Peter, fastening his eyes upon him with John, said, Look on us" (Acts 3:4; cf. 11:6); (4) "looked up steadfastly": "But he [Stephen], being full of the Holy Ghost, looked up

stedfastly into heaven, and saw the glory of God, and Jesus standing on the right hand of God" (Acts 7:55); (5), "earnestly beholding": "And Paul, earnestly beholding the council, said, Men and brethren, I have lived in all good conscience before God until this day" (Act 23:1); (6) "steadfastly behold": "But if the ministration of death, written and engraven in stones, was glorious, so that the children of Israel could not stedfastly behold the face of Moses for the glory of his countenance; which glory was to be done away" (2 Cor 3:7); and (7) in Lk 4:20, "eyes . . . were fastened": "And He closed the book, and He gave it again to the minister, and sat down. And the eyes of all them that were in the synagogue were fastened on Him." Syn. for (1) - (7): 308, 352, 578, 872, 991, 1689, 1896, 1914, 1980, 1983, 2300, 2334, 3706, 3708, 3879, 4017, 4648. (8) *Atenizo* [from *atenes,* "strained, intent"], also denotes "to gaze upon," "beholding earnestly," or "steadfastly": "The same heard Paul speak: who stedfastly beholding (*atenizo*) him, and perceiving that he had faith to be healed" (Acts 14:9; cf. 23:1). Syn.for (8): 333, 991, 1689, 1896, 2029, 2300, 2334, 2657, 2734, 3708. See: BAGD—119d; THAYER—83b.

817. **ἄτερ** {2x} **atĕr**, *at'-er;* a particle prob. akin to *427; aloof,* i.e. *apart* from (lit. or fig.):—in the absence of {1x}, without {1x}.

This word means (1) "without" in Lk 22:35, "without purse"; and (2) in Lk 22:6 "in the absence of the multitude." See: BAGD—120a; THAYER—83b.

818. **ἀτιμάζω** {6x} **atimazō**, *at-im-ad'-zo;* from *820;* to *render infamous,* i.e. (by impl.) *contemn* or *maltreat:*—despise {1x}, dishonour {3x}, suffer shame {1x}, treat shamefully {1x}.

Atimazo, as a verb, means "to dishonor, put to shame. (1) It is translated "treat shamefully": "And again he sent another servant: and they beat him also, and entreated him shamefully, and sent him away empty" (Lk 20:11). (2) *Atimazo* signifies to dishonour, treat shamefully, insult, whether (2a) in word: "Jesus answered, I have not a devil; but I honour my Father, and ye do dishonour me" (Jn 8:49) or (2b) deed: "And again he sent unto them another servant; and at him they cast stones, and wounded him in the head, and sent him away shamefully handled" (Mk 12:4). Syn.: 150, 152, 808, 819, 1788, 1791, 2617, 3856. See: BAGD— 120a; THAYER—83b.

819. **ἀτιμία** {7x} **atimia**, *at-ee-mee'-ah;* from *820; infamy,* i.e. (subj.) comparative indignity, (obj.) *disgrace:*—dishonour {4x}, reproach {1x}, shame {1x}, vile {1x}.

(1) This word means to lower down from a place of honor. *Atimia*, as a noun, signifies (2) "shame, disgrace": "For this cause God gave them up unto vile affections (*aitimia*): for even their women did change the natural use into that which is against nature" (Rom 1:26, lit., "(passions) of shame"); cf. 1 Cor 11:14; (3) "dishonor": "But in a great house there are not only vessels of gold and of silver, but also of wood and of earth; and some to honour, and some to dishonour (*aitimia*)" (2 Ti 2:20), (3a) where the idea of disgrace or "shame" does not attach to the use of the word; (3b) the meaning is that while in a great house some vessels are designed for purposes of honor, others have no particular honor attached to their use (the prefix *"a"* simply negates the idea of honor). Syn.: 150, 152, 808, 818, 1788, 1791, 2617, 3856. See: BAGD—120a; THAYER—83b.

820. **ἄτιμος** {4x} **atimŏs**, *at'-ee-mos;* from *1* (as a neg. particle) and *5092;* (neg.) *unhonoured* or (pos.) *dishonoured:*—despised {1x}, without honour {2x}, less honourable {1x} [*comparative degree*].

(1) This word stresses that no honor is present to lower. (2) It means "without honor" and is translated (2a) as a verb in 1 Cor 4:10 "are despised"; lit., "(we are) without honor"; and (2b) "without honor" in Mt 13:57; Mk 6:4; and (2c) "less honourable" in 1 Cor 12:23. Syn.: 819. See: BAGD—120b; THAYER—83c.

821. **ἀτιμόω** {1x} **atimŏō**, *at-ee-mŏ'-o;* from *820;* used like *818,* to *maltreat:*—handle shamefully {1x}.

This word means to dishonour, mark with disgrace, Mk 12:4. See: BAGD—120b; THAYER—83c.

822. **ἀτμίς** {2x} **atmis**, *at-mece';* from the same as *109; mist:*—vapour {2x}.

Atmis is used (1) of "smoke," Acts 2:19; (2) figuratively of human life, Jas 4:14. See: BAGD—120b; THAYER—83c.

823. **ἄτομος** {1x} **atŏmŏs**, *at'-om-os;* from *1* (as a neg. particle) and the base of *5114; uncut,* i.e. (by impl.) *indivisible* [an *"atom"* of time]:—moment {1x}.

This word means lit. "indivisible" [from *a*, negative, and *temno*, "to cut"; Eng., "atom"]; hence it denotes "a moment," 1 Cor 15:52. See: BAGD—120b; THAYER—83c.

824. **ἄτοπος** {3x} **atŏpŏs**, *at'-op-os;* from *1* (as a neg. particle) and *5117; out of place,* i.e. (fig.) *improper, injurious, wicked:*—amiss {1x}, harm {1x}, unreasonable {1x}.

(1) This word means lit., "out of place" and denotes unbecoming, not befitting. (2) It is rendered "amiss" in the malefactor's testimony of Christ, Lk 23:41; (3) "harm"in Acts 28:6, of the expected effect of the viper's attack upon Paul; and (4) "unreasonable" in 2 Th 3:2 of men capable of outrageous conduct. See: BAGD—120c; THAYER—83c.

825. **Ἀττάλεια** {1x} **Attalĕia**, *at-tal'-i-ah;* from Ἄτταλος **Attalŏs** (a king of Pergamus); *Attaleia,* a place in Pamphylia:—Attalia {1x}. See: BAGD—120c; THAYER—83d.

826. **αὐγάζω** {1x} **augazō**, *ŏw-gad'-zo;* from *827;* to *beam* forth (fig.):—shine {1x}.

This word means "to shine" and is used metaphorically of the light of dawn, in 2 Cor 4:4. See: TDNT—1:507, 87; BAGD—120c; THAYER—83d.

827. **αὐγή** {1x} **augē**, *ŏwg'-ay;* of uncert. der.; a *ray* of light, i.e. (by impl.) *radiance, dawn:*—break of day {1x}.

This word means "brightness, bright, shining, as of the sun"; hence, "the beginning of daylight" and is translated "break of day" in Acts 20:11. See: BAGD—120d; THAYER—83d.

828. **Αὔγουστος** {1x} **Augŏustŏs**, *ŏw'-goos-tos;* from Lat. ["august"]; *Augustus,* a title of the Rom. emperor:—Augustus {1x}. See: BAGD—120d; THAYER—83d.

829. **αὐθάδης** {2x} **authadēs**, *ŏw-thad'-ace;* from *846* and the base of *2237; self-pleasing,* i.e. *arrogant:*—self-willed {2x}.

Authades means self-pleasing and denotes one who, dominated by self-interest, and inconsiderate of others, arrogantly asserts his own will. He asserts his own rights, regardless of the rights of others. With no motive at all he is quick to act contrary to the feelings of others (Titus 1:7; 2 Pet 2:10). Syn.: 5367. See: TDNT—1:508, 87; BAGD—120d; THAYER—83d.

830. **αὐθαίρετος** {2x} **authairĕtŏs**, *ŏw-thah'-ee-ret-os;* from *846* and the same as *140; self-chosen,* i.e. (by impl.) *voluntary:*—willing of (one's)self {2x}.

This word means "to choose, self-chosen, voluntary, of one's own accord" and occurs (1) in 2 Cor 8:3 of the churches of Macedonia as to their gifts for the poor saints in Judea, and (2) of Titus in his willingness to go and exhort the church in Corinth concerning the matter 2 Cor 8:17. See: BAGD—121a; THAYER—84a.

831. αὐθεντέω {1x} **authĕntĕō**, ἕντης **hĕntēs** *aw-than-teh'-o* (a *worker*); to *act of oneself*, i.e. (fig.) *dominate:*—usurp authority over {1x}.

This word means "to exercise authority on one's own account, to domineer over" and is used in 1 Ti 2:12 "to usurp authority over." See: BAGD—121a; THAYER—84a.

832. αὐλέω {3x} **aulĕō**, *ŏw-leh'-o;* from *836;* to play the *flute:*—to pipe {3x}.

This word means "to play on an *aulos*" [a flute-like instrument] and is used in Mt 11:17; Lk 7:32; 1 Cor 14:7. See: BAGD—121b; THAYER—84a.

833. αὐλή {12x} **aulē**, *ŏw-lay';* from the same as *109;* a *yard* (as open to the *wind*); by impl. a *mansion:*—palace {7x}, hall {2x}, sheepfold + 4163 {1x}, fold {1x}, court {1x}.

Aule is primarily an uncovered space around a house, enclosed by a wall, where the stables were; hence, describes **(1)** the courtyard of a house (Rev 11:2); **(2)** the courts in the dwellings of well-to-do folk, which usually had two: **(2a)** one exterior, between the door and the street (Mk 14:68), and the other **(2b)** interior, surrounded by the buildings of the dwellings (Mt 26:69; Mk 14:66). Syn.: 60. See: BAGD—121b; THAYER—84a.

834. αὐλητής {2x} **aulētēs**, *ŏw-lay-tace';* from *832;* a *flute-player:*—minstrel {1x}, piper {1x}.

This word means "a flute-player" and occurs **(1)** in Mt 9:23 "minstrel" and **(2)** Rev 18:22 "pipers." See: BAGD—121b; THAYER—84b.

835. αὐλίζομαι {2x} **aulizŏmai**, *ŏw-lid'-zom-ahee;* mid. voice from *833;* to *pass the night* (prop. in the open air):—abide {1x}, lodge {1x}.

This word means "to lodge," originally "to lodge in the *aule*, or courtyard" and is said of shepherds and flocks; hence, **(1)** to pass the night in the open air, as did the Lord, Lk 21:37; and **(2)** "to lodge in a house," [in the courtyard?] as of His visit to Bethany, Mt 21:17. See: BAGD—121c; THAYER—84b.

836. αὐλός {1x} **aulŏs**, *ŏw-los';* from the same as *109;* a *flute* (as blown):—a pipe {1x}.

This word means "a flute" and occurs in 1 Cor 14:7. Syn.: 832, 834. See: BAGD—121c; THAYER—84c.

837. αὐξάνω {22x} **auxanō**, *ŏwx-an'-o;* a prol. form of a primary verb; to *grow* ("*wax*"), i.e. *enlarge* (lit. or fig., act. or pass.):—grow {12x}, increase {7x}, give the increase {2x}, grow up {1x}.

This word means "to grow or increase" of the growth of that which lives, naturally or spiritually, and is used transitively, signifying to make to increase, said **(1)** of giving the increase, 1 Cor 3:6, 7; 2 Cor 9:10, the effect of the work of God, according to the analogy of His operations in nature; **(2)** "to grow, become greater" e.g. of plants and fruit, Mt 6:28; **(3)** used in the passive voice in Mt 13:32 and Mk 4:8, "increase"; **(4)** in the active in Lk 12:27; 13:19; **(4a)** of the body, Lk 1:80; 2:40; **(4b)** of Christ, Jn 3:30, "increase"; **(4c)** of the work of the gospel of God, Acts 6:7, "increased"; 12:24; 19:20; **(4d)** of people, Acts 7:17; **(4e)** of faith, 2 Cor 10:15 (passive voice, "is increased"); **(4f)** of believers individually, Eph 4:15; Col 1:6; 1 Pet 2:2; 2 Pet 3:18; **(4g)** of the church, Col 2:19; **(4h)** of churches, Eph 2:21. See: TDNT—8:517,*; BAGD—121c; THAYER—84c.

838. αὔξησις {2x} **auxēsis**, *ŏwx'-ay-sis;* from *837; growth:*—increase {2x}.

This word expresses growth in the "body of Christ", the church, Eph 4:16, Col 2:9. See: BAGD—122a; THAYER—84d.

839. αὔριον {15x} **auriŏn**, *ŏw'-ree-on;* from a der. of the same as *109* (mean. a *breeze*, i.e. the morning *air*); prop. *fresh*, i.e. (adv. with ellipsis of *2250*) *to-morrow:*—tomorrow {9x}, morrow {5x}, next day {1x}.

Aurion is an adverb denoting "tomorrow," is used **(1)** with this meaning in Mt 6:30; Lk 12:28; 13:32, 33; Acts 23:15, 20; 25:22; 1 Cor 15:32; Jas 4:13, **(2)** with the word *hemera*, "day," understood and translated as a noun, "(the) morrow," Mt 6:34 [twice]; Lk 10:35; Acts 4:3 "next day"; 4:5; Jas 4:14. See: BAGD—122a; THAYER—84d.

840. αὐστηρός {2x} **austērŏs**, *ŏw-stay-ros';* from a (presumed) der. of the same as *109* (mean. *blown*); *rough* (prop. as a *gale*), i.e. (fig.) *severe:*—austere {2x}.

Austeros means to dry up [Eng., "austere"] and primarily denotes stringent to the taste, like new wine not matured by age, unripe fruit; hence, harsh, severe, Lk 19:21–22. Syn.: Synonymous with *austeros*, but to be distinguished from it, is *skleros* (4642 from *skello*, "to be dry"). It was applied to that which lacks moisture, and so is rough and disageeable to the touch, and hence came to denote "harsh, stern, hard." It is used by Mt 25:24 to describe the unprofitable servant's remark concerning his master. *Austeros* (*840*) is derived from a word having to do with the taste, *skleros* "with the touch." *Austeros* is not necessarily a term of reproach, whereas *skleros* is always so, and indicates a harsh, even inhuman character. *Austeros* is "rather the exaggeration of a virtue pushed too far, than an absolute vice." *Skleros*

is used of the character of a man, Mt 25:24; of a saying, Jn 6:60; of the difficulty and pain of kicking against the ox-goads, Acts 9:5; 26:14; of rough winds, Jas 3:4 and of harsh speeches, Jude 15. See: BAGD—122b; THAYER—84d.

841. αὐτάρκεια {2x} **autarkeia,** *ŏw-tar'-ki-ah;* from *842; self-satisfaction,* i.e. (abstr.) *contentedness,* or (concr.) a *competence:*—contentment {1x}, sufficiency {1x}.

Autarkeia, as a noun, means **(1)** "contentment, satisfaction with what one has": "But godliness with contentment is great gain" (1 Ti 6:6); or **(2)** "sufficiency": "And God is able to make all grace abound toward you; that ye, always having all sufficiency in all things, may abound to every good work" (2 Cor 9:8). Syn.: 714, 842, 2425, 4909. See: TDNT—1:466, 78; BAGD—122b; THAYER—84d.

842. αὐτάρκης {1x} **autarkēs,** *ŏw-tar'-kace;* from *846* and *714; self-complacent,* i.e. *contented:*—content {1x}.

Autarkes, as an adjective, means "self-sufficient, adequate, needing no assistance"; hence, "content": "Not that I speak in respect of want: for I have learned, in whatsoever state I am, therewith to be content" (Phil 4:11). Syn.: 714, 841, 2425, 4909. See: TDNT—1:466, 78; BAGD—122b; THAYER—85a.

843. αὐτοκατάκριτος {1x} **autŏkatakritŏs,** *ŏw-tok-at-ak'-ree-tos;* from *846* and a der. or *2632; self-condemned:*—condemned of self {1x}.

Autokatakritos, as an adjective, means "self-condemned" i.e., on account of doing himself what he condemns in others: "Knowing that he that is such is subverted, and sinneth, being condemned of himself" (Titus 3:11). Syn.: 176, 2607, 2613, 2631, 2632, 2633, 2917, 2919, 2920. See: TDNT—3:952, 469; BAGD—122c; THAYER—85a.

844. αὐτόματος {2x} **autŏmatŏs,** *ŏw-tom'-at-os;* from *846* and the same as *3155; self-moved; moved by one's own impulse* ["automatic"], i.e. *spontaneous:*—of (one's) self {1x}, of (one's) own accord {1x}.

(1) This word comes from "self," and a root *ma—,* signifying "desire" and denotes of oneself, moved by one's own impulse. **(2)** It occurs in **(2a)** Mk 4:28, of the power of the earth to produce plants and fruits of itself; **(2b)** Acts 12:10, of the door which opened of its own accord. Syn.: 4861. See: BAGD—122c; THAYER—85a.

845. αὐτόπτης {1x} **autŏptēs,** *ŏw-top'-tace;* from *846* and *3700; self-seeing,* i.e. an *eyewitness:*—eye-witness {1x}.

This word signifies "seeing with one's own

eyes," Lk 1:2. See: TDNT—5:373, 706; BAGD—122c; THAYER—85a.

846. αὐτός {5118x} **autŏs,** *av-rŏs';* αὖ **au** [perh. akin to the base of *109* through the idea of a *baffling* wind] (*backward*); the refl. pron. *self,* used (alone or in the comp. *1438*) of the third pers., and (with the proper pers. pron.) of the other persons:—him {1947x}, them {1148x}, her {195x}, it {152x}, not tr. {36x}, misc. {1676x} = itself, one, the other, (mine) own, said, ([self-], the) same, ([him-, my-, thy-]) self, [your-] selves, she, that, their (-s), themselves, there [-at, -by, -in, -into, -of, -on, -with], they, (these) things, this (man), those, together, very, which. See: BAGD—122c; THAYER—85b. comp. *848.*

847. αὐτοῦ {4x} **autŏu,** *ŏw-too';* gen. (i.e. possessive) of *846,* used as an adv. of location; prop. belonging to the *same* spot, i.e. *in this* (or *that*) *place:*—there {3x}, here {1x}.

This word is the genitive case of *autos,* "self," and signifies **(1)** "here" in Mt 26:36 and **(2)** "there" in Acts 15:34; 18:19; 21:4. See: BAGD—124a; THAYER—87b.

848. αὐτοῦ {5x} **hautŏu,** *how-too';* contr. for *1438; self* (in some oblique case or refl. relation):—himself {3x}, themself {1x}, them {1x}. See: BAGD—212c; THAYER—87b.

849. αὐτόχειρ {1x} **autŏchĕir,** *ŏw-tokh'-ire;* from *846* and *5495; self-handed,* i.e. doing *personally:*—with . . . own hands {1x}.

Autocheir is a noun and is used in the plural in Acts 27:19, "with their own hands." See: BAGD—124a; THAYER—87d.

850. αὐχμηρός {1x} **auchmĕrŏs,** *owkh-may-ros';* αὐχμός **auchmŏs** [prob. from a base akin to that of *109*] (*dust,* as *dried* by wind); prop. *dirty,* i.e. (by impl.) *obscure:*—dark {1x}.

Auchmeros means dry, murky, dark, squalid (2 Pet 1:19). Syn.: 2217, 4652, 4653, 4654, 4655, 4656.

See: BAGD—124b; THAYER—87d.

851. ἀφαιρέω {10x} **aphairĕō,** *af-ahee-reh'-o;* from *575* and *138; to remove* (lit. or fig.):—cut off {2x}, smite off {1x}, take away {7x}.

This word means "to take away, remove," is translated **(1)** "cut off" in Mk 14:47; and Lk 22:50; **(2)** "smote off" in Mt 26:51; and **(3)** "take away" in Lk. 1:25; 10:42; 16:3; Rom 11:27; Heb 10:4; Rev 22:19 (twice). See: BAGD—124b; THAYER—87d.

852. ἀφανής {1x} **aphanēs,** *af-an-ace';* from *1* (as a neg. particle) and *5316;*

non-apparent, hidden, unseen:—that is not manifest {1x}.

This word denotes "unseen, hidden," Heb 4:13, "not manifest." See: BAGD—124c; THAYER—88a.

853. ἀφανίζω {5x} **aphanizō**, *af-an-id'-zo;* from *852;* to *render unappar- ent,* i.e. (act.) *consume (becloud),* or (pass.) *dis- appear (be destroyed):*—corrupt {2x}, disfigure {1x}, perish {1x}, vanish away {1x}.

This word means lit., "to cause to disappear, put out of sight," came to mean "to do away with" and is **(1)** said of the destructive work of moth and rust, to deprive of lustre, render unsightly, corrupt, Mt 6:19–20. It is also ren- dered **(2)** "perish" in Acts 13:41; **(3)** "disfigure" in Mt 6:16; and **(4)** "vanish away" in Jas 4:14. See: BAGD—124c; THAYER—88a.

854. ἀφανισμός {1x} **aphanismŏs**, *af-an-is- mos';* from *853;* disappear- ance, i.e. (fig.) *abrogation:*—vanish away {1x}.

This word means "to cause to appear" and in the negative [*a*, negative, *phaino*] to "vanish away" and occurs in Heb 8:13; the word is sug- gestive of abolition. See: BAGD—124d; THAYER—88a.

855. ἄφαντος {1x} **aphantŏs**, *af'-an-tŏs;* from *1* (as a neg. particle) and a der. of *5316; non-manifested,* i.e. *invisible:*—van- ished out of sight + 575 {1x}.

This word means lit., "to cause to disappear, put out of sight," came to mean "to do away with" [*a*, negative, *phaino*, "to cause to ap- pear"], said of the destructive work of moth and rust, Mt 6:19–20; the corruption being complete. See: BAGD—124d; THAYER—88a.

856. ἀφεδρών {2x} **aphĕdrōn**, *af-ed-rone';* from a compound of *575* and the base of *1476;* a place of *sitting apart,* i.e. a *privy:*—draught {2x}.

This word means "a latrine, a sink, drain," a place where the human waste discharges are dumped, a privy, sink, toilet and is found in Mt 15:17 and Mk 7:19. See: BAGD—124d; THAYER—88b.

857. ἀφειδία {1x} **aphĕidia**, *af-i-dee'-ah;* from a compound of *1* (as a neg. par- ticle) and *5339; unsparingness,* i.e. *austerity (ascetism):*—neglecting {1x}.

Apheidia stresses unsparing treatment, sever- ity, ascetic discipline (Col 2:23). See: BAGD— 124d; THAYER—88b.

858. ἀφελότης {1x} **aphĕlŏtēs**, *af-el-ot'-ace;* from a compound of *1* (as a neg. particle) and φέλλος **phĕllŏs** (in the sense of a *stone* as *stubbing* the foot); *smoothness,* i.e. (fig.) *simplicity:*—singleness {1x}.

This word denotes "simplicity," Acts 2:46, "singleness, unworldly simplicity"; the idea here is that of an unalloyed benevolence ex- pressed in act. See: BAGD—124d; THAYER— 88b.

859. ἄφεσις {17x} **aphĕsis**, *af'-es-is;* from *863; freedom;* (fig.) *pardon:*—deliv- erance {1x}, forgiveness {6x}, liberty {1x}, re- mission {9x}.

(1) *Aphesis* denotes a release, from bondage, imprisonment, liberation from captivity and remission of debt. **(2)** *Aphesis,* as a noun, de- notes "a release, from bondage, imprisonment" and in Lk 4:18 it is used of "liberation" from captivity: "The Spirit of the Lord is upon me, because He hath anointed me to preach the gospel to the poor; He hath sent me to heal the brokenhearted, to preach deliverance to the captives, and recovering of sight to the blind, to set at liberty (*aphesis*) them that are bruised." **(3)** It also means forgiveness or pardon, of sins (letting them go as if they had never been com- mitted), remission of the penalty, Mt 26:28; Eph 1:7. Syn.: 325, 525, 629, 591, 1325, 1560, 1659, 1807, 1929, 3086, 3860, 4506, 5483. Syn.: 3929. See: TDNT—1:509, 88; BAGD—125a; THAYER—88b.

860. ἀφή {2x} **haphē**, *haf-ay';* from *680;* prob. a *ligament* (as *fastening*):—joint {2x}.

This word means "a ligature, joint, a place where a ligament joins muscle to bone," and occurs in Eph 4:16 and Col 2:19. See: BAGD— 125a; THAYER—88c.

861. ἀφθαρσία {8x} **aphtharsia**, *af-thar-see'- ah;* from *862; incorruptibil- ity;* gen. *unending existence;* (fig.) *genuine- ness:*—immortality {2x}, incorruption {4x}, sincerity {2x}.

This word means "incorruption," and is used **(1)** of the resurrection body, 1 Cor 15:42, 50, 53–54; **(2)** of a condition associated with glory and honor and life, including perhaps a moral significance, immortality, Rom 2:7; 2 Ti 1:10; **(3)** of love to Christ, that which is sincere and undiminishing, "sincerity" Eph 6:24 and Titus 2:7. See: TDNT—9:93, 1259; BAGD—125b; THAYER—88c.

862. ἄφθαρτος {7x} **aphthartŏs**, *af'-thar-tos;* from *1* (as a neg. particle) and a der. of *5351; undecaying* (in essence or continuance):—not corruptible {1x}, incor- ruptible {4x}, uncorruptible {1x}, immortal {1x}.

This word means "not liable to corruption or decay, incorruptible" and is used of **(1)** God, Rom 1:23; 1 Ti 1:17 "immortal"; **(2)** the raised dead, 1 Cor 15:52; **(3)** rewards given to the

Greek

saints hereafter, metaphorically described as a "crown," 1 Cor 9:25; **(4)** the eternal inheritance of the saints, 1 Pet 1:4; **(5)** the Word of God, as "incorruptible" seed, 1 Pet 1:23; **(6)** a meek and quiet spirit, metaphorically spoken of as "incorruptible" apparel, 1 Pet 3:4. See: TDNT— 9:93, 1259; BAGD—125b; THAYER—88c.

863. ἀφίημι {146x} **aphiēmi**, *af-ee'-ay-mee;* from *575* and ἵημι **hiēmi** (to *send;* an intens. form of εἶμι **ĕimi**, to *go*); to *send forth*, in various applications (as follow):—leave {52x}, forgive {47x}, suffer {14x}, let {8x}, forsake {6x}, let alone {6x}, misc. {13x} = cry, lay aside, omit, put (send) away, remit, yield up.

This word means **(1)** to send away: **(1a)** to bid going away or depart, **(1a1)** a crowd (Mt 13:36), **(1a2)** of a husband divorcing his wife (1 Cor 7:11–13); **(1b)** to send forth, yield up, to expire (Mt 27:50; Mk 15:37); **(1c)** to let go, let alone, let be: **(1c1)** to disregard (Mt 15:14), **(1c2)** to leave, not to discuss now, (a topic), used of teachers, writers and speakers (Heb 6:1), **(1c3)** to omit, neglect (Mt 23:23); **(1d)** to let go, give up a debt, forgive, to remit (Jn 20:23); **(1e)** to give up, keep no longer (Rev 2:4); **(2)** to permit, allow, not to hinder, to give up a thing to a person (Mk 10:14; Lk 18:16; Jn 11:34); **(3)** to leave, go way from one: **(3a)** in order to go to another place (Mt 22:22; 26:44), **(3b)** to depart from any one (Mt 4:11), **(3c)** to depart from one and leave him to himself so that all mutual claims are abandoned (Mt 4:22; Mk 1:20), **(3d)** to desert wrongfully (Mt 26:56; Mk 14:50); **(3e)** to go away leaving something behind (Mt 5:24; Jn 4:28); **(3f)** to leave one by not taking him as a companion (Mt 24:40; Lk 17:34); **(3g)** to leave one dying, leave behind one (Mt 22:25); **(3h)** to leave so that what is left may remain, leave remaining (Mt 24:2; Mk 13:2); **(3i)** abandon, leave destitute (Acts 14: 17). See: TDNT—1:509, 88; BAGD—125c; THAYER— 88d.

864. ἀφικνέομαι {1x} **aphiknĕŏmai**, *af-ik-neh'-om-ahee;* from *575* and the base of *2425;* to *go* (i.e. *spread*) *forth* (by rumor):—come abroad {1x}.

This word means "to arrive at a place," is used in Rom 16:19, "come abroad" (of the obedience of the saints): "For your obedience is come abroad unto all men. I am glad therefore on your behalf: but yet I would have you wise unto that which is good, and simple concerning evil." See: BAGD—126c; THAYER—89c.

865. ἀφιλάγαθος {1x} **aphilagathŏs**, *af-il-ag'-ath-os;* from *1* (as a neg. particle) and *5358; hostile to virtue:*—despiser of those that are good {1x}.

This word means opposed to goodness and good men, 2 Ti 3:3. See: TDNT—1:18, 3; BAGD— 126c; THAYER—89c.

866. ἀφιλάργυρος {2x} **aphilargurŏs**, *af-il-ar'-goo-ros;* from *1* (as a neg. particle) and *5366; unavaricious; free from the love of money:*—without covetousness {1x}, not covetous.

This word means "without covetousness, free from the love of money" in Heb 13:5 and 1 Ti 3:3. See: BAGD—126c; THAYER—89c.

867. ἄφιξις {1x} **aphixis**, *af'-ix-is;* from *864;* prop. *arrival*, i.e. (by impl.) *departure:*—departing {1x}.

Etymologically, this word means to come far enough, reach; the departure being regarded in relation to the end in view (Acts 20:29). See: BAGD—126d; THAYER—89d.

868. ἀφίστημι {15x} **aphistēmi**, *af-is'-tay-mee;* from *575* and *2476;* to *remove*, i.e. (act.) *instigate* to revolt; usually (refl.) to *desist, desert*, etc.:—depart {10x}, draw away {1x}, fall away {1x}, away {1x}, refrain {1x}, withdraw self {1x}.

This word means in the active voice, **(1)** used transitively, signifies "to cause to depart, to cause to revolt," Acts 5:37; **(2)** used intransitively, "to stand off, or aloof, or to depart from anyone," Lk 4:13; 13:27; Acts 5:38 "refrain from"; 12:10; 15:38; 19:9; 22:29; 2 Cor 12:8; **(3)** metaphorically, "to fall away," 2 Ti 2:19; **(3a)** in the middle voice, "to withdraw or absent oneself from," Lk 2:37; **(3b)** to "apostatize," Lk 8:13; 1 Tim 4:1; Heb 3:12. **(4)** *Aphistem* also means "depart": "And she was a widow of about fourscore and four years, which departed not from the temple, but served God with fastings and prayers night and day" (Lk 2:37). Syn.: 307, 385, 392, 501, 502, 645, 1096, 1670, 1448, 1828, 2020, 2464, 4317, 4334, 4358, 4685, 4951, 5288, 5289. See: TDNT—1:512, 88; BAGD—126d; THAYER—89d.

869. ἄφνω {3x} **aphnō**, *af'-no;* adv. from *852* (contr.); *unawares*, i.e. *unexpectedly:*—suddenly {3x}.

Aphno, as an adverb, means "suddenly": "And suddenly there came a sound from heaven as of a rushing mighty wind, and it filled all the house where they were sitting" (Acts 2:2; cf. 16:26; 28:6). Syn.: 160, 1810, 1819. See: BAGD—127a; THAYER—89d.

870. ἀφόβως {4x} **aphŏbōs**, *af-ob'-oce;* adv. from a compound of *1* (as a neg. particle) and *5401; fearlessly:*—without fear {4x}.

This word means "without fear" and is

found in Lk 1:74; 1 Co 16:10; Phil 1:14; Jude 12. See: BAGD—127a; THAYER—89d.

871. ἀφομοιόω {1x} **aphŏmŏiŏō**, *af-om-oy-ŏ'-o;* from *575* and *3666;* to *assimilate* closely:—make like {1x}.

This word means "to make like" and is used in Heb 7:3, of Melchizedek as "made like" the Son of God, i.e., in the facts related and withheld in the Genesis record. See: TDNT—5:198, 684; BAGD—127b; THAYER—89d.

872. ἀφοράω {2x} **aphŏraō**, *af-or-ah'-o;* from *575* and *3708;* to *consider* attentively:—see {1x}, look {1x}.

Aphorao, as a verb, means "to look away from one thing so as to see another," "to concentrate the gaze upon": "Looking (*aphorao*) unto Jesus the author and finisher of our faith" (Heb 12:2; cf. Phil 2:23). Syn.: 308, 352, 578, 816, 991, 1689, 1896, 1914, 1980, 1983, 2300, 2334, 3706, 3708, 3879, 4017, 4648. See: BAGD—127b; THAYER—90a.

873. ἀφορίζω {10x} **aphŏrizō**, *af-or-id'-zo;* from *575* and *3724;* to *set off* by boundary, i.e. (fig.) *limit, exclude, appoint,* etc.:—divide {1x}, separate {8x}, sever {1x}.

This word means lit., "to mark off by boundaries or limits" [*apo,* "from," *horizo,* "to determine, mark out"] and denotes **(1)** "to separate", Mt 25:32 (first occurrence); Lk 6:22; Acts 13:2; 19:9; Rom 1:1; 2 Cor 6:17; Gal 1:15; 2:12; **(2)** "to sever", Mt 13:49; and **(3)** "to divide", Mt 25:32 (second occurrence). See: TDNT—5:454, 728; BAGD—127b; THAYER—90a.

874. ἀφορμή {7x} **aphŏrmē**, *af-or-may';* from a compound of *575* and *3729;* a *starting*-point, i.e. (fig.) an *opportunity:*—occasion {7x}.

Aphorme properly is a starting point and was used to denote a base of operations in war. It is used of **(1)** the Law providing sin with a base of operations for its attack upon the soul (Rom 7:8, 11); **(2)** the irreproachable conduct of the Apostle providing his friends with a base of operations against his detractors (2 Cor 5:12); **(3)** by refusing temporal support at Corinth he deprived these detractors of their base of operations against him (2 Cor 11:12); **(4)** Christian freedom is not to provide a base of operations for the flesh (Gal 5:13); **(5)** unguarded behavior on the part of young widows would provide Satan with a base of operations against the faith (1 Ti 5:14). See: TDNT—5:472, 730; BAGD—127c; THAYER—90b.

875. ἀφρίζω {2x} **aphrizō**, *af-rid'-zo;* from *876;* to *froth* at the mouth (in epilepsy):—foam {2x}.

This word denotes "to foam at the mouth", Mk 9:18, 20. Syn.: 1890. See: BAGD—127c; THAYER—90b.

876. ἀφρός {1x} **aphrŏs**, *af-ros';* appar. a primary word; *froth,* i.e. *slaver:*—the one foameth again + *3326* {1x}.

This word means "foam," and occurs in Lk 9:39, where it is used with the preposition *meta,* "with," lit., "(teareth him) with (accompanied by) foam." See: BAGD—127d; THAYER—90b.

877. ἀφροσύνη {4x} **aphrŏsunē**, *af-ros-oo'-nay;* from *878; senselessness,* i.e. (euphem.) *egotism;* (mor.) *recklessness:*—foolishly + 1722 {2x}, foolishness {1x}, folly {1x}.

This word means "senselessness," is translated **(1)** "foolishness" in Mk 7:22; **(2)** "folly" in 2 Cor 11:1; and **(3)** "foolishly" in 2 Cor 11:17, 21. See: TDNT—9:220, 1277; BAGD—127d; THAYER—90b.

878. ἄφρων {11x} **aphrōn**, *af'-rone;* from *1* (as a neg. particle) and *5424;* prop. *mindless,* i.e. *stupid,* (by impl.) *ignorant,* (spec.) *egotistic,* (practically) *rash,* or (mor.) *unbelieving:*—fool {8x}, foolish {2x}, unwise {1x}.

Aphron signifies without reason, want of mental sanity and sobriety, a reckless and inconsiderate habit of mind; the lack of common sense perception of the reality of things natural and spiritual or the imprudent ordering of one's life in regard to salvation. It is translated **(1)** "foolish" or "foolish ones" in Rom 2:20; 1 Cor 15:36; 2 Cor 11:16 (twice); 19 (contrasted with *phronimos,* "prudent"); 12:6, 11; 1 Pet 2:15; **(2)** "fool/fools" in Lk 11:40; 12:20; and **(3)** "unwise" in Eph 5:17. Syn.: 453, 801, 877, 3472, 3474. See: TDNT—9:220, 1277; BAGD—127d; THAYER—90b.

879. ἀφυπνόω {1x} **aphupnŏō**, *af-oop-nŏ'-o;* from a compound of *575* and *5258;* prop. to *become awake,* i.e. (by impl.) to *drop* (off) in slumber:—fall asleep {1x}.

This word means "to fall asleep" and is used of natural "sleep," Lk 8:23, of the Lord's falling "asleep" in the boat on the lake of Galilee. See: TDNT—8:545, 1233; BAGD—127d; THAYER—90c.

880. ἄφωνος {4x} **aphōnŏs**, *af'-o-nos;* from *1* (as a neg. particle) and *5456; voiceless,* i.e. *mute* (by nature or choice); fig. *unmeaning:*—dumb {3x}, without signification {1x}.

Aphonos, as an adjective, literally means "voiceless, or soundless" [*a,* negative, and *phone,* "a sound"], and has reference **(1)** to voice: "The place of the scripture which He

read was this, He was led as a sheep to the slaughter; and like a lamb dumb before his shearer, so opened he not his mouth" (Acts 8:32; cf. 1 Cor 12:2; 2 Pet 2:16). **(2)** In 1 Cor 14:10 it is used metaphorically of the significance of voices or sounds, "without signification": "There are, it may be, so many kinds of voices in the world, and none of them is without signification." Syn.: *Aphonos* (*880*), lit., "voiceless, or soundless" has reference to voice, while *alalos* (*216*) has reference to words. See also: 216, 2974, 4623. See: BAGD—128a; THAYER—90c.

881. **Ἀχάζ** {2x} **Achaz,** *akh-adz';* of Heb. or. [271]; *Achaz,* an Isr.:—*Achaz* {2x}. See: BAGD—128a; THAYER—90c.

882. **Ἀχαΐα** {11x} **Achaïa,** *ach-ah-ee'-ah;* of uncert. der.; *Achaia* (i.e. *Greece*), a country of Europe:—*Achaia* {11x}. See: BAGD—128a; THAYER—90d.

883. **Ἀχαϊκός** {2x} **Achaïkŏs,** *ach-ah-ee-kos';* from *882;* an *Achaïan; Achaicus,* a Chr.:—Achaicus {2x}. See: BAGD—128b; THAYER—90d.

884. **ἀχάριστος** {2x} **acharistŏs,** *ach-ar'-is-tos;* from *1* (as a neg. particle) and a presumed der. of *5483; thankless,* i.e. *ungrateful:*—unthankful {2x}.
    This word denotes "ungrateful, thankless", Lk 6:35; 2 Ti 3:2. See: TDNT—9:372, 1298; BAGD—128b; THAYER—90d.

885. **Ἀχείμ** {2x} **Achĕim** or Ἀχίμ **Achim,** *akh-ime';* prob. of Heb. or. [comp. 3137]; *Achim,* an Isr.:—*Achim* {2x}. See: BAGD—128b; THAYER—90d.

886. **ἀχειροποίητος** {3x} **achĕirŏpŏiētŏs,** *akh-i-rop-oy'-ay-tos;* from *1* (as a neg. particle) and *5499; unmanufactured,* i.e. *inartificial:*—made without hands {2x}, not made with hands {1x}.
    This word means "not made by hands" and is said **(1)** of an earthly temple, Mk 14:58; **(2)** of the resurrection body of believers, metaphorically as a house, 2 Cor 5:1; **(3)** metaphorically, of spiritual circumcision, Col 2:11. See: TDNT—9:436, 1309; BAGD—128b; THAYER—90d.

887. **ἀχλύς** {1x} **achlus,** *akh-looce';* of uncert. der.; *dimness* of sight, i.e. (prob.) a *cataract:*—mist {1x}.
    This word means "a mist," especially a dimness of the eyes, is used in Acts 13:11. "In the single place of its NT use it attests the accuracy in the selection of words, and not least of medical words, which 'the beloved physician' so often displays. For him it expresses the mist of darkness . . . which fell on the sorcerer Elymas,

being the outward and visible sign of the inward spiritual darkness which would be his portion for a while in punishment for his resistance to the truth." See: BAGD—128b; THAYER—90d.

888. **ἀχρεῖος** {2x} **achrĕiŏs,** *akh-ri'-os;* from *1* (as a neg. particle) and a der. of *5534* [comp. *5532*]; *useless,* i.e. (euphem.) *unmeritorious:*—unprofitable {2x}.
    Achreios, as an adjective, means "useless" [5532 - *chreia,* "use"], "unprofitable": "And cast ye the unprofitable servant into outer darkness: there shall be weeping and gnashing of teeth" (Mt 25:30; cf. Lk 17:10). Syn.: *Achreios,* positively hurtful, is more distinctly negative than *achrestos* (*890*). See also: 255, 512, 889, 890. See: BAGD—128c; THAYER—91a.

889. **ἀχρειόω** {1x} **achrĕiŏō,** *akh-ri-ŏ'-o;* from *888;* to *render useless,* i.e. *spoil:*—become unprofitable {1x}.
    Achreoo, or *achreioo,* as a verb, means "to make useless": "They are all gone out of the way, they are together become unprofitable; there is none that doeth good, no, not one" (Rom 3:12, in the passive voice). Syn.: 255, 512, 888, 890. See: BAGD—128c; THAYER—91a.

890. **ἄχρηστος** {1x} **achrēstŏs,** *akh'-race-tos;* from *1* (as a neg. particle) and *5543; inefficient,* i.e. (by impl.) *detrimental:*—unprofitable {1x}.
    Achrestos, as an adjective, means "unprofitable, unserviceable" (5543 - *chrestos,* "serviceable"), is said of Onesimus, antithetically to (2173 - *euchrestos,* "profitable"): "Which in time past was to thee unprofitable (*achrestos*), but now profitable (*euchrestos*) to thee and to me" (Philem 11). Syn.: *Achreios* (*888*), positively hurtful, is more distinctly negative than *achrestos.* See also: 255, 512, 888, 889. See: BAGD—128c; THAYER—91a.

891. **ἄχρι** {49x} **achri,** *akh'-ree;* or ἄχρις **achris,** *akh'-rece;* akin to *206* (through the idea of a *terminus*); (of time) *until* or (of place) *up to:*—until {14x}, unto {13x}, till {3x}, till + 3739 + 302 {3x}, until + 3739 {2x}, while + 3739 {2x}, even to {2x}, misc. {7x} = as far as, for, in, into. See: BAGD—128d; THAYER—91b. comp. *3360.*

892. **ἄχυρον** {2x} **achurŏn,** *akh'-oo-ron;* perh. remotely from χέω **chĕō** (to *shed* forth); *chaff* (as *diffusive*):—chaff {2x}.
    Chaff is the stalk of the grain from which the kernels have been beaten out, or the straw broken up by a threshing machine (Mt 3:12; Lk 3:17). See: BAGD—129a; THAYER—91d.

893. **ἀψευδής** {1x} **apsĕudēs,** *aps-yoo-dace';* from *1* (as a neg. particle) and

5579; veracious; free from falsehood:—that cannot lie {1x}.

This word denotes "free from falsehood" truthful, Titus 1:2, of God, "who cannot lie." See: TDNT—9:594, 1339; BAGD—129c; THAYER—91d.

894. **ἄψινθος** {2x} **apsinthŏs,** *ap'-sin-thos;* of uncert. der.; *wormwood* (as a type of *bitterness,* i.e. [fig.] *calamity*):—wormwood {2x}.

This word means a plant both bitter and deleterious, and growing in desolate places, figuratively suggestive of "calamity" (Lam 3:15) and injustice (Amos 5:7), and is used in Rev 8:11 (twice; in the 1st part as a proper name). See: BAGD—129c; THAYER—91d.

895. **ἄψυχος** {1x} **apsuchŏs,** *ap'-soo-khos;* from *1* (as a neg. particle) and *5590; lifeless,* i.e. *inanimate* (mechanical):—without life {1x}.

This word means denotes "lifeless inanimate" "without life": "And even things without life giving sound, whether pipe or harp, except they give a distinction in the sounds, how shall it be known what is piped or harped?"(1 Cor 14:7). See: BAGD—129c; THAYER—91d.

B

896. **Βάαλ** {1x} **Baal,** *bah'-al;* of Heb. or. [1168]; *Baal,* a Phœnician deity (used as a symbol of idolatry):—*Baal* {1x}. See: BAGD—129b; THAYER—92a.

897. **Βαβυλών** {12x} **Babulōn,** *bab-oo-lone';* of Heb. or. [894]; *Babylon,* the capital of Chaldæa (lit. or fig. [as a type of tyranny]):—*Babylon* {12x}. See: TDNT—1:514, 89; BAGD—129b; THAYER—92b.

898. **βαθμός** {1x} **bathmŏs,** *bath-mos';* from the same as *899;* a *step,* i.e. (fig.) *grade* (of dignity):—degree {1x}.

This word means denotes "a step," primarily of a threshold or stair, and figuratively, means "a standing, a stage in a career, position, degree," 1 Ti 3:13, of faithful deacons. See: BAGD—130a; THAYER—92d.

899. **βάθος** {9x} **bathŏs,** *bath'-os;* from the same as *901; profundity,* i.e. (by impl.) *extent;* (fig.) *mystery:*—depth {5x}, deep {1x}, deep + 2596 {1x}, deepness {1x}, deep thing {1x}.

Bathos is used **(1)** naturally, in Mt 13:5: "Some fell upon stony places, where they had not much earth: and forthwith they sprung up, because they had no deepness of earth"; (cf. Mk 4:5; Lk 5:4, of "deep" water; Rom 8:39 contrasted with "height"); **(2)** metaphorically, in

(2a) Rom 11:33, of God's wisdom and knowledge; in **(2b)** 1 Cor 2:10, of God's counsels; in **(3)** Eph 3:18 of the dimensions of the sphere of the activities of God's counsels, and of the love of Christ which occupies that sphere; in **(4)** 2 Cor 8:2, of "deep" poverty; and in **(5)** Rev 2:24 of the depths of Satan. Syn.: 1037. See: TDNT—1:517, 89; BAGD—130a; THAYER—92d.

900. **βαθύνω** {1x} **bathunō,** *bath-oo'-no;* from *901;* to *deepen:*—dig deep + 4626 {1x}.

This word means "to deepen, make deep," is used in Lk 6:48 ("digged deep"). The original has two separate verbs, *skapto,* "to dig," and *bathuno;* therefore, "digged and went deep." See: BAGD—130b; THAYER—92d.

901. **βαθύς** {3x} **bathus,** *bath-oos';* from the base of *939; profound* (as *going down*), lit. or fig.:—deep {2x}, very early in the morning + 3722 {1x}.

Bathus is said **(1)** in Jn 4:11, of a deep well; **(2)** in Acts 20:9, of deep sleep; and **(3)** in Lk 24:1 of very early [deep in darkness, the early hours of] the morning. See: BAGD—130b; THAYER—93a.

902. **βαΐον** {1x} **baïŏn,** *bah-ee'-on;* a diminutive of a der. prob. of the base of *939;* a palm *twig* (as *going* out far):—branch {1x}.

This word means "a branch of the palm tree," Jn 12:13. See: BAGD—130c; THAYER—93a.

903. **Βαλαάμ** {3x} **Balaam,** *bal-ah-am';* of Heb. or. [1109]; *Balaam,* a Mesopotamian (symbolic of a false teacher):—*Balaam* {3x}. See: TDNT—1:524, 91; BAGD—130c; THAYER—93a.

904. **Βαλάκ** {1x} **Balak,** *bal-ak';* of Heb. or. [1111]; *Balak,* a Moabite:—*Balac* {1x}. See: BAGD—130c; THAYER—93b.

905. **βαλάντιον** {4x} **balantiŏn,** *bal-an'-tee-on;* prob. remotely from *906* (as a *depository*); a *pouch* (for money):—purse {3x}, bag {1x}.

This word means "a money-box or purse" and is found in Luke's Gospel, four times, 10:4; 12:33 ("bag"); 22:35-36. See: TDNT—1:525, 91; BAGD—130d; THAYER—93b.

906. **βάλλω** {125x} **ballō,** *bal'-lo;* a primary verb; to *throw* (in various applications, more or less violent or intense):—cast {86x}, put {13x}, thrust {5x}, cast out {4x}, lay {3x}, lie {2x}, misc. {12x} = arise, ✗ dung, pour, send, strike, throw (down).

This word means **(1)** with force and effort:

(1a) to smite someone with slaps, to buffet (Mk 14:65); and (1b) to apprehend someone (Jn 7:44); (2) without force and effort: (2a) to throw or let go of a thing without caring where it falls: to scatter, to throw, cast into (Mt 27:35; Mk 15:24); (2b) to give over to one's care uncertain about the result (Mt 25:27); (2c) to pour (Mt 19:17; Mk 2:22: Lk 5:37). See: TDNT—1:526, 91; BAGD—130d; THAYER—93b. comp. 4496.

907. βαπτίζω {80x} **baptizō**, bap-tid'-zo; from a der. of 911; to make overwhelmed (i.e. fully wet); used only (in the N.T.) of ceremonial ablution, espec. (tech.) of the ordinance of Chr. baptism:—baptize {76x}, wash {2x}, baptist {1x}, baptized + 2258 {1x}.

Baptizo means to baptize and is used of (1) washing oneself (Lk 11:38); (2) the rite performed by John the Baptist who called upon the people to repent that they might receive remission of sins. Those who obeyed came confessing their sins, thus acknowledging their unfitness to be in the Messiah's coming kingdom (Acts 1:5; 11:16; 19:4). (3) Distinct from (2) is the baptism enjoined by Christ (Mt 28:19), a baptism to be undergone by believers, thus witnessing to their identification with Him in death, burial and resurrection (Acts 19:5; 1 Cor 1:13–17). (4) The phrase in Mt 28:19, "baptizing them into the Name" would indicate that the baptized person was closely bound to, or became the property of, the one into whose name he was baptized. (5) In Acts 22:16 it is used in the middle voice, in the command given to Saul of Tarsus, "arise and be baptized," the significance of the middle voice form being "get thyself baptized."

(6) The experience of those who were in the ark at the time of the Flood was a figure or type of the facts of spiritual death, burial, and resurrection, Christian baptism being an antitupon, "a corresponding type," a "like figure," (1 Pet 3:21). (7) Likewise the nation of Israel was figuratively baptized (1 Cor 10:2). (8) The verb is used metaphorically also in two distinct senses: (8a) of baptism by the Holy Spirit, which took place on the Day of Pentecost, showing eternal association with and bound to the Holy Spirit; (8b) of the calamity which would come upon the nation of the Jews, a baptism of the fire of divine judgment for rejection of the will and word of God (Mt 3:11; Lk 3:16). See: TDNT—1:529, 92; BAGD—131c; THAYER—94a.

908. βάπτισμα {22x} **baptisma**, bap'-tis-mah; from 907; baptism (tech. or fig.):—baptism {22x}.

Baptisma means baptism consisting of the processes of immersion, submersion and emergence and is used (1) of John's baptism (2) of Christian baptism; (3) of the overwhelming afflictions and judgments to which the Lord voluntarily submitted on the cross (Lk 12:50); (4) of the sufferings His followers would experience, not of a vicarious character, but in fellowship with the sufferings of their Master (Mk 10:38–39). Syn.: 909, 910. See: TDNT—1:545, 92; BAGD—132c; THAYER—94d.

909. βαπτισμός {4x} **baptismŏs**, bap-tis-mos'; from 907; ablution (cerem. or Chr.):—washing {3x}, baptism {1x}.

Baptismos, as distinct from baptisma (908 - the ordinance), is used (1) of the ceremonial washing of articles (Mk 7:4, 8; Heb 9:10). (2) It is translated "baptisms" in Heb 6:2. Syn.: 908. See: TDNT—1:545, 92; BAGD—132d; THAYER—95a.

910. Βαπτιστής {14x} **Baptistēs**, bap-tis-tace'; from 907; a baptizer, as an epithet of Christ's forerunner:—Baptist {14x}.

This word is used only of John the Baptist, and only in the Synoptics. See: TDNT—1:545, 92; BAGD—132d; THAYER—95b.

911. βάπτω {3x} **baptō**, bap'-to; a primary verb; to overwhelm, i.e. cover wholly with a fluid; in the NT only in a qualified or special sense, i.e. (lit.) to moisten (a part of one's person), or (by impl.) to stain (as with dye):—dip {3x}.

This word means "to immerse, dip" and also signified "to dye," which is suggested in Rev 19:13, of the Lord's garment "dipped (i.e. dyed) in blood." It is elsewhere translated "to dip," Lk 16:24; Jn 13:26. See: TDNT—1:529, 92; BAGD—132d; THAYER—95b.

912. Βαραββᾶς {11x} **Barabbas**, bar-ab-bas'; of Chald. or. [1347 and 5]; son of Abba; Bar-abbas, an Isr.:—Barabbas {11x}. See: BAGD—133a; THAYER—95b.

913. Βαράκ {1x} **Barak**, bar-ak'; of Heb. or. [1301]; Barak, an Isr.:—Barak {1x}. See: BAGD—133a; THAYER—95c.

914. Βαραχίας {1x} **Barachias**, bar-akh-ee'-as; of Heb. or. [1296]; Barachias (i.e. Berechijah), an Isr.:—Barachias {1x}. See: BAGD—133a; THAYER—95c.

915. βάρβαρος {6x} **barbarŏs**, bar'-bar-os; of uncert. der.; a foreigner (i.e. non-Greek):—barbarian {5x}, barbarous {1x}.

Barbaros properly meant (1) "one whose speech is rude, or harsh"; the word is onomatopoeic, indicating in the sound the uncouth character represented by the repeated syllable "bar-bar." (2) Hence it signified one who

speaks a strange or foreign language (1 Cor 14:11). **(3)** It then came to denote any foreigner ignorant of the Greek language and culture. **(4)** After the Persian war it acquired the sense of rudeness and brutality. **(5)** In Acts 28:2, 4, it is used unreproachfully of the inhabitants of Malta, who were of Phoenician origin. **(6)** So in Rom 1:14, where it stands in distinction from Greeks, and in implied contrast to both Greeks and Jews. **(7)** Cf. the contrasts in Col 3:11, where all such distinctions are shown to be null and void in Christ. See: TDNT—1:546, 94; BAGD—133b; THAYER—95c.

916. βαρέω {6x} **barĕō**, *bar-eh′-o; from 926;* to *weigh* down (fig.):—be heavy {3x}, be pressed {1x}, be burdened {1x}, be charged {1x}.

Bareo is used of **(1)** the effects of drowsiness: "And He came and found them asleep again: for their eyes were heavy *(bareo)*" (Mt 26:43; cf. Mk 14:40; Lk 9:32); **(2)** of the believer's present physical state in the body: "For we that are in this tabernacle do groan, being burdened: not for that we would be unclothed, but clothed upon, that mortality might be swallowed up of life" (2 Cor 5:4 "burdened"); **(3)** of persecution: "For we would not, brethren, have you ignorant of our trouble which came to us in Asia, that we were pressed out of measure, above strength, insomuch that we despaired even of life" (2 Cor 1:8 "pressed" out of measure); and **(4)** of a charge upon material resources: "If any man or woman that believeth have widows, let them relieve them, and let not the church be charged; that it may relieve them that are widows indeed" (1 Ti 5:16 "charged"). Syn.: 922, 1912, 2599, 2655. See: TDNT—1:558, 95; BAGD—133c; THAYER—95d.

917. βαρέως {2x} **barĕōs**, *bar-eh′-oce; adv. from 926; heavily, with difficulty* (fig.):— dull {2x}.

This word means "heavily, with difficulty" and is used with *akouo,* "to hear," in Mt 13:15, and Acts 28:27 [from Is 6:10], lit., "to hear heavily, to be dull of hearing." See: BAGD— 133c; THAYER—95d.

918. Βαρθολομαῖος {4x} **Barthŏlŏmaiŏs**, *bar-thol-om-ah′-yos; of* Chald. or. [1247 and 8526]; *son of Tolmai; Bartholomæus,* a Chr. apostle:—Bartholomew {4x}. See: BAGD—133d; THAYER—95d.

919. Βαριησοῦς {1x} **Bariēsŏus**, *bar-ee-ay-sooce′; of* Chald. or. [1247 and 3091]; *son of Jesus* (or *Joshua*); *Bar-jesus,* an Isr.:—Barjesus {1x}. See: BAGD—133d; THAYER—96a.

920. Βαριωνᾶς {1x} **Bariōnas**, *bar-ee-oo-nas′; of* Chald. or. [1247 and 3124]; *son of Jonas* (or *Jonah*); *Bar-jonas,* an Isr.:— Barjona {1x}. See: BAGD—133d; THAYER— 96a.

921. Βαρνάβας {29x} **Barnabas**, *bar-nab′-as; of* Chald. or. [1247 and 5029]; *son of Nabas* (i.e. *prophecy*); *Barnabas,* an Isr.:— Barnabas {29x}. See: BAGD—133d; THAYER— 96a.

922. βάρος {6x} **barŏs**, *bar′-os;* prob. from the same as *939* (through the notion of *going* down; comp. *899*); *weight;* in the N.T. only fig. a *load, abundance, authority:*— burden {4x}, burdensome + 1722 {1x}, weight {1x}.

This word denotes **(1)** "a weight, anything pressing on one physically," Mt 20:12, or **(2)** "that makes a demand on one's resources," whether **(2a)** material, 1 Th 2:6 (to be burdensome), or **(2b)** spiritual, Gal 6:2; Rev 2:24, or **(2c)** religious, Acts 15:28. **(3)** In one place it metaphorically describes the future state of believers as "an eternal weight of glory," 2 Cor 4:17. See: TDNT—1:553, 95; BAGD—133d; THAYER—96a.

923. Βαρσαβᾶς {2x} **Barsabas**, *bar-sab-as′; of* Chald. or. [1247 and prob. 6634]; *son of Sabas* (or *Tsaba*); *Bar-sabas,* the name of two Isr.:—Joseph {1x}, Judas {1x}. See: BAGD—134a; THAYER—96b.

924. Βαρτιμαῖος {1x} **Bartimaiŏs**, *bar-tim-ah′-yos; of* Chald. or. [1247 and 2931]; *son of Timæus* (or the *unclean*); *Bartimæus,* an Isr.:—Bartimaeus {1x}. See: BAGD— 134a; THAYER—96b.

925. βαρύνω {1x} **barunō**, *bar-oo′-no; from 926;* to *burden, weighed down* (fig.):—be overcharged {1x}.

This word means to weigh down, overcharge and is used in Lk 21:34: "And take heed to yourselves, lest at any time your hearts be overcharged *(baruno)* with surfeiting, and drunkenness, and cares of this life, and so that day come upon you unawares." See: BAGD—134b; THAYER—96b.

926. βαρύς {6x} **barus**, *bar-ooce′; from the same as 922; weighty,* i.e. (fig) *burdensome, grave:*—grievous {3x}, heavy {1x}, weighty {1x}, weightier {1x}.

This word **(1)** denotes "heavy, burdensome"; **(2)** it is always used metaphorically in the NT, and is **(3)** translated **(3a)** "heavy" in Mt 23:4, of Pharisaical ordinances; **(3b)** in the comparative degree "weightier," Mt 23:23, of details of the law of God; **(3c)** "grievous," metaphorically **(3c1)** of wolves, in Acts 20:29; **(3c2)** of charges,

Acts 25:7; **(3c3)** negatively of God's commandments, 1 Jn 5:3 (causing a burden on him who fulfills them); and **(4)** in 2 Cor. 10:10, "weighty," of Paul's letters. See: TDNT—1:556, 95; BAGD—134b; THAYER—96b.

927. βαρύτιμος {1x} **barutimŏs**, *bar-oo'-tim-os;* from *926* and *5092;* highly *valuable:*—very precious {1x}.

This word means "of great value, exceeding precious" [*barus*, "weighty," *time*, value] and is used in Mt 26:7. See: BAGD—134b; THAYER—96b.

928. βασανίζω {12x} **basanizō**, *bas-an-id'-zo;* from *931;* to *torture:*—torment {8x}, pain {1x}, toss {1x}, vex {1x}, toil {1x}.

Basanizo, as a verb, properly signifies in Greek **(1)** "to test by rubbing on the touchstone" [*basanos*, "a touchstone"], then, **(1a)** "to question by applying torture"; hence **(1b)** "to vex, torment"; **(2)** in the NT in the passive voice, **(2a)** "to be harassed, **(2b)** distressed"; **(2c)** it is said of men struggling in a boat against wind and waves: "But the ship was now in the midst of the sea, tossed (*basanizo*) with waves: for the wind was contrary" (Mt 14:24; Mk 6:48, toiling). Syn.: 318, 2347, 2669, 4660, 4729, 4730, 4928. See: TDNT—1:561, 96; BAGD—134c; THAYER—96c.

929. βασανισμός {6x} **basanismŏs**, *bas-an-is-mos';* from *928;* *torment:*—torment {6x}.

This word describes the results of divine judgments, torment, in Rev 9:5 (twice); 14:11; 18:7, 10, 15. See: TDNT—1:561, 96; BAGD—134c; THAYER—96c.

930. βασανιστής {1x} **basanistēs**, *bas-an-is-tace';* from *928;* a *torturer:*—tormentor {1x}.

One who elicits information by torture and is used of jailors (Mt 18:34). See: TDNT—1:561, 96; BAGD—134d; THAYER—96d.

931. βάσανος {3x} **basanŏs**, *bas'-an-os;* perh. remotely from the same as *939* (through the notion of *going* to the bottom); a *touch-stone*, i.e. (by anal.) *torture:*—torment {3x}.

This word means **(1)** a touchstone, which is a black siliceous stone used to test the purity of gold or silver by the color of the streak produced on it by rubbing it with either metal; hence **(2)** "torment" because of strong force being exerted and was used of the rack or instrument of torture by which one is forced to divulge the truth. **(3)** In the NT it speaks of torture, torment, acute pains **(3a)** of physical diseases, Mt 4:24; and **(3b)** of those in hell after

death, Lk 16:23, 28. See: TDNT—1:561, 96; BAGD—134d; THAYER—96d.

932. βασιλεία {162x} **basilĕia**, *bas-il-i'-ah;* from *935;* prop. *royalty*, i.e. (abstr.) *rule*, or (concr.) a *realm* (lit. or fig.):—kingdom (of God) {71x}, kingdom (of heaven) {32x}, kingdom (general or evil) {20x}, (Thy or Thine) kingdom {6x}, His kingdom {6x}, the kingdom {5x}, (My) kingdom {4x}, misc. {18x} = kingdom, + reign.

Basileia is primarily an abstract noun, **(1)** denoting **(1a)** "sovereignty, royal power, dominion," e.g., Rev 17:18: "And the woman which thou sawest is that great city, which reigneth over the kings of the earth"; then, **(1b)** by metonymy, a concrete noun, denoting the territory or people over whom a king rules: "Again, the devil taketh Him up into an exceeding high mountain, and sheweth Him all the kingdoms of the world, and the glory of them" (Mt 4:8; Mk 3:24).

(2) It is used especially of the "kingdom" of God and of Christ. The kingdom of God is **(2a)** the sphere of God's rule: "For the kingdom is the LORD'S: and He is the governor among the nations" (Ps 22:28; cf. 145:13; Dan 4:25; Lk 1:52; Rom 13:1, 2). **(2b)** Since, however, this earth is the scene of universal rebellion against God, (e.g., Lk 4:5, 6; 1 Jn 5:19; Rev 11:15–18), the "kingdom" of God is the sphere in which, at any given time, His rule is acknowledged. **(2c)** God has not relinquished His sovereignty in the face of rebellion, demoniac and human, but has declared His purpose to establish it: "And in the days of these kings shall the God of heaven set up a kingdom, which shall never be destroyed: and the kingdom shall not be left to other people, but it shall break in pieces and consume all these kingdoms, and it shall stand for ever" (Dan 2:44; cf. 7:14; 1 Cor 15:24, 25). **(2d)** Meantime, seeking willing obedience, He gave His law to a nation and appointed kings to administer His "kingdom" over it, 1 Chr 28:5. **(2e)** Israel, however, though declaring still a nominal allegiance shared in the common rebellion, Is 1:2–4, and, after they had rejected the Son of God, Jn 1:11 (cf. Mt 21:33–43), were "cast away," Rom 11:15, 20, 25. **(2f)** Henceforth God calls upon men everywhere, without distinction of race or nationality, to submit voluntarily to His rule. **(2g)** Thus the "kingdom" is said to be "in mystery" now, Mk 4:11, that is, it does not come within the range of the natural powers of observation, Lk 17:20, but is spiritually discerned, Jn 3:3 (cf. 1 Cor 2:14). **(2h)** When, hereafter, God asserts His rule universally, Christ will return to establish His earthly rule; then the "kingdom" will be in glory of the rebuilt Davidic, messianic kingdom, that is, it

will be manifest to all; cf. Mt 25:31–34; Phil 2:9–11; 2 Ti 4:1, 18.

(3) Thus, speaking generally, references to the kingdom fall into two classes, **(3a)** the first, in which it is viewed as present and involving suffering for those who enter it, 2 Th 1:5; **(3b)** the second, in which it is viewed as future and is associated with reward, Mt 25:34, and glory, 13:43. See also Acts 14:22. **(4)** The fundamental principle of the kingdom is declared in the words of the Lord spoken in the midst of a company of Pharisees, "the kingdom of God is in the midst of you," Lk 17:21, that is, where the King is, there is the kingdom. **(5)** Thus at the present time and so far as this earth is concerned, where the King is and where His rule is acknowledged, is, **(5a)** first, in the heart of the individual believer, Acts 4:19; Eph 3:17; 1 Pet 3:15; and **(5b)** then in the churches of God, 1 Cor. 12:3, 5, 11; 14:37; cf. Col. 1:27. **(6)** Now, the King and His rule being refused, **(6a)** those who enter the kingdom of God are brought into conflict with all who disown its allegiance, as well as with the desire for ease, and the dislike of suffering and unpopularity, natural to all. **(6b)** On the other hand, subjects of the kingdom are the objects of the care of God, Mt 6:33, and of the rejected King, Heb 13:5.

(7) Entrance into the kingdom of God is by the new birth, Mt 18:3; Jn 3:5, for nothing that a man may be by nature, or can attain to by any form of self-culture, avails in the spiritual realm. **(7a)** And as the new nature, received in the new birth, is made evident by obedience, **(7b)** it is further said that only such as do the will of God shall enter into His kingdom, Mt 7:21, where, **(7c)** however, the context shows that the reference is to the future, as in 2 Pet 1:10, 11. Cf. also 1 Cor 6:9, 10; Gal 5:21; Eph 5:5. **(8)** The expression "kingdom of God" occurs four times in Matthew, "kingdom of [from] the heavens" usually taking its place. **(8a)** The latter (cf. Dan 4:26) does not occur elsewhere in NT, but **(8b)** see 2 Ti 4:18, "His heavenly kingdom." **(9)** This kingdom is identical with **(9a)** the kingdom of the Father (cf. Mt 26:29 with Mk 14:25), and **(9b)** with the kingdom of the Son (cf. Lk 22:30).

(10) Thus there is but one kingdom, variously described: **(10a)** of the Son of Man, Mt 13:41; **(10b)** of Jesus, Rev 1:9; **(10c)** of Christ Jesus, 2 Ti 4:1; **(10d)** "of Christ and God," Eph 5:5; **(10e)** "of our Lord, and of His Christ," Rev 11:15; **(10f)** "of our God, and the authority of His Christ," Rev 12:10; **(10g)** "of the Son of His love," Col 1:13. **(11)** Concerning the future, the Lord taught His disciples to pray, "Thy kingdom come," Mt 6:10, where the verb is in the

point tense, precluding the notion of gradual progress and development, and implying a sudden establishment of the kingdom as declared in 2 Th 2:8. **(12)** Concerning the present, that a man is of the kingdom of God is not shown in the punctilious observance of ordinances, which are external and material, but in the deeper matters of the heart, which are spiritual and essential, viz., "righteousness, and peace, and joy in the Holy Spirit," Rom 14:17."

(13) With regard to the expressions "the kingdom of God" and the "kingdom of the heavens," while they are often used interchangeably, it does not follow that in every case they mean exactly the same and are quite identical. **(13a)** The apostle Paul often speaks of the kingdom of God, not dispensationally but morally, e.g., in Rom 14:17; 1 Cor 4:20, but never so of the kingdom of heaven. **(13b)** "God" is not the equivalent of "the heavens." He is everywhere and above all dispensations, whereas 'the heavens' are distinguished from the earth, until the kingdom comes in judgment and power and glory (Rev 11:15) when rule in heaven and on earth will be one. **(13c)** While, then, the sphere of the kingdom of God and the kingdom of heaven are at times identical, yet the one term cannot be used indiscriminately for the other. **(13d)** In the "kingdom of heaven" (32 times in Mt), heaven is in antithesis to earth, and the phrase is stressing the originating point for the kingdom. It will come from heaven (Jn 18:36), not raised up from the earth. **(13e)** In the "kingdom of God", in its broader aspect, God is in antithesis to "man" or "the world," and **(13e1)** the term signifies the entire sphere of God's rule and action in relation to the world. **(13e2)** It has a moral and spiritual force and is a general term for the kingdom at any time. The kingdom of [from, genitive of source] heaven is always the kingdom of God, but the kingdom of God is not limited to the kingdom of heaven, until in their final form, they become identical, e.g., Jn 3:5; Rev 11:15; Rev 12:10. See: TDNT— 1:579, 97; BAGD—134d; THAYER—96d.

933. **βασίλειον** {1x} **basilĕiŏn**, *bas-il´-i-on; neut. of 934; a palace:* — king's court + 3588 {1x}.

Basileion is an adjective meaning "royal" and signifies, in the neuter plural, "a royal palace," translated "kings' courts" in Lk 7:25. See: BAGD—136a; THAYER—98a.

934. **βασίλειος** {1x} **basilĕiŏs**, *bas-il´-i-os; from 935; kingly* (in nature):— royal {1x}.

This word means royal, kingly, regal and occurs in 1 Pet 2:9: "But ye are a chosen generation,

a royal priesthood, an holy nation, a peculiar people; that ye should shew forth the praises of Him who hath called you out of darkness into His marvelous light." See: TDNT—1:591, 97; BAGD—136a; THAYER—98a.

935. βασιλεύς {118x} **basilĕus**, *bas-il-yooce';*
prob. from *939* (through the notion of a *foundation* of power); a *sovereign* (abstr., rel., or fig.):—king {82x}, King (of Jews) {21x}, King (God or Christ) {11x}, King (of Israel) {4x}.

Basileus, as a noun, means **(1)** "a king" e.g., **(1a)** Mt 1:6, and is used of the Roman emperor in 1 Pet 2:13, 17 (a command of general application); **(1b)** of Herod the Tetrarch, Mt 14:9; **(1c)** of Christ, **(1c1)** as the "King" of the Jews, e.g., Mt 2:2; 27:11, 29, 37; **(1c2)** as the "King" of Israel, Mk 15:32; Jn 1:49; 12:13; **(1c3)** as "King of kings," Rev 17:14; 19:16; **(1c4)** as "the King" in judging nations and men at the establishment of the millennial kingdom, Mt 25:34, 40; **(2)** of God, **(2a)** "the great King," Mt 5:35; **(2b)** "the King eternal, incorruptible, invisible," 1 Tim 1:17; **(2c)** "King of kings" 1 Ti 6:15. **(3)** Christ's "kingship" **(3a)** was predicted in the OT, e.g., Ps 2:6, and **(3b)** in the NT, e.g., Lk 1:32, 33; **(3c)** He came as such e.g., Mt 2:2; Jn 18:37; **(3d)** was rejected and died as such, Lk 19:14; Mt 27:37; **(3e)** is now a "King" Priest, after the order of Melchizedek, Heb 5:6; 7:1, 17; and **(3f)** will reign for ever and ever, Rev 11:15. Syn.: 934, 937. See: TDNT—1:576, 97; BAGD—136a; THAYER—98a.

936. βασιλεύω {21x} **basilĕuō**, *bas-il-yoo'-o;*
from *935;* to *rule* (lit. or fig.):—reign {20x}, king {1x}.

Basileuo, as a verb, means "to reign" and is used **(1)** literally, **(1a)** of God, Rev 11:17; 19:6, in each of which the aorist tense (in the latter, translated "reigneth") is "ingressive," stressing the point of entrance; **(1b)** of Christ, Lk 1:33; 1 Cor 15:25; Rev 11:15; as rejected by the Jews, Lk 19:14, 27; **(1c)** of the saints, hereafter, 1 Cor 4:8 (2nd part), where the apostle, casting a reflection upon the untimely exercise of authority on the part of the church at Corinth, anticipates the due time for it in the future; Rev 5:10; 20:4, where the aorist tense is not simply of a "point" character, but "constative," that is, regarding a whole action as having occurred, without distinguishing any steps in its progress (in this instance the aspect is future); 5:6; 22:5; **(1d)** of earthly potentates, Mt 2:22; 1 Ti 6:15, where "kings" is, lit., "them that reign"; **(2)** metaphorically, **(2a)** of believers, Rom 5:17, where "shall reign in life" indicates the activity of life in fellowship with Christ in His sovereign power, reaching its fullness

hereafter; 1 Cor 4:8 (1st part), of the carnal pride that laid claim to a power not to be exercised until hereafter; **(2b)** of divine grace, Rom 5:21; **(2c)** of sin, Rom 5:21; 6:12; **(2d)** of death, Rom 5:14, 17. Syn.: 4821. See: TDNT—1:590, 97; BAGD—136c; THAYER—98b.

937. βασιλικός {5x} **basilikŏs**, *bas-il-ee-kos';*
from *935; regal* (in relation), i.e. (lit.) belonging to (or befitting) the sovereign (as land, dress, or a *courtier*), or (fig.) *preeminent:*—nobleman {2x}, royal {2x}, king's country + 3588 {1x}.

This word means "royal, belonging to a king," is used **(1)** in Acts 12:20 with "country" understood, "their country was fed from the king's," lit., "the royal [country], the "king's country." **(2)** It is also translated "nobleman," Jn 4:46, 49; and **(3)** "royal" (robes), Acts 12:21; "royal [law]," Jas 2:8. See: TDNT—1:591, 97; BAGD—136d; THAYER—98c.

938. βασίλισσα {4x} **basilissa**, *bas-il'-is-sah;*
fem. from *936;* a *queen:*—queen {4x}.

Basilissa is the feminine of *basileus,* "a king," is used **(1)** of the "Queen of Sheba," Mt 12:42; Lk 11:31; **(2)** of "Candace," Acts 8:27; **(3)** metaphorically, of "Babylon," Rev 18:7. See: TDNT—1:590, 97; BAGD—137a; THAYER—98c.

939. βάσις {1x} **basis**, *bas'-ece;* from βαίνω
bainō (to *walk*); a *pace* ("base"), i.e. (by impl.) the *foot:*—foot (sole of) {1x}.

This word means lit., "a step"; hence denotes that with which one steps, "a foot," and is used in the plural in Acts 3:7. See: BAGD—137a; THAYER—98d.

940. βασκαίνω {1x} **baskainō**, *bas-kah'-ee-no;*
akin to *5335;* to *malign,* i.e. (by extens.) to *fascinate* (by false representations):—bewitch {1x}.

This word means primarily, "to slander, to prate about anyone"; then "to bring evil on a person by feigned praise, or mislead by an evil eye, and so to charm, bewitch" [Eng., "fascinate" is connected] and is used figuratively in Gal 3:1, of leading into evil doctrine. See: TDNT—1:594, 102; BAGD—137a; THAYER—98d.

941. βαστάζω {27x} **bastazō**, *bas-tad'-zo;* perh.
remotely der. from the base of *939* (through the idea of *removal*); to *lift,* lit. or fig. (*endure, declare, sustain, receive,* etc.):—bear {23x}, carry {3x}, take up {1x}.

Bastazo signifies "to support as a burden." It is used with the meaning **(1)** "to take up," as in picking up anything stones, Jn 10:31; **(2)** "to carry" **(2a)** something, Mt 3:11; Mk 14:13; Lk

7:14; 22:10; Acts 3:2; 21:35; Rev 17:7; **(2b)** "to carry" on one's person, Lk 10:4; Gal 6:17; **(2c)** in one's body, Lk 11:27; **(2d)** "to bear" a name in testimony, Acts 9:15; **(2e)** metaphorically, of a root "bearing" branches, Rom 11:18; **(3)** "to bear" a burden, whether **(3a)** physically, as of the cross, Jn 19:17, or **(3b)** metaphorically in respect of sufferings endured in the cause of Christ, Lk 14:27; Rev 2:3; **(3c)** it is said of physical endurance, Mt 20:12; **(3d)** of sufferings "borne" on behalf of others, Mt 8:17; Rom 15:1; Gal 6:2; **(3e)** of spiritual truths not able to be "borne," Jn 16:12; **(3f)** of the refusal to endure evil men, Rev 2:2; **(3g)** of religious regulations imposed on others, Acts 15:10; **(3h)** of the burden of the sentence of God to be executed in due time, Gal 5:10; **(3i)** of the effect at the judgment seat of Christ, to be "borne" by the believer for failure in the matter of discharging the obligations of discipleship, Gal 6:5; **(4)** to "bear" by way of carrying off, Jn 12:6; 20:15. Syn.: 4064, 5342. See: TDNT—1:596, 102; BAGD—137b; THAYER—98d.

942. **βάτος** {5x} **batŏs,** *bat'-os;* of uncert. der.; a *brier* shrub:—bush {4x}, bramble bush {1x}.

Batos denotes **(1)** "a bramble bush," as in Lk 6:44. **(2)** In Mk 12:26 and Lk 20:37 the phrase "in the place concerning the bush" signifies in that part of the book of Exodus concerning the "burning bush." See also Acts 7:30, 35. See: BAGD—137c; THAYER—99b.

943. **βάτος** {1x} **batŏs,** *bat'-os;* of Heb. or. [1324]; a *bath,* or measure for liquids:—measure {1x}.

Batos, as a noun, denotes a bath, a Jewish liquid measure (the equivalent of an ephah), containing between 8 and 9 gallons, Lk 16:6. Syn.: 280, 488, 2884, 3313, 3354, 3358, 4057, 4568, 5234, 5249, 5518. See: BAGD—137c; THAYER—99b.

944. **βάτραχος** {1x} **batrachŏs,** *bat'-rakh-os;* of uncert. der.; a *frog:*—frog {1x}.

Batrachos is mentioned in Rev 16:13 only. See: BAGD—137d; THAYER—99b.

945. **βαττολογέω** {1x} **battŏlŏgĕō,** *bat-tol-og-eh'-o;* from Βάττος **Battŏs** (a proverbial stammerer) and *3056;* to *stutter,* i.e. (by impl.) to *prate* tediously:—use vain repetitions {1x}.

This word means "to repeat idly" and is used in Mt 6:7, "use (not) vain repetitions"; the meaning "to stammer" is scarcely to be associated with this word. It denotes meaningless and mechanically repeated phrases, the reference being to pagan (not Jewish) modes of

prayer. See: TDNT—1:597, 103; BAGD—137d; THAYER—99b.

946. **βδέλυγμα** {6x} **bdĕlugma,** *bdel'-oog-mah;* from *948;* a *detestation,* i.e. (spec.) *idolatry:*—abomination {6x}.

Bdelugma denotes **(1)** an "object of disgust, an abomination." **(2)** This is said of the image to be set up by Antichrist, Mt 24:15; Mk 13:14; **(3)** of that which is highly esteemed amongst men, in contrast to its real character in the sight of God, Lk 16:15. The constant association with idolatry suggests that what is highly esteemed among men constitutes an idol in the human heart. **(4)** In Rev 21:27, entrance is forbidden into the Holy City on the part of the unclean, or one who "maketh an abomination and a lie." **(5)** It is also used of the contents of the golden cup in the hand of the evil woman described in Rev 17:4, and of the name ascribed to her in the following verse. See: TDNT—1:598, 103; BAGD—137d; THAYER—99b.

947. **βδελυκτός** {1x} **bdĕluktŏs,** *bdel-ook-tos';* from *948; detestable,* i.e. (spec.) *idolatrous:*—abominable {1x}.

Bdeluktos is used in Titus 1:16 and is said of deceivers who profess to know God, but deny Him by their works. See: TDNT—1:598, 103; BAGD—138a; THAYER—99c.

948. **βδελύσσω** {2x} **bdĕlussō,** *bdel-oos'-so;* from a (presumed) der. of βδέω **bdĕō** (to *stink*); to *be disgusted,* i.e. (by impl.) *detest* (esp. of idolatry):—abhor {1x}, abominable {1x}.

This word means "to render foul" [from *bdeo,* "to stink"], "to cause to be abhorred" and is used in the middle voice, signifying "to turn oneself away from" (as if from a stench); hence, **(1)** "to detest, abhor" Rom 2:22. **(2)** In Rev 21:8 it denotes "to be abominable." See: TDNT—1:598,*; BAGD—138a; THAYER—99d.

949. **βέβαιος** {9x} **bĕbaiŏs,** *beb'-ah-yos;* from the base of *939* (through the idea of *basality*); *stable* (lit. or fig.):—stedfast {4x}, sure {2x}, firm {1x}, of force {1x}, more sure {1x}.

This word means "firm, steadfast, secure" and is translated **(1)** "firm" in Heb 3:6, of the maintenance of the boldness of the believer's hope; and **(2)** "steadfast" in Heb 3:14 "the beginning of our confidence"; 2 Cor 1:7; Heb 2:2; 6:19. It is also translated **(3)** "sure" in Rom 4:16, **(4)** "of force" in Heb 9:17; and **(5)** "more sure" in 2 Pet 1:10, 19. Syn.: 4731. See: TDNT—1:600, 103; BAGD—138b; THAYER—99d.

950. **βεβαιόω** {8x} **bĕbaiŏō,** *beb-ah-yŏ'-o;* from *949;* to *stabilitate* (fig.):—confirm {5x}, establish {2x}, stablish {1x}.

This word means "to make firm, establish, make secure" (the connected adjective *bebaios* signifies "stable, fast, firm"), and is used of "confirming, stablishing, establishing" **(1)** a word, Mk 16:20; **(2)** promises, Rom 15:8; **(3)** the testimony of Christ, 1 Cor 1:6; **(4)** the saints by the Lord Jesus Christ, 1 Cor 1:8; **(5)** the saints by God, 2 Cor 1:21 ("stablisheth"); **(6)** in faith, Col 2:7; **(7)** the salvation spoken through the Lord and "confirmed" by the apostles, Heb 2:3; **(8)** the heart by grace, Heb 13:9 ("stablished"). "Establish" means to build up from without; "stablish" means to build up from within. See: TDNT—1:600, 103; BAGD—138c; THAYER—99d.

951. βεβαίωσις {2x} **běbaiōsis**, *beb-ah'-yo-sis;* from *950; stabiliment:—*confirmation {2x}.

Bebaiosis is used in two senses **(1)** "of firmness, establishment," said of the "confirmation" of the gospel, Phil 1:7; and **(2)** "of authoritative validity imparted," said of the settlement of a dispute by an oath to produce confidence, Heb 6:16. The word is found frequently in the papyri of the settlement of a business transaction. See: TDNT—1:600, 103; BAGD—138d; THAYER—100a.

952. βέβηλος {5x} **běbēlos**, *beb'-ay-los;* from the base of *939* and βηλός **bēlŏs** (a *threshold*); *accessible* (as by *crossing the door-way*), i.e. (by impl. of Jewish notions) *heathenish, wicked:—*profane {4x}, profane person {1x}.

(1) This word suggests a trodden and trampled spot that is open to the causal step of every intruder or careless passer-by. **(2)** This word means primarily, "permitted to be trodden, accessible"; hence, "unhallowed, profane" [opposite to *hieros*, "sacred"], and is used of **(2a)** persons, 1 Ti 1:9; Heb 12:16; **(2b)** things, 1 Ti 4:7; 6:20; 2 Ti 2:16. **(3)** "The natural antagonism between the profane and the holy or divine grew into a moral antagonism. . . . Accordingly *bebelos* is that which lacks all relationship or affinity to God." Syn.: 2839. See: TDNT—1:604, 104; BAGD—138d; THAYER—100a.

953. βεβηλόω {2x} **běbēlŏō**, *beb-ay-lŏ'-o;* from *952;* to *desecrate:—*profane {2x}.

This word means primarily, "to cross the threshold"; hence, "to profane, pollute" and occurs in Mt 12:5 and Acts 24:6. See: TDNT—1:605, 104; BAGD—138d; THAYER—100a.

954. Βεελζεβούλ {7x} **Běělzěbŏul**, *beh-el-zeb-ool';* of Chald. or. [by parody on 1176]; *dung-god; Beelzebul*, a name of Satan:—Beelzebub {7x}. See: TDNT—1:605, 104; BAGD—139a; THAYER—100a.

955. Βελίαλ {1x} **Bělial**, *bel-ee'-al;* or Βελιάρ **Beliar**, *bel-ee'-ar* of Heb. or. [1100]; *worthlessness; Belial,* as an epithet of Satan:—*Belial* {1x}.

Belial (*955*) is a word **(1)** frequently used in the Old Testament, with various meanings, especially in the books of Samuel, where it is found nine times. See also Deut 13:13; Judg 19:22; 20:13; 1 Kin 21:10, 13; 2 Chr 13:7. **(2)** Its original meaning was either "worthlessness" or "hopeless ruin." **(3)** It also had the meanings of "extreme wickedness and destruction," the latter indicating the destiny of the former. **(4)** In the period between the OT and the NT it came to be a proper name for Satan. There may be an indication of this in Nahum 1:15, where the word translated "the wicked one" is *Belial.* **(5)** The oldest form of the word is "Beliar," possibly from a phrase signifying "Lord of the forest," or perhaps simply a corruption of the form "*Belial.*" **(6)** In the NT, in 2 Cor 6:15, it is set in contrast to Christ and represents a personification of the system of impure worship connected especially with the cult of Aphrodite. See: TDNT—1:607, 104; BAGD—139a; THAYER—100c.

956. βέλος {1x} **bělŏs**, *bel'-os;* from *906;* a *missile,* i.e. *spear* or *arrow:—*dart {1x}.

Belos denotes "a missile, an arrow, javelin, dart", Eph 6:16. See: TDNT—1:608, 104; BAGD—139b; THAYER—100c.

957. βελτίον {1x} **běltiŏn**, *bel-tee'-on;* neut. of a comparative of a der. of *906* (used for the comparative of *18*); *better:—*very well {1x}. See: BAGD—139b.100c.

958. Βενιαμίν {4x} **Běniamin**, *ben-ee-am-een';* of Heb. or. [1144]; *Benjamin,* an Isr.:—Benjamin {4x}. See: BAGD—139b; THAYER—100c.

959. Βερνίκη {3x} **Běrnikē**, *ber-nee'-kay;* from a provincial form of *5342* and *3529; victorious; Bernicè,* a member of the *Herodian family:-* Bernice {3x}. See: BAGD—139c; THAYER—100c.

960. Βέροια {2x} **Běrŏia**, *ber'-oy-ah;* perh. a provincial from a der. of *4008* [*Perœa,* i.e. the region *beyond* the coast-line]; *Berœa,* a place in Macedonia:—Berea {2x}. See: BAGD—139c; THAYER—100c.

961. Βεροιαῖος {1x} **Běrŏiaiŏs**, *ber-oy-ah'-yos;* from *960;* a *Berœœan* or native of Beræa:—of Berea {1x}. See: BAGD—139c; THAYER—100c.

962. **Βηθαβαρά** {1x} **Bēthabara**, *bay-thab-ar-ah';* of Heb. or. [1004 and 5679]; *ferry-house; Bethabara* (i.e. *Bethab-arah*), a place on the Jordan:—Bethabara {1x}. See: BAGD—139c; THAYER—100d.

963. **Βηθανία** {11x} **Bēthania**, *bay-than-ee'-ah;* of Chald. or.; *date-house; Beth-any,* a place in Pal.:—Bethany {11x}. See: BAGD—139d; THAYER—100d.

964. **Βηθεσδά** {1x} **Bēthĕsda**, *bay-thes-dah';* of Chald. or. [compound of 1004 and 2617]; *house of kindness; Beth-esda,* a pool in Jerusalem:—*Bethesda* {1x}. See: BAGD—139d; THAYER—100d.

965. **Βηθλεέμ** {8x} **Bēthlĕĕm**, *bayth-leh-em';* of Heb. or. [1036]; *Bethleem* (i.e. *Beth-lechem*), a place in Pal.:—Bethlehem {8x}. See: BAGD—140a; THAYER—101a.

966. **Βηθσαϊδά** {7x} **Bēthsaïda**, *bayth-sahee-dah';* of Chald. or. [compound of 1004 and 6719]; *fishing-house; Bethsaïda,* a place in Pal.:—*Bethsaida* {7x}. See: BAGD—140a; THAYER—101a.

967. **Βηθφαγή** {3x} **Bēthphagē**, *bayth-fag-ay';* of Chald. or. [compound of 1004 and 6291]; *fig-house; Beth-phage',* a place in Pal.:—*Bethphage* {3x}. See: BAGD—140b; THAYER—101b.

968. **βῆμα** {12x} **bēma**, *bay'-ma;* from the base of *939; a step,* i.e. *foot-breath;* by impl. a *rostrum,* i.e. a *tribunal:*—judgment seat {10x}, throne {1x}, to set (one's) foot on + 4128 {1x}.

Bema primarily means a step, a pace (Acts 7:5) and was used **(1)** to denote a raised place or platform, reached by steps, where was the place of assembly; from the platform orations were made. **(2)** It is used of the divine tribunal before which all believers are hereafter to stand (Rom 14:10). **(3)** In 2 Cor 5:10 it is called the judgment seat of Christ, to whom the Father has given all judgment (Jn 5:22, 27). **(3a)** At this *bema* believers are to be made manifest, that each may "receive the things done in (or through) the body," according to what he has done, "whether it be good or bad." **(3b)** There they will receive rewards for their faithfulness to the Lord. For all that has been contrary in their lives to His will they will suffer loss (1 Cor 3:15). **(3c)** This judgment seat is to be distinguished from **(3c1)** the premillennial, earthly throne of Christ (Mt 25:31), and **(3c2)** the postmillennial Great White Throne (Rev 20:11), at which only "the unsaved dead" will appear. See: BAGD—140b; THAYER—101b.

969. **βήρυλλος** {1x} **bĕrullŏs**, *bay'-rool-los;* of uncert. der.; a *"beryl":*—beryl {1x}.

Beryl is a precious stone of a sea-green color (Rev. 21:20; cf. Ex 28:20). See: BAGD—140b; THAYER—101c.

970. **βία** {4x} **bia**, *bee'-ah;* prob. akin to *979* (through the idea of *vital* activity); *force:*—violence {4x}.

This word denotes "force, violence" and is said **(1)** of men, Acts 5:26; 21:35; 24:7; and **(2)** of waves, Acts 27:41. See: BAGD—140c; THAYER—101c.

971. **βιάζω** {2x} **biazō**, *bee-ad'-zo;* from *970;* to *force,* i.e. (refl.) to *crowd one-self* (into), or (pass.) to *be seized:*—suffer violence {1x}, press {1x}.

Biazo, in the middle voice "means to press violently" or "force one's way into" and is translated **(1)** "presseth" in Lk 16:16, "entereth violently," a meaning confirmed by the papyri, speaking of "those who (try to) force their way in" and **(2)** in Mt 11:12 "suffereth violence": "And from the days of John the Baptist until now the kingdom of heaven suffereth violence, and the violent take it by force." See: TDNT—1:609,*; BAGD—140b; THAYER—101c.

972. **βίαιος** {1x} **biaiŏs**, *bee'-ah-yos;* from *970; violent:*—mighty {1x}.

This word is translated "mighty" in Acts 2:2: "And suddenly there came a sound from heaven as of a rushing mighty (*biaios*) wind, and it filled all the house where they were sitting." See: BAGD—141a; THAYER—101d.

973. **βιαστής** {1x} **biastēs**, *bee-as-tace';* from *971;* a *forceful man,* i.e. (fig.) *energetic:*—violent {1x}.

This word means "a forceful or violent man" and is used in Mt 11:12. See: TDNT—1:613, 105; BAGD—141a; THAYER—101d.

974. **βιβλιαρίδιον** {4x} **bibliaridiŏn**, *bib-lee-ar-id'-ee-on;* a dimin. of *975;* a *booklet:*—little book {4x}.

Bibliaridion is diminutive of *biblion* (975) and is always rendered "little book" in Rev 10:2, 8, 9–10. See: BAGD—141a; THAYER—101d.

975. **βιβλίον** {32x} **biblĭon**, *bib-lee'-on;* a dimin. of *976;* a *roll:*—book {29x}, bill {1x}, scroll {1x}, writing {1x}.

This word means primarily "a small book, a scroll, or any sheet on which something has been written"; hence, in connection with *apostasion,* "divorce," signifies "a writing of divorcement," Mt 19:7; Mk 10:4. See: TDNT—1:617, 106; BAGD—141b; THAYER—101d.

976. βίβλος {13x} **biblŏs**, *bib'-los;* prop. the inner *bark* of the papyrus plant, i.e. (by impl.) a *sheet* or *scroll* of writing:— book {13x}.

Biblos was the inner part, or rather the cellular substance, of the stem of the papyrus (Eng. "paper"). It came to denote the paper made from this bark in Egypt, and then a written "book," roll, or volume. It is used in referring to **(1)** "books" of Scripture, the "book," or scroll, of Matthew's Gospel, Mt 1:1; **(2)** the Pentateuch, as the "book" of Moses, Mk 12:26; **(3)** Isaiah, as "the book of the words of Isaiah," Lk 3:4; **(4)** the Psalms, Lk 20:42 and Acts 1:20; **(5)** "the prophets," Acts 7:42; **(6)** to "the Book of Life," Phil 4:3; Rev 3:5; 20:15. **(7)** Once only it is used of secular writings, Acts 19:19. See: TDNT—1:615, 106; BAGD—141c; THAYER—102a.

977. βιβρώσκω {1x} **bibrōskō**, *bib-ro'-sko;* a redupl. and prol. form of an obs. primary verb [perh. caus. of *1006*]; to *eat:*—eat {1x}.

This word means "to eat" and is derived from a root, *bor,* "to devour." Syn.: In Jn 6:5 *phago* (*5315*) intimates nothing about a full supply; whereas, *bibrosko* (6:13), indicates that the people had been provided with a big meal, of which they had partaken eagerly. See also: 1089, 2068, 2719, 2880, 5176, 5315. See: BAGD—141c; THAYER—102a.

978. Βιθυνία {2x} **Bithunia**, *bee-thoo-nee'-ah;* of uncert. der.; *Bithynia,* a region of Asia:—Bithynia {2x}. See: BAGD—141d; THAYER—102a.

979. βίος {11x} **biŏs**, *bee'-os;* a primary word; *life,* i.e. (lit.) the present state of existence; by impl. the means of *livelihood:*—life {5x}, living {5x}, good {1x}.

Bios denotes **(1)** "life, lifetime", Lk 8:14; 1 Ti 2:2; 2 Ti 2:4; 1 Pet 4:3; 1 Jn 2:16; **(2)** "livelihood, living, means of living", Mk 12:44; Lk 8:43; 15:12, 30; 21:4; and is translated **(3)** "good" in 1 Jn 3:17: "But whoso hath this world's good, and seeth his brother have need, and shutteth up his bowels of compassion from him, how dwelleth the love of God in him?" Syn.: 2222. See: TDNT—2:832, 290; BAGD—141d; THAYER—102b.

980. βιόω {1x} **biŏō**, *bee-ŏ'-o;* from *979;* to *spend* existence:—live {1x}.

Bioo, as a verb, means "to spend life, to pass one's life": "That he no longer should live the rest of his time in the flesh to the lusts of men, but to the will of God" (1 Pet 4:2). Syn.: 326, 390, 1236, 2198, 2225, 4176, 4800, 5225. See: TDNT—2:832, 280; BAGD—142a; THAYER—102b.

981. βίωσις {1x} **biōsis**, *bee'-o-sis;* from *980; living* (prop. the act, by impl. the mode):—manner of life {1x}.

This word means "to spend one's life, to live" and denotes "a manner of living and acting, way of life," Acts 26:4. See: BAGD—142a; THAYER—102b.

982. βιωτικός {3x} **biōtikŏs**, *bee-o-tee-kos';* from a der. of *980; relating to* the present *existence:*—things pertaining to this life {1x}, things that pertain to this life {1x}, of this life {1x}.

Biotikos means "pertaining to life" (*bios*) and is translated **(1)** "of this life" in Lk 21:34; **(2)** with reference to cares; in 1 Cor 6:3 "(things) that pertain to this life"; and **(3)** 1 Cor 6: 4, "(things) pertaining to this life," i.e., matters of this world, concerning which Christians at Corinth were engaged in public lawsuits one with another; such matters were to be regarded as relatively unimportant in view of the great tribunals to come under the jurisdiction of saints hereafter. See: BAGD—142a; THAYER—102b.

983. βλαβερός {1x} **blabĕrŏs**, *blab-er-os';* from *984; injurious:*—hurtful {1x}.

Blaberos signifies "hurtful" in 1 Ti 6:9, said of lusts. See: BAGD—142b; THAYER—102b.

984. βλάπτω {2x} **blaptō**, *blap'-to;* a primary verb; prop. to *hinder,* i.e. (by impl.) to *injure, mar do damage to:*—hurt {2x}.

Blapto signifies **(1)** "to injure, mar, do damage to," Mk 16:18, "shall (in no wise) hurt (them)"; and **(2)** in Lk 4:35, "hurt him not." Syn.: *Adikeo* (*91*) stresses the unrighteousness of the act, *blapto* stresses the injury done. See: BAGD—142b; THAYER—102c.

985. βλαστάνω {4x} **blastanō**, *blas-tan'-o;* from βλαστός **blastŏs** (a *sprout*); to *germinate;* by impl. to *yield* fruit:—spring up {2x}, bud {1x}, bring forth {1x}.

Blastano, as a verb, means "to bud, spring up" and is translated "brought forth" [i.e., "caused to produce"] in Jas 5:18: "And he [Elijah] prayed again, and the heaven gave rain, and the earth brought forth her fruit." Cf. Mt 13:26; Mk 4:27; Heb 9:4. See: BAGD—142b; THAYER—102c.

986. Βλάστος {1x} **Blastŏs**, *blas'-tos;* perh. the same as the base of *985; Blastus,* an officer of Herod Agrippa:—Blastus {1x}. See: BAGD—142c; THAYER—102c.

987. βλασφημέω {35x} **blasphēmĕō**, *blas-fay-meh'-o;* from *989;* to *vilify;* spec. to *speak impiously:*—blaspheme {17x}, speak evil of {10x}, rail on {2x}, blasphemer

{1x}, speak blasphemy {1x}, blasphemously {1x}, misc. {3x} = defame, revile.

(1) This word means to use speech to bring down another's value, honor, due-respect; to injure another's reputation in the eyes of others. **(1a)** *Blasphemeo*, as a verb, means "to blaspheme, rail at or revile" and is used **(1b)** in a general way, of any contumelious speech, reviling, calumniating, railing at, etc., as of those who railed at Christ, e.g., Mt 27:39; Mk 15:29; Lk 22:65; 23:39; **(2)** of those who speak contemptuously of God or of sacred things, e.g.; Mt 9:3; Mk 3:28; Rom 2:24; 1 Ti 1:20; 6:1; Rev 13:6; 16:9, 11, 21; **(2a)** "hath spoken blasphemy," Mt 26:65; **(2b)** "rail at," 2 Pet 2:10; Jude 8, 10; **(2c)** "railing," 2 Pet 2:12; **(2d)** "slanderously reported," Rom 3:8; **(2e)** "be evil spoken of," Rom 14:16; 1 Cor 10:30; 2 Pet 2:2; **(2f)** "speak evil of," Titus 3:2; 1 Pet 4:4; **(2g)** "being defamed," 1 Cor 4:13. **(3)** The verb (in the present participial form) is translated **(3a)** "blasphemers" in Acts 19:37; **(3b)** in Mk 2:7, "speaketh blasphemies." **(4)** As to Christ's teaching concerning "blasphemy" against the Holy Spirit, e.g., Mt 12:32, that anyone, with the evidence of the Lord's power before His eyes, should declare it to be Satanic, exhibited a condition of heart beyond divine illumination and therefore hopeless. Divine forgiveness would be inconsistent with the moral nature of God. As to the Son of Man, in His state of humiliation, there might be misunderstanding, but not so with the Holy Spirit's power demonstrated. This sin can not be committed today; only during the days of His incarnation. See: TDNT—1:621, 107; BAGD—142c; THAYER—102c.

988. **βλασφημία** {19x} **blasphēmia**, *blas-fay-me'-ah;* from *989; vilification* (espec. against God):—blasphemy {16x}, railing {2x}, evil speaking {1x}.

Blasphemia is **(1)** translated **(1a)** "blasphemy, blasphemies" sixteen times; **(1b)** "a railing, railings" in 1 Ti 6:4, Jude 9; and **(1c)** "evil speaking" in Eph 4:31. **(2)** The word "blasphemy" is practically confined to speech defamatory of the Divine Majesty. See: TDNT—1:621, 107; BAGD—143a; THAYER—102d.

989. **βλάσφημος** {5x} **blasphēmŏs**, *blas'-fay-mos;* from a der. of *984* and *5345; scurrilous,* i.e. *calumnious* (against man), or (spec.) *impious* (against God):—blasphemous {2x}, blasphemer {2x}, railing {1x}.

Blasphemos means "abusive, speaking evil" and is translated **(1)** "blasphemous," in Acts 6:11, 13; **(2)** "a blasphemer," 1 Ti 1:13; 2 Ti 3:2;

and **(3)** "railing," 2 Pet 2:11. See: TDNT—1:621, 107; BAGD—143a; THAYER—103a.

990. **βλέμμα** {1x} **blemma**, *blem'-mah;* from *991; vision* (prop. concr.; by impl. abstr.):—seeing {1x}.

This word means primarily, "a look, a glance" and denotes "sight, seeing," 2 Pet 2:8. See: BAGD—143b; THAYER—103a.

991. **βλέπω** {135x} **blĕpō**, *blep'-o;* a primary verb; to *look* at (lit. or fig.):—see {90x}, take heed {12x}, behold {10x}, beware {4x}, look on {4x}, look {3x}, beware of {3x}, misc. {9x} = lie, perceive, regard, sight.

Blepo, as a verb, means primarily, "to have sight, to see," then, "observe, discern, perceive," frequently implying special contemplation, and is rendered **(1)** "to look back" (Lk 9:62); **(2)** Jn 13:22 "(the disciples) looked (one on another)"; **(3)** "beheld" (Acts 1:9); **(4)** Acts 3:4 "look (on us)"; **(5)** Eph 5:15 "see (that ye walk circumspectly)"; **(6)** Rev 11:9 and 18:9 "shall see." Syn. for **(1) - (5):** 308, 352, 578, 816, 872, 1689, 1896, 1914, 1980, 1983, 2300, 2334, 3706, 3708, 3879, 4017, 4648.

(7) *Blepo*, is used of bodily, mental vision, and also, **(7a)** "to perceive": "Therefore speak I to them in parables: because they seeing (*blepo*) see not (*blepo*); and hearing they hear not, neither do they understand" (e.g., Mt 13:13); and **(7b)** "to take heed": "But take ye heed (*blepo*): behold, I have foretold you all things" (e.g., Mk 13:23, 33). **(7c)** It indicates greater vividness than *horao* (*3708*), expressing a more intent, earnest contemplation **(7d)** in Lk 6:41 of "beholding" the mote in a brother's eye; **(7e)** in Lk 24:12 of "beholding" the linen clothes in the empty tomb; **(7f)** in Acts 1:9 of the gaze of the disciples when the Lord ascended; **(7g)** The greater earnestness is sometimes brought out by the rendering "regardest": "And they [Pharisees] sent out unto Him their disciples with the Herodians, saying, Master, we know that thou art true, and teachest the way of God in truth, neither carest thou for any man: for thou regardest (*blepo*) not the person of men" (Mt 22:16). Syn. for **(7a-g):** 333, 816, 1689, 1896, 2029, 2300, 2334, 2657, 2734, 3708. See: TDNT—5:315, 706; BAGD—143b; THAYER—103a. comp. *3700.*

992. **βλητέος** {2x} **blētĕŏs**, *blay-teh'-os;* from *906;* fit *to be cast* (i.e. *applied*):—must be put {2x}.

Bleteos means that which must be put, placed specifically: "And no man putteth (*bleteos*) new wine into old bottles: else the new wine doth burst the bottles, and the wine is spilled, and the bottles will be marred: but new

wine must be put into new bottles" (cf. Lk 5:38). See: BAGD—144a; THAYER—103d.

993. Βοανεργές {1x} **Bŏanĕrgĕs**, *bŏ-an-erg-es'*; of Chald. or. [1123 and 7266]; *sons of commotion; Boänerges*, an epithet of two of the Apostles:—*Boanerges* {1x}. See: BAGD—144a; THAYER—103d.

994. βοάω {11x} **bŏaō**, *bŏ-ah'-o*; appar. a prol. form of a primary verb; *to halloo*, i.e. *shout* (for help or in a tumultuous way):—cry {11x}.

Boao, as a verb, signifies **(1)** "to raise a cry" whether **(1a)** of joy (Gal 4:27), or **(1b)** vexation (Acts 8:7); **(2)** "to speak with a strong voice" (Mt 3:3; Mk 1:3; 15:34; Lk 3:4; Jn 1:23; Acts 17:6); **(3)** "to cry out for help" (Lk 18:7, 38). Syn.: *Kaleo* (*2564*), denotes "to call out for any purpose," *boao* (*994*), "to cry out as an expression of feeling," *krazo* (*2896*), to cry out loudly." *Kaleo* suggests intelligence, *boao*, sensibilities, *krazo*, instincts. See also: 310, 349, 994, 995, 1916, 2019, 2896, 2905, 2906, 5455. See: TDNT—1:625, 108; BAGD—144b; THAYER—103d.

995. βοή {1x} **bŏē**, *bŏ-ay'*; from *994;* a *halloo*, i.e. *call* (for aid, etc.):—cry {1x}.

Boe, as a noun, means especially "a cry for help" and is found in Jas 5:4: "Behold, the hire of the labourers who have reaped down your fields, which is of you kept back by fraud, crieth (*krazo – 2896*): and the cries (*boe*) of them which have reaped are entered into the ears of the Lord of sabaoth." Syn.: 310, 349, 994, 1916, 2019, 2896, 2905, 2906, 5455. See: BAGD—144c; THAYER—104a.

996. βοήθεια {2x} **bŏēthĕia**, *bŏ-ay'-thi-ah*; from *998; aid;* spec. a rope or chain for *frapping* a vessel:—help {2x}.

Boetheia denotes **(1)** "an answer to a cry for help": "Let us therefore come boldly unto the throne of grace, that we may obtain mercy, and find grace to help (*boetheia*) in time of need", Heb. 4:16 literally, "(grace) unto (timely) help"; and **(2)** in Acts 27:17, where the plural is used, the term is nautical, "frapping": "Which when they had taken up, they used helps (*boetheia*), undergirding the ship; and, fearing lest they should fall into the quicksands, strake sail, and so were driven." Frapping means to use ropes or chains to wrap around a ship to prevent its demise. See: TDNT—1:628, 108; BAGD—144c; THAYER—104a.

997. βοηθέω {8x} **bŏēthĕō**, *bŏ-ay-theh'-o;* from *998;* to *aid* or *relieve:*—help {6x}, succour {2x}.

This word means "to come to the aid of anyone, to succour" and is used in Mt 15:25; Mk

9:22, 24; Acts 16:9; 21:28; 2 Cor 6:2, "did I succour"; Heb 2:18, "to succour"; Rev 12:16. See: TDNT—1:628, 108; BAGD—144c; THAYER—104a.

998. βοηθός {1x} **bŏēthŏs**, *bŏ-ay-thos';* from *995* and θέω **thĕō** (to *run*); a *succorer:*—helper {1x}.

Boethos is an adjective and is used as a noun in Heb 13:6 of God as the helper of His saints: "So that we may boldly say, The Lord is my helper, and I will not fear what man shall do unto me." See: TDNT—1:628, 108; BAGD—144d; THAYER—104b.

999. βόθυνος {3x} **bŏthunŏs**, *both'-oo-nos;* akin to *900;* a *hole* (in the ground); spec. a *cistern:*—ditch {2x}, pit {1x}.

Bothunos is any kind of "deep hole or pit" and is translated **(1)** "ditch" in Mt 15:14 and Lk 6:39, and **(2)** "pit" in Mt 12:11. See: BAGD—144d; THAYER—104b.

1000. βολή {1x} **bŏlē**, *bol-ay';* from *906;* a *throw* (as a measure of distance):—cast {1x}.

This word means a short throw, cast: "And He was withdrawn from them about a stone's cast, and kneeled down, and prayed" (Lk 22:41). See: BAGD—144d; THAYER—104b.

1001. βολίζω {2x} **bŏlizō**, *bol-id'-zo;* from *1002;* to *heave* the lead:—sound {2x}.

This word means "to heave the lead, sounding-lead" to take soundings, occurs in Acts 27:28 (twice). See: BAGD—144d; THAYER—104b.

1002. βολίς {1x} **bŏlis**, *bol-ece';* from *906;* a *missile*, i.e. *javelin:*—dart {1x}. See: BAGD—144d; THAYER—104b.

1003. Βοόζ {3x} **Bŏŏz**, *bŏ-oz';* of Heb. or. [1162]; *Booz*, (i.e. *Boäz*), an Isr.:—*Booz* {3x}. See: BAGD—145a; THAYER—104b.

1004. Βόρβορος {1x} **bŏrbŏrŏs**, *bor'-bor-os;* of uncert. der.; *mud:*—mire {1x}.

This word means "mud, filth" and occurs in 2 Pet. 2:22. See: BAGD—145a; THAYER—104c.

1005. Βορρᾶς {2x} **borrhas**, *bor-hras';* of uncert. der.; the *north* (prop. wind):—north {2x}.

This word means primarily Boreas, the North Wind and came to denote the "north" (cf. "Borealis"), Lk 13:29; Rev 21:13. See: BAGD—145b; THAYER—104c.

1006. βόσκω {9x} **bŏskō**, *bos'-ko;* a prol. form of a primary verb [comp. *977,*

1016]; to *pasture;* by extens. to, *fodder;* refl. to *graze:*—feed {2x}, keep {1x}.

This word means (1) "to feed" and is primarily used of a herdsman [from *boo,* "to nourish," the special function being to provide food; the root is *bo,* found in *boter,* "a herdsman or herd," and *botane,* "fodder, pasture"]. Its uses are (2) literal, Mt 8:30; 33; Mk. 5:14; Lk 8:34; in Mk 5:11 and Lk 8:32, "feeding"; Lk 15:15; (3) metaphorical, of spiritual ministry, Jn 21:15, 17. Syn.: 4165. *Bosko* simply means to feed; whereas, *poimein (4165)* refers to the whole office of shepherd: guiding, guarding, folding, and providing pasture (Rev 2:27; 19:15). See: BAGD—145b; THAYER—104c.

1007. Βοσόρ {1x} **Bŏsŏr,** *bos-or';* of Heb. or. [1160]; *Bosor* (i.e. *Beör),* a Moabite:—*Bosor* {1x}. See: BAGD—145b; THAYER—104c.

1008. βοτάνη {1x} **bŏtanē,** *bot-an'-ay;* from *1006; herbage* (as if for *grazing):*—herb {1x}.

This word means an herb fit for fodder, green herb, growing plant, Heb 6:7. See: BAGD—145b; THAYER—104c.

1009. βότρυς {1x} **bŏtrus,** *bot'-rooce;* of uncert. der.; a *bunch* (of grapes):— (vine) cluster (of the vine) {1x}.

This word means "a cluster, or bunch, bunch of grapes" and is found in Rev 14:18. Syn.: *Staphule, (4718)* "a bunch of grapes, the ripe cluster," stresses the individual grapes themselves within the cluster; whereas *botrus* stresses the cluster. See: BAGD—145c; THAYER—104d.

1010. βουλευτής {2x} **bŏulĕutēs,** *bool-yoo-tace';* from *1011;* an *adviser,* i.e. (spec.) a *councillor* or member of the Jewish Sanhedrin:—counsellor {2x}.

Joseph of Arimathaea is described as "a councillor of honorable estate," Mk 15:43; cf. Lk 23:50. See: BAGD—145c; THAYER—104d.

1011. βουλεύω {8x} **bŏulĕuō,** *bool-yoo'-o;* from *1012;* to *advise,* i.e. (refl.) *deliberate,* or (by impl.) *resolve:*—consult {2x}, take counsel {1x}, determine {1x}, be minded {2x}, purpose {2x}.

Bouleuo, used in the middle voice, means (1) "to consult, consider," Lk 14:31; Jn 12:10; (2) "take counsel", Act 5:33; (3) "determine", Acts 15:37; (4) "be minded", Acts 27:39; and (5) "purpose", 2 Cor 1:17. See: BAGD—145c; THAYER—104d.

1012. βουλή {12x} **bŏulē,** *boo-lay';* from *1014; volition,* i.e. (obj.) *advice,* or (by impl.) *purpose:*—+ advise + 5087 {1x}, counsel {10x}, will {1x}.

Boule comes from a root meaning "a will,"

hence "a counsel, a piece of advice." The word is used (1) of the counsel of God in Lk 7:30; Acts 2:23; 4:28; 13:36; 20:27; Eph 1:11; Heb 6:17; and in other passages, (2) of the counsel of men, Lk 23:51; Acts 27:12, 42; 1 Cor 4:5. Syn.: *Boule* is to be distinguished from *gnome (1106); boule* is the result of determination, *gnome* is the result of knowledge. See: BAGD—145d; THAYER—104d.

1013. βούλημα {2x} **bŏulēma,** *boo'-lay-mah;* from *1014;* a *resolve:*—purpose {1x}, will {1x}.

This word means "a purpose or will, a deliberate intention" and occurs (1) as "purpose" in Acts 27:43: "But the centurion, willing to save Paul, kept them from their purpose; and commanded that they which could swim should cast themselves first into the sea, and get to land"; and (2) "will" in Rom 9:19: "Thou wilt say then unto me, Why doth He yet find fault? For who hath resisted His will?" See: TDNT— 1:636, 108; BAGD—145d; THAYER—105a.

1014. βούλομαι {34x} **bŏulŏmai,** *boo'-lom-ahee;* mid. voice of a primary verb.; to *"will,"* i.e. (refl.) *be willing:*—will {15x}, would {11x}, be minded {2x}, intend {2x}, be disposed {1x}, be willing {1x}, list {1x}, of his own will {1x}.

This word means "to wish, to will deliberately," and expresses strongly the deliberate exercise of the will. See: TDNT—1:629, 108; BAGD—146a; THAYER—105a. comp. *2309.*

1015. βουνός {2x} **bŏunŏs,** *boo-nos';* prob. of for. or.; a *hillock:*—hill {2x}.

Bounos means "a mound, heap, height," is translated (1) "hill" in Lk 3:5; (2) "hills" in Lk 23:30. See: BAGD—146c; THAYER—105b.

1016. βοῦς {8x} **bŏus,** *booce;* prob. from the base of *1006;* an *ox* (as *grazing),* i.e. an animal of that species ("beef"):—ox {8x}.

This word means denotes an "ox" or "a cow," Lk 13:15; 14:5, 19; Jn 2:14–15; 1 Cor 9:9 (twice); 1 Ti 5:18. Syn.: 5022. See: BAGD— 146c; THAYER—105b.

1017. βραβεῖον {2x} **brabĕiŏn,** *brab-i'-on;* from βραβεύς **brabĕus** (an *umpire;* of uncert. der.); an *award* (of arbitration), i.e. (spec.) a *prize* in the public games:— prize {2x}.

Brabeion is "a prize bestowed in connection with the games." (1) In 1 Cor 9:24, is used metaphorically of "the reward" to be obtained hereafter by the faithful believer; and (2) in Phil 3:14; the preposition *eis,* "unto," indicates the position of the goal. The "prize" is not "the high calling," but will be bestowed in virtue of, and relation to, it, the heavenly calling, (cf.

Heb 3:1), which belongs to all believers and directs their minds and aspirations heavenward; for the "prize" see especially 2 Ti 4:7, 8. See: TDNT—1:638, 110; BAGD—146d; THAYER—105b.

1018. βραβεύω {1x} **brabĕuō**, *brab-yoo'-o;* from the same as *1017;* to *arbitrate,* i.e. (gen.) to *govern* (fig. *prevail*):— rule {1x}.

This word properly means to act as an umpire (*brabeus*); hence, generally, to arbitrate, decide (Col 3:15) representing "the peace of God" as deciding all matters in the hearts of believers; some regard the meaning as that of simply directing, controlling, "ruling." See: TDNT—1:637, 110; BAGD—146d; THAYER—105c.

1019. βραδύνω {2x} **bradunō**, *brad-oo'-no;* from *1021;* to *delay;* to be *slow:*—be slack {1x}, tarry {1x}.

Braduno used intransitively signifies "to be slow, to tarry" and is said **(1)** negatively of God, 2 Pet 3:9, "is (not) slack"; and **(2)** in 1 Ti 3:15 is translated "(if) I tarry." See: BAGD—147a; THAYER—105c.

1020. βραδυπλοέω {1x} **braduplŏĕō**, *brad-oo-plŏ-eh'-o;* from *1021* and a prol. form of *4126;* to *sail slowly:*—sail slowly {1x}.

Braduploeo means "to sail slowly" (*bradus,* "slow," *plous,* "a voyage") and occurs in Acts 27:7: "And when we had sailed slowly many days, and scarce were come over against Cnidus, the wind not suffering us, we sailed under Crete, over against Salmone." See: BAGD—147a; THAYER—105c.

1021. βραδύς {3x} **bradus**, *brad-ooce';* of uncert. aff.; *slow;* fig. *dull:*—slow {3x}. Syn.: 692, 3576.

Bradus is used **(1)** twice in Jas 1:19, in an exhortation to "be slow to speak" and "slow to wrath"; and **(2)** in Lk 24:25, metaphorically of the understanding. Syn.: *Bradus* means slow, *nothros* (3576) means sluggish, and *argos* (692) means idle. See: BAGD—147a; THAYER—105c.

1022. βραδύτης {1x} **bradutēs**, *brad-oo'-tace;* from *1021; tardiness:*—slackness {1x}.

This word means "slowness" and is rendered "slackness" in 2 Pet 3:9. See: BAGD—147a. 105d.

1023. βραχίων {3x} **brachiōn**, *brakh-ee'-own;* prop. comp. of *1024,* but appar. in the sense of βράσσω **brassō** (to *wield*); the *arm,* i.e. (fig.) *strength:*—arm {3x}.

Brachion is the shorter part of the arm, from the shoulder to the elbow and is used metaphorically to denote strength, power; always in the NT of the power of God (Lk 1:51; Jn 12:38; Acts 13:17). See: TDNT—1:639, 110; BAGD—147b; THAYER—105d.

1024. βραχύς {7x} **brachus**, *brakh-ooce';* of uncert. aff.; *short* (of time, place, quantity, or number):—few words {1x}, a little {4x}, a little space {1x}, a little while {1x}.

Brachus denotes **(1)** "short," **(1a)** in regard to time, e.g., Heb 2:7; or **(1b)** distance, Acts 27:28; **(2)** "few," in regard to quantity, Heb 13:22, lit., "by means of few," i.e., "in few words." See: BAGD—147b; THAYER—105d.

1025. βρέφος {8x} **brĕphŏs**, *bref'-os;* of uncert. affin.; an *infant* (prop. unborn) lit. or fig.:—babe {5x}, young child {1x}, child {1x}, infant {1x}.

Brephos denotes **(1)** "an unborn child," as in Lk 1:41, 44; **(2)** "a newborn child, or an infant still older," Lk 2:12, 16; 18:15; Acts 7:19; 2 Ti 3:15; 1 Pet 2:2. Syn.: 3516. See: TDNT—5:636, 759; BAGD—147b; THAYER—105d.

1026. βρέχω {7x} **brĕchō**, *brekh'-o;* a primary verb; to *moisten* (espec. by a shower):—send rain {1x}, rain + 5205 {1x}, rain {3x}, wash {2x}.

Brecho signifies **(1)** "to wash," Lk 7:38, 44; **(2)** "to send rain," Mt 5:45; **(3)** to rain, Lk 17:29 (of fire and brimstone); **(4)** Jas 5:17, used literally (twice); **(5)** Rev 11:6, lit., "(that) rain rain (not)." See: BAGD—147c; THAYER—105d.

1027. βροντή {12x} **brŏntē**, *bron-tay';* akin to βρέμω **brĕmō** (to *roar*); *thunder:*—thunder {8x}, thundering {4x}.

Bronte means **(1)** literal thunder signaling a storm, Rev. 4:5; 6:1; 8:5; 10:3, 4; 11:19; 14:2; 16:18; 19:6. **(2)** In Mk 3:17 "sons of thunder" is the interpretation of *Boanerges,* the name applied by the Lord to James and John; their fiery disposition is seen in 9:38 and Lk 9:54. See: TDNT—1:640, 110; BAGD—147d; THAYER—106a.

1028. βροχή {2x} **brŏchē**, *brokh-ay';* from *1026; rain:*—rain {2x}.

This word means lit., "a wetting," hence, "rain" and is used in Mt 7:25, 27. See: BAGD—147d; THAYER—106a.

1029. βρόχος {1x} **brŏchŏs**, *brokh'-os;* of uncert. der.; a *noose:*—snare {1x}.

Brochos is "a noose, slipknot, halter," is used metaphorically in 1 Cor 7:35, "a snare." See: BAGD—147d; THAYER—106a.

1030. βρυγμός {7x} **brugmŏs**, *broog-mos';* from *1031;* a *grating* (of the teeth):— gnashing {7x}.

Brugmos denotes "gnashing" ("of teeth" being added), Mt 8:12; 13:42, 50; 22:13; 24:51; 25:30; Lk 13:28. See: TDNT—1:641, 110; BAGD—147d; THAYER—106a.

1031. **βρύχω** {1x} **bruchō**, *broo'-kho;* a primary verb; to *grate* the teeth (in pain or rage):—gnash {1x}.

Brucho means primarily, "to bite or eat greedily" and denotes "to grind or gnash with the teeth," Acts 7:54. See: TDNT—1:641, 110; BAGD—148a; THAYER—106b.

1032. **βρύω** {1x} **bruō**, *broo'-o;* a primary verb; to be full to bursting, *to swell* out, i.e. (by impl.) to *gush:*—send forth {1x}.

Bruo means "to be full to bursting," was used of the earth in producing vegetation, of plants in putting forth buds; in Jas 3:11 it is said of springs gushing with water, "(doth the fountain) send forth . . . ?" See: BAGD—148a; THAYER—106b.

1033. **βρῶμα** {17x} **brōma**, *bro'-mah;* from the base of *977; food* (lit. or fig.), espec. (cer.) articles allowed or forbidden by the Jewish law:—meat {16x}, victuals {1x}.

Broma frequently translated "meat," and always so except in Mt 14:15, "victuals." See: TDNT—1:642, 111; BAGD—148a; THAYER—106b.

1034. **βρώσιμος** {1x} **brōsimŏs**, *bro'-sim-os;* from *1035; eatable:*—meat {1x}.

Brosimos signifying "eatable," is found in Lk 24:41: "And while they yet believed not for joy, and wondered, He said unto them, Have ye here any meat?" "Meat" is defined in vs. 42 as broiled fish and honeycomb. See: BAGD—148b; THAYER—106c.

1035. **βρῶσις** {11x} **brōsis**, *bro'-sis;* from the base of *977;* (abstr.) *eating* (lit. or fig.); by extens. (concr.) *food* (lit. or fig.):—eating {1x}, morsel of meat {1x}, food {1x}, meat {6x}, rust {2x}.

Brosis denotes **(1)** "the act of eating," e.g., Rom 14:17; **(2)** is said of rust, Mt 6:19–20; or, more usually **(3)** "that which is eaten, food, meat," Jn 4:32; 6:27, 55; Col 2:16; Heb 12:16 ("morsel of meat"); **(4)** "food," 2 Cor 9:10; **(5)** "eating," 1 Cor 8:4. See: TDNT—1:642, 111; BAGD—148b; THAYER—106c.

1036. **βυθίζω** {2x} **buthizō**, *boo-thid'-zo;* from *1037;* to *sink;* by impl. to *drown:*—begin to sink {1x}, drown {1x}.

This word means "to plunge into the deep, to sink" [*buthos*, "bottom, the deep, the sea", akin to *bathos*, "depth," and *abussos*, "bottomless," and Eng., "bath,"] and is used **(1)** in Lk 5:7 of the "sinking" of a boat; and **(2)** meta-

phorically in 1 Ti 6:9, of the effect of foolish and hurtful lusts, which "drown men in destruction and perdition." See: BAGD—148c; THAYER—106c.

1037. **βυθός** {1x} **buthŏs**, *boo-thos';* a var. of *899; depth,* i.e. (by impl.) the *sea:*—deep {1x}.

Buthos, "a depth," is used in the NT only in the natural sense, of the sea 2 Cor 11:25. See: BAGD—148c; THAYER—106c.

1038. **βυρσεύς** {3x} **bursĕus**, *boorce-yooce';* from βύρσα **bursa** (a *hide*); a *tanner:*—tanner {1x}.

Burseus is "a tanner" (from *bursa*, "a hide"), and occurs in Acts 9:43; 10:6, 32. See: BAGD—148d; THAYER—106d.

1039. **βύσσινος** {4x} **bussinŏs**, *boos'-see-nos;* from *1040;* made of *linen* (neut. a linen *cloth*):—fine linen {4x}.

Bussinos is an adjective denoting "made of fine linen." This is used **(1)** of the clothing of the mystic Babylon, Rev 18:12; 16, and **(2)** of the suitable attire of the Lamb's wife, Rev 19:8, 14, figuratively describing "the righteous acts of the saints." The presumption of Babylon is conspicuous in that she arrays herself in that which alone befits the bride of Christ. See: BAGD—148d; THAYER—106d.

1040. **βύσσος** {2x} **bussŏs**, *boos'-sos;* of Heb. or. [948]; white *linen:*—fine linen {2x}.

Bussos is "fine linen," made from a special species of flax. **(1)** In Lk 16:19 it is the clothing of the "rich man"; and **(2)** it is one of the products of mystery Babylon, Rev 18:12. See: BAGD—148d; THAYER—106d.

1041. **βῶμος** {1x} **bōmŏs**, *bo'-mos;* from the base of *939;* prop. a *stand,* i.e. (spec.) an *altar:*—altar {1x}.

Bomos is properly, "an elevated place" and always denotes either a pagan "altar" or an "altar" reared without divine appointment. In the NT the only place where this is found is Acts 17:23, as this is the only mention of such. Syn.: *Bomos* refers to the heathen altar and *thysiasterion* (2379) refers to the altar of the true God. See: BAGD—148d; THAYER—106d.

Γ

1042. **γαββαθά** {1x} **gabbatha**, *gab-bath-ah';* of Chald. or. [comp. 1355]; *the knoll; gabbatha,* a vernacular term for the Roman tribunal in Jerusalem:—Gabbatha {1x}. See: BAGD—149a; THAYER—107a.

1043. **Γαβριήλ** {2x} **Gabriĕl**, *gab-ree-ale';* of Heb. or. [1403]; *Gabriel,* an

archangel:—*Gabriel* {2x}. See: BAGD—149a; THAYER—107b.

1044. γάγγραινα {1x} **gaggraina**, *gang'-grahee-nah;* from γραίνω **grainō** (to *gnaw*); an *ulcer* ("gangrene"); an eating sore:—canker {1x}.

Gaggraina is "an eating sore," spreading corruption and producing mortification, is used, in 2 Ti 2:17, of errorists in the church, who, pretending to give true spiritual food, produce spiritual gangrene ("canker"). See: BAGD—149a; THAYER—107b.

1045. Γάδ {1x} **Gad**, *gad;* of Heb. or. [1410]; *Gad*, a tribe of Isr.:—*Gad* {1x}. See: BAGD—149a; THAYER—107b

1046. Γαδαρηνός {3x} **Gadarēnŏs**, *gad-ar-ay-nos';* from Γαδαρά (a town E. of the Jordan); a *Gadarene* or inhab. of Gadara:—Gadarene {3x}. See: BAGD—149a; THAYER—107b.

1047. γάζα {1x} **gaza**, *gad'-zah;* of for. or.; a *treasure:*—treasure {1x}.

Gaza signifies "royal treasure" and occurs in Acts 8:27. See: BAGD—149b; THAYER—107c.

1048. Γάζα {1x} **Gaza**, *gad'-zah;* of Heb. or. [5804]; *Gazah* (i.e. *Azzah*), a place in Pal.:—*Gaza* {1x}. See: BAGD—149b; THAYER—107c.

1049. γαζοφυλάκιον {5x} **gazŏphulakiŏn**, *gad-zof-oo-lak'-ee-on;* from *1047* and *5438;* a *treasure-house*, i.e. a court in the temple for the collection-boxes:—treasury {5x}.

This word comes from *gaza*, "a treasure," *phulake*, "a guard," is used by Josephus for a special room in the women's court in the temple in which gold and silver bullion was kept. This seems to be referred to in Jn 8:20; in Mk 12:41 (twice), 43 and Lk 21:1. It is used of the trumpet-shaped or ram's-horn-shaped chests, into which the temple offerings of the people were cast. There were 13 chests, six for such gifts in general, seven for distinct purposes. Syn.: 2878. See: BAGD—149b; THAYER—107d.

1050. Γάϊος {5x} **Gaïŏs**, *gah'-ee-os;* of Lat. or.; *Gâus* (i.e. *Caius*), a Chr.:—Gaius (of Corinth) {2x}, Gaius (of Macedonia) {1x}, Gaius (of Derbe) {1x}, Gaius (a Christian) {1x}. See: BAGD—149c; THAYER—108a.

1051. γάλα {5x} **gala**, *gal'-ah;* of uncert. aff.; *milk* (fig.):—milk {5x}.

Gala is used **(1)** literally (1 Cor 9:7) and **(2)** metaphorically, **(2a)** of rudimentary spiritual teaching (1 Cor 3:2; Heb 5:12, 13; 1 Pet 2:2).

(2b) The nourishment may be understood as of that spiritually rational nature which, acting through the regenerate mind, develops spiritual growth. God's Word is not given so that it is impossible to understand it, or that it requires a special class of men to interpret it; its character is such that the Holy Spirit who gave it can unfold its truths even to the young convert (cf. 1 Jn 2:27). See: TDNT—1:645, 111; BAGD—149c; THAYER—108b.

1052. Γαλάτης {2x} **Galatēs**, *gal-at'-ace;* from *1053;* a *Galatian* or inhab. of Galatia:—Galatians {2x}. See: BAGD—149d; THAYER—108b.

1053. Γαλατία {4x} **Galatia**, *gal-at-ee'-ah;* of for. or.; *Galatia*, a region of Asia:—Galatia {4x}. See: BAGD—149d; THAYER—108b.

1054. Γαλατικός {2x} **Galatikŏs**, *gal-at-ee-kos';* from *1053; Galatic* or relating to Galatia:—of Galatia {2x}. See: BAGD—150a; THAYER—108b.

1055. γαλήνη {3x} **Galēnē**, *gal-ay'-nay;* of uncert. der.; *tranquillity:*—calm {3x}. See: BAGD—150b; THAYER—108b.

1056. Γαλιλαία {63x} **Galilaia**, *gal-il-ah'-yah;* of Heb. or. [1551]; *Galilœa* (i.e. the heathen *circle*), a region of Pal.:—Galilee {63x}. See: BAGD—150b; THAYER—108c.

1057. Γαλιλαῖος {11x} **Galilaiŏs**, *gal-ee-lah'-yos;* from *1056; Galilœan* or belonging to Galilæa:—Galilæan {8x}, of Galilee {3x}. See: BAGD—150c; THAYER—108c.

1058. Γαλλίων {3x} **Galliōn**, *gal-lee'-own;* of Lat. or.; *Gallion* (i.e. *Gallio*), a Roman officer:—Gallio {3x}. See: BAGD—150c; THAYER—108d.

1059. Γαμαλιήλ {2x} **Gamaliēl**, *gam-al-ee-ale';* of Heb. or. [1583]; *Gamaliel* (i.e. *Gamliel*), an Isr.:—Gamaliel {2x}. See: BAGD—150c; THAYER—108d.

1060. γαμέω {29x} **gaměō**, *gam-eh'-o;* from *1062;* to *wed* (of either sex):—marry {24x}, married {3x}, marry a wife {2x}.

This word means "to marry" and is used **(1)** of "the man," Mt 5:32; 19:9, 10; 22:25 ("married a wife"); v. 30; 24:38; Mk 6:17; 10:11; 12:25; Lk 14:20; 16:18; 17:27, ("married wives"); 20:34, 35; 1 Cor 7:28 (1st part); v. 33; **(2)** of "the woman," **(2a)** in the active voice, Mk 10:12; 1 Cor 7:28 (last part); ver. 34; 1 Ti 5:11, 14; **(2b)** in the passive voice, 1 Cor 7:39; **(3)** of "both sexes," 1 Cor 7:9, 10, 36; 1 Ti 4:3. See: TDNT—1:648, 111; BAGD—150d; THAYER—108d.

1061. **γαμίσκω** {1x} **gamiskō,** *gam-is'-ko;* from *1062;* to *espouse* (a daughter to a husband):—give in marriage {1x}. See: BAGD—151b; THAYER—109a.

1062. **γάμος** {16x} **gamŏs,** *gam'-os;* of uncert. aff.; *nuptials:*—marriage {9x}, wedding {6x}.

This word means "a wedding," especially a wedding "feast." It is used **(1)** in the plural in the following passages: Mt 22:2, 3, 4, 9 (in verses 11, 12, it is used in the singular, in connection with the wedding garment); 25:10; Lk 12:36; 14:8; **(2)** in the following it signifies a wedding itself, Jn 2:1, 2; Heb 13:4; and **(3)** figuratively in Rev 19:7, of the marriage of the Lamb; in v. 9 it is used in connection with the supper, the wedding supper, not the wedding itself, as in v. 7. See: TDNT—1:648, 111; BAGD—151b; THAYER—109b.

1063. **γάρ** {1067x} **gar,** *gar;* a primary particle; prop. assigning a *reason* (used in argument, explanation or intensification; often with other particles):—for {1027x}, not tr {12x}, misc. {28x}, = and, as, because (that), but, even, indeed, no doubt, seeing, then, therefore, verily, what, why, yet. See: BAGD—151c; THAYER—109b.

1064. **γαστήρ** {9x} **gastēr,** *gas-tare';* of uncert. der.; the *stomach;* by anal. the *matrix;* fig. a *gourmand:*—be with child + 1722 + 2192 {5x}, with child + 1722 + 2192 {2x}, womb {1x}, belly {1x}.

This word means womb or be with child. But in Titus 1:12, by synecdoche (a figure of speech in which the part is put for the whole, or vice versa), it is used to denote "gluttons" ("bellies"). See: BAGD—152c; THAYER—110d.

1065. **γέ** {11x} **gĕ,** *gheh;* a primary particle of *emphasis* or *qualification* (often used with other particles pref.):—yet {2x}, at least {1x}, beside {1x}, doubtless {1x}, not tr {6x}. See: BAGD—152d; THAYER—110d.

1066. **Γεδεών** {1x} **Gĕdĕōn,** *ghed-eh-own';* of Heb. or. [1439]; *Gedeon* (i.e. *Gid[e]on*), an Isr.:—*Gedeon* (Gideon) {1x}. See: BAGD—153b; THAYER—111c.

1067. **γέεννα** {12x} **gĕĕnna,** *gheh'-en-nah;* of Heb. or. [1516 and 2011]; *valley of* (the son of) *Hinnom; ge-henna* (or *Ge-Hinnom*), a valley of Jerusalem, used (fig.) as a name for the place (or state) of everlasting punishment:—hell {9x}, hell fire + 3588 + 4442 {3x}.

Geenna **(1)** represents the Hebrew Ge-Hinnom (the valley of Tophet); **(2)** it is found twelve times in the NT, eleven of which are in

the Synoptics, in every instance as uttered by the Lord Himself. **(2a)** He who says to his brother, Thou fool will be in danger of "the hell of fire," Mt 5:22; **(2b)** it is better to pluck out (a metaphorical description of irrevocable law) an eye that causes its possessor to stumble, than that his "whole body be cast into hell," Mt 5:29; similarly with the hand, v. 30; **(2c)** in Mt 18:8, 9, the admonitions are repeated, with an additional mention of the foot; here, too, the warning concerns the person himself (for which obviously the "body" stands in chapt. 5); **(2d)** in Mt 18: 8, "the eternal fire" is mentioned as the doom, the character of the region standing for the region itself, the two being combined in the phrase "the hell of fire," Mt 18: 9. **(2e)** To the passage in Mt 18, that in Mk 9:43–47, is parallel; here to the word "hell" are applied the extended descriptions "the unquenchable fire" and "where their worm dieth not and the fire is not quenched."

(3) That God, "after He hath killed, hath power to cast into hell," **(3a)** is assigned as a reason why He should be feared with the fear that keeps from evil doing, Lk 12:5; **(3b)** the parallel passage to this in Mt 10:28 declares, not the casting in, but the doom which follows, namely, the destruction (not the loss of being, but of well-being) of "both soul and body." **(4)** In Mt 23 the Lord denounces the scribes and Pharisees, who in proselytizing a person "make him two-fold more a son of hell" than themselves (v. 15), **(4a)** the phrase here being expressive of moral characteristics, and **(4b)** declares the impossibility of their escaping "the judgment of hell," v. 33. **(5)** In Jas 3:6 "hell" is described as the source of the evil done by misuse of the tongue; here the word stands for the powers of darkness, whose characteristics and destiny are those of "hell." **(6)** For terms descriptive of "hell," see e.g., Mt 13:42; 25:46; Phil 3:19; 2 Th 1:9; Heb 10:39; 2 Pet 2:17; Jude 13; Rev 2:11; 19:20; 20:6, 10, 14; 21:8. **(7)** The verb *tartaroo,* translated "cast down to hell" in 2 Pet 2:4, signifies to consign to Tartarus, which is neither Sheol nor hades nor hell, but the place where those angels whose special sin is referred to in that passage are confined "to be reserved unto judgment"; the region is described as "pits of darkness." See: TDNT—1:657, 113; BAGD—153; THAYER—111c.

1068. **Γεθσημανῆ** {2x} **Gĕthsēmanē,** *gheth-say-man-ay';* of Chald. or. [comp. 1660 and 8081]; *oil-press; Gethsemane,* a garden near Jerusalem:—*Gethsemane* {2x}. See: BAGD—153b.111d.

1069. **γείτων** {4x} **gĕitōn,** *ghi'-tone;* from 1093; a *neighbour* (living in the same

land and probably adjoining one's *ground*); by impl. a *friend*:—neighbour {4x}.

Geiton is literally "one living in the same land" and denotes "a neighbor," always plural in the NT, Lk 14:12; 15:6, 9; Jn 9:5. See: BAGD—153c; THAYER—112a.

1070. γελάω {2x} **gĕlaō**, *ghel-ah'-o;* of uncert. aff.; to *laugh* (as a sign of joy or satisfaction):—laugh {2x}.

Gelao means "to laugh," is found in Lk 6:21, 25. This signifies loud laughter in contrast to demonstrative weeping. Syn.: 1071, 2606. See: TDNT—1:658, 113; BAGD—153c; THAYER—112a.

1071. γέλως {1x} **gĕlōs**, *ghel'-oce;* from *1070; laughter* (as a mark of gratification):—laughter {1x}. Syn.: 1070, 2606. See: TDNT—1:658, 113; BAGD—153c; THAYER—112a.

1072. γεμίζω {9x} **gĕmizō**, *ghem-id'-zo;* tran. from *1073;* to *fill* entirely:—fill {7x}, be full {1x}, fill . . . fill {1x}.

Gemizo means "to fill or load full" and is **(1)** used of a boat, Mk 4:37; **(2)** a sponge, Mk 15:36; **(3)** a house, Lk 14:23; **(4)** the belly, Lk 15:16; **(5)** waterpots, Jn 2:1; **(6)** baskets, 6:13; **(7)** bowls, with fire, Rev 8:5; **(8)** the temple, with smoke, Rev 15:8. See: BAGD—153c; THAYER—112a.

1073. γέμω {11x} **gĕmō**, *ghem'-o;* a primary verb; to *swell* out, i.e. *be full*:— be full {3x}, full {8x}.

Gemo means **(1)** "to be full, to be heavily laden with," was primarily used of a ship; **(2)** it is chiefly used in the NT of evil contents, such as **(2a)** extortion and excess, Mt 23:25; **(2b)** dead men's bones, Mt 23:27; **(2c)** extortion and wickedness, Lk 11:39; **(2d)** cursing, Rom 3:14; **(2e)** blasphemy, Rev 17:3; **(2f)** abominations, Rev 17: 4; **(2g)** of divine judgments, Rev 15:7; 21:9; **(2h)** of good things, Rev 4:6, 8; 5:8. See: BAGD—153d; THAYER—112a.

1074. γενεά {42x} **gĕnĕa**, *ghen-eh-ah';* from (a presumed der. of) *1085;* a *generation;* by impl. an *age* (the period or the persons):—age {2x}, generation {37x}, nation {1x}, time {2x}.

Genea, connected with *ginomai* (*1096*), "to become," primarily **(1)** signifies "a begetting, or birth"; hence, that which has been begotten, a family; **(1a)** or successive members of a genealogy (Mt 1:17), or **(1b)** of a race of people, possessed of similar characteristics, pursuits, etc., of a bad character: "Then Jesus answered and said, O faithless and perverse generation (*1074*), how long shall I be with you?" (Mt 17:17; cf. Mk 9:19; Lk 9:41; 16:8; Acts 2:40); or **(1c)** of

the whole multitude of men living at the same time: "Verily I say unto you, This generation shall not pass, till all these things be fulfilled" (Mt 24:34; cf. Mk 13:30; Lk 1:48; 21:32; Phil 2:15), and **(1d)** especially of those of the Jewish race living at the same period: "But whereunto shall I liken this generation? It is like unto children sitting in the markets, and calling unto their fellows" (Mt 11:16). **(2)** Transferred from people to the time in which they lived, the word came to mean "an age," i.e., a period ordinarily occupied by each successive generation, say, of thirty or forty years: "Who in times (*genea*) past suffered all nations to walk in their own ways" (Acts 14:16; cf. 15:21; Eph 3:5; Col 1:26). **(3)** In Eph 3:21 *genea* is combined with aion (*165*) in a remarkable phrase in a doxology: **(3a)** "Unto him be glory in the church by Christ Jesus throughout all ages, world without end. Amen." **(3b)** The word *genea* is to be distinguished from *aion,* as not denoting a period of unlimited duration. Syn.: 165, 166, 2244, 2250, 5046, 5230. See: TDNT—1:662, 114; BAGD—153d; THAYER—112b.

1075. γενεαλογέω {1x} **gĕnĕalŏgĕō**, *ghen-eh-al-og-eh'-o;* from *1074* and *3056;* to *reckon by generations,* i.e. *trace in genealogy:*—count (one's) descent {1x}.

This word means "to reckon or trace a genealogy" and is used, in the passive voice, of Melchizedek in Heb 7:6 "whose descent" is not counted." See: TDNT—1:665, 114; BAGD—154b; THAYER—112c.

1076. γενεαλογία {2x} **gĕnĕalŏgia**, *ghen-eh-al-og-ee'-ah;* from the same as *1075; tracing by generations,* i.e. "*genealogy*":—genealogy {2x}.

This word is used in 1 Ti 1:4 and Titus 3:9, with reference to such "genealogies" as are found in Philo, Josephus and the book of Jubilees, by which Jews traced their descent from the patriarchs and their families, and perhaps also to Gnostic "genealogies" and orders of aeons and spirits. Amongst the Greeks, as well as other nations, mythological stories gathered round the birth and "genealogy" of their heroes. Probably Jewish "genealogical" tales crept into Christian communities. Hence the warnings to Timothy and Titus. See: TDNT—1:663, 114; BAGD—154b; THAYER—112c.

1077. γενέσια {2x} **gĕnĕsia**, *ghen-es'-ee-ah;* neut. plur. of a der. of *1078; birthday* ceremonies:—birthday {2x}.

This word primarily denoted "the festivities of a birthday, a birthday feast," and is found in Mt 14:6 and Mk 6:21. See: BAGD—154c; THAYER—112d.

1078. **γένεσις** {3x} **genesis**, *ghen'-es-is;* from the same as *1074; nativity;* fig. *nature:*—generation {1x}, nature {1x}, natural {1x}.

Genesis denotes "an origin, a lineage, or birth" **(1)** translated "generation" in Mt 1:1; **(2)** "nature" in Jas 3:6; and **(3)** "natural" in Jas 1:23, describing the face with which one is born. See: BAGD—154d; THAYER—112d.

1079. **γενετή** {1x} **gĕnĕtē**, *ghen-et-ay;* fem. of a presumed der. of the base of *1074; birth:*—birth {1x}.

This word means "a being born, or the hour of birth" and is used in Jn 9:1 of a man born blind. See: BAGD—155a; THAYER—112d.

1080. **γεννάω** {97x} **gĕnnaō**, *ghen-nah'-o;* from a var. of *1085;* to *procreate* (prop. of the father, but by extens. of the mother); fig. to *regenerate:*—begat {49x}, be born {39x}, bear {2x}, gender {2x}, bring forth {1x}, be delivered {1x}, conceive {1x}, make {1x}, spring {1x}.

Gennao, as a verb, **(1)** means "to beget" and in the passive voice means "to be born." **(2)** It is chiefly used of men "begetting" children (Mt 1:2–16). **(3)** A woman "brings forth" a child, "is delivered" (Lk 1:57) or "bares" the child (Lk 1:13; 23:29). **(4)** The child is said to "be born" (Jn 16:21). **(5)** In Gal 4:24, it is used allegorically, to contrast Jews under bondage to the Law, and spiritual Israel to contrast the natural birth of Ishmael and the supernatural birth of Isaac. **(6)** In Mt 1:20 it is used of conception, "that which is conceived in her." **(7)** It is used of the act of God in the birth of Christ, (Acts 13:33; Heb 1:5; 5:5, quoted from Ps 2:7, none of which indicate that Christ became the Son of God at His birth). **(8)** It is used metaphorically **(8a)** in the writings of the apostle John, of the gracious act of God in conferring upon those who believe the nature and disposition of "children," imparting to them spiritual life (Jn 3:3, 5, 7; 1 Jn 2:29; 3:9; 4:7; 5:1, 4, 18); **(8b)** of one who by means of preaching the gospel becomes the human instrument in the impartation of spiritual life (1 Cor 4:15; Philem 10); **(8c)** in 2 Pet 2:12 with reference to the evil men whom the apostle describes as "natural brute beasts"; **(9)** in the sense of gendering strife (2 Ti 2:23). **(10)** Beget in English means to bring into a special relationship. The "be" is intensive and "get" means to bring to one's self. Jesus, as the "only begotten of the Father" means that even though He had the unique and equal relationship within the Trinity in eternity past, He took upon Himself the likeness of sinful flesh, dwelt among men, was tempted in all ways, yet without sin, submitted to the death on the cross,

was raised on the third day, and ascended to the right hand of the Father. He was always uniquely related to the Father, but even more so now as He is the only unique Son of God, the only sacrifice to remove sins and restore fallen man to God. **(11)** In Jn 3:3, 5, 7, the adverb *anothen* (509) "anew, or from above," accompanies the simple verb *gennao*. Syn.: 313, 616, 738, 1084, 1085, 1626, 5088. See: TDNT—1:665, 114; BAGD—155b; THAYER—113a.

1081. **γέννημα** {9x} **gĕnnēma**, or γένημα **gĕnēma**, *ghen'-nay-mah;* from *1080; offspring;* by anal. *produce* (lit. or fig.):—fruit {5x}, generation {4x}.

This word means "to beget" and denotes "the offspring of men and animals," Mt 3:7; 12:34; 23:33; Lk 3:7. See: TDNT—1:672, 114; BAGD—155d; THAYER—113c.

1082. **Γεννησαρέτ** {3x} **Gĕnnēsarĕt**, *ghen-nay-sar-et';* of Heb. or. [comp. 3672]; *Gennesaret* (i.e. *Kinnereth*), a lake and plain in Pal.:—*Gennesaret* {3x}. See: BAGD—156a; THAYER—113c.

1083. **γέννησις** {2x} **gĕnnēsis**, *ghen'-nay-sis;* from *1080; nativity:*—birth {2x}.

Gennesis is "a birth, begetting, producing" and is used in Mt 1:18 and Lk 1:14. See: BAGD—156a.113d.

1084. **γεννητός** {2x} **gĕnnētŏs**, *ghen-nay-tos';* from *1080; born:*—that is born {2x}.

Gennetos, as an adjective, is translated "born" and is used in Mt 11:11: "Verily I say unto you, Among them that are born of women there hath not risen a greater than John the Baptist" (cf. Lk 7:28 - a periphrasis for "men," and suggestive of frailty). Syn.: 313, 616, 738, 1080, 1085, 1626, 5088. See: TDNT—1:672, 114; BAGD—156a; THAYER—113d.

1085. **γένος** {21x} **gĕnŏs**, *ghen'-os;* from *1096; "kin"* (abstr. or concr., lit. or fig., indiv. or collect.):—kind {5x}, kindred {3x}, offspring {3x}, nation {2x}, stock {2x}, born {2x}, diversity {1x}, country {1x}, countryman {1x}, generation {1x}.

Genos, as a noun, means "a generation, kind, stock," is used in the dative case, with the article, to signify "by race": "And found a certain Jew named Aquila, born (*genos*) in Pontus" (Acts 18:2; cf. v. 24). Syn.: 313, 616, 738, 1080, 1084, 1626, 5088. See: TDNT—1:684, 117; BAGD—156b; THAYER—113d.

1086. **Γεργεσηνός** {1x} **Gĕrgĕsēnŏs**, *gher-ghes-ay-nos';* of Heb. or. [1622]; a *Gergesene* (i.e. *Girgashite*) or one of

the aborigines of Pal.:—Gergesenes {1x}. See: BAGD—156d; THAYER—114a.

1087. γερουσία {1x} **gĕrŏusia**, *gher-oo-see'-ah;* from *1088;* the *eldership,* i.e. (collect.) the Jewish *Sanhedrin:*—senate {1x}.

This word means "a council of elders" (from *geron,* "an old man," a term which early assumed a political sense among the Greeks, the notion of age being merged in that of dignity), is used in Acts 5:21, apparently epexegetically of the preceding word *sunedrion,* "council," the Sanhedrin. See: BAGD—156d; THAYER—114b.

1088. γέρων {1x} **gĕrōn**, *gher'-own;* of uncert. aff. [comp. *1094*]; *aged:*—old {1x}.

Geron denotes "an old man", Jn 3:4. See: BAGD—157a; THAYER—114b.

1089. γεύομαι {15x} **gĕuŏmai**, *ghyoo'-om-ahee;* a primary verb; to *taste;* by impl. to *eat;* fig. to *experience* (good or ill):—eat {3x}, taste {12x}.

Geuomai means primarily, "to cause to taste, to give one a taste of," is used in the middle voice and denotes (1) "to taste," its usual meaning; (2) "to take food, to eat," Acts 10:10; 20:11; 23:14. See: TDNT—1:675, 117; BAGD—157a; THAYER—114b.

1090. γεωργέω {1x} **gĕōrgĕō**, *gheh-or-gheh'-o;* from *1092;* to *till* (the soil):—dress {1x}.

This word means "to till the ground," is used in the passive voice in Heb 6:7, "by whom [the earth] is dressed." See: BAGD—157b; THAYER—114c.

1091. γεώργιον {1x} **gĕōrgiŏn**, *gheh-ore'-ghee-on;* neut. of a (presumed) der. of *1092; cultivable,* i.e. a *farm:*—husbandry {1x}.

Georgion denotes "tillage, cultivation, husbandry," 1 Cor 3:9, where the local church is described under this metaphor ("tillage"), suggestive of the diligent toil of the apostle and his fellow missionaries, both in the ministry of the gospel, and the care of the church at Corinth; suggestive, too, of the effects in spiritual fruitfulness. See: BAGD—157b; THAYER—114c.

1092. γεωργός {19x} **gĕōrgŏs**, *gheh-ore-gos';* from *1093* and the base of *2041;* a *land-worker,* i.e. *farmer:*—husbandman {19x}.

Georgos from *ge,* "land, ground," and *ergo* (or *erdo*), "to do" [Eng., "George"], denotes (1) "a husbandman," a tiller of the ground, 2 Ti 2:6; Jas 5:7; (2) "a vinedresser," Mt 21:33–35,

38, 40, 41; Mk 12:1, 2, 7, 9; Lk 20:9, 10, 14, 16; Jn 15:1, where Christ speaks of the Father as the "Husbandman," Himself as the Vine, His disciples as the branches, the object being to bear much fruit, life in Christ producing the fruit of the Spirit, i.e., character and ways in conformity to Christ. See: BAGD—157b; THAYER—114c.

1093. γῆ {252x} **gē**, *ghay;* contr. from a primary word; *soil;* by extension a *region,* or the solid part or the whole of the *terrene* globe (incl. the occupants in each application):—earth 188, land {42x}, ground {18x}, country {2x}, world {1x}, earthly + 1537 + 3588 {1x}.

Ge denotes (1) "earth as arable land," e.g., Mt 13:5, 8, 23; (2) in 1 Cor 15:47 it is said of the "earthly" material of which "the first man" was made, suggestive of frailty; (3) "the earth as a whole, the world," (3a) in contrast, whether to the heavens, e.g., Mt 5:18, 35, or (3b) to heaven, the abode of God, e.g., Mt 6:19, where the context suggests the "earth" as a place characterized by mutability and weakness; (3c) in Col 3:2 the same contrast is presented by the word "above"; (4) in Jn 3:31 ("of the earth, earthly") it describes one whose origin and nature are "earthly" and whose speech is characterized thereby, in contrast with Christ as the One from heaven; (5) in Col 3:5 the physical members are said to be "upon the earth," as a sphere where, as potential instruments of moral evils, they are, by metonymy, spoken of as the evils themselves; (6) "the inhabited earth," e.g., Lk 21:35; Acts 1:8; 8:33; 10:12; 11:6; 17:26; 22:22; Heb 11:13; Rev 13:8. (7) In the following the phrase "on the earth" signifies "among men," Lk 12:49; 18:8; Jn 17:4, (8) "a country, territory," e.g. Lk 4:25; Jn 3:22; (9) "the ground," e.g., Mt 10:29; Mk 4:26, "(into the) ground"; (10) "land," e.g., Mk 4:1; Jn 21:8–9, 11. (11) Cf. Eng. words beginning with ge—, e.g., "geodetic," "geodesy," "geology," "geometry," "geography." Syn.: 3625. See: TDNT—1:677, 116; BAGD—157c; THAYER—114d.

1094. γῆρας {1x} **gēras**, *ghay'-ras;* akin to *1088; senility:*—old age {1x}. See: BAGD—157d; THAYER—115a.

1095. γηράσκω {2x} **gēraskō**, *ghay-ras'-ko;* from *1094;* to *be senescent:*—be old {1x}, wax old {1x}.

Gerasko signifies (1) "to grow old," Jn 21:18 ("when thou shalt be old") and (2) Heb 8:13 ("that which . . . waxeth old"). See: BAGD—158a; THAYER—115a.

1096. γίνομαι {678x} **ginŏmai**, *ghin'-om-ahee;* a prol. and mid. voice

form of a primary verb; to *cause to be* ("gen"-
erate), i.e. (refl.) to *become* (*come into being*),
used with great latitude (lit., fig., intens.,
etc.):—be {255x}, come to pass {82x}, be made
{69x}, be done {63x}, come {52x}, become {47x},
God forbid + 3361 {15x}, arise {13x}, have {5x},
be fulfilled {3x}, be married to {3x}, be preferred {3x}, not tr {14x}, vr done {2x}, misc. {4x}
= be assembled, befall, behave self, be brought
(to pass), continue, be divided, draw, be ended,
fall, be finished, follow, be found, grow, happen, be kept, be ordained to be, partake, pass,
be performed, be published, require, seem, be
showed, X soon as it was, sound, be taken, be
turned, use, wax, will, would, be wrought.

    Ginomai, as a verb, means "to become, to
come into existence" and is used in the sense of
I. "taking place after" and translated **(1)** "there
followed" (Rev 8:7; cf. 11:15, 19). **(2)** It is translated "by means of [a death] having taken
place": "And for this cause He is the mediator
of the new testament, that by means of death,
for the redemption of the transgressions that
were under the first testament, they which are
called might receive the promise of eternal inheritance" (Heb 9:15), referring, not to the circumstances of a testamentary disposition, but
to the sacrifice of Christ as the basis of the
New Covenant. Syn.: 190, 201, 402, 1377, 1502,
1811, 1837, 1872, 2614, 2628, 3877, 4042, 4870,
5117, 5247, 5564, 5602. **II. It can also be translated "arise": (1)** of a great tempest on the sea
(Mt 8:24; Mk 4:37); **(2)** of persecution (Mt 13:21;
Mk 4:17, this might be translated "taketh
place"); **(3)** of a tumult (Mt 27:24, kjv, "made");
(4) of a flood (Lk 6:48); **(5)** a famine (Lk 15:14);
(6) a questioning (Jn 3:25); **(7)** a murmuring
(Acts 6:1); **(8)** a stir in the city (Acts 19:23); **(9)** a
dissension (Acts 23:7); **(10)** a great clamor (Acts
23:9). Syn.: 305, 393, 450, 1326, 1453, 1525,
1817, 4911. See: TDNT—1:681, 117; BAGD—
158a; THAYER—115b.

1097. γινώσκω {223x} **ginōskō**, *ghin-oce'-ko;*
             a prol. form of a primary
verb; to "*know*" (absolutely) in a great variety
of applications and with many impl. (as follow,
with others not thus clearly expressed):—know
{196x}, perceive {9x}, understand {8x}, misc.
{10x} = allow, be aware (of), feel, have knowledge, be resolved, can speak, be sure.

    Ginosko (*1097*) signifies **(1)** "to be taking in
knowledge, to come to know, recognize, understand," or "to understand completely," e.g., Mk
13:28, 29; Jn 13:12; 15:18; 21:17; 2 Cor 8:9; Heb
10:34; 1 Jn 2:5; 4:2, 6 (twice), 7, 13; 5:2, 20;
(2) in its past tenses it frequently means "to
know in the sense of realizing," the aorist or
point tense usually indicating definiteness, Mt
13:11; Mk 7:24; Jn 7:26; in 10:38 "that ye may

know (aorist tense) and understand, (present
tense)"; 19:4; Acts 1:7; 17:19; Rom 1:21; 1 Cor
2:11 (2nd part), 14; 2 Cor 2:4; Eph 3:19; 6:22;
Phil 2:19; 3:10; 1 Th 3:5; 2 Ti 2:19; Jas 2:20; 1 Jn
2:13 (twice), 14; 3:6; 4:8; 2 Jn 1; Rev 2:24; 3:3,
9. **(3)** In the passive voice, it often signifies "to
become known," e.g., Mt 10:26; Phil 4:5. **(4)** In
the sense of complete and absolute understanding on God's part, it is used, e.g., in Lk
16:15; Jn 10:15 (of the Son as well as the Father); 1 Cor 3:20. **(5)** In Lk 12:46 it is rendered
"He is . . . aware."

    (6) In the NT *ginosko* frequently indicates
a relation between the person "knowing" and
the object known; in this respect, what is
"known" is of value or importance to the one
who knows, and hence the establishment of
the relationship, e.g., especially **(6a)** of God's
"knowledge," 1 Cor 8:3, "if any man love God,
the same is known of Him"; **(6b)** Gal 4:9, "to be
known of God"; here the "knowing" suggests
approval and bears the meaning "to be approved"; so in 2 Ti 2:19; cf. Jn 10:14, 27; **(6c)** The
same idea of appreciation as well as "knowledge" underlies several statements concerning
the "knowledge" of God and His truth on the
part of believers, e.g., Jn 8:32; 14:20, 31; 17:3;
Gal 4:9 (1st part); 1 Jn 2:3–13, 14; 4:6, 8, 16;
5:20; **(6c1)** such "knowledge" is obtained, not
by mere intellectual activity, but by operation
of the Holy Spirit consequent upon acceptance
of Christ. **(6c2)** Nor is such "knowledge" marked
by finality; see e.g., 2 Pet 3:18. **(7)** The verb is
also used to convey the thought of connection
or union, as between man and woman, Mt 1:25;
Lk 1:34. **(8)** *Ginosko*, as a verb, means "to know
by observation and experience" is translated
"to know" (to learn - Mk 15:45; Jn 12:9). Syn.:
See discussion under *oida* (*1492*); *epiginosko*
(*1921*). See also: 198, 1097, 1107, 1110, 1492,
1921, 1467, 1922, 1987, 3129, 3453. See:
TDNT—1:689, 119; BAGD—160d; THAYER—
117b.

1098. γλεῦκος {1x} **gleukŏs**, *glyoo'-kos;* akin
             to *1099; sweet* wine, i.e.
(prop.) *must* (fresh juice), but used of the more
saccharine (and therefore highly inebriating)
fermented *wine:*—new wine {1x}.

    Gleukos denotes sweet "new wine," or must,
Acts 2:13, where the accusation shows that it
was intoxicant and must have been undergoing
fermentation some time. See: BAGD—162a;
THAYER—118c.

1099. γλυκύς {4x} **glukus**, *gloo-koos';* of un-
             cert. aff.; *sweet* (i.e. not bitter
nor salt)[cf. glucose]:—sweet {3x}, fresh {1x}.

    This word occurs in Jas 3:11, 12 ("fresh"

in this verse); Rev 10:9, 10. See: BAGD—162a; THAYER—118c.

1100. γλῶσσα {50x} **glōssa**, *gloce-sah';* of uncert. aff.; the *tongue;* by impl. a *language* (spec., one naturally unacquired):—tongue {50x}.

Glossa is used of **(1)** the "tongues . . . like as of fire" which appeared at Pentecost; **(2)** "the tongue," as an organ of speech, e.g., Mk 7:33; Rom 3:13; 14:11; 1 Cor 14:9; Phil 2:11; Jas 1:26; 3:5, 6, 8; 1 Pet 3:10; 1 Jn 3:18; Rev 16:10; **(3)** "a language," **(3a)** coupled with *phule,* "a tribe," *laos,* "a people," *ethnos,* "a nation," seven times in the Apocalypse, 5:9; 7:9; 10:11; 11:9; 13:7; 14:6; 17:15; **(3b)** the supernatural gift of speaking in another language without its having been learnt; in Acts 2:4–13 the circumstances are recorded from the viewpoint of the hearers; to those in whose language the utterances were made it appeared as a supernatural phenomenon; to others, the stammering of drunkards; what was uttered was not addressed primarily to the audience but consisted in recounting "the mighty works of God"; cf. 2:46; **(3c)** in 1 Cor, chapters 12 and 14, the use of the gift of "tongues" is mentioned as exercised in the gatherings of local churches; 12:10 speaks of the gift in general terms, and couples with it that of "the interpretation of tongues"; chapt. 14 gives instruction concerning the use of the gift, the paramount object being the edification of the church; unless the "tongue" was interpreted the speaker would speak "not unto men, but unto God,"; 14:2; he would edify himself alone, v. 4, unless he interpreted, v. 5, in which case his interpretation would be of the same value as the superior gift of prophesying, as he would edify the church, vv. 4–6; he must pray that he may interpret, v. 13; if there were no interpreter, he must keep silence, v. 28, for all things were to be done "unto edifying," v. 26. "If I come . . . speaking with tongues, what shall I profit you," says the apostle (expressing the great object in all oral ministry), "unless I speak to you either by way of revelation, or of knowledge, or of prophesying, or of teaching?" (v. 6). "Tongues" were for a sign, not to believers, but to unbelievers, v. 22, and especially to unbelieving Jews (see v. 21): cf. the passages in the Acts.

(4) There is no evidence of the continuance of this gift after apostolic times nor indeed in the later times of the apostles themselves; this provides confirmation of the fulfillment in this way of 1 Cor 13:8, that this gift would cease in the churches, just as would "prophecies" and "knowledge" in the sense of knowledge received by immediate supernatural power (cf. 14:6).

The completion of the Holy Scriptures has provided the churches with all that is necessary for individual and collective guidance, instruction, and edification. Syn.: 1258, 2804. See: TDNT—1:689, 119; BAGD—162b; THAYER—118c.

1101. γλωσσόκομον {2x} **glōssŏkŏmŏn**, *glocesok'-om-on;* from *1100* and the base of *2889;* prop. a *case* (to keep mouthpieces of wind-instruments in) i.e. (by extens.) a *casket* or (spec.) *purse:*—bag {2x}.

This word denotes "a small box" for any purpose, but especially a "casket or purse," to keep money in. It is used of the "bag" which Judas carried, Jn 12:6; 13:29. See: BAGD—162d; THAYER—119a.

1102. γναφεύς {1x} **gnaphĕus**, *gnaf-yuce';* by var. for a der. from κνάπτω **knaptō** (to *tease* cloth); a *cloth-dresser:*—fuller {1x}. See: BAGD—162d; THAYER—119a.

1103. γνήσιος {4x} **gnēsiŏs**, *gnay'-see-os;* from the same as *1077; legitimate* (of birth), i.e. *genuine:*—own {2x}, sincerity {1x}, true {1x}.

Gnesios, as an adjective, means primarily "lawfully begotten"; hence, "true, genuine, sincere" and is used **(1)** in the apostle's exhortation to his "true yoke-fellow": "And I intreat thee also, true yokefellow, help those women which laboured with me in the gospel, with Clement also, and with other my fellow-labourers, whose names are in the book of life" (Phil 4:3). It also speaks of **(2)** the "sincerity of love", 2 Cor 8:8; and **(3)** "one's own son", 1 Ti 1:2 and Titus 1:4. Syn.: 225, 226, 227, 228, 230, 1104. See: TDNT—1:727, 125; BAGD—162d; THAYER—119a.

1104. γνησίως {1x} **gnēsiŏs**, *gnay-see'-oce;* adv. from *1103; genuinely,* i.e. *really:*—naturally {1x}.

Gnesios, as an adverb, means "sincerely, honorably" and is rendered "naturally": "For I have no man likeminded, who will naturally care for your state" (Phil 2:20). Syn.: 225, 226, 227, 228, 230, 1103. See: BAGD—163a; THAYER—119a.

1105. γνόφος {1x} **gnŏphŏs**, *gnof'-os;* akin to *3509; gloom* (as of a storm):—blackness {1x}.

Gnophos in Heb 12:18 denotes "blackness, gloom," seems to have been associated with the idea of a tempest and is related to *skotos,* "darkness." Syn.: 887, 2217, 4655. See: BAGD—163a; THAYER—119b.

1106. γνώμη {9x} **gnōmē**, *gno'-may;* from *1097; cognition,* i.e. (subj.) *opinion,* or (obj.) *resolve* (counsel, consent, etc.):—judg-

ment {3x}, mind {2x}, purpose + 1096 {1x}, advice {1x}, will {1x}, agree + 4160 + 3391 {1x}.

This word comes from "to know, perceive" and (1) firstly means "the faculty or knowledge, reason"; then, (2) "that which is thought or known, one's mind." (3) Under this heading there are various meanings: (3a) a view, judgment, opinion, 1 Cor 1:10; Philem 14; Rev 17:13, 17; (3b) an opinion as to what ought to be done, either (3b1) by oneself, and so a resolve, or purpose, Acts 20:3; or (3b2) by others, and so, judgment, advice, 1 Cor 7:25, 40; 2 Cor 8:10. Syn.: *Boule* (*1012*) is to be distinguished from *gnome; boule* is the result of determination, *gnome* is the result of knowledge. See: TDNT—1:717, 119; BAGD—163a.; THAYER—119b.

1107. **γνωρίζω** {24x} **gnōrizō**, *gno-rid'-zo;* from a der. of *1097;* to *make known;* subj. to *know:*—make known {16x}, declare {4x}, certify {1x}, give to understand {1x}, do to wit {1x}, wot {1x}.

Gnorizo signifies (1) "to come to know, discover, know," Phil 1:22, "I wot (not)," i.e., "I know not," "I have not come to know"; (2) "to make known," whether (2a) communicating things before "unknown," Lk 2:15; Jn 15:15, "I have made known"; 17:26; Acts 2:28; 7:13 (1st part); Rom 9:22, 23; 16:26 (passive voice); 2 Cor 8:1, "we do (you) to wit"; Eph 1:9; 3:3, 5, 10 (all three in the passive voice); 6:19, 21; Col 1:27; 4:7, 9, "shall declare"; 2 Pet 1:16; or (2b) reasserting things already "known," 1 Cor 12:3, "I give (you) to understand" (the apostle reaffirms what they knew); 15:1, (2b1) of the gospel; Gal 1:11 (he reminds them of what they well knew, the ground of his claim to apostleship); (2b2) Phil 4:6 (passive voice), of requests to God. This word signifies (3) to come to know, discover, know (Phil 1:22) and (4) to make known (Lk 2:15, 17). Syn.: 1097, 1110, 1492, 1921, 1467, 1922, 1987. See: TDNT—1:718, 119; BAGD—163b; THAYER—119b

1108. **γνῶσις** {29x} **gnōsis**, *gno'-sis;* from *1097; knowing* (the act), i.e. (by impl.) *knowledge:*—knowledge {28x}, science {1x}.

This word means primarily "a seeking to know, an enquiry, investigation" and denotes, in the NT, "knowledge," especially of spiritual truth; it is used (1) absolutely, in Lk 11:52; Rom 2:20; 15:14; 1 Cor 1:5; 8:1 (twice), 7, 10, 11; 13:2, 8; 14:6; 2 Cor 6:6; 8:7; 11:6; Eph 3:19; Col 2:3; 1 Pet 3:7; 2 Pet 1:5, 6; (2) with an object: in respect of (2a) God, 2 Cor 2:14; 10:5; (2b) the glory of God, 2 Cor 4:6; (2c) Christ Jesus, Phil 3:8; 2 Pet 3:18; (2d) salvation, Lk 1:77; (3) subjectively, (3a) of God's "knowledge," Rom

11:33; (3b) the word of "knowledge," 1 Cor 12:8; (3c) "knowledge" falsely so called, 1 Ti 6:20. Syn.: *Epignosis* (*1903*) is the complete comprehension after the first knowledge [*gnosis*]. Something that is known before is now more familiar; a more exact viewing of an object previously seen from a distance. The small portion of knowledge [*gnosis*] is improved upon and it is seen more strongly and clearly. See also: 1922, 4678, 4907, 5428, 5826. See: TDNT—1:689, 119; BAGD—163d; THAYER—119c.

1109. **γνώστης** {1x} **gnōstēs**, *gnoce'-tace;* from *1097;* a *knower:*—expert {1x}.

A *gnostes* is "one who knows" and denotes "an expert, a connoisseur," Acts 26:3. See: BAGD—164b; THAYER—119d.

1110. **γνωστός** {12x} **gnōstos**, *gnoce-tos';* from *1097;* well-*known:*—acquaintance {2x}, (which may be) known {12x}, notable {1x}.

Gnostos signifies "known, or knowable"; hence, "one's acquaintance"; it is used in this sense, in the plural, in Lk 2:44 and 23:49. See: TDNT—1:718, 119; BAGD—164b; THAYER—119d.

1111. **γογγύζω** {8x} **gŏgguzō**, *gong-good'-zo;* of uncert. der.; to *grumble:*—murmur {8x}. Syn.: 1112, 1234, 1690.

This word means "to mutter, murmur, grumble, say anything in a low tone", an onomatopoeic word, representing the significance by the sound of the word, as in the word "murmur" itself, (1) is used of the laborers in the parable of the householder, Mt 20:11; (2) of the scribes and Pharisees, against Christ, Lk 5:30; (3) of the Jews, Jn 6:41, 43; (4) of the disciples, Jn 6:61; (5) of the people, Jn 7:32 (of debating secretly); (6) of the Israelites, 1 Cor 10:10 (twice), where it is also used in a warning to believers. See: TDNT—1:728, 125; BAGD—164b; THAYER—120a.

1112. **γογγυσμός** {4x} **gŏggusmŏs**, *gong-goos-mos';* from *1111;* a *grumbling:*—grudging {1x}, murmuring {3x}.

This word means "a murmuring, muttering" and is used (1) in the sense of secret debate among people, Jn 7:12; (2) of displeasure or complaining (more privately than in public), said of Grecian Jewish converts against Hebrews, Acts 6:1; (3) in general admonitions, Phil 2:14; 1 Pet 4:9, "grudging." Syn.: 1234, 1690. See: TDNT—1:735, 125; BAGD—164c; THAYER—120a.

1113. **γογγυστής** {1x} **gŏggustēs**, *gong-goos-tace';* from *1111;* a *grumbler:*—murmurer {1x}.

A *goggustes* is "a murmurer", i.e. "one who complains" and is used in Jude 16, especially perhaps of utterances against God (see v. 15). See: TDNT—1:737, 125; BAGD—164c; THAYER—120b.

1114. **γόης** {1x} **gŏēs**, *go'-ace;* from γοάω **gŏaō** (to *wail*); prop. a *wizard* (as *muttering* spells), i.e. (by impl.) an *imposter:*—seducer {1x}.

Goes primarily denotes "a wailer"; hence, from the howl in which spells were chanted, "a wizard, sorcerer, enchanter," and hence, "a juggler, cheat, impostor," rendered "impostors" in 2 Ti 3:13 "seducers"; possibly the false teachers referred to practiced magical arts; cf. v. 8. See: TDNT—1:737, 126; BAGD—164d; THAYER—120b.

1115. **Γολγοθᾶ** {3x} **Golgŏtha**, *gol-goth-ah';* of Chald. or. [comp. 1538]; *the skull; Golgotha*, a knoll near Jerusalem:—Golgotha {3x}. See: BAGD—164d; THAYER—120b.

1116. **Γόμορρα** {5x} **Gŏmŏrrha**, *gom'-or-hrhah;* of Heb. or. [6017]; *Gomorrha* (i.e. *'Amorah*), a place near the Dead Sea:—Gomorrha {5x}. See: BAGD—164d; THAYER—120b.

1117. **γόμος** {3x} **gŏmŏs**, *gom'-os;* from *1073;* a *load* (as *filling*), i.e. (spec.) a *cargo*, or (by extens.) *wares:*—burden {1x}, merchandise {2x}.

This word means "full, or heavy," and denotes (1) "the lading of freight of a ship," Acts 21:3, or (2) "merchandise conveyed in a ship," and so "merchandise in general," Rev 18:11–12. See: BAGD—164d; THAYER—120c.

1118. **γονεύς** {19x} **gŏnĕus**, *gon-yooce';* from the base of *1096;* a *parent:*—parents {19x}.

A *goneus* is "a begetter, a father" and is used (1) in the plural in the NT, Mt 10:21; Mk 13:12; (2) six times in Lk (in Lk 2:43 "Joseph and His mother"); (3) six in Jn; (4) elsewhere, Rom 1:30; 2 Cor 12:14 (twice); Eph 6:1; Col 3:20; 2 Ti 3:2. See: BAGD—165a; THAYER—120c.

1119. **γόνυ** {12x} **gŏnu**, *gon-oo';* of uncert. aff.; the *"knee":*—knee {7x}, kneel + 5087 + 3588 {5x}.

A *gonu* is "a knee" (Latin, *genu* cf. genuflect) and is used (1) metaphorically in Heb 12:12, where the duty enjoined is that of "courageous self-recovery in God's strength;" (2) literally, (2a) of the attitude of a suppliant, Lk 5:8; Eph 3:14; (2b) of veneration, Rom 11:4; 14:11; Phil 2:10; (2c) in mockery, Mk 15:19. See: TDNT—1:738, 126; BAGD—165a; THAYER—120c.

1120. **γονυπετέω** {4x} **gŏnupĕtĕō**, *gon-oo-pet-eh'-o;* from a compound of *1119* and the alt. of *4098;* to *fall* on the *knee:*—kneel down to {2x}, bow the knee {1x}, kneel to {1x}.

This word denotes (1) "to bow the knees, kneel," from *gonu* (see above) and *pipto*, "to fall prostrate," the act of one imploring aid, Mt 17:14; Mk 1:40; (2) of one expressing reverence and honor, Mk 10:17; (3) in mockery, Mt 27:29. See: TDNT—1:738, 126; BAGD—165b; THAYER—120c.

1121. **γράμμα** {15x} **gramma**, *gram'-mah;* from *1125;* a *writing*, i.e. a *letter, note, epistle, book*, etc.; plur. *learning:*—letter {9x}, bill {2x}, writing {1x}, learning {1x}, scripture {1x}, written + 1722 {1x}. See: TDNT—1:761, 128; BAGD—165b; THAYER—120d.

1122. **γραμματεύς** {67x} **grammatĕus**, *grammat-yooce';* from *1121;* a *writer*, i.e. (professionally) *scribe* or *secretary:*—scribe {66x}, town-clerk {1x}.

Grammateus (1) denotes a scribe, a man of letters, a teacher of the law. (2) They are connected with the Pharisees, (2a) with whom they virtually formed one party (Lk 5:21), (2b) sometimes with the chief priests (Mt 2:4; Mk 8:31; 10:33). (3) They were considered naturally qualified to teach in the synagogues (Mk 1:22). (4) They were ambitious of honor (Mt 23:5–11), (4a) which they demanded especially from their pupils, and (4b) which was readily granted them, as well as by the people generally. (5) Like Ezra (cf. Ezra 7:12), the scribes were found originally among the priests and Levites. (6) The priests being the official interpreters of the Law, the scribes became an independent company. (7) Though they never held political power, they became leaders of the people. (8) Their functions regarding the Law were (8a) to teach it, (8b) develop it, and (8c) use it in connection with the Sanhedrin and various local courts. (9) They also occupied themselves with the sacred writings both historical and didactic. (10) They attached the utmost importance to ascetic elements, by which the nation was especially separated from the Gentiles. (10a) In their regime piety was reduced to external formalism. (10b) Only that was of value which was governed by external precept. (10c) Life under them became a burden; (10c1) they themselves sought to evade certain of their own precepts (Mt 23:16; Lk 11:46); (10c2) by their traditions the Law, instead of being a help in moral and spiritual life, became an instrument for preventing true

access to God (Lk 11:52). See: TDNT—1:740, 127; BAGD—165d; THAYER—121a.

1123. γραπτός {1x} **graptŏs**, *grap-tos';* from *1125; inscribed* (fig.):—written {1x}. See: BAGD—166a; THAYER—121b.

1124. γραφή {51x} **graphē**, *graf-ay';* from *1125; a document*, i.e. holy *Writ* (or its contents or a statement in it):—scripture {51x}.

Graphe, as a verb, means "to write" [Eng., "graph," "graphic," etc.], primarily denotes "a drawing, painting"; then "a writing," **(1)** of the OT Scriptures, **(1a)** in the plural, **(1a1)** the whole, e.g., Mt 21:42; 22:29; Jn 5:39; Acts 17:11; 18:24; **(1a2)** Rom 1:2, where "the prophets" comprises the OT writers in general; 15:4; **(1a3)** Rom 16:26, lit., "prophetic writings," expressing the character of all the Scriptures; **(1b)** in the singular in reference to a particular passage, e.g., Mk 12:10; Lk 4:21; Jn 2:22; 10:35 (though applicable to all); 19:24, 28, 36, 37; 20:9; Acts 1:16; 8:32, 35; Rom 4:3; 9:17; 10:11; 11:2; Gal 3:8, 22; 4:30; 1 Ti 5:18, where the 2nd quotation is from Lk 10:7, from which it may be inferred that the apostle included Luke's Gospel as "Scripture" alike with Deuteronomy, from which the first quotation is taken; **(1c)** in reference to the whole, e.g. Jas 4:5; **(1c1)** in 2 Pet 1:20, "no prophecy of Scripture," a description of all, **(1c2)** with special application to the OT in the next verse; **(2)** of the OT Scriptures (those accepted by the Jews as canonical) and all those of the NT which were to be accepted by Christians as authoritative, 2 Ti 3:16; these latter were to be discriminated from the many forged epistles and other religious "writings" already produced and circulated in Timothy's time. Such discrimination would be directed by the fact that "all Scripture," is inspired by God, and is profitable for the purposes mentioned. **(3)** The Scriptures are frequently personified by the NT writers (as by the Jews, Jn 7:42), **(3a)** as speaking with divine authority, e.g., Jn 19:37; Rom 4:3; 9:17, where the Scripture is said to speak to Pharaoh, giving the message actually sent previously by God to him through Moses; Jas 4:5; **(3b)** as possessed of the sentient quality of foresight, and the active power of preaching, Gal 3:8, where the Scripture mentioned was written more than four centuries after the words were spoken. **(4)** The Scripture, in such a case, stands for its divine Author with an intimation that it remains perpetually characterized as the living voice of God. **(5)** This divine agency is again illustrated in Gal 3:22 (cf. v. 10 and Mt 11:13). Syn.: 1121. See: TDNT—1:749, 128; BAGD—166a; THAYER—121b.

1125. γράφω {209x} **graphō**, *graf'-o;* a primary verb; to *"grave,"* espec. to *write;* fig. to *describe:*—write {206x}, writing {1x}, describe {1x}, vr write {1x}. See: TDNT—1:742, 128; BAGD—166c; THAYER—121c.

1126. γραώδης {1x} **graōdēs**, *grah-o'-dace;* from γραύς **graus** (an *old woman*) and *1491; crone-like*, i.e. *silly:*—old wives' {1x}.

Graodes is an adjective, signifying "old-womanish" and is said of fables, in 1 Ti 4:7. See: BAGD—167b; THAYER—122b.

1127. γρηγορέω {23x} **grēgŏrĕuō**, *gray-gor-yoo'-o;* from *1453;* to *keep awake*, i.e. *watch* (lit. or fig.):—watch {21x}, wake {1x}, be vigilant {1x}.

Gregoreuo, as a verb, has **(1)** the meaning of vigilance and expectancy as contrasted with laxity and indifference. **(2)** It translated "wake" in 1 Th 5:10. **(2a)** It is not used in the metaphorical sense of "to be alive"; here **(2b)** it is set in contrast with *katheudo*, "to sleep," which is never used by the apostle with the meaning "to be dead." **(3)** All believers will live together with Christ from the time of the Rapture described in ch. 4; **(3a)** for all have spiritual life now, **(3b)** though their spiritual condition and attainment vary considerably. **(4)** Those who are lax and fail to be watchful will suffer loss (1 Cor 3:15; 9:27; 2 Cor 5:10, e.g.), but the apostle is not here dealing with that aspect of the subject. **(5)** What he does make clear is that **(5a)** the Rapture of believers seven years before the second coming of Christ will depend solely on the death of Christ for them, and not upon their spiritual condition. **(5b)** The Rapture is not a matter of reward, but of salvation. See: TDNT—2:338, 195; BAGD—167b; THAYER—122b.

1128. γυμνάζω {4x} **gumnazō**, *goom-nad'-zo;* from *1131;* to *practise naked* (in the games), i.e. *train* (fig.):—exercise {4x}.

Gumnazo **(1)** primarily means to exercise naked (from *gumnos*, "naked"); then, **(2)** generally, of **(2a)** exercise, training the body or mind [Eng., "gymnastic"] with a view to godliness (1 Ti 4:7); **(2b)** of exercising the senses, so as to discern good and evil (Heb 5:14); **(2c)** of the effect of chastening, the spiritual "exercise producing the fruit of righteousness" (Heb 2:11); **(2d)** of certain evil teachers with hearts exercised in covetousness (2 Pet 2:14). Syn.: 1129. See: TDNT—1:775, 133; BAGD—167c; THAYER—1128c.

1129. γυμνασία {1x} **gumnasia**, *goom-nas-ee'-ah;* from *1128; training*, i.e. (fig.) *asceticism:*—exercise {1x}.

Gumnasia primarily denotes "gymnastic

exercise", 1 Ti 4:8, where the immediate reference is probably not to mere physical training for games but to discipline of the body such as that to which the apostle refers in 1 Cor 9:27, though there may be an allusion to the practices of asceticism and/or separation. See: TDNT—1:775, 133; BAGD—167d; THAYER—122c.

1130. **γυμνητεύω** {1x} **gumnēteuō,** *goom-nayt-yoo'-o* or γυμνιτεύω **gum-niteuo,** *goom-niyt-yoo'-o;* from a der. of *1131;* to *strip,* i.e. (refl.) *go poorly clad:*—be naked {1x}.

This word means "to be naked or scantily clad" and is used in 1 Cor. 4:11: "Even unto this present hour we [the apostles] both hunger, and thirst, and are naked, and are buffeted, and have no certain dwelling place." See: BAGD—167d; THAYER—122d.

1131. **γυμνός** {15x} **gumnŏs,** *goom-nos';* of uncert. aff.; *nude* (absol. or rel., lit. or fig.):—naked {14x}, bare {1x}.

Gumnos, "naked," is once translated "bare," 1 Cor 15:37, where, used of grain, the meaning is made clearer by understanding the phrase by "a bare grain." See: TDNT—1:773, 133; BAGD—167d; THAYER—122d.

1132. **γυμνότης** {3x} **gumnŏtēs,** *goom-not'-ace;* from *1131; nudity* (absol. or comp.):—nakedness {3x}.

Gumnotes, "nakedness" is used (1) of "want of sufficient clothing," Rom 8:35; 2 Cor 11:27; and (2) metaphorically, of "the nakedness of the body," said of the condition of a local church, Rev 3:18. See: TDNT—1:775, 133; BAGD—168a; THAYER—122d.

1133. **γυναικάριον** {1x} **gunaikariŏn,** *goo-nahee-kar'-ee-on;* a dimin. from *1135;* a *little* (i.e. *foolish) woman:*—silly woman {1x}.

Gunaikarion, a diminutive of gune (1135), a "little woman," is used contemptuously in 2 Ti 3:6, "a silly woman." See: BAGD—168b; THAYER—123a.

1134. **γυναικεῖος** {1x} **gunaikĕiŏs,** *goo-nahee-ki'-os;* from *1135; feminine:*—wife {1x}.

Gunaikeios, an adjective denoting "womanly, female," is used as a noun in 1 Pet 3:7, "wife." See: BAGD—168b; THAYER—123a.

1135. **γυνή** {221x} **gunē,** *goo-nay';* prob. from the base of *1096;* a *woman;* spec. a *wife:*—wife {129x}, woman {92x}.

Gune is (1) a woman of any age, whether a virgin, or married, or a widow; or (2) a "wife," e.g., Mt 1:20; 1 Cor 7:3, 4; and (3) in 1 Ti 3:11, "women," the reference is to the "wives" of dea-

cons. See: TDNT—1:776, 134; BAGD—168b; THAYER—123a.

1136. **Γώγ** {1x} **Gōg,** *gogue;* of Heb. or. [1463];
Gog, a symb. name for some future Antichrist:—*Gog* {1x}. See: TDNT—1:789, 136; BAGD—168d; THAYER—123c.

1137. **γωνία** {9x} **gōnia,** *go-nee'-ah;* prob. akin to *1119;* an *angle:*—corner {8x}, quarter {1x}.

Gonia, "an angle", signifies (1) "an external angle," as (1a) of the "corner" of a street, Mt 6:5; or (1b) of a building, Mt 21:42; Mk 12:10; Lk 20:17; Acts 4:11; 1 Pet 2:7, "the corner stone or head-stone of the corner"; or (1c) the four extreme limits of the earth, Rev 7:1; 20:8; (2) "an internal corner," a secret place, Acts 26:26. See: TDNT—1:791, 137; BAGD—168d; THAYER—123c.

Δ

1138. **Δαβίδ** {59x} **Dabid,** *dab-eed';* of Heb. or. [1732]; *Dabid* (i.e. *David),* the Isr. king:—David {59x}. See: TDNT—8:478,*; BAGD—169a; THAYER—123b.

1139. **δαιμονίζομαι** {13x} **daimŏnizŏmai,** *dahee-mon-id'-zom-ahee;* mid. voice from *1142;* to *be exercised by a demon:*—possessed with devils {4x}, possessed with the devil {3x}, of the devils {2x}, vexed with a devil {1x}, possessed with a devil {1x}, have a devil {1x}. See: TDNT—2:19, 137; BAGD—169a; THAYER—123b.

1140. **δαιμόνιον** {60x} **daimŏniŏn,** *dahee-mon'-ee-on;* neut. of a der. of *1142;* a *demonic being;* by extens. a *deity:*—devil {59x}, god {1x}. See: TDNT—2:1, 137; BAGD—169a; THAYER—123d.

1141. **δαιμονιώδης** {1x} **daimŏniōdēs,** *dahee-mon-ee-o'-dace;* from *1140* and *1142; demon-like:*—devilish {1x}. See: TDNT—2:20, 137; BAGD—169d; THAYER—124b.

1142. **δαίμων** {5x} **daimōn,** *dah'-ee-mown;* from δαίω **daiō** (to *distribute* fortunes); a *demon* or supernatural spirit (of a bad nature):—devils {4x}, devil {1x}. See: TDNT—2:1, 137; BAGD—169d; THAYER—124d.

1143. **δάκνω** {1x} **daknō,** *dak'-no;* a prol. form of a primary root; to *bite,* i.e. (fig.) *thwart:*—bite {1x}. See: BAGD—169d; THAYER—124c.

1144. **δάκρυ** {11x} **dakru,** *dak'-roo;* or
δάκρυον dakruŏn, *dak'-roo-on;* of uncert. affin.; a *tear:*—tear {11x}.

Tear drops from the eyes. See: BAGD—170a;
THAYER—124c.

1145. δακρύω {1x} **dakruō**, *dak-roo'-o;* from
1144; to *shed tears:*—weep {1x}.
See: BAGD—170a; THAYER—124c. comp. *2799.*

1146. δακτύλιος {1x} **daktuliŏs**, *dak-too'-
lee-os;* from *1147;* a *finger-
ring:*—ring {1x}. See: BAGD—170a; THAYER—
124c.

1147. δάκτυλος {8x} **daktulŏs**, *dak'-too-los;*
prob. from *1176;* a *finger:*—
finger {8x}. See: TDNT—2:20, 140; BAGD—
170a; THAYER—124c.

1148. Δαλμανουθά {1x} **Dalmanŏutha**, *dal-
man-oo-thah';* prob. of
Chald. or.; *Dalmanūtha*, a place in Pal.:—Dalmanutha {1x}. See: BAGD—170b; THAYER—
124c.

1149. Δαλματία {1x} **Dalmatia**, *dal-mat-ee'-
ah;* prob. of for. der.; *Dal-
matia*, a region of Europe:—*Dalmatia* {1x}.
See: BAGD—170b; THAYER—124d.

1150. δαμάζω {4x} **damazō**, *dam-ad'-zo;* a
var. of an obs. primary of the
same mean.; to *tame:*—tame {4x}. See: BAGD—
170b; THAYER—124d.

1151. δάμαλις {1x} **damalis**, *dam'-al-is;* prob.
from the base of *1150;* a *heifer*
(as *tame*):—heifer {1x}. See: BAGD—170a;
THAYER—124d.

1152. Δάμαρις {1x} **Damaris**, *dam'-ar-is;* prob.
from the base of *1150;* perh.
gentle; Damaris, an Athenian woman:—*Damaris* {1x}. See: BAGD—170c; THAYER—124d.

1153. Δαμασκηνός {1x} **Damaskēnŏs**, *dam-
as-kay-nos';* from *1154;*
a *Damascene* or inhab. of Damascus:—Damascenes {1x}. See: BAGD—170c; THAYER—
124d.

1154. Δαμασκός {15x} **Damaskŏs**, *dam-as-
kos';* of Heb. or. [1834]; *Da-
mascus*, a city of Syria:—Damascus {15x}. See:
BAGD—170c; THAYER—125a.

1155. δανείζω {4x} **danĕizō**, *dan-ayd'-zo;* or

δανίζω danizō, *dan-ide'-zo* from *1156;*
to *loan* on interest; refl. to *borrow:*—lend {3x}, borrow {1x}. See: BAGD—
170d; THAYER—125a.

1156. δάνειον {1x} **danĕiŏn**, *dan'-i-on;* from
δάνος **danŏs** (a *gift*); prob.
akin to the base of *1325;* a *loan:*—debt {1x}.
See: BAGD—170d; THAYER—125a.

1157. δανειστής {1x} **danĕistēs**, *dan-ice-tace';*
or

δανιστής danistēs, *dan-iys-tace'* from
1155; a *lender:*—creditor {1x}.
This is one who lends money to another on
credit. See: BAGD—170d; THAYER—125a.

1158. Δανιήλ {2x} **Daniēl**, *dan-ee-ale';* of Heb.
or. [1840]; *Daniel*, an Isr.:—
Daniel {2x}. See: BAGD—170d; THAYER—
125b.

1159. δαπανάω {5x} **dapanaō**, *dap-an-ah'-o;*
from *1160;* to *expend*, i.e. (in
a good sense) to *incur cost*, or (in a bad one)
to *waste:*—spend {3x}, be at charges with {1x},
consume {1x}. See: BAGD—171a; THAYER—
125b.

1160. δαπάνη {1x} **dapanē**, *dap-an'-ay;* from
δάπτω **daptō** (to *devour*); *ex-
pense* (as *consuming*):—cost {1x}. See: BAGD—
171a; THAYER—125b.

1161. δέ {2870x} **dĕ**, *deh;* a primary particle
(adversative or continuative); *but,
and*, etc.:—but {1237x}, and {935x}, now {166x},
then {132x}, also {18x}, yet {16x}, yea {13x}, so
{13x}, moreover {13x}, nevertheless {11x}, for
{4x}, even {3x}, misc. {9x}, not tr {300x}. See:
BAGD—171c; THAYER—125b.

1162. δέησις {19x} **dĕēsis**, *deh'-ay-sis;* from
1189; a *petition:*—prayer {12x},
supplication {6x}, request {1x}. Syn.: 155, 1783,
2171, 2428, 5335.
Deesis is prayer for particular benefits and
proseuche (*4335*) is prayer in general. See:
TDNT—2:40, 144; BAGD—171d; THAYER—
126a.

1163. δεῖ {106x} **dĕi**, *die;* third pers. sing. act.
present of *1210;* also δεόν **dĕŏn**,
deh-on'; neut. act. part. of the same; both used
impers.; *it is* (*was*, etc.) *necessary* (as *binding*):—must {58x}, ought {32x}, must needs {5x},
should {4x}, misc. {7x} = behoved, be meet, (be)
need (-ful). See: TDNT—2:21, 140; BAGD—
172a; THAYER—126b.

1164. δεῖγμα {1x} **dĕigma**, *dīgh'-mah;* from
the base of *1166;* a *specimen*
(as *shown*):—example {1x}. See: BAGD—172c;
THAYER—126d.

1165. δειγματίζω {1x} **dĕigmatizō**, *dīgh-
mat-id'-zo;* from *1164;* to
exhibit:—make a show {1x}. See: TDNT—2:31,
141; BAGD—172c; THAYER—126d.

1166. δεικνύω {31x} **dĕiknuō**, *dike-noo'-o;* a
prol. form of an obs. primary
of the same mean.; to *show* (lit. or fig.):—show

{31x}. Syn.: 322, 1731. See: TDNT—2:25,*; BAGD—172d; THAYER—126d.

1167. **δειλία** {1x} **dĕilia**, *di-lee'-ah;* from *1169; timidity:*—fear {1x}.

The word denotes cowardice, unmanliness, and timidity (2 Ti 1:7). Syn.: 2124, 5401. See: BAGD—173a; THAYER—127a.

1168. **δειλιάω** {1x} **dĕiliaō**, *di-lee-ah'-o;* from *1167;* to *be timid:*—be afraid {1x}. See: BAGD—173a; THAYER—127a.

1169. **δειλός** {3x} **dĕilŏs**, *di-los';* from δέος **dĕŏs** (*dread*); *timid,* i.e. (by impl.) *faithless:*—fearful {3x}. See: BAGD—173a; THAYER—127a.

1170. **δεῖνα** {1x} **dĕina**, *di'-nah;* prob. from the same as *1171* (through the idea of forgetting the name as *fearful,* i.e. *strange*); *so and so* (when the person is not specified):—such a man {1x}. See: BAGD—173a; THAYER—127b.

1171. **δεινῶς** {2x} **dĕinōs**, *di-noce';* adv. from a der. of the same as *1169; terribly,* i.e. *excessively:*—grievously {1x}, vehemently {1x}. See: BAGD—173b; THAYER—127b.

1172. **δειπνέω** {4x} **dĕipnĕō**, *dipe-neh'-o;* from *1173;* to *dine,* i.e. take the principal (or evening) meal:—sup {3x}, supper {1x}. See: TDNT—2:34, 143; BAGD—173b; THAYER—127b.

1173. **δεῖπνον** {16x} **dĕipnŏn**, *dipe'-non;* from the same as *1160; dinner,* i.e. the chief meal (usually in the evening):—supper {13x}, feast {3x}. See: TDNT—2:34, 143; BAGD—173b; THAYER—127b.

1174. **δεισιδαιμονέστερος** {1x} **dĕisidaimŏn-ĕstĕrŏs**, *dice-ee-dahee-mon-es'-ter-os;* the comparative of a der. of the base of *1169* and *1142; more religious* than others:—too superstitious {1x}.

This person has a conceit that God is well-pleased by an overdoing in external things and observances and laws of men's own making. Syn.: 2126, 2152, 2318, 2357. See: TDNT—2:20; BAGD—173d; THAYER—127c.

1175. **δεισιδαιμονία** {1x} **dĕisidaimŏnia**, *dice-ee-dahee-mon-ee'-ah;* from the same as *1174; relig.:*—superstition {1x}. See: TDNT—2:20, 137; BAGD—173c; THAYER—127c.

1176. **δέκα** {27x} **dĕka**, *dek'-ah;* a primary number; *ten:*—ten {24x}, eighteen + 2532 + 3638 {3x}. See: TDNT—2:36, 143; BAGD—173d; THAYER—127d.

1177. **δεκαδύο** {2x} **dĕkaduŏ**, *dek-ad-oo'-o;* from *1176* and *1417; two* and *ten,* i.e. *twelve:*—twelve {2x}. See: BAGD—174a; THAYER—127d.

1178. **δεκάπεντε** {3x} **dĕkapĕntĕ**, *dek-ap-en'-teh;* from *1176* and *4002; ten* and *five,* i.e. *fifteen:*—fifteen {3x}. See: BAGD—174a; THAYER—127d.

1179. **Δεκάπολις** {3x} **Dĕkapŏlis**, *dek-ap'-ol-is;* from *1176* and *4172;* the *ten-city* region; the *Decapolis,* a district in Syria:—Decapolis {3x}. See: BAGD—174a; THAYER—127d.

1180. **δεκατέσσαρες** {5x} **dĕkatĕssarĕs**, *dek-at-es'-sar-es;* from *1176* and *5064; ten* and *four,* i.e. *fourteen:*—fourteen {5x}. See: BAGD—174a; THAYER—128a.

1181. **δεκάτη** {4x} **dĕkatē**, *dek-at'-ay;* fem. of *1182;* a *tenth,* i.e. as a percentage or (tech.) *tithe:*—tithe {2x}, tenth part {1x}, tenth {1x}. See: BAGD—174a; THAYER—128a.

1182. **δέκατος** {3x} **dĕkatŏs**, *dek'-at-os;* ordinal from *1176; tenth:*—tenth {3x}. See: BAGD—174a; THAYER—128a.

1183. **δεκατόω** {2x} **dĕkatŏō**, *dek-at-ŏ'-o;* from *1181;* to *tithe,* i.e. to *give* or *take a tenth:*—receive tithes {1x}, pay tithes {1x}. See: BAGD—174b; THAYER—128a.

1184. **δεκτός** {5x} **dĕktŏs**, *dek-tos';* from *1209; approved;* (fig.) *propitious:*—accepted {3x}, acceptable {2x}. See: TDNT—2:58, 146; BAGD—174b; THAYER—128a.

1185. **δελεάζω** {3x} **dĕlĕazō**, *del-eh-ad'-zo;* from the base of *1388;* to *entrap,* i.e. (fig.) *delude:*—entice {1x}, beguile {1x}, allure {1x}.

This word means to catch using bait. See: BAGD—174b; THAYER—128b.

1186. **δένδρον** {26x} **dĕndrŏn**, *den'-dron;* prob. from δρύς **drus** (an *oak*); a *tree:*—tree {26x}. See: BAGD—174c; THAYER—128b.

1187. **δεξιολάβος** {1x} **dĕxiŏlabŏs**, *dex-ee-ol-ab'-os;* from *1188* and *2983;* a *guardsman* (as if *taking the right hand*) or light-armed soldier:—spearmen {1x}. See: BAGD—174c; THAYER—128b.

1188. **δεξιός** {53x} **dĕxiŏs**, *dex-ee-os';* from *1209;* the *right* side or (fem.) *hand* (as that which usually *takes*):—right hand {39x}, right {12x}, right side {2x}. See:

TDNT—2:37, 143; BAGD—174c; THAYER—128c.

1189. δέομαι {22x} **dĕŏmai**, *deh'-om-ahee;* mid. voice of *1210;* to *beg* (as *binding oneself*), i.e. *petition:*—pray {12x}, beseech {9x}, make request {1x}. See: TDNT—2:40, 144; BAGD—175a; THAYER—129a. comp. *4441.*

     δεόν dĕŏn. See *1163.*

1190. Δερβαῖος {1x} **Dĕrbaiŏs**, *der-bah'-ee-os;* from *1191;* a *Derbæan* or inhab. of Derbe:—of Derbe {1x}. See: BAGD—175c; THAYER—129b.

1191. Δέρβη {3x} **Dĕrbē**, *der-bay';* of for. or.; *Derbe'*, a place in Asia Minor:— *Derbe* {3x}. See: BAGD—175c; THAYER—129b.

1192. δέρμα {1x} **dĕrma**, *der'-mah;* from *1194;* a *hide:*—skin + 122 {1x}. See: BAGD—175c; THAYER—129b.

1193. δερμάτινος {2x} **dĕrmatinŏs**, *der-mat'-ee-nos;* from *1192;* made of *hide:*—leathern {1x}, of a skin {1x}. See: BAGD—175c; THAYER—129b.

1194. δέρω {15x} **dĕrō**, *der'-o;* a primary verb; prop. to *flay*, i.e. (by impl.) to *scourge*, or (by anal.) to *thrash:*—beat {12x}, smite {3x}. See: BAGD—175d; THAYER—129b.

1195. δεσμεύω {2x} **dĕsmĕuō**, *des-myoo'-o;* from a (presumed) der. of *1196;* to *be a binder* (*captor*), i.e. to *enchain* (a prisoner), to *tie on* (a load):—bind {2x}. See: BAGD—175d; THAYER—129c.

1196. δεσμέω {1x} **dĕsmĕō**, *des-meh'-o;* from *1199;* to *tie*, i.e. *shackle:*— bind {1x}. See: BAGD—175d; THAYER—129c.

1197. δέσμη {1x} **dĕsmē**, *des-may';* from *1196;* a *bundle:*—bundle {1x}. See: BAGD—176a; THAYER—129c.

1198. δέσμιος {16x} **dĕsmiŏs**, *des'-mee-os;* from *1199;* a *captive* (as *bound*):—prisoner {14x}, be in bonds {1x}, in bonds {1x}.

Desmios, as a noun, means "a binding" and **(1)** denotes "a prisoner in bonds" (Acts 25:14; Heb 13:3, "them that are in bonds"). **(2)** Paul speaks of himself as a prisoner of Christ (Eph 3:1; 2 Ti 1:8; Philem 1, 9; Eph 4:1 "in the Lord"). Syn.: 254, 1199, 4886. See: TDNT—2:43, 145; BAGD—176a; THAYER—129c.

1199. δεσμόν {20x} **dĕsmŏn**, *des-mon';* or

     δεσμός dĕsmŏs, *des-mos';* neut. and masc. respectively from *1210;*

a *band*, i.e. *ligament* (of the body) or *shackle* (of a prisoner); fig. an *impediment* or *disability:*— bond {15x}, band {3x}, string {1x}, chain {1x}.

Desmos, as a noun, **(1)** is usually found in the plural, either masculine or neuter; **(1a)** it stands thus for the actual "bonds" which bind a prisoner (Lk 8:29; Acts 16:26; 20:23 the only three places where the neuter plural is used; 22:30); **(1b)** the masculine plural stands frequently in a figurative sense for "a condition of imprisonment:" "Even as it is meet for me to think this of you all, because I have you in my heart; inasmuch as both in my bonds (*demos*), and in the defence and confirmation of the gospel, ye all are partakers of my grace" (Phil 1:7; cf. vv. 13–16, i.e., "so that my captivity became manifest as appointed for the cause of Christ"; Col 4:18; 2 Ti 2:9; Philem 10, 13; Heb 10:34). **(2)** In Mk 7:35 "the bond (KJV, string)" stands metaphorically for "the infirmity which caused an impediment in his speech." **(3)** So in Lk 13:16, of the infirmity of the woman who was bowed together. Syn.: 254, 1198, 4886. See: TDNT—2:43; BAGD—176a; THAYER—129d.

1200. δεσμοφύλαξ {3x} **dĕsmŏphulax**, *des-mof-oo'-lax;* from *1199* and *5441;* a *jailer* (as *guarding* the *prisoners*):— keeper of the prison {2x}, jailor {1x}. See: BAGD—176b; THAYER—129d.

1201. δεσμωτήριον {4x} **dĕsmōtēriŏn**, *des-mo-tay'-ree-on;* from a der. of *1199* (equiv. to *1196*); a *place of bondage*, i.e. a *dungeon:*—prison {4x}. See: BAGD—176b; THAYER—130a.

1202. δεσμώτης {2x} **dĕsmōtēs**, *des-mo'-tace;* from the same as *1201;* (pass.) a *captive:*—prisoner {2x}. See: BAGD—176b; THAYER—130a.

1203. δεσπότης {10x} **dĕspŏtēs**, *des-pot'-ace;* perh. from *1210* and πόσις **pŏsis** (a *husband*); an absolute *ruler* ("despot"):—Lord {5x}, master {5x}.

A man is a *despotes* to his slaves, but a *kurios* (*2962*) to his wife and children. He exercises an unrestricted power and domination, with no limitations or restraints. Syn.: 2962. See: TDNT—2:44, 145; BAGD—176c; THAYER—130a.

1204. δεῦρο {9x} **dĕurŏ**, *dyoo'-ro;* of uncert. aff.; *here;* used also imperative *hither!;* and of time, *hitherto:*—come {6x}, come hither {2x}, hitherto + 891 + 3588 {1x}. See: BAGD—176c; THAYER—130a.

1205. δεῦτε {13x} **dĕutĕ**, *dyoo'-teh;* from *1204* and an imper. form of εἰμι **ĕimi**

(to *go*); *come hither!:*—come {12x}, follow + 3694 {1x}. See: BAGD—176d; THAYER—130b.

1206. **δευτεραῖος** {1x} **děutěraiŏs,** *dyoo-ter-ah'-yos;* from *1208; secondary,* i.e. (spec.) on the *second* day:—next day {1x}. See: BAGD—177a; THAYER—130b.

1207. **δευτερόπρωτος** {1x} **děutěrŏprōtŏs,** *dyoo-ter-op'-ro-tos;* from *1208* and *4413; second-first,* i.e. (spec.) a designation of the Sabbath immediately after the Paschal week (being the *second* after Passover day, and the *first* of the seven Sabbaths intervening before Pentecost):—second . . . after the first {1x}. See: BAGD—177a; THAYER—130b.

1208. **δεύτερος** {47x} **děutěrŏs,** *dyoo'-ter-os;* as the comp. of *1417;* (ordinal) *second* (in time, place, or rank; also adv.):—second {34x}, the second time + 1537 {4x}, the second time {4x}, again + 1537 {2x}, again {1x}, secondarily {1x}, afterward {1x}. See: BAGD—177a; THAYER—130c.

1209. **δέχομαι** {59x} **děchŏmai,** *dekh'-om-ahee;* mid. voice of a primary verb; to *receive* (in various applications, lit. or fig.):—receive {52x}, take {4x}, accept {2x}, take up {1x}.

This word signifies to accept by a deliberate and ready reception of what is offered (1 Th 2:13). *Dechomai,* as a verb, means "to receive by deliberate and ready reception of what is offered" and is used of **(1)** taking with the hand, taking hold, taking hold of or up: "Then took (*dechomai*) he (Simeon) Him up in his arms, and blessed God, and said" (Lk 2:28; cf. 16:6, 7; 22:17; Eph 6:17); **(2)** "receiving," said **(2a)** of a place "receiving" a person, of Christ into the heavens: "Whom the heaven must receive until the times of restitution of all things, which God hath spoken by the mouth of all his holy prophets since the world began" (Acts 3:21); or **(2b)** of persons in giving access to someone as a visitor: "Then when He was come into Galilee, the Galilaeans received Him, having seen all the things that He did at Jerusalem at the feast: for they also went unto the feast" (Jn 4:45; cf. 2 Cor 7:15; Gal 4:14; Col 4:10); **(3)** by way of giving hospitality: "And whosoever shall not receive (*dechomai*) you, nor hear your words, when ye depart out of that house or city, shake off the dust of your feet" (Mt 10:14; cf. 10: 40 [four times], 41 [twice]; 18:5; Mk 6:11; 9:37; Lk 9:5, 48, 53; 10:8, 10; 16:4, 9 of reception "into the eternal tabernacles," said of followers of Christ who have used "the mammon of unrighteousness" to render assistance to "make . . . friends of" others); **(4)** of Rahab's reception of the spies: "By faith the harlot Rahab perished not with them that believed not, when she had received (*dechomai*) the spies with peace" (Heb 11:31); **(5)** of the reception, by the Lord, of the spirit of a departing believer: "And they stoned Stephen, calling upon God, and saying, Lord Jesus, receive my spirit" (Acts 7:59); **(6)** of "receiving" a gift: "Praying us with much intreaty that we would receive the gift, and take upon us the fellowship of the ministering to the saints" (2 Cor 8:4);

(7) of the favorable reception of testimony and teaching: **(7a)** "They on the rock are they, which, when they hear, receive the word with joy; and these have no root, which for a while believe, and in time of temptation fall away" (Lk 8:13; cf. Acts 8:14; 11:1; 17:11; 1 Cor 2:14; 2 Cor 8:17; 1 Th 1:6; 2:13, where *paralambano* (*3880*) is used in the 1st part, "ye received," *dechomai* in the 2nd part, "ye accepted," RV (KJV, "received"), the former refers to the ear, the latter, adding the idea of appropriation, to the heart; Jas 1:21); **(7b)** in 2 Th 2:10 receiving "the love of the truth, i.e., love for the truth (cf. Mt 11:14 "if ye are willing to receive it" an elliptical construction frequent in Greek writings); **(8)** of "receiving," by way of bearing with, enduring: "I say again, Let no man think me a fool; if otherwise, yet as a fool receive me, that I may boast myself a little" (2 Cor 11:16);

(9) of "receiving" by way of getting: "As also the high priest doth bear me witness, and all the estate of the elders: from whom also I received letters unto the brethren, and went to Damascus, to bring them which were there bound unto Jerusalem, for to be punished" (Acts 22:5; cf. 28:21, of becoming partaker of benefits, Mk 10:15; Lk 18:17; Acts 7:38; 2 Cor 6:1; 11:4; Phil 4:18). Syn.: There is a certain distinction between *lambano* (*2983*) and *dechomai* (*1209*) in that in many instances *lambano* suggests a self-prompted taking, whereas *dechomai* more frequently indicates "a welcoming or an appropriating reception." See also: 324, 353, 354, 568, 588, 618, 1523, 1926, 2210, 2865, 2975, 2983, 3028, 3335, 3336, 3858, 3880, 3970, 4327, 4355, 4356, 4380, 4381, 4382, 5562, 5264, 5274. See: TDNT—2:50, 146; BAGD—177b; THAYER—130d.

1210. **δέω** {44x} **děō,** *deh'-o;* a primary verb; to *bind* (in various applications, lit. or fig.):—bind {37x}, be in bonds {1x}, knit {1x}, tie {4x}, wind {1x}. See: TDNT—2:60, 148; BAGD—177c; THAYER—131b. See also *1163, 1189.*

1211. **δή** {6x} **dē,** *day;* prob. akin to *1161;* a particle of emphasis or explicitness; *now, then,* etc.:—also {1x}, and {1x}, doubtless

{1x}, now {1x}, therefore {1x}, not tr {1x}. See: BAGD—178b; THAYER—131c.

1212. **δῆλος** {4x} **dēlŏs**, *day'-los;* of uncert. der.; *clear:*—bewray + 4160 {1x}, certain {1x}, evident {1x}, manifest {1x}.

This word signifies visible, clear to the mind, evident (Gal. 3:11; 1 Cor 15:27). See: BAGD—178b; THAYER—131d.

1213. **δηλόω** {7x} **dēlŏō**, *day-lŏ'-o;* from *1212;* to *make plain* (by words):—declare {3x}, show {1x}, signify {3x}. See: TDNT—2:61, 148; BAGD—178c; THAYER—131d.

1214. **Δημᾶς** {3x} **Dēmas**, *day-mas';* prob. for *1216; Demas,* a Chr.:—*Demas* {3x}. See: BAGD—178c; THAYER—132a.

1215. **δημηγορέω** {1x} **dēmēgŏrĕō**, *day-may-gor-eh'-o;* from a compound of *1218* and *58;* to *be a people-gatherer,* i.e. to *address* a public assembly:—make an oration {1x}. See: BAGD—178d; THAYER—132a.

1216. **Δημήτριος** {3x} **Dēmētriŏs**, *day-may'-tree-os;* from Δημήτηρ **Dēmētēr** (*Ceres*); *Demetrius,* the name of an Ephesian and of a Chr.:—*Demetrius* {3x}. See: BAGD—178d; THAYER—132a.

1217. **δημιουργός** {1x} **dēmiŏurgŏs**, *day-me-oor-gos';* from *1218* and *2041;* a *worker* for the *people,* i.e. *mechanic* (spoken of the *Creator*):—maker {1x}.

This word emphasizes the power of a Divine creator. Syn.: 5079. See: TDNT—2:62, 149; BAGD—178d; THAYER—132a.

1218. **δῆμος** {4x} **dēmŏs**, *day'-mos;* from *1210;* the *public* (as *bound* together socially):—people {4x}.

Demos is an assembly of people gathered together with consent of the law and for mutual benefit; an assembled group of people actively exercising their rights as citizens. Syn.: 1484, 2992, 3793. See: TDNT—2:63, 149; BAGD—179a; THAYER—132b.

1219. **δημόσιος** {4x} **dēmŏsiŏs**, *day-mos'ee-os;* from *1218; public;* (fem. sing. dat. case as adv.) *in public:*—common {1x}, openly {1x}, publicly {2x}. See: BAGD—179a; THAYER—132b.

1220. **δηνάριον** {16x} **dēnariŏn**, *day-nar'-ee-on;* of Lat. or.; a *denarius* (or *ten asses*):—pence {9x}, penny {5x}, pennyworth {2x}. See: BAGD—179b; THAYER—132b.

1221. **δήποτε** {1x} **dēpŏtĕ**, *day'-pot-eh;* from *1211* and *4218;* a particle of generalization; *indeed, at any time:*—whatso-

ever + 3769 {1x}. See: BAGD—179b; THAYER—132b.

1222. **δήπου** {1x} **dēpŏu**, *day'-poo;* from *1211* and *4225;* a particle of asseveration; *indeed doubtless:*—verily {1x}. See: BAGD—179b; THAYER—132c.

1223. **διά** {647x} **dia**, *dee-ah';* a primary prep. denoting the *channel* of an act; *through* (in very wide applications, local, causal, or occasional):—by {241x}, through {88x}, with {16x}, for {58x}, for . . . sake {47x}, therefore + 5124 {44x}, for this cause + 5124 {14x}, because {53x}, misc. {86x} = after, always, among, at, to avoid, briefly, fore, from, in, by occasion of, of, by reason of, that, thereby, though, throughout, to, wherefore, within. In composition it retains the same general import. See: TDNT—2:65, 149; BAGD—179b; THAYER—132c.

Δία Dia. See *2203.*

1224. **διαβαίνω** {3x} **diabainō**, *dee-ab-ah'-ee-no;* from *1223* and the base of *939;* to *cross:*—come over {1x}, pass {1x}, pass through {1x}. See: BAGD—181c; THAYER—135a.

1225. **διαβάλλω** {1x} **diaballō**, *dee-ab-al'-lo;* from *1223* and *906;* (fig.) to *traduce:*—accuse {1x}.

Diaballo, as a verb, is used in Lk 16:1, in the passive voice, literally **(1)** signifies "to hurl across" (*dia,* "through," *ballo,* "to throw"), and suggests a verbal assault: "And he said also unto his disciples, There was a certain rich man, which had a steward; and the same was accused unto him that he had wasted his goods." **(2)** It stresses the act rather than the author of the accusation, as in the case of *aitia* (*156*) and *kategoria* (*2724*). Syn.: 156, 157, 1458, 1462, 1908, 2723, 2724, 4811. See: TDNT—2:71, 150; BAGD—181d; THAYER—135a.

1226. **διαβεβαιόομαι** {2x} **diabĕbaiŏŏmai**, *dee-ab-eb-ahee-ŏ'-om-ahee;* mid. voice of a compound of *1223* and *950;* to *confirm thoroughly* (by words), i.e. *asseverate:*—affirm {1x}, affirm constantly {1x}. See: BAGD—181d; THAYER—135a.

1227. **διαβλέπω** {2x} **diablĕpō**, *dee-ab-lep'-o;* from *1223* and *991;* to *look through,* i.e. *recover* full *vision:*—see clearly {2x}. See: BAGD—181d; THAYER—135b.

1228. **διάβολος** {38x} **diabŏlŏs**, *dee-ab'-ol-os;* from *1225;* a *traducer;* spec. *Satan* [comp. 7854]:—false accuser {2x}, devil {35x}, slanderer {1x}. See: TDNT—2:72, 150; BAGD—182a.135b.

1229. **διαγγέλλω** {3x} **diaggĕllō**, *de-ang-gel'-lo;* from *1223* and the base of *32;* to *herald thoroughly:*—declare {1x}, preach {1x}, signify {1x}. See: TDNT—1:67, 10; BAGD—182b; THAYER—135c.

1230. **διαγίνομαι** {3x} **diaginŏmai**, *dee-ag-in'-om-ahee;* from *1223* and *1096;* to *elapse meanwhile:*—after {1x}, be past {1x}, be spent {1x}. See: BAGD—182b; THAYER—135c.

1231. **διαγινώσκω** {2x} **diaginōskō**, *dee-ag-in-o'-sko;* from *1223* and *1097;* to *know thoroughly,* i.e. *ascertain exactly:*—(would) enquire {1x}, know the uttermost {1x}. See: BAGD—182b; THAYER—135c.

1232. **διαγνωρίζω** {1x} **diagnōrizō**, *dee-ag-no-rid'-zo;* from *1123* and *1107;* to *tell abroad:*—make known abroad {1x}. See: BAGD—182b; THAYER—135d.

1233. **διάγνωσις** {1x} **diagnōsis**, *dee-ag'-no-sis;* from *1231;* (magisterial) *examination* ("diagnosis"):—hearing {1x}. See: BAGD—182c; THAYER—135d.

1234. **διαγογγύζω** {2x} **diagŏgguzō**, *dee-ag-ong-good'-zo;* from *1223* and *1111;* to *complain throughout* a crowd:—murmur {2x}. See: TDNT—1:735, 125; BAGD—182c; THAYER—135d.

1235. **διαγρηγορέω** {1x} **diagrēgŏrĕō**, *dee-ag-ray-gor-eh'-o;* from *1223* and *1127;* to *waken thoroughly:*—be awake {1x}. See: BAGD—182c; THAYER—135d.

1236. **διάγω** {2x} **diagō**, *dee-ag'-o;* from *1223* and *71;* to *pass* time or life:—lead a life + 979 {1x}, living {1x}.

Diago is used of time in the sense of passing a life: **(1)** 1 Ti 2:2 "[prayer] For kings, and for all that are in authority; that we may lead (*diago*) a quiet and peaceable life in all godliness and honesty"; and **(2)** in Titus 3:3 "For we ourselves also were sometimes foolish, disobedient, deceived, serving divers lusts and pleasures, living (*diago*) in malice and envy, hateful, and hating one another." Syn.: 326, 390, 980, 2198, 2225, 4176, 4800, 5225. See: BAGD—182c; THAYER—135d.

1237. **διαδέχομαι** {1x} **diadĕchŏmai**, *dee-ad-ekh'-om-ahee;* from *1223* and *1209;* to *receive in turn,* i.e. (fig.) *succeed to:*—come after {1x}. See: BAGD—182c; THAYER—136a.

1238. **διάδημα** {3x} **diadēma**, *dee-ad-ay-mah;* from a compound of *1223* and

1210; a "*diadem*" (as *bound about* the head):—crown {3x}.

It is always the symbol of kingly or imperial dignity; whereas a *stephanos* (*4735*) is the victor's crown. See: BAGD—182d; THAYER—136a. comp. *4735*.

1239. **διαδίδωμι** {5x} **diadidōmi**, *dee-ad-id'-o-mee;* from *1223* and *1325;* to *give throughout* a crowd, i.e. *deal out;* also to *deliver* over (as to a successor):—make distribution {1x}, distribute {2x}, divide {1x}, give {1x}. See: BAGD—182d; THAYER—136a.

1240. **διάδοχος** {1x} **diadŏchŏs**, *dee-ad'-okh-os;* from *1237;* a *successor* in office:—come into (one's) room {1x}. See: BAGD—182d; THAYER—136b.

1241. **διαζώννυμι** {3x} **diazōnnumi**, *dee-az-own'-noo-mee;* from *1223* and *2224;* to *gird tightly:*—gird {3x}.

Diazonnumi, as a verb, means "to gird round," i.e., firmly [*dia,* "throughout," used intensively], is used **(1)** of the Lord's act in "girding" Himself with a towel: "He riseth from supper, and laid aside His garments; and took a towel, and girded (*diazonnumi*) Himself. After that He poureth water into a bason, and began to wash the disciples' feet, and to wipe them with the towel wherewith He was girded (*diazonnimi*)" (Jn 13:4–5), and **(2)** of Peter's girding himself with his coat: "Therefore that disciple whom Jesus loved saith unto Peter, It is the Lord. Now when Simon Peter heard that it was the Lord, he girt (*diazonnumi*) his fisher's coat unto him, (for he was naked,) and did cast himself into the sea" (Jn 21:7). Syn.: 328, 2224, 4024. See: TDNT—5:302, 702; BAGD—182d; THAYER—136b.

1242. **διαθήκη** {33x} **diathēkē**, *dee-ath-ay'-kay;* from *1303;* prop. a *disposition,* i.e. (spec.) a *contract* (espec. a devisory *will*):—covenant {20x}, testament {13x}. See: TDNT—2:106, 157; BAGD—183a; THAYER—136b.

1243. **διαίρεσις** {3x} **diairĕsis**, *dee-ah'-ee-res-is;* from *1244;* a *distinction* or (concr.) *variety:*—difference {1x}, diversity {2x}. See: TDNT—1:184, 27; BAGD—1243c; THAYER—137a.

1244. **διαιρέω** {2x} **diairĕō**, *dee-ahee-reh'-o;* from *1223* and *138;* to *separate,* i.e. *distribute:*—divide {2x}.

Diaireo means to divide into parts, to distribute (Lk 15:12; 1 Cor 12:11). See: TDNT—1:184, 27; BAGD—183c; THAYER—137b.

1245. **διακαθαρίζω** {2x} **diakatharizō**, *dee-ak-ath-ar-id'-zo;* from

1223 and *2511;* to *cleanse perfectly, completely,* i.e. (spec.) *winnow:—*thoroughly purged {2x}. See: BAGD—183d; THAYER—137b.

1246. διακατελέγχομαι {1x} **diakatĕlĕgchŏmai,** *dee-ak-at-el-eng'-khom-ahee;* mid. voice from *1223* and a compound of *2596* and *1651;* to *prove downright,* i.e. *confute:—*convince {1x}. See: BAGD—184a; THAYER—137b.

1247. διακονέω {37x} **diakŏnĕō,** *dee-ak-on-eh'-o;* from *1249;* to *be an attendant,* i.e. *wait upon* (menially or as a host, friend, or [fig.] teacher); techn. to *act as a* Chr. *deacon:—*minister unto {15x}, serve {10x}, minister {7x}, misc. {5x} = administer, use the office of a deacon. See: TDNT—2:81, 152; BAGD—184a; THAYER—137b.

1248. διακονία {34x} **diakŏnia,** *dee-ak-on-ee'-ah;* from *1249; attendance* (as a servant, etc.); fig. (eleemosynary) *aid,* (official) *service* (espec. of the Chr. teacher, or techn. of the *diaconate):—*ministry {16x}, ministration {6x}, ministering {3x}, misc. {9x} = administer, office, relief, servicing. See: TDNT—2:87, 152; BAGD—184b; THAYER—137d.

1249. διάκονος {31x} **diakŏnŏs,** *dee-ak'-on-os;* prob. from an obs. διάκω **diakō** (to *run* on errands; comp. *1377);* an *attendant,* i.e. (gen.) a *waiter* (at table or in other menial duties); spec. a Chr. *teacher* and *pastor* (tech. a *deacon* or *deaconess):—*deacon {3x}, minister {20x}, servant {8x}.

This word focuses on the servant in his activity for the work and not his relation to a person. *Doulos* (*1401*) stresses relationship. Syn.: 1401, 2324, 3610, 5257. See: TDNT—2:88, 152; BAGD—184c; THAYER—138a.

1250. διακόσιοι {8x} **diakŏsiŏi,** *dee-ak-os'-ee-oy;* from *1364* and *1540; two hundred:—*two hundred {8x}. See: BAGD—185a; THAYER—138c.

1251. διακούομαι {1x} **diakŏuŏmai,** *dee-ak-oo'-om-ahee;* mid. voice from *1223* and *191;* to *hear throughout,* i.e. *patiently listen* (to a prisoner's plea):—hear {1x}.

Diakouo, as a verb, means "to hear through, hear fully" and is used technically, of "hearing" judicially (Acts 23:35 of Felix in regard to the charges against Paul). Syn.: 189, 191, 1522, 1873, 1874, 3878, 4257. See: BAGD—185; THAYER—138c.

1252. διακρίνω {19x} **diakrinō,** *dee-ak-ree'-no;* from *1223* and *2919;* to *separate thoroughly,* i.e. (lit. and refl.) to *with-*

draw from, or (by impl.) *oppose;* fig. to *discriminate* (by impl. *decide),* or (refl.) *hesitate:—*doubt {5x}, judge {3x}, discern {2x}, contend {2x}, waver {2x}, misc. {5x} = make (to) differ, difference, be partial, stagger.

Diakrino is rendered "to waver" (Rom 4:20; Jas 1:6 twice). See: TDNT—3:946, 469; BAGD—185a; THAYER—138c.

1253. διάκρισις {3x} **diakrisis,** *dee-ak'-ree-sis;* from *1252;* judicial *estimation:—*discern {1x}, discerning {1x}, disputation {1x}. See: TDNT—3:949, 469; BAGD—185b; THAYER—139a.

1254. διακωλύω {1x} **diakōluō,** *dee-ak-o-loo'-o;* from *1223* and *2967;* to *hinder altogether,* i.e. *utterly prohibit:—*forbid {1x}. See: BAGD—185c; THAYER—139a.

1255. διαλαλέω {2x} **dialalĕō,** *dee-al-al-eh'-o;* from *1223* and *2980;* to *talk throughout* a company, i.e. *converse* or (gen.) *publish:—*commune {1x}, noise abroad {1x}. See: BAGD—185c; THAYER—139a.

1256. διαλέγομαι {13x} **dialĕgŏmai,** *dee-al-eg'-om-ahee;* mid. voice from *1223* and *3004;* to *say thoroughly,* i.e. *discuss* (in argument or exhortation):—dispute {6x}, preach {1x}, preach unto {1x}, reason {2x}, reason with {2x}, speak {1x}.

Dialegomai primarily denotes to ponder, resolve in one's mind. See: TDNT—2:93, 155; BAGD—185c; THAYER—139a.

1257. διαλείπω {1x} **dialĕipō,** *dee-al-i'-po;* from *1223* and *3007;* to *leave off in the middle,* i.e. *intermit:—*cease {1x}. See: TDNT—4:194; BAGD—185d; THAYER—139b.

1258. διάλεκτος {6x} **dialĕktŏs,** *dee-al'-ek-tos;* from *1256;* a (mode of) discourse, i.e. "*dialect*":—language {1x}, tongue {5x}. See: BAGD—185d; THAYER—139b.

1259. διαλλάσσω {1x} **diallassō,** *dee-al-las'-so;* from *1223* and *236;* to *change thoroughly,* i.e. (ment.) to *conciliate:—*reconcile {1x}. See: TDNT—1:253, 40; BAGD—186a; THAYER—139b.

1260. διαλογίζομαι {16x} **dialŏgizŏmai,** *dee-al-og-id'-zom-ahee;* from *1223* and *3049;* to *reckon thoroughly,* i.e. (gen.) to *deliberate* (by reflection or discussion):—reason {11x}, dispute {1x}, cast in the mind {1x}, muse {1x}, think {1x}, consider {1x}. See: TDNT—2:95, 155; BAGD—186a; THAYER—139c.

1261. διαλογισμός {14x} **dialŏgismŏs,** *dee-al-og-is-mos';* from *1260; discussion,* i.e. (internal) *consideration* (by

impl. *purpose*), or (external) *debate:*—dispute
{1x}, doubtful {1x}, doubting {1x}, imagination
{1x}, reasoning {9x}, thought {1x}. See: TDNT—
2:96, 155; BAGD—186a; THAYER—139c.

1262. **διαλύω** {1x} **dialuō**, *dee-al-oo'-o;* from
          1223 and *3089;* to *dissolve*
utterly:—scatter {1x}. See: BAGD—186b;
THAYER—139d.

1263. **διαμαρτύρομαι** {15x} **diamarturŏmai**,
                          dee-am-ar-too'-rom-
ahee; from *1223* and *3140;* to *attest* or *protest
earnestly,* or (by impl.) *hortatively:*—charge
{3x}, testify (unto) {11x}, witness {1x}. See:
TDNT—4:510, 564; BAGD—186c; THAYER—
139d.

1264. **διαμάχομαι** {1x} **diamachŏmai**, *dee-
          am-akh'-om-ahee;* from
1223 and *3164;* to *fight fiercely* (in altercation):—
strive {1x}. See: BAGD—186c; THAYER—140a.

1265. **διαμένω** {5x} **diamĕnō**, *dee-am-en'-o;*
          from *1223* and *3306;* to *stay
constantly* (in being or relation):—continue
{3x}, remain {2x}. See: BAGD—186c; THAYER—
140a.

1266. **διαμερίζω** {12x} **diamĕrizō**, *dee-am-
          er-id'-zo;* from *1223* and
3307; to *partition thoroughly* (lit. in distribution, fig. in dissension):—cloven {1x}, divide
{5x}, part {6x}. See: BAGD—186d; THAYER—
140b.

1267. **διαμερισμός** {1x} **diamĕrismŏs**, *dee-am-
          er-is-mos';* from *1266; dis-
union* (of opinion and conduct):—division {1x}.
See: BAGD—186d; THAYER—140b.

1268. **διανέμω** {1x} **dianĕmō**, *dee-an-em'-o;*
          from *1223* and the base of
3551; to *distribute,* i.e. (of information) to *disseminate:*—spread {1x}. See: BAGD—186d;
THAYER—140b.

1269. **διανεύω** {1x} **dianĕuō**, *dee-an-yoo'-o;*
          from *1223* and *3506;* to *nod*
(or *express* by signs) *across* an intervening
space:—beckoned + 2258 {1x}. See: BAGD—
187a; THAYER—140b.

1270. **διανόημα** {1x} **dianŏēma**, *dee-an-o'-
          ay-mah;* from a compound
of *1223* and *3539;* something *thought through,*
i.e. a *sentiment:*—thought {1x}. See: TDNT—
4:968, 636; BAGD—187a; THAYER—140c.

1271. **διάνοια** {13x} **dianŏia**, *dee-an'-oy-ah;*
          from *1223* and *3563; deep
thought,* prop. the faculty (*mind* or its *disposition*), by impl. its exercise:—imagination {1x},

mind {9x}, understanding {3x}. See: TDNT—
4:963, 636; BAGD—187a; THAYER—140c.

1272. **διανοίγω** {8x} **dianŏigō**, *dee-an-oy'-
                    go;* from *1223* and *455;* to
open thoroughly, lit. (as a first-born) or fig.
(to *expound*):—open {8x}. See: BAGD—187b;
THAYER—140c.

1273. **διανυκτερεύω** {1x} **dianuktĕrĕuō**, *dee-
                    an-ook-ter-yoo'-o;* from
1223 and a der. of *3571;* to *sit up the whole
night:*—continued all night + 2258 {1x}. See:
BAGD—187b; THAYER—140d.

1274. **διανύω** {1x} **dianuō**, *dee-an-oo'-o;* from
          1223 and ἀνύω **anuō** (to *effect*);
to *accomplish thoroughly:*—finish {1x}. See:
BAGD—187b; THAYER—140d.

1275. **διαπαντός** {7x} **diapantŏs**, *dee-ap-
                    an-tos';* from *1223* and the
genit. of *3956; through all* the time, i.e. (adv.)
constantly:—alway {2x}, always {3x}, continually {2x}. See: BAGD—187c; THAYER—140d.

1276. **διαπεράω** {6x} **diapĕraō**, *dee-ap-er-
                    ah'-o;* from *1223* and a der.
of the base of *4008;* to *cross entirely:*—go over
{1x}, pass {1x}, pass over {3x}, sail over {1x}.
See: BAGD—187c; THAYER—140d.

1277. **διαπλέω** {1x} **diaplĕō**, *dee-ap-leh'-o;*
          from *1223* and *4126;* to *sail
through, across:*—sail over {1x}. See: BAGD—
187c; THAYER—141a.

1278. **διαπονέω** {2x} **diapŏnĕō**, *dee-ap-on-
                    eh'-o;* from *1223* and a der.
of *4192;* to *toil through,* i.e. (pass.) *be worried:*—be grieved {2x}. See: BAGD—187c;
THAYER—141a.

1279. **διαπορεύομαι** {5x} **diapŏrĕuŏmai**, *dee-
                    ap-or-yoo'-om-ahee;*
from *1223* and *4198;* to *travel through:*—went
through {3x}, in (one's) journey {1x}, pass by
{1x}. See: BAGD—187d; THAYER—141a.

1280. **διαπορέω** {5x} **diapŏrĕō**, *dee-ap-or-eh'-o;*
          from *1223* and *639;* to *be
thoroughly nonplussed:*—be in doubt {1x},
doubt {2x}, be much perplexed {1x}, be perplexed {1x}.

  Diaporeo signifies to be thoroughly perplexed, amounting to despair, at a loss as to
what to do; without resources to solve the
problem. See: BAGD—187d; THAYER—141a.

1281. **διαπραγματεύομαι** {1x} **diapragma-
                    tĕuŏmai**, *dee-ap-
rag-mat-yoo'-om-ahee;* from *1223* and *4231;* to
thoroughly occupy oneself, i.e. (tran. and by

impl.) to *earn* in business:—gain by trading {1x}. See: TDNT—6:641, 927; BAGD—187d; THAYER—141b.

1282. **διαπρίω** {2x} **diapriō**, *dee-ap-ree'-o;* from *1223* and the base of *4249;* to *saw asunder,* i.e. (fig.) to *exasperate:*—cut {1x}, be cut to the heart {1x}. See: BAGD—187d; THAYER—141b.

1283. **διαρπάζω** {4x} **diarpazo**, *dee-ar-pad'-zo;* from *1223* and *726;* to *seize asunder,* i.e. *plunder:*—spoil {4x}. See: BAGD—188a; THAYER—141b.

1284. **διαρρήσσω** {5x} **diarrhēssō**, *dee-ar-hrayce'-so;* from *1223* and *4486;* to *tear asunder:*—break {2x}, rend {3x}. See: BAGD—188a; THAYER—141b.

1285. **διασαφέω** {1x} **diasaphēo**, *dee-as-af-eh'-o;* from *1223* and σαφής **saphēs** (*clear*); to *clear thoroughly, explain fully,* i.e. (fig.) *declare:*—tell unto {1x}. See: BAGD—188b; THAYER—141c.

1286. **διασείω** {1x} **diaseiō**, *dee-as-i'-o;* from *1223* and *4579;* to *shake thoroughly, violently,* i.e. (fig.) to *intimidate:*—do violence to {1x}. See: BAGD—188b; THAYER—141c.

1287. **διασκορπίζω** {9x} **diaskorpizo**, *dee-as-kor-pid'-zo;* from *1223* and *4650;* to *dissipate,* i.e. (gen.) to *rout* or *separate;* spec., to *winnow;* fig. to *squander:*—disperse {1x}, scatter {2x}, scatter abroad {2x}, strew {2x}, waste {2x}. See: TDNT—7:418, 1048; BAGD—188b; THAYER—141c.

1288. **διασπάω** {2x} **diaspaō**, *dee-as-pah'-o;* from *1223* and *4685;* to *draw apart,* i.e. *sever* or *dismember:*—pluck asunder {1x}, pull in pieces {1x}. See: BAGD—188c; THAYER—141d.

1289. **διασπείρω** {3x} **diaspĕirō**, *dee-as-pi'-ro;* from *1223* and *4687;* to *sow throughout,* i.e. (fig.) *distribute* in foreign lands:—scatter abroad {3x}. See: BAGD—188c; THAYER—141d.

1290. **διασπορά** {3x} **diaspŏra**, *dee-as-por-ah';* from *1289; dispersion,* i.e. (spec. and concr.) the (converted) Isr. *resident* in Gentile countries:—dispersed {1x}, which are scattered abroad {1x}, scattered {1x}. See: TDNT—2:98, 156; BAGD—188c; THAYER—141d.

1291. **διαστέλλομαι** {8x} **diastĕllŏmai**, *dee-as-tel'-lom-ahee;* mid. voice from *1223* and *4724;* to *set* (oneself) *apart* (fig. *distinguish*), i.e. (by impl.) to *enjoin:*—charge {6x}, give commandment {1x}, be com-

manded {1x}. See: TDNT—7:591; BAGD—188d; THAYER—142a.

1292. **διάστημα** {1x} **diastēma**, *dee-as'-tay-mah;* from *1339;* an *interval:*—space {1x}. See: BAGD—188d; THAYER—142a.

1293. **διαστολή** {3x} **diastŏlē**, *dee-as-tol-ay';* from *1291;* a *variation:*—difference {2x}, distinction {1x}. See: TDNT—7:592, 1074; BAGD—188d; THAYER—142a.

1294. **διαστρέφω** {7x} **diastrĕphō**, *dee-as-tref'-o;* from *1223* and *4762;* to *distort, twist,* i.e. (fig.) *misinterpret,* or (morally) *corrupt:*—perverse {4x}, pervert {2x}, turn away {1x}. See: TDNT—7:717, 1093; BAGD—189a; THAYER—142a.

1295. **διασώζω** {8x} **diasōzō**, *dee-as-odze'-o;* from *1223* and *4982;* to *save thoroughly,* i.e. (by impl. or anal.) to *cure, preserve, rescue,* etc.:—escape {2x}, save {2x}, make perfectly whole {1x}, escape safe {1x}, bring safe {1x}, heal {1x}. See: BAGD—189a; THAYER—142b.

1296. **διαταγή** {2x} **diatagē**, *dee-at-ag-ay';* from *1299; arrangement,* i.e. *institution:*—disposition {1x}, ordinance {1x}. See: TDNT—8:36, 1156; BAGD—189b; THAYER—142b.

1297. **διάταγμα** {1x} **diatagma**, *dee-at'-ag-mah;* from *1299;* an *arrangement,* i.e. (authoritative) *edict:*—commandment {1x}.

Diatagma signifies that which is imposed by decree or law (Heb 11:23). It stresses the concrete character of the commandment. See: BAGD—189b; THAYER—142c.

1298. **διαταράσσω** {1x} **diatarassō**, *dee-at-ar-as'-so;* from *1223* and *5015;* to *disturb wholly,* i.e. *agitate* (with alarm):—trouble {1x}. See: BAGD—189b; THAYER—142c.

1299. **διατάσσω** {16x} **diatassō**, *dee-at-as'-so;* from *1223* and *5021;* to *arrange thoroughly,* i.e. (spec.) *institute, prescribe,* etc.:—command {7x}, appoint {4x}, ordain {3x}, set in order {1x}, give order {1x}.

Diatasso, a verb, a strengthened form of *tasso* (*5021*) [*dia,* "through," intensive], frequently denotes "to arrange, appoint, prescribe" **(1)** what was "appointed" for tax collectors to collect: "And he said unto them, Exact no more than that which is appointed you" (Lk 3:13); **(2)** of the tabernacle, as "appointed" by God for Moses to make: "Our fathers had the tabernacle of witness in the wilderness, as He had appointed, speaking

unto Moses, that he should make it according to the fashion that he had seen" (Acts 7:44); **(3)** of the arrangements "appointed" by Paul with regard to himself and his travelling companions: "And we went before to ship, and sailed unto Assos, there intending to take in Paul: for so had he appointed, minding himself to go afoot" (Acts 20:13);

(4) of what the apostle "ordained" in all the churches in regard to marital conditions: "But as God hath distributed to every man, as the Lord hath called every one, so let him walk. And so ordain I in all churches" (1 Cor 7:17); **(5)** of what the Lord "ordained" in regard to the support of those who proclaimed the gospel: "Even so hath the Lord ordained that they which preach the gospel should live of the gospel" (1 Cor 9:14); **(6)** of the Law as divinely "ordained," or administered, through angels, by Moses,: "Wherefore then serveth the law? It was added because of transgressions, till the seed should come to whom the promise was made; and it was ordained by angels in the hand of a mediator" (Gal 3:19). See: TDNT—8:34, 1156; BAGD—189c; THAYER—142c.

1300. διατελέω {1x} **diatĕlĕō**, *dee-at-el-eh'-o;* from *1223* and *5055;* to *accomplish thoroughly,* i.e. (subj.) to *persist:—* continue {1x}.

Diatelo means to bring through to an end. See: BAGD—189c; THAYER—142d.

1301. διατηρέω {2x} **diatērĕō**, *dee-at-ay-reh'-o;* from *1223* and *5083;* to *watch thoroughly,* i.e. (pos. and tran.) to *observe* strictly, or (neg. and refl.) to *avoid* wholly:—keep {2x}. See: TDNT—8:151, 1174; BAGD—189d; THAYER—142d.

1302. διατί {27x} **diati**, *dee-at-ee';* from *1223* and *5101; through what* cause?, i.e. *why?:—*wherefore {4x}, why {23x}. See: BAGD—189d; THAYER—142d.

1303. διατίθεμαι {7x} **diatithĕmai**, *dee-at-ith'-em-ahee;* mid. voice from *1223* and *5087;* to *put apart,* i.e. (fig.) *dispose* (by assignment, compact, or bequest):—appoint {2x}, make {3x}, testator {2x}.

Diatithemi, a verb, a strengthened form of tithemi (*5087*) [*dia*, "through," intensive], is **(1)** used in the middle voice only. **(2)** It means to arrange, dispose of, one's own affairs **(2a)** of something that belongs to one: The Lord used it of His disciples with reference to the kingdom which is to be theirs hereafter, and of Himself in the same respect, as that which has been "appointed" for Him by His Father: "And I appoint (*diatithemi*) unto you a kingdom, as My Father hath appointed (*diatithemi*) unto Me" (Lk 22:29); **(2b)** to make a covenant, enter

into a covenant, with one, Acts 3:25; Heb 8:10; 10:16; **(3)** be the person who disposes of through covenant, a testator, Heb 9:16, 17. See: TDNT—2:104, 157; BAGD—189d; THAYER—142d.

1304. διατρίβω {10x} **diatribō**, *dee-at-ree'-bo;* from *1223* and the base of *5147;* to *wear through* (time), i.e. *remain:—* abide {5x}, be {1x}, continue {2x}, tarry {2x}.

Diatribo means lit., "to wear through by rubbing, to wear away" and **(1)** when used of time, "to spend or pass time, to stay, continue" Jn 11:54; Acts 15:35; elsewhere it means **(2)** "abiding, abode" Acts 12:19; 14:3, 28; 16:12; 20:6; **(3)** "had been" Acts 25:14; **(4)** "tarry" Jn 3:22; Acts 25:6. See: BAGD—190a; THAYER—143a.

1305. διατροφή {1x} **diatrŏphē**, *dee-at-rof-ay';* from a compound of *1223* and *5142; nourishment:—*food {1x}.

This word means "sustenance, food," suggesting a sufficient supply and is used in 1 Ti 6:8. See: BAGD—190a; THAYER—143a.

1306. διαυγάζω {1x} **diaugazō**, *dee-ow-gad'-zo;* from *1223* and *826;* to *glimmer* (through), i.e. *break* (as day):—dawn {1x}.

Diaugazo describes the breaking of daylight upon the darkness of night, metaphorically in 2 Pet 1:19, of the shining of spiritual light into the heart. A probable reference is to the day to be ushered in at the second coming of Christ: "until the Day gleam through the present darkness, and the Light-bringer dawn in your hearts." See: BAGD—190a; THAYER—143a.

1307. διαφανής {1x} **diaphanēs**, *dee-af-an-ace';* from *1223* and *5316; appearing through,* i.e. "*diaphanous*":—transparent {1x}. See: BAGD—190b; THAYER—143a.

1308. διαφέρω {13x} **diaphĕrō**, *dee-af-er'-o;* from *1223* and *5342;* to *bear through,* i.e. (lit.) *transport;* usually to *bear apart,* i.e. (obj.) to *toss about* (fig. *report*); subj. to "*differ*," or (by impl.) *surpass:—*be better {3x}, be of more value {2x}, differ from {2x}, should carry {1x}, publish {1x}, drive up and down {1x}, misc. {3x} = be (more) excellent, make matter.

This word used **(1)** transitively, means "to carry through", Mk 11:16; Acts 13:49; 27:27 ("driven to and fro"); **(2)** intransitively, **(2a)** "to differ," Rom 2:18; Gal 2:6; Phil 1:10; **(2b)** "to excel, be better," e.g., Mt 6:26; 10:31 ("of more value"); 12:12; Lk 12:7, 24; Rom 2:18; 1 Cor

15:41; Gal 4:1; Phil 1:10. See: BAGD—190b; THAYER—143b.

1309. διαφεύγω {1x} **diaphĕugō**, *dee-af-yoo'-go;* from *1223* and *5343;* to *flee through,* i.e. *escape:*—escape {1x}.

Diapheugo means lit., "to flee through," is used of the "escaping" of prisoners from a ship, Acts 27:42. See: BAGD—190c; THAYER—143c.

1310. διαφημίζω {3x} **diaphēmizō**, *dee-af-ay-mid'-zo;* from *1223* and a der. of *5345;* to *report thoroughly,* i.e. *divulgate:*—spread abroad (one's) fame {1x}, be commonly reported {1x}, blaze abroad {1x}.

This word means "to spread broad, commonly reported" (*dia*, "throughout," *phemizo*, "to speak"), and is so translated in Mt 9:31; 28:15 ("commonly reported"); Mk 1:45 ("blaze abroad"). See: BAGD—190c; THAYER—143c.

1311. διαφθείρω {6x} **diaphthĕirō**, *dee-af-thi'-ro;* from *1225* and *5351;* to *rot thoroughly,* i.e. (by impl.) to *ruin* (pass. *decay* utterly, fig. *pervert*):—corrupt {2x}, destroy {3x}, perish {1x}.

This word, derived from *dia*, "through," intensive, and *phtheiro* (*5351*), "to corrupt utterly, through and through," is **(1)** said of men "of corrupt in mind," whose wranglings result from the doctrines of false teachers, 1 Ti 6:5. **(2)** It is translated "corrupteth," in Lk 12:33, of the work of a moth; **(3)** in Rev 8:9, of the effect of divine judgments hereafter upon navigation; **(4)** in 11:18, of the divine retribution of destruction upon those who have destroyed the earth; **(5)** in 2 Cor 4:16 it is translated "perish," said of the human body. See: TDNT—9:93, 1259; BAGD—190c; THAYER—143c.

1312. διαφθορά {6x} **diaphthŏrá**, *dee-af-thor-ah';* from *1311; decomposition and decay:*—corruption {6x}.

Diaphthora, an intensified form of *phtheiro* (*5351*), "utter or thorough corruption," referring in the NT to physical decomposition and decay, is used **(1)** six times, five of which refer, negatively, to the body of God's "Holy One," after His death, which body, by reason of His absolute holiness, could not see "corruption," Acts 2:27, 31; 13:34–35, 37; **(2)** once it is used of a human body, that of David, which, by contrast, saw "corruption," Acts 13:36. See: TDNT—9:93, 1259; BAGD—190d; THAYER—143d.

1313. διάφορος {4x} **diaphŏrŏs**, *dee-af'-or-os;* from *1308; varying;* also *surpassing:*—differing {1x}, divers {1x}, more excellent {2x}.

Diaphoros signifies "varying in kind, differ-

ent, diverse." It is used **(1)** of spiritual gifts, Rom 12:6; and **(2)** of ceremonial washings, Heb 9:10 ("divers"); and in the **(3)** comparative degree of *diaphoros,* "excellent," it is used twice, **(3a)** in Heb 1:4, "more excellent (name)," and **(3b)** Heb 8:6, "more excellent (ministry)." See: TDNT—9:62, 1259; BAGD—190d; THAYER—143d.

1314. διαφυλάσσω {1x} **diaphulassō**, *dee-af-oo-las'-so;* from *1223* and *5442;* to *guard thoroughly,* i.e. *protect:*—keep {1x}.

Diaphulasso, a strengthened form of *phulasso* (*5442*), (*dia*, "through," used intensively), "to guard carefully, defend, to keep" is found in Lk 4:10. See: BAGD—191a; THAYER—143d.

1315. διαχειρίζομαι {2x} **diachĕirizŏmai**, *dee-akh-i-rid'-zom-ahee;* from *1223* and a der. of *5495;* to *handle thoroughly,* i.e. *lay* violent *hands* upon:—kill {1x}, slay {1x}.

This word means primarily, "to have in hand, manage" and is used in the middle voice, in the sense of "laying hands on" with a view to "kill," or of actually "killing," Acts 5:30, "ye slew"; 26:21, "to kill." See: BAGD—191a; THAYER—143d.

1316. διαχωρίζομαι {1x} **diachōrizŏmai**, *dee-akh-o-rid'-zom-ahee;* from *1223* and the mid. voice of *5563;* to *remove* (oneself) *wholly,* i.e. *retire:*—depart {1x}.

This word means lit., "to unloose, undo" and signifies "to depart," in the sense of "departing" from life, Phil 1:23, a metaphor drawn from loosing moorings preparatory to setting sail, or, according to some, from breaking up an encampment, or from the unyoking of baggage animals. See: BAGD—191a; THAYER—144a.

1317. διδακτικός {2x} **didaktikŏs**, *did-ak-tik-os';* from *1318; instructive* ("didactic"):—This word means apt to teach {2x}. "skilled in teaching" and is translated "apt to teach" in 1 Tim 3:2; 2 Ti 2:24. See: TDNT—2:165, 161; BAGD—191b; THAYER—144a.

1318. διδακτός {3x} **didaktŏs**, *did-ak-tos';* from *1321;* (subj.) *instructed,* or (obj.) *communicated* by teaching:—taught {1x}, which . . . teacheth {2x}.

This word means primarily "what can be taught," then, "taught," is used **(1)** of persons, Jn 6:45; **(2)** of things, 1 Cor 2:13 (twice), "(not in words which man's wisdom) teacheth, (but which the Spirit) teacheth," lit., "(not in words) taught (of man's wisdom, but) taught (of the

Spirit)." See: TDNT—2:165, 161; BAGD—191b; THAYER—144a.

1319. διδασκαλία {21x} **didaskalia**, *did-as-kal-ee'-ah;* from *1320; instruction* (the function or the information; that which is taught):—doctrine {19x}, learning {1x}, teaching {1x}.

This word denotes **(1)** "that which is taught, doctrine," Mt 15:9; Mk 7:7; Eph 4:14; Col 2:22; 1 Ti 1:10; 4:1, 6; 6:1, 3; 2 Ti 4:3; Titus 1:9 ("doctrine," in last part of verse); 2:1, 10; **(2)** "teaching, instruction," Rom 12:7, "teaching"; 15:4, "learning," 1 Ti 4:13 "doctrine"; v. 16 "the doctrine,"; 5:17 "doctrine"; 2 Ti 3:10, 16 (ditto); Titus 2:7, "thy doctrine." See: TDNT—2:160, 161; BAGD—191c; THAYER—144a.

1320. διδάσκαλος {58x} **didaskalŏs**, *did-as'-kal-os;* from *1321;* an *instructor* (gen. or spec.):—Master (Jesus) {40x}, teacher {10x}, master {7x}, doctor {1x}.

This word means a teacher and in the NT one who teaches concerning the things of God, and the duties of man **(1)** one who is fitted to teach, or thinks himself so, Heb 5:12; Rom 2:20; **(2)** the teachers of the Jewish religion, Lk 2:46; Jn 3:10; **(3)** of those who by their great power as teachers draw crowds around them **(3a)** John the Baptist, Lk 3:12, **(3b)** Jesus, Jn 1:38; 3:2; 8:4; **(4)** of the apostles, and of Paul, 1 Ti 2:7; 2 Ti 1:11; **(5)** of those who in the religious assemblies of the Christians, undertook the work of teaching, with the special assistance of the Holy Spirit, 1 Cor 12:28; Eph 4:11; Acts 13:1; **(6)** of false teachers among Christians, 2 Ti 4:3. See: TDNT—2:148, 161; BAGD—191c; THAYER—144b.

1321. διδάσκω {97x} **didaskō**, *did-as'-ko;* a prol. (caus.) form of a primary verb δάω **daō** (to *learn*); to *teach* (in the same broad application):—teach {93x}, taught + 2258 {4x}.

This word denotes to cause to learn, to effect learning. This word means is used **(1)** absolutely, "to give instruction," e.g., Mt 4:23; 9:35; Rom 12:7; 1 Cor 4:17; 1 Ti 2:12; 4:11; **(2)** transitively, with an object, whether **(2a)** persons, e.g., Mt 5:2; 7:29, and frequently in the Gospels and Acts, or **(2b)** things "taught," e.g., Mt 15:9; 22:16; Acts 15:35; 18:11; **(2c)** both persons and things, e.g., Jn 14:26; Rev 2:14, 20. See: TDNT—2:135, 161; BAGD—192a; THAYER—144b.

1322. διδαχή {30x} **didachē**, *did-akh-ay';* from *1321; instruction* (the act or the matter):—doctrine {29x}, hath been taught {1x}.

This word denotes "teaching," either **(1)** that which is taught, e.g., Mt 7:28 "doctrine"; Titus 1:9; Rev 2:14–15, 24, or **(2)** the act of teaching, instruction, e.g., Mk 4:2 "doctrine"; Rom 16:17. See: TDNT—2:163, 161; BAGD—192b; THAYER—144d.

1323. δίδραχμον {2x} **didrachmŏn**, *did'-rakh-mon;* from *1364* and *1406;* a *double drachma* (*didrachm*):—tribute {1x}, tribute money {1x}.

This word means "a half-shekel" (i.e., *dis*, "twice," *drachme*, "a drachma," the coin mentioned in Lk 15:8, 9), was the amount of the tribute in the 1st cent., A.D., due from every adult Jew for the maintenance of the temple services, Mt 17:24 (twice). See: BAGD—192c; THAYER—145a.

1324. Δίδυμος {3x} **Didumŏs**, *did'-oo-mos;* prol. from *1364; double,* i.e. *twin; Didymus,* a Chr.:—Didymus {1x}. See: BAGD—192c; THAYER—145a.

1325. δίδωμι {413x} **didōmi**, *did'-o-mee;* a prol. form of a primary verb (which is used as an altern. in most of the tenses); to *give* (used in a very wide application, prop. or by impl., lit. or fig.; greatly modified by the connection):—give {365x}, grant {10x}, put {5x}, shew {4x}, deliver {2x}, make {2x}, misc. {25x} = adventure, bestow, bring forth, commit, hinder, minister, number, offer, have power, receive, set, smite (+ with the hand), strike (+ with the palm of the hand), suffer, take, utter, yield. See: TDNT—2:166, 166; BAGD—192c; THAYER—145a.

1326. διεγείρω {7x} **diĕgĕirō**, *dee-eg-i'-ro;* from *1223* and *1453;* to *wake fully;* i.e. *arouse* (lit. or fig.):—arise {2x}, awake {2x}, raise {1x}, stir up {2x}.

Diegeiro, as a verb, signifies "to rouse, to awaken from sleep." **(1)** In Mt 1:24, "Joseph being raised from sleep," the passive participle is, lit., "being aroused." **(2)** In Mk 4:39 "he arose," the lit. rendering is "he being awakened." **(3)** In Jn 6:18 "the sea arose" the imperfect tense of the passive voice is used, and is understood as "the sea was being aroused." Syn. for **(1)** - **(3)**: 305, 393, 450, 1096, 1453, 1525, 1817, 4911. **(4)** *Diegeiro* also means "stir up": "Yea, I think it meet, as long as I am in this tabernacle, to stir you up by putting you in remembrance" (2 Pet 1:13; cf. 3:1). Syn. for **(4)**: 329, 383, 387, 1892, 2042, 3947, 3951, 4531, 4579, 4787, 4797, 5017. See: BAGD—193d; THAYER—147a.

1327. διέξοδος {1x} **diĕxŏdŏs**, *dee-ex'-od-os;* from *1223* and *1841;* an *outlet through,* i.e. prob. an open *square* (from which roads diverge):—highway + 3598 + 3588 {1x}. In Mt 22:9, the word is translated "high-

ways," "the partings of the highways, the cross-roads." See: TDNT—5:103, 666; BAGD—194a; THAYER—147b.

1328. **διερμηνευτής** {1x} **diĕrmēnĕutēs**, *dee-er-main-yoo-tace';* from *1329;* an *explainer:*—interpreter {1x}. See: TDNT—2:661, 256; BAGD—194b; THAYER—147c.

1329. **διερμηνεύω** {6x} **diĕrmēnĕuō**, *dee-er-main-yoo'-o;* from *1223* and *2059;* to *explain thoroughly,* by impl. to *translate:*—expound {1x}, interpret {4x}, interpretatioin {1x}.

This word means "to interpret fully" (*dia* "through," intensive, *hermeneuo,* "to interpret"); (Eng., "hermeneutics"), and is translated, **(1)** "He expounded" in Lk 24:27; **(2)** in Acts 9:36, "by interpretation," lit., "being interpreted"; see also **(3)** 1 Cor 12:30; 14:5, 13, 27. See: TDNT—2:661, 256; BAGD—194b; THAYER—147c.

1330. **διέρχομαι** {43x} **diĕrchŏmai**, *dee-er'-khom-ahee;* from *1223* and *2064;* to come or go through; to *traverse* (lit.):—pass {8x}, pass through {7x}, go {7x}, go over {3x}, go through {2x}, walk {2x}, vr to go {1x}, misc. {13x} come, depart, go about, go abroad, go everywhere, go throughout, pass (by, over, throughout), pierce through, travel.

This word means to go through, pass through **(1)** to go, walk, journey, pass through a place, Mt 12:43; 19:24; **(2)** to travel the road which leads through a place, go, pass, travel through a region, Lk 19:1; Acts 12:10; 13:6; **(3)** to go different places, of people, to go abroad, Acts 8:4, 40; 13:14; **(4)** of a report, to spread, go abroad, Lk 5:15. See: TDNT—2:676, 257; BAGD—194c; THAYER—147c.

1331. **διερωτάω** {1x} **diĕrōtaō**, *dee-er-o-tah'-o;* from *1223* and *2065;* to *question throughout,* i.e. *ascertain* by interrogation:—make enquiry for {1x}.

Dierotao means "to find by inquiry, to inquire through to the end" (*dia,* intensive, *erotao,* "to ask") and is used in Acts 10:17. See: BAGD—194d; THAYER—148a.

1332. **διετής** {1x} **diĕtēs**, *dee-et-ace';* from *1364* and *2094;* of *two years* (in age):—two years old {1x}. See: BAGD—194d; THAYER—148a.

1333. **διετία** {2x} **diĕtia**, *dee-et-ee'-a;* from *1332;* a space of *two years* (*biennium*):—two years {2x}. See: BAGD—194d; THAYER—148a.

1334. **διηγέομαι** {8x} **diēgĕŏmai**, *dee-aygeh'-om-ahee;* from *1223* and

2233; to *relate fully:*—declare {3x}, shew {1x}, tell {4x}.

This word means to conduct a narration through to the end; hence, denotes to recount, to relate in full (Mk 5:16; Lk 8:39; 9:10). See: BAGD—195a; THAYER—148a.

1335. **διήγεσις** {1x} **diēgĕsis**, *dee-ayg'-es-is;* or διήγησις **diēgēsis** *dee-ayg'-es-is;* from *1334;* a *recital:*—declaration {1x}.

Diegesis is translated "a declaration" in Lk 1:1 and denotes a "narrative," ("to set out in detail, recount). See: TDNT—2:909, 303; BAGD—195a; THAYER—148b.

1336. **διηνεκές** {4x} **diēnĕkĕs**, *dee-ay-nek-es';* neut. of a compound of *1223* and a der. of an alt. of *5342; carried through,* i.e. (adv. with *1519* and *3588* pref.) *perpetually:*—+ continually + 1519 {2x}, for ever + 1591 {2x}. See: BAGD—195a; THAYER—148b.

1337. **διθάλασσος** {1x} **dithalassŏs**, *dee-thal'-as-sos;* from *1364* and *2281; having two seas,* i.e. a *sound* with a double outlet:—where two seas meet {1x}.

This word means primarily "divided into two seas," then, "dividing the sea," as of a reef or rocky projection running out into the "sea," Acts 27:41. See: BAGD—195a; THAYER—148b.

1338. **διϊκνέομαι** {1x} **diïknĕŏmai**, *dee-ik-neh'-om-ahee;* from *1223* and the base of *2425;* to *reach through,* i.e. *penetrate:*—pierce {1x}.

This word means "to go through, penetrate" and is used of the power of the Word of God, in Heb 4:12, "piercing." See: BAGD—195b; THAYER—148b.

1339. **διΐστημι** {3x} **diïstēmi**, *dee-is'-tay-mee;* from *1223* and *2476;* to *stand apart,* i.e. (refl.) to *remove, intervene:*—after the space of . . . {1x}, go further {1x}, be parted {1x}.

Diistemi means "to set apart, separate" (*dia,* "apart," *histemi,* "to cause to stand"), and is used **(1)** in the active voice in Lk 24:51, "was parted"; and is translated **(2)** "after the space of . . .", Lk 22:59; and **(3)** "gone . . . further", Acts 27:28). See: BAGD—195b; THAYER—148b.

1340. **διϊσχυρίζομαι** {2x} **diïschurizŏmai**, *dee-is-khoo-rid'-zom-ahee;* from *1223* and a der. of *2478;* to *stout it through,* i.e. *asseverate:*—confidently affirm {1x}, constantly affirm {1x}.

This word primarily signifies "to lean upon," hence, "to affirm stoutly, assert vehemently,"

Lk 22:59; Acts 12:15. See: BAGD—195b; THAYER—148c.

1341. **δικαιοκρισία** {1x} **dikaiŏkrisia**, *dik-ah-yok-ris-ee'-ah;* from *1342* and *2920;* a *just sentence:*—righteous judgment {1x}. See: TDNT—2:224, 168; BAGD—195c; THAYER—148c.

1342. **δίκαιος** {81x} **dikaiŏs**, *dik'-ah-yos;* from *1349; equitable* (in character or act); by impl. *innocent, holy* (absol. or rel.):—righteous {41x}, just {33x}, right {5x}, meet {2x}.

Dikaios denotes **(1)** righteous, a state of being right, or right conduct, judged whether by the divine standard, or according to human standards, of what is right. **(2)** Said of God, it designates the perfect agreement between His nature and His acts (in which He is the standard for all men). It is used in the broad sense, **(3)** of persons: **(3a)** of God (Jn 17:25; Rom 3:26; 1 Jn 1:9; 2:29); **(3b)** of Christ (Acts 3:14; 7:52; 2 Ti 4:8; 1 Pet 3:18); **(3c)** of men (Mt 1:19; Lk 1:6; Rom 1:17); **(4)** of things: **(4a)** blood [metaphorical] (Mt 23:35); **(4b)** Christ's judgment (Jn 5:30); **(4c)** any circumstance, fact or deed (Mt 20:4; Lk 12:57; Acts 4:19); **(4d)** the commandment [the Law] (Rom 7:12); **(4e)** works (1 Jn 3:12); **(4f)** the ways of God (Rev 15:3). Syn.: 1346, 1738. See: TDNT—2:182, 168; BAGD—195c; THAYER—148c.

1343. **δικαιοσύνη** {92x} **dikaiŏsunē**, *dik-ah-yos-oo'-nay;* from *1342; equity* (of character or act); spec. (Chr.) *justification:*—righteousness {92x}.

Dikaiosune is the character or quality of being right or just. **(1)** It denotes an attribute of God (Rom 3:5). **(2)** It is found in the sayings of the Lord Jesus **(2a)** of whatever is right or just in itself that conforms to the revealed will of God (Mt 5:6, 10, 20; Jn 16:8, 10); **(2b)** whatever has been appointed by God to be acknowledged and obeyed by man (Mt 3:15; 21:32); **(2c)** the sum total of the requirements of God (Mt 6:33); **(2d)** religious duties (Mt 6:1–15): distinguished as **(2d1)** almsgiving, man's duty to his neighbor (6: 2–4), **(2d2)** prayer—his duty to God (vv. 5–15), and **(2d3)** fasting—the duty of self-control (vv. 16–18).

(3) It is used of that gracious gift of God to men **(3a)** whereby all who believe on the Lord Jesus Christ are brought into right relationship with God. **(3b)** This righteousness is unattainable by obedience to any law, or by any merit of man's own, or any other condition than that of faith in Christ. **(3c)** The man who trusts in Christ becomes "the righteousness of God in Him," (2 Cor 5:21), i.e., becomes in Christ all that God requires a man to be, all that he could

never be in himself. **(4)** Righteousness is not said to be imputed to the believer save in the sense that faith is imputed (reckoned) for righteousness (Rom 4:6, 11). **(5)** The faith thus exercised brings the soul into vital union with God in Christ, and inevitably produces righteousness of life, that is, conformity to the will of God. Syn.: 1345. See: TDNT—2:192, 168; BAGD—196b; THAYER—149b.

1344. **δικαιόω** {40x} **dikaiŏō**, *dik-ah-yŏ'-o;* from *1342;* to *render* (i.e. *show* or *regard* as) *just* or *innocent:*—be freed {1x}, justify {37x}, justifier {1x}, be righteous {1x}.

Dikaioo, as a verb, means primarily "to deem to be right," and signifies, in the NT, **(1)** "to show to be right or righteous"; in the passive voice, to be justified, Mt 11:19; Lk 7:35; Rom 3:4; 1 Ti 3:16; **(2)** "to declare to be righteous, to pronounce righteous," **(2a)** by man, **(2a1)** concerning God, Lk 7:29; **(2a2)** concerning himself, Lk 10:29; 16:15; **(2b)** by God concerning men, who are declared to be righteous before Him on certain conditions laid down by Him.

(3) Ideally the complete fulfillment of the law of God would provide a basis of "justification" in His sight, Rom 2:13. **(3a)** But no such case has occurred in mere human experience, and therefore no one can be "justified" on this ground, Rom 3:9–20; Gal 2:16; 3:10, 11; 5:4. **(3b)** From this negative presentation in Rom 3, the apostle proceeds to show that, consistently with God's own righteous character, and with a view to its manifestation, He is, through Christ, as "a propitiation . . . by (*en,* "instrumental") His blood," 3:25, "justification" being the legal and formal acquittal from guilt by God as Judge, the pronouncement of the sinner as righteous, who believes on the Lord Jesus Christ. **(3c)** In v. 24, "being justified" is in the present continuous tense, indicating the constant process of "justification" in the succession of those who believe and are "justified." **(3d)** In 5:1, "being justified" is in the aorist, or point, tense, indicating the definite time at which each person, upon the exercise of faith, was justified. **(3e)** In 8:1, "justification" is presented as "no condemnation." That "justification" is in view here is confirmed by the preceding chapters and by verse 34. **(3f)** In 3:26, the word rendered "Justifier" is the present participle of the verb, lit., "justifying"; similarly in 8:33 (where the article is used), "God that justifieth," is, more lit., "God is the (One) justifying," with stress upon the word "God."

(4) "Justification" is primarily and gratuitously by faith, subsequently and evidentially by works. **(4a)** In regard to "justification" by

works, the so-called contradiction between James and the apostle Paul is only apparent. There is harmony in the different views of the subject. **(4a1)** Paul has in mind Abraham's attitude toward God, his acceptance of God's word. This was a matter known only to God. The Romans epistle is occupied with the effect of this God-ward attitude, not upon Abraham's character or actions, but upon the contrast between faith and the lack of it, namely, unbelief, cf. Rom 11:20. **(4a2)** James (2:21–26) is occupied with the contrast between faith that is real and faith that is false, a faith barren and dead, which is not faith at all. **(4b)** Again, the two writers have before them different epochs in Abraham's life—**(4b1)** Paul, the event recorded in Gen 15, **(4b2)** James, that in Gen 22. **(4c)** Contrast the words "believed" in Gen 15:6 and "obeyed" in 22:18. **(4d)** Further, the two writers use the words "faith" and "works" in somewhat different senses. **(4d1)** With Paul, faith is acceptance of God's word; with **(4d2)** James, it is acceptance of the truth of certain statements about God, (v. 19), which may fail to affect one's conduct. **(4e)** Faith, as dealt with by Paul, results in acceptance with God., i.e., "justification," and is bound to manifest itself. If not, as James says "Can that faith save him?" (v. 14). **(4f)** With Paul, works are dead works, with James they are life works. The works of which Paul speaks could be quite independent of faith: those referred to by James can be wrought only where faith is real, and they will attest its reality. **(4g)** So with righteousness, or "justification": Paul is occupied with a right relationship with God, James, with right conduct. Paul testifies that the ungodly can be "justified" by faith, James that only the right-doer is "justified." See: TDNT—2:211, 168; BAGD—197c; THAYER—150b.

1345. **δικαίωμα** {10x} **dikaiōma,** *dik-ah'-yo-mah;* from *1344;* an *equitable deed;* by impl. a *statute* or *decision:*— judgment {2x}, justification {1x}, ordinance {3x}, righteousness {4x}.

Dikaioma has three distinct meanings, and seems best described comprehensively as "a concrete expression of righteousness"; it is a declaration that a person or thing is righteous, and hence, broadly speaking, it represents the expression and effect of *dikaiosis* (*1347*). It signifies **(1)** "an ordinance, judgment", Lk 1:6; **(1a)** Rom 1:32, judgment, i.e., what God has declared to be right, referring to His decree of retribution; **(1b)** Rom 2:26, "righteousness of the Law" (i.e., righteous requirements enjoined by the Law); **(1c)** so 8:4, collectively, the precepts of the Law, all that it demands as right;

(1d) in Heb 9:1, 10, ordinances connected with the tabernacle ritual; **(2)** "a sentence of acquittal," by which God acquits men of their guilt, on the conditions **(2a)** of His grace in Christ, through His expiatory sacrifice, **(2b)** the acceptance of Christ by faith, Rom 5:16; **(2c)** "a righteous act," Rom 5:18, "(through one) act of righteousness," **(2c1)** not the act of "justification," nor **(2c2)** the righteous character of Christ (*dikaioma* does not signify character, as does *dikaiosune*, righteousness), but **(2c3)** the death of Christ, as an act accomplished consistently with God's character and counsels; **(2c4)** this is clear as being in antithesis to the "one trespass" in the preceding statement. **(2d)** Some take the word here as meaning a decree of righteousness, as in v. 16; the death of Christ could indeed be regarded as fulfilling such a decree, but as the apostle's argument proceeds, the word, as is frequently the case, passes from one shade of meaning to another, and **(2d1)** here stands not for a decree, but **(2d2)** an act; so in Rev 15:4, "righteous judgments", and 19:8, "righteousness (acts) of the saints." See: TDNT—2:219, 168; BAGD—198a; THAYER—151b.

1346. **δικαίως** {5x} **dikaiōs,** *dik-ah'-yoce;* adv. from *1342; equitably:*— justly {2x}, to righteousness {1x}, righteously {2x}.

This adverb means "justly, righteously, in accordance with what is right," and is said **(1)** of God's judgment, 1 Pet 2:23; **(2)** of men, Lk 23:41, "justly;" 1 Cor 15:34 "righteousness"; 1 Th 2:10; Titus 2:12. See: BAGD—198b; THAYER—151c.

1347. **δικαίωσις** {2x} **dikaiōsis,** *dik-ah'-yo-sis;* from *1344; acquittal* (for Christ's sake):—justification {2x}.

Dikaiosis denotes "the act of pronouncing righteous, justification, acquittal"; its precise meaning is determined by that of the verb *dikaioo,* "to justify" (*1344*); **(1)** it is used twice in Romans, and there alone in the NT, signifying the establishment of a person as just by acquittal from guilt. **(2)** In Rom 4:25 the phrase "for our justification," is, lit., "because of our justification" (parallel to the preceding clause "for our trespasses," i.e., because of trespasses committed), and means, not with a view to our "justification," but because all that was necessary on God's part for our "justification" had been effected in the death of Christ. On this account He was raised from the dead. The propitiation being perfect and complete, His resurrection was the confirmatory counterpart. **(3)** In 5:18, "justification of life" means "justification which results in life" (cf. v. 21). That

God "justifies" the believing sinner on the ground of Christ's death, involves His free gift of life. See: TDNT—2:223, 168; BAGD—198b; THAYER—151c.

1348. δικαστής {3x} **dikastēs**, *dik-as-tace';* from a der. of *1349;* a *judger:—* judge {3x}.

Dikastes denotes "a judge", Lk 12:14; Acts 7:27, 35. Syn.: While *dikastes* is a forensic term, *krites* (*2923*) "gives prominence to the mental process." The *dikastes* acted as a juryman, the *krites* being the presiding "judge." See: BAGD—198b; THAYER—151c.

1349. δίκη {4x} **dikē**, *dee'-kay;* prob. from *1166; right* (as self-*evident*), i.e. *justice* (the principle, a decision, or its execution):—judgment {1x}, punish + 5099 {1x}, vengeance {2x}.

Dike means primarily "custom, usage," came to denote "what is right"; then, "a judicial hearing"; hence, "the execution of a sentence," **(1)** "punished," 2 Th 1:9; **(2)** "judgment", Acts 25:15; **(3)** Jude 7, "vengeance". Some feel that in Acts 28:4 ("vengeance") should be personified to denote the goddess Justice or Nemesis (Lat., *Justitia*), who the Melita folk supposed was about to inflict the punishment of death upon Paul by means of the viper. See: TDNT—2:178, 168; BAGD—198c; THAYER—151d.

1350. δίκτυον {12x} **diktuŏn**, *dik'-too-on;* prob. from a primary verb δίκω **dikō** (to *cast*); a *seine* (for fishing):—net {12x}.

Diktuon, a general term for a "net," occurs in Mt 4:20–21; Mk 1:18–19; Lk 5:2, 4–6; Jn 21:6, 8, 11 [twice]. Syn.: 293, 4522. See 293 for discussion. See: BAGD—198c; THAYER—151d.

1351. δίλογος {1x} **dilŏgŏs**, *dil'-og-os;* from *1364* and *3056; equivocal,* i.e. telling a different story:—double-tongued {1x}.

Dilogos primarily means saying the same thing twice, or given to repetition; hence, saying a thing to one person and giving a different view of it to another, double-tongued (1 Ti 3:8). See: BAGD—198d; THAYER—151d.

1352. διό {53x} **diŏ**, *dee-ŏ';* from *1223* and *3739; through which* thing, i.e. *consequently:*—for which cause {2x}, therefore {10x}, wherefore {41x}. See: BAGD—198d; THAYER—152a.

1353. διοδεύω {2x} **diŏdĕuō**, *dee-od-yoo'-o;* from *1223* and *3593;* to *travel through:*—go throughout {1x}, pass through {1x}.

Diodeuo means "to travel throughout or along" and is used in **(1)** Lk 8:1, of "going throughout" cities and villages; and **(2)** of "passing through" towns, Acts 17:1. See: BAGD—198d; THAYER—152a.

1354. Διονύσιος {1x} **Diŏnusiŏs**, *dee-on-oo'-see-os;* from Διόνυσος **Diŏnusŏs** (*Bacchus*); *reveller; Dionysius,* an Athenian:—Dionysius {1x}. See: BAGD—199a; THAYER—152a.

1355. διόπερ {3x} **diŏpĕr**, *dee-op'-er;* from *1352* and *4007; on which very account:*—wherefore {3x}. See: BAGD—199a; THAYER—152a.

1356. διοπετής {1x} **diŏpĕtēs**, *dee-op-et'-ace;* from the alt. of *2203* and the alt. of *4098; sky-fallen* (i.e. an *aerolite*):—which fell down from Jupiter {1x}. See: BAGD—199a; THAYER—152a.

1357. διόρθωσις {1x} **diŏrthōsis**, *dee-or'-tho-sis;* from a compound of *1223* and a der. of *3717,* mean. to *straighten thoroughly; rectification,* i.e. (spec.) the Messianic *restoration:*—reformation {1x}.

Diorthosis means properly **(1)** "a making straight" and denotes a "reformation" or reforming, Heb 9:10. **(2)** The word has the meaning of a right arrangement, right ordering, and what is here indicated is a time when the imperfect, the inadequate, would be superseded by a better order of things. See: TDNT—5:450, 727; BAGD—199a; THAYER—152b.

1358. διορύσσω {4x} **diŏrussō**, *dee-or-oos'-so;* from *1223* and *3736;* to *penetrate* burglariously:—break through {2x}, be broken up {1x}, be broken through {1x}.

This word means lit., "to dig through" and is used of the act of thieves in "breaking" into a house, Mt 6:19, 20; 24:43; Lk 12:39. See: BAGD—199b; THAYER—152b.

Διός Diŏs. See *2203.*

1359. Διόσκουροι {1x} **Diŏskŏurŏi**, *dee-os'-koo-roy;* from the alt. of *2203* and a form of the base of *2877; sons of Jupiter,* i.e. the twins *Dioscuri:*—Castor and Pollux {1x}. See: BAGD—199b; THAYER—152b.

1360. διότι {22x} **diŏti**, *dee-ot'-ee;* from *1223* and *3754; on the very account that,* or *inasmuch as:*—because {10x}, for {8x}, because that {3x}, therefore {1x}. See: BAGD—199b; THAYER—152c.

1361. Διοτρεφής {1x} **Diŏtrĕphēs**, *dee-ot-ref-ace';* from the alt. of *2203* and *5142; Jove-nourished; Diotrephes,* an opponent of Christianity:—Diotrephes {1x}. See: BAGD—199c; THAYER—152c.

1362. **διπλοῦς** {4x} **diplŏus**, *dip-looce';* or
διπλόος **diploos**, *dip-loce'*
from *1364* and (prob.) the base of *4119; two-fold:*—double {3x}, two-fold more {1x}.

Diplous denotes **(1)** "twofold, double," 1 Ti
5:17; Rev 18:6 (twice). **(2)** The comparative degree *diploteron* (neuter) is used adverbially in
Mt 23:15, "twofold more." See: BAGD—199c;
THAYER—152c.

1363. **διπλόω** {1x} **diplŏō**, *dip-lŏ'-o;* from *1362;*
to *render twofold:*—double {1x}.

Diploo signifies "to double, to repay or render twofold," Rev 18:6. See: BAGD—199d;
THAYER—152c.

1364. **δίς** {6x} **dis**, *dece;* adv. from *1417;
twice:*—again {2x}, twice {4x}.

Dis, the ordinary numeral adverb signifying
twice, is rendered **(1)** "again" in Phil 4:16, "ye
sent once and again unto my need," and **(2)** in
1 Th 2:18, where Paul states that he would have
come to the Thessalonians "once and again,"
that is, twice at least he had attempted to do
so. See: BAGD—199d; THAYER—152d.

Δίς **Dis**. See *2203.*

1365. **διστάζω** {2x} **distazō**, *dis-tad'-zo;* from
1364; prop. to *duplicate,* i.e.
(ment.) to *waver* (in opinion):—doubt {2x}.

Distazo means to stand in two ways implying uncertainty which way to take (Mt
14:31; 28:17). See: BAGD—200a; THAYER—
152d.

1366. **δίστομος** {3x} **distŏmŏs**, *dis'-tom-os;*
from *1364* and *4750;* double-edged:*—with two edges {1x}, two-edged
{2x}.

Distomos, lit., "double-mouthed, two-edged,"
is used of a sword with two edges, Heb 4:12;
Rev 1:16; 2:12. See: BAGD—200a; THAYER—
152d.

1367. **δισχίλιοι** {1x} **dischilĭoi**, *dis-khil'-ee-oy;* from *1364* and *5507; two
thousand:*—two thousand {1x}. See: BAGD—
200a; THAYER—153a.

1368. **διυλίζω** {1x} **diulizō**, *dee-oo-lid'-zo;*
from *1223* and ὑλίζω **hulizō**,
hoo-lid'-zo (to *filter*); to *strain out:*—strain at
{1x}.

Diulizo primarily denotes "to strain thoroughly" (*dia,* "through," intensive, *hulizo,* "to
strain"), then, "to strain at," as through a sieve
or strainer, as in the case of wine, so as to remove the unclean midge, Mt 23:24. It is correctly translated "strain at" and not "strained
out" as the stress is on the point of focus. The
Pharisees habitually focused not on the life
and joy in the wine itself, but focused on the

insignificant (cf. tithing the mint, anise, and
cumin, Mt 23:23). Their focus was the gnat so
they strained at the gnat, not strain the wine
to enjoy the immenseness of its purity. See:
BAGD—200d; THAYER—153a.

1369. **διχάζω** {1x} **dichazō**, *dee-khad'-zo;* from
a der. of *1364;* to *make apart,*
i.e. *sunder* (fig. *alienate*):—set at variance {1x}.

Dichazo, "to cut apart, divide in two," is
used metaphorically in Mt 10:35, "to set at
variance." See: BAGD—200b; THAYER—153a.

1370. **διχοστασία** {3x} **dichŏstasia**, *dee-khos-tas-ee'-ah;* from a der. of
1364 and *4714; disunion,* i.e. (fig.) *dissension:*—
division {2x}, sedition {1x}.

Dichostasia means lit., "a standing apart"
(*dicha,* "asunder, apart," *stasis,* "a standing"),
hence "a dissension, division," is translated **(1)**
"seditions" in Gal 5:20; and **(2)** "divisions" in
Rom 16:17; 1 Cor 3:3. See: TDNT—1:514, 88;
BAGD—200b; THAYER—153a.

1371. **διχοτομέω** {2x} **dichŏtŏmĕō**, *dee-khot-om-eh'-o;* from a compound
of a der. of *1364* and a der. of τέμνω **tĕmnō** (to
cut); to *bisect,* i.e. (by extens.) to *flog* severely:—cut asunder {1x}, cut in sunder {1x}.

This word means lit., "to cut into two parts":
(1) Mt 24:51, "to cut asunder," and **(2)** Lk 12:46,
"cut in sunder." **(2a)** Some take the reference
to be to the mode of punishment by which
criminals and captives were "cut" in two; others, on account of the fact that in these passages the delinquent is still surviving after the
treatment, take the verb to denote "to cut up"
by scourging, to scourge severely, the word being used figuratively, denoting "cutting" future
recurrences of the crime from the criminal.
(2b) As to Mt 24:51, it has been remarked that
the "cutting asunder" was an appropriate punishment for one who had lived a double life.
(2c) In both passages the latter part of the
sentence applies to retribution beyond this
life. See: TDNT—2:225, 177; BAGD—200c;
THAYER—153a.

1372. **διψάω** {16x} **dipsaō**, *dip-sah'-o;* from a
var. of *1373;* to *thirst* for (lit. or
fig.):—(be, be athirst {3x}, thirst {10x}, thirsty
{3x}.

Dipsao is used **(1)** in the natural sense, e.g.,
Mt 25:35, 37, 42; in v. 44, "athirst" (lit., "thirsting"); Jn 4:13, 15; 19:28; Rom 12:20; 1 Cor 4:11;
Rev 7:16; **(2)** figuratively, of spiritual "thirst,"
Mt 5:6; Jn 4:14; 6:35; 7:37; in Rev 21:6 and
22:17, "that is athirst." See: TDNT—2:226, 177;
BAGD—200c; THAYER—153b.

Greek

1373. **δίψος** {1x} **dipsŏs,** *dip'-sos;* of uncert. aff.; *thirst:*—thirst {1x}.

This word means "thirst" and occurs in 2 Cor 11:27. See: TDNT—2:226; BAGD—200d; THAYER—153b.

1374. **δίψυχος** {2x} **dipsuchŏs,** *dip'-soo-khos;* from *1364* and *5590; two-spirited,* i.e. *vacillating* (in opinion or purpose):—double minded {2x}.

Dipsuchos lit. means "two-souled", hence, "double-minded," Jas 1:8; 4:8. This person lives one life for himself and lives another for God. See: TDNT—9:665, 1342; BAGD—201a; THAYER—153b.

1375. **διωγμός** {10x} **diōgmŏs,** *dee-ogue-mos';* from *1377; persecution:*—persecution {10x}.

Diogmos means persecution and occurs in Mt 13:21; Mk 4:17; 10:30; Acts 8:1; 13:50; Rom 8:35; 2 Cor 12:10; 2 Th 1:4; 2 Ti 3:11 (twice). See: BAGD—201a; THAYER—153c.

1376. **διώκτης** {1x} **diōktēs,** *dee-oke'-tace;* from *1377;* a *persecutor:*—persecutor {1x}. See: TDNT—2:229; BAGD—201b; THAYER—153c.

1377. **διώκω** {44x} **diōkō,** *dee-o'-ko;* a prol. (and caus.) form of a primary verb δίω **diō** (to *flee;* comp. the base of *1169* and *1249*); to *pursue* (lit. or fig.); by impl. to *persecute:*—persecute {28x}, follow after {6x}, follow {4x}, suffer persecution {3x}, ensue {1x}, given to {1x}, press toward {1x}.

Dioko, as a verb, denotes **(1)** "to drive away" (Mt 23:34); **(2)** "to pursue without hostility, to follow, follow after," said **(2a)** of righteousness (Rom 9:30); **(2b)** the Law (Rom 9:31; 12:13); **(3)** literally, "pursuing" (as one would a calling), **(3a)** the things which make for peace (Rom 14:19); **(3b)** love (1 Cor 14:1); **(3c)** that which is good (1 Th 5:15); **(3d)** righteousness, godliness, faith, love, patience, meekness (1 Ti 6:11); **(3e)** righteousness, faith, love, peace (2 Ti 2:22); **(3f)** peace and sanctification (Heb 12:14); **(3g)** peace (1 Pet 3:11). Syn.: 190, 1096, 1811, 1872, 2614, 2628, 3877, 4870. See: TDNT—2:229, 177; BAGD—201b; THAYER—153c.

1378. **δόγμα** {5x} **dŏgma,** *dog'-mah;* from the base of *1380;* a *law* (civil, cerem. or eccl.):—decree {3x}, ordinance {2x}.

Dogma is transliterated in English, primarily denoting an opinion or judgment; hence, an opinion expressed with authority, a doctrine, ordinance, decree (Lk 2:1; Acts 16:4; 17:7; Eph 2:15; Col 2:14). See: TDNT—2:230, 178; BAGD—201c; THAYER—153d.

1379. **δογματίζω** {1x} **dŏgmatizō,** *dog-mat-id'-zo;* from *1378;* to *pre-*

scribe by statute, i.e. (refl.) to *submit* to cer. *rule:*—be subject to ordinances {1x}.

This word means "to decree," and signifies, in the middle voice, "to subject oneself to an ordinance," Col 2:20. See: TDNT—2:230, 178; BAGD—201d; THAYER—154a.

1380. **δοκέω** {63x} **dŏkĕō,** *dok-eh'-o;* a prol. form of a primary verb, δόκω **dŏkō,** *dok'-o* (used only in an alt. in certain tenses; comp. the base of *1166*) of the same mean.; to *think;* by impl. to *seem* (truthfully or uncertainly):—think {33x}, seem {13x}, suppose {7x}, seem good {3x}, please {2x}, misc. {5x} = be accounted, of own pleasure, be of reputation, trow.

This refers to a person's subjective mental estimate or opinion about something. A person's *doxa* (*1391*) may be right or wrong since it always involves the possibility of error [except when used of Jesus]. It always signifies a subjective estimate of a thing, not the objective appearance and qualities the thing actually possesses. Syn.: 5316. See: TDNT—2:232, 178; BAGD—201d; THAYER—154b.

1381. **δοκιμάζω** {23x} **dŏkimazō,** *dok-im-ad'-zo;* from *1384;* to *test* (lit. or fig.); by impl. to *approve:*—prove {10x}, try {4x}, approve {3x}, discern {2x}, allow {2x}, like {1x}, examine {1x}.

This word means "to prove with a view to approving," and is **(1)** twice translated by the verb "to allow" in Rom 14:22, and **(2)** "have been approved," 1 Th 2:4, of being qualified to be entrusted with the gospel; **(3)** in Rom 1:28, with the negative. Syn.: 3985. See: TDNT—2:255, 181; BAGD—202c; THAYER—154c.

1382. **δοκιμή** {7x} **dŏkimē,** *dok-ee-may';* from the same as *1384; test* (abstr. or concr.); by impl. *trustiness:*—proof {3x}, experience {2x}, trial {1x}, experiment {1x}.

Dokime means **(1)** "the process of proving"; it is **(2)** rendered "experiment" in 2 Cor 9:13; **(3)** in 2 Cor 8:2 "trial"; **(4)** "the effect of proving, approval, experience," Rom 5:4 (twice); **(5)** "proof" in 2 Cor 2:9; 13:3 and Phil 2:22. See: TDNT—2:255, 181; BAGD—202d; THAYER—154d.

1383. **δοκίμιον** {2x} **dŏkimiŏn,** *dok-im'-ee-on;* neut. of a presumed der. of *1382;* a *testing;* by impl. *trustworthiness:*—trial {1x}, trying {1x}.

Dokimion, "a test, a proof," is rendered **(1)** "trying" in Jas 1:3; **(2)** the same phrase is used in 1 Pet 1:7 "the trial of your faith," where the meaning probably is "that which is approved [i.e., as genuine] in your faith." See: TDNT—2:255, 181; BAGD—203a; THAYER—155a.

1384. δόκιμος {7x} **dŏkimŏs,** *dok'-ee-mos;* from *1380;* prop. *acceptable* (*current* after assayal), i.e. *approved:*—approved {6x}, tried {1x}. See: TDNT—2:255, 183; BAGD—203a; THAYER—155a.

1385. δοκός {6x} **dŏkŏs,** *dok-os';* from *1209* (through the idea of *holding* up); a *stick* of timber:—beam {6x}.
Dokos, "a beam," was the heavy rafters holding up the ceiling. The Lord used it metaphorically, in contrast to a mote, "of a great fault, or vice," Mt 7:3–5; Lk 6:41–42. See: BAGD—203a; THAYER—155a.

    δόκω δŏkō. See *1380.*

1386. δόλιος {1x} **dŏliŏs,** *dol'-ee-os;* from *1388; guileful:*—deceitful {1x}.
Dolios, "deceitful," is used in 2 Cor 11:13, of false apostles as "deceitful workers." See: BAGD—203b; THAYER—155a.

1387. δολιόω {1x} **dŏliŏō,** *dol-ee-ŏ'-o;* from *1386;* to *be guileful:*—use deceit {1x}.
Dolioo means to lure using bait and is translated "have used deceit" in Rom 3:13. See: BAGD—203b; THAYER—155b.

1388. δόλος {12x} **dŏlŏs,** *dol'-os;* from an obs. primary verb, δέλλω **dĕllō** (prob. mean. to *decoy;* comp. *1185*); a *trick* (*bait*), i.e. (fig.) *wile:*—craft {1x}, deceit {2x}, guile {7x}, subtilty {2x}.
Dolos, primarily, "a bait," is rendered **(1)** "craft" in Mk 14:1; **(2)** "guile" Jn 1:47; 2 Co 12:16; 1 Th 2:3; 1 Pet 2:1; 2:22; 3:10; Rev 14:5 and **(3)** "subtilty" in Mt 26:4; Acts 13:10; and **(4)** "deceit" in Mk 7:22; Rom 1:29. See: BAGD—203b; THAYER—155b.

1389. δολόω {1x} **dŏlŏō,** *dol-ŏ'-o;* from *1388;* to *ensnare,* i.e. (fig.) *adulterate:*—handle deceitfully {1x}.
Doloo signifies to ensnare; hence, to corrupt, especially by mingling the truths of the Word of God with false doctrines or notions, and so handling it deceitfully (2 Cor 4:2). It focuses on the falsifying, not the motives for falsifying. See: BAGD—203b; THAYER—155b.

1390. δόμα {4x} **dŏma,** *dom'-ah;* from the base of *1325;* a *present:*—gift {4x}.
Doma lends greater stress to the concrete character of the gift than to its beneficent nature (Mt 7:11; Lk 11:13; Eph 4:8; Phil 4:17). See: BAGD—203c; THAYER—155b.

1391. δόξα {168x} **dŏxa,** *dox'-ah;* from the base of *1380; glory* (as very apparent), in a wide application (lit. or fig., obj. or subj.):—dignity {2x}, glory {145x}, glorious {10x}, honour {6x}, praise {4x}, worship {1x}.

Doxa, "glory," primarily signifies an opinion, estimate, and hence, the honor resulting from a good opinion. It is used **(1)** of the nature and acts of God in self-manifestation, i.e., **(1a)** what He essentially is and does, as exhibited in whatever way he reveals Himself in these respects, and particularly in the person of Christ, in whom essentially His "glory" has ever shone forth and ever will do, Jn 17:5, 24; Heb 1:3; **(1b)** it was exhibited in the character and acts of Christ in the days of His flesh, Jn 1:14; Jn 2:11; at Cana both His grace and His power were manifested, and these constituted His "glory", so also in the resurrection of Lazarus, Jn 11:4, 40; **(1c)** the "glory" of God was exhibited **(1c1)** in the resurrection of Christ, Rom 6:4, and **(1c2)** in His ascension and exaltation, 1 Pet 1:21, **(1c3)** likewise on the Mount of Transfiguration, 2 Pet 1:17. **(1d)** In Rom 1:23 His "everlasting power and divinity" are spoken of as His "glory," i.e., His attributes and power as revealed through creation; **(1e)** in Rom 3:23 the word denotes the manifested perfection of His character, especially His righteousness, of which all men fall short; **(1f)** in Col 1:11 "the might of His glory" signifies the might which is characteristic of His "glory"; **(1g)** in Eph 1:6, 12, 14, "the praise of the glory of His grace" and "the praise of His glory" signify the due acknowledgement of the exhibition of His attributes and ways; **(1h)** in Eph 1:17, "the Father of glory" describes Him as the source from whom all divine splendor and perfection proceed in their manifestation, and to whom they belong;

(2) of the character and ways of God as exhibited through Christ to and through believers, 2 Cor 3:18 and 4:6; **(3)** of the state of blessedness into which believers are to enter hereafter through being brought into the likeness of Christ, e.g., Rom 8:18, 21; Phil 3:21; 1 Pet 5:1, 10; Rev 21:11; **(4)** brightness or splendor, **(4a)** supernatural, **(4a1)** emanating from God (as in the *shekinah* "glory," in the pillar of cloud and in the Holy of Holies, e.g., Ex 16:10; 25:22); Lk 2:9; Acts 22:11; Rom 9:4; 2 Cor 3:7; Jas 2:1; **(4a2)** in Titus 2:13 it is used of Christ's return, "the appearing of the glory of the great God and our Savior Jesus Christ"; **(4b)** natural, as of the heavenly bodies, 1 Cor 15:40, 41; **(5)** of good reputation, praise, honor, Lk 14:10 "worship"; Jn 5:41 "honor"; 7:18; 8:50; 12:43 "praise"; 2 Cor 6:8 "honor"; Phil 3:19; Heb 3:3; **(5a)** in 1 Cor 11:7, of man as representing the authority of God, and of woman as rendering conspicuous the authority of man; **(5b)** in 1 Th 2:6, "glory" probably stands, by metonymy, for material gifts, an honorarium,

since in human estimation "glory" is usually expressed in things material.

(6) The word is used in **(6a)** ascriptions of praise to God, e.g. Lk 17:18; Jn 9:24, "praise"; Acts 12:23; **(6b)** as in doxologies (lit., "glory-words"), e.g., Lk 2:14; Rom 11:36; 16:27; Gal 1:5; Rev 1:6. **(7)** *Doxa* also denotes always a good opinion, praise, honor, glory, an appearance commanding respect, magnificence, excellence, manifestation of glory; hence, of angelic powers, in respect of their state as commanding recognition (dignities—2 Pet 2:10; Jude 8). Syn.: 1741. See: TDNT—2:233, 178; BAGD—203c; THAYER—155c.

1392. **δοξάζω** {62x} **dŏxazō**, *dox-ad'-zo;* from *1391;* to *render* (or *esteem*) *glorious* (in a wide application):—glorify {54x}, honour {3x}, have glory {2x}, magnify {1x}, make glorious {1x}, full of glory {1x}.

Doxazo, as a verb, primarily denotes in the NT **(1)** "to magnify, extol, praise", especially of "glorifying"; **(1a)** God, i.e., ascribing honor to Him, acknowledging Him as to His being, attributes and acts, i.e., His glory, e.g., Mt 5:16; 9:8; 15:31; Rom 15:6, 9; Gal 1:24; 1 Pet 4:16; **(1b)** the Word of the Lord, Acts 13:48; **(1c)** the Name of the Lord, Rev 15:4; **(1d)** also of "glorifying" oneself, Jn 8:54; Rev 18:7; **(2)** "to do honor to, to make glorious," e.g., Rom 8:30; 2 Cor 3:10; 1 Pet 1:8, "full of glory," passive voice (lit., "glorified"); **(2a)** said of Christ, e.g., Jn 7:39; 8:54 "honor" and "honoreth"; **(2b)** of the Father, e.g., Jn 13:31, 32; 21:19; 1 Pet 4:11; **(2c)** of "glorifying" one's ministry, Rom 11:13, "magnify"); **(2d)** of a member of the body, 1 Cor 12:26, "be honored."

(3) As the glory of God is the revelation and manifestation of all that He has and is, it is said of a Self-revelation in which God manifests all the goodness that is His, Jn 12:28. **(3a)** So far as it is Christ through whom this is made manifest, He is said to glorify the Father, Jn 17:1, 4; or the Father is glorified in Him, 13:31; 14:13; **(3b)** and Christ's meaning is analogous when He says to His disciples, "Herein is My Father glorified, that ye bear much fruit; and so shall ye be My disciples," Jn 15:8. **(3c)** When *doxazo* is predicated of Christ, it means simply that His innate glory is brought to light, is made manifest; cf. Jn 11:4; so 7:39; 12:16, 23; 13:31; 17:1, 5. **(3d)** It is an act of God the Father in Him. . . . As the revelation of the Holy Spirit is connected with the glorification of Christ, Christ says regarding Him, 'He shall glorify Me," Jn 16:14. Syn.: 1740, 4888. See: TDNT—2:253, 178; BAGD—204c; THAYER—157a.

1393. **Δορκάς** {2x} **Dŏrkas**, *dor-kas'; gazelle; Dorcas,* a Chr. woman:—*Dorcas* {2x}. See: BAGD—204d; THAYER—157b.

1394. **δόσις** {2x} **dŏsis**, *dos'-is;* from the base of *1325;* a *giving;* by impl. (concr.) a *gift:*—gift {1x}, giving {1x}.

Dosis denotes, properly, **(1)** "the act of giving," Phil 4:15, euphemistically referring to "gifts" as a matter of debt and credit accounts; then, **(2)** objectively, "a gift," Jas 1:17. See: BAGD—204d; THAYER—157b.

1395. **δότης** {1x} **dŏtēs**, *dot'-ace;* from the base of *1325;* a *giver:*—giver {1x}.

Dotes is used in 2 Cor 9:7 of him who gives cheerfully (hilariously) and is thereby loved of God. See: BAGD—205a; THAYER—157c.

1396. **δουλαγωγέω** {1x} **dŏulagōgĕō**, *doo-lag-ogue-eh'-o;* from a presumed compound of *1401* and *71;* to *be a slave-driver,* i.e. to *enslave* (fig. *subdue*):—bring into subjection {1x}.

This word means "to bring into bondage" and is used in 1 Cor 9:27, concerning the body. The stress is on mastery of the body's carnal desires; hence, subjection. See: TDNT—2:279, 182; BAGD—205a; THAYER—157c.

1397. **δουλεία** {5x} **dŏulĕia**, *doo-li'-ah;* from *1398; slavery* (cerem. or fig.):—bondage {5x}.

Douleia, primarily "the condition of being a slave," came to denote any kind of bondage, as, e.g., **(1)** of the condition of creation, Rom 8:21; **(2)** of that fallen condition of man himself which makes him dread God, Rom 8:15, and **(3)** fear death, Heb 2:15; and **(4)** of the condition imposed by the Mosaic Law, Gal 4:24; 5:1. See: TDNT—2:261, 182; BAGD—205a; THAYER—157c.

1398. **δουλεύω** {25x} **dŏulĕuō**, *dool-yoo'-o;* from *1401;* to *be a slave* to (lit. or fig., invol. or vol.):—serve {18x}, be in bondage {4x}, do service {3x}.

Douleuo, "to serve as a slave, to be a slave, to be in bondage," is frequently used without any association of slavery, e.g., Acts 20:19; Rom 6:6; 7:6; 12:11; Gal 5:13. See: TDNT—2:261, 182; BAGD—205a; THAYER—157d.

1399. **δούλη** {3x} **dŏulē**, *doo'-lay;* fem. of *1401;* a *female slave* (invol. or vol.):—handmaid {1x}, handmaiden {2x}. See: TDNT—2:261, 182; BAGD—205c; THAYER—157d.

1400. **δοῦλον** {2x} **dŏulŏn**, *doo'-lon;* neut. of *1401; subservient:*—servant {1x}. See: BAGD—205c; THAYER—157d.

1401. **δοῦλος** {125x} **dŏulŏs**, *doo'-los;* from *1210;* a *slave* (lit. or fig., invol. or vol.; frequently, therefore in a qualified sense of *subjection* or *subserviency*):—bond {6x}, bondman {1x}, servant {118x}.

(1) The *doulos* was properly the "bond man," one who was in a permanent relation of servitude to another one whose will was completely subject to the will of another. **(2)** He was a *doulos* apart from any service he rendered at any given moment. The focus is on the relationship, not the service [see 1249]. **(3)** This word means "a slave," originally the lowest term in the scale of servitude, came also to mean **(3a)** "one who gives himself up to the will of another," e.g., 1 Cor 7:23; Rom 6:17, 20, and **(3b)** became the most common and general word for "servant," as in Mt 8:9, without any idea of bondage. **(4)** In calling himself, however, a "bondslave of Jesus Christ," e.g., Rom 1:1, the apostle Paul intimates **(4a)** that he had been formerly a "bondslave" of Satan, and **(4b)** that, having been bought by Christ, he was now a willing slave, bound to his new Master. Syn.: *Diakonos* (*1249*) is, generally speaking, to be distinguished from *doulos* (*1401*), "a bond-servant, slave"; *diakonos* views a servant in relationship to his work, *doulos* views him in relationship to his master. See, e.g., Mt 22:2-14; those who bring in the guests (vv. 3-4, 6, 8, 10) are douloi those who carry out the king's sentence (v. 13) are diakonoi. See also: 2324, 3610, 5257. See: TDNT—2:261, 182; BAGD—205c; THAYER—157d.

1402. **δουλόω** {8x} **dŏulŏō**, *doo-lŏ'-o;* from *1401;* to *enslave* (lit. or fig.):—become servant {2x}, bring into bondage {2x}, be under bondage {1x}, given {1x}, make servant {1x}, in bondage {1x}.

Douloo signifies **(1)** "to make a slave of, to bring into bondage," Acts 7:6; 1 Cor 9:19; **(2)** in the passive voice, "to be brought under bondage," 2 Pet 2:19; **(3)** "to be held in bondage," Gal 4:3 (lit., "were reduced to bondage"); **(4)** Titus 2:3, "of being enslaved to wine"; **(5)** Rom 6:18, "of service to righteousness" (lit., "were made bondservants"). **(6)** As with the purchased slave there were no limitations either in the kind or the time of service, so the life of the believer is to be lived in continuous obedience to God. See: TDNT—2:279, 182; BAGD—206b; THAYER—158b.

1403. **δοχή** {2x} **dŏchē**, *dokh-ay';* from *1209;* a *reception,* i.e. convivial *entertainment:*—feast {2x}.

Doche is "a reception feast, a banquet", Lk 5:29; 14:13. See: TDNT—2:54, 146; BAGD—206b; THAYER—158b.

1404. **δράκων** {13x} **drakōn**, *drak'-own;* prob. from an alt. form of δέρκομαι **dĕrkŏmai** (to *look*); a fabulous kind of *serpent* (perh. as supposed to *fascinate*):—dragon {13x}.

Drakon denoted also a large serpent, so called because of its keen power of sight (from a root *derke,* signifying "to see"). Thirteen times in the Apocalypse it is used of the devil 12:3-4, 7, 9, 13, 16-17; 13:2, 4, 11; 16:13; 20:2. See: TDNT—2:281, 186; BAGD—206b; THAYER—158b.

1405. **δράσσομαι** {1x} **drassŏmai**, *dras'-som-ahee;* perh. akin to the base of *1404* (through the idea of *capturing*); to *grasp,* i.e. (fig.) *entrap:*—take {1x}.

This word means "to grasp with the hand, take hold of," and is used metaphorically in 1 Cor 3:19, "taketh (the wise in their craftiness)." See: BAGD—206c; THAYER—158c.

1406. **δραχμή** {3x} **drachmē**, *drakh-may';* from *1405;* a *drachma* or (silver) coin (as *handled*):—piece {2x}, piece of silver {1x}.

A *drachma,* firstly, is **(1)** as much as one can hold in the hand (connected with *drassomai,* "to grasp with the hand, lay hold of," 1 Cor 3:19), then, **(2)** "a coin," nearly equal to the Roman *denarius,* is translated **(2a)** "pieces of silver" in Lk 15:8, 1st part; **(2b)** "piece," Lk 15:8, 2nd part and v. 9. See: BAGD—206c; THAYER—158c.

δρέμω drĕmō. See *5143.*

1407. **δρέπανον** {8x} **drĕpanŏn**, *drep'-an-on;* from δρέπω **drĕpō** (to *pluck*); a gathering *hook* (espec. for harvesting):—sickle {8x}.

A *drepanon* is "a pruning hook, a sickle, a hooked vine knife" and occurs in Mk 4:29; Rev 14:14, 15, 16, 17, 18 (twice), 19. See: BAGD—206d; THAYER—158c.

1408. **δρόμος** {3x} **drŏmŏs**, *drom'-os;* from the alt. of *5143;* a *race,* i.e. (fig.) *career:*—course {3x}.

Dromos properly means a running, a race; hence, metaphorically, denotes a career, course of occupation, or of life (Acts 13:25; 20:24; 2 Ti 4:7). See: TDNT—8:233, 1189; BAGD—206d; THAYER—158c.

1409. **Δρούσιλλα** {1x} **Drŏusilla**, *droo'-sil-lah;* a fem. dimin. of *Drusus* (a Rom. name); *Drusilla,* a member of the Herodian family:—Drusilla {1x}. See: BAGD—207a; THAYER—158c.

δύμι dumi. See *1416.*

1410. **δύναμαι** {210x} **dunamai**, *doo'-nam-ahee;* of uncert. aff.; to *be able*

or *possible:*—can (could) {100x}, cannot + 3756 {45x}, be able {37x}, may (might) {18x}, able {3x}, misc. {7x} = be possible, be of power.

Dunamai means to be able, to have power, whether by (1) virtue of one's own ability and resources (Rom 15:14); or (2) through a state of mind, or through favorable circumstances (1 Th 2:6); or (3) by permission of law or custom (Acts 24:8, 11); or (4) simply to be able, powerful (Mt 3:9; 2 Ti 3:15). See: TDNT—2:284, 186; BAGD—207a; THAYER—158d.

1411. **δύναμις** {120x} **dunamis**, *doo'-nam-is;* from *1410;* force (lit. or fig.); spec. miraculous *power* (usually by impl. a *miracle* itself):—power {77x}, mighty work {11x}, strength {7x}, miracle {7x}, might {4x}, virtue {3x}, mighty {2x}, misc. {9x} = ability, abundance, meaning, mightily, worker of miracles, violence.

Dunamis almost always points to new and higher forces that have entered and are working in this lower world of ours. It is (1) "power, ability," physical or moral, as residing in a person or thing; (2) "power in action," as, e.g., when put forth in performing miracles. (3) It occurs 118 times in the NT. (4) It is sometimes used of the miracle or sign itself, the effect being put for the cause, e.g., Mk 6:5, frequently in the Gospels and Acts. (5) In 1 Cor 14:11 it is rendered "meaning." Syn.: 1741, 2297, 3167, 3861, 4592, 5059. See: TDNT—2:284, 186; BAGD—207b; THAYER—159a.

1412. **δυναμόω** {1x} **dunamŏō**, *doo-nam-ŏ'-o;* from *1411;* to *enable:*—strengthen {1x}.

This word means "to make strong, confirm, strengthen" and occurs in Col 1:11. See: TDNT—2:284, 186; BAGD—208c; THAYER—160a.

1413. **δυνάστης** {3x} **dunastēs**, *doo-nas'-tace;* from *1410;* a *ruler* or *officer:*—of great authority {1x}, mighty {1x}, Potentate {1x}.

Dunastes signifies "a potentate, a high officer"; (1) in Acts 8:27, of a high officer, it is rendered "of great authority"; (2) in Lk 1:52, "the mighty"; (3) in 1 Ti 6:15 it is said of God ("Potentate"). See: TDNT—2:284, 186; BAGD—208c; THAYER—160a.

1414. **δυνατέω** {1x} **dunatĕō**, *doo-nat-eh'-o;* from *1415;* to *be efficient* (fig.):—be mighty {1x}.

Dunateo signifies "to be mighty, to show oneself powerful," Rom 4:14; 2 Cor 9:8; 13:3. See: TDNT—2:284, 186; BAGD—208c; THAYER—160a.

1415. **δυνατός** {35x} **dunatŏs**, *doo-nat-os';* from *1410;* powerful or capa-

ble (lit. or fig.); neut. *possible:*—possible {13x}, able {10x}, mighty {6x}, strong {3x}, could {1x}, power {1x}, mighty man {1x}.

Dunatos signifies "powerful." See, e.g., Rom 4:21; 9:22; 11:23; 12:18; 15:1; 1 Cor 1:26; 2 Cor 9:8. See: TDNT—2:284, 186; BAGD—208c; THAYER—160b.

1416. **δύνω** {2x} **dunō**, *doo'-no;* or

   δῦμι **dumi**, *doo'-mee;* prol. forms of an obsolete primary δύω **duō**, *doo'-o* (to *sink*); to go "*down*":—set {2x}.

Dumi, "to sink into," is used (1) of the "setting" of the sun, Mk 1:32, "did set"; (2) Lk 4:40, "was setting." The sun, moon and stars were conceived of as sinking into the sea when they set. See: TDNT—2:318, 192; BAGD—209a; THAYER—160b.

1417. **δύο** {135x} **duŏ**, *doo'-ŏ;* a primary numeral; "*two*":—two {122x}, twain {10x}, both {2x}, two and two + 303 {1x}.

Duo is rendered (1) "twain" in Mt 5:41; 19:5, 6; 21:31; 27:21, 51; Mk 10:8 (twice); 15:38; Eph 2:15; (2) in 1 Cor 6:16 and Eph 5:31 "two"; (3) in Jn 20:4; Rev 19:20. See: BAGD—209a; THAYER—160c.

1418. **δυσ-** {0x} **dus-**, *doos;* a primary inseparable particle of uncert. der.; used only in composition as a pref.; *hard,* i.e. *with difficulty:*—+ hard, + grievous, *etc.;* THAYER—160d.

1419. **δυσβάστακτος** {2x} **dusbastaktŏs**, *doos-bas'-tak-tos;* from *1418* and a der. of *941;* oppressive:—grievous to be borne {2x}.

This word means "hard to be borne" (from *dus,* an inseparable prefix, like Eng. "mis-," and "un-," indicating "difficulty, injuriousness, opposition," etc., and *bastazo,* "to bear"), is used in Lk 11:46 and Mt 23:4, "grievous to be borne." See: BAGD—209b; THAYER—160d.

1420. **δυσεντερία** {1x} **dusĕntĕria**, *doos-en-ter-ee'-ah;* from *1418* and a comp. of *1787* (mean. a *bowel*); a "*dysentery*":—bloody flux {1x}.

Dusenteria, [whence Eng., "dysentery"] is translated "bloody flux" in Acts 28:8. (*Enteron* denotes an "intestine".) See: BAGD—209c; THAYER—160d.

1421. **δυσερμήνευτος** {1x} **dusĕrmēnĕutŏs**, *doos-er-mane'-yoo-tos;* from *1418* and a presumed der. of *2059; difficult of explanation:*—hard to be uttered {1x}. See: BAGD—209c; THAYER—160d.

1422. **δύσκολος** {1x} **duskŏlŏs**, *doos'-kol-os;* from *1418* and κόλον **kŏlŏn**

(*food*); prop. *fastidious about eating* (*peevish*), i.e. (gen.) *impracticable:*—hard {1x}.

This word primarily means "hard to satisfy with food, difficulty, opposition, injuriousness"; hence, "difficult," Mk 10:24, of the "difficulty," for those who trust in riches, to enter into the kingdom of God. See: BAGD—209c; THAYER—161a.

1423. **δυσκόλως** {3x} **duskŏlōs**, *doos-kol'-oce;* adv. from *1422; impracticably:*—hardly {3x}.

Duskolos, the adverbial form of "hard," is used in Mt 19:23; Mk 10:23; Lk 18:24 of the danger of riches. See: BAGD—209d; THAYER—161a.

1424. **δυσμή** {5x} **dusmē**, *doos-may';* from *1416;* the sun-*set*, i.e. (by impl.) the *western* region:—west {5x}.

Dusme, "the quarter [north, south, east, west] where sun sets"; hence, "the west," occurs in Mt 8:11; 24:27; Lk 12:54 (some regard this as the sunset); 13:29; Rev 21:13. See: BAGD—209d; THAYER—161a.

1425. **δυσνόητος** {1x} **dusnŏētŏs**, *doos-no'-ay-tos;* from *1418* and a der. of *3539; difficult of perception:*—hard to be understood {1x}. See: TDNT—4:963, 636; BAGD—209d; THAYER—161b.

1426. **δυσφημία** {1x} **dusphēmia**, *doos-fay-mee'-ah;* from a compound of *1418* and *5345; defamation:*—evil report {1x}. See: BAGD—209d; THAYER—161b.

       δύω duō. See *1416.*

1427. **δώδεκα** {72x} **dōdĕka**, *do'-dek-ah;* from *1417* and *1176; two* and *ten*, i.e. a *dozen:*—twelve {72x}.

Dodeka is used **(1)** frequently in the Gospels for the twelve apostles, and in Acts 6:2; 1 Cor 15:5; Rev 21:14b; **(2)** of the tribes of Israel, Mt 19:28; Lk 22:30; Jas 1:1; Rev 21:12c (cf. 7:5–8; 12:1); **(3)** in various details relating to the heavenly Jerusalem, Rev 21:12–21; 22:2. **(4)** The number in general is regarded as suggestive of divine administration. See: TDNT—4:963, 636; BAGD—210a; THAYER—161b.

1428. **δωδέκατος** {1x} **dōdĕkatŏs**, *do-dek'-at-os;* from *1427; twelfth:*—twelfth {1x}. See: TDNT—2:321, 192; BAGD—210b; THAYER—161b.

1429. **δωδεκάφυλον** {1x} **dōdĕkaphulŏn**, *do-dek-af'-oo-lon;* from *1427* and *5443;* the *commonwealth* of Israel:—twelve tribes {1x}. See: TDNT—2:321, 192; BAGD—210b; THAYER—161b.

1430. **δῶμα** {7x} **dōma**, *do'-mah;* from δέμω **dĕmō** (to *build*); prop. an *edifice*, i.e. (spec.) a *roof:*—housetop {7x}.

Doma denotes a housetop. **(1)** The housetop was flat, and **(2)** guarded by a low parapet wall (cf. Deut 22:8). **(3)** It was much frequented and used: **(3a)** for proclamations (Mt 10:27; Lk 12:3); **(3b)** for prayer (Acts 10:9). **(4)** The housetop could be reached by stairs outside the building. **(5)** External flight from the housetop in time or danger is enjoined (Mt 24:17; Mk 13:15; Lk 17:31). See: BAGD—210b; THAYER—161c.

1431. **δωρεά** {11x} **dōrĕa**, *do-reh-ah';* from *1435;* a *gratuity:*—gift {11x}.

Dorea denotes a free gift, stressing its gratuitous character and it is always used in the NT of a spiritual or supernatural gift (Jn 4:10; Acts 8:20; 11:17; Rom 5:15; 2 Cor 9:15; Eph 3:7; Heb 6:4). See: TDNT—2:166, 166; BAGD—210b; THAYER—161c.

1432. **δωρεάν** {9x} **dōrĕan**, *do-reh-an';* acc. of *1431* as adv.; *gratuitously* (lit. or fig.):—freely {6x}, without a cause {1x}, in vain {1x}, for nought {1x}.

Dorean, lit., "as a gift, gratis," (connected with *doron*, "a gift"), is rendered **(1)** "without a cause," Jn 15:25; **(2)** "for nought," 2 Cor 11:7; Gal 2:21; 2 Th 3:8; **(3)** "freely," Mt 10:8; Rom 3:24; Rev 21:6; 22:17. See: TDNT—2:167, 166; BAGD—210c; THAYER—161d.

1433. **δωρέομαι** {3x} **dōrĕŏmai**, *do-reh'-om-ahee;* mid. voice from *1435;* to *bestow* gratuitously:—give {3x}.

Doreomai, used in the middle voice means "to bestow, make a gift of": "And when he [Pilate] knew it of the centurion, he gave the body [of Jesus] to Joseph" (Mk 15:45; cf. 2 Pet 1:3, 4). See: TDNT—2:166, 166; BAGD—210d; THAYER—161d.

1434. **δώρημα** {2x} **dōrēma**, *do'-ray-mah;* from *1433;* a *bestowment:*—gift {2x}.

Dorema, translated "gift" in Jas 1:17 is thus distinguished, as the thing given, from the preceding word in the verse, *dosis* (*1394*), "the act of giving"; elsewhere in Rom 5:16. Syn.: *Dorema* is the thing given; whereas, *dosis* (*1394*) is the act of giving. See: TDNT—2:166, 166; BAGD—210d; THAYER—161d.

1435. **δῶρον** {19x} **dōrŏn**, *do'-ron;* a *present;* spec. a *sacrifice:*—gift {18x}, offering {1x}.

Doron means to give and is used of gifts **(1)** presented as an expression of honor (Mt 2:11); **(2)** for the support of the temple and the needs of the poor (Mt 15:5; Mk 7:11; Lk 21:1, 4); **(3)** offered to God (Mt 5:23, 24; 8:4; Heb 5:1; 8:3); **(4)** of salvation by grace as the gift of God (Eph

2:8); **(5)** of presents for mutual celebration of an occasion (Rev 11:10). Syn.: *1390, 1394, 1431, 1434, 5486.* See: TDNT—2:166, 166; BAGD—210d; THAYER—161d.

E

1436. ἔα {2x} **ĕa,** *eh'-ah;* appar. imper. of *1439;* prop. *let* it *be,* i.e. (as interj.) *aha!:*—let alone {2x}.

An interjection of surprise, fear and anger, was the cry of the man with the spirit of an unclean demon (Lk 4:34). See: BAGD—211a; THAYER—162a.

1437. ἐάν {275x} **ĕan,** *eh-an';* from *1487* and *302;* a *conditional* particle; *in case* that, *provided,* etc.; often used in connection with other particles to denote *indefiniteness* or *uncertainty:*—if {200x}, whosoever + 3769 {14x}, whatsoever + 3739 {16x}, though {14x}, misc. {31x} = before, but, except, whithersoever, whensoever, whether (or), to whom, soever. See: BAGD—211a; THAYER—162a. See *3361.*

ἐάν μή ĕan mē. See *3361* and *3362.*

1438. ἑαυτοῦ {339x} **hĕautŏu,** *heh-ow-too'* (incl. all other cases); from a refl. pron. otherwise obs. and the gen. (dat. or acc.) of *846; him-* (*her-, it-, them-,* also [in conjunction with the pers. pron. of the other persons] *my-, thy-, our-, your-*) *self* (*selves*), etc.:— himself {110x}, themselves {57x}, yourselves {36x}, ourselves {20x}, his {19x}, their {15x}, itself {9x}, misc. {73x} = alone, her (own self), his (own), itself, one (to) another, our (thine) own (selves), + that she had, their (own, own selves), they, thyself, you, your (own, own conceits, own selves). See: BAGD—211d; THAYER—163b.

1439. ἐάω {13x} **ĕaō,** *eh-ah'-o;* of uncert. aff.; to *let be,* i.e. *permit* or *leave* alone:—suffer {9x}, let alone {1x}, leave {1x}, let {1x}, commit {1x}.

Eao signifies **(1)** "let alone", Acts 5:38; **(2)** "to leave," Acts 23:32, of "leaving" horsemen; **(3)** Acts 27:40, of "committing (themselves)" unto the sea; **(4)** "to suffer" in Mt 24:43; Lk 4:41; 22:51; Acts 14:16; 16:7; 19:30; 28:4; 1 Cor 10:13; Rev 2:20; **(5)** "to let" Acts 27:32. See: BAGD—212c; THAYER—163c. See also *1436.*

1440. ἑβδομήκοντα {5x} **hĕbdŏmēkŏnta,** *heb-dom-ay'-kon-tah;* from *1442* and a modified form of *1176; seventy:*— seventy {2x}, three score and ten {1x}, three score and fifteen + 4002 {1x}. See: TDNT— 2:627, 249; BAGD—212d; THAYER—163d.

1441. ἑβδομηκοντάκις {1x} **hĕbdŏmēkŏn-takis,** *heb-dom-ay-kon-tak-is';* multiple adv. from *1440; seventy times:*—seventy times {1x}.

Having a possible allusion to the Genesis story (4:24) is highly probable: Jesus pointedly sets against the natural man's craving for seventy-sevenfold revenge the spiritual man's ambition to exercise the privilege of seventy-sevenfold forgiveness. The Lord's reply "until seventy times seven" was indicative of completeness, the absence of any limit, and was designed to turn away Peter's mind from a merely numerical standard. God's forgiveness is limitless; so should man's be. See: TDNT— 2:627, 249; BAGD—213a; THAYER—163d.

1442. ἕβδομος {9x} **hĕbdŏmŏs,** *heb'-dom-os;* ord. from *2033; seventh:*— seventh {9x}. This word occurs in Jn 4:52; Heb 4:4 (twice); Jude 14; Rev 8:1; 10:7; 11:15; 16:17; 21:20. See: TDNT—2:627, 249; BAGD— 213a.163d; THAYER—163d.

1443. Ἐβέρ {1x} **Ĕbĕr,** *eb'-er;* of Heb. or. [5677]; *Eber,* a patriarch:—*Eber* {1x}. See: BAGD—213a; THAYER—163d.

1444. Ἑβραϊκός {1x} **Hĕbraïkŏs,** *heb-rah-ee-kos';* from *1443; Hebraïc* or the *Jewish* language:—Hebrew (Aramaic) {1x}. See: TDNT—3:356, 372; BAGD—213a; THAYER—163d.

1445. Ἑβραῖος {5x} **Hĕbraiŏs,** *heb-rah'-yos;* from *1443;* a *Hebræan* (i.e. Hebrew) or *Jew:*—Hebrew {5x}. See: TDNT— 3:356, 372; BAGD—213b; THAYER—163d.

1446. Ἑβραΐς {3x} **Hĕbraïs,** *heb-rah-is';* from *1443;* the *Hebraistic* (i.e. *Hebrew*) or *Jewish* (*Chaldee*) language:—Hebrew (Aramaic) {3x}. See: TDNT—3:356, 372; BAGD— 213b; THAYER—163d.

1447. Ἑβραϊστί {6x} **Hĕbraïsti,** *heb-rah-is-tee';* adv. from *1446; Hebraistically* or in the Jewish (Chaldee) language:— in the Hebrew tongue {3x}, in the Hebrew {2x}, in Hebrew {1x}. See: TDNT—3:356, 372; BAGD— 213c; THAYER—164b.

1448. ἐγγίζω {43x} **ĕggizō,** *eng-id'-zo;* from *1451;* to make *near,* i.e. (refl.) *approach:*—draw nigh {12x}, be at hand {9x}, come nigh {8x}, come near {5x}, draw near {4x}, misc. {5x} = approach, be nigh.

Engizo, as a verb, means "to come near, draw nigh" and is translated **(1)** "approacheth": "Sell that ye have, and give alms; provide yourselves bags which wax not old, a treasure in the heavens that faileth not, where no thief approacheth, neither moth corrupteth" (Lk

12:33); **(2)** "approaching": "Not forsaking the assembling of ourselves together, as the manner of some is; but exhorting one another: and so much the more, as ye see the day approaching" (Heb 10:25; cf. Lk 18:35; 19:29, 37); **(3)** "was come nigh": "And it came to pass, that, as I made my journey, and was come nigh unto Damascus about noon . . ." (Acts 22:6); **(4)** "came nigh": "Now when He came nigh to the gate of the city" (Lk 7:12); **(5)** "came near": "And as he journeyed, he came near Damascus" (Acts 9:3). **(6)** It also means "to draw near, to approach," and is used **(6a)** of place and position, **(6a1)** literally and physically, Mt 21:1; Mk 11:1; Lk 12:33; 15:25; **(6a2)** figuratively, of drawing near to God, Mt 15:8; Heb 7:19; Jas 4:8; **(6b)** of time, with reference to things that are imminent, as **(6b1)** the kingdom of heaven, Mt 3:2; 4:17; 10:7; **(6b2)** the kingdom of God, Mk 1:15; Lk 10:9, 11; **(6b3)** the time of fruit, Mt 21:34; **(6b4)** the desolation of Jerusalem, Lk 21:8; **(6b5)** redemption, Lk 21:28; **(6b6)** the fulfillment of a promise, Acts 7:17; **(6b7)** the Day of Christ in contrast to the present night of the world's spiritual darkness, Rom 13:12; Heb 10:25; **(6b8)** the coming of the Lord, Jas 5:8; **(6b9)** the end of all things, 1 Pet 4:7. **(7)** It is also said of one who was drawing near to death, Phil 2:30. Syn.: 307, 385, 392, 501, 502, 645, 868, 1670, 1828, 2020, 2464, 4317, 4334, 4358, 4685, 4951, 5288, 5289. See: TDNT—2:330, 194; BAGD—213c; THAYER—164b.

1449. ἐγγράφω {2x} **ĕggraphō**, *eng-graf'-o;* from *1722* and *1125;* to "*engrave,*" i.e. *inscribe:*—write (in) {2x}.

Eggrapho denotes "to write in," Lk 10:20; 2 Cor 3:2, 3. See: TDNT—1:769, 128; BAGD—213d; THAYER—164c.

1450. ἔγγυος {1x} **ĕgguŏs**, *eng'-goo-os;* from *1722* and γυῖον **guiŏn** (a *limb*); *pledged* (as if *articulated* by a member), i.e. a *bondsman:*—surety {1x}.

Enguos primarily signifies the bail who personally answers for anyone, whether with his life or his property. In Heb 7:22 it refers to Jesus, the personal guarantee of the terms of the new and better covenant, secured on the ground of His perfect sacrifice (v. 27). See: TDNT—2:329, 194; BAGD—214a; THAYER—164d.

1451. ἐγγύς {30x} **ĕggus**, *eng-goos';* from a primary verb ἄγχω **agchō** (to *squeeze* or *throttle;* akin to the base of *43*); *near* (lit. or fig., of place or time):—nigh {13x}, at hand {6x}, nigh at hand {4x}, near {4x}, from {1x}, nigh unto {1x}, ready {1x}.

Engus means "near, nigh" and is translated **(1)** "nigh": **(1a)** of a place: "And as they heard

these things, He added and spake a parable, because He was nigh to Jerusalem" (Lk 19:11; Jn 6:19, 23; metaphorically in Rom 10:8; Eph 2:13, 17); **(1b)** of time: "Now learn a parable of the fig tree; When his branch is yet tender, and putteth forth leaves, ye know that summer is nigh" (Mt 24:32–33; cf. Lk 21:30–31); **(1c)** as a preposition **(1c1)** Heb 6:8 "nigh unto (a curse)" and **(1c2)** Heb 8:13 "nigh unto (vanishing away)." **(2)** It is translated "near" [of place] in Jn 3:23 and 11:54. **(3)** The difference between "near" and "nigh" is one of focus. **(3a)** When the speaker is focusing on the two objects, and not the distance separating the two objects, he uses "near." The listener focuses on the two objects becoming closer to each other. **(3b)** When the speaker is focusing on the distance separating the two objects as lessening, he uses "nigh." The listener/reader focuses on the distance lessening, not the two objects. Syn.: 316, 1448, 1452, 4139, 4317, 4334. See: TDNT—2:330, 194; BAGD—214a; THAYER—164d.

1452. ἐγγύτερον {1x} **ĕggutĕron**, *eng-goo'-ter-on;* neut. of the comp. of *1451; nearer:*—nearer {1x}.

Enguteron is the comparative degree of *engus* (*1451*) and the neuter of the adjective *enguteros* and is used adverbially in Rom 13:11: "And that, knowing the time, that now it is high time to awake out of sleep: for now is our salvation nearer (*enguteron*) than when we believed." Syn.: 316, 1451, 1448, 1451, 4139, 4317, 4334. See: BAGD—214a; THAYER—165a.

1453. ἐγείρω {141x} **ĕgĕirō**, *eg-i'-ro;* prob. akin to the base of *58* (through the idea of *collecting* one's faculties); to *waken* (tran. or intr.), i.e. *rouse* (lit. from sleep, from sitting or lying, from disease, from death; or fig. from obscurity, inactivity, ruins, nonexistence):—rise {36x}, raise {28x}, arise {27x}, raise up {23x}, rise up {8x}, rise again {5x}, raise again {4x}, misc. {10x} awake, lift up, rear up, arise, stand, take up.

Egeiro, as a verb, is frequently used in the NT in the sense **(1)** of "raising" (active voice), or "rising" (middle and passive voices): **(1a)** from sitting, lying, sickness: "When he arose, he took the young child and his mother by night, and departed into Egypt" (Mt 2:14; cf. 9:5, 7, 19; Jas 5:15; Rev 11:1); **(1b)** of causing to appear, or, in the passive, appearing, or raising up so as to occupy a place in the midst of people: "And think not to say within yourselves, We have Abraham to our father: for I say unto you, that God is able of these stones to raise up children unto Abraham" (Mt 3:9; cf. Mk 13:22; Acts 13:22). It is thus said of Christ in Acts 13:23:

"Of this man's seed hath God according to His promise raised unto Israel a Saviour, Jesus"; **(2)** of rousing, stirring up, or "rising" against: "For nation shall rise against nation, and kingdom against kingdom:" (Mt 24:7; cf. Mk 13:8;

(3) of "raising buildings" (Jn 2:19-20); **(4)** of "raising or rising" from the dead: **(4a)** of Christ (Mt 16:21); and **(4b)** of Christ's "raising" the dead (Mt 11:5; cf. Mk 5:41; Lk 7:14; Jn 12:1, 9, 17); **(4c)** of the act of the disciples (Mt 10:8); **(4d)** of the resurrection of believers (Mt 27:52; Jn 5:21; 1 Cor 15:15-16, 29, 32, 35, 42-44 52; 2 Cor 1:9; 4:14); **(4e)** of unbelievers (Mt 12:42). Syn.: *Egeiro* (*1453*) stands in contrast to *anistemi* (*450* - when used with reference to resurrection) in this respect, that *egeiro* is frequently used both in the transitive sense of "raising up" and the intransitive of "rising," whereas *anistemi* is comparatively infrequent in the transitive use. See also: 305, 393, 450, 1096, 1326, 1525, 1817, 4911. See: TDNT—2:333, 195; BAGD—214c; THAYER—165a.

1454. **ἔγερσις** {1x} **ĕgĕrsis**, *eg'-er-sis;* from *1453;* a *resurgence* (from death):— resurrection {1x}.

Egersis, "a rousing, an excitation", is used of the "resurrection" of Christ, in Mt 27:53. See: TDNT—2:337, 195; BAGD—215b; THAYER—165d.

1455. **ἐγκάθετος** {1x} **ĕgkathĕtŏs**, *eng-kath'-et-os;* from *1722* and a der. of *2524; subinduced,* i.e. surreptitiously *suborned* as a lier-in-wait:—spy {1x}.

Egkathetos, an adjective denoting "suborned to lie in wait, one who is bribed by others to entrap a man by crafty words" is used as a plural noun in Lk 20:20, "spies." See: BAGD—215a; THAYER—165d.

1456. **ἐγκαίνια** {1x} **ĕgkainia**, *eng-kah'-ee-nee-ah;* neut. plur. of a presumed compound from *1722* and *2537; innovatives,* i.e. (spec.) *renewal* (of relig. services after the Antiochian interruption):—feast of dedication {1x}.

Egkainia, in the sense of "dedication," became used particularly for the annual eight days' feast beginning on the 25th of Chisleu (mid. of Dec.), instituted by Judas Maccabaeus, 164 B.C., to commemorate the cleansing of the temple from the pollutions of Antiochus Epiphanes; hence it was called the Feast of the Dedication, Jn 10:22. This feast could be celebrated anywhere. The lighting of lamps was a prominent feature; hence the description "Feast of Lights." Jn 9:5 may also refer to this. See: BAGD—215b; THAYER—165d.

1457. **ἐγκαινίζω** {2x} **ĕgkainizō**, *eng-kahee-nid'-zo;* from *1456;* to *renew,* i.e. *inaugurate:*—consecrate {1x}, dedicate {1x}.

Egkainizo, primarily means "to make new, to renew"; then, **(1)** to initiate or "dedicate," Heb 9:18, with reference to the first covenant, as not "dedicated" without blood; **(2)** in Heb 10:20, of Christ's "consecration" of the new and living way ("consecrated"). See: TDNT—3:453, 388; BAGD—215b; THAYER—166a.

1458. **ἐγκαλέω** {7x} **ĕgkalĕō**, *eng-kal-eh'-o;* from *1722* and *2564;* to *call in* (as a debt or demand), i.e. *bring to account* (*charge, criminate,* etc.):—accuse {4x}, implead {1x}, call in question {1x}, lay anything to the charge {1x}.

Egkaleo, as a verb, means **(1)** "to bring a charge against, or **(2)** to come forward as an accuser against." **(3)** It literally denotes "to call in" (*en,* "in," *kaleo,* "to call"), **(3a)** i.e., "to call (something) in or against (someone)"; hence, **(3b)** "to call to account, to accuse, to implead": "Wherefore if Demetrius, and the craftsmen which are with him, have a matter against any man, the law is open, and there are deputies: let them implead (*egkaleo*) one another" (Acts 19:38); **(3c)** "accused": "For we are in danger to be called in question (*egkaleo*) for this day's uproar, there being no cause whereby we may give an account of this concourse" (Acts 19:40; 23:28-29; 26:2, 7); **(3d)** "shall lay to the charge": "Who shall lay any thing to the charge (*egkaleo*) of God's elect? It is God that justifieth" (Rom 8:33). Syn.: 156, 157, 1225, 1462, 1908, 2723, 2724, 4811. See: TDNT—3:496, 394; BAGD—215c; THAYER—166b.

1459. **ἐγκαταλείπω** {9x} **ĕgkatalĕipō**, *eng-kat-al-i'-po;* from *1722* and *2641;* to *leave behind in* some place, i.e. (in a good sense) *let remain over,* or (in a bad sense) to *desert:*—forsake {7x}, leave {2x}.

Egkataleipo denotes **(1)** "to leave behind, among, leave surviving," Rom 9:29; **(2)** "to forsake, abandon, leave in straits, or helpless," said **(2a)** by, or of, Christ, Mt 27:46; Mk 15:34; Acts 2:27; **(2b)** of men, 2 Cor 4:9; 2 Ti 4:10, 16; **(2c)** by God, Heb 13:5; **(2d)** of things, by Christians (negatively), Heb 10:25. See: BAGD—215d; THAYER—166b.

1460. **ἐγκατοικέω** {1x} **ĕgkatŏikĕō**, *eng-kat-oy-keh'-o;* from *1722* and *2730;* to *settle down in* a place, i.e. *reside:*—dwell among {1x}. See: BAGD—216a; THAYER—166c.

1461. **ἐγκεντρίζω** {6x} **ĕgkĕntrizō**, *eng-ken-trid'-zo;* from *1722* and a der. of *2759;* to *prick in,* i.e. *ingraft:*—graff {1x}, graft in {4x}, graft into {1x}.

Egkentrizo denotes "to graft in" to insert a slip of a cultivated tree into a wild one. In Rom 11:17, 19, 23, 24, however, the metaphor is used "contrary to nature" (v. 24), of grafting a wild olive branch (the Gentile) into the good olive tree (the Jews); that unbelieving Jews (branches of the good tree) were broken off that Gentiles might be grafted in, afforded no occasion for glorying on the part of the latter. Jew and Gentile alike must enjoy the divine blessings by faith alone. So Jews who abide not in unbelief shall, as "the natural branches, be grafted into their own olive tree." See: BAGD—216a; THAYER—166c.

1462. **ἔγκλημα** {2x} **ĕgklēma,** *eng'-klay-mah; from 1458;* an *accusation,* i.e. *offence* alleged:—laid to (one's) charge {1x}, crime laid against (one) {1x}.

Egklema is "an accusation made in public," but not necessarily before a tribunal. **(1)** That is the case in Acts 23:29: "Whom I perceived to be accused of questions of their law, but to have nothing laid to his charge (*egklema*) worthy of death or of bonds." **(2)** In Acts 25:16 it signifies a matter of complaint, a crime: "To whom I answered, It is not the manner of the Romans to deliver any man to die, before that he which is accused have the accusers face to face, and have licence to answer for himself concerning the crime (*egklema*) laid against him." Syn.: 156, 157, 1225, 1458, 1908, 2723, 2724, 4811. See: TDNT—3:496, 394; BAGD—216b; THAYER—166c.

1463. **ἐγκομβόομαι** {1x} **ĕgkŏmbŏŏmai,** *eng-kom-bŏ'-om-ahee;* mid. voice from *1722* and κομβόω **kŏmbŏŏ** (to *gird*); to *engirdle* oneself (for labor), i.e. fig. (the apron being a badge of servitude) to *wear* (in token of mutual deference):—be clothed with {1x}.

Egkomboomai, "to gird oneself with a thing, be clothed with": "Likewise, ye younger, submit yourselves unto the elder. Yea, all of you be subject one to another, and be clothed with humility: for God resisteth the proud, and giveth grace to the humble"(1 Pet 5:5). Syn.: 294, 1737, 1746, 1902, 2439, 4016. See: TDNT—2:339, 196; BAGD—216b; THAYER—166d.

1464. **ἐγκοπή** {1x} **ĕgkŏpē,** *eng-kop-ay'; from 1465;* a *hindrance:*—✕ hinder {1x}.

Egkope is literally a cut in a road to impede an enemy's advance and is used in 1 Cor 9:12, with *didomi,* "to give," "(lest) we should hinder." See: TDNT—3:855, 453; BAGD—216b; THAYER—166d.

1465. **ἐγκόπτω** {4x} **ĕgkŏptō,** *eng-kop'-to; from 1722* and *2875;* to *cut*

into, i.e. (fig.) *impede, detain:*—hinder {3x}, be tedious unto {1x}.

Egkepto, lit., "to cut into" (*en,* "in," *kopto,* "to cut"), was used of "impeding" persons by breaking up the road, or by placing an obstacle sharply in the path; hence, **(1)** metaphorically, of "detaining" a person unnecessarily, Acts 24:4; **(2)** of "hindrances" in the way of reaching others, Rom 15:22; **(3)** or returning to them, 1 Th 2:18; **(4)** of "hindering" progress in the Christian life, Gal 5:7, where the significance virtually is "who broke up the road along which you were travelling so well?"; **(5)** of "hindrances" to the prayers of husband and wife, through low standards of marital conduct, 1 Pet 3:7. See: TDNT—3:855, 453; BAGD—216c; THAYER—166d.

1466. **ἐγκράτεια** {4x} **ĕgkratĕia,** *eng-krat'-i-ah;* from *1468; self-control* (espec. *continence*):—temperance {4x}.

Egkrateia is the virtue of one who masters his desires and passions, esp. his sensual appetites. **(1)** It comes from *kratos,* "strength," and occurs in Acts 24:25; Gal 5:23; 2 Pet 1:6 (twice), in all of which it is rendered "temperance." **(2)** To render it self-control in Gal 5:23 is contradictory. If one has contol of self, the Spirit's ministry is needless. **(3)** The various powers bestowed by God upon man are capable of abuse; the right use demands the controlling power of the will under the operation of the Spirit of God. **(4)** In Acts 24:25 the word follows "righteousness," which represents God's claims, self-control, even in the non-Christian, being man's response thereto. **(5)** In 2 Pet 1:6, it follows "knowledge," suggesting that what is learned requires to be put into practice. See: TDNT—2:339, 196; BAGD—216c; THAYER—166d.

1467. **ἐγκρατεύομαι** {2x} **ĕgkratĕuŏmai,** *eng-krat-yoo'-om-ahee;* mid. voice from *1468;* to *exercise self-restraint* (in diet and chastity):—can not contain {1x}, be temperate {1x}.

This is the opposite of 1466. *Egkrateuomai,* "power, strength," lit., "to have power over oneself," is rendered **(1)** "(if) they have (not) continency, can not contain" (i.e., are lacking in self-control), in 1 Cor 7:9; **(2)** in 1 Cor 9:25, "is temperate." See: TDNT—2:339, 196; BAGD—216c; THAYER—167a.

1468. **ἐγκρατής** {1x} **ĕgkratēs,** *eng-krat-ace'; from 1722* and *2904; strong in* a thing (*masterful*), i.e. (fig. and refl.) *self-controlled* (in appetite, etc.):—temperate {1x}.

Egkrates denotes "exercising self-control," and is rendered "temperate" in Titus 1:8. See:

TDNT—2:339, 196; BAGD—216d; THAYER—167a.

1469. ἐγκρίνω {1x} ĕgkrinō, *eng-kree'-no;* from *1722* and *2919;* to *judge in,* i.e. *count* among:—make of the number {1x}.

(1) *Egkrino* means to judge one worthy of being admitted to a certain class. (2) *Egkrino,* "to reckon among" is translated "to number . . . (ourselves) with" in 2 Cor 10:12 of the apostle's dissociation of himself and his fellow missionaries from those who commended themselves. See: TDNT—3:951, 469; BAGD—216d; THAYER—167a.

1470. ἐγκρύπτω {2x} ĕgkruptō, *eng-kroop'-to;* from *1722* and *2928;* to *conceal in,* i.e. *incorporate, mingle with:*—hid in {2x}. See: BAGD—216d; THAYER—167b.

1471. ἔγκυος {1x} ĕgkuŏs, *eng'-koo-os;* from *1722* and the base of *2949; swelling in*side, i.e. *pregnant:*—great with child {1x}. See: BAGD—216d; THAYER—167b.

1472. ἐγχρίω {1x} ĕgchriō, *eng-khree'-o;* from *1722* and *5548;* to *rub in* (oil), i.e. *besmear:*—anoint {1x}.

Egchrio, as a verb, means primarily "to rub in," hence, "to besmear, to anoint," and is used metaphorically in the command to the church in Laodicea to "anoint" their eyes with eye salve (Rev 3:18). Syn.: 218, 2025, 3462, 5545, 5548. See: BAGD—217a; THAYER—167b.

1473. ἐγώ {370x} ĕgō, *eg-o'*; a primary pron. of the first pers. *I* (only expressed when emphatic):—I {365x}, my {2x}, me {2x}, not tr {1x}. For the other cases and the plur. see *1691, 1698, 1700, 2248, 2249, 2254, 2257,* etc. See: TDNT—2:343, 196; BAGD—217a.; THAYER—167b.

1474. ἐδαφίζω {1x} ĕdaphizō, *ed-af-id'-zo;* from *1475;* to *raze:*—lay even with the ground {1x}. See: BAGD—217c; THAYER—167d.

1475. ἔδαφος {1x} ĕdaphŏs, *ed'-af-os;* from the base of *1476;* a *basis* (*bottom*), i.e. the *soil:*—ground {1x}.

Edaphos, "a bottom, base," is used of the "ground" in Acts 22:7, suggestive of that which is level and hard. See: BAGD—217d; THAYER—168a.

1476. ἐδραῖος {3x} hĕdraiŏs, *hed-rah'-yos;* from a der. of ἕζομαι hĕzŏmai (to *sit*); *sedentary,* i.e. (by impl.) *immovable:*—settled {2x}, stedfast {1x}.

Hedraios primarily denotes "seated"; hence, "steadfast," metaphorical of moral fixity, 1 Cor

7:37; 15:58; Col 1:23. See: TDNT—2:362, 200; BAGD—217d; THAYER—168a.

1477. ἑδραίωμα {1x} hĕdraiōma, *hed-rah'-yomah;* from a der. of *1476;* a *support,* i.e. (fig.) *basis:*—ground {1x}.

Edraioma, "a support, bulwark, stay" (from *hedraios,* "steadfast, firm"; from *hedra,* "a seat"), is translated "ground" in 1 Ti 3:15 (said of a local church; that upon which one can build because it dispenses Christ's words, the rock, upon which one builds his life, cf. Mt 7:24–25; 16:18; Lk 6:48; 8:6). See: TDNT—2:362, 200; BAGD—218a; THAYER—168a.

1478. Ἐζεκίας {2x} ezĕkias, *ed-zek-ee'-as;* of Heb. or. [2396]; *Ezekias* (i.e. *Hezekiah*), an Isr.:—*Ezekias* {2x}. See: BAGD—218a; THAYER—168a.

1479. ἐθελοθρησκεία {1x} ethĕlŏthrēskĕia, *eth-el-oth-race-ki'-ah;* from *2309* and *2356; voluntary* (*arbitrary* and *unwarranted*) *piety,* i.e. *sanctimony:*—will worship {1x}.

Ethelothreskeia occurs in Col 2:23 and means voluntarily adopted worship, not that which is imposed by others, but which one affects himself. See: TDNT—3:155, 337; BAGD—218a; THAYER—168a.

ἐθέλω ethĕlō. See *2309.*

1480. ἐθίζω {1x} ethizō, *eth-id'-zo;* from *1485;* to *accustom,* i.e. (neut. pass. part.) *customary:*—custom {1x}.

Ethizo signifies "to accustom," or in the passive voice, "to be accustomed." In the participial form it is equivalent to a noun, "custom, Lk 2:27. See: BAGD—218b; THAYER—168b.

1481. ἐθνάρχης {1x} ethnarchēs, *eth-nar'-khace;* from *1484* and *746;* the *governor* [not king] *of a district:*—governor {1x}.

Ethnarches is translated "governor" in 2 Cor 11:32. It describes normally the ruler of a nation possessed of separate laws and customs among those of a different race. Eventually it denoted a ruler of a province, superior to a tetrarch, but inferior to a king (e.g., Aretas). See: BAGD—218b; THAYER—168b.

1482. ἐθνικός {2x} ĕthnikŏs, *eth-nee-kos';* from *1484; national* ("*ethnic*"), i.e. (spec.) a *Gentile:*—heathen {1x}, heathen man {1x}.

Ethnikos is used as noun, and translated (1) "heathen" in Mt 6:7; (2) "an heathen man" in Mt 18:17. TDNT—2:372, 201; BAGD—218b; THAYER—168b.

1483. ἐθνικῶς {1x} ĕthnikōs, *eth-nee-koce';* adv. from *1482; as a Gentile:*—

after the manner of Gentiles {1x}. See: BAGD—218b; THAYER—168c.

1484. ἔθνος {164x} **ĕthnŏs**, *eth'-nos;* prob. from *1486;* a *race* (as of the same *habit*), i.e. a *tribe;* spec. a *foreign* (*non-Jewish*) one (usually by impl. *pagan*):—Gentiles {93x}, heathen {5x}, nation {64x}, people {2x}.

Ethnos denotes, firstly, "a multitude or company"; then, "a multitude of people of the same nature or genus, a nation, people"; **(1)** it is used in the singular, of the Jews, e.g., Lk 7:5; 23:2; Jn 11:48, 50–52; **(2)** in the plural, of nations (Heb., *goiim*) other than Israel, e.g., Mt 4:15; Rom 3:29; 11:11; 15:10; Gal 2:8; **(3)** occasionally it is used of Gentile converts in distinction from Jews, e.g., Rom 11:13; 16:4; Gal 2:12, 14; Eph 3:1. See: TDNT—2:364, 201; BAGD—218b; THAYER—168c.

1485. ἔθος {12x} **ĕthŏs**, *eth'-os;* from *1486;* a *usage* (prescribed by habit or law):—custom {7x}, manner {4x}, be wont {1x}.

Ethos, as a noun, means "a habit, custom" and is translated **(1)** "manner": "Then took they the body of Jesus, and wound it in linen clothes with the spices, as the manner of the Jews is to bury" Jn 19:40; cf. Acts 15:1; 25:16; Heb 10:25. It denotes **(2)** "a custom, usage, prescribed by law," Lk 1:9; 2:42; Acts 6:14; 16:21; 21:21; 26:2; 28:17; **(3)** "wont", Lk 22:39. Syn.: 195, 2239, 3634, 3668, 3697, 3779, 4169, 4187, 4217, 4459, 5158, 5159, 5179, 5615. See: TDNT—2:372, 202; BAGD—218d; THAYER—168d.

1486. ἔθω {4x} **ĕthō**, *eth'-o;* a primary verb; to *be used* (by habit or conventionality); neut. perfect part. *usage:*—be wont {2x}, - as his custom was + 2596 + 3588 {1x}, as his manner was + 2596 + 3588 {1x}.

Etho, "to be accustomed" is used **(1)** in the passive participle as a noun, signifying "a custom, a manner" Lk 4:16; Acts 17:2; and **(2)** in Mt 7:15 and Mk 10:1, "was wont." See: BAGD—219a; THAYER—168d.

1487. εἰ {{290x} **ĕi**, *i;* a primary particle of conditionality; *if, whether, that,* etc.:—if {242x}, whether {20x}, that {6x}, not tr {19x}, forasmuch as {1x}, although {1x}, whether {1x}. Often used in connection or composition with other particles, espec. as in *1489, 1490, 1499, 1508, 1509, 1512, 1513, 1536, 1537.* See also *1437.* See: BAGD—219a; THAYER—169a.

1488. εἶ {92x} **ĕi**, *i;* second pers. sing. present of *1510;* thou *art:*—art {81x}, be {11x}. See: BAGD—223a [under 1510]; THAYER—175c [1510].

1489. εἴγε {5x} **ĕigĕ**, *i'-gheh;* from *1487* and *1065; if indeed, seeing that, unless,* (with neg.) *otherwise:*—if {2x}, if so be that {2x}, yet {1x}. See: BAGD—220a; THAYER—172c.

1490. εἰ δὲ μή(γε) {14x} **ĕi dĕ mē(gĕ)** *i deh may'-(gheh);* from *1487, 1161,* and *3361* (sometimes with *1065* added); *but if not:*—or else {3x}, else {4x}, if not {2x}, if otherwise {2x}, if not {1x}, or else {1x}, otherwise {1x}. See: BAGD—220a; THAYER—111b.

1491. εἶδος {5x} **ĕidŏs**, *i'-dos;* from *1492;* a *view,* i.e. *form* (lit. or fig.):—appearance {1x}, fashion {1x}, shape {2x}, sight {1x}.

Eidos, as a noun, means properly "that which strikes the eye, that which is exposed to view," signifies **(1)** the "external appearance, form, or shape," and in this sense is used **(1a)** of the Holy Spirit in taking bodily form, as a dove, Lk 3:22; **(1b)** of Christ, Lk 9:29, "And as He prayed, the fashion (*eidos*) of His countenance was altered, and His raiment was white and glistering" (Lk 9:29); **(1c)** Christ used it, negatively, of God the Father, when He said "Ye have neither heard His voice at any time, nor seen His form," Jn 5:37. **(1d)** Thus it is used with reference to each person of the Trinity. **(1e)** Probably the same meaning attaches to the word in the apostle's statement, "We walk by faith, not by sight (*eidos*)," 2 Cor 5:7, **(1f)** where *eidos* can scarcely mean the act of beholding, but the visible "appearance" of things which are set in contrast to that which directs faith. **(1g)** The believer is guided, then, not only by what he beholds but by what he knows to be true though it is invisible. **(2)** It has a somewhat different significance in 1 Th 5:22, in the exhortation, "Abstain from every appearance of evil," i.e., every sort or kind of evil, even that which can allow onlookers to think one is participating in evil. See: TDNT—2:373, 202; BAGD—221b; THAYER—172d.

1492. εἴδω {666x} **ĕidō**, *i'-do;* a primary verb; used only in certain past tenses, the others being borrowed from the equiv. *3700* and *3708;* prop. to *see* (lit. or fig.); by impl. (in the perf. only) to *know by perception:*—know {282x}, cannot tell + 3756 {8x}, know how {7x}, wist {6x}, see {314x}, behold {16x}, look {5x}, perceive {5x}, vr see {3x}, vr know {1x}, misc. {19x}, be aware, consider, have knowledge, knowledge, be sure, tell, understand, wot.

Oida (Perf. of *eido*), as a verb, "to see,"**(1)** is a perfect tense with a present meaning, **(2)** signifying, primarily, "to have seen or perceived"; hence, "to know, to have knowledge of," whether absolutely, **(2a)** as in divine knowledge, e.g., Mt

Greek

6:8, 32; Jn 6:6, 64; 8:14; 11:42; 13:11; 18:4; 2 Cor
11:31; 2 Pet 2:9; Rev 2:2, 9, 13, 19; 3:1, 8, 15;
(2b) or in the case of human "knowledge," to
know from observation, e.g., 1 Th 1:4, 5; 2:1;
2 Th 3:7. Syn.: The differences between *ginosko*
(*1097*) and *oida* (*1492*) demand consideration:
(A) *ginosko,* frequently suggests inception or
progress in "knowledge," while *oida* suggests
fullness of "knowledge," e.g., **(A1)** Jn 8:55, "ye
have not known Him" (*ginosko*), i.e., begun to
"know," "but I know Him" (*oida*), i.e., "know
Him perfectly"; **(A2)** Jn 13:7, "What I do thou
knowest not now," i.e. Peter did not yet perceive (*oida*) its significance, "but thou shalt understand," i.e., "get to know (*ginosko*),
hereafter"; **(A3)** Jn 14:7, "If ye had known Me"
(*ginosko*), i.e., "had definitely come to know
Me," "ye would have known My Father also"
(*oida*), i.e., "would have had perception of":
"from henceforth ye know Him" (*ginosko*), i.e.,
having unconsciously been coming to the Father, as the One who was in Him, they would
now consciously be in the constant and progressive experience of "knowing" Him; **(A4)** in
Mk 4:13, "Know ye not (*oida*) this parable? and
how shall ye know (*ginosko*) all the parables?";
the intimation being that the first parable is
a leading and testing one; **(B)** while *ginosko*
frequently implies an active relation between
the one who "knows" and the person or thing
"known" *oida* expresses the fact that the object
has simply come within the scope of the
"knower's" perception; **(B1)** thus in Mt 7:23 "I
never knew you" (*ginosko*) suggests "I have
never been in approving connection with you,"
whereas **(B2)** in Mt 25:12, "I know you not"
(*oida*) suggests "you stand in no relation to
Me." See also: 1097, 1107, 1110, 1492, 1921,
1467, 1922, 1987. See: TDNT—5:116, 673;
BAGD—220c; THAYER—172d. comp. *3700.*

1493. εἰδωλεῖον {1x} **ĕĭdōlĕiŏn,** *i-do-li′-on;*
                    neut. of a presumed der. of
1497; an *image-fane:*—idol's temple {1x}. See:
TDNT—2:379, 202; BAGD—221b; THAYER—
174c.

1494. εἰδωλόθυτον {10x} **ĕĭdōlŏthutŏn,** *i-do-*
                    loth′-oo-ton; neut. of a
compound of *1497* and a presumed der. of *2380;*
an *image-sacrifice,* i.e. part of an *idolatrous
offering:*—things offered unto idols {4x}, things
offered in sacrifice to idols {3x}, things sacrificed unto idols {2x}, meats offered to idols
{1x}.
    This word is an adjective signifying "sacri-
ficed to idols" (*eidolon*–1497, and *thuo*–2380,
"to sacrifice"), Acts 15:29; 21:25; 1 Cor 8:1, 4,
7, 10; 10:19, 28; Rev 2:14, 20 (in these the RV

and KJV both have "sacrificed"). See: TDNT—
2:378, 202; BAGD—221b; THAYER—174c.

1495. εἰδωλολατρεία {4x} **ĕĭdōlŏlatrĕia,** *i-do-*
                    lol-at-ri′-ah; from *1497*
and *2999; image-worship* (lit. or fig.):—idolatry {4x}.
    Eidololatreia, whence Eng., "idolatry," and
(1) is found in 1 Cor 10:14; Gal 5:20; Col 3:5;
and, in the plural, in 1 Pet 4:3. **(2)** Heathen
sacrifices were sacrificed to devils, 1 Cor 10:19.
(2a) There was a dire reality in the cup and
table of devils and in the involved communion
with devils. **(2b)** In Rom 1:22–25, "idolatry,"
the sin of the mind against God (Eph 2:3), and
immorality, sins of the flesh, are associated,
and are traced to lack of the acknowledgment
of God and of gratitude to Him. **(2c)** An "idolater" is a slave to the depraved ideas his idols
represent, Gal 4:8, 9; and thereby, to divers
lusts, Titus 3:3. See: TDNT—2:379, 202; BAGD—
221c; THAYER—174c.

1496. εἰδωλολάτρης {7x} **ĕĭdōlŏlatrēs,** *i-do-*
                    lol-at′-race; from *1497*
and the base of *3000;* an *image-(servant* or)
worshipper (lit. or fig.):—idolater {7x}.
    Eidololatres, an "idolater" (from *eidolon,*
and *latris,* "a hireling"), is **(1)** found in 1 Cor
5:10, 11; 6:9; 10:7. **(2)** The warning is to believers against turning away from God to idolatry,
whether openly or secretly, consciously or unconsciously; Eph 5:5; Rev 21:8; 22:15. See:
TDNT—2:379, 202; BAGD—221c; THAYER—
174c.

1497. εἴδωλον {11x} **ĕĭdōlŏn,** *i′-do-lon;* from
                    1491; an *image* (i.e. for wor-
ship); by impl. a heathen *god,* or (plur.) the
worship of such:—idol {11x}.
    Eidolon, primarily **(1)** "a phantom or like-
ness" (from *eidos,* "an appearance"), means
(1a) lit., "that which is seen", or **(1b)** "an idea,
fancy," **(2)** denotes in the NT **(2a)** "an idol," an
image to represent a false god, Acts 7:41; 1 Cor
12:2; Rev 9:20; **(2b)** "the false god" worshiped
in an image, Acts 15:20; Rom 2:22; 1 Cor 8:4,
7; 10:19; 2 Cor 6:16; 1 Th 1:9; 1 Jn 5:21. **(3)** The
corresponding Heb. word denotes "vanity," cf.
Jer 14:22; 18:15; "thing of nought," Lev 19:4, cf.
Eph 4:17. **(4)** Hence what represented a deity to
the Gentiles, was to Paul a "vain thing," Acts
14:15; "nothing in the world," 1 Cor 8:4; 10:19.
(5) Jeremiah describes the idol, 10:5; cf. Is 44:9–
20; Hab 2:18, 19; and the psalmist, 115:4–8,
etc., are all equally scathing. **(6)** It is important
to notice, however, that in each case the people
of God are addressed. **(7)** When he speaks to
idolaters, Paul, knowing that no man is won
by ridicule, adopts a different line, Acts 14:15–

18; 17:16, 21–31. See: TDNT—2:375, 202; BAGD—221c; THAYER—174d.

1498. **εἴην** {12x} ĕiēn, *i'-ane;* optative (i.e. English subjunctive) present of *1510* (incl. the other pers.); *might (could, would,* or *should) be:*—should be {3x}, be {3x}, meant {2x}, might be {1x}, should mean {1x}, wert {1x}, not tr {1x}. See: BAGD—222d; THAYER—175c.

1499. **εἰ καί** {22x} ĕi kai, *i kahee;* from *1487* and *2532; if also* (or *even):*— though {14x}, if {4x}, and if {2x}, if that {1x}, if also {1x}. See: BAGD—220a; THAYER—171b.

1500. **εἰκῇ** {7x} ĕikē, *i-kay';* prob. From *1502* (through the idea of *failure*); *idly,* i.e. *without a reason* (or *effect*):—in vain {5x}, without a cause {1x}, vainly {1x}.

Eike denotes **(1)** "without cause," Mt 5:22; **(2)** "vainly," Col 2:18; **(3)** "to no purpose," "in vain," Rom 13:4; 1 Cor 15:2; Gal 3:4 (twice); 4:11. See: TDNT—2:380, 203; BAGD—221d; THAYER—174d.

1501. **εἴκοσι** {12x} ĕikŏsi, *i'-kos-ee;* of uncert. aff.; a *score:*—twenty {12x}. See: BAGD—222a; THAYER—174d.

1502. **εἴκω** {1x} ĕikō, *i'-ko;* appar. a primary verb; prop. to *be weak,* i.e. *yield:*— give place {1x}.

Eiko, as a verb, means "to yield, give way" and is rendered "gave place": "To whom we gave place by subjection, no, not for an hour; that the truth of the gospel might continue with you" (Gal 2:5). Syn.: 201, 402, 1096, 3837, 4042, 5117, 5247, 5564, 5602. See: BAGD—222b; THAYER—175a.

1503. **εἴκω** {2x} ĕikō, *i'-ko;* appar. a primary verb [perh. akin to *1502* through the idea of *faintness* as a copy]; to *resemble:*— be like {2x}. See: BAGD—222b; THAYER—175a.

1504. **εἰκών** {23x} ĕikōn, *i-kone';* from *1503;* a *likeness,* i.e. (lit.) *statue, profile,* or (fig.) *representation, resemblance:*—image {23x}.

(1) This word always refers to a prototype that it resembles and from which it is drawn; an imitation of an archtype. **(1a)** *Eikon* denotes "an image"; **(1b)** the word involves the two ideas of representation and manifestation. **(2)** The idea of a perfect likeness does not lie in the word itself, but must be sought from the context; the following instances clearly show any distinction between the imperfect and the perfect likeness. **(3)** The word is used **(3a)** of an "image" or a coin (not a mere likeness), Mt 22:20; Mk 12:16; Lk 20:24; **(3b)** so of a statue

or similar representation (more than a resemblance), Rom 1:23; Rev 13:14, 15 (thrice); 14:9, 11; 15:2; 16:2; 19:20; 20:4; **(3c)** of the descendants of Adam as bearing his image, 1 Cor 15:49, each a representation derived from the prototype; **(3d)** of subjects relative to things spiritual, Heb 10:1, negatively of the Law as having "a shadow of the good things to come, not the very image of the things," i.e., not the essential and substantial form of them; the contrast has been likened to the difference between a statue and the shadow cast by it;

(4) of the relations between God the Father, Christ, and man, **(4a)** of man as he was created as being a visible representation of God, 1 Cor 11:7, a being corresponding to the original; **(4a1)** the condition of man as a fallen creature has not entirely effaced the "image"; **(4a2)** he is still suitable to bear responsibility, he still has Godlike qualities, such as love of goodness and beauty, none of which are found in a mere animal; **(4a3)** in the Fall man ceased to be a perfect vehicle for the representation of God; **(4a4)** God's grace in Christ will yet accomplish more than what Adam lost; **(4b)** of regenerate persons, in being moral representations of what God is, Col 3:10; cf. Eph 4:24; **(4c)** of believers, in their glorified state, not merely as resembling Christ but representing Him, Rom 8:29; 1 Cor 15:49; here the perfection is the work of divine grace; believers are yet to represent, not something like Him, but what He is in Himself, both in His spiritual body and in His moral character;

(5) of Christ in relation to God, **(5a)** 2 Cor 4:4, "the image of God," i.e., essentially and absolutely the perfect expression and representation of the Archetype, God the Father; **(5b)** in Col 1:15, "the image of the invisible God" gives the additional thought suggested by the word "invisible," that Christ is the visible representation and manifestation of God to created beings; **(5c)** the likeness expressed in this manifestation is involved in the essential relations in the Godhead, and is therefore unique and perfect; "he that hath seen Me hath seen the Father," Jn 14:9. **(5d)** The epithet "invisible" . . . must not be confined to the apprehension of the bodily senses, but will include the cognizance of the inward eye also. Syn.: 3667, 3669. See: TDNT—2:381, 203; BAGD—222b; THAYER—175a.

1505. **εἰλικρίνεια** {3x} ĕilikrinĕia, *i-lik-ree'-ni-ah;* from *1506; clearness,* i.e. (by impl.) *purity* (fig.):—sincerity {3x}.

Eilikrineia denotes "sincerity, purity"; it is described **(1)** metaphorically in 1 Cor 5:8 as "unleavened (bread)"; in **(2)** 2 Cor 1:12, "(godly) sincerity," it describes a quality possessed by

God, as that which is to characterize the conduct of believers; **(3)** in 2 Cor 2:17 it is used of the rightful ministry of the Scriptures. See: TDNT—2:397, 206; BAGD—222d; THAYER—175b.

1506. εἰλικρινής {2x} **ĕilikrinēs**, *i-lik-ree-nace';* from εἵλη **hĕilē** (the sun's *ray*) and *2919; judged by sunlight,* i.e. tested as *genuine* (fig.):—pure {1x}, sincere {1x}.

Eilikrines, signifies "unalloyed, pure"; and it was used of unmixed substances; **(1)** in the NT it is used of moral and ethical "purity," Phil 1:10, "sincere"; and **(2)** in 2 Pet 3:1 "pure." **(3)** Some regard the etymological meaning as "tested by the sunlight" Syn.: This Christian virtue will exclude all double-mindedness (Jas 1:8; 4:8), the eye that is not single (Mt 6:22), and all hypocrisies (1 Pet 2:1). It refers to the Christian freedom from falsehoods, while *katharos* (*2513*) refers to the Christian's freedom from defilements of the flesh and the world. See: TDNT—2:397, 206; BAGD—222d; THAYER—175b

1507. εἰλίσσω {1x} **hĕilissō**, *hi-lis'-so;* a prol. form of a primary but defective verb εἵλω **hĕilō** (of the same mean.); to *coil* or *wrap:*—roll together {1x}. See: BAGD—222d; THAYER—175b. See also *1667.*

1508. εἰ μή {91x} **ĕi mē**, *i-may';* from *1487* and *3361; if not:*—but {53x}, save {16x}, except {6x}, if not {5x}, not tr {1x}, misc. {1x}. See: BAGD—220a; THAYER—171c.

1509. εἰ μή τι {3x} **ĕi mē ti**, *i-may'-tee;* from *1508* and the neut. of *5100; if not somewhat:*—except {3x}. See: BAGD—220b; THAYER—172a.

1510. εἰμί {146x} **ĕimi**, *i-mee';* the first pers. sing. present ind.; a prol. form of a primary and defective verb; I *exist* (used only when emphatic):—I am + 1473 {74x}, am {55x}, it is I + 1473 {6x}, be {2x}, I was + 1473 {1x}, have been {1x}, not tr {7x}. See: BAGD—222d; THAYER—175c. See also *1488, 1498, 1511, 2258, 2071, 2070, 2075, 2076, 2771, 2468, 5600, 5607.*

1511. εἶναι {126x} **ĕinai**, *i'-nahee;* present infin. from *1510;* to *exist:*—to be {33x}, be {28x}, was {15x}, is {14x}, am {7x}, are {6x}, were {4x}, not tr {11x}, misc. {8x} = come, × lust after, × please well, there is. See: BAGD—223a; THAYER—176c.

εἵνεκεν hĕinĕkĕn. See *1752.*

1512. εἴ περ {6x} **ĕi pĕr**, *i-per;* from *1487* and *4007; if perhaps:*—if so be that

{3x}, though {1x}, seeing {1x}, if so be {1x}. See: BAGD—226a; 220b; THAYER—180c; 172a.

1513. εἴ πως {4x} **ĕi pōs**, *i-poce;* from *1487* and *4458; if somehow:*—if by any means {4x} See: BAGD—220b; THAYER—172a.

1514. εἰρηνεύω {4x} **ĕirēnĕuō**, *i-rane-yoo'-o;* from *1515;* to *be* (act) *peaceful:*—have peace {1x}, live peaceably {1x}, live in peace {1x}, be at peace {1x}.

Eireneuo means primarily, "to bring to peace, reconcile" and denotes in the NT, "to keep peace or to be at peace": in **(1)** Mk 9:50 the Lord bids the disciples "be at peace" with one another, gently rebuking their ambitious desires; **(2)** in Rom 12:18 "live peaceably", the limitation "if it be possible, as much as in you lieth," seems due to the phrase "with all men," but is not intended to excuse any evasion of the obligation imposed by the command; **(3)** in 2 Cor 13:11 it is rendered "live in peace," a general exhortation to believers; **(4)** in 1 Th 5:13, "be at peace (among yourselves). See: TDNT—2:417, 207; BAGD—227a; THAYER—182a.

1515. εἰρήνη {92x} **ĕirēnē**, *i-ray'-nay;* prob. from a primary verb εἴρω **ĕirō** (to *join*); *peace* (lit. or fig.); by impl. *prosperity:*—one {1x}, peace {89x}, quietness {1x}, rest {1x}.

Eirene **(1)** occurs in each of the books of the NT, save 1 Jn and save in Acts 7:26 ["(at) one again"]. **(2)** It describes **(2a)** harmonious relationships between men, Mt 10:34; Rom 14:19; **(2b)** between nations, Lk 14:32; Acts 12:20; Rev 6:4; **(2c)** friendliness, Acts 15:33; 1 Cor 16:11; Heb 11:31; **(2d)** freedom from molestation, Lk 11:21; 19:42; Acts 9:31 "rest"; 16:36; **(2e)** order, in the state, Acts 24:2 "quietness"; **(2f)** order in the churches, 1 Cor 14:33; **(2g)** the harmonized relationships between God and man, accomplished through the gospel, Acts 10:36; Eph 2:17; **(2h)** the sense of rest and contentment consequent thereon, Mt 10:13; Mk 5:34; Lk 1:79; 2:29; Jn 14:27; Rom 1:7; 3:17; 8:6; **(2i)** in certain passages this idea is not distinguishable from the last, Rom 5:1. See: TDNT—2:400, 207; BAGD—227b; THAYER—182a.

1516. εἰρηνικός {2x} **ĕirēnikŏs**, *i-ray-nee-kos';* from *1515; pacific;* by impl. *salutary:*—peaceable {2x}.

Eirenikos denotes "peaceful." It is used **(1)** of the fruit of righteousness, Heb 12:11, "peaceable" (or "peaceful") because it is produced in communion with God the Father, through His chastening; and **(2)** of "the wisdom that is from above," Jas 3:17. See: TDNT—2:418, 207; BAGD—228a; THAYER—182d.

1517. εἰρηνοποιέω {1x} ĕirēnŏpŏiĕō, *i-ray-nop-oy-eh'-o;* from *1518;* to *be a peace-maker,* i.e. (fig.) to *harmonize:—* make peace {1x}. See: TDNT—2:419, 207; BAGD—228a; THAYER—183a.

1518. εἰρηνοποιός {1x} ĕirēnŏpŏiŏs, *i-ray-nop-oy-os';* from *1515* and *4160; pacificatory,* i.e. (subj.) *peaceable:—*peace-makers {1x}. See: TDNT—2:419, 207; BAGD—228a; THAYER—183a.

εἴρω ĕirō. See *1515, 4483, 5346.*

1519. εἰς {1773x} ĕis, *ice;* a primary prep.; *to* or *into* (indicating the point reached or entered), of place, time, or (fig.) purpose (result, etc.); also in adv. phrases:—into {573x}, to {281x}, unto {207x}, for {140x}, in {138x}, on {58x}, toward {29x}, against {26x}, misc. {321x} = [abundant-] ly, among, as, at, [back-] ward, before, by, concerning, continual, far more exceeding, for [intent, purpose], fore, forth, in (among, at, unto, so much that,), to the intent that, of one mind, never, of, upon, perish, set at one again, (so) that, therefore (unto), throughout, till, to be, to the end, (here) until, [where] fore, with. Often used in composition with the same general import, but only with verbs (etc.) expressing motion (lit. or fig.). See: TDNT—2:420, 211; BAGD—228a; THAYER—183a.

1520. εἷς {271x} hĕis, *hice;* (incl. the neut. [etc.] ἕν hĕn); a primary numeral; *one:—*one {229x}, a {9x}, other {6x}, some {6x}, not tr {4x}, misc. {17x} any, a certain, + abundantly, man, one another, only.
Heis, the first cardinal numeral, masculine (feminine and neuter nominative forms are *mia* and *hen,* respectively), is used to signify **(1)** "one" in contrast to many, e.g., Mt 25:15; Rom 5:18, "the offense of one", Adam's transgression, in contrast to the "one act of righteousness," i.e., the death of Christ; **(2)** metaphorically, "union" and "concord," e.g., Jn 10:30; 11:52; 17:11, 21–22; Rom 12:4–5; Phil 1:27; **(3)** emphatically, **(3a)** a single ("one"), to the exclusion of others, e.g., Mt 21:24; Rom 3:10; 1 Cor 9:24; 1 Ti 2:5 (twice); **(3b)** "one, alone," e.g., Mk 2:7, "only"; 10:18; Lk 18:19; **(3c)** "one and the same," e.g., Rom 3:30; "God is one," i.e., there is not "one" God for the Jew and one for the Gentile; **(3d)** cf. Gal 3:20, which means that in a promise there is no other party; 1 Cor 3:8; 11:5; 12:11; 1 Jn 5:8 (lit., "and the three are into one," i.e., united in "one" and the same witness);
(4) a certain "one," **(4a)** in the same sense as the indefinite pronoun *tis,* e.g., Mt 8:19, "a certain (scribe)"; 19:16, "one;" in Rev 8:13 "one (eagle)"; **(4b)** *heis tis* are used together in Lk 22:50; Jn 11:49; **(5)** distributively, with *hek-*

astos, **(5a)** "each," i.e., "every one," e.g., Lk 4:40; Acts 2:6, "every man" (lit., "every one"); **(5b)** in the sense of "one . . . and one," e.g., Jn 20:12; **(5c)** or "one" . . . followed by *allos* or *heteros,* "the other," e.g., Mt 6:24; **(5d)** or by a second *heis,* e.g., Mt 24:40; Jn 20:12; in Rom 12:5 *heis* is preceded by *kata (kath)* in the sense of "severally (members) one (of another)," "every one . . . one"; cf. Mk 14:19; **(5e)** in 1 Th 5:11 the phrase in the 2nd part, "each other," "one another", is, lit., "one the one"; **(6)** as an ordinal number, equivalent to *protos,* "first," in the phrase "the first day of the week," lit. and idiomatically, "one of sabbaths," signifying "the first day after the sabbath," e.g., Mt 28:1; Mk 16:2; Acts 20:7; 1 Cor 16:2. See: TDNT—2:434, 214; BAGD—230d; THAYER—186b.

1521. εἰσάγω {10x} ĕisagō, *ice-ag'-o;* from *1519* and *71;* to *introduce* (lit. or fig.):—bring in {5x}, bring {4x}, lead {1x}. See: BAGD—232b; THAYER—187c.

1522. εἰσακούω {5x} ĕisakŏuō, *ice-ak-oo'-o;* from *1519* and *191;* to *listen to:—*hear {5x}.
Eisakouo, as a verb, means "to listen to" and has two meanings: **(1)** "to hear and to obey" (1 Cor 14:21 - "they will not hear"); **(2)** "to hear so as to answer" of God's answer to prayer (Mt 6:7; Lk 1:13; Acts 10:31; Heb 5:7). Syn.: 189, 191, 1251, 1873, 1874, 3878, 4257. See: TDNT—1:222, 34; BAGD—232b; THAYER—187c.

1523. εἰσδέχομαι {1x} ĕisdĕchŏmai, *ice-dekh'-om-ahee;* from *1519* and *1209;* to *take into* one's favor:—receive {1x}.
Eisdechomai, as a verb, means "to receive into" and is used only in 2 Cor 6:17, where the verb does not signify "to accept," but "to admit": "Wherefore come out from among them, and be ye separate, saith the Lord, and touch not the unclean thing; and I will receive (*eisdechomai*) you" [as antithetic to "come ye out" cf. Is 52:11 with Zeph 3:20]. Syn.: 324, 353, 354, 568, 588, 618, 1209, 1926, 2210, 2865, 2975, 2983, 3028, 3335, 3336, 3858, 3880, 3970, 4327, 4355, 4356, 4380, 4381, 4382, 5562, 5264, 5274. See: TDNT—2:57, 146; BAGD—232c; THAYER—187c.

1524. εἴσειμι {4x} ĕisĕimi, *ice'-i-mee;* from *1519* and εἶμι ĕimi (to *go*); to *enter:—*entered {1x}, went {2x}, went into {1x}.
Eiseimi, means **(1)** "to go into" Acts 3:3, **(2)** "entered" Acts 21:26; and **(3)** "went" Acts 21:18. Heb 9:6. See: BAGD—232c; THAYER—187d.

Greek

1525. **εἰσέρχομαι** {198x} **ĕisĕrchŏmai**, *ice-er'-khom-ahee;* from *1519* and *2064;* to *enter* (lit. or fig.):—enter {107x}, go {22x}, come in {19x}, go in {18x}, enter in {17x}, come {14x}, arise {1x}.

Eiserchomai, as a verb, means **(1)** literally "to go in, to enter" and is **(2)** once rendered "arose," metaphorically, with reference to a reasoning among the disciples which of them should be the greatest (Lk 9:46). Syn.: 305, 393, 450, 1096, 1326, 1453, 1817, 4911. See: TDNT—2:676, 257; BAGD—232d; THAYER—187d.

1526. **εἰσί** {163x} **ĕisi**, *i-see';* third pers. plur. present ind. of *1510;* they *are:*—are {135x}, be {14x}, were {7x}, have {2x}, not tr {1x}, misc. {4x} = agree, is. See: BAGD—223a; THAYER—175c.

1527. **εἱ̑ςκαθ'εἱ̑ς** {2x} **hĕis kath̆ hĕis**, *hice kath hice;* from *1520* repeated with *2596* inserted; *severally:*—one by one {2x}.

This phrase means "one by one, one after the other", Mk 14:19; Jn 8:9. See: BAGD—232b; THAYER—187b.

1528. **εἰσκαλέω** {1x} **ĕiskalĕō**, *ice-kal-eh'-o;* from *1519* and *2564;* to *invite* in:—call in {1x}. See: TDNT—3:496, 394; BAGD—233b; THAYER—188c.

1529. **εἴσοδος** {5x} **ĕisŏdŏs**, *ice'-od-os;* from *1519* and *3598;* an *entrance* (lit. or fig.):—coming {1x}, entering in {1x}, entrance in {1x}, to enter into + 1519 {1x}, entrance {1x}.

Eisodos, "an entrance, an entering in," is **(1)** once translated "coming," Acts 13:24, of the coming of Christ into the nation of Israel. For its meaning "entrance" **(2)** see 1 Th 1:9; 2:1; Heb 10:19; 2 Pet 1:11. See: TDNT—5:103, 666; BAGD—233b; THAYER—189c.

1530. **εἰσπηδάω** {2x} **ĕispēdaō**, *ice-pay-dah'-o;* from *1519* and πηδάω **pēdaō** (to *leap*); to *rush in:*—ran in {1x}, sprang in {1x}.

Eispedao means **(1)** "sprang in," occurs in Acts 16:29; and **(2)** "ran in" in Acts 14:14. See: BAGD—233c; THAYER—188c.

1531. **εἰσπορεύομαι** {17x} **ĕispŏrĕuŏmai**, *ice-por-yoo'-om-ahee;* from *1519* and *4198;* to *enter* (lit. or fig.):—enter {9x}, enter in {5x}, come in {3x}.

Eisporeuomai, "to go into," found only in the Synoptics and Acts, is translated **(1)** "entered, entereth" in Mt 15:16; Mk 1:21; 6:56; 7:19; 11:2; Lk 8:16; 22:10; Acts 3:2; **(2)** "entering in" Mk 4:19; 5:40; 7:15; 7:18; Lk 19:20; Acts 8:3; **(3)** "come in" Lk 11:33; Acts 9:28; 28:30. See:

TDNT—6:578, 915; BAGD—233c; THAYER—188c.

1532. **εἰστρέχω** {1x} **ĕistrĕchō**, *ice-trekh'-o;* from *1519* and *5143;* to *hasten inward:*—run in {1x}. See: BAGD—233d; THAYER—188d.

1533. **εἰσφέρω** {7x} **ĕisphĕrō**, *ice-fer'-o;* from *1519* and *5342;* to *carry inward* (lit. or fig.):—bring {3x}, bring in {2x}, lead into {2x}.

Eisphero denotes **(1)** "to bring to", Lk 5:19; Acts 17:20; **(2)** "to bring into", Lk 5:18; 1 Ti 6:7; Heb 13:11; and **(3)** "lead into", Mt 6:13; Lk 11:4. See: TDNT—9:64, 1252; BAGD—233d; THAYER—188d.

1534. **εἶτα** {16x} **ĕita**, *i'-tah;* of uncert. aff.; a particle of *succession* (in time or logical enumeration), *then, moreover:*—then {11x}, after that {3x}, afterward {1x}, furthermore {1x}.

Eita which is chiefly used of time or enumerations, signifying "then" or "next," is once used in argument, signifying furthermore, Heb 12:9. See: BAGD—233d; THAYER—188d. See also *1899*.

1535. **εἴτε** {65x} **ĕitĕ**, *i'-teh;* from *1487* and *5037; if too:*—or {33x}, whether {28x}, or whether {3x}, if {1x}. See: BAGD—234a; 220b; THAYER—172c.

1536. **εἴ τις** {79x} **ĕi tis**, *i tis;* from *1487* and *5100; if any:*—if any man {35x}, if any {19x}, if a man {8x}, if any thing {6x}, if ought {3x}, whosoever {2x}, misc. {6x} he that, whether any. See: BAGD—220b; THAYER—172c.

1537. **ἐκ** {921x} **ĕk**, *ek* or

ἐξ **ĕx**, *ex;* a primary prep. denoting *origin* (the point *whence* motion or action proceeds), *from, out* (of place, time, or cause; lit. or fig.; direct or remote):—of {367x}, from {181x}, out of {162x}, by {55x}, on {34x}, with {25x}, misc. {97x} = after, among, are, at, betwixt, beyond, by the means of, exceedingly, (abundantly above), for (th), grudgingly, heartily, heavenly, hereby, very highly, in, . . . ly, (because, by reason) of, off (from), out among, out from, over, since, thenceforth, through, unto, vehemently, without. Often used in composition, with the same general import; often of completion. See: BAGD—234b; THAYER—189a.

1538. **ἕκαστος** {83x} **hĕkastŏs**, *hek'-as-tos;* as if a superl. of ἕκας **hĕkas** (*afar*); *each* or *every:*—every man {39x}, every one {20x}, every {17x}, misc. {7x} any, both, each (one), every woman, particularly.

This word means "each" or "every," is used of any number separately, either **(1)** as an adjective qualifying a noun, **(1a)** e.g., Lk 6:44; Jn 19:23; Heb 3:13, where "day by day," is, lit., "according to each day"; **(1b)** or, more emphatically with *heis*, "one," in Mt 26:22; Lk 4:40; 16:5; Acts 2:3, 6, 20:31; 1 Cor 12:18; Eph 4:7, 16 "every"; Col 4:6; 1 Th. 2:11; 2 Th 1:3; **(2)** as a distributive pronoun, **(2a)** e.g., Acts 4:35; Rom 2:6; Gal 6:4; in Phil 2:4, it is used in the plural; Rev 6:11. **(2b)** The repetition in Heb 8:11 is noticeable "every man" (i.e., everyone). **(3)** Prefixed by the preposition **(3a)** *ana*, "apiece" (a colloquialism), it is used, with stress on the individuality, in Rev 21:21, of the gates of the heavenly city, "every several gate"; **(3b)** in Eph 5:33, preceded by *kath' hena*, "by one," it signifies "each (one) his own." See: BAGD—236c; THAYER—192a.

1539. ἑκάστοτε {1x} **hĕkastŏtĕ**, *hek-as'-tot-eh;* as if from *1538* and *5119;* at *every time:*—always {1x}.

Ekastote, "always," is used in 2 Pet 1:15. "Always" stresses "all ways, in all manners"; and "alway" stresses "all the time, all along the way without interruption." See: BAGD—236d; THAYER—192b.

1540. ἑκατόν {17x} **hĕkatŏn**, *hek-at-on';* of uncert. aff.; a *hundred:*—hundred {15x}, hundredfold {2x}.

Ekaton is an indeclinable numeral, denotes **(1)** "a hundred," e.g., Mt 18:12, 28; **(2)** it also signifies "a hundredfold," Mt 13:8, 23, signifying the complete productiveness of sown seed. **(3)** In the passage in Mk 4:8, 20 the phrase is, lit., "in thirty and in sixty and in a hundred." **(4)** In Mk 6:40 it is used with the preposition *kata*, in the phrase "by hundreds." **(5)** It is followed by other numerals in Jn 21:11; Acts 1:15; Rev 7:4; 14:1, 3; 21:17. See: BAGD—236d; THAYER—192b.

1541. ἑκατονταετης {1x} **hĕkatŏntaĕtēs**, *hek-at-on-tah-et'-ace;* from *1540* and *2094; centenarian:*—hundred years old {1x}. See: BAGD—236d; THAYER—192b.

1542. ἑκατονταπλασίων {3x} **hĕkatŏntaplasiōn**, *hek-at-on-ta-plah-see'-own;* from *1540* and a presumed der. of *4111;* a *hundred times, a hundred times as much:*—hundredfold {3x}. See: BAGD—237a; THAYER—192c.

1543. ἑκατοντάρχης {21x} **hĕkatŏntarchēs**, *hek-at-on-tar'-khace;* or

ἑκατόνταρχος **hĕkatŏntarchŏs**, *hek-at-on'-tar-khos;* from *1540* and *757;* the *captain of one hundred*

men:—centurion {21x}. See: BAGD—237a; THAYER—192c.

1544. ἐκβάλλω {82x} **ĕkballō**, *ek-bal'-lo;* from *1537* and *906;* to *eject* (lit. or fig.):—cast out {45x}, cast {11x}, bring forth {3x}, pull out {3x}, send forth {3x}, misc. {17x} = drive (out), expel, leave, pluck, take out, thrust out, put forth, put out, send away, send out. See: TDNT—1:527, 91; BAGD—237b; THAYER—192d.

1545. ἔκβασις {2x} **ĕkbasis**, *ek'-bas-is;* from a compound of *1537* and the base of *939* (mean. to *go out*); an *exit* (lit. or fig.):—end {1x}, way to escape {1x}.

Ekbasis denotes **(1)** "a way out", 1 Cor 10:13, "way of escape"; or **(2)** an "end", Heb 13:7. See: BAGD—237d; THAYER—193b.

1546. ἐκβολή {1x} **ĕkbŏlē**, *ek-bol-ay';* from *1544; ejection*, i.e. (spec.) a *throwing overboard* of the cargo:—lighten the ship + 4060 {1x}.

Ekbole, lit., "a throwing out" denotes "a jettison, a throwing out of cargo," Acts 27:18, lit., "they made a throwing out." See: BAGD—238a; THAYER—193b.

1547. ἐκγαμίζω {5x} **ĕkgamizō**, *ek-gam-id'-zo;* from *1537* and a form of *1061* [comp. *1548*]; to *marry off* a daughter:—give in marriage {5x}. See: BAGD—238a; THAYER—193b.

1548. ἐκγαμίσκω {2x} **ĕkgamiskō**, *ek-gam-is'-ko;* from *1537* and *1061;* the same as *1547:*—give in marriage {2x}. See: BAGD—238a; THAYER—193b.

1549. ἔκγονον {1x} **ĕkgŏnŏn**, *ek'-gon-on;* neut. of a der. of a compound of *1537* and *1096;* a *descendant*, i.e. (spec.) *grandchild:*—nephew {1x}.

Ekgonon, an adjective, denoting "born of" (*ek*, "from," *ginomai*, "to become or be born"), was used as a noun, signifying "a child"; in the plural, descendants, "nephews" 1 Ti 5:4. See: BAGD—238a; THAYER—193c.

1550. ἐκδαπανάω {1x} **ĕkdapanaō**, *ek-dap-an-ah'-o;* from *1537* and *1159;* to *expend* (wholly), i.e. (fig.) *exhaust:*—spend {1x}.

Ekdapanao lit., "to spend out", "to spend entirely," is used in 2 Cor 12:15, in the passive voice, with reflexive significance, "to spend oneself out (for others)," "will . . . be spent." See: BAGD—238b; THAYER—193c.

1551. ἐκδέχομαι {8x} **ĕkdĕchŏmai**, *ek-dekh'-om-ahee;* from *1537* and *1209;* to *accept from* some source, i.e. (by impl.)

to *await:*—wait for {3x}, look for {2x}, tarry for {1x}, expect {1x}, wait {1x}.

Ekdechomai lit. and primarily means **(1)** "to take or receive from"; hence **(2)** denotes "to await, expect," the only sense of the word in the NT; **(3)** it suggests a reaching out in readiness to receive something; **(3a)** "expecting," Heb 10:13; **(3b)** to wait for, Jn 5:3; Acts 17:16; Jas 5:7; **(3c)** "tarry for", 1 Cor 11:33; **(3d)** "wait", 1 Pet 3:20; **(3e)** "look for," 1 Cor 16:11; Heb 11:10. See: TDNT—2:56, 146; BAGD—238b; THAYER—193c.

1552. **ἔκδηλος** {1x} **ĕkdēlŏs**, *ek'-day-los;* from *1537* and *1212; wholly evident:*—manifest {1x}. See: BAGD—238b; THAYER—192c.

1553. **ἐκδημέω** {3x} **ĕkdēmĕō**, *ek-day-meh'-o;* from a compound of *1537* and *1218;* to *emigrate; to be away from people,* i.e. (fig.) *vacate* or *quit:*—be absent {3x}.

Ekdemeo, lit., "to be away from people" (*ek,* "from," or "out of," *demos,* "people"), came to mean "to go abroad, depart, be absent." The apostle Paul uses it to speak of departing from the body as the earthly abode of the spirit, 2 Cor 5:6–9: **(1)** of being here in the body and absent from the Lord (v. 6), or **(2)** of being absent from the body and present with the Lord (v. 8). **(3)** Its other occurrence is in v. 9. See: TDNT—2:63, 149; BAGD—238b; THAYER—193d.

1554. **ἐκδίδωμι** {4x} **ĕkdidōmi**, *ek-did-o'-mee;* from *1537* and *1325;* to *give forth for one's advantage,* i.e. (spec.) to *lease:*—let forth {1x}, let out {1x}.

Ekdidomi, primarily, "to give out, give up, surrender" denotes "to let out for hire." In the NT it is used, in the middle voice, with the meaning in the parable of the husbandman and his vineyard **(1)** "to let out to one's advantage", Mt 21:33, 41; Mk 12:1; or **(2)** "let forth . . ." Lk 20:9. See: BAGD—238c; THAYER—193d.

1555. **ἐκδιηγέομαι** {2x} **ĕkdiēgĕŏmai**, *ek-dee-ayg-eh'-om-ahee;* from *1537* and a compound of *1223* and *2233;* to *narrate* through wholly:—declare {2x}.

Ekdiegeomai, properly means "to narrate in full," and came to denote, "to tell, declare wholly", Acts 13:41; 15:3. See: BAGD—238c; THAYER—193d.

1556. **ἐκδικέω** {6x} **ĕkdikĕō**, *ek-dik-eh'-o;* from *1558;* to *vindicate, retaliate, punish:*—avenge {5x}, revenge {1x}.

Ekdikeo, (*ek,* "from," *dike,* "justice") i.e., that which proceeds from justice, means **(1)** "to vindicate a person's right" in the parable of the unjust judge, Lk 18:3, 5, of the "vindication"

of the rights of the widow; **(2)** with the meaning **(2a)** "to avenge a thing," it is used in Rev 6:10 and 19:2, of the act of God in "avenging" the blood of the saints; **(2b)** in 2 Cor 10:6, of the apostle's readiness to use his apostolic authority in punishing disobedience on the part of his readers; **(2c)** in Rom 12:19 of "avenging" oneself, against which the believer is warned. See: TDNT—2:442, 215; BAGD—238c; THAYER—193d.

1557. **ἐκδίκησις** {9x} **ĕkdikēsis**, *ek-dik'-ay-sis;* from *1556; vindication, retribution:*—vengeance {4x}, avenge + 4060 {3x}, revenge {1x}, punishment {1x}.

Ekdikesis, "vengeance," is used **(1)** with the verb *poieo,* "to make," i.e., to avenge, in Lk 18:7–8; Acts 7:24; **(2)** twice it is used in statements that "vengeance" belongs to God, Rom 12:19; Heb 10:30. **(3)** In 2 Th 1:8 it is said of the act of divine justice which will be meted out to those who know not God and obey not the gospel, when the Lord comes in flaming fire at His second advent. In the divine exercise of judgment there is no element of vindictiveness, nothing by way of taking revenge. **(4)** In Lk 21:22, it is used of the "days of vengeance" upon the Jewish people; **(5)** in 1 Pet 2:14, of civil governors as those who are sent of God "for punishment on evildoers"; **(6)** in 2 Cor 7:11, of the "revenge" of believers, in their godly sorrow for wrong doing. See: TDNT—2:445, 215; BAGD—238d; THAYER—194a.

1558. **ἔκδικος** {2x} **ĕkdikŏs**, *ek'-dik-os;* from *1537* and *1349;* carrying *justice out,* i.e. a *punisher:*—revenger {1x}, avenger {1x}.

Ekdikos, primarily, "without law," then, "one who exacts a penalty from a person, an avenger, a punisher," is used **(1)** in Rom 13:4 of a civil authority in the discharge of his function of executing wrath on the evildoer, a "revenger"; **(2)** in 1 Th 4:6, of God as the avenger of the one who wrongs his brother, here particularly in the matter of adultery. See: TDNT—2:444, 215; BAGD—238d; THAYER—194a.

1559. **ἐκδιώκω** {2x} **ĕkdiōkō**, *ek-dee-o'-ko;* from *1537* and *1377;* to *pursue out, to chase away,* i.e. *expel* or *persecute* implacably:—persecute {2x}.

Ekdioko, "to chase away, drive out," oppress with calamities, **(1)** is used in 1 Th 2:15 "have persecuted"; and **(2)** Lk 11:49 of the persecution of God's prophets. See: BAGD—239a; THAYER—194a.

1560. **ἔκδοτος** {1x} **ĕkdŏtŏs**, *ek'-dot-os;* from *1537* and a der. of *1325; given out* or *over,* i.e. *surrendered:*—delivered {1x}.

Ekdotos, as a verbal adjective [participle] means literally "given up" [*ek*, "out of," *didomi*, "to give"], "delivered up" (to enemies, or to the power or will of someone), is used of Christ in Acts 2:23: "Him, being delivered by the determinate counsel and foreknowledge of God, ye have taken, and by wicked hands have crucified and slain." Syn.: 325, 525, 629, 591, 859, 1325, 1659, 1807, 1929, 3086, 3860, 4506, 5483. See: BAGD−239a; THAYER−194b.

1561. ἐκδοχή {1x} ĕkdŏchē, *ek-dokh-ay';* from *1551; expectation:*−looking for {1x}.

Ekdoche, "looking for expectedly" is used in Heb 10:27 "looking for" judgment. See: BAGD−239a; THAYER−194b.

1562. ἐκδύω {5x} ĕkduō, *ek-doo'-o;* from *1537* and the base of *1416;* to cause to *sink out* of, i.e. (spec. as of clothing) to *divest:*−strip {2x}, take off from {2x}, unclothe {1x}.

Ekduo, "to take off, strip off," is used especially of clothes, and rendered **(1)** "to strip" in Mt 27:28; Lk 10:30, **(2)** to take off, Mt 27:31; Mk 15:20; and **(3)** figuratively, 2 Cor 5:4, "unclothed" (middle voice), of putting off the body at death (the believer's state of being unclothed does not refer to the body in the grave but to the spirit, which awaits the "body of glory" at the resurrection). See: TDNT−2:318, 192; BAGD−239a; THAYER−194b.

1563. ἐκεῖ {98x} ĕkĕi, *ek-i';* of uncert. aff.; *there;* by extens. *thither:*−there {86x}, thither {7x}, not tr {3x}, misc. {3x} thitherward, (to) yonder (place). "There" has reference to a specific location away from the speaker; whereas, "thither" is a non-specific location somewhere away from the speaker. See: BAGD−239b; THAYER−194b.

1564. ἐκεῖθεν {27x} ĕkĕithĕn, *ek-i'-then;* from *1563; thence:*−thence {16x}, from thence {9x}, from that place {1x}, there {1x}.

"Thence" denotes time and place; "from thence" stresses place, with a hint of no return. See: BAGD−239b; THAYER−194c.

1565. ἐκεῖνος {251x} ĕkĕinŏs, *ek-i'-nos;* from *1563; that* one (or [neut.] thing); often intensified by the art. prefixed:−that {99x}, those {40x}, he {40x}, the same {20x}, they {14x}, misc. {38x} it, the other, selfsame, their, them, this.

Ekeinos denotes "that one, that person"; its use marks special distinction, favorable or unfavorable; this form of emphasis should always be noted; e.g., **(1)** Jn 2:21 "(But) He (spake)"; **(2)** 5:19, "(what things soever) He (doeth)"; 7:11; 2 Cor 10:18, lit., "for not he that commen-

deth himself, he (*ekeinos*) is approved"; **(3)** 2 Ti 2:13, "He (in contrast to "we") abideth faithful"; **(4)** 1 Jn 3:3, "(even as) He (is pure)"; **(5)** 1 Jn 5:5, "He (was manifested)"; **(6)** 1 Jn 5:7, "He (is righteous)"; **(7)** 1 Jn 5:16, "He laid down"; **(8)** 1 Jn 4:17, "(as) He (is)." See: BAGD−239b; THAYER−194c. See also *3778.*

1566. ἐκεῖσε {2x} ĕkĕisĕ, *ek-i'-seh;* from *1563; thither:*−there {2x}. See: BAGD−240; THAYER−195b.

1567. ἐκζητέω {7x} ĕkzētĕō, *ek-zay-teh'-o;* from *1537* and *2212;* to *search out*, i.e. (fig.) *investigate, crave, demand,* (by Heb.) *worship:*−require {2x}, seek after {2x}, diligently {1x}, seek carefully {1x}, enquire {1x}.

Ekzeteo, as a verb, signifies **(1)** "to seek out (*ek*) or after, to search for": **(1a)** "There is none that understandeth, there is none that seeketh after God" (Rom 3:11); **(1b)** the Lord: "That the residue of men might seek after the Lord, and all the Gentiles, upon whom My name is called, saith the Lord, who doeth all these things" (Acts 15:17; cf. Heb 11:6; 12:17; 1 Pet 1:10, followed by *exeraunao*, "to search diligently"; **(2)** "to require or demand": "That the blood of all the prophets, which was shed from the foundation of the world, may be required (*ekzeteo*) of this generation; from the blood of Abel unto the blood of Zacharias, which perished between the altar and the temple: verily I say unto you, It shall be required (*ekzeteo*) of this generation" (Lk 11:50, 51). Syn.: 327, 1934, 2206, 2212, 3713. See: TDNT−2:894, 300; BAGD−240a; THAYER−195b.

1568. ἐκθαμβέω {4x} ĕkthambĕō, *ek-tham-beh'-o;* from *1569;* to *astonish* utterly:−be affrighted {2x}, sore amazed {1x}, greatly amazed {1x}.

This word means to throw into terror or amazement; to alarm thoroughly, to terrify or astound and is used in the passive sense, **(1)** "to be amazed, affrighted," Mk 16:5−6; **(2)** Mk 9:15, "were greatly amazed"; **(3)** Mk 14:33, "to be sore amazed." See: TDNT−3:4,*; BAGD−240b; THAYER−195c.

1569. ἔκθαμβος {1x} ĕkthambŏs, *ek'-tham-bos;* from *1537* and *2285;* utterly *astounded:*−greatly wondering {1x}.

A strengthened form of *thambos* is found in Acts 3:11. The intensive force of the word is brought out by the rendering "greatly wondering." See: TDNT−3:4, 312; BAGD−240b; THAYER−195c.

1570. ἔκθετος {1x} ĕkthĕtŏs, *ek'-thet-os;* from *1537* and a der. of *5087; put*

out, i.e. *exposed* to perish:—cast out {1x}. See: BAGD—240b; THAYER—195c.

1571. ἐκκαθαίρω {2x} ĕkkathairō, *ek-kath-ah'-ee-ro;* from *1537* and *2508;* to *cleanse thoroughly:*—purge {1x}, purge out {1x}.

Ekkathairo, "to cleanse out, cleanse thoroughly," is said **(1)** of "purging" out leaven, 1 Cor 5:7; and **(2)** in 2 Ti 2:21, of "purging" oneself from those who utter "profane babblings," vv. 16–18. See: TDNT—3:430, 381; BAGD—240b; THAYER—195c.

1572. ἐκκαίω {1x} ĕkkaiō, *ek-kah'-yo;* from *1537* and *2545;* to *inflame* deeply:—burn {1x}.

Ekkaio, lit., "to burn out," in the passive voice, "to be kindled, burn up," is used of the lustful passions of men, Rom 1:27. See: BAGD—240c; THAYER—195d.

1573. ἐκκακέω {6x} ĕkkakĕō, *ek-kak-eh'-o* or ἐγκακέω egkakeō *eng-kak-eh'-o;* from *1537* and *2556;* to *be* (*bad* or) *weak*, i.e. (by impl.) to *fail* (in heart); to lose courage:—faint {4x}, be weary {2x}.

Ekkakeo, "to lack courage, lose heart, be fainthearted", is said **(1)** of prayer, Lk 18:1; **(2)** of gospel ministry, 2 Cor 4:1, 16; **(3)** of the effect of tribulation, Eph 3:13; **(4)** as to well doing, 2 Th 3:13, "be not weary"; **(5)** as to reaping, Gal 6:9. See: TDNT 3:486,*; BAGD—240c; THAYER—195d.

1574. ἐκκεντέω {2x} ĕkkĕntĕō, *ek-ken-teh'-o;* from *1537* and the base of *2759;* to *transfix:*—pierce {2x}.

Ekkenteo, "to pierce" [Christ], Jn 19:37; Rev 1:7. See: TDNT—2:446, 216; BAGD—240c; THAYER—195d.

1575. ἐκκλάω {3x} ĕkklaō, *ek-klah'-o;* from *1537* and *2806;* to *exscind:*—break off {3x}.

Ekklao, "to break off," is used metaphorically of branches, Rom 11:17, 19–20. See: BAGD—240c; THAYER—195d.

1576. ἐκκλείω {2x} ĕkklĕiō, *ek-kli'-o;* from *1537* and *2808;* to *shut out* (lit. or fig.):—exclude {2x}.

Ekkleio, "to shut out" is said **(1)** of glorying in works as a means of justification, Rom 3:27; **(2)** of Gentiles, who by Judaism would be "excluded" from salvation and Christian fellowship, Gal 4:17. See: BAGD—240d; THAYER—195d.

1577. ἐκκλησία {118x} ĕkklēsia, *ek-klay-see'-ah;* from a compound of *1537* and a der. of *2564;* a *calling out,* i.e. (concr.) a popular *meeting,* espec. a religious *congrega-*

tion (Jewish *synagogue,* or Chr. community of members on earth or saints in heaven or both):—assembly {3x}, church {115x}.

(1) This word stresses a group of people called out for a special purpose. **(1a)** It designated the new society of which Jesus was the founder, being as it was a society knit together by the closest spiritual bonds and altogether independent of space. **(1b)** *Ekklesia,* from *ek,* "out of," and *klesis,* "a calling" (*kaleo,* "to call"), was used among the Greeks of a body of citizens "gathered" to discuss the affairs of state, Acts 19:39. **(2)** In Acts 7:38 it is used of Israel; in 19:32, 41, of a riotous mob. **(3)** It has two applications to companies of Christians, **(3a)** to the whole company of the redeemed throughout the present era, the company of which Christ said, "I will build My church," Mt 16:18, and which is further described as "the church which is His body," Eph 1:22; 5:23, **(3b)** in the singular number (e.g., Mt 18:17), to a company consisting of professed believers, e.g., Acts 20:28; 1 Cor 1:2; Gal 1:13; 1 Th 1:1; 2 Th 1:1; 1 Ti 3:5, and in the plural, with reference to churches in a district. **(4)** In Acts 9:31 "churches" point to a district. Syn.: 3831, 4864. See: TDNT—3:501, 394; BAGD—40d; THAYER—195d.

1578. ἐκκλίνω {3x} ĕkklinō, *ek-klee'-no;* from *1537* and *2827;* to *deviate,* i.e. (absolutely) to *shun* (lit. or fig.), or (rel.) to *decline* (from piety):—avoid {1x}, eschew {1x}, go out of the way {1x}.

Ekklino, "to turn away from, to turn aside," lit., "to bend out of" (*ek,* "out," *klino,* "to bend"), is **(1)** used in Rom 3:12, of the sinful condition of mankind, "gone out of the way"; **(2)** in Rom 16:17, of turning away from those who cause offenses and occasions of stumbling "avoid"; **(3)** in 1 Pet 3:11 of turning away from evil, "eschew." See: BAGD—240c; THAYER—196c.

1579. ἐκκολυμβάω {1x} ĕkkŏlumbaō, *ek-kol-oom-bah'-o;* from *1537* and *2860;* to *escape* by *swimming:*—swim out {1x}. See: BAGD—241d; THAYER—196c.

1580. ἐκκομίζω {1x} ĕkkŏmizō, *ek-kom-id'-zo;* from *1537* and *2865;* to *bear forth* (to burial):—carry out {1x}. See: BAGD—241d; THAYER—196c.

1581. ἐκκόπτω {11x} ĕkkŏptō, *ek-kop'-to;* from *1537* and *2875;* to *exscind;* fig. to *frustrate:*—cut off {4x}, hewn down {3x}, cut down {2x}, cut out {1x}, be hindered {1x}.

Ekkopto, "to cut down," is used **(1)** literally, **(1a)** "hewn down", Mt 3:10; 7:19; Lk 3:9; **(1b)** "cut down", Lk 13:7, 9; **(2)** metaphorically, **(2a)** of "cutting off" from spiritual blessing, Rom

11:22, 24; **(2b)** of "cutting off" an offending body part, Mt 5:30; 18:8 **(3)** of depriving persons of an occasion for something, 2 Cor 11:12; and **(4)** "to hinder" prayers ["cut off" from reaching God] 1 Pet 3:7. See: TDNT—3:857, 453; BAGD—241d; THAYER—196c.

1582. **ἐκκρέμαμαι** {1x} **ĕkkrĕmamai**, *ek-krem'-am-ahee;* mid. voice from *1537* and *2910;* to *hang upon* the lips of a speaker, i.e. *listen closely:*—be very attentive {1x}. See: TDNT—3:915, 468; BAGD—242a; THAYER—196d.

1583. **ἐκλαλέω** {1x} **ĕklalĕō**, *ek-lal-eh'-o;* from *1537* and *2980;* to *divulge:*—tell {1x}.

Eklaleo, "to speak out" is translated "tell" in Acts 23:22. See: BAGD—242a; THAYER—196d.

1584. **ἐκλάμπω** {1x} **ĕklampō**, *ek-lam'-po;* from *1537* and *2989;* to *be resplendent:*—shine forth {1x}. See: TDNT—4:16, 497; BAGD—242a; THAYER—196d.

1585. **ἐκλανθάνομαι** {1x} **ĕklanthanŏmai**, *ek-lan-than'-om-ahee;* mid. voice from *1537* and *2990;* to *be* utterly *oblivious* of:—forget {1x}. See: BAGD—242b; THAYER—196d.

1586. **ἐκλέγομαι** {21x} **ĕklĕgŏmai**, *ek-leg'-om-ahee;* mid. voice from *1537* and *3004* (in its primary sense); to *select:*—make choice {1x}, choose {19x}, choose out {1x}.

Eklegomai, "to pick out, select," means, in the middle voice, "to choose for oneself," not necessarily implying the rejection of what is not chosen, but "choosing" with the subsidiary ideas of kindness or favor or love, Mk 13:20; Lk 6:13; 10:42; 14:7; Jn 6:70; 13:18; 15:16, 19; Acts 1:2, 24; 6:5; 13:17; 15:7 "made choice"; 15:22, 25; 1 Cor 1:27–28; Eph 1:4; Jas 2:5. See: TDNT—4:144, 505; BAGD—242b; THAYER—196d.

1587. **ἐκλείπω** {3x} **ĕklĕipō**, *ek-li'-po;* from *1537* and *3007;* to *omit,* i.e. (by impl.) *cease* (*die*):—fail {3x}.

Ekleipo, "to leave out", used intransitively, means "to leave off, cease, fail"; **(1)** it is said of the cessation of earthly life, Lk 16:9; **(2)** of faith, Lk 22:32; **(3)** of the years of Christ, Heb 1:12. See: BAGD—242c; THAYER—197a.

1588. **ἐκλεκτός** {23x} **ĕklĕktŏs**, *ek-lek-tos';* from *1586; select, chosen out;* by impl. *favorite:*—chosen {16x}, elect {7x}.

Eklektos, signifies "chosen out, select," e.g., Mt 22:14; Lk 23:35; Rom 16:13; Rev 17:14; 1 Pet 2:4, 9. See: TDNT—4:181, 505; BAGD—242d; THAYER—197b.

1589. **ἐκλογή** {7x} **ĕklŏgē**, *ek-log-ay';* from *1586;* (divine) *selection* (abstr. or concr.):—chosen {1x}, election {6x}.

Ekloge, "a picking out, choosing", is translated **(1)** "chosen" in Acts 9:15, lit., "he is a vessel of choice unto Me." **(2)** In the six other places where this word is found it is translated "election", Rom 9:11; 11:5; 11:7; 11:28; 1:4; 2 Pet 1:10. See: TDNT—4:176, 505; BAGD—243a; THAYER—197c.

1590. **ἐκλύω** {6x} **ĕkluō**, *ek-loo'-o;* from *1537* and *3089;* to *relax* (lit. or fig.):—faint {5x}, faint + 2258 {1x}.

Ekluo, denotes (a) "to loose, release" (*ek,* "out," *luo,* "to loose"); (b) "to unloose," as a bow-string, "to relax," and so, "to enfeeble," and is used in the passive voice with the significance "to be faint, grow weary," **(1)** of the body, Mt 9:36; 15:32; Mk 8:3; **(2)** of the soul, Gal 6:9 (last clause), in discharging responsibilities in obedience to the Lord; **(3)** in Heb 12:3, of becoming weary in the strife against sin; **(4)** in Heb 13:5, under the chastening hand of God. See: BAGD—243b; THAYER—197d.

1591. **ἐκμάσσω** {5x} **ĕkmassō**, *ek-mas'-so;* from *1537* and the base of *3145;* to *knead out,* i.e. (by anal.) to *wipe dry:*—wipe {5x}.

Ekmasso, "to wipe out" (*ek*), "wipe dry," is used **(1)** of "wiping" tears from Christ's feet, Lk 7:38, 44; Jn 11:2; 12:3; **(2)** of Christ's "wiping" the disciples' feet, Jn 13:5. See: BAGD—243b; THAYER—198a.

1592. **ἐκμυκτηρίζω** {2x} **ĕkmuktĕrizō**, *ek-mook-ter-id'-zo;* from *1537* and *3456;* to *sneer* outright at:—deride {2x}.

Ekmukterizo, "to hold up the nose in derision at" (*ek,* "from," used intensively, *mukterizo,* "to mock;* from *mukter,* "the nose"), is translated "derided" **(1)** in Lk 16:14, of the Pharisees in their derision of Christ on account of His teaching; **(2)** in Lk 23:35, of the mockery of Christ on the cross by the rulers of the people. See: TDNT—4:176, 505; BAGD—243b; THAYER—198a.

1593. **ἐκνεύω** {1x} **ĕknĕuō**, *ek-nyoo'-o;* from *1537* and *3506;* (by anal.) to *slip off,* i.e. quietly *withdraw:*—convey self away {1x}.

Ekneuo, primarily, "to bend to one side, to turn aside"; then "to take oneself away, withdraw," is found in Jn 5:13, of Christ's "conveying" Himself away from one place to another. Some have regarded the verb as having the same meaning as *ekneo,* "to escape," as from peril, "slip away secretly"; but the Lord did not leave the place where He had healed

the paralytic in order to escape danger, but to avoid the applause of the throng. See: BAGD— 243b; THAYER—198a.

1594. ἐκνήφω {1x} ĕknēphō, ek-nay'-fo; from 1537 and 3525; (fig.) to rouse (oneself) out of stupor:—awake {1x}.

In 1 Cor 15:34 eknepho means to awake up righteously and sin not, suggesting a return to soberness of mind from the stupor consequent upon the influence of evil doctrine. TDNT— 4:941, 633; BAGD—243b; THAYER—198b.

1595. ἐκούσιον {1x} hĕkŏusiŏn, hek-oo'-see-on; neut. of a der. from 1635; voluntariness:—willingly + 2596 {1x}. See: TDNT—2:470; BAGD—243b; THAYER—198b.

1596. ἐκουσίως {2x} hĕkŏusiŏs, hek-oo-see'-oce; adv. from the same as 1595; voluntarily:—wilfully {1x}, willingly {1x}.

Hekousios denotes "voluntarily, willingly," (1) Heb 10:26, (of sinning) "willfully"; and (2) in 1 Pet 5:2, "willingly" (of exercising oversight over the flock of God). See: TDNT—221; BAGD— 243c; THAYER—198b.

1597. ἔκπαλαι {2x} ĕkpalai, ek'-pal-ahee; from 1537 and 3819; long ago, for a long while:—of a long time {1x}, of old {1x}.

Ekpalai, is translated (1) "from of old" in 2 Pet 3:5; and (2) "of a long time" in 2 Pet 2:3. See: BAGD—243c; THAYER—198b.

1598. ἐκπειράζω {4x} ĕkpĕirazō, ek-pi-rad'-zo; from 1537 and 3985; to test thoroughly:—tempt {4x}.

Ekpeirazo, an intensive form, is used (1) in Christ's quotation from Deut 6:16, in reply to the devil, Mt 4:7; Lk 4:12; (2) in 1 Cor 10:9 "Christ": "Neither let us tempt Christ, as some of them also tempted, and were destroyed of serpents"; (3) of the lawyer who "tempted" Christ, Lk 10:25. See: TDNT—6:23, 822; BAGD—243c; THAYER—198b.

1599. ἐκπέμπω {2x} ĕkpĕmpō, ek-pem'-po; from 1537 and 3992; to despatch:—sent away {1x}, being sent forth {1x}.

Ekpempo denotes "to send forth", (1) Acts 13:4, "being sent forth"; and (2) Acts 17:10, "sent away." See: BAGD—243c; THAYER— 198c.

ἐκπερισσοῦ ĕkpĕrissŏu. See 1537 and 4053.

1600. ἐκπετάννυμι {1x} ĕkpĕtannumi, ek-pet-an'-noo-mee; from 1537 and a form of 4072; to fly out like a sail, i.e. (by anal.) to extend:—stretch forth {1x}.

Ekpetannumi, "to spread out" (as a sail), is rendered in Rom 10:21, "I have stretched forth". See: BAGD—243d; THAYER—198c.

1601. ἐκπίπτω {14x} ĕkpiptō, ek-pip'-to; from 1537 and 4098; to drop away; spec., be driven out of one's course; fig. to lose, become inefficient:—fall {7x}, fall off {2x}, be cast {1x}, take none effect {1x}, fall away {1x}, fail {1x}, vr fallen {1x}.

This word means literally (1) to fall out of, to fall down from, to fall off Acts 12:7; (2) metaphorically, (2a) to fall from a thing, to lose it Gal 5:4; 2 Pet 3:17; (2b) to perish, to fall from a place from which one cannot keep; fall from its position, 1 Cor 13:8; (2c) to fall powerless, to fall to the ground, be without effect; of the divine promise of salvation Rom 9:6. See: TDNT—6:167, 846; BAGD—243d; THAYER— 198c.

1602. ἐκπλέω {3x} ĕkplĕō, ek-pleh'-o; from 1537 and 4126; to depart by ship:—sail {1x}, sail away {1x}, sail thence {1x}.

This means to depart by ship, Acts 15:39; 18:18; 20:6. See: BAGD—244a; THAYER— 198d.

1603. ἐκπληρόω {1x} ĕkplērŏō, ek-play-rŏ'-o; from 1537 and 4137; to accomplish entirely:—fulfill {1x}. See: TDNT— 6:307, 867; BAGD—244a; THAYER—198d.

1604. ἐκπλήρωσις {1x} ĕkplērōsis, ek-play'-ro-sis; from 1603; completion:—accomplishment {1x}. See: TDNT— 6:308, 867; BAGD—244b; THAYER—198d.

1605. ἐκπλήσσω {13x} ĕkplēssō, ek-place'-so; from 1537 and 4141; to strike with astonishment:—be amazed {3x}, be astonished {10x}.

Ekplesso signifies "to be exceedingly struck in mind, to be astonished", e.g., Mt 19:25; Lk 2:48; 9:43. Syn.: (A) Ekplesso (1605) means "to be astonished", prop. to be struck with terror, of a sudden and startling alarm; but like our "astonish" in popular use, often employed on comparatively slight occasions. (B) Ptoeo (4422) signifies "to terrify", to agitate with fear. (C) Tremo (5141) "to tremble", predominately physical; and (D) phobeo (5399) denotes "to fear", the general term; often used of a protracted state. See: BAGD—244b; THAYER—198d.

1606. ἐκπνέω {3x} ĕkpnĕō, ek-pneh'-o; from 1537 and 4154; to expire:— give up the ghost {3x}.

Ekpneo, lit., "to breathe out", "to expire," is used in the NT, without an object, "soul" or "life" being understood, Mk 15:37, 39, and Lk 23:46, of the death of Christ. In Mt 27:50 and Jn 19:30, where different verbs are used, the

act is expressed in a way which stresses it as of His own volition. See: TDNT—6:452, 876; BAGD—244b; THAYER—199a.

1607. ἐκπορεύομαι {35x} **ĕkpŏrĕuŏmai,** *ek-por-yoo'-om-ahee;* from *1537* and *4198;* to *depart, be discharged, proceed, project:*—proceed {10x}, go out {6x}, go {5x}, come {4x}, depart {3x}, go forth {2x}, vr go forth {1x}, misc. {4x} come (forth, out of), issue.

Ekporeuomai, "from," in the middle and passive, "to proceed from or forth," more expressive of a definite course than simply "to go forth," is translated **(1)** "departed," in Mt 20:29; Mk 6:11; Acts 25:4; **(2)** "that which cometh" in Mk 7:20; **(3)** It is frequently translated by the verb "to proceed," and is often best so rendered Eph 4:29; Rev 11:5; and **(4)** "issued" in Rev 9:17–18. See: TDNT—6:578, 915; BAGD—244b; THAYER—199a.

1608. ἐκπορνεύω {1x} **ĕkpŏrnĕuō,** *ek-porn-yoo'-o;* from *1537* and *4203;* to *be utterly unchaste:*—give self over to fornication {1x}.

Ekporneuo, (a strengthened form of *porneuo, ek,* used intensively), "to give oneself up to fornication," implies excessive indulgence, Jude 7. See: 6:579, 918; BAGD—244d; THAYER—199b.

1609. ἐκπτύω {1x} **ĕkptuō,** *ek-ptoo'-o;* from *1537* and *4429;* to *spit out,* i.e. (fig.) *spurn:*—reject {1x}.

Ekptuo, "to spit out" i.e., "to abominate, loathe," is used in Gal 4:14, "rejected" where the sentence is elliptical: "although my disease repelled you, you did not refuse to hear my message." See: TDNT—2:448, 216; BAGD—244d; THAYER—199b.

1610. ἐκριζόω {4x} **ĕkrizŏō,** *ek-rid-zŏ'-o;* from *1537* and *4492;* to *uproot:*—pluck up by the root {2x}, root up {2x}.

Ekrizoo, "to pluck up by the roots" (*ek,* "out," *rhiza,* "a root"), is so translated **(1)** in Jude 12 (figuratively), Lk 17:6; **(2)** "root up," Mt 13:29; "shall be rooted up," 15:13. See: TDNT—6:991, 985; BAGD—244d; THAYER—199c.

1611. ἔκστασις {7x} **ĕkstasis,** *ek'-stas-is;* from *1839;* a *displacement* of the mind, i.e. *bewilderment,* "ecstasy":—be amazed + 3083 {2x}, amazement {1x}, astonishment {1x}, trance {3x}.

Ekstasis is, lit., a standing out [Eng. "ecstasy"] and was said of any displacement, and especially, with reference to the mind, of that alteration of the normal condition by which the person is thrown into a state of surprise or fear, or both; **(1)** or again, in which a person is so transported out of his natural state that he falls into a trance (Acts 10:10; 11:5; 22:17). As

to the other meanings: **(2)** "astonishment", see Mk 5:42 and Lk 5:26; but **(3)** "amazed"in Mk 16:8; Lk 5:26; and **(4)** "amazement" in Acts 3:10. Syn.: 1568, 1569, 2285. See: TDNT—2:449, 217; BAGD—245a; THAYER—199c.

1612. ἐκστρέφω {1x} **ĕkstrĕphō,** *ek-stref'-o;* from *1537* and *4762;* to *pervert* (fig.):—subvert {1x}.

The word means to turn inside out, to change entirely and is used metaphorically in Titus 3:11. See: BAGD—245b; THAYER—199d.

1613. ἐκταράσσω {1x} **ĕktarassō,** *ek-tar-as'-so;* from *1537* and *5015;* to *disturb wholly:*—exceedingly trouble {1x}. See: BAGD—245b; THAYER—199d.

1614. ἐκτείνω {16x} **ĕktĕinō,** *ek-ti'-no;* from *1537* and τείνω **tĕinō** (to *stretch*); to *extend:*—cast {1x}, put forth {3x}, stretch forth {10x}, stretch out {2x}.

Ekteino means **(1)** "to stretch forth," is so rendered in Mt 12:13 (twice); 49; 14:31; Mk 3:5 (first part), Lk 6:10; Lk 22:53; Jn 21:18; Acts 4:30; 26:1 **(2)** "put forth" in Mt 8:3; Mk 1:41; Lk 5:13; **(3)** "cast" in Acts 27:30; and **(4)** "stretch out" in Mt 26:51; Mk 3:5 (second part). See: TDNT—2:460, 219; BAGD—245b; THAYER—199d.

1615. ἐκτελέω {2x} **ĕktĕlĕō,** *ek-tel-eh'-o;* from *1537* and *5055;* to *complete fully:*—finish {2x}.

Ekteleo literally means, "to finish out," i.e., "completely" (*ek,* "out," intensive), and is used in Lk 14:29, 30. See: BAGD—245c; THAYER—200a.

1616. ἐκτένεια {1x} **ĕktĕnĕia,** *ek-ten-i'-ah;* from *1618; intentness (of mind):*—instantly + 1722 {7x}. See: TDNT—2:464, 219; BAGD—245c; THAYER—200a.

1617. ἐκτενέστερον {1x} **ĕktĕnĕstĕrŏn,** *ek-ten-es'-ter-on;* neut. of the comparative of *1618; more intently:*—more earnestly {1x}.

Ektenesteron, the comparative degree, used as an adverb in this neuter form, denotes "more earnestly, fervently," Lk 22:44. See: TDNT—2:463, 219; BAGD—245c; THAYER—200a.

1618. ἐκτενής {2x} **ĕktĕnēs,** *ek-ten-ace';* from *1614; intent:*—without ceasing {1x}, fervent {1x}.

Ektenes denotes "strained, stretched out"; hence, **(1)** metaphorically, "fervent," 1 Pet 4:8; and **(2)** the adverb, "without ceasing" in Acts 12:5. See: TDNT—2:463, 219; BAGD—245c; THAYER—200a.

Greek

1619. ἐκτενῶς {1x} **ĕktĕnōs,** *ek-ten-oce';* adv. from *1618; intently:*—fervently {1x}.

In 1 Pet 1:22, "fervently"; the idea suggested is that of not relaxing in effort and acting in a right spirit. See: BAGD—245d; THAYER—200a.

1620. ἐκτίθημι {4x} **ĕktithēmi,** *ek-tith'-ay-mee;* from *1537* and *5087;* to *expose;* fig. to *declare:*—cast out {1x}, expound {3x}.

Ektithemi, "to set out, expose" is used **(1)** literally, Acts 7:21; **(2)** metaphorically, in the middle voice, to set forth, "expound," **(2a)** of circumstances, Acts 11:4; **(2b)** of the way of God, Acts 18:26; **(2c)** of the kingdom of God, Acts 28:23. See: BAGD—245d; THAYER—200a.

1621. ἐκτινάσσω {4x} **ĕktinassō,** *ek-tin-as'-so;* from *1537* and τινάσσω *tinassō* (to *swing*); to *shake* violently:—shake {1x}, shake off {3x}.

Ektinasso, "to shake out," is used **(1)** of "shaking off" the dust from the feet, Mt 10:14; Mk 6:11; Acts 13:51; **(2)** of "shaking out" one's raiment, Acts 18:6. See: BAGD—245d; THAYER—200b.

1622. ἐκτός {9x} **ĕktŏs,** *ek-tos';* from *1537;* the *exterior;* fig. (as a prep.) *aside from, besides:*—out of {2x}, outside {1x}, other than {1x}, without {1x}, be excepted {1x}, except + 1508 {1x}, unless + 1508 {1x}, but + 1508 {1x}.

Ektos, an adverb, lit., "outside," is used with *ei me,* as an extended conjunction signifying **(1)** "except", in 1 Cor 14:5; **(2)** in 1 Cor 15:2 "unless"; **(3)** in 1 Ti 5:19 "but." **(4)** It has the force of a preposition in the sense of **(4a)** "without" in 1 Cor 6:18; **(4b)** "out of" in 2 Cor 12:2–3; **(4c)** "other than" in Acts 26:22; **(4d)** in 1 Cor 15:27 "excepted." **(5)** For its use as a noun see Mt 23:26, "(the) outside of." See: BAGD—246a; THAYER—200b.

1623. ἕκτος {14x} **hĕktŏs,** *hek'-tos;* ordinal from *1803; sixth:*—sixth {14x}. See: BAGD—246a; THAYER—200b.

1624. ἐκτρέπω {5x} **ĕktrĕpō,** *ek-trep'-o;* from *1537* and the base of *5157;* to *deflect,* i.e. *turn away* (lit. or fig.):—turn aside {2x}, avoid {1x}, turn {1x}, turn out of the way {1x}.

Ektrepo, lit., "to turn or twist out," is used **(1)** in the passive voice in Heb 12:13, "that which is lame be not turned out of the way" (or rather, "put out of joint"); **(2)** in the sense of the middle voice (though passive in form) of turning aside, or turning away from, 2 Ti 4:4

"shall be turned unto fables; **(3)** in 1 Ti 1:6, of those who, having swerved from the faith, have turned aside unto vain talking; **(4)** in 1 Ti 5:15, of those who have turned aside after Satan; **(5)** in 6:20, of "avoiding" profane babblings and oppositions of the knowledge which is falsely so called. See: BAGD—246b; THAYER—200c.

1625. ἐκτρέφω {2x} **ĕktrĕphō,** *ek-tref'-o;* from *1537* and *5142;* to *rear up* to maturity, i.e. (gen.) to *cherish* or *train:*—bring up {1x}, nourish {1x}.

This word means **(1)** "to nourish (up to maturity)" Eph 5:29; or **(2)** "bring up (to maturity)", Eph 6:4. See: BAGD—246c; THAYER—200c.

1626. ἔκτρωμα {1x} **ĕktrōma,** *ek'-tro-mah;* from a compound of *1537* and τιτρώσκω *titrōskō* (to *wound*); a *miscarriage* (*abortion*), i.e. (by anal.) *untimely birth:*—born out of due time {1x}.

Ektroma, as a noun, denotes "an abortion, an untimely birth": "And last of all He was seen of me also, as of one born out of due time" (1 Cor 15:8). The apostle likens himself to "one born out of due time"; i.e., in point of time, inferior to the rest of the apostles, as an immature birth comes short of a mature one. Syn.: 313, 616, 738, 1080, 1084, 1085, 5088. See: TDNT—2:465, 220; BAGD—246c; THAYER—200d.

1627. ἐκφέρω {7x} **ĕkphĕrō,** *ek-fer'-o;* from *1537* and *5342;* to *bear out* (lit. or fig.):—bear {1x}, bring forth {2x}, carry forth {1x}, carry out {3x}.

Ekphero is used, literally, **(1)** "of carrying something forth, or out," **(1a)** e.g., a garment, Lk 15:22; **(1b)** sick folk, Acts 5:15; **(1c)** a corpse, Acts 5:6; 9–10; **(1d)** of the impossibility of "carrying" anything out from this world at death, 1 Ti 6:7. **(2)** It is also used of the earth, in "bringing forth" produce, Heb. 6:8. See: BAGD—246d; THAYER—200d.

1628. ἐκφεύγω {7x} **ĕkphĕugō,** *ek-fyoo'-go;* from *1537* and *5343;* to *flee out:*—escape {5x}, flee {2x}.

This word means "to flee out of a place" and is said **(1)** of the "escape" of prisoners, Acts 16:27; **(2)** of Sceva's sons, "fleeing" from the man with an evil spirit, Acts 19:16; **(3)** of Paul's escape from Damascus, 2 Cor 11:33; **(4)** elsewhere with reference to the judgments of God, Lk 21:36; Rom 2:3; Heb 2:3; 12:25; 1 Th 5:3. See: BAGD—246d; THAYER—200d.

1629. ἐκφοβέω {1x} **ĕkphŏbĕō,** *ek-fob-eh'-o;* from *1537* and *5399;* to *frighten utterly away:*—terrify {1x}. See: BAGD—247a; THAYER—201a.

1630. **ἔκφοβος** {2x} **ĕkphŏbŏs,** *ek'-fob-os;* from *1537* and *5401; frightened out* of one's wits: sore afraid {1x}, exceedingly fear + 1510 {1x}.

Ekphobos signifies "frightened outright" **(1)** Heb 12:21 (with *eimi,* "I am"), "I exceedingly fear"; **(2)** Mk 9:6, "sore afraid." See: BAGD—247a; THAYER—201a.

1631. **ἐκφύω** {2x} **ĕkphuō,** *ek-foo'-o;* from *1537* and *5453;* to *sprout up:*—put forth {2x}.

This word means "to cause to grow out, put forth" (*ek,* "out," *phuo,* "to bring forth, produce, beget"), and is used of the leaves of a tree, Mt 24:32; Mk 13:28, "putteth forth." See: BAGD—247b; THAYER—201a.

1632. **ἐκχέω** {28x} **ĕkchĕō,** *ek-kheh'-o;* or (by var.)

ἐκχύνω ĕkchunō, *ek-khoo'-no;* from *1537;* and χέω **chĕō** (to *pour*); to *pour forth;* fig. to *bestow:*—pour out {12x}, shed {4x}, shed forth {1x}, spill {1x}, run out {1x}, shed {5x}, run greedily {1x}, shed abroad {1x}, gush out {1x}, spill {1x}.

This word means "to pour out" and is used **(1)** of Christ's act as to the changers' money, Jn 2:15; **(2)** of the Holy Spirit, Acts 2:17, 18, 33, "He hath . . . shed forth"); Titus 3:6 "shed"); **(3)** of the emptying of the contents of the "vials" of divine wrath, Rev 16:1–4, 8, 10, 12, 17; **(4)** of the shedding of the blood of saints by the foes of God, Acts 22:20; Rev 16:6 "shed". See: TDNT—2:467, 220; BAGD—247b; THAYER—201a.

1633. **ἐκχωρέω** {1x} **ĕkchōrĕō,** *ek-kho-reh'-o;* from *1537* and *5562;* to *depart:*—depart out {1x}.

Ekchoreo signifies "to depart out", "to leave a place" in the sense of fleeing from," Lk 21:21 (twice). See: BAGD—247c; THAYER—201c.

1634. **ἐκψύχω** {3x} **ĕkpsuchō,** *ek-psoo'-kho;* from *1537* and *5594;* to *expire:*—give up the ghost {2x}, yield up the ghost {1x}.

Ekpsucho means "to expire," lit., "to breathe out the soul (or life), to give up the ghost" (*ek,* "out," *psuche,* "the soul"), and is used in Acts 5:5, 10; 12:23. See: BAGD—247c; THAYER—201c.

1635. **ἑκών** {2x} **hĕkōn,** *hek-own';* of uncert. aff.; *voluntary:*—willingly {2x}.

Hekon "of free will, willingly," occurs **(1)** in Rom 8:20 "willingly"; **(2)** 1 Cor 9:17 "willingly." See: TDNT—2:469, 221; BAGD—247d; THAYER—201c.

1636. **ἐλαία** {15x} **ĕlaia,** *el-ah'-yah;* fem. of a presumed der. from an obsolete primary; an *olive* (the tree or the fruit):—olives {11x}, olive tree {3x}, olive berries {1x}.

This word denotes **(1)** "an olive tree," Rom 11:17, 24; Rev 11:4 (plural); **(2)** the Mount of Olives was so called from the numerous olive trees there, and indicates the importance attached to such; the Mount is mentioned in the NT in connection only with the Lord's life on earth, Mt 21:1; 24:3; 26:30; Mk 11:1; 13:3; 14:26; Lk 19:37; 22:39; Jn 8:1; **(3)** "an olive," Jas 3:12 "olive berries." See: BAGD—247d; THAYER—201c.

1637. **ἔλαιον** {11x} **ĕlaiŏn,** *el'-ah-yon;* neut. of the same as *1636;* olive *oil:*—oil {11x}.

In the NT the uses mentioned were **(1)** for lamps, in which the "oil" is a symbol of the Holy Spirit, Mt 25:3–4, 8; **(2)** as a medicinal agent, for healing, Lk 10:34; **(3)** for anointing at feasts, Lk 7:46; **(4)** on festive occasions, Heb 1:9, where the reference is probably to the consecration of kings; **(5)** as an accompaniment of miraculous power, Mk 6:13, or of the prayer of faith, Jas 5:14. **(6)** For its general use in commerce, see Lk 16:6; Rev 6:6; 18:13. Syn.: **(A)** *Muron* denotes "ointment." **(A1)** The distinction between this and *elaion,* "oil," is observable in Lk 7:46 in Christ's reproof of the Pharisee who, while desiring Him to eat with him, failed in the ordinary marks of courtesy; **(A2)** "My head with oil (*1637 - elaion*) thou didst not anoint (*aleipho*), but she hath anointed (*aleipho*) My feet with ointment" (*3464 - muron*). **(B)** It is used of normal, yet inexpensive courtesies; whereas, *muron (3464)* is seen as costly and rare. See also: 218, 3464, 5548. See: TDNT—2:470, 221; BAGD—247d; THAYER—201d.

1638. **ἐλαιών** {1x} **ĕlaiōn,** *el-ah-yone';* from *1636;* an *olive-orchard,* i.e. (spec.) the *Mt. of Olives:*—Olivet {1x}. See: BAGD—248a; THAYER—201d.

1639. **Ἐλαμίτης** {1x} **Ĕlamitēs,** *el-am-ee'-tace;* of Heb. or. [5867]; an *Elamite* or Persian:—*Elamites* {1x}. See: BAGD—248a; THAYER—202a.

1640. **ἐλάσσων** {4x} **ĕlassōn,** *el-as'-sone;* or

ἐλάττων ĕlattōn *el-at-tone';* comparative of the same as *1646; smaller* (in size, quantity, age or quality):—less {1x}, under {1x}, worse {1x}, younger {1x}.

Elatton serves as a comparative degree of *mikros,* "little" and denotes "less" in **(1)** quality, as of wine, Jn 2:10, "worse;" **(2)** age, Rom 9:12, "younger"; **(3)** 1 Ti 5:9, "under" neuter,

adverbially; **(4)** rank, Heb 7:7. See: TDNT—4:648, 593; BAGD—248b; THAYER—202a.

1641. **ἐλαττονέω** {1x} **ĕlattŏnĕō**, *el-at-ton-eh-o;* from *1640;* to *diminish,* i.e. *fall short:*—have lack {1x}.

This word means "to be less" (from *elatton,* "less"), is translated "had no lack," 2 Cor 8:15, the circumstance of the gathering of the manna being applied to the equalizing nature of cause and effect in the matter of supplying the wants of the needy. See: BAGD—248d; THAYER—202a.

1642. **ἐλαττόω** {3x} **ĕlattŏō**, *el-at-tŏ'-o;* from *1640;* to *lessen* (in rank or influence):—decrease {1x}, make lower {2x}.

Elattoo signifies "to make less or inferior, in quality, position or dignity"; **(1)** "madest . . . lower" and "hast made . . . lower," in Heb 2:7, 9. **(2)** In Jn 3:30, it is used in the middle voice, in John the Baptist's "I must decrease," indicating the special interest he had in his own "decrease," i.e., in authority and popularity. See: BAGD—248b; THAYER—202b.

1643. **ἐλαύνω** {5x} **ĕlaunō**, *el-ŏw'-no;* a prol. form of a primary verb (obsolete except in certain tenses as an altern. of this) of uncert. affin; to *push, drive, impel, urge on* (as wind, oars or demoniacal power):—carry {1x}, drive {2x}, row {2x}.

Elauno signifies "to drive, impel, urge on." It is used **(1)** of "rowing," Mk 6:48 and Jn 6:19; **(2)** of the act of a demon upon a man, Lk 8:29; **(3)** of the power of winds upon ships, Jas 3:4; and **(4)** of storms upon mists, 2 Pet 2:17 "carried." See: BAGD—248c; THAYER—202b.

1644. **ἐλαφρία** {1x} **ĕlaphria**, *el-af-ree'-ah;* from *1645; levity, not taking things seriously* (fig.), i.e. *fickleness:*—lightness {1x}. See: BAGD—248c; THAYER—202b.

1645. **ἐλαφρός** {2x} **ĕlaphrŏs**, *el-af-ros';* prob. akin to *1643* and the base of *1640; light,* i.e. *easy; not heavy:*—light {2x}.

This word means "light in weight, easy to bear," is used **(1)** of the burden imparted by Christ, Mt 11:30; **(2)** of affliction, 2 Cor 4:17. See: BAGD—248c; THAYER—202b.

1646. **ἐλάχιστος** {13x} **ĕlachistŏs**, *el-akh'-is-tos;* superl. of ἔλαχυς **ĕlachus** (*short*); used as equiv. to *3398; least* (in size, amount, dignity, etc.):—least {9x}, very little {1x}, very small {2x}, smallest {1x}.

Elachistos, "least," is a superlative degree formed from the word *elachus,* "little," the place of which was taken by *mikros* (the comparative degree being *elasson,* "less"); it is used of **(1)** size, Jas 3:4; **(2)** amount; of the management of affairs, Lk 16:10 (twice), 19:17, "very

little"; **(3)** importance, 1 Cor 6:2, "smallest (matters)"; **(4)** authority: of commandments, Mt 5:19; **(5)** estimation, **(5a)** as to persons, Mt 5:19 (2nd part); 25:40, 45; 1 Cor 15:9; **(5b)** as to a town, Mt 2:6; **(5c)** as to activities or operations, Lk 12:26; 1 Cor 4:3, "a very small thing." See: TDNT—4:648, 593; BAGD—248d; THAYER—202b.

1647. **ἐλαχιστότερος** {1x} **ĕlachistŏtĕrŏs**, *el-akh-is-tot'-er-os;* comparative of *1646; far less:*—less than the least {1x}. See: BAGD—248d; THAYER—202c.

1648. **Ἐλεάζαρ** {2x} **Ĕlĕazar**, *el-eh-ad'-zar;* of Heb. or. [499]; *Eleazar,* an Isr.:—*Eleazar* {2x}. See: BAGD—249a; THAYER—202c.

1649. **ἔλεγξις** {1x} **ĕlĕgxis**, *el'-eng-xis;* from *1651; refutation,* i.e. *reproof:*—rebuke + 2192 {1x}. See: TDNT—2:476, 221; BAGD—249a; THAYER—202c.

1650. **ἔλεγχος** {2x} **ĕlĕgchŏs**, *el'-eng-khos;* from *1651; proof, conviction:*—evidence {1x}, reproof {1x}.

Elegchos, "a reproof", is found in 2 Ti 3:16 and in Heb 11:1, "evidence." See: TDNT—2:476, 221; BAGD—249a; THAYER—202d.

1651. **ἐλέγχω** {17x} **ĕlĕgchō**, *el-eng'-kho;* of uncert. aff.; to *confute, admonish:*—reprove {6x}, rebuke {5x}, convince {4x}, tell (one's) fault {1x}, convict {1x}.

(1) This word means to rebuke another with the truth so that the person confesses, or at least is convicted of his sin. Although convicted, he may not be convinced. **(2)** The world will be convicted by the Holy Spirit (Jn 16:8) but not all will change. **(3)** Jesus was charged with sin (Mt 9:3; Jn 9:16) but none convicted nor convinced Him of sin (Jn 8:46). It signifies **(4)** "to convict, confute, refute," usually with the suggestion of putting the convicted person to shame; **(5)** see Mt 18:15, where more than telling the offender his fault is in view; **(6)** it is used of "convicting" of sin, Jn 8:46; **(7)** gainsayers in regard to the faith, Titus 1:9; **(8)** transgressors of the Law, Jas 2:9; Jn 8:9; **(9)** "to convince," 1 Cor 14:24, for the unbeliever is there viewed as being reproved for, or "convicted" of, his sinful state; so in Lk 3:19; **(10)** it is used of reproving works, Jn 3:20; Eph 5:11, 13; 1 Ti 5:20; 2 Ti 4:2; Titus 1:13; 2:15; all these speak of reproof by word of mouth. **(11)** In Heb 12:5 and Rev 3:19, the word is used of reproving by action. Syn.: 156, 1650, 2008. See: TDNT—2:473, 221; BAGD—249b; THAYER—202d.

1652. ἐλεεινός {2x} ĕlĕĕinŏs, *el-eh-i-nos'; from 1656; pitiable:*—miserable {2x}.

Here the idea is probably that of a combination of "misery" and pitiableness. Misearable comes from "miser," one who has the means available to relieve his pain, but chooses not to take advantage of it; hence, miserable, and one to be pitied. See: BAGD—249c; THAYER—203a.

1653. ἐλεέω {31x} ĕlĕĕō, *el-eh-eh'-o; from 1656; to compassionate* (by word or deed, spec., by divine grace):—have mercy on {14x}, obtain mercy {8x}, shew mercy {2x}, have compassion {1x}, have compassion on {1x}, have pity on {1x}, have mercy {1x}, have mercy upon {1x}, receive mercy {1x}.

Eleeo (*1653*), as a verb, signifies, **(1)** in general, "to feel sympathy with the misery of another," and especially sympathy manifested in act, **(1a)** in the active voice, "to have pity or mercy on, to show mercy" to, e.g., Mt 9:27; 15:22; 17:15; 18:33; 20:30, 31; Rom 9:15, 16, 18; 11:32; 12:8; Phil 2:27; Jude 22, 23; **(1b)** in the passive voice, "to have pity or mercy shown one, to obtain mercy," Mt 5:7; Rom 11:30, 31; 1 Cor 7:25; 2 Cor 4:1; 1 Ti 1:13, 16; 1 Pet 2:10. Syn.: *Eleeo* means to feel sympathy with the misery of another, esp. such sympathy as manifests itself in act, less freq. in word. *Oiktirmos* (*3628*) denotes the inward feeling of compassion which abides in the heart. A criminal begs 1653 of his judge; but hopeless suffering is often the object of 3628. See also: 1655, 1656, 2433, 2436, 3627, 3628, 3629, 4698. See: TDNT—2:477, 222; BAGD—249c; THAYER—203a.

1654. ἐλεημοσύνη {14x} ĕlĕēmŏsunē, *el-eh-ay-mos-oo'-nay; from 1656; compassionateness,* i.e. (as exercised toward the poor) *beneficence,* or (concr.) a *benefaction:*—alms {13x}, almsdeeds {1x}.

Eleemosune, connected with *eleemon,* "merciful," signifies **(1)** "mercy, pity, particularly in giving alms," Mt 6:1, 2–4; Acts 10:2; 24:17; **(2)** the benefaction itself, the "alms" (the effect for the cause), Lk 11:41; 12:33; Acts 3:2–3, 10; 9:36, "alms-deeds"; 10:2, 4, 31. See: TDNT—2:485, 222; BAGD—249d; THAYER—203b.

1655. ἐλεήμων {2x} ĕlĕēmōn, *el-eh-ay'-mone; from 1653; compassionate* (actively):—merciful {2x}.

Eleemon, as an adjective, means "merciful," not simply possessed of pity but actively compassionate, is used **(1)** of Christ as a High Priest, Heb 2:17, and **(2)** of those who are like God, Mt 5:7. Syn.: 1653, 1656, 2433, 2436, 3627, 3628, 3629, 4698. See: TDNT—2:485, 222; BAGD—250a; THAYER—203c.

1656. ἔλεος {28x} ĕlĕŏs, *el'-eh-os; of uncert. aff.; compassion* (human or divine, espec. active):—mercy {28x}.

Summary: *Eleos* is the free gift for the forgiveness of sins and is related to the misery that sins brings. God's tender sense of our misery displays itself in His efforts to lessen and entirely remove it—efforts that are hindered and defeated only by man's continued perverseness. Grace removes guilt, mercy removes misery. *Eleos* **(1)** is the outward manifestation of pity; it assumes need on the part of him who receives it, and resources adequate to meet the need on the part of him who shows it. **(2)** It is used **(2a)** of God, **(2a1)** who is rich in mercy, Eph 2:4, and **(2a2)** who has provided salvation for all men, Titus 3:5, for Jews, Lk 1:72, and Gentiles, Rom 15:9. **(3)** He is merciful to those who fear him, Lk 1:50, for they also are compassed with infirmity, and He alone can succor them. **(4)** Hence they are to pray boldly for mercy, **(4a)** Heb 4:16, and if for themselves, **(4b)** it is seemly that they should ask for mercy for one another, Gal 6:16; 1 Ti 1:2.

(5) When God brings His salvation to its issue at the Second Coming of Christ, His people will obtain His mercy, 2 Ti 1:16; Jude 21; **(6)** It is used of men; for since God is merciful to them, He would have them show mercy to one another, Mt 9:13; 12:7; 23:23; Lk 10:37; Jas 2:13. **(7)** Wherever the words mercy and peace are found together they occur in that order, except in Gal 6:16. Mercy is the act of God, peace is the resulting experience in the heart of man. Grace describes God's attitude toward the lawbreaker and the rebel; mercy is His attitude toward those who are in distress. **(8)** In the order of the manifestation of God's purposes of salvation grace must go before mercy . . . only the forgiven may be blessed. . . . From this it follows that in each of the apostolic salutations where these words occur, grace precedes mercy, 1 Ti 1:2; 2 Ti 1:2; Titus 1:4; 2 Jn 3. Syn.: 1653, 1655, 2433, 2436, 3627, 3628, 3629, 4698. See: TDNT—2:477, 222; BAGD—250a; THAYER—203c.

1657. ἐλευθερία {11x} ĕlĕuthĕria, *el-yoo-ther-ee'-ah; from 1658; freedom* (legitimate or licentious, chiefly mor. or cerem.):—liberty {11x}.

Eleutheria, as a noun, means "liberty" and is **(1)** so rendered in Gal 5:1, "in the liberty wherewith Christ hath made us free." **(2)** The combination of the noun with the verb stresses the completeness of the act. **(3)** Not to bring us into another form of bondage did Christ liberate us from that in which we were born, but in order to make us free from bondage. **(4)** The word is twice rendered "liberty" in Gal 5:13.

The phraseology is that of manumission from slavery, which among the Greeks was effected by a legal fiction, according to which the manumitted slave was purchased by a god; as the slave could not provide the money, the master paid it into the temple treasury in the presence of the slave, a document being drawn up containing the words "for freedom." No one could enslave him again, as he was the property of the god. Hence the word *apeleutheros,* "a freed man." **(5)** The word is also translated "liberty" in 1 Pet 2:16. **(6)** In 2 Cor 3:17 the word denotes "liberty" of access to the presence of God. See: TDNT—2:487, 224; BAGD—250c; THAYER—204a.

1658. ἐλεύθερος {23x} ĕlĕuthĕrŏs, *el-yoo'-ther-os;* prob. from the alt. of *2064; unrestrained* (to *go* at pleasure), i.e. (as a citizen) *not a slave* (whether *freeborn* or *manumitted*), or (gen.) *exempt* (from obligation or liability):—free {18x}, freeman {1x}, free woman {3x}, at liberty {1x}.

Eleutheros, as an adjctive, means primarily of "freedom to go wherever one likes," is used of **(1)** "freedom from restraint and obligation" in general, Mt 17:26; Rom 7:3; 1 Cor 7:39, of the second marriage of a woman; 9:1, 19; 1 Pet 2:16; **(2)** from the Law, Gal 4:26; **(3)** from sin, Jn 8:36; **(4)** with regard to righteousness, Rom 6:20 (i.e., righteousness laid no sort of bond upon them, they had no relation to it); **(5)** in a civil sense, "free" from bondage or slavery, Jn 8:33; 1 Cor 7:21, 22 (second part); 12:13; Gal 3:28; Eph 6:8; Rev 13:16; 19:18; **(6)** as a noun, "free (man)," Col 3:11; Rev 6:15; **(7)** "freewoman," Gal 4:22, 23, 30, 31. See: TDNT—2:487, 224; BAGD—250d; THAYER—204a.

1659. ἐλευθερόω {7x} ĕlĕuthĕrŏō, *el-yoo-ther-o'-o;* from *1658;* to *liberate,* i.e. (fig.) to *exempt* (from mor., cerem. or mortal liability):—deliver {1x}, make free {6x}.

Eleutheroo, as a verb, means "to set free" is translated **(1)** "deliver": "Because the creature itself also shall be delivered from the bondage of corruption into the glorious liberty of the children of God" (Rom 8:21). **(2)** In six other places it is translated "make free": "And ye shall know the truth, and the truth shall make you free" (Jn 8:32; cf. 8:36; Rom 6:18, 22; 8:2; Gal 5:1). **(3)** *Eleutheroo,* as a verb, means "to make free" and is used of deliverance from **(3a)** sin, Jn 8:32, 36; Rom 6:18, 22; **(3b)** the Law, Rom 8:2; Gal 5:1; **(3c)** the bondage of corruption, Rom 8:21. Syn.: 325, 525, 629, 591, 859, 1325, 1560, 1659, 1807, 1929, 3086, 3860, 4506, 5483. See: TDNT—2:487, 224; BAGD—250d; THAYER—204b.

ἐλεύθω ĕlĕuthō. See *2064.*

1660. ἔλευσις {1x} ĕlĕusis, *el'-yoo-sis;* from the alt. of *2064;* an *advent:*—coming {1x}. See: TDNT—2:675, 257; BAGD—251a; THAYER—204c.

1661. ἐλεφάντινος {1x} ĕlĕphantinŏs, *el-ef-an'-tee-nos;* from ἔλεφας ĕlĕphas (an "*elephant*"); *elephantine,* i.e. (by impl.) composed of *ivory:*—of ivory {1x}. See: BAGD—251a; THAYER—204c.

1662. Ἐλιακείμ {3x} Ĕliakĕim, *el-ee-ak-ehm'* or Ἐλιακίμ Ĕliakim *el-ee-ak-ime';* of Heb. or. [471]; *Eliakim,* an Isr.:—Eliakim {3x}. See: BAGD—251b; THAYER—204c.

1663. Ἐλιέζερ {1x} Ĕliĕzĕr, *el-ee-ed'-zer;* of Heb. or. [461]; *Eliezer,* an Isr.:—Eliezer {1x}. See: BAGD—251b; THAYER—204c.

1664. Ἐλιούδ {2x} Ĕliŏud, *el-ee-ood';* of Heb. or. [410 and 1935]; *God of majesty; Eliud,* an Isr.:—Eliud {2x}. See: BAGD—251b; THAYER—204c.

1665. Ἐλισάβετ {9x} Ĕlisabĕt, *el-ee-sab'-et;* of Heb. or. [472]; *Elisabet,* an Israelitess:—Elisabeth {9x}. See: BAGD—251b; THAYER—204c.

1666. Ἐλισσαῖος {1x} Ĕlissaiŏs, *el-is-sah'-yos;* of Heb. or. [477]; *Elissæus,* an Isr.:—Elissæus {1x}. See: BAGD—251b; THAYER—204c.

1667. ἐλίσσω {1x} hĕlissō, *hel-is'-so;* a form of *1507;* to *coil* or *wrap:*—fold up {1x}. See: BAGD—251b; THAYER—204d.

1668. ἕλκος {3x} hĕlkŏs, *hel'-kos;* prob. from *1670;* an *ulcer* (as if drawn together):—sore {3x}.

Elkos, "a sore" or "ulcer" (primarily a wound with a discharge), occurs in Lk 16:21; Rev 16:2, 11. See: BAGD—251c; THAYER—204d.

1669. ἑλκόω {1x} hĕlkŏō, *hel-ko'-o;* from *1668;* to *cause to ulcerate,* i.e. (pass.) *be ulcerous:*—full of sores {1x}.

Helkoo, "to wound, to ulcerate," is used in the passive voice, signifying "to suffer from sores," to be "full of sores," Lk 16:20 (perfect participle). See: BAGD—251c; THAYER—204d.

1670. ἑλκύω {8x} hĕlkuō, *hel-koo'-o;* or

ἕλκω hĕlkō, *hel'-ko;* prob. akin to *138;* to *drag* (lit. or fig.):—draw {8x}.

Helko, as a verb, is translated **(1)** "to draw": "And all the city was moved, and the people ran together: and they took Paul, and drew him out of the temple: and forthwith the doors were shut" (Acts 21:30; cf. Jas 2:6). **(2)** It differs from

suro (4951), as "drawing" does from violent "dragging." **(2a)** This less violent significance, **(2b)** usually present in *helko,* but always absent from *suro,* **(3)** is seen in the metaphorical use of *helko,* to signify "drawing" by inward power, by divine impulse, Jn 6:44; 12:32. **(4)** It is used of a more vigorous action, **(4a)** in Jn 18:10, of "drawing" a sword; **(4b)** in Acts 16:19; 21:30, of forcibly "drawing" men to or from a place; so in Jas 2:6. Syn.: It is used of "drawing" a net, Jn 21:6, 11. **(A)** At vv. 6 and 11 *helko* (or *helkuo*) is used; for there a drawing of the net to a certain point is intended; by the disciples to themselves in the ship, by Peter to himself upon the shore. **(B)** But at v. 8 *helko* gives place to *suro (4951)*: for nothing is there intended but the dragging of the net, which had been fastened to the ship, after it through the water. Syn.: 307, 385, 392, 501, 502, 645, 868, 1448, 1828, 2020, 2464, 4317, 4334, 4358, 4685, 4951, 5288, 5289. See: TDNT–2:503, 227; BAGD–251c; THAYER–204d. comp. *1667.*

1671.ˈ**Ελλάς** {1x} **Hĕllas,** *hel-las';* of uncert. aff.; *Hellas* (or *Greece*), a country of Europe:–Greece {1x}. See: TDNT–2:504, 227; BAGD–251d; THAYER–205a.

1672. ˝**Ελλην** {27x} **Hĕllēn,** *hel'-lane;* from *1671;* a *Hellen (Grecian)* or inhab. of Hellas; by extens. a *Greek-speaking* person, espec. a *non-Jew:*–Gentile {7x}, Greek {20x}.

Hellen **(1)** originally denoted the early descendants of Thessalian Hellas; then, **(2)** Greeks as opposed to barbarians, Rom 1:14. **(3)** It became applied to such Gentiles as spoke the Greek language, e.g., Gal 2:3; 3:28. **(4)** Since that was the common medium of intercourse in the Roman Empire, Greek and Gentile became more or less interchangeable terms, "Gentiles," e.g., Jn 7:35; Rom 2:9, 10; 3:9; 1 Cor 10:32, where the local church is distinguished from Jews and Gentiles; 12:13. See: TDNT–2:504, 227; BAGD–251d; THAYER–205a.

1673.ˈ**Ελληνικός** {2x} **Hĕllēnikŏs,** *hel-lay-nee-kos';* from *1672; Hellenic,* i.e. *Grecian* (in language):–Greek {2x}. See: TDNT–2:504, 227; BAGD–252a; THAYER–205b.

1674.ˈ**Ελληνίς** {2x} **Hĕllēnis,** *hel-lay-nis';* fem. of *1672;* a *Grecian* (i.e. *non-Jewish*) woman:–Greek {2x}. See: TDNT–2:504, 227; BAGD–252a; THAYER–205b.

1675.ˈ**Ελληνιστής** {3x} **Hĕllēnistēs,** *hel-lay-nis-tace';* from a der. of *1672;* a *Hellenist* or Greek-speaking Jew:–Grecian {3x}. See: TDNT–2:504, 227; BAGD–252b; THAYER–205b.

1676.ˈ**Ελληνιστί** {2x} **Hĕllēnisti,** *hel-lay-nis-tee';* adv. from the same as *1675; Hellenistically,* i.e. in the Grecian language:–Greek {2x}. See: TDNT–2:504, 227; BAGD–252b; THAYER–205b.

1677. **ἐλλογέω** {2x} **ĕllŏgĕō,** *el-log-eh'-o;* from *1722* and *3056* (in the sense of account); to *reckon in,* i.e. *attribute:*–impute {1x}, put on (one's) account {1x}.

Ellogeo, **(1)** "to put to a person's account," Philem 18, is used **(2)** of sin in Rom 5:13, "impute." See: TDNT–2:516, 229; BAGD–252b; THAYER–205b.

ἔλλομαι hĕllŏmai. See *138.*

1678. ˈ**Ελμωδάμ** {1x} **Elmōdam,** *el-mo-dam';* of Heb. or. [perh. for *486*]; *Elmodam,* an Isr.:–*Elmodam* {1x}. See: BAGD–252c; THAYER–205c.

1679. **ἐλπίζω** {32x} **ĕlpizō,** *el-pid'-zo;* from *1680;* to *expect* or *confide:*–trust {18x}, hope {10x}, hope for {2x}, things hoped for {1x}, vr hope {1x}.

Elpizo, as a verb, means **(1)** "to hope," e.g., **(1a)** Jn 5:45, "Moses, on whom ye have set your hope"; **(1b)** 2 Cor 1:10, "on whom we have set our hope"; so in 1 Ti 4:10; 5:5; 6:17; see also, e.g., Mt 12:21; Lk 24:21; Rom 15:12, 24. **(2)** The verb is followed by three prepositions: **(2a)** *eis,* rendered "on" in Jn 5:45; the meaning is really "in" as in 1 Pet 3:5, "who hoped in God"; the "hope" is thus said to be directed to, and to center in, a person; **(2b)** *epi,* "on," Rom 15:12, "in Him shall the Gentiles trust (hope)"; so 1 Ti 4:10; 5:5; **(2c)** *en,* "in," 1 Cor 15:19, "we have hoped in Christ," the preposition expresses that Christ is not simply the ground upon whom, but the sphere and element in whom, the "hope" is placed. The form of the verb (the perfect participle with the verb to be, lit., "are having hoped") stresses the character of those who "hope," more than the action; "hope" characterizes them, showing what sort of persons they are. Syn.: 560, 1680, 4276. See: BAGD–252c; THAYER–205c.

1680. **ἐλπίς** {54x} **ĕlpis,** *el-pece';* from a primary **ἔλπω ĕlpō** (to *anticipate,* usually with pleasure); *expectation* (abstr. or concr.) or *confidence:*–faith {1x}, hope {53x}.

Elpis, as a noun in the NT, "favorable and confident expectation, a forward look with assurance." **(1)** It has to do with the unseen and the future, Rom 8:24, 25. **(2)** "Hope" describes **(2a)** the anticipation of good (the most frequent significance), e.g., Titus 1:2; 1 Pet 1:21; **(2b)** the ground upon which "hope" is based, Acts 16:19; Col 1:27, "Christ in you the hope of

glory"; **(2c)** the object upon which the "hope" is fixed, e.g., 1 Ti 1:1.

(3) Various phrases are used with the word "hope," in Paul's epistles and speeches: **(3a)** Acts 23:6, "the hope and resurrection of the dead"; this has been regarded as a *hendiadys* (one by means of two), i.e., the "hope" of the resurrection; but the *kai*, "and," is epexegetic, defining the "hope," namely, the resurrection; **(3b)** Acts 26:6, 7, "the hope of the promise (i.e., the fulfillment of the promise) made unto the fathers"; **(3c)** Gal 5:5, "the hope of righteousness"; i.e., the believer's complete conformity to God's will, at the coming of Christ; **(3d)** Col 1:23, "the hope of the gospel," i.e., the "hope" of the fulfillment of all the promises presented in the gospel; cf. 1:5; **(3e)** Rom 5:2, "(the) hope of the glory of God," i.e., as in Titus 2:13, "the blessed hope and appearing of the glory of our great God and Savior Jesus Christ"; cf. Col 1:27; **(3f)** 1 Th 5:8, "the hope of salvation," i.e., of the rapture of believers, to take place at the opening of the Parousia of Christ; **(3g)** Eph 1:18, "the hope of His (God's) calling," i.e., the prospect before those who respond to His call in the gospel; **(3h)** Eph 4:4, "the hope of your calling," regarded from the point of view of the called; **(3i)** Titus 1:2, and 3:7, "the hope of eternal life," i.e., the full manifestation and realization of that life which is already the believer's possession; **(3j)** Acts 28:20, "the hope of Israel," i.e., the expectation of the coming of the Messiah.

(4) In Eph 1:18; 2:12 and 4:4, the "hope" is objective. **(5)** The objective and subjective use of the word need to be distinguished, in Rom 15:4, e.g., the use is subjective. **(6)** In the NT three adjectives are descriptive of "hope": **(6a)** "good," 2 Th 2:16; **(6b)** "blessed," Titus 2:13; **(6c)** "living," 1 Pet 1:3; **(6d)** Heb 7:19, "a better hope," i.e., additional to the commandment, which became disannulled (v. 18), a hope centered in a new priesthood. **(7)** In Rom 15:13 God is spoken of as "the God of hope," i.e., He is the author, not the subject, of it. **(8)** "Hope" is a factor in endurance, Rom 8:24; it finds its expression in endurance under trial, which is the effect of waiting for the coming of Christ, 1 Th 1:3; **(9)** it is "an anchor of the soul," staying it amidst the storms of this life, Heb 6:18, 19; **(10)** it is a purifying power, "every one that hath this hope set on Him (Christ) purifieth himself, even as He is pure," 1 Jn 3:3 (the apostle John's one mention of "hope"). **(11)** The phrase "full assurance of hope," Heb 6:11 expresses the completeness of its activity in the soul. Syn.: 560, 1679, 4276. See: TDNT—2:517, 229; BAGD—252d; THAYER—205d.

1681. Ἐλύμας {1x} **Élumas**, *el-oo'-mas;* of for. or.; *Elymas,* a wizard:— Elymas {1x}. See: BAGD—253c; THAYER—206b.

1682. ἐλωΐ {2x} **ĕlōï**, *el-o-ee';* of Chald. or. [426 with pron. suff.] *my God:—* Eloi {2x} See: BAGD—253d.; THAYER—206c.

1683. ἐμαυτοῦ {37x} **ĕmautŏu**, *em-ŏw-too';* gen. compound of *1700* and *846; of myself* (so likewise the dat.

ἐμαυτῷ **ĕmautōi**, *em-ow-to';* and acc.

ἐμαυτόν **ĕmautŏn**, *em-ow-ton'*):—myself {29x}, me {4x}, mine own self {2x}, mine own {1x}, I myself {1x}. See: BAGD—253d; THAYER—206c.

1684. ἐμβαίνω {18x} **ĕmbainō**, *em-ba'-hee-no;* from *1722* and the base of *939;* to *walk on*, i.e. *embark* (aboard a vessel), *reach* (a pool):—enter {8x}, come {2x}, get {2x}, go {2x}, take + 1519 {2x}, go up {1x}, step in {1x}. See: BAGD—254a; THAYER—206c.

1685. ἐμβάλλω {1x} **ĕmballō**, *em-bal'-lo;* from *1722* and *906;* to *throw on,* i.e. (fig.) *subject to* (eternal punishment):—cast into {1x}. See: BAGD—254a; THAYER—206c.

1686. ἐμβάπτω {3x} **ĕmbaptō**, *em-bap'-to;* from *1722* and *911;* to *whelm on*, i.e. *wet* (a part of the person, etc.) by contact with a fluid:—dip {3x}. See: BAGD—254b; THAYER—206d.

1687. ἐμβατεύω {1x} **ĕmbatĕuō**, *em-bat-yoo'-o;* from *1722* and a presumed der. of the base of *939;* equiv. to *1684;* to *intrude on* (fig.):—intrude into {1x}.

Embateuo, in Col 2:18 perhaps used in this passage as a technical term of the mystery religions, denoting the entrance of the initiated into the new life. See: TDNT—2:535, 232; BAGD—254b; THAYER—206d.

1688. ἐμβιβάζω {1x} **ĕmbibazō**, *em-bib-ad'-zo;* from *1722* and βιβάζω bibazō (to *mount;* caus. of *1684);* to *place on,* i.e. *transfer* (aboard a vessel):—put in {1x}. See: BAGD—254c; THAYER—207a.

1689. ἐμβλέπω {12x} **ĕmblĕpō**, *em-blep'-o;* from *1722* and *991;* to *look on,* i.e. (rel.) to *observe* fixedly, or (absolutely) to *discern* clearly:—behold {5x}, look upon {4x}, see {1x}, gaze up {1x}, can see {1x}.

Emblepo, as a verb, means "to look at" and **(1)** is translated "to look upon": "And Jesus looking upon them saith, With men it is impossible, but not with God" (Mk 10:27; cf. 14:67; Lk 22:61; Jn 1:36). **(2)** This verb implies a close, penetrating "look," as distinguished from *epi-*

blepo (*1914*) and *epeidon* (*1896*). Syn. for **(1) - (2)**: 308, 352, 578, 816, 872, 991, 1896, 1914, 1980, 1983, 2300, 2334, 3706, 3708, 3879, 4017, 4648. *Emblepo*, **(3)** [*en*, "in" (intensive)], expresses "earnest looking" e.g., in the Lord's command to "behold" the birds of the heaven, with the object of learning lessons of faith from them: "Behold the fowls of the air: for they sow not, neither do they reap, nor gather into barns; yet your heavenly Father feedeth them. Are ye not much better than they?" (Mt 6:26. cf. 19:26; Mk 8:25; 10:21, 27; 14:67; Lk 20:17; 22:61; Jn 1:36; of the Lord's looking upon Peter, Jn 1:42; Acts 1:11; 22:11). Syn. for **(3)**: 333, 816, 991, 1896, 2029, 2300, 2334, 2657, 2734, 3708. See: BAGD—254c; THAYER—207a.

1690. **ἐμβριμάομαι** {5x} **ĕmbrimaŏmai**, *em-brim-ah'-om-ahee;* from *1722* and βριμάομαι **brimaŏmai** (to *snort* with anger); to have *indignation on*, i.e. (tran.) to *blame*, (intr.) to *sigh* with chagrin, (spec.) to sternly *enjoin:*—straitly charge {2x}, groan {2x}, murmur against {1x}.

Embrimaomai, from *en*, "in," intensive, and *brime*, "strength," **(1)** primarily signifies "to snort with anger, as of horses." **(2)** Used of men it signifies "to fret, to be painfully moved"; then, **(3)** "to express indignation against"; hence, "to rebuke sternly, to charge strictly," Mt 9:30; Mk 1:43; **(4)** it is rendered "murmured against" in Mk 14:5; and **(5)** "groaned" in Jn 11:33; "groaning" in v. 38. See: BAGD—254d; THAYER—207a.

1691. **ἐμέ** {88x} **ĕmĕ**, *em-eh';* a prol. form of *3165; me:*—me {83x}, I {2x}, my {2x}, myself {1x}. See: BAGD—217a; [see 1423]; THAYER—207 bottom.

1692. **ἐμέω** {1x} **ĕmĕō**, *em-eh'-o;* of uncert. aff.; to *vomit:*—(will) spue {1x}. See: BAGD—254d; THAYER—207b.

1693. **ἐμμαίνομαι** {1x} **ĕmmainŏmai**, *em-mah'-ee-nom-ahee;* from *1722* and *3105;* to *rave on, furious, exceedingly mad against*, i.e. *rage at:*—be mad against {1x}. See: BAGD—255a; THAYER—207b.

1694. **Ἐμμανουήλ** {1x} **Ĕmmanŏuēl**, *em-man-oo-ale';* of Heb. or. [6005]; *God with us; Emmanuel*, a name of Christ:—Emmanuel {1x}. See: BAGD—255a; THAYER—207b.

1695. **Ἐμμαούς** {1x} **Ĕmmaŏus**, *em-mah-ooce';* prob. of Heb. or. [comp. 3222]; *Emmaüs*, a place in Pal.:—Emmaus {1x}. See: BAGD—255a; THAYER—207b.

1696. **ἐμμένω** {3x} **ĕmmĕnō**, *em-men'-o;* from *1722* and *3306;* to *stay in* the same place, i.e. (fig.) *persevere:*—continue {3x}.

Emmeno, "to remain in", is used of "continuing" **(1)** in the faith, Acts 14:22; **(2)** in the Law, Gal 3:10; **(3)** in God's covenant, Heb 8:9. See: TDNT—4:576, 581; BAGD—255b; THAYER—207c.

1697. **Ἐμμόρ** {1x} **Ĕmmŏr**, *em-mor';* of Heb. or. [2544]; *Emmor* (i.e. *Chamor*), a Canaanite:—Emmor {1x}. See: BAGD—255b; THAYER—207c.

1698. **ἐμοί** {95x} **ĕmŏi**, *em-oy';* a prol. form of *3427; to me:*—I {6x}, me {86x}, mine {2x}, my {1x}. See: BAGD—217a, c; [1473]; THAYER—207c.

1699. **ἐμός** {78x} **ĕmŏs**, *em-os';* from the oblique cases of *1473* (*1698, 1700, 1691*); *my:*—my {50x}, mine {12x}, mine own {11x}, of me {4x}, I {1x}. See: BAGD—255c; THAYER—207c.

1700. **ἐμοῦ** {109x} **ĕmŏu**, *em-oo';* a prol. form of *3450; of me:*—me {97x}, mine {1x}, my {11x}. See: BAGD—255c; THAYER—207c.

1701. **ἐμπαιγμός** {1x} **ĕmpaigmŏs**, *emp-aheeg-mos';* from *1702; derision:*—mocking {1x}. See: TDNT—5:635, 758; BAGD—255d; THAYER—207d.

1702. **ἐμπαίζω** {13x} **ĕmpaizō**, *emp-aheed'-zo;* from *1722* and *3815;* to *jeer at*, i.e. *deride:*—mock {13x}.

Empaizo, a compound of *paizo*, "to play like a child" (*pais*), "to sport, jest," prefixed by *en*, "in" or "at," is used **(1)** only in the Synoptics, and, in every instance, of the "mockery" of Christ, **(1a)** except in Mt 2:16 (there in the sense of deluding, or deceiving, of Herod by the wise men) and **(1b)** in Lk 14:29, of ridicule cast upon the one who after laying a foundation of a tower is unable to finish it. **(2)** The word is used **(2a)** prophetically by the Lord, of His impending sufferings, Mt 20:19; Mk 10:34; Lk 18:32; **(2b)** of the actual insults inflicted upon Him by the men who had taken Him from Gethsemane, Lk 22:63; **(2b1)** by Herod and his soldiers, Lk 23:11; **(2b2)** by the soldiers of the governor, Mt 27:29, 31; Mk 15:20; Lk 23:36; **(2b3)** by the chief priests, Mt 27:41; Mk 15:31. See: TDNT—5:630, 758; BAGD—255d; THAYER—207d.

1703. **ἐμπαίκτης** {2x} **ĕmpaiktēs**, *emp-aheek-tace';* from *1702;* a *derider*, i.e. (by impl.) a *false teacher:*—mockers {1x}, scoffers {1x}.

Empaiktes, "a mocker" is used **(1)** in 2 Pet 3:3, "scoffers"; and **(2)** Jude 18, "mockers." See:

TDNT—5:635, 758; BAGD—255d; THAYER—208a.

1704. ἐμπεριπατέω {1x} **ĕmpĕripatĕō**, *em-per-ee-pat-eh'-o;* from 1722 and 4043; to *perambulate on* a place, i.e. (fig.) to *be occupied among* persons:—walk in {1x}.

Emperipateo, "to walk about in, or among" is used in 2 Cor 6:16, of the activities of God in the lives of believers. See: TDNT—5:940, 804; BAGD—256a; THAYER—208a.

1705. ἐμπίπλημι {5x} **ĕmpiplēmi**, *em-pip'-lay-mee;* or

ἐμπλήθω ĕmplēthō, *em-play'-tho;* from 1722 and the base of 4118; to *fill in* (*up*), i.e. (by impl.) to *satisfy* (lit. or fig.):—fill {4x}, be full {1x}.

Empletho, "to fill full, to satisfy," is used **(1)** of "filling" the hungry, Lk 1:53; Jn 6:12; **(2)** "filling hearts", Acts 14:17; **(3)** of the abundance of the rich, Lk 6:25; **(4)** metaphorically, of a company of friends, Rom 15:24, "filled." See: TDNT—6:128, 840; BAGD—256a; THAYER—208a.

1706. ἐμπίπτω {7x} **ĕmpiptō**, *em-pip'-to;* from 1722 and 4098; to *fall on*, i.e. (lit.) to *be entrapped by*, or (fig.) *be overwhelmed with:*—fall among (into) {7x}.

Empipto, "to fall into, or among" is used **(1)** literally, Mt 12:11; 10:36; 14:5; **(2)** metaphorically, **(2a)** into condemnation, 1 Ti 3:6; **(2b)** reproach, 3:7; **(2c)** temptation and snare, 6:9; **(2d)** the hands of God in judgment, Heb 10:13. See: BAGD—256b; THAYER—208b.

1707. ἐμπλέκω {2x} **ĕmplĕkō**, *em-plek'-o;* from 1722 and 4120; to *entwine*, i.e. (fig.) *involve* with:—entangle (one's) self with {1x}, entangle therein + 5125 {1x}.

Empleko, "to weave in" (*en*, "in," *pleko*, "to weave"), hence, metaphorically, to be involved, entangled in, is used **(1)** in the passive voice in 2 Ti 2:4, "entangleth himself;" **(2)** 2 Pet 2:20, "are entangled." See: BAGD—256c; THAYER—208b.

ἐμπλήθω ĕmplēthō. See *1705*.

1708. ἐμπλοκή {1x} **ĕmplŏkē**, *em-plok-ay';* from 1707; elaborate *braiding* of the hair:—plaiting {1x}. See: BAGD—256c; THAYER—208b.

1709. ἐμπνέω {1x} **ĕmpnĕō**, *emp-neh'-o;* from 1722 and 4154; to *inhale*, i.e. (fig.) to *be animated by* (*bent upon*):—breathe out {1x}.

Empneo, lit., "to breathe in, or on," is used in Acts 9:1, indicating that threatening and slaughter were, so to speak, the elements from which Saul drew and expelled his breath. See:

TDNT—6:452, 876; BAGD—256c; THAYER—208b.

1710. ἐμπορεύομαι {2x} **ĕmpŏrĕuŏmai**, *em-por-yoo'-om-ahee;* from 1722 and 4198; to *travel in* (a country as a pedlar), i.e. (by impl.) to *trade:*—buy and sell {2x}, make merchandise {1x}.

This word primarily signifies "to travel," especially for business; then, **(1)** "to traffic, trade," Jas 4:13; then, **(2)** "to make a gain of, make merchandise of," 2 Pet 2:3. See: BAGD—256d; THAYER—208c.

1711. ἐμπορία {1x} **ĕmpŏria**, *em-por-ee'-ah;* fem. from 1713; *commerce*, *business, trade, traffic:*—merchandise {1x}. That which is sold in an *emporion* (1712). See: BAGD—256d; THAYER—208c.

1712. ἐμπόριον {1x} **ĕmpŏriŏn**, *em-por'-ee-on;* neut. from 1713; a *mart* ("*emporium*"):—merchandise {1x}.

Emporion denotes "a trading place, exchange" (Eng., "emporium"), Jn 2:16, "(a house) of merchandise." See: BAGD—257a; THAYER—208c.

1713. ἔμπορος {5x} **ĕmpŏrŏs**, *em'-por-os;* from 1722 and the base of 4198; a (wholesale) *tradesman:*—merchant {5x}.

Emporos denotes "a person on a journey" (*poros*, "a journey"), "a passenger on shipboard"; then, "a merchant," Mt 13:45; Rev 18:3, 11, 15, 23. See: BAGD—257a; THAYER—208c.

1714. ἐμπρήθω {1x} **ĕmprēthō**, *em-pray'-tho;* from 1722 and πρήθω **prēthō** (to *blow* a flame); to *enkindle*, i.e. *set on fire:*—burn up {1x}. See: BAGD—no listing; THAYER—208d.

1715. ἔμπροσθεν {48x} **ĕmprŏsthĕn**, *em'-pros-then;* from 1722 and 4314; *in front of* (in place [lit. or fig.] or time):—before {41x}, in (one's) sight {2x}, of {1x}, against {1x}, in the sight of {1x}, in the presence of {1x}, at {1x}. See: BAGD—257a; THAYER—208d.

1716. ἐμπτύω {6x} **ĕmptuō**, *emp-too'-o;* from 1722 and 4429; to *spit at* or *on:*—spit upon {2x}, spit on {2x}, spit {2x}. See: BAGD—257c; THAYER—209a.

1717. ἐμφανής {2x} **ĕmphanēs**, *em-fan-ace';* from a compound of 1722 and 5316; *apparent in* self:—show openly + 1325 + 1096 {1x}, manifest {1x}.

Emphanes is used **(1)** literally in Acts 10:40; and **(2)** metaphorically in Rom 10:20, "(I was made) manifest." See: BAGD—257c; THAYER—209b.

1718. ἐμφανίζω {10x} **ĕmphanizō**, *em-fan-id'-zo;* from 1717; to *exhibit*

(in person) or *disclose* (by words):—inform {3x}, be manifest {2x}, appear {2x}, signify {1x}, show {1x}, declare plainly {1x}.

Emphanizo, from *en,* "in," intensive, and *phaino,* "to shine," is used, either **(1)** of "physical manifestation," Mt 27:53; Heb 9:24; cf. Jn 14:22, or, **(2)** metaphorically, of "the manifestation of Christ" by the Holy Spirit in the spiritual experience of believers who abide in His love, Jn 14:21. **(3)** It has another, secondary meaning, "to make known, signify, inform." This is confined to the Acts, where it is used five times, 23:15, 22; 24:1; 25:2, 15. **(4)** There is perhaps a combination of the two meanings in Heb 11:14, i.e., to declare by oral testimony and to "manifest" by the witness of the life. See: TDNT—9:7, 1244; BAGD—257d; THAYER—209b.

1719. **ἔμφοβος** {6x} **ĕmphŏbŏs,** *em'-fob-os;* from *1722* and *5401; in fear,* i.e. *alarmed:*—afraid {3x}, affrighted {2x}, tremble + 1096 {1x}.

Emphobos, lit., "in fear" means **(1)** "afraid" Lk 24:5; Acts 10:4; 22:9; **(2)** "affrighted" Lk 24:37; Rev 11:13; and **(3)** "trembled" Acts 24:25. See: BAGD—257d; THAYER—209b.

1720. **ἐμφυσάω** {1x} **ĕmphusaō,** *em-foo-sah'-o;* from *1722* and φυσάω **phusaō** (to *puff*) [comp. *5453*]; to *blow at* or *on:*—breathe on {1x}. See: TDNT—2:536, 232; BAGD—258a; THAYER—209b.

1721. **ἔμφυτος** {1x} **ĕmphutŏs,** *em'-foo-tos;* from *1722* and a der. of *5453; implanted* (fig.):—engrafted {1x}. See: BAGD—258a; THAYER—209c.

1722. **ἐν** {{2782x}} **ĕn,** *en;* a primary prep. denoting (fixed) *position* (in place, time or state), and (by impl.) *instrumentality* (medially or constructively), i.e. a relation of *rest* (intermediate between *1519* and *1537*); *"in,"* at, (up-) on, by, etc.:—in {1874x}, by {141x}, with {134x}, among {117x}, at {112x}, on {46x}, through {37x}, misc. {321x} about, after, against, almost, altogether, as, before, between, hereby, by all means, for (. . . sake of), give self wholly to, herein, into, inwardly, mightily, (because) of, upon, [open-] ly, outwardly, one, quickly, shortly, [speedi-] ly, that, there (-in, -on), throughout, (un-) to (-ward), under, when, where (-with), while, within. Often used in compounds, with substantially the same import; rarely with verbs of motion, and then not to indicate direction, except (elliptically) by a separate (and different) prep. See: TDNT—2:537, 233; BAGD—258b; THAYER—209c.

1723. **ἐναγκαλίζομαι** {2x} **ĕnagkalizŏmai,** *en-ang-kal-id'-zom-ahee;* from *1722* and a der. of *43;* to *take in* one's *arms,* i.e. *embrace:*—take in (one's) arms {1x}, take up in (one's) arms {1x}. See: BAGD—261c; THAYER—213b.

1724. **ἐνάλιος** {1x} **ĕnaliŏs,** *en-al'-ee-os;* from *1722* and *251; in the sea,* i.e. *marine:*—things in the sea {1x}.

Enalios, "in the sea," lit., "of, or belonging to, the salt water" (from *hals,* "salt"), occurs in Jas 3:7. See: BAGD—261d; THAYER—213b.

1725. **ἔναντι** {1x} **ĕnanti,** *en'-an-tee;* from *1722* and *473; in front* (i.e. fig. *presence*) *of:*—before {1x}. See: BAGD—261d; THAYER—213b.

1726. **ἐναντίον** {5x} **ĕnantiŏn,** *en-an-tee'-on;* neut. of *1727;* (adv.) *in the presence* (*view*) *of:*—before {4x}, in the sight of {1x}.

Enantion, virtually an adverb, is used as a preposition signifying **(1)** "in the presence of, in the sight of," Mk 2:12; Lk 20:26; Acts 7:10; 8:32; **(2)** "in the judgment of," Lk 24:9. See: BAGD—261d; THAYER—213b.

1727. **ἐναντίος** {8x} **ĕnantiŏs,** *en-an-tee'-os;* from *1725; opposite;* fig. *antagonistic:*—(over) against {2x}, contrary {6x}.

Enantios, "over against" is used primarily **(1)** of place, Mk 15:39; **(2)** of an opposing wind, Mt 14:24; Mk 6:48; Acts 27:4; **(3)** metaphorically, opposed as an adversary, antagonistic, Acts 26:9; 1 Th 2:15; Titus 2:8; Acts 28:17, "against." See: BAGD—262a; THAYER—213b.

1728. **ἐνάρχομαι** {2x} **ĕnarchŏmai,** *en-ar'-khom-ahee;* from *1722* and *756;* to *commence on:*—begun {2x}.

This word means lit., "to begin in" is used in **(1)** Gal 3:3 ("having begun in the Spirit"), to refer to the time of conversion; **(2)** similarly in Phil 1:6, "He which began a good work in you." The *en* may be taken in its literal sense in these places. See: BAGD—262b; THAYER—213c.

1729. **ἐνδεής** {1x} **ĕndĕēs,** *en-deh-ace';* from a compound of *1722* and *1210* (in the sense of *lacking*); *deficient in:*—lacked {1x}. See: BAGD—262c; THAYER—213d.

1730. **ἔνδειγμα** {1x} **ĕndĕigma,** *en'-dighe-mah;* from *1731;* an *indication* (concr.):—manifest token {1x}.

Endeigma, "a plain token, a proof" is used in 2 Th 1:5 "a manifest token," said of the patient endurance and faith of the persecuted saints at Thessalonica, affording proof to themselves of their new life, and a guarantee of the vindication by God of both Himself and them. See: BAGD—262c; THAYER—213d.

1731. ἐνδείκνυμι {12x} ĕndĕiknumi, *en-dike'-noo-mee;* from *1722* and *1166;* to *indicate* (by word or act):—show {9x}, show forth {1x}, do {1x}, vr show {1x}.

This word signifies **(1)** "to show forth, prove" (middle voice), said **(1a)** of God as to **(1a1)** His power, Rom 9:17; **(1a2)** His wrath, 9:22; **(1a3)** the exceeding riches of His grace, Eph 2:7; **(1b)** of Christ, as to His longsuffering, 1 Ti 1:16; **(1c)** of Gentiles, as to "the work of the Law written in their hearts," Rom 2:15; **(1d)** of believers, as to the proof of **(1d1)** their love, 2 Cor 8:24; **(1d2)** all good fidelity, Titus 2:10; **(1d3)** meekness, 3:2; **(1d4)** love toward God's Name, Heb 6:10; **(1d5)** diligence in ministering to the saints, v. 11; **(2)** "to manifest by evil acts," 2 Ti 4:14, "did (me much evil)." See: BAGD—262c; THAYER—213d.

1732. ἔνδειξις {4x} ĕndĕixis, *en'-dike-sis;* from *1731; a pointing out; indication* (abstr.):—to declare + 1519 {1x}, to declare + 4214 {1x}, proof {1x}, evident token {1x}.

Endeixis, "a showing, pointing out" is translated **(1)** "to declare" God's righteousness, in Rom 3:25–26; **(2)** "proof" in 2 Cor 8:24; and **(3)** in Phil 1:28, "an evident token." See: BAGD—262d; THAYER—213d.

1733. ἔνδεκα {6x} hĕndĕka, *hen'-dek-ah;* from (the neut. of) *1520* and *1176;* *one* and *ten,* i.e. *eleven:*—eleven {6x}. See: BAGD—262d; THAYER—213d.

1734. ἐνδέκατος {3x} hĕndĕkatŏs, *hen-dek'-at-os;* ord. from *1733; eleventh:*—eleventh {3x}. See: BAGD—262d; THAYER—214a.

1735. ἐνδέχεται {1x} ĕndĕchĕtai, *en-dekh'-et-ahee;* third pers. sing. present of a compound of *1722* and *1209;* (impers.) *it is accepted in,* i.e. *admitted (possible); is (not) admissible:*—it can be {1x}. See: BAGD—262d; THAYER—214a.

1736. ἐνδημέω {3x} ĕndēmĕō, *en-day-meh'-o;* from a compound of *1722* and *1218;* to *be in* one's own *country,* i.e. *home* (fig.):—be at home {1x}, be present {1x}, present {1x}.

Endemeo, lit., "to be among one's people" (*en,* "in," *demos,* "people"; *endemos,* "one who is in his own place or land"), is used **(1)** metaphorically of the life on earth of believers, 2 Cor 5:6, "at home (in the body)"; **(2)** in v. 8 of the life in heaven of the spirits of believers, after their decease, "present (with the Lord)"; **(3)** in v. 9, "present" refers again to the life on earth. **(4)** In each verse the verb is contrasted with *ekdemeo,* "to be away from home, to be

absent"; **(4a)** in v. 6, "we are absent," i.e., away from "home" (from the Lord); **(4b)** in v. 8, "to be absent" (i.e., away from the "home" of the body); **(4c)** so in v. 9, "absent." **(5)** The implication in being "at home with the Lord" after death is a testimony against the doctrine of the unconsciousness of the spirit, when freed from the natural body. See: TDNT—2:63, 149 BAGD—263a; THAYER—214a.

1737. ἐνδιδύσκω {2x} ĕndiduskō, *en-did-oos'-ko;* a prol. form of *1746;* to *invest* (with a garment):—clothed in {1x}, wear {1x}.

Endidusko, as a verb, means "to wear clothes, be clothed" [the termination,—*sko* suggests the beginning or progress of the action]. The verb is used **(1)** in the middle voice in Lk 16:19: "There was a certain rich man, which was clothed in purple and fine linen, and fared sumptuously every day." **(2)** It is used in Lk 8:27 of a devil-possessed man: "And when He (Jesus) went forth to land, there met Him out of the city a certain man, which had devils long time, and ware no clothes, neither abode in any house, but in the tombs." Syn.: 294, 1463, 1746, 1902, 2439, 4016. See: BAGD—263a; THAYER—214a.

1738. ἔνδικος {2x} ĕndikŏs, *en'-dee-kos;* from *1722* and *1349; in* the *right,* i.e. *equitable:*—just {2x}.

Endikos is said **(1)** of the condemnation of those who say "Let us do evil, that good may come," Rom 3:8; **(2)** of the recompense of reward of transgressions under the Law, Heb 2:2. See: BAGD—263b; THAYER—214a.

1739. ἐνδόμησις {1x} ĕndŏmēsis, *en-dom'-ay-sis;* from a compound of *1722* and a der. of the base of *1218;* a *housing in* (*residence*), i.e. *structure:*—building {1x}. See: BAGD—263b; THAYER—214a.

1740. ἐνδοξάζω {2x} ĕndŏxazō, *en-dox-ad'-zo;* from *1741;* to *glorify:*—glorify {2x}.

Endoxazo signifies, in the passive voice, "to be glorified," i.e., to exhibit one's glory; it is said **(1)** of God, regarding His saints in the future, 2 Th 1:10, and **(2)** of the name of the Lord Jesus as "glorified" in them in the present, v. 12. See: TDNT—2:254, 178; BAGD—263b; THAYER—214.

1741. ἔνδοξος {4x} ĕndŏxŏs, *en'-dox-os;* from *1722* and *1391; in glory,* i.e. *splendid,* (fig.) *noble:*—glorious {2x}, gorgeously {1x}, honourable {1x}.

Endoxos signifies **(1)** "held in honor", "of high repute," 1 Cor 4:10, "are honorable"); **(2)** "splendid, glorious," said **(2a)** of apparel, Lk

7:25, "gorgeously"; **(2b)** of the works of Christ, Lk 13:17; **(2c)** of the church, Eph 5:27. See: TDNT−2:254, 178; BAGD−263b; THAYER− 214b.

1742. **ἔνδυμα** {8x} **ĕnduma**, *en'-doo-mah;* from *1746; apparel* (espec. the outer *robe*):−clothing {1x}, garment {2x}, raiment {5x}.

In the NT it is used **(1)** of John the Baptist's raiment, Mt 3:4; **(2)** of raiment in general, Mt 6:25, 28; Lk 12:23; **(3)** metaphorically, **(3a)** of sheep's clothing, Mt 7:15; **(3b)** of a wedding garment, Mt 22:11–12; **(3c)** of the raiment of the angel at the tomb of the Lord after His resurrection, Mt 28:3. See: BAGD−263c.214b.

1743. **ἐνδυναμόω** {8x} **ĕndunamŏō**, *en-doo-nam-ŏ'-o;* from *1722* and *1412;* to *empower:*−be strong {2x}, was strong {1x}, strengthen {2x}, increase in strength {1x}, enable {1x}, be made strong {1x}.

Endunamoo, "to make strong" (*en,* "in," *dunamis,* "power"), "to strengthen," is rendered **(1)** "was strong" in Rom 4:20; **(2)** "be strong," Eph 6:10; 2 Ti 2:1; **(3)** "were made strong," Heb 11:34; **(4)** "increased . . . in strength" in Acts 9:22; **(5)** "which strengtheneth" in Phil 4:13; 2 Ti 4:17 "strengthened"; **(6)** "hath enabled" in 1 Ti 1:12, more lit., "instrengthened," "inwardly strengthened," suggesting strength in soul and purpose. See: TDNT−2:284, 186; BAGD−263d; THAYER−214b.

1744. **ἐνδύνω** {1x} **ĕndunō**, *en-doo'-no;* from *1772* and *1416;* to *sink* (by impl. *wrap* [comp. *1746*]) on, i.e. (fig.) *sneak:*− creep {1x}.

Enduno means properly, "to envelop in" (*en,* "in," *duno,* "to enter"), "to put on," as of a garment, has the secondary and intransitive significance of "creeping into, insinuating oneself into," and is found with this meaning in 2 Tim 3:6. See: BAGD−263d; THAYER−214c.

1745. **ἔνδυσις** {1x} **ĕndusis**, *en'-doo-sis;* from *1746; investment* with clothing:−putting on {1x}. See: BAGD−263d; THAYER−214d.

1746. **ἐνδύω** {29x} **ĕnduō**, *en-doo'-o;* from *1722* and *1416* (in the sense of *sinking* into a garment); to *invest* with clothing (lit. or fig.):−put on {18x}, clothed with {2x}, clothed in {2x}, have on {2x}, clothe with {1x}, be endued {1x}, arrayed in {1x}, be clothed {1x}, vr put on {1x}.

Enduo, as a verb, signifies "to enter into, get into," as into clothes, "to put on" (Mk 1:6; 24:49; 2 Cor 5:3; Rev 1:13; 19:14). This word means literally to sink into (clothing), put on, clothe one's self. Syn.: 294, 1463, 1737, 1902,

2439, 4016. See: TDNT−2:319, 192; BAGD− 264a; THAYER−214d.

ἐνέγκω ĕnĕgkō. See *5342*.

1747. **ἐνέδρα** {1x} **ĕnĕdra**, *en-ed'-rah;* fem. from *1722* and the base of *1476;* an *ambuscade, lying in wait, an ambush,* i.e. (fig.) murderous *purpose:*−a laying wait + 4060 {1x}. See: BAGD−264c; THAYER−215a. See also *1749*.

1748. **ἐνεδρεύω** {2x} **ĕnĕdrĕuō**, *en-ed-ryoo'-o;* from *1747;* to *lurk,* i.e. (fig.) *plot a trap or plan for* assassination:−to lay in wait for {1x}, lay wait for {1x}. Cf. Lk 11:54; Acts 23:21. See: BAGD−264c; THAYER− 215a.

1749. **ἔνεδρον** {1x} **ĕnĕdrŏn**, *en'-ed-ron;* neut. of the same as *1747;* an *ambush,* i.e. (fig.) murderous *design:*−lying in wait {1x}. See: BAGD−264C; THAYER−215a.

1750. **ἐνειλέω** {1x} **ĕnĕilĕō**, *en-i-leh'-o;* from *1772* and the base of *1507;* to *enwrap:*−wrap in {1x}.

Eneileo, "to roll in, wind in," is used in Mk 15:46, of "winding" the cloth around the Lord's body, "wrapped." See: BAGD−264C; THAYER− 215a.

1751. **ἔνειμι** {1x} **ĕnĕimi**, *en'-i-mee;* from *1772* and *1510;* to *be within* (neut. part. plur.):−such things as (one) has {1x}. See: BAGD−264c; THAYER−215a. See also *1762*.

1752. **ἕνεκα** {25x} **hĕnĕka**, *hen'-ek-ah;* or

ἕνεκεν hĕnĕkĕn, *hen'-ek-en;* or

εἵνεκεν hĕinĕkĕn, *hi'-nek-en;* of uncert. aff.; *on account of:*−for . . . sake {14x}, for . . . cause {5x}, for {2x}, because + 3739 {1x}, wherefore + 5101 {1x}, by reason of {1x}, that . . . might {1x}. See: BAGD−264d; THAYER−215b.

1753. **ἐνέργεια** {8x} **ĕnĕrgĕia**, *en-erg'-i-ah;* from *1756; efficiency* ("energy"):−operation {1x}, strong {1x}, effectual working {2x}, working {4x}.

Energeia (Eng., "energy") is used **(1)** of the "power" of God, **(1a)** in the resurrection of Christ, Eph 1:19; Col 2:12, "operation"; **(1b)** in the call and enduement of Paul, Eph 3:7; Col 1:29; **(1c)** in His retributive dealings in sending "strong delusion, a working of error" upon those under the rule of the Man of Sin who receive not the love of the truth, but have pleasure in unrighteousness, 2 Th 2:11; **(2)** of the "power" of Christ **(2a)** generally, Phil 3:21; **(2b)** in the church, individually, Eph 4:16; **(2c)** of the power of Satan in energizing the Man of Sin in his "parousia," 2 Th 2:9, "coming." See:

TDNT—2:652, 251; BAGD—265a; THAYER—215b.

1754. ἐνεργέω {21x} **ĕnĕrgĕō**, *en-erg-eh'-o;* from *1756;* to *be active, efficient:*—work {12x}, show forth (one's) self {2x}, wrought {1x}, be effectual {1x}, effectually work {1x}, effectual fervent {1x}, work effectually in {1x}, be might in {1x}, to do {1x}.

Energeo, lit., "to work in", "to be active, operative," is used of **(1)** God, 1 Cor 12:6; Gal 2:8; 3:5; Eph 1:11, 20; 3:20; Phil 2:13a; Col 1:29; **(2)** the Holy Spirit, 1 Cor 12:11; **(3)** the Word of God, 1 Th 2:13 (middle voice; "effectually worketh"); **(4)** supernatural power, undefined, Mt 14:2; Mk 6:14; **(5)** faith, as the energizer of love, Gal 5:6; **(6)** the example of patience in suffering, 2 Cor 1:6; **(7)** death (physical) and life (spiritual), 2 Cor 4:12; **(8)** sinful passions, Rom 7:5; **(9)** the spirit of the Evil One, Eph 2:2; **(10)** the mystery of iniquity, 2 Th 2:7. See: TDNT—2:652, 251; BAGD—265b; THAYER—215c.

1755. ἐνέργημα {2x} **ĕnĕrgēma**, *en-erg'-ay-mah;* from *1754;* an *effect; what is wrought:*—operation {1x}, working {1x}. See: TDNT—2:652, 251; BAGD—265c; THAYER—215d.

1756. ἐνεργής {3x} **ĕnĕrgēs**, *en-er-gace';* from *1722* and *2041; active, operative:*—effectual {2x}, powerful {1x}.

Energes, lit., "in work" (cf. Eng., "energetic"), is used **(1)** of the Word of God, Heb 4:12, "powerful"; **(2)** of a door for the gospel, 1 Cor 16:9, "effectual"; **(3)** of faith, Philem 6, "effectual." See: TDNT—2:652, 251; BAGD—265d; THAYER—215d.

1757. ἐνευλογέω {2x} **ĕnĕulŏgĕō**, *en-yoo-log-eh'-o;* from *1722* and *2127;* to *confer a benefit on:*—bless {2x}. Cf. Acts 3:25, and Gal 3:8. See: TDNT—2:765, 275; BAGD—265d; THAYER—215d.

1758. ἐνέχω {3x} **ĕnĕchō**, *en-ekh'-o;* from *1722* and *2192;* to *hold in* or *upon,* i.e. ensnare; by impl. to *keep a grudge:*—entangle with {1x}, have a quarrel against {1x}, urge {1x}.

Enecho, "to hold in," is said **(1)** of being "entangled" in a yoke of bondage, such as Judaism, Gal 5:1; **(2)** with the meaning to set oneself against, be urgent against, said of the plotting of Herodias against John the Baptist, Mk 6:19, "had a quarrel against"; **(3)** of the effort of the scribes and Pharisees to provoke the Lord to say something which would provide them with a ground of accusation against Him, Lk 11:53, "to urge." See: TDNT—2:828, 286; BAGD—265d; THAYER—216a.

1759. ἐνθάδε {8x} **ĕnthadĕ**, *en-thad'-eh;* from a prol. form of *1722;* prop. *within,* i.e. (of place) *here, hither:*—there {1x}, hither {4x}, here {3x}. See: BAGD—266a; THAYER—216a.

1760. ἐνθυμέομαι {3x} **ĕnthumĕŏmai**, *en-thoo-meh'-om-ahee;* from a compound of *1722* and *2372;* to *be inspirited,* i.e. *think on, ponder:*—think {3x}.

Enthumeomai, "to reflect on, ponder," is used in Mt 1:20; 9:4; Acts 10:19. Syn.: 3541. See: TDNT—3:172, 339; BAGD—266a; THAYER—216b.

1761. ἐνθύμησις {4x} **ĕnthumēsis**, *en-thoo'-may-sis;* from *1760; deliberation:*—device {1x}, thoughts {3x}.

This word denotes a cogitation, an inward reasoning and intentions, strong feelings, passion; generally, with evil surmising or supposition. The word is translated **(1)** "device" in Acts 17:29, of man's production of images; elsewhere, **(2)** "thoughts," Mt 9:4; 12:25; Heb 4:12. Syn.: 3540. See: TDNT—3:172, 339; BAGD—266b; THAYER—216b.

1762. ἔνι {6x} **ĕni**, *en'-ee;* contr. for the third pers. sing. pres. ind. of *1751;* impers. *there is* in or among:—be {1x}, there is {4x}. Cf. Gal 3:28 (thrice); Col 3:11; Jas 1:17. See: BAGD—266b; THAYER—216b.

1763. ἐνιαυτός {14x} **ĕniautŏs**, *en-ee-ŏw-tos';* prol. from a primary ἔνος **ĕnŏs** (a *year*); a *year:*—year {14x}.

Eniautos, originally "a cycle of time," is used **(1)** of a particular time marked by an event, e.g., Lk 4:19; Jn 11:49, 51; 18:13; Gal 4:10; Rev 9:15; **(2)** to mark a space of time, Acts 11:26; 18:11; Jas 4:13; 5:17; **(3)** of that which takes place every year, Heb 9:7; with *kata* Heb 9:25; 10:1, 3. See: BAGD—266b; THAYER—216c.

1764. ἐνίστημι {7x} **ĕnistēmi**, *en-is'-tay-mee;* from *1722* and *2476;* to *place on* hand, i.e. (refl.) impend, (part.) be *instant:*—come {1x}, be at hand {1x}, present {3x}, things present {2x}.

Enistemi, "to set in," or, in the middle voice and perfect tense of the active voice, "to stand in, be present," is used of the present **(1)** in contrast with the past, Heb 9:9; **(2)** in contrast to the future, Rom 8:38; 1 Cor 3:22; Gal 1:4, "present"; **(3)** 1 Cor 7:26, where "the present distress" is set in contrast to both the past and the future; **(4)** 2 Th 2:2, "is at hand"; the saints at Thessalonica, owing to their heavy afflictions, were possessed of the idea that "the day of (the) Christ" had begun; this mistake the apostle corrects; 2 Ti 3:1, "shall come." **(5)** It

is also understood as "to be present or to be imminent," and is rendered "shall come" in 2 Ti 3:1; here expressing permanence, "shall settle in (upon you)." See: TDNT—2:543, 234; BAGD—266d; THAYER—216c.

1765. ἐνισχύω {2x} **ĕnischuō**, *en-is-khoo'-o;* from *1722* and *2480;* to *invigorate* (tran. or refl.):—strengthen {2x}. Cf. Lk 22:43 and Acts 9:19. See: BAGD—266d; THAYER—216d.

1766. ἔννατος {10x} **ĕnnatŏs**, *en'-nat-os;* ord. from *1767;* *ninth:*—ninth {10x}.

The ninth hour corresponds to our 3 o'clock in the afternoon, for the sixth hour of the Jews coincides with the twelfth of the day as divided by our method, and the first hour of the day is 6 A.M. to us. See: BAGD—267a; THAYER—216d.

1767. ἐννέα {1x} **ĕnnĕa**, *en-neh'-ah;* a primary number; *nine:*—nine {1x}. See: BAGD—267a; THAYER—216d.

1768. ἐννενηκονταεννέα {4x} **ĕnnĕnēkŏntaĕnnĕa**, *en-nen-ay-kon-tah-en-neh'-ah;* from a (tenth) multiple of *1767* and *1767* itself; *ninety-nine:*—ninety and nine {4x}. See: BAGD—267a; THAYER—216b.

1769. ἐννεός {1x} **ĕnnĕŏs**, *en-neh-os';* from *1770;* *dumb* (as *making signs*), i.e. *silent* from astonishment:—speechless {1x}. See: BAGD—267a; THAYER—217a.

1770. ἐννεύω {1x} **ĕnnĕuō**, *en-nyoo'-o;* from *1722* and *3506;* to *nod at,* i.e. *beckon* or *communicate by gesture:*—make signs {1x}. See: BAGD—267a; THAYER—217a.

1771. ἔννοια {2x} **ĕnnŏia**, *en'-noy-ah;* from a compound of *1722* and *3563;* *thoughtfulness,* i.e. moral *understanding:*—intent {1x}, mind {1x}.

This word primarily means a thinking, idea, consideration and denotes purpose, intention, design (Heb 4:12-"intents;" 1 Pet 4:1- "mind"). See: TDNT—4:968, 636; BAGD—267a; THAYER—217a.

1772. ἔννομος {2x} **ĕnnŏmŏs**, *en'-nom-os;* from *1722* and *3551;* (subj.) *legal,* or (obj.) *subject* to:—lawful {1x}, under law {1x}.

This word means what is within the range of law and is translated **(1)** "lawful" in Acts 19:39, of the legal tribunals in Ephesus; and **(2)** "under the law" in relation to Christ, 1 Cor 9:21, where it is contrasted with *anomos.* The word as used by the apostle suggests not merely the condition of being under "law," but the intimacy of a relation established in the loyalty of a will devoted to his Master. See:

TDNT—4:1087, 646; BAGD—267b; THAYER—217b.

1773. ἔννυχον {1x} **ĕnnuchŏn**, *en'-noo-khon;* neut. of a compound of *1722* and *3571;* (adv.) *by night; very early, still night:*—a great while before day + *3129* {1x}. See: BAGD—267b; THAYER—217b.

1774. ἐνοικέω {6x} **ĕnŏikĕō**, *en-oy-keh'-o;* from *1722* and *3611;* to *inhabit* (fig.):—dwell in {6x}.

This word means literally to dwell in and is used, with a spiritual significance only, of the indwelling of **(1)** God in believers (2 Cor 6:16); **(2)** the Holy Spirit (Rom 8:11; 2 Ti 1:14); **(3)** the Word of Christ (Col 3:16); **(4)** faith (2 Ti 1:5); **(5)** sin in the believer (Rom 7:17). See: BAGD—267b; THAYER—217b.

1775. ἑνότης {2x} **hĕnŏtēs**, *hen-ot-ace';* from *1520;* *oneness,* i.e. (fig.) *unanimity:*—unity {2x}. Cf. Eph 4:3, 13. See: BAGD—267c; THAYER—217c.

1776. ἐνοχλέω {1x} **ĕnŏchlĕō**, *en-okh-leh'-o;* from *1722* and *3791;* to *crowd in,* i.e. (fig.) to *annoy:*—trouble {1x}. See: BAGD—267d; THAYER—217c.

1777. ἔνοχος {10x} **ĕnŏchŏs**, *en'-okh-os;* from *1758;* *liable* to (a condition, penalty or imputation):—in danger of {5x}, guilty of {4x}, subject to {1x}. See: TDNT—4:1087, 646; BAGD—267d; THAYER—217c.

1778. ἔνταλμα {3x} **ĕntalma**, *en'-tal-mah;* from *1781;* an *injunction,* i.e. relig. *precept:*—commandment {3x}.

Entalma marks more especially "the thing commanded, a commission"; in Mt 15:9; Mk 7:7; Col 2:22, "commandments." Syn.: *Entole* (*1785*), the most frequent term, denotes an injunction, charge, precept, commandment and is used of moral and religious precepts (Mt 5:19; Acts 17:15; Rom 7:8–13). *Diatagma* (*1297*) signifies that which is imposed by decree or law (Heb 11:23) and stresses the concrete character of the commandment more than *epitage* (*2003*). *Epitage* stresses the authoritativeness of the command (Rom 16:26; 1 Cor 7:6, 25). *Entalma* (*1778*) marks more especially the thing commanded, a commission (Mt 15:9; Mk 7:7; Col 2:22). See: BAGD—268b; THAYER—218a.

1779. ἐνταφιάζω {2x} **ĕntaphiazō**, *en-taf-ee-ad'-zo;* from a compound of *1722* and *5028;* to *inswathe* with cerements for interment:—bury {1x}, burial {1x}.

Entaphiazo, "to prepare a body for burial," is used of any provision for this purpose, Mt

26:12; Jn 19:40 "to bury." See: BAGD—268b; THAYER—218a.

1780. ἐνταφιασμός {2x} ĕntaphiasmŏs, *en-taf-ee-as-mos'*; from *1779; preparation* for interment:—burying {2x}.

Entaphiasmos, lit. "an entombing" (from *en*, "in," *taphos*, "a tomb"), "burying," occurs in Mk 14:8; Jn 12:7. See: BAGD—268b; THAYER—218a.

1781. ἐντέλλομαι {17x} ĕntĕllŏmai, *en-tel'-lom-ahee;* from *1722* and the base of *5056;* to *enjoin:*—command {10x}, give commandment {3x}, give charge {2x}, enjoin {1x}, charge {1x}.

Entellomai signifies "to enjoin upon, to charge with"; it is used in the middle voice in the sense **(1)** of commanding, Mt 19:7; 28:20; Mk 10:3; 13:34; Jn 8:5; 15:14, 17; Acts 13:47; Heb 9:20; 11:22, "gave commandment." **(2)** It is translated by the verb "to charge, to give charge", Mt 4:6; 17:9; Lk 4:10. See: TDNT—2:544, 234; BAGD—268b; THAYER—218a.

1782. ἐντεῦθεν {13x} ĕntĕuthĕn, *ent-yoo'-then;* from the same as *1759; hence* (lit. or fig.); (repeated) *on both sides:*—hence {6x}, on either side + 2534 {4x}, from hence {3x}. See: BAGD—268c; THAYER—218b.

1783. ἔντευξις {2x} ĕntĕuxis, *ent'-yook-sis;* from *1793;* an *interview,* i.e. (spec.) *supplication:*—intercession {1x}, prayer {1x}.

Enteuxis primarily denotes a lighting upon, a meeting with; then, a conversation; and hence, a petition. It is a technical term for approaching a king, and so for boldy approaching God in intimate intercession and prayer [seeking the presence and hearing of God on behalf of others] (1 Ti 2:1; 4:5). Syn.: 155, 1162, 1793, 2169, 2171, 2428, 4335, 5241. See: TDNT—8:244, 1191; BAGD—268d; THAYER—218b.

1784. ἔντιμος {5x} ĕntimŏs, *en'-tee-mos;* from *1722* and *5092; valued* (fig.):—dear {1x}, more honourable {1x}, precious {2x}, in reputation {1x}.

Entimos, "held in honor", **(1)** "precious, dear," is found in Lk 7:2, of the centurion's servant; **(2)** Lk 14:8, "more honorable"; **(3)** Phil 2:29, "reputation", **(4)** of devoted servants of Christ, in 1 Pet 2:4, 6, "precious," of stones, metaphorically. See: BAGD—268d; THAYER—218b.

1785. ἐντολή {71x} ĕntŏlē, *en-tol-ay';* from *1781; injunction,* i.e. an authoritative *prescription:*—commandment {69x}, precept {2x}. See: TDNT—2:545, 234; BAGD—269a; THAYER—218c.

1786. ἐντόπιος {1x} ĕntŏpiŏs, *en-top'-ee-os;* from *1722* and *5117;* a *resident:*—of that place {1x}. See: BAGD—269b; THAYER—218d.

1787. ἐντός {2x} ĕntŏs, *en-tos';* from *1722; inside* (adverb or noun):—within {2x}.

Entos, an adverb denoting "within," is once used with the article, as a noun, **(1)** of "the inside (of the cup and of the platter)," Mt 23:26, "that which is within etc."; elsewhere, **(2)** "among, in your midst," Lk 17:21. See: BAGD—269b; THAYER—218d.

1788. ἐντρέπω {9x} ĕntrĕpō, *en-trep'-o;* from *1722* and the base of *5157;* to *invert,* i.e. (fig. and refl.) in a good sense, to *respect;* or in a bad one, to *confound:*—reverence {4x}, regard {2x}, be ashamed {2x}, shame {1x}.

Entrepo, "to turn in" (*en*, "in," *trepo,* "to turn"), is **(1)** metaphorically used of "putting to shame," e.g., 1 Cor 4:14; **(2)** in the middle voice, "to reverence," in Mt 21:37; Mk 12:6; Lk 20:13; Heb 12:9; **(3)** "to regard" Lk 18:2, 4; **(4)** "to put to shame," in the passive voice, to be ashamed, that is, to turn one upon himself and so produce a feeling of "shame," a wholesome "shame" which involves a change of conduct, 1 Cor 4:14; 2 Th 3:14; Titus 2:8, the only places where it has this meaning. See: BAGD—269c; THAYER—219a.

1789. ἐντρέφω {1x} ĕntrĕphō, *en-tref'-o;* from *1722* and *5142;* (fig.) to *educate:*—nourish up in {1x}.

Entrepho, "to train up, nurture," is used metaphorically, in the passive voice, in 1 Ti 4:6, of being "nourished" in the faith. See: BAGD—269d; THAYER—219a.

1790. ἔντρομος {3x} ĕntrŏmŏs, *en'-trom-os;* from *1722* and *5156; terrified:*—tremble + 1096 {1x}, trembling {1x}, quake {1x}.

Entromos, "trembling with fear" (*en,* "in," intensive, and *tremo,* "to tremble, quake"; Eng., "tremor," etc.), is **(1)** in Acts 7:32, "trembled"; **(2)** Acts 16:29, "trembling (for fear)"; **(3)** in Heb 12:21, "quake." See: BAGD—269d; THAYER—219a.

1791. ἐντροπή {2x} ĕntrŏpē, *en-trop-ay';* from *1788; confusion:*—shame {2x}.

Entrope is a turning in upon oneself producing a recoil—based on a wholesome shame—from what is unseemly or vile (1 Cor 6:5; 15:34). Syn.: 127, 152. See: BAGD—269d; THAYER—219b.

1792. ἐντρυφάω {1x} ĕntruphaō, *en-troo-fah'-o;* from *1722* and *5171;*

to *revel in; live in luxury:*—sporting themselves {1x}.

Entruphao means to live in luxury, live delicately or luxuriously, to revel in, to take delight in; 2 Pe 2:13. See: BAGD—270a; THAYER—219b.

1793. **ἐντυγχάνω** {5x} **ĕntugchanō,** *en-toong-khan'-o; from 1722 and 5177;* to *chance upon,* i.e. (by impl.) *confer with;* by extens. to *entreat* (in favor or against):—deal with {1x}, make intercession {4x}.

Entugchano means primarily to fall in with, meet with in order to converse; then, to make petition, especially to make intercession, plead with a person **(1)** either for others: **(1a)** the Holy Spirit for the saints (8:27); **(1b)** Christ praying for the saints (Rom 8:34; Heb 7:25); or **(2)** against others: **(2a)** Paul (Acts 25:24); **(2b)** Israel by Elijah (Rom 11:2). Syn.: 1792, 5241. See: TDNT—8:242, 1191; BAGD—270a; THAYER—219b.

1794. **ἐντυλίσσω** {3x} **ĕntulissō,** *en-too-lis'-so; from 1722 and* τυλίσσω **tulissō** (to *twist;* prob. akin to *1507*); to *entwine,* i.e. *wind* up in; roll up:—wrap in {2x}, wrap together {1x}.

Entulisso, "to wrap up, roll round or about," is translated **(1)** "wrapped together" in Jn 20:7, of the cloth or "napkin" that had been wrapped around the head of the Lord before burial. "Wrapped together," might suggest that this cloth had been "rolled" or wrapped up and put in a certain part of the tomb at the Lord's resurrection, whereas, as with the body wrappings, the head cloth was lying as it had been "rolled" round His head, an evidence, to those who looked into the tomb, of the fact of His resurrection without any disturbance of the wrappings either by friend or foe or when the change took place. **(2)** It is followed by *en,* "in," and translated "wrapped" in Mt 27:59; Lk 23:53. See: BAGD—270b; THAYER—219b.

1795. **ἐντυπόω** {1x} **ĕntupŏō,** *en-too-pŏ'-o; from 1722 and a der. of 5179;* to *enstamp,* i.e. *engrave:*—engrave {1x}. See: BAGD—270b; THAYER—219c.

1796. **ἐνυβρίζω** {1x} **ĕnubrizo,** *en-oo-brid'-zo; from 1722 and 5195;* to *insult:*—do despite unto {1x}.

This word means to treat insultingly; to insult; the insulting disdain of one who considers himself superior (Heb 10:29). See: TDNT—8:295, 1200; BAGD—270b; THAYER—219c.

1797. **ἐνυπνιάζομαι** {2x} **ĕnupniazŏmai,** *en-oop-nee-ad'-zom-ahee;* mid. voice from *1798;* to *dream:*—dreams {1x}, filthy dreamers {1x}.

This word is used **(1)** in the passive voice in a phrase which means "shall be given up to dream by dreams [shall dream dreams]" and is used in Acts 2:17; **(2)** metaphorically in Jude 8, of being given over to sensuous dreamings and so defiling the flesh. See: TDNT—8:545, 1233; BAGD—270b; THAYER—219c.

1798. **ἐνύπνιον** {1x} **ĕnupniŏn,** *en-oop'-nee-on; from 1722 and 5258;* something seen *in sleep,* i.e. a *dream* (*vision* in a dream):—dream {1x}. See: TDNT—8:545, 1233; BAGD—270c; THAYER—219c.

1799. **ἐνώπιον** {97x} **ĕnōpiŏn,** *en-o'-pee-on;* neut. of a compound of *1722* and a der. of *3700; in* the *face* of (lit. or fig.):—before {64x}, in the sight of {16x}, in the presence of {7x}, in (one's) sight {5x}, in (one's) presence {2x}, to {1x}, not tr {2x}. See: BAGD—270c; THAYER—219c.

1800. **Ἐνώς** {1x} **Ēnōs,** *en-oce'; of Heb. or.* [583]; *Enos* (i.e. *Enosh*), a patriarch:—*Enos* {1x}. See: BAGD—271a; THAYER—220b.

1801. **ἐνωτίζομαι** {1x} **ĕnōtizŏmai,** *en-o-tid'-zom-ahee;* mid. voice from a compound of *1722* and *3775;* to take *in one's ear,* i.e. to *listen:*—hearken {1x}. See: TDNT—5:559, 744; BAGD—271a; THAYER—220a.

1802. **Ἐνώχ** {3x} **Ēnōch,** *en-oke'; of Heb. or.* [2585]; *Enoch* (i.e. *Chanok*), an antediluvian:—*Enoch* {3x}. See: TDNT—2:556, 237; BAGD—271a; THAYER—220c.

ἐξ ĕx. See *1537.*

1803. **ἕξ** {13x} **hĕx,** *hex;* a primary numeral; *six:*—six {13x}. See: BAGD—271b; THAYER—220c.

1804. **ἐξαγγέλλω** {1x} **ĕxaggĕllō,** *ex-ang-el'-lo; from 1537 and the base of 32;* to *publish,* i.e. *celebrate:*—shew forth {1x}.

This word means to tell out, proclaim abroad, to publish completely; it indicates a complete proclamation and is rendered "show forth" in 1 Pet 2:9. See: TDNT—1:69, 10; BAGD—271b; THAYER—220d.

1805. **ἐξαγοράζω** {4x} **ĕxagŏrazō,** *ex-ag-or-ad'-zo; from 1537 and 59;* to *buy up,* i.e. *ransom;* fig. to *rescue* from loss (*improve* opportunity):—redeem {4x}.

Exagorazo, as a verb, is a strengthened form of *agorazo* (59 - "to buy"), and denotes "to buy out," especially of purchasing a slave with a view to his freedom. **(1)** It is used in Gal 3:13 and 4:5, **(1a)** of the deliverance by Christ of Christians from the Law and its curse. **(1b)** Christ paid the ransom to God in order to satisfy the

demands of His holy character. **(2)** It is used in the middle voice, "to buy up for oneself": "Redeeming the time, because the days are evil" (Eph 5:16). **(2a)** "Redeeming the time," where "time" is *kairos*, "a season," a time in which something is seasonable, i.e., **(2b)** making the most of every opportunity, turning each to the best advantage since none can be recalled if missed (Col 4:5). Syn.: **(A)** *Agorazo* (59) means to purchase; the slave has a new owner but is still unsure of his future. **(B)** *Exagorazo* means to purchase out implying a new master and at least the slave knows he will not be sold again. **(C)** *Apolutrosis* (629) means to purchase and set totally free. See also: 3084, 3085. See: TDNT—1:124, 19; BAGD—271b.

1806. ἐξάγω {13x} **ĕxagō**, *ex-ag'-o;* from *1537* and *71;* to *lead forth:*—lead out {6x}, bring out {5x}, bring forth {1x}, fetch out {1x}. See: BAGD—271c; THAYER—220d.

1807. ἐξαιρέω {8x} **ĕxairĕō**, *ex-ahee-reh'-o;* from *1537* and *138;* act. to *tear out;* mid. voice to *select;* fig. to *release:*—deliver {5x}, pluck out {2x}, rescue {1x}.

Exaireo, as a verb, means literally **(1)** "to take out" and denotes, in the middle voice, "to take out for oneself," hence, "to deliver, to rescue," the person who does so having a special interest in the result of his act. Thus it is used, in Gal 1:4, of the act of God in "delivering" believers "out of this present evil world" the middle voice indicating His pleasure in the issue of their "deliverance": "Who gave Himself for our sins, that He might deliver (*exaireo*) us from this present evil world, according to the will of God and our Father." **(2)** It signifies to "deliver" by rescuing **(2a)** from danger: "And when Peter was come to himself, he said, Now I know of a surety, that the Lord hath sent his angel, and hath delivered me out of the hand of Herod, and from all the expectation of the people of the Jews" (Acts 12:11; cf. 23:27; 26:17); **(2b)** from bondage: "And delivered him [Joseph] out of all his afflictions, and gave him favour and wisdom in the sight of Pharaoh king of Egypt; and he made him governor over Egypt and all his house" (Acts 7:10; cf. 7:34. **(3)** It also means "to pluck out of": "And if thy right eye offend thee, pluck it out, and cast it from thee: for it is profitable for thee that one of thy members should perish, and not that thy whole body should be cast into hell" (Mt 5:29; cf. 18:9). Syn.: 325, 525, 629, 591, 859, 1325, 1560, 1659, 1929, 3086, 3860, 4506, 5483. See: BAGD—271d.; THAYER—221a.

1808. ἐξαίρω {2x} **ĕxairō**, *ex-ah'-ee-ro;* from *1537* and *142;* to *remove:*—put away {1x}, take away {1x}.

Exairo means to put away from the midst of and is used of church discipline (1 Cor 5:2, 13). See: BAGD—272a; THAYER—221a.

1809. ἐξαιτέομαι {1x} **ĕxaitĕŏmai**, *ex-ahee-teh'-om-ahee;* mid. voice from *1537* and *154;* to *demand* (for trial):—desire {1x}. See: TDNT—1:194,*; BAGD—272a; THAYER—221a.

1810. ἐξαίφνης {5x} **ĕxaiphnēs**, *ex-ah'-eef-nace;* from *1537* and the base of *160; of a sudden* (*unexpectedly*):—suddenly {5x}.

Exaiphnes, as an adverb, a strengthened form, is translated "suddenly": "Lest coming suddenly he find you sleeping" (Mk 13:36; cf. Lk 2:13; 9:39; Acts 9:3; 22:6). Syn.: 160, 869, 1819. See: BAGD—272b; THAYER—220b. comp. *1819.*

1811. ἐξακολουθέω {3x} **ĕxakŏlŏuthĕō**, *ex-ak-ol-oo-theh'-o;* from *1537* and *190;* to *follow out the end,* i.e. (fig.) to *imitate, obey,* yield to:—follow {3x}.

Exakoloutheo, as a verb, means "to follow up, or out to the end" and is used metaphorically, and only by the apostle Peter in his second epistle: **(1)** in 1:16, of cunningly devised fables; **(2)** 2:2 of lascivious doings; **(3)** 2:15, of the way of Balaam. Syn.: 190, 1096, 1377, 1872, 2614, 2628, 3877, 4870. See: TDNT—1:215, 33; BAGD—272b; THAYER—221b.

1812. ἐξακόσιοι {2x} **hĕxakŏsiŏi**, *hex-ak-os'-ee-oy;* plur. ordinal from *1803* and *1540; six hundred:*—six hundred {2x}. See: BAGD—272b; THAYER—221c.

1813. ἐξαλείφω {5x} **ĕxalĕiphō**, *ex-al-i'-fo;* from *1537* and *218;* to *smear out,* i.e. *obliterate* (*erase* tears, fig. *pardon* sin):—blot out {3x}, wipe away {2x}.

This word means to wipe and signifies to wash, or to smear completely; hence, metaphorically, in the sense of removal, to wipe away, wipe off, obliterate: **(1)** sins (Acts 3:19); **(2)** writing (Col 2:14); **(3)** of a name in a book (Rev 3:5); and **(4)** of tears (Rev 7:17; 21:4). See: BAGD—272c; THAYER—221c.

1814. ἐξάλλομαι {1x} **ĕxallŏmai**, *ex-al'-lom-ahee;* from *1537* and *242;* to *spring forth:*—leap up {1x}. See: BAGD—272c; THAYER—221c.

1815. ἐξανάστασις {1x} **ĕxanastasis**, *ex-an-as'-tas-is;* from *1817;* a *rising from* death:—resurrection {1x}. See: TDNT—1:371, 60; BAGD—272d; THAYER—221c.

1816. ἐξανατέλλω {2x} **ĕxanatĕllō**, *ex-an-at-el'-lo;* from *1537* and

393; to *start up out* of the ground, i.e. *germinate:*—spring up {2x}. Cf. Mt. 13:5; Mk 4:5. See: BAGD—272d; THAYER—221c.

1817. ἐξανίστημι {3x} **ĕxanistēmi,** *ex-an-is'-tay-mee;* from *1537* and *450;* obj. to *produce,* i.e. (fig.) *beget;* subj. to *arise,* i.e. (fig.) *object:*—raise up {2x}. rise up {1x}.

Exanistemi, as a verb, is a strengthened form of *anistemi* (*450*) and signifies (1) "to raise up": "Master, Moses wrote unto us, If a man's brother die, and leave his wife behind him, and leave no children, that his brother should take his wife, and raise up seed unto his brother" (Mk 12:19; Lk 20:28); (2) intransitively, "to rise up": "But there rose up certain of the sect of the Pharisees which believed, saying, That it was needful to circumcise them" (Acts 15:5). Syn.: 305, 393, 450, 1096, 1326, 1453, 1525, 4911. See: TDNT—1:368, 60; BAGD—272d; THAYER—221d.

1818. ἐξαπατάω {5x} **ĕxapataō,** *ex-ap-at-ah'-o;* from *1537* and *538;* to *seduce wholly:*—beguile {1x}, deceive {4x}.

Exapatao, a strengthened form, is rendered (1) "beguile," 2 Cor 11:3; literally "as the serpent thoroughly beguiled Eve." It is translated (2) "deceive" and speaks (2a) of the influence of sin, Rom 7:11; (2b) of self-deception, 1 Cor 3:18; (2c) of evil men who cause divisions, Rom 16:18; (2d) of deceitful teachers, 2 Th 2:3. See: TDNT—1:384, 65; BAGD—273a; THAYER—221d.

1819. ἐξάπινα {1x} **ĕxapina,** *ex-ap'-ee-nah;* from *1537* and a der. of the same as *160; of* a *sudden,* i.e. *unexpectedly:*—suddenly {1x}.

Exapina, as an adverb, occurs in Mk 9:8: "And suddenly (*exapina*), when they had looked round about, they saw no man any more, save Jesus only with themselves." Syn.: 160, 869, 1810. See: BAGD—273a; THAYER—221d. comp. *1810.*

1820. ἐξαπορέομαι {2x} **ĕxapŏrĕŏmai,** *ex-ap-or-eh'-om-ahee;* mid. voice from *1537* and *639;* to *be utterly at a loss,* i.e. *despond:*—in despair {1x}, despair {1x}.

Exaporeomai means to be utterly without a way, without a way through, to be quite at a loss, without resource, in despair. It is used (1) in 2 Cor 1:8 to despair of life; and (2) in 2 Cor 4:8, in the sentence "perplexed, but not in despair." See: BAGD—273a; THAYER—221d.

1821. ἐξαποστέλλω {11x} **ĕxapŏstĕllō,** *ex-ap-os-tel'-lo;* from *1537* and *649;* to *send away forth,* i.e. (on a mission) to *despatch,* or (peremptorily) to *dismiss:*—send

{2x}, send away {4x}, send forth {4x}, send out {1x}.

Exapostello denotes (1) "to send forth": (1a) of the Son by God the Father, Gal 4:4; (1b) of the Holy Spirit, Gal 4:6; (1c) an angel, Acts 12:11; (1d) the ancestors of Israel, Acts 7:12; (1e) Paul to the Gentiles, Acts 22:21; (2) "to send away," Lk 1:53; 20:10, 11; Acts 9:30; 11:22; 17:14. See: TDNT—1:406, 67; BAGD—273a; THAYER—221d.

1822. ἐξαρτίζω {2x} **ĕxartizō,** *ex-ar-tid'-zo;* from *1537* and a der. of *739;* to *finish out* (time); fig. to *equip fully* (a teacher):—accomplish + 1096 {1x}, thoroughly furnish {1x}.

Exartizo, "to fit out," means (1) "to furnish completely," 2 Ti 3:17, or (2) "to accomplish," Acts 21:5, there said of a number of days, as if to render the days complete by what was appointed for them. See: TDNT—1:475, 80; BAGD—273c; THAYER—222a.

1823. ἐξαστράπτω {1x} **ĕxastraptō,** *ex-as-trap'-to;* from *1537* and *797;* to *lighten forth,* i.e. (fig.) to *be radiant* (of very white garments):—glistening {1x}.

Exastrapto stresses the source of light is from Christ Himself; He was not reflecting light (Lk 9:29). See: BAGD—273d; THAYER—222a.

1824. ἐξαυτῆς {6x} **ĕxautēs,** *ex-ow'-tace;* from *1537* and the gen. sing. fem. of *846* (*5610* being understood); *from that* hour, i.e. *instantly:*—by and by {1x}, immediately {3x}, presently {1x}, straightway {1x}. See: BAGD—273d; THAYER—222b.

1825. ἐξεγείρω {2x} **ĕxĕgĕirō,** *ex-eg-i'-ro;* from *1537* and *1453;* to *rouse fully,* i.e. (fig.) to *resuscitate* (from death), *release* (from infliction):—raise up {2x}.

Exegeiro, is used (1) of the "resurrection" of believers, 1 Cor 6:14 [2nd part]; (2) of "raising" a person to public position, Rom 9:17, said of Pharaoh by God. See: TDNT—2:338, 195; BAGD—273d; THAYER—222b.

1826. ἔξειμι {4x} **ĕxĕimi,** *ex'-i-mee;* from *1537* and εἶμι **ĕimi** (to *go*); to *issue,* i.e. *leave* (a place), *escape* (to the shore):—depart {2x}, get [*to land*]{1x}, gone out {1x}.

Exeimi, "to go out" is rendered (1) "gone out" in Acts 13:42; (2) in Acts 27:43, "get," of mariners getting to shore; (3) in Acts 17:15, "departed"; and in Acts 20:7, "to depart." See: BAGD—273d; THAYER—222b.

1827. ἐξελέγχω {1x} **ĕxĕlĕgchō,** *ex-el-eng'-kho;* from *1537* and *1651;* to

convict fully, i.e. (by impl.) to *punish:*—convince {1x}.

Exelegcho, an intensive form, "to convince thoroughly," is used of the Lord's future "conviction" of the ungodly, Jude 15. A person can be convicted by a court, but not convinced within himself that he is guilty. A person can also be convinced of wrong doing, but no outside power convicts. See: BAGD—274a; THAYER—222b.

1828. ἐξέλκω {1x} **ĕxĕlkō,** *ex-el'-ko;* from 1537 and 1670; to *drag forth,* i.e. (fig.) to *entice* (to sin):—draw away {1x}.

Exelko, as a verb, means "to draw away, or lure forth" and is used metaphorically in Jas 1:14, of being "drawn away" by lust. As in hunting or fishing the game is "lured" from its haunt, so man's lust "allures" him from the safety of his self-restraint. Syn.: 307, 385, 392, 501, 502, 645, 868, 1448, 1670, 2020, 2464, 4317, 4334, 4358, 4685, 4951, 5288, 5289. See: BAGD—274a; THAYER—222b.

1829. ἐξέραμα {1x} **ĕxĕrama,** *ex-er'-am-ah;* from a compound of 1537 and a presumed ἐράω **ĕraō** (to *spue*); *vomit,* i.e. *food disgorged:*—vomit {1x}. See: BAGD—274b; THAYER—222c.

1830. ἐξερευνάω {1x} **ĕxĕrĕunaō,** *ex-er-yoo-nah'-o;* from 1537 and 2045; to *explore* (fig.):—search diligently {1x}. See: TDNT—2:655, 255; BAGD—274b; THAYER—222c.

1831. ἐξέρχομαι {222x} **ĕxĕrchŏmai,** *ex-er'-khom-ahee;* from 1537 and 2064; to *issue* (lit. or fig.):—go out {60x}, come {34x}, depart {28x}, go {25x}, go forth {25x}, come out {23x}, come forth {9x}, misc. {18x} = escape, get out, go (abroad, away, thence), proceed (forth), spread abroad. See: TDNT—2:678, 257; BAGD—274b; THAYER—222c.

1832. ἔξεστι {32x} **ĕxĕsti,** *ex'-es-tee* or ἔξεστιν **exestin,** *ex'-es-teen;* third pers. sing. pres. ind. of a compound of 1537 and 1510; so also

ἐξόν **ĕxŏn,** *ex-on';* neut. pres. part. of the same (with or without some form of 1510 expressed); impers. *it is right* (through the fig. idea of *being out* in public):—be lawful {29x}, let {1x}, ✕ mayest {2x}.

Exesti, an impersonal verb, signifying **(1)** "it is permitted, it is lawful" (or interrogatively, "is it lawful?"), **(2)** occurs most frequently in the synoptic Gospels and the Acts; **(2a)** elsewhere in Jn 5:10; 18:31; 1 Cor 6:12; 10:23; 2 Cor 12:4; Acts 2:29 it is rendered "let me (speak)," lit., "it being permitted"; **(2b)** in Acts 8:37, "thou mayest," lit., "it is permitted;" 16:21; **(2c)** in

21:37, "may I," lit., "is it permitted?" See: TDNT—2:560, 238; BAGD—275b; THAYER—223c.

1833. ἐξετάζω {3x} **ĕxĕtazō,** *ex-et-ad'-zo;* from 1537 and ἐτάζω **ĕtazō** (to *examine*); to *search out; test thoroughly* (by questions), i.e. *ascertain* or *interrogate:*—ask {1x}, enquire {1x}, search {1x}.

Exetazo, "to search out" (*ek,* "out," intensive, *etazo,* "to examine"), is translated **(1)** "ask," in Jn 21:12; **(2)** in Mt 2:8, "search"; and **(3)** Mt 10:11 "inquire." See: BAGD—275c; THAYER—223d.

1834. ἐξηγέομαι {6x} **ĕxēgĕŏmai,** *ex-ayg-eh'-om-ahee;* from 1537 and 2233; to *consider out* (aloud), i.e. *rehearse, unfold:*—declare {5x}, tell {1x}.

This word means **(1)** to lead out and signifies to make known, rehearse declare, tell (Lk 24:35; Acts 10:8; 15:12, 14; 21:19). **(2)** In John 1:18, in the sentence "He hath declared Him," means to unfold in teaching, to declare by making known. See: TDNT—2:908, 303; BAGD—275d; THAYER—223d.

1835. ἐξήκοντα {9x} **hĕxēkŏnta,** *hex-ay'-kon-tah;* the tenth multiple of 1803; *sixty:*—sixty {3x}, sixtyfold {1x}, threescore {5x}. See: BAGD—276a; THAYER—223d.

1836. ἑξῆς {5x} **hĕxēs,** *hex-ace';* from 2192 (in the sense of *taking hold of,* i.e. *adjoining*); *successive:*—next {1x}, next day {1x}, day after {1x}, day following {1x}, morrow {1x}.

Hexes denotes "after" with the significance of a succession of events, an event following next in order after another, Lk 7:11; 9:37; Acts 21:1; 25:17; 27:18. See: BAGD—276a; THAYER—223d.

1837. ἐξηχέομαι {1x} **ĕxēchĕŏmai,** *ex-ay-kheh'-om-ahee;* mid. voice from 1537 and 2278; to *"echo" forth,* i.e. *resound* (*be* generally *reported*):—sound forth {1x}.

Execheomai, "to sound forth as a trumpet" or "thunder" is used in 1 Th 1:8, "sounded forth," passive voice, lit., "has been sounded out." See: BAGD—276a; THAYER—224a.

1838. ἕξις {1x} **hĕxis,** *hex-is;* from 2192; *habit,* i.e. (by impl.) *experience, practice:*—use {1x}. See: BAGD—276b; THAYER—224a.

1839. ἐξίστημι {17x} **ĕxistēmi,** *ex-is'-tay-mee;* from 1537 and 2476; to *put* (*stand*) *out* of wits, i.e. *astound,* or (refl.) *become astounded, insane:*—be amazed {5x}, be astonished {6x}, bewitch {2x}, be beside

(one's) self {2x}, make astonished {1x}, wonder {1x}.

This word means to throw out of position, displace: **(1)** to amaze, Mt 12:23; Mk 2:12; 6:51; Acts 2:7; 9:21; **(2)** be astonished, Mk 5:42; Lk 2:47; 8:56; Acts 2:12; 10:45; 12:16 **(3)** bewitch, Acts 8:9, 11; **(4)** make astonished, Lk 24:22; **(5)** wonder, throw into wonderment, Act 8:13; and **(6)** to be out of one's mind, besides one's self, insane, Mk 3:21; 2 Cor 5:13. Syn.: 1611, 2285. See: TDNT—2:459, 217; BAGD—276b; THAYER—224a.

1840. **ἐξισχύω** {1x} **ĕxischuō**, *ex-is-khoo'-o;* from *1537* and *2480;* to *have full strength,* i.e. *be entirely competent:*—be able {1x}. See: BAGD—276c; THAYER—224b.

1841. **ἔξοδος** {3x} **ĕxŏdŏs**, *ex'-od-os;* from *1537* and *3598;* an *exit,* i.e. (fig.) *death:*—decease {2x}, departing {1x}.

Exodos, lit. signifies "a way out" (*ex,* "out," *hodos,* "a way"); hence, "a departure," especially from life, **(1)** "a decease"; **(1a)** in Lk 9:31, of the Lord's decease, "which He was about to accomplish"; **(1b)** in 2 Pet 1:15, of Peter's death; **(2)** "departure" from Egypt in Heb 11:22. See: TDNT—5:103, 666; BAGD—276c; THAYER—224b.

1842. **ἐξολοθρεύω** {1x} **ĕxŏlŏthrĕuō**, *ex-ol-oth-ryoo'-o;* from *1537* and *3645;* to *extirpate:*—destroy {1x}.

Exolothreuo, "to destroy utterly, to slay wholly," is found in Acts 3:23, to the "destruction" of one who would refuse to hearken to the voice of God through Christ. See: TDNT—5:170, 681; BAGD—276b; THAYER—224b.

1843. **ἐξομολογέω** {11x} **ĕxŏmŏlŏgĕō**, *ex-om-ol-og-eh'-o;* from *1537* and *3670;* to *acknowledge* or (by impl. of *assent*) *agree fully:*—confess {8x}, thank {2x}, promise {1x}.

Exomologeo, intensive, "to confess forth," i.e., "freely, openly," is used **(1)** "of a public acknowledgment or confession of sins," Mt 3:6; Mk 1:5; Acts 19:18; Jas 5:16; **(2)** "to profess or acknowledge openly," Mt 11:25 (translated "thank," but indicating the fuller idea); Phil 2:11; Rev 3:5; **(3)** "to confess by way of celebrating, giving praise," Rom 14:11; 15:9. **(4)** In Lk 10:21, it is translated "I thank," the true meaning being "I gladly acknowledge." **(5)** In Lk 22:6 it signifies "promised." See: TDNT—5:199, 687; BAGD—277a; THAYER—224c.

ἐξόν **ĕxŏn**. See *1832*.

1844. **ἐξορκίζω** {1x} **ĕxŏrkizō**, *ex-or-kid'-zo;* from *1537* and *3726;* to *extract an oath,* i.e. *conjure:*—adjure {1x}. See:

TDNT—5:464, 729; BAGD—277b; THAYER—224c.

1845. **ἐξορκιστής** {1x} **ĕxŏrkistēs**, *ex-or-kis-tace';* from *1844; one that binds by an oath* (or *spell*), i.e. (by impl.) an "*exorcist*" (*conjurer*):—exorcist {1x}. See: TDNT—5:464, 729; BAGD—277b; THAYER—224d.

1846. **ἐξορύσσω** {2x} **ĕxŏrussō**, *ex-or-oos'-so;* from *1537* and *3736;* to *dig out,* i.e. (by extens.) to *extract* (an eye), *remove* (roofing):—break up {1x}, pluck out {1x}.

Exorusso, "to dig out" is used **(1)** of the "breaking up" of part of a roof, Mk 2:4, and, **(2)** in a vivid expression, of plucking out the eyes, Gal 4:15. See: BAGD—277c; THAYER—224c.

1847. **ἐξουδενόω** {1x} **ĕxŏudĕnŏō**, *ex-oo-den-ŏ'-o;* from *1537* and a der. of the neut. of *3762;* to *make utterly nothing of,* i.e. *despise:*—set at nought {1x}. See: BAGD—277c. See also *1848;* THAYER—224d.

1848. **ἐξουθενέω** {11x} **ĕxŏuthĕnĕō**, *ex-oo-then-eh'-o;* a var. of *1847* and mean. the same:—contemptible {1x}, despise {6x}, least esteemed {1x}, set at nought {3x}.

Exoutheneo, "to make of no account" (*ex,* "out," *oudeis,* "nobody") means "to regard as nothing, to despise utterly, to treat with contempt." This is usually translated to **(1)** "set at nought," Lk 23:11; Acts 4:11; Rom 14:10; **(2)** "despise", Lk 18:9; Rom 14:3; 1 Cor 1:28; 16:11; Gal 4:14; 1 Th 5:20; **(3)** "contemptible", 2 Cor 10:10; and **(4)** "least esteemed", 1 Cor 6:4. **(4a)** It is used, not in a contemptuous sense, **(4b)** but of Gentile judges, before whom the saints are not to go to law with one another, such magistrates having no place, and therefore being "of no account" in the church. **(4c)** The apostle is not speaking of any believers as "least esteemed." See: BAGD—277c; THAYER—225a.

1849. **ἐξουσία** {103x} **ĕxŏusia**, *ex-oo-see'-ah;* from *1832* (in the sense of *ability*); *privilege,* i.e. (subj.) *force, capacity, competency, freedom,* or (obj.) *mastery* (concr. *magistrate, superhuman, potentate, token of control*), delegated *influence:*—power {69x}, authority {29x}, right {2x}, liberty {1x}, jurisdiction {1x}, strength {1x}.

Exousia, as a noun, denotes **(1)** "authority" (from the impersonal verb *exesti,* "it is lawful"). **(2)** From the meaning of "leave or permission," or liberty of doing as one pleases, **(2a)** it passed to that of "the ability or strength with which one is endued," **(2b)** then to that of the

Greek

"power of authority," the right to exercise power, e.g., Mt 9:6; 21:23; 2 Cor 10:8; **(2c)** or "the power of rule or government," the power of one whose will and commands must be obeyed by others, e.g., Mt 28:18; Jn 17:2; Jude 25; Rev 12:10; 17:13; **(2d)** more specifically of apostolic "authority," 2 Cor 10:8; 13:10; **(3)** the "power" **(3a)** of judicial decision, Jn 19:10; **(3b)** of "managing domestic affairs," Mk 13:34. **(4)** By metonymy, or name-change (the substitution of a suggestive word for the name of the thing meant), it stands for "that which is subject to authority or rule," Lk 4:6 "power"; **(5)** or, as with the English "authority," "one who possesses authority, a ruler, magistrate," Rom 13:1–3; Lk 12:11; Titus 3:1; **(6)** or "a spiritual potentate," e.g., Eph 3:10; 6:12; Col 1:16; 2:10, 15; 1 Pet 3:22. **(7)** In 1 Cor 11:10 it is used of the veil with which a woman is required to cover herself in an assembly or church, as a sign of the Lord's "authority" over the church. See: TDNT—2:562, 238; BAGD—277d; THAYER—225a.

1850. ἐξουσιάζω {4x} **ĕxŏusiazō**, *ex-oo-see-ad'-zo;* from *1849;* to *control:*—exercise authority upon {1x}, bring under the power of {1x}, have power of {2x}.

Exousiazo, as a verb, means **(1)** exercise authority upon, Gentile rulers, Lk 22:25; **(2)** bring under the power of a thing, 1 Cor 6:12, "All are within my power; but I will not put myself under the power of any one of all things;" **(3)** have power of one's body in proper marital relationships, 1 Cor 7:4 (twice). See: TDNT—2:574, 238; BAGD—279a; THAYER—225d.

1851. ἐξοχή {1x} **ĕxŏchē**, *ex-okh-ay';* from a compound of *1537* and *2192* (mean. to *stand out*); *prominence* (fig.):—principal + 2596 {1x}.

Exoche describes men of eminence, excellence, superiority, Acts 25:23. See: BAGD—279a; THAYER—226a.

1852. ἐξυπνίζω {1x} **ĕxupnizō**, *ex-oop-nid'-zo;* from *1853;* to *waken:*—awake out of sleep {1x}. See: TDNT—8:545, 1233; BAGD—279b; THAYER—226a.

1853. ἔξυπνος {1x} **ĕxupnŏs**, *ex'-oop-nos;* from *1537* and *5258; fully awake:*—wake out of sleep + 1096 {1x}. See: TDNT—8:545, 1233; BAGD—279b; THAYER—226a.

1854. ἔξω {65x} **ĕxō**, *ex'-o;* adv. from *1537; out (-side, of doors),* lit. or fig.:—without {23x}, out {16x}, out of {15x}, forth {8x}, outward {1x}, strange {1x}, away {1x}. See: TDNT—2:575, 240; BAGD—279b; THAYER—226a.

1855. ἔξωθεν {11x} **ĕxōthĕn**, *ex'-o-then;* from *1854; external (-ly):*—without {4x}, outside {2x}, from without {2x}, outward {2x}, outwardly {1x}.

Exothen is an adverb and properly signifies "from without." See: BAGD—279d; THAYER—226b.

1856. ἐξωθέω {2x} **ĕxōthĕō**, *ex-o-theh'-o;* or

ἐξώθω **ĕxōthō**, *ex-o'-tho;* from *1537* and ὠθέω **ōthĕō** (to *push*); to *expel;* by impl. to *propel:*—drive out {1x}, thrust in {1x}. Cf. Acts 7:45, 27:39. See: BAGD—280a; THAYER—226c.

1857. ἐξώτερος {3x} **ĕxōtĕrŏs**, *ex-o'-ter-os;* comp. of *1854; exterior:*—outer {3x}. Cf. Mt 8:12; 22:13; 25:30. See: BAGD—280a; THAYER—226c.

1858. ἑορτάζω {1x} **hĕŏrtazō**, *heh-or-tad'-zo;* from *1859;* to *observe a festival:*—keep the feast {1x}.

Heortazo in 1 Cor 5:8 is not the Lord's Supper, nor the Passover, but has reference to the continuous life of the believer as a festival or holy day, in freedom from "the leaven of malice and wickedness, but with the unleavened bread of sincerity and truth." See: BAGD—280a; THAYER—226c.

1859. ἑορτή {27x} **hĕŏrtē**, *heh-or-tay';* of uncert. aff.; a *festival, especially of the Jews:*—feast {26x}, holyday {1x}.

Heorte, "a feast or festival," is used **(1)** especially of those of the Jews, and particularly of the Passover; **(2)** the word is found mostly in John's Gospel (seventeen times); apart from the Gospels it is used in this way only in Acts 18:21; **(3)** in a more general way, in Col 2:16, "holy day." See: BAGD—280b; THAYER—226c.

1860. ἐπαγγελία {53x} **ĕpaggĕlia**, *ep-ang-el-ee'-ah;* from *1861;* an *announcement* (for information, assent or pledge; espec. a divine *assurance* of good):—message {52x}, promise {1x}.

Epangelia, as a noun, is **(1)** primarily a law term, **(1a)** denoting "a summons" and **(1b)** also meant "an undertaking to do or give something, a promise." **(2)** Except in Acts 23:21 it is used only of the "promises" of God. **(3)** It frequently stands for the thing "promised," and so signifies a gift graciously bestowed, not a pledge secured by negotiation; thus, **(3a)** in Gal 3:14, "the promise of the Spirit" denotes "the promised Spirit", cf. Lk 24:49; Acts 2:33 and Eph 1:13; **(3b)** in Heb 9:15, "the promise of the eternal inheritance" is "the promised eternal inheritance." **(3c)** On the other hand, in Acts 1:4, "the promise of the Father," is the "promise" made by the Father. **(4)** In Gal 3:16, the

plural "promises" is used because **(4a)** the one "promise" to Abraham was variously repeated (cf. Gen 12:1–3; 13:14–17; 15:18; 17:1–14; 22:15–18), and because **(4b)** it contained the germ of all subsequent "promises"; cf. Rom 9:4; Heb 6:12; 7:6; 8:6; 11:17; **(4c)** Gal 3 is occupied with showing that the "promise" was conditional upon faith and not upon the fulfillment of the Law. The Law was later than, and inferior to, the "promise," and did not annul it, v. 21; cf. 4:23, 28.

(5) Again, in Eph 2:12, "the covenants of the promise" does not indicate different covenants, but a covenant often renewed, all centering in Christ as the "promised" Messiah-Redeemer, and comprising the blessings to be bestowed through Him. **(6)** In 2 Cor 1:20 the plural is used of every "promise" made by God: cf. Heb 11:33; in 7:6, of special "promises" mentioned. **(7)** For other applications of the word, see, e.g., Eph 6:2; 1 Ti 4:8; 2 Ti 1:1; Heb 4:1; 2 Pet 3:4, 9; 1 Jn 1:5. **(8)** The occurrences of the word in relation to Christ and what centers in Him may be arranged under the headings **(8a)** the contents of the "promise," e.g., Acts 26:6; Rom 4:20; 1 Jn 2:25; **(8b)** the heirs, e.g., Rom 9:8; 15:8; Gal 3:29; Heb 11:9; **(8c)** the conditions, e.g., Rom 4:13, 14; Gal 3:14–22; Heb 10:36. See: TDNT–2:576, 240; BAGD–280c; THAYER–226d.

1861. ἐπαγγέλλω {15x} **ĕpaggĕllō**, *ep-ang-el'-lo;* from *1909* and the base of *32;* to *announce upon* (refl.), i.e. (by impl.) to *engage* to do something, to *assert* something respecting oneself:—profess {2x}, make promise {2x}, promise {11x}.

Epangello, as a verb, means "to announce, proclaim," has in the NT the two meanings "to profess" and "to promise," each used in the middle voice; of "promises" **(1)** of God, Acts 7:5; Rom 4:21; in Gal 3:19, passive voice; Titus 1:2; Heb 6:13; 10:23; 11:11; 12:26; Jas 1:12; 2:5; 1 Jn 2:25; **(2)** made by men, Mk 14:11; 2 Pet 2:19. See: TDNT–2:576, 240; BAGD–280d; THAYER–227b.

1862. ἐπάγγελμα {2x} **ĕpaggĕlma**, *ep-ang'-el-mah;* from *1861;* a *self-committal* (by *assurance* of conferring some good):—a promise {2x}.

Epangelma denotes "a promise made," 2 Pet 1:4; 3:13. See: TDNT–2:585, 240; BAGD–281a; THAYER–227c.

1863. ἐπάγω {3x} **ĕpagō**, *ep-ag'-o;* from *1909* and *71;* to *superinduce*, i.e. *inflict* (an evil), *charge* (a crime):—bring {1x}, bring upon {1x}, bring in upon {1x}.

This word means to cause something to be-fall one, usually something evil, Acts 5:28; 2 Pet 2:1, 5. See: BAGD–281b; THAYER–227c.

1864. ἐπαγωνίζομαι {1x} **ĕpagōnizŏmai**, *ep-ag-o-nid'-zom-ahee;* from *1909* and *75;* to *struggle for:*—earnestly contend for {1x}.

This word signifies to contend about a thing, as a combatant. The word "earnestly" is added to convey the intensive force of the preposition (Jude 3). See: TDNT–1:134, 20; BAGD–281b; THAYER–227c.

1865. ἐπαθροίζω {1x} **ĕpathrŏizō**, *ep-ath-roid'-zo;* from *1909* and ἀθροίζω **athrŏizō** (to *assemble*); to *accumulate:*—gather thick together {1x}. See: BAGD–281b; THAYER–227c.

1866. Ἐπαίνετος {1x} **Ĕpainĕtŏs**, *ep-a'-hee-net-os;* from *1867; praised;* *Epœnetus*, a Chr.:—Epenetus {1x}. See: BAGD–281c; THAYER–227d.

1867. ἐπαινέω {6x} **ĕpainĕō**, *ep-ahee-neh'-o;* from *1909* and *134;* to *applaud:*—commend {1x}, laud {1x}, praise {4x}. See: BAGD–281c; THAYER–227d.

1868. ἔπαινος {11x} **ĕpainŏs**, *ep'-ahee-nos;* from *1909* and the base of *134; laudation;* concr. a *commendable* thing:—praise {11x}.

Epainos denotes "approbation, commendation, praise"; it is used **(1)** of those on account of, and by reason of, whom as God's heritage, "praise" is to be ascribed to God, in respect of His glory (the exhibition of His character and operations), Eph 1:12; **(1a)** in 1:14, of the whole company, the church, viewed as "God's own possession"; **(1b)** in 1:6, with particular reference to the glory of His grace towards them; **(1c)** in Phil 1:11, as the result of "the fruits of righteousness" manifested in them through the power of Christ; **(2)** of "praise" bestowed by God, **(2a)** upon the Jew spiritually (Judah = "praise"), Rom 2:29; **(2b)** bestowed upon believers hereafter at the judgment seat of Christ, 1 Cor 4:5 (where the definite article indicates that the "praise" will be exactly in accordance with each person's actions); **(2c)** as the issue of present trials, "at the revelation of Jesus Christ," 1 Pet 1:7; **(3)** of whatsoever is "praiseworthy," Phil 4:8; **(4)** of the approbation by churches of those who labor faithfully in the ministry of the gospel, 2 Cor 8:18; **(5)** of the approbation of well-doers by human rulers, Rom 13:3; 1 Pet 2:14. Syn.: *133*. See: TDNT–2:586, 242; BAGD–281c; THAYER–227d.

1869. ἐπαίρω {19x} **ĕpairō**, *ep-ahee'-ro;* from *1909* and *142;* to *raise up* (lit.

or fig.):—lift up {15x}, exalt (one's) self {2x}, take up {1x}, hoisted up {1x}.

Epairo, as a verb, means "to lift up" and is said **(1)** literally, **(1a)** of a sail, Acts 27:40; **(1b)** hands, Lk 24:50; 1 Ti 2:8; **(1c)** heads, Lk 21:28; **(1d)** eyes, Mt 17:8; Lk 6:20; 16:23, 18:13; Jn 4:35; 6:5; 17:1; **(1e)** the voice, Lk 11:27; Acts 2:14; 14:11; 22:22; **(1f)** a foresail, Acts 27:40; **(2)** metaphorically, **(2a)** of "exalting" oneself, being "lifted up" with pride, 2 Cor 10:5; 11:20 "exalteth himself"; **(2b)** of the heel, Jn 13:18, as of one "lifting" up the foot before kicking; the expression indicates contempt and violence; **(3)** in the passive voice, Acts 1:9, of Christ's ascension, "was taken up." See: TDNT—1:186, 28; BAGD—281d; THAYER—227d.

1870. ἐπαισχύνομαι {11x} **ĕpaischunŏmai**, *ep-ahee-skhoo'-nom-ahee;* from *1909* and *153;* to *feel shame for* something:—be ashamed {11x}.

Epaischunomai, as a verb, means "the feeling of shame arising from something that has been done." It is said of being "ashamed" **(1)** of persons, Mk 8:38; Lk 9:26; **(2)** the gospel, Rom 1:16; **(3)** former evil doing, Rom 6:21; **(4)** "the testimony of our Lord," 2 Ti 1:8; **(5)** suffering for the gospel, 2 Ti 1:12; **(6)** rendering assistance and comfort to one who is suffering for the gospel's sake, 2 Ti 1:16. **(7)** It is used in Hebrews of Christ **(7a)** in calling those who are sanctified His brethren, Heb 2:11; and **(7b)** of God in His not being "ashamed" to be called the God of believers, Heb 11:16. See: TDNT—1:189,*; BAGD—282a; THAYER—228a.

1871. ἐπαιτέω {1x} **ĕpaitĕō**, *ep-ahee-teh'-o;* from *1909* and *154;* to *ask for:*—beg {1x}. See: BAGD—282b; THAYER—228b.

1872. ἐπακολουθέω {4x} **ĕpakŏlouthĕō**, *ep-ak-ol-oo-theh'-o;* from *1909* and *190;* to *accompany:*—follow {3x}, follow after {1x}.

Epakoloutheo, as a verb, means "to follow after, close upon" and is used of signs "following" the preaching of the gospel (Mk 16:20); **(2)** of "following" good works (1 Ti 5:10); **(3)** of sins "following" after those who are guilty of them (1 Ti 5:24); **(4)** of "following" the steps of Christ (1 Pet 2:21). Syn.: 190, 1096, 1377, 1811, 2614, 2628, 3877, 4870. See: TDNT—1:215, 33; BAGD—282b; THAYER—228b.

1873. ἐπακούω {1x} **ĕpakŏuō**, *ep-ak-oo'-o;* from *1909* and *191;* to *hearken* (favorably) *to:*—hear {1x}.

Epakouo, as a verb, means "to listen to, hear with favor, at or upon an occasion" and is used in 2 Cor 6:2: "For he saith, I have heard (*epakouo*) thee in a time accepted, and in the day

of salvation have I succoured thee: behold, now is the accepted time; behold, now is the day of salvation." Syn.: 189, 191, 1251, 1522, 1874, 3878, 4257. See: TDNT—1:222, 34; BAGD—282c; THAYER—228b.

1874. ἐπακροάομαι {1x} **ĕpakrŏaŏmai**, *ep-ak-rŏ-ah'-om-ahee;* from *1909* and the base of *202;* to *listen* (intently) *to:*—hear {1x}.

Epakroaomai, as a verb, means "to listen attentively to" and is used in Acts 16:25: "(the prisoners) were listening to (them)." Syn.: 189, 191, 1251, 1522, 1873, 3878, 4257. See: BAGD—282c; THAYER—228b.

1875. ἐπάν {3x} **ĕpan**, *ep-an';* from *1909* and *302;* a particle of indef. contemporaneousness; *whenever, as soon as:*—when {3x}. See: BAGD—282c; THAYER—228c.

1876. ἐπάναγκες {1x} **ĕpanagkĕs**, *ep-an'-ang-kes;* neut. of a presumed compound of *1909* and *318;* (adv.) *on necessity,* i.e. *necessarily:*—necessary {1x}. See: BAGD—282d; THAYER—228c.

1877. ἐπανάγω {3x} **ĕpanagō**, *ep-an-ag'-o;* from *1909* and *321;* to *lead up on,* i.e. (tech.) to *put out* (to sea); (intr.) to *return:*—launch out {1x}, thrust out {1x}, return {1x}.

Epanago, as a verb, means **(1)** "to bring up or back" [primarily a nautical term for "putting to sea"], (cf. Lk 5:3, 4); and **(2)** is used intransitively in Mt 21:18: "Now in the morning as He returned into the city, He hungered." Syn.: 344, 360, 390, 1880, 1994, 5290. See: BAGD—282d; THAYER—228c.

1878. ἐπαναμιμνήσκω {1x} **ĕpanamimnēskō**, *ep-an-ah-mim-nace'-ko;* from *1909* and *363;* to *remind of again,* to *recall to mind again:*—put in mind {1x}. See: BAGD—282d; THAYER—228c.

1879. ἐπαναπαύομαι {2x} **ĕpanapauŏmai**, *ep-an-ah-pŏw'-om-ahee;* mid. voice from *1909* and *373;* to *settle on;* lit. (*remain*) or fig. (*rely*):—rest in {1x}, rest upon {1x}.

Epanapauomai, "to cause to rest," is used in the middle voice, metaphorically, signifying **(1)** "to rest upon" in Lk 10:6 and **(2)** "rest in" in Rom 2:17. See: TDNT—1:351,*; BAGD—282d; THAYER—228c.

1880. ἐπανέρχομαι {2x} **ĕpanĕrchŏmai**, *ep-an-er'-khom-ahee;* from *1909* and *424;* to *come up on,* i.e. *return:*—come (back) again {1x}, return {1x}.

In Lk 19:15, *epanerchomai*, as a verb, means "returned": "And it came to pass, that when he

was returned, having received the kingdom. . . ."
(cf. Lk 10:35). Syn.: 344, 360, 390, 1877, 1994,
5290. See: BAGD–283a; THAYER–228d.

1881. ἐπανίσταμαι {2x} **ĕpanistamai**, *ep-*
an-is'-tam-ahee; mid.
voice from *1909* and *450;* to *stand up on,* i.e.
(fig.) to *attack:*–rise up against {2x}. Cf. Mt 10:31;
Mk 13:12. See: BAGD–283a; THAYER–228d.

1882. ἐπανόρθωσις {1x} **ĕpanŏrthōsis**, *ep-an-*
or'-tho-sis; from a com-
pound of *1909* and *461;* a *straightening up*
again, i.e. (fig.) *rectification (reformation):*–
correction {1x}.

   Epanorthosis, lit., "a restoration to an upright or right state", hence, "correction," is used
of the Scripture in 2 Ti 3:16, referring to im-
provement of life and character. See: TDNT–
5:450, 727; BAGD–283a; THAYER–228d.

1883. ἐπάνω {20x} **ĕpanō**, *ep-an'-o;* from *1909*
and *507; up above,* i.e. *over* or *on*
(of place, amount, rank, etc.):–over {6x}, on {4x},
thereon + 846 {3x}, upon {3x}, above {3x}, more
than {1x}. See: BAGD–283b; THAYER–228d.

1884. ἐπαρκέω {3x} **ĕparkĕō**, *ep-ar-keh'-o;*
from *1909* and *714;* to *avail*
for, i.e. *help:*–relieve {3x}.

   Eparkeo signifies to be strong enough for
and so to ward off or to aid, to relieve (1 Tim
5:10, 16, 16). See: BAGD–283c; THAYER–
229a.

1885. ἐπαρχία {2x} **ĕparchia**, *ep-ar-khee'-ah*
or ἐπαρχεία **ĕparchĕia**, *ep-*
ar-khi'-ah; from a compound of *1909* and *757*
(mean. a *governor* of a district, "eparch"); a
special *region* of government, i.e. a Roman
præfecture:–province {2x}.

   Eparcheia, or *eparchia,* was a technical term
for the administrative divisions of the Roman
Empire. The original meaning was the district
within which a magistrate, whether consul or
pretor, exercised supreme authority. The
"province" mentioned in Acts 23:34 and 25:1
was assigned to the jurisdiction of an *eparchos,*
"a prefect or governor." See: BAGD–283c;
THAYER–229a.

1886. ἔπαυλις {1x} **ĕpaulis**, *ep'-ŏw-lis;* from
1909 and an equiv. of *833;* a
hut over the head, i.e. a *dwelling:*–habitation
{1x}. See: BAGD–283d; THAYER–229b.

1887. ἐπαύριον {17x} **ĕpauriŏn**, *ep-ow'-ree-*
on; from *1909* and *839;* oc-
curring *on* the *succeeding* day, i.e. (*2250* being
implied) *to-morrow:*–morrow {7x}, next day {6x},
day following {2x}, next day after {1x}, morrow
after {1x}. See: BAGD–283d; THAYER–229b.

1888. ἐπαυτοφώρῳ {1x} **ĕpautŏphōrōi**, *ep-*
ow-tof-o'-ro; from *1909*
and *846* and (the dat. sing. of) a der. of φώρ
phōr (a *thief); in theft itself,* i.e. (by anal.) *in*
actual crime:–in the very act {1x}. See: BAGD–
124a; THAYER–229b.

1889. Ἐπαφρᾶς {3x} **Ĕpaphras**, *ep-af-ras';*
contr. from *1891; Epaphras,*
a Chr.:–*Epaphras* {3x}. See: BAGD–283d;
THAYER–229b.

1890. ἐπαφρίζω {1x} **ĕpaphrizō**, *ep-af-rid'-zo;*
from *1909* and *875;* to *foam*
upon, i.e. (fig.) to *exhibit* (a vile passion):–
foam out {1x}.

   This word is used metaphorically in Jude
13, of the impious libertines, who had crept in
among the saints, and "foamed" out their own
shame with swelling words; i.e. the refuse
borne on the crest of waves and cast up on the
beach. See: BAGD–283d; THAYER–229b.

1891. Ἐπαφρόδιτος {3x} **Ĕpaphrŏditŏs**, *ep-*
af-rod'-ee-tos; from *1909*
(in the sense of *devoted* to) and Ἀφροδίτη **Aph-**
rŏditē (*Venus); Epaphroditus,* a Chr.:–Epaphroditus {3x}. See: BAGD–284a; THAYER–
229c. comp. *1889.*

1892. ἐπεγείρω {2x} **ĕpĕgĕirō**, *ep-eg-i'-ro;*
from *1909* and *1453;* to *rouse*
upon, i.e. (fig.) to *excite* against:–raise {1x},
stir up {1x}.

   Epegeiro, as a verb, means "stirred up": "But
the unbelieving Jews stirred up the Gentiles,
and made their minds evil affected against the
brethren" (Acts 14:2). Syn.: 329, 383, 387, 1326,
2042, 3947, 3951, 4531, 4579, 4787, 4797, 5017.
See: BAGD–284a; THAYER–229c.

1893. ἐπεί {27x} **ĕpĕi**, *ep-i';* from *1909* and
1487; thereupon, i.e. *since* (of time
or cause):–because {7x}, otherwise {4x}, for
then {3x}, else {3x}, seeing {3x}, forasmuch as
{2x}, for that {1x}, misc. {4x} = seeing that,
since, when. See: BAGD–284a; THAYER–
229c.

1894. ἐπειδή {11x} **ĕpĕidē**, *ep-i-day';* from
1893 and *1211; since now,* i.e.
(of time) *when,* or (of cause) *whereas:*–for {3x},
because {2x}, seeing {2x}, forasmuch as {1x}, after
that {1x}, since {1x}, for that {1x}. See: BAGD–
284b; THAYER–229c.

1895. ἐπειδήπερ {1x} **ĕpĕidēpĕr**, *ep-i-day'-*
per; from *1894* and *4007;*
since indeed (of cause):–forasmuch {1x}. See:
BAGD–284b; THAYER–229d.

1896. ἐπεῖδον {2x} **ĕpĕidŏn**, *ep-i'-don;* and
other moods and persons of
the same tense; from *1909* and *1492;* to *regard*

Greek

(favorably or otherwise):—behold {1x}, look upon {1x}.

Epeidon, as a verb, denotes "to look upon" (1) favorably: "Thus hath the Lord dealt with me in the days wherein He looked on me, to take away my reproach among men" (Lk 1:25); or (2) unfavorably: "And now, Lord, behold (epeidon) their threatenings: and grant unto thy servants, that with all boldness they may speak thy word" (Acts 4:29). Syn.: 308, 352, 578, 816, 872, 991, 1689, 1914, 1980, 1983, 2300, 2334, 3706, 3708, 3879, 4017, 4648. See: BAGD—284b; THAYER—229d.

1897. ἐπείπερ {1x} ĕpĕipĕr, ep-i'-per; from 1893 and 4007; since indeed (of cause):—seeing {1x}. See: BAGD—284c; THAYER—229d.

1898. ἐπεισαγωγή {1x} ĕpĕisagōgē, ep-ice-ag-o-gay'; from a compound of 1909 and 1521; a superintroduction, a bringing in besides, in addition:—bringing in {1x}.

The word literally means to bring something in and upon (Heb 7:19). See: BAGD—284c; THAYER—230a.

1899. ἔπειτα {16x} ĕpĕita, ep'-i-tah; from 1909 and 1534; thereafter:—after that {4x}, afterward(s) {3x}, then {9x}. See: BAGD—284c; THAYER—230a.

1900. ἐπέκεινα {1x} ĕpĕkĕina, ep-ek'-i-nah; from 1909 and (the acc. plur. neut. of) 1565; upon those parts of, i.e. on the further side of:—beyond {1x}. See: BAGD—284d; THAYER—230b.

1901. ἐπεκτείνομαι {1x} ĕpĕktĕinŏmai, ep-ek-ti'-nom-ahee; mid. voice from 1909 and 1614; to stretch (oneself) forward upon:—reach forth unto {1x}. See: BAGD—284d; THAYER—230b.

1902. ἐπενδύομαι {2x} ĕpĕnduŏmai, ep-en-doo'-om-ahee; mid. voice from 1909 and 1746; to invest upon oneself:—be clothed upon {2x}.

Ependuo, as a verb, used in the middle voice, "to cause to be put on over, to be clothed upon": "For in this we groan, earnestly desiring to be clothed upon with our house which is from heaven" (2 Cor 5:2; cf. v. 4, of the future spiritual body of the redeemed). Syn.: 294, 1463, 1737, 1746, 2439, 4016. See: TDNT—2:320,*; BAGD—284d; THAYER—230b.

1903. ἐπενδύτης {1x} ĕpĕndutēs, ep-en-doo'-tace; from 1902; a wrapper, i.e. outer garment:—fisher's coat {1x}. See: BAGD—285a; THAYER—230b.

1904. ἐπέρχομαι {10x} ĕpĕrchŏmai, ep-er'-khom-ahee; from 1909 and 2064; to supervene, i.e. arrive, occur, impend, attack, (fig.) influence:—come {6x}, come upon {2x}, come on {1x}, come thither {1x}. See: TDNT—2:680, 257; BAGD—285a; THAYER—230b.

1905. ἐπερωτάω {59x} ĕpĕrōtaō, ep-er-o-tah'-o; from 1909 and 2065; to ask for, i.e. inquire, seek:—ask {53x}, demand {2x}, desire {1x}, ask question {1x}, question {1x}, ask after {1x}.

Due to the prefixed preposition (ἐπι) the asking is intensified and approximates a demand (Lk 2:46; 3:14; 6:9; 17:20). See: TDNT—2:687, 262; BAGD—285b; THAYER—230c.

1906. ἐπερώτημα {1x} ĕpĕrōtēma, ep-er-o'-tay-mah; from 1905; an inquiry:—answer {1x}. See: TDNT—2:688, 262; BAGD—285c; THAYER—230d.

1907. ἐπέχω {5x} ĕpĕchō, ep-ekh'-o; from 1909 and 2192; to hold upon, i.e. (by impl.) to retain; (by extens.) to detain; (with impl. of 3563) to pay attention to:—mark {1x}, give heed unto {1x}, stay {1x}, hold forth {1x}, take heed unto {1x}.

(1) This word literally means to hold upon; then to direct towards, to give attention to; so thus is rendered "gave heed" (Acts 3:5; 1 Ti 4:16). (2) It also signifies "to hold out" (2a) Phil 2:16, of the word of life; then, (2b) "to hold one's mind towards, to observe," translated "marked" in Lk 14:7, of the Lord's observance of those who chose the chief seats. See: BAGD—285c; THAYER—231a.

1908. ἐπηρεάζω {3x} ĕpērĕazō, ep-ay-reh-ad'-zo; from a comp. of 1909 and (prob.) ἀρειά arĕia (threats); to insult, slander:—despitefully use {2x}, falsely accuse {1x}.

Epereazo, as a verb, has its (1) more ordinary meaning "to insult, treat abusively, despitefully": "Bless them that curse you, and pray for them which despitefully use you" (Lk 6:28), and (2) has the forensic significance "to accuse falsely": "Having a good conscience; that, whereas they speak evil of you, as of evildoers, they may be ashamed that falsely accuse (epereazo) your good conversation in Christ" (1 Pet 3:16). Syn.: 156, 157, 1225, 1458, 1462, 2723, 2724, 4811. See: BAGD—285d; THAYER—221b.

1909. ἐπί {895x} ĕpi, ep-ee'; a primary prep.; prop. mean. superimposition (of time, place, order, etc.), as a relation of distribution [with the gen.], i.e. over, upon, etc.; of rest (with the dat.) at, on, etc.; of direction (with the acc.) toward, upon, etc.:—on {196x}, in {120x}, upon {159x}, unto {41x}, to {41x}, misc.

{338x} = about (the times), above, after, against, among, as long as (touching), at, beside, ✕ have charge of, (be-, [where-])fore, into, (because) of, over, (by, for) the space of, through (-out), toward, with. In compounds it retains essentially the same import, *at, upon,* etc. (lit. or fig.). See: BAGD—285d; THAYER—221b.

1910. **ἐπιβαίνω** {6x} **ĕpibainō,** *ep-ee-bah'-ee-no;* from *1909* and the base of *939;* to *walk upon,* i.e. *mount, ascend, embark, arrive:*—sit {1x}, come {1x}, go aboard {1x}, take + *1519* {1x}, come into {1x}, enter into {1x}.

Epibaino, as a verb, means "sitting upon": "Tell ye the daughter of Sion, Behold, thy King cometh unto thee, meek, and sitting upon an ass, and a colt the foal of an ass" (Mt 21:5). Cf. Acts 20:18; 221:2, 6; 25:1; 27:2. Syn.: 339, 345, 347, 377, 2516, 2521, 2621, 2523, 2625, 4775, 4776, 4873. See: BAGD—289d; THAYER—236a.

1911. **ἐπιβάλλω** {18x} **ĕpiballō,** *ep-ee-bal'-lo;* from *1909* and *906;* to *throw upon* (lit. or fig., tran. or refl.; usually with more or less force); spec. (with *1438* implied) to *reflect;* impers. to *belong to:*—lay {8x}, put {3x}, lay on {1x}, beat {1x}, cast on {1x}, think thereon {1x}, fall {1x}, stretch forth {1x}, cast upon {1x}. See: TDNT—1:528, 91; BAGD—289d; THAYER—236b.

1912. **ἐπιβαρέω** {3x} **ĕpibarĕō,** *ep-ee-bar-eh'-o;* from *1909* and *916;* to *be heavy upon,* i.e. (pecuniarily) to *be expensive to;* fig. to *be severe toward:*—be chargeable to {1x} be chargeable unto {1x}, overcharge {1x}.

Epibareo, "to burden heavily," is said **(1)** of material resources, **(1a)** "be chargeable unto", 1 Th 2:9; **(1b)** "be chargeable to", 2 Th 3:8; **(2)** of the effect of spiritual admonition and discipline, 2 Cor 2:5, "overcharge." See: BAGD—290b; THAYER—236c.

1913. **ἐπιβιβάζω** {3x} **ĕpibibazō,** *ep-ee-bee-bad'-zo;* from *1909* and a redupl. deriv. of the base of *939* [comp. *307*]; to *cause to mount* (an animal):—set on {2x}, set thereon {1x}.

Epibibazo, "to place upon," is used of causing persons to mount animals for riding, Lk 10:34; 19:35; Acts 23:24. See: BAGD—290b; THAYER—236c.

1914. **ἐπιβλέπω** {3x} **ĕpiblĕpō,** *ep-ee-blep'-o;* from *1909* and *991;* to *gaze at* (with favor, pity or partiality):—look upon {1x}, regard {1x}, have respect to {1x}.

Epiblepo, as a verb, means "to look upon" and is used **(1)** of favorable regard: "For He hath regarded the low estate of His handmaiden: for, behold, from henceforth all gener-

ations shall call me blessed" (Lk 1:48 of the low estate of the Virgin Mary); **(2)** in a request to the Lord to "look" upon an afflicted son: "And, behold, a man of the company cried out, saying, Master, I beseech thee, look upon my son: for he is mine only child" (Lk 9:38); **(3)** of having a partial regard, respect, for the well-to-do: "And ye have respect to him that weareth the gay clothing, and say unto him, Sit thou here in a good place; and say to the poor, Stand thou there, or sit here under my footstool" (Jas 2:3). Syn.: 308, 352, 578, 816, 872, 991, 1689, 1896, 1980, 1983, 2300, 2334, 3706, 3708, 3879, 4017, 4648. See: BAGD—290b; THAYER—236c.

1915. **ἐπίβλημα** {4x} **ĕpiblēma,** *ep-ib'-lay-mah;* from *1911;* a *patch:*—piece {4x}.

Epiblema primarily denotes "that which is thrown over, a cover" (*epi,* "over," *ballo,* "to throw"); then, "that which is put on, or sewed on, to cover a rent, a patch," Mt 9:16; Mk 2:21; Lk 5:36 (twice). See: BAGD—290c; THAYER—236d.

1916. **ἐπιβοάω** {1x} **ĕpibŏaō,** *ep-ee-bo-ah'-o;* from *1909* and *994;* to *ex-claim against:*—cry {1x}.

Epiboao, as a verb, [*epi,* "upon," intensive], means "to cry out, exclaim vehemently" and is used in Acts 25:24: "And Festus said, King Agrippa, and all men which are here present with us, ye see this man, about whom all the multitude of the Jews have dealt with me, both at Jerusalem, and also here, crying that he ought not to live any longer." Syn.: 310, 349, 994, 995, 2019, 2896, 2905, 2906, 5455. See: BAGD—290c; THAYER—236d.

1917. **ἐπιβουλή** {4x} **ĕpibŏulē,** *ep-ee-boo-lay';* from a presumed compound of *1909* and *1014;* a *plan against* someone, i.e. a *plot:*—lying in wait {1x}, lay wait for + *1096* {1x}, lay wait + *3195* + *2071* {1x}, - laying await {1x}.

Epiboule, lit., "a plan against" (*epi,* "against," *boule,* "a counsel, plan"), is translated "laying await" and "lying in wait" in Acts 9:24; 20:3, 19; 23:30. See: BAGD—290c; THAYER—236d.

1918. **ἐπιγαμβρεύω** {1x} **ĕpigambrĕuō,** *ep-ee-gam-bryoo'-o;* from *1909* and a der. of *1062;* to *form affinity with,* i.e. (spec.) in a levirate way:—marry {1x}.

Epigambreuo, "to take to wife after" (*epi,* "upon," *gambros,* "a connection by marriage"), signifies "to marry" (of a deceased husband's next of kin, Mt 22:24). See: BAGD—290c; THAYER—236d.

Greek

1919. ἐπίγειος {7x} ĕpigĕiŏs, *ep-ig'-i-os;* from *1909* and *1093; worldly* (phys. or mor.):—earthly {4x}, in earth {1x}, terrestrial {2x}.

Epigeios, "on earth" (*epi,* "on," *ge,* "the earth"), is rendered **(1)** "earthly" in Jn 3:12; 2 Cor 5:1; Phil 3:19; Jas 3:15; **(2)** in Phil 2:10, "in earth"; and **(3)** "terrestrial" in 1 Cor 15:40 (twice). See: TDNT—1:680, 116; BAGD—290c; THAYER—236d.

1920. ἐπιγίνομαι {1x} ĕpiginŏmai, *ep-ig-in'-om-ahee;* from *1909* and *1096;* to *arrive upon,* i.e. *spring up* (as a wind):—blew {1x}.

In Acts 28:13, *epiginomai,* "to come on," is used of the springing up of a wind, "blew." See: BAGD—290d; THAYER—236a.

1921. ἐπιγινώσκω {42x} ĕpiginōskō, *ep-ig-in-oce'-ko;* from *1909* and *1097;* to *know upon* some mark, i.e. *recognize;* by impl. to *become fully acquainted with,* to *acknowledge:*—know {30x}, acknowledge {5x}, perceive {3x}, take knowledge of {2x}, have knowledge of {1x}, know well {1x}.

Epiginosko denotes **(1)** "to observe, fully perceive, notice attentively, discern, recognize"; **(1a)** it suggests generally a directive, a more special, recognition of the object "known" than does *ginosko* (*1097*); **(1b)** it also may suggest advanced "knowledge" or special appreciation; thus, in Rom 1:32, "knowing the ordinance of God" (*epiginosko*) means "knowing full well," whereas in verse 21 "knowing God" (*ginosko*) simply suggests that they could not avoid the perception. **(1c)** Sometimes *epiginosko* implies a special participation in the object "known," and gives greater weight to what is stated; thus in Jn 8:32, "ye shall know the truth," *ginosko* is used, whereas in 1 Ti 4:3, "them that believe and know the truth," *epiginosko* lays stress on participation in the truth. **(1d)** Cf. the stronger statement in Col 1:6 (*epiginosko*) with that in 2 Cor 8:9 (*ginosko*), and the two verbs in 1 Cor 13:12, "now I know in part (ginosko); but then shall I know (*epiginosko*) even as also I have been known (*epiginosko*)," "a knowledge" which perfectly unites the subject with the object; **(1e)** It also signifies **(1e1)** "to know thoroughly" (*epi* "intensive," *ginosko,* "to know"); **(1e2)** "to recognize a thing to be what it really is, to acknowledge," 1 Cor 14:37; 16:18; 2 Cor 1:13–14; **(2)** "to discover, ascertain, determine," **(2a)** e.g., Lk 7:37; 23:7; Acts 9:30; 19:34; 22:29; 28:1; **(2b)** *epignosis* is "knowledge directed towards a particular object, perceiving, discerning," whereas *gnosis* (*1108*) is knowledge in the abstract. Syn.: 1097, 1107, 1110, 1492, 1467, 1922, 1987, 4267. See: TDNT—1:689, 119; BAGD—291a; THAYER—237a.

1922. ἐπίγνωσις {20x} ĕpignōsis, *ep-ig'-no-sis;* from *1921; recognition,* i.e. (by impl.) full *discernment, acknowledgement:*—knowledge {16x}, acknowledging {3x}, acknowledgement {1x}.

(1) *Epignosis* is the complete comprehension after the first knowledge (*gnosis* – 1108) of a matter. **(1a)** It is bringing one to be better acquainted with something known previously; a more exact viewing of something beheld before. *Epignosis* denotes **(1b)** "exact or full knowledge, discernment, recognition," and **(1c)** is a strengthened form of *gnosis,* expressing a fuller or a full "knowledge," **(1d)** a greater participation by the "knower" in the object "known," thus more powerfully influencing him. **(1e)** It is not found in the Gospels and Acts. **(1f)** Paul uses it 15 times (16 if Heb 10:26 is included) out of the 20 occurrences; Peter 4 times, all in his 2nd epistle. **(1g)** Contrast Rom 1:28 (*epignosis*) with the simple verb in v. 21. **(2)** It is used with reference **(2a)** to God in Rom 1:28; 10:2; Eph 1:17; Col 1:10; 2 Pet 1:3; **(2b)** God and Christ, 2 Pet 1:2; **(2c)** Christ, Eph 4:13; 2 Pet 1:8; 2:20; **(2d)** the will of the Lord, Col 1:9; **(2e)** every good thing, Philem 6 "acknowledging"; **(2f)** the truth, 1 Ti 2:4; Col 2:2 "to the acknowledgment of"), lit., "into a full knowledge." **(3)** It is used without the mention of an object in Phil 1:9; Col 3:10. Syn.: 1097, 1107, 1108, 1110, 1492, 1921, 1467, 1922, 1987, 4678, 5428. See: TDNT—1:689, 119; BAGD—291b; THAYER—237b.

1923. ἐπιγραφή {5x} ĕpigraphē, *ep-ig-raf-ay';* from *1924;* an *inscription:*—superscription {5x}.

Epigraphe, lit., "an overwriting" (*epi,* "over," *grapho,* "to write") (the meaning of the anglicized Latin word "superscription"), denotes **(1)** "an inscription, a title." **(2)** On Roman coins the emperor's name was inscribed, Mt 22:20; Mk 12:16; Lk 20:24. **(3)** In the Roman Empire, in the case of a criminal on his way to execution, a board on which was inscribed the cause of his condemnation was carried before him or hung round his neck; the inscription was termed a "title" (*titlos*). **(3a)** The four Evangelists state that at the crucifixion of Christ the title was affixed to the cross, Mk 15:26, and Lk (23:38), call it a "superscription"; Mk says it was "written over" (*epigrapho,* the corresponding verb). Matthew calls it "His accusation"; John calls it "a title" (a technical term). **(3b)** The wording varies: the essential words are the same, and the variation serves to authenticate the narratives, showing that each evangelist

wrote separate but complementary details of
the account to present a complete picture. See:
BAGD—291c; THAYER—237c.

1924. **ἐπιγράφω** {5x} **ĕpigraphō**, *ep-ee-graf'-o;*
from *1909* and *1125;* to *in-
scribe* (phys. or ment.):—write {2x}, write over
{1x}, write thereon {1x}, with this inscription +
1722 + 3639 {1x}.

　　Epigrapho, "to write upon, inscribe" (*epi*,
"upon," *grapho*, "to write"), is usually rendered
(1) by the verb "to write upon, over, or in,"
Mk 15:26; Heb 8:10; 10:16; Rev 21:12; **(2)** it is
translated by a noun phrase in Acts 17:23,
"(with this) inscription," lit., "(on which) had
been inscribed." See: BAGD—291c; THAYER—
237c.

1925. **ἐπιδείκνυμι** {9x} **ĕpidĕiknumi**, *ep-ee-
dike'-noo-mee;* from *1909*
and *1166;* to *exhibit* (phys. or ment.):—shew
{9x}.

　　(1) This words means to bring forth to view,
to show, to furnish to be looked at, to produce
what may looked at. **(2)** It signifies **(2a)** "to
exhibit, display," Mt 16:1; 22:19; 24:1; Lk 17:14;
24:40; **(2b)** in the middle voice, "to display,"
with a special interest in one's own action, Acts
9:39; **(3)** "to point out, prove, demonstrate," Acts
18:28; Heb 6:17. See: BAGD—291d; THAYER—
237d.

1926. **ἐπιδέχομαι** {2x} **ĕpidĕchŏmai**, *ep-ee-
dekh'-om-ahee;* from *1909*
and *1209;* to *admit* (as a guest or [fig.] teacher):—
receive {2x}.

　　Epidechomai, as a verb, means literally "to
accept besides, to receive" and is used in the
sense **(1)** of accepting in 3 Jn 9: "I wrote unto
the church: but Diotrephes, who loveth to have
the preeminence among them, receiveth (*epidechomai*) us not"; **(2)** and in 3 Jn 10 in the
sense of "receiving" with hospitality: "Wherefore, if I come, I will remember his [Diotre-
phes'] deeds which he doeth, prating against
us with malicious words: and not content therewith, neither doth he himself receive (*epidechomai*) the brethren, and forbiddeth them that
would, and casteth them out of the church." Syn.:
324, 353, 354, 568, 588, 618, 1209, 1523, 2210,
2865, 2975, 2983, 3028, 3335, 3336, 3858, 3880,
3970, 4327, 4355, 4356, 4380, 4381, 4382, 5562,
5264, 5274. See: BAGD—292a; THAYER—237d.

1927. **ἐπιδημέω** {2x} **ĕpidēmĕō**, *ep-ee-day-
meh'-o;* from a compound
of *1909* and *1218;* to *make oneself at home*, i.e.
(by extens.) to *reside* (in a foreign country):—[be]
dwelling (which were) there {1x}, stranger {1x}.

　　Epidemeo means to be a sojourner or a foreign resident, among any people, in any country,

Acts 2:10; 17:21. See: BAGD—292a; THAYER—
237d.

1928. **ἐπιδιατάσσομαι** {1x} **ĕpidiatassŏmai**,
*ep-ee-dee-ah-tas'-
som-ahee;* mid. voice from *1909* and *1299;* to
appoint besides, i.e. *supplement* (as a codi-
cil):—add to {1x}.

　　Epidiatassomai, lit., "to arrange in addition"
(*epi*, "upon," *dia*, "through," *tasso*, "to arrange"), is used in Gal 3:15 ("addeth," or rather,
"ordains something in addition"). If no one
does such a thing in the matter of a human
covenant, how much more is a covenant made
by God inviolable! The Judaizers by their "addition" violated this principle, and, by proclaiming the divine authority for what they
did, they virtually charged God with a breach
of promise. He gave the Law, indeed, but neither in place of the promise nor to supplement
it. See: BAGD—292b; THAYER—238a.

1929. **ἐπιδίδωμι** {11x} **ĕpididōmi**, *ep-ee-did'-
o-mee;* from *1909* and *1325;*
to *give over* (by hand or surrender):—give {7x},
deliver {1x}, offer {1x}, let drive + 5342 {1x},
deliver unto {1x}.

　　Epididomi signifies **(1)** "to give by handing,
to hand" (*epi*, "over"), e.g., Mt 7:9, 10; Lk 11:11
(twice), 12; **(1a)** cf. Lk 4:17; 24:30, here of the
Lord's act in "handing" the broken loaf to the
two at Emmaus, an act which was the means
of the revelation of Himself as the crucified
and risen Lord; **(2)** of the "delivering" of the
epistle from the elders at Jerusalem to the
church at Antioch, Acts 15:30; **(3)** in Lk 11:12,
"to give" (*epi*, "over," in the sense of "instead
of"), is translated "will he offer"; **(4)** "to give
in, give way," Acts 27:15, "let drive" of the ship
by the wind; **(5)** "to give upon or in addition,"
as from oneself to another, hence, "to deliver
over unto," is used of the "delivering" of the
roll of Isaiah to Christ in the synagogue, "And
there was delivered unto Him the book of the
prophet Esaias. And when He had opened the
book, He found the place where it was written"
(Lk 4:17). Syn.: 325, 525, 629, 591, 859, 1325,
1560, 1659, 1807, 3086, 3860, 4506, 5483. See:
BAGD—292b; THAYER—238a.

1930. **ἐπιδιορθόω** {1x} **ĕpidiŏrthŏō**, *ep-ee-
dee-or-thŏ'-o;* from *1909*
and a der. of *3717;* to *straighten further*, i.e.
(fig.) *arrange additionally*:—set in order {1x}.

　　This word is used in Titus 1:5, in the sense
of setting right again what was defective, a
commission to Titus not to add to what the
apostle himself had done, but to restore what
had fallen into disorder since the apostle had
labored in Crete; this is suggested by the *epi*.
See: BAGD—292b; THAYER—238a

1931. ἐπιδύω {1x} ĕpiduō, *ep-ee-doo'-o;* from *1909* and *1416;* to *set* fully (as the sun):—go down {1x}.

Epiduo, signifies "to go down," and is said of the sun in Eph 4:26; i.e., put wrath away before sunset. See: BAGD—292c; THAYER—238a.

1932. ἐπιείκεια {2x} ĕpiĕikĕia, *ep-ee-i'-ki-ah;* from *1933; suitableness,* i.e. (by impl.) *equity, mildness:*—clemency {1x}, gentleness {1x}.

This word suggests "sweet reasonableness", is translated "clemency" in Acts 24:4; elsewhere, in 2 Cor 10:1, of the gentleness of Christ. It refers to the sort of moderation that recognizes that it is impossible for formal laws to anticipate and provide for all possible cases. It rectifies and redresses the injustices of justice; a correction of the law where law falls short on account of generalities. God remembers we are but dust and deals with us accordingly [cf. Ps 103:10]; expecting us to treat others as He has treated us (Mt 18:23; Eph 4:32). Syn.: 4236. See: TDNT—2:588, 243; BAGD—292c; THAYER—238a.

1933. ἐπιεικής {5x} ĕpiĕikēs, *ep-ee-i-kace';* from *1909* and *1503; appropriate,* i.e. (by impl.) *mild:*—gentle {3x}, moderation {1x}, patient {1x}.

Epieikes, an adjective (from *epi,* used intensively, and *eikos,* "reasonable"), denotes **(1)** "seemly, fitting"; hence, "equitable, fair, moderate, forbearing, not insisting on the letter of the law"; **(2)** it expresses that considerateness that looks "humanely and reasonably at the facts of a case"; **(3)** it is rendered **(3a)** "patient" in 1 Ti 3:3, in contrast to contentiousness; **(3b)** "gentle," **(3b1)** in Titus 3:2, in association with meekness, **(3b2)** in Jas 3:17, as a quality of the wisdom from above, and **(3b3)** in 1 Pet 2:18, in association with the good; **(4)** it is used as a noun with the article in Phil 4:5, and translated "moderation," not going to the extremes. See: TDNT—2:588, 243; BAGD—292c; THAYER—238b.

1934. ἐπιζητέω {14x} ĕpizētĕō, *ep-eed-zay-teh'-o;* from *1909* and *2212;* to *search* (*inquire*) *for;* intens. to *demand,* to *crave:*—seek after {5x}, seek {3x}, desire {3x}, seek for {2x}, enquire {1x}.

Epizeteo, as a verb, means "to seek after" (directive, *epi,* "towards"), and is translated: **(1)** "to seek after", Mt 6:32; 12:39; 16:4; Mk 8:12; Lk 12:30; **(2)** "to seek", Lk 11:29; Heb 11:14; 13:14; **(3)** "desired": **(3a)** "Which was with the deputy of the country, Sergius Paulus, a prudent man; who called for Barnabas and Saul, and desired (*epizeteo*) to hear the word of God"

(Acts 13:7); **(3b)** "desire": "Not because I desire a gift: but I desire fruit that may abound to your account" Phil 4:17 (twice); **(4)** "seeketh for", Rom 11:7; Acts 12:19 "sought"; **(5)** "enquire": "But if ye enquire (*epizeteo*) any thing concerning other matters, it shall be determined in a lawful assembly" (Acts 19:39). Syn.: 327, 1567, 2206, 2212, 3713. See: TDNT—2:895, 300; BAGD—292d; THAYER—238b.

1935. ἐπιθανάτιος {1x} ĕpithanatiŏs, *ep-ee-than-at'-ee-os;* from *1909* and *2288;* doomed to *death:*—appointed to death {1x}.

Epithanatios, as an adjective, means "appointed to death" and is said of the apostles (1 Cor 4:9): "For I think that God hath set forth us the apostles last, as it were appointed to death: for we are made a spectacle unto the world, and to angels, and to men." Syn.: 336, 337, 520, 2288, 2289, 5054. See: BAGD—292d; THAYER—238b.

1936. ἐπίθεσις {4x} ĕpithĕsis, *ep-ith'-es-is;* from *2007;* an *imposition* (of hands officially):—laying on {3x}, putting on {1x}.

Epithesis means a laying on, and is used **(1)** of the laying on of the apostles' hands accompanied by the impartation of the Holy Spirit in outward demonstration, **(1a)** in the cases of those in Samaria who had believed (Acts 8:18); **(1b)** such supernatural manifestations were signs especially intended to give witness to Jews as to the facts of Christ and the faith, **(1c)** they were thus temporary; **(1d)** there is no record of their continuance after the time and circumstances narrated in Acts 19, **(1e)** nor was the gift delegated by the apostles to others; **(2)** of the similar act by the elders of a church on occasions when a member of a church was set apart for a particular work, having given evidence of qualifications necessary for it, as in the case of Timothy (1 Ti 4:14); **(3)** of the impartation of a spiritual gift through the laying on of the hands of the apostle Paul (2 Ti 1:6). **(4)** The principle underlying the act was that of identification on the part of him who did it with the animal or person upon whom the hands were laid. See: TDNT—8:159, 1176; BAGD—293a; THAYER—238b.

1937. ἐπιθυμέω {16x} ĕpithumĕō, *ep-ee-thoo-meh'-o;* from *1909* and *2372;* to *set* the *heart upon,* i.e. *long* for (rightfully or otherwise):—covet {3x}, desire {8x}, would fain {1x}, lust {1x}, lust after {1x}.

Epithumeo, "to fix the desire upon" (*epi,* "upon," used intensively, *thumos,* "passion"), whether things good or bad; hence, translated **(1)** "desire", "to desire earnestly" stresses the

inward impulse rather than the object desired, Mt 13:17 of good men, for good things; Lk 16:21 "desiring"; 17:22; 22:15 of the Lord Jesus, "I have desired"; 1 Ti 3:1; Heb 6:11; 1 Pet 1:12 of the holy angels; Rev 9:6 of men to die; **(2)** "covet", "to fix the desire upon" whether things good or bad; hence, "to long for, lust after, covet," is used with the meaning "to covet evilly" in Acts 20:33, of "coveting money and apparel"; cf. Rom 7:7; 13:9 a Ten Commandment; **(3)** "lust", 1 Cor 10:6; Gal 5:17 used of the Holy Spirit against the flesh; Jas 4:2; **(4)** "lust after", Mt 5:28; **(5)** "fain", "to set one's heart upon, desire," is translated "would fain" in Lk 15:16, of the Prodigal Son. See: TDNT—3:168, 339; BAGD—293a; THAYER—238c.

1938. **ἐπιθυμητής** {1x} **ĕpithumētēs,** *ep-ee-thoo-may-tace';* from *1937;* a *craver:*—lust after + 1510 {1x}.

Epithumetes, literally is "a luster after" and is translated in 1 Cor 10:6, in verbal form, "should not lust after." See: TDNT—3:172, 339; BAGD—293b; THAYER—238d.

1939. **ἐπιθυμία** {38x} **ĕpithumia,** *ep-ee-thoo-mee'-ah;* from *1937;* a *longing* (espec. for what is forbidden):—concupiscence {3x}, desire {3x}, lust {31x}, lust after {1x}.

(1) This word stresses the lust, craving, longing, or desire for what is usually forbidden. It refers to the whole world of active lusts and desires—to all that the *sarx* (*4561*) as the seat of desires and the natural appetites impels. **(2)** Concupiscence is an irrational longing for pleasure, "unbridled lust." *Epithumia,* as a noun, means "a desire, craving, longing, mostly of evil desires," frequently translated "lust," is used in the following, **(3)** of good "desires": **(3a)** of the Lord's "wish" concerning the last Passover, Lk 22:15, **(3b)** of Paul's "desire" to be with Christ, Phil 1:23; **(3c)** of his "desire" to see the saints at Thessalonica again, 1 Th 2:17. **(4)** With regard to evil "desires," **(4a)** "concupiscence" in Rom 7:8; Col 3:5; 1 Th 4:5; **(4b)** in Rom 6:12 the injunction against letting sin reign in our mortal body to obey the "lust" thereof, refers to those evil desires which are ready to express themselves in bodily activity. **(4c)** They are equally the "lusts" of the flesh, Rom 13:14; Gal 5:16, 24; Eph 2:3; 2 Pet 2:18; 1 Jn 2:16, a phrase which describes the emotions of the soul, the natural tendency towards things evil. **(4d)** Such "lusts" are not necessarily base and immoral, they may be refined in character, but are evil if inconsistent with the will of God. **(5)** Other descriptions besides those already mentioned are:—lusts: **(5a)** "of the mind," Eph 2:3; **(5b)** "evil (desire)," Col 3:5; **(5c)** "the passion of," 1 Th 4:5; **(5d)** "foolish and hurtful,"

1 Ti 6:9; **(5e)** "youthful," 2 Ti 2:22; **(5f)** "divers," 2 Ti 3:6 and Titus 3:3; **(5g)** "their own," 2 Ti 4:3; 2 Pet 3:3; Jude 16; **(5h)** "worldly," Titus 2:12; **(5i)** "his own," Jas 1:14; **(5j)** "your former," 1 Pet 1:14; **(5k)** "fleshly," 1 Pet 2:11; **(5l)** "of men," 1 Pet 4:2; **(5m)** "of defilement," 2 Pet 2:10; **(5n)** "of the eyes," 1 Jn 2:16; **(5o)** of the world ("thereof"), Jn 2:17; **(5p)** "their own ungodly," Jude 18. Syn.: *Epithumia* is the more comprehensive term, including all manner of "lusts and desires"; *pathema* (*3804*) denotes suffering; in the passage in Gal 5:17f the sufferings are those produced by yielding to the flesh; *pathos* (*3806*) points more to the evil state from which "lusts" spring. See: TDNT—3:168, 339; BAGD—293b; THAYER—238d.

1940. **ἐπικαθίζω** {2x} **ĕpikathizō,** *ep-ee-kath-id'-zo;* from *1909* and *2523;* to cause to sit upon; *seat upon:*—set on {2x}. See: BAGD—293d; THAYER—239a.

1941. **ἐπικαλέομαι** {32x} **ĕpikalĕŏmai,** *ep-ee-kal-eh'-om-ahee;* mid. voice from *1909* and *2564;* to *entitle;* by impl. to *invoke* (for aid, worship, testimony, decision, etc.):—call on {7x}, be (one's) surname {6x}, be surnamed {5x}, call upon {4x}, appeal unto {4x}, call {4x}, appeal to {1x}, appeal {1x}.

Epikaleomai means to call upon and has the meaning **(1)** "appeal" in the middle voice, which suggests a special interest on the part of the doer of an action in that in which he is engaged; Stephen died "calling upon the Lord" (Acts 7:59). **(2)** In the more strictly legal sense the word is used only of Paul's appeal to Caesar (Acts 25:11–12, 21, etc.). See: TDNT—3:496,*; BAGD—294a; THAYER—239a.

1942. **ἐπικάλυμα** {1x} **ĕpikaluma,** *ep-ee-kal'-oo-mah;* from *1943;* a *covering,* i.e. (fig.) *pretext:*—cloke {1x}. See: BAGD—294b; THAYER—239c.

1943. **ἐπικαλύπτω** {1x} **ĕpikaluptō,** *ep-ee-kal-oop'-to;* from *1909* and *2572;* to *conceal,* i.e. (fig.) *forgive:*—cover {1x}. See: BAGD—294c; THAYER—239c.

1944. **ἐπικατάρατος** {3x} **ĕpikataratŏs,** *ep-ee-kat-ar'-at-os;* from *1909* and a der. of *2672; imprecated,* i.e. *execrable:*—accursed {3x}.

Epikataratos, as an adjective, means "cursed, accursed, exposed to divine vengeance, lying under God's curse": "For as many as are of the works of the law are under the curse (*katara* – *2671*): for it is written, Cursed (*epikataratos*) is every one that continueth not in all things which are written in the book of the law to do them" (Gal 3:10; cf. vs 13; Jn 7:49). Syn.: 331, 332, 685, 2551, 2652, 2653, 2671, 2672. See:

TDNT—1:451, 75; BAGD—294c; THAYER—239d.

1945. ἐπίκειμαι {7x} **ĕpikĕimai**, *ep-ik'-i-mahee;* from *1909* and *2749;* to *rest upon* (lit. or fig.):—press upon {1x}, be instant {1x}, lie {1x}, be laid thereon {1x}, lie on {1x}, be laid upon {1x}, be imposed on {1x}.

Epikeimai denotes "to be placed on, to lie on," **(1)** literally, **(1a)** as of the stone on the sepulchre of Lazarus, Jn 11:38; **(1b)** of the fish on the fire of coals, Jn 21:9; **(2)** figuratively, **(2a)** of a tempest (to press upon), Acts 27:20; **(2b)** of a necessity laid upon the apostle Paul, 1 Cor 9:16; **(2c)** of the pressure of the multitude upon Christ to hear Him, Lk 5:1, "pressed upon"; **(2d)** of the insistence of the chief priests, rulers and people that Christ should be crucified, Lk 23:23, "were instant"; **(2e)** of carnal ordinances "imposed" under the Law until a time of reformation, brought in through the High Priesthood of Christ, Heb 9:10. See: TDNT—3:655, 425; BAGD—294c; THAYER—239d.

1946. Ἐπικούρειος {1x} **Ĕpikŏurĕiŏs**, *ep-ee-koo'-ri-os* or Ἐπικούριος **Ĕpikŏuriŏs**, *ep-ee-koo'-ree-os;* from Ἐπίκουρος **Ĕpikŏurŏs** [comp. *1947*] (a noted philosopher); an *Epicurean* or follower of Epicurus:—Epicurea {1x}. See: BAGD—294d; THAYER—239d.

1947. ἐπικουρία {1x} **ĕpikŏuria**, *ep-ee-koo-ree'-ah;* from a compound of *1909* and a (prol.) form of the base of *2877* (in the sense of *servant*); *assistance:*—help {1x}.

This word strictly denotes such aid as is rendered by an *epikouros,* "an ally, an auxiliary"; Paul uses it in his testimony to Agrippa, "having therefore obtained the help that is from God" (Acts 26:22). See: BAGD—294d; THAYER—239d.

1948. ἐπικρίνω {1x} **ĕpikrinō**, *ep-ee-kree'-no;* from *1909* and *2919;* to *adjudge:*—give sentence {1x}. See: BAGD—295a; THAYER—240a.

1949. ἐπιλαμβάνομαι {19x} **ĕpilambanŏmai**, *ep-ee-lam-ban'-om-ahee;* mid. voice from *1909* and *2983;* to *seize* (for help, injury, attainment, or any other purpose; lit. or fig.):—take {7x}, take by {3x}, catch {2x}, take on {2x}, lay hold on {2x}, take hold of {2x}, lay hold upon {1x}.

Epilambanomai, **(1)** in the middle voice, "to lay hold of, take hold of," is used **(1a)** literally, e.g., Mk 8:23; Lk 9:47; 14:4; **(1b)** metaphorically, e.g., **(1b1)** Heb 8:9, "(I, God) took them (by the hand)"; **(1b2)** Lk 20:20, 26, of taking "hold" of Christ's words; **(1b3)** in Lk 23:26 and Acts 21:33, of laying "hold" of persons; **(1b4)** in 1 Ti 6:12, 19, of laying "hold" on eternal life, i.e.,

practically appropriating all the benefits, privileges and responsibilities involved in the possession of it; **(1b5)** in Heb 2:16, "He took on"; **(2)** it is translated "caught" in Acts 16:19. See: TDNT—4:9,*; BAGD—295a; THAYER—240a.

1950. ἐπιλανθάνομαι {8x} **ĕpilanthanŏmai**, *ep-ee-lan-than'-om-ahee;* mid. voice from *1909* and *2990;* to *lose out* of mind; by impl. to *neglect:*—be forgetful of {1x}, forget {7x}.

Epilanthanomai, "to forget, or neglect" (*epi,* "upon," used intensively), is said **(1)** negatively **(1a)** of God, indicating His remembrance of sparrows, Lk 12:6, and **(1b)** of the work and labor of love of His saints, Heb 6:10; **(2)** of the disciples regarding taking bread, Mt 16:5; Mk 8:14; **(3)** of Paul regarding "the things which are behind," Phil 3:13; **(4)** of believers, **(4a)** as to entertaining strangers, Heb 13:2; **(4b)** and as to doing good and communicating, Heb 13:16; **(5)** of a person who after looking at himself in a mirror, forgets what kind of person he is, Jas 1:24. See: BAGD—295b; THAYER—240b.

1951. ἐπιλέγομαι {2x} **ĕpilĕgŏmai**, *ep-ee-leg'-om-ahee;* mid. voice from *1909* and *3004;* to *surname, select:*—call {1x}, choose {1x}.

This word means "to call in addition," i.e., by another name besides that already intimated (Jn 5:2). By extension, in Acts 15:40 Paul named Silas as his traveling companion in the place of Barnabas. See: BAGD—295c; THAYER—240b.

1952. ἐπιλείπω {1x} **ĕpilĕipō**, *ep-ee-li'-po;* from *1909* and *3007;* to *leave upon,* i.e. (fig.) to *be insufficient for:*—fail {1x}.

This word means not enough to suffice for a purpose and is said of insufficient time (Heb 11:32). See: BAGD—295c; THAYER—240b.

1953. ἐπιλησμονή {1x} **ĕpilēsmŏnē**, *ep-ee-lace-mon-ay';* from a der. of *1950; negligence:*—× forgetful {1x}.

(1) This word implies that the person has the necessary information to accomplish a task, but fails to recall it in time to act on it. **(2)** It means "forgetfulness" and is used in Jas 1:25, "a forgetful hearer", "a hearer that forgetteth," lit., "a hearer of forgetfulness," i.e., a hearer characterized by "forgetfulness." See: BAGD—295d; THAYER—240c.

1954. ἐπίλοιπος {1x} **ĕpilŏipŏs**, *ep-il'-oy-pos;* from *1909* and *3062; left over,* i.e. *remaining:*—rest {1x}.

Epiloipos, signifying "still left, left over", is used in the neuter with the article in 1 Pet 4:2, "the rest (of your time)." See: BAGD—295d; THAYER—240c.

1955. ἐπίλυσις {1x} **ĕpilusis**, *ep-il'-oo-sis;* from *1956; explanation,* i.e. *application:*—interpretation {1x}.

This word means to loose, solve, explain and denotes a solution, explanation, lit., "a release." In 2 Pet 1:20, "(of private) interpretation"; i.e., the writers of Scripture did not put their own construction upon the "Godbreathed" words they wrote. See: TDNT—4:337, 543; BAGD—295d; THAYER—240c.

1956. ἐπιλύω {2x} **ĕpiluō**, *ep-ee-loo'-o;* from *1909* and *3089;* to *solve further,* i.e. (fig.) to *explain, decide:*—determine {1x}, expound {1x}.

Literally, this word means to loosen upon, and denotes **(1)** to solve, expound in Mk 4:34; and **(2)** to settle a controversy in Acts 19:39. See: TDNT—4:337, 543; BAGD—295d; THAYER—240c.

1957. ἐπιμαρτυρέω {1x} **ĕpimartŭrĕō**, *ep-ee-mar-too-reh'-o;* from *1909* and *3140;* to *attest further,* i.e. *corroborate:*—testify {1x}.

Epimartureo, to bear witness to, establish by testimony, is rendered "testifying" in 1 Pet 5:12. See: TDNT—4:508, 564; BAGD—296a; THAYER—240c.

1958. ἐπιμέλεια {1x} **ĕpimĕlĕia**, *ep-ee-mel'-i-ah;* from *1959; carefulness,* i.e. kind *attention (hospitality):*—refresh (one's) self + 5177 {1x}.

Epimeleia, in the middle voice, means to care for, give attention to one's self, Acts 27:3. See: BAGD—296a; THAYER—240d.

1959. ἐπιμελέομαι {3x} **ĕpimĕlĕŏmai**, *ep-ee-mel-eh'-om-ahee;* mid. voice from *1909* and the same as *3199;* to *care for* (phys. or otherwise):—take care of {3x}.

This word signifies to take care of, involving forethought and provision (*epi* indicating "the direction of the mind toward the object cared for"). **(1)** Lk 10:34–35 of the Good Samaritan's care for the wounded man; **(2)** and in 1 Ti 3:5 of a bishop's (or overseer's) care of a church—a significant association of ideas. See: BAGD—296a; THAYER—240d.

1960. ἐπιμελῶς {1x} **ĕpimĕlōs**, *ep-ee-mel-oce';* adv. from a der. of *1959; carefully:*—diligently {1x}. See: BAGD—296a; THAYER—240d.

1961. ἐπιμένω {18x} **ĕpimĕnō**, *ep-ee-men'-o;* from *1909* and *3306;* to *stay over,* i.e. *remain* (fig. *persevere):*—tarry {7x}, continue in {5x}, continue {2x}, abide {2x}, abide in {1x}, abide still {1x}.

Epimeno is a strengthened form of *meno* [3306] (*epi,* "intensive"), indicating **(1)** per-

severance in continuing, whether **(1a)** in evil (Rom 6:1; 11:23), or **(1b)** good (Rom 11:22; 1 Ti 4:16). **(2)** It also means to abide, continue, and is translated "to tarry" in Acts 10:48; 21:4, 10; 28:12, 14; 1 Cor 16:7, 8; Gal 1:18, "abode". **(3)** Lit. "to remain on," i.e., in addition to (*epi,* "upon," and *meno*), "to continue long, still to abide," *epimeno* is used of "continuing" **(3a)** to ask, Jn 8:7; **(3b)** to knock, Acts 12:16; **(3c)** in the grace of God, Acts 13:43; **(3d)** in sin, Rom 6:1; **(3e)** in God's goodness, Rom 11:22; **(3f)** in unbelief, Rom 11:23 "abide"; **(3g)** in the flesh, Phil 1:24; **(3h)** in the faith, Col 1:23; **(3i)** in doctrine, 1 Ti 4:16. See: BAGD—296b; THAYER—240d.

1962. ἐπινεύω {1x} **ĕpinĕuō**, *ep-een-yoo'-o;* from *1909* and *3506;* to *nod at,* i.e. (by impl.) to *assent:*—consent {1x}. See: BAGD—296c; THAYER—241a.

1963. ἐπίνοια {1x} **ĕpinŏia**, *ep-in'-oy-ah;* from *1909* and *3563; attention* of the mind, i.e. (by impl.) *purpose:*—thought {1x}. See: BAGD—296c; THAYER—241a.

1964. ἐπιορκέω {1x} **ĕpiŏrkĕō**, *ep-ee-or-keh'-o;* from *1965;* to *commit perjury:*—forswear (one's) self {1x}.

Epiorkeo signifies "to swear falsely, to undo one's swearing, forswear oneself", Mt 5:33. Forswear means to take an oath to fulfill an event before the event occurs, yet being unable to fulfill the vow when the event does happen. Do not swear ahead of time what you may not be able to fulfill. Cf. 1965. See: TDNT—5:466, 729; BAGD—296d; THAYER—241a.

1965. ἐπίορκος {1x} **ĕpiŏrkŏs**, *ep-ee'-or-kos;* from *1909* and *3727; on oath,* i.e. (falsely) a *forswearer:*—perjured person {1x}. Cf. 1964 for discussion. See: TDNT—5:466, 729; BAGD—296d; THAYER—241a.

1966. ἐπιοῦσα {5x} **ĕpiŏusa**, *ep-ee-oo'-sah;* fem. sing. part. of a compound of *1909* and εἶμι **ĕimi** (to *go); supervening,* i.e. (*2250* or *3571* being expressed or implied) the *ensuing* day or night:—following {2x}, next day {2x}, next {1x}. See: BAGD—96d; THAYER—241a.

1967. ἐπιούσιος {2x} **ĕpiŏusiŏs**, *ep-ee-oo'-see-os;* perh. from the same as *1966; tomorrow's;* but more prob. from *1909* and a der. of the pres. part. fem. of *1510; for subsistence,* i.e. *needful:*—daily {2x}.

This word is derived from [1909] *epi,* and [1510] *eimi,* "to go" and means (bread) for going on, i.e., for the morrow and after, or (bread) coming (for us). The added *semeron* [4594] "today," i.e., the prayer is to be for bread that suffices for this day and next, so that the mind

may conform to Christ's warning against anxiety for the morrow. See: TDNT—2:590, 243; BAGD—296d; THAYER—241a.

1968. ἐπιπίπτω {13x} **ĕpipiptō,** *ep-ee-pip'-to;* from *1909* and *4098;* to *embrace* (with affection) or *seize* (with more or less violence; lit. or fig.):—fall {10x}, fall on {1x}, press {1x}, lie {1x}.

Epipipto, "to fall upon", is used **(1)** literally, Mk 3:10, "pressed upon"; Acts 20:10, 37; **(2)** metaphorically, **(2a)** of fear, Lk 1:12; Acts 19:17; Rev 11:11; **(2b)** reproaches, Rom 15:3; **(2c)** of the Holy Spirit, Acts 8:16; 10:44; 11:15. See: BAGD—297c; THAYER—241c.

1969. ἐπιπλήσσω {1x} **ĕpiplēssō,** *ep-ee-place'-so;* from *1909* and *4141;* to *chastise,* i.e. (with words) to *upbraid:*—rebuke {1x}.

Epiplesso, "to strike at" (*epi,* "upon" or "at," *plesso*), "to strike, smite", to strike upon, beat upon, to chastise with words, to chide, upbraid, rebuke and is used in the injunction against "rebuking" an elder, 1 Ti 5:1. See: BAGD—297d; THAYER—241d.

1970. ἐπιπνίγω {1x} **ĕpipnigō,** *ep-ee-pnee'-go;* from *1909* and *4155;* to *throttle upon,* i.e. (fig.) *overgrow:*—choke {1x}. See: BAGD—679d [4155]; THAYER—231b [1901] + 524a [4155].

1971. ἐπιποθέω {9x} **ĕpipŏthĕō,** *ep-ee-poth-eh'-o;* from *1909* and ποθέω **pŏthĕō** (to *yearn*); to *dote upon,* i.e. *intensely crave* possession (lawfully or wrongfully):—greatly desire {2x}, long {1x}, earnestly desire {1x}, long after {1x}, greatly long after {1x}, lust {1x}, desire {1x}, longed after + 2258 {1x}.

Epipotheo, "to long for greatly", is translated **(1)** "I long," in Rom 1:11; **(2)** in 2 Cor 5:2, "earnestly desiring"; **(3)** in 1 Th 3:6 and 2 Ti 1:4, "desiring greatly"; **(4)** to long after, in 2 Cor 9:14; Phil 1:8; 2:26; **(5)** to long for, in 1 Pet 2:2, "desire"; **(6)** Jas 4:5, "long." See: BAGD—297d; THAYER—241d.

1972. ἐπιπόθησις {2x} **ĕpipŏthēsis,** *ep-ee-poth'-ay-sis;* from *1971;* a *longing for:*—earnestly desire {1x}, vehemently desire {1x}. Cf. 2 Cor 7:7, 11. See: BAGD—298a; THAYER—242a.

1973. ἐπιπόθητος {1x} **ĕpipŏthētŏs,** *ep-ee-poth'-ay-tos;* from *1909* and a der. of the latter part of *1971;* *yearned upon,* i.e. *greatly loved:*—longed for {1x}. See: BAGD—298a; THAYER—242a.

1974. ἐπιποθία {1x} **ĕpipŏthia,** *ep-ee-poth-ee'-ah;* from *1971; intense longing:*—great desire {1x}. See: BAGD—298a; THAYER—242a.

1975. ἐπιπορεύομαι {1x} **ĕpipŏrĕuŏmai,** *ep-ee-por-yoo'-om-ahee;* from *1909* and *4198;* to *journey further,* i.e. *travel on* (reach):—come {1x}.

Epiporeuomai, "to travel or journey to a place" is translated "were come [resorted]" in Lk 8:4. See: BAGD—298a; THAYER—242a.

1976. ἐπιρράπτω {1x} **ĕpirrhaptō,** *ep-ir-hrap'-to;* from *1909* and the base of *4476;* to *stitch upon,* i.e. *fasten* with the needle:—sew on {1x}. See: BAGD—298a; THAYER—242a.

1977. ἐπιρρίπτω {2x} **ĕpirrhiptō,** *ep-ir-hrip'-to;* from *1909* and *4496;* to *throw upon* (lit. or fig.):—cast upon {2x}.

Epirrhipto, "to cast upon," means **(1)** lit., "of casting garments on a colt," Lk 19:35; **(2)** figuratively, "of casting care upon God," 1 Pet 5:7. See: TDNT—6:991, 987; BAGD—298b; THAYER—242a.

1978. ἐπίσημος {2x} **ĕpisēmŏs,** *ep-is'-ay-mos;* from *1909* and some form of the base of *4591; remarkable,* i.e. (fig.) *eminent:*—notable {1x}, of note {1x}.

This word means having a mark on it, marked, stamped, coined. *Episemos* primarily meant "bearing a mark," e.g., of money "stamped, coined"; it is used in the NT, metaphorically, **(1)** in a good sense, Rom 16:7, "of note, illustrious," said of Andronicus and Junias; **(2)** in a bad sense, Mt 27:16, "notable," of the prisoner Barabbas. See: TDNT—7:267, 1015; BAGD—298b; THAYER—242a.

1979. ἐπισιτισμός {1x} **ĕpisitismŏs,** *ep-ee-sit-is-mos';* from a compound of *1909* and a der. of *4621;* a *provisioning,* i.e. (concr.) *food:*—victuals {1x}. See: BAGD—298c; THAYER—242b.

1980. ἐπισκέπτομαι {10x} **ĕpiskĕptŏmai,** *ep-ee-skep'-tom-ahee;* mid. voice from *1909* and the base of *4649;* to *inspect,* i.e. (by impl.) to *select;* by extens. to *go to see, relieve:*—look out {1x}, visit {10x}.

Episkeptomai, as a verb, means "to visit," and has the meaning of "seeking out," and is rendered "look ye out": primarily, "to inspect" ("to look upon, care for, exercise oversight"), and **(1)** signifies **(1a)** "to visit" with help, of the act of God, Lk 1:68, 78; 7:16; Acts 15:14; Heb 2:6; **(1b)** "to visit" the sick and afflicted, Mt 25:36, 43; Jas 1:27; **(1c)** "to go and see," "pay a visit to," Acts 7:23; 15:36; **(1d)** "to look out" certain men for a purpose, Acts 6:3; **(2)** it has the meaning of "seeking out," and is rendered "look ye out"

in Acts 6:3: "Wherefore, brethren, look ye out among you seven men of honest report, full of the Holy Ghost and wisdom." Syn.: 308, 352, 578, 816, 872, 991, 1689, 1896, 1914, 1983, 2300, 2334, 3706, 3708, 3879, 4017, 4648. See: TDNT— 2:599, 244; BAGD—298d; THAYER—242b.

1981. ἐπισκηνόω {1x} **ĕpiskēnŏō**, *ep-ee-skay-nŏ'-o;* from *1909* and *4637;* to *tent upon,* i.e. (fig.) *abide with:*—rest upon {1x}.

Episkenoo "to spread a tabernacle over" (*epi,* "upon," *skene,* "a tent"), is used metaphorically in 2 Cor 12:9, "may rest upon (me)", "cover," "spread a tabernacle over." See: TDNT—7:386, 1040; BAGD—298d; THAYER—242c.

1982. ἐπισκιάζω {5x} **ĕpiskiazō**, *ep-ee-skee-ad'-zo;* from *1909* and a der. of *4639;* to *cast a shade upon,* i.e. (by anal.) to *envelop* in a haze of brilliancy; fig. to *invest* with preternatural influence:—overshadow {5x}.

From a vaporous cloud that casts a shadow the word is transferred to a shining cloud surrounding and enveloping persons with brightness. **(1)** Used of the Holy Spirit exerting creative energy upon the womb of the virgin Mary and impregnating it (Lk 1:35); a use of the word which seems to have been drawn from the familiar OT idea of a cloud as symbolising the immediate presence and power of God. It is used **(2)** of the bright cloud at the Transfiguration, Mt 17:5; Mk 9:7; Lk 9:34; **(3)** of the apostle Peter's shadow upon the sick, Acts 5:15. See: TDNT—7:399, 1044; BAGD—298d; THAYER—242c.

1983. ἐπισκοπέω {2x} **ĕpiskŏpĕō**, *ep-ee-skop-eh'-o;* from *1909* and *4648;* to *oversee;* by impl. to *beware:*—look diligently {1x}, take the oversight {1x}.

Episkopeo, as a verb, means literally "to look upon" and is rendered **(1)** "looking carefully/ diligently": "Looking diligently lest any man fail of the grace of God" (Heb 12:15, *epi* being probably intensive here); and **(2)** "to exercise the oversight, to visit, care for": "Feed the flock of God which is among you, taking the oversight thereof, not by constraint, but willingly" (1 Pet 5:2). Syn.: 308, 352, 578, 816, 872, 991, 1689, 1896, 1914, 1980, 2300, 2334, 3706, 3708, 3879, 4017, 4648. See: TDNT—2:599, 244; BAGD—298d; THAYER—242d.

1984. ἐπισκοπή {4x} **ĕpiskŏpē**, *ep-is-kop-ay';* from *1980; inspection* (for relief); by impl. *superintendence;* spec., the Chr. "*episcopate*":—the office of a bishop {1x}, bishoprick {1x}, visitation {2x}.

(1) This word expresses that act by which God looks into and searches out the ways, deeds, and character of men in order to adjudge them their lot accordingly, whether joyous or sad; and by extension the role of the bishop within the local church. Besides its meaning, **(2)** "visitation," e.g., 1 Pet 2:12, it is rendered **(3)** "office," in Acts 1:20, "bishoprick"; and **(4)** in 1 Ti 3:1 "the office of a bishop," lit., "(if any one seeketh) overseership." See: TDNT—2:606, 244; BAGD—299a; THAYER—242d.

1985. ἐπίσκοπος {7x} **ĕpiskŏpŏs**, *ep-is'-kop-os;* from *1909* and *4649* (in the sense of *1983*); a *superintendent,* i.e. Chr. officer in general charge of a (or the) church (lit. or fig.):—bishop {6x}, overseer {1x}.

Episkopos is translated **(1)** "bishop" in Phil 1:1; 1 Ti 3:2; Titus 1:7; 3:15; 1 Pet 2:25; and **(2)** "overseer" in Acts 20:28. See: TDNT—2:608, 244; BAGD—299b; THAYER—243a.

1986. ἐπισπάομαι {1x} **ĕpispaŏmai**, *ep-ee-spah'-om-ahee;* from *1909* and *4685;* to *draw over,* i.e. (with *203* impl.) *efface* the mark of *circumcision* (by recovering with the foreskin):—become uncircumcised {1x}. See: BAGD—299d; THAYER—243a.

1987. ἐπίσταμαι {14x} **ĕpistamai**, *ep-is'-tam-ahee;* appar. a mid. voice of *2186* (with *3563* implied); to *put* the mind *upon,* i.e. *comprehend,* or *be acquainted with:*—know {13x}, understand {1x}.

Epistamai, "to know, know of, understand" is used **(1)** in Mk 14:68, "understand," which follows *oida* "I (neither) know"; and translated **(2)** "know" most frequently in the Acts, 10:28; 15:7; 18:25; 19:15, 25; 20:18; 22:19; 24:10; 26:26; **(3)** elsewhere, 1 Ti 6:4; Heb 11:8; Jas 4:14; Jude 10. Syn.: 1097, 1107, 1110, 1492, 1921, 1467, 1922, 1987. See: BAGD—300a; THAYER—243b.

1988. ἐπιστάτης {7x} **ĕpistatēs**, *ep-is-tat'-ace;* from *1909* and a presumed der. of *2476;* an *appointee over,* i.e. *commander* (*teacher*):—Master {7x}.

It is used by the disciples in addressing the Lord, in recognition of His authority rather than His instruction, Lk 5:5; 8:24 (twice), 45; 9:33, 49; 17:13. See: TDNT—2:622, 248; BAGD—300b; THAYER—243c.

1989. ἐπιστέλλω {3x} **ĕpistĕllō**, *ep-ee-stel'-lo;* from *1909* and *4724;* to *enjoin* (by writing), i.e. (gen.) to *communicate by letter* (for any purpose):—write {1x}, write unto {1x}, write a letter unto {1x}.

Epistello denotes "to send a message by letter, to write word" (*stello,* "to send"; Eng., "epistle"), Acts 15:20; 21:25; Heb 13:22. See:

TDNT—7:593, 1074; BAGD—300c; THAYER—243c.

1990. ἐπιστήμων {1x} **ĕpistēmōn**, *ep-ee-stay'-mone;* from *1987; intelligent:*—endued with knowledge {1x}.

This person is intelligent, experienced, and one having the knowledge of an expert, Jas 3:13. See: BAGD—300c; THAYER—243d.

1991. ἐπιστηρίζω {4x} **ĕpistērizō**, *ep-ee-stay-rid'-zo;* from *1909* and *4741;* to *support further,* i.e. *reestablish:*—confirm {3x}, strengthen {1x}.

(1) This word means to make to lean upon, and thus to strengthen through support. It is used of **(2)** "confirming" souls, Acts 14:22, **(2a)** brethren, Acts 15:32; **(2b)** churches, Acts 15:41; **(2c)** disciples, Acts 18:23. See: TDNT—7:653, 1085; BAGD—300d; THAYER—243d.

1992. ἐπιστολή {24x} **ĕpistŏlē**, *ep-is-tol-ay';* from *1989;* a *written message:*—epistle {15x}, letter {9x}.

Epistole, primarily "a message" (from epistello, "to send to"), hence, "a letter, an epistle," is used **(1)** in the singular, e.g., Acts 15:30; **(2)** in the plural, e.g., Acts 9:2; 2 Cor 10:10. **(3)** Epistle is a less common word for a letter. A letter affords a writer more freedom, both in subject and expression, than does a formal treatise. A letter is usually occasional, that is, it is written in consequence of some circumstance which requires to be dealt with promptly. The style of a letter depends largely on the occasion that calls it forth. **(4)** A broad line is to be drawn between the letter and the epistle. The letter is essentially a spontaneous product dominated throughout by the image of the reader, his sympathies and interests, instinct also with the writer's own soul: it is virtually one half of an imaginary dialogue, the suppressed responses of the other party shaping the course of what is actually written. The epistle has a general aim, addressing all and sundry whom it may concern: it is like a public speech and looks towards publication. **(5)** In 2 Pet 3:16 the apostle includes the Epistles of Paul as part of the God-breathed Scriptures. See: TDNT—7:593, 1074; BAGD—300d; THAYER—243d.

1993. ἐπιστομίζω {1x} **ĕpistŏmizō**, *ep-ee-stom-id'-zo;* from *1909* and *4750;* to put something *over* the *mouth,* i.e. (fig.) to *silence:*—stop mouths {1x}. See: BAGD—301a; THAYER—243d.

1994. ἐπιστρέφω {39x} **ĕpistrĕphō**, *ep-ee-stref'-o;* from *1909* and *4762;* to *revert* (lit., fig. or mor.):—turn {16x}, be converted {6x}, return {6x}, turn about {4x}, turn again {3x}, misc. {4x} = come (go) again.

Epistrepho, as a verb, means "to turn about," or "towards" and is translated **(1)** "to return": "Then he [a demon] saith, I will return into my house from whence I came out; and when he is come, he findeth it empty, swept, and garnished", Mt 12:44; cf. 24:18; Mk 13:16 "turn back again"; Lk 2:39; 8:55, "came again"; 17:31; Acts 15:36 "go again." **(2)** It also denotes **(2a)** "to make to turn towards", Lk 1:16, 17; Jas 5:19, 20 (to convert); **(2b)** intransitively, "to turn oneself round," e.g., **(2b1)** in the passive voice, Mk 5:30; **(2b2)** in the active voice, Mt 13:15, "be converted"; Acts 11:21; 14:15; 15:19; 1 Th 1:9, "ye turned," indicating an immediate and decisive change, consequent upon a deliberate choice; conversion is a voluntary act in response to the presentation of truth. Syn.: 344, 360, 390, 1880, 1877, 5290. See: TDNT—7:722, 1093; BAGD—301a; THAYER—243d.

1995. ἐπιστροφή {1x} **ĕpistrŏphē**, *ep-is-trof-ay';* from *1994; reversion,* i.e. mor. *revolution:*—conversion {1x}.

This word means a turning about, or round, conversion (Acts 15:3). The word implies a turning and a turning from; corresponding to these are faith and repentance; cf. "turned to God from idols" (1 Th 1:9). Divine grace is the efficient cause, human agency the responding effect. See: TDNT—7:722, 1093; BAGD—301c; THAYER—244a.

1996. ἐπισυνάγω {7x} **ĕpisunagō**, *ep-ee-soon-ag'-o;* from *1909* and *4863;* to *collect upon* the same place:—gather {2x}, gather together {5x}.

Episunago "to gather together," suggesting stress upon the place at which the "gathering" is made, is said **(1)** of a hen and her chickens, Mt 23:37; and so of the Lord's would-be protecting care of the people of Jerusalem; cf. Lk 13:34; **(2)** of the "gathering" together of the elect, Mt 24:31; Mk 13:27; **(3)** of the "gathering" together of a crowd, Mk 1:33; Lk 12:1. See: BAGD—301c; THAYER—244b.

1997. ἐπισυναγωγή {2x} **ĕpisunagōgē**, *ep-ee-soon-ag-o-gay';* from *1996;* a *complete collection;* spec. a Chr. *meeting* (for worship):—assembling together {1x}, gathering together {1x}.

Episunagoge, "a gathering together," is used in **(1)** 2 Th 2:1, of the "rapture" of the saints; and for **(2)** Heb 10:25, of the "gatherings" of believers on earth during the present period. See: TDNT—7:841, 1107; BAGD—301d; THAYER—244b.

1998. ἐπισυντρέχω {1x} **ĕpisuntrĕchō**, *ep-ee-soon-trekh'-o;* from *1909* and *4936;* to *hasten together upon* one place (or a particular occasion):—come running

together {1x}. See: BAGD—301d; THAYER—244b.

1999. ἐπισύστασις {2x} **ĕpisustasis,** *ep-ee-soo'-stas-is;* from the mid. voice of a compound of *1909* and *4921;* a *conspiracy,* i.e. *concourse* (riotous or friendly):—that which comes upon {1x}, a raising up + *4060* {1x}.

This word primarily means a stopping, halting (as of soldiers), then, **(1)** an incursion, onset, rush, pressure, a coming upon, 2 Cor 11:28, "Beside those things that are without, that which cometh upon me daily, the care of all the churches" describing the "pressure" or onset due to the constant call upon the apostle for all kinds of help, advice, counsel, exhortation, decisions as to difficulties, disputes, etc. **(2)** The other occurrence of the word is in Acts 24:12, "stirring up, raising", lit. "making a stir." See: BAGD—301d; THAYER—244b.

2000. ἐπισφαλής {1x} **ĕpisphalēs,** *ep-ee-sfal-ace';* from a compound of *1909* and σφάλλω **sphallō** (to *trip*); fig. *insecure:*—dangerous {1x}.

This word literally means "prone to fall"; hence, "insecure, dangerous" as in Acts 27:9. See: BAGD—302a; THAYER—244b.

2001. ἐπισχύω {1x} **ĕpischuō,** *ep-is-khoo'-o;* from *1909* and *2480;* to *avail further,* i.e. (fig.) *insist stoutly:*—be the more fierce {1x}. See: BAGD—302a; THAYER—244c.

2002. ἐπισωρεύω {1x} **ĕpisōrĕuō,** *ep-ee-so-ryoo'-o;* from *1909* and *4987;* to *accumulate further,* i.e. (fig.) *seek* additionally:—heap {1x}.

Episoreuo, "to heap upon" or "together," is used metaphorically in 2 Ti 4:3 of appropriating a number of teachers to suit the liking of those who do the gathering. See: TDNT—7:1094, 1150; BAGD—302a; THAYER—244c.

2003. ἐπιταγή {7x} **ĕpitagē,** *ep-ee-tag-ay';* from *2004;* an *injunction* or *decree;* by impl. *authoritativeness:*—authority {1x}, commandment {6x}.

Epitage stresses "the authoritativeness of the command"; **(1)** it is used in Rom 16:26; 1 Cor 7:6, 25; 2 Cor 8:8; 1 Ti 1:1; Titus 1:3; 2:15. It is also **(2)** an injunction (from *epi,* "upon," *tasso,* "to order"), and is once rendered "authority," Titus 2:15. See: TDNT—8:36, 1156; BAGD—302a; THAYER—244c.

2004. ἐπιτάσσω {10x} **ĕpitassō,** *ep-ee-tas'-so;* from *1909* and *5021;* to *arrange upon,* i.e. *order:*—charge {1x}, command {8x}, enjoin {1x}.

This word signifies to appoint over, put in charge; then, "to put upon one as a duty, to

enjoin" and is translated **(1)** "charge" in Mk 9:25; **(2)** "command" in Mk 1:27; 6:27; 6:39; Lk 4:36; 8:25, 31; 14:22; Acts 23:2; and **(3)** "enjoin" in Philem 8. See: BAGD—302b; THAYER—244c.

2005. ἐπιτελέω {11x} **ĕpitĕlĕō,** *ep-ee-tel-eh'-o;* from *1909* and *5055;* to *fulfill further* (or *completely*), i.e. *execute;* by impl. to *terminate, undergo:*—perform {3x}, perfect {2x}, accomplish {2x}, finish {1x}, performance {1x}, make {1x}, do {1x}.

Epiteleo, intensive, is a strengthened form in the sense of "accomplishing." **(1)** The fuller meaning is "to accomplish perfectly"; **(1a)** "performed" in Rom 15:28; **(1b)** "perfecting" in 2 Cor 7:1; **(1c)** "complete" in 2 Cor 8:6 and 11; **(1d)** "performance" in the latter part of this 11th verse; **(1e)** "perfected" in Gal 3:3; **(1f)** "perfect" in Phil 1:6. **(2)** In Heb 8:5 "make," with regard to the tabernacle. **(3)** In Heb 9:6 and in 1 Pet 5:9 it is translated "accomplish." See: TDNT—8:61, 1161; BAGD—302b; THAYER—244c.

2006. ἐπιτήδειος {1x} **ĕpitēdĕiŏs,** *ep-ee-tay'-di-os;* from ἐπιτηδές **ĕp-itēdĕs** (*enough*); *serviceable,* i.e. (by impl.) *requisite:*—things which are needful {1x}.

Epitedeios denotes needful, esp. of the necessities of life, Jas 2:16. See: BAGD—302d; THAYER—244d.

2007. ἐπιτίθημι {42x} **ĕpitithēmi,** *ep-ee-tith'-ay-mee;* from *1909* and *5087;* to *impose* (in a friendly or hostile sense):—lay on {10x}, lay {7x}, put {6x}, lay upon {4x}, put on {3x}, put upon {2x}, set {2x}, not tr {1x}, misc. {7x} = add unto, lade, + surname, × wound.

Epitithemi, as a verb, means **(1)** "to add to, lay upon," and is used of **(1a)** "laying" hands on the sick, for healing, Mt 9:18; 19:13, "put"; 19:15; Mk 5:23; 6:5; 7:32; 8:23, "put"; so in v. 25; 16:18; Lk 4:40; 13:13; Acts 6:6; 8:17, 19; 9:12 and 17, "putting"; 13:3; 19:6; 28:8; Rev. 1:17; **(1b)** of "laying" hands on a person by way of public recognition, 1 Ti 5:22; **(1c)** of a shepherd's "laying" a sheep on his shoulders, Lk 15:5; **(1d)** of laying" the cross on Christ's shoulders, Lk 23:26; **(1e)** of "laying" on stripes, Acts 16:23; **(1f)** wood on a fire, Acts 28:3; **(1g)** metaphorically, **(1g1)** of "laying" burden's on men's shoulders, Mt 23:4; **(1g2)** similarly of "giving" injunctions, Acts 15:28 (cf. "put . . . upon" in v. 10). **(2)** In Acts 28:10 it is translated "they laded (us) with" [put on board with us]. **(3)** It is also translated "to put, or set" and is used **(3a)** of the placing over the head of Christ on the cross "His accusation," Mt 27:37, "set up"; **(3b)** of attacking a person, Acts 18:10, "shall set on." **(4)** It has a secondary and somewhat

infrequent meaning, "to add to," and is found in this sense in **(4a)** Mk 3:16–17, lit., "He added the name Peter to Simon," "He added to them the name Boanerges," and **(4b)** Rev 22:18, where the word is set in contrast to "take away from" (v. 19). See: TDNT—8:159, 1176; BAGD—302a; THAYER—244d.

2008. ἐπιτιμάω {29x} **ĕpitimaō,** *ep-ee-tee-mah'-o;* from *1909* and *5091;* to *tax upon,* i.e. *censure* or *admonish;* by impl. *forbid:*—straitly charge {1x}, charge {4x}, rebuke {24x}.

Epitimao, as a verb, signifies **(1)** to put honour upon (*epi,* upon, *time,* honour); honor being derived from the root "to be heavy" hence to weigh down upon someone, to exert pressure upon. **(2)** To judge, to find fault with, rebuke; hence to charge, or rather, to charge strictly (*epi,* intensive), **(2a)** e.g., Mt 12:16; Mk 3:12, "charged much"; Mk 8:30; 10:48; **(2b)** "to rebuke"; except for 2 Ti 4:2 and Jude 9, it is confined in the NT to the Synoptic Gospels, where it is frequently used of the Lord's rebukes to **(2b1)** evil spirits, e.g., Mt 17:18; Mk 1:25; 9:25; Lk 4:35, 41; 9:42; **(2b2)** winds, Mt 8:26; Mk 4:39; Lk 8:24; **(2b3)** fever, Lk 4:39; **(2b4)** disciples, Mk 8:33; Lk 9:55; contrast Lk 19:39. **(2c)** For rebukes by others see Mt 16:22; 19:13; 20:31; Mk 8:32; 10:13; 10:48, "charged"; Lk 17:3; 18:15, 39; 23:40. **(3)** One may rebuke a person without convicting that person of any fault. In such a case either there is no fault (so the rebuke is unnecessary or unjust), or although there is a fault, the rebuke does not cause the offender to admit it. Syn.: Thus the distinction between *epitimao* and *elencho* (*1651*) lies in the possibility of rebuking for sin without convincing of sin. See also: 156, 1650, 1651. See: TDNT—2:623, 249 BAGD—303b; THAYER—245b.

2009. ἐπιτιμία {1x} **ĕpitimia,** *ep-ee-tee-mee'-ah;* from a compound of *1909* and *5092;* prop. *esteem,* i.e. *citizenship;* used (in the sense of *2008*) of a *penalty:*—punishment {1x}.

(1) *Epitimia* in the NT denotes "penalty, punishment," 2 Cor 2:6. **(2)** Originally it signified the enjoyment of the rights and privileges of citizenship; then it became used of the estimate fixed by a judge on the infringement of such rights, and hence, in general, a "penalty." See: TDNT—2:627, 249; BAGD—303c; THAYER—245c.

2010. ἐπιτρέπω {19x} **ĕpitrĕpō,** *ep-ee-trep'-o;* from *1909* and the base of *5157;* to *turn over* (*transfer*), i.e. *allow:*—suffer {10x}, permit {4x}, give leave {2x}, give liberty {1x}, give license {1x}, let {1x}.

Epitrepo, as a verb, lit. denotes "to turn to" (*epi,* "upon, to," *trepo,* "to turn"), and so **(1)** "to permit, give leave, send," **(1a)** of Christ's permission to the unclean spirits to enter the swine, Mk 5:13; in Lk 8:32, "suffer" and "suffered"); **(1b)** in Jn 19:38, of Pilate's permission to Joseph to take away the body of the Lord; **(1c)** in Acts 21:39, of Paul's request to the chief captain to permit him to address the people, "suffer"; **(1d)** in Acts 21:40, "he had given him licence"; **(2)** "to entrust," signifies "to permit," Acts 26:1; 1 Cor 14:34; 16:7; 1 Ti 2:12, "suffer"; Heb 6:3; **(3)** is rendered "to suffer" in Mt 8:21; Mk 10:4; Lk 9:59; Acts 28:16; Lk 9:61 "let"; Acts 21:39; Mt 8:31. See: BAGD—303c; THAYER—245c.

2011. ἐπιτροπή {1x} **ĕpitrŏpē,** *ep-ee-trop-ay';* from *2010;* *permission,* i.e. (by impl.) full *power:*—commission {1x}.

This word denotes a turning over (to another), a referring of a thing to another, and so a committal of full powers, a commission (Acts 26:12). See: BAGD—303d; THAYER—245c.

2012. ἐπίτροπος {3x} **ĕpitrŏpŏs,** *ep-it'-rop-os;* from *1909* and *5158* (in the sense of *2011*); a *commissioner,* i.e. domestic *manager, guardian:*—steward {2x}, tutor {1x}.

An *epitropos,* literally, is one to whose care something is committed and is rendered **(1)** "tutors" in Gal 4:2; and **(2)** "steward" Mt 20:8 and Lk 8:3. See: BAGD—303d; THAYER—245c.

2013. ἐπιτυγχάνω {5x} **ĕpitugchanō,** *ep-ee-toong-khan'-o;* from *1909* and *5177;* to *chance upon,* i.e. (by impl.) to *attain:*—obtain {1x}. Cf. Rom 11:7 (twice); Heb 6:15; 11:33; Jas 4:2. See: BAGD—303d.

2014. ἐπιφαίνω {4x} **ĕpiphainō,** *ep-ee-fah'-ee-no;* from *1909* and *5316;* to *shine upon,* i.e. *become* (lit.) *visible* or (fig.) *known:*—appear {3x}, give light {1x}.

Epiphaino is used **(1)** in the active voice with the meaning "to give light," Lk 1:79; **(2)** in the passive voice, "to appear, become visible." It is said of heavenly bodies, e.g., the stars, Acts 27:20; **(3)** metaphorically, of things spiritual, **(3a)** the grace of God, Titus 2:11; **(3b)** the kindness and the love of God, Titus 3:4. See: TDNT—9:7, 1244; BAGD—304a; THAYER—245d.

2015. ἐπιφάνεια {6x} **ĕpiphanĕia,** *ep-if-an'-i-ah;* from *2016;* a *manifestation,* i.e. (spec.) the *advent* of Christ (past or future):—appearing {5x}, brightness {1x}.

Epiphaneia is often used of the glorious manifestation of Christ—not only that which has already taken place during and through His earthly ministry, but also that illustrious

return from heaven to earth to occur in the future. **(1)** "Epiphany," lit., "a shining forth," was used of the "appearance" of a god to men, and of an enemy to an army in the field, etc. In the NT it occurs of **(2)** the advent of the Savior when the Word became flesh, 2 Ti 1:10; **(3)** the coming of the Lord Jesus into the air to the meeting with His saints, 1 Ti 6:14; 2 Ti 4:1, 8; **(4)** the shining forth of the glory of the Lord Jesus "as the lightning cometh forth from the east, and is seen even unto the west," Mt 24:27, immediately consequent on the unveiling, *apokalupsis,* of His *Parousia,* His return, in the air with His saints, 2 Th 2:8; Titus 2:13. Syn.: 602, 5321. See: TDNT—9:7, 1244; BAGD—304a; THAYER—245d.

2016. **ἐπιφανής** {1x} **ĕpiphanēs,** *ep-if-an-ace'; from 2014; conspicuous,* i.e. (fig.) *memorable:—*notable {1x}.

Epiphanes denotes conspicuous, manifest, illustrious is translated "notable" in Acts 2:20, of the great Day of the Lord. See: TDNT—9:7, 1244; BAGD—304b; THAYER—246a.

2017. **ἐπιφαύω** {1x} **ĕpiphauō,** *ep-ee-fŏw'-o;* a form of *2014;* to *illuminate* (fig.):—give light {1x}.

This word means to shine forth and is rendered "shall give . . . light," in Eph 5:14 of the glory of Christ, illumining the believer who fulfills the conditions, so that being guided by His "light" he reflects His character. See: TDNT—9:310,*; BAGD—304a; THAYER—246a.

2018. **ἐπιφέρω** {5x} **ĕpipherō,** *ep-ee-fer'-o;* from *1909* and *5342;* to *bear upon* (or *further*), i.e. *adduce* (pers. or judicially [*accuse, inflict*]), *superinduce:—*add {1x}, bring {2x}, bring against {1x}, take {1x}.

Epiphero signifies **(1)** "to bring upon, or to bring against," Acts 25:18; Jude 9; **(2)** "to impose, inflict, visit upon," Rom 3:5; **(3)** "to bring", Acts 19:12; and **(4)** "to add", Phil 1:16. See: BAGD—304c; THAYER—246a.

2019. **ἐπιφωνέω** {3x} **ĕpiphōnĕō,** *ep-ee-fo-neh'-o;* from *1909* and *5455;* to *call at* something, i.e. *exclaim:—*cry {1x}, cry against {1x}, give a shout {1x}.

Epiphoneo, as a verb, signifies "to shout" either **(1)** against: "But they cried, saying, Crucify him, crucify him"(Lk 23:21; 22:24), or **(2)** in acclamation: "And the people gave a shout, saying, It is the voice of a god, and not of a man" (Acts 12:22). Syn.: 310, 349, 994, 995, 1916, 2896, 2905, 2906, 5455. See: BAGD—304d; THAYER—246b.

2020. **ἐπιφώσκω** {2x} **ĕpiphōskō,** *ep-ee-foce'-ko;* a form of *2017;* to begin to *grow light:—*begin to dawn {1x}, ✕ draw on {1x}.

Epiphosko, as a verb, means "to dawn" (lit., "to make to shine upon"), and is said of the approach of the Sabbath: "And that day was the preparation, and the sabbath drew on" (Lk 23:54 – "drew on/began to dawn"; cf. Mt 28:1). Syn.: 307, 385, 392, 501, 502, 645, 868, 1448, 1670, 1828, 2464, 4317, 4334, 4358, 4685, 4951, 5288, 5289. See: TDNT—9:310, 1293; BAGD—304d; THAYER—246b.

2021. **ἐπιχειρέω** {3x} **ĕpichĕirĕō,** *ep-ee-khi-reh'-o;* from *1909* and *5495;* to put the *hand upon,* i.e. *undertake:—*go about {1x}, take in hand {1x}, take upon {1x}.

This word occurs **(1)** in Lk 1:1, "have taken in hand"; **(2)** in Acts 9:29, "they went about"; **(3)** in Acts 19:13, "took upon them." See: BAGD—304d; THAYER—246b.

2022. **ἐπιχέω** {1x} **ĕpichĕō,** *ep-ee-kheh'-o;* from *1909* and χέω **chĕō** (to pour);—to *pour upon:—*pour in {1x}.

The wounds being deep needed ointment poured "in" in order to cleanse. See: BAGD—305a; THAYER—246b.

2023. **ἐπιχορηγέω** {5x} **ĕpichŏrēgĕō,** *ep-ee-khor-ayg-eh'-o;* from *1909* and *5524;* to *furnish besides,* i.e. fully *supply,* (fig.) *aid* or *contribute:—*add {1x}, minister {2x}, minister nourishment {1x}, minister unto {1x}.

This word means "to supply, to minister" and is translated **(1)** "add to" in 2 Pet 1:5; and **(2)** "minister", 2 Cor 9:10; Gal 3:5; Col 2:19; 2 Pet 1:5, "add"; 1:11. See: BAGD—305a; THAYER—246b.

2024. **ἐπιχορηγία** {2x} **ĕpichŏrēgia,** *ep-ee-khor-ayg-ee'-ah;* from *2023; contribution:—*supply {1x}.

Epichoregia, "a full supply," occurs in **(1)** Eph 4:16, "supplieth," lit., "by the supply of every joint," metaphorically of the members of the church, the body of which Christ is the Head, and **(2)** Phil 1:19, "the supply (of the Spirit of Jesus Christ)," i.e., "the bountiful supply"; here "of the Spirit" may be taken either in the subjective sense, the Giver, or the objective, the Gift. See: BAGD—305b; THAYER—246c.

2025. **ἐπιχρίω** {2x} **ĕpichriō,** *ep-ee-khree'-o;* from *1909* and *5548;* to *smear over:—*anoint {1x}, anoint + 1909 {1x}.

Epichrio, as a verb, means primarily, "to rub on" and is used of the blind man whose eyes Christ "anointed," and indicates the manner in

which the "anointing" was done: "When He had thus spoken, He spat on the ground, and made clay of the spittle, and He anointed the eyes of the blind man with the clay" (Jn 9:6; cf. v. 11). Syn.: 218, 1472, 3462, 5545, 5548. See: BAGD—305b; THAYER—246c.

2026. ἐποικοδομέω {8x} ĕpŏikŏdŏmĕō, *ep-oy-kod-om-eh'-o;* from *1909* and *3618;* to *build upon,* i.e. (fig.) to *rear up:*—build up {3x}, build thereon {1x}, build thereupon {2x}, build {2x}. Cf. 1 Cor 3:10 (twice), 12, 14; Eph 2:20; Jude 20; or up, Acts 20:32; Col 2:7. See: TDNT—5:147, 674; BAGD—305b; THAYER—246c.

2027. ἐποκέλλω {1x} ĕpŏkĕllō, *ep-ok-el'-lo;* from *1909* and ὀκέλλω ŏkĕllō (to *urge*); to *drive upon* the shore, i.e. to *beach* a vessel:—run aground {1x}. See: BAGD—305c; THAYER—246d.

2028. ἐπονομάζω {1x} ĕpŏnŏmazō, *ep-on-om-ad'-zo;* from *1909* and *3687;* to *name further,* to *surname,* i.e. *denominate:*—call {1x}. See: TDNT—5:282, 694; BAGD—305c; THAYER—246d.

2029. ἐποπτεύω {2x} ĕpŏptĕuō, *ep-opt-yoo'-o;* from *1909* and a der. of *3700;* to *inspect,* i.e. *watch:*—behold {2x}.

Epopteuo, [from *epi,* "upon," and a form of *horao*], "to see," is used of "witnessing as a spectator, or overseer": "Having your conversation honest among the Gentiles: that, whereas they speak against you as evildoers, they may by your good works, which they shall behold (*epopteuo*), glorify God in the day of visitation" (1 Pet 2:12; cf. 3:2). Syn.: 333, 816, 991, 1689, 1896, 2300, 2334, 2657, 2734, 3708. See: TDNT—5:373, 706; BAGD—305c; THAYER—246d.

2030. ἐπόπτης {1x} ĕpŏptēs, *ep-op'-tace;* from *1909* and a presumed der. of *3700;* a *looker-on:*—eye-witness {1x}.

Epoptes, as a noun, means "an eye-witness": "For we have not followed cunningly devised fables, when we made known unto you the power and coming of our Lord Jesus Christ, but were eyewitnesses (*epoptes*) of His majesty" (2 Pet 1:16). Syn.: 333, 816, 991, 1689, 1896, 2029, 2300, 2334, 2657, 2734, 3708. See: TDNT—5:373, 706; BAGD—305d; THAYER—246d.

2031. ἔπος {1x} ĕpŏs, *ep'-os;* from *2036;* a *word:*—say + 2036 {1x}. See: BAGD—305d; THAYER—246d.

2032. ἐπουράνιος {20x} ĕpŏuraniŏs, *ep-oo-ran'-ee-os;* from *1909* and

3772; above the *sky:*—celestial {2x}, in heaven {1x}, heavenly {16x}, high {1x}.

Epouranios (2032), as a noun, means "heavenly," what pertains to, or is in, heaven (*epi,* in the sense of "pertaining to," not here, "above"). It is used **(1)** of God the Father, Mt 18:35; **(2)** of the place where Christ "sitteth at the right hand of God" (i.e., in a position of divine authority), Eph 1:20; and **(2a)** of the present position of believers in relationship to Christ, Eph 2:6; **(2b)** where they possess "every spiritual blessing," 1:3; **(3)** of Christ as "the Second Man," and all those who are related to Him spiritually, 1 Cor 15:48; **(4)** of those whose sphere of activity or existence is above, or in contrast to that of earth, **(4a)** of "principalities and powers," Eph 3:10; **(4b)** of "spiritual hosts of wickedness," Eph 6:12, "in high places"; **(5)** of the Holy Spirit, Heb 6:4; **(6)** of "heavenly things," **(6a)** as the subjects of the teaching of Christ, Jn 3:12, and **(6b)** as consisting of the spiritual and "heavenly" sanctuary and "true tabernacle" and all that appertains thereto in relation to Christ and His sacrifice as antitypical of the earthly tabernacle and sacrifices under the Law, Heb 8:5; 9:23; **(7)** of the "calling" of believers, Heb 3:1; **(8)** of heaven as the abode of the saints, **(8a)** "a better country" than that of earth, Heb 11:16, and **(8b)** of the spiritual Jerusalem, Heb 12:22; **(9)** of the kingdom of Christ in its future manifestation, 2 Ti 4:18; **(10)** of all beings and things, animate and inanimate, that are "above the earth," Phil 2:10; **(11)** of the resurrection and glorified bodies of believers, 1 Cor 15:49; **(12)** of the "heavenly orbs," 1 Cor 15:40 ("celestial," twice, and so rendered here only). Syn.: 3321, 3770, 3771, 3772. See: TDNT—5:538, 736; BAGD—305d; THAYER—247a.

2033. ἑπτά {87x} hĕpta, *hep-tah';* a primary number; *seven:*—seven {86x}, seventh {1x}. See: TDNT—2:627, 249; BAGD—306b; THAYER—247b.

2034. ἑπτάκις {4x} hĕptakis, *hep-tak-is';* adv. from *2033; seven times:*—seven times {4x}. See: TDNT—2:627, 249; BAGD—306b; THAYER—247b.

2035. ἑπτακισχίλιοι {1x} hĕptakischiliŏi, *hep-tak-is-khil'-ee-oy;* from *2034* and *5507; seven times a thousand:*—seven thousand {1x}. See: TDNT—2:627, 249; BAGD—306c; THAYER—247b.

2036. ἔπω {977x} ĕpō, *ep'-o;* a primary verb (used only in the def. past tense, the others being borrowed from *2046, 4483,* and *5346*); to *speak* or *say* (by word or writing):—say {859x}, speak {57x}, tell {41x}, command {8x}, bid {5x}, vr say {1x}, misc. {6x} =

answer, bring word, call, grant. See: BAGD—468a; THAYER—247b. Comp. *3004.*

2037. Ἔραστος {3x} Ĕrastŏs, *er'-as-tos;* from ἐράω ĕraō (to *love); beloved; Erastus,* a Chr.:—Erastus {3x}. See: BAGD—306c; THAYER—247b.

ἐραυνάω ĕraunaō. See *2045.*

2038. ἐργάζομαι {39x} ĕrgazŏmai, *er-gad'-zom-ahee;* mid. voice from *2041;* to *toil* (as a task, occupation, etc.), (by impl.) *effect, be engaged in* or *with,* etc.:—work {22x}, wrought {7x}, do {3x}, minister about {1x}, forbear working + 3361 {1x}, labour for {1x}, labour {1x}, commit {1x}, trade by {1x}, trade {1x}.

This word is used **(1)** intransitively, e.g., Mt 21:28; Jn 5:17; 9:4 (2nd part); Rom 4:4, 5; 1 Cor 4:12; 9:6; 1 Th 2:9; 4:11; 2 Th 3:8, 10–12; **(2)** transitively, **(2a)** "to work something, produce, perform," e.g., Mt 26:10, "she hath wrought"; Jn 6:28, 30; 9:4 (1st part); Acts 10:35; 13:41; Rom 2:10; 13:10; 1 Cor 16:10; Gal 6:10; Eph 4:28; Heb 11:33; 2 Jn 8; **(2b)** "to earn by working, work for," Jn 6:27, "labor"; **(3)** it is translated by the verb "to commit" (of committing sin), in Jas 2:9. See: TDNT—2:635, 251; BAGD—306d; THAYER—247b.

2039. ἐργασία {6x} ĕrgasia, *er-gas-ee'-ah;* from *2040; occupation, a business;* by impl. *profit, pains:*—craft {1x}, diligence {1x}, gain {3x}, work {1x}.

Ergasia, **(1)** lit., "a working" (akin to *ergon,* "work"), is indicative of a process, in contrast to the concrete, *ergon,* e.g., Eph 4:19, lit., "unto a working" (contrast *ergon* in v. 12); **(2)** "craft," Acts 19:25; **(3)** or gain got by "work," Acts 16:16, 19; 19:24; **(4)** endeavor, pains, "diligence," Lk 12:58. See: TDNT—2:635, 251; BAGD—307c; THAYER—247d.

2040. ἐργάτης {16x} ĕrgatēs, *er-gat'-ace;* from *2041; a toiler;* fig. a *teacher:*—labourer {10x}, worker {3x}. workmen {3x}.

An *ergates* (*2040*), akin to *ergazomai,* "to work," and *ergon,* "work," denotes **(1)** "a field laborer, a husbandman," Mt 9:37, 38; 20:1, 2, 8; Lk 10:2 (twice); Jas 5:4; **(2)** "a workman, laborer," in a general sense, Mt 10:10; Lk 10:7; Acts 19:25; 1 Ti 5:18; and it is used **(3)** of false apostles and evil teachers, 2 Cor 11:13; Phil 3:2, **(4)** of a servant of Christ, 2 Ti 2:15; **(5)** of evildoers, Lk 13:27. See: TDNT—2:635, 251; BAGD—307c; THAYER—248a.

2041. ἔργον {176x} ĕrgŏn, *er'-gon;* from a primary (but obs.) ἔργω ĕrgō (to *work*); *toil* (as an effort or occupation); by impl. an *act:*—deed {22x}, doing {1x}, labour {1x},

work {152x}. See: TDNT—2:635, 251; BAGD—307d; THAYER—248a.

2042. ἐρεθίζω {2x} ĕrĕthizō, *er-eth-id'-zo;* from a presumed prol. form of *2054;* to *stimulate* (espec. to anger):—provoke {2x}.

Erethizo, as a verb, means "to excite, stir up, provoke," is used **(1)** in a good sense in 2 Cor 9:2, "hath provoked"; **(2)** in an evil sense in Col 3:21, "provoke." Syn.: 329, 383, 387, 1326, 1892, 3947, 3951, 4531, 4579, 4787, 4797, 5017. See: BAGD—308d; THAYER—249a.

2043. ἐρείδω {1x} ĕrĕidō, *er-i'-do;* of obscure aff.; to *prop,* i.e. (refl.) *get fast:*—stick fast {1x}. See: BAGD—308d; THAYER—249a.

2044. ἐρεύγομαι {1x} ĕrĕugŏmai, *er-yoog'-om-ahee;* of uncert. aff.; to *belch,* i.e. (fig.) to *speak outloud:*—utter {1x}. See: BAGD—308d; THAYER—249a.

2045. ἐρευνάω {6x} ĕrĕunaō, *er-yoo-nah'-o* or ἐραυνάω ĕraunaō, *er-ouw-nah'-o;* appar. from *2046* (through the idea of *inquiry*); to *seek,* i.e. (fig.) to *investigate:*—search {6x}.

Ereunao, "to search, examine," is used **(1)** of God, as "searching" the heart, Rom 8:27; **(2)** of Christ, similarly, Rev 2:23; **(3)** of the Holy Spirit, as "searching" all things, 1 Cor 2:10, acting in the spirit of the believer; **(4)** of the OT prophets, as "searching" their own writings concerning matters foretold of Christ, testified by the Spirit of Christ in them, 1 Pet 1:11; **(5)** of the Jews, as commanded by the Lord to "search" the Scriptures, Jn 5:39; **(6)** of Nicodemus as commanded similarly by the chief priests and Pharisees, Jn 7:52. See: TDNT—2:655, 255; BAGD—306c; THAYER—249a.

2046. ἐρέω {71x} ĕrĕō, *er-eh'-o;* prob. a fuller form of *4483;* an alternate for *2036* in cert. tenses; to *utter,* i.e. *speak* or *say:*—call {1x}, say {57x}, speak {7x}, speak of {2x}, tell {4x}. See: TDNT—2:655, 255; BAGD—468a; 735a; THAYER—562a [4483].

2047. ἐρημία {4x} ĕrēmia, *er-ay-mee'-ah;* from *2048; solitude* (concr.):—desert {1x}, wilderness {3x}.

Eremia, primarily "a solitude, an uninhabited place," in contrast to a town or village, is **(1)** translated "deserts" in Heb 11:38; **(2)** "the wilderness" in Mt 15:33, "a desert place," in Mk 8:4; **(3)** "wilderness" in 2 Cor 11:26. **(4)** It does not always denote a barren region, void of vegetation; it is often used of a place uncultivated, but fit for pasturage. See: TDNT—2:657, 255; BAGD—308d; THAYER—249b.

2048. ἔρημος {50x} ĕrēmŏs, *er'-ay-mos;* of uncert. aff.; *lonesome,* i.e. (by impl.) *waste* (usually as a noun, 5561 being implied):—desert {13x}, desolate {4x}, solitary {1x}, wilderness {32x}. See: TDNT—2:657, 255; BAGD—309a; THAYER—249b.

2049. ἐρημόω {5x} ĕrēmŏō, *er-ay-mŏ'-o;* from 2048; to *lay waste* (lit. or fig.):— bring to desolation {2x}, desolate {1x}, come to nought {1x}, make desolate {1x}.

Eremoo signifies "to make desolate, lay waste." From the primary sense of "making quiet" comes that of "making lonely." It is used only in the passive voice in the NT; **(1)** in Rev 17:16, "shall make desolate" is, lit., "shall make her desolated"; in **(2)** Rev 18:17, 19, "is made desolate"; **(3)** in Mt 12:25 and Lk 11:17, "is brought to desolation." See: TDNT—2:657, 255; BAGD—309b; THAYER—249c.

2050. ἐρήμωσις {3x} ĕrēmōsis, *er-ay'-mo-sis;* from 2049; *despolia-tion:*—desolation {3x}.

Eremosis denotes "desolation," **(1)** in the sense of "making desolate," e.g., in the phrase "the abomination of desolation," Mt 24:15; Mk 13:14; the genitive is objective, "the abomination that makes desolate"; **(2)** with stress upon the effect of the process, Lk 21:20, with reference to the "desolation" of Jerusalem. See: TDNT—2:660, 255; BAGD—309b; THAYER—249c.

2051. ἐρίζω {1x} ĕrizō, *er-id'-zo;* from 2054; to *wrangle:*—strive {1x}.

Erizo means to wrangle, engage in strife used to describe the calm temper of Jesus in contrast with the vehemence of the Jewish doctors wrangling together about tenets and practices in Mt 12:19. See: BAGD—309b; THAYER—249c.

2052. ἐριθεία {7x} ĕrithĕia, *er-ith-i'-ah;* perh. as the same as 2042; prop. *in-trigue,* i.e. (by impl.) *faction:*—contention {1x}, contentious {1x}, strife {5x}.

Eritheia denotes **(1)** "ambition, self-seeking, rivalry," self-will being an underlying idea in the word; hence it denotes "party-making." **(1a)** Seeking to win followers creates factions. **(1b)** Factions are the result of jealousy. **(1c)** It is derived, not from *eris,* "strife," but from *er-ithos,* "a hireling"; hence the meaning of "seeking to win followers," "strifes, factions," 2 Cor 12:20; not improbably the meaning here is rivalries, or base ambitions (all the other words in the list express abstract ideas rather than factions); cf. Gal 5:20; Phil 1:17,(v. 16, "contention"); Phil 2:3 "strife"; Jas 3:14, 16; **(2)** in Rom 2:8 it is translated as an adjective, "conten-

tious." **(2a)** The order "strife, jealousy, wrath, faction," is the same in 2 Cor 12:20 and **(2b)** Gal 5:20. See: TDNT—2:660, 256; BAGD—309b; THAYER—249c.

2053. ἔριον {2x} ĕriŏn, *er'-ee-on;* of obscure aff.; *wool:*—wool {2x}. Cf. Heb 9:19; Rev 1:14. See: BAGD—309c; THAYER—249d.

2054. ἔρις {9x} ĕris, *er'-is;* of uncert. aff.; a *quar-rel,* i.e. (by impl.) *wrangling:*—contention {2x}, debate {2x}, strife {4x}, variance {1x}.

Eris, "strife, contention," is the **(1)** expression of "enmity," Rom 1:29, "debate"; 13:13; 1 Cor 1:11, "contentions"; 3:3; 2 Cor 12:20, "debates"; Gal 5:20, "variance"; Phil 1:15; 1 Ti 6:4; Titus 3:9, "contentions". **(2)** The stress in this word is on rivalry. See: BAGD—309c; THAYER—249d.

2055. ἐρίφιον {1x} ĕriphiŏn, *er-if'-ee-on;* from 2056; a *kidling,* i.e. (gen.) *goat* (symbol. *wicked* person):—goat {1x}.

This diminutive of *eriphos* [2056] is in Mt 25:33. Its use is purely figurative and where the application is made, though metaphorically, the change to the diminutive is suggestive of the contempt which those so described bring upon themselves by their refusal to assist the needy. See: BAGD—309d; THAYER—249d.

2056. ἔριφος {2x} ĕriphŏs, *er'-if-os;* perh. from the same as 2053 (through the idea of *hairiness);* a *kid* or (gen.) *goat:*—goat {1x}, kid {1x}. Cf. Mt 25:32; Lk 15:29. See: BAGD—309d; THAYER—249d.

2057. Ἑρμᾶς {1x} Hĕrmas, *her-mas';* prob. from 2060; *Hermas,* a Chr.:—Hermas {1x}. See: BAGD—309d; THAYER—250a.

2058. ἑρμηνεία {2x} hĕrmēnĕia, *her-may-ni'-ah;* from the same as 2059; *translation:*—interpretation {2x}.

Hermeneia is interpretation of what has been spoken more or less obscurely by others, 1 Cor 12:10; 14:26. See: TDNT—2:661, 256; BAGD—310a; THAYER—250a.

2059. ἑρμηνεύω {4x} hĕrmēnĕuō, *her-mayn-yoo'-o;* from a presumed der. of 2060 (as the god of language); to *trans-late:*—by interpretation {3x}, being interpreted {1x}.

(1) *Hermes,* the Greek name of the pagan god Mercury, was regarded as the messenger of the gods. **(2)** *Hermeneuo,* denotes "to explain, interpret" (Eng., "hermeneutics"), and is used of explaining the meaning of words in a different language: **(2a)** Jn 1:38, "Siloam," interpreted as "sent"; **(2b)** Heb 7:2, Melchizedec, "by

interpretation," lit., "being interpreted," King of righteousness; **(2c)** Jn 1:42, "Cephas, which is by interpretation, a stone"; and **(2d)** Jn 1:38, "rabbi . . . being interpreted master." See: TDNT—2:661, 256; BAGD—310a; THAYER—250a.

2060. Ἑρμῆς {2x} **Hĕrmēs,** *her-mace';* perh. from *2046; Hermes,* the name of the messenger of the Gr. deities; also of a Chr.:—*Hermes* {1x}, Mercurious {1x}.

See 2059 for why Paul, being the chief speaker, was called *Hermes* by those at Lystra, Acts 14:12. See: BAGD—310a; THAYER—250a.

2061. Ἑρμογένης {1x} **Hĕrmŏgĕnēs,** *her-mog-en'-ace;* from *2060* and *1096; born of Hermes; Hermogenes,* an apostate Chr.:—*Hermogenes* {1x}. See: BAGD—310b; THAYER—250a.

2062. ἑρπετόν {4x} **hĕrpĕtŏn,** *her-pet-on';* neut. of a der. of ἕρπω **hĕrpō** (to *creep*); a *reptile,* i.e. (by Heb. [comp. 7431]) a small *animal:*—creeping thing {3x}, serpent {1x}.

Herpeton signifies "a creeping thing" and is translated **(1)** "serpents" in Jas 3:7 (which form only one of this genus); **(2)** it is set in contrast to quadrupeds and birds, Acts 10:12; 11:6; Rom 1:23. See: BAGD—310b; THAYER—250b.

2063. ἐρυθρός {2x} **ĕruthrŏs,** *er-oo-thros';* of uncert. aff.; *red,* i.e. (with *2281*) the *Red* Sea:—red {2x}. Cf. Acts 7:36; Heb 11:29. See: BAGD—310b; THAYER—250b.

2064. ἔρχομαι {643x} **ĕrchŏmai,** *er'-khom-ahee;* mid. voice of a primary verb (used only in the present and imperfect tenses, the others being supplied by a kindred [mid. voice]

     ἐλεύθομαι **ĕlĕuthŏmai,** *el-yoo'-thom-ahee;* or [act.]

     ἔλθω **ĕlthō,** *el'-tho;* which do not otherwise occur); to *come* or *go* (in a great variety of applications, lit. and fig.):—come {616x}, go {13x}, vr come {1x}, misc. {13x} = accompany, appear, bring, enter, fall out, grow, × light, × next, pass, resort, be set. See: TDNT—2:666, 257; BAGD—310b; THAYER—250b.

2065. ἐρωτάω {58x} **ĕrōtaō,** *er-o-tah'-o;* appar. from *2046* [comp. *2045*]; to *interrogate;* by impl. to *request:*—ask {23x}, beseech {14x}, pray {14x}, desire {16x}, intreat {1x}.

Erotao more frequently suggests **(1)** that the petitioner is on a footing of equality or famil-

iarity that lends authority to the request with the person whom he intreats. It is used **(1a)** of a king in making request from another king (Lk 14:32); **(1b)** of the Pharisee who desired Christ that He would eat with him, indicating the inferior conception he had of Christ (Lk 7:36). **(2)** It is significant that the Lord Jesus never used *aiteo* (*154*) in the matter of making request to the Father. The consciousness of His equal dignity, of His potent and prevailing intercession, speaks out in this, that as often as He asks, or declares that He will ask anything of the Father, it is always *erotao,* an asking, that is, upon equal terms (Jn 14:16; 16:26; 17:9, 15, 20). **(3)** Martha, on the contrary, plainly reveals her poor unworthy conception of His person, that . . . she ascribes that *aiteo* to Him which He never ascribes to Himself (Jn 11:22). Syn.: 154, 1833, 1905, 4441. See: TDNT—2:685, 262; BAGD—311d; THAYER—252b.

2066. ἐσθής {7x} **ĕsthēs,** *es-thace';* from ἕν-νυμι **hĕnnumi** (to *clothe*); *dress:*—apparel {3x}, clothing {2x}, raiment {1x}, robe {1x}.

This word usually suggests good clothing as compared to common. See: BAGD—312b; THAYER—252c.

2067. ἔσθησις {1x} **ĕsthēsis,** *es'-thay-sis;* from a der. of *2066; clothing* (concr.):—garment {1x}. See: BAGD—312b; THAYER—252c; THAYER—252c.

2068. ἐσθίω {65x} **ĕsthiō,** *es-thee'-o;* strengthened for a primary ἔδω **ĕdō** (to *eat*); used only in certain tenses, the rest being supplied by *5315;* to *eat* (usually lit.):—devour {1x}, eat {63x}, live {1x}. See: TDNT—2:689, 262; BAGD—312b; THAYER—252c.

2069. Ἐσλί {1x} **Ĕsli,** *es-lee';* of Heb. or. [prob. for 454]; *Esli,* an Isr.:—*Esli* {1x}. See: BAGD—313b; THAYER—253b.

2070. ἐσμέν {53x} **ĕsmĕn,** *es-men';* first pers. plur. ind. of *1510;* we *are:*—are {49x}, have hope + 1679 {1x}, was {1x}, be {1x}, have our being {1x}. See: BAGD—222d [1510]; THAYER—175c [1510].

2071. ἔσομαι {188x} **ĕsŏmai,** *es'-om-ahee;* future of *1510; will be:*—shall be {151x}, will be {9x}, be {6x}, shall have {6x}, shall come to pass {4x}, shall {4x}, not tr {1x}, misc. {7x} = should be, × may have, × fall, what would follow, × live long, × sojourn. See: BAGD—223a [1510]; THAYER—175c [1510].

2072. ἔσοπτρον {2x} **ĕsŏptrŏn,** *es'-op-tron;* from *1519* and a presumed der. of *3700;* a *mirror* (for *looking into*):—glass {2x}. Cf. 1 Cor 13:12 and Jas 1:23. See: TDNT—

2:696, 27/264; BAGD—313b; THAYER—253b. Syn.: ????.

2073. ἑσπέρα {3x} hĕspĕra, *hes-per'-ah;* fem. of an adj. ἑσπερός hĕspĕrŏs (*evening*); the *eve* (5610 being implied):—evening {2x}, eventide {1x}. Cf. Lk 24:29; Acts 4:3, "eventide"; 28:23. See: BAGD—313c; THAYER—253b.

2074. Ἐσρώμ {3x} Ĕsrōm, *es-rome;* of Heb. or. [2696]; *Esrom* (i.e. *Chetsron*), an Isr.:—*Esrom* {3x}. See: BAGD—313d; THAYER—253b.

2075. ἐστέ {92x} ĕstĕ, *es-teh';* second pers. plur. pres. ind. of 1510; ye *are:*—are {82x}, be {5x}, is {2x}, belong to {1x}, have been {1x}, not tr {1x}. See: BAGD—222d [1510]; THAYER—175c [1510].

2076. ἐστί {910x} ĕsti, *es-tee';* third pers. sing. pres. ind. of 1510; he (she or it) *is;* also (with neut. plur.) they *are:*—is {752x}, are {51x}, was {29x}, be {25x}, have {11x}, not tr {15x}, vr is {1x}, misc. {27x} = belong, call, ✗ can [-not], come, consisteth, ✗ dure for a while, + follow, (that) is (to say), make, meaneth, ✗ must needs, + profit, + remaineth, + wrestle. See: BAGD—222d [1510]; THAYER—175c [1510].

2077. ἔστω {16x} ĕstō, *es'-to;* second pers. sing. pres. imper. of 1510; *be* thou; also

ἔστωσαν ĕstōsan, *es'-to-san;* third pers. of the same; *let* them *be:*—let be {10x}, be {5x}, not tr {1x}. See: BAGD—222d [1510]; THAYER—175c [1510].

2078. ἔσχατος {54x} ĕschatŏs, *es'-khat-os;* a superl. prob. from 2192 (in the sense of *contiguity*); *farthest, final* (of place or time):—last {46x}, lowest {2x}, uttermost {2x}, last state {2x}, ends {1x}, latter end {1x}.

Eschatos, "last, utmost, extreme," is used **(1)** of place, e.g., Lk 14:9, 10, "lowest;" Acts 1:8 and 13:47, "uttermost part;" **(2)** of rank, e.g., Mk 9:35; **(3)** of time, relating either to persons or things, e.g., Mt 5:26, "the uttermost (farthing)"; **(4)** of apostles as "last" in the program of a spectacular display, Mt 20:8, 12, 14; Mk 12:6, 22; 1 Cor 4:9; **(5)** 1 Cor 15:45, "the last Adam"; **(6)** of the "last" state of persons, Rev 2:19; Mt 12:45; Lk 11:26; 2 Pet 2:20, "the latter end"; **(7)** of Christ as the Eternal One, Rev 1:11, 17; 2:8; 22:13;

(8) in eschatological phrases as follows: **(8a)** "the last day," a comprehensive term including both **(8a1)** the time of the resurrection of the redeemed, Jn 6:39, 40, 44, 54 and 11:24, and **(8a2)** the ulterior time of the judgment of the

unregenerate, at the Great White Throne, Jn 12:48; **(8b)** "the last days," Acts 2:17, a period relative to the supernatural manifestation of the Holy Spirit at Pentecost and the resumption of the divine interpositions in the affairs of the world at the end of the present age, before "the great and notable Day of the Lord," which will usher in the messianic kingdom; **(8c)** in 2 Ti 3:1, "the last days" refers to the close of the present age of world conditions; **(8d)** in Jas 5:3, the phrase "for the last days" refers both to the period preceding the Roman overthrow of the city and the land in A.D. 70, and to the closing part of the age in consummating acts of Gentile persecution including "the time of Jacob's trouble" (cf. vv. 7, 8); **(8e)** in 1 Pet 1:5, "the last time" refers to the time of the Lord's second advent; **(8f)** in 1 Jn 2:18,"the last time" and, in Jude 18, "the last time" signify the present age previous to the Second Advent.

(9) In Heb 1:2, "in these last days", the reference is to the close of the period of the testimony of the prophets under the Law, terminating with the presence of Christ and His redemptive sacrifice and its effects, **(9a)** the perfect tense "hath spoken" indicating the continued effects of the message embodied in the risen Christ; **(9b)** so in 1 Pet 1:20, "in these last times." See: TDNT—2:697, 264; BAGD—313d; THAYER—253b.

2079. ἐσχάτως {1x} ĕschatōs, *es-khat'-oce;* adv. from 2078; *finally,* i.e. (with 2192) *at the extremity* of life:—point of death + 2292 {1x}.

This word means extreme, to be in the last gasp, at the point of death, Mk 5:23. See: BAGD—314; THAYER—254a.

2080. ἔσω {8x} ĕsō, *es'-o;* from 1519; *inside* (as prep. or adj.):—within {3x}, in {1x}, inner {1x}, into {1x}, inward {1x}, not tr. {1x}.

Eso is an adverb connected with *eis,* "into," and is translated **(1)** "inner" in Eph 3:16; **(2)** after verbs of motion, it denotes "into," Mk 15:16; **(3)** after verbs of rest, "within," Jn 20:26; Acts 5:23; 1 Cor 5:12 (i.e., "within" the church); **(4)** "in", Mt 26:58; **(5)** "inward", Rom 7:22. See: TDNT—2:698, 265; BAGD—314b; THAYER—254a.

2081. ἔσωθεν {14x} ĕsōthĕn, *es'-o-then;* from 2080; *from inside;* also used as equiv. to 2080 (*inside*):—within {7x}, from within {3x}, inward part {1x}, inwardly {1x}, inward man {1}, without {1x}.

Esothen is an adverb denoting "from within," or "within," and is **(1)** used with the article, as a noun, of the inner being, the secret

intents of the heart, which, the Lord declared, God made, as well as the visible physical frame, Lk 11:40. **(2)** In Lk 11:39, it is rendered "inward part"; **(3)** in Mt 7:15 it has its normal use as an adverb, "inwardly"; also translated **(4)** "within", Mt 23:25, 27, 28; 2 Cor 7:5; Rev 4:8; 5:1; **(5)** "from within," Mk 7:21, 23; Lk 11:7; "inward man", 2 Cor 4:16. See: BAGD—314b; THAYER—254a.

2082. ἐσώτερος {2x} **ĕsōtĕrŏs**, *es-o'-ter-os;* comparative of *2080; interior:*—inner {1x}, within {1x}.

Esoteros, the comparative degree, denotes **(1)** "inner," Acts 16:24 (of a prison); **(2)** Heb 6:19, with the article, and practically as a noun, "that which is within (the veil)," lit., "the inner (of the veil)." See: BAGD—314c; THAYER—254b.

2083. ἑταῖρος {4x} **hĕtairŏs**, *het-ah'-ee-ros;* from ἔτης **ĕtēs** (a *clansman*); a *comrade:*—fellow {1x}, friend {3x}.

Hetairos, "a companion, comrade," is translated **(1)** "fellows" in Mt 11:16. The word is used only by Matthew and is translated **(2)** "friend" in 20:13; 22:12; 26:50. See: TDNT—2:699, 265; BAGD—314c; THAYER—254b.

2084. ἑτερόγλωσσος {1x} **hĕtĕrŏglōssŏs**, *het-er-og'-loce-sos;* from *2087* and *1100; other-tongued,* i.e. a *foreigner:*—other tongue {1x}. See: TDNT—1:726, 123; BAGD—314d; THAYER—254b.

2085. ἑτεροδιδασκαλέω {2x} **hĕtĕrŏdidaskalĕō**, *het-er-od-id-as-kal-eh'-o;* from *2087* and *1320;* to *instruct differently:*—teach other doctrine {1x}, teach otherwise {1x}.

This word means to teach a different doctrine (*heteros,* different, to be distinguished from *allos,* another of the same kind), and is used in 1 Ti 1:3; 6:3 of what is contrary to the faith. See: TDNT—2:163, 161; BAGD—314d; THAYER—254b.

2086. ἑτεροζυγέω {1x} **hĕtĕrŏzugĕō**, *het-er-od-zoog-eh'-o;* from a compound of *2087* and *2218;* to *yoke* up *differently,* i.e. (fig.) to *associate discordantly:*—unequally yoked together with {1x}. See: TDNT—2:901, 301; BAGD—314d; THAYER—254b.

2087. ἕτερος {99x} **hĕtĕrŏs**, *het'-er-os;* of uncert. aff.; (an-, the) *other* or *different:*—another {43x}, other {42x}, other thing {3x}, some {2x}, next day {2x}, misc. {7x} = altered, else, one, strange.

This word means "another": i.e. one not of the same nature, form, class, kind, different. See: TDNT—2:702, 265; BAGD—315a; THAYER—254b.

2088. ἑτέρως {1x} **hĕtĕrōs**, *het-er'-oce;* adv. from *2087; differently:*—otherwise {1x}. See: BAGD—315c; THAYER—254d.

2089. ἔτι {117x} **ĕti**, *et'-ee;* perh. akin to *2094; "yet," still* (of time or degree):—yet {52x}, more {34x}, any more {5x}, still {4x}, further {4x}, longer {3x}, misc. {15x} = after that, also, ever, (t-) henceforth (more), hereafter, anyone), now. See: BAGD—315c; THAYER—254d.

2090. ἑτοιμάζω {40x} **hĕtŏimazō**, *het-oy-mad'-zo;* from *2092;* to *prepare:*—prepare {29x}, provide {1x}, make ready {10x}.

Hetoimazo, as a verb, means "to prepare, make ready," is used **(1)** absolutely, e.g., Mk 14:15; Lk 9:52; **(2)** with an object, e.g., of those things which are ordained **(2a)** by God, such as future positions of authority, Mt 20:23; **(2a1)** the coming kingdom, 25:34; **(2a2)** salvation personified in Christ, Lk 2:31; **(2a3)** future blessings, 1 Cor 2:9; **(2a4)** a city, Heb 11:16; **(2a5)** a place of refuge for the Jewish remnant, Rev 12:6; **(2a6)** divine judgments on the world, Rev 8:6; 9:7, 15; 16:12; **(2a7)** eternal fire, for the devil and his angels, Mt 25:41; **(2b)** by Christ: a place in heaven for His followers, Jn 14:2, 3; **(3)** of human "preparation" for the Lord, e.g., Mt 3:3; 26:17, 19; Lk 1:17 ("make ready"), 76; 3:4; 9:52 ("to make ready"); 23:56; Rev 19:7; 21:2; **(4)** in 2 Ti 2:21, of "preparation" of oneself for "every good work"; **(5)** of human "preparations" for human objects, e.g., Lk 12:20, "thou hast provided"; Acts 23:23; Philem 22. See: TDNT—2:704, 266; BAGD—316a; THAYER—255b. comp. *2680.*

2091. ἑτοιμασία {1x} **hĕtŏimasia**, *het-oy-mas-ee'-ah;* from *2090; preparation:*—preparation {1x}.

In Eph 6:15, the gospel itself is to be the firm footing of the believer, his walk being worthy of it and therefore a testimony in regard to it. See: TDNT—2:704, 266; BAGD—316c; THAYER—255c.

2092. ἕτοιμος {17x} **hĕtŏimŏs**, *het'-oy-mos;* from an old noun ἔτεος **hĕtĕŏs** (*fitness*); *adjusted,* i.e. *ready:*—ready {14}, prepared {1x}, readiness {1x}, make ready to (one's) hand {1x}.

Hetoimos denotes **(1)** "preparation"; it is found in Eph 6:15, of having the feet shod with the "preparation" of the gospel of peace; it also has the meaning of firm footing (foundation); if that is the meaning in Eph 6:15, the gospel itself is to be the firm footing of the believer, his walk being worthy of it and therefore a testimony in regard to it. It also means **(2)** "ready"

and is used **(2a)** of persons, Mt 24:44; 25:10; Lk 12:40; 22:33; Acts 23:15, 21; Titus 3:1; 1 Pet 3:15; **(2b)** of things, Mt 22:4 (2nd part), 8; Mk 14:15, "prepared"; Lk 14:17; Jn 7:6; 2 Cor 9:5; 10:16, "things made ready"; 1 Pet 1:5. See: TDNT—2:704, 266; BAGD—316c; THAYER— 255c.

2093. ἑτοίμως {3x} **hĕtŏimōs**, *het-oy'-moce;* adv. from *2092; in readi-ness:*—ready {3x}. Cf. Acts 21:13; 2 Cor. 12:14; 1 Pet. 4:5. See: BAGD—316d; THAYER—256d.

2094. ἔτος {49x} **ĕtŏs**, *et'-os;* appar. a pri-mary word; a *year:*—year {4x}. See: BAGD—316d; THAYER—256d.

2095. εὖ {6x} **ĕu**, *yoo;* neut. of a primary εὖς **ĕus** (*good*); (adv.) *well:*—good {1x}, well {3x}, well done {2x}. See: BAGD—317b; THAYER—256a.

2096. Εὖα {2x} **Ĕua**, *yoo'-ah;* of Heb. or. [2332]; *Eua* (or *Eva*, i.e. *Chavvah*), the first woman:—Eve {2x}. See: BAGD—317b; THAYER—256b.

2097. εὐαγγελίζω {55x} **ĕuaggĕlizō**, *yoo-ang-ghel-id'-zo;* from *2095* and *32;* to *announce good* news ("evangelize") es-pec. the gospel:—preach {23x}, preach the gos-pel {22x}, bring good tidings {2x}, show glad tidings {2x}, bring glad tidings {1x}, declare {1x}, declare glad tidings {1x}, misc. {3x}.

Euangelizo, as a verb, means "to bring or an-nounce glad tidings" (Eng., "evangelize"), is used **(1)** in the active voice in Rev 10:7, "declared" and 14:6, "to preach"; **(2)** in the passive voice, **(2a)** of matters to be proclaimed as "glad tid-ings," Lk 16:16; Gal 1:11; 1 Pet 1:25; **(2b)** of persons to whom the proclamation is made, Mt 11:5; Lk 7:22; Heb 4:2, 6; 1 Pet 4:6; **(3)** in the middle voice, especially of the message of sal-vation, **(3a)** with a personal object, either **(3a1)** of the person preached, e.g., Acts 5:42; 11:20; Gal 1:16, or, **(3a2)** with a preposition, of the persons evangelized, e.g., Acts 13:32, "declare glad tidings"; Rom 1:15; Gal 1:8; **(3b)** with an impersonal object, e.g., **(3b1)** "the word," Acts 8:4; **(3b2)** "good tidings," Acts 8:12; **(3b3)** "the word of the Lord," Acts 15:35; **(3b4)** "the gos-pel," 1 Cor 15:1; 2 Cor 11:7; **(3b5)** "the faith," Gal 1:23; **(3b6)** "peace," Eph 2:17; **(3b7)** "the unsearchable riches of Christ, 3:8. Syn.: 4283. See: TDNT—2:707,*; BAGD—317b; THAYER—256b.

2098. εὐαγγέλιον {77x} **ĕuaggĕliŏn**, *yoo-ang-ghel'-ee-on;* from the same as *2097;* a *good message,* i.e. the *gospel:*—gos-pel {46x}, gospel of Christ {11x}, gospel of God {7x}, gospel of the kingdom {3x}, misc. {10x}.

Euangelion **(1)** originally denoted a reward for good tidings; **(1a)** later, the idea of reward dropped, and **(1b)** the word stood for "the good news" itself. **(1c)** The Eng. word "gospel," i.e. "good message," is the equivalent of *euangel-ion* (Eng., "evangel"). **(1d)** In the NT it denotes the "good tidings" of the kingdom of God and of salvation through Christ, to be received by faith, on the basis of His expiatory death, His burial, resurrection, and ascension, e.g., Acts 15:7; 20:24; 1 Pet 4:17; **(1e)** Apart from those references and those in the Gospels of Matthew and Mark, and Rev 14:6, the noun is confined to Paul's epistles. **(2)** The apostle uses it of two associated yet distinct things, **(2a)** of the basic facts of the death, burial and resurrection of Christ, e.g., 1 Cor 15:1–3; the "gospel" is viewed historically; **(2b)** of the interpretation of these facts, e.g., Rom 2:16; Gal 1:7, 11; 2:2; the gospel is viewed doctrinally, with reference to the in-terpretation of the facts, as is sometimes indi-cated by the context.

(3) The following phrases describe the sub-jects or nature or purport of the message; it is the "gospel" of **(3a)** God, Mk 1:14; Rom 1:1; 15:16; 2 Cor 11:7; 1 Th 2:2, 9; 1 Pet 4:17; **(3b)** God, concerning His Son, Rom 1:1–3; **(3c)** His Son, Rom 1:9; **(3d)** Jesus Christ, the Son of God, Mk 1:1; **(3e)** our Lord Jesus, 2 Th 1:8; **(3f)** Christ, Rom 15:19, etc.; **(3g)** the glory of Christ, 2 Cor 4:4; **(3h)** the grace of God, Acts 20:24; **(3i)** the glory of the blessed God, 1 Ti 1:11; **(3j)** your salvation, Eph 1:13; **(3k)** peace, Eph 6:15. **(4)** Cf. also **(4a)** "the gospel of the kingdom," Mt 4:23; 9:35; 24:14; **(4b)** "an eternal gospel," Rev 14:6. **(5)** In Gal 2:14, "the truth of the gospel" de-notes, not the true "gospel," but the true teach-ing of it, in contrast to perversions of it. See: TDNT—2:721, 267; BAGD—317d; THAYER—257a.

2099. εὐαγγελιστής {3x} **ĕuaggĕlistēs**, *yoo-ang-ghel-is-tace';* from *2097;* a *preacher* of the gospel:—evangelist {3x}.

Euangelistes denotes a "preacher of the gos-pel," Acts 21:8; Eph 4:11, which makes clear the distinctiveness of the function in the churches; 2 Ti 4:5. See: TDNT—2:736, 267; BAGD—318c; THAYER—257c.

2100. εὐαρεστέω {3x} **ĕuarĕstĕō**, *yoo-ar-es-teh'-o;* from *2101;* to *grat-ify entirely:*—please {2x}, be well pleased {1x}

Euaresteo, **(1)** in the active voice, Heb 11:5, "he pleased"; **(2)** so 11: 6; in the passive voice, Heb 13:16. See: TDNT—1:456, 77; BAGD—318c; THAYER—257d.

2101. εὐάρεστος {9x} **ĕuarĕstŏs**, *yoo-ar'-es-tos;* from *2095* and *701;*

fully agreeable:—acceptable {4x}, well pleasing {3x}, please well + 1510 {1x}, accepted {1x}.

Euarestos is translated **(1)** "acceptable" Rom 12:1, 2; 14:8; Eph 5:10; Heb 13:1; **(2)** "well pleasing" Phil 4:18; Col 3:20; **(3)** "please well" Titus 2:9; **(4)** "accepted" 2 Cor 5:9. See: TDNT—1:456, 77; BAGD—318d; THAYER—257d.

2102. **εὐαρέστως** {1x} **ĕuarĕstōs,** *yoo-ar-es'-toce;* adv. from *2101; quite agreeably:*—acceptably {1x}.

Euarestos means in a manner well pleasing to one, acceptable, so as to please, Heb 12:28. See: BAGD—318d; THAYER—257d.

2103. **Εὔβουλος** {1x} **Ĕubŏulŏs,** *yoo'-boo-los;* from *2095* and *1014; good-willer; Eubulus,* a Chr.:—Eubulus {1x}. See: BAGD—319a; THAYER—257d.

2104. **εὐγένης** {3x} **ĕugĕnēs,** *yoog-en'-ace;* from *2095* and *1096; well born,* i.e. (lit.) *high* in rank, or (fig.) *generous:*—nobleman + 444 {1x}, more noble {1x}, noble {1x}.

Eugenes, an adjective, lit., "well born" (*eu,* "well," and *genos,* "a family, race"), **(1)** signifies "more noble," Acts 17:11; 1 Cor 1:26; and **(2)** is used with *anthropos,* "a man," i.e., "a nobleman," in Lk 19:12. See: BAGD—319a; THAYER—257d.

2105. **εὐδία** {1x} **ĕudia,** *yoo-dee'-ah;* fem. from *2095* and the alternate of *2203* (as the god of the weather); a *clear sky,* i.e. *fine weather:*—fair weather {1x}. See: BAGD—319a; THAYER—258a.

2106. **εὐδοκέω** {21x} **ĕudŏkĕō,** *yoo-dok-eh'-o;* from *2095* and *1380; to think well* of, i.e. *approve* (an act); spec., to *approbate* (a person or thing):—be well pleased {7x}, please {5x}, have pleasure {4x}, be willing {2x}, be (one's) good pleasure {1x}, take pleasure {1x}, think good {1x}.

Eudokeo signifies **(1)** "to be well pleased, to think it good" not merely an understanding of what is right and good as in *dokeo,* but stressing the willingness and freedom of an intention or resolve regarding what is good, e.g., Lk 12:32, "it is (your Father's) good pleasure"; so Rom 15:26, 27; 1 Cor 1:21; Gal 1:15; Col 1:19; 1 Th 2:8, "we were willing"; **(2)** "to be well pleased with," or "take pleasure in," e.g., Mt 3:17; 12:18; 17:5; 1 Cor 10:5; 2 Cor 12:10; 2 Th 2:12; Heb 10:6, 8, 38; 2 Pet 1:17. See: TDNT—2:738, 273; BAGD—319b; THAYER—258a.

2107. **εὐδοκία** {9x} **ĕudŏkia,** *yoo-dok-ee'-ah;* from a presumed compound of *2095* and the base of *1380; satisfaction,* i.e. (subj.) *delight,* or (obj.) *kindness, wish, pur-*

pose:—good pleasure {4x}, good will {2x}, seem good + 1096 {2x}, desire {1x}.

Eudokia, lit., "good pleasure", implies a gracious purpose, a good object being in view, with the idea of a resolve, showing the willingness with which the resolve is made. It is often translated **(1)** "good pleasure," e.g., Eph 1:5, 9; Phil 2:13; 2 Th 1:11; **(2)** in Phil 1:15, "good will"; **(3)** in Rom 10:1, "desire." **(4)** It is used of God in Mt 11:26 "seemed good"; Lk 2:14; 10:21; Eph 1:5, 9; Phil 2:13. See: TDNT—2:742, 273; BAGD—319c; THAYER—258b.

2108. **εὐεργεσία** {2x} **ĕuĕrgĕsia,** *yoo-erg-es-ee'-ah;* from *2110; benefi-cence* (gen. or spec.):—benefit {1x}, good deed done {1x}. Cf. Acts 4:9, "good deed," and 1 Ti 6:2, "benefit." See: TDNT—2:654, 251; BAGD—319d; THAYER—258c.

2109. **εὐεργετέω** {1x} **ĕuĕrgĕtĕō,** *yoo-erg-et-eh'-o;* from *2110; to be phil-anthropic:*—doing good {1x}.

Euergeteo, as a verb, means "to bestow a benefit, to do good": "How God anointed Jesus of Nazareth with the Holy Ghost and with power: Who went about doing good, and healing all that were oppressed of the devil; for God was with Him" (Acts 10:38). See: TDNT—2:654, 251; BAGD—320a; THAYER—258c.

2110. **εὐεργέτης** {1x} **ĕuĕrgĕtēs,** *yoo-erg-et'-ace;* from *2095* and the base of *2041;* a *worker of good,* i.e. (spec.) a *philanthropist:*—benefactor {1x}. See: TDNT—2:654, 251; BAGD—320a; THAYER—258c.

2111. **εὔθετος** {3x} **ĕuthĕtŏs,** *yoo'-thet-os;* from *2095* and a der. of *5087; well placed,* i.e. (fig.) *appropriate:*—fit {2x}, meet {1x}.

Euthetos means "ready for use, fit, well adapted," lit., "well placed" (*eu,* "well," *tithemi,* "to place"), and is used **(1)** of persons, Lk 9:62, negatively, of one who is not fit for the kingdom of God; **(2)** of things, **(2a)** Lk 14:35, of salt that has lost its savor; **(2b)** rendered "meet" in Heb 6:7, of herbs. See: BAGD—320b; THAYER—258c.

2112. **εὐθέως** {80x} **ĕuthĕōs,** *yoo-theh'-oce;* adv. from *2117; directly,* i.e. *at once* or *soon:*—immediately {35x}, straightway {32x}, forthwith {7x}, misc. {6x} = anon, as soon as, shortly. See: BAGD—320b; THAYER—258d.

2113. **εὐθυδρομέω** {2x} **ĕuthudrŏmĕō,** *yoo-thoo-drom-eh'-o;* from *2117* and *1408; to lay a straight course,* i.e. *sail direct:*—(come) with a straight course {2x}. Cf.

Acts 16:11; 21:1. See: BAGD—320d; THAYER—258d.

2114. εὐθυμέω {3x} **ĕuthumĕō**, *yoo-thoo-meh'-o;* from *2115;* to *cheer up,* i.e. (intr.) *be cheerful;* neut. comparative (adv.) *more cheerfully:*—be of good cheer {2x}, be merry {1x}. *Euthumeo* signifies, in the active voice, "to put in good spirits, to make cheerful" (*eu,* "well," *thumos,* "passion"); or **(1)** intransitively, "to be cheerful", Acts 27:22, 25; and **(2)** Jas 5:13 "merry". See: BAGD—320d; THAYER—258d.

2115. εὔθυμος {2x} **ĕuthumŏs**, *yoo'-thoo-mos;* from *2095* and *2372;* in *fine spirits,* i.e. *cheerful:*—of good cheer {1x}, the more cheerfully {1x}. Cf. Act 24:10; 27:36. See: BAGD—320d; THAYER—258d.

2116. εὐθύνω {2x} **ĕuthunō**, *yoo-thoo'-no;* from *2117;* to *straighten* (*level*); tech. to *steer:*—governor + 3588 {1x}, make straight {1x}.
   Euthuno is used **(1)** of the directing of a ship by the steersman, Jas 3:4 (A governor is one who guides straight); **(2)** metaphorically, of making "straight" the way of the Lord, Jn 1:23. See: BAGD—320d; THAYER—258d.

2117. εὐθύς {16x} **ĕuthus**, *yoo-thoos';* perh. from *2095* and *5087; straight,* i.e. (lit.) *level,* or (fig.) *true;* adv. (of time) *at once:*—straight {5x}, right {3x}, immediately {3x}, straightway {2x}, anon {1x}, by and by {1x}, forthwith {1x}. See: BAGD—321a,b; THAYER—259a.

2118. εὐθύτης {1x} **ĕuthutēs**, *yoo-thoo'-tace;* from *2117; rectitude:*—righteousness {1x}. See: BAGD—321b; THAYER—259a.

2119. εὐκαιρέω {3x} **ĕukairĕō**, *yoo-kahee-reh'-o;* from *2121;* to *have good time,* i.e. *opportunity* or *leisure:*—have leisure {1x}, have convenient time {1x}, spend time {1x}.
   Eukaireo, as a verb, means "to have time or leisure or convenient time" and is translated **(1)** "he shall have convenient time": "As touching our brother Apollos, I greatly desired him to come unto you with the brethren: but his will was not at all to come at this time; but he will come when he shall have convenient time" (1 Cor 16:12). It is also translated **(2)** "they had . . . leisure" in Mk 6:31; and **(3)** in Acts 17:21, "spent their time." Syn.: 170, 2120, 2540, 5117. See: BAGD—321b; THAYER—259a.

2120. εὐκαιρία {2x} **ĕukairia**, *yoo-kahee-ree'-ah;* from *2121;* a *favorable occasion:*—opportunity {2x}.

Eukairia, as a noun, means "a fitting time, opportunity": "And from that time he sought opportunity to betray him" (Mt 26:16; cf. Lk 22:6). Syn.: 170, 2119, 2540, 5117. See: TDNT—3:462, 389; BAGD—321; THAYER—259b.

2121. εὔκαιρος {2x} **ĕukairŏs**, *yoo'-kahee-ros;* from *2095* and *2540; well-timed,* i.e. *opportune:*—convenient {1x}, in time of need {1x}.
   Eukairos, lit., "well-timed" (*eu,* "well," *kairos,* "a time, season"), hence signifies "timely, opportune, convenient"; it is said **(1)** of a certain day, Mk 6:21; elsewhere, **(2)** Heb 4:16, "in time of need." See: TDNT—3:462, 389; BAGD—321c; THAYER—259b.

2122. εὐκαίρως {2x} **ĕukairōs**, *yoo-kah'-ee-roce;* adv. from *2121; opportunely:*—conveniently {1x}, in season {1x}.
   Eukairos, as an adverb, means **(1)** "in season": "Preach the word; be instant in season, out of season (*akairos*); reprove, rebuke, exhort with all longsuffering and doctrine" (2 Ti 4:2); or **(2)** "conveniently": "And when they heard it, they were glad, and promised to give him money. And he sought how he might conveniently betray him" (Mk 14:11). Syn.: 171, 2540, 3641, 4340, 5550, 5610. See: BAGD—321c; THAYER—259b.

2123. εὐκοπώτερος {7x} **ĕukŏpōtĕrŏs**, *yoo-kop-o'-ter-os;* comp. of a compound of *2095* and *2873; better for toil,* i.e. *more facile:*—easier {7x}.
   Eukopoteros, the comparative degree of *eukopos,* "easy, with easy labor" (*eu,* "well," *kopos,* "labor"), hence, of that which is "easier to do," is found in the Synoptics only, Mt 9:5; 19:24; Mk 2:9; 10:25; Lk 5:23; 16:17; 18:25. See: BAGD—321d; THAYER—259b.

2124. εὐλάβεια {2x} **ĕulabĕia**, *yoo-lab'-i-ah;* from *2126;* prop. *caution,* i.e. (religiously) *reverence* (*piety*); by impl. *dread* (concr.):—godly fear {1x}, feared {1x}.
   In general, this word means apprehension, but especially holy fear, that mingled fear and love which, combined, constitute the piety of man toward God; the OT places its emphasis on the fear, the NT . . . on the love, though there was love in the fear of God's saints then, as there must be fear in their love now. It signifies, firstly, "caution"; then, **(1)** "fear", Heb 5:7; and **(2)** "godly fear," Heb 12:28, "apprehension, but especially holy fear." Syn.: 1167, 5401. See: TDNT—2:751, 275; BAGD—321d; THAYER—259b.

2125. εὐλαβέομαι {2x} **ĕulabĕŏmai**, *yoo-lab-eh'-om-ahee;* mid. voice from *2126;* to *be circumspect,* i.e. (by impl.) to

be apprehensive; religiously to *reverence:* — moved with fear {1x}, fear {1x}.

This word means to be cautious, to beware and signifies to act with the reverence produced by holy fear (Heb 11:7); moved with godly fear. It also speaks of human fear of something happening, Acts 23:10. See: TDNT—2:751,*; BAGD—321d; THAYER—259c.

2126. **εὐλαβής** {3x} **ĕulabēs,** *yoo-lab-ace';* from *2095* and *2983; taking well (carefully),* i.e. *circumspect* (religiously, *pious*):—devout {3x}.

Literally, this word means taking hold well, cautious; and signifies careful as to the realization of the presence and claims of God, reverencing God, pious, devout (Lk 2:25; Acts 2:5; 8:2) which manifests itself in caution and carefulness in human relationships. This one is an anxious and scrupulous worshiper who never changes or omits anything because he is afraid of offending. Syn.: 1174, 2152, 2318, 2357. See: TDNT—2:751,*; BAGD—322a; THAYER—259c.

2127. **εὐλογέω** {44x} **ĕulŏgĕō,** *yoo-log-eh'-o;* from a compound of *2095* and *3056;* to *speak well of,* i.e. (religiously) to *bless (thank* or *invoke a benediction upon, prosper):*—bless {43x}, praise {1x}.

Eulogeo literally means to speak well of and signifies **(1)** to praise, to celebrate with praises, of that which is addressed to God, acknowledging His goodness, with desire for His glory (Lk 1:64; 2:28; Jas 3:9); **(2)** to invoke blessings upon a person (Lk 6:28; Rom 12:14); **(3)** to consecrate/bless a thing with solemn prayers, to ask God's blessing on a thing (Lk 9:16; 1 Cor 10:16); **(4)** to cause to prosper, to make happy, to bestow blessings on, said of God (Acts 3:26; Gal 3:9; Eph 1:3). Syn.: 1757, 2128, 2129. See: TDNT—2:754, 275; BAGD—322b; THAYER—259d.

2128. **εὐλογητός** {8x} **ĕulŏgētŏs,** *yoo-log-ay-tos';* from *2127; adorable:*—blessed (said of God) {8x}. This word is only applied to God, Mk 14:61; Lk 1:68; Rom 1:25; 9:5; 2 Cor 1:3; 11:31; Eph 1:3; 1 Pet 1:3. See: TDNT—2:764, 275; BAGD—322c; THAYER—260a.

2129. **εὐλογία** {16x} **ĕulŏgia,** *yoo-log-ee'-ah;* from the same as *2127; fine speaking,* i.e. *elegance of language; commendation ("eulogy"),* i.e. (reverentially) *adoration; religiously benediction;* by impl. *consecration;* by extens. *benefit* or *largess:*—blessing {11x}, bounty {2x}, bountifully + 1909 {2x}, fair speech {1x}.

Eulogia, lit., "good speaking, praise," is used of **(1)** God and Christ, Rev 5:12–13; 7:12; **(2)** of

the invocation of blessings, benediction, Heb 12:17; Jas 3:10; **(3)** of the giving of thanks, 1 Cor 10:16; **(4)** of a blessing, a benefit bestowed, Rom 15:29; Gal 3:14; Eph 1:3; Heb 6:7; **(5)** of a monetary gift sent to needy believers, 2 Cor 9:5–6; **(6)** in a bad sense, of fair speech, Rom 16:18, where it is joined with *chrestologia,* "smooth speech," the latter relating to the substance, *eulogia* to the expression. See: TDNT—2:754, 275; BAGD—322d; THAYER—260b.

2130. **εὐμετάδοτος** {1x} **ĕumĕtadŏtŏs,** *yoo-met-ad'-ot-os;* from *2095* and a presumed der. of *3330; good at imparting,* i.e. *liberal:*—ready to distribute {1x}. See: BAGD—323a; THAYER—260c.

2131. **Εὐνίκη** {1x} **Ĕunikē,** *yoo-nee'-kay;* from *2095* and *3529; victorious; Eunice,* a Jewess:—Eunice {1x}. See: BAGD—323b; THAYER—260c.

2132. **εὐνοέω** {1x} **ĕunŏĕō,** *yoo-no-eh'-o;* from a compound of *2095* and *3563;* to *be well-minded, well disposed, of a peaceable spirit,* i.e. *reconcile:*—agree {1x}. See: TDNT—4:971, 636; BAGD—323b; THAYER—260c.

2133. **εὔνοια** {2x} **ĕunŏia,** *yoo'-noy-ah;* from the same as *2132; kindness;* euphem. *conjugal duty:*—benevolence {1x}, good will {1x}.

Eunoia, "good will" is rendered **(1)** "benevolence" in 1 Cor 7:3; and **(2)** "good will" in Eph 6:7, "good will." See: TDNT—4:971, 636; BAGD—323b; THAYER—260c.

2134. **εὐνουχίζω** {2x} **ĕunŏuchizō,** *yoo-noo-khid'-zo;* from *2135;* to *castrate* (fig. *live unmarried*):—make . . . eunuch {2x}. Cf. Mt 19:12 (thrice). See: TDNT—2:765, 277; BAGD—323c; THAYER—260d.

2135. **εὐνοῦχος** {8x} **ĕunŏuchŏs,** *yoo-noo'-khos;* from εὐνή **ĕunē** (a *bed*) and *2192;* a *castrated* person (such being employed in Oriental bed-chambers); by extens. an *impotent* or *unmarried* man; by impl. a *chamberlain (state-officer):*—eunuch {8x}.

Eunouchos denotes **(1)** "an emasculated man, a eunuch," Mt 19:12; **(2)** in the 3rd instance in that Mt 19:12, "one naturally incapacitated for, or voluntarily abstaining from, wedlock"; **(3)** one such, in a position of high authority in a court, "a chamberlain," Acts 8:27–39 (5 times). See: TDNT—2:765, 277; BAGD—323c; THAYER—260d.

2136. **Εὐοδία** {1x} **Ĕuŏdia,** *yoo-od-ee'-ah;* from the same as *2137; fine travelling; Euodia,* a Chr. woman:—Euodias {1x}. See: BAGD—323d; THAYER—260d.

2137. εὐοδόω {4x} ĕuŏdŏō, *yoo-od-ŏ'-o;* from a compound of *2095* and *3598;* to *help* on the *road,* i.e. (pass.) *succeed in reaching;* fig. to *succeed* in business affairs:—prosper {3x}, have a prosperous journey {1x}.

Euodoo, "to help on one's way" (*eu,* "well," and *hodos*), is used in the passive voice with the meaning **(1)** "to have a prosperous journey"; so Rom 1:10; and **(2)** "to prosper", 1 Cor 16:2; 3 Jn 2. See: TDNT—5:109, 666; BAGD—323d; THAYER—260d.

2138. εὐπειθής {1x} ĕupĕithēs, *yoo-pi-thace';* from *2095* and *3982; good* for *persuasion,* i.e. (intr.) *compliant:*—easy to be intreated {1x}.

Eupeithes, "well persuaded" (*eu,* "well," *peithomai,* "to obey, to be persuaded"), "compliant," is translated "easy to be intreated" in Jas 3:17, said of the wisdom that is from above. Heavenly wisdom is unchanging, well-persuaded of its own unchangeableness (cf. wisdom in the Prov). Heavenly wisdom can be freely approached, is not rigid, but is open to discussion (compliant), will not waver but will attempt in gentleness to persuade. See: BAGD—324a; THAYER—261a.

2139. εὐπερίστατος {1x} ĕupĕristatŏs, *yoo-per-is'-tat-os;* from *2095* and a der. of a presumed compound of *4012* and *2476; well standing around,* i.e. (a *competitor*) *thwarting* (a racer) in every direction (fig. of sin in gen.):—which doth so easily beset {1x}.

It describes the sin of unbelief skillfully surrounding and as having advantage in favor of its prevailing, Heb 12:1. See: BAGD—324a; THAYER—261a.

2140. εὐποιΐα {1x} ĕupŏiïa, *yoo-poy-ee'-ah;* from a compound of *2095* and *4160; well-doing,* i.e. *beneficence:*—to do good {1x}.

Eupoiia, means "beneficence, doing good," and is translated as a verb, "to do good" in Heb 13:16: "But to do good and to communicate forget not: for with such sacrifices God is well pleased." See: BAGD—324a; THAYER—261a.

2141. εὐπορέω {1x} ĕupŏrĕō, *yoo-por-eh'-o;* from a compound of *2090* and the base of *4197;* (intr.) to *be good* for *passing* through, i.e. (fig.) *have* pecuniary *means:*—his ability + *5100* {1x}.

Euporeo, lit., "to journey well" (*eu,* "well," *poreo,* "to journey"), hence, "to prosper," is translated "according to (his) ability", "as he has been blessed in his life's journey", in Acts 11:29. See: BAGD—324b; THAYER—261b.

2142. εὐπορία {1x} ĕupŏria, *yoo-por-ee'-ah;* from the same as *2141;* pecu-niary *resources:*—wealth {1x}. See: BAGD—324b; THAYER—261b.

2143. εὐπρέπεια {1x} ĕuprĕpĕia, *yoo-prep'-i-ah;* from a compound of *2095* and *4241; good suitableness,* i.e. *gracefulness:*—grace {1x}.

This word means outward comeliness, goodly appearance, shapeliness, and beauty and is said of the outward appearance of the flower of the grass (Jas 1:11). See: BAGD—324b; THAYER—261b.

2144. εὐπρόσδεκτος {5x} ĕuprŏsdĕktŏs, *yoo-pros'-dek-tos;* from *2095* and a der. of *4327; well-received,* i.e. *approved, favorable:*—acceptable {2x}, accepted {3x}.

This word is a strong form and signifies a very favorable acceptance (Rom 15:16, 31; 2 Cor 6:2; 8:12; 1 Pet 2:5). See: TDNT—2:58, 146; BAGD—324c; THAYER—261b.

2145. εὐπρόσεδρος {1x} ĕuprŏsĕdrŏs, *yoo-pros'-ed-ros;* from *2095* and the same as *4332; sitting well toward,* i.e. (fig.) *assiduous* (neut. *diligent service*):—that (one) may attend upon + *4314* + *3588* {1x}.

Euprosedros, lit., "sitting well beside", i.e., sitting constantly by, and so applying oneself diligently to, anything, is used in 1 Cor 7:35, with *pros,* "upon," "that ye may attend upon." See: BAGD—324c; THAYER—261b.

2146. εὐπροσωπέω {1x} ĕuprŏsōpĕō, *yoo-pros-o-peh'-o;* from a compound of *2095* and *4383;* to *be of good countenance,* i.e. (fig.) to *make a display:*—make a fair show {1x}.

Euprosopeo denotes "to look well, make a fair show" (*eu,* "well," *prosopon,* "a face"), and is used in Gal 6:12, "to make a fair show (in the flesh)," i.e., "to make a display of religious zeal." See: TDNT—6:779, 950; BAGD—324d; THAYER—261b.

2147. εὑρίσκω {178x} hĕuriskō, *hyoo-ris'-ko;* a prol. form of a primary

εὕρω hĕurō, *hyoo'-ro;* which (together with another cognate form

εὑρέω hĕurĕō, *hyoo-reh'-o*) is used for it in all the tenses except the present and imperfect; to *find* (lit. or fig.):—find {174x}, get {1x}, obtain {1x}, perceive {1x}, see {1x}. See: TDNT—2:769,*; BAGD—324d; THAYER—261c.

2148. Εὐροκλύδων {1x} Ĕurŏkludōn, *yoo-rok-loo'-dohn;* from Εὖρος Ĕurŏs (the *east* wind) and *2830;* a *storm from the East* (or Southeast), i.e. (in modern phrase) a *Levanter:*—Euroklydon {1x}. See: BAGD—325d; THAYER—262b.

2149. εὐρύχωρος {1x} **ĕuruchōrŏs,** *yoo-roo'-kho-ros;* from εὐρύς **ĕurus** (*wide*) and *5561; spacious:*—broad {1x}. See: BAGD—326a; THAYER—262c.

2150. εὐσέβεια {15x} **ĕusĕbĕia,** *yoo-seb'-i-ah;* from *2152; piety;* spec. the *gospel* scheme:—godliness {14x}, holiness {1x}.

(1) It is from *eu,* "well," and *sebomai,* "to be devout," denotes that piety which, characterized by a Godward attitude, does that which is well-pleasing to Him. (1a) This and the corresponding verb and adverb are frequent in the Pastoral Epistles, but do not occur in previous epistles of Paul. (1b) The apostle Peter has the noun four times in his 2nd epistle, 1:3, 6, 7; 3:11. (1c) Elsewhere it occurs in Acts 3:12; 1 Ti 2:2; 3:16; 4:7, 8; 6:3, 5, 6, 11; 2 Ti 3:5; Titus 1:1. (2) In 1 Ti 6:3 "the doctrine which is according to godliness" signifies that which is consistent with "godliness," in contrast to false teachings; (3) in Titus 1:1, "the truth which is according to godliness" is that which is productive of "godliness"; (4) in 1 Ti 3:16, "the mystery of godliness" is "godliness" as embodied in, and communicated through, the truths of the faith concerning Christ; (5) in 2 Pet 3:11, the word is in the plural, signifying acts of "godliness." See: TDNT—7:175, 1010; BAGD—326a; THAYER—262c.

2151. εὐσεβέω {2x} **ĕusĕbĕō,** *yoo-seb-eh'-o;* from *2152;* to *be pious,* i.e. (toward God) to *worship,* or (toward parents) to *respect* (*support*):—show piety {1x}, worship {1x}.

Eusebeo, "to reverence, to show piety" towards any to whom dutiful regard is due and is used (1) in 1 Ti 5:4 of the obligation on the part of children to express in a practical way their dutifulness "towards their own family"; (2) in Acts 17:23 of worshiping God. See: TDNT—7:175, 1010; BAGD—326b; THAYER—262c.

2152. εὐσεβής {4x} **ĕusĕbēs,** *yoo-seb-ace';* from *2095* and *4576; well-reverent,* i.e. *pious:*—devout {3x}, godly {1x}.

The root of this word—*seb*—signifies sacred awe and describes reverence exhibited especially in actions; reverence or awe well directed. In the NT it is used (1) "devout", of a pious attitude towards God, Acts 10:2, 7; 22:12; (2) "godly," in 2 Pet 2:9. Syn.: 1174, 2126, 2318, 2357. See: TDNT—7:175, 1010; BAGD—326b; THAYER—262d.

2153. εὐσεβῶς {2x} **ĕusĕbōs,** *yoo-seb-oce';* adv. from *2152; piously:*—godly {2x}.

This word denotes "piously, godly"; it is used with the verb "to live" (of manner of life) in 2 Ti 3:12; Titus 2:12. See: BAGD—326c; THAYER—262d.

2154. εὔσημος {1x} **ĕusēmŏs,** *yoo'-say-mos;* from *2095* and the base of *4591; well indicated,* i.e. (fig.) *significant:*—easy to be understood {1x}.

Eusemos primarily denotes "conspicuous" or "glorious", then, "distinct, clear to understanding," "easy to be understood" well marked, clear and definite, distinct, 1 Cor 14:9. See: TDNT—2:770, 278; BAGD—32c; THAYER—262d.

2155. εὔσπλαγχνος {2x} **ĕusplagchnŏs,** *yoo'-splangkh-nos;* from *2095* and *4698; well compassioned,* i.e. *sympathetic:*—pitiful {1x}, tender-hearted {1x}.

This word denotes "compassionate, tenderhearted," lit., "of good heartedness" and is translated (1) "pitiful" in 1 Pet 3:8, and (2) "tender-hearted" in Eph 4:32. See: TDNT—7:548, 1067; BAGD—326d; THAYER—262d.

2156. εὐσχημόνως {3x} **ĕuschēmŏnōs,** *yoo-skhay-mon'-oce;* adv. from *2158; decorously:*—decently {1x}, honestly {2x}.

This word denotes "gracefully, becomingly, in a seemly manner" (*eu,* "well," *schema,* "a form, figure"); and is translated (1) "honestly," (1a) in Rom 13:13, in contrast to the shamefulness of Gentile social life; and (1b) in 1 Th 4:12, the contrast is to idleness and its concomitant evils and the resulting bad testimony to unbelievers; (2) in 1 Cor 14:40, "decently," where the contrast is to disorder in oral testimony in the churches. See: BAGD—327a; THAYER—262d.

2157. εὐσχημοσύνη {1x} **ĕuschēmŏsunē,** *yoo-skhay-mos-oo'-nay;* from *2158; decorousness:*—comeliness {1x}.

This word depicts charm or elegance of figure, external beauty, decorum, modesty, seemliness, of external charm, comeliness, 1 Cor 12:23. See: BAGD—327a; THAYER—262d.

2158. εὐσχήμων {5x} **ĕuschēmōn,** *yoo-skhay'-mone;* from *2095* and *4976; well-formed,* i.e. (fig.) *decorous, noble* (in rank):—comely {2x}, honourable {3x}.

This word stresses (1) "comely", elegant figure, shapely, graceful, bearing one's self becomingly in speech or behaviour; or by extension, 1 Cor 7:35; 12:24; and (2) "honourable", of good standing, influential, wealthy, respectable, Mk 15:43; Acts 13:50; 17:12. See: TDNT—2:770, 278; BAGD—327a; THAYER—263a.

2159. εὐτόνως {2x} **ĕutŏnōs,** *yoo-ton'-oce;* adv. from a compound of *2095* and

a der. of τείνω **tĕinō** (to *stretch*); *in a well-strung manner*, i.e. (fig.) *intensely* (in a good sense, *cogently;* in a bad one, *fiercely*):—mightily {1x}, vehemently {1x}.

This word means "vigorously, vehemently" and is translated (1) "mightily" in Acts 18:28, of the power of Apollos in "confuting" the Jews; and (2) in Lk 23:10 it is rendered "vehemently." See: BAGD–327b; THAYER–263a.

2160. **εὐτραπελία** {1x} **ĕutrapĕlia**, *yoo-trap-el-ee'-ah;* from a compound of *2095* and a der. of the base of *5157* (mean. *well-turned*, i.e. *ready at repartee, jocose*); *witticism*, i.e. (in a vulgar sense) *ribaldry:*—jesting {1x}.

Paul did not use this method which in its common, worldly sense means something that turns easily, of something that adapts itself to the shifting circumstances of the hour, to the moods and conditions of those around it, Eph 5:4. Syn.: 148, 3437. See: BAGD–327c; THAYER–263a.

2161. **Εὔτυχος** {1x} **Ĕutuchŏs**, *yoo'-too-khos;* from *2095* and a der. of *5177; well-fated*, i.e. *fortunate; Eutychus,* a young man:—Eutychus {1x}. See: BAGD–327c; THAYER–263b.

2162. **εὐφημία** {1x} **ĕuphēmia**, *yoo-fay-mee'-ah;* from *2163; good language* ("*euphemy*"), i.e. *praise* (*repute*):—good report {1x}. See: BAGD–327c; THAYER–263b.

2163. **εὔφημος** {1x} **ĕuphēmŏs**, *yoo'-fay-mos;* from *2095* and *5345; well spoken of,* i.e. *reputable:*—of good report {1x}. See: BAGD–327c; THAYER–263b.

2164. **εὐφορέω** {1x} **ĕuphŏrĕō**, *yoo-for-eh'-o;* from *2095* and *5409;* to *bear well*, i.e. *be fertile:*—bring forth plentifully {1x}. See: BAGD–327c; THAYER–263b.

2165. **εὐφραίνω** {14x} **ĕuphrainō**, *yoo-frah'-ee-no;* from *2095* and *5424;* to *put* (mid. or pass. *be*) *in a good* frame of *mind*, i.e. *rejoice:*—rejoice {6x}, be merry {3x}, make merry {3x}, fare {1x}, make glad {1x}.

Euphraino, as a verb, means "to cheer, gladden," is translated (1) "rejoice", Acts 2:26; 7:41; Rom 15:10; Gal 4:7; Rev 12:12; 18:20; (2) "be merry", Lk 12:19; 15:23, 24; (3) "make merry", Lk 15:29, 32; Rev 11:10; (4) "fared", Lk 16:19; (5) "make glad", 2 Cor 2:2. Syn.: 21, 5463. See: TDNT–2:772, 278; BAGD–327c; THAYER–263b.

2166. **Εὐφράτης** {2x} **Ĕuphratēs**, *yoo-frat'-ace;* of for. or. [comp. 6578]; *Euphrates,* a river of Asia:—*Euphrates* {2x}. See: BAGD–328a; THAYER–263c.

2167. **εὐφροσύνη** {2x} **ĕuphrŏsunē**, *yoo-fros-oo'-nay;* from the same as *2165; joyfulness:*—gladness {1x}, joy {1x}.

Euphrosune, "good cheer, joy, mirth, gladness of heart" is rendered (1) "joy" in Acts 2:28, and (2) "gladness" in Acts 14:17. See: TDNT–2:772, 278; BAGD–328a; THAYER–263c.

2168. **εὐχαριστέω** {39x} **ĕucharistĕō**, *yoo-khar-is-teh'-o;* from *2170;* to *be grateful,* i.e. (act.) to *express gratitude* (toward); spec. to *say grace* at a meal:—give thanks {26x}, thank {12x}, be thankful {1x}.

Eucharisteo, as a verb, means "to give thanks," (1) is said of Christ, Mt 15:36; 26:27; Mk 8:6; 14:23; Lk 22:17, 19; Jn 6:11, 23; 11:41; 1 Cor 11:24; (2) of the Pharisee in Lk 18:11 in his self-complacent prayer; (3) "giving thanks" is used by Paul (3a) at the beginning of all his epistles, except 2 Cor, Gal, 1 Ti, 2 Ti, and Titus, (3b) for his readers, Rom 1:8; Eph 1:16; Col 1:3; 1 Th 1:2; 2 Th 1:3 (cf. 2:13); virtually so in Philem 4; (3c) for fellowship shown, Phil 1:3; (3d) for God's gifts to them, 1 Cor 1:4; (4) is recorded (4a) of Paul elsewhere, Acts 27:35; 28:15; Rom 7:25; 1 Cor 1:14; 14:18; (4b) of Paul and others, Rom 16:4; 1 Th 2:13; (4c) of himself, representatively, as a practice, 1 Cor 10:30; (4d) of others, Lk 17:16; Rom 14:6 (twice); 1 Cor 14:17; Rev 11:17; (4e) is used in admonitions to the saints, the Name of the Lord Jesus suggesting His character and example, Eph 5:20; Col 1:12; 3:17; 1 Th 5:18; (4f) as the expression of a purpose, 2 Cor 1:11; (4g) negatively of the ungodly, Rom 1:21. (5) "Thanksgiving" is the expression of joy Godward, and is therefore the fruit of the Spirit (Gal 5:22); believers are encouraged to abound in it (e.g., Col 2:7). Syn.: 437, 1843, 2169. See: TDNT–9:407, 1298; BAGD–328a; THAYER–263c.

2169. **εὐχαριστία** {15x} **ĕucharistia**, *yoo-khar-is-tee'-ah;* from *2170; gratitude;* act. *grateful language* (to God, as an act of worship):—thanksgiving {9x}, giving of thanks {3x}, thanks {2x}, thankfulness {1x}.

(1) This prayer expresses the grateful acknowledgement of past mercies as distinct from seeking future ones. *Eucharistia* denotes (2) "gratitude," "thankfulness," Acts 24:3; (3) "giving of thanks, thanksgiving," 1 Cor 14:16; 2 Cor 4:15; 9:11, 12 (plur.); Eph 5:4; Phil 4:6; Col 2:7; 4:2; 1 Th 3:9 ("thanks"); 1 Ti 2:1 (plur.); 4:3, 4; Rev 4:9, "thanks"; 7:12. Syn.: 155, 1162, 1783, 2171, 2428. See: TDNT–9:407, 1298; BAGD–328c; THAYER–264a.

2170. **εὐχάριστος** {1x} **ĕucharistŏs**, *yoo-khar'-is-tos;* from *2095* and a der. of *5483; well favored,* i.e. (by impl.) *grateful:*—thankful {1x}.

(1) This word stresses mindful of favours. **(2)** It means primarily, "gracious, agreeable" then "grateful, thankful," and is so used in Col 3:15. See: TDNT—9:407, 1298; BAGD—329a; THAYER—264a.

2171. **εὐχή** {3x} **ĕuchē**, *yoo-khay';* from *2172;* prop. a *wish,* expressed as a *petition* to God, or in *votive* obligation:—prayer {1x}, vow {2x}.

The concept of the vow or dedicated thing is more present than prayer in this word. *Euche* denotes **(1)** "a prayer," Jas 5:15; and **(2)** "a vow," Acts 18:18 and 21:23. See: TDNT—2:775, 279; BAGD—329b; THAYER—264a.

2172. **εὔχομαι** {7x} **ĕuchŏmai**, *yoo'-khom-ahee;* mid. voice of a primary verb; to *wish;* by impl. to *pray* to God:—wish {3x}, pray {2x}, can wish {1x}, I would to God {1x}.

Euchomai, **(1)** "to pray (to God)," is used with this meaning in 2 Cor 13:7, Jas 5:16. Even when it is translated **(2)** "wish", Acts 27:29; 2 Cor 13:9; 3 Jn 1:2; **(3)** "can wish", Rom 9:3; **(4)** "I would to God," Acts 26:29, the indication is that "prayer" is involved. See: TDNT—2:775, 279; BAGD—329b; THAYER—264b.

2173. **εὔχρηστος** {3x} **ĕuchrēstŏs**, *yoo'-khrays-tos;* from *2095* and *5543; easily used,* i.e. *useful:*—profitable {2x}, meet for use {1x}.

This word means easy to make use of, useful and is translated **(1)** "profitable", 2 Ti 4:11; Philem 11; and **(2)** "meet for use", 2 Ti 2:21. See: BAGD—329c; THAYER—264b.

2174. **εὐψυχέω** {1x} **ĕupsuchĕō**, *yoo-psoo-kheh'-o;* from a compound of *2095* and *5590;* to *be in good spirits,* i.e. *feel encouraged:*—be of good comfort {1x}.

This word means to be of good courage, to be of a cheerful spirit, Phil 2:19. See: BAGD—329d; THAYER—264b.

2175. **εὐωδία** {3x} **ĕuōdia**, *yoo-o-dee'-ah;* from a compound of *2095* and a der. of *3605; good-scentedness,* i.e. *fragrance:*—sweet savour {1x}, sweet smell {1x}, sweet smelling {1x}.

Euodia, "fragrance" is used metaphorically **(1)** of those who in the testimony of the gospel are to God "a sweet savor of Christ," 2 Cor 2:15; **(2)** of the giving up of His life by Christ for us, an offering and a sacrifice to God for an odor of "a sweet smelling savor," Eph 5:2; and **(3)** of material assistance sent to Paul from the church at Philippi "(an odor) of a sweet smell," Phil 4:18. In all three instances the fragrance is that which ascends to God through the person, and as a result of the sacrifice, of Christ. See:

TDNT—2:808, 285; BAGD—329d; THAYER—264b.

2176. **εὐώνυμος** {10x} **ĕuōnumŏs**, *yoo-o'-noo-mos;* from *2095* and *3686;* prop. *well-named* (*good-omened*), i.e. the *left* (which was the *lucky* side among the pagan Greeks); neut. as adv. *at the left* hand:—left {5x}, on the left hand {4x}, left foot {1x}. See: BAGD—39d; THAYER—264c.

2177. **ἐφάλλομαι** {1x} **ĕphallŏmai**, *ef-al'-lom-ahee;* from *1909* and *242;* to *spring upon:*—leap on {1x}. See: BAGD—330a; THAYER—264c.

2178. **ἐφάπαξ** {5x} **ĕphapax**, *ef-ap'-ax;* from *1909* and *530; upon one occasion* (only):—(at) once (for all) {5x}.

Ephapax a strengthened form signifies **(1)** "once (for all)," Rom 6:10; Heb 7:27; 9:12; 10:10; **(2)** "at once," 1 Cor 15:6. See: TDNT—1:383, 64; BAGD—330a; THAYER—264d.

2179. **Ἐφεσῖνος** {1x} **Ĕphēsinŏs**, *ef-es-ee'-nos;* from *2181; Ephesine,* or situated at Ephesus:—of Ephesus {1x}. See: BAGD—330a; THAYER—264d.

2180. **Ἐφέσιος** {7x} **Ĕphēsiŏs**, *ef-es'-ee-os;* from *2181;* an *Ephesian* or inhab. of Ephesus:—Ephesian {6x}, of Ephesus {1x}. See: BAGD—330b; THAYER—264d.

2181. **Ἔφεσος** {15x} **Ĕphēsŏs**, *ef'-es-os;* prob. of for. or.; *Ephesus,* a city of Asia Minor:—Ephesus {15x}. See: BAGD—330b; THAYER—264d.

2182. **ἐφευρέτης** {1x} **ĕphĕurĕtēs**, *ef-yoo-ret'-ace;* from a compound of *1909* and *2147;* a *discoverer,* i.e. *contriver:*—inventor {1x}. See: BAGD—330b; THAYER—265a.

2183. **ἐφημερία** {2x} **ĕphēmĕria**, *ef-ay-mer-ee'-ah;* from *2184; diurnality,* i.e. (spec.) the quotidian *rotation* or *class* of the Jewish priests' service at the temple, as distributed by families:—course {2x}. Cf. Lk 1:5, 8. See: BAGD—330c; THAYER—265a.

2184. **ἐφήμερος** {1x} **ĕphēmĕrŏs**, *ef-ay'-mer-os;* from *1909* and *2250; for a day* ("ephemeral"), i.e. *diurnal* (*happening each day*):—daily {1x}. See: BAGD—330c; THAYER—265a.

2185. **ἐφικνέομαι** {2x} **ĕphiknĕŏmai**, *ef-ik-neh'-om-ahee;* from *1909* and a cognate of *2240;* to *arrive upon,* i.e. *extend to:*—reach {2x}. Cf. 2 Cor 10:13, 14. See: BAGD—330c; THAYER—265b.

2186. **ἐφίστημι** {21x} **ĕphistēmi**, *ef-is'-tay-mee;* from *1909* and *2476;* to

stand upon, i.e. *be present* (in various applications, friendly or otherwise, usually lit.);— come upon {6x}, come {4x}, stand {3x}, stand by {3x}, misc. {5x} = assault, be at hand (instant), present. See: BAGD—330d; THAYER—265b.

2187. **'Εφραίμ** {1x} **Ĕphraïm,** *ef-rah-im';* of Heb. or. [669 or better 6085]; *Ephraïm,* a place in Pal.:—*Ephraim* {1x}. See: BAGD—331a; THAYER—265b.

2188. **ἐφφαθά** {1x} **ĕphphatha,** *ef-fath-ah';* of Chald. or. [6606]; *be opened!:—Ephphatha* {1x}. See: BAGD—331b; THAYER—265c.

2189. **ἔχθρα** {6x} **ĕchthra,** *ekh'-thrah;* fem. of *2190; hostility;* by impl. a reason for *opposition:*—enmity {5x}, hatred {1x}.

Echthra is rendered **(1)** "enmity" in Lk 23:12; Rom 8:7; Eph 2:15–16; Jas 4:4; and **(2)** "hatred", Gal 5:20. **(3)** It is the opposite of *agape,* "love." See: TDNT—2:815, 285; BAGD—331b; THAYER—265c.

2190. **ἐχθρός** {32x} **ĕchthrŏs,** *ekh-thros';* from a primary ἔχθω **ĕchthō** (to *hate*); *hateful* (pass. *odious,* or act. *hostile*); usually as a noun, an *adversary* (espec. *Satan*):—enemy {30x}, foe {2x}.

Echthros, an adjective, primarily denoting "hated" or "hateful" hence, in the active sense, denotes "hating, hostile." It is used as a noun signifying an "enemy," adversary, and is said **(1)** of the devil, Mt 13:39; Lk 10:19; **(2)** of death, 1 Cor 15:26; **(3)** of the professing believer who would be a friend of the world, thus making himself an enemy of God, Jas 4:4; **(4)** of men who are opposed **(4a)** to Christ, Mt 13:25, 28; 22:44; Mk 12:36; Lk 19:27; 20:43; Acts 2:35; Rom 11:28; Phil 3:18; Heb 1:13; 10:13; or **(4b)** to His servants, Rev 11:5, 12; **(4c)** to the nation of Israel, Lk 1:71, 74; 19:43; **(5)** of one who is opposed to righteousness, Acts 13:10; **(6)** of Israel in its alienation from God, Rom 11:28; **(7)** of the unregenerate in their attitude toward God, Rom 5:10; Col 1:21; **(8)** of believers in their former state, 2 Th 3:15; **(9)** of foes, Mt 5:43–44; 10:36; Lk 6:27, 35; Rom 12:20; 1 Cor 15:25; **(10)** of the apostle Paul because he told converts "the truth," Gal 4:16. See: TDNT— 2:811, 285; BAGD—331b; THAYER—265c.

2191. **ἔχιδνα** {5x} **ĕchidna,** *ekh'-id-nah;* of uncert. or.; an *adder* or other poisonous snake (lit. or fig.):—viper {5x}.

Echidna is probably a generic term for "poisonous snakes." It is rendered "viper" **(1)** of the actual creature, Acts 28:3; **(2)** metaphorically in Mt 3:7; 12:34; 23:33; Lk 3:7. See: TDNT— 2:815, 286; BAGD—331d; THAYER—265d.

2192. **ἔχω** {712x} **ĕchō,** *ekh'-o;* (incl. an alt. form

σχέω schĕō, *skheh'-o;* used in certain tenses only); a primary verb; to *hold* (used in very various applications, lit. or fig., direct or remote; such as *possession; ability, contiguity, relation,* or *condition*):—have {613x}, be {22x}, need + 5532 {12x}, vr have {2x}, misc {63x} = accompany, + begin to amend, can (+ -not), × conceive, count, diseased, do + eat, + enjoy, + fear, following, hold, keep, + lack, + go to law, lie, + must needs, + of necessity, next, + recover, + reign, + rest, return, × sick, take for, + tremble, + uncircumcised, use.

This word stresses that one has the means to accomplish a task. See: TDNT—2:816, 286; BAGD—331d; THAYER—365d.

2193. **ἕως** {148x} **hĕōs,** *heh'-oce;* of uncert. aff.; a conjunc., prep. and adv. of continuance, *until* (of time and place):—till {28x}, unto {27x}, until {25x}, to {16x}, till + 3739 {11x}, misc. {41x} = even (until, unto), (as) far (as), how long, (hither-, up) to, while (-s). See: BAGD—334b; THAYER—268a.

Z

2194. **Ζαβουλών** {3x} **Zabŏulōn,** *dzab-oo-lone';* of Heb. or. [2074]; *Zabulon* (i.e. *Zebulon*), a region of Pal.:—Zabulon {3x}. See: BAGD—335b; THAYER—269a.

2195. **Ζακχαῖος** {3x} **Zakchaiŏs,** *dzak-chah'-ee-yos;* of Heb. or. [comp. 2140]; *Zacchœus,* an Isr.:—Zacchæus {3x}. See: BAGD—335b; THAYER—269a.

2196. **Ζαρά** {1x} **Zara,** *dzar-ah';* of Heb. or. [2226]; *Zara,* (i.e. *Zerach*), an Isr.:— Zara {1x}. See: BAGD—335d; THAYER—269a.

2197. **Ζαχαρίας** {11x} **Zacharias,** *dzakh-ar-ee'-as;* of Heb. or. [2148]; *Zacharias* (i.e. *Zechariah*), the name of two Isr.:—*Zacharias* {11x}. See: BAGD—335d; THAYER—269a.

2198. **ζάω** {143x} **zaō,** *dzah'-o;* a primary verb; to *live* (lit. or fig.):—live {117x}, be alive {9x}, alive {6x}, quick {4x}, lively {3x}, not tr {1x}, vr live {1x}, life {1x}, lifetime {1x}.

Zao, as a verb, means "to live, be alive" and is used in the NT of **(1)** God: "And Simon Peter answered and said, Thou art the Christ, the Son of the living God" Mt 16:16; cf. Jn 6:57; Rom 14:11; **(2)** the Son in Incarnation: "He that eateth My flesh, and drinketh My blood, dwelleth in Me, and I in him" (Jn 6:57); **(3)** the Son in Resurrection: "Yet a little while, and the world seeth Me no more; but ye see Me: because I live,

ye shall live also" (Jn 14:19; cf. Acts 1:3; Rom 6:10; 2 Cor 13:4; Heb 7:8); **(4)** spiritual life: "As the living Father hath sent Me, and I live by the Father: so he that eateth Me, even he shall live by Me" (Jn 6:57; cf. Rom 1:17; 8:13b; Gal 2:19, 20; Heb 12:9); **(5)** the present state of departed saints: "For He is not a God of the dead, but of the living: for all live unto Him" (Lk 20:38; 1 Pet 4:6); **(6)** the hope of resurrection: "Blessed be the God and Father of our Lord Jesus Christ, which according to His abundant mercy hath begotten us again unto a lively hope by the resurrection of Jesus Christ from the dead" (1 Pet 1:3);

(7) the resurrection **(7a)** of believers: "Who died for us, that, whether we wake or sleep, we should live together with Him" (1 Th 5:10; cf. Jn 5:25; Rev 20:4), and **(7b)** of unbelievers: "But the rest of the dead lived not again until the thousand years were finished. This is the first resurrection" (Rev 20:5); **(8)** the way of access to God through the Lord Jesus Christ: "By a new and living way, which He hath consecrated for us, through the veil, that is to say, His flesh" (Heb 10:20); **(9)** the manifestation of divine power in support of divine authority; "For though He was crucified through weakness, yet He liveth by the power of God. For we also are weak in Him, but we shall live with Him by the power of God toward you" (2 Cor 13:4b; cf. 12:10; 1 Cor 5:5); **(10)** bread: "I am the living bread which came down from heaven: if any man eat of this bread, he shall live for ever: and the bread that I will give is my flesh, which I will give for the life of the world" (Jn 6:51 figurative of the Lord Jesus); **(11)** a stone "To Whom coming, as unto a living stone, disallowed indeed of men, but chosen of God, and precious" (1 Pet 2:4 figurative of the Lord Jesus); **(12)** water: "Jesus answered and said unto her, If thou knewest the gift of God, and who it is that saith to thee, Give me to drink; thou wouldest have asked of him, and he would have given thee living water" (Jn 4:10 figurative of the Holy Spirit; 7:38); **(13)** a sacrifice: "I beseech you therefore, brethren, by the mercies of God, that ye present your bodies a living sacrifice, holy, acceptable unto God, which is your reasonable service" (Rom 12:1 figurative of the believer); **(14)** stones: "Ye also, as lively stones, are built up a spiritual house, an holy priesthood, to offer up spiritual sacrifices, acceptable to God by Jesus Christ" (1 Pet 2:5 figurative of the believer); **(15)** the oracles, *logion,* word, *logos,* of God: "This is he [Moses], that was in the church in the wilderness with the angel which spake to him in the mount Sina, and with our fathers: who received the lively

oracles to give unto us" (Acts 7:38; cf. Heb 4:12; 1 Pet 1:23);

(16) the physical life of men: "For this we say unto you by the word of the Lord, that we which are alive and remain unto the coming of the Lord shall not prevent them which are asleep" (1 Th 4:15; Mt 27:63; Acts 25:24; Rom 14:9; Phil 1:21 in the infinitive mood used as a noun with the article, "living", 22; 1 Pet 4:5); **(17)** the maintenance of physical life: "But He answered and said, It is written, Man shall not live by bread alone, but by every word that proceedeth out of the mouth of God" (Mt 4:4; cf. 1 Cor 9:14); **(18)** the duration of physical life: "And deliver them who through fear of death were all their lifetime subject to bondage" (Heb 2:15); **(19)** the enjoyment of physical life: "For now we live, if ye stand fast in the Lord" (1 Th 3:8); **(20)** the recovery of physical life from the power of disease: "And besought Him greatly, saying, My little daughter lieth at the point of death: I pray thee, come and lay thy hands on her, that she may be healed; and she shall live" (Mk 5:23; cf. Jn 4:50);

(21) the recovery of physical life from the power of death: "While He spake these things unto them, behold, there came a certain ruler, and worshipped Him, saying, My daughter is even now dead: but come and lay thy hand upon her, and she shall live" (Mt 9:18; cf. Acts 9:41; Rev 20:5); **(22)** the course, conduct, and character of men: **(22a)** good: "Which knew me from the beginning, if they would testify, that after the most straitest sect of our religion I lived a Pharisee" (Acts 26:5; cf. 2 Ti 3:12; Titus 2:12); **(22b)** evil: "And not many days after the younger son gathered all together, and took his journey into a far country, and there wasted his substance with riotous living" (Lk 15:13; cf. Rom 6:2; 8:13a; 2 Cor 5:15b; Col 3:7); **(22c)** undefined: "For I was alive without the law once: but when the commandment came, sin revived, and I died" (Rom 7:9; 14:7; Gal 2:14); **(22d)** restoration after alienation: "It was meet that we should make merry, and be glad: for this thy brother was dead, and is alive again; and was lost, and is found" (Lk 15:32).

(23) In 1 Th 5:10, to live means to experience that change, 1 Cor 15:51, which is to be the portion of all in Christ who will be alive upon the earth at the Parousia of the Lord Jesus, cf. Jn 11:25, and which corresponds to the resurrection of those who had previously died in Christ, 1 Cor 15:52–54. **(24)** *Zao* is translated **(24a)** "quick": "And He commanded us to preach unto the people, and to testify that it is He which was ordained of God to be the Judge of quick and dead" (Acts 10:42; cf. 2 Ti 4:1; 1 Pet 4:5); and **(24b)** "living": "For the word of

Greek

God is quick, and powerful, and sharper than any two-edged sword, piercing even to the dividing asunder of soul and spirit, and of the joints and marrow, and is a discerner of the thoughts and intents of the heart" (Heb 4:12). Quick implies the ability to respond immediately to God's word and living stresses the ongoing nature of His word; it is just as effective today as tomorrow. Syn.: 326, 390, 980, 1236, 2225, 4176, 4800, 5225. See: TDNT—2:832, 290; BAGD—336a; THAYER—269c.

2199. Ζεβεδαῖος {12x} Zĕbĕdaiŏs, dzeb-ed-ah'-yos; of Heb. or. [comp. 2067]; Zebedœus, an Isr.:—Zebedee {12x}. See: BAGD—337b; THAYER—270d.

2200. ζεστός {3x} zĕstŏs, dzes-tos'; from 2204; boiled, i.e. (by impl.) calid (fig. fervent):—hot {3x}.

Zestos means "boiling hot" (from zeo, "to boil, be hot, fervent"; cf. Eng., "zest"), and is used, metaphorically, in Rev 3:15 (twice), 16. See: TDNT—2:876, 296; BAGD—337b; THAYER—270d.

2201. ζεῦγος {2x} zĕugŏs, dzyoo'-gos; from the same as 2218; a couple, i.e. a team (of oxen yoked together) or brace (of birds tied together):—yoke {1x}, pair {1x}.

Zeugos "a yoke" is used (1) of beasts, Lk 14:19; and (2) of a pair of anything; in Lk 2:24, of turtledoves. See: BAGD—337b; THAYER—270d.

2202. ζευκτηρία {1x} zĕuktēria, dzook-tay-ree'-ah; fem. of a der. (at the second stage) from the same as 2218; a fastening (tiller-rope):—band {1x}. See: BAGD—337b; THAYER—271a.

2203. Ζεύς {2x} Zĕus, dzyooce; of uncert. aff.; in the oblique cases there is used instead of it a (prob. cognate) name.

Δίς Dis, deece, which is otherwise obs.; Zeus or Dis (among the Latins Jupiter or Jove), the supreme deity of the Greeks:—Jupiter {2x}. Cf. Acts 14:12, 13. See: BAGD—337c; THAYER—271a.

2204. ζέω {2x} zĕō, dzeh'-o; a primary verb; to be hot (boil, of liquids; or glow, of solids), i.e. (fig.) be fervid (earnest):—be fervent {1x}, fervent {1x}.

Zeo "to be hot, to boil" (Eng. "zeal" is akin), is metaphorically used of "fervency" of spirit, Acts 18:25; Rom 12:11. See: TDNT—2:875, 296; BAGD—337c; THAYER—271a.

2205. ζῆλος {17x} zēlŏs, dzay'-los; from 2204; prop. heat, i.e. (fig.) "zeal" (in a favorable sense, ardor; in an unfavorable one, jealousy, as of a husband [fig. of God], or an enemy, malice):—zeal {6x}, envying {5x}, indignation {2x}, envy {1x}, fervent mind {1x}, jealousy {1x}, emulation {1x}.

Zelos may be a favorable term but usually is used of evil. When considering good it is an honorable emulation and consequent imitation of that which is excellent. In an evil sense envy is tormented by another's good fortune and is active and aggressive to diminish the good in another; usually accompanied by petty complaining and fault finding. See: TDNT—2:877, 297; BAGD—337d; THAYER—271a.

2206. ζηλόω {12x} zēlŏō, dzay-lŏ'-o or ζηλεύω zēlĕuō dzay-loo'-o; from 2205; to have warmth of feeling for or against:—zealously affect {2x}, move with envy {2x}, envy {1x}, be zealous {1x}, affect {1x}, desire {1x}, covet {1x}, covet earnestly {1x}, misc. {2x}.

Zeloo, as a verb, in Gal 4:17, 18 means "they zealously seek," "ye may seek," "to be zealously sought": "They zealously affect (zeloo) you, but not well; yea, they would exclude you, that ye might affect them. But it is good to be zealously (zeloo) affected always in a good thing, and not only when I am present with you." Syn.: 327, 1567, 1934, 2212, 3713. See: TDNT—2:882, 297; BAGD—338a; THAYER—271b.

2207. ζηλωτής {5x} zēlōtēs, dzay-lo-tace'; from 2206; a "zealot":—zealous {5x}.

Zelotes is used adjectivally, of "being zealous" (1) "of the Law," Acts 21:20; (2) "toward God," lit., "of God," Acts 22:3; (3) "of spiritual gifts," 1 Cor 14:12, i.e., for exercise of spiritual gifts; (4) "of/for the traditions of my fathers," Gal 1:14, of Paul's loyalty to Judaism before his conversion; (5) "of good works," Titus 2:14. See: TDNT—2:882, 297; BAGD—338a; THAYER—271c.

2208. Ζηλωτής {2x} Zēlōtēs, dzay-lo-tace'; the same as 2207; a Zealot, i.e. (spec.) partisan for Jewish political independence:—Zelotes {2x}. See: TDNT—2:882, 297; BAGD—338b; THAYER—271c.

2209. ζημία {4x} zēmia, dzay-mee'-ah; prob. akin to the base of 1150 (through the idea of violence); detriment:—damage {1x}, loss {3x}.

Zemia is used (1) in Acts 27:10, "damage", and "loss", Acts 27:21, of ship and cargo; (2) in Phil 3:7, 8 of the apostle's estimate of the things which he formerly valued, and of all things on account of "the excellency of the knowledge of Christ Jesus." (3) This is loss actively incurred. See: TDNT—2:888, 299; BAGD—338c; THAYER—271d.

2210. **ζημιόω** {6x} **zēmióō**, *dzay-mee-ŏ'-o;*
       from *2209;* to *injure*, i.e. (refl.
or pass.) to *experience detriment:*—be cast
away {1x}, receive damage {1x}, lose {2x}, suffer
loss {2x}.

(1) What is in view here is the act of forfeit-
ing what is of the greatest value, not the casting away by divine judgment, though that is
involved, but losing or penalizing one's own
self, with spiritual and eternal loss: "For what
is a man profited, if he shall gain the whole
world, and lose his own soul? or what shall a
man give in exchange for his soul?" (Mt 16:26;
cf. Mk 8:36; Lk 9:25; cf. Phil 3:8). **(2)** In 2 Cor
7:9 *zemioo* is translated "ye might receive damage": "Now I rejoice, not that ye were made
sorry, but that ye sorrowed to repentance: for
ye were made sorry after a godly manner, that
ye might receive damage by us in nothing"; also
(3) "to suffer loss", 1 Cor 3:15. Syn.: 324, 353,
354, 568, 588, 618, 1209, 1523, 1926, 2865,
2975, 2983, 3028, 3335, 3336, 3858, 3880, 3970,
4327, 4355, 4356, 4380, 4381, 4382, 5562, 5264,
5274. See: TDNT—2:888, 299; BAGD—338c;
THAYER—272a.

2211. **Ζηνᾶς** {1x} **Zēnas**, *dzay-nas';* prob.
       contr. from a poetic form of
2203 and *1435; Jove-given; Zenas*, a Chr.:—*Zenas* {1x}. See: BAGD—338c; THAYER—272a.

2212. **ζητέω** {119x} **zētéō**, *dzay-teh'-o;* of un-
       cert. aff.; to *seek* (lit. or fig.);
spec. (by Heb.) to *worship* (God), or (in a bad
sense) to *plot* (against life):—seek {100x}, seek
for {5x}, go about {4x}, desire {3x}, misc. {7x} =
be about, endeavour, enquire (for), require.

Zeteo, as a verb, signifies **(1)** "to seek, to
seek for": "Ask, and it shall be given you; seek,
and ye shall find; knock, and it shall be opened
unto you" (Mt 7:7; cf. 7:88; 13:45; Lk 24:5; Jn
6:24); **(1a)** of plotting against a person's life:
"Saying, Arise, and take the young child and
His mother, and go into the land of Israel: for
they are dead which sought the young child's
life" (Mt 2:20; Acts 21:31; Rom 11:3); **(1b)** metaphorically, to "seek" by thinking, to "seek" how
to do something, or what to obtain: "And the
scribes and chief priests heard it, and sought
how they might destroy Him: for they feared
Him, because all the people was astonished at
His doctrine" (Mk 11:18; Lk 12:29; **(1c)** to "seek"
to ascertain a meaning: "Now Jesus knew that
they were desirous to ask him, and said unto
them, Do ye enquire (*zeteo*) among yourselves
of that I said, A little while, and ye shall not see
me: and again, a little while, and ye shall see
me?" (Jn 16:19); **(1d)** to "seek" God: "That they
should seek the Lord, if haply they might feel

after him, and find him, though he be not far
from every one of us" (Acts 17:27; Rom 10:20);
(2) "to seek or strive after, endeavor, to desire": "While He yet talked to the people, behold, his mother and his brethren stood without,
desiring (*zeteo*) to speak with him" (Mt 12:46,
47; Lk 9:9; Jn 7:19; Rom 10:3); **(3)** of "seeking"
the kingdom of God and His righteousness, in
the sense of coveting earnestly, striving after:
"But seek ye first the kingdom of God, and his
righteousness; and all these things shall be added
unto you" (Mt 6:33; Col 3:1; 1 Pet 3:11); **(4)** "to
require or demand": "And He sighed deeply in
His spirit, and saith, Why doth this generation
seek after a sign? verily I say unto you, There
shall no sign be given unto this generation"
(Mk 8:12; Lk 11:29; 1 Cor 4:2; 2 Cor 13:3). Syn.:
327, 1567, 1934, 2206, 3713, 4441. See: TDNT—
2:892, 300; BAGD—338d; THAYER—272a.

2213. **ζήτημα** {5x} **zētēma**, *dzay'-tay-mah;*
       from *2212;* a *search* (prop.
concr.), i.e. (in words) a *debate:*—question {5x}.
This word denotes questions about the Law, Acts
15:2; 18:15; 23:29; 25:19; 26:3. See: BAGD—
339b; THAYER—272c.

2214. **ζήτησις** {6x} **zētēsis**, *dzay'-tay-sis;* from
       2212; a *searching* (prop. the
act), i.e. a *dispute* or its *theme:*—question {6x}.

Zetesis denotes, firstly, "a seeking" (*zeteo,*
"to seek"), then, "a debate, dispute, questioning, questions", Jn 3:25; Acts 15:2, 7; Acts 25:20;
1 Ti 1:4; 6:4; 2 Ti 2:23; Titus 3:9. See: TDNT—
2:893, 300; BAGD—339b; THAYER—272c.

2215. **ζιζάνιον** {8x} **zizaniŏn**, *dziz-an'-ee-on;*
       of uncert. or.; *darnel* or false
grain:—tares {8x}.

Zizanion is a kind of darnel growing in the
grain fields, as tall as wheat and barley, and
resembling wheat in appearance, except the seeds
are black. It was credited among the Jews with
being degenerate wheat. The seeds are poisonous to man and herbivorous animals, producing sleepiness, nausea, convulsions and even
death (they are harmless to poultry). The plants
can be separated out, but the custom, as in the
parable, is to leave the cleaning out till near
the time of harvest (Mt 13:25–27, 29, 30, 36, 38,
40). See: BAGD—339c; THAYER—272c.

2216. **Ζοροβάβελ** {3x} **Zŏrŏbabĕl**, *dzor-ob-
       ab'-el;* of Heb. or. [2216];
Zorobabel (i.e. *Zerubbabel*), an Isr.:—*Zorobabel*
{3x}. See: BAGD—339c; THAYER—272d.

2217. **ζόφος** {4x} **zŏphŏs**, *dzof'-os;* akin to
       the base of *3509; gloom of the
netherworld* (as shrouding like a *cloud*):—
blackness {1x}, darkness {2x}, mist {1x}.

Zophos always signifies the darkness of that

shadowy land where there is no light, but only visible darkness, and translated (1) "blackness", Jude 13; (2) "darkness", 2 Pet 2:4; Jude 6; and (3) "mist", 2 Pet 2:17. See: TDNT—2:893, 300; BAGD—339d; THAYER—272d.

2218. ζυγός {6x} zugŏs, dzoo-gos'; from the root of ζεύγνυμι zĕugnumi (to join, espec. by a "yoke"); a coupling, i.e. (fig.) servitude (a law or obligation); also (lit.) the beam of the balance (as connecting the scales):—pair of balances {1x}, yoke {5x}.

Zugos is "a yoke," serving to couple two things together, is used (1) metaphorically, (1a) of submission to authority, Mt 11:29, 30, of Christ's "yoke," not simply imparted by Him but shared with Him; (1b) of bondage, Acts 15:10 and Gal 5:1, of bondage to the Law as a supposed means of salvation; (1c) of bond service to masters, 1 Ti 6:1; (2) to denote "a balance, a pair of scales," Rev 6:5. See: TDNT—2:896, 301; BAGD—339d; THAYER—272d.

2219. ζύμη {13x} zumē, dzoo'-may; prob. from 2204; ferment (as if boiling up):—leaven {13x}.

Zume is leaven, sour dough, in a high state of fermentation and was used in making bread. It required time to fulfill the process. Leaven paints the picture of being bred of corruption, coming from previous evil, and spreading through the mass of that in which it is mixed; and therefore, symbolizing the pervasive character of evil. It is used (1) metaphorically (1a) of corrupt doctrine, of error as mixed with the truth (Mt 16:6; Lk 13:21; 1 Cor 5:7, 8 twice); (1b) of the kingdom of heaven (Mt 13:33; 16:11, 12; Mk 8:15 [twice]; Lk 12:1), but does not mean that the kingdom is leaven. The same statement, as made in other parables, shows that it is the whole parable which constitutes the similitude of the kingdom; the history of Christendom confirms the fact that the pure meal of the doctrine of Christ has been adulterated with error; (1c) of corrupt practices (Mk 8:15; 1 Cor 5:7, 8); and (2) literally, (2a) of leaven (Lk 13:21; 1 Cor 5:6); (2b) of corrupt practice (Mt 16:12; 1 Cor 5:6), and (2c) corrupt doctrine (Gal 5:9). Syn.: 2220. See: TDNT—2:902, 302; BAGD—340a; THAYER—273a.

2220. ζυμόω {4x} zumŏō, dzoo-mŏ'-o; from 2219; to cause to ferment:—to leaven {4x}.

(1) This verb stresses mixing leaven with dough so as to make it ferment. (2) It signifies "to leaven, to act as leaven," (2a) passive voice in Mt 13:33 and Lk 13:21; (2b) active voice in 1 Cor 5:6 and Gal 5:9. See: TDNT—2:902, 302; BAGD—340a; THAYER—273b.

2221. ζωγρέω {2x} zōgrĕō, dzogue-reh'-o; from the same as 2226 and 64; to take alive (make a prisoner of war), i.e. (fig.) to capture or ensnare:—take captive {1x}, catch {1x}.

Zogreo, as a verb, (from zoos, "alive," and agreuo, "to hunt or catch"), (1) literally signifies "to take men alive": "And so was also James, and John, the sons of Zebedee, which were partners with Simon. And Jesus said unto Simon, Fear not; from henceforth thou shalt catch men" (Lk 5:10 - there of the effects of the work of the gospel). (2) In 2 Ti 2:26 it is said of the power of Satan to lead men astray: "and that they may recover themselves out of the snare of the devil (having been taken captive by him)." Syn.: 161, 162, 163, 164. See: BAGD—340b; THAYER—273b.

2222. ζωή {134x} zōē, dzo-ay'; from 2198; life (lit. or fig.):—life {133x}, lifetime {1x}.

Zoe means (1) life in the absolute sense, (1a) life as God has it, which the Father has in Himself, and (1a1) which He gave to the Incarnate Son to have in Himself (Jn 5:26), and (1a2) which the Son manifested in the world (1 Jn 1:2). (1a3) From this life man has become alienated in consequence of the Fall (Eph 4:18), and (1a4) of this life men become partakers through faith in the Lord Jesus Christ (Jn 3:15), (1a4i) who becomes its Author to all such as trust in Him (Acts 3:15), and (1a4ii) who is therefore said to be 'the life' of the believer (Col 3:4), because (1a4iii) the life that He gives He maintains (Jn 6:35, 63). (1b) Eternal life is (1b1) the present actual possession of the believer because of his relationship with Christ (Jn 5:24; 1 Jn 3:14), and (1b2) that it will one day extend its domain to the sphere of the body is assured by the resurrection of Christ (2 Cor 5:4; 2 Ti 1:10). (1c) This life is not merely a principle of power and mobility, however, for it has moral associations which are inseparable from it: holiness and righteousness.

Zoe also means (2) life as a principle of that (2a) which is the common possession of all animals and men by nature (Acts 17:25; 1 Jn 5:16), and of that (2b) describing the present sojourn of man upon the earth with reference to its duration (Lk 16:25; 1 Cor 15:19). (3) "This life" is a term equivalent to "the gospel," "the faith," "Christianity" (Acts 5:20). Syn.: 979, 5590. While zoe is life intensive, bios (979) is life extensive; and psuche (5590) is the individual life, the living being, whereas zoe is the life of that being (cf. Ps 66:9; Jn 10:10–11). See: TDNT—2:832, 290; BAGD—340; THAYER—273b. comp. 5590.

2223. ζώνη {8x} zōnē, *dzo'-nay;* prob. akin to the base of *2218;* a *belt;* by impl. a *pocket:*—girdle {6x}, purse {2x}.

Zone denotes **(1)** "a belt or girdle," Mt 3:4; Mk 1:6; Acts 21:11; Rev 1:13; 15:6; **(2)** it was often hollow, and hence served as a purse, Mt 10:9; Mk 6:8. See: TDNT—5:302, 702; BAGD—341b; THAYER—274c.

2224. ζώννυμι {2x} zōnnumi, *dzone'-noo-mi;* from *2223;* to *bind about* (espec. with a belt):—gird {2x}.

Zonnumi, as a verb, means "to gird" in the middle voice, "to gird oneself," is used of the long garments worn in the east: "Verily, verily, I say unto thee, When thou wast young, thou girdedst (*zonnumi*) thyself, and walkedst whither thou wouldest: but when thou shalt be old, thou shalt stretch forth thy hands, and another shall gird (*zonnumi*) thee, and carry thee whither thou wouldest not" (Jn 21:18). Syn.: 328, 1241, 4024. See: TDNT—5:302, 702; BAGD—341c; THAYER—274c.

2225. ζωογονέω {2x} zōŏgŏnĕō, *dzo-og-on-eh'-o;* from the same as *2226* and a der. of *1096;* to *engender alive,* i.e. (by anal.) to *rescue* (pass. *be saved*) from death:—live {1x}, preserve {1x}.

Zoogoneo, as a verb, denotes **(1)** "to preserve alive": "Whosoever shall seek to save his life shall lose it; and whosoever shall lose his life shall preserve it" (Lk 17:33); and **(2)** in Acts 7:19 "live," negatively of the efforts of Pharaoh to destroy the babes in Israel: "The same dealt subtilly with our kindred, and evil entreated our fathers, so that they cast out their young children, to the end they might not live." Syn.: 326, 390, 980, 1236, 2198, 4176, 4800, 5225. See: TDNT—2:873, 290; BAGD—341c; THAYER—274c.

2226. ζῶον {23x} zōŏn, *dzo'-on;* neut. of a der. of *2198;* a *live* thing, i.e. an *animal:*—beast {23x}.

(1) All creatures that live on earth, including man, are *zoon.* **(1a)** This word primarily denotes "a living being" (*zoe,* "life"). **(1b)** The Eng., "animal," is the equivalent, stressing the fact of life as the characteristic feature. **(2)** In Heb 13:11 it is translated "beasts" (cf. 2 Pet 2:12 and Jude 10). **(3)** In the Apocalypse, where the word is found some 20 times, and always of those beings which stand before the throne of God, who give glory and honor and thanks to Him, 4:6, and act in perfect harmony with His counsels, 5:14; 6:1–7, e.g., the word "beasts" is signifying that not only are these creatures "living" they are also on the upper end of the life scale; neither small animals, nor men. Syn.:

2342. See: TDNT—2:873, 290; BAGD—341c; THAYER—274c.

2227. ζωοποιέω {12x} zōŏpŏiĕō, *dzo-op-oy-eh'-o;* from the same as *2226* and *4160;* to *(re-) vitalize* (lit. or fig.):—make alive {1x}, give life {2x}, quicken {9x}.

Zoopoieo, as a verb, means "to make alive, cause to live, quicken" (from *zoe,* "life," and *poieo,* "to make"), is used as follows: **(1)** of God as the bestower **(1a)** of every kind of life in the universe, 1 Ti 6:13; and, particularly, **(1b)** of resurrection life, Jn 5:21; Rom 4:17; **(2)** of Christ, who also is the bestower of resurrection life, Jn 5:21 (2nd part); 1 Cor 15:45; cf. v. 22; **(3)** of the resurrection of Christ in "the body of His glory," 1 Pet 3:18; **(4)** of the power of reproduction inherent in seed, which presents a certain analogy with resurrection, 1 Cor 15:36; **(5)** of the "changing," or "fashioning anew," of the bodies of the living, which corresponds with, and takes place at the same time as, the resurrection of the dead in Christ, Rom 8:11; **(6)** of the impartation of spiritual life, and the communication of spiritual sustenance generally, Jn 6:63; 2 Cor 3:6; Gal 3:2. **(7)** "Quicken" means to enable to respond to His voice immediately. Once born again and indwelt by the Holy Ghost, one does not have to wait to be able to respond. Response comes fully and instaneously. Syn.: 979, 981, 982, 2222. See: TDNT—2:874, 290; BAGD—341d; THAYER—274d.

H

2228. ἤ {357x} ē, *ay;* a primary particle of distinction between two connected terms; disjunctive, *or;* comparative, *than:*—or {259x}, than {38x}, either {8x}, or else {5x}, nor {5x}, not tr {22x}, misc. {20x} = and, but (either), neither, except it be, rather, save, that, what, yea. Often used in connection with other particles. See: BAGD—342a; THAYER—275a. comp. especially *2235, 2260, 2273.*

2229. ἤ {1x} ē, *ay;* an adv. of *confirmation;* perh. intens. of *2228;* used only (in the N.T.) before *3303; assuredly:*—surely + 3375 {1x}. See: BAGD—343a; THAYER—275a.

ἥ hē. See *3588.*

ἥ hē See *3739.*

ᾗ ῃ̈ See *5600.*

2230. ἡγεμονεύω {2x} hēgĕmŏnĕuō, *hayg-em-on-yoo'-o;* from *2232;* to *act as ruler:*—be governor {2x}.

The root of this word stresses leading the way, Lk 2:2; 3:1. See: BAGD—343a; THAYER—275d.

2231. ἡγεμονία {1x} hēgĕmŏnia, *hayg-em-on-ee'-ah;* from *2232; government,* i.e. (in time) official *term:*—reign {1x}. See: BAGD—343b; THAYER—275d.

2232. ἡγεμών {22x} hēgĕmōn, *hayg-em-ohn';* from *2233;* a *leader,* i.e. *chief* person (or fig. place) of a province:—governor {19x}, prince {1x}, ruler {2x}.

Hegemon is a term used **(1)** for rulers generally [leader of any kind, a guide, ruler, prefect, chief, general, commander, sovereign] (Mk 13:9; 1 Pet 2:14); or **(2)** for the Roman procurators, referring, in the Gospels to **(2a)** Pontius Pilate (Mt 27:2; Lk 20:20); **(2b)** Felix (Acts 23:26). **(2c)** Technically the procurator was **(2c1)** a financial official under a proconsul or proprietor, for collecting the imperial revenues, but **(2c2)** entrusted also with magisterial powers for decisions of questions relative to the revenues. **(2c3)** In certain provinces, of which Judea was one (the procurator of which was dependent on the legate of Syria), he was the general administrator and supreme judge, with sole power of life and death. **(2d)** Such a governor was a person of high social standing. Felix, however, was an ex-slave, a freedman, and his appointment to Judea could not but be regarded by the Jews as an insult to the nation. **(2e)** The headquarters of the governor of Judea was Caesarea, which was made a garrison town. Syn.: 1481, 2233, 3623. See: BAGD—343b; THAYER—275d.

2233. ἡγέομαι {28x} hēgĕŏmai, *hayg-eh'-om-ahee;* mid. voice of a (presumed) strengthened form of *71;* to *lead,* i.e. *command* (with official authority); fig. to *deem,* i.e. *consider:*—count {10x}, think {4x}, esteem {3x}, have rule over {3x}, be governor {2x}, misc. {6x} = account, (be) chief, judge, suppose. See: TDNT—2:907, 303; BAGD—343c; THAYER—276a.

2234. ἡδέως {3x} hēdĕōs, *hay-deh'-oce;* adv. from a der. of the base of *2237; sweetly,* i.e. (fig.) *with pleasure:*—gladly {3x}.

Hedeos, as an adverb, means "gladly" and is used in Mk 6:20; 12:37; and 2 Cor 11:19. Syn.: 780, 2236. See: BAGD—343d; THAYER—276c.

2235. ἤδη {59x} ēdē, *ay'-day;* appar. from *2228* (or possibly *2229*) and *1211; even now:*—now {37x}, already {17x}, yet {2x}, even now {1x}, by this time {1x}, now already {1x}.

Ede is always used of time and means now, at (or by) this time, sometimes in the sense of now already. See: BAGD—344a; THAYER—276c.

2236. ἥδιστα {2x} hēdista, *hay'-dis-tah;* neut. plur. of the superl. of the same

as *2234; with great pleasure:*—most gladly {1x}, very gladly {1x}.

Hedista, as an adverb, means "most gladly, most delightedly, with great relish," and is rendered **(1)** "most gladly" in 2 Cor 12:9, and **(2)** "very gladly" in 2 Cor 12:15. Syn.: 780, 2234. See: BAGD—344a; THAYER—276c.

2237. ἡδονή {5x} hēdŏnē, *hay-don-ay';* from ἁνδάνω handanō (to *please*); sensual *delight;* by impl. *desire:*—lusts {2x}, pleasure {3x}.

Hedone, "pleasure," is used of the gratification of the natural desire or sinful desires and is translated **(1)** "lusts" Jas 4:1, 3; and **(2)** "pleasure", Lk 8:14 plural; Titus 3:3 plural; 2 Pet 2:13. See: TDNT—2:909, 303; BAGD—344b; THAYER—276c.

2238. ἡδύοσμον {2x} hēduŏsmŏn, *hay-doo'-os-mon;* neut. of the compound of the same as *2234* and *3744;* a *sweet-scented* plant, i.e. *mint:*—mint {2x}. Cf. Mt 23:23; Lk 11:42. See: BAGD—344b; THAYER—276d.

2239. ἦθος {1x} ēthŏs, *ay'-thos;* a strengthened form of *1485; usage,* i.e. (plur.) moral *habits:*—manners {1x}.

'Ethos, as a noun, means "a custom, manner" and occurs in the plural in 1 Cor 15:33: "Be not deceived: evil communications corrupt good manners" [i.e., ethical conduct, morals]. Syn.: 195, 1485, 3634, 3668, 3697, 3779, 4169, 4187, 4217, 4459, 5158, 5159, 5179, 5615. See: BAGD—344c; THAYER—276d.

2240. ἥκω {27x} hēkō, *hay'-ko;* a primary verb; to *arrive,* i.e. *be present* (lit. or fig.):—to come {27x}.

Heko means **(1)** "to come, to be present" **(2)** "to come upon, of time and events," Mt 24:14; Jn 2:4; 2 Pet 3:10; Rev 18:8; **(3)** metaphorically, "to come upon one, of calamitous times, and evils," Mt 23:36; Lk 19:43. See: TDNT—2:926, 306; BAGD—344c; THAYER—276d.

2241. ἠλί {2x} ēli, *ay-lee'* or ἐλοι ĕloi *ay-lo'-ee;* of Heb. or. [410 with pron. suff.]; *my God:*—Eli {2x}. See: BAGD—345a; THAYER—277a.

2242. Ἡλί {1x} Hēli, *hay-lee';* of Heb. or. [5941]; *Heli* (i.e. *Eli*), an Isr.:—Heli {1x}. See: BAGD—345a; THAYER—277a.

2243. Ἡλίας {30x} Hēlias, *hay-lee'-as;* of Heb. or. [452]; *Helias* (i.e. *Elijah*), an Isr.:—Elias {30x}. See: TDNT—2:928, 306; BAGD—345a; THAYER—277a.

2244. ἡλικία {8x} hēlikia, *hay-lik-ee'-ah;* from the same as *2245; maturity* (in years or size):—age {3x}, stature {5x}.

Helikia, as a noun, primarily "an age," as

a certain length of life, came to mean **(1)** "a particular time of life," as when a person is said to be "of age": **(1a)** "But by what means he now seeth, we know not; or who hath opened his eyes, we know not: he is of age; ask him: he shall speak for himself" (Jn 9:21, cf. v 23), or **(1b)** beyond a certain stage of life: "Through faith also Sara herself received strength to conceive seed, and was delivered of a child when she was past age, because she judged him faithful who had promised" (Heb 11:11); **(2)** elsewhere only "of stature": "Which of you by taking thought can add one cubit unto his stature (*helikia*)?" (Mt 6:27; cf. Lk 2:52; 12:25; 19:3; Eph 4:13). Syn.: 165, 166, 1074, 2250, 5046, 5230. See: TDNT—2:941, 308; BAGD—345a; THAYER—277b.

2245. ἡλίκος {2x} **hēlikŏs**, *hay-lee'-kos;* from
　　　ἡλιξ **hēlix** (a *comrade*, i.e. one of the same age); *as big as*, i.e. (interjectively) *how much:*—how great {1x}, what great {1x}.

Helikos primarily denotes "as big as, as old as"; then, as an indirect interrogation, "what, what size, how great, how small" (the context determines the meaning), said **(1)** of a spiritual conflict, Col 2:1, "what great (conflict) I have"; **(2)** of much wood as kindled by a little fire, Jas 3:5 "how great a matter (wood is kindled by) how small (a fire)." See: BAGD—345c; THAYER—277c.

2246. ἥλιος {32x} **hēliŏs**, *hay'-lee-os;* from
　　　ἕλη **hĕlē** (a *ray;* perh. akin to the alt. of *138*); the *sun;* by impl. *light:*—+ east {2x}, sun {30x}.

Helios is used **(1)** as a means of the natural benefits of light and heat (Mt 5:45) and power (Rev 1:16); **(2)** of its qualities of brightness and glory (Mt 13:43; 17:2; Acts 26:13; 1 Cor 15:41; Rev 10:1; 12:1); **(3)** as a means of destruction (Mt 13:6; Jas 1:11); **(4)** of physical misery (Rev 7:16); and **(5)** as a means of judgment (Mt 24:29; Mk 13:24; Lk 21:25; 23:45; Acts 2:20; Rev 6:12; 8:12; 9:2; 16:8). See: BAGD—345c; THAYER—277c.

2247. ἧλος {2x} **hēlŏs**, *hay'-los;* of uncert.
　　　aff.; a *stud,* i.e. *spike:*—nails {2x}. Cf. Jn 20:25 twice. See: BAGD—345d; THAYER—277c.

2248. ἡμᾶς {178x} **hēmas**, *hay-mas';* acc. plur.
　　　of *1473; us:*—us {148x}, we {25x}, our {2x}, us-ward + *1519* {2x}, not tr {1x}. See: BAGD—217a [1473]; THAYER—167b [1473].

2249. ἡμεῖς {127x} **hēmeis**, *hay-mice';* nom.
　　　plur. of *1473; we* (only used when emphat.):—us {3x}, we {123x}, we ourselves {1x}. See: BAGD—217a [1473]; THAYER—277c; 167b [1473].

2250. ἡμέρα {389x} **hēmĕra**, *hay-mer'-ah;* fem.
　　　(with *5610* impl.) of a der. of

ἧμαι **hēmai** (to *sit;* akin to the base of *1476*) mean. *tame,* i.e. *gentle; day,* i.e. (lit.) the time space between dawn and dark, or the whole 24 hours (but several days were usually reckoned by the Jews as inclusive of the parts of both extremes); fig. a *period* (always defined more or less clearly by the context):—day {355x}, daily + *2596* {15x}, time {3x}, not tr {2x}, misc. {14x} = age, + alway, midday, + for ever, judgment, while, years.

Hemera, as a noun, means "a day," is rendered "age," "of a great age" (lit., "advanced in many days") in Lk 2:36: "And there was one Anna, a prophetess, the daughter of Phanuel, of the tribe of Aser: she was of a great age, and had lived with an husband seven years from her virginity." Syn.: 165, 166, 1074, 2244, 5046, 5230. See: TDNT—2:943, 309; BAGD—345d; THAYER—277c.

2251. ἡμέτερος {9x} **hēmĕtĕrŏs**, *hay-met'-er-*
　　　os; from *2349; our:*—our {8x}, your {1x}. See: BAGD—347d; THAYER—279b.

2252. ἤμην {16x} **ēmēn**, *ay'-mane;* a prol. form
　　　of *2349;* I *was:*—was {13x}, I imprisoned + *1473* + *5439* {1x}, I was + *1473* {1x}, should be {1x}. See: BAGD—343a [2229]; THAYER—279c. [*Sometimes unexpressed*].

2253. ἡμιθανής {1x} **hēmithanēs**, *hay-mee-*
　　　than-ace'; from a presumed compound of the base of *2255* and *2348; half dead,* i.e. *entirely exhausted:*—half dead {1x}. See: BAGD—348a; THAYER—279c.

2254. ἡμῖν {177x} **hēmin**, *hay-meen';* dat.
　　　plur. of *1473; to* (or *for, with, by*) *us:*—us {161x}, we {13x}, our {2x}, for us {1x}. See: BAGD—217a; THAYER—167b [1473].

2255. ἥμισυ {5x} **hēmisu**, *hay'-mee-soo;* neut.
　　　of a der. from an inseparable pref. akin to *260* (through the idea of *partition* involved in *connection*) and mean. *semi-;* (as noun) *half:*—half {5x}.

Hemisu, an adjective, is used **(1)** as such in the neuter plural, in Lk 19:8, lit., "the halves (of my goods)"; **(2)** as a noun, in the neuter sing., "the half," Mk 6:23; "half (a time)," Rev 12:14; "half," 11:9, 11. See: BAGD—348a; THAYER—279c.

2256. ἡμιώριον {1x} **hēmiōriŏn**, *hay-mee-o'-*
　　　ree-on; from the base of *2255* and *5610;* a *half-hour:*—half an hour {1x}. See: BAGD—348a; THAYER—279d.

2257. ἡμῶν {410x} **hēmōn**, *hay-mone';* gen.
　　　plur. of *1473; of* (or *from*) *us:*—our {313x}, us {82x}, we {12x}, not tr {1x}, misc. {2x}. See: BAGD—217a; THAYER—167b [1473].

Greek

2258. ἦν {455x} **ēn**, *ane;* imperf. of *1510; I* (*thou,* etc.) *was* (*wast* or *were*):— was {266x}, were {115x}, had been {12x}, had {11x}, taught + 1321 {4x}, stood + 2476 {4x}, vr was {1x}, misc {41x} = + agree, be, × have (+ charge of), hold, use. See: BAGD—222d; THAYER—175c [1510].

2259. ἡνίκα {2x} **hēnika**, *hay-nee'-kah;* of uncert. aff.; *at which time:*— when {2x}. Cf. 2 Cor 3:15, 16. See: BAGD— 348b; THAYER—279d.

2260. ἤπερ {1x} **ēpĕr**, *ay'-per;* from *2228* and *4007; than at all* (or *than perhaps, than indeed*):—than {1x}. See: BAGD— 348b; THAYER—279d.

2261. ἤπιος {2x} **ēpiŏs**, *ay'-pee-os;* prob. from *2031;* prop. *affable,* i.e. *mild* or *kind:*—gentle {2x}.

(1) In 1 Th 2:7, the apostle uses *epios* of the conduct of himself and his fellow missionaries towards the converts at Thessalonica (cf. 2 Cor. 11:13, 20); and **(2)** in 2 Ti 2:24, of the conduct requisite for a servant of the Lord. See: BAGD—348b; THAYER—279d.

2262. Ἤρ {1x} **Ēr**, *ayr;* of Heb. or. [6147]; *Er,* an Isr.:—Er {1x}. See: BAGD—348b; THAYER—279d.

2263. ἤρεμος {1x} **ērĕmŏs**, *ay'-rem-os;* perh. by transposition from *2048* (through the idea of *stillness*); *tranquil:*—quiet {1x}.

Eremos means quiet, tranquil, occurs in 1 Ti 2:2 and indicates tranquility arising from without. See: BAGD—348b; THAYER—279d.

2264. Ἡρώδης {44x} **Hērōdēs**, *hay-ro'-dace;* compound of ἤρως **hērōs** (a "*hero*") and *1491; heroic; Herod,* the name of four Jewish kings:—Herod, Antipas {27x}, Herod, the Great {11x}, Herod Agrippa {6x}. See: BAGD—348c; THAYER—280a.

2265. Ἡρωδιανοί {3x} **Hērōdianŏi**, *hay-ro-dee-an-oy';* plur. of a der. of *2264; Herodians,* i.e. partisans of Herod:—Herodians {3x}. See: BAGD—348d; THAYER—280d.

2266. Ἡρωδιάς {6x} **Hērōdias**, *hay-ro-dee-as';* from *2264; Herodias,* a woman of the Herodian family:—Herodias {6x}. See: BAGD—348d; THAYER—280d.

2267. Ἡρωδίων {1x} **Hērōdiōn**, *hay-ro-dee'-ohn;* from *2264; Herodion,* a Chr.:— *Herodion* {1x}. See: BAGD—348d; THAYER— 281a.

2268. Ἡσαΐας {21x} **Hēsaïas**, *hay-sah-ee'-as;* of Heb. or. [3470]; *Hesaias* (i.e. *Jeshajah*), an Isr.:—Esaias {21x}. See: BAGD— 348d; THAYER—281a.

2269. Ἠσαῦ {3x} **Ēsau**, *ay-sow';* of Heb. or. [6215]; *Esau,* an Edomite:—*Esau* {3x}. See: TDNT—2:953, 311; BAGD—349a; THAYER—281b.

2270. ἡσυχάζω {5x} **hēsuchazō**, *hay-soo-khad'-zo;* from the same as *2272;* to *keep still* (intr.), i.e. *refrain* from labor, meddlesomeness or speech:—cease {1x}, hold (one's) peace {1x}, be quiet {1x}, rest {1x}.

Hesuchazo, "to be quiet, still, at rest," is said **(1)** of Paul's friends in Caesarea, in "ceasing" to persuade him not to go to Jerusalem, Acts 21:14; **(2)** it is used of silence ("held their peace") in Lk 14:4 and Acts 11:18. It is translated **(3)** "rested" in Lk 23:56 and **(4)** "quiet" in 1 Th 4:11. See: BAGD—349a; THAYER—281b.

2271. ἡσυχία {4x} **hēsuchia**, *hay-soo-khee'-ah;* fem. of *2272;* (as noun) *stillness,* i.e. desistance from bustle or language:— quietness {1x}, silence {3x}.

Hesuchia denotes **(1)** "quietness," 2 Th 3:12; it is translated **(2)** "silence" **(2a)** 1 Ti 2:11, 12; and **(2b)** in Acts 22:2, "(they kept the more) silence," lit., "they kept quietness the more." See: BAGD—349b; THAYER—281b.

2272. ἡσύχιος {2x} **hēsuchiŏs**, *hay-soo'-khee-os;* a prol. form of a compound prob. of a der. of the base of *1476* and perh. *2192;* prop. *keeping* one's *seat* (*sedentary*), i.e. (by impl.) *still* (*undisturbed, undisturbing*):— peaceable {1x}, quiet {1x}.

(1) This word indicates tranquility arising from within, causing no disturbance to others. **(2)** It is translated **(2a)** "peaceable" in 1 Ti 2:2; and **(2b)** "quiet" in 1 Pet 3:4, where it is associated with "meek," and is to characterize the spirit or disposition. See: BAGD—349c; THAYER—281c.

2273. ἤτοι {1x} **ētŏi**, *ay'-toy;* from *2228* and *5104; either indeed:*—whether {1x}. See: BAGD—349c; THAYER—281c.

2274. ἡττάω {3x} **hēttaō**, *hayt-tah'-o;* from the same as *2276;* to *make worse,* i.e. *vanquish* (lit. or fig.); by impl. to *rate lower:*—be inferior {1x}, overcome {2x}.

Hettao, "to be less or inferior," is used in the passive voice, and translated **(1)** "ye were inferior," in 2 Cor 12:13, i.e., were treated with less consideration than other churches, through his independence in not receiving gifts from them. **(2)** In 2 Pet 2:19, 20 it signifies to be overcome, in the sense of being subdued and enslaved. See: BAGD—349c; THAYER—281c.

2275. ἥττημα {2x} **hēttēma**, *hayt'-tay-mah;* from *2274;* a *deterioration,* i.e. (obj.) *failure* or (subj.) *loss:*—diminishing {1x}, fault {1x}.

Hettema primarily means "a lessening, a decrease, diminution," denotes "a loss." **(1)** It is used of the "loss" sustained by the Jewish nation in that they had rejected God's testimonies and His Son and the gospel, **(1a)** Rom 11:12, the reference being not only to national diminution but to spiritual "loss"; "diminishing." **(1b)** Here the contrasting word is *pleroma,* "fullness." **(2)** In 1 Cor 6:7 the reference is to the spiritual "loss" sustained by the church at Corinth because or their discord and their litigious ways in appealing to the world's judges, "fault." **(2a)** The preceding adverb "altogether" shows the comprehensiveness of the "defect"; **(2b)** the "fault" affected the whole church, and was "an utter detriment." See: BAGD—349c; THAYER—281d.

2276. ἥττον {2x} **hēttŏn,** *hate'-ton;* neut. of comp. of ἥκα **hēka** (*slightly*) used for that of *2556; worse* (as noun); by impl. *less* (as adv.):—less {1x}, worse {1x}.

Hetton, "less, inferior," used in the neuter, after *epi,* "for," is translated **(1)** "worse" in 1 Cor 11:17; and **(2)** in 2 Cor 12:15 the neuter, used adverbially, is translated "the less." See: BAGD—397c; THAYER—281d.

2277. ἤτω {2x} **ētō,** *ay'-to;* third pers. sing. imper. of *1510; let him* (or *it*) *be:*—let . . . be {2x}. See: BAGD—222d; THAYER—175c [1510].

2278. ἠχέω {2x} **ēchĕō,** *ay-kheh'-o;* from *2279; to make a* loud *noise,* i.e. *reverberate:*—roaring {1x}, sounding {1x}.

Echeo occurs **(1)** in 1 Cor 13:1, "sounding (brass)"; and **(2)** "a noise" or "sound" (Eng., "echo"), is used of the "roaring" of the sea in Lk 21:25, "(the sea and the waves) roaring." See: BAGD—349c; THAYER—281d,

2279. ἦχος {3x} **ēchŏs,** *ay'-khos;* of uncert. aff.; a loud or confused *noise* ("*echo*"), i.e. *roar;* fig. a *rumor:*—fame {1x}, sound {2x}.

Echos "a noise, report, sound," is translated **(1)** "fame," in Lk 4:37; and **(2)** "sound" in Acts 2:2; Heb 12:19. See: BAGD—349d; THAYER—281d.

Θ

2280. Θαδδαῖος {2x} **Thaddaiŏs,** *thad-dah'-yos;* of uncert. or.; *Thaddæus,* one of the apostles:—Thaddæus {2x}. See: BAGD—350a; THAYER—282a.

2281. θάλασσα {92x} **thalassa,** *thal'-as-sah;* prob. prol. from *251;* the *sea* (gen. or spec.):—sea {92x}.

Thalassa, as a noun, is used **(1)** chiefly liter-ally, e.g., **(1a)** "the Red Sea," Acts 7:36; 1 Cor 10:1; Heb 11:29; **(1b)** the "sea" of Galilee or Tiberias, Mt 4:18; 15:29; Mk 6:48, 49, where the acts of Christ testified to His deity; Jn 6:1; 21:1; **(1c)** in general, e.g., Lk 17:2; Acts 4:24; Rom 9:27; Rev 16:3; 18:17; 20:8, 13; 21:1; **(1d)** in combination, Mt 18:6; **(2)** metaphorically, of "the ungodly men" described in Jude 13 (cf. Is 57:20); **(3)** symbolically, **(3a)** in the apocalyptic vision of "a glassy sea like unto crystal," Rev 4:6, emblematic of the fixed purity and holiness of all that appertains to the authority and judicial dealings of God; **(3b)** in 15:2, the same, "mingled with fire," and, standing on it, those who had "come victorious from the beast" (ch. 13); **(3c)** of the wild and restless condition of nations, Rev 13:1 (see 17:1, 15), where "he stood" refers to John; **(3d)** from the midst of this state arises the beast, symbolic of the final Gentile power dominating the federated nations of the Roman world (see Dan, chs. 2, 7, etc.). Syn.: 989, 1337, 1724, 3864, 3882. See: BAGD—350a; THAYER—282a.

2282. θάλπω {2x} **thalpō,** *thal'-po;* prob. akin to θάλλω **thallō** (to *warm*); to *brood,* i.e. (fig.) to *foster:*—cherish {2x}.

Thalpo primarily means **(1)** "to heat, to soften by heat"; **(1a)** then, "to keep warm," as of birds covering their young with their feathers, cf. Deut 22:6t.; **(2)** metaphorically, "to cherish with tender love, to foster with tender care," **(2a)** in Eph 5:29 of Christ and the church; **(2b)** in 1 Th 2:7 of the care of the saints at Thessalonica by the apostle and his associates, as of a nurse for her children. See: BAGD—350b; THAYER—282b.

2283. Θάμαρ {1x} **Thamar,** *tham'-ar;* of Heb. or. [8559]; *Thamar* (i.e. *Tamar*), an Israelitess:—Thamar {1x}. See: BAGD—350c; THAYER—282c.

2284. θαμβέω {4x} **thambĕō,** *tham-beh'-o;* from *2285; to stupefy* (with surprise), i.e. *astound:*—be amazed {2x}, be astonished {2x}.

Thambeo is translated **(1)** "be amazed" in Mk 1:27; 10:32; and **(2)** "be astonished" Mk 10:24; Acts 9:6. **(3)** Amazement comes first, then settled amazement equals astonished, and settled astonishment equals astonied, cf. *2285.* See: TDNT—3:4, 312; BAGD—350c; THAYER—282c.

2285. θάμβος {3x} **thambŏs,** *tham'-bos;* akin to an obs. τάφω **taphō** (to *dumbfound*); *stupefaction* (by surprise), i.e. *astonishment:*—be amazed + 1096 {1x}, be astonished + 4023 {1x}, wonder {1x}.

This word means amazement, wonder and is probably connected with a root signifying to

render immovable; it is frequently associated with terror as well as astonishment (Lk 4:36; 5:9; Acts 3:10). See: TDNT—3:4, 312; BAGD—350c; THAYER—282c.

2286. θανάσιμος {1x} **thanasimŏs,** *than-as'-ee-mos;* from *2288; fatal,* i.e. *poisonous:*—deadly {1x}.

This word means belonging to death, or partaking of the nature of death: "They shall take up serpents; and if they drink any deadly thing, it shall not hurt them; they shall lay hands on the sick, and they shall recover" (Mk 16:18). See: BAGD—350d; THAYER—282c.

2287. θανατήφορος {1x} **thanatēphŏrŏs,** *than-at-ay'-for-os;* from (the fem. form of) *2288* and *5342; death-bearing,* i.e. *fatal:*—deadly {1x}.

This word means death-bearing, deadly: "But the tongue can no man tame; it is an unruly evil, full of deadly poison" (Jas 3:8). See: BAGD—350d; THAYER—282c.

2288. θάνατος {119x} **thanatŏs,** *than'-at-os;* from *2348;* (prop. an adj. used as a noun) *death* (lit. or fig.):—× deadly {2x}, (be . . .) death {117x}.

Thanatos, death, has the basic meaning of separation of **(1)** the soul (the spiritual part of man) from the body (the material part), the latter ceasing to function and turning to dust (Jn 11:13; Heb 2:15; 5:7; 7:23); **(2)** man from God; **(2a)** Adam died on the day he disobeyed God (cf. Gen 2:17); and hence **(2b)** all mankind are born in the same spiritual condition (Rom 5:12, 14, 17, 21), **(2c)** from which, however, those who believe in Christ are delivered (Jn 5:24; 1 Jn 3:14). **(3)** Death is the opposite of life; it never denotes nonexistence. **(4)** As spiritual life is conscious existence in communion with God, so spiritual death is conscious existence in separation from God. **(5)** Death, in whichever of the above-mentioned senses it is used, is **(5a)** always, in Scripture, viewed as the penal consequence of sin, and **(5b)** since sinners alone are subject to death (Rom 5:12), **(5c)** it was as the Bearer of sin that the Lord Jesus submitted thereto on the Cross (1 Pet 2:24). **(5d)** And while the physical death of the Lord Jesus was of the essence of His sacrifice, it was not the whole. **(5e)** The darkness symbolized, and His cry expressed, the fact that He was left alone in the universe, He was forsaken (Mt 27:45–46). Syn.: 336, 615, 1935, 2289, 5054. See: TDNT—3:7, 312; BAGD—350d; THAYER—282d.

2289. θανατόω {11x} **thanatŏō,** *than-at-ŏ'-o;* from *2288;* to *kill* (lit. or fig.):—put to death {4x}, cause to be put to death {3x}, kill {2x}, become dead {1x}, mortify {1x}.

Thanatoo, as a verb, means **(1)** "to put to death" (Mt 10:21; cf. Mk 13:12; Lk 21:16) and is translated "shall . . . cause (them) to be put to death" literally, "shall put (them) to death." **(2)** It is used of the death of Christ in Mt 26:59; 27:1; Mk 14:55 and 1 Pet 3:18. **(3)** In Rom 7:4 (passive voice) it is translated "ye . . . are become dead," with reference to the change from bondage to the Law to union with Christ; **(3a)** cf. in 8:13, "mortify" of the act of the believer in regard to the deeds of the body; **(3b)** in 8:36, "are killed" (so in 2 Cor 6:9). Syn.: 336, 337, 520, 1935, 2288, 5054. See: TDNT—3:21, 312; BAGD—351c; THAYER—283c.

θάνω thanō. See *2348.*

2290. θάπτω {11x} **thaptō,** *thap'-to;* a primary verb; to *celebrate funeral rites,* i.e. *inter:*—bury {11x}.

Thapto occurs **(1)** generally, in Mt. 8:21, 22; Lk 9:59, 60; **(2)** of the rich man, Lk 16:22; **(3)** of David, Acts 2:29; **(4)** of Ananias, Acts 5:6, and Sapphira, 9–10; **(5)** of John the baptizer, Mt 14:12; **(6)** of Christ's "burial," 1 Cor 15:4. See: BAGD—351d; THAYER—283d.

2291. Θάρα {1x} **Thara,** *thar'-ah;* of Heb. or. [8646]; *Thara* (i.e. *Terach*), the father of Abraham:—*Thara* {1x}. See: BAGD—351d; THAYER—283d.

2292. θαρρέω {6x} **tharrhĕō,** *thar-hreh'-o;* another form for *2293;* to *exercise courage:*—be bold {2x}, be confident {1x}, confident {1x}, have confidence {1x}, boldly {1x}.

The root of this word means "to be warm" [warmth of temperament being associated with confidence; cf. Eng. "he had cold feet" implying a lack of courage]; hence, **(1)** "to be confident", 2 Cor 5:6, 8; **(2)** 2 Cor 7:16 "to have confidence"; **(3)** 2 Cor 10:1, 2 "to be bold"; **(4)** Heb 13:6 "boldly"; (lit., "being courageous"). See: TDNT—3:25, 315; BAGD—352a; THAYER—283d. comp. *5111.*

2293. θαρσέω {8x} **tharsĕō,** *thar-seh'-o;* from *2294;* to *have courage:*—be of good cheer {5x}. be of good comfort {3x}.

This word means "to be of good courage, of good cheer" (*tharsos,* "courage, confidence"), and is used only in the imperative mood, in the NT; **(1)** "be of good cheer", Mt 9:2; 14:27; Mk 6:50; Jn 16:33; Acts 23:11; and **(2)** "be of good comfort", Mt 9:22; Mk 10:49; Lk 8:48. See: TDNT—3:25, 315; BAGD—352a; THAYER—283d. Comp. *2292.*

2294. θάρσος {1x} **tharsŏs,** *thar'-sos;* akin (by transp.) to θράσος **thrasŏs** (*daring*); *boldness* (subj.):—courage {1x}. See: BAGD—352a; THAYER—283d.

2295. θαῦμα {1x} **thauma,** *thŏu'-mah;* appar. from a form of *2300; wonder* (prop. concr.; but by impl. abstr.):—admiration {1x}.

Thauma, "a wonder" (akin to *theaomai,* "to gaze in wonder"), is found in Rev 17:6 "admiration", said of John's astonishment at the vision of the woman described as Babylon the Great. See: TDNT—3:27, 316; BAGD—352a; THAYER—283d.

2296. θαυμάζω {47x} **thaumazō,** *thŏu-mad'-zo;* from *2295;* to *wonder;* by impl. to *admire:*—marvel {29x}, wonder {14x}, have in admiration {1x}, admire {1x}, marvelled + 2258 {1x}, vr wonder {1x}.

This word means to wonder, wonder at, marvel, to be wondered at, and hence, to be had in admiration. See: TDNT—3:27, 316; BAGD—352b; THAYER—284a.

2297. θαυμάσιος {1x} **thaumasiŏs,** *thŏu-mas'-ee-os;* from *2295; wondrous,* i.e. (neut. as noun) a *miracle:*—wonderful thing {1x}.

Thaumasios is admiration and astonishment provoked by a miracle: "And when the chief priests and scribes saw the wonderful things that He did, and the children crying in the temple, and saying, Hosanna to the Son of David; they were sore displeased" (Mt 21:15). Syn.: 1411, 1741, 3167, 3861, 4592, 5259. See: TDNT—3:27, 316; BAGD—352d; THAYER—284b.

2298. θαυμαστός {7x} **thaumastŏs,** *thŏw-mas-tos';* from *2296; wondered* at, i.e. (by impl.) *wonderful:*—marvel {1x}, marvellous {5x}, marvelous thing {1x}.

Thaumastos, is translated **(1)** "marvellous" and is said **(1a)** of the Lord's doing in making the rejected Stone the Head of the corner, Mt 21:42; Mk 12:11; **(1b)** of the spiritual light into which believers are brought, 1 Pet 2:9; **(1c)** of the vision of the seven angels having the seven last plagues, Rev 15:1; **(1d)** of the works of God, Rev 15:3; **(2)** "a marvellous thing", of the erstwhile [former] blind man's astonishment that the Pharisees knew not from whence Christ had come, and yet He had given him sight, Jn 9:30 and translated **(3)** "marvel": "And no marvel; for Satan himself is transformed into an angel of light", 2 Cor 11:14. See: TDNT—3:27, 316; BAGD—352d; THAYER—284b.

2299. θεά {3x} **thĕa,** *theh-ah';* fem. of *2316;* a female *deity:*—goddess {3x}. Cf. Acts 19:27, 35, 37. See: BAGD—353a; THAYER—284c.

2300. θεάομαι {24x} **thĕaŏmai,** *theh-ah'-om-ahee;* a prol. form of a primary verb; to *look* closely at, i.e. (by impl.) *perceive* (lit. or fig.); by extens. to *visit:*—see {20x}, behold {2x}, look {1x}, look upon {1x}.

(1) *Theaomai,* as a verb, means "to behold" [of careful contemplation], and is translated **(1a)** "looking" (Jn 4:35, of "looking" on the fields); and **(1b)** "looked upon" (1 Jn 1:1, of the apostles' personal experiences of Christ in the days of His flesh, and the facts of His Godhood and Manhood). **(2)** *Theaomai* also means "to behold, view attentively, contemplate," in the sense of a wondering regard. **(2a)** It signifies a more earnest contemplation than the ordinary verbs for "to see," "a careful and deliberate vision which interprets . . . its object," and **(2b)** is more frequently rendered "behold": "And the women also, which came with him from Galilee, followed after, and beheld the sepulchre, and how His body was laid" (Lk 23:55; cf. Jn 1:14; 1:32; Acts 1:11; 1 Jn 1:1(more than merely seeing); 4:12, 14). Syn.: 308, 333, 352, 578, 816, 872, 991, 1689, 1896, 1914, 1980, 1983, 2029, 2334, 2657, 2734, 3700, 3706, 3708, 3879, 4017, 4648. See: TDNT—5:315, 706; BAGD—353a; THAYER—284c.

2301. θεατρίζω {1x} **thĕatrizō,** *theh-at-rid'-zo;* from *2302;* to *expose as a spectacle:*—make a gazing stock {1x}.

This word means to bring upon the stage, to set forth as a spectacle, and to expose to contempt, Heb 10:33. See: TDNT—3:42,*; BAGD—353c; THAYER—284d.

2302. θέατρον {3x} **thĕatrŏn,** *theh'-at-ron;* from *2300;* a *place for public show* ("theatre"), i.e. general *audience-room;* by impl. a *show* itself (fig.):—spectacle {1x}, theatre {2x}.

Theatron, akin to *theaomai,* "to behold," denotes **(1)** "a theater" (used also as a place of assembly), Acts 19:29, 31; and **(2)** "a spectacle, a show," metaphorically in 1 Cor 4:9. See: TDNT—3:42, 318; BAGD—353c; THAYER—284d.

2303. θεῖον {7x} **thĕiŏn,** *thi'-on;* prob. neut. of *2304* (in its orig. sense of *flashing*); *sulphur:*—brimstone {7x}.

Theion originally denoted "fire from heaven." It is connected with sulphur. Places touched by lightning were called *theia,* and, as lightning leaves a sulphurous smell, and sulphur was used in pagan purifications, it received the name of *theion* Lk 17:29; Rev 9:17–18; 14:10; 19:20; 20:10; 21:8. See: TDNT—3:122,*; BAGD—353c; THAYER—284d.

2304. θεῖος {3x} **thĕiŏs,** *thi'-os;* from *2316; godlike* (neut. as noun, *divinity*):—divine {2x}, Godhead {1x}.

Theios means **(1)** divine and is used **(1a)** of the power of God (2 Pet 1:3), and **(1b)** of His

nature (2 Pet 1: 4), both of which proceed from Himself. **(2)** In Acts 17:29 it is used as a noun with the definite article, to denote the God-head, the Deity, the one true God. See: TDNT—3:122, 322; BAGD—353d; THAYER—285a.

2305. **θειότης** {1x} **thĕiŏtēs**, *thi-ot'-ace;* from *2304; divinity* (abstr.):—God-head {1x}.

Theiotes (Rom 1:20), Godhead, is derived from *theios* (2304), and is to be distinguished from *theotes* (2320 - Col 2:9). In Rom 1:20 the apostle is declaring how much of God may be known from the revelation of Himself which He has made in the creation, from those ves-tiges of Himself which men may everywhere trace in the world around them. Yet it is not the personal God whom any man may learn to know by these aids; He can be known only by the revelation of Himself in His Son. In Col 2:9, Paul is declaring that in the Son there dwells all the fullness of absolute Godhead; they were no mere rays of divine glory which gilded Him, lighting up His Person for a season and with a splendor not His own; but He was, and is, absolute and perfect God; and the apos-tle uses *theotes* (2320) to express this essential and personal Godhead of the Son. *Theotes* (2320) indicates the divine essence of Godhood, the personality of God; *theiotes* (2305), the at-tributes of God, His divine nature and proper-ties. See: TDNT—3:123, 322; BAGD—354a; THAYER—285a.

2306. **θειώδης** {1x} **thĕiŏdēs**, *thi-o'-dace;* from *2303* and *1491; sulphur-like,* i.e. *sulphurous:*—brimstone {1x}. See: BAGD—354a; THAYER—285a.

θελέω **thĕlĕō**. See *2309.*

2307. **θέλημα** {64x} **thĕlēma**, *thel'-ay-mah;* from the prol. form of *2309; a determination* (prop. the thing), i.e. (act.) *choice* (spec. *purpose, decree;* abstr. *volition*) or (pass.) *inclination:*—desire {1x}, pleasure {1x}, will {62x}.

(1) What one wishes or has determined shall be done, Lk 12:47, Jn 5:30; 1 Cor 7:37; and speaks **(1a)** of the purpose of God to bless man-kind through Christ, Acts 22:14; Eph 1:9; Col 1:9; **(1b)** of what God wishes to be done by us, **(1b1)** Rom 12:2; Col 4:12; 1 Pet 4:2; **(1b2)** especially His commands, precepts, Acts 13:22; **(2)** of one's will, choice, inclination, desire, pleasure. Jn 1:13; Eph 2:13 plural. See: TDNT—3:52, 318; BAGD—354b; THAYER—285a.

2308. **θέλησις** {1x} **thĕlēsis**, *thel'-ay-sis;* from *2309; determination* (prop. the act), i.e. *option:*—will {1x}.

Thelesis denotes "a willing, a wishing", Heb

2:4. See: TDNT—3:62, 318; BAGD—354c; THAYER—285c.

2309. **θέλω** {210x} **thĕlō**, *thel'-o;* or ἐθέλω **ĕth-ĕlō**, *eth-el'-o;* in certain tenses θελέω **thĕlĕō**, *thel-eh'-o;* and ἐθελέω **ĕthĕlĕō**, *eth-el-eh'-o;* which are otherwise obs.; appar. strengthened from the alt. form of *138;* to *de-termine* (as an act. *option* from subj. impulse; whereas *1014* prop. denotes rather a pass. *ac-quiescence* in obj. considerations), i.e. *choose* or *prefer* (lit. or fig.); by impl. to *wish*, i.e. *be inclined* to (sometimes adv. *gladly*); impers. for the future tense, to *be about to;* by Heb. to *de-light in:*—will/would {159x}, will/would have {16x}, desire {13x}, desirous {3x}, list {3x}, to will {2x}, misc. {4x}.

This word stresses to will, to wish, implying volition and purpose, frequently a determina-tion, have in mind, intend, to be resolved or determined; usually rendered "to will." See: TDNT—3:44, 318; BAGD—354d; THAYER—285c.

2310. **θεμέλιος** {16x} **thĕmĕliŏs**, *them-el'-ee-os;* from a der. of *5087;* some-thing *put* down, i.e. a *substruction* (of a build-ing, etc.), (lit. or fig.):—foundation {16x}.

Themelios is properly an adjective denoting "belonging to a foundation" (connected with *tithemi*, "to place"). It is used **(1)** as a noun, with *lithos*, "a stone," understood, in Lk 6:48, 49; 14:29; Heb 11:10; Rev 21:14, 19; **(2)** as a neuter noun in Acts 16:26, and metaphorically, **(2a)** of "the ministry of the gospel and the doc-trines of the faith," Rom 15:20; 1 Cor 3:10, 11, 12; Eph 2:20, where the "of" is not subjective (i.e., consisting of the apostles and prophets), but objective, (i.e., laid by the apostles, etc.); so in 2 Ti 2:19, where "the foundation of God" is "the foundation laid by God,"—not the church (which is not a "foundation"), but Christ Him-self, upon whom the saints are built; Heb 6:1; **(2b)** "of good works, 1 Ti 6:19. See: TDNT—3:63, 322; BAGD—355d; THAYER—286d.

2311. **θεμελιόω** {6x} **thĕmĕliŏō**, *them-el-ee-o'-o;* from *2310;* to *lay a ba-sis* for, i.e. (lit.) *erect,* or (fig.) *consolidate:*—lay the foundation {1x}, found {2x}, ground {2x}, settle {1x}.

Themelioo, "to lay a foundation, to found" is used **(1)** literally, **(1a)** "lay the foundation", Heb 1:10; **(1b)** "founded", Mt 7:25; Lk 6:48; and **(2)** metaphorically, **(2a)** "grounded", Eph 3:17 in love; Col 1:23 in the faith; **(2b)** "settle" 1 Pet 5:10. See: TDNT—3:63, 322; BAGD—356a; THAYER—287a.

2312. **θεοδίδακτος** {1x} **thĕŏdidaktŏs**, *theh-od-id'-ak-tos;* from *2316*

and *1321; divinely instructed:*—taught of God {1x}.

Theodidaktos, "God-taught" occurs in 1 Th 4:9, lit., "God-taught (persons)"; while the missionaries had "taught" the converts to love one another, God had Himself been their Teacher. See: TDNT—3:121, 322; BAGD—356b; THAYER—287b.

2312. **θεολόγος** {1x} **thĕŏlŏgŏs,** *theh-ol-og'-os;* from *2316* and *3004;* a "*theologian*":—divine {1x}. See: BAGD—356b; THAYER—287b.

2313. **θεομαχέω** {1x} **thĕŏmachĕō,** *theh-o-makh-eh'-o;* from *2314;* to *resist deity:*—fight against God {1x}. See: TDNT—4:528, 573; BAGD—356c; THAYER—287b.

2314. **θεόμαχος** {1x} **thĕŏmachŏs,** *theh-om'-akh-os;* from *2316* and *3164;* an *opponent of deity:*—to fight against God {1x}.

Theomachos, "to fight against God" occurs in Acts 5:39 and literally means "god-fighters" (Acts 5:39). See: TDNT—4:528, 573; BAGD—356c; THAYER—287b.

2315. **θεόπνευστος** {1x} **thĕŏpnĕustŏs,** *theh-op'-nyoo-stos;* from *2316* and a presumed der. of *4154; divinely breathed in:*—given by inspiration of God {1x}.

This word means "inspired by God" (*theos,* "God," *pneuo,* "to breathe"), is used in 2 Ti 3:16, of the Scriptures as distinct from non-inspired writings. See: TDNT—6:453, 876; BAGD—356c; THAYER—287c.

2316. **θεός** {1343x} **thĕŏs,** *theh'-os;* of uncert. aff.; a *deity,* espec. (with *3588*) the supreme *Divinity;* fig. a *magistrate;* by Heb. *very:*—God {1320x}, god {13x}, godly {3x}, God-ward + *4214* {2x}, misc. {5x} = ✕ exceeding.

Theos, as a noun, means **I.** in the polytheism of the Greeks, denoted "a god or deity," e.g., Acts 14:11; 19:26; 28:6; 1 Cor 8:5; Gal 4:8. **II.** **(1)** Hence the word was appropriated by Jews and retained by Christians to denote "the one true God." **(1a)** In the OT "God" comes from the Hebrew words *Elohim* and *Yahweh,* the former indicating His power and preeminence, the latter His unoriginated, immutable, eternal and self-sustained existence. **(1b)** In the NT, these and all the other divine attributes are predicated of Him. To Him are ascribed, e.g., **(1b1)** His unity, or monism, e.g., Mk 12:29; 1 Ti 2:5; **(1b2)** self-existence, Jn 5:26; **(1b3)** immutability, Jas 1:17; **(1b4)** eternity, Rom 1:20; **(1b5)** universality, Mt 10:29; Acts 17:26–28; **(1b6)** almighty power, Mt 19:26; **(1b7)** infinite knowledge, Acts 2:23; 15:18; Rom 11:33; **(1b8)** cre-

ative power, Rom 11:36; 1 Cor 8:6; Eph 3:9; Rev 4:11; 10:6; **(1b9)** absolute holiness, 1 Pet 1:15; 1 Jn 1:5; **(1b10)** righteousness, Jn 17:25; **(1b11)** faithfulness, 1 Cor 1:9; 10:13; 1 Th 5:24; 2 Th 3:3; 1 Jn 1:9; **(1b12)** love, 1 Jn 4:8, 16; **(1b13)** mercy, Rom 9:15, 18; **(1b14)** truthfulness, Titus 1:2; Heb 6:18. **(2)** The divine attributes are likewise indicated or definitely predicated of Christ, e.g., Mt 20:18–19; Jn 1:1–3; 1:18; 5:22–29; 8:58; 14:6; 17:22–24; 20:28; Rom 1:4; 9:5; Phil 3:21; Col 1:15; 2:3; Titus 2:13; Heb 1:3; 13:8; 1 Jn 5:20; Rev 22:12, 13. **(3)** Also of the Holy Spirit, e.g., Mt 28:19; Lk 1:35; Jn 14:16; 15:26; 16:7–14; Rom 8:9, 26; 1 Cor 12:11; 2 Cor 13:14.

(4) *Theos* is used **(4a)** with the definite article, **(4b)** without (i.e., as an anarthrous noun). **(4c)** The English may or may not have need of the article in translation. But that point cuts no figure in the Greek idiom. Thus in Acts 27:23 ("of [the] God whose I am,") the article points out the special God whose Paul is, and is to be preserved in English. In the very next verse (*ho theos*) we in English do not need the article. **(4d) John 1:1** As to this latter it is usual to employ the article with a proper name, when mentioned a second time. **(4e)** There are, of course, exceptions to this, as when the absence of the article serves to lay stress upon, or give precision to, the character or nature of what is expressed in the noun. **(4e1)** A notable instance of this is in Jn 1:1, "and the Word was God"; here a double stress is on *theos,* by the absence of the article and by the emphatic position. To translate it literally, "a god was the Word," is entirely misleading. Moreover, that "the Word" is the subject of the sentence, exemplifies the rule that the subject is to be determined by its having the article when the predicate is an-arthrous (without the article). **(4e2)** In Rom 7:22, in the phrase "the law of God," both nouns have the article; in v. 25, neither has the article. This is in accordance with a general rule that if two nouns are united by the genitive case (the "of" case), either both have the article, or both are without. Here, in the first instance, both nouns, "God" and "the law" are definite, whereas in v. 25 the word "God" is not simply titular; the absence of the article stresses His character as lawgiver. **(4e3)** Where two or more epithets are applied to the same person or thing, one article usually serves for both (the exceptions being when a second article lays stress upon different aspects of the same person or subject, e.g., Rev 1:17).

(5) Titles: In the following titles God is described by certain of His attributes; the God **(5a)** of glory, Acts 7:2; **(5b)** of peace, Rom 15:33; 16:20; Phil 4:9; 1 Th 5:23; Heb 13:20; **(5c)** of love and peace, 2 Cor 13:11; **(5d)** of patience and

comfort, Rom 15:5; **(5e)** of all comfort, 2 Cor
1:3; **(5f)** of hope, Rom 15:13; **(5g)** of all grace,
1 Pet 5:10. **(5h)** These describe Him, not as in
distinction from other persons, but as the
source of all these blessings; hence the employment of the definite article. **(5i)** In such phrases
as "the God of a person," e.g., Mt 22:32, the
expression marks the relationship in which the
person stands to God and God to him. **(6)** The
phrase "the things of God" (translated literally
or otherwise) stands for **(6a)** His interests, Mt
16:23; Mk 8:33; **(6b)** His counsels, 1 Cor 2:11;
(6c) things which are due to Him, Mt 22:21; Mk
12:17; Lk 20:25. **(7)** The phrase "things pertaining to God," Rom 15:17; Heb 2:17; 5:1, describes,
in the Heb passages, the sacrificial service of
the priest; in the Rom passage the gospel ministry as an offering to God.
    III. (1) The word is used of divinely ap-
pointed judges in Israel, as representing God
in His authority, Jn 10:34, quoted from Ps 82:6,
which indicates that God Himself sits in judgment on those whom He has appointed. **(2)** The
application of the term to **(2a)** the devil, 2 Cor
4:4, and **(2b)** the belly, Phil 3:19, virtually
places these instances under **I.** See: TDNT—
3:65, 322; BAGD—356d; THAYER—287c.

2317. θεοσέβεια {1x} **thĕŏsĕbĕia**, *theh-os-
eb'-i-ah;* from *2318; devout-
ness,* i.e. *piety:* — godliness {1x}.
    Theosebia denotes "the fear or reverence
of God, a reverence for God's goodness", 1 Ti
2:10. See: TDNT—3:123, 331; BAGD—358b;
THAYER—288c.

2318. θεοσεβής {1x} **thĕŏsĕbēs**, *theh-os-eb-
ace';* from *2316* and *4576; rev-
erent of God,* i.e. *pious:* — worshipper of God
{1x}.
    Theosebes denotes "reverencing God" (*theos,*
"God," *sebomai*), and is rendered "a worshipper of God" in Jn 9:31. Syn.: 1174, 2126, 2152,
2357. See: TDNT—3:123, 331; BAGD—358b;
THAYER—288c.

2319. θεοστυγής {1x} **thĕŏstugēs**, *theh-os-
too-gace';* from *2316* and
the base of *4767; hateful to God,* i.e. *impious:* —
haters of God {1x}.
    These people are exceptionally impious and
wicked and act out their wickedness by hating
God, Rom 1:30. See: BAGD—358c; THAYER—
288c.

2320. θεότης {1x} **thĕŏtēs**, *theh-ot'-ace;* from
2316; divinity (abstr.): — god-
head {1x}.
    This word stresses deity, the state of being
God [see 2305 for full discussion]. See: TDNT—
3:119, 322; BAGD—358c; THAYER—288c.

2321. Θεόφιλος {2x} **Thĕŏphilŏs**, *theh-of'-
il-os;* from *2316* and *5384;
friend of God; Theophilus,* a Chr.: — Theophilus
{2x}. See: BAGD—358d; THAYER—288d.

2322. θεραπεία {4x} **thĕrapĕia**, *ther-ap-i'-ah;*
from *2323; attendance* (spec.
medical, i.e. *cure*); fig. and collec. *domestics:* —
healing {2x}, household {2x}.
    Therapeia primarily denotes **(1)** "household",
a place where one's servants render constant
care and attention, Mt 24:45; Lk 12:42; and then,
(2) "medical service, healing" (Eng., "therapy"),
Lk 9:11; Rev 22:2, of the effects of the leaves of
the tree of life, perhaps here with the meaning
"health." See: TDNT—3:131, 331; BAGD—358d;
THAYER—288d.

2323. θεραπεύω {44x} **thĕrapĕuō**, *ther-ap-
yoo'-o;* from the same as
2324; to *wait upon* menially, i.e. (fig.) to *adore*
(God), or (spec.) to *relieve* (of disease): — cure
{5x}, heal {38x}, worship {1x}.
    Therapeuo primarily signifies "to serve as a
therapon, an attendant"; then, "to care for the
sick, to treat, cure, heal" (Eng., "therapeu-
tics"). It is translated **(1)** many times "heal"
and chiefly used in Mt and Lk, once in Jn
(5:10), and, after the Acts, only Rev 13:3, 12.
(2) Taking the idea of service, it is translated
"worshipped", Acts 17:25. **(3)** Applying the
healing aspect it is translated "cure", Mt 17:16,
18; Lk 7:21; 9:1; Jn 5:10; Acts 28:9. See: TDNT—
3:128, 331; BAGD—359a; THAYER—288d.

2324. θεράπων {1x} **thĕrapōn**, *ther-ap'-ohn;*
appar. a part. from an other-
wise obs. der. of the base of *2330;* a menial
attendant (as if *cherishing*): — servant {1x}.
    Therapon means to serve, be an attendant,
a servant, and is a term used of Moses (Heb 3:5)
discharging the duties committed to him by
God from a more confidential position, offering a freer service, and possessing a higher dignity than a *doulos* (*1401*). Syn.: 1401, 1249, 3610,
5257. See: TDNT—3:132, 331; BAGD—359b;
THAYER—289a.

2325. θερίζω {21x} **thĕrizō**, *ther-id'-zo;* from
2330 (in the sense of the *crop*);
to *harvest:* — reap {21x}.
    Therizo, "to reap" (akin to *theros,* "summer,
harvest"), is used **(1)** literally, Mt 6:26; 25:24,
26; Lk 12:24; 19:21, 22; Jas 5:4 2nd part), "have
reaped"; **(2)** figuratively or in proverbial expressions, **(2a)** Jn 4:36 (twice), 37, 38, with immediate reference to bringing Samaritans into
the kingdom of God, in regard to which the
disciples would enjoy the fruits of what Christ
Himself had been doing in Samaria; the Lord's
words are, however, of a general application in
respect of such service; **(2b)** in 1 Cor 9:11, with

reference to the right of the apostle and his fellow missionaries to receive material assistance from the church, a right which he forbore to exercise; **(2c)** in 2 Cor 9:6 (twice), with reference to rendering material help to the needy, either "sparingly" or "bountifully," the "reaping" being proportionate to the sowing; **(2d)** in Gal 6:7, 8 (twice), of "reaping" corruption, **(2d1)** with special reference, according to the context, to that which is naturally short-lived, transient (though the statement applies to every form of sowing to the flesh), and **(2d2)** of "reaping" eternal life (characteristics and moral qualities being in view), **(2d3)** as a result of sowing "to the Spirit," the reference probably being to the new nature of the believer, which is, however, under the controlling power of the Holy Spirit, v. 9, **(2d4)** the "reaping" (the effect of well doing) being accomplished, to a limited extent, in this life, but in complete fulfillment at and beyond the judgment seat of Christ; **(2d5)** diligence or laxity here will then produce proportionate results; **(2e)** in Rev 14:15 (twice), 16, figurative of the discriminating judgment divinely to be fulfilled at the close of this age, when the wheat will be separated from the tares (see Mt 13:30). See: TDNT—3:132, 332; BAGD—359b; THAYER—289a.

2326. **θερισμός** {13x} **thĕrismŏs**, *ther-is-mos';* from *2325; reaping,* i.e. the *crop:*—harvest {13x}.

Therismos, akin to *therizo,* "to reap," is used **(1)** of "the act of harvesting," Jn 4:35; **(2)** "the time of harvest," figuratively, Mt 13:30, 39; Mk 4:29; **(3)** "the crop," figuratively, Mt 9:37, 38; Lk 10:2; Rev 14:15. **(4)** The beginning of "harvest" varied according to natural conditions, but took place on the average about the middle of April in the eastern lowlands of Palestine, in the latter part of the month in the coast plains and a little later in high districts. **(4a)** Barley "harvest" usually came first and then wheat. **(4b)** "Harvesting" lasted about seven weeks, and was the occasion of festivities. See: TDNT—3:133, 332; BAGD—359c; THAYER—289b.

2327. **θεριστής** {2x} **thĕristēs**, *ther-is-tace';* from *2325;* a *harvester:*—reaper {2x}.

Theristes, "a reaper" (akin to *therizo,* see above), is used of angels in Mt 13:30, 39. See: BAGD—359c; THAYER—289b.

2328. **θερμαίνω** {6x} **thĕrmainō**, *ther-mah'-ee-no;* from *2329;* to *heat* (oneself):—warm (one's) self {5x}, be warmed {1x}.

Thermaino, "to warm, heat" (Eng. "thermal," etc.), when used in the middle voice, signifies **(1)** "to warm oneself," Mk 14:54, 67; Jn

18:18 (twice), 25; and **(2)** "be warmed", Jas 2:16. See: BAGD—359c; THAYER—289b.

2329. **θέρμη** {1x} **thĕrmē**, *ther'-may;* from the base of *2330; warmth:*—heat {1x}. See: BAGD—359c; THAYER—289c.

2330. **θέρος** {3x} **thĕrŏs**, *ther'-os;* from a primary θέρω **thĕrō** (to *heat*); prop. *heat,* i.e. *summer:*—summer {3x}.

Theros, akin to *thero,* "to heat," occurs in Mt 24:32; Mk 13:28; Lk 21:30. See: BAGD—359d; THAYER—289c.

2331. **Θεσσαλονικεύς** {6x} **Thĕssalŏnikĕus**, *thes-sal-on-ik-yoos';* from *2332;* a *Thessalonican,* i.e. inhab. of Thessalonice:—Thessalonians {5x}, of Thessalonica {1x}. See: BAGD—359d; THAYER—289c.

2332. **Θεσσαλονίκη** {5x} **Thĕssalŏnikē**, *thes-sal-on-ee'-kay;* from Θεσσαλός **Thĕssalŏs** (a *Thessalian*) and *3529; Thessalonice,* a place in Asia Minor:—Thessalonica {5x}. See: BAGD—359d; THAYER—289c.

2333. **Θευδᾶς** {1x} **Thĕudas**, *thyoo-das';* of uncert. or.; *Theudas,* an Isr.:—Theudas {1x}. See: BAGD—359d; THAYER—289c.

   θέω thĕŏ. See *5087.*

2334. **θεωρέω** {57x} **thĕōrĕō**, *theh-o-reh'-o;* from a der. of *2300* (perh. by add. of *3708*); to *be a spectator* of, i.e. *discern,* (lit., fig. [*experience*] or intens. [*acknowledge*]):—see {40x}, behold {11x}, perceive {4x}, consider {1x}, look on {1x}.

This word means **(1)** to be a spectator, look at, behold, view attentively, take a view of, survey, to view mentally, consider; and **(2)** to see, to perceive with the eyes, to enjoy the presence of one, to discern, to ascertain, find out by seeing. **(3)** *Theoreo,* as a verb, means "to look at, gaze at, behold" and is translated "looking on": "There were also women looking on afar off" (Mk 15:40). Syn. for **(1)** - **(3):** 308, 352, 578, 816, 872, 991, 1689, 1896, 1914, 1980, 1983, 2300, 3706, 3708, 3879, 4017, 4648. *Theoreo,* also [from *theoros,* "a spectator"], as a verb, is used **(4)** of one who looks at a thing with interest and for a purpose, usually indicating the careful observation of details: "And Mary Magdalene and Mary the mother of Joses beheld where He was laid" (Mk 15:47; cf. Lk 10:18; 23:35; Jn 20:6; so in verses 12 and 14); **(5)** "consider": "Now consider how great this man was, unto whom even the patriarch Abraham gave the tenth of the spoils" (Heb 7:4). **(6)** It is used of experience, in the sense of partaking of: "Verily, verily, I say unto you, If a man keep my saying, he shall never see (*theoreo*) death" (Jn 8:51; cf. 17:24). Syn. for **(4)** - **(6):** 333, 816, 991, 1689,

1896, 2029, 2300, 2657, 2734, 3700, 3708. See: TDNT—5:315, 706; BAGD—360a; THAYER— 289d.

2335. θεωρία {1x} **thēōria**, *theh-o-ree'-ah;* from the same as *2334; spectatorship,* i.e. (concr.) a *spectacle:*—sight {1x}.

Theoria, as a noun, denotes "a spectacle, a sight": "And all the people that came together to that sight (*theoria*), beholding the things which were done, smote their breasts, and returned" (Lk 23:48 – the crucifixion). See: BAGD—360b; THAYER—290b.

2336. θήκη {1x} **thēkē**, *thay'-kay;* from *5087;* a *receptacle,* i.e. *scabbard:*—sheath {1x}.

Theke, "a place to put something in", "a receptacle, chest, case," is used of the "sheath" of a sword, Jn 18:11. See: BAGD—360b; THAYER— 290b.

2337. θηλάζω {6x} **thēlazō**, *thay-lad'-zo;* from θηλή **thēlē** (the *nipple*); to *suckle,* (by impl.) to *suck:*—give suck {4x}, suck {1x}, suckling {1x}.

Thelazo, from *thele,* "a breast," is used **(1)** of the mother, "to suckle, give suck" Mt 24:19; Mk 13:17; Lk 21:23; 23:29; **(2)** of the young, "sucklings," Mt 21:16; and **(3)** "to suck," Lk 11:27, "hast sucked." See: BAGD—60c; THAYER—290b.

2338. θῆλυς {5x} **thēlus**, *thay'-loos;* from the same as *2337; female:*—female {3x}, woman {2x}.

Thelus, an adjective (from *thele,* "a breast"), is used in the form *thelu* (grammatically neuter) **(1)** as a noun, "female," in Mt 19:4; Mk 10:6; Gal 3:28; **(2)** in the feminine form *theleia,* in Rom 1:26, "women"; v. 27 "woman." See: BAGD—360c; THAYER—290b.

2339. θήρα {1x} **thēra**, *thay'-rah;* from θήρ **thēr** (a wild *animal,* as *game*); *hunting,* i.e. (fig.) *destruction:*—trap {1x}.

This word denotes a hunting, chase, then, a prey; hence, figuratively, preparing destruction by a net or trap (Rom 11:9). See: BAGD— 360d; THAYER—290b.

2340. θηρεύω {1x} **thēreuō**, *thay-ryoo'-o;* from *2339;* to *hunt* (an animal), i.e. (fig.) to *carp at:*—catch {1x}.

Thereuo, "to hunt or catch wild beasts" (*therion,* "a wild beast"), is used by Luke metaphorically, of the Pharisees and Herodians in seeking to catch Christ in His talk, Lk 11:54. See: BAGD—360d; THAYER—290c.

2341. θηριομαχέω {1x} **thēriŏmachĕō**, *thay-ree-om-akh-eh'-o;* from a compound of *2342* and *3164;* to *be a beast-fighter* (in the gladiatorial show), i.e. (fig.) to

encounter (furious men):—fight with wild beasts {1x}.

This word signifies "to fight with wild beasts", 1 Cor 15:32. Some think that the apostle was condemned to fight with wild beasts; if so, he would scarcely have omitted it from 2 Cor 11:23–end. Moreover, he would have lost his status as a Roman citizen. Probably he uses the word figuratively of contending with ferocious men. Ignatius so uses it in his Ep. to the Romans. See: BAGD—360d; THAYER—290c.

2342. θηρίον {46x} **thēriŏn**, *thay-ree'-on;* dimin. from the same as *2339;* a *dangerous animal:*—beast {42x}, venomous beast {1x}, wild beast {3x}.

Therion, **(1)** to be distinguished from *zoon,* almost invariably denotes "a wild beast." **(2)** In Acts 28:4, "venomous beast" is used of the viper which fastened on Paul's hand. **(3)** The idea of a "beast" of prey is not always present. Once, in Heb 12:20, it is used of the animals in the camp of Israel, such, e.g., as were appointed for sacrifice. *Therion,* in the sense of wild "beast," is used in the Apocalypse for the two antichristian potentates who are destined to control the affairs of the nations with satanic power in the closing period of the present era, 11:7; 13:1–18; 14:9, 11; 15:2; 16:2, 10, 13; 17:3–17; 19:19–20; 20:4, 10. Syn.: *Zoon (2226)* means a living creature; whereas, *therion* means a beast. *Zoon* stresses the vital element, *therion* the bestial. See: TDNT—3:133, 333; BAGD— 361a; THAYER—290c.

2343. θησαυρίζω {8x} **thēsaurizō**, *thay-sŏw-rid'-zo;* from *2344;* to *amass* or *reserve* (lit. or fig.):—lay up {3x}, in store {1x}, lay up treasure {1x}, treasure up {1x}, heap treasure together {1x}, keep in store {1x}.

Thesaurizo, "to lay up, store up" (akin to *thesauros,* "a treasury, a storehouse, a treasure"), is used **(1)** of "laying" up treasures, **(1a)** on earth, Mt 6:19; **(1b)** in heaven, Mt 16:20; **(1c)** in the last days, Jas 5:3, "ye have heaped treasure together"; **(2)** in Lk 12:21, "that layeth up treasure (for himself)"; **(3)** in 1 Cor 16:2, of money for needy ones (here the present participle is translated "in store," lit. "treasuring" or "storing," the "laying by" translating the preceding verb *tithemi*); **(4)** in 2 Cor 12:14, negatively, of children for parents; **(5)** metaphorically, of "laying" up wrath, Rom 2:5, "treasurest up." **(6)** In 2 Pet 3:7 the passive voice is used of the heavens and earth as "stored up" for fire, "kept in store." See: TDNT—3:138, 333; BAGD— 361b; THAYER—290d.

2344. θησαυρός {18x} **thēsaurŏs**, *thay-sow-ros';* from *5087;* a *deposit,* i.e. *wealth* (lit. or fig.):—treasure {18x}.

This word denotes (1) "a place of safe keeping" (possibly akin to *tithemi*, "to put"), (1a) "a casket," Mt 2:11; (1b) "a storehouse," Mt 13:52; (1c) used metaphorically of the heart, Mt 12:35, twice, "out of the treasure"; Lk 6:45; (2) "a treasure," Mt 6:19, 20, 21; 13:44; Lk 12:33, 34; Heb 11:26; (2a) "treasure" (in heaven or the heavens), Mt 19:21; Mk 10:21; Lk 18:22; (2b) in these expressions (which are virtually equivalent to that in Mt 6:1, "with your Father which is in heaven") the promise does not simply refer to the present life, but looks likewise to the hereafter; (3) in 2 Cor 4:7 it is used of "the light of the knowledge of the glory of God in the face of Jesus Christ," descriptive of the gospel, as deposited in the earthen vessels of the persons who proclaim it (cf. v. 4); (4) in Col 2:3, of the wisdom and knowledge hidden in Christ. See: TDNT—3:136, 333; BAGD—361c; THAYER—290d.

2345. **θιγγάνω** {3x} **thigganō**, *thing-gan'-o;* a prol. form of an obs. primary θίγω **thigō** (to *finger*); to *manipulate,* i.e. *have to do with;* by impl. to *injure:*—handle {1x}, touch {2x}.

This word signifies "to touch, to handle" and is translated (1) "handle" in Col 2:21: "Touch (*hapto*) not; taste not; handle (*thigganō*) not". It is translated (2) "touch" in (2a) Heb 12:20, of a beast's touching Mount Sinai; and (2b) "to touch by way of injuring," Heb 11:28. See: BAGD—361d; THAYER—291a.

2346. **θλίβω** {10x} **thlibō**, *thlee'-bo;* akin to the base of *5147;* to *crowd* (lit. or fig.):—afflict {3x}, narrow {1x}, throng {1x}, suffer tribulation {1x}, trouble {4x}.

Thlibo, "to suffer affliction, to be troubled," has reference to sufferings due to the pressure of circumstances, or the antagonism of persons. It is translated (1) "afflict", 2 Cor 1:6; 1 Ti 5:10; Heb 11:37; (2) "narrow", Mt 7:14; (3) "throng", Mk 3:9; (4) "suffer tribulation", 1 Th 3:4; (5) "trouble", 2 Cor 4:8; 7:5; 2 Th 1:6, 7. (6) Both the verb and the noun, when used of the present experience of believers, refer almost invariably to that which comes upon them from without. See: TDNT—3:139, 334; BAGD—362a; THAYER—291a.

2347. **θλίψις** {45x} **thlipsis**, *thlip'-sis;* from *2346; pressure* (lit. or fig.):—tribulation {21x}, affliction {17x}, trouble {3x}, anguish {1x}, persecution {1x}, burdened {1x}, to be afflicted + *1519* {1x}.

This word primarily means "a pressing, pressure", anything which burdens the spirit. (1) In two passages in Paul's Epistles it is used of future retribution, in the way of "affliction," Rom 2:9; 2 Th 1:6. (2) In Mt 24:9 "to be af-

flicted". (3) It is coupled (3a) with *stenochoria* (*4730*), "anguish," in Rom 2:9; 8:35; (3b) with *ananke* (*318*), "distress," 1 Th 3:7; (3c) with *diogmos* (*1375*), "persecution," Mt 13:21; Mk 4:17; 2 Th 1:4. (4) It is used of the calamities of war, Mt 24:21, 29; Mk 13:19, 24; (5) of want, 2 Cor 8:13, lit., "distress for you"; Phil 4:14 (cf. 1:16); Jas 1:27; (6) of the distress of woman in childbirth, Jn 16:21; (7) of persecution, Acts 11:19; 14:22; 20:23; 1 Th 3:3, 7; Heb 10:33; Rev 2:10; 7:14; (8) of the "afflictions" of Christ, from which (His vicarious sufferings apart) His followers must not shrink, whether sufferings of body or mind, Col 1:24; (9) of sufferings in general, 1 Cor 7:28; 1 Th 1:6. Syn.: *4730.* See: TDNT—3:139, 334; BAGD—362b; THAYER—291a.

2348. **θνήσκω** {13x} **thnēskō**, *thnay'-sko;* a strengthened form of a simpler primary θάνω **thanō**, *than'-o* (which is used for it only in certain tenses); to *die* (lit. or fig.):—be dead {10x}, die {1x}, dead man {1x}, dead {1x}.

(1) This word means to die (in the perf. tense, "to be dead"), and (1a) is always used of physical death, (1b) except in 1 Ti 5:6, where it is metaphorically used of the loss of spiritual life. (2) The noun *thanatos* (*2288*) and the verb *thanatoo* (*2230*) are connected; the root probably signifying the breathing out of the last breath. See: TDNT—3:7, 312; BAGD—362c; THAYER—291b.

2349. **θνητός** {6x} **thnētŏs**, *thnay-tos';* from *2348; liable to die:*—mortal {5x}, mortality + *3588* {1x}.

Thnetos, "subject or liable to death, mortal" (akin to *thnesko,* "to die"), is translated (1) "mortal" (1a) in Rom 6:12, of the body, where it is called "mortal," not simply because it is liable to death, but because it is the organ in and through which death carries on its death-producing activities; (1b) in Rom 8:11 where the stress is on the liability to death, and the quickening is not reinvigoration but the impartation of life at the time of the Rapture, as in 1 Cor 15:53, 54; and (1c) in 2 Cor 4:11, it is applied to the flesh, which stands, not simply for the body, but the body as that which consists of the element of decay, and is thereby death-doomed. (2) Christ's followers are in this life delivered unto death, (2a) that His life may be manifested in that which naturally is the seat of decay and death. (2b) That which is subject to suffering is that in which the power of Him who suffered here is most manifested. (3) It is translated "mortality" in 2 Cor 5:4. See: TDNT—3:21, 312; BAGD—362d; THAYER—291c.

2350. **θορυβέω** {4x} **thŏrubĕō**, *thor-oo-beh'-o;* from *2351;* to *be in tumult,* i.e.

disturb, clamor:—make ado {1x}, make a noise {1x}, set on an uproar {1x}, trouble (one's) self {1x}.

"To make an uproar, to throw into confusion, or to wail tumultuously," is rendered (1) "make . . . ado," in Mk 5:39; (2) "making a noise" in Mt. 9:23; (3) "set . . . on an uproar" in Acts 17:5; and (4) "trouble . . . yourselves" in Acts 20:10. See: BAGD—362d; THAYER—291c.

2351. θόρυβος {7x} **thŏrubŏs,** *thor'-oo-bos;* from the base of *2360;* a *disturbance:*—tumult {4x}, uproar {3x}.

Thorubos, "a noise, uproar, tumult," is rendered (1) "tumult" in Mt 27:24; Mk 5:38; Acts 21:34; 24:18; and (2) "uproar" in Mt 26:5; Mk 14:2; Acts 20:1. See: BAGD—363a; THAYER—291c.

2352. θραύω {1x} **thrauō,** *thrŏw'-o;* a primary verb; to *crush:*—bruise {1x}.

This word means to smite through, shatter and in Lk 4:18, "them that are bruised," i.e., broken by calamity. See: BAGD—363; THAYER—291d. Syn.: 4486.

2353. θρέμμα {1x} **thrĕmma,** *threm'-mah;* from *5142;* stock (as *raised* on a farm):—cattle {1x}.

The word means whatever is fed or nourished, raised by man (Jn 4:12). See: BAGD—363b; THAYER—291d.

2354. θρηνέω {4x} **thrēnĕō,** *thray-neh'-o;* from *2355;* to *bewail:*—lament {2x}, mourn {2x}.

(1) This word means to break out into a wailing composed of unstudied words or may take a more elaborate form like a poem (cf. 2 Sa 1:17). *Threneo,* "to lament, wail" (akin to *threnos,* "a lamentation, a dirge"), is translated (2) "lament" (2a) in a general sense, of the disciples during the absence of the Lord, Jn 16:20; and (2b) of those who sorrowed for the sufferings and the impending crucifixion of the Lord, Lk 23:27. It is translated (3) "mourn, mourning" as for the dead, Mt 11:17, "have mourned"; Lk 7:32. Syn.: 2857, 3076, 3996. See: TDNT—3:148, 335; BAGD—363b; THAYER—291d.

2355. θρῆνος {1x} **thrēnŏs,** *thray'-nos;* from the base of *2360; wailing:*—lamentation {1x}. See: TDNT—3:148, 335; BAGD—363b; THAYER—291d.

2356. θρησκεία {4x} **thrēskĕia,** *thrace-ki'-ah;* from a der. of *2357;* ceremonial *observance:*—religion {3x}, worshipping {1x}.

Threskeia signifies religion in its external aspect, religious worship, especially the ceremonial service of religion. It is used of the religion (1) of the Jews (Acts 26:5); (2) of the

worshiping of angels (Col 2:18) (2a) which they themselves repudiate (Rev 22:8, 9); (2b) there was an officious parade of humility in selecting these lower beings as intercessors rather than appealing directly to the throne of grace; (3) in Jas 1:26, 27 the contrast is set forth between that which is unreal and deceptive, and the pure religion which consists in visiting the fatherless and widows in their affliction and in keeping oneself unspotted from the world. He is not herein affirming . . . these offices to be the sum total, nor yet the great essentials, of true religion, but declares them to be the body, the *threskeia,* of which godliness, or the love of God, is for the informing soul. See: TDNT—3:155, 337; BAGD—363b; THAYER—292a.

2357. θρῆσκος {1x} **thrēskŏs,** *thrace'-kos;* prob. from the base of *2360;* ceremonious in worship (as *demonstrative*), i.e. *pious:*—religious {1x}.

This word denotes religious, careful of the externals of divine service (Jas 1:26). Syn.: 1174, 2126, 2152, 2318, 2356. See: TDNT—3:155, 337; BAGD—363d; THAYER—292a.

2358. θριαμβεύω {2x} **thriambĕuō,** *three-am-byoo'-o;* from a prol. compound of the base of *2360;* and a der. of *680* (mean. a *noisy iambus,* sung in honor of Bacchus); to *make an acclamatory procession,* i.e. (fig.) to *conquer* or (by Heb.) to *give victory:*—cause to triumph {1x},triumph over {1x}.

Thriambeuo (*2358*) denotes (1) "to cause to triumph," used of a conqueror with reference to the vanquished, 2 Cor 2:14. Theodoret paraphrases it "He leads us about here and there and displays us to all the world." This is in agreement with evidences from various sources. Those who are led are not captives exposed to humiliation, but are displayed as the glory and devoted subjects of Him who leads (see the context). This is so even if there is a reference to a Roman "triumph." On such occasions the general's sons, with various officers, rode behind his chariot (Livy, xlv. 40). But there is no necessary reference here to a Roman "triumph." The main thought is that of the display, "in Christ" being the sphere; its evidences are the effects of gospel testimony. (2) In Col 2:15 ("triumph over") the circumstances and subjects are quite different, and relate to Christ's victory over spiritual foes at the time of His death; accordingly the reference may be to the triumphant display of the defeated. See: TDNT—3:159, 337; BAGD—363d; THAYER—292b.

2359. θρίξ {15x} **thrix,** *threeks;* gen. τριχός **trichŏs,** etc.; of uncert. der.; *hair:*—hair {15x}.

Thrix denotes the "hair," whether of beast,

as of the camel's "hair" (1) which formed the raiment of John the Baptist, Mt 3:4; Mk 1:6; (2) or of man. Regarding the latter (2a) it is used to signify the minutest detail, as that which illustrates the exceeding care and protection bestowed by God upon His children, Mt 10:30; Lk 12:7; 21:18; Acts 27:34; (2b) as the Jews swore by the "hair," the Lord used the natural inability to make one "hair" white or black, as one of the reasons for abstinence from oaths, Mt 5:36; (2c) while long "hair" is a glory to a woman, and to wear it loose or disheveled is a dishonor, yet the woman who wiped Christ's feet with her "hair" (in place of the towel which Simon the Pharisee omitted to provide), despised the shame in her penitent devotion to the Lord (slaves were accustomed to wipe their masters' feet), Lk 7:38, 44; see also Jn 11:2; 12:3; (2d) the dazzling whiteness of the head and "hair" of the Son of Man in the vision of Rev 1:14 is suggestive of the holiness and wisdom of "the Ancient of Days"; (2e) the long "hair" of the spirit-beings described as locusts in Rev 9:8 is perhaps indicative of their subjection to their satanic master (cf. 1 Cor 11:10); (2f) Christian women are exhorted to refrain from adorning their "hair" for outward show, 1 Pet 3:3.

(3) Goat's hair was used in tentmaking, as, e.g., in the case of Paul's occupation, Acts 18:3; the haircloth of Cilicia, his native province, was noted, being known in commerce as *cilicium*. Syn.: 2863, 2864, 5155. See: BAGD—363d; THAYER—292b.

2360. **θροέω** {3x} **thrŏĕō**, *thrŏ-eh'-o;* from θρέομαι **thrĕŏmai** to *wail;* to *clamor,* to *cry aloud,* i.e. (by impl.) to *frighten:—* trouble {3x}.

Throeo, "to make an outcry" (*throos,* "a tumult"), is used in the passive voice, Mt 24:6; Mk 13:7; Lk 24:37; 2 Th 2:2. See: TDNT—3:159, 337; BAGD—364a; THAYER—292b.

2361. **θρόμβος** {1x} **thrŏmbŏs**, *throm'-bos;* perh. from *5142* (in the sense of *thickening*); a *clot:—*great drop {1x}.

Thrombos, "a large, thick drop of clotted blood" (etymologically akin to *trepho,* "to curdle"), is used in Lk 22:44, in the plural, in the narrative of the Lord's agony in Gethsemane. See: BAGD—364a; THAYER—292c.

2362. **θρόνος** {61x} **thrŏnŏs**, *thron'-os;* from θράω **thraō** (to *sit*); a *stately seat* ("throne"); by impl. *power or authority* or (concr.) a *potentate:—*seat {7x}, throne {54x}.

Thronos, as a noun, means "a throne, a seat of authority," is used of the "throne" (1) of God, e.g., Mt 5:34; 23:22; Acts 7:49; Heb 4:16, "the throne of grace," i.e., from which grace proceeds;

8:1; 12:2; Rev 1:4; 3:21 (2nd part); 4:2 (twice); 5:1; frequently in Rev; 21:3; (2) of Christ, e.g. (2a) Heb 1:8; Rev 3:21 (1st part); 22:3; (2b) His seat of authority in the Millennium, Mt 19:28 (1st part); (3) by metonymy for angelic powers, Col 1:16; (4) of the apostles in millennial authority, Mt 19:28 (2nd part); Lk 22:30; (5) of the elders in the heavenly vision, Rev 4:4 (2nd and 3rd parts), "seats"; so 11:16; (6) of David, Lk 1:32; Acts 2:30; (7) of Satan, Rev 2:13, "seat"; (8) of "the beast," the final and federal head of the revived Roman Empire, Rev 13:2; 16:10. See: TDNT—3:160, 338; BAGD—364b; THAYER—292c.

2363. **Θυάτειρα** {4x} **Thuatĕira**, *thoo-at'-i-rah;* of uncert. der.; *Thyatira,* a place in Asia Minor:—Thyatira {4x}. See: BAGD—364c; THAYER—292d.

2364. **θυγάτηρ** {29x} **thugatĕr**, *thoo-gat'-air;* appar. a primary word [comp. "daughter"]; a *female child,* or (by Heb.) *descendant* (or *inhabitant*):—daughter {29x}.

Thugater means a daughter and is used of (1) the natural relationship; (2) spiritual relationship to God (2 Cor 6:18); (3) the inhabitants of a city or region (Mt 21:5; Jn 12:15); (4) the women who followed Christ to Calvary (Lk 23:28); (5) women of Aaron's posterity (Lk 1:5); (6) a female descendant of Abraham (Lk 13:16). Syn.: 2365, 3933. See: BAGD—364d; THAYER—292d.

2365. **θυγάτριον** {2x} **thugatriŏn**, *thoo-gat'-ree-on;* diminutive from *2364;* a *daughterling:—*little daughter {1x}, young daughter {1x}. Cf. Mk 5:23; 7:25. See: BAGD—365a; THAYER—293a.

2366. **θύελλα** {1x} **thuĕlla**, *thoo'-el-lah;* from *2380* (in the sense of *blowing*) a sudden storm, a whirlwind:—tempest {1x}.

(1) This word often refers to a wilder and fiercer natural phenomenon than *lailaps* (*2978*) and refers to the conflicted mingling of many opposing winds; (2) a sudden storm, tempest, whirlwind, Heb 12:18. Syn.: 417, 2978, 4151, 4157. See: BAGD—365a; THAYER—293a.

2367. **θύϊνος** {1x} **thuïnŏs**, *thoo'-ee-nos;* from a der. of *2380* (in the sense of *blowing;* denoting a certain *fragrant* tree); made of *citron*-wood:—thyine {1x}.

Thuinos is akin to *thuia,* or *thua,* an African aromatic and coniferous tree; in Rev 18:12 it describes a wood which formed part of the merchandise of Babylon; it was valued by Greeks and Romans for tables, being hard, durable and fragrant ("sweet"). See: BAGD—365a; THAYER—293a.

2368. **θυμίαμα** {6x} **thumiama**, *thoo-mee'-am-ah;* from *2370;* an *aroma,*

i.e. fragrant *powder* burnt in relig. service; by impl. the *burning* itself:—incense {4x}, odour {2x}.

This word denotes "fragrant stuff for burning, incense" (from *thuo*, "to offer in sacrifice"). It is translated **(1)** "incense" Lk 1:10, 11; Rev 8:3, 4 signifying "frankincense"; and **(2)** by metonomy ["odour" for what produces it], Rev 5:8; 18:13 both times in plural. **(3)** In connection with the tabernacle, the "incense" was to be prepared from stacte, onycha, and galbanum, with pure frankincense, an equal weight of each; imitation for private use was forbidden. See: BAGD—365a; THAYER—293a.

2369. θυμιαστήριον {1x} **thumiastēriŏn**, *thoo-mee-as-tay'-ree-on;* or

θυμιατήριον thumiatērion, *thoo-mee-a-tay'-ree-on;* from a der. of *2370;* a *place of fumigation*, i.e. the *altar of incense* (in the Temple):—censer {1x}. This is a vessel for burning incense (Heb 9:4). See: BAGD—365b; THAYER—293a.

2370. θυμιάω {1x} **thumiaō**, *thoo-mee-ah'-o;* from a der. of *2380* (in the sense of *smoking*); to *fumigate*, i.e. *offer* aromatic *fumes:*—burn incense {1x}. See: BAGD—365b; THAYER—293b.

2371. θυμομαχέω {1x} **thumŏmachĕō**, *thoo-mom-akh-eh'-o;* from a presumed compound of *2372* and *3164;* to *be in a furious fight*, i.e. (fig.) to *be exasperated:*—be highly displeased {1x}.

Thumomacheo, means lit., "to fight with great animosity," "to be very angry, to be highly displeased," is said of Herod's "displeasure" with the Tyrians and Sidonians in Acts 12:20. See: BAGD—365b; THAYER—293b.

2372. θυμός {18x} **thumŏs**, *thoo-mos';* from *2380; passion* (as if *breathing* hard):—fierceness {2x}, indignation {1x}, wrath {15x}.

Thumos, "hot anger, wrath, passion," is translated **(1)** "wrath" in Lk 4:28; Acts 19:28; Gal 5:20; Eph 4:31; Col 3:8; Heb 11:27; Rev 12:12; 14:8, 10, 19; 15:1, 7; 16:1; 18:3; "wraths" in 2 Cor 12:20; **(2)** "fierceness" in Rev 16:19; 19:15; of the wrath of God; and **(3)** "indignation" Rom 2:8. Syn.: *Thumos* is incipient displeasure fermenting in the mind. *Orge* (3709) takes over when *thumos* has subsided and longs for revenge and desires to injure the one causing the harm. See also: 3950. See: TDNT—3:167, 339; BAGD—365b; THAYER—293b. comp. *5590.*

2373. θυμόω {1x} **thumŏō**, *tho-mŏ'-o;* from *2372;* to *put in a passion*, i.e. *enrage:*—be wroth {1x}.

Thumoo signifies "to be very angry" (from *thumos*, "wrath, hot anger"), "to be stirred into

passion," Mt 2:16, of Herod (passive voice). See: BAGD—365c; THAYER—293c.

2374. θύρα {39x} **thura**, *thoo'-rah;* appar. a primary word [comp. "door"]; a *portal* or entrance (the opening or the closure, lit. or fig.):—door {38x}, gate {1x}.

Thura, "a door, gate" is used **(1)** literally, e.g., Mt 6:6; 27:60; **(2)** metaphorically, **(2a)** of Christ, Jn 10:7, 9; **(2b)** of faith, by acceptance of the gospel, Acts 14:27; **(2c)** of "openings" for preaching and teaching the Word of God, 1 Cor 16:9; 2 Cor 2:12; Col 4:3; Rev 3:8; **(2d)** of "entrance" into the kingdom of God, Mt 25:10; Lk 13:24–25; **(2e)** of Christ's "entrance" into a repentant believer's heart, Rev 3:20; **(2f)** of the nearness of Christ's second advent, Mt 24:33; Mk 13:29; **(2g)** of "access" to behold visions relative to the purposes of God, Rev 4:1. It is translated "gate" in Acts 3:2. See: TDNT—3:173, 340; BAGD—365d; THAYER—293d.

2375. θυρεός {1x} **thurĕŏs**, *thoo-reh-os';* from *2374;* a large oblong *shield* (as *door*-shaped):—shield {1x}.

Thureos formerly meant "a stone for closing the entrance of a cave"; then, "a shield," large and oblong, protecting every part of the soldier; the word is used metaphorically of faith, Eph 6:16, which the believer is to take up "in (*en* in the original) all" (all that has just been mentioned), i.e., as affecting the whole of his activities. See: TDNT—5:312, 702; BAGD—366a; THAYER—294a.

2376. θυρίς {2x} **thuris**, *thoo-rece';* a diminutive from *2374;* an *aperture*, i.e. *window:*—window {2x}.

Thuris, a diminutive of *thura* (2374), "a door," occurs in Acts 20:9; 2 Cor 11:33. See: BAGD—366a; THAYER—294a.

2377. θυρωρός {4x} **thurōrŏs**, *thoo-ro-ros';* from *2374* and οὖρος **ŏurŏs** (a *watcher*); a *gate-warden:*—that keeps the door {2x}, porter {2x}.

A *thuroros*, "a door-keeper" (*thura*, "a door," *ouros*, "a guardian"), is translated **(1)** "porter" in Mk 13:34; Jn 10:3; and **(2)** it is used of a female in Jn 18:16, 17, translated "(her) that kept the door." See: BAGD—366a; THAYER—294a.

2378. θυσία {29x} **thusia**, *thoo-see'-ah;* from *2380; sacrifice* (the act or the victim, lit. or fig.):—sacrifice {29x}.

Thusia primarily denotes "the act of offering"; then, objectively, "that which is offered" **(1)** of idolatrous "sacrifice," Acts 7:41; **(2)** of animal or other "sacrifices," as offered under the Law, Mt 9:13; 12:7; Mk 9:49; 12:33; Lk 2:24; 13:1; Acts 7:42; 1 Cor 10:18; Heb 5:1; 7:27; 8:3;

9:9; 10:1, 5, 8, 11; 11:4; **(3)** of Christ, in His "sacrifice" on the cross, Eph 5:2; Heb 9:23, where the plural anti-typically comprehends the various forms of Levitical "sacrifices" in their typical character; Heb 9:26; 10:12, 26; **(4)** metaphorically, **(4a)** of the body of the believer, presented to God as a living "sacrifice," Rom 12:1; **(4b)** of faith, Phil 2:17; **(4c)** of material assistance rendered to servants of God, Phil 4:18; **(4d)** of praise, Heb 13:15; **(4e)** of doing good to others and communicating with their needs, Heb 13:16; **(4f)** of spiritual "sacrifices" in general, offered by believers as a holy priesthood, 1 Pet 2:5. Syn.: 2380. See: TDNT—3:180, 342; BAGD—366b; THAYER—

2379. **θυσιαστήριον** {23x} **thusiastērion**, *thoo-see-as-tay'-ree-on;* from a der. of *2378;* a *place of sacrifice,* i.e. an *altar* (spec. or gen., lit. or fig.):—altar {23x}.

(1) This word is derived from *thuciazo,* "to sacrifice." **(2)** Accordingly it denotes an "altar" for the sacrifice of victims, though it was also used for the "altar" of incense, e.g., Lk 1:11. **(3)** In the NT this word is reserved for the "altar" of the true God, Mt 5:23–24; 23:18–20, 35; Lk 11:51; 1 Cor 9:13; 10:18, in contrast to *bomos (1041).* Syn.: This is the altar to the one true God; whereas, *bomos (1041)* is a heathen altar. See: TDNT—3:180, 342; BAGD—366c; THAYER—294c.

2380. **θύω** {14x} **thuō**, *thoo'-o;* a primary verb; prop. to *rush* (*breathe* hard, *blow, smoke*), i.e. (by impl.) to *sacrifice* (prop. by fire, but gen.); by extens. to *immolate* (*slaughter* for any purpose):—kill {8x}, sacrifice {3x}, do sacrifice {2x}, slay {1x}.

This word primarily denotes "to offer first-fruits to a god"; then **(1)** "to sacrifice by slaying a victim," Acts 14:13, 18, to do sacrifice; 1 Cor 10:20, to sacrifice; 1 Cor 5:7, "hath been sacrificed," of the death of Christ as our Passover; **(2)** "to slay, kill," Mt 22:4; Mk 14:12; Lk 15:23, 27, 30; 22:7; Jh 10:10; Acts 10:13; 11:7. See: TDNT—3:180, 342; BAGD—367a; THAYER—294c.

2381. **Θωμᾶς** {12x} **Thōmas**, *tho-mas';* of Chald. or. [comp. 8380]; *the twin; Thomas,* a Chr.:—*Thomas* {12x}. See: BAGD—367c; THAYER—294d.

2382. **θώραξ** {5x} **thōrax**, *tho'-rax;* of uncert. aff.; the *chest* ("*thorax*"), i.e. (by impl.) a *corslet:*—breast-plate {5x}.

Thorax, primarily, "the breast," denotes "a breastplate or corselet," consisting of two parts and protecting the body on both sides, from the neck to the middle. **(1)** It is used metaphorically **(1a)** of righteousness, Eph 6:14; **(1b)** of faith and love, 1 Th 5:8, with perhaps a sugges-

tion of the two parts, front and back, which formed the coat of mail (an alternative term for the word in the NT sense); **(2)** elsewhere in Rev 9:9, 17. See: TDNT—5:308, 702; BAGD—367c; THAYER—294d.

I

2383. **Ἰάειρος** {2x} **Iaĕirŏs**, *ee-ah'-i-ros;* or

Ἰάϊρος Iairŏs, *ee-ahee'-ros;* of Heb. or. [2971]; *Jaïrus* (i.e. *Jair*), an Isr.:—Jairus {2x}. See: BAGD—367b; THAYER—295b.

2384. **Ἰακώβ** {27x} **Iakōb**, *ee-ak-obe';* of Heb. or. [3290]; *Jacob* (i.e. *Ja'akob*), the progenitor of the Isr.:—also an Isr.:—Jacob {27x}. See: TDNT—*, 344; BAGD—367b; THAYER—295b.

2385. **Ἰάκωβος** {42x} **Iakōbŏs**, *ee-ak'-o-bos;* the same as *2384* Græcized; *Jacobus,* the name of three Isr.:—James (son of Zebedee) {21x}, James (son of Alphaeus) {4x}, James (half-brother of Jesus) {17x}. See: BAGD—367d; THAYER—295b.

2386. **ἴαμα** {3x} **iama**, *ee'-am-ah;* from *2390;* a *cure* (the effect):—healing {3x}.

Iama formerly signified "a means of healing"; in the NT, "a healing" (the result of the act), used in the plural, in 1 Cor 12:9, 28 plural, 30; of divinely imparted gifts in the churches in apostolic times. See: TDNT—3:194, 344; BAGD—368a; THAYER—295d.

2387. **Ἰαμβρῆς** {1x} **Iambrēs**, *ee-am-brace';* of Eg. or.; *Jambres,* an Eg.:—Jambres {1x}. See: TDNT—3:192, 344; BAGD—368b; THAYER—295d.

2388. **Ἰαννά** {1x} **Ianna**, *ee-an-nah';* prob. of Heb. or. [comp. 3238]; *Janna,* an Isr.:—Janna {1x}.368b; THAYER—296a.

2389. **Ἰαννῆς** {1x} **Iannēs**, *ee-an-nace';* of Eg. or.; *Jannes,* an Eg.:—Jannes {1x}. See: TDNT—3:192, 344; BAGD—368b; THAYER—296a.

2390. **ἰάομαι** {28x} **iaŏmai**, *ee-ah'-om-ahee;* mid. voice of appar. a primary verb; to *cure* (lit. or fig.):—heal {26x}, make whole {2x}.

Iaomai, "to heal," is used **(1)** of physical treatment 22 times; **(1b)** in Mt 5:28; Acts 9:34, "made whole"; **(2)** figuratively, of spiritual "healing," Mt 13:15; Jn 12:40; Acts 28:27; Heb 12:13; 1 Pet 2:24; possibly, Jas 5:16 includes both **(1)** and **(2)**. **(3)** Luke, the physician, uses the word fifteen times. See: TDNT—3:194, 344; BAGD—368b; THAYER—296a.

2391. **'Ιάρεδ** {1x} **Iarĕd**, *ee-ar'-ed* or

'Ιάρετ **Iaret**, *ee-ar'-et;* of Heb. or. [3382]; *Jared* (i.e. *Jered*), an antediluvian:—Jared {1x}. See: BAGD—368c; THAYER—296b.

2392. **ἴασις** {3x} **iasis**, *ee'-as-is;* from *2390; curing* (the act):—cures {1x}, to heal + 1519 {1x}, healing {1x}.

Iasis, "a healing, a cure" (akin to *iaomai*, "to heal," and *iatros*, "a physician"), is **(1)** used in the plural, "cures", in Lk 13:32; **(2)** in Acts 4:22, "healing", **(3)** in Acts 4:30 with the preposition *eis* "unto," lit., "unto healing," translated "to heal." See: TDNT—3:194, 344; BAGD—368c; THAYER—296b.

2393. **ἴασπις** {4x} **iaspis**, *ee'-as-pis;* prob. of for. or. [see 3471]; *"jasper,"* a gem:—jasper {4x}.

Jasper is a precious stone of various colours (some are purple, others blue, others green, and others the colour of brass (Rev 4:3; 21:11, 18, 19). See: BAGD—368d; THAYER—296b.

2394. **'Ιάσων** {5x} **Iasōn**, *ee-as'-oan;* future act. part. masc. of *2390; about to cure; Jason,* a Chr.:—Jason {5x}. See: BAGD—368d; THAYER—296b.

2395. **ἰατρός** {7x} **iatrŏs**, *ee-at-ros';* from *2390;* a *physician:*—physician {7x}.

Iatros, akin to *iaomai*, "to heal," "a physician," occurs in Mt 9:12; Mk 2:17; 5:26; Lk 4:23; 5:31; 8:43; Col 4:14. See: TDNT—3:194, 344; BAGD—368d; THAYER—296b.

2396. **ἴδε** {27x} **idĕ**, *id'-eh;* second pers. sing. imper. act. of *1492;* used as an interj. to denote *surprise; lo!:*—behold {22x}, lo {3x}, look {1x}, see {1x}.

Ide and idou (2396 and 2400) are imperative moods, active and middle voices, respectively, of eidon (*1492*), to see, calling attention to what may be seen or heard or mentally apprehended in any way, **(1)** regularly rendered "behold." **(2)** It is used as an interjection, addressed either to one or many persons, e.g., Mt 25:20, 22, 25; Jn 1:29, 36, 47; Gal 5:2, the only occurrence outside Matthew, Mark and John. See: BAGD—369b; THAYER—296b.

2397. **ἰδέα** {1x} **idĕa**, *id-eh'-ah;* from *1492;* a *sight* [comp. fig. "idea"], i.e. *aspect:*—countenance {1x}.

This word is concerned with outward form, external appearance, one's aspect, one's looks. It is the sight occurring to the eyes, not to the thing itself but to the thing as it is seen. Syn.: *Morphe* (*3444*) means form, *schema* (*4976*) means fashion, and *idea* means appearance. See:

TDNT—2:373, 202; BAGD—369c; THAYER—296c.

2398. **ἴδιος** {113x} **idiŏs**, *id'-ee-os;* of uncert. aff.; *pertaining to self,* i.e. one's *own;* by impl. *private* or *separate:*—his own {48x}, their own {13x}, privately {8x}, apart {7x}, your own {6x}, his {5x}, own {5x}, not tr {1x}, misc. {20x} = × his acquaintance, when they were alone, aside, due, his (proper, several), home, (her, our, thine) own (business), proper, severally. See: BAGD—369c; THAYER—296d.

2399. **ἰδιώτης** {5x} **idiōtēs**, *id-ee-o'-tace;* from *2398;* a *private* person, i.e. (by impl.) an *ignoramus* (comp. "idiot"):—ignorant {1x}, rude {1x}, unlearned {3x}.

Idiotes, as a noun, primarily means **(1)** "a private person" in contrast to a state official, hence, "a person without professional knowledge, unskilled, uneducated, unlearned," is translated **(1a)** "unlearned" in 1 Cor 14:16, 23, 24, of those who have no knowledge of the facts relating to the testimony borne in and by a local church; **(1b)** "rude" in 2 Cor 11:6, of the apostle's mode of speech in the estimation of the Corinthians;

(2) "ignorant men" in Acts 4:13, of the speech of the apostle Peter and John in the estimation of the rulers, elders and scribes in Jerusalem. Syn.: While *agrammatoi* (*62*) refers to being unacquainted with rabbinical book learning, *idiotai* would signify laymen, in contrast with the religious officials. The apostles were accused of not having that learning gained by mingling with people who have important affairs to transact. Sources of learning are from God Himself or from books and people (literature and politics). One is *agrammatos* when he has not shared in the first; he is *idiotes* when not sharing in the second. The word became a derogatory word because the Greeks felt one's highest education consisted in public life and to purposely withdraw from it was unthinkable. See also: 50, 51, 52, 56, 2990. See: TDNT—3:215, 348; BAGD—370c; THAYER—297b.

2400. **ἰδού** {219x} **idŏu**, *id-oo';* second pers. sing. imper. mid. voice of *1492;* used as imper. *lo!;*—behold {181x}, lo {29x}, see {3x}.

Ide and *idou* (2396 and 2400) are imperative moods, active and middle voices, respectively, of *eidon* (*1492*), to see, calling attention to what may be seen or heard or mentally apprehended in any way, regularly rendered "behold." See: BAGD—370d; THAYER—297c.

2401. **'Ιδουμαία** {1x} **Idŏumaia**, *id-oo-mah'-yah;* of Heb. or. [123]; *Idumæa* (i.e. *Edom*), a region E. (and S.) of Pal.:—

Idumæa {1x}. See: BAGD—371b; THAYER—297d.

2402. **ἱδρώς** {1x} **hidrōs**, *hid-roce';* a strengthened form of a primary ἵδος **idŏs** (*sweat*); *perspiration:*—sweat {1x}. See: BAGD—371c; THAYER—298a.

2403. **Ἰεζαβήλ** {1x} **Iĕzabēl**, *ee-ed-zab-ale';* of Heb. or. [348]; *Jezabel* (i.e. *Jezebel*), a Tyrian woman (used as a synonym of a termagant or false teacher):—Jezabel {1x}. See: TDNT—3:217, 348; BAGD—371c; THAYER—298a.

2404. **Ἱεράπολις** {1x} **Hiĕrapŏlis**, *hee-er-ap'-ol-is;* from *2413* and *4172; holy city; Hierapolis,* a place in Asia Minor:—Hierapolis {1x}. See: BAGD—371c; THAYER—298a.

2405. **ἱερατεία** {2x} **hiĕratĕia**, *hee-er-at-i'-ah;* from *2407; priestliness,* i.e. the *sacerdotal function:*—office of the priesthood {1x}, priest's office {1x}. Cf. Lk 1:9; Heb 7:5. See: TDNT—3:251, 349; BAGD—371d; THAYER—298b.

2406. **ἱεράτευμα** {2x} **hiĕratĕuma**, *hee-er-at'-yoo-mah;* from *2407;* the *priestly fraternity,* i.e. *sacerdotal order* (fig.):—priesthood {2x}.

This word means a body of priests consisting of all believers, the whole church (not a special order from among them), called "a holy priesthood," (1 Pet 2:5); "a royal priesthood," (1 Pet 2:9); the former term is associated with offering spiritual sacrifices, the latter with the royal dignity of showing forth the Lord's excellencies. See: TDNT—3:249, 349; BAGD—371d; THAYER—298b.

2407. **ἱερατεύω** {1x} **hiĕratĕuō**, *hee-er-at-yoo'-o;* prol. from *2409;* to *be a priest,* i.e. *perform his functions:*—execute the priest's office {1x}. See: TDNT—3:248, 349; BAGD—371d; THAYER—298b.

2408. **Ἰερεμίας** {2x} **Hiĕrĕmias**, *hee-er-em-ee'-as;* of Heb. or. [3414]; *Hieremias* (i.e. *Jermijah*), an Isr.:—Jeremias {1x}, Jeremy {1x}. See: TDNT—3:218,*; BAGD—371d; THAYER—298b.

2409. **ἱερεύς** {32x} **hiĕrĕus**, *hee-er-yooce';* from *2413;* a *priest* (lit. or fig.):—high priest {1x}, priest {31x}.

Hiereus refers to one who offers sacrifice and has the charge of things pertaining thereto and is used **(1)** of a priest of the pagan god Zeus (Acts 14:13); **(2)** of Jewish priests (Mt 8:4; 12:4, 5; Lk 1:5); **(3)** of believers (Rev 1:6; 5:10; 1 Pet 2:5, 9), **(3a)** constituting **(3a1)** a kingdom of priests (Rev 1:6), **(3a2)** a holy priesthood

(1 Pet 2:5), and **(3a3)** royal (1 Pet 2: 9), **(3b)** not a special sacerdotal class in contrast to the laity; **(3c)** all believers are commanded to offer the sacrifices (Rom 12:1; Phil 2:17; 4:18; Heb 13:15, 16; 1 Pet 2:5); **(4)** of Christ (Heb 5:6; 7:11, 15, 17, 21; 8:4); **(5)** of Melchizedek, as the foreshadower of Christ (Heb 7:1, 3). Syn.: 749. See: TDNT—3:257, 349; BAGD—372a; THAYER—298c.

2410. **Ἱεριχώ** {7x} **Hiĕrichō**, *hee-er-ee-kho';* of Heb. or. [3405]; *Jericho,* a place in Pal.:—Jericho {7x}. See: BAGD—372b; THAYER—298c.

2411. **ἱερόν** {71x} **hiĕrŏn**, *hee-er-on';* neut. of *2413;* a *sacred* place, i.e. the entire precincts (whereas *3485* denotes the central *sanctuary* itself) of the *temple* (at Jerusalem or elsewhere):—temple {71x}

Hieron, the neuter of the adjective *hieros,* "sacred," is used as a noun denoting "a sacred place, a temple," **(1)** that of Artemis (Diana), Acts 19:27; **(2)** that in Jerusalem, Mk 11:11, signifying the entire building with its precincts, or some part thereof, as distinct from the *naos,* "the inner sanctuary"; **(3)** apart from the Gospels and Acts, it is mentioned only in 1 Cor 9:13. **(4)** Christ taught in one of the courts, to which all the people had access. **(5)** *Hieron* is never used figuratively. **(6)** The temple mentioned in the Gospels and Acts was begun by Herod in 20 B.C., and destroyed by the Romans in A.D. 70. Syn.: 3485. See: TDNT—3:230, 349; BAGD—372b; THAYER—298d.

2412. **ἱεροπρεπής** {1x} **hiĕrŏprĕpēs**, *hee-er-op-rep-ace';* from *2413* and the same as *4241; reverent:*—as becometh holiness {1x}.

Hieroprepes, from *hieros,* "sacred," with the adjectival form of *prepo,* denotes "suited to a sacred character, that which is befitting in persons, actions or things consecrated to God," Titus 2:3, "as becometh holiness." Syn.: 38, 40, 41, 42, 3741, 3742, 3743. See: TDNT—3:253, 349; BAGD—372d; THAYER—299b.

2413. **ἱερός** {2x} **hiĕrŏs**, *hee-er-os';* of uncert. aff.; *sacred:*—holy {2x}.

This word means sacred, consecrated to deity, pertaining to God; the sacred Scriptures, because inspired by God, treating of divine things and therefore to be devoutly revered, translated "holy" (1 Cor 9:13; 2 Ti 3:15). See: TDNT—3:221, 349; BAGD—372d; THAYER—299b.

2414. **Ἱεροσόλυμα** {59x} **Hiĕrŏsŏluma**, *hee-er-os-ol'-oo-mah;* of Heb. or. [3389]; *Hierosolyma* (i.e. *Jerushalaïm*), the capital of Pal.:—Jerusalem {5x}. See: TDNT—

7:292, 1028; BAGD—372d; THAYER—299b. comp. *2419.*

2415. Ἱεροσολυμίτης {2x} Hiĕrŏsŏlumitēs, *hee-er-os-ol-oo-mee'-tace;* from *2414;* a *Hierosolymite,* i.e. inhab. of Hierosolyma:—of Jerusalem {2x}. See: TDNT—7:292, 1028; BAGD—373b; THAYER—299d.

2416. ἱεροσυλέω {1x} hiĕrŏsuleō, *hee-er-os-ool-eh'-o;* from *2417;* to *be a temple-robber* (fig.):—commit sacrilege {1x}.

This word means to commit sacrilege, to rob a temple and in Rom 2:22, the meaning is, thou who abhorrest idols and their contamination, doest yet not hesitate to plunder their shrines and copy their ways. See: TDNT—3:255, 349; BAGD—373c; THAYER—299d.

2417. ἱερόσυλος {1x} hiĕrŏsulŏs, *hee-er-os'-oo-los;* from *2411* and *4813;* a *temple-despoiler:*—robber of churches {1x}.

In Acts 19:37 this word is used by the Roman town clerk generally of an assembly of religious people and not to the gathering of Christians. See: TDNT—3:256, 349; BAGD—373c; THAYER—300a.

2418. ἱερουργέω {1x} hiĕrŏurgĕō, *hee-er-oorg-eh'-o;* from a compound of *2411* and the base of *2041;* to *be a temple-worker,* i.e. *officiate as a priest* (fig.):—minister {1x}.

Hierourgeo means to minister in priestly service, a sacrificing priest and is used by Paul metaphorically of his ministry of the gospel (Rom 15:16); the offering connected with his priestly ministry is "the offering up of the Gentiles," i.e., the presentation of Gentile converts to God. Syn.: 1247, 1249, 3011. See: TDNT—3:251, 349; BAGD—373c; THAYER—300a.

2419. Ἱερουσαλήμ {83x} Hiĕrŏusalēm, *hee-er-oo-sal-ame';* of Heb. or. [3389]; *Hierusalem* (i.e. *Jerushalem*), the capital of Pal.:—Jerusalem {83x}. See: TDNT—7:292, 1028; BAGD—373c; THAYER—300a. comp. *2414.*

2420. ἱερωσύνη {4x} hiĕrŏsunē, *hee-er-o-soo'-nay;* from *2413; sacredness,* i.e. (by impl.) the *priestly office:*—priesthood {4x}.

Hierosune, "a priesthood," signifies the office, quality, rank and ministry of "a priest," Heb 7:11, 12, 14, 24, where the contrasts between the Levitical "priesthood" and that of Christ are set forth. See: TDNT—3:247, 349; BAGD—373c; THAYER—300a.

2421. Ἰεσσαί {5x} Iĕssai, *es-es-sah'-ee;* of Heb. or. [3448]; *Jessae* (i.e. *Jis-hai*), an Isr.:—Jesse {5x}. See: BAGD—373d; THAYER—300a.

2422. Ἰεφθάε {1x} Iĕphthaĕ, *ee-ef-thah'-eh;* of Heb. or. [3316]; *Jephthaë* (i.e. *Jiphtach*), an Isr.:—Jephthah {1x}. See: BAGD—373d; THAYER—300b.

2423. Ἰεχονίας {2x} Iĕchŏnias, *ee-ekh-on-ee'-as;* of Heb. or. [3204]; *Jechonias* (i.e. *Jekonjah*), an Isr.:—Jechonias {2x}. See: BAGD—373d; THAYER—300b.

2424. Ἰησοῦς {975x} Iēsŏus, *ee-ay-sooce';* of Heb. or. [3091]; *Jesus* (i.e. *Jehoshua*), the name of our Lord and two (three) other Isr.:—Jesus {972x}, Jesus (Joshua) {2x}, Jesus (Justus) {1x}. See: TDNT—3:284, 360; BAGD—373d; THAYER—300b.

2425. ἱκανός {41x} hikanŏs, *hik-an-os';* from ἵκω hikō [ἱκάνω hikanō or ἱκνέομαι hiknĕŏmai, akin to *2240*] (to *arrive*); *competent* (as if *coming* in season), i.e. *ample* (in amount) or *fit* (in character):—many}, much {6x}, worthy {5x}, long {4x}, sufficient {3x}, misc. {12x} = able, + content, enough, good, great, large, meet, security, sore.

(1) *Hikanos,* as an adjective, means "sufficient" and is used with *poieo* (*4160* - "to do") in Mk 15:15 and is translated "to content (the multitude)," i.e., to do sufficient to satisfy them: "And so Pilate, willing to content the people, released Barabbas unto them, and delivered Jesus, when he had scourged him, to be crucified." (2) This word translated "able," is to be distinguished from *dunatos* (*1415*) which means possessing power; *hikanos* means sufficient power. (3) When said of things it signifies enough: "And they said, Lord, behold, here are two swords. And he said unto them, It is enough" (Lk 22:38); (4) when said of persons, it means competent, worthy: "To the one we are the savour of death unto death; and to the other the savour of life unto life. And who is sufficient for these things?" (2 Cor 2:16; cf. 3:5; 2 Ti 2:2). Syn.: 714, 841, 842, 4909. See: TDNT—3:293, 361; BAGD—374b; THAYER—300c.

2426. ἱκανότης {1x} hikanŏtēs, *hik-an-ot'-ace;* from *2425; ability:*—sufficiency {1x}.

This word means sufficient power, ability or competency to do a thing (2 Cor 3:5). See: TDNT—3:293, 361; BAGD—374d; THAYER—300d.

2427. ἱκανόω {2x} hikanŏō, *hik-an-ŏ'-o;* from *2425;* to *enable,* i.e. *qualify:*—make able {1x}, make meet {1x}.

Hikanoo, "to render fit, meet, to make sufficient," is translated (1) "hath made . . . meet" in Col 1:12; and (2) "hath made able" in 2 Cor

3:6. See: TDNT−3:293, 361; BAGD−374d; THAYER−300d.

2428. ἱκετηρία {1x} **hikĕtēria,** *hik-et-ay-ree'-ah;* from a der. of the base of *2425* (through the idea of *approaching* for a favor); *intreaty:*—supplication {1x}.

Hiketeria is the feminine form of the adjective *hiketerios,* denoting "of a suppliant," and used as a noun, formerly "an olive branch" carried by a suppliant (*hiketes*), then later, "a supplication," used in Heb 5:7. See: TDNT−3:296, 362; BAGD−375a; THAYER−301a.

2429. ἱκμάς {1x} **hikmas,** *hik-mas';* of uncert aff.; *dampness:*—moisture {1x}. See: BAGD−375a; THAYER−301a.

2430. Ἰκόνιον {6x} **Ikŏniŏn,** *ee-kon'-ee-on;* perh. from *1504; image-like; Iconium,* a place in Asia Minor:—Iconium {6x}. See: BAGD−375b; THAYER−30a.

2431. ἱλαρός {1x} **hilarŏs,** *hil-ar-os';* from the same as *2436; propitious* or *merry* ("*hilarious*"), i.e. *prompt* or *willing:*—cheerful {1x}.

This word signifies that readiness of mind, that joyousness, which is prompt to do anything (2 Cor 9:7). See: TDNT−3:297, 362; BAGD−375b; THAYER−301a.

2432. ἱλαρότης {1x} **hilarŏtēs,** *hil-ar-ot'-ace;* from *2431; alacrity:*—cheerfulness {1x}. See: TDNT−3:297, 362; BAGD−375b; THAYER−301b.

2433. ἱλάσκομαι {2x} **hilaskŏmai,** *hil-as'-kom-ahee;* mid. voice from the same as *2436;* to *conciliate,* i.e. (tran.) to *atone* for (sin), or (intr.) *be propitious:*—be merciful {1x}, make reconciliation for {1x}.

Hilaskomai **(1)** was used amongst the Greeks with the significance "to make the gods propitious, to appease, propitiate," inasmuch as their good will was not conceived as their natural attitude, but something to be earned first. **(2)** This use of the word is foreign to the Greek Bible, with respect to God whether in the Sept. or in the NT. **(3)** It is never used of any act whereby man brings God into a favorable attitude or gracious disposition. **(4)** It is God who is "propitiated" by the vindication of His holy and righteous character, whereby through the provision He has made in the vicarious and expiatory sacrifice of Christ, He has so dealt with sin that He can show mercy to the believing sinner in the removal of his guilt and the remission of his sins. **(5)** Thus in Lk 18:13 it signifies "to be propitious" or "merciful to" (with the person as the object of the verb), and in Heb 2:17 "to expiate, to make reconciliation" (the object of the verb being sins).

(6) Through the "propitiatory" sacrifice of Christ, he who believes upon Him is by God's own act delivered from justly deserved wrath, and comes under the covenant of grace. **(7)** Never is God said to be reconciled, a fact itself indicative that the enmity exists on man's part alone, and that it is man who needs to be reconciled to God, and not God to man. **(8)** God is always the same and, since He is Himself immutable, His relative attitude does change towards those who change. **(9)** He can act differently towards those who come to Him by faith, and solely on the ground of the "propitiatory" sacrifice of Christ, not because He has changed, but because He ever acts according to His unchanging righteousness. **(10)** The expiatory work of the Cross is therefore the means whereby the barrier which sin interposes between God and man is broken down. **(11)** By the giving up of His sinless life sacrificially, Christ annuls the power of sin to separate between God and the believer. **(12)** Man has forfeited his life on account of sin and God has provided the one and only way whereby eternal life could be bestowed, namely, by the voluntary laying down of His life by His Son, under divine retribution. Of this the former sacrifices appointed by God were foreshadowings. Syn.: 1653, 1655, 1656, 2436, 3627, 3628, 3629, 4698. See: TDNT−3:301, 362; BAGD−375c; THAYER−301b.

2434. ἱλασμός {2x} **hilasmŏs,** *hil-as-mos';* *atonement,* i.e. (concr.) an *expiator:*—propitiation {2x}.

Hilasmos (*2434*), akin to *hileos* ("merciful, propitious"), signifies "an expiation, a means whereby sin is covered and remitted." **(1)** It is used in the NT of Christ Himself as "the propitiation," in 1 Jn 2:2 and 4:10, **(1a)** signifying that He Himself, through Him alone, the violated holiness and righteousness of God by man's sin has been propitiated [satisfied]. This is the personal means through which God shows mercy to the sinner who believes on Christ as the One thus provided. **(1b)** In the former passage He is described as "the propitiation for our sins; and not for ours only, but also for the sins of the whole world." **(1c)** Provision is made for the whole world, so that no one is, by divine predetermination, excluded from the scope of God's mercy; **(1d)** the efficacy of the "propitiation," however, is made actual for those who believe. **(1e)** In 4:10, the fact that God "sent His Son to be the propitiation for our sins," is shown to be the great expression of God's love toward man, and the reason why Christians should love one another. See: TDNT−3:301, 362; BAGD−375c; THAYER−301b.

2435. **ἱλαστήριον** {2x} **hilastēriŏn**, *hil-as-tay'-ree-on;* neut. of a der. of *2433;* an *expiatory* (place or thing), i.e. (concr.) an atoning *victim,* or (spec.) the *lid* of the Ark (in the Temple):—mercyseat {1x}, propitiation {1x}.

Hilasterion (2435), is regarded as the neuter of an adjective signifying "propitiatory." **(1)** It is used for the lid of the ark in Heb 9:5. **(2)** Elsewhere in the NT it occurs only in Rom 3:25, where it is used of Christ Himself. **(3)** Christ, through His expiatory death, is the personal means by whom God shows the mercy of His justifying grace to the sinner who believes. **(4)** His "blood" stands for the voluntary giving up of His life, by the shedding of His blood in expiatory sacrifice under divine judgment righteously due to us as sinners, faith being the sole condition on man's part. **(5)** By metonymy, "blood" is sometimes put for "death," inasmuch as, blood being essential to life, Lev 17:11, when the blood is shed life is given up, that is, death takes place. The fundamental principle on which God deals with sinners is expressed in the words "apart from shedding of blood," i.e., unless a death takes place, "there is no remission" of sins, Heb 9:22.

(6) But whereas the essential of the type lay in the fact that blood was shed, the essential of the antitype lies in this, that the blood shed was that of Christ. Hence, in connection with Jewish sacrifices, "the blood" is mentioned without reference to the victim from which it flowed, but in connection with the great antitypical sacrifice of the NT the words "the blood" never stand alone; the One Who shed the blood is invariably specified, for it is the Person that gives value to the work; the saving efficacy of the death depends entirely upon the fact that He Who died was the Son of God. See: TDNT—3:318, 362; BAGD—375d.301c.

2436. **ἵλεως** {2x} **hileōs**, *hil'-eh-oce;* perh. from the alt. form of *138; cheerful* (as *attractive*), i.e. *propitious;* adv. (by Heb.) God be *gracious!,* i.e. (in averting some calamity) *far* be it:—be it far {1x}, merciful {1x}.

Hileos, as an adjective, means "propitious, merciful." **(1)** The quality expressed by it there essentially appertains to God, though man is undeserving of it. **(2)** It is used only of God, Heb 8:12; **(3)** in Mt 16:22, "Be it far from Thee" (Peter's word to Christ) may have the meaning, "(God) have mercy on Thee," lit., "propitious to Thee" so that what You said will not happen. Syn.: 1653, 1655, 1656, 2433, 3627, 3628, 3629, 4698. See: TDNT—3:300, 362; BAGD—376a; THAYER—301d.

2437. **Ἰλλυρικόν** {1x} **Illurikŏn**, *il-loo-ree-kon';* neut. of an adj. from a name of uncert. der.: (the) *Illyrican* (shore), i.e. (as a name itself) *Illyricum,* a region of Europe:—Illyricum {1x}. See: BAGD—376a.301d.

2438. **ἱμάς** {4x} **himas**, *hee-mas';* perh. from the same as *260;* a *strap,* i.e. (spec.) the *tie* (of a sandal) or the *lash* (of a scourge):—latchet {3x}, thong {1x}.

Himas denotes "a thong, strap," whether **(1)** for binding prisoners, Acts 22:25, "(the) thongs" or **(2)** for fastening sandals, Mk 1:7; Lk 3:16; Jn 1:27. Among the Orientals everything connected with the feet and shoes is defiled and debasing, and the stooping to unfasten the dusty latchet is the most insignificant in such service. See: BAGD—376b; THAYER—302a.

2439. **ἱματίζω** {2x} **himatizō**, *him-at-id'-zo;* from *2440;* to *dress:*—clothe {2x}.

Himatizo as a verb, means "to put on raiment": "And they come to Jesus, and see him that was possessed with the devil, and had the legion, sitting, and clothed *(himatizo),* and in his right mind: and they were afraid" (Mk 5:15; cf. Lk 8:35). Syn.: 294, 1463, 1737, 1746, 1902, 4016. See: BAGD—376b; THAYER—302a.

2440. **ἱμάτιον** {61x} **himatiŏn**, *him-at'-ee-on;* neut. of a presumed der. of ἕννυμι **ĕnnumi** (to *put on*); a *dress* (inner or outer):—garment {30}, raiment {12x}, clothes {12x}, cloke {2x}, robe {2x}, vesture {2x}, apparel {1x}.

Himation, a diminutive of *heima,* "a robe," was used especially of an outer cloak or mantle thrown over the *chiton (5509),* and in **(1)** general of raiment, "apparel" in 1 Pet 3:3; **(2)** in the plural, "clothes" (the "cloke" and the tunic), e.g., Mt 17:2; 26:65; 27:31, 35; **(3)** "an outer garment," is rendered "vesture" in Rev 19:13, 16. See: BAGD—376b; THAYER—302a.

2441. **ἱματισμός** {6x} **himatismŏs**, *him-at-is-mos';* from *2439; clothing:*—vesture {2x}, apparel {2x}, raiment {1x}, array {1x}.

Himatismos, in form a collective word, denoting "vesture, garments," is used **(1)** generally of "costly or stately raiment," the apparel of kings, of officials, etc. **(1a)** See Lk 7:25, where "gorgeously apparelled" is, lit., "in gorgeous vesture." **(1b)** See also Acts 20:33 and 1 Ti 2:9, "costly raiment." **(2)** This is the word used of the Lord's white and dazzling raiment on the Mount of Transfiguration, Lk 9:29. **(3)** It is also used of His *chiton (5509),* His undergarment for which the soldiers cast lots, Jn 19:23–24, **(4)** "vesture" in Mt 27:35. See: BAGD—376d; THAYER—302b.

2442. ἱμείρομαι {1x} **himĕirŏmai,** *him-i'-rom-ahee;* mid. voice from ἵμ-ερος **himĕrŏs** (a *yearning;* of uncert. aff.); to *long for:*—be affectionately desirous {1x}.

Himeiromai, "to have a strong affection for, a yearning after," is found in 1 Th 2:8, "being affectionately desirous of you." It is probably derived from a root indicating remembrance. See: TDNT—5:176,*; BAGD—376d; THAYER—302b.

2443. ἵνα {621x} **hina,** *hin'-ah;* prob. from the same as the former part of *1438* (through the *demonstrative* idea; comp. *3588*); in order *that* (denoting the *purpose* or the *result*):—that {536x}, to {69x}, for to {8x}, not translated {1x}, misc. {7x} = albeit, because, lest, so as. See: TDNT—3:323, 366; BAGD—376d; THAYER—302b. comp. *3363.*

ἵνα μή hina mē. See *3363.*

2444. ἱνατί {6x} **hinati,** *hin-at-ee';* from *2443* and *5101;* for *what* reason?, i.e. *why?:*—wherefore {1x}, why {5x}. See: BAGD—378c; THAYER—305a.

2445. Ἰόππη {10x} **Iŏppē,** *ee-op'-pay;* of Heb. or. [3305]; *Joppe* (i.e. *Japho*), a place in Pal.:—Joppa {10x}. See: BAGD—378d; THAYER—305a.

2446. Ἰορδάνης {15x} **Iŏrdanēs,** *ee-or-dan'-ace;* of Heb. or. [3383]; the *Jordanes* (i.e. *Jarden*), a river of Pal.:—Jordan {15x}. See: TDNT—6:608, 921; BAGD—378d; THAYER—305b.

2447. ἰός {3x} **iŏs,** *ee-os';* perh. from εἶμι **ĕimi** (to *go*) or ἵημι **hiēmi** (to *send*); *rust* (as if *emitted* by metals); also *venom* (as *emitted* by serpents):—poison {2x}, rust {1x}.

This word denotes something active as **(1)** rust, as acting on metals, affecting their nature (Jas 5:3); **(2)** poison, as of asps, acting destructively on living tissues, figuratively **(2a)** of the evil use of the lips as the organs of speech (Rom 3:13); **(2b)** so of the tongue (Jas 3:8). See: TDNT—3:334, 368; BAGD—378d; THAYER—305b.

2448. Ἰουδά {1x} **Iŏuda,** *ee-oo-dah';* of Heb. or. [3063 or perh. 3194]; *Judah* (i.e. *Jehudah* or *Juttah*), a part of (or place in) Pal.:—Judah {1x}. See: BAGD—379b; THAYER—305b.

2449. Ἰουδαία {44x} **Iŏudaia,** *ee-oo-dah'-yah;* fem. of *2453* (with *1093* impl.); the *Judæan* land (i.e. *Judæa*), a region of Pal.:—Judæa {42x}, Jewry {2x}. See: TDNT—3:356, 372; BAGD—379a; THAYER—305c.

2450. Ἰουδαΐζω {1x} **Iŏudaïzō,** *ee-oo-dah-id'-zo;* from *2453;* to *become a Judæan,* i.e. "*Judaize*":—live as the Jews {1x}.

This word means to adopt Jewish customs and rites, practices and manners, imitate the Jews, Judaise, observe the ritual law of the Jews (Gal 14). See: TDNT—3:356, 372; BAGD—379b; THAYER—305d.

2451. Ἰουδαϊκός {1x} **Iŏudaïkŏs,** *ee-oo-dah-ee-kos';* from *2453; Judaïc,* i.e. *resembling a Judæan:*—Jewish {1x}. See: TDNT—3:356, 372; BAGD—379b; THAYER—305d.

2452. Ἰουδαϊκῶς {1x} **Iŏudaïkōs,** *ee-oo-dah-ee-koce';* adv. from *2451; Judaïcally* or *in a manner resembling a Judæan:*—as do the Jews {1x}. See: BAGD—379b; THAYER—305d.

2453. Ἰουδαῖος {198x} **Iŏudaiŏs,** *ee-oo-dah'-yos;* from *2448* (in the sense of *2455* as a country); *Judæan,* i.e. belonging to *Jehudah:*—Jew {193x}, of Judea {3x}, Jewess {2x}.

This word means Jewish, **(1)** belonging to the Jewish race, or **(1a)** Jewish as respects to birth, race, religion. *Ioudaios* is used **(1b)** adjectively, with the lit. meaning, "Jewish," **(1c)** sometimes with the addition **(1c1)** of *aner,* "a man," Acts 10:28; 22:3; **(1c2)** in Acts 21:39 with *anthropos;* **(1c3)** in Acts 13:6, lit., "a Jewish false-prophet"; **(1c4)** in Jn 3:22, with the word *chora,* "land" or "country," signifying "Judean," lit., "Judean country"; used by metonymy for the people of the country; **(2)** as a noun, "a Jew, Jews," e.g., Mt 2:2; Mk 7:3. **(2a)** The name "Jew" is primarily tribal (from Judah). **(2b)** It is first found in 2 Kin 16:6, as distinct from Israel, of the northern kingdom. **(2c)** After the Captivity it was chiefly used to distinguish the race from Gentiles, e.g., Jn 2:6; Acts 14:1; Gal 2:15, where it denotes Christians of "Jewish" race; **(2d)** it distinguishes Jews **(2d1)** from Samaritans, in Jn 4:9; **(2d2)** from proselytes, in Acts 2:10. **(2e)** The word is most frequent in John's Gospel and the Acts; in the former it especially denotes the typical representatives of Jewish thought contrasted with believers in Christ . . . or with other Jews of less pronounced opinions, e.g., Jn 3:25; 5:10; 7:13; 9:22; **(2f)** such representatives were found, generally, in opposition to Christ; in the Acts they are chiefly those who opposed the apostles and the gospel. **(3)** In Rom 2:28, 29 the word is used of ideal "Jews," i.e., "Jews" in spiritual reality, believers, whether "Jews" or Gentiles by natural birth. **(4)** The feminine, "Jewess," is found in Acts 16:1; 24:24. **(5)** It also denotes Judea, e.g., Mt 2:1; Lk 1:5;

Jn 4:3, the word "country" being understood. **(6)** In Lk 23:5 and Jn 7:1, "Jewry." See: TDNT— 3:356, 372; BAGD—379b; THAYER—305d.

2454. Ἰουδαϊσμός {2x} **Iŏudaismŏs,** *ee-oo-dah-is-mos';* from *2450;* "*Judaïsm*", i.e. the *Jewish faith* and usages:— Jews' religion {2x}.

This word denotes the Jews religion (Gal 1:13, 14) and stands, not for their religious beliefs, but for their religious practices, not as instituted by God, but as developed and extended from these by the traditions of the Pharisees and scribes. See: TDNT—3:356, 372; BAGD— 379d; THAYER—306b.

2455. Ἰουδάς {45x} **Iŏudas,** *ee-oo-das';* of Heb. or. [3063]; *Judas* (i.e. *Jehudah*), the name of ten Isr.; also of the posterity of one of them and its region:—Judas (Iscariot) {22x}, Juda (Son of Jacob) {7x}, Judah (Son of Jacob) {1x}, Judas (Son of Jacob) {2x}, Judas (Brother of James) {3x}, Jude (Brother of James) {1x}, Judas Barsabas {3x}, Juda (Ancestors of Jesus {2x}, misc. {4x}. See: BAGD—379d; THAYER— 306b.

2456. Ἰουλία {1x} **Iŏulia,** *ee-oo-lee'-ah;* fem. of the same as *2457; Julia,* a Chr. woman:—Julia {1x}. See: BAGD—380b; THAYER—306d.

2457. Ἰούλιος {2x} **Iŏuliŏs,** *ee-oo'-lee-os;* of Lat. or.; *Julius,* a centurion:— Julius {2x}. See: BAGD—380b; THAYER— 306d.

2458. Ἰουνίας {1x} **Iŏunias,** *ee-oo-nee'-as;* of Lat. or.; *Junias,* a Chr.:— Junias {1x}. See: BAGD—380b; THAYER— 306d.

2459. Ἰοῦστος {3x} **Iŏustŏs,** *ee-ooce'-tos;* of Lat. or. ("*just*"); *Justus,* the name of three Chr.:—Justus (of Corinth) {1x}, Justus (surnamed Barsabas) {1x}, Justus (Jesus, a fellow worker of Paul) {1x}. See: BAGD— 380b; THAYER—306d.

2460. ἱππεύς {2x} **hippĕus,** *hip-yooce';* from *2462;* an *equestrian,* i.e. member of a *cavalry* corps.:—horseman {2x}. Cf. Acts 23:23, 32. See: BAGD—306d; THAYER— 380c.

2461. ἱππικόν {1x} **hippikŏn,** *hip-pee-kon';* neut. of a der. of *2462;* the *cavalry* force:—horsemen {1x}.

Hippikon is an adjective signifying "of a horse" or "of horsemen, equestrian," is used as a noun denoting "horsemen," in Rev 9:16, "horsemen," numbering "two hundred thousand thousand." See: BAGD—380c; THAYER—306d.

2462. ἵππος {16x} **hippŏs,** *hip'-pos;* of uncert. aff.; a *horse:*—horse {16x}.

Hippos, **(1)** has fifteen occurrences in the Apocalypse, **(1a)** seen in visions in 6:2, 4, 5, 8; 9:7, 9, 17 (twice); 14:20; 19:11, 14, 19, 21; and **(1b)** otherwise in 18:13; 19:18. **(2)** It also occurs in Jas 3:3. See: TDNT—3:336, 369; BAGD—380c; THAYER—306d.

2463. ἶρις {2x} **iris,** *ee'-ris;* perh. from *2046* (as a symbol of the female *messenger* of the pagan deities); a *rainbow* ("*iris*"):—rainbow {2x}.

(1) This rainbow "round about the throne, like an emerald to look upon" (Rev 4:3) is emblematic of the fact that, in the exercise of God's absolute sovereignty and perfect counsels, He will remember His covenant concerning the earth (cf. Gen 9:9–17). **(2)** In Rev 10:1, "a rainbow," suggests a connection with the scene in 4:3. See: TDNT—3:339, 369; BAGD— 380d; THAYER—306d.

2464. Ἰσαάκ {20x} **Isaak,** *ee-sah-ak';* of Heb. or. [3327]; *Isaac* (i.e. *Jitschak*), the son of Abraham:—Isaac {20x}. See: TDNT 3:191,*; BAGD—380d; THAYER—306d.

2465. ἰσάγγελος {1x} **isaggĕlŏs,** *ee-sang'-el-los;* from *2470* and *32; like an angel,* i.e. *angelic:*—equal unto the angels {1x}. See: TDNT—1:87, 12; BAGD—380d; THAYER— 307a.

2466. Ἰσαχάρ {1x} **Isachar,** *ee-sakh-ar';* of Heb. or. [3485]; *Isachar* (i.e. *Jissaskar*), a son of Jacob (fig. his desc.):—Issachar {1x}. See: BAGD—381d; THAYER—307a.

2467. ἴσημι {2x} **isēmi,** *is'-ay-mee;* assumed by some as the base of cert. irreg. forms of *1492;* to *know:*—know {2x}. See: BAGD—220c; THAYER—307a.

2468. ἴσθι {5x} **isthi,** *is'-thee;* second pers. imper. present of *1510; be* thou:— be thou {1x}, be {1x}, agree + 2132 {1x}, give thyself wholly to + 1722 {1x}, not tr {1x}. See: BAGD—380d; THAYER—175c [see 1510].

2469. Ἰσκαριώτης {11x} **Iskariōtēs,** *is-kar-ee-o'-tace;* of Heb. or. [prob. 377 and 7149]; *inhabitant of Kerioth; Iscariotes* (i.e. *Keriothite*), an epithet of Judas the traitor:—Iscariot {11x}. See: BAGD—380d; THAYER—307a.

2470. ἴσος {8x} **isŏs,** *ee'-sos;* prob. from *1492* (through the idea of *seeming*); *similar* (in amount and kind):—equal {4x}, agree together + 2258 {2x}, as much {1x}, like {1x}.

This word, translated "equal," is used with the verb "to be," signifying "to agree" (Mk 14:56, 59); lit., "their thought was not equal

one with the other." See: TDNT—3:343, 370; BAGD—381a; THAYER—307b.

2471. ἰσότης {3x} **isŏtēs,** *ee-sot'-ace; likeness* (in condition or proportion); by impl. *equity:*—equal {1x}, equality {2x}.

Isotes, "equality", is translated **(1)** "equality" in 2 Cor 8:14, twice; and **(2)** in Col 4:1, with the article, "that which is . . . equal," (lit., "the equality,"), i.e., equity, fairness, what is equitable. See: TDNT—3:343, 370; BAGD—381b; THAYER—307b.

2472. ἰσότιμος {1x} **isŏtimŏs,** *ee-sot'-ee-mos; from 2470 and 5092; of equal value* or *honor:*—like precious {1x}.

Isotimos, "of equal value, held in equal honor" (*isos,* "equal," and *time,* is used in 2 Pet 1:1, "a like precious (faith)." See: TDNT—3:343, 370; BAGD—381b; THAYER—307b.

2473. ἰσόψυχος {1x} **isŏpsuchŏs,** *ee-sop'-soo-khos; from 2470 and 5590; of similar spirit:*—likeminded {1x}.

Isopsuchos, lit., "of equal soul" (*isos,* "equal," *psuche,* "the soul"), is rendered "likeminded" in Phil 2:20. See: BAGD—381b; THAYER—307b.

2474. Ἰσραήλ {70x} **Israēl,** *is-rah-ale'; of Heb. or.* [3478]; *Israel* (i.e. *Jisrael*), the adopted name of Jacob, incl. his desc. (lit. or fig.):—Israel {70x}. See: TDNT—3:356, 372; BAGD—381c; THAYER—307b.

2475. Ἰσραηλίτης {9x} **Israēlitēs,** *is-rah-ale-ee'-tace; from 2474; an* "Israelite", i.e. desc. of Israel (lit. or fig.):—Israel {5x}, Israelite {4x}.

Syn.: *Hebraios* (1445) refers to a Hebrew-speaking as contrasted to a Greek-speaking or Hellenizing Jew, and *Ioudaios* (2453) refers to the Jew nationalistically in distinction from Gentiles, and *Israelites,* the most majestic title of all, refers to a Jew as a member of the theocracy and heir of the promises. The first word refers to his language, the second to his nationality, and the third to his theocratic privileges and glorious vocation. See: TDNT—3:356, 372; BAGD—381d; THAYER—307c.

2476. ἵστημι {158x} **histēmi,** *his'-tay-mee; a* prol. form of a primary στάω **staō,** *stah'-o* (of the same mean., and used for it in certain tenses); to *stand* (tran. or intr.), used in various applications (lit. or fig.):—stand {116x}, set {11x}, establish {5x}, stand still {4x}, stand by {3x}, vr stand {2x}, misc. {17x} = abide, appoint, bring, continue, covenant, hold up, lay, present, stanch.

Histemi, as a verb, usually means "to cause to stand, to set." Rarely it can mean "to appoint": "Because He hath appointed (*histemi*)

a day, in the which He will judge the world in righteousness by that man whom He hath ordained; whereof he hath given assurance unto all men, in that he hath raised Him from the dead" (Acts 17:31 of the day in which God will judge the world by Christ). **(2)** In Acts 1:23, with reference to Joseph and Barnabas, these were simply singled out, in order that it might be made known which of them the Lord had chosen: "And they appointed two, Joseph called Barsabas, who was surnamed Justus, and Matthias." The Lord then chose by lots which one He wanted. See: TDNT—7:638, 1082; BAGD—381d; THAYER—307d. comp. *5087.*

2477. ἱστορέω {1x} **histŏrĕō,** *his-tor-eh'-o; from a der. of 1492; to be knowing* (*learned*), i.e. (by impl.) to *visit* for information (*interview*):—see {1x}.

Historeo, from *histor,* "one learned in anything," denotes "to visit" in order to become acquainted with, "to see", Gal 1:18. See: TDNT—3:391, 377; BAGD—383a; THAYER—308d.

2478. ἰσχυρός {27x} **ischurŏs,** *is-khoo-ros'; from 2479; forcible* (lit. or fig.):—mighty {10x}, strong {9x}, strong man {5x}, boisterous {1x}, powerful {1x}, valiant {1x}.

Ischuros, "strong, mighty," as an adjective, is used of **(1)** persons: **(1a)** God, Rev 18:8; **(1b)** angels, Rev 5:2; 10:1; 18:21; **(1c)** men, Mt 12:29 (twice) and parallel passages; Heb 11:34, "valiant"; 19:18, "mighty"; metaphorically, **(1d)** the church at Corinth, 1 Cor 4:10, where the apostle reproaches them ironically with their unspiritual and self-complacent condition; **(1e)** of young men in Christ spiritually strong, through the Word of God, to overcome the evil one, 1 Jn 2:14; of **(2)** things: **(2a)** wind, Mt 14:30 "boisterous"; **(2b)** famine, Lk 15:14; **(2c)** things in the mere human estimate, 1 Cor 1:27; **(2d)** Paul's letters, 2 Cor 10:10; **(2e)** the Lord's crying and tears, Heb 5:7; **(2f)** consolation, Heb 6:18; **(2g)** Babylon, Rev 18:10; **(2h)** thunderings, Rev 19:6. It is translated "boisterous" in Mt 14:30. See: TDNT—3:397, 378; BAGD—383a; THAYER—309a.

2479. ἰσχύς {11x} **ischus,** *is-khoos'; from a der. of* ἴς **is** (*force; comp.* ἔσχον **ĕschŏn,** a form of *2192*); *forcefulness* (lit. or fig.):—strength {4x}, power {2x}, might {2x}, ability {1x}, mightily + 1722 {1x}, mighty {1x}.

Ischus, "to have, to hold" denotes "ability, force, strength"; **(1)** "strength" in 1 Pet 4:11. **(2)** In Eph 1:19 and 6:10, it is said of the strength of God bestowed upon believers, the phrase "the power of His might" indicating strength afforded by power. **(3)** In 2 Th 1:9, "the glory of His might" signifies the visible expression of the inherent personal power of the Lord Jesus.

It is said of angels in 2 Pet 2:11 (cf. Rev 18:2, "mightily"). **(4)** It is ascribed to God in Rev 5:12 and 7:12. **(5)** In Mk 12:30, 33, and Lk 10:27 it describes the full extent of the power wherewith we are to love God. Syn.: 970, 1411, 1753, 1849, 2904. See: TDNT—3:397, 378; BAGD—383c; THAYER—309b.

2480. ἰσχύω {29x} **ischuō**, *is-khoo'-o;* from *2479;* to *have* (or *exercise*) *force* (lit. or fig.):—can (could) {9x}, be able {6x}, avail {3x}, prevail {3x}, be whole {2x}, cannot + 3756 {1x}, can do {1x}, may {1x}, be good {1x}, be of strength {1x}, + much work {1x}.

(1) *Ischuo,* means "to be strong, to have efficacy, force or value" and is said of salt, negatively, "it is good for nothing": "Ye are the salt of the earth: but if the salt have lost his savour, wherewith shall it be salted? it is thenceforth good (*2480*) for nothing, but to be cast out, and to be trodden under foot of men" (Mt 5:13). **(2)** This word denotes to be strong, to prevail and indicates a more forceful strength or ability than *dunamai* (*1410*) and in Jas 5:16 it is rendered "availeth much" (i.e., "prevails greatly"). See: TDNT—3:397, 378; BAGD—383d; THAYER—309b.

2481. ἴσως {1x} **isōs**, *ee'-soce;* adv. from *2470; likely,* i.e. *perhaps:*—it may be {1x}. See: BAGD—384a; THAYER—309c.

2482. Ἰταλία {5x} **Italia**, *ee-tal-ee'-ah;* prob. of for. or.; *Italia,* a region of Europe:—Italy {5x}. See: BAGD—384a; THAYER—309c.

2483. Ἰταλικός {1x} **Italikŏs**, *ee-tal-ee-kos';* from *2482; Italic,* i.e. belonging to Italia:—Italian {1x}. See: BAGD—384a; THAYER—309c.

2484. Ἰτουραία {1x} **Itŏuraia**, *ee-too-rah'-yah;* of Heb. or. [3195]; *Ituræa* (i.e. *Jetur*), a region of Pal.:—Ituræa {1x}. See: BAGD—384a; THAYER—309c.

2485. ἰχθύδιον {2x} **ichthudiŏn**, *ikh-thoo'-dee-on;* dimin. from *2486;* a *petty fish:*—little fish {1x}, small fish {1x}. Cf. Mt 15:34; Mk 8:7. See: BAGD—384b; THAYER—309d.

2486. ἰχθύς {20x} **ichthus**, *ikh-thoos';* of uncert. aff.; a *fish:*—fish {20x}. *Ichthus* denotes "a fish," Mt 7:10; Mk 6:38, etc.; apart from the Gospels, only in 1 Cor 15:39. See: BAGD—384b; THAYER—309d.

2487. ἴχνος {3x} **ichnŏs**, *ikh'-nos;* from ἰκνέομαι **iknĕomai** (to *arrive;* comp. *2240);* a *track* (fig.):—step {3x}.

This word denotes a footstep, a track and is used metaphorically of the steps **(1)** of Christ's

conduct (1 Pet 2:21); **(2)** of Abraham's faith (Rom 4:12); **(3)** of identical conduct in carrying on the work of the gospel (2 Cor 12:18). See: TDNT—3:402, 379; BAGD—384b; THAYER—309d.

2488. Ἰωάθαμ {2x} **Iōatham**, *ee-o-ath'-am;* of Heb. or. [3147]; *Joatham* (i.e. *Jotham*), an Isr.:—Joatham {2x}. See: BAGD—384c; THAYER—309d.

2489. Ἰωάννα {2x} **Iōanna**, *ee-o-an'-nah;* fem. of the same as *2491; Joanna,* a Chr.:—Joanna {2x}. See: BAGD—384c; THAYER—309d.

2490. Ἰωαννᾶς {1x} **Iōannas**, *ee-o-an-nas';* a form of *2491; Joannas,* an Isr.:—Joannas {1x}. See: BAGD—384c; THAYER—309d.

2491. Ἰωάννης {133x} **Iōannēs**, *ee-o-an'-nace;* of Heb. or. [3110]; *Joannes* (i.e. *Jochanan*), the name of four Isr.:—John (the Baptist) {92x}, John (the apostle) {36x}, John (Mark) {4x}, John (the chief priest) {1x}. See: BAGD—384d; THAYER—309d.

2492. Ἰώβ {1x} **Iōb**, *ee-obe';* of Heb. or. [347]; *Job* (i.e. *Ijob*), a patriarch:—Job {1x}. See: BAGD—385a; THAYER—310c.

2493. Ἰωήλ {1x} **Iōēl**, *ee-o-ale';* of Heb. or. [3100]; *Joel,* an Isr.:—Joel {1x}. See: BAGD—385b; THAYER—310c.

2494. Ἰωνάν {1x} **Iōnan**, *ee-o-nan'* or Ἰωναμ **Ionam**, *ee-o-nam';* prob. for *2491* or *2495; Jonan,* an Isr.:—Jonan (Jonam) {1x}. See: BAGD—385b; THAYER—310c.

2495. Ἰωνᾶς {13x} **Iōnas**, *ee-o-nas';* of Heb. or. [3124]; *Jonas* (i.e. *Jonah*), the name of two Isr.:—Jonas (the prophet) {9x}, Jona (father of Peter) {4x}. See: TDNT—3:406, 380; BAGD—385b; THAYER—310d.

2496. Ἰωράμ {2x} **Iōram**, *ee-o-ram';* of Heb. or. [3141]; *Joram,* an Isr.:—Joram {2x}. See: BAGD—385c; THAYER—310d.

2497. Ἰωρείμ {1x} **Iōrĕim**, *ee-o-rime'* or Ἰωρίμ **Iōrim**, *ee-o-reem';* perh. for *2496; Jorim,* an Isr.:—Jorim {1x}. See: BAGD—385c; THAYER—310d.

2498. Ἰωσαφάτ {2x} **Iōsaphat**, *ee-o-saf-at';* of Heb. or. [3092]; *Josaphat* (i.e. *Jehoshaphat*), an Isr.:—Josaphat {2x}. See: BAGD—385c; THAYER—310d.

2499. Ἰωσή {1x} **Iōsē**, *ee-o-say';* gen. of *2500; Jose,* an Isr.:—Jose (son of Eliezer) {1x}. See: BAGD—385c; THAYER—310d.

2500. Ἰωσῆς {6x} **Iōsēs**, *ee-o-sace';* perh. for *2501; Joses,* the name of two Isr.:—

Joses (brother of James) {3x}, Joses (brother of Jesus) {2x}, Joses (Barnabas) {1x}. See: BAGD— 385d; THAYER—310d. comp. *2499.*

2501. Ἰωσήφ {35x} Iōsēph, *ee-o-safe';* of Heb. or. [3130]; *Joseph,* the name of seven Isr.:—Joseph (husband of Mary) {16x}, Joseph (son of Jacob) {9x}, Joseph of Arimathaea {6x}, Joseph (son of Judas) {1x}, Joseph of Barsabas {1x}, Joseph (son of Jonan) {1x}, Joseph (son of Mattathias) {1x}. See: BAGD— 385d; THAYER—311a.

2502. Ἰωσίας {2x} Iōsias, *ee-o-see'-as;* of Heb. or. [2977]; *Josias* (i.e. *Joshiah*), an Isr.:—Josias {2x}. See: BAGD—386a; THAYER—311c.

2503. ἰῶτα {1x} iōta, *ee-o'-tah;* of Heb. or. [the tenth letter of the Heb. alphabet]; *"iota,"* the name of the eighth letter of the Greek alphabet, put (fig.) for a very small part of anything:—jot {1x}.

Iota is from the Heb. *yod,* the smallest Hebrew letter, and is mentioned by the Lord in Mt 5:18, together with *keraia* (*2762*) a little horn, a tittle, the point or extremity which distinguishes certain Hebrew letters from others, to express the fact that not a single item of the Law will pass away or remain unfulfilled. See: BAGD—386a; THAYER—311c.

K

2504. κἀγώ {72x} kagō, *kag-o';* from *2532* and *1473* (so also the dat.)

κἀμοί kamŏi, *kam-oy';* and acc.

κἀμέ kamĕ, *kam-eh';* and (or *also, even,* etc.) *I,* (*to*) *me:*—and I {34x}, I also {17x}, so I {4x}, I {4x}, even I {3x}, me also {3x}, misc. {7x} = (even so) I (in like wise), both me. See: BAGD—386a; THAYER—311b.

2505. καθά {1x} katha, *kath-ah';* from *2596* and the neut. plur. of *3739; according to which* things, i.e. *just as:*—as {1x}. See: BAGD—386b; THAYER—311d.

2506. καθαίρεσις {3x} kathairĕsis, *kath-ah'-ee-res-is;* from *2507; demolition;* fig. *extinction:*—destruction {2x}, pulling down {1x}.

Kathairesis, "a taking down, a pulling down," is used three times in 2 Cor and is translated **(1)** "destruction" in 10:8; 13:10; and **(2)** "pulling down" in 10:4. See: TDNT—3:412, 381; BAGD— 386b; THAYER—311d.

2507. καθαιρέω {9x} kathairĕō, *kath-ahee-reh'-o;* from *2596* and *138* (incl. its alt.); to *lower* (or with violence) *demolish* (lit. or fig.):—take down {4x}, destroy

{2x}, put down {1x}, pull down {1x}, cast down {1x}.

Kathaireo, kata, "down," *haireo,* means **(1)** "to take, to cast down, demolish," in 2 Cor 10:5, of strongholds and imaginations; **(2)** and "He hath put down" the mighty in Lk 1:52. **(3)** It is translated "to destroy" in Acts 13:19; and in Acts 19:27, "should be destroyed." **(4)** It is translated "I will pull down" in Lk 12:18. **(5)** It denotes "to take down" (*kata*), besides its meaning of "putting down by force," was the technical term for the "removal" of the body after crucifixion, Mk 15:36, 46; Lk 23:53; Acts 13:29. See: TDNT—3:411, 380; BAGD—386c; THAYER— 311d.

2508. καθαίρω {2x} kathairō, *kath-ah'-ee-ro;* from *2513;* to *cleanse,* i.e. (spec.) to *prune;* fig. to *expiate:*—purge {2x}.

Kathairo means to cleanse, of filth impurity, **(1)** to prune trees and vines from useless shoots, Jn 15:2 "purgeth"; and **(2)** metaphorically purging worshipers from guilt, Heb 10:2. See: TDNT—3:413, 381; BAGD—386d; THAYER— 312a.

2509. καθάπερ {13x} kathapĕr, *kath-ap'-er;* from *2505* and *4007; exactly as:*—as {7x}, even as {5x}, as well as {1x}. See: BAGD—387a; THAYER—312a.

2510. καθάπτω {1x} kathaptō, *kath-ap'-to;* from *2596* and *680;* to *seize upon:*—fasten on {1x}.

Kathapto, "to fasten on, lay hold of, attack," is used of the serpent which fastened on Paul's hand, Acts 28:3. See: BAGD—387a; THAYER— 312b.

2511. καθαρίζω {30x} katharizō, *kath-ar-id'-zo;* from *2513;* to *cleanse* (lit. or fig.):—cleanse {16x}, make clean {5x}, be clean {3x}, purge {3x}, purify {3x}.

Katharizo signifies to **(1)** make clean, to cleanse **(1a)** literally, from **(1a1)** physical stains and dirt (Mt 23:25); **(1a2)** disease (Mt 8:2); **(1b)** in a moral sense, from **(1b1)** the defilement of sin (Acts 15:9; 2 Cor 7:1; Heb 9:14; Jas 4:8), **(1b2)** the guilt of sin (Eph 5:26; 1 Jn 1:7); **(2)** to pronounce clean in a Levitical sense (Mk 7:19; Acts 10:15; 11:9); **(3)** to consecrate by cleansings (Heb 9:22, 23; 10:2). Syn.: *1245, 2512, 2514.* See: TDNT—3:413, 381; BAGD—387b; THAYER— 312b.

2512. καθαρισμός {7x} katharismŏs, *kath-ar-is-mos';* from *2511;* a *washing* off, i.e. (cer.) *ablution,* (mor.) *expiation:*— cleansing {2x}, purifying {2x}, be purged {1x}, purge + *4060* {1x}, purification {1x}.

This word denotes "cleansing," **(1)** both the action and its results, in the Levitical sense,

Mk 1:44; Lk 2:22, "purification"; Lk 5:14, "cleansing"; Jn 2:6; 3:25, "purifying"; (2) in the moral sense, from sins, Heb 1:3; 2 Pet 1:9. See: TDNT—3:429, 381; BAGD—387d; THAYER—312c.

2513. **καθαρός** {28x} **katharŏs**, *kath-ar-os';* of uncert. aff.; *clean* (lit. or fig.):— clean {10x}, clear {1x}, pure {17x}.

Katharos means free from impure admixture, without blemish, spotless and is used **(1)** physically (Mt 23:26; 27:59); **(2)** figuratively, (Jn 13:10) where the Lord teaches that one who has been entirely cleansed needs not radical renewal, but only to be cleansed from every sin into which he may fall (Jn 15:3; Heb 10:22); **(3)** in a Levitical sense (Rom 14:20; Titus 1:15 – pure); **(4)** ethically, with the significance free from corrupt desire, from guilt (Mt 5:8; Jn 13:10–11; 1 Ti 1:5; 3:9); and **(5)** in a combined Levitical and ethical sense ceremonially (Lk 11:41). Syn.: *Eilikrines* (*1506*) refers to the Christian's freedom from falsehoods. *Katharos* refers to the Christian's freedom from the defilements of the flesh and the world. See: TDNT—3:413, 381; BAGD—388a; THAYER—312d.

2514. **καθαρότης** {1x} **katharŏtēs**, *kath-ar-ot'-ace;* from *2513; cleanness* (cer.):—purifying {1x}.

This word means "cleanness, purity," and is used in the Levitical sense in Heb 9:13. See: TDNT—3:413, 381; BAGD—388b; THAYER—313a.

2515. **καθέδρα** {3x} **kathĕdra**, *kath-ed'-rah;* from *2596* and the same as *1476;* a *bench* (lit. or fig.):—seat {3x}.

This word is used of the exalted seat occupied by men of eminent rank or influence. [cf. Eng. cathedral]. *Kathedra*, from *kata*, "down," and *hedra*, "a seat," denotes "a seat", Mt 21:12; Mk 11:15; of teachers, Mt 23:2. See: BAGD—388b; THAYER—313a.

2516. **καθέζομαι** {6x} **kathĕzŏmai**, *kath-ed'-zom-ahee;* from *2596* and the base of *1476;* to *sit down:*—sit {6x}.

Kathezomai, as a verb, means "to sit (down)": "In that same hour said Jesus to the multitudes, Are ye come out as against a thief with swords and staves for to take me? I sat daily (*kathezomai*) with you teaching in the temple, and ye laid no hold on me" (Mt 26:55; cf. Lk 2:46; Jn 4:6; 11:20; 20:12; Acts 6:15). Syn.: 339, 345, 347, 377, 1910, 2521, 2621, 2623, 2625, 4775, 4776, 4873. See: TDNT—3:440, 386; BAGD—388c; THAYER—313a.

2517. **καθεξῆς** {5x} **kathĕxēs**, *kath-ex-ace';* from *2596* and *1836; there-*

after, i.e. *consecutively;* as a noun (by ellip. of noun) a *subsequent* person or time:—in order {2x}, afterward {1x}, after {1x}, by order {1x}.

Kathexes means one after another, successively, in order, Lk 1:3; 8:1; Acts 3:24; 11:4; 18:23. See: BAGD—388d; THAYER—313a.

2518. **καθεύδω** {22x} **kathĕudō**, *kath-yoo'-do;* from *2596* and εὕδω **hĕudō** (to *sleep*); to lie *down* to *rest,* i.e. (by impl.) to *fall asleep* (lit. or fig.):—(be a-) sleep {22x}.

Katheudo means to go to sleep and is **(1)** chiefly used of natural sleep (1 Th 5:7); **(2)** figuratively of death: "He said unto them, Give place: for the maid is not dead, but sleepeth. And they laughed Him to scorn", (Mt 9:24; cf. Mk 5:39; Lk 8:52); **(3)** of carnal indifference to spiritual things on the part of believers (Eph 5:14; 1 Th 5:6, 10); **(4)** and in Mk 13:36 of a condition of insensibility to divine things involving conformity to the world. Syn.: 2837. See: TDNT—3:431, 384; BAGD—388d; THAYER—313b.

2519. **καθηγητής** {3x} **kathēgētēs**, *kath-ayg-ay-tace';* from a compound of *2596* and *2233;* a *guide,* i.e. (fig.) a *teacher:*—master {3x}.

This word is properly a guide and denotes a master, a teacher, one who can guide the learner (Mt 23:8, 10 twice). See: BAGD—388d; THAYER—313b.

2520. **καθήκω** {2x} **kathēkō**, *kath-ay'-ko;* from *2596* and *2240;* to *reach to,* i.e. (neut. of pres. act. part., fig. as adj.) *becoming:*—convenient {1x}, fit {1x}.

Katheko, "to be fitting, [not] convenient" is so translated **(1)** in Rom 1:28; "(not) convenient"; and **(2)** in Acts 22:22, "it is (not) fit." See: TDNT—3:437, 385; BAGD—389a; THAYER—313b.

2521. **κάθημαι** {89x} **kathēmai**, *kath'-ay-mahee;* from *2596;* and ἦμαι **hēmai** (to *sit;* akin to the base of *1476*); to *sit down;* fig. to *remain, reside:*—sit {82x}, sit down {3x}, sit by {2x}, be set down {1x}, dwell {1x}.

Kathemai, as a verb, is used **(1)** of the natural posture: "And as Jesus passed forth from thence, he saw a man, named Matthew, sitting at the receipt of custom: and He saith unto him, Follow Me. And he arose, and followed Him" (Mt 9:9, most frequently in the Apocalypse, some 32 times; frequently in the Gospels and Acts; elsewhere only in 1 Cor 14:30; Jas 2:3 [twice]; **(2)** and of Christ's position of authority on the throne of God: "If ye then be risen with Christ, seek those things which are above, where Christ sitteth on the right hand of God" (Col 3:1; cf. Heb 1:13; Mt 22:44; 26:64 and parallel passages in Mark and Luke, and Acts 2:34); **(3)** often as antecedent or successive to,

or accompanying, another act: "And Jesus departed from thence, and came nigh unto the sea of Galilee; and went up into a mountain, and sat down there" (Mt 15:29; 27:36; Mk 2:14; 4:1); **(4)** metaphorically in Mt 4:16: "The people which sat in (*kathemai*) darkness saw great light; and to them which sat (*kathemai*) in the region and shadow of death light is sprung up"; **(5)** of inhabiting a place (translated "dwell"): "For as a snare shall it come on all them that dwell on the face of the whole earth" (Lk 21:35; cf. Lk 1:79). Syn.: 339, 345, 347, 377, 1910, 2516, 2621, 2523, 2625, 4775, 4776, 4873. See: TDNT—3:440, 386; BAGD—389b; THAYER—313b.

2522. **καθημερινός** {1x} **kathēmĕrinŏs**, *kath-ay-mer-ee-nos'*; from *2596* and *2250; quotidian:*—daily {1x}.

This word means, lit., "according to" (*kata*) "the day" (*hemera*), "day by day, daily," Acts 6:1. See: BAGD—389d; THAYER—313d.

2523. **καθίζω** {48x} **kathizō**, *kath-id'-zo;* another (act.) form for *2516;* to *seat down,* i.e. *set* (fig. *appoint*); intr. to *sit* (down); fig. to *settle* (*hover, dwell*):—. sit {26x}, sit down {14x}, set {2x}, be set {2x}, be set down {2x}, continue {1x}, tarry {1x}.

Kathizo, as a verb, is used **(1)** transitively, "to make sit down": "Therefore being a prophet, and knowing that God had sworn with an oath to him [David], that of the fruit of his loins, according to the flesh, he would raise up Christ to sit on his throne" (Acts 2:30); **(2)** intransitively, "to sit down, was set": "And seeing the multitudes, He went up into a mountain: and when He was set, His disciples came unto Him" (Mt 5:1; 19:28; 20:21, 23; 23:2; 25:31; 26:36; Mk 11:2, 7; 12:41; Lk 14:28, 31; 16:6; Jn 19:13; Acts 2:3, of the tongues of fire; 8:31; 1 Cor 10:7; 2 Th 2:4, "he takes his seat" as, e.g., in Mk 16:19; Rev 3:21 [twice]). Syn.: 339, 345, 347, 377, 1910, 2516, 2521, 2621, 2625, 4775, 4776, 4873. See: TDNT—3:440, 386; BAGD—389d; THAYER—313d.

2524. **καθίημι** {4x} **kathiēmi**, *kath-ee'-ay-mee;* from *2596;* and ἵημι **hiēmi** (to *send*); to *lower:*—let down {4x}.

Kathiemi, "to send," or "let down" (*kata,* "down," *hiemi,* "to send"), is translated "to let down," with reference to **(1)** the paralytic in Lk 5:19; **(2)** Saul of Tarsus, Acts 9:25; **(3)** the great sheet in Peter's vision, 10:11 and 11:5. See: BAGD—390b; THAYER—314a.

2525. **καθίστημι** {22x} **kathistēmi**, *kath-is'-tay-mee;* from *2596* and *2476;* to *place down* (permanently), i.e. (fig.) to *designate, constitute, convoy:*—make {8x},

make ruler {6x}, ordain {3x}, be {2x}, appoint {1x}, conduct {1x}, set {1x}.

Kathistemi, as a verb, a strengthened form of *histemi* (*2476*), **(1)** usually signifies "to appoint a person to a position." **(2)** In this sense the verb is often translated "to make" or "to set," in appointing a person to a place of authority, **(2a)** a servant over a household: "Who then is a faithful and wise servant, whom his lord hath made ruler (*kathistemi*) over his household, to give them meat in due season?" (Mt 24:45; cf. 25:47; 25:21, 23; Lk 12:42, 44); **(2b)** a judge: "And he said unto him, Man, who made me a judge or a divider over you?" (Lk 12:14; cf. Acts 7:27, 35); **(2c)** a governor: "And delivered him (Joseph) out of all his afflictions, and gave him favour and wisdom in the sight of Pharaoh king of Egypt; and he made him governor over Egypt and all his house" (Acts 7:10); **(2d)** man by God over the work of His hands: "Thou madest him a little lower than the angels; thou crownedst him with glory and honour, and didst set him over the works of thy hands" (Heb 2:7).

(3) It is rendered "appoint," with reference to the so-called seven deacons in Acts 6:3: "Wherefore, brethren, look ye out among you seven men of honest report, full of the Holy Ghost and wisdom, whom we may appoint over this business." **(4)** Titus was to "ordain" elders in every city in Crete where there were churches: "For this cause left I thee in Crete, that thou shouldest set in order the things that are wanting, and ordain elders in every city, as I had appointed thee" (Titus 1:5). Not a formal ecclesiastical ordination is in view, but the "appointment," for the recognition of the churches, of those who had already been raised up and qualified by the Holy Spirit, and had given evidence of this in their life and service. **(5)** It is used of the priests of old: "For every high priest taken from among men is ordained (*kathistemi*) for men in things pertaining to God, that he may offer both gifts and sacrifices for sins" (Heb 5:1; cf. 7:28; 8:3). See: TDNT—3:444, 387; BAGD—390b; THAYER—314b.

2526. **καθό** {4x} **kathŏ**, *kath-o';* from *2596* and *3739; according to which* thing, i.e. *precisely as, in proportion as:*—according to {2x}, as {1x}, inasmuch as {1x}. See: BAGD—390d; THAYER—314c.

2526. **καθολικός** {2x} **kathŏlikŏs**, *kath-ol-ee-kos';* from *2527; universal:*—general {2x}. See: BAGD—390d; THAYER—314c.

2527. **καθόλου** {1x} **kathŏlŏu**, *kath-ol'-oo;* from *2596* and *3650; on the whole,* i.e. *entirely:*—at all {1x}.

This word means wholly, entirely, at all: "And they called them, and commanded them not to speak at all (*katholikos*) nor teach in the name of Jesus", Acts 4:18. See: BAGD—391a; THAYER—314c.

2528. καθοπλίζω {1x} **kathŏplizō**, *kath-op-lid'-zo;* from *2596;* and *3695;* to *equip fully* with armor:—arm {1x}.

Kathoplizo is an intensive form, "to furnish fully with arms," *kata*, "down," intensive, *hoplon,* "a weapon," Lk 11:21, lit., "a strong man fully armed." See: BAGD—391a; THAYER—314d.

2529. καθοράω {1x} **kathŏraō**, *kath-or-ah'-o;* from *2596* and *3708;* to *behold fully,* i.e. (fig.) *distinctly apprehend:—* clearly see {1x}.

This word literally means to look down, see from above, view from on high; and hence, to see thoroughly, perceive clearly, understand, Rom 1:20. See: TDNT—5:379, 706; BAGD—391a; THAYER—314d.

2530. καθότι {5x} **kathŏti**, *kath-ot'-ee;* from *2596;* and *3739* and *5100; according to which certain* thing, i.e. *as far* (or *inasmuch*) *as:*—because {2x}, forsomuch as {1x}, as {1x}, according as {1x}.

Kathoti, from *kata,* "according to," and *hoti,* "that," lit., **(1)** "because that," Lk 1:7; **(2)** "forsomuch as", Lk 19:9; **(3)** "because", Acts 2:24; **(4)** "as", Acts 2:45; and **(5)** "according as", Acts 4:35. See: BAGD—319b; THAYER—314d.

2531. καθώς {182x} **kathōs**, *kath-oce';* from *2596* and *5613; just* (or *inasmuch*) *as, that:*—as {138x}, even as {36x}, according as {4x}, when {1x}, according to {1x}, how {1x}, as well as + *2532* {1x}. See: BAGD—391b; THAYER—314d.

2532. καί {9280x} **kai**, *kahee;* appar. a primary particle, having a *copulative* and sometimes also a *cumulative* force; *and, also, even, so, then, too,* etc.; often used in connection (or composition) with other particles or small words:—and {8182x}, also {515x}, even {108x}, both {43x}, then {20x}, so {18x}, likewise {13x}, not tr. {354x}, vr and {1x}, misc. {46x} = but, for, if, indeed, moreover, or, that, therefore, when, yet. See: BAGD—391d; THAYER—315b.

2533. Καϊάφας {9x} **Kaïaphas**, *kah-ee-af'-as;* of Chald. or.; *the dell; Câaphas* (i.e. *Cajepha*), an Isr.:—Caiaphas {9x}. See: BAGD—393d; THAYER—317a.

2534. καίγε {1x} **kaigĕ**, *kah'-ee-gheh;* from *2532* and *1065; and at least* (or *even, indeed*):—and at least {1x}. See: BAGD—394a;153a; THAYER—317c.

2535. Κάϊν {3x} **Kaïn**, *kah'-in;* of Heb. or. [7014]; *Cân,* (i.e. *Cajin*), the son of Adam:—Cain {3x}. See: TDNT—1:6,*; BAGD—394a; THAYER—317c.

2536. Καϊνάν {2x} **Kaïnan**, *kah-ee-nan'* or

Καϊνάμ Kaïnam *kah-ee-nam';* of Heb. or. [7018]; *Cânan* (i.e. *Kenan*), the name of two patriarchs:—Cainan {2x}. See: BAGD—394a; THAYER—317d.

2537. καινός {44x} **kainŏs**, *kahee-nos';* of uncert. aff.; *new* (espec. in *freshness;* while *3501* is prop. so with respect to *age*):— new {44x}.

Kainos denotes **(1)** "new," of that which is unaccustomed or unused, not "new" in time, recent, but "new" as to form or quality, of different nature from what is contrasted as old. **(2)** The "new tongues," *kainos,* of Mk 16:17 are the "other tongues," *heteros,* of Acts 2:4. These languages, however, were "new" and "different," not in the sense that they had never been heard before, or that they were new to the hearers, for it is plain from v. 8 that this is not the case; they were new languages to the speakers, different from those in which they were accustomed to speak. **(3)** The new things that the gospel brings for present obedience and realization are: **(3a)** a new covenant, Mt 26:28; **(3b)** a new commandment, Jn 13:34; **(3c)** a new creative act, Gal 6:15; **(3d)** a new creation, 2 Cor 5:17; **(3e)** a new man, i.e., a new character of manhood, spiritual and moral, after the pattern of Christ, Eph 4:24; **(3f)** a new man, i.e., "the church which is His (Christ's) body," Eph 2:15.

(4) The new things that are to be received and enjoyed hereafter are: **(4a)** a new name, the believer's, Rev 2:17; **(4b)** a new name, the Lord's, Rev 3:12; **(4c)** a new song, Rev 5:9; **(4d)** a new heaven and a new earth, Rev 21:1; **(4e)** the new Jerusalem, Rev 3:12; 21:2; **(4f)** "And He that sitteth on the Throne said, Behold, I make all things new," Rev 21:5. Syn.: *Kainos* denotes new primarily in reference to quality, the fresh, unworn, a condition; whereas, *neos* (*3501*) denotes the new primarily in reference to time, the young, recent, appearing for the first time. See: TDNT—3:447, 388; BAGD—394a; THAYER—317d.

2538. καινότης {2x} **kainŏtēs**, *kahee-not'-ace;* from *2537; renewal* (fig.):— newness {2x}.

Kainotes, akin to *kainos,* is used in the phrases **(1)** "newness of life," Rom 6:4, i.e., life of a new quality; the believer, being a new creation (2 Cor 5:17), is to behave himself consistently with this in contrast to his former manner of life; **(2)** "newness of spirit," RV, Rom 7:6, said of the believer's manner of serving the

Lord. While the phrase stands for the new life of the quickened spirit of the believer, it is impossible to dissociate this (in an objective sense) from the operation of the Holy Spirit, by whose power the service is rendered. See: TDNT—3:450, 388; BAGD—394c; THAYER—318a.

2539. **καίπερ** {6x} **kaipĕr**, *kah'-ee-per;* from *2532* and *4007;* and *indeed,* i.e. *nevertheless* or *notwithstanding:*—and yet {1x}, although {5x}. See: BAGD—394c; THAYER—318a.

2540. **καιρός** {87x} **kairŏs**, *kahee-ros';* of uncert. aff.; an *occasion,* i.e. *set* or *proper* time:—time {64x}, season {13x}, opportunity {2x}, due time {2x}, always + 1722 + 3956 {2x}, not tr {1x}, a while {3x}.

Kairos, as a noun, means **(1)** primarily, "due measure, fitness, proportion," **(2)** is used in the NT to signify "a season, a time, a period" possessed of certain characteristics, **(3)** and is frequently rendered **(3a)** "time" or "times": "At that time Jesus answered and said, I thank thee, O Father, Lord of heaven and earth, because thou hast hid these things from the wise and prudent, and hast revealed them unto babes" (Mt 11:25; 12:1; 14:1; 21:34; Mk 11:13; Acts 3:19; 7:20; 17:26; Rom 3:26; 5:6; 9:9; 13:11; 1 Cor 7:5; Gal 4:10; 1 Th 2:17); **(3b)** literally, "for a season (of an hour)": "And now ye know what withholdeth that he might be revealed in his time [*kairos*]" (2 Th 2:6); **(3c)** "always" [lit. "at all seasons"]: "Praying always (*kairos*) with all prayer and supplication in the Spirit, and watching thereunto with all perseverance and supplication for all saints" (Eph 6:18); **(3d)** "in due times": "But hath in due times manifested his word through preaching, which is committed unto me according to the commandment of God our Saviour" (Titus 1:3).

(4) The characteristics of a period are exemplified in the use of the term with regard **(4a)** to harvest (Mt 13:30); **(4b)** reaping (Gal 6:9); **(4c)** punishment (Mt 8:29); **(4d)** discharging duties (Lk 12:42); **(4e)** opportunity for doing anything, whether **(4e1)** good (Mt 26:18; cf. Gal 6:10 ("opportunity"); Eph 5:16); or **(4e2)** evil (Rev 12:12); **(4f)** the fulfillment of prophecy (Lk 1:20; Acts 3:19; 1 Pet 1:11); **(4g)** a time suitable for a purpose (Lk 4:13, lit., "until a season"; cf. 2 Cor 6:2). Syn.: *Chronos* (*5550*) is simply time as such or the succession of moments together, length. *Kairos* is a favorable opportunity, time as it brings forth its several events. See also: 171, 2122, 3641, 4340, 5550, 5610. See: TDNT—3:455, 389; BAGD—394c; THAYER—318b.

2541. **Καῖσαρ** {30x} **Kaisar**, *kah'-ee-sar;* of Lat. or.; *Cæsar,* a title of the Rom. emperor:—Cæsar {30x}. See: BAGD—395d; THAYER—319c.

2542. **Καισάρεια** {17x} **Kaisarĕia**, *kahee-sar'-i-a;* from *2541; Cæsaria,* the name of two places in Pal.:—Caesarea (of Palestine) {15x}, Caesarea (Philippi) {2x}. See: BAGD—396a; THAYER—319b.

2543. **καίτοι** {1x} **kaitŏi**, *kah'-ee-toy;* from *2532* and *5104; and yet,* i.e. *nevertheless:*—although {1x}. See: BAGD—396a; THAYER—319c.

2544. **καίτοιγε** {3x} **kaitŏigĕ**, *kah'-ee-toyg-eh;* from *2543* and *1065; and yet indeed,* i.e. *although really:*—nevertheless {1x}, though {2x}. See: BAGD—396b; THAYER—319c.

2545. **καίω** {12x} **kaiō**, *kah'-yo;* appar. a primary verb; to *set on fire,* i.e. *kindle* or (by impl.) *consume:*—burn {10x}, did burn + 2258 {1x}, light {1x}.

Kaio, "to set fire to, to light"; **(1)** in the passive voice, "to be lighted, to burn," Mt 5:15; Jn 15:6; 1 Cor 13:3; Heb 12:18; Rev 4:5; 8:8, 10; 19:20; 21:8; **(2)** is used metaphorically of the heart, Lk 24:32; **(3)** of spiritual light, Lk 12:35; Jn 5:35; **(4)** it is translated "do (men) light" in Mt 5:15. See: TDNT—3:464, 390; BAGD—396b; THAYER—319c.

2546. **κἀκεῖ** {11x} **kakĕi**, *kak-i';* from *2532* and *1563; likewise in that place:*—and there {9x}, there also {1x}, thither also {1x}. See: BAGD—396c; THAYER—319d.

2547. **κἀκεῖθεν** {9x} **kakĕithĕn**, *kak-i'-then;* from *2532* and *1564; likewise from that place* (or *time*):—and from thence {5x}, and thence {2x}, and afterward {1x}, thence also {1x}. See: BAGD—396d; THAYER—319d.

2548. **κἀκεῖνος** {23x} **kakĕinŏs**, *kak-i'-nos;* from *2532* and *1565; likewise that* (or *those*):—and he {4x}, and they {3x}, he also {3x}, and them {2x}, and the other {2x}, and him {2x}, they also {2x}, him also {1x}, misc. {4x}. See: BAGD—396d; THAYER—319d.

2549. **κακία** {11x} **kakia**, *kak-ee'-ah;* from *2556; badness,* i.e. (subj.) *depravity,* or (act.) *malignity,* or (pass.) *trouble:*—malice {6x}, maliciousness {2x}, evil {1x}, wickedness {1x}, naughtiness {1x}.

This word basically means badness in quality, an evil mindset, and works itself out **(1)** in malignity, malice [the shrewd and deceitful calculation of doing harm], ill-will, desire to injure; **(2)** wickedness, depravity that is not ashamed to break laws; and **(3)** evil, trouble; it denotes **(4)** "wickedness, depravity, malignity,"

e.g., Acts 8:22, "wickedness"; **(4a)** Rom 1:29, "maliciousness"; **(4b)** in Jas 1:21, "naughtiness"; **(4c)** "the evil of trouble, affliction," Mt 6:34, only, and here alone translated "evil." **(5)** "Badness in quality" (the opposite of *arete*, "excellence"), "the vicious character generally" is also translated "malice" in 1 Cor 5:8; 14:20; Eph 4:31; Col 3:8; Titus 3:3; 1 Pet 2:1; 1 Pet 2:16. Syn.: 4190, 5337. See: TDNT—3:482, 391; BAGD—397a; THAYER—320a.

2550. κακοήθεια {1x} **kakŏēthĕia**, *kak-ŏē-ay'-thi-ah;* from a compound of 2556 and 2239; *bad character,* i.e. (spec.) *mischievousness:*—malignity {1x}.

Lit., this word means bad manner or character; hence, an evil disposition that tends to put the worst construction on everything, malice, malevolence, craftiness (Rom 1:29). This *kakoetheia,* the evil that we find in ourselves, makes us ready to suspect that evil exists in others. See: TDNT—3:485, 391; BAGD—397b; THAYER—320a.

2551. κακολογέω {4x} **kakŏlŏgĕō**, *kak-ol-og-eh'-o;* from a compound of 2556 and 3056; *to revile:*—curse {2x}, speak evil of {2x}.

Kakologeo, as a verb, means "to speak evil" and is translated **(1)** "to curse": "For God commanded, saying, Honour thy father and mother: and, He that curseth father or mother, let him die the death" (Mt 15:4; cf. Mk 7:10); and **(2)** "to speak evil of father and mother," not necessarily "to curse," is what the Lord intended; Mk 9:39 and Acts 19:9. Syn.: 331, 332, 685, 1944, 2652, 2653, 2671, 2672.See: TDNT—3:468, 391; BAGD—397b; THAYER—320a.

2552. κακοπάθεια {1x} **kakŏpathĕia**, *kak-op-ath'-i-ah;* from a compound of 2556 and 3806; *hardship:*—suffering affliction {1x}.

This word, from *kakos,* "evil," and *pascho,* "to suffer" is rendered "suffering affliction" in Jas 5:10. See: TDNT—5:936, 798; BAGD—397b; THAYER—320b.

2553. κακοπαθέω {4x} **kakŏpathĕō**, *kak-op-ath-eh'-o;* from the same as 2552; *to undergo hardship:*—endure hardness {1x}, suffer trouble {1x}, endure affliction {1x}, be afflicted {1x}.

This word from *kakos,* "evil," *pathos,* "suffering," signifies "to suffer hardship." It is translated **(1)** "endure hardness", 2 Ti 2:3; **(2)** "suffer trouble", 2 Ti 2:9; **(3)** "endure afflictions", 2 Ti 4:5; and **(4)** "afflicted", Jas 5:13. See: TDNT—5:936, 798; BAGD—397c; THAYER—320b.

2554. κακοποιέω {4x} **kakŏpŏiĕō**, *kak-op-oy-eh'-o;* from 2555; *to be a bad-doer,* i.e. (obj.) to *injure,* or (gen.) to *sin:*—do evil {3x}, evil doing {1x}.

This word signifies **(1)** "to do evil", Mk 3:4; Lk 6:9; 3 Jn 11, "doeth evil"; and **(2)** in 1 Pet 3:17, "evil doing." See: TDNT—3:485, 391; BAGD—397c; THAYER—320b.

2555. κακοποιός {5x} **kakŏpŏiŏs**, *kak-op-oy-os';* from 2556 and 4160; a *bad-doer;* (spec.) a *criminal:*—evil-doer {4x}, malefactor {1x}.

Kakopoios, properly the masculine gender of the adjective, denotes an **(1)** "evil-doer" (*kakon,* "evil," *poieo,* "to do"), 1 Pet 2:12, 14; 3:16; 4:15; and **(2)** "malefactor" in Jn 18:30. See: TDNT—3:485, 391; BAGD—397c; THAYER—320c.

2556. κακός {51x} **kakŏs**, *kak-os';* appar. a primary word; *worthless* (*intrinsically,* such; whereas *4190* prop. refers to *effects*), i.e. (subj.) *depraved,* or (obj.) *injurious:*—evil {40x}, evil things {3x}, harm {2x}, that which is evil + 3458 {2x}, wicked {1x}, ill {1x}, bad {1x}, noisome {1x}.

Kakos indicates the lack in a person or thing of those qualities which should be possessed and means bad in character **(1)** morally, by way of thinking, feeling or acting (Mk 7:21; 1 Cor 15:33; Col 3:5; 1 Ti 6:10; 1 Pet 3:9); **(2)** in the sense of what is injurious or baneful: **(2a)** the tongue as a restless evil (Jas 3:8); **(2b)** evil beasts (Titus 1:12); **(3)** harm (Acts 16:28). **(4)** *Kakon,* the neuter adjective, is used with the article, as a noun, e.g., Acts 23:9; Rom 7:21; Heb 5:14; in the plural, "evil things," e.g., 1 Cor 10:6; 1 Ti 6:10, "all kinds of evil."

(5) It stands for "whatever is evil in character, base," its use broadly divided as follows: **(5a)** of what is morally or ethically "evil," whether **(5b)** of persons, e.g., Mt 21:41; 24:48; Phil 3:2; Rev 2:2, or **(5c)** qualities, emotions, passions, deeds, e.g., Mk 7:21; Jn 18:23, 30; Rom 1:30; 3:8; 7:19, 21; 13:4; 14:20; 16:19; 1 Cor 13:5; 2 Cor 13:7; 1 Th 5:15; 1 Ti 6:10; 2 Ti 4:14; 1 Pet 3:9, 12; **(5d)** of what is injurious, destructive, baneful, pernicious, e.g., Lk 16:25; Acts 16:28; 28:5; Titus 1:12; Jas 3:8; Rev 16:2. Syn.: *Kakos,* in distinction (wherever the distinction is observable) from *poneros* (*4190*), which indicates "what is evil in influence and effect, malignant." *Kakos* is the wider term and often covers the meaning of *poneros. Kakos* is antithetic to *kalos* (*2570*), "fair, advisable, good in character," and to *agathos* (*18*), "beneficial, useful, good in act"; hence it denotes what is useless, incapable, bad; *poneros* is essentially antithetic to *chrestos* (*5543*), "kind, gracious, serviceable"; hence it

denotes what is destructive, injurious, evil. As evidence that *poneros* and *kakos* have much in common, though still not interchangeable, each is used of thoughts, cf. Mt 15:19 with Mk 7:21; of speech, Mt 5:11 with 1 Pet 3:10; of actions, 2 Ti 4:18 with 1 Th 5:15; of man, Mt 18:32 with 24:48. See also: 2554, 2559, 2560. See: TDNT—3:469, 391; BAGD—397d; THAYER—320c.

2557. κακοῦργος {4x} **kakŏurgŏs,** *kak-oor'- gos;* from 2556 and the base of 2041; a *wrong-doer,* i.e. *criminal:*—evil-doer {1x}, malefactor {3x}.

Kakourgos, an adjective, lit., "evil-working" (*kakos,* "evil," *ergon,* "work"), is used as a noun, translated **(1)** "malefactor(-s)" in Lk 23:32, 33, 39, and **(2)** in 2 Ti 2:9, "evil doer." See: TDNT—3:484, 391; BAGD—398b; THAYER—320d.

2558. κακουχέω {2x} **kakŏuchĕō,** *kak-oo- kheh'-o;* from a presumed compound of 2556 and 2192; to oppress, plague, *maltreat:*—which suffer adversity {1x}, torment {1x}.

Kakoucheo, from *kakos,* "evil," and *echo,* "to have," signifies, in the passive voice, **(1)** "to suffer ill, to be maltreated, tormented," Heb 11:37, "tormented"; and **(2)** Heb 13:3, "suffer adversity." See: BAGD—398b; THAYER—320d.

2559. κακόω {6x} **kakŏō,** *kak-ŏ'-o;* from 2556; to *injure;* fig. to *exasperate:*— make evil affected {1x}, entreat evil {2x}, harm {1x}, hurt {1x}, vex {1x}.

Kakoo, as a verb, means "to ill-treat," and is rendered "to entreat evil" in Acts 7:6, 19; "made (them) evil affected," 14:2. See: TDNT—3:484, 391; BAGD—398b; THAYER—320d.

2560. κακῶς {16x} **kakōs,** *kak-oce';* from 2556; *badly* (phys. or mor.):—be sick + 2192 {7x}, be diseased + 2192 {2x}, evil {2x}, grievously {1x}, sore {1x}, miserable {1x}, amiss {1x}, sick people + 2192 {1x}.

Kakos, "badly, evilly," is used in the physical sense, **(1)** "to be sick," e.g., Mt 4:24; Mk 1:32, 34; Lk 5:31. **(2)** In Mt 21:41 this adverb is used with the adjective, "He will miserably destroy those miserable men," more lit., "He will evilly destroy those men (evil as they are)," with stress on the adjective; **(3)** in the moral sense, "to speak evilly," Jn 18:23; Acts 23:5. It is translated **(4)** "amiss" "evil," is translated "amiss, evilly" in Jas 4:3. **(5)** It denotes "badly, ill," is translated "grievously (vexed)," in Mt 15:22. See: TDNT—4:1091,*; BAGD—398c; THAYER—321a.

2561. κάκωσις {1x} **kakōsis,** *kak'-o-sis;* from 2559; *maltreatment:*—affliction {1x}. See: BAGD—398c; THAYER—321a.

2562. καλάμη {1x} **kalamē,** *kal-am'-ay;* fem. of 2563; a *stalk* of grain after the ears have been cut off, i.e. (collect.) *stubble:*— stubble {1x}. See: BAGD—398c; THAYER—321a.

2563. κάλαμος {12x} **kalamŏs,** *kal'-am-os;* or uncert. aff.; a *reed* (the plant or its stem, or that of a similar plant); by impl. a *pen:*—pen {1x}, reed {11x}.

This word denotes **(1)** "the reed" mentioned in Mt 11:7; 12:20; Lk 7:24; the same as the Heb., *qaneh* (among the various reeds in the OT), e.g., Is 42:3, from which Mt 12:20 is quoted (cf. Job 40:21; Eze 29:6, "a reed with jointed, hollow stalk"); **(2)** "a reed staff, staff," Mt 27:29, 30, 48; Mk 15:19; **(3)** "a measuring reed or rod," Rev 11:1; 21:15, 16; **(4)** "a writing reed, a pen," 3 Jn 13. See: BAGD—398d; THAYER—321a.

2564. καλέω {146x} **kalĕō,** *kal-eh'-o;* akin to the base of 2753; to "call" (prop. aloud, but used in a variety of applications, dir. or otherwise):—call {125x}, bid {16x}, be so named {1x}, named + 3686 {1x}, misc. {3x} = (whose, whose sur-) name (was [called]).

Kaleo is used **(1)** with a personal object, **(1a)** "to call anyone, summon," e.g., Mt 20:8; 25:14; **(1b)** it is used particularly of the divine call to partake of the blessings of redemption, e.g., Rom 8:30; 1 Cor 1:9; 1 Th 2:12; Heb 9:15; **(2)** of nomenclature or vocation, "to call by a name, to name"; in the passive voice, "to be called by a name, to bear a name." Thus it suggests either vocation or destination; the context determines which, e.g., Rom 9:25–26; **(3)** it is also translated "surname," in Acts 15:37. **(4)** This word means to call and often means to bid in the sense of invite (Mt 22:3–4, 8, 9; Lk 14:7–10, 13). Syn.: *Boao* (994) means to cry out as a manifestation of feeling, esp. a cry for help; *kaleo* (2564) to cry out for a purpose; *krazo* (2896) means to cry out harshly, often of inarticulate and brutish sound; and *kraugazo* (2905), an intensive of (2896) and denotes to cry coarsely, in contempt. (2564) suggests intelligence; (994) sensibilities; and (2896) instincts. See: TDNT—3:487, 394; BAGD—398d; THAYER—321b.

2565. καλλιέλαιος {1x} **kalliĕlaiŏs,** *kal-le- el'-ah-yos;* from the base of 2566 and 1636; a *cultivated olive* tree, i.e. a *domesticated* or *improved* one:—good olive tree {1x}.

Kallielaios is the garden olive as opposed to the wild olive, Rom 11:24. See: BAGD—400a; THAYER—322a.

2566. **καλλιον** {1x} **kalliŏn,** *kal-lee'-on;* neut. of the (irreg.) comp. of *2570;* (adv.) *better* than many:—very well {1x}.

Being in the comparative form it is to be understood as "better." See: BAGD—400a; THAYER—322a.

2567. **καλοδιδάσκαλος** {1x} **kalŏdidaskalŏs,** *kal-od-id-as'-kal-os;* from *2570* and *1320;* a *teacher of* the *right:*—teacher of good things {1x}. See: TDNT—2:159, 161; BAGD—400a; THAYER—322b.

2568. **Καλοὶ Λιμένες** {1x} **Kalŏi Limĕnĕs,** *kal-oy' lee-men'-es;* plur. of *2570* and *3040; Good Harbors,* i.e. *Fairhaven,* a bay of Crete:—Fair Havens {1x}. See: BAGD—400a; THAYER—322a.

2569. **καλοποιέω** {1x} **kalŏpŏiĕō,** *kal-op-oy-eh'-o;* from *2570* and *4160;* to *do well,* i.e. live virtuously:—well doing {1x}.

Kalopoieo, "to do well, excellently, act honorably, act uprightly" (*kalos,* "good," *poieo,* "to do"), occurs in 2 Th 3:13. See: BAGD—400b; THAYER—322b.

2570. **καλός** {102x} **kalŏs,** *kal-os';* of uncert. aff.; prop. *beautiful,* but chiefly (fig.) *good* (lit. or mor.), i.e. *valuable* or *virtuous* (for *appearance* or *use,* and thus distinguished from *18,* which is prop. *intrinsic):*—good {83x}, better {7x}, honest {5x}, meet {2x}, goodly {2x}, fair {1x}, well {1x}, worthy {1x}.

This word denotes something is **(1)** beautiful, handsome to look at, shapely, magnificent; **(2)** good, excellent in its nature and characteristics, and therefore well adapted to its ends, praiseworthy, noble; **(3)** beautiful by reason of purity of heart and life, and hence praiseworthy; morally good, noble; or **(4)** honourable, conferring honour which effects the mind agreeably, comforting and confirming.

Definition: *Kalos,* as an adjective, denotes that which is intrinsically "good," and so, "goodly, fair, beautiful," as **(1)** of that which is well adapted to its circumstances or ends: **(1a)** fruit: "And now also the axe is laid unto the root of the trees: therefore every tree which bringeth not forth good fruit is hewn down, and cast into the fire" (Mt 3:10); **(1b)** a tree: "Either make the tree good, and his fruit good; or else make the tree corrupt, and his fruit corrupt: for the tree is known by his fruit" (Mt 12:33); **(1c)** ground: "But other fell into good ground, and brought forth fruit, some an hundredfold, some sixtyfold, some thirtyfold" (Mt 13:8; cf. vs 23); **(1d)** fish: "Which, when it was full, they drew to shore, and sat down, and gathered the good into vessels, but cast the bad away" (Mt 13:48); **(1e)** the Law: "If then I do that which I would not, I consent unto the Law

that it is good" (Rom 7:16; cf. 1 Ti 1:8); **(1f)** every creature of God: "For every creature of God is good, and nothing to be refused, if it be received with thanksgiving" (1 Ti 4:4); **(1g)** a faithful minister of Christ and the doctrine he teaches: "If thou put the brethren in remembrance of these things, thou shalt be a good minister of Jesus Christ, nourished up in the words of faith and of good doctrine, whereunto thou hast attained" (1 Ti 4:6);

(2) of that which is ethically good, right, noble, honorable: "But it is good to be zealously affected always in a good thing, and not only when I am present with you" (Gal 4:18; cf. 1 Ti 5:10, 25; 6:18; Titus 2:7, 14; 3:8, 14). **(3)** Christians are to **(3a)** "take thought for things honest" (*kalos*): "Providing for honest things, not only in the sight of the Lord, but also in the sight of men" (2 Cor 8:21); **(3b)** not to be weary in well doing (Gal 6:9); **(3c)** to hold fast "that which is good" (1 Th 5:21); **(3d)** to be zealous of good works (Titus 2:14); **(3d1)** to maintain them (Titus 3:8); **(3d2)** to provoke to them (Heb 10:24); **(3d3)** to bear testimony by them (1 Pet 2:12).

Syn.: **(A)** *Kalos* and *agathos* (*18*) occur together in Lk 8:15: "But that on the good (*kalos*) ground are they, which in an honest (*kalos*) and good (*agathos*) heart, having heard the word, keep it, and bring forth fruit with patience." An "honest" (*kalos*) heart is one that has a right attitude before God and a "good" (*agathos*) heart is one that, instead of working ill to a neighbor, acts beneficially towards him. **(B)** In Rom 7:18, "in me . . . dwelleth no good thing" (*agathos*) signifies that in him is nothing capable of doing "good," and hence he lacks the power "to do that which is good" (*kalos*). **(C)** In 1 Th 5:15, "follow after that which is good" (*agathos*), the "good" is that which is beneficial; in v. 21, "hold fast that which is good (*kalos*)," the "good" describes the intrinsic value of the teaching. See also: 5543. See: TDNT—3:536, 402; BAGD—400b; THAYER—322b.

2571. **κάλυμμα** {4x} **kaluma,** *kal'-oo-mah;* from *2572;* a *cover,* i.e. *vail:*—vail {4x}.

Kaluma, "a covering," is used **(1)** of the "vail" which Moses put over his face when descending Mount Sinai, thus preventing Israel from beholding the glory, 2 Cor 3:13; **(2)** metaphorically of the spiritually darkened vision suffered retributively by Israel, until the conversion of the nation to their Messiah takes place, 2 Cor 3:14, 15, 16. See: TDNT—3:558, 405; BAGD—400d; THAYER—322d.

2572. **καλύπτω** {8x} **kaluptō,** *kal-oop'-to;* akin to *2813* and *2928;* to *cover* up (lit. or fig.):—cover {5x}, hide {3x}.

Kalupto signifies **(1)** "to cover," Mt 8:24; 10:26; Lk 8:16; 23:30; 1 Pet 4:8; **(2)** to hide in Jas 5:20; 2 Cor 4:3 (twice). See: TDNT—3:536, 405; BAGD—401a; THAYER—323a.

2573. καλῶς {37x} **kalōs**, *kal-oce';* adv. from *2570; well* (usually mor.):—well {30x}, good {2x}, full well {1x}, very well {1x}, misc. {3x} = in a good place {1x}, honestly {1x}, recover {1x}.

Kalos, "finely", is usually translated **(1)** "well," indicating what is done rightly, in the Epistles it is most frequent in 1 Ti (3:4, 12, 13; 5:17); **(2)** twice it is used as an exclamation of approval, Mk 12:32; Rom 11:20. See: BAGD—401b; THAYER—323a.

2574. κάμηλος {6x} **kamēlŏs**, *kam'-ay-los;* of Heb. or. [1581]; a *"camel"*:—camel {6x}.

Kamelos, from a Hebrew word signifying "a bearer, carrier," is used in proverbial statements to indicate **(1)** "something almost or altogether impossible," Mt 19:24; Mk 10:25; Lk 18:25; and **(2)** "the acts of a person who is careful not to sin in trivial details, but pays no heed to more important matters," Mt 23:24; **(3)** its hair being used for clothing, Mt 3:4; Mk 1:7. See: TDNT—3:592, 413; BAGD—401c; THAYER—323b.

2575. κάμινος {4x} **kaminŏs**, *kam'-ee-nos;* prob. from *2545;* a *furnace:*—furnace {4x}.

Kaminos, "an oven, furnace, kiln" (whence Lat. *caminus*, Eng., chimney), used for smelting, or for burning earthenware, occurs in Mt 13:42, 50; Rev 1:15; 9:2. See: BAGD—401d; THAYER—323c.

2576. καμμύω {2x} **kammuō**, *kam-moo'-o;* from a compound of *2596* and the base of *3466;* to *shut down,* i.e. *close* the eyes:—close {2x}.

This word denotes "to close down"; hence, "to shut the eyes," Mt 13:15 and Acts 28:27, in each place of the obstinacy of Jews in their opposition to the gospel. See: BAGD—402a; THAYER—323c.

2577. κάμνω {3x} **kamnō**, *kam'-no;* appar. a primary verb; prop. to *toil,* i.e. (by impl.) to *tire* (fig. *faint, sicken*):—faint {1x}, sick {1x}, be wearied {1x}.

This word primarily signifies to work; then, as the effect of continued labor, to be weary. It is used **(1)** in Heb 12:3 of becoming weary; **(2)** in Jas 5:15 of sickness; and **(3)** in Rev 2:3 of fainting. See: BAGD—402a; THAYER—323c.

2578. κάμπτω {4x} **kamptō**, *kamp'-to;* appar. a primary verb; to *bend:*—bow {4x}.

Kampto means to bend, bow the knee (the knees) or one's self and is used of worshipers who bend in honour of one in religious veneration (Rom 11:4; 14:11; Eph 3:14; Phil 2:10). See: TDNT—3:594, 413; BAGD—402b; THAYER—323d.

2579. κἄν {13x} **kan**, *kan;* from *2532* and *1437; and* (or *even*) *if:*—though {4x}, and if {3x}, if but {2x}, also if {1x}, at the least {1x}, and if so much as {1x}, yet {1x}. See: BAGD—402c; THAYER—323d.

2580. Κανᾶ {4x} **Kana**, *kan-ah';* of Heb. or. [comp. 7071]; *Cana,* a place in Pal.:—Cana {4x}. See: BAGD—402c; THAYER—324a.

2581. Κανανίτης {2x} **Kananitēs**, *kan-an-ee'-tace;* of Chald. or. [comp. 7067]; *zealous; Cananitës,* an epithet:—Canaanite {2x}. See: BAGD—402d; THAYER—324a, 324b.

2582. Κανδάκη {1x} **Kandakē**, *kan-dak'-ay;* of for. or.; *Candacë,* an Eg. queen:—Candace {1x}. See: BAGD—402d; THAYER—324b.

2583. κανών {5x} **kanōn**, *kan-ohn';* from κάνη **kanē** (a straight *reed,* i.e. *rod*); a *rule* ("canon"), i.e. (fig.) a *standard* (of faith and practice); by impl. a *boundary,* i.e. (fig.) a *sphere* (of activity):—line {4x}, rule {1x}.

Kanon **(1)** originally denoted a straight rod used as a ruler or measuring instrument, or, in rare instances, the beam of a balance; **(2)** the secondary notion being either **(2a)** of keeping anything straight, as of a rod used in weaving, or **(2b)** of testing straightness, as a carpenter's rule; hence, **(2c)** its metaphorical use to express what serves to measure or determine anything. **(3)** In general the word thus came to serve for anything regulating the actions of men, as a standard or principle, Phil 3:16. **(3a)** In Gal 6:16 are those who make what is stated in vv. 14 and 15 their guiding line in the matter of salvation through faith in Christ alone, apart from works, whether following the principle themselves or teaching it to others. **(3b)** In 2 Cor 10:13, 15, 16, province signifies the limits of the responsibility in gospel service as measured and appointed by God. See: TDNT—3:596, 414; BAGD—403a; THAYER—324b.

2584. Καπερναούμ {16x} **Kapĕrnaŏum**, *kap-er-nah-oom';* of Heb. or. [prob. 3723 and 5151]; *Capernaüm* (i.e. *Capha-nachum*), a place in Pal.:—Capernaum {16x}. See: BAGD—403a; 426b; THAYER—324c.

2585. καπηλεύω {1x} **kapēlĕuō**, *kap-ale-yoo'-o;* from κάπηλος **kapēlŏs** (a

huckster); to *retail,* i.e. (by impl.) to *adulterate* (fig.):—corrupt {1x}.

This word means to be a retailer, to peddle, to hucksterize; hence, intentionally to get base gain by dealing in anything, to do anything for sordid personal advantage (2 Cor 2:17). Syn.: 1389. See: TDNT—3:603, 415; BAGD—403a; THAYER—324d.

2586. **καπνός** {13x} **kapnŏs,** *kap-nos';* of uncert. aff.; *smoke:*—smoke {13x}.

Kapnos, "smoke," occurs in Acts 2:19 and 12 times in the Apocalypse. See: BAGD—403b; THAYER—325a.

2587. **Καππαδοκία** {2x} **Kappadŏkia,** *kappad-ok-ee'-ah;* of for. or.; *Cappadocia,* a region of Asia Minor:—Cappadocia {2x}. See: BAGD—403b; THAYER—325a.

2588. **καρδία** {160x} **kardia,** *kar-dee'-ah;* prol. from a primary κάρ **kar** (Lat. *cor,* "*heart*"); the *heart,* i.e. (fig.) the *thoughts* or *feelings* (*mind*); also (by anal.) the *middle:*—heart {159x}, broken hearted + 4937 {1x}.

Kardia (cf. Eng., "cardiac") is the heart, **(1)** the chief organ of physical life, and occupies the most important place in the human system. **(2)** By an easy transition the word came to stand for man's entire mental and moral activity, both the rational and the emotional elements. **(3)** It is used figuratively for the hidden springs of the personal life: **(3a)** the seat of total depravity, the principle in the center of man's inward life that defiles all he does (Mt 15:19, 20; and **(3b)** it is the sphere of divine influence (Rom 2:15; Acts 15:9; "the hidden man," 1 Pet 3:4, the real man). It represents the true character but conceals it. **(4)** It denotes **(4a)** the seat of physical life (Acts 14:17; Jas 5:5); **(4b)** the seat of moral nature and spiritual life: **(4b1)** the seat of grief (Jn 14:1; Rom 9:2; 2 Cor 2:4); **(4b2)** joy (Jn 16:22; Eph 5:19); **(4b3)** the desires (Mt 5:28; 2 Pet 2:14); **(4b4)** the affections (Lk 24:32; Acts 21:13); **(4b5)** the perceptions (Jn 12:40; Eph 4:18); **(4b6)** the thoughts (Mt 9:4; Heb 4:12); **(4b7)** the understanding (Mt 13:15; Rom 1:21); **(4b8)** the reasoning powers (Mk 2:6; Lk 24:38); **(4b9)** the imagination (Lk 1:51); **(4b10)** conscience (Acts 2:37; 1 Jn 3:20); **(4b11)** the intentions (Heb 4:12, cf. 1 Pet 4:1); **(4b12)** purpose (Acts 11:23; 2 Cor 9:7); **(4b13)** the will (Rom 6:17; Col 3:15); and **(4b14)** faith (Mk 11:23; Rom 10:10; Heb 3:12). See: TDNT—3:605, 415; BAGD—403b; THAYER—325a.

2589. **καρδιογνώστης** {2x} **kardiŏgnōstēs,** *kar-dee-og-noce'-tace;* from *2588* and *1097;* a *heart-knower:*—which knowest the hearts {2x}.

Kardiognostes, "a knower of hearts" (*kardia*

and *ginosko,* "to know"), is used in Acts 1:24; 15:8. See: TDNT—3:613, 415; BAGD—404c; THAYER—326b.

2590. **καρπός** {66x} **karpŏs,** *kar-pos';* prob. from the base of *726; fruit* (as *plucked*), lit. or fig.:—fruit {66x}.

Karpos, as a noun, means "fruit" and is used **(1)** of the fruit of trees, fields, the earth, that which is produced by the inherent energy of a living organism (Mt 7:17; Jas 5:7, 18; **(2)** plural (Lk 12:17; 2 Ti 2:6; **(3)** of the human body: "And she spake out with a loud voice, and said, Blessed art thou among women, and blessed is the fruit of thy womb" Lk 1:42; Acts 2:30); **(4)** metaphorically, **(4a)** of works or deeds, "fruit" being the visible expression of power working inwardly and invisibly, the character of the "fruit" being evidence of the character of the power producing it: "Ye shall know them by their fruits. Do men gather grapes of thorns, or figs of thistles?" (Mt 7:16). **(4b)** As the visible expressions of hidden lusts are the works of the flesh, so the invisible power of the Holy Spirit in those who are brought into living union with Christ (Jn 15:2–8, 16) produces "the fruit of the Spirit" (Gal 5:22 the singular form suggesting the unity of the character of the Lord as reproduced in them, namely, "love, joy, peace, longsuffering, kindness, goodness, faithfulness, meekness, temperance," all in contrast with the confused and often mutually antagonistic "works of the flesh"). **(5)** So in Phil 1:11 "fruit of righteousness." In Heb 12:11, "the fruit of righteousness" is described as "peaceable fruit," the outward effect of divine chastening;

(6) "the fruit of righteousness is sown in peace" (Jas 3:18, i.e., the seed contains the fruit; those who make peace produce a harvest of righteousness); **(7)** "fruit of the light" (Eph 5:9 is seen in "goodness and righteousness and truth," as the expression of the union of the Christian with God; **(7a)** for God is good (Mk 10:18), **(7b)** the Son is "the righteous One" (Acts 7:52), **(7c)** the Spirit is "the Spirit of truth" (Jn 16:13). **(8)** Fruit speaks of advantage, profit, consisting **(8a)** of converts as the result of evangelistic ministry (Jn 4:36; Rom 1:13; Phil 1:22; **(8b)** of sanctification, through deliverance from a life of sin and through service to God (Rom 6:22), in contrast to **(8c)** the absence of anything regarded as advantageous as the result of former sins (Rom 6: 21); **(8d)** of the reward for ministration to servants of God (Phil 4:17); **(8e)** of the effect of making confession to God's name by the sacrifice of praise (Heb 13:15). Syn.: 175, 2592, 2593, 3703, 5352. See: TDNT—3:614, 416; BAGD—404c; THAYER—326b; THAYER—326b.

2591. Κάρπος {1x} **Karpŏs,** *kar'-pos;* perh. for *2590; Carpus,* prob. a Chr.:—Carpus {1x}. See: BAGD—404b; THAYER—326b.

2592. καρποφορέω {8x} **karpŏphŏrĕō,** *kar-pof-or-eh'-o;* from *2593;* to *be fertile* (lit. or fig.):—bring forth fruit {6x}, bear fruit {1x}, be fruitful {1x}.

Karpophoreo, as a verb, "to bear or bring forth fruit" is used in the natural sense, of the "fruit of the earth," **(1)** "bring forth fruit", metaphorically, of conduct or that which takes effect in conduct": "And these are they which are sown on good ground; such as hear the word, and receive it, and bring forth fruit, some thirtyfold, some sixty, and some an hundred" (Mk 4:20, 28; cf. Lk 8:15; Rom 7:4, 5 the latter, of evil "fruit," borne "unto death," of activities resulting from a state of alienation from God); Col 1:6 (in the middle voice); **(2)** "to bear fruit", Mt 13:23; and **(3)** "to be fruitful", Col 1:10. See: TDNT—3:616, 416; BAGD—405a; THAYER—326c.

2593. καρποφόρος {1x} **karpŏphŏrŏs,** *kar-pof-or'-os;* from *2590* and *5342; fruitbearing* (fig.):—fruitful {1x}.

Karpophoros, as an adjective, denotes "fruitful": "Nevertheless he left not himself without witness, in that he did good, and gave us rain from heaven, and fruitful seasons, filling our hearts with food and gladness" (Acts 14:17). Syn.: 175, 2590, 2592, 3703, 5352. See: BAGD—405b; THAYER—326d.

2594. καρτερέω {1x} **kartĕrĕō,** *kar-ter-eh'-o;* from a der. of *2904* (transp.); to *be strong,* i.e. (fig.) *steadfast* (*patient*):—endure {1x}.

Kartereo, "to be steadfast, patient," is used in Heb 11:27, "endured," of Moses in relation to Egypt. See: TDNT—3:617, 417; BAGD—405b; THAYER—326d.

2595. κάρφος {6x} **karphŏs,** *kar'-fos;* from κάρφω **karphō** (to *wither*); a dry *twig* or *straw:*—mote {6x}.

Karphos, "a small, dry stalk, a twig, a bit of dried stick", or "a tiny straw or bit of wool," such as might fly into the eye, is used metaphorically of a minor fault, Mt 7:3, 4, 5; Lk 6:41, 42 (twice), in contrast with *dokos* (*1385*), "a beam supporting the roof of a building." See: BAGD—405c; THAYER—326d.

2596. κατά {480x} **kata,** *kat-ah';* a primary particle; (prep.) *down* (in place or time), in varied relations (according to the case [gen., dat. or acc.] with which it is joined):— according to {107x}, after {61x}, against {58x}, in {36x}, by {27x}, daily + 2250 {15x}, as {11x},

misc. {165x} = about, (when they were) X alone, among, and, X apart, (even, like) as (concerning, pertaining to touching), X aside, at, before, beyond, by, to the charge of, [charita-] bly, concerning, + covered, down, every, (+ far more) exceeding, X more excellent, for, from . . . to, godly, after the manner of, + by any means, beyond (out of) measure, X mightily, more, X natural, of (up-) on (X part), out (of every), over against, (+ your) X own, + particularly, so, through (-oughout, oughout every), thus, (un-) to (-gether, -ward), X uttermost, where (-by), with. In composition it retains many of these applications, and frequently denotes *opposition, distribution,* or *intensity.* See: BAGD—405c; THAYER—326d.

2597. καταβαίνω {81x} **katabainō,** *kat-ab-ah'-ee-no;* from *2596* and the base of *939;* to *descend* (lit. or fig.):—come down {41x}, descend {18x}, go down {17x}, fall down {1x}, step down {1x}, get down {1x}, fall {1x}, vr come down {1x}.

Inherent within this word is someone or something leaving a positionally higher position and arriving at a lower one. See: TDNT—1:522, 90; BAGD—408b; THAYER—329c.

2598. καταβάλλω {3x} **kataballō,** *kat-ab-al'-lo;* from *2596* and *906;* to *throw down:*—cast down {2x}, lay {1x}.

Kataballo signifies **(1)** "cast down," **(1a)** 2 Cor 4:9: "Persecuted, but not forsaken; cast down, but not destroyed"; **(1b)** "the casting down of Satan", Rev 12:10; and **(2)** Heb 6:1: "Therefore leaving the principles of the doctrine of Christ, let us go on unto perfection; not laying [down] again the foundation of repentance from dead works, and of faith toward God"; and See: BAGD—408d; THAYER—329d.

2599. καταβαρέω {1x} **katabarĕō,** *kat-ab-ar-eh'-o;* from *2596* and *916;* to *impose upon:*—burden {1x}.

Katabareo means to weigh down, to overload and is used of material weight (metaphorically, 2 Cor 12:16). See: BAGD—408d; THAYER—330a.

2600. κατάβασις {1x} **katabasis,** *kat-ab'-as-is;* from *2597;* a *declivity:*—a descent {1x}.

Katabasis stresses the "way down," Lk 19:37; whereas, *katabaino* (*2597*) stresses the activity of descending. See: BAGD—409a; THAYER—330a.

2601. καταβιβάζω {2x} **katabibazō,** *kat-ab-ib-ad'-zo;* from *2596* and a der. of the base of *939;* to *cause to go down,* i.e. *precipitate:*—bring down {1x}, thrust down {1x}.

Katabibazo, as a verb, means in the active

voice, "to cause to go down" and is used in the passive in the sense of **(1)** "being brought down, thrust down": "And thou, Capernaum, which art exalted to heaven, shalt be thrust down to hell" (Lk 10:15); **(2)** "go down": "And thou, Capernaum, which art exalted unto heaven, shalt be brought down (*katabibazo*) to hell: for if the mighty works, which have been done in thee, had been done in Sodom, it would have remained until this day" (Mt 11:23). See: BAGD— 409a; THAYER—330a.

2602. **καταβολή** {11x} **katăbŏlē**, *kat-ab-ol-ay';* from *2598;* a *deposition,* i.e. *founding;* fig. *conception:*—to conceive + 1519 {1x}, foundation {10x}.

Literally, *katabole* means "a casting down," is used **(1)** of "conceiving seed," the injection or depositing of the virile semen in the womb, Heb 11:11; **(2)** of "a foundation," as that which is laid down, or in the sense of founding; metaphorically, of "the foundation of the world"; in this respect two phrases are used, **(2a)** "from the foundation of the world," Mt 13:35; 25:34; Lk 11:50; Heb 4:3; 9:26; Rev 13:8; 17:8; **(2b)** "before the foundation of the world," Jn 17:24; Eph 1:4; 1 Pet 1:20. The latter phrase looks back to the past eternity. See: TDNT—3:620, 418; BAGD—409a; THAYER—330a.

2603. **καταβραβεύω** {1x} **katabrabĕuō**, *kat-ab-rab-yoo'-o;* from *2596* and *1018* (in its orig. sense); to *award* the price *against,* i.e. (fig.) to *defraud* (of salvation):— beguile of (one's) reward {1x}.

Katabrabeuo means to defraud or beguile of the prize of victory; occurs in Col 2:18, said of false teachers who would frustrate the faithful adherence of the believers to the truth, causing them to lose their reward. See: BAGD—409b; THAYER—330b.

2604. **καταγγελεύς** {1x} **kataggĕleus**, *kat-ang-gel-yooce';* from *2605;* a *proclaimer:*—setter forth {1x}.

Kataggeleus, "a proclaimer, herald" (akin to *katangello,* "to proclaim"), is used in Acts 17:18, "a setter forth (of strange gods)." See: TDNT—1:70, 10; BAGD—409b; THAYER— 330c.

2605. **καταγγέλλω** {17x} **kataggĕllō**, *kat-ang-gel'-lo;* from *2596* and the base of *32;* to *proclaim, promulgate:*—declare {2x}, preach {10x}, shew {3x}, speak of {1x}, teach {1x}.

Kataggello, lit., "to report down" (*kata,* intensive), means to lay it down firmly, accurately, and in order. It is translated **(1)** "to preach" in Acts 4:2; 13:5, 38; 15:36; 17:3, 13; 1 Cor 9:14; Col 1:28; **(2)** "to declare" in Acts 17:23; 1 Cor 2:1; **(3)** "to shew" Acts 16:17; 26:23;

1 Cor 11:26, "shew"; in the last passage the partaking of the elements at the Lord's Supper is a "showing forth" of His death, a "visual" detailing of it; **(4)** "to teach", Acts 16:21; and **(5)** "speak of" in Rom 1:8. See: TDNT—1:70, 10; BAGD—409b; THAYER—330c.

2606. **καταγελάω** {3x} **katagĕlaō**, *kat-ag-el-ah'-o;* to *laugh down,* i.e. *deride:*—laugh to scorn {3x}.

Katagelao denotes "to laugh scornfully at," (*kata,* "down," used intensively), and signifies derisive laughter, Mt 9:24; M 5:40; Lk 8:53. See: TDNT—1:658, 113; BAGD—409c; THAYER— 330c.

2607. **καταγινώσκω** {3x} **kataginōskō**, *kat-ag-in-o'-sko;* from *2596* and *1097;* to *note against,* i.e. *find fault with:*— blame {1x}, condemn {2x}.

Kataginosko, as a verb, means "to know something against" (*kata,* "against," *ginosko,* "to know by experience"), hence, "to think ill of, to condemn" and is said, **(1)** in Gal 2:11, of Peter's conduct, he being "self-condemned" as the result of an exercised and enlightened conscience, and "condemned" in the sight of others: "But when Peter was come to Antioch, I withstood him to the face, because he was to be blamed." **(2)** so of "self-condemnation" due to an exercise of heart: "For if our heart condemn us, God is greater than our heart, and knoweth all things. Beloved, if our heart condemn us not, then have we confidence toward God" (1 Jn 3:20–21). Syn.: 176, 273, 274, 298, 299, 338, 410, 423, 843, 2613, 2631, 2632, 2633, 2917, 2919, 2920, 3201, 3469. See: TDNT— 1:714, 119; BAGD—409d; THAYER—330c.

2608. **κατάγνυμι** {4x} **katagnumi**, *kat-ag'-noo-mee;* from *2596* and the base of *4486;* to *rend in pieces,* i.e. *crack apart:*—break {4x}.

Katagnumi, (*kata,* "down", intensive), is used **(1)** of the "breaking" of a bruised reed, Mt 12:20, and **(2)** of the "breaking" of the legs of those who were crucified, Jn 19:31, 32, 33. See: BAGD—409d; THAYER—330d.

2609. **κατάγω** {10x} **katagō**, *kat-ag'-o;* from *2596* and *71;* to *lead down;* spec. to *moor* a vessel:—bring down {5x}, land {2x}, bring {1x}, bring forth {1x}, touch {1x}.

Katago, as a verb, means **(1)** "to bring down": "Which when the brethren knew, they brought him down (*katago*) to Caesarea, and sent him forth to Tarsus" (Acts 9:30; cf. 22:30; 23:15, 20; Rom 10:6); **(2)** "to bring forth": "And when I would have known the cause wherefore they accused him, I brought him forth (*katago*) into their council" (Acts 23:28); **(3)** of ships, "to bring to land": "And when they had brought

their ships to land, they forsook all, and followed Him" (Lk 5:11); **(4)** "to land", Acts 21:3 (make land, arrive at land); and **(5)** "to touch", Acts 27:3 (to briefly land). See: BAGD—410a; THAYER—330d.

2610. καταγωνίζομαι {1x} **katagōnizŏmai,** *kat-ag-o-nid'-zom-ahee;* from *2596* and *75;* to *struggle against,* i.e. (by impl.) to *overcome:*—subdue {1x}.

This word means primarily, "to struggle against" (*kata,* "against," *agon,* "a contest"), came to signify "to conquer," Heb 11:33, "subdued." See: TDNT—1:134, 20; BAGD—410a; THAYER—330d.

2611. καταδέω {1x} **katadĕō,** *kat-ad-eh'-o;* from *2596* and *1210;* to *tie down,* i.e. *bandage* (a wound):—bind up {1x}.

Katadeo, (*kata,* "down," *deo* "to bind or tie down, or bind up"), is used in Lk 10:34 of the act of the good Samaritan: "And went to him, and bound up (*katadeo*) his wounds, pouring in oil and wine, and set him on his own beast, and brought him to an inn, and took care of him." The man evidently had broken bones which were "bound" in a sort of cast. See: BAGD—410b; THAYER—331a.

2612. κατάδηλος {1x} **katadēlŏs,** *kat-ad'-ay-los;* from *2596* intens. and *1212; manifest:*—far more evident {1x}.

Kadadelos, "quite manifest, evident, thoroughly clear, plain" is used in Heb 7:15, "more evident". See: BAGD—410b; THAYER—331a.

2613. καταδικάζω {5x} **katadikazo,** *kat-ad-ik-ad'-zo;* from *2596* and a der. of *1349;* to *adjudge against,* i.e. *pronounce guilty:*—condemn {5x}.

Katadikazo, as a verb, signifies "to exercise right or law against anyone"; hence, "to pronounce judgment, to condemn": "But if ye had known what this meaneth, I will have mercy, and not sacrifice, ye would not have condemned the guiltless" (Mt 12:7; cf. 12: 37; Lk 6:37 twice; Jas 5:6). Syn.: 176, 843, 2607, 2631, 2632, 2633, 2917, 2919, 2920. See: TDNT—3:621, 418; BAGD—410b; THAYER—331a.

2614. καταδιώκω {1x} **katadiōkō,** *kat-ad-ee-o'-ko;* from *2596* and *1377;* to *hunt down,* i.e. *search for:*—follow after {1x}.

Katadioko, as a verb, means "to follow up or closely," with the determination to find (*kata,* "down," intensive, giving the idea of a hard, persistent search, and *dioko* - 1377), "followed after (Him)," is said of the disciples in going to find the Lord who had gone into a desert place to pray (Mk 1:36). Syn.: 190, 1096, 1377, 1811, 1872, 2628, 3877, 4870. See: BAGD—410c; THAYER—331a.

2615. καταδουλόω {2x} **katadŏulŏō,** *kat-ad-oo-lŏ'-o;* from *2596* and *1402;* to *enslave utterly:*—bring into bondage {2x}. Cf. 2 Cor 11:20; Gal 2:4. See: TDNT—2:279, 182; BAGD—410c; THAYER—331b.

2616. καταδυναστεύω {2x} **katadunastĕuō,** *kat-ad-oo-nas-tyoo'-o;* from *2596* and a der. of *1413;* to *exercise dominion against,* i.e. *oppress:*—oppress {2x}.

This word denotes "to exercise power over" (*kata,* "down," *dunastes,* "a potentate": *dunamai* "to have power"), "to oppress," is used, **(1)** in the passive voice, in Acts 10:38; **(2)** in the active, in Jas 2:6. See: BAGD—410c; THAYER—331b.

2617. καταισχύνω {13x} **kataischunō,** *kat-ahee-skhoo'-no;* from *2596* and *153;* to *shame down,* i.e. *disgrace* or (by impl.) *put to the blush:*—ashamed {7x}, confound {3x}, dishonour {2x}, shame {1x}.

Kataischuno, as a verb, means **(1)** "to put to shame": "What? have ye not houses to eat and to drink in? or despise ye the church of God, and shame (*kataischuno*) them that have not? What shall I say to you? shall I praise you in this? I praise you not" (1 Cor 11:22; cf. Lk 13:17; Rom 5:5; 9:33; 10:11; 1 Cor 11:22; 2 Cor 7:14; 9:4; 1 Pet 3:16). It is translated **(2)** "confound": "But God hath chosen the foolish things of the world to confound the wise; and God hath chosen the weak things of the world to confound the things which are mighty" (1 Cor 1:27 twice; cf. 1 Pet 2:6); "dishonour", 1 Cor 11:4, 5. Syn.: 150, 152, 181, 808, 818, 819, 1788, 1791, 3856, 4797, 4799. See: TDNT—1:189, 29; BAGD—410d; THAYER—331b.

2618. κατακαίω {12x} **katakaiō,** *kat-ak-ah'-ee-o;* from *2596* and *2545;* to *burn down* (to the ground), i.e. *consume wholly:*—burn {7x}, burn up {4x}, burn utterly {1x}.

Katakaio, signifies "to burn up, burn utterly," as of **(1)** chaff, Mt 3:12; Lk 3:17; **(2)** tares, Mt 13:30, 40; **(3)** the earth and its works, 2 Pet 3:10; **(4)** trees and grass, Rev 8:7 (twice). **(5)** This form should be noted in Acts 19:19; 1 Cor 3:15; Heb 13:11; Rev 17:16. In each place the full rendering "burn utterly" might be used, as in Rev 18:8. See: BAGD—411a; THAYER—331c.

2619. κατακαλύπτω {3x} **katakaluptō,** *kat-ak-al-oop'-to;* from *2596* and *2572;* to *cover wholly,* i.e. *veil:*—cover {3x}.

In 1 Cor 11:4 "having his head covered" is, lit., "having (something) down the head" signifying that hair that hangs down is too long for a man, and consequently hair that does not hang down on a woman is too short. See: TDNT—3:561, 405; BAGD—411a; THAYER—331c.

Greek

2620. **κατακαυχάομαι** {4x} **katakauchaŏmai**, *kat-ak-ŏw-khah'-om-ahee;* from *2596* and *2744;* to *exult against* (i.e. *over*):—boast {1x}, boast against {1x}, glory {1x}, rejoice against {1x}.

(1) This word means to glory against, to exult over, to boast one's self to the injury of a person. (2) It signifies (2a) "to boast against, exult over," Rom 11:18 (twice); (2b) "rejoiceth against" Jas 2:13; (2c) Jas 3:14, "glory (not)." See: TDNT—3:653, 423; BAGD—411b; THAYER—331c.

2621. **κατάκειμαι** {11x} **katakĕimai**, *kat-ak'-i-mahee;* from *2596* and *2749;* to *lie down,* i.e. (by impl.) *be sick;* spec. to *recline* at a meal:—lie {6x}, sit at meat {3x}, keep {1x}, sat down + *2258* {1x}.

Katakeimai, as a verb, means "to lie down" and is used (1) of "reclining at a meal", Mk 2:15; 14:3; Lk 5:29; 1 Cor 8:10; (2) "to lie down" is used of the sick, Mk 1:30; 2:4; Lk 5:25; Jn 5:3, 6; Acts 28:8; (3) in Acts 9:33 it is rendered "had kept (his bed)," lit., "lying (on a bed)." Syn.: 339, 345, 347, 377, 1910, 2516, 2521, 2523, 2625, 4775, 4776, 4873. See: TDNT—3:655, 425; BAGD—411c; THAYER—331a.

2622. **κατακλάω** {2x} **kataklaō**, *kat-ak-lah'-o;* from *2596* and *2806;* to *break down,* i.e. *divide into pieces:*—break {2x}.

Kataklao is used in Mk 6:41 and Lk 9:16, of Christ's "breaking" loaves for the multitudes. See: BAGD—411c; THAYER—331d.

2623. **κατακλείω** {2x} **kataklĕiō**, *kat-ak-li'-o;* from *2596* and *2808;* to *shut down* (in a dungeon), i.e. *incarcerate:*—shut up {2x}.

Katakleio, lit., "to shut down" (the *kata* has, however, an intensive use; cf. Eng. "lock down"), signifies "to shut up in confinement," Lk 3:20; Acts 26:10. See: BAGD—411c; THAYER—331d.

2624. **κατακληροδοτέω** {1x} **kataklērŏdŏtĕō**, *kat-ak-lay-rod-ot-eh'-o;* from *2596* and a der. of a compound of *2819* and *1325;* to *be a giver of lots to each,* i.e. (by impl.) to *apportion an estate:*—divide by lot {1x}. See: BAGD—411d; THAYER—331d.

2625. **κατακλίνω** {3x} **kataklinō**, *kat-ak-lee'-no;* from *2596* and *2827;* to *recline down,* i.e. (spec.) to *take a place* at table:—sit down {1x}, sit at meat {1x}, make sit down {1x}.

Kataklino, as a verb, is used only in connection with meals (1) in the active voice, "to make recline": "For they were about five thousand men. And He said to His disciples, Make them sit down by fifties in a company" (Lk 9:14);

(2) in the passive voice, "to recline, sat down to meat": "When thou art bidden of any man to a wedding, sit not down (*kataklino*) in the highest room; lest a more honourable man than thou be bidden of him" (Lk 14:8; cf. 24:30). Syn.: 339, 345, 347, 377, 1910, 2516, 2521, 2621, 2523, 4775, 4776, 4873. See: BAGD—411d; THAYER—332a.

2626. **κατακλύζω** {1x} **katakluzō**, *kat-ak-lood'-zo;* from *2596* and the base of *2830;* to *dash (wash) down,* i.e. (by impl.) to *deluge:*—overflow {1x}.

Katakluzo, "to inundate, to submerge, deluge, overwhelm with water" (*kata,* "down," *kluzo,* "to wash" or "dash over," said, e.g., of the sea), is used in the passive voice in 2 Pet 3:6, of the Flood. See: BAGD—411d; THAYER—332a.

2627. **κατακλυσμός** {4x} **kataklusmŏs**, *kat-ak-looce-mos';* from *2626;* an *inundation:*—flood {4x}.

This word is used of the "flood" in Noah's time, Mt 24:38, 39; Lk 17:27; 2 Pet 2:5; 2 Pet 3:6. See: BAGD—411d; THAYER—332a.

2628. **κατακολουθέω** {2x} **katakŏlŏuthĕō**, *kat-ak-ol-oo-theh'-o;* from *2596* and *190;* to *accompany closely:*—follow {1x}, follow after {1x}.

Katakoloutheo, as a verb, means "to follow behind or intently after" and is used (1) of the women on their way to Christ's tomb (Lk 23:55); (2) of the demon-possessed maid in Philippi in "following" the missionaries (Acts 16:17). Syn.: 190, 1096, 1377, 1811, 1872, 2614, 3877, 4870. See: BAGD—412a; THAYER—332b.

2629. **κατακόπτω** {1x} **katakŏptō**, *kat-ak-op'-to;* from *2596* and *2875;* to *chop down,* i.e. *mangle:*—cut {1x}.

Katakopto, lit., to cut down, cut in pieces" (*kata,* "down," intensive), Mk 5:5, of the devil possessed man, who had many deep wounds/cuts from stumbling among the sharp stones of the graveyard. See: BAGD—412a; THAYER—332b.

2630. **κατακρημνίζω** {1x} **katakrēmnizō**, *kat-ak-rame-nid'-zo;* from *2596* and a der. of *2911;* to *precipitate down:*—cast down headlong {1x}.

Katakremnizo signifies "to throw over a precipice" (*kata,* "down," *kremnos,* "a steep bank," etc.), said of the purpose of the people of Nazareth to destroy Christ, Lk 4:29. See: BAGD—412a; THAYER—332b.

2631. **κατάκριμα** {3x} **katakrima**, *kat-ak'-ree-mah;* from *2632;* an *adverse sentence* (the verdict):—condemnation {3x}.

Katakrima, as a noun, is "the sentence pro-

nounced, the condemnation" with a suggestion of the punishment following: "And not as it was by one that sinned, so is the gift: for the judgment was by one to condemnation (*katakrima*), but the free gift is of many offences unto justification" (Rom 5:16; cf. 5:18; 8:1). Syn.: 176, 843, 2607, 2613, 2632, 2633, 2917, 2919, 2920. See: TDNT—3:951, 469; BAGD—412a; THAYER—332b.

2632. **κατακρίνω** {19x} **katakrinō**, *kat-ak-ree'- no;* from 2596 and 2919; to *judge against,* i.e. *sentence:*—condemn {17x}, damn {2x}.

    Katakrino, as a verb, **(1)** signifies "to give judgment against, pass sentence upon"; hence, "to condemn," implying **(1a)** the fact of a crime (Rom 2:1; 14:23; 2 Pet 2:6); **(1b)** the imputation of a crime, as in the "condemnation" of Christ by the Jews (Mt 20:18; Mk 14:64). **(2)** It is used metaphorically of "condemning" by a good example: "The men of Nineveh shall rise in judgment with this generation, and shall condemn it: because they repented at the preaching of Jonas; and, behold, a greater than Jonas is here. The queen of the south shall rise up in the judgment with this generation, and shall condemn it: for she came from the uttermost parts of the earth to hear the wisdom of Solomon; and, behold, a greater than Solomon is here" (Mt 12:41–42; cf. Lk 11:31–32; Heb 11:7). **(3)** In Rom 8:3, God's "condemnation" of sin is set forth in that Christ, His own Son, sent by Him to partake of human nature (sin apart) and to become an offering for sin, died under the judgment due to our sin. Syn.: 176, 843, 2607, 2613, 2631, 2633, 2917, 2919, 2920. See: TDNT— 3:951, 469; BAGD—412a; THAYER—332b.

2633. **κατάκρισις** {2x} **katakrisis**, *kat-ak'- ree-sis;* from 2632; *sentencing adversely* (the act):—condemn {1x}, condemnation {1x}.

    Katakrisis, as a noun, denotes "a judgment against, condemnation," with the suggestion of the process leading to it, as **(1)** of "the ministration of condemnation" (2 Cor 3:9); **(2)** in 2 Cor 7:3 "to condemn," more lit., "with a view to condemnation." Syn.: 176, 843, 2607, 2613, 2631, 2632, 2917, 2919, 2920. See: TDNT—3:951, 469; BAGD—332c; THAYER—332c.

2634. **κατακυριεύω** {4x} **katakurieuō**, *kat- ak-oo-ree-yoo'-o;* from 2596 and 2961; to *lord against,* i.e. *control, subjugate:*—exercise dominion over {1x}, overcome {1x}, be lord over {1x}, exercise lordship over {1x}.

    Katakurieul, "to exercise, or gain, dominion over, to lord it over," is used of **(1)** the "lordship" of Gentile rulers, Mt 20:25, "exercise do-

minion"; **(2)** Mk 10:42, "exercise lordship over"; **(3)** the power of devils over men, Acts 19:16, "overcame"; **(4)** of the evil of elders in "lording" it over the saints under their spiritual care, 1 Pet 5:3. See: TDNT—3:1098, 486; BAGD—412c; THAYER—332c.

2635. **καταλαλέω** {5x} **katalaleō**, *kat-al-al- eh'-o;* from 2637; to *be a traducer,* i.e. to *slander:*—speak against {1x}, speak evil of {4x}.

    This word means to speak against one, to criminate, and is translated **(1)** "speak against", 1 Pet 2:12; 3:16; and **(2)** "speak evil of", Jas 4:1 (thrice). See: TDNT—4:3, 495; BAGD—412c; THAYER—332c.

2636. **καταλαλιά** {2x} **katalalia**, *kat-al-al- ee'-ah;* from 2637; *defamation:*—backbiting {1x}, evil speaking {1x}.

    Katalalia is translated **(1)** "evil speaking" in 1 Pet 2:1; **(2)** "backbiting" in 2 Cor 12:20. See: TDNT—4:3, 495; BAGD—412d; THAYER— 332d.

2637. **κατάλαλος** {1x} **katalalŏs**, *kat-al'-al-os;* from 2596 and the base of 2980; *talkative against,* i.e. a *slanderer:*—backbiter {1x}. See: TDNT—4:3, 495; BAGD—412d; THAYER—332d.

2638. **καταλαμβάνω** {15x} **katalambanō**, *kat- al-am-ban'-o;* from 2596 and 2983; to *take eagerly,* i.e. *seize, possess,* etc. (lit. or fig.):—take {3x}, apprehend {3x}, comprehend {2x}, come upon {1x}, attain {1x}, find {1x}, overtake {1x}, obtain {1x}.

    Katalambano properly signifies to lay hold of; then, to lay hold of so as to possess as one's own, to appropriate. Hence it has the twofold meaning of to apprehend: **(1)** to seize upon, take possession of **(1a)** with a beneficial effect **(1a1)** laying hold of the righteousness which is of faith (Rom 9:30 - not there a matter of attainment, but of appropriation); **(1a2)** of the obtaining of a prize (1 Cor 9:24); **(1a3)** of the apostle's desire to apprehend, or lay hold of that for which he was apprehended by Christ (Phil 3:12–13); **(1b)** with a detrimental effect **(1b1)** of demon power (Mk 9:18); **(1b2)** of human action in seizing upon a person (Jn 8:3–4); **(1b3)** metaphorically, with the added idea of overtaking, **(1b3a)** of spiritual darkness in coming upon people (Jn 12:35); **(1b3b)** of the Day of the Lord, in suddenly coming upon unbelievers as a thief (1 Th 5:4); **(2)** to lay hold of with the mind, to understand, perceive **(2a)** metaphorically, **(2a1)** of darkness with regard to light (Jn 1:5); **(2a2)** of mental perception (Acts 4:13; 10:34; 25:25; Eph 3:18). Syn.: 4084. See: TDNT—4:9, 495; BAGD—412d; THAYER—332d.

Greek

2639. καταλέγω {1x} **katalĕgō**, *kat-al-eg'-o;* from *2596* and *3004* (in its orig. mean.); to *lay down,* i.e. (fig.) to *enroll:*—take into the number {1x}. See: BAGD—413b; THAYER—333a.

2640. κατάλειμμα {1x} **katalĕimma**, *kat-al'-ime-mah;* from *2641;* a *remainder,* i.e. (by impl.) a *few:*—remnant {1x}. See: TDNT—4:194, 523; BAGD—413c; THAYER—333a.

2641. καταλείπω {25x} **katalĕipō**, *kat-al-i'-po;* from *2596* and *3007;* to *leave down,* i.e. *behind;* by impl. to *abandon, have remaining:*—forsake {2x}, leave {22x}, reserve {1x}.

(1) This word usually denotes to forsake, to purposely leave a person or thing by ceasing to care for it, to abandon, leave in the lurch. *Kataleipo,* a strengthened form of *leipo,* signifies (2) "to leave", (2a) "to leave behind", e.g., Mt 4:13; (2b) "to leave remaining, reserve," e.g., Lk 10:40; (2c) "to leave," in the sense of "abandoning", Mk 10:7; 14:52; Lk 15:4; Eph 5:31; (3) "to forsake," in the sense of abandoning, in Heb 11:27; 2 Pet 2:15; (4) "reserved", in the sense of permanently set aside; left, Rom 11:4. See: TDNT—4:194, 523; BAGD—413c; THAYER—333a.

2642. καταλιθάζω {1x} **katalithazō**, *kat-al-ith-ad'-zo;* from *2596* and *3034;* to *stone down,* i.e. *to death:*—stone {1x}.

Katalithazo, an intensive form of *lithazo,* "to cast stones at, overwhelm with stones" occurs in Lk 20:6. See: TDNT—4:267, 533; BAGD—413d; THAYER—333b.

2643. καταλλαγή {4x} **katallagē**, *kat-al-lag-ay';* from *2644; exchange* (fig. *adjustment*), i.e. *restoration* to (the divine) favor:—atonement {1x}, reconciliation {2x}, reconciling {1x}.

(1) This word denotes an adjustment of a difference, reconciliation, restoration to favour, especially the restoration of the favour of God to sinners that repent and put their trust in the expiatory/propitiatory death of Christ. Man changes and is reconciled. God does not change. (2) It is translated (2a) "atonement" in Rom 5:11, signifying that sinners are made "at one" with God; and in the NT so much more is given the believer in Christ; (2b) "reconciliation" 2 Cor 5:18, 19; (2c) "reconciling", Rom 11:15. (3) Man receives Christ as his Saviour, he is reconciled, has received the reconciliation, and is "at one" with God. Reconciliation stresses the process, atonement stresses the end result of the process. Syn.: *Hilasmos* (*2434*), [expiation and propitiation] and *apolytrosis* (*629*) have fundamentally a single benefit—namely, the restitu-

tion of a lost sinner. It is *apoltrosis* in reference to an enemy, and *katallage* in respect to God. And here these terms *hilasmos* and *katallage,* again differ. *Hilasmos* (propitiation) removes an offense against God; *katallage* (reconciliation) has two fronts and removes (a) God's displeasure toward us (2 Cor 5:19) and (b) our alienation from God (2 Cor 5:20). See: TDNT—1:258, 40; BAGD—414a; THAYER—333b.

2644. καταλλάσσω {6x} **katallassō**, *kat-al-las'-so;* from *2596* and *236;* to *change mutually,* i.e. (fig.) to *compound a difference:*—reconcile {6x}.

Katallasso properly denotes (1) to change, exchange; hence, of persons, to change from enmity to friendship, to reconcile. (2) With regard to the relationship between God and man, (2a) reconciliation is what God accomplishes, (2a1) exercising His grace towards sinful man (2a2) on the ground of the death of Christ in propitiatory sacrifice under the judgment due to sin (2 Cor 5:18–20). (2b) By reason of this (2b1) men in their sinful condition and alienation from God (2b2) are invited to be reconciled to Him; that is to say, to change their attitude, and accept the provision God has made, (2b3) whereby their sins can be remitted and they themselves be justified in His sight in Christ. (2c) What we do receive is the result, namely, reconciliation.

(3) The removal of God's wrath does not contravene His immutability. (3a) He always acts according to His unchanging righteousness and lovingkindness, and (3b) it is because He changes not that His relative attitude does change towards those who change. (4) Not once is God said to be reconciled. (4a) The enmity is alone on our part. (4b) It was we who needed to be reconciled to God, not God to us, and (4c) it is propitiation, which His righteousness and mercy have provided, that makes the reconciliation possible to those who receive it. (5) The hostility is not on the part of God, but of man. Syn.: 604, 1259, 2643. *Diallasso* (1259 - only in Mt 5:24) is never used in this connection, but always *katallasso,* because the former word denotes mutual concession after mutual hostility, an idea absent from *katallasso.* See: TDNT—1:254, 40; BAGD—414a; THAYER—333c.

2645. κατάλοιπος {1x} **katalŏipŏs**, *kat-al'-oy-pos;* from *2596* and *3062; left down* (*behind*), i.e. *remaining* (plur. the *rest*):—residue {1x}.

Kataloipos, an adjective denoting "left remaining" (*kata,* "after, behind," *leipo,* "to leave"), is translated "residue" in Acts 15:17, cf. Amos 9:12. See: BAGD—414b; THAYER—333d.

2646. **κατάλυμα** {3x} **kataluma**, *kat-al'-oo-mah;* from *2647;* prop. a *dissolution* (breaking up of a journey), i.e. (by impl.) a *lodging-place:*—guest chamber {2x}, inn {1x}.

Kataluma signifies **(1)** an inn, lodging-place (Lk 2:7); or **(2)** a guest-room (Mk 14:14; Lk 22:11). The word lit. signifies a loosening down, used of the place where travelers and their beasts untied their packages, belts and sandals. See: TDNT—4:338, 543; BAGD—414b; THAYER—333d.

2647. **καταλύω** {17x} **kataluō**, *kat-al-oo'-o;* from *2596* and *3089;* to *loosen down (disintegrate),* i.e. (by impl.) to *demolish* (lit. or fig.); spec. [comp. *2646*] to *halt* for the night:—destroy {9x}, throw down {3x}, lodge {1x}, guest {1x}, come to nought {1x}, overthrow {1x}, dissolve {1x}.

Kataluo, "to destroy utterly, to overthrow completely," is rendered **(1)** "destroy," **(1a)** the Law, in Mt 5:17, twice; **(1b)** the temple, in Mt 26:61; 27:40; Mk 13:2; 14:58; 15:29; Lk 21:6; **(1c)** Jerusalem, (temple only) in Acts 6:14; **(1d)** the Law as a means of justification, in Gal 2:18; **(1e)** in Rom 14:20, of the marring of a person's spiritual well-being; **(1f)** in Acts 5:38 and 39 of the failure of purposes; **(1g)** in 2 Cor 5:1, of the death of the body ("dissolved"). It is also translated **(2)** "throw down", Mt 24:2; Mk 13:2; **(3)** "lodge", Lk 9:12, of a traveler "throwing down" his luggage; **(4)** "guest", Lk 19:7, one who has "thrown down" his luggage in a lodge; **(5)** "come to nought", Acts 5:38; **(6)** "overthrow", Acts 5:39; and **(7)** "dissolve", 2 Cor 5:1, the earthly body. See: TDNT—4:338, 543; BAGD—414b; THAYER—334a.

2648. **καταμανθάνω** {1x} **katamanthanō**, *kat-am-an-than'-o;* from *2596* and *3129;* to *learn thoroughly,* i.e. (by impl.) to *note carefully:*—consider {1x}.

This word means to note accurately, consider well, to learn thoroughly through careful examination (Mt 6:28). See: TDNT—4:414, 552; BAGD—414d; THAYER—334b.

2649. **καταμαρτυρέω** {4x} **katamartureō**, *kat-am-ar-too-reh'-o;* from *2596* and *3140;* to *testify against:*—witness against {4x}.

Katamartureo, as a verb, denotes "to witness against": "And the high priest arose, and said unto Him, Answerest thou nothing? what is it which these witness against thee?" (Mt 26:62; cf. 27:13; Mk 14:60; 15:4). Syn.: 267, 3140, 3141, 3142, 3143, 3144, 4828, 4901, 5571, 5576, 5577. See: TDNT—4:508, 564; BAGD—414d; THAYER—334b.

2650. **καταμένω** {1x} **katamĕnō**, *kat-am-en'-o;* from *2596* and *3306;* to *stay fully,* i.e. *reside:*—abide + 2258 {1x}.

Katameno is used in Acts 1:13 and may signify "constant residence," but more probably indicates "frequent resort." See: BAGD—414d; THAYER—334b.

2651. **καταμόνας** {2x} **katamŏnas**, *kat-am-on'-as;* from *2596* and acc. plur. fem. of *3441* (with *5561* impl.); *according to sole* places, i.e. (adv.) *separately:*—alone {2x}.

Katamonas signifies apart, in private, alone (Mk 4:10; Lk 9:18). See: BAGD—414d; THAYER—334b.

2652. **κατανάθεμα** {1x} **katanathĕma**, *kat-an-ath'-em-ah;* from *2596* (intens.) and *331;* an *imprecation:*—a curse {1x}.

Katanathema, as a noun, is stronger than *anathema (331),* and denotes, by metonymy, "an accursed thing" (the object "cursed" being put for the "curse" pronounced): "And there shall be no more curse: but the throne of God and of the Lamb shall be in it; and His servants shall serve Him" (Rev 22:3). Syn.: 331, 332, 685, 1944, 2552, 2653, 2671, 2672. See: TDNT—1:354,*; BAGD—414d; THAYER—334b.

2653. **καταναθεματίζω** {1x} **katanathĕmatizō**, *kat-an-ath-em-at-id'-zo;* from *2596* (intens.) and *332;* to *imprecate:*—to curse {1x}.

Katanathematizo, a strengthened form of *anathematizo (332),* as a verb, denotes "to utter curses against": "Then began he [Peter] to curse and to swear, saying, I know not the man" (Mt 26:74). Syn.: 331, 332, 685, 1944, 2551, 2652, 2671, 2672. See: TDNT—1:355,*; BAGD—414d; THAYER—334b.

2654. **καταναλίσκω** {1x} **katanaliskō**, *kat-an-al-is'-ko;* from *2596* and *355;* to *consume utterly:*—consume {1x}.

Katanalisko, "to consume utterly, wholly" *(kata,* intensive), is said, in Heb 12:29, of God as "a consuming fire." See: BAGD—414d; THAYER—334b.

2655. **καταναρκάω** {3x} **katanarkaō**, *kat-an-ar-kah'-o;* from *2596* and ναρκάω **narkaō** (to *be numb*); to *grow utterly torpid,* i.e. (by impl.) *slothful* (fig. *expensive*):—be burdensome {2x}, be chargeable {1x}.

This word means to be a burden, to be burdensome, primarily signifying to be numbed or torpid, to grow stiff *(narke* is the torpedo or cramp fish, which benumbs anyone who touches it); hence, to be idle to the detriment of another person, like a useless limb. It is translated **(1)** "be chargeable", 2 Cor 11:9; and

(2) "be burdensome", 2 Cor 12:13–14. See: BAGD–414d; THAYER–334b.

2656. κατανεύω {1x} **katanĕuō**, *kat-an-yoo'-o;* from *2596* and *3506;* to *nod down* (*toward*), i.e. (by anal.) to *make signs* to:—beckon {1x}.

Kataneuo means to nod to, make a sign, to indicate to another by a nod and is used of the fishermen-partners in Lk 5:7, as they held the full nets with both hands they beckoned with frantic nods of their heads for their friends to assist them. See: BAGD–415a; THAYER–334c.

2657. κατανοέω {14x} **katanŏĕō**, *kat-an-o-eh'-o;* from *2596* and *3539;* to *observe fully:*—behold {4x}, consider {7x}, discover {1x}, perceive {2x}.

Katanoeo, as a verb, a strengthened form of *noeo*, "to perceive, understand fully, consider closely" (*kata*, intensive), denotes "the action of the mind in apprehending certain facts about a thing"; hence, translated **(1)** "behold," Acts 7:31–32; Jas 1:23–24; **(2)** "consider" **(2a)** the beam in one's own eye, Mt 7:3; **(2b)** of carefully "considering" the ravens, Lk 12:24; **(2c)** the lilies, Lk 12:27; **(2d)** of Peter's full "consideration" of his vision, Acts 11:6; **(2e)** of Abraham's careful "considering" of his own body, and Sarah's womb, as dead, and yet accepting by faith God's promise, Rom 4:19; **(2f)** of "considering" fully the Apostle and High Priest of our confession, Heb 3:1; **(2g)** of thoughtfully "considering" one another to provoke unto love and good works, Heb 10:24; **(3)** "discover," Acts 27:39; **(4)** "perceive," **(4a)** the beam in one's eye, Lk 6:41; **(4b)** of Jesus' perceiving the chief priests' craftiness, Lk 20:23. Syn.: 333, 816, 991, 1689, 1896, 2029, 2300, 2334, 2734, 3708. See: TDNT–4:973, 636; BAGD–415a; THAYER–334c.

2658. καταντάω {13x} **katantaō**, *kat-an-tah'-o;* from *2596* and a der. of *473;* to *meet against*, i.e. *arrive* at (lit. or fig.):—attain {2x}, come {11x}.

Katantao, "to come to, arrive at", is translated **(1)** "to come", **(1a)** literally, of locality, Acts 16:1; 18:19, 24; 20:15; 21:7; 25:13; 26:7; 28:13; **(1b)** metaphorically, **(1b1)** in 1 Cor 10:11 "upon whom the ends of the world are come", the metaphor is apparently that of an inheritance as coming down or descending to an heir, the "ends" (*tele* being the spiritual revenues (cf. Mt 17:25, revenues derived from taxes, and Rom 13:7, where the singular, *telos*, "custom," is used); the inheritance metaphor is again seen in 1 Cor 14:36, of the coming (or descending) of the Word of God to the Corinthians; and **(1b2)** to come in the sense of attain, Eph 4:13,

of "attaining" to the unity of the faith and of the knowledge of the Son of God. It is also translated **(2)** "to attain", in the sense of arriving completely at, **(2a)** in Acts 27:12, to the city of Phinece; **(2b)** Phil 3:11, of the paramount aims of the apostle's life, "if by any means," he says, "I might attain unto the resurrection from the dead," not the physical resurrection, which is assured to all believers hereafter, but to the present life of identification with Christ in His resurrection. See: TDNT–3:623, 419; BAGD–415d; THAYER–334c.

2659. κατάνυξις {1x} **katanuxis**, *kat-an'-oox-is;* from *2660;* a *prickling* (sensation, as of the limbs *asleep*), i.e. (by impl. [perh. by some confusion with *3506* or even with *3571*]) *stupor* (*lethargy*):—slumber {1x}.

Katanuxis, literally means "a pricking" (akin to *katanusso*, "to strike" or "prick violently," Acts 2:37), and is used in Rom 11:8, "slumber." This word describes the prickly, numb, tingling feeling one has when a limb [hand, foot, leg, etc.] "falls asleep." In the Jews' case their eyes and ears slumber. The Jews are still "wide awake" but their abilities to respond through their eyes and ears is hampered by "being asleep, slumbering, a deep sleep." See: TDNT–3:626, 419; BAGD–415c; THAYER–334d.

2660. κατανύσσω {1x} **katanussō**, *kat-an-oos'-so;* from *2596* and *3572;* to *pierce thoroughly*, i.e. (fig.) to *agitate* violently ("sting to the quick"):—prick {1x}.

Katanusso, primarily, "to strike or prick violently, to stun," is used of strong emotion, in Acts 2:37 (passive voice), "they were pricked (in their heart)." See: TDNT–3:626, 419; BAGD–415c; THAYER–334d.

2661. καταξιόω {4x} **kataxiŏō**, *kat-ax-ee-ŏ'-o;* from *2596* and *515;* to *deem entirely deserving:*—account worthy {2x}, count worthy {2x}.

Kataxioo denotes "to account worthy" (*kata*, "intensive", *axios*, "worthy"), "to judge, account worthy," Lk 20:35; 21:36; Acts 5:41; 2 Th 1:5. See: TDNT–1:380, 63; BAGD–415c; THAYER–335a.

2662. καταπατέω {5x} **katapatĕō**, *kat-ap-at-eh'-o;* from *2596* and *3961;* to *trample down;* fig. to *reject* with disdain:—trample {1x}, tread down {1x}, tread underfoot {2x}, tread {1x}.

Katapateo, "to tread down, trample under foot," is used **(1)** literally, Mt 5:13; 7:6; Lk 8:5; 12:1; **(2)** metaphorically, of "treading under foot" the Son of God, Heb 10:29, i.e., turning away from Him, to indulge in willful sin. See: TDNT–5:940, 804; BAGD–415d; THAYER–335a.

2663. **κατάπαυσις** {9x} **katapausis**, *kat-ap'-ow-sis;* from *2664; reposing down,* i.e. (by Heb.) *abode:*—rest {9x}.

Katapausis, "rest, repose"; is used **(1)** of God's "rest," Acts 7:49; Heb 3:11, 18; 4:1, 3 (twice), 5, 11; **(2)** in a general statement, applicable to God and man, Heb 4:10. **(3)** God's rest is entered when the believer is confidently assured within and outwardly lives peaceably in the assurance of God's daily provisions. See: TDNT—3:628, 419; BAGD—415d; THAYER—335a.

2664. **καταπαύω** {4x} **katapauō**, *kat-ap-ŏw'-o;* from *2596* and *3973;* to *settle down,* i.e. (lit.) to *colonize,* or (fig.) to (*cause to*) *desist:*—cease {1x}, give rest {1x}, rest {1x}, restrain {1x}.

Katapauo signifies "to cause to cease, restrain", and is translated **(1)** "restrained in Acts 14:18; **(2)** "rest" in Heb 4:4; **(3)** "give rest" in Heb 4:8; and **(4)** intransitively, "ceased" in Heb 4:10. See: TDNT—3:627, 419; BAGD—416a; THAYER—334b.

2665. **καταπέτασμα** {6x} **katapĕtasma**, *kat-ap-et'-as-mah;* from a compound of *2596* and a congener of *4072;* something *spread thoroughly,* i.e. (spec.) the door *screen* (to the Most Holy Place) in the Jewish temple:—veil {6x}.

Katapetasma, lit., "that which is spread out" (*petannumi*) "before" (*kata*), hence, "a veil," is used **(1)** of the inner "veil" of the tabernacle, Heb 6:19; 9:3; **(2)** of the corresponding "veil" in the temple, Mt 27:51; Mk 15:38; Lk 23:45; **(3)** metaphorically of the "flesh" of Christ, Heb 10:20, i.e., His body which He gave up to be crucified, thus by His expiatory death providing a means of the spiritual access of believers, the "new and living way," into the presence of God. See: TDNT—3:628, 420; BAGD—416b; THAYER—335b.

2666. **καταπίνω** {7x} **katapinō**, *kat-ap-ee'-no;* from *2596* and *4095;* to *drink down,* i.e. *gulp entire* (lit. or fig.):—devour {1x}, drown {1x}, swallow {4x}, swallow up {1x}.

Katapino, from *kato,* "down," intensive, *pino,* "to drink," **(1)** in 1 Pet 5:8 is translated "devour," of Satan's activities against believers. **(2)** The meaning "to swallow" is found in Mt 23:24; 1 Cor 15:54; 2 Cor 2:7; 5:4; Heb 11:29; Rev 12:16. See: TDNT—6:158, 841; BAGD—416b; THAYER—335c.

2667. **καταπίπτω** {2x} **katapiptō**, *kat-ap-ip'-to;* from *2596* and *4098;* to *fall down:*—fall {1x}, fall down {1x}. Cf. Acts 26:14; 28:6. See: TDNT—6:169, 846; BAGD—416c; THAYER—335d.

2668. **καταπλέω** {1x} **kataplĕō**, *kat-ap-leh'-o;* from *2596* and *4126;* to *sail down from the high seas* upon a place, i.e. to *land* at:—arrive {1x}.

Katapleo denotes "to sail down" (*kata,* "down," *pleo,* "to sail"), i.e., from the high sea to the shore, Lk 8:26. See: BAGD—416d; THAYER—335d.

2669. **καταπονέω** {2x} **kataponĕō**, *kat-ap-on-eh'-o;* from *2596* and a der. of *4192;* to *labor down,* i.e. *wear with toil* (fig. *harass*):—oppress {1x}, vex {1x}.

Kataponeo, as a verb, means primarily, **(1)** "to tire down with toil, exhaust with labor" [*kata,* "down," *ponos,* "labor"], hence signifies **(1a)** "to afflict, oppress"; **(1b)** in the passive voice, "to be oppressed, much distressed." **(2)** It is translated **(2a)** "oppressed": "And seeing one *of them* suffer wrong, he (Moses) defended *him,* and avenged him that was oppressed, and smote the Egyptian" (Acts 7:24), and **(2b)** "sore distressed/vexed": "And delivered just Lot, vexed with the filthy conversation of the wicked" (2 Pet 2:7). Syn.: 318, 928, 2347, 4660, 4729, 4730, 4928. See: BAGD—416d; THAYER—335d.

2670. **καταποντίζω** {2x} **katapŏntizō**, *kat-ap-on-tid'-zo;* from *2596* and a der. of the same as *4195;* to *plunge down,* i.e. *submerge:*—drown {1x}, sink {1x}.

Katapontizo, "to throw into the sea" (*kata,* "down," *pontos,* "the open sea"), in the passive voice, "to be sunk in, to be drowned," is translated **(1)** "were drowned," in Mt 18:6; and in **(2)** Mt 14:30, "(beginning) to sink." See: BAGD—417a; THAYER—335d.

2671. **κατάρα** {6x} **katara**, *kat-ar'-ah;* from *2596* (intens.) and *685; imprecation, execration:*—curse {3x}, cursed {2x}, cursing {1x}.

Katara, (*kata,* "down," intensive), denotes **(1)** an "execration, imprecation, curse," uttered out of malevolence, Jas 3:10; 2 Pet 2:14; or **(2)** pronounced by God in His righteous judgment, as upon a land doomed to barrenness, Heb 6:8; **(3)** upon those who seek for justification by obedience, in part or completely, to the Law, Gal 3:10, 13; in this 13th verse it is used concretely of Christ, as having "become a curse" for us, i.e., by voluntarily undergoing on the cross the appointed penalty of the "curse." He thus was identified, on our behalf, with the doom of sin. See: TDNT—1:449, 75; BAGD—417a; THAYER—335d.

2672. **καταράομαι** {6x} **kataraŏmai**, *kat-ar-ah'-om-ahee;* mid. voice from *2671;* to *execrate;* by anal. to *doom:*—curse {6x}.

Kataraomai, as a verb, primarily signifies

"to pray against, to wish evil against a person or thing"; hence "to curse": "Then shall he say also unto them on the left hand, Depart from me, ye cursed, into everlasting fire, prepared for the devil and his angels" (Mt 25:41; cf. Mk 11:21; Lk 6:28; Rom 12:14; Jas 3:9). Syn.: 331, 332, 685, 1944, 2551, 2652, 2653, 2671. See: TDNT—1:448, 75; BAGD—417a; THAYER—336a.

2673. **καταργέω** {27x} **katargĕō**, *kat-arg-eh'-o;* from *2596* and *691;* to *be* (*render*) *entirely* idle (*useless*), lit. or fig.:—destroy {5x}, do away {3x}, abolish {3x}, cumber {1x}, loose {1x}, cease {1x}, fall {1x}, deliver {1x}, misc. {11x} = become (make) of no (none, without) effect, bring (come) to nought, put away (down), vanish away, make void.

Katargeo, as a verb, means lit., "to reduce to inactivity" (*kata*, "down," *argos*, "inactive"), is translated **(1)** "abolish" in Eph 2:15; 2 Ti 1:10; 2 Cor 3:13. In this and similar words not loss of being is implied, but loss of well-being. **(1a)** The barren tree was cumbering the ground, making it useless for the purpose of its existence, Lk 13:7; **(1b)** the unbelief of the Jews could not "make of none effect" the faithfulness of God, Rom 3:3; **(1c)** the preaching of the gospel could not "make of none effect" the moral enactments of the Law, Rom 3:31; **(1d)** the Law could not make the promise of "none effect," Rom 4:14; Gal 3:17; **(1e)** the effect of the identification of the believer with Christ in His death is to render inactive his body in regard to sin, Rom 6:6; **(1f)** the death of a woman's first husband discharges her from the law of the husband, that is, it makes void her status as his wife in the eyes of the law, Rom 7:2; **(1g)** in that sense the believer has been discharged from the Law, Rom 7:6; **(1h)** God has chosen things that are not "to bring to nought things that are," i.e., to render them useless for practical purposes, 1 Cor 1:28; **(1i)** the princes of this world are "brought to nought," i.e., their wisdom becomes ineffective, Rom 2:6; **(1j)** the use for which the human stomach exists ceases with man's death, Rom 6:13; **(1k)** knowledge, prophesyings, and that which was in part were to be "done away," 1 Cor 13:8, 10, i.e., they were to be rendered of no effect after their temporary use was fulfilled; **(1l)** when the apostle became a man he did away with the ways of a child, 1 Cor 13:11; **(1m)** God is going to abolish all rule and authority and power, i.e., He is going to render them inactive, 1 Cor 15:24; **(1n)** the last enemy that shall be abolished, or reduced to inactivity, is death, 1 Cor 15: 26; **(1o)** the glory shining in the face of Moses, "was passing away," 2 Cor 3:7, **(1p)** the transitoriness of its character being of a special significance,

2 Cor 3:11, 13; **(1q)** the veil upon the heart of Israel is "done away" in Christ, 2 Cor 3:14; **(1r)** those who seek justification by the Law are "severed" from Christ, they are rendered inactive in relation to Him, Gal 5:4; **(1s)** the essential effect of the preaching of the Cross would become inoperative by the preaching of circumcision, 2 Cor 5:11; **(1t)** by the death of Christ the barrier between Jew and Gentile is rendered inoperative as such, Eph 2:15; **(1u)** the Man of Sin is to be reduced to inactivity by the manifestation of the Lord's Parousia with His people, 2 Th 2:8; **(1v)** Christ has rendered death inactive for the believer, 2 Ti 1:10, death becoming the means of a more glorious life, with Christ; **(1w)** the devil is to be reduced to inactivity through the death of Christ, Heb 2:14. **(2)** It is translated "cumber" in Lk 13:7. See: TDNT—1:452, 76; BAGD—417b; THAYER—336a.

2674. **καταριθμέω** {1x} **katarithmĕō**, *kat-ar-ith-meh'-o;* from *2596* and *705;* to *reckon among:*—number with {1x}. See: BAGD—417c; THAYER—336b.

2675. **καταρτίζω** {13x} **katartizo**, *kat-ar-tid'-zo;* from *2596* and a der. of *739;* to *complete thoroughly,* i.e. *repair* (lit. or fig.) or *adjust:*—perfect {2x}, make perfect {2x}, mend {2x}, be perfect {2x}, fit {1x}, frame {1x}, prepare {1x}, restore {1x}, perfectly joined together {1x}.

Katartizo, "to render fit, complete" (*artios*), is used **(1)** of mending nets, Mt 4:21; Mk 1:19, and is translated **(2)** "restore" in Gal 6:1. **(3)** It does not necessarily imply, however, that that to which it is applied has been damaged, though it may do so, as in these passages; it signifies, rather, right ordering and arrangement, Heb 11:3, "framed"; **(4)** it points out the path of progress, as in Mt 21:16; Lk 6:40; cf. 2 Cor 13:9; Eph 4:12, where corresponding nouns occur. **(5)** It indicates the close relationship between character and destiny, Rom 9:22, "fitted", where the middle voice signifies that those referred to "fitted" themselves for destruction, as illustrated in the case of Pharaoh, who self-hardened his own heart. **(6)** It expresses the pastor's desire for the flock, **(6a)** in prayer, Heb 13:21, and **(6b)** in exhortation, 1 Cor 1:10, "perfectly joined"; 2 Cor 13:11, **(6c)** as well as his conviction of God's purpose for them, 1 Pet 5:10. **(7)** It is used of the Incarnation of the Word in Heb 10:5, "prepare" quoted from Ps 40:6, where it is apparently intended to describe the unique creative act involved in the Virgin Birth, Lk 1:35. **(8)** In 1 Th 3:10 it means to supply what is necessary, as

the succeeding words show. See: TDNT—1:475, 80; BAGD—417d; THAYER—336c.

2676. κατάρτισις {1x} **katartisis**, *kat-ar'-tis-is;* from *2675; thorough equipment* (subj.):—perfection {1x}.

This word means making a fit and is used figuratively in an ethical sense in 2 Cor 13:9, implying a process leading to consummation. See: TDNT—1:475, 80; BAGD—418a; THAYER—336d.

2677. καταρτισμός {1x} **katartismŏs**, *kat-ar-tis-mos';* from *2675; complete furnishing* (obj.):—perfecting {1x}.

This word means "a fitting or preparing fully," Eph 4:12. See: TDNT—1:475, 80; BAGD—418a; THAYER—336d.

2678. κατασείω {4x} **kataseiō**, *kat-as-i'-o;* from *2596* and *4579;* to *sway downward,* i.e. *make a signal usually with the hand:*—beckon {4x}.

Kataseio, lit., "to shake down" (*kata,* "down," *seio,* "to shake"), of shaking the hand, of waving, expresses a little more vigorously the act of "beckoning," Acts 12:17; 13:16; 19:33; 21:40. Syn.: *Neuo* and its compounds have primary reference to a movement of the head; *kataseio,* to that of the hand. See also 2656. See: BAGD—418a; THAYER—336d.

2679. κατασκάπτω {2x} **kataskaptō**, *kat-as-kap'-to;* from *2596* and *4626;* to *undermine,* i.e. (by impl.) *destroy:*—dig down {1x}, ruin {1x}.

This verb means to dig under, dig down under the foundation so as to topple, demolish, and destroy and is found **(1)** in Rom 11:3, of altars, and in **(2)** Acts 15:16, "ruins," lit., "the things dug down." See: BAGD—418b; THAYER—336d.

2680. κατασκευάζω {11x} **kataskĕuazō**, *kat-ask-yoo-ad'-zo;* from *2596* and a der. of *4632;* to *prepare thoroughly* (prop. by extern. *equipment;* whereas *2090* refers rather to intern. *fitness*); by impl. to *construct, create:*—build {3x}, make {1x}, ordain {1x}, prepare {6x}.

Kataskeuazo, "to prepare, make ready" (*kata,* used intensively, *skeue,* "equipment"), and is translated **(1)** "prepare" in Mt 11:10; Mk 1:2; Lk 1:17; 7:27; Heb 11:7; 1 Pet 3:20; **(2)** "were . . . ordained" in Heb 9:6; and **(3)** "made" in Heb 9:2; and **(4)** "build" in Heb 3:3, 4 twice. See: BAGD—418b; THAYER—336d.

2681. κατασκηνόω {4x} **kataskēnŏō**, *kat-as-kay-nŏ'-o;* from *2596* and *4637;* to *camp down,* i.e. *haunt;* fig. to *remain:*—lodge {3x}, rest {1x}.

Literally, *kataskenoo* means to pitch one's

tent, and is translated **(1)** "lodge" (Mt 13:32; Mk 4:32; Lk 13:19); and **(2)** "rest" in Acts 2:26. See: TDNT—7:387, 1040; BAGD—418c; THAYER—337a.

2682. κατασκήνωσις {2x} **kataskēnōsis**, *kat-as-kay'-no-sis;* from *2681;* an *encamping,* i.e. (fig.) a *perch:*—nest {2x}.

This word means properly "an encamping, taking up one's quarters," then, "a lodging, abode" (*kata,* "down over," *skene,* "a tent"), is used of birds' "nests" in Mt 8:20 and Lk 9:58. See: BAGD—418c; THAYER—337a.

2683. κατασκιάζω {1x} **kataskiazō**, *kat-as-kee-ad'-zo;* from *2596* and a der. of *4639;* to *overshade,* i.e. *cover:*—shadow {1x}.

Kataskiazo, lit., "to shadow down," is used of the cherubim of glory above the mercy seat casting their shadow down upon it, Heb 9:5, "shadowing." See: BAGD—418d; THAYER—337a.

2684. κατασκοπέω {1x} **kataskŏpĕō**, *kat-as-kop-eh'-o;* from *2685;* to *be a sentinel,* i.e. to *inspect* insidiously:—spy out {1x}.

This word means to view closely, spy out, search out with a view to plotting against and overthrowing (Gal 2:4). See: TDNT—7:416, 1047; BAGD—418d; THAYER—337b.

2685. κατάσκοπος {1x} **kataskŏpŏs**, *kat-as'-kop-os;* from *2596* (intens.) and *4649* (in the sense of a *watcher*); a *reconnoiterer:*—a spy {1x}.

One who does 2684 is a *kataskopos,* Heb 11:31. See: TDNT—7:417, 1047; BAGD—418d; THAYER—337b.

2686. κατασοφίζομαι {1x} **katasŏphizŏmai**, *kat-as-of-id'-zom-ahee;* mid. voice from *2596* and *4679;* to *be crafty against,* i.e. *circumvent:*—deal subtilly (subtly) with {1x}.

This word means to circumvent by artifice or fraud, to conquer by subtle devices; to outwit, to deal craftily with (Acts 7:19). See: BAGD—418d; THAYER—337b.

2687. καταστέλλω {2x} **katastĕllō**, *kat-as-tel'-lo;* from *2596* and *4724;* to *put down,* i.e. *quell:*—appease {1x}, quiet {1x}.

Katastello means to put or keep down one who is roused or incensed, to repress, restrain, appease, quiet and is translated **(1)** in the passive voice, "to be quiet, or to be quieted" in Acts 19:36, lit., "to be quieted"; and **(2)** in the active voice in Acts 19:35, "appeased." See:

TDNT−7:595, 1074; BAGD−419a; THAYER− 337b.

2688. κατάστημα {1x} **katastēma**, *kat-as'-tay-mah;* from *2525;* prop. a *position* or *condition,* i.e. (subj.) *demeanor:*−behaviour {1x}.

Katastema denotes "a condition, or constitution of anything, or deportment", Titus 2:3. See: BAGD−419a; THAYER−337b.

2689. καταστολή {1x} **katastŏlē**, *kat-as-tol-ay';* from *2687;* a *deposit,* i.e. (spec.) *costume:*−apparel {1x}.

Katastole, "to send or let down, to lower", connected with *katastello* (*kata,* "down," *stello,* "to send"), was primarily a garment let down; hence, "dress, attire," in general (cf. *stole,* a loose outer garment worn by kings and persons of rank,−Eng., "stole"); 1 Ti 2:9, "apparel." See: TDNT−7:595, 1074; BAGD−419a; THAYER−337b.

2690. καταστρέφω {2x} **katastrĕphō**, *kat-as-tref'-o;* from *2596* and *4762;* to *turn* upside *down,* i.e. *upset:*−overthrow {2x}.

Katastrepho, lit. and primarily, "to turn down" or "turn over," as, e.g., the soil, denotes to "overturn, overthrow," Mt 21:12; Mk 11:15. See: TDNT−7:715, 1093; BAGD−419a; THAYER−337c.

2691. καταστρηνιάω {1x} **katastrēniaō**, *kat-as-tray-nee-ah'-o;* from *2596* and *4763;* to *become voluptuous against:*−begin to wax wanton against {1x}.

Used only once, 1 Ti 5:11: "But the younger widows refuse: for when they have begun to wax wanton against Christ, they will marry . . ." Wanton means to be undisciplined [to the vows of widowhood and receiving care from being on the church's support list]. These young widows will slowly over time ["wax"] desire support from a husband [not condemned, just stated] and they will beome undisciplined in their vows contained in being put on the list; hence, against Christ as their sole support through His church. To prevent this natural desire leading to an uncomfortable situation for the local church, let the younger widows marry. See: TDNT−3:631, 420; BAGD−419b; THAYER−337c.

2692. καταστροφή {2x} **katastrŏphē**, *kat-as-trof-ay';* from *2690;* an *overturn* ("catastrophe"), i.e. *demolition;* fig. *apostasy:*−overthrow {1x}, subverting {1x}.

Katastrophe, lit., "a turning down" (*kata,* "down," *strophe,* "a turning"; Eng., "catastrophe"), is used **(1)** literally, 2 Pet 2:6, "overthrow" (of cities); and **(2)** metaphorically, 2 Ti

2:14 "subverting," i.e., the "overthrowing" of faith. See: TDNT−7:715, 1093; BAGD−419b; THAYER−337c.

2693. καταστρώννυμι {1x} **katastrŏnnumi**, *kat-as-trone'-noo-mee;* from *2596* and *4766;* to *strew down,* i.e. (by impl.) to *prostrate* (*slay*):−overthrow {1x}.

These unbelieving Israelites were slain (*katastronnumi*) and strewn over the wilderness [and buried] over the forty years (1 Cor 10:5). See: BAGD−419b; THAYER−337c.

2694. κατασύρω {1x} **katasurō**, *kat-as-oo'-ro;* from *2596* and *4951;* to *drag down,* i.e. *arrest* judicially:−hale {1x}.

Katasuro means to pull down and drag away forcibly to stand before a judge (Lk 12:58). See: BAGD−419b; THAYER−337d.

2695. κατασφάττω {1x} **katasphattō**, *kat-as-fat'-to;* from *2596* and *4969;* to *kill down,* i.e. *slaughter:*−slay {1x}.

This word stresses to kill off, to slaughter all the disobedient (Lk 19:27). See: BAGD−419c; THAYER−337d.

2696. κατασφραγίζω {1x} **katasphragizō**, *kat-as-frag-id'-zo;* from *2596* and *4972;* to *seal closely and securely:*−to seal {1x}.

In Rev 5:1 the book/scroll is securely sealed (*kata,* intensive) by seven seals. See: TDNT−7:939, 1127; BAGD−419c; THAYER−337d.

2697. κατάσχεσις {2x} **kataschĕsis**, *kat-as'-khes-is;* from *2722;* a *holding down,* i.e. *occupancy:*−possession {2x}.

Kataschesis, primarily "a holding back", then, "a holding fast," denotes "a possession," Acts 7:5, or "taking possession," v. 45, with the article, lit., "in the (i.e., their) taking possession." See: BAGD−419c; THAYER−337d.

2698. κατατίθημι {3x} **katatithēmi**, *kat-at-ith'-ay-mee;* from *2596* and *5087;* to *place down,* i.e. *deposit* (lit. or fig.):−do {1x}, lay {1x}, shew {1x}.

This word means to deposit, lay up, to lay down, (*kata*), is translated **(1)** "lay" in Mk 15:46 of the act of Joseph of Arimathaea in "laying" Christ's body in the tomb; **(2)** "do", Acts 25:9, doing the Jews a pleasure; and **(3)** "shew", Acts 24:27, to shew the Jews a pleasure. See: BAGD−419c; THAYER−337d.

2699. κατατομή {1x} **katatŏmē**, *kat-at-om-ay';* from a compound of *2596* and τέμνω **tĕmnō** (to *cut*); a *cutting down* (*off*), i.e. *mutilation* (ironically):−concision {1x}.

Katatome, lit., "a cutting off" (*kata,* "down," *temno,* "to cut"), "a mutilation," is a term found

in Phil 3:2, there used by the Apostle, by a *paranomasia* (play on words), contemptuously, for the Jewish circumcision with its Judaistic influence, in contrast to the true spiritual circumcision. See: TDNT—8:109, 1169; BAGD—419d; THAYER—338a. comp. *609.*

2700. κατατοξεύω {1x} **katatŏxĕuō,** *kat-at-ox-yoo'-o;* from *2596* and a der. of *5115;* to *shoot down* with an arrow or other missile:—thrust through {1x}. See: BAGD—419d; THAYER—338a.

2701. κατατρέχω {1x} **katatrĕchō,** *kat-at-rekh'-o;* from *2596* and *5143;* to *run down,* i.e. *hasten* from a tower:—run down (from) {1x}. See: BAGD—419d; THAYER—338a.

καταφάγω kataphagō. See *2719.*

2702. καταφέρω {3x} **kataphĕrō,** *kat-af-er'-o;* from *2596* and *5342* (incl. its alt.); to *bear down,* i.e. (fig.) *overcome* (with drowsiness); spec. to *cast* a vote:—fall {1x}, give {1x}, sink down {1x}.

Kataphero, "to bring down or against" (*kata,* "down"), **(1)** of Eutychus **(1a)** "fallen down" into a deep sleep, Acts 26:10 (first reference), and **(2)** being "borne down" with sleep, Acts 20:9 (second reference), he fell from the window to the street below; and **(3)** it is used of casting a ballot or "giving" a vote in Acts 26:10. See: BAGD—419d; THAYER—338a.

2703. καταφεύγω {2x} **kataphĕugō,** *kat-af-yoo'-go;* from *2596* and *5343;* to *flee down* (*away*):—flee {2x}.

Katapheugo, "to flee for refuge" (*kata,* used intensively), is used **(1)** literally in Acts 14:6; and **(2)** metaphorically in Heb 6:18, of "fleeing" for refuge to lay hold upon hope. See: BAGD—420a; THAYER—338b.

2704. καταφθείρω {2x} **kataphthĕirō,** *kat-af-thi'-ro;* from *2596* and *5351;* to *spoil entirely,* i.e. (lit.) to *destroy;* or (fig.) to *deprave:*—corrupt {1x}, utterly perish {1x}.

Kataphtheiro is said **(1)** of men who are reprobate concerning the faith, "corrupt in mind", 2 Ti 3:8; and **(2)** men who will "utterly perish", 2 Pet 2:12. See: TDNT—9:93, 1259; BAGD—420a; THAYER—338b.

2705. καταφιλέω {6x} **kataphilĕō,** *kat-af-ee-leh'-o;* from *2596* and *5368;* to *kiss earnestly:*—kiss {6x}.

Kataphileo denotes "to kiss fervently" (*kata,* intensive); the stronger force of this verb has been called in question, but the change from *phileo* to *kataphileo* in Mt 26:49 and Mk 14:45 can scarcely be without significance, and the

act of the traitor was almost certainly more demonstrative than the simple kiss of salutation. So with the kiss of genuine devotion, Lk 7:38, 45; 15:20; Acts 20:37, in each of which this verb is used. See: TDNT—9:114, 1262; BAGD—420b; THAYER—338b.

2706. καταφρονέω {9x} **kataphrŏnĕō,** *kat-af-ron-eh'-o;* from *2596* and *5426;* to *think against,* i.e. *disesteem:*—despise {9x}.

This verb denotes to think little of, slightly of, or nothing of another lit., "to think down upon or against anyone" (*kata,* "down," *phren,* "the mind"), hence signifies "to think slightly of, to despise," Mt 6:24; 18:10; Lk 16:13; Rom 2:4; 1 Cor 11:22; 1 Ti 4:12; 6:2; Heb 12:2; 2 Pet 2:10. See: TDNT—3:631, 421; BAGD—420b; THAYER—338c.

2707. καταφρονητής {1x} **kataphrŏntēs,** *kat-af-ron-tace';* from *2706;* a *contemner:*—despiser {1x}.

Kataphrontes, lit., "one who thinks down against," hence, "a despiser" is found in Acts 13:41. See: TDNT—3:632, 421; BAGD—420c; THAYER—338c.

2708. καταχέω {2x} **katachĕō,** *kat-akh-eh'-o;* from *2596* and χέω **chĕō** (to *pour*); to *pour down* (*out*):—pour {2x}.

Katacheo, "to pour down upon" (*kata,* "down," *cheo,* "to pour"), is used in Mt 26:7 and Mk 14:3, of ointment. See: BAGD—420c; THAYER—338c.

2709. καταχθόνιος {1x} **katachthŏniŏs,** *kat-akh-thon'-ee-os;* from *2596* and χθών **chthōn** (the *ground*); *subterranean,* i.e. *infernal* (belonging to the world of departed spirits):—under the earth {1x}. See: TDNT—3:633, 421; BAGD—420d; THAYER—338c.

2710. καταχράομαι {2x} **katachraŏmai,** *kat-akh-rah'-om-ahee;* from *2596* and *5530;* to *overuse,* i.e. *misuse:*—abuse {2x}.

Katachraomai, lit., "to use overmuch" (*kata,* "down," intensive, *chraomai,* "to use"), is found in 1 Cor 7:31, with reference to the believer's use [over use] of the world, and 1 Cor 9:18, "abuse." See: BAGD—420d; THAYER—338d.

2711. καταψύχω {1x} **katapsuchō,** *kat-ap-soo'-kho;* from *2596* and *5594;* to *cool down* (*off*), i.e. *refresh:*—cool {1x}. See: BAGD—421a; THAYER—338d.

2712. κατείδωλος {1x} **katĕidōlŏs,** *kat-i'-do-los;* from *2596* (intens.) and *1497; utterly idolatrous:*—wholly

given to idolatry {1x}. See: TDNT—2:379, 202; BAGD—412a; THAYER—338d.

κατελεύθω katělěuthō. See 2718.

2713. **κατέναντι** {5x} **katěnanti**, *kat-en'-an-tee;* from *2596* and *1725; directly opposite:*—before {1x}, over against {4x}.

Katenanti, (*kata,* "down," lit., "down over against"), is used (1) of locality, "over against", e.g., Mk 11:2; 13:3; Lk 19:30; (2) as "before", "in the sight of", Rom 4:17. See: BAGD—421b; THAYER—338d.

κατενέγκω katěněgkō. See 2702.

2714. **κατενώπιον** {5x} **katěnōpiŏn**, *kat-en-o'-pee-on;* from *2596* and *1799; dir. in front of:*—before {2x}, in sight of {1x}, in (one's) sight {1x}, before the presence of {1x}.

Katenopion signifies "right over against, opposite", always in reference to God: (1) "before", (1a) "before (God)", 2 Cor 12:19; (1b) "before" (God as Judge), Eph 1:4; (2) "in the sight of (God)", 2 Cor 2:17 (3) "in His sight", Col. 1:22; (4) "before the presence of (His glory)", Jude 24. See: BAGD—421b; THAYER—339a.

2715. **κατεξουσιάζω** {2x} **katěxŏusiazō**, *kat-ex-oo-see-ad'-zo;* from *2596* and *1850;* to *have* (*wield*) *full privilege over:*—exercise authority upon {2x}. Cf. Mt 20:25; Mk 10:42. See: TDNT—2:575, 238; BAGD—421c; THAYER—339a.

2716. **κατεργάζομαι** {24x} **katěrgazŏmai**, *kat-er-gad'-zom-ahee;* from *2596* and *2038;* do *work fully,* i.e. *accomplish;* by impl. to *finish, fashion:*—work {15x}, do {5x}, do deed {1x}, to perform {1x}, cause {1x}, work out {1x}.

(1) This word usually means to work out, i.e. to do that from which something results, to bring about, to result in. (2) It is an emphatic form and signifies "to work out, achieve, effect by toil," rendered "to work" (past tense, "wrought") in Rom 1:27; 4:15 (the Law brings men under condemnation and so renders them subject to divine wrath); 5:3; 7:8, 13; 15:18; 2 Cor 4:17; 5:5; 7:10, 11; 12:12; Phil 2:12, where "your own salvation" refers especially to freedom from strife and vainglory; Jas 1:3, 20; 1 Pet 4:3. (3) It has various translations of "do": (3a) Rom 2:9 "doeth", (3b) Rom 7:15, 17, "I do", (3c) Rom 7:20, "I that do", (3d) 1 Cor 5:3, "done." (4) In Eph 6:13 "having done (all)". See: TDNT—3:634, 421; BAGD—421c; THAYER—339a.

2717. Because of some changes in the numbering system (while the original work was in progress) no Greek words were cited for 2717 or 3203-3302. These numbers were dropped altogether. This will not cause any problems in Strong's numbering system. No Greek words have been left out. Because so many other reference works use this numbering system, it has not been revised. If it were revised, much confusion would certainly result.

2718. **κατέρχομαι** {13x} **katěrchŏmai**, *kat-er'-khom-ahee;* from *2596* and *2064* (incl. its alt.); to *come* (or *go*) *down* (lit. or fig.):—come down {5x}, come {3x}, go down {2x}, depart {1x}, descend {1x}, land {1x}.

This word means "to come down" (*kata,* "down"), and is translated (1) "come down", Lk 4:31; 9:37; Acts 9:32; 15:1; 21:10; (2) "come", Acts 11:27; 18:5; 27:5; (3) "go down", Acts 8:5; 12:19; (4) "depart", Acts 13:4; (5) "descend", Jas 3:15; (6) "landed", Acts 18:22. See: BAGD—422a; THAYER—339b.

2719. **κατεσθίω** {15x} **katěsthiō**, *kat-es-thee'-o;* from *2596* and *2068* (incl. its alt.); to *eat down,* i.e. *devour* (lit. or fig.):—devour {10x}, eat up {3x}, devour up {2x}.

Katesthio denotes (1) "to consume by eating, to devour," said of birds, Mt 13:4; Mk 4:4; Lk 8:5; (1a) of the dragon, Rev 12:4; (1b) of a prophet, "eating" up a book, suggestive of spiritually "eating" and digesting its contents, Rev 10:9 (cf. Eze 2:8; 3:1–3; Jer 15:16); (2) metaphorically, (2a) "to squander, to waste," Lk 15:30; (2b) "to consume" one's physical powers by emotion, Jn 2:17; (2c) "to devour" by forcible appropriation, as of widows' property, Mt 23:14; Mk 12:40; (2d) "to demand maintenance," as false apostles did to the church at Corinth, 2 Cor 11:20; (2e) "to exploit or prey on one another," Gal 5:15, where "bite . . . devour . . . consume" form a climax, the first two describing a process, the last the act of swallowing down; (2f) to "destroy" by fire, Rev 11:5; 20:9. See: BAGD—422a; THAYER—339b.

2720. **κατευθύνω** {3x} **katěuthunō**, *kat-yoo-thoo'-no;* from *2596* and *2116;* to *straighten fully,* i.e. (fig.) *direct:*—guide {1x}, direct {2x}.

This word means to make straight, remove all hindrances in order to guide or direct (Lk 1:79; 1 Th 3:11; 2 Th 3:5). See: BAGD—422b; THAYER—339c.

2721. **κατεφίστημι** {1x} **katěphistēmi**, *kat-ef-is'-tay-mee;* from *2596* and *2186;* to *stand over against,* i.e. *rush upon* (*assault*):—make insurrection against {1x}. See: BAGD—422c; THAYER—339d.

2722. **κατέχω** {19x} **katěchō**, *kat-ekh'-o;* from *2596* and *2192;* to *hold*

down (*fast*), in various applications (lit. or fig.):—hold {3x}, hold fast {3x}, keep {2x}, possess {2x}, stay {1x}, take {1x}, have {1x}, make {1x}, misc. {5x} = let, retain, seize on, withhold.

This word stresses holding fast in order to hinder the course or progress of something or someone. This word means "to hold firmly, hold fast" and is rendered **(1)** "keep" in 1 Cor 11:2; **(2)** "hold fast" in 1 Th 5:21; Heb 3:6; 10:23; **(3)** "hold" in Heb 3:14; Rom. 1:18, of unrighteous men who restrain the spread of truth by their unrighteousness, **(4)** "held" in Rom 7:6 of the Law as that which had "held" in bondage those who through faith in Christ were made dead to it as a means of life; **(5)** "to hold fast, hold back," signifies "to possess," in 1 Cor 7:30 and 2 Cor 6:10. See: TDNT—2:829, 286; BAGD—422c; THAYER—339d.

2723. **κατηγορέω** {22x} **katēgŏrĕō**, *kat-ay-gor-eh'-o;* from *2725;* to be a *plaintiff,* i.e. to *charge* with some offence:—accuse {21x}, object {1x}.

Kategoreo, as a verb, means "to speak against, accuse" is used **(1)** in a general way, "to accuse": "Which shew the work of the law written in their hearts, their conscience also bearing witness, and their thoughts the mean while accusing or else excusing one another" (Rom 2:15); and more specifically **(2)** before a judge: "And, behold, there was a man which had his hand withered. And they asked him, saying, Is it lawful to heal on the sabbath days? that they might accuse him" (Mt 12:10). Syn.: *Aitiama* (*157*) means to accuse with primary reference to the ground of the accusation; the crime, *egklema* (*1462*) means to make a verbal assault which reaches its goal, and *katagoreo* (*2723*) means to accuse formally before a tribunal, bring a charge against publicly. See also: 156, 157, 1225, 1458, 1462, 1908, 2724, 4811. See: TDNT—3:637, 422; BAGD—423a; THAYER—340a.

2724. **κατηγορία** {4x} **katēgŏria**, *kat-ay-gor-ee'-ah;* from *2725;* a *complaint* ("category"), i.e. criminal *charge:*—accusation {3x}, accused {1x}.

Kategoria (*2724*), means **(1)** "an accusation": "Pilate then went out unto them, and said, What accusation bring ye against this man?" (Jn 18:29; cf. 1 Ti 5:19; Titus 1:6). **(2)** This noun and the verb *kategoreo* (2723 - "to accuse"), and the participle *kategoros* (from 2723 - "an accuser"), all have chiefly to do with judicial procedure, as distinct from *diaballo* (1225 - "to slander"). **(3)** It is derived from *agora,* "a place of public speaking," prefixed by *kata,* "against"; hence, it signifies a speaking against a person before a public tribunal. It is the op-

posite to *apologia* (*626*), "a defense." Syn.: 156, 157, 1225, 1458, 1462, 1908, 2723, 4811. See: TDNT—3:637, 422; BAGD—423c; THAYER—340c.

2725. **κατήγορος** {7x} **katēgŏrŏs**, *kat-ay'-gor-os;* from *2596* and *58; against* one in the *assembly,* i.e. a *complainant* at law; spec. *Satan:*—accuser {7x}.

A *kategoros* is "an accuser," and is used in Jn 8:10; Acts 23:30, 35; 24:8; 25:16, 18. In Rev 12:10, it is used of Satan. See: TDNT—3:636, 422; BAGD—423c; THAYER—340c.

2726. **κατήφεια** {1x} **katēphĕia**, *kat-ay'-fi-ah;* from a compound of *2596* and perh. a der. of the base of *5316* (mean. *downcast* in look); *demureness,* i.e. (by impl.) *sadness:*—heaviness {1x}.

Katapheia denotes a downcast look, expressive of sorrow; hence, "dejection, heaviness"; it is used in Jas. 4:9. See: BAGD—423c; THAYER—340c.

2727. **κατηχέω** {8x} **katēchĕō**, *kat-ay-kheh'-o;* from *2596* and *2279;* to *sound down* into the ears, i.e. (by impl.) to *indoctrinate* ("catechize") or (gen.) to *apprise* of:—inform {2x}, instruct {3x}, teach {3x}.

(1) This word indicates verbal instruction which is "sounded down into the student's ears," and then repeated by the student to assure learning has taken place [cf. Eng. catechize]. *Katecheo* primarily denotes "to resound" (*kata,* "down," *echos* "a sound"); then, "to sound down the ears, to teach by word of mouth, instruct, inform" (Eng., "catechize, catechumen"); it is rendered, **(2)** in the passive voice, by the verb "to inform," in Acts 21:21, 24. Here it is used of the large numbers of Jewish believers at Jerusalem whose zeal for the Law had been stirred by information of accusations made against the apostle Paul, as to certain anti-Mosaic teaching he was supposed to have given the Jews. **(3)** It also denotes "to teach orally, inform, instruct," is translated by the verb "to instruct" in Lk 1:4; Acts 18:25; Rom 2:18; **(4)** is rendered "to teach" in 1 Cor 14:19; Gal 6:6 (twice). See: TDNT—3:638, 422; BAGD—423d; THAYER—340d.

2728. **κατιόω** {1x} **katiŏō**, *kat-ee-ŏ'-o;* from *2596* and a der. of *2447;* to *rust down,* i.e. *corrode:*—canker {1x}.

A canker is an ulcer-like sore, erupting from below the surface, like rust erupts in metal. See: TDNT—3:334; BAGD—424a; THAYER—340d.

2729. **κατισχύω** {2x} **katischuō**, *kat-is-khoo'-o;* from *2596* and *2480;* to *overpower:*—prevail {1x}, prevail against {1x}.

This word means to be strong to another's detriment, to prevail against, to be superior in strength, to overcome, to prevail. *Katischuo*, "to be strong against" is used **(1)** in Mt 16:18, negatively of the gates of hades not "prevailing against" Christ's church; and **(2)** in Lk 23:23, of the voices of the chief priests, rulers and people "prevailed" over Pilate regarding the crucifixion of Christ. See: TDNT—3:397, 378; BAGD—424a; THAYER—340d.

2730. **κατοικέω** {47x} **katŏikĕō,** *kat-oy-keh'-o;* from *2596* and *3611;* to *house permanently,* i.e. *reside* (lit. or fig.):—dwell {42x}, dweller {2x}, inhabitant {1x}, inhabiters {2x}

This frequent verb properly signifies "to settle down in a dwelling, to dwell fixedly in a place." Besides its literal sense, it is used of **(1)** the "indwelling" of the totality of the attributes and powers of the Godhead in Christ, Col 1:19; 2:9; **(2)** the "indwelling" of Christ in the hearts of believers ("may make a home in your hearts"), Eph 3:17; **(3)** the "dwelling" of Satan in a locality, Rev 2:13; **(4)** the future "indwelling" of righteousness in the new heavens and earth, 2 Pet 3:13. It is translated **(5)** "dwellers" in Acts 1:19; 2:9; **(6)** "inhabitants" in Rev 17:2; and **(7)** "inhabiters" in Rev 8:13 and 12:12. See: TDNT—5:153, 674; BAGD—424a; THAYER—341a.

2731. **κατοίκησις** {1x} **katŏikēsis,** *kat-oy'-kay-sis;* from *2730;* residence (prop. the act; but by impl. concr. the mansion):—a dwelling {1x}. See: BAGD—424c; THAYER—341b.

2732. **κατοικητήριον** {2x} **katŏikētēriŏn,** *kat-oy-kay-tay'-ree-on;* from a der. of *2730;* a *dwelling-place:*—habitation {2x}.

Katoiketerion, (*kata,* "down," used intensively), implying permanency, is used **(1)** in Eph 2:22 of the church as the dwelling place of the Holy Spirit; **(2)** in Rev 18:2 of Babylon, figuratively, as the dwelling place of devils. See: TDNT—5:155, 674; BAGD—424c; THAYER—341b.

2733. **κατοικία** {1x} **katŏikia,** *kat-oy-kee'-ah; residence* (prop. the condition; but by impl. the abode itself):—habitation {1x}.

Katoikia is "a settlement, colony, dwelling" (*kata,* and *oikos,* see above), is used in Acts 17:26, of the localities divinely appointed as the dwelling places of the nations. See: BAGD—424c; THAYER—341b.

2734. **κατοπτρίζομαι** {1x} **katŏptrizŏmai,** *kat-op-trid'-zom-ahee;* mid. voice from a compound of *2596* and a der.

of *3700* [comp. *2072*]; to *mirror oneself,* i.e. to *see reflected* (fig.):—behold as in a glass {1x}.

Katoptrizo, as a verb, signifies in the middle voice "beholding as in a glass": "But we all, with open face beholding as in a glass the glory of the Lord, are changed into the same image from glory to glory, even as by the Spirit of the Lord" (2 Cor 3:18). Syn.: 333, 816, 991, 1689, 1896, 2029, 2300, 2334, 2657, 3708. See: TDNT—2:696, 264; BAGD—424d; THAYER—341c.

2735. **κατόρθωμα** {1x} **katŏrthōma,** *kat-or'-tho-mah;* from a compound of *2596* and a der. of *3717* [comp. *1357*]; something *made fully upright,* i.e. (fig.) *rectification* (spec. *good* public *administration*):—a very worthy deed {1x}. See: BAGD—424d; THAYER—341c.

2736. **κάτω** {11x} **katō,** *kat'-o;* also (comparative)

κατωτέρω katōtĕrō, *kat-o-ter'-o;* [comp. *2737*]; adv. from *2596; downwards:*—beneath {3x}, bottom {2x}, down {5x}, under {1x}. See: TDNT—3:640, 422; BAGD—425a; THAYER—341c.

2737. **κατώτερος** {1x} **katōtĕrŏs,** *kat-o'-ter-os;* comparative from *2736; inferior* (locally, of Hades):—lower {1x}. See: TDNT—3:640, 422; BAGD—425a; THAYER—341d.

2738. **καῦμα** {2x} **kauma,** *kŏw'-mah;* from *2545;* prop. a *burn* (concr.), but used (abstr.) of a *glow:*—heat {2x}.

This word denotes painful and hurtful heat and signifies "the result of burning," or "the heat produced," Rev 7:16; 16:9. See: TDNT—3:642, 423; BAGD—425a; THAYER—341d.

2739. **καυματίζω** {4x} **kaumatizō,** *kŏw-mat-id'-zo;* from *2738;* to *burn:*—scorch {4x}.

This word means "to scorch" (from *kauma,* "heat"), and is used **(1)** of seed that had not much earth, Mt 13:6; Mk 4:6; **(2)** of men, stricken retributively by the sun's heat, Rev 16:8, 9. See: TDNT—3:643, 423; BAGD—341d.

2740. **καῦσις** {1x} **kausis,** *kŏw'-sis;* from *2545; burning* (the act):—be burned + *1519* {1x}. See: TDNT—3:643, 423; BAGD—425b; THAYER—341d.

2741. **καυσόω** {2x} **kausŏō,** *kŏw-sŏ'-o;* from *2740;* to *set on fire:*—with fervent heat {2x}.

Kausoo was used as a medical term, of "a fever"; in the NT, "to burn with great heat", and is said of the future destruction of the natural elements, 2 Pet 3:10, 12, "with fervent

heat," passive voice, lit. "being burned." See: TDNT—3:644,*; BAGD—425b; THAYER— 342a.

2742. **καύσων** {3x} **kausōn**, *kŏw'-sone;* from *2741;* a *glare:*—(burning) heat {3x}.

Kauson denotes "a burning heat" (from *kaio*, "to burn"; cf. Eng., "caustic," "cauterize"), Mt 20:12; Lk 12:55 "heat"; in Jas 1:11, "a burning heat." See: TDNT—3:644, 423; BAGD—425c; THAYER—342a.

2743. **καυτηριάζω** {1x} **kautēriazō**, *kŏw-tay-ree-ad'-zo* or

     καυστηριάζω **kaustēriazō** *kŏws-tay-ree-ad'-zo;* from a der. of *2545;* to *brand* ("*cauterize*"), i.e. (by impl.) to *render unsensitive* (fig.):—sear with a hot iron {1x}.

This word means "to burn in with a branding iron" (cf. Eng., "caustic") and is found in 1 Ti 4:2. The reference is to apostates whose consciences are "branded" with the effects of their sin. See: TDNT—3:644,*; BAGD—425c; THAYER—342a.

2744. **καυχάομαι** {38x} **kauchaŏmai**, *kŏw-khah'-om-ahee;* from some (obsolete) base akin to that of αὐχέω **auchĕō** (to *boast*) and *2172;* to *vaunt* (in a good or a bad sense):—glory {23x}, boast {8x}, rejoice {4x}, make boast {2x}, joy {1x}.

Kauchaomai means "to boast or glory," is translated **(1)** "to boast" (see, e.g., Rom 2:17, 23; 2 Cor 7:14; 9:2; 10:8, 13, 15, 16); **(2)** it is used **(2a)** of "vaingloriying," e.g., 1 Cor 1:29; 3:21; 4:7; 2 Cor 5:12; 11:12, 18; Eph 2:9; **(2b)** of "valid glorying," e.g., Rom 5:2, "rejoice"; 5:3; 1 Cor 1:31; 2 Cor 9:2; 10:8, 12:9; Gal 6:14; Phil 3:3 and Jas 1:9, "rejoice". See: TDNT—3:645, 423; BAGD—425c; THAYER—342b.

2745. **καύχημα** {11x} **kauchēma**, *kŏw'-khay-mah;* from *2744;* a *boast* (prop. the obj.; by impl. the act) in a good or a bad sense:—rejoicing {4x}, to glory {3x}, glorying {2x}, boasting {1x}, rejoice {1x}.

Kauchema denotes **(1)** "that in which one glories, a matter or ground of glorying," Rom 4:2 and Phil 2:16; **(2)** in the following the meaning is likewise "a ground of glorying": 1 Cor 5:6; 9:15, "glorying," 16, "to glory of"; Gal 6:4, "rejoicing"; Phil 1:26; Heb 3:6. **(3)** In 2 Cor 5:12 and 9:3 the word denotes the boast itself, yet as distinct from the act. See: TDNT—3:645, 423; BAGD—426a; THAYER—342c.

2746. **καύχησις** {12x} **kauchēsis**, *kŏw'-khay-sis;* from *2744; boasting* (prop.

the act; by impl. the obj.), in a good or a bad sense:—boasting {6x}, whereof I may glory {1x}, glorying {1x}, rejoicing {4x}.

Kauchesis denotes "the act of boasting," Rom 3:27; 15:17, "whereof I may glory"; 1 Cor 15:31; 2 Cor 1:12; 7:4, 14 "boasting"; 8:24; 11:10, and 17; 1 Th 2:19 "rejoicing"; Jas 4:16. See: TDNT—3:645, 423; BAGD—426b; THAYER—342d.

2747. **Κεγχρεαί** {3x} **Kĕgchrĕai**, *keng-khreh-a'-hee;* prob. from κέγχρος **kĕgchrŏs** (*millet*); *Cenchreæ*, a port of Corinth:—Cenchrea {3x}. See: BAGD—426c; THAYER—342d.

2748. **Κεδρών** {1x} **Kĕdrōn**, *ked-rone';* of Heb. or. [6939]; *Cedron* (i.e. *Kidron*), a brook near Jerusalem:—Cedron {1x}. See: BAGD—426c; THAYER—342d.

2749. **κεῖμαι** {26x} **kĕimai**, *ki'-mahee;* mid. voice of a primary verb; to *lie* outstretched (lit. or fig.):—lie {9x}, be laid {6x}, be set {6x}, be appointed {1x}, be {1x}, be made {1x}, laid up {1x}, there {1x}.

Keimai, as a verb, means "to lie" and is used **(1)** in 1 Th 3:3 of the "appointment" of affliction for faithful believers: "That no man should be moved by these afflictions: for yourselves know that we are appointed (*keima*) thereunto." **(2)** It is rendered "set" in Lk 2:34: "And Simeon blessed them, and said unto Mary his mother, Behold, this child is set (*keima*) for the fall and rising again of many in Israel; and for a sign which shall be spoken against" (cf. Phil 1:17; The verb is a perfect tense, used for the perfect passive of *tithemi*, "to place," "I have been placed," i.e., "I lie."). See: TDNT—3:654, 425; BAGD—426c; THAYER—343a. comp. *5087.*

2750. **κειρία** {1x} **kĕiria**, *ki-ree'-ah;* of uncert. aff.; a *swathe*, i.e. *winding-sheet:*—graveclothes {1x}.

Keiria denotes, firstly, "a band" either for a bed girth, or bed sheets themselves; then, "the swathings wrapped round a corpse"; it is used in the plural in Jn 11:44. See: BAGD—427a; THAYER—343b.

2751. **κείρω** {4x} **kĕirō**, *ki'-ro;* a primary verb; to *shear:*—shear {3x}, shearer {1x}.

Keiro is used **(1)** of "shearing sheep," Acts 8:32, "shearer," lit., "the (one) shearing": **(2)** in the middle voice, "to have one's hair cut off, be shorn," Acts 18:18; 1 Cor 11:6 (twice). See: BAGD—427a; THAYER—343b.

Greek

2752. **κέλευμα** {1x} **kĕlĕuma**, *kel'-yoo-mah*
or
κέλευσμα **kĕlĕusma**, *kel'-yoos-mah;*
from 2753; a *cry* of incitement:—shout {1x}.

This word means "a call, summons, shout of command" (akin to *keleuo*, "to command"), is used in 1 Th 4:16 of the "shout" with which the Lord will descend from heaven at the time of the rapture of the saints to meet Him in the air. The "shout" is not here said to be His actual voice, though this indeed will be so (Jn 5:28). See: TDNT—3:656,*; BAGD—427b; THAYER—343b.

2753. **κελεύω** {27x} **kĕlĕuō**, *kel-yoo'-o;* from a primary κέλλω **kĕllō** (to *urge* on); "hail;" to *incite* by word, i.e. *order:*—command {24x}, at (one's) command {1x}, give commandment {1x}, bid {1x}.

This word means "to urge, incite, order," Mt 14:9, 19; 15:35; 18:25; 27:58, 64; Lk 18:40; Acts 4:15. See: BAGD—427b; THAYER—343b.

2754. **κενοδοξία** {1x} **kĕnŏdŏxia**, *ken-od-ox-ee'-ah;* from 2755; *empty glorying,* i.e. *self-conceit:*—vain-glory {1x}.

This word stresses groundless self-esteem, empty pride, a vain opinion. See: TDNT—3:662, 426; BAGD—427c; THAYER—343d.

2755. **κενόδοξος** {1x} **kĕnŏdŏxŏs**, *ken-od'-ox-os;* from 2756 and 1391; *vainly glorifying,* i.e. *self-conceited:*—desirous of vain-glory {1x}.

This word denotes one who is glorying without reason, conceited, vain glorious, eager for empty glory, Phil 2:3. See: TDNT—3:662, 426; BAGD—427d; THAYER—343d.

2756. **κενός** {18x} **kĕnŏs**, *ken-os';* appar. a primary word; *empty* (lit. or fig.):—vain {9x}, in vain {4x}, empty {4x}, vain things {1x}.

This word denotes that which is empty, implies hollowness, and is devoid of contents. There is the absence of good, but also the presence of evil because man's moral nature permits no vacuum (Jas 2:20). *Kenos* expresses the "hollowness" of anything, the "absence" of that which otherwise might be possessed. It is used **(1)** literally, Mk 12:3; Lk 1:53; 20:10–11; **(2)** metaphorically, **(2a)** of imaginations, Acts 4:25; **(2b)** of words which convey erroneous teachings, Eph 5:6; **(2c)** of deceit, Col 2:8; **(2d)** of a person whose professed faith is not accompanied by works, Jas 2:20; **(2e)** negatively, concerning the grace of God, 1 Cor 15:10; **(2f)** of refusal to receive it, 2 Cor 6:1; **(2g)** of faith, 1 Cor 15:14; **(2h)** of preaching and other forms of Christian activity and labor, 1 Cor 15:58; Gal

2:2; Phil 2:16; 1 Th 2:1; 3:5. Syn.: The synonymous word *mataios* (3152), "vain," signifies "void" of result, it marks the aimlessness of anything. The vain (*kenos*) man in Jas 2:20 is one who is "empty" of divinely imparted wisdom; in 1:26 the vain (*mataios*) religion is one that produces nothing profitable. *Kenos* stresses the absence of quality, *mataios*, the absence of useful aim or effect. See: TDNT—3:659, 426; BAGD—427d; THAYER—343d.

2757. **κενοφωνία** {2x} **kĕnŏphōnia**, *ken-of-o-nee'-ah;* from a presumed compound of 2756 and 5456; *empty sounding,* i.e. *fruitless discussion:*—vain babblings {2x}.

This word signifies empty discussion, discussion on useless subjects (1 Ti 6:20; 2 Ti 2:16). See: BAGD—428a; THAYER—343d.

2758. **κενόω** {5x} **kĕnŏō**, *ken-ŏ'-o;* from 2756; to *abase, neutralize:*—make void {2x}, make of none effect {1x}, make of no reputation {1x}, be in vain {1x}.

(1) *Kenoo* means to neutralize or to take that which has positivie effects and renders them neutral; making negative is not within the definition of the word. It is translated **(2)** "should be made of none effect" in 1 Cor 1:17, to neutralize the effects of preaching the cross of Christ; **(3)** of Christ, "making Himself of no reputation", Phil 2:7, He did not effect His own reputation, but left it up to God; **(3)** of faith, being made "void", of no effect, if the promise of salvation is earned by works of the Law, Rom 4:14; **(4)** of the apostle Paul's glorying in the gospel ministry, 1 Cor 9:15; **(5)** of his glorying on behalf of the church at Corinth, 2 Cor 9:3, would "be in vain", of no effect, if the Corinthians failed in the offering. See: TDNT—3:661, 426; BAGD—428a; THAYER—344a.

2759. **κέντρον** {5x} **kĕntrŏn**, *ken'-tron;* from κεντέω **kĕntĕō** (to *prick*); a *point* ("centre"), i.e. a *sting* (fig. *poison*) or *goad* (fig. divine *impulse*):—prick {2x}, sting {3x}.

Kentron from *kenteo*, "to prick," denotes **(1)** "a sting," **(1a)** literally, Rev 9:10; **(1b)** metaphorically, of sin as the "sting" of death, 1 Cor 15:55, 56; **(2)** "a prick," Acts 9:5; 26:14, said of the promptings and conscience "stings" which Saul of Tarsus felt before conversion, possibly at approving and witnessing the stoning death of Stephen. See: TDNT—3:663, 427; BAGD—428b; THAYER—344a.

2760. **κεντυρίων** {3x} **kĕnturiōn**, *ken-too-ree'-ohn;* of Lat. or.; a *centurion,* i.e. *captain* of one hundred soldiers:—centurion {3x}. Cf. Mk 14: 39, 44–45. See: BAGD—428c; THAYER—344a.

2761. κενῶς {1x} **kĕnōs,** *ken-oce';* adv. from 2756; *vainly,* i.e. *to no purpose:*—in vain {1x}. See: BAGD—428c; THAYER—344a.

2762. κεραία {2x} **kĕraia,** *ker-ah'-yah;* fem. of a presumed der. of the base of *2768;* something *horn-like,* i.e. (spec.) the *apex* of a Heb. letter (fig. the least *particle*):—tittle {2x}.

Keraia, "a little horn" (*keras,* "a horn"), was used to denote the small stroke distinguishing one Hebrew letter from another. The rabbis attached great importance to these; hence the significance of the Lord's statements in Mt 5:18 and Lk 16:17, charging the Pharisees with hypocrisy, because, while professing the most scrupulous reverence to the Law, they violated its spirit. See: BAGD—428d; THAYER—344b.

2763. κεραμεύς {3x} **kĕramĕus,** *ker-am-yooce';* from *2766;* a *potter:*—potter {3x}.

Kerameus, "a potter" is used **(1)** in connection with the "potter's field," Mt 27:7, 10; and **(2)** illustratively of the "potter's" right over the clay, Rom 9:21, where the introductory "or" suggests the alternatives that either there must be a recognition of the absolute discretion and power of God, or a denial that the "potter" has power over the clay. There is no suggestion of the creation of sinful beings, or of the creation of any simply in order to punish them. What the passage sets forth is God's right to deal with sinful beings according to His own counsel. See: BAGD—428d; THAYER—344b.

2764. κεραμικός {1x} **kĕramikŏs,** *ker-am-ik-os';* from *2766; made of clay,* i.e. *earthen:*—of a potter {1x}. See: BAGD—428; THAYER—344b.

2765. κεράμιον {2x} **kĕramiŏn,** *ker-am'-ee-on;* neut. of a presumed der. of *2766;* an *earthenware* vessel, i.e. *jar:*—pitcher {2x}.

Keramion, "an earthen vessel", "a jar" or "jug," occurs in Mk 14:13; Lk 22:10. See: BAGD—428d; THAYER—344b.

2766. κέραμος {1x} **kĕramŏs,** *ker'-am-os;* prob. from the base of *2767* (through the idea of *mixing* clay and water); *earthenware,* i.e. a *tile* (by anal. a thin *roof* or *awning*):—tiling {1x}.

This word means "potter's clay," or "an earthen vessel," denotes in the plural "tiling" in Lk 5:19. See: BAGD—429a; THAYER—344b.

2767. κεράννυμι {3x} **kĕrannumi,** *ker-an'-noo-mee;* a prol. form of a more primary κεράω **kĕraō,** *ker-ah'-o* (which is used in certain tenses); to *mingle,* i.e. (by impl.) to *pour* out (for drinking):—fill {2x}, pour out {1x}.

Kerannumi, "to mix, to mingle," chiefly of the diluting of wine, implies "a mixing of two things, so that they are blended and form a compound, as in wine and water. It is translated "fill, filled" in Rev 18:6 (twice); and "poured out" in Rev 14:10. See: BAGD—429a; THAYER—344c. comp. *3396.*

2768. κέρας {11x} **kĕras,** *ker'-as;* from a primary κάρ **kar** (the *hair* of the head); a *horn* (lit. or fig.):—horn {11x}.

Keras, "a horn," is used in the plural, as the symbol of strength, **(1)** in the apocalyptic visions; **(1a)** on the head of the Lamb as symbolic of Christ, Rev 5:6; **(1b)** on the heads of beasts as symbolic of national potentates, Rev 12:3; 13:1, 11; 17:3, 7, 12, 16 (cf. Dan 7:8; 8:9; Zec 1:18, etc.); **(1c)** at the corners of the golden altar, Rev 9:13 (cf. Ex 30:2; the horns were of one piece with the altar, as in the case of the brazen altar, 27:2, and were emblematic of the efficacy of the ministry connected with it); **(2)** metaphorically, in the singular, "a horn of salvation," Lk 1:69. See: TDNT—3:669, 428; BAGD—429b; THAYER—344d.

2769. κεράτιον {1x} **kĕratiŏn,** *ker-at'-ee-on;* neut. of a presumed der. of *2768;* something *horned,* i.e. (spec.) the *pod* of the carob-tree:—husk {1x}.

Keration, used in the plural in Lk 15:16, of carob pods, given to swine, and translated "husks." See: BAGD—429b; THAYER—344d.

κεράω kĕraō. See 2767.

2770. κερδαίνω {17x} **kĕrdainō,** *ker-dah'-ee-no;* from *2771;* to *gain* (lit. or fig.):—gain {13x}, win {2x}, get gain {1x}, vr gain {1x}.

Kerdaino signifies **(1)** literally, **(1a)** "to gain something," Mt 16:26; 25:17, 20, 22; Mk 8:36; Lk 9:25; **(1b)** "to get gain, make a profit," Jas 4:13; **(2)** metaphorically, "to win persons," said **(2a)** of "gaining" an offending brother who by being told privately of his offense, and by accepting the representations, is won from alienation and from the consequences of his fault, Mt 18:15; **(2b)** of winning souls into the kingdom of God **(2b1)** by the gospel, 1 Cor 9:19, 20 (twice), 21, 22, or **(2b2)** by godly conduct, 1 Pet 3:1; **(2c)** of so practically appropriating Christ to oneself that He becomes the dominating power in and over one's whole being and circumstances, Phil 3:8; **(3)** "to gain things," said of getting injury and loss, Acts 27:21. See: TDNT—3:672, 428; BAGD—429c; THAYER—345a.

Greek

2771. **κέρδος** {3x} **kĕrdŏs,** *ker'-dos;* of uncert. aff.; *gain* (pecuniary or gen.):—gain {2x}, lucre {1x}.

Kerdos, "gain", is translated **(1)** "gain" in Phil 1:21; 3:7; and **(2)** "lucre" in Titus 1:11. See: TDNT—3:672, 428; BAGD—429c; THAYER—345a.

2772. **κέρμα** {1x} **kĕrma,** *ker'-mah;* from *2751;* a *clipping* (bit), i.e. (spec.) a *coin:*—money {1x}.

Kerma, primarily "a slice", hence, "a small coin, change," is used in the plural in Jn 2:15, "the changers' money," probably considerable heaps of small coins for making change. See: BAGD—429d; THAYER—345b.

2773. **κερματιστής** {1x} **kĕrmatistēs,** *ker-mat-is-tace';* from a der. of *2772;* a *handler of coins,* i.e. *money-broker:*—changer of money {1x}.

In the court of the Gentiles, in the temple precincts, were the seats of those who sold selected and approved animals for sacrifice, and other things. The magnitude of this traffic had introduced the bankers' or brokers' business, Jn 2:14. See: BAGD—429d; THAYER—345b.

2774. **κεφάλαιον** {2x} **kĕphalaiŏn,** *kef-al'-ah-yon;* neut. of a der. of *2776;* a *principal* thing, i.e. *main point;* spec. an *amount* (of money):—sum {2x}.

This word, akin to the adjective *kephalaios,* "belonging to the head," and *kephale,* "the head," denotes **(1)** the chief point, principal thing, or the "total of what has been said to this point" in a subject, Heb 8:1; and **(2)** in Acts 22:28 (of principal, as to money), "(a great) sum." See: BAGD—429d; THAYER—345b.

2775. **κεφαλαιόω** {1x} **kĕphalaiŏō,** *kef-al-ahee-ŏ'-o;* from the same as *2774;* (spec.) to *strike on the head:*—wound in the head {1x}. See: BAGD—430a; THAYER—345c.

2776. **κεφαλή** {76x} **kĕphalē,** *kef-al-ay';* prob. from the primary κάπτω **kaptō** (in the sense of *seizing*); the *head* (as the part most readily *taken* hold of), lit. or fig.:—head {76x}.

Kephale, besides its natural significance, is used figuratively **(1)** in Rom 12:20, of heaping coals of fire on a "head"; **(2)** in Acts 18:6, "Your blood be upon your own heads," i.e., "your blood-guiltiness rest upon your own persons," a mode of expression frequent in the OT, and perhaps here directly connected with Eze 3:18, 20; 33:6, 8; see also Lev 20:16; 2 Sa 1:16; 1 Kin 2:37; **(3)** of Christ in relation to the church, Eph 1:22; 4:15; 5:23; Col 1:18; 2:19; **(4)** of Christ in relation to principalities and powers, Col 2:10. **(5)**

metaphorically, of the authority or direction of God in relation to Christ, of Christ in relation to believing men, of the husband in relation to the wife, 1 Cor 11:3; **(6)** it is used of Christ as the foundation of the spiritual building set forth by the temple, with its "corner stone," Mt 21:42; **(7)** symbolically also of the imperial rulers of the Roman power, as seen in the apocalyptic visions, Rev 13:1, 3; 17:3, 7, 9. See: TDNT—3:673, 429; BAGD—430a; THAYER—345c.

2777. **κεφαλίς** {1x} **kĕphalis,** *kef-al-is';* from *2776;* prop. a *knob,* i.e. (by impl.) a *roll* (by extens. from the *end* of a stick on which the MS. was rolled):—volume {1x}. See: BAGD—430c; THAYER—345d.

2778. **κῆνσος** {4x} **kēnsŏs,** *kane'-sos;* of Lat. or.; prop. an *enrollment* ("*census*"), i.e. (by impl.) a *tax:*—tribute {4x}.

Kensos is literally a census (among the Romans, denoting a register and valuation of property in accordance with which taxes were paid), in the NT the tax or tribute levied on individuals and to be paid yearly, Mt 17:25; 22:17, 19; Mk 12:14. Taxes were collected from all to fund the normal expenses of the government. Custom was charged to strangers in the land. Tribute was paid by a conquered people in order to remain in good standing with the conquering army. It is above the normal levied taxes. Taxes are levied, tribute is paid somewhat ironically to the conquerors to maintain favor. See: BAGD—430d; THAYER—345d.

2779. **κῆπος** {5x} **kēpŏs,** *kay'-pos;* of uncert. aff.; a *garden:*—garden {5x}.

Kepos, "a garden," occurs **(1)** in Lk 13:19, in one of the Lord's parables; **(2)** in Jn 18:1, 26, of the garden of Gethsemane; **(3)** in Jn 19:41, of the garden near the place of the Lord's crucifixion. See: BAGD—430d; THAYER—346a.

2780. **κηπουρός** {1x} **kēpŏurŏs,** *kay-poo-ros';* from *2779* and οὖρος **ŏurŏs** (a *warden*); a *garden-keeper,* i.e. *gardener:*—gardener {1x}. See: BAGD—430d; THAYER—346a.

2781. **κηρίον** {7} **kēriŏn,** *kay-ree'-on;* dimin. from κηός **kēŏs** (*wax*); a *cell* for honey, i.e. (collect.) the *comb:*—honeycomb + *3193* {1x}. See: BAGD—430d; THAYER—346a.

2782. **κήρυγμα** {8x} **kērugma,** *kay'-roog-mah;* from *2784;* a *proclamation* (espec. of the gospel; by impl. the *gospel* itself):—preaching {8x}.

Kerugma, as a noun, means "a proclamation by a herald" and denotes "a message, a preaching" (the substance of what is "preached" as

distinct from the act of "preaching"), Mt 12:41; Lk 11:32; Rom 16:25; 1 Cor 1:21; 2:4; 15:14; 2 Ti 4:17; Titus 1:3. See: TDNT—3:714, 430; BAGD—430d; THAYER—346a.

2783. κῆρυξ {3x} **kērux**, *kay'-roox;* from *2784;* a *herald*, i.e. of divine truth (espec. of the gospel):—preacher {3x}.

Kerux, "a herald", is used **(1)** of the "preacher" of the gospel, 1 Ti 2:7; 2 Ti 1:11; and **(2)** of Noah, as a "preacher" of righteousness, 2 Pet 2:5. See: TDNT—3:683, 430; BAGD—431a; THAYER—346b.

2784. κηρύσσω {61x} **kērussō**, *kay-roos'-so;* of uncert. aff.; to *herald* (as a public *crier*), espec. divine truth (the gospel):— preach {51x}, publish {5x}, proclaim {2x}, preached + 2258 {2x}, preacher {1x}.

Kerusso signifies **(1)** "to be a herald," or, in general, "to proclaim," e.g., Mt 3:1; Mk 1:45, "publish"; in Lk 4:18, "to preach"; so verse 19; Lk 12:3; Acts 10:37; Rom 2:21; Rev 5:2; **(2)** "to preach the gospel as a herald," e.g., Mt 24:14; Mk 13:10, "be published"; 14:9; 16:15, 20; Lk 8:1; 9:2; 24:47; Acts 8:5; 19:13; 28:31; Rom 10:14, present participle, lit., "(one) preaching," "a preacher"; 10:15 (1st part); 1 Cor 1:23; 15:11, 12; 2 Cor 1:19; 4:5; 11:4; Gal 2:2; Phil 1:15; Col 1:23; 1 Th 2:9; 1 Ti 3:16; **(3)** "to preach the word," 2 Ti 4:2 (of the ministry of the Scriptures, with special reference to the gospel). Syn.: 2097, 2782, 3955, 4283, 4296. See: TDNT—3:697, 430; BAGD—431b; THAYER—346b.

2785. κῆτος {1x} **kētŏs**, *kay'-tos;* prob. from the base of *5490;* a huge *fish* (as *gaping* for prey):—whale {1x}. See: BAGD—431d; THAYER—346d.

2786. Κηφᾶς {6x} **Kēphas**, *kay-fas';* of Chald. or. [comp. 3710]; *the Rock; Cephas* (i.e. *Kepha*), a surname of Peter:—Cephas {6x}. See: TDNT—6:100, 835; BAGD—431d.

2787. κιβωτός {6x} **kibōtŏs**, *kib-o-tos';* of uncert. der.; a *box*, i.e. the sacred *ark* and that of Noah:—ark {6x}.

Kibotos, "a wooden box, a chest," is used of **(1)** Noah's vessel, Mt 24:38; Lk 17:27; Heb 11:7; 1 Pet 3:20; **(2)** the "ark" of the covenant in the tabernacle, Heb 9:4; **(3)** the "ark" seen in vision in the heavenly temple, Rev 11:19. See: BAGD—431d; THAYER—346d.

2788. κιθάρα {4x} **kithara**, *kith-ar'-ah;* of uncert. aff.; a *lyre:*—harp {4x}.

Kithara denotes "a lyre" or "harp"; it is described by Josephus as an instrument of ten strings, played by a plectrum (a smaller instrument was played by the hand); it is mentioned

in 1 Cor 14:7; Rev 5:8; 14:2; 15:2. See: BAGD—432a; THAYER—347a.

2789. κιθαρίζω {2x} **kitharizō**, *kith-ar-id'-zo;* from *2788;* to *play on a lyre:*— to harp {2x}.

Kitharizo signifies "to play on the harp," 1 Cor 14:7; Rev 14:2. See: BAGD—432a; THAYER—347a.

2790. κιθαρῳδός {2x} **kitharōdŏs**, *kith-ar-o'-dos;* from *2788* and a der. of the same as *5603;* a *lyre-singer* (*-player*), i.e. *harpist:*—harper {2x}.

Kitharodos denotes "one who plays and sings to the lyre" (from *kithara*, "a lyre," and *aoidos*, "a singer"), Rev 14:2; 18:22. See: BAGD—432a; THAYER—347a.

2791. Κιλικία {8x} **Kilikia**, *kil-ik-ee'-ah;* prob. of for. or.; *Cilicia*, a region of Asia Minor:—Cilicia {8x}. See: BAGD—432a; THAYER—346a.

2792. κινάμωμον {1x} **kinamōmŏn**, *kin-am'-o-mon;* of for. or. [comp. 7076]; *cinnamon:*—cinnamon {1x}. See: BAGD—432a; THAYER—347b.

2793. κινδυνεύω {4x} **kinduneuō**, *kin-doon-yoo'-o;* from *2794;* to *undergo peril:*—be in danger {2x}, be in jeopardy {1x}, stand in jeopardy {1x}.

Kinduneuo properly signifies "to run a risk, face danger," but is used in the NT in the sense of **(1)** "being in danger," Acts 19:27, 40. It is translated **(2)** "were in jeopardy" in Lk 8:23, and **(3)** "stand we in jeopardy," 1 Cor 15:30. See: BAGD—432b; THAYER—347b.

2794. κίνδυνος {9x} **kindunŏs**, *kin'-doo-nos;* of uncert. der.; *danger:*— peril {9x}. Cf. Rom 8:35; 2 Cor 11:26. See: BAGD—432b; THAYER—347b.

2795. κινέω {8x} **kĭnĕō**, *kin-eh'-o;* from κίω-κιο (poetic for εἰμι **ĕimi**, to *go*); to *stir* (tran.), lit. or fig.:—move {4x}, wag {2x}, remove {1x}, mover {1x}.

Kineo, as a verb, means "to set in motion, move" and is used **(1)** of wagging the head (Mt 27:39; Mk 15:29); **(2)** of the general activity of the human being: "For in him we live, and move (*2795*), and have our being" (Acts 17:28); **(3)** of the "moving" of mountains: "And the heaven departed as a scroll when it is rolled together; and every mountain and island were moved out of their places" (Rev 6:14, in the sense of removing, as in Rev 2:5, of removing a lampstand [there figuratively of causing a local church to be discontinued]; **(4)** figuratively, of exciting, stirring up feelings and passions: "And all the city was moved, and the people

ran together: and they took Paul, and drew him out of the temple: and forthwith the doors were shut" (Acts 21:30 [passive voice]; cf. 24:5, "a mover"); **(5)** of "moving burdens": "For they bind heavy burdens and grievous to be borne, and lay them on men's shoulders; but they themselves will not move them with one of their fingers" (Mt 23:4). Syn.: 277, 383, 761, 2796, 3334, 4525, 4531, 4579, 4787, 5342. See: TDNT—3:718, 435; BAGD—432c; THAYER—347b.

2796. κίνησις {1x} **kinēsis**, *kin'-ay-sis;* from *2795;* a *stirring:*—moving {1x}.

Kinesis, as a noun, means "a moving" and is found in Jn 5:3: "In these lay a great multitude of impotent folk, of blind, halt, withered, waiting for the moving of the water." Syn.: 277, 383, 761, 2795, 3334, 4525, 4531, 4579, 4787, 5342. See: BAGD—432d; THAYER—347c.

2797. Κίς {1x} **Kis**, *kis;* of Heb. or. [7027]; *Cis* (i.e. *Kish*), an Isr.:—Cis {1x}. See: BAGD—432d; THAYER—347c.

κίχρημι kichrēmi. See *5531.*

2798. κλάδος {11x} **kladŏs**, *klad'-os;* from *2806;* a small tender *twig* or *bough* (as if broken off):—branch {11x}.

Klados, properly a young tender shoot, "broken off" for grafting, is used for any kind of branch, Mt 13:32; 21:8; 24:32; Mk 4:32; 13:28; Lk 13:19; the descendants of Israel, Rom 11:16–19, 21. See: TDNT—3:720,*; BAGD—433a; THAYER—347c.

2799. κλαίω {40x} **klaiō**, *klah'-yo;* of uncert. aff.; to *sob*, i.e. *wail* aloud (whereas *1145* is rather to *cry* silently):—bewail {1x}, weep {39x}.

Klaio is used of **(1)** "any loud expression of grief," especially in mourning for the dead, Mt 2:18; Mk 5:38, 39; 16:10; Lk 7:13; 8:52 (twice); Jn 11:31, 33 (twice); 20:11 (twice), 13, 15; Acts 9:39; **(2)** otherwise, e.g., in exhortations, Lk 23:28; Rom 12:15; Jas 4:9; 5:1; **(3)** negatively, "weep not," Lk 7:13; 8:52; 23:28; Rev 5:5 (cf. Acts 21:13); **(4)** in Acts 18:9, "bewail." Syn.: *Alalazo* (*214*) means to wail in oriental style, to howl in a consecrated, semi-liturgical fashion. *Dakruo* (*1145*) means to shed tears, weep silently. *Threneo* (*2354*) means to give formal expression to grief, to sing a dirge. *Klaio* (*2799*) means to weep audibly, cry as a child. *Odurmos* (*3602*) means to give verbal expression to grief, to lament. *Stenazo* (*4727*) means to express grief by inarticulate or semi-articulate sounds, to groan. See: TDNT—3:722, 436; BAGD—433a.

2800. κλάσις {2x} **klasis**, *klas'-is;* from *2806; fracture* (the act):—breaking {2x}.

Klasis, "a breaking", is used in Lk 24:35 and Acts 2:42, of the "breaking" of bread. See: TDNT—3:726, 437; BAGD—433b; THAYER—347d.

2801. κλάσμα {9x} **klasma**, *klas'-mah;* from *2806;* a *piece* (*bit*):—broken {2x}, fragment {7x}.

Klasma is always used of remnants of food and translated **(1)** "broken", Mt 5:37; Mk 8:8; and **(2)** "fragments", Mt 14:20; Mk 6:43; 8:19, 20; Lk 9:17; Jn 6:12, 13. See: TDNT—3:726, 437; BAGD—433b; THAYER—347d.

2802. Κλαύδη {1x} **Klaudē**, *klŏw'-day* or

Καύδη Kaudē *kŏw'-day;* of uncert. der.; *Claude*, an island near Crete:—Clauda (Cauda) {1x}. See: BAGD—433b; THAYER—347d.

2803. Κλαυδία {1x} **Klaudia**, *klŏw-dee'-ah;* fem. of *2804; Claudia*, a Chr. woman:—Claudia {1x}. See: BAGD—433c; THAYER—348a.

2804. Κλαύδιος {3x} **Klaudiŏs**, *klŏw'-dee-os;* of Lat. or.; *Claudius*, the name of two Romans:—Claudius (Caesar) {2x}, Claudius (Lysias) {1x}. See: BAGD—433c; THAYER—348a.

2805. κλαυθμός {9x} **klauthmŏs**, *klŏwth-mos';* from *2799; lamentation:*—wailing {2x}, weeping {1x}.

This word denotes "weeping, crying," Mt 2:18; 8:12; 13:42, "wailing"; 13:50, "wailing"; 22:13; 24:51; 25:30; Lk 13:28; Acts 20:37, "wept." See: TDNT—3:725, 436; BAGD—433c; THAYER—348a.

2806. κλάω {15x} **klaō**, *klah'-o;* a primary verb; to *break* (spec. of bread):—break {15x}.

This word means "to break, to break off pieces," is used of "breaking bread," **(1)** of the Lord's act in providing for people, Mt 14:19; 15:36; Mk 8:6, 19; **(2)** of the "breaking of bread" in the Lord's Supper, Mt 26:26; Mk 14:22; Lk 22:19; Acts 20:7; 1 Cor 10:16; 11:24; **(3)** of an ordinary meal, Acts 2:46; 20:11; 27:35; **(4)** of the Lord's act in giving evidence of His resurrection, Lk 24:30. See: TDNT—3:726, 437; BAGD—433d; THAYER—348a.

2807. κλείς {6x} **klĕis**, *klice;* from *2808;* a *key* (as *shutting* a lock), lit. or fig.:—key {6x}.

Kleis, "a key," is used metaphorically **(1)** of "the keys of the kingdom of heaven," which the Lord committed to Peter, Mt 16:19, by which

he would open the door of faith, as he did to Jews at Pentecost, and to Gentiles in the person of Cornelius, acting as one commissioned by Christ, through the power of the Holy Spirit; he had precedence over his fellow disciples, not in authority, but in the matter of time, on the ground of his confession of Christ (v. 16); equal authority was committed to them (18:18); **(2)** of "the key of knowledge," Lk 11:52, i.e., knowledge of the revealed will of God, by which men entered into the life that pleases God; this the religious leaders of the Jews had presumptuously "taken away," so that they neither entered in themselves, nor permitted their hearers to do so; **(3)** of "the keys of death and of hades," Rev 1:18, indicative of the authority of the Lord over the bodies and souls of men; **(4)** of "the key of David," Rev 3:7, a reference to Is 22:22, speaking of the deposition of Shebna and the investiture of Eliakim, in terms evidently messianic, the metaphor being that of the right of entrance upon administrative authority; the mention of David is symbolic of complete sovereignty; **(5)** of "the key of the pit of the abyss," Rev 9:1; here the symbolism is that of competent authority; the pit represents a shaft or deep entrance into the region, from whence issued smoke, symbolic of blinding delusion; **(6)** of "the key of the abyss," Rev 20:1; this is to be distinguished from (5): the symbolism is that of the complete supremacy of God over the region of the lost, in which, by angelic agency, Satan is destined to be confined for a thousand years. See: TDNT—3:744, 439; BAGD—433d; THAYER—348b.

2808. **κλείω** {16x} **klĕiō,** *kli'-o;* a primary verb; to *close* (lit. or fig.):—shut {12x}, shut up {4x}.

Kleio is used **(1)** of things material, Mt 6:6; 25:10; Lk 11:7; Jn 20:19, 26; Acts 5:23; 21:30; Rev 20:3; figuratively, 21:25; **(2)** metaphorically, **(2a)** of the kingdom of heaven, Mt 23:13; **(2b)** of heaven, with consequences of famine, Lk 4:25; Rev 11:6; **(2c)** of compassion, 1 Jn 3:17, "bowels of compassion"; **(2d)** of the blessings accruing from the promises of God regarding David, Rev 3:7; **(2e)** of a door for testimony, Rev 3:8. See: BAGD—434a; THAYER—348b.

2809. **κλέμμα** {1x} **klĕmma,** *klem'-mah;* from *2813; stealing* (prop. the thing stolen, but used of the act):—theft {1x}. See: BAGD—434b; THAYER—348c.

2810. **Κλεόπας** {1x} **Klĕŏpas,** *kleh-op'-as;* prob. contr. from Κλεόπα-τρος **Klĕŏpatrŏs** (compound of *2811* and *3962*); *Cleopas,* a Chr.:—Cleopas {1x}. See: BAGD—434b; THAYER—348c.

2811. **κλέος** {1x} **klĕŏs,** *kleh'-os;* from a short. form of *2564; renown* (as if *being called*):—glory {1x}.

The word is derived from a root signifying hearing; hence, the meaning reputation, good report, fame, renown (1 Pet 2:20). See: BAGD—434b; THAYER—348c.

2812. **κλέπτης** {16x} **klĕptēs,** *klep'-tace;* from *2813;* a *stealer* (lit. or fig.):—thief {16x}.

Kleptes is used **(1)** literally, Mt 6:19, 20; 24:43; Lk 12:33, 39; Jn 10:1, 10; 12:6; 1 Cor 6:10; 1 Pet 4:15; **(2)** metaphorically of "false teachers," Jn 10:8; **(3)** figuratively, **(3a)** of the personal coming of Christ, in a warning to a local church, with most of its members possessed of mere outward profession and defiled by the world, Rev 3:3; **(3b)** in retributive intervention to overthrow the foes of God, 16:15; **(4)** of the day of the Lord, in divine judgment upon the world, 2 Pet 3:10 and 1 Th 5:2, 4; there is no reference to the time of the coming, only to the manner of it. The use of the present tense instead of the future emphasizes the certainty of the coming. The unexpectedness of the coming of the thief, and the unpreparedness of those to whom He comes, are the essential elements in the figure. Syn.: A kleptes uses deception while the *lestes* (*3027*) is a robber who plunders, audaciously snatching away that which is another's. See: TDNT—3:754, 441; BAGD—434b; THAYER—348c.

2813. **κλέπτω** {13x} **klĕptō,** *klep'-to;* a primary verb; to *filch:*—steal {13x}.

Klepto, "to steal," akin to *kleptes,* "a thief" (cf. Eng., "kleptomania"), occurs in Mt 6:19, 20; 19:18; 27:64; 28:13; Mk 10:19; Lk 18:20; Jn 10:10; Rom 2:21 (twice); 13:9; Eph 4:28 (twice). See: TDNT—3:754, 441; BAGD—434c; THAYER—348c.

2814. **κλῆμα** {4x} **klēma,** *klay'-mah;* from *2806;* a *limb* or *shoot* (as if *broken* off):—branch {4x}.

Klema denotes a tender, flexible branch, especially the shoot of a vine, a vine sprout (Jn 15:2, 4, 5, 6). See: TDNT—3:757, 441; BAGD—434c; THAYER—348d.

2815. **Κλήμης** {1x} **Klēmēs,** *klay'-mace;* of Lat. or.; *merciful; Clemes* (i.e. *Clemens*), a Chr.:—Clement {1x}. See: BAGD—434c; THAYER—348d.

2816. **κληρονομέω** {18x} **klērŏnŏmĕō,** *klay-ron-om-eh'-o;* from *2818;* to *be an heir* to (lit. or fig.):—be heir {2x}, obtain by inheritance {1x}, inherit {15x}.

Introduction: *Kleronomeo* strictly means

"to receive by lot" (*kleros*, "a lot," *nemomai*, "to possess"); then, in a more general sense, "to possess oneself of, to receive as one's own, to obtain." The following list shows how in the NT the idea of inheriting broadens out to include all spiritual good provided through and in Christ, and particularly all that is contained in the hope grounded on the promises of God. The verb is used of the following objects: **(1)** birthright, that into the possession of which one enters in virtue of sonship, not because of a price paid or of a task accomplished, Gal 4:30; Heb 1:4; 12:17; **(2)** that which is received as a gift, in contrast with that which is received as the reward of law-keeping, Heb 1:14; 6:12 ("through," i.e., "through experiences that called for the exercise of faith and patience," but not "on the ground of the exercise of faith and patience."); **(3)** that which is received on condition of obedience to certain precepts, 1 Pet 3:9, and of faithfulness to God amidst opposition, Rev 21:7; **(4)** the reward of that condition of soul which forbears retaliation and self-vindication, and expresses itself in gentleness of behavior, Mt 5:5. The phrase "inherit the earth" or "land" occurs several times in OT. See especially Ps 37:11, 22;

(5) the reward (in the coming age, Mk 10:30) of the acknowledgment of the paramountcy of the claims of Christ, Mt 19:29. In the three accounts given of this incident, see Mk 10:17–31; Lk 18:18–30, the words of the question put to the Lord are, in Matthew, "that I may have," in Mark and Luke, "that I may inherit." In the report of the Lord's word to Peter in reply to his subsequent question, Matthew has "inherit eternal life," while Mark and Luke have "receive eternal life." It seems to follow that the meaning of the word "inherit" is here ruled by the words "receive" and "have," with which it is interchanged in each of the three Gospels, i.e., the less common word "inherit" is to be regarded as equivalent to the more common words "receive" and "have." Cf. Luke 10:25. Note: In regard to (5), the word clearly signifies entrance into eternal life without any previous title; it will not bear the implication that a child of God may be divested of his "inheritance" by the loss of his right of succession. **(6)** The reward of those who have shown kindness to the "brethren" of the Lord in their distress during the tribulatioin, Mt 25:34; **(7)** the kingdom of God, which the morally corrupt cannot "inherit," 1 Cor 6:9, 10, the "inheritance" of which is likewise impossible to the present physical constitution of man, 1 Cor 15:50; **(8)** incorruption, impossible of "inheritance" by corruption, 1 Cor 15:50. See: TDNT—3:767, 442; BAGD—434d; THAYER—348d.

2817. κληρονομία {14x} **klērŏnŏmia**, *klay-ron-om-ee'-ah;* from *2818;* heirship, i.e. (concr.) a *patrimony* or (gen.) a *possession:*—inheritance {14x}.

Kleronomia, "a lot", properly "an inherited property, an inheritance." **(1)** It is always rendered inheritance in NT, but only in a few cases in the Gospels has it the meaning ordinarily attached to that word in English, i.e., that into possession of which the heir enters only on the death of an ancestor. **(2)** The NT usage may be set out as follows: **(2a)** that property in real estate which in ordinary course passes from father to son on the death of the former, Mt 21:38; Mk 12:7; Lk 12:13; 20:14; **(2b)** a portion of an estate made the substance of a gift, Acts 7:5; Gal 3:18, which also is to be included under **(2c)**; in Gal 3:18, "if the inheritance is of the Law," the word "inheritance" stands for "the title to the inheritance;" **(2c)** the prospective condition and possessions of the believer in the new order of things to be ushered in at the return of Christ, Acts 20:32; Eph 1:14; 5:5; Col 3:24; Heb 9:15; 1 Pet 1:4; **(2d)** what the believer will be to God in that age, Eph 1:18. See: TDNT—3:767, 442; BAGD—435a; THAYER—349a.

2818. κληρονόμος {15x} **klērŏnŏmŏs**, *klay-ron-om'-os;* from *2819* and the base of *3551* (in its orig. sense of *partitioning,* i.e. [refl.] *getting* by apportionment); a *sharer by lot,* i.e. *inheritor* (lit. or fig.); by impl. a *possessor:*—heir {15x}. See: TDNT—3:767, 442; BAGD—435b; THAYER—349b.

2819. κλῆρος {13x} **klērŏs**, *klay'-ros;* prob. from *2806* (through the idea of using *bits* of wood, etc., for the purpose); a *die* (for drawing chances); by impl. a *portion* (as if so secured); by extens. an *acquisition* (espec. a *patrimony,* fig.):—heritage {1x}, inheritance {2x}, lot {8x}, part {2x}.

Kleros, (whence Eng., "clergy"), denotes **(1)** "a lot," given or cast (the latter as a means of obtaining divine direction), Mt 27:35 twice; Mk 15:24; Lk 23:24; Jn 19:24; Acts 1:26 twice; **(2)** "a person's share" in anything, Acts 1:17, "part"; 8:21, "lot"; **(3)** "a charge" (lit., "charges") "allotted," to elders, 1 Pet 5:3, "(God's) heritage"; the figure is from portions of lands allotted to be cultivated; **(4)** "an inheritance" Acts 26:18; Col 1:12. See: TDNT—3:758, 442; BAGD—435b; THAYER—349c.

2820. κληρόω {1x} **klērŏō**, *klay-rŏ'-o;* from *2819;* to *allot,* i.e. (fig.) to *assign* (a privilege):—obtain an inheritance {1x}. See: TDNT—3:764, 442; BAGD—435d; THAYER—349d.

2821. **κλῆσις** {11x} **klēsis,** *klay'-sis;* from a shorter form of *2564;* an *invitation* (fig.):—calling {10x}, vocation {1x}.

Klesis, "a calling", **(1)** is always used in the NT of that "calling" the origin, nature and destiny of which are heavenly (the idea of invitation being implied); **(2)** it is used especially of God's invitation to man to accept the benefits of salvation, Rom 11:29; 1 Cor 1:26; 7:20 (said there of the condition in which the "calling" finds one); Eph 1:18, "His calling"; Phil 3:14, the "high calling"; 2 Th 1:11 and 2 Pet 1:10, "your calling"; 2 Ti 1:9, a "holy calling"; Heb 3:1, a "heavenly calling"; Eph 4:1, "the vocation wherewith ye were called"; 4:4, "in one hope of your calling." See: TDNT—3:491, 394; BAGD—435d; THAYER—349d.

2822. **κλητός** {11x} **klētŏs,** *klay-tos';* from the same as *2821; invited,* i.e. *appointed,* or (spec.) a *saint:*—called {11x}.

Kletos, "called, invited," is used, **(1)** "of the call of the gospel," Mt 20:16; 22:14, not there "an effectual call," as in the Epistles, Rom 1:1, 6–7; 8:28; 1 Cor 1:2, 24; Jude 1; Rev 17:14; **(2)** in Rom 1:7 and 1 Cor 1:2 the meaning is "saints by calling"; **(3)** of "an appointment to apostleship," Rom 1:1; 1 Cor 1:1. See: TDNT—3:494, 394; BAGD—436a; THAYER—350a.

2823. **κλίβανος** {2x} **klibanŏs,** *klib'-an-os;* of uncert. der.; an earthen *pot* used for baking in:—oven {2x}.

Klibanos is mentioned in Mt 6:30 and Lk 12:28. The form of "oven" commonly in use in the east indicates the kind in use as mentioned in Scripture. A hole is sunk in the ground about 3 feet deep and somewhat less in diameter. The walls are plastered with cement. A fire is kindled inside, the fuel being grass, or dry twigs, which heat the oven rapidly and blacken it with smoke and soot (see Lam 5:10). When sufficiently heated the surface is wiped, and the dough is molded into broad thin loaves, placed one at a time on the wall of the "oven" to fit its concave inner circle. The baking takes a few seconds. Such ovens are usually outside the home, and often the same "oven" serves for several families (Lev 26:26). An "oven" of this sort is doubtless referred to in Ex 8:3. See: BAGD—436b; THAYER—350b.

2824. **κλίμα** {3x} **klima,** *klee'-mah;* from *2827;* a *slope,* i.e. (spec.) a *"clime"* or *tract* of country:—part {1x}, region {2x}.

Klima, primarily "an incline, slope" (Eng., "clime, climate"), is used **(1)** of "parts", Rom 15:23; and **(2)** of "regions", 2 Cor 11:10; Gal 1:21. See: BAGD—436b; THAYER—350b.

2825. **κλίνη** {10x} **klinē,** *klee'-nay;* from *2827;* a *couch* (for sleep, sickness, sitting or eating):—bed {9x}, table {1x}.

Kline, akin to *klino,* "to lean" (Eng., "recline, incline" etc.), **(1)** "a bed," e.g., Mk 7:30, also denotes **(2)** a "couch" **(2a)** for reclining at meals, Mk 4:21, or **(2b)** a "couch" for carrying the sick, Mt 9:2, 6. **(3)** The metaphorical phrase "to cast into a bed," Rev 2:22, signifies to afflict with disease (or possibly, to lay on a bier); **(4)** in Mk 7:4, "tables." See: BAGD—436b; THAYER—350c.

2826. **κλινίδιον** {2x} **klinidiŏn,** *kleen-eed'-ee-on;* neut. of a presumed der. of *2825;* a *pallet* or *little couch:*—bed {2x}.

Klinidion, "a small bed," a diminutive form of *kline,* "a bed" (from *klino,* "to incline, recline"), is used in Lk 5:19, 24 of the "bed" (*kline,* in v. 18) on which the palsied man was brought. See: BAGD—436c; THAYER—350c.

2827. **κλίνω** {7x} **klinō,** *klee'-no;* a primary verb; to *slant* or *slope,* i.e. *incline* or *recline* (lit. or fig.):—bow {1x}, bow down {1x}, be far spent {1x}, lay {2x}, turn to flight {1x}, wear away {1x}.

Klino, "to incline, to bow down," is used **(1)** of the women who in their fright "bowed" their faces to the earth at the Lord's empty tomb, Lk 24:5; **(2)** of the act of the Lord on the cross immediately before giving up His Spirit. What is indicated in the statement "He bowed His head," is not the helpless dropping of the head after death, but the deliberate putting of His head into a position of rest, Jn 19:30. The verb is deeply significant here. The Lord reversed the natural order. The same verb is used in His statement in Mt 8:20 and Lk 9:58, "the Son of Man hath not where to lay His head." **(3)** It is used, too, of the decline of day, Lk 9:12; 24:29; **(4)** of turning enemies to flight, Heb 11:34. See: BAGD—436c; THAYER—350c.

2828. **κλισία** {1x} **klisia,** *klee-see'-ah;* from a der. of *2827;* prop. *reclination,* i.e. (concr. and spec.) a *party* at a meal:—company {1x}.

It is found in the plural in Lk 9:14 signifying companies reclining at a meal. See: BAGD—436d; THAYER—350d.

2829. **κλοπή** {2x} **klŏpē,** *klop-ay';* from *2813;* *stealing:*—theft {2x}. Cf. Matt. 15:19; Mark 7:22. See: BAGD—436d; THAYER—350d.

2830. **κλύδων** {2x} **kludōn,** *kloo'-dohn;* from κλύζω **kluzō** (to *billow* or *dash* over); a *surge* of the sea (lit. or fig.):—raging {1x}, wave {1x}.

Kludon "a billow, a dashing or surging

wave, a surge, a violent agitation" (akin to *kluzo,* "to wash over"), said of the sea; translated (1) "raging" in Lk 8:24; and (2) "wave" in Jas 1:6. Syn.: *Kludon* (*2949*) denotes a wave, suggesting uninterrupted successions; and *kuma* (*2830*) denotes a billow, surge, suggesting size and extension. Both are figuratively used of words suggesting the same definitions. See: BAGD—436d; THAYER—350d.

2831. **κλυδωνίζομαι** {1x} **kludōnizŏmai,** *kloo-do-nid'-zom-ahee;* mid. voice from *2830;* to *surge,* i.e. (fig.) to *fluctuate:*—toss to and fro {1x}.

This word signifies "to be tossed by billows" (*kludon,* "a billow"); metaphorically, in Eph 4:14 it speaks of an unsettled condition of mind influenced and agitated by one false teaching and another, and characterized by that immaturity which lacks the firm conviction begotten by the truth. See: BAGD—436d; THAYER—350d.

2832. **Κλωπᾶς** {1x} **Klōpas,** *klo-pas';* of Chald. or. (corresp. to *256*); *Clopas,* an Isr.:—Clopas {1x}. See: BAGD—436d; THAYER—351a.

2833. **κνήθω** {1x} **knēthō,** *knay'-tho;* from a primary κνάω **knaō** (to *scrape*); to *scratch,* i.e. (by impl.) to *tickle:*—× itching {1x}.

Knetho, "to scratch, tickle," is used in the passive voice, metaphorically, of an eagerness to hear, in 2 Ti 4:3, lit., "itched (as to the hearing)," of those who, not enduring sound doctrine, heap to themselves teachers who teach what they are "itching" to hear." See: BAGD—437a; THAYER—351a.

2834. **Κνίδος** {1x} **Knidŏs,** *knee'-dos;* prob. of for. or.; *Cnidus,* a place in Asia Minor:—Cnidus {1x}. See: BAGD—437a; THAYER—351a.

2835. **κοδράντης** {2x} **kŏdrantēs,** *kod-ran'-tace;* of Lat. or.; a *quadrans,* i.e. the fourth part of an as:—farthing {2x}.

This coin equals about ⅜ of a cent, Mt 5:26; Mk 12:42. See: BAGD—437a; THAYER—351a.

2836. **κοιλία** {23x} **kŏilia,** *koy-lee'-ah;* from κοῖλος **kŏilŏs** (*"hollow"*); a *cavity,* i.e. (spec.) the *abdomen;* by impl. the *matrix;* fig. the *heart:*—belly {11x}, womb {12x}.

Koilia, from *koilos,* "hollow", denotes the entire physical cavity, but most frequently was used to denote (1) "the womb", Mt 19:12; Lk 1:15, 41, 42, 44; 2:21; 11:27; 23:29; Jn 3:4; Acts 3:2; 14:8; Gal 1:15; (2) When translated "belly"

it represents the whole belly, the entire cavity, the upper [i.e. stomach] and the lower belly being distinguished; (2a) the lower belly, the lower region, the receptacle of the excrement, Mt 15:17; Mk 7:19; (2b) the gullet, Mt 12:40; Lk 15:16; and (3) to be given up to the pleasures of the palate, to gluttony, Rom 16:18; Phil 3:19; it also (4) stands metaphorically for the innermost part of man, the soul, the heart, seat of thought, feeling, choice, Jn 7:38. See: TDNT—3:786, 446; BAGD—437b; THAYER—351b.

2837. **κοιμάω** {18x} **kŏimaō,** *koy-mah'-o;* from *2749;* to *put to sleep,* i.e. (pass. or refl.) to *slumber;* fig. to *decease:*—sleep {10x}, fall asleep {4x}, be asleep {2x}, fall on sleep {1x}, be dead {1x}.

Koimaomai is used of (1) natural sleep (Mt 28:13; Lk 22:45; Jn 11:12); (2) the death of the body, but only of such as are Christ's; (3) yet never of Christ Himself, though He is the first-fruits of them that have fallen asleep (1 Cor 15:20); (4) of saints who departed before Christ came (Mt 27:52; Acts 13:36); (5) of Lazarus, while Christ was yet upon the earth (Jn 11:11); (6) of believers since the Ascension (1 Th 4:13–15; Acts 7:60; 1 Cor 7:39; 11:30; 15:6, 18, 51; 2 Pet 3:4). (7) This metaphorical use of the word sleep is appropriate, because of the similarity in appearance between a sleeping body and a dead body; restfulness and peace normally characterize both. As the sleeper does not cease to exist while his body sleeps, so the dead person continues to exist despite his absence from the region in which those who remain can communicate with him, and that, as sleep is known to be temporary, so the death of the body will be found to be. See: BAGD—437c; THAYER—351b.

2838. **κοίμησις** {1x} **kŏimēsis,** *koy'-may-sis;* from *2837; sleeping,* i.e. (by impl.) *repose:*—taking of rest {1x}.

Koimesis, "a resting, reclining", is used in Jn 11:13, of natural sleep, translated "taking of rest." See: BAGD—437d; THAYER—351c.

2839. **κοινός** {12x} **kŏinŏs,** *koy-nos';* prob. from *4862; common,* i.e. (lit.) shared by all or several, or (cer.) *profane:*—common {7x}, defiled {1x}, unclean {3x}, unholy {1x}.

(1) This word means "common" from the idea of coming into contact with everything, not separated in the least. (2) *Koinos,* as an adjective, means "common," and is translated "unclean": "I know, and am persuaded by the Lord Jesus, that there is nothing unclean of itself: but to him that esteemeth any thing to be unclean, to him it is unclean" (Rom 14:14 (thrice). *Koinos* (*2834*) denotes "common, be-

longing to several" (Lat., *communis*), said **(3)** of things had in common, Acts 2:44; 4:32; **(3a)** of faith, Titus 1:4; **(3b)** of salvation, Jude 3; it stands in contrast to *idios*, "one's own"; **(4)** "ordinary, belonging to the generality, as distinct from what is peculiar to the few", hence the application to religious practices of Gentiles in contrast with those of Jews; **(4a)** or of the ordinary people in contrast with those of the Pharisees; hence the meaning "unhallowed, profane," Levitically unclean (Lat., *profanus*), said **(4b)** of hands, Mk 7:2, "defiled"; **(4c)** of animals, ceremonially unclean, Acts 10:14; 11:8; **(4d)** of a man, Acts 10:28; **(4e)** of meats, Rom 14:14, "unclean"; **(4f)** of the blood of the covenant, as viewed by an apostate, Heb 10:29, "unholy"; **(4g)** of everything unfit for the Holy City, Rev 21:27.

　　Syn.: 167, 169, 952, 2840, 3394. See: TDNT—3:789, 447; BAGD—438a; THAYER—351c.

2840. κοινόω {15x} **kŏinŏō**, *koy-nŏ'-o;* from 2839; to *make* (or *consider*) *profane* (ceremon.):—call common {2x}, defile {11x}, pollute {1x}, unclean {1x}.

　　Koinoo, as a verb, means **(1)** to make *koinos* (2839), "to defile," **(2)** is translated "unclean": "For if the blood of bulls and of goats, and the ashes of an heifer sprinkling the unclean, sanctifieth to the purifying of the flesh:" (Heb 9:13), **(3)** where the perfect participle, passive, is used with the article, hence "them that have been defiled." Syn.: 167, 169, 2839, 3394. See: TDNT—3:809, 447; BAGD—438b; THAYER—351d.

2841. κοινωνέω {8x} **kŏinōnĕō**, *koy-no-neh'-o;* from 2844; to *share* with others (obj. or subj.):—communicate {2x}, distribute {1x}, be partaker {5x}.

　　Koinoneo is used in two senses, **(1)** "to have a share in," Rom 15:27; 1 Ti 5:22; Heb 2:14; 1 Pet 4:13; 2 Jn 11; **(2)** "to give a share to, go shares with," Rom 12:13, "distributing"; Gal 6:6, "communicate"; Phil 4:15, "did communicate"; it is also translated **(3)** "to be partaker of" **(3a)** in 1 Ti 5:22; Heb 2:14, 1st part, "are partakers of"; **(3b)** 1 Pet 4:13; 2 Jn 11, "is partaker of"; **(3c)** in the passive voice in Rom 15:27, "have been made partakers of." See: TDNT—3:797, 447; BAGD—438c; THAYER—351d.

2842. κοινωνία {20x} **kŏinōnia**, *koy-nohn-ee'-ah;* from 2844; *partnership,* i.e. (lit.) *participation,* or (social) *intercourse,* or (pecuniary) *benefaction:*—fellowship {12x}, communion {4x}, communication {1x}, distribution {1x}, contribution {1x}, to communicate {1x}.

　　Koinonia, "a having in common (*koinos*),

partnership, fellowship" denotes **(1)** the share which one has in anything, a participation, fellowship recognized and enjoyed; thus it is used of the common experiences and interests of Christian men, Acts 2:42; Gal 2:9; **(2)** of participation in the knowledge of the Son of God, 1 Cor 1:9; **(3)** of sharing in the realization of the effects of the blood (i.e., the death) of Christ and the body of Christ, as set forth by the emblems in the Lord's Supper, 1 Cor 10:16; **(4)** of participation in what is derived from the Holy Spirit, 2 Cor 13:14; Phil 2:1; **(5)** of participation in the sufferings of Christ, Phil 3:10; **(6)** of sharing in the resurrection life possessed in Christ, and so of fellowship with the Father and the Son, 1 Jn 1:3, 6–7; **(7)** negatively, of the impossibility of "communion" between light and darkness, 2 Cor 6:14; **(8)** fellowship manifested in acts, the practical effects of fellowship with God, **(8a)** wrought by the Holy Spirit in the lives of believers as the outcome of faith, Philem 6, and **(8b)** finding expression in joint ministration to the needy, Rom 15:26; 2 Cor 8:4; 9:13; Heb 13:16, and **(8c)** in the furtherance of the Gospel by gifts, Phil 1:5. **(9)** It is translated **(9a)** "fellowship", Acts 2:42; 1 Cor 1:9; 2 Cor 8:4; Gal 2:9; Eph 3:9; Phil 1:5; 2:1; 3:10; 1 Jn 1:3 (twice); 1;6, 7; **(9b)** "communion", 1 Cor 10:16 (twice); 2 Cor 6:14; 13:14; **(9c)** "communication", Philem 6; **(9d)** "distribution", 2 Cor 9:13; **(9e)** "contribution", Rom 15:26; **(9f)** "to communicate", Heb 13:16. See: TDNT—3:797, 447; BAGD—438d; THAYER—352a.

2843. κοινωνικός {1x} **kŏinōnikŏs**, *koy-no-nee-kos';* from 2844; *communicative,* i.e. (pecuniarily) *liberal:*—willing to communicate {1x}.

　　This word denotes social, sociable, ready and apt to form and maintain communion and fellowship; inclined to make others sharers in one's possessions, inclined to impart, free in giving, liberal, 1 Ti 6:18. See: TDNT—3:809, 447; BAGD—439c; THAYER—352b.

2844. κοινωνός {10x} **kŏinōnŏs**, *koy-no-nos';* from 2839; a *sharer,* i.e. *associate:*—companion {1x}, ✕ fellowship {1x}, partaker {5x}, partner {3x}.

　　Koinonos, "having in common," is rendered **(1)** "are partakers with (the altar),"—the altar standing by metonymy for that which is associated with it—in 1 Cor 10:18, and **(2)** in 10: 20, "have fellowship with (devils)." **(3)** It is translated **(3a)** "companion", Heb 10:33; **(3b)** "✕ fellowship", 1 Cor 10:20; **(3c)** "partaker", Mt 23:30; 1 Cor 10:18; 2 Cor 1:7; 1 Pet 5:1; 2 Pet 1:4; **(3d)** "partner", Lk 5:10; 2 Cor 8:23; Philem 7. See: TDNT—3:797, 447; BAGD—439d; THAYER—352b.

2845. **κοίτη** {4x} **kŏitē,** *koy'-tay;* from *2749;* a *couch;* by extens. *cohabitation;* by impl. the male *sperm:*—bed {2x}, chambering {1x}, × conceive {1x}.

Koite, primarily "a place for lying down", denotes **(1)** a "bed," Lk 11:7; the marriage "bed," Heb 13:4; **(2)** in Rom 13:13, it is used of sexual intercourse. **(3)** By metonymy, the cause standing for the effect, it denotes conception, Rom 9:10. See: BAGD—440a; THAYER—352c.

2846. **κοιτών** {1x} **kŏitōn,** *koy-tone';* from *2845;* a *bedroom:*—+ chamberlain + 1909 {1x}.

Koiton denotes the officer who is over the bed chamber, the chamberlain, Acts 12:20. See: BAGD—440b; THAYER—352d.

2847. **κόκκινος** {6x} **kŏkkinŏs,** *kok'-kee-nos;* from *2848* (from the *kernel*-shape of the insect); *crimson*-colored:—scarlet {4x}, scarlet colour {1x}, scarlet coloured {1x}.

Kokkinos is derived from *kokkos,* used of the "berries" (clusters of the eggs of an insect) collected from the *ilex coccifera;* the color, however, is obtained from the *cochineal* insect, which attaches itself to the leaves and twigs of the *coccifera* oak; another species is raised on the leaves of the *cactus ficus.* The Arabic name for this insect is *qirmiz,* whence the word "crimson." It is used **(1)** of "scarlet" wool, Heb 9:19; **(1a)** cf. in connection with the cleansing of a leper, Lev 14:4, 6, "scarlet"; **(1b)** with the offering of the red heifer, cf. Num 19:6; **(2)** of the robe put on Christ by the soldiers, Mt 27:28; **(3)** of the "beast" seen in symbolic vision in Rev 17:3, "scarlet-colored"; **(4)** of the clothing of the "woman" as seen sitting on the "beast," Rev 17:4; **(5)** of part of the merchandise of Babylon, Rev 18:12; **(6)** figuratively, of the glory of the city itself, Rev 18:16; the neuter is used in the last three instances. See: TDNT—3:812, 450; BAGD—440b; THAYER—352d.

2848. **κόκκος** {6x} **kŏkkŏs,** *kok'-kos;* appar. a primary word; a *kernel* of seed:—corn {1x}, grain {6x}.

Kokkos denotes "a grain," Mt 13:31; 17:20; Mk 4:31; Lk 13:19; 17:6; Jn 12:24 "corn"; 1 Cor 15:37. See: TDNT—3:810, 450; BAGD—440c; THAYER—352d.

2849. **κολάζω** {2x} **kŏlazō,** *kol-ad'-zo;* from κόλος **kŏlos** (*dwarf*); prop. to *curtail,* i.e. (fig.) to *chastise* (or *reserve* for infliction):—punish {2x}.

Kolos primarily denotes "to curtail, prune, dock" (from *kolos,* "docked"); then, "to check, restrain, punish"; it is used in the **(1)** middle voice in Acts 4:21; **(2)** passive voice in 2 Pet 2:9, "to be punished", "being punished", a futu-

rative present tense. See: TDNT—3:814, 451; BAGD—440c; THAYER—352d.

2850. **κολακεία** {1x} **kŏlakĕia,** *kol-ak-i'-ah;* from a der. of κόλαξ **kŏlax** (a *fawner*); *flattery:*—× flattering {1x}.

Kolakeia is used in 1 Th 2:5 of flattering words, adopted as a cloak of covetousness, i.e., words which flattery uses, not simply as an effort to give pleasure, but with motives of self-interest. See: TDNT—3:817, 451; BAGD—440d; THAYER—353a.

2851. **κόλασις** {2x} **kŏlasis,** *kol'-as-is;* from *2849;* penal *inflicton:*—punishment {1x}, torment {1x}.

(1) *Kolasis* stresses the punishment aspect of judgment. **(2)** *Kolasis,* "punishment," is used in **(2a)** Mt 25:46, "(eternal) punishment," and **(2b)** 1 Jn 4:18, "(fear hath) torment", which there describes a process, not merely an effect; this kind of fear is expelled by perfect love; where God's love is being perfected in us, it gives no room for the fear of meeting with His reprobation; the "torment/punishment" referred to is the immediate consequence of the sense of sin, not a holy awe but a slavish fear, the negation of the enjoyment of love. Syn.: 5098. See: TDNT—3:816, 451; BAGD—440d; THAYER—353a.

2852. **κολαφίζω** {5x} **kŏlaphizō,** *kol-af-id'-zo;* from a der. of the base of *2849;* to *rap* with the fist:—buffet {5x}.

Kolaphizo signifies "to strike with clenched hands, to buffet with the fist" (*kolaphos,* "a fist"), Mt 26:67; Mk 14:65; 1 Cor 4:11; 2 Cor 12:7; 1 Pet 2:20. See: TDNT—3:818, 451; BAGD—441a; THAYER—353b.

2853. **κολλάω** {11x} **kŏllaō,** *kol-lah'-o;* from κόλλα **kŏlla** ("*glue*"); to *glue,* i.e. (pass. or refl.) to *stick* (fig.):—join (one's) self {4x}, cleave {3x}, be joined {2x}, keep company {1x}, vr reach {1x}.

Kollao, "to join fast together, to glue, cement," is **(1)** primarily said of metals and other materials (from *kolla,* "glue"). **(2)** In the NT it is used only in the passive voice, with reflexive force, in the sense of **(2a)** "cleaving unto," as of cleaving to one's wife, Mt 19:5; 1 Cor 6:16–17, "joined." **(2b)** In Lk 10:11 it is used of the "cleaving" of dust to the feet; **(2c)** in Acts 5:13; 8:29; 9:26; 10:28; 17:34, in the sense of becoming associated with a person so as to company with him, or be on his side, said, in the last passage, of those in Athens who believed; **(2d)** in Rom 12:9, ethically, of "cleaving" to that which is good; **(2e)** in Rev 18:5, metaphorically, Babylon "has sinned to high heaven", so severe are her sins they, "when piled high" reach and

cleave even unto heaven itself. See: TDNT—3:822, 452; BAGD—441c; THAYER—353b.

2854. κολλούριον {1x} **kŏllŏuriŏn,** *kol-loo'-ree-on;* neut. of a presumed der. of κολλύρα **kŏllura** (a *cake;* prob akin to the base of *2853*); prop. a *poultice* (as made of or in the form of *crackers*), i.e. (by anal.) a *plaster:*—eyesalve {1x}.

Kollourion, an "eye-salve," shaped like a roll, is used in Rev 3:18, of the true knowledge of one's condition and of the claims of Christ. See: BAGD—441d; THAYER—353c.

2855. κολλυβιστής {3x} **kŏllubistēs,** *kol-loo-bis-tace';* from a presumed der. of κόλλυβος **kŏllubŏs** (a small *coin;* prob. akin to *2854*); a *coin-dealer:*—money-changer {2x}, changer {1x}.

A *kollubos* is a "a small coin or rate of change" (*koloboo* signifies "to cut off, to clip, shorten," Mt 24:22), and denotes "a money-changer," lit., money-clipper, Mt 21:12; Mk 11:15; Jn 2:15 "changers." See: BAGD—442a; THAYER—353c.

2856. κολοβόω {4x} **kŏlŏbŏō,** *kol-ob-ŏ'-o;* from a der. of the base of *2849;* to *dock,* i.e. (fig.) *abridge:*—shorten {4x}.

Koloboo denotes to cut off, amputate; hence, to curtail, shorten, said of the shortening by God of the time of the great tribulation (Mt 24:22, twice; Mk 13:20, twice). See: TDNT—3:823, 452; BAGD—442a; THAYER—353d.

2857. Κολοσσαί {1x} **Kŏlŏssai,** *kol-os-sah'-ee;* appar. fem. plur. of κολοσσός **kŏlŏssŏs** ("*colossal*"); *Colossæ,* a place in Asia Minor:—Colosse {1x}. See: BAGD—442b; THAYER—353d.

2858. Κολοσσαεύς {1x} **Kŏlŏssaĕus,** *kol-os-sayoos';* from *2857;* a *Colossæan,* (i.e. inhab. of Colossæ:—Colossian {1x}. See: BAGD—442a; THAYER—353d.

2859. κόλπος {6x} **kŏlpŏs,** *kol'-pos;* appar. a primary word; the *bosom;* by anal. a *bay:*—bosom {5x}, creek {1x}.

Kolpos signifies **(1)** "the front of the body between the arms"; hence, to recline in the "bosom" was said of one who so reclined at table that his head covered, as it were, the "bosom" of the one next to him, Jn 13:23. Hence, **(2)** figuratively, **(2a)** it is used of a place of blessedness with another, as with Abraham in paradise, Lk 16:22–23 (plural in v. 23), from the custom of reclining at table in the "bosom," a place of honor; **(2b)** of the Lord's eternal and essential relation with the Father, in all its blessedness and affection as intimated in the phrase, "The only begotten Son, which is in the bosom of the Father" (Jn 1:18); **(3)** "of the bosom of a gar-

ment, the hollow formed by the upper forepart of a loose garment, bound by a girdle and used for carrying or keeping things"; thus figuratively of repaying one liberally, Lk 6:38; cf. Is 65:6; Jer 39:18; **(4)** "of an inlet of the sea," because of its shape, like a bosom, Acts 27:39. By analogy a creek is a small inlet as seen from the sea that narrows by the "arms" of the land on each of its sides. See: TDNT—3:824, 452; BAGD—442b; THAYER—353d.

2860. κολυμβάω {1x} **kŏlumbaō,** *kol-oom-bah'-o;* from κόλυμβος **kŏlumbŏs** (a *diver*); to *plunge* into water:—swim {1x}. See: BAGD—442c; THAYER—354b.

2861. κολυμβήθρα {5x} **kŏlumbēthra,** *kol-oom-bay'-thrah;* from *2860;* a *diving-place,* i.e. *pond* for bathing (or swimming):—pool {5x}.

This word denotes "a pool large enough to swim in, a swimming pool," (akin to *kolumbao,* "to swim," Acts 27:43; Jn 5:2, 4, 7; 9:7, 11. See: BAGD—442c; THAYER—354b.

2862. κολωνία {1x} **kŏlōnia,** *kol-o-nee'-ah;* of Lat. or.; a Rom. "*colony*" for veterans:—colony {1x}.

Philippi was a Roman military colony (Acts 16:12), a watch tower of the Roman state. It possessed the right of Roman freedom, and of holding the soil under Roman law, as well as exemption from poll-tax and tribute. See: BAGD—442c; THAYER—354b.

2863. κομάω {2x} **kŏmaō,** *kom-ah'-o;* from *2864;* to *wear tresses* of hair:—have long hair {2x}.

Komao signifies "to let the hair grow long, to wear long hair," a glory to a woman, a dishonor to a man (as taught by nature), 1 Cor 11:14, 15. See: BAGD—442d; THAYER—354b.

2864. κόμη {1x} **kŏmē,** *kom'-ay;* appar. from the same as *2865;* the *hair* of the head (*locks,* as *ornamental,* and thus differing from *2359;* which prop. denotes merely the *scalp*):—hair {1x}.

Kome is used only of "human hair," but not in the NT of the ornamental. The word is found in 1 Cor 11:15, where the context shows that the "covering" provided in the long "hair" of the woman is as a veil, a sign of subjection to authority, as indicated in the headships spoken of in vv. 1–10. Syn.: *Thrix (2359)* is the anatomical or physical term for hair; whereas, *kome (2864)* designates the hair as an ornament, the notion of length being only secondary and suggested. See: BAGD—442d; THAYER—354b.

2865. κομίζω {10x} **kŏmizō,** *kom-id'-zo;* from a primary κομέω **kŏmĕō** (to *tend,* i.e. take care of); prop. to *provide* for,

i.e. (by impl.) to *carry* off (as if from harm; generally *obtain*):—bring {1x}, receive {10x}.

Komizo, as a verb, denotes **(1)** "to bear, carry": "And, behold, a woman in the city, which was a sinner, when she knew that Jesus sat at meat in the Pharisee's house, brought an alabaster box of ointment" (Lk 7:37); **(2)** in the middle voice, "to bear for oneself" hence **(2a)** "to receive": "For ye have need of patience, that, after ye have done the will of God, ye might receive (*komizo*) the promise" (Heb 10:36; cf. 11:39; 1 Pet 1:9; 5:4; 2 Pet 2:13); **(2b)** "to receive back, recover": "Thou oughtest therefore to have put my money to the exchangers, and then at my coming I should have received (*komizo*) mine own with usury" (Mt 25:27; cf. Heb 11:19; metaphorically, of requital 2 Cor 5:10; Col 3:25); **(2c)** of "receiving back again" by the believer at the judgment seat of Christ hereafter, for wrong done in this life: "But he that doeth wrong shall receive for the wrong which he hath done: and there is no respect of persons" (Col 3:25); **(2d)** Eph 6:8 of "receiving," on the same occasion, "whatsoever good thing each one doeth": "Knowing that whatsoever good thing any man doeth, the same shall he receive of the Lord, whether he be bond or free." Syn.: 324, 353, 354, 568, 588, 618, 1209, 1523, 1926, 2210, 2975, 2983, 3028, 3335, 3336, 3858, 3880, 3970, 4327, 4355, 4356, 4380, 4381, 4382, 5562, 5264, 5274. See: BAGD—442d; THAYER—354c.

2866. **κομψότερον** {1x} **kŏmpsŏtĕrŏn**, *komp-sot'-er-on;* neut. comparative of a der. of the base of *2865* (mean. prop. *well dressed,* i.e. *nice*); fig. *convalescent:*—began to amend + *2192* {1x}. See: BAGD—443a; THAYER—354d.

2867. **κονιάω** {2x} **kŏniaō**, *kon-ee-ah'-o;* from κονία **kŏnia** (*dust;* by anal. *lime*); to *whitewash:*—whiten {2x}.

Koniao, from *konia*, "dust, lime," denotes "to whiten, whitewash," **(1)** of tombs, Mt 23:27; **(2)** figuratively of a hypocrite, Acts 23:3. See: TDNT—3:827, 453; BAGD—443a; THAYER—354d.

2868. **κονιορτός** {5x} **kŏniŏrtŏs**, *kon-ee-or-tos';* from the base of *2867* and ὄρνυμι **ŏrnumi** (to "*rouse*"); *pulverulence* (as *blown* about):—dust {5x}.

Koniortos, "raised or flying dust" (*konia*, "dust," *ornumi*, "to stir up"), is found in Mt 10:14; Lk 9:5; 10:11; Acts 13:51; 22:23. See: BAGD—443b; THAYER—355a.

2869. **κοπάζω** {3x} **kŏpazō**, *kop-ad'-zo;* from *2873;* to *tire,* i.e. (fig.) to *relax:*—cease {3x}.

Kopazo, "to cease through being spent with toil, to cease raging" (from *kopos*, "labor, toil," *kopiao*, "to labor"), is said of the wind only, Mt 14:32; Mk 4:39; 6:51. See: BAGD—443b; THAYER—355a.

2870. **κοπετός** {1x} **kŏpĕtŏs**, *kop-et-os';* from *2875; mourning* (prop. by *beating* the breast):—lamentation {1x}. See: TDNT—3:830, 453; BAGD—443b; THAYER—355a.

2871. **κοπή** {1x} **kŏpē**, *kop-ay';* from *2875; cutting,* i.e. *carnage:*—slaughter {1x}.

Kope, "a stroke" (akin to *kopto*, "to strike, to cut"), signifies "a decisive smiting in battle," in Heb 7:1. See: BAGD—443c; THAYER—355a.

2872. **κοπιάω** {23x} **kŏpiaō**, *kop-ee-ah'-o;* from a der. of *2873;* to *feel fatigue;* by impl. to *work hard:*—bestow labour {3x}, labour {16x}, toil {3x}, be wearied {1x}.

This word **(1)** means **(1a)** to grow weary, tired, exhausted with toil or burdens or grief and **(1b)** to labour with wearisome effort, bodily labour, toiling and is translated: **(2)** "bestow labour", Jn 4:38; Rom 16:6; Gal 4:11; **(3)** "labour", Mt 11:28; Jn 4:38 (2nd part); Acts 20:35; Rom 16:12 (twice); 1 Cor 4:12; 15:10; 16:16; Eph 4:28; Phil 2:16; Col 1:29; 1 Th 5:12; 1 Ti 4:10; 5:17; 2 Ti 2:6; Rev 2:3; **(4)** "toil", Mt 6:28; Lk 5:5; 12:27; **(5)** "be wearied", Jn 4:6. See: TDNT—3:827, 453; BAGD—443c; THAYER—355a.

2873. **κόπος** {19x} **kŏpŏs**, *kop'-os;* from *2875;* a *cut,* i.e. (by anal.) *toil* (as *reducing* the strength), lit. or fig.; by impl. *pains:*—labour {13x}, trouble + *3830* {5x}, weariness {1x}.

Kopos means "a striking, beating", then, "toil resulting in weariness, laborious toil, trouble." It is translated **(1)** "labor" or "labors" in Jn 4:38; 1 Cor 3:8; 15:58; 2 Cor 6:5; 10:15; 11:23; 1 Th 1:3; 2:9; 3:5; 2 Th 3:8; Heb 6:10; Rev 2:2; 14:13. **(2)** In the following the noun is used as the object of the verb *parecho*, "to afford, give, cause," the phrase being rendered "to trouble," lit., "to cause toil or trouble," **(2a)** to embarrass a person by giving occasion for anxiety, as some disciples did to the woman with the ointment, perturbing her spirit by their criticisms, Mt 26:10; Mk 14:6; or **(2b)** by distracting attention or disturbing a person's rest, as the importunate friend did, Lk 11:7; 18:5; **(3)** in Gal 6:17, "let no man trouble me," the apostle refuses, in the form of a peremptory prohibition, to allow himself to be distracted further by the Judaizers, through their proclamation of a false gospel and by their malicious attacks upon himself; and **(4)** "weariness", 2 Cor 11:27. Syn.: *Kopos* (*4192*) gives prominence to the effort, work as requiring force, which begins the weariness

from excessive labor. *Mochthos* (*3449*) refers to the final state of fatigue. *Ponos* (*4192*) refers to the hardship. See: TDNT—3:827, 453; BAGD—443d; THAYER—355b.

2874. κοπρία {2x} **kŏpria,** *kop-ree'-ah;* from κόπρος **kŏprŏs** (*ordure;* perh. akin to *2875*); *manure:*—dung + 906 {1x}, dunghill {1x}.

Kopria, "manure," **(1)** Lk 13:8, used in the plural with *ballo,* "to throw," is translated by the verb "to dung" and **(2)** in Lk 14:35 "a dunghill,." See: TDNT—3:827, 453; BAGD—443d; THAYER—355c.

2875. κόπτω {8x} **kŏptō,** *kop'-to;* a primary verb; to "*chop;*" spec. to *beat* the breast in grief:—cut down {2x}, lament {2x}, mourn {2x}, bewail {1x}, wail {1x}.

Kopto, primarily, "to beat, smite"; then, "to cut off," is translated **(1)** literally to "cut down" branches from trees, Mt 21:8; Mk 11:8; also **(2)** in the middle voice, of beating oneself, beating the breast, as a token of grief; hence, "lamented," Mt 11:17; Rev 18:9; and **(3)** "mourn", Mt 24:30; **(4)** "bewail", in Lk 8:52; 23:27; and **(5)** in Rev 1:7 "wail." Syn.: 2354, 3079, 3996. See: TDNT—3:830, 453; BAGD—444a; THAYER—355d. comp. the base of *5114*.

2876. κόραξ {1x} **kŏrax,** *kor'-ax;* perh. from *2880;* a *crow* (from its *voracity*):—raven {1x}. See: BAGD—444b; THAYER—355d.

2877. κοράσιον {8x} **kŏrasiŏn,** *kor-as'-ee-on;* neut. of a presumed der. of κόρη **kŏrē** (a *maiden*); a (little) *girl:*—damsel {6x}, maid {2x}.

Korasion, a diminutive of *kore,* "a girl," denotes "a little girl"; in the NT it is used only in familiar conversation: **(1)** "damsel", Mt 14:11; Mk 5:41–42; 6:22, 28 (twice); and **(2)** "maid", Mt 9:24–25. See: BAGD—444b; THAYER—355d.

2878. κορβᾶν {2x} **kŏrban,** *kor-ban';* and

κορβανᾶς **kŏrbanas,** *kor-ban-as';* of Heb. and Chald. or. respectively [7133]; a votive *offering* and *the offering;* a consecrated *present* (to the Temple fund); by extens. (the latter term) the *Treasury* itself, i.e. the room where the contribution boxes stood:—Corban {1x}, treasury {1x}.

Korban signifies **(1)** "an offering," and was a Hebrew term for any sacrifice, whether by the shedding of blood or otherwise [not used in the NT]; **(2)** "a gift offered to God," Corban, Mk 7:11; and **(3)** "treasury", the place where offerings were stored, Mt 27:6. **(4)** Jews were much addicted to rash vows; a saying of the rabbis was, "It is hard for the parents, but the

law is clear, vows must be kept." See: TDNT—3:860, 459; BAGD—444b; THAYER—355d.

2879. Κορέ {1x} **Kŏrĕ,** *kor-eh';* of Heb. or. [7141]; *Corë* (i.e. *Korach*), an Isr.:—Core {1x}. See: BAGD—444c; THAYER—356a.

2880. κορέννυμι {2x} **kŏrĕnnumi,** *kor-en'-noo-mee;* a primary verb; to *cram,* i.e. *glut* or *sate:*—eat enough {1x}, full {1x}.

This word means "to satiate, to satisfy," as with food, is used in the middle voice **(1)** in Acts 27:38, "had eaten enough"; and **(2)** in 1 Cor 4:8, "ye are filled." See: BAGD—444c; THAYER—356a.

2881. Κορίνθιος {4x} **Kŏrinthiŏs,** *kor-in'-thee-os;* from *2882;* a *Corinthian,* i.e. inhab. of Corinth:—Corinthian {4x}. See: BAGD—444d; THAYER—356a.

2882. Κόρινθος {7x} **Kŏrinthŏs,** *kor'-in-thos;* of uncert. der.; *Corinthus,* a city of Greece:—Corinth {7x}. See: BAGD—444d; THAYER—356a.

2883. Κορνήλιος {10x} **Kŏrnēliŏs,** *kor-nay'-lee-os;* of Lat. or.; *Cornelius,* a Rom.:—Cornelius {10x}. See: BAGD—444d; THAYER—356b.

2884. κόρος {1x} **kŏrŏs,** *kor'-os;* of Heb. or. [3734]; a *cor,* i.e. a spec. measure:—measure {1x}.

Koros, as a noun, denotes a *cor,* the largest Hebrew dry measure (ten *ephahs*), containing about 11 bushels, Lk 16:7; the hundred "measures" amounted to a very considerable quantity. Syn.: 280, 488, 943, 3313, 3354, 3358, 4057, 4568, 5234, 5249, 5518. See: BAGD—444d; THAYER—356b.

2885. κοσμέω {10x} **kŏsmĕō,** *kos-meh'-o;* from *2889;* [cf. Eng. cosmetic]; to *put in* proper *order,* i.e. *decorate* (lit. or fig.); spec. to *snuff* (a wick):—adorn {5x}, garnish {4x}, trim {1x}.

Kosmeo, primarily "to arrange, to put in order" (Eng., "cosmetic"), hence, **(1)** "to adorn, to ornament," **(1a)** one's person, 1 Ti 2:9; 1 Pet 3:5; Rev 21:2; **(1b)** metaphorically, of "adorning a doctrine", Titus 2:10; **(1c)** the "temple", Lk 21:5; it is also **(2)** translated by the verb "to garnish" **(2a)** "rooms" in Mt 12:44; **(2b)** "tombs", Mt 23:29; **(2c)** "buildings", Lk 11:25; Rev 21:19; and denotes **(3)** trimming lamps, Mt 25:7. See: TDNT—3:867, 459; BAGD—445a; THAYER—356b.

2886. κοσμικός {2x} **kŏsmikŏs,** *kos-mee-kos';* from *2889* (in its second. sense); *terrene* ("*cosmic*"), lit. (*mundane*) or fig. (*corrupt*):—worldly {2x}.

Kosmikos is used **(1)** in Heb 9:1 of the tabernacle as worldly (i.e., made of mundane materials, adapted to this visible world, local and transitory); and **(2)** in Titus 2:12, ethically, of worldly lusts or desires which have the character of this present corrupt age. See: TDNT—3:897, 459; BAGD—445b; THAYER—356c.

2887. **κόσμιος** {2x} **kŏsmiŏs**, *kos'-mee-os;* from 2889 (in its primary sense); *orderly,* i.e. *decorous:*—of good behaviour {1x}, modest {1x}.

(1) This word stresses well-ordered in earthly life, seemly, modest. **(2)** The stress is outward appearance and is translated **(2a)** "of good behavior" in 1 Ti 3:2 and **(2b)** "modest" in 1 Ti 2:9. See: TDNT—3:895, 459; BAGD—445c; THAYER—356c.

2888. **κοσμοκράτωρ** {1x} **kŏsmŏkratōr**, *kos-mok-rat'-ore;* from 2889 and 2902; a *world-ruler,* an epithet of Satan:—ruler {1x}.

Kosmokrator, plural in its only use, denotes rulers of this world and the context of Eph 6:12 ("the rulers of the darkness of this world") shows that not earthly potentates are indicated, but spirit powers, who, under the permissive will of God, and in consequence of human sin, exercise satanic and therefore antagonistic authority over the world in its present condition of spiritual darkness and alienation from God. Syn.: 746, 758, 4173. See: TDNT—3:913, 466; BAGD—445c; THAYER—356d.

2889. **κόσμος** {187x} **kŏsmŏs**, *kos'-mos;* prob. from the base of 2865; orderly *arrangement,* i.e. *decoration;* by impl. the *world* (in a wide or narrow sense, incl. its inhab., lit. or fig. [mor.]):—adorning {1x}, world {186x}.

Kosmos is first a harmonious arrangement or order, then by extension, adornment or decoration, and came to denote the world, or the universe, as that which is divinely arranged. It came to mean anyone not of the *ekklasia* (1577). *Kosmos,* primarily "order, arrangement, ornament, adornment" is used to denote **(1)** the "earth," e.g., Mt 13:35; Jn 21:25; Acts 17:24; Rom 1:20 (probably here the universe: it had this meaning among the Greeks, owing to the order observable in it); 1 Ti 6:7; Heb 4:3; 9:26; **(2)** the "earth" in contrast with Heaven, 1 Jn 3:17 (perhaps also Rom 4:13); **(3)** by metonymy, the "human race, mankind," e.g., Mt 5:14; Jn 1:9, 10; 3:16, 17 (thrice), 19; 4:42, and frequently in Rom, 1 Cor and 1 Jn; **(4)** "Gentiles" as distinguished from Jews, e.g., Rom 11:12, 15; **(5)** the "present condition of human affairs," in alienation from and opposition to

God, e.g., Jn 7:7; 8:23; 14:30; 1 Cor 2:12; Gal 4:3; 6:14; Col 2:8; Jas 1:27; 1 Jn 4:5 (thrice); 5:19; **(6)** the "sum of temporal possessions," Mt 16:26; 1 Cor 7:31 (1st part); **(7)** metaphorically, of the "tongue" as "a world (of iniquity)," Jas 3:6, expressive of magnitude and variety. Syn.: 165, 3625. See: TDNT—3:868, 459; BAGD—445d; THAYER—356d.

2890. **Κούαρτος** {1x} **Kŏuartŏs**, *koo'-ar-tos;* of Lat. or. (*fourth*); *Quartus,* a Chr.:—Quartus {1x}. See: BAGD—447b; THAYER—358a.

2891. **κοῦμι** {1x} **kŏumi**, *koo'-mee* or κουμ **koum**, *koom';* of Chald. origin [6966]; *cumi* (i.e. *rise!*):—cumi {1x}. See: BAGD—447b; THAYER—358a.

2892. **κουστωδία** {3x} **kŏustōdia**, *koos-to-dee'-ah;* of Lat. or.; "*custody,*" i.e. a Rom. *sentry:*—watch {3x}.

Koustodia, "a guard," (Latin, *custodia,* Eng., "custodian"), is used of the soldiers who "guarded" Christ's sepulchre, Mt 27:65, 66 and 28:11, and is translated, ". . . a watch," "(setting a) watch," and ". . . the watch." This was the Temple guard, stationed under a Roman officer in the tower of Antonia, and having charge of the high priestly vestments. Hence the significance of Pilate's words "Ye have a guard." A Roman guard was made up of four to sixteen solders. In combat, they would form a square, and were able to hold off a much larger force. See: BAGD—447b; THAYER—358a.

2893. **κουφίζω** {1x} **kŏuphizō**, *koo-fid'-zo;* from κοῦφος **kŏuphŏs** (*light* in weight); to *unload:*—lighten {1x}.

Kouphizo, "to make light, lighten", denotes "slight, light, empty", and is used of "lightening" the ship, in Acts 27:38. See: BAGD—447b; THAYER—358a.

2894. **κόφινος** {6x} **kŏphinŏs**, *kof'-ee-nos;* of uncert. der.; a (small) *basket:*—basket {6x}.

A *kophinos* was "a wicker basket," originally containing a certain measure of capacity, Mt 14:20; 16:9; Mk 6:43; 8:19; Lk 9:17; Jn 6:13. See: BAGD—447c; THAYER—358a.

2895. **κράββατος** {12x} **krabbatŏs**, *krab'-bat-os;* prob. of for. or.; a *mattress:*—bed {11x}, couch {1x}.

This word denotes a small, one-person pallet or mattress for the poor (Mk 2:4, 9, 11–12; 6:55; Jn 5:8–11). See: BAGD—447c; THAYER—358a.

2896. **κράζω** {59x} **krazō**, *krad'-zo;* a primary verb; prop. to "*croak*" (as a ra-

ven) or *scream*, i.e. (gen.) to *call* aloud (*shriek, exclaim, intreat*):—cry {40x}, cry out {19x}.

Krazo, as a verb, means "to cry out," used especially of the "cry" of the raven; then, (1) of any inarticulate cries, from fear, pain etc.and in the NT (1a) of the shouts of the children in the Temple: "And when the chief priests and scribes saw the wonderful things that he did, and the children crying in the temple, and saying, Hosanna to the Son of David; they were sore displeased" (Mt 21:15); (1b) of the people who shouted for Christ to be crucified (Mat 27:23; Mk 15:13–14); (1c) of the "cry" of Christ on the cross at the close of His sufferings (Mt 27:50; Mk 15:39). (2) Elsewhere: (2a) In John's Gospel it is used three times, out of the six, of Christ's utterances, 7:28, 37; 12:44. (2b) In the Acts it is not used of "cries" of distress, but chiefly of the shouts of opponents; (2c) in the Apocalypse, chiefly of the utterances of heavenly beings concerning earthly matters; (2d) in Rom 8:15 and Gal 4:6, of the appeal of believers to God the Father; (2e) in Rom 9:27, of a prophecy concerning Israel; (2f) in Jas 5:4, metaphorically, of hire kept back by fraud. Syn.: *Kaleo* (*2564*), denotes "to call out for any purpose," *boao* (*994*), "to cry out as an expression of feeling," *krazo* (*2896*), to cry out loudly." *Kaleo* suggests intelligence, *boao*, sensibilities, *krazo*, instincts. See also: 310, 349, 994, 995, 1916, 2019, 2905, 2906, 5455. See: TDNT—3:898, 465; BAGD—447c; THAYER—358b.

2897. κραιπάλη {1x} **kraipalē**, *krahee-pal'-ay;* prob. from the same as *726;* prop. a *headache* (as a *seizure* of pain) from drunkenness, i.e. (by impl.) a *debauch* (by anal. a *glut*):—surfeiting {1x}.

This word signifies the giddiness and headache resulting from excessive wine-bibbing, a drunken nausea; the disgust and loathing that arises from drinking too much wine, "surfeiting", Lk 21:34. Syn.: 239. See: BAGD—448a; THAYER—358c.

2898. κρανίον {4x} **kraniŏn**, *kran-ee'-on;* dimin. of a der. of the base of *2768;* a *skull* ("*cranium*"):—Calvary {1x}, skull {3x}.

Kranion is a head (Eng., cranium) and denotes a skull (Latin *calvaria*) with the corresponding Aramaic word being *Golgotha* (Mt 27:33; Mk 15:22; Lk 23:33; Jn 19:17). See: BAGD—448a; THAYER—358d.

2899. κράσπεδον {5x} **kraspĕdŏn**, *kras'-ped-on;* of uncert. der.; a *margin*, i.e. (spec.) a *fringe* or *tassel*:—border {3x}, hem {2x}.

Kraspedon was primarily the extremity or prominent part of a thing, an edge; hence the fringe of a garment, or a little fringe hanging

down from the edge of the mantle or cloak. The Jews had these attached to their mantles to remind them of the Law (cf. Num 15:38–39; Deut 22:12; Zec 8:23). It is translated (1) of the edge of Christ's garment, (1a) "hem", in Mt 9:20; 14:36; and (1b) "border" in Mk 6:56; Lk 8:44; (2) it refers to the edge of the scribes' and Pharisees' garments in Mt 23:5. See: TDNT—3:904, 466; BAGD—448b; THAYER—358d.

2900. κραταιός {1x} **krataiŏs**, *krat-ah-yos';* from *2904; powerful:*—mighty {1x}. See: TDNT—3:912, 466; BAGD—448b; THAYER—358d.

2901. κραταιόω {4x} **krataiŏŏ**, *krat-ah-yŏ'-o;* from *2900;* to *empower*, i.e. (pass.) *increase in vigor:*—be strengthened {1x}, be strong {1x}, wax strong {2x}.

Krataioo, "to strengthen," is rendered (1) "to be strengthened" in Eph 3:16; (2) "be strong" in 1 Cor 16:30; and (3) "wax strong" in Lk 1:80; 2:40.

Wax denotes growing strong slowly; not a sudden influx of power. See: TDNT—3:912, 466; BAGD—448b; THAYER—358d.

2902. κρατέω {47x} **kratěō**, *krat-eh'-o;* from *2904;* to *use strength*, i.e. *seize* or *retain* (lit. or fig.):—hold {12x}, take {9x}, lay hold on {8x}, hold fast {5x}, take by {4x}, lay hold upon {2x}, lay hand on {2x}, misc. {5x} = keep, obtain, retain.

Krateo, as a verb, means "to be strong, mighty, to prevail," (1) is most frequently rendered "to lay or take hold on" (1a) literally, e.g., Mt 12:11; 14:3; 18:28 and 21:46, "laid hands on"; 22:6, "took"; 26:55, "took"; 28:9, "held by"; Mk 3:21; 6:17; 12:12; 14:51; Acts 24:6, "took"; Rev 20:2; (1b) metaphorically, of "laying hold of the hope of the Lord's return," Heb 6:18; (2) also signifies "to hold" or "hold fast," i.e., firmly, (2a) literally, Mt 26:48; Acts 3:11; Rev. 2:1; (2b) metaphorically, of "holding fast a tradition or teaching," (2b1) in an evil sense, Mk 7:3, 4, 8; Rev 2:14, 15; (2b2) in a good sense, 2 Th 2:15; Rev 2:25; 3:11; (2c) of "holding" Christ, i.e., practically apprehending Him, as the head of His church, Col 2:19; (2d) a confession, Heb 4:14; (2e) the name of Christ, i.e., abiding by all that His name implies, Rev 2:13; (2f) of restraint, Lk 24:16, "(their eyes) were holden"; (2g) of the winds, Rev 7:1; (2h) of the impossibility of Christ's being "holden" of death, Acts 2:24. Syn.: 1949, 2192, 2722, 4912. See: TDNT—3:910, 466; BAGD—448c; THAYER—359a.

2903. κράτιστος {4x} **kratistŏs**, *krat'-is-tos;* superl. of a der. of *2904; strongest*, i.e. (in dignity) *very honorable:*—most excellent {2x}, most noble {2x}.

Kratistos, "mightiest, noblest, best," the

superlative degree of *kratos* (*2904*), "strong", is used as a title of honor and respect, **(1)** "most excellent," Lk 1:3 (Theophilus was quite possibly a man of high rank); and **(2)** "most noble" (Acts 23:26; 24:3; 26:25). See: BAGD—449a; THAYER—359b.

2904. κράτος {12x} **kratŏs**, *krat'-os;* perh. a primary word; *vigor* ["great"] (lit. or fig.):—dominion {4x}, might + 2596 {1x}, power {6x}, strength {1x}.

Kratos, "force, strength, might," more especially "manifested power," is derived from a root which means "to perfect, to complete"; "creator" is probably connected. It signifies **(1)** "dominion," and is so rendered frequently in doxologies, 1 Pet 4:11; 5:11; Jude 25; Rev 1:6; **(2)** "mightily" in Acts 19:20; **(3)** "power" in Eph 1:19 (last part); 6:10; Col 1:11; 1 Ti 6:16; Heb 2:14; Rev 5:13; and **(4)** "strength" in Lk 1:51. Syn.: *Bia* (*970*) means force, effective, often oppressive power exhibiting itself in single deeds of violence. *Dunamis* (*1411*) expresses power, natural ability, general and inherent. *Energeia* (*1753*) denotes working, power in exercise, operative power. *Exousia* (*1849*) is primarily liberty of action; then authority—either as delegated power, or as unrestrained, arbitrary power. *Ischus* (*2479*) expresses strength, power, (especially physical) as an endowment. *Kratos* (*2904*) means might, relative and manifested power —chiefly of God. See: TDNT—3:905, 466; BAGD—449a; THAYER—358a.

2905. κραυγάζω {7x} **kraugazō**, *krŏw-gad'-zo;* from *2906;* to *clamor:*— cry {4x}, cry out {3x}.

Kraugazo, a stronger form of *krazo* (*2896*), means "to make a clamor or outcry": "He shall not strive, nor cry (*kraugazo*); neither shall any man hear his voice in the streets" (Mt 12:19, in a prophecy from Isaiah of Christ; Jn 11:43; 18:40; 19:6, 15; Acts 22:23). Syn.: 310, 349, 994, 995, 1916, 2019, 2896, 2906, 5455. See: TDNT—3:898, 465; BAGD—449b; THAYER—359c.

2906. κραυγή {6x} **kraugē**, *krŏw-gay';* from *2896;* an *outcry* (in notification, tumult or grief):—clamour {1x}, cry {3x}, crying {2x}.

Krauge, as a noun, is translated **(1)** "cry, crying": "And at midnight there was a cry made, Behold, the bridegroom cometh; go ye out to meet him" (Mt 25:6; cf. Acts 23:9; Heb 5:7; Rev 14:18; 21:4); and **(2)** "clamour" (Eph 4:31). Syn.: 310, 349, 994, 995, 1916, 2019, 2896, 2905, 5455. See: 2896 for discussion. See: TDNT—3:898, 465; BAGD—449c; THAYER—359d.

2907. κρέας {2x} **krĕas**, *kreh'-as;* perh. a primary word; (butcher's) *meat:*— flesh {2x}.

Kreas denotes flesh in the sense of animal meat and may only refer to animals sacrificed to idols. It is used only in the plural (Rom 14:21; 1 Cor 8:13). See: BAGD—449c; THAYER—359d.

2908. κρεῖσσον {1x} **krĕissŏn**, *krice'-son;* neut. of an alt. form of *2909;* (as noun) *better*, i.e. *greater advantage:*—better {1x}. See: BAGD—449d; THAYER—359d.

2909. κρείττων {19x} **krĕittōn**, *krite'-tohn;* comparative of a der. of *2904;* *stronger*, i.e. (fig.) *better*, i.e. *nobler:*—best {1x}, better {18x}.

Kreitton, from *kratos* (*2904*) means strong (which denotes power in activity and effect), is used 12 times in Hebrews, and indicates what is **(1)** advantageous or useful (1 Cor 7:9, 38; 11:17; Heb 11:40; 12:24); or **(2)** excellent (Heb. 1:4; 6:9; 7:7, 19, 22; 8:6; 9:23; 10:34; 11:16, 35). See: BAGD—449d; THAYER—359d.

2910. κρεμάννυμι {7x} **krĕmannumi**, *kreman'-noo-mee;* a prol. form of a primary verb; to *hang:*—hang {7x}.

Kremannumi 1s used **(1)** transitively in Acts 5:30; 10:39 of Jesus being hanged on a tree; **(2)** in the passive voice, **(2a)** in Mt 18:6, of a millstone about a neck, and **(2b)** in Lk 23:39, of the malefactors hanging on crosses beside Jesus; **(3)** intransitively, in the middle voice, **(3a)** in Mt 22:40, of the dependence of "the Law and the prophets" (i.e., that which they enjoin) upon the one great principle of love to God and one's neighbor (as a door "hangs" on a hinge, or as articles "hang" on a nail); **(3b)** in Acts 28:4, of the serpent "hanging" from Paul's hand; **(3c)** in Gal 3:13 with reference to Christ's hanging on a tree (Deut 21:23). Syn.: 1582. See: TDNT—3:915, 468; BAGD—450a; THAYER—359d.

2911. κρημνός {3x} **krēmnŏs**, *krame-nos';* from *2910; overhanging*, i.e. a *precipice:*—steep place {3x}.

Kremnos, "a steep bank" (akin to *kremannumi*, "to hang"), occurs in Mt 8:32; Mk 5:13; Lk 8:33, "a steep place." See: BAGD—450b; THAYER—360a.

2912. Κρής {3x} **Krēs**, *krace;* from *2914;* a *Cretan*, i.e. inhab. of Crete:— Crete {1x}, Cretians {2x}. See: BAGD—450b; THAYER—360a.

2913. Κρήσκης {1x} **Krēskēs**, *krace'-kace;* of Lat. or.; *growing; Cresces* (i.e. *Crescens*), a Chr.:—Crescens {1x}. See: BAGD—450a; THAYER—360a.

2914. Κρήτη {5x} **Krētē**, *kray'-tay;* of uncert. der.; *Cretë*, an island in the

Mediterranean:—Crete {5x}. See: BAGD—450c; THAYER—360b.

2915. κριθή {1x} **krithē,** *kree-thay';* of uncert. der.; *barley:*—barley {1x}. See: BAGD—450c; THAYER—360b.

2916. κρίθινος {2x} **krithĭnŏs,** *kree'-thee-nos;* from *2915;* consisting of *barley:*—barley {2x}. See: BAGD—450c; THAYER—360b.

2917. κρῖμα {28x} **krima,** *kree'-mah;* from *2919;* a *decision* (the function or the effect, for or against ["crime"]):—judgment {13x}, damnation {7x}, condemnation {5x}, be condemned {1x}, go to law + 2192 {1x}, avenge + 2919 {1x}.

Krima, as a noun, denotes **(1)** "the sentence pronounced, a verdict, a condemnation, the decision resulting from an investigation" (Mk 12:40; Lk 23:40; 1 Ti 3:6; Jude 4); it is used **(1a)** of a decision passed on the faults of others, Mt 7:2; **(1b)** of "judgment" by man upon Christ, Lk 24:20; **(1c)** of God's "judgment" upon men, e.g., Rom 2:2, 3; 3:8; 5:16; 11:33; 13:2; 1 Cor 11:29; Gal 5:10; Heb 6:2; Jas 3:1; through Christ, e.g., Jn 9:39; **(1d)** of the right of "judgment," Rev 20:4; **(2)** "the process of judgment leading to a decision" (1 Pet 4:17). **(3)** In Lk 24:20, "to be condemned" translates the phrase *eis krima,* "unto condemnation" (i.e., unto the pronouncement of the sentence of "condemnation"). **(4)** In these (Rom 11:33; 1 Cor 11:34; Gal 5:10; Jas 3:1) **(4a)** the process leading to a decision and **(4b)** the pronouncement of the decision, the verdict, are to be distinguished. **(5)** In 1 Cor 6:7 the word means a matter for judgment, a lawsuit: "Now therefore there is utterly a fault among you, because ye go to law (*krima*) one with another. Why do ye not rather take wrong? why do ye not rather suffer yourselves to be defrauded?" Syn.: 176, 843, 2607, 2613, 2631, 2632, 2633, 2919, 2920. See: TDNT—3:942, 469; BAGD—450c; THAYER—360b.

2918. κρίνον {2x} **krinŏn,** *kree'-non;* perh. a prim word; a *lily:*—lily {2x}.

Krinon occurs in Mt 6:28 and Lk 12:27; in the former the Lord speaks of "the lilies of the field"; the "lily" referred to was a flower of rich color, probably including the gladiolus and iris species. The former "grow among the grain, often overtopping it and illuminating the broad fields with their various shades of pinkish purple to deep violet purple and blue. . . . Anyone who has stood among the wheat fields of Galilee . . . will see at once the appropriateness of our Savior's allusion. They all have a reedy stem, which, when dry, would make such fuel as is used in the ovens. The beautiful irises . . . have gorgeous flowers, and would

suit our Savior's comparison even better than the above. But they are plants of pasture grounds and swamps, and seldom found in grain fields. If, however, we understand by 'lilies of the field' simply wild lilies, these would also be included in the expression. Our Savior's comparison would then be like a 'composite photograph,' a reference to all the splendid colors and beautiful shapes of the numerous wild plants comprehended under the name 'lily'." See: BAGD—451a; THAYER—60d.

2919. κρίνω {114x} **krinō,** *kree'-no;* prop. to *distinguish,* i.e. *decide* (mentally or judicially); by impl. to *try, condemn, punish:*—judge {88x}, determine {7x}, condemn {5x}, go to law {2x}, call in question {2x}, esteem {2x}, misc. {8x} = avenge, conclude, damn, decree, ordain, sentence to, think.

Krino, as a verb, means "to distinguish, choose, give an opinion upon, judge," sometimes denotes "to condemn": "For they that dwell at Jerusalem, and their rulers, because they knew him not, nor yet the voices of the prophets which are read every sabbath day, they have fulfilled them in condemning him" (Acts 13:27; cf. Rom 2:27). To separate, put asunder, to pick out, select, choose, hence, **(1)** to approve, esteem, to prefer, Rom 14:5; **(2)** to be of opinion, deem, think, Lk 7:43; Acts 15:19; 1 Cor 11:13; 2 Cor 5:14; **(3)** to determine, resolve, decree, 1 Cor 7:37; Acts 16:4; **(4)** to judge, **(4a)** to pronounce an opinion concerning right and wrong, **(4a1)** in a forensic sense, Jn 7:51; 18:31; Acts 23:3; 24:6; **(4a2)** to pronounce judgment, to subject to censure, Jn 8:16, 26; 1 Cor 10:15; **(5)** to rule, govern; Mt 19:28; Lk 22:30. Syn.: 176, 843, 2607, 2613, 2631, 2632, 2633, 2917, 2920. See: TDNT—3:921, 469; BAGD—451b; THAYER—360d.

2920. κρίσις {48x} **krisis,** *kree'-sis;* decision (subj. or obj., for or against); by extens. a *tribunal;* by impl. *justice* (spec. divine *law*):—accusation {2x}, condemnation {2x}, damnation {3x}, judgment {41x}.

Krisis, as a noun, **(1)** denotes "the process of investigation, the act of distinguishing and separating" [as distinct from *krima* (*2917*)]; hence "a judging, a passing of judgment upon a person or thing." **(2)** It has a variety of meanings, such as **(2a)** judicial authority (Jn 5:22, 27); **(2b)** justice (Acts 8:33); **(2c)** a tribunal (Mt 5:21–22); **(2d)** a trial (Jn 5:24; 2 Pet 2:4); **(2e)** a judgment (2 Pet 2:11; Jude 9); **(2f)** by metonymy, the standard of judgment, just dealing (Mt 12:18, 20; 23:23; Lk 11:42); **(2g)** divine judgment executed (2 Th 1:5; Rev 16:7). **(3)** Sometimes it has the meaning "condemnation," and is virtually equivalent to *krima* (*2917*) - see Mt

23:33; Jn 3:19; Jas 5:12. Syn.: 176, 843, 2607, 2613, 2631, 2632, 2633, 2917, 2919. See: TDNT—3:941, 469; BAGD—452c; THAYER—361d.

2921. Κρίσπος {2x} **Krispŏs,** *kris'-pos;* of Lat. or.; *"crisp"; Crispus,* a Corinthian:—Crispus {2x}. See: BAGD—453b; THAYER—362b.

2922. κριτήριον {3x} **kritēriŏn,** *kree-tay'-ree-on;* neut. of a presumed der. of 2923; a *rule* of judging (*"criterion"*), i.e. (by impl.) a *tribunal:*—to judge {1x}, judgment {1x}, judgment seat {1x}.

Kriterion is primarily "a means of judging" (akin to *krino,* "to judge": Eng., "criterion"), then, a tribunal, law court, or "lawsuit," and is translated **(1)** "to judge" in 1 Cor 6:2; **(2)** "judgment" in 1 Cor 6:4; and **(3)** "(human) judgment seats" in Jas 2:6. See: TDNT—3:943, 469; BAGD—453b; THAYER—362b.

2923. κριτής {1x} **kritēs,** *kree-tace';* from 2919; a *judge* (gen. or spec.):—judge {1x}.

Krites, "a judge", is used **(1)** of God, Heb 12:23, where the order in the original is "to a Judge who is God of all"; this is really the significance; it suggests that He who is the Judge of His people is at the same time their God; that is the order in 10:30; the word is also used of God in Jas 4:12; **(2)** of Christ, Acts 10:42; 2 Ti 4:8; Jas 5:9; **(3)** of a ruler in Israel in the times of the Judges, Acts 13:20; **(4)** of a Roman procurator, Acts 24:10; **(5)** of those whose conduct provides a standard of "judging," Mt 12:27; Lk 11:19; **(6)** in the forensic sense, of one who tries and decides a case, Mt 5:25 (twice); 12:58 (twice); 18:2; 18:6 (lit., "the judge of unrighteousness," expressing subjectively His character); Acts 18:15; **(7)** of one who passes, or arrogates to himself, judgment on anything, Jas 2:4; 4:11. Syn.: *Dikastes (1348)* is the more dignified and official term; whereas, *krites (2923)* gives prominence to the mental process, whether the judge is a magistrate or not. See: TDNT—3:943, 469; BAGD—453c; THAYER—362b.

2924. κριτικός {1x} **kritikŏs,** *krit-ee-kos';* from 2923; *decisive ("critical"),* i.e. *discriminative:*—discerner {1x}.

Kritikos signifies that which relates to judging, fit for, or skilled in, judging (Eng., critical), and found in Heb 4:12, of the Word of God as quick to discern the thoughts and intents of the heart, i.e., discriminating and passing judgment on the thoughts, intents, and feelings. See: TDNT—3:943, 469; BAGD—453d; THAYER—362c.

2925. κρούω {9x} **krŏuō,** *kroo'-o;* appar. a primary verb; to *rap:*—knock.

Krouo, "to strike, knock," is used in the NT of "knocking" at a door, **(1)** literally, Lk 12:36; Acts 12:13, 16; **(2)** figuratively, Mt 7:7, 8; Lk 11:9, 10 (of importunity in dealing with God); 13:25; Rev 3:20. See: TDNT—3:954, 475; BAGD—453d; THAYER—362c.

2926. κρυπτή {1x} **kruptē,** *kroop-tay';* fem. of 2927; a *hidden* place, i.e. *cellar ("crypt"):*—secret place {1x}.

Krupte, (Eng., "crypt"), "a covered way or vault" (akin to *kruptos,* "hidden, secret"), is used in Lk 11:33, of lighting a lamp and putting it "in a cellar." See: TDNT—3:957, 476; BAGD—454a; THAYER—362c.

2927. κρυπτός {19x} **kruptŏs,** *kroop-tos';* from 2928; *concealed,* i.e. *private:*—secret {12x}, hid {3x}, hidden {3x}, inwardly {1x}.

Kruptos, "secret, hidden" (akin to *krupto,* "to hide"), Eng., "crypt," "cryptic," etc., is used as an adjective and rendered **(1)** "secret" **(1a)** in Lk 8:17, in the neuter, with *en,* "in," as an adverbial phrase, "in secret," **(1b)** with the article, Mt 6:4, 6, 18 twice in each verse, **(1c)** without the article, Jn 7:4, 10; 18:20; **(1d)** in the neuter plural, with the article, "the secrets **(1d1)** (of men)," Rom 2:16; **(1d2)** of the heart, 1 Cor 14:25; **(1e)** in Lk 11:33, "a secret place"; and is translated **(2)** "hid" in Mt 10:26; Mk 4:22; Lk 12:2 (last part); **(3)** "hidden" in **(3a)** 1 Cor 4:5, "hidden (things of darkness)"; **(3b)** 2 Cor 4:2, "hidden (things of shame)"; **(3c)** 1 Pet 3:4, "hidden (man of the heart)"; and **(4)** "inwardly" in Rom 2:29. See: TDNT—3:957, 476; BAGD—454a; THAYER—362d.

2928. κρύπτω {16x} **kruptō,** *kroop'-to;* a primary verb; to *conceal* (prop. by *covering*):—hide {11x}, hide (one's) self {2x}, keep secret {1x}, secretly {1x}, hidden {1x}.

Krupto, "to cover, conceal, keep secret" (Eng., "crypt," "cryptic," etc.), is translated **(1)** "hide, hid" **(1a)** literally, Mt 5:14; 13:44 twice; 25:18; 25:25; Heb 11:23; Rev 6:15, 16; **(1b)** metaphorically, e.g., Lk 18:34; 19:42; Col 3:3; 1 Ti 5:25; **(2)** "hid himself", Jn 8:59; 12:36; **(3)** "kept secret" in Mt 13:35; **(4)** "secretly" in Jn 19:38 [perfect participle, passive voice, lit., "(but) having been hidden"], referring to Nicodemus as having been a "secret" disciple of Christ; and **(5)** "hidden" in Rev 2:17. See: TDNT—3:957, 476; BAGD—454b; THAYER—362d.

2929. κρυσταλλίζω {1x} **krustallizō,** *kroos-tal-lid'-zo;* from 2930; to *make* (i.e. intr. *resemble*) ice ("crystallize"):—

be clear as crystal {1x}. See: BAGD—454d; THAYER—363a.

2930. κρύσταλλος {2x} **krustallŏs**, *kroos'-tal-los;* from a der. of κρύος **kruos** (*frost*); *ice,* i.e. (by anal.) rock, a precious stone, "*crystal*":—crystal {2x}. See: BAGD—454d; THAYER—363a.

2931. κρυφῆ {1x} **kruphē**, *kroo-fay';* adv. from *2928; privately:*—in secret {1x}. See: TDNT—3:957, 476; BAGD—454d; THAYER—363a.

2932. κτάομαι {7x} **ktaŏmai**, *ktah'-om-ahee;* a primary verb; to *get,* i.e. *acquire* (by any means; *own*):—obtain {1x}, possess {3x}, provide {1x}, purchase {2x}.

Ktaomai means "to procure for oneself, acquire, obtain,"and is translated **(1)** "obtained" in Acts 22:28; **(2)** "to possess" in Lk 18:12; 21:19 where the probable meaning is "ye shall gain the mastery over your souls," i.e., instead of giving way to adverse circumstances; 1 Th 4:4; **(3)** "provide" in Mt 10:9; and **(4)** "purchased", "to procure for oneself, get, gain, acquire" in Acts 1:18, 8:20. See: BAGD—455a; THAYER—363b.

2933. κτῆμα {4x} **ktēma**, *ktay'-mah;* from *2932;* an *acquirement,* i.e. *estate:*—possession {4x}.

Ktema denotes "a possession, property," Mt 19:22; Mk 10:22; Acts 2:45; 5:1. See: BAGD—455b; THAYER—363b.

2934. κτῆνος {4x} **ktēnŏs**, *ktay'-nos;* from *2932; property,* i.e. (spec.) a domestic *animal:*—beast {4x}.

Ktenos signifies, **(1)** a "beast" of burden, Lk 10:34; Acts 23:24; and **(2)** "beasts" of any sort, apart from those signified by *therion* (2432), 1 Cor 15:39; Rev 18:13. Syn.: 2432. See: BAGD—455b; THAYER—363b.

2935. κτήτωρ {1x} **ktētōr**, *ktay'-tore;* from *2932;* an *owner:*—possessor {1x}. See: BAGD—455c; THAYER—363b.

2936. κτίζω {14x} **ktizō**, *ktid'-zo;* prob. akin to *2932* (through the idea of *proprietorship* of the *manufacturer*); to *fabricate,* i.e. *found* (*form* orig.):—create {12x}, Creator {1x}, make {1x}.

Ktizo signifies, in Scripture, "to create," always of the act of God, whether **(1)** in the natural creation, Mk 13:19; Rom 1:25 (where the title "The Creator" translates the article with the aorist participle of the verb); 1 Cor 11:9; Eph 3:9; Col 1:16; 1 Ti 4:3; Rev 4:11; 10:6, or **(2)** in the spiritual creation, Eph 2:10, 15; 4:24; Col 3:10. See: TDNT—3:1000, 481; BAGD—455c; THAYER—363b.

2937. κτίσις {19x} **ktisis**, *ktis'-is;* from *2936;* orig. *formation* (prop. the act; by impl. the thing, lit. or fig.):—building {1x}, creation {6x}, creature {11x}, ordinance {1x}.

Ktisis, primarily "the act of creating," or "the creative act in process," and is translated **(1)** "building" in Heb 9:11; **(2)** "creation" in Mk 10:16; 13:19; Rom 1:20; 8:22; Gal 6:15 the creative act of God, whereby a man is introduced into the blessing of salvation, in contrast to circumcision done by human hands, which the Judaizers claimed was necessary to that end; 2 Cor 5:17 the reference is to what the believer is in Christ; in consequence of the creative act he has become a new creature; 2 Pet 3:4; Rev 3:14; **(3)** "creature" in Mk 16:15 mankind in general; Rom 1:25; 8:19, 20, 21, 39; Gal 6:15; Col 1:15; 23 mankind in general; Heb 4:13; **(4)** "ordinance" in 1 Pet 2:13 used of human actions. See: TDNT—3:1000, 481; BAGD—455d; THAYER—363c.

2938. κτίσμα {4x} **ktisma**, *ktis'-mah;* from *2936;* an orig. *formation* (concr.), i.e. *product* (created thing):—creature {4x}.

Ktisma has the concrete sense, "the created thing, the creature, the product of the creative act," 1 Ti 4:4; Jas 1:18; Rev 5:13; 8:9. See: TDNT—3:1000, 481; BAGD—456b; THAYER—363d.

2939. κτιστής {1x} **ktistēs**, *ktis-tace';* from *2936;* a *founder,* i.e. *God* (as author of all things):—Creator {1x}. See: TDNT—3:1000, 481; BAGD—456b; THAYER—364a.

2940. κυβεία {1x} **kubĕia**, *koo-bi'-ah;* from κύβος **kubŏs** (a "*cube,*" i.e. *die* for playing); *gambling,* i.e. (fig.) *artifice* or *fraud:*—sleight {1x}.

Metaphorically, *kubos* is used for the deception of men, because dice players sometimes cheated and defrauded their fellow players. It denotes "dice playing" (from *kubos,* "a cube, a die as used in gaming"); hence, metaphorically, "trickery, sleight," Eph 4:14. The Eng. word is connected with "sly" ("not with slight"). See: BAGD—456c; THAYER—364a.

2941. κυβέρνησις {1x} **kubĕrnēsis**, *koo-ber'-nay-sis;* from κυβερνάω **kubĕrnaō** (of Lat. or., to *steer*); *pilotage,* i.e. (fig.) *directorship* (in the church):—government {1x}.

Kubernesis means to guide (whence Eng., "govern") and denotes **(1)** steering, pilotage; and **(2)** metaphorically, governments or governings, said of those who act as guides in a local church (1 Cor 12:28). See: TDNT—3:1035, 486; BAGD—456c; THAYER—364a.

2942. **κυβερνήτης** {2x} **kubĕrnētēs**, *koo-ber-nay'-tace;* from the same as *2941; helmsman,* i.e. (by impl.) *captain:*—shipmaster {1x}, master {1x}.

Kubernetes, "the pilot or steersman of a ship," or, metaphorically, "a guide or governor" (akin to *kubernao,* "to guide": Eng., "govern" is connected; cf. *kubernesis,* "a steering, pilotage," 1 Cor 12:28, "governments"), is translated **(1)** "master" in Acts 27:11; and **(2)** "shipmaster" in Rev 18:17. See: BAGD—456c; THAYER—364a.

2943. **κυκλόθεν** {4x} **kuklŏthĕn,** *koo-kloth'-en;* adv. from the same as *2945; from* the *circle,* i.e. *all around:*—round about {3x}, about {1x}.

Kuklothen, "round about, or all round" (from *kuklos,* "a circle, cycle"), is found in the Apocalypse only: **(1)** "round about", Rev 4:3, 4; 5:11; and **(2)** "about" 4: 8. See: BAGD—456c; THAYER—364a.

κυκλός kuklŏs. See *2945.*

2944. **κυκλόω** {5x} **kuklŏō,** *koo-klŏ'-o;* from the same as *2945;* to *encircle,* i.e. *surround:*—compass about {2x}, compass {1x}, come round about {1x}, stand round about {1x}.

Kukloo, "to compass, to encircle, surround" (Eng., "cycle"), is translated **(1)** "compassed about" in **(1a)** Rev 20:9, of a camp surrounded by foes; **(1b)** Heb 11:30 of Jericho; **(2)** "compassed" in Lk 21:20 as of a city "compassed" by armies, Lk 21:20; Heb 11:30; **(3)** "came round about," in Jn 10:24; and **(4)** "stood round about" in Acts 14:20. See: BAGD—456d; THAYER—364b.

2945. **κύκλω** {7x} **kuklŏi,** *koo'-klo;* as if dat. of κύκλος **kuklŏs** (a *ring,* "cycle"; akin to *2947);* i.e. *in a circle* (by impl. of *1722),* i.e. (adv.) *all around:*—round about {7x}.

Kuklo, the dative case of *kuklos* (*2945*), means "round about," lit., "in a circle", Mk 3:34; 6:6, 36; Lk 9:12; Rom 15:19; Rev 4:6; 5:11; 7:11. See: BAGD—456d; THAYER—364b.

2946. **κύλισμα** {1x} **kulisma,** *koo'-lis-mah;* from *2947;* a *wallow* (the effect of *rolling),* i.e. *filth:*—wallowing {1x}. See: BAGD—457b; THAYER—364b.

2947. **κυλίω** {1x} **kuliŏō,** *koo-lee-ŏ'-o;* from the base of *2949* (through the idea of *circularity;* comp. *2945, 1507);* to *roll about; roll along:*—wallow {1x}. See: BAGD—457b; THAYER—364c.

2948. **κυλλός** {4x} **kullŏs,** *kool-los';* from the same as *2947; rocking about,* i.e. *crippled* (*maimed,* in feet or hands):—maimed {4x}.

Kullos denotes "crooked, crippled"; translated "maimed" in Mt 15:30, 31; 18:8; Mk 9:43. See: BAGD—457b; THAYER—364c.

2949. **κῦμα** {5x} **kuma,** *koo'-mah;* from κύω **kuō** (to *swell* [with young], i.e. *bend, curve);* a *billow* (as *bursting* or *toppling*):—wave {5x}.

Kuo, "to be pregnant, to swell, swelling in order to break forth with force", is used **(1)** literally in the plural, Mt 8:24; 14:24; Mk 4:37; Acts 27:41; **(2)** figuratively, Jude 13 of the impulse of restless men, tossed to and fro by their raging passions. Syn.: *Kludon* (*2830*) denotes a wave, suggesting uninterrupted successions; and *kuma* (*2949*) denotes a billow, surge, suggesting size and extension. Both are figuratively used of words suggesting the same definitions. See: BAGD—457c; THAYER—364c.

2950. **κύμβαλον** {1x} **kumbalŏn,** *koom'-bal-on;* from a der. of the base of *2949;* a *"cymbal"* (as *hollow*):—cymbal {1x}.

Kumbalon, "a cymbal," was so called from its shape (akin to *kumbos,* "a hollow basin," *kumbe,* "a cup"), and was made of bronze, two being struck together, 1 Cor 13:1. It was noted for its loud, sharp, attention-getting sound. See: TDNT—3:1037, 486; BAGD—457c; THAYER—364c.

2951. **κύμινον** {1x} **kuminŏn,** *koo'-min-on;* of for. or. [comp. *3646*]; *dill* or *fennel* ("cummin"):—cummin {1x}.

Cumin is a cultivated plant in Palestine with seeds that have a bitter warm taste and an aromatic flavor. See: BAGD—457c; THAYER—364d.

2952. **κυνάριον** {4x} **kunariŏn,** *koo-nar'-ee-on;* neut. of a presumed der. of *2965;* a *puppy:*—dog {4x}.

Kunarion, "a little dog, a puppy," is used in Mt 15:26–27; Mk 7:27, 28. See: TDNT—3:1104, 494; BAGD—457d; THAYER—364d.

2953. **Κύπριος** {3x} **Kupriŏs,** *koo'-pree-os;* from *2954;* a *Cyprian* (*Cypriot*), i.e. inhab. of Cyprus:—of Cyprus {3x}. See: BAGD—457d; THAYER—364d.

2954. **Κύπρος** {5x} **Kuprŏs,** *koo'-pros;* of uncert. or.; *Cyprus,* an island in the Mediterranean:—Cyprus {5x}. See: BAGD—457d; THAYER—364d.

2955. **κύπτω** {3x} **kuptō,** *koop'-to;* prob. from the base of *2949;* to *bend* forward:—stoop {2x}, stoop down {1x}.

Kupto, "to bow the head, stoop down," occurs in Mk 1:7; Jn 8:6, 8. See: BAGD—458a; THAYER—364d.

2956. **Κυρηναῖος** {6x} **Kurēnaiŏs,** *koo-ray-nah'-yos;* from *2957;* i.e. *Cyrenæan,* i.e. inhab. of Cyrene:—of Cyrene {3x}, Cyrenian {3x}. See: BAGD—458a; THAYER—364d.

2957. **Κυρήνη** {1x} **Kurēnē,** *koo-ray'-nay;* of uncert. der.; *Cyrenë,* a region of Africa:—Cyrene {1x}. See: BAGD—458a; THAYER—364d.

2958. **Κυρήνιος** {1x} **Kurēniŏs,** *koo-ray'-nee-os;* of Lat. or.; *Cyrenius* (i.e. *Quirinus*), a Rom.:—Cyrenius {1x}. See: BAGD—458b; THAYER—365a.

2959. **Κυρία** {2x} **Kuria,** *koo-ree'-ah;* fem. of *2962; Cyria,* a Chr. woman:—lady {2x}.

Kuria is the person addressed in 2 Jn 1 and 5. This is probably a reference to the church itself. See: TDNT—3:1095, 486; BAGD—458b; THAYER—365b.

2960. **κυριακός** {2x} **kuriakŏs,** *koo-ree-ak-os';* from *2962; belonging to* the *Lord* (Jehovah or Jesus):—Lord's {2x}.

Kuriakos, from *kurios,* signifies "pertaining to a lord or master"; in the NT, is used only of Christ; **(1)** in 1 Cor 11:20, of the Lord's Supper, or the Supper of the Lord; and **(2)** in Rev 1:10, of the Day of the Lord; which may be a reference to Sunday, the day observed by the early church in honor of the resurrection. See: TDNT—3:1095, 486; BAGD—458c; THAYER—365b.

2961. **κυριεύω** {7x} **kuriĕuō,** *koo-ree-yoo'-o;* from *2962;* to *rule:*—have dominion over {4x}, exercise lordship over {1x}, be Lord of {1x}, lords {1x}.

Kurieus, "to be lord over, rule over, have dominion over" is used of **(1)** divine authority over men, Rom 14:9, "(He might) be Lord"; **(2)** human authority over men, Lk 22:25, "exercise lordship over"; **(3)** 1 Ti 6:15, "lords"; **(4)** the permanent immunity of Christ from the "dominion" of death, Rom 6:9; **(5)** the deliverance of the believer from the "dominion" of sin, Rom 6:14; **(6)** the "dominion" of law over men, Rom 7:1; **(7)** the "dominion" of a person over the faith of other believers, 2 Cor 1:24. See: BAGD—458d; THAYER—365b.

2962. **κύριος** {748x} **kuriŏs,** *koo'-ree-os;* from κῦρος **kurŏs** (*supremacy*); *supreme* in authority, i.e. (as noun) *controller;* by impl. *Mr.* (as a respectful title):—Lord {667x}, lord {54x}, master {11x}, sir {6x}, Sir {6x}, God {4x}.

The *kurios* wielded a limited moral authority which took into consideration the good of those over whom it is exercised. *Kurios,* prop-

erly an adjective, signifying "having power" (*kuros*) or "authority," is used as a noun, variously translated in the NT, Lord, master, Master, owner, Sir, a title of wide significance, occurring in each book of the NT save Titus and the epistles of John. It is used **(1)** of an owner, as in Lk 19:33, cf. Mt 20:8; Acts 16:16; Gal 4:1; or **(2)** of one who has the disposal of anything, as the Sabbath, Mt 12:8; **(3)** of a master, i.e., one to whom service is due on any ground, Mt 6:24; 24:50; Eph 6:5; **(4)** of an Emperor or King, Acts 25:26; Rev 17:14; **(5)** of idols, ironically, 1 Cor 8:5, cf. Is 26:13; **(6)** as a title of respect addressed to **(6a)** a father, Mt 21:30, **(6b)** a husband, 1 Pet 3:6, **(6c)** a master, Mt 3:27; Lk 13:8, **(6d)** a ruler, Mt 27:63, **(6e)** an angel, Acts 10:4; Rev 7:14; **(7)** as a title of courtesy addressed to a stranger, Jn 12:21; 20:15; Acts 16:30; **(8)** from the outset of His ministry this was a common form of address to the Lord Jesus, alike **(8a)** by the people, Mt 8:2; Jn 4:11, and **(8b)** by His disciples, Mt 8:25; Lk 5:8; Jn 6:68; **(9)** *kurios* is the NT representative of Heb. Jehovah (LORD in Eng. versions), see Mt 4:7; Jas 5:11, e.g., **(9a)** of adon, Lord, Mt 22:44, and **(9b)** of Adonay, Lord, Mt 1:22; **(9c)** it also occurs for Elohim, God, 1 Pet 1:25.

(10) Christ Himself assumed the title, Mt 7:21, 22; 9:38; 22:41–45; Mk 5:19 (cf. Ps 66:16; the parallel passage, Lk 8:39, has "God"); Lk 19:31; Jn 13:13, apparently intending it in the higher senses of its current use, and at the same time suggesting its OT associations. **(11)** His purpose did not become clear to the disciples until after His resurrection, and the revelation of His deity consequent thereon. Thomas, when he realized the significance of the presence of a mortal wound in the body of a living man, immediately joined with it the absolute title of Deity, saying, "My Lord and my God," Jn 20:28. Thereafter, except in Acts 10:4 and Rev 7:14, there is no record that *kurios* was ever again used by believers in addressing any save God and the Lord Jesus; cf Acts 2:47 with 4:29, 30. **(12)** How soon and how completely the lower meaning had been superseded is seen in Peter's declaration in his first sermon after the resurrection, "God hath made Him—Lord," Acts 2:36, and that in the house of Cornelius, "He is Lord of all," Acts 10:36, cf. Deut 10:14; Mt 11:25; Acts 17:24. **(13)** In Peter's writings the implications of his early teaching are confirmed and developed. **(13a)** Thus Ps 34:8, 'O taste and see that Jehovah is good,' is applied to the Lord Jesus, 1 Pet 2:3, and **(13b)** "Jehovah of Hosts, Him shall ye sanctify," Is 8:13, becomes "sanctify in your hearts Christ as Lord," 1 Pet 3:15.

(14) So also James who uses *kurios* alike of God, Jas 1:7 (cf. v. 5); 3:9; 4:15; 5:4, 10, 11, and

of the Lord Jesus, 1:1 (where the possibility that *kai* is intended epexegetically, i.e. = even, cf. 1 Th 3:11, should not be overlooked); 2:1 (lit., "our Lord Jesus Christ of glory," cf. Ps 24:7; 29:3; Acts 7:2; 1 Cor 2:8); 5:7, 8, while the language of 4:10; 5:15, is equally applicable to either **(15)** Jude, v. 4, speaks of "our only— Lord, Jesus Christ," and immediately, v. 5, uses "Lord" of God as he does later, vv. 9, 14. **(16)** Paul ordinarily uses *kurios* of the Lord Jesus, 1 Cor 1:3, e.g., but also on occasion, of God, in quotations from the OT, 1 Cor 3:20, e.g., and in his own words, 1 Cor 3:5, cf. v. 10. It is equally appropriate to either in 1 Cor 7:25; 2 Cor 3:16; 8:21; 1 Th 4:6, and if 1 Cor 11:32 is to be interpreted by 10:21, 22, the Lord Jesus is intended, but if by Heb 12:5–9, then *kurios* here also = God. 1 Ti 6:15, 16 is probably to be understood of the Lord Jesus, cf. Rev 17:14.

(17) Though John does not use "Lord" in his Epistles, and though, like the other Evangelists, he ordinarily uses the personal Name in his narrative, yet he occasionally speaks of Him as "the Lord," Jn 4:1; 6:23; 11:2; 20:20; 21:12. The full significance of this association of Jesus with God under the one appellation, "Lord," is seen when it is remembered that these men belonged to the only monotheistic race in the world. To associate with the Creator one known to be a creature, however exalted, though possible to Pagan philosophers, was quite impossible to a Jew. It is not recorded that in the days of His flesh any of His disciples either addressed the Lord, or spoke of Him, by His personal Name. Where Paul has occasion to refer to the facts of the gospel history he speaks of what the Lord Jesus said, Acts 20:35, and did, 1 Cor 11:23, and suffered, 1 Th 2:15; 5:9, 10. It is our Lord Jesus who is coming, 1 Th 2:19, etc. In prayer also the title is given, 3:11; Eph 1:3; the sinner is invited to believe on the Lord Jesus, Acts 16:31; 20:21, and the saint to look to the Lord Jesus for deliverance, Rom 7:24, 25, and in the few exceptional cases in which the personal Name stands alone a reason is always discernible in the immediate context.

(18) The title "Lord," as given to the Savior, in its full significance rests upon the resurrection, Acts 2:36; Rom 10:9; 14:9, and is realized only in the Holy Spirit, 1 Cor 12:3. Syn.: There is a degree of truth in the saying "a man is a *despot* (*1203*) to his slaves, but a *kurios* to his wife and children." See also: 1203, 3175. See: TDNT—3:1039, 486; BAGD—458d; THAYER— 365b.

2963. **κυριότης** {4x} **kuriŏtēs**, *koo-ree-ot'-ace;* from *2962; mastery,* i.e. (concr. and collect.) *rulers:*—dominion {3x}, government {1x}.

Kuriotes denotes "lordship" (*kurios,* "a lord"), "power, dominion," whether angelic or human and is translated **(1)** "dominion" Eph 1:21; Col 1:16; Jude 1:8; and **(2)** "government" 2 Pet 2:10. In Eph and Col it indicates a grade in the angelic orders, in which it stands second. See: TDNT—3:1039, 486; BAGD—460d; THAYER— 366c.

2964. **κυρόω** {2x} **kurŏō**, *koo-rŏ'-o;* from the same as *2962;* to *make authoritative,* i.e. *ratify:*—confirm {2x}.

Kuroo, "to make valid, ratify, impart authority or influence" (from *kuros,* "might," *kurios,* "mighty, a head, as supreme in authority"), is translated "confirm" and used of confirming **(1)** love, 2 Cor 2:8; and **(2)** a human covenant, Gal 3:15. See: TDNT—3:1098, 486; BAGD—461a; THAYER—366d.

2965. **κύων** {5x} **kuōn**, *koo'-ohn;* a primary word; a *dog* ["*hound*"] (lit. or fig.):—dog {5x}.

Kuon is used in two senses, **(1)** natural, Mt 7:6; Lk 16:21; 2 Pet 2:22; and **(2)** metaphorically, dogs are ungodly men with impure minds exercising immoral ways which will exclude them from the New Jerusalem, Phil 3:2; Rev 22:15. **(3)** The Jews used the term of Gentiles, under the idea of ceremonial impurity. See: TDNT— 3:1101,; BAGD—461b; THAYER—366d.

2966. **κῶλον** {1x} **kōlŏn**, *ko'-lon;* from the base of *2849;* a *limb* of the body (as if *lopped*):—carcase (carcass) {1x}.

Kolon **(1)** specifically is a member of a body, particularly the more external and prominent members esp. the feet and **(2)** extension a dead body, corpse, inasmuch as the members of a corpse are loose and fall apart (Heb 3:17). See: BAGD—461b; THAYER—366d.

2967. **κωλύω** {23x} **kōluō**, *ko-loo'-o;* from the base of *2849;* to *estop,* i.e. *prevent* (by word or act):—forbid {17x}, hinder {2x}, withstand {1x}, keep from {1x}, let {1x}, not suffer {1x}.

Koluo, "to hinder, restrain, withhold, forbid" (akin to *kolos,* "docked, lopped, clipped"), is most usually translated **(1)** "to forbid" in Mt 19:14; Mk 9:38, 39; Mk 10:14; Lk 6:29; 9:49, 50; 18:16; 23:2; Acts 10:47; 16:6; 24:23; 1 Cor 14:39; 1 Th 2:16; 1 Ti 4:3; 2 Pet 2:16; 3 Jn 1:10; **(2)** "to hinder" in Lk 11:52; Acts 8:36; **(3)** "withstand" in Acts 11:17; **(4)** "kept (them) from" in Acts 27:43; **(5)** "was let" in Rom 1:13; and **(6)** "were not suffered" in Heb 7:23. See: BAGD—461b; THAYER—366d.

2968. **κώμη** {28x} **kōmē**, *ko'-may;* from *2749;* a *hamlet* (as if *laid* down):—town {11x}, village {17x}.

A hamlet is a few small houses in the country. A village is a larger group of houses in the country, loosely organized, and without walls. A country town is larger than a village, usually somewhat isolated, more organized, having city officials or representatives, a synagogue, and usually has no walls. Normally a town is somewhat near a city. A city is usually organized and walled and increases in complexity as the population increases. In the Scriptures there are villages, towns, and cities. Syn.: 2969. See: BAGD–461d; THAYER–367a.

2969. **κωμόπολις** {1x} **kōmŏpŏlis**, *ko-mop'-ol-is;* from *2968* and *4172;* an unwalled *city:*–town {1x}.

Komopolis is a larger village, still unwalled, and loosely organized, Mk 1:38. Syn.: 2968. See: BAGD–461d; THAYER–367b.

2970. **κῶμος** {3x} **kōmŏs**, *ko'-mos;* from *2749;* a *carousal* (as if *letting loose*):–revelling {2x}, rioting {1x}.

Summary: *Komos* unites the concepts of rioting and revelry and usually involves a nocturnal and riotous procession of half-drunken and frolicsome fellows who after supper parade through the streets with torches and music in honor of some deity, and sing and play before houses of male and female friends; hence used generally of feasts and drinking parties that are protracted till late at night and indulge in revelry. It is used **(1)** in the plural, Rom 13:13, translated by the singular, "rioting"; and translated **(2)** "reveling" in Gal 5:21 and 1 Pet 4:3, "revelings." Syn.: 2897, 3178, 3632, 4224. See: BAGD–461d; THAYER–462a.

2971. **κώνωψ** {1x} **kōnōps**, *ko'-nopes;* appar. a der. of the base of *2759* and a der. of *3700;* a *mosquito* (from its *stinging proboscis*):–gnat {1x}.

Konops probably denotes the winegnat or midge which breeds in fermenting or evaporating wine (Mt 23:24). See: BAGD–462a.

2972. **Κῶς** {1x} **Kōs**, *koce;* of uncert. or.; *Cos,* an island in the Mediterranean:–Coos {1x}. See: BAGD–462a; THAYER–367c.

2973. **Κωσάμ** {1x} **Kōsam**, *ko-sam';* of Heb. or. [comp. *7081*]; *Cosam* (i.e. *Kosam*) an Isr.:–Cosam {1x}. See: BAGD–367c; THAYER–462a.

2974. **κωφός** {14x} **kōphŏs**, *ko-fos';* from *2875; blunted,* i.e. (fig.) of hearing (*deaf*) or speech (*dumb*):–deaf {5x}, dumb {8x}, speechless {1x}.

Kophos, as an adjective, (akin to *kopto*, "to beat," and *kopiao*, "to be tired") signifies "blunted, dull," as of a weapon; it denotes **(1)** "blunted or dulled in tongue" and is trans-

lated "dumb": "As they went out, behold, they brought to Him a dumb man possessed with a devil" in Mt 9:32, 33; 12:22 twice; 15:30, 31. The man had his ability to speak "blunted" by the devil. When **(2)** "blunted in hearing" it is translated "deaf," Mt 11:5; Mk 7:32, 37; Mk 9:25; Lk 7:22; 11:14 twice. It is also translated **(3)** "speechless" in Lk 1:22. Syn.: 216, 880, 4623. See: BAGD–462a; THAYER–367d.

Λ

2975. **λαγχάνω** {4x} **lagchanō**, *lang-khan'-o;* a prol. form of a primary verb, which is only used as an alt. in certain tenses; to *lot,* i.e. *determine* (by impl. *receive*) espec. by lot:–his lot be {1x}, cast lots {1x}, obtain {2x}.

Lagchano, as a verb, means "to obtain by lot" in Acts 1:17: "For he [Judas Iscariot] was numbered with us, and had obtained part of this ministry." *Lagchano* denotes "to draw lots, to obtain by casting lots" and is translated **(1)** "his lot" in Lk 1:9; lit., "he received by lot," i.e., by divine appointment; **(2)** "cast lots" in Jn 19:24; and **(3)** "obtained" in **(3a)** Acts 1:17, of the portion "allotted" by the Lord to His apostles in their ministry; and in **(3b)** 2 Pet 1:1, "that have obtained (a like precious faith)," i.e., by its being "allotted" to them, not by acquiring it for themselves, but by divine grace (an act independent of human control, as in the casting of "lots"). Syn.: 324, 353, 354, 568, 588, 618, 1209, 1523, 1926, 2210, 2865, 2983, 3028, 3335, 3336, 3858, 3880, 3970, 4327, 4355, 4356, 4380, 4381, 4382, 5562, 5264, 5274. See: TDNT–4:1, 495; BAGD–462a; THAYER–367b.

2976. **Λάζαρος** {15x} **Lazarŏs**, *lad'-zar-os;* prob. of Heb. or. [499]; *Lazarus* (i.e. *Elazar*), the name of two Isr.:–Lazarus {11x}, Lazarus (the poor man) {4x}. See: BAGD–462b.

2977. **λάθρα** {4x} **lathra**, *lath'-rah;* adv. from *2990; privately:*–privily {3x}, secretly {1x}.

Lathra means "secretly, covertly" (from a root *lath*– indicating "unnoticed, unknown," seen in *lanthano,* "to escape notice," *lethe,* "forgetfulness"), and is translated **(1)** "privily" in Mt 1:19; 2:7; Acts 16:37; and **(2)** "secretly" in Jn 11:28. See: BAGD–462c; THAYER–367d.

2978. **λαῖλαψ** {3x} **lailaps**, *lah'-ee-laps;* of uncert. der.; a *whirlwind* (*squall*):–storm {2x}, tempest {1x}.

Lailaps refers to a formidable squall, a storm raging back and forth unstably, breaking forth from dark clouds and accompanied by torrential rains and is translated **(1)** "storm" in Mk 4:37; Lk 8:23; and **(2)** "tempest" in 2 Pet

2:17. Syn.: 417, 2366, 4151, 4157. See: BAGD—462d; THAYER—368a.

2979. **λακτίζω** {2x} **laktizō,** *lak-tid'-zo;* from adv. λάξ **lax** (*heelwise*); to *recalcitrate:*—kick {2x}.

This word means to kick forcefully with the heel (Acts 9:5; 26:14). See: TDNT—4:3, 495; BAGD—463a; THAYER—368a.

2980. **λαλέω** {296x} **laleō,** *lal-eh'-o;* a prol. form of an otherwise obs. verb; to *talk,* i.e. *utter* words:—speak {244x}, say {15x}, tell {12x}, talk {11x}, preach {6x}, utter {4x}, vr speak {1x}, misc. {3x}.

This word focuses on the articulated, distinct sound of the formed word in human language. Syn.: 2981, 3004. See: TDNT—4:69, 505; BAGD—463a; THAYER—368a. comp. *3004.*

2981. **λαλιά** {4x} **lalia,** *lal-ee-ah';* from *2980; talk:*—saying {1x}, speech {3x}.

Lalia focuses not on the speaker but on the condition of the hearer to receive the word spoken. *Lalia* requires an open heart to receive the spoken word. It denotes "talk, a particular dialect of speech" and is translated **(1)** "speech" Mt 26:73; Mk 14:70; Jn 8:43; and **(2)** "saying" Jn 4:42. Syn.: 2980, 3004. See: BAGD—464a; THAYER—369b.

2982. **λαμά** {2x} **lama,** *lam-ah';* or

λαμμᾶ lamma, *lam-mah';* or

λεμά lĕma, *leh-mah';* of Heb. or Aramaic orig. [4100 with prep. pref.]; *lama* (i.e. *why*):—*lama* {2x}. See: BAGD—464a; THAYER—370a.

2983. **λαμβάνω** {263x} **lambanō,** *lam-ban'-o;* a prol. form of a primary verb, which is used only as an alt. in certain tenses; to *take* (in very many applications, lit. and fig. [properly obj. or act., to *get hold* of; whereas *1209* is rather subj. or pass., to *have offered* to one; while *138* is more violent, to *seize* or *remove*]):—receive {133x}, take {106x}, have {3x}, catch {3x}, not tr {1x}, misc. {7x} = accept, + be amazed, assay, attain, bring, × when I call, come on (× unto), + forget, hold, obtain.

Lambano, as a verb, denotes either "to take" or "to receive," **(1)** literally, **(1a)** without an object, in contrast to asking: "For every one that asketh receiveth (*lambano*); and he that seeketh findeth; and to him that knocketh it shall be opened" (Mt 7:8; cf. Mk 11:24); **(1b)** in contrast to giving: (Mt 10:8; cf. Acts 20:35); **(1c)** with objects, whether **(1c1)** things: "But he shall receive (*lambano*) an hundredfold now in this time, houses, and brethren, and sisters, and mothers, and children, and lands, with persecutions; and in the world to come eternal

life" (Mk 10:30; cf. Jn 13:30; Acts 9:19; 1 Cor 9:25); or **(1c2)** persons: "Then they willingly received Him into the ship: and immediately the ship was at the land whither they went" (Jn 6:21; cf. 13:20; 16:14; 2 Jn 10; Mk 14:65);

(2) metaphorically, **(2a)** of the word of God: "But he that received the seed into stony places, the same is he that heareth the word, and *anon* with joy receiveth it" (Mt 13:20; cf. Mk 4:16); **(2b)** of the sayings of Christ: "He that rejecteth me, and receiveth not My words, hath one that judgeth him: the word that I have spoken, the same shall judge him in the last day" (Jn 12:48); **(2c)** of the witness of Christ: "Verily, verily, I say unto thee, We speak that we do know, and testify that we have seen; and ye receive not our witness" (Jn 3:11); **(2d)** of a hundredfold in this life, and eternal life in the world to come: "But he shall receive an hundredfold now in this time, houses, and brethren, and sisters, and mothers, and children, and lands, with persecutions; and in the world to come eternal life" (Mk 10:30); **(2e)** of mercy: "Let us therefore come boldly unto the throne of grace, that we may obtain mercy, and find grace to help in time of need" (Heb 4:16); **(2f)** of a person: "And they asked Him, saying, Master, we know that thou sayest and teachest rightly, neither acceptest (*lambano*) thou the person of any, but teachest the way of God truly" (Lk 20:21; cf. Gal 2:6 "accepteth," an expression used in the OT either in the sense of being gracious or kind to a person [Gen 19:21; 32:20], or negatively in the sense of being impartial [Lev 19:15; Deut 10:17]. Syn.: There is a certain distinction between *lambano* (*2983*) and *dechomai* (*1209*) in that in many instances *lambano* suggests a self-prompted taking, whereas *dechomai* more frequently indicates "a welcoming or an appropriating reception." See also: 324, 353, 354, 568, 588, 618, 1209, 1523, 1926, 2210, 2865, 2975, 3028, 3335, 3336, 3858, 3880, 3970, 4327, 4355, 4356, 4380, 4381, 4382, 5562, 5264, 5274. See: TDNT—4:5, 495; BAGD—464a; THAYER—371c.

2984. **Λάμεχ** {1x} **Lamĕch,** *lam'-ekh;* of Heb. or. [3929]; *Lamech* (i.e. *Lemek*), a patriarch:—*Lamech* {1x}. See: BAGD—465c; THAYER—371c.

λαμμᾶ lamma. See *2982.*

2985. **λαμπάς** {9x} **lampas,** *lam-pas';* from *2989;* a "*lamp*" or *flambeau:*—lamp {7x}, light {1x}, torch {1x}.

(1) *Lampas* denotes a light, frequently fed, like a lamp with oil from a little vessel used for that purpose; they held little oil and would frequently need replenishing. **(2)** It is translated **(2a)** "lamp" in Mt 25:1, 3, 4, 7, 8; Rev 4:5; 8:10; **(2b)** "light" in Acts 20:8; and **(2c)** "torch"

in Jn 18:3, i.e. larger lamps. Syn.: 3088, 5338, 5457, 5458. See: TDNT—4:16, 497; BAGD—465c; THAYER—371c.

2986. λαμπρός {9x} **lamprŏs,** *lam-pros';* from the same as *2985; radiant;* by anal. *limpid;* fig. *magnificent* or *sumptuous* (in appearance):—bright {2x}, goodly {2x}, white {2x}, gorgeous {1x}, gay {1x}, clear {1x}.

   Lampros, "shining, brilliant, bright," is used **(1)** of the clothing of an angel, Acts 10:30 and Rev 15:6; **(2)** symbolically, "white" of the clothing **(2a)** of the saints, Rev 19:8; and angels, Rev 15:6; **(3)** of Christ **(3a)** as the Morning Star, Rev 22:16, "bright"; and of His appearance to Saul on the Damascus road, Acts 10:30, "bright"; **(4)** of the water of life, Rev 22:1, "clear." It is translated **(5)** "gorgeous" of the robe put on Jesus by Herod, Lk 23:11. **(6)** The clothing of the favored rich man is described as **(6a)** "gay", Jas 2:2; and **(6b)** "goodly", Jas 2:3. **(7)** "Goodly" also refers to the destroyed merchandise of Babylon, Rev 18:14. See: TDNT—4:16, 497; BAGD—465d; THAYER—371c.

2987. λαμπρότης {1x} **lamprŏtēs,** *lam-prot'-ace;* from *2986; brilliancy:*—brightness {1x}. See: BAGD—466a; THAYER—371c.

2988. λαμπρῶς {1x} **lamprōs,** *lam-proce';* adv. from *2986; brilliantly,* i.e. fig. *luxuriously:*—sumptuously {1x}. See: BAGD—466a; THAYER—371d.

2989. λάμπω {7x} **lampō,** *lam'-po;* a primary verb; to *beam,* i.e. *radiate* brilliancy (lit. or fig.):—give light {1x}, shine {6x}.

   Lampo, "to give the light of a torch," is rendered **(1)** "giveth light" in Mt 5:15; and **(2)** "to shine (as a torch)" in Mt 5:16, 17:2; Lk 17:24; Acts 12:7; 2 Cor 4:6 (twice). See: TDNT—4:16, 497; BAGD—466a; THAYER—371d.

2990. λανθάνω {6x} **lanthanō,** *lan-than'-o;* a prol. form of a primary verb, which is used only an alt. in certain tenses; to *lie hid* (lit. or fig.); often used adv. *unwittingly:*—be hid {3x}, be ignorant of {2x}, unawares {1x}.

   Lanthano, "to escape notice, to be hidden from," is rendered **(1)** "be hid" in **(1a)** Mk 7:24 "(could not) be hid", of Christ; "was (not) hid"; **(1b)** Lk 8:47, of the woman with the issue of blood; "was (not) hid"; and **(1c)** Acts 26:26, of the facts concerning Christ; the sentence might be rendered "none of these things has escaped (are hidden from) the king's notice"; **(2)** "be ignorant of" in **(2a)** 2 Pet 3:5, "they willingly are ignorant of": "For this they willingly are ignorant of, that by the word of God the heavens were of old, and the earth standing out of

the water and in the water", **(2b)** 2 Pet 3:8, "be not ignorant of", "let this one thing not escape your notice"; and **(3)** "unawares" in Heb 13:2 of entertaining angels unawares. Syn.: 50, 51, 52, 56, 2399. See: TDNT—4:16, 497; BAGD—371d; THAYER—466b.

2991. λαξευτός {1x} **laxeutŏs,** *lax-yoo-tos';* from a compound of λᾶς **las** (a *stone*) and the base of *3584* (in its orig. sense of *scraping*); *rock-quarried:*—hewn in stone {1x}. See: BAGD—466c; THAYER—371d.

2992. λαός {143x} **laŏs,** *lah-os';* appar. a primary word; a *people* (in general; thus differing from *1218,* which denotes one's *own* populace):—people {143x}.

   Laos is used of **(1)** "the people at large," especially of people assembled, e.g., Mt 27:25; Lk 1:21; 3:15; Acts 4:27; **(2)** "a people of the same race and language," e.g., **(2a)** Rev 5:9; in the plural, e.g., Lk 2:31; Rom 15:11; Rev 7:9; 11:9; **(2b)** especially of Israel, e.g., Mt 2:6; 4:23; Jn 11:50; Acts 4:8; Heb 2:17; **(2b1)** in distinction from their rulers and priests, e.g., Mt 26:5; Lk 20:19; Heb 5:3; **(2b2)** in distinction from Gentiles, e.g., Acts 26:17, 23; Rom 15:10; **(3)** of Christians as the people of God, e.g., Acts 15:14; Titus 2:14; Heb 4:9; 1 Pet 2:9. Syn.: 1218, 1484, 3793. See: TDNT—4:29, 499; BAGD—466c; THAYER—372a.

2993. Λαοδίκεια {6x} **Laŏdikĕia,** *lah-od-ik'-i-ah;* from a compound of *2992* and *1349; Laodicia,* a place in Asia Minor:—Laodicea {6x}. See: BAGD—466c; THAYER—371d.

2994. Λαοδικεύς {2x} **Laŏdikĕus,** *lah-od-ik-yooce';* from *2993;* a *Laodicean,* i.e. inhab. of Laodicia:—Laodicean {2x}. See: BAGD—466c; THAYER—372a.

2995. λάρυγξ {1x} **larugx,** *lar'-oongks;* of uncert. der.; the *throat* ("*larynx*"):—throat {1x}.

   This word is used metaphorically of the instrument or organ of speech (Rom 3:13). See: TDNT—4:57, 503; BAGD—467b; THAYER—372b.

2996. Λασαία {1x} **Lasaia,** *las-ah'-yah;* of uncert. or.; *Lasæa,* a place in Crete:—Lasea {1x}. See: BAGD—467b; THAYER—372c.

2997. λάσκω {1x} **laschō,** *las'-kho;* a strengthened form of a primary verb, which only occurs in this and another prol. form as alt. in certain tenses; to *crack* open (from a fall):—burst asunder {1x}.

   Lascho primarily means to crack, or crash and denotes to burst asunder with a crack,

crack open, always of making a noise (Acts 1:18). See: BAGD—467b; THAYER—372c.

2998. λατομέω {2x} **latŏmĕō**, *lat-om-eh'-o;* from the same as the first part of *2991* and the base of *5114;* to hew out stones, *to quarry:*—hew {2x}.

Latomeo signifies "to hew out stones" (from *latomos*, "a stone-cutter"; *las*, "a stone," *temno*, "to cut"), and is used of the sepulchre which Joseph of Arimathaea had "hewn" out of a rock for himself, where the body of the Lord was buried, Mt 27:60; Mk 15:46. See: BAGD—467b; THAYER—372c.

2999. λατρεία {5x} **latrĕia**, *lat-ri'-ah;* from *3000; ministration* of God, i.e. *worship:*—divine service {1x}, service {4x}.

Latreia means to serve primarily and denotes **(1)** specifically, the service of God according to the requirements of the Levitical Law ("divine service" - Rom 9:4; Heb 9:1, 6); and **(2)** generally, a sense of service to God (Jn 16:2; Rom 12:1). Syn.: 3000, 3008. See: TDNT—4:58, 503; BAGD—467b; THAYER—372d.

3000. λατρεύω {21x} **latrĕuō**, *lat-ryoo'-o;* from λάτρις **latris** (a hired *menial*); to *minister* (to God), i.e. *render,* relig. *homage:*—serve {16x}, do the service {1x}, worship {3x}, worshipper {1x}.

Latreuo, primarily "to work for hire" (akin to *lataris,* "a hired servant"), signifies **(1)** to worship, **(2)** to "serve"; in the latter sense it is used of service **(2a)** to God, Mt 4:10; Lk 1:74 ("without fear"); 4:8; Acts 7:7; 24:14, "worship"; 26:7; 27:23; Rom 1:9 ("with my spirit"); 2 Ti 1:3; Heb 9:14; 12:28, "we may serve"; Rev 7:15; **(2b)** to God and Christ ("the Lamb"), Rev 22:3; **(2c)** in the tabernacle, Heb 8:5; 13:10; **(2d)** to "the host of heaven," Acts 7:42, "to worship"; **(2e)** to "the creature," instead of the Creator, Rom 1:25, of idolatry. It is translated **(3)** "to worship" in Phil 3:3, "(which) worship (God in the spirit)"; "to worship" in Acts 7:42; 24:14; and **(4)** "(the) worshipers" in Heb 10:2, present participle, lit., "(the ones) worshiping." Syn.: 2999, 3008. See: TDNT—4:58, 503; BAGD—467c; THAYER—372d.

3001. λάχανον {4x} **lachanŏn**, *lakh'-an-on;* from λαχαίνω **lachainō** (to *dig*); a *vegetable:*—herb {4x}.

Lachanon denotes a garden herb, a vegetable, in contrast to wild plants (Mt 13:32; Mk 4:32; Lk 11:42; Rom 14:2). See: TDNT—4:65, 504; BAGD—467d; THAYER—373a.

3002. Λεββαῖος {1x} **Lĕbbaiŏs**, *leb-bah'-yos;* of uncert. or.; *Lebbæus,* a Chr.:—Lebbæus {1x}. See: BAGD—467d; THAYER—373a.

3003. λεγεών {4x} **lĕgĕōn**, *leg-eh-ohn'* or **λεγιών lĕgiōn**, *leg-ee-ohn';* of Lat. or.; a *"legion,"* i.e. Rom. *regiment* (fig.):—legion {4x}.

This word means **(1)** specifically, a *legion,* a body of soldiers whose number differed at different times, and in the time of Augustus seems to have consisted of 6826 men: 6100 foot soldiers, and 726 horsemen (Mt 26:53); and **(2)** more generally a large number (Mk 5:9, 15; Lk 8:30). See: TDNT—4:68, 505; BAGD—467d; THAYER—373a.

3004. λέγω {1343x} **lĕgō**, *leg'-o;* a primary verb; prop. to *"lay"* forth, i.e. (fig.) *relate* (in words [usually of systematic or set *discourse;* whereas *2036* and *5346* generally refer to an *individual* expression or speech respectively; while *4483* is prop. to *break silence* merely, and *2980* means an *extended* or random harangue]); by impl. to *mean:*—say {1184x}, speak {61x}, call {48x}, tell {33x}, misc. {17x} = ask, bid, boast, describe, give out, name, put forth, shew, utter.

(1) *Lego* focuses on the words that are uttered, the thought of the mind which is correlative to the spoken word as their necessary condition; the bringing together of words into a sentence. **(2)** *Lego* occasionally signifies "to ask," as of an inquiry, the reason being that *lego* is used for every variety of speaking, e.g., Acts 25:20, "I asked whether he would come to Jerusalem." Syn.: 154, 155, 350, 1833, 1905, 2065, 2980, 2981, 4441. See: TDNT—4:69, 505; BAGD—468a; THAYER—373b.

3005. λεῖμμα {1x} **lĕimma**, *lime'-mah;* from *3007;* a *remainder:*—remnant {1x}.

Leimma "that which is left" (akin to *leipo,* "to leave"), "a remnant," is used in Rom 11:5, "there is a remnant," more lit., "there has come to be a remnant," i.e., there is a spiritual "remnant" saved by the gospel from the midst of apostate Israel. While in one sense there has been and is a considerable number, yet, compared with the whole nation, past and present, the "remnant" is small, and as such is an evidence of God's electing grace (see v. 4). See: TDNT—4:194, 523; BAGD—470b; THAYER—375b.

3006. λεῖος {1x} **lĕiŏs**, *li'-os;* appar. a primary word; *smooth,* i.e. *"level":*—smooth {1x}.

Leios literally means "smooth" and occurs in Lk 3:5, prophetically and figuratively (or literally) of the topographical changes that incur to insure the full view of the Messiah; mountains lowered, valleys filled. It may speak of the lowering of spiritual pride and the raising

of humility necessary to receive Him. See: TDNT—4:193, 523; BAGD—470b; THAYER—375b.

3007. λείπω {6x} **lĕipō,** *li'-po;* a primary verb; to *leave,* i.e. (intr. or pass.) to *fail* or *be absent:*—lack {2x}, be wanting {2x}, want + 1722 {1x}, be destitute {1x}.

Leipo, "to leave," denotes **(1)** transitively, **(1a)** in the passive voice, "to be left behind, to lack," **(1a1)** Jas 1:4, "ye may be wanting in (nothing)"; **(1a2)** Jas 1:5, "lacketh"; **(1a3)** Jas 2:15, "be . . . destitute"; **(2)** intransitively, **(2a)** active voice, **(2a1)** Lk 18:22, "(one thing) thou) lackest," is, lit., "(one thing) is lacking (to thee)"; **(2a2)** Titus 1:5, "(the things) that were wanting"; **(2a3)** Titus 3:13, "(that nothing) be wanting." See: BAGD—470b; THAYER—375c.

3008. λειτουργέω {3x} **lĕitŏurgĕō,** *li-toorg-eh'-o;* from *3011;* to be a *public servant,* i.e. (by anal.) to *perform* relig. or charitable *functions* (*worship, obey, relieve*):—minister {3x}.

(1) Basically, this word means to serve at one's own expense; free service, nothing expected in return. The service is the focus and then the office. **(2)** In the NT it is used **(2a)** of the prophets and teachers in the church at Antioch, who "ministered to the Lord," Acts 13:2; **(2b)** of the duty of churches of the Gentiles to "minister" in "carnal things" to the poor Jewish saints at Jerusalem, in view of the fact that the former had "been made partakers" of the "spiritual things" of the latter, Rom 15:27; **(2c)** of the official service of priests and Levites under the Law, Heb 10:11. See: TDNT—4:215, 526; BAGD—470c; THAYER—375c.

3009. λειτουργία {6x} **lĕitŏurgia,** *li-toorg-ee'-ah;* from *3008; public function* (as priest ["liturgy"] or almsgiver):—ministration {1x}, ministry {2x}, service {3x}.

Leitourgia is used in the NT of "sacred ministrations," **(1)** priestly, Lk 1:23; Heb 8:6; 9:21; **(2)** figuratively, of the practical faith of the members of the church at Philippi regarded as priestly sacrifice, upon which the apostle's lifeblood might be poured out as a libation, Phil 2:17; **(3)** of the "ministration" of believers one to another, regarded as priestly service, 2 Cor 9:12; Phil 2:30. See: TDNT—4:215, 526; BAGD—471a; THAYER—375d.

3010. λειτουργικός {1x} **lĕitŏurgikŏs,** *li-toorg-ik-os';* from the same as *3008; functional publicly* ("liturgic"); i.e. *beneficent:*—ministering {1x}.

Leitourgikos is related to the performance of service, employed in ministering, Heb 1:14. See: TDNT—4:231, 526; BAGD—471b; THAYER—376a.

3011. λειτουργός {5x} **lĕitŏurgŏs,** *li-toorg-os';* from a der. of *2992* and *2041;* a *public servant,* i.e. a *functionary* in the Temple or Gospel, or (gen.) a *worshipper* (of God) or *benefactor* (of man):—minister {4x}, he that ministers {1x}.

In the NT it is used **(1)** of Christ, as a "Minister of the sanctuary" (in the heavens), Heb 8:2; **(2)** of angels, Heb 1:7 (Ps 104:4); **(3)** of the apostle Paul, in his evangelical ministry, fulfilling it as a serving priest, Rom 15:16; that he used it figuratively and not in an ecclesiastical sense, is obvious from the context; **(4)** of Epaphroditus, as ministering to Paul's needs on behalf of the church at Philippi, Phil 2:25; here, representative service is in view; **(5)** of earthly rulers, who though they do not all act consciously as servants of God, yet discharge functions which are the ordinance of God, Rom 13:6. See: TDNT—4:229, 526; BAGD—471b; THAYER—377c.

3012. λέντιον {2x} **lĕntiŏn,** *len'-tee-on;* of Lat. or.; a *"linen"* cloth, i.e. *apron:*—towel {2x}.

Lention denotes "a linen cloth or towel" (Lat., *linteum*), as used by the Lord, Jn 13:4, 5; it was commonly used by servants in a household. See: BAGD—471c; THAYER—376b.

3013. λεπίς {1x} **lĕpis,** *lep-is';* from λέπω **lĕpō** (to *peel*); a *flake:*—scale {1x}. See: TDNT—4:232, 529; BAGD—471c; THAYER—376b.

3014. λέπρα {4x} **lĕpra,** *lep'-rah;* from the same as *3013; scaliness,* i.e. *"leprosy":*—leprosy {4x}.

Lepra, akin to *lepros* (*3015*), **(1)** is mentioned in Mt 8:3; Mk 1:42; Lk 5:12, 13. **(2)** In the removal of other maladies the verb "to heal" (*iaomai*) is used, but in the removal of "leprosy," the verb "to cleanse" (*katharizo*), save in the statement concerning the Samaritan, Lk 17:15, "when he saw that he was healed." Mt 10:8 and Lk 4:27 indicate that the disease was common in the nation. Only twelve cases are recorded in the NT, but these are especially selected. For the Lord's commands to the leper mentioned in Mt 8 and to the ten in Lk 17, see Lev 14:2–32. See: TDNT—4:233, 529; BAGD—471d; THAYER—376b.

3015. λεπρός {9x} **lĕprŏs,** *lep-ros';* from the same as *3014; scaly,* i.e. *leprous* (a *leper*):—leper {9x}.

Lepros, an adjective, characterized by an eruption of rough scaly patches; later, "leprous," but chiefly used as a noun, "a leper," Mt

8:2; 10:8; 11:5; Mk 1:40; Lk 4:27; 7:22; 17:12; especially of Simon mentioned in Mt 26:6; Mk 14:3. See: TDNT—4:233, 529; BAGD—472a; THAYER—376b.

3016. **λεπτόν** {3x} **lĕptŏn**, *lep-ton';* neut. of a der. of the same as *3013;* something *scaled (light),* i.e. a small *coin:*—mite {3x}.

Lepton denotes a small copper coin, proverbially the smallest Jewish coin. It was valued at 1/8th of the Roman *as,* and the 1/128th part of the *denarious:* its legal value was about one third of an English farthing, ½ cent American money. See: TDNT—4:233,*; BAGD—472a; THAYER—376c.

3017. **Λευΐ** {5x} **Lĕuï**, *lyoo-ee';* of Heb. or. [3878]; *Levi,* the name of three Isr.:—Levi {5x}. See: TDNT—4:234, 529; BAGD—472; THAYER—376c. comp. *3018.*

3018. **Λευΐς** {3x} **Lĕuïs**, *lyoo-is';* a form of *3017; Lewis* (i.e. *Levi*), a Chr.:—Levi {3x}. See: TDNT—4:234, 529; BAGD—472a; THAYER—376c.

3019. **Λευΐτης** {3x} **Lĕuïtēs**, *lyoo-ee'-tace;* from *3017;* a *Levite,* i.e. desc. of Levi:—Levite {3x}. See: TDNT—4:239, 530; BAGD—472b; THAYER—376d.

3020. **Λευϊτικός** {1x} **Lĕuïtikŏs**, *lyoo-it-ee-kos';* from *3019; Levitic,* i.e. relating to the Levites:—Levitical {1x}. See: BAGD—472b; THAYER—376d.

3021. **λευκαίνω** {2x} **lĕukainō**, *lyoo-kah'-ee-no;* from *3022;* to *whiten:*—make white {1x}, whiten {1x}.

Leukaino, "to whiten, make white", is used in Mk 9:3; figuratively in Rev 7:14. See: TDNT—4:241, 530; BAGD—472b; THAYER—376d.

3022. **λευκός** {25x} **lĕukŏs**, *lyoo-kos';* from λύκη **lukē**, ("*light*"); *white:*—white {25x}.

Luke is used of **(1)** clothing (sometimes in the sense of "bright"), Mt 17:2; 28:3; Mk 9:3; 16:5; Lk 9:29; Jn 20:12; Acts 1:10; symbolically, Rev 3:4, 5, 18; 4:4; 6:11; 7:9, 13; 19:14 (2nd part); **(2)** hair, Mt 5:36; Christ's head and hair (in a vision; cf. Dan 7:9), Rev 1:14 (twice); **(3)** ripened grain, Jn 4:35; **(4)** a stone, Rev 2:17, an expression of the Lord's special delight in the overcomer, the new name on it being indicative of a secret communication of love and joy; **(5)** a horse (in a vision), Rev 6:2; 19:11–14 (1st part); **(6)** a cloud, Rev 14:14; **(7)** the throne of God, Rev 20:11. See: TDNT—4:241, 530; BAGD—472b; THAYER—376d.

3023. **λεών** {9x} **lĕōn**, *leh-ohn';* a primary word; a "*lion*":—lion {9x}.

Leon occurs **(1)** in 2 Ti 4:17, **(1a)** probably figurative of the imminent peril of death, the figure being represented by the whole phrase, not by the word "lion" alone; **(1b)** some suppose the reference to be to the lions of the amphitheater; **(1c)** the Greek commentators regarded the "lion" as Nero; **(1d)** others understand it to be Satan. **(1e)** The language not improbably recalls that of Ps 22:21, and Dan 6:20. **(2)** The word is used metaphorically, too, in Rev 5:5, where Christ is called "the Lion of the tribe of Judah." **(3)** Elsewhere it has the literal meaning, Heb 11:33; 1 Pet 5:8; Rev 4:7; 9:8, 17; 10:3; 13:2. **(4)** Taking the OT and NT occurrences the allusions are to the three great features of the "lion," **(4a)** its majesty and strength, indicative of royalty, e.g., Prov 30:30, **(4b)** its courage, e.g., Prov 28:1, **(4c)** its cruelty, e.g., Ps 22:13. See: TDNT—4:251, 531; BAGD—472d; THAYER—377a.

3024. **λήθη** {1x} **lēthē**, *lay'-thay;* from *2990; forgetfulness:*—forget + 3083 {1x}. See: BAGD—472d; THAYER—377a.

3025. **ληνός** {5x} **lēnŏs**, *lay-nos';* appar. a primary word; a *trough,* i.e. winevat:*—winepress {4x}, winepress + 3631 {1x}.

Lenos denotes "a trough or vat," used especially for the treading of grapes, Mt 21:33. Not infrequently they were dug out in the soil or excavated in a rock, as in the rock vats in Palestine today. In Rev 14:19, 20 (twice) and 19:15 (where *oinos* is added, lit. "the winepress of the wine") the word is used metaphorically with reference to the execution of divine judgment upon the gathered foes of the Jews at the close of this age preliminary to the establishment of the millennial kingdom. See: TDNT—4:254, 531; BAGD—473a.

3026. **λῆρος** {1x} **lērŏs**, *lay'-ros;* appar. a primary word; *twaddle,* i.e. an *incredible* story:—idle tale.

Leros denotes an incredible tale in that it is foolish talk, nonsense, lacking credibility (Lk 24:11). See: BAGD—473a; THAYER—377b.

3027. **ληστής** {15x} **lēstēs**, *lace-tace';* from ληΐζομαι **leizomai** (to *plunder*); a *brigand:*—robber {4x}, thief {11x}.

Lestes, "a robber, brigand" (akin to *leia,* "booty"), "one who plunders openly and by violence" (in contrast to *kleptes,* "a thief"), is translated **(1)** "robber" or "robbers", Jn 10:1, 8, 18:40; 2 Cor 11:26; and **(2)** "thief" or "thieves" in Mt 21:13; 26:55; 27:38, 44; Mk 11:17; 14:48; 15:27; Lk 10:30, 36; 19:46; 22:52. Syn.: A *lestes* is a robber, a brigand, one who plunders openly and by violence; whereas the

kleptes, (2812), a thief, denotes one who steals by stealth. See: TDNT—4:257, 532; BAGD—473a; THAYER—377b.

3028. λῆμψις {1x} **lēmpsis,** *lemp'-sis;* from 2983; *receipt* (the act):—a receiving {1x}.

Lempsis, as a noun, means "a receiving" and is used in Phil 4:15: "Now ye Philippians know also, that in the beginning of the gospel, when I departed from Macedonia, no church communicated with me as concerning giving and receiving (*lempsis*), but ye only." Syn.: 324, 353, 354, 568, 588, 618, 1209, 1523, 1926, 2210, 2865, 2975, 2983, 3335, 3336, 3858, 3880, 3970, 4327, 4355, 4356, 4380, 4381, 4382, 5562, 5264, 5274. See: BAGD—473a; THAYER—377b.

3029. λίαν {14x} **lian,** *lee'-an;* of uncert. aff.; *much* (adv.):—exceeding {5x}, greatly {4x}, very chiefest + 5228 {2x}, great {1x}, sore {1x}, very {1x}.

Lian, "very, exceedingly," is translated **(1)** "exceeding" in Mt 2:16; 4:8; 8:28; Mk 9:3; Lk 23:8; **(2)** "greatly" **(2a)** in Mt 27:14, of wonder, **(2b)** 2 Ti 4:15, of opposition; **(2c)** 2 Jn 3 and 3 Jn 4, of joy; **(3)** "very chiefest" in 2 Cor 11:5; 12:11; **(4)** "great" in Mk 1:35; **(5)** "sore" in Mk 6:51 of amazement; and **(6)** "very" in Mk 16:2. See: BAGD—473a; THAYER—377b.

3030. λίβανος {2x} **libanŏs,** *lib'-an-os;* of for. or. [3828]; the *incense*-tree, i.e. (by impl.) *incense* itself:—frankincense {2x}. Cf. Mt 2:11; Rev 18:13. See: TDNT—4:263, 533; BAGD—473c; THAYER—377c.

3031. λιβανωτός {2x} **libanōtŏs,** *lib-an-o-tos';* from 3030; *frankincense,* i.e. (by extens.) a *censer* for burning it:—censer {2x}.

A *libanotos* is a vessel in which to burn incense," Rev 8:3, 5. See: TDNT—4:263, 533; BAGD—473d; THAYER—317a.

3032. Λιβερτῖνος {1x} **Libĕrtinŏs,** *lib-er-tee'-nos;* of Lat. or.; a Rom. *freedman:*—Libertine {1x}. See: TDNT—4:265, 533; BAGD—473d; THAYER—377c.

3033. Λιβύη {1x} **Libuē,** *lib-oo'-ay;* prob. from 3047; *Libye,* a region of Africa:—Libya {1x}. See: BAGD—473d; THAYER—377d.

3034. λιθάζω {8x} **lithazō,** *lith-ad'-zo;* from 3037; to *lapidate:*—to stone {8x}.

This word [cf. 3036] is used for throwing stones at someone, to pelt one in order to wound, frighten away, or kill him; most contexts seem to indicate intent to kill, Jn 10:31–33; 11:8; Acts 5:26; 14:19; 2 Cor 11:25; Heb 11:37. See: TDNT—4:267, 533; BAGD—473d; THAYER—377d.

3035. λίθινος {3x} **lithinŏs,** *lith-ee'-nos;* from 3037; *stony,* i.e. made of *stone:*—of stone {3x}. Cf. Jn 2:6; 2 Cor 3:3; Rev 9:20. See: TDNT—4:268, 534; BAGD—474a; THAYER—378a.

3036. λιθοβολέω {9x} **lithŏbŏlĕō,** *lith-ob-ol-eh'-o;* from a compound of 3037 and 906; to *throw stones,* i.e. *lapidate:*—stone {8x}, cast stones {1x}.

Lithoboleo, "to pelt with stones", "to stone to death." This word seems to carry the idea of casting stones to kill (exception – Mk 12:4), not just frighten or hurt [cf. 3034]. It occurs in Mt 21:35; 23:37; Lk 13:34; Jn 8:5; Acts 7:58, 59; 14:5; Heb 12:20. See: TDNT—4:267, 533; BAGD—474a; THAYER—378a.

3037. λίθος {60x} **lithŏs,** *lee'-thos;* appar. a primary word; a *stone* (lit. or fig.):—stone {49x}, one stone {4x}, another {4x}, stumbling stone + 4348 {2x}, mill stone + 3457 {1x}.

Lithos is used **(1)** literally, of **(1a)** the "stones" of the ground, e.g., Mt 4:3, 6; 7:9; **(1b)** "tombstones," e.g., Mt 27:60, 66; **(1c)** "building stones," e.g., Mt 21:42; **(1d)** "a millstone," Lk 17:2; cf. Rev 18:21; **(1e)** the "tables (or tablets)" of the Law, 2 Cor 3:7; **(1f)** "idol images," Acts 17:29; **(1g)** the "treasures" of commercial Babylon, Rev 18:12, 16; **(2)** metaphorically, of **(2a)** Christ, Rom 9:33; 1 Pet 2:4, 6, 8; **(2b)** believers, 1 Pet 2:5; **(2c)** spiritual edification by scriptural teaching, 1 Cor 3:12; **(2d)** the adornment of the foundations of the wall of the spiritual and heavenly Jerusalem, Rev 21:19; **(2e)** the adornment of religious Babylon, Rev 17:4; **(3)** figuratively, of Christ, Rev 4:3; 21:11, where "light" stands for "Light-giver." It is also translated **(4)** one stone, Mt 24:2 first reference; Mk 13:2 first reference; Lk 19:44; 21:6 both first reference; **(5)** another, Mt 24:2 second reference; Mk 13:2 second reference; Lk 19:44; 21:6 both second reference; **(6)** stumbling stone + 4348, Rom 9:32, 33; **(7)** mill stone + 3457, Mk 9:42. See: TDNT—4:268, 534; BAGD—474b; THAYER—378a.

3038. λιθόστρωτος {1x} **lithŏstrōtŏs,** *lith-os'-tro-tos;* from 3037 and a der. of 4766; *stone-strewed,* i.e. a tessellated *mosaic* on which the Rom. tribunal was placed:—Pavement {1x}.

This word is an adjective, denoting "paved with stones" (*lithos,* "a stone," and *stronnuo,* "to spread"), especially of tessellated work, is used as a noun in Jn 19:13, of a place near the Praetorium in Jerusalem, called *Gabbatha,* a

Greek transliteration of an Aramaic word. See: BAGD—474d; THAYER—378b.

3039. λικμάω {2x} **likmaō,** *lik-mah'-o;* from λικμός **likmŏs,** the equiv. of λίκνον **liknŏn** (a winnowing *fan* or basket); to *winnow,* i.e. (by anal.) to *triturate:*—grind to powder {2x}.

Likmao, as a verb, means "to winnow," as of grain, by throwing it up against the wind, to scatter the chaff and straw; hence has the meaning "to scatter," as chaff or dust, and is translated "will grind... to powder" (Mt 21:44; Lk 20:18). See: TDNT—4:280, 535; BAGD—474d; THAYER—378c.

3040. λιμήν {3x} **limēn,** *lee-mane';* appar. a primary word; a *harbor:*—haven {2x}, the fair havens + 2570 {1x}.

This is a place called "Fair Haven", Acts 27:8, 12. See: BAGD—475a; THAYER—378c. comp. *2568.*

3041. λίμνη {10x} **limnē,** *lim'-nay;* prob. from *3040* (through the idea of nearness of shore); a *pond* (large or small):—lake {10x}.

This word, "a lake," is used **(1)** in the Gospels, only by Lk, of the Sea of Galilee, Lk 5:2; 8:22, 23, 33, called Gennesaret in 5:1 (Mt and Mk use *thalassa,* "a sea"); **(2)** of the "lake" of fire, Rev 19:20; 20:10, 14, 15; 21:8. Lake Gennesaret is the western most "indention" of the Sea of Galilee. See: BAGD—475a; THAYER—378c.

3042. λιμός {12x} **limŏs,** *lee-mos';* prob. from *3007* (through the idea of *destitution*); a *scarcity* of food:—dearth {2x}, famine {7x}, hunger {3x}.

Limos has the meanings "famine" and "hunger" and is translated **(1)** "dearth", Acts 7:11; 11:28; **(2)** "famine", Mt 24:7; Mk 13:8; Lk 4:25; 15:14; 21:11; Rom 8:35; Rev 18:8; **(3)** hunger" Lk 15:17; 2 Cor 11:27; Rev 6:8. See: TDNT—6:12, 820; BAGD—475a; THAYER—378c.

3043. λίνον {2x} **linŏn,** *lee'-non;* prob. a primary word; *flax,* i.e. (by impl.) "*linen*":—flax {1x}, linen {1x}.

Linon primarily denotes **(1)** "flax" (Eng., "linen"); then, that which is made of it, "a wick of a lamp," Mt 12:20; and **(2)** "linen" in Rev 15:6. See: BAGD—475b; THAYER—378d.

3044. Λῖνος {1x} **Linŏs,** *lee'-nos;* perh. from *3043;* Linus, a Chr.:—Linus {1x}. See: BAGD—475c; THAYER—378d.

3045. λιπαρός {1x} **liparŏs,** *lip-ar-os';* from λίπος **lipŏs** (*grease*); *fat,* i.e. (fig.) *sumptuous:*—dainty {1x}.

Liparos properly signifies "oily, or anointed with oil" (from *lipos,* "grease," connected with *aleipho,* "to anoint"); it is said of things which pertain to delicate and sumptuous living; hence, "dainty," Rev 18:14. See: BAGD—475c; THAYER—378d.

3046. λίτρα {2x} **litra,** *lee'-trah;* of Lat. or. [*libra*]; a *pound* in weight:—pound {2x}.

In the NT it is used as a measure of weight, a pound, Jn 12:3; 19:39. See: BAGD—475d; THAYER—378d.

3047. λίψ {1x} **lips,** *leeps;* prob. from λείβω **lĕibō** (to *pour* a "libation"); the *south* (-west) wind (as bringing rain, i.e. (by extens.) the *south* quarter):—southwest {1x}.

Lips denotes "the S.W. wind," Acts 27:13, which blows towards the N.E. See: BAGD—475d; THAYER—378d.

3048. λογία {2x} **lŏgia,** *log-ee'-ah* or λογεία **lŏgĕia,** *log-i'-ah;* from *3056* (in the commercial sense); a *contribution:*—collection {1x}, gathering {1x}.

Logeia, "to collect," is translated **(1)** "collection" in 1 Cor 16:1 and **(2)** "gathering" in 1 Cor 16:2. See: TDNT—4:282,*; BAGD—475d; THAYER—379a.

3049. λογίζομαι {41x} **lŏgizŏmai,** *log-id'-zom-ahee;* mid. voice from *3056;* to *take an inventory,* i.e. *estimate* (lit. or fig.):—think {9x}, impute {8x}, reckon {6x}, count {5x}, account {4x}, suppose {2x}, reason {1x}, number {1x}, misc. {5x} = conclude, + despise, esteem, lay.

Logizomai primarily signifies **(1)** "to reckon," whether by calculation or imputation, e.g., Gal 3:6; then, **(2)** to deliberate, and so to "account", Rom 8:36; "esteemeth", Rom 14:14; Jn 11:50; 1 Cor 4:1; Heb 11:19; "consider"; Acts 19:27; 1 Pet 5:12. **(3)** It is used of love in 1 Cor 13:5, as not "thinking" of evil. **(4)** In 2 Cor 3:5 the apostle uses it in repudiation of the idea that he and fellow-servants of God are so self-sufficient as to "think anything" as from themselves, i.e., as to attribute anything to themselves. Cf. 12:6. **(5)** In 2 Ti 4:16 it is used of laying to, charging a person's "account" as a charge against him. **(6)** Imputation has three steps: **(6a)** the collecting of all charges and remissions; **(6b)** the totaling of these debits and credits; **(6c)** the placing of the balance or credit on one's account. See: TDNT—4:284, 536; BAGD—475d; THAYER—379a.

3050. λογικός {2x} **lŏgikŏs,** *log-ik-os';* from *3056; rational* ("*logical*"):—reasonable {1x}, of the word {1x}.

Logikos pertains to the reasoning faculty,

reasonable, rational and is used **(1)** of the service rendered by believers in presenting their bodies a living sacrifice. The sacrifice is to be in accordance with the spiritual intelligence of those who are new creatures in Christ and are mindful of the mercies of God; in contrast to those offered by ritual and compulsion (Rom 12:1). **(2)** The word signifies a rationale affecting the soul (1 Pet 2:2). **(3)** It pertains to "the reasoning faculty, reasonable, rational," and is used **(3a)** in Rom 12:1, of the service (*latreia*) to be rendered by believers in presenting their bodies "a living sacrifice, holy, acceptable to God." The sacrifice is to be intelligent, in contrast to those offered by ritual and compulsion; the presentation is to be in accordance with the spiritual intelligence of those who are new creatures in Christ and are mindful of "the mercies of God." **(3b)** It is found also in 1 Pet 2:2, "(milk) of the word" and so here the nourishment may be understood as of that spiritually rational nature which, acting through the regenerate mind, develops spiritual growth. God's Word is not given so that it is impossible to understand it, or that it requires a special class of men to interpret it; its character is such that the Holy Spirit who gave it can unfold its truths even to the young convert. See: TDNT—4:142, 505; BAGD—476c; THAYER—379c.

3051. **λόγιον** {4x} **lŏgiŏn**, *log'-ee-on;* neut. of *3052;* an *utterance* (of God):—oracle {4x}.

Logion, "a word, narrative, statement," denotes "a divine response or utterance, an oracle"; it is used of **(1)** the contents of the Mosaic Law, Acts 7:38; **(2)** all the written utterances of God through OT writers, Rom 3:2; **(3)** the substance of Christian doctrine, Heb 5:12; **(4)** the utterances of God through Christian teachers, 1 Pet 4:11. See: TDNT—4:137, 505; BAGD—476c; THAYER—379c.

3052. **λόγιος** {1x} **lŏgiŏs**, *log'-ee-os;* from *3056; fluent*, i.e. an *orator:*—eloquent {1x}.

Logios, from *logos*, "a word," primarily meant "learned, a man skilled in literature and the arts." In Acts 18:24, it is translated "eloquent," said of Apollos, who had stores of "learning" and could express it convincingly. See: TDNT—4:136, 505; BAGD—476d; THAYER—379d.

3053. **λογισμός** {2x} **lŏgismŏs**, *log-is-mos';* from *3049; computation*, i.e. (fig.) *reasoning* (*conscience, conceit*):—imagination {1x}, thought {1x}.

Logismos, "a reasoning, a thought" (akin to *logizomai*, "to count, reckon"), is translated **(1)** "thoughts" in Rom 2:15, suggestive of evil in-

tent, not of mere reasonings; **(2)** "imaginations" in 2 Cor 10:5. The word suggests the contemplation of actions as a result of the verdict of conscience. See: TDNT—4:284, 536; BAGD—476d; THAYER—380a.

3054. **λογομαχέω** {1x} **lŏgŏmachĕō**, *log-om-akh-eh'-o;* from a compound of *3056* and *3164;* to *be disputatious* (on trifles):—to strive about words {1x}.

This word means to wrangle about empty and trifling matters, 2 Ti 2:14. See: TDNT—4:143, 505; BAGD—477a; THAYER—380a.

3055. **λογομαχία** {1x} **lŏgŏmachia**, *log-om-akh-ee'-ah;* from the same as *3054; disputation* about trifles ("*logomachy*"):—a strife of words {1x}.

Logomachia denotes "a dispute about words" (*logos*, "a word," *mache*, "a fight"), or about trivial things, 1 Ti 6:4, "strifes." See: TDNT—4:143, 505; BAGD—477a; THAYER—380a.

3056. **λόγος** {330x} **lŏgŏs**, *log'-os;* from *3004;* something *said* (incl. the *thought*); by impl. a *topic* (subject of discourse), also *reasoning* (the mental faculty) or *motive;* by extens. a *computation;* spec. (with the art. in John) the Divine *Expression* (i.e. *Christ*):—word {218x}, saying {50x}, account {8x}, speech {8x}, Word (Christ) {7x}, thing {5x}, not tr {2x}, misc. {32x} = cause, communication, × concerning, doctrine, fame, × have to do, intent, matter, mouth, preaching, question, reason, + reckon, remove, shew, × speaker, talk, + none of these things move me, tidings, treatise, utterance, work.

Logos denotes **I.** "the expression of thought"—not the mere name of an object—**(1)** as embodying a conception or idea, e.g., Lk 7:7; 1 Cor 14:9, 19; **(2)** a saying or statement, **(2a)** by God, e.g., Jn 15:25; Rom 9:9; 9:28, "work"; Gal 5:14; Heb 4:12; **(2b)** by Christ, e.g., Mt 24:35 (plur.); Jn 2:22; 4:41; 14:23 (plur.); 15:20. In connection with (2a) and (2b) the phrase "the word of the Lord," i.e., the revealed will of God (very frequent in the OT), is used **(2b1)** of a direct revelation given by Christ, 1 Th 4:15; **(2b2)** of the gospel, Acts 8:25; 13:49; 15:35, 36; 16:32; 19:10; 1 Th 1:8; 2 Th 3:1; **(2b3)** in this respect it is the message from the Lord, delivered with His authority and made effective by His power (cf. Acts 10:36); **(2b4)** for other instances relating to the gospel see Acts 13:26; 14:3; 15:7; 1 Cor 1:18; 2 Cor 2:17; 4:2; 5:19; 6:7; Gal 6:6; Eph 1:13; Phil 2:16; Col 1:5; Heb 5:13; **(2b5)** sometimes it is used as the sum of God's utterances, e.g., Mk 7:13; Jn 10:35; Rev 1:2, 9; **(3)** discourse, speech, of instruction, etc., e.g., Acts 2:40; 1 Cor 2:13; 12:8; 2 Cor 1:18; 1 Th 1:5; 2 Th 2:15; Heb 6:1;

(4) doctrine, e.g., Mt 13:20; Col 3:16; 1 Ti 4:6; 2 Ti 1:13; Titus 1:9; 1 Jn 2:7.

II. "The Personal Word," a title of the Son of God; this identification is substantiated by the statements of doctrine in Jn 1:1–18, declaring in verses 1 and 2 **(1)** His distinct and superfinite personality, **(2)** His relation in the Godhead (pros, "with," not mere company, but the most intimate communion), **(3)** His deity; in v. 3, His creative power; in v. 14, His incarnation ("was made flesh," expressing His voluntary act), the reality and totality of His human nature, and His glory "as of the only begotten from the Father", the absence of the article in each place lending stress to the nature and character of the relationship; His was the *shekinah* glory in open manifestation; v. 18 consummates the identification: "the only begotten Son, which is in the bosom of the Father, He hath declared Him," thus fulfilling the significance of the title "*Logos*," the "Word," the personal manifestation, not of a part of the divine nature, but of the whole deity (see image). The title is used also in 1 Jn 1, "the Word of life" combining the two declarations in Jn 1:1 and 4 and Rev 19:13. Syn.: The significance of *rhema* (4487) as distinct from *logos* is exemplified in the injunction to take "the sword of the Spirit, which is the word of God," Eph 6:17; here the reference is not to the whole Bible as such, but to the individual scripture which the Spirit brings to our remembrance for use in time of need, a prerequisite being the regular storing of the mind with Scripture. See: TDNT—4:69, 505; BAGD—477a; THAYER—380a.

3057. **λόγχη** {1x} **lŏgchē,** *long'-khay;* perh. a primary word; a "*lance*":—spear {1x}.

Logche is primarily "a spearhead," then, "a lance or spear," and occurs in Jn 19:34. See: BAGD—479b; THAYER—382a.

3058. **λοιδορέω** {4x} **lŏidŏrĕō,** *loy-dor-eh'-o;* from *3060;* to *reproach,* i.e. *vilify:*—revile {4x}.

Loidoreo denotes "to abuse, revile," Jn 9:28; Acts 23:4; 1 Cor 4:12; 1 Pet 2:23 (1st clause). See: TDNT—4:293, 538; BAGD—479c.

3059. **λοιδορία** {3x} **lŏidŏria,** *loy-dor-ee'-ah;* from *3060;* slander or *vituperation:*—railing {2x}, to speak reproachfully + 5484 {1x}.

Loidoria, "abuse, railing, reviling," is rendered **(1)** "railing" in 1 Pet 3:9 (twice); and **(2)** "to speak reproachfully" in 1 Ti 5:14. See: TDNT—4:293, 538; BAGD—479c; THAYER—382b.

3060. **λοίδορος** {2x} **lŏidŏrŏs,** *loy'-dor-os;* from λοιδός **lŏidŏs** (*mischief*); *abusive,* i.e. a *blackguard:*—railer {1x}, reviler {1x}.

Loidoros, an adjective denoting "reviling, railing" is used as a noun, **(1)** "a railer," 1 Cor 5:11 and **(2)** "railers" in 1 Cor 6:10. See: TDNT—4:293, 538; BAGD—479c; THAYER—382b.

3061. **λοιμός** {3x} **lŏimŏs,** *loy'-mos;* of uncert. aff.; a *plague* (lit. the *disease,* or fig. a *pest*):—pestilence {1x}, pestilent {1x}.

This word denotes **(1)** a pestilence, any deadly infectious malady (Lk 21:11; Mt 24:7); and **(2)** metaphorically, a pestilent fellow, one who spreads a deadly infection (Acts 24:5). See: BAGD—479d; THAYER—382b.

3062. **λοιποί** {41x} **lŏipŏi,** *loy-poy';* masc. plur. of a der. of *3007; remaining* ones:—other {15x}, rest {12x}, others {7x}, remnant {4x}, residue {1x}, which remains {1x}, other things {1x}. **(1)** other, in Mt 25:11; Lk 18:11; 24:10; Acts 17:9; Rom 1:13; 1 Cor 9:5; 15:37; 2 Cor 12:13; 13:2; Gal 2:13; Eph 4:17; Phil 1:13; 4:3; 2 Pet 3:16; Rev 8:13; **(2)** rest, in Mt 27:49; Lk 12:26; 24:9; Acts 2:37; 5:13; 27:44; Rom 11:7; 1 Cor 7:12; 11:34; Rev 2:24; 9:20; 20:5; **(3)** others, in Lk 8:9; Acts 28:9; Eph 2:3; 1 Th 4:13; 5:6; 1 Ti 5:20; **(4)** remnant, in Mt 22:6; Rev 11:13; 12:17; 19:21; **(5)** residue {1x}, in Mk 16:13, plural; **(6)** which remains, in Rev 3:2; and **(7)** other things, in Mk 4:19. See: BAGD—479d; THAYER—382b.

3063. **λοιπόν** {14x} **lŏipŏn,** *loy-pon';* neut. sing. of the same as *3062;* something *remaining* (adv.):—finally {5x}, now {2x}, then {1x}, besides {1x}, moreover + 1161 + 3739 {1x}, it remains + 2076 {1x}, furthermore {1x}, henceforth {1x}, from henceforth {1x}.

Loipon is the neuter of the adjective *loipos,* remaining (which is used in its different genders as a noun, "the rest"), and is used either with the article or without, to signify "finally," lit., "for the rest." The apostle Paul uses it frequently in the concluding portion of his epistles, introducing practical exhortations, not necessarily implying that the letter is drawing to a close, but marking a transition in the subject matter, as in Phil 3:1, where the actual conclusion is for the time postponed and the farewell injunctions are resumed in 4:8. It is translated **(1)** finally, in 2 Cor 13:11; Eph 6:10; Phil 3:1; 4:8; 2 Th 3:1; **(2)** now, in Mt 26:45; Mk 14:41; **(3)** then, in Acts 27:20; **(4)** besides, in 1 Cor 1:16; **(5)** moreover + 1161 + 3739, in 1 Cor 4:2; **(6)** it remains + 2076, in 1 Cor 7:29; **(7)** furthermore, in 1 Th 4:1; **(8)** henceforth, in 2 Ti 4:8; **(9)** from henceforth, in Heb 10:13. See: BAGD—479d; THAYER—382b.

3064. λοιποῦ {1x} **lŏipŏu,** *loy-poo';* gen. sing. of the same as *3062; remaining* time:—from henceforth {1x}.

Loipou means hereafter, for the future, Gal 6:17. See: BAGD—480a; THAYER—382b.

3065. Λουκᾶς {4x} **Lŏukas,** *loo-kas';* contr. from Lat. *Lucanus; Lucas,* a Chr.:—Lucas {2x}, Luke {2x}. See: BAGD—480b; THAYER—382c.

3066. Λούκιος {2x} **Lŏukiŏs,** *loo'-kee-os;* of Lat. or.; *illuminative; Lucius,* a Chr.:—Lucius {2x}. See: BAGD—480c; THAYER—382d.

3067. λουτρόν {2x} **lŏutrŏn,** *loo-tron';* from *3068;* a *bath,* i.e. (fig.), *baptism:*—washing {2x}.

Loutron, "a bath, a laver" (akin to *louo* – 3068), is used **(1)** metaphorically of the Word of God, as the instrument of spiritual cleansing, Eph 5:26; and **(2)** in Titus 3:5, of "the washing of regeneration." Syn.: 2354, 2875, 3996. See: TDNT—4:295, 538; BAGD—480c; THAYER—382d.

3068. λούω {6x} **lŏuō,** *loo'-o;* a primary verb; to *bathe* (the *whole* person; whereas *3538* means to wet a *part* only, and *4150* to wash, cleanse *garments* exclusively):—wash {6x}. Syn.: 3538, 4150.

Louo signifies "to bathe, to wash the body," **(1)** active voice, Acts 9:37; 16:33; **(2)** passive voice, Jn 13:10, "washed" [completely]; Heb 10:22, lit., "having been washed as to the body," metaphorical of the effect of the Word of God upon the activities of the believer; **(3)** middle voice, 2 Pet 2:22; **(4)** Rev 1:5, we are washed from our sins by His blood. See: TDNT—4:295, 538; BAGD—480d; THAYER—382d.

3069. Λύδδα {3x} **Ludda,** *lud'-dah;* of Heb. or. [3850]; *Lydda* (i.e. *Lod*), a place in Pal.:—Lydda {3x}. See: BAGD—481a; THAYER—383a.

3070. Λυδία {2x} **Ludia,** *loo-dee'-ah;* prop. fem. of Λύδιος **Ludiŏs** [of for. or.] (a *Lydian,* in Asia Minor); *Lydia,* a Chr. woman:—Lydia {2x}. See: BAGD—481b; THAYER—383a.

3071. Λυκαονία {1x} **Lukaŏnia,** *loo-kah-on-ee'-ah;* perh. remotely from *3074; Lycaonia,* a region of Asia Minor:—Lycaonia {1x}. See: BAGD—481b; THAYER—383a.

3072. Λυκαονιστί {1x} **Lukaŏnisti,** *loo-kah-on-is-tee';* adv. from a der. of *3071; Lycaonistically,* i.e. in the language of the Lycaonians:—in the speech of Lycaonia {1x}. See: BAGD—481b; THAYER—383b.

3073. Λυκία {1x} **Lukia,** *loo-kee'-ah;* prob. remotely from *3074; Lycia,* a province of Asia Minor:—Lycia {1x}. See: BAGD—481b; THAYER—383b.

3074. λύκος {6x} **lukŏs,** *loo'-kos;* perh. akin to the base of *3022* (from the *whitish* hair); a *wolf:*—wolf {6x}.

Lukos is **(1)** figuratively literal in Jn 10:12 twice; and **(2)** metaphorically, *lukos* speaks of cruel, greedy, rapacious, destructive men (Mt 7:15; 10:16; Lk 10:3; Acts 20:29). See: TDNT—4:308, 540; BAGD—481b; THAYER—383b.

3075. λυμαίνομαι {1x} **lumainŏmai,** *loo-mah'-ee-nom-ahee;* mid. voice from a prob. der. of *3089* (mean. *filth*); prop. to *soil,* i.e. (fig.) *insult* (*maltreat*):—make havock of {1x}.

This word means to affix a stigma to, to dishonour, spot, defile, to treat shamefully or with injury, to ravage, devastate, ruin, Acts 8:3. See: TDNT—4:312, 540; BAGD—481c; THAYER—383b.

3076. λυπέω {26x} **lupěō,** *loo-peh'-o;* from *3077;* to *distress;* refl. or pass. to *be sad:*—be sorrowful {6x}, grieve {6x}, make sorry {6x}, be sorry {3x}, sorrow {3x}, cause grief {1x}, be in heaviness {1x}.

Lupeo denotes **(1)** in the active voice, **(1a)** "to cause pain, or grief, to distress, grieve," e.g., 2 Cor 2:2 (twice, active and passive voices); **(1b)** 2 Cor 2:5 (twice), "have caused grief," and "grieved"; **(1c)** 2 Cor 7:8, "made (you) sorry"; **(1d)** Eph 4:30, of grieving the Holy Spirit of God (as indwelling the believer); **(2)** in the passive voice, **(2a)** "to be grieved, to be made sorry, to be sorry, sorrowful," e.g., Mt 14:9, "(the king) was sorry"; **(2b)** Mk 10:22, "(went away) grieved"; **(2c)** Jn 21:17, "(Peter) was grieved"; **(2d)** Rom 14:15, "(if . . . thy brother) is grieved"; **(2e)** 2 Cor 2:4, "(not that) ye should be grieved." See: TDNT—4:313, 540; BAGD—481c; THAYER—383b.

3077. λύπη {16x} **lupē,** *loo'-pay;* appar. a primary word; *sadness:*—sorrow {11x}, heaviness {2x}, grievous {1x}, grudging + 1537 {1x}, grief {1x}.

Lupe, as a noun, means "grief, sorrow" and is translated **(1)** "sorrow": "And when he rose up from prayer, and was come to his disciples, he found them sleeping for sorrow," (Lk 22:45; cf. Jn 16:6, 20–22; 2 Cor 2:3, 7; 7:10 [twice]; Phil 2:27 [twice]) or **(2)** "heaviness": "That I have great heaviness (*lupe*) and continual sorrow (3601 – *odune*) in my heart" (Rom 9:2; cf. 2 Cor 2:1). Syn.: 253, 3076, 3600, 3601, 3997, 4036, 5604. See: TDNT—4:313, 540; BAGD—482a; THAYER—383c.

3078. **Λυσανίας** {1x} **Lusanias,** *loo-san-ee'-as;* from *3080* and ἀνία **ania** (*trouble*); *grief-dispelling; Lysanias,* a governor of Abilene:—Lysanias {1x}. See: BAGD—482b; THAYER—383c.

3079. **Λυσίας** {3x} **Lusias,** *loo-see'-as;* of uncert. aff.; *Lysias,* a Rom.:—Lysias {3x}. See: BAGD—482b; THAYER—384a.

3080. **λύσις** {1x} **lusis,** *loo'-sis;* from *3089;* a *loosening,* i.e. (spec.) *divorce:*—to be loosed {1x}. See: BAGD—482b; THAYER—384a.

3081. **λυσιτελεῖ** {1x} **lusitĕlĕi,** *loo-sit-el-i';* third pers. sing. pres. ind. act. of a der. of a compound of *3080* and *5056;* impers. it *answers* the *purpose,* i.e. *is advantageous:*—it is better {1x}.

Lusitelei signifies "to indemnify, pay expenses, pay taxes" (from *luo,* "to loose," *telos,* "toll, custom"); hence, "to be useful, advantageous, to be better" Lk 17:2. See: BAGD—482b; THAYER—384a.

3082. **Λύστρα** {6x} **Lustra,** *loos'-trah;* of uncert. or.; *Lystra,* a place in Asia Minor:—Lystra {6x}. See: BAGD—482c; THAYER—384a.

3083. **λύτρον** {2x} **lutrŏn,** *loo'-tron;* from *3089;* something to *loosen* with, i.e. a redemption *price* (fig. *atonement*):—ransom {2x}.

Lutron, lit., "a means of loosing" (from *luo,* "to loose"), and **(1)** in the OT where it is always used to signify "equivalence." Thus it is used of the "ransom" **(1a)** for a life, e.g., Ex 21:30, **(1b)** of the redemption price of a slave, e.g., Lev 19:20, **(1c)** of land, Lev 25:24, **(1d)** of the price of a captive, Is 45:13.

(2) In the NT it **(2a)** occurs in Mt 20:28 and Mk 10:45, where it is used of Christ's gift of Himself as "a ransom for many." **(2b)** Christ paid the ransom to God, to satisfy violated holiness and righteousness. He did not pay the ransom to Satan or to some impersonal power such as death, or evil. That Christ gave up His life in expiatory sacrifice under God's judgment upon sin and thus provided a "ransom" whereby those who receive Him on this ground obtain deliverance from the penalty due to sin, is what Scripture teaches. **(2c)** What the Lord states in the two passages mentioned involves this essential character of His death. In these passages the preposition is *anti,* which has a vicarious significance, indicating that the "ransom" holds good for those who, accepting it as such, no longer remain in death since Christ suffered death in their stead. **(2d)** The change of preposition in 1 Ti 2:6, where the word *antilutron.*

Substitutionary "ransom," is used, is significant. There the preposition is *huper,* "on behalf of," and the statement is made that He "gave Himself a ransom for all," indicating that the "ransom" was provisionally universal, while being of a vicarious character. **(2e)** Thus the three passages consistently show that while the provision was universal, for Christ died for all men, yet it is actual for those only who accept God's conditions, and who are described in the Gospel statements as "the many." **(2f)** The giving of His life was the giving of His entire person, and while His death under divine judgment was alone expiatory, it cannot be dissociated from the character of His life which, being sinless, gave virtue to His death and was a testimony to the fact that His death must be of a vicarious nature. See: TDNT—4:328 & 4:340, 543; BAGD—482c; THAYER—384a.

3084. **λυτρόω** {3x} **lutrŏō,** *loo-trŏ'-o;* from *3083;* to *ransom* (lit. or fig.):—redeem {3x}.

Lutroo, as a verb, means "to release on receipt of ransom" and **(1)** is used **in the middle voice,** signifying "to release by paying a ransom price, to redeem" **(1a)** in the natural sense of delivering: "But we trusted that it had been He which should have redeemed Israel: and beside all this, to day is the third day since these things were done" (Lk 24:21 - of setting Israel free from the Roman yoke); **(1b)** in a spiritual sense: "Who gave Himself for us, that He might redeem us from all iniquity, and purify unto Himself a peculiar people, zealous of good works" (Titus 2:14 - of the work of Christ in "redeeming" men "from all iniquity" (*anomia* - 459 "lawlessness," the bondage of self-will which rejects the will of God); **(1c) in the passive voice,** "ye were redeemed," from a vain manner of life, i.e., from bondage to tradition: "Forasmuch as ye know that ye were not redeemed with corruptible things, as silver and gold, from your vain conversation received by tradition from your fathers" (1 Pet 1:18). **(2)** In both instances the death of Christ is stated as the means of "redemption." Syn.: *Exagorazo* (*1805*) does not signify the actual "redemption," but the price paid with a view to it. *Lutroo* signifies the actual "deliverance," the setting at liberty. See also: 629, 3085. See: TDNT—4:349, 543; BAGD—482d; THAYER—384a.

3085. **λύτρωσις** {3x} **lutrōsis,** *loo'-tro-sis;* from *3084;* a *ransoming* (fig.):—redeemed + 4160 {1x}, redemption {2x}.

Lutrosis, as a noun, means "a redemption" and is used **(1)** in the general sense of "deliverance," of the nation of Israel (Lk 1:68; 2:38; and

(2) of "the redemptive work" of Christ (Heb 9:12), bringing deliverance through His death, from the guilt and power of sin. Syn.: 625. See: TDNT—4:351, 543; BAGD—483; THAYER—384b.

3086. **λυτρωτής** {1x} **lutrōtēs**, *loo-tro-tace';* from *3084;* a *redeemer* (fig.):—deliverer {1x}.

Lutrotes, as a noun, means "a redeemer, one who releases" and is translated "deliverer" in Acts 7:35: "This Moses whom they refused, saying, Who made thee a ruler and a judge? the same did God send to be a ruler and a deliverer by the hand of the angel which appeared to him in the bush." Syn.: 325, 525, 629, 591, 859, 1325, 1560, 1659, 1807, 1929, 3860, 4506, 5483. See: TDNT—4:351, 543; BAGD—483a; THAYER—384b.

3087. **λυχνία** {12x} **luchnia**, *lookh-nee'-ah;* from *3088;* a *lamp-stand* (lit. or fig.):—candlestick {12x}.

This is the stand ["the stick"] upon which a portable light sits [is stuck]; not the candle [the light producer] itself [see 3088]. See: TDNT—4:324, 542; BAGD—483a; THAYER—384b.

3088. **λύχνος** {14x} **luchnŏs**, *lookh'-nos;* from the base of *3022;* a portable *lamp* or other *illuminator* (lit. or fig.):—candle {8x}, light {6x}.

Luchnos, "candle," is a portable "lamp" usually set on a stand (see 3087); the word is used **(1)** literally, Mt 5:15; Mk 4:21; Lk 8:16; 11:33, 36; 15:8; Rev 18:23; 22:5; **(2)** metaphorically, **(2a)** of Christ as the Lamb, Rev 21:23, "the light"; **(2b)** of John the Baptist, Jn 5:35, "a . . . light"; **(2c)** "light" of the eye/body, Mt 6:22, and Lk 11:34; **(2d)** of spiritual readiness, Lk 12:35 "lights be burning"; **(2e)** of "the word of prophecy," 2 Pet 1:19 "a light shining". See: TDNT—4:324, 542; BAGD—483b; THAYER—384c.

3089. **λύω** {43x} **luō**, *loo'-o;* a primary verb; to *"loosen"* (lit. or fig.):—loose {27x}, break {5x}, unloose {3x}, destroy {2x}, dissolve {2x}, put off {1x}, melt {1x}, break up {1x}, break down {1x}.

Luo denotes **(1)** "to loose, unbind, release," **(1a1)** of things, e.g., in Mk 1:7 "shoes"; **(1a2)** of animals, e.g., Mt 21:2; **(1a3)** of persons, e.g., Jn 11:44; Acts 22:30; **(1a4)** of Satan, Rev 20:3, 7; and **(1a5)** angels, Rev 9:14, 15; **(1b)** metaphorically, **(1b1)** of one diseased, Lk 13:16; **(1b2)** of the marriage tie, 1 Cor 7:27; **(1c)** "to loosen, break up, dismiss, dissolve, destroy"; in this sense it is translated "to loose" in **(1c1)** Acts 2:24, of the pains of death; **(1c2)** in Rev 5:2, of the seals of a roll; **(2)** "breaking, destructively," e.g., **(2a)** of "breaking" commandments, not only infringing them, but loosing the force of them,

rendering them not binding, Mt 5:19; Jn 5:18; **(2b)** of "breaking" the Law of Moses, Jn 7:23; **(2c)** Scripture, Jn 10:35; **(2d)** non-destructively, a congregation, Acts 13:43; **(3)** "unloose" in Mk 1:7; Lk 3:16; Jn 1:27; **(4)** "destroy" in **(4a)** in 1 Jn 3:8, of the works of the devil; and **(4b)** Jn 2:19 of Christ's body figuratively called "temple"; **(5)** "dissolve" in 2 Pet 3:11–12, of the earth and its elements; **(6)** "put off" in Acts 7:33; **(7)** "melt" in 2 Pet 3: 10; **(8)** "break up" in Acts 27:41, of the "breaking up" of a ship; **(9)** "break down" in Eph 2:14, of the "breaking down" of the middle wall of partition, Eph 2:14. See: TDNT—2:60 & 4:328, 543; BAGD—483c; THAYER—384d. comp. *4486.*

3090. **Λωΐς** {1x} **Lōïs**, *lo-ece';* of uncert. or.; *Loïs,* a Chr. woman:—*Lois* {1x}. See: BAGD—484c; THAYER—385c.

3091. **Λώτ** {4x} **Lōt**, *lote;* of Heb. or. [3876]; *Lot,* a patriarch:—*Lot* {4x}. See: BAGD—484c; THAYER—385c.

M

3092. **Μααθ** {1x} **Maath**, *mah-ath';* prob. of Heb. or.; *Maath,* an Isr.:—*Maath* {1x}. See: BAGD—484b; THAYER—385b.

3093. **Μαγδαλά** {1x} **Magdala**, *mag-dal-ah';* of Chald. or. [comp. 4026]; *the tower; Magdala* (i.e. *Migdala*), a place in Pal.:—*Magdala* {1x}. See: BAGD—484b; THAYER—385b.

3094. **Μαγδαληνή** {12x} **Magdalēnē**, *mag-dal-ay-nay';* fem. of a der. of *3093;* a female *Magdalene,* i.e. inhab. of Magdala:—*Magdalene* {12x}. See: BAGD—484b; THAYER—385d.

3095. **μαγεία** {1x} **mageia**, *mag-i'-ah;* from *3096;* "magic":—sorcery {1x}.

Mageia, "the magic art," is used in the plural in Acts 8:11, "sorceries. See: TDNT—4:359, 547; BAGD—484b; THAYER—385d.

3096. **μαγεύω** {1x} **mageuō**, *mag-yoo'-o;* from *3097;* to *practice magic:*—use sorcery {1x}.

Mageuo, "to practice magic," Acts 8:9, "used sorcery," is used as in 3095, of Simon Magus. See: TDNT—4:359, 547; BAGD—484d; THAYER—385d.

3097. **μάγος** {6x} **magŏs**, *mag'-os;* of for. or. [7248]; a *Magian,* i.e. Oriental astrologer, *scientist;* by impl. a *magician:*—sorcerer {2x}, wise man {4x}.

Magos, denotes **(1)** "a wizard, sorcerer, a pretender to magic powers, a professor of the

arts of witchcraft," Acts 13:6, 8, where Bar-Jesus was the Jewish name, *Elymas,* an Arabic word meaning "wise." Hence the name Magus, "the magician," originally applied to Persian priests. **(2)** It also denotes "a Magian," one of a sacred caste, originally Median, who apparently conformed to the Persian religion while retaining their old beliefs; it is used in the plural, Mt 2:1, 7, 16 (twice), "wise men." See: TDNT—4:356, 547; BAGD—484d; THAYER—385d.

3098. Μαγώγ {1x} **Magōg,** *mag-ogue';* of Heb. or. [4031]; *Magog,* a for. nation, i.e. (fig.) an Antichristian party:—*Magog* {1x}. See: TDNT—1:789,*; BAGD—485b; THAYER—386a.

3099. Μαδιάν {1x} **Madian,** *mad-ee-on'* or

Μαδιάμ **Madiam,** *mad-ee-on';* of Heb. origin [4080]; *Madian* (i.e. *Midian*), a region of Arabia:—*Madian* {1x}. See: BAGD—485b; THAYER—386a.

3100. μαθητεύω {4x} **mathētĕuō,** *math-ayt-yoo'-o;* from *3101;* intr. to *become a pupil;* tran. to *disciple,* i.e. enroll as scholar:—be disciple {1x}, instruct {1x}, teach {2x}.

Matheteuo is used **(1)** in the active voice, intransitively, in some mss., in Mt 27:57, in the sense of being the "disciple" of a person; **(2)** Mt 13:52, "which is instructed." **(3)** It is used in the transitive sense in the active voice in **(3a)** Mt 28:19, "teach", and **(3b)** Acts 14:21, "taught." See: TDNT—4:461, 552; BAGD—485c; THAYER—386a.

3101. μαθητής {269x} **mathētēs,** *math-ay-tes';* from *3129; a learner,* i.e. *pupil:*—disciple {269x}.

Mathetes, lit., "a learner" (from *manthano,* "to learn," from a root *math*—, indicating thought accompanied by endeavor), in contrast to *didaskalos,* "a teacher"; hence it denotes "one who follows one's teaching," as **(1)** the "disciples" **(1a)** of John, Mt 9:14; **(1b)** of the Pharisees, Mt 22:16; **(1c)** of Moses, Jn 9:28; **(2)** it is used of the "disciples" of Jesus **(2a)** in a wide sense, of Jews who became His adherents, Jn 6:66; Lk 6:17, some being secretly so, Jn 19:38; **(2b)** especially of the twelve apostles, Mt 10:1; Lk 22:11, e.g.; **(3)** of all who manifest that they are His "disciples" by abiding in His Word, Jn 8:31, cf. 13:35; 15:8; **(4)** in the Acts, of those who believed upon Him and confessed Him, 6:1–2, 7; 14:20, 22, 28; 15:10; 19:1, etc. **(5)** A "disciple" was not only a pupil, but an adherent; hence they are spoken of as imitators of their teacher; cf. Jn 8:31; 15:8. Syn.: 3102, 4827. See: TDNT—4:415, 552; BAGD—485c; THAYER—386a.

3102. μαθήτρια {1x} **mathētria,** *math-ay'-tree-ah;* fem. from *3101;* a female *pupil:*—disciple {1x}.

Mathatria, "a female disciple," is said of Tabitha, Acts 9:36. See: TDNT—4:460, 552; BAGD—486a; THAYER—386b.

3103. Μαθουσάλα {1x} **Mathŏusala,** *math-oo-sal'-ah;* of Heb. or. [4968]; *Mathusala* (i.e. *Methushelach*), an antediluvian:—Mathusala {1x}. See: BAGD—486b; THAYER—386b.

3104. Μαϊνάν {1x} **Maïnan,** *mahee-nan';* prob. of Heb. or.; *Maïnan,* an Isr.:—Mainan {1x}. See: BAGD—486b; THAYER—386b.

3105. μαίνομαι {5x} **mainŏmai,** *mah'-ee-nom-ahee;* mid. voice from a primary μάω **maō** (to *long* for; through the idea of insensate *craving*); to *rave* as a "maniac":—be mad {4x}, be beside (one's) self {1x}.

Mainomai, "to be mad, to rave", is said **(1)** of one who so speaks that he appears to be out of his mind, out of himself, beside himself, Acts 26:24, translated "thou art beside thyself"; **(2)** of one is said "to be mad" in Jn 10:20; Acts 12:15; 26:24, 25; 1 Cor 14:23. See: TDNT—4:360, 548; BAGD—486b; THAYER—386c.

3106. μακαρίζω {2x} **makarizō,** *mak-ar-id'-zo;* from *3107;* to *beatify,* i.e. *pronounce* (or *esteem*) *fortunate:*—call blessed {1x}, count happy {1x}.

Makarizo, from a root *mak,* meaning "large, lengthy," found also in *makros,* "long," *mekos,* "length," hence denotes "to pronounce happy, blessed", Lk 1:48 and Jas 5:11. See: TDNT—4:362, 548; BAGD—486a; THAYER—386c.

3107. μακάριος {50x} **makariŏs,** *mak-ar'-ee-os;* a prol. form of the poet. μάκαρ **makar** (mean. the same); supremely *blest;* by extens. *fortunate, well off:*—blessed {44x}, happy {5x}, happier {1x}.

Makarios is used **(1)** in the beatitudes in Mt 5 and Lk 6, is especially frequent in the Gospel of Luke, and is found seven times in Revelation, 1:3; 14:13; 16:15; 19:9; 20:6; 22:7, 14. **(2)** It is said of God twice, 1 Ti 1:11; 6:15. **(3)** In the beatitudes the Lord indicates not only the characters that are "blessed," but the nature of that which is the highest good. See: TDNT—4:362, 548; BAGD—486c; THAYER—386c.

3108. μακαρισμός {3x} **makarismŏs,** *mak-ar-is-mos';* from *3106; beatification,* i.e. *attribution of good fortune:*—blessedness {3x}.

Mararismos denotes "a declaration of blessedness, a felicitation"; it is translated **(1)** "blessedness" in Gal 4:15; the Galatian converts had

counted themselves happy when they heard and received the gospel from Paul; he asks them rhetorically what had become of that spirit which had animated them; **(2)** the word is rendered "blessing" in Rom 4:6, 9. See: TDNT—4:362, 548; BAGD—487a; THAYER—386c.

3109. **Μακεδονία** {24x} **Makĕdŏnia,** *mak-ed-on-ee′-ah;* from *3110; Macedonia,* a region of Greece:—Macedonia {24x}. See: BAGD—487b; THAYER—386c.

3110. **Μακεδών** {5x} **Makĕdōn,** *mak-ed′-ohn;* of uncert. der.; a *Macedon (Macedonian),* i.e. inhab. of Macedonia:—of Macedonia {4x}, Macedonian {1x}. See: BAGD—487b; THAYER—386b.

3111. **μάκελλον** {1x} **makĕllŏn,** *mak′-el-lon;* of Lat. or. [*macellum*]; a *butcher's stall, meat market* or *provision-shop:*—shambles {1x}.

Due to the unkempt nature of the slaughter house, the benches upon which the meat was sold [Lat. shambles] became synonymous with anything disorderly. A plan, drawn by Lietzmann, of a forum in Pompeii, shows both the slaughterhouse and the meat shop next to the chapel of Caesar. Some of the meat which had been used for sacrificial purposes was afterwards sold in the markets. The apostle enjoins upon the believer to enter into no inquiry, so as to avoid the troubling of conscience, 1 Cor 10:25; (contrast v. 28). See: TDNT—4:370, 549; BAGD—487b; THAYER—386d.

3112. **μακράν** {10x} **makran,** *mak-ran′;* fem. acc. sing. of *3117 (3598* being impl.); *at a distance* (lit. or fig.):—far {4x}, afar off {2x}, good way off {1x}, far hence {1x}, great way off {1x}, far off {1x}.

Makran, a feminine adjective, from *macros,* **(1)** "far," Mt 8:20 "a good way"; **(2)** "a long way off," is used with *eis,* "unto," in Acts 2:39, "afar off." **(3)** With the article, in Eph 2:13, 17, it signifies "the (ones) far off." It also denotes **(4)** "a long way, far," **(4a)** literally, Mt 8:30; Lk 7:6; 15:20; Jn 21:8; Acts 17:27; 22:21; **(4b)** metaphorically, "far (from the kingdom of God)," Mk 12:34; **(4c)** in spiritual darkness, Acts 2:39; Eph 2:13, 17; **(5)** "a good (or great) way off," Mt 8:30; Lk 15:20. See: TDNT—4:372, 549; BAGD—487c; THAYER—386b.

3113. **μακρόθεν** {14x} **makrŏthĕn,** *mak-roth′-en;* adv. from *3117; from a distance* or *afar:*—afar off {13x}, from far {1x}. See: TDNT—4:372, 549; BAGD—487d; THAYER—387a.

3114. **μακροθυμέω** {10x} **makrŏthumĕō,** *mak-roth-oo-meh′-o;* from the same as *3116;* to *be long-spirited,* i.e. (obj.) *forbearing* or (subj.) *patient:*—be patient {3x}, have patience {2x}, have long patience {1x}, bear long {1x}, suffer long {1x}, be longsuffering {1x}, patiently endure {1x}.

Makrothumeo is **(1)** to be of a long spirit, not to lose heart; **(2)** to persevere patiently and bravely in enduring misfortunes and troubles; **(3)** to be patient in bearing the offenses and injuries of others and to be mild and slow in avenging; **(4)** to be longsuffering, slow to anger, slow to punish. **(5)** It means "to be long-tempered" (*makros,* "long," *thumos,* "temper"), and is translated **(5a)** "to be patient" in 1 Th 5:14; Jas 5:7 first part; Jas 5:8; **(5b)** "to have patience," Mt 18:26, 29; **(5c)** "have long patience" in Jas 5:7, second part; **(5d)** "bear long with " in Lk 18:7; **(5e)** "suffereth long" in 1 Cor 13:4; **(5f)** "be longsuffering" in 2 Pet 3:9; **(5g)** "after he had patiently endured" in Heb 6:15. See: TDNT—4:374, 550; BAGD—488a; THAYER—387a.

3115. **μακροθυμία** {14x} **makrŏthumia,** *mak-roth-oo-mee′-ah;* from the same as *3116; longanimity,* i.e. (obj.) *forbearance* or (subj.) *fortitude:*—longsuffering {12x}, patience {2x}. "forbearance, patience, longsuffering" (*makros,* "long," *thumos,* "temper"), is usually rendered **(1)** "longsuffering," Rom 2:4; 9:22; 2 Cor 6:6; Gal 5:22; Eph 4:2; Col 1:11; 3:12; 1 Ti 1:16; 2 Ti 3:10; 4:2; 1 Pet 3:20; 2 Pet 3:15; **(2)** "patience" in Heb. 6:12 and Jas. 5:10. **(3)** One who possesses *makrothumia* has the power to avenge but refrains from doing so. Syn.: 463, 5281. See: TDNT—4:374, 550; BAGD—488b; THAYER—387b.

3116. **μακροθυμώς** {1x} **makrŏthumōs,** *mak-roth-oo-moce′;* adv. of a compound of *3117* and *2372; with long (enduring) temper,* i.e. *leniently:*—patiently {1x}. See: TDNT—4:387, 550; BAGD—488b; THAYER—387c.

3117. **μακρός** {5x} **makrŏs,** *mak-ros′;* from *3372; long* (in place [*distant*] or time [neut. plur.]):—far {2x}, long {3x}.

Makros is used **(1)** of space and time, long, said of prayers, in Mt 23:14, Mk 12:40; Lk 20:47; **(2)** of distance, "far, far" distant, Lk 15:13; 19:12. See: BAGD—488c; THAYER—387c.

3118. **μακροχρόνιος** {1x} **makrŏchrŏniŏs,** *mak-rokh-ron′-ee-os;* from *3117* and *5550; long-timed,* i.e. *long-lived:*—live long {1x}. See: BAGD—488c; THAYER—387d.

3119. μαλακία {3x} **malakia**, *mal-ak-ee'-ah;* from *3120; softness,* i.e. *enervation* (*debility*):—disease {3x}.

Malakia means infirmity, debility, bodily weakness, sickness found in Matthew only (4:23; 9:35; 10:1). See: TDNT—4:1091, 655; BAGD—488c; THAYER—387b.

3120. μαλακός {4x} **malakŏs**, *mal-ak-os';* of uncert. aff.; *soft,* i.e. *fine* (clothing); fig. a *catamite:*—effeminate {1x}, soft {3x}.

Malakos is used (1) of raiment, Mt 11:8 (twice); Lk 7:25; (2) metaphorically, in a bad sense, 1 Cor 6:9, "effeminate," not simply of a male who practices forms of lewdness, but persons in general, who are guilty of addiction to sins of the flesh, voluptuous. See: BAGD—488d; THAYER—387d.

3121. Μαλελεήλ {1x} **Malĕlĕēl**, *mal-el-eh-ale';* of Heb. or. [4111]; *Maleleël* (i.e. *Mahalalel*), an antediluvian:—Maleleel {1x}. See: BAGD—488d; THAYER—387d.

3122. μάλιστα {12x} **malista**, *mal'-is-tah;* neut. plur. of the superl. of an appar. primary adv. μάλα **mala** (*very*); (adv.) *most* (*in the greatest degree*) or *particularly:*—specially {5x}, especially {4x}, chiefly {2x}, most of all {1x}.

Malista, "most, most of all, above all", "very, very much," is the superlative of *mala,* "very much" and is translated (1) "specially," Acts 25:26; 1 Ti 4:10; 5:8; Titus 1:10; Philem 16; (2) "especially" in Acts 26:3; Gal 6:10; 1 Ti 5:17; 2 Ti 4:13; (3) "chiefly" in 2 Pet 2:10; Phil 4:22; (4) in Acts 20:38, "most of all." "Specially" and "especially" both describe something as distinct, attention–getting and unique in relation to another. Especially is an intensified form which may, according to context, denote preeminence. Both draw attention to source; special having to do within a circle of influence; whereas, especially implies an outside influence. See: BAGD—488d; THAYER—387d.

3123. μᾶλλον {85x} **mallŏn**, *mal'-lon;* neut. of the comparative of the same as *3122;* (adv.) *more* (*in a greater degree*) or *rather:*—more {34x}, rather {33x}, the more {12x}, better + 2570 {2x}, misc. {4x}.

Mallon, the comparative degree of *mala,* "very, very much," is used (1) of increase, "more," (1a) with qualifying words, with *pollo,* "much," e.g., Mk 10:48, "the more (a great deal)"; Rom 5:15, 17, "(much) more"; Phil 2:12 (ditto); (1b) with *poso,* "how much," e.g., Lk 12:24; Rom 11:12; (1c) with *tosouto,* "by so much," Heb 10:25; (2) without a qualifying word, by way of comparison, "the more," e.g.,

(2a) Lk 5:15, "so much the more"; (2b) Jn 5:18, "the more"; Acts 5:14; Phil 1:9; 1 Th 4:1, 10, "more and more"; (2c) in Acts 20:35, by a periphrasis, it is translated "more (blessed)"; (2d) in Gal 4:27, "more (than)," lit., "rather (than)"; (3) with qualifying words, similarly to, e.g., Mk 7:36. (4) It is also translated "rather": e.g., Mt 10:6, 28; 1 Cor 14:1, 5; (4a) sometimes followed by "than," with a connecting particle, e.g., Mt 18:13 ("more than"); (4b) or without, e.g., Jn 3:19; Acts 4:19, "more"; (4c) in 1 Cor 9:12, "rather"; 12:22, "more"; 2 Cor 3:9; Philem 16; (4d) in 2 Pet 1:10, "the rather." See: BAGD—489a; THAYER—387d.

3124. Μάλχος {1x} **Malchŏs**, *mal'-khos;* of Heb. or. [4429]; *Malchus,* an Isr.:—Malchus {1x}. See: BAGD—489d; THAYER—388c.

3125. μάμμη {1x} **mammē**, *mam'-may;* of nat. or. ["mammy"]; a *grandmother:*—grandmother {1x}. See: BAGD—490a; THAYER—388c.

3126. μαμμωνᾶς {4x} **mammōnas** *mam-mo-nas',* or

μαμωνᾶς **mamōnas** *mam-o-nas';* of Chald. or. (*confidence,* i.e. *wealth,* personified); *mammonas,* i.e. *avarice* (deified):—mammon {4x}.

Mamonas, a common Aramaic word for "riches," akin to a Hebrew word signifying "to be firm, steadfast" (whence "Amen"), hence, "that which is to be trusted"; it is personified in Mt 6:24; Lk 16:9, 11, 13. See: TDNT—4:388, 552; BAGD—490a; THAYER—388d.

3127. Μαναήν {1x} **Manaēn**, *man-ah-ane';* of uncert. or.; *Manaën,* a Chr.:—Manaen {1x}. See: BAGD—490a; THAYER—388d.

3128. Μανασσῆς {3x} **Manassēs**, *man-as-sace';* of Heb. or. [4519]; *Mannasses* (i.e. *Menashsheh*), an Isr.:—Manasses {3x}. See: BAGD—490b; THAYER—388d.

3129. μανθάνω {25x} **manthanō**, *man-than'-o;* prol. from a primary verb, another form of which, μαθέω **mathĕo**, is used as an alt. in cert. tenses; to *learn* (in any way):—learn {24x}, understand {1x}.

Manthano, as a verb, denotes (1) "to learn" [akin to *mathetes* - 3101, "a disciple"), "to increase one's knowledge," or "be increased in knowledge," frequently "to learn by inquiry, or observation" (e.g., Mt 9:13; 11:29; 24:32; Mk 13:28; Jn 7:15; Rom 16:17; 1 Cor 4:6; 14:35; Phil 4:9; 2 Ti 3:14; Rev 14:3); (2) said of "learning" Christ (Eph 4:20), not simply the doctrine of Christ, but Christ Himself, a process not

merely of getting to know the person but of so applying the knowledge as to walk differently from the rest of the Gentiles; **(3)** "to ascertain" (Acts 23:27 KJV, "understood"); **(4)** Gal 3:2, "This only would I learn from you," perhaps with a tinge of irony in the enquiry, the answer to which would settle the question of the validity of the new Judaistic gospel they were receiving; **(5)** "to learn by use and practice, to acquire the habit of, be accustomed to," (e.g., Phil 4:11; 1 Ti 5:4, 13; Titus 3:14; Heb 5:8). Syn.: 198, 1097, 3453. See: TDNT—4:390, 552; BAGD—490b; THAYER—388d.

3130. **μανία** {1x} **mania**, *man-ee'-ah;* from *3105; craziness:*—[+ make] × mad {1x}.

Mania, transliterated into English, denotes "frenzy, madness," Acts 26:24 "(thy much learning doth make thee) mad." See: BAGD—490d; THAYER—389b.

3131. **μάννα** {5x} **manna**, *man'-nah;* of Heb. or. [4478]; *manna* (i.e. *man*), an edible wafer:—*manna* {5x}.

Manna, as a noun, means **(1)** the supernaturally provided food for Israel during their wilderness journey (for details see Ex 16 and Num 11). **(2)** It is described in Ps 78:24, 25 as "the corn of heaven" and "angels' food" and in 1 Cor 10:3, as "spiritual meat." **(3)** The vessel appointed to contain it, as a perpetual memorial, was of gold, Heb 9:4, with Ex 16:33. **(4)** The Lord speaks of it as being typical of Himself, the true Bread from Heaven, imparting eternal life and sustenance to those who by faith partake spiritually of Him, Jn 6:31–35. **(5)** The "hidden manna" is promised as one of the rewards of the overcomer, Rev 2:17; it is thus suggestive of the moral excellence of Christ in His life on earth, hid from the eyes of men, by whom He was "despised and rejected"; the path of the overcomer is a reflex of His life. See: TDNT—4:462, 563; BAGD—490d; THAYER—389b.

3132. **μαντεύομαι** {1x} **mantĕuŏmai**, *mant-yoo'-om-ahee;* from a der. of *3105* (mean. a *prophet,* as supposed to *rave* through *inspiration*); to *divine,* i.e. *utter spells* (under pretense of foretelling):—by soothsaying {1x}.

This word refers to the tumult of the mind, to the fury or temporary madness of those who were supposedly possessed by the god during the time they uttered their message. It is the art of heathen divination, Acts 16:16. Syn.: 4395. See: BAGD—491a; THAYER—389c.

3133. **μαραίνω** {1x} **marainō**, *mar-ah'-ee-no;* of uncert. aff.; to *extinguish* (as fire), i.e. (fig. and pass.) to *pass away:*—fade away {1x}.

Maraino, as a verb, in the active voice, means "to quench, waste, wear out"; in the passive, "to waste away" Jas 1:11, of the "fading" away of a rich man, as illustrated by the flower of the field. Syn.: 262, 263. See: BAGD—491b; THAYER—389d.

3134. **μαρὰν ἀθά** {1x} **maran atha**, *mar-an' ath-ah';* of Chald. or. (mean. *our Lord has come*); *maranatha,* i.e. an exclamation of the approaching *divine judgment:*—Maran-atha {1x}.

Maran-atha, **(1)** an expression used in 1 Cor 16:22, **(2)** is the Greek spelling for two Aramaic words, **(3)** formerly supposed by some to be an imprecatory utterance or "a curse reinforced by a prayer," an idea contrary to the intimations conveyed by its use in early Christian documents, e.g., "The Teaching of the Apostles," a document of the beginning of the 2nd cent., and in the "Apostolic Constitutions" (vii. 26), where it is used as follows: "Gather us all together into Thy Kingdom which Thou hast prepared. *Maranatha,* Hosanna to the Son of David; blessed is He that cometh, etc." **(4)** The first part, ending in 'n,' signifies "Lord"; as to the second part, the Fathers regarded it as a past tense, "has come." Modern expositors take it as equivalent to a present, "cometh," or future, "will come." Certain Aramaic scholars regard the last part as consisting of *tha,* and regard the phrase as an ejaculation, "Our Lord, come," or "O Lord, come."

(5) The character of the context, however, indicates that the apostle is making a statement rather than expressing a desire or uttering a prayer. **(6)** As to the reason why it was used, most probably it was a current proclamation among early Christians, as embodying the consummation of their desires. **(7)** At first the title *Marana* or *Maran,* used in speaking to and of Christ was no more than the respectful designation of the Teacher on the part of the disciples. After His resurrection they used the title of or to Him as applied to God, but it must here be remembered that the Aramaic-speaking Jews did not, save exceptionally, designate God as "Lord"; so that in the "Hebraist" section of the Jewish Christians the expression "our Lord" (*Marana*) was used in reference to Christ only. See: TDNT—4:466, 563; BAGD—491b; THAYER—389d.

3135. **μαργαρίτης** {9x} **margaritēs**, *mar-gar-ee'-tace;* from μάργ-αρος **margarŏs** (a pearl-*oyster*); a *pearl:*—pearl {9x}.

Margarite, "a pearl" (Eng., Margaret), occurs in Mt 7:6 (proverbially and figuratively); 13:45, 46; 1 Ti 2:9; Rev 17:4; 18:12, 16; 21:21 (twice). See: TDNT—4:472, 564; BAGD—91c; THAYER—389d.

3136. Μάρθα {13x} **Martha,** *mar'-thah;* prob. of Chald. or. (mean. *mistress*); *Martha,* a Chr. woman:—*Martha* {13x}. See: BAGD—491c; THAYER—389d.

3137. Μαρία {54x} **Maria,** *mar-ee'-ah;* or

Μαριάμ Mariam, *mar-ee-am';* of Heb. or. [4813]; *Maria* or *Mariam* (i.e. *Mirjam*), the name of six Chr. females:— Mary the mother of Jesus {19x}, Mary Magdalene {13x}, Mary the sister of Martha {11x}, Mary the mother of James {9x}, Mary the mother of John Mark {1x}, Mary of Rome {1x}. See: BAGD—491d; THAYER—389d.

3138. Μάρκος {5x} **Markŏs,** *mar'-kos;* of Lat. or.; *Marcus,* a Chr.:—Marcus {3x}, Mark {5x}. See: BAGD—492b; THAYER—390b.

3139. μάρμαρος {1x} **marmarŏs,** *mar'-mar-os;* from μαρμαίρω **marmairō,** (to *glisten*); *marble* (as sparkling *white*):— marble {1x}.

Marmaros primarily denoted any "glistering stone" (from *maraino,* "to glisten"); hence, "marble," Rev 18:12. See: BAGD—492c; THAYER—390c.

μάρτυρ martur. See *3144.*

3140. μαρτυρέω {79x} **martureō,** *mar-too-reh'-o;* from *3144;* to *be a witness,* i.e. *testify* (lit. or fig.):—bear witness {25x}, testify {19x}, bear record {13x}, witness {5x}, be a witness {2x}, give testimony {2x}, have a good report {2x}, misc. {11x} = charge, give [*evidence*], (obtain, of) good (honest) report, be well reported of.

Martureo, as a verb, denotes **(1)** "to be a *martus*" (*3144*), or "to bear witness to," sometimes rendered "to testify"; **(1a)** It means to affirm that one has seen or heard or experienced something, or **(1b)** that he knows it because taught by divine revelation or inspiration. **(2)** It is used of the witness **(2a)** of God the Father **(2a1)** to Christ: "There is another that beareth witness of me; and I know that the witness which he witnesseth of me is true" (Jn 5:32, cf. v. 37; 8:18; 1 Jn 5:9, 10; **(2a2)** to others: "And when He had removed him, He raised up unto them David to be their king; to whom also He gave testimony, and said, I have found David the son of Jesse, a man after mine own heart, which shall fulfill all my will" (Acts 13:22; cf. 15:8; Heb 11:2, 4 [twice], 5, 39);

(3) of Christ: "Verily, verily, I say unto thee, We speak that we do know, and testify that we have seen; and ye receive not our witness" (Jn 3:11, cf. v. 32; 4:44; 5:31; 7:7; 8:13, 14, 18; 13:21; 18:37; Acts 14:3; 1 Ti 6:13; Rev 22:18, 20); **(4)** of the Holy Spirit to Christ: "But when the Comforter is come, whom I will send unto you from the Father, even the Spirit of truth, which proceedeth from the Father, He shall testify of me" (Jn 15:26; cf. Heb 10:15; 1 Jn 5:7, 8); **(5)** of the Scriptures, to Christ: "Search the scriptures; for in them ye think ye have eternal life: and they are they which testify of me" (Jn 5:39; cf. Heb 7:8, 17); **(6)** of the works of Christ, to Himself, and of the circumstances connected with His death: "But I have greater witness than that of John: for the works which the Father hath given me to finish, the same works that I do, bear witness of me, that the Father hath sent me" (Jn 5:36; cf. 10:25; 1 Jn 5:8);

(7) of prophets and apostles, **(7a)** to the righteousness of God: "But now the righteousness of God without the law is manifested, being witnessed by the law and the prophets" (Rom 3:21); **(7b)** to Christ: "The same [John the baptizer] came for a witness, to bear witness of the Light, that all men through him might believe" (Jn 1:7, 8, 15, 32, 34; 3:26; 15:27; 19:35; 21:24; Acts 10:43; 23:11; 1 Cor 15:15; 1 Jn 1:2; 4:14; Rev 1:2); **(7c)** to doctrine: "Having therefore obtained help of God, I continue unto this day, witnessing both to small and great, saying none other things than those which the prophets and Moses did say should come" (Acts 26:22); **(7d)** to the Word of God: "[John, the apostle] Who bare record of the word of God, and of the testimony of Jesus Christ, and of all things that he saw" (Rev 1:2); **(7e)** of others, concerning Christ: "And all bare Him witness, and wondered at the gracious words which proceeded out of His mouth. And they said, Is not this Joseph's son?" (Lk 4:22; cf. Jn 4:39; 12:17); **(7f)** of believers to one another: "Ye yourselves bear me [John the baptizer] witness, that I said, I am not the Christ, but that I am sent before Him" (Jn 3:28; cf. 2 Cor 8:3; Gal 4:15; Col 4:13; 3 Jn 3, 6, 12); **(7g)** of the apostle Paul concerning Israel (Rom 10:2); **(7h)** of an angel, to the churches (Rev 22:16); **(7i)** of unbelievers, **(7i1)** concerning themselves: "Wherefore ye be witnesses unto yourselves, that ye are the children of them which killed the prophets" (Mt 23:31); **(7i2)** concerning Christ: "Jesus answered him, If I have spoken evil, bear witness of the evil: but if well, why smitest thou me?" (Jn 18:23); **(7i3)** concerning others: "And needed not that any should testify of man: for He knew what was in man" (Jn 2:25; cf. Acts 22:5; 26:5);

(8) *Martureo* means "to give a good report, to approve of": "Wherefore, brethren, look ye out among you seven men of honest report (*martureo*), full of the Holy Ghost and wisdom, whom we may appoint over this business" (Acts 6:3; cf. 10:22; 16:2; 22:12; 1 Ti 5:10; 3 Jn 12). Syn.: 267, 2649, 3141, 3142, 3143, 3144, 4828, 4901, 5571, 5576, 5577. See: TDNT— 4:474, 564; BAGD—492c; THAYER—390c.

3141. μαρτυρία {37x} **marturia,** *mar-too-ree'-ah;* from *3144; evidence* given (judicially or gen.):—record {7x}, report {1x}, testimony {14x}, witness {15x}.

Marturia, as a noun, means "witness, evidence, testimony," is rendered **(1)** "record" in Jn 1:19; 8:13, 14; 19:35; 1 Jn 5:10b, 11, 12; **(2)** "report" in 1 Ti 3:7; **(3)** "testimony" in Jn 3:32, 33; 5:34; 8:17; 21:24; Acts 22:18; Rev 1:2, 9; 6:9; 11:7; 12:11, 17; 19:10 (twice); and **(4)** "witness" in Mk 14:55, 56, 59; Lk 22:71; Jn 1:7; 3:11, 32; 5:31, 32, 36; Titus 1:13; 1 Jn 5:9 (thrice), 10a. **(5)** In Rev 19:10, "the testimony of Jesus" is objective, the "testimony" or witness given to Him (cf. 1:2, 9; as to those who will bear it, see Rev 12:17). The statement "the testimony of Jesus is the spirit of prophecy," is to be understood in the light, e.g., of the "testimony" concerning Christ and Israel in the Psalms, which will be used by the godly Jewish remnant in the coming time of "Jacob's Trouble." All such "testimony" centers in and points to Christ. Syn.: 267, 2649, 3142, 3140, 3143, 3144, 4828, 4901, 5571, 5576, 5577. See: TDNT—4:474, 564; BAGD—493c; THAYER—391c.

3142. μαρτύριον {20x} **marturiŏn,** *mar-too'-ree-on;* neut. of a presumed der. of *3144;* something *evidential,* i.e. (gen.) *evidence* given or (spec.) the *Decalogue* (in the sacred Tabernacle):—to be testified {1x}, testimony {15x}, witness {4x}.

Marturion, as a noun, means "a testimony, witness," and is translated **(1)** "to be testified" in 1 Ti 2:6; **(2)** predominantly "testimony"; and **(3)** "witness" in Mt 24:14; Acts 4:33; 7:44; Jas 5:3. **(4)** In 2 Th 1:10, "our testimony among you," refers to the fact that the missionaries, besides proclaiming the truths of the gospel, had borne witness to the power of these truths. **(4a)** *Kerugma,* "the thing preached, the message," is objective, having especially to do with the effect on the hearers; **(4b)** *marturion* is mainly subjective, having to do especially with the preacher's personal experience. **(5)** In 1 Ti 2:6 "to be testified in due time", i.e., in the times divinely appointed for it, namely, the present age, from Pentecost till the church is complete. **(6)** In Rev 15:5, in the phrase, "the temple of the tabernacle of the testimony in

Heaven," the "testimony" is the witness to the rights of God, denied and refused on earth, but about to be vindicated by the exercise of the judgments under the pouring forth of the seven bowls or vials of divine retribution. Syn.: 267, 2649, 3140, 3141, 3143, 3144, 4828, 4901, 5571, 5576, 5577. See: TDNT—4:474, 564; BAGD—493d; THAYER—391d.

3143. μαρτύρομαι {3x} **marturŏmai,** *mar-too'-rom-ahee;* mid. voice from *3144;* to *be adduced* as a *witness,* i.e. (fig.) to *obtest* (in affirmation or exhortation):—take to record {1x}, testify {2x}.

Marturomai, as a verb, strictly meaning "to summon as a witness," signifies "to affirm solemnly, adjure," and is used in the middle voice only, rendered **(1)** "I take . . . to record" (Acts 20:26); and **(2)** "testify" (Gal 5:3; Eph 4:17). Syn.: 267, 2649, 3140, 3141, 3142, 3144, 4828, 4901, 5571, 5576, 5577. See: TDNT—4:510, 564; BAGD—494a; THAYER—392b.

3144. μάρτυς {34x} **martus,** *mar'-toos;* of uncert. aff.; a *witness* (lit. [judicially] or fig. [gen.]); by anal. a "*martyr*":—martyr {3x}, record {2x}, witness {29x}.

Martus or *martur* (whence Eng., "martyr," one who bears "witness" by his death) **(1)** denotes "one who can or does aver what he has seen or heard or knows"; it is used **(2)** of God: "For God is my witness, whom I serve with my spirit in the gospel of his Son, that without ceasing I make mention of you always in my prayers" (Rom 1:9; cf. 2 Cor 1:23; Phil 1:8; 1 Th 2:5, 10); of Christ, Rev 1:5; 3:14; **(3)** of those who "witness" for Christ by their death (Acts 22:20; Rev 2:13; Rev 17:6); **(4)** of the interpreters of God's counsels, yet to "witness" in Jerusalem in the times of the Antichrist (Rev 11:3); **(5)** in a forensic sense: "But if he will not hear thee, then take with thee one or two more, that in the mouth of two or three witnesses every word may be established" (Mt 18:16; 26:65; Mk 14:63; Acts 6:13; 7:58; 2 Cor 13:1; 1 Ti 5:19; Heb 10:28); **(6)** in a historical sense: "Truly ye bear witness that ye allow the deeds of your fathers: for they indeed killed them, and ye build their sepulchres" (Lk 11:48; cf. 24:48; Acts 1:8, 22; 2:32; 3:15; 5:32; 10:39, 41; 13:31; 22:15; 26:16; 1 Th 2:10; 1 Ti 6:12; 2 Ti 2:2; Heb 12:1, "[a cloud] of witnesses," here of those mentioned in ch. 11, those whose lives and actions testified to the worth and effect of faith, and whose faith received "witness" in Scripture; 1 Pet 5:1). Syn.: 267, 2649, 3140, 3141, 3142, 3143, 4828, 4901, 5571, 5576, 5577. See: TDNT—4:474, 564; BAGD—494b; THAYER—392b.

3145. μασσάομαι {1x} **massaōmai,** *mas-sah'-om-ahee;* from a primary

μάσσω **massō** (to *handle* or *squeeze*); to bite or *chew:*—gnaw {1x}. See: TDNT—4:514, 570; BAGD—392c; THAYER—392c.

3146. μαστιγόω {7x} **mastigŏō**, *mas-tig-ŏ'-o;* from *3148;* to *flog* (lit. or fig.):—to scourge {7x}.

Matigoo is used of (1) Jewish "scourgings" of (1a) Christ, in Mt 20:19; Mk 10:34; Lk 18:33; Jn 19:1; (1b) "apostles", in Mt 10:17; and (1c) "prophets", in Mt 23:34; (1d) "believers", metaphorically, in Heb 12:6, of the "chastening" by the Lord administered in love to His spiritual sons. (2) The Jewish method of "scourging," as described in the *Mishna*, was by the use of three thongs of leather, the offender receiving thirteen stripes on the bare breast and thirteen on each shoulder, the "forty stripes save one," as administered to Paul five times (2 Cor 11:24). See: TDNT—4:515, 571; BAGD—495a; THAYER—392c.

3147. μαστίζω {1x} **mastizō**, *mas-tid'-zo;* from *3149;* to *whip* (lit.):—to scourge {1x}. See: TDNT—4:515, 571; BAGD—495a; THAYER—392d.

3148. μάστιξ {6x} **mastix**, *mas'-tix;* prob. from the base of *3145* (through the idea of *contact*); a *whip* (lit. the Rom. *flagellum* for criminals; fig. a *disease*):—plague {4x}, scourging {2x}.

Mastix is "a whip, scourge," is used (1) literally, with the meaning (1a) "scourging," in Acts 22:24, of the Roman method, (1b) in Heb 11:36, of the "sufferings" of saints in the OT times. Among the Hebrews the usual mode, legal and domestic, was that of beating with a rod (2 Cor 11:25); (2) metaphorically, of "disease" or "suffering, a scourge, plague, a calamity, misfortune", Mk 3:10; 5:29, 34; Lk 7:21. See: TDNT—4:518, 571; BAGD—495c; THAYER—392d.

3149. μαστός {3x} **mastŏs**, *mas-tos';* from the base of *3145;* a (prop. female) *breast* (as if *kneaded* up):—pap {3x}. Cf. Lk 11:27; 23:29; Rev 1:13. See: BAGD—495b; THAYER—392d.

3150. ματαιολογία {1x} **mataiŏlŏgia**, *mat-ah-yol-og-ee'-ah;* from *3151; random talk,* i.e. *babble:*—vain jangling {1x}. See: TDNT—4:524, 571; BAGD—495c; THAYER—392d.

3151. ματαιολόγος {1x} **mataiŏlŏgŏs**, *mat-ah-yol-og'-os;* from *3152* and *3004;* an *idle* (i.e. *senseless* or *mischievous*) *talker,* i.e. a *wrangler:*—vain talker {1x}.

This one is an idle talker, one who utters empty senseless things, 1 Ti 1:6. See: TDNT—4:524, 571; BAGD—495c; THAYER—392d.

3152. μάταιος {6x} **mataiŏs**, *mat'-ah-yos;* from the base of *3155; empty,* i.e. (lit.) *profitless,* or (spec.) an *idol:*—vain {5x}, vanities {1x}.

(1) *Mataios* denotes communication that is devoid of force, truth, success, result; it is useless, of no purpose. (2) It stresses aimlessness and vanity of anything that does not have God. (3) It means "void of result," is used of (3a) idolatrous practices, Acts 14:15, "vanities"; (3b) the thoughts of the wise, 1 Cor 3:20, "vain"; (3c) faith, if Christ is not risen, 1 Cor 15:17; (3d) questionings, strifes, etc., Titus 3:9; (3e) religion, with an unbridled tongue, Jas 1:26; (3f) manner of life, 1 Pet 1:18. Syn.: *Mataios* (*3152*), "vain," signifies "void" of result, it marks the aimlessness of anything. The vain (*kenos* - 2756) man in Jas 2:20 is one who is "empty" of divinely imparted wisdom; in 1:26 the vain (*mataios*) religion is one that produces nothing profitable. *Kenos* stresses the absence of quality, *mataios,* the absence of useful aim or effect. See: TDNT—4:519, 571; BAGD—495c; THAYER—392d.

3153. ματαιότης {3x} **mataiŏtēs**, *mat-ah-yot'-ace;* from *3152; inutility;* fig. *transientness;* mor. *depravity:*—vanity {3x}.

This word stresses emptiness as to results and is used (1) of the creation (Rom 8:20) as failing of the results designed, owing to sin; (2) of the mind which governs the manner of life of the Gentiles (Eph 4:17); and (3) of the great swelling words of false teachers (2 Pet 2:18). See: TDNT—4:523, 571; BAGD—495d; THAYER—393a.

3154. ματαιόω {1x} **mataiŏō**, *mat-ah-yŏ'-o;* from *3152;* to *render* (pass. *become*) *foolish, empty,* i.e. (mor.) *wicked* or (spec.) *idolatrous:*—become vain {1x}. See: TDNT—4:523, 571; BAGD—495d; THAYER—393a.

3155. μάτην {2x} **matēn**, *mat'-ane;* accus. of a der. of the base of *3145* (through the idea of tentative *manipulation,* i.e. unsuccessful *search,* or else of *punishment*); *folly,* i.e. (adv.) to *no purpose:*—in vain {2x}.

Maten, "a fault, a folly," signifies "in vain, to no purpose," Mt 15:9; Mk 7:7. See: TDNT—4:523, 571; BAGD—495d; THAYER—393a.

3156. Ματθαῖος {5x} **Matthaiŏs**, *mat-thah'-yos;* or

Ματθαῖος **Maththaiŏs**, *math-thah'-yos;* a short. form of *3161; Matthæus* (i.e. *Matthitjah*), an Isr. and a Chr.:—Matthew {5x}. See: BAGD—496a; THAYER—393b.

3157. **Ματθάν** {2x} **Matthan,** *mat-than';* of Heb. or. [4977]; *Matthan* (i.e. *Mattan*), an Isr.:—*Matthan* {2x}. See: BAGD—496a; THAYER—393b.

3158. **Ματθάτ** {2x} **Matthat,** *mat-that';* or

Μαθθάτ **Maththat,** *math-that';* prob. a short. form of *3161; Matthat* (i.e. *Mattithjah*), the name of two Isr.:—Mathat {2x}. See: BAGD—496a; THAYER—393c.

3159. **Ματθίας** {2x} **Matthias** *mat-thee'-as,* or **Μαθθίας** **Maththias,** *math-thee'-as;* appar. a short. form of *3161; Matthias* (i.e. *Mattithjah*), an Isr.:—*Matthias* {2x}. See: BAGD—496a; THAYER—393c.

3160. **Ματταθά** {1x} **Mattatha,** *mat-tath-ah';* prob. a short. form of *3161* [comp. 4992]; *Mattatha* (i.e. *Mattithjah*), an Isr.:—*Mattatha* {1x}. See: BAGD—496a; THAYER—393c.

3161. **Ματταθίας** {2x} **Mattathias,** *mat-tath-ee'-as;* of Heb. or. [4993]; *Mattathias* (i.e. *Mattithjah*), an Isr. and a Chr.:—*Mattathias* {2x}. See: BAGD—496b; THAYER—393c.

3162. **μάχαιρα** {29x} **machaira,** *makh'-ahee-rah;* prob. fem. of a presumed der. of *3163; a knife,* i.e. *dirk;* fig. *war,* judicial *punishment:*—sword {29x}.

Machaira is a short sword, long knife, or dagger (Mt 26:47, 51, 52) and is used metaphorically and by metonomy **(1)** for ordinary violence, or dissensions, that destroy peace (Mt 10:34); **(2)** as the instrument of a magistrate or judge (Rom 13:4); **(3)** of the Word of God, "the sword of the Spirit," (Eph 6:17). Syn.: *Rhomphaia* (*4501*) denotes a large sword occuring **(A)** literally (Rev 6:8); **(B)** metaphorically, as the instrument **(B1)** of anguish (Lk 2:35); **(B2)** of judgment (Rev 1:16; 2:12, 16; 19:15, 21), probably figurative of the Lord's judicial utterances. See: TDNT—4:524, 572; BAGD—496b; THAYER—393c.

3163. **μάχη** {4x} **machē,** *makh'-ay;* from *3164; a battle,* i.e. (fig.) *controversy:*—fighting {2x}, strife {1x}, striving {1x}.

Mache are contentions that may involve armed conflict, but usually do not. *Mache,* "a fight, strife", is always used in the plural in the NT, and translated **(1)** "fightings" in 2 Cor 7:5; Jas 4:1; **(2)** "strivings" in Titus 3:9; and **(3)** "strifes" in 2 Ti 2:23. Syn.: *Mache* is the battle and *polemos* (*4171*) is the war. See: TDNT—4:527, 573; BAGD—496c; THAYER—394a.

3164. **μάχομαι** {4x} **machŏmai,** *makh'-om-ahee;* mid. voice of an appar.

primary verb; to *war,* i.e. (fig.) to *quarrel, dispute:*—fight {1x}, strive {3x}.

Machomai, "to fight," is rendered **(1)** "fightings," in Jas 4:2; and **(2)** "strive": **(2a)** "strive" in 2 Ti 2:24; **(2b)** "strove" in Jn 6:52; Acts 7:26. See: TDNT—4:527, 573; BAGD—496c; THAYER—394a.

3165. **μέ** {301x} **mĕ,** *meh;* a short. (and prob. orig.) form of *1691; me:*—*me* {262x}, I {37x}, my {1x}, not tr {1x}. See: BAGD—[1473] 217a; THAYER—167b.

3166. **μεγαλαυχέω** {1x} **mĕgalauchĕō,** *meg-al-ow-kheh'-o;* from a compound of *3173* and αὐχέω **auchĕō,** (to *boast;* akin to *837* and *2744*); to *talk big,* i.e. *be grandiloquent* (*arrogant, egotistic*):—boast great things {1x}.

This word means to lift up the neck; hence, to boast and indicates any kind of haughty speech which stirs up strife or provokes others (Jas 3:5). See: BAGD—496c; THAYER—394a.

3167. **μεγαλεῖος** {2x} **mĕgalĕiŏs,** *meg-al-i'-os;* from *3173; magnificent,* i.e. (neut. plur. as noun) a conspicuous *favor,* or (subj.) *perfection:*—great things {1x}, wonderful works {1x}.

(1) *Megaleios* are outpourings of the greatness of God's power and glory leaving the observer full of wonder. **(2)** In Acts 2:11, the adjective *megaleios,* "magnificent," in the neuter plural with the article, is rendered "the wonderful works" (of God). **(3)** In Lk 1:49 Mary proclaims what "great things" God had done for her. Syn.: 1411, 1741, 2297, 3861, 4192, 5259. See: TDNT—4:541, 573; BAGD—496d; THAYER—394b.

3168. **μεγαλειότης** {3x} **mĕgalĕiŏtēs,** *meg-al-i-ot'-ace;* from *3167; superbness,* i.e. *glory* or *splendor:*—magnificence {1x}, majesty {1x}, mighty power {1x}.

Megaleiotes denotes "splendor, magnificence" (from *megaleios,* "magnificent," mighty," Acts 2:11, *megas,* "great"), and is translated **(1)** "magnificence" in Acts 19:27, of the splendor of the goddess Diana. **(2)** In Lk 9:43, "mighty power"; and **(3)** in 2 Pet 1:16, "majesty." See: TDNT—4:541, 573; BAGD—496d; THAYER—394b.

3169. **μεγαλοπρεπής** {1x} **mĕgalŏprĕpēs,** *meg-al-op-rep-ace';* from *3173* and *4241; befitting greatness* or *magnificence* (*majestic*):—excellent {1x}.

Megaloprepes signifies "magnificent, majestic, that which is becoming to a great man" (from *megas,* "great," and *prepo,* "to be fitting or becoming"), in 2 Pet 1:17, "excellent." See:

TDNT—4:542, 573; BAGD—497a; THAYER—394a.

3170. **μεγαλύνω** {8x} **mĕgalunō**, *meg-al-oo'-no;* from *3173;* to *make* (or *declare*) *great,* i.e. *increase* or (fig.) *extol:*—enlarge {2x}, magnify {5x}, shew great {1x}.

Megaluno denotes "to make great" (from *megas,* "great"), and is translated (1) "enlarge" in Mt 23:5; 2 Cor 10:15; (2) "to magnify" in Lk 1:46; Acts 5:13; 10:46; 19:17; Phil 1:20; and (3) "shew great" in Lk 1:58 "had showed great (mercy)." See: TDNT—4:543, 573; BAGD—497b; THAYER—394b.

3171. **μεγάλως** {1x} **mĕgalōs**, *meg-al'-oce;* adv. from *3173; much:*—greatly {1x}. See: BAGD—497b; THAYER—394b.

3172. **μεγαλωσύνη** {3x} **mĕgalōsunē**, *meg-al-o-soo'-nay;* from *3173; greatness,* i.e. (fig.) *divinity* (often God himself):—Majesty {2x}, majesty {1x}.

Megalosune, from *megas,* "great," denotes "greatness, majesty"; it is used of God the Father, signifying (1) His greatness and dignity, in (1a) Heb 1:3, "the Majesty (on high)", (1b) Heb 8:1, "the Majesty (in the Heavens)"; and (2) in an ascription of praise acknowledging the attributes of God in Jude 25. See: TDNT—4:544, 573; BAGD—497b; THAYER—394c.

3173. **μέγας** {195x} **mĕgas**, *meg'-as;* [incl. the prol. forms, fem.

μεγάλη mĕgalē, plur.

μεγάλοι mĕgalŏi, etc.; comp. also *3176, 3187*]; *big* (lit. or fig. in a very wide application):—great {150x}, loud {33x}, misc. {12x} = (+ fear) exceedingly, high, large, mighty, + (be) sore (afraid), strong, X to years.

Megas is used (1) of external form, size, measure, e.g., of (1a) a stone, Mt 27:60; (1b) fish, Jn 21:11; (2) of degree and intensity, e.g., (2a) of fear, Mk 4:41; (2b) wind, Jn 6:18; Rev 6:13, "mighty"; (3) of a circumstance, 1 Cor 9:11; 2 Cor 11:15; (4) in Rev 5:2, 12, "loud", of a voice; (5) of rank, whether of persons, e.g., (5a) God, Titus 2:13; (5b) Christ as a "great Priest," Heb 10:21; (5c) Diana, Acts 19:27, (5d) Simon Magus, Acts 8:9 "(some) great one"; (5e) in the plural "great ones," Mt 20:25; Mk 10:42, those who hold positions of authority in Gentile nations; (6) or of things, e.g., a mystery, Eph 5:32; Acts 8:8, of joy; (7) of intensity, as, e.g., (7a) of the force of a voice, e.g., Mt 27:46, 50; (7b) "loud" in Rev 5:2, 12; 6:10; 7:2, 10; 8:13; 10:3; 12:10; 14:7, 9, 15, 18. See: TDNT—4:529, 573; BAGD—497c; THAYER—394c.

3174. **μέγεθος** {1x} **mĕgĕthŏs**, *meg'-eth-os;* from *3173; magnitude* (fig.):—greatness {1x}. See: TDNT—4:544, 573; BAGD—498c; THAYER—395c.

3175. **μεγιστᾶνες** {3x} **mĕgistanĕs**, *meg-is-tan'-es;* plur. from *3176; grandees:*—great men {2x}, lords {1x}.

Megistanes, akin to *megistos,* "greatest," the superlative degree of *megas,* "great," denotes "chief men, nobles", it is rendered (1) "lords" in Mk 6:21, of nobles in Herod's entourage; (2) "great men" in Rev 6:15 and 18:23. See: BAGD—498c; THAYER—395c.

3176. **μέγιστος** {1x} **mĕgistŏs**, *meg'-is-tos;* superl. of *3173; greatest* or *very great:*—exceeding great {1x}. See: BAGD—498d; THAYER—395c.

3177. **μεθερμηνεύω** {7x} **mĕthĕrmēnĕuō**, *meth-er-mane-yoo'-o;* from *3326* and *2059;* to *explain over,* i.e. *translate:*—being interpreted {6x}, be by interpretation {1x}.

Methermeneuo, "to change or translate from one language to another, to interpret," is always used in the passive voice in the NT, "being interpreted," of interpreting (1) names, (1a) Immanuel, Mt 1:23, "God with us"; (1b) Golgotha, Mk 15:22, "the place of a skull"; (1c) Barnabas, Acts 4:36, "the son of consolation"; (1d) in Acts 13:8, of *Elymas,* the verb is rendered "is . . . by interpretation," lit., "is interpreted"; (1e) Jn 1: 41 Messiah, interpreted as "Christ"; (2) it is used of interpreting or translating sentences in Mk 5:41; 15:34. See: BAGD—498c; THAYER—395c.

3178. **μέθη** {3x} **mĕthē**, *meth'-ay;* appar. a primary word; an *intoxicant,* i.e. (by impl.) *intoxication:*—drunkenness {3x}.

Methe "strong drink" (akin to *methu,* "wine"), denotes "drunkenness, habitual intoxication," Lk 21:34; Rom 13:13; Gal 5:21. Syn.: 2897, 2970, 3632, 4224. See: TDNT—4:545, 576; BAGD—498d; THAYER—395d.

3179. **μεθίστημι** {5x} **mĕthistēmi**, *meth-is'-tay-mee;* or (1 Cor. 13:2)

μεθιστάνω mĕthistanō, *meth-is-tan'-o;* from *3326* and *2476;* to *transfer,* i.e. *carry away, depose* or (fig.) *exchange, seduce:*—put out {1x}, remove {2x}, translate {1x}, turn away {1x}.

This word means to transpose, transfer, remove from one place to another, is used transitively in the sense of causing "to remove", specifically (1) of change of situation or place, in 1 Cor 13:2, of "removing" mountains; (2) to remove from the office of a steward, Lk 16:4; or (3) to depart from life, to die, in Acts 13:22, of the "removing" of King Saul, by bring-

ing about his death. See: BAGD−498d; THAYER−395d.

3180. μεθοδεία {2x} **mĕthŏdĕia**, *meth-od-i'-ah;* from a compound of *3326* and *3593* [comp. "method"]; *travelling over,* i.e. *travesty* (*trickery*):—wile {1x}, lie in wait {1x}.

Methodeia denotes "craft, deceit" (*meta,* "after," *hodos,* "a way"), "a cunning device, a wile," and is translated **(1)** "wiles (of error)" in Eph 4:14, "they lie in wait (to deceive)", lit., "with a view to the craft (singular) of deceit"; **(2)** in Eph 6:11, "the wiles (plural) of the devil. See: TDNT−5:102, 666; BAGD−499a; THAYER−395d.

3181. μεθόριος {1x} **mĕthŏriŏs**, *meth-or'-ee-os;* from *3326* and *3725;* *bounded alongside,* i.e. *contiguous* (neut. plur. as noun, *frontier*):—border {1x}. See: BAGD−499b; THAYER−396a.

3182. μεθύσκω {3x} **mĕthuskō**, *meth-oos'-ko;* a prol. (tran.) form of *3184;* to *intoxicate:*—be drunk {1x}, be drunken {2x}.

Methusko signifies "to make drunk, or to grow drunk" (an inceptive verb, marking the process or the state), "to become intoxicated," Lk 12:45; Eph 5:18; 1 Th 5:7a. See: TDNT−4:545,*; BAGD−499b; THAYER−396a.

3183. μέθυσος {2x} **mĕthusŏs**, *meth'-oo-sos;* from *3184; tipsy,* i.e. (as noun) a *sot:*—drunkard {2x}.

Methusos, "drunken", is used as noun, **(1)** in the singular, in 1 Cor 5:11, "drunkard", and **(2)** in the plural, in 1 Cor 6:10, "drunkards." See: TDNT−4:545, 576; BAGD−499b; THAYER−396a.

3184. μεθύω {7x} **mĕthuō**, *meth-oo'-o;* from another form of *3178;* to *drink* to *intoxication,* i.e. *get drunk:*—be drunken {5x}, have well drunk {1x}, be made drunk {1x}.

Metheuo, is used **(1)** in Jn 2:10 in the passive voice, and is translated "have well drunk." **(2)** It signifies "to be drunk with wine", originally it denoted simply "a pleasant drink." **(2a)** The verb is used of "being intoxicated" in Mt 24:49; Acts 2:15; 1 Cor 11:21; 1 Th 5:7b; **(2b)** metaphorically, of the effect upon men of partaking of the abominations of the Babylonish system, Rev 17:2; **(2c)** of being in a state of mental "intoxication," through the shedding of men's blood profusely, Rev 17:6. See: TDNT−4:545, 576; BAGD−499c; THAYER−396a.

3185. μεῖζον {1x} **mĕizŏn**, *mide'-zon;* neut. of *3187;* (adv.) in *greater* degree:—the more {1x}. See: BAGD−499d; THAYER−394b [*3173*].

3186. μειζότερος {1x} **mĕizŏtĕrŏs**, *mide-zot'-er-os;* continued comparative of *3187; still larger* (fig.):—greater {1x}. See: BAGD−499d; THAYER−396b.

3187. μείζων {45x} **mĕizōn**, *mide'-zone;* irreg. comparative of *3173; larger* (lit. or fig. spec. in age):—greater {34x}, greatest {9x}, elder {1x}, more {1x}.

Meizon is the comparative degree of *megas,* translated **(1)** "greater", e.g., Mt 11:11; in Jas 3:1, "the greater condemnation"; it is used in the neuter plural in John 1:50, "greater things"; in 14:12, "greater works" (lit., "greater things." **(2)** It is used of age, and translated "elder" in Rom 9:12, with reference to Esau and Jacob. **(3)** In Mt 20:31, the neuter of *meizon,* used as an adverb, is translated "the more." It also expresses the superlative and is translated **(4)** "greatest" in Mt 13:32, "the greatest among"; cf. Mt 18:1, 4; 23:11; Mk 9:34; Lk 9:46; 22:24, 26; 1 Cor 13:13. See: BAGD−499d; THAYER−396b.

3188. μέλαν {3x} **mĕlan**, *mel'-an;* neut. of *3189* as noun; *ink:*—ink {3x}.

Melan, the neuter of the adjective *melas,* "black" (*3189*), denotes "ink," 2 Cor 3:3; 2 Jn 12; 3 Jn 13. See: BAGD−499d; THAYER−396b.

3189. μέλας {3x} **mĕlas**, *mel'-as;* appar. a primary word; *black:*—black {3x}; Cf. Mt 5:36; Rev 6:5, 12. See: BAGD−499d; THAYER−396b.

3190. Μελεᾶς {1x} **Mĕlĕas**, *mel-eh-as';* of uncert. or.; *Meleas,* an Isr.:—Meleas {1x}. See: BAGD−500a; THAYER−396b.

μέλει mĕlĕi. See *3199*.

3191. μελετάω {3x} **mĕlĕtaō**, *mel-et-ah'-o;* from a presumed der. of *3199;* to *take care of,* i.e. (by impl.) *revolve* in the mind:—imagine {1x}, premeditate {1x}, meditate {1x}.

Meletao signifies "to care for, attend carefully" (from *melete,* "care"); **(1)** in 1 Ti 4:15, "meditate"; **(2)** in Acts 4:25, "imagine"; **(3)** in Mk 13:11, "premeditate." See: BAGD−500b; THAYER−396b.

3192. μέλι {4x} **mĕli**, *mel'-ee;* appar. a primary word; *honey:*—honey {4x}.

Meli occurs with the adjective *agrios,* **(1)** "wild," in Mt 3:4; Mk 1:6; **(2)** in Rev 10:9, 10, as an example of sweetness. **(3)** As "honey" is liable to ferment, it was precluded from offerings to God, Lev 2:11. The liquid "honey" mentioned in Ps 19:10 and Prov 16:24 is regarded as the best; a cruse of it was part of the present

brought to Ahijah by Jeroboam's wife, 1 Kin 14:3. See: TDNT—4:552, 577; BAGD—500c; THAYER—396c.

3193. μελίσσιος {1x} **mělissiŏs**, *mel-is'-see-os;* from *3192; relating to honey,* i.e. *bee* (comb):—honeycomb + 2781 {1x}. See: BAGD—500d; THAYER—396c.

3194. Μελίτη {1x} **Mělitē**, *mel-ee'-tay;* of uncert. or.; *Melita,* an island in the Mediterranean:—Melita {1x}. See: BAGD—500d; THAYER—396c.

3195. μέλλω {110x} **mĕllō**, *mel'-lo;* a strengthened form of *3199* (through the idea of *expectation*); to *intend,* i.e. *be about* to be, do, or suffer something (of persons or things, espec. events; in the sense of *purpose, duty, necessity, probability, possibility,* or *hesitation*):—shall {25x}, should {20x}, would {9x}, to come {9x}, will {7x}, things to come {4x}, not tr {3x}, misc. {33x} = about, after that, be (almost), intend, was to (be), mean, mind, be at the point, (be) ready, + return, tarry, which was for, be yet.

Mello signifies **(1)** "of intention, to be about to do something," e.g., Acts 3:3; 18:14; 20:3; Heb 8:5; **(2)** "of certainty, compulsion or necessity, to be certain to act," e.g., Jn 6:71. It is used **(3)** of purpose. It is rendered simply by "shall" or "should" (which frequently represent elsewhere part of the future tense of the verb) in the following: Mt 16:27 (1st part), lit., "is about to come"; 17:12, 22; 20:22; 24:6; Mk 13:4 (2nd part); Lk 9:44; 21:7 (2nd part); v. 36; Acts 23:3; 24:15; 26:2; Rom 4:24; 8:13 (1st part); v. 18; 2 Ti 4:1; Heb 1:14; 10:27; Jas 2:12; 1 Pet 5:1; Rev 1:19; 2:10 (1st and 2nd parts); 3:10; 17:8 (1st part); **(4)** "should" e.g., Mk 10:32; Lk 19:11; 22:23; 24:21; Jn 6:71; 7:39; 11:51; 12:4, 33; 18:32; Acts 11:28; 23:27; 1 Th 3:4; Rev 6:11. See: BAGD—500d; THAYER—396d.

3196. μέλος {34x} **mĕlŏs**, *mel'-os;* of uncert. aff.; a *limb* or *part* of the body:—member {34x}.

Melos, as a noun, means "a limb of the body," is used **(1)** literally, Mt 5:29–30; Rom 6:13 (twice), 19 (twice); 7:5, 23 (twice); 12:4 (twice); 1 Cor 12:12 (twice), 14, 18–20, 22, 25–26 (twice); Jas 3:5, 6; 4:1; **(2)** in Col 3:5, "mortify therefore your members which are upon the earth"; since our bodies and their "members" belong to the earth, and are the instruments of sin, they are referred to as such (cf. Mt 5:29–30; Rom 7:5, 23); **(2a)** the putting to death is not physical, but ethical; as the physical "members" have distinct individualities, so those evils, of which the physical "members" are agents, are by analogy regarded as examples of the way in which the "members" work if not put to death;

(2b) this is not precisely the same as "the old man," v. 9, i.e., the old nature, though there is a connection;

(3) metaphorically, of believers **(3a)** as members of Christ, 1 Cor 6:15 (1st part); of one another, Rom 12:5 (as with the natural illustration, so with the spiritual analogy, there is not only vital unity, and harmony in operation, but diversity, all being essential to effectivity; the unity is not due to external organization but to common and vital union in Christ); there is stress in v. 5 upon "many" and "in Christ" and "members;" **(3b)** 1 Cor 12:27 of the "members" of a local church as a body; **(3c)** Eph 4:25 of the "members" of the whole church as the mystical body of Christ; **(3d)** in 1 Cor 6:15 (2nd part), of one who practices fornication. See: TDNT—4:555, 577; BAGD—501d; THAYER—397b.

3197. Μελχί {2x} **Mělchi**, *mel-khee';* of Heb. or [4428 with pron. suffix *my king*]; *Melchi* (i.e. *Malki*), the name of two Isr.:—Melchi {2x}. See: BAGD—502a; THAYER—397b.

3198. Μελχισεδέκ {9x} **Mělchisĕdĕk**, *mel-khis-ed-ek';* of Heb. or. [4442]; *Melchisedek* (i.e. *Malkitsedek*), a patriarch:—Melchisedec {9x}. See: TDNT—4:568,*; BAGD—502a; THAYER—397b.

3199. μέλω {10x} **mĕlō**, *mel'-o;* a primary verb; to *be of interest* to, i.e. to *concern* (only third pers. sing. pres. ind. used impers. *it matters*):—take care {1x}, care {9x}.

Melei, the third person sing. of *melo,* used impersonally, signifies that "something is an object of care," especially the care of forethought and interest, rather than anxiety, Mt 22:16; Mk 4:38; 12:14; Lk 10:40; Jn 10:13; 12:6; Acts 18:17; 1 Cor 7:21, 9:9, (God does "care" for oxen, but there was a divinely designed significance in the OT passage, relating to the service of preachers of the gospel); 1 Pet 5:7. See: BAGD—500d [3195]; THAYER—396b.

3200. μεμβράνα {1x} **mĕmbrana**, *mem-bran'-ah;* of Lat. or. ("*membrane*"); a (written) sheep-*skin:*—parchment {1x}.

Membrana is a Latin word, properly an adjective, from *membrum,* "a limb," but denoting "skin, parchment." The Eng. word "parchment" is a form of *pergamena,* an adjective signifying "of Pergamum," the city in Asia Minor where "parchment" was either invented or brought into use. The word *membrana* is found in 2 Ti 4:13, where Timothy is asked to bring to the apostle "the books, especially the parchments." The writing material was prepared from the skin of the sheep or goat. The skins were first soaked in lime for the purpose of removing the hair, and then shaved, washed,

dried, stretched and ground or smoothed with fine chalk or lime and pumice stone. The finest kind is called "vellum," and is made from the skins of calves or kids. See: BAGD—502a; THAYER—397c.

3201. μέμφομαι {3x} **mĕmphŏmai**, *mem'-fom-ahee;* mid. voice of an appar. primary verb; to *blame:*—find fault {3x}.

Memphomai, as a verb, means "to find fault": "And when they saw some of his disciples eat bread with defiled, that is to say, with unwashen, hands, they found fault" (Mk 7:2; cf. Rom 9:19; Heb 8:8). Syn.: 273, 274, 298, 299, 338, 410, 423, 2607, 3469. See: TDNT—4:571, 580; BAGD—502b; THAYER—397c.

3202. μεμψίμοιρος {1x} **mĕmpsimŏirŏs**, *mem-psim'-oy-ros;* from a presumed der. of *3201* and μοῖρα **mŏira**, *(fate;* akin to the base of *3313*); *blaming fate,* i.e. *querulous (discontented):*—complainer {1x}.

This word denotes one who complains of his lot, his station in life; hence, discontented, querulous, repining, blaming someone else (Jude 16). See: TDNT—4:571, 580; BAGD—502c; THAYER—397c.

3203–3302. Because of some changes in the numbering system (while the original work was in progress) no Greek words were cited for *2717* or *3203–3302.* These numbers were dropped altogether. This will not cause any problems in Strong's numbering system. No Greek words have been left out. Because so many other reference works use this numbering system, it has not been revised. If it were revised, much confusion would certainly result.

3303. μέν {194x} **mĕn**, *men;* a primary particle; prop. ind. of *affirmation* or *concession (in fact);* usually followed by a contrasted clause with *1161 (this* one, the *former,* etc):—indeed {22x}, verily {14x}, truly {12x}, not tr {142x}, misc. {4x}. Often compounded with other particles in an *intens.* or *asseverative* sense.

Men, a conjunctive particle (originally a form of *men,* "verily, truly," found in Heb 6:14 is usually related to an adversative conjunction or particle, like *de,* in the following clause, which is placed in opposition to it. Frequently it is untranslatable; sometimes it is rendered "indeed," e.g., Mt 3:11; 13:32; 17:11 "truly"; 20:23; 26:41; Mk 1:8; 9:12 "verily." See: BAGD—502c; THAYER—397c.

3304. μενοῦνγε {4x} **mĕnŏungĕ**, *men-oon'-geh* or

   μενοῦν mĕnŏun, *men-oon'* or

   μενοῦν γε mĕnŏun ge *men-oon' geh;* from *3203* and *3767* and

1065; so then at least:—yea rather {1x}, nay but {1x}, yea verily {1x}, yea doubtless {1x}.

Menounge, "nay rather," is rendered **(1)** "yea rather" in Lk 11:28; **(2)** "nay but" in Rom 9:20; **(3)** "yea verily" in Rom 10:18; and **(4)** "yea doubtless" in Phil 3:8. See: BAGD—503c; THAYER—399a.

3305. μέντοι {8x} **mĕntŏi**, *men'-toy;* from *3303* and *5104; indeed though,* i.e. *however:*—yet {2x}, nevertheless {2x}, howbeit {1x}, but {1x}, not tr {2x}.

This word is translated **(1)** "yet", in Jn 4:27; 20:5; **(2)** "nevertheless" in Jn 12:42; 2 Ti 2:19; **(3)** "howbeit" in Jn 7:13; **(4)** "but" in Jn 21:4; **(5)** not tr in Jas 2:8; Jude 8. See: BAGD—593c; THAYER—399a.

3306. μένω {120x} **mĕnō**, *men'-o;* a primary verb; to *stay* (in a given place, state, relation or expectancy):—abide {61x}, remain {16x}, dwell {15x}, continue {11x}, tarry {9x}, endure {3x}, misc. {5x} = "to abide," be present, stand, × thine own.

It is translated "abide" and used **(1)** of place, **(1a)** literally, e.g., Mt 10:11, **(1b)** metaphorically, is said **(1b1)** of God, 1 Jn 4:15; **(1b2)** Christ, Jn 6:56; 15:4, etc.; **(1b3)** the Holy Spirit, Jn 1:32–33; 14:17; **(1b4)** believers, Jn 6:56; 15:4; 1 Jn 4:15, etc.; **(1b5)** the Word of God, 1 Jn 2:14; **(1b6)** the truth, 2 Jn 2, etc.; **(2)** of time; it is said **(2a)** of believers, Jn 21:22–23; Phil 1:25; 1 Jn 2:17; **(2b)** Christ, Jn 12:34; Heb 7:24; **(2c)** the Word of God, 1 Pet 1:23; **(2d)** sin, Jn 9:41; **(2e)** cities, Mt 11:23; Heb 13:14; **(2f)** bonds and afflictions, Acts 20:23; **(3)** of qualities; **(3a)** faith, hope, love, 1 Cor 13:13; **(3b)** Christ's love, Jn 15:10; **(3c)** afflictions, Acts 20:23; **(3d)** brotherly love, Heb 13:1; **(3e)** the love of God, 1 Jn 3:17; **(3f)** the truth, 2 Jn 2. **(4)** It is translated "to remain," e.g., Mt 11:23; Lk 10:7; Jn 1:33; 9:41; 15:16; 19:31; Acts 5:4 (twice); 27:41; 1 Cor 7:11; 15:6; 2 Cor 3:11, 14; 9:9; Heb 12:27; 1 Jn 3:9. **(5)** It is translated "to dwell," in Jn 1:38–39; 6:56; 14:10, 17; Acts 28:16. **(6)** It is translated "to tarry," in Mt 26:38; Mk 14:34; Lk 24:29; Jn 4:40; Acts 9:43; 18:20; 20:5, 15. See: TDNT—4:574, 581; BAGD—503c; THAYER—399b.

3307. μερίζω {14x} **mĕrizō**, *mer-id'-zo;* from *3313;* to *part,* i.e. (lit.) to *apportion, bestow, share,* or (fig.) to *disunite, differ:*—divide {9x}, distribute {2x}, deal {1x}, be difference between {1x}, give part {1x}.

Merizo, akin to *meros,* hence, "to distribute, divide out, deal out to, a part, to part, divide into," in the middle voice means "to divide anything with another, to share with." The usual meaning is **(1)** "to divide," Mt 12:25 (twice), 26; Mk 3:24–26 (thrice); 6:41; Lk 12:13; 1 Cor 1:13;

(2) "hath distributed" in 1 Cor 7:17; 2 Cor 10:13; **(3)** "hath dealt" in Rom 12:3; **(4)** "be difference between" in 1 Cor 7:34; **(5)** "gave a part" in Heb 7:2. See: BAGD–504c; THAYER–399d.

3308. **μέριμνα** {6x} **měrimna**, *mer'-im-nah;* from *3307* (through the idea of *distraction*); *solicitude:*—care {6x}.

Merimna, probably connected with *merizo,* "to draw in different directions, distract," hence signifies "that which causes this, a care, especially an anxious care," Mt 13:22; Mk 4:19; Lk 8:14; 21:34; 2 Cor 11:28; 1 Pet 5:7. See: TDNT–4:589, 584; BAGD–504d; THAYER–400a.

3309. **μεριμνάω** {19x} **měrimnaō**, *mer-im-nah'-o;* from *3308;* to *be anxious* about:—take thought {11x}, care {5x}, be careful {2x}, have care {1x}.

Merimnao signifies **(1)** "to be anxious about, to have a distracting care," e.g., Mt 6:25, 27, 28, 31, 34; Lk 12:11, 22, 25, 26 "take thought"; 10:19; Lk 10:41 "careful"; 12:11; **(2)** to be careful for, 1 Cor 7:32–34; **(3)** to have a care for, 1 Cor 12:25; **(4)** to care for, Phil 2:20; **(5)** "be anxious", Phil 4:6. See: TDNT–4:589, 584; BAGD–505a; THAYER–400b.

3310. **μερίς** {5x} **měris**, *mer-ece';* fem. of *3313;* a *portion,* i.e. *province, share* or (abstr.) *participation:*—part {4x}, to be partaker + 1519 {1x}.

Meris, denotes **(1)** "a part" or "portion," **(1a)** Lk 10:42; Acts 8:21; 2 Cor 6:15; **(1b)** "a district" or "division," Acts 16:12; **(2)** in Col 1:12, "partakers," lit., "unto the part of." See: BAGD–505a; THAYER–400b.

3311. **μερισμός** {2x} **měrismŏs**, *mer-is-mos';* from *3307;* a *separation* or *distribution:*—dividing asunder {1x}, gift {1x}.

Merismos primarily denotes "a division, partition" (*meros,* "a part"); hence, **(1)** "a distribution," Heb 2:4, "gifts"; **(2)** "a dividing or separation", Heb 4:12, "dividing asunder." See: BAGD–505c; THAYER–400c.

3312. **μεριστής** {1x} **měristēs**, *mer-is-tace';* from *3307;* an *apportioner* (*administrator*):—divider {1x}. See: BAGD–505d; THAYER–400c.

3313. **μέρος** {43x} **měrŏs**, *mer'-os;* from an obs. but more primary form of μείρομαι **měirŏmai** (to *get* as a *section* or *allotment*); a *division* or *share* (lit. or fig. in a wide application):—part {24x}, portion {3x}, coast {3x}, behalf {2x}, respect {2x}, misc. {9x} = course, craft, particular (+ -ly), partly, piece, side, some sort (-what).

Meros denotes **(1)** "a part, portion," **(1a)** of the whole, e.g., Jn 13:8; Rev 20:6; 22:19; **(1b)**

hence, "a lot" or "destiny," e.g., Rev 21:8; **(1c)** in Mt 24:51 and Lk 12:46, "portion"; **(2)** "a part" as opposite to the whole, e.g., Lk 11:36; Jn 19:23; 21:6, "side"; Acts 5:2; 23:6; Eph 4:16; Rev 16:19; **(2a)** a party, Acts 23:9; the divisions of a province, e.g., Mt 2:22; Acts 2:10; **(2b)** the regions belonging to a city, e.g., Mt 15:21, "coasts"; 16:13; Acts 19:1; Mk 8:10; **(2c)** "the lower parts of the earth," Eph 4:9; this phrase means the regions beneath the earth; **(3)** "a class," or "category" (with *en,* in, "in respect of"), Col 2:16; "in this respect," 2 Cor 3:10; 9:3; 1 Pet 4:16, "in this behalf"; **(4)** used with the preposition *apo,* "from," with the meaning "in some sort": "Nevertheless, brethren, I have written the more boldly unto you in some sort (*meros*), as putting you in mind, because of the grace that is given to me of God" (Rom 15:15). Syn.: 280, 488, 943, 2884, 3354, 3358, 4057, 4568, 5234, 5249, 5518. See: TDNT–4:594, 585; BAGD–505d; THAYER–400d.

3314. **μεσημβρία** {2x} **měsēmbria**, *mes-ame-bree'-ah;* from *3319* and *2250; midday;* by impl. the *south:*—noon {1x}, south {1x}.

The south, Acts 8:26, is the direction from which the most glaring sunlight comes; like the noon, Acts 22:6, day sun. See: BAGD–506d; THAYER–401a.

3315. **μεσιτεύω** {1x} **měsitěuō**, *mes-it-yoo'-o;* from *3316;* to *interpose* (as arbiter), i.e (by impl.) to *ratify* (as surety):—confirm {1x}.

Mesiteuo means to act as a mediator between litigating or covenanting parties, to accomplish something by interposing between two parties, and then seeing the agreement is carried out; hence, to confirm, make firm between them, Heb 6:17. See: TDNT–4:598, 585; BAGD–506d; THAYER–401b.

3316. **μεσίτης** {6x} **měsitēs**, *mes-ee'-tace;* from *3319;* a *go-between,* i.e. (simply) an *internunciator,* or (by impl.) a *reconciler* (*intercessor*):—mediator {6x}.

Mesites, as a noun, means lit., "a go-between" (from *mesos,* "middle," and *eimi,* "to go"), is used in two ways in the NT, **(1)** "one who mediates" between two parties with a view to producing peace, as in 1 Ti 2:5, **(1a)** though more than mere "mediatorship" is in view, **(1b)** for the salvation of men necessitated that the Mediator should Himself possess the nature and attributes of Him towards whom He acts, and should likewise participate in the nature of those for whom He acts (sin apart); **(1c)** only by being possessed both of deity and humanity could He comprehend the claims of the one and the needs of the other;

(1d) further, the claims and the needs could be met only by One who, Himself being proved sinless, would offer Himself an expiatory sacrifice on behalf of men; **(1e)** "one who acts as a guarantee" so as to secure something which otherwise would not be obtained. **(1f)** Thus in Heb 8:6; 9:15; 12:24 Christ is the Surety of "the better covenant," "the new covenant," guaranteeing its terms for His people.

(2) In Gal 3:19 Moses is spoken of as a "mediator," and the statement is made that "a mediator is not a mediator of one," v. 20, that is, of one party. **(2a)** Here the contrast is between the promise given to Abraham and the giving of the Law. **(2b)** The Law was a covenant enacted between God and the Jewish people, requiring fulfillment by both parties. **(2c)** But with the promise to Abraham, all the obligations were assumed by God, which is implied in the statement, "but God is one." See: TDNT—4:598, 585; BAGD—506d; THAYER—401b.

3317. μεσονύκτιον {4x} **mĕsŏnuktiŏn,** *mes-on-ook'-tee-on;* neut. of compound of *3319* and *3571; midnight* (espec. as a watch):—midnight {4x}.

Mesonuktion, an adjective denoting "at, or of, midnight," is used as a noun in Mk 13:35; Lk 11:5; Acts 16:25; 20:7. See: BAGD—507a; THAYER—401c.

3318. Μεσοποταμία {2x} **Mĕsŏpŏtamia,** *mes-op-ot-am-ee'-ah;* from *3319* and *4215; Mesopotamia* (as lying between the Euphrates and the Tigris; comp. *763*), a region of Asia:—Mesopotamia {2x}. See: BAGD—507b; THAYER—401c.

3319. μέσος {61x} **mĕsŏs,** *mes'-os;* from *3326; middle* (as an adj. or [neut.] noun):—midst {41x}, among {6x}, from among + *1537* {5x}, midnight + *3571* {2x}, ✕ before then {1x}, between {1x}, + forth {1x}, midday {1x}, way {1x}.

Mesos, an adjective denoting "middle, in the middle or midst," is used in the following, in which the English requires a phrase, and the adjectival rendering must be avoided: **(1)** Lk 22:55, "Peter sat in the midst of them," lit., "a middle one of (them)"; **(2)** Lk 23:45, of the rending of the veil "in the midst"; here the adjective idiomatically belongs to the verb "was rent," and is not to be taken literally, as if it meant "the middle veil"; **(3)** Jn 1:26, "in the midst of you (standeth One)", lit., "a middle One"; **(4)** Acts 1:18, where the necessity of avoiding the lit. rendering is obvious. See: BAGD—507b; THAYER—401c.

3320. μεσότοιχον {1x} **mĕsŏtŏichŏn,** *mes-ot'-oy-khon;* from *3319* and *5109;* a *partition* (fig.):—middle wall {1x}.

Mesotoichon, "a partition wall" (*mesos,* "middle"), occurs in Eph 2:14, figuratively of the separation of Gentile from Jew in their unregenerate state, a partition demolished by the Cross for both on acceptance of the gospel. See: TDNT—4:625, 589; BAGD—508a; THAYER—402b.

3321. μεσουράνημα {3x} **mĕsŏuranēma,** *mes-oo-ran'-ay-mah;* from a presumed compound of *3319* and *3772; mid-sky:*—midst of heaven {3x}.

This word denotes the highest point in the heavens, which the sun occupies at noon, where what is done can be seen and heard by all (Rev 8:13; 14:6; 19:17). See: BAGD—508a; THAYER—402b.

3322. μεσόω {1x} **mĕsŏō,** *mes-ŏ'-o;* from *3319;* to *form* the *middle,* i.e. (in point of time), to *be half-way* over:—be about the midst {1x}.

Mesoo, "to be in the middle," is used of time in Jn 7:14, translated "when it was . . . the midst (of the feast)," lit., "(the feast) being in the middle" or about half over. See: BAGD—508b; THAYER—402b.

3323. Μεσσίας {2x} **Mĕssias,** *mes-see'-as;* of Heb. or. [*4899*]; the *Messias* (i.e. *Mashiach*), or Christ:—*Messias* {2x}. See: TDNT 9:493, 1322; BAGD—508b; THAYER—402c.

3324. μεστός {8x} **mĕstŏs,** *mes-tos';* of uncert. der.; *replete* (lit. or fig.):—full {8x}.

Mestos, probably akin to a root signifying "to measure," hence conveys the sense of "having full measure," **(1)** of material things, **(1a)** a vessel, Jn 19:29; **(1b)** a net, 21:11; **(2)** metaphorically, of thoughts and feelings, exercised **(2a)** in evil things, hypocrisy, Mt 23:28; **(2b)** envy, murder, strife, deceit, malignity, Rom 1:29; **(2c)** the utterances of the tongue, Jas 3:8; **(2d)** adultery, 2 Pet 2:14; **(3)** in virtues, **(3a)** goodness, Rom 15:14; **(3b)** mercy, etc, Jas 3:17. See: BAGD—508b; THAYER—402c.

3325. μεστόω {1x} **mĕstŏō,** *mes-tŏ'-o;* from *3324;* to *replenish,* i.e. (by impl.) to *intoxicate:*—fill {1x}. See: BAGD—508c; THAYER—402c.

3326. μετά {473x} **mĕta,** *met-ah';* a primary prep. (often used adv.); prop. denoting *accompaniment;* "*amid*" (local or causal); modif. variously according to the case (gen. *association,* or acc. *succession*) with which it is joined; occupying an intermediate position between *575* or *1537* and *1519* or *4314;* less intimate than *1722* and less close than *4862*):—with {345x}, after {88x}, among {5x},

hereafter + 5023 {4x}, afterward + 5023 {4x}, against {4x}, not tr {1x}, misc {32x} = X that he again, X and, + follow, hence, in, of, (up-) on, + our, X and setting, since, (un-) to, + together, when, without. Often used in composition, in substantially the same relations of *participation* or *proximity*, and *transfer* or *sequence*. See: TDNT—7:766, 1102; BAGD—508c; THAYER—402c.

3327. μεταβαίνω {12x} **mĕtabainō**, *met-ab-ah'-ee-no;* from 3326 and the base of 939; to *change place:*—depart {7x}, go {1x}, pass {2x}, remove {2x}.

Metabaino is rendered "to depart" in Mt 8:34; 11:1; 12:9; 15:29; Jn 7:3; 13:1; Acts 18:7; **(2)** "go" in Lk 10:7; **(3)** "pass" in Jn 5:24; 1 Jn 3:14; **(4)** "remove" in Mt 17:20 (twice). See: TDNT—1:523, 90; BAGD—510c; THAYER—404d.

3328. μεταβάλλω {1x} **mĕtaballō**, *met-ab-al'-lo;* from 3326 and 906; to *throw over,* i.e. (mid. voice fig.) to *turn about* in opinion:—change (one's) mind {1x}.

The emphasis of this word seems to be on the quickness of the change; literally, "thrown over with" (Acts 28:6). See: BAGD—510d; THAYER—404d.

3329. μετάγω {2x} **mĕtagō**, *met-ag'-o;* from 3326 and 71; to *lead over,* i.e. *transfer* (*direct*):—turn about {2x}.

Metago literally means "to move from one side to another," is rendered "to turn about" in Jas 3:3, 4. See: BAGD—510d; THAYER—404d.

3330. μεταδίδωμι {5x} **mĕtadidōmi**, *met-ad-id'-o-mee;* from 3326 and 1325; to *give over,* i.e. *share:*—give {2x}, impart {3x}.

(1) This word stresses giving something that is part of and precious to the giver, as if part of the giver resides within the gift. **(2)** It means "to give a share of, impart" (*meta,* "with"), as distinct from "giving." **(2a)** The apostle Paul speaks of "sharing" some spiritual gift with Christians at Rome, Rom 1:11, "that I may impart," and exhorts those who minister in things temporal, to do so as "sharing," and **(2b)** that generously, 12:8, "he that giveth"; so in Eph 4:28; Lk 3:11; **(3)** in 1 Th 2:8 he speaks of himself and his fellow missionaries as having been well pleased to impart to the converts both God's gospel and their own souls (i.e., so "sharing" those with them as to spend themselves and spend out their lives for them). See: BAGD—510d; THAYER—404d.

3331. μετάθεσις {3x} **mĕtathĕsis**, *met-ath'-es-is;* from 3346; *transp.,* i.e. *transferral* (to heaven), *disestablishment* (of

a law):—change {1x}, removing {1x}, translation {1x}.

(1) This word stresses the permanency of the change. **(2)** *Metathesis,* "a transposition, or a transference from one place to another" (from *meta,* implying "change," and *tithemi* "to put"), **(2a)** has the meaning of "change" in Heb 7:12, **(2b)** in connection with the necessity of a "change" of the Law (or, as margin, law), if the priesthood is changed. **(3)** It is rendered "translation" in Heb 11:5, and **(4)** "removing" in Heb 12:27. See: TDNT—8:161, 1176; BAGD—511a; THAYER—405a.

3332. μεταίρω {2x} **mĕtairō**, *met-ah'-ee-ro;* from 3326 and 142; to *betake* oneself, i.e. *remove* (locally):—depart {2x}.

(1) A permanent removal without returning is implied. *Metairo,* "to make a distinction, to remove, to lift away" (in its transitive sense), is used intransitively in the NT, signifying **(2)** "to depart," and is said **(2a)** of Christ, in Mt 13:53; 19:1. **(2b)** It could be well understood as "removed." See: BAGD—511a; THAYER—405a.

3333. μετακαλέω {4x} **mĕtakalĕō**, *met-ak-al-eh'-o;* from 3326 and 2564; to *call elsewhere,* i.e. *summon:*—call {1x}, call for {1x}, call hither {1x}, call to (one's) self {1x}.

Metakaleo stresses calling someone from one place to another, especially to summon, to call to one's self (Acts 7:14; 10:32; 20:17; 24:25). See: TDNT—3:496, 394; BAGD—511a; THAYER—405a.

3334. μετακινέω {1x} **mĕtakinĕō**, *met-ak-ee-neh'-o;* from 3326 and 2795; to *stir* to a place *elsewhere,* i.e. *remove* (fig.):—move away {1x}.

Metakineo, as a verb, in the middle voice, means **(1)** "to remove oneself, shift" and is translated in the passive in Col 1:23: "be . . . not moved away (from the hope of the gospel)." **(2)** This word literally means to be stirred by external stimuli and then moving from one place or position to another. Syn.: 277, 383, 761, 2795, 2796, 4525, 4531, 4579, 4787, 5342. See: TDNT—3:720, 435; BAGD—511b; THAYER—405a.

3335. μεταλαμβάνω {6x} **mĕtalambanō**, *met-al-am-ban'-o;* from 3326 and 2983; to *participate;* generally to *accept* (and use):—eat {1x}, have {1x}, be partaker {2x}, receive {1x}, take {1x}.

Metalambano, as a verb, means "to have or get a share of, partake of" and is rendered **(1)** "receiveth": "For the earth which drinketh in the rain that cometh oft upon it, and bringeth forth herbs meet for them by whom it is dressed, receiveth (*metalambano*) blessing

from God" (Heb 6:7). It also is translated **(2)** "did eat," in Acts 2:46; **(3)** "have" in Acts 24:25; **(4)** "be partaker" in 2 Ti 2:6; Heb 12:10; and **(5)** "take" in Acts 27:23. Syn.: 324, 353, 354, 568, 588, 618, 1209, 1523, 1926, 2210, 2865, 2975, 2983, 3028, 3336, 3858, 3880, 3970, 4327, 4355, 4356, 4380, 4381, 4382, 5562, 5264, 5274. See: TDNT—4:10, 495; BAGD—511b; THAYER—405b.

3336. **μετάλημψις** {1x} **mĕtalēmpsis**, *met-al'-ampe-sis;* from *3335;* *participation:*—to be received + 1519 {1x}.

Metalempsis, as a noun, means "a participation, taking, receiving" and is used in 1 Ti 4:3, in connection with food, "to be received," literally, "with a view to [*eis*] reception: "Forbidding to marry, and commanding to abstain from meats, which God hath created to be received (*metalempsis*) with thanksgiving of them which believe and know the truth." Syn.: 324, 353, 354, 568, 588, 618, 1209, 1523, 1926, 2210, 2865, 2975, 2983, 3028, 3335, 3858, 3880, 3970, 4327, 4355, 4356, 4380, 4381, 4382, 5562, 5264, 5274. See: TDNT—4:10, 495; BAGD—511c; THAYER—405b.

3337. **μεταλλάσσω** {2x} **mĕtallassō**, *met-al-las'-so;* from *3326* and *236;* to *exchange:*—change {2x}.

This word means totally to surrender one thing for another; hence, change—give one thing for another, and exchange, meaning a supposedly equivalent swap (Rom 1:25–26). See: TDNT—1:259, 40; BAGD—511c; THAYER—405b.

3338. **μεταμέλομαι** {6x} **mĕtamĕlŏmai**, *met-am-el'-lom-ahee;* from *3326* and the mid. voice of *3199;* to *care afterwards,* i.e. *regret:*—repent {5x}, repent (one's) self {1x}.

Metamelomai, as a verb, means "to regret, to repent one," stresses a change of the will which results in change in single individual actions and is translated "to repent": "For though I made you sorry with a letter, I do not repent, though I did repent: for I perceive that the same epistle hath made you sorry, though it were but for a season" (2 Cor 7:8 [twice]). Syn.: 278. cf. 3340 for discussion. See: TDNT—4:626, 589; BAGD—511c; THAYER—405b.

3339. **μεταμορφόω** {4x} **mĕtamŏrphŏō**, *met-am-or-fŏ'-o;* from *3326* and *3445;* to *transform* (lit. or fig. "metamorphose"):—change {1x}, transfigure {2x}, transform {1x}.

Metamorphoo, as a verb, means "to change into another form" (*meta,* implying change, and *morphe,* "form"), is used in the passive voice **(1)** of Christ's "transfiguration," Mt 17:2;

Mk 9:2; Lk (in 9:29) avoids this term, which might have suggested to Gentile readers the metamorphoses of heathen gods, and uses the phrase *egeneto heteron,* "was altered", lit., "became (*ginomai*) different (*heteros*)"; **(2)** of believers, Rom 12:2, "be ye transformed," the obligation being to undergo a complete change which, under the power of God, will find expression in character and conduct; *morphe* lays stress on the inward change, *schema* (see the preceding verb in that verse, *suschematizo*) lays stress on the outward; the present continuous tenses indicate a process; **(3)** 2 Cor 3:18 describes believers as being "changed into the same image" (i.e., of Christ in all His moral excellencies), the change being effected by the Holy Spirit. See: TDNT—4:755, 607; BAGD—511d; THAYER—405c.

3340. **μετανοέω** {34x} **mĕtanŏĕō**, *met-an-ŏ-eh'-o;* from *3326* and *3539;* to *think differently* or *afterwards,* i.e. *reconsider* (mor. *feel compunction*):—repent {34x}.

Metanoeo, lit., "to perceive afterwards" (*meta,* "after," implying "change," *noeo,* "to perceive"; *nous,* "the mind, the seat of moral reflection"), in contrast to *pronoeo,* "to perceive beforehand," hence signifies **(1)** "to change one's mind or purpose," **(1a)** always, in the NT, involving a change for the better, an amendment, and always, **(1b)** except in Lk 17:3, 4, of "repentance" from sin. **(2)** The word is found in the Synoptic Gospels (in Lk, nine times), in Acts five times, in the Apocalypse twelve times, eight in the messages to the churches, 2:5 (twice), 16, 21 (twice), "she repented not" (2nd part); 3:3, 19 (the only churches in those chapters which contain no exhortation in this respect are those at Smyrna and Philadelphia); **(3)** elsewhere only in 2 Cor 12:21. **(4)** The three steps found in *metanoeo* is **(4a)** new knowledge, **(4b)** regret for the previous course, displeasure with self, and **(4c)** a change of action. Syn.: *Metamellomai* (*3338*) refers to an emotional change, *metanoeo* to a change of choice; (*3338*) has reference to particulars, (*3340*) to the entire life; (*3338*) signifies nothing but regret even amounting to remorse, (*3340*) that reversal of moral purpose known as repentance. See: TDNT—4:975, 636; BAGD—511d; THAYER—405c.

3341. **μετάνοια** {24x} **mĕtanŏia**, *met-an'-oy-ah;* from *3340;* (subj.) *compunction* (for guilt, incl. *reformation*); by impl. *reversal* (of [another's] decision):—repentance {24x}.

Metanoia, as a noun, means "afterthought, change of mind, repentance," and **(1)** is used of "repentance" from sin or evil, except in Heb

12:17, where the word "repentance" seems to mean, not simply a change of Isaac's mind, but such a change as would reverse the effects of his own previous state of mind. Esau's birthright-bargain could not be recalled; it involved an irretrievable loss. **(2)** As regards "repentance" from sin, **(2a)** the requirement by God on man's part is set forth, e.g., in Mt 3:8; Lk 3:8; Acts 20:21; 26:20; **(2b)** the mercy of God in giving "repentance" or leading men to it is set forth, e.g., in Acts 5:31; 11:18; Rom 2:4; 2 Ti 2:25.

(3) In the OT, "repentance" **(3a)** with reference to sin is not so prominent as that change of mind or purpose, out of pity for those who have been affected by one's action, or in whom the results of the action have not fulfilled expectations, a "repentance" attributed both to God and to man, e.g., Gen 6:6; Ex 32:14 (that this does not imply anything contrary to God's immutability, but that the aspect of His mind is changed toward an object that has itself changed. **(3b)** In the NT the subject chiefly has reference to "repentance" from sin, and this change of mind involves both a turning from sin and a turning to God. **(3b1)** The parable of the Prodigal Son is an outstanding illustration of this. **(3b2)** Christ began His ministry with a call to "repentance," Mt 4:17, but the call is addressed, not as in the OT to the nation, but to the individual. **(3b3)** In the Gospel of John, as distinct from the Synoptic Gospels, referred to above, "repentance" is not mentioned, even in connection with John the Baptist's preaching; in John's Gospel and 1st epistle the effects are stressed, e.g., in the new birth, and, generally, in the active turning from sin to God by the exercise of faith (Jn 3:3; 9:38; 1 Jn 1:9), as in the NT in general. See: TDNT—4:975, 636; BAGD—512c; THAYER—405d.

3342. **μεταξύ** {9x} **mĕtaxu**, *met-ax-oo';* from *3326* and a form of *4862; betwixt* (of place or pers.); (of time) as adj. *intervening*, or (by impl.) *adjoining:*—between {6x}, mean while {2x}, next {1x}.

Metaxu, "in the midst, or between", is used as a preposition, **(1)** of mutual relation, Mt 18:15; Acts 15:9; Rom 2:15, "the meanwhile" lit., "between one another"; **(2)** of place, Mt 23:35; Lk 11:51; 16:26; Acts 12:6; **(3)** of time, "meanwhile," Jn 4:31. **(4)** In Acts 13:42, "the next Sabbath" implies "in the week between," the literal rendering. See: BAGD—512d; THAYER—406b.

3343. **μεταπέμπω** {8x} **mĕtapĕmpō**, *met-ap-emp'-o;* from *3326* and *3992;* to *send* from *elsewhere*, i.e. (mid. voice)

to *summon* or *invite:*—call for {2x}, send for {6x}.

Metapempo, "to send after or for" (*meta,* "after," *pempo,* "to send"), in the middle voice, understood as "to fetch": **(1)** Peter, Acts 10:5, "call for", 22, "send for"; 29, "sent for"; 11:13, "call for"; and **(2)** Paul, Acts 24:24, "sent for"; 24:26, "sent for"; Acts 25:3, "send for." See: BAGD—513b; THAYER—406b.

3344. **μεταστρέφω** {3x} **mĕtastrĕphō**, *met-as-tref'-o;* from *3326* and *4762;* to *turn across*, i.e. *transmute* or (fig.) *corrupt:*—pervert {1x}, turn {2x}.

This word means to transform into something of an opposite character: **(1)** the Judaizers perverting the gospel of Christ (Gal 1:7); **(2)** the sun into darkness (Acts 2:20); **(3)** laughter into mourning and joy to heaviness (Jas 4:9). See: TDNT—7:729, 1093; BAGD—513b; THAYER—406b.

3345. **μετασχηματίζω** {5x} **mĕtaschēmatizō**, *met-askh-ay-mat-id'-zo;* from *3326* and a der. of *4976;* to *transfigure* or *disguise;* fig. to *apply* (by accommodation):—transform {2x}, transfer in a figure {1x}, transform (one's) self {1x}, change {1x}.

Metaschematizo, "to change in fashion or appearance" (*meta,* "after," here implying change, *schema*), is rendered **(1)** "shall change" in Phil 3:21, of the bodies of believers as changed or raised at the Lord's return; **(2)** in 2 Cor 11:13, 14, 15, to transform, of Satan and his human ministers, false apostles; **(3)** in 1 Cor 4:6 it is used by way of a rhetorical device, with the significance of transferring by a figure. Syn.: *Metamorphoo* (*3339*) refers to the permanent state to which a change takes place; whereas, *metaschematizo* (*3345*) refers to the transient condition from which a change happens. See: TDNT—7:957, 1129; BAGD—513b; THAYER—406c.

3346. **μετατίθημι** {6x} **mĕtatithēmi**, *met-at-ith'-ay-mee;* from *3326* and *5087;* to *transfer*, i.e. (lit.) *transport,* (by impl.) *exchange* (refl.) *change sides,* or (fig.) *pervert:*—carry over {1x}, change {1x}, remove {1x}, translate {2x}, turn {1x}.

Metatithemi, "to place among, put in another place" (*meta,* implying "change," and *tithemi,* "to put"), **(1)** "to remove a person or thing from one place to another", e.g., in Acts 7:16, "were carried over." It is also translated: **(2)** "to change", is said of priesthood, Heb 7:12; **(3)** "to change oneself," signifies, in the middle voice, and is so used in Gal 1:6 "(I marvel that) ye are . . . removed"; the present tense suggests that the defection of the Galatians from the

truth was not yet complete and would continue unless they changed their views. The middle voice indicates that they were themselves responsible for their decision, rather than the Judaizers who had influenced them. **(4)** "to translate" in Heb 11:5 (twice); and **(5)** "turning (the grace of God)" in Jude 4. See: TDNT—8:161, 1176; BAGD—513c; THAYER—406d.

3347. μετέπειτα {1x} **mĕtĕpĕita**, *met-ep'-i-tah;* from *3326* and *1899; thereafter:*—afterward {1x}.

Metepeita, "afterwards," without necessarily indicating an order of events is found in Heb 12:17. See: BAGD—514a; THAYER—406d.

3348. μετέχω {8x} **mĕtĕchō**, *met-ekh'-o;* from *3326* and *2192;* to *share* or *participate;* by impl. *belong* to, *eat* (or *drink):*—be partaker {5x}, pertain {1x}, take part {1x}, use {1x}.

Metecho, "to partake of, share in" (*meta*, "with," *echo*, "to have"), is translated **(1)** "be partaker of", **(1a)** lit "of partaking" in 1 Cor 9:10; **(1b)** "be partakers of" in 9:12; so in 10:17, 21; **(1c)** in 10:30 "partake"; **(2)** in Heb 2:14, "took part of", Christ "partook of" flesh and blood; **(3)** in Heb 5:13, metaphorically, of receiving elementary spiritual teaching, "useth of (milk)"; **(4)** in Heb 7:13, it is said of Christ (the antitype of Melchizedek) as "pertaineth to" another tribe than that of Levi. See: TDNT—2:830, 286; BAGD—514a; THAYER—406d.

3349. μετεωρίζω {1x} **mĕtĕōrizō**, *met-eh-o-rid'-zo;* from a compound of *3326* and a collat. form of *142* or perh. rather *109* (comp. "meteor"); to *raise in mid-air,* i.e. (fig.) *suspend* (pass. *fluctuate* or *be anxious):*—be of doubtful mind {1x}.

Meteorizo, from *meteoros* (Eng., "meteor"), signifying "in mid air, raised on high," was primarily used of putting a ship out to sea, or of "raising" fortifications, or of the "rising" of the wind. In the OT, it is used, e.g., in Mic 4:1, of the "exaltation" of the Lord's house; in Eze 10:16, of the "lifting" up of the wings of the cherubim; in Obad 4, of the "mounting" up of the eagle; in the NT metaphorically, of "being anxious," through a "distracted" state of mind, of "wavering" between hope and fear, Lk 12:29, "neither be ye of doubtful mind", addressed to those who have little faith. See: TDNT—4:630,*; BAGD—514a; THAYER—407a.

3350. μετοικεσία {4x} **mĕtŏikĕsia**, *met-oy-kes-ee'-ah;* from a der. of a compound of *3326* and *3624;* a *change of abode by force,* i.e. (spec.) *expatriation:*—carrying away into {2x}, carried away to {1x}, be brought to {1x}.

Metoikesia, "a change of abode, or a carrying away by force" (*meta,* implying "change," *oikia,* "a dwelling"), is used only of the carrying away to Babylon, Mt 1:11–12, 17. See: BAGD—514b; THAYER—407b.

3351. μετοικίζω {2x} **mĕtŏikizō**, *met-oy-kid'-zo;* from the same as *3350;* to *transfer* as a *settler* or *captive,* i.e *colonize* or *exile:*—carry away {1x}, remove into {1x}.

Metoikizo is used of the removal of Abraham into Canaan, Acts 7:4, and of the carrying of Judah into Babylon, 7:43. See: BAGD—514b; THAYER—407b.

3352. μετοχή {1x} **mĕtŏchē**, *met-okh-ay';* from *3348; participation,* i.e. *intercourse:*—fellowship {1x}. a sharing, communion, fellowship in 2 Cor 6:4. See: BAGD—514c; THAYER—407c.

3353. μέτοχος {6x} **mĕtŏchŏs**, *met'-okh-os;* from *3348; participant,* i.e. (as noun) a *sharer;* by impl. an *associate:*—fellow {1x}, partaker {4x}, partner {1x}.

Metochos, properly an adjective, signifying "sharing in, partaking of," is translated **(1)** "partners" in Lk 5:7; **(2)** "partakers" in Heb 3:1, 14; 6:4; 12:8; and **(3)** "fellows" in Heb 1:9, of those who share in a heavenly calling, or have held, or will hold, a regal position in relation to the earthly, messianic kingdom. See: TDNT—2:830, 286; BAGD—514c; THAYER—407c.

3354. μετρέω {10x} **mĕtrĕō**, *met-reh'-o;* from *3358;* to *measure* (i.e. ascertain in size by a fixed standard); by impl. to *admeasure* (i.e. allot by rule); fig. to *estimate:*—measure {7x}, mete {3x}.

Metreo, as a verb, means "to measure" and is used **(1)** of space, number, value: "And there was given me a reed like unto a rod: and the angel stood, saying, Rise, and measure the temple of God, and the altar, and them that worship therein" (Rev 11:1, cf. 11:2; 21:15, 16, 17); **(2)** metaphorically: **(2a)** "measuring [one's] self": "For we dare not make ourselves of the number, or compare ourselves with some that commend themselves: but they measuring themselves by themselves, and comparing themselves among themselves, are not wise" (2 Cor 10:12); **(2b)** in the sense of "measuring" out, giving by "measure": "For with what judgment ye judge, ye shall be judged: and with what measure ye mete (*metreo*), it shall be measured to you again" (Mt 7:2; cf. Mk 4:24; Lk 6:38). Syn.: 280, 488, 943, 2884, 3313, 3358,

4057, 4568, 5234, 5249, 5518. See: TDNT—4:632, 590; BAGD—514c; THAYER—497c.

3355. μετρητής {1x} **mĕtrētēs**, *met-ray-tace'*; from *3354;* a *measurer*, i.e. (spec.) a certain standard *measure* of capacity for liquids:—firkin {1x}.

A liquid measure containing somewhat less than nine English gallons or about 40 liters, Jn 2:6. See: BAGD—514d; THAYER—407d.

3356. μετριοπαθέω {1x} **mĕtriŏpathĕō**, *met-ree-op-ath-eh'-o;* from a compound of the base of *3357* and *3806;* to *be moderate in passion,* i.e. *gentle* (to *treat indulgently*):—have compassion {1x}.

(1) This word means to be affected moderately or in due measure, yet preserving moderation in the passions, especially anger or grief. **(2)** This word means "to treat with mildness, or moderation, to bear gently with" (*metrios,* "moderate," and *pascho,* "to suffer"), is used in Heb 5:2. **(3)** The idea is that of not being unduly disturbed by the faults and ignorance of others or rather perhaps of feeling in some measure, in contrast to the full feeling with expressed in the verb *sumpatheo* in 4:15, with reference to Christ as the High Priest. See: TDNT—5:938, 798; BAGD—514d; THAYER—407d.

3357. μετρίως {1x} **mĕtriōs**, *met-ree'-oce;* adv. from a der. of *3358; moderately,* i.e. *slightly:*—a little {1x}. See: BAGD—515a; THAYER—407d.

3358. μέτρον {13x} **mĕtrŏn**, *met'-ron;* an appar. primary word; a *measure* ("*metre*"), lit. or fig.; by impl. a limited *portion* (*degree*):—a measure {13x}.

Metron denotes **(1)** "that which is used for measuring, a measure," **(1a)** of "a vessel" figuratively: "Fill ye up then the measure of your fathers" (Mt 23: 32; cf. Lk 6:38 [twice]; **(1b)** in Jn 3:34, with the preposition *ek*, "He giveth not the Spirit unto Him" by measure." **(1b1)** Not only had Christ the Holy Spirit without "measure," but God so gives the Spirit through Him to others. **(1b2)** It is the ascended Christ who gives the Spirit to those who receive His testimony and set their seal to this, that God is true. **(1b3)** The Holy Spirit is imparted neither by degrees, nor in portions, as if He were merely an influence, He is bestowed personally upon each believer, at the time of the New Birth; **(2)** of "a graduated rod or rule for measuring," **(2a)** figuratively: "For with what judgment ye judge, ye shall be judged: and with what measure ye mete, it shall be measured to you again" (Mt 7:2; cf. Mk 4:24); **(2b)** literally: "And He that talked with me had a golden reed to measure the city, and the gates thereof, and the wall thereof" (Rev 21:15);

(3) "that which is measured, a determined extent, a portion measured off": **(3a)** of faith: "For I say, through the grace given unto me, to every man that is among you, not to think of himself more highly than he ought to think; but to think soberly, according as God hath dealt to every man the measure of faith" (Rom 12:3; cf. 2 Cor 10:13 [twice]; **(3b)** of grace: "But unto every one of us is given grace according to the measure of the gift of Christ" (Eph 4:7), the gift of grace is "measured" and given according to the will of Christ; whatever the endowment, His is the bestowment and the adjustment; **(3c)** Eph 4:13 "the measure (of the stature of the fullness of Christ)," the standard of spiritual stature being the fullness which is essentially Christ's; **(3d)** Eph 4:16, "according to the working in due measure of each several part," i.e., according to the effectual working of the ministration rendered in due "measure" by every part. Syn.: 280, 488, 943, 2884, 3313, 3354, 4057, 4568, 5234, 5249, 5518. See: TDNT—4:632, 590; BAGD—515a; THAYER—408a.

3359. μέτωπον {8x} **mĕtōpŏn**, *met'-o-pon;* from *3326* and ὤψ **ōps** (the *face*); the *forehead* (as *opposite*, the *countenance*):—forehead {8x}.

Metopon, from *meta,* "with," and *ops,* "an eye," occurs only in the Apocalypse, 7:3; 9:4; 13:16; 14:1, 9; 17:5; 20:4; 22:4. See: TDNT—4:635, 591; BAGD—515b; THAYER—408a.

3360. μέχρι {17x} **mĕchri** *mekh'-ree;* or

μεχρίς **mĕchris**, *mekh-ris';* from *3372; as far as,* i.e. *up to* a certain point (as a prep. of extent [denoting the *terminus,* whereas *891* refers espec. to the *space* of time or place intervening] or a conjunc.):—unto {7x}, until {7x}, till {1x}, to {1x}, till + 3739 {1x}. See: BAGD—515b; THAYER—408b.

3361. μή {674x} **mē**, *may;* a primary particle of qualified *negation* (whereas *3756* expresses an absolute denial); (adv.) *not,* (conjunc.) *lest;* also (as an interrog. implying a neg. answer [whereas *3756* expects an *affirmative* one]) *whether:*—not {487x}, no {44x}, that not {21x}, God forbid + 1096 {15x}, lest {14x}, neither {7x}, no man + 5100 {6x}, but {3x}, none {3x}, not translated {51x}, misc. {23x} = any, ✕ forbear, + lack, never, nor, nothing, untaken, without. Often used in compounds in substantially the same relations. See also *3362, 3363, 3364, 3372, 3373, 3375, 3378.* See: BAGD—515d; THAYER—408b.

3362. ἐὰν μή {60x} **ĕan mē**, *eh-an' may;* i.e. *1437* and *3361; if not,* i.e. *unless:*—except {33x}, if not {16x}, whosoever not

+ 3739 {5x}, but {3x}, if no {1x}, not {1x}, before {1x}. See: BAGD—515d; 211c [1437]; THAYER—408d.

3363. ἵνα μή {97x} **hina mē** *hin'-ah may;* i.e. *2443* and *3361; in order* (or *so*) *that not:*—that not {45x}, lest {43x}, that . . . no {6x}, that nothing + 5100 {1x}, albeit not {1x}, so that not {1x}. See: BAGD—516a; THAYER—302c.

3364. οὐ μή {94x} **ŏu mē**, *oo may;* i.e. *3756* and *3361;* a double neg. streng. the denial; *not at all:*—not {56x}, in no wise {6x}, no {6x}, never + 1519 + 165 + 3588 {6x}, no more at all + 2089 {5x}, not tr. {1x}, misc. {14x} = any more, by any (no) means, neither, in no case, nor ever. See: BAGD—517c; THAYER—411b. comp. *3378*.

3365. μηδαμῶς {2x} **mēdamōs**, *may-dam-oce';* adv. from a compound of *3361* and ἀμός **amŏs** (*somebody*); *by no means:*—not so {2x}. See: BAGD—517d; THAYER—411b.

3366. μηδέ {57x} **mēdě**, *may-deh';* from *3361* and *1161; but not, not even;* in a continued negation, *nor:*—neither {32x}, nor {18x}, not {3x}, nor yet {1x}, not once {1x}, no not {1x}, not so much as {1x}. See: BAGD—517d; THAYER—411b.

3367. μηδείς {91x} **mēdĕis**, *may-dice';* incl. the irreg. fem. μηδεμία **mēdĕ-mia** *may-dem-ee'-ah;* and the neut. μηδέν **mēdĕn**, *may-den';* from *3361* and *1520; not even one* (man, woman, thing):—no man {32x}, nothing {27x}, no {16x}, none {6x}, not {1x}, anything {2x} misc. {7x} = not (at all, any man, a whit), + without delay.

This form is found, not in direct negative statements, but **(1)** in warnings, prohibitions, etc., e.g., Mt 27:19; Acts 19:36; **(2)** in expressions conveying certain impossibilities, e.g., Acts 4:21; **(3)** comparisons, e.g., 2 Cor 6:10; **(4)** intimating a supposition to the contrary, 1 Ti 6:4; **(5)** adverbially, e.g., 2 Cor 11:5, "not a whit." See: BAGD—518a; THAYER—411c.

3368. μηδέποτε {1x} **mēdĕpŏtě**, *may-dep'-ot-eh;* from *3366* and *4218; not even ever:*—never {1x}. See: BAGD—518b; THAYER—412a.

3369. μηδέπω {1x} **mēdĕpō**, *may-dep'-o;* from *3366* and *4452; not even yet:*—not as yet {1x}. See: BAGD—518b; THAYER—412a.

3370. Μῆδος {1x} **Mēdŏs**, *may'-dos;* of for. or. [comp. *4074*]; a *Median,* or in-hab. of Media:—Mede {1x}. See: BAGD—518b; THAYER—412a.

3371. μηκέτι {21x} **mēkĕti**, *may-ket'-ee;* from *3361* and *2089; no fur-ther:*—no more {7x}, no longer {4x}, henceforth not {2x}, no {1x}, no . . . henceforward {1x}, hereafter {1x}, misc. {5x} = any longer, not any more.

Meketi means "no more, no longer," but generally **(1)** suggests what is a matter of thought or supposition, whereas *eti* refers to what is a matter of fact. **(2)** It is rendered **(2a)** "any longer" in Acts 25:24; **(2b)** "no lon-ger," in Mk 2:2, "no (room)"; **(2c)** 2 Cor 5:15, "not henceforth"; **(2d)** Eph 4:14, "no more"; 4:17, "henceforth . . . not"; **(2e)** "no longer", 1 Th 3:1, 5; 1 Ti 5:23; 1 Pet 4:2. See: BAGD—518c; THAYER—412a.

3372. μῆκος {3x} **mēkŏs**, *may'-kos;* prob. akin to *3173; length* (lit. or fig.):—length {3x}.

Mekos, "length," from the same root as *makros,* "long", occurs in Eph 3:18 and Rev 21:16 (twice). See: BAGD—518c; THAYER—412b.

3373. μηκύνω {1x} **mēkunō**, *may-koo'-no;* from *3372;* to *lengthen,* i.e. (mid. voice) to *enlarge:*—grow up {1x}.

Mekuno, "to grow long, lengthen, extend" (from *mekos,* "length"), is used of the "growth" of plants, in Mk 4:27. See: BAGD—518d; THAYER—412b.

3374. μηλωτή {1x} **mēlōtē**, *may-lo-tay';* from μῆλον **mēlŏn**, (a *sheep*); a *sheep-skin:*—sheepskin {1x}. See: TDNT—4:637, 591; BAGD—518d; THAYER—412b.

3375. μήν {1x} **mēn**, *mane;* a stronger form of *3303;* a particle of affirmation (only with *2229*); *assuredly:*—surely + 2229 {1x}. See: BAGD—518d; THAYER—412c.

3376. μήν {18x} **mēn**, *mane;* a primary word; a *month:*—month {18x}.

Men, connected with *mene,* "the moon," akin to a Sanskrit root *ma—*, "to measure" (the Sanskrit *masa* denotes both moon and month, cf, e.g., Lat. *mensis,* Eng., "moon" and "month," the moon being in early times the measure of the "month"). **(1)** The interval be-tween the 17th day of the second "month" (Gen 7:11) and the 17th day of the seventh "month," is said to be 150 days (8:3, 4), i.e., five months of 30 days each; hence the year would be 360 days (cf. Dan 7:25; 9:27; 12:7 with Rev 11:2–3; 12:6, 14; 13:5; whence we conclude that 3½ years or 42 months = 1260 days, i.e., one year = 360 days); this was the length of the old Egyp-tian year; later, five days were added to corre-spond to the solar year. The Hebrew year was

as nearly solar as was compatible with its commencement, coinciding with the new moon, or first day of the "month." This was a regular feast day, Num 10:10; 28:11–14; the Passover coincided with the full moon (the 14th of the month Abib). **(2)** Except in Gal 4:10; Jas 5:17; Rev 9:5, 10, 15; 11:2; 13:5; 22:2, the word is found only in Luke's writings, Lk 1:24, 26, 36, 56; 4:25; Acts 7:20; 18:11; 19:8; 20:3; 28:11, examples of Luke's care as to accuracy of detail. Syn.: 5072, 5150. See: TDNT—4:638, 591; BAGD—518d; THAYER—412c.

3377. **μηνύω** {4x} **mēnuō**, *may-noo′-o;* prob. from the same base as *3145* and *3415* (i.e. μάω **maō**, to *strive*); to *disclose* (through the idea of ment. *effort* and thus calling to *mind*), i.e. *report, declare, intimate:*—shew {3x}, tell {1x}.

Menuo, "to disclose, make known" (what was secret), is rendered **(1)** "to show" in Lk 20:37; 1 Cor 10:28; in a forensic sense, Jn 11:57; and **(2)** Acts 23:30, "it was told." See: BAGD—519a; THAYER—412c.

3378. **μὴ οὐκ** {6x} **mē ŏuk**, *may ook;* i.e. *3361* and *3756;* as interrog. and neg. *is it not that?:*—not {6x}. See: BAGD—519b; 517b; THAYER—412c. comp. *3364.*

3379. **μήποτε** {25x} **mēpŏtĕ**, *may′-pot-eh;* or

μή ποτε **mē pŏtĕ**, *may pot′-eh;* from *3361* and *4218; not ever;* also *if* (or *lest*) *ever* (or *perhaps*):—lest {12x}, lest at any time {7x}, whether or not {1x}, lest haply + *2443* {1x}, if peradventure {1x}, no . . . not at all {1x}, not tr {1x}.

Mepote, lit., "lest ever," **(1)** "lest haply," e.g., Lk 14:29, of laying a foundation, with the possibility of being unable to finish the building; **(2)** Acts 5:39, of the possibility of being found fighting against God; **(3)** Heb 3:12, "lest " of the possibility of having an evil heart of unbelief; **(4)** "lest at any time", e.g., Mt 4:6; 5:25; 13:15; Mk 4:12; Lk 4:11; 21:34; Heb 2:1; **(5)** in 2 Ti 2:25, "if peradventure"; **(6)** in Jn 7:26, "Do." See: BAGD—519b; THAYER—412d.

3380. **μήπω** {2x} **mēpō**, *may′-po;* from *3361* and *4452; not yet:*—not yet {2x}. Cf. Rom 9:11; Heb 9:8. See: BAGD—519c; THAYER—413b.

3381. **μήπως** {12x} **mēpōs**, *may′-poce;* or

μή πως **mē pōs**, *may poce;* from *3361* and *4458; lest somehow:*—lest {5x}, lest by any means {3x}, lest perhaps {1x}, lest haply {1x}, lest by some means {1x}, lest that by any means {1x}. See: BAGD—519c; THAYER—413b.

3382. **μηρός** {1x} **mērŏs**, *may-ros′;* perh. a primary word; a *thigh:*—thigh {1x}.

Meros occurs in Rev 19:16; Christ appears there in the manifestation of His judicial capacity and action hereafter as the executor of divine vengeance upon the foes of God; His name is spoken of figuratively as being upon His "thigh" (where the sword would be worn; cf. Ps 45:3), emblematic of His strength to tread down His foes, His action being the exhibition of His divine attributes of righteousness and power. See: BAGD—519d; THAYER—413c.

3383. **μήτε** {37x} **mētĕ**, *may′-teh;* from *3361* and *5037; not too,* i.e. (in continued negation) *neither* or *nor;* also, *not even:*—neither {20x}, nor {15x}, so much as {1x}, or {1x}. See: BAGD—519d; THAYER—413c.

3384. **μήτηρ** {85x} **mētēr**, *may′-tare;* appar. a primary word; a *"mother"* (lit. or fig., immed. or remote):—mother {85x}.

Meter is used **(1)** of the natural relationship (e.g., Mt 1:18; 2 Ti 1:5); **(2)** figuratively, **(2a)** of "one who takes the place of a mother," (Mt 12:49, 50; Mk 3:34, 35; Jn 19:27; Rom 16:13; 1 Ti 5:2); **(2b)** of "the heavenly and spiritual Jerusalem" (Gal 4:26, which is "free" not bound by law imposed externally, as under the Law of Moses), "which is our mother", i.e., of Christians, the metropolis, mother-city, used allegorically, just as the capital of a country is "the seat of its government, the center of its activities, and the place where the national characteristics are most fully expressed; **(3)** symbolically, of "Babylon" (Rev 17:5), as the source from which has proceeded the religious harlotry of mingling pagan rites and doctrines with the Christian faith. **(4)** Note: In Mk 16:1 the article, followed by the genitive case of the name "James," the word "mother" being omitted, is an idiomatic mode of expressing the phrase "the mother of James." See: TDNT—4:642, 592; BAGD—520a; THAYER—413d.

3385. **μήτι** {15x} **mēti**, *may′-tee;* from *3361* and the neut. of *5100; whether at all:*—not {2x}, not tr. {13x} [*the particle usually not expressed, except by the form of the question*]. See: BAGD—520b; THAYER—413d.

3386. **μήτιγε** {1x} **mētigĕ**, *may′-tig-eh;* from *3385* and *1065; not at all then,* i.e. *not to say* (*the rather still*):—how much more {1x}. See: BAGD—520b; THAYER—414a.

3387. **μήτις** {4x} **mētis**, *may′-tis;* or

μή τις **mē tis** *may tis;* from *3361* and *5100; whether any:*—any {2x}, any man {1x}, not tr. {1x} [*sometimes unexpressed except by the simple interrogative*

form of the sentence]. See: BAGD—517b [3361]; THAYER—414a.

3388. **μήτρα** {2x} **mētra**, *may'-trah;* from *3384;* the *matrix:*—womb {2x}.

Metra, the matrix (akin to *meter* "a mother"), occurs in Lk 2:23; Rom. 4:19. See: BAGD—520b; THAYER—414a.

3389. **μητραλῴας** {1x} **mētralŏias**, *may-tral-o'-as* or

μετρολῴας **mĕtrolŏias**, *may-trol-o'-as;* from *3384* and the base of *257;* a *mother-thresher,* i.e. *matricide:*—murderers of mothers {1x}.

Metroloas, or *metraloas* denotes "a matricide" (1 Tim 1:9 "murderers of mothers"). See: BAGD—520c; THAYER—414a.

3390. **μητρόπολις** {1x} **mētrŏpŏlis**, *may-trop'-ol-is;* from *3384* and *4172;* a *mother city,* i.e. *"metropolis":*—chiefest city {1x}. See: BAGD—520c; THAYER—414a.

3391. **μία** {79x} **mia**, *mee'-ah;* irreg. fem. of *1520; one* or *first:*—one {62x}, first {8x}, a certain {4x}, a {3x}, the other {1x}, agree + 4160 + 1106 {1x}. See: BAGD—230d [1520]; THAYER—414a.

3392. **μιαίνω** {5x} **miainō**, *me-ah'-ee-no;* perh. a primary verb; to *sully* or *taint,* i.e. *contaminate* (cer. or mor.):—defile {5x}.

Miaino, primarily, "to stain, to tinge or dye with another color," as in the staining of a glass, hence, "to pollute, contaminate, soil, defile," is used (1) of "ceremonial defilement," Jn 18:28; cf. Lev 22:5, 8; Num 19:13, 20; (2) of "moral defilement," Titus 1:15 (twice); (3) Heb 12:15; "of moral and physical defilement," Jude 8. Syn.: *Miaino* (*3392*) means to stain, and differs from *moluno* (*3435*), to smear, not only in its primary and outward sense, but in the circumstance that (like Eng. "stain") it may be used in good part, while 3435 has no worthy reference. See: TDNT—4:644, 593; BAGD—520d; THAYER—414a.

3393. **μίασμα** {1x} **miasma**, *mee'-as-mah;* from *3392* ("*miasma*"); (mor.) *foulness* (prop. the effect):—pollution {1x}.

Miasma denotes the vices of the ungodly which contaminate a person in his interaction with the world, 2 Pet 2:20. See: TDNT—4:646, 593; BAGD—521a; THAYER—414b.

3394. **μιασμός** {1x} **miasmŏs**, *mee-as-mos';* from *3392;* (mor.) *contamination* (prop. the act of defiling):—uncleanness {1x}.

Miasmos, (1) primarily denotes "the act of

defiling," the process, in contrast to the "defiling" thing (*3393*). (2) *Miasmos,* as a noun, is rendered "uncleanness" in 2 Pet 2:10: "But chiefly them that walk after the flesh in the lust of uncleanness (*miasmos*), and despise government. Presumptuous are they, selfwilled, they are not afraid to speak evil of dignities." Syn.: 167, 169, 2839, 2840. See: TDNT—4:647, 593; BAGD—521a; THAYER—414b.

3395. **μίγμα** {1x} **migma**, *mig'-mah;* from *3396;* a *compound:*—mixture {1x}. See: BAGD—521a; THAYER—414c.

3396. **μίγνυμι** {4x} **mignumi**, *mig'-noo-mee;* a primary verb; to *mix:*—mingle {4x}.

Mignumi, "to mix, mingle" (from a root *mik;* Eng., "mix" is akin), is always in the NT translated "to mingle," Mt 27:34; Lk 13:1; Rev 8:7; 15:2. Syn.: *Keramos* (*2766*) denotes in a strict sense, mixing as combines the ingredients into a new compound, chemical mixture, inseparable. *Mignumi* denotes such a mixture as merely blending or intermingling of them promiscuously, as in a mechanical mixture; hence, separable. See: BAGD—521a; 499c; THAYER—414c.

3397. **μικρόν** {16x} **mikrŏn**, *mik-ron';* masc. or neut. sing. of *3398* (as noun); a *small* space of *time* or *degree:*—a little while {9x}, a little {6x}, a while {1x}.

Mikron, the neuter of *mikros* (*3398*) is used adverbially (1) of distance, Mt 26:39; Mk 14:35; (2) of quantity, 2 Cor 11:1, 16; (3) of time, Mt 26:73, "a while"; Mk 14:70; Jn 13:33, "a little while", 14:19; 16:16–19; Heb 10:37, with the repeated *hoson,* "how very," lit., "a little while, how very, how little!" See: BAGD—521b; THAYER—414c.

3398. **μικρός** {30x} **mikrŏs**, *mik-ros';* incl. the comp.

μικρότερος **mikrŏtĕrŏs**, *mik-rot'-er-os;* appar. a primary word; *small* (in size, quantity, number or (fig.) dignity):—least {6x}, less {2x}, little {14x}, small {6x}.

Mikron, "little, small" (the opposite of *megos,* "great"), is used (1) of persons, with regard to (1a) station, or age, in the singular, Mk 15:40, of James "the less", possibly referring to age; Lk 19:3; in the plural, "little" ones, Mt 18:6, 10, 14; Mk 9:42; (1b) rank or influence, e.g., Mt 10:42 (see context); Acts 8:10; 26:22, "small," as in Rev 11:18; 13:16; 19:5, 18; 20:12; (2) of things, with regard to (2a) size, e.g., Jas 3:5; (2b) quantity, Lk 12:32; 1 Cor 5:6; Gal 5:9; Rev 3:8; (2c) time, Jn 7:33; 12:35; Rev 6:11; 20:3.

See: TDNT—4:648, 593; BAGD—521b; THAYER—414c.

3399. Μίλητος {3x} **Milētŏs**, *mil'-ay-tos;* of uncert. or.; *Miletus,* a city of Asia Minor:—Miletus {2x}, Miletum {1x}. See: BAGD—521d; THAYER—414d.

3400. μίλιον {1x} **miliŏn**, *mil'-ee-on;* of Lat. or.; a *thousand* paces, i.e. a *"mile":*—mile {1x}.

A mile, among the Romans, is the distance of a thousand paces or eight stadia, about 1.5 km [somewhat less than our mile], Mt 5:41. See: BAGD—521d; THAYER—414d.

3401. μιμέομαι {4x} **mimĕŏmai**, *mim-eh'-om-ahee;* mid. voice from μῖμος**mimŏs** (a *"mimic"*); to *imitate:*—follow {4x}.

(1) This verb is always used in exhortations, and always in the continuous tense, suggesting a constant habit or practice. **(2)** *Mimeomai,* "a mimic, an actor" (Eng., "mime," etc.), is translated "to follow," **(2a)** of imitating the conduct of missionaries, 2 Th 3:7, 9; **(2b)** the faith of spiritual guides, Heb 13:7; **(2c)** that which is good, 3 Jn 11. See: TDNT—4:659, 594; BAGD—521d; THAYER—414d.

3402. μιμητής {7x} **mimētēs**, *mim-ay-tace';* from *3401;* an *imitator:*—follower {7x}.

Mimetes, "a follower," is always used in a good sense in the NT. **(1)** In 1 Cor 4:16; 11:1; Eph 5:1; Heb 6:12, it is used in exhortations, accompanied by the verb *ginomai,* "to be, become," and in the continuous tense (except in Heb 6:12, where the aorist or momentary tense indicates a decisive act with permanent results); **(2)** in 1 Th 1:6; 2:14, the accompanying verb is in the aorist tense, referring to the definite act of conversion in the past. **(3)** These instances, coupled with the continuous tenses referred to, teach that what we became at conversion we must diligently continue to be thereafter. See: TDNT—4:659, 594; BAGD—522a; THAYER—415a.

3403. μιμνήσκω {2x} **mimnēskō**, *mim-nace'-ko;* a prol. form of *3415* (from which some of the tenses are borrowed); to *remind,* i.e. (mid. voice) to *recall to mind:*—be mindful {1x}, remember {1x}.

Mimnesko, from the older form *mnaomai,* in the active voice signifies "to remind"; in the middle voice, "to remind oneself of," hence, "to remember, to be mindful of"; the later form is found only in the present tense, **(1)** in Heb 2:6, "are mindful of," and **(2)** 13:3, "remember." **(3)** By comparison, the perfect tense in 1 Cor 11:2 and in 2 Ti 1:4, "being mindful of", is used

with a present meaning. **(4)** See also **(4a)** Lk 1:54, "in remembrance of"; **(4b)** 2 Pet 3:2, "be mindful of"; **(4c)** Rev 16:19 (passive voice), "came in remembrance". **(4d)** The passive voice is used also in Acts 10:31, "are had in remembrance." See: BAGD—522b; THAYER—415a.

3404. μισέω {42x} **misĕō**, *mis-eh'-o;* from a primary μῖσος **misŏs** (*hatred*); to *detest* (espec. to *persecute*); by extens. to *love less:*—hate {41x}, hateful {1x}.

Miseo, as a verb, means "to hate," is used especially **(1)** of malicious and unjustifiable feelings towards others, whether towards the innocent or by mutual animosity, e.g., Mt 10:22; 24:10; Lk 6:22, 27; 19:14; Jn 3:20, of "hating" the light (metaphorically); 7:7; 15:18, 19, 23–25; Titus 3:3; 1 Jn 2:9, 11; 3:13, 15; 4:20; Rev 18:2, where "hateful" translates the perfect participle passive voice of the verb, lit., "hated," or "having been hated"; **(2)** of a right feeling of aversion from what is evil; **(2a)** said of wrongdoing, Rom 7:15; **(2b)** iniquity, Heb 1:9; **(2c)** "the garment (figurative) spotted by the flesh," Jude 23; **(2d)** "the works of the Nicolaitans," Rev 2:6, 15;

(3) of relative preference for one thing over another, by way of expressing either aversion from, or disregard for, the claims of one person or thing relatively to those of another, **(3a)** Mt 6:24, and Lk 16:13, as to the impossibility of serving two masters; **(3b)** Lk 14:26, as to the claims of parents relatively to those of Christ; **(3c)** Jn 12:25, of disregard for one's life relatively to the claims of Christ; **(3d)** Eph 5:29, negatively, of one's flesh, i.e. of one's own, and therefore a man's wife as one with him; **(3e)** Rom 9:13, of God "hating" Esau. No emotions are involved here, just God's sovereign choice. **(4)** In 1 Jn 3:15, he who "hates" his brother is called a murderer; for the sin lies in the inward disposition, of which the act is only the outward expression. Syn.: 2189, 2319, 4767. See: TDNT—4:683, 597; BAGD—522c; THAYER—415b.

3405. μισθαποδοσία {3x} **misthapŏdŏsia**, *mis-thap-od-os-ee'-ah;* from *3406; requital* (good or bad):—recompence of reward {3x}.

This noun stands for payment of wages due, recompence. Cf. Heb 22:2; 10:35; 11:26. See: TDNT—4:695, 599; BAGD—523a; THAYER—415c.

3406. μισθαποδότης {1x} **misthapŏdŏtēs**, *mis-thap-od-ot'-ace;* from *3409* and *591;* a *renumerator:*—rewarder {1x}. See: TDNT—4:695, 599; BAGD—523a; THAYER—415c.

3407. **μίσθιος** {2x} **misthiŏs,** *mis'-thee-os;* from *3408;* a *wage-earner:—* hired servant {2x}.

Misthios, an adjective, signifying "a hired servant," is used in Lk 15:17, 19. See: TDNT—4:695, 599; BAGD—523a; THAYER—415c.

3408. **μισθός** {29x} **misthŏs,** *mis-thos';* appar. a primary word; *pay* for services (lit. or fig.), good or bad:—hire {3x}, reward {24x}, wages {2x}.

Misthos, primarily "wages, hire," and then, generally, "reward," **(1)** received in this life, Mt 5:46; 6:2, 5, 16; Rom 4:4; 1 Cor 9:17, 18; of evil "rewards," Acts 1:18; **(2)** to be received hereafter, Mt 5:12; 10:41 (twice), 42; Mk 9:41; Lk 6:23, 35; 1 Cor 3:8, 14; 2 Jn 8; Rev 11:18; 22:12. See: TDNT—4:695, 599; BAGD—523b; THAYER—415c.

3409. **μισθόω** {2x} **misthŏō,** *mis-thŏ'-o;* from *3408;* to *let* out for wages, i.e. (mid. voice) to *hire:—*hire {2x}.

Misthoo, "to let out for hire," is used in the middle voice, signifying "to hire, to engage the services of anyone by contract," Mt 20:1, 7. See: TDNT—4:695, 599; BAGD—523d; THAYER—415d.

3410. **μίσθωμα** {1x} **misthōma,** *mis'-tho-mah;* from *3409;* a *rented* building:—hired house {1x}.

Misthoma, primarily, "a price, a hire" (akin to *misthos,* "wages, hire" and *misthoo,* "to let out for hire") is used in Acts 28:30 to denote "a hired dwelling." See: BAGD—523d; THAYER—415d.

3411. **μισθωτός** {4x} **misthōtŏs,** *mis-tho-tos';* from *3409;* a *wage-worker* (good or bad):—hired servant {1x}, hireling {3x}.

Misthotos, an adjective denoting "hired," is used as a noun, signifying "one who is hired," **(1)** "hired servants," Mk 1:20; **(2)** "hireling," Jn 10:12, 13 twice; here, it expresses, not only one who has no real interest in his duty (that may or may not be present in its use in Mk 1:20), but one who is unfaithful in the discharge of it; that sense attaches always to the word rendered "hireling." See: TDNT—4:695, 599; BAGD—523d; THAYER—415d.

3412. **Μιτυλήνη** {1x} **Mitulēnē,** *mit-oo-lay'-nay;* for μυτιλήνη **muti-lēnē,** *(abounding in shell-fish);* Mitylene (or Mytilene), a town on the island of Lesbos:—Mitylene {1x}. See: BAGD—524a; THAYER—415d.

3413. **Μιχαήλ** {2x} **Michaēl,** *mikh-ah-ale';* of Heb. or. [4317]; *Michaël,* an archangel:—*Michael* {2x}. See: BAGD—524a; THAYER—415d.

3414. **μνᾶ** {9x} **mna,** *mnah;* of Lat. or.; a *mna* (i.e. *mina*), a certain *weight:—*pound {9x}.

In the NT, a weight and sum of money equal to 100 drachmae, one talent was 100 pounds, a pound equaled 10⅓ oz. (300 gm) and occurs in Lk 19:13, 16 (twice), 18 (twice), 20, 24 (twice), 25. See: BAGD—524a; THAYER—416a.

3415. **μνάομαι** {21x} **mnaŏmai,** *mnah'-om-ahee;* mid. voice of a der. of *3306* or perh. of the base of *3145* (through the idea of *fixture* in the mind or of mental *grasp*); to *bear in mind,* i.e. *recollect;* by impl. to *reward* or *punish:—*remember {16x}, be mindful {2x}, be had in remembrance {1x}, in remembrance {1x}, come in remembrance {1x}. See: BAGD—524b; THAYER—416a. comp. *3403.*

3416. **Μνάσων** {1x} **Mnasōn,** *mnah'-sohn;* of uncert. or.; *Mnason,* a Chr.:—*Mnason* {1x}. See: BAGD—524b; THAYER—416a.

3417. **μνεία** {7x} **mnĕia,** *mni'-ah;* from *3415* or *3403; recollection;* by impl. *recital:—*mention {4x}, remembrance {3x}.

Mneia, "remembrance, mention" (akin to *mimnesko,* "to remind, remember"), is always used in connection with prayer, and translated **(1)** "mention" in Rom 1:9; Eph 1:16; 1 Th 1:2; Philem 4, in each of which it is preceded by the verb to make; **(2)** "remembrance" in Phil 1:3; 1 Th 3:6; 2 Ti 1:3. See: TDNT—4:678, 596; BAGD—524b; THAYER—416a.

3418. **μνῆμα** {7x} **mnēma,** *mnay'-mah;* from *3415;* a *memorial,* i.e. sepulchral *monument (burial-place):—*grave {1x}, sepulchre {4x}, tomb {2x}.

This word first signified "a memorial" or "record of a thing or a dead person," then "a sepulchral monument," and hence "a tomb"; **(1)** it is rendered "graves" in Rev 11:9; **(2)** "tomb" or "tombs" in Mk 5: 5; Lk 8:27; and **(3)** "sepulcher" in Lk 23:53; 24:1; Acts 2:29; 7:16. See: TDNT—4:679, 596; BAGD—524c; THAYER—416a.

3419. **μνημεῖον** {42x} **mnēmĕiŏn,** *mnay-mi'-on;* from *3420;* a *remembrance,* i.e. cenotaph *(place of interment):—*grave {8x}, sepulchre {29x}, tomb {5x}.

Mnemeion, primarily denotes **(1)** "a memorial" (akin to *mnaomai,* "to remember"), then, **(1a)** "a monument" (the significance of the word rendered "sepulchres," in Lk 11:47), **(1b)** anything done to preserve the memory of things and persons; **(2)** it usually denotes a

tomb, and is translated either "tomb" or "sepulchre" or "grave." **(3)** Apart from the Gospels, it is found only in Acts 13:29. Among the Hebrews it was generally a cavern, closed by a door or stone, often decorated. Cf. Mt 8:28; 27:60; 23:29; Mk 5:2; 6:29. Syn.: In English, a sepulchre is a general term designating a place for safekeeping, especially for safekeeping a dead body and may be decorated with something as a memorial, Mt 23:29. A grave is also a general word for a place where a dead body is placed, but usually implying going/digging down into the earth, Mt 27:52. [cf. "the sea was his grave"]. A tomb is secured grave, usually implying something above ground, like a cave, where the body is sealed and lain with some kind of "memorial" marker placed upon it, Mt 27:60. See: TDNT—4:680, 596; BAGD—524c; THAYER—416b.

3420. **μνήμη** {1x} **mnēmē,** *mnay'-may;* from *3403; memory:—*remembrance {1x}.

Mneme denotes "a memory" (akin to *mnaomai*), "remembrance, mention," 2 Pet 1:15, "remembrance"; here, however, it is used with *poieo,* "to make" (middle voice), and some suggest that the meaning is "to make mention." See: TDNT—4:679, 596; BAGD—524d; THAYER—416b.

3421. **μνημονεύω** {21x} **mnēmŏnĕuō,** *mnay-mon-yoo'-o;* from a der. of *3420;* to *exercise memory,* i.e. *recollect;* by impl. to *punish;* also to *rehearse:—*make mention {1x}, be mindful {1x}, remember {19x}.

Mnemoneul signifies **(1)** "to call to mind, remember"; **(1a)** it is used absolutely in Mk 8:18; **(1b)** everywhere else it has an object, **(2)** persons, Lk 17:32; Gal 2:10; **(2a)** 2 Ti 2:8; Paul was not reminding Timothy (nor did he need to) that Christ was raised from the dead, **(2b)** what was needful for him was to "remember" (to keep in mind) the One who rose, the Source and Supplier of all his requirements; **(3)** things, e.g., Mt 16:9; Jn 15:20; 16:21; Acts 20:35; Col 4:18; 1 Th 1:3; 2:9; Heb 11:15, "had been mindful of"; 13:7; Rev 18:5; **(4)** a clause, representing a circumstance, etc., Jn 16:4; Acts 20:31; Eph 2:11; 2 Th 2:5; Rev 2:5; 3:3; **(5)** in Heb 11:22 it signifies "to make mention of." See: TDNT—4:682, 596; BAGD—525a; THAYER—416b.

3422. **μνημόσυνον** {3x} **mnēmŏsunŏn,** *mnay-mos'-oo-non;* from *3421;* a *reminder* (*memorandum*), i.e. *record:—*memorial {3x}.

This noun denotes a memorial, that which keeps alive the memory of someone or some-

thing (Mt 26:13; Mk 14:9; Acts 10:4). See: BAGD—525b; THAYER—416c.

3423. **μνηστεύω** {3x} **mnēstĕuō,** *mnace-tyoo'-o;* from a der. of *3415;* to *give a souvenir* (engagement present), i.e. *betroth:—*espouse {3x}.

Mneustos, in the active voice, signifies "to woo a woman and ask for her in marriage"; in the NT, only in the passive voice, "to be promised in marriage, to be betrothed," Mt 1:18; Lk 1:27; 2:5, "espoused". See: BAGD—525c; THAYER—416c.

3424. **μογιλάλος** {1x} **mŏgilalŏs,** *mog-il-al'-os;* from *3425* and *2980;* *hardly talking,* i.e. *dumb* (*tongue-tied*):—having an impediment in his speech.

Mogilalos denotes "speaking with difficulty" (*mogis,* "hardly," *laleo,* "to talk"), "stammering," Mk 7:32. See: BAGD—525c; THAYER—416d.

3425. **μόγις** {1x} **mŏgis,** *mog'-is;* adv. from a primary μόγος **mŏgŏs,** (*toil*); *with difficulty:—*hardly {1x}.

Mogis, "with labor, pain, trouble" (akin to *mogos,* "toil"), Lk 9:39. See: TDNT—4:735, 606; BAGD—525d; THAYER—416d.

3426. **μόδιος** {3x} **mŏdiŏs,** *mod'-ee-os;* of Lat. or.; a *modius,* i.e. certain measure for things dry (the quantity or the utensil):—bushel {3x}.

Modios was a dry measure containing about a peck, Mt 5:15; Mk 4:21; Lk 11:33. See: BAGD—525d; THAYER—416d.

3427. **μοί** {240x} **mŏi,** *moy;* the simpler form of *1698; to me:—*me {218x}, my {11x}, I {10x}, mine {1x}. See: BAGD—255b [1698]; THAYER—207c [1698].

3428. **μοιχαλίς** {7x} **mŏichalis,** *moy-khal-is';* a prol. form of the fem. of *3432;* an *adulteress* (lit. or fig.):—adulterous {3x}, adulteress {3x}, adultery {1x}.

Moichalis, "an adulteress," is used **(1)** in the natural sense, 2 Pet 2:14; Rom 7:3; **(2)** in the spiritual sense, Jas 4:4. **(3)** As in Israel the breach of their relationship with God through their idolatry, was described as "adultery" or "harlotry" (e.g., Eze 16:15; 23:43), so believers who cultivate friendship with the world, thus breaking their spiritual union with Christ, are spiritual "adulteresses," having been spiritually united to Him as wife to husband, Rom 7:4. **(4)** It is used adjectively to describe the Jewish people in transferring their affections from God, Mt 12:39; 16:4; Mk 8:38. **(5)** In 2 Pet 2:14, "adultery." See: TDNT—4:729, 605; BAGD—526a; THAYER—416d.

3429. **μοιχάω** {6x} **mŏichaō**, *moy-khah'-o;* from *3432;* (mid. voice) to *commit adultery:*—commit adultery {6x}.

Moichao, used in the middle voice in the NT, is said **(1)** of men in Mt 5:32; 19:9; Mk 10:11; **(2)** of women in Mk 10:12. See: TDNT—4:729, 605; BAGD—526a; THAYER—417a.

3430. **μοιχεία** {4x} **mŏichĕia**, *moy-khi'-ah;* from *3431; adultery:*—adultery {4x}. Mt 15:19; Mk 7:21; Jn 8:3; Gal 5:19. See: TDNT—4:729, 605; BAGD—526b; THAYER—417a.

3431. **μοιχεύω** {14x} **mŏichĕuō**, *moy-khyoo'-o;* from *3432;* to *commit adultery:*—commit adultery {13x}, in adultery {1x}.

Moicheuo, is used in Mt 5:27–28; 19:18; Mk 10:19; Lk 16:18; 18:20; Jn 8:4; Rom 2:22; 13:9; Jas 2:11; in Rev 2:22, metaphorically, of those who are by a Jezebel's solicitations drawn away to idolatry. See: TDNT—4:729, 605; BAGD—526a; THAYER—417b.

3432. **μοιχός** {4x} **mŏichŏs**, *moy-khos';* perh. a primary word; a (male) *paramour;* fig. *apostate:*—adulterer {4x}.

Moichos denotes one "who has unlawful intercourse with the spouse of another" **(1)** literally, Lk 18:11; 1 Cor 6:9; Heb 13:4; **(2)** metaphorically, Jas 4:4. See: TDNT—4:729, 605; BAGD—526d; THAYER—417b.

3433. **μόλις** {6x} **mŏlis**, *mol'-is;* prob. by var. for *3425; with difficulty:*—scarce {2x}, scarcely {2x}, hardly {1x}, have much work + 2480 {1x}.

Molis signifies "with difficulty, hardly" (from *molos,* "toil"). **(1)** In Lk 9:39, it is rendered "hardly," of the "difficulty" in the departure of a devil. **(2)** In Acts 27:7, 8, 16, it has three different renderings, "scarce," "hardly," and "much work," respectively. **(3)** For its other meanings, "scarce, scarcely," see Acts 14:18; Rom 5:7; 1 Pet 4:18. See: TDNT—4:735, 606; BAGD—526d; THAYER—417b.

3434. **Μολόχ** {1x} **Mŏlŏch**, *mol-okh';* of Heb. or. [4432]; *Moloch* (i.e. *Molek*), an idol:—*Moloch* {1x}. See: BAGD—526d; THAYER—417b.

3435. **μολύνω** {3x} **mŏlunō**, *mol-oo'-no;* prob. from *3189;* to *soil* (fig.):—defile {3x}.

(1) Both the literal and figurative meanings of *moluno* are negative. **(2)** It properly denotes "to besmear," as with mud or filth, "to befoul." **(3)** It is used in the figurative sense, **(3a)** of a conscience "defiled" by sin, 1 Cor 8:7; **(3b)** of believers who have kept themselves (their "garments") from "defilement," Rev 3:4, and **(3c)** of those who have not "soiled" themselves

by adultery or fornication, Rev 14:4. See: TDNT—4:736, 606; BAGD—526d; THAYER—417c.

3436. **μολυσμός** {1x} **mŏlusmŏs**, *mol-oos-mos';* from *3435;* a *stain;* i.e. (fig.) *immorality:*—filthiness {1x}.

Molsumos denotes "defilement," in the sense of an action by which anything is "defiled," 2 Cor 7:1. See: TDNT—4:737, 606; BAGD—527a; THAYER—417c.

3437. **μομφή** {1x} **mŏmphē**, *mom-fay';* from *3201; blame,* i.e. (by impl.) a *fault:*—quarrel {1x}.

Momphe denotes "blame" (akin to *mempho-mai*), "an occasion of complaint," Col 3:13, "quarrel." See: TDNT—4:571, 580; BAGD—527a; THAYER—417d.

3438. **μονή** {2x} **mŏnē**, *mon-ay';* from *3306;* a *staying,* i.e. *residence* (the act or the place):—abode {1x}, mansion {1x}.

Mone, "an abode", is found in **(1)** Jn 14:2, "mansions" (cf. Eng. "manse", a dwelling place for a minister), and **(2)** Jn 14:23, "abode." See: TDNT—4:579, 581; BAGD—527a; THAYER—417d.

3439. **μονογενής** {9x} **mŏnŏgĕnēs**, *mon-og-en-ace';* from *3441* and *1096; only-born,* i.e. *sole:*—only {2x}, only begotten {6x}, only child {1x}.

Monogenes is translated **(1)** "only" in **(1a)** Lk 7:12 of the widow of Nain's son; **(1b)** Lk 8:42 of Jairus' daughter; **(2)** "only begotten" **(2a)** of Jesus in Jn 1:14, 18; 3:16, 18; 1 Jn 4:9; **(2b)** of Isaac in Heb 11:17; and **(3)** "only child" in Lk 9:38 of the devil-possessed child. **(4)** With reference to Christ, the phrase "the only begotten of (from) the Father," Jn 1:14, indicates that as the Son of God He was the sole representative of the Being and character of the One who sent Him. **(4a)** In the original the definite article is omitted both before "only begotten" and before "Father," and its absence in each case serves to lay stress upon the characteristics referred to in the terms used. **(4b)** The apostle's object is to demonstrate what sort of glory it was that he and his fellow apostles had seen. **(4c)** That he is not merely making a comparison with earthly relationships is indicated by *para,* "from." **(4d)** The glory was that of a unique relationship and the word "begotten" does not imply a beginning of His Sonship. **(4e)** It suggests relationship indeed, but must be distinguished from generation as applied to man.

(5) We can only rightly understand the term "the only begotten" when used of the Son, in the sense of un-originated relationship. **(5a)** The begetting is not an event of time, however remote, but a fact irrespective of time. **(5b)** The

Christ did not become, but necessarily and eternally is the Son. He, a Person, possesses every attribute of pure Godhood. **(5c)** This necessitates eternity, absolute being; in this respect He is not 'after' the Father. **(6)** The expression also suggests the thought of the deepest affection, as in the case of the OT word *yachid,* variously rendered, **(6a)** "only one," Gen 22:2, 12; **(6b)** "only son," Jer 6:26; Amos 8:10; Zec 12:10; **(6c)** "only beloved," Prov 4:3, and **(6d)** "darling," Ps 22:20; 35:17. **(7)** In Jn 1:18 the clause "the only begotten son, which is in the bosom of the Father," expresses both His eternal union with the Father in the Godhead and the ineffable intimacy and love between them, the Son sharing all the Father's counsels and enjoying all His affections. **(8)** In Jn 3:16 the statement, "God so loved the world that He gave His only begotten son," must not be taken to mean that Christ became the only begotten son by incarnation. **(8a)** The value and the greatness of the gift lay in the Sonship of Him who was given. **(8b)** His Sonship was not the effect of His being given. **(9)** In Jn 3:18 the phrase "the name of the only begotten son of God" lays stress upon the full revelation of God's character and will, His love and grace, as conveyed in the name of One who, being in a unique relationship to Him, was provided by Him as the object of faith. **(10)** In 1 Jn 4:9 the statement "God hath sent His only begotten son into the world" **(10a)** does not mean that God sent out into the world one who at His birth in Bethlehem had become His Son. **(10b)** Cf. the parallel statement, "God sent forth the Spirit of His Son," Gal 4:6, which could not mean that God sent forth One who became His Spirit when He sent Him. See: TDNT—4:737, 606; BAGD—527b; THAYER—417d.

3440. **μόνον** {66x} **mŏnŏn**, *mon'-on;* neut. of *3441* as adv.; *merely:*—alone {3x}, but {1x}, only {62x}. See: BAGD—527c, 528a; THAYER—418b.

3441. **μόνος** {47x} **mŏnŏs**, *mon'-os;* prob. from *3306; remaining,* i.e. *sole* or *single;* by impl. *mere:*—alone {21x}, only {24x}, by themselves {2x}. See: BAGD—527c; THAYER—418b.

3442. **μονόφθαλμος** {2x} **mŏnŏphthalmŏs**, *mon-of'-thal-mos;* from *3441* and *3788; one-eyed:*—with one eye {2x}.

Monophthalmos, "one-eyed, deprived of one eye", is used in the Lord's warning in Mt 18:9; Mk 9:47. See: BAGD—528b; THAYER—418c.

3443. **μονόω** {1x} **mŏnŏō**, *mon-ŏ'-o;* from *3441;* to *isolate,* i.e. *bereave:*—be desolate {1x}.

Monoo, "to leave alone" (akin to *monos,* "alone"), is used in 1 Ti 5:5, in the passive voice, but translated "desolate," lit., "was made desolate" or "left desolate." See: BAGD—528b; THAYER—418c.

3444. **μορφή** {3x} **mŏrphē**, *mor-fay';* perh. from the base of *3313* (through the idea of *adjustment* of parts); *shape;* fig. *nature:*—form {3x}.

Morphe denotes **(1)** "the special or characteristic form or feature" of a person or thing; **(2)** it is used with particular significance in the NT, only of Christ, **(2a)** in Phil 2:6, "being in the form of God," and **(2b)** 2:7 "taking the form of a servant." **(3)** An excellent definition of the word is: *morphe* is therefore properly the nature or essence, not in the abstract, but as actually subsisting in the individual, and retained as long as the individual itself exists. . . . **(3a)** Thus in the passage before us *morphe Theou* is the Divine nature actually and inseparably subsisting in the Person of Christ. . . . **(3b)** For the interpretation of "the form of God" it is sufficient to say that **(3b1)** it includes the whole nature and essence of Deity, and is inseparable from them, since they could have no actual existence without it; and **(3b2)** that it does not include in itself anything "accidental" or separable, such as particular modes of manifestation, or conditions of glory and majesty, which may at one time be attached to the "form," at another separated from it.... **(4)** The true meaning of *morphe* in the expression "form of God" is confirmed by its recurrence in the corresponding phrase, "form of a servant." It is universally admitted that the two phrases are directly antithetical, and that "form" must therefore have the same sense in both. **(5)** The definition above mentioned applies to its use in Mk 16:12, as to the particular ways in which the Lord manifested Himself. Syn.: 2397. *Morphe* (*3444*) is intrinsic and essential; *schema* (*4976*) is that which is outward. See: TDNT—4:742, 607; BAGD—528b; THAYER—418c.

3445. **μορφόω** {1x} **mŏrphŏō**, *mor-fŏ'-o;* from the same as *3444;* to *fashion* (fig.):—form {1x}.

Morphoo refers, not to the external and transient, but to the inward and real; it is used in Gal 4:19, expressing the necessity of a change in character and conduct to correspond with inward spiritual condition, so that there may be moral conformity to Christ. See:

TDNT—4:752, 607; BAGD—528c; THAYER—418d.

3446. μόρφωσις {2x} **mŏrphōsis**, *mor'-fo-sis;* from *3445; formation*, i.e. (by impl.) *appearance* (an outward *semblance* or [concr.] *formula*):—form {2x}.

Morphosis, "a form or outline," denotes, in the NT, "an image or impress, an outward semblance," **(1)** Rom 2:20, of knowledge of the truth; **(2)** 2 Ti 3:5, of godliness. Syn.: It is thus to be distinguished from *morphe;* it is used in almost the same sense as *schema*, "fashion", but is not so purely the outward "form" as *schema* is. See: TDNT—4:754, 607; BAGD—528c; THAYER—419a.

3447. μοσχοποιέω {1x} **mŏschŏpŏiĕō**, *mos-khop-oy-eh'-o;* from *3448* and *4160;* to *fabricate* the image of a *bullock:*—make a calf {1x}. See: BAGD—528c; THAYER—419a.

3448. μόσχος {6x} **mŏschŏs**, *mos'-khos;* prob. strengthened for ὄσχος **ŏschŏs** (a *shoot*); a young *bullock:*—calf {6x}.

Moschos primarily denotes "anything young," whether plants or the offspring of men or animals, the idea being that which is tender and delicate; hence "a calf, young bull, heifer," Lk 15:23, 27, 30; Heb 9:12, 19; Rev 4:7. See: TDNT—4:760, 610; BAGD—528c; THAYER—419a.

3449. μόχθος {3x} **mŏchthŏs**, *mokh'-thos;* from the base of *3425; toil*, i.e. (by impl.) *sadness:*—painfulness {1x}, travail {2x}.

Mochtos, "labor, involving painful effort," is rendered **(1)** "travail" in 1 Th 2:9 and 2 Th 3:8 where it stresses the toil involved in the work; and **(2)** "painfulness" in 2 Cor 11:27. Syn.: 2873, 4192. See: BAGD—528d; THAYER—419a.

3450. μοῦ {587x} **mŏu**, *moo;* the simpler form of *1700; of me:*—my {501x}, me {52x}, mine {19x}, I {11x}, mine own {4x}. See: BAGD—255c [1700]; THAYER—167b [1473].

3451. μουσικός {1x} **mŏusikŏs**, *moo-sik-os';* from Μοῦσα **Mŏusa**, (a *Muse*); *"musical"*, i.e. (as noun) a *minstrel:*—musician {1x}.

Mousikos is found in Rev 18:22, "musicians"; inasmuch as other instrumentalists are mentioned, some word like "musicians" is necessary to make the distinction. Primarily the word denoted "devoted to the Muses" (the nine goddesses who presided over the principal departments of letters), and was used of anyone devoted to or skilled in arts and sciences, or "learned" implying the skill necessary to play

an instrument; to make music. See: BAGD—528d; THAYER—419a.

3452. μυελός {1x} **muĕlŏs**, *moo-el-os';* perh. a primary word; the *marrow:*—marrow {1x}.

Muelos, "marrow," occurs in Heb 4:12, where, by a natural metaphor, the phraseology changes from the material to the spiritual. See: BAGD—528d; THAYER—419b.

3453. μυέω {1x} **muĕō**, *moo-eh'-o;* from the base of *3466;* to *initiate*, i.e. (by impl.) to *teach:*—instruct {1x}.

Mueo, as a verb, means "to initiate into mysteries" is translated "I am instructed" [passive voice, perfect tense] (Phil 4:12). Mysteries are not only for the initiated or special privileged people. In the NT it denotes one to whom God has revealed further details of His plan for all times; details previously only known to Him. Syn.: 198, 1097, 3129. See: TDNT—4:828, 615; BAGD—529a; THAYER—419b.

3454. μῦθος {5x} **muthŏs**, *moo'-thos;* perh. from the same as *3453* (through the idea of *tuition*); a *tale*, i.e. *fiction* (*"myth"*):—fable {5x}.

(1) *Muthos* is that which is a simple account which attempts to explain reality; yet is unreal and fabricated, having only the appearance of truth, no truth actually contained therein. **(2)** It primarily signifies "speech, conversation." The first syllable comes from a root *mu—*, signifying "to close, keep secret, be dumb"; whence, *muo*, "to close" (eyes, mouth) and *musterion*, "a secret, a mystery"; hence, "a story, narrative, fable, fiction" (Eng., "myth"). **(3)** The word is used of gnostic errors and of Jewish and profane fables and genealogies, "fables", in 1 Ti 1:4; 4:7; 2 Ti 4:4; Titus 1:14; of fiction, in 2 Pet 1:16. See: TDNT—4:762, 610; BAGD—529a; THAYER—419b.

3455. μυκάομαι {1x} **mukaŏmai**, *moo-kah'-om-ahee;* from a presumed der. of μύζω **muzō** (to *"moo"*); to *bellow* (*roar*):—roar {1x}.

This word formerly was used of oxen, an onomatopoeic word, "to low, bellow," is used of a lion, Rev 10:3, roaring as a sign of conquering and to instill fear. See: BAGD—529b; THAYER—419b.

3456. μυκτηρίζω {1x} **muktērizō**, *mook-tay-rid'-zo;* from a der. of the base of *3455* (mean. *snout*, as that whence *lowing* proceeds); to *make mouths* at, i.e. *ridicule:*—mock {1x}.

Mukterizo, from *mukter*, "the nose," hence, "to turn up the nose at, sneer at, treat with contempt," is used in the passive voice in Gal

Greek

6:7, where the statement "God is not mocked" does not mean that men do not mock Him, they do; the apostle vividly contrasts the essential difference between God and man. It is impossible to impose upon Him who discerns the thoughts, the mockings and intents of the heart. See: TDNT—4:796, 614; BAGD—529b; THAYER—419c.

3457. **μυλικός** {1x} **mulikŏs**, *moo-lee-kos';* from *3458; belonging to a mill:*—millstone + 3037 {1x}. See: BAGD—529b; THAYER—419c.

3458. **μύλος** {4x} **mulŏs**, *moo'-los;* prob. ultimately from the base of *3433* (through the idea of *hardship*); a "*mill*", i.e. (by impl.) a *grinder* (*millstone*):—millstone + 3684 {2x}, millstone {2x}.

Mulos denotes **(1)** "a handmill," consisting of two circular stones, one above the other, the lower being fixed. From the center of the lower a wooden pin passes through a hole in the upper, into which the grain is thrown, escaping as flour between the stones and falling on a prepared material below them. The handle is inserted into the upper stone near the circumference. Small stones could be turned by one woman (millgrinding was a work deemed fit only for women and slaves; cf. Judg 16:21); larger ones were turned by two (cf. Mt 24:41, under mill), or more. **(2)** Still larger ones were turned by an ass (*onikos*), **(2a)** Mt 18:6, "a millstone" ("a millstone turned by an ass"), indicating the immediate and overwhelming drowning of one who causes one young believer to stumble; **(2b)** "a stone of a mill," as in Lk 17:2; Rev 18:22. See: BAGD—529b; THAYER—419c.

3459. **μύλων** {1x} **mulōn**, *moo'-lone;* from *3458;* a *mill-house:*—mill {1x}.

Mulon denotes "a mill house," where the millstone is, Mt 24:41. See: BAGD—529c; THAYER—419c.

3460. **Μύρα** {1x} **Mura**, *moo'-rah;* of uncert. der.; *Myra,* a place in Asia Minor:—Myra {1x}. See: BAGD—529c; THAYER—419d.

3461. **μυρίας** {9x} **murias**, *moo-ree'-as;* from *3463;* a *ten-thousand;* by extens. a "*myriad*" or indef. number:—ten thousand times ten thousand {2x}, two hundred thousand thousand + 1417 {2x}, innumerable multitude {1x}, ten thousand {1x}, innumerable company {1x}, fifty thousand + 3902 {1x}, thousands {1x}.

Murias denotes either "ten thousand," or, "indefinitely, a myriad, a numberless host," in the plural, Acts 19:19; lit. "five ten-thousands,"

Rev 5:11; 9:16; in the following, used of vast numbers, Lk 12:1, "an innumerable multitude"; Acts 21:20, "thousands"; Heb 12:22, "innumerable hosts"; Jude 14, "ten thousands." See: BAGD—529c; THAYER—419d.

3462. **μυρίζω** {1x} **murizō**, *moo-rid'-zo;* from *3464;* to *apply* (perfumed) *unguent* to:—anoint {1x}.

Murizo, as a verb, is used of "anointing" the body for burial: (Mk 14:8). Syn.: 218, 1472, 1637, 2025, 3464, 5545, 5548. See: TDNT—4:800, 615; BAGD—529d; THAYER—419d.

3463. **μύριοι** {3x} **muriŏi**, *moo'-ree-oi;* plur. of an appar. primary word (prop. mean. *very many*); *ten thousand;* by extens. *innumerably* many:—ten thousand {3x}. See: BAGD—529d; THAYER—419d.

3464. **μύρον** {14x} **murŏn**, *moo'-ron;* prob. of for. or. [comp. 4753, 4666]; "*myrrh*", i.e. (by impl.) fragrent and *perfumed oil:*—ointment {14x}.

Muron, a word derived by the ancients from *muro,* "to flow," or from *murra,* "myrrh-oil" (it is probably of foreign origin; see myrrh). The "ointment" is mentioned in the NT in connection with **(1)** the anointing of the Lord on the occasions recorded in Mt 26:7, 9, 12; Mk 14:3–4; Lk 7:37–38, 46; Jn 11:2; 12:3 (twice), 5. **(2)** The alabaster cruse mentioned in the passages in Mt, Mk and Lk was the best of its kind, and the spikenard was one of the costliest of perfumes. **(3)** "Ointments" were used in preparing a body for burial, Lk 23:56 ("ointments"). **(4)** Of the act of the woman mentioned in Mt 26:6–13, the Lord said, "she did it to prepare Me for burial"; her devotion led her to antedate the customary ritual after death, by showing both her affection and her understanding of what was impending. **(5)** For the use of the various kinds of "ointments" as articles of commerce, see Rev 18:13. Syn.: *Muron,* denotes "ointment." The distinction between this and *elaion,* "oil," is observable in Lk 7:46 in Christ's reproof of the Pharisee who, while desiring Him to eat with him, failed in the ordinary marks of courtesy; "My head with oil (1637 - *elaion*) thou didst not anoint (*aleipho*), but she hath anointed (*aleipho*) My feet with ointment" (3464 - *muron*). Syn. 3462. See: TDNT—4:800, 615; BAGD—529d; THAYER—419d.

3465. **Μυσία** {2x} **Musia**, *moo-see'-ah;* of uncert. or.; *Mysia,* a region of Asia Minor:—Mysia {2x}. See: BAGD—530a; THAYER—429a.

3466. **μυστήριον** {27x} **mustēriŏn**, *moos-tay'-ree-on;* from a der. of μύω **muō** (to *shut* the mouth); a *secret* or "*mys-*

tery" (through the idea of *silence* imposed by *initiation* into relig. rites):—mystery {27x}.

Musterion, (1) in the NT it denotes, not the mysterious (as with the Eng. word), but that which, being outside the range of unassisted natural apprehension, can be made known only by divine revelation, and is made known in a manner and at a time appointed by God, and to those only who are illumined by His Spirit. (1a) In the ordinary sense a "mystery" implies knowledge withheld; (1b) its scriptural significance is truth revealed. Hence the terms especially associated with the subject are "made known," "manifested," "revealed," "preached," "understand," "dispensation." (2) The definition given above may be best illustrated by the following passage: "Even the mystery which hath been hid from ages and from generations, but now is made manifest to His saints" (Col 1:26).

(3) It is used of: (3a) spiritual truth generally, as revealed in the gospel, 1 Cor 13:2; 14:2 [cf. 1 Ti 3:9]. (3a1) Among the ancient Greeks "the mysteries" were religious rites and ceremonies practiced by secret societies into which any one who so desired might be received. (3a2) Those who were initiated into these "mysteries" became possessors of certain knowledge, which was not imparted to the uninitiated, and were called "the perfected," cf. 1 Cor 2:6–16 where the apostle has these "mysteries" in mind and presents the gospel in contrast thereto; here "the perfected" are, of course the believers, who alone can perceive the things revealed; (3b) Christ, who is God Himself revealed under the conditions of human life, Col 2:2; 4:3, and submitting even to death, 1 Cor 2:1, 7, but raised from among the dead, 1 Ti 3:16, that the will of God to coordinate the universe in Him, and subject it to Him, might in due time be accomplished, Eph 1:9 (cf. Rev 10:7), as is declared in the gospel, Rom 16:25; Eph 6:19; (3c) the church, which is Christ's body, i.e., the union of redeemed men with God in Christ, Eph 5:32 [cf. Col 1:27]; (3d) the rapture into the presence of Christ of those members of the church which is His body who shall be alive on the earth at His Parousia, 1 Cor 15:51; (3e) the operation of those hidden forces that either retard or accelerate the kingdom of Heaven (i.e., of God), Mt 13:11; Mk 4:11; (3f) the cause of the present condition of Israel, Rom 11:25; (3g) the spirit of disobedience to God, 2 Th 2:7; Rev 17:5, 7, cf. Eph 2:2. (3h) To these may be added the seven local churches, and their angels, seen in symbolism, Rev 1:20; (3i) the ways of God in grace, Eph 3:9. (3j) The word is used in a comprehensive way in 1 Cor

4:1. See: TDNT—4:802, 615; BAGD—530a; THAYER—420a.

3467. μυωπάζω {1x} muōpazō, *moo-ope-ad'-zo;* from a compound of the base of *3466* and ὤψ ōps (the *face;* from *3700*); to *shut* the *eyes*, i.e. *blink* (*see indistinctly*):— cannot see far off {1x}.

Muopazo, "to be short-sighted" (*muo*, "to shut," *ops*, "the eye"; cf. Eng., "myopy," "myopic"), occurs in 2 Pet 1:9, "and cannot see afar off"; this does not contradict the preceding word "blind," it qualifies it; he of whom it is true is blind in that he cannot discern spiritual things, he is near-sighted in that he is occupied in regarding worldly affairs. See: BAGD—531a; THAYER—420c.

3468. μώλωψ {1x} mōlōps, *mo'-lopes;* from μῶλος mōlōs, ("*moil;*" prob. akin to the base of *3433*) and prob. ὤψ ōps), (the *face;* from *3700*); a *mole* ("black eye") or *blow-mark:*—stripe {1x}.

Molops, "a bruise, a wound from a stripe," is used in 1 Pet 2:24 (from the OT of Is 53:5), lit., in the original, "by whose bruise," not referring to Christ's scourging, but figurative of the stroke of divine judgment administered vicariously to Him on the cross (a comforting reminder to these Christian servants, who were not infrequently buffeted, v. 20, by their masters). See: TDNT—4:829, 619; BAGD—531a; THAYER—420c.

3469. μωμάομαι {2x} mōmaŏmai, *mo-mah'-om-ahee;* from *3470;* to *carp* at, i.e. *censure* (*discredit*):—blame {2x}.

Momaomai, as a verb, means "to find fault with, to blame, or calumniate" is used (1) of the ministry of the gospel: "Giving no offence in any thing, that the ministry be not blamed [*momaomai*]" (2 Cor 6:3); and (2) of the ministration of financial help: "Avoiding this, that no man should blame [*momaomai*] us in this abundance which is administered by us" (2 Cor 8:20). Syn.: 273, 274, 298, 299, 338, 410, 423, 2607, 3201. See: BAGD—531a; THAYER—420c.

3470. μῶμος {1x} mōmŏs, *mo'-mos;* perh. from *3201; a flaw* or *blot*, i.e. (fig.) *disgraceful* person:—blemish {1x}.

Momos signifies "a shame, a moral disgrace," metaphorical of the licentious, 2 Pet 2:13. See: TDNT—4:829, 619; BAGD—531a; THAYER—420c.

3471. μωραίνω {4x} mōrainō, *mo-rah'-ee-no;* from *3474;* to *become insipid;* fig. to *make* (pass. *act*) as a *simpleton:*— become a fool {1x}, make foolish {1x}, lose savour {2x}.

Moraino is used **(1)** in the causal sense, "to make foolish," 1 Cor 1:20; **(2)** in the passive sense, "to become foolish," Rom 1:22; **(3)** in Mt 5:13 and Lk 14:34 it is said of salt that has lost its flavor, becoming tasteless, having lost the ability to make thirsty for spiritual truth and to preserve from further corruption. When salt is damp it clumps and looses its properties, much like when the believers "clump" and fail to give thirst to the world for Christ and fail to stop its ever-encroaching evil. See: TDNT— 4:832, 620; BAGD—531b; THAYER—420c.

3472. μωρία {5x} **mōria,** *mo-ree'-ah;* from *3474; silliness,* i.e. *absurdity:—* foolishness {5x}.

Moria denotes "foolishness", and is used in 1 Cor 1:18, 21, 23; 2:14; 3:19. See: TDNT— 4:832, 620; BAGD—531b; THAYER—420d.

3473. μωρολογία {1x} **mōrŏlŏgia,** *mo-rol-og-ee'-ah;* from a compound of *3474* and *3004; silly talk,* i.e. *buffoonery:—* foolish talking {1x}.

Morologia, (from *moros,* "foolish, dull, stupid," and *lego*), is used in Eph 5:4; **(1)** it denotes more than mere idle "talk"; it is "that talk of fools which is foolishness and sin together." **(2)** Even though foolish, what is said is still sin. Syn.: 148, 2160. See: TDNT—4:832, 620; BAGD—531b; THAYER—420d.

3474. μωρός {13x} **mōrŏs,** *mo-ros';* prob. from the base of *3466; dull* or *stupid* (as if *shut* up), i.e. *heedless,* (mor.) *blockhead,* (appar.) *absurd:—*fool {5x}, foolish {7x}, foolishness {1x}.

Moros primarily denotes **(1)** "dull, sluggish" (from a root *muh,* "to be silly"); hence, "stupid, foolish"; **(2)** it is used **(2a)** of persons, **(2a1)** Mt 5:22, "Thou fool"; here the word means morally worthless, a scoundrel, a more serious reproach than *"Raca"*; the latter scorns a man's mind and calls him stupid; *moros* scorns his heart and character; hence the Lord's more severe condemnation; **(2a2)** in Mt 7:26, "a foolish man"; 23:17, 19, "fools"; 25:2, 3, 8, "foolish"; **(2a3)** in 1 Cor 3:18, "a fool"; **(2a4)** the apostle Paul uses it of himself and his fellow-workers, in 1 Cor 4:10, "fools" (i.e., in the eyes of opponents); **(2b)** of things, **(2b1)** 2 Ti 2:23, "foolish and ignorant questionings"; so Titus 3:9; **(2b2)** in 1 Cor 1:25, "the foolishness of God," not *moria,* "foolishness" as a personal quality, but adjectively, that which is considered by the ignorant as a "foolish" policy or mode of dealing, lit., "the foolish (thing)"; so in v. 27, "the foolish (things) of the world." See: TDNT— 4:832, 620; BAGD—531c; THAYER—420d.

3475. Μωσεύς {80x} **Mōsĕus,** *moce-yoos';* or

Μωσῆς **Mōsēs,** *mo-sace';* or

Μωϋσῆς **Mŏësēs,** *mo-oo-sace';* of Heb. or.; [4872]; *Moseus, Moses,* or *Moüses* (i.e. *Mosheh*), the Heb. lawgiver:—*Moses* {80x}. See: TDNT—4:848, 622; BAGD— 531d; THAYER—420d.

N

3476. Ναασσών {3x} **Naassōn,** *nah-as-sone';* of Heb. or. [5177]; *Naasson* (i.e. *Nachshon*), an Isr.:—*Naasson.* See: BAGD—532a; THAYER—421b.

3477. Ναγγαί {1x} **Naggai,** *nang-gah'-ee;* prob. of Heb. or. [comp. *5052*]; *Nangœ* (i.e. perh. *Nogach*), an Isr.:—Nagge {1x}. See: BAGD—532a; THAYER—421b.

3478. Ναζαρέθ {12x} **Nazarĕth,** *nad-zar-eth';* or

Ναζαρέτ **Nazarĕt,** *nad-zar-et';* of uncert. der.; *Nazareth* or *Nazaret,* a place in Pal.:—*Nazareth* {12x}. See: BAGD—532a; THAYER—421b.

3479. Ναζαρηνός {4x} **Nazarēnŏs,** *nad-zar-ay-nos';* from *3478; a Nazarene,* i.e. inhab. of Nazareth:—of Nazareth {4x}. See: TDNT—4:874, 625; BAGD—532b; THAYER—422a.

3480. Ναζωραῖος {15x} **Nazōraiŏs,** *nad-zo-rah'-yos;* from *3478; a Nazorœan,* i.e. inhab. of Nazareth; by extens. a *Christian:—*Nazarene {2x}, of Nazareth {13x}. See: TDNT—4:874, 625; BAGD—532b; THAYER—422a.

3481. Ναθάν {1x} **Nathan,** *nath-an',* or

Ναθάμ **Natham,** *nath-am';* of Heb. or. [5416]; *Nathan,* an Isr.:—*Nathan* {1x}. See: BAGD—532d; THAYER—422b.

3482. Ναθαναήλ {6x} **Nathanaēl,** *nath-an-ah-ale';* of Heb. or. [5417]; *Nathanaël* (i.e. *Nathanel*), an Isr. and Chr.:—*Nathanael* {6x}. See: BAGD—532d; THAYER— 422b.

3483. ναί {34x} **nai,** *nahee;* a primary particle of strong affirmation; *yes:—*yea {23x}, even so {5x}, yes {3x}, truth {1x}, verily {1x}, surely {1x}.

Nai, a particle of strong affirmation, is used **(1)** in answer to a question, Mt 9:28; 11:9; 13:51; 17:25; 21:16; Lk 7:26; Jn 11:27; 21:15, 16; Acts 5:8; 22:27; Rom 3:29; **(2)** in assent to an assertion, Mt 15:27, "truth"; Mk 7:28; Rev 14:13; 16:7, "even so"; **(3)** in confirmation of an asser-

tion, Mt 11:26 and Lk 10:21 "even so"; Lk 11:51, "verily"; 12:5; Philem 20; **(4)** in solemn asseveration, Rev 1:7 "even so"; 22:20, "surely"; **(5)** in repetition for emphasis, Mt 5:37; 2 Cor 1:17; Jas 5:12; **(6)** singly in contrast to *ou*, "nay," 2 Cor 1:18, 19 (twice), 20, "(the) yea." See: BAGD—532d; THAYER—422b.

3484. **Ναΐν** {1x} **Naïn**, *nah-in'*; prob. of Heb. or. [comp. 4999]; *Naïn*, a place in Pal.:—*Nain* {1x}. See: BAGD—533b; THAYER—422c.

3485. **ναός** {46x} **naŏs**, *nah-os'*; from a primary ναίω **naiō** (to *dwell*); a *fane, shrine, temple:*—shrine {1x}, temple {45x}.

Naos, "a shrine or sanctuary," was used **(1)** among the heathen, to denote the shrine containing the idol, Acts 17:24; 19:24 (in the latter, miniatures); **(2)** among the Jews, the sanctuary in the "temple," **(2a)** into which only the priests could lawfully enter, e.g., Lk 1:9, 21, 22; **(2b)** Christ, as being of the tribe of Judah, and thus not being a priest while upon the earth (Heb 7:13, 14; 8:4), did not enter the *naos;* **(2c)** by Christ metaphorically, of His own physical body, Jn 2:19, 21; **(3)** in apostolic teaching, metaphorically, **(3a)** of the church, the mystical body of Christ, Eph 2:21; **(3b)** of a local church, 1 Cor 3:16, 17; 2 Cor 6:16; **(3c)** of the present body of the individual believer, 1 Cor 6:19; **(3d)** of the "temple" seen in visions in the Apocalypse, 3:12; 7:15; 11:19; 14:15, 17; 15:5, 6, 8; 16:1, 17; **(3e)** of the Lord God Almighty and the Lamb, as the "temple" of the new and heavenly Jerusalem, Rev 21:22. Syn.: *Hieron* (*2411*) refers to the whole sacred enclosure including the outer courts, porches, and porticoes (Mt 26:55; Lk 21:37; Jn 8:20). *Naos* refers to the temple itself, the proper habitation of God (Acts 7:38; 17:24; Mt 27:5). See: TDNT—4:880, 625; BAGD—533b; THAYER—422c. Comp *2411.*

3486. **Ναούμ** {1x} **Naŏum**, *nah-oom';* of Heb. or. [5151]; *Naüm* (i.e. *Nachum*), an Isr.:—Naum {1x}. See: BAGD—534a; THAYER—422d.

3487. **νάρδος** {2x} **nardŏs**, *nar'dos;* of for. or. [comp. 5373]; *"nard":*—spikenard + 4101 {2x}.

Nardos is "a fragrant oil," procured from the stem of an Indian plant. The Arabs call it the "Indian spike [hence, spikenard]." The adjective *pistikos* is attached to it in the NT, Mk 14:3; Jn 12:3; *pistikos,* i.e., the *Pistacia Terebinthus,* which grows in Cyprus, Syria, Palestine, etc., and yields a resin of very fragrant odor, and in such inconsiderable quantities as to be very costly. *Nard* was frequently mixed with aromatic ingredients . . . so when scented

with the fragrant resin of the *pistake* it would quite well be called *nardos pistakes.* The oil used for the anointing of the Lord's head was worth about L/12, and must have been of the most valuable kind. See: BAGD—534a; THAYER—423a.

3488. **Νάρκισσος** {1x} **Narkissŏs**, *nar'-kis-sos;* a flower of the same name, from νάρκη **narkē** (*stupefaction,* as a "narcotic"); *Narcissus,* a Rom.:—Narcissus {1x}. See: BAGD—534b; THAYER—423a.

3489. **ναυαγέω** {2x} **nauagĕō**, *nŏw-ag-eh'-o;* from a compound of *3491* and *71;* to *be shipwrecked* (*stranded,* "navigate"), lit. or fig.:—make shipwreck {1x}, suffer shipwreck {1x}.

Nauageo signifies **(1)** literally, "to suffer shipwreck" (*naus,* "a ship," *agnumi,* "to break"), 2 Cor 11:25; **(2)** metaphorically, "to make shipwreck," 1 Ti 1:19, "concerning the faith," as the result of thrusting away a good conscience. See: TDNT—4:891, 627; BAGD—534b; THAYER—423a.

3490. **ναύκληρος** {1x} **nauklērŏs**, *nŏw'-klay-ros;* from *3491* and *2819* ("clerk"); a *captain:*—owner of a ship {1x}. See: BAGD—534b; THAYER—423b.

3491. **ναῦς** {1x} **naus**, *nŏwce;* from νάω **naō** or νέω **nĕō** (to *float*); a *boat* (of any size):—ship {1x}. See: BAGD—534c; THAYER—423b.

3492. **ναύτης** {3x} **nautēs**, *now'-tace;* from *3491;* a *boatman,* i.e. *seaman:*—sailor {1x}, shipman {1x}.

Nautes, "a seaman, mariner, sailor" (from *naus,* "a ship," Eng., "nautical"), is translated **(1)** "shipmen" in Acts 27:27, 30; and **(2)** "sailors" in Rev 18:17. See: BAGD—534c; THAYER—423b.

3493. **Ναχώρ** {1x} **Nachōr**, *nakh-ore';* of Heb. or. [5152]; *Nachor,* the grandfather of Abraham:—*Nachor* {1x}. See: BAGD—534c; THAYER—423b.

3494. **νεανίας** {5x} **nĕanias**, *neh-an-ee'-as;* from a der. of *3501;* a *youth* (up to about forty years):—young man {5x}.

Neanias, "a young man," occurs in Acts 7:58; 20:9; 23:17, 18; 23:22. See: BAGD—534c; THAYER—423b.

3495. **νεανίσκος** {10x} **nĕaniskŏs**, *neh-an-is'-kos;* from the same as *3494;* a *youth* (under forty):—young man {10x}.

Neaniskos, a diminutive of *3494,* "a youth, a young man," occurs in Mt 19:20, 22; Mk 14:51 twice; 16:5; Lk 7:14; Acts 2:17; 5:10 (i.e., attendants); 1 Jn 2:13, 14, of the second branch of

the spiritual family. See: BAGD—534c; THAYER—423b.

3496. Νεάπολις {1x} **Nĕapŏlis,** *neh-ap'-ol-is;* from *3501* and *4172; new town; Neäpolis,* a place in Macedonia:— *Neapolis* {1x}. See: BAGD—534c, 536b; THAYER—423c.

3497. Νεεμάν {1x} **Nĕĕman,** *neh-eh-man'* or

Ναιμάν Naïman, *nah-ee-man';* of Heb. or. [5283]; *Neëman* (i.e. *Naaman*), a Syrian:—Naaman {1x}. See: BAGD—534d, 533b; THAYER—423c.

3498. νεκρός {132x} **nĕkrŏs,** *nek-ros';* from an appar. primary νέκυς **nĕkus** (a *corpse*); *dead* (lit. or fig.; also as noun):—dead {132x}.

Nekros is used of (1) the death of the body, cf. Jas 2:26, its most frequent sense; (2) the actual spiritual condition of unsaved men, Mt 8:22; Jn 5:25; Eph 2:1, 5; 5:14; Phil 3:11; Col 2:13; cf. Lk 15:24; (3) the ideal spiritual condition of believers in regard to sin, Rom 6:11; (4) a church in declension, inasmuch as in that state it is inactive and barren, Rev 3:1; (5) sin, which apart from law cannot produce a sense of guilt, Rom 7:8; (6) the body of the believer in contrast to his spirit, Rom 8:10; (7) the works of the Law, inasmuch as, however good in themselves, Rom 7:13, they cannot produce life, Heb 6:1; 9:14; (8) the faith that does not produce works, Jas 2:17, 26; cf. v. 20. See: TDNT—4:892, 627; BAGD—534d.

3499. νεκρόω {3x} **nĕkrŏō,** *nek-rŏ'-o;* from *3498;* to *deaden,* i.e. (fig.) to *subdue:*—be dead {2x}, mortify {1x}.

Nekroo, "to put to death," is used (1) in the active voice in the sense of destroying the strength of, depriving of power, with reference to the evil desires which work in the body, Col 3:5. (2) In the passive voice it is used of Abraham's body as being "as good as dead," Rom 4:19 with Heb 11:12. Syn.: 2289. See: TDNT—4:894, 627; BAGD—533c; THAYER—424a.

3500. νέκρωσις {2x} **nĕkrōsis,** *nek'-ro-sis;* from *3499; decease;* fig. *impotency:*—deadness {1x}, dying {1x}.

Nekrosis, "a putting to death", is rendered (1) "dying" in 2 Cor 4:10; (2) "deadness" in Rom 4:19, i.e., the state of being virtually "dead." See: TDNT—4:895, 627; BAGD—535c; THAYER—424a.

3501. νέος {24x} **nĕŏs,** *neh'-os;* incl. the comparative νεώτερος **nĕŏtĕrŏs,** *neh-o'-ter-os;* a primary word; *"new",* i.e. (of persons) *youthful,* or (of things) *fresh;* fig. *regenerate:*—new {11x}, younger {7x}, young man

{2x}, new man {1x}, young women {1x}, younger man {1x}, young {1x}.

Neos (*3501*) signifies (1) "new" in respect of time, that which is recent; it is used (1a) of the young, and so translated, especially the comparative degree "younger"; (1b) accordingly what is *neos* may be a reproduction of the old in quality or character. (2) *Neos* and *kainos* (*2537*) are sometimes used of the same thing, but there is a difference, as already indicated. (2a) Thus the "new man" in Eph 2:15 (*kainos*) is "new" in differing in character; so in 4:24; (2b) but the "new man" in Col 3:10 (*neos*) stresses the fact of the believer's "new" experience, recently begun, and still proceeding. (2c) "The old man in him . . . dates as far back as Adam; a new man has been born, who therefore is fitly so called" [i.e., *neos*].

(3) The "New" Covenant in Heb 12:24 is "new" (*neos*) compared with the Mosaic, nearly fifteen hundred years before; it is "new" (*kainos*) compared with the Mosaic, which is old in character, ineffective, 8:8, 13; 9:15. (4) The "new" wine of Mt 9:17; Mk 2:22; Lk 5:37–39, is *neos,* as being of recent production; the "new" wine of the kingdom, Mt 26:29; Mk 14:25, is *kainos,* since it will be of a different character from that of this world. (5) The rendering "new" (*neos*) is elsewhere used metaphorically in 1 Cor 5:7, "a new lump." (6) This word in the feminine plural, denotes "young women," Titus 2:4. Syn.: *Kainos* (*2537*) denotes the new primarily in reference to quality, the fresh, unworn; whereas, *neos* denotes the new primarily in reference to time, the young, recent. See: TDNT—4:896, 628; BAGD—535d; THAYER—424b.

3502. νεοσσός {1x} **nĕŏssŏs,** *neh-os-sos'* or

νοσσός nossos, *nos-sos';* from *3501;* a *youngling* (*nestling*):—young {1x}. See: BAGD—536c, 543d; THAYER—424b.

3503. νεότης {5x} **nĕŏtēs,** *neh-ot'-ace;* from *3501; newness,* i.e. *youthfulness:*—youth {5x}.

Neotes, from *neos,* "new," occurs in Mk 10:20; Lk 18:21; Acts 26:4; 1 Ti 4:12; Mt 19:20). See: BAGD—536c; THAYER—424b.

3504. νεόφυτος {1x} **nĕŏphutŏs,** *neh-of'-oo-tos;* from *3501* and a der. of *5453; newly planted,* i.e. (fig.) a *young convert* ("*neophyte*"):—novice {1x}.

Neophutos, an adjective, lit., "newly-planted" (from *neos,* "new," and *phuo,* "to bring forth, produce"), denotes "a new convert, neophyte, novice," 1 Ti 3:6, of one who by inexperience is unfitted to act as a bishop or overseer in a church. See: BAGD—536c; THAYER—424b.

3505. Νέρων {1x} **Nĕrōn,** *ner'-ohn;* of Lat. or.; *Neron* (i.e. *Nero*), a Rom. emperor:—Nero {1x}. See: BAGD—536c; THAYER—424c.

3506. νεύω {2x} **nĕuō,** *nyoo'-o;* appar. a primary verb; to *"nod,"* i.e. (by anal.) *signal:*—beckon {2x}.

Literally, *neuo* means to give a nod, to signify by a nod and **(1)** is used in Jn 13:24 of Peter's beckoning to John to ask the Lord of whom He had been speaking; and **(2)** in Acts 24:10 of the intimation given by Felix to Paul to speak. See: BAGD—536d; THAYER—424c.

3507. νεφέλη {26x} **nĕphĕlē,** *nef-el'-ay;* from *3509;* prop. *cloudiness,* i.e. (concr.) a *cloud:*—cloud {26x}.

Nephele, "a definitely shaped cloud, or masses of clouds possessing definite form," is used, besides the physical element, **(1)** of the "cloud" on the mount of transfiguration, Mt 17:5; **(2)** of the "cloud" which covered Israel in the Red Sea, 1 Cor 10:1–2; **(3)** of "clouds" seen in the Apocalyptic visions, Rev 1:7; 10:1; 11:12; 14:14–16; **(4)** metaphorically in 2 Pet 2:17, of the evil workers there mentioned. See: TDNT—4:902, 628; BAGD—536d; THAYER—424c.

3508. Νεφθαλείμ {3x} **Nĕphthalĕim,** *nef-thal-ime';* of Heb. or. [5321]; *Nephthaleim* (i.e. *Naphthali*), a tribe in Pal.:—Nephthalim {3x}. See: BAGD—537a; THAYER—424c.

3509. νέφος {1x} **nĕphŏs,** *nef'-os;* appar. a primary word; a *cloud:*—cloud {1x}.

Nephos denotes "a cloudy, shapeless mass covering the heavens"; hence, metaphorically, of "a dense multitude, a throng," Heb 12:1. See: TDNT—4:902, 628; BAGD—537a; THAYER—424d.

3510. νεφρός {1x} **nĕphrŏs,** *nef-ros';* of uncert. aff.; a *kidney* (plur.), i.e. (fig.) the inmost *mind:*—reins {1x}.

Nephros is literally a kidney, usually in the plural, and is used metaphorically of the inmost thoughts, feelings, purposes, and will of the soul (Rev 2:23). So called because the two ureters from the kidneys to the bladder resemble reins (cf. Ps 7:9; Jer 11:20; 17:10; 20:12). See: TDNT—4:911, 630; BAGD—537a; THAYER—424d.

3511. νεωκόρος {1x} **nĕōkŏrŏs,** *neh-o-kor'-os;* from a form of *3485* and κορέω **kŏrĕō** (to *sweep*); a *temple-servant,* i.e. (by impl.) a *votary:*—worshipper {1x}.

This word appears from coins still extant, it was an honourary title [temple-keeper or temple-warden] of certain cities, esp. in Asia Minor, or in which some special worship of some deity or even some deified human ruler had been established; used of Ephesus (Acts 19:35). See: BAGD—537b; THAYER—424d.

3512. νεωτερικός {1x} **nĕōtĕrikŏs,** *neh-o-ter'-ik-os;* from the comparative of *3501; appertaining to younger* persons, i.e. *juvenile:*—youthful {1x}. See: BAGD—537b; THAYER—425a.

νεώτερος **nĕōtĕrŏs.** See *3501.*

3513. νή {1x} **nē,** *nay;* prob. an intens. form of *3483;* a particle of attestation (accompanied by the obj. invoked or appealed to in confirmation); *as sure as:*—I protest by {1x}. See: BAGD—537b; THAYER—425a.

3514. νήθω {2x} **nēthō,** *nay'-tho;* from νέω **nĕō** (of like mean.); to *spin:*—spin {2x}.

This word means to spin as in making cloth, and is found in Mt 6:28 and Lk 12:27, of the lilies of the field. See: BAGD—537c; THAYER—425b.

3515. νηπιάζω {1x} **nēpiazō,** *nay-pee-ad'-zo;* from *3516;* to *act* as a *babe,* i.e. (fig.) *innocently:*—be a child {1x}. See: TDNT—4:912, 631; BAGD—537c; THAYER—425b.

3516. νήπιος {14x} **nēpiŏs,** *nay'-pee-os;* from an obs. particle νη- **nē-** (implying *negation*) and *2031; not speaking,* i.e. an *infant* (*minor*); fig. a *simple-minded* person, an *immature* Christian:—babe {6x}, child {7x}, childish {1x}.

(1) Literally, a *nepios* was one without the power of speech, a little child; he can make sounds but not articulate speech. **(1a)** *Nepios,* lit., "without the power of speech," denotes "a little child," the literal meaning having been lost in the general use of the word. It is used **(1b)** of "infants," Mt 21:16; **(2)** metaphorically, of the unsophisticated in mind and trustful in disposition, Mt 11:25 and Lk 10:21, where it stands in contrast to the wise; **(2a)** of those who are possessed merely of natural knowledge, Rom 2:20; **(2b)** of those who are carnal, and have not grown, as they should have done, in spiritual understanding and power, the spiritually immature, 1 Cor 3:1; **(2c)** those who are so to speak partakers of milk, and "without experience of the word of righteousness," Heb 5:13; **(2d)** of the Jews, who, while the Law was in force, were in a state corresponding to that of childhood, or minority, just as the word "infant" is used of a minor, in English law, Gal 4:3, "children"; **(2e)** of believers in an immature condition, impressionable and liable to be imposed upon instead of being in a state of

spiritual maturity, Eph 4:14, "children." **(3)** "Immaturity" is always associated with this word. Syn.: 1025. See: TDNT—4:912, 631; BAGD—537c; THAYER—425b.

3517. Νηρεύς {1x} **Nērĕus,** *nare-yoos';* appar. from a der. of the base of *3491* (mean. *wet*); *Nereus,* a Chr.:—*Nereus* {1x}. See: BAGD—538a; THAYER—425b.

3518. Νηρί {1x} **Nēri,** *nay-ree';* of Heb. or. [5374]; *Neri* (i.e. *Nerijah*), an Isr.:—*Neri* {1x}. See: BAGD—538a; THAYER—425b.

3519. νησίον {1x} **nēsiŏn,** *nay-see'-on;* dimin. of *3520;* a small island, an *islet:*—island {1x}.
This is a small island, Cauda (Acts 27:16). See: BAGD—538a; THAYER—425b.

3520. νῆσος {9x} **nēsŏs,** *nay'-sos;* prob. from the base of *3491;* an *island:*—island {6x}, isle {3x}.
Nasos, "an island," occurs in Acts 13:6 "isle"; 27:26; 28:1, 7, 9, 11 "isle"; Rev 1:9 "isle"; 6:14; 16:20. See: BAGD—538a; THAYER—425b.

3521. νηστεία {8x} **nēstĕia,** *nace-ti'-ah;* from *3522; abstinence* (from lack of food, or vol. and relig.); spec. the *fast* of the Day of Atonement:—fast {7x}, fasting {1x}.
Nesteia, "a fasting, fast" (from *ne,* a negative prefix, and *esthio,* "to eat"), is used **(1)** of voluntary abstinence from food, Mt 17:21; Mk 9:29; Lk 2:37; Acts 14:23; **(1a)** "fasting" had become a common practice among Jews, and **(1b)** was continued among Christians; **(2)** in Acts 27:9, "the Fast" refers to the Day of Atonement, Lev 16:29; that time of the year would be one of dangerous sailing; **(3)** of involuntary abstinence (perhaps voluntary is included), consequent upon trying circumstances, 2 Cor 6:5; 11:27. See: TDNT—4:924, 632; BAGD—538; THAYER—425b.

3522. νηστεύω {21x} **nēstĕuō,** *nace-tyoo'-o;* from *3523;* to *abstain* from food (relig.):—fast {21x}.
Nesteuo, as a verb, means "to fast, to abstain from eating", and is used **(1)** of voluntary "fasting," Mt. 4:2; 6:16, 17, 18; 9:14, 15; Mk 2:18, 19, 20; Lk 5:33, 34, 35; 18:12; Acts 13:2, 3. **(2)** Some of these passages show that teachers to whom scholars or disciples were attached gave them special instructions as to "fasting." Christ taught the need of purity and simplicity of motive. **(3)** The answers of Christ to the questions of the disciples of John and of the Pharisees reveal His whole purpose and method. No doubt He and His followers observed such a fast as that on the Day of Atone-

ment, but He imposed no frequent "fasts" in addition. What He taught was suitable to the change of character and purpose which He designed for His disciples. His claim to be the Bridegroom, Mt 9:15, and the reference there to the absence of "fasting," virtually involved a claim to be the Messiah (cf. Zec 8:19). Syn.: 777, 3521, 3523. See: TDNT—4:924, 632; BAGD—538b; THAYER—425c.

3523. νῆστις {2x} **nēstis,** *nace'-tis;* from the insep. neg. particle νη- **nē-,** (*not*) and *2068; not eating,* i.e. *abstinent* from food (relig.):—fasting {2x}.
Nestis, "not eating", "fasting," is used of lack of food, Mt 15:32; Mk 8:3. See: TDNT—4:924, 632; BAGD—538c; THAYER—425d.

3524. νηφάλεος {3x} **nēphalĕŏs,** *nay-fal'-eh-os;* or
νηφάλιος nēphaliŏs, *nay-fal'-ee-os;* from *3525;* sober, i.e. (fig.) *circumspect:*—sober {2x}, vigilant {1x}.
Naphalios means **(1)** to abstain from wine or any substance that could cloud one's judgment. It is translated **(2)** "vigilant" in 1 Ti 3:2; and **(3)** in 1 Ti 3:11 and Titus 2:2, "sober." Syn.: 3525. See: TDNT—4:939, 633; BAGD—538d; THAYER—425d.

3525. νήφω {6x} **nēphō,** *nay'-fo;* of uncert. aff.: to *abstain* from wine (*keep sober*), i.e. (fig.) *be discreet:*—be sober {4x}, watch {2x}.
Nepho signifies **(1)** "to be free from the influence of intoxicants"; **(2)** in the NT, metaphorically, it does not in itself imply watchfulness, but is used **(3)** in association with it, 1 Th 5:6, 8; 2 Ti 4:5; 1 Pet 1:13; 4:7, "watch"; 5:8. See: TDNT—4:936, 633; BAGD—538d; THAYER—425d.

3526. Νίγερ {1x} **Nigĕr,** *neeg'-er;* of Lat. or.; *black; Niger,* a Chr.:—*Niger* {1x}. See: BAGD—539a; THAYER—425D.

3527. Νικάνωρ {1x} **Nikanōr,** *nik-an'-ore;* prob. from *3528; victorious; Nicanor,* a Chr.:—Nicanor {1x}. See: BAGD—539a; THAYER—425d.

3528. νικάω {28x} **nikaō,** *nik-ah'-o;* from *3529;* to *subdue* (lit. or fig.):—overcome {24x}, conquer {2x}, prevail {1x}, get the victory {1x}.
Nikao is used **(1)** of God, Rom 3:4 (a law term); **(2)** of Christ, Jn 16:33; Rev 3:21; 5:5; 17:14; **(3)** of His followers, Rom 12:21 (2nd part); 1 Jn 2:13–14; 4:4; 5:4–5; Rev 2:7, 11, 17, 26; 3:5, 12, 21; 12:11; 15:2; 21:7; **(4)** of faith, 1 Jn 5:4; **(5)** of evil (passive voice), Rom 12:21; **(6)** of predicted human potentates, Rev 6:2;

11:7; 13:7. See: TDNT—4:942, 634; BAGD—539a. THAYER—425d.

3529. **νίκη** {1x} **nikē,** *nee′-kay;* appar. a primary word; *conquest* (abstr.), i.e. (fig.) the *means of success:*—victory {1x}. See: TDNT—4:942, 634; BAGD—539c; THAYER—426a.

3530. **Νικόδημος** {5x} **Nikŏdēmŏs,** *nik-od′-ay-mos;* from *3534* and *1218; victorious* among his *people; Nicodemus,* an Isr.:—Nicodemus {5x}. See: TDNT—4:942, 634; BAGD—539c; THAYER—426b.

3531. **Νικολαΐτης** {2x} **Nikŏlaïtēs,** *nik-ol-ah-ee′-tace;* from *3532;* a *Nicolaïte,* i.e. adherent of *Nicolaüs:*—Nicolaitans {2x}. See: BAGD—539; THAYER—426b.

3532. **Νικόλαος** {1x} **Nikŏlaŏs,** *nik-ol′-ah-os;* from *3534* and *2992; victorious* over the *people; Nicolaüs,* a heretic:—Nicolaus {1x}. See: BAGD—539d; THAYER—426b.

3533. **Νικόπολις** {2x} **Nikŏpŏlis,** *nik-op′-ol-is;* from *3534* and *4172; victorious city; Nicopolis,* a place in Macedonia:—Nicopolis {2x}. See: BAGD—539d; THAYER—426b.

3534. **νῖκος** {4x} **nikŏs,** *nee′-kos;* from *3529;* a *conquest* (concr.), i.e. (by impl.) *triumph:*—victory {4x}.

Nikos, as a noun, means victory, utterly vanquished one's foes, is used in Mt 12:20; 1 Cor 15:54, 55, 57. See: TDNT—4:942, 634; BAGD—539d; THAYER—426c.

3535. **Νινευΐ** {1x} **Nineŭï,** *nin-yoo-ee′;* of Heb. or. [5210]; *Ninevi* (i.e. *Nineveh*), the capital of Assyria:—Nineve {1x}. See: BAGD—540a; THAYER—426c.

3536. **Νινευΐτης** {2x} **Nineŭïtēs,** *nin-yoo-ee′-tace;* from *3535;* a *Ninevite,* i.e. inhab. of Nineveh:—of Nineve {1x}, Ninevite {1x}. See: BAGD—540a; THAYER—429d.

3537. **νιπτήρ** {1x} **niptēr,** *nip-tare′;* from *3538;* a *ewer:*—bason {1x}.

Nipter, the vessel into which the Lord poured water to wash the disciples' feet, was "a large ewer," Jn 13:5. The word is connected with the verb *nipto,* "to wash." See: BAGD—540a; THAYER—426d.

3538. **νίπτω** {17x} **niptō,** *nip′-to;* to *cleanse* (espec. the hands or the feet or the face); cerem. to *perform ablution:*—wash {17x}.

(1) This word is only used of washing part of the body, **(1a)** literally, Jn 13:5–6, 8, 12, 14 (twice); **(1b)** in 1 Ti 5:10, including the figura-

tive sense; **(2)** in the middle voice, to wash oneself, Mt 6:17; 15:2; Mk 7:3; Jn 9:7, 11, 15; 13:10. Syn.: 3068, 4150. See: TDNT—4:946, 635; BAGD—540B; THAYER—426D. comp. *3068.*

3539. **νοιέω** {14x} **nŏiěō,** *noy-eh′-o;* from *3563*

νοέω **nŏěō** *no-eh′-o;* to *exercise* the *mind, (observe),* i.e. (fig.) to *comprehend, heed:*—consider {1x}, perceive {2x}, think {1x}, understand {10x}.

Noieo, "to perceive with the mind," as distinct from perception by feeling, is so used **(1)** in Mt 15:17, "understand"; 16:9, 11; 24:15 (here rather perhaps in the sense of considering) and parallels in Mk (not in Lk); Jn 12:40; Rom 1:20; 1 Ti 1:7; Heb 11:3; **(2)** in Eph 3:4, "may understand"; 3:20, "think"; 2 Ti 2:7, "consider." See: TDNT—4:948, 636; BAGD—540B; THAYER—426D.

3540. **νόημα** {8x} **nŏēma,** *nŏ′-ay-mah;* from *3539;* a *perception,* i.e. *purpose,* or (by impl.) the *intellect, disposition,* itself:—device {1x}, mind {8x}, thought {1x}.

Noema denotes "thought, that which is thought out" (cf. *noeo,* "to understand"); hence, "a purpose, device"; translated **(1)** "devices" in 2 Cor 2:11; **(2)** "minds" in 2 Cor 3:14; 4:4; 11:3; **(3)** in 2 Cor 10:5, "thought"; **(4)** in Phil 4:7, "minds." See: TDNT—4:960, 636; BAGD—540d; THAYER—427a.

3541. **νόθος** {1x} **nŏthŏs,** *noth′-os;* of uncert. aff.; a *spurious* or *illegitimate* son:—bastard {1x}.

Nothos denotes an illegitimate child, one born out of lawful wedlock (Heb 12:8). See: BAGD—540d. See: TDNT—4:960, 636; BAGD—427a; THAYER—427a.

3542. **νομή** {2x} **nŏmē,** *nom-ay′;* fem. from the same as *3551; pasture,* i.e. (the act) *feeding* (fig. *spreading* of a gangrene), or (the food) *pasturage:*—eat + 2192 {1x}, pasture {1x}.

Noma denotes **(1)** "pasture, pasturage," figuratively in Jn 10:9; **(2)** "grazing, feeding," figuratively in 2 Ti 2:17, of the doctrines of false teachers, lit., "their word will have feeding as a gangrene." See: BAGD—541a; THAYER—427a.

3543. **νομίζω** {15x} **nŏmizō,** *nom-id′-zo;* from *3551;* prop. to *do by law (usage),* i.e. to *accustom* (pass. *be usual*); by extens. to *deem* or *regard:*—suppose {9x}, think {5x}, be wont {1x}.

Nomizo, "to consider, suppose, think," is rendered **(1)** "to suppose" in Mt 20:10; Lk 2:34; 3:23; Acts 7:25; 14:19; 16:27; 21:29; 1 Ti 6:5; in 1 Cor 7:26; Acts 16:13, "to suppose," "(where) we supposed (there was a place of prayer)";

(2) this word also signifies "to practice a custom" (*nomos*) and is commonly so used by Greek writers; "was wont (to be made)" in Acts 16:13; **(3)** it is rendered "to think" in Mt 5:17; 10:34; Acts 8:20; 17:29; 1 Cor 7:36. See: BAGD—541a; THAYER—427b.

3544. νομικός {9x} **nŏmikŏs**, *nom-ik-os'*; from *3551; according* (or *pertaining) to law*, i.e. *legal* (cer.); as noun, an *expert in* the (Mosaic) *law:*—about the law {1x}, lawyer {8x}.

Nomikos, an adjective, "learned in the law", is used as a noun, **(1)** "a lawyer," Mt 22:35; Lk 7:30; 10:25; 11:45, 46, 52; 14:3; Titus 3:13, where Zenas is so named. **(2)** As there is no evidence that he was one skilled in Roman jurisprudence, the term may be regarded in the usual NT sense as applying to one skilled in the Mosaic Law. **(3)** The usual name for a scribe is *grammateus*, a man of letters; for a doctor of the law, *nomo didaskalos*, a comparison of Lk 5:17 with v. 21 and Mk 2:6 and Mt 9:3 shows that the three terms were used synonymously, and did not denote three distinct classes. **(3a)** The scribes were originally simply men of letters, students of Scripture, and the name first given to them contains in itself no reference to the law; in course of time, however, they devoted themselves mainly, though by no means exclusively, to the study of the law. They became jurists rather than theologians, and received names which of themselves called attention to that fact. **(3b)** Some would doubtless devote themselves more to one branch of activity than to another; but a "lawyer" might also be a "doctor," and the case of Gamaliel shows that a "doctor" might also be a member of the Sanhedrin, Acts 5:34. See: TDNT—4:1088, 646; BAGD—541b.

3545. νομίμως {2x} **nŏmimŏs**, *nom-im'-oce;* adv. from a der. of *3551; legitimately* (spec. agreeably to the rules of the lists):—lawfully {2x}.

Nomimos, "lawfully," is used **(1)** in 1 Ti 1:8, "the Law is good, if a man use it lawfully," i.e., agreeably to its design; the meaning here is that, while no one can be justified or obtain eternal life through its instrumentality, the believer is to have it in his heart and to fulfill its requirements; walking "not after the flesh but after the spirit," Rom 8:4, he will "use it lawfully." **(2)** In 2 Ti 2:5 it is used of contending in the games and adhering to the rules. See: TDNT—4:1088, 646; BAGD—541c; THAYER—427b.

3546. νόμισμα {1x} **nŏmisma**, *nom'-is-mah;* from *3543; what is reckoned* as of value (after the Lat. *numisma*), i.e. current *coin:*—money {1x}.

Nomisma, primarily "that which is established by custom" (*nomos*, "a custom, law"), hence, "the current coin of a state, currency," is found in Mt 22:19, "(tribute) money." See: BAGD—541d; THAYER—427b.

3547. νομοδιδάσκαλος {3x} **nŏmŏdidaskalŏs**, *nom-od-id-as'-kal-os;* from *3551* and *1320;* an *expounder of* the (Jewish) *law*, i.e. a *Rabbi:*—doctor of the law {2x}, teacher of the law {1x}.

This word means **(1)** "a teacher of the Law", with reference to the doctors of the Mosaic Law, Lk 5:17; Acts 5:34; **(2)** also of those who went about among Christians, professing to be instructors of the Law, 1 Ti 1:7. See: TDNT—2:159, 161; BAGD—541d; THAYER—427c.

3548. νομοθεσία {1x} **nŏmŏthĕsia**, *nom-oth-es-ee'-ah;* from *3550; legislation* (spec. the *institution of* the Mosaic *code*):—giving of the law {1x}.

This word denotes "legislation, lawgiving", Rom 9:4, "(the) giving of the law." See: TDNT—4:1089, 646; BAGD—541d; THAYER—427c.

3549. νομοθετέω {2x} **nŏmŏthĕtĕō**, *nom-oth-et-eh'-o;* from *3550;* to *legislate*, i.e. (pass.) to *have* (the Mosaic) *enactments* injoined, *be sanctioned* (by them):—establish {1x}, receive the law {1x}.

This word means "to ordain by law, to enact" (*nomos*, "a law," *tithemi*, "to put"), is used in the passive voice, and rendered **(1)** "established" in Heb 8:6; **(2)** in 7:11, used intransitively, it is rendered "received the law." See: TDNT—4:1090, 646; BAGD—541d; THAYER—427c.

3550. νομοθέτης {1x} **nŏmŏthĕtēs**, *nom-oth-et'-ace;* from *3551* and a der. of *5087;* a *legislator:*—lawgiver {1x}.

This word means "a lawgiver" and occurs in Jas 4:12, of God, as the sole "Lawgiver"; therefore, to criticize the Law is to presume to take His place, with the presumption of enacting a better law. See: TDNT—4:1090, 646; BAGD—542a; THAYER—427c.

3551. νόμος {197x} **nŏmŏs**, *nom'-os;* from a primary νέμω **nĕmō**, (to *parcel* out, espec. *food* or *grazing* to animals); *law* (through the idea of prescriptive *usage*), gen. (*regulation*), spec. (of Moses [incl. the volume]; also of the Gospel), or fig. (a *principle*):—law {197x}.

Nomos, in the NT is used **(1)** of "law" in general, **(1a)** e.g., Rom 2:12, 13, expressing a general principle relating to "law"; **(1b)** 3:27, "By what manner of law?" i.e., "by what sort of principle (has the glorying been excluded)?"; **(1c)** 5:13, referring to the period between Ad-

am's trespass and the giving of the Law; **(1d)** 7:1 against those graces which constitute the fruit of the Spirit "there is no law," Gal 5:23; **(1e)** the ostensible aim of the law is to restrain the evil tendencies natural to man in his fallen estate, yet in experience law finds itself not merely ineffective, it actually provokes those tendencies to greater activity. The intention of the gift of the Spirit is to constrain the believer to a life in which the natural tendencies shall have no place, and to produce in him their direct contraries. Law, therefore, has nothing to say against the fruit of the Spirit; hence the believer is not only not under law, ver. 18, the law finds no scope in his life, inasmuch as, and in so far as, he is led by the Spirit. **(2)** of a force or influence impelling to action, Rom 7:21, 23 (1st part), "a different law";

(3) of the Mosaic Law, the "law" of Sinai, **(3a)** with the definite article, e.g., Mt 5:18; Jn 1:17; Rom 2:15, 18, 20, 26, 27; 3:19; 4:15; 7:4, 7, 14, 16, 22; 8:3, 4, 7; Gal 3:10, 12, 19, 21, 24; 5:3; Eph 2:15; Phil 3:6; 1 Ti 1:8; Heb 7:19; Jas 2:9; **(3b)** without the article, thus stressing the Mosaic Law in its quality as "law," e.g., Rom 2:14 (1st part); 5:20; 7:9, where the stress in the quality lies in this, that "the commandment which was unto (i.e., which he thought would be a means of) life," he found to be "unto (i.e., to have the effect of revealing his actual state of) death"; 10:4; 1 Cor 9:20; Gal 2:16, 19, 21; 3:2, 5, 10 (1st part), 11, 18, 23; 4:4, 5, 21 (1st part); 5:4, 18; 6:13; Phil 3:5, 9; Heb 7:16; 9:19; Jas 2:11; 4:11; (in regard to the statement in Gal 2:16, that "a man is not justified by the works of the Law," the absence of the article before *nomos* indicates the assertion of a principle, "by obedience to law," but evidently the Mosaic Law is in view. Here the apostle is maintaining that submission to circumcision entails the obligation to do the whole "Law." Circumcision belongs to the ceremonial part of the "Law," but, while the Mosaic Law is actually divisible into the ceremonial and the moral, no such distinction is made or even assumed in Scripture. The statement maintains the freedom of the believer from the "law" of Moses in its totality as a means of justification);

(4) by metonymy, of the books which contain the "law," **(4a)** of the Pentateuch, e.g., Mt 5:17; 12:5; Lk 16:16; 24:44; Jn 1:45; Rom 3:21; Gal 3:10; **(4b)** of the Psalms, Jn 10:34; 15:25; **(4c)** of the Psalms, Isaiah, Ezekiel and Daniel, 12:34, the Psalms and Isaiah, Rom 3:19 (with vv. 10–18); Isaiah, 1 Cor 14:21; **(5)** from all this it may be inferred that "the law" in the most comprehensive sense was an alternative title to "The Scriptures."

(6) The following phrases specify "laws" of various kinds; **(6a)** "the law of Christ," Gal 6:2, i.e., **(6a1)** either given by Him (as in the Sermon on the Mount and in Jn 13:14, 15; 15:4), or **(6a2)** the "law" or principle by which Christ Himself lived (Mt 20:28; Jn 13:1); these are not actual alternatives, for the "law" imposed by Christ was always that by which He Himself lived in the "days of His flesh." He confirmed the "Law" as being of divine authority (cf. Mt 5:18); yet He presented a higher standard of life than perfunctory obedience to the current legal rendering of the "Law," a standard which, without annulling the "Law," He embodied in His own character and life (see, e.g., Mt 5:21–48; this breach with legalism is especially seen in regard to the ritual or ceremonial part of the "Law" in its wide scope); He showed Himself superior to all human interpretations of it; **(6b)** "a law of faith," Rom 3:27, i.e., a principle which demands only faith on man's part; **(6c)** "the law of my mind," Rom 7:23, that principle which governs the new nature in virtue of the new birth; **(6d)** "the law of sin," Rom 7:23, the principle by which sin exerts its influence and power despite the desire to do what is right; **(6e)** "of sin and death," 8:2, death being the effect; **(6f)** "the law of liberty," Jas 1:25; 2:12, a term comprehensive of all the Scriptures, not a "law" of compulsion enforced from without, but meeting with ready obedience through the desire and delight of the renewed being who is subject to it; into it he looks, and in its teaching he delights; he is "under law (*ennomos*, "in law," implying union and subjection) to Christ," 1 Cor 9:21; cf, e.g., Ps 119:32, 45, 97; 2 Cor 3:17; **(6g)** "the royal law," Jas 2:8, i.e., the "law" of love, royal in the majesty of its power, the "law" upon which all others hang, Mt 22:34–40; Rom 13:8; Gal 5:14; **(6h)** "the law of the Spirit of life," Rom 8:2, i.e., the animating principle by which the Holy Spirit acts as the imparter of life (cf. Jn 6:63); **(6i)** "a law of righteousness," Rom 9:31, i.e., a general principle presenting righteousness as the object and outcome of keeping a "law," particularly the "Law" of Moses (cf. Gal 3:21); **(6j)** "the law of a carnal commandment," Heb 7:16, i.e., the "law" respecting the Aaronic priesthood, which appointed men conditioned by the circumstances and limitations of the flesh.

(7) In the Epistle to the Hebrews the "Law" is treated of especially in regard to the contrast between the Priesthood of Christ and that established under the "law" of Moses, and in regard to access to God and to worship. In these respects the "Law" "made nothing perfect," 7:19. There was "a disannulling of a foregoing commandment . . . and a bringing in of a better

hope." This is established under the "New Covenant," a covenant instituted on the basis of "better promises," 8:6. **(8)** In Gal 5:3, the statement that to receive circumcision constitutes a man a debtor to do "the whole Law," views the "Law" as made up of separate commands, each essential to the whole, and predicates the unity of the "Law"; in v. 14, the statement that "the whole law" is fulfilled in the one commandment concerning love, views the separate commandments as combined to make a complete "law." **(9)** In Rom 8:3, "what the law could not do," is lit., "the inability (*adunaton*, the neuter of the adjective *adunatos*, 'unable,' used as a noun) of the Law"; this may mean either "the weakness of the Law" or "that which was impossible for the Law"; the latter is preferable; the significance is the same in effect; the "Law" could neither give freedom from condemnation nor impart life. See: TDNT—4:1022, 646; BAGD—542b; THAYER—427d.

3552. **νοσέω** {1x} **nŏsĕō**, *nos-eh'-o;* from *3554;* to *be sick,* i.e. (by impl. of a diseased appetite) to *hanker* after (fig. to *harp* upon):—dote {1x}.

Noseo signifies "to be ill, to be ailing," whether in body or mind; hence, "to be taken with such a morbid interest in a thing as is tantamount to a disease, to dote," 1 Ti 6:4. The primary meaning of "*dote*" is to be foolish (cf. Jer 50:36), the evident meaning of *noseo,* in this respect, is "to be unsound." See: TDNT—4:1091, 655; BAGD—543c; THAYER—429c.

3553. **νόσημα** {1x} **nŏsēma**, *nos'-ay-ma;* from *3552;* an *ailment:*—disease {1x}. See: TDNT—4:1091, 655; BAGD—543c; THAYER—429a.

3554. **νόσος** {12x} **nŏsŏs**, *nos'-os;* of uncert. aff.; a *malady* (rarely fig. of mor. *disability*):—disease {6x}, infirmity {1x}, sickness {5x}.

Nosos is the regular word for **(1)** "sickness" in Mt 4:23; 8:17; 9:35; 10:1; Mk 3:15; **(2)** "disease" in Mt 4:24; Mk 1:34; Lk 4:40; 6:17; 9:1; Acts 19:12; and **(3)** "infirmities" in Lk 7:21. See: TDNT—4:1091, 655; BAGD—543c; THAYER—429a.

3555. **νοσσιά** {1x} **nŏssia**, *nos-see-ah';* from *3502;* a *brood* (of chickens):—brood {1x}.

Nossia is primarily, "a nest" and denotes "a brood," Lk 13:34. See: BAGD—543d; THAYER—429a.

3556. **νοσσίον** {1x} **nŏssiŏn**, *nos-see'-on;* dimin. of *3502;* a *birdling:*—chicken {1x}. See: BAGD—543d; THAYER—429a.

3557. **νοσφίζομαι** {3x} **nŏsphizŏmai**, *nos-fid'-zom-ahee;* mid. voice from **νοσφί nŏsphi** (*apart* or *clandestinely*); to *sequestrate,* for oneself, i.e. *embezzle:*—keep back {2x}, purloin {1x}.

This word means "to set apart, remove," signifies, **(1)** in the middle voice, "to set apart for oneself, to purloin," and is rendered "purloining" in Titus 2:10; **(2)** "kept back" (and "keep") in Acts 5:2, 3, of the act of Ananias and his wife in "retaining" part of the price of the land. See: BAGD—543d; THAYER—429b.

3558. **νότος** {7x} **nŏtŏs**, *not'-os;* of uncert. aff.; the *south* (-*west*) *wind;* by extens. the *southern quarter* itself:—south {4x}, south wind {3x}.

Notos denotes **(1)** the south wind (Lk 12:55; Acts 27:13; 28:13); **(2)** south as a direction (Lk 13:29; Rev 21:13); **(3)** the South as a region (Mt 12:42; Lk 11:31). See: BAGD—544a; THAYER—429b.

3559. **νουθεσία** {3x} **nŏuthĕsia**, *noo-thes-ee'-ah;* from *3563* and a der. of *5087;* calling *attention* to, i.e. (by impl.) mild *rebuke* or *warning:*—admonition {3x}.

Literally, this word means a putting in mind, and is used of **(1)** the purpose of the Scriptures (1 Cor 10:11); **(2)** of that which is ministered by the Lord (Eph 6:4); and **(3)** of that which is to be administered for the correction of one who creates trouble in the church (Titus 3:10). Syn.: *Nouthesia* is the training by word, whether of encouragement, or, if necessary, by reproof or remonstrance. *Paideia* (*3809*) stresses training by act, though both words are used in each respect. See: TDNT—4:1019, 636; BAGD—544b; THAYER—429b.

3560. **νουθετέω** {8x} **nŏuthĕtĕō**, *noo-thet-eh'-o;* from the same as *3559;* to *put in mind,* i.e. (by impl.) to *caution* or *reprove* gently:—admonish {4x}, warn {4x}.

Noutheteo (*3560*) means "to put in mind, admonish," **(1)** "to warn" in Acts 20:31; 1 Cor 4:14; Col 1:28 "warning"; 1 Th 5:14 "warn"; and **(2)** "to admonish" in Rom 15:14; Col 3:16; 1 Th 5:12; 2 Th 3:15. **(3)** The difference between "admonish" and "teach" seems to be that, whereas the former has mainly in view the things that are wrong and call for warning, the latter has to do chiefly with the impartation of positive truth, cf. Col 3:16; they were to let the Word of Christ dwell richly in them, so that they might be able **(3a)** to teach and "admonish" one another, and **(3b)** to abound in the praises of God. **(4)** Admonition differs from remonstrance, in that the former is warning based on instruction; the latter may be little more than expostulation. For example, though

Eli remonstrated with his sons, 1 Sa 2:24, he failed to admonish them, 3:13. Pastors and teachers in the churches are thus themselves admonished, i.e., instructed and warned, by the Scriptures, 1 Cor 10:11, so to minister the Word of God to the saints, that, naming the Name of the Lord, they shall depart from unrighteousness, 2 Ti 2:19. Syn.: 3560, 3867, 5537. See: TDNT—4:1019, 636; BAGD—544b; THAYER—429b.

3561. νουμηνία {1x} **nŏumēnia**, *noo-may-nee'-ah;* fem. of a compound of *3501* and *3376* (as noun by impl. of *2250*); the festival of *new moon:*—new moon {1x}.

This word, denoting "a new moon" (*neos*, "new," *men*, "a month"), is (1) used in Col 2:16, of a Jewish festival. (2) Judaistic tradition added special features in the liturgy of the synagogue in connection with the observance of the first day of the month, the new "moon" time. (3) In the OT see Num 29:6; 1 Sa 20:27; Hos 5:7. (4) For the connection with feast days see Lev 23:24; Num 10:10; 29:1; Ps 81:31. See: TDNT—4:638,*; BAGD—544b; THAYER—429b.

3562. νουνεχῶς {1x} **nŏunĕchōs**, *noon-ekh-oce';* adv. from a comp. of the acc. of *3563* and *2192;* in a *mind-having* way, i.e. *prudently:*—discreetly {1x}.

Nounechos, lit., "mindpossessing" (*nous*, "mind, understanding," *echo*, "to have"), hence denotes "discreetly, sensibly prudently," Mk 12:34. See: TDNT—2:816,*; BAGD—544b; THAYER—429c.

3563. νοῦς {24x} **nŏus**, *nooce;* prob. from the base of *1097;* the *intellect*, i.e. *mind* (divine or human; in thought, feeling, or will); by impl. *meaning:*—mind {21x}, understanding {3x}.

Nous, as a noun, means "mind," denotes, (1) speaking generally, the seat of reflective consciousness, comprising the faculties of perception and understanding, and those of feeling, judging and determining. (2) Its use in the NT may be analyzed as follows: it denotes (2a) the faculty of knowing, the seat of the understanding, Lk 24:45; Rom 1:28; 14:5; 1 Cor 14:15, 19; Eph 4:17; Phil 4:7; Col 2:18; 1 Ti 6:5; 2 Ti 3:8; Titus 1:15; Rev 13:18; 17:9; (2b) counsels, purpose, Rom 11:34 (of the "mind" of God); (2b1) Rom 12:2; 1 Cor 1:10; 2:16, twice of the thoughts and counsels of God, (2b2) of Christ, a testimony to His Godhood; Eph 4:23; (2b3) 2 Th 2:2, where it stands for the determination to be steadfast amidst afflictions, through the confident expectation of the day of rest and recompense mentioned in the first chapter; (3) the new nature, which belongs to the believer by reason of the new birth, Rom 7:23, 25, where it is contrasted with "the flesh," the principle of evil which dominates fallen man. Syn.: 363, 1271, 1771, 3540, 5279, 5436, 5427. See: TDNT—4:951, 636; BAGD—544c; THAYER—429c. comp. *5590*.

3564. Νυμφᾶς {1x} **Numphas**, *noom-fas';* prob. contr. for a compound of *3565* and *1435; nymph-given* (i.e. *-born*); *Nymphas*, a Chr.:—Nymphas {1x}. See: BAGD—545a; THAYER—429d.

3565. νύμφη {8x} **numphē**, *noom-fay';* from a primary but obs. verb νύπτω **nuptō**, (to *veil* as a bride; comp. Lat. "*nupto*," to *marry*); a young *married* woman (as *veiled*), incl. a *betrothed* girl; by impl. a *son's wife:*—bride {5x}, daughter in law {3x}.

Numphe means a bride, or young wife (Jn 3:29; Rev 18:23; 21:2, 9; 22:17) who was led veiled from her home to the bridegroom; hence, the secondary meaning of daughter-in-law (Mt 10:35; Lk 12:53). See: TDNT—4:1099, 657; BAGD—545b; THAYER—429d.

3566. νυμφίος {16x} **numphiŏs**, *noom-fee'-os;* from *3565;* a *bridegroom* (lit. or fig.):—bridegroom {16x}. See: TDNT—4:1099, 657; BAGD—545b; THAYER—429d.

3567. νυμφών {3x} **numphōn**, *noom-fohn';* from *3565;* the *bridal* room:—bridechamber {3x}.

Numphion signifies (1) "the room or dining hall in which the marriage ceremonies were held," Mt 22:10; (2) "the chamber containing the bridal bed," "the sons of the bridechamber" being the friends of the bridegroom, who had the charge of providing what was necessary for the nuptials, Mt 9:15; Mk 2:19; Lk 5:34. See: BAGD—545b; THAYER—430a.

3568. νῦν {139x} **nun**, *noon;* a primary particle of present time; "*now*" (as adv. of date, a transition or emphasis); also as noun or adj. *present* or *immediate:*—now {121x}, present {4x}, henceforth {4x}, this + *3588* {3x}, this time {2x}, misc. {5x} = + hereafter, of late, soon.

Nun is used (1) of time, the immediate present, whether in contrast (1a) to the past, e.g., Jn 4:18; Acts 7:52, or (1b) to the future, e.g., Jn 12:27; Rom 11:31; (1c) sometimes with the article, singular or plural, e.g., Acts 4:29; 5:38; (2) of logical sequence, often partaking also of the character of (*1*), "now therefore, now however," as it is, e.g., Lk 11:39; Jn 8:40; 9:41; 15:22, 24; 1 Cor 5:11. See: TDNT—4:1106, 658; BAGD—545c; THAYER—430a. See also *3569, 3570*.

3569. **τανῦν** {5x} **tanun,** *tan-oon';* or

τὰ νῦν **ta nun** *tah noon;* from neut.
plur. of *3588* and *3568; the*
things *now,* i.e. (adv.) *at present:*—but now {1x},
now {4x}. See: BAGD—546a; THAYER—430a.

3570. **νυνί** {{20x} **nuni,** *noo-nee';* a prol. form
of *3568* for emphasis; *just now:*—
now {20x}.
Nuni, a strengthened form of *nun* (*3569*) is
used (1) of time, e.g., Acts 24:13; Rom 6:22;
15:23, 25; (2) with logical import, e.g., Rom
7:17. See: BAGD—546b; THAYER—430d.

3571. **νύξ** {65x} **nux,** *noox;* a primary word;
"night" (lit. or fig.):—night {63x},
midnight + *3319* {2x}.
Nux is used (1) literally, (1a) of "the alter-
nating natural period to that of the day," e.g.,
Mt 4:2; 12:40; 2 Ti 1:3; Rev 4:8; (1b) of "the
period of the absence of light," the time in which
something takes place, e.g., Mt 2:14; 27:64; Lk
2:8; Jn 3:2; 7:50; Acts 5:19; 9:25; (1c) of "point
of time," e.g., Mt 14:30; Lk 12:20; Acts 27:23;
(1d) of "duration of time," e.g., Lk 2:37; 5:5;
Acts 20:31; 26:7; (2) metaphorically, (2a) of "the
period of man's alienation from God," Rom
13:12; 1 Th 5:5, lit., "not of night," where "of"
means 'belonging to;' cf. "of the Way"; Acts 9:2;
(2b) "of shrinking back" and "of faith," Heb
10:39, marg.; (2c) of "death," as the time when
work ceases, Jn 9:4. See: TDNT—4:1123, 661;
BAGD—546b; THAYER—431a.

3572. **νύσσω** {1x} **nussō,** *noos'-so;* appar. a primary word; to *prick* ("nudge"):—
pierce {1x}.
Nusso means to pierce or pierce through,
often of inflicting severe or deadly wounds, is
used of the piercing of the side of Christ (Jn
19:34). See: BAGD—547a; THAYER—431c.

3573. **νυστάζω** {2x} **nustazō,** *noos-tad'-zo;*
from a presumed der. of
3506; to *nod,* i.e. (by impl.) to *fall asleep;* fig.
to *delay:*—slumber {2x}.
Nustazo denotes "to nod in sleep" (akin to
neuo, "to nod"), "fall asleep," and is used (1) of
natural slumber, Mt 25:5; (2) metaphorically in
2 Pet 2:3, negatively, of the destruction awaiting
false teachers. See: BAGD—547a; THAYER—
431c.

3574. **νυχθήμερον** {1x} **nuchthēmĕrŏn,** *nookh-
thay'-mer-on;* from *3571*
and *2250;* a *day-and-night,* i.e. full *day* of
twenty-four hours:—a night and day {1x}.
This word is an adjective denoting "lasting a
night and a day" (from *nux,* "night," and *hemera,*
"a day"), and is used in 2 Cor 11:25, in the
neuter gender, as a noun, the object of the verb

poieo, to do, lit., "I have done a night-and-a-
day." See: BAGD—547a; THAYER—431c.

3575. **Νῶε** {8x} **Nŏĕ,** *no'-eh;* of Heb. or. [5146];
Noë, (i.e. *Noäch*), a patriarch:—
Noe {5x}, Noah {3x}. See: BAGD—547c;
THAYER—431c.

3576. **νωθρός** {2x} **nōthrŏs,** *no-thros';* from a
der. of *3541; sluggish,* i.e. (lit.)
lazy, or (fig.) *stupid:*—dull {1x}, slothful {1x}.
Nothros, "slow, sluggish, indolent, dull" is
translated (1) "dull" in Heb 5:11 (in connection
with the noun, *akoe,* "hearing"; lit., "in hear-
ings"); (2) "slothful," in Heb 6:12. Syn.: In Lk
24:25 "slow (of heart)" translates the synonymous word *bradus* (*917*). *Bradus* differs from
nothros in that no moral fault or blame is necessarily involved in it; so far indeed is it from
this, that of the three occasions on which it is
used in the NT two are in honor; for to be
"slow" to evil things, to rash speaking, or to
anger (Jas 1:19, twice), is a grace, and not the
contrary. . . . There is a deeper, more inborn
sluggishness implied in *nothros,* and this
bound up as it were in the very life. Syn.: 692,
1021. See: TDNT—4:1126, 661; BAGD—547c;
THAYER—431d.

3577. **νῶτος** {1x} **nōtŏs,** *no'-tos;* of uncert.
aff.; the *back:*—back {1x}.
Notos, "the back," signifying "to bend,
curve" is used in Rom 11:10. See: BAGD—547c;
THAYER—431d.

Ξ

3578. **ξενία** {2x} **xĕnia,** *xen-ee'-ah;* from *3581;*
hospitality, i.e. (by impl.) a *place
of entertainment:*—lodging {2x}.
Xenia denotes "hospitality, entertainment" and
by metonymy, "a place of entertainment, a lodging-
place," Acts 28:23; Philem 22. See: TDNT—5:1,
661; BAGD—547b; THAYER—3578b.

3579. **ξενίζω** {10x} **xĕnizō,** *xen-id'-zo;* from
3581; to *be a host* (pass. a
guest); by impl. *be* (*make, appear*) *strange:*—
entertain {1x}, lodge {6x}, think it strange {2x},
strange {1x}.
This word signifies to receive as a guest,
rendered (1) lodged (Acts 28:7); (2) have entertained (Heb 13:2); and (3) to be astonished by
the strangeness of a thing (Acts 17:20; 1 Pet
4:4, 12). When one lodges in a place the host
sees that the guests are entertained, i.e. have
no thoughts for needs. The root for entertain
means to hold and in order to take the traveler's mind off his cares the host provides that
which is new and unfamiliar to the guest;

hence, strange. See: TDNT—5:1, 661; BAGD—547d; THAYER—431d.

3580. ξενοδοχέω {1x} xĕnŏdŏchĕō, *xen-od-okh-eh'-o;* from a compound of *3581* and *1209;* to *be hospitable:*—lodge strangers {1x}. See: TDNT—5:1, 661; BAGD—548a; THAYER—432a.

3581. ξένος {14x} xĕnŏs, *xen'-os;* appar. a primary word; *for.* (lit. *alien,* or fig. *novel*); by impl. a *guest* or (vice-versa) *entertainer:*—host {1x}, strange {3x}, stranger {10x}.

Xenos denotes **(1)** one who receives and entertains another hospitably, the one with whom he stays or lodges, a host, Rom 16:23; **(2)** "stranger" in Mt 25:35, 38, 43, 44; 27:7; Acts 17:21 plural; Eph 2:12, 19; Heb 11:13; 3 Jn 1:5; and **(3)** "strange" in Acts 17:18; Heb 13:9; 1 Pet 4:2, "served" by the "host". See: TDNT—5:1, 661; BAGD—548a; THAYER—432a.

3582. ξέστης {2x} xĕstēs, *xes'-tace;* as if from ξέω xĕō, (prop. to *smooth;* by impl. [of *friction*] to *boil* or *heat*); a *vessel* (as *fashioned* or for *cooking*) [or perh. by corruption from the Lat. *sextarius,* the *sixth* of a modius, i.e. about a *pint*], i.e. (spec.) a *measure* for liquids or solids, (by anal. a *pitcher*):—pot {2x}. See: BAGD—548b; THAYER—432b.

3583. ξηραίνω {16x} xērainō, *xay-rah'-ee-no;* from *3584;* to *desiccate;* by impl. to *shrivel,* to *mature:*—wither away {6x}, wither {5x}, dry up {3x}, pine away {1x}, be ripe {1x}.

Xeraino means "to dry up, wither" and is translated "to wither," **(1)** of plants, Mt 13:6; 21:19, 20; Mk 4:6; 11:20, "dried up", 21; Lk 8:6; Jn 15:6; Jas 1:11; 1 Pet 1:24; **(2)** of the body, Mk 3:1, 3, a "withered hand"; 5:29 of blood; **(3)** of "ripened" crops: "And another angel came out of the temple, crying with a loud voice to him that sat on the cloud, Thrust in thy sickle, and reap: for the time is come for thee to reap; for the harvest of the earth is ripe" (Rev 14:15); **(4)** "pineth away" in Mk 9:18; and **(5)** "dried up" of the Euphrates river, Rev 16:12. Syn.: 187, 3860. See: BAGD—548c; THAYER—432b.

3584. ξηρός {7x} xērŏs, *xay-ros';* from the base of *3582* (through the idea of *scorching*); *arid;* by impl. *shrunken, earth* (as opposed to *water*):—withered {4x}, dry {1x}, dry land {1x}, land {1x}.

Xeros is used **(1)** naturally, of "dry" land, Heb 11:29; or of land in general, Mt 23:15, "land"; or **(2)** of physical infirmity, "withered," Mt 12:10; Lk 6:6, 8; Jn 5:3; **(3)** figuratively, in Lk 23:31, "dry", with reference to the spiritual "barrenness" of the Jews, in contrast to the character

of the Lord. Cf. Ps 1:3; Is 56:3; Eze 17:24; 20:47. See: BAGD—548c; THAYER—432c.

3585. ξύλινος {2x} xulinŏs, *xoo'-lin-os;* from *3586;* wooden:—of wood {2x}. See: BAGD—549a; THAYER—432c.

3586. ξύλον {19x} xulŏn, *xoo'-lon;* from another form of the base of *3582;* timber (as fuel or material); by impl. a *stick, club* or *tree* or other wooden art. or substance:—staff {5x}, stocks {1x}, tree {10x}, wood {3x}.

Xulon, "wood, a piece of wood, anything made of wood" is used, with the rendering **(1)** "tree," in Lk 23:31, where "the green tree" refers either to Christ, figuratively of all His living power and excellencies, or to the life of the Jewish people while still inhabiting their land, in contrast to "the dry," a figure fulfilled in the horrors of the Roman massacre and devastation in A.D. 70 (cf. the Lord's parable in Lk 13:6–9; see Eze 20:47, and cf. 21:3); **(2)** of "the cross," the tree being the *stauros,* the upright pale or stake to which Romans nailed those who were thus to be executed, Acts 5:30; 10:39; 13:29; Gal 3:13; 1 Pet 2:24; **(3)** of "the tree of life," Rev. 2:7; 22:2 (twice), 14, 19, "book"; and **(4)** "a cudgel" or "staff," the plural being "staves" in Mt 26:47, 55; Mk 14:43, 48; Lk 22:52. See: TDNT—5:37, 665; BAGD—549a; THAYER—432c.

3587. ξυράω {3x} xuraō, *xoo-rah'-o;* from a der. of the same as *3586* (mean. a *razor*); to *shave* or "*shear*" the hair:—shave {3x}.

Xurao, a late form of *xureo,* or *xuro,* from *xuron,* "a razor," occurs in Acts 21:24 (middle voice), in connection with a vow (cf. Num 6:2–18; Acts 18:18); 1 Cor 11:5, 6 (2nd part in each). See: BAGD—549c; THAYER—432d.

O

3588. ὁ {543x} hŏ, *hŏ;* incl. the fem.

ἡ hē, *hay;* and the neut.

τό tŏ, *tŏ;* in all their inflections; the def. art.; *the* (sometimes to be supplied, at others omitted, in English idiom):—which {413x}, who {79x}, the things {11x}, the son {8x}, misc. {32x} = the, this, that, one, he, she, it, etc. See: BAGD—549b; THAYER—433a.

ὅ hŏ. See *3739.*

3589. ὀγδοήκοντα {2x} ŏgdŏēkŏnta, *og-dŏ-ay'-kon-tah;* from *3590;* ten times eight:—fourscore {2x}. Cf. Lk 2:37; 16:7. See: BAGD—552d; THAYER—437b.

3590. ὄγδοος {5x} ŏgdŏŏs, *og'-dŏ-os;* from *3638;* the *eighth:*—eighth {5x}.

Greek

Cf. Lk 1:59; Acts 7:8; 2 Pet 2:5; Rev 17:11; 21:20. See: BAGD—552d; THAYER—437b.

3591. ὄγκος {1x} **ŏgkŏs**, *ong'-kos;* prob. from the same as *43;* a *mass* (as *bending* or *bulging* by its load), i.e. *burden* (*hindrance*):—weight {1x}. Syn.: *Baros* (*922*) refers to weight, *ogkos* (*3591*) to bulk, and either may be oppressive; *922* is a load in so far as it is heavy, *phortion,* (*5413*) a burden in so far as it is borne; hence *5413* may be either heavy or light. See: TDNT—5:41, 666; BAGD—553a; THAYER—437b.

3592. ὅδε {12x} **hŏdĕ**, *hod'-eh;* incl. the fem.

ἥδε hēdĕ, *hay'-deh;* and the neut.

τόδε tŏdĕ, *tod'-e;* from *3588* and *1161;* the *same,* i.e. *this* or *that* one (plur. *these* or *those*); often used as pers. pron.:—these things {7x}, thus {1x}, after this manner {1x}, he {1x}, she {1x}, such {1x}. See: BAGD—553a; THAYER—437b.

3593. ὁδεύω {1x} **hŏdĕuō**, *hod-yoo'-o;* from *3598;* to *travel:*—journey {1x}.

Hodeuo, "to be on the way, journey" (from *hodos,* "a way"), the simplest form of the verbs denoting "to journey," is used in the parable of the good Samaritan, Lk 10:33. See: BAGD—553b; THAYER—437c.

3594. ὁδηγέω {5x} **hŏdēgĕō**, *hod-ayg-eh'-o;* from *3595;* to *show* the *way* (lit. or fig. [*teach*]):—guide {2x}, lead {3x}.

This word means "to lead the way", and is used **(1)** literally, "lead", **(1a)** of "guiding" the blind, in Mt 15:14; Lk 6:39; **(1b)** of "guiding" unto fountains of waters of life, Rev 7:17; **(2)** figuratively, in **(2a)** Jn 16:13, of "guidance" into the truth by the Holy Spirit; **(2b)** in Acts 8:31, of the interpretation of Scripture. See: TDNT—5:97, 666; BAGD—553b; THAYER—437c.

3595. ὁδηγός {5x} **hŏdēgŏs**, *hod-ayg-os';* from *3598* and *2233;* a *conductor* (lit. or fig. [*teacher*]):—guide {4x}, leader {1x}.

Hodegos, "a leader on the way" (*hodos,* "a way," *hegeomai,* "to lead"), "a guide," is used **(1)** literally, in Acts 1:16; **(2)** figuratively, Mt 15:14, "leaders"; Mt 23:16, 24, "guides"; Rom 2:19, "a guide." See: TDNT—5:97, 666; BAGD—553c; THAYER—437d.

3596. ὁδοιπορέω {1x} **hŏdŏipŏrĕō**, *hod-oy-por-eh'-o;* from a compound of *3598* and *4198;* to *be a wayfarer,* i.e. *travel:*—go on (one's) journey {1x}. See: BAGD—553d; THAYER—437d.

3597. ὁδοιπορία {2x} **hŏdŏipŏria**, *hod-oy-por-ee'-ah;* from the same as *3596; travel:*—journey {1x}, journeyings {1x}.

Hodoiporia, "a wayfaring, journeying" (*hodos,* and *poros,* "a way, a passage"), is used **(1)** of the Lord's journey to Samaria, Jn 4:6, and **(2)** of Paul's "journeyings," 2 Cor 11:26. See: BAGD—553d; THAYER—437d.

3598. ὁδός {102x} **hŏdŏs**, *hod-os';* appar. a primary word; a *road;* by impl. a *progress* (the route, act or distance); fig. a *mode* or *means:*—way {83x}, way side {8x}, journey {6x}, highway {3x}, misc. {2x}.

Hodos denotes **(1)** "a natural path, road, way," **(1a)** frequent in the Synoptic Gospels; **(1b)** elsewhere, e.g., Acts 8:26; 1 Th 3:11; Jas 2:25; Rev. 16:12; **(2)** "a traveler's way" (see journey); **(3)** metaphorically, of "a course of conduct," or "way of thinking," e.g., **(3a)** of righteousness, Mt 21:32; 2 Pet 2:21; **(3b)** of God, Mt 22:16, and parallels, i.e., **(3b1)** the "way" instructed and approved by God; so Acts 18:26 and Heb 3:10, **(3b2)** "My ways" (cf. Rev 15:3); **(3c)** of the Lord, Acts 18:25; **(3d)** that leads **(3d1)** "that leadeth to destruction," Mt 7:13; **(3d2)** ". . . unto life," 7:14; **(3d3)** of peace, Lk 1:79; Rom 3:17; **(4)** of Paul's "ways" in Christ, 1 Cor 4:17 (plural); **(5)** "more excellent" **(5a)** of love, 1 Cor 12:31; **(5b)** of truth, 2 Pet 2:2; **(6)** of the right "way," 2 Pet 2:15; **(7)** of Balaam (id.), of Cain, Jude 11; **(8)** of a "way" consisting in what is from God, e.g., **(8a)** of life, Acts 2:28 (plural); **(8b)** of salvation, Acts 16:17; **(9)** personified, of Christ as the means of access to the Father, Jn 14:6; **(10)** of the course followed and characterized by the followers of Christ, Acts 9:2; 19:9, 23; 24:22. See: TDNT—5:42, 666; BAGD—553d; THAYER—437d.

3599. ὀδούς {12x} **ŏdŏus**, *od-ooce;* perh. from the base of *2068;* a *"tooth":*—tooth {12x}.

Odous is used in the **(1)** sing. in Mt 5:38 (twice); **(2)** elsewhere in the plural, **(2a)** of "the gnashing of teeth," the gnashing being expressive of anguish and indignation, Mt 8:12; 13:42, 50; 22:13; 24:51; 25:30; Mk 9:18; Lk 13:28; Acts 7:54; and **(2b)** in Rev 9:8, of the beings seen in a vision and described as locusts. See: BAGD—555a; THAYER—437d.

3600. ὀδυνάω {4x} **ŏdunaō**, *od-oo-nah'-o;* from *3601;* to *grieve:*—sorrow {2x}, torment {2x}.

Odunao, verb, means "to cause pain" and is used in the middle voice: "And when they saw him, they were amazed: and his mother said unto him, Son, why hast thou thus dealt with us? behold, thy father and I have sought thee sorrowing (*odunao*)" (Lk 2:48; cf. Lk 16:24–25

"tormented", Acts 20:38 "sorrowing"). Syn.: 253, 3076, 3077, 3601, 3997, 4036, 5604. See: TDNT—5:115,*; BAGD—555a; THAYER—438c.

3601. ὀδύνη {2x} **ŏdunē**, *od-oo'-nay;* from *1416; grief* (as *dejecting*):—sorrow {2x}.

Odune, as a noun, means "pain, consuming grief, distress" **(1)** of heart: "That I have great heaviness and continual sorrow in my heart" (Rom 9:2); or **(2)** "sorrows" as a result of loving money: "For the love of money is the root of all evil: which while some coveted after, they have erred from the faith, and pierced themselves through with many sorrows" (1 Ti 6:10). Syn.: 253, 3076, 3077, 3600, 3997, 4036, 5604. See: TDNT—5:115, 673; BAGD—555b; THAYER—438d.

3602. ὀδυρμός {2x} **ŏdurmŏs**, *od-oor-mos';* from a der. of the base of *1416; moaning,* i.e. *lamentation:*—mourning {2x}.

Odurmos, "lamentation, mourning," is translated "mourning" in Mt 2:18 and 2 Cor 7:7. See: TDNT—5:116, 673; BAGD—555b.438d; THAYER—438d.

3603. ὅ ἐστι {11x} **hŏ esti**, *hŏ es-tee'* or

ὅ ἐστιν hŏ estin, *hŏ es-teen';* from the neut. of *3739* and the third pers. sing. pres. ind. of *1510; which is:*—which is {5x}, that is {3x}, that is to say {1x}, which make {1x}, called {1x}. See: BAGD—596b [3603]; THAYER—455b [3739].

3604. Ὀζίας {2x} **Ŏzias**, *od-zee'-as;* of Heb. or. [5818]; *Ozias* (i.e. *Uzziah*), an Isr.:—*Ozias* {2x}. See: BAGD—555b; THAYER—438d.

3605. ὄζω {1x} **ŏzō**, *od'-zo;* a primary verb (in a strengthened form); to *scent* (usually an ill "odor"):—stink {1x}. See: BAGD—555c; THAYER—438d.

3606. ὅθεν {15x} **hŏthĕn**, *hoth'-en;* from *3739* with the directive enclitic of source; *from which* place or source or cause (adv. or conjunc.):—wherefore {4x}, from whence {3x}, whereupon {3x}, where {2x}, whence {1x}, from thence {1x}, whereby {1x}. See: BAGD—555c; THAYER—439a.

3607. ὀθόνη {2x} **ŏthŏnē**, *oth-on'-ay;* of uncert. aff.; a *linen* cloth, i.e. (espec.) a *sail:*—sheet {2x}.

Othone primarily denoted "fine linen," later, "a sheet," Acts 10:11; 11:5. See: BAGD—555c; THAYER—439a.

3608. ὀθόνιον {5x} **ŏthŏniŏn**, *oth-on'-ee-on;* neut. of a presumed der. of *3607;* a linen *bandage:*—linen clothes {5x}.

Othonion, "a piece of fine linen," is used **(1)** in the plural, of the strips of cloth with which the body of the Lord was bound, Lk 24:12; Jn 19:40; 20:5, 6, 7. **(2)** The word is a diminutive of *othone* (*3607*) "a sheet." See: BAGD—555c; THAYER—439a.

3609. οἰκεῖος {3x} **ŏikĕiŏs**, *oy-ki'-os;* from *3624; domestic*, i.e. (as noun), a *relative, adherent:*—of the household {2x}, of (one's) own house {1x}.

Oikeios primarily signifies "of, or belonging to, a house," hence, "of persons, one's household, or kindred," as in **(1)** 1 Ti 5:8 "house"; in **(2)** Eph 2:19, "the household of God" denotes the company of the redeemed; in **(3)** Gal 6:10, it is called "the household of the faith." See: TDNT—5:134, 674; BAGD—556d; THAYER—439a.

3610. οἰκέτης {5x} **ŏikĕtēs**, *oy-ket'-ace;* from *3611;* a fellow *resident*, i.e. menial *domestic:*—household servant {1x}, servant {4x}.

An *oiketes* was one of the family, of the household, but not necessarily born in the home and translated **(1)** "household servant" in Acts 10:7; and **(2)** "servant" in Lk 16:13; Rom 14:4; Philem 25; 1 Pet 2:18. Syn.: 1249, 1401, 2324, 5257. See: BAGD—557a; THAYER—439b.

3611. οἰκέω {9x} **ŏikĕō**, *oy-keh'-o;* from *3624;* to *occupy a house,* i.e. *reside* (fig. *inhabit, remain, inhere*); by impl. to *cohabit:*—dwell {9x}.

Oikeo, "to dwell" (from *oikos*, "a house"), "to inhabit as one's abode." It is used **(1)** of God as "dwelling" in light, 1 Ti 6:16; **(2)** of the "indwelling" of the Spirit of God in the believer, Rom 8:9, 11, or in a church, 1 Cor 3:16; **(3)** of the "indwelling" of sin, Rom 7:17, 20; **(4)** of the absence of any good thing in the flesh of the believer, Rom 7:18; **(5)** of the "dwelling" together of those who are married, 1 Cor 7:12-13. See: TDNT—5:135, 674; BAGD—557a; THAYER—439b. See also *3625.*

3612. οἴκημα {1x} **ŏikĕma**, *oy'-kay-mah;* from *3611;* a *tenement*, i.e. (spec.) a *jail:*—prison {1x}. See: BAGD—557a; THAYER—439c.

3613. οἰκητήριον {2x} **ŏikētēriŏn**, *oy-kay-tay'-ree-on;* neut. of a presumed der. of *3611* (equiv. to *3612*); a *residence* (lit. or fig.):—habitation {1x}, house {1x}.

Oiketerion, "a habitation" (from *oiketer,* "an inhabitant," and *oikos*, "a dwelling"), is used in **(1)** Jude 6, of the heavenly region appointed

by God as the dwelling place of angels; **(2)** in 2 Cor 5:2, "house," figuratively of the spiritual bodies of believers when raised or changed at the return of the Lord. See: TDNT—5:155, 674; BAGD—357b; THAYER—439c.

3614. οἰκία {95x} **ŏikia**, *oy-kee'-ah;* from *3624;* prop. *residence* (abstr.), but usually (concr.) an *abode* (lit. or fig.); by impl. a *family* (espec. *domestics*):—house {92x}, at home {1x}, household {1x}, from the house {1x}.

(1) *Oikos* denoted the whole estate, *oikia* stood for the dwelling only; this distinction was largely lost in later Greek. In the NT it denotes **(2)** "a house, a dwelling," e.g., **(2a)** Mt 2:11; 5:15; 7:24–27; 2 Ti 2:20; 2 Jn 10; **(2b)** it is not used of the tabernacle or the temple; **(3)** metaphorically, the heavenly abode, spoken of by the Lord as "My Father's house," Jn 14:2, the eternal dwelling place of believers; **(4)** the body as the dwelling place of the soul, 2 Cor 5:1; **(5)** similarly the resurrection body of believers, 2 Cor 5:1; **(6)** property, e.g., Mk 12:40; **(7)** by metonymy, the inhabitants of a house, a household, e.g., Mt 12:25; Jn 4:53; 1 Cor 16:15. See: TDNT—5:131, 674; BAGD—557b; THAYER—439c.

3615. οἰκιακός {2x} **ŏikiakŏs**, *oy-kee-ak-os';* from *3614; familiar,* i.e. (as noun) *relatives:*—they (them) of (his own) household {2x}. Cf. Mt 10:25, 36. See: BAGD—557d; THAYER—439d.

3616. οἰκοδεσποτέω {1x} **ŏikŏdĕspŏtĕō**, *oy-kod-es-pot-eh'-o;* from *3617;* to *be* the *head of* (i.e. *rule*) a *family:*—guide the house {1x}. See: TDNT—2:49, 145; BAGD—558a; THAYER—439d.

3617. οἰκοδεσπότης {12x} **ŏikŏdĕspŏtēs**, *oy-kod-es-pot'-ace;* from *3624* and *1203; the head of a family:*—householder {4x}, goodman of the house {4x}, master of the house {3x}, goodman {1x}.

The goodman, master of the house, oversees all of the goods in a house and is translated **(1)** "householder" in Mt 13:27; 13:52; 20:1; 21:13; **(2)** "goodman of the house" in Mt 20:11; 24:43; Mk 14:14; Lk 12:39; **(3)** "master of the house" in Mt 10:25; Lk 13:25; 14:21; and **(4)** "goodman" in Lk 22:11. See: TDNT—2:49, 145; BAGD—558a; THAYER—439d.

3618. οἰκοδομέω {39x} **ŏikŏdŏmĕō**, *oy-kod-om-eh'-o;* from the same as *3619;* to *be* a *house-builder,* i.e. *construct* or (fig.) *confirm:*—build {24x}, edify {7x}, builder {5x}, build up {1x}, be in building {1x}, embolden {1x}.

Oikodomeo, as a verb, means lit., "to build a house" (*oikos,* "a house," *domeo,* "to build"),

hence, to build anything, **(1)** e.g., Mt 7:24; Lk 4:29; 6:48; Jn 2:20; **(1a)** usually signifies "to build," whether literally, or figuratively; **(1b)** the present participle, lit., "the (ones) building," is used as a noun, "the builders," in Mt 21:42; Mk 12:10; Lk 20:17; Acts 4:11; 1 Pet 2:7; **(2)** is used metaphorically, in the sense of "edifying," promoting the spiritual growth and development of character of believers, by teaching or by example, suggesting such spiritual progress as the result of patient labor. It is said **(2a)** of the effect of this upon local churches, Acts 9:31; 1 Cor 14:4; **(2b)** of the individual action of believers towards each other, 1 Cor 8:1; 10:23; 14:17; 1 Th 5:11; **(3)** of an individual in regard to himself, 1 Cor 14:4. **(4)** In 1 Cor 8:10, where it is translated "emboldened," the apostle uses it with pathetic irony, of the action of a brother in "building up" his brother who had a weak conscience, causing him to compromise his scruples; "strengthened," or "confirmed," would be suitable renderings. See: TDNT—5:136, 674; BAGD—558a; THAYER—439d.

3619. οἰκοδομή {18x} **ŏikŏdŏmē**, *oy-kod-om-ay';* fem. (abstr.) of a compound of *3624* and the base of *1430; architecture,* i.e. (concr.) a *structure;* fig. *confirmation:*—edifying {7x}, building {6x}, edification {4x}, wherewith (one) may edify {1x}.

Oikodome denotes "a building, or edification" and is used **(1)** literally, e.g., Mt 24:1; Mk 13:1–2; **(2)** figuratively, e.g., **(2a)** Rom 14:19 (lit., "the things of building up"); Rom 15:2; **(2b)** of a local church as a spiritual building, 1 Cor 3:9, or **(2c)** the whole church, the body of Christ, Eph 2:21. **(3)** It expresses the strengthening effect **(3a)** of teaching, 1 Cor 14:3, 5, 12, 26; 2 Cor 10:8; 12:19; 13:10, or **(3b)** other ministry, Eph 4:12, 16, 29 (the idea conveyed is progress resulting from patient effort). **(4)** It is also used of the believer's resurrection body, 2 Cor 5:1. See: TDNT—5:144, 674; BAGD—558d; THAYER—440b.

3620. οἰκοδομία {1x} **ŏikŏdŏmia**, *oy-kod-om-ee'-ah;* from the same as *3619; confirmation:*—edifying {1x}.

Oidodomia is used of building up another, edifying, 1 Ti 1:4. See: BAGD—559c; THAYER—440c.

3621. οἰκονομέω {1x} **ŏikŏnŏmĕō**, *oy-kon-om-eh'-o;* from *3623;* to *manage* (a house, i.e. an estate):—be steward {1x}. See: BAGD—559c; THAYER—440c.

3622. οἰκονομία {7x} **ŏikŏnŏmia**, *oy-kon-om-ee'-ah;* from *3623; administration* (of a household or estate); spec. a

(relig.) "*economy*":—dispensation {4x}, stewardship {3x}.

Oikonomia (*3622*) (1) primarily signifies "the management of a household or of household affairs" (*oikos*, "a house," *nomos*, "a law"); (1a) then the management or administration of the property of others, and so (1b) "a stewardship," Lk 16:2–4; (2) elsewhere only in the epistles of Paul, who applies it (2a) to the responsibility entrusted to him of preaching the gospel, 1 Cor 9:17 "dispensation"; (2b) to the stewardship committed to him "to fulfill the Word of God," the fulfillment being the unfolding of the completion of the divinely arranged and imparted cycle of truths which are consummated in the truth relating to the church as the body of Christ, Col 1:25 "dispensation"; (2c) so in Eph 3:2, of the grace of God given him as a stewardship ("dispensation") in regard to the same "mystery"; (3) in Eph 1:10 and 3:2, it is used of the arrangement or administration by God, by which in "the fullness of the times" (or seasons) God will sum up all things in the heavens and on earth in Christ. (4) A "dispensation" is not a period or epoch, but a mode of dealing, an arrangement or administration of affairs; but by metonomy, dispensation is applied to that period of time (not clearly demarked in the Scriptures) wherein God deals specifically with man, giving him a special stewardship to administer. (5) A steward oversees another's goods and dispenses them in accordance with the Master's desires. See: TDNT—5:151, 674; BAGD—559c; THAYER—440d.

3623. οἰκονόμος {10x} ŏikŏnŏmŏs, *oy-kon-om'-os;* from *3624* and the base of *3551;* a *house-distributor* (i.e. *manager*), or *overseer,* i.e. an employee in that capacity; by extens. a fiscal *agent* (*treasurer*); fig. a preacher (of the gospel):—chamberlain {1x}, governor {1x}, steward {8x}.

Oikonomos primarily denoted "the manager of a household or estate" (*oikos,* "a house," *nemo,* "to arrange"), (1) "a steward" (such were usually slaves or freedmen), Lk 12:42; 16:1, 3, 8; 1 Cor 4:2; Gal 4:2, "governors"; (2) in Rom 16:23, the "the chamberlain" of a city; (3) it is used metaphorically, in the wider sense, of a "steward" in general, (3a) of preachers of the gospel and teachers of the Word of God, 1 Cor 4:1; (3b) of elders or bishops in churches, Titus 1:7; (3c) of believers generally, 1 Pet 4:10. See: TDNT—5:149, 674; BAGD—560a; THAYER—440d.

3624. οἶκος {114x} ŏikŏs, *oy'-kos;* of uncert. aff.; a *dwelling* (more or less extens., lit. or fig.); by impl. a *family* (more or less related, lit. or fig.):—house {104x}, household

{3x}, home + *1519* {2x}, at home + *1722* {2x}, temple {3x}.

Oikos denotes (1) "a house, a dwelling," e.g., Mt 9:6, 7; 11:8; it is used of (1a) the tabernacle, as the house of God, Mt 12:4, and the temple similarly, e.g., Mt 21:13; Lk 11:51, "temple"; Jn 2:16, 17; (1b) called by the Lord "your house" in Mt 23:38 and Lk 13:35; (2) metaphorically of Israel as God's house, Heb 3:2, 5, where "His house" is not Moses', but God's; (3) of believers, similarly, Heb 3:6, where Christ is spoken of as "over God's House"; Heb 10:21; 1 Pet 2:5; 4:17; (4) of the body, Mt 12:44; Lk 11:24; (5) by metonymy, of the members of a household or family, e.g., Lk 10:5; Acts 7:10; 11:14; 1 Ti 3:4, 5, 12; 2 Ti 1:16; 4:19, "household"; Titus 1:11 (plural); (6) of a local church, 1 Ti 3:15; (7) of the descendants of Jacob (Israel) and David, e.g., Mt 10:6; Lk 1:27, 33; Acts 2:36; 7:42. See: TDNT—5:119, 674; BAGD—560b; THAYER—441a.

3625. οἰκουμένη {15x} ŏikŏumĕnē, *oy-kou-men'-ay;* fem. part. pres. pass. of *3611* (as noun, by impl. of *1093*); *land,* i.e. the (terrene part of the) *globe;* spec. the Rom. *empire:*—earth {1x}, world {14x}.

Oidouomene, (1) "the inhabited earth", is used (1a) of the whole inhabited world, Mt 24:14; Lk 4:5; 21:26; Rom 10:18; Heb 1:6; Rev 3:10; 16:14; (1b) by metonymy, of its inhabitants, Acts 17:31; Rev 12:9; (2) of the Roman Empire, (2a) the world as viewed by the writer or speaker, Lk 2:1; Acts 11:28; 24:5; (2b) by metonymy, of its inhabitants, Acts 17:6; 19:27; (3) the inhabited world in a coming age, Heb 2:5. See: TDNT—5:157, 674; BAGD—561b; THAYER—441d.

3626. οἰκουρός {1x} ŏikŏurŏs, *oy-koo-ros'* or

οἰκουργός ŏikŏurgŏs, *oy-koor-gos';* from *3624* and οὖρος ŏurŏs (a *guard;* be "ware"); a *stayer at home,* i.e. *domestically inclined* (a "good housekeeper"):—keeper at home {1x}.

This word means "working at home" (*oikos,* and a root of *ergon,* "work"), is used in Titus 2:5, "workers at home", in the injunction given to elder women regarding the training of the young women. See: BAGD—561c; THAYER—442a.

3627. οἰκτείρω {2x} ŏiktĕirō, *oyk-ti'-ro;* also (in certain tenses) prol.

οἰκτερέω ŏiktĕrĕō, *oyk-ter-eh'-o;* from οἶκτος ŏiktŏs, (*pity*); to *exercise pity:*—have compassion on {1x}, have compassion {1x}.

This verb means to have pity, a feeling of distress through the ills of others, Rom

9:15. See: TDNT—5:159,*; BAGD—561d; THAYER—442a.

3628. οἰκτιρμός {5x} **ŏiktirmŏs**, *oyk-tir-mos';* from and stronger than *3627; pity:*—mercy {5x}.

This word means "the viscera, the inward parts," as the seat of emotion, **(1)** the "heart," Phil 2:1; Col 3:12, "bowels of mercies". **(2)** In Heb 10:28 it is used with *choris*, "without," (lit., "without compassions"). **(3)** It is translated "mercies" in Rom 12:1 and 2 Cor 1:3. Syn.: *Eleeo* (*1653*) means to feel sympathy with the misery of another, esp. such sympathy as manifests itself in act, less freq. in word. *Oiktirmos* (*3628*) denotes the inward feeling of compassion which abides in the heart. A criminal begs 1653 of his judge; but hopeless suffering is often the object of 3628. See: TDNT—5:159, 680; BAGD—561d; THAYER—442b. See also: 1653, 1655, 1656, 2433, 2436, 3627, 3629, 4698.

3629. οἰκτίρμων {3x} **ŏiktirmōn**, *oyk-tir'-mone;* from *3627; compassionate:*—merciful {2x}, of tender mercy {1x}.

This word means "pitiful, compassionate for the ills of others" and is used **(1)** twice in Lk 6:36, "merciful" (of the character of God, to be expressed in His people); and **(2)** Jas 5:11, "of tender mercy." See: TDNT—5:159, 680; BAGD—561d; THAYER—442b. Syn.: 1653, 1655, 1656, 2433, 2436, 3627, 3628, 4698.

οἶμαι ŏimai. See *3633*.

3630. οἰνοπότης {2x} **ŏinŏpŏtēs**, *oy-nop-ot'-ace;* from *3631* and a der. of the alt. of *4095;* a *tippler:*—winebibber {2x}.

Oinopotes designates a wine drinker (Mt 11:19; Lk 7:34). See: BAGD—562a; THAYER—442b.

3631. οἶνος {33x} **ŏinŏs**, *oy'-nos;* a primary word (or perh. of Heb. origin [3196]); *"wine"* (lit. or fig.):—wine {32x}, winepress + 3125 {1x}.

Oinos is the general word for "wine." **(1)** The mention of the bursting of the wineskins, Mt 9:17; Mk 2:22; Lk 5:37, implies fermentation. See also Eph 5:18 (cf. Jn 2:10; 1 Ti 3:8; Titus 2:3). **(2)** In Mt 27:34 it is translated "vinegar" the result of complete fermentation. **(3)** The drinking of "wine" could be a stumbling block and the apostle enjoins abstinence in this respect, as in others, so as to avoid giving an occasion of stumbling to a brother, Rom 14:21. Contrast 1 Ti 5:23, which has an entirely different connection. **(4)** The word is used metaphorically **(4a)** of the evils ministered to the nations by religious Babylon, 14:8; 17:2; 18:3; **(4b)** of the contents of the cup of divine wrath upon the nations and Babylon, Rev 14:10; 16:19;

19:15. See: TDNT—5:162, 680; BAGD—562a; THAYER—442b.

3632. οἰνοφλυγία {1x} **ŏinŏphlugia**, *oy-nof-loog-ee'-ah;* from *3631* and a form of the base of *5397;* an *overflow* (or surplus) of *wine,* i.e. *vinolency* (*drunkenness*):—excess of wine {1x}.

(1) This word means an insatiate desire for wine and refers to debauchery, an extravagant indulgence on alcoholic beverages that may permanently damage the body. **(2)** In 1 Pet 4:3, *oinophlugia,* means "drunkenness, debauchery" [from *oinos,* "wine," *phluo,* "to bubble up, overflow"] and is rendered "excess of wine": "For the time past of our life may suffice us to have wrought the will of the Gentiles, when we walked in lasciviousness, lusts, excess of wine, revellings, banquetings, and abominable idolatries." Syn.: 2897, 2970, 3178, 4224. See: BAGD—562c; THAYER—442c.

3633. οἴομαι {3x} **ŏiŏmai**, *oy'-om-ahee;* or (shorter)

οἶμαι ŏimai, *oy'-mahee;* mid. voice appar. from *3634;* to *make like* (oneself), i.e. *imagine* (*be of* the *opinion*):—suppose {2x}, think {1x}.

Oiomai signifies "to expect, imagine, suppose"; it is rendered **(1)** "to suppose" in Jn 21:25; and **(2)** "think" in Jas 1:7; Phil 1:16, "thinking." Syn.: *Dokeo* (*1380*) refers to the subjective judgment, which may or may not conform to the fact. *Hegeomai* (*2233*) refers to the actual external appearance, generally correct, but possibly deceptive. *Hegeomai* (*2233*) and *nomizo* (*3543*) denote a belief resting not on one's inner feeling or sentiment, but on the due consideration of external grounds, and the weighing and comparing of facts. *Dokeo* (*1380*) and *oiomai* (*3633*), on the other hand, describe a subjective judgment growing out of inclination or a view of facts in their relation to us. *Hegeomai* denotes a more deliberate and careful judgment than *nomizo* (*3543*); *oiomai* (*3633*) having a subjective judgment which has feeling rather than thought (*dokeo* –1380) for its ground. See: BAGD—562c; THAYER—442c.

3634. οἶος {15x} **hŏiŏs**, *hoy'-os;* prob. akin to *3588, 3739,* and *3745; such* or *what sort* of (as a correl. or exclamation); espec. the neut. (adv.) with neg. not *so:*—such as {6x}, as {3x}, which {2x}, what manner {1x}, so as {1x}, what manner of man {1x}, what {1x}.

Hoios, a relative pronoun, signifying "what sort of or manner of" (1 Th 1:5; Lk 9:55). Syn.: 195, 1485, 2239, 3668, 3697, 3779, 4169, 4187,

4217, 4459, 5158, 5159, 5179, 5615. See: BAGD—561c; THAYER—442c.

οἴω ŏiō. See 5342.

3635. ὀκνέω {1x} ŏknĕō, ok-neh'-o; from ὄκνος ŏknŏs, (hesitation); to be slow (fig. loath):—delay {1x}.

Okneo, as a verb, means "to shrink, to be loath or slow to do a thing, to hesitate, delay": ". . . the disciples had heard that Peter was there, they sent unto him two men, desiring him that he would not delay to come to them" (Acts 9:38). Syn.: 311, 5549. See: BAGD—563a; THAYER—442d.

3636. ὀκνηρός {3x} ŏknērŏs, ok-nay-ros'; from 3635; tardy, i.e. indolent; (fig.) irksome:—grievous {1x}, slothful {2x}.

This word means "shrinking, timid" (from okneo, "to shrink, delay"), is used (1) negatively in Phil 3:1, "grievous", i.e., "I do not hesitate"; and (2) in Mt 25:26, and Rom 12:11, "slothful." See: TDNT—5:166, 681; BAGD—563a; THAYER—442d.

3637. ὀκταήμερος {1x} ŏktaēmĕrŏs, ok-tah-ay'-mer-os; from 3638 and 2250; an eight-day old person or act:—the eighth day {1x}.

Oktaemeros, an adjective, signifying an "eighth-day" person or thing, "eight days old" (okto, and hemera, "a day"), is used in Phil 3:5. This, and similar numerical adjectives not found in the NT, indicate duration rather than intervals. The apostle shows, by his being an "eighth-day" person as to circumcision, that his parents were neither Ishmaelites (circumcised in their thirteenth year) nor other Gentiles, converted to Judaism (circumcised on becoming Jews). See: BAGD—563a; THAYER—442d.

3638. ὀκτώ {9x} ŏktō, ok-to'; a primary numeral; "eight":—eight {6x}, eighteen + 1176 + 2532 {3x}. See: BAGD—563a; THAYER—443a.

3639. ὄλεθρος {4x} ŏlĕthrŏs, ol'-eth-ros; from a primary ὄλλυμι ŏllumi (to destroy; a prol. form); ruin, i.e. death, punishment:—destruction {4x}.

Olethros, "ruin, destruction," always translated "destruction," is used (1) in 1 Cor 5:5, of the effect upon the physical condition of an erring believer for the purpose of his spiritual profit; (2) in 1 Th 5:3 and 2 Th 1:9, of the effect of the divine judgments upon men at the ushering in of the Day of the Lord and the revelation of the Lord Jesus; (3) in 1 Ti 6:9, of the consequences of the indulgence of the flesh, referring to physical "ruin" and possibly that of the whole being, the following word apoleia stressing the final, eternal and irrevocable character of the ruin. See: TDNT—5:168, 681; BAGD—563b; THAYER—443a.

3640. ὀλιγόπιστος {5x} ŏligŏpistŏs, ol-ig-op'-is-tos; from 3641 and 4102; incredulous, i.e. lacking confidence (in Christ):—of little faith {5x}.

Literally, this word means little of faith and is used only by the Lord as a tender rebuke (1) for anxiety (Mt 6:30; Lk 12:28); or (2) for fear (Mt 8:26; 14:31; 16:8). See: TDNT—6:174, 849; BAGD—563b; THAYER—443a.

3641. ὀλίγος {43x} ŏligŏs, ol-ee'-gos; of uncert. aff.; puny (in extent, degree, number, duration or value); espec. neut. (adv.) somewhat:—few {14x}, (a) little {7x}, small {5x}, few things {4x}, almost + 1722 {2x}, a while {2x}, misc. {9x} = brief [-ly], + long, a season, short.

Oligon, as an adverb, is used of number quantity, and size, and denotes (1) "few, little, small, slight," e.g., Mt 7:14; 9:37; 15:34; 20:16; (2) neuter plural, "a few things," Mt 25:21, 23; Rev 2:14, 20; (3) in Eph 3:3, the phrase en oligo, in brief, is translated "in a few words"; also translated (4) "for a season": "Wherein ye greatly rejoice, though now for a season, if need be, ye are in heaviness through manifold temptations" (1 Pet 1:6). Syn.: 171, 2122, 2540, 4340, 5550, 5610. See: TDNT—5:171, 682; BAGD—563c; THAYER—443a.

3642. ὀλιγόψυχος {1x} ŏligŏpsuchŏs, ol-ig-op'-soo-khos; from 3641 and 5590; little-spirited, i.e. faint-hearted:—feebleminded {1x}.

Oligopsuchos, lit., "small-souled" (oligos, "small," psuche, "the soul"), denotes "despondent"; then, "fainthearted," 1 Th 5:14, "feebleminded." See: TDNT—9:665, 1342; BAGD—564a; THAYER—443b.

3643. ὀλιγωρέω {1x} ŏligōrĕō, ol-ig-o-reh'-o; from a compound of 3641 and ὥρα ōra ("care"); to have little regard, for, i.e. to disesteem:—despise {1x}. See: BAGD—564a; THAYER—443b.

3644. ὀλοθρευτής {1x} ŏlŏthrĕutēs, ol-oth-ryoo-tace'; from 3645; a ruiner, i.e. (spec.) a venomous serpent:—destroyer {1x}. See: TDNT—5:169, 681; BAGD—564b; THAYER—443c.

3645. ὀλοθρεύω {1x} ŏlŏthrĕuō, ol-oth-ryoo'-o; from 3639; to spoil, i.e. slay:—destroy {1x}. See: TDNT—5:167,*; BAGD—564b; THAYER—443c.

3646. ὁλοκαύτωμα {3x} **hŏlŏkautōma,** *hol-ok-ŏw'-to-mah;* from a der. of a compound of *3650* and a der. of *2545;* a *wholly-consumed* sacrifice ("holocaust"):— (whole) burnt offering {3x}.

This word denotes "a whole burnt offering" (*holos,* "whole," *kautos,* for *kaustos,* a verbal adjective from *kaio,* "to burn"), i.e., "a victim," the whole of which is burned (cf. Ex 30:20; Lev 5:12; 23:8, 25, 27). It is used in Mk 12:33, by the scribe who questioned the Lord as to the first commandment in the Law and in Heb 10:6, 8. See: BAGD—564b; THAYER—443c.

3647. ὁλοκληρία {1x} **hŏlŏklēria,** *hol-ok-lay-ree'-ah;* from *3648; integrity,* i.e. phys. *wholeness:*—perfect soundness {1x}.

This word speaks of an unimpaired condition of the body, in which all its members are healthy and fit for use; good health, Acts 3:16. See: TDNT—3:767, 442; BAGD—564c; THAYER—443c.

3648. ὁλόκληρος {2x} **hŏlŏklērŏs,** *hol'-ok'-lay-ros;* from *3650* and *2819; complete* in every *part,* i.e. perfectly *sound* (in body):—entire {1x}, whole {1x}.

This word refers to that which retains all that was initially allotted to it and implies completion and wholeness in all its parts and is used ethically in 1 Th 5:23, indicating that every grace present in Christ should be manifested in the believer; so Jas 1:4. Syn.: 739, 5046. See: TDNT—3:766, 442; BAGD—564c; THAYER—443d.

3649. ὀλολύζω {1x} **ŏlŏluzō,** *ol-ol-ood'-zo;* a redupl. primary verb; to *"howl"* or *"halloo",* i.e. *shriek:*—howl {1x}.

Ololuzo is an onomatopoeic verb (expressing its significance in its sound) meaning to cry aloud [Eng., howl] and was primarily used of crying aloud to the gods, with Jas 5:1 being an exhortation to the godless rich. See: TDNT—5:173, 682; BAGD—564c; THAYER—443d.

3650. ὅλος {112x} **hŏlŏs,** *hol'-os;* a primary word; *"whole"* or *"all",* i.e. *complete* (in extent, amount, time or degree), espec. (neut.) as noun or adv.:—all {65x}, whole {43x}, every whit {2x}, altogether {1x}, throughout + 1223 {1x}. See: TDNT—5:174, 682; BAGD—564c; THAYER—443d.

3651. ὁλοτελής {1x} **hŏlŏtĕlēs,** *hol-ot-el-ace';* from *3650* and *5056; complete* to the *end,* i.e. *absolutely perfect:*—wholly {1x}.

Holoteles, "wholly," 1 Th 5:23, is lit., "whole-complete", i.e., "through and through"; the apostle's desire is that the sanctification of the believer may extend to every part of his being. See: TDNT—5:175, 682; BAGD—565a.; THAYER—444b.

3652. Ὀλυμπᾶς {1x} **Olumpas,** *ol-oom-pas';* prob. a contr. from Ὀλυμπιόδωρος **Olumpiŏdōrŏs,** (*Olympian-bestowed,* i.e. *heaven-descended*); *Olympas,* a Chr.:— Olympas {1x}. See: BAGD—565a; THAYER—444b.

3653. ὄλυνθος {1x} **ŏlunthŏs,** *ol'-oon-thos;* of uncert. der.; an *unripe* (because out of season) *fig:*—untimely fig {1x}. See: TDNT—7:751, 1100; BAGD—565a; THAYER—444b.

3654. ὅλως {4x} **hŏlōs,** *hol'-oce;* adv. from *3650; completely,* i.e. *altogether;* (by anal.) *everywhere;* (neg.) not *by any means:*—at all {2x}, commonly {1x}, utterly {1x}.

Holos, "all, whole," is translated **(1)** "commonly" in 1 Cor 5:1; **(2)** in 1 Cor 6:7 it is translated "utterly"; **(3)** in 1 Cor 15:29, "at all" as in Mt 5:34. See: BAGD—565b; THAYER—444b.

3655. ὄμβρος {1x} **ŏmbrŏs,** *om'-bros;* of uncert. aff.; a thunder *storm:*—shower {1x}.

Ombros denotes a heavy shower, a storm of rain (Lk 12:54). See: BAGD—565b; THAYER—444b.

3656. ὁμιλέω {4x} **hŏmilĕō,** *hom-il-eh'-o;* from *3658;* to *be in company* with, i.e. (by impl.) to *converse:*—commune {1x}, commune with {1x}, talk {2x}. Cf. Lk 24:14, 15; Acts 20:11; 24:26. See: BAGD—565c; THAYER—444c.

3657. ὁμιλία {1x} **hŏmilia,** *hom-il-ee'-ah;* from *3658; companionship* ("homily"), i.e. (by impl.) *intercourse:*—communication {1x}.

Homilia, "an association of people, those who are of the same company" (*homos,* "same"), is used in 1 Cor 15:33, "(evil) communications." See: BAGD—565c; THAYER—444d.

3658. ὅμιλος {1x} **hŏmilŏs,** *hom'-il-os;* from the base of *3674* and a der. of the alt. of *138* (mean. a *crowd*); *association together,* i.e. a *multitude:*—company {1x}. See: BAGD—565d; THAYER—444d.

3659. ὄμμα {1x} **ŏmma,** *om'-mah;* from *3700;* a *sight,* i.e. (by impl.) the *eye:*—eye {1x}. See: BAGD—565d; THAYER—444d.

3660. ὀμνύω {27x} **ŏmnuō,** *om-noo'-o;* a prol. form of a primary but obsolete ὄμω **ŏmō,** for which another prol. form ὀμόω **ŏmŏō** *om-ŏ'-o* is used in certain tenses; to *swear,* i.e. *take* (or *declare on*) *oath:*—swear {27x}.

Omnuo is used of "affirming or denying by an oath," **(1)** e.g., Mt 26:74; Mk 6:23; Lk 1:73; Heb 3:11, 18; 4:3; 7:21; accompanied by that by which one swears, **(2)** e.g., Mt 5:34, 36; 23:16; Heb 6:13, 16; Jas 5:12; Rev 10:6. See: TDNT—5:176, 683; BAGD—565d; THAYER—444d.

3661. **ὀμοθυμαδόν** {12x} **hŏmŏthumadŏn**, *hom-oth-oo-mad-on';* adv. from a compound of the base of *3674* and *2372; unanimously:*—with one accord {11x}, with one mind {1x}.

Homothumadon, "of one accord" (from *homos,* "same," *thumos,* "mind"), **(1)** occurs eleven times, **(1)** ten in the Acts, 1:14; 2:46; 4:24; 5:12; 7:57; 8:6; 12:20; 15:25; 18:12, 19:29, and the other **(2)** in Rom 15:6, "with one mind." See: TDNT—5:185, 684; BAGD—566c; THAYER—445a.

3662. **ὀμοιάζω** {1x} **hŏmŏiazō**, *hom-oy-ad'-zo;* from *3664;* to *resemble:*—agree thereto {1x}. See: BAGD—566c; THAYER—445a.

3663. **ὀμοιοπαθής** {2x} **hŏmŏiŏpathēs**, *hom-oy-op-ath-ace';* from *3664* and the alt. of *3958; similarly affected:*—of like passions {1x}, subject to like passions {1x}.

Homoiopathes, "of like feelings or affections", is rendered **(1)** "of like passions" in Acts 14:15; and **(2)** in Jas 5:17, "subject to like passions." See: TDNT—5:938, 798; BAGD—566c; THAYER—445a.

3664. **ὄμοιος** {47x} **hŏmŏiŏs**, *hom'-oy-os;* from the base of *3674; similar* (in appearance or character):—like {47x}.

Homios, "like, resembling, such as, the same as," is used **(1)** of appearance or form Jn 9:9; Rev 1:13, 15; 2:18; 4:3 (twice), 6, 7; 9:7 (twice), 10, 19; 11:1; 13:2, 11; 14:14; **(2)** of ability, condition, nature, Mt 22:39; Acts 17:29; Gal 5:21, "such like," lit., "and the (things) similar to these"; 1 Jn 3:2; Rev 13:4; 18:18; 21:11, 18; **(3)** of comparison in parables, Mt 13:31, 33, 44, 45, 47; 20:1; Lk 13:18, 19, 21; **(4)** of action, thought, etc. Mt 11:16; 13:52; Lk 6:47, 48, 49; 7:31, 32; 12:36; Jn 8:55; Jude 7. See: TDNT—5:186, 684; BAGD—566; THAYER—445b.

3665. **ὀμοιότης** {2x} **hŏmŏiŏtēs**, *hom-oy-ot'-ace;* from *3664; resemblance:*—like as + 2596 {1x}, similitude {1x}. Cf. Heb 4:15; 7:15. See: TDNT—5:189, 684; BAGD—567a; THAYER—445b.

3666. **ὀμοιόω** {15x} **hŏmŏiŏō**, *hom-oy-ŏ'-o;* from *3664;* to *assimilate,* i.e. *compare;* pass. to *become similar:*—liken {9x}, make like {2x}, be like {2x}, in the likeness of {1x}, resemble {1x}.

Homioo, "to make like", is used **(1)** especially in the parables, **(1a)** with the significance of comparing, "likening," or, in the passive voice, "being likened," Mt 7:24, 26; 11:16; 13:24; 18:23; 22:2; 25:1; Mk 4:30; Lk 7:31; 13:18, "resemble"; v. 20; **(1b)** in several of these instances the point of resemblance is not a specific detail, but the whole circumstances of the parable; **(2)** of making "like," or, in the passive voice, of being made or becoming "like," Mt 6:8; Acts 14:11, "in the likeness of (men)," lit., "being made like" (aorist participle, passive); Rom 9:29; Heb 2:17, of Christ in being "made like" unto His brethren, i.e., in partaking of human nature, apart from sin (cf. v. 14). See: TDNT—5:188, 684; BAGD—567b; THAYER—445c.

3667. **ὀμοίωμα** {6x} **hŏmŏiōma**, *hom-oy'-o-mah;* from *3666;* a *form;* abstr. *resemblance:*—made like to {1x}, likeness {3x}, shape {1x}, similitude {1x}.

(1) The main stress of this word is on the outward similarities with nothing being considered about the inward realities. **(2)** This resemblance is an accidental one like two eggs and not a derived resemblance like a statue resembles its model (see *eikon* – 1504). The key word is similar, like in appearance without considering the essence. **(3)** This word denotes "that which is made like something, a resemblance," **(3a)** in the concrete sense, Rev 9:7, "shapes"; **(3b)** in the abstract sense, Rom 1:23, "(into an image) made like to"; **(3b1)** the association here of the two words *homoioma* and *eikon* serves to enhance the contrast between the idol and "the glory of the incorruptible God," and **(3b2)** is expressive of contempt; **(3c)** in Rom 5:14, "(the) similitude of Adam's transgression"; **(3d)** in Rom 6:5, "(the) likeness (of His death); **(3e)** in Rom 8:3, "(the) likeness (of sinful flesh); **(3f)** in Phil 2:7, "the likeness of men." **(3g)** The expression "likeness of men" does not of itself imply, still less does it exclude or diminish, the reality of the nature which Christ assumed. That . . . is declared in the words "form of a servant." Paul justly says *in the likeness of men,* because, in fact, Christ, although certainly perfect Man (Rom 5:15; 1 Cor 15:21; 1 Ti 2:5), was, by reason of the Divine nature present in Him, not simply and merely man . . . but the Incarnate Son of God. Syn.: 1504, 3669. See: TDNT—5:191, 684; BAGD—567c; THAYER—445c.

3668. **ὀμοίως** {30x} **hŏmŏiŏs**, *hom-oy'-oce;* adv. from *3664; similarly:*—likewise {28x}, moreover + 1161 {1x}, so {1x}.

Homoios, signifies "likewise, in like manner, equally" in Mt 26:35; 27:41; Mk 4:16; Lk 5:33; 6:31; 10:32; 10:37; 17:28, 31; 22:36; Jn 5:19; 6:11; 21:13; Rom 1:27; Jas 2:25; 1 Pet 5:5.

Syn.: 195, 1485, 2239, 3634, 3697, 3779, 4169, 4187, 4217, 4459, 5158, 5159, 5179, 5615. See: BAGD—568d; THAYER—445c. Mt 26:35; Lk 5:33; 6:31; 10:37; 17:28, 31; 22:36; Jn 6:11; 21:13; Rom 1:27; 1 Pet 5:5.

3669. ὁμοίωσις {1x} **hŏmŏiōsis,** *hom-oy'-o-sis;* from *3666; assimilation,* i.e. *resemblance:*—similitude {1x}. Syn.: 3667, 1504. See: TDNT—5:190, 684; BAGD—568a; THAYER—445d.

3670. ὁμολογέω {24x} **hŏmŏlŏgĕō,** *hom-ol-og-eh'-o;* from a compound of the base of *3674* and *3056; to assent,* i.e. *covenant, acknowledge:*—confess {17x}, profess {3x}, promise {1x}, give thanks {1x}, confession is made {1x}, acknowledgeth {1x}.

Homologeo, lit., "to speak the same thing" (*homos,* "same," *lego,* "to speak"), "to assent, accord, agree with," denotes, **(1)** "to confess, declare, admit," Jn 1:20; e.g., Acts 24:14; Heb 11:13; **(2)** "to confess by way of admitting oneself guilty of what one is accused of, the result of inward conviction," 1 Jn 1:9; **(3)** "to declare openly by way of speaking out freely, such confession being the effect of deep conviction of facts," Mt 7:23; 10:32 (twice) and Lk 12:8; Jn 9:22; 12:42; Acts 23:8; Rom 10:9–10 ("confession is made"); 1 Ti 6:12; Titus 1:16; 1 Jn 2:23; 4:2, 15; 2 Jn 7; **(4)** "to confess by way of celebrating with praise," Heb 13:15; **(5)** "to promise," Mt 14:7.

(6) In Mt 10:32 and Lk 12:8 the construction of this verb with *en,* "in," followed by the dative case of the personal pronoun, has a special significance, namely, to "confess" in a person's name, the nature of the "confession" being determined by the context, the suggestion being to make a public "confession." Thus the statement, "every one . . . who shall confess Me (lit. "in Me," i.e., in My case) before men, him (lit., "in him," i.e., in his case) will I also confess before My Father," conveys the thought of "confessing" allegiance to Christ as one's Master and Lord, and, on the other hand, of acknowledgment, on His part, of the faithful one as being His worshiper and servant, His loyal follower; this is appropriate to the original idea in *homologeo* of being identified in thought or language. See: TDNT—5:199, 687; BAGD—568a; THAYER—446a.

3671. ὁμολογία {6x} **hŏmŏlŏgia,** *hom-ol-og-ee'-ah;* from the same as *3670; acknowledgment:*—confession {1x}, profession {4x}, professed {1x}.

Homologia denotes "confession, by acknowledgment of the truth," 2 Cor 9:13; 1 Ti 6:12–13; Heb 3:1; 4:14; 10:23; 1 Ti 6:13). See: TDNT—5:199, 687; BAGD—568d; THAYER—446b.

3672. ὁμολογουμένως {1x} **hŏmŏlŏgŏumĕnōs,** *hom-ol-og-ŏw-men'-oce;* adv. of pres. pass. part. of *3670; confessedly:*—without controversy {1x}. See: TDNT—5:199, 687; BAGD—569a; THAYER—446c.

3673. ὁμότεχνος {1x} **hŏmŏtĕchnŏs,** *hom-ot'-ekh-nos;* from the base of *3674* and *5078;* a *fellow-artificer:*—of the same craft {1x}. See: BAGD—569b; THAYER—446c.

3674. ὁμοῦ {3x} **hŏmŏu,** *hom-oo';* gen. of ὁμός **hŏmŏs,** (the *same;* akin to *260*) as adv.; *at* the *same* place or time:—together {3x}.

Homou, used in connection with place, and is used **(1)** with the idea of together at the same place: "So they ran both together: and the other disciple did outrun Peter, and came first to the sepulchre" (Jn 20:4); **(2)** without reference to place, Jn 4:36; 21:2. Syn.: *Hama (260)* stresses the temporal, being together at the same time. See: BAGD—569b; THAYER—446c.

3675. ὁμόφρων {1x} **hŏmŏphrōn,** *hom-of'-rone;* from the base of *3674* and *5424; like-minded,* i.e. *harmonious:*—of one mind {1x}. See: BAGD—569c; THAYER—446c.

ὁμόω **ŏmŏō.** See *3660.*

3676. ὅμως {3x} **hŏmōs,** *hom'-oce;* adv. from the base of *3674; at* the *same* time, i.e. (conjunc.) *notwithstanding, yet still:*—and even {1x}, nevertheless {1x}, though it be but {1x}.

Homos, "yet, nevertheless," is translated **(1)** "and even" in 1 Cor 14:7; **(2)** elsewhere **(2a)** Jn 12:42, "nevertheless"; **(2b)** Gal 3:15, "though it be but." See: BAGD—569c; THAYER—446c.

3677. ὄναρ {6x} **ŏnar,** *on'-ar;* of uncert. der.; a *dream:*—dream {6x}.

An onar is a vision in sleep in distinction from a waking vision (Mt 1:20; 2:12–13, 19, 22; 27:19). See: TDNT—5:220, 690; BAGD—569d; THAYER—446d.

3678. ὀνάριον {1x} **ŏnariŏn,** *on-ar'-ee-on;* neut. of a presumed der. of *3688;* a *little ass:*—young ass {1x}. See: TDNT—5:283, 700; BAGD—570a; THAYER—446d.

ὀνάω **ŏnaō.** See *3685.*

3679. ὀνειδίζω {10x} **ŏnĕidizō,** *on-i-did'-zo;* from *3681; to defame,* i.e. *rail at, chide, taunt:*—upbraid {3x}, reproach {3x}, revile {2x}, cast in (one's) teeth {1x}, suffer reproach {1x}.

Oneidizo signifies **(1)** in the active voice, "to reproach, upbraid," Mt 5:11, "shall revile"; 11:20, "to upbraid"; 27:44, "cast . . . in (His)

teeth"; Mk 15:32, "reviled"; 16:14 "upbraided"; Lk 6:22 "shall reproach", Rom 15:3; Jas 1:5, "upbraideth"; **(2)** in the passive voice, "to suffer reproach, be reproached," 1 Ti 4:10; 1 Pet 4:14. See: TDNT—5:239, 693; BAGD—570a; THAYER—446d.

3680. ὀνειδισμός {5x} ŏnĕidismŏs, *on-i-dis-mos'; from 3679; contumely:*—reproach {5x}.

This word means "a reproach, defamation" and is used in Rom 15:3; 1 Ti 3:7; Heb 10:33; 11:26; 13:13. See: TDNT—5:241, 693; BAGD—570b; THAYER—446d.

3681. ὄνειδος {1x} ŏnĕidŏs, *on'-i-dos;* prob. akin to the base of 3686; *notoriety,* i.e. a *taunt (disgrace):*—a reproach {1x}. See: TDNT—5:238, 693; BAGD—570b; THAYER—447a.

3682. Ὀνήσιμος {4x} Ŏnēsimŏs, *on-ay'-sim-os;* from 3685; *profitable; Onesimus,* a Chr.:—Onesimus {4x}. See: BAGD—570c; THAYER—447a.

3683. Ὀνησίφορος {2x} Ŏnēsiphŏrŏs, *on-ay-sif'-or-os;* from a der. of 3685 and 5411; *profit-bearer; Onesiphorus,* a Chr.:—Onesiphorus {2x}. See: BAGD—570c; THAYER—447a.

3684. ὀνικός {2x} ŏnikŏs, *on-ik-os';* from 3688; *belonging to* an *ass,* i.e. *large* (so as to be turned by an ass):—millstone + 3458 {2x}. See: BAGD—570c; THAYER—447a.

3685. ὀνίνημι {1x} ŏninēmi, *on-in'-ay-mee;* a prol. form of an appar. primary verb

ὄνομαι ŏnŏmai, to *slur);* for which another prol. form (ὀνάω ŏnaō) is used as an alt. in some tenses [unless indeed it be ident. with the base of 3686 through the idea of *notoriety*]; to *gratify,* i.e. (mid. voice) to *derive pleasure* or *advantage* from:—have joy {1x}.

Oninemi, "to benefit, profit," in the middle voice, "to have profit, derive benefit," is translated "let me have joy" in Philem 20; the apostle is doubtless continuing his credit and debit metaphors and using the verb in the sense of "profit." See: BAGD—570d; THAYER—447a.

3686. ὄνομα {230x} ŏnŏma, *on'-om-ah;* from a presumed der. of the base of 1097 (comp. 3685); a *"name"* (lit. or fig.) [*authority, character*]:—name {194x}, named {28x}, called {4x}, surname + 2007 {2x}, named + 2564 {1x}, not tr {1x}.

Onoma, as a noun, is used **I.** in general of the "name" by which a person or thing is called, e.g., **(1)** Mk 3:16, 17, "(He) surnamed,"

lit., "(He added) the name"; **(2)** Mk 14:32, lit., "(of which) the name (was)"; Lk 1:63; Jn 18:10; **(2a)** sometimes translated "named," e.g., **(2a1)** Lk 8:5, "named (Zacharias)," lit., "by name"; **(2a2)** in the same verse, "named (Elizabeth)," lit., "the name of her," an elliptical phrase, with "was" understood; **(3)** Acts 8:9, "called," 10:1; **(4)** the "name" is put for the reality in Rev 3:1; **(5)** in Phil 2:9, the "Name" represents "the title and dignity" of the Lord, as in Eph 1:21 and Heb 1:4; **II.** for all that a "name" implies, of authority, character, rank, majesty, power, excellence, etc., of everything that the "name" covers: **(1)** of the "Name" of God as expressing His attributes, etc., e.g., Mt 6:9; Lk 1:49; Jn 12:28; 17:6, 26; Rom 15:9; 1 Ti 6:1; Heb 13:15; Rev 13:6; **(2)** of the "Name" of Christ, e.g., Mt 10:22; 19:29; Jn 1:12; 2:23; 3:18; Acts 26:9; Rom 1:5; Jas 2:7; 1 Jn 3:23; 3 Jn 7; Rev 2:13; 3:8;

(3) also the phrases rendered "in the name"; these may be analyzed as follows: **(3a)** representing the authority of Christ, e.g., Mt 18:5 (with *epi,* "on the ground of My authority"); **(3a1)** so Mt 24:5 (falsely) and parallel passages; **(3a2)** as substantiated by the Father, Jn 14:26; 16:23; **(3b)** in the power of (with *en,* "in"), e.g., Mk 16:17; Lk 10:17; Acts 3:6; 4:10; 16:18; Jas 5:14; **(3c)** in acknowledgement or confession of, e.g., Acts 4:12; 8:16; 9:27, 28; **(3d)** in recognition of the authority of (sometimes combined with the thought of relying or resting on), Mt 18:20; cf. 28:19; Acts 8:16; 9:2 (*eis,* "into"); Jn 14:13; 15:16; Eph 5:20; Col 3:17; **(3e)** owing to the fact that one is called by Christ's "Name" or is identified with Him, e.g. **(3e1)** 1 Pet 4:14 (with *en,* "in"); **(3e2)** with *heneken,* "for the sake of," e.g., Mt 19:29; **(3e3)** with *dia,* "on account of," Mt 10:22; 24:9; Mk 13:13; Lk 21:17; Jn 15:21; 1 Jn 2:12; Rev 2:3; **III.** as standing, by metonymy, for "persons," Acts 1:15; Rev 3:4; 11:13. Syn.: 3687. See: TDNT—5:242, 694; BAGD—570d; THAYER—447a.

3687. ὀνομάζω {10x} ŏnŏmazō, *on-om-ad'-zo;* from 3686; to *name,* i.e. *assign an appellation;* by extens. to *utter, mention, profess:*—call {2x}, name {8x}.

Onomazo denotes **(1)** "to name," "mention," or "address by name," **(1a)** Acts 19:13, "to call"; **(1b)** in the passive voice, Rom 15:20; Eph 1:21; 5:3; to make mention of the "Name" of the Lord in praise and worship, 2 Ti 2:19; **(2)** "to name, call, give a name to," **(2a)** Lk 6:13, 14; **(2b)** passive voice, 1 Cor 5:11, "is called"; **(2c)** Eph 3:15; 1 Cor 5:1, "is named." See: TDNT—5:282, 694; BAGD—573d; THAYER—448d.

3688. ὄνος {6x} ŏnŏs, *on'-os;* appar. a primary word; a *donkey:*—an ass

{6x}. See: TDNT—5:283, 700; BAGD—574a; THAYER—448d.

3689. ὄντως {10x} **ŏntōs**, *on'-toce;* adv. of the oblique cases of *5607; really:—* certainly {1x}, clean {1x}, indeed {6x}, of a truth {1x}, verily {1x}. See: BAGD—574a; THAYER—448d.

3690. ὄξος {7x} **ŏxŏs**, *ox-os;* from *3691; vinegar,* i.e. *sour* wine:—vinegar {7x}.

Oxos denotes "sour wine," the ordinary drink of laborers and common soldiers; it is used in the four Gospels of the "vinegar" offered to the Lord at His crucifixion, Mt 27:34, 48; Mk 15:36; Lk 23:36; Jn 19:29, 30. This, which the soldiers offered before crucifying, was refused by Him, as it was designed to alleviate His sufferings. See: TDNT—5:288, 701; BAGD—574b; THAYER—449a.

3691. ὀξύς {8x} **ŏxus**, *ox-oos';* prob. akin to the base of *188* ["*acid*"]; *keen;* by anal. *rapid:*—sharp {7x}, swift {1x}.

Oxus denotes **(1)** "sharp", said **(1a)** of a sword, Rev 1:16; 2:12; 19:15; **(1b)** of a sickle, Rev 14:14, 17, 18 (twice); and **(2)** of motion, "swift," Rom 3:15. See: BAGD—574a; THAYER—449a.

3692. ὀπή {2x} **ŏpē**, *op-ay';* prob. from *3700;* a *hole* (as if for light), i.e. *cavern;* by anal. a *spring* (of water):—cave {1x}, place {1x}.

Ope denotes "a hole, an opening," **(1)** such as a fissure in a rock, Heb 11:38, a "cave"; and in **(2)** Jas 3:11, the "place" of the orifice of a fountain. See: BAGD—574d; THAYER—449a.

3693. ὄπισθεν {7x} **ŏpisthĕn**, *op'-is-then;* from ὄπις **ŏpis**, (*regard;* from *3700*) with enclitic of source; *from the rear* (as a secure *aspect*), i.e. *at* the *back* (adv. and prep. of place or time):—after {2x}, backside {1x}, behind {4x}.

Opisthen, "behind," is used only of place, e.g., **(1)** "behind" in Mt 9:20; Mk 5:27; Lk 8:44; Rev 4:6; **(2)** as a preposition, **(2a)** Mt 15:23; Lk 23:26, "after"; **(2b)** in Rev 5:1, "backside." See: TDNT—5:289, 702; BAGD—574d; THAYER—449b.

3694. ὀπίσω {36x} **ŏpisō**, *op-is'-o;* from the same as *3693* with enclitic of direction; *to the back,* i.e. *aback* (as adv. or prep. of time or place; or as noun):—after {22x}, behind {6x}, back + 1519 + 3588 {5x}, back {1x}, follow {1x}, backward + 1519 + 3588 {1x}.

Opiso, connected with *hepomai,* "to follow," is used adverbially, of place, with the meaning "back," "backward," in the phrase *eis ta opiso,* lit., "unto the things behind," in Mk 13:16; Lk 9:62; 17:31; Jn 6:66; 18:6; 20:14. Cf. Phil 3:13,

"the things which are behind." See: TDNT—5:289, 702; BAGD—575a; THAYER—449b.

3695. ὁπλίζω {1x} **hŏplizō**, *hop-lid'-zo;* from *3696;* to *equip* (with weapons [mid. voice and fig.]):—arm (one's) self with {1x}.

Hopilizo, "to arm oneself," is used in 1 Pet 4:1, in an exhortation "to arm" ourselves with the same mind as that of Christ in regard to His sufferings. See: TDNT—5:294, 702; BAGD—575c; THAYER—449c.

3696. ὅπλον {6x} **hŏplŏn**, *hop'-lon;* prob. from a primary ἕπω **hĕpō** (to be *busy* about); an *implement,* or *utensil* or *tool* (lit. or fig., espec. offensive for war):—armour {2x}, instrument {2x}, weapon {2x}.

Hoplon, originally any tool or implement for preparing a thing, became used in the plural for "weapons of warfare." **(1)** Once in the NT it is used of actual weapons, Jn 18:3; elsewhere, **(2)** metaphorically, of **(2a)** the members of the body as instruments of unrighteousness and as instruments of righteousness, Rom 6:13; **(2b)** the "armor" of light, Rom 13:12; **(2c)** the "armor" of righteousness, 2 Cor 6:7; **(2d)** the weapons of the Christian's warfare, 2 Cor 10:4. See: TDNT—5:292, 702; BAGD—575c; THAYER—449d.

3697. ὁποῖος {5x} **hŏpŏiŏs**, *hop-oy'-os;* from *3739* and *4169;* of *what* kind that, i.e. *how* (*as*) *great* (*excellent*) (spec. as an indef. correl. to the antecedent def. *5108* of quality):—what manner of {1x}, such as {1x}, of what sort {1x}, whatsoever + 4118 {1x}, what manner of man {1x}.

Hopoios is rendered **(1)** "what manner of" in 1 Th 1:9; **(2)** "of what sort" in 1 Cor 3:13; **(3)** "such as" in Acts 26:29; **(4)** "whatsoever" in Gal 2:6; and **(5)** "what manner of man" in Jas 1:24. Syn.: 195, 1485, 2239, 3634, 3668, 3779, 4169, 4187, 4217, 4459, 5158, 5159, 5179, 5615. See: BAGD—575d; THAYER—449d.

3698. ὁπότε {1x} **hŏpŏtĕ**, *hop-ot'-eh;* from *3739* and *4218; what* (-ever) *then,* i.e. (of time) *as soon as:*—when {1x}. See: BAGD—576a; THAYER—449d.

3699. ὅπου {82x} **hŏpŏu**, *hop'-oo;* from *3739* and *4225; what* (-ever) *where,* i.e. *at whichever* spot:—where {58x}, whither {9x}, wheresoever + 302 {3x}, whithersoever + 302 {4x}, wheresoever + 1437 {2x}, whereas {2x}, not tr {1x}, in what place {3x}. See: BAGD—576a; THAYER—449d.

3700. ὀπτάνομαι {58x} **ŏptanŏmai**, *op-tan'-om-ahee;* a (mid. voice) prol. form of the primary (mid. voice)

    ὄπτομαι ŏptŏmai, *op'-tom-ahee;* which is used for it in certain tenses;

and both as alternate of *3708;* to *gaze* (i.e. with wide-open eyes, as at something remarkable; and thus differing from *991,* which denotes simply *voluntary* observation; and from *1492,* which expresses merely mechanical, passive or casual vision; while *2300,* and still more emphatically its intensive *2334,* signifies an earnest but more continued *inspection;* and *4648* a watching *from a distance*):—see {37x}, appear {17x}, look {2x}, show (one's) self {1x}, being seen {1x}.

Optomai, "to see" (from *ops,* "the eye"; cf. Eng. "optical," etc.), in the passive sense, "to be seen, to appear," is used **(1)** objectively, with reference to the person or thing seen, e.g., 1 Cor 15:5–8, "was seen"; **(2)** subjectively, with reference **(2a)** to an inward impression or a spiritual experience, Jn 3:36, or **(2b)** a mental occupation, Acts 18:15, "look to it"; **(3)** cf. Mt 27:4, 24, "see (thou) to it," "see (ye) to it," throwing responsibility on others. **(4)** *Optomai* is to be found in dictionaries under the word *horao,* "to see"; it supplies some forms that are lacking in that verb. See: TDNT—5:315, 706; BAGD—576c; THAYER—450b.

3701. ὀπτασία {4x} **ŏptasia,** *op-tas-ee'-ah;* from a presumed der. of *3700; visuality,* i.e. (concr.) an *apparition:*—vision {4x}.

Optasia, from *optano,* "to see, a coming into view," denotes a "vision" in Lk 1:22; 24:23; Acts 26:19; 2 Cor 12:1. See: TDNT—5:372, 706; BAGD—576c; THAYER—450b.

ὄπτομαι ŏptŏmai. See *3700.*

3702. ὀπτός {1x} **ŏptŏs,** *op-tos';* from an obs. verb akin to ἕπσω **hĕpsō** (to "*steep*"); *cooked,* i.e. *roasted:*—broiled {1x}.

Optos, (from *optao,* "to cook, roast"), is said of food prepared by fire, Lk 24:42. See: BAGD—576c; THAYER—450b.

3703. ὀπώρα {1x} **ŏpōra,** *op-o'-rah;* appar. from the base of *3796* and *5610;* prop. *even-tide* of the (summer) season (*dog-days*), i.e. (by impl.) *ripe fruit:*—fruit {1x}.

Opora as a noun, primarily denotes "late summer or early autumn," i.e., late July, all August and early September. Since that is the time of "fruit-bearing," the word was used, by metonymy, for the "fruits" themselves: "And the fruits that thy soul lusted after are departed from thee, and all things which were dainty and goodly are departed from thee, and thou shalt find them no more at all" (Rev 18:14). Syn.: 175, 2590, 2592, 2593, 5352. See: BAGD—576c; THAYER—450b.

3704. ὅπως {56x} **hŏpōs,** *hop'-oce;* from *3739* and *4459; what* (-ever) *how,* i.e.

in the *manner that* (as adv. or conjunc. of coincidence, intentional or actual):—that {45x}, how {4x}, to {4x}, so that {1x}, when {1x}, because {1x}. See: BAGD—576d; THAYER—450c.

3705. ὅραμα {12x} **hŏrama,** *hor'-am-ah;* from *3708; something gazed at,* i.e. a *spectacle* (espec. supernatural):—sight {1x}, vision {11x}.

Horama, as a noun, signifies "that which is seen" and denotes **(1)** "a spectacle, sight," Mt 17:9; Acts 7:31 ("sight"); **(2)** "an appearance, vision," Acts 9:10, 12; 10:3, 17, 19; 11:5; 12:9; 16:9, 10; 18:9. Syn.: *Horama* (*3705*) the noun, signifies that which is seen, *horasis* (*3706*) the act of seeing. See: TDNT—5:371, 706; BAGD—577b; THAYER—451a.

3706. ὅρασις {4x} **hŏrasis,** *hor'-as-is;* from *3708;* the act of *gazing,* i.e. (external) an *aspect* or (intern.) an inspired *appearance:*—in sight {1x}, look upon {1x}, vision {2x}.

Horasis, as a noun, denotes **(1)** a vision: "And thus I saw the horses in the vision, and them that sat on them" (Rev 9:17; cf. Acts 2:17); and **(2)** to look upon [in appearance], in sight: "And He that sat was to look upon (*horasis*) like a jasper and a sardine stone: and there was a rainbow round about the throne, in sight (*horasis*) like unto an emerald" (Rev 4:3). Syn.: *Horama* (*3705*) the noun, signifies that which is seen, *horasis,* the verb, (*3706*) the act of seeing. See also: 308, 352, 578, 816, 872, 991, 1689, 1896, 1914, 1980, 1983, 2300, 2334, 3708, 3879, 4017, 4648. See: TDNT—5:370, 706; BAGD—577c; THAYER—451a.

3707. ὁρατός {1x} **hŏratŏs,** *hor-at-os';* from *3708; gazed at,* i.e. (by impl.) *capable of being seen:*—visible {1x}. See: TDNT—5:368, 706; BAGD—577c.

3708. ὁράω {59x} **hŏraō,** *hor-ah'-o;* prop. to *stare* at [comp. *3700*], i.e. (by impl.) to *discern* clearly (phys. or ment.); by extens. to *attend* to; by Heb. to *experience;* pass. to *appear:*—behold {1x}, perceive {1x}, see {51x}, take heed {5x}. not tr. {1x}.

Horao, as a verb, is said **(1)** of bodily vision: "He saith unto them, How many loaves have ye? go and see" (e.g., Mk 6:38; Jn 1:18, 46); **(2)** of mental perception: "But as it is written, To whom He was not spoken of, they shall see (*horao*): and they that have not heard shall understand" (e.g., Rom 15:21; Col 2:18); **(3)** of taking heed: "And Jesus saith unto him, See (*horao*) thou tell no man; but go thy way, shew thyself to the priest, and offer the gift that Moses commanded, for a testimony unto them" (e.g., Mt 8:4; 1 Th 5:15); **(4)** of experience, as **(4a)** of

death: "And it was revealed unto him by the Holy Ghost, that he should not see (*horao*) death, before he had seen the Lord's Christ" (Lk 2:26; cf. Heb 11:5), **(4b)** life: "He that believeth on the Son hath everlasting life: and he that believeth not the Son shall not see (*horao*) life; but the wrath of God abideth on him" (Jn 3:36); **(4c)** corruption: "Because thou wilt not leave My soul in hell, neither wilt thou suffer thine Holy One to see (*horao*) corruption" (Acts 2:27); **(5)** of caring for: "Saying, I have sinned in that I have betrayed the innocent blood. And they said, What is that to us? see (*horao*) thou to that" (Mt 27:4). Syn.: 333, 816, 991, 1689, 1896, 2029, 2300, 2334, 2657, 2734. See: TDNT—5:368, 706; BAGD—577d; THAYER—451b.

3709. ὀργή {36x} **ŏrgē**, *or-gay'*; from *3713*; prop. *desire* (as a *reaching* forth or *excitement* of the mind), i.e. (by anal.) violent *passion* (*ire*, or [justifiable] *abhorrence*); by impl. *punishment:*—anger {3x}, indignatio {1x}, vengeance {1x}, wrath {31x}.

Orge, originally any "natural impulse, or desire, or disposition," came to signify "anger," as the strongest of all passions. It is used of **(1)** the wrath of man, Eph 4:31; Col 3:8; 1 Ti 2:8; Jas 1:19–20; **(2)** the displeasure of human governments, Rom 13:4–5; **(3)** the sufferings of the Jews at the hands of the Gentiles, Lk 21:23; **(4)** the terrors of the Law, Rom 4:15; **(5)** the "anger" of the Lord Jesus, Mk 3:5; **(6)** God's "anger" with Israel in the wilderness, in a quotation from the OT, Heb 3:11; 4:3; **(7)** God's present "anger" with the Jews nationally, Rom 9:22; 1 Th 2:16; **(8)** His present "anger" with those who disobey the Lord Jesus in His gospel, Jn 3:36; **(9)** God's purposes in judgment, Mt 3:7; Lk 3:7; Rom 1:18; 2:5, 8; 3:5; 5:9; 12:19; Eph 2:3; 5:6; Col 3:6; 1 Th 1:10; 5:9. Syn.: cf. 2372 for discussion; 3950. See: TDNT—5:382, 716; BAGD—578d; THAYER—452a.

3710. ὀργίζω {8x} **ŏrgizō**, *or-gid'-zo*; from *3709*; to *provoke* or *enrage*, i.e. (pass.) *become exasperated:*—be angry {5x}, be wroth {3x}.

Orgizo, "to provoke, to arouse to anger," is used in the middle voice in the eight places where it is found, and signifies "to be angry, wroth." It is said **(1)** of individuals, in Mt 5:22; 18:34; 22:7; Lk 14:21; 15:28, and Eph 4:26; **(2)** of nations, Rev 11:18; **(3)** of Satan as the dragon, Rev 12:17. See: TDNT—5:382,*; BAGD—579c; THAYER—452c.

3711. ὀργίλος {1x} **ŏrgilŏs**, *org-ee'-los*; from *3709; irascible:*—soon angry {1x}. See: TDNT—5:382, 716; BAGD—579d; THAYER—452c.

3712. ὀργυιά {2x} **ŏrguia**, *org-wee-ah'*; from *3713;* a *stretch* of the arms, i.e. a *fathom:*—fathom {2x}.

A fathom is the distance across the chest from the tip of one middle finger to the tip of the other when the arms are outstretched, 5 to 6 feet (2 m), Acts 27:28 twice. See: BAGD—579d; THAYER—452c.

3713. ὀρέγομαι {3x} **ŏrĕgŏmai**, *or-eg'-om-ahee;* mid. voice of appar. a prol. form of an obs. primary [comp. *3735*]; to *stretch* oneself, i.e. *reach* out after (*long* for):—covet after {1x}, desire {2x}.

Oregomai, as a verb, means "to reach out, or after," is used in the middle voice, and is translated "desireth": "This is a true saying, If a man desire the office of a bishop, he desireth a good work" (1 Ti 3:1; cf. 6:10; Heb 11:16). Syn.: 327, 1567, 1934, 2206, 2212. See: TDNT—5:447, 727; BAGD—579d; THAYER—452d.

3714. ὀρεινός {2x} **ŏrĕinŏs**, *or-i-nos;* from *3735; mountainous,* i.e. (fem. by impl. of *5561*) the *Highlands* (of Judæa):—hill country {2x}.

Oreinos, "hilly" (from *oros*, "a hill, mountain"), is translated "hill country" in Lk 1:39, 65. See: BAGD—580a; THAYER—452d.

3715. ὄρεξις {1x} **ŏrĕxis**, *or'-ex-is;* from *3713; excitement* of the mind, i.e. *longing* after:—lust {1x}.

Orexis denotes an irrational longing, "a reaching" or "stretching after" (akin to *oregomai*, "to stretch oneself out, reach after"), a general term for every kind of desire, is used in Rom 1:27, "lust." Syn.: 1939, 3730, 3806. See: TDNT—5:447, 727; BAGD—580a; THAYER—452d.

3716. ὀρθοποδέω {1x} **ŏrthŏpŏdĕō**, *or-thop-od-eh'-o;* from a compound of *3717* and *4228;* to *be straight-footed,* i.e. (fig.) to *go directly* forward:—walk uprightly {1x}. See: TDNT—5:451, 727; BAGD—580a; THAYER—452d.

3717. ὀρθός {2x} **ŏrthŏs**, *or-thos';* prob. from the base of *3735; right* (as *rising*), i.e. (perpendicularly) *erect* (fig. *honest*), or (horizontally) *level* or *direct:*—straight {1x}, upright {1x}.

Orthos, "to walk in a straight path" (*orthos*, "straight," *pous*, "a foot"), is used **(1)** metaphorically in Gal 2:14, signifying a "course of conduct" by which one leaves a straight track for others to follow ("walked . . . uprightly"); and **(2)** Peter's command to the cripple to not only stand but to walk in a straight line, without staggering, signifying complete healing. See: TDNT—5:449, 727; BAGD—580b; THAYER—453a.

Greek

3718. ὀρθοτομέω {1x} **ŏrthŏtŏmĕō,** *or-thot-om-eh'-o;* from a compound of *3717* and the base of *5114,* to *make* a *straight cut,* i.e. (fig.) to *dissect (expound) correctly* (the divine message):—rightly divide {1x}.

Orthotomeo, lit., "to cut straight" (*orthos,* "straight," *temno,* "to cut"), is found in 2 Ti 2:15, "rightly dividing" (the word of truth); the meaning passed from the idea of cutting or "dividing," to the more general sense of "rightly dealing with a thing." What is intended here is not "dividing" Scripture from Scripture, but teaching Scripture accurately, carefully discerning each nuance. See: TDNT—8:111, 1169; BAGD—580b; THAYER—453a.

3719. ὀρθρίζω {1x} **ŏrthrizō,** *or-thrid'-zo;* from *3722;* to *use* the *dawn,* i.e. (by impl.) to *repair betimes:*—come early in the morning {1x}.

Orthizo, "to do anything early in the morning," is translated "came early in the morning," in Lk 21:38. See: BAGD—580c; THAYER—453a.

3720. ὀρθρινός {1x} **ŏrthrinŏs,** *or-thrin-os';* from *3722;* relating to the *dawn,* i.e. *matutinal* (as an epithet of Venus, espec. brilliant in the early day):—morning {1x}. See: BAGD—580c; THAYER—453b.

3721. ὄρθριος {1x} **ŏrthriŏs,** *or'-three-os;* from *3722;* in the *dawn,* i.e. up at *day-break:*—early {1x}. See: BAGD—580c; THAYER—453b.

3722. ὄρθρος {3x} **ŏrthrŏs,** *or'-thros;* from the same as *3735; dawn* (as *sun-rise, rising* of light); by extens. *morn:*—early in the morning {3x}.

Orthros, "daybreak," denotes "early in the morning," Lk 24:1; Jn 8:2; and Acts 5:21. See: BAGD—580c; THAYER—453b.

3723. ὀρθῶς {4x} **ŏrthōs,** *or-thoce';* adv. from *3717;* in a *straight* manner, i.e. (fig.) *correctly* (also mor.):—plain {1x}, right {1x}, rightly {2x}. See: BAGD—580d; THAYER—453b.

3724. ὁρίζω {8x} **hŏrizō,** *hor-id'-zo;* from *3725;* to *mark* out or *bound* ("horizon"), i.e. (fig.) to *appoint, decree, specify:*—determine {2x}, ordain {2x}, as it was determined + *2596* + *3588* {1x}, declare {1x}, limit {1x}, determine {1x}.

Horizo, [Eng., "horizon"], as a verb, means literally "to mark by a limit," hence, "to determine, ordain" and is used **(1)** of Christ as ordained of God to be a judge of the living and the dead: "Because He hath appointed a day, in the which He will judge the world in righteousness by that man whom He hath ordained (*horizo*); whereof He hath given assurance unto all men, in that He hath raised him from the

dead" (Acts 17:31); **(2)** of His being "marked out" as the Son of God: "And declared (*horizo*) to be the Son of God with power, according to the spirit of holiness, by the resurrection from the dead" (Rom 1:4); **(3)** of divinely appointed seasons: "And hath made of one blood all nations of men for to dwell on all the face of the earth, and hath determined (*horizo*) the times before appointed, and the bounds of their habitation" (Acts 17:26). See: TDNT—5:452, 728; BAGD—580d; THAYER—453b.

3725. ὅριον {11x} **hŏriŏn,** *hor'-ee-on;* neut. of a der. of an appar. primary ὅρος **hŏrŏs** (a *bound* or *limit*); a *boundary*-line, i.e. (by impl.) a *frontier (region):*—border {1x}, coast {10x}.

Horion, "the border of a country or district" (cf. Eng., "horizon"), is always used in the plural and translated **(1)** "borders" in Mt 4:13; **(2)** "coasts" in Mt 2:16; 4:13; 8:34; 15:22, 39; 19:1; Mk 5:17; 7:31 (twice); 10:1; Acts 13:50. See: BAGD—581b; THAYER—453c.

3726. ὁρκίζω {3x} **hŏrkizō,** *hor-kid'-zo;* from *3727;* to *put on oath,* i.e. *make swear;* by anal. to solemnly *enjoin:*—adjure {2x}, charge {1x}.

Orkizo, "to cause to swear, to lay under the obligation of an oath", **(1)** "adjure" in Mk 5:7; Acts 19:13, and **(2)** "charge" in 1 Th 5:27. See: TDNT—5:462, 729; BAGD—581b; THAYER—453c.

3727. ὅρκος {10x} **hŏrkŏs,** *hor'-kos;* from ἕρκος **hĕrkŏs,** (a *fence;* perh. akin to *3725);* a *limit,* i.e. (sacred) *restraint* (spec. an *oath):*—oath {10x}.

Horkos is primarily equivalent to *herkos,* "a fence, an enclosure, that which restrains a person"; hence, "an oath." **(1)** The Lord's command in Mt 5:33 was a condemnation of the minute and arbitrary restrictions imposed by the scribes and Pharisees in the matter of adjurations, by which God's name was profaned. **(2)** The injunction is repeated in Jas 5:12. **(3)** The language of the apostle Paul, e.g., in Gal 1:20 and 1 Th 5:27 was not inconsistent with Christ's prohibition, read in the light of its context. **(4)** Contrast the "oaths" mentioned in Mt 14:7, 9; 26:72; Mk 6:26. **(5)** Heb 6:16 refers to the confirmation of a compact among men, guaranteeing the discharge of liabilities; in their disputes "the oath is final for confirmation." This is referred to in order to illustrate the greater subject of God's "oath" to Abraham, confirming His promise; cf. Lk 1:73; Acts 2:30. See: TDNT—5:457, 729; BAGD—581c; THAYER—453d.

3728. ὁρκωμοσία {4x} hŏrkōmŏsia, hor-ko-
        mos-ee'ah; from a com-
pound of 3727 and a der. of 3660; asseveration
on oath:—oath {4x}.
  This word denotes "an affirmation on oath."
This is used in Heb 7:20–21 (twice), 28, of the
establishment of the priesthood of Christ, the
Son of God, appointed a priest after the order
of Melchizedek, and "perfected for evermore."
See: TDNT—5:463, 729; BAGD—581d;
THAYER—453d.

3729. ὁρμάω {5x} hŏrmaō, hor-mah'-o; from
        3730; to start, spur or urge on,
i.e. (refl.) to dash or plunge:—run violently
{3x}, run {1x}, rush {1x}.
  Hormao, "to set in motion, urge on," but
intransitively "to hasten on, rush," is always
translated (1) "ran violently," Mt 8:32; Mk 5:13;
Lk 8:33; (2) "ran," Acts 7:57; (3) "rushed", Acts
19:29. See: TDNT—5:467, 730; BAGD—581d;
THAYER—453d.

3730. ὁρμή {2x} hŏrmē, hor-may'; of uncert.
        aff.; a violent impulse, i.e. on-
set:—assault {1x}, not tr. {1x}.
  This word stresses the purpose and intention, an impulse of the mind or soul, a person's
reason compelling him to act; sometimes the
action going unfulfilled, Acts 14:5. Syn.: 1939,
3715, 3806. See: TDNT—5:467, 730; BAGD—
581d; THAYER—453d.

3731. ὅρμημα {1x} hŏrmēma, hor'-may-mah;
        from 3730; an attack, i.e. (abstr.)
precipitancy:—violence {1x}. See: TDNT—
5:467, 730; BAGD—581d; THAYER—453d.

3732. ὄρνεον {3x} ŏrnĕŏn, or'-neh-on; neut.
        of a presumed der. of 3733; a
birdling:—bird {1x}, fowl {2x}. Cf. Rev 18:2;
19:17, 21. See: BAGD—581d; THAYER—454a.

3733. ὄρνις {2x} ŏrnis, or'-nis; prob. from a
        prol. form of the base of 3735; a
bird (as rising in the air), i.e. (spec.) a hen (or
female domestic fowl):—hen {2x}. Cf. Mt 23:37;
Lk 13:34. See: BAGD—582a; THAYER—454a.

3734. ὁροθεσία {1x} hŏrŏthĕsia, hor-oth-es-
        ee'-ah; from a compound of
the base of 3725 and a der. of 5087; a limit-
placing, i.e. (concr.) boundary-line:—bound
{1x}. See: BAGD—582a; THAYER—454a.

3735. ὄρος {65x} ŏrŏs, or'-os; prob. from an
        obs. ὄρω ŏrō (to rise or "rear;"
perh. akin to 142; comp. 3733); a mountain (as
lifting itself above the plain):—hill {3x}, mount
{21x}, mountain {41x}
  Oros is used (1) without specification, e.g.,
Lk 3:5 (distinct from bounos, "a hill"); Jn 4:20;

(2) of "the Mount of Transfiguration," Mt 17:1,
9; Mk 9:2, 9; Lk 9:28, 37, "hill"; 2 Pet 1:18; (3) of
"Zion," Heb 12:22; Rev 14:1; (4) of "Sinai," Acts
7:30, 38; Gal 4:24, 25; Heb 8:5; 12:20; (5) of "the
Mount of Olives," Mt 21:1; 24:3; Mk 11:1; 13:3;
Lk 19:29, 37; 22:39; Jn 8:1; Acts 1:12; (6) of "the
hill districts as distinct from the lowlands,"
especially of the hills above the Sea of Galilee,
e.g., Mt 5:1; 8:1; 18:12; Mk 5:5; (7) of "the mountains on the east of Jordan" and "those in the
land of Ammon" and "the region of Petra," etc.,
Mt 24:16; Mk 13:14; Lk 21:21; (8) proverbially,
"of overcoming difficulties, or accomplishing
great things," 1 Cor 13:2; cf. Mt 17:20; 21:21;
Mk 11:23; (9) symbolically, of "a series of the
imperial potentates of the Roman dominion,
past and future," Rev 17:9. See: TDNT—5:475,
732; BAGD—582b; THAYER—454a.

3736. ὀρύσσω {3x} ŏrussō, or-oos'-so; appar.
        a primary verb; to "burrow" in
the ground, i.e. dig:—dig {3x}.
  Orusso, "to dig, dig up soil, dig a pit," is said
(1) of a place for a winepress, Mt 21:33; Mk 12:1;
(2) of "digging" a pit for hiding something, Mt
25:15. See: BAGD—582d; THAYER—454b.

3737. ὀρφανός {2x} ŏrphanŏs, or-fan-os'; of
        uncert. aff.; bereaved ("or-
phan"), i.e. parentless:—comfortless {1x}, fatherless {1x}.
  Orphanos, (Eng., "orphan"), signifies "bereft of parents or of a father." (1) In Jas 1:27 it
is translated "fatherless." (2) It was also used
in the general sense of being "friendless or desolate." In Jn 14:18 the Lord uses it of the relationship between Himself and His disciples, He
having been their guide, teacher and protector;
"comfortless." See: TDNT—5:487, 734; BAGD—
583a; THAYER—454b.

3738. ὀρχέομαι {4x} ŏrchĕŏmai, or-kheh'-
        om-ahee; mid. voice from
ὄρχος ŏrchŏs (a row or ring); to dance (from
the ranklike or regular motion):—dance {4x}.
  Orcheomai, (cf. Eng., "orchestra"), probably
originally signified "to lift up," as of the feet;
hence, "to leap with regularity of motion."
(1) It is always used in the middle voice, Mt
11:17; 14:6; Mk 6:22; Lk 7:32. (2) The performance by the daughter of Herodias is the only
clear instance of artistic dancing. See: BAGD—
583b; THAYER—454b.

3739. ὅς {1393x} hŏs, hos; incl. fem.

  ἥ hē, hay; and neut.

  ὅ hŏ hŏ; prob. a primary word (or perh.
        a form of the art. 3588); the rel. (some-
times demonstr.) pron., who, which, what,
that:—which {395x}, whom {262x}, that {129x},
who {84x}, whose {53x}, what {42x}, that which

{20x}, whereof {13x}; misc. {430x} = one, (an-, the) other, some, etc. See: BAGD—583b; THAYER—454b. See also 3757.

3740. ὁσάκις {3x} **hŏsakis,** *hos-ak'-is;* multiple adv. from *3739; how* (i.e. with *302, so) many times* as:—as often as + 302 {1x}, as often as + 1437 {1x}, as often as + 302 {1x}. See: BAGD—585b; THAYER—456b.

3741. ὅσιος {8x} **hŏsiŏs,** *hos'-ee-os;* of uncert. aff.; prop. *right* (by intrinsic or divine character; thus distinguished from *1342,* which refers rather to *human* statutes and relations; from *2413,* which denotes formal *consecration;* and from *40,* which relates to *purity* from defilement), i.e. *hallowed* (*pious, sacred, sure*):—holy {4x}, Holy One {2x}, mercies {1x}, shall be {1x}.

(1) *Hosios* means undefiled by sin, free from wickedness, religiously observing every moral obligation, pure holy, pious. **(2)** This is one who reverences God's everlasting ordinances and admits his obligations to them. **(3)** *Hosios,* as an adjective, signifies "religiously right, holy," as opposed to what is unrighteous or polluted. **(4)** It is commonly associated with righteousness. **(5)** It is used **(5a)** of God (Rev 15:4; 16:5); and **(5b)** of the body of the Lord Jesus (Acts 2:27; 13:35, citations from Ps 16:10); **(5c)** and of certain promises made to David, which could be fulfilled only in the resurrection of the Lord Jesus (Acts 13:34). **(6)** In 1 Ti 2:8 and Titus 1:8, it is used of the character of Christians. Syn.: 38, 40, 41, 42, 3742, 3743. See: TDNT—5:489, 734; BAGD—585c; THAYER—456b.

3742. ὁσιότης {2x} **hŏsiŏtēs,** *hos-ee-ot'-ace;* from *3741; piety:*—holiness {2x}.

Hosiotes denotes that quality of "holiness" **(1)** which is manifested in those who have regard equally to grace and truth; **(1a)** it involves a right relation to God; **(2)** it is used in Lk 1:75 and Eph 4:24, and in each place is associated with righteousness. Syn.: 38, 40, 41, 42, 2412, 3741, 3743.See: TDNT—5:493, 734; BAGD—585d; THAYER—456c.

3743. ὁσίως {1x} **hŏsiōs,** *hos-ee-oce';* adv. from *3741; piously:*—holily {1x}.

Hosios, as an adverb, means **(1)** pure from evil conduct, and observant of God's will. **(2)** It is used in 1 Th 2:10 of the conduct of the apostle and his fellow missionaries: "Ye are witnesses, and God also, how holily and justly and unblameably we behaved ourselves among you that believe." Syn.: 38, 40, 41, 42, 2412, 3741, 3742. See: TDNT—5:489, 734; BAGD—585d; THAYER—456c.

3744. ὀσμή {6x} **ŏsmē,** *os-may';* from *3605; fragrance* (lit. or fig.):—odour {2x}, savour {4x}.

Osme, "a smell, an odor", is translated **(1)** "odour" in Jn 12:3; **(2)** it is used metaphorically in Eph 5:2, "a sweet smelling savor," of the effects God-ward of the sacrifice of Christ; **(3)** in Phil 4:18 of the effect of sacrifice, on the part of those in the church at Philippi, who sent material assistance to the apostle in his imprisonment. **(4)** The word is translated "savor" in 2 Cor 2:14, 16 (twice). See: TDNT—5:493, 735; BAGD—586a; THAYER—456c.

3745. ὅσος {115x} **hŏsŏs,** *hos'-os;* by redupl. from *3739; as* (*much, great, long,* etc.) *as:*—as many as {24x}, whatsoever {9x}, that {9x}, whatsoever things {8x}, whatsoever + 302 {7x} as long as {5x}, how great things {5x}, what {4x}, misc. {37x} = all (that), as much as, how great (many, much), [in-] as much as, so many as, that (ever), the more, those things, wheresoever, wherewithsoever, which, × while, who (-soever). See: BAGD—586b; THAYER—456c.

3746. ὅσπερ {1x} **hŏspĕr,** *hos'-per;* from *3739* and *4007; who especially:*—whomsoever {1x}. See: BAGD—586c; 585a; THAYER—457a.

3747. ὀστέον {5x} **ŏstĕŏn,** *os-teh'-on;* or contr.

ὀστοῦν ŏstŏun, *os-toon';* of uncert. aff.; a *bone:*—bone {5x}. Cf. Mt 23:27; Lk 24:39; Jn 19:36; Heb 11:22. See: BAGD—586c; THAYER—457a.

3748. ὅστις {154x} **hŏstis,** *hos'-tis;* incl. the fem.

ἥτις hētis, *hay'-tis;* and the neut.

ὅ,τι hŏ,ti, *hot'-ee;* from *3739* and *5100; which some,* i.e. *any that;* also (def.) *which same:*—which {82x}, who {30x}, whosoever {12x}, that {8x}, whatsoever + 302 {4x}, whosoever + 302 {3x}, whatsoever + 3956 + 302 {2x}, misc {13x} = × and (they), (such) as, (they) that, in that they, whereas ye, they which. See: BAGD—586d; THAYER—457b. comp. *3754.*

3749. ὀστράκινος {2x} **ŏstrakinŏs,** *os-tra'-kin-os;* from ὄστρακον **ŏstrakŏn,** ["oyster"] (a *tile,* i.e. *terra cotta); earthen-ware,* i.e. *clayey;* by impl. *frail:*—of earth {1x}, earthen {1x}.

Ostrakinos signifies "made of earthenware or clay" (from *ostrakon,* "baked clay, potsherd, shell"; akin to *osteon,* "a bone"), translated **(1)** 2 Ti 2:20, "of earth"; **(2)** 2 Cor 4:7, "earthen." See: BAGD—587c; THAYER—457d.

3750. ὄσφρησις {1x} **ŏsphrēsis**, *os'-fray-sis;*
from a der. of *3605; smell*
(the sense):—smelling {1x}. See: BAGD—587c;
THAYER—457d.

3751. ὀσφύς {8x} **ŏsphus**, *os-foos';* of uncert.
aff.; the *loin* (extern.), i.e. the
hip; intern. (by extens.) *procreative power:*—
loins {8x}.

(1) The loins are the hips plus the lower abdomen regarded as the center of strength and
procreative power. **(2)** It is used **(2a)** in the natural sense in Mt 3:4; Mk 1:6; **(2b)** as "the seat
of generative power," Heb 7:5, 10; **(3)** metaphorically in Acts 2:30; **(4)** metaphorically,
(4a) of girding the "loins" in readiness for active service for the Lord, Lk 12:35; **(4b)** the
same, with truth, Eph 6:14, i.e., bracing up
oneself so as to maintain perfect sincerity and
reality as the counteractive in Christian character against hypocrisy and falsehood; **(4c)** of
girding the "loins" of the mind, 1 Pet 1:13, suggestive of the alertness necessary for sobriety
and for setting one's hope perfectly on "the grace
to be brought . . . at the revelation of Jesus
Christ" (the present participle, "girding," is introductory to the rest of the verse). See: TDNT—
5:496, 736; BAGD—587d; THAYER—457d.

3752. ὅταν {123x} **hŏtan**, *hot'-an;* from *3753*
and *302; whenever* (implying *hy-
pothesis* or more or less *uncertainty*); also caus.
(conjunc.) *inasmuch as:*—when {116x}, as soon
as {2x}, as long as {1x}, that {1x}, whensoever
{1x}, while {1x}, till + 1508 {1x}. See: BAGD—
587d; THAYER—458a.

3753. ὅτε {105x} **hŏtĕ**, *hot'-eh;* from *3739* and
5037; at *which* (thing) *too,* i.e.
when:—when {97x}, while {2x}, as soon as {2x},
after that {2x}, after {1x}, that {1x}. See:
BAGD—588b; THAYER—458c.

ὅ, τε **hŏ, tĕ**, *hŏ,t'-eh;* also fem.

ἥ, τε **hē, tĕ**, *hay'-teh;* and neut.

τό, τε **tŏ, tĕ**, *tot'-eh;* simply the art.
3588 followed by *5037;* so writ-
ten (in some editions) to distinguish them from
3752 and *5119.*

3754. ὅτι {1293x} **hŏti**, *hot'-ee;* neut. of *3748*
as conjunc.; demonst. *that* (some-
times redundant); caus. *because:*—that {612x},
for {264x}, because {173x}, how that {21x}, how
{11x}, misc. {212x} = as concerning that, as
though, because that, for that, in that, though,
why. See: BAGD—588c; THAYER—458d.

3755. ὅτου {6x} **hŏtŏu**, *hot'-oo;* for the gen.
of *3748* (as adverb); during *which
same* time, i.e. *whilst:*—not tr. {6x}. See:
BAGD—587c; THAYER—460a.

3756. οὐ {1453x} **ŏu**, *oo;* also (before a vowel)

οὐκ **ŏuk**, *ook;* and (before an aspirate)

οὐχ **ŏuch**, *ookh;* a primary word; the
absolute neg. [comp. *3361*] adv.; *no*
or *not:*—not {1214x}, no {136x}, cannot + 1410
{55x}, misc. {48x} = + long, nay, neither, never,
no man, none, + nothing, + special, unworthy,
when, + without, + yet but. See: BAGD—589a;
THAYER—460b. See also *3364, 3372.*

3757. οὗ {27x} **hŏu**, *hoo;* gen. of *3739* as adv.;
at *which* place, i.e. *where:*—where
{22x}, whither {2x}, when {1x}, wherein {1x},
whithersoever + 1437 {1x}. See: BAGD—589d;
THAYER—460b.

3758. οὐά {1x} **ŏua**, *oo-ah';* a primary exclamation of surprise; "*ah*":—ah {1x}.
Ouä, an interjection of derision and insult,
is translated "Ha!" in Mk 15:29. See: BAGD—
591a; THAYER—461c.

3759. οὐαί {47x} **ŏuai**, *oo-ah'-ee;* a primary
exclamation of grief; "*woe*":—
alas {6x}, woe {41x}.
Ouai, **(1)** an interjection, is used **(1a)** in denunciation, Mt 11:21; 18:7 (twice); eight times
in ch. 23; 24:19; 26:24; Mk 13:17; 14:21; Lk 6:24,
25 (twice), 26; 10:13; six times in ch. 11; 17:1;
21:23; 22:22; 1 Cor 9:16; Jude 11; Rev 8:13
(thrice); 12:12; **(1b)** as a noun, Rev 9:12 (twice);
11:14 (twice); **(2)** in grief, "alas," Rev 18:10, 16, 19
(twice in each). See: BAGD—591a; THAYER—
461c.

3760. οὐδαμῶς {1x} **ŏudamōs**, *oo-dam-oce';*
adv. from (the fem.) of *3762;
by no means:*—not {1x}.
This word denotes "by no means, in no
wise," Mt 2:6. See: BAGD—591b; THAYER—
461d.

3761. οὐδέ {137x} **ŏudĕ**, *oo-deh';* from *3756*
and *1161; not however,* i.e. *nei-
ther, nor, not even:*—neither {69x}, nor {31x},
not {10x}, no not {8x}, not so much as {2x}, then
not {1x}, not tr. {1x}, misc {14x} = neither
indeed, never, no more, no not, + nothing, such
as. See: BAGD—591c; THAYER—461d.

3762. οὐδείς {236x} **ŏudĕis**, *oo-dice';* incl.
fem.

οὐδεμία **ŏudĕmia**, *oo-dem-ee'-ah;* and
neut.

οὐδέν **ŏudĕn**, *oo-den';* from *3761* and
1520; not even one (man, woman
or thing), i.e. *none, nobody, nothing:*—no man
{94x}, nothing {68x}, none {27x}, no {24x}, any
man {3x}, any {3x}, man {2x}, neither any man
{2x}, misc. {13x} = aught, man, neither any
(thing), never (man), none of these things), not

(any, at all), nought. See: BAGD—591d; THAYER—462b.

3763. **οὐδέποτε** {16x} **ŏudĕpŏtĕ,** *oo-dep'-ot-eh;* from *3761* and *4218; not even at any time,* i.e. *never at all:*—never {14x}, neither at any time {1x}, nothing at any time + 3856 {1x}.

This word, (from *oude,* "not even," and *pote,* "at any time"), is used **(1)** in definite negative statements, e.g., Mt 7:23; 1 Cor 13:8; Heb 10:1, 11, or **(2)** questions, e.g., Mt 21:16, 42; **(3)** in Lk 15:29 (1st part), "neither . . . at any time"; "never" (2nd part). See: BAGD—592b; THAYER—462d.

3764. **οὐδέπω** {5x} **ŏudĕpō,** *oo-dep'-o;* from *3761* and *4452; not even yet:*—never before {1x}, never yet {1x}, nothing yet {1x}, not yet {1x}, as yet not {1x}. See: BAGD—592c; THAYER—462d.

3765. **οὐκέτι** {47x} **ŏukĕti,** *ook-et'-ee;* also (separately)

οὐκ ἔτι **ŏuk ĕti,** *ook et'-ee;* from *3756* and *2089; not yet, no longer:*—no more {29x}, any more {3x}, now not {2x}, misc. {13x} = after that (not), not any more, henceforth (hereafter) not, no longer, not as yet (now), now no more, yet (not).

Ouketi, "no more, no longer", is rendered **(1)** "no more" in Mk 7:12, **(2)** Jn 15:15, "henceforth not", **(3)** Rom 14:15, "now . . . not", **(4)** Gal 2:20, "yet not", **(5)** Gal 3:25; 4:7, "no more", and **(6)** Philem 16, "not now". See: BAGD—592c; THAYER—462d.

3766. **οὐκοῦν** {1x} **ŏukŏun,** *ook-oon';* from *3756* and *3767; is it not therefore* that, i.e. (affirmatively) *hence* or *so:*—then {1x}. See: BAGD—592d; THAYER—463a.

3767. **οὖν** {526x} **ŏun,** *oon;* appar. a primary word; (adv.) *certainly,* or (conjunc.) *accordingly:*—therefore {263x}, then {197x}, so {18x}, and {11x}, now {9x}, wherefore {8x}, but {5x}, r. {9x}, misc. {6x} = but, so likewise then, verily. See: BAGD—592d; THAYER—463b.

3768. **οὔπω** {23x} **ŏupō,** *oo'-po;* from *3756* and *4452; not yet:*—not yet {20x}, hitherto . . . not {1x}, as yet {1x}, no . . . as yet {1x}. See: BAGD—593c; THAYER—464b.

3769. **οὐρά** {5x} **ŏura,** *oo-rah';* appar. a primary word; a *tail:*—tail {5x}.

Oura, "the tail of an animal," occurs in Rev 9:10 (twice), 19; 12:4. See: BAGD—593c; THAYER—464b.

3770. **οὐράνιος** {6x} **ŏuraniŏs,** *oo-ran'-ee-os;* from *3772; celestial,* i.e. *belonging to* or *coming from* the *sky:*—heavenly {6x}.

Ouranios, signifying "of heaven, heavenly," is used **(1)** as an appellation of God the Father, **(1a)** Mt 6:14, 26, 32, "your heavenly Father"; **(1b)** 15:13, "My heavenly Father"; **(2)** as descriptive of the holy angels, Lk 2:13; **(3)** of the vision seen by Paul, Acts 26:19. See: TDNT—5:536, 736; BAGD—593c; THAYER—464b.

3771. **οὐρανόθεν** {2x} **ŏuranŏthĕn,** *oo-ran-oth'-en;* from *3772* and the enclitic of source; *from* the *sky:*—from heaven {2x}.

Ouranothen, denoting "from heaven," is used of **(1)** the aerial heaven, Acts 14:17; **(2)** heaven, as the uncreated sphere of God's abode, Acts 26:13. See: TDNT—5:542, 736; BAGD—593d; THAYER—464c.

3772. **οὐρανός** {284x} **ŏuranŏs,** *oo-ran-os';* perh. from the same as *3735* (through the idea of *elevation*); the *sky;* by extens. *heaven* (as the abode of God); by impl. *happiness, power, eternity;* spec. the *gospel* (*Christianity*):—heaven {268x}, air {10x}, sky {5x}, heavenly + 1537 {1x}.

Ouranos, is used in the NT **(1)** of "the aerial heavens," e.g., Mt 6:26; 8:20; Acts 10:12; 11:6 "air"; Jas 5:18; **(2)** "the sidereal" (i.e. the starry heavens), e.g., Mt 24:29, 35; Mk 13:25, 31; Heb 11:12, "sky"; Rev 6:14; 20:11; **(3)** they, (*1*) and (*2*), **(3a)** were created by the Son of God, Heb 1:10, as also **(3b)** by God the Father, Rev 10:6; **(4)** "the eternal dwelling place of God," Mt 5:16; 12:50; Rev 3:12; 11:13; 16:11; 20:9. **(5)** From thence the Son of God descended to become incarnate, Jn 3:13, 31; 6:38, 42. **(6)** In His ascension Christ "passed through the heavens," Heb 4:14, **(7)** He "ascended far above all the heavens," Eph 4:10, and was "made higher than the heavens," Heb 7:26; **(8)** He "sat down on the right hand of the throne of the Majesty in heavens," Heb 8:1; **(9)** He is "on the right hand of God," having gone into heaven, 1 Pet 3:22. **(10)** Since His ascension it is the scene of His present life and activity, e.g., Rom 8:34; Heb 9:24.

(11) From thence the Holy Spirit descended at Pentecost, 1 Pet 1:12. **(12)** It is the abode of the angels, e.g., Mt 18:10; 22:30; cf. Rev 3:5. **(13)** Thither Paul was "caught up," whether in the body or out of the body, he knew not, 2 Cor 12:2. **(14)** It is to be the eternal dwelling place of the saints in resurrection glory, 2 Cor 5:1. **(15)** From thence Christ will descend to the air **(15a)** to receive His saints at the Rapture, 1 Th 4:16; Phil 3:20, 21, and **(15b)** will subsequently come with His saints and with His holy angels at His second advent, Mt 24:30; 2 Th 1:7. **(16)** In the present life "heaven" is the region of the spiritual citizenship of believers, Phil 3:20. **(17)** The present "heavens," with the earth, are to

pass away, 2 Pet 3:10, "being on fire," v. 12 (see v. 7); Rev 20:11, and **(18)** new "heavens" and earth are to be created, 2 Pet 3:13; Rev 21:1, with Is 65:17. **(19)** In Lk 15:18, 21, "heaven" is used, by metonymy, for God. See: TDNT— 5:497, 736 BAGD—593d; THAYER—464c.

3773. Οὐρβανός {1x} **Ŏurbanŏs**, *oor-ban-os';* of Lat. or.; *Urbanus (of the city, "urbane"),* a Chr.:—Urbane {1x}. See: BAGD—595c; THAYER—465d.

3774. Οὐρίας {1x} **Ŏurias**, *oo-ree'-as;* of Heb. or. [223]; *Urias* (i.e. *Urijah*), a Hittite:—Urias {1x}. See: TDNT—3:1,*; BAGD— 595c; THAYER—465d.

3775. οὖς {37x} **ŏus**, *ooce;* appar. a primary word; the *ear* (phys. or ment.):— ear {37x}.

Ous is used **(1)** of the physical organ (Lk 4:21; Acts 7:57); **(1a)** in Acts 11:22, in the plural with *akouo,* "to hear," lit., "was heard into the ears of someone," i.e., came to the knowledge of, similarly, in the singular, Mt 10:27, in familiar private conversation; **(1b)** in Jas 5:4 the phrase is used with *eiserchomai (1525),* "to enter into"; **(1c)** in Lk 1:44, with *ginomai (1096),* "to become, to come"; **(1d)** in Lk 12:3, with *lalein (2980),* "to speak" and pros, "to"; **(2)** metaphorically, of the faculty of perceiving with the mind, understanding and knowing (Mt 13:16); **(3)** frequently with *akouo (191),* "to hear" (Mt 11:15; 13:9, 43); **(3a)** Rev 2 and 3, at the close of each of the messages to the churches; **(3b)** in Mt 13:15 and Acts 28:27, with *bareos (917),* "heavily," of being slow to understand and **(3c)** with a negative: "Having eyes, see ye not? and having ears, hear ye not? and do ye not remember?" (Mk 8:18; cf. Rom 11:8); **(3d)** in Lk 9:44 the lit. meaning is "put those words into your ears," i.e., take them into your mind and keep them there; **(3e)** in Acts 7:51 it is used with *aperitmetos (564),* "uncircumcised." **(4)** As seeing is metaphorically associated with conviction, so hearing is with obedience [*hupakoe* - 5219, lit., "hearing under"; the Eng., "obedience" is etymologically "hearing over against," i.e., with response in the hearer]. Syn.: 189, 5621. See: TDNT—5:543, 744; BAGD— 595c; THAYER—465d.

3776. οὐσία {2x} **ŏusia**, *oo-see'-ah;* from the fem. of *5607; substance,* i.e. *property (possessions):*—goods {1x}, substance {1x}.

Ousia, derived from a present participial form of *eimi,* "to be," denotes "substance, property," and is translated **(1)** Lk 15:12, "goods", and **(2)** 15:13, "substance." See: BAGD—596a; THAYER— 466a.

3777. οὔτε {94x} **ŏutĕ**, *oo'-teh;* from *3756* and *5037; not too,* i.e. *neither* or *nor;* by anal. *not even:*—neither {44x}, nor {40x}, nor yet {4x}, no not {1x}, not {1x}, yet not {1x}, misc. {3x} = none, nothing. See: BAGD—596a; THAYER—466b.

3778. οὗτος {355x} **hŏutŏs**, *hoo'-tos;* incl. nom. masc. plur.

  οὗτοι hŏutŏi, *hoo'-toy;* nom. fem. sing.

  αὕτη hautē, *hŏw'-tay;* and nom. fem. plur.

  αὗται hautai, *hŏw'-tahee;* from the art. *3588* and *846; the he (she* or *it),* i.e. *this* or *that* (often with art. repeated):— this {157x}, these {59x}, he {31x}, the same {28x}, this man {25x}, she {12x}, they {10x}, misc. {33x} = he it was that, hereof, it, such as, this (same, woman), which, who. See: BAGD— 596b; THAYER—466c.

3779. οὕτω {213x} **hŏutō**, *hoo'-to;* or (before a vowel)

  οὕτως hŏutōs, *hoo'-toce;* adv. from *3778; in this way* (referring to what precedes or follows):—so {164x}, thus {17x}, even so {9x}, on this wise {6x}, likewise {4x}, after this manner {3x}, misc. {10x} = after that, in this manner, as, for all that, no more, on this fashion, so in like manner, what.

Houtos or *houto,* as an averb, means "thus, in this way" and is rendered "after this manner" (Mt 6:9; 1 Pet 3:5; Rev 11:5). Syn.: 195, 1485, 2239, 3634, 3668, 3697, 4169, 4187, 4217, 4459, 5158, 5159, 5179, 5615. See: BAGD— 597c; THAYER—468a.

3780. οὐχί {56x} **ŏuchi**, *oo-khee';* intens. of *3756; not indeed:*—not {46x}, nay {5x}, not {4x}, not so {1x}. See: BAGD—598b; THAYER—469a.

3781. ὀφειλέτης {7x} **ŏphĕilĕtēs**, *of-i-let'-ace;* from *3784;* an *ower,* i.e. person *indebted;* fig. a *delinquent;* mor. a *transgressor* (against God):—debtor {5x}, which owed {1x}, sinner {1x}.

This word means one who owes anything to another," primarily in regard to money; **(1)** in Mt 18:24, "who owed" (lit., "one was brought, a debtor to him of ten thousand talents"). The slave could own property, and so become a "debtor" to his master, who might seize him for payment. **(2)** It is used metaphorically, **(2a)** of a person who is under an obligation, Rom 1:14, **(2a1)** of Paul, in the matter of preaching the gospel; **(2a2)** in Rom 8:12, of believers, to mortify the deeds of the body; **(2a3)** in Rom 15:27, of gentile believers, to assist afflicted Jewish believers; **(2a4)** in Gal 5:3, of those who would

be justified by circumcision, to do the whole Law; **(2b)** of those who have not yet made amends to those whom they have injured, Mt 6:12, "our debtors"; **(2c)** of some whose disaster was liable to be regarded as a due punishment, Lk 13:4, "sinners." See: TDNT—5:565, 746; BAGD—598b; THAYER—469a.

3782. ὀφειλή {2x} **ŏphĕilē,** *of-i-lay';* from *3784; indebtedness,* i.e. (concr.) a *sum* owed; fig. *obligation,* i.e. (conjugal) *duty:*—debt {1x}, due {1x}.

Opheile, "that which is owed", is translated **(1)** "debt" in Mt 18:32; **(2)** in the plural, "dues", Rom 13:7. See: TDNT—5:564, 746; BAGD—598c; THAYER—469b.

3783. ὀφείλημα {2x} **ŏphĕilēma,** *of-i'-lay-mah;* from (the alt. of) *3784; something owed,* i.e. (fig.) a *due;* mor. a *fault:*—debt {2x}.

Opheilema, expressing a "debt" more concretely, is used **(1)** literally, of that which is legally due, Rom 4:4; **(2)** metaphorically, of sin as a "debt," because it demands expiation, and thus payment by way of punishment, Mt 6:12. See: TDNT—5:565, 746; BAGD—598c; THAYER—469b.

3784. ὀφείλω {36x} **ŏphĕilō,** *of-i'-lo;* or (in certain tenses) its prol. form

ˈφειλέω ŏphĕilĕō, *of-i-leh'-o;* prob. from the base of *3786* (through the idea of *accruing*); to *owe* (pecuniarily); fig. to *be under obligation (ought, must, should);* mor. to *fail* in duty:—ought {15x}, owe {7x}, be bound {2x}, be (one's) duty {2x}, be a debtor {1x}, be guilty {1x}, be indebted 1, misc. {7x} = behove, (must) need (-s), should. Syn.: *Dei (1165)* expresses a logical necessity, *opheilo (3784),* a moral obligation; cf. *chre (5534),* Jas 3:10, "ought," which expresses a need resulting from the fitness of things. See: TDNT—5:559, 746; BAGD—598d; THAYER—469b. See also *3785.*

3785. ὄφελον {4x} **ŏphĕlŏn,** *of'-el-on;* first pers. sing. of a past tense of *3784; I ought (wish),* i.e. (interj.) *oh that!:*—I would {2x}, I would to God {1x}, would to God {1x}. See: BAGD—599a; THAYER—469c.

3786. ὄφελος {3x} **ŏphĕlŏs,** *of'-el-os;* from ὀφέλλω **ŏphĕllō,** (to *heap* up, i.e. *accumulate* or *benefit*); *gain:*—it advantageth {1x}, it profiteth {2x}.

Ophello, "to increase," comes from a root signifying "to increase"; hence, "advantage, profit"; it is rendered as a verb in its three occurrences: **(1)** 1 Cor 15:32, "advantageth"; **(2)** Jas 2:14, 16, "What (is) the profit?" See: BAGD—599b; THAYER—469d.

3787. ὀφθαλμοδουλεία {2x} **ŏphthalmŏdŏulĕia,** *of-thal-mod-oo-li'-ah;* from *3788* and *1397; sight-labor,* i.e. that needs watching *(remissness):*—eye-service {2x}.

This is service performed [only] under the master's eyes for the master's eye usually stimulates to greater diligence and his absence, on the other hand, renders sluggish, Eph 6:6 and Col 3:22. See: TDNT—2:280, 182; BAGD—599b; THAYER—469d.

3788. ὀφθαλμός {101x} **ŏphthalmŏs,** *of-thal-mos';* from *3700;* the *eye* (lit. or fig.); by impl. *vision;* fig. *envy* (from the jealous side-glance):—eye {101x}, sight {1x}.

Ophthalmos, akin to *opsis,* "sight," probably from a root signifying "penetration, sharpness" (cf. Eng., "ophthalmia," etc.), is used **(1)** of the physical organ, e.g., Mt 5:38; **(1a)** of restoring sight, e.g., Mt 20:33; **(1b)** of God's power of vision, Heb 4:13; 1 Pet 3:12; **(1c)** of Christ in vision, Rev 1:14; 2:18; 19:12; **(1d)** of the Holy Spirit in the unity of Godhood with Christ, Rev 5:6; **(2)** metaphorically, **(2a)** of ethical qualities, evil, Mt 6:23; Mk 7:22 (by metonymy, for envy); **(2b)** singleness of motive, Mt 6:22; Lk 11:34; **(2c)** as the instrument of evil desire, "the principal avenue of temptation," 1 Jn **(2d)** of adultery, 2 Pet 2:14; **(3)** metaphorically, **(3a)** of mental vision, Mt 13:15; Jn 12:40; Rom 11:8; Gal 3:1; **(3b)** by gospel-preaching Christ had been, so to speak, placarded before their "eyes"; **(3c)** the question may be paraphrased, "What evil teachers have been malignly fascinating you?"; **(3d)** Eph 1:18, of the "eyes of the heart," as a means of knowledge. See: TDNT—5:375, 706; BAGD—599b; THAYER—470a.

3789. ὄφις {14x} **ŏphis,** *of'-is;* prob. from *3700* (through the idea of *sharpness* of vision); a *snake,* fig. (as a type of sly cunning) an artful *malicious* person, espec. *Satan:*—serpent {14x}.

(1) The characteristics of the "serpent" as alluded to in Scripture **(1a)** are mostly evil (though Mt 10:16 refers to its caution in avoiding danger); **(1b)** its treachery, cf. Gen 49:17; 2 Cor 11:3; **(1c)** its venom, cf. Ps 58:4; 1 Cor 10:9; Rev 9:19; **(1d)** its skulking, cf. Job 26:13; **(1e)** its murderous proclivities, e.g., Ps 58:4; Prov 23:32; Eccl 10:8, 11; Amos 5:19; Mk 16:18; Lk 10:19; **(2)** the Lord used the word metaphorically of the scribes and Pharisees, Mt 23:33 (cf. *echidna,* "viper," in Mt 3:7; 12:34). **(3)** The general aspects of its evil character are intimated in the Lord's rhetorical question in Mt 7:10 and Lk 11:11. **(4)** Its characteristics are concentrated in the arch-adversary of God and man, the devil, metaphorically described as the serpent, 2 Cor 11:3; Rev 12:9, 14, 15; 20:2. **(5)**

The brazen "serpent" lifted up by Moses was symbolical of the means of salvation provided by God, in Christ and His vicarious death under the divine judgment upon sin, Jn 3:14. **(6)** While the living "serpent" symbolizes sin in its origin, hatefulness, and deadly effect, the brazen "serpent" symbolized the bearing away of the curse and the judgment of sin; the metal was itself figurative of the righteousness of God's judgment. See: TDNT—5:566, 748; BAGD—600a; THAYER—470b.

3790. ὀφρύς {1x} **ŏphrus,** *of-roos';* perh. from *3700* (through the idea of the shading or proximity to the organ of *vision*); the eye-"*brow*" or *forehead,* i.e. (fig.) the *brink* of a precipice:—brow {1x}. See: BAGD—600b; THAYER—470c.

3791. ὀχλέω {2x} **ŏchlĕō,** *okh-leh'-o;* from *3793;* to *mob,* i.e. (by impl.) to *harass:*—vex {2x}.

Ochleo means to disturb, trouble and is used in the passive voice, of being troubled, molested, vexed by evil spirits (Lk 6:18; Acts 5:16). See: BAGD—600c; THAYER—470c.

3792. ὀχλοποιέω {1x} **ŏchlŏpŏiĕō,** *okh-lop-oy-eh'-o;* from *3793* and *4160;* to *make a crowd,* i.e. *raise a* public *disturbance:*—gather a company {1x}. See: BAGD—600c; THAYER—470c.

3793. ὄχλος {175x} **ŏchlŏs,** *okh'los;* from a der. of *2192* (mean. a *vehicle*); a disorganized *throng* (as *borne* along); by impl. the *rabble;* by extens. a *class* of people; fig. a *riot:*—people {82x}, multitude {79x}, press {5x}, company {7x}, number of people {1x}, number {1x}.

Ochlos is used **(1)** frequently in the four Gospels and the Acts; elsewhere only in Rev. 7:9; 17:15; 19:1, 6; **(2)** it denotes **(2a)** "a crowd or multitude of persons, a throng," e.g., Mt 14:14, 15; 15:33; **(2b)** often in the plural, e.g., Mt 4:25; 5:1; **(2c)** with *polus,* "much" or "great," it signifies **(2c1)** "a great multitude," e.g., Mt 20:29, or **(2c2)** "the common people," Mk 12:37, perhaps preferably "the mass of the people." The mass of the people was attracted to Him (for the statement "heard Him gladly" cf. what is said in Mk 6:20 of Herod Antipas concerning John the Baptist; **(2c3)** in Jn 12:9, "the people" stands in contrast with their leaders (v. 10); Acts 24:1 "crowd"; **(3)** "the populace, an unorganized multitude," in contrast to *demos,* "the people as a body politic," e.g., Mt 14:5; 21:26; Jn 7:12 (2nd part); **(4)** in a more general sense, **(4a)** "the company of His disciples" e.g., Lk 6:17; **(4b)** Acts 1:15, "the number of names"; **(4c)** Acts 24:18, "multitude." Syn.:

1218, 1484, 2992, 3793. See: TDNT—5:582, 750; BAGD—600c; THAYER—470c.

3794. ὀχύρωμα {1x} **ŏchurōma,** *okh-oo'-ro-mah;* from a remote der. of *2192* (mean. to *fortify,* through the idea of *holding* safely); a *castle* (fig. *argument*):—stronghold {1x}.

Ochurmoa, "a stronghold, fortress" (akin to *ochuroo,* "to make firm"), is used metaphorically in 2 Cor 10:4, of those things in which mere human confidence is imposed. See: TDNT—5:590, 752; BAGD—601a; THAYER—471a.

3795. ὀψάριον {5x} **ŏpsariŏn,** *op-sar'-ee-on;* neut. of a presumed der. of the base of *3702;* a *relish* to other food (as if cooked *sauce*), i.e. (spec.) *fish* (presumably salted and dried as a condiment):—fish {4x}, small fish {1x}.

Opsarion is a diminutive of *opson* (3702 - cooked meat), or a relish, a dainty dish, especially of fish or little fish (Jn 6:9, "small fishes"; 6:11; 21:9, 10, 13). See: BAGD—601b; THAYER—471a.

3796. ὀψέ {3x} **ŏpsĕ,** *op-seh';* from the same as *3694* (through the idea of *backwardness*); (adv.) *late* in the day; by extens. *after the close* of the day:—in the end {1x}, even {1x}, at even {1x}.

Opse, "long after, late, late in the day, at evening" (in contrast to *proi,* "early," e.g., Mt 20:1), is used **(1)** practically as a noun in Mk 11:11, lit., "the hour being at eventide"; 11:19; 13:35; **(2)** in Mt 28:1 it is rendered "in the end of." See: BAGD—601b; THAYER—471b.

3797. ὄψιμος {1x} **ŏpsimŏs,** *op'-sim-os;* from *3796; later,* i.e. *vernal* (showering):—latter {1x}.

Opsimos denotes "late," or "latter," and is used of "the latter rain" in Jas 5:7; this rain falls in March and April, just before the harvest, in contrast to the early rain, in October. See: BAGD—601c; THAYER—471c.

3798. ὄψιος {15x} **ŏpsiŏs,** *op'-see-os;* from *3796; late;* fem. (as noun) *afternoon* (early eve) or *nightfall* (later eve):—even {8x}, evening {4x}, in the evening + 1096 {1x}, eventide + 5610 {1x}, at even + 1096 {1x}.

Opsios, the feminine of the adjective *opsios,* "late," **(1)** used as a noun, denoting "evening," with *hora,* "understood", is found seven times in Mt, five in Mk, two in Jn, and in these places only in the NT. **(2)** The word really signifies the "late evening," the latter of the two "evenings" as reckoned by the Jews, the first from 3 p.m. to sunset, the latter after sunset; this is the usual meaning. It is used, however, of both, e.g., Mk 1:32. See: BAGD—601c; THAYER—471c.

3799. ὄψις {3x} **ŏpsis**, *op'-sis;* from *3700;* prop. *sight* (the act), i.e. (by impl) the *visage*, an extern. *show:*—appearance {1x}, countenance {1x}, face {1x}.

Opsis, (from *ops*, "the eye," connected with *horao*, "to see", primarily denotes "seeing, sight"; hence, **(1)** "the face, the countenance," Jn 11:44 ("face"); **(2)** Rev 1:16 ("countenance"); **(3)** the outward "appearance," the look, Jn 7:24, only here, of the outward aspect of a person. See: BAGD—601d; THAYER—471d.

3800. ὀψώνιον {4x} **ŏpsōniŏn**, *op-so'-nee-on;* neut. of a presumed der. of the same as *3795; rations* for a soldier, i.e. (by extens.) his *stipend* or *pay:*—wages {3x}, charges {1x}.

Opsonion, (from *opson*, "meat," and *oneomai*, "to buy"), primarily signified whatever is brought to be eaten with bread provisions, supplies for an army, soldier's pay, translated **(1)** "charges," 9:7, of the service of a soldier. **(2)** It is rendered "wages" in Lk 3:14; Rom 6:23; 2 Cor 11:8. See: TDNT—5:591, 752; BAGD—602a; THAYER—471d.

3801. ὁ ὢν καὶ ὁ ἦν καὶ ὁ ἐρχόμενος {15x} **hŏ ōn kai hŏ ēn kai hŏ ĕrchŏmĕnŏs**, *hŏ own kahee hŏ ane kahee hŏ erkhom'-en-os;* a phrase combining *3588* with the pres. part. and imperf. of *1510* and the pres. part. of *2064* by means of *2532; the one being and the one that was and the one coming,* i.e. *the Eternal,* as a divine epithet of Christ:—which is {2x}, and which was {2x}, and which is to come {2x}, which art {2x}, and wast {2x}, which was {1x}, and is {1x}, and is to come {1x}, and art to come {1x}, and shall be {1x}. See: BAGD—not listed; THAYER—not listed.

Π

3802. παγιδεύω {1x} **pagidĕuō**, *pag-id-yoo'-o;* from *3803;* to *ensnare* (fig.):—entangle {1x}.

Pagideuo, "to entrap, lay snares for" (from *pagis*, "anything which fixes or grips," hence, "a snare"), **(1)** is used in Mt 22:15, of the efforts of the Pharisees to "entangle" the Lord in His speech. **(2)** Metaphorically, *pagideuo* speaks of the attempt to elicit from one some remark which can be turned into an accusation against him. See: TDNT—5:595, 752; BAGD—602a; THAYER—472a.

3803. παγίς {5x} **pagis**, *pag-ece';* from *4078;* a *trap* (as *fastened* by a noose or notch); fig. a *trick* or *statagem* (*temptation*):—snare {5x}.

Pagis, "a trap, a snare" (akin to *pegnumi*, "to fix," and *pagideuo*, "to ensnare", is used

metaphorically of **(1)** the allurements to evil by which the Devil "ensnares" one, 1 Ti 3:7; 2 Ti 2:26; **(2)** seductions to evil, which "ensnare" those who "desire to be rich," 1 Ti 6:9; **(3)** the evil brought by Israel upon themselves by which the special privileges divinely granted them and centering in Christ, became a "snare" to them, their rejection of Christ and the gospel being the retributive effect of their apostasy, Rom 11:9; **(4)** of the sudden judgments of God to come upon those whose hearts are "overcharged with surfeiting, and drunkenness, and cares of this life," Lk 21:35. See: TDNT—5:593, 752; BAGD—602a; THAYER—472a.

Πάγος Pagŏs. See *697.*

3804. πάθημα {16x} **pathēma**, *path'-ay-mah;* from a presumed der. of *3806;* something *undergone*, i.e. *hardship* or *pain;* subj. an *emotion* or *influence:*—affection {1x}, affliction {3x}, motion {1x}, suffering {11x}.

Pathema, from *pathos*, "suffering," signifies "affliction." **(1)** The word is frequent in Paul's epistles and is found three times in Hebrews, four in 1 Pet; and it is used **(2)** of "afflictions", Rom 8:18, etc.; **(3)** of Christ's "sufferings", 1 Pet 1:11; 5:1; Heb 2:9; **(4)** of those as shared by believers, 2 Cor 1:5; Phil 3:10; 1 Pet 4:13; 5:1; **(5)** of "an evil emotion, passion", Rom 7:5; Gal 5:24. **(6)** The connection between the two meanings is that the emotions, whether good or evil, **(6a)** were regarded as consequent upon external influences exerted on the mind (cf. the two meanings of the English "passion"). It expresses in sense **(6b)** the uncontrolled nature of evil desires, in contrast to *epithumia*, the general and comprehensive term, lit., "what you set your heart upon." **(7)** Its concrete character is seen in Heb 2:9. See: TDNT—5:930, 798; BAGD—602b; THAYER—472a.

3805. παθητός {1x} **pathētŏs**, *path-ay-tos';* from the same as *3804; liable* (i.e. *doomed*) to experience *pain:*—suffer {1x}.

Pathetos denotes "one who has suffered," or "subject to suffering," or "destined to suffer", endued with the capacity of suffering, capable of feeling; and hence, subject to the necessity of suffering; it is used in the last sense of the "suffering" of Christ, Acts 26:23. See: TDNT—5:924, 798; BAGD—602d; THAYER—472b.

3806. πάθος {3x} **pathŏs**, *path'-os;* from the alt. of *3958;* prop. *suffering* ("*pathos*"), i.e. (subj.) a *passion* (espec. *concupiscence*):—inordinate affection {1x}, affection {1x}, lust {1x}.

(1) This word primarily denotes whatever one experiences in any way which affects him; hence, an affection of the mind which stimulates a passionate desire, capricious delight,

the disease of passion, and is always used in a bad sense; primarily denotes whatever one suffers or experiences in any way; hence, "an affection of the mind, a passionate desire." **(2)** Used by the Greeks of either good or bad desires, it is always used in the NT of the latter, **(2a)** Rom 1:26, "(vile) affections"; **(2b)** Col 3:5, "inordinate affection"; **(2c)** 1 Th 4:5, "lust." Syn.: 1939, 3715, 3730. See: TDNT—5:926, 798; BAGD—602d; THAYER—472c.

πάθω **pathō**. See *3958*.

3807. **παιδαγωγός** {3x} **paidagōgŏs**, *pahee-dag-o-gos';* from *3816* and a redupl. form of *71;* a *boy-leader,* i.e. a servant whose office it was to take the children to school; (by impl. [fig.] a *tutor* ["*pœda-gogue*"]):—instructor {1x}, schoolmaster {2x}.

This word means "a guide," or "guardian" or "trainer of boys," lit., "a child-leader" (*pais,* "a boy, or child," *ago,* "to lead"), "a tutor," is translated **(1)** "instructors" in 1 Cor 4:15; here the thought is that of pastors rather than teachers; **(2)** in Gal 3:24, 25, "schoolmaster", but here the idea of instruction is absent. **(2a)** In this and allied words the idea is that of training, discipline, not of impartation of knowledge. **(2b)** The *paidagogos* was not the instructor of the child; he exercised a general supervision over him and was responsible for his moral and physical well-being. **(2c)** Thus understood, *paidagogos* is appropriately used with "kept in ward" and "shut up," whereas to understand it as equivalent to "teacher" introduces an idea entirely foreign to the passage, and throws the Apostle's argument into confusion. See: TDNT—5:596, 753; BAGD—603a; THAYER—472d.

3808. **παιδάριον** {2x} **paidariŏn**, *pahee-dar'-ee-on;* neut. of a presumed der. of *3816;* a *little boy:*—child {1x}, lad {1x}.

Paidarion, a diminutive of *pais,* is used **(1)** of "boys and girls," in Mt 11:16, and **(2)** a "lad" in Jn 6:9. Syn.: *Paidarion* (*3808*) refers to a child up to his first school years. *Paidion* (*3813*) refers exclusively to little children. *Paidiske* (*3814*) refers to female in late childhood and early youth. *Pais* (*3816*) refers to a child of any age. *Teknon* (*5043*) gives prominence to physical and outward aspects of parentage. *Huios* (*5207*) gives prominence to the inward, ethical, legal aspects of parentage. *Pais* (*3816*) and *teknon* (*5043*) denote a child as respects to descent and age, reference to the later being more prominent in the former word, to descent in *paidion* (*3813*); but the period *pais* (*3816*) covers is not sharply defined. See: TDNT—5:636, 759; BAGD—603b; THAYER—472d.

3809. **παιδεία** {6x} **paidĕia**, *pahee-di'-ah;* from *3811; tutorage,* i.e. *education* or *training;* by impl. disciplinary *correction:*—chastening {3x}, chastisement {1x}, instruction {1x}, nurture {1x}.

Paideia denotes "the training of a child, including instruction"; hence, "discipline, correction," "chastening," and is translated **(1)** in Eph 6:4, "nurture", suggesting the Christian discipline that regulates character; and **(2)** "chastening" in Heb 12:5, 7; **(3)** "chastisement" in Heb 12:8; and **(4)** in 2 Ti 3:16, "instruction. Syn.: 3559. See: TDNT—5:596, 753; BAGD—603b; THAYER—472d.

3810. **παιδευτής** {2x} **paidĕutēs**, *pahee-dyoo-tace';* from *3811;* a *trainer,* i.e. *teacher* or (by impl.) *discipliner:*—which corrected {1x}, instructor {1x}.

Paideutes has two meanings, corresponding to the two meanings of the verb *paideuo* (*3811*) from which it is derived, **(1)** "a teacher, preceptor, corrector," Rom 2:20, "instructor", and **(2)** [the one] "which corrected", "a chastiser," Heb 12:9. See: TDNT—5:596, 753; BAGD—603d; THAYER—473a.

3811. **παιδεύω** {13x} **paidĕuō**, *pahee-dyoo'-o;* from *3816;* to *train* up a child, i.e. *educate,* or (by impl.) *discipline* (by punishment):—chasten {6x}, chastise {2x}, instruct {1x}, learn {2x}, teach {2x}.

Paideuo primarily denotes "to train children," suggesting the broad idea of education (*pais,* "a child"), and is translated **(1)** "learned" in Acts 7:22; **(2)** "taught" in Acts 22:3; **(3)** "teaching" in Titus 2:12, here of a training gracious and firm; grace, which brings salvation, employs means to give us full possession of it; hence, **(4)** "to chastise," this being part of the training, whether **(4a)** by correcting with words, reproving, and admonishing, 1 Ti 1:20; 2 Ti 2:25, or **(4b)** by "chastening" by the infliction of evils and calamities, 1 Cor 11:32; 2 Cor. 6:9; Heb 12:6–7, 10; Rev 3:19. **(5)** The verb also has the meaning "to chastise with blows, to scourge," said of the command of a judge, Lk 23:16, 22. See: TDNT—5:596, 753; BAGD—603d; THAYER—473a.

3812. **παιδιόθεν** {1x} **paidiŏthĕn**, *pahee-dee-oth'-en;* adv. (of *source*) from *3813; from infancy:*—of a child {1x}. See: BAGD—604a; THAYER—473b.

3813. **παιδίον** {51x} **paidiŏn**, *pahee-dee'-on;* neut. dimin. of *3816;* a *child-ling* (of either sex), i.e. (prop.) an infant, or (by extens.) a half-grown *boy* or girl; fig. an *immature* Chr.:—child {25x}, little child {12x}, young child {10x}, damsel {4x}.

Paidion, a diminutive of *pais,* **(1)** signifies

"a little or young child"; **(1a)** it is used of an infant just born, Jn 16:21, **(1b)** of a male child recently born, e.g., Mt 2:8; Heb 11:23; **(1c)** of a more advanced child, Mk 9:24; **(1d)** of a son, Jn 4:49; **(1e)** of a girl, Mk 5:39, 40, 41; **(1f)** in the plural, of "children," e.g., Mt 14:21. **(2)** It is used metaphorically **(2a)** of believers who are deficient in spiritual understanding, 1 Cor 14:20, and **(2b)** in affectionate and familiar address by the Lord to His disciples, almost like the Eng., "lads," Jn 21:5; **(2c)** by the apostle John to the youngest believers in the family of God, 1 Jn 2:13, 18; there it is to be distinguished from *teknia,* which term he uses in addressing all his readers. Syn.: *Paidarion* (*3808*) refers to a child up to his first school years. *Paidion* (*3813*) refers exclusively to little children. *Paidiske* (*3814*) refers to a female in late childhood and early youth. *Pais* (*3816*) refers to a child of any age. *Teknon* (*5043*) gives prominence to physical and outward aspects of parentage. *Huios* (*5207*) gives prominence to the inward, ethical, legal aspects of parentage. *Pais* (*3816*) and *teknon* (*5043*) denote a child as respects to descent and age, reference to the later being more prominent in the former word, to descent in *paidion* (*3813*); but the period *pais* (*3816*) covers is not sharply defined. See: TDNT—5:636, 759; BAGD—604a; THAYER—473b.

3814. παιδίσκη {13x} **paidiskē,** *pahee-dis'-kay;* fem. dimin. of *3816;* a *girl,* i.e. (spec.) a *female slave* or *servant:*—damsel {4x}, bondwomen {4x}, maid {3x}, maiden {1x}, bondmaid {1x}.

Syn.: *Paidarion* (*3808*) refers to a child up to his first school years. *Paidion* (*3813*) refers exclusively to little children. *Paidiske* (*3814*) refers to a female in late childhood and early youth. *Pais* (*3816*) refers to a child of any age. *Teknon* (*5043*) gives prominence to physical and outward aspects of parentage. *Huios* (*5207*) gives prominence to the inward, ethical, legal aspects of parentage. *Pais* (*3816*) and *teknon* (*5043*) denote a child as respects to descent and age, reference to the later being more prominent in the former word, to descent in *paidion* (*3813*); but the period *pais* (*3816*) covers is not sharply defined. See: BAGD—604b; THAYER—473c.

3815. παίζω {1x} **paizō,** *paheed'-zo;* from *3816;* to *sport* (to play as a boy):—play {1x}.

Paizo, properly, "to play as a child" (*pais*), hence denotes "to play" as in dancing and making merry, 1 Cor 10:7. See: TDNT—5:625, 758; BAGD—604c; THAYER—473c.

3816. παῖς {24x} **pais,** *paheece;* perh. from *3817;* a *boy* (as often *beaten* with impunity), or (by anal.) a *girl,* and (gen.) a *child;* spec. a *slave* or *servant* (espec. a *minister* to a king; and by eminence to God):—servant {10x}, child {7x}, son (Christ) {2x}, son {1x}, manservant {1x}, maid {1x}, maiden {1x}, young man {1x}.

Syn.: *Paidarion* (*3808*) refers to a child up to his first school years; *paidion* (*3813*) refers exclusively to little children; *paidiske* (*3814*) refers to late childhood and early youth; *pais* (*3816*) stresses the age of the child and refers to a child of any age, not clearly defined; *teknon* (*5043*) stresses descent and gives prominence to physical and outward aspects of parentage; *huios* (*5207*) gives prominence to the inward, ethical, legal aspects of parentage. See: BAGD—604c; THAYER—473d.

3817. παίω {5x} **paiō,** *pah'-yo;* a primary verb; to *hit* (as if by a single blow and less violently than *5180*); spec. to *sting* (as a scorpion):—smite {4x}, strike {1x}.

(1) This verb means to strike, not kill. **(2)** All who are killed are smitten, but not all who are smitten are killed. **(3)** This word signifies "to strike or smite" **(3a)** with the hand or fist, Mt 26:68; Lk 22:64; **(3b)** with a sword, Mk 14:47; Jn 18:10, "struck"; **(3c)** with a sting, Rev 9:5, "striketh." See: BAGD—605b; THAYER—474a.

3818. Πακατιανή {1x} **Pakatianē,** *pak-at-ee-an-ay';* fem. of an adj. of uncert. der.; *Pacatianian,* a section of Phrygia:—Pacatiana {1x}. See: BAGD—605c; THAYER—474b.

3819. πάλαι {6x} **palai,** *pal'-ahee;* prob. another form for *3825* (through the idea of *retrocession*); (adv.) *formerly,* or (by rel.) *sometime since;* (ellip. as adj.) *ancient:*—long ago {1x}, any while {1x}, a great while ago {1x}, old {1x}, in time past {1x}, of old {1x}.

Palai denotes "long ago, of old," **(1)** Heb 1:1, "in time past"; **(2)** in Jude 4, "of old"; **(3)** it is used as an adjective in 2 Pet 1:9, "(his) old (sins)," lit., "his sins of old"; **(4)** "long ago" in Mt 11:12; **(5)** "any while" Mk 15:44; **(6)** "a great while ago" Lk 10:13. See: TDNT—5:717, 769; BAGD—605c; THAYER—474b.

3820. παλαιός {19x} **palaiŏs,** *pal-ah-yos';* from *3819; antique,* i.e. *not recent, worn out:*—old {18x}, old wine {1x}.

Palaios, (Eng., "paleontology," etc.), "of what is of long duration, old in years," etc., **(1)** a garment, wine (in contrast to *neos,* new), Mt 9:16:17; Mk 2:21–22 (twice); Lk 5:36–37, 39 (twice); **(2)** of the treasures of divine truth, Mt

13:52 (compared with *kainos*); **(3)** of what belongs to the past, e.g., the believer's former self before his conversion, his "old man," "old" because it has been superseded by that which is new, Rom 6:6; Eph 4:22 (in contrast to *kainos*); Col 3:9 (in contrast to *neos*); **(4)** of the covenant in connection with the Law, 2 Cor 3:14; **(5)** of leaven, metaphorical of moral evil, 1 Cor 5:7, 8 (in contrast to *neos*); **(6)** of that which was given long ago and remains in force, an "old" commandment, 1 Jn 2:7 (twice), that which was familiar and well known in contrast to that which is fresh. Syn.: In *palaios (3820)* the simple idea of time dominates, while *archaios (744)* often carries with it a suggestion of nature or original character. *Palaios* is out of date, antiquated; and *arachaios* is old in the sense of more or less worn out (Mt 9:16–17). See: TDNT—5:717, 769; BAGD—605d; THAYER—474b.

3821. παλαιότης {1x} **palaiŏtēs,** *pal-ah-yot'-ace;* from *3820; antiquatedness:*—oldness {1x}.

This word occurs in Rom 7:6 of the letter of the law with its rules of conduct, mere outward conformity to which has yielded place in the believer's service to a response to the inward operation of the Holy Spirit. The word is contrasted with *kainotes* (2538 – newness). See: TDNT—5:720, 769; BAGD—606a; THAYER—474c.

3822. παλαιόω {4x} **palaiŏō,** *pal-ah-yŏ'-o;* from *3820;* to *make* (pass. *become*) *worn out,* or *declare obs.:*—decay {1x}, make old {1x}, wax old {2x}.

(1) As wax candles are dipped layer upon layer, this word expresses graduality. **(2)** *Palaioo* "to make old" (*palaios*), is translated in **(2a)** Heb 8:13, first use **(2a1)** "hath made . . . old," **(2a2)** second use (passive voice), "decayeth"; and **(3)** "wax old" in Lk 12:33 and Heb 1:11. See: TDNT—5:720, 769; BAGD—606a.

3823. πάλη {1x} **palē,** *pal'-ay;* from πάλλω **pallō,** (to *vibrate;* another form for *906); wrestling:*—+ wrestle {1x}.

Pallo, "a wrestling" (akin to *pallo,* "to sway, vibrate"), is used figuratively in Eph 6:12, of the spiritual conflict engaged in by believers, "(we) wrestle." See: TDNT—5:721, 770; BAGD—606a; THAYER—474c.

3824. παλιγγενεσία {2x} **paliggĕnĕsia,** *pal-ing-ghen-es-ee'-ah;* from *3825* and *1078;* (spiritual) *rebirth* (the state or the act), i.e. (fig.) spiritual *renovation;* spec. Messianic *restoration:*—regeneration {2x}.

(1) The new birth and regeneration do not represent successive stages in spiritual experience; they refer to the same event but view it in different aspects. **(2)** The new birth stresses the communication of spiritual life in contrast to antecedent spiritual death; regeneration stresses the inception of a new state of things in contrast with the old.

(3) This word means "new birth" (*palin,* "again," *genesis,* "birth"), and is used of "spiritual regeneration," **(3a)** Titus 3:5, involving the communication of a new life, the two operating powers to produce which are **(3a1)** "the word of truth," Jas 1:18; 1 Pet 1:23, and **(3a2)** the Holy Spirit, Jn 3:5, 6; **(3b)** the *loutron,* "the laver, the washing," is explained in Eph 5:26, "having cleansed it by the washing (*loutron*) of water with the word." Syn.: *Anakainosis (342)* is the result of *paliggenesia.* The *paliggenesia* is that free act of God's mercy and power by which He removes the sinner from the kingdom of darkness and places him in the kingdom of light; it is that act by which God brings him from death to life. In the act itself (rather than the preparations for it), the recipient is passive, just as a child has nothing to do with his own birth. *Anakainos,* by contrast, is the gradual conforming of the person to the new spiritual world in which he now lives, the restoration of the divine image. In this process the person is not passive but is a fellow worker with God. See: TDNT—1:686, 117; BAGD—606a; THAYER—474d.

3825. πάλιν {142x} **palin,** *pal'-in;* prob. from the same as *3823* (through the idea of *oscillatory* repetition); (adv.) *anew,* i.e. (of place) *back,* (of time) *once more,* or (conjunc.) *furthermore* or *on the other hand:*—again {142x}.

Palin, the regular word for "again," is used chiefly in two senses, **(1)** with reference to repeated action; **(2)** rhetorically, in the sense **(2a)** of "moreover" or "further," indicating a statement to be added in the course of an argument, e.g., Mt 5:33; or **(2b)** with the meaning "on the other hand, in turn," Lk 6:43; 1 Cor 12:21; 2 Cor 10:7; 1 Jn 2:8. **(3)** In the first chapter of Hebrews, **(3a)** v. 5, *palin* simply introduces an additional quotation; in **(3b)** v. 6 this is not so. That is to say, *palin* is here set in contrast to the time when God *first* brought His Son into the world. This statement, then, refers to the future second advent of Christ. **(4)** The word is used far more frequently in the Gospel of John than in any other book in the New Testament. See: BAGD—606c; THAYER—475a.

3826. παμπληθεί {1x} **pamplēthĕi,** *pam-play-thi';* dat. (adv.) of a compound of *3956* and *4128; in full multitude,* i.e.

concertedly or *simultaneously:*—all at once {1x}. See: BAGD—607b; THAYER—475c.

3827. πάμπολυς {1x} **pampŏlus,** *pam-pol-ooce;* from *3956* and *4183; full many,* i.e. *immense:*—very great {1x}. See: BAGD—607b; THAYER—475c.

3828. Παμφυλία {5x} **Pamphulia,** *pam-fool-ee'-ah;* from a compound of *3956* and *5443; every-tribal,* i.e. *heterogeneous* (*5561* being impl.); *Pamphylia,* a region of Asia Minor:—Pamphylia {5x}. See: BAGD—607b; THAYER—475c.

3829. πανδοχεῖον {1x} **pandŏchĕiŏn,** *pan-dokh-i'-on;* neut. of a presumed compound of *3956* and a der. of *1209; all-receptive,* i.e. a public *lodging*-place (*caravanserai* or *khan*):—inn {1x}.

Pandocheion, lit., "a place where all are received" (*pas,* "all," *dechomai,* "to receive"), denotes "a house for the reception of strangers," a *caravanserai,* translated "inn," in Lk 10:34, in the parable of the good Samaritan. Cattle and beasts of burden could be sheltered there. See: BAGD—607c; THAYER—475d.

3830. πανδοχεύς {1x} **pandŏchĕus,** *pan-dokh-yoos';* from the same as *3829;* an *innkeeper* (*warden of a caravanserai*):—host {1x}.

Pandocheus, lit., "one who receives all" (*pas,* "all," *dechomai,* "to receive"), denotes "an innkeeper, host," Lk 10:35. See: BAGD—475d; THAYER—607d.

3831. πανήγυρις {1x} **panēguris,** *pan-ay'-goo-ris;* from *3956* and a der. of *58;* a *mass-meeting,* i.e. (fig.) *universal companionship:*—gen. assembly {1x}.

The *paneguris* refers to that solemn assembly gathered for festal rejoicing used in Heb 12:23 to represent the church in heaven whose earthly toil and suffering has forever passed away (cf. Rev 21:4). See: TDNT—5:722, 770; BAGD—607d.

3832. πανοικί {1x} **panŏiki,** *pan-oy-kee'* or

πανοικεί **panŏikei,** *pan-oy-ki'* adv. from *3956* and *3624; with the whole family:*—with all his house {1x}. See: BAGD—607d; THAYER—475d.

3833. πανοπλία {3x} **panŏplia,** *pan-op-lee'-ah;* from a compound of *3956* and *3696; full armor* ("panoply"):—all . . . armour {1x}, whole armour {2x}.

Panoplia, lit., "all armor, full armor" (*pas,* "all," *hoplon,* "a weapon"), is used **(1)** of literal "armor," Lk 11:22; **(2)** of the spiritual helps supplied by God for overcoming the tempta-

tions of the devil, Eph 6:11, 13. See: TDNT—5:295, 702; BAGD—607d.

3834. πανουργία {5x} **panŏurgia,** *pan-oorg-ee'-ah;* from *3835; adroitness,* i.e. (in a bad sense) *trickery* or *sophistry:*—cunning craftiness {1x}, craftiness {3x}, subtilty (subtlety) {1x}.

Panourgia literally means all-working, able to do everything; hence, high discerning which works itself out in unscrupulous conduct, craftiness. It is always used in a bad sense, Lk 20:23; 1 Cor 3:19; 2 Cor 4:2; 11:3; Eph 4:14, "cunning craftiness." See: TDNT—5:722, 770; BAGD—608a; THAYER—476a.

3835. πανοῦργος {1x} **panŏurgŏs,** *pan-oor'-gos;* from *3956* and *2041; all-working,* i.e. *adroit* (*shrewd*):—crafty {1x}.

Panourgos, "cunning, crafty," is found in 2 Cor 12:16, where the apostle speaks ironically or is really quoting an accusation made against him by his detractors. Syn.: 3834 for discussion. See: TDNT—5:722, 770; BAGD—608a; THAYER—476a.

3836. πανταχόθεν {1x} **pantachŏthĕn,** *pan-takh-oth'-en;* adv. (of *source*) from *3837; from all* directions:—from every quarter {1x}. See: BAGD—608b; THAYER—476b.

3837. πανταχοῦ {7x} **pantachŏu,** *pan-takh-oo';* gen. (as adv. of *place*) of a presumed der. of *3956; universally:*—in all places {1x}, everywhere {6x}.

Pantachou, as an adverb is translated **(1)** "everywhere" in **(1a)** Mk 16:20, of preaching; **(1b)** Lk 9:6, of healing; **(1c)** Acts 17:30, of a divine command for repentance; **(1d)** Acts 28:22, of disparagement of Christians; **(1e)** 1 Cor 4:17, of apostolic teaching; **(2)** in Acts 24:3, it is rendered "in all places": "We accept it always, and in all places, most noble Felix, with all thankfulness." Syn.: 201, 402, 1096, 1502, 4042, 5117, 5247, 5564, 5602. See: BAGD—608b; THAYER—476b.

3838. παντελής {2x} **pantĕlēs,** *pan-tel-ace';* an adverb of manner from *3956* and *5056; full-ended,* i.e. *entire* (neut. as noun, *completion*):—in no wise + *1519* + *3588* {1x}, uttermost {1x}.

Panteles, the neuter of the adjective *panteles,* "complete, perfect," used with *eis to* ("unto the"), is translated **(1)** "to the uttermost" in Heb 7:25, where the meaning is "finally and completely in all ways"; **(2)** in Lk 13:11 (negatively), "in no wise." See: TDNT—8:66, 1161; BAGD—608c; THAYER—476b.

3839. **πάντη** {1x} **pantē**, *pan'-tay;* adv. (of *manner*) from *3956; wholly:*— always {1x}.

This word means everywhere, wholly, in all respects, in every way and is found in Acts 24:3. See: BAGD—608d; THAYER—476b.

3840. **παντόθεν** {2x} **pantŏthĕn**, *pan-toth'-en;* adv. (of *source*) from *3956; from* (i.e. *on*) *all* sides:—on every side {1x}, round about {1x}.

Pantothen, "from all sides," is translated **(1)** in Lk 19:43, "on every side"; and **(2)** in Heb 9:4, "round about." See: BAGD—608d; THAYER—476b.

3841. **παντοκράτωρ** {10x} **pantŏkratōr**, *pan-tok-rat'-ore;* from *3956* and *2904;* the *all-ruling,* i.e. *God* (as absolute and universal *sovereign*):—Almighty {9x}, Omnipotent {1x}.

Pantokrator, "almighty, or ruler of all" (*pas,* "all," *krateo,* "to hold, or to have strength"), is used of God only, and is found, **(1)** in the Epistles, only in 2 Cor 6:18, where the title is suggestive in connection with the context; **(2)** elsewhere only in the Apocalypse, 1:8; 4:8; 11:17; 15:3; 16:7, 14; 19:6, "omnipotent"; 19:15; 21:22. See: TDNT—3:914, 466; BAGD—608d; THAYER—476b.

3842. **πάντοτε** {42x} **pantŏtĕ**, *pan'-tot-eh;* from *3956* and *3753; every when,* i.e. *at all* times:—always {29x}, ever {6x}, alway {5x}, evermore {2x}.

Pantote, "at all times, always" (akin to *pas,* "all"), is translated **(1)** "always", Mt 26:11; Mk 14:7 (twice); Lk 18:1; Jn 8:29; 11:42; 12:8 (twice); 18:20 (second part); Rom 1:9; 1 Cor 1:4; 15:58; 2 Cor 2:14; 4:10; 5:6; 9:8; Gal 4:18; Eph 5:20; Phil 1:4, 20; 2:12; Col 1:3; 4:12; 1 Th 1:2; 3:6; 2 Th 1:3, 11; Philem 4; **(2)** "always", Phil 4:4; Col 4:6; 1 Th 2:16; 2 Th 2:13; **(3)** "ever", Lk 15:31; Jn 18:20 (first part); 1 Th 4:7; 5:15; 2 Ti 3:7; Heb 7:25; and **(4)** "evermore", Jn 6:34; 7:6, 1 Th 5:16. **(5)** "Always" stresses manner: "all ways, all means" and **(6)** "alway" stresses time, "all the way." See: BAGD—609b; THAYER—476c.

3843. **πάντως** {9x} **pantōs**, *pan'-toce;* adv. from *3956; entirely;* spec. *at all events,* (with neg. following) *in no event:*— by all means {2x}, altogether {2x}, surely {1x}, must needs + 1163 {1x}, no doubt {1x}, in no wise {1x}, at all {1x}.

Pantos, when used **(1)** without a negative, signifies **(1a)** "wholly, entirely, by all means," Acts 18:21; 1 Cor 9:22; **(1b)** "altogether," 1 Cor 9:10; **(1c)** "surely," Lk 4:23; Acts 28:4. **(1d)** In Acts 21:22 it is translated "needs" (lit., "by all means"). **(2)** With a negative it signifies "in no

wise," Rom 3:9; 1 Cor 5:10; 16:12 (at all). See: BAGD—609b; THAYER—476c.

3844. **παρά** { {200x} **para**, *par-ah';* a primary prep.; prop. *near;* i.e. (with gen.) *from beside* (lit. or fig.), (with dat.) *at* (or *in*) the *vicinity* of (object or subject), (with acc.) to the *proximity* with (local [espec. *beyond* or *opposed* to] or causal [*on account* of]):—of {51x}, with {42x}, from {24x}, by . . . side {15x}, at {12x}, than {11x}, misc. {45x} = above, against, among, before, by, contrary to, ✕ friend, + give [such things as they], + that [she] had, ✕ his, in, more than, nigh unto, out of, past, save, in the sight of, then, [there-] fore.

(1) In compounds it retains the same variety of application. **(2)** It has the meaning "contrary to" in Acts 18:13; Rom 11:24; 16:17; **(3)** "other than" in Gal 1:8. See: TDNT—5:727, 771; BAGD—609c; THAYER—476d.

3845. **παραβαίνω** {4x} **parabainō**, *par-ab-ah'-ee-no;* from *3844* and the base of *939;* to *go contrary* to, i.e. *violate* a command:—transgression {3x}, fall by transgression {1x}.

Parabaino, lit., "to go aside" (*para*), hence "to go beyond," **(1)** is chiefly used metaphorically **(1a)** of "transgressing" the tradition of the elders, Mt 15:2; **(1b)** the commandment of God, Mt 15:3; and **(2)** in Acts 1:25, of Judas, "by transgression fell." **(3)** *Parabaino* means to overstep, disregard an accepted boundary either on purpose or neglect; to violate. Syn.: 3847. See: TDNT—5:736, 772; BAGD—611c; THAYER—478c.

3846. **παραβάλλω** {2x} **paraballō**, *par-ab-al'-lo;* from *3844* and *906;* to *throw alongside,* i.e. (refl.) to *reach* a place, or (fig.) to *liken:*—arrive {1x}, compare {1x}.

Paraballo, "to place side by side, to set forth," and the noun *parabole* (Eng., "parable"), **(1)** occur in Mk 4:30, "with what comparison shall we compare it?" **(2)** This word means to put one thing by the side of another for the sake of comparison. See: BAGD—611d; THAYER—478d.

3847. **παράβασις** {7x} **parabasis**, *par-ab'-as-is;* from *3845; viola-tion:*—breaking {1x}, transgression {6x}.

(1) *Parabasis* is the act of excessive and enormous transgression of a stated law or a given commandment. **(2)** This word means primarily "a going aside," then, "an overstepping," is used metaphorically to denote "transgression" (always of a breach of law): **(2a)** of Adam, Rom 5:14; **(2b)** of Eve, 1 Ti 2:14; **(2c)** negatively, where there is no law, since "transgression" implies the violation of law, none having been enacted between Adam's

"transgression" and those under the Law, Rom 4:15; **(2d)** of "transgressions" of the Law, Gal 3:19, where the statement "it was added because of transgressions" is best understood according to Rom 4:15; 5:13 and 5:20; the Law does not make men sinners, but makes them "transgressors"; hence sin becomes "exceeding sinful," Rom 7:7, 13. Conscience thus had a standard external to itself; by the Law men are taught their inability to yield complete obedience to God, that thereby they may become convinced of their need of a Savior; **(3)** in Rom 2:23, "breaking (the Law)"; Heb 2:2; 9:15. Syn.: 51, 265, 266, 458, 2275, 3876, 3892, 3900. See: TDNT—5:739, 772; BAGD—611d; THAYER—478d.

3848. **παραβάτης** {5x} **parabatēs**, *par-ab-at'-ace;* from *3845;* a *violator:*— breaker {1x}, transgress {1x}, transgressor {3x}.

A *parabates* is "a transgressor", and is translated **(1)** "breaker," Rom 2:25. **(2)** in Rom 2:27 "dost transgress"; and **(3)** "transgressor" in Gal 2:18; Jas 2:9, plural, 11. Syn.: 3847. See: TDNT—5:740, 772; BAGD—612a; THAYER—479a.

3849. **παραβιάζομαι** {2x} **parabiazōmai**, *par-ab-ee-ad'-zom-ahee;* from *3844* and the mid. voice of *971;* to *force contrary* to (nature), i.e. *compel* (by entreaty):—constrain {2x}.

Parabiazomai, as a verb, primarily denotes "to employ force contrary to nature and right, to compel by using force" [*para,* "alongside," intensive, *biazo,* "to force"], and is used only of "constraining" by entreaty, **(1)** as the two going to Emmaus did to Christ: "But they constrained Him, saying, Abide with us: for it is toward evening, and the day is far spent. And He went in to tarry with them" (Lk 24:29); and **(2)** as Lydia did to Paul and his companions: "And when she was baptized, and her household, she besought us, saying, If ye have judged me to be faithful to the Lord, come into my house, and abide there. And she constrained us" (Acts 16:15). Syn.: 315, 317, 4912. See: BAGD—612a; THAYER—479a.

3850. **παραβολή** {50x} **parabŏlē**, *par-ab-ol-ay';* from *3846;* a *similitude* ("*parable*"), i.e. (symbol.) *fictitious narrative* (of common life conveying a mor.), *apothegm* or *adage:*—comparison {1x}, figure {2x}, parable {46x}, proverb {1x}.

Parabole, as a noun, lit. denotes "a placing beside" (akin to *paraballo,* "to throw" or "lay beside, to compare"). **(1)** It signifies "a placing of one thing beside another" with a view to comparison (some consider that the thought of comparison is not necessarily contained in the

word). **(2)** In the NT it is found outside the gospels, only in Heb 9:9 and 11:19. **(3)** It is generally used of a somewhat lengthy utterance or narrative drawn from nature or human circumstances, the object of which is to set forth a spiritual lesson, e.g., those in Mt 13 and Synoptic parallels; **(3a)** sometimes it is used of a short saying or proverb, e.g., Mt 15:15; Mk 3:23; 7:17; Lk 4:23; 5:36; 6:39. **(3b)** It is the lesson that is of value; the hearer must catch the analogy if he is to be instructed (this is true also of a proverb). **(3c)** Such a narrative or saying, dealing with earthly things with a spiritual meaning, is distinct from a fable, which attributes to things what does not belong to them in nature.

(4) Christ's "parables" most frequently convey truths connected with the subject of the kingdom of God. **(4a)** His withholding the meaning from His hearers as He did from the multitudes, Mt 13:34, was a divine judgment upon the unworthy. A parable hides the truth from unbelievers and reveals the truth to the soft hearted, the fourth soil in the parable of "the sower", Mt 13:1f. **(5)** Two dangers are to be avoided in seeking to interpret the "parables" in Scripture, **(5a)** that of ignoring the important features, and **(5b)** that of trying to make all the details mean something. Syn.: 3942. See: TDNT—5:744, 773; BAGD—612b; THAYER—479b.

3851. **παραβουλεύομαι** {1x} **parabŏuleuŏmai**, *par-ab-ool-yoo'-om-ahee* or

παραβολεύομαι **parabŏleuŏmai**, *par-ab-ol-yoo'-om-ahee* from *3844,* and the mid. voice of *1011;* to *misconsult,* i.e. *disregard:*—not (to) regard (-ing) {1x}.

Literally, this verb means to throw aside; hence, to expose oneself to danger, to hazard one's life as said of Ephaphroditus (Phil 2:30). See: BAGD—613a; THAYER—479c.

3852. **παραγγελία** {5x} **paraggēlia**, *par-ang-gel-ee'-ah;* from *3853;* a *mandate:*—charge {2x}, commandment {2x}, straitly {1x}.

This word means "a proclamation, a command or commandment," and is strictly used of commands received from a superior and transmitted to others. It is rendered **(1)** "charge" in Acts 16:24; 1 Ti 1:18; **(2)** "commandment" in 1 Ti 1:5; 1 Th 4:2, plural; and **(3)** "straitly" in Acts 5:28, literally meaning "Did we not command you with a command?" See: TDNT—5:761, 776; BAGD—613a; THAYER—479d.

3853. **παραγγέλλω** {31x} **paraggēllō**, *par-ang-gel'-lo;* from *3844*

and the base of *32;* to *transmit a message,* i.e. (by impl.) to *enjoin:*—command {20x}, charge {6x}, give commandment {1x}, give charge {1x}, declare {1x}, give in charge {1x}, vr. command {1x}.

This word means "to announce beside" (*para,* "beside," *angello,* "to announce"), "to pass on an announcement," hence denotes "to give the word, order, give a charge, command", e.g., Mk 6:8; Lk 8:29; 9:21; Acts 5:28; 2 Th 3:4, 6, 10, 12. Syn.: *Entellomai (1781)* means to enjoin, is used esp. of those whose office or position invests them with claims, and points rather to the contents of the command, cf our instruction. *Keleuo (2753)* means to command and designates verbal orders, coming usually from a superior. *Paraggello (3853)* means to charge, and is used esp. of the order of a military commander to his troops. *Tasso (5021)* means to assign a post to, with a suggestion of duties connected with it, often used of military appointments. *Paraggello (3853)* differs from *entellomai (1781)* in denoting fixed and abiding obligations rather than specific or occasional instructions, duties arising from the office rather than coming from the personal will of a superior. See: TDNT—5:761, 776; BAGD—613b; THAYER—479d.

3854. **παραγίνομαι** {37x}　**paraginŏmai,** *par-ag-in'-om-ahee;* from *3844* and *1096;* to *become near,* i.e. *approach (have arrived);* by impl. to *appear* on the scene publicly:—come {35x}, go {1x}, be present {1x}.

This word means to come forth, make one's public appearance such as John the baptizer, Mt 3:1. See: BAGD—613c; THAYER—479d.

3855. **παράγω** {10x} **paragō,** *par-ag'-o;* from *3844* and *71;* to *lead near,* i.e. (refl. or intr.) to *go along* or *away:*—pass by {5x}, pass away {2x}, pass forth {1x}, depart {1x}, pass {1x}.

Parago, used intransitively, means (1) "to pass by" (*para,* "by, beside"), and is so translated everywhere in the Gospels, except in Mt 9:27, "departed." (2) Outside the Gospels it is used in its other meaning, "to pass away," 1 Cor 7:31; 1 Jn 2:8 "past", 17. (3) It also means "to pass by, pass away," in Mt 9:9, "passed forth", and (4) is used in the middle voice in 1 Jn 2:8, "is past", (4a) of the "passing" of spiritual darkness through the light of the gospel, and (4b) in 1 Jn 2:17 of the world. See: TDNT—1:129, 20; BAGD—613d; THAYER—480a.

3856. **παραδειγματίζω** {2x} **paradĕigmatizō,** *par-ad-igue-mat-id'-zo;* from *3844* and *1165;* to *show alongside* (the public), i.e. *expose to infamy:*—

make a public example {1x}, put to an open shame {1x}.

Paradeigmatizo, as a verb, signifies "to set forth as an example" (*para,* "beside," *deiknumi,* "to show"), and is used (1) in Mt 1:19: "Then Joseph, her husband, being a just man, and not willing to make her a public example (*paradeigmatizo*), was minded to put her away privily." (2) It is also used in Heb 6:6, "put (Christ) to open shame" by the apostate Christians. Syn.: 150, 152, 808, 818, 819, 1788, 1791, 2617. See: TDNT—2:32, 141; BAGD—614a; THAYER—480b.

3857. **παράδεισος** {3x} **paradĕisŏs,** *par-ad'-i-sos;* of Oriental or. [comp. 6508]; a *park,* i.e. (spec.) an *Eden* (place of future happiness, "*paradise*"):—paradise {3x}.

Paradeisos, "paradise" is found: (1) In Lk 23:43, the promise of the Lord to the repentant robber was fulfilled the same day; (1a) Christ, at His death, having committed His spirit to the Father, went in spirit immediately into heaven itself, the dwelling place of God. (1b) The Lord's mention of the place as "paradise" must have been a great comfort to the malefactor because it expressed the sum total of blessedness. (2) Thither the apostle Paul was caught up, 2 Cor 12:4, spoken of as "the third heaven" (v. 3 does not introduce a different vision), (2a) beyond the heavens of the natural creation. (2b) The same region is mentioned in Rev 2:7, where the "tree of life," the figurative antitype of that in Eden, held out to the overcomer, is spoken of as being in "the Paradise of God" as in Gen 2:8. (3) In the OT see (3a) Neh 2:8; Eccl 2:5; Song 4:13. (3b) It is also used of (3b1) the garden of Eden, Gen 2:8, and (3b2) in other respects, e.g., Num 24:6; Is 1:30; Jer 29:5; Eze 31:8–9. See: TDNT—5:765, 777; BAGD—614a; THAYER—480b.

3858. **παραδέχομαι** {5x} **paradĕchŏmai,** *par-ad-ekh'-om-ahee;* from *3844* and *1209;* to *accept near,* i.e. receive with approval, *admit* or (by impl.) *delight* in:—receive {5x}.

Paradechomai, as a verb, means "to receive or admit with approval" and is used (1) of persons: "For whom the Lord loveth He chasteneth, and scourgeth every son whom He receiveth" (Heb 12:6); (2) of things: "And these are they which are sown on good ground; such as hear the word, and receive it, and bring forth fruit, some thirtyfold, some sixty, and some an hundred" (Mk 4:20; cf. Acts 16:21; 22:18; 1 Ti 5:9). Syn.: 324, 353, 354, 568, 588, 618, 1209, 1523, 1926, 2210, 2865, 2975, 2983, 3028, 3335, 3336, 3880, 3970, 4327, 4355, 4356, 4380, 4381,

4382, 5562, 5264, 5274. See: BAGD—614b; THAYER—480d.

3859. **παραδιατριβή** {1x} **paradiatribē,** *par-ad-ee-at-ree-bay';* from a compound of *3844* and *1304; misemployment,* i.e. *meddlesomeness:*—perverse disputing {1x}.

This word denotes a constant or incessant wrangling, to wear out, suggesting the attrition or wearing effect of contention, "perverse disputings", 1 Ti 6:5. See: BAGD—614b; THAYER—480d.

3860. **παραδίδωμι** {121x} **paradidōmi,** *par-ad-id'-o-mee;* from *3844* and *1325;* to *surrender,* i.e. to deliver over to another to keep, *yield up, intrust, transmit:*—deliver {53x}, betray {40x}, deliver up {10x}, give {4x}, give up {4x}, give over {2x}, commit {2x}, misc. {6x} = bring forth, cast, hazard, put in prison, recommend.

Paradidomi, as a verb, means "to deliver over": **(1)** "But God be thanked, that ye were the servants of sin, but ye have obeyed from the heart that form of doctrine which was delivered you" (Rom 6:17). **(2)** In Rom 8:32 it is used of God in "delivering" His Son to expiatory death: "He that spared not His own Son, but delivered Him up for us all, how shall He not with Him also freely give us all things?" (cf. Rom 4:25; Mk 9:31); **(3)** of Christ in "delivering" Himself up: "I am crucified with Christ: nevertheless I live; yet not I, but Christ liveth in me: and the life which I now live in the flesh I live by the faith of the Son of God, who loved me, and gave Himself for me" (Gal 2:20; cf. Eph 5:2, 25).

(4) *Pardidomi* also means "to give over, commit, deliver" and also signifies "is brought forth": "But when the fruit is brought forth, immediately he putteth in the sickle, because the harvest is come" (Mk 4:29 – the grain is ready to be given over the table as food). **(5)** It is also translated "to betray" (*para,* "up," *didomi,* "to give"), lit., "to give over," and is used either **(5a)** in the sense of delivering a person or thing to be kept by another, to commend, e.g., Acts 28:16; **(5b)** to deliver to prison or judgment, e.g., Mt 4:12; 1 Ti 1:20; **(5c)** to deliver over treacherously by way of "betrayal," Mt 17:22; 26:16; Jn 6:64 etc.; **(5d)** to hand on, deliver, e.g., 1 Cor 11:23; **(5e)** to allow of something being done, said of the ripening of fruit, Mk 4:29. Syn.: 187, 325, 525, 629, 591, 859, 1325, 1560, 1659, 1807, 1929, 3583, 4506, 5483. See: TDNT—2:169, 166; BAGD—614b; THAYER—480d.

3861. **παράδοξος** {1x} **paradŏxŏs,** *par-ad'-ox-os;* from *3844* and *1391*

(in the sense of *seeming*); *contrary to expectation,* i.e. *extraordinary* ("*paradox*"):—strange {1x}.

Paradoxos (Lk 5:26) describes miracles not previously seen (cf. Mk 2:12); hence "strange" and thus they are beside and beyond people's opinions and expectations. Syn.: 1411, 1741, 2297, 3167, 6592, 5059. See: TDNT—2:255, 178; BAGD—615d; THAYER—481d.

3862. **παράδοσις** {13x} **paradŏsis,** *par-ad'-os-is;* from *3860; transmission,* i.e. (concr.) a *precept;* spec. the Jewish *traditionary law:*—ordinance {1x}, tradition {12x}.

Paradosis, "a handing down or on" (akin to *paradidomi,* "to hand over, deliver"), denotes "a tradition," and hence, by metonymy, **(1)** "the teachings of the rabbis," interpretations of the Law, which was thereby made void in practice, Mt 15:2, 3, 6; Mk 7:3, 5, 8, 9, 13; Gal 1:14; Col 2:8; **(2)** of "apostolic teaching," 1 Cor 11:2, "ordinances", of instructions concerning the gatherings of believers (instructions of wider scope than ordinances in the limited sense); **(3)** in 2 Th 2:15, of Christian doctrine in general, where the apostle's use of the word constitutes a denial that what he preached originated with himself, and a claim for its divine authority; **(4)** in 2 Th 3:6, it is used of instructions concerning everyday conduct. See: TDNT—2:172, 166; BAGD—615d; THAYER—481d.

3863. **παραζηλόω** {4x} **parazēlŏō,** *par-ad-zay-lŏ'-o;* from *3844* and *2206;* to *stimulate alongside,* i.e. *excite to rivalry:*—provoke to emulation {1x}, provoke to jealousy {3x}.

Parazeloo, "to provoke to jealousy" (*para,* "beside," used intensively, is found **(1)** in Rom 10:19 and 11:11, of God's dealings with Israel through his merciful dealings with Gentiles; **(2)** in Rom 11:14, "I may provoke to emulation", of the apostle's evangelical ministry to Gentiles with a view to stirring his fellow nationals to a sense of their need and responsibilities regarding the gospel; **(3)** in 1 Cor 10:22, of the provocation of God on the part of believers who compromise their divine relationship by partaking of the table of demons; **(4)** in Gal 5:20, of the works of the flesh. See: TDNT—2:881, 297; BAGD—616a; THAYER—482a.

3864. **παραθαλάσσιος** {1x} **parathalassiŏs,** *par-ath-al-as'-see-os;* from *3844* and *2281; along* the *sea,* i.e. *maritime* (*lacustrine*):—upon the sea coast {1x}. See: BAGD—616a; THAYER—482a.

3865. **παραθεωρέω** {1x} **parathēōreō,** *par-ath-eh-o-reh'-o;* from *3844* and *2334;* to *overlook* or *disregard:*—neglect {1x}.

Paratheoreo, primarily, "to examine side by side, compare" (*para,* "beside," *theoreo,* "to look at"), hence, "to overlook, to neglect," is used in Acts 6:1, of the "neglect" of widows in the daily ministration in Jerusalem. See: BAGD—616b; THAYER—482a.

3866. παραθήκη {1x} **parathēkē,** *par-ath-ay'-kay;* from *3908;* a *deposit,* i.e. (fig.) *trust:*—that . . . committed {1x}.

Paratheke, "a putting with, a deposit" (*para,* "with," *tithemi,* "to put"), is found in 2 Ti 1:12, "that which I have committed unto Him." See: TDNT—8:162, 1176; BAGD—616b; THAYER—482b.

3867. παραινέω {2x} **parainĕō,** *par-ahee-neh'-o;* from *3844* and *134;* to *mispraise,* i.e. *recommend* or *advise* (a different course):—admonish {1x}, exhort {1x}.

Paraineo, "to admonish by way of exhorting or advising," is found in Acts 27:9, "Paul admonished them", and v. 22, "and now I exhort you", based on the admonition to put what I said into action. See: BAGD—616b; THAYER—482b.

3868. παραιτέομαι {11x} **paraitĕŏmai,** *par-ahee-teh'-om-ahee;* from *3844* and the mid. voice of *154;* to *beg off,* i.e. *deprecate, decline, shun:*—avoid {1x}, make excuse {1x}, excuse {2x}, intreat {1x}, refuse {1x}, reject {1x}.

Pariteomai, lit., "to ask aside" (*para,* "aside," *aiteo,* "to ask"), signifies **(1)** "to entreat (that) not," Heb 12:19; **(2)** "to refuse, decline, avoid," 1 Ti 4:7; 5:11; 2 Ti 2:23; Titus 3:10; Heb 12:25; **(3)** "to beg off, ask to be excused," Lk 14:18–19. See: TDNT—1:195, 30; BAGD—616c; THAYER—482b.

3869. παρακαθίζω {1x} **parakathizō,** *par-ak-ath-id'-zo;* from *3844* and *2523;* to *sit down near:*—sit {1x}.

Parakathezomai, as a verb, means "to sit down beside" and in a passive voice form occurs in Lk 10:39: "And she had a sister called Mary, which also sat (*parakathezomai*) at Jesus' feet, and heard His word." Syn.: 339, 345, 347, 377, 1910, 2516, 2521, 2621, 2523, 2625, 4775, 4776, 4873. See: BAGD—616d; THAYER—482c.

3870. παρακαλέω {109x} **parakalĕō,** *par-ak-al-eh'-o;* from *3844* and *2564;* to *call near,* i.e. *invite, invoke* (by *imploration, hortation* or *consolation*):—beseech {43x}, comfort {23x}, exhort {21x}, desire {8x}, pray {6x}, intreat {3x}, vr besought {1x}, misc. {4x} = call for, (give) exhort (-ation).

Parakaleo, the most frequent word with this meaning, lit. denotes "to call to one's side,"

hence, "to call to one's aid." It is used for every kind of calling to a person which is meant to produce a particular effect, hence, with various meanings, such as "comfort, exhort, desire, call for," in addition to its significance "to beseech," which has a stronger force than *aiteo.* See: TDNT—5:773, 778; BAGD—617a; THAYER—482c.

3871. παρακαλύπτω {1x} **parakaluptō,** *par-ak-al-oop'-to;* from *3844* and *2572;* to *cover alongside,* i.e. *veil* (fig.):—hide {1x}.

Parakalupto, "to conceal thoroughly" (*para,* "beside," intensive, *kalupto,* "to hide"), is found in Lk 9:45, of "concealing" from the disciples the fact of the delivering up of Christ. See: BAGD—617d; THAYER—483b.

3872. παρακαταθήκη {2x} **parakatathēkē,** *par-ak-at-ath-ay'-kay;* from a compound of *3844* and *2698;* something *put down alongside,* i.e. a *deposit* (sacred *trust*):—that (thing) which is committed (un-) to (trust) + 3588 {2x}.

A deposit, a trust or thing consigned to one's faithful keeping; used of the correct knowledge and pure doctrine of the gospel, to be held firmly and faithfully, and to be conscientiously delivered unto others; 1 Ti 6:20; 2 Ti 1:14. See: TDNT—8:162, 1176; BAGD—617d; THAYER—483b.

3873. παράκειμαι {2x} **parakĕimai,** *par-ak'-i-mahee;* from *3844* and *2749;* to *lie near,* i.e. *be at hand* (fig. *be prompt* or *easy*):—be present {2x}.

Parakeimai, "to lie beside" (*para,* and *keimai,* "to lie"), "to be near," is translated "is present" in Rom 7:18, 21. See: TDNT—3:656, 425; BAGD—617d; THAYER—483b.

3874. παράκλησις {29x} **paraklēsis,** *par-ak'-lay-sis;* from *3870;* *imploration, hortation, solace:*—comfort {6x}, consolation {14x}, exhortation {8x}, intreaty {1x}.

Paraklesis, means "a calling to one's side" (*para,* "beside," *kaleo,* "to call"); hence, **(1)** either "an exhortation, or consolation, comfort," e.g., Lk 2:25 (here "looking for the consolation of Israel" is equivalent to waiting for the coming of the Messiah); 6:24; Acts 9:31; Rom 15:4–5; 1 Cor 14:3, "exhortation"; 2 Cor 1:3, 4–7; 7:4, 7, 13; 2 Th 2:16; Philem 7. **(2)** In 2 Th 2:16 it combines encouragement with alleviation of grief; **(3)** "consolation", Lk 2:25; 6:24; Acts 4:36; 15:31; Heb 6:18; in Acts 4:36. See: TDNT—5:773, 778; BAGD—618a; THAYER—483b.

3875. **παράκλητος** {5x} **paraklētŏs,** *par-ak′-lay-tos;* an *intercessor, consoler:*—advocate {1x}, comforter {4x}.

Parakletos is the one summoned, called to one's side, esp. called to one's aid and is used of **(1)** Christ in his exaltation at God's right hand, pleading with God the Father for the pardon of our sins (1 Jn 2:1); and **(2)** the Holy Spirit destined to take the place of Christ with the apostles (after Christ's ascension to the Father), to lead them to a deeper knowledge of the gospel truth, and give them divine strength needed to enable them to undergo trials and persecutions on behalf of the divine kingdom (Jn 14:16;14:26; 15:26; 16:7). See: TDNT—5:800, 782; BAGD—618b; THAYER—483c.

3876. **παρακοή** {3x} **parakŏē,** *par-ak-ŏ-ay′;* from *3878; inattention,* i.e. (by impl.) *disobedience:*—disobedience {3x}.

(1) Carelessness in attitude is the precursor of actual disobedience, the mind and will both wavering. Primarily, *parakoe,* means "hearing amiss" (*para,* "aside," *akouo,* "to hear"), hence signifies "a refusal to hear"; hence, **(2)** "an act of disobedience," Rom 5:19; 2 Cor 10:6; Heb 2:2. Syn.: It is broadly to be distinguished from *apeitheia* as an act from a condition, though *parakoe* itself is the effect, in transgression, of the condition of failing or refusing to hear. **(3)** In the OT "disobedience" is frequently described as "a refusing to hear," e.g., Jer 11:10; 35:17; cf. Acts 7:57. Syn.: 51, 265, 266, 458, 2275, 3847, 3892, 3900. See: TDNT—1:223, 34; BAGD—618d; THAYER—483d.

3877. **παρακολουθέω** {4x} **parakŏlŏuthĕō,** *par-ak-ol-oo-theh′-o;* from *3844* and *190;* to *follow near,* i.e. (fig.) *attend* (as a result), *trace out, conform* to:—attain {1x}, follow {1x}, fully know {1x}, have understanding {1x}.

Parakoleutheo, as a verb, literally signifies "to follow close up, or side by side," hence, "to accompany, to conform to" and is used of **(1)** signs accompanying "them that believe" (Mk 16:17); **(2)** of tracing the course of facts (Lk 1:3); **(3)** of "following" good doctrine (1 Ti 4:6); **(4)** similarly of "following" teaching so as to practice it: "But thou hast fully known (*parakoloutheo*) my doctrine, manner of life, purpose, faith, longsuffering, charity, patience," (2 Ti 3:10). Syn.: 190, 1096, 1377, 1811, 1872, 2614, 2628, 4870. See: TDNT—1:215, 33; BAGD—618d; THAYER—484a.

3878. **παρακούω** {2x} **parakŏuō,** *par-ak-oo′-o;* from *3844* and *191;* to *mishear,* i.e. (by impl.) to *disobey:*—neglect to hear {2x}.

Parakouo primarily signifies "to overhear,

---

hear amiss or imperfectly" (*para,* "beside, amiss"); then (in the NT) "to hear without taking heed, to neglect to hear," Mt 18:17 (twice). It seems obvious that the Lord paid no attention to those from the ruler's house and their message that his daughter was dead. Syn.: 189, 191, 1251, 1522, 1873, 1874, 3876, 4257. See: TDNT—1:223, 34; BAGD—619a; THAYER—484a.

3879. **παρακύπτω** {5x} **parakuptō,** *par-ak-oop′-to;* from *3844* and *2955;* to *bend beside,* i.e. *lean over* (so as to *peer within*):—look (into) {2x}, stoop down {3x}.

Parakupto, as a verb, means literally and primarily "to stoop sideways" and denotes **(1)** "to stoop to look into": "Then arose Peter, and ran unto the sepulchre; and stooping down, he beheld the linen clothes" (Lk 24:12 "stooping and looking in"); **(2)** metaphorically in Jas 1:25, of "looking" into the perfect law of liberty; and **(3)** in 1 Pet 1:12 of things which the angels desire "to look into." Syn.: 308, 352, 578, 816, 872, 991, 1689, 1896, 1914, 1980, 1983, 2300, 2334, 3706, 3708, 4017, 4648. See: TDNT—5:814, 784; BAGD—619b; THAYER—484a.

3880. **παραλαμβάνω** {50x} **paralambanō,** *par-al-am-ban′-o;* from *3844* and *2983;* to *receive near,* i.e. *associate with* oneself (in any familiar or intimate act or relation); by anal. to *assume* an office; fig. to *learn:*—take {30x}, receive {15x}, take unto {2x}, take up {2x}, take away {1x}.

Paralambano, "to receive from another" (*para,* "from beside"), signifies **(1)** "to receive," e.g., in Mk 7:4; Jn 1:11; 14:3; 1 Cor 11:23; 15:1, 3; Gal 1:9, 12; Phil 4:9; Col 2:6; 4:17; 1 Th 2:13 (1st part); 4:1; 2 Th 3:6; Heb 12:28. It also denotes **(2)** "to take to (or with) oneself," **(2a)** of "taking" a wife, e.g., Mt 1:20, 24; **(2b)** of "taking" a person or persons with one, e.g., Mt 2:13, 14, 20, 21; 4:5, 8; **(2c)** of devils, Mt 12:45; **(2d)** of Christ and His disciples, Mt 17:1; 20:17; Mk 9:2; 10:32; 14:33; **(2e)** of witnesses, Mt 18:16; **(2f)** of the removal of persons from the earth in judgment, when "the Son of Man is revealed," Mt 24:40, 41; Lk 17:34, 35 (cf. the means of the removal of corruption, in v. 37); **(2g)** of the "taking" of Christ by the soldiers for scourging, Mt 27:27, and to crucifixion, Jn 19:16; **(2h)** see also Acts 15:39; 16:33; 21:24, 26, 32; 23:18. See: TDNT—4:11, 495; BAGD—619b; THAYER—484b.

3881. **παραλέγομαι** {2x} **paralĕgŏmai,** *par-al-eg′-om-ahee;* from *3844* and the mid. voice of *3004* (in its orig.

sense); (spec.) to *lay* one's course *near,* i.e. *sail past:*—pass {1x}, sail by {1x}.

This word is used, in the middle voice, as a nautical term, **(1)** "to sail past," Acts 27:8, **(2)** "coasting along"; Acts 27:13, "sailed by." See: BAGD—619d; THAYER—484d.

3882. **παράλιος** {1x} **paraliŏs,** *par-al'-ee-os;* from *3844* and *251; beside* the *salt* (*sea*), i.e. *maritime:*—sea coast {1x}. See: BAGD—620a; THAYER—484d.

3883. **παραλλαγή** {1x} **parallagē,** *par-al-lag-ay';* from a compound of *3844* and *236; transmutation* (of phase or orbit), i.e. (fig.) *fickleness:*—variableness {1x}.

Parallage denotes, in general, "a change" (Eng., "parallax," the difference between the directions of a body as seen from two different points), "a transmission" from one condition to another; it occurs in Jas 1:17, "variableness", and speaks of God's immutability. See: BAGD—620a; THAYER—484d.

3884. **παραλογίζομαι** {2x} **paralŏgizŏmai,** *par-al-og-id'-zom-ahee;* from *3844* and *3049;* to deceive by false reasoning, *misreckon,* i.e. *delude:*—beguile {1x}, deceive {1x}.

Paralogizomai means lit. and primarily, "to reckon wrong," hence means "to reason falsely" (*para,* "from, amiss," *logizomai,* "to reason") or "to deceive by false reasoning"; translated **(1)** "beguile" in Col 2:4, and **(2)** Jas 1:22 "deceive." See: BAGD—620b; THAYER—484d.

3885. **παραλυτικός** {10x} **paralutikŏs,** *par-al-oo-tee-kos';* from a der. of *3886;* as if *dissolved,* i.e. *"paralytic":*—sick of palsy {9x}, (one) that has the palsy {1x}.

This one is suffering from the relaxing of the nerves of one's side; hence, disabled, weak of limb "paralytic, sick of the palsy," is found in Mt 4:24; 8:6; 9:2 (twice), 6; Mk 2:3, 4, 5, 9, 10. See: BAGD—620b; THAYER—484d.

3886. **παραλύω** {5x} **paraluŏ,** *par-al-oo'-o;* from *3844* and *3089;* to *loosen beside,* i.e. *relax* (perf. pass. part. *paralyzed* or *enfeebled*):—sick of the palsy {2x}, taken with palsy {2x}, feeble {1x}.

Paraluo, lit., "to loose from the side," hence, "to set free," is used in the passive voice of "being enfeebled by a paralytic stroke, palsied," **(1)** Lk 5:18, "taken with a palsy"; 5:24 (ditto); Acts 8:7 (ditto); **(2)** Lk 9:33, "was sick of the palsy"; **(3)** Heb 12:12, "feeble." Syn.: 3885. See: BAGD—620b; THAYER—484d.

3887. **παραμένω** {3x} **paramĕnō,** *par-am-en'-o;* from *3844* and *3306;* to *stay near,* i.e. *remain beside* (lit. *tarry;* or fig.

be *permanent, persevere*):—abide {1x}, continue {2x}.

Parameno, "to remain beside" (*para,* "beside"), "to continue near," came to signify simply "to continue," **(1)** e.g., negatively, of the Levitical priests, Heb 7:23. **(2)** In 1 Cor 16:6 the apostle uses this word to express his desire to winter with the Corinthians. **(3)** In Jas 1:25, of steadfast continuance in the law of liberty. See: TDNT—4:577,   581;   BAGD—620c; THAYER—485a.

3888. **παραμυθέομαι** {4x} **paramuthĕŏmai,** *par-am-oo-theh'-om-ahee;* from *3844* and the mid. voice of a der. of *3454;* to *relate near,* i.e. (by impl.) *encourage, console:*—comfort {4x}

This word means "to soothe, console, encourage," and is translated "comfort" in Jn 11:19, 31; 1 Th 2:11 and 5:14, as the sense there is that of stimulating to the earnest discharge of duties. See: TDNT—5:816, 784; BAGD—620d; THAYER—485a.

3889. **παραμυθία** {1x} **paramuthia,** *par-am-oo-thee'-ah;* from *3888; consolation* (prop. abstr.):—comfort {1x}.

Primarily, *paramutha* is an address spoken closely to someone; hence, denoting consolation and comfort with a great degree of tenderness (1 Cor 14:3). See: TDNT—5:816, 784; BAGD—620d; THAYER—485a.

3890. **παραμύθιον** {1x} **paramuthiŏn,** *par-am-oo'-thee-on;* neut. of *3889; consolation* (prop. concr.):—comfort {1x}.

Paramuthion stresses the instrument as used by the agent, Phil 2:1. Syn.: *Paramuthion* (*3890*) has the same meaning as 3889, the difference being that *paramuthia* (*3889*) stresses the process or progress of the act, *paramuthion* emphasizing the instrument of comfort used by the agent. See: TDNT—5:816, 784; BAGD—620d; THAYER—485b.

3891. **παρανομέω** {1x} **paranŏmĕō,** *par-an-om-eh'-o;* from a compound of *3844* and *3551;* to *be opposed to law,* i.e. to *transgress:*—contrary to law {1x}.

Paranomeo, "to transgress law" (*para,* "contrary to," and *nomos*), is used in the present participle in Acts 23:3, and translated "contrary to the law," lit., "transgressing the law." See: TDNT—4:1091, 646; BAGD—621a; THAYER—485b.

3892. **παρανομία** {1x} **paranŏmia,** *par-an-om-ee'-ah;* from the same as *3891; transgression:*—iniquity {1x}.

A person who commits *paranomia* is one living contrary to a stated law, not one who has no law as a guide (2 Pet 2:16). Syn.: 51, 265,

266, 458, 2275, 3847, 3876, 3900. See: TDNT—4:1090, 646; BAGD—621a; THAYER—485b.

3893. παραπικραίνω {1x} **parapikrainō,**
par-ap-ik-rah'-ee-no;
from *3844* and *4087;* to *embitter alongside,* i.e.
(fig.) to *exasperate:*—provoke {1x}.

Parapikraino, "to embitter, provoke", occurs in Heb 3:16 of provoking God. See: TDNT—6:125, 839; BAGD—621a; THAYER—485b.

3894. παραπικρασμός {2x} **parapikrasmŏs,**
*par-ap-ik-ras-
mos';* from *3893; irritation:*—provocation {2x}.

Parapikrasmos, from *para,* "amiss" or "from," used intensively, and *pikraino,* "to make bitter" (*pikros,* "sharp, bitter"), "provocation," occurs in Heb 3:8, 15. See: TDNT—6:125, 839; BAGD—621b; THAYER—485b.

3895. παραπίπτω {1x} **parapiptō,** *par-ap-
ip'-to;* from *3844* and *4098;* to *fall aside,* i.e. (fig.) to *apostatize:*—fall away {1x}.

Parpipto means properly, "to fall in one's way" (*para,* "by"), and signifies "to fall away" (from adherence to the realities and facts of the faith), Heb 6:6. See: TDNT—6:170, 846; BAGD—621b; THAYER—485c.

3896. παραπλέω {1x} **paraplĕō,** *par-ap-
leh'-o;* from *3844* and *4126;*
to *sail near:*—sail by {1x}. See: BAGD—621; THAYER—485c.

3897. παραπλήσιον {1x} **paraplēsiŏn,** *par-
ap-lay'-see-on;* neut. of a compound of *3844* and the base of *4139* (as adv.); *close by,* i.e. (fig.) *almost:*—nigh unto {1x}.

This word denotes beside, near, nearly resembling and has reference to death because it stresses the person is drawing near to that state when the body is lifeless (Phil 2:27). See: BAGD—621c; THAYER—485c.

3898. παραπλησίως {1x} **paraplēsiŏs,** *par-
ap-lay-see'-oce;* adv. from the same as *3897; in a manner near by,* i.e. (fig.) *similarly:*—likewise {1x}.

Paraplesios, from *para,* "beside," and the adjective *plesios,* "near" (akin to the adverb *pelas,* "near, hard by"), is used in Heb 2:14, "likewise", expressing the true humanity of Christ in partaking of flesh and blood. See: BAGD—621c; THAYER—485c.

3899. παραπορεύομαι {5x} **parapŏrĕuŏmai,**
*par-ap-or-yoo'-om-
ahee;* from *3844* and *4198;* to *travel near:*—go {1x}, pass {1x}, pass by {3x}.

This word means primarily, "to go beside,

accompany" (*para,* "beside," *poreuomai,* "to proceed"), and denotes **(1)** "to go past, pass by," Mt 27:39; **(2)** Mk 9:30, "passed through"; 11:20; 15:29; **(3)** in Mk 2:23, "going . . . through." See: BAGD—621d; THAYER—485c.

3900. παράπτωμα {23x} **paraptōma,** *par-
ap'-to-mah;* from *3895;* a *side-slip* (*lapse* or *deviation*), i.e. (unintentional) *error* or (willful) *transgression:*—fall {2x}, fault, {2x} offence {7x}, sin {3x}, trespass {9x}.

(1) Primarily, this word means a false step, a blunder; hence, a lapse from uprightness, a sin, a moral trespass, misdeed; a downfall, a falling down along side of the correct path (Rom 11:11–12). **(1a)** *Paraptoma,* as a noun, (akin to *parapipto,* "to fall away," Heb 6:6), means lit., "a fall beside," used ethically, denotes **(1b)** "a trespass," a deviation, from uprightness and truth, Mt 6:14, 15 (twice); 18:35; Mk 11:25, 26; **(2)** in Romans **(2a)** 4:25, "for (i.e., because of) our trespasses"; **(2b)** 5:15 (twice), where the trespass is that of Adam (in contrast to the free gift of righteousness), **(2c)** 5:16, where "of many trespasses" expresses a contrast of quantity; the condemnation resulted from one "trespass," the free gift is "of (*ek,* expressing the origin, and throwing stress upon God's justifying grace in Christ) many trespasses"; **(2d)** 5:17, introducing a contrast between legal effects and those of divine grace; **(2e)** 5:18, "through one offense," is contrasted with "one act of righteousness"; this is important, the difference is not between one man's "trespass" and Christ's righteousness, but between two acts, that of Adam's "trespass" and the vicarious death of Christ. Syn.: *Paraptoma,* and *hamartema* (264 - "a sinful deed") are closely associated, with regard to their primary meanings: *parabasis* seems to be a stronger term, as the breach of a known law. Syn.: 51, 265, 266, 458, 2275, 3847, 3876, 3892. See: TDNT—6:170, 846; BAGD—621d; THAYER—485d.

3901. παραρρυέω {1x} **pararrhuĕō,** *par-ar-
hroo-eh'-o;* from *3844* and the alternate of *4482;* to *glide by, flow by,* i.e. (fig.) carelessly *pass* (*miss*):—let slip {1x}.

(1) The significance of this word is to find oneself flowing, gliding, or passing by without giving due heed to a thing. **(2)** It means lit., "to flow past, glide by" (*para,* "by," *rheo,* "to flow"), and is used in Heb 2:1, where the significance is to find oneself "flowing" or "passing by," without giving due heed to a thing, here "the things that were heard," or perhaps the salvation of which they spoke; "let them slip." See: BAGD—621d; THAYER—485d.

3902. παράσημος {1x} **parasēmŏs,** *par-as'-ay-mos;* from *3844* and the base of *4591; side-marked,* i.e. *labelled* (with a *badge* [*figure-head*] of a ship):—sign {1x}.

Parasmos, an adjective meaning "marked at the side" (*para,* "beside," *sema,* "a mark"), is used in Acts 28:11 as a noun denoting the figurehead of a vessel. See: BAGD—622a; THAYER—486a.

3903. παρασκευάζω {4x} **paraskĕuazō,** *par-ask-yoo-ad'-zo;* from *3844* and a der. of *4632; to furnish aside,* i.e. *get ready:*—make ready {1x}, prepare oneself {1x}, be ready {1x}, ready {1x}.

This word means "to prepare, make ready" (*para,* "beside"), is used (1) of making ready a meal, Acts 10:10; (2) in the middle voice, of "preparing" oneself for war, 1 Cor 14:8; (3) in the passive voice, of (3a) "preparing" an offering for the needy, 2 Cor 9:2, "was ready"; (3b) 2 Cor 9:3, "ye may be ready." See: BAGD—622a; THAYER—486a.

3904. παρασκευή { {6x} **paraskĕuē,** *par-ask-yoo-ay';* as if from *3903; readiness:*—preparation.

Paraskeue denotes "preparation, equipment." (1) The day on which Christ died is called (1a) "the Preparation" in Mk 15:42; Jn 19:31; (1b) in Jn 19:42 "the Jews' Preparation"; (1c) in 19:14 it is described as "the Preparation of the Passover"; (1d) in Lk 23:54, RV, "the day of the preparation (and the sabbath drew on)." (2) The same day is in view in Mt 27:62, where the events recorded took place on "that followed the day of the preparation." The reference would be to the 6th day of the week. The title arose from the need of preparing food etc. for the Sabbath. Apparently it was first applied only to the afternoon of the 6th day; later, to the whole day. (3) In regard to the phraseology in Jn 19:14, many hold this to indicate the "preparation" for the paschal feast. It probably means "the Preparation day," and thus falls in line with the Synoptic Gospels. See: TDNT—7:1, 989; BAGD—622b; THAYER—486a.

3905. παρατείνω {1x} **paratĕinō,** *par-at-i'-no;* from *3844* and τείνω **tĕinō** (to stretch); to *extend along,* i.e. *prolong* (in point of time):—continue {1x}.

Parateino, "to stretch out along" (*para,* "along," *teino,* "to stretch"), is translated "continued" in Acts 20:7, of Paul's discourse. See: BAGD—622c; THAYER—486b.

3906. παρατηρέω {6x} **paratĕrĕō,** *par-at-ay-reh'-o;* from *3844* and *5083; to inspect alongside,* i.e. *note insidiously* or *scrupulously:*—watched {4x}, observe {1x}, watched + 2258 {1x}.

Paratereo, "to observe," especially with sinister intent, is rendered (1) "to watch" in Mk 3:2; Lk 6:7; 14:1; 20:20; Acts 9:24. (2) This verb also means to watch closely, observe narrowly, used in Gal 4:10, where the middle voice suggests that their religious observance of days, etc. was not from disinterested motives, but with a view to their own advantage. See: TDNT—8:146, 1174; BAGD—622c; THAYER—486b.

3907. παρατήρησις {1x} **paratērēsis,** *par-at-ay'-ray-sis;* from *3906; inspection,* i.e. *ocular evidence:*—observation {1x}.

Parateresis is attentive watching and is used in Lk 17:20, of the manner in which the kingdom of God (i.e., the operation of the spiritual kingdom in the hearts of men) does not come in such a manner that it can be watched with the eyes; not with outward show. See: TDNT—8:148, 1174; BAGD—622d; THAYER—486c.

3908. παρατίθημι {19x} **paratithēmi,** *par-at-ith'-ay-mee;* from *3844* and *5087; to place alongside,* i.e. *present* (food, truth); by impl. to *deposit* (as a trust or for protection):—set before {9x}, commit {3x}, commend {3x}, put forth {2x}, commit the keeping of {1x}, allege {1x}.

Paratithemi means (1) "to place beside", "to put forth," (1a) of a parable, Mt 13:24, 31; (1b) "to set before," of food, Mk 6:41; 8:6 (twice), 7; Lk 9:16; 10:8; 11:6; Acts 16:34; 1 Cor 10:27. It is also translated (2) "to entrust, commit to one's charge," in Lk 12:48, "committed"; 1 Ti 1:18; 2 Ti 2:2; 1 Pet 4:19, "commit the keeping"; (3) "to commend" in Lk 23:46; Acts 14:23; 20:32; and (4) "alleging" in Acts 17:3. See: TDNT—8:162, 1176; BAGD—622d; THAYER—486c.

3909. παρατυγχάνω {1x} **paratugchanō,** *par-at-oong-khan'-o;* from *3844* and *5177; to chance near,* i.e. *fall in with:*—meet with {1x}.

Paratugchano, "to happen to be near or present, to chance to be by" (*para,* "beside, near," *tunchano,* "to happen"), occurs in Acts 17:17, "met with (him)." See: BAGD—623a; THAYER—486d.

3910. παραυτίκα {1x} **parautika,** *par-ŏw-tee'-kah;* from *3844* and a der. of *846; at* the *very* instant, i.e. *momentary:*—but for a moment {1x}.

Parautika, "at the same circumstances," is used adjectivally in 2 Cor 4:17 and translated "which is but for a moment"; the meaning is

not, however, simply that of brief duration, but that which is present with us now or immediate (*para*, "beside with"), in contrast to the future glory; the clause is, lit., "for the present lightness (i.e., 'light burden,' the adjective *elaphron*, 'light,' being used as a noun) of (our) affliction." See: BAGD—623b; THAYER—486b.

3911. παραφέρω {3x} **paraphĕrō**, *par-af-er'-o;* from *3844* and *5342* (incl. its alt. forms); to *bear along* or *aside*, i.e. *carry off* (lit. or fig.); by impl. to *avert:*—remove {1x}, take away {2x}.

Paraphero, lit., "to bring to or before" (*para*, "beside," *phero*, "to carry"), "to take or carry away," is translated "take away" in the Lord's prayer in Gethsemane, Mk 14:36; Lk 22:42. See: BAGD—623b; THAYER—486d.

3912. παραφρονέω {1x} **paraphrŏnĕō**, *par-af-ron-eh'-o;* from *3844* and *5426;* to *misthink*, i.e. *be insane* (*silly*):— as a fool {1x}.

This word literally means to be beside oneself, to be deranged, out of one's senses, void of understanding, insane (2 Cor 11:23). See: BAGD—623c; THAYER—486d.

3913. παραφρονία {1x} **paraphrŏnia**, *par-af-ron-ee'-ah;* from *3912;* *insanity*, i.e. *foolhardiness:*—madness {1x}.

This word means madness; literally, contrary to the mind, speaking as mindless (2 Pet 2:16). See: BAGD—623c; THAYER—486d.

3914. παραχειμάζω {4x} **parachĕimazō**, *par-akh-i-mad'-zo;* from *3844* and *5492;* to *winter near*, i.e. *stay* with over the *rainy* season:—to winter {4x}.

Paracheimazo denotes "to winter at a place", Acts 27:12 (2nd part); 28:11; 1 Cor 16:6; Titus 3:12. See: BAGD—623c; THAYER—487a.

3915. παραχειμασία {1x} **parachĕimasia**, *par-akh-i-mas-ee'-ah;* from *3914;* a *wintering* over:—winter in {1x}. See: BAGD—623d; THAYER—487a,

3916. παραχρῆμα {19x} **parachrēma**, *par-akh-ray'-mah;* from *3844* and *5536* (in its orig. sense); *at the thing* itself, i.e. *instantly:*—immediately {13x}, straight way {3x}, forthwith {1x}, presently {1x}, soon {1x}.

Parachrema, lit., "with the matter (or business) itself" (*para*, "with," *chrema*, "a business," or "event"), and so, **(1)** "immediately," Lk 1:64; 4:39; 5:25; 8:44, 47; 13:13; 18:43; 19:11; 22:60; Acts 3:7; 12:23; 13:11; 16:26; it is thus used by Luke only, save for the two instances in Matthew. **(2)** It is also rendered "presently" in Mt 21:19; **(3)** "forthwith" in Acts 9:18; **(4)** "soon" in Mt 21:20; and **(5)** "straightway"

in Lk 8:55; Acts 5:10; 16:33. See: BAGD—623d; THAYER—487a.

3917. πάρδαλις {1x} **pardalis**, *par'-dal-is;* fem. of πάρδος **pardŏs** (a *panther*); a *leopard:*—leopard {1x}.

Pardalis denotes "a leopard or a panther," an animal characterized by swiftness of movement and sudden spring, in Dan 7:6 symbolic of the activities of Alexander the Great, and the formation of the Grecian kingdom, the third seen in the vision there recorded. In Rev 13:2 the imperial power, described there also as a "beast," is seen to concentrate in himself the characteristics of those mentioned in Dan 7. See: BAGD—623d; THAYER—487a.

3918. πάρειμι {23x} **parĕimi**, *par'-i-mee;* from *3844* and *1510* (incl. its various forms); to *be near*, i.e. *at hand;* neut. pres. part. (sing.) *time being*, or (plural) *property:*—be present {9x}, come {7x}, present {3x}, be present here {1x}, be here {1x}, such things as one hath + 3588 {1x}, he that lacketh + 3361 + 3739 {1x}.

Pareimi signifies **(1)** "to be by, at hand or present," **(1a)** of persons, e.g., Lk 13:1; Acts 10:33; 24:19; 1 Cor 5:3; 2 Cor 10:2, 11; Gal 4:18, 20; **(1b)** of things, **(1b1)** Jn 7:6, of a particular season in the Lord's life on earth, "is (not yet) come," or "is not yet at hand"; **(1b2)** Heb 12:11, of chastening "(for the) present" (the neuter of the present participle, used as a noun); **(1b3)** in Heb 13:5 "such things as ye have" is, lit., "the things that are present"; **(1b4)** 2 Pet 1:12, of the truth "the present truth," i.e. the truth which is now with you, not as if of special doctrines applicable to a particular time; **(1b5)** in 2 Pet 1:9 "he that lacketh" is lit., "to whom are not present"; **(2)** "to have arrived or come," Mt 26:50, "thou art come"; Jn 11:28; Acts 10:21; Col 1:6. See: TDNT—5:858, 791; BAGD—624a; THAYER—487b.

3919. παρεισάγω {1x} **parĕisagō**, *par-ice-ag'-o;* from *3844* and *1521;* to *lead in aside*, i.e. *introduce surreptitiously:*—privily bring in {1x}.

Pareisago, as a verb, means "to bring in privily" [lit., "to bring in beside"], "to introduce secretly": "But there were false prophets also among the people, even as there shall be false teachers among you, who privily shall bring in (*pareisago*) damnable heresies, even denying the Lord that bought them, and bring upon themselves swift destruction" (2 Pet 2:1). See: TDNT—5:824, 786; BAGD—624c; THAYER—487c.

3920. παρείσακτος {1x} **parĕisaktŏs**, *par-ice'-ak-tos;* from *3919;*

smuggled in:—unawares brought in {1x}. *Pare-isaktos,* See: TDNT—5:824, 786; BAGD—624c; THAYER—487c.

3921. παρεισδύνω {1x} **parĕisdunō,** *par-ice-doo'-no;* from *3844* and a compound of *1519* and *1416;* to *settle in alongside,* i.e. *lodge stealthily:*—creep in unawares {1x}. See: BAGD—624d; THAYER—487c.

3922. παρεισέρχομαι {2x} **parĕisĕrchŏmai,** *par-ice-er'-khom-ahee;* from *3844* and *1525;* to *come in alongside,* i.e. *supervene additionally* or *stealthily:*—come in privily {1x}, enter {1x}.

This word means lit., "to come in" (*eis*) "beside or from the side" (*para*) so as to be present with, and is used **(1)** in the literal sense, of the "coming" in of the Law in addition to sin, Rom 5:20; **(2)** in Gal 2:4, of false brethren, suggesting their "coming" in by stealth. See: TDNT—2:682, 257; BAGD—624d; THAYER—487c.

3923. παρεισφέρω {1x} **parĕisphĕrō,** *par-ice-fer'-o;* from *3844* and *1533;* to *bear in alongside,* i.e. *introduce simultaneously:*—give {1x}.

This word means "to bring in besides" (*para,* "besides," *eis,* "in," *phero,* "to bring"), means "to add," 2 Pet 1:5, "giving" (all your diligence) representing the intensive force of the verb. See: BAGD—625a; THAYER—487d.

3924. παρεκτός {3x} **parĕktŏs,** *par-ek-tos';* from *3844* and *1622; near outside,* i.e. *besides:*—except {1x}, saving {1x}, without {1x}.

Parektos, (a strengthened form *ektos,* and *para,* beside), is used **(1)** as an adverb, signifying "without," 2 Cor 11:28; lit., "the things without," i.e., the things happening without; **(2)** as a preposition signifying **(2a)** "except" in Mt 5:32, and **(2b)** "saving" in Acts 26:29 except. See: BAGD—625a; THAYER—487d.

3925. παρεμβολή {10x} **parĕmbŏlē,** *par-em-bol-ay';* from a compound of *3844* and *1685;* a *throwing in beside (juxtaposition),* i.e. (spec.) *battle-array, encampment* or *barracks* (tower Antonia):—army {1x}, camp {3x}, castle {6x}.

This word means lit., "a casting in among, an insertion" (*para,* "among," *ballo,* "to throw"), and was a military term. **(1)** In the NT it denotes the distribution of troops in army formation, "armies," **(1a)** Heb 11:34; a camp, as of the Israelites, Ex 19:17; 29:14; 32:17; hence, **(1b)** in Heb 13:11, 13, of Jerusalem, since the city was to the Jews what the camp in the wilderness had been to the Israelites; **(1c)** in Rev 20:9, the "armies" or camp of the saints, at the close of the millennium. **(2)** It also denoted a castle or barracks, the defensible part of the royal estate: Acts 21:34, 37; 22:24; 23:10, 16, 32. See: BAGD—625b; THAYER—487d.

3926. παρενοχλέω {1x} **parĕnŏchlĕō,** *par-en-okh-leh'-o;* from *3844* and *1776;* to *harass further,* i.e. *annoy:*—trouble {1x}. See: BAGD—625c; THAYER—488a.

3927. παρεπίδημος {3x} **parepidēmŏs,** *par-ep-id'-ay-mos;* from *3844* and the base of *1927;* an *alien alongside,* i.e. a *resident foreigner:*—pilgrim {2x}, stranger {1x}.

This word is an adjective signifying "sojourning in a strange place, away from one's own people" (*para,* "from," expressing a contrary condition, and *epidemeo,* "to sojourn"; *demos,* "a people"), and is used **(1)** of OT saints, Heb 11:13, "pilgrims" (coupled with *xenos,* "a foreigner"); **(2)** of Christians, 1 Pet 1:1, "strangers scattered"; the word is stressing those Christians scattered in Pontus, etc., and applied metaphorically of those to whom heaven is their own country, and who are sojourners on earth. See: TDNT—2:64, 49; BAGD—625d; THAYER—488a.

3928. παρέρχομαι {31x} **parĕrchŏmai,** *par-er'-khom-ahee;* from *3844* and *2064;* to *come near* or *aside,* i.e. to *approach* (*arrive*), *go by* (or *away*), (fig.) *perish* or *neglect,* (caus.) *avert:*—pass away {12x}, pass {10x}, pass by {3x}, pass over {1x}, transgress {1x}, past {1x}, go {1x}, come forth {1x}, come {1x}.

Parerchomai, from *para,* "by," *erchomai,* "to come" or "go," denotes **(1)** literally, "to pass, pass by," **(1a)** of persons, Mt 8:28; Mk 6:48; Lk 18:37; Acts 16:8; **(1b)** of things, Mt 26:39, 42; **(1c)** of time, Mt 14:15; Mk 14:35; Acts 27:9, "past"; 1 Pet 4:3; **(2)** metaphorically, **(2a)** "to pass away, to perish," Mt 5:18; 24:34, 35; Mk 13:30, 31; Lk 16:17; 21:32, 33; 2 Cor 5:17; Jas 1:10; 2 Pet 3:10; **(2b)** "to pass by, disregard, neglect, pass over," Lk 11:42; 15:29, "transgressed." **(3)** For the meaning "to come forth or come," see Lk 12:37; 17:7. See: TDNT—2:681, 257; BAGD—625d; THAYER—488b.

3929. πάρεσις {1x} **parĕsis,** *par'-es-is;* from *2935; prætermission,* i.e. *toleration:*—remission {1x}.

Paresis primarily means a letting go, a dismissal and denotes a passing by, a suspension of judgment or withholding of punishment (Rom 3:25) with reference to sins committed previously up to the propitiatory sacrifice of Christ; the passing by not being a matter of divine disregard but of forbearance. Syn.:

859. See: TDNT—1:509, 88; BAGD—626b; THAYER—488c.

3930. **παρέχω** {16x} **parĕchō**, *par-ekh'-o;* from 3844 and 2192; to *hold near,* i.e. *present, afford, exhibit, furnish occasion:*—trouble + 2873 {5x}, give {3x}, bring {2x}, shew {2x}, do for {1x}, keep {1x}, minister {1x}, offer {1x}.

Parecho, as a verb, means usually, "to offer, furnish, supply" [lit., "to have near"], (1) "to bring, in the sense of supplying": "And it came to pass, as we went to prayer, a certain damsel possessed with a spirit of divination met us, which brought (*parecho*) her masters much gain by soothsaying" (Acts 16:16; cf. 19:24). (2) In the active voice, signifies "to afford, furnish, provide, supply" (lit., "to hold out or towards"); and is translated (2a) "hath given" in Acts 17:31; (2b) "giveth" in 1 Ti 6:17 (in the sense of affording); and (2c) in Col 4:1, "give." See: BAGD—626b; THAYER—488c.

3931. **παρηγορία** {1x} **parēgŏria**, *par-ay-gor-ee'-ah;* from a compound of 3844 and a der. of 58 (mean. to *harangue* an assembly); an *address alongside,* i.e. (spec.) *consolation:*—comfort {1x}.

This word primarily means an addressing, an address; hence, denotes a soothing, a solace (Col 4:11). A verbal form of the word signifies medicines which allay irritation (Eng., paregoric). See: BAGD—626d; THAYER—488d.

3932. **παρθενία** {1x} **parthĕnia**, *par-then-ee'-ah;* from 3933; *maidenhood:*—virginity {1x}. See: BAGD—626d; THAYER—489a.

3933. **παρθένος** {14x} **parthĕnŏs**, *par-then'-os;* of unknown or.; a *maiden;* by impl. an unmarried *daughter:*—virgin {14x}.

Parthenos is used (1) of "the Virgin Mary," Mt 1:23; Lk 1:27; (2) of the ten "virgins" in the parable, Mt 25:1, 7, 11; (3) of the "daughters" of Philip the evangelist, Acts 21:9; (4) those concerning whom the apostle Paul gives instructions regarding marriage, 1 Cor 7:25, 28, 34; in vv. 36, 37, 38, the subject passes to that of "virgin daughters", which almost certainly formed one of the subjects upon which the church at Corinth sent for instructions from the apostle; one difficulty was relative to the discredit which might be brought upon a father (or guardian), if he allowed his daughter or ward to grow old unmarried. The interpretation that this passage refers to a man and woman already in some kind of relation by way of a spiritual marriage and living together in a vow of virginity and celibacy is untenable if only in view of the phraseology of the passage;

(5) figuratively, of "a local church" in its relation to Christ, 2 Cor 11:2; (6) literally of virgin young men, Rev 14:4. See: TDNT—5:826, 786; BAGD—627a; THAYER—489a.

3934. **Πάρθος** {1x} **Parthŏs**, *par'-thos;* prob. of for. or.; a *Parthian,* i.e. inhab. of Parthia:—Parthian {1x}. See: BAGD—627b; THAYER—489b.

3935. **παρίημι** {1x} **pariēmi**, *par-ee'-ay-mi;* from 3844 and ἵημι **hiēmi,** (to *send*); to *let by,* i.e. *relax:*—hang down {1x}.

Pareiemi means relaxed, unstrung, weakened, exhausted; hence, hanging down, Heb 12:12. See: TDNT—1:509, 88; BAGD—627c.

3936. **παρίστημι** {42x} **paristēmi**, *par-is'-tay-mee;* or prol.

παριστάνω paristanō *par-is-tan'-o;* from 3844, and 2476; *stand beside,* i.e. (tran.) to *exhibit, proffer,* (spec.) *recommend,* (fig.) *substantiate;* or (intr.) to *be at hand* (or *ready*), *aid:*—stand by {13x}, present {9x}, yield {5x}, shew {2x}, stand {2x}, misc. {11x} = assist, bring before, command, commend, give presently, prove, provide.

Paristano, (1) intransitively, denotes (1a) "to stand by or beside" in Mk 14:47, 69, 70; 15:35, 39; Lk 19:24; Jn 18:22; 19:26; Acts 1:10; 9:39; 23:2, 4; 27:23; (1b) in Acts 27:24, "stand before"; (1c) in Acts 4:10, "doth . . . stand here"; (1d) in Lk 1:19, "stand"; (1e) Rom 14:10, "we shall . . . stand before" (middle voice); (1f) 2 Ti 4:17, "stood with"; (2) used transitively, "to place beside" (*para,* "by," *histemi,* "to set"), (2a) "to present," e.g., Lk 2:22; Acts 1:3, "He shewed (Himself)"; 9:41; 23:33; Rom 6:13 (2nd part), "yield"; so 6:19 (twice); 12:1; 2 Cor 4:14; 11:2; Eph 5:27; Col 1:22, 28; 2 Ti 2:15, "shew." See: TDNT—5:837, 788; BAGD—627c; THAYER—489b.

3937. **Παρμενᾶς** {1x} **Parmĕnas**, *par-men-as';* prob. by contr. for Παρμενίδης **Parmĕnidēs** (a der. of a compound of 3844 and 3306); *constant; Parmenas,* a Chr.:—Parmenas {1x}. See: BAGD—628c; THAYER—489d.

3938. **πάροδος** {1x} **parŏdŏs**, *par'-od-os;* from 3844 and 3598; a *byroad,* i.e. (act.) a *route:*—way {1x}. See: BAGD—628d; THAYER—488b.

3939. **παροικέω** {2x} **parŏikĕō**, *par-oy-keh'-o;* from 3844 and 3611; to *dwell near,* i.e. *reside* as a *foreigner:*—sojourn in {1x}, be a stranger {1x}.

Paroikeo denotes "to dwell beside, among or by" (*para,* "beside," *oikeo,* "to dwell"); then, "to dwell in a place as a *paroikos,* a stranger"

(*3941*), (1) Lk 24:18, "art thou (only) a stranger?" [*monos,* "alone," is an adjective, not an adverb]; (2) in Heb 11:9, "he sojourned." See: TDNT— 5:841, 788; BAGD—628d; THAYER—489d.

3940. **παροικία** {2x} **paroĭkia,** *par-oy-kee'-ah;* from *3941; foreign residence:*—sojourning here {1x}, dwelt as strangers {1x}.

Paroikia denotes (1) "a sojourning," Acts 13:17, lit., "in the sojourning," translated "dwelt as strangers"; and (2) in 1 Pet 1:17, "sojourning here." See: TDNT—5:841, 788; BAGD—629a; THAYER—490a.

3941. **πάροικος** {4x} **paroĭkŏs,** *par'-oy-kos;* from *3844* and *3624;* having a *home near,* i.e. (as noun) a *by-dweller (alien resident):*—foreigner {1x}, sojourn {1x}, stranger {2x}.

Paroidos, as a noun, "a sojourner," is (1) used with *eimi,* "to be," in Acts 7:6, "should sojourn"; (2) in Acts 7:29, "stranger"; in 1 Pet 2:11, "strangers"; (3) in Eph 2:19, "foreigners." See: TDNT—5:841, 788; BAGD—629a; THAYER—490a.

3942. **παροιμία** {5x} **paroĭmia,** *par-oy-mee'-ah;* from a compound of *3844* and perh. a der. of *3633;* appar. a state *alongside of supposition,* i.e. (concr.) an *adage;* spec. an enigmatical or fictitious *illustration:*—parable {1x}, proverb {4x}.

Paraoimia is (1) a saying out of the usual course or deviating from the usual manner of speaking; (2) any dark saying (2a) which shadows forth some didactic truth, esp. a symbolic or figurative saying; (2b) speech or discourse in which a thing is illustrated by the use of similes and comparisons. (3) It is translated "parable" in Jn 10:6; and "proverb" in Jn 16:25 twice; 16:29; 2 Pet 2:2. See: TDNT—5:854, 790; BAGD—629b; THAYER—490b.

3943. **πάροινος** {2x} **paroĭnŏs,** *par'-oy-nos;* from *3844* and *3631;* staying *near wine,* i.e. *tippling* (a *toper):*—given to wine {2x}.

Paroinos, as an adjective, literally means "tarrying at wine, given to wine" (1 Ti 3:3; Titus 1:7 with the secondary sense, of the effects of wine-bibbing, viz., abusive brawling). Syn.: 269. See: BAGD—629b; THAYER—490b.

3944. **παροίχομαι** {1x} **paroĭchŏmai,** *par-oy'-khom-ahee;* from *3844* and οἴχομαι **ŏichŏmai** (to *depart*); to *escape along,* i.e. *be gone:*—past {1x}.

Paroichomai, "to have passed by, to be gone by," is used in Acts 14:16, of past generations, "(in times) past." See: BAGD—629b; THAYER—490b.

3945. **παρομοιάζω** {1x} **parŏmŏiazō,** *par-om-oy-ad'-zo;* from *3946;* to *resemble:*—be like unto {1x}.

This word is used in Mt 23:27 (perhaps with intensive force), in the Lord's comparison of the scribes and Pharisees to whitened sepulchers. See: TDNT—5:199, 684; BAGD—629b; THAYER—490b.

3946. **παρόμοιος** {2x} **parŏmŏiŏs,** *par-om'-oy-os;* from *3844* and *3664; alike nearly,* i.e. *similar:*—like things {2x}.

Paromoios "much like" is used in Mk 7:8, 13, in the neuter plural, "(many such) like things." See: TDNT—5:198, 684; BAGD—629b; THAYER—490c.

3947. **παροξύνω** {2x} **parŏxunō,** *par-ox-oo'-no;* from *3844* and a der. of *3691;* to *sharpen alongside,* i.e. (fig.) to *exasperate:*—easily provoked {1x}, stir {1x}.

Paroxuno, as a verb, primarily, means "to sharpen" and is used metaphorically, signifying "to rouse to anger, to provoke," (1) in the passive voice, in Acts 17:16: "Now while Paul waited for them at Athens, his spirit was stirred in him, when he saw the city wholly given to idolatry"; and (2) "was stirred" in 1 Cor 13:5. Syn.: 329, 383, 387, 1326, 1892, 2042, 3951, 4531, 4579, 4787, 4797, 5017. See: TDNT—5:857, 791; BAGD—629c; THAYER—490c.

3948. **παροξυσμός** {2x} **parŏxusmŏs,** *par-ox-oos-mos';* from *3947* ("*paroxysm*"); *incitement* (to good), or *dispute* (in anger):*—contention . . . so sharp {1x}, provoke unto + 1519 {1x}.

Paroxusmos, lit., "a sharpening," hence "a sharpening of the feeling, or action" (*para,* "beside," intensive, *oxus,* "sharp"), denotes (1) an incitement, a sharp contention, Acts 15:39, the effect of irritation; and (2) elsewhere in Heb 10:24, "provoke," unto love. See: TDNT—5:857, 791; BAGD—629c; THAYER—490c.

3949. **παροργίζω** {2x} **parŏrgizō,** *par-org-id'-zo;* from *3844* and *3710;* to *anger alongside,* i.e. *enrage:*—anger {1x}, provoke to wrath {1x}.

Parorgizo is "to arouse to wrath, provoke"; (1) Rom 10:19, "will I anger"; (2) Eph 6:4, "provoke to wrath." See: TDNT—5:382, 716; BAGD—62d; THAYER—490c.

3950. **παροργισμός** {1x} **parŏrgismŏs,** *par-org-is-mos';* from *3949; rage:*—wrath {1x}.

Parorgismos occurs when irritation, exasperation, and embitterment attach themselves to righteous anger and makes it sin (Eph 4:26).

Syn.: 2372, 3209. See: TDNT—5:382, 716; BAGD—629d; THAYER—490d.

3951. **παροτρύνω** {1x} **parŏtrunō**, *par-ot-roo'-no;* from *3844* and ὀτρύνω **ŏtrunō** (to *spur*); to *urge along*, i.e. *stimulate* (to hostility):—stir up {1x}.

Parotruno, as a verb, [from *para,* used intensively, beyond measure, and *otruno*], means "to urge on, rouse": "But the Jews stirred up the devout and honourable women, and the chief men of the city, and raised persecution against Paul and Barnabas, and expelled them out of their coasts" (Acts 13:50). Syn.: 329, 383, 387, 1326, 1892, 2042, 3947, 4531, 4579, 4787, 4797, 5017. See: BAGD—629d; THAYER—490d.

3952. **παρουσία** {24x} **parŏusia**, *par-oo-see'-ah;* from the present part. of *3918;* a *being near,* i.e. *advent* (often, *return;* spec. of Christ to punish Jerusalem, or finally the wicked); (by impl.) phys. *aspect:*—coming {22x}, presence {2x}.

Parousia is used **(1)** to describe the presence of Christ with His disciples on the Mount of Transfiguration (2 Pet 1:16). **(2)** When used of the return of Christ, at the rapture of the church, it signifies, not merely His momentary coming for His saints in the rapture, but His presence with them from that moment until His revelation and manifestation to the world in His second coming. **(3)** In some passages the word **(3a)** gives prominence to the beginning of that period, the course of the period being implied (1 Cor 15:23; 1 Th 4:15; 5:23; 2 Th 2:1; Jas 5:7–8; 2 Pet 3:4). **(3b)** In some, the course is prominent (Mt 24:3, 37; 1 Th 3:13; 1 Jn 2:28); **(3c)** in others the conclusion of the period (Mt 24:27; 2 Th 2:8). See: TDNT—5:858, 791; BAGD—629d; THAYER—490d.

3953. **παροψίς** {2x} **parŏpsis**, *par-op-sis';* from *3844* and the base of *3795;* a *side-dish* (the receptacle):—platter {2x}.

This word, (*para,* "beside," *opson,* "cooked"), means **(1)** firstly, "a side dish of dainties" in Mt 23:26; **(2)** then, "the dish itself" in Mt 23:25. See: BAGD—630b; THAYER—491a.

3954. **παῤῥησία** {31x} **parrhēsia**, *par-rhay-see'-ah;* from *3956* and a der. of *4483; all out-spokenness,* i.e. *frankness, bluntness, publicity;* by impl. *assurance:*—boldness {8x}, confidence {6x}, openly {4x}, plainly {4x}, openly + 1722 {2x}, boldly + 1722 {1x}, misc. {6x} = × freely, plainness.

This word (from *pas,* "all," *rhesis,* "speech") denotes **(1)** primarily, **(1a)** "freedom of speech, unreservedness of utterance," Acts 4:29, 31;

2 Cor 3:12; 7:4; Philem 8; or **(1b)** "to speak without ambiguity, plainly," Jn 10:24; **(1c)** or "without figures of speech," Jn 16:25; **(2)** "the absence of fear in speaking boldly; hence, confidence, cheerful courage, boldness, without any connection necessarily with speech"; "boldness" in the following; Acts 4:13; Eph 3:12; 1 Ti 3:13; Heb 3:6; 4:16; 10:19, 35; 1 Jn 2:28; 3:21; 4:17; 5:14; **(3)** the deportment by which one becomes conspicuous, Jn 7:4; 11:54, acts openly, or secures publicity, Col 2:15. See: TDNT—5:871, 794; BAGD—639c; THAYER—491a.

3955. **παῤῥησιάζομαι** {9x} **parrhēsiazŏmai**, *par-hray-see-ad'-zom-ahee;* mid. voice from *3954;* to *be frank* in utterance, or *confident* in spirit and demeanor:—speak boldly {4x}, preach boldly {1x}, be bold {1x}, wax bold {1x}, boldly {1x}, freely {1x}.

This word means "to speak boldly, or freely," and primarily had reference to speech, but acquired the meaning of "being bold, or waxing bold," 1 Th 2:2; in Acts 13:46, the aorist participle here signifies "waxing bold"; Acts 9:27, 29, "preached boldly"; 18:26, "speak boldly"; 19:8, "spake boldly; 26:26, "speak freely." See: TDNT—5:871, 794; BAGD—631a; THAYER—491b.

3956. **πᾶς** {1243x} **pas** *pas;* incl. all the forms of declension; appar. a primary word; *all, any, every,* the *whole:*—all {748x}, all things {170x}, every {117x}, all men {41x}, whosoever {31x}, everyone {28x}, whole {12x}, all manner of {11x}, every man {11x}, no + 3756 {9x}, every thing {7x}, any {7x}, whatsoever {6x}, whosoever + 3739 + 302 {3x}, always + 1223 {3x}, daily + 2250 {2x}, any thing {2x}, no + 3361 {2x}, not tr {7x}, misc. {26x} = all means, any one, × daily, + ever, everyway, as many as, × thoroughly, whole. See: TDNT—5:886, 795; BAGD—631b; THAYER—491b.

3957. **πάσχα** {29x} **pascha**, *pas'-khah;* of Chald. or. [comp. 6453]; the *Passover* (the meal, the day, the festival or the special sacrifices connected with it):—Easter {1x}, Passover {28x}.

Pascha is the Greek spelling of the Aramaic word for the Passover, from the Hebrew *pasach,* "to pass over, to spare," a feast instituted by God in commemoration of the deliverance of Israel from Egypt, and anticipatory of the expiatory sacrifice of Christ. The word signifies **(1)** "the Passover Feast," e.g., Mt 26:2; Jn 2:13, 23; 6:4; 11:55; 12:1; 13:1; 18:39; 19:14; Acts 12:4; Heb 11:28; **(2)** by metonymy, **(2a)** "the Paschal Supper," Mt 26:18, 19; Mk 14:16; Lk 22:8, 13; **(2b)** "the Paschal lamb," e.g., Mk 14:12 (cf.

Ex 12:21); Lk 22:7; **(2c)** "Christ Himself," 1 Cor 5:7. **(3)** It is also translated "Easter" which etymologically arises from the Anglo-Saxon *eastre* which is derived from *east* which means "to shine, to dawn, to spring forth" and is an excellent designation for the resurrection of Jesus Christ. Unfortunately the pagans also had a holiday which corresponded. See: TDNT—5:896, 797; BAGD—633b; THAYER—493d.

3958. **πάσχω** {42x} **paschō**, *pas'-kho;* incl. the forms

πάθω (**pathō**, *path'-o*) and

πένθω (**pěnthō**, *pen'-tho*), used only in certain tenses for it; appar. a primary verb; to *experience* a sensation or impression (usually painful):—suffer {39x}, be vexed {1x}, passion + 3588 {1x}, feel {1x}.

Pascho, "to suffer," is used **I.** of the "sufferings" of Christ **(1)** at the hands of men, e.g., Mt 16:21; 17:12; 1 Pet 2:23; **(2)** in His expiatory and vicarious sacrifice for sin, Heb 9:26; 13:12; 1 Pet 2:21; 3:18; 4:1; **(3)** including both (*1*) and (*2*), Lk 22:15; 24:26, 46; Acts 1:3, "passion"; 3:18; 17:3; Heb 5:8; **(4)** by the antagonism of the evil one, Heb 2:18; **II.** of human "suffering" **(1)** of followers of Christ, Acts 9:16; 2 Cor 1:6; Gal 3:4; Phil 1:29; 1 Th 2:14; 2 Th 1:5; 2 Ti 1:12; 1 Pet 3:14, 17; 5:10; Rev 2:10; **(1a)** in identification with Christ in His crucifixion, as the spiritual ideal to be realized, 1 Pet 4:1; **(1b)** in a wrong way, 4:15; **(2)** of others, physically, **(2a)** as the result of demoniacal power, Mt 17:15, "is (sore) vexed"; cf. Mk 5:26; **(2b)** in a dream, Mt 27:19; **(2c)** through maltreatment, Lk 13:2; 1 Pet 2:19, 20; **(2d)** by a serpent (negatively), Acts 28:5, "felt"; **(3)** of the effect upon the whole body through the "suffering" of one member, 1 Cor 12:26, with application to a church. See: TDNT—5:904, 798; BAGD—633d; THAYER—494b.

3959. **Πάταρα** {1x} **Patara**, *pat'-ar-ah;* prob. of for. or.; *Patara*, a place in Asia Minor:—*Patara* {1x}. See: BAGD—634c; THAYER—494c.

3960. **πατάσσω** {10x} **patassō**, *pat-as'-so;* prob. prol. from *3817;* to *knock* (gently or with a weapon or fatally):—smite {9x}, strike {1x}.

Patasso, "to strike, smite," is used **I.** literally, of giving a blow with the hand, or fist or a weapon, Mt 26:51, "struck"; Lk 22:49, 50; Acts 7:24; 12:7; **II.** metaphorically, **(1)** of judgment meted out to Christ, Mt 26:31; Mk 14:27; **(2)** of the infliction of disease, by an angel, Acts 12:23; **(3)** of plagues to be inflicted upon men by two divinely appointed witnesses, Rev 11:6;

(4) of judgment to be executed by Christ upon the nations, Rev 19:15, the instrument being His Word, described as a sword. See: TDNT—5:939, 804; BAGD—634d; THAYER—494c. comp. *5180.*

3961. **πατέω** {5x} **patěō**, *pat-eh'-o;* from a der. prob. of *3817* (mean. a "*path*"); to *trample* (lit. or fig.):—tread {3x}, tread down {1x}, tread under foot {1x}.

Pateo is used **(1)** intransitively and figuratively of "treading" upon serpents, Lk 10:19; **(2)** transitively, of "treading" on, down or under, **(2a)** of the desecration of Jerusalem by its foes, Lk 21:24; Rev 11:2; **(2b)** of the avenging, by the Lord in person hereafter, of this desecration and of the persecution of the Jews, in divine retribution, metaphorically spoken of as the "treading" of the winepress of God's wrath, Rev 14:20; 19:15 (cf. Is 63:2, 3). See: TDNT—5:940, 804; BAGD—634d; THAYER—494d.

3962. **πατήρ** {419x} **patēr**, *pat-ayr';* appar. a primary word; a "*father*" (lit. or fig., near or more remote):—Father {268x}, father {150x}.

Pater, from a root signifying "a nourisher, protector, upholder" (Lat., *pater*, Eng., "father," are akin), is used **(1)** of the nearest ancestor, e.g., Mt 2:22; **(2)** of a more remote ancestor, the progenitor of the people, a "forefather," e.g., Mt 3:9; 23:30; 1 Cor 10:1; the patriarchs, 2 Pet 3:4; **(3)** one advanced in the knowledge of Christ, 1 Jn 2:13; **(4)** metaphorically, of the originator of a family or company of persons animated by the same spirit as himself, as **(4a)** of Abraham, Rom 4:11, 12, 16, 17, 18, or **(4b)** of Satan, Jn 8:38, 41, 44; **(5)** of one who, as a preacher of the gospel and a teacher, stands in a "father's" place, caring for his spiritual children, 1 Cor 4:15 (not the same as a mere title of honor, which the Lord prohibited, Mt 23:9); **(6)** of the members of the Sanhedrin, as of those who exercised religious authority over others, Acts 7:2; 22:1;

(7) of God in relation **(7a)** to those who have been born anew (Jn 1:12, 13), and **(7b)** so are believers, Eph 2:18; 4:6 (cf. 2 Cor 6:18), and **(7c)** imitators of their "Father," Mt 5:45, 48; 6:1, 4, 6, 8, 9, etc. **(7d)** Christ never associated Himself with them by using the personal pronoun "our"; **(7d1)** He always used the singular, "My Father," His relationship being unoriginated and essential, whereas theirs is by grace and regeneration, e.g., Mt 11:27; 25:34; Jn 20:17; Rev 2:27; 3:5, 21; **(7d2)** so the apostles spoke of God as the "Father" of the Lord Jesus Christ, e.g., Rom 15:6; 2 Cor 1:3; 11:31; Eph 1:3; Heb 1:5; 1 Pet 1:3; Rev 1:6;

(8) of God, as the "Father" **(8a)** of lights,

i.e., the source or giver of whatsoever provides illumination, physical and spiritual, Jas 1:17; **(8b)** of mercies, 2 Cor 1:3; **(8c)** of glory, Eph 1:17; **(9)** of God, as Creator, Heb 12:9 (cf. Zec 12:1). **(10)** Whereas the everlasting power and divinity of God are manifest in creation, His "Fatherhood" in spiritual relationship through faith is the subject of NT revelation, and waited for the presence on earth of the Son, Mt 11:27; Jn 17:25. The spiritual relationship is not universal, Jn 8:42, 44 (cf. Jn 8:12 and Gal 3:26). See: TDNT—5:945, 805; BAGD—635a; THAYER—494d.

3963. Πάτμος {1x} **Patmŏs,** *pat'-mos;* of uncert. der.; *Patmus,* an islet in the Mediterranean:—*Patmos* {1x}. See: BAGD—636c; THAYER—495c.

3964. πατραλῴας {1x} **patralōias,** *pat-ral-o'-as* πατρολῴας **patrŏlŏias,** *pat-rol-o'-as;* from *3962* and the same as the latter part of *3389;* a *parricide:*—murderer of fathers {1x}. See: BAGD—636c; THAYER—495d.

3965. πατριά { {3x} **patria,** *pat-ree-ah';* as if fem. of a der. of *3962;* paternal *descent,* i.e. (concr.) a *group* of families or a whole *race (nation):*—family {1x}, kindred {1x}, lineage {1x}.

Patria, primarily "an ancestry, lineage," signifies in the NT "a family or tribe"; it is used **(1)** of the "family" of David, Lk 2:4, "lineage"; **(2)** in the wider sense of "nationalities, races," Acts 3:25, "kindreds"; **(3)** in Eph 3:15, "the whole family," the reference being to all those who are spiritually related to God the Father, He being the author of their spiritual relationship to Him as His children, they being united to one another in "family" fellowship. See: TDNT—5:1015, 805; BAGD—636d; THAYER—495d.

3966. πατριάρχης {4x} **patriarchēs,** *pat-ree-arkh'-ace;* from *3965* and *757;* a *progenitor* ("patriarch"):—patriarch {4x}. See: BAGD—636d; THAYER—496a.

3967. πατρικός {1x} **patrikŏs,** *pat-ree-kos';* from *3962; paternal,* i.e. *ancestral:*—of (one's) fathers {1x}.

Patrikos, from *patria,* "a family," and *archo,* "to rule," is found in Acts 2:29; 7:8, 9; Heb 7:4. See: TDNT—5:1021, 805; BAGD—636d; THAYER—496a.

3968. πατρίς {8x} **patris,** *pat-rece';* from *3962;* a *father-land,* i.e. *native town;* (fig.) heavenly *home:*—of (one's) own country {5x}, country {3x}.

Patris primarily signifies "one's fatherland, native country, of one's own town," Mt 13:54,

57; Mk 6:1, 4; Lk 4:23–24; Jn 4:44; Heb 11:14. See: BAGD—636d; THAYER—496a.

3969. Πατρόβας {1x} **Patrŏbas,** *pat-rob'-as;* perh. contr. for Πατρόβιος **Patrŏbiŏs** (a compound of *3962* and *979*); *father's life; Patrobas,* a Chr.:—*Patrobas* {1x}. See: BAGD—637a; THAYER—496a.

3970. πατροπαράδοτος {1x} **patrŏparadŏtŏs,** *pat-rop-ar-ad'-ot-os;* from *3962* and a der. of *3860* (in the sense of *handing over* or *down); traditionary:*—received by tradition from (one's) fathers {1x}.

Patroparadotos, as a verb, means in 1 Pet 1:18 "received by tradition from your fathers": "Forasmuch as ye know that ye were not redeemed with corruptible things, as silver and gold, from your vain conversation received by tradition from your fathers." Syn.: 324, 353, 354, 568, 588, 618, 1209, 1523, 1926, 2210, 2865, 2975, 2983, 3028, 3335, 3336, 3858, 3880, 4327, 4355, 4356, 4380, 4381, 4382, 5562, 5264, 5274. See: BAGD—637a; THAYER—496b.

3971. πατρῷος {3x} **patrōiŏs,** *pat-ro'-os;* from *3962; paternal,* i.e. *hereditary:*—of (one's) fathers {2x}, of the fathers {1x}.

Patroos signifies "of one's fathers," or "received from one's fathers" in Acts 22:3; 24:14; 28:17. See: TDNT—5:1014,*; BAGD—637b; THAYER—496b.

3972. Παῦλος {164x} **Paulŏs,** *pŏw'-los;* of Lat. or.; *(little;* but remotely from a der. of *3973,* mean. the same); *Paulus,* the name of a Rom. and of an apostle:—Paul {163x}, Paulus (the deputy) {1x}. See: BAGD—637b; THAYER—496b.

3973. παύω {15x} **pauō,** *pŏw'-o;* a primary verb ("pause"); to *stop* (tran. or intr.), i.e. *restrain, quit, desist, come to an end:*—cease {15x}, leave {2x}, refrain {1x}.

Pauo, "to stop, to make an end," is used chiefly in the middle voice in the NT, signifying "to come to an end, to take one's rest, a willing cessation" (in contrast to the passive voice which denotes a forced cessation), **(1)** Lk 5:4, of a discourse; **(2)** Lk 8:24, of a storm; **(3)** Lk 11:1, of Christ's prayer; **(4)** Acts 5:42, of teaching and preaching; **(5)** Acts 6:13, of speaking against; **(6)** Acts 13:10, of evil doing; **(7)** Acts 20:1, of an uproar; **(8)** Acts 20:31, of admonition; **(9)** Acts 21:32, of a scourging; **(10)** 1 Cor 13:8, of tongues; **(11)** Eph 1:16, of giving thanks; **(12)** Col 1:9, of prayer; **(13)** Heb 10:2, of sacrifices; **(14)** 1 Pet 4:1, of "ceasing" from sin. **(15)** It is used in the active voice in 1 Pet 3:10, "let him cause his tongue to cease from evil." See: BAGD—638a; THAYER—496d.

3974. Πάφος {2x} **Paphŏs**, *paf'-os;* of uncert. der.; *Paphus*, a place in Cyprus:—*Paphos* {2x}. See: BAGD—638b; THAYER—497a.

3975. παχύνω {2x} **pachunō**, *pakh-oo'-no;* from a der. of *4078* (mean. *thick);* to *thicken*, i.e. (by impl.) to *fatten* (fig. *stupefy* or *render callous):*—wax gross {2x}.

Pachuno, from *pachus*, "thick," signifies "to thicken, fatten"; **(1)** in the passive voice, "to grow fat"; metaphorically said of the heart, to wax gross or dull, Mt 13:15; Acts 28:27. **(2)** "Wax" denotes slowly, thin layer by thin layer, until thick and hardened. See: TDNT— 5:1022, 816; BAGD—638b; THAYER—497a.

3976. πέδη {3x} **pĕdē**, *ped'-ay;* ultimately from *4228;* a *shackle* for the feet:—fetter {3x}.

Pede, "a fetter" (akin to *peza*, "the instep," and *pous*, "a foot"; cf. Eng. prefix *ped-*), occurs in Mk 5:4, twice, and Lk 8:29. See: BAGD— 638c; THAYER—497b.

3977. πεδινός {1x} **pĕdinŏs**, *ped-ee-nos';* from a der. of *4228* (mean. the *ground); level* (as easy for the *feet):*—plain + 5117 {1x}. See: BAGD—638c; THAYER—497b.

3978. πεζεύω {1x} **pĕzĕuō**, *ped-zyoo'-o;* from the same as *3979;* to *foot* a journey, i.e. *travel* by land:—go afoot {1x}.

Pezeuo is to travel on foot (not on horseback or in carriage), or (if opp. to going by sea) by land, Acts 20:13. See: BAGD—638d; THAYER—497b.

3979. πεζῇ {2x} **pĕzēi**, *ped-zay';* dat. fem. of a der. of *4228* (as adv.); *foot-wise*, i.e. by *walking:*—afoot {1x}, on foot {1x}. See: BAGD—638d; THAYER—497b.

3980. πειθαρχέω {4x} **pĕitharchĕō**, *pi-tharkh-eh'-o;* from a compound of *3982* and *757;* to *be persuaded* by a *ruler*, i.e. (gen.) to *submit* to authority; by anal. to *conform* to advice:—hearken {1x}, obey {2x}, to obey magistrates {1x}.

This word means "to obey one in authority" and is translated **(1)** "obey" in Acts 5:29, 32; **(2)** Titus 3:1, "to obey magistrates"; and **(3)** in Acts 27:21, "hearkened." See: TDNT—6:9, 818; BAGD—638d; THAYER—497b.

3981. πειθός {1x} **pĕithŏs**, *pi-thos';* from *3982; persuasive:*—enticing {1x}.

Peithos, "apt to persuade" (from *peitho*, "to persuade"), is used in 1 Cor 2:4, "enticing." See: TDNT—6:8, 818; BAGD—639a; THAYER— 497c.

3982. πείθω {55x} **pĕithō**, *pi'-tho;* a primary verb; to *convince* (by argument, true or false); by anal. to *pacify* or *conciliate* (by other fair means); refl. or pass. to *assent* (to evidence or authority), to *rely* (by inward certainty):—persuade {22x}, trust {8x}, obey {7x}, have confidence {6x}, believe {3x}, be confident {2x}, misc. {7x} = agree, assure, wax confident, make friend, yield.

Peitho, **(1)** in the active voice, signifies "to apply persuasion, to prevail upon or win over, to persuade," bringing about a change of mind by the influence of reason or moral considerations, e.g., in Mt 27:20; 28:14; Acts 13:43; 19:8; **(2)** in the passive voice, "to be persuaded, believe", e.g., Lk 16:31; 20:6; Acts 17:4, "believed"; 21:14; 26:26; Rom 8:38; 14:14; 15:14; 2 Ti 1:5, 12; Heb 6:9; 11:13; 13:18, "trust." **(3)** *Peitho*, intransitively, in the perfect and pluperfect active, "to have confidence, trust," is rendered "to trust" in Mt 27:43; Mk 10:24; Lk 11:22; 18:9; 2 Cor 1:9; 10:7; Phil 2:24; 3:4; Heb 2:13; in the present middle, Heb 13:18. **(4)** It also means "to persuade, to win over," in the passive and middle voices, "to be persuaded, to listen to, to obey," is **(4a)** so used with this meaning, in the middle voice, e.g., in Acts 5:36–37 (in v. 40, passive voice, "they agreed"); Rom 2:8; Gal 5:7; Heb 13:17; Jas 3:3. **(4b)** The "obedience" suggested is not by submission to authority, but resulting from persuasion. Syn.: *Peitho* and *pisteuo*, "to trust," **(A)** are closely related etymologically; **(B)** the difference in meaning is that the former implies the obedience that is produced by the latter, cf. Heb 3:18–19, where the disobedience of the Israelites is said to be the evidence of their unbelief Faith is of the heart, invisible to men; **(C)** obedience is of the conduct and may be observed. **(D)** When a man obeys God he gives the only possible evidence that in his heart he believes God. **(E)** Of course it is persuasion of the truth that results in faith (we believe because we are persuaded that the thing is true, a thing does not become true because it is believed), **(F)** but *peitho* in NT suggests an actual and outward result of the inward persuasion and consequent faith. See: TDNT—6:1, 818; BAGD—639a; THAYER—497c.

3983. πεινάω {23x} **pĕinaō**, *pi-nah'-o;* from the same as *3993* (through the idea of pinching *toil; "pine");* to *famish* (absol. or comp.); fig. to *crave:*—hunger {10x}, be an hungred {9x}, be hungry {3x}, hungry {1x}.

Peinao, "to hunger, be hungry, hungered," is used **(1)** literally, **(1a)** e.g., Mt 4:2; 12:1; 21:18; Rom 12:20; 1 Cor 11:21, 34; Phil 4:12; Rev 7:16; **(1b)** Christ identifies Himself with His saints in speaking of Himself as suffering in their suf-

ferings in this and other respects, Mt 25:35, 42; **(2)** metaphorically, Mt 5:6; Lk 6:21, 25; Jn 6:35. See: TDNT—6:12, 820; BAGD—640a; THAYER—498a.

3984. πεῖρα {2x} **pĕira,** *pi'-rah;* from the base of *4008* (through the idea of *piercing*); a *test,* i.e. *attempt, experience:—* assay + 2983 {1x}, trial {1x}.

Peira, "a making trial, an experiment," is used with *lambano,* "to receive or take," **(1)** in Heb 11:29, rendered "assaying," and **(2)** Heb 11:36, in the sense of "having experience of" (akin to *peirao,* "to assay, to try"), "had trial." See: TDNT—6:23, 822; BAGD—640a; THAYER—498b.

3985. πειράζω {39x} **pĕirazō,** *pi-rad'-zo;* from *3984;* to *test* (obj.), i.e. *endeavor, scrutinize, entice, discipline:*—assay {1x}, examine {1x}, go about {1x}, prove {1x}, tempt {29x}, tempter {2x}, try {4x}.

(1) Testing will cause its recipients to appear as what they always have been. This is predominantly, though not exclusively, the sense of *peirazo.* **(2)** Nothing in the word requires it to refer to a trial given with the intention of entangling the person in sins. **(3)** *Peirazo* properly means to make an experience of, to pierce or search into, or to attempt (Acts 16:7, 24:6). **(4)** It also signifies testing whose intention was to discover whether a person or thing was good or evil or strong or weak (Mt 16:1; 19:3; 22:18); or **(5)** if the outcome already was known to the tester, to reveal the same to the one being tested (2 Cor 13:5). **(6)** Sinners are said to tempt God, when they put Him to the test by refusing to believe His word until He manifests His power. **(7)** God tempts people only in the sense of self-knowledge and so that they may and often do emerge from testing holier, humbler, and stronger than they were before. **(8)** *Peirazo* applied also to the solicitations and suggestions of Satan, the tempter (Mt 4:3; 1 Th 3:5), putting one to a test with the intentions and the desire that the proved may not turn out approved, but reprobate, and break down under the test. Satan never proves in order to approve, nor tests that he may accept. Syn.: 1381. See: TDNT—6:23, 822; BAGD—640b; THAYER—498b.

3986. πειρασμός {21x} **pĕirasmŏs,** *pi-ras-mos';* from *3985;* a putting to *proof* (by experiment [of good], *experience* [of evil], solicitation, discipline or provocation); by impl. *adversity:*—temptation {19x}, temptations {1x}, ✕ try {1x}.

Peirasmos is used of "trials" with a beneficial purpose and effect, **(1)** of "trials" or "temptations," divinely permitted or sent, Lk 22:28;

Acts 20:19; Jas 1:2; 1 Pet 1:6; 4:12, "to try"; 2 Pet 2:9 (singular); Rev 3:10, "temptation"; **(2)** in Jas 1:12, "temptation" used in the widest sense; **(2a)** with a good or neutral significance, Gal 4:14, of Paul's physical infirmity, "a temptation" to the Galatian converts, of such a kind as to arouse feelings of natural repugnance; **(3)** of "trials" of a varied character, **(3a)** Mt 6:13 and Lk 11:4, where believers are commanded to pray not to be led into such by forces beyond their own control; **(3b)** Mt 26:41; Mk 14:38; Lk 22:40, 46, where they are commanded to watch and pray against entering into "temptations" by their own carelessness or disobedience; in all such cases God provides "the way of escape"; **(3c)** 1 Cor 10:13 (where *peirasmos* occurs twice). **II.** Of "trial" definitely designed to lead to wrong doing, "temptation," Lk 4:13; 8:13; 1 Ti 6:9; **III.** Of "trying" or challenging God, by men, Heb 3:8. See: TDNT—6:23, 822; BAGD—640d; THAYER—498d.

3987. πειράω {3x} **pĕiraō,** *pi-rah'-o;* from *3984;* to *test* (subj.), i.e. (refl.) to *attempt:*—assay {1x}, go about {1x}, vr tempted {1x}.

(1) to make a trial of, to attempt, Acts 9:26, of Saul [Paul] attempting to join himself to the Jerusalem disciples; **(2)** to test, to make trial of one, put him to proof, Acts 26:21, of the Jews attempting to gain a case against Paul that would allow for them to kill him; and **(3)** in particular, to attempt to induce one to commit some (esp. carnal) crime, Heb 4:15, of Christ being tempted in all points as we are. See: TDNT—6:23, 822; BAGD—641a; THAYER—499a.

3988. πεισμονή {1x} **pĕismŏnē,** *pice-mon-ay';* from a presumed der. of *3982; persuadableness,* i.e. *credulity:*—persuasion {1x}.

In Gal 5:8 the meaning is this influence that has won you over, or that seems likely to do so. See: TDNT—6:9, 818; BAGD—641b; THAYER—499b.

3989. πέλαγος {2x} **pĕlagŏs,** *pel'-ag-os;* of uncert. aff.; deep or open *sea,* i.e. the *main:*—depth {1x}, sea {1x}.

Pelagos is the vast uninterrupted expanse of open water as distinguished from a sea broken by islands and shut in by coasts and headlines. It primarily suggests the breadth of the open sea, Acts 27:5, and sometimes its depth, Mt 18:6. Syn.: 2281. See: BAGD—641b; THAYER—499b.

3990. πελεκίζω {1x} **pĕlĕkizō,** *pel-ek-id'-zo;* from a der. of *4141* (mean. an *axe*); to *chop* off (the head), i.e. *truncate:*—

behead {1x}. See: BAGD—641c; THAYER—499b.

3991. πέμπτος {4x} **pĕmptŏs**, *pemp'-tos;* from *4002; fifth:*—fifth {4x}. See: BAGD—641c; THAYER—499c.

3992. πέμπω {81x} **pĕmpō**, *pem'-po;* appar. a primary verb; to *dispatch* (from the subj. view or point of *departure,* whereas ἵημι **hiēmi** [as a stronger form of εἰμι **ĕimi**] refers rather to the obj. point or *terminus ad quem,* and *4724* denotes prop. the *orderly* motion involved), espec. on a temporary errand; also to *transmit, bestow,* or *wield:*—send {77x}, thrust in {2x}, again send {2x}.

Pempo, "to send," is used **(1)** of persons: **(1a)** Christ, by the Father, Lk 20:13; Jn 4:34; 5:23, 24, 30, 37; 6:38, 39, (40), 44; 7:16, 18, 28, 33; 8:16, 18, 26, 29; 9:4; 12:44, 45, 49; 13:20 (2nd part); 14:24; 15:21; 16:5; Rom 8:3; **(1b)** the Holy Spirit, Jn 14:26; 15:26; 16:7; **(1c)** Elijah, Lk 4:26; **(1d)** John the Baptist, Jn 1:33; **(1e)** disciples and apostles, e.g., Mt 11:2; Jn 20:21; **(1f)** servants, e.g., Lk 20:11, 12; **(1g)** officials, Mt 14:10; **(1h)** messengers, e.g., Acts 10:5, 32, 33; 15:22, 25; 2 Cor 9:3; Eph 6:22; Phil 2:19, 23, 25; 1 Th 3:2, 5; Titus 3:12; **(1i)** a prisoner, Acts 25:25, 27; **(1j)** potentates, by God, 1 Pet 2:14; **(1k)** an angel, Rev 22:16; **(1l)** demons, Mk 5:12; **(2)** of things, Acts 11:29; Phil 4:16; 2 Th 2:11; Rev 1:11; 11:10; 14:15, 18, "thrust in." Syn.: *Pempo* is a more general term than *apostello; apostello* usually suggests official or authoritative sending. A comparison of the usages mentioned above shows how nearly (in some cases practically quite) interchangeably they are used, and yet on close consideration the distinction just mentioned is discernible; in the Gospel of John, cf. *pempo* in 5:23, 24, 30, 37, *apostello* in 5:33, 36, 38; *pempo* in 6:38, 39, 44, *apostello* in 6:29, 57; the two are not used simply for the sake of variety of expression. *Pempo* is not used in the Lord's prayer in Jn 17, whereas *apostello* is used six times. See: TDNT—1:398, 67; BAGD—641d; THAYER—499c.

3993. πένης {1x} **pĕnēs**, *pen'-ace;* from a primary πένω **pĕnō**, (to *toil* for daily subsistence); *starving,* i.e. *indigent:*—poor {1x}.

Penes, "a laborer" (akin to *penomai,* "to work for one's daily bread"), is translated "poor" in 2 Cor 9:9. Syn.: *Penes* is one who is so poor he earns his bread by daily labour; whereas, *ptochos* (*4434*) is one who only obtains his living by begging. See: TDNT—6:37, 824; BAGD—642c; THAYER—499d. comp. *4434.*

3994. πενθερά {6x} **pĕnthĕra**, *pen-ther-ah';* fem. of *3995;* a *wife's mother:*—mother in law {3x}, wife's mother {3x}.

Penthera, the feminine of *pentheros* ("a father-in-law"), is translated **(1)** "mother in law" Mt 8:14; 10:35; Lk 12:53 twice; and **(2)** "wife's mother" in Mk 1:30; Lk 4:38. See: BAGD—642c; THAYER—500a.

3995. πενθερός {1x} **pĕnthĕrŏs**, *pen-ther-os';* of uncert. aff.; a *wife's father:*—father in law {1x}. See: BAGD—642c; THAYER—500a.

3996. πενθέω {10x} **pĕnthĕō**, *pen-theh'-o;* from *3997;* to *grieve* (the feeling or the act):—mourn {7x}, bewail {1x}, wail {2x}.

(1) *Pentheo* means to mourn, bewail primarily for the dead, but also includes any other passionate lamenting; a grief so all-emcompassing that it cannot be hidden. This word means "to mourn for, lament," and is used **(1)** of mourning in general, Mt 5:4; 9:15; Lk 6:25; **(2)** of sorrow for the death of a loved one, Mk 16:10; **(3)** of "mourning" for the overthrow of Babylon and the Babylonish system, Rev 18:11, 15, "wailing"; v. 19 wailing; **(4)** of sorrow for sin or for condoning it, Jas 4:9; 1 Cor 5:2; **(5)** of grief for those in a local church who show no repentance for evil committed, 2 Cor 12:21, "bewail." Syn.: 2354, 2875, 3076. See: TDNT—6:40, 825; BAGD—642c; THAYER—500a.

3997. πένθος {5x} **pĕnthŏs**, *pen'-thos;* strengthened from the alt. of *3958; grief:*—mourning {2x}, sorrow {3x}.

Penthos is translated **(1)** "mourning" in Jas 4:9; Rev 18:8; and **(2)** "sorrow": "How much she hath glorified herself, and lived deliciously, so much torment and sorrow [*penthos*] give her: for she saith in her heart, I sit a queen, and am no widow, and shall see no sorrow [*penthos*]" (Rev 18:7 twice; cf. 21:4). Syn.: 253, 3076, 3077, 3600, 3601, 4036, 5604. See: TDNT—6:40, 825; BAGD—642d; THAYER—500a.

3998. πενιχρός {1x} **pĕnichrŏs**, *pen-ikh-ros';* prol. from the base of *3993; necessitous:*—poor {1x}. See: TDNT—6:40, 824; BAGD—642d; THAYER—500a.

3999. πεντακίς {1x} **pĕntakis**, *pen-tak-ece';* mult. adv. from *4002; five times:*—five times {1x}. See: BAGD—643a; THAYER—500b.

4000. πεντακισχίλιοι {6x} **pĕntakischiliŏi**, *pen-tak-is-khil'-ee-oy;* from *3999* and *5507; five times a thousand:*—five thousand {6x}. See: BAGD—643a; THAYER—500b.

4001. **πεντακόσιοι** {2x} **pĕntakŏsiŏi,** *pen-tak-os'-ee-oy;* from *4002* and *1540; five hundred:*—five hundred {2x}. See: BAGD—643a; THAYER—500b.

4002. **πέντε** {38x} **pĕntĕ,** *pen'-teh;* a primary number; *"five":*—five {36x}, three score and fifteen + 1440 {1x}, fifty thousand + 3461 {1x}. See: BAGD—643a; THAYER—500b.

4003. **πεντεκαιδέκατος** {1x} **pĕntĕkaidĕkatŏs,** *pen-tek-ahee-dek'-at-os;* from *4002* and *2532* and *1182; five and tenth:*—fifteenth {1x}. See: BAGD—643a; THAYER—500b.

4004. **πεντήκοντα** {7x} **pĕntēkŏnta,** *pen-tay'-kon-tah;* mult. of *4002; fifty:*—fifty {7x}. See: BAGD—643b; THAYER—500a.

4005. **πεντηκοστή** {3x} **pĕntēkŏstē,** *pen-tay-kos-tay';* fem. of the ord. of *4004; fiftieth* (*2250* being impl.) from Passover, i.e. the festival of *"Pentecost":*—Pentecost {3x}.

Pentekoste, an adjective denoting "fiftieth," is used as a noun, with "day" understood, i.e., the "fiftieth" day after the Passover, counting from the second day of the Feast, Acts 2:1; 20:16; 1 Cor 16:8. See: TDNT—6:44, 826; BAGD—643b; THAYER—500b.

4006. **πεποίθησις** {6x} **pĕpŏithēsis,** *pep-oy'-thay-sis;* from the perfect of the alt. of *3958; reliance:*—confidence {5x}, trust {1x}.

Pepoitesis, akin to *peitho,* denotes "persuasion, assurance, confidence," and is translated **(1)** "confidence" in 2 Cor 1:15; 8:22; 10:2; Eph 3:12; Phil 3:4; and **(2)** "trust" in 2 Cor 3:4. See: TDNT—6:7, 818; BAGD—643b; THAYER—500b.

4007. **περ** {4x} **pĕr,** *per;* from the base of *4008;* an enclitic particle significant of *abundance* (*thoroughness*), i.e. *emphasis; much, very* or *ever:*—whomsoever + 3739 {1x}, not tr {3x}. See: BAGD—643c; THAYER—500c.

4008. **πέραν** {23x} **pĕran,** *per'-an;* appar. acc. of an obs. der. of πείρω **pĕirō,** (to *"pierce"*); *through* (as adv. or prep.), i.e. *across:*—other side {10x}, beyond {7x}, over {3x}, on the other side {2x}, farther side {1x}.

This word means "on the other side, across," is **(1)** used with the definite article, signifying the regions "beyond," the opposite shore, Mt 8:18 etc. **(2)** With verbs of going it denotes direction toward and "beyond" a place, e.g., Jn 10:40. **(3)** It frequently indicates "beyond," of locality, without a verb of direction, Mt 16:5;

Mk 10:1; Jn 1:28; 3:26. **(4)** As an adverb, it signifies "beyond, on the other side" and is used **(4a)** as a preposition and translated "on the other side of," e.g., in Mk 5:1; Lk 8:22; Jn 6:1; 6:22, 25; **(4b)** as a noun with the article, e.g., Mt 8:18, 28; 14:22; 16:5. See: BAGD—643d; THAYER—500c.

4009. **πέρας** {4x} **pĕras,** *per'-as;* from the same as *4008;* an *extremity:*—end {2x}, utmost part {1x}, uttermost part {1x}.

Peras, "a limit, boundary" (from *pera,* "beyond"), is used **(1)** of space, chiefly in the plural, in **(1a)** Mt 12:42, "uttermost parts"; **(1b)** Lk 11:31, "utmost"; **(1c)** Rom 10:18 "ends"; **(2)** of the termination of something occurring in a period, Heb 6:16, "an end" said of strife. See: BAGD—644a; THAYER—500d.

4010. **Πέργαμος** {2x} **Pĕrgamŏs,** *per'-gam-os;* from *4444; fortified; Pergamus,* a place in Asia Minor:—*Pergamos* {2x}. See: BAGD—644b; THAYER—500d.

4011. **Πέργη** {3x} **Pĕrgē,** *perg'-ay;* prob. from the same as *4010;* a *tower; Perga,* a place in Asia Minor:—Perga {3x}. See: BAGD—644b; THAYER—501a.

4012. **περί** {331x} **pĕri,** *per-ee';* from the base of *4008;* prop. *through* (all over), i.e. *around;* fig. *with respect* to; used in various applications, of place, cause or time (with the gen. denoting the *subject* or *occasion* or *superlative* point; with the acc. the *locality, circuit, matter, circumstance* or general *period*):—of {148x}, for {61x}, concerning {40x}, about {31x}, as touching {8x}, touching {3x}, whereof + 3739 {3x}, not tr {4x}, misc {33x} = (there-) about, above, against, at, on behalf of, X and his company, which concern, X how it will go with, there of, on, over, pertaining (to), for sake, X (e-) state, whereby, wherein, with. In composition it retains substantially the same meaning of circuit (*around*), excess (*beyond*), or completeness (*through*). See: TDNT—6:53, 827; BAGD—644b; THAYER—501a.

4013. **περιάγω** {6x} **pĕriagō,** *per-ee-ag'-o;* from *4012* and *71;* to *take around* (as a companion); refl. to *walk around:*—compass {1x}, go about {3x}, go round about {1x}, lead about {1x}.

Periago, **(1)** "to lead about" is found in 1 Cor 9:5; or **(2)** intransitively, "to go about, to go up and down" and is so used in Mt 4:23; 9:35; Mk 6:6 "go round about"; Acts 13:11; **(3)** "to compass regions" Mt 23:15. See: BAGD—645c; THAYER—502a.

4014. **περιαιρέω** {4x} **pĕriairĕō,** *per-ee-ahee-reh'-o;* from *4012* and *138* (incl. its alt.); to *remove* all *around,* i.e. *unveil,*

cast off (anchor); fig. to *expiate:*—take away {3x}, take up {1x}.

Periaireo, "to take away that which surrounds" is used (1) literally, of "having taken up" the anchors from the different sides of the ship, Acts 27:40; (2) metaphorically, (2a) of "taking away" the veil off the hearts of Israel, 2 Cor 3:16; (2b) of hope of rescue, Acts 27:20; (2c) of sins (negatively), Heb 10:11. See: BAGD—645d; THAYER—502b.

4015. **περιαστράπτω** {2x}   **pĕriastraptō,**
                                 per-ee-as-trap'-to;
from *4012* and *797;* to *flash* all *around,* i.e. *to envelop in light:*—shine round {1x}, shine round about {1x}.

Periastrapto, "to flash around, shine round about" (*peri,* and *astrape,* "shining brightness"), is used in Acts 9:3 and 22:6 of the same circumstance as in 26:13, of the heavenly light shining around Saul [Paul] on the Damascus road. See: BAGD—645d; THAYER—502b.

4016. **περιβάλλω** {24x}   **pĕriballō,** *per-ee-bal'-lo;* from *4012* and *906;* to *throw* all *around,* i.e. *invest* (with a palisade or with clothing):—clothe {7x}, clothed with {4x}, array {3x}, array in {3x}, clothe in {3x}, cast about {3x}, put on {1x}.

Periballo, as a verb, (in 23 of the 24 uses) means (1) "to cast around or about, to put on, array," or, in the middle and passive voices, "to clothe oneself": "Naked, and ye clothed me: I was sick, and ye visited me" (Mt 25:36; cf. vv. 38, 43). (2) It is most frequent in the Apocalypse, where it is found some 12 times. (3) In Lk 19:43 it is used of "casting" up a bank or palisade against a city, "shall cast a trench about thee." A palisade is built by digging a large trench. Syn.: 294, 1463, 1737, 1746, 1902, 2439. See: BAGD—646a; THAYER—502b.

4017. **περιβλέπω** {7x}   **pĕriblĕpō,** *per-ee-blep'-o;* from *4012* and *991;* to *look* all *around:*—look round about {3x}, look round about upon {2x}, look round about on {2x}.

Periblepo, as a verb, means "to look about, or round about, on" and is used in the middle voice: "And when He had looked round about on them with anger" (Mk 3:5; cf. 3:34, 5:32; 9:8; 10:23; 11:11; Lk 6:10). Syn.: 308, 352, 578, 816, 872, 991, 1689, 1896, 1914, 1980, 1983, 2300, 2334, 3706, 3708, 3879, 4648. See: BAGD—646b; THAYER—502c.

4018. **περιβόλαιον** {2x} **pĕribŏlaiŏn,** *per-ib-ol'-ah-yon;* neut. of a presumed der. of *4016;* something *thrown around* one, i.e. a *mantle, veil:*—covering {1x}, vesture {1x}.

Peribolaion, lit. denotes "something thrown

around" (*peri,* "around," *ballo,* "to throw"); hence, (1) "a veil, covering," 1 Cor 11:15; or (2) "a mantle around the body, a vesture," Heb 1:12. See: BAGD—646c; THAYER—502c.

4019. **περιδέω** {1x} **pĕridĕō,** *per-ee-deh'-o;* from *4012* and *1210;* to *bind around* one, i.e. *enwrap:*—bind about {1x}.

Perodeo, (*peri,* "around," with "to bind around"), is used in Jn 11:44 of the napkin around the face of Lazarus. See: BAGD—646c; THAYER—502d.

περιδρέμω **pĕridrĕmō.** See *4063.*

περιέλλω **pĕriĕllō.** See *4014.*

περιέλθω **pĕriĕlthō.** See *4022.*

4020. **περιεργάζομαι** {1x} **pĕriĕrgazŏmai,** *per-ee-er-gad'-zom-ahee;* from *4012* and *2038;* to *work* all *around,* i.e. *bustle about* (*meddle*):—be a busybody {1x}.

This word literally means to be working round about, instead of at one's own business and signifies to take more pains than enough about a thing, to waste one's labor, to be meddling with, trifling in needless useless matters, or bustling about, overbusied in other people's matters (2 Th 3:11). See: BAGD—646d; THAYER—502d.

4021. **περίεργος** {2x} **pĕriĕrgŏs,** *per-ee'-er-gos;* from *4012* and *2041;* *working* all *around,* i.e. *officious* (*meddlesome,* neut. plur. *magic*):—busybody {1x}, curious arts {1x}.

This word means busy (1) about trifles and neglectful of important matters, esp. busy about other folks' affairs, a busybody (1 Ti 5:13); and (2) with things that are impertinent and superfluous, the curious arts (Acts 19:9). "Curious" is derived from "care" and means devoting much time and energy to learn and master matters that are less than eternal. Syn.: 4020. See: BAGD—646d; THAYER—502b.

4022. **περιέρχομαι** {4x} **pĕriĕrchŏmai,** *per-ee-er'-khom-ahee;* from *4012* and *2064* (incl. its alt.); to *come* all *around,* i.e. *stroll, vacillate, veer:*—fetch a compass {1x}, vagabond {1x}, wandering about {2x}.

Perierchomai means "to go about" (*peri,* "about," *erchomai,* "to go"), and is said (1) of "navigating a ship under difficulty owing to contrary winds," Acts 28:13, "we fetched a compass." (2) In 1 Ti 5:13 and Heb 11:37, *perierchomai* means "to go about or around," is translated "to wander about." It is also translated "vagabond", one who wanders about, Acts 19:13. See: TDNT—2:682, 257; BAGD—646d; THAYER—502d.

Greek

4023. περιέχω {3x} **pĕrĭĕchō,** *per-ee-ekh'-o;* from *4012* and *2192;* to *hold* all *around,* i.e. *include, clasp* (fig.):—be astonished + 2285 {1x}, after this manner + 5126 + 5176 {1x}, be contained {1x}.

Pericho literally means to have all around, to completely hold all around, and denotes **(1)** to contain, enclose (1 Pet 2:6); **(2)** after this manner, completely following this manner, lit. "having this form" (Acts 23:25); and **(3)** astonished, as the person is completely seized by an event (Lk 5:9). See: BAGD—647a; THAYER—502d.

4024. περιζώννυμι {7x} **pĕrizōnnumi,** *per-id-zone'-noo-mee;* from *4012* and *2224;* to *gird* all *around,* i.e. (middle or passive voice) to *fasten on one's belt* (lit. or fig.):—gird (one's) self {3x}, be girded about {1x}, have girded {1x}, have girded about {1x}, be girt {1x}.

Perizonnumi, as a verb, means "to gird around or about," and is used **(1)** literally, **(1a)** of "girding" oneself for service: "Blessed are those servants, whom the lord when he cometh shall find watching: verily I say unto you, that he shall gird himself, and make them to sit down to meat, and will come forth and serve them" (Lk 12:37; 17:8); **(2)** for rapidity of movement: "And the angel said unto him, Gird thyself, and bind on thy sandals" (Acts 12:8); **(3)** figuratively, of the condition for service on the part of the followers of Christ: "Let your loins be girded about, and your lights burning" (Lk 12:35; cf. Eph 6:14); **(4)** emblematically, **(4a)** of Christ's priesthood: "And in the midst of the seven candlesticks one like unto the Son of man, clothed with a garment down to the foot, and girt about the paps with a golden girdle" (Rev 1:13, indicative of majesty of attitude and action, the middle voice suggesting the particular interest taken by Christ in "girding" Himself thus); and **(4b)** so of the action of the angels: "And the seven angels came out of the temple, having the seven plagues, clothed in pure and white linen, and having their breasts girded with golden girdles" (Rev 15:6). Syn.: 328, 1241, 2224. See: TDNT—5:302, 702; BAGD—647b; THAYER—503a.

4025. περίθεσις {1x} **pĕrithĕsis,** *per-ith'-es-is;* from *4060; a putting* all *around,* i.e. *decorating* oneself with:—wearing {1x}.

Perithesis, "a putting around or on" (*peri,* "around," *tithemi,* "to put"), is used in 1 Pet 3:3 of "wearing" of gold. See: BAGD—647; THAYER—503b.

4026. περιΐστημι {4x} **pĕriistēmi,** *per-ee-is'-tay-mee;* from *4012* and *2476;* to *stand* all *around,* i.e. (near) to *be a bystander,* or (aloof) to *keep away* from:—avoid {1x}, shun {1x}, stand by {1x}, stand round about {1x}.

Periistemi **(1)** in the active voice means to stand by or around about (Jn 11:42; Acts 25:7); and **(2)** in the middle voice means to turn oneself about for the purpose of avoiding or shunning something; **(2a)** profane babblings (2 Ti 2:16); **(2b)** foolish questions, genealogies, strife, etc. (Titus 3:9). See: BAGD—647c; THAYER—503b.

4027. περικάθαρμα {1x} **pĕrikatharma,** *per-ee-kath'-ar-mah;* from a compound of *4012* and *2508;* something *cleaned* off all *around,* i.e. *refuse* (fig.):—filth {1x}.

This word denotes "offscouring, refuse" (lit., "cleanings," i.e., that which is thrown away in cleansing; from *perikathairo,* "to purify all around," i.e., completely. It is used in 1 Cor 4:13 "the filth of the world" representing the most abject and despicable men, the scum or rubbish of humanity. See: TDNT—3:430, 381; BAGD—647d; THAYER—503b.

4028. περικαλύπτω {3x} **pĕrikaluptō,** *per-ee-kal-oop'-to;* from *4012* and *2572;* to *cover* all *around,* i.e. *entirely* (the face, a surface):—blindfold {1x}, cover {1x}, overlay {1x}.

This word means "to cover around" (*peri,* "around"), e.g., the face, and so, to blindfold, is translated **(1)** "cover" in Mk 14:65, of the face of Jesus in His scourging and mocking by the soldiers; **(2)** "blindfold" in Lk 22:64 of the same event; and **(3)** in Heb 9:4, it signifies "to overlay" of the gold on the ark of the covenant. See: BAGD—647d; THAYER—503c.

4029. περίκειμαι {5x} **pĕrikĕimai,** *per-ik'-i-mahee;* from *4012* and *2749;* to *lie* all *around,* i.e. *enclose, encircle, hamper* (lit. or fig.):—be hanged {2x}, be bound with {1x}, be compassed with {1x}, be compassed about with + 2192 {1x}.

Perikeimai, lit., "to lie around" (*peri,* "around," *keimai,* "to lie"), "to be compassed," is used **(1)** of binding fetters around a person, Acts 28:20; **(2)** in Mk 9:42, and Lk 17:2, to hang about a person's neck; **(3)** in Heb 5:2, to compass about, metaphorically of infirmities; and **(4)** in Heb 12:1, of those who have witness borne to their faith. See: TDNT—3:656, 425; BAGD—647d; THAYER—503c.

4030. περικεφαλαία {2x} **pĕrikĕphalaia,** *per-ee-kef-al-ah'-yah;* fem. of a compound of *4012* and *2776; encirclement* of the *head,* i.e. a *helmet:*—helmet {2x}.

This word (from *peri*, "around," and *kephale*, "a head") is used **(1)** figuratively in Eph 6:17, with reference to salvation, and **(2)** 1 Th 5:8, where it is described as "the hope of salvation." **(3)** The head is regarded here as standing for the seat of the intellect which has been enlightened by the Holy Spirit to comprehend all the aspects of salvation portrayed in the others parts of the armor. **(3a)** In Eph 6:17 salvation is a present experience of the Lord's deliverance of believers as those who are engaged in spiritual conflict; **(3b)** in 1 Th 5:8, the hope is that of the Lord's return, which encourages the believer to resist the spirit of the age in which he lives. See: TDNT—5:314, 702; BAGD—648a; THAYER—503d.

4031. περικρατής {1x} **pĕrikratēs**, *per-ee-krat-ace';* from *4012* and *2904; strong* all *around,* i.e. a *master* (*manager*):—+ come by {1x}.

This adjective signifies having full command of; it is used with *ginomai* (1096 —to become) and translated "to come by" (Acts 27:16). [cf. Eng. "How did you come by that new home?]. See: BAGD— 648b; THAYER—503d.

4032. περικρύπτω {1x} **pĕrikruptō**, *per-ee-kroop'-to;* from *4012* and *2928;* to *conceal* all *around,* i.e. *entirely:*—hide {1x}.

Perikrupto signifies "to hide by placing something around, to conceal entirely, to keep hidden" (*peri*, "around," used intensively), Lk 1:24, where Elizabeth "hid" her pregnancy by wearing large clothing. See: BAGD— 648b; THAYER—503d.

4033. περικυκλόω {1x} **pĕrikuklŏō**, *per-ee-koo-klŏ'-o;* from *4012* and *2944;* to *encircle* all *around,* i.e. *blockade completely:*—compass round {1x}. See: BAGD—648b; THAYER—503d.

4034. περιλάμπω {2x} **pĕrilampō**, *per-ee-lam'-po;* from *4012* and *2989;* to *illuminate* all *around,* i.e. *invest with a halo:*—shine round about {2x}.

Perilampo, "to shine around", is used **(1)** in Lk 2:9, "shone round about," of the glory of the Lord; so **(2)** in Acts 26:13, of the light from heaven upon Saul of Tarsus. See: TDNT—4:16, 497; BAGD—648c; THAYER—503d.

4035. περιλείπω {2x} **pĕrilĕipō**, *per-ee-li'-po;* from *4012* and *3007;* to *leave* all *around,* i.e. (pass.) *survive:*—remain {2x}.

Perileipo, "to leave over," used in the middle voice, is translated "remain" in 1 Th 4:15, 17, where it stands for the living believers at the coming (the beginning of the Parousia) of Christ. See: TDNT—4:194,*; BAGD—648c; THAYER—503d.

4036. περίλυπος {5x} **pĕrilupŏs**, *per-il'-oo-pos;* from *4012* and *3077; grieved* all *around,* i.e. *intensely sad:*—exceeding sorrowful {2x}, very sorrowful {2x}, exceeding sorry {1x}.

Perilupos, as an adjective, means "very sad, deeply grieved" and is translated "exceedingly sorrowful": "Then saith He unto them, My soul is exceeding sorrowful, even unto death: tarry ye here, and watch with Me" (Mt 26:38; cf. Mk 14:34; Mk 6:26; Lk 18:23, 24). Syn.: 253, 3076, 3077, 3600, 3601, 3997, 5604. See: TDNT—4:323, 540; BAGD—648c; THAYER—503d.

4037. περιμένω {1x} **pĕrimĕnō**, *per-ee-men'-o;* from *4012* and *3306;* to *stay around,* i.e. *await:*—wait for {1x}.

Perimeno means to await an event, Acts 1:4, of "waiting" for the Holy Spirit, "the promise of the Father." See: TDNT—4:578, 581; BAGD—648c; THAYER—503d.

4038. πέριξ {1x} **pĕrix**, *per'-ix;* adv. from *4012;* all *around,* i.e. (as an adj.) *circumjacent:*—round about {1x}.

This word means round about: the neighbouring cities, Acts 5:16. See: BAGD—648d; THAYER—504a.

4039. περιοικέω {1x} **pĕriŏikĕō**, *per-ee-oy-keh'-o;* from *4012* and *3611;* to *reside around,* i.e. *be a neighbor:*—dwell round about {1x}. See: BAGD—648d; THAYER—504a.

4040. περίοικος {1x} **pĕriŏikŏs**, *per-ee'-oy-kos;* from *4012* and *3624; housed around,* i.e. *neighboring* (ellip. used as a noun):—neighbour {1x}. See: BAGD—648d; THAYER—504a.

4041. περιούσιος {1x} **pĕriŏusiŏs**, *per-ee-oo'-see-os;* from the pres. part. fem. of a compound of *4012* and *1510; being beyond* usual, i.e. *special* (one's *own possession):*—peculiar {1x}.

Periousios, "of one's own possession, one's own," qualifies the noun *laos,* "people," in Titus 2:14, "peculiar", a people selected by God from the other nations for His own possession. See: TDNT—6:57, 828; BAGD—648d; THAYER—504a.

4042. περιοχή {1x} **pĕriŏchē**, *per-ee-okh-ay';* from *4023;* a *being held around,* i.e. (concr.) a *passage* (of Scripture, as *circumscribed):*—a place {1x}.

Perioche, as a noun, in reference to a writing or book, "a portion or passage of its con-

tents": "The place of the scripture which he read was this, He was led as a sheep to the slaughter; and like a lamb dumb before his shearer, so opened he not his mouth" (Acts 8:32). Syn.: 201, 402, 1096, 1502, 3837, 5117, 5247, 5564, 5602. See: BAGD−648d; THAYER−504a.

4043. περιπατέω {96x} **pĕripatĕō,** *per-ee-pat-eh'-o;* from *4012* and *3961;* to *tread* all *around,* i.e. *walk* at large (espec. as proof of ability); fig. to *live, deport oneself, follow* (as a companion or votary):− walk {93x}, go {1x}, walk about {1x}, be occupied {1x}. See: TDNT−5:940, 804; BAGD− 649a; THAYER−504b.

4044. περιπείρω {1x} **pĕripĕirō,** *per-ee-pi'-ro;* from *4012* and the base of *4008;* to *penetrate entirely,* i.e. *transfix* (fig.):−pierce through {1x}.

Peripeiro means to put on a spit; hence, to pierce and is used metaphorically in 1 Ti 6:10 of torturing one's soul with many sorrows, "have pierced (themselves) through." See: BAGD−649d; THAYER−504d.

4045. περιπίπτω {3x} **pĕripiptō,** *per-ee-pip'-to;* from *4012* and *4098;* to *fall* into something all *around,* i.e. *light among* or *upon, be surrounded with:*−fall among {1x}, fall into {2x}.

Peripipto, "to fall around", hence signifies to "fall" in with, or among, to light upon, come across, and is translated **(1)** "fall among" in Lk 10:30, "among (robbers)"; and **(2)** "fall into" in Acts 27:41, **(2a)** "falling into", a part of a shore; and **(2b)** "fall into" in Jas 1:2, into temptation (i.e., trials). See: TDNT−6:173, 846; BAGD− 649d; THAYER−504d.

4046. περιποιέομαι {2x} **pĕripŏiĕŏmai,** *per-ee-poy-eh'-om-ahee;* mid. voice from *4012* and *4160;* to *make around oneself,* i.e. *acquire* (*buy*):−purchase {2x}.

This word signifies "to gain" or "get for one-self, purchase"; middle voice in Acts 20:28 and 1 Ti 3:13. See: BAGD−650a; THAYER−504d.

4047. περιποίησις {5x} **pĕripŏiēsis,** *per-ee-poy'-ay-sis;* from *4046;* *acquisition* (the act or the thing); by extens. *preservation:*−purchased possession {1x}, to obtain + 1519 {1x}, obtaining {1x}, saving {1x}, peculiar + 1519 {1x}.

Peripoiesis, lit., "a making around" (*peri,* "around," *poieo,* "to do or make"), denotes **(1)** "the act of obtaining" anything, **(1a)** "to obtain", as of salvation, deliverence; 1 Th 5:9; **(1b)** "obtaining" salvation in its completeness, the glory of Christ; **(2)** "a thing acquired, an acquisition, possession," Eph 1:14, "(God's own) possession"; **(3)** 1 Pet 2:9, "a peculiar

(people);" cf. Is 43:21; **(4)** preservation, this may be the meaning in Heb 10:39, "saving." See: BAGD−650a; THAYER−504d.

4048. περιρρήγνυμι {1x} **pĕrirrhēgnumi,** *per-ir-hrayg'-noo-mee;* from *4012* and *4486;* to *tear* all *around,* i.e. *completely away:*−rend off {1x}.

This word means "to tear off all round" and is said of garments in Acts 16:22. See: BAGD− 650b; THAYER−505a.

4049. περισπάω {1x} **pĕrispaō,** *per-ee-spah'-o;* from *4012* and *4685;* to *drag* all *around,* i.e. (fig.) to *distract* (with care):−cumber {1x}.

Perispao literally means to draw around, to draw away, to distract and is used in the passive voice in the sense of being overoccupied about a thing; cumbered (Lk 10:40). See: BAGD−650b; THAYER−505a.

4050. περισσεία {4x} **pĕrissĕia,** *per-is-si'-ah;* from *4052;* *surplusage,* i.e. *superabundance:*−abundance {2x}, abundantly {1x}, superfluity {1x}.

Perisseia is an exceeding measure, something above the ordinary and is used **(1)** of the abundance of grace (Rom 5:17); **(2)** of the abundance of joy (2 Cor 8:2); **(3)** of the extension of the apostle's sphere of service through the practical fellowship of the saints at Corinth (2 Cor 10:15); and **(4)** metaphorically in Jas 1:21 of overflowing ["superfluity of"] wickedness. See: TDNT−6:63, 828; BAGD−650c; THAYER−505a.

4051. περίσσευμα {5x} **pĕrissĕuma,** *per-is'-syoo-mah;* from *4052;* a *surplus,* or *superabundance:*−abundance {4x}, that was left over and above {1x}.

Perisseuma denotes **(1)** "abundance" in a slightly more concrete form; **(1a)** 2 Cor 8:13−14, where it stands for the gifts in kind supplied by the saints. **(1b)** In Mt 12:34 and Lk 6:45 it is used of the "abundance" of the heart; **(2)** in Mk 8:8, of the broken pieces left after feeding the multitude "that was left"). See: TDNT−6:63, 828; BAGD−650c; THAYER−505b.

4052. περισσεύω {39x} **pĕrissĕuō,** *per-is-syoo'-o;* from *4053;* to *superabound* (in quantity or quality), *be in excess, be superfluous;* also (tran.) to *cause to superabound* or *excel:*−abound {17x}, abundance {3x}, remain {3x}, exceed {2x}, increase {2x}, be left {1x}, redound {1x}, misc. {10x} = be more abundant, be the better, enough and to spare, excel.

Perisseuo is used **I.** intransitively **(1)** "of exceeding a certain number, or measure, to be over, to remain," of the fragments after feeding the multitude (cf. *perisseuma*), Lk 9:17; Jn

6:12–13; (2) "to exist in abundance"; (2a) as of wealth, Lk 12:15; 21:4; (2b) of food, Lk 15:17. In this sense it is used also (2c) of consolation, 2 Cor 1:5; (2d) of the effect of a gift sent to meet the need of saints, 2 Cor 9:12; (2e) of rejoicing, Phil 1:26; (3) of what comes or falls to the lot of a person in large measure, (3a) as of the grace of God and the gift by the grace of Christ, Rom 5:15, (3b) of the sufferings of Christ, 2 Cor 1:5. (3c) In Mk 12:44 and Lk 21:4, "abundance." (4) "to redound to, or to turn out abundantly for something," as (4a) of the liberal effects of poverty, 2 Cor 8:2; (4b) in Rom 3:7, argumentatively of the effects of the truth of God, as to whether God's truthfulness becomes more conspicuous and His glory is increased through man's untruthfulness; (4c) of numerical increase, Acts 16:5. (5) "to be abundantly furnished, to abound in a thing," (5a) as of material benefits, Lk 12:15; (5b) Phil 4:18 of spiritual gifts; (6) 1 Cor 14:12, or "to be preeminent, to excel, to be morally better off," as regards partaking of certain meats; (7) 1 Cor 8:8, "are we the better"; (8) "to abound" (8a) in hope, Rom 15:13; (8b) the work of the Lord, 1 Cor 15:58; (8c) faith and grace, 2 Cor 8:7; (8d) thanksgiving, Col 2:7; (8e) walking so as to please God, Phil 1:9; 1 Th 4:1, 10; (8f) of righteousness, Mt 5:20; (8g) of the gospel, as the ministration of righteousness 2 Cor 3:9, "exceed." II. It is used transitively, in the sense of (1) "to make to abound," e.g., to provide a person richly so that he has "abundance," as (1a) of spiritual truth, Mt 13:12; (1b) the right use of what God has entrusted to us, Mt 25:29; (1c) the power of God in conferring grace, 2 Cor 9:8; (2) Eph 1:8; to "make abundant" or to cause to excel, (2a) as of the effect of grace in regard to thanksgiving, 2 Cor 4:15; (2b) His power to make us "to abound" in love, 1 Th 3:12. See: TDNT—6:58, 828; BAGD—650c; THAYER—505b.

4053. περισσός {10x} pĕrissŏs, per-is-sos'; from 4012 (in the sense of beyond); superabundant (in quantity) or superior (in quality); by impl. excessive; adv. (with 1537) violently; neut. (as noun) preeminence:— more {2x}, beyond measure {1x}, vehemently + 1537 {1x}, more abundantly {1x}, advantage {1x}, superfluous {1x}, very highly + 5228 + 1537 {1x}, exceeding abundantly above + 5228 + 1537 {1x}, exceeding + 5228 + 1537 {1x}.

Perissos, "abundant," is translated (1) "advantage" in Rom 3:1; (2) "superfluous" in 2 Cor 9:1. (3) It also means "what is above and over, superadded," hence came to denote "what is superior and advantageous," Rom 3:1, "advantage" in a comparison between Jew and Gentile; only here with this meaning. (4) It is

translated "more," e.g., in Mt 5:37–47 and (5) in Jn 10:10 the neuter form is rendered "more abundantly." See: TDNT—6:61, 828; BAGD—651b; THAYER—505d.

4054. περισσότερον {4x} pĕrissŏtĕrŏn, per-is-sot'-er-on; neut. of 4055 (as adv.); in a more superabundant way:—more abundantly {2x}, a great deal {1x}, far more {1x}.

This word is the neuter of the comparative degree of perissos, "more abundant," is translated (1) "more abundantly" in 1 Cor 15:10; Heb 6:17; (2) "a great deal" in Mk 7:36; (3) "far more" in Heb 7:15. See: BAGD—651c; THAYER—506a.

4055. περισσότερος {12x} pĕrissŏtĕrŏs, per-is-sot'-er-os; comp. of 4053; more superabundant (in number, degree or character):—more {4x}, greater {3x}, more abundant {3x}, much more {1x}, overmuch {1x}.

Perissoteros, the comparative degree of perissos (4053) is translated as follows: (1) "more" in Mt 11:9; Lk 12:4, 48; 2 Cor 10:8; (2) "greater" in Mt 23:14; Mk 12:40; Lk 20:47; (3) in 1 Cor 12:23 twice, 24, "more abundant"; (4) in 2 Cor 2:7, "overmuch"; and (5) "much more" in Lk 7:26. See: BAGD—651c; THAYER—506 bottom of page; go to 505d [4053].

4056. περισσοτέρως {13x} pĕrissŏtĕrŏs, per-is-sot-er'-oce; adv. from 4055; more superabundantly:—more abundantly {4x}, more exceedingly {2x}, more abundant {2x}, much more {1x}, more frequent {1x}, the rather {1x}, exceedingly {1x}, the more earnest {1x}. See: BAGD—651d; THAYER—506 bottom of page; go to 505d [4053].

4057. περισσῶς {3x} pĕrissŏs, per-is-soce'; adv. from 4053; superabundantly:—exceedingly {1x}, out of measure {1x}, the more {1x}.

Perissos, as an adverb, is translated (1) "exceedingly" in Acts 26:11; (2) "the more" in Mt 27:23; and (3) "out of measure": "And they were astonished out of measure, saying among themselves, Who then can be saved?" (Mk 10:26). Syn.: 280, 488, 943, 2884, 3313, 3354, 3358, 4568, 5234, 5249, 5518. See: BAGD—651d; THAYER—506a.

4058. περιστερά {10x} pĕristĕra, per-is-ter-ah'; of uncert. der.; a pigeon:—dove {9x}, pigeon {1x}.

Peristera denotes "a dove or pigeon," Mt 3:16; 10:16 (indicating its proverbial harmlessness); 21:12; Mk 1:10; 11:15; Lk 2:24 (pigeons"); 3:22; Jn 1:32; 2:14, 16. See: TDNT—6:63, 830; BAGD—651d; THAYER—506b.

4059. περιτέμνω {18x} **pĕritĕmnō**, *per-ee-tem'-no;* from *4012* and the base of *5114;* to *cut around,* i.e. (spec.) to *circumcise:*—circumcise {18x}.

Peritemno, as a verb, means "to circumcise" and is used **(1)** literally, **(1a)** being circumcised (Lk 1:59; 2:21); **(1b)** of receiving circumcision (Gal 5:2–3; 6:13); **(2)** metaphorically, of spiritual circumcision (Col 2:11). Syn.: 203, 564, 1986, 4061. See: TDNT—6:72, 831; BAGD—652b; THAYER—506b.

4060. περιτίθημι {8x} **pĕritithēmi**, *per-ee-tith'-ay-mee;* from *4012* and *5087;* to *place around;* by impl. to *present:*—put on {3x}, put upon {1x}, set about {1x}, put about {1x}, bestow upon {1x}, hedge around + 5318 {1x}. See: BAGD—652c; THAYER—506b.

4061. περιτομή {36x} **pĕritŏmē**, *per-it-om-ay';* from *4059; circumcision* (the rite, the condition or the people, lit. or fig.):—✗ circumcised {1x}, circumcision {35x}.

Peritome, as a noun, literally means "a cutting round, circumcision" and **(1)** was a rite enjoined by God upon Abraham and his male descendants and dependents, as a sign of the covenant made with him (Gen 17; Acts 7:8; Rom 4:11). **(2)** Hence Israelites termed Gentiles "the uncircumcised" (cf. Judg 15:18; 2 Sa 1:20). So in the NT, but without the suggestion of contempt (e.g., Rom 2:26; Eph 2:11). **(3)** The rite had a moral significance (cf. Ex 6:12, 30, where it is metaphorically applied to the lips; so to the ear, Jer 6:10, and the heart, Deut 30:6; Jer 4:4. Cf. Jer 9:25–26). **(3a)** It refers to the state of "circumcision" (Rom 2:25–28; 3:1; 4:10; 1 Cor 7:19; Gal 5:6; 6:15; Col 3:11). **(3b)** In the economy of grace no account is taken of any ordinance performed on the flesh; the old racial distinction is ignored in the preaching of the gospel, and faith is the sole condition upon which the favor of God in salvation is to be obtained (Rom 10:11–13; 1 Cor 7:19; cf. Rom 4:9–12).

(4) Upon the preaching of the gospel to, and the conversion of, Gentiles, a sect of Jewish believers arose who argued that the gospel, without the fulfillment of "circumcision," would make void the Law and make salvation impossible (Acts 15:1). **(4a)** Hence this party was known as "the circumcision" (Acts 10:45; 11:2; Gal 2:12; Col 4:11; Titus 1:10—the term being used by metonymy, the abstract being put for the concrete, as with the application of the word to Jews generally, Rom 3:30; 4:9, 12; 15:8; Gal 2:7–9; Eph 2:11). **(4b)** It is used metaphorically and spiritually of believers with reference **(4b1)** to the act (Col 2:11; Rom 2:29);

(4b2) to the condition (Phil 3:3). Syn.: 203, 564, 1986, 4059. See: TDNT—6:72, 831; BAGD—652d; THAYER—506c.

4062. περιτρέπω {1x} **pĕritrĕpō**, *per-ee-trep'-o;* from *4012* and the base of *5157;* to *turn around,* i.e. (ment.) to *craze:*—make mad + 3130 + 1519 {1x}. See: BAGD—653a; THAYER—506d.

4063. περιτρέχω {1x} **pĕritrĕchō**, *per-ee-trekh'-o;* from *4012* and *5143* (incl. its alt.); to *run around,* i.e. *traverse:*—run through {1x}. See: BAGD—653a; THAYER—506d.

4064. περιφέρω {5x} **pĕriphĕrō**, *per-ee-fer'-o;* from *4012* and *5342;* to *convey around,* i.e. *transport hither and thither:*—bear about {1x}, carry about {4x}.

Periphero, "about," signifies "to carry about, or bear about," and is used **(1)** literally, **(1a)** of carrying the sick Mk 6:55; or **(1b)** of physical sufferings endured in fellowship with Christ, 2 Cor 4:10; **(2)** metaphorically, of being "carried" about by different evil doctrines, Eph 4:14; Heb 13:9; Jude 12. See: BAGD—653b; THAYER—506d.

4065. περιφρονέω {1x} **pĕriphrŏnĕō**, *per-ee-fron-eh'-o;* from *4012* and *5426;* to *think beyond,* i.e. *depreciate* (*contemn*):—despise {1x}.

Literally, this word means **(1)** to think round a thing, to turn over in the mind, to have thoughts beyond, to consider or examine on all sides, i.e. carefully, thoroughly; **(2)** to exalt one's self in thought above a person or a thing; hence, **(3)** to feel contempt for, to despise (Titus 2:15). See: TDNT—3:663, 421; BAGD—653b; THAYER—507a.

4066. περίχωρος {10x} **pĕrichōrŏs**, *per-ikh'-o-ros;* from *4012* and *5561;* *around* the *region,* i.e. *circumjacent* (as noun, with *1093* impl. *vicinity*):—region round about {5x}, country round about {3x}, country about {1x}, region that lieth around about {1x}.

Perichoros, signifies **(1)** "country round about," Lk 8:37; **(2)** "country about," Lk 3:3; **(3)** in Mt 14:35 and Lk 4:37, "country round about"; **(4)** Mt 3:5; Mk 1:28; Lk 4:14; 7:17; Acts 14:6. See: BAGD—653c; THAYER—507a.

4067. περίψωμα {1x} **pĕripsōma**, *per-ip'-so-mah* or

περίψημα **pĕripsēma**,
per-ip'-say-mah; from a compound of *4012* and ψάω *psaō* (to *rub*); something *brushed* all *around,* completely *wiped off* all around, i.e. *off-scrapings* (fig. *scum*):—offscouring {1x}.

Peripsema, "that which is wiped off" (akin to *peripsao,* "to wipe off all round"; *peri,* "around," *psao,* "to wipe"), hence, "offscouring," is used metaphorically in 1 Cor 4:13. This and the synonymous word *perikatharma,* "refuse, rubbish," "were used especially of condemned criminals of the lowest classes, who were sacrificed as expiatory offerings because of their degraded life. See: TDNT—6:84,*; BAGD—653c; THAYER—507a.

4068. π**ερπερεύομαι** {1x} **pĕrpĕrĕuŏmai,** *per-per-yoo'-om-ahee;* mid. voice from πέρπερος **pĕrpĕrŏs** (*braggart;* perh. by redupl. of the base of *4008*); to *boast:*—vaunt itself {1x}.

This word means to boast one's self, give a self display, employing rhetorical embellishments in extolling one's self excessively, "to boast or vaunt oneself" and is used in 1 Cor 13:4, negatively of love. See: TDNT—6:93, 833; BAGD—653d; THAYER—507b.

4069. Π**ερσίς** {1x} **Pĕrsis,** *per-sece';* a *pers.* woman; *Persis,* a Chr. female:—Persis {1x}. See: BAGD—653d; THAYER—507b.

4070. π**έρυσι** {2x} **pĕrusi,** *per'-oo-si;* adv. from *4009;* the *by-gone,* i.e. (as noun) *last year:*—a year ago + 572 {2x}. Cf. 2 Cor 8:10; 9:2. See: BAGD—653d; THAYER—507b.

π**ετάομαι pĕtaŏmai.** See *4072.*

4071. π**ετεινόν** {14x} **pĕtĕinŏn,** *pet-i-non';* neut. of a der. of *4072;* a *flying* animal, i.e. *bird:*—bird {5x}, fowl {9x}. See: BAGD—654a; THAYER—507c.

4072. π**έτομαι** {5x} **pĕtŏmai,** *pet'-om-ahee;* or prol.

π**ετάομαι pĕtaŏmai,** *pet-ah'-om-ahee;* or contr. πτάομαι **ptaŏmai,** *ptah'-om-ahee;* mid. voice of a primary verb; to *fly:*—fly {3x}, flying {2x}. See: BAGD—654a; THAYER—507c.

4073. π**έτρα** {16x} **pĕtra,** *pet'-ra;* fem. of the same as *4074;* a (mass of) *rock* (lit. or fig.):—rock {16x}.

Petra denotes **(1)** a mass of rock (Mt 7:24, 25; 27:51, 60; Mk 15:46; Lk 6:48) as distinct from **(2)** *petros* (*4074*), **(2a)** a detached stone or boulder, or **(2b)** a stone that might be thrown or easily moved. See: TDNT—6:95, 834; BAGD—654a; THAYER—507c.

4074. Π**έτρος** {162x} **Pĕtrŏs,** *pet'-ros;* appar. a primary word; a (piece of) *rock* (larger than *3037*); as a name, *Petrus,* an apostle:—Peter {161x}, rock {1x}. See: TDNT—

6:100, 835; BAGD—654d; THAYER—507d. comp. *2786.*

4075. π**ετρώδης** {4x} **pĕtrōdēs,** *pet-ro'-dace;* from *4073* and *1491; rocklike,* i.e. *rocky:*—stony place {2x}, stony ground {2x}.

Petrodes, "rock-like" (*petra,* "a rock," *eidos,* "a form, appearance"), is used of "rock" underlying shallow soil, **(1)** Mt 13:5, 20, "stony places"; **(2)** Mk 4:5, 16, "stony ground." See: BAGD—655c; THAYER—508b.

4076. π**ήγανον** {1x} **pēganŏn,** *pay'-gan-on;* from *4078; rue* (from its *thick* or *fleshy* leaves):—rue {1x}.

Peganon is a shrubby plant with yellow flowers and a heavy smell, cultivated for medicinal purposes (Lk 11:42). See: BAGD—655d; THAYER—508b.

4077. π**ηγή** {12x} **pēgē,** *pay-gay';* prob. from *4078* (through the idea of *gushing* plumply); a *fount* (lit. or fig.), i.e. *source* or *supply* (of water, blood, enjoyment) (not necessarily the orig. spring):—fountain {8x}, well {4x}.

Pege, "a spring or fountain," is used of **(1)** "an artificial well," fed by a spring, Jn 4:6; **(2)** metaphorically (in contrast to such a well), "the indwelling Spirit of God," Jn 4:14; **(3)** "springs," metaphorically in 2 Pet 2:17, "wells" (without water, spoken of apostate teachers); **(4)** "natural fountains or springs," Jas 3:11, 12; Rev 8:10; 14:7; 16:4; **(5)** metaphorically, "eternal life and the future blessings accruing from it," Rev 7:17; 21:6; **(6)** "a flow of blood," Mk 5:29. See: TDNT—6:112, 837; BAGD—655d; THAYER—508b.

4078. π**ήγνυμι** {1x} **pēgnumi,** *payg'-noo-mee;* a prol. form of a primary verb (which in its simpler form occurs only as an alt. in certain tenses); to *fix* ("peg"), i.e. (spec.) to *set up* (a tent):—to pitch {1x}. See: BAGD—656a; THAYER—508b.

4079. π**ηδάλιον** {2x} **pēdaliŏn,** *pay-dal'-ee-on;* neut. of a (presumed) der. of πηδόν **pēdŏn** (the *blade* of an oar; from the same as *3976*); a "*pedal,*" i.e. *helm:*—rudder {1x}, helm {1x}.

Pedalion, "a rudder" (akin to *pedos,* "the blade of an oar"), occurs in **(1)** Jas 3:4, "helm"; and **(2)** Acts 27:40, plural, "the rudder (bands)." **(3)** The *pedalia* were actually steering paddles, two of which were used as "rudders" in ancient ships. See: BAGD—656a; THAYER—508b.

4080. π**ηλίκος** {2x} **pēlikŏs,** *pay-lee'-kos;* a quantitative form (the fem.) of the base of *4225; how much* (as an indef.),

i.e. in size or (fig.) dignity:—how great {1x}, how large {1x}.

Pelikos, primarily a direct interrogative, "how large? how great?" is used in exclamations, indicating magnitude, in **(1)** Gal 6:11, of letter characters; in **(2)** Heb 7:4, metaphorically, of the distinguished character of Melchizedek. See: BAGD—656b; THAYER—508c.

4081. πηλός {6x} pēlŏs, *pay-los';* perh. a primary word; *clay:*—clay {6x}.

Pelos, "clay," especially such as was used by a mason or potter, is used **(1)** of moist "clay," in Jn 9:6, 11, 14–15, in connection with Christ's healing the blind man; in **(2)** Rom 9:21, of potter's "clay," as to the potter's right over it as an illustration of the prerogatives of God in His dealings with sinful men. See: TDNT—6:118, 838; BAGD—656b; THAYER—508c.

4082. πήρα {6x} pēra, *pay'-rah;* of uncert. aff.; a *wallet* or leather *pouch* for food:—scrip {6x}.

Pera, "a traveler's leather bag or pouch for holding provisions," is translated "scrip", Mt 10:10; Mk 6:8; Lk 9:3; 10:4; 22:35, 36. See: TDNT—6:119, 838; BAGD—656c; THAYER—508c.

4083. πῆχυς {4x} pēchus, *pay'-khoos;* of uncert. aff.; the *fore-arm,* i.e. (as a measure) a *cubit:*—cubit {4x}.

A *pechus* is a measure of length equal to distance from the joint of the elbow to the tip of the middle finger [i.e. about 18 inches, or .5 m] (Mt 6:27; Lk 12:25; Jn 21:8; Rev 21:17). See: BAGD—656d; THAYER—508c.

4084. πιάζω {12x} piazō, *pee-ad'-zo;* prob. another form of *971;* to *squeeze,* i.e. *seize* (gently by the hand [*press*], or officially [*arrest*], or in hunting [*capture*]):—apprehend {2x}, catch {2x}, lay hand on {1x}, take {7x}.

Poiazo, "to lay hold of," with the suggestion of firm pressure or force, **(1)** is used in John, six times of efforts to seize Christ and is always rendered "take" in 7:30, 32, 44; 10:39; 11:57. **(2)** It is translated "laid hands on" in 8:20. **(3)** In Acts 12:4 and 2 Cor 11:32 it is translated respectively "apprehended" and "apprehend." **(4)** In Rev 19:20, "taken", it is used of the seizure of the Beast and the False Prophet. **(5)** In Jn 21:3, 10 it is used of catching fish, "caught." **(6)** Elsewhere in Acts 3:7, "took." See: BAGD—657a; THAYER—508d. comp. *4085.*

4085. πιέζω {1x} piĕzō, *pee-ed'-zo;* another form for *4084;* to *pack:*—press down {1x}.

Piezo, "to press down together," is used in Lk 6:38, "pressed down," of the character of

the measure given in return for giving. See: BAGD—657b; THAYER—508d.

4086. πιθανολογία {1x} pithanŏlŏgia, *pith-an-ol-og-ee'-ah;* from a compound of a der. of *3982* and *3056; persuasive language:*—enticing words {1x}. See: BAGD—657b; THAYER—508d.

4087. πικραίνω {4x} pikrainō, *pik-rah'-ee-no;* from *4089;* to *embitter* (lit. or fig.):—be bitter {2x}, make bitter {2x}.

Pikraino signifies, **(1)** in the active voice, "to be bitter," Col 3:19, or "to embitter, irritate, or to make bitter," Rev 10:9; **(2)** the passive voice, "to be made bitter," is used in Rev 8:11; 10:10. See: TDNT—6:122, 839; BAGD—657b; THAYER—508d.

4088. πικρία {4x} pikria, *pik-ree'-ah;* from *4089; acridity* (espec. *poison*), lit. or fig.:—bitterness {4x}.

Pikria denotes "bitterness." **(1)** It is used in Acts 8:23, metaphorically, of a condition of extreme wickedness, "gall of bitterness" or "bitter gall"; **(2)** in Rom 3:14, of evil speaking; **(3)** in Eph 4:31, of "bitter" hatred; **(4)** in Heb 12:15, in the same sense, metaphorically, of a root of "bitterness," producing "bitter" fruit. See: TDNT—6:122, 839; BAGD—657c; THAYER—509a.

4089. πικρός {2x} pikrŏs, *pik-ros';* perh. from *4078* (through the idea of *piercing*); *sharp* (*pungent*), i.e. *acrid* (lit. or fig.):—bitter {2x}.

Pikros, meaning "to cut, to prick," hence, lit., "pointed, sharp, keen, pungent to the sense of taste, smell, etc.," is found in Jas 3:11, 14. In v. 11 it has its natural sense, with reference to water; in v. 14 it is used metaphorically of jealousy. See: TDNT—6:122, 839; BAGD—657c; THAYER—509a.

4090. πικρῶς {2x} pikrŏs, *pik-roce';* adv. from *4089; bitterly,* i.e. (fig.) *violently:*—bitterly {2x}.

Pikros, "bitterly," is used of the poignant grief of Peter's weeping for his denial of Christ, Mt 26:75; Lk 22:62. See: BAGD—657d; THAYER—509a.

4091. Πιλᾶτος {55x} Pilatŏs, *pil-at'-os;* of Lat. or.; *close-pressed,* i.e. *firm; Pilatus,* a Rom.:—Pilate {55x}. See: BAGD—657d; THAYER—509b.

πίμπλημι pimplēmi. See *4130.*

4092. **πίμπρημι** {1x} **pimprēmi**, *pim'-pray-mee;* a redupl. and prol. form of a primary

πρέω prĕō, *preh'-o;* which occurs only as an alt. in certain tenses); to *fire*, i.e. *burn* (fig. and pass. *become inflamed* with fever):—be (✗ should have) swollen {1x}. See: BAGD—658b; THAYER—509d.

4093. **πινακίδιον** {1x} **pinakidiŏn**, *pin-ak-id'-ee-on;* dimin. of *4094;* a *tablet* (for writing on):—writing table {1x}. See: BAGD—658b; THAYER—509d.

4094. **πίναξ** {5x} **pinax**, *pin'-ax;* appar. a form of *4109;* a *plate:*—charger {4x}, platter {1x}.

Pinax is primarily a board or plank and came to denote various articles of wood, [cf. "cutting boards"] upon which meat was sliced; hence, a wooden platter, a charger (Mt 14:8, 11; Mk 6:25, 28; Lk 11:39). See: BAGD—658c; THAYER—509d.

4095. **πίνω** {75x} **pinō**, *pee'-no;* a prol. form of

πίω piō, *pee'-o;* which (together with another form πόω **pŏō**, *pŏ'-o;* occurs only as an alt. in certain tenses; to *imbibe* (lit. or fig.):—drink {68x}, drink of {7x}.

Pino, as a verb, means "to drink," and is used chiefly in the Gospels and in 1 Cor, whether literally (most frequently), or figuratively, **(1)** of "drinking" of the blood of Christ, in the sense of receiving eternal life, through His death, Jn 6:53–54, 56; **(2)** of "receiving" spiritually that which refreshes, strengthens and nourishes the soul, Jn 7:37; **(3)** of "deriving" spiritual life from Christ, Jn 4:14, as Israel did typically, 1 Cor 10:4; **(4)** of "sharing" in the sufferings of Christ humanly inflicted, Mt 20:22–23; Mk 10:38–39; **(5)** of "participating" in the abominations imparted by the corrupt religious and commercial systems emanating from Babylon, Rev 18:3; **(6)** of "receiving" divine judgment, through partaking unworthily of the Lord's Supper, 1 Cor 11:29; **(7)** of "experiencing" the wrath of God, Rev 14:10; 16:6; **(8)** of the earth's "receiving" the benefits of rain, Heb 6:7. Syn.: 3184, 4213, 4222, 4844, 5202. See: TDNT—6:135, 840; BAGD—658c; THAYER—510a.

4096. **πιότης** {1x} **piŏtēs**, *pee-ot'-ace;* from πίων **piōn**, (*fat;* perh. akin to the alt. of *4095* through the idea of *repletion*); *plumpness*, i.e. (by impl.) *richness* (*oiliness*):—fatness {1x}.

Piotes, from *pion*, "fat," from a root which signifies "swelling," is used metaphorically in Rom 11:17. The gentile believer had become a sharer in the spiritual life and blessing bestowed by divine covenant upon Abraham and his descendants as set forth under the figure of "the root of (not 'and') the 'fatness' of the olive tree." See: BAGD—659a; THAYER—510b.

4097. **πιπράσκω** {9x} **pipraskō**, *pip-ras'-ko;* a redupl. and prol. form of

πράω praō, *prah'-o;* (which occurs only as an alt. in certain tenses); contr. from περάω **pĕraō** (to *traverse;* from the base of *4008*); to *traffic* (by *travelling*), i.e. *dispose* of as merchandise or into slavery (lit. or fig.):—sell {9x}.

Piprasko, from an earlier form, *perao*, "to carry across the sea for the purpose of selling or to export," is used **(1)** literally, Mt 13:46; 18:25; 26:9; Mk 14:5; Jn 12:5; Acts 2:45; 4:34; 5:4; **(2)** metaphorically, Rom 7:14, "sold under sin," i.e., as fully under the domination of sin as a slave is under his master; the statement evinces an utter dissatisfaction with such a condition; it expresses, not the condemnation of the unregenerate state, but the evil of bondage to a corrupt nature, involving the futility of making use of the Law as a means of deliverance. See: TDNT—6:160, 846; BAGD—659a; THAYER—510b.

4098. **πίπτω** {90x} **piptō**, *pip'-to;* a redupl. and contr. form of πέτω **pĕtō**, *pet'-o;* (which occurs only as an alt. in certain tenses); prob. akin to *4072* through the idea of *alighting;* to *fall* (lit. or fig.):—fail {1x}, fall {69x}, fall down {19x}, light on {1x}.

Pipto, "to fall," is used **(1)** of descent, to "fall" down from, e.g., Mt 10:29; 13:4; **(2)** of a lot, Acts 1:26; **(3)** of "falling" under judgment, Jas 5:12 (cf. Rev 18:2); **(4)** of persons in the act of prostration, to prostrate oneself, **(4a)** e.g., Mt 17:6; Jn 18:6; Rev 1:17; **(4b)** in homage and worship, e.g., Mt 2:11; Mk 5:22; Rev 5:14; 19:4; **(5)** of things, "falling" into ruin, or failing, e.g., Mt 7:25; Heb 11:30; **(6)** of "falling" in judgment upon persons, as of the sun's heat, Rev 7:16, "light"; **(7)** of persons, in "falling" morally or spiritually, Rom 14:4; 1 Cor 10:8, 12; Rev 2:5; **(8)** Lk 16:17, "fail", of one tittle of the Law to fail. See: TDNT—6:161, 846; BAGD—659b; THAYER—510b.

4099. **Πισιδία** {2x} **Pisidia**, *pis-id-ee'-ah;* prob. of for. or.; *Pisidia*, a region of Asia Minor:—Pisidia {2x}. See: BAGD—660b; THAYER—511b.

4100. **πιστεύω** {248x} **pistĕuō**, *pist-yoo'-o;* from *4102;* to *have faith* (in, upon, or with respect to, a person or thing), i.e. *credit;* by impl. to *entrust* (espec. one's spiritual

well-being to Christ):—believe {239x}, commit
unto {4x}, commit to (one's) trust {1x}, be committed unto {1x}, be put in trust with {1x}, be
commit to one's trust {1x}, believer {1x}.

Pisteuo means not just to believe, but also
to be persuaded of; and hence, to place confidence in, to trust, and signifies, in this sense
of the word, reliance upon, not mere credence,
hence it is translated "commit unto", "commit
to one's trust", "be committed unto", etc. See:
TDNT—6:174, 849; BAGD—660b; THAYER—
511b.

4101. **πιστικός** {2x} **pistikŏs,** *pis-tik-os';*
from *4102; trustworthy,* i.e.
genuine (unadulterated):—spikenard + 3487
{2x}.

Spikenard is the head or spike of the nard
plant from which was extracted and purified a
juice of delicious odour which was used (either
pure or mixed) in the preparation of a most
precious ointment. Pure, unmixed, unadulterated spikenard was described as *pistikos.* See:
BAGD—662b; THAYER—512d.

4102. **πίστις** {244x} **pistis,** *pis'-tis;* from
3982; persuasion, i.e. *credence;*
mor. *conviction* (of *relig.* truth, or the truthfulness of God or a relig. teacher), espec. *reliance*
upon Christ for salvation; abstr. *constancy* in
such profession; by extension, the system of
religious (gospel) *truth* itself:—faith {239x}, assurance {1x}, believe + 1537 {1x}, belief {1x},
them that believe {1x}, fidelity {1x}.

Pistis is **(1)** conviction of the truth of anything, belief; of a conviction or belief respecting man's relationship to God and divine
things, generally with the included idea of
trust and holy fervour born of faith and joined
with it. It is related **(1a)** to God with the conviction that God exists and is the creator and
ruler of all things, the provider and bestower of
eternal salvation through Christ; **(1b)** to Christ
with a strong and welcome conviction or belief
that Jesus is the Messiah, through whom we
obtain eternal salvation in the kingdom of
God. **(2)** It includes all of the religious beliefs
of Christians ["the faith" – 1 Ti 1:2; 4:1]. **(3)**
Pistis is used of belief with the predominate
idea of trust (or confidence) whether in God or
in Christ, springing from faith in the same.
(4) It speaks of fidelity, faithfulness. **(5)** It describes the character of one who can be relied
on. See: TDNT—6:174, 849; BAGD—662b;
THAYER—512d.

4103. **πιστός** {67x} **pistŏs,** *pis-tos';* from
3982; obj. *trustworthy;* subj.
trustful:—faithful {53x}, believe {6x}, believe in
{2x}, true {2x}, faithfully {1x}, believer {1x},
sure {1x}; not tr {1x}.

Pistos, **(1)** in the active sense means "believing, trusting" in Gal 3:9; Acts 16:1; 2 Cor 6:15;
(2) in the passive sense, "trusty, faithful, trustworthy" in 1 Th 5:24; 2 Th 3:3. **(3)** It is translated **(3a)** "believer" in 2 Cor 6:15; **(3b)**
"believers" in 1 Ti 4:12; **(3c)** in 1 Ti 5:16, "if any
woman that believeth," lit. "if any believing
woman." **(3d)** So in 1 Ti 6:2, "believing masters." **(3e)** In 1 Pet 1:21, "do believe in God";
(3f) In Jn 20:27 it is translated "believing." See:
TDNT—6:174, 849; BAGD—664c; THAYER—
514b.

4104. **πιστόω** {1x} **pistŏō,** *pis-tŏ'-o;* from
4103; to *assure:*—assure of
{1x}.

Pistoo, "to trust or give assurance to" has a
secondary meaning, in the passive voice, "to be
assured of," 2 Ti 3:14. See: TDNT—6:174, 849;
BAGD—665b; THAYER—514c.

4105. **πλανάω** {39x} **planaō,** *plan-ah'-o;* from
4106; to (prop. *cause* to) *roam*
(from safety, truth, or virtue):—deceive {24x},
err {6x}, go astray {5x}, seduce {2x}, wander
{1x}, be out of the way {1x}.

Planao, in the passive form sometimes
means **(1)** "to go astray, wander," Mt 18:12;
1 Pet 2:25; Heb 11:38; **(2)** frequently active, "to
deceive, by leading into error, to seduce," e.g.,
Mt 24:4, 5, 11, 24; Jn 7:12; 1 Jn 3:7. **(3)** In Rev
12:9 the present participle is used with the definite article, as a title of the devil, "the deceiver," lit., "the deceiving one." **(4)** Often it has
the sense of "deceiving oneself," e.g., 1 Cor 6:9;
15:33; Gal 6:7; or **(5)** Jas 1:16, "do not err." See:
TDNT—6:228, 857; BAGD—665b; THAYER—
514d.

4106. **πλάνη** {39x} **planē,** *plan'-ay;* fem. of
4108 (as abstr.); obj. *fraudu-
lence;* subj. a *straying* from orthodoxy or
piety:—deceive {24x}, err {6x}, go astray {5x},
seduce {2x}, wander {1x}, be out of the way {1x}.

(1) Literally, plane means a wandering
whereby those who are led astray roam hither
and thither and is always used of mental straying, wrong opinion, error in morals or religion, 2 Th 2:11, "delusion." **(2)** It is akin to
planao, "a wandering, a forsaking of the right
path," (see Jas 5:20), whether **(2a)** in doctrine,
2 Pet 3:17; 1 Jn 4:6, or **(2b)** in morals, Rom 1:27;
2 Pet 2:18; Jude 11; **(3)** though, in Scripture,
doctrine and morals are never divided by any
sharp line. **(4)** "Errors" in doctrine are not infrequently the effect of relaxed morality, and
vice versa. See: TDNT—6:228, 857; BAGD—
665d; THAYER—514d.

4107. **πλανήτης** {1x} **planētēs,** *plan-ay'-tace;*
from *4108;* a *rover* ("planet"),
i.e. (fig.) an *erratic* teacher:—wandering {1x}.

Planetes, "a wanderer" (Eng., "planet"), is used metaphorically in Jude 13, of the evil teachers there mentioned as "wandering (stars)." See: TDNT—6:228, 857; BAGD—666a; THAYER—515a.

4108. πλάνος {5x} **planŏs,** *plan'-os;* of uncert. aff.; *roving* (as a *tramp*), i.e. (by impl.) an *impostor* or *misleader:*—deceiver {4x}, seducing {1x}.

Planos, properly, an adjective, signifying **(1)** "wandering, or leading astray, seducing," 1 Ti 4:1, "seducing (spirits)", used as a noun, it denotes **(2)** an impostor of the vagabond type, and so any kind of "deceiver" or corrupter, Mt 27:63; 2 Cor 6:8; 2 Jn 7 (twice), in the last of which the accompanying definite article necessitates the translation "the deceiver." See: TDNT—6:228, 857; BAGD—666a; THAYER—515a.

4109. πλάξ {3x} **plax,** *plax;* from *4111;* a *moulding-board,* i.e. *flat* surface ("*plate*", or *tablet,* lit. or fig.):—table {3x}.

Plax primarily denotes anything flat and broad; hence, a flat stone, a small table, i.e., a tablet, 2 Cor 3:3 twice; Heb 9:4. See: BAGD—666a; THAYER—515a.

4110. πλάσμα {1x} **plasma,** *plas'-mah;* from *4111;* something *moulded:*—thing formed {1x}. See: TDNT—6:254, 862; BAGD—666b; THAYER—515b.

4111. πλάσσω {2x} **plassō,** *plas'-so;* a primary verb; to *mould,* i.e. *shape* or *fabricate:*—form {2x}.

Plasso, "to mold, to shape," was used of the artist who wrought in clay or wax (Eng., "plastic," "plasticity"), and occurs in Rom 9:20; 1 Ti 2:13. See: TDNT—6:254, 862; BAGD—666c; THAYER—515b.

4112. πλαστός {1x} **plastŏs,** *plas-tos';* from *4111; moulded,* i.e. (by impl.) *artificial* or (fig.) *fictitious* (*false*):—feigned {1x}.

Plastos primarily denotes formed, molded; then, metaphorically, made up, fabricated, feigned (2 Pet 2:3). See: TDNT—6:262, 862; BAGD—666c; THAYER—515b.

4113. πλατεῖα {9x} **platĕia,** *plat-i'-ah;* fem. of *4116;* a *wide* "*plat*" or "*place*", i.e. open *square:*—street {9x}.

Plateia, as a noun, means "a broad way, a street" (Mt 6:5; 12:19; Lk 10:10; 13:26; 14:21; Acts 5:15; Rev 11:8; 21:21; 22:2). Syn.: 296, 4505. See: BAGD—666d; THAYER—515b.

4114. πλάτος {4x} **platŏs,** *plat'-os;* from *4116; width:*—breadth {4x}.

This word denotes "breadth," Eph 3:18;

Rev 20:9; 21:16, twice. See: BAGD—666d; THAYER—515b.

4115. πλατύνω {3x} **platunō,** *plat-oo'-no;* from *4116;* to *widen* (lit. or fig.):—make broad {1x}, enlarge {2x}.

Platuno, connected with *plak,* "a flat, broad surface," signifies "to make broad"; said **(1)** of phylacteries, Mt 23:5; **(2)** used figuratively in 2 Cor 6:11, 13, "to be enlarged," in the ethical sense, of the heart. See: BAGD—667a; THAYER—515b.

4116. πλατύς {1x} **platus,** *plat-oos';* from *4111;* spread out "*flat*" ("plot"), i.e. *broad:*—wide {1x}.

Platus denotes "breadth," Eph 3:18; Rev 20:9; 21:16 (twice). See: BAGD—667b; THAYER—515c.

4117. πλέγμα {1x} **plĕgma,** *pleg'-mah;* from *4120;* a *plait* (of hair):—broidered hair {1x}.

Plegma signifies what is woven and is used in 1 Ti 2:9, of broided hair. See: BAGD—667a; THAYER—515c.

πλεῖον plĕiŏn. See *4119.*

4118. πλεῖστος {3x} **plĕistŏs,** *plice'-tos;* irreg. superl. of *4183;* the *largest number* or *very large:*—very great {1x}, most {2x}.

Pleistos, the superlative degree of *polus,* is used **(1)** as an adjective in Mt 21:8, "a very great"; **(2)** in the neuter, with the article, adverbially, "at the most", Mt 11:20; 1 Cor 14:27. See: BAGD—689d; THAYER—515c.

4119. πλείων {56x} **plĕiōn,** *pli-own;* neut.

πλεῖον plĕiŏn, *pli'-on;* or

πλέον plĕŏn, *pleh'-on;* comparative of *4183; more* in quantity, number, or quality; also (in plur.) the *major portion:*—more {23x}, many {12x}, greater {5x}, further + 1909 {3x}, most {2x}, more part {2x}, not tr {1x}, misc. {8x} = X above, + exceed, yet but. See: BAGD—667b; THAYER—515c.

4120. πλέκω {3x} **plĕkō,** *plek'-o;* a primary word; to *twine* or *braid:*—plait {3x}.

Pleko, "to weave, twist, plait," is used of the crown of thorns inflicted on Christ, Mt 27:29; Mk 15:17; Jn 19:2. See: BAGD—667b; THAYER—516a.

πλέον plĕŏn. See *4119.*

4121. πλεονάζω {9x} **plĕŏnazō,** *pleh-on-ad'-zo;* from *4119;* to *do, make* or *be more,* i.e. *increase* (tran. or intr.); by extens. to *superabound:*—abound {6x},

abundant {1x}, make to increase {1x}, have over {1x}.

This word, from *pleion,* or *pleon,* "more" (greater in quantity), akin to *pleo,* "to fill," signifies, **(1)** intransitively, "to superabound," **(1a)** of a trespass or sin, Rom 5:20; **(1b)** of grace, Rom 6:1; 2 Cor 4:15; **(1c)** of spiritual fruit, Phil 4:17; **(1d)** of love, 2 Th 1:3; **(1e)** of various fruits, 2 Pet 1:8; **(1f)** of the gathering of the manna, 2 Cor 8:15, "had . . . over"; **(2)** transitively, "to make to increase," 1 Th 3:12. See: TDNT— 6:263, 864; BAGD—667b; THAYER—516a.

4122. **πλεονεκτέω** {5x} **plĕŏnĕktĕō,** *pleh-on-ek-teh'-o;* from *4123;* to *be covetous,* i.e. (by impl.) to *over-reach:*— get an advantage {1x}, defraud {2x}, make a gain {2x}.

(1) This word always signifies an unfair advantage, never used positively. This word means lit., "to seek to get more" (*pleon,* "more," *echo,* "to have"); hence, "to get an advantage of, to take advantage of." **(2)** In 2 Cor 7:2, "defrauded"; **(3)** in 1 Th 4:6, "defraud." It is also translated **(4)** "get an advantage" in 2 Cor 2:11, of Satan's effort to gain an "advantage" over the church, through their neglect to restore the backslider; and **(5)** "make a gain" in 2 Cor 12:17–18. See: TDNT—6:266, 864; BAGD— 667c; THAYER—516b.

4123. **πλεονέκτης** {4x} **plĕŏnĕktēs,** *pleh-on-ek'-tace;* from *4119* and *2192; holding (desiring) more,* i.e. *eager for gain (avaricious,* hence, a *defrauder):*—covetous {4x}.

This word means lit., "(eager) to have more", i.e., to have what belongs to others; hence, "greedy of gain, covetous" in 1 Cor 5:10– 11; 6:10; Eph 5:5, "covetous man." See: TDNT—6:266, 864; BAGD—667c; THAYER— 516b.

4124. **πλεονεξία** {10x} **plĕŏnĕxia,** *pleh-on-ex-ee'-ah;* from *4123;* *ava-rice,* i.e. (by impl.) *fraudulency, extortion:*— covetousness {8x}, covetous practices {1x}, greediness {1x}.

Pleonexia, "covetousness," lit., "a desire to have more" (*pleon,* "more," *echo,* "to have"), **(1)** always in a bad sense, is used in **(2)** a general way in Mk 7:22 (plural, lit., "covetings," i.e., various ways in which "covetousness" shows itself); Rom 1:29; Eph 5:3; 1 Th 2:5. **(3)** Elsewhere it is used, **(3a)** of material posses-sions, Lk 12:15; 2 Pet 2:3; 2 Cor 9:5, a gift which betrays the giver's unwillingness to bestow what is due; **(3b)** of sensuality, **(3b1)** Eph 4:19, "greediness"; **(3b2)** Col 3:5, where it is called "idolatry"; **(3b3)** 2 Pet 2:14, "covetous prac-tices." Syn.: **(A)** *Pleonexia* is the more active

sin, *philargyria* (*5365*) the more passive. *Pleonexia* refers to having more with the desire to have more, seeking to possess what is not possessed. *Philargyria* refers to seeking to re-tain what is possessed and, through accumula-tion, to multiplying what is possessed. *Pleonexia* often implies bold and aggressive methods of acquisition; it frequently refers to behavior that is as free in scattering and squandering as it was eager and unscrupulous in acquiring. *Pleonexia* often squanders what he has seized. **(B)** The main distinction between *pleonexia* (*4124*) and *philarguria* (*5365*) is be-ing that between "covetousness" and avarice, the former having a much wider and deeper sense, being "the genus of which *philarguria* is the species." The "covetous" man is often cruel as well as grasping, while the avaricious man is simply miserly and stinting. See: TDNT— 6:266, 864; BAGD—667d; THAYER—516b.

4125. **πλευρά** {5x} **plĕura,** *plyoo-rah';* of un-cert. aff.; a *rib,* i.e. (by extens.) *side:*—side {5x}.

Pleura, "a side" (cf. Eng., "pleurisy"), is used **(1)** of the "side" of Christ, into which the spear was thrust, Jn 19:34; 20:20, 25, 27; **(2)** elsewhere, in Acts 12:7, of Peter's side. See: BAGD—668a; THAYER—516b.

4126. **πλέω** {5x} **plĕō,** *pleh'-o;* another form for

    πλεύω plĕuō, *plyoo'-o;* which is used as an alt. in certain tenses; prob. a form of *4150* (through the idea of *plunging* through the water); to *pass* in a vessel:—to sail {5x}. See: BAGD—668a; THAYER—516c. See also *4130.*

4127. **πληγή** {21x} **plēgē,** *play-gay';* from *4141;* a *stroke;* by impl. a *wound;* fig. a *calamity:*—plague {12x}, stripe {5x}, wound (-ed) {4x}.

A *plege* is a stripe, wound and is used by extension of a public calamity, heavy afflic-tion, a plague (e.g. Rev 9:20; 11:6; 15:1). See: BAGD—667a; THAYER—516c.

4128. **πλῆθος** {32x} **plēthŏs,** *play'-thos;* from *4130;* a *fulness,* i.e. a *large number, throng, populace:*—bundle {1x}, com-pany {1x}, multitude {30x}.

Plethos, lit., "a fullness," hence, "a large company, a multitude," is used **(1)** of things: **(1a)** of fish, Lk 5:6; Jn 21:6; **(1b)** of sticks ("bun-dle"), Acts 28:3; **(1c)** of stars and of sand, Heb 11:12; **(1d)** of sins, Jas 5:20; 1 Pet 4:8; **(2)** of persons, **(2a)** a "multitude": **(2a1)** of people, e.g., Mk 3:7, 8; Lk 6:17; Jn 5:3; Acts 14:1; **(2a2)** of angels, Lk 2:13; **(2b)** with the article, the whole number, the "multitude," the populace,

e.g., Lk 1:10; 8:37; Acts 5:16; 19:9; 23:7; **(2c)** a particular company, e.g., **(2c1)** of disciples, Lk 19:37; Acts 4:32; 6:2, 5; 15:30; **(2c2)** of elders, priests, and scribes, Acts 23:7; **(2c3)** of the apostles and the elders of the church in Jerusalem, Acts 15:12. See: TDNT—6:274, 866; BAGD—668b; THAYER—516c.

4129. πληθύνω {12x} **plēthunō,** *play-thoo'-no;* from another form of *4128;* to *increase* (tran. or intr.):—abound {1x}, multiply {11x}.

Plethuno, used **(1)** transitively, denotes **(1a)** "to cause to increase, to multiply," 2 Cor 9:10; Heb 6:14 (twice); **(1b)** in the passive voice, "to be multiplied," Mt 24:12, "(iniquity) shall abound"; Acts 6:7; 7:17; 9:31; 12:24; 1 Pet 1:2; 2 Pet 1:2; Jude 2; **(2)** intransitively, it denotes "to be multiplying," Acts 6:1, "was multiplied." See: TDNT—6:279, 866; BAGD—669a; THAYER—516d.

4130. πλήθω {24x} **plēthō,** *play'-tho;* a prol. form of a primary πλέω **plēŏ,** *pleh'-o* (which appears only as an alt. in certain tenses and in the redupl. form πίμπλημι **pimplēmi**); to *"fill"* (lit. or fig. [*imbue, influence, supply*]); spec. to *fulfil* (time):—fill {18x}, accomplish {4x}, furnish {1x}, full . . . come {1x}.

This word is used **(1)** of things; **(1a)** boats, with fish, Lk 5:7; **(1b)** a sponge, with vinegar, Mt 27:48; Jn 19:29; **(1c)** a city, with confusion, Acts 19:29; **(1d)** a wedding, with guests, Mt 22:10; **(2)** of persons (only in Luke's writings): **(2a)** with the Holy Spirit, Lk 1:15, 41, 67; Acts 2:4; 4:8, 31; 9:17; 13:9; **(2b)** with emotions: **(2b1)** wrath, Lk 4:28; **(2b2)** fear, Lk 5:26; **(2b3)** madness, Lk 6:11; **(2b4)** wonder, amazement, Acts 3:10; **(2b5)** indignation, Acts 5:17; and **(2b6)** Acts 13:45. **(3)** It is translated "accomplished" in Lk 1:23; 2:6, 21–22. See: TDNT—6:128,*; BAGD—658a; THAYER—516d.

4131. πλήκτης {2x} **plēktēs,** *plake'-tace;* from *4141;* a *smiter,* i.e. *pugnacious (quarrelsome):*—striker {2x}.

This person is a bruiser, one ready to deliver a blow; a pugnacious, contentious, quarrelsome person, 1 Ti 3:3; Titus 1:7. See: BAGD—669; THAYER—519d.

4132. πλήμμύρα {1x} **plēmmura,** *plame-moo'-rah;* prol. from *4130;* *flood-tide,* i.e. (by anal.) a *freshet:*—flood {1x}. See: BAGD—669b; THAYER—517a.

4133. πλήν {31x} **plēn,** *plane;* from *4119;* *moreover (besides),* i.e. *albeit, save that, rather, yet:*—but {14x}, nevertheless {8x}, notwithstanding {4x}, but rather {2x}, except {1x}, than {1x}, save {1x}. See: BAGD—669b; THAYER—517b.

4134. πλήρης {17x} **plērēs,** *play'-race;* from *4130; replete,* or *covered* over; by anal. *complete:*—full {17x}.

Pleres denotes "full," **(1)** in the sense of "being filled," **(1a)** materially, Mt 14:20; 15:37; Mk 8:19, said of baskets "full" of bread crumbs; **(1b)** of leprosy, Lk 5:12; **(1c)** spiritually, of the Holy Spirit, Lk 4:1; Acts 6:3; 7:55; 11:24; **(1d)** grace and truth, Jn 1:14; **(1e)** faith, Acts 6:5; **(1f)** grace and power, Acts 6:8; **(1g)** of the effects of spiritual life and qualities, seen in good works, Acts 9:36; **(1h)** in an evil sense, of guile and villany, Acts 13:10; **(1i)** wrath, Acts 19:28; **(2)** in the sense of "being complete," **(2a)** "full corn in the ear," Mk 4:28; **(2b)** of a reward hereafter, 2 Jn 8. See: TDNT—6:283, 867; BAGD—669d; THAYER—517b.

4135. πληροφορέω {5x} **plērŏphŏrĕŏ,** *play-rof-or-eh'-o;* from *4134* and *5409;* to *carry out fully* (in evidence), i.e. *completely assure* (or *convince*), *entirely accomplish:*—be fully persuaded {2x}, be most surely believed {1x}, be fully known {1x}, make full proof of {1x}.

This word means "to bring in full measure, to fulfill," also signifies **(1)** "to be fully persuaded" **(1a)** Rom 4:21, of Abraham's faith. **(1b)** In Rom 14:5 it is said of the apprehension of the will of God. **(1c)** In these two places it is used subjectively, with reference to an effect upon the mind. It is also understood **(2)** "to fulfill entirely," **(2a)** of circumstances relating to Christ, Lk 1:1, "are most surely believed"; **(2b)** of evangelical ministry, 2 Ti 4:5, "make full proof"; so **(2c)** in 2 Ti 4:17, "fully known." See: TDNT—6:309, 867; BAGD—670b; THAYER—517b.

4136. πληροφορία {4x} **plērŏphŏria,** *play-rof-or-ee'-ah;* from *4135; entire confidence:*—full assurance {3x}, assurance {1x}.

This word means "a fullness, abundance," also means "full assurance, entire confidence"; lit., a "full-carrying" (*pleros,* "full," *phero,* "to carry"). It is translated **(1)** "full assurance" in Heb 6:11, the engrossing effect of the expectation of the fulfillment of God's promises; **(2)** In 1 Th 1:5 it describes the willingness and freedom of spirit enjoyed by those who brought the gospel to Thessalonica, "much assurance"; **(3)** in Col 2:2, the freedom of mind and confidence resulting from an understanding in Christ, "full assurance"; **(4)** in Heb 10:22, the character of the faith by which we are to draw near to God, "full assurance." See: TDNT—6:310, 867; BAGD—670c; THAYER—517c.

4137. πληρόω {90x} **plērŏō,** *play-rŏ'-o;* from *4134;* to *make replete,* i.e. (lit.)

to *cram* (a net), *level* up (a hollow), or (fig.) to *furnish* (or *imbue, diffuse, influence*), *satisfy, execute* (an office), *finish* (a period or task), *verify* (or *coincide* with a prediction), etc.:— fulfil {51x}, fill {19x}, be full {7x}, complete {2x}, end {2x}, misc. {9x} = accomplish, ✕ after, expire, fully preach, perfect, supply.

Pleroo signifies **(1)** "to fill" and is used **(1a)** of things: **(1a1)** a net, Mt 13:48; **(1a2)** a building, Jn 12:3; Acts 2:2; **(1a3)** a city, Acts 5:28; **(1a4)** needs, Phil 4:19, "supply"; **(1a5)** metaphorically, of valleys, Lk 3:5; **(1a6)** figuratively, of a measure of iniquity, Mt 23:32; **(1b)** of persons: **(1b1)** of the members of the church, the body of Christ, as filled by Him, Eph 1:23, "all things in all the members"; 4:10; in Eph 3:19, of their being filled "into" (*eis*), "with" (all the fullness of God); of their being "made full" in Him, Col 2:10, "complete"; **(1b2)** of Christ Himself: with wisdom, in the days of His flesh, Lk 2:40; with joy, in His return to the Father, Acts 2:28; **(1b3)** of believers: with the Spirit, Eph 5:18; with joy, Acts 13:52; 2 Ti 1:4; with joy and peace, Rom 15:13; with knowledge, Rom 15:14; with comfort, 2 Cor 7:4; with the fruits of righteousness, Phil 1:11 (Gk. "fruit"); with the knowledge of God's will, Col 1:9; with abundance through material supplies by fellow believers, Phil 4:18; **(1b4)** of the hearts of believers as the seat of emotion and volition, Jn 16:6 (sorrow); Acts 5:3 (deceitfulness); **(1b5)** of the unregenerate who refuse recognition of God, Rom 1:29;

(2) "to fulfill, complete," **(2a)** of time, e.g., **(2a1)** Mk 1:15; Lk 21:24; Jn 7:8, "full come"; **(2a2)** Acts 7:23, "he was full forty years old", lit., "the time of forty years was fulfilled to him"; **(2a3)** Acts 7:30, "were expired"; **(2a4)** Acts 9:23; 24:27, "after two years"; **(2b)** "fulfill" **(2b1)** of number, Rev 6:11; **(2b2)** of good pleasure, 2 Th 1:11; **(2b3)** of joy, Phil 2:2; **(2b4)** in the passive voice, "to be fulfilled," Jn 3:29 and 17:13; **(2b5)** of obedience, 2 Cor 10:6; **(2b6)** of works, Rev 3:2; **(2b7)** of the future Passover, Lk 22:16; **(2b8)** of sayings, prophecies, etc., e.g., Mt. 1:22 (twelve times in Mt, two in Mk, four in Lk, eight in Jn, two in Acts); Jas 2:23; **(3)** in Col 1:25 the word signifies to preach "fully," to complete the ministry of the gospel appointed. See: TDNT—6:286, 867; BAGD—670c; THAYER—517c.

4138. πλήρωμα {17x} **plērōma**, *play'-ro-mah;* from *4137; repletion* or *completion*, i.e. (subj.) what *fills* (as contents, supplement, copiousness, multitude), or (obj.) what is *filled* (as container, performance, period):—fulness {13x}, full {1x}, fulfilling {1x}, which is put in to fill up {1x}, pierce that filled up {1x}.

Pleroma denotes "fullness," that of which a thing is "full"; it is thus used **(1)** of the grace and truth manifested in Christ, Jn 1:16; **(2)** of all His virtues and excellencies, Eph 4:13; Rom 15:29; **(3)** the conversion and restoration of Israel, Rom 11:12; **(4)** the completion of the number of Gentiles who receive blessing through the gospel, Rom 11:25; **(5)** the complete products of the earth, 1 Cor 10:26; **(6)** the end of an appointed period, Gal 4:4; Eph 1:10; **(7)** God, in the completeness of His being, Eph 3:19; Col 1:19; 2:9; **(8)** the church as the complement of Christ, Eph 1:23. **(9)** In Mk 6:43, "basketfuls." See: TDNT—6:298, 867; BAGD—672a; THAYER—518c.

4139. πλησίον {17x} **plēsiŏn**, *play-see'-on;* neut. of a der. of πέλας **pĕlas** (near); (adv.) *close* by; as noun, a *neighbor,* i.e. *fellow* (as man, countryman, Chr. or friend):— near {16x}, neighbour {1x}.

(1) The neuter of the adjective *plesios* (from *pelas,* "near"), is used as an adverb accompanied by the article, lit., "the (one) near"; hence, one's "neighbor", "Then cometh He to a city of Samaria, which is called Sychar, near to the parcel of ground that Jacob gave to his son Joseph" (Jn 4:5). **(2)** This word has a wider range of meaning than that of the Eng. word "neighbor." There were no farmhouses scattered over the agricultural areas of Palestine; the populations, gathered in villages, went to and fro to their toil. Hence domestic life was touched at every point by a wide circle of neighborhood. The terms for neighbor were therefore of a very comprehensive scope. This may be seen from the chief characteristics of the privileges and duties of neighborhood as set forth in Scripture, **(2a)** its helpfulness, e.g., Prov 27:10; Lk 10:36; **(2b)** its intimacy, e.g., Lk 15:6, 9; Heb 8:11; **(2c)** its sincerity and sanctity, e.g., Ex 22:7, 10; Prov 3:29; 14:21; Rom 13:10; 15:2; Eph 4:25; Jas 4:12. **(3)** The NT quotes and expands the command in Lev 19:18, "to love one's neighbor as oneself"; see, e.g., Mt 5:43; 19:19; 22:39; Mk 12:31, 33; Lk 10:27; Gal 5:14; Jas 2:8; see also Acts 7:27. Syn.: 316, 1448, 1451, 1452, 4317, 4334. See: TDNT—6:311, 872; BAGD—672c; THAYER—518d.

4140. πλησμονή {1x} **plēsmŏnē**, *place-mon-ay';* from a presumed der. of *4130;* a *filling* up, i.e. (fig.) *gratification:*— satisfying {1x}.

This word means "a filling up, satiety" (akin to *pimplemi,* "to fill"), is translated "satisfying (of the flesh)" in Col 2:23. It can be understood as "yet not really of any value to remedy indulgence of the flesh." A possible meaning is, "of

no value in attempts at asceticism." Some regard it as indicating that the ascetic treatment of the body is not of any honor to the satisfaction of the flesh (the reasonable demands of the body): this interpretation is unlikely. The following paraphrase well presents the contrast between the asceticism which "practically treats the body as an enemy, and the Pauline view which treats it as a potential instrument of a righteous life": ordinances, "which in fact have a specious look of wisdom (where there is no true wisdom), by the employment of self-chosen acts of religion and humility (and) by treating the body with brutality instead of treating it with due respect, with a view to meeting and providing against over-indulgence of the flesh. See: TDNT— 6:131, 840; BAGD—673a; THAYER—519a.

4141. **πλήσσω** {1x} **plēssō**, *place'-so;* appar. another form of *4111* (through the idea of *flattening* out); to *pound,* i.e. (fig.) to *inflict* with (calamity):—smite {1x}.

This word means "a plague, stripe, wound," is used figuratively of the effect upon sun, moon and stars, after the sounding of the trumpet by the fourth angel, in the series of divine judgments upon the world hereafter, Rev 8:12. See: BAGD—673a; THAYER—519a. comp. *5180.*

4142. **πλοιάριον** {6x} **plŏiariŏn**, *ploy-ar'-ee-on;* neut. of a presumed der. of *4143;* a *boat:*—boat {3x}, little ship {2x}, small ship {1x}. See: BAGD—673b; THAYER—519b.

4143. **πλοῖον** {67x} **plŏiŏn**, *ploy'-on;* from *4126;* a *sailer,* i.e. *vessel:*—ship {66x}, shipping {1x}. See: BAGD—673b; THAYER—519b.

4144. **πλόος** {3x} **plŏŏs**, *plŏ'-os;* from *4126;* a *sail,* i.e. *navigation:*—course {1x}, sailing {1x}, voyage {1x}. See: BAGD—673c; THAYER—519b.

4145. **πλούσιος** {28x} **plŏusiŏs**, *ploo'-see-os;* from *4149; wealthy;* fig. *abounding* with:—rich {28x}.

This word means "rich, wealthy," is used **(1)** literally, **(1a)** adjectivally (with a noun expressed separately) in Mt 27:57; Lk 12:16; 14:12; 16:1, 19; (without a noun), 18:23; 19:2; **(1b)** as a noun, singular, a "rich" man (the noun not being expressed), Mt 19:23, 24; Mk 10:25; 12:41; Lk 16:21, 22; 18:25; Jas 1:10, 11, "the rich," "the rich (man)"; plural, Mk 12:41, lit., "rich (ones)"; Lk 6:24; 21:1; 1 Ti 6:17, "(them that are) rich," lit., "(the) rich"; Jas 2:6; 5:1; Rev 6:15 and 13:16; **(2)** metaphorically, **(2a)** of God, Eph 2:4, "in mercy"; **(2b)** of Christ, 2 Cor 8:9;

(2c) of believers, Jas 2:5; **(2d)** Rev 2:9, of spiritual "enrichment" generally; **(2e)** Rev 3:17, of a false sense of "enrichment." See: TDNT— 6:318, 873; BAGD—673c; THAYER—519b.

4146. **πλουσίως** {4x} **plŏusiōs**, *ploo-see'-oce;* adv. from *4145; copiously:*— abundantly {2x}, richly {2x}.

Plousios, connected with *ploutos,* "riches," is used of **(1)** the gift of the Holy Spirit, "abundantly, Titus 3:6; **(2)** entrance into the coming kingdom, "abundantly" in 2 Pet 1:11; **(3)** the indwelling of the Word of Christ, "richly" in Col 3:16; and of **(4)** material benefits, "richly" in 1 Ti 6:17. See: BAGD—673d; THAYER— 519c.

4147. **πλουτέω** {12x} **plŏutĕō**, *ploo-teh'-o;* from *4148;* to *be* (or *become*) *wealthy* (lit. or fig.):—be rich {7x}, be made rich {2x}, rich {1x}, wax rich {1x}, be increased with goods {1x}.

This word means "to be rich," in the aorist or point tense, "to become rich," is used **(1)** literally, Lk 1:53, "the rich," present participle, lit., "(ones or those) being rich"; 1 Ti 6:9, 18; Rev 18:3, 15, 19; **(2)** metaphorically, **(2a)** of Christ, Rom 10:12, the passage stresses the fact that Christ is Lord; **(2b)** of the "enrichment" of believers through His poverty, 2 Cor 8:9, expressing completeness, with permanent results; **(2c)** so in Rev 3:18, where the spiritual "enrichment" is conditional upon righteousness of life and conduct; **(2d)** of a false sense of "enrichment," 1 Cor 4:8, "ye are rich"; Rev 3:17, perfect tense, "I am . . . increased with goods." See: TDNT—6:318, 873; BAGD—673d; THAYER—519c.

4148. **πλουτίζω** {3x} **plŏutizō**, *ploo-tid'-zo;* from *4149;* to *make wealthy* (fig.):—enrich {2x}, make rich {1x}.

This word means "to make rich" (from *ploutos,* "wealth, riches"), is used metaphorically, **(1)** of spiritual "riches," in 1 Cor 1:5, "ye were enriched"; **(2)** 2 Cor 6:10, "making rich"; **(3)** 2 Cor 9:11, "being enriched." See: TDNT— 6:318, 873; BAGD—674a; THAYER—519c.

4149. **πλοῦτος** {22x} **plŏutŏs**, *ploo'-tos;* from the base of *4130; wealth* (as *fulness*), i.e. (lit.) *money, possessions,* or (fig.) *abundance, richness,* (spec.) valuable *bestowment:*—riches {22x}.

Ploutos is used in the singular **(1)** of material "riches," used evilly, Mt 13:22; Mk 4:19; Lk 8:14; 1 Ti 6:17; Jas 5:2; Rev 18:17; **(2)** of spiritual and moral "riches," **(2a)** possessed by God and exercised toward men, **(2a1)** Rom 2:4, "of His goodness and forbearance and longsuffering"; **(2a2)** Rom 9:23 and Eph 3:16, "of His glory" (i.e., of its manifestation in grace toward

believers); **(2a3)** Rom 11:33, of His wisdom and knowledge; **(2a4)** Eph 1:7 and 2:7, "of His grace"; **(2a5)** Eph 1:18, "of the glory of His inheritance in the saints"; **(2a6)** Eph 3:8, "of Christ"; **(2a7)** Phil 4:19, "in glory in Christ Jesus"; **(2b)** to be ascribed to Christ, Rev 5:12; **(2c)** of the effects of the gospel upon the Gentiles, Rom 11:12 (twice); **(2d)** of the full assurance of understanding in regard to the mystery of God, even Christ, Col 2:2; **(2e)** of the liberality of the churches of Macedonia, 2 Cor 8:2, where "the riches" stands for the spiritual and moral value of their liberality; **(2f)** of "the reproach of Christ" in contrast to this world's treasures, Heb 11:26. See: TDNT—6:318, 873; BAGD—674b; THAYER—519c.

4150. πλύνω {1x} **pluno̅**, *ploo'-no;* a prol. form of an obs. πλύω **pluo̅**, (to *"flow"*); to *"plunge,"* i.e. *launder* clothing:—wash {1x}.

Pluno is used of washing only inanimate objects, garments (Rev 7:14). Syn.: 3068, 3538. See: BAGD—674c; THAYER—519d.

4151. πνεῦμα {385x} **pnĕuma**, *pnyoo'-mah;* from *4154;* a *current* of air, i.e. *breath* (*blast*) or a *breeze;* by anal. or fig. a *spirit,* i.e. (human) the rational *soul,* (by impl.) *vital principle,* ment. *disposition,* etc., or (superhuman) an *angel, demon,* or (divine) *God,* Christ's *spirit,* the Holy *Spirit:*—Spirit {111x}, Holy Ghost {89x}, Spirit (of God) {13x}, Spirit (of the Lord) {5x}, (My) Spirit {3x}, Spirit (of truth) {3x}, Spirit (of Christ) {2x}, human (spirit) {49x}, (evil) spirit {47x}, spirit (general) {26x}, spirit {8x}, (Jesus' own) spirit {6x}, (Jesus' own) ghost {2x}, misc. {21x} = life, spiritual, spiritually, wind.

Syn.: This word is rarely used of wind, but when so used it is known for its strength, vigor, and force (Jn 3:8; Acts 2:2; 27:40). *Pnoe* (*4157*) by contrast is a gentle breeze, a quiet and calm exhalation. Comp. 417, 2366, 2978, 4157, 5590. See: TDNT—6:332, 876; BAGD—674c; THAYER—520a.

4152. πνευματικός {26x} **pnĕumatikŏs**, *pnyoo-mat-ik-os';* from *4151; non-carnal,* i.e. (humanly) *ethereal* (as opposed to gross), or (demoniacally) a *spirit* (concr.), or (divinely) *supernatural, regenerate, religious:*—spiritual {26x}.

Pneumatikos always connotes the ideas of invisibility and of power. It does not occur in the OT or in the Gospels; it is in fact an after-Pentecost word. In the NT it is used as follows: **(1)** the angelic hosts, lower than God but higher in the scale of being than man in his natural state, are "spiritual hosts," Eph 6:12; **(2)** things that have their origin with God, and

which, therefore, are in harmony with His character, as His law is, are "spiritual," Rom 7:14; **(3)** "spiritual" is prefixed to the material type in order to indicate that what the type sets forth, not the type itself, is intended, 1 Cor 10:3, 4; **(4)** the purposes of God **(4a)** revealed in the gospel by the Holy Spirit, 1 Cor 2:13a; and the words in which that revelation is expressed, are "spiritual"; matching, or combining, spiritual things with spiritual words; **(4b)** "spiritual songs" are songs of which the burden is the things revealed by the Spirit, Eph 5:19; Col 3:16; **(4c)** "spiritual wisdom and understanding" is wisdom in, and understanding of, those things, Col 1:9;

(5) men in Christ who walk so as to please God are "spiritual," Gal 6:1; 1 Cor 2:13b, 15; 3:1; 14:37; **(6)** the whole company of those who believe in Christ is a "spiritual house," 1 Pet 2:5a; **(7)** the blessings that accrue to regenerate men at this present time are called "spiritualities," Rom 15:27; 1 Cor 9:11; **(8)** "spiritual blessings," Eph 1:3; **(9)** "spiritual gifts," Rom 1:11; **(10)** the activities Godward of regenerate men are "spiritual sacrifices," 1 Pet 2:5b; **(11)** their appointed activities in the churches are also called "spiritual gifts," lit., "spiritualities," 1 Cor 12:1; 14:1; **(12)** the resurrection body of the dead in Christ is "spiritual," i.e., such as is suited to the heavenly environment, 1 Cor 15:44;

(13) all that is produced and maintained among men by the operations of the Spirit of God is "spiritual," 1 Cor 15:46. . . . The spiritual man is one who walks by the Spirit both in the sense of Gal 5:16 and in that of 5:25, and who himself manifests the fruit of the Spirit in his own ways. According to the Scriptures, the "spiritual" state of soul is normal for the believer, but to this state all believers do not attain, nor when it is attained is it always maintained. Thus the apostle, in 1 Cor 3:1–3, suggests a contrast between this spiritual state and that of the babe in Christ, i.e., of the man who because of immaturity and inexperience has not yet reached spirituality, and that of the man who by permitting jealousy, and the strife to which jealousy always leads, has lost it. The spiritual state is reached by diligence in the Word of God and in prayer; it is maintained by obedience and self-judgment. Such as are led by the Spirit are spiritual, but, of course, spirituality is not a fixed or absolute condition, it admits of growth; indeed growth in "the grace and knowledge of our Lord and Savior Jesus Christ," 2 Pet 3:18, is evidence of true spirituality. See: TDNT—6:332, 876; BAGD—678b; THAYER—523c. comp. *5591.*

4153. πνευματικῶς {2x} **pnĕumatikōs**, *pnyoo-mat-ik-oce'*; adv. from *4152; non-physical*, i.e. *divinely, figuratively:*—spiritually {2x}. Cf. 1 Cor 2:14; Rev. 11:8. See: BAGD—679b; THAYER—523d.

4154. πνέω {7x} **pnĕō**, *pneh'-o;* a primary word; to *breathe* hard, i.e. *breeze:*—to blow {6x}, wind {1x}. See: TDNT—6:452, 876; BAGD—679c; THAYER—524a. comp. *5594.*

4155. πνίγω {2x} **pnigō**, *pnee'-go;* strengthened from *4154;* to *wheeze,* i.e. (cause. by impl.) to *throttle* or *strangle* (*drown*):—choke {1x}, take by the throat {1x}.

Pnigo is used, in the passive voice, **(1)** of "perishing by drowning," Mk 5:13; **(2)** in the active, "to seize a person's throat, to throttle," Mt 18:28. See: TDNT—6:455, 895; BAGD—679d; THAYER—524a.

4156. πνικτός {3x} **pniktŏs**, *pnik-tos';* from *4155; throttled,* i.e. (neut. concr.) an animal *choked* to death (*not bled*):—strangled {3x}. See: TDNT—6:455, 895; BAGD—679d; THAYER—524a.

4157. πνοή {2x} **pnŏē**, *pno-ay';* from *4154; respiration,* a *breeze:*—breath {1x}, wind {1x}.

Pnoe, akin to pneo, "to blow," lit., "a blowing," signifies **(1)** "breath, the breath of life," Acts 17:25; and **(2)** "wind," Acts 2:2. Syn.: *Pneuma* (*4151*) stresses strength, vigor, and force (Jn 3:8; Acts 2:2; 27:40). *Pnoe* (*4157*) by contrast is a gentle breeze, a quiet and calm exhalation. Comp. 417, 2366, 2978, 4151, 5590. See: TDNT—6:453, 876; BAGD—680b; THAYER—524a.

4158. ποδήρης {1x} **pŏdērēs**, *pod-ay'-race;* from *4228* and another element of uncert. aff.; a *dress* (*2066* impl.) *reaching* the *ankles:*—garment down to the foot {1x}. Syn.: 2440, 2441, 4749, 5509, 5511. See: BAGD—680b; THAYER—524a.

4159. πόθεν {28x} **pŏthĕn**, *poth'-en;* from the base of *4213* with enclitic adverb of origin; *from which* (as interr.) or *what* (as rel.) place, state, source or cause:—whence {28x}. See: BAGD—680b; THAYER—524b.

4160. ποιέω {579x} **pŏiĕō**, *poy-eh'-o;* appar. a prol. form of an obs. primary; to *make* or *do* (in a very wide application, more or less dir.):—do {357x}, make {113x}, bring forth {14x}, commit {9x}, cause {9x}, work {8x}, shew {5x}, bear {4x}, keep {4x}, fulfil {3x}, deal {2x}, perform {2x}, not tr {3x}, misc. {43x}, vr do {3x} = abide, + agree, appoint, X avenge, + band together, be, + bewray, cast out, + content, con-

tinue, + without any delay, doing, execute, exercise, gain, give, have, hold, X journeying, + lay wait, + lighten the ship, X mean, + none of these things move me, observe, ordain, provide, + have purged, purpose, put, + raising up, X secure, shew, X shoot out, spend, take, tarry, + transgress the law, yield.

Poieo, as a verb, means "to make, to do" and is used of the bringing forth of fruit: "Bring forth therefore fruits meet for repentance" (Mt 3:8, cf. 10; 7:17, 18). Syn.: cf. 4238 for discussion. See: TDNT—6:458, 895; BAGD—680d; THAYER—524b.

4161. ποίημα {2x} **pŏiēma**, *poy'-ay-mah;* from *4160;* a *product,* i.e. *fabric* (lit. or fig.):—thing that is made {1x}, workmanship {1x}. Cf. Rom 1:20; Eph 2:10. See: TDNT—6:458, 895; BAGD—683b; THAYER—527b.

4162. ποίησις {1x} **pŏiēsis**, *poy'-ay-sis;* from *4160; action,* i.e. *performance* (of the law):—deed {1x}. See: TDNT—6:458, 895; BAGD—683b; THAYER—527b.

4163. ποιητής {6x} **pŏiētēs**, *poy-ay-tace';* from *4160;* a *performer;* spec. a "*poet*":—doer {5x}, poet {1x}.

Poietes signifies **(1)** "a doer," Rom 2:13; Jas 1:22–23, 25; 4:11. **(2)** Its meaning "poet" is found in Acts 17:28. A poet is one who "makes" a writing, not just reports or narrates. See: TDNT—6:458, 895; BAGD—683b; THAYER—527b.

4164. ποικίλος {10x} **pŏikilŏs**, *poy-kee'-los;* of uncert. der.; *motley,* i.e. *various* in character:—divers {8x}, manifold {2x}.

Poikilos denotes "particolored, variegated" hence **(1)** "divers," Mt 4:24; Mk 1:34; Lk 4:40; 2 Ti 3:6; Titus 3:3; Heb 2:4; 13:9; Jas 1:2; and **(2)** in 1 Pet 1:6 and 4:10, "manifold." See: TDNT—6:484, 901; BAGD—683c; THAYER—527b.

4165. ποιμαίνω {11x} **pŏimainō**, *poy-mah'-ee-no;* from *4166;* to *tend* as a shepherd (or fig. *superviser*):—feed {6x}, feed cattle {1x}, rule {4x}.

(1) Poimaino refers to the whole process of shepherding: guiding, guarding, folding, and providing pasture. It means "to act as a shepherd" (from *poimen,* "a shepherd"), is used **(2)** literally, Lk 17:7, "feeding cattle"; 1 Cor 9:7, **(3)** metaphorically, "to tend, to shepherd"; said **(3a)** of Christ Mt 2:6, "shall rule"; **(3b)** of those who act as spiritual shepherds under Him, Jn 21:16, "feed", so 1 Pet 5:2; Acts 20:28, "to feed"; **(3c)** of base shepherds, Jude 12. **(4)** It is also translated "to rule" in Rev 2:27; 12:5; 19:15, all indicating that the governing power exercised

by the Shepherd is to be of a firm character. **(5)** Cattle is the word for any four-footed beast, usually domesticated. THAYER—1006. See: TDNT—6:485, 901; BAGD—683d; THAYER—527c.

4166. ποιμήν {18x} **pŏimēn**, *poy-mane';* of uncert. aff.; a *shepherd* (lit. or fig.):—shepherd {15x}, Shepherd {2x}, pastor {1x}.

Poimen, "a shepherd, one who tends herds or flocks" (not merely one who feeds them), is used **(1)** metaphorically of Christian "pastors," Eph 4:11. **(2)** "Pastors" guide as well as feed the flock, cf. Acts 20:28, which with 20:17, indicates that this was the service committed to elders (overseers or bishops); so also in 1 Pet 5:1, 2, "tend the flock . . . exercising the oversight"; this involves tender care and vigilant superintendence. See: TDNT—6:485, 901; BAGD—684a; THAYER—527c.

4167. ποίμνη {5x} **pŏimnē**, *poym'-nay;* contr. from *4165;* a *flock* (lit. or fig.):—flock {4x}, fold {1x}.

A flock is a group of animals, possibly mixed [sheep and goats] but a fold contains only one kind of animal. See: TDNT—6:499, 901; BAGD—684c; THAYER—527d.

4168. ποίμνιον {5x} **pŏimniŏn**, *poym'-nee-on;* neut. of a presumed der. of *4167;* a *flock,* i.e. (fig.) *group* (of believers):—flock {5x}. Syn.: 4167. See: TDNT—6:499, 901; BAGD—684c; THAYER—527d.

4169. ποῖος {34x} **pŏiŏs**, *poy'-os;* from the base of *4226* and *3634;* individualizing interr. (of character) *what* sort of, or (of number) *which* one:—what {27x}, which {4x}, what things {1x}, what way {1x}, what manner of {1x}.

Poios, as an adjective, means "of what sort" is translated **(1)** "by what [manner of] death" (Jn 21:19); **(2)** "what [manner of] house" (Acts 7:49); **(3)** "what [manner of] law" (Rom 3:27); **(4)** "what [manner of] body" (1 Cor 15:35). Syn.: 195, 1485, 2239, 3634, 3668, 3697, 3779, 4187, 4217, 4459, 5158, 5159, 5179, 5615. See: BAGD—684c; THAYER—527d.

4170. πολεμέω {7x} **pŏlĕmĕō**, *pol-em-eh'-o;* from *4171;* to *be* (engaged) in *warfare,* i.e. to *battle* (lit. or fig.):—fight {3x}, make war {3x}, war {1x}.

Polemeo, (Eng., "polemics"), "to fight, to make war," is used **(1)** literally, "fought", Rev 12:7 (twice); 13:4; 17:14; 19:11; **(2)** metaphorically, Rev 2:16; and **(3)** hyperbolically, Jas 4:2. Syn.: *Polemeo* is the war and *mache* (*3163*) refers to the battles of which *polemeo* is made.

See: TDNT—6:502, 904; BAGD—685a; THAYER—527d.

4171. πόλεμος {18x} **pŏlĕmŏs**, *pol'-em-os;* from πέλομαι **pĕlŏmai**, (to *bustle*); *warfare* (lit. or fig.; a single encounter or a series):—battle {5x}, fight {1x}, war {12x}. See: TDNT—6:502, 904; BAGD—685a; THAYER—528a.

4172. πόλις {164x} **pŏlis**, *pol'-is;* prob. from the same as *4171,* or perh. from *4183;* a *town* (prop. with walls, of greater or less size):—city {164x}.

(1) A *polis* is primarily a town enclosed with a wall. **(2)** It is used of the heavenly Jerusalem, the abode and community of the redeemed, Heb 11:10, 16; 12:22; 13:14. **(3)** In the Apocalypse it signifies the visible capital of the heavenly kingdom, as destined to descend to earth in a coming age e.g., Rev 3:12; 21:2, 14, 19. **(4)** By metonymy the word stands for the inhabitants, as in the English use, e.g., Mt 8:34; 12:25; 21:10; Mk 1:33; Acts 13:44. See: TDNT—6:516, 906; BAGD—685b; THAYER—528a.

4173. πολιτάρχης {2x} **pŏlitarchēs**, *pol-it-ar'-khace;* from *4172* and *757;* a *town-officer,* i.e. *magistrate:*—ruler of the city {2x}.

This word means "a ruler of a city" (*polis,* "a city," *archo,* "to rule"), "a politarch," is used in Acts 17:6, 8, of the magistrates in Thessalonica, before whom the Jews, with a mob of market idlers, dragged Jason and other converts, under the charge of showing hospitality to Paul and Silas, and of treasonable designs against the emperor. Thessalonica was a "free" city and the citizens could choose their own politarchs. The accuracy of Luke has been vindicated by the use of the term, for while classical authors use the terms *poliarchos* and *politarchos* of similar "rulers," the form used by Luke is supported by inscriptions discovered at Thessalonica. See: BAGD—686a; THAYER—528c.

4174. πολιτεία {2x} **pŏlitĕia**, *pol-ee-ti'-ah;* from *4177* ("*polity*"); *citizenship;* concr. a *community:*—commonwealth {1x}, freedom {1x}.

Politeia signifies **(1)** "the relation in which a citizen stands to the state, the condition of a citizen, citizenship," Acts 22:28, "with a great sum obtained I this freedom." While Paul's "citizenship" of Tarsus was not of advantage outside that city, yet his Roman "citizenship" availed throughout the Roman Empire and, besides private rights, included **(1a)** exemption from all degrading punishments; **(1b)** a right of appeal to the emperor after a sentence; **(1c)** a right to be sent to Rome for trial before the

emperor if charged with a capital offense. It is also **(2)** "a civil polity, the condition of a state, a commonwealth," said of Israel, Eph 2:12. See: TDNT—6:516, 906; BAGD—686a; THAYER—528c.

4175. πολίτευμα {1x} **pŏlitĕuma,** *pol-it'-yoo-mah;* from *4176;* a *community,* i.e. (abstr.) *citizenship* (fig.):—conversation {1x}.

To converse is to go back and forth with another; hence, by extension how one goes back and forth in life, Phil 3:20. See: TDNT—6:516, 906; BAGD—686b; THAYER—528c.

4176. πολιτεύομαι {2x} **pŏlitĕuŏmai,** *pol-it-yoo'-om-ahee;* mid. voice of a der. of *4177;* to *behave* as a citizen (fig.):—let (one's) conversation be {1x}, live {1x}.

Politeuo, as a verb, means "to be a citizen (polites), to live as a citizen" and is used metaphorically of conduct as in accordance with the characteristics of the heavenly community; **(1)** in Acts 23:1: "And Paul, earnestly beholding the council, said, Men and brethren, I have lived (*politeuo*) in all good conscience before God until this day"; and **(2)** in Phil 1:27, "Only let your conversation (*politeuo*) be as it becometh the gospel of Christ: that whether I come and see you, or else be absent, I may hear of your affairs, that ye stand fast in one spirit, with one mind striving together for the faith of the gospel." Syn.: 326, 390, 980, 1236, 2198, 2225, 4800, 5225. See: TDNT—6:516, 906; BAGD—686c; THAYER—528d.

4177. πολίτης {3x} **pŏlitēs,** *pol-ee'-tace;* from *4172;* a *townsman:*—citizen {3x}.

Polites, "a member of a city or state, or the inhabitant of a country or district," Lk 15:15, is used elsewhere in Lk 19:14, Acts 21:39. See: TDNT—6:516, 906; BAGD—686d; THAYER—528d.

4178. πολλάκις {18x} **pŏllakis,** *pol-lak'-is;* mult. adv. from *4183; many times,* i.e. *frequently:*—often {7x}, oft {5x}, ofttimes {3x}, oftentimes {3x}. See: BAGD—686d; THAYER—529a.

4179. πολλαπλασίων {1x} **pŏllaplasiōn,** *pol-lap-las-ee'-ohn;* from *4183* and prob. a der. of *4120; manifold,* i.e. (neut. as noun) *very much more:*—manifold more {1x}. See: BAGD—686d; THAYER—529a.

4180. πολυλογία {1x} **pŏlulŏgia,** *pol-oo-log-ee'-ah;* from a compound of *4183* and *3056; loquacity,* i.e. *prolixity:*—much speaking {1x}. See: TDNT—6:545, 911; BAGD—687b; THAYER—529a.

4181. πολυμέρως {1x} **pŏlumĕrōs,** *pol-oo-mer'-oce;* adv. from a compound of *4183* and *3313; in many portions,* i.e. *variously* as to time and agency (*piecemeal*):—at sundry times {1x}.

This word means by many portions, by many times and in many ways, yet all connected. It is related to "asunder," to break one item into many pieces; hence, all of God's means of revelation still have Him, the One God, as their source. See: BAGD—687b; THAYER—529a.

4182. πολυποίκιλος {1x} **pŏlupŏikilŏs,** *pol-oo-poy'-kil-os;* from *4183* and *4164; much variegated,* i.e. *multifarious:*—manifold {1x}. See: TDNT—6:485, 901; BAGD—687b; THAYER—529a.

4183. πολύς {365x} **pŏlus,** *pol-oos';* incl. the forms from the alt. πολλός **pŏllŏs;** (sing.) *much* (in any respect) or (plural) *many;* neut. (sing.) as adv. *largely;* neut. (plural) as adv. or noun *often, mostly, largely:*—many {210x}, much {73x}, great {59x}, misc {23x} = abundant, + altogether, common, + far (passed, spent), long, oft (-en [-times]), plenteous, sore, straitly. See: TDNT—6:536,*; BAGD—687c; THAYER—529a. comp. *4118, 4119.*

4184. πολύσπλαγχνος {1x} **pŏlusplagchnŏs,** *pol-oo'-splankh-nos;* from *4183* and *4698* (fig.); *full of pity, extremely compassionate:*—very pitiful {1x}.

This word denotes "very pitiful" or "full of pity" (*polus,* "much," *splanchnon,* "the heart"; in the plural, "the affections"), occurs in Jas 5:11. See: TDNT—7:548, 1067; BAGD—689d; THAYER—530b.

4185. πολυτελής {3x} **pŏlutĕlēs,** *pol-oo-tel-ace';* from *4183* and *5056; extremely expensive:*—costly {1x}, very precious {1x}, of great price {1x}.

This word means primarily, "the very end or limit" (from *polus,* "much," *telos,* "revenue"), with reference to price, of highest "cost," very expensive, is said **(1)** of spikenard, Mk 14:3, "very pressure"; **(2)** raiment, 1 Ti 2:9, "costly"; and **(3)** metaphorically, of a meek and quiet spirit, 1 Pet 3:4, "of great price." See: BAGD—690a; THAYER—530b.

4186. πολύτιμος {2x} **pŏlutimŏs,** *pol-oot'-ee-mos;* from *4183* and *5092; extremely valuable:*—very costly {1x}, of great price {1x}.

This word means lit., "of great value" and is used **(1)** of a pearl, Mt 13:46, "of great price";

and **(2)** of spikenard, Jn 12:3, "very costly." See: BAGD—690a; THAYER—530b.

4187. **πολυτρόπως** {1x} **pŏlutrŏpōs**, *pol-oot-rop'-oce;* adv. from a compound of *4183* and *5158; in many ways,* i.e. *variously* as to method or form:—in divers manners {1x}.

Polutropos, as an adverb, literally means "much turning, in many ways (or manners)" and is rendered "in divers manners" (Heb 1:1). Syn.: 195, 1485, 2239, 3634, 3668, 3697, 3779, 4169, 4217, 4459, 5158, 5159, 5179, 5615. See: BAGD—690b; THAYER—530b.

4188. **πόμα** {2x} **pŏma**, *pom'-ah;* from the alt. of *4095;* the thing drunk, a *beverage:*—a drink {2x}.

Poma denotes "the thing drunk" in 1 Cor 10:4; Heb 9:10. See: TDNT—6:145, 840; BAGD—690b; THAYER—530b.

4189. **πονηρία** {7x} **pŏnēria**, *pon-ay-ree'-ah;* from *4190; depravity,* i.e. (spec.) *malice;* plur. (concr.) *plots, sins:*—iniquity {1x}, wickedness {6x}.

Poneria denotes **(1)** "wickedness," and is so translated in Mt 22:18; Mk 7:22 (plural); Lk 11:39; Rom 1:29; 1 Cor 5:8; Eph 6:12; and **(2)** in Acts 3:26, "iniquities." Syn.: *Kakia (2549)* denotes a vicious disposition; whereas *poneria (4189)* denotes the active exercise of a vicious disposition. See: TDNT—6:562, 912; BAGD—690c; THAYER—530b.

4190. **πονηρός** {76x} **pŏnērŏs**, *pon-ay-ros';* from a der. of *4192; hurtful,* i.e. *evil* (prop. in effect or influence, and thus differing from *2556,* which refers rather to *essential* character, as well as from *4550,* which indicates *degeneracy* from original virtue); fig. *calamitous;* also (pass.) *ill,* i.e. *diseased;* but espec. (mor.) *culpable,* i.e. *derelict, vicious, facinorous;* neut. (sing.) *mischief, malice,* or (plural) *guilt;* masc. (sing.) the *devil,* or (plural) *sinners:*—evil {51x}, wicked {10x}, wicked one {6x}, evil things {2x}, misc. {7x} = bad, grievous, harm, lewd, malicious, wickedness.

Poneros is connected with *ponos (4192)* and means labor and expresses especially **(1)** the active form of evil. It is used **(1a)** of thoughts (Mt 15:19); **(1b)** of speech (Mt 5:11); **(1c)** of acts (2 Ti 4:18). **(2)** *Poneros* alone is used **(2a)** of Satan (Mt 5:37); and **(2b)** of demons (Lk 7:21). This word also denotes "labor, toil," and denotes "evil that causes labor, pain, sorrow, malignant evil" being used **(3)** with the meaning bad, worthless, **(3a)** in the physical sense, Mt 7:17–18; **(3b)** in the moral or ethical sense, "evil," wicked; **(3b1)** of persons, e.g., Mt 7:11; Lk 6:45; Acts 17:5; 2 Th 3:2; 2 Ti 3:13; **(3b2)** of "evil" spirits, e.g., Mt 12:45; Lk 7:21; Acts

19:12–13, 15–16; **(3b3)** of a generation, Mt 12:39, 45; 16:4; Lk 11:29; **(3b4)** of things, e.g., Mt 5:11; 6:23; 20:15; Mk 7:22; Lk 11:34; Jn 3:19; 7:7; Acts 18:14; Gal 1:4; Col 1:21; 1 Ti 6:4; 2 Ti 4:18; Heb 3:12; 10:22; Jas 2:4; 4:16; 1 Jn 3:12; 2 Jn 11; 3 Jn 10; **(4)** with the meaning toilsome, painful, Eph 5:16; 6:13; Rev 16:2. Syn.: Where *kakos (2556)* and *poneros* are put together, *kakos* is always put first and signifies bad in character, base and *poneros* means bad in effect, malignant (1 Cor 5:8; Rev 16:2). *Kakos* has a wider meaning, *poneros* a stronger meaning. Comp. 5337. See: TDNT—6:546, 912; BAGD—690d; THAYER—650c. See also *4191.*

4191. **πονηρότερος** {2x} **pŏnērŏtĕrŏs**, *pon-ay-rot'-er-os;* comp. of *4190; more evil:*—more wicked {2x}. See: BAGD—690d; THAYER—650c.

4192. **πόνος** {3x} **pŏnŏs**, *pon'-os;* from the base of *3993; toil,* i.e. (by impl.) *anguish:*—pain {3x}.

Ponos refers to labor that demands the greatest exertion if one is to accomplish a task. It denotes "the consequence of toil," viz., distress, suffering, pain, Rev 16:10, 11; 21:4. Syn.: 2873, 3449. See: BAGD—691c; THAYER—531a.

4193. **Ποντικός** {1x} **Pŏntikŏs**, *pon-tik-os';* from *4195;* a *Pontican,* i.e. native of Pontus:—born in Pontus {1x}. See: BAGD—691d; THAYER—531a.

4194. **Πόντιος** {4x} **Pŏntiŏs**, *pon'-tee-os;* of Lat. or.; appar. *bridged; Pontius,* a Rom.:—Pontius [Pilate]{4x}. See: BAGD—691d; THAYER—531a.

4195. **Πόντος** {2x} **Pŏntŏs**, *pon'-tos;* a *sea; Pontus,* a region of Asia Minor:—Pontus {2x}. See: BAGD—691d; THAYER—531a.

4196. **Πόπλιος** {2x} **Pŏpliŏs**, *pop'-lee-os;* of Lat. or.; appar. *"popular";* *Poplius* (i.e. *Publius*), a Rom.:—Publius {2x}. See: BAGD—692a; THAYER—530a.

4197. **πορεία** {2x} **pŏrĕia**, *por-i'-ah;* from *4198; travel* (by land); fig. (plural) *proceedings,* i.e. *career:*—journeying + 4160 {1x}, ways {1x}.

This word refers **(1)** to a purposeful journey, Lk 13:22; and **(2)** describes the purposeful ways a rich man lives his life, Jas 1:11. See: BAGD—692a; THAYER—531b.

4198. **πορεύομαι** {154x} **pŏrĕuŏmai**, *por-yoo'-om-ahee;* mid. voice from a der. of the same as *3984; to traverse,* i.e. *travel* (lit. or fig.; espec. to *remove* [fig. *die*], *live,* etc.):—go {117x}, depart {11x}, walk {9x},

go (one's) way {8x}, misc. {9x} = (make a, take a) journey.

Syn.: **(A)** *Erchomai* (*2064*) denotes motion or progress generally, and of any sort, hence to "come" and arrive at, as well as "to go." **(B)** *Bathmos* (*898*) primarily signifies "to walk", "take steps", picturing the mode of motion; to "go away." **(C)** *Poreuomai* (*4198*) expresses motion in general, often confined within certain limits, or giving prominence to the bearing; hence the regular word for the march of an army. **(D)** *Choreo* (*5562*) always emphasizes the idea of separation, change of place, and does not, like e.g. 4198, note the external and perceptible motion. See: TDNT—6:566, 915; BAGD—692b; THAYER—531b.

4199. **πορθέω** {3x} **pŏrthĕō**, *por-theh'-o;* prol. from πέρθω **pĕrthō**, (to *sack*); to *ravage* (fig.):—destroy {2x}, waste {1x}.

Portheo, "to destroy, ravage, lay waste," is used of the persecution inflicted by Saul of Tarsus on the church in Jerusalem, **(1)** Acts 9:21, and Gal 1:23, "destroyed"; **(2)** Gal 1:13, "wasted." See: BAGD—693a; THAYER—531d.

4200. **πορισμός** {2x} **pŏrismŏs**, *por-is-mos';* from a der. of πόρος **pŏrŏs** (a *way*, i.e. *means*); *furnishing*, (*procuring*), i.e. (by impl.) *money-getting* (*acquisition*):—gain {2x}.

This word primarily denotes "a providing" (akin to *porizo*, "to procure"), then, "a means of gain," 1 Ti 6:5; 6:6. See: BAGD—693a; THAYER—531d.

4201. **Πόρκιος** {1x} **Pŏrkiŏs**, *por'-kee-os;* of Lat. or.; appar. *swinish; Porcius*, a Rom.:—Porcius {1x}. See: BAGD—693a; THAYER—531d.

4202. **πορνεία** {26x} **pŏrnĕia**, *por-ni'-ah;* from *4203; harlotry* (incl. *adultery* and *incest*); fig. *idolatry:*—fornication {26x}.

Porneis is used **(1)** of "illicit sexual intercourse," in Jn 8:41; Acts 15:20, 29; 21:25; 1 Cor 5:1; 6:13, 18; 2 Cor 12:21; Gal 5:19; Eph 5:3; Col 3:5; 1 Th 4:3; Rev 2:21; 9:21; in the plural in 1 Cor 7:2; **(2)** in Mt 5:32 and 19:9 it stands for, or includes, adultery; it is distinguished from it in 15:19 and Mk 7:21; **(3)** metaphorically, of "the association of pagan idolatry with doctrines of, and professed adherence to, the Christian faith," Rev 14:8; 17:2, 4; 18:3; 19:2. See: TDNT—6:579, 918; BAGD—693b; THAYER—531d.

4203. **πορνεύω** {8x} **pŏrnĕuō**, *porn-yoo'-o;* from *4204;* to *act the harlot,* i.e. (lit.) *indulge* unlawful *lust* (of either sex), or

(fig.) *practice idolatry:*—commit {1x}, commit fornication {7x}.

Porneuo, "to commit fornication," is used **(1)** literally, Mk 10:19; 1 Cor 6:18; 10:8; Rev 2:14, 20; **(2)** metaphorically, Rev 17:2; 18:3, 9. See: TDNT—6:579, 918; BAGD—693c; THAYER—532a.

4204. **πόρνη** {12x} **pŏrnē**, *por'-nay;* fem. of *4205; a strumpet;* fig. an *idolater:*—harlot {8x}, whore {4x}.

(1) A woman who sells her body for sexual uses is **(1a)** a prostitute, a harlot (a hirelot), one who yields herself to defilement for the sake of gain; or **(1b)** any woman indulging in unlawful sexual intercourse, usually driven by lust, maybe for gain. **(2)** Metaphorically, it is used of Babylon, the chief seat of idolatry. See: TDNT—6:579, 918; BAGD—693c; THAYER—532b.

4205. **πόρνος** {10x} **pŏrnŏs**, *por'-nos;* from πέρνημι **pĕrnēmi**, (to *sell;* akin to the base of *4097*); a (male) *prostitute* (as *venal*), i.e. (by anal.) a *debauchee* (*libertine*):—fornicator {5x}, whoremonger {5x}.

Pornos denotes "a man who indulges in fornication, **(1)** a fornicator" 1 Cor 5:9, 10, 11; 6:9; Heb 12:16; or **(2)** a "whoremonger" in Eph 5:5; 1 Ti 1:10; Heb 13:4; Rev 21:8; 22:15. See: TDNT—6:579, 918; BAGD—693d; THAYER—532b.

4206. **πόρρω** {3x} **pŏrrhō**, *por'-rho;* adv. from *4253; forwards,* i.e. *at a distance:*—far {2x}, a great way off {1x}. Cf. Mt 15:8; Lk 14:32; 24:28. See: BAGD—693d; THAYER—532c. See also 4207.

4207. **πόρρωθεν** {2x} **pŏrrhōthĕn**, *por'-rho-then;* from *4206* with adv. enclitic of source; *from far,* or (by impl.) *at a distance,* i.e. *distantly:*—afar off {2x}. Cf. Lk 17:12; Heb 11:13. See: BAGD—693d; THAYER—532c.

4208. **πορρωτέρω** {1x} **pŏrrhōtĕrō**, *por-rho-ter'-o;* adv. comparative of *4206; further,* i.e. *a greater distance:*—farther {1x}. See: BAGD—694a; 693d; THAYER—532c.

4209. **πορφύρα** {5x} **pŏrphura**, *por-foo'-rah;* of Lat. or.; the *"purple"* mussel, i.e. (by impl.) the *red-blue* color itself, and finally a garment dyed with it:—purple {5x}. Cf. Mk 15:17, 20; Lk 16:19; Rev 18:12. See: BAGD—694a; THAYER—532c.

4210. **πορφυρόπωλις** {1x} **pŏrphurŏpŏlis**, *por-foo-rop'-o-lis;* fem. of a compound of *4209* and *4453;* a *female trader in purple* cloth:—seller of purple {1x}. See: BAGD—694a; THAYER—532c.

4211. πορφυροῦς {3x} pŏrphurŏus, *por-foo-rooce';* from *4209; pur-pureal,* i.e. *bluish red:*—purple {3x}. Cf. Jn 19:2, 5; Rev 18:16. See: BAGD—694b; THAYER—532c.

4212. ποσάκις pŏsakis, *pos-ak'-is;* mult. from *4214; how many times:*—how oft {1x}, how often {2x}. Cf. Mt 18:21; 23:37; Lk 13:34. See: BAGD—694b; THAYER—532c.

4213. πόσις {3x} pŏsis, *pos'-is;* from the alt. of *4095;* a *drinking* (the act), i.e. (concr.) a *draught:*—drink {3x}.

Posis suggests "the act of drinking and that which is drunk," Jn 6:55; Rom 14:17; Col 2:16. See: TDNT—6:145, 841; BAGD—694b; THAYER—532d.

4214. πόσος {27x} pŏsŏs, *pos'-os;* from an obs. πός pŏs, (*who, what*) and *3739;* interr. pron. (of amount) *how much* (*large, long* or [plural] *many*):—how much {13x}, how many {9x}, how many things {2x}, what {1x}, how long {1x}, how great {1x}. See: BAGD—694b; THAYER—532d.

4215. ποταμός {16x} pŏtamŏs, *pot-am-os';* prob. from a der. of the alt. of *4095* (comp. *4224*); a *current, brook* or *freshet* (as *drinkable*), i.e. *running water:*—flood {4x}, river {9x}, stream {2x}, water {1x}.

Potamos denotes **(1)** "a stream," Lk 6:48, 49; **(2)** "a flood or floods," Mt 7:25, 27; **(3)** "a river," **(3a)** natural, Mk 1:5; Acts 16:13; 2 Cor 11:26, "waters"; Rev 8:10; 9:14; 16:4, 12; **(3b)** symbolical, Rev 12:15 (1st part), "flood"; so 12:16; 22:1, 2 (cf. Gen 2:10; Eze 47); **(3c)** figuratively, Jn 7:38, the effects of the operation of the Holy Spirit in and through the believer. See: TDNT—6:595, 921; BAGD—694c; THAYER—532d.

4216. ποταμοφόρητος {1x} pŏtamŏphŏrētŏs, *pot-am-of-or'-ay-tos;* from *4215* and a der. of *5409; river-borne,* i.e. *overwhelmed by a stream:*—carried away of the flood {1x}. See: TDNT—6:607, 921; BAGD—694d; THAYER—532d.

4217. ποταπός {7x} pŏtapŏs, *pot-ap-os';* appar. from *4219* and the base of *4226;* interrog. *whatever,* i.e. of *what possible* sort:—what manner of {4x}, what {1x}, what manner of man {1x}, what manner of person {1x}.

Potapos, as an adjective, means primarily "what manner" **(1)** of man" (Mt 8:27); **(2)** persons (2 Pet 3:11); **(3)** Mk 13:1: "And as he went out of the temple, one of his disciples saith unto him, Master, see what manner (*potapos*) of stones and what (*potapos*) buildings are

here!"; **(4)** salutation (Lk 1:29); **(5)** woman (Lk 7:39); **(6)** love (1 Jn 3:1). Syn.: 195, 1485, 2239, 3634, 3668, 3697, 3779, 4169, 4187, 4459, 5158, 5159, 5179, 5615. See: BAGD—694d; THAYER—532d.

4218. πότε {19x} pŏtĕ, *pot'-eh;* from the base of *4226* and *5037;* interr. adv., at *what time:*—when {12x}, how long + 2193 {7x}. See: BAGD—695a; THAYER—533a.

4219. ποτέ {32x} pŏtĕ, *pot-eh';* from the base of *4225* and *5037;* indef. adv., at *some time, ever:*—in time past {5x}, at any time {4x}, in times past {3x}, sometimes {3x}, sometime {3x}, once {2x}, not tr {3x}, misc. {9x} = at length (the last), (+ n-) ever, in the old time, when. See: BAGD—695a; THAYER—533a.

4220. πότερον {1x} pŏtĕrŏn, *pot'-er-on;* neut. of a comparative of the base of *4226;* interr. as adv., *which* (of two), i.e. *is it* this or that:—whether {1x}. See: BAGD—695b; THAYER—533b.

4221. ποτήριον {33x} pŏtēriŏn, *pot-ay'-ree-on;* neut. of a der. of the alt. of *4095;* a *drinking-vessel;* by extens. the contents thereof, i.e. a *cupful* (*draught*); fig. a *lot* or *fate:*—cup {33x}.

Poterion, a diminutive of *poter,* denotes, primarily, a "drinking vessel"; hence, "a cup" **(1)** literal, as, e.g., in Mt 10:42. **(1a)** The "cup" of blessing, 1 Cor 10:16, is so named from the third "cup" in the Jewish Passover feast, over which thanks and praise were given to God. **(1b)** This connection is not to be rejected on the ground that the church at Corinth was unfamiliar with Jewish customs. That the contrary was the case, see 5:7; **(2)** figurative, of one's lot or experience, joyous or sorrowful **(2a)** frequent in the Psalms; cf. Ps 116:18, "cup of salvation"; **(2b)** in the NT it is used most frequently **(2b1)** of the sufferings of Christ, Mt 20:22–23; 26:39; Mk 10:38–39; 14:36; Lk 22:42; Jn 18:11; **(2b2)** also of the evil deeds of Babylon, Rev 17:4; 18:6; **(2b3)** of divine punishments to be inflicted, Rev 14:10; 16:19. See: TDNT—6:148, 841; BAGD—695b; THAYER—533b.

4222. ποτίζω {15x} pŏtizō, *pot-id'-zo;* from a der. of the alt. of *4095;* to *furnish drink, irrigate:*—give to drink {4x}, give drink {4x}, water {3x}, make to drink {2x}, watering {1x}, feed {1x}.

Potizo, "to give to drink, to make to drink," is used **(1)** in the material sense, in Mt. 10:42, 25:35, 37, 42 (here of "ministering" to those who belong to Christ and thus doing so virtually to Him); 27:48; Mk 9:41; 15:36; Lk 13:15

("to watering"); Rom 12:20; 1 Cor 3:7-8; **(2)** figuratively, with reference to "teaching" of an elementary character, 1 Cor 3:2, "I fed (you with milk)"; **(3)** of "spiritual watering by teaching" the Word of God, 1 Cor 3:6; **(4)** of being "provided" and "satisfied" by the power and blessing of the Spirit of God, 1 Cor 12:13; **(5)** of the effect upon the nations of "partaking" of the abominable mixture, provided by Babylon, of paganism with details of the Christian faith, Rev 14:8. See: TDNT—6:159, 841; BAGD—695d; THAYER—533c.

4223. Ποτίολοι {1x} **Pŏtiŏlŏi**, *pot-ee'-ol-oy;* of Lat. or.; *little wells,* i.e. *mineral springs; Potioli* (i.e. *Puteoli*), a place in Italy:—Puteoli {1x}. See: BAGD—696a; THAYER—533c.

4224. πότος {1x} **pŏtŏs**, *pot'-os;* from the alt. of *4095;* a *drinking-bout* or *carousal:*—banqueting {1x}.
Potos is a drinking bout, a banquet; not necessarily excessiveness, though it does provide that opportunity. Syn.: 2897, 2970, 3178, 3632. See: TDNT—6:145, 841; BAGD—696a; THAYER—533d.

4225. πού {3x} **pŏu**, *poo;* gen. of an indef. pron. πός **pŏs** (*some*) otherwise obs. (comp. *4214*); as adv. of place, *somewhere,* i.e. *nearly:*—about {1x}, a certain place {2x}.
Pou, an indefinite particle, signifying "somewhere, somewhere about, nearly," **(1)** has a limiting force, with numerals, e.g., Rom 4:19. **(2)** In referring to a passage in the OT, it is translated in Heb 2:6 and 4:4. By not mentioning the actual passage referred to, the writer acknowledged the familiar acquaintance of his readers with the OT. Also, when Hebrews was written the Scriptures had not been broken down into chapters and verses; hence, "in a certain place." See: BAGD—696a; THAYER—533d.

4226. ποῦ {47x} **pŏu**, *poo;* gen. of an interr. pron. πός **pŏs**, (*what*) otherwise obs. (perh. the same as *4225* used with the rising slide of inquiry); as adv. of place; *at* (by impl. to) *what* locality:—where {10x}, whither {47x}. Where is specific, whither, non-specific. See: BAGD—696b; THAYER—533d.

4227. Πούδης {1x} **Pŏudēs**, *poo'-dace;* of Lat. or.; *modest; Pudes* (i.e. *Pudens*), a Chr.:—Pudens {1x}. See: BAGD—696c; THAYER—533d.

4228. πούς {93x} **pŏus**, *pooce;* a primary word; a *"foot"* (fig. or lit.):—foot {85x}, footstool + 5286 {8x}.
Pous, **(1)** besides its literal meaning, is used, **(2)** by metonymy, of "a person in motion," Lk

1:79; Acts 5:9; Rom 3:15; 10:15; Heb 12:13. **(3)** It is used in phrases expressing subjection, 1 Cor 15:27; **(3a)** of the humility and receptivity of discipleship, Lk 10:39; Acts 22:3; **(3b)** of obeisance and worship, e.g., Mt 28:9; **(3c)** of scornful rejection, Mt 10:14; Acts 13:51. **(4)** Washing the "feet" of another betokened the humility of the service and the comfort of the guest, and was a feature of hospitality, Lk 7:38; Jn 13:5; 1 Ti 5:10 (here figuratively). See: TDNT—6:624, 925; BAGD—696c; THAYER—534a.

4229. πρᾶγμα {11x} **pragma**, *prag'-mah;* from *4238;* that which has been done, a *deed;* by impl. an *affair;* by extens. an *object* (material):—business {1x}, matter {3x}, thing {6x}, work {1x}.
Pragma, akin to *prasso,* "to do," denotes **(1)** "that which has been done, a deed," translated **(1a)** "things" in Lk 1:1, **(1b)** "matter" in 2 Cor 7:11; **(2)** "that which is being done, an affair," translated "matter" in Rom 16:2, "business"; 1 Cor. 6:1, in a forensic sense, "a lawsuit"; **(3)** 1 Th 4:6, "in the matter," i.e., the "matter" under consideration, which, as the preceding words show, is here the sin of adultery. See: TDNT—6:638, 927; BAGD—697a; THAYER—534b.

4230. πραγματεία {1x} **pragmatĕia**, *prag-mat-i'-ah;* from *4231;* a *transaction,* i.e. *negotiation:*—affair {1x}.
Pragmateia is a deed and denotes a business, occupation, the prosecution of any affair; and in the plural, pursuits, affairs of life (2 Ti 2:4). See: TDNT—6:640, 927; BAGD—697b; THAYER—534b.

4231. πραγματεύομαι {1x} **pragmatĕuŏmai**, *prag-mat-yoo'-om-ahee;* from *4229;* to *busy oneself* with, i.e. to *trade:*—occupy {1x}.
This word means to be engaged in a business, hence, occupied totally, Lk 19:13. See: TDNT—6:641, 927; BAGD—697b; THAYER—534b.

4232. πραιτώριον {8x} **praitōriŏn**, *prahee-to'-ree-on;* of Lat. or.; the *prætorium* or governor's *court-room* (sometimes incl. the whole *edifice* and *camp*):—judgment hall {4x}, hall of judgment {1x}, common hall {1x}, praetorium {1x}, palace {1x}.
Praitorion is translated **(1)** "common hall" in Mt 27:27, "palace"; **(2)** "Praetorium" in Mk 15:16; **(3)** "hall of judgment" or "judgment hall" in Jn 18:28, 33; 19:9; Acts 23:35; **(4)** "palace", Phil 1:13. See: BAGD—697c; THAYER—534c.

4233. πράκτωρ {2x} **praktōr,** *prak'-tor;* from a der. of *4238;* a *practiser,* i.e. (spec.) an official *collector:*—officer {2x}.

An officer of justice of the lower order whose business it is to inflict punishment (Lk 12:58). See: TDNT—6:642, 927; BAGD—697d; THAYER—534d.

4234. πρᾶξις {6x} **praxis,** *prax'-is;* from *4238; practice,* i.e. (concr.) an *act;* by extens. a *function:*—deed {4x}, office {1x}, work {1x}.

Praxis denotes "a doing, transaction, a deed the action of which is looked upon as incomplete and in progress" (cf. *prasso,* "to practice"); **(1)** in Mt 16:27, "works"; and **(2)** "deed"; Lk 23:51; Acts 19:18; Rom 8:13; Col 3:9. **(3)** In Rom 12:4 it denotes an "action," business, or function, translated "office." See: TDNT—6:642, 927; BAGD—697d; THAYER—534d.

4235. πρᾷος {1x} **praiŏs,** *prah'-os;* a form of *4239,* used in certain parts; *gentle,* i.e. *humble:*—meek {1x}.

Praos is mildness of disposition, gentleness of spirit, meekness. Meekness toward God is that disposition of spirit in which we accept His dealings with us as good, and therefore without disputing or resisting. The meek man truly acknowledges himself as a sinner among sinners and this knowledge of his own sin teaches him to meekly endure the provocations of others and not to withdraw from the burdens their sins may impose on him (Gal 6:1; 2 Ti 2:25; Titus 3:2). The meek are those wholly relying on God rather than their own strength to defend them against injustice. Thus, meekness toward evil people means knowing God is permitting the injuries they inflict, that He is using them to purify His elect, and that He will deliver His elect in His time (cf. Is 41:17, Lk 18:1–8). Gentleness or meekness is the opposite of self-assertiveness and self-interest. It stems from trust in God's goodness and control over the situation. The gentle person is not occupied with self at all. This is a work of the Holy Spirit, not of the human will (Gal 5:23). Syn.: 1932, 5912. See: BAGD—698b; THAYER—534d.

4236. πραότης {9x} **praiŏtēs,** *prah-ot'-ace;* from *4235; gentleness,* by impl. *humility:*—meekness {9x}. See: BAGD—698b; 699a; THAYER—535a.

4237. πρασιά {1x} **prasia,** *pras-ee-ah';* perh. from πράσον **prason** (a *leek,* and so an *onion-patch*); a *garden plot,* i.e. (by impl. of reg. *beds*) a *row* (repeated in plur. by Heb., to indicate an arrangement):—in ranks {1x}. See: BAGD—698b; THAYER—535a.

4238. πράσσω {38x} **prassō,** *pras'-so;* a primary verb; to "*practice*", i.e. *perform repeatedly* or *habitually* (thus differing from *4160,* which prop. refers to a *single* act); by impl. to *execute, accomplish,* etc.; spec. to *collect* (dues), *fare* (personally):—do {28x}, commit {5x}, exact {1x}, require {1x}, deed {1x}, keep {1x}, use arts {1x}.

(1) *Prasso* signifies "to practice," though this is not always to be pressed. **(2)** The apostle John, in his epistles, uses the continuous tenses of *poieo,* to indicate a practice, the habit of doing something, e.g., 1 Jn 3:4, 8, 9, "committeth" and "commit." He uses *prasso* twice in the Gospel, 3:20 and 5:29. **(3)** Generally speaking, in Paul's epistles *poieo* denotes "an action complete in itself," while *prasso* denotes "a habit." Again, *poieo* stresses the accomplishment, e.g., "perform," in Rom 4:21; *prasso* stresses the process leading to the accomplishment, e.g., "doer," in 2:25. In Rom 2:3 he who does, *poieo,* the things mentioned, is warned against judging those who practice them, *prasso.* The distinction in Jn 3:20–21 is noticeable: "Every one that doeth (*prasso,* practiceth) ill . . . he that doeth (*poieo*) the truth." While we cannot draw the regular distinction, that *prasso* speaks of doing evil things, and *poieo* of doing good things, yet very often "where the words assume an ethical tinge, there is a tendency to use the verbs with this distinction. Syn.: *Poieo* (*4160*) denotes to do and *prasso* (*4238*) denotes to practice. *Poieo* (*4160*) designates performance, *prasso* designates an intended, earnest, and habitual performance; *poieo* denotes merely productive action, *prasso* denotes definitely directed action; *poieo* points to the action result and *prasso* points to the scope and character of the result. See: TDNT—6:632, 927; BAGD—698b; THAYER—535a.

4239. πραΰς {3x} **praës,** *prah-ooce';* appar. a primary word; *gentle, mild,* i.e. (by impl.) *humble:*—meek {3x}. See: TDNT—6:645, 929; BAGD—698d; THAYER—535c. See also *4235.*

4240. πραΰτης {3x} **praëtēs,** *prah-oo'-tace;* from *4239; mildness,* i.e. (by impl.) *humility:*—meekness {3x}.

Praetes denotes "meekness." In its use in Scripture, in which it has a fuller, deeper significance than in nonscriptural Greek writings, it consists not in a person's "outward behavior only; nor yet in his relations to his fellow-men; as little in his mere natural disposition. Rather it is an inwrought grace of the soul; and the exercises of it are first and chiefly toward God. It is that temper of spirit in which we accept His dealings with us as good, and

therefore without disputing or resisting; it is closely linked with the word *tapeinophrosune* [humility], and follows directly upon it, Eph 4:2; Col 3:12. It is only the humble heart which is also the meek, and which, as such, does not fight against God and more or less struggle and contend with Him. This meekness, however, being first of all a meekness before God, is also such in the face of men, even of evil men, out of a sense that these, with the insults and injuries which they may inflict, are permitted and employed by Him for the chastening and purifying of His elect.

In Gal 5:23 it is associated with *enkrateia*, "self-control." The meaning of *prautes* is not readily expressed in English, for the terms meekness, mildness, commonly used, suggest weakness and pusillanimity to a greater or less extent, whereas *prautes* does nothing of the kind. Nevertheless, it is difficult to find a rendering less open to objection than 'meekness'; 'gentleness' has been suggested, but as *prautes* describes a condition of mind and heart, and as 'gentleness' is appropriate rather to actions, this word is no better than that used in both English versions. It must be clearly understood, therefore, that the meekness manifested by the Lord and commended to the believer is the fruit of power. The common assumption is that when a man is meek it is because he cannot help himself; but the Lord was "meek" because he had the infinite resources of God at His command.

Described negatively, meekness is the opposite of self-assertiveness and self-interest; it is equanimity of spirit that is neither elated nor cast down, simply because it is not occupied with self at all. In 2 Cor 10:1 the apostle appeals to the "meekness . . . of Christ." Christians are charged to show "all meekness toward all men," Titus 3:2, for meekness becomes "God's elect," Col 3:12. To this virtue the "man of God" is urged; he is to "follow after meekness" for his own sake, 1 Ti 6:11, and in his service, and more especially in his dealings with the "ignorant and erring," he is to exhibit "a spirit of meekness," 1 Cor 4:21, and Gal 6:1; even "they that oppose themselves" are to be corrected in meekness, 2 Ti 2:25. James exhorts his "beloved brethren" to "receive with meekness the implanted word," 1:21. Peter enjoins "meekness" in setting forth the grounds of the Christian hope, 1 Pet 3:15. See: TDNT—6:645, 929; BAGD—699a; THAYER—535c.

4241. πρέπω {7x} **prĕpō**, *prep'-o;* appar. a primary verb; to *tower* up (*be conspicuous*), i.e. (by impl.) to *be suitable* or *proper* (third pers. sing. pres. ind., often used

impers., it is *fit* or *right*):—become {6x}, comely {1x}.

Prepo means "to be conspicuous among a number, to be eminent, distinguished by a thing," hence, "to be becoming, seemly, fit." **(1)** The adornment of good works "becometh women professing godliness," 1 Ti 2:10. **(2)** Those who minister the truth are to speak "the things which befit the sound doctrine," Titus 2:1. **(3)** Christ, as a High Priest "became us," Heb 7:26. **(4)** In the impersonal sense, it signifies "it is fitting, it becometh," Mt 3:15; 1 Cor 11:13; Eph 5:3; Heb 2:10. See: BAGD—699b; THAYER—535c.

4242. πρεσβεία {2x} **prĕsbĕia**, *pres-bi'-ah;* from *4243; seniority* (*eldership*), i.e. (by impl.) an *embassy* (concr. *ambassadors*):—ambassage {1x}, message {1x}.

Presbeia denotes **(1)** to be elder or eldest, prior in birth or age; and **(2)** to be an ambassador (2 Cor 5:20; Eph 6:20; Philem 9). There is a suggestion that to be an ambassador for Christ involves the experience suggested by the word elder. See: BAGD—699b; THAYER—535c.

4243. πρεσβεύω {2x} **prĕsbĕuō**, *pres-byoo'-o;* from the base of *4245;* to be a *senior,* i.e. (by impl.) *act as a representative* (fig. *preacher*):—be an ambassador {2x}.

Presbeuo, "to be an ambassador," 2 Cor 5:20, and Eph 6:20. There is a suggestion that to be an "ambassador" for Christ involves the experience suggested by the word "elder." Elder men were chosen as "ambassadors." See: TDNT—6:681, 931; BAGD—699c; THAYER—535d.

4244. πρεσβυτέριον {3x} **prĕsbutĕriŏn**, *presboo-ter'-ee-on;* neut. of a presumed der. of *4245;* the *order of elders,* i.e. (spec.) Isr. *Sanhedrin* or Chr. "*presbytery*":—elders {1x}, estate of elders {1x}, presbytery {1x}.

Presbuterion, "an assembly of aged men," denotes **(1)** the Council or Senate among the Jews, Lk 22:66; Acts 22:5; **(2)** the "elders" or bishops in a local church, 1 Ti 4:14, "the presbytery." See: TDNT—6:651, 931; BAGD—699c; THAYER—535d.

4245. πρεσβύτερος {67x} **prĕsbutĕrŏs**, *presboo'-ter-os;* comparative of πρέσβυς **prĕsbus** (*elderly*); *older;* as noun, a *senior;* spec. an Isr. *Sanhedrist* (also fig. member of the celestial council) or Chr. "*presbyter*":—elder {64x}, old man {1x}, eldest {1x}, elder woman {1x}.

Presbuteros, an adjective, the comparative degree of *presbus,* "an old man, an elder," is used **(1)** of age, whether **(1a)** of the "elder" of

two persons, Lk 15:25, or more, Jn 8:9, "the eldest", or **(1b)** of a person advanced in life, a senior, Acts 2:17; **(1c)** in Heb 11:2, the "elders" are the forefathers in Israel so in Mt 15:2; Mk 7:3, 5; **(1d)** the feminine of the adjective is used of "elder" women in the churches, 1 Ti 5:2, not in respect of position but in seniority of age; **(2)** of rank or positions of responsibility, **(2a)** among Gentiles, as in Gen 50:7; Num 22:7, **(2b)** in the Jewish nation, **(2b1)** firstly, those who were the heads or leaders of the tribes and families, as of the seventy who assisted Moses, Num 11:16; Deut 27:1, and those assembled by Solomon; **(2b2)** secondly, members of the San-hedrin, consisting of the chief priests, "elders" and scribes, learned in Jewish law, e.g., Mt 16:21; 26:47; **(2c)** thirdly, those who managed public affairs in the various cities, Lk 7:3;

(3) in the Christian churches those who, be-ing raised up and qualified by the work of the Holy Spirit, were appointed to have the spiri-tual care of, and to exercise oversight over, the churches. To these the term "bishops," *episko-poi,* or "overseers," is applied (see Acts 20, v. 17 with v. 28, and Titus 1:5 and 7), the latter term indicating the nature of their work *presbuteroi* their maturity of spiritual experience. The di-vine arrangement seen throughout the NT was for a plurality of these to be appointed in each church, Acts 14:23; 20:17; Phil 1:1; 1 Ti 5:17; Titus 1:5. The duty of "elders" is described by the verb *episkopeo.* They were appointed ac-cording as they had given evidence of fulfilling the divine qualifications, Titus 1:6 to 9; cf. 1 Ti 3:1–7 and 1 Pet 5:2; **(4)** the twenty-four "elders" enthroned in heaven around the throne of God, Rev 4:4, 10; 5:5–14; 7:11, 13; 11:16; 14:3; 19:4. The number twenty-four is representative of earthly conditions. The word "elder" is no-where applied to angels. See: TDNT—6:651, 931; BAGD—699d; THAYER—535d.

4246. πρεσβύτης {3x} **prĕsbutēs**, *pres-boo'-tace;* from the same as *4245;* an *old man:*—aged {1x}, aged man {1x}, old man {1x}.

The noun is found in **(1)** Lk 1:18, "an old man"; **(2)** Titus 2:2, "aged men," and **(3)** Philem 9, "an old man." See: TDNT—6:683, 931; BAGD—700d; THAYER—536b.

4247. πρεσβῦτις {1x} **prĕsbutis**, *pres-boo'-tis;* fem. of *4246;* an *old woman:*—aged woman {1x}. See: BAGD—700d; THAYER—536b.

πρήθω **prēthō**. See *4092.*

4248. πρηνής {1x} **prēnēs**, *pray-nace';* from *4253; leaning (falling) forward* ("*prone*"), i.e. *head foremost:*—headlong {1x}. See: BAGD—700d; THAYER—536b.

4249. πρίζω {1x} **prizō**, *prid'-zo;* a strength-ened form of a primary πρίω **priō**, (to *saw*); to *saw* in two:—saw asunder {1x}. See: BAGD—701a; THAYER—536b.

4250. πρίν {14x} **prin**, *prin;* adv. from *4253; prior, sooner:*—before {11x}, be-fore that {2x}, ere {1x}. See: BAGD—701a; THAYER—536b.

4251. Πρίσκα {1x} **Priska**, *pris'-kah;* of Lat. or.; fem. of *Priscus, ancient; Priska,* a Chr. woman:—Prisca {1x}. See: BAGD—701b; THAYER—536c. See also *4252.*

4252. Πρίσκιλλα {5x} **Priskilla**, *pris'-kil-lah;* dimin. of *4251; Pris-cilla* (i.e. *little Prisca*), a Chr. woman:—Priscilla {5x}. See: BAGD—701d; THAYER—536c.

4253. πρό {48x} **prŏ**, *prŏ;* a primary prep.; "*fore*", i.e. *in front of, prior* (fig. *superior*) *to:*—before {44x}, above {2x}, above . . . ago {1x}, or ever {1x}. See: TDNT—6:683, 935; BAGD—701c; THAYER—536d. In composition it retains the same significations.

4254. προάγω {18x} **prŏagō**, *prŏ-ag'-o;* from *4253* and *71; to lead forward* (magisterially); intr. to *precede* (in place or time [part. *previous*]):—go before {14x}, bring forth {2x}, went before + *2258* {1x}, bring out {1x}.

Proago, as a verb, means "to bring, go be-fore, or lead forth": "And when Herod would have brought him forth (*proago*), the same night Peter was sleeping between two soldiers, bound with two chains: and the keepers before the door kept the prison" (Acts 12:6; cf.16:30; 25:26). See: TDNT—1:130, 20; BAGD—702a; THAYER—537a.

4255. προαιρέομαι {1x} **prŏairĕŏmai**, *prŏ-ahee-reh'-om-ahee;* from *4253* and *138; to choose* for oneself *before* an-other thing (*prefer*), i.e. (by impl.) to *propose* (*intend*):—purpose {1x}.

This word means "to bring forth or for-ward," or, in the middle voice, "to take by choice, prefer, purpose," is translated "He pur-posed" in 2 Cor 9:7. See: BAGD—702b; THAYER—537b.

4256. προαιτιάομαι {1x} **prŏaitiaŏmai**, *prŏ-ahee-tee-ah'-om-ahee;* from *4253* and a der. of *156; to accuse already,* i.e. *previously charge:*—prove before {1x}.

Proaitiaomai denotes "to prove before-hand": "What then? are we better than they? No, in no wise: for we have before proved (*pro-aitiaomai*) both Jews and Gentiles, that they

4257. προακούω {1x} **prŏakŏuō,** *prŏ-ak-oo'-o;* from *4253* and *191;* to *hear already,* i.e. *anticipate:*—hear before {1x}.

Proakouo, as a verb, signifies "to hear before": "For the hope which is laid up for you in heaven, whereof ye heard before in the word of the truth of the gospel", Col 1:5—the preposition, *pro,* contrasts what they heard before, the true gospel, with the false gospel of their recent teachers. Syn.: 189, 191, 1251, 1522, 1873, 1874, 3878. See: BAGD—702c; THAYER—537b.

4258. προαμαρτάνω {2x} **prŏamartanō,** *prŏ-am-ar-tan'-o;* from *4253* and *264;* to *sin previously* (to conversion):—sin already {1x}, heretofore sin {1x}.

Proamartano, as a verb, means "to sin previously": "And lest, when I come again, my God will humble me among you, and that I shall bewail many which have sinned already (*proamartano*), and have not repented of the uncleanness and fornication and lasciviousness which they have committed" (2 Cor 12:21; cf. 13:2). Syn.: 264, 265, 266, 361. See: BAGD—702c; THAYER—537c.

4259. προαύλιον {1x} **prŏauliŏn,** *prŏ-ŏw'-lee-on;* neut. of a presumed compound of *4253* and *833;* a *forecourt,* i.e. *vestibule* (*alley-way*):—porch {1x}.

Proaulion, "the exterior court" or "vestibule," between the door and the street, in the houses of well-to-do folk, Mk 14:68, "porch." See: BAGD—702d; THAYER—537c.

4260. προβαίνω {5x} **prŏbainō,** *prob-ah'-ee-no;* from *4253* and the base of *939;* to *walk forward,* i.e. *advance* (lit. or in years):—be well stricken {2x}, go on {1x}, go farther {1x}, be of . . . age + 2250 + 1722 {1x}.

Probaino, "to go on, forwards, advance," is used (1) of locality, Mt 4:21; Mk 1:19; (2) metaphorically use with reference to age, Lk 1:7, 18; 2:36. See: BAGD—702d; THAYER—537c.

4261. προβάλλω {2x} **prŏballō,** *prob-al'-lo;* from *4253* and *906;* to *throw forward,* i.e. *push to the front, germinate:*—put forward {1x}, shoot forth {1x}.

It is used (1) of plants shooting forth leaves, Lk 21:30; and (2) of Paul being thrust forward to defend himself, Acts 19:33. See: BAGD—702d; THAYER—537c.

4262. προβατικός {1x} **prŏbatikŏs,** *prob-at-ik-os';* from *4263; relating to sheep,* i.e. (a *gate*) through which they were led into Jerusalem:—sheep (market) {1x}. See: BAGD—703a; THAYER—537d.

4263. πρόβατον {41x} **prŏbatŏn,** *prob'-at-on;* prob. neut. of a presumed. der. of *4260; something that walks forward* (a *quadruped*), i.e. (spec.) a *sheep* (lit. or fig.):—sheep {40x}, sheepfold + 833 {1x}.

Probaton, from *probaino,* "to go forward," i.e., of the movement of quadrupeds, was used among the Greeks of small cattle, sheep and goats; in the NT, of "sheep" only **(1)** naturally, e.g., Mt 12:11, 12; **(2)** metaphorically, **(2a)** of those who belong to the Lord, the lost ones of the house of Israel, Mt 10:6; **(2b)** of those who are under the care of the Good Shepherd, e.g., Mt 26:31; Jn 10:1, lit., "the fold of the sheep," and vv. 2–27; 21:16; Heb 13:20; **(2c)** of those who in a future day, at the introduction of the millennial kingdom, have shown kindness to His persecuted earthly people in their great tribulation, Mt 25:33; **(2d)** of the clothing of false shepherds, Mt 7:15; **(3)** figuratively, by way of simile, **(3a)** of Christ, Acts 8:32; **(3b)** of the disciples, e.g., Mt 10:16; **(3c)** of true followers of Christ in general, Rom 8:36; **(3d)** of the former wayward condition of those who had come under His Shepherd care, 1 Pet 2:25; **(3e)** of the multitudes who sought the help of Christ in the days of His flesh, Mt 9:36; Mk 6:34. See: TDNT—6:689, 936; BAGD—703a; THAYER—537d.

4264. προβιβάζω {2x} **prŏbibazō,** *prob-ib-ad'-zo;* from *4253* and a redupl. form of *971;* to *force forward,* i.e. *bring to the front, instigate:*—draw {1x}, before instruct {1x}.

Probibazo, as a verb, means "to draw, to bring or drag forward": "And they drew Alexander out of the multitude" (Acts 19:33). It is also used of Herodias' daughter being "before instructed," thrust forward by her mother; possibly indicating a reluctance, Mt 14:8. Syn.: 307, 385, 392, 501, 502, 645, 868, 1448, 1670, 1828, 2020, 4317, 4334, 4358, 4685, 4951, 5288, 5289. See: BAGD—703c; THAYER—538a.

4265. προβλέπω {1x} **prŏblĕpō,** *prob-lep'-o;* from *4253* and *991;* to *look out beforehand,* i.e. *furnish in advance:*—provide {1x}. See: BAGD—703c; THAYER—538a.

4266. προγίνομαι {1x} **prŏginŏmai,** *prog-in'-om-ahee;* from *4253* and *1096;* to *be already,* i.e. *have previously transpired:*—be past {1x}.

Proginomai, "to happen before" is used in Rom 3:25, "that are past", of sins committed in times previous to the atoning sacrifice of Christ. See: BAGD—703c; THAYER—538a.

4267. προγινώσκω {5x} **prŏginōskō,** *prog-in-oce'-ko;* from *4253* and *1097;* to *know beforehand,* i.e. *foresee:*—

foreknow {2x}, foreordain {1x}, know {1x}, know before {1x}.

Proginosko, "to know beforehand," is used **(1)** of the divine "foreknowledge" **(1a)** concerning believers, Rom 8:29; **(1b)** Israel, 11:2; **(1c)** Christ as the Lamb of God, 1 Pet 1:20, "foreordained"; **(2)** of human previous "knowledge," **(2a)** of a person, Acts 26:5, "which knew"; **(2b)** of facts, 2 Pet 3:17. Syn.: 1097, 1107, 1110, 1492, 1921, 1467, 1922, 1987. See: TDNT—1:715, 119; BAGD—703d; THAYER—538a.

4268. πρόγνωσις {2x} **prŏgnōsis**, *prog'-no-sis;* from *4267;* forethought:—foreknowledge {2x}.

"Foreknowledge" is one aspect of omniscience; it is implied in God's warnings, promises and predictions. See Acts 15:18. God's "foreknowledge" involves His electing grace, but this does not preclude human will. He "foreknows" the exercise of faith which brings salvation. The apostle Paul stresses especially the actual purposes of God rather than the ground of the purposes, see, e.g., Gal 1:16; Eph 1:5, 11. The divine counsels will ever be unthwartable. See: TDNT—1:715, 119; BAGD—703d; THAYER—538b.

4269. πρόγονος {2x} **prŏgŏnŏs**, *prog'-on-os;* from *4266;* an *ancestor, (grand-) parent:*—forefather {1x}, parent {1x}.

This word is used as a noun in the plural, **(1)** 2 Ti 1:3, "forefathers"; **(2)** in 1 Ti 5:4, "parents." See: BAGD—704a; THAYER—538b.

4270. προγράφω {5x} **prŏgraphō**, *prog-raf'-o;* from *4253* and *1125;* to *write previously;* fig. to *announce, prescribe:*—write {1x}, write aforetime {1x}, write afore {1x}, evidently set forth {1x}, before ordain {1x}.

This word is used **(1)** in Rom 15:4 first time, "written aforetime"; second time, "written"; **(2)** in Gal 3:1, "evidently set forth"; **(3)** in Eph 3:3, "wrote before time"; and **(4)** in Jude 4, "before ordained." See: TDNT—1:770, 128; BAGD—704a; THAYER—538b.

4271. πρόδηλος {3x} **prŏdēlŏs**, *prod'-ay-los;* from *4253* and *1212;* plain *before* all men, i.e. *obvious:*—evident {1x}, manifest beforehand {1x}, open beforehand {1x}.

This word is used **(1)** in Heb 7:14 in the sense of "clearly evident"; **(2)** in 1 Ti 5:24, "open beforehand"; and **(3)** in 1 Ti 5:25, "manifest beforehand." See: BAGD—704b; THAYER—538c.

4272. προδίδωμι {1x} **prŏdidōmi**, *prod-id'-o-mee;* from *4253* and

1325; to *give before* the other party has given:—first give {1x}. See: BAGD—704c; THAYER—538c.

4273. προδότης {3x} **prŏdŏtēs**, *prod-ot'-ace;* from *4272* (in the sense of *giving forward* into another's [the enemy's] hands); a *surrender:*—betrayer {1x}, traitor {2x}.

This word is translated **(1)** "betrayers" in Acts 7:52; **(2)** "traitor," in Lk 6:16; and "traitors" in 2 Ti 3:4. See: BAGD—704c; THAYER—538c.

προδρέμω prŏdrĕmō. See *4390.*

4274. πρόδρομος {1x} **prŏdrŏmŏs**, *prod'-rom-os;* from the alt. of *4390;* a *runner ahead,* i.e. *scout* (fig. *precursor*):—forerunner {1x}. See: TDNT—8:235, 1189; BAGD—704c; THAYER—538c.

4275. προείδω {2x} **prŏĕidō**, *pro-i'-do;* from *4253* and *1492; foresee:*—foresee {1x}, saw before {1x}.

Oreido is used **(1)** of David, as foreseeing Christ, in Acts 2:31, "seeing before"; and **(2)** in Gal 3:8 it is said of the Scripture, personified, personal activity being attributed to it by reason of its divine source (cf. v. 22). "What saith the Scripture?" was a common formula among the Rabbis. See: TDNT—5:381,*; BAGD—704c; 709a; THAYER—538d.

προειρέω prŏĕirĕō. See *4280.*

4276. προελπίζω {1x} **prŏĕlpizō**, *prŏ-el-pid'-zo;* from *4253* and *1679;* to *hope in advance* of other confirmation:—first trust {1x}. See: TDNT—2:534, 229; BAGD—705a; THAYER—538d.

4277. προέπω {3x} **prŏĕpō**, *prŏ-ep'-o;* from *4253* and *2036;* to *say before* the event, *say already,* to *predict:*—speak before {1x}, tell in time past {1x}, forewarn {1x}. See: BAGD—none listed; THAYER—none listed. comp. *4280.*

4278. προενάρχομαι {2x} **prŏĕnarchŏmai**, *prŏ-en-ar'-khom-ahee;* from *4253* and *1728;* to *commence already:*—begin {1x}, begin before {1x}. See: BAGD—705b; THAYER—538d.

4279. προεπαγγέλλομαι {1x} **prŏĕpaggĕllŏmai**, *prŏ-ep-ang-ghel'-lom-ahee;* mid. voice from *4253* and *1861;* to *promise of old:*—promise afore {1x}. See: TDNT—2:586, 240; BAGD—705b; THAYER—539a.

4280. προερέω {9x} **prŏĕrĕō**, *prŏ-er-eh'-o;* from *4253* and *2046;* used as alt. of *4277;* to *say already, predict:*—say before

{4x}, tell before {2x}, speak before {2x}, foretell {1x}. See: BAGD—not listed; THAYER—not listed.

4281. προέρχομαι {9x} **prŏĕrchŏmai**, *prŏ-er'-khom-ahee;* from *4253* and *2064* (incl. its alt.); to *go onward, precede* (in place or time):—go before {5x}, go farther {1x}, go forward {1x}, outgo {1x}, pass on {1x}. See: BAGD—705b; THAYER—539a.

4282. προετοιμάζω {2x} **prŏĕtŏimazō**, *pro-et-oy-mad'-zo;* from *4253* and *2090;* to *fit* up *in advance* (lit. or fig.):—ordain before {1x}, prepare afore {1x}. See: TDNT—2:704, 266; BAGD—705d; THAYER—539a.

4283. προευαγγελίζομαι {1x} **prŏĕuaggĕlizŏmai**, *prŏ-yoo-ang-ghel-id'-zom-ahee;* mid. voice from *4253* and *2097;* to *announce* glad news *in advance:*—preach before the gospel {1x}. See: TDNT—2:737, 267; BAGD—705d; THAYER—539b.

4284. προέχομαι {1x} **prŏĕchŏmai**, *prŏ-ekh-om-ahee;* mid. voice from *4253* and *2192;* to *hold* oneself *before* others, i.e. (fig.) to *excel:*—be better {1x}.

This word means to have before or in advance of another, to have pre-eminence over another, to excel, surpass; and hence, be better, to be intrinsically better before the comparison is made, Rom 3:9. See: TDNT—6:692, 937; BAGD—705d; THAYER—539b.

4285. προηγέομαι {1x} **prŏēgĕŏmai**, *prŏ-ay-geh'-om-ahee;* from *4253* and *2233;* to *lead the way* for others, i.e. *show deference:*—prefer {1x}.

This word is used in Rom 12:10, in the sense of taking the lead in showing deference one to another, "(in honor) preferring one another." See: TDNT—2:908, 303; BAGD—706a; THAYER—539b.

4286. πρόθεσις {12x} **prŏthĕsis**, *proth'-es-is;* from *4388;* a *setting forth,* i.e. (fig.) *proposal* (*intention*); spec. the *show*bread (in the Temple) as *exposed* before God:—purpose {8x}, shewbread + *740* {4x}.

Prothesis, "a setting forth" (used of the "shewbread"), "a purpose", is used **(1)** of the "purposes of God," Rom 8:28; 9:11; Eph 1:11; 3:11; 2 Ti 1:9; **(2)** of "human purposes," as to things **(2a)** material, Acts 27:13; **(2b)** spiritual, Acts 11:23; 2 Ti 3:10. One puts forth his purpose first, then acts. God put forth the shewbread daily to demonstrate His purpose; He would provide daily bread. See: TDNT—8:164, 1176; BAGD—706a; THAYER—539a.

4287. προθέσμιῇ {1x} **prŏthĕsmiŏs**, *prothes'-mee-os;* from *4253* and a der. of *5087; fixed beforehand,* i.e. (fem. with *2250* implied) a *designated* day:—time appointed {1x}.

Prothesmia, as a verb, means "appointed": "But is under tutors and governors until the time appointed of the father" (Gal 4:2). See: BAGD—706c; THAYER—539c.

4288. προθυμία {5x} **prŏthumia**, *proth-oo-mee'-ah;* from *4289; predisposition,* i.e. *alacrity:*—forwardness of mind {1x}, readiness {1x}, readiness of mind {1x}, ready mind {1x}, willing mind {1x}.

This word connotes zeal, spirit, eagerness, inclination, readiness of mind, implying action to surely follow. See: TDNT—6:697, 937; BAGD—706c; THAYER—539d.

4289. πρόθυμος {3x} **prŏthumŏs**, *proth'-oo-mos;* from *4253* and *2372; forward* in *spirit,* i.e. *predisposed;* neut. (as noun) *alacrity:*—ready {2x}, willing {1x}. Cf. Mt 26:41; Mk 14:38; Rom 1:15. See: TDNT—6:694, 937; BAGD—706c; THAYER—539d.

4290. προθύμως {1x} **prŏthumōs**, *proth-oo'-moce;* adv. from *4289; with alacrity:*—of a ready mind {1x}.

This word implies a ready mind, a desire to do what is right for the flock, and actions that follow. See: BAGD—706d; THAYER—539d.

4291. προΐστημι {8x} **prŏïstēmi**, *prŏ-is'-tay-mee;* from *4253* and *2476;* to *stand before,* i.e. (in rank) to *preside,* or (by impl.) to *practice:*—maintain {2x}, be over {1x}, rule {5x}. See: TDNT—6:700,*; BAGD—707a; THAYER—539d.

4292. προκαλέομαι {1x} **prŏkalĕŏmai**, *prok-al-eh'-om-ahee;* mid. voice from *4253* and *2564;* to *call forth to oneself* (*challenge*), i.e. (by impl.) to *irritate:*—provoke {1x}.

This word means to call forth as to a contest; hence to stir up what is evil in another (Gal 5:26). See: TDNT—3:496,*; BAGD—707b; THAYER—540a.

4293. προκαταγγέλλω {4x} **prŏkataggĕllō**, *prok-at-ang-ghel'-lo;* from *4253* and *2605;* to *announce beforehand,* i.e. *predict, promise:*—foretell {1x}, have notice before {1x}, shew before {1x}.

This verb implies previous verbal communication of a message. See: TDNT—1:70, 10; BAGD—707b; THAYER—540a.

4294. προκαταρτίζω {1x} **prŏkatartizō**, *prok-at-ar-tid'-zo;* from *4253* and *2675;* to *prepare in advance:*—

make up beforehand {1x}. See: BAGD—707c; THAYER—540a.

4295. πρόκειμαι {5x} **prŏkĕimai**, *prok'-i-mahee;* from *4253* and *2749;* to *lie before* the view, i.e. (fig.) to *be present* (to the mind), to *stand forth* (as an example or reward):—be set before {3x}, be first {1x}, be set forth {1x}.

This word signifies **(1)** "to be set before", and is so rendered in **(1a)** Heb 6:18 of the hope of the believer; **(1b)** 12:1, of the Christian race; **(1c)** Heb 12:2. 2, of the joy "set" before Christ in the days of His flesh and at His death; **(2)** "to be set forth," said of Sodom and Gomorrah, in Jude 7. **(3)** It is used elsewhere in 2 Cor 8:12, "first" a willing mind. See: TDNT—3:656, 425; BAGD—707c; THAYER—540a.

4296. προκηρύσσω {2x} **prŏkērussō**, *prok-ay-rooce'-so;* from *4253* and *2784;* to *herald* (i.e. *proclaim*) *in advance:*—preach before {1x}, preach first {1x}. See: TDNT—3:717, 430; BAGD—707d; THAYER—540a.

4297. προκοπή {3x} **prŏkŏpē**, *prok-op-ay';* from *4298; progress,* i.e. *advancement* (subj. or obj.):—furtherance {2x}, profit {1x}. See: TDNT—6:703, 939; BAGD—707d; THAYER—540b.

4298. προκόπτω {6x} **prŏkŏptō**, *prok-op'-to;* from *4253* and *2875;* to *drive forward* (as if by beating), i.e. (fig. and intr.) to *advance* (in amount, to *grow;* in time, to *be well along*):—increase {2x}, proceed {1x}, profit {1x}, be far spent {1x}, wax {1x}.

(1) This word stresses a steady and incremental progress. This word means lit., "to strike forward, cut forward a way," i.e., to make progress, is translated **(2)** "increased" in Lk 2:52, of the Lord Jesus; **(3)** in Gal 1:14 "profited", of Paul's former progress in the Jews' religion; **(4)** in Rom 13:12, "is far spent," of the "advanced" state of the "night" of the world's spiritual darkness; **(5)** in 2 Ti 2:16, "will increase unto more [ungodliness]," of profane babblings; **(6)** in 2 Ti 3:9, "shall proceed no further," of the limit divinely to be put to the doings of evil men; **(7)** in 2 Ti 3:13, of the progress of evil men and impostors, "shall wax," lit., "shall advance to the worse." See: TDNT—6:703, 939 BAGD—707d; THAYER—540b.

4299. πρόκριμα {1x} **prŏkrima**, *prok'-ree-mah;* from a compound of *4253* and *2919;* a *prejudgment* (*prejudice*), i.e. *prepossession:*—prefer one before another {1x}.

Prokrima denotes prejudging, to judge beforehand (1 Ti 5:21), preferring one person, another being put aside by unfavorable judgment

due to partiality. See: TDNT—3:953, 469; BAGD—708a; THAYER—540c.

4300. προκυρόω {1x} **prŏkurŏō**, *prok-oo-rŏ'-o;* from *4253* and *2964;* to *ratify previously:*—confirm before {1x}.

Prokuroo, "to confirm or ratify before," is said of the divine confirmation of a promise given originally to Abraham, Gen 12, and "confirmed" by the vision of the furnace and torch, Gen 15, by the birth of Isaac, Gen 21, and by the oath of God, Gen 22, all before the giving of the Law, Gal 3:17. See: TDNT—3:1100, 494; BAGD—708b; THAYER—540c.

4301. προλαμβάνω {3x} **prŏlambanō**, *prol-am-ban'-o;* from *4253* and *2983;* to *take in advance,* i.e. (lit.) *eat before* others have an opportunity; (fig.) to *anticipate, surprise:*—come aforehand {1x}, overtake {1x}, take before {1x}.

Prolambano, "to anticipate" (*pro,* "before," *lambano,* "to take"), is used **(1)** of the act of Mary, in Mk 14:8; **(2)** of forestalling the less favored at a social meal, 1 Cor 11:21; **(3)** of being "overtaken" in any trespass, Gal 6:1, where the meaning is not that of detecting a person in the act, but of his being caught by the trespass, through his being off his guard (see 5:21 and contrast the premeditated practice of evil in 5:26). See: TDNT—4:14, 495; BAGD—708b; THAYER—540c.

4302. προλέγω {3x} **prŏlĕgō**, *prol-eg'-o;* from *4253* and *3004;* to *say beforehand,* i.e. *predict, forewarn:*—foretell {2x}, tell before {1x}. See: BAGD—708b; THAYER—540c.

4303. προμαρτύρομαι {1x} **prŏmarturŏmai**, *prom-ar-too'-rom-ahee;* from *4253* and *3143;* to *be a witness in advance,* i.e. *predict:*—testify beforehand {1x}. See: TDNT—4:510, 564; BAGD—708c; THAYER—540d.

4304. προμελετάω {1x} **prŏmĕlĕtaō**, *prom-el-et-ah'-o;* from *4253* and *3191;* to *premeditate:*—meditate before {1x}. See: BAGD—708c; THAYER—540d.

4305. προμεριμνάω {1x} **prŏmĕrimnaō**, *prom-er-im-nah'-o;* from *4253* and *3309;* to *care* (anxiously) *in advance:*—take thought beforehand {1x}. See: TDNT—4:589, 584; BAGD—708c; THAYER—540d.

4306. προνοέω {3x} **prŏnŏĕō**, *pron-ŏ-eh'-o;* from *4253* and *3539;* to *consider in advance,* i.e. *look out for beforehand* (act. by way of *maintenance* for others; mid. voice by way of *circumspection* for oneself):—

provide {1x}, provide for {2x}. Cf. 1 Ti 5:8; Rom 12:17; 2 Cor 8:21. See: TDNT—4:1009, 636; BAGD—708c; THAYER—540d.

4307. πρόνοια {2x} **prŏnŏia**, *pron'-oy-ah;* from *4306; forethought,* i.e. provident *care* or *supply:*—providence {1x}, provision {1x}. See: TDNT—4:1011, 636; BAGD—708d; THAYER—540d.

4308. προοράω {2x} **prŏŏraō**, *prŏ-or-ah'-o;* from *4253* and *3708;* to *behold in advance,* i.e. (act.) to *notice* (another) *previously,* or (mid. voice) to *keep in* (one's own) *view:*—foresee {1x}, see before {1x}.

Proorao is used with reference **(1)** to the past, of seeing a person before, Acts 21:29; **(2)** to the future, in the sense of "foreseeing" a person or thing, Acts 2:25, with reference to Christ and the Father, "saw before" (here the middle voice is used). See: TDNT—5:381, 706; BAGD—709a; THAYER—540d.

4309. προορίζω {6x} **prŏŏrizō**, *prŏ-or-id'-zo;* from *4253* and *3724;* to *limit in advance,* i.e. (fig.) *predetermine:*—determine before {1x}, ordain {1x}, predestinate {4x}.

This word denotes "to mark out beforehand, to determine before, foreordain"; **(1)** in Acts 4:28, "determined before"; **(2)** so in 1 Cor 2:7, "ordained", **(3)** in Rom 8:29–30 and Eph 1:5, 11, "predestinate." See: TDNT—5:456, 728; BAGD—709b; THAYER—541a.

4310. προπάσχω {1x} **prŏpaschō**, *prop-as'-kho;* from *4253* and *3958;* to *undergo* hardship *previously:*—suffer before {1x}. See: TDNT—5:924, 798; BAGD—709b; THAYER—541a.

4311. προπέμπω {9x} **prŏpĕmpō**, *prop-em'-po;* from *4253* and *3992;* to *send forward,* i.e. *escort* or *aid* in travel:—bring on (one's) way {4x}, bring (forward) on (one's) journey {3x}, conduct forth {1x}, accompany {1x}.

Propempo, as a verb, means "to send forth, to bring on one's way" and means "to send forward"; hence of assisting a person on a journey **(1)** in the sense of fitting him out with the requisites for it, **(1a)** Rom 15:24 and 1 Cor 16:6, and v. 11. **(1b)** So in 2 Cor 1:16 and Titus 3:13, and **(1c)** of John's exhortation to Gaius concerning traveling evangelists, "whom thou wilt do well to set forward on their journey worthily of God," 3 Jn 6. **(2)** While personal "accompaniment" is not excluded, practical assistance seems to be generally in view, as indicated by Paul's word to Titus to set forward Zenas and Apollos on their journey and to see "that nothing be wanting unto them." In regard to the parting of Paul from the elders of Ephesus

at Miletus, personal "accompaniment" is especially in view, perhaps not without the suggestion of assistance, Acts 20:38; "accompaniment" is also indicated in 21:5; "they all with wives and children brought us on our way, till we were out of the city." In Acts 15:3, both ideas perhaps are suggested. See: BAGD—709b; THAYER—541a.

4312. προπετής {2x} **prŏpĕtēs**, *prop-et-ace';* from a compound of *4253* and *4098; falling forward,* i.e. *headlong* (fig. *precipitate*):—heady {1x}, rashly {1x}.

Propetes lit. means "falling forwards" (from *pro,* "forwards," and *pipto,* "to fall"); it is used metaphorically to signify "precipitate, rash, reckless," and is said **(1)** of persons, 2 Ti 3:4; "headstrong" is the appropriate understanding; **(2)** of things, Acts 19:36, "(nothing) rashly." See: BAGD—709c; THAYER—541b.

4313. προπορεύομαι {2x} **prŏpŏrĕuŏmai**, *prop-or-yoo'-om-ahee;* from *4253* and *4198;* to *precede* (as guide or herald):—go {1x}, go before {1x}. See: BAGD—709c; THAYER—541b.

4314. πρός {726x} **prŏs**, *pros;* a strengthened form of *4253;* a prep. of direction; *forward to,* i.e. *toward* (with the gen. *the side of,* i.e. *pertaining to;* with the dat. *by the side of,* i.e. *near to;* usually with the acc., the place, time, occasion, or respect, which is the *destination* of the relation, i.e. *whither* or *for* which it is predicated):—unto {340x}, to {203x}, with {43x}, for {25x}, against {24x}, among {20x}, at {11x}, not tr {6x}, vr to {1x}, misc. {53x} = about, according to, because of, before, between, ([where-]) by, X at thy house, in, for intent, nigh unto, of, which pertain to, that, to (the end that), + together, to ([you]) -ward, within. In composition it denotes essentially the same applications, namely, motion *toward,* accession *to,* or nearness *at.* See: TDNT—6:720, 942; BAGD—709c; THAYER—541b.

4315. προσάββατον {1x} **prŏsabbatŏn**, *pros-ab'-bat-on;* from *4253* and *4521;* a *fore-sabbath,* i.e. the *Sabbath-eve:*—day before the sabbath {1x}. See: BAGD—711a; THAYER—543c. comp. *3904.*

4316. προσαγορεύω {1x} **prŏsagŏrĕuō**, *pros-ag-or-yoo'-o;* from *4314* and a der. of *58* (mean to *harangue*); to *address,* i.e. *salute* by *name:*—call {1x}. See: BAGD—711b; THAYER—543d.

4317. προσάγω {4x} **prŏsago**, *pros-ag'-o;* from *4314* and *71;* to *lead toward,* i.e. (tran.) to *conduct near* (*summon, present*), or (intr.) to *approach:*—bring {3x}, draw near {1x}.

Prosago, as a verb, used **(1)** transitively, means "to bring to": "And Jesus answering said, O faithless and perverse generation, how long shall I be with you, and suffer you? Bring thy son hither" (Lk 9:41; cf. Acts 16:20; 1 Pet 3:18); **(2)** intransitively, "to draw near": "But when the fourteenth night was come, as we were driven up and down in Adria, about midnight the shipmen deemed that they drew near to some country" (Acts 27:27). Syn.: 307, 385, 392, 501, 502, 645, 868, 1448, 1670, 1828, 2020, 4264, 4334, 4358, 4685, 4951, 5288, 5289. See: TDNT−1:131, 20; BAGD−711b; THAYER−543d.

4318. προσαγωγή {3x} **prŏsagōgē**, *pros-ag-ogue-ay';* from *4317* (comp. 72); *admission:*−access {3x}.

Prosagoge, lit., "a leading or bringing into the presence of" (*pros,* "to," *ago,* "to lead"), denotes "access," with which is associated the thought of freedom to enter through the assistance or favor of another. It is used three times, **(1)** Rom 5:2, of the "access" which we have by faith, through our Lord Jesus Christ, into grace; **(2)** Eph 2:18, of our "access" in one Spirit through Christ, unto the Father; **(3)** Eph 3:12, of the same "access," there said to be "in Christ," and which we have "in confidence through our faith in Him." This "access" involves the acceptance which we have in Christ with God, and the privilege of His favor toward us. See: TDNT−1:133, 20; BAGD−711c; THAYER−544a.

4319. προσαιτέω {3x} **prŏsaitĕō**, *pros-ahee-teh'-o;* from *4314* and *154;* to *ask repeatedly* (*importune*), i.e. *solicit:*−beg {3x}.

Prosaiteo, lit., "to ask besides" (*pros,* "toward," used intensively, and *aiteo*), "to ask earnestly, to importune, continue asking," is said of the blind beggar in Mk 10:46; Lk 18:35; Jn 9:8. See: BAGD−711c; THAYER−544a.

4320. προσαναβαίνω {1x} **prŏsanabainō**, *pros-an-ab-ah'-ee-no;* from *4314* and *305;* to *ascend farther,* i.e. *be promoted* (*take an upper [more honorable] seat):*−go up {1x}. See: BAGD−711c; THAYER−544a.

4321. προσαναλίσκω {1x} **prŏsanaliskō**, *pros-an-al-is'-ko;* from *4314* and *355;* to *expend further:*−spend {1x}. See: BAGD−711c; THAYER−544a.

4322. προσαναπληρόω {2x} **prŏsanaplērŏō**, *pros-an-ap-lay-ro'-o;* from *4314* and *378;* to *fill up further,* i.e. *furnish fully:*−supply {2x}.

Prosanapleroo, "to fill up by adding to, to

supply fully", is translated **(1)** "supplieth" in 2 Cor 9:12; and **(2)** in 11:9, "supplied." See: BAGD−711d; THAYER−544b.

4323. προσανατίθημι {2x} **prŏsanatithēmi**, *pros-an-at-ith'-ay-mee;* from *4314* and *394;* to *lay up in addition,* i.e. (mid. voice and fig.) to *impart* or (by impl.) to *consult:*−in conference add {1x}, confer {1x}.

This word means lit., "to lay upon in addition," and came to be used in the sense of putting oneself before another, for the purpose of consulting him; hence simply "to consult, to take one into counsel, to confer." **(1)** With this meaning it is used only in Gal 1:16. This less intensive word may have been purposely used there by the apostle to suggest that he described to his fellow apostles the character of his teaching, not to obtain their approval or their advice concerning it, but simply that they might have the facts of the case before them on which they were shortly to adjudicate. **(2)** It was also used to signify "to communicate, to impart." With this meaning it is used only in Gal 2:6, in the middle voice, the suggestion being to "add" from one's store of things. In regard to his visit to Jerusalem the apostle says "those who were of repute in conference added" nothing to me, that is to say, they neither modified his teaching nor "added" to his authority. See: TDNT−1:353, 57; BAGD−711d; THAYER−544b.

4324. προσαπειλέω {1x} **prŏsapĕilĕō**, *pros-ap-i-leh'-o;* from *4314* and *546;* to *menace additionally:*−threaten further {1x}. See: BAGD−711d; THAYER−544b.

4325. προσδαπανάω {1x} **prŏsdapanaō**, *pros-dap-an-ah'-o;* from *4314* and *1159;* to *expend additionally:*−spend more {1x}. See: BAGD−712a; THAYER−544b.

4326. προσδέομαι {1x} **prŏsdĕŏmai**, *pros-deh'-om-ahee;* from *4314* and *1189;* to *require additionally,* i.e. *want further:*−need {1x}. See: TDNT−2:41, 143; BAGD−712a; THAYER−544c.

4327. προσδέχομαι {14x} **prŏsdĕchŏmai**, *pros-dekh'-om-ahee;* from *4314* and *1209;* to *admit* (to intercourse, hospitality, credence, or [fig.] endurance); by impl. to *await* (with confidence or patience):−look for {4x}, wait for {3x}, receive {3x}, waited for + 2258 {1x}, allow {1x}, take {1x}, accept {1x}.

Prosdechomai, as a verb, means "to receive to oneself, to receive favorably," also "to look

for, wait for," is used **(1)** of "receiving": "And the Pharisees and scribes murmured, saying, This man receiveth sinners, and eateth with them" (Lk 15:2; cf. Rom 16:2; Phil 2:29). It also means "to receive favorably," denoting "to expect," and is rendered **(2)** "to look for," e.g., in Lk 2:38; 23:51; Titus 2:13; Jude 21. **(3)** It is translated "allow" in Acts 24:15. Syn.: 324, 353, 354, 568, 588, 618, 1209, 1523, 1926, 2210, 2865, 2975, 2983, 3028, 3335, 3336, 3858, 3880, 3970, 4355, 4356, 4380, 4381, 4382, 5562, 5264, 5274. See: TDNT—2:57, 146; BAGD—712b; THAYER—544c.

4328. **προσδοκάω** {16x} **prŏsdŏkaō**, *pros-dok-ah'-o;* from *4314* and δοκεύω **dŏkĕuō** (to watch); to *anticipate* (in thought, hope or fear); by impl. to *await:*—look for {8x}, waited for + 2258 {2x}, expect {1x}, be in expectation {1x}, look {1x}, look when {1x}, waiting for {1x}, tarry {1x}. See: TDNT—6:725, 943; BAGD—712c; THAYER—544c.

4329. **προσδοκία** {2x} **prŏsdŏkia**, *pros-dok-ee'-ah;* from *4328;* apprehension (of evil); by impl. *infliction* anticipated:—expectation {1x}, looking after {1x}.

Proskokia, "a watching for, expectation", is used in the NT only of the "expectation" of evil, **(1)** Lk 21:26, "looking for," regarding impending calamities; **(2)** Acts 12:11, "the expectation" of the execution of Peter. See: TDNT—6:725, 943; BAGD—712c; THAYER—544d.

προσδρέμω prŏsdrĕmō. See *4370.*

4330. **προσεάω** {1x} **prŏseaō**, *pros-eh-ah'-o;* from *4314* and *1439;* to *permit further* progress:—suffer {1x}. See: BAGD—712d; THAYER—544d.

4331. **προσεγγίζω** {1x} **prŏsĕggizō**, *pros-eng-ghid'-zo;* from *4314* and *1448;* to *approach near:*—come nigh {1x}. See: TDNT—2:330, 194; BAGD—712d; THAYER—544d.

4332. **προσεδρεύω** {1x} **prŏsĕdrĕuō**, *pros-ed-ryoo'-o;* from a compound of *4314* and the base of *1476;* to *sit near,* i.e. *attend* as a servant:—wait at {1x}. See: BAGD—712d; THAYER—544d.

4333. **προσεργάζομαι** {1x} **prŏsĕrgazŏmai**, *pros-er-gad'-zom-ahee;* from *4314* and *2038;* to *work additionally,* i.e. (by impl.) *acquire besides:*—gain {1x}. See: BAGD—713a; THAYER—544d.

4334. **προσέρχομαι** {86x} **prŏsĕrchŏmai**, *pros-er'-khom-ahee;* from *4314* and *2064* (incl. its alt.); to *approach,* i.e. (lit.) *come near, visit,* or (fig.) *worship, as-*

sent to:—come {30x}, come to {25x}, come unto {19x}, go to {3x}, go unto {2x}, draw near {2x}, misc. {5x} = come thereunto, consent, go near.

Proserchomai, as a verb, is translated **(1)** "draw near": "Let us draw near with a true heart in full assurance of faith" (Heb 10:22); **(2)** "drew near": "When Moses saw *it,* he wondered at the sight: and as he drew near to behold it, the voice of the Lord came unto him" (Acts 7:31); **(3)** "come boldly": "Let us therefore come boldly unto the throne of grace" (Heb 4:16); and "come": "Wherefore He is able also to save them to the uttermost that come (*proserchomai*) unto God by him, seeing He ever liveth to make intercession for them" (Heb 7:25). Syn.: 307, 316, 385, 392, 501, 502, 645, 868, 1448, 1451, 1452, 1670, 1828, 2020, 4139, 4264, 4317, 4358, 4685, 4951, 5288, 5289. See: TDNT—2:683, 257; BAGD—713a; THAYER—545a.

4335. **προσευχή** {37x} **prŏsĕuchē**, *pros-yoo-khay';* from *4336;* *prayer* (*worship*); by impl. an *oratory* (*chapel*):—pray earnestly + 3346 {1x}, prayer {36x}.

Proseuche denotes **(1)** "prayer" (to God), the most frequent term, e.g., Mt 21:22; **(1a)** Lk 6:12, where the phrase is not to be taken literally as if it meant, "the prayer of God" (subjective genitive), but objectively, "prayer to God." **(1b)** In Jas 5:17, "He prayed with prayer [fervently]," (a Hebraistic form); Eph 6:18; Phil 4:6; 1 Ti 2:1; 5:5; **(2)** "a place of prayer," Acts 16:13, 16, a place outside the city wall. Syn.: *Deesis* (*1162*) is petitionary, *proseuche* (*4335*) is a word of sacred character, being limited to prayer to God, whereas *deesis* (*1162*) may also be used of a request addressed to man. *Enteuxis* (*1783*) expresses confiding access to God, *deesis* (*1162*) gives prominence to the expression of personal need. *Proseuche* (*4335*) refers to the element of devotion, *enteuxis* (*1783*) to that of childlike confidence, by representing prayer as the heart's conversation with God. Several *aitemata* (*155*) make up one *proseuche* (*4335*). See: TDNT—2:807, 279; BAGD—713b; THAYER—545b.

4336. **προσεύχομαι** {87x} **prŏsĕuchŏmai**, *pros-yoo'-khom-ahee;* from *4314* and *2172;* to *pray to God,* i.e. *supplicate, worship:*—pray {83x}, make prayer {3x}, pray for {1x}.

Proseuchomai, "to pray," is **(1)** always used of "prayer" to God, and **(2)** is the most frequent word in this respect, **(3)** especially in the Synoptists and Acts, once in **(3a)** Rom 8:26; **(3b)** in Eph 6:18; **(3c)** in Phil 1:9; **(3d)** in 1 Ti 2:8; **(3e)** in Heb 13:18; **(3f)** in Jude 20. See: TDNT—2:807, 279; BAGD—713d; THAYER—545d.

4337. προσέχω {24x} **prŏsĕchō**, *pros-ekh'-o;* from *4314* and *2192;* (fig.) to *hold* the mind (*3563* impl.) *toward*, i.e. *pay attention to, be cautious about, apply oneself* to, *adhere to:*—beware {7x}, give heed to {5x}, take heed to {3x}, give heed unto {1x}, take heed {1x}, take heed unto {1x}, take heed whereunto + 3739 {1x}, misc. {5x} = be given to, have regard. *Prosecho* suggests devotion of thought and effort to a thing. See: BAGD—714b; THAYER—546a.

4338. προσηλόω {1x} **prŏsēlŏō**, *pros-ay-lŏ'-o;* from *4314* and a der. of *2247;* to *peg to*, i.e. *spike* fast:—nail to {1x}.

Proseloo, "to nail to", is used in Col 2:14, in which the figure of a bond (ordinances of the Law) is first described as cancelled, and then removed; the idea in the verb itself is not that of the cancellation, to which the taking out of the way was subsequent, but of nailing up the removed thing in triumph to the cross. The death of Christ not only rendered the Law useless as a means of salvation, but gave public demonstration that it was so. See: BAGD—714d; THAYER—546c.

4339. προσήλυτος {4x} **prŏsēlutŏs**, *pros-ay'-loo-tos;* from the alt. of *4334;* an *arriver* from a for. region, i.e. (spec.) an *acceder* (*convert*) to Judaism ("*proselyte*"):—proselyte {4x}.

Proselutos, akin to *proserchomai*, "to come to," primarily signifies "one who has arrived, a stranger"; in the NT it is used **(1)** of converts to Judaism, or foreign converts to the Jewish religion, Mt 23:15; Acts 2:10; 6:5; 13:43. **(2)** There seems to be no connection necessarily with Palestine, for in Acts 2:10 and 13:43 it is used of those who lived abroad. See: TDNT—6:727, 943; BAGD—715a; THAYER—546c.

4340. πρόσκαιρος {4x} **prŏskairŏs**, *pros'-kahee-ros;* from *4314* and *2540;* for the *occasion* only, i.e. *temporary:*—dureth for awhile {1x}, endure for a time {1x}, for a season {1x}, temporal {1x}.

Proskairos, as an adjective, means "temporary, transient" and is rendered "for a season": "Choosing rather to suffer affliction with the people of God, than to enjoy the pleasures of sin for a season" (Heb 11:25; cf. Mt 13:21; Mk 4:17; 2 Cor 4:18). Syn.: 171, 2122, 2540, 3641, 5550, 5610. See: TDNT—3:463, 389; BAGD—715b; THAYER—546d.

4341. προσκαλέομαι {30x} **prŏskalĕŏmai**, *pros-kal-eh'-om-ahee;* mid. voice from *4314* and *2564;* to *call toward oneself*, i.e. *summon, invite:*—call {7x}, call for {2x}, call to {1x}, call unto {20x}.

This word signifies **(1)** "to call to oneself, to

bid to come"; it is used only in the middle voice, e.g., Mt 10:1; Acts 5:40; Jas 5:14; **(2)** "God's call to Gentiles through the gospel," Acts 2:39; **(3)** the divine call in entrusting men with the preaching of the gospel," Acts 13:2; 16:10. See: TDNT—3:500,*; BAGD—715c; THAYER—546d.

4342. προσκαρτερέω {10x} **prŏskartĕrĕō**, *pros-kar-ter-eh'-o;* from *4314* and *2594;* to *be earnest toward*, i.e. (to a thing) to *persevere, be constantly* diligent, or (in a place) to *attend* assiduously all the exercises, or (to a person) to *adhere* closely to (as a servitor):—continue {4x}, continue instant {1x}, continue steadfastly {1x}, attend continually {1x}, give (one's) self continually {1x}, wait on {1x}, wait on continually {1x}.

This word means lit., "to be strong toward" (*pros*, "toward," used intensively, and *kartereo*, "to be strong"), "to endure in, or persevere in, to be continually steadfast with a person or thing," is used of "continuing" **(1)** in prayer with others, Acts 1:14; Rom 12:12; Col 4:2; **(2)** in the apostles' teaching, Acts 2:42; **(3)** in the Temple, Acts 2:46, the adverb representing the intensive preposition; **(4)** in prayer and the ministry, Acts 6:4; **(5)** of Simon Magus with Philip, Acts 8:13. **(6)** In Mk 3:9 and Acts 10:7, it signifies "to wait on"; **(7)** in Rom 13:6, to attend "continually" upon. See: TDNT—3:618, 417; BAGD—715c; THAYER—547a.

4343. προσκαρτέρησις {1x} **prŏskartĕrēsis**, *pros-kar-ter'-ay-sis;* from *4342;* persistency:—perseverance {1x}. See: TDNT—3:619, 417; BAGD—715d; THAYER—547b.

4344. προσκεφάλαιον {1x} **prŏskĕphalaiŏn**, *pros-kef-al'-ahee-on;* neut. of a presumed compound of *4314* and *2776;* something *for the head*, i.e. a *cushion:*—pillow {1x}. See: BAGD—715d; THAYER—547b.

4345. προσκληρόω {1x} **prŏsklērŏō**, *pros-klay-rŏ'-o;* from *4314* and *2820;* to *give* a common *lot to*, i.e. (fig.) to *associate with:*—consort with {1x}.

Literally, *proskleroo* means to assign by lot, to allot (Acts 17:4), consorted with, imparting to the passive voice (the form of the verb there) a middle voice significance, i.e., "they joined themselves to," or "threw in their lot with." The passive voice significance can be retained by translating (in the stricter sense of the word), "they were allotted" (i.e., by God) to Paul and Silas, as followers or disciples. See: TDNT—3:765, 442; BAGD—716a; THAYER—547b.

4346. **πρόσκλισις** {1x} **prŏsklisis**, *pros'-klis-is;* from a compound of *4314* and *2827;* a *leaning toward,* i.e. (fig.) *proclivity (favoritism):*—partiality {1x}. See: BAGD—716a; THAYER—547c.

4347. **προσκολλάω** {4x} **prŏskŏllaō**, *pros-kol-lah'-o;* from *4314* and *2853;* to *glue to,* i.e. (fig.) to *adhere:*—cleave {2x}, be joined {1x}, join (one's) self {1x}.

Inherent within this word are two aspects with the second aspect being stressed. In order to cleave, one must first make a clean break; hence, cleave as in to cut. Then once cleanly separated a joining is easy, Mt 19:5; Mk 10:7; Acts 5:36; Eph 5:31. See: TDNT—3:823, 452; BAGD—716a; THAYER—547c.

4348. **πρόσκομμα** {6x} **prŏskŏmma**, *pros'-kom-mah;* from *4350;* a *stub,* i.e. (fig.) *occasion of apostasy:*—stumbling stone + 3037 {2x}, stumbling block {2x}, stumbling {1x}, offence {1x}.

Proskomma, "an obstacle against which one may dash his foot" (akin to *proskopto,* "to stumble" or "cause to stumble"; *pros,* "to or against," *kopto,* "to strike"), is translated **(1)** "offence" in Rom 14:20, **(2)** in Rom 14:13, "a stumblingblock," of the spiritual hindrance to another by a selfish use of liberty; so in 1 Cor 8:9. **(3)** It is used of Christ, in Rom 9:32, 33, "a stumblingstone," and **(4)** 1 Pet 2:8, "a stone of stumbling." See: TDNT—6:745, 946; BAGD—716b; THAYER—547c.

4349. **προσκοπή** {1x} **prŏskŏpē**, *pros-kop-ay';* from *4350;* a *stumbling,* i.e. (fig. and concr.) *occasion of sin:*—offence {1x}.

Proskope occurs in 2 Cor 6:3, "offence", and means something which leads others into error or sin. See: TDNT—6:745, 946; BAGD—716b; THAYER—547d.

4350. **προσκόπτω** {8x} **prŏskŏptō**, *pros-kop'-to;* from *4314* and *2875;* to *strike at,* i.e. *surge against* (as water); spec. to *stub on,* i.e. *trip up* (lit. or fig.):—beat upon {1x}, dash {2x}, stumble {3x}, stumble at {2x}.

Proskopto, "to strike against," is used of "stumbling," **(1)** physically, Jn 11:9, 10; **(2)** metaphorically, **(2a)** of Israel in regard to Christ, whose Person, teaching, and atoning death, and the gospel relating thereto, were contrary to all their ideas as to the means of righteousness before God, Rom 9:32; 1 Pet 2:8; **(2b)** of a brother in the Lord in acting against the dictates of his conscience, Rom 14:21; **(3)** is once used of a storm "beating" upon a house, Mt 7:27; and **(4)** used once of "dash", Mt 4:6, of

Christ's foot against a stone. See: TDNT—6:745, 946; BAGD—716b; THAYER—547d.

4351. **προσκυλίω** {2x} **prŏskuliō**, *pros-koo-lee'-o;* from *4314* and *2947;* to *roll toward,* i.e. *block against:*—roll (to) {2x}.

This word means "to roll up or to" and is used in Mt 27:60 and Mk 15:46 of the sepulchre stone. See: BAGD—716c; THAYER—548a.

4352. **προσκυνέω** {60x} **prŏskunĕō**, *pros-koo-neh'-o;* from *4314* and a probable der. of *2965* (mean. to *kiss,* like a dog *licking* his master's hand); to *fawn* or *crouch to,* i.e. (lit. or fig.) *prostrate* oneself in homage (do *reverence* to, *adore*):—worship {60x}.

This word means "to make obeisance, do reverence to" (from *pros,* "towards," and *kuneo,* "to kiss"), is the most frequent word rendered "to worship." It is used of an act of homage or reverence **(1)** to God, e.g., Mt 4:10; Jn 4:21–24; 1 Cor 14:25; Rev 4:10; 5:14; 7:11; 11:16; 19:10 (2nd part) and 22:9; **(2)** to Christ, e.g., Mt 2:2, 8, 11; 8:2; 9:18; 14:33; 15:25; 20:20; 28:9, 17; Jn 9:38; Heb 1:6, in a quotation from the Sept. of Deut 32:43, referring to Christ's second advent; **(3)** to a man, Mt 18:26; **(4)** to the Dragon, by men, Rev 13:4; **(5)** to the Beast, his human instrument, Rev 13:4, 8, 12; 14:9, 11; **(6)** the image of the Beast, Rev 13:15; 14:11; 16:2; **(7)** to demons, Rev 9:20; **(8)** to idols, Acts 7:43. See: TDNT—6:758, 948; BAGD—716c; THAYER—548a.

4353. **προσκυνητής** {1x} **prŏskunētēs**, *pros-koo-nay-tace';* from *4352;* an *adorer:*—worshipper {1x}. See: TDNT—6:766, 948; BAGD—717b; THAYER—548c.

4354. **προσλαλέω** {2x} **prŏslalĕō**, *pros-lal-eh'-o;* from *4314* and *2980;* to *talk to,* i.e. *converse with:*—speak to {1x}, speak with {1x}. Cf. Acts 13:43 and 28:20. See: BAGD—717b; THAYER—548c.

4355. **προσλαμβάνω** {14x} **prŏslambanō**, *pros-lam-ban'-o;* from *4314* and *2983;* to *take to* oneself, i.e. *use* (food), *lead* (aside), *admit* (to friendship or hospitality):—receive {7x}, take {5x}, take unto {2x}.

Proslambano, as a verb, denotes "to take to oneself" or **(1)** "to receive," always in the middle voice, signifying a special interest on the part of the receiver, suggesting a welcome: "And the barbarous people shewed us no little kindness: for they kindled a fire, and received (*proslambano*) us every one, because of the present rain, and because of the cold" (Acts 28:2; cf. Rom 14:1, 3; 15:7; Philem 12, 17). It

also means **(2)** "to take to oneself" and is used **(2a)** of food, Acts 27:33–36; **(2b)** of persons, **(2b1)** of Peter's act toward Christ, Mt 16:22; Mk 8:32; **(2b2)** for evil purposes, Acts 17:5; **(2b3)** for good purposes, Acts 18:26. Syn.: 324, 353, 354, 568, 588, 618, 1209, 1523, 1926, 2210, 2865, 2975, 2983, 3028, 3335, 3336, 3858, 3880, 3970, 4327, 4356, 4380, 4381, 4382, 5562, 5264, 5274. See: TDNT—4:15, 495; BAGD—717b; THAYER—548c.

4356. πρόσληψις {1x} **prŏslēpsis**, *pros'-lape-sis;* from *4355;* ad-mission:—receiving {1x}.

Proslepsis, as a noun, is used in Rom 11:15 of the restoration of Israel: "For if the casting away of them be the reconciling of the world, what shall the receiving (*4356*) of them be, but life from the dead?" Syn.: 324, 353, 354, 568, 588, 618, 1209, 1523, 1926, 2210, 2865, 2975, 2983, 3028, 3335, 3336, 3858, 3880, 3970, 4327, 4355, 4380, 4381, 4382, 5562, 5264, 5274. See: TDNT—4:15, 495; BAGD—717c; THAYER—548d.

4357. προσμένω {6x} **prŏsmĕnō**, *pros-men'-o;* from *4314* and *3306;* to *stay further,* i.e. *remain* in a place, with a person; fig. to *adhere* to, *persevere* in:—abide still {1x}, be with {1x}, cleave unto {1x}, con-tinue in {1x}, tarry {1x}, continue with {1x}.

Prosmeno, "to abide still longer, continue with" is used **(1)** of place, Mt 15:32; Mk 8:2, "been with"; Acts 18:18, "tarried"; 1 Ti 1:3, "abide still"; **(2)** metaphorically, "of cleaving unto a person," Acts 11:23, indicating persis-tent loyalty; **(3)** of continuing in a thing, 1 Ti 5:5. See: TDNT—4:579, 581; BAGD—717c; THAYER—548d.

4358. προσορμίζω {1x} **prŏsŏrmizō**, *pros-or-mid'-zo;* from *4314* and a der. of the same as *3730* (mean. to *tie* [*anchor*] or *lull*); to *moor to,* i.e. (by impl.) *land at:*—draw to the shore {1x}.

Prosormizo, as a verb, means "to bring a ship (or boat) to anchor, cast anchor, land at a place" is translated "drew to the shore": "And when they had passed over, they came into the land of Gennesaret, and drew to the shore" (Mk 6:53). Syn.: 307, 385, 392, 501, 502, 645, 868, 1448, 1670, 1828, 2020, 4264, 4317, 4334, 4685, 4951, 5288, 5289. See: BAGD—717d; THAYER—548d.

4359. προσοφείλω {1x} **prŏsŏphĕilō**, *pros-of-i'-lo;* from *4314* and *3784;* to *be indebted additionally:*—to owe be-sides {1x}.

This word is used in Philem 19, "thou owest (to me even thine own self) besides," i.e., "thou owest me already as much as Onesimus" debt, and in addition even thyself" (not "thou owest me much more"). See: BAGD—717d; THAYER—549a.

4360. προσοχθίζω {2x} **prŏsŏchthizō**, *pros-okh-thid'-zo;* from *4314* and a form of ὀχθέω **ŏchthĕō** (to *be vexed* with something irksome); to *feel indignant at:*—be grieved with {2x}.

Prosochthizo means "to be wroth or dis-pleased with" and is used in Heb 3:10, 17. Grieved means to become inactive. God with-drew His active hand from them; yet always maintained sovereignty and providence. See: BAGD—717d; THAYER—549a.

4361. πρόσπεινος {1x} **prŏspĕinŏs**, *pros'-pi-nos;* from *4314* and the same as *3983; hungering further,* i.e. *intensely hungry:*—very hungry {1x}. See: BAGD—718a; THAYER—549a.

4362. προσπήγνυμι {1x} **prŏspēgnumi**, *pros-payg'-noo-mee;* from *4314* and *4078;* to *fasten to,* i.e. (spec. on a cross):—crucify {1x}.

Prospegnumi, "to fix or fasten to anything" (*pros,* "to," *pegnumi,* "to fix"), is used of the "crucifixion" of Christ, Acts 2:23. See: BAGD—718a; THAYER—549b.

4363. προσπίπτω {8x} **prŏspiptō**, *pros-pip'-to;* from *4314* and *4098;* to *fall toward,* i.e. (gently) *prostrate* oneself (in supplication or homage), or (violently) to *rush* upon (in storm):—fall down before {5x}, beat upon {1x}, fall down at {1x}, fall {1x}.

Prospipto "to fall toward anything" (*pros,* "toward"), "to strike against," is said **(1)** of "wind," Mt 7:25; **(2)** it also signifies to "fall" down at one's feet, "fall" prostrate before, Mk 3:11; 5:33; 7:25; Lk 5:8; 8:28, 47; Acts 16:29. See: BAGD—718a; THAYER—549b.

4364. προσποιέομαι {2x} **prŏspŏiĕŏmai**, *pros-poy-eh'-om-ahee;* mid. voice from *4314* and *4160;* to *do forward for oneself,* i.e. *pretend* (as if about to do a thing):—make as though {2x}. See: BAGD—718b; THAYER—549b.

4365. προσπορεύομαι {1x} **prŏspŏrĕuŏmai**, *pros-por-yoo'-om-ahee;* from *4314* and *4198;* to *journey toward,* i.e. *approach* [not the same as *4313*]:—come unto {1x}. See: BAGD—718b; THAYER—549c.

4366. προσρήγνυμι {2x} **prŏsrēgnumi**, *pros-rayg'-noo-mee;* from *4314* and *4486;* to *tear toward,* i.e. *burst upon* (as a tempest or flood):—beat vehemently against {1x}, beat vehemently upon {1x}. See: BAGD—not listed; THAYER—549c.

4367. προστάσσω {7x} **prŏstassō**, *pros-tas'-so;* from *4314* and *5021;* to *arrange toward,* i.e. (fig.) *enjoin:*—bid {1x}, command {6x}.

(1) This word is a mild command stressing that the one giving the command arranges the life of the receiver for the near future. (2) It denotes "to arrange or set in order toward" (*pros,* "toward," *tasso,* "to arrange"); hence "to prescribe, give command," Mt 1:24, "bidden"; 8:4; 21:6; Mk 1:44; Lk 5:14; Acts 10:33, 48. TDNT—8:37, 1156; BAGD—718c; THAYER—549c.

4368. προστάτις {1x} **prŏstatis**, *pros-tat'-is;* fem. of a der. of *4291;* a *patroness,* i.e. *assistant:*—succourer {1x}.

Prostatis is the feminine form of *prostates* and denotes a protectress, a patroness. It is used metaphorically of Phoebe (Rom 16:2) and is a word of dignity. It indicates the high esteem with which she was regarded, as one who had been a protectress of many. *Prostates* was the title of a citizen in Athens, who had the responsibility of seeing to the welfare of resident aliens who were without civic rights. Among the Jews it signified a wealthy patron of the community. See: BAGD—718d; THAYER—549c.

4369. προστίθημι {18x} **prŏstithēmi**, *pros-tith'-ay-mee;* from *4314* and *5087;* to *place additionally,* i.e. *lay beside, annex, repeat:*—add {11x}, again send + 3892 {2x}, give more {1x}, increase {1x}, proceed further {1x}, lay unto {1x}, speak to any more {1x}. See: TDNT—8:167, 1176; BAGD—718d; THAYER—549d.

4370. προστρέχω {3x} **prŏstrĕchō**, *pros-trekh'-o;* from *4314* and *5143* (incl. its alt.); to *run toward,* i.e. *hasten* to meet or join:—run {1x}, run thither to {1x}, run to {1x}. Cf. Mk 9:15; 10:17; Acts 8:30. See: BAGD—719b; THAYER—550a.

4371. προσφάγιον {1x} **prŏsphagiŏn**, *pros-fag'-ee-on;* neut. of a presumed der. of a compound of *4314* and *5315;* something *eaten in addition* to bread, i.e. a *relish* (spec. *fish;* comp. *3795):*—meat {1x}.

This word is not so broad a word as "something to eat" but stresses something small in addition to bread; hence, relish, usually small fish, Mk 8:14. See: BAGD—719c; THAYER—550a.

4372. πρόσφατος {1x} **prŏsphatŏs**, *pros'-fat-os;* from *4253* and a der. of *4969; previously (recently) slain (fresh),* i.e. (fig.) *lately made:*—new {1x}. See: TDNT—6:766, 950; BAGD—719c; THAYER—550a.

4373. προσφάτως {1x} **prŏsphatōs**, *pros-fat'-oce;* adv. from *4372; recently:*—lately {1x}. See: TDNT—6:766, 950; BAGD—719c; THAYER—550a.

4374. προσφέρω {48x} **prŏsphĕrō**, *pros-fer'-o;* from *4314* and *5342* (incl. its alt.); to *bear toward,* i.e. *lead to, tender* (espec. to God), *treat:*—offer {22x}, bring unto {10x}, bring to {4x}, bring {3x}, offer up {3x}, offer unto {1x}, offer to {1x}, deal with {1x}, do {1x}, present unto {1x}, put to {1x}.

Prosphero, as a verb, means (1) "to bring (in addition)": "And so he that had received five talents came and brought (*prosphero*) other five talents, saying, Lord, thou deliveredst unto me five talents: behold, I have gained beside them five talents more" (Mt 25:20); (2) "to bring unto": "Therefore if thou bring (*prosphero*) thy gift to the altar, and there rememberest that thy brother hath ought against thee" (Mt 5:23; Mk 10:13); (3) "to offer": "Leave there thy gift before the altar, and go thy way; first be reconciled to thy brother, and then come and offer (*prosphero*) thy gift" (Mt 5:24). See: TDNT—9:65, 1252; BAGD—719c; THAYER—550a.

4375. προσφιλής {1x} **prŏsphilēs**, *pros-fee-lace';* from a presumed compound of *4314* and *5368; friendly toward,* i.e. *acceptable:*—lovely {1x}. See: BAGD—720b; THAYER—550c.

4376. προσφορά {9x} **prŏsphŏra**, *pros-for-ah';* from *4374; presentation;* concr. an *oblation* (bloodless) or *sacrifice:*—offering {8x}, offering up {1x}.

Prosphora, lit., "a bringing to", hence an "offering," in the NT a sacrificial "offering," (1) of Christ's sacrifice, Eph 5:2; Heb 10:10 (of His body); 10:14; negatively, of there being no repetition, 10:18; (2) of "offerings" under, or according to, the Law, Acts 21:26; Heb 10:5, 8; (3) of gifts in kind conveyed to needy Jews, Acts 24:17; (4) of the presentation of believers themselves (saved from among the Gentiles) to God, Rom 15:16, "offering up." See: TDNT—9:68, 1252; BAGD—720b; THAYER—550c.

4377. προσφωνέω {7x} **prŏsphōnĕō**, *pros-fo-neh'-o;* from *4314* and *5455;* to *sound toward,* i.e. *address, exclaim, summon:*—call {2x}, call unto {1x}, call to {1x}, speak {1x}, speak to {1x}, speak unto {1x}.

Prosphoneo, "to address, call to," is rendered (1) "spake to" (or "to") in Lk 23:20; Acts 21:40; 22:2; (2) "to call unto" (or "to") in Mt 11:16; Lk 6:13; 7:32; 13:12. See: BAGD—720c; THAYER—550d.

4378. πρόσχυσις {1x} **prŏschusis**, *pros'-khoo-sis;* from a comp. of *4314*

and χέω **chĕō** (to *pour*); a *shedding forth,* i.e. *affusion:*—sprinkling {1x}. See: BAGD—720c; THAYER—550d.

4379. προσψαύω {1x} **prŏspsauō**, *prospsŏw'-o;* from *4314* and ψαύω **psauō** (to *touch slightly*); to *impinge,* i.e. *lay a finger on and touch slightly* (in order to relieve):—touch {1x}. See: BAGD—720c; THAYER—550d.

4380. προσωποληπτέω {1x} **prŏsōpŏlēptĕō**, *pros-o-pol-ape-teh'-o;* from *4381;* to *favor an individual,* i.e. *show partiality:*—have respect to persons {1x}.

(1) This word means to respect the person based on the external conditions of the man, i.e. his wealth, fame, looks, etc. in contrast to his inward character. **(2)** *Prosopolepteo,* as a verb, means "to have respect of persons" and is found in Jas 2:9: "But if ye have respect to persons, ye commit sin, and are convinced of the law as transgressors." Syn.: 324, 353, 354, 568, 588, 618, 1209, 1523, 1926, 2210, 2865, 2975, 2983, 3028, 3335, 3336, 3858, 3880, 3970, 4327, 4355, 4356, 4381, 4382, 5562, 5264, 5274. See: TDNT—6:779, 950; BAGD—720c; THAYER—550d.

4381. προσωπολήπτης {1x} **prŏsōpŏlēptēs**, *pros-o-pol-ape'-tace;* from *4383* and *2983;* an *accepter* of *a face* (*individual*), i.e. (spec.) one *exhibiting partiality:*—respecter of persons {1x}.

Prosopoleptes, as a noun, means "respecter of persons" and is found in Acts 10:34: "Then Peter opened *his* mouth, and said, Of a truth I perceive that God is no respecter of persons." Syn.: 324, 353, 354, 568, 588, 618, 1209, 1523, 1926, 2210, 2865, 2975, 2983, 3028, 3335, 3336, 3858, 3880, 3970, 4327, 4355, 4356, 4380, 4382, 5562, 5264, 5274. See: TDNT—6:779, 950; BAGD—720d; THAYER—550d.

4382. προσωποληψία {4x} **prŏsōpŏlēpsia**, *pros-o-pol-ape-see'-ah;* from *4381; partiality,* i.e. *favoritism:*—respect of persons {4x}.

(1) *Prosopolepsia,* as a noun, means "respect of persons" and is found in Rom 2:11: "For there is no respect of persons with God" (cf. Eph 6:9; Col 3:25; Jas 2:1). **(2)** It denotes "respect of persons, partiality", the fault of one who, when responsible to give judgment, has respect to the position, rank, popularity, or circumstances of men, instead of their intrinsic conditions, preferring the rich and powerful to those who are not so. Syn.: 324, 353, 354, 568, 588, 618, 1209, 1523, 1926, 2210, 2865, 2975, 2983, 3028, 3335, 3336, 3858, 3880, 3970, 4327, 4355, 4356, 4380, 4381, 5562, 5264, 5274. See:

TDNT—6:779, 950; BAGD—720d; THAYER—551a.

4383. πρόσωπον {78x} **prŏsōpŏn**, *pros'-o-pon;* from *4314* and ὤψ **ōps** (the *visage,* from *3700*); the *front,* (as being *toward view*), i.e. the *countenance, aspect, appearance, surface;* by impl. *presence, person:*—face {55x}, person {7x}, presence {7x}, countenance {3x}, not tr {1x}, misc. {5x} = (outward) appearance, × before, fashion.

Prosopon, (pros, "toward," *ops,* "an eye"), lit., "the part round the eye, the face," denotes "the countenance," lit., "the part toward the eyes" (from *pros,* "toward," *ops,* "the eye"), and is used **(1)** of the "face," Mt 6:16–17; Rev 12:14; **(1a)** 2 Cor 3:7, 2nd part, "countenance"; **(1b)** in 2 Cor 5:12; 10:7, "outward appearance", the phrase is figurative of superficial judgment; **(2)** of the look i.e., the "face," which by its various movements affords an index of inward thoughts and feelings. e g., Lk 9:51, 53; 1 Pet 3:12, used of the face of the Lord; **(3)** the presence of a person, the "face" being the noblest part, e.g., **(3a)** Acts 3:13, "in the presence of"; **(3b)** Acts 5:41; 2 Th 1:9, "presence"; **(3c)** came to signify the presentation of the whole person (translated "person," of "persons", e.g., in Mt 22:16; Mk 12:14; Lk 20:21; 2 Cor 1:11; 2 Cor 2:10; Gal 2:6; Jude 16. **(3d)** Acts 3:13; 1 Th 2:17 (first part), "presence";

(4) the person himself, e.g., Gal 1:22; 1 Th 2:17 (second part); **(5)** the appearance one presents by his wealth or poverty, his position or state, Mt 22:16; Mk 12:14; Gal 2:6; Jude 16; **(6)** the outward appearance of inanimate things, Mt 16:3; Lk 12:56; 21:35; Acts 17:26. **(7)** "To spit in a person's face" was an expression of the utmost scorn and aversion, e.g., Mt 26:67 (cf. 27:30; Mk 10:34; Luke 18:32). **(8)** Cf. the expression in OT passages, as **(8a)** Gen 19:21, where it is said by God of Lot, and **(8b)** Gen 33:10, where it is said by Jacob of Esau; **(8c)** see also Deut 10:17 ("persons"), Lev 19:15 ("person"). **(9)** It also signifies the presence of a company, Acts 5:41. See: TDNT—6:768, 950; BAGD—720d; THAYER—551a.

4384. προτάσσω {1x} **prŏtassō**, *prot-as'-so;* from *4253* and *5021;* to *pre-arrange,* i.e. *prescribe:*—before appoint {1x}.

Protasso, as a verb, means "to appoint before" and is used in Acts 17:26 of the seasons arranged by God for nations, and the bounds of their habitation: "And hath made of one blood all nations of men for to dwell on all the face of the earth, and hath determined the times before appointed, and the bounds

of their habitation." See: BAGD—721d; THAYER—552a.

4385. προτείνω {x} **prŏtĕinō**, *prot-i'-no;* from *4253* and τείνω **tĕinō** (to *stretch*); to *protend*, i.e. *tie prostrate* (for scourging):—bind {x}.

Proteino, lit., "to stretch forth" (*pro*, "forth," *teino*, "to stretch"), is used in Acts 22:25, "they bound"; in reference to the preparations made for scourging, probably, to stretch the body forward, to make it tense for severe punishment. See: BAGD—721d; THAYER—721d; THAYER—552a.

4386. πρότερον {10x} **prŏtĕrŏn**, *prot'-er-on;* neut. of *4387* as adv. (with or without the art.); *previously:*—before + 3588 {3x}, first {2x}, former {2x}, before {2x}, at the first + 3588 {1x}.

Proteron, the comparative of *pro*, "before, aforetime," as being definitely antecedent to something else, is more emphatic than *pote* in this respect. See, e.g., Jn 6:62; 7:50; 9:8; 2 Cor 1:13; Gal 4:13; 1 Ti 1:13; Heb 4:6; 7:27; 10:32; 1 Pet 1:14. See: BAGD—721d; THAYER—552a.

4387. πρότερος {1x} **prŏtĕrŏs**, *prot'-er-os;* comp. of *4253; prior* or *previous:*—former {1x}. See: BAGD—721d; THAYER—552a.

4388. προτίθημι {3x} **prŏtithĕmo**, *prot-ith'-em-ahee;* mid. voice from *4253* and *5087;* to *place before*, i.e. (for oneself) to *exhibit;* (to oneself) to *propose* (*determine*):—purpose {2x}, set forth {1x}.

Protithemi, "to set before, set forth", is used **(1)** in Rom 3:25, "set forth," middle voice, which lays stress upon the personal interest which God had in so doing. **(2)** It is also found in Rom 1:13, "I purposed"; and Eph 1:9, "He purposed (in Him)." See: TDNT—8:164, 1176; BAGD—722b; THAYER—552b.

4389. προτρέπομαι {1x} **prŏtrĕpŏmai**, *prot-rep'-om-ahee;* mid. voice from *4253* and the base of *5157;* to *turn forward* for oneself, i.e. *encourage:*—exhort {1x}.

This word means "to urge forward, persuade," and is used in Acts 18:27 in the middle voice, "exhorting" indicating their particular interest in giving Apollos the "encouragement" mentioned. See: BAGD—722b; THAYER—552c.

4390. προτρέχω {2x} **prŏtrĕchō**, *prot-rekh'-o;* from *4253* and *5143* (incl. its alt.); to *run forward*, i.e. *outstrip, precede:*—outrun {1x}, run before {1x}.

Protrecho, primarily, "to run forward" (*pro*, "forward" or "before," *trecho*, "to run"), is

(1) used with *tachion*, "more quickly," in Jn 20:4, "did outrun"), lit., "ran forward more quickly"; **(2)** in Lk 19:4, "he ran before." See: BAGD—722b; THAYER—552c.

4391. προϋπάρχω {2x} **prŏĕparchō**, *prŏ-oop-ar'-kho;* from *4253* and *5225;* to *exist before*, i.e. (adv.) to *be* or *do* something *previously:*—be before {1x}, be be foretime {1x}.

This word means "to exist before, or be beforehand" and is found **(1)** in Lk 23:12, "be before"; and **(2)** Acts 8:9, "be beforetime." See: BAGD—722c; THAYER—552c.

4392. πρόφασις {7x} **prŏphasis**, *prof'-as-is;* from a compound of *4253* and *5316;* an *outward showing*, i.e. *pretext:*—cloke {2x}, colour {1x}, pretence {3x}, shew {1x}.

Prophases, either from *pro*, "before," and *phaino*, "to cause to appear, shine," or, more probably, from *pro*, and *phemi*, "to say," is rendered **(1)** "cloke" (of covetousness) in Jn 15:22; 1 Th 2:5; **(2)** "pretence" in Mt 23:14; Mk 12:40; Phil 1:18; **(3)** "shew" in Lk 20:47; and **(4)** "colour" in Acts 27:30. **(5)** It signifies the assuming of something so as to disguise one's real motives. See: BAGD—722c; THAYER—552c.

4393. προφέρω {2x} **prŏphĕrō**, *prof-er'-o;* from *4253* and *5342;* to *bear forward*, i.e. *produce:*—bring forth {2x}.

Prophero, as a verb, denotes "to bring forth": "A good man out of the good treasure of his heart bringeth forth that which is good; and an evil man out of the evil treasure of his heart bringeth forth that which is evil: for of the abundance of the heart his mouth speaketh" (Lk 6:45, twice). See: BAGD—722d; THAYER—552c.

4394. προφητεία {19x} **prŏphētĕia**, *prof-ay-ti'-ah;* from *4396* ("*prophecy*"); *prediction* (scriptural or other):—prophecy {16x}, prophesying {3x}.

(1) Prophecy is not necessarily, nor even primarily, fore-telling. **(2)** It is the declaration of that which cannot be known by natural means (Mt 26:68), **(3)** it emanates from God and is the forth-telling of the will of God, whether with reference to the past, the present, or the future (Rev 10:11; 11:3). **(4)** It signifies "the speaking forth of the mind and counsel of God" (*pro*, "forth," *phemi*, "to speak"); **(5)** in the NT it is used **(5a)** of the gift, e.g., Rom 12:6; 1 Cor 12:10; 13:2; **(5b)** either of the exercise of the gift or of that which is "prophesied," e.g., Mt 13:14; 1 Cor 13:8; 14:6, 22 and 1 Th 5:20, "prophesying(s)"; 1 Ti 1:18; 4:14; 2 Pet 1:20, 21; Rev 1:3; 11:6; 19:10; 22:7, 10, 18, 19. See: TDNT—6:781, 952; BAGD—722d; THAYER—552d.

4395. προφητεύω {28x} **prŏphēteuō**, *prof-ate-yoo'-o;* from *4396;* to *foretell* events, *divine, speak* under *inspiration, exercise* the prophetic office:—prophesy {28x}. Syn.: see 3132 for discussion.

This word means "to be a prophet, to prophesy," and is used **(1)** with the primary meaning of telling forth the divine counsels, e.g., Mt 7:22; 26:68; 1 Cor 11:4, 5; 13:9; 14:1, 3–5, 24, 31, 39; Rev 11:3; **(2)** of foretelling the future, e.g., Mt 15:7; Jn 11:51; 1 Pet 1:10; Jude 14. See: TDNT—6:781, 952; BAGD—723a; THAYER—552d.

4396. προφήτης {149x} **prŏphētēs**, *prof-ay'-tace;* from a compound of *4253* and *5346;* a *foreteller* ("*prophet*"); by anal. an *inspired speaker;* by extens. a *poet:*—prophet {149x}.

Prophetes, "one who speaks forth or openly", "a proclaimer of a divine message." **I. In the OT,** it is the translation **(1)** of the word *roeh,* "a seer"; 1 Sa 9:9, indicating that the "prophet" was one who had immediate conversation with God. **(2)** It also translates the word *nabhi,* meaning "either one in whom the message from God springs forth" or "one to whom anything is secretly communicated." **(3)** Hence, in general, "the prophet" was one upon whom the Spirit of God rested, Num 11:17–29, one to whom and through whom God speaks, Num 12:2; Amos 3:7, 8. **(4)** In the case of the OT prophets their messages were very largely the proclamation of the divine purposes of salvation and glory to be accomplished in the future; the "prophesying" of the NT "prophets" was both a preaching of the divine counsels of grace already accomplished and the foretelling of the purposes of God in the future.

II. In the NT the word is used **(1)** of "the OT prophets," e.g., Mt 5:12; Mk 6:15; Lk 4:27; Jn 8:52; Rom 11:3; **(2)** of "prophets in general," e.g., Mt 10:41; 21:46; Mk 6:4; **(3)** of "John the Baptist," Mt 21:26; Lk 1:76; **(4)** of "prophets in the churches," e.g., Acts 13:1; 15:32; 21:10; 1 Cor 12:28, 29; 14:29, 32, 37; Eph 2:20; 3:5; 4:11; **(5)** of "Christ, **(5a)** as the afore-promised Prophet," e.g., Jn 1:21; 6:14; 7:40; Acts 3:22; 7:37, or, **(5b)** without the article, and, without reference to the Old Testament, Mk 6:15; Lk 7:16; in Lk 24:19 it is used with *aner,* "a man"; Jn 4:19; 9:17; **(6)** of "two witnesses" yet to be raised up for special purposes, Rev 11:10, 18; **(7)** of "the Cretan poet Epimenides," Titus 1:12; **(8)** by metonymy, of "the writings of prophets," e.g., Lk 24:27; Acts 8:28. Syn.: 4394. See: TDNT—6:781, 952; BAGD—723b; THAYER—553b.

4397. προφητικός {2x} **prŏphētikŏs**, *prof-ay-tik-os';* from *4396;* pertaining to a foreteller ("*prophetic*"):—of prophecy {1x}, of the prophets {1x}

Prophetikos, "of or relating to prophecy," or "proceeding from a prophet, prophetic," is used **(1)** of the OT Scriptures, Rom 16:26, "of the prophets," lit., "(by) prophetic (Scriptures)"; **(2)** 2 Pet 1:19, "the word of prophecy (made more sure)," i.e., confirmed by the person and work of Christ ("a more sure, etc."), lit., "the prophetic word." Syn.: 4394. See: TDNT—6:781, 952; BAGD—724b; THAYER—554a.

4398. προφῆτις {2x} **prŏphētis**, *prof-ay'-tis;* fem. of *4396;* a *female foreteller* or an *inspired woman:*—prophetess {2x}.

Prophetis, the feminine of *prophetes,* is used of Anna, Lk 2:36; of the self-assumed title of "the woman Jezebel" in Rev 2:20. See: TDNT—6:781, 952; BAGD—724b; THAYER—554a.

4399. προφθάνω {1x} **prŏphthanō**, *prof-than'-o;* from *4253* and *5348;* to *get* an *earlier start of,* i.e. *anticipate:*—prevent {1x}.

Prevent is derived from Latin, *pre* – before, and *venir,* to go; hence, to go before, precede in time. See: TDNT—9:88, 1258; BAGD—724b; THAYER—554a.

4400. προχειρίζομαι {2x} **prŏchĕirizŏmai**, *prokh-i-rid'-zom-ahee;* mid. voice from *4253* and a der. of *5495;* to *handle* for oneself *in advance,* i.e. (fig.) to *purpose:*—choose {1x}, make {1x}.

Procheirizo, as a verb, signifies **(1)** in the middle voice, "to take into one's hand, to determine, appoint beforehand," translated "appointed": "And he said, The God of our fathers hath chosen (*procheirizo*) thee, that thou shouldest know his will, and see that Just One, and shouldest hear the voice of his mouth" (Acts 22:14); and **(2)** "to make, to appoint": "But rise, and stand upon thy feet: for I have appeared unto thee for this purpose, to make (*procheirizo*) thee a minister and a witness both of these things which thou hast seen, and of those things in the which I will appear unto thee" (Acts 26:16). See: TDNT—6:862,*; BAGD—724c; THAYER—554b.

4401. προχειροτονέω {1x} **prŏchĕirŏtŏnĕō**, *prokh-i-rot-on-eh'-o;* from *4253* and *5500;* to *elect in advance:*—choose before {1x}.

This word signifies "to choose before," Acts 10:41, where it is used of a choice made before by God. See: BAGD—724c; THAYER—554b.

4402. Πρόχορος {1x} **Prŏchŏrŏs**, *prokh'-or-os;* from *4253* and *5525;* before the *dance; Prochorus*, a Chr.:—*Prochorus* {1x}. See: BAGD—724c; THAYER—554b.

4403. πρύμνα {3x} **prumna**, *proom'-nah;* fem. of πρυμνύς **prumnus** (*hindmost*); the *stern* of a ship:—hinder part {1x}, hinder part of ship {1x}, stern {1x}. Cf. Mk 4:38; Acts 27:29, 41. See: BAGD—724d; THAYER—554b.

4404. πρωΐ { {1x} **prōï**, *pro-ee';* adv. from *4253;* at *dawn;* by impl. the *daybreak* watch:—in the morning {5x}, early in the morning {2x}, early {2x}, morning {1x}.

Proi is the fourth watch of the night, from 3 o'clock in the morning until 6 o'clock approximately. This word means "early in the day, at morn." **(1)** In Mk 16:2, it is translated "early in the morning"; **(2)** in Mk 16:9 and Jn 18:28; 20:1, "early"; **(3)** in Mt 16:3; 20:1; 21:18; Mk 1:35; 11:20; 13:35; 15:1, "in the morning"; **(4)** in Acts 28:23, "(from) morning." See: BAGD—724d; THAYER—554b.

4405. πρωΐα {4x} **prōïa**, *pro-ee'-ah;* fem. of a der. of *4404* as noun; *daydawn:*—early {1x}, morning {3x}.

Proia, "early, at early morn" (from *pro*, "before"), is used **(1)** as a noun in the feminine form *proia*, "morning" in Mt 21:18; 27:1; Jn 18:28; 21:4. Its adjectival force is retained by regarding it as qualifying the noun *hora*, "an hour," i.e., "at an early hour." See: BAGD—724d; THAYER—554c.

4406. πρώϊμος {1x} **prōïmŏs**, *pro'-ee-mos;* from *4404;* dawning, i.e. (by anal.) *autumnal* (showering, the first of the rainy season in October):—early {1x}. See: BAGD—725a; 706d; THAYER—554c.

4407. πρωϊνός {1x} **prōïnŏs**, *pro-ee-nos';* from *4404;* pertaining to the *dawn,* i.e. *matutinal:*—morning {1x}.

This adjective qualifies *aster,* "star," in Rev 2:28. That Christ will give to the overcomer "the morning star" indicates a special interest for such in Himself. For Israel He will appear as "the sun of righteousness"; as the "morning" Star which precedes the dawn, He will appear for the rapture of the church. See: BAGD—725a; THAYER—554c.

4408. πρῶρα {2x} **prōra**, *pro'-ra;* fem. of a presumed der. of *4253* as noun; the *prow,* i.e. forward part of a vessel:—forepart {1x}, foreship {1x}. See: BAGD—725a; THAYER—554c.

4409. πρωτεύω {1x} **prōtĕuō**, *prote-yoo'-o;* from *4413;* to *be first* (in rank or influence):—have the preeminence {1x}. See: TDNT—6:881, 965; BAGD—725a; THAYER—554d.

4410. πρωτοκαθεδρία {4x} **prōtŏkathĕdria**, *pro-tok-ath-ed-ree'-ah;* from *4413* and *2515;* a *sitting first* (in the front row), i.e. *preeminence* in council:—chief seat {2x}, highest seat {1x}, uppermost seat {1x}.

This word means "a sitting in the first or chief seat" (*protos*, "first," *kathedra,* "a seat"), and is found in Mt 23:6; Mk 12:39; Lk 11:43; 20:46. See: TDNT—6:870, 965; BAGD—725b; THAYER—554d.

4411. πρωτοκλισία {5x} **prōtŏklisia**, *pro-tok-lis-ee'-ah;* from *4413* and *2828;* a *reclining first* (in the place of honor) at the dinner-bed, i.e. *preeminence* at meals:—chief room {2x}, highest room {1x}, uppermost room {2x}.

Protoklisia, "the first reclining place, the chief place at table" (from *protos*, and *klisia,* "a company reclining at a meal"; cf. *klino,* "to incline"), is found in Mt 23:6; Mk 12:39; Lk 14:7–8; 20:46. Room signifies a place or position of total and complete authority. To take over another's room is to exercise total control over what the previous one held. To be in one's stead, by comparison, is to replace another, but not with the same extent of authority. See: TDNT—6:870, 965; BAGD—725b; THAYER—554d.

4412. πρῶτον {60x} **prōtŏn**, *pro'-ton;* neut. of *4413* as adv. (with or without *3588*); *firstly* (in time, place, order, or importance):—first {51x}, at the first + 3588 {2x}, first of all {2x}, misc. {5x} = before, at the beginning, chiefly.

Proton, the neuter of the adjective *protos* (the superlative degree of *pro*, "before"), signifies "first, or at the first," **(1)** in order of time, e.g., Lk 10:5; Jn 18:13; 1 Cor 15:46; 1 Th 4:16; 1 Ti 3:10; **(2)** in enumerating various particulars, e.g., Rom 3:2; 1 Cor 11:18; 12:28; Heb 7:2; Jas 3:17. **(3)** It is translated "before" in Jn 15:18. See: TDNT—6:868, 965; BAGD—725b; THAYER—554d.

4413. πρῶτος {105x} **prōtŏs**, *pro'-tos;* contr. superl. of *4253; foremost* (in time, place, order or importance):—first {85x}, chief {9x}, first day {2x}, former {2x}, misc. {7x} = before, beginning, best.

Protos, the superlative degree of *pro,* "before," is used **I.** "of time or place," **(1)** as a noun, e.g., Lk 14:18; Rev 1:17; **(1a)** opposite to "the last," in the neuter plural, Mt 12:45; Lk 11:26; 2 Pet 2:20; **(1b)** in the neuter singular, opposite to "the second," Heb 10:9; **(1c)** in 1 Cor 15:3,

en protois, lit., "in the first (things, or matters)" denotes "first of all"; **(2)** as an adjective, e.g., Mk 16:9, used with "day" understood, lit., "the first (day) of (i.e., after) the Sabbath," in which phrase the "of" is objective, not including the Sabbath, but following it; **(2a)** in Jn 20:4, 8; Rom 10:19, e.g., equivalent to an English adverb; **(2b)** in Jn 1:15, lit., "first of me," i.e., "before me" (of superiority); **II.** "of rank or dignity," denotes "the first," whether in time or place. **(1)** It is translated "chief" in Mk 6:21, **(1a)** of men of Galilee; **(1b)** in Acts 13:50, of men in a city; **(1c)** in Acts 28:7, of the "chief" man in the island of Melita; **(1d)** in Acts 17:4, of "chief" women in a city; **(1e)** in Acts 28:17, of Jews; **(1f)** in 1 Ti 1:15–16, of a sinner. **(1g)** Cf. Mt 20:27; Mk 10:44; Lk 19:47; Acts 16:12; 25:2. See: TDNT—6:865, 965; BAGD—725b; THAYER—554d.

4414. **πρωτοστάτης** {1x} **prōtŏstatēs**, *pro-tos-tat'-ace;* from *4413* and *2476;* one *standing first* in the ranks, i.e. a *captain* (*champion*):—ringleader {1x}.

Protostates, "one who stands first" (*protos*, "first," *histemi*, "to cause to stand"), was used of soldiers, one who stands in the front rank; hence, metaphorically, "a leader," Acts 24:5. See: BAGD—725c; THAYER—555c.

4415. **πρωτοτόκια** {1x} **prōtŏtŏkia**, *pro-tot-ok'-ee-ah;* from *4416;* *primogeniture* (as a privilege):—birthright {1x}.

(1) *Prototokia* is the right or advantages of the firstborn son. **(2)** This word means a birthright" (from *protos*, "first," *tikto*, "to beget"), and is found in Heb 12:16, with reference to Esau (cf. *prototokos*, firstborn). The "birthright" involved preeminence and authority, Gen 27:29; 49:3. Another right was that of the double portion, Deut 21:17; 1 Chr 5:1–2. Connected with the "birthright" was the progenitorship of the Messiah. Esau transferred his "birthright" to Jacob for a paltry mess of pottage, profanely despising this last spiritual privilege, Gen 25 and 27. In the history of the nation God occasionally set aside the "birthright," to show that the objects of His choice depended not on the will of the flesh, but on His own authority. Thus Isaac was preferred to Ishmael, Jacob to Esau, Joseph to Reuben, David to his elder brethren, Solomon to Adonijah. See: TDNT—6:871, 965; BAGD—725c; THAYER—555d.

4416. **πρωτότοκος** {9x} **prōtŏtŏkŏs**, *pro-tot-ok'-os;* from *4413* and the alt. of *5088;* *first-born* (usually as noun, lit. or fig.):—first begotten {2x}, firstborn {7x}.

Firstborn is used **(1)** of Christ as born of the Virgin Mary (Mt 1:25; Lk 2:7); **(2)** of His relationship to the Father, expressing His priority to, and preeminence over, creation, not in the sense of being the first to be born. It is used of superiority of position (cf. Ex 4:22; Deut 21:16, 17). **(3)** Chronologically, the four passages relating to Christ as firstborn, first begotten, may be set forth thusly: **(3a)** Col 1:15, where His eternal relationship with the Father is in view, and the clause means both that He was the firstborn before all creation and that He Himself produced creation (the genitive case being objective, as v. 16 makes clear); **(3b)** Col 1:18 and Rev 1:5, in reference to His resurrection; **(3c)** Rom 8:29, His being firstborn among those living by faith alone in God the Father; **(3d)** Heb 1:6, first begotten, stresses His superior position, His preeminence over all; His second advent in contrast to His first advent, at His birth, being implied. See: TDNT—6:871, 965; BAGD—726c; THAYER—555d.

4417. **πταίω** {5x} **ptaiō**, *ptah'-yo;* a form of *4098;* to *trip,* i.e. (fig.) to *err, sin, fail* (of salvation):—fall {1x}, offend {3x}, stumble {1x}.

Ptaio, "to cause to stumble," signifies, intransitively, "to stumble," used **(1)** metaphorically in Rom 11:11; **(2)** with moral significance in Jas 2:10 and 3:2 (twice), "offend"; **(3)** in 2 Pet 1:10, "fall." See: TDNT—6:883, 968; BAGD—727a; THAYER—556b.

4418. **πτέρνα** {1x} **ptĕrna**, *pter'-nah;* of uncert. der.; the *heel* (fig.):—heel {1x}.

Pterna is found in Jn 13:18, where the Lord quotes from Ps 41:9; the metaphor is that of tripping up an antagonist in wrestling. See: BAGD—727b; THAYER—556b.

4419. **πτερύγιον** {2x} **ptĕrugiŏn**, *pter-oog'-ee-on;* neut. of a presumed der. of *4420;* a *winglet,* i.e. (fig.) *extremity* (top corner):—pinnacle {2x}.

This wing/pinnacle has been regarded **(1)** as the apex of the sanctuary, **(2)** the top of Solomon's porch, or **(3)** the top of the Royal Portico, which Josephus describes as of tremendous height (*Antiq.* xv. 11.5). Cf. Mt 4:5; Lk 49. See: BAGD—727b; THAYER—556b.

4420. **πτέρυξ** {5x} **ptĕrux**, *pter'-oox;* from a der. of *4072* (mean. a *feather*); a *wing as of a bird:*—wing {5x}.

Pterux is used **(1)** of birds, Mt 23:37; Lk 13:34; **(2)** symbolically in Rev 12:14, "two wings of a great eagle", suggesting the definiteness of the action, the "wings" indicating rapidity and protection, an allusion, perhaps, to Ex 19:4 and Deut 32:11, 12; **(3)** of the "living

creatures" in a vision, Rev 4:8; 9:9. See: BAGD−727b; THAYER−556c.

4421. πτηνόν {1x} ptēnŏn, *ptay-non';* contr. for *4071;* a *bird:*−bird {1x}. See: BAGD−727c; THAYER−556c.

4422. πτοέω {2x} ptŏĕō, *ptŏ-eh'-o;* prob. akin to the alt. of *4098* (through the idea of causing to *fall*) or to *4072* (through that of causing to *fly* away); to *scare:*−terrify {2x}.

Ptoeo, "to terrify," is used in the passive voice, Lk 21:9; 24:37. Syn.: **(A)** *Ekplesso* (*1605*) means "to be astonished", prop. to be struck with terror, of a sudden and startling alarm; but like our "astonish" in popular use, often employed on comparatively slight occasions. **(B)** *Ptoeo* (*4422*) signifies "to terrify", to agitate with fear. **(C)** *Tremo* (*5141*) "to tremble", predominately physical; and **(D)** *phobeo* (*5399*) denotes "to fear", the general term; often used of a protracted state. See: BAGD−727c; THAYER−556c.

4423. πτόησις {1x} ptŏēsis, *ptŏ'-ay-sis;* from *4422; alarm:*−amazement {1x}. See: BAGD−727c; THAYER−556c.

4424. Πτολεμαΐς {1x} Ptŏlĕmaïs, *ptol-em-ah-is';* from Πτολεμαῖος Ptŏlĕmaiŏs (*Ptolemy,* after whom it was named); *Ptolemaïs,* a place in Pal.:−*Ptolemais* {1x}. See: BAGD−727c; THAYER−556c.

4425. πτύον {2x} ptuŏn, *ptoo'-on;* from *4429;* a *winnowing-fork* (as *scattering* like spittle):−fan {2x}.

Ptuon denotes a winnowing shovel or fan with which grain is thrown up against the wind, in order to separate the chaff (Mt 3:12; Lk 3:17). See: BAGD−727c; THAYER−556d.

4426. πτύρω {1x} pturō, *ptoo'-ro;* from a presumed der. of *4429* (and thus akin to *4422*); to *frighten:*−terrify {1x}. See: BAGD−727d; THAYER−556d.

4427. πτύσμα {1x} ptusma, *ptoos'-mah;* from *4429; saliva:*−spittle {1x}. See: BAGD−727d; THAYER−556d.

4428. πτύσσω {1x} ptussō, *ptoos'-so;* prob. akin to πετάννυμι pĕtannumi, (to *spread;* and thus appar. allied to *4072* through the idea of *expansion,* and to *4429* through that of *flattening;* comp. *3961*); to *fold,* i.e. *furl, roll up* a scroll:−close {1x}.

This word means "to fold, double up," and is used of a scroll of parchment, Lk 4:20. See: BAGD−727d; THAYER−556d.

4429. πτύω {3x} ptuō, *ptoo'-o;* a primary verb (comp. *4428*); to *spit:*−spit {3x}.

Cf. Mk 7:33; 8:23; Jn 9:6. See: BAGD−727d; THAYER−556d.

4430. πτῶμα {5x} ptōma, *pto'-mah;* from the alt. of *4098;* a *ruin,* i.e. (spec.) lifeless *body* (*corpse, carrion*):−dead body {3x}, carcase {1x}, corpse {1x}.

Ptoma denotes, lit., "a fall" (akin to *pipto,* "to fall"); hence, "that which is fallen, a corpse," Mt 14:12; 24:28, "carcase"; Mk 6:29; 15:45, "corpse"; Rev 11:8−9, "dead bodies." See: TDNT−6:166, 846; BAGD−727d; THAYER−557a.

4431. πτῶσις {2x} ptōsis, *pto'-sis;* from the alt. of *4098;* a *crash,* i.e. *downfall* (lit. or fig.):−fall {2x}.

Ptosos, "a fall", is used **(1)** literally, of the "overthrow of a building," Mt 7:27; **(2)** metaphorically, Lk 2:34, of the spiritual "fall" of those in Israel who would reject Christ. See: TDNT−6:167, 846; BAGD−728a; THAYER−557a.

4432. πτωχεία {3x} ptōchĕia, *pto-khi'-ah;* from *4433; beggary,* i.e. *indigence* (lit. or fig.):−poverty {3x}.

Ptocheia, "destitution" is used **(1)** of the "poverty" which Christ voluntarily experienced on our behalf, 2 Cor 8:9; **(2)** of the destitute condition of saints in Judea, 2 Cor 8:2; **(3)** of the condition of the church in Smyrna, Rev 2:9, where the word is used in a general sense. See: TDNT−6:885, 969; BAGD−728a; THAYER−557a.

4433. πτωχεύω {1x} ptōchĕuō, *pto-khyoo'-o;* from *4434;* to *be a beggar,* i.e. (by impl.) to *become indigent* (fig.):−become poor {1x}. See: TDNT−6:885, 969; BAGD−728a; THAYER−557a.

4434. πτωχός {34x} ptōchŏs, *pto-khos';* from πτώσσω ptōssō, to *crouch;* akin to *4422* and the alt. of *4098*); a *beggar* (as *cringing*), i.e. *pauper* (strictly denoting absolute or public *mendicancy,* although also used in a qualified or relative sense; whereas *3993* prop. means only *straitened* circumstances in private), lit. (often used as a noun) or fig. (*distressed*):−beggar {2x}, beggarly {1x}, poor {30x}, poor man {1x}.

Ptochos, an adjective describing "one who crouches and cowers," is used **(1)** as a noun, "a beggar" (from *ptosso,* "to cower down or hide oneself for fear"), e.g., Lk 14:13, 21 ("poor"); 16:20, 22; **(2)** as an adjective, "beggarly" in Gal 4:9, i.e., poverty-stricken, powerless to enrich, metaphorically descriptive of the religion of the Jews. Syn.: While **(A)** *prosaites* (*4319*) is descriptive of a "beggar," and stresses his "begging," *ptochos* stresses his poverty-stricken

condition. **(B)** *Penes* (*3993*) is one who is so poor he earns his bread by daily labour; whereas, *ptochos* (*4434*) is one who only obtains his living by begging. See: TDNT—6:885, 969; BAGD—728b; THAYER—557b.

4435. **πυγμή** {1x} **pugmē,** *poog-may';* from a primary πύξ **pux** (the *fist,* as a weapon); the clenched *hand,* i.e. (only in dat. as adverb) *with* the *fist* (hard *scrubbing*):—oft {1x}.

The dative case of *pugme* is a fist, and literally, means "with the fist" (one hand being rubbed with the clenched fist of the other, a metaphorical expression for thoroughly, diligently, oft, in contrast to what is superficial (Mk 7:3). See: TDNT—6:915, 973; BAGD—728c; THAYER—557c.

4436. **Πύθων** {1x} **Puthōn,** *poo'-thone;* from Πυθώ **Puthō** (the name of the region where Delphi, the seat of the famous *oracle,* was located); a *Python,* i.e. (by anal. with the supposed *diviner* there) *inspiration* (*soothsaying*):—divination {1x}.

Puthon, (Eng., "python"), in Greek mythology was the name of the Pythian serpent or dragon, dwelling in Pytho, at the foot of mount Parnassus, guarding the oracle of Delphi, and slain by Apollo. Thence the name was transferred to Apollo himself. Later the word was applied to diviners or soothsayers, regarded as inspired by Apollo. Since devils are the agents inspiring idolatry, 1 Cor 10:20, the young woman in Acts 16:16 was possessed by a devil instigating the cult of Apollo, and thus had "a spirit of divination." See: TDNT—6:917,*; BAGD—728d; THAYER—557c.

4437. **πυκνός** {3x} **puknŏs,** *pook-nos';* from the same as *4635; clasped* (*thick*), i.e. (fig.) *frequent;* neut. plur. (as adv.) *frequently:*—often {2x}, oftener {1x}. Cf. Lk 5:3; Acts 24:26; 1 Ti 5:23. See: BAGD—729a; THAYER—557d.

4438. **πυκτεύω** {1x} **puktĕō,** *pook-teh'-o;* from a der. of the same as *4435;* to *box* (with the fist), i.e. *contend* (as a boxer) at the games (fig.):—fight {1x}. See: BAGD—729c; THAYER—557d.

4439. **πύλη** {10x} **pulē,** *poo'-lay;* appar. a primary word; a *gate,* i.e. the leaf or wing of a folding *entrance* (lit. or fig.):—gate {10x}.

Pule is used **(1)** literally, for a larger sort of gate in the wall either of a city or palace or temple (Lk 7:12; Acts 3:10; 9:24; 12:10; Heb 13:12); and **(2)** metaphorically, of the gates at the entrances of the ways leading to life and to destruction (Mt 7:13 twice, 14; Lk 13:24).

(3) The importance and strength of gates made them viewed as synonymous with power; figuratively of hell's power, Mt 16:18. **(4)** By metonymy, the gates stood for those who held government and administered justice there. See: TDNT—6:921, 974; BAGD—729b; THAYER—557d.

4440. **πυλών** {18x} **pulōn,** *poo-lone';* from *4439;* a *gate-way, door-way* of a building or city; by impl. a *portal* or *vestibule:*—gate {17x}, porch {1x}.

(1) *Pulon* is a large gate of a palace or the front part of a house, into which one enters through the gate, porch. **(2)** It primarily signifies **(2a)** "a porch or vestibule," e.g., Mt 26:71; Lk 16:20; Acts 10:17; 12:13, 14; **(2b)** then, the "gateway" or "gate tower" of a walled town, Acts 14:13; Rev 21:12, 13, 15, 21, 25; 22:14. See: TDNT—6:921, 974; BAGD—729c; THAYER—558a.

4441. **πυνθάνομαι** {12x} **punthanŏmai,** *poon-than'-om-ahee;* mid. voice prol. from a primary πύθω **puthō** (which occurs only as an alt. in certain tenses); to *question,* i.e. *ascertain* by inquiry (as a matter of *information* merely; and thus differing from *2065,* which prop. means a *request* as a favor; and from *154,* which is strictly a *demand* for something due; as well as from *2212,* which implies a *search* for something hidden; and from *1189,* which involves the idea of urgent *need*); by impl. to *learn* (by casual intelligence):—ask {7x}, demand {2x}, enquire {2x}, understand {1x}.

Punthanomai, as a verb, means **(1)** to ask by way of inquiry, not by way of making a request for something, **(2)** is found in the Gospels and the Acts, five times in the former, seven in the latter. **(3)** In Mt 2:4 it is translated "demanded": "And when he had gathered all the chief priests and scribes of the people together, he demanded of them where Christ should be born" (cf. Acts 21:33). **(4)** It is translated "enquired" in Mt 2:4; Jn 4:52; Acts 23:20; **(5)** in Acts 21:33, "demanded"; **(6)** in Lk 15:26; 18:36; Jn 13:24; Acts 4:7; 10:18, 29; 23:19, "asked"; and **(7)** in Acts 23:34 it denotes "when (he) understood." Syn.: 154, 155, 350, 1833, 1905, 2065, 3004. See: BAGD—729c; THAYER—558a.

4442. **πῦρ** {74x} **pur,** *poor;* a primary word; "*fire*" (lit. or fig., spec. *lightning*):—fiery {1x}, fire {73x}.

Pur is used (besides its ordinary natural significance): **(1)** of the holiness of God, which consumes all that is inconsistent therewith, Heb 10:27; 12:29; cf. Rev 1:14; 2:18; 10:1; 15:2; 19:12; **(1a)** similarly of the holy angels as His

ministers, Heb 1:7; **(1b)** in Rev 3:18 it is symbolic of that which tries the faith of saints, producing what will glorify the Lord; **(2)** of the divine judgment, testing the deeds of believers, at the judgment seat of Christ 1 Cor 3:13 and 15; **(3)** of the fire of divine judgment upon the rejectors of Christ, Mt 3:11 (where a distinction is to be made between the baptism of the Holy Spirit at Pentecost and the "fire" of divine retribution; Acts 2:3 could not refer to baptism); Lk 3:16;

(4) of the judgments of God at the close of the present age previous to the establishment of the kingdom of Christ in the world, 2 Th 1:8; Rev 18:8; **(5)** of the "fire" of hell, to be endured by the ungodly hereafter, Mt 5:22; 13:42, 50; 18:8, 9; 25:41; Mk 9:43, 48; Lk 3:17; **(6)** of human hostility both to the Jews and to Christ's followers, Lk 12:49; **(7)** as illustrative of retributive judgment upon the luxurious and tyrannical rich, Jas 5:3; **(8)** of the future overthrow of the Babylonish religious system at the hands of the Beast and the nations under him, Rev 17:16; **(9)** of turning the heart of an enemy to repentance by repaying his unkindness by kindness, Rom 12:20; **(10)** of the tongue, as governed by a "fiery" disposition and as exercising a destructive influence over others, Jas 3:6; **(11)** as symbolic of the danger of destruction, Jude 23. See: TDNT—6:928, 975; BAGD—729d; THAYER—558a.

4443. **πυρά** {2x} **pura**, *poo-rah';* from *4442;* a fire (concr.):—fire {2x}.

Pura denotes a heap of fuel collected to be set on fire [Eng., pyre], Acts 28:2, 3. See: BAGD—730c; THAYER—558c.

4444. **πύργος** {4x} **purgŏs**, *poor'-gos;* appar. a primary word (*"burgh"*); a tower or castle:—tower {4x}.

Purgos is used **(1)** of "a watchtower in a vineyard," Mt 21:33; Mk 12:1; **(2)** probably, too, in Lk 14:28 (cf. Is 5:2); in Lk 13:4, of the "tower in Siloam." See: TDNT—6:953, 980; BAGD—730d; THAYER—538c.

4445. **πυρέσσω** {2x} **purĕssō**, *poo-res'-so;* from *4443;* to be on fire, i.e. (spec.) to have a fever:—be sick of a fever {2x}. Cf. Matt. 8:14; Mark 1:30. See: TDNT—6:956, 981; BAGD—730d; THAYER—538c.

4446. **πυρετός** {6x} **purĕtŏs**, *poo-ret-os';* from *4445;* inflamed, i.e. (by impl.) feverish (as noun, *fever*):—fever {6x}.

Puretos, "feverish heat" (from *pur,* "fire"), hence, "a fever," occurs in Mt 8:15; Mk 1:31; Jn 4:52; Acts 28:8; in Lk 4:38, with *megas,* "great, a high fever"; v. 39. Luke, as a physician, uses the medical distinction by which the ancients classified fevers into great and little. See:

TDNT—6:956, 981; BAGD—730d; THAYER—558c.

4447. **πύρινος** {1x} **purinŏs**, *poo'-ree-nos;* from *4443;* fiery, i.e. (by impl.) flaming:—of fire {1x}. See: TDNT—6:951, 975; BAGD—731a; THAYER—558d.

4448. **πυρόω** {6x} **purŏō**, *poo-rŏ'-o;* from *4442;* to kindle, i.e. (pass.) to be ignited, glow (lit.), be refined (by impl.), or (fig.) to be inflamed (with anger, grief, lust):—burn {3x}, fiery {1x}, be on fire {1x}, try {1x}.

Puroo, from *pur,* "fire, to glow with heat," is said **(1)** of the feet of the Lord, in the vision in Rev 1:15; **(2)** it is translated "fiery" in Eph 6:16 (of the darts of the evil one); **(3)** used metaphorically of the emotions, in 1 Cor 7:9; 2 Cor 11:29; **(4)** elsewhere literally, of the heavens, 2 Pet 3:12; **(5)** of gold, Rev 3:18. See: TDNT—6:948, 975; BAGD—731a; THAYER—558d.

4449. **πυρράζω** {2x}   **purrhazō**, *poor-hrad'-zo;* from *4450;* to redden (intr.):—be red {2x}. See: BAGD—731b; THAYER—558d.

4450. **πυρρός** {2x} **purrhŏs**, *poor-hros';* from *4442; fire-like,* i.e. (spec.) flame-colored:—red {2x}.

This word means "to be fiery red", is used of the sky, Mt 16:2, 3. See: TDNT—6:952, 975; BAGD—731c; THAYER—559a.

4451. **πύρωσις** {3x} **purōsis**, *poo'-ro-sis;* from *4448; ignition,* i.e. (spec.) smelting (fig. conflagration, calamity as a test):—burning {2x}, trial {1x}.

Purosis is used **(1)** literally in Rev 18:9, 18; **(2)** metaphorically in 1 Pet 4:12, "fiery trial." See: TDNT—6:950, 975; BAGD—731c; THAYER—559a.

4452. **-πω** {0x} **-pō**, *po;* another form of the base of *4458;* an enclitic particle of indefiniteness; *yet, even;* used only in composition. See *3369, 3380, 3764, 3768, 4455.* See: BAGD—not listed; cf. 732d [4458]; THAYER—413b [3380].

4453. **πωλέω** {22x} **pōlĕō**, *po-leh'-o;* prob. ultimately from πέλομαι **pĕlŏmai** (to be busy, to trade); to barter (as a pedlar), i.e. to sell:—sell {21x}, whatever is sold {1x}.

Poleo, "to exchange or barter, to sell," is used in the latter sense in the NT, six times in Mt, three in Mk, six in Lk; in Jn only in connection with the cleansing of the Temple by the Lord, Jn 2:14, 16; in Acts only in connection with the disposing of property for distribution among the community of believers, 4:34, 37;

5:1; elsewhere, 1 Cor 10:25; Rev 13:17. See: BAGD—731c; THAYER—559a.

4454. πῶλος {12x} **pōlŏs**, *po'-los;* appar. a primary word; a *"foal"* or *"filly"*, i.e. (spec.) a *young ass:*—colt {12x}.

Polos, "a foal," whether "colt or filly," had the general significance of "a young creature"; in Mt 21:2, and parallel passages, "an ass's colt." See: TDNT—6:959, 981; BAGD—731d; THAYER—559b.

4455. πώποτε {6x} **pōpŏtĕ**, *po'-pot-e;* from *4452* and *4218; at any time,* i.e. (with neg. particle) *at no time:*—at any time {3x}, yet never + 3762 {1x}, never {1x}, never + 3364 {1x}. See: BAGD—732a; THAYER—559b.

4456. πωρόω {5x} **pōrŏō**, *po-rŏ'-o;* appar. from πῶρος **pōrŏs**, (a kind of *stone*); to *petrify*, i.e. (fig.) to *indurate* (render *stupid* or *callous*):—blind {2x}, harden {3x}.

Poroo signifies "to harden" (from *poros,* "a thick skin, a hardening"), "to make hard, callous, to petrify", is used **(1)** metaphorically, **(1a)** of the heart, Mk 6:52; 8:17; Jn 12:40; **(1b)** of the mind (or thoughts), 2 Cor 3:14, of those in Israel who refused the revealed will and ways of God in the gospel, as also in Rom 11:7, "blinded", in both places. See: TDNT—5:1025, 816; BAGD—732a; THAYER—559b.

4457. πώρωσις {3x} **pōrŏsis**, *po'-ro-sis;* from *4456; stupidity* or *callousness:*—blindness {2x}, hardness {1x}.

Porosis, primarily means "a covering with a callus," **(1)** in Rom 11:25 and Eph 4:18, "blindness"; **(2)** in Mk 3:5, "hardness." **(3)** It is metaphorical of a dulled spiritual perception. See: TDNT—5:1025, 816; BAGD—732a; THAYER—559b.

4458. -πώς {16x} **-pōs**, *poce;* adv. from the base of *4225;* an enclitic particle of indefiniteness of manner; *somehow* or *anyhow;* used only in composition:—by any means {8x}, by some means {1x}, perhaps {1x}, haply {1x}, not tr {5x}.

This word means "at all, somehow, in any way," and is used after the conjunction **(1)** *ei,* "if," meaning "if by any means," e.g., Acts 27:12; Rom 1:10; 11:14; Phil 3:11; **(2)** *me,* "lest, lest by any means," e.g., 1 Cor 8:9; 9:27; 2 Cor 2:7, "perhaps"; 9:4, "haply"; 11:3; 12:20; Gal 2:2; 4:11, "lest"; 3:5, "lest by some means." See: BAGD—732d; THAYER—560c. See *1513, 3381.* comp. *4459.*

4459. πῶς {103x} **pōs**, *poce;* adv. from the base of *4226;* an interr. particle of manner; *in what way?* (sometimes the question is indirect, *how?*); also as exclamation, *how much!:*—how {99x}, by what means {2x}, after

what manner {1x}, that {1x}. [*Occasionally unexpressed in English*].

Pos (*4459*), "how," is translated "after what manner" in Acts 20:18. Syn.: 195, 1485, 2239, 3634, 3668, 3697, 3779, 4169, 4187, 4217, 5158, 5159, 5179, 5615. See: BAGD—732b; THAYER—559c.

P

4460. Ῥαάβ {2x} **Rhaab**, *hrah-ab';* of Heb. or. [7343]; *Raab* (i.e. *Rachab*), a Canaanitess:—Rahab {2x}. See: BAGD—733a; THAYER—560b. See also *4477.*

4461. ῥαββί {17x} **rhabbi**, *hrab-bee';* of Heb. or. [7227 with pron. suff.); *my master,* i.e *Rabbi,* as an official title of honor:—Master (Christ) {9x}, Rabbi (Christ) {5x}, rabbi {3x}.

Rhabbi was an Aramaic word signifying "my master," a title of respectful address to Jewish teachers. The Aramaic word *rabbei,* transliterated into Greek, is explicitly recognized as the common form of address to Christ, Mt 26:25. **(1)** It is translated "Master"; Mt 26:25, 49; Mk 9:5; 11:21; 14:45; Jn 4:31; 9:2; 11:8. **(2)** In other passages, "Rabbi," Mt 23:7–8; Jn 1:38, 49; 3:2, 26; 6:25. See: TDNT—6:961, 982; BAGD—733a; THAYER—560b.

4462. ῥαββονί {2x} **rhabbŏni**, *hrab-bon-ee';* or

ῥαββουνί **rhabbŏuni**, *hrab-boo-nee';* of Chald. or.; corresp. to *4461:*—Lord (Christ) {1x}, Rabboni (Christ) {1x}.

(1) In its use in the NT the pronominal force of the suffix is apparently retained (contrast Rabbi - 4461); **(2)** it is found in **(2a)** Mk 10:51, "Lord"), addressed to Christ by blind Bartimaeus, and **(2b)** in Jn 20:16 by Mary Magdalene, where it is interpreted by *didaskalos,* "Master." This title is said to be Galilean; hence it would be natural on the lips of a woman of Magdala. It does not differ materially from "Rabbi." See: TDNT—6:962, 982; BAGD—733a; THAYER—560b.

4463. ῥαβδίζω {2x} **rhabdizō**, *hrab-did'-zo;* from *4464;* to *strike with a stick,* i.e. *bastinado:*—beat {1x}, beat with rods {1x}.

Rhabdizo is the verbal form of *rhabdos* (*4464*), "a rod, or staff," Acts 16:22; 2 Cor 11:25. See: TDNT—6:970, 982; BAGD—733b; THAYER—560c.

4464. ῥάβδος {12x} **rhabdŏs**, *hrab'-dos;* from the base of *4474;* a *stick* or *wand* (as a *cudgel,* a *cane* or a *baton* of royalty):—rod {6x}, sceptre {2x}, staff {4x}.

Rhabdos, "a staff, rod, scepter," is used **(1)** of Aaron's "rod," Heb 9:4; **(2)** a staff used on a journey, Mt 10:10, "staves"; so Lk 9:3; Mk 6:8, "staff"; Heb 11:21, "staff"; **(3)** a ruler's staff, a "scepter," Heb 1:8 (twice); elsewhere **(4)** a "rod," Rev 2:27; 12:5; 19:15; **(5)** a "rod" for chastisement (figuratively), 1 Cor 4:21; **(6)** a measuring rod, Rev 11:1. See: TDNT—6:966, 982; BAGD—733b; THAYER—560d.

4465. ῥαβδοῦχος {2x} **rhabdŏuchŏs,** *hrab-doo'-khos;* from *4464* and *2192;* a *rod-* (the Lat. *fasces) holder,* i.e. a Rom. *lictor* (*constable* or *executioner*):—serjeant {2x}. [now spelled sergeant—Acts 16:35, 38].

The duty of these officials was to attend Roman magistrates to execute their orders, especially administering punishment by scourging or beheading; they carried as their sign of office the *fasces* (whence "Fascist"), a bundle of rods with an axe inserted. See: TDNT—6:971, 982; BAGD—733c; THAYER—560d.

4466. Ῥαγαύ {1x} **Rhagau,** *hrag-ŏw';* of Heb. or. [7466]; *Ragaü* (i.e. *Reu*), a patriarch:—*Ragau* {1x}. See: BAGD—733c; THAYER—560d.

4467. ῥαδιούργημα {1x} **rhadiŏurgēma,** *hrad-ee-oorg'-ay-mah;* from a comp. of ῥᾳδιος **rhadiŏs** (*easy,* i.e. *reckless*) and *2041; easy-going behavior,* i.e. (by extens.) a *crime:*—lewdness {1x}.

Lewdness does not always mean public indecency. It can mean acts of villainy. See: TDNT—6:972, 983; BAGD—733c; THAYER—561a.

4468. ῥᾳδιουργία {1x} **rhadiŏurgia,** *hrad-ee-oorg-ee'-a;* from the same as *4467; recklessness,* i.e. (by extens.) *malignity:*—mischief {1x}. See: TDNT—6:972, 983; BAGD—733c; THAYER—561a.

4469. ῥακά {1x} **rhaka,** *hrak-ah';* of Chald. or. [comp. 7386]; O *empty* one, i.e. thou *worthless* (as a term of utter vilification):—*Raca* {1x}.

(1) *Rhaka* is an Aramaic word akin to the Heb. *req,* "empty," the first *a* being due to a Galilean change. **(2)** It was a word of utter contempt, signifying "empty," intellectually rather than morally, "empty-headed," like Abimelech's hirelings, Judg 9:4, and the "vain" man of Jas 2:20. **(3)** As condemned by Christ, Mt 5:22, it was worse than being angry, inasmuch as an outrageous utterance is worse than a feeling unexpressed or somewhat controlled in expression; it does not indicate such a loss of self-control as the word rendered "fool," a godless, moral reprobate. See: TDNT—6:973, 983; BAGD—733d; THAYER—561a.

4470. ῥάκος {2x} **rhakŏs,** *hrak'-os;* from *4486;* a "*rag,*" i.e. *piece* of cloth:—cloth {2x}.

Rakos denotes "a ragged garment, or a piece of cloth torn off, a rag"; hence, a piece of undressed "cloth," Mt 9:16; Mk 2:21. See: BAGD—734a; THAYER—561a.

4471. Ῥαμά {1x} **Rhama,** *hram-ah';* of Heb. or. [7414]; *Rama* (i.e. *Ramah*), a place in Pal.:—*Rama* {1x}. See: BAGD—734a; THAYER—561b.

4472. ῥαντίζω {4x} **rhantizō,** *hran-tid'-zo;* from a der. of ῥαίνω **rhainō** (to *sprinkle*); to *render besprinkled,* i.e. *asperse* (cerem. or fig.):—sprinkle {4x}.

Rhaino, "to sprinkle", is used **(1)** in the active voice in Heb 9:13, of "sprinkling" with blood the unclean, a token of the efficacy of the expiatory sacrifice of Christ, His blood signifying the giving up of His life in the shedding of His blood (cf. 9:22) under divine judgment upon sin (the voluntary act to be distinguished from that which took place after His death in the piercing of His side); so again in vv. 19, 21; **(2)** in Heb 10:22, passive voice, of the purging (on the ground of the same efficacy) of the hearts of believers from an evil conscience. This application of the blood of Christ is necessary for believers, in respect of their committal of sins, which on that ground receive forgiveness, 1 Jn 1:9. See: TDNT—6:976, 984; BAGD—734a; THAYER—561d.

4473. ῥαντισμός {2x} **rhantismŏs,** *hran-tis-mos';* from *4472; aspersion* (cerem. or fig.):—sprinkling {2x}.

Rhantismos is used of the "sprinkling" of the blood of Christ, in Heb 12:24 and 1 Pet 1:2, an allusion to the use of the blood of sacrifices, appointed for Israel, typical of the sacrifice of Christ. See: TDNT—6:976, 984; BAGD—734b; THAYER—561b.

4474. ῥαπίζω {2x} **rhapizō,** *hrap-id'-zo;* from a der. of a primary ῥέπω **rhĕpō** (to *let fall,* "*rap*"); to *slap:*—smite {1x}, smite with the palm of the hand {1x}.

Rhapizo, primarily "to strike with a rod" (*rhapis,* "a rod"), then, "to strike the face with the palm of the hand or the clenched fist," which is its usage in Mt 5:39; 26:67. See: BAGD—734b; THAYER—561c. comp. *5180.*

4475. ῥάπισμα {3x} **rhapisma,** *hrap'-is-mah;* from *4474;* a *slap:*—strike with the palm of (one's) hand + 906 {1x}, strike with the palm of (one's) hand + 1325 {1x}, smite with (one's) hand + 1325 {1x}.

Rhapisma is **(1)** "a blow with a rod or staff," **(2)** "a blow with the hand, a slap or cuff," is

found in three places; **(2a)** of the maltreatment of Christ by the officials or attendants of the high priest, Mk 14:65, "did strike Him with the palms of their hands"; **(3)** that they received, or took, Him would indicate their rough handling of Him; Jn 18:22 and 19:3. So with the corresponding verb *rhapizo* (*4475*), in Mt 26:67. The soldiers subsequently beat Him with a reed, 27:30, where *tupto*, "to beat," is used. See: BAGD—734c; THAYER—561c.

4476. ῥαφίς {3x} **rhaphis**, *hraf-ece';* from a primary ῥάπτω **rhaptō** (to *sew;* perh. rather akin to the base of *4474* through the idea of *puncturing*); a *needle:*—needle {3x}.
Rhapis, denotes a sharp point, hence, "a needle," Lk 18:25. *Note:* The idea of applying "the needle's eye" to small gates seems to be a modern one; there is no ancient trace of it. The Lord's object in the statement is to express human impossibility and there is no need to endeavor to soften the difficulty by taking the needle to mean anything more than the ordinary instrument. An attempt is sometimes made to explain the words as a reference to the small door, a little over 2 feet square, in the large heavy gate of a walled city. This mars the figure without materially altering the meaning, and receives no justification from the language and traditions of Palestine. See: BAGD—734c; THAYER—561c.

4477. Ῥαχάβ {1x} **Rhachab**, *hrakh-ab';* from the same as *4460; Rachab,* a Canaanitess:—*Rachab* {1x}. See: TDNT—3:1, 311; BAGD—734c; THAYER—561c.

4478. Ῥαχήλ {1x} **Rhachēl**, *hrakh-ale';* of Heb. or. [*7354*]; *Rachel,* the wife of Jacob:—Rachel {1x}. See: BAGD—734d; THAYER—561d.

4479. Ῥεβέκκα {1x} **Rhĕbĕkka**, *hreb-bek'-kah;* of Heb. or. [*7259*]; *Rebecca* (i.e. *Ribkah*), the wife of Isaac:—Rebecca {1x}. See: BAGD—734d; THAYER—561d.

4480. ῥέδα {1x} **rhĕda**, *hred'-ah;* of Lat. or.; a *rheda,* i.e. four-wheeled *carriage* (*wagon* for riding):—chariot {1x}. See: BAGD—734d; THAYER—561d.

4481. Ῥεμφάν {1x} **Rhĕmphan**, *hrem-fan'* or

Ῥαιφάν **Rhaiphan**, *hrahee-fan';* by incorrect transliteration for a word of Heb. of [*3594*]; *Remphan* (i.e. *Kijun*), an Eg. idol:—*Remphan* {1x}. See: BAGD—735a; THAYER—561d.

4482. ῥέω {1x} **rheō**, *hreh'-o;* a primary verb; for some tenses of which a prol. form

ῥεύω **rhĕuō**, *hryoo'-o* is used; to *flow* ("*run*"; as water):—flow {1x}.
Rheo, "to flow," is used figuratively in Jn 7:38 of the Holy Spirit, acting in and through the believer. See: BAGD—735a; THAYER—561d.

4483. ῥέω {26x} **rheō**, *hreh'-o;* for certain tenses of which a prol. form

ἐρέω **ĕrĕō**, *er-eh'-o;* is used; and both as alt. for *2036;* perh. akin (or ident.) with *4482* (through the idea of *pouring* forth); to *utter,* i.e. *speak* or *say:*—speak {12x}, say {9x}, speak of {3x}, command {1x}, make {1x}. See: BAGD—735a; THAYER—562a. comp. *3004.*

4484. Ῥήγιον {1x} **Rhēgiŏn**, *hrayg'-ee-on;* of Lat. or.; *Rhegium,* a place in Italy:—*Rhegium* {1x}. See: BAGD—735a; THAYER—562a.

4485. ῥῆγμα {1x} **rhēgma**, *hrayg'-mah;* from *4486;* something *torn,* i.e. a *fragment* (by impl. and abstr. a *fall*):—ruin {1x}.
Rhegma denotes "a cleavage, fracture"; by metonymy, that which is broken, "a ruin," Lk 6:49. See: BAGD—735a; THAYER—562a.

4486. ῥήγνυμι {7x} **rhēgnumi**, *hrayg'-noo-mee;* or

ῥήσσω **rhēssō**, *hrace'-so;* both prol. forms of ῥήκω **rhēkō** (which appears only in certain forms, and is itself prob. a strengthened form of ἄγνυμι **agnumi** [see in *2608*]); to "*break*", "*wreck*" or "*crack*", i.e. (espec.) to *sunder* (by *separation* of the parts; *2608* being its intensive [with the prep. in composition], and *2352* a *shattering* to minute fragments; but not a *reduction* to the constituent particles, like *3089*) or *disrupt, lacerate;* by impl. to *convulse* (with *spasms*); fig. to *give vent* to joyful emotions:—burst {2x}, tear {1x}, rend {1x}, break {1x}, break forth {1x}, throw down {1x}.
Rhesso, "to tear, rend, as of garments, etc.," is translated **(1)** "break" in Mt 9:17, of wineskins; **(2)** "burst" in Mk 2:22 and Lk 5:37; **(3)** "break forth" in Gal 4:27. It is also translated **(4)** "rend" in Mt 7:6; **(5)** "teareth" in Mk 9:18; and **(6)** "throw down" in Lk 9:42. Syn.: *Thrauo* (*2352*) means to shatter and is suggestive of many fragments and minute dispersion. *Katagnumi* (*2608*) means to break and denotes the destruction of a thing's unity or completeness. *Rhegnumi* (*4486*) means to rend asunder and makes pointed reference to the separation

of the parts. See: BAGD−735a; THAYER−
562a.

4487. ῥῆμα {70x} **rhēma**, *hray'-mah;* from
            4483; an *utterance* (indiv., col-
lect. or spec.); by impl. a *matter* or *topic* (espec.
of narration, command or dispute); with a neg.
naught whatever:−word {56x}, saying {9x},
thing {3x}, no thing + 3756 {1x}, not tr {1x}.

Rhema, **(1)** in the singular, "a word," e.g.,
Mt 12:36; 27:14; 2 Cor 12:4; 13:1; Heb 12:19;
(2) in the plural, speech, discourse, e.g., Jn 3:34;
8:20; Acts 2:14; 6:11, 13; 11:14; 13:42; 26:25;
Rom 10:18; 2 Pet 3:2; Jude 17; **(3)** it is used of
the gospel in Rom 10:8 (twice), 17, "the word
of God"; 10:18; 1 Pet 1:25 (twice); **(4)** of a statement, command, instruction, e.g., Mt 26:75; Lk
1:37, 38; Acts 11:16; Heb 11:3. Syn.: The significance of *rhema* (as distinct from *logos*) is exemplified in the injunction to take "the sword
of the Spirit, which is the word of God," Eph
6:17; here the reference is not to the whole
Bible as such, but to the individual scripture
which the Spirit brings to our remembrance
for use in time of need, a prerequisite being the
regular storing of the mind with Scripture. See:
TDNT−4:69, 505; BAGD−735b; THAYER−
562b.

4488. ῾Ρησά {1x} **Rhēsa**, *hray-sah';* prob. of
            Heb. or. [appar. for 7509]; *Resa*
(i.e. *Rephajah*), an Isr.:−*Rhesa* {1x}. See:
BAGD−735d; THAYER−563a.

4489. ῥήτωρ {1x} **rhētōr**, *hray'-tore;* from
            4483; a *speaker,* i.e. (by impl.) a
forensic *advocate:*−orator {1x}.

Rhetor, "to say" (cf. Eng., "rhetoric"), denotes "a public speaker, an orator," Acts 24:1,
of Tertullus. Such a person, distinct from the
professional lawyer, was hired, as a professional speaker, to make a skillful presentation
of a case in court. His training was not legal
but rhetorical. See: BAGD−735d; THAYER−
563a.

4490. ῥητῶς {1x} **rhētōs**, *hray-toce';* adv.
            from a der. of *4483;* out-
spokenly, i.e. *distinctly:*−expressly {1x}.

Rhetos, meaning "in stated terms" (from
rhetos, "stated, specified"; from *rheo,* or *ero,*
"to say"; cf. *rhema,* "a word"), is used in 1 Ti
4:1, "expressly." See: BAGD−736a; THAYER−
563a.

4491. ῥίζα {17x} **rhiza**, *hrid'-zah;* appar. a
            primary word; a *"root"* (lit. or
fig.):−root {17x}.

Rhiza is used **(1)** in the natural sense, Mt
3:10; 13:6, 21; Mk 4:6, 17, 11:20; Lk 3:9; 8:13;
(2) metaphorically of "cause, origin, source,"
said **(2a)** of persons, ancestors, Rom 11:16, 17,

18 (twice); **(2b)** of things, **(2b1)** evils, 1 Ti 6:10,
of the love of money as a "root" of all "evil");
(2b2) bitterness, Heb 12:15; **(3)** of that which
springs from a "root," a shoot, said of offspring,
Rom 15:12; Rev 5:5; 22:16. See: TDNT−6:985,
985; BAGD−736a; THAYER−563a.

4492. ῥιζόω {2x} **rhizŏō**, *hrid-zŏ'-o;* from
            4491; to cause to take *root* (fig.
become stable):−root {2x}.

Rhizoo, "to cause to take root," is used metaphorically in the passive voice **(1)** in Eph 3:17,
of being "rooted" in love; **(2)** Col 2:7, in Christ,
i.e., in the sense of being firmly planted, or
established. See: TDNT−6:990, 985; BAGD−
736b; THAYER−563b.

4493. ῥιπή {1x} **rhipē**, *hree-pay';* from *4496;*
            a *jerk* (of the eye, i.e. [by anal.]
an *instant*):−twinkling {1x}.

Rhipe, akin to *rhipto,* "to hurl," was used of
any rapid movement, e.g., the throw of a javelin, the rush of wind or flame; in 1 Cor 15:52 of
the "twinkling" of an eye. See: BAGD−736b;
THAYER−563b.

4494. ῥιπίζω {1x} **rhipizo**, *hrip-id'-zo;* from
            a der. of *4496* (mean. a *fan* or
bellows); to *breeze up,* i.e. (by anal.) to *agitate*
(into waves):−toss {1x}.

Rhipizo, primarily "to fan a fire" (*rhipis,* "a
fan," cf. *rhipe,* "twinkling"), then, "to make a
breeze," is used in the passive voice in Jas 1:6,
"tossed," of the raising of waves by the wind.
See: BAGD−736b; THAYER−563b.

4495. ῥιπτέω {1x} **rhiptĕō**, *hrip-teh'-o;* from
            a der. of *4496;* to *toss* up:−cast
off {1x}. See: TDNT−6:991,*; BAGD−736c;
THAYER−563c.

4496. ῥίπτω {7x} **rhiptō**, *hrip'-to;* a primary
            verb (perh. rather akin to the
base of *4474,* through the idea of sudden *motion*); to *fling* (prop. with a quick *toss,* thus
differing from *906,* which denotes a *deliberate*
hurl; and from τείνω **tĕinō**, [see in *1614*],
which indicates an *extended* projection); by
qualification, to *deposit* (as if a load); by extens. to *disperse:*−cast down {2x}, cast {2x},
scatter abroad {1x}, cast out {1x}, throw {1x}.

Rhipto denotes "to throw with a sudden
motion, to jerk, cast forth"; **(1)** "cast down," Mt
15:30 and 27:5; **(2)** "thrown down," Lk 4:35;
(3) "cast," Lk 17:2; **(4)** in Acts 27:19 "cast out,"
of the tackling of a ship; **(5)** in Acts 17:29
"cast", of anchors; **(6)** in Mt 9:36, "scattered
abroad," said of sheep. See: TDNT−6:991, 987;
BAGD−736c; THAYER−563c.

4497. ῾Ροβοάμ {2x} **Rhŏbŏam**, *hrob-ŏ-am';* of
            Heb. or. [7346]; *Roboäm* (i.e.

Rechabam), an Isr.:—Roboam {2x}. See: BAGD—736d; THAYER—563d.

4498.´**Ρόδη** {1x} **Rhŏdē,** *hrod'-ay;* prob. for ῥοδή **rhŏdē,** (a *rose*); *Rodē,* a servant girl:—Rhoda {1x}. See: BAGD—736d; THAYER—563d.

4499.´**Ρόδος** {1x} **Rhŏdŏs,** *hrod'-os;* prob. from ῥόδον **rhŏdŏn,** (a *rose*); *Rhodus,* an island of the Mediterranean:—Rhodes {1x}. See: BAGD—737a; THAYER—563d.

4500. **ῥοιζηδόν** {1x} **rhŏizēdŏn,** *hroyd-zay-don';* adv. from a der. of ῥοῖζος **rhŏizŏs** (a *whir*); *whizzingly,* i.e. *with a crash:*—with a great noise {1x}.

Rhoizedon is from a root which means the whistling of an arrow signifying with a rushing sound, as of roaring flames, and is used in 2 Pet 3:10 of the future passing away of the heavens. See: BAGD—737a; THAYER—563d.

4501. **ῥομφαία** {7x} **rhŏmphaia,** *hrom-fah'-yah;* prob. of for. or.; a *sabre,* i.e. a long and broad *cutlass* (any *weapon* of the kind, lit. or fig.):—sword {7x}.

Rhomphaia denoted a sword of large size and occurs **(1)** literally in (Rev 6:8); **(2)** metaphorically, as the instrument of anguish (Lk 2:35); **(3)** of judgment (Rev 1:16; 2:12, 16; 19:15, 21), probably figurative of the Lord's judicial utterances. See: TDNT—6:993, 987; BAGD—737a; THAYER—564a.

4502.´**Ρουβήν** {1x} **Rhŏubēn,** *hroo-bane';* of Heb. or. [7205]; *Ruben* (i.e. *Reuben*), an Isr.:—Reuben {1x}. See: BAGD—737b; THAYER—564a.

4503.´**Ρούθ** {1x} **Rhŏuth,** *hrooth;* of Heb. or. [7327]; *Ruth,* a Moabitess:—Ruth {1x}. See: TDNT—3:1, 311; BAGD—737b; THAYER—564a.

4504.´**Ρούφος** {2x} **Rhŏuphŏs,** *hroo'-fos;* of Lat. or.; *red; Rufus,* a Chr.:—Rufus {2x}. See: BAGD—737b; THAYER—564a.

4505. **ῥύμη** {4x} **rhumē,** *hroo'-may;* prol. from *4506* in its orig. sense; an *alley* or *avenue* (as crowded):—lane {1x}, street {3x}.

Rhume, "a narrow road lane or street", is translated **(1)** "streets" in Mt 6:2; "street" in Acts 9:11; 12:10; and **(2)** "lanes" in Lk 14:21, "Then the master of the house being angry said to his servant, Go out quickly into the streets and lanes of the city, and bring in hither the poor, and the maimed, and the halt, and the blind." Syn.: 296, 4113. See: BAGD—737c; THAYER—564b.

4506. **ῥύομαι** {18x} **rhuŏmai,** *hroo'-om-ahee;* mid. voice of an obs. verb, akin to *4482* (through the idea of a *current;* comp. *4511*); to *rush* or *draw* (for oneself), i.e. *rescue:*—deliver {17x}, Deliverer {1x}.

Rhuomai, as a verb, means **(1)** "to rescue from, to preserve from," and so, **(1a)** "to deliver," the word by which it is regularly translated, **(1b)** with the idea of "rescue from" as predominant in *rhuomai:* "He trusted in God; let him deliver him now, if he will have him: for he said, I am the Son of God" (Mt 27:43). **(2)** In Rom 11:26 the present participle is used with the article, as a noun, **(2a)** "the Deliverer": "And so all Israel shall be saved: as it is written, There shall come out of Sion the Deliverer, and shall turn away ungodliness from Jacob." **(2b)** In 1 Th 1:10, Christ is similarly spoken of, "our Deliverer," that is, from the retributive calamities with which God will visit men at the end of the present age. From that wrath believers are to be "delivered."

(3) The verb is used **(3a)** with *apo,* "away from": "And lead us not into temptation, but deliver us from (*rhuomai apo*) evil: For thine is the kingdom, and the power, and the glory, for ever. Amen" (Mt 6:13; Lk 11:4; Rom 15:31; 2 Th 3:2; 2 Ti 4:18); and **(3b)** with *ek,* "from, out of": "That He would grant unto us, that we being delivered out of (*rhuomai ek*) the hand of our enemies might serve Him without fear" (Lk 1:74; cf. Rom 7:24; 2 Cor 1:10; Col 1:13 from bondage; in 2 Pet 2:9 from temptation; in 2 Ti 3:11 from persecution); **(3c)** but *ek* is used of ills impending: "Who delivered us from so great a death, and doth deliver: in whom we trust that He will yet deliver us" (2 Cor 1:10); and **(3d)** in 2 Ti 4:17 *ek* indicates that the danger was more imminent than in v. 18, where *apo* is used: "Notwithstanding the Lord stood with me, and strengthened me; that by me the preaching might be fully known, and that all the Gentiles might hear: and I was delivered out (*rhuomai ek*) of the mouth of the lion. 18 And the Lord shall deliver me from (*rhuomai apo*) every evil work, and will preserve me unto his heavenly kingdom: to whom be glory for ever and ever. Amen."

(4) Accordingly the meaning "out of the midst of": "And to wait for His Son from heaven, whom He raised from the dead, even Jesus, which delivered us from the wrath to come" (1 Th 1:10). Syn.: 325, 525, 629, 591, 859, 1325, 1560, 1659, 1807, 1929, 3086, 3860, 5483. See: TDNT—6:998, 988; BAGD—737c; THAYER—737c.

4507. **ῥυπαρία** {1x} **rhuparia,** *hroo-par-ee'-ah;* from *4508; dirtiness* (mor.):—filthiness {1x}.

Rhuparia means to make filthy, befoul, to defile, to dishonor (Jas 1:21). See: BAGD— 738a; THAYER—564c.

4508. ῥυπαρός {1x} **rhuparŏs**, *hroo-par-os';* from *4509; dirty,* i.e. (rel.) *cheap* or *shabby;* mor. *wicked:*—vile {1x}. See: BAGD—738a; THAYER—564c.

4509. ῥύπος {1x} **rhupŏs**, *hroo'-pos;* of uncert. aff.; *dirt,* i.e. (mor.) *depravity:*—filth {1x}. See: BAGD—738a; THAYER—564c.

4510. ῥυπόω {2x} **rhupŏō**, *hroo-pŏ'-o;* from *4509;* to *soil,* i.e. (intr.) to *become dirty* (mor.):—be filthy {2x}. See: BAGD—738b; THAYER—564b.

4511. ῥύσις {3x} **rhusis**, *hroo'-sis;* from *4506* in the sense of its congener *4482;* a *flux* (of blood):—issue {3x}.

Rhusis, "a flowing" (akin to *rheo,* "to flow"), "an issue," is used in Mk 5:25; Lk 8:43, 44. See: BAGD—738b; THAYER—564c.

4512. ῥυτίς {1x} **rhutis**, *hroo-tece';* from *4506;* a *fold* (as *drawing* together), i.e. a *wrinkle* (espec. on the face):—wrinkle {1x}.

Rhutis, from an obsolete verb *rhuo,* signifying "to draw together," occurs in Eph 5:27, describing the flawlessness of the complete church, as the result of the love of Christ in giving Himself up for it, with the purpose of presenting it to Himself hereafter. See: BAGD—738b; THAYER—564d.

4513. Ῥωμαϊκός {1x} **Rhōmaïkŏs**, *hro-mah-ee-kos';* from *4514; Romaïc,* i.e. *Lat.:*—Latin {1x}. See: BAGD—738c; THAYER—564d.

4514. Ῥωμαῖος {13x} **Rhōmaiŏs**, *hro-mah'-yos;* from *4516; Romœan,* i.e. *Roman* (as noun):—Roman {12x}, of Rome {1x}.

This word occurs in Jn 11:48; Acts 2:10, ("of Rome"); 16:21, 37, 38; 22:25, 26, 27, 29; 23:27; 25:16; 28:17. See: BAGD—738c; THAYER—564d.

4515. Ῥωμαϊστί {1x} **Rhōmaïsti**, *hro-mah-is-tee';* adv. from a presumed der. of *4516; Romaïstically,* i.e. *in the Latin* language:—Latin {1x}.

This word is an adverb, "in Latin," occurs in Jn 19:20. See: BAGD—738c; THAYER—564d.

4516. Ῥώμη {14x} **Rhōmē**, *hro'-may;* from the base of *4517; strength; Roma,* the capital of Italy:—Rome {14x}. See: BAGD—738c; THAYER—564d.

4517. ῥώννυμι {2x} **rhōnnumi**, *hrone'-noo-mee;* prol. from ῥώομαι **rhŏō-mai** (to *dart;* prob. akin to *4506*); to *strengthen,* i.e. (impers. pass.) *have health* (as a parting exclamation, *good-bye*):—farewell {2x}.

Rhonnumi, "to strengthen, to be strong," is used in the imperative mood as a formula at the end of letters, signifying "Farewell," Acts 15:29; 23:30. See: BAGD—738d; THAYER—565a.

Σ

4518. σαβαχθάνι {2x} **sabachthani**, *sab-akh-than-ee';* of Chald. or [7662 with pron. suff.]; *thou hast left me; sabachthani* (i.e. *shebakthani*), a cry of distress:—sabachthani {2x}.

Literally "thou hast forsaken me", Mt 27:46; Mk 15:34. See: BAGD—738b; THAYER—565b.

4519. σαβαώθ {2x} **sabaōth**, *sab-ah-owth';* of Heb. or. [6635 in fem. plur.]; *armies; sabaoth* (i.e. *tsebaoth*), a military epithet of God:—sabaoth {2x}.

Sabaoth is the transliteration of a Hebrew word which denotes "hosts" or "armies," Rom 9:29; Jas 5:4. While the word "hosts" probably had special reference to angels, the title "the LORD of hosts" became used to designate Him as the One who is supreme over all the innumerable hosts of spiritual agencies, or of what are described as "the armies of heaven." Eventually it was used as equivalent to "the LORD all-sovereign." See: BAGD—738b; THAYER—565b.

4520. σαββατισμός {1x} **sabbatismŏs**, *sabbat-is-mos';* from a der. of *4521;* a *"sabbatism,"* i.e. (fig.) the *repose* of Christianity (as a type of heaven):—rest {1x}.

Sabbath-keeping," is used in Heb 4:9, "a keeping of a sabbath"; here the sabbath-keeping is the perpetual sabbath "rest" to be enjoyed uninterruptedly by believers in their fellowship with the Father and the Son, in contrast to the weekly Sabbath under the Law. Because this sabbath "rest" is the "rest" of God Himself, 4:10, its full fruition is yet future, though believers now enter into it. In whatever way they enter into divine "rest," that which they enjoy is involved in an indissoluble relation with God. See: TDNT—7:34, 989; BAGD—739a; THAYER—565c.

4521. σάββατον {68x} **sabbatŏn**, *sab'-bat-on;* of Heb. or. [7676]; the *Sabbath* (i.e. *Shabbath*), or day of weekly *repose* from secular avocations (also the observance or institution itself); by extens. a *se'nnight,* i.e. the interval between two Sab-

baths; likewise the plural in all the above applications:—sabbath {22x}, sabbath day {37x}, week {9x}.

(1) The root means "to cease, desist" (Heb., *shabath*); **(2)** the doubled *b* has an intensive force, implying a complete cessation or a making to cease, probably the former. **(3)** The idea is not that of relaxation or refreshment, but cessation from activity. **(4)** The observation of the seventh day of the week, enjoined upon Israel, was a sign between God and His earthly people, based upon the fact that after the six days of creative operations He rested, cf. Ex 31:16, 17, with 20:8–11. **(5)** The OT regulations were developed and systematized to such an extent that they became a burden upon the people (who otherwise rejoiced in the rest provided) and a byword for absurd extravagance. **(6)** Two treatises of the Mishna (the *Shabbath* and *Erubin*) are entirely occupied with regulations for the observance; so with the discussions in the Gemara, on rabbinical opinions.

(7) The effect upon current opinion explains the antagonism roused by the Lord's cures wrought on the "Sabbath," e.g., Mt 12:9–13; Jn 5:5–16, and explains the fact that on a "Sabbath" the sick were brought to be healed after sunset, e.g., Mk 1:32. **(8)** According to rabbinical ideas, the disciples, by plucking ears of corn (Mt 12:1; Mk 2:23), and rubbing them (Lk 6:1), broke the "sabbath" in two respects; for to pluck was to reap, and to rub was to thresh. **(9)** The Lord's attitude towards the "sabbath" was by way of freeing it from these vexatious traditional accretions by which it was made an end in itself, instead of a means to an end (Mk 2:27). **(10)** In the Epistles the only direct mentions are in **(10a)** Col 2:16, "sabbath days", where it is listed among things that were "a shadow of the things to come" (i.e., of the age introduced at Pentecost), and in **(10b)** Heb 4:4–11, where the perpetual *sabbatismos* is appointed for believers; **(10c)** inferential references are in Rom 14:5 and Gal 4:9–11. **(11)** For the first three centuries of the Christian era the first day of the week was never confounded with the "sabbath"; the confusion of the Jewish and Christian institutions was due to declension from apostolic teaching. See: TDNT—7:1, 989; BAGD—739a; THAYER—565c.

4522. **σαγήνη** {1x} **sagēnē**, *sag-ay'-nay;* from a der. of σάττω **sattō** (to *equip*) mean. *furniture,* espec. a *pack-saddle* (which in the E. is merely a bag of *netted* rope); a *"seine"* for fishing:—net {1x}.

Sagene denotes "a dragnet, a seine"; two modes were employed with this, either by its being let down into the water and drawn together in a narrowing circle, and then into the boat, or as a semicircle drawn to the shore, Mt 13:47. Syn.: 293, 1350. Syn.: **(A)** *Sagene* is the long-drawn net or sweep net. **(B)** *Diktyon* (*1350*) is the general terms for nets. **(C)** *Amphiblestron* (*293*) is the circular casting net. See: BAGD—739c; THAYER—566b.

4523. **Σαδδουκαῖος** {14x} **Saddŏukaiŏs**, *sad-doo-kah'-yos;* prob. from *4524;* a *Sadducœan* (i.e. *Tsadokian*), or follower of a certain heretical Isr.:—Sadducee {14x}. Syn.: See discussion under Pharisse, (*5330*). See: TDNT—7:35, 992; BAGD—739d; THAYER—566b.

4524. **Σαδώκ** {2x} **Sadōk**, *sad-oke';* of Heb. or. [6659]; *Sadoc* (i.e. *Tsadok*), an Isr.:—Sadoc {2x}. See: BAGD—739d; THAYER—566c.

4525. **σαίνω** {1x} **sainō**, *sah'-ee-no;* akin to *4579;* to *wag* (as a dog its tail fawningly), i.e. (gen.) to *shake* (fig. *disturb*):—move {1x}

Saino, as a verb, means properly, of dogs, "to wag the tail"; hence, metaphorically of persons, "to disturb, disquiet," 1 Th 3:3, passive voice, "(that no man) be moved (by these afflictions)." Syn.: 277, 383, 761, 2795, 2796, 3334, 4531, 4579, 4787, 5342. See: TDNT—7:54, 994; BAGD—740a; THAYER—566c.

4526. **σάκκος** {4x} **sakkŏs**, *sak'-kos;* of Heb. or. [8242]; *"sack"-cloth*, i.e. *mohair* (the material or garments made of it, worn as a sign of grief):—sackcloth {4x}.

Sakkos, "a warm material woven from goat's or camel's hair," and **(1)** hence of a dark color, Rev 6:12. **(2)** It was used for garments worn as **(2a)** expressing mourning or penitence, Mt 11:21; Lk 10:13, or **(2b)** for purposes of prophetic testimony, Rev 11:3. See: TDNT—7:56, 995; BAGD—740a; THAYER—566d.

4527. **Σαλά** {1x} **Sala**, *sal-ah';* of Heb. or. [7974]; *Sala* (i.e. *Shelach*), a patriarch:—*Sala* {1x}. See: BAGD—740b; THAYER—566d.

4528. **Σαλαθιήλ** {3x} **Salathiēl**, *sal-ath-ee-ale';* of Heb. or. [7597]; *Salathiël* (i.e. *Sheältiël*), an Isr.:—Salathiel {3x}. See: BAGD—740b; THAYER—566d.

4529. **Σαλαμίς** {1x} **Salamis**, *sal-am-ece';* prob. from *4535* (from the *surge* on the shore); *Salamis,* a place in Cyprus:—*Salamis* {1x}. See: BAGD—740b; THAYER—567a.

4530. **Σαλείμ** {1x} **Salĕim**, *sal-ime';* prob. from the same as *4531; Salim,* a place in Pal.:—Salim {1x}. See: BAGD—740d; THAYER—567a.

4531. σαλεύω {15x} **salĕuō**, *sal-yoo'-o;* from *4535;* to *waver,* i.e. *agitate, rock, topple* or (by impl.) *destroy;* fig. to *disturb, incite:*—shake {10x}, move {1x}, shake together {1x}, that are shaken {1x}, which cannot be shaken + 3361 {1x}, stir up {1x}.

Saleuo, as a verb, means I. "to shake," properly of the action of stormy wind, then, "to render insecure, stir up," is rendered (1) "I should (not) be moved" in Acts 2:25, in the sense of being cast down or shaken from a sense of security and happiness, said of Christ, in a quotation from Ps 16:8. (2) It also means "to agitate, shake," primarily of the action of stormy winds, waves, etc., is used (2a) literally, (2a1) of a reed, Mt 11:7; Lk 7:24; (2a2) a vessel, "shaken" in filling, Lk 6:38; (2a3) a building, Lk 6:48; Acts 4:31; 16:26; (2a4) the natural forces of the heavens and heavenly bodies, Mt 24:29; Mk 13:25; Lk 21:26; (2a5) the earth, Heb 12:26, "shook"; (2b) metaphorically, (2b1) of "shaking" so as to make insecure, Heb 12:27 (twice); (2b2) of casting down from a sense of security, Acts 2:25, "I should (not) be moved"; (2b3) to stir up (a crowd), Acts 17:13; (2b4) to unsettle, 2 Th 2:2, "(to the end that) ye be not (quickly) shaken (from your mind)," i.e., from their settled conviction and the purpose of heart begotten by it, as to the return of Christ before the Day of the Lord begins; the metaphor may be taken from the loosening of a ship from its moorings by a storm. Syn. for I: 277, 383, 761, 2795, 2796, 3334, 4525, 4579, 4787, 5342.
II. *Saleuo,* also means "stirred up": "But when the Jews of Thessalonica had knowledge that the word of God was preached of Paul at Berea, they came thither also, and stirred up the people" (Acts 17:13). Syn. for II: 329, 383, 387, 1326, 1892, 2042, 3947, 3951, 4579, 4787, 4797, 5017. See: TDNT—7:65, 996; BAGD—740c; THAYER—567a.

4532. Σαλήμ {2x} **Salēm**, *sal-ame';* of Heb. or. [8004]; *Salem* (i.e. *Shalem*), a place in Pal.:—*Salem* {2x}. See: BAGD—740d; THAYER—567b.

4533. Σαλμών {3x} **Salmōn**, *sal-mone';* of Heb. or. [8012]; *Salmon,* an Isr.:—*Salmon* {3x}. See: BAGD—740d; THAYER—567b.

4534. Σαλμώνη {1x} **Salmōnē**, *sal-mo'-nay;* perh. of similar or. to *4529; Salmone,* a place in Crete:—*Salmone* {1x}. See: BAGD—740d; THAYER—567b.

4535. σάλος {1x} **salŏs**, *sal'-os;* prob. from the base of *4525;* a *vibration,* i.e. (spec.) *billow:*—wave {1x}.
Salos denotes "a tossing," especially the rolling swell of the sea, Lk 21:25, "waves." See: BAGD—741a; THAYER—567c.

4536. σάλπιγξ {11x} **salpigx**, *sal'-pinx;* perh. from *4535* (through the idea of *quavering* or *reverberation*); a *trumpet:*—trump {2x}, trumpet {9x}.
Salpigx is used (1) of the natural instrument, 1 Cor 14:8; (2) of the supernatural accompaniment of divine interpositions, (2a) at Sinai, Heb 12:19; (2b) of the acts of angels at the second advent of Christ, Mt 24:31; (2c) of their acts in the period of divine judgments preceding this, Rev 8:2, 6, 13; 9:14; (2d) of a summons to John to the presence of God, Rev 1:10; 4:1; (2e) of the act of the Lord in raising from the dead the saints who have fallen asleep and changing the bodies of those who are living, at the Rapture of all to meet Him in the air, 1 Cor 15:52, where "the last trump" is a military allusion, familiar to Greek readers, and has no connection with the series in Rev 8:6 to 11:15; there is a possible allusion to Num 10:2–6, with reference to the same event, 1 Th 4:16, "the (lit., a) trump of God" (the absence of the article suggests the meaning "a trumpet such as is used in God's service"). See: BAGD—741a; THAYER—567c.

4537. σαλπίζω {12x} **salpizō**, *sal-pid'-zo;* from *4536;* to *trumpet,* i.e. *sound a blast* (lit. or fig.):—sound {10x}, sound of a trumpet {1x}, trumpet sounds {1x}.
Salpizo, "to sound a trumpet" (*salpinx*), occurs in Mt 6:2; 1 Cor 15:52, "the trumpet shall sound"; Rev 8:6–8, 10, 12, 13; 9:1, 13; 10:7; 11:15. See: TDNT—7:71, 997; BAGD—741a; THAYER—567c.

4538. σαλπιστής {1x} **salpistēs**, *sal-pis-tace';* from *4537;* a *trumpeter:*—trumpeter {1x}. See: TDNT—7:71, 997; BAGD—741b; THAYER—567d.

4539. Σαλώμη {2x} **Salōmē**, *sal-o'-may;* prob. of Heb. or. [fem. from 7965]; *Salome'* (i.e. *Shelomah*), an Israelitess:—*Salome* {2x}. See: BAGD—741b; THAYER—567d.

4540. Σαμάρεια {11x} **Samarĕia**, *sam-ar'-i-ah;* of Heb. or. [8111]; *Samaria* (i.e. *Shomeron*), a city and region of Pal.:—*Samaria* {11x}. See: TDNT—7:88, 999; BAGD—741b; THAYER—567d.

4541. Σαμαρείτης {9x} **Samarĕitēs**, *sam-ar-i'-tace* or

Σαμαρίτης Samaritēs, *sam-ar-ee'-tace;* from *4540;* a *Samarite,* i.e. inhab. of Samaria:—Samaritan {9x}. See: TDNT—7:88, 999; BAGD—741c; THAYER—568a.

4542. Σαμαρεῖτις {2x} **Samarĕitis**, *sam-ar-i'-tis* or

Σαμαρῖτις Samaritis, *sam-ar-ee'-tis* fem. of *4541;* a *Samaritess,* i.e. woman of Samaria:—of Samaria {2x}. See: TDNT—7:88, 999; BAGD—741d; THAYER—568c.

4543. Σαμοθρᾴκη {1x} **Samŏthrakē**, *sam-oth-rak'-ay;* from *4544* and Θρᾴκη **Thrakē** (*Thrace*); *Samo-thrace'* (*Samos of Thrace*), an island in the Mediterranean:—Samothracia {1x}. See: BAGD—741d; THAYER—568c.

4544. Σάμος {1x} **Samŏs**, *sam'-os;* of uncert. aff.; *Samus,* an island of the Mediterranean:—*Samos* {1x}. See: BAGD—741d; THAYER—568c.

4545. Σαμουήλ {3x} **Samŏuēl**, *sam-oo-ale';* of Heb. or. [8050]; *Samuel* (i.e. *Shemuel*), an Isr.:—Samuel {3x}. See: BAGD—741d; THAYER—568c.

4546. Σαμψών {1x} **Sampsōn**, *samp-sone';* of Heb. or. [8123]; *Sampson* (i.e. *Shimshon*), an Isr.:—Samson {1x}. See: BAGD—742a; THAYER—568c.

4547. σανδάλιον {2x} **sandaliŏn**, *san-dal'-ee-on;* neut. of a der. of σάνδαλον **sandalŏn** (a "*sandal*"; of uncert. or.); a *slipper* or *sole-pad:*—sandal {2x}. Cf. Mark 6:9; Acts 12:8.

The sandal usually had a wooden sole bound on by straps round the instep and ankle (Mk 6:9; Acts 12:8). See: TDNT—5:310, 702; BAGD—742a; THAYER—568d.

4548. σανίς {1x} **sanis**, *san-ece';* of uncert. aff.; a *plank:*—board {1x}. See: BAGD—742a; THAYER—568d.

4549. Σαούλ {9x} **Saŏul**, *sah-ool';* of Heb. or. [7586]; *Saül* (i.e. *Shaül*), the Jewish name of *Paul:*—Saul (Paul) {8x}, Saul (son of Cis) {1x}. See: BAGD—742a; THAYER—568d. comp. *4569.*

4550. σαπρός {8x} **saprŏs**, *sap-ros';* from *4595; rotten,* i.e. *worthless* (lit. or mor.):—bad {8x}, corrupt {1x}.

Primarily, *sapros* speaks of vegetable and animal substances, expresses what is of poor quality, unfit for use, putrid. It is said of (1) a tree and its fruit (Mt 7:17–18; 12:33; Lk 6:43); (2) certain fish (Mt 13:48 - "bad"); and (3) defiling speech (Eph 4:29). See: TDNT—7:94, 1000; BAGD—742b; THAYER—568d. comp. *4190.*

4551. Σάπφιρα {1x} **Sapphĕirē**, *sap-fi'-ray;* fem. of *4552; Sapphirë,* an Israelitess:—Sapphira {1x}. See: BAGD—742b; THAYER—569a.

4552. σάπιρος {1x} **sapphĕirŏs**, *sap'-fi-ros;* of Heb. or. [5601]; a "*sapphire*" or *lapis-lazuli* gem:—sapphire {1x}.

(1) It was one of the stones in the high priest's breastplate, cf. Ex 28:18; 39:11; (2) as an intimation of its value see Job 28:16; Eze 28:13. (3) The sapphire has various shades of blue and ranks next in hardness to the diamond. See: BAGD—742c; THAYER—569a.

4553. σαργάνη {1x} **sarganē**, *sar-gan'-ay;* appar. of Heb. or. [8276]; a *basket* (as *interwoven* or *wicker-*work:—basket {1x}.

Sargene denotes (1) "a braided rope or band," (2) "a large basket made of ropes, or a wicker "basket" made of entwined twigs, 2 Cor 11:33. (3) That the "basket" in which Paul was let down from a window in Damascus is spoken of by Luke as a *spuris,* and by Paul himself as a *sargane,* is quite consistent, the two terms being used for the same article. See: BAGD—742c; THAYER—569a.

4554. Σάρδεις {3x} **Sardĕis**, *sar'-dice;* plur. of uncert. der.; *Sardis,* a place in Asia Minor:—Sardis {3x}. See: BAGD—742c; THAYER—569a.

4555. σάρδινος {1x} **sardinŏs**, *sar'-dee-nos;* from the same as *4556; sardine* (*3037* being impl.), i.e. a gem, so called:—sardine {1x}.

(1) There are two special varieties, one a yellowish brown, the other a transparent red (like a cornelian). (2) It denotes "the sardian stone." *Sardius* is the word in Rev 4:3, where it formed part of the symbolic appearance of the Lord on His throne, setting forth His glory and majesty in view of the judgment to follow. (3) The beauty of the stone, its transparent brilliance, the high polish of which it is susceptible, made it a favorite among the ancients. (4) It forms the sixth foundation of the wall of the heavenly Jerusalem, Rev 21:20. See: BAGD—742c; THAYER—569a.

4556. σάρδιον {1x} **sardiŏs**, *sar'-dee-os;* prop. an adj. from an uncert. base; *sardian* (*3037* being impl.), i.e. (as noun) the gem so called:—sardius {1x}. See: BAGD—742d; THAYER—569b.

4557. σαρδόνυξ {1x} **sardŏnux**, *sar-don'-oox;* from the base of *4556* and ὄνυξ **ŏnux** (the *nail* of a finger; hence, the "*onyx*" stone); a "*sardonyx*", i.e. the gem so called:—sardonyx {1x}.

(1) A *sardonyx* is a precious stone marked by the red colors of the carnelian (sard) and

the white of the onyx. **(2)** *Saradonux,* a name which indicates the formation of the gem, a layer of sard, and a layer of onyx, marked by the red of the sard and the white of the onyx. **(3)** It was used among the Romans both for cameos and for signets. **(4)** It forms the fifth foundation of the wall of the heavenly Jerusalem, Rev 21:20. See: BAGD – 742d; THAYER – 569b.

4558. **Σάρεπτα** {1x} **Sarĕpta,** *sar'-ep-tah;* of Heb. or. [6886]; *Sarepta* (i.e. *Tsarephath*), a place in Pal.: — *Sarepta* {1x}. See: BAGD – 742d; THAYER – 569b.

4559. **σαρκικός** {11x} **sarkikŏs,** *sar-kee-kos';* from *4561; pertaining to flesh,* i.e. (by extens.) *bodily, temporal,* or (by impl.) *animal, unregenerate:* — carnal {9x}, fleshly {2x}.

Sarkikos, flesh, signifies **(1)** having the nature of flesh, **(1a)** i.e., sensual, controlled by animal appetites, governed by human nature, instead of by the Spirit of God (1 Cor 3:3); **(1b)** having its seat in the animal nature, or excited by it (1 Pet 2:11 – fleshly); **(1c)** as the equivalent of human with the added idea of weakness, figuratively of the weapons of spiritual warfare: i.e. of the flesh, carnal (2 Cor 10:4); or **(1d)** with the idea of unspirituality, of human wisdom, fleshly (2 Cor 1:12); **(2)** pertaining to the flesh, i.e., the body (Rom 15:27; 1 Cor 9:11); **(3)** "pertaining to the natural, transient life of the body," Heb 7:16, "a carnal commandment"; **(4)** given up to the flesh, Rom 7:14, "I am carnal sold under sin"; 1 Cor 3:1. **(5)** In regard to 1 Pet 2:11, *sarkikos* describes the lusts which have their source in man's corrupt and fallen nature, and the man is *sarkikos* who allows to the flesh a place which does not belong to it of right; **(6)** in 1 Cor 3:1, 3–4 *sarkikos* is an accusation graver than *sarkinos* would have been. The Corinthian saints were making no progress, and they were anti-spiritual in respect of the particular point with which the apostle was there dealing. Syn.: S*arkikos* describes the lusts which have their source in man's corrupt and fallen nature, and the man is *sarkikos* who allows to the flesh a place which does not belong to it of right (1 Pet 2:11). *Sarkinos* stresses the material; *sarkikos* the quality. Syn.: 4560, 5591. See: TDNT – 7:98, 1000; BAGD – 742d; THAYER – 569b.

4560. **σάρκινος** {1x} **sarkinŏs,** *sar'-kee-nos;* from *4561; similar to flesh,* i.e. (by anal.) *soft:* — fleshly {1x}.

Sarkinos means "consisting of flesh," 2 Cor 3:3, "fleshy tables of the heart." Syn.: See discussion under 4559. See: TDNT – 7:98, 1000; BAGD – 743a; THAYER – 569c.

4561. **σάρξ** {151x} **sarx,** *sarx;* prob. from the base of *4563; flesh* (as *stripped* of the skin), i.e. (strictly) the *meat* of an animal (as *food*), or (by extens.) the *body* (as opposed to the soul [or spirit], or as the symbol of what is external, or as the means of kindred), or (by impl.) *human nature* (with its frailties [phys. or mor.] and passions), or (spec.) a *human being* (as such): — flesh {147x}, carnal {2x}, carnally minded + 5427 {1x}, fleshly {1x}.

Sarx means **(1)** the substance of the body whether of beasts or of men (1 Cor 15:39); **(2)** the human body (2 Cor 10:3a; Gal 2:20; Phil 1:22); **(3)** by synecdoche, of mankind, in the totality of all that is essential to manhood, i.e., spirit, soul, and body, (Mt 24:22; Jn 1:13; Rom 3:20); **(4)** by synecdoche, of the holy humanity of the Lord Jesus, in the totality of all that is essential to manhood, i.e., spirit, soul, and body (Jn 1:14; 1 Ti 3:16; 1 Jn 4:2; 2 Jn 7; in Heb 5:7, "the days of His flesh," i.e., His past life on earth in distinction from His present life in resurrection; **(5)** by synecdoche, for the complete person (Jn 6:51–57; 2 Cor 7:5; Jas 5:3);

(6) the weaker element in human nature (Mt 26:41; Rom 6:19; 8:3a); **(7)** the unregenerate state of men (Rom 7:5; 8:8, 9); **(8)** the seat of sin in man, but this is not the same thing as in the body (2 Pet 2:18; 1 Jn 2:16); **(9)** the lower and temporary element in the Christian (Gal 3:3; 6:8, and in religious ordinances, Heb 9:10); **(10)** the natural attainments of men (1 Cor 1:26; 2 Cor 10:2, 3b); **(11)** circumstances (1 Cor 7:28; the externals of life, 2 Cor 7:1; Eph 6:5; Heb 9:13); **(12)** by metonymy, the outward and seeming as contrasted with the spirit, the inward and real, (Jn 6:63; 2 Cor 5:16); **(13)** natural relationship, **(13a)** consanguine (1 Cor 10:18; Gal 4:23), or **(13b)** marital (Mt 19:5). See: TDNT – 7:98, 1000; BAGD – 743b; THAYER – 569d.

4562. **Σαρούχ** {1x} **Sarŏuch** *sa-rooch',* or

Σερούχ **Sĕrŏuch,** *seh-rooch';* of Heb. or. [8286]; *Saruch* (i.e. *Serug*), a patriarch: — Saruch {1x}. See: BAGD – 744d; 747c; THAYER – 571d.

4563. **σαρόω** {3x} **sarŏō,** *sar-ŏ'-o;* from a der. of σαίρω **sairō** (to *brush* off; akin to *4951*); mean. a *broom;* to *sweep:* — sweep {3x}. Cf. Mt. 12:44; Lk 11:25; 15:8. See: BAGD – 744d; THAYER – 571d.

4564. **Σάρρα** {4x} **Sarrha,** *sar'-hrah;* of Heb. or. [8283]; *Sarra* (i.e. *Sarah*), the wife of Abraham: — Sara {2x}, Sarah {2x}. See: BAGD – 744d; THAYER – 571d.

4565. **Σάρων** {1x} **Sarōn,** *sar'-one;* of Heb. or. [8289]; *Saron* (i.e. *Sharon*), a

district of Pal.:—*Saron* {1x}. See: BAGD—744d; THAYER—571d.

4566. Σατάν {1x} **Satan**, *sat-an';* of Heb. or. [7854]; *Satan,* i.e. the *devil:—* Satan {1x}. See: TDNT—7:151,*; BAGD—744d; THAYER—571d. comp. 4567.

4567. Σατανᾶς {36x} **Satanas**, *sat-an-as';* of Chald. or. corresp. to *4566* (with the def. aff.); *the accuser,* i.e. the *devil:—* Satan {36x}.

Satanas, a Greek form derived from the Heb, *Satan*), "an adversary," is used **(1)** of an angel of Jehovah in Num 22:22 (the first occurrence of the Word in the OT); **(2)** of men, e.g., 1 Sa 29:4; Ps 38:20; 71:13; four in Ps 109; **(3)** of "*Satan,*" the devil, some seventeen or eighteen times in the OT; in Zec 3:1, where the name receives its interpretation, "to resist him." **(4)** In the NT the word is always used of "*Satan,*" the adversary **(4a)** of God and Christ, e.g., Mt 4:10; 12:26; Mk 1:13; 3:23, 26; 4:15; Lk 4:8; 11:18; 22:3; Jn 13:27; **(4b)** of His people, e.g., Lk 22:31; Acts 5:3; Rom 16:20; 1 Cor 5:5; 7:5; 2 Cor 2:11; 11:14; 12:7; 1 Th 2:18; 1 Ti 1:20; 5:15; Rev 2:9, 13 (twice), 24; 3:9; **(4c)** of mankind, Lk 13:16; Acts 26:18; 2 Th 2:9; Rev 12:9; 20:7. **(5)** His doom, sealed at the Cross, is foretold in its stages in Lk 10:18; Rev 20:2, 10.

(6) Believers are assured of victory over him, Rom 16:20. **(7)** The appellation was given by the Lord to Peter, as a "*Satan*-like" man, on the occasion when he endeavored to dissuade Him from death, Mt 16:23; Mk 8:33. **(8)** "*Satan*" is not simply the personification of evil influences in the heart, for he tempted Christ, in whose heart no evil thought could ever have arisen (Jn 14:30; 2 Cor 5:21; Heb 4:15); **(9)** moreover, his personality is asserted in both the OT and the NT, and especially in the latter, whereas if the OT language was intended to be figurative, the NT would have made this evident. See: TDNT—7:151, 1007; BAGD—744d; THAYER—571d.

4568. σάτον {2x} **satŏn**, *sat'-on;* of Heb. or. [5429]; a certain *measure* for things dry:—measure {2x}.

Saton, as a noun, is a Hebrew dry measure (Heb., *seah*), about a peck and a half, Mt 13:33; Lk 13:21; "three measures" would be the quantity for a baking (cf. Gen 18:6; Judg 6:19; 1 Sa 1:24; the "ephah" of the last two passages was equal to three *sata*). Syn.: 280, 488, 943, 2884, 3313, 3354, 3358, 4057, 5234, 5249, 5518. See: BAGD—745b; THAYER—572a.

4569. Σαῦλος {17x} **Saulŏs**, *sŏw'-los;* of Heb. or., the same as *4549; Saulus*

(i.e. *Shaül*), the Jewish name of *Paul:*—Saul {17x}. See: BAGD—745b; THAYER—572b.

σαυτοῦ sautŏu.etc. See 4572.

4570. σβέννυμι {8x} **sbĕnnumi**, *sben'-noo-mee;* a prol. form of an appar. primary verb; to *extinguish* (lit. or fig.):—go out {1x}, quench {7x}.

Sbennumi is used **(1)** of "quenching" fire or things on fire, Mt 12:20, quoted from Is 42:3, **(1a)** figurative of the condition of the feeble, Heb 11:34; **(1b)** in the passive voice, **(1b1)** Mt 25:8, of torches, "are gone out", lit., "are being quenched"; **(1b2)** of the retributive doom hereafter of sin unrepented of and unremitted in this life, Mk 9:44, 46, 48; **(2)** metaphorically, **(2a)** of "quenching" the fire-tipped darts of the evil one, Eph 6:16; **(2b)** of "quenching" the Spirit, by hindering His operations in oral testimony in the church gatherings of believers, 1 Th 5:19. **(2c)** The peace, order, and edification of the saints were evidence of the ministry of the Spirit among them, 1 Cor 14:26, 32, 33, 40, but if, through ignorance of His ways, or through failure to recognize, or refusal to submit to, them, or through impatience with the ignorance or self-will of others, the Spirit were quenched, these happy results would be absent. For there was always the danger that the impulses of the flesh might usurp the place of the energy of the Spirit in the assembly, and the endeavor to restrain this evil by natural means would have the effect of hindering His ministry also. Apparently then, this injunction was intended to warn believers against the substitution of a mechanical order for the restraints of the Spirit. See: TDNT—7:165, 1009; BAGD—745b; THAYER—572b.

4571. σέ {197x} **sĕ**, *seh;* acc. sing. of *4771; thee:*—thee {178x}, thou {16x}, thy house {1x}, not tr {2x}. See: BAGD—772a [4771]; THAYER—591c [4771].

4572. σεαυτοῦ {40x} **sĕautŏu**, *seh-ŏw-too';* gen. from *4571* and *846;* also dat. of the same,

σεαυτῷ **sĕautŏi**, *seh-ŏw-to';* and acc.

σεαυτόν **sĕautŏn**, *seh-ŏw-ton';* likewise contr.

σαυτοῦ **sautŏu**, *sŏw-too';*

σαυτῷ **sautŏi**, *sŏw-to';* and

σαυτόν **sautŏn**, *sŏw-ton';* respectively; *of* (*with, to*) *thyself:*—thyself {35x}, thine own self {2x}, thou thyself {1x}, thee {1x}, thy {1x}. See: BAGD—745c; THAYER—572b.

4573. σεβάζομαι {1x} **sĕbazŏmai**, *seb-ad'-zom-ahee;* mid. voice from a der. of *4576;* to *venerate,* i.e. *adore:—*worship {1x}.

This word means to worship religiously; through religious practices, Rom 1:25. See: TDNT—7:172, 1010; BAGD—745c; THAYER—572c.

4574. σέβασμα {3x} **sĕbasma**, *seb'-as-mah;* from *4573;* something *adored,* i.e. an *object of worship* (god, altar, etc):—devotion {1x}, that is worshipped {2x}.

(1) It denotes "an object of worship", Acts 17:23; **(2)** in 2 Th 2:4, "that is worshipped"; every object of "worship," whether the true God or pagan idols, will come under the ban of the Man of Sin. See: TDNT—7:173, 1010; BAGD—745d; THAYER—572c.

4575. σεβαστός {3x} **sĕbastŏs**, *seb-as-tos';* from *4573;* venerable *(august),* i.e. (as noun) a title of the Rom. *emperor,* or (as adj.) *imperial:—*Augustus {3x}.

Sebastos, "august, reverent," the masculine gender of an adjective (from *sebas,* "reverential awe"), became used as the title of the Roman emperor, Acts 25:21, 25, "Augustus"; then, taking its name from the emperor, it became a title of honor applied to certain legions or cohorts or battalions, marked for their valor, Acts 27:1. See: TDNT—7:174, 1010; BAGD—745d; THAYER—572c.

4576. σέβομαι {10x} **sĕbŏmai**, *seb'-om-ahee;* mid. voice of an appar. primary verb; to feel awe, to *revere,* i.e. *adore:—*devout {3x}, religious {1x}, worship {6x}.

Sebomai, "to revere," stressing the feeling of awe or devotion, is used of **(1)** "worship" **(1a)** to God, Mt 15:9; Mk 7:7; Acts 16:14; 18:7, 13; **(1b)** to a goddess, Acts 19:27. It also denotes "to feel awe," whether before God or man, "to worship," is translated **(2)** "devout," in Acts 13:50; 17:4, 17; and **(3)** "religious" in Acts 13:43. See: TDNT—7:169, 1010; BAGD—746a; THAYER—572d.

4577. σειρά { {1x} **sĕira**, *si-rah';* prob. from *4951* through its congener εἴρω **ĕirō** (to *fasten;* akin to *138*); a *chain,* (as *binding* or *drawing*):—chain {1x}. See: BAGD—746b; THAYER—572d.

4578. σεισμός {14x} **sĕismŏs**, *sice-mos';* from *4579;* a *commotion,* i.e. (of the air), a *gale* (of the ground), an *earthquake:—*earthquake {13x}, tempest {1x}.

Seismos, "a shaking, a shock," from *seio,* "to move to and fro, to shake," chiefly with the idea of concussion (Eng., "seismic," "seismology," "seismometry"), is used **(1)** of a "tempest"

in the sea, Mt 8:24; **(2)** of "earthquakes," Mt 24:7; 27:54; 28:2; Mk 13:8; Lk 21:11; Acts 16:26; Rev 6:12; 8:5; 11:13 (twice), 19; 16:18 (twice). See: TDNT—7:196, 1014; BAGD—746b; THAYER—572d.

4579. σείω {5x} **sĕiō**, *si'-o;* appar. a primary verb; to *rock* (*vibrate,* prop. sideways or to and fro), i.e. (gen.) to *agitate* (in any direction; cause to *tremble*); fig. to throw into a *tremor* (of fear or concern):—move {1x}, quake {1x}, shake {3x}.

Sio, as a verb, means "to shake, move to and fro," usually of violent concussion [Eng., "seismic," "seismograph," "seismology"], and is said **(1)** of the earth as destined to be shaken by God (Heb 12:26); **(2)** of a local convulsion of the earth, at the death of Christ (Mt 27:51 "did quake"); **(3)** of a fig tree (Rev 6:13); **(4)** metaphorically, to stir up with fear or some other emotion, **(4a)** Mt 21:10 of the people of a city: "And when He was come into Jerusalem, all the city was moved, saying, Who is this?"; **(4b)** Mt 28:4 of the keepers or watchers, at the Lord's tomb ("did shake"). Syn.: 277, 383, 761, 2795, 2796, 3334, 4525, 4531, 4787, 5342. See: TDNT—7:196, 1014; BAGD—746c; THAYER—573a.

4580. Σεκοῦνδος {1x} **Sĕkŏundŏs**, *sek-oon'-dos;* of Lat. or.; "*second*"; *Secundus,* a Chr.:—Secundus {1x}. See: BAGD—746c; THAYER—573a.

4581. Σελεύκεια {1x} **Sĕlĕukĕia**, *sel-yook'-i--ah;* from Σέλευκος **Sĕlĕukŏs**, (*Seleucus,* a Syrian king); *Seleuceia,* a place in Syria:—Seleucia {1x}. See: BAGD—746d; THAYER—573a.

4582. σελήνη {9x} **sĕlēnē**, *sel-ay'-nay;* from σέλας **sĕlas**, (*brilliancy;* prob. akin to the alt. of *138,* through the idea of *attractiveness*); the *moon:—*moon {9x}.

Selene, from *selas,* "brightness" (the Heb. words are *yareach,* "wandering," and *lebanah,* "white"), **(1)** occurs in Mt 24:29; Mk 13:24; Lk 21:25; Acts 2:20; 1 Cor 15:41; Rev 6:12; 8:12; 12:1; 21:23. **(2)** In Rev 12:1, "the moon under her feet" is suggestive of derived authority, just as her being clothed with the sun is suggestive of supreme authority, everything in the symbolism of the passage centers in Israel. In Rev 6:12 the similar symbolism of the sun and "moon" is suggestive of the supreme authority over the world, and of derived authority, at the time of the execution of divine judgments upon nations at the close of the present age. See: BAGD—746d; THAYER—573a.

4583. σεληνιάζομαι {2x} **sĕlēniazŏmai**, *sel-ay-nee-ad'-zom-ahee;*

middle or passive voice from a presumed der. of *4582;* to *be moon-struck,* i.e. *crazy:*—be a lunatick {2x}.

　Seleniazomai, lit., "to be moon struck" (from *selene,* "the moon"), is used in the passive voice with active significance, "*lunatick,*" Mt 4:24; 17:15; the corresponding English word is "lunatic." Epilepsy was supposed to be influenced by the moon. See: BAGD—746d; THAYER—573b.

4584. Σεμεΐ { {1x} **Sĕmëï,** *sem-eh-ee'* or

　Σεμεΐν Sĕmëïn, *sem-eh-een'* of Heb. or. [8096]; *Semeï* (i.e. *Shimi*), an Isr.:—Semei {1x}. See: BAGD—746d; THAYER—573b.

4585. σεμίδαλις {1x} **sĕmidalis,** *sem-id'-al-is;* prob. of for. origin; fine wheaten *flour:*—fine flour {1x}. See: BAGD—746b; THAYER—573b.

4586. σεμνός {4x} **sĕmnŏs,** *sem-nos';* from *4576; venerable,* i.e. *honorable:*—grave {3x}, honest {1x}.

　(1) One who is *semnos* is well ordered in his earthly life and has a grace and dignity derived from his heavenly citizenship. **(2)** There is something majestic and awe-inspiring about one who is *semnos;* he does not repel but invites and attracts. **(3)** It first denoted "reverend, august, venerable" (akin to *sebomai,* "to reverence"); then, **(4)** "serious, grave," whether **(4a)** of persons, 1 Ti 3:8, 11 (deacons and their wives); Titus 2:2 (aged men); or **(4b)** things, Phil 4:8, "honest." **(5)** It denotes what inspires reverence and awe. **(6)** The word points to seriousness of purpose and to self-respect in conduct. Syn.: 2412, 2887. See: TDNT—7:191, 1010; BAGD—746d; THAYER—573b.

4587. σεμνότης {3x} **sĕmnŏtēs,** *sem-not'-ace;* from *4586; venerableness,* i.e. *probity:*—gravity {2x}, honesty {1x}.

　(1) *Semnotes* is the characteristic of a person that entitles him to reverence and respect, dignity, majesty, and sanctity. **(2)** It denotes "venerableness, dignity, honesty"; **(2a)** it is a necessary characteristic of the life and conduct of Christians, 1 Ti 2:2, "honesty" which flows from a life of gravity; **(2b)** a qualification of a bishop or overseer in a church, in regard to his children, 1 Ti 3:4, "gravity"; **(2c)** a necessary characteristic of the teaching imparted by a servant of God, Titus 2:7, "gravity." See: TDNT—7:191, 1010; BAGD—747a; THAYER—573b.

4588. Σέργιος {1x} **Sĕrgiŏs,** *serg'-ee-os;* of Lat. or.; *Sergius,* a Rom.:—Sergius (Paulus) {1x}. See: BAGD—747b; THAYER—573b.

4589. Σήθ {1x} **Sēth,** *sayth;* of Heb. or. [8352]; *Seth* (i.e. *Sheth*), a patriarch:—Seth {1x}. See: BAGD—747c; THAYER—573b.

4590. Σήμ {1x} **Sēm,** *same;* of Heb. or. [8035]; *Sem* (i.e. *Shem*), a patriarch:—Sem {1x}. See: BAGD—747c; THAYER—573c.

4591. σημαίνω {6x} **sēmainō,** *say-mah'-ee-no;* from σῆμα **sēma** (a *mark;* of uncert. der.); to make a sign, *indicate:*—signify {6x}.

　'*Semaino,* "to give a sign, indicate" (*sema,* "a sign"), "to signify," is so translated in Jn 12:33; 18:32; 21:19; Acts 11:28; 25:27; Rev 1:1, where perhaps the suggestion is that of expressing by signs. See: TDNT—7:262, 1015; BAGD—747c; THAYER—573c.

4592. σημεῖον {77x} **sēmĕïŏn,** *say-mi'-on;* neut. of a presumed der. of the base of *4591;* an *indication,* espec. cerem. or supernat.:—miracle {23x}, sign {50x}, token {1x}, wonder {3x}.

　(1) *Semeion* is a manifest deed, having in itself an explanation of something hidden and secret. **(2)** It denotes "a sign, mark, indication, token," is used **(2a)** of that which distinguished a person or thing from others, e.g., Mt 26:48; Lk 2:12; Rom 4:11; 2 Cor 12:12 (1st part); 2 Th 3:17, "token," i.e., his autograph attesting the authenticity of his letters; **(2b)** of a "sign" as a warning or admonition, e.g., Mt 12:39, "the sign of (i.e., consisting of) the prophet Jonas"; 16:4; Lk 2:34; 11:29, 30; **(2c)** of miraculous acts, "miracles", **(2c1)** as tokens of divine authority and power, e.g., Mt 12:38, 39 (1st part); Jn 2:11, 23; 3:2; 4:54; 6:2, 14, 26; 7:31; 9:16; 10:41; 11:47; 12:18, 37; 20:30; in 1 Cor 1:22, "the Jews ask for a sign" indicates that the apostles were met with the same demand from Jews as Christ had been. Signs were vouchsafed in plenty, signs of God's power and love, but these were not the signs which they sought. They wanted signs of an outward messianic kingdom, of temporal triumph, of material greatness for the chosen people. With such cravings the gospel of a "crucified Messiah" was to them a stumblingblock indeed, 1 Cor 14:22; **(2c2)** by devils, Rev 16:14; **(2c3)** by false teachers or prophets, indications of assumed authority, e.g., Mt 24:24; Mk 13:22; **(2c4)** by Satan through his special agents, 2 Th 2:9; Rev 13:13, 14; 19:20; **(2c5)** of tokens portending future events, e. g., Mt 24:3, where "the sign of the Son of Man" signifies, subjectively, that the Son of Man is Himself the "sign" of what He is about to do; Mk 13:4; Lk 21:7, 11, 25; Acts 2:19; Rev 12:1; 3; 15:1.

　(3) "Signs" confirmatory of what God had accomplished in the atoning sacrifice of Christ,

His resurrection and ascension, and of the sending of the Holy Spirit, were given to the Jews for their recognition, as at Pentecost, and supernatural acts by apostolic ministry, as well as by the supernatural operations in the churches, such as the gift of tongues and prophesyings; there is no record of the continuance of these latter after the circumstances recorded in Acts 19:1–20. Syn.: 1411, 1741, 2297, 3167, 3861, 5059. See: TDNT—7:200, 1015; BAGD—747d; THAYER—573c.

4593. σημειόω {1x} sēmĕiŏō, *say-mi-ŏ'-o;* from *4592;* to *distinguish,* i.e. *mark* (for avoidance):—to note {1x}.

Semeioo means to mark, to note and being in the middle voice stresses to note for oneself; an injunction to take cautionary note of one who refuses obedience to the apostle's word (2 Th 3:14). See: TDNT—7:265, 1015; BAGD—748d; THAYER—574a.

4594. σήμερον {41x} sēmĕrŏn, *say'-mer-on;* neut. (as adv.) of a presumed compound of the art. *3588* (τ changed to ς) and *2250;* on *the* (i.e. *this*) *day* (or *night* current or just passed); gen. *now* (i.e. at *present, hitherto*):—this day {22x}, to day {18x}, this + 3588 {1x}.

Semeron, an adverb, is **(1)** used frequently in **(1a)** Mt, Lk; and **(1b)** in Acts it is always rendered "this day"; **(1c)** in Heb **(1c1)** 1:5; 5:5, "to day", in the same quotation; **(1c2)** "today" in 3:7, 13, 15; 4:7 (twice); 13:8; also Jas 4:13. **(2)** The clause containing *semeron* is **(2a)** sometimes introduced by the conjunction *hoti,* "that," e.g., Mk 14:30; Lk 4:21; 19:9; **(2b)** sometimes without the conjunction, e.g., Lk 22:34; 23:43, where "today" is to be attached to the next statement, "shalt thou be with Me"; there are no grammatical reasons for the insistence that the connection must be with the statement "Verily I say unto thee." **(3)** In Rom 11:8 and 2 Cor 3:14, 15, the lit. rendering is "unto the today day." **(4)** In Heb 4:7, the "today" of Ps 95:7 is evidently designed to extend to the present period of the Christian faith. See: TDNT—7:269, 1024; BAGD—749a; THAYER—574a.

4595. σήπω {1x} sēpō, *say'-po;* appar. a primary verb; to *putrefy,* i.e. (fig.) *perish:*—be corrupted {1x}.

(1) The verb is derived from a root signifying to rot off, drop to pieces. **(2)** It signifies "to make corrupt, to destroy"; in the passive voice with middle sense, "to become corrupt or rotten, to perish," said of riches, Jas 5:2, of the gold and silver of the luxurious rich who have ground down their laborers. See: TDNT—7:94, 1000; BAGD—749b; THAYER—574b.

4596. σηρικός {1x} sērikŏs, *say-ree-kos'* or

σιρικός sirikŏs, *see-ree-kos';* from Σήρ **Sēr** (an Indian tribe from whom *silk* was procured; hence, the name of the *silkworm*); *Seric,* i.e. *silken* (neut. as noun, a *silky* fabric):—silk {1x}. See: BAGD—749b; 751d; THAYER—574b.

4597. σής {3x} sēs, *sace;* appar. of Heb. or. [5580]; a clothes *moth:*—moth {3x}. *Ses* denotes "a clothes moth," Mt 6:19, 20; Lk 12:33. See: TDNT—7:275, 1025; BAGD—749b; THAYER—574c.

4598. σητόβρωτος {1x} sētŏbrōtŏs, *say-tob'-ro-tos;* from *4597* and a der. of *977;* *moth-eaten:*—motheaten {1x}. See: TDNT—7:275, 1025; BAGD—749c; THAYER—574c.

4599. σθενόω {1x} sthĕnŏō, *sthen-ŏ'-o;* from σθένος sthĕnŏs, (bodily *vigor;* prob. akin to the base of *2476*); to *strengthen,* i.e. (fig.) *confirm* (in spiritual knowledge and power):—strengthen {1x}. See: BAGD—749c; THAYER—574c.

4600. σιαγών {2x} siagōn, *see-ag-one';* of uncert. der.; the *jaw*-bone, i.e. (by impl.) the *cheek* or side of the face:—cheek {2x}. Cf. Mt 5:39; Lk 6:29. See: BAGD—749c; THAYER—574c.

4601. σιγάω {9x} sigaō, *see-gah'-o;* from *4602;* to *keep silent* (tran. or intr.):—hold (one's) peace {4x}, keep silence {3x}, keep close {1x}, keep secret {1x}.

Sigao signifies **(1)** used intransitively, **(1a)** "to be silent" (from *sige,* "silence"), translated "to hold one's peace," in Lk 20:26; Acts 12:17; 15:13; 1 Cor 14:34; **(1b)** "kept silence", Acts 15:12; 1 Cor 14:28, 30; **(1c)** "kept close" in Lk 9:36; **(2)** used transitively, "to keep secret"; in the passive voice, "to be kept secret," Rom 16:25. See: BAGD—749c; THAYER—574c.

4602. σιγή {2x} sigē, *see-gay';* appr. from σίζω sizō (to *hiss,* i.e. *hist* or *hush*); *silence:*—silence {2x}.

Sige occurs in **(1)** Acts 21:40; and **(2)** Rev 8:1, where the "silence" is introductory to the judgments following the opening of the seventh seal. See: BAGD—749d; THAYER—574c. comp. *4623.*

4603. σιδήρεος {5x} sidērĕŏs, *sid-ay'-reh-os;* from *4604;* made *of iron:*—of iron {4x}, iron {1x}.

Sidereos "of iron," occurs in **(1)** Acts 12:10, of an iron gate; and **(2)** "of iron," Rev 2:27; 9:9; 12:5; 19:15. See: BAGD—750a; THAYER—574d.

4604. σίδηρος {1x} **sidērŏs,** *sid'-ay-ros;* of uncert. der.; *iron:*—iron {1x}. See: BAGD—750a; THAYER—574d.

4605. Σιδών {11x} **Sidōn,** *sid-one';* of Heb. or. [6721]; *Sidon* (i.e. *Tsidon*), a place in Pal.:—*Sidon* {11x}. See: BAGD—750a; THAYER—574d.

4606. Σιδώνιος {1x} **Sidōniŏs,** *sid-o'-nee-os;* from *4605;* a *Sidonian,* i.e. inhab. of Sidon:—of Sidon {1x}. See: BAGD—750b; THAYER—574d.

4607. σικάριος {1x} **sikariŏs,** *sik-ar'-ee-os;* of Lat. or.; a *dagger-man* or *assassin;* a *freebooter* (Jewish *fanatic* outlawed by the Romans):—murderer {1x}.

The *sikarios* derived his name from the sica, a short sword that he wore and was prompt to use; he was a hired mercernary or swordsman. They were hired assassins. Concealing their short swords under their garments and mingling with the crowd at the great feasts, the *sicari* would stab their enemies and then join the bystanders in exclamations of horror, thus effectively averting suspicion from themselves, Acts 21:38. Syn.: 443, 5406. See: TDNT—7:278, 1026; BAGD—750b; THAYER—574d. comp. *5406.*

4608. σίκερα {1x} **sikĕra,** *sik'-er-ah;* of Heb. or. [7941]; an *intoxicant,* i.e. intensely fermented *liquor:*—strong drink {1x}.

Sikera is strong drink, an intoxicating beverage, different from wine; it was an artificial product, made of a mixture of sweet ingredients, whether derived from grain and vegetables, or from the juice of fruits (dates), or a decoction of honey (Lk 1:15). See: BAGD—750b; THAYER—574d.

4609. Σίλας {13x} **Silas,** *see'-las;* contr. for *4610;* *Silas,* a Chr.:—*Silas* {13x}. See: BAGD—750c; THAYER—575a.

4610. Σιλουανός {4x} **Silŏuanŏs,** *sil-oo-an-os';* of Lat. or.; *"silvan;"* *Silvanus,* a Chr.:—Silvanus {4x}. See: BAGD—750c; THAYER—575b. comp. *4609.*

4611. Σιλωάμ {3x} **Silōam,** *sil-o-am';* of Heb. or. [7975]; *Siloam* (i.e. *Shiloäch*), a pool of Jerusalem:—*Siloam* {3x}. See: BAGD—750d; THAYER—575b.

4612. σιμικίνθιον {1x} **simikinthiŏn,** *sim-ee-kin'-thee-on;* of Lat. or.; a *semicinctium* or *half-girding,* i.e. narrow covering (*apron*):—apron {1x}.

Simikinthion, "a thing girded round half the body" (Latin, *semicinctium*), was a narrow apron, or linen covering, worn by workmen

and servants, Acts 19:12. See: BAGD—751a; THAYER—575c.

4613. Σίμων {75x} **Simōn,** *see'-mone;* of Heb. or. [8095]; *Simon* (i.e. *Shimon*), the name of nine Isr.:—*Simon* (Peter) {49x}, *Simon* (Zelotes) {4x}, *Simon* (father of Judas) {4x}, *Simon* (Magus) {4x}, *Simon* (the tanner) {4x}, *Simon* (the Pharisee) {3x}, *Simon* (of Cyrene) {3x}, *Simon* (brother of Jesus) {2x}, *Simon* (the leper) {2x}. See: BAGD—751a; THAYER—575c. comp. *4826.*

4614. Σινά {4x} **Sina,** *see-nah';* of Heb. or. [5514]; *Sina* (i.e. *Sinai*), a mountain in Arabia:—*Sina* {2x}, Sinai {2x}. See: TDNT—7:282, 1026; BAGD—751c; THAYER—575d.

4615. σίναπι {5x} **sinapi,** *sin'-ap-ee;* perh. from σίνομαι **sinŏmai** (to *hurt,* i.e. *sting*); *mustard* (the plant):—mustard seed {5x}.

(1) *Sinapi* is mustard, the name of a plant **(1a)** which in oriental countries grows from a very small seed and attains to the height of a tree, 10 feet (3 m) and more; **(1b)** hence a very small quantity of a thing is likened to a mustard seed, and also a thing which grows to a remarkable size. **(2)** It is translated "mustard seed" in the NT. **(2a)** The conditions to be fulfilled by the mustard are that it should be a familiar plant, with a very small seed, Mt 17:20; Lk 17:6, sown in the earth, growing larger than garden herbs, Mt 13:31, having large branches, Mk 4:31, attractive to birds, Lk 13:19. **(2b)** The cultivated mustard is *sinapis nigra.* The seed is well known for its minuteness. The mustards are annuals, reproduced with extraordinary rapidity. **(3)** The translation in Mt 13:32, "greatest among herbs" should be noted. **(3a)** As the parable indicates, Christendom presents a sort of Christianity that has become conformed to the principles and ways of the world, and the world has favored this debased Christianity. **(3b)** Contrast the testimony of the NT, e.g., in Jn 17:14; Gal 6:14; 1 Pet 2:11; 1 Jn 3:1. See: TDNT—7:287, 1027; BAGD—751c; THAYER—575d.

4616. σινδών {6x} **sindōn,** *sin-done';* of uncert. (perh. for.) or.; *byssos,* i.e. bleached *linen* (the cloth or a garment of it):—linen cloth {3x}, linen {2x}, fine linen {1x}.

(1) *Sindon* is a linen cloth, esp. that which was fine and costly, in which the bodies of the dead were wrapped. **(2)** It was "a fine linen cloth, an article of domestic manufacture" (Prov 31:24) used **(2a)** as a garment or wrap, the "linen cloth" of Mk 14:51, 52; **(2b)** as shrouds or winding sheets, Mt 27:59; Mk 15:46, "linen"; Lk 23:53. See: BAGD—751c; THAYER—576a.

4617. σινιάζω {1x} **siniazō**, *sin-ee-ad'-zo;* from σινίον **siniŏn**, (a sieve); to *riddle* (fig.):—sift {1x}.

Siniazo means to sift, shake in a sieve; figuratively, by inward agitation to try one's faith to the verge of overthrow (Lk 22:31). See: TDNT—7:291, 1028; BAGD—751d; THAYER—576b.

σῖτα sita. See *4621.*

4618. σιτευτός {3x} **sitĕutŏs**, *sit-yoo-tos';* from a der. of *4621; grain-fed,* i.e. *fattened:*—fatted {3x}.

The fatted calf was one isolated and grain-fed to fatten in order to secure tender meat for feasts, Lk 15:23, 37, 30. See: BAGD—752a; THAYER—576b.

4619. σιτιστός {1x} **sitistŏs**, *sit-is-tos';* from a der. of *4621; grained,* i.e. *fatted:*—fatling {1x}. See: BAGD—752a; THAYER—576b.

4620. σιτομέτρον {1x} **sitŏmĕtrŏn**, *sit-om'-et-ron;* from *4621* and *3358;* a *grain-measure,* i.e. (by impl.) *ration* (*allowance* of food):—portion of meat {1x}. See: BAGD—752a; THAYER—576b.

4621. σῖτος {14x} **sitŏs**, *see'-tos;* plur. irreg. neut.

σῖτα sita, *see'-tah;* of uncert. der.; *grain*, espec. *wheat:*—corn {2x}, wheat {12x}.

(1) *Sita* speaks of any grain in which is the hard seed of any cereal plant; especially wheat; [corn in Eng. is generic for grain]. **(2)** *Sitos* is "wheat, corn"; in the plural, "grain," is translated **(2a)** "corn" in Mk 4:28; Acts 7:12; and **(2b)** "wheat" in Mt 3:12; 13:25, 29–30; Lk 3:17; 16:7; 22:31; Jn 12:24; Acts 27:38; 1 Cor 15:37; Rev 6:6; 18:13. See: BAGD—752b; THAYER—576b.

4622. Σιών {7x} **Siōn**, *see-own';* of Heb. or. [6726]; *Sion* (i.e. *Tsijon*), a hill of Jerusalem; fig. the *church* (militant or triumphant):—*Sion* {7x}. See: TDNT—7:292, 1028; BAGD—752b; THAYER—576c.

4623. σιωπάω {11x} **siōpaō**, *see-o-pah'-o;* from σιωπή **siōpē**, (*silence,* i.e. a *hush;* prop. *muteness,* i.e. *involuntary* stillness, or *inability* to speak; and thus differing from *4602,* which is rather a voluntary *refusal* or *indisposition* to speak, although the terms are often used synonymously); to *be dumb* (but not *deaf* also, like *2974* prop.); fig. to *be calm* (as *quiet* water):—hold (one's) peace {9x}, peace {1x}, dumb {1x}.

Siopao, "to be silent or still, to keep silence" (from *siope,* "silence"), is translated **(1)** "to

hold one's peace," in Mt 20:31; 26:63; Mk 3:4; 4:39; 10:48; 14:61; Lk 18:39; 19:40; Acts 18:9; **(2)** in the Lord's command to the sea, in Mk 4:39, it is translated "peace (be still)"; **(3)** in Lk 1:20, "dumb", is used of Zacharias' "dumbness": "And, behold, thou shalt be dumb, and not able to speak, until the day that these things shall be performed, because thou believest not my words, which shall be fulfilled in their season." Syn.: 216, 880, 2974. See: BAGD—752c; THAYER—576d.

4624. σκανδαλίζω {30x} **skandalizō**, *skandal-id'-zo* ("scandalize"); from *4625;* to *entrap,* i.e. *trip* up (fig. *stumble* [tran.] or *entice* to sin, apostasy or displeasure):—make to offend {2x}, offend {28x}.

Skandalizo means **(1)** to put a stumbling block or impediment in the way, upon which another may trip and fall; **(1a)** metaph. to offend; **(1b)** to entice to sin; **(1c)** to cause a person to begin to distrust and desert one whom he ought to trust and obey; **(1c1)** to cause to fall away; **(1c2)** to be offended in one, i.e. to see in another what I disapprove of and what hinders me from acknowledging his authority; **(1c3)** to cause one to judge unfavorably or unjustly of another. **(2)** Since one who stumbles or whose foot gets entangled feels annoyed, *skandalizo* also means **(2a)** to cause one displeasure at a thing; or **(2b)** to make indignant. **(3)** It signifies "to put a snare or stumblingblock in the way," always **(3a)** metaphorically in the NT: **(3b)** 14 times in Mt, 8 in Mk, twice in Lk, twice in Jn; **(3c)** elsewhere in 1 Cor 8:13 (twice) and 2 Cor 11:29; Rom 14:21. See: TDNT—7:339, 1036; BAGD—752d; THAYER—576d.

4625. σκάνδαλον {15x} **skandalŏn**, *skan'-dal-on* ("scandal"); prob. from a der. of *2578;* a *trap-stick* (*bent* sapling), i.e. *snare* (fig. *cause* of displeasure or sin):—offence {9x}, stumbling block {3x}, occasion of stumbling {1x}, occasion to fall {1x}, thing that offends {1x}.

Skandalon, **(1)** originally was "the name of the part of a trap to which the bait is attached, hence, the trap or snare itself, as **(1a)** in Rom 11:9, "stumblingblock," quoted from Ps 69:22, and **(1b)** in Rev 2:14, for Balaam's device was rather a trap for Israel than a stumblingblock to them, and **(1c)** in Mt 16:23, for in Peter's words the Lord perceived a snare laid for Him by Satan. **(2)** In NT *skandalon* is always used metaphorically, and **(2a)** ordinarily of anything that arouses prejudice, or **(2b)** becomes a hindrance to others, or **(2c)** causes them to fall by the way. **(2d)** Sometimes the hindrance is in itself good, and those stumbled by it are the wicked. Thus it is used **(2d1)** of Christ in Rom

Greek

9:33, "(a rock) of offense"; cf. 1 Pet 2:8; 1 Cor 1:23, "stumblingblock"), and **(2d2)** of His cross, Gal 5:11; **(2d3)** of the "table" provided by God for Israel, Rom 11:9; **(2e)** of that which is evil, e.g., **(2e1)** Mt 13:41, "things that offend", lit., "all stumblingblocks"; **(2e2)** Mt 18:7, "occasions of stumbling" and "occasion"; Lk 17:1; **(2e3)** Rom 14:13, "an occasion to fall", said of such a use of Christian liberty as proves a hindrance to another; **(2e4)** Rom 16:17, "offences", said of the teaching of things contrary to sound doctrine; **(2e5)** 1 Jn 2:10, "occasion of stumbling," of the absence of this in the case of one who loves his brother and thereby abides in the light. Love, then, is the best safeguard against the woes pronounced by the Lord upon those who cause others to stumble. See: TDNT—7:339, 1036; BAGD—753a; THAYER—577a.

4626. **σκάπτω** {3x} **skaptō**, *skap'-to;* appar. a primary verb; to *dig:*—dig {3x}.

Skapto, primarily, "to dig, by way of hollowing out," hence, denotes "to dig." The root *skap* is seen in *skapane,* "a spade," *skapetos,* "a ditch," *skaphe,* "a boat," and in Eng., "scoop, skiff, and ship" (i.e., something hollowed out). The verb is found in Lk 6:48; 13:8; 16:3. See: BAGD—753b; THAYER—577b.

4627. **σκάφη** {3x} **skaphē**, *skaf'-ay;* a *"skiff"* (as if *dug* out), or *yawl* (carried aboard a large vessel for landing):—boat {3x}.

Skaphe is, lit., "anything dug or scooped out" (from *skapto,* "to dig"), "as a trough, a tub, and hence a light boat, or skiff, a boat belonging to a larger vessel," Acts 27:16, 30, 32. See: BAGD—753c; THAYER—577c.

4628. **σκέλος** {3x} **skĕlŏs**, *skel'-os;* appar. from σκέλλω **skĕllō**, (to *parch;* through the idea of *leanness*); the *leg* (as *lank*):—leg {3x}.

Skello, "the leg from the hip downwards," is used only of the breaking of the "legs" of the crucified malefactors, to hasten their death, Jn 19:31–33; a customary act, not carried out in the case of Christ, in fulfillment of Ex 12:46; Num 9:12. The practice was known as *skelokopia* (from *kopto,* "to strike"), or, in Latin, *crurifragium* (from *crus,* "a leg," and *frango,* "to break"). See: BAGD—753c; THAYER—577c.

4629. **σκέπασμα** {1x} **skĕpasma**, *skep'-as-mah;* from a der. of σκέπας **skĕpas** (a *covering;* perh. akin to the base of *4649,* through the idea of *noticeableness*); *clothing:*—raiment {1x}.

Skepasma, "a covering" (*skepazo,* "to cover"), strictly, "a roofing," then, "any kind of

shelter or covering," is used in the plural in 1 Ti 6:8, "raiment", outer clothing which covers others. See: BAGD—753d; THAYER—577c.

4630. **Σκευᾶς** {1x} **Skĕuas**, *skyoo-as';* appar. of Lat. or.; *left-handed; Scevas* (i.e. *Scœvus*), an Isr.:—Sceva {1x}. See: BAGD—753d; THAYER—577c.

4631. **σκευή** {1x} **skĕuē**, *skyoo-ay';* from *4632; furniture,* i.e. spare *tackle:*—tackling {1x}. See: BAGD—754a; THAYER—577c.

4632. **σκεῦος** {23x} **skĕuŏs**, *skyoo'-os;* of uncert. aff.; a *vessel, implement, equipment* or *apparatus* (lit. or fig. [spec. a *wife* as contributing to the usefulness of the husband]):—goods {2x}, sail {1x}, stuff {1x}, vessel {19x}.

Skeuos is used **(1)** of "a vessel or implement" of various kinds, Mk 11:16; Lk 8:16; Jn 19:29; Acts 10:11, 16; 11:5; 27:17 (a sail); Rom 9:21; 2 Ti 2:20; Heb 9:21; Rev 2:27; 18:12; **(2)** of "goods or household stuff," Mt 12:29 and Mk 3:27, "goods"; Lk 17:31, "stuff"; **(3)** of "persons," **(3a)** for the service of God, **(3a1)** Acts 9:15, "a (chosen) vessel"; **(3a2)** 2 Ti 2:21, "a vessel (unto honor)"; **(3b)** the "subjects" of divine wrath, Rom 9:22; **(3c)** the "subjects" of divine mercy, Rom 9:23; **(3d)** the human frame, **(3d1)** 2 Cor 4:7; **(3d2)** perhaps 1 Th 4:4; **(3d3)** a husband of his wife, 1 Pet 3:7; **(3d4)** of the wife, probably, 1 Th 4:4; **(3d5)** while the exhortation to each one "to possess himself of his own vessel in sanctification and honor" is regarded by some as referring to the believer's body [cf Rom 6:13; 1 Cor 9:27], the view that the "vessel" signifies the wife, and that the reference is to the sanctified maintenance of the married state, is supported by the facts that in 1 Pet 3:7 the same word *time,* "honor," is used with regard to the wife, again in Heb 13:4, *timios,* "honorable" is used in regard to marriage; further, the preceding command in 1 Th 4 is against fornication, and the succeeding one (v. 6) is against adultery. See: TDNT—7:358, 1038; BAGD—754a; THAYER—577c.

4633. **σκηνή** {20x} **skēnē**, *skay-nay';* appar. akin to *4632* and *4639;* a *tent* or cloth hut (lit. or fig.):—habitation {1x}, tabernacle {19x}.

Skene, "a tent, booth, tabernacle," is used of **(1)** tents as dwellings, Mt 17:4; Mk 9:5; Lk 9:33; Heb 11:9, "tabernacles"; **(2)** the Mosaic tabernacle, Acts 7:44; Heb 8:5; 9:8, 21, termed "tabernacle", where the people were called to meet God; the outer part 9:2, 6; the inner sanctuary, 9:3; **(3)** the heavenly prototype, Heb 8:2; 9:11; Rev 13:6; 15:5; 21:3 (of its future descent); **(4)** the eternal abodes of the saints, Lk 16:9,

"habitations"; **(5)** the Temple in Jerusalem, as continuing the service of the tabernacle, Heb 13:10; **(6)** the house of David, i.e., metaphorically of his people, Acts 15:16; **(7)** the portable shrine of the god Moloch, Acts 7:43. See: TDNT—7:368, 1040; BAGD—754c; THAYER—577d.

4634. σκηνοπηγία {1x} **skēnŏpēgia**, *skay-nop-ayg-ee'-ah;* from *4636* and *4078;* the *Festival of Tabernacles* (so called from the custom of erecting booths for temporary homes):—tabernacles {1x}.

Skenopegia, properly "the setting up of tents or dwellings", represents the word "tabernacles" in "the feast of tabernacles," Jn 7:2. **NOTE:** This feast, one of the three pilgrimage feasts in Israel, is called "the feast of ingathering" in Ex 23:16; 34:22; it took place at the end of the year, and all males were to attend at the "tabernacle" with their offerings. In Lev 23:34; Deut 16:13, 16; 31:10; 2 Chr 8:13; Ezra 3:4 (cf. Neh 8:14–18), it is called "the feast of tabernacles" (or "booths," *sukkoth*), and was appointed for seven days at Jerusalem from the 15th to the 22nd Tishri (approximately October), to remind the people that their fathers dwelt in these in the wilderness journeys. Cf. Num 29:15–38, especially v. 35–38, for the regulations of the eighth or "last day, the great day of the feast" (Jn 7:37). See: TDNT—7:390, 1040; BAGD—754d; THAYER—578b.

4635. σκηνοποιός {1x} **skēnŏpŏiŏs**, *skay-nop-oy-os';* from *4633* and *4160;* a *manufacturer of tents:*—tentmaker {1x}. See: TDNT—7:393, 1040; BAGD—755a; THAYER—578c.

4636. σκῆνος {2x} **skēnŏs**, *skay'-nos;* from *4633;* a *hut* or temporary residence, i.e. (fig.) the human *body* (as the abode of the spirit):—tabernacle {2x}.

Skenos is used metaphorically of the body as the "tabernacle" of the soul, 2 Cor 5:1, 4; stressing the temporary nature of the body. See: TDNT—7:381, 1040; BAGD—755b; THAYER—578c.

4637. σκηνόω {5x} **skēnŏō**, *skay-nŏ'-o;* from *4636;* to *tent* or *encamp,* i.e. (fig.) to *occupy* (as a mansion) or (spec.) to *reside* (as God did in the Tabernacle of old, a symbol of protection and communion):—dwell {5x}.

Skenoo, "to pitch a tent" (*skene*), "to tabernacle," is translated **(1)** "dwelt," in Jn 1:14; **(2)** in Rev 7:15, "shall dwell"; **(3)** in Rev 12:12; 13:6; 21:3, "dwell." See: TDNT—7:385, 1040; BAGD—755c; THAYER—578c.

4638. σκήνωμα {3x} **skēnōma**, *skay'-no-mah;* from *4637;* an *encampment,* i.e. (fig.) the *Temple* (as God's residence), the *body* (as a tenement for the soul):—tabernacle {3x}.

Skenoma, "a booth," or "tent pitched", is used **(1)** of the Temple as God's dwelling, as that which David desired to build, Acts 7:46, "tabernacle"; and **(2)** metaphorically of the body as a temporary tabernacle, 2 Pet 1:13, 14. See: TDNT—7:383, 1040; BAGD—755c; THAYER—578d.

4639. σκιά {7x} **skia**, *skee-ah';* appar. a primary word; "*shade*" or a shadow (lit. or fig. [darkness of *error* or an *adumbration*]):—shadow {7x}.

Skia is used **(1)** of "a shadow," **(1a)** caused by the interception of light, Mk 4:32; Acts 5:15; **(1b)** metaphorically of the darkness and spiritual death of ignorance, Mt 4:16; Lk 1:79; **(2)** of "the image" or "outline" cast by an object, **(2a)** Col 2:17, of ceremonies under the Law; **(2b)** of the tabernacle and its appurtenances and offerings, Heb 8:5; **(3)** of these as appointed under the Law, Heb 10:1. See: TDNT—7:394, 1044; BAGD—755d; THAYER—578d.

4640. σκιρτάω {3x} **skirtaō**, *skeer-tah'-o;* akin to σκαίρω **skairō**, (to *skip*); to *jump,* i.e. sympathetically *move* (as the *quickening* of a fetus):—leap {2x}, leap for joy {1x}.

Skiptao, "to leap," is found **(1)** in Lk 1:4, and 6:23, there translated "leap for joy"; **(2)** in Lk 1:44 the words "for joy" are expressed separately. See: TDNT—7:401, 1046; BAGD—755d; THAYER—578d.

4641. σκληροκαρδία {3x} **sklērŏkardia**, *sklay-rok-ar-dee'-ah;* fem. of a compound of *4642* and *2588;* *hardheartedness,* i.e. (spec.) *destitution of* (spiritual) *perception:*—hardness of heart {3x}.

Sklerokardia, "hardness of heart" (*skleros,* "hard," and *kardia*), is used in Mt 19:8; Mk 10:5; 16:14. See: TDNT—3:613, 415; BAGD—756a; THAYER—579a.

4642. σκληρός {6x} **sklērŏs**, *sklay-ros';* from the base of *4628; dry,* i.e. *hard* or *tough* (fig. *harsh, severe*):—fierce {1x}, hard {5x}.

(1) *Skleros* is applied to someone who takes a serious approach to life and is rough, harsh, inhuman, uncivil and intractable in his moral nature. **(2)** *Skleros* is used **(2a)** of the character of a man, Mt 25:24; **(2b)** of a saying, Jn 6:60; **(2c)** of the difficulty and pain of kicking against the ox-goads, Acts 9:5; 26:14; **(2d)** of rough winds, Jas 3:4 and **(2e)** of harsh speeches, Jude 15. **(3)** In Jas 3:4, *skleros,* "hard, rough,

violent," is said of winds, "fierce." Syn.: Synonymous with *austeros* (*840*) but to be distinguished from it, is *skleros* (from *skello*, "to be dry"). *Austeros* was applied to that which lacks moisture, and so is rough and disageeable to the touch, and hence came to denote "harsh, stern, hard." It is used by Matthew to describe the unprofitable servant's remark concerning his master, in the parable corresponding to that in Lk 19. *Austeros* is derived from a word having to do with the taste, *skleros,* "with the touch." *Austeros* is not necessarily a term of reproach, whereas *skleros* is always so, and indicates a harsh, even inhuman character. *Austeros* is rather the exaggeration of a virtue pushed too far, than an absolute vice. See: TDNT—5:1028, 816; BAGD—756a; THAYER—579a.

4643. σκληρότης {1x} **sklērŏtēs,** *sklay-rot'-ace;* from *4642; callousness,* i.e. (fig.) *stubbornness:*—hardness {1x}. See: TDNT—5:1028, 816; BAGD—756b; THAYER—579a.

4644. σκληροτράχηλος {1x} **sklērŏtrachē-lŏs,** *sklay-rot-rakh'-ay-los;* from *4642* and *5137; hardnaped,* i.e. (fig.) *obstinate:*—stiffnecked {1x}. See: TDNT—5:1029, 816; BAGD—756b; THAYER—579a.

4645. σκληρύνω {6x} **sklērunō,** *sklay-roo'-no;* from *4642;* to *indurate,* i.e. (fig.) *render stubborn:*—harden {6x}.

(1) This word stresses that the nape of the neck stiffens and thus renders the head in an unbending position. *Skleruno,* "to make dry or hard", is used (2) in Acts 19:9 of men hardened against the gospel; (2a) in Rom 9:18, illustrated by the case of Pharaoh, who first persistently "hardened" his heart (see Ex 7:13, 22; 8:19, all producing the retributive "hardening" by God, after His much long-suffering, 9:12); (2b) in Heb 3:8, 13, 15; 4:7, warnings against the "hardening" of the heart. See: TDNT—5:1030, 816; BAGD—756b; THAYER—579b.

4646. σκολιός {4x} **skŏliŏs,** *skol-ee-os';* from the base of *4628; warped,* i.e. *winding;* fig. *perverse:*—crooked {2x}, froward {1x}, untoward {1x}.

Skolios, "curved, crooked," was especially used (1) of a way, Lk 3:5, with spiritual import; (2) it is set in contrast to *orthos* and *euthus,* "straight"; metaphorically, of what is morally "crooked," perverse, froward, (2a) of people belonging to a particular generation, Acts 2:40, "untoward"; Phil 2:15; (2b) of tyrannical or unjust masters, 1 Pet 2:18, "froward"; in this sense it is set in contrast to *agathos,* "good." See: TDNT—7:403, 1046; BAGD—756b; THAYER—579b.

4647. σκόλοψ {1x} **skŏlŏps,** *skol'-ops;* perh. from the base of *4628* and *3700; withered* at the *front,* i.e. a *point* or *prickle* (fig. a bodily *annoyance* or *disability*):—thorn {1x}.

Skolops, as a noun, originally denoted "anything pointed" and is used (1) 2 Cor 12:7, of the apostle's "thorn in the flesh." (2) His language indicates that it was physical, painful, humiliating. (3) It was also the effect of divinely permitted satanic antagonism. (4) The verbs are in the present tense, signifying recurrent action, indicating a constantly repeated attack. (5) What is stressed is not the metaphorical size, but the acuteness of the suffering and its effects. (6) Attempts to connect this with the circumstances of Acts 14:19 and Gal 4:13 are speculative. Syn.: 173, 174.See: TDNT—7:409, 1047; BAGD—756c; THAYER—579b.

4648. σκοπέω {6x} **skŏpĕō,** *skop-eh'-o;* from *4649;* to take *aim* at (*spy*), i.e. (fig.) *regard:*—consider {1x}, take heed {1x}, look at {1x}, look on {1x}, mark {2x}.

Skopeo, as a verb, means "to look at, consider" [Eng., "scope"], implying mental consideration, and is rendered (1) "while we look . . . at": "While we look not at the things which are seen, but at the things which are not seen" (2 Cor 4:18); and (2) "looking on": "Look not every man on (*skopeo*) his own things, but every man also on the things of others" (Phil 2:4). (3) It is translated "mark" in (3a) Rom 16:17, of a warning against those who cause divisions, and (3b) in Phil 3:17, of observing those who walked after the example of the apostle and his fellow workers, so as to follow their ways. (4) In Lk 11:35, "to look," is translated "take heed (that)." (5) It is translated "consider" in Gal 6:1. Syn.: 308, 352, 578, 816, 872, 991, 1689, 1896, 1914, 1980, 1983, 2300, 2334, 3706, 3708, 3879, 4017. See: TDNT—7:414, 1047; BAGD—756d; THAYER—579a. comp. *3700.*

4649. σκοπός {1x} **skŏpŏs,** *skop-os'* ("scope"); from σκέπτομαι **skĕptŏmai** (to *peer* about ["skeptic"]; perh. akin to *4626* through the idea of *concealment;* comp. *4629*); a *watch* (*sentry* or *scout*), i.e. (by impl.) a *goal:*—mark {1x}.

Skopos is primarily a watcher (Eng., scope) denoting a mark on which to fix the eye and is used metaphorically of an aim or object (Phil 3:14). See: TDNT—7:413, 1047; BAGD—756d; THAYER—579c.

4650. σκορπίζω {5x} **skŏrpizō,** *skor-pid'-zo;* appar. from the same as *4651* (through the idea of *penetrating*); to *dissipate,* i.e. (fig.) *put to flight, waste, be liberal:*—

disperse abroad {1x}, scatter {3x}, scatter abroad {1x}.

Skorpizo means "to scatter" (probably from a root, *skarp-*, signifying "to cut asunder," akin to *skorpios*, "a scorpion"), and is used (1) in Mt 12:30, "scattereth abroad"; (2) "scatter" in Lk 11:23; Jn 10:12; 16:32; (3) and in 2 Cor 9:9, "he hath dispersed abroad." See: TDNT—7:418, 1048; BAGD—757a; THAYER—579c.

4651. σκορπίος {5x} **skŏrpiŏs**, *skor-pee'-os;* prob. from an obs. σκέρπω **skĕrpō** (perh. strengthened from the base of *4649,* and mean. to *pierce*); a "*scorpion*" (from its *sting*):—scorpion {5x}.

The *skorpios* is (1) a small animal (the largest of the several species is 6 in. long) like a lobster, but with a long tail, at the end of which is its venomous sting; the pain, the position of the sting, and the effect are mentioned in Rev 9:3, 5, 10. (2) The Lord's rhetorical question as to the provision of a scorpion instead of an egg (Lk 11:12), is (2a) an allusion to the egg-like shape of the creature when at rest; and (2b) an indication of the abhorrence with which it is regarded. (3) In Lk 10:19 the Lord's assurance to the disciples of the authority given them by Him to tread upon serpents and scorpions (3a) conveys the thought of victory over spiritually antagonistic forces, the powers of darkness, (3b) as is shown by His reference to the power of the enemy and by the context (Lk 10:17, 20). See: BAGD—757a; THAYER—579d.

4652. σκοτεινός {3x} **skŏtĕinŏs**, *skot-i-nos';* from *4655; opaque,* i.e. (fig.) *benighted:*—dark {1x}, full of darkness {2x}.

Skotemos, "full of darkness, or covered with darkness," is (1) translated "dark" in Lk 11:36; (2) "full of darkness" in Mt 6:23 and Lk 11:34, where the physical condition is figurative of the moral. See: TDNT—7:423, 1049; BAGD—757b; THAYER—579d.

4653. σκοτία {16x} **skŏtia**, *skot-ee'-ah;* from *4655; dimness, obscurity* (lit. or fig.):—dark {2x}, darkness {14x}.

Skotia is used (1) of physical darkness, "dark," Jn 6:17, lit., "darkness had come on," and 20:1, lit., "darkness still being"; (2) of secrecy, in general, whether what is done therein is good or evil, Mt 10:27; Lk 12:3; (3) of spiritual or moral "darkness," emblematic of sin, as a condition of moral or spiritual depravity, Mt 4:16; Jn 1:5; 8:12; 12:35, 46; 1 Jn 1:5; 2:8-9, 11. See: TDNT—7:423, 1049; BAGD—757b; THAYER—580a.

4654. σκοτίζω {8x} **skŏtizō**, *skot-id-zo;* from *4655;* to deprive of light, to *obscure* (lit. or fig.):—darken {8x}.

Skotizo, "to deprive of light, to make dark," is used in the NT in the passive voice only, (1) of the heavenly bodies Mt 24:29; Mk 13:24; Rev 8:12; (2) metaphorically, (2a) of the mind, Rom 1:21; 11:10; Lk 23:45. See: TDNT—7:423, 1049; BAGD—757c; THAYER—580a.

4655. σκότος {32x} **skŏtŏs**, *skot'-os;* from the base of *4639; shadiness,* i.e. *obscurity* (lit. or fig.):—darkness {32x}.

Skotos is the exact opposite of *phos* (5457—light). It is a neuter noun used in the NT as the equivalent of *skotia* (*4653*): (1) of "physical darkness," Mt 27:45; 2 Cor 4:6; (2) of "intellectual darkness," Rom 2:19; (3) of "blindness," Acts 13:11; (4) by metonymy, of the "place of punishment," e.g., Mt 8:12; 2 Pet 2:17; Jude 13; (5) metaphorically, of "moral and spiritual darkness," e.g., Mt 6:23; Lk 1:79; 11:35; Jn 3:19; Acts 26:18; 2 Cor 6:14; Eph 6:12; Col 1:13; 1 Th. 5:4-5; 1 Pet 2:9; 1 Jn 1:6; (6) by metonymy, of "those who are in moral or spiritual darkness," Eph 5:8; (7) of "evil works," Rom 13:12; (8) Eph 5:11, of the "evil powers that dominate the world"; (9) Lk 22:53 "of secrecy." (10) While *skotos* is used more than twice as many times as *skotia* in the NT, (10a) the apostle John uses *skotos* only once, 1 Jn 1:6, but *skotia* 15 times out of the 18. (10b) With the exception of the significance of secrecy, darkness is always used in a bad sense. Moreover the different forms of darkness are so closely allied, being either cause and effect, or else concurrent effects of the same cause, that they cannot always be distinguished; 1 Jn 1:5; 2:8, e.g., are passages in which both spiritual and moral darkness are intended. Syn.: 887, 1105, 2217. See: TDNT—7:423, 1049; BAGD—757c; THAYER—580b.

4656. σκοτόω {1x} **skŏtŏō**, *skot-ŏ'-o;* from *4655;* to *obscure* or *blind* (lit. or fig.):—be full of darkness {1x}. See: TDNT—7:423, 1049; BAGD—758a; THAYER—580c.

4657. σκύβαλον {1x} **skubalŏn**, *skoo'-bal-on;* neut. of a presumed der. of *1519* and *2965* and *906;* what is *thrown to* the *dogs,* i.e. *refuse* (*ordure*):—dung {1x}.

Skubalon denotes "refuse," whether (1) "excrement," that which is cast out from the body, or (2) "the leavings of a feast," that which is thrown away from the table. Judaizers counted gentile Christians as dogs, while they themselves were seated at God's banquet. The apostle, reversing the image, counts the Judaistic ordinances as refuse upon which their advocates feed, Phil 3:8. See: TDNT—7:445, 1052; BAGD—758a; THAYER—580c.

4658. Σκύθης {1x} **Skuthēs**, *skoo'-thace;* prob. of for. or.; a *Scythene* or *Scythian,* i.e. (by impl.) a *savage:*—Scythian {1x}. See: TDNT—7:447, 1053; BAGD—758b; THAYER—580c.

4659. σκυθρωπός {2x} **skuthrōpŏs**, *skoo-thro-pos';* from σκυθρός **skuthrŏs**, *(sullen)* and a der. of *3700; angry-visaged,* i.e. *gloomy* or affecting a *mournful* appearance:—of a sad countenance {1x}, sad {1x}.

This word describes **(1)** the Emmaus road travelers, Lk 24:17; and **(2)** the sad countenance of the hypocritical faster, Mt 6:16. See: TDNT—7:450, 1053; BAGD—758b; THAYER—580c.

4660. σκύλλω {3x} **skullō**, *skool'-lo;* appar. a primary verb; to *flay,* i.e. (fig.) to *harass:*—trouble {2x}, trouble (one's) self {1x}.

Skullo, as a verb, primarily signifies **(1)** "to skin, to flay"; then **(1a)** "to rend, mangle"; hence, **(1b)** "to vex, trouble, annoy": "While He yet spake, there came from the ruler of the synagogue's *house certain* which said, Thy daughter is dead: why troublest *(skullo)* thou the Master any further?" (Mk 5:35; cf. Lk 7:6; 8:49). Syn.: 318, 928, 2347, 2669, 4729, 4730, 4928. See: BAGD—758b; THAYER—580d.

4661. σκῦλον {1x} **skulŏn**, *skoo'-lon;* neut. from *4660;* something *stripped* (as a *hide),* i.e. *booty:*—spoils {1x}.

Skulon are the weapons and valuables stripped off from an enemy, "spoils", Lk 11:22. See: BAGD—758b; THAYER—580d.

4662. σκωληκόβρωτος {1x} **skōlēkŏbrōtŏs**, *sko-lay-kob'-ro-tos;* from *4663* and a der. of *977; worm-eaten,* i.e. *diseased with maggots:*—eaten of worms {1x}. See: TDNT—7:456, 1054; BAGD—758c; THAYER—580d.

4663. σκώληξ {3x} **skōlēx**, *sko'-lakes;* of uncert. der.; a *grub, maggot* or *earth-worm:*—worm {3x}.

A *skolex* is a worm, specifically that kind which preys upon dead bodies (Mk 9:44, 46, 48). See: TDNT—7:452, 1054; BAGD—758c; THAYER—580d.

4664. σμαράγδινος {1x} **smaragdinŏs**, *smar-ag'-dee-nos;* from *4665;* consisting *of emerald:*—emerald {1x}.

This word denotes consisting of emerald green in color and character and is descriptive of the rainbow round about the throne (Rev 4:3). See: BAGD—758c; THAYER—581a.

4665. σμάραγδος {1x} **smaragdŏs**, *smar'-ag-dos;* of uncert. der.; the *emerald* or green gem so called:—emerald {1x}.

This is a transparent precious stone noted especially for its light green color occupying the first place in the second row on the high priest's breastplate, Ex 28:18. Tyre imported it from Syria, Eze 27:16. It is one of the foundations of the heavenly Jerusalem, Rev 21:19. The name was applied to other stones of a similar character, such as the carbuncle. See: BAGD—758c; THAYER—581a.

4666. σμύρνα {2x} **smurna**, *smoor'-nah;* appar. strengthened for *3464; myrrh:*—myrrh {2x}.

Smurna, whence the name "Smyrna," a word of Semitic origin, Heb., *mor,* from a root meaning "bitter," is **(1)** a gum resin from a shrubby tree, which grows in Yemen and neighboring regions of Africa; **(2)** the fruit is smooth and somewhat larger than a pea. **(3)** The color of myrrh varies from pale reddish-yellow to reddish-brown or red. **(4)** The taste is bitter, and the substance astringent, acting as an antiseptic and a stimulant. **(5)** It was used as a perfume, Ps 45:8, where the language is symbolic of the graces of the Messiah; Prov 7:17; Song 1:13; 5:5; **(6)** it was one of the ingredients of the "holy anointing oil" for the priests, Ex 30:23; **(7)** it was used also for the purification of women, Est 2:12; **(8)** for embalming, John 19:39; **(9)** it was one of the gifts of the Magi, Mt 2:11. See: TDNT—7:457, 1055; BAGD—758d; THAYER—581a.

4667. Σμύρνα {1x} **Smurna**, *smoor'-nah;* the same as *4666; Smyrna,* a place in Asia Minor:—Smyrna {1x}. See: BAGD—759a; THAYER—581a.

4668. Σμυρναῖος {1x} **Smurnaiŏs**, *smoor-nah'-yos;* from *4667;* a *Smyrnæan:*—in Smyrna {1x}. See: BAGD—759a; THAYER—581b.

4669. σμυρνίζω {1x} **smurnizō**, *smoor-nid'-zo;* from *4667;* to *tincture with myrrh,* i.e. *embitter* (as a narcotic):—mingle with myrrh {1x}.

Smurnizo is used transitively in the NT, with the meaning **(1)** "to mingle or drug with myrrh," Mk 15:23; **(2)** the mixture was doubtless offered to deaden the pain; **(3)** Matthew's word "gall" suggests that "myrrh" was not the only ingredient. **(4)** Christ refused to partake of any such means of alleviation; He would retain all His mental power for the complete fulfillment of the Father's will. See: TDNT—7:458, 1055; BAGD—759a; THAYER—581b.

Greek

4670. Σόδομα {10x} **Sŏdŏma**, *sod'-om-ah;* plur. of Heb. or. [5467]; *Sodoma* (i.e. *Sedom*), a place in Pal.:—Sodom {9x}, Sodoma {1x}. See: BAGD—759a; THAYER—581b.

4671. σοί {221x} **sŏi**, *soy;* dat. of *4771; to thee:*—thee {200x}, thou {14x}, thy {4x}, thine own {1x}, not tr {2x}. See: BAGD— 772a [4771]; THAYER—591c [4771].

4672. Σολομών or Σολομῶν {12x} **Sŏlŏmōn**, *sol-om-one';* of Heb. or. [8010]; *Solomon* (i.e. *Shelomoh*), the son of David:—*Solomon* {12x}. See: TDNT— 7:459, 1055; BAGD—759b; THAYER—581b.

4673. σορός {1x} **sŏrŏs**, *sor-os';* prob. akin to the base of *4987;* a *funereal receptacle* (*urn, coffin*), i.e. (by anal.) a *bier:*— bier {1x}.
Soros (1) originally denoted a receptacle for containing the bones of the dead, "a cinerary urn"; (2) then "a coffin," Gen 50:26; Job 21:32; (3) then, "the funeral couch or bier" on which the Jews bore their dead to burial, Lk 7:14. See: BAGD—759b; THAYER—581c.

4674. σός {27x} **sŏs**, *sos;* from *4771; thine:*— thy {13x}, thine {9x}, thine own {3x}, thy goods {1x}, thy friends {1x}. See: BAGD—759b; THAYER—581c.

4675. σοῦ { {498x} **sŏu**, *soo;* gen. of *4771; of thee, thy:*—thy {358x}, thee {76x}, thine {50x}, thine own {7x}, thou {6x}, not tr {1x}. See: BAGD—772a [4771]; THAYER— 591c [4771].

4676. σουδάριον {4x} **sŏudariŏn**, *soo-dar'-ee-on;* of Lat. or.; a *sudarium* (*sweat-cloth*), i.e. *towel* (for wiping the perspiration from the face, or binding the face of a corpse):—handkerchief {1x}, napkin {3x}.
Soudarion, a Latin word, *sudarium* (from *sudor*, "sweat"), denotes (1) "a cloth for wiping the face," etc., Lk 19:20, "napkin"; Acts 19:12, "handkerchief"; (2) "a headcovering for the dead," Jn 11:44, "napkin"; 20:7, "napkin." (3) In Lk 19:20 the reference may be to a towel or any kind of linen cloth or even a sort of headdress, any of which might be used for concealing money. See: BAGD—759c; THAYER—581c.

4677. Σουσάννα {1x} **Sŏusanna**, *soo-san'-nah;* of Heb. or. [7799 fem.]; *lily; Susannah* (i.e. *Shoshannah*), an Israelitess:—Susanna {1x}. See: BAGD—759c; THAYER—581d.

4678. σοφία {51x} **sŏphia**, *sof-ee'-ah;* from *4680; wisdom* (higher or lower, worldly or spiritual):—wisdom {51x}.
Sophia means (1) broad and full of intelligence; it is used of the knowledge of very diverse matters. There is (2) the wisdom which belongs to men, human wisdom (Lk 2:40, 52); specifically (2a) varied knowledge of things human and divine, acquired by acuteness and experience, and summed up in maxims and proverbs (Mt 12:42); (2b) science and learning (Acts 7:22); (2c) the act of interpreting dreams and always giving the sagest advice (Acts 7:10); (2d) the intelligence evinced in discovering the meaning of some mysterious number or vision (Rev 13:18; 17:9); (2e) skill in the management of affairs (Acts 6:3); (2f) devout and proper prudence in intercourse with men not disciples of Christ (Col 4:5); (2g) skill and discretion in imparting Christian truth (Col 1:28; 3:16); and (2h) the knowledge and practice of the requisites for godly and upright living (Jas 1:5; 3:13, 17). *Sophia* also includes (3) supreme intelligence, such as belongs (3a) to God (Rom 16:27), and (3b) to Christ (Jude 25). (4) This word also denotes the wisdom of God as evinced in forming and executing counsels in the formation and government of the world and the scriptures (Rom 11:33).
(5) It is used with reference (5a) to God, Rom 11:33; 1 Cor 1:21, 24; 2:7; Eph 3:10; Rev 7:12; (5b) Christ, Mt 13:54; Mk 6:2; Lk 2:40, 52; 1 Cor 1:30; Col 2:3; Rev 5:12; (5c) "wisdom" personified, Mt 11:19; Lk 7:35; 11:49; (5d) human "wisdom" (5d1) in spiritual things, Lk 21:15; Acts 6:3, 10; 7:10; 1 Cor 2:6 (1st part); 12:8; Eph 1:8, 17; Col 1:9, "(spiritual) wisdom," 28; 3:16; 4:5; Jas 1:5; 3:13, 17; 2 Pet 3:15; Rev 13:18; 17:9; (5d2) in the natural sphere, Mt 12:42; Lk 11:31; Acts 7:22; 1 Cor 1:17, 19, 20, 21 (twice), 22; 2:1, 4, 5, 6 (2nd part), 13; 3:19; 2 Cor 1:12; Col 2:23; (5d3) in its most debased form, Jas 3:15, "earthly, sensual, devilish." Syn.: (A) *Gnosis* (*1108*) denotes knowledge by itself, chiefly to the apprehension of truths. (B) *Epignosis* (*1922*) is greater and more accurate knowledge; complete comprehension which is intuitive and perfect (1 Cor 13:12). (C) *Sophia* (*4678*) denotes a mental excellence of the highest sense, to details with wisdom as exhibited in action, and adding the power of reasoning about wisdom's details by tracing their relationships. (D) *Sunesis* (*4907*) stresses the critical, apprehending and the bearing of things. (E) *Phronesis* (*5428*) is practical, suggesting lines of action. See also: 1922. See: TDNT— 7:465, 1056; BAGD—581d; THAYER—581d.

4679. σοφίζω {2x} **sŏphizō**, *sof-id'-zo;* from *4680;* to *render wise;* in a sinister acceptation, to *form* "*sophisms*", i.e. *continue plausible error:*—cunningly devised {1x}, make wise {1x}.
Sophizo from *sophos*, "wise" (1) in the ac-

tive voice signifies "to make wise," 2 Ti 3:15.
(2) In the middle voice it means "to play the
sophist, to devise cleverly", it is used with this
meaning in the passive voice in 2 Pet 1:16,
"cunningly devised fables." See: TDNT—7:527,
1056; BAGD—760b; THAYER—582c.

4680. σοφός {22x} **sŏphŏs**, *sof-os';* akin to
σαφής **saphēs**, (*clear*); *wise* (in
a most gen. application):—wise {22x}.

Sophos is used of (1) God, Rom 16:27; 1 Ti
1:17; Jude 25; (2) the comparative degree, *so-
photeros*, occurs in 1 Cor 1:25, where "foolishness" is simply in the human estimate;
(3) spiritual teachers in Israel, Mt 23:34; (4) believers endowed with spiritual and practical
wisdom, Rom 16:19; 1 Cor 3:10; 6:5; Eph 5:15;
Jas 3:13; (5) Jewish teachers in the time of
Christ, Mt 11:25; Lk 10:21; (6) the naturally
learned, Rom 1:14, 22; 1 Cor 1:19, 20, 26, 27;
3:15–20. Syn.: (A) *Sophos* denotes one who is
wise, skilled, an expert. (B) *Sunetos* (*4908*)
means intelligent, and denotes one who can
put things together, who has insight and comprehension. (C) *Phronimos* (*5429*) means prudent, and denotes primarily one who has quick
and correct perceptions; hence, discreet, circumspect. See: TDNT—7:465, 1056; BAGD—
760b; THAYER—582c.

4681. Σπανία {2x} **Spania**, *span-ee'-ah;*
prob. of for. or.; *Spania*, a re-
gion of Europe:—Spain {2x}. See: BAGD—
760c; THAYER—582d.

4682. σπαράσσω {4x} **sparassō**, *spar-as'-so;*
prol. from σπαίρω **spairō**
(to *gasp;* appar. strengthened from *4685*,
through the idea of *spasmodic* contraction); to
mangle, i.e. *convulse* with epilepsy:—rend {1x},
tear {3x}.

Sparasso denotes (1) "to tear, convulse" in
Mk 1:26; 9:20, 26; (2) "rent" in Lk 9:39. See:
BAGD—760d; THAYER—582d.

4683. σπαργανόω {2x} **sparganŏō**, *spar-
gan-ŏ'-o;* from σπάργα-
νον **sparganŏn**, (a *strip;* from a der. of the base
of *4682* mean. to *strap* or *wrap* with strips); to
swathe (an infant after the Oriental custom):—
wrap in swaddling clothes {2x}.

Sparganoo, "to swathe" (from *sparganon,* "a
swathing band"), signifies "to wrap in swaddling clothes" in Lk 2:7, 12. The idea that the
word means "rags" is without foundation. See:
BAGD—760d; THAYER—582d.

4684. σπαταλάω {2x} **spatalaō**, *spat-al-ah'-o;*
from σπατάλη **spatalē**,
(*luxury*); to *be voluptuous:*—live in pleasure
{1x}, be wanton {1x}.

Wanton means undisciplined. *Spatalao* con-

cerns extravagance and wastefulness. This
word means "to live riotously," and is translated (1) "liveth in pleasure" in 1 Ti 5:6; (2)
"been wanton" in Jas 5:5. Syn.: (A) *Spatalao* is
pictured by the prodigal son (Lk 15:13); (B)
tryphao (*5171*) by the rich man who fared
sumptuously every day (Lk 16:19), and (C)
strenao (*4763*) by the Great Whore, Babylon,
who "lived deliciously", Rev 18:7, 9. See:
BAGD—761a; THAYER—583a.

4685. σπάω {2x} **spaō**, *spah'-o;* a primary verb;
to *draw:*—draw {1x}, draw out
{1x}.

Spao, as a verb, means "to draw or pull"
and is used, in the middle voice of "drawing"
a sword from its sheath (Mk 14:47; Acts 16:27).
Syn.: 307, 385, 392, 501, 502, 645, 868, 1448,
1670, 1828, 2020, 4264, 4317, 4334, 4358, 4951,
5288, 5289. See: BAGD—761a; THAYER—
583a.

4686. σπεῖρα {7x} **spĕira**, *spi'-rah;* of immed.
Lat. or., but ultimately a der.
of *138* in the sense of its cognate *1507;* a *coil*
(*spira,* "spire"), i.e. (fig.) a *mass* of men (a Rom.
military *cohort;* also [by anal.] a *squad* of Levitical janitors):—band {7x}.

(1) Band, generically, means that which is
sufficient to completely surround and accomplish the job assigned. (2) *Speira,* primarily
"anything round," and so "whatever might be
wrapped round a thing, a twisted rope," came
to mean "a body of men at arms," and was the
equivalent of the Roman *manipulus.* It was also
used for a larger body of men, a cohort, about
600 infantry, commanded by a tribune. It is
confined to its military sense. It is used for a
"band" (1) of soldiers in Mt 27:27; Mk 15:16;
Acts 10:1; 21:31; 27:1; and (2) of men in Jn 18:3;
18:12. See: BAGD—761a; THAYER—583a.

4687. σπείρω {54x} **spĕirō**, *spi'-ro;* prob.
strengthened from *4685*
(through the idea of *extending*); to *scatter,* i.e.
sow (lit. or fig.):—sower {44x}, sower {6x}, receive seed {4x}.

Speiro, "to sow seed," is used (1) literally,
especially in the Synoptic Gospels; elsewhere,
1 Cor 15:36, 37; 2 Cor 9:10, "the sower", (2) metaphorically, (2a) in proverbial sayings, e.g., Mt
13:3, 4; Lk 19:21, 22; Jn 4:37; 2 Cor 9:6; (2b) in
the interpretation of parables, e.g., Mt 13:19–
23 (in these vv., "received seed"); (2c) otherwise
as follows: (2c1) of "sowing" spiritual things in
preaching and teaching, 1 Cor 9:11; (2c2) of the
interment of the bodies of deceased believers,
1 Cor 15:42–44; (2c3) of ministering to the necessities of others in things temporal (the harvest being proportionate to the "sowing"),
2 Cor 9:6, 10; (2c4) of "sowing" to the flesh,

Gal 6:7, 8 ("that" in v. 7 is emphatic, "that and that only," what was actually "sown"); in v. 8, *eis*, "unto," signifies "in the interests of"; **(2c5)** of the "fruit of righteousness" by peacemakers, Jas 3:18. See: TDNT—7:536, 1065; BAGD—761b; THAYER—583b.

4688. **σπεκουλάτωρ** {1x} **spĕkŏulatōr**, *spek-oo-lat′-ore;* of Lat. or.; a *speculator,* i.e. military *scout* (*spy* or [by extens.] *life-guardsman*):—executioner {1x}.

Spekoulator, primarily denotes a lookout officer, or "scout; but, under the emperors, a member of the bodyguard [one who looked out for the welfare of his superior and had the power of execution]; these were employed as messengers, watchers and executioners; ten such officers were attached to each legion; such a guard was employed by Herod Antipas, (Mk 6:27). See: BAGD—761c; THAYER—583c.

4689. **σπένδω** {2x} **spĕndō**, *spen′-do;* appar. a primary verb; to *pour* out as a libation, i.e. (fig.) to *devote* (one's life or blood, as a sacrifice) ("*spend*"):—be ready to be offered {1x}, be offered {1x}.

Spendo, "to pour out as a drink offering, make a libation," is used **(1)** figuratively in the passive voice in Phil 2:17, "be offered." **(2)** In 2 Ti 4:6, "I am already being offered", the apostle is referring to his approaching death, upon the sacrifice of his ministry. See: TDNT—7:528,*; BAGD—761c; THAYER—583d.

4690. **σπέρμα** {44x} **spĕrma**, *sper′-mah;* from *4687;* something *sown,* i.e. *seed* (incl. the male "*sperm*"); by impl. *offspring;* spec. a *remnant* (fig. as if kept over for planting):—issue {1x}, seed {43x}.

Sperma,. akin to *speiro,* "to sow" (Eng., "sperm," "spermatic," etc.), has the following usages, **(1)** agricultural and botanical, e.g., Mt 13:24, 27, 32; 1 Cor 15:38; 2 Cor 9:10; **(2)** physiological, Heb 11:11;

(3) metaphorical and by metonymy for "offspring, posterity," **(3a)** of natural offspring, e.g., Mt 22:24, 25, "issue"; Jn 7:42; 8:33, 37; Acts 3:25; Rom 1:3; 4:13, 16, 18; 9:7 (twice), 8, 29; 11:1; 2 Cor 11:22; Heb 2:16; 11:18; Rev 12:17; Gal 3:16, 19, 29; **(3b)** Gal 3:16 "He saith not, and to seeds, as of many; but as of one, and to thy seed, which is Christ," **(3b1)** quoted from Gen 13:15 and 17:7, 8, there is especial stress on the word "seed," as referring to an individual (here, Christ) in fulfillment of the promises to Abraham—a unique use of the singular. **(3b2)** While the plural form "seeds," promises to Abraham—a unique use of the singular. **(3b3)** While the plural form "seeds," neither in Hebrew nor in Greek, would have been natural any more than in English (it is not so

used in Scripture of human offspring; its plural occurrence is in 1 Sa 8:15, of crops), **(3b4)** yet if the divine intention had been to refer to Abraham's natural descendants, another word could have been chosen in the plural, such as "children"; **(3b5)** all such words were, however, set aside, "seed" being selected as one that could be used in the singular, with the purpose of showing that the "seed" was Messiah. **(3b6)** Some of the rabbis had even regarded "seed," e.g., in Gen 4:25 and Is 53:10, as referring to the Coming One. **(3b7)** Descendants were given to Abraham by other than natural means, so that through him Messiah might come, and the point of the apostle's argument is that since the fulfillment of the promises of God is secured alone by Christ, they only who are "in Christ" can receive them;

(4) of spiritual offspring, **(4a)** Rom 4:16, 18; 9:8; here "the children of the promise are reckoned for a seed" points, firstly, to Isaac's birth as being not according to the ordinary course of nature but by divine promise, and, secondly, by analogy, to the fact that all believers are children of God by spiritual birth; Gal 3:29. **(4b)** As to 1 Jn 3:9, "his seed abideth in him," it is possible to understand this as meaning that children of God (His "seed") abide in Him, and "doth not commit sin." The present tense signifies continually sinning. Alternatively, the "seed" signifies the principle of spiritual life as imparted to the believer, which abides in him without possibility of removal or extinction; the child of God remains eternally related to Christ, he who lives in sin has never become so related, he has not the principle of life in him. This meaning suits the context and the general tenor of the Epistle. See: TDNT—7:536, 1065; BAGD—761d; THAYER—583d.

4691. **σπερμολόγος** {1x} **spĕrmŏlŏgŏs**, *sper-mol-og′-os;* from *4690* and *3004;* a *seed-picker* (as the crow), i.e. (fig.) a *sponger, loafer* (spec. a *gossip* or *trifler* in talk):—babbler {1x}.

This word is translated "a babbler" in Acts 17:18. Primarily an adjective, **(1)** it came to be used as a noun signifying a crow, or some other bird, picking up seeds. **(2)** Then it seems to have been used of a man accustomed to hang about the streets and markets, picking up scraps which fall from loads; hence a parasite, who lives at the expense of others, a hanger-on. **(3)** Metaphorically it became used of a man who picks up scraps of information and retails them secondhand, a plagiarist, or of those who make a show, in unscientific style, of knowledge obtained from misunderstanding lectures. See: BAGD—762b; THAYER—584b.

4692. σπεύδω {6x} spĕudō, spyoo'-do; prob.
strengthened from 4228; to
"speed" ("study"), i.e. urge on (diligently or
earnestly); by impl. to await eagerly:—make
haste {3x}, haste {1x}, haste unto {1x}, with
haste {1x}.

Speudo denotes (1) intransitively, "with
haste" in Lk 2:16; 19:5, "make haste"; 19:6,
"made haste"; Acts 20:16, "he hasted"; 22:18,
"make haste"; (2) transitively, "to desire earnestly, hasting" in 2 Pet 3:12, "hasting unto"
(the day of God), i.e., in our practical fellowship with God as those who are appointed by
Him as instruments through prayer and service
for the accomplishment of His purposes, purposes which will be unthwartably fulfilled
both in time and manner of accomplishment.
In this way the earnest desire will find its fulfillment. See: BAGD—762b; THAYER—584b.

4693. σπήλαιον {6x} spēlaiŏn, spay'-lah-yon;
neut. of a presumed der. of
σπέος spĕŏs (a grotto); a cavern; by impl. a
hiding-place or resort:—cave {1x}, den {5x}.

Spelaion, "a grotto, cavern, den" (Lat., spel-
unca), (1) "cave" in Jn 11:38, is said of the grave
of Lazarus; (2) "dens" in Heb 11:38 and Rev
6:15; (3) in the Lord's rebuke concerning the
defilement of the temple, Mt 21:13; Mk 11:17;
Lk 19:46, "den" is used. See: BAGD—762c;
THAYER—582c.

4694. σπιλάς {1x} spilas, spee-las'; of uncert.
der.; a ledge or reef of rock in
the sea:—spot {1x}.

A spilas is a rock or reef over which the sea
dashes (Jude 12), spots metaphorically stressing the quick, unsuspecting, and pointed destruction upon the life of a believer, rendered
by men whose conduct is a danger to others.
See: BAGD—762c; THAYER—584c.

4695. σπίλος {2x} spilŏs, spee'-los; of uncert.
der.; a stain or blemish, i.e.
(fig.) defect, disgrace:—spot {1x}, defile {1x}.

Spilos, "a spot or stain," is used metaphorically (1) of moral blemish, Eph 5:27; (2) of lascivious and riotous persons, 2 Pet 2:13. Syn.:
Spilas (4695) refers to a hidden location which
can destroy a life; whereas spilos refers to a
subtle intaking from an impure source which
can equally destroy a life. Both externally and
internally, destruction can come. See: BAGD—
762d; THAYER—584c.

4696. σπιλόω {2x} spilŏō, spee-lŏ'-o; from
4696; to stain or soil (lit. or
fig.):—defile {1x}, spot {1x}.

Spilo means to make a stain or spot and so
to defile and is used (1) in Jas 3:6 of the defiling
effects of an evil use of the tongue; and (2) in
Jude 23 spotted refers to moral defilement.

Syn.: 4696. See: BAGD—762d; THAYER—
584c.

4697. σπλαγχνίζομαι {12x} splagchnizŏmai, splangkh-nid'-
zom-ahee; mid. voice from 4698; to have the
bowels yearn, i.e. (fig.) feel sympathy, to pity:—
have compassion {7x}, be moved with compassion {5x}.

This word means "to be moved as to one's
inwards (splanchna), to be moved with compassion, to yearn with compassion," and is frequently recorded (1) of Christ toward the
multitude and toward individual sufferers, Mt
9:36; 14:14; 15:32; 18:27; 20:34; Mk 1:41; 6:34;
8:2; Lk 7:13; 10:33; (2) Mk 9:22 of the appeal
of a father for a devil-possessed son; and (3) of
the father in the parable of the Prodigal Son,
Lk 15:20. See: TDNT—7:548, 1067; BAGD—
762d; THAYER—584d.

4698. σπλάγχνον {11x} splagchnŏn, splangkh'-
non; prob. strengthened
from σπλήν splēn (the "spleen"); an intestine,
(plural); fig. pity or sympathy:—bowels {9x},
inward affection {1x}, tender mercy + 1656 {1x}.

(1) Splagchnon are the bowels which were
regarded by the Hebrews as the seat of the tender affections. (2) It is used always in the plural,
and properly denotes "the physical organs of
the intestines," and is once used in this respect,
Acts 1:18. The word is rendered (3) "tender mercy"
in Lk 1:78; (4) "bowels" in 2 Cor 6:12; Phil 1:8;
2:1; Col 3:12; Philem 7, 12, 20; 1 Jn 3:17; and
(5) "inward affection" in 2 Cor 7:15. See: TDNT—
7:548, 1067; BAGD—763a; THAYER—584d.

4699. σπόγγος {3x} spŏggŏs, spong'-gos; perh.
of for. or.; a "sponge":—spunge
{3x}.

Spoggos was the medium by which vinegar
was carried to the mouth of Christ on the cross,
Mt 27:48; Mk 15:36; Jn 19:29. See: BAGD—
763b; THAYER—585a.

4700. σποδός {3x} spŏdŏs, spod-os'; of uncert.
der.; ashes:—ashes {3x}.

Spodos, "ashes", is found three times,
(1) twice in association with sackcloth, Mt
11:21 and Lk 10:13, as tokens of grief (cf. Est.
4:1, 3; Is 58:5; 61:3; Jer 6:26; Jonah 3:6); (2) of
the ashes resulting from animal sacrifices, Heb
9:13. See: BAGD—763b; THAYER—585b.

4701. σπορά {1x} spŏra, spor-ah'; from 4687;
a sowing, i.e. (by impl.) parent-
age:—seed {1x}.

Spora denotes "seed sown," 1 Pet 1:23, of
human offspring. See: TDNT—7:536, 1065;
BAGD—763b; THAYER—585b.

Greek

4702. σπόριμος {3x} **spŏrimŏs**, *spor'-ee-mos;* from *4703; sown,* i.e. (neut. plur.) a planted *field:*—corn {1x}, cornfield {2x}.

(1) Corn speaks of any type grain. *Sporimos,* lit., "sown, or fit for sowing" (*speiro* "to sow, scatter seed"), denotes, in the plural, **(2)** "sown fields, fields of grain, cornfields," Mt 12:1, "corn"; Mk 2:23; Lk 6:1. See: TDNT—7:536, 1065; BAGD—763b; THAYER—585b.

4703. σπόρος {5x} **spŏrŏs**, *spor'-os;* from *4687;* a *scattering* (of seed), i.e. (concr.) *seed* (as sown):—seed {4x}, seed sown {1x}.

Sporos properly "a sowing," denotes "seed sown," **(1)** natural, Mk 4:26, 27; Lk 8:5, 11; **(2)** the natural being figuratively applied to the Word of God; 2 Cor 9:10 (1st part); metaphorically of material help to the needy, 2 Cor 9:10 (2nd part), "seed sown." See: TDNT—7:536, 1065; BAGD—763b; THAYER—585b.

4704. σπουδάζω {11x} **spŏudazō**, *spoo-dad'-zo;* from *4710;* to *use speed,* i.e. to *make effort, be prompt* or *earnest:*—endeavour {3x}, do diligence {2x}, be diligent {2x}, give diligence {1x}, be forward {1x}, labour {1x}, study {1x}.

Spoudazo signifies "to hasten to do a thing, to exert oneself, endeavor, give diligence"; **(1)** "was forward" in Gal 2:10, of remembering the poor; **(2)** "endeavoring": **(2a)** in Eph 4:3, of keeping the unity of the Spirit, **(2b)** in 1 Th 2:17, of going to see friends, "endeavored", **(2c)** in 2 Pet 1:15, of enabling believers to call Scripture truth to remembrance, "endeavour"; **(3)** "do thy diligence" in 2 Ti 4:9; 4:21; **(4)** "study" in 2 Ti 2:15; **(5)** "be diligent": **(5a)** in Titus 3:12, **(5b)** in 2 Pet 3:14, of being found in peace without fault and blameless, when the Lord comes; **(6)** "let us labor": **(6a)** in Heb 4:11, of keeping continuous Sabbath rest, **(6b)** in 2 Pet 1:10, of making our calling and election sure. See: TDNT—7:559, 1069; BAGD—763c; THAYER—585b.

4705. σπουδαῖος {1x} **spŏudaiŏs**, *spoo-dah'-yos;* from *4710; prompt, energetic, earnest:*—diligent {1x}. See: TDNT—7:559, 1069; BAGD—763c; THAYER—585b.

4706. σπουδαιότερον {1x} **spŏudaiŏtĕrŏn**, *spoo-dah-yot'-er-on;* neut. of *4707* as adv.; *more earnestly* than others, i.e. very *promptly:*—very diligently {1x}. See: BAGD—763c; THAYER—585b.

4707. σπουδαιότερος {2x} **spŏudaiŏtĕrŏs**, *spoo-dah-yot'-er-os;* comparative of *4705; more prompt, more earnest:*—more diligent {1x}, more forward {1x}.

Spoudaioteros is the comparative degree of

spoude (*4710*) and is translated "more diligent" in 2 Cor 8:22; and "more forward" in 2 Cor 8:17. See: BAGD—763c; THAYER—585b.

4708. σπουδαιοτέρως {1x} **spŏudaiŏtĕrōs**, *spoo-dah-yot-er'-oce;* adv. from *4707; more speedily,* i.e. *sooner* than otherwise:—more carefully {1x}.

This is the comparative adverb of *spoude* (*4710*) and signifies "the more carefully" in Phil 2:28. See: BAGD—763c; THAYER—585b.

4709. σπουδαίως {2x} **spŏudaiōs**, *spoo-dah'-yoce;* adv. from *4705; earnestly, promptly:*—diligently {1x}, instantly {1x}.

Spoudaios "speedily, earnestly, diligently" is translated **(1)** "instantly" in Lk 7:4; and **(2)** "diligently" in Titus 3:13. See: BAGD—763d; THAYER—585b.

4710. σπουδή {12x} **spŏudē**, *spoo-day';* from *4692; "speed",* i.e. (by impl.) *despatch, eagerness, earnestness:*—diligence {5x}, haste {2x}, business {1x}, care {1x}, forwardness {1x}, earnest care {1x}, carefulness {1x}.

Spoude, "earnestness, zeal," or sometimes **(1)** "the haste accompanying this," Mk 6:25; Lk 1:39, is translated **(2)** "diligence" in Rom 12:8; 2 Cor 8:7; Heb 6:11; 2 Pet 1:5; Jude 3; **(3)** "carefulness" in 2 Cor 7:11; **(4)** "care" in 2 Cor 7:12; **(5)** "business" in Rom 12:11; **(6)** "forwardness" in 2 Cor 8:8; and **(7)** "earnest care" in 2 Cor 8:16. See: TDNT—7:559, 1069; BAGD—763d; THAYER—585c.

4711. σπυρίς {5x} **spuris**, *spoo-rece';* from *4687* (as *woven*); a *hamper* or *lunch-receptacle:*—basket {5x}.

Spuris denotes a reed basket, plaited, a capacious kind of hamper, sometimes large enough to hold a man (Mt 15:37; 16:10; Mk 8:8, 20; Acts 9:25). See: BAGD—764a; THAYER—585c.

4712. στάδιον {6x} **stadiŏn**, *stad'-ee-on;* or masc. (in plur.) στάδιος **stadiŏs**, *stad'-ee-os;* from the base of *2476,* (as *fixed*); a *stade* or certain measure of distance; by impl. a *stadium* or *race-course:*—furlong {5x}, race {1x}.

Stadion denotes **(1)** a stadium, i.e., a measure of length, 600 Greek feet, or one-eighth of a Roman mile, a space or distance of about 600 feet or 185 m (Lk 24:13; Jn 6:19; 11:18; Rev 14:20; 21:16; and **(2)** a race course, the length of the Olympic course (1 Cor 9:24). See: BAGD—764a; THAYER—585c.

4713. στάμνος {1x} **stamnŏs**, *stam'-nos;* from the base of *2476* (as *station-*

ary); a *jar* or earthen *tank:*—pot {1x}. See: BAGD—764b; THAYER—585d.

4714. στάσις {9x} **stasis**, *stas'-is;* from the base of *2476;* a *standing* (prop. the act), i.e. (by anal.) *position* (*existence*); by impl. a popular *uprising;* fig. *controversy:*—sedition {3x}, dissension {3x}, insurrection {1x}, ✕ standing {1x}, uproar {1x}.

Stasis, akin to *histemi,* "to stand," denotes **(1)** "a standing, stability" in Heb 9:8, "(while as the first tabernacle) is yet standing"; **(2)** "an insurrection" in Mk 15:7; **(3)** "sedition" in Lk 23:19, 25; Acts 24:5; **(4)** "uproar" in Acts 19:40; and **(5)** "a dissension, Acts 15:2; 23:7, 10. See: TDNT—7:559, 1069; BAGD—764c; THAYER—585d.

4715. στατήρ {1x} **statēr**, *stat-air';* from the base of *2746;* a *stander* (*standard* of value), i.e. (spec.) a *stater* or certain coin:—piece of money {1x}.

By the time recorded in Mt 17:24; the value was about three shillings, and would pay the Temple tax for two persons. See: BAGD—764c; THAYER—586a.

4716. σταυρός {28x} **staurŏs**, *stŏw-ros';* from the base of *2476;* a *stake* or *post* (as *set* upright), i.e. (spec.) a *pole* or *cross* (as an instrument of capital punishment); fig. *exposure to death,* i.e. *self-denial;* by impl. the *atonement* of Christ:—cross {28x}.

Stauros denotes **(1)** "the cross, or stake itself," e.g., Mt 27:32; **(2)** "the crucifixion suffered," e.g., 1 Cor 1:17–18, where "the preaching of the cross," stands for the gospel; **(3)** Gal 5:11, where crucifixion is metaphorically used of the renunciation of the world, that characterizes the true Christian life; Gal 6:12, 14; Eph 2:16; Phil 3:18. **(4)** The judicial custom by which the condemned person carried his stake to the place of execution, was applied by the Lord to those sufferings by which His faithful followers were to express their fellowship with Him, e.g., Mt 10:38. See: TDNT—7:572, 1071; BAGD—764d; THAYER—586a.

4717. σταυρόω {46x} **staurŏō**, *stŏw-rŏ'-o;* from *4716;* to *impale* on the cross; fig. to *extinguish* (*subdue*) passion or selfishness:—crucify {46x}.

Stauroo signifies **(1)** "the act of crucifixion," e.g., Mt 20:19; **(2)** metaphorically, "the putting off of the flesh with its passions and lusts," a condition fulfilled in the case of those who are "in Christ Jesus," Gal 5:24; **(3)** so of the relationship between the believer and the world, Gal 6:14. See: TDNT—7:581, 1071; BAGD—765b; THAYER—586b.

4718. σταφυλή {3x} **staphulē**, *staf-oo-lay';* prob. from the base of *4735;* a *cluster* of grapes (as if *intertwined*):—grapes {3x}.

Staphule, "a bunch of grapes, the ripe cluster," stresses the individual grapes themselves, Mt 7:16; Lk 6:44; Rev 14:18. Syn.: *Staphule,* (*4718*) "a bunch of grapes, the ripe cluster" stressing the individual grapes themselves within the cluster. See: BAGD—765c; THAYER—586c.

4719. στάχυς {5x} **stachus**, *stakh'-oos;* from the base of *2476;* a *head* of grain (as *standing* out from the stalk):—ear {2x}, ear of corn {3x}.

Stachus means "an ear of grain," Mt 12:1; Mk 2:23; 4:28; Lk 6:1. See: BAGD—765d; THAYER—586c.

4720. Στάχυς {1x} **Stachus**, *stakh'-oos;* the same as *4719; Stachys,* a Chr.:—Stachys {1x}. See: BAGD—765d; THAYER—586d.

4721. στέγη {3x} **stĕgē**, *steg'-ay;* strengthened from a primary τέγος **tĕgŏs** (a "*thatch*" or "*deck*" of a building); a *roof:*—roof {3x}.

Stege, "a covering" (*stego,* "to cover"), denotes **(1)** "a roof," Mk 2:4; **(2)** said of entering a house, Mt 8:8; Lk 7:6. See: BAGD—765d; THAYER—586d.

4722. στέγω {4x} **stĕgō**, *steg'-o;* from *4721;* to *roof* over, i.e. (fig.) to *cover* with silence (*endure* patiently):—can forbear {2x}, bear {1x}, suffer {1x}.

Stego means primarily to protect, or preserve by covering; hence **(1)** means to keep off something which threatens, to bear up against, to hold out against, and so to endure, bear, forbear (1 Cor 9:12). **(2)** The idea of supporting what is placed upon a thing is prominent in 1 Th 3:1, 5; 1 Cor 13:7). See: TDNT—7:585, 1073; BAGD—765d; THAYER—586d.

4723. στεῖρος {4x} **stĕirŏs**, *sti'-ros;* a contr. from *4731* (as *stiff* and *unnatural*); "*sterile*":—barren {4x}.

Steiros means hard, firm [Eng., "sterile"] and signifies barren, not bearing children. It is used with **(1)** the natural significance (Lk 1:7, 36; 23:29); and **(2)** a spiritual significance (Gal 4:27). See: BAGD—766a; THAYER—586d.

4724. στέλλω {2x} **stĕllō**, *stel'-lo;* prob. strengthened from the base of *2476;* prop. to *set* fast ("*stall*"), i.e. (fig.) to *repress* (refl. *abstain* from associating with):—avoid {1x}, withdraw (one's) self {1x}.

Stello, "to place," sometimes signifies, in the middle voice, "to take care against a thing," **(1)** "to avoid," 2 Cor 8:20; and **(2)** in 2 Th 3:6,

"of withdrawing from a person." See: TDNT— 7:588, 1074; BAGD—766a.

4725. στέμμα {1x} **stĕmma**, *stem'-mah;* from the base of *4735;* a *wreath* for show to prepare for sacrifice:—garland {1x}.

Stemma denotes "a wreath" (from *stepho,* "to put around, enwreath"), as used in sacrifices, Acts 14:13. See: BAGD—766a; THAYER—587a.

4726. στεναγμός {2x} **stĕnagmŏs**, *sten-ag-mos';* from *4727;* a *sigh:*—groaning {2x}.

Stenagmos, **(1)** in Acts 7:34, is used in a quote from Ex 2:24 of the children of Israel groaning in Egypt; **(2)** in Rom 8:26, in the plural, of the intercessory groanings of the Holy Spirit. See: TDNT—7:600, 1076; BAGD—766b; THAYER—587a.

4727. στενάζω {6x} **stĕnazō**, *sten-ad'-zo;* from *4728;* to *make* (intr. *be*) *in straits,* i.e. (by impl.) to *sigh, murmur, pray* inaudibly:—with grief {1x}, groan {3x}, grudge {1x}, sigh {1x}.

Stenazo, "to groan" (of an inward, unexpressed feeling of sorrow), is translated **(1)** "with grief" in Heb 13:17. **(2)** It is rendered "sighed" in Mk 7:34; **(3)** "groan," in Rom 8:23; 2 Cor 5:2, 4; and **(4)** "grudge" in Jas 5:9. Syn.: **(A)** *Alalazo* (*214*) means to wail in oriental style, to howl in a consecrated, semi-liturgical fashion. **(B)** *Dakruo* (*1145*) means to shed tears, weep silently. **(C)** *Threneo* (*2354*) means to give formal expression to grief, to sing a dirge. **(D)** *Klaio* (*2799*) denotes to weep audibly, cry as a child. **(E)** *Odurmos* (*3602*) means to give verbal expression to grief, to lament. **(F)** *Stenazo* (*4727*) denotes to express grief by inarticulate or semi-articulate sounds, to groan. See: TDNT—7:600, 1076; BAGD—766b; THAYER—587a.

4728. στενός {3x} **stĕnŏs**, *sten-os';* prob. from the base of *2476; narrow* (from obstacles *standing* close about):—strait {3x}.

Stenos is used figuratively in Mt 7:13, 14; Lk 13:24; of the gate which provides the entrance to eternal life; narrow because it runs counter to natural inclinations. Syn.: *Stenochoreo* (*4729*) means to be straitened and *stenochoria* (*4730*) means narrowness, anguish, distress. See: TDNT—7:604, 1077; BAGD—766b; THAYER—587b.

4729. στενοχωρέω {3x} **stĕnŏchōrĕō**, *sten-okh-o-reh'-o;* from the same as *4730;* to *hem* in closely, i.e. (fig.) *cramp:*—distress {1x}, straiten {2x}.

This word means lit., "to crowd into a nar-

row space," or, in the passive voice "to be pressed for room," hence, metaphorically, **(1)** "to be straitened," 2 Cor 6:12 twice; and **(2)** "distressed" in 2 Cor 4:8. See: TDNT— 7:604, 1077; BAGD—766c; THAYER—587b.

4730. στενοχωρία {4x} **stĕnŏchōria**, *sten-okh-o-ree'-ah;* from a compound of *4728* and *5561; narrowness of room,* i.e. (fig.) *calamity:*—anguish {1x}, distress {3x}.

(1) *Stenochoria* refers to confined space and the consequent painfulness; narrow straits. This word means lit., "narrowness of place" (*stenos,* "narrow," *chora,* "a place"), metaphorically came to mean the "distress arising from that condition, anguish." **(2)** It is used in the plural, of various forms of "distress" in 2 Cor 6:4; 12:10; Rom 8:35, and **(3)** of "anguish" in Rom 2:9. **(4)** The opposite state, is of being in a large place, and so metaphorically in a state of joy. Syn.: 2347. See: TDNT—7:604, 1077; BAGD—766c; THAYER—587b.

4731. στερεός {4x} **stĕrĕŏs**, *ster-eh-os';* from *2476; stiff,* i.e. *solid, stable* (lit. or fig.):—stedfast {1x}, strong {2x}, sure {1x}.

Stereos, "solid, hard, stiff," is translated **(1)** "sure" in 2 Ti 2:19, "(foundation of God standeth) sure"; **(2)** "strong (meat)" in Heb 5:12, 14; and **(3)** "steadfast" in 1 Pet 5:9. See: TDNT—7:609, 1077; BAGD—766d; THAYER—587b.

4732. στερεόω {3x} **stĕrĕŏō**, *ster-eh-ŏ'-o;* from *4731;* to *solidify,* i.e. *confirm* (lit. or fig.):—establish {1x}, receive strength {1x}, make strong {1x}.

Steroo, "to make firm, or solid" (akin to *stereos,* "hard, firm, solid"; cf Eng., "stereotype"), is used only in Acts, **(1)** physically, **(1a)** 3:7, "received strength"; **(1b)** 3:16, "hath made strong"; **(2)** metaphorically, of establishment in the faith, 16:5, "established." See: TDNT— 7:609, 1077; BAGD—766d; THAYER—587c.

4733. στερέωμα {1x} **stĕrĕōma**, *ster-eh'-o-mah;* from *4732;* something *established,* i.e. (abstr.) *confirmation* (*stability*):—stedfastness {1x}.

Stereoma, primarily "a support, foundation," denotes "strength, steadfastness," Col 2:5. See: TDNT—7:609, 1077; BAGD—766d; THAYER—587c.

4734. Στεφανᾶς {4x} **Stĕphanas**, *stef-an-as';* prob. contr. for στεφανωτός **stĕphanōtŏs** (*crowned;* from *4737*); *Stephanas,* a Chr.:—*Stephanas* {4x}. See: BAGD—767a; THAYER—587c.

4735. στέφανος {18x} **stĕphanŏs**, *stef'-an-os;* from an appar. primary στέφω **stĕphō** (to *twine* or *wreathe*); a *chaplet,* (as a badge of royalty, a prize in the public games or a symbol of honor gen.; but more conspicuous and elaborate than the simple *fillet, 1238*), lit. or fig.:—crown {18x}.

Stephanos, primarily, "that which surrounds, as a wall or crowd" (from *stepho,* "to encircle"), denotes **(1)** "the victor's crown," the symbol of triumph in the games or some such contest; hence, by metonymy, a reward or prize; **(2)** "a token of public honor" for distinguished service, military prowess, etc., or of nuptial joy, or festal gladness, especially at the parousia of kings. **(3)** It was woven as a garland of oak, ivy, parsley, myrtle, or olive, or in imitation of these in gold. **(4)** In some passages the reference to the games is clear, **(4a)** 1 Cor 9:25; 2 Ti 4:8 ("crown of righteousness"); it may be so in **(4b)** 1 Pet 5:4, where the fadeless character of "the crown of glory" is set in contrast to the garlands of earth. **(5)** In other passages it stands as an emblem **(5a)** of life, joy, reward and glory, Phil 4:1; 1 Th 2:19; Jas 1:12 ("crown of life "); Rev 2:10; 3:11; 4:4, 10; **(5b)** of triumph, Rev 6:2; 9:7; 12:1; 14:14. **(6)** It is used of "the crown of thorns" which the soldiers plaited and put on Christ's head, Mt 27:29; Mk 15:17; Jn 19:2, 5. **(6a)** At first sight this might be taken as an alternative for *diadema,* "a kingly crown", but considering the blasphemous character of that masquerade, and the materials used, obviously *diadema* would be quite unfitting and the only alternative was *stephanos.* Syn.: *Diadema (1238)* is a crown as a badge of royalty; whereas *stephanos* is the badge of victory in the games of civic worth, of military valour, of nuptial joy, of festive gladness. See: TDNT—7:615, 1078; BAGD—767a; THAYER—587d.

4736. Στέφανος {7x} **Stĕphanŏs**, *stef'-an-os;* the same as *4735; Stephanus,* a Chr.:—Stephen {7x}. See: BAGD—767a; THAYER—587d.

4737. στεφανόω {3x} **stephanŏō**, *stef-an-ŏ'-o;* from *4735;* to *adorn with* an honorary *wreath* (lit. or fig.):—crown {3x}.

Stephanoo, "to crown," conforms in meaning to *stephanos;* **(1)** it is used of the reward of victory in the games, in 2 Ti 2:5; **(2)** of the glory and honor bestowed by God upon man in regard to his position in creation, Heb 2:7; **(3)** of the glory and honor bestowed upon the Lord Jesus in His exaltation, Heb 2:9. See: TDNT—7:615, 1078; BAGD—767c; THAYER—587d.

4738. στῆθος {5x} **stēthŏs**, *stay'-thos;* from *2476* (as *standing* prominently); the (entire extern.) *bosom,* i.e. *chest:*—breast {5x}.

Stethos, connected with *histemi,* "to stand," i.e., that which stands out, is used **(1)** of mourners in smiting the "breast," Lk 18:13; 23:48; **(2)** of John in reclining on the "breast" of Christ, Jn 13:25; 21:20; **(3)** of the "breasts" of the angels in Rev 15:6. See: BAGD—767d; THAYER—588a.

4739. στήκω {8x} **stēkō**, *stay'-ko;* from the perfect tense of *2476;* to *be stationary,* i.e. (fig.) to *persevere:*—stand {2x}, stand fast {6x}.

Steko is used **(1)** literally, Mk 11:25; **(2)** figuratively, **(2a)** Rom 14:4; **(2b)** of "standing fast," 1 Cor 16:13, "in the faith," i.e., by adherence to it; **(2c)** Gal 5:1, in freedom from legal bondage; **(2d)** Phil 1:27, "in one spirit"; **(2e)** Phil 4:1 and 1 Th 3:8, "in the Lord," i.e., in the willing subjection to His authority; **(2f)** 2 Th 2:15, in the apostle's teaching. See: TDNT—7:636, 1082; BAGD—767d; THAYER—588a.

4740. στηριγμός {1x} **stērigmŏs**, *stay-rig-mos';* from *4741; stability* (fig.):—stedfastness {1x}.

Sterigmos, "a setting firmly, supporting," then "fixedness, steadfastness" (akin to *sterizo,* "to establish"), is used in 2 Pet 3:17. See: TDNT—7:653, 1085; BAGD—768a; THAYER—588b.

4741. στηρίζω {13x} **stērizō**, *stay-rid'-zo;* from a presumed der. of *2476* (like *4731*); to *set fast,* i.e. (lit.) to *turn resolutely* in a certain direction, or (fig.) to *confirm:*—stablish {6x}, establish {3x}, strengthen {2x}, fix {1x}, stedfastly set {1x}.

Establish is to find the source of building from without; to stablish, the source is from within. *Sterizo,* "to fix, make fast, to set" (from *sterix,* "a prop"), is used **(1)** of "establishing" or "stablishing" (i.e., the confirmation) of persons; **(1a)** the apostle Peter was called by the Lord to "establish" his brethren, Lk 22:32, translated "strengthen"; **(1b)** Paul desired to visit Rome that the saints might be "established," Rom 1:11; cf. Acts 8:23; **(1c)** so with Timothy at Thessalonica, 1 Th 3:2; **(2)** the "confirmation" of the saints is the work of God, Rom 16:25, "to stablish (you)"; 1 Th 3:13, "stablish (your hearts)"; 2 Th 2:17, "stablish them (in every good work and word)"; 1 Pet 5:10, "stablish"; **(3)** the means used to reflect the "confirmation" is the ministry of the Word of God, 2 Pet 1:12, "are established (in the truth which is with you)"; **(4)** James exhorts Christians to "stablish" their hearts, Jas 5:8; cf. Rev

Greek

3:2. **(5)** The character of this "confirmation" may be learned from its use in Lk 9:51, "steadfastly set"; 16:26, "fixed." **(6)** Neither the laying on of hands nor the impartation of the Holy Spirit is mentioned in the NT in connection with either of these words, or with the synonymous verb *bebaioo* (see 1 Cor 1:8; 2 Cor 1:21, etc.). See: TDNT—7:653, 1085; BAGD—768a; THAYER—588b.

4742. στίγμα {1x} **stigma**, *stig'-mah;* from a primary στίζω **stizō** (to "*stick*", i.e. *prick*); a *mark* incised or punched (for recognition of ownership), i.e. (fig.) *scar* of service:—mark {1x}.

Stigma denotes "a tattooed mark" or "a mark burnt in, a brand", translated "marks" in Gal 6:17. **(1)** It is probable that the apostle refers to the physical sufferings he had endured since he began to proclaim Jesus as Messiah and Lord [e.g., at Lystra and Philippi]. **(2)** It is probable, too, that this reference to his scars was intended to set off the insistence of the Judaizers upon a body-mark which cost them nothing. Over against the circumcision they demanded as a proof of obedience to the law he set the indelible tokens, sustained in his own body, of his loyalty to the Lord Jesus. As to the origin of the figure, it was indeed customary for a master to brand his slaves, but this language does not suggest that the apostle had been branded by His Master. Soldiers and criminals also were branded on occasion; but to neither of these is the case of Paul as here described analogous. The religious devotee branded himself with the peculiar mark of the god whose cult he affected; so was Paul branded with the marks of his devotion to the Lord Jesus. It is true such markings were forbidden by the law, Lev 19:28, but then Paul had not inflicted these on himself. "The marks of Jesus" cannot be taken to be the marks which the Lord bears in His body in consequence of the Crucifixion; they were different in character. See: TDNT—7:657, 1086; BAGD—768c; THAYER—588c.

4743. στιγμή {1x} **stigmē**, *stig-may';* fem. of *4742;* a *point* of time, i.e. an *instant:*—moment {1x}. See: BAGD—768c; THAYER—588d.

4744. στίλβω {1x} **stilbō**, *stil'-bo;* appar. a primary verb; to *gleam*, i.e. *flash* intensely:—shining {1x}. See: TDNT—7:665, 1087; BAGD—768d; THAYER—588d.

4745. στοά {4x} **stŏa**, *stŏ-ah';* prob. from *2476;* a *colonnade* or interior *piazza:*—porch {4x}.

(1) A *stoa* is a portico, a covered colonnade where people can stand or walk protected from the weather and the heat of the sun. *Stoa,* "a portico," is used **(2)** of the "porches" at the pool of Bethesda, Jn 5:2; **(3)** of the covered colonnade in the Temple, called Solomon's "porch," Jn 10:23; Acts 3:11; 5:12 a portico on the eastern side of the temple. **(4)** This and the other "porches" existent in the time of Christ were almost certainly due to Herod's restoration. See: BAGD—768d; THAYER—588d.

4746. στοιβάς {1x} **stŏibas**, *stoy-bas'* or στιβάς **stibas**, *stee-bas';* from a primary στείβω **stĕibō** (to "*step*" or "*stamp*"); a *spread* (as if *tramped* flat) of loose materials for a couch, i.e. (by impl.) a *bough* of a tree so employed:—branch {1x}. See: BAGD—768d, 768b; THAYER—588d, 588c.

4747. στοιχεῖον {7x} **stŏichĕiŏn**, *stoy-khi'-on;* neut. of a presumed der. of the base of *4748;* something *orderly* in arrangement, i.e. (by impl.) a *serial* (*basal, fundamental, initial*) constituent (lit.), proposition (fig.):—element {4x}, principle {1x}, rudiment {2x}.

Stoicheion used in the plural, primarily signifies **(1)** any first things from which others in a series, or a composite whole take their rise. The word denotes **(1a)** an element, a first principle; or **(1b)** the letters of the alphabet, as elements of speech. **(2)** It is used of **(2a)** the substance of the material world (2 Pet 3:10, 12); **(2b)** the delusive speculations of gentile cults and of Jewish theories, **(2b1)** treated as elementary principles, "the rudiments of the world," (Col 2:8), **(2b2)** spoken of as "philosophy and vain deceit"; **(2b3)** these were presented as superior to faith in Christ; **(3)** the rudimentary principles of religion, Jewish or Gentile, also **(3a)** described as "the rudiments of the world" (Col 2:20), and **(3b)** as "weak and beggarly rudiments" (Gal 4:3, 9); **(4)** the elementary principles (the A, B, C's . .) of the OT, as a revelation from God (Heb 5:12). See: TDNT—7:670, 1087; BAGD—768d; THAYER—588d.

4748. στοιχέω {5x} **stŏichĕō**, *stoy-kheh'-o;* from a der. of στείχω **stĕichō** (to *range* in regular line); to *march,* in (military) rank (*keep step*), i.e. (fig.) to *conform* to virtue and piety:—walk {4x}, walk orderly {1x}.

Stoicheo, from *stoichos,* "a row," signifies "to walk in line," and is used metaphorically of "walking" in relation to others; **(1)** in Acts 21:24, it is translated "walkest orderly"; **(2)** in Rom 4:12, "walk (in . . . steps)"; **(3)** in Gal 5:25 it is used of walking "in the Spirit", in an exhortation to keep step with one another in submission of heart to the Holy Spirit, and therefore of keeping step with Christ, the great

means of unity and harmony in a church; **(4)** in Gal 6:16 it is used of walking by the rule expressed in vv. 14, 15; **(5)** in Phil 3:16 the reference is to the course pursued by the believer who makes "the prize of the high calling" the object of his ambition. See: TDNT—7:666, 1087; BAGD—769c; THAYER—589b.

4749. στολή {9x} **stŏlē**, *stol-ay';* from *4724; equipment,* i.e. (spec.) a *"stole"* or long-fitting *gown* possibly with a train (as a mark of dignity):—robe {5x}, long clothing {1x}, long garment {1x}, them + 848 {1x}, long robe {1x}. Syn.: 2440, 2441, 4158, 5509, 5511.

(1) A *stole* was a long sweeping stately robe that reached to the feet and was a garment of special solemnity, richness, and beauty. *Stole,* (Eng., "stole"), denotes any "stately robe," a long garment reaching to the feet or with a train behind. **(2)** It is used **(2a)** of the long clothing in which the scribes walked, making themselves conspicuous in the eyes of men, Mk 12:38; Lk 20:46; **(2b)** of the robe worn by the young man in the Lord's tomb, Mk 16:5; **(2c)** of the best or, rather, the chief robe, which was brought out for the returned prodigal, Lk 15:22; **(2d)** five times in the Apocalypse, as to glorified saints, 6:11; 7:9, 13–14; 22:14. See: TDNT—7:687, 1088; BAGD—769c; THAYER—589c.

4750. στόμα {79x} **stŏma**, *stom'-a;* prob. strengthened from a presumed der. of the base of *5114;* the *mouth* (as if a *gash* in the face); by impl. *language* (and its relations); fig. an *opening* (in the earth); spec. the *front* or *edge* (of a weapon):—edge {2x}, face {4x}, mouth {73x}.

(1) When "mouth" is used for the edge of the sword it refers, by figure, to the mouth of the river, the shallow, "sharper" edge of the water as it is emitted and flows deeper and wider, Lk 21:24; Heb 11:34. It is akin to *stomachos* (which originally meant "a throat, gullet"), is used **(2)** of "the mouth" **(2a)** of man, e.g., Mt 15:11; **(2b)** of animals, e.g., Mt 17:27; 2 Ti 4:17 (figuratively); Heb 11:33; Jas 3:3; Rev 13:2 twice; **(3)** figuratively of "inanimate things," **(3a)** of the "edge" of a sword, Lk 21:24; Heb 11:34; **(3b)** of the earth, Rev 12:16; **(4)** figuratively, of the "mouth," as the organ of speech, **(4a)** of Christ's words, e.g., Mt 13:35; Lk 11:54; Acts 8:32; 22:14; 1 Pet 2:22; **(4b)** of human words, **(4b1)** e.g., Mt 18:16; 21:16; Lk 1:64; Rev 14:5; **(4b2)** as emanating from the heart, Mt 12:34; Rom 10:8, 9; **(4c)** of prophetic ministry through the Holy Spirit, Lk 1:70; Acts 1:16; 3:18; 4:25; **(4d)** of the destructive policy of two world potentates at the end of this age, Rev 13:2, 5, 6; 16:13 (twice); **(4e)** of shameful speak-

ing, Eph 4:29 and Col 3:8; **(4f)** of the devil speaking as a dragon or serpent, Rev 12:15, 16; 16:13; **(4g)** figuratively, in the phrase "face to face" (lit., "mouth to mouth"), 2 Jn 12; 3 Jn 14; **(4h)** metaphorically, of "the utterances of the Lord, in judgment," 2 Th 2:8; Rev 1:16; 2:16; 19:15, 21; **(4i)** of His judgment upon a local church for its lukewarmness, Rev 3:16; **(4j)** by metonymy, for "speech," Mt 18:16; Lk 19:22; 21:15; 2 Cor 13:1. Syn.: 1366. See: TDNT—7:692, 1089; BAGD—769d; THAYER—589c.

4751. στόμαχος {1x} **stŏmachŏs**, *stom'-akh-os;* from *4750;* an *orifice* (the *gullet*), i.e. (spec.) the *"stomach"*:—stomach {1x}. See: BAGD—770b; THAYER—590a.

4752. στρατεία {2x} **stratĕia**, *strat-i'-ah;* from *4754;* military *service,* i.e. (fig.) the apostolic *career* (as one of hardship and danger):—warfare {2x}. Cf. 2 Cor 10:4; 1 Ti 1:18. See: TDNT—7:701, 1091; BAGD—770b; THAYER—590a.

4753. στράτευμα {8x} **stratĕuma**, *strat'-yoo-mah;* from *4754;* an *armament,* i.e. (by impl.) a body of *troops* (more or less extensive or systematic):—army {6x}, soldier {1x}, men of war {1x}.

Strateuma denotes **(1)** "an army" of any size, large or small, Mt 22:7; Acts 23:27; Rev 9:16; 19:14, 19 (twice); **(2)** a company of soldiers, such as Herod's bodyguard, Lk 23:11, "men of war", or **(3)** the soldiers of a garrison, Acts 23:10. See: TDNT—7:701, 1091; BAGD—770b; THAYER—590b.

4754. στρατεύομαι {7x} **stratĕuŏmai**, *strat-yoo'-om-ahee;* mid. voice from the base of *4756;* to *serve* in a military campaign; fig. to *execute the apostolate* (with its arduous duties and functions), to *contend* with carnal inclinations:—soldier {1x}, goeth to warfare {1x}, war {5x}.

Strateuomai, used in the middle voice, "to make war" (from *stratos,* "an encamped army"), is translated **(1)** "to war", metaphorically, of spiritual "conflict," in 2 Cor 10:3; 1 Ti 1:18; 2 Ti 2:4; Jas 4:1; 1 Pet 2:11. It is used **(2)** literally **(2a)** of "serving as a soldier," Lk 3:14, "soldiers"; **(2b)** 1 Cor 9:7, "(who) goeth a warfare." See: TDNT—7:701, 1091; BAGD—770b; THAYER—590b.

4755. στρατηγός {10x} **stratēgŏs**, *strat-ay-gos';* from the base of *4756* and 71 or *2233;* a *general,* i.e. (by impl. or anal.) a (military) *governor* (*prætor*), the chief (*præfect*) of the (Levitical) temple-wardens:—captain {5x}, magistrate {5x}.

Strategos, originally the commander of an army (from *stratos,* "an army," and *ago,* "to

lead"), came to denote (1) "a civil commander, a governor", the highest magistrate, or any civil officer in chief command, Acts 16:20, 22, 35–36, 38; also (2) the "chief captain" of the Temple, himself a Levite, having command of the Levites who kept guard in and around the Temple, Lk 22:4, 52; Acts 4:1; 5:24, 26. Cf. Jer 20:1. See: TDNT—7:701, 1091; BAGD—770c; THAYER—590b.

4756. στρατία {2x} **stratia**, *strat-ee'-ah;* fem. of a der. of στρατός **stratŏs**, (an *army;* from the base of *4766,* as *encamped*); *camp-likeness,* i.e. an *army,* i.e. (fig.) the *angels,* the celestial *luminaries:*—host {2x}.

Stratia, "an army," is used (1) of angels, Lk 2:13; (2) of stars, Acts 7:42. See: TDNT—7:701, 1091; BAGD—770d; THAYER—590c.

4757. στρατιώτης {26x} **stratiōtēs**, *strat-ee-o'-tace;* from a presumed der. of the same as *4756;* a *camper-out,* i.e. a (common) *warrior* (lit. or fig.):—soldier {26x}.

Stratiotes, "a soldier," is used (1) in the natural sense, e.g., Mt 8:9; 27:27; 28:12; Mk 15:16; Lk 7:8; 23:36; six times in John; thirteen times in Acts; not again in the NT; (2) metaphorically of one who endures hardship in the cause of Christ, 2 Ti 2:3. See: TDNT—7:701, 1091; BAGD—770d; THAYER—590c.

4758. στρατολογέω {1x} **stratŏlŏgĕō**, *strat-ol-og-eh'-o;* from a compound of the base of *4756* and *3004* (in its orig. sense); to *gather* (or *select*) as a *warrior,* i.e. *enlist* in the army:—choose to be a soldier {1x}. See: TDNT—7:701, 1091; BAGD—770d; THAYER—590c.

4759. στρατοπεδάρχης {1x} **stratŏpĕdarchēs**, *strat-op-ed-ar'-khace;* from *4760* and *757;* a *ruler of an army,* i.e. (spec.) a Prætorian *præfect:*—captain of the guard {1x}. See: BAGD—771a; THAYER—590d.

4760. στρατόπεδον {1x} **stratŏpĕdŏn**, *strat-op'-ed-on;* from the base of *4756* and the same as *3977;* a *camping-ground,* i.e. (by impl.) a body of *troops:*—army {1x}.

Stratopedon, from stratos, "a military host," pedon, "a plain," strictly denotes "an army encamped, a camp"; in Lk 21:20, of the soldiers who were to be encamped about Jerusalem in fulfillment of the Lord's prophecy concerning the destruction of the city; the phrase might be translated "by camps" (or encampments). See: TDNT—7:701, 1091; BAGD—771a; THAYER—590d.

4761. στρεβλόω {1x} **strĕblŏō**, *streb-lŏ'-o;* from a der. of *4762;* to *wrench,* i.e. (spec.) to *torture* (by the rack), but only fig. to *pervert:*—wrest {1x}.

Strebloo, "to twist, to torture" (from *streble,* "a winch" or "instrument of torture," and akin to *strepho,* "to turn"), is used metaphorically in 2 Pet 3:16, of "wresting" the Scriptures on the part of the ignorant and unsteadfast. See: BAGD—771a; THAYER—590d.

4762. στρέφω {19x} **strĕphō**, *stref'-o;* strengthened from the base of *5157;* to *twist,* i.e. *turn* quite around or *reverse* (lit. or fig.):—turn {11x}, turn (one's) self {2x}, turn (one) {1x}, turn again {1x}, turn back again {1x}, turn (one) about {1x}, be converted {1x}, vr turn {1x}.

Strepho, denotes (1) in the active voice, (1a) "to turn" (something), Mt 5:39; (1b) reflexively, "to turn oneself, to turn the back to people," said of God, Acts 7:42; (2) "to turn one thing into another," Rev 11:6 (the only place where this word occurs after the Acts); (3) in the passive voice, (3a) used reflexively, "to turn oneself," e.g. Mt 7:6; Jn 20:14, 16; (3b) metaphorically, Mt 18:3, "(except) ye . . . be converted." See: TDNT—7:714, 1093; BAGD—771a; THAYER—590d.

4763. στρηνιάω {1x} **strēniaō**, *stray-nee-ah'-o;* from a presumed der. of *4764;* to *be luxurious:*—live deliciously {1x}.

(1) Streniao refers to the insolence of wealth, to the wantonness and petulance that result from being full and lacking nothing, but there is a power and vigor to this wealth. (2) Streniao, "to run riot," is rendered "lived deliciously" in Rev 18:7, 8. Syn.: 4684, 5171. See: BAGD—771c; THAYER—591a.

4764. στρῆνος {1x} **strēnŏs**, *stray'-nos;* akin to *4731;* a "straining", "strenuousness" or "strength", i.e. (fig.) *luxury* (*voluptuousness*):—delicacy {1x}.

Strenos stresses the results of one who strains at labor and has excess to purchase above the ordinary; hence, a delicacy. See: BAGD—771c; THAYER—591a.

4765. στρουθίον {4x} **strŏuthiŏn**, *stroo-thee'-on;* dimin. of στρουθός **strŏuthŏs** (a *sparrow*); a *little sparrow:*—sparrow {4x}.

Strouthion, a diminutive of strouthos, "a sparrow," occurs in Mt 10:29, 31; Lk 12:6, 7. Being a diminutive stresses that God takes care of even the smallest of the small. See: TDNT—7:730, 1096; BAGD—771c; THAYER—591a.

4766. στρώννυμι {7x} **strōnnumi**, *strone'-noo-mee;* or simpler

στρωννύω **strōnnuō**, *strone-noo'-o;* prol. from a still simpler

στρόω **strŏō**, *strŏ'-o* (used only as an alt. in certain tenses; prob. akin to *4731* through the idea of *positing*); to *"strew"*, i.e. *spread* (as a carpet or couch):—make (one's) bed {1x}, furnish {2x}, spread {2x}, strew {2x}.

Stronnumi, "to spread," is used **(1)** of "furnishing a room," Mk 14:15; Lk 22:12; **(2)** of "making a bed," Acts 9:34; **(3)** "strawed" in Mt 21:8, second use; Mk 11:8, second use; and **(4)** "to spread," in Mt 21:8, first use; Mk 11:8, first use. See: BAGD—771c; THAYER—591b.

4767. στυγνητός {1x} **stugnētŏs**, *stoog-nay-tos';* from a der. of an obs. appar. primary στύγω **stugō** (to *hate*); *hated,* i.e. *odious:*—hateful {1x}. See: BAGD—771d; THAYER—591b.

4768. στυγνάζω {2x} **stugnazō**, *stoog-nad'-zo;* from the same as *4767;* to *render gloomy,* i.e. (by impl.) *glower* (*be overcast* with clouds, or *sombreness* of speech):—lower {1x}, be sad {1x}. See: BAGD—771d; THAYER—591b.

4769. στύλος {4x} **stulŏs**, *stoo'-los;* from στύω **stuō** (to *stiffen; prop.* akin to the base of *2476);* a *post* (*"style"),* i.e. (fig.) *support:*—pillar {4x}. See: TDNT—7:732, 1096; BAGD—772a; THAYER—591b.

4770. Στωϊκός {1x} **Stōïkŏs**, *sto-ik-os';* from *4745;* a *"Stoïc"* (as occupying a particular porch in Athens), i.e. adherent of a certain philosophy:—Stoicks {1x}. See: BAGD—772a; THAYER—591c.

4771. σύ {178x} **su**, *soo;* the pers. pron. of the second pers. sing.; *thou:*—thou {178x}. See: BAGD—772a; THAYER—591c. See also *4571, 4671, 4675;* and for the plur. *5209, 5210, 5213, 5216.*

4772. συγγένεια {3x} **suggĕnĕia**, *soong-ghen'-i-ah;* from *4773;* relationship, i.e. (concr.) *relatives:*—kindred {3x}. See: TDNT—7:736, 1097; BAGD—772c; THAYER—592a.

4773. συγγενής {12x} **suggĕnēs**, *soong-ghen-ace';* from *4862* and *1085;* a *relative* (by blood); by extens. a fellow *countryman:*—cousin {2x}, kin {1x}, kinsfolk {2x}, kinsman {7x}. See: TDNT—7:736, 1097; BAGD—772c; THAYER—592a.

4774. συγγνώμη {1x} **suggnōmē**, *soong-gno'-may;* from a com-pound of *4862* and *1097; fellow knowledge,* i.e. *concession:*—permission {1x}. See: TDNT—1:716, 119; BAGD—773a; THAYER—592a.

4775. συγκάθημαι {2x} **sugkathēmai**, *soong-kath'-ay-mahee;* from *4862* and *2521;* to *seat oneself* in company *with:*—sat + 2258 {1x}, sit with {1x}.

Sunkathemai, as a verb, means "to sit with" and occurs in Mk 14:54: "And Peter followed Him afar off, even into the palace of the high priest: and he sat with the servants, and warmed himself at the fire" (cf. Acts 26:30). Syn.: 339, 345, 347, 377, 1910, 2516, 2521, 2621, 2523, 2625, 4776, 4873. See: BAGD—773a; THAYER—592b.

4776. συγκαθίζω {2x} **sugkathizō**, *soong-kath-id'-zo;* from *4862* and *2523;* to *give* (or *take*) *a seat* in company *with:*—make sit together {1x}, be set down together {1x}.

Sunkathizo, as a verb, denotes **(1)** transitively, "to make to sit together": "And hath raised us up together, and made us sit together in heavenly places in Christ Jesus" (Eph 2:6); and **(2)** intransitively, "were set down": "And when they had kindled a fire in the midst of the hall, and were set down together, Peter sat down among them" (Lk 22:55). Syn.: 339, 345, 347, 377, 1910, 2516, 2521, 2621, 2523, 2625, 4775, 4873. See: TDNT—7:787, 1102; BAGD—773b; THAYER—592b.

4777. συγκακοπαθέω {1x} **sugkakŏpathĕō**, *soong-kak-op-ath-eh'-o;* from *4862* and *2553;* to *suffer hardship* in company *with:*—be partaker of afflictions {1x}. See: TDNT—5:936, 798; BAGD—773b; THAYER—592b.

4778. συγκακουχέω {1x} **sugkakŏuchĕō**, *soong-kak-oo-kheh'-o;* from *4862* and *2558;* to *maltreat* in company *with,* i.e. (pass.) *endure persecution together:*—suffer affliction with {1x}. See: BAGD—773b; THAYER—592c.

4779. συγκαλέω {8x} **sugkalĕō**, *soong-kal-eh'-o;* from *4862* and *2564;* to *convoke:*—call together {8x}.

Sugkaleo signifies "to call together," Mk 15:16; Lk 9:1; 15:6, 9; 23:13; Acts 5:21; 10:24; 28:17. See: TDNT—3:496, 394; BAGD—773b; THAYER—592c

4780. συγκαλύπτω {1x} **sugkaluptō**, *soong-kal-oop'-to;* from *4862* and *2572;* to *conceal altogether:*—cover {1x}. See: TDNT—7:743, 1098; BAGD—773b; THAYER—592c.

4781. συγκάμπτω {1x} **sugkamptō**, *soong-kamp'-to;* from *4862* and *2578;* to *bend together,* i.e. (fig.) to *afflict:*—bow down {1x}.

Sugkampto signifies "to bend completely together, to bend down by compulsory force," Rom 11:10. See: BAGD—773b; THAYER—592c.

4782. συγκαταβαίνω {1x} **sugkatabainō**, *soong-kat-ab-ah'-ee-no;* from *4862* and *2597;* to *descend* in company *with:*—go down with {1x}. See: BAGD—773c; THAYER—592c.

4783. συγκατάθεσις {1x} **sugkatathĕsis**, *soong-kat-ath'-es-is;* from *4784;* a *deposition* (of sentiment) in company *with,* i.e. (fig.) *accord* with:—agreement {1x}. See: BAGD—773c; THAYER—592d.

4784. συγκατατίθεμαι {1x} **sugkatatithĕmai**, *soong-kat-at-ith'-em-ahee;* mid. from *4862* and *2698;* to *deposit* (one's vote or opinion) in company *with,* i.e. (fig.) to *accord* with:—consented + 2258 {1x}.

This word means lit., "to put or lay down together with" (*sun,* "with," *kata,* "down," *tithemi,* "to put"), was used of depositing one's vote in an urn; hence, "to vote for, agree with, consent to." It is said negatively of Joseph of Arimathaea, who had not "consented" to the counsel and deed of the Jews, Lk 23:51 (middle voice). See: BAGD—773c; THAYER—592d.

4785. συγκαταψηφίζω {1x} **sugkatapsēphizō**, *soong-kat-aps-ay-fid'-zo;* from *4862* and a compound of *2596* and *5585;* to *count down* in company *with,* i.e. *enroll among:*—number with {1x}. See: TDNT—9:604,*; BAGD—773c; THAYER—592d.

4786. συγκεράννυμι {2x} **sugkĕrannumi**, *soong-ker-an'-noo-mee;* from *4862* and *2767;* to *commingle,* i.e. (fig.) to *combine* or *assimilate:*—mix with {1x}, temper together {1x}. See: BAGD—773d; THAYER—592d.

4787. συγκινέω {1x} **sugkinĕō**, *soong-kin-eh'-o;* from *4682* and *2795;* to *move together,* i.e. (spec.) to *excite* as a mass (to sedition):—stir up {1x}.

Sunkineo, as a verb, means "to move together" [*sun,* "together," *kineo,* "to move"], "to stir up, excite," and is used metaphorically in Acts 6:12: "And they stirred up the people, and the elders, and the scribes, and came upon him, and caught him, and brought him to the council." Syn.: 329, 383, 387, 1326, 1892, 2042, 3947, 3951, 4531, 4579, 4797, 5017. See: BAGD—773d; THAYER—593a.

4788. συγκλείω {4x} **sugklĕiō**, *soong-kli'-o;* from *4862* and *2808;* to *shut together,* i.e. *include* or (fig.) *embrace* in a common subjection to:—conclude {2x}, inclose {1x}, shut up {1x}.

Subkleio, "to shut together, shut in on all sides" (*sun,* "with," *kleio,* "to shut"), is used **(1)** of a catch of fish, Lk 5:6; **(2)** metaphorically, **(2a)** "shut up" unto faith, Gal 5:23; **(2b)** "concluded" that all are under sin, **(2b1)** Gal 5:22; and **(2b2)** in Rom 11:32, of God's dealings with Jew and Gentile, in that He has "concluded all unto disobedience, that He might have mercy upon all." **(2c)** There is no intimation in this of universal salvation. **(2d)** The meaning, from the context, is that God has ordered that all should be convicted of disobedience without escape by human merit, that He might display His mercy, and has offered the gospel without national distinction, and that when Israel is restored, He will, in the resulting millennium, show His mercy to all nations. See: TDNT—7:744, 1098; BAGD—774a; THAYER—593a.

4789. συγκληρονόμος {4x} **sugklērŏnŏmŏs**, *soong-klay-ron-om'-os;* from *4862* and *2818;* a *co-heir,* i.e. (by anal.) *participant in common:*—fellow heirs {1x}, joint heirs {1x}, heirs together {1x}, heirs with {1x}.

This word means "a joint-heir, co-inheritor", and is translated **(1)** "heirs with" of Isaac and Jacob as participants with Abraham in the promises of God, Heb 11:9; **(2)** "heirs together" of husband and wife who are also united in Christ, 1 Pet 3:7; **(3)** "fellow heirs" of Gentiles who believe, as participants in the gospel with Jews who believe, Eph 3:6; and **(4)** "joint heirs", of all believers as prospective participants with Christ in His glory, as recompense for their participation in His sufferings, Rom 8:17. See: TDNT—3:767 & 7:787, 442 & 1102; BAGD—774a; THAYER—593b.

4790. συγκοινωνέω {3x} **sugkŏinōnĕō**, *soong-koy-no-neh'-o;* from *4862* and *2841;* to *share* in company *with,* i.e. *co-participate* in:—communicate with {1x}, have fellowship with {1x}, be partaker of {1x}.

This word means "to share together with", and is translated **(1)** "communicated with" in Phil 4:14; **(2)** "have fellowship with" in Eph 5:11; **(3)** "be . . . partakers of" in Rev 18:4. The thought is that of sharing with others what one has, in order to meet their needs. See: TDNT—3:797, 447; BAGD—774b; THAYER—593b.

4791. συγκοινωνός {4x} **sugkŏinōnŏs**, *soong-koy-no-nos';* from *4862* and *2844;* a *co-participant:*—companion {1x},

partaker {1x}, partaker +1096 {1x}, partaker with {1x}.

This word denotes "partaking jointly with" and is found in **(1)** Rom 11:17, "partakest"; **(2)** 1 Cor 9:23, "a partaker with"; **(3)** Phil 1:7, "partakers (of my grace)"; **(4)** Rev 1:9, "companion with (you in the tribulation, etc.)." See: TDNT—3:797, 447; BAGD—774b; THAYER—593b.

4792. συγκομίζω {1x} **sugkŏmizō**, *soong-kom-id'-zo;* from *4862* and *2865;* to *convey together,* i.e. *collect* or *bear away in company with* others:—carry {1x}. See: BAGD—774c; THAYER—593b.

4793. συγκρίνω {3x} **sugkrinō**, *soong-kree'-no;* from *4862* and *2919;* to *judge* of one thing in connection *with* another, i.e. *combine* (spiritual ideas with appropriate expressions) or *collate* (one person with another by way of contrast or resemblance):—compare among {1x}, compare with {2x}.

Sugkrino denotes "to join fitly, to combine", **(1)** 1 Cor 2:13, "comparing" either **(1a)** in the sense of combining spiritual things with spiritual, adapting the discourse to the subject, under the guidance of the Holy Spirit, or **(1b)** communicating spiritual things by spiritual things or words, or in the sense of interpreting spiritual things to spiritual men; **(2)** "to place together; hence, judge or discriminate by comparison, compare, with or among," 2 Cor 10:12 (twice). See: TDNT—3:953, 469; BAGD—774d; THAYER—593c.

4794. συγκύπτω {1x} **sugkuptō**, *soong-koop'-to;* from *4862* and *2955;* to *stoop altogether,* i.e. *be completely overcome* by:—bow together {1x}. See: BAGD—775a; THAYER—593c.

4795. συγκυρία {1x} **sugkuria**, *soong-koo-ree'-ah;* from a compound of *4862* and κυρέω **kurĕō**, (to *light* or *happen;* from the base of *2962*); *concurrence,* i.e. *accident:*—chance {1x}.

Sugkuria literally means a meeting together with, a coincidence of circumstances, a happening and is translated "chance" (Lk 10:31). But concurrence of events is what the word signifies, rather than chance. English chance is used here similarly to purchasing a chance on a raffle. One is seeking the ticket which concurs with the winning number. See: BAGD—775a; THAYER—593d.

4796. συγχαίρω {7x} **sugchairō**, *soong-khah'-ee-ro;* from *4862* and *5463;* to *sympathize in gladness, congratulate:*—rejoice in {1x}, rejoice with {6x}.

Sugchairo, "to rejoice with", is used **(1)** of

"rejoicing" together in the recovery of what was lost, Lk 15:6, 9; **(2)** in suffering in the cause of the gospel, Phil 2:17 (2nd part), 18; **(3)** in the joy of another, Lk 1:58; **(4)** in the honor of fellow believers, 1 Cor 12:26; **(5)** in the triumph of the truth, 1 Cor 13:6, "rejoiceth in." See: TDNT—9:359, 1298; BAGD—775a; THAYER—593d.

4797. συγχέω {5x} **sugchĕō**, *soong-kheh'-o;* or

    συγχύνω sugchunō, *soong-khoo'-no;* from *4862* and χέω **chĕō** (to *pour*) or its alt.; to *commingle,* promiscuously, i.e. (fig.) to *throw* (an assembly) *into disorder,* to *perplex* (the mind):—confound {2x}, confuse {1x}, stir up {1x}, be in an uproar {1x}.

Sugcheo, as a verb, means literally "to pour together, commingle," hence, **(1)** said of persons, means "to trouble or confuse, to stir up": "Some therefore cried one thing, and some another: for the assembly was confused (*sugcheo*); and the more part knew not wherefore they were come together" (Acts 19:32—said of the mind); **(2)** "was in an uproar" (Acts 21:31); **(3)** "stirred up": "And when the seven days were almost ended, the Jews which were of Asia, when they saw him in the temple, stirred up all the people, and laid hands on him" (Acts 21:27); **(4)** "confounded": "Now when this was noised abroad, the multitude came together, and were confounded, because that every man heard them speak in his own language" (Acts 2:6; cf. 9:22). Syn.: 181, 329, 383, 387, 1326, 1892, 2042, 2617, 3947, 3951, 4531, 4579, 4787, 4799, 5017. See: BAGD—775a; THAYER—593d.

4798. συγχράομαι {1x} **sugchraŏmai**, *soong-khrah'-om-ahee;* from *4862* and *5530;* to *use jointly,* i.e. (by impl.) to *hold intercourse in common:*—have dealings with {1x}. See: BAGD—775b; THAYER—594a.

4799. σύγχυσις {1x} **sugchusis**, *soong'-khoo-sis;* from *4797; commixture,* i.e. (fig.) riotous *disturbance:*—confusion {1x}.

Sunchusis, as a noun, means "a pouring or mixing together"; hence "a disturbance, confusion, a tumultuous disorder, as of riotous persons": "And the whole city was filled with confusion: and having caught Gaius and Aristarchus, men of Macedonia, Paul's companions in travel, they rushed with one accord into the theatre" (Acts 19:29). Syn.: 181, 2617, 4797. See: BAGD—775c; THAYER—594a.

4800. συζάω {3x} **suzaō**, *sood-zah'-o;* from *4862* and *2198;* to *continue to live in common with,* i.e. *co-survive* (lit. or fig.):—live with {3x}.

Sunzao, as a verb, means "to live together with": "Now if we be dead with Christ, we believe that we shall also live with him" (Rom 6:8; cf. 2 Ti 2:11; 2 Cor 7:3). Syn.: 326, 390, 980, 1236, 2198, 2225, 4176, 5225. See: TDNT— 7:787, 1102; BAGD—775c; THAYER—594a.

4801. συζεύγνυμι {2x} **suzĕugnumi,** *sood-zyoog'-noo-mee;* from *4862* and the base of *2201;* to *yoke together,* i.e. (fig.) *conjoin* (in marriage):—join together {2x}. Cf. Mt 19:6; Mk 10:9. See: BAGD—775c; THAYER— 594a.

4802. συζητέω {10x} **suzētĕō,** *sood-zay-teh'-o;* from *4862* and *2212;* to investigate *jointly,* i.e. *discuss, controvert, cavil:—* question with {2x}, question {2x}, question one with another {1x}, enquire {1x}, dispute with {1x}, dispute {1x}, reason together {1x}, reason {1x}.

This word means "to search together", "to discuss, dispute," is translated **(1)** "question with" in Mk 8:11; 9:16; **(2)** "question" in Mk 1:27; 9:14; **(3)** "question one with another" in Mk 9:10; **(4)** "enquire" in Lk 22:23; **(5)** "dispute with" in Acts 6:9; **(6)** "dispute" in Acts 9:29; **(7)** "reason together" in Mk 12:28; and **(8)** "reason" in Lk 24:15. See: TDNT—7:747, 1099; BAGD—775d; THAYER—594a.

4803. συζήτησις {3x} **suzētēsis,** *sood-zay'-tay-sis;* from *4802; mutual questioning,* i.e. *discussion:—*disputation {1x}, disputing {1x}, reasoning {1x}. Cf. Acts 15:2, 7; 28:29. See: TDNT—7:748, 1099; BAGD—775d; THAYER—594b.

4804. συζητητής {1x} **suzētētēs,** *sood-zay-tay-tace';* from *4802;* a *disputant,* i.e. *sophist:—*disputer {1x}.

Suzetetes, from *sun,* "with," *zeteo,* "to seek," denotes "a disputer," 1 Cor 1:20, where the reference is especially to a learned "disputant," a sophist. See: TDNT—7:748, 1099; BAGD— 775d; THAYER—594b.

4805. σύζυγος {1x} **suzugŏs,** *sood'-zoo-gos;* from *4801; co-yoked,* i.e. (fig.) as noun, a *colleague;* prob. rather as a proper name; *Syzygus,* a Chr.:—yokefellow {1x}. See: TDNT—7:748, 1099; BAGD—775a; THAYER—594b.

4806. συζωοποιέω {2x} **suzōŏpŏiĕō,** *sood-zo-op-oy-eh'-o;* from *4862* and *2227;* to *reanimate conjointly* with (fig.):— quicken together with {1x}, quicken together {1x}.

(1) Quicken means to make a person able to respond immediately to spiritual stimuli; neither growth nor time is necessary before one is capable of walking in the Spirit. **(2)** It is used

in Eph 2:5; Col 2:13, of the spiritual life with Christ, imparted to believers at their conversion. See: TDNT—7:787, 1102; BAGD—776a; THAYER—594c.

4807. συκάμινος {1x} **sukaminŏs,** *soo-kam'-ee-nos;* of Heb. or. [8256] in imitation of *4809;* a *sycamore*-fig tree:—sycamine tree {1x}.

The sycamine tree has the form and foliage of the mulberry, but fruit resembling the fig; probably mimics the *sycamore* (*4809*) in appearance, Lk 17:6. See: TDNT—7:758, 1100; BAGD—776a; THAYER—594c.

4808. συκῆ {16x} **sukē,** *soo-kay';* from *4810;* a *fig-tree:—*fig tree {16x}. *Suke,* "a fig tree," is found in Mt 21:19, 20, 21; 24:32; Mk 11:13, 20, 21; 13:28; Lk 13:6, 7; 21:29; Jn 1:48, 50, Jas 3:12; Rev 6:13. *Note:* A "fig tree" with leaves must have young fruits already, or it will be barren for the season. The first figs ripen in late May or early June. The tree in Mk 11:13 should have had fruit, unripe indeed, but existing. In some lands "fig trees" bear the early fruit under the leaves and the later fruit above the leaves. In that case the leaves were a sign that there should have been fruit, unseen from a distance, underneath the leaves. The condemnation of this fig tree lay in the absence of any sign of fruit. See: TDNT—7:751, 1100; BAGD—776b; THAYER—594c.

4809. συκομωραία {1x} **sukŏmōraia,** *soo-kom-o-rah'-yah;* from *4810* and μόρον **mŏrŏn** (the *mulberry*); the "*sycamore*"- fig tree:—*sycamore* tree {1x}. See: TDNT— 7:758,*; BAGD—776b; THAYER—594c. comp. *4807.*

4810. σῦκον {4x} **sukŏn,** *soo'-kon;* appar. a primary word; a *fig:—*fig {4x}.

Sukon denotes "the ripe fruit of a *suke,* a fig-tree" and is found in Mt 7:16; Mk 11:13; Lk 6:44; Jas 3:12. See: TDNT—7:751, 1100; BAGD—776b; THAYER—594d.

4811. συκοφαντέω {2x} **sukŏphantĕō,** *soo-kof-an-teh'-o;* from a compound of *4810* and a der. of *5316;* to *be a fig-informer* (reporter of the law forbidding the exportation of figs from Greece), "*sycophant*", i.e. (gen. and by extens.) to *defraud* (*exact* unlawfully, *extort*):—accuse falsely {1x}, take by false accusation {1x}.

Sukophanteo, as a verb, means **(1)** "to accuse wrongfully" in Lk 3:14; and **(2)** "to exact money wrongfully, to take anything by false accusation" in Lk 19:8. **(3)** The word is derived from *sukon,* "a fig," and *phaino,* "to show." **(3a)** At Athens a man whose business it was to give information against anyone who might be

detected exporting figs out of the province is said to have been called a *sukophantes.* **(3b)** Probably, however, the word was used to denote one who brings figs to light by shaking the tree, and then in a metaphorical sense one who makes rich men yield up their fruit by "false accusation." **(3c)** Hence in general parlance it was used to designate "a malignant informer," one who accused from love of gain. Syn.: 156, 157, 1225, 1458, 1462, 1908, 2723, 2724. See: TDNT—7:759, 1100; BAGD—776c; THAYER—594d.

4812. συλαγωγέω {1x} **sulagōgĕō**, *soo-lag-ogue-eh'-o;* from the base of *4813* and (the redupl. form of) *71;* to *lead* away as *booty,* i.e. (fig.) *seduce:*—spoil {1x}.

Sulagogeo means to carry off as spoil, lead captive. The false teacher, through his philosophy and vain deceit, would carry them off as so much booty (Col 2:8). See: BAGD—776c; THAYER—594d.

4813. συλάω {1x} **sulaō**, *soo-lah'-o;* from a der. of **σύλλω sullō** (to *strip;* prob. akin to *138;* comp. *4661*); to *despoil:*—rob {1x}. See: BAGD—776c; THAYER—595a.

4814. συλλαλέω {6x} **sullalĕō**, *sool-lal-eh'-o;* from *4862* and *2980;* to *talk together,* i.e. *converse:*—talk with {2x}, talk {1x}, speak {1x}, commune with {1x}, confer {1x}. See: BAGD—776d; THAYER—595a.

4815. συλλαμβάνω {16x} **sullambanō**, *sool-lam-ban'-o;* from *4862* and *2983;* to *clasp,* i.e. *seize* (*arrest, capture*); spec. to *conceive* (lit. or fig.); by impl. to *aid:*— catch {1x}, conceive {5x}, help {2x}, take {8x}.

This word means "to seize, take," and is rendered **(1)** "to take" **(1a)** Jesus in Mt 26:55; Mk 14:48; Lk 22:54; Jn 18:12; Acts 1:16; **(1b)** a large draught of fish in Lk 5:9; **(1c)** Peter in Acts 12:3; and **(1d)** Paul in Acts 23:27; **(2)** "catch" in "Acts 26:21; **(3)** "conceive", **(3a)** Elisabeth in Lk 1:24, 36; **(3b)** Mary in Lk 1:31; **(3c)** Jesus in Lk 2:21; **(3d)** "lust" in Jas 1:15; and **(4)** "help" in Lk 5:7; Phil 4:3. See: TDNT—7:759, 1101; BAGD—776d; THAYER—595a.

4816. συλλέγω {8x} **sullĕgō**, *sool-leg'-o;* from *4862* and *3004* in its orig. sense; to *collect:*—gather {5x}, gather up {2x}, gather together {1x}.

(1) This word denotes to gather up, to collect in order to carry off. This word means "to collect, gather up or out" (*sun,* "with" *lego,* "to pick out"), is said of "gathering" **(2)** grapes and figs, Mt 7:16; Lk 6:44; **(3)** tares, Mt 13:28, 29, 30, 40; **(4)** good fish, Mt 13:48; and **(5)** "all things that cause stumbling, and them that do

iniquity," Mt 13:41. See: BAGD—777a; THAYER—595b.

4817. συλλογίζομαι {1x} **sullŏgizŏmai**, *sool-log-id'-zom-ahee;* from *4862* and *3049;* to *reckon together* (with oneself), i.e. *deliberate:*—reason with {1x}.

This word stresses to bring together accounts, reckon up, compute; and to reckon within one's self, to reason (Lk 20:5) [cf. Eng. "syllogism"]. See: BAGD—777a; THAYER—595b.

4818. συλλυπέω {1x} **sullupĕō**, *sool-loop-eh'-o;* from *4862* and *3076;* to *afflict jointly,* i.e. (pass.) *sorrow at* (on account of) someone:—be grieved {1x}.

Sullupeo is used in the passive voice in Mk 3:5, "to be grieved" or afflicted together with a person, said of Christ's "grief" at the hardness of heart of those who criticized His healing on the Sabbath day; it here seems to suggest the sympathetic nature of His grief because of their self-injury. Some suggest that the *sun* indicates the mingling of "grief" with His anger. See: TDNT—4:323,*; BAGD—777a; THAYER—595b.

4819. συμβαίνω {8x} **sumbainō**, *soom-bah'-ee-no;* from *4862* and the base of *939;* to *walk* (fig. *transpire*) *together,* i.e. *concur* (*take place*):—happen unto {4x}, happen {2x}, befell, {1x}, so it was {1x}.

Sumbaino literally means to walk with the feet near together; hence, to walk together, come together, arrive at the same point at the same time. Therefore, figuratively, of things which fall out at the same time, to happen, turn out, come to pass. It is translated **(1)** "happen unto" in Mk 10:32; Acts 3:10; 1 Pet 4:12; 2 Pet 2:22; **(2)** "happen" in Lk 24:14; 1 Cor 10:11; **(3)** "befell" in Acts 20:19; and **(4)** "so it was" in Acts 21:35. See: BAGD—777b; THAYER—595b.

4820. συμβάλλω {6x} **sumballō**, *soom-bal'-lo;* from *4862* and *906;* to *combine,* i.e. (in speaking) to *converse, consult, dispute,* (mentally) to *consider,* (by impl.) to *aid,* (personally) to *join, attack:*—confer {1x}, encounter {1x}, help {1x}, make {1x}, meet with {1x}, ponder {1x}. See: BAGD—777b; THAYER—595c.

4821. συμβασιλεύω {2x} **sumbasilĕuō**, *soom-bas-il-yoo'-o;* from *4862* and *936;* to *be co-regent* (fig.):—reign with {2x}.

Sumbasileuo, "to reign together with", is used of the future "reign" of believers together and with Christ in the kingdom of God in manifestation, 1 Cor 4:8 (3rd part); of those who

endure, 2 Ti 2:12. See: TDNT—1:591 & 7:787, 1102; BAGD—777c; THAYER—595d.

4822. συμβιβάζω {6x} **sumbibazō**, *soom-bib-ad'-zo;* from *4862* and βι-βάζω **bibazō** (to *force;* caus. [by redupl.] of the base of *939*); to *drive together,* i.e. *unite* (in association or affection), (mentally) to *infer, show, teach:*—compact {1x}, assuredly gather {1x}, intrust {1x}, knit together {2x}, prove {1x}. See: TDNT—7:763, 1101; BAGD—777d; THAYER—595d.

4823. συμβουλεύω {5x} **sumbŏulĕuō**, *soom-bool-yoo'-o;* from *4862* and *1011;* to *give* (or *take*) *advice jointly,* i.e. *recommend, deliberate* or *determine:*—consult {1x}, give counsel {1x}, take counsel {1x}, counsel together {1x}, take counsel together {1x}. See: BAGD—777d; THAYER—596a.

4824. συμβούλιον {8x} **sumbŏuliŏn**, *soom-boo'-lee-on;* neut. of a presumed der. of *4825; advisement;* spec. a *deliberative* body, i.e. the provincial *assessors* or lay-court:—consultation {1x}, counsel {5x}, council {2x}.

Sumboulion, "a uniting in counsel" (*sun*, "together," *boule,* "counsel, advice"), denotes **(1)** "counsel" which is given, taken and acted upon, e.g., Mt 12:14, "held a council"; 22:15; 27:1, 7; 28:12; Mk 3:6; 15:1, "consultation"; hence **(2)** "a council," an assembly of counsellors or persons in consultation, Acts 25:12, of the "council" with which Festus conferred concerning Paul. **(3)** The governors and procurators of provinces had a board of advisers or assessors, with whom they took "counsel," before pronouncing judgment. See: BAGD—778a; THAYER—596a.

4825. σύμβουλος {1x} **sumbŏulŏs**, *soom'-boo-los;* from *4862* and *1012;* a *consultor,* i.e. *adviser:*—counsellor {1x}. See: BAGD—778b; THAYER—596b.

4826. Συμεών {7x} **Sumĕōn**, *soom-eh-one';* from the same as *4613; Symeon* (i.e. *Shimon*), the name of five Isr.:—Simeon {6x}, Simon Peter {1x}. See: BAGD—778b; THAYER—596b.

4827. συμμαθητής {1x} **summathētēs**, *soom-math-ay-tace';* from a compound of *4862* and *3129;* a *co-learner* (of Christianity):—fellowdisciples {1x}. See: TDNT—4:460, 552; BAGD—778b; THAYER—596b.

4828. συμμαρτυρέω {4x} **summarturĕō**, *soom-mar-too-reh'-o;* from *4862* and *3140;* to *testify jointly,* i.e. *corroborate* by (concurrent) *evidence:*—testify unto {1x}, also bear witness {2x}, bear witness with {1x}.

Summartureo, as a verb, is translated **(1)** "to bear witness with" in Rom 2:15; 8:16; 9:1; and **(2)** "testify" in Rev 22:18. Syn.: 267, 2649, 3140, 3141, 3142, 3143, 3144, 4901, 5571, 5576, 5577. See: TDNT—4:508, 564; BAGD—778b; THAYER—596c.

4829. συμμερίζομαι {1x} **summĕrizŏmai**, *soom-mer-id'-zom-ahee;* mid. voice from *4862* and *3307;* to *share jointly,* i.e. *participate* in:—be partaker with {1x}.

This word means primarily, "to distribute in shares" (*sun,* "with," *meros,* "a part"), in the middle voice, "to have a share in," is used in 1 Cor 9:13, "are partakers with (the altar)," i.e., they feed with others on that which, having been sacrificed, has been placed upon an altar; so the believer feeds upon Christ (who is the altar in Heb 13:10). See: BAGD—778c; THAYER—596c.

4830. συμμέτοχος {2x} **summĕtŏchŏs**, *soom-met'-okh-os;* from *4862* and *3353;* a *co-participant:*—partaker {2x}. Cf. Eph 3:6; 5:7. See: TDNT—2:830, 286; BAGD—778c; THAYER—596c.

4831. συμμιμητής {1x} **summimētēs**, *soom-mim-ay-tace';* from a presumed compound of *4862* and *3401;* a *co-imitator,* i.e. *fellow votary:*—follower together {1x}. See: TDNT—4:659, 594; BAGD—778c; THAYER—596d.

4832. σύμμορφος {2x} **summŏrphŏs**, *soom-mor-fos';* from *4862* and *3444; jointly formed,* i.e. (fig.) *similar:*—conformed to {1x}, fashioned like unto {1x}.

Summorphos signifies "having the same form as another, conformed to"; **(1)** of the "conformity" of children of God "to the image of His Son," Rom 8:29; **(2)** of their future physical "conformity" to His body of glory, Phil 3:21. See: TDNT—7:787, 1102; BAGD—778d; THAYER—596d.

4833. συμμορφόω {1x} **summŏrphŏō**, *soom-mor-fŏ'-o;* from *4832;* to *render like,* i.e. (fig.) to *assimilate:*—make conformable unto {1x}.

Summorphoo, "to make of like form with another person or thing, to render like" (*sun,* "with," *morphe,* "a form"), is found in Phil 3:10 (in the passive participle of the verb), "becoming conformed" (or "growing into conformity") to the death of Christ, indicating the practical apprehension of the death of the carnal self, and fulfilling his share of the sufferings following upon the sufferings of Christ; becoming less dependent upon self and more dependent

upon Him. See: BAGD—778d; THAYER—596d.

4834. συμπαθέω {2x} **sumpathĕō**, *soom-path-eh'-o;* from *4835;* to *feel* "*sympathy*" with, i.e. (by impl.) to *commiserate:*—have compassion {1x}, be touched with a feeling of {1x}. Cf. Heb 4:15; 10:34. See: TDNT—5:935, 798; BAGD—778d; THAYER—596d.

4835. συμπαθής {1x} **sumpathēs**, *soom-path-ace';* from *4841; having a fellow-feeling* ("*sympathetic*"), i.e. (by impl.) *mutually commiserative:*—having compassion one of another {1x}. See: TDNT—5:935, 798; BAGD—779a; THAYER—596d.

4836. συμπαραγίνομαι {2x} **sumparaginŏmai**, *soom-par-ag-in'-om-ahee;* from *4862* and *3854;* to *be present together,* i.e. to *convene;* by impl. to *appear in aid:*—come together {1x}, stand with {1x}. Cf. Lk 23:48; 2 Ti 4:16. See: BAGD—779a; THAYER—596d.

4837. συμπαρακαλέω {1x} **sumparakalĕō**, *soom-par-ak-al-eh'-o;* from *4862* and *3870;* to *console jointly:*—comfort together {1x}. See: BAGD—779a; THAYER—97a.

4838. συμπαραλαμβάνω {4x} **sumparalam-banō**, *soom-par-al-am-ban'-o;* from *4862* and *3880;* to *take along in company:*—take with {4x}.

The word denotes "to take along with oneself," as a companion, Acts 12:25; 15:37, 38; Gal 2:1. See: BAGD—779a; THAYER—597a.

4839. συμπαραμένω {1x} **sumparamĕnō**, *soom-par-am-en'-o;* from *4862* and *3887;* to *remain in company,* i.e. *still live:*—continue with {1x}. See: BAGD—779a; THAYER—597a.

4840. συμπάρειμι {1x} **sumparĕimi**, *soom-par'-i-mee;* from *4862* and *3918;* to *be at hand together,* i.e. *now present:*—be here present with {1x}. See: BAGD—779d; THAYER—597a.

4841. συμπάσχω {2x} **sumpaschō**, *soom-pas'-kho;* from *4862* and *3958* (incl. its alt.); to *experience pain jointly* or of the *same kind* (spec. *persecution;* to "*sympathize*"):—suffer with {2x}.

Sumpascho, "to suffer with", is used **(1)** in Rom 8:17 of "suffering" with Christ; and **(2)** in 1 Cor 12:26 of joint "suffering" in the members of the body. See: TDNT—5:925 & 7:787, 798 & 1102; BAGD—779b; THAYER—597a.

4842. συμπέμπω {2x} **sumpĕmpō**, *soom-pem'-po;* from *4862* and *3992;* to *dispatch in company:*—send with {2x}. Cf. 2 Cor 8:18, 22. See: BAGD—779b; THAYER—597b.

4843. συμπεριλαμβάνω {1x} **sumpĕrilam-banō**, *soom-per-ee-lam-ban'-o;* from *4862* and a compound of *4012* and *2983;* to *take by enclosing altogether,* i.e. *earnestly throw the arms about one:*—embrace {1x}. See: BAGD—779c; THAYER—597b.

4844. συμπίνω {1x} **sumpinō**, *soom-pee'-no;* from *4862* and *4095;* to *partake a beverage in company:*—drink with {1x}. See: BAGD—779c; THAYER—597b.

4845. συμπληρόω {3x} **sumplērŏō**, *soom-play-rŏ'-o;* from *4862* and *4137;* to *implenish completely,* i.e. (of space) to *swamp* (a boat), or (of time) to *accomplish* (pass. be *complete*):—be fully come {1x}, be come {1x}, fill up {1x}.

Sumpleroo, "to fill completely" (*sun,* "with," intensive), is used, in the passive voice, **(1)** of time to be fulfilled or completed, **(1a)** Lk 9:51, "the days were well-nigh come"; **(1b)** Acts 2:1, "the day . . . was fully come". **(2)** In Lk 8:23, it is used in the active voice, of the filling of a boat in a storm. See: TDNT—6:308, 867; BAGD—779c; THAYER—597b.

4846. συμπνίγω {5x} **sumpnigō**, *soom-pnee'-go;* from *4862* and *4155;* to *strangle completely,* i.e. (lit.) to *drown,* or (fig.) to *crowd:*—choke {4x}, throng {1x}.

Sumpnigo gives the suggestion of **(1)** "choking together", i.e., by crowding, Mt 13:22; Mk 4:7, 19; Lk 8:14. **(2)** It is used in Lk 8:42, of the crowd that thronged the Lord, almost, so to speak, to suffocation. See: TDNT—6:455, 895; BAGD—779d; THAYER—597b.

4847. συμπολίτης {1x} **sumpŏlitēs**, *soom-pol-ee'-tace;* from *4862* and *4177; a native of the same town,* i.e. (fig.) *co-religionist* (*fellow-Christian*):—fellow-citizens {1x}. See: BAGD—780a; THAYER—597b.

4848. συμπορεύομαι {4x} **sumpŏrĕuŏmai**, *soom-por-yoo'-om-ahee;* from *4862* and *4198;* to *journey together;* by impl. to *assemble:*—go with {3x}, resort {1x}.

This word means "to go together with" and is used **(1)** in Mk 10:1, "resort"; and **(2)** "go with" in Lk 7:11; 14:25; 24:15. See: BAGD—780a; THAYER—597c.

4849. συμπόσιον {1x} **sumpŏsiŏn**, *soom-pos'-ee-on;* neut. of a der. of the

alt. of *4844;* a *drinking*-party ("*symposium*"), i.e. (by extens.) a *room* of guests:—company {1x}.

In Mk 6:39 the noun is repeated, in the plural, by way of an adverbial and distributive phrase, *sumposia sumposia,* lit., "companies-companies" (i.e., by companies). See: BAGD—780a; THAYER—579c.

4850. **συμπρεσβύτερος** {1x} **sumprĕsbut-ĕrŏs**, *soom-pres-boo'-ter-os;* from *4862* and *4245;* a *co-presbyter:*—presbyter, also an elder {1x}. See: TDNT—6:651, 931; BAGD—780a; THAYER—597c.

συμφάγω sumphagō. See *4906.*

4851. **συμφέρω** {17x} **sumphĕrō**, *soom-fer'-o;* from *4862* and *5342* (incl. its alt.); to *bear together* (*contribute*), i.e. (lit.) to *collect,* or (fig.) to *conduce;* espec. (neut. part. as a noun) *advantage:*—be expedient {7x}, profit {4x}, be profitable {3x}, bring together {1x}, be better {1x}, be good {1x}.

Sumphero, signifies **(1)** transitively, lit., "to bring together" (*sun,* "with," *phero,* "to bring"), **(2)** intransitively, "to be an advantage, profitable, expedient"; it is used mostly impersonally, **(2a)** "it is (it was) expedient", so in Mt 19:10, "it is (not) good"; Jn 11:50; 16:7; 18:14; 1 Cor 6:12; 10:23; 2 Cor 8:10; 12:1; **(2b)** "it is profitable," Mt 5:29–30; 18:6; Acts 20:20; **(2c)** "to profit withal," 1 Cor 12:7; **(2d)** in Heb 12:10, used in the neuter of the present participle with the article as a noun, "for (our) profit." See: TDNT—9:69, 1252; BAGD—780b; THAYER—597c.

4852. **σύμφημι** {1x} **sumphĕmi**, *soom'-fay-mee;* from *4862* and *5346;* to *say jointly,* i.e. *assent to:*—consent unto {1x}. See: BAGD—780c; THAYER—579d.

4853. **συμφυλέτης** {1x} **sumphulĕtēs**, *soom-foo-let'-ace;* from *4862* and a der. of *5443;* a *co-tribesman,* i.e. *native of the same country:*—countryman {1x}.

Sumphuletes, lit., "a fellow-tribesman" (*sun,* "with," *phule,* "a tribe, race, nation, people"), hence, one who is of the same people, a fellow-countryman, is found in 1 Th 2:14. See: BAGD—780c; THAYER—579d.

4854. **σύμφυτος** {1x} **sumphutŏs**, *soom'-foo-tos;* from *4862* and a der. of *5453; grown* along *with* (*connate*), i.e. (fig.) closely *united* to:—planted together {1x}.

This word is found only in Rom 6:5, "planted together," indicating the union of the believer with Christ in experiencing spiritually "the likeness of His death." See: TDNT—7:786, 1102; BAGD—780d; THAYER—597d.

4855. **συμφύω** {1x} **sumphuō,** *soom-foo'-o;* from *4862* and *5453;* pass. to *grow jointly:*—spring up with {1x}. See: BAGD—780d; THAYER—598a.

4856. **συμφωνέω** {6x} **sumphōnĕō**, *soom-fo-neh'-o;* from *4859;* to be *harmonious,* i.e. (fig.) to *accord* (*be suitable, concur*) or *stipulate* (by compact):—agree {3x}, agree together {1x}, agree with {2x}.

Sumphoneo, lit., "to sound together" (*sun,* "together," *phone,* "a sound"), i.e., "to be in accord, primarily of musical instruments," is used in the NT of the "agreement" **(1)** of persons concerning a matter, Mt 18:19; 20:2, 13; Acts 5:9; **(2)** of the writers of Scripture, Acts 15:15; **(3)** of things that are said to be congruous in their nature, Lk 5:36. See: TDNT—9:304, 1287; BAGD—780d; THAYER—598a.

4857. **συμφώνησις** {1x} **sumphōnēsis**, *soom-fo'-nay-sis;* from *4856; accordance:*—concord {1x}.

This word literally means a sounding together, to agree (2 Cor 6:15) [Eng., symphony]. See: TDNT—9:304, 1287; BAGD—781a; THAYER—598b.

4858. **συμφωνία** {1x} **sumphōnia**, *soom-fo-nee'-ah;* from *4859; unison* of sound ("*symphony*"), i.e. a *concert* of instruments (harmonious *note*):—music {1x}. See: TDNT—9:304, 1287; BAGD—81a; THAYER—598b.

4859. **σύμφωνος** {1x} **sumphōnŏs**, *soom'-fo-nos;* from *4862* and *5456; sounding together* (*alike*), i.e. (fig.) *accordant* (neut. as noun, *agreement*):—consent {1x}. See: TDNT—9:304, 1287; BAGD—781b; THAYER—598b.

4860. **συμψηφίζω** {1x} **sumpsēphizō**, *soom-psay-fid'-zo;* from *4862* and *5585;* to *compute jointly:*—count {1x}. See: TDNT—9:604, 1341; BAGD—781b; THAYER—598b.

4861. **σύμψυχος** {1x} **sumpsuchŏs**, *soom'-psoo-khos;* from *4862* and *5590; co-spirited,* i.e. *similar in sentiment:*—likeminded {1x}. See: BAGD—781b; THAYER—598b.

4862. **σύν** {125x} **sun,** *soon;* a primary prep. denoting *union; with* or *together* (but much closer than *3326* or *3844*), i.e. by association, companionship, process, resemblance, possession, instrumentality, addition, etc.:—with {123x}, beside {1x}, accompany + *2064* {1x}. [In composition, it has similar applications, including *completeness.*] See: TDNT—7:766, 1102; BAGD—781c; THAYER—598b.

4863. συνάγω {62x} **sunagō,** *soon-ag'-o;* from *4862* and *71;* to *lead together,* i.e. *collect* or *convene;* spec. to *entertain* (hospitably):—gather {15x}, be gathered together {12x}, gather together {9x}, come together {6x}, be gathered {4x}, be assembled {3x}, take in {3x}, misc. {10x} = + accompany, bestow, lead into, resort, take in. See: BAGD—782a; THAYER—599d.

4864. συναγωγή { {57x} **sunagōgē,** *soon-ag-o-gay';* from (the redupl. form of) *4863;* an *assemblage* of persons; spec. a Jewish *"synagogue"* (the meeting or the place); by anal. a Christian *church:*—assembly {1x}, congregation {1x}, *synagogue* {55x}. Syn.: 1577, 3831.

(1) *Sunagoge* originally meant just a gathering or bringing together of people, yet in the NT it became specifically the gathering place for the Jews, Jewish proselytes, and God-fearers. (2) This word means properly "a bringing together" (*sun,* "together," *ago,* "to bring"), denoted (3) "a gathering of things, a collection," then, (3a) of "persons, an assembling, of Jewish religious gatherings," e.g., Acts 9:2; (3b) an assembly of Christian Jews, Jas 2:2; (3c) a company dominated by the power and activity of Satan, Rev 2:9; 3:9; (4) by metonymy, "the building" in which the gathering is held, e.g. Mt 6:2; Mk 1:21. (5) The origin of the Jewish *"synagogue"* is probably to be assigned to the time of the Babylonian exile. Having no temple, the Jews assembled on the Sabbath to hear the Law read, and the practice continued in various buildings after the return. Cf. Ps 74:8. See: TDNT—7:798, 1108; BAGD—782d; THAYER—600a.

4865. συναγωνίζομαι {1x} **sunagōnizŏmai,** *soon-ag-o-nid'-zom-ahee;* from *4862* and *75;* to *struggle* in company *with,* i.e. (fig.) to *be a partner (assistant):*—strive together with {1x}. See: BAGD—783b; THAYER—600c.

4866. συναθλέω {2x} **sunathlĕō,** *soon-ath-leh'-o;* from *4862* and *118;* to *wrestle* in company *with,* i.e. (fig.) to *seek jointly:*—labour with {1x}, strive together for {1x}. Cf. Phil 1:27; 4:3. See: TDNT—1:167, 25; BAGD—783b; THAYER—600c.

4867. συναθροίζω {3x} **sunathrŏizō,** *soon-ath-royd'-zo;* from *4862* and ἀθροίζω **athrŏizō** (to *hoard*); to *convene:*—call together {1x}, gather together {2x}. Acts 12:12; 19:25. See: BAGD—783b; THAYER—600c.

4868. συναίρω {3x} **sunairō,** *soon-ah'-ee-ro;* from *4862* and *142;* to *make*

up together, i.e. (fig.) to *compute and settle* (an account):—reckon {1x}, reckon + 3056 {1x}, take {1x}. See: BAGD—783c; THAYER—600c.

4869. συναιχμάλωτος {3x} **sunaichmalōtŏs,** *soon-aheekh-mal'-o-tos;* from *4862* and *164;* a *co-captive:*—fellow-prisoner {3x}.

Sunaichmalotos, "a fellow prisoner," primarily "one of fellow captives in war" (from *aichme,* "a spear," and *haliskomai,* "to be taken" at spear point), is used by Paul (1) of Andronicus and Junias, Rom 16:7; (2) of Epaphras, Philem 23; (3) of Aristarchus, Col 4:10. See: TDNT—1:195, 31; BAGD—783c; THAYER—600d.

4870. συνακολουθέω {2x} **sunakŏlŏuthĕō,** *soon-ak-ol-oo-theh'-o;* from *4862* and *190;* to *accompany:*—follow {2x}.

Sunakoloutheo, as a verb, means "to follow along with, to accompany a leader" and is found (1) in Mk 5:37: "And He suffered no man to follow Him, save Peter, and James, and John the brother of James"; (2) Lk 23:49, of the women who "followed with" Christ from Galilee. Syn.: 190, 1096, 1377, 1811, 1872, 2614, 2628, 3877. See: TDNT—1:216, 33; BAGD—600d; THAYER—600d.

4871. συναλίζω {1x} **sunalizō,** *soon-al-id'-zo;* from *4862* and ἀλίζω **halizō** (to *throng*); to *accumulate,* i.e. *convene:*—assemble together {1x}.

Sunalizo, "to gather together, to assemble," with the suggestion of a crowded meeting (*sun,* "with," *halizo,* "to crowd, or mass:" the corresponding adjective is *hales,* "thronged"), is used in Acts 1:4. See: BAGD—783d; THAYER—600d.

4872. συναναβαίνω {2x} **sunanabainō,** *soon-an-ab-ah'-ee-no;* from *4862* and *305;* to *ascend* in company *with:*—come up with {2x}. Cf. Mk 15:41; Acts 13:31. See: BAGD—784b; THAYER—601a.

4873. συνανάκειμαι {9x} **sunanakĕimai,** *soon-an-ak'-i-mahee;* from *4862* and *345;* to *recline* in company *with* (at a meal):—sit at meat with {4x}, sit with {2x}, sit together with {1x}, sit down with {1x}, sit at table with {1x}. Cf. Mt 9:10; 14:9; Mk 2:15; 6:22, 26; Lk 7:49; 14:10, 15; Jn 12:2). Syn.: 339, 345, 347, 377, 1910, 2516, 2521, 2621, 2523, 2625, 4775, 4776. See: TDNT—3:654, 425; BAGD—784b; THAYER—601a.

4874. συναναμείγνυμι {3x} **sunanamignumi,** *soon-an-am-ig'-noo-mee;* from *4862* and a compound of *303* and *3396;* to *mix up together,* i.e. (fig.) *associate with:*—have company with {1x}, keep company

{1x}, with {1x}. Cf. 1 Cor 5:9, 11; 2 Thess. 3:14. See: TDNT—7:852, 1113; BAGD—784b; THAYER—601a.

4875. συναναπαύομαι {1x} **sunanapauŏmai,** *soon-an-ap-ŏw'-om-ahee;* mid. voice from *4862* and *373;* to *recruit oneself* in company *with:*—refresh with {1x}. See: BAGD—784b; THAYER—601a.

4876. συναντάω {6x} **sunantaō,** *soon-an-tah'-o;* from *4862* and a der. of *473;* to *meet with, of events;* fig. to *occur:*—befall {1x}, meet {5x}.

Sunantao, "to meet with," lit., "to meet together with" is used **(1)** literally in Lk 9:37; 22:10; Acts 10:25; Heb 7:1, 10; **(2)** metaphorically in Acts 20:22 ("shall befall"). See: BAGD—784c; THAYER—601b.

4877. συνάντησις {1x} **sunantēsis,** *soon-an'-tay-sis;* from *4876;* a *meeting with:*—meet + 1519 {1x}. See: BAGD—784c; THAYER—601b.

4878. συναντιλαμβάνομαι {2x} **sunantilam-banŏmai,** *soon-an-tee-lam-ban'-om-ahee;* from *4862* and *482;* to *take* hold of *opposite together,* i.e. *co-operate (assist):*—help {2x}.

This word signifies "to take hold with at the side for assistance"; hence, "to take a share in, help in bearing, to help in general." **(1)** It is used, in the middle voice in Martha's request to the Lord to bid her sister help her, Lk 10:40; **(2)** and of the ministry of the Holy Spirit in helping our infirmities, Rom 8:26. See: TDNT—1:375, 62; BAGD—784c; THAYER—601b.

4879. συναπάγω {3x} **sunapagō,** *soon-ap-ag'-o;* from *4862* and *520;* to *take off together,* i.e. *transport with (seduce,* pass. *yield):*—carry away with {1x}, lead away with {1x}, condescend {1x}.

Sunapago, "to carry away with", is used **(1)** in a bad sense, **(1a)** "was carried away" in Gal 2:13 and **(1b)** "being led away" in 2 Pet 3:17; **(2)** "condescend" in a good sense in Rom 12:16. Condescend means to lower one's self down in order to be led along with those around you. See: BAGD—784d; THAYER—601b.

4880. συναποθνήσκω {3x} **sunapŏthnēskō,** *soon-ap-oth-nace'-ko;* from *4862* and *599;* to *decease* (lit.) in company *with,* or (fig.) similarly *to:*—be dead with {1x}, die with {2x}.

Sunapothnesko, "to die with, to die together," is used **(1)** literally of association in physical "death," Mk 14:31; **(2)** in 2 Cor 7:3, the apostle declares that his love to the saints

makes separation impossible, whether in life or in "death." **(3)** It is used once of association spiritually with Christ in His "death," 2 Ti 2:11. See: TDNT—3:7 & 7:786, 312 & 1102; BAGD—784d; THAYER—601b.

4881. συναπόλλυμι {1x} **sunapŏllumi,** *soon-ap-ol'-loo-mee;* from *4862* and *622;* to *destroy* (middle or passive voice *be slain)* in company *with:*—perish with {1x}. See: BAGD—785a; THAYER—601c.

4882. συναποστέλλω {1x} **sunapŏstĕllō,** *soon-ap-os-tel'-lo;* from *4862* and *649;* to *despatch* (on an errand) in company *with:*—send with {1x}. See: BAGD—785a; THAYER—601c.

4883. συναρμολογέω {2x} **sunarmŏlŏgĕō,** *soon-ar-mol-og-eh'-o;* from *4862* and a der. of a compound of *719* and *3004* (in its orig. sense of *laying);* to *render close-jointed together,* i.e. *organize compactly:*—be fitly framed together {1x}, be fitly joined together {1x}.

Sunarmologeo, "to fit or frame together" *(sun,* "with," *harmos,* "a joint, in building," and *lego,* "to choose"), is used **(1)** metaphorically of the various parts of the church as a building, Eph 2:21, "fitly framed together"; **(2)** also of the members of the church as the body of Christ, Eph 4:16, "fitly framed . . . together." See: TDNT—7:855, 1114; BAGD—785b; THAYER—601c.

4884. συναρπάζω {4x} **sunarpazo,** *soon-ar-pad'-zo;* from *4862* and *726;* to *snatch together,* i.e. *seize:*—catch {4x}.

Sunarpazo, *(sun,* used intensively, and *arpazo,* "to snatch, to seize, to keep a firm grip of"), is used only by Luke, and translated **(1)** "caught" in Lk 8:29, of devil-possession; **(2)** in Acts 6:12, of the act of the elders and scribes in seizing Stephen; and **(3)** of the crowd catching Gaius in Acts 19:29. **(4)** In Acts 27:15, it is used of the effects of wind upon a ship. See: BAGD—785b; THAYER—601c.

4885. συναυξάνω {1x} **sunauxanō,** *soon-ŏwx-an'-o;* from *4862* and *837;* to *increase (grow up) together:*—grow together {1x}. See: BAGD—785b; THAYER—601c.

4886. σύνδεσμος {4x} **sundĕsmŏs,** *soon'-des-mos;* from *4862* and *1199;* a *joint tie,* i.e. *ligament,* (fig.) *uniting principle, control:*—band {1x}, bond {3x}.

Sundesmos, as a noun, means "that which binds together" and is said of **(1)** "the bond of iniquity" (Acts 8:23); **(2)** "the bond of peace" (Eph 4:3); **(3)** "the bond of perfectness" (Col 3:14 figurative of the ligaments of the body);

(4) "bands" (Col 2:19, figuratively of the bands which unite the church, the body of Christ). Syn.: 254, 1198, 1199. See: TDNT—7:856, 1114; BAGD—785b; THAYER—601d.

4887. συνδέω {1x} **sundĕō**, *soon-deh'-o;* from *4862* and *1210;* to *bind with,* i.e. (pass.) *be a fellow-prisoner* (fig.):— be bound with {1x}. See: BAGD—785c; THAYER—601d.

4888. συνδοξάζω {1x} **sundŏxazō**, *soon-dox-ad'-zo;* from *4862* and *1392;* to *exalt* to dignity in company (i.e. *similarly*) *with:*—glorify together {1x}. See: TDNT—2:253 & 7:787, 178 & 1102; BAGD—785d; THAYER—602a.

4889. σύνδουλος {10x} **sundŏulŏs**, *soon'-doo-los;* from *4862* and *1401;* a *co-slave,* i.e. *servitor* or *ministrant of the same master* (human or divine):—fellow-servant {10x}.

Sundoulos, "a fellow servant," is used **(1)** of natural conditions, Mt 18:28, 29, 31, 33; 24:49; **(2)** of "servants" of the same divine Lord, Col 1:7; 4:7; Rev 6:11; **(3)** of angels, Rev 19:10; 22:9. See: TDNT—2:261, 182; BAGD—785d; THAYER—602a.

συνδρέμω **sundrĕmō**. See *4936*.

4890. συνδρομή {1x} **sundrŏmē**, *soon-drom-ay';* from (the alt. of) *4936;* a *running together,* i.e. (riotous) *concourse:*—run together + 1096 {1x}. See: BAGD—785d; THAYER—602a.

4891. συνεγείρω {3x} **sunĕgĕirō**, *soon-eg-i'-ro;* from *4862* and *1453;* to *rouse* (from death) in company *with,* i.e. (fig.) to *revivify* (spiritually) in resemblance to:— raise up together {1x}, rise with {2x}.

Sunergeiro, "to raise together", is used **(1)** of the believer's spiritual resurrection with Christ, Eph 2:6; **(2)** passive voice in Col 2:12, "ye are risen"; so Col 3:1. See: TDNT—7:786, 1102; BAGD—785d; THAYER—602a.

4892. συνέδριον {22x} **sunĕdriŏn**, *soon-ed'-ree-on;* neut. of a presumed der. of a compound of *4862* and the base of *1476;* a *joint session,* i.e. (spec.) the Jewish *San-hedrin;* by anal. a subordinate *tribunal:*—council {22x}.

Sunedrion, properly, "a settling together" (*sun,* "together," *hedra,* "a seat"), hence, **(1)** "any assembly or session of persons deliberating or adjusting," Mt 10:17; Mk 13:9; Jn 11:47; **(2)** in particular, it denoted **(2a)** "the *Sanhedrin*," the Great Council at Jerusalem, consisting of 71 members, namely, prominent members of the families of the high priest, el-

ders and scribes. The Jews trace the origin of this to Num 11:16. The more important causes came up before this tribunal. The Roman rulers of Judea permitted the *Sanhedrin* to try such cases, and even to pronounce sentence of death, with the condition that such a sentence should be valid only if confirmed by the Roman procurator. **(2b)** In Jn 11:47, it is used of a meeting of the *Sanhedrin;* in Acts 4:15, of the place of meeting. See: TDNT—7:860, 1115; BAGD—786a; THAYER—602b.

4893. συνείδησις {32x} **sunĕidēsis**, *soon-i'-day-sis;* from a prol. form of *4894; co-perception,* i.e. moral *conscious-ness:*—conscience {32x}.

Summary: *Suneidesis* literally means "a knowing," a co-knowledge with one's self, the witness borne to one's conduct by conscience, that faculty by which we apprehend the will of God, as that which is designed to govern our lives. The word is stressing that we receive input from our surroundings [temptations, decision-making events, etc.] and we are driven to make a decision. We compare what we know with our conscience [*con* – "with", *science* – "knowledge"], our knowledge base about this input. If we follow our conscience we act according to what we know to be true about the situation and the consequences/blessings of our decision. We can violate our conscience by overriding that knowledge.

Discussion: This word means lit., "a know-ing with" (*sun,* "with," *oida,* "to know"), i.e., "a co-knowledge (with oneself), the witness borne to one's conduct by conscience, that faculty by which we apprehend the will of God, as that which is designed to govern our lives"; hence **(1)** the sense of guiltiness before God, Heb 10:2; **(2)** that process of thought which distinguishes what it considers morally good or bad, commending the good, condemning the bad, and so prompting to do the former, and avoid the latter, Rom 2:15 (bearing witness with God's law); 9:1; 2 Cor 1:12; **(3)** acting in a certain way because "conscience" requires it, Rom 13:5; **(3a)** so as not to cause scruples of "conscience" in another, 1 Cor 10:28–29; **(3b)** not calling a thing in question unnecessarily, as if conscience demanded it, 1 Cor 10:25, 27;

(4) "commending oneself to every man's conscience," 2 Cor 4:2; cf. 5:11. **(5)** There may be a "conscience" not strong enough to distinguish clearly between the lawful and the unlawful, 1 Cor 8:7, 10, 12. **(6)** The phrase "con-science toward God," in 1 Pet 2:19, signifies a "conscience" so controlled by the apprehension of God's presence that the person realizes that griefs are to be borne in accordance with His

will. **(7)** Heb 9:9 teaches that sacrifices under the Law could not so perfect a person that he could regard himself as free from guilt. **(8)** For various descriptions of "conscience" see: **(8a)** "good . . . before God" in Acts 23:1; 1 Ti 1:5, 19; Heb 13:18; 1 Pet 3:16, 21; **(8b)** "void of offence"in Acts 24:16; **(8c)** "weak" in 1 Cor 8:7, second part; **(8d)** "pure" in 1 Ti 3:9; 2 Ti 1:3; **(8e)** "seared" in 1 Ti 4:2; **(8f)** "defiled" in Titus 1:15; **(8g)** "purge . . . from dead works" in Heb 9:14; and **(8h)** "evil" in Heb 10:22. See: TDNT— 7:898, 1120; BAGD—786c; THAYER—602c.

4894. **συνεῖδω** {4x} **sunĕidō**, *soon-i'-do;* from *4862* and *1492;* to *see completely;* used (like its primary) only in two past tenses, respectively mean. to *understand* or *become aware,* and to *be conscious* or (clandestinely) *informed of:*—consider {1x}, know {1x}, be privy {1x}, be ware of {1x}.

Sunoida, a perfect tense with a present meaning, denotes **(1)** "to share the knowledge of, be privy to," Acts 5:2; **(2)** "to be conscious of," especially of guilty consciousness, 1 Cor 4:4, "I know nothing by myself." It is also translated **(3)** "consider" in Acts 12:12; and **(4)** "were ware of" in Acts 14:6. Syn.: 1097, 1107, 1110, 1492, 1921, 1467, 1922, 1987. See: TDNT— 7:898,*; BAGD—787a; THAYER—603b.

4895. **σύνειμι** {2x} **sunĕimi**, *soon'-i-mee;* from *4862* and *1510* (incl. its various inflections); to *be in company with,* i.e. *present* at the time:—be with {2x}. See: BAGD—787a; THAYER—603b.

4896. **σύνειμι** {1x} **sunĕimi**, *soon'-i-mee;* from *4862* and εἶμι **ĕimi** (to *go*); to *assemble:*—gather together {1x}. See: BAGD—787a; THAYER—603b.

4897. **συνεισέρχομαι** {2x} **sunĕisĕrchŏmai**, *soon-ice-er'-khom-ahee;* from *4862* and *1525;* to *enter* in company *with:*—go in with {1x}, go with into {1x}. Cf. 6:22; 18:15. See: BAGD—787a; THAYER— 603b.

4898. **συνέκδημος** {2x} **sunĕkdēmŏs**, *soon-ek'-day-mos;* from *4862* and the base of *1553;* a *co-absentee* from home, i.e. *fellow-traveller:*—companion in travel {1x}, travel with {1x}. Cf. Acts 19:29; 2 Cor 8:19. See: BAGD—787a; THAYER—603b.

4899. **συνεκλεκτός** {1x} **sunĕklĕktŏs**, *soon-ek-lek-tos';* from a compound of *4862* and *1586; chosen* in company *with,* i.e. *co-elect (fellow Christian):*—elected together with {1x}. See: BAGD—787b; THAYER—603c.

4900. **συνελαύνω** {1x} **sunĕlaunō**, *soon-el-ow'-no;* from *4862* and *1643;* to *drive together,* i.e. (fig.) *exhort* (to reconciliation):—set at one again + 1515 + 1519 {1x}. See: BAGD—787b; THAYER—603c.

4901. **συνεπιμαρτυρέω** {1x} **sunĕpimarturĕō**, *soon-ep-ee-mar-too-reh'-o;* from *4862* and *1957;* to *testify further jointly,* i.e. *unite in adding evidence:*—also bear witness {1x}.

Sunepimartureo, as a verb, denotes "to join in bearing witness with others": "God also bearing *them* witness, both with signs and wonders, and with divers miracles, and gifts of the Holy Ghost, according to his own will?" (Heb 2:4). Syn.: 267, 2649, 3140, 3141, 3142, 3143, 3144, 4828, 5571, 5576, 5577.See: TDNT—4:508, 564; BAGD—787b; THAYER— 603c.

4902. **συνέπομαι** {1x} **sunĕpŏmai**, *soon-ep'-om-ahee;* mid. voice from *4862* and a primary ηἕπω **hĕpō** (to *follow*); to *attend (travel)* in company *with:*—accompany {1x}.

Sunepomai, lit., "to follow with" (*sun,* "with," *hepomai,* "to follow"), came to mean simply "to accompany," Acts 20:4, distinguishing Paul as the leader of those following/accompanying. See: BAGD—787c; THAYER— 603c.

4903. **συνεργέω** {5x} **sunĕrgĕō**, *soon-erg-eh'-o;* from *4904;* to *be a fellow-worker,* i.e. *co-operate:*—work with {2x}, help with {1x}, workers together {1x}, work together {1x}. Cf. Mk 16:20; Rom 8:28; 1 Cor 16:16; 2 Cor 6:1; Jas 2:22. See: TDNT—7:871, 1116; BAGD—787c; THAYER—603c.

4904. **συνεργός** {13x} **sunĕrgŏs**, *soon-er-gos';* from a presumed compound of *4862* and the base of *2041;* a *co-laborer,* i.e. *coadjutor:*—fellowlabourer {4x}, helper {3x}, fellowhelper {2x}, fellowworkers {1x}, workfellow {1x}, labourer together with {1x}, companion in labour {1x}. Cf. Rom 16:3, 9, 21; 1 Cor 3:9; 2 Cor 1:24; 8:23; Phil 2:25; 4:3; Col 4:11; 1 Th 3:2; Philem 1, 24; 3 Jn 1:8. See: TDNT—7:871, 1116; BAGD—787d; THAYER—603b.

4905. **συνέρχομαι** {32x} **sunĕrchŏmai**, *soon-er'-khom-ahee;* from *4862* and *2064;* to *convene, depart* in company *with, associate* with, or (spec.) *cohabit* (conjugally):—come together {18x}, go with {4x}, come with {2x}, resort {2x}, come {2x}, come with + 2258 {1x}, company with {1x}, accompany {1x}, assemble with {1x}. See: TDNT—2:684, 257; BAGD—788a; THAYER—604a.

4906. συνεσθίω {5x} **sunĕsthiō**, *soon-es-thee'-o;* from *4862* and *2068* (incl. its alt.); to *take food* in company *with:*—eat with {5x}. Cf. Lk 15:2; Acts 10:41; 11:3; 1 Cor 5:11; Gal 2:12. See: BAGD—788b; THAYER—604b.

4907. σύνεσις {7x} **sunĕsis**, *soon'-es-is;* from *4920;* a mental *putting together,* i.e. *intelligence* or (concr.) the *intellect:*—knowledge {1x}, understanding {6x}.

(1) *Sunesis* suggests quickness of apprehension, the penetrating consideration which precedes action. *Sunesis*, "to set together, to understand," denotes **(2)** "the understanding, the mind or intelligence," Mk 12:33; Lk 2:47; 1 Cor 1:19; Eph 3:4, "knowledge"; Col 1:9; 2:2; 2 Ti 2:7. Syn.: **(A)** *Gnosis* (*1108*) denotes knowledge by itself and applies chiefly to the apprehension of truths. **(B)** *Sophia* (*4678*) denotes wisdom as exhibited in action and adds the power of reasoning about them and tracing their relationships. It is a mental excellence of the highest sense, to details. **(C)** *Sunesis* (*4907*) denotes critical, apprehending the bearing of things. **(D)** *Phronesis* (*5428*) denotes practical, suggesting lines of action. See: TDNT—7:888, 1119; BAGD—788c; THAYER—604b.

4908. συνετός {4x} **sunĕtŏs**, *soon-et'-os;* from *4920;* mentally *put* (or *putting*) *together,* i.e. *sagacious:*—prudent {4x}.

Sunetos signifies "intelligent, sagacious, understanding" (akin to *suniemi,* "to perceive"), translated "prudent" in Mt 11:25; Lk 10:21; Acts 13:7; 1 Cor 1:19. Prudence is applied wisdom. Syn.: cf. 4907 for discussion. See: TDNT—7:888, 1119; BAGD—788d; THAYER—604b. comp. *5429.*

4909. συνευδοκέω {6x} **sunĕudŏkĕō**, *soon-yoo-dok-eh'-o;* from *4862* and *2106;* to *think well of in common,* i.e. *assent* to, *feel gratified with:*—consent unto {2x}, be pleased {2x}, allow {1x}, have pleasure in {1x}.

Suneudokeo, as a verb, means lit., "to think well with" (*sun,* "with," *eu,* "well," *dokeo,* "to think"), to take pleasure with others in anything, to approve of, to assent, is used **(1)** in Lk 11:48, of "allowing" the evil deeds of predecessors; **(2)** in Rom 1:32, of "have pleasure" in doing evil; **(3)** in Acts 8:1; 22:20, of "consenting" to the death of another. All these are cases of "consenting" to evil things. In 1 Cor 7:12–13, it is used of an unbelieving wife's "being pleased" to dwell with her converted husband, and of an unbelieving husband's "consent" to dwell with a believing wife. Syn.: 714, 841, 842, 2425. See: BAGD—788d; THAYER—604b.

4910. συνευωχέω {2x} **sunĕuōchĕō**, *soon-yoo-o-kheh'-o;* from *4862* and

a der. of a presumed compound of *2095* and a der. of *2192* (mean. to *be in good condition,* i.e. [by impl.] to *fare well,* or *feast*); to *entertain* sumptuously in company *with,* i.e. (middle or passive voice) to *revel together:*—feast with {2x}. Cf. 2 Pet 2:13 and Jude 12. See: BAGD—789a; THAYER—604c.

4911. συνεφίστημι {1x} **sunĕphistēmi**, *soon-ef-is'-tay-mee;* from *4862* and *2186;* to *stand up together against,* i.e. to *resist* (or *assault*) *jointly:*—rise up together {1x}.

Sunephistemi, as a verb, means "to rise up together" and is used in Acts 16:22, of the "rising up" of a multitude against Paul and Silas. Syn.: 305, 393, 450, 1096, 1326, 1453, 1525, 1817. See: BAGD—789a; THAYER—604c.

4912. συνέχω {12x} **sunĕchō**, *soon-ekh'-o;* from *4862* and *2192;* to *hold together,* i.e. to *compress* (the ears, with a crowd or siege) or *arrest* (a prisoner); fig. to *compel, perplex, afflict, preoccupy:*—be taken with {3x}, throng {1x}, straiten {1x}, keep in {1x}, hold {1x}, stop {1x}, press {1x}, lie sick of {1x}, constrain {1x}, be in a strait {1x}.

Sunecho, as a verb, means "to hold together, confine, secure, to hold fast" [*sun* "together," *echo,* "to have or hold"], "to constrain," and is said **(1)** of the effect of the word of the Lord upon Paul: "And when Silas and Timotheus were come from Macedonia, Paul was pressed in the spirit (*sunecho*), and testified to the Jews that Jesus was Christ" (Acts 18:5); **(2)** of the effect of the love of Christ: "For the love of Christ constraineth us; because we thus judge, that if one died for all, then were all dead" (2 Cor 5:14); **(3)** of being taken with a disease: "And His fame went throughout all Syria: and they brought unto Him all sick people that were taken (*sunecho*) with divers diseases and torments, and those which were possessed with devils, and those which were lunatick, and those that had the palsy; and he healed them" (Mt 4:24; cf. Lk 4:38; Acts 28:8); **(4)** taken with fear: "Then the whole multitude of the country of the Gadarenes round about besought Him to depart from them; for they were taken with great fear: and He went up into the ship, and returned back again" (Lk 8:37); **(5)** of thronging or holding in a person: "And Jesus said, Who touched me? When all denied, Peter and they that were with Him said, Master, the multitude throng thee and press thee, and sayest thou, Who touched me?" (Lk 8:45); **(6)** being straitened: "But I have a baptism to be baptized with; and how am I straitened till it be accomplished!" (Lk 12:50); **(7)** being in a strait betwixt two: "For I am in a strait betwixt

two, having a desire to depart, and to be with Christ; which is far better" (Phil 1:23); **(8)** keeping a city in on every side: "For the days shall come upon thee, that thine enemies shall cast a trench about thee, and compass thee round, and keep thee in on every side" (Lk 19:43); **(9)** keeping a tight hold on a person, as the men who seized the Lord Jesus did, after bringing Him into the High Priest's house: "And the men that held Jesus mocked him, and smote him" (Lk 22:63); **(10)** of stopping the ears in refusal to listen: "Then they cried out with a loud voice, and stopped their ears, and ran upon him [Stephen] with one accord" (Acts 7:57). Syn.: 315, 317, 3849. See: TDNT—7:877, 1117; BAGD—789a; THAYER—604c.

4913. συνήδομαι {1x} **sunēdŏmai**, *soon-ay'-dom-ahee;* mid. voice from *4862* and the base of *2237;* to *rejoice in with* oneself, i.e. *feel satisfaction* concerning:—delight {1x}.

　　Sunedomai, lit., "to rejoice with (anyone), to delight in (a thing) with (others)," signifies "to delight with oneself inwardly in a thing," in Rom 7:22. See: BAGD—789c; THAYER—604d.

4914. συνήθεια {2x} **sunēthĕia**, *soon-ay'-thi-ah;* from a compound of *4862* and *2239; mutual habituation,* i.e. *usage:*—custom {2x}.

　　Sunetheia denotes **(1)** "a custom, customary usage" in Jn 18:39; 1 Cor 11:16. See: BAGD—789c; THAYER—604d.

4915. συνηλικιώτης {1x} **sunēlikiōtēs**, *soon-ay-lik-ee-o'-tace;* from *4862* and a der. of *2244;* a *co-aged* person, i.e. *alike* in years:—equal {1x}. See: BAGD—789d; THAYER—605a.

4916. συνθάπτω {2x} **sunthaptō**, *soon-thap'-to;* from *4862* and *2290;* to *inter* in company *with,* i.e. (fig.) to *assimilate* spiritually (to Christ by a sepulture as to sin):—bury with {2x}. Cf. Rom 6:4; Col 2:12. See: TDNT—7:786, 1102; BAGD—789d; THAYER—605a.

4917. συνθλάω {2x} **sunthlaō**, *soon-thlah'-o;* from *4862* and θλάω **thlaō** (to *crush*); to *dash together,* i.e. *shatter:*—break {2x}. Cf. Mt 21:44 and Lk 20:18. See: BAGD—790a; THAYER—605a.

4918. συνθλίβω {2x} **sunthlibō**, *soon-thlee'-bo;* from *4862* and *2346;* to *compress,* i.e. *crowd* on all sides:—throng {2x}. Cf. Mk 5:24, 31. See: BAGD—790a; THAYER—605a.

4919. συνθρύπτω {1x} **sunthruptō**, *soon-throop'-to;* from *4862* and θρύπτω **thruptō** (to *crumble*); to *crush together,* i.e. (fig.) to *dispirit:*—break {1x}. See: BAGD—790a; THAYER—605a.

4920. συνίημι {26x} **suniēmi**, *soon-ee'-ay-mee;* from *4862* and ἵημι **hiēmi** (to *send*); to *put together,* i.e. (mentally) to *comprehend;* by impl. to *act piously:*—consider {1x}, understand {24x}, be wise {1x}.

　　Suneimi, primarily, "to bring or set together," is used metaphorically **(1)** of "perceiving, understanding, uniting", so to speak, the perception with what is perceived, e.g., Mt 13:13–15, 19, 23, 51; 15:10; 16:12; 17:13, and similar passages in Mk and Lk; Acts 7:25 (twice); 28:26, 27; in Rom 3:11, the present participle, with the article, is used as a noun, lit., "there is not the understanding (one)," in a moral and spiritual sense; Rom 15:21; 2 Cor 10:12, "are (not) wise"; Eph 5:17, "understand." It is translated **(2)** "consider" in Mk 6:52; and **(3)** "be wise" in 2 Cor 10:12. See: TDNT—7:888, 1119; BAGD—790a; THAYER—605b.

4921. συνιστάω {16x} **sunistaō**, *soon-is-tah'-o;* or (strengthened)

　　συνιστάνω **sunistanō**, *soon-is-tan'-o;* or

　　συνίστημι **sunistēmi**, *soon-is'-tay-mee;* from *4862* and *2476* (incl. its collat. forms); to *set together,* i.e. (by impl.) to *introduce* (favorably), or (fig.) to *exhibit;* intr. to *stand near,* or (fig.) to *constitute:*—commend {10x}, approve {2x}, consist {1x}, make {1x}, stand {1x}, stand with {1x}. See: TDNT—7:896, 1120; BAGD—790c; THAYER—605c.

4922. συνοδεύω {1x} **sunŏdĕuō**, *soon-od-yoo'-o;* from *4862* and *3593;* to *travel* in company *with:*—journey with {1x}. See: BAGD—791c; THAYER—605d.

4923. συνοδία {1x} **sunŏdia**, *soon-od-ee'-ah;* from a compound of *4862* and *3598* ("synod"); *companionship* on a journey, i.e. (by impl.) a *caravan:*—company {1x}.

　　Sunodia, lit., "a way or journey together" (*sun,* "with," *hodos,* "a way"), denotes, by metonymy, "a company of travelers", travelers bound together only by destination; in Lk 2:44, of the company from which Christ was missed by Joseph and Mary. See: BAGD—791a; THAYER—605d.

4924. συνοικέω {1x} **sunŏikĕō**, *soon-oy-keh'-o;* from *4862* and *3611;* to *reside together* (as a family):—dwell together {1x}. See: BAGD—791c; THAYER—605d.

4925. συνοικοδομέω {1x} **sunŏikŏdŏmĕō**, *soon-oy-kod-om-eh'-o;* from

4862 and *3618;* to *construct,* i.e. (pass.) to *compose* (in company with other Christians, fig.):— build together {1x}. See: TDNT—5:148, 674; BAGD—791c; THAYER—606a.

4926. συνομιλέω {1x} **sunŏmilĕō**, *soon-om-il-eh'-o;* from *4862* and *3656;* to *converse* mutually:—talk with {1x}. See: BAGD—791c; THAYER—606a.

4927. συνομορέω {1x} **sunŏmŏrĕō**, *soon-om-or-eh'-o;* from *4862* and a der. of a compound of the base of *3674* and the base of *3725;* to *border together,* i.e. *adjoin:*—join hard + 2251 {1x}. See: BAGD—791c; THAYER—606a.

4928. συνοχή {2x} **sunŏchē**, *soon-okh-ay';* from *4912; restraint,* i.e. (fig.) *anxiety:*—anguish {1x}, distress {1x}.

Sunoche literally means, a holding together, or compressing and was used of the narrowing of a way. It is found only in its metaphorical sense, of straits, distress, anguish **(1)** Lk 21:25—distress of nations, and **(2)** 2 Cor 2:4— anguish of heart. See: TDNT—7:886, 1117; BAGD—791d; THAYER—606a.

4929. συντάσσω {2x} **suntassō**, *soon-tas-so;* from *4862* and *5021;* to *arrange jointly,* i.e. (fig.) to *direct:*—appoint {2x}.

Suntasso, as a verb, means literally "to arrange together with", hence "to appoint, prescribe" and is used **(1)** Mt 26:19 of what the Lord "appointed" for His disciples: "And the disciples did as Jesus had appointed them; and they made ready the passover" and **(2)** in Mt 27:10, in a quotation concerning the price of the potter's field: "And gave them for the potter's field, as the Lord appointed me." See: BAGD—791d; THAYER—606a.

4930. συντέλεια {6x} **suntĕlĕia**, *soon-tel'-i-ah;* from *4931; entire completion,* i.e. *consummation* (of a dispensation):—end {6x}.

Sunteleia signifies "a bringing to completion together" (*sun* "with," *teleo,* "to complete"), marking the "completion" or consummation of the various parts of a scheme. It is used **(1)** in Mt 13:39–40, 49; 24:3; 28:20, "the end of the world", **(1a)** not denoting a termination, but the heading up of events to the appointed climax. **(1b)** *Aion* is not the world, but a period or epoch or era in which events take place on the world. **(2)** In Heb 9:26, the word translated "world" is in the plural, and the phrase is "the end of the world." It was at the heading up of all the various epochs appointed by divine counsels that Christ was manifested (i.e., in His Incarnation) "to put away sin by the

sacrifice of Himself. See: TDNT—8:64, 1161; BAGD—792a; THAYER—606b.

4931. συντελέω {7x} **suntĕlĕō**, *soon-tel-eh'-o;* from *4862* and *5055;* to *complete entirely;* gen. to *execute* (lit. or fig.):—end {4x}, finish {1x}, fulfil {1x}, make {1x}.

Sunteleo means to end together, bring quite to an end and is said **(1)** of the completion of a period of days (Lk 4:2; Acts 21:27); **(2)** of completing something; of the Lord ending His discourse (Mt 7:28); **(3)** of God **(3a)** in finishing a work (Rom 9:28), and **(3b)** in making a new covenant (Heb 8:8); **(4)** of the fulfillment of things foretold (Mk 13:4); **(5)** of the devil's temptation of the Lord (Lk 4:13). See: TDNT— 8:62, 1161; BAGD—792a; THAYER—606b.

4932. συντέμνω {2x} **suntĕmnō**, *soon-tem'-no;* from *4862* and the base of *5114;* to *contract* by cutting, i.e. (fig.) *do concisely* (*speedily*):—cut short {1x}, short {1x}.

Suntemno, lit., "to cut together" signifies "to make contract by cutting, to cut short"; thus, to bring to an end or accomplish speedily; it is said of a prophecy or decree, Rom 9:28 (twice). See: BAGD—792c; THAYER—606c.

4933. συντηρέω {4x} **suntērĕō**, *soon-tay-reh'-o;* from *4862* and *5083;* to *keep closely together,* i.e. (by impl.) to *conserve* (from ruin); ment. to *remember* (and *obey*):— keep {1x}, observe {1x}, preserve {2x}.

Suntereo denotes "to preserve, keep safe, keep close" (*sun,* "together with," used intensively), **(1)** in Lk 2:19, of the mother of Jesus in regard to the words of the shepherds; **(2)** in Mk 6:20 it is used of Herod's preservation of John the Baptist from Herodias, by "watching over/ out" for him, "observed (him)"; **(3)** in Mt 9:17; Lk 5:38, of the preservation of wineskins. See: TDNT—8:151, 1174; BAGD—792c; THAYER— 606c.

4934. συντίθημι {4x} **suntithĕmai**, *soon-tith'-em-ahee;* mid. voice from *4862* and *5087;* to *place jointly,* i.e. (fig.) to *consent* (*bargain, stipulate*), *concur:*—agree {2x}, assent {1x}, covenant {1x}.

Suntithemi, lit., "to put together" (*sun,* "with," *tithemi,* "to put"), in the middle voice, means "to make an agreement, or to assent to"; translated **(1)** "covenanted" in Lk 22:5; **(2)** "agreed" in Jn 9:22, and **(3)** Acts 23:20; "assented" in Acts 24:9. See: BAGD—72d; THAYER—606c.

4935. συντόμως {1x} **suntŏmōs**, *soon-tom'-oce;* adv. from a der. of *4932; concisely* (*briefly*):—a few words {1x}. See: BAGD—792d; THAYER—606d.

Greek

4936. συντρέχω {3x} **suntrĕchō**, *soon-trekh'-o;* from 4862 and 5143 (incl. its alt.); to *rush together* (hastily *assemble*) or *headlong* (fig.):—run {1x}, run together {1x}, run with {1x}.

Suntrecho, "to run together with", is used **(1)** literally, Mk 6:33; Acts 3:11; **(2)** metaphorically, 1 Pet 4:4, of "running" a course of evil with others. See: BAGD—793a; THAYER—606d.

4937. συντρίβω {8x} **suntribō**, *soon-tree'-bo;* from 4862 and the base of 5147; to *crush completely,* i.e. to *shatter* (lit. or fig.):—bruise {3x}, break {2x}, broken to shivers {1x}, brokenhearted + 2588 {1x}, break in pieces {1x}.

The stress in this word is harm inflicted by a quick blow. *Subtribo,* lit., "to rub together," and so "to shatter, shiver, break in pieces by crushing," is said **(1)** of the bruising of a reed, Mt 12:20; **(2)** the "breaking" of fetters in pieces, Mk 5:4; **(3)** the "breaking" of **(3a)** an alabaster cruse, Mk 14:3; **(3b)** an earthenware vessel, Rev 2:27; **(4)** of the physical bruising of a person possessed by a devil, Lk 9:39; **(5)** concerning Christ, "a bone of Him shall not be broken," Jn 19:36; **(6)** metaphorically of the crushed condition of a "broken-hearted" person, Lk 4:18; **(7)** of the eventual crushing of Satan, Rom 16:20. Syn.: 4938. See: TDNT—7:919, 1124; BAGD—793b; THAYER—606d.

4938. σύντριμμα {1x} **suntrimma**, *soon-trim'-mah;* from 4937; *concussion* or utter *fracture* (prop. concr.), i.e. complete *ruin:*—destruction {1x}.

This word stresses a destruction incurred through long-term rubbing or wearing away. It is used metaphorically of destruction in Rom 3:16, which, in a passage setting forth the sinful state of mankind in general, suggests the wearing process of the effects of cruelty. Syn.: 4937. See: TDNT—7:919, 1124; BAGD—793c; THAYER—607a.

4939. σύντροφος {1x} **suntrŏphŏs**, *soon'-trof-os;* from 4862 and 5162 (in a pass. sense); a *fellow-nursling,* i.e. *comrade:*—brought up with {1x}. See: BAGD—793c; THAYER—607a.

4940. συντυγχάνω {1x} **suntugchanō**, *soon-toong-khan'-o;* from 4862 and 5177; to *chance together,* i.e. *meet* with (*reach*):—come at {1x}.

Suntugchano, "to meet with" (*sun,* "with," and *tunchano,* "to reach"), is rendered "to come at" in Lk 8:19, (of the efforts of Christ's mother and brethren to get at Him through a crowd). See: BAGD—793c; THAYER—607b.

4941. Συντύχη {1x} **Suntuchē**, *soon-too'-khay;* from 4940; an *accident; Syntyche,* a Chr. female:—*Syntyche* {1x}. See: BAGD—793d; THAYER—607a.

4942. συνυποκρίνομαι {1x} **sunupŏkrinŏmai**, *soon-oo-pok-rin'-om-ahee;* from 4862 and 5271; to *act hypocritically* in concert *with:*—dissemble with {1x}.

Sunupokrinomai, (*sun,* "with," *hupokrinomai,* "to join in acting the hypocrite") is pretending to act from one motive, whereas another motive really inspires the act. So in Gal 2:13, Peter with other believing Jews, in separating from believing Gentiles at Antioch, pretended that the motive was loyalty to the Law of Moses, whereas it was really fear of the Judaizers. See: TDNT—8:559, 1235; BAGD—793d; THAYER—607b.

4943. συνυπουργέω {1x} **sunupŏurgĕō**, *soon-oop-oorg-eh'-o;* from 4862 and a der. of a compound of 5259 and the base of 2041; to *be a co-auxiliary,* i.e. *assist:*—help together {1x}. See: BAGD—793b; THAYER—607b.

4944. συνωδίνω {1x} **sunōdinō**, *soon-o-dee'-no;* from 4862 and 5605; to *have* (parturition) *pangs* in company (concert, simultaneously) *with,* i.e. (fig.) to *sympathize* (in expectation of relief from suffering):—travail in pain together {1x}. See: BAGD—793b; THAYER—607b.

4945. συνωμοσία {1x} **sunōmŏsia**, *soon-o-mos-ee'-ah;* from a compound of 4862 and 3660; being leagued by oath, a *swearing together,* i.e. (by impl.) a *plot:*—conspiracy {1x}. See: BAGD—793d; THAYER—607b.

4946. Συράκουσαι {1x} **Surakŏusai**, *soo-rak'-oo-sahee;* plur. of uncert. der.; *Syracuse,* the capital of Sicily:—Syracuse {1x}. See: BAGD—794a; THAYER—607c.

4947. Συρία {8x} **Suria**, *soo-ree'-ah;* prob. of Heb. or. [6865]; *Syria* (i.e. *Tsyria* or *Tyre*), a region of Asia:—Syria {8x}. See: BAGD—794a; THAYER—607c.

4948. Σύρος {1x} **Surŏs**, *soo'-ros;* from the same as 4947; a *Syran* (i.e. prob. *Tyrian*), a native of Syria:—Syrian {1x}. See: BAGD—794b; THAYER—607c.

4949. Συροφοίνισσα {1x} **Surŏphŏinissa**, *soo-rof-oy'-nis-sah;* fem. of a compound of 4948 and the same as 5403; a *Syro-phœnician* woman, i.e. a female

native of Phœnicia in Syria:—Syrophenician {1x}. See: BAGD—794b; THAYER—607c.

4950. Σύρτις {1x} **surtis**, *soor'-tis;* from *4951;* a *shoal* (from the sand *drawn* thither by the waves), i.e. the *Syrtis* Major or great bay on the N. coast of Africa:— quicksands {1x}. See: BAGD—794c; THAYER—607d.

4951. σύρω {5x} **surō**, *soo'-ro;* prob. akin to *138;* to *trail:*—drag {1x}, draw {3x}, hale {1x}.

Suro, as a verb, means "to drag, to hale, to draw" and is translated (1) "drag": "And the other disciples came in a little ship; . . . dragging the net with fishes" (Jn 21:8); (2) "haling, violently dragging": "As for Saul, he made havock of the church, entering into every house, and haling men and women committed them to prison" (Acts 8:3). It is also translated (3) "to draw" in Acts 14:19; 17:6; Rev 12:4. Syn.: It is used of "drawing" a net, Jn 21:6, 11: (A) At vv. 6 and 11 *helko* (or *helkuo*) is used; for there a drawing of the net to a certain point is intended; by the disciples to themselves in the ship, by Peter to himself upon the shore. (B) But at v. 8 *helko* gives place to *suro* (*4951*): for nothing is there intended but the dragging of the net, which had been fastened to the ship, after it through the water. See also: 307, 385, 392, 501, 502, 645, 868, 1448, 1670, 1828, 2020, 4264, 4317, 4334, 4358, 4685, 5288, 5289. See: BAGD—794c; THAYER—607d.

4952. συσπαράσσω {1x} **susparassō**, *soos-par-as'-so;* from *4862* and *4682;* to *rend completely,* i.e. (by anal.) to *convulse* violently:—tare (tear) {1x}. See: BAGD—794c; THAYER—608a.

4953. σύσσημον {1x} **sussēmŏn**, *soos'-say-mon;* neut. of a compound of *4862* and the base of *4591;* a *sign in common,* i.e. preconcerted *signal:*—token {1x}.

Sussemon, "a fixed sign or signal, agreed upon with others", is used in Mk 14:44, "a token." See: TDNT—7:269, 1015; BAGD—794d; THAYER—608a.

4954. σύσσωμος {1x} **sussōmŏs**, *soos'-so-mos;* from *4862* and *4983;* of a *joint body,* i.e. (fig.) a *fellow-member* of the Chr. community:—of the same body {1x}. See: TDNT—7:1024, 1140; BAGD—794d; THAYER—608a.

4955. συστασιαστής {1x} **sustasiastēs**, *soos-tas-ee-as-tace';* from a compound of *4862* and a der. of *4714;* a *fellow-insurgent,* a *rebel,* a *revolutionist:*—make insurrection with {1x}. See: BAGD—794d; THAYER—608a.

4956. συστατικός {2x} **sustatikŏs**, *soos-tat-ee-kos';* from a der. of *4921; introductory,* i.e. *recommendatory:*—of commendation {2x}. See: BAGD—795a; THAYER—608a.

4957. συσταυρόω {5x} **sustaurŏō**, *soos-tow-rŏ'-o;* from *4862* and *4717;* to *impale* in company *with* (lit. or fig.):— crucify with {5x}.

Sustauroo, "to crucify with" (*su-,* "for," *sun,* "with"), is used (1) of actual "crucifixion" in company with another, Mt 27:44; Mk 15:32; Jn 19:32; (2) metaphorically, of spiritual identification with Christ in His death, Rom 6:6 and Gal 2:20. See: TDNT—7:786, 1102; BAGD—795a; THAYER—608b.

4958. συστέλλω {2x} **sustĕllō**, *soos-tel'-lo;* from *4862* and *4724;* to *send* (*draw*) *together,* i.e. *enwrap* (*enshroud* a corpse for burial), *contract* (an interval):— short {1x}, wind up {1x}.

Sustello, is used (1) literally, Acts 5:6; and (2) metaphorically, 1 Cor 7:29. Short means to wind things up; "time is short, things are being wound up." Stress is on events winding around and upon themselves (1 Cor 7:29). See: TDNT—7:596, 1074; BAGD—795a; THAYER—608b.

4959. συστενάζω {1x} **sustĕnazō**, *soos-ten-ad'-zo;* from *4862* and *4727;* to *moan jointly,* i.e. (fig.) *experience a common calamity:*—groan together {1x}. See: TDNT—7:600, 1076; BAGD—795b; THAYER—608b.

4960. συστοιχέω {1x} **sustŏichĕō**, *soos-toy-kheh'-o;* from *4862* and *4748;* to *file together* (as soldiers in ranks), i.e. (fig.) to *correspond* to:—answer to {1x}.

Sustoicheo, lit., "to be in the same line or row with" (*sun,* "with," *stoichos,* "a row"), is translated "answereth to" in Gal 4:25. See: TDNT—7:669, 1087; BAGD—795b; THAYER—608b.

4961. συστρατιώτης {2x} **sustratiōtēs**, *soos-trat-ee-o'-tace;* from *4862* and *4757;* a *co-campaigner,* i.e. (fig.) an *associate* in Chr. toil:—fellowsoldier {2x}.

Sustratiotes is used metaphorically in Phil 2:25 and Philem 2, of fellowship in Christian service. See: TDNT—7:701, 1091; BAGD—795b; THAYER—608c.

4962. συστρέφω {1x} **sustrĕphō**, *soos-tref'-o;* from *4862* and *4762;* to *twist together,* i.e. *collect* (a bundle, a crowd):— gather {1x}. See: BAGD—795c; THAYER—608c.

Greek

4963. συστροφή {2x} **sustrŏphē**, *soos-trof-ay';* from *4962;* a *twisting together,* i.e. (fig.) a secret *coalition,* riotous *crowd:*—+ band together {1x}, concourse {1x}.

Sustrophe, "a turning together" (*sun,* "with," *trepo,* "to turn"), signifies **(1)** that which is rolled together; hence, a dense mass of people, "a concourse", people bound together by a common course of action, Acts 19:40. **(2)** It is translated "band together" in Acts 23:12; again a group bound together by a common course of action, to kill Paul. See: BAGD—795c; THAYER—608c.

4964. συσχηματίζω {2x} **suschēmatizō**, *soos-khay-mat-id'-zo;* from *4862* and a der. of *4976;* to *fashion alike,* i.e. *conform* to the same pattern (fig.):—conform to {1x}, fashion (one's) self according to {1x}.

Suschematizo, "to fashion or shape one thing like another," is translated **(1)** "conformed to" in Rom 12:2; **(2)** "fashioning ones self according to" in 1 Pet 1:14. **(3)** This word could not be used of inward transformation. Syn.: **(A)** *Summorphos* (*4832*) stresses inward conformity and describes what is the essence in character and thus complete or durable, not merely a form or outline. **(B)** *Suschematizo* (*4964*) stresses outward conformity and means to shape one thing like another and describes what is transitory, changeable, and unstable. See: BAGD—795c; THAYER—608c.

4965. Συχάρ {1x} **Suchar**, *soo-khar';* of Heb. or. [7941]; *Sychar* (i.e. *Shekar*), a place in Pal.:—Sychar {1x}. See: BAGD—795d; THAYER—608d.

4966. Συχέμ {2x} **Suchĕm**, *soo-khem';* of Heb. or. [7927]; *Sychem* (i.e. *Shekem*), the name of a Canaanite and of a place in Pal.:—Sychem (city in Ephraim) {1x}, Sychem (son of Emmor) {1x}. See: BAGD—795d; THAYER—609a.

4967. σφαγή {3x} **sphagē**, *sfag-ay';* from *4969;* butchery (of animals for food or sacrifice, or [fig.] of men [*destruction*]):—slaughter {3x}.

Sphage expresses slaughter **(1)** within a strain of sorrow (Acts 8:32); **(2)** within a strain of triumph (Rom 8:36); and **(3)** in Jas 5:5 the luxurious rich are getting wealth by injustice, spending it on their pleasures, and are fattening themselves like sheep unconscious of their doom. See: TDNT—7:935, 1125; BAGD—795d; THAYER—609a.

4968. σφάγιον {1x} **sphagiŏn**, *sfag'-ee-on;* neut. of a der. of *4967;* a *victim* (in sacrifice):—slain beast {1x}. See: BAGD—796a; THAYER—609b.

4969. σφάζω {10x} **sphazō**, *sfad'-zo;* a primary verb; to *butcher* (espec. an animal for food or in sacrifice) or (gen.) to *slaughter,* or (spec.) to *maim* (violently):—kill {1x}, slay {8x}, wound {1x}.

Sphazo, "to slay," especially of victims for sacrifice is used **(1)** of taking human life, 1 Jn 3:12 (twice); Rev 6:4, "kill"; in 13:3, probably of assassination, "wounded (to death)"; 18:24; **(2)** of Christ, as the Lamb of sacrifice, Rev 5:6, 9, 12; 6:9; 13:8. See: TDNT—7:925, 1125; BAGD—796a; THAYER—609b.

4970. σφόδρα {11x} **sphŏdra**, *sfod'-rah;* neut. plur. of σφοδρός **sphŏdrŏs**, (*violent;* of uncert. der.) as adv.; *vehemently,* i.e. in a *high degree, much:*—exceeding {4x}, very {3x}, greatly {2x}, exceedingly {1x}, sore {1x}.

Sphodra, properly the neuter plural of *sphodros,* "excessive, violent" (from a root indicating restlessness), translated **(1)** "exceeding" in Mt 2:10; 17:23; 26:22; Rev 16:21; **(2)** "very" in Mt 18:31; Mk 16:4; Lk 18:23; **(3)** "greatly" in Mt 27:54; Act 6:7; **(4)** "exceedingly" in Mt 19:25; and **(5)** "sore" in Mt 17:6. Sore means to exceed normal feelings. See: BAGD—796a; THAYER—609b.

4971. σφοδρῶς {1x} **sphŏdrōs**, *sfod-roce';* adv. from the same as *4970; very much:*—exceedingly {1x}. See: BAGD—796b; THAYER—609b.

4972. σφραγίζω {27x} **sphragizō**, *sfrag-id'-zo;* from *4973;* to *stamp* (with a signet or private mark) for security or preservation (lit. or fig.); by impl. to *keep secret,* to *attest:*—seal {22x}, set to (one's) seal {1x}, stop {1x}, seal up {1x}, set a seal {1x}, vr seal {1x}.

Spragizo, "to seal", is used to indicate **(1)** security and permanency, **(1a)** of Jesus' sepulcher, Mt 27:66; **(2)** of the doom of Satan, fixed and certain, Rev 20:3; **(3)** in Rom 15:28, "when . . . I have . . . sealed to them this fruit"; the metaphor stresses the sacred formalities of the transaction and guarantees the full complement of the contents; **(4)** secrecy and security and the postponement of disclosure, Rev 10:4; in a negative command Rev 22:10; **(5)** ownership and security, together with destination, Rev 7:3, 4, 5; **(6)** the same three indications [(*1*) through (*3*) above] are conveyed in Eph 1:13, **(6a)** in the metaphor of the "sealing" of believers by the gift of the Holy Spirit, upon believing, i.e., at the time of their regeneration; **(6b)** the idea of destination is stressed by the phrase "the Holy Spirit of promise" (see also v. 14); **(6c)** so Eph 4:30, "ye were sealed unto the day of redemption"; so in 2 Cor 1:22, where the middle voice intimates the special interest

of the Sealer in His act; **(7)** authentication by the believer (by receiving the witness of the Son) of the fact that "God is true," Jn 3:33; **(8)** authentication by God in sealing the Son as the Giver of eternal life Jn 6:27. See: TDNT— 7:939, 1127; BAGD—796b; THAYER—609b.

4973. **σφραγίς** {16x} **sphragis**, *sfrag-ece';* prob. strengthened from *5420;* a *sig-net* (as *fencing* in or protecting from misappro-priation); by impl. the *stamp* impressed (as a mark of privacy, or genuineness), lit. or fig.:— seal {16x}.

Sphragis denotes **(1)** "a seal" or "signet," Rev 7:2, "the seal of the living God," **(1a)** an emblem of ownership and security, here com-bined with that of destination (as in Eze 9:4), **(1b)** the persons to be "sealed" being secured from destruction and marked for reward; **(2)** "the impression" of a "seal" or signet, **(2a)** literal, a "seal" on a book or roll, combin-ing with the ideas of security and destination those of secrecy and postponement of disclo-sures, Rev 5:1, 2, 5, 9; 6:1, 3, 5, 7, 9, 12; 8:1; **(2b)** metaphorical, **(2b1)** Rom 4:11, said of "cir-cumcision," as an authentication of the righ-teousness of Abraham's faith, and an external attestation of the covenant made with him by God; the rabbis called circumcision "the seal of Abraham"; **(2b2)** in 1 Cor 9:2, of converts as a "seal" or authentication of Paul's apostleship; **(2b3)** in 2 Ti 2:19, "the firm foundation of God standeth, having this seal, The Lord knoweth them that are His", indicating ownership, au-thentication, security and destination"; and, Let every one that nameth the Name of the Lord depart from unrighteousness," indicating a ratification on the part of the believer of the determining counsel of God concerning him; **(3)** Rev 9:4 distinguishes those who will be found without the "seal" of God on their fore-heads. See: TDNT—7:939, 1127; BAGD—796c; THAYER—609d.

4974. **σφυρόν** {1x} **sphurŏn**, *sfoo-ron';* neut. of a presumed der. prob. of the same as σφαῖρα **sphaira** (a *ball*, *"sphere;"* com-pare the fem. σφῦρα **sphura**, a *hammer*); the *ankle* (as *globular*):—ankle bone {1x}. See: BAGD—797a; THAYER—609d.

4975. **σχεδόν** {3x} **schĕdŏn**, *skhed-on';* neut. of a presumed der. of the alt. of *2192* as adv.; *nigh*, i.e. *nearly:*—almost {3x}.

Schedon is used either **(1)** of locality, Acts 19:26, or **(2)** of degree, Acts 13:44; Heb 9:22. See: BAGD—797a; THAYER—609d.

σχέω **schĕŏ**. See *2192*.

4976. **σχῆμα** {2x} **schēma**, *skhay'-mah;* from the alt. of *2192;* a *figure* (as a

mode or *circumstance*), i.e. (by impl.) extern. *condition:*—fashion {2x}.

Schema, "a figure, fashion", is translated **(1)** "fashion" in 1 Cor 7:31, of the world, signi-fying that which comprises the manner of life, actions, etc. of humanity in general; **(2)** in Phil 2:8 it is used of the Lord in His being found "in fashion" as a man, and signifies what He was in the eyes of men, the entire outwardly perceptible mode and shape of His existence, just as the preceding words *morphe*, "form," and *homoioma*, "likeness," describe what He was in Himself as man. Men saw in Christ a human form, bearing, language, action, mode of life . . . in general the state and relations of a human being, so that in the entire mode of His appearance He made Himself known and was recognized as a man. Syn.: *Morphe* (*3444*) "form" differs from *schema* (*4976*) "fig-ure, shape, fashion", as that which is intrinsic and essential, from that which is outward and accidental. In Phil *2:7 morphe* relates to the complete form or nature of a servant; and *schema* to the external form, or human body in 2:8. See: TDNT—7:954, 1129; BAGD—797b; THAYER—610a.

4977. **σχίζω** {10x} **schizō**, *skhid'-zo;* appar. a primary verb; to *split* or *sever* (lit. or fig.):—break {1x}, divide {2x}, open {1x}, rend {5x}, make a rent {1x}.

Schizo, **(1)** "to split, to rend open," is said **(1a)** of the veil of the temple, Mt 27:51; Mk 15:38; Lk 23:45; **(1b)** the rending of rocks, Mt 27:51; **(1c)** a garment, Lk 5:36, "make a rent"; Jn 19:24; **(2)** "to break", a net, Jn 21:11; **(3)** in the passive voice, metaphorically, of a crowd being divided into factions, Acts 14:4; 23:7; **(4)** the opening of the heavens, Mk 1:10;. See: TDNT—7:959, 1130; BAGD—797b; THAYER— 610a.

4978. **σχίσμα** {8x} **schisma**, *skhis'-mah;* from *4977;* a *split* or *gap* ("*schism*"), lit. or fig.:—division {5x}, rent {2x}, schism {1x}.

Schisma, (Eng., "schism"), denotes **(1)** "a cleft, a rent," Mt 9:16; Mk 2:21, then, **(2)** meta-phorically, "a division dissension," Jn 7:43; 9:16; 10:19; 1 Cor 1:10; 11:18; **(3)** in 1 Cor 12:25 it is translated "schism." See: TDNT—7:963, 1130; BAGD—797c; THAYER—610a.

4979. **σχοινίον** {2x} **schŏiniŏn**, *skhoy-nee'-on;* dimin. of σχοῖνος **schŏinŏs** (a *rush* or *flag*-plant; of uncert. der.); a *rushlet*, i.e. *grass-withe* or *tie* (gen.):—small cord {1x}, rope {1x}.

Schoinion, "a cord or rope," a diminutive of *schoinos*, "a rush, bulrush," meant a "cord" made of rushes; it denotes **(1)** "a small cord,"

Jn 2:15 (plural), **(2)** "a rope," Acts 27:32. See: BAGD—797d; THAYER—610b.

4980. **σχολάζω** {2x} **schŏlazō**, *skhol-ad'-zo; from 4981;* to *take a holiday,* i.e. *be at leisure* for (by impl. *devote oneself* wholly to); fig. to *be vacant* (of a house):— empty {1x}, give self {1x}.

Scholazo literally means leisure and is used **(1)** of persons who have time for anything; hence, can consequently be totally occupied with something else (1 Cor 7:5); and **(2)** of things left empty because attention is absorbed elsewhere (Mt 12:44). See: BAGD—797d; THAYER—610b.

4981. **σχολή** {1x} **schŏlē**, *skhol-ay';* prob. fem. of a presumed der. of the alt. of *2192;* prop. *loitering* (as a *withholding* of oneself from work) or *leisure,* i.e. (by impl.) a "*school*" (as *vacation* from phys. employment):—school {1x}.

Schole (whence Eng., "school") primarily denotes "leisure," then, "that for which leisure was employed, a disputation, lecture"; hence, by metonymy, "the place where lectures are delivered, a school," Acts 19:9. See: BAGD—798a; THAYER—610b.

4982. **σῴζω** {110x} **sōzō**, *sode'-zo;* from a primary **σῶς** **sōs** (contr. for obs. *σάος* **saŏs**, "*safe*"); to *save,* i.e. *deliver* or *protect* (lit. or fig.):—save {93x}, make whole {9x}, heal {3x}, be whole {2x}, misc. {3x} = preserve, do well.

Sozo, "to save," is used (as with the noun *soteria,* "salvation") **(1)** of material and temporal deliverance **(1a)** from danger, suffering, etc., e.g., Mt 8:25; Mk 13:20; Lk 23:35; Jn 12:27; 1 Ti 2:15; 2 Ti 4:18, "preserve"; Jude 5; **(1b)** from sickness, Mt 9:22, "made . . . whole"; so Mk 5:34; Lk 8:48; Jas 5:15; **(2)** of the spiritual and eternal salvation granted immediately by God to those who believe on the Lord Jesus Christ, **(2a)** e.g., Acts 2:47, "such as should be saved"; 16:31; Rom 8:24, "we are saved"; Eph 2:5, 8; 1 Ti 2:4; 2 Ti 1:9; Titus 3:5; **(2b)** of human agency in this, Rom 11:14; 1 Cor 7:16; 9:22; **(3)** of the present experiences of God's power to deliver from the bondage of sin, **(3a)** e.g., Mt 1:21; Rom 5:10; 1 Cor 15:2; Heb 7:25; Jas 1:21; 1 Pet 3:21; **(3b)** of human agency in this, 1 Ti 4:16;

(4) of the future deliverance of believers at the second coming of Christ for His saints, being deliverance from the wrath of God to be executed upon the ungodly at the close of this age and from eternal doom, e.g., Rom 5:9; **(5)** of the deliverance of the nation of Israel at the

second advent of Christ, e.g., Rom 11:26; **(6)** inclusively for all the blessings bestowed by God on men in Christ, e.g., Lk 19:10; Jn 10:9; 1 Cor 10:33; 1 Ti 1:15; **(7)** of those who endure to the end of the time of the Great Tribulation, Mt 10:22; Mk 13:13; **(8)** of the individual believer, who, though losing his reward at the judgment seat of Christ hereafter, will not lose his salvation, 1 Cor 3:15; 5:5; **(9)** of the deliverance of the nations at the millennium, Rev 21:24. See: TDNT—7:965, 1132; BAGD—798a; THAYER—610b.

4983. **σῶμα** {146x} **sōma**, *so'-mah;* from *4982;* the *body* (as a *sound* whole), used in a very wide application, lit. or fig.:— bodily {1x}, body {144x}, slave {1x}.

Soma is "the body as a whole, the instrument of life," whether **(1)** of man **(1a)** living, e.g., Mt 6:22, or **(1b)** dead, Mt 27:52; or **(1c)** in resurrection, 1 Cor 15:44; or **(2)** of beasts, Heb 13:11; **(3)** of grain, 1 Cor 15:37–38; **(4)** of the heavenly hosts, 1 Cor 15:40. **(5)** In Rev 18:13 it is translated "slaves." In its figurative uses the essential idea is preserved. **(6)** Sometimes the word stands, by *synecdoche,* for "the complete man," Mt 5:29; 6:22; Rom 12:1; Jas 3:6; Rev 18:13. **(7)** Sometimes the person is identified with his or her "body," Acts 9:37; 13:36, and this is so even of the Lord Jesus, Jn 19:40 with 42. **(8)** The "body" is not the man, for he himself can exist apart from his "body," 2 Cor 12:2–3. **(9)** The "body" is an essential part of the man and therefore the redeemed are not perfected till the resurrection, Heb 11:40; no man in his final state will be without his "body," Jn 5:28– 29; Rev 20:13. **(10)** The word is also used for physical nature, as distinct **(10a)** from *pneuma,* "the spiritual nature," e.g., 1 Cor 5:3, and **(10b)** from *psuche,* "the soul," e.g., 1 Th 5:23. **(10c)** *Soma,* "body," and *pneuma,* "spirit," may be separated; *pneuma* and *psuche,* "soul," can only be distinguished." **(11)** It is also used metaphorically, of the mystic body of Christ, with **(11a)** reference to the whole church, e.g., Eph 1:23; Col 1:18, 22, 24; **(11b)** also of a local church, 1 Cor 12:27. See: TDNT—7:1024, 1140; BAGD—799a; THAYER—611a.

4984. **σωματικός** {2x} **sōmatikŏs**, *so-mat-ee-kos';* from *4983; corporeal* or *physical:*—bodily {2x}.

Somatikos, "bodily," is used **(1)** in Lk 3:22, of the Holy Spirit in taking a bodily shape; **(2)** in 1 Ti 4:8 of bodily exercise. See: TDNT— 7:1024, 1140; BAGD—800b; THAYER—611d.

4985. **σωματικῶς** {1x} **sōmatikōs**, *so-mat-ee-koce';* adv. from *4984; corporeally* or *physically:*—bodily {1x}. See: BAGD—800b; THAYER—611d.

4986. Σώπατρος {1x} **Sōpatrŏs**, *so'-pat-ros;*
from the base of *4982* and
3962; of a *safe father; Sopatrus,* a Chr.:—*Sopa-*
ter {1x}. See: BAGD—800b; THAYER—612a.
comp. *4989.*

4987. σωρεύω {2x} **sōrĕuō**, *sore-yoo'-o;* from
　　　　　another form of *4673;* to *pile*
up (lit. or fig.):—heap {1x}, laden {1x}.

　Soreuo, "to heap one thing on another," is
said (1) of "heaping" coals of fire on the head,
Rom 12:20; in (2) 2 Ti 3:6 it is used metaphorically of women "laden" (or overwhelmed) with
sins. See: TDNT—7:1094, 1150; BAGD—800c;
THAYER—612a.

4988. Σωσθένης {2x} **Sōsthěnēs**, *soce-then'-*
　　　　　ace; from the base of *4982*
and that of *4599; of safe strength; Sosthenes,*
a Chr.:—*Sosthenes* {2x}. See: BAGD—800c;
THAYER—612a.

4989. Σωσίπατρος {1x} **Sōsipatrŏs**, *so-sip'-*
　　　　　at-ros; prol. for *4986;*
Sosipatrus, a Chr.:—*Sosipater* {1x}. See:
BAGD—800c; THAYER—612a.

4990. σωτήρ {24x} **sōtēr**, *so-tare';* from *4982;*
　　　　　a *deliverer,* i.e. God or Christ:—
Saviour {24x}.

　Soter, "a savior, deliverer, preserver," is used
(1) of God, Lk 1:47; 1 Ti 1:1; 2:3; 4:10 (in the
sense of "preserver," since He gives "to all life
and breath and all things"); Titus 1:3; 2:10; 3:4;
Jude 25; (2) of Christ, Lk 2:11; Jn 4:42; Acts
5:31; 13:23 (of Israel); Eph 5:23 (the sustainer
and preserver of the church, His "body"); Phil
3:20 (at His return to receive the Church to
Himself); 2 Ti 1:10 (with reference to His incarnation, "the days of His flesh"); Titus 1:4 (a
title shared, in the context, with God the Father); 2:13, "God and our Savior Jesus Christ";
Titus 3:6; 2 Pet 1:1, "our Savior Jesus Christ;
as in the parallel in 2 Pet 1: 11, "our Lord and
Savior Jesus Christ"; these passages are therefore a testimony to His deity; 2 Pet 2:20; 3:2, 18;
1 Jn 4:14. See: TDNT—7:1003, 1132; BAGD—
800d; THAYER—612a.

4991. σωτηρία {45x} **sōtēria**, *so-tay-ree'-ah;*
　　　　　fem. of a der. of *4990* as
(prop. abstr.) noun; *rescue* or *safety* (phys. or
mor.):—salvation {40x}, the (one) be saved {1x},
deliver + 1325 {1x}, health {1x}, saving {1x},
that (one) be saved + 1519 {1x}.

　Soteria denotes "deliverance, preservation,
salvation." "Salvation" is used in the NT (1) of
material and temporal deliverance from danger and apprehension, (1a) national, Lk 1:69,
71; Acts 7:25, "deliverance"; (1b) personal, as
from (1b1) the sea, Acts 27:34, "health"; (1b2)
prison, Phil 1:19; (1b3) the flood, Heb 11:7;

(1b4) of the spiritual and eternal deliverance
granted immediately by God to those who accept His conditions of repentance and faith in
the Lord Jesus, in whom alone it is to be obtained, Acts 4:12, and upon confession of Him
as Lord, Rom 10:10; for this purpose the gospel
is the saving instrument, Rom 1:16; Eph 1:13;
(1c) of the present experience of God's power
to deliver from the bondage of sin, e.g., (1c1)
Phil 2:12, where the special, though not the
entire, reference is to the maintenance of peace
and harmony; 1 Pet 1:9; (1c2) this present experience on the part of believers is virtually
equivalent to sanctification; (1c3) for this purpose, God is able to make them wise, 2 Ti 3:15;
(1c4) they are not to neglect it, Heb 2:3; (1d) of
the future deliverance of believers at the Parousia of Christ for His saints, a salvation which
is the object of their confident hope, e.g., Rom
13:11; 1 Th 5:8, and v. 9, where "salvation" is
assured to them, as being deliverance from the
wrath of God destined to be executed upon the
ungodly at the end of this age, 1 Th 1:10; 2 Th
2:13; Heb 1:14; 9:28; 1 Pet 1:5; 2 Pet 3:15;
　(2) of the deliverance of the nation of Israel
at the second advent of Christ at the time of "the
epiphany (or shining forth) of His Parousia"
(2 Th 2:8); Lk 1:71; Rev 12:10; (3) inclusively,
to sum up all the blessings bestowed by God
on men in Christ through the Holy Spirit, e.g.,
2 Cor 6:2; Heb 5:9; 1 Pet 1:9, 10; Jude 3; (4) occasionally, as standing virtually for the Savior,
e.g., Lk 19:9; cf. Jn 4:22; (5) in ascriptions of
praise to God, Rev 7:10, and as that which it
is His prerogative to bestow, Rev 19:1. See:
TDNT—7:965, 1132; BAGD—801b; THAYER—
612c.

4992. σωτήριον {5x} **sōtēriŏn**, *so-tay'-ree-on;*
　　　　　neut. of the same as *4991* as
(prop. concr.) noun; *defender* or (by impl.) *de-*
fence:—salvation {4x}, that brings salvation {1x}.

　Soterion, the neuter of the adjective, is used
as (1) a noun in Lk 2:30; 3:6; Titus 2:11, in each
of which it virtually stands for the Savior as
in Acts 28:28, (2) in Eph 6:17, for the helmet of
"salvation." See: TDNT—7:1021, 1132; BAGD—
801d; THAYER—612d.

4993. σωφρονέω {6x} **sōphrŏněō**, *so-fron-eh'-o;*
　　　　　from *4998;* to *be of sound*
mind, i.e. *sane,* (fig.) *moderate:*—be in right
mind {2x}, be sober {2x}, be sober minded {1x},
soberly {1x}.

　Sophreno signifies (1) "to be of sound
mind," or "in one's right mind, sober-minded"
(*sozo,* "to save," *phren,* "the mind"), Mk 5:15
and Lk 8:35, "in his right mind"; 2 Cor 5:13,
"we be sober"; (2) "to be temperate, self-controlled," Titus 2:6, "to be sober-minded"; (3)

1 Pet 4:7, "be ye sober"; see also Rom 12:3. See: TDNT—7:1097, 1150; BAGD—802a; THAYER—612d.

4994. σωφρονίζω {1x} **sōphrŏnizō**, *so-fron-id'-zo;* from *4998;* to *make of sound mind,* i.e. (fig.) to *discipline* or *correct:*—teach to be sober {1x}.

This word denotes to be of sound mind, to recall to one's senses, restore one to his senses, to moderate, control, curb, disciple, to hold one to his duty, to admonish, to exhort earnestly, Titus 2:4 encompasses the cultivation of sound judgment and prudence. See: TDNT—7:1104, 1150; BAGD—802a; THAYER—613a.

4995. σωφρονισμός {1x} **sōphrŏnismŏs**, *so-fron-is-mos';* from *4994; discipline,* i.e. *self-control:*—sound mind {1x}.

Literally this word means saving the mind through admonishing and calling to soundness of mind and to self-control (2 Ti 1:7). See: TDNT—7:1104, 1150; BAGD—802b; THAYER—613a.

4996. σωφρόνως {1x} **sōphrŏnōs**, *so-fron'-oce;* adv. from *4998; with sound mind,* i.e. *moderately:*—soberly {1x}.

Sophronos occurs in Titus 2:12 and suggests the exercise of that self-restraint that governs all passions and desires, enabling the believer to be conformed to the mind of Christ. See: BAGD—802c; THAYER—613c.

4997. σωφροσύνη {3x} **sōphrŏsunē**, *so-fros-oo'-nay;* from *4998; soundness of mind,* i.e. (lit.) *sanity* or (fig.) *self-control:*—soberness {1x}, sobriety {2x}.

Sophrosune refers to having complete control over the passions and desires so that they are lawful and reasonable; a certain curtailment and regulation of passions, both removing those that are improper and excessive and also arranging those that are necessary to the proper time and in moderation, Acts 26:25; 1 Ti 2:9, 15. Syn.: 127. See: TDNT—7:1097, 1150; BAGD—802c; THAYER—613c.

4998. σώφρων {4x} **sōphrōn**, *so'-frone;* from the base of *4982* and that of *5424; safe* (*sound*) in *mind,* i.e. *self-controlled* (*moderate* as to opinion or passion):—discreet {1x}, sober {2x}, temperate {1x}.

Sophron, "of sound mind self-controlled", is translated **(1)** "sober," in 1 Ti 3:2; Titus 1:8; **(2)** 1 Ti 2:2, "temperate; and **(3)** in 1 Ti 2:5, "discreet." See: TDNT—7:1097, 1150; BAGD—802c.

T

τα' ta. def. art. See *3588.* See: BAGD—549b; THAYER—433a.

4999. Ταβέρναι {1x} **Tabĕrnai**, *tab-er'-nahee* or **Ταβερνῶν Tabĕrnōn**, *tab-er-non';* plur. of Lat. or.; *huts* or *wooden-walled* buildings; *Tabernæ:*—taverns {1x}. See: BAGD—802b; THAYER—613b.

5000. Ταβιθά {2x} **Tabitha**, *tab-ee-thah';* of Chald. or. [comp. 6646]; *the gazelle; Tabitha* (i.e. *Tabjetha*), a Chr. female:—*Tabitha* {2x}. See: BAGD—802b; THAYER—613b.

5001. τάγμα {1x} **tagma**, *tag'-mah;* from *5021; something orderly in arrangement* (a *troop*), i.e. (fig.) a *series* or *succession:*—order {1x}.

Tagma, signifying "that which has been arranged in order," was especially a military term, denoting "a company"; it is used metaphorically in 1 Cor 15:23 of the various classes of those who have part in the first resurrection. See: TDNT—8:31, 1156; BAGD—802d; THAYER—613b.

5002. τακτός {1x} **taktŏs**, *tak-tos';* from *5021; arranged,* i.e. *appointed* or *stated:*—set {1x}.

Taktos, an adjective (from *tasso*), "ordered, fixed, set," is said of an appointed day, in Acts 12:21. See: BAGD—803a; THAYER—613d.

5003. ταλαιπωρέω {1x} **talaipōrĕō**, *tal-ahee-po-reh'-o;* from *5005;* to *be wretched,* i.e. *realize* one's own *misery:*—be afflicted {1x}.

Talaiporeo, "to be afflicted," is used in Jas 4:9, in the middle voice ("afflict yourselves"). It is derived from *tlao,* "to bear, undergo," and *poros,* "a hard substance, a callus," which metaphorically came to signify that which is miserable. See: BAGD—803a; THAYER—613d.

5004. ταλαιπωρία {2x} **talaipōria**, *tal-ahee-po-ree'-ah;* from *5005; wretchedness,* i.e. *calamity:*—misery {2x}.

Talaiporia, "hardship, suffering, distress" (akin to *talaiporos,* "wretched," Rom 7:24; Rev 3:17. See: BAGD—803b; THAYER—613d.

5005. ταλαίπωρος {2x} **talaipōrŏs**, *tal-ah'-ee-po-ros;* from the base of *5007* and a der. of the base of *3984; enduring trial,* i.e. *miserable:*—wretched {2x}.

Talaiporos, "distressed, miserable, wretched," is used in Rom 7:24 and Rev 3:17. See: BAGD—803b; THAYER—614a.

5006. ταλαντιαῖος {1x} **talantiaiŏs**, *tal-an-tee-ah'-yos;* from *5007; talent-like* in weight:—weight of a talent {1x}.

A talent of silver weighed about 100 pounds (45 kg) and a talent of gold, 200 pounds (91 kg). See: BAGD—803b; THAYER—614a.

5007. τάλαντον {15x} **talantŏn**, *tal'-an-ton;* neut. of a presumed der. of the orig. form of τλάω **tlaō** (to *bear;* equiv. to *5342*); a *balance* (as *supporting* weights), i.e. (by impl.) a certain *weight* (and thence a *coin* or rather *sum* of money) or "*talent*":—talent {15x}.

Talanton, originally "a balance," then, "a talent in weight," was hence "a sum of money" in gold or silver equivalent to a "talent." The Jewish "talent" contained 3,000 shekels of the sanctuary, e.g., Ex 30:13 (about 114 lbs.). In NT times the "talent" was not a weight of silver, but the Roman-Attic "talent," comprising 6,000 *denarii* or *drachmas,* and equal to about L/240. It is mentioned in Matthew only, 18:24; 25:15, 16, 20 (four times), 22 (thrice), 24, 25, 28 (twice). In 18:24 the vastness of the sum, 10,000 talents (L/2,400,000), indicates the impossibility of man's clearing himself, by his own efforts, of the guilt which lies upon him before God. See: BAGD—803c; THAYER—614a.

5008. ταλιθά {1x} **talitha**, *tal-ee-thah';* of Chald. or. [comp. 2924]; *the fresh,* i.e. young *girl; talitha* (*O maiden*):—talitha {1x}. See: BAGD—803c; THAYER—614b.

5009. ταμεῖον {4x} **tamĕiŏn**, *tam-i'-on;* neut. contr. of a presumed der. of ταμίας **tamias** (a *dispenser* or *distributor;* akin to τέμνω **tĕmnō**, to *cut*); a *dispensary* or *magazine,* i.e. a chamber on the ground-floor or interior of an Oriental house (gen. used for *storage* or *privacy,* a spot for retirement):—secret chamber {1x}, closet {2x}, storehouse {1x}.

Tameion denotes, firstly, "a store-chamber," then, "any private room, secret chamber," (1) Mt 6:6; Lk 12:3, "closet"; (2) Mt 24:26, "secret chambers"; (3) Lk 12:24, "storehouse" of birds. See: BAGD—803c; THAYER—614b.

τανῦν tanun. See *3568*.

5010. τάξις {10x} **taxis**, *tax'-is;* from *5021;* reg. *arrangement,* i.e. (in time) fixed *succession* (of rank or character), official *dignity:*—order {10x}.

Taxis, "an arranging, arrangement, order" (akin to *tasso,* "to arrange, draw up in order"), is used in (1) Lk 1:8 of the fixed succession of the course of the priests; (2) of due "order," in contrast to confusion, in the gatherings of a local church, 1 Cor 14:40; (3) of the general condition of the local church, Col 2:5 (some give it a military significance here); (4) of the divinely appointed character or nature of a priesthood, of Melchizedek, as foreshadowing that of Christ, Heb 5:6, 10; 6:20; 7:11, where also the character of the Aaronic priesthood is set in contrast also in 7:11, second part; Heb 7:17, 21. See: BAGD—803d; THAYER—614b.

5011. ταπεινός {8x} **tapĕinŏs**, *tap-i-nos';* of uncert. der.; *depressed,* i.e. (fig.) *humiliated* (in circumstances or disposition):—of low degree {2x}, humble {2x}, base {1x}, cast down {1x}, of low estate {1x}, lowly {1x}.

Primarily *tapeinos* means that which is low, and does not rise far from the ground; hence, metaphorically, it signifies lowly, of no degree. It is translated (1) "of low degree" in Lk 1:52; Jas 1:9; (2) "humble" in Jas 4:6; 1 Pet 5:5; (3) "base" in 2 Cor 10:1; (4) "cast down" in 2 Cor 7:6; (5) "of low estate" in Rom 12:16; and (6) "lowly" in Mt 11:29. See: TDNT—8:1, 1152; BAGD—804a; THAYER—614c.

5012. ταπεινοφροσύνη {7x} **tapĕinŏphrŏsunē**, *tap-i-nof-ros-oo'-nay;* from a compound of *5011* and the base of *5424; humiliation of mind,* i.e. *modesty:*—humility {3x}, humbleness of mind {1x}, humility of mind {1x}, lowliness {1x}, lowliness of mind {1x}.

This virtue, a fruit of the gospel, exists when a person through most genuine self-evaluation deems himself worthless. It involves evaluating ourselves as small because we are so. The humble person is not stressing his sinfulness, but his creatureliness, of absolute dependence, of possessing nothing and of receiving all things from God.

Tapeinophrosune, "lowliness of mind", is rendered (1) "humility of mind" in Acts 20:19; (2) in Eph 4:2, "lowliness"; (3) in Phil 2:3, "lowliness of mind"; (4) in Col 2:18, 23, of a false "humility"; (5) in Col 3:12, "humbleness of mind"; (6) 1 Pet 5:5, "humility." Syn.: 4236. See: TDNT—8:1, 1152; BAGD—804c; THAYER—614c.

5013. ταπεινόω {14x} **tapĕinŏō**, *tap-i-nŏ'-o;* from *5011;* to *depress;* fig. to *humiliate* (in condition or heart):—abase {5x}, bring low {1x}, humble {6x}, humble (one's) self {2x}.

Tapeinoo signifies "to make low, bring low," (1) of bringing to the ground, making level, reducing to a plain, as in Lk 3:5; (2) metaphorically (2a) in the active voice, to bring to a humble condition, "to abase," 2 Cor 11:7, and (2b) in the passive, "to be abased," Phil 4:12; in Mt 23:12; Lk 14:11; 18:14. (3) It is translated "humble yourselves" (3a) in the middle voice sense in Jas 4:10; 1 Pet 5:6; (3b) "humble," in Mt 18:4; 2 Cor 12:21 and Phil 2:8. See: TDNT—8:1, 1152; BAGD—804c; THAYER—614d.

5014. ταπείνωσις {4x} **tapĕinōsis**, *tap-i'-no-sis;* from *5013; depression* (in rank or feeling):—humiliation {1x}, be made low {1x}, low estate {1x}, vile {1x}.

Tepeinosis denotes "abasement, humiliation, low estate" (from *tapeinos*, "lowly"), **(1)** Lk 1:48, "low estate"; **(2)** Acts 8:33, "humiliation"; **(3)** Phil 3:21, "vile"; **(4)** Jas 1:10, "is made low," lit., "in his low estate. See: TDNT—8:1, 1152; BAGD—805a; THAYER—615a.

5015. ταράσσω {17x} **tarassō,** *tar-as'-so;* of uncert. aff.; to *stir* or *agitate* (*roil* water):—trouble {17x}.

Tarasso, akin to *tarache* (*5016*), is used **(1)** in a physical sense, Jn 5:4, 7; **(2)** metaphorically, **(2a)** of the soul and spirit of the Lord, Jn 11:33; **(2b)** of the hearts of disciples, Jn 14:1, 27; **(2c)** of the minds of those in fear or perplexity, Mt 2:3; 14:26; Mk 6:50; Lk 1:12; 24:38; 1 Pet 3:14; **(2d)** of subverting the souls of believers, by evil doctrine, Acts 15:24; Gal 1:7; 5:10; **(2e)** of stirring up a crowd, Acts 17:8. See: BAGD—805b; THAYER—615a.

5016. ταραχή {2x} **tarachē,** *tar-akh-ay';* fem. from *5015; disturbance,* i.e. (of water) *roiling,* or (of a mob) *sedition:*—troubles {1x}, troubling {1x}.

Tarache, "an agitation, disturbance, trouble," is found in Mk 13:8 (plur.) and Jn 5:4. See: BAGD—805c; THAYER—615b.

5017. τάραχος {2x} **tarachŏs,** *tar'-akh-os;* masc. from *5015;* a *disturbance,* i.e. (popular) *tumult:*—stir {2x}.

Tarachos, as a noun, is rendered "stir": "Now as soon as it was day, there was no small stir among the soldiers, what was become of Peter" (Acts 12:18; cf. 19:23). Syn.: 329, 383, 387, 1326, 1892, 2042, 3947, 3951, 4531, 4579, 4787, 4797. See: BAGD—805c; THAYER—615b.

5018. Ταρσεύς {2x} **Tarsĕus,** *tar-syoos';* from *5019;* a *Tarsean,* i.e. native of Tarsus:—of Tarsus {2x}. See: BAGD—805c; THAYER—615b.

5019. Ταρσός {3x} **Tarsŏs,** *tar-sos';* perh. the same as ταρσός **tarsŏs** (a *flat* basket); *Tarsus,* a place in Asia Minor:—Tarsus {3x}. See: BAGD—805d; THAYER—615b.

5020. ταρταρόω {1x} **tartarŏō,** *tar-tar-ŏ'-o;* from Τάρταρος **Tartarŏs,** (the deepest *abyss* of Hades); to *incarcerate* in eternal torment:—cast down to hell {1x}. See: BAGD—805d; THAYER—615c.

5021. τάσσω {8x} **tassō,** *tas'-so;* a prol. form of a primary verb (which latter appears only in certain tenses); to *arrange* in an orderly manner, i.e. *assign* or *dispose* (to a certain position or lot):—addict {1x}, appoint {3x}, determine {1x}, ordain {2x}, set {1x}.

Tasso, as a verb, means "to place in order, arrange," and signifies **(1)** "to appoint" of the place where Christ had "appointed" a meeting with His disciples after His resurrection: "Then the eleven disciples went away into Galilee, into a mountain where Jesus had appointed them" (Mt 28:16); **(2)** of positions of military and civil authority over others, whether **(2a)** "appointed" by men: "For I also am a man set (*tasso*) under authority, having under me soldiers, and I say unto one, Go, and he goeth; and to another, Come, and he cometh; and to my servant, Do this, and he doeth it" (Lk 7:8), or **(2b)** by God: "Let every soul be subject unto the higher powers. For there is no power but of God: the powers that be are ordained of God" (Rom 13:1).

It signifies **(3)** to be "ordained." **(3a)** It is said of those who, having believed the gospel, "were ordained to eternal life": "And when the Gentiles heard this, they were glad, and glorified the word of the Lord: and as many as were ordained to eternal life believed" (Acts 13:48). **(3b)** The house of Stephanas at Corinth had "addicted" themselves to the ministry of the saints: "I beseech you, brethren, ye know the house of Stephanas, that it is the firstfruits of Achaia, and that they have addicted (*tasso*) themselves to the ministry of the saints" (1 Cor 16:15). Syn.: **(A)** *Entellomai* (*1781*) means to enjoin, is used esp. of those whose office or position invests them with claims, and points rather to the contents of the command, cf "our instruction." **(B)** *Keleuo* (*2753*) means to command, designates verbal orders, coming usually from a superior. **(C)** *Paraggello* (*3853*) means to charge, and is used esp. of the order of a military commander to his troops. *Tasso* means to assign a post to, with a suggestion of duties connected with it, often used of military appointments. **(D)** *Paraggello* (*3853*) differs from *entellomai* (*1781*) in denoting fixed and abiding obligations rather than specific or occasional instructions, duties arising from the office rather than coming from the personal will of a superior. See: TDNT—8:27, 1156; BAGD—805d; THAYER—615c.

5022. ταῦρος {4x} **taurŏs,** *tow'-ros;* appar. a primary word [comp. 8450, "*steer*"]; a *bullock:*—bull {2x}, ox {2x}.

Tauros is translated **(1)** "oxen" in Mt 22:4 and Acts 14:13; **(2)** "bulls" in Heb 9:13 and 10:4. See: BAGD—806b; THAYER—615d.

5023. ταῦτα {247x} **tauta,** *tŏw'-tah;* nominative or acc. neut. plur. of *3778; these* things:—these things {158x}, these {26x}, thus {17x}, that {7x}, these words {7x}, this {6x}, afterwards + 3326 {4x}, misc. {22x} = follow, + hereafter, ✗ him, the same, so, such, then, they,

those. See: BAGD—549b [3778]; THAYER—466c [3778].

5024. **ταὐτά** {4x} **tauta**, *tŏw-tah';* neut. plur. of *3588* and *846* as adv.; in *the same* way:—even thus {1x}, like {1x}, like manner {1x}, so {1x}. See: BAGD—806b; THAYER—615d.

5025. **ταὐταις** {21x} **tautais**, *tŏw'-taheece;* and

ταὐτας **tautas**, *tŏw'-tas;* dat. and acc. fem. plur. respectively of *3778; (to* or *with* or *by,* etc.) *these:*—hence {1x}, that {1x}, then {1x}, these {12x}, those {6x}. See: BAGD—596b [3778]; THAYER—466c [3778].

5026. **ταὐτῃ** {122x} tautȩ̄, *tŏw'-tay;* and

ταὐτην **tautēn**, *tŏw'-tane;* and

ταὐτης **tautēs**, *tŏw'-tace;* dat., acc., and gen. respectively of the fem. sing. of *3778; (toward* or *of) this:*—this {105x}, that {4x}, the same {4x}, misc. {9x} = her, + hereof, it, + thereby. See: BAGD—596b [3778]; THAYER—466c [3778].

5027. **ταφή** {1x} **taphē**, *taf-ay';* fem. from *2290; burial* (the act):—bury + 1519 {1x}. See: BAGD—806b; THAYER—616a.

5028. **τάφος** {7x} **taphŏs**, *taf'-os;* masc. from *2290; a grave* (the place of interment):—sepulchre {6x}, tomb {1x}.

Taphos, akin to *thapto,* "to bury," originally "a burial," then, "a place for burial", **(1)** "a *sepulchre"* in Mt 23:27; 27:61, 64, 66; 28:1; **(2)** "tomb" in Mt 23:29; and **(3)** metaphorically, Rom 3:13, *"sepulchre."* See: BAGD—806b; THAYER—616a.

5029. **τάχα** {2x} **tacha**, *takh'-ah;* as if neut. plur. of *5036* (adv.); *shortly,* i.e. (fig.) *possibly:*—peradventure {1x}, perhaps {1x}.

Tacha, primarily "quickly" (from *tachus,* "quick"), signifies **(1)** "peradventure" in Rom 5:7; and **(2)** in Philem 15, "perhaps." See: BAGD—806c; THAYER—616a.

5030. **ταχέως** {10x} **tachĕōs**, *takh-eh'-oce;* adv. from *5036; briefly,* i.e. (in time) *speedily,* or (in manner) *rapidly:*—hastily {1x}, quickly {2x}, shortly {4x}, soon {2x}, suddenly {1x}.

Tacheos in 1 Ti 5:22 carries the idea of quickly/hastily: "Lay hands suddenly (*tacheos*) on no man, neither be partaker of other men's sins: keep thyself pure." Syn.: 160, 869, 1810, 1819. See: BAGD—806d; THAYER—616a.

5031. **ταχινός** {2x} **tachinŏs**, *takh-ee-nos';* from *5034; curt,* i.e. *impending:*—shortly {1x}, swift {1x}.

Tachinos, "of swift approach," is used **(1)** in

2 Pet 1:14, "shortly", lit., "(the putting off of my tabernacle is) swift," i.e., "imminent"; **(2)** in 2 Pet 2:1, "swift (destruction)." See: BAGD—807a; THAYER—616a.

5032. **τάχιον** {5x} **tachiŏn**, *takh'-ee-on;* neut. sing. of the comp. of *5036* (as adv.); *more swiftly,* i.e. (in manner) *more rapidly,* or (in time) *more speedily:*—shortly {2x}, quickly {1x}, outrun + 4390 {1x}, the sooner {1x}.

Tachion, the comparative degree of *tachus* is translated **(1)** "quickly" in Jn 13:27; **(2)** "out(-ran)" in Jn 20:4; **(3)** "shortly" in 1 Ti 3:14 and Heb 13:23; **(4)** in Heb 13:19, "(the) sooner." See: BAGD—807a; THAYER—616a.

5033. **τάχιστα** {1x} **tachista**, *takh'-is-tah;* neut. plur. of the superl. of *5036* (as adv.); *most quickly,* i.e. (with *5613* pref.) *as soon* as possible:—with all speed + 5613 {1x}. See: BAGD—807a; THAYER—616b.

5034. **τάχος** {7x} **tachŏs**, *takh'-os;* from the same as *5036; a brief* space (of time), i.e. (with *1722* pref.) in *haste:*—shortly + 1722 {4x}, quickly + 1722 {2x}, speedily + 1722 {1x}. Cf. Lk 18:8; Acts 12:7; 22:18; 25:4; Rom 16:20; Rev 1:1; 22:6. See: BAGD—807a; THAYER—616b.

5035. **ταχύ** {13x} **tachu**, *takh-oo';* neut. sing. of *5036* (as adv.); *shortly,* i.e. *without delay, soon,* or (by surprise) *suddenly,* or (by impl. of ease) *readily:*—lightly {1x}, quickly {12x}.

Tachu, the neuter of *tachus,* "swift, quick," signifies **(1)** "quickly," Mt 5:25; 28:7, 8; Lk 15:22; Jn 11:29; Rev 2:5, 16; 3:11; 11:14; 22:7, 12, 20; and **(2)** in Mk 9:39, "lightly". See: BAGD—807b; THAYER—616b.

5036. **ταχύς** {1x} **tachus**, *takh-oos';* of uncert. aff.; *fleet,* i.e. (fig.) *prompt* or *ready:*—swift {1x}. See: BAGD—807b; THAYER—616b.

5037. **τὲ** {209x} **tĕ**, *teh;* a primary particle (enclitic) of connection or addition; *both* or *also* (prop. as correl. of *2532*):—and {130x}, both {36x}, then {2x}, whether {1x}, even {1x}, also {1x}, not tr {38x}. Often used in composition, usually as the latter part. See: BAGD—807b; THAYER—616b.

5038. **τεῖχος** {9x} **tĕichŏs**, *ti'-khos;* akin to the base of *5088; a wall* (as *formative* of a house):—wall {9x}.

Teichos, "a wall," especially one around a town, is used **(1)** literally, Acts 9:25; 2 Cor 11:33; Heb 11:30; **(2)** figuratively, of the "wall" of the heavenly city, Rev 21:12, 14, 15, 17, 18, 19. Syn.: A *teichos* is a wall around a city and

may also double as the outer wall of a house. A *toichos* (5109) is specifically a wall around a city. See: BAGD—808a; THAYER—617b.

5039. **τεκμήριον** {1x} **tĕkmēriŏn,** *tek-may'-ree-on;* neut. of a presumed der. of τεκμάρ **tĕkmar** (a *goal* or fixed *limit*); a *token* (as *defining* a fact), i.e. *criterion* of certainty:—infallible proof {1x}.

Tekmerion denotes that from which something is surely and plainly known; indubitable evidence, a proof, Acts 1:3. See: BAGD—808a; THAYER—617b.

5040. **τεκνίον** {9x} **tĕkniŏn,** *tek-nee'-on;* dimin. of 5043; an *infant,* i.e. (plur. fig.) *darlings* (Chr. *converts*):—little children {9x}.

(1) *Teknion,* only figuratively and always in the plural, is a term of kindly address by teachers to their disciples under circumstances requiring a tender appeal, e.g., **(1a)** of Christ to the Twelve just before His death, Jn 13:33; **(1b)** the apostle John used it in warning believers against spiritual dangers, 1 Jn 2:1, 12, 28; 3:7, 18; 4:4; 5:21; **(1c)** Paul, because of the deadly errors of Judaism assailing the Galatian churches, Gal 4:19. See: TDNT—5:636, 759; BAGD—808a; THAYER—617b.

5041. **τεκνογονέω** {1x} **tĕknŏgŏnĕō,** *tek-nog-on-eh'-o;* from a compound of 5043 and the base of 1096; to *be a child-bearer,* i.e. *parent* (*mother*):—bear children {1x}. See: BAGD—808a; THAYER—617c.

5042. **τεκνογονία** {1x} **tĕknŏgŏnia,** *tek-nog-on-ee'-ah;* from the same as 5041; *childbirth* (*parentage*), i.e. (by impl.) *maternity* (the performance of *maternal duties*):—childbearing {1x}. See: BAGD—808b; THAYER—617c.

5043. **τέκνον** {99x} **tĕknŏn,** *tek'-non;* from the base of 5098; a *child* (as *produced*):—child {77x}, daughter {1x}, son {21x}.

Teknon, "a child" (akin to *tikto,* "to beget, bear"), is used in both the natural and the figurative senses. Figuratively, *teknon* is used of "children" of **(1)** God, Jn 1:12; **(2)** light, Eph 5:8; **(3)** obedience, 1 Pet 1:14; **(4)** a promise, Rom 9:8; Gal 4:28; **(5)** the devil, 1 Jn 3:10; **(6)** wrath, Eph 2:3; **(7)** cursing, 2 Pet 2:14; **(8)** spiritual relationship, 2 Ti 2:1; Philem 10. Syn.: **(A)** *Paidarion* (3808) refers to a child up to his first school years. **(B)** *Paidion* (3813) refers exclusively to little children. **(C)** *Paidiske* (3814) refers to a female in late childhood and early youth. **(D)** *Pais* (3816) refers to a child of any age. **(E)** *Teknon* (5043) gives prominence to physical and outward aspects of parentage. **(F)**

Huios (5207) gives prominence to the inward, ethical, legal aspects of parentage, the dignity and character of the relationship. *Pais* (3816) and *teknon* (5043) denote a child as respects to descent and age, reference to the later being more prominent in the former word, to descent in *paidion* (3813); but the period *pais* (3816) covers is not sharply defined. See: TDNT—5:636, 759; BAGD—808b; THAYER—617c.

5044. **τεκνοτροφέω** {1x} **tĕknŏtrŏphĕō,** *tek-not-rof-eh'-o;* from a compound of 5043 and 5142; to *be a child-rearer,* i.e. *fulfil* the duties of a *female parent:*—bring up children {1x}. See: BAGD—808d; THAYER—618b.

5045. **τέκτων** {2x} **tĕktōn,** *tek'-tone;* from the base of 5098; an *artificer* (as *producer* of fabrics), i.e. (spec.) a *craftsman* in wood:—carpenter {2x}. Cf. Mt 13:55; Mk 6:3. See: BAGD—809a; THAYER—618b.

5046. **τέλειος** {19x} **tĕlĕiŏs,** *tel'-i-os;* from 5056; *complete* (in various applications of labor, growth, ment. and mor. character, etc.); neut. (as noun, with 3588) *completeness:*—of full age {1x}, man {1x}, perfect {17x}.

Teleios means **(1)** brought to its end, finished; wanting nothing necessary to completeness, perfect (Jas 1:4); **(2)** consummate human integrity and virtue (Rom 12:2); **(3)** *Teleios,* as an adjective means "complete, perfect," men full grown, adult, of full age, mature [from *telos,* "an end,"] and is translated "of full age": "But strong meat belongeth to them that are of full age, even those who by reason of use have their senses exercised to discern both good and evil" (Heb 5:14). **(4)** It also means "perfect": signifies "having reached its end" (*telos*), "finished, complete perfect." It is used **(4a)** of persons, **(4a1)** primarily of physical development, then, with ethical import, "fully grown, mature," 1 Cor 2:6; 14:20; Eph 4:13; Phil 3:15; Col 1:28; 4:12; in Heb 5:14, "of full age"; **(4a2)** "complete," conveying the idea of goodness without necessary reference to maturity or what is expressed under **(4a1)** Mt 5:48; 19:21; Jas 1:4 (2nd part); 3:2. **(4a3)** It is used thus of God in Mt 5:48; **(4b)** of "things, complete, perfect," Rom 12:2; **(4b1)** 1 Cor 13:10 (referring to the complete revelation of God's will and ways, whether in the completed Scriptures or in the hereafter); **(4b2)** Jas 1:4 (of the work of patience); v. 25; 1 Jn 4:18. Syn.: **(A)** One who is *holokleros* (3648) has preserved, or regained, his completeness. **(B)** One who is *teleios* has attained the moral end for which he was intended, namely to be a man in Christ. **(C)** *Arios*

(739) refers not only to the presence of all the parts that are necessary for completeness but also to the further adaptation and aptitude of these parts for their assigned purpose (2 Ti 34:17). See also: 165, 166, 739, 1074, 2244, 2250, 3648, 5230. See: TDNT−8:67, 1161; BAGD−809a; THAYER−618b.

5047. **τελειότης** {2x} **tĕlĕiŏtēs**, *tel-i-ot'-ace;* from *5046;* (the state) *completeness* (ment. or mor.):—perfection {1x}, perfectness {1x}.

Teleiotes denotes much the same as *teleiosis* (5050), but stressing perhaps the actual accomplishment of the end in view (Col 3:14, perfectness; Heb 6:1 perfection). See: TDNT−8:78, 1161; BAGD−809c; THAYER−618c.

5048. **τελειόω** {24x} **tĕlĕiŏō**, *tel-i-ŏ'-o;* from *5046;* to *complete,* i.e. (lit.) *accomplish,* or (fig.) *consummate* (in character):—make perfect {12x}, perfect {4x}, finish {4x}, fulfil {2x}, be perfect {1x}, consecrate {1x}.

The main distinction between *teleo* (5055) and *teleioo* is that *teleo* more frequently signifies to fulfill, *teleioo,* more frequently, to make perfect. See: TDNT−8:79, 1161; BAGD−809d; THAYER−618d.

5049. **τελείως** {1x} **tĕlĕiōs**, *tel-i'-oce;* adv. from *5046; completely,* i.e. (of hope) *without wavering*:—to the end {1x}.

Teleios signifies having reached its end, finished, complete perfect." See: BAGD−810b; THAYER−619a.

5050. **τελείωσις** {2x} **tĕlĕiōsis**, *tel-i'-o-sis;* from *5448;* (the act) *completion,* i.e. (of prophecy) *verification,* or (of expiation) *absolution:*—perfection {1x}, performance {1x}.

Teleiosis denotes "a fulfillment, completion, perfection, an end accomplished as the effect of a process," **(1)** Heb 7:11, "perfection"; **(2)** in Lk 1:45, "performance." See: TDNT−8:84, 1161; BAGD−810a; THAYER−619a.

5051. **τελειωτής** {1x} **tĕlĕiōtēs**, *tel-i-o-tace';* from *5048;* a *completer,* i.e. *consummater:* —finisher {1x}.

Jesus, the one who has in His own person raised faith to its perfection and so set before us the highest example of faith, Heb 12:2. See: TDNT−8:86, 1161; BAGD−810c; THAYER−619b.

5052. **τελεσφορέω** {1x} **tĕlĕsphŏrĕō**, *tel-es-for-eh'-o;* from a compound of *5056* and *5342;* to *be a bearer to completion* (maturity), i.e. to *ripen* fruit (fig.):—bring fruit to perfection {1x}. See: BAGD−810c; THAYER−619b.

5053. **τελευτάω** {12x} **tĕlĕutaō**, *tel-yoo-tah'-o;* from a presumed der. of *5055;* to *finish* life (by impl. of *979*), i.e. *expire* (*demise*):—be dead {3x}, decease {1x}, die {8x}.

Teleutao, "to end" (from *telos,* "an end"), hence, "to end one's life," is used **(1)** of the "death" of the body, Mt 2:19; 9:18; 15:4, where "die the death" means "surely die"; Mk 7:10; Mt 22:25, "deceased"; Lk 7:2; Acts 2:29; 7:15; Heb 11:22; **(2)** of the gnawings of conscience in self reproach, under the symbol of a worm, Mk 9:44, 46, 48. See: BAGD−810c; THAYER−619b.

5054. **τελευτή** {1x} **tĕlĕutē**, *tel-yoo-tay';* from *5053; decease:*—death {1x}.

Teleute, as a noun, means "an end, limit"; hence, "the end of life, death," is used of the "death" of Herod (Mt 2:15). Syn.: 336, 337, 520, 1935, 2288, 2289. See: BAGD−810c; THAYER−619b.

5055. **τελέω** {26x} **tĕlĕō**, *tel-eh'-o;* from *5056;* to *end,* i.e. *complete, execute, conclude, discharge* (a debt):—finish {8x}, fulfil {7x}, accomplish {4x}, pay {2x}, perform {1x}, expire {1x}, make an end {1x}, fill up {1x}, go over {1x}.

Frequently this word signifies, not merely to terminate a thing, but to carry out a thing to the full. See: TDNT−8:57, 1161; BAGD−810d; THAYER−619c.

5056. **τέλος** {42x} **tĕlŏs**, *tel'-os;* from a primary τέλλω **tĕllō**, (to *set out* for a def. point or *goal*); prop. the point aimed at as a *limit,* i.e. (by impl.) the *conclusion* of an act or state (*termination* [lit., fig. or indef.], *result* [immed., ultimate or prophetic], *purpose*; spec. an *impost* or *levy* (as *paid*):—end {35x}, custom {3x}, uttermost {1x}, finally {1x}, ending {1x}, by (one's) continual + 1519 {1x}.

Telos means an end, a termination, whether of time or purpose, denotes, in its secondary significance, what is paid for public ends, a toll, tax, custom (Mt 17:25). See: TDNT−8:49, 1161; BAGD−811b; THAYER−619d. comp. *5411.*

5057. **τελώνης** {22x} **tĕlōnēs**, *tel-o'-nace;* from *5056* and *5608;* a *tax-farmer,* i.e. *collector* of public *revenue:*—publican {22x}.

(1) *Telones* primarily denoted "a farmer of the tax" (from *telos,* "toll, custom, tax"), then, as in the NT, a subsequent subordinate of such, who collected taxes in some district, "a tax gatherer"; such were naturally hated intensely by the people; **(2)** they are classed **(2a)** with "sinners," Mt 9:10, 11; 11:9; Mk 2:15, 16; Lk 5:30; 7:34; 15:1; **(2b)** with harlots, Mt 21:31, 32; **(2c)** with "the Gentile," Mt 5:47; 18:17. See also

Mt 5:46; 10:3; Lk 3:12; 5:27, 29; 7:29; 18:10, 11, 13. See: TDNT—8:88, 1166; BAGD—812b; THAYER—620c.

5058. τελώνιον {3x} **tĕlōniŏn,** *tel-o'-nee-on;* neut. of a presumed der. of 5057; a *tax-gatherer's* place of business:—receipt of custom {3x}.

Telonion denotes "a custom-house," for the collection of the taxes, Mt 9:9; Mk 2:14; Lk 5:27. See: BAGD—812c; THAYER—620c.

5059. τέρας {16x} **tĕras,** *ter'-as;* of uncert. aff.; a *prodigy* or *omen:*—wonder {16x}.

Wonders are manifested as **(1)** divine operations in thirteen occurrences (9 times in Acts); **(2)** three times they are ascribed to the work of Satan through human agents, Mt 24:24; Mk 13:22 and 2 Th 2:9. Syn.: **(A)** *Teras* denotes something strange causing the beholder to marvel and is always used in the plural, always rendered "wonders," and generally follows **(B)** *semeia* (4592, signs). A sign is intended to appeal to the understanding, a wonder appeals to the imagination, **(C)** *dunamis* (1411, a power) indicates its source as supernatural. See also: 1411, 1741, 2297, 3167, 3861, 4592. See: TDNT—8:113, 1170; BAGD—812c; THAYER—620d.

5060. Τέρτιος {1x} **Tĕrtiŏs,** *ter'-tee-os;* of Lat. or.; *third; Tertius,* a Chr.:—Tertius {1x}. See: BAGD—813a; THAYER—620d.

5061. Τέρτυλλος {2x} **Tĕrtullŏs,** *ter'-tool-los;* of uncert. der.; *Tertullus,* a Rom.:—Tertullus {2x}. See: BAGD—813a; THAYER—620d.

τέσσαρα tĕssara. See *5064.*

5062. τεσσαράκοντα {22x} **tĕssarakŏnta,** *tes-sar-ak'-on-tah;* the decade of *5064; forty:*—forty {22x}. See: TDNT—8:135, 1172; BAGD—813a; THAYER—620d.

5063. τεσσαρακονταετής {2x} **tĕssarakŏntaĕtēs,** *tes-sar-ak-on-tah-et-ace';* from 5062 and 2094; *of forty years* of age:—of forty years {1x}, forty years old {1x}. See: TDNT—8:135, 1172; BAGD—813b; THAYER—620d.

5064. τέσσαρες {42x} **tĕssarĕs,** *tes'-sar-es;* neut.

τέσσαρα tĕssara, *tes'-sar-ah;* a plur. number; *four:*—four {42x}. See: TDNT—8:127, 1172; BAGD—813b; THAYER—612a.

5065. τεσσαρεσκαιδέκατος {2x} **tĕssarĕskaidĕkatŏs,** *tes-sar-es-kahee-dek'-at-os;* from *5064* and *2532* and *1182; fourteenth:*—fourteenth {2x}. See: BAGD—813b; THAYER—621a.

5066. τεταρταῖος {1x} **tĕtartaiŏs,** *tet-ar-tah'-yos;* from *5064;* pertaining to the *fourth* day:—four days {1x}. See: TDNT—8:127, 1172; BAGD—813c; THAYER—621a.

5067. τέταρτος {10x} **tĕtartŏs,** *tet'-ar-tos;* ord. from *5064; fourth:*—four {1x}, fourth {9x}. See: TDNT—8:127, 1172; BAGD—813a; THAYER—621a.

5068. τετράγωνος {1x} **tĕtragōnŏs,** *tet-rag'-o-nos;* from *5064* and *1137; four-cornered,* i.e. *square:*—foursquare {1x}. See: BAGD—813c; THAYER—621a.

5069. τετράδιον {1x} **tĕtradiŏn,** *tet-rad'-ee-on;* neut. of a presumed der. of τέτρας **tĕtras** (a *tetrad;* from *5064*); a *quaternion,* or squad (picket) of four Rom. soldiers:—quaternion {1x}.

A *tetradion* is a group of four and occurs in Acts 12:4. A quaternion was a set of four men occupied in the work of a guard, two soldiers being chained to the prisoner and two keeping watch; alternatively one of the four watched while the other three slept. The night was divided into four watches of three hours each; there would be one quaternion for each watch by day and by night. See: BAGD—813d; THAYER—621b.

5070. τετρακισχίλιοι {5x} **tĕtrakischiliŏi,** *tet-rak-is-khil'-ee-oy;* from the mult. adv. of *5064* and *5507; four times a thousand:*—four thousand {5x}. See: BAGD—813d; THAYER—621b.

5071. τετρακόσιοι {4x} **tĕtrakŏsiŏi,** *tet-rak-os'-ee-oy;* neut. τετρακόσια **tĕtrakŏsia,** *tet-rak-os'-ee-ah;* plur. from *5064* and *1540; four hundred:*—four hundred {4x}. See: BAGD—813d; THAYER—621b.

5072. τετράμηνον {1x} **tĕtramēnŏn,** *tet-ram'-ay-non;* neut. of a compound of *5064* and *3376;* a *four months'* space:—four months {1x}. See: BAGD—813d; THAYER—621b.

5073. τετραπλόος {1x} **tĕtraplŏŏs,** *tet-rap-lŏ'-os;* from *5064* and a der. of the base of *4118; quadruple:*—fourfold {1x}. See: BAGD—813d; THAYER—621b.

5074. τετράπους {3x} **tĕtrapŏus,** *tet-rap'-ooce;* from *5064* and *4228;* a *quadruped:*—fourfooted beast {3x}. Cf. Acts 10:12; 11:6; Rom 1:23. See: BAGD—814a; THAYER—621b.

5075. τετραρχέω {3x} **tĕtrarchĕō,** *tet-rar-kheh'-o;* from *5076;* to be a *tetrarch:*—be tetrarch {1x}, tetrarch {2x}.

This word means to be a *tetrarch* and occurs in Lk 3:1 (thrice), of Herod Antipas, his brother Philip and Lysanias. Antipas and Philip each inherited a fourth part of his father's [Herod the Great] dominions. See: BAGD—814a; THAYER—621c.

5076. τετράρχης {4x} **tĕtrarchēs,** *tet-rar'-khace;* from *5064* and *757;* the *ruler of a fourth* part of a country ("*tetrarch*"):—tetrarch {4x}.

Tetarches denotes "one of four rulers" (*tetra,* "four," *arche,* "rule"), properly, "the governor of the fourth part of a region"; hence, "a dependent princeling," or "any petty ruler" subordinate to kings or ethnarchs; in the NT, Herod Antipas, Mt 14:1; Lk 3:19; 9:7; Acts 13:1. See: BAGD—814a; THAYER—621c.

τεύχω tĕuchō. See *5177.*

5077. τεφρόω {1x} **tĕphrŏō,** *tef-rŏ'-o;* from τέφρα **tephra,** (*ashes*); to *incinerate,* i.e. *consume:*—turn to ashes {1x}. See: BAGD—814b; THAYER—621c.

5078. τέχνη {3x} **tĕchnē,** *tekh'-nay;* from the base of *5088;* art (as *productive*), i.e. (spec.) a *trade,* or (gen.) *skill:*—art {1x}, craft {1x}, occupation {1x}.

Techne, "an art, handicraft, trade," is used (1) in Acts 17:29, of the art; (2) in Acts 18:3, of a trade or craft, "occupation"; and (3) in Rev 18:22, "craft" (cf. *technites,* "a craftsman," Eng., "technical"). See: BAGD—814b; THAYER—621d.

5079. τεχνίτης {4x} **tĕchnitēs,** *tekh-nee'-tace;* from *5078;* an *artisan;* fig. a *founder (Creator):*—builder {1x}, craftsman {3x}.

Technites, "an artificer, artisan, one who does a thing by rules of art", "a craftsman," is translated (1) "craftsman" in Acts 19:24, 38 and Rev 18:22. (2) It is found elsewhere in Heb. 11:10, "builder", viewing God as "moulding and fashioning . . . the materials which He called into existence." Syn.: *Demiourgos* (*1217*) recognizes God as the Maker of all things and emphasizes the power of the divine creator. *Technites* stresses the artistic side of creation, His manifold wisdom, the infinite variety and beauty of His handiwork. See: BAGD—814b; THAYER—621d.

5080. τήκω {1x} **tēkō,** *tay'-ko;* appar. a primary verb; to *liquefy:*—melt {1x}. See: BAGD—814b; THAYER—621d.

5081. τηλαυγῶς {1x} **tēlaugōs,** *tay-lŏw-goce';* adv. from a compound of a der. of *5056* and *827;* in a *far-shining* manner, i.e. *plainly:*—clearly {1x}.

Telaugos (from *tele,* "afar," and *auge,* "radiance") signifies "conspicuously, or clearly," Mk 8:25, of the sight imparted by Christ to one who had been blind. See: BAGD—814c; THAYER—621d.

5082. τηλικοῦτος {4x} **tēlikŏutŏs,** *tay-lik-oo'-tos;* fem.

τηλικαύτη tēlikautē, *tay-lik-ŏw'-tay;* from a compound of *3588* with *2245* and *3778;* such as this, i.e. (in [fig.] magnitude) so *vast:*—so great {3x}, so mighty {1x}.

This word means so great and is used of things only: (1) "so great" (1a) a death (2 Cor 1:10); (1b) salvation (Heb 2:3); (1c) ships (Jas 3:4); and (2) "so mighty" an earthquake (Rev 16:18). See: BAGD—814c; THAYER—621d.

5083. τηρέω {75x} **tērĕō,** *tay-reh'-o;* from τερός **tĕrŏs,** (a *watch;* perh. akin to *2334*); to *guard* (from *loss* or *injury,* prop. by keeping *the eye* upon; and thus differing from *5442,* which is prop. to *prevent* escaping; and from *2892,* which implies a *fortress* or full military lines of apparatus), i.e. to *note* (a prophecy; fig. to *fulfil* a command); by impl. to *detain* (in custody; fig. to *maintain*); by extens. to *withhold* (for personal ends; fig. to *keep unmarried*):—keep {57x}, reserve {8x}, observe {4x}, watch {2x}, preserve {2x}, keeper {1x}, hold fast {1x}.

Tereo denotes (1) "to watch over, preserve, keep, watch," e.g., Acts 12:5, 6; 16:23; in (1a) in Acts 25:21, "reserved"; (1b) the present participle is translated "keepers" in Mt 28:4, lit. "the keeping (ones)"; (2) it is used of the "keeping" power of God the Father and Christ, exercised (2a) over His people, Jn 17:11, 12, 15; 1 Th 5:23, "preserved"; 1 Jn 5:18, where "he that is begotten of God," "keepeth himself"; Jude 1, "preserved in Jesus Christ", Rev 3:10; (2b) of their inheritance, 1 Pet 1:4 "reserved"; (2c) of judicial reservation by God in view of future doom, 2 Pet 2:4, 9, 17; 3:7; Jude 6, 13; (3) of "keeping" (3a) the faith, 2 Ti 4:7; (3b) the unity of the Spirit, Eph 4:3; (3c) oneself, 2 Cor 11:9; 1 Ti 5:22; (3d) Jas 1:27; figuratively, one's garments, Rev 16:15; (4) "to observe, to give heed to," (4a) as of keeping commandments, etc., e.g., Mt 19:17; Jn 14:15; 15:10; 17:6; Jas 2:10; 1 Jn 2:3, 4, 5; 3:22, 24; 5:2, 3; Rev 1:3; 2:26; 3:8, 10; 12:17; 14:12; 22:7, 9. Syn.: (A) *Tereo* (*5083*) means to watch or keep and expresses watchful care and is suggestive of present possession. (B) *Phulasso* (*5442*) means to guard and indicates safe custody and often implies assault from without; 5083 may mark the result of which 5442 is

the means. See: TDNT—8:140, 1174; BAGD—814c; THAYER—622a.

5084. τήρησις {3x} **tērēsis**, *tay'-ray-sis;* from *5083;* a *watching,* i.e. (fig.) *observance,* or (concr.) a *prison:*—a hold {1x}, prison {1x}, keeping {1x}.

Teresis translated **(1)** "hold" in Acts 4:3, **(2)** "prison" in Acts 5:18 signifies "a watching, guarding"; hence, "imprisonment, ward" (from *tereo,* "to watch, keep"); and **(3)** "a keeping," as of commandments, 1 Cor 7:19. See: TDNT—8:146, 1174; BAGD—815c; THAYER—622c.

Τῇ te, **τήν** tēn, **τῆς** tēs. See *3588.*

5085. Τιβεριάς {3x} **Tibĕrias**, *tib-er-ee-as';* from *5086; Tiberias,* the name of a town and a lake in Pal.:—*Tiberias* {3x}. See: BAGD—815c; THAYER—622c.

5086. Τιβέριος {1x} **Tibĕriŏs**, *tib-er'-ee-os;* of Lat. or.; prob. *pertaining to the* river *Tiberis* or *Tiber; Tiberius,* a Rom. emperor:—Tiberius {1x}. See: BAGD—815c; THAYER—622d.

5087. τίθημι {96x} **tithēmi**, *tith'-ay-mee;* a prol. form of a primary

θέω thĕo, *theh'-o* (which is used only as alt. in certain tenses); to *place* (in the widest application, lit. and fig.; prop. in a pass. or horizontal posture, and thus different from *2476,* which prop. denotes an upright and active position, while *2749* is prop. refl. and utterly prostrate):—lay {28x}, put {18x}, lay down {12x}, make {10x}, appoint {6x}, kneel down + 1119 + 3588 {5x}, misc. {17x} = + advise, bow, commit, conceive, give, ordain, purpose, set (forth), settle, sink down.

Tithemi, as a verb, means "to put" is used of "appointment" to any form of service. **(1)** Christ used it of His followers: "Ye have not chosen me, but I have chosen you, and ordained *(tithemi)* you, that ye should go and bring forth fruit, and that your fruit should remain: that whatsoever ye shall ask of the Father in my name, he may give it you" (Jn 15:16). **(2)** The verb is used by Paul of his service in the ministry of the gospel: "And I thank Christ Jesus our Lord, who hath enabled me, for that he counted me faithful, putting *(tithemi)* me into the ministry" (1 Ti 1:12; cf. 2:7; 2 Ti 1:11); **(3)** of the overseers, or bishops, in the local church at Ephesus, as those "appointed" by the Holy Ghost, to tend the church of God: "Take heed therefore unto yourselves, and to all the flock, over the which the Holy Ghost hath made *(tithemi)* you overseers, to feed the church of God, which he hath purchased with his own blood" (Acts 20:28);

(4) of the Son of God, as appointed heir of all things: "Hath in these last days spoken unto us by His Son, whom He hath appointed *(tithemi)* heir of all things, by whom also He made the worlds" (Heb 1:2). **(5)** It is also used of "appointment" to punishment, **(5a)** as of the unfaithful servant: "And shall cut him asunder, and appoint *(tithemi)* him his portion with the hypocrites: there shall be weeping and gnashing of teeth" (Mt 24:51; cf. Lk 12:46); **(5b)** of unbelieving Israel: "And a stone of stumbling, and a rock of offence, even to them which stumble at the word, being disobedient: whereunto also they were appointed *(titnemi)*" (1 Pet 2:8; cf. 2 Pet 2:6). See: TDNT—8:152, 1176; BAGD—815d; THAYER—622d.

5088. τίκτω {19x} **tiktō**, *tik'-to;* a strengthened form of a primary τέκω **tekō**, *tek'-o* (which is used only as alt. in certain tenses); to *produce* (from seed, as a mother, a plant, the earth, etc.), lit. or fig.:—bring forth {9x}, be delivered {5x}, be born {3x}, be in travail {1x}, bear {1x}.

Tikto, as a verb, means **(1)** "to bring forth": "Now Elisabeth's full time came that she should be delivered; and she brought forth a son" (Lk 1:57; cf. Jn 16:21; Heb 11:11; Rev 12:2, 4), or **(2)** "to be born" **(2a)** said of the Child (Mt 2:2; Lk 2:11), and **(2b)** is used metaphorically in Jas 1:15 of lust as bringing forth sin. Syn.: 313, 616, 738, 1080, 1084, 1085, 1626. See: BAGD—816d; THAYER—623d.

5089. τίλλω {3x} **tillō**, *til'-lo;* perh. akin to the alt. of *138,* and thus to *4951;* to *pull* off:—pluck {3x}.

Tillo is used of "plucking off ears of corn," Mt 12:1; Mk 2:23; Lk 6:1. See: BAGD—817a; THAYER—623d.

5090. Τιμαῖος {1x} **Timaiŏs**, *tim'-ah-yos;* prob. of Chald. or. [comp. 2931]; *Timæus* (i.e. *Timay*), an Isr.:—Timæus {1x}. See: BAGD—817a; THAYER—624a.

5091. τιμάω {21x} **timaō**, *tim-ah'-o;* from *5093;* to *prize,* i.e. *fix* a *valuation* upon; by impl. to *revere:*—honour {19x}, value {2x}.

Timao, "to honor", is used of **(1)** valuing Christ at a price by Judas as thirty pieces of silver, Mt 27:9 twice; **(2)** "honoring" a person: **(2a)** the "honor" done by Christ to the Father, Jn 8:49; **(2b)** "honor" bestowed by the Father upon him who serves Christ, Jn 12:26; **(2c)** the duty of all to "honor" the Son equally with the Father, Jn 5:23, 4 times; **(2d)** the duty of children to "honor" their parents, Mt 15:4, 6; 19:19; Mk 7:10; 10:19; Lk 18:20; Eph 6:2; **(2e)** the duty of Christians to "honor" the king, and all men, 1 Pet 2:17 twice; **(2f)** the respect and material assistance to be given to widows "that are wid-

ows indeed," 1 Ti 5:3; **(2g)** the "honor" done to Paul and his companions by the inhabitants of Melita, Acts 28:10; **(2h)** mere lip profession of "honor" to God, Mt 15:8: Mk 7:6. See: TDNT— 8:169, 1181; BAGD—817a; THAYER—624a.

5092. τιμή {43x} **timē**, *tee-may'; from 5099; a value, i.e. money paid, or* (concr. and collect.) *valuables; by anal. esteem* (espec. of the highest degree), or the *dignity* itself:— honour {35x}, precious {1x}, price {8x}, sum {1x}.

    Time, primarily "a valuing," hence, objectively, **(1)** "a price paid or received," e.g., Mt 27:6, 9; Acts 4:34; 5:2, 3; 7:16, "sum"; 19:19; 1 Cor 6:20; 7:23; **(2)** of "the preciousness of Christ" unto believers, 1 Pet 2:7, i.e., the honor and inestimable value of Christ as appropriated by believers, who are joined, as living stones, to Him the cornerstone; **(3)** in the sense of value, of human ordinances, valueless against the indulgence of the flesh, or, perhaps of no value in attempts at asceticism, Col 2:23; **(4)** "honor, esteem," **(4a)** used in ascriptions of worship **(4a1)** to God, 1 Ti 1:17; 6:16; Rev 4:9, 11; 5:13; 7:12; **(4a2)** to Christ, Rev 5:12, 13; **(4b)** bestowed upon Christ by the Father, Heb 2:9; 2 Pet 1:17; **(4c)** bestowed upon man, Heb 2:7; **(4d)** bestowed upon Aaronic priests, Heb 5:4; **(4e)** to be the reward hereafter of "the proof of faith" on the part of tried saints, 1 Pet 1:7; **(4f)** used of the believer who as a vessel is "meet for the Master's use," 2 Ti 2:21; **(4g)** to be the reward of patience in well-doing, Rom 2:7, and of working good (a perfect life to which man cannot attain, so as to be justified before God thereby), Rom 2:10; **(4h)** to be given to all to whom it is due, Rom 13:7 (see 1 Pet 2:17); **(4i)** as an advantage to be given by believers one to another instead of claiming it for self, Rom 12:10; **(4j)** to be given to elders that rule well ("double honor"), 1 Ti 5:17 (here the meaning may be an honorarium); **(4k)** to be given by servants to their master, 1 Ti 6:1; **(4l)** to be given to wives by husbands, 1 Pet 3:7; **(4m)** said of the husband's use of the wife, in contrast to the exercise of the passion of lust, 1 Th 4:4 (some regard the "vessel" here as the believer's body); **(4n)** of that bestowed upon; parts of the body, 1 Cor 12:23, 24; **(4o)** of that which belongs to the builder of a house in contrast to the house itself, Heb 3:3; **(4p)** of that which is not enjoyed by a prophet in his own country, Jn 4:44; **(4q)** of that bestowed by the inhabitants of Melita upon Paul and his fellow-passengers, in gratitude for his benefits of healing, Acts 28:10; **(4r)** of the festive honor to be possessed by nations, and brought into the Holy City, the heavenly Jerusalem, Rev 21:24, 26; **(4s)** of honor bestowed upon things inani-

mate, a potter's vessel, Rom 9:21; 2 Ti 2:20. See: TDNT—8:169, 1181; BAGD—817b; THAYER—624a.

5093. τίμιος {14x} **timŏs**, *tim'-ee-os;* including the comparative

    τιμιώτερος **timiōtĕrŏs**, *tim-ee-o'-ter-os;* and the superlative

    τιμιώτατος **timiōtatŏs**, *tim-ee-o'-tat-os; from 5092; valuable,* i.e. (obj.) *costly,* or (subj.) *honored, esteemed,* or (fig.) *beloved:*—precious {8x}, most precious {2x}, more precious {1x}, dear {1x}, honourable {1x}, had in reputation {1x}.

    Timios, from *time,* "honor, price," signifies **(1)** primarily, "accounted as of great price, precious, costly," **(1a)** 1 Cor 3:12; Rev 17:4; 18:12, 16; 21:19, and **(1b)** in the superlative degree, Rev 18:12; 21:11; **(1c)** the comparative degree is found in 1 Pet 1:7; **(2)** in the metaphorical sense, "held in honor, esteemed, very dear," **(2a)** Acts 5:34, "had in reputation"; so **(2b)** in Heb 13:4, "marriage is honorable"; **(2c)** Acts 20:24, "dear," negatively of Paul's estimate of his life; **(2d)** Jas. 5:7, "precious" (of fruit); **(2e)** 1 Pet 1:19, "precious" (of the blood of Christ); **(2f)** 2 Pet 1:4, "precious" (of God's promises). See: BAGD—818a; THAYER—624b.

5094. τιμιότης {1x} **timiŏtēs**, *tim-ee-ot'-ace; from 5093; expensiveness,* i.e. (by impl.) *magnificence:*—costliness {1x}. See: BAGD—818b; THAYER—624c.

5095. Τιμόθεος {28x} **Timŏthĕŏs**, *tee-moth'-eh-os; from 5092 and 2316; dear to God; Timotheus,* a Chr.:—Timotheus {19x}, Timothy {9x}. See: BAGD—818b; THAYER—624c,

5096. Τίμων {1x} **Timōn**, *tee'-mone; from 5092; valuable; Timon,* a Chr.:— Timon {1x}. See: BAGD—818c; THAYER— 624c.

5097. τιμωρέω {2x} **timōrĕŏ**, *tim-o-reh'-o; from* a comp. of *5092* and οὖρος ŏurŏs (a *guard*); prop. to *protect,* one's *honor,* i.e. to *avenge* (*inflict a penalty*):—punish {2x}.

    Timoreo, primarily, "to help," then, "to avenge" (from *time,* "value, honor," and *ouros,* "a guardian"), i.e., "to help" by redressing injuries, is used **(1)** in the active voice in Acts 26:11, "I punished"; **(2)** passive voice in Acts 22:5, lit., "(that) they may be punished." See: BAGD—818c; THAYER—624c.

5098. τιμωρία {1x} **timōria**, *tee-mo-ree'-ah; from 5097; vindication,* i.e. (by impl.) a *penalty:*—punishment {1x}.

    Timoria emphasizes the vindictive character of punishment that satisfied the inflicter's

sense of outraged justice and that defended his own honor or that of the violated law, Heb 10:29. Syn.: 2851. See: BAGD—818d; THAYER—624d.

5099. **τίνω** {1x} **tinō**, *tee'-no;* strengthened for a primary

τίω **tiō**, *tee'-o* (which is only used as an alt. in certain tenses); to *pay* a price, i.e. as a *penalty:*—be punished with + 1349 {1x}. See: BAGD—818d; THAYER—625d.

5100. **τίς** {450x} **tis**, *tis;* an enclit. indef. pron.; *some* or *any* person or object:—certain {104x}, some {73x}, any man {55x}, any {38x}, one {34x}, man {34x}, anything {24x}, a {9x}, certain man {7x}, something {6x}, somewhat {6x}, ought {5x}, some man {4x}, certain thing {2x}, nothing + 3756 {2x}, divers {2x}, he {2x}, thing {2x}, another {2x}, not tr {17x}, misc. {22x} = divers, + partly (+ that no-) thing, what (-soever), X wherewith, whom [-soever], whose ([-soever]). See: BAGD—819d; THAYER—625d.

5101. **τίς** {538x} **tis**, *tis;* prob. emphat. of *5100;* an interrog. pron., *who, which* or *what* (in direct or indirect questions):—what {260x}, who {102x}, why {67x}, whom {25x}, which {17x}, misc. {67x} = every man, how (much), + no (-ne, thing), where ([-by, -fore, -of, -unto, -with, -withal]), whether, whose. See: BAGD—818d; THAYER—624d.

5102. **τίτλος** {2x} **titlŏs**, *tit'-los;* of Lat. or.: a *titulus* or *"title"* (*placard*):— title {2x}.

Titlos is an inscription giving the accusation or crime for which a criminal suffered (Jn 19:19, 20). See: BAGD—820d; THAYER—627a.

5103. **Τίτος** {15x} **Titŏs**, *tee'-tos;* of Lat. or. but uncert. signif.; *Titus*, a Chr.:— Titus {15x}. See: BAGD—820d; THAYER—627b.

τίω **tiō**. See *5099.*

τό **tŏ**. See *3588.*

5104. **τοί** {0x} **tŏi**, *toy;* prob. for the dat. of *3588;* an enclit. particle of *asseveration* by way of contrast; *in sooth:*—[used only with other particles in comp. as 2544, 3305, 5105, 5106, etc.]. See: BAGD—821a; THAYER—433a [3588].

5105. **τοιγαροῦν** {2x} **tŏigarŏun**, *toy-gar-oon';* from *5104* and *1063* and *3767; truly for then*, i.e. *consequently:*— therefore {1x}, wherefore {1x}. See: BAGD—821a; THAYER—627b.

τοίγε **tŏigĕ**. See *2544.*

5106. **τοίνυν** {4x} **tŏinun**, *toy'-noon;* from *5104* and *3568; truly now*, i.e. *accordingly:*—then {1x}, therefore {3x}. See: BAGD—821b; THAYER—627b.

5107. **τοιόσδε** {1x} **tŏiŏsdĕ**, *toy-os'-deh;* (incl. the other inflections); from a der. of *5104* and *1161; such-like then*, i.e. *so great:*—such {1x}. See: BAGD—821b; THAYER—627c.

5108. **τοιοῦτος** {61x} **tŏiŏutŏs**, *toy-oo'-tos;* (incl. the other inflections); from *5104* and *3778; truly this*, i.e. *of this sort* (to denote character or individuality):—such {39x}, such thing {11x}, such an one {8x}, like {1x}, such a man {1x}, such a fellow {1x}. See: BAGD—821b; THAYER—627c.

5109. **τοῖχος** {1x} **tŏichŏs**, *toy'-khos;* another form of *5038;* a *wall:*— wall {1x}.

A *toichos* is especially a wall of a house, is used figuratively in Acts 23:3, "(thou whited) wall." Syn.: A *teichos* is a wall around a city and may also double as the outer wall of a house. A *toichos* (*5109*) is specifically a wall around a city. See: BAGD—821c; THAYER—627d.

5110. **τόκος** {2x} **tŏkŏs**, *tok'-os;* from the base of *5088; interest* on money loaned (as a *produce*):—usury {2x}.

Tokos primarily means a bringing forth, birth; then, an offspring and is used metaphorically of the produce of money lent out (Mt 25:27; Lk 19:23). Usury can imply charging an exorbitant rate of interest; not so in *tokos*. See: BAGD—821d; THAYER—627d.

5111. **τολμάω** {16x} **tŏlmaō**, *tol-mah'-o;* from τόλμα **tŏlma**, (*boldness;* prob. itself from the base of *5056* through the idea of *extreme* conduct); to *venture* (obj. or in *act;* while *2292* is rather subj. or in *feeling*); by impl. to be *courageous:*—be bold {4x}, boldly {1x}, dare {4x}, durst {7x}.

Tolmao signifies to dare to do, or to bear, something terrible or difficult; hence, to be bold, to bear oneself boldy, deal boldly. Syn.: It is translated be bold in 2 Cor 10:2 as contrasted with *tharreo* (*2292*) in verse 1. *Tharreo* denotes confidence in one's own powers, and has reference to character; *tolmao* denotes boldness in undertaking and has reference to manifestation. See: TDNT—8:181, 1183; BAGD—821d.

5112. **τολμηρότερον** {1x} **tŏlmērŏtĕrŏn**, *tol-may-rot'-er-on;* neut. of the comparative of a der. of the base of *5111* (as adv.); *more daringly*, i.e. *with greater confidence* than otherwise:—the more boldly {1x}.

Greek

See: TDNT—8:181,*; BAGD—822a; THAYER—628a.

5113.　τολμητής {1x} **tŏlmētēs**, *tol-may-tace';* from *5111;* a *daring* (*audacious*) man:—presumptuous {1x}.

Tolmetes means daring and is used in 2 Pet 2:10 of shameless and irreverent daring. See: TDNT—8:181, 1183; BAGD—822a; THAYER—628a.

5114.　τομώτερος {1x} **tŏmōtĕrŏs**, *tom-o'-ter-os;* comparative of a der. of the primary τέμνω **tĕmnō** (to *cut;* more comprehensive or decisive than *2875,* as if by a *single* stroke; whereas that implies repeated blows, like *hacking*); *more keen:*—sharper {1x}. See: BAGD—822a; THAYER—628a.

5115.　τόξον {1x} **tŏxŏn**, *tox'-on;* from the base of *5088;* a *bow* (appar. as the simplest fabric):—a bow {1x}.

Toxon is a bow as in "bow and arrow", Rev 6:2. See: BAGD—822b; THAYER—628a.

5116.　τοπάζιον {1x} **tŏpaziŏn**, *top-ad'-zee-on;* neut. of a presumed der. (alt.) of τόπαζος **tŏpazŏs** (a "*topaz*"; of uncert. or.); a gem, prob. the *chrysolite:*—topaz {1x}.

Topazion is mentioned in Rev 21:20, as the ninth of the foundation stones of the wall of the heavenly Jerusalem; the stone is of a yellow color (though there are topazes of other colors) and is almost as hard as the diamond. It has the power of double refraction, and when heated or rubbed becomes electric. See: BAGD—822b; THAYER—628a.

5117.　τόπος {92x} **tŏpŏs**, *top'-os;* appar. a primary word; a *spot* (gen. in *space,* but limited by occupancy; whereas *5561* is a larger but part. *locality*), i.e. *location* (as a position, home, tract, etc.); fig. *condition, opportunity;* spec. a *scabbard:*—place {80x}, room {5x}, quarter {2x}, licence {1x}, coast {1x}, where {1x}, plain + 3977 {1x}, rock + 5138 {1x}.

Topos, as a noun, [Eng., "topic," "topography"] is used of a specific "region" or "locality." It is translated **(1)** "room": **(1a)** "And she brought forth her firstborn son, and wrapped him in swaddling clothes, and laid him in a manger; because there was no room for them in the inn" (Lk 2:7; cf. 14:22); **(1b)** of a place which a person or thing occupies, a couch at table: "And he that bade thee and him come and say to thee, Give this man place; and thou begin with shame to take the lowest room" (Lk 14:9, cf. v. 10); **(2)** of the destiny of Judas Iscariot: "That he may take part of this ministry and apostleship, from which Judas by transgression fell, that he might go to his own place (*topos*)" (Acts 1:25); **(3)** of the condition of the "unlearned" or non-gifted in a church gathering: "Else when thou shalt bless with the spirit, how shall he that occupieth the room (*topos*) of the unlearned say Amen at thy giving of thanks, seeing he understandeth not what thou sayest?" (1 Cor 14:16); **(4)** the sheath of a sword: "Then said Jesus unto him, Put up again thy sword into his place (*topos*): for all they that take the sword shall perish with the sword" (Mt 26:52); **(5)** a place in a book: "And there was delivered unto him the book of the prophet Esaias. And when he had opened the book, he found the place (*topos*) where it was written" (Lk 4:17; cf. Rev 2:5; 6:14; 12:8); **(6)** metaphorically, of **(6a)** "condition, occasion, opportunity, licence": "To whom I answered, It is not the manner of the Romans to deliver any man to die, before that he which is accused have the accusers face to face, and have licence (*topos*) to answer for himself concerning the crime laid against him" (Acts 25:16; cf. Rom 12:19; Eph 4:27). Syn.: **(A)** *Topos* is a place, indefinite; a portion of space viewed in reference to its occupancy, or as appropriated to itself. **(B)** *Chora* (*5561*) is region, country, extensive; space, yet unbounded. **(C)** *Chorion* (*5564*) parcel of ground, circumscribed; a definite portion of space viewed as enclosed or complete in itself. See also: 170, 201, 402, 1096, 1502, 2119, 2120, 2540, 3837, 4042, 5247, 5561, 5564, 5602. See: TDNT—8:187, 1184; BAGD—822b; THAYER—628a.

5118.　τοσοῦτος {21x} **tŏsŏutŏs**, *tos-oo'-tos;* from τόσος **tŏsŏs**, (*so much;* appar. from *3588* and *3739*) and *3778* (including its variations); so *vast as this,* i.e. *such* (in quantity, amount, number or space):—so much {7x}, so great {5x}, so many {4x}, so long {2x}, as large {1x}, these many {1x}, so many things {1x}. See: BAGD—823b; THAYER—628d.

5119.　τότε {159x} **tŏtĕ**, *tot'-eh;* from (the neut. of) *3588* and *3753; the when,* i.e. *at the time* that (of the past or future, also in consecution):—then {149x}, that time {4x}, when {1x}, not tr {5x}.

Tote, a demonstrative adverb of time, denoting "at that time," is used **(1)** of concurrent events, e.g., Mt 2:17; Gal 4:8, "at that time"; v. 29, "then"; 2 Pet 3:6,"(the world) that then was," lit., "(the) then (world)"; **(2)** of consequent events, "then, thereupon," e.g., Mt 2:7; Lk 11:26; 16:16, "since" that time; Jn 11:14; Acts 17:14; **(3)** of things future, e.g., Mt 7:23; 24:30 (twice), 40; eight times in ch. 25; 1 Cor 4:5; Gal 6:4; 1 Th 5:3; 2 Th 2:8. **(4)** It occurs 90 times in Matthew, more than in all the

rest of the NT together. See: BAGD — 823d; THAYER — 629a.

5120. τοῦ tŏu, *too;* prop. the gen. of *3588;* sometimes used for *5127; of this person:*—his {1x}. See: BAGD — 549b [3588]; THAYER — 433a [3588].

5121. τοὐναντίον {3x} **tŏunantiŏn,** *too-nan-tee'-on;* contr. for the neut. of *3588* and *1726; on the contrary:*—contrariwise {3x}. Cf. 2 Cor 2:7; Gal 2:7; 1 Pet 3:9. See: BAGD — 824a; THAYER — 629c.

5122. τοὔνομα {1x} **tŏunŏma,** *too'-no-mah;* contr. for the neut. of *3588* and *3686; the name* (is):—named {1x}.
Literally, translated this word is "of the name" = named. See: BAGD — 824a; THAYER — 629c.

5123. τουτέστι {17x} **tŏutĕsti,** *toot-es'-tee;* contr. for *5124* and *2076; that is:*—that is {12x}, that is to say {5x}. See: BAGD — 824a; THAYER — 629c.

5124. τοῦτο {320x} **tŏutŏ,** *too'-tŏ;* neut. sing. nom. or acc. of *3778; that thing:*—this {199x}, therefore + 1223 {44x}, that {25x}, for this cause + 1223 {14x}, wherefore + 1223 {7x}, it {5x}, not tr. {1x}, misc. {25x} = here [-unto], partly, self [-same], so, the same, thereunto], thus. See: BAGD — 549b [3588]; THAYER — 466c [3778].

5125. τούτοις {19x} **tŏutŏis,** *too'-toice;* dat. plur. masc. or neut. of *3778; to (for, in, with* or *by)* these (persons or things):—these {7x}, these things {3x}, this {2x}, such {1x}, them {1x}, therein {1x}, therewith {1x}, those {1x}, therewith + 1909 {1x}, not tr. {1x} = such, them, there [-in, -with], these, those. See: BAGD — 549b [3588]; THAYER — 466c [3778].

5126. τοῦτον {64x} **tŏutŏn,** *too'-ton;* acc. sing. masc. of *3778; this* (person, as obj. of verb or prep.):—this {39x}, him {18x}, that {4x}, this fellow {2x}, the same {1x}. See: BAGD — 549b [3778]; THAYER — 466c [3778].

5127. τούτου {7x} **tŏutŏu,** *too'-too;* gen. sing. masc. or neut. of *3778; of (from* or *concerning) this* (person or thing):—this {64x}, that {4x}, him {2x}, thus {1x}, thereabout + 4012 {1x}, it {1x}, thenceforth {1x}, hereby {1x}, here {1x}, + such manner of {1x}. See: BAGD — 549b [3778]; THAYER — 466c [3778].

5128. τούτους {27x} **tŏutŏus,** *too'-tooce;* acc. plur. masc. of *3778; these* (persons, as obj. of verb or prep.):—these {17x},

them {7x}, these men {1x}, this {1x}, such {1x}. See: BAGD — 549b [3778]; THAYER — 466c [3778].

5129. τούτῳ {89x} **tŏutō̧,** *too'-to;* dat. sing. masc. or neut. of *3778; to (in, with* or *by) this* (person or thing):—this {59x}, him {10x}, hereby + 1722 {8x}, herein + 1722 {7x}, misc. {5x} = one, the same, there [-in], this. See: BAGD — 549b [3778]; THAYER — 466c [3778].

5130. τούτων {69x} **tŏutōn,** *too'-tone;* gen. plur. masc. or neut. of *3778; of (from* or *concerning) these* (persons or things):—these {38x}, these things {21x}, such {2x}, these matters {1x}, such matters {1x}, those {1x}, not tr {1x}, their {1x}, they {1x}, this {1x}, sort {1x}. See: BAGD — 549b [3778]; THAYER — 466c [3778].

5131. τράγος {4x} **tragŏs,** *trag'-os;* from the base of *5176; a he-goat* (as a *gnawer):*—goat {4x}.
Tragos denotes "a hegoat," Heb 9:12, 13, 19; 10:4, the male prefiguring the strength by which Christ laid down His own life in expiatory sacrifice. See: BAGD — 824b; THAYER — 629c.

5132. τράπεζα {15x} **trapĕza,** *trap'-ed-zah;* prob. contr. from *5064* and *3979; a table* or *stool* (as being *four-legged),* usually for food (fig. a *meal);* also a *counter* for money (fig. a broker's *office* for loans at interest):—table {13x}, bank {1x}, meat {1x}.
Trapeza is used of **(1)** "a dining table," Mt 15:27; Mk 7:28; Lk 16:21; 22:21, 30; **(2)** "the table of shewbread," Heb 9:2; **(3)** by metonymy, of "what is provided on the table" (the word being used of that with which it is associated), Acts 16:34; **(3a)** Rom 11:9 (figurative of the special privileges granted to Israel and centering in Christ); **(3b)** 1 Cor 10:21 (twice), "the Lord's table," denoting all that is provided for believers in Christ on the ground of His death (and thus expressing something more comprehensive than the Lord's Supper); **(3c)** "the table of demons," denoting all that is partaken of by idolaters as the result of the influence of demons in connection with their sacrifices; **(4)** "a moneychanger's table," Mt 21:12; Mk 11:15; Jn 2:15; **(5)** "a bank," Lk 19:23; **(6)** by metonymy for "the distribution of money," Acts 6:2. See: TDNT — 8:209, 1187; BAGD — 824b; THAYER — 629c.

5133. τραπεζίτης {1x} **trapĕzitēs,** *trap-ed-zee'-tace;* from *5132; a money-broker* or *banker:* —exchanger {1x}. See: BAGD — 824d; THAYER — 629d.

5134. τραῦμα {1x} **trauma,** *trŏw'-mah;* from the base of τιτρώσκω **titrōskō,** (to *wound;* akin to the base of *2352, 5147, 5149,* etc.); a *wound:*—wound {1x}. See: BAGD — 824d; THAYER — 629d.

5135. τραυματίζω {2x} **traumatizō**, *trŏw-mat-id'-zo; from 5134;* to *inflict a wound:*—to wound {2x}.

Traumatizo occurs in Lk 20:12 and Acts 19:16. See: BAGD—824d; THAYER—629d.

5136. τραχηλίζω {1x} **trachēlizō**, *trakh-ay-lid'-zo; from 5137;* to *seize* by *the throat* or *neck,* i.e. to *expose* the *gullet* of a victim for killing (gen. to *lay bare*):—opened {1x}.

Trachelizo, "to seize and twist the neck" (from *trachelos,* "the throat"), was used of wrestlers, in the sense of taking by the throat. The word is found in Heb 4:13, "opened." The literal sense of the word seems to be "with the head thrown back and the throat exposed." See: BAGD—824d; THAYER—629d.

5137. τράχηλος {7x} **trachēlŏs**, *trakh'-ay-los;* prob. from 5143 (through the idea of *mobility*); the *throat (neck),* i.e. (fig.) *life:*—neck {7x}.

Trachelos is used **(1)** literally **(1a)** of that which holds up the head (Mt 18:6; Mk 9:42; Lk 17:2); **(1b)** of being embraced (Lk 15:20; Acts 20:37); **(2)** metaphorically, in Acts 15:10 of putting a yoke upon; **(3)** figuratively, in Rom 16:4, singular in the original, "laid down their neck," indicating that Prisca and Aquila in some way had risked their lives for the apostle. See: BAGD—825a; THAYER—630a.

5138. τραχύς {2x} **trachus**, *trakh-oos';* perh. strengthened from the base of 4486 (as if *jagged* by rents); *uneven, rocky (reefy):*—rock + 5117 {1x}, rough {1x}.

Trachus, **(1)** "rough, uneven," is used of paths, Lk 3:5; **(2)** of rocky places, Acts 27:29. See: BAGD—825a; THAYER—630a.

5139. Τραχωνῖτις {1x} **Trachōnitis**, *trakh-o-nee'-tis; from* a der. of *5138; rough* district; *Trachonitis,* a region of Syria:—Trachonitis {1x}. See: BAGD—825b; THAYER—630a.

5140. τρεῖς {69x} **trĕis**, *trice;* neut.

τρία **tria**, *tree'-ah;* or

τριῶν **triōn**, *tree-on';* a primary (plural) number; "*three*":—three {69x}. See: TDNT—8:216, 1188; BAGD—825b; THAYER—630a.

5141. τρέμω {4x} **trĕmō**, *trem'-o;* strengthened from a primary τρέω **trĕō** (to "*dread,*" "*terrify*"); to "*tremble*" or *fear:*—be afraid {1x}, trembling {3x}.

Tremo, "to tremble, especially with fear," is used in Mk 5:33; Lk 8:47; Acts 9:6; 2 Pet 2:10, "they are (not) afraid." Syn.: **(A)** *Ekplesso (1605)* means "to be astonished", prop. to be

struck with terror, of a sudden and startling alarm; but like our "astonish" in popular use, often employed on comparatively slight occasions. **(B)** *Ptoeo (4422)* signifies "to terrify", to agitate with fear. **(C)** *Tremo (5141)* "to tremble", predominately physical; and **(D)** *phobeo (5399)* denotes "to fear", the general term; often used of a protracted state. See: BAGD—825b; THAYER—630a.

5142. τρέφω {8x} **trĕphō**, *tref'-o;* a primary verb (prop. θρέφω **thrĕphō**; but perhaps strengthened from the base of 5157 through the idea of *convolution*); prop. to *stiffen,* i.e. *fatten* (by impl. to *cherish* [with food, etc.], *pamper, rear):*—bring up {1x}, feed {4x}, nourish {3x}.

Trepho, as a verb, means "to rear, bring up" and signifies **(1)** "to make to grow, bring up, rear," Lk 4:16, "brought up"; **(2)** "to nourish, feed," Mt 6:26; 25:37; Lk 12:24; Acts 12:20; Rev 12:6, 14; **(3)** "to fatten," as of fattening animals, Jas 5:5, "ye have nourished (your hearts)." See: BAGD—825c; THAYER—630a.

5143. τρέχω {20x} **trĕchō**, *trekh'-o;* appar. a primary verb (prop. θρέχω **thrĕchō**; comp. 2359); which uses δρέμω **drĕmō**, *drem'-o* (the base of 1408) as alt. in certain tenses; to *run* or *walk hastily* (lit. or fig.):—have course {1x}, run {19x}.

Trecho, "to run," is used **(1)** in the Gospels the literal meaning alone is used, **(1a)** e.g., Mt 27:48 (*dramon,* an aorist participle, from an obsolete verb *dramo,* but supplying certain forms absent from *trecho,* lit., "having run, running," expressive of the decisiveness of the act); **(1b)** the same form in the indicative mood is used, e.g., in Mt 28:8; **(2)** elsewhere in 1 Cor 9:24 (twice in 1st part); Rev 9:9, "running"; **(3)** metaphorically, **(3a)** from the illustration of "runners" in a race, of either swiftness or effort to attain an end, Rom 9:16, indicating that salvation is not due to human effort, but to God's sovereign right to exercise mercy; **(3b)** of persevering activity in the Christian course with a view to obtaining the reward, **(3b1)** 1 Cor 9:24 (2nd part), and v. 26, **(3b2)** so Heb 12:1; **(3c)** in Gal 2:2 **(3c1)** (1st part), "(lest) I should run," continuous present tense referring to the activity of the special service of his mission to Jerusalem; **(3c2)** (2nd part), "had run," aorist tense, expressive of the continuous past, referring to the activity of his antagonism to the Judaizing teachers at Antioch, and his consent to submit the case to the judgment of the church in Jerusalem; **(3d)** in Gal 5:7 of the erstwhile faithful course doctrinally of the Galatian believers; **(3e)** in Phil 2:16, of the apostle's manner of life among the Philippian believers;

(3f) in 2 Th 3:1, of the free and rapid progress of "the word of the Lord." See: TDNT—8:226, 1189; BAGD—825d; THAYER—630b.

5144. τριάκοντα {11x} **triakŏnta**, *tree-ak'-on-tah;* the decade of *5140; thirty:—*thirty {9x}, thirtyfold {2x}. See: BAGD—826a; THAYER—630b.

5145. τριακόσιοι {2x} **triakŏsiŏi**, *tree-ak-os'-ee-oy;* plur. from *5140* and *1540; three hundred:—*three hundred {2x}.
Triakosioi occurs in Mk 14:5 and Jn 12:5. See: BAGD—826a; THAYER—630c.

5146. τρίβολος {2x} **tribŏlŏs**, *trib'-ol-os;* from *5140* and *956;* prop. a *crow-foot* (*three-pronged* obstruction in war), i.e. (by anal.) a *thorny* plant (*caltrop):—*brier {1x}, thistle {1x}.
Tribolos occurs in **(1)** Mt 7:16 "thistle" and **(2)** Heb 6:8 "briers." Thistle is the plant which produces the briers. See: BAGD—826a; THAYER—630c.

5147. τρίβος {3x} **tribŏs**, *tree'-bos;* from τρίβω **tribō** (to "*rub*"; akin to τείρω **tĕirō**, τρύω **truō**, and the base of *5131, 5134*); a *rut*, or worn *track:—*path {3x}.
Tribos, "a beaten track" (akin to *tribo,* "to rub, wear down"), "a path," is used in Mt 3:3; Mk 1:3; Lk 3:4. See: BAGD—826b; THAYER—630c.

5148. τριετία {1x} **triĕtia**, *tree-et-ee'-ah;* from a compound of *5140* and *2094;* a *three years' period* (*triennium):—*space of three years {1x}. See: BAGD—826b; THAYER—630c.

5149. τρίζω {1x} **trizō**, *trid'-zo;* appar. a primary verb; to *creak* (*squeak*), i.e. (by anal.) to *grate* the teeth (in frenzy):—gnash {1x}.
Trizo, as a verb, primarily used of the sounds of animals, "to chirp, cry, squeak," came to signify "to grind or gnash with the teeth," Mk 9:18. When the teeth are ground in gnashing they produce a squeaking sound. See: BAGD—826b; THAYER—630c.

5150. τρίμηνον {1x} **trimēnŏn**, *trim'-ay-non;* neut. of a compound of *5140* and *3376* as noun; a *three months'* space:—three months {1x}. See: BAGD—826b; THAYER—630c.

5151. τρίς {12x} **tris**, *trece;* adv. from *5140; three times:—*three times {1x}, thrice {11x}. See: TDNT—8:216, 1188; BAGD—826b; THAYER—630c.

5152. τρίστεγον {1x} **tristĕgŏn**, *tris'-teg-on;* neut. of a compound of *5140* and *4721* as noun; a *third roof* (*story*):—

third loft {1x}. See: BAGD—826c; THAYER—630d.

5153. τρισχίλιοι {1x} **trischiliŏi**, *tris-khil'-ee-oy;* from *5151* and *5507; three times a thousand:—*three thousand {1x}. See: BAGD—826c; THAYER—630d.

5154. τρίτος {57x} **tritŏs**, *tree'-tos;* ord. from *5140; third;* neut. (as noun) a *third part,* or (as adv.) a (or the) *third* time, *thirdly:—*third {56x}, thirdly {1x}. See: TDNT—8:216, 1188; BAGD—826c; THAYER—630d.

τρίχες triches, etc. See *2359.*

5155. τρίχινος {1x} **trichinŏs**, *trikh'-ee-nos;* from *2359; hairy,* i.e. made *of hair* (*mohair*):—of hair {1x}. See: BAGD—827a; THAYER—630d.

5156. τρόμος {5x} **trŏmŏs**, *trom'-os;* from *5141;* a "*trembling*", i.e. quaking with *fear:* —tremble + *2192* {1x}, trembling {4x}.
Tromos means to be with fear and trembling, used to describe the anxiety of one who distrusts his ability completely to meet all requirements, but religiously does his utmost to fulfill his duty. This word means "a trembling", and occurs in Mk 16:8; 1 Cor 2:3; 2 Cor 7:15; Eph 6:5; Phil 2:12. See: BAGD—827a; THAYER—630d.

5157. τροπή {1x} **trŏpē**, *trop-ay';* from an appar. primary τρέπω **trĕpō**, to *turn*); a *turn* ("*trope*"), i.e. the revolving of a planet, a *revolution* (fig. *variation*):—turning {1x}. See: BAGD—827a; THAYER—631a.

5158. τρόπος {13x} **trŏpŏs**, *trop'-os;* from the same as *5157;* a *turn,* i.e. (by impl.) *mode* or *style* (espec. with prep. or rel. pref. as adv. *like*); fig. *deportment* or *character:—*as + *3739* {3x}, even as + *2596* + *3739* {2x}, way {2x}, means {2x}, even as + *3739* {1x}, in like manner as + *3639* {1x}, manner {1x}, conversation {1x}.
Tropos, as a noun, means "a turning, fashion, manner, character, way of life" and is translated "manner" **(1)** in Acts 1:11, with reference to the Lord's ascension and return, and **(2)** in Jude 7, of the similarity of the evil of those mentioned in vv. 6 and 7. Syn.: 195, 1485, 2239, 3634, 3668, 3697, 3779, 4169, 4187, 4217, 4459, 5159, 5179. See: BAGD—827b; THAYER—631a.

5159. τροποφορέω {1x} **trŏpŏphŏrĕō**, *trop-of-or-eh'-o;* from *5158* and *5409; to endure* one's *habits:—*suffer (one's) manners {1x}.
Tropophoreo, as a verb, means "to bear another's manners" is translated "suffered He

(their) manners" in Acts 13:18. Syn.: 195, 1485, 2239, 3634, 3668, 3697, 3779, 4169, 4187, 4217, 4459, 5158, 5179, 5615. See: BAGD—827c; THAYER—631a.

5160. **τροφή** {16x} **trŏphē**, *trof-ay';* from *5142; nourishment* (lit. or fig.); by impl. *rations (wages):*—meat {11x}, food {2x}, some meat {2x}, not tr {1x}.

Trophe denotes "nourishment, food" (akin to *trepho,* "to rear, nourish, feed"); **(1)** it is used literally, in the Gospels, Acts and Jas 2:15; **(2)** metaphorically, in Heb 5:12, 14, "(strong) meat," i.e., deeper subjects of the faith than that of elementary instruction. **(3)** The word is rendered "meat"; e.g., Mt 3:4; 6:25; 10:10; 24:45; Lk 12:23; Jn 4:8; Acts 2:46, "did eat their meat"; 27:33, 34, 36; and **(4)** "food" in Acts 9:19; 14:17 and Jas 2:15. Food is the general term for all nourishments [soups, liquids, gelatins, etc]. Meat refers to solid food which requires chewing. See: BAGD—827d; THAYER—631b.

5161. **Τρόφιμος** {3x} **Trŏphĭmŏs**, *trof'-ee-mos;* from *5160; nutritive; Trophimus,* a Chr.:—Trophimus {3x}. See: BAGD—827d; THAYER—631b.

5162. **τροφός** {1x} **trŏphŏs**, *trof-os';* from *5142;* a *nourisher,* i.e. *nurse:*—nurse {1x}.

Trophos translated "nurse" in 1 Th 2:7, there denotes a "nursing" mother, as is clear from the statement "cherisheth her own children"; this is also confirmed by the word *epios,* "gentle" (in the same verse), which was commonly used of the kindness of parents toward children. See: BAGD—827d; THAYER—631b.

5163. **τροχιά** {1x} **trŏchia**, *trokh-ee-ah';* from *5164;* a *track* (as a wheel-*rut*), i.e. (fig.) a *course* of conduct:—path {1x}.

Trochia, "the track of a wheel" (*trochos,* "a wheel"; *trecho,* "to run") hence, "a track, path," is used figuratively in Heb 12:13. See: BAGD—828a; THAYER—631b.

5164. **τροχός** {1x} **trŏchŏs**, *trokh-os';* from *5143;* a *wheel* (as a *runner*), i.e. (fig.) a *circuit* of phys. effects:—course {1x}.

Trochos is literally a wheel and is translated "course" in Jas 3:6 with metaphorical reference to the round of human activity, as a glowing axle would set on fire the whole wooden wheel. See: BAGD—828a; THAYER—631b.

5165. **τρύβλιον** {2x} **trublĭon**, *troob'-lee-on;* neut. of a presumed der. of uncert. aff.; a *bowl somewhat deep:*—dish {2x}.

Trublion denotes "a bowl," somewhat deep, Mt 26:23; Mk 14:20; See: BAGD—828b; THAYER—631b.

5166. **τρυγάω** {3x} **trugaō**, *troo-gah'-o;* from a der. of τρύγω **trugō** (to *dry*) mean. ripe *fruit* (as if *dry*); to *collect* the vintage:—gather {3x}.

Truago signifies "to gather in," of harvest, vintage, ripe fruits (*truge* denotes "fruit," etc., gathered in autumn), **(1)** Lk 6:44, of grapes (last part); **(2)** metaphorically, **(2a)** of the clusters of "the vine of the earth," Rev 14:18; **(2b)** of that from which they are "gathered", Rev 14:19. See: BAGD—828b; THAYER—631c.

5167. **τρυγών** {1x} **trugōn**, *troo-gone';* from τρύζω **truzō** (to *murmur;* akin to *5149,* but denoting a *duller* sound); a *turtle-dove* (as *cooing*):—turtle-dove {1x}. See: TDNT—6:63, 830; BAGD—828b; THAYER—631c.

5168. **τρυμαλιά** {2x} **trumalia**, *troo-mal-ee-ah';* from a der. of τρύω **truō** (to *wear,* away; akin to the base of *5134, 5147* and *5176*); an *orifice,* i.e. needle's *eye:*—eye {2x}. Cf. Mk 10:25; Lk 18:25. See: BAGD—828b; THAYER—631c. comp. *5169.*

5169. **τρύπημα** {1x} **trupēma**, *troo'-pay-mah;* from a der. of the base of *5168;* an *aperture,* i.e. a needle's *eye:*—eye {1x}. This "eye" is smaller than in 5168. See: BAGD—828c; THAYER—631c.

5170. **Τρύφαινα** {1x} **Truphaina**, *troo'-fahee-nah;* from *5172; luxurious; Tryphæna,* a Chr. woman:—Tryphena {1x}. See: BAGD—828c; THAYER—631c.

5171. **τρυφάω** {1x} **truphaō**, *troo-fah'-o;* from *5172;* to *indulge in luxury:*—live in pleasure {1x}.

Truphao concerns itself with the softness of a luxurious life. Syn.: 4684, 4763. See: BAGD—828c; THAYER—631c.

5172. **τρυφή** {2x} **truphē**, *troo-fay';* from θρύπτω **thruptō** (to *break* up or [fig.] *enfeeble,* espec. the mind and body by indulgence); *effeminacy,* i.e. *luxury* or *debauchery:*—delicately {1x}, riot {1x}.

Truphe is used **(1)** with *en,* in the phrase *en truphe,* "luxuriously," "delicately," Lk 7:25, and denotes effeminacy, softness; **(2)** "to riot" in 2 Pet 2:13, lit., "counting reveling in the day time a pleasure." See: BAGD—828d; THAYER—631d.

5173. **Τρυφῶσα** {1x} **Truphōsa**, *troo-fo'-sah;* from *5172; luxuriating; Tryphosa,* a Chr. female:—Tryphosa {1x}. See: BAGD—828d; THAYER—631d.

5174. **Τρωάς** {6x} **Trōas**, *tro-as';* from Τρός **Trŏs** (a *Trojan*); the *Troad* (or plain of Troy), i.e. *Troas,* a place in Asia Minor:—Troas {6x}. See: BAGD—829a; THAYER—631d.

Greek

5175. Τρωγύλλιον {1x} **Trōgulliŏn,** *tro-gool'-lee-on;* of uncert. der.; *Trogyllium,* a place in Asia Minor:—Trogyllium {1x}. See: BAGD—829a; THAYER—631d.

5176. τρώγω {6x} **trōgō,** *tro'-go;* probably strengthened from a collateral form of the base of *5134* and *5147* through the idea of *corrosion* or *wear;* or perh. rather of a base of *5167* and *5149* through the idea of a *crunching* sound; to *gnaw* or *chew,* i.e. (gen.) to *eat:*—eat {6x}.

Trogo, primarily, "to gnaw, to chew," **(1)** stresses the slow process; it is used **(2)** metaphorically of the habit of spiritually feeding upon Christ, Jn 6:54, 56–58 (the aorists here do not indicate a definite act, but view a series of acts seen in perspective); **(3)** of the constant custom of "eating" in certain company, Jn 13:18; **(4)** of a practice unduly engrossing the world, Mt 24:38. **(5)** In Jn 6, the change in the Lord's use from the verb *esthio (phago)* to the stronger verb *trogo,* is noticeable. The more persistent the unbelief of His hearers, the more difficult His language and statements became. In vv. 49 to 53 the verb *phago* is used; in 54, 58, *trogo* (in v. 58 it is put into immediate contrast with *phago*). See: TDNT—8:236, 1191; BAGD—829b; THAYER—631d.

5177. τυγχάνω {13x} **tugchanō,** *toong-khan'-o;* prob. for an obs. τύχω **tuchō** (for which the mid. voice of another alt. τεύχω **tĕuchō** [to *make ready* or *bring to pass*] is used in certain tenses; akin to the base of *5088* through the idea of *effecting;* prop. to *affect;* or (spec.) to *hit* or *light upon* (as a mark to be reached), i.e. (tran.) to *attain* or *secure* an object or end, or (intr.) to *happen* (as if *meeting* with); but in the latter application only impers. (with *1487*), i.e. *perchance;* or (pres. part.) as adj. *usual* (as if commonly *met with,* with *3756,* *extraordinary*), neut. (as adv.) *perhaps;* or (with another verb) as adv. by *accident (as it were):*—obtain {5x}, be {1x}, chance {1x}, little {1x}, enjoy {1x}, may be {1x}, not tr {1x}, misc. {2x} = X refresh . . . self, + special.

Tugchano, "to meet with, light upon," also signifies "to obtain, attain to, reach, get" (with regard to things), translated "to obtain" **(1)** in Acts 26:22, of "the help that is from God"; **(2)** 2 Ti 2:10, of "the salvation which is in Christ Jesus with eternal glory"; **(3)** Heb 8:6, of the ministry obtained by Christ; **(4)** Heb 11:35, of "a better resurrection." See: TDNT—8:238, 1191; BAGD—829b; THAYER—632a. comp. *5180.*

5178. τυμπανίζω {1x} **tumpanizō,** *toom-pan-id'-zo;* from a der. of *5180* (mean. a *drum,* "*tympanum*"); to *stretch on an* instrument of *torture* resembling a drum, and thus *beat* to death:—torture {1x}.

Tumpanizo primarily denotes "to beat a drum" (*tumpanon,* "a kettledrum," Eng., "tympanal," "tympanitis," "tympanum"), hence, "to torture by beating, to beat to death," Heb 11:35. See: BAGD—829; THAYER—632b.

5179. τύπος {16x} **tupŏs,** *too'-pos;* from *5180;* a *die* (as *struck*), i.e. (by impl.) a *stamp* or *scar;* by anal. a *shape,* i.e. a *statue,* (fig.) *style* or *resemblance;* spec. a *sampler* ("*type*"), i.e. a *model* (for imitation) or *instance* (for warning):—ensample {5x}, print {2x}, figure {2x}, example {2x}, pattern {2x}, fashion {1x}, manner {1x}, form {1x}.

Tupos, primarily denoted "a blow" (from a root *tupto,* "to strike"), and is translated **(1)** "ensample" in 1 Cor 10:11; Phil 3:17; 1 Th 1:7; 2 Th 3:9; 1 Pet 5:3; **(2)** "print" in Jn 20:25 twice; **(3)** "figure" in Acts 7:43; Rom 5:14; **(4)** "example" in 1 Cor 10:6; 1 Ti 4:12; **(5)** "pattern" in Titus 2:7; Heb 8:5; **(6)** "fashion" in Acts 7:44; **(7)** "manner" in Acts 23:25; and **(8)** "form" in Rom 6:17. Syn.: 195, 1485, 2239, 3634, 3668, 3697, 3779, 4169, 4187, 4217, 4459, 5158, 5159, 5615. See: TDNT—8:246, 1193; BAGD—829d; THAYER—632b.

5180. τύπτω {14x} **tuptō,** *toop'-to;* a primary verb (in a strengthened form); to "*thump*", i.e. *cudgel* or *pummel* (prop. with a stick or *bastinado*), but in any case by *repeated* blows; thus differing from *3817* and *3960,* which denote a [usually single] blow with the hand or any instrument, or *4141* with the *fist* [or a *hammer*], or *4474* with the *palm;* as well as from *5177,* an *accidental* collision); by impl. to *punish;* fig. to *offend* (the conscience):—beat {3x}, smite {9x}, strike {1x}, wound {1x}.

Tupto (from a root *tup,* meaning "a blow," *tupos,* "a figure or print:" Eng., "type") denotes "to smite, strike, or beat," **(1)** usually not with the idea of giving a thrashing as with *dero.* **(2)** It frequently signifies a "blow" of violence, and, when used in a continuous tense, indicates a series of "blows." **(2a)** In Mt 27:30 the imperfect tense signifies that the soldiers kept on striking Christ on the head. **(2b)** So Mk 15:19; Lk 22:64. In that verse the word *paio,* "to smite," is used of the treatment given to Christ (*dero* in the preceding verse). **(2c)** The imperfect tense of the verb is again used in Acts 18:17, of the beating given to Sosthenes. Cf. Acts 21:32, which has the present participle. **(3)** It is used in the metaphorical sense of "wounding," in 1 Cor 8:12. **(4)** It is also translated "to strike, smite, beat," is rendered "to smite" in Mt 24:49; 27:30; Mk 15:19; Lk 6:29; 18:13; 22:64 (1st part); 23:48; Acts 23:2, 3

(twice). See: TDNT—8:260, 1195; BAGD—
830b; THAYER—632d.

5181. **Τύραννος** {1x} **Turannŏs,** *too'-ran-nos;*
　　　　a provincial form of the der.
of the base of *2962;* a *"tyrant"*; *Tyrannus,* an
Ephesian:—Tyrannus {1x}. See: BAGD—830c;
THAYER—632d.

5182. **τυρβάζω** {1x} **turbazō,** *toor-bad'-zo;* from
　　　　τύρβη **turbē,** (Lat. *turba,* a
crowd; akin to *2351*); to *make "turbid",* i.e.
disturb:—trouble {1x}. See: BAGD—830d;
THAYER—632d.

5183. **Τύριος** {1x} **Turiŏs,** *too'-ree-os;* from
　　　　5184; a *Tyrian,* i.e. inhab.
of Tyrus:—of Tyre {1x}. See: BAGD—830d;
THAYER—632d.

5184. **Τύρος** {11x} **Turŏs,** *too'-ros;* of Heb. or.
　　　　[6865]: *Tyrus* (i.e. *Tsor*), a place
in Pal.:—Tyre {11x}. See: BAGD—830d;
THAYER—633a.

5185. **τυφλός** {53x} **tuphlŏs,** *toof-los';* from
　　　　5187; opaque (as if *smoky*), i.e.
(by anal.) *blind* (phys. or ment.):—blind {44x},
blind man {9x}.
　　Tuphlos, "blind," is (1) used both physically
and metaphorically, chiefly in the Gospels;
(2) elsewhere four times; (2a) physically, Acts
13:11; (2b) metaphorically, Rom 2:19; 2 Pet 1:9;
Rev 3:17. (3) The word is frequently used as a
noun, signifying "a blind man." See: TDNT—
8:270, 1196; BAGD—830d; THAYER—633a.

5186. **τυφλόω** {3x} **tuphlŏō,** *toof-lŏ'-o;* from
　　　　5185; to *make blind,* i.e. (fig.)
to *obscure:*—to blind {3x}.
　　Tuphloo, "to blind" (from a root *tuph—,* "to
burn, smoke"; cf. *tuphos,* "smoke"), is used
metaphorically, of the dulling of the intellect,
Jn 12:40; 2 Cor 4:4; 1 Jn 2:11. Cf. "cloudy thinking, not thinking clearly." See: TDNT—8:270,
1196; BAGD—831a; THAYER—633a.

5187. **τυφόω** {3x} **tuphŏō,** *toof-ŏ'-o;* from a
　　　　der. of *5188;* to envelop with
smoke, i.e. (fig.) to *inflate* with self-conceit:—
high-minded {1x}, be lifted up with pride {1x},
be proud {1x}.
　　Tuphoo, properly means "to wrap in smoke"
(from *tuphos,* "smoke"; metaphorically, for
"conceit"); it is used in the passive voice, metaphorically (1) in 1 Ti 3:6, "lifted up with pride";
(2) so 1 Ti 6:4, "proud," and (3) 2 Ti 3:4, "highminded." Cf. "having one's head in the clouds,
minding heavenly directives." See: BAGD—
831a; THAYER—633c.

5188. **τύφω** {1x} **tuphō,** *too'-fo;* appar. a pri-
　　　　mary verb; to make a *smoke,* i.e.
slowly *consume* without flame:—smoke {1x}.

　　Tupho, "to raise a smoke" (akin to *tuphoo,*
"to puff up with pride), is used in the passive
voice in Mt 12:20, "smoking (flax)," lit.,
"caused to smoke," of the wick of a lamp which
has ceased to burn clearly, about to go out,
figurative of mere nominal religiousness without the Spirit's power. See: BAGD—831c;
THAYER—633c.

5189. **τυφωνικός** {1x} **tuphōnikŏs,** *too-fo-*
　　　　nee-kos'; from a der. of
5188; stormy (as if *smoky*):—tempestuous {1x}.
See: BAGD—831c; THAYER—633c.

5190. **Τυχικός** {7x} **Tuchikŏs,** *too-khee-kos';*
　　　　from a der. of *5177; fortu-
itous,* i.e. *fortunate; Tychicus,* a Chr.:—Tychicus {7x}. See: BAGD—831c; THAYER—633c.

Υ

5191. **ὑακίνθινος** {1x} **huakinthinŏs,** *hoo-ak-*
　　　　in'-thee-nos; from *5192; "hy-
acinthine"* or *"jacinthine",* i.e. deep *blue:*—jacinth
{1x}. See: BAGD—831b; THAYER—633b.

5192. **ὑάκινθος** {1x} **huakinthŏs,** *hoo-ak'-in-
thos;* of uncert. der.; the *"hy-
acinth"* or *"jacinth",* i.e. some gem of a deep
blue color, prob. the *zirkon:*—jacinth {1x}. See:
BAGD—831b; THAYER—633b.

5193. **ὑάλινος** {3x} **hualinŏs,** *hoo-al'-ee-nos;*
　　　　from *5194; glassy,* i.e. *trans-
parent:*—of glass {3x}. See: BAGD—831d;
THAYER—633b.

5194. **ὕαλος** {2x} **hualŏs,** *hoo'-al-os;* perh.
　　　　from the same as *5205* (as being
transparent like *rain*); *glass:*—glass {2x}.
　　Hualos signifies "glassy, made of glass",
Rev 4:6; 15:2 (twice). See: BAGD—831d;
THAYER—633b.

5195. **ὑβρίζω** {5x} **hubrizō,** *hoo-brid'-zo;* from
　　　　5196; to *exercise violence,* i.e.
abuse:—use despitefully {1x}, reproach {1x},
entreat shamefully {1x}, entreat spitefully {2x}.
　　Hubrizo means (1) to be insolent, to behave
insolently, wantonly, outrageously; (2) to act
insolently and shamefully toward one, to treat
shamefully (Mt 22:6, "entreated spitefully"; Lk
18:32, "spitefully entreated"; Acts 14:5, "use
despitefully"); (3) of one who injures another
by speaking evil of him (Lk 11:45, "reproachest"; but in this case Jesus spoke the
truth, which the lawyers took as reproach); and
(4) 1 Th 2:2, "shamefully treated." See: TDNT—
8:295, 1200; BAGD—831d; THAYER—633d.

5196. **ὕβρις** {3x} **hubris,** *hoo'-bris;* from *5228;
insolence* (as *over*-bearing), i.e.

insult, injury:—harm {1x}, hurt {1x}, reproach {1x}.

Hubris primarily denotes "wantonness, insolence": then, "an act of wanton violence, an outrage, injury," **(1)** 2 Cor 12:10, "reproaches" (more than reproach is conveyed by the term); **(2)** metaphorically **(2a)** of a loss by sea, Acts 27:10, "hurt," and **(2b)** Acts 27:21, "harm." See: TDNT—8:295, 1200; BAGD—832a; THAYER—633d.

5197. **ὑβριστής** {2x} **hubristēs,** *hoo-bris-tace';* from *5195;* a violent, insolent man; an *insulter,* i.e. *maltreater:*—despiteful {1x}, injurious {1x}.

(1) *Hubristes* denotes insolent wrongdoing for the sheer pleasure of inflicting pain on others, not out of revenge or a similar motive. **(2)** His contempt for others results in acts of wantonness and outrage. It is translated **(1)** "despiteful" in Rom 1:30; and **(2)** "injurious" in 1 Ti 1:13. Syn.: 213, 5244. See: TDNT—8:295, 1200; BAGD—832a; THAYER—633d.

5198. **ὑγιαίνω** {12x} **hugiainō,** *hoog-ee-ah'-ee-no;* from *5199;* to *have* sound health, i.e. *be well* (in body); fig. to be *uncorrupt* (*true* in doctrine):—sound {6x}, be sound {1x}, be whole {1x}, whole {1x}, wholesome {1x}, be in health {1x}, safe and sound {1x}.

Hugiaino, "to be healthy, sound in health" (Eng., "hygiene," etc.), translated **(1)** "safe and sound" in Lk 15:27, is used **(2)** metaphorically **(2a)** of doctrine, 1 Ti 1:10; 2 Ti 4:3; Titus 1:9; 2:1; **(2b)** of words, 1 Ti 6:3, "wholesome"; 2 Ti 1:13; **(2c)** "in the faith," Titus 1:13; **(2d)** "in faith," Titus 2:2. See: TDNT—8:308, 1202; BAGD—832b; THAYER—634a.

5199. **ὑγιής** {14x} **hugiēs,** *hoog-ee-ace';* from the base of *837; healthy,* i.e. *well* (in body); fig. *true* (in doctrine):—sound {1x}, whole {13x}.

Hugies is used **(1)** especially in the Gospels of making sick folk "whole," Mt 12:13; 15:31; Mk 3:5; 5:34; Lk 6:10; Jn 5:4, 6, 9, 11, 14, 15; 7:23; **(2)** also Acts 4:10; **(3)** of "sound (speech)," Titus 2:8. See: TDNT—8:308, 1202; BAGD—832c; THAYER—634a.

5200. **ὑγρός** {1x} **hugrŏs,** *hoo-gros';* from the base of *5205; wet* (as if with *rain*), i.e. (by impl.) *sappy* (*fresh*):—green {1x}.

Hugros denotes "wet, moist" (the opposite of *xeros,* "dry"); said of wood, sappy, "green," Lk 23:31, i.e., if they thus by the fire of their wrath treated Christ, the guiltless, holy, the fruitful, what would be the fate of the perpetrators, who were like the dry wood, exposed to the fire of divine wrath. See: BAGD—832c; THAYER—634b.

5201. **ὑδρία** {3x} **hudria,** *hoo-dree-ah';* from *5204;* a *water-jar,* i.e. *receptacle* for family supply:—water-pot {3x}. Cf. John 2:6, 7; 4:28. See: BAGD—832c; THAYER—634b.

5202. **ὑδροποτέω** {1x} **hudrŏpŏtĕō,** *hoo-drop-ot-eh'-o;* from a compound of *5204* and a der. of *4095;* to *be a water-drinker,* i.e. to *abstain from vinous beverages:*—drink water {1x}. See: BAGD—832d; THAYER—634b.

5203. **ὑδρωπικός** {1x} **hudrōpikŏs,** *hoo-dro-pik-os';* from a compound of *5204* and a der. of *3700* (as if *looking watery*); to be "*dropsical*":—have the dropsy {1x}.

Hudropikos, "dropsical, suffering from dropsy" (*hudrops,* "dropsy"), is found in Lk 14:2, the only instance recorded of the healing of this disease by the Lord. See: BAGD—832d; THAYER—634b.

5204. **ὕδωρ** {79x} **hudōr,** *hoo'-dore;* gen.,

ὕδατος hudatŏs, *hoo'-dat-os,* etc.; from the base of *5205; water* (as if *rainy*) lit. or fig.:—water {79x}.

Hudor, whence Eng. prefix, "hydro-," is used **(1)** of the natural element, **(1a)** frequently in the Gospels; **(1b)** in the plural especially in the Apocalypse; **(1c)** elsewhere, e.g., Heb 9:19; Jas 3:12; **(2)** in 1 Jn 5:6, that Christ "came by water and blood," refers to, in view of the order of the words and the prepositions here used, to His baptism in Jordan and His death on the cross. Jesus the Son of God came on His mission by, or through, "water" and blood, namely, at His baptism, when He publicly entered upon His mission and was declared to be the Son of God by the witness of the Father, and at the cross, when He publicly closed His witness; the apostle's statement thus counteracts the doctrine of the Gnostics that the divine *Logos* united Himself with the man Jesus at His baptism, and left him at Gethsemane. On the contrary, He who was baptized and He who was crucified was the Son of God throughout in His combined deity and humanity.

(3) The word "water" is in Jn 3:5, in view of the preposition *ek,* "out of," the truth conveyed by baptism, this being the expression, not the medium, the symbol, not the cause, of the believer's identification with Christ in His death, burial and resurrection. So the new birth is, in one sense, the setting aside of all that the believer was according to the flesh, for it is evident that there must be an entirely new beginning. **(4)** "The water of life," Rev 21:6 and 22:1, 17, is emblematic of the maintenance of spiritual life in perpetuity. **(5)** In Rev 17:1 "the waters" are symbolic of nations, peoples, etc.

See: TDNT—8:314, 1203; BAGD—832d; THAYER—634b.

5205. ὑετός {6x} **huĕtŏs**, *hoo-et-os';* from a primary ὕω **huō**, (to *rain*); *rain,* espec. a *shower:*—rain {6x}.

Huetos, from *huo,* "to rain," is used especially, but not entirely, of "showers," and is found in Acts 14:17; 28:2; Heb 6:7; Jas 5:7; 5:18; Rev 11:6. See: BAGD—833b; THAYER—634c.

5206. υἱοθεσία {5x} **huiŏthĕsia**, *hwee-oth-es-ee'-ah;* from a presumed compound of *5207* and a der. of *5087;* the *placing* as a *son,* i.e. *adoption* (fig. Chr. *sonship* in respect to God):—adoption {3x}, adoption of children {1x}, adoption of sons {1x}.

Huiothesia, (from *huios,* "a son," and *thesis,* "a placing," akin to *tithemi*), "to place," **(1)** signifies the place and condition of a son given to one to whom it does not naturally belong. **(2)** The word is used by the apostle Paul only. **(3)** In Rom 8:15, believers are said to have received "the Spirit of adoption," that is, the Holy Spirit who, given as the firstfruits of all that is to be theirs, produces in them the realization of sonship and the attitude belonging to sons. **(4)** In Gal 4:5 they are said to receive "the adoption of sons," i.e., sonship bestowed in distinction from a relationship consequent merely upon birth; here two contrasts are presented, **(4a)** between the sonship of the believer and the unoriginated sonship of Christ, **(4b)** between the freedom enjoyed by the believer and bondage, whether of Gentile natural condition, or of Israel under the Law. **(5)** In Eph 1:5 they are said to have been foreordained unto "adoption as sons" through Jesus Christ, "adoption of children." God does "adopt" believers as children and they are begotten as such by His Holy Spirit through faith. **(6)** "Adoption" is a term involving the dignity of the relationship of believers as sons; it is not a putting into the family by spiritual birth, but a putting into the position of sons. **(7)** In Rom 8:23 the "adoption" of the believer is set forth as still future, as it there includes the redemption of the body, when the living will be changed and those who have fallen asleep will be raised. **(8)** In Rom 9:4 "adoption" is spoken of as belonging to Israel, in accordance with the statement in Ex 4:12, "Israel is My Son." Cf. Hos 11:1. Israel was brought into a special relation with God, a collective relationship, not enjoyed by other nations, cf. Deut 14:1; Jer 31:9. See: TDNT—8:397, 1206; BAGD—833b; THAYER—634c.

5207. υἱός {382x} **huiŏs**, *hwee-os';* appar. a primary word; a *"son"* (sometimes of animals), used very widely of immed. remote or fig. kinship:—son(s) {85x}, Son of Man + 444 {87x}, Son of God + 2316 {49x}, child(ren) {49x}, Son {42x}, his Son + 848 {21x}, Son of David + 1138 {15x}, my beloved Son + 27 + 3350 {7x}, thy Son + 4575 {5x}, only begotten Son + 3339 {3x}, his (David's) son + 846 {3x}, firstborn son + 4316 {2x}, foal {4x}.

(1) Primarily this word stresses the quality and essence of one so resembling another that distinctions between the two are indiscernible (Heb 1:2–3). It is used in the NT of **(2)** male offspring, Jn 9:18–20; Gal 4:30; **(2a)** legitimate, as opposed to illegitimate offspring, Heb 12:8; **(2b)** descendants, without reference to sex, Rom 9:27; **(2c)** friends attending a wedding, Mt 9:15; **(2d)** those who enjoy certain privileges, Acts 3:25; **(2e)** those who act in a certain way, whether **(2e1)** evil, Mt 23:31, or **(2e2)** good, Gal 3:7; **(2f)** those who manifest a certain character, whether **(2f1)** evil, Acts 13:10; Eph 2:2, or **(2f2)** good, Lk 6:35; Acts 4:36; Rom 8:14; **(2g)** the destiny that corresponds with the character, whether **(2g1)** evil, Mt 23:15; Jn 17:12; 2 Th 2:3, or **(2g2)** good, Lk 20:36; **(2h)** the dignity of the relationship with God whereinto men are brought by the Holy Spirit when they believe on the Lord Jesus Christ, Rom 8:19; Gal 3:26.

(3) The Apostle John does not use *huios,* "son," of the believer, he reserves that title for the Lord; but he does use *teknon,* "child," as in his Gospel, Jn 1:12; 1 Jn 3:1, 2; Rev 21:7 (*huios*) is a quotation from 2 Sa 7:14. **(4)** The Lord Jesus used *huios* in a very significant way, as **(4a)** in Mt 5:9, "Blessed are the peacemakers, for they shall be called the sons of God," and **(4b)** vv. 44, 45, "Love your enemies, and pray for them that persecute you; that ye may be (become) sons of your Father which is in heaven." **(4c)** The disciples were to do these things, not in order that they might become children of God, but that, being children (note "your Father" throughout), they might make the fact manifest in their character, might "become sons." See also 2 Cor 6:17, 18. **(5)** As to moral characteristics, the following phrases are used: **(5a)** sons of God, Mt 5:9, 45; Lk 6:35; **(5b)** sons of the light, Lk 16:8; Jn 12:36; **(5c)** sons of the day, 1 Th 5:5; **(5d)** sons of peace, Lk 10:6; **(5e)** sons of this world, Lk 16:8; **(5f)** sons of disobedience, Eph 2:2; **(5g)** sons of the evil one, Mt 13:38, cf. "of the devil," Acts 13:10; **(5h)** son of perdition, Jn 17:12; 2 Th 2:3.

(6) It is also used to describe characteristics other than moral, as: **(6a)** sons of the resurrection, Lk 20:36; **(6b)** sons of the Kingdom, Mt 8:12; 13:38; **(6c)** sons of the bridechamber, Mk 2:19; **(6d)** sons of exhortation, Acts 4:36; **(6e)** sons of thunder, *Boanerges,* Mk 3:17. Syn.: **(A)** *Paidarion* (*3808*) refers to a child up to his

first school years. **(B)** *Paidion* (*3813*) refers exclusively to little children. **(C)** *Paidiske* (*3814*) refers to a female in late childhood and early youth. **(D)** *Pais* (*3816*) refers to a child of any age. **(E)** *Teknon* (*5043*) gives prominence to physical and outward aspects of parentage. **(F)** *Huios* (*5207*) gives prominence to the inward, ethical, legal aspects of parentage. *Pais* (*3816*) and *teknon* (*5043*) denote a child as respects to descent and age, reference to the later being more prominent in the former word, to descent in *paidion* (*3813*); but the period *pais* (*3816*) covers is not sharply defined. See: TDNT—8:334, 1206; BAGD—833c; THAYER—634d.

5208. **ὕλη** {1x} **hulē,** *hoo'-lay;* perh. akin to *3586*; a *forest,* spec. of felled wood, i.e. (by impl.) *fuel:*—matter {1x}.

Matter is derived from "material" and signifies any combustible substance. See: BAGD—836a; THAYER—636d.

5209. **ὑμᾶς** {437x} **humas,** *hoo-mas';* acc. pl. of *5210; you* (as the obj. of a verb or prep.):—you {376x}, ye {42x}, for your sakes + 1223 {9x}, not tr {1x}, misc. {9x} = youward, your (+ own). See: BAGD—772a [4771]; THAYER—636d; 591c [4771].

5210. **ὑμεῖς** {243x} **humĕis,** *hoo-mice';* irreg. plur. of *4771; you* (as subj. of verb):—ye {236x}, ye yourselves {1x}, you {1x}, not tr {5x}. See: BAGD—836a; 772a [4771]; THAYER—636d; 591c [4771].

5211. **Ὑμέναιος** {2x} **Humĕnaiŏs,** *hoo-me-n-ah'-yos;* from Ὑμήν **Humēn,** (the god of *weddings*); "hymenœal"; *Hymenœus,* an opponent of Christianity:—Hymenæus {2x}. See: BAGD—836a; THAYER—636d.

5212. **ὑμέτερος** {10x} **humĕtĕrŏs,** *hoo-met'-er-os;* from *5210; yours,* i.e. *pertaining to you:*—your {7x}, yours {2x}, your own {1x}. See: BAGD—836a; THAYER—637a.

5213. **ὑμῖν** {621x} **humin,** *hoo-min';* irreg. dat. pl. of *5210; to* (*with* or *by*) *you:*—you {597x}, ye {14x}, your {6x}, not tr {1x}, yourselves {3x}. See: BAGD—772a [4771; THAYER—637a; 591c [4771].

5214. **ὑμνέω** {4x} **humnĕō,** *hoom-neh'-o;* from *5215; to hymn,* i.e. sing a relig. ode; by impl. to *celebrate* (God) in song:—sing a hymn {2x}, sing praise unto {2x}.

Humneo is used **(1)** transitively, Mt 26:30; Mk 14:26, where the "hymn" was that part of the *Hallel* consisting of Psalms 113—118; **(2)** intransitively, where the verb itself is rendered "to sing praises" or "praise," Acts 16:25;

Heb 2:12. See: TDNT—8:489, 1225; BAGD—836b; THAYER—637a.

5215. **ὕμνος** {2x} **humnŏs,** *hoom'-nos;* appar. from a simpler (obs.) form of ὑδέω **hudĕō,** (to *celebrate;* prob. akin to *103;* comp. *5567*); a "*hymn*" or relig. ode (one of the Psalms):—hymn {2x}.

Humnos denotes "a song of praise addressed to God" (Eng., "hymn"), Eph 5:19; Col 3:16. Syn.: *Ode* (*5603*) is the generic term containing praises, exhortations and other admonitions. *Psalmos* (*5568*) and *humnos* (*5215*) are specific, the former designating a song which took its general character from the OT Psalms and is usually accompanied by some musical instrument, although not restricted to them; the later a song of praise with or without instrumental accompaniment; the generic term for a song; hence the accompanying adjective "spiritual." See: TDNT—8:489, 1225; BAGD—836b; THAYER—637b.

5216. **ὑμῶν** {583x} **humōn,** *hoo-mone';* gen. pl. of *5210;* of (*from* or *concerning*) *you:*—your {348x}, you {203x}, ye {9x}, yours {5x}, not tr {1x}, misc. {17x}. See: BAGD—772a [4771]; THAYER—637b; 591c [4771].

5217. **ὑπάγω** {81x} **hupagō,** *hoop-ag'-o;* from *5259* and *71;* to *lead* (oneself) *under,* i.e. *withdraw* or *retire* (as if *sinking* out of sight), lit. or fig.:—go {55x}, go (one's) way {17x}, go away {3x}, get thee {3x}, depart {2x}, get thee hence {1x}. See: TDNT—8:504, 1227; BAGD—836c; THAYER—637b.

5218. **ὑπακοή** {15x} **hupakŏē,** *hoop-ak-ŏ-ay';* from *5219; attentive hearkening,* i.e. (by impl.) *compliance* or *submission:*—obedience {11x}, obedient {1x}, to make obedient + 1519 {1x}, to obey + 1519 {1x}, obeying {1x}.

Hupakoe, "obedience" (*hupo,* "under," *akouo,* "to hear"), is used **(1)** in general, Rom 6:16 (1st part), "(to) obey"; here "obedience" is not personified, as in the next part of the verse, "servants . . . of obedience", but is simply shown to be the effect of the presentation mentioned; **(2)** of the fulfillment of apostolic counsels, 2 Cor 7:15; 10:6; Philem 21; **(3)** of the fulfillment of God's claims or commands, **(3a)** Rom 1:5 and 16:26, "obedience of faith," which grammatically is objective, obedient to the faith. Faith is one of the main subjects of the Epistle, and is the initial act of obedience in the new life [justification], as well as an essential characteristic thereof [sanctification]; **(3b)** Rom 6:16 (2nd part); **(3c)** Rom 15:18, "(to make) obedient"; 16:19; **(3d)** 1 Pet 1:2, 14, "obedient (children)", characterized by "obedience"; **(3e)** 1 Pet 1:22, "obeying (the truth)";

(4) of "obedience" to Christ (objective), 2 Cor 10:5; **(5)** of Christ's "obedience," **(5a)** Rom 5:19 (referring to His death; cf. Phil 2:8); **(5b)** Heb. 5:8, which refers to His delighted experience in constant "obedience" to the Father's will (not to be understood in the sense that He learned to obey). "Learned" means to experience firsthand and by experience make it one's own. See: TDNT—1:224, 34; BAGD—837a; THAYER—637d.

5219. ὑπακούω {21x} **hupakŏuō,** *hoop-ak-oo'-o;* from *5259* and *191;* to *hear under* (as a *subordinate*), i.e. to *listen attentively;* by impl. to *heed* or *conform* to a command or authority:—hearken {1x}, be obedient to {2x}, obey {18x}.

Hupakouo, "to listen, attend" (as in Acts 12:13), and so, "to submit, to obey," is used of "obedience" **(1)** to God, Heb 5:9; 11:8; **(2)** to Christ, by natural elements, Mt 8:27; Mk 1:27; 4:41; Lk 8:25; **(3)** to disciples of Christ, Lk 17:6; **(4)** to the faith, Acts 6:7; **(5)** to the gospel, Rom 10:16; 2 Th 1:8; **(6)** to Christian doctrine, Rom 6:17 (as to a form or mold of teaching); **(7)** to apostolic injunctions, Phil 2:12; 2 Th 3:14; **(8)** to Abraham by Sarah, 1 Pet 3:6; **(9)** to parents by children, Eph 6:1; Col 3:20; **(10)** to masters by servants, Eph 6:5; Col 3:22; **(11)** to sin, Rom 6:12; **(12)** in general, Rom 6:16. See: TDNT—1:223, 34; BAGD—837b; THAYER—638a.

5220. ὕπανδρος {1x} **hupandrŏs,** *hoop'-an-dros;* from *5259* and *435;* in subjection *under* a man, i.e. a *married* woman:—which hath an husband {1x}.

Hupandros, lit., "under (i.e. subject to) a man," married, and therefore, according to Roman law under the legal authority of the husband, occurs in Rom 7:2, "that hath a husband." See: BAGD—837c; THAYER—638a.

5221. ὑπαντάω {5x} **hupantaō,** *hoop-an-tah'-o;* from *5259* and a der. of *473;* to *go opposite* (*meet*) *under* (*quietly*), i.e. to *encounter, fall in with:*—go and meet {1x}, meet {4x}.

(1) *Hupantao* means to go to meet, to meet and may imply in military reference, a hostile meeting. **(2)** It is used in Mt 8:28; Lk 8:27; Jn 11:20, 30; 12:18. See: TDNT—3:625, 419; BAGD—837d; THAYER—638a.

5222. ὑπάντησις {1x} **hupantēsis,** *hoop-an'-tay-sis;* from *5221;* an *encounter* or *concurrence* (with *1519* for infin. in order to *fall in with*):—meeting + 1519 {1x}. See: TDNT—3:625, 419; BAGD—837d; THAYER—638b.

5223. ὕπαρξις {2x} **huparxis,** *hoop'-arx-is;* from *5225; existency* or *pro-* *prietorship,* i.e. (concr.) *property, wealth:*—goods {1x}, substance {1x}.

Huparix primarily, "subsistence," then, "substance, property, goods" (akin to *huparcho,* "to exist, be, belong to"), is translated **(1)** "goods" in Acts 2:45; **(2)** "substance" in Heb 10:34. See: BAGD—837d; THAYER—638b.

5224. ὑπάρχοντα {14x} **huparchŏnta,** *hoop-ar'-khon-tah;* neut. plur. of pres. part. act. of *5225* as noun; things *extant* or *in hand,* i.e. *property* or *possessions:*—goods {7x}, that (one) has {4x}, things which (one) possesses {2x}, substance {1x}. See: BAGD—838a; THAYER—638b.

5225. ὑπάρχω {48x} **huparchō,** *hoop-ar'-kho;* from *5259* and *756;* to *begin under* (*quietly*), i.e. *come into existence* (*be present* or *at hand*); expletively, to *exist* (as copula or subordinate to an adj., part., adv. or prep., or as auxil. to principal verb):—be {42x}, have {2x}, live {1x}, after {1x}, not tr {2x}.

Huparcho, as a verb, **(1)** means "to be in existence, to be" and is translated "live (delicately)": "But what went ye out for to see? A man clothed in soft raiment? Behold, they which are gorgeously apparelled, and live delicately (*huparcho*), are in kings' courts" (Lk 7:25). **(2)** *Huparacho* is highlighted in Phil 2:6, concerning the deity of Christ. The phrase "being (existing) in the form (*morphe* - 3444, the essential and specific form and character) of God," carries with it two facts: **(2a)** of the antecedent Godhood of Christ, previous to His incarnation, and **(2b)** the continuance of His Godhood at and after the event of His birth. **(3)** It is translated "there be" in 1 Cor 11:18. Cf. Lk 16:14; 23:50; Acts 2:30; 3:2; 17:24; 22:3. Syn.: 326, 390, 980, 1236, 2198, 2225, 4176, 4800. See: BAGD—838a; THAYER—638b.

5226. ὑπείκω {1x} **hupĕikō,** *hoop-i'-ko;* from *5259* and εἴκω **ĕikō** (to *yield,* be "*weak*"); to *surrender:*—submit (one's) self {1x}.

Hupeiko, "to retire, withdraw" (*hupo,* under, *eiko,* "to yield"), hence, "to yield, submit, to pull one's self back in order to submit," is used metaphorically in Heb 13:17, of "submitting" to spiritual guides in the churches. See: BAGD—838b; THAYER—638c.

5227. ὑπεναντίος {2x} **hupĕnantiŏs,** *hoop-en-an-tee'-os;* from *5259* and *1727; under* (*covertly*) *contrary to,* i.e. *opposed* or (as noun) an *opponent:*—adversaries, contrary {1x}.

(1) The intensive force is due to the preposition *hupo.* **(2)** It is translated **(2a)** "contrary to," in Col 2:14, of ordinances; and **(2b)** in Heb

10:27, "adversaries." In each place a more violent form of opposition is suggested than in the case of *enantios* (1727). See: BAGD—838b; THAYER—638c.

5228. ὑπέρ {160x} **hupĕr**, *hoop-er'*; a primary prep.; *"over"*, i.e. (with the gen.) of place, *above, beyond, across,* or causal, *for* the sake of, *instead, regarding;* with the acc. *superior to,* more *than:*—for {104x}, of {12x}, above {12x}, for (one's) sake {8x}, on (one's) behalf {3x}, more than {3x}, in (one's) stead {2x}, than {2x}, very chiefest + 3029 {2x}, beyond {1x}, to {1x}, over {1x}, more {1x}, exceedingly abundantly + 1537 + 4053 {1x}, exceedingly + 1537 + 4053 {1x}, very highly + 1537 + 4053 {1x}, misc. {5x} = by, concerning, + very highly, to (-ward), very. [In composition, it retains many of the above applications.] See: BAGD—838b; THAYER—638d.

5229. ὑπεραίρομαι {3x} **hupĕrairŏmai**, *hoop-er-ah'-ee-rom-ahee;* mid. voice from *5228* and *142;* to *raise* oneself *over,* i.e. (fig.) to *become haughty:*—exalt (one's) self {1x}, be exalted above measure {2x}.

Huperairomai is used in the middle voice, of exalting oneself exceedingly (2 Cor 12:7; 2 Th 2:4). See: BAGD—839d; THAYER—640a.

5230. ὑπέρακμος {1x} **hupĕrakmŏs**, *hoop-er'-ak-mos;* from *5228* and the base of *188; beyond* the *"acme"*, i.e. fig. (of a daughter) *past* the *bloom* (*prime*) of youth:—+ pass the flower of (her) age + 5610 {1x}.

Huperakmos as an adjective in 1 Cor 7:36 is rendered "past the flower of her age"; more lit., "beyond the bloom or flower (acme) of life." Syn.: 165, 166, 1074, 2244, 2250, 5046. See: BAGD—839d; THAYER—640b.

5231. ὑπεράνω {3x} **hupĕranō**, *hoop-er-an'-o;* from *5228* and *507; above* upward, i.e. *greatly higher* (in place or rank):—far above {2x}, over {1x}. Cf. Eph 1:21; 4:10; Heb 9:5. See: BAGD—840a; THAYER—640b.

5232. ὑπεραυξάνω {1x} **hupĕrauxanō**, *hoop-er-ŏwx-an'-o;* from *5228* and *837;* to *increase above* ordinary degree:—grow exceedingly {1x}.

Huperauxano, "to increase beyond measure", is used of faith and love, in their living and practical effects, 2 Th 1:3. Syn.: *Huperauxano* implies an internal, organic growth, as of a tree; whereas, *pleonazo* (4121) at the end of 2 Th 1:3, implies a diffusive or expansive character, as of a flood irrigating the land. See: TDNT—8:517, 1229; BAGD—840a; THAYER—640b.

5233. ὑπερβαίνω {1x} **hupĕrbainō**, *hoop-er-bah'-ee-no;* from *5228* and the base of *939;* to *transcend,* i.e. (fig.) to *overreach:*—go beyond {1x}.

Huperbaino is used metaphorically and rendered go beyond in 1 Th 4:6, i.e., of overstepping the limits separating chastity from licentiousness, sanctification from sin. See: TDNT—5:743, 772; BAGD—840a; THAYER—640b.

5234. ὑπερβαλλόντως {1x} **hupĕrballŏntōs**, *hoop-er-bal-lon'-toce;* adv. from pres. part. act. of *5235; excessively:*—above measure {1x}.

Huperballontos, as an adverb, means "beyond measure" and is rendered "above measure": "Are they ministers of Christ? (I speak as a fool) I am more; in labours more abundant, in stripes above measure, in prisons more frequent, in deaths oft" (2 Cor 11:23). Syn.: 280, 488, 943, 2884, 3313, 3354, 3358, 4057, 4568, 5249, 5518. See: TDNT—8:520, 1230; BAGD—840a; THAYER—640b.

5235. ὑπερβάλλω {5x} **hupĕrballō**, *hoop-er-bal'-lo;* from *5228* and *906;* to *throw beyond* the usual mark, i.e. (fig.) to *surpass* (only act. part. *supereminent*):—exceeding {3x}, excel {1x}, pass {1x}.

Huperballo, "to throw over or beyond" (*huper*, "over," *ballo*, "to throw"), is translated **(1)** "exceeding" in 2 Cor 9:14; Eph 1:19; Eph 2:19; **(2)** "excel" in 2 Cor 3:10; and **(3)** "pass" in Eph 3:19. See: TDNT—8:520, 1230; BAGD—840b; THAYER—640c.

5236. ὑπερβολή {7x} **hupĕrbŏlē**, *hoop-er-bol-ay';* from *5235;* a *throwing beyond* others, i.e. (fig.) *supereminence;* adv. (with *1519* or *2596*) *pre-eminently:*—exceeding + 2596 {1x}, more excellent +2596 {1x}, out of measure + 2596 {1x}, beyond measure + 2596 {1x}, excellency {1x}, abundance {1x}, exceeding + 1519 {1x}.

Huperbole, "a throwing beyond" (*huper*, "over," *ballo*, "to throw"), denotes "excellence, exceeding greatness," **(1)** "excellency"of the power of God in His servants, 2 Cor 4:7; **(2)** "abundance" of the revelations given to Paul, 2 Cor 12:7; **(3)** with the preposition *kata*, the phrase signifies "exceeding," Rom 7:13; **(4)** "more excellent," 1 Cor 12:31; **(5)** "out of measure," 2 Cor 1:8; **(6)** "beyond measure," Gal 1:13; and, in a more extended phrase, **(7)** "far more exceedingly," 2 Cor 4:17. See: TDNT—8:520, 1230; BAGD—840b; THAYER—640c.

5237. ὑπερείδω {1x} **hupĕrĕidō**, *hoop-er-i'-do;* from *5228* and *1492;* to *overlook,* i.e. *not punish:*—wink at {1x}.

Hupereido, "to overlook", is used in Acts 17:30, "winked at", i.e., God bore with them without interposing by way of punishment,

though the debasing tendencies of idolatry necessarily developed themselves; means to overlook momentarily. See: BAGD—840c; 841d; THAYER—640c.

5238. ὑπερέκεινα {1x} **hupĕrĕkĕina**, *hoop-er-ek'-i-nah;* from *5228* and the neut. plur. of *1565; above those* parts, i.e. *still farther:*—beyond {1x}.

Huperekeina means beyond: the regions lying beyond the country of one's residence, 2 Cor 10:16. See: BAGD—840c; THAYER—640c.

5239. ὑπερεκτείνω {1x} **hupĕrĕktĕinō**, *hoop-er-ek-ti'-no;* from *5228* and *1614;* to *extend inordinately:*—stretch beyond {1x} See: TDNT—2:465, 219; BAGD—840d; THAYER—640d.

5240. ὑπερεκχύνω {1x} **hupĕrĕkchunō**, *hoop-er-ek-khoo'-no;* from *5228* and the alt. form of *1632;* to *pour out over,* i.e. (pass.) to *overflow:*—run over {1x}. See: BAGD—840d; THAYER—640d.

ὑπερεκπερισσοῦ hupĕrĕkpĕrissŏu. See *5228* and *1537* and *4053.*

5241. ὑπερεντυγχάνω {1x} **hupĕrĕntugchanō**, *hoop-er-en-toong-khan'-o;* from *5228* and *1793;* to *intercede on behalf of:*—make intercession for {1x}. See: TDNT—8:238, 1191; BAGD—840d; THAYER—640d.

5242. ὑπερέχω {5x} **hupĕrĕchō**, *hoop-er-ekh'-o;* from *5228* and *2192;* to *hold* oneself *above,* i.e. (fig.) to *excel;* part. (as adj. or neut. as noun) *superior, superiority:*—better {1x}, excellency {1x}, higher {1x}, pass {1x}, supreme {1x}.

Huperecho lit. means "to hold or have above" (*huper,* "above," *echo,* "to hold"); hence, metaphorically, to be superior to, **(1)** to be better than, Phil 2:3; **(2)** 1 Pet 2:13, "supreme," in reference to kings; **(3)** in Rom 13:1, "higher"; **(4)** Phil 3:8, "excellency," more strictly "the surpassing thing (namely, the knowledge of Christ)"; **(5)** in Phil 4:7, passeth. See: TDNT—8:523, 1230; BAGD—840d; THAYER—640d.

5243. ὑπερηφανία {1x} **hupĕrēphania**, *hoop-er-ay-fan-ee'-ah;* from *5244;* *haughtiness:*—pride {1x}.

Huperephania describes the character of one who, with a swollen estimate of his own powers or merits, looks down on others and even treats them with insolence and contempt (Mk 7:22). See: TDNT—8:525, 1231; BAGD—841a; THAYER—640a.

5244. ὑπερήφανος {5x} **hupĕrēphanŏs**, *hoop-er-ay'-fan-os;* from *5228*

and *5316; appearing above* others (*conspicuous*), i.e. (fig.) *haughty:*—proud {5x}.

(1) *Huperephanos* is one who compares himself (secretly or openly) with others and lifts himself above them. **(2)** His arrogance consists in claiming honor for himself. His comparing himself is not the sin; it is his sin that causes him to compare. **(3)** This word is always used in the evil sense of arrogant, disdainful, haughty (Rom 1:30; 2 Ti 3:2; Lk 1:51). **(4)** In Jas 4:6 and 1 Pet 5:5 it is in opposition to *tapeinos* (5012 - humble, lowly). Syn.: 213, 5197. See: TDNT—8:525, 1231; BAGD—841b; THAYER—641a.

ὑπερλίαν hupĕrlian. See *5228* and *3029.*

5245. ὑπερνικάω {1x} **hupĕrnikaō**, *hoop-er-nik-ah'-o;* from *5228* and *3528;* to *vanquish beyond,* i.e. *gain* a decisive *victory:*—more than conquer {1x}.

Hupernikao, "to be more than conqueror", "to gain a surpassing victory," is found in Rom 8:37, lit., "we are hyper-conquerors," i.e., we are pre-eminently victorious. See: TDNT—4:942, 634; BAGD—841c; THAYER—641b.

5246. ὑπέρογκος {2x} **hupĕrŏgkŏs**, *hoop-er'-ong-kos;* from *5228* and *3591; bulging over,* i.e. (fig.) *insolent:*—great swelling {2x}.

Huperogkos, an adjective denoting "of excessive weight or size," is used metaphorically in the sense of "immoderate," especially of arrogant speech, in the neuter plural, virtually as a noun, 2 Pet 2:18; Jude 16, "great swelling words." See: BAGD—841c; THAYER—641b.

5247. ὑπεροχή {2x} **hupĕrŏchē**, *hoop-er-okh-ay';* from *5242; prominence,* i.e. (fig.) *superiority* (in rank or character):—authority {1x}, excellency {1x}.

Huperoche, primarily, "a projection, eminence," as a mountain peak, hence, metaphorically, "pre-eminence, superiority, excellency," is once rendered **(1)** "authority," 1 Ti 2:2, of the position of magistrates; **(2)** in 1 Cor 2:1, "excellency" (of speech). Syn.: 201, 402, 1096, 1502, 3837, 4042, 5117, 5564, 5602. See: TDNT—8:523, 1230; BAGD—841d; THAYER—641b.

5248. ὑπερπερισσεύω {2x} **hupĕrpĕrissĕuō**, *hoop-er-per-is-syoo'-o;* from *5228* and *4052;* to *super-abound:*—abound much more {1x}, exceeding {1x}.

Huperperisseuo signifies **(1)** "to abound exceedingly," Rom 5:20, of the operation of grace; **(2)** 2 Cor 7:4, in the middle voice, of the apostle's joy in the saints. See: TDNT—6:58, 828; BAGD—841d; THAYER—641b.

5249. ὑπερπερισσῶς {1x} **hupĕrpĕrissōs**, *hoop-er-per-is-soce';* from *5228*

and *4057; superabundantly,* i.e. *exceedingly:*—beyond measure {1x}.

Huperperissos, as an adverb, and is translated "beyond measure": "And were beyond measure astonished, saying, He hath done all things well: he maketh both the deaf to hear, and the dumb to speak" (Mk 7:37). Syn.: 280, 488, 943, 2884, 3313, 3354, 3358, 4057, 4568, 5234, 5518. See: BAGD—842a; THAYER—641c.

5250. **ὑπερπλεονάζω** {1x} **hupĕrplĕŏnazō**, *hoop-er-pleh-on-ad'-zo;* from *5228* and *4121;* to *superabound:*—be exceeding abundant {1x}. See: TDNT—6:263, 864; BAGD—842a; THAYER—641c.

5251. **ὑπερυψόω** {1x} **hupĕrupsŏō**, *hoop-er-oop-so'-o;* from *5228* and *5312;* to *elevate above* others, i.e. *raise* to the *highest* position:—highly exalt {1x}. See: TDNT—8:606, 1241; BAGD—842a; THAYER—641c.

5252. **ὑπερφρονέω** {1x} **hupĕrphrŏnĕō**, *hoop-er-fron-eh'-o;* from *5228* and *5426;* to *esteem* oneself *overmuch,* i.e. *be vain* or *arrogant:*—think more highly {1x}. See: BAGD—842a; THAYER—641c.

5253. **ὑπερῷον** {4x} **hupĕrōŏn**, *hoop-er-o'-on;* neut. of a der. of *5228;* a *higher* part of the house, i.e. apartment in the *third story:*—upper chamber {3x}, upper room {1x}. Cf. Acts 1:13; 9:37, 39; 20:8. See: BAGD—842b; THAYER—641a.

5254. **ὑπέχω** {1x} **hupĕchō**, *hoop-ekh'-o;* from *5259* and *2192;* to *hold* oneself *under,* i.e. *endure* with patience:—suffer {1x}. See: BAGD—842b; THAYER—641d.

5255. **ὑπήκοος** {3x} **hupĕkŏŏs**, *hoop-ay'-kŏ-os;* from *5219; attentively listening,* i.e. (by impl.) *submissive:*—obedient {2x}, obey + 1096 {1x}.

Hupekoos, "obedient" "giving ear, subject," occurs **(1)** in Acts 7:39, "(would not) obey"; **(2)** 2 Cor 2:9, "obedient"; **(3)** Phil 2:8, where "obedience" was not to death but to the Father. See: TDNT—1:224, 34; BAGD—842b; THAYER—641d.

5256. **ὑπηρετέω** {3x} **hupĕrĕtĕō**, *hoop-ay-ret-eh'-o;* from *5257;* to *be a subordinate,* i.e. (by impl.) *subserve:*—minister {1x}, minister unto {1x}, serve {1x}.

Hupereteo, "to do the service of a *huperetes*", properly, "to serve as a rower on a ship," is used **(1)** of David, as serving the counsel of God in his own generation, Acts 13:36, "served"; expressive of the lowly character of his service for God; **(2)** of Paul's toil in working with his hands, and his readiness to avoid any pose of ecclesiastical superiority, Acts 20:34, "minis-

tered unto"; **(3)** of the service permitted to Paul's friends to render to him, Acts 24:23, "minister." See: TDNT—8:530, 1231; BAGD—842c; THAYER—641d.

5257. **ὑπηρέτης** {20x} **hupērĕtēs**, *hoop-ay-ret'-ace;* from *5259* and a der. of ἐρέσσω **ĕrĕssō** (to *row*); an *under-oarsman,* i.e. (gen.) *subordinate (assistant, sexton, constable):*—minister {5x}, officer {11x}, servant {4x}.

Hupertes, properly "an under rower" *(hupo,* "under," *eretes,* "a rower"), as distinguished from *nautes,* "a seaman" (a meaning which lapsed from the word), hence came to denote "any subordinate acting under another's direction"; **(1)** in Lk 4:20, "minister" signifies the attendant at the synagogue service; **(2)** in Acts 13:5, it is said of John Mark, "minister;" **(3)** in Acts 26:16, "a minister," it is said of Paul as a servant of Christ in the gospel; so **(4)** in 1 Cor 4:1, where the apostle associates others with himself, as Apollos and Cephas, as "ministers of Christ." **(5)** It is translated "servants" in Mt 26:58; Mk 14:54, 65; Jn 18:36. Syn.: **(A)** *Diakonos (1249)* represents the servant in his activity for the work; not in his relation, either servile, as that of the **(B)** *douloo (1402),* or more voluntary, as in the case of **(C)** *therapon (2324),* to a person. A *douloo* is opposed to a *diakonos* and denotes a bondman, one who sustains a permanent servile relation to another. A *therapon* is the voluntary performer of services, whether as a freeman or a slave; it is a nobler tenderer word than *douloo.* **(D)** A *huperetes (5257)* suggests subordination. *Oiketes (3610)* is a household servant. See: TDNT—8:530, 1231; BAGD—842c; THAYER—641d.

5258. **ὕπνος** {6x} **hupnŏs**, *hoop'-nos;* from an obs. primary (perh. akin to *5259* through the idea of *subsilience*); *sleep,* i.e. (fig.) spiritual *torpor:*—sleep {6x}.

(1) *Hupnos* is never used of death. **(2)** In five places in the NT it is used of physical "sleep", Mt 1:24; Lk 9:32; Jn 11:13; Acts 20:9; and **(3)** in Rom 13:11, metaphorically, of a slumbering state of soul, i.e., of spiritual conformity to the world, out of which believers are warned to awake. See: TDNT—8:545, 1233; BAGD—843a; THAYER—642a.

5259. **ὑπό** {230x} **hupŏ**, *hoop-ŏ';* a primary prep.; *under,* i.e. (with the gen.) of place *(beneath),* or with verbs (the agency or means, *through);* (with the acc.) of place (whither [*underneath*] or where [*below*] or time (when [*at*]):—of {116x}, by {42x}, under {48x}, with {14x}, in {1x}, not tr {6x}, misc. {3x} = among, from. [In composition, it retains the same general applications, espec. of *inferior* position or

condition, and spec. *covertly* or *moderately.*]
See: BAGD—843a; THAYER—642a.

5260. ὑποβάλλω {1x} hupŏballō, *hoop-ob-al'-lo;* from *5259* and *906;* to
throw in *stealthily,* i.e. *introduce* by collusion:—suborn {1x}.

Hupoballo primarily means to throw or put under, to subject, denoting to suggest, whisper, prompt; hence, to instigate, suborn (Acts 6:11). To suborn in the legal sense is to procure a person who will take a false oath. The idea of making suggestions is probably present in this use of the word. See: BAGD—843d; THAYER—642d.

5261. ὑπογραμμός {1x} hupŏgrammŏs, *hoop-og-ram-mos';* from a compound of *5259* and *1125;* an *underwriting,* i.e. *copy* for imitation (fig.):—example {1x}.

This word literally means an under-writing, to trace letters for copying by scholars; hence, a writing-copy, including all the letters of the alphabet, given to beginners as an aid in learning to draw them; an example. In 1 Pet 2:21 it is said of what Christ left for believers, by His sufferings (not expiatory, but exemplary), that they might "follow His steps." See: TDNT—1:772, 128; BAGD—843d; THAYER—642d.

5262. ὑπόδειγμα {6x} hupŏdĕigma, *hoop-od'-igue-mah;* from *5263;*
an *exhibit* for imitation or warning (fig. *specimen, adumbration*):—ensample {1x}, example {4x}, pattern {1x}.

Hupodeigma, (from *hupo,* "under," *deiknumi,* "to show"), properly denotes "what is shown below or privately"; it is translated **(1)** "example," **(1a)** Heb 8:5; a sign suggestive of anything, the delineation or representation of a thing, and so, a figure, "copy"; **(1b)** an example **(1b1)** for imitation, Jn 13:15; Jas 5:10; **(1b2)** for warning, Heb 4:11; **(3)** in Heb 9:23, "patterns"; and **(4)** in 2 Pet 2:6, "ensample." An "example" is a sample taken from without the group; an "ensample" from within the group. See: TDNT—2:32, 141; BAGD—844a; THAYER—642d.

5263. ὑποδείκνυμι {6x} hupŏdĕiknumi, *hoop-od-ike'-noo-mee;* from *5259* and *1166;* to *exhibit under* the eyes, i.e. (fig.) to *exemplify* (*instruct, admonish*):—show {3x}, forewarn {1x}, warn {2x}.

Hupodeinumi primarily means **(1)** to show by placing under (i.e. before) the eyes; **(2)** to show by words and arguments, i.e. to teach/warn **(2a)** with the infinitive of the thing (Mt 3:7; Lk 3:7); **(2b)** by use of figure followed by indirect discourse (Lk 6:47; 12:5); **(2c)** to show or teach by one's example (Acts 20:35); and **(3)** to show by making known future things, Acts 9:16. See: BAGD—844b; THAYER—643a.

5264. ὑποδέχομαι {4x} hupŏdĕchŏmai, *hoop-od-ekh'-om-ahee;* from
5259 and *1209;* to *admit under* one's roof, i.e. *entertain* hospitably:—receive {4x}.

Hupodechomai, as a verb, denotes "to receive under one's roof, receive as a guest, entertain hospitably": "Now it came to pass, as they went, that he entered into a certain village: and a certain woman named Martha received (*hupodechomai*) Him into her house" (Lk 10:38; cf. 19:6; Acts 17:7; Jas 2:25). Syn.: 324, 353, 354, 568, 588, 618, 1209, 1523, 1926, 2210, 2865, 2975, 2983, 3028, 3335, 3336, 3858, 3880, 3970, 4327, 4355, 4356, 4380, 4381, 4382, 5562, 5274. See: BAGD—844b; THAYER—643a.

5265. ὑποδέω {3x} hupŏdĕō, *hoop-od-eh'-o;* from *5259* and *1210;* to *bind under* one's feet, i.e. *put on* shoes or sandals:—bind on {1x}, be shod with {1x}, shod {1x}.

Hupodeo, "to bind underneath," is used **(1)** of binding of sandals, Acts 12:8; rendered **(2)** "shod" in Mk 6:9 and Eph 6:15. See: TDNT—5:310, 702; BAGD—844b; THAYER—643a.

5266. ὑπόδημα {10x} hupŏdēma, *hoop-od'-ay-mah;* from *5265;* something *bound under* the feet, i.e. a *shoe* or *sandal:*—shoe {10x}. See: TDNT—5:310, 702; BAGD—844c; THAYER—643b.

5267. ὑπόδικος {1x} hupŏdikŏs, *hoop-od'-ee-kos;* from *5259* and *1349;* under sentence, i.e. (by impl.) *condemned:*—guilty {1x}.

Hupodikos, "brought to trial, answerable to" (*hupo,* "under," *dike,* "justice"), Rom 3:19, is translated "guilty", the decision of the court. See: TDNT—8:557, 1235; BAGD—844c; THAYER—643b.

5268. ὑποζύγιον {2x} hupŏzugiŏn, *hoop-od-zoog'-ee-on;* neut. of a compound of *5259* and *2218;* an animal *under* the yoke (*draught-beast*), i.e. (spec.) a *donkey:*—ass {2x}.

Hupozugion, lit., "under a yoke" (*hupo,* "under," *zugos,* "a yoke"), is used **(1)** as an alternative description of the same animal, in Mt 21:5, where both words are found together, "Behold, thy king cometh unto thee, meek and riding upon an ass (*onos*), and upon a colt the foal of an ass (*hupozugion*)." It was upon the colt that the Lord sat, Jn 12:14. **(2)** In 2 Pet 2:16, it is used of Balaam's "ass." See: BAGD—844d; THAYER—643b.

5269. ὑποζώννυμι {1x} hupŏzōnnumi, *hoop-od-zone'-noo-mee;* from
5259 and *2224;* to *gird under,* i.e. *frap* (a vessel with cables across the keel, sides and deck):—undergirding {1x}.

Hupozonnumi is used in Acts 27:17 of bracing the timbers of a vessel by means of strong ropes. See: BAGD—844d; THAYER—643b.

5270. ὑποκάτω {9x} **hupŏkatō**, *hoop-ok-at'-o;* from *5259* and *2736; down under,* i.e. *beneath:*—under {9x}.

Hupokato, an adverb signifying "under," is used as a preposition and rendered "under" in Mk 6:11; 7:28; Lk 8:16; Heb 2:8; Rev 5:3, 13; 6:9; 12:1; "underneath" in Mt 22:44; Jn 1:50, "under." See: BAGD—844d; THAYER—643c.

5271. ὑποκρίνομαι {1x} **hupŏkrinŏmai**, *hoop-ok-rin'-om-ahee;* mid. voice from *5259* and *2919;* to *decide* (*speak* or *act*) *under* a false part, i.e. (fig.) *dissemble* (*pretend*):—feign {1x}.

Hupokrinomai primarily denotes "to answer"; then, "to answer on the stage, play a part," and so, metaphorically, "to feign, pretend," Lk 20:20. See: TDNT—8:559, 1235; BAGD—845a; THAYER—643c.

5272. ὑπόκρισις {7x} **hupŏkrisis**, *hoop-ok'-ree-sis;* from *5271; acting under* a feigned part, i.e. (fig.) *deceit* ("*hypocrisy*"):—condemnation {1x}, dissimulation {1x}, hypocrisy {5x}.

(1) *Hupokrisis* is primarily a reply and came to mean the acting of a stage player because such a one answered another in prepared dialogue; hence the meaning dissembling or pretense (Gal 2:13). It primarily denotes "a reply, an answer" (akin to *hupokrinomai,* "to answer"); then, "play-acting," as the actors spoke in dialogue; hence, "pretence, hypocrisy"; it is translated **(2)** "hypocrisy" in Mt 23:28; Mk 12:15; Lk 12:1; 1 Ti 4:2; the plural in 1 Pet 2:1; and **(3)** "condemnation" in Jas 5:12. See: TDNT—8:559, 1235; BAGD—845a; THAYER—643c.

5273. ὑποκριτής {20x} **hupŏkritēs**, *hoop-ok-ree-tace';* from *5271;* an *actor under* an assumed character (*stage-player*), i.e. (fig.) a *dissembler* ("*hypocrite*"):—hypocrite {20x}. See: TDNT—8:559, 1235; BAGD—845b; THAYER—643c.

5274. ὑπολαμβάνω {4x} **hupŏlambanō**, *hoop-ol-am-ban'-o;* from *5259* and *2983;* to *take* from *below,* i.e. *carry upward;* fig. to *take up,* i.e. *continue* a discourse or topic; ment. to *assume* (*presume*):—answer {1x}, receive {1x}, suppose {2x}.

This word means to take up in order to raise, to bear on high; **(1)** to take up and carry away: "And when He had spoken these things, while they beheld, He was taken up; and a cloud received Him out of their sight" (Acts 1:9); **(2)** to take up where another left off, follow in speech, in order either to reply to or controvert

or supplement what another has said: "And Jesus answering (*hupolambano*) said, A certain man went down from Jerusalem to Jericho, and fell among thieves, which stripped him of his raiment, and wounded him, and departed, leaving him half dead" (Lk 10:30); **(3)** to take up in the mind, to assume, suppose: "Simon answered and said, I suppose that he, to whom he forgave most. And He said unto him, Thou hast rightly judged" (Lk 7:43; Acts 2:15). Syn.: 324, 353, 354, 568, 588, 618, 1209, 1523, 1926, 2210, 2865, 2975, 2983, 3028, 3335, 3336, 3858, 3880, 3970, 4327, 4355, 4356, 4380, 4381, 4382, 5562, 5264. See: TDNT—4:15, 495; BAGD—845b; THAYER—643d.

5275. ὑπολείπω {1x} **hupŏlěipō**, *hoop-ol-i'-po;* from *5295* and *3007;* to *leave under* (*behind*), i.e. (pass.) to *remain* (*survive*):—be left {1x}.

Hupoleipo, "to leave remaining"; lit., "to leave under", is used in the passive voice in Rom 11:3, of a survivor. See: TDNT—4:194,*; BAGD—845c; THAYER—643d.

5276. ὑπολήνιον {1x} **hupŏlēniŏn**, *hoop-ol-ay'-nee-on;* neut. of a presumed compound of *5259* and *3025;* vessel or receptacle *under* the *press,* i.e. lower *wine-vat:*—winefat {1x}.

Hupolenion denotes "a vessel or trough beneath a winepress," to receive the juice, Mk 12:1, "a place for . . . the wine-fat." See: TDNT—4:254, 531; BAGD—845c; THAYER—643d.

5277. ὑπολιμπάνω {1x} **hupŏlimpanō**, *hoop-ol-im-pan'-o;* a prol. form for *5275;* to *leave behind,* i.e. *bequeath:*—leave {1x}. See: BAGD—845d; THAYER—644a.

5278. ὑπομένω {17x} **hupŏměnō**, *hoop-om-en'-o;* from *5259* and *3306;* to *stay under* (*behind*), i.e. *remain;* fig. to *undergo,* i.e. *bear* (trials), *have fortitude, persevere:*—endure {11x}, take patiently {2x}, tarry behind {1x}, abide {1x}, patient {1x}, suffer {1x}.

Hupomeno denotes "to abide under, to bear up courageously" **(1)** under suffering, Mt 10:22; 24:13; Mk 13:13; Rom 12:12, translated "patient"; 1 Cor 13:7; 2 Ti 2:10, 12, "suffer"; Heb 10:32; 12:2–3, 7; Jas 1:12; 5:11; 1 Pet 2:20, "ye shall take it patiently." It has its other significance, **(2)** "to tarry, wait for, await," in Lk 2:43; Acts 17:14. See: TDNT—4:581, 581; BAGD—845d; THAYER—644a.

5279. ὑπομιμνήσκω {7x} **hupŏmimnēskō**, *hoop-om-im-nace'-ko;* from *5259* and *3403;* to *remind quietly,* i.e. *suggest* to the (mid. voice, one's own) memory:—put in remembrance {3x}, remember {2x}, bring

to remembrance {1x}, put in mind {1x}. See: BAGD–846a; THAYER–644b.

5280. **ὑπόμνησις** {3x} **hupŏmnēsis,** *hoop-om'-nay-sis;* from *5279;* a *reminding* or (refl.) *recollection:*—remembrance {2x}, put in remembrance {1x}.

Syn.: *Anamnesis* (*364*) denotes an unassisted recalling, *hupomnesis* (*5280*) a remembrance prompted by another. See: TDNT–1:348, 56; BAGD–846b; THAYER–644b.

5281. **ὑπομονή** {32x} **hupŏmŏnē,** *hoop-om-on-ay';* from *5278;* cheerful (or hopeful) *endurance, constancy:*—patience {29x}, enduring {1x}, patient continuance {1x}, patient waiting {1x}.

Hupomone, lit., "an abiding under" (*hupo,* "under," *meno,* "to abide"), is almost invariably rendered "patience." "Patience", which **(1)** grows only in trial, Jas 1:3 may be passive, i.e., = "endurance," as, **(1a)** in trials, generally, Lk 21:19 (which is to be understood by Mt 24:13), cf. Rom 12:12; Jas 1:12; **(1b)** in trials incident to service in the gospel, 2 Cor 6:4; 12:12; 2 Ti 3:10; **(1c)** under chastisement, which is trial viewed as coming from the hand of God our Father, Heb 12:7; **(1d)** under undeserved affliction, 1 Pet 2:20; or active, i.e. = "persistence, perseverance," as **(1e)** in well doing, Rom 2:7, "patient continuance"; **(1f)** in fruit bearing, Lk 8:15; **(1g)** in running the appointed race, Heb 12:1. **(2)** Patience perfects Christian character, **(2a)** Jas 1:4, and **(2b)** fellowship in the patience of Christ is therefore the condition upon which believers are to be admitted to reign with Him, 2 Ti 2:12; Rev 1:9. **(2c)** For this patience believers are "strengthened with all power," Col 1:11, "through His Spirit in the inward man," Eph 3:16. **(3)** In 2 Th 3:5, the phrase "the patience waiting for Christ." **(4)** In Rev 3:10, "the word of My patience" is the word which tells of Christ's patience, and its effects in producing "patience" on the part of those who are His (see above on 2 Th 3:5). Syn.: *Hupomone* (*5281*) is the temper which does not easily succumb under suffering, *makrothumia* (*3115*) is the self restraint which does not hastily retaliate a wrong. *Hupomone* is opposed to cowardice or despondency, *makrothumia* to wrath and revenge. See: TDNT–4:581, 581; BAGD–846b; THAYER–644c.

5282. **ὑπονοέω** {3x} **hupŏnŏĕō,** *hoop-on-ŏ-eh'-o;* from *5259* and *3539;* to *think under* (*privately*), i.e. to *surmise* or *conjec.:*—think {1x}, suppose {1x}, deem {1x}.

Huponoeo, "to suppose, conjecture, surmise," is translated **(1)** "deemed" in Acts 27:27; **(2)** in Acts 13:25, "think ye"; and **(3)** in Acts

25:18, "supposed." See: TDNT–4:1017, 636; BAGD–846d; THAYER–644c.

5283. **ὑπόνοια** {1x} **hupŏnŏia,** *hoop-on'-oy-ah;* from *5282;* *suspicion:*—surmising {1x}. See: TDNT–4:1017, 636; BAGD–846d; THAYER–644d.

5284. **ὑποπλέω** {2x} **hupŏplĕō,** *hoop-op-leh'-o;* from *5259* and *4126;* to *sail under* the lee of:—sail under {2x}. Cf 27:4, 7. See: BAGD–846d; THAYER–644d.

5285. **ὑποπνέω** {1x} **hupŏpnĕō,** *hoop-op-neh'-o;* from *5259* and *4154;* to *breathe gently,* i.e. *breeze:*—blow softly {1x}. See: BAGD–846d; THAYER–644d.

5286. **ὑποπόδιον** {9x} **hupŏpŏdiŏn,** *hoop-op-od'-ee-on;* neut. of a compound of *5259* and *4228;* something *under* the *feet,* i.e. a *foot-rest* (fig.):—footstool + 4228 {8x}, footstool {1x}.

Huupopodion (from *hupo,* "under," and *pous,* "a foot"), is used **(1)** literally in Jas 2:3, **(2)** metaphorically, **(2a)** of the earth as God's "footstool," Mt 5:35; **(2b)** of the foes of the Lord, Mt 22:44; Mk 12:36, Lk 20:43; Acts 2:35; 7:49; Heb 1:13; 10:13. See: BAGD–846d; THAYER–644d.

5287. **ὑπόστασις** {5x} **hupŏstasis,** *hoop-os'-tas-is;* from a compound of *5259* and *2476;* a *setting under* (*support*), i.e. (fig.) concr. *essence,* or abstr. *assurance* (obj. or subj.):—confidence {2x}, confident {1x}, person {1x}, substance {1x}.

Hupostasis, lit., "a standing under" (*hupo,* "under," *stasis,* "a standing"), "that which stands, or is set, under, a foundation, beginning"; hence, **(1)** the quality of confidence which leads one to stand under, endure, or undertake anything, 2 Cor 9:4; 11:17; Heb 3:14. **(2)** In Heb it signifies "substance" in Heb 11:1; and **(3)** "Person" in Heb 1:3. This Person is the Lord Jesus, the substance, the essence, of God Himself, the One in whom all confidence resides. See: TDNT–8:572, 1237; BAGD–847a; THAYER–644d.

5288. **ὑποστέλλω** {4x} **hupŏstĕllō,** *hoop-os-tel'-lo;* from *5259* and *4724;* to *withhold under* (*out of sight*), i.e. (refl.) to *cower* or *shrink,* (fig.) to *conceal* (*reserve*):—draw back {1x}, keep back {1x}, shun {1x}, withdraw {1x}.

Hupostello, as a verb, means "to draw back, withdraw," [the prefix *hupo,* "underneath," suggestive of stealth]. **(1)** It is perhaps a metaphor from lowering a sail and so slackening the course, and hence of being remiss in holding the truth; **(2)** in the active voice, rendered

"withdrew/draw back": "For before that certain came from James, he did eat with the Gentiles: but when they were come, he [Peter] withdrew and separated himself, fearing them which were of the circumcision" (Gal 2:12); **(3)** in the middle voice, "draw back": "Now the just shall live by faith: but if any man draw back, My soul shall have no pleasure in him" (Heb 10:38). Syn.: 307, 385, 392, 501, 502, 645, 868, 1448, 1670, 1828, 2020, 4264, 4317, 4334, 4358, 4685, 4951, 5289. See: TDNT—7:597, 1074; BAGD—847b; THAYER—645a.

5289. ὑποστολή {1x} **hupŏstŏlē,** *hoop-os-tol-ay';* from 5288; *shrinkage (timidity),* i.e. (by impl.) *apostasy:*—of them that draw back {1x}.

Hupostole, as a noun, is translated "of them who draw back": "But we are not of them who draw back unto perdition; but of them that believe to the saving of the soul" (Heb 10:39). Syn.: 307, 385, 392, 501, 502, 645, 868, 1448, 1670, 1828, 2020, 4264, 4317, 4334, 4358, 4685, 4951, 5288. See: TDNT—7:599, 1074; BAGD—847c; THAYER—645b.

5290. ὑποστρέφω {35x} **hupŏstrĕphō,** *hoop-os-tref'-o;* from 5259 and 4762; to *turn under (behind),* i.e. to *return* (lit. or fig.):—return {28x}, return again {3x}, turn back {1x}, turn again {1x}, return back again {1x}, come again {1x}.

Hupostrepho, as a verb, means "to turn behind or back" and is translated "to return": "And when He returned, He found them asleep again, (for their eyes were heavy,) neither wist they what to answer Him" (Mk 14:40; Lk 1:56; 2:20, 43; v. 45 "turned back again", 4:1, 14; 7:10; 8:37; 10:17; 11:24 "I will turn back"; 17:18; 19:12; 23:48, 56; Acts 1:12; 12:25; 13:13; 13:34; 20:3; 21:6; 22:17, "was come again"; 23:32; Gal 1:17; Heb 7:1). Syn.: 344, 360, 390, 1880, 1877, 1994. See: BAGD—847c; THAYER—645b.

5291. ὑποστρώννυμι {1x} **hupŏstrōnnumi,** *hoop-os-trone'-noo-mee;* from 5259 and 4766; to *strew underneath* (the feet as a carpet):—spread {1x}. See: BAGD—847d; THAYER—645c.

5292. ὑποταγή {4x} **hupŏtagē,** *hoop-ot-ag-ay';* from 5293; *subordination:*—subjection {4x}.

Hupotage, "subjection," occurs in 2 Cor 9:13; Gal 2:5; 1 Ti 2:11; 3:4. See: TDNT—8:46, 1156; BAGD—847d; THAYER—645c.

5293. ὑποτάσσω {40x} **hupŏtassō,** *hoop-ot-as'-so;* from 5259 and 5021; to *subordinate;* refl. to *obey:*—put under {6x}, be subject unto {6x}, be subject to {5x}, submit (one's) self unto {5x}, submit (one's) self to {3x},

be in subjection unto {2x}, put in subjection under {1x}, misc. {12x} = be under obedience (obedient), subdue unto.

(1) This was originally a Greek military term meaning to arrange [troop divisions] in a military fashion under the command of a leader. **(2)** In non-military use, it was a voluntary attitude of giving in, cooperating, assuming responsibility, and carrying a burden. **(3)** It denotes **(3a)** "to put in subjection, to subject, to put under" in Rom 8:20 (twice); 1 Cor 15:27 (thrice), 28 (3rd clause); Eph 1:22; Heb 2:8 (4th clause); **(3b)** in 1 Cor 15:28 (1st clause), "be subdued"; **(3c)** in Phil 3:21, "subdue"; **(3d)** in Heb 2:5, "hath . . . put in subjection"; **(4)** in the middle or passive voice, to subject oneself, to obey, be subject to, **(4a)** Lk 2:51; 10:17, 20; **(4b)** Rom 8:7; 10:3, "have (not) submitted themselves"; 13:1, 5; **(4c)** 1 Cor 14:34, "be under obedience"; 15:28 (2nd clause); 16:16, "submit, etc."; so Col 3:18; **(4d)** Eph 5:21, "submitting, etc."; 5:22, 24, "is subject"; **(4e)** Titus 2:5, 9, "be obedient"; 3:1, "to be subject"; **(4f)** Heb 12:9, "be in subjection"; Jas 4:7, "submit yourselves"; so **(4g)** 1 Pet 2:13, 18; so 3:1, 5, 22, "being made subject"; 5:5, "submit yourselves"; also in the 2nd part. See: TDNT—8:39, 1156; BAGD—847d; THAYER—645c.

5294. ὑποτίθημι {2x} **hupŏtithēmi,** *hoop-ot-ith'-ay-mee;* from 5259 and 5087; to *place underneath,* i.e. (fig.) to *hazard,* (refl.) to *suggest:*—lay down {1x}, put in remembrance {1x}.

Hupotithemi, "to place under, lay down", is used metaphorically **(1)** in Rom 16:4, of risking one's life, "laid down" (their own necks). **(2)** In the middle voice in 1 Ti 4:6 it is used of "putting" persons in mind, "in remembrance." See: BAGD—848b; THAYER—645d.

5295. ὑποτρέχω {1x} **hupŏtrĕchō,** *hoop-ot-rekh'-o;* from 5259 and 5143 (incl. its alt.); to *run under,* i.e. (spec.) to *sail past:*—run under {1x}. See: BAGD—848b; THAYER—645d.

5296. ὑποτύπωσις {2x} **hupŏtupōsis,** *hoop-ot-oop'-o-sis;* from a compound of 5259 and a der. of 5179; *typification under (after),* i.e. (concr.) a *sketch* (fig.) for imitation:—form {1x}, pattern {1x}.

Hupotuposis, "an outline, sketch," akin to *hupotupoo,* "to delineate," is used metaphorically to denote **(1)** a "pattern," in 1 Ti 1:16; and **(2)** 2 Ti 1:13, "form." See: TDNT—8:246, 1193; BAGD—848c; THAYER—645d.

5297. ὑποφέρω {3x} **hupŏphĕrō,** *hoop-of-er'-o;* from 5259 and 5342; to *bear from underneath,* i.e. (fig.) to *undergo* hardship:—bear {1x}, endure {2x}.

Hupophero, lit., "to bear up under," is rendered by **(1)** "bear," as 1 Cor 10:13; and **(2)** of "enduring" **(2a)** persecutions, 2 Ti 3; **(2b)** grief, 1 Pet 2:19. See: BAGD—848c; THAYER—645d.

5298. ὑποχωρέω {2x} **hupŏchōrĕō**, *hoop-okh-o-reh'-o;* from *5259* and *5562;* to *vacate down*, i.e. *retire*, i.e. *retire* quietly suggesting privacy:—go aside {1x}, withdraw self + 2258 {1x}.

Hupochoreo, "to go back, retire" (*hupo*, "under," suggesting privacy), **(1)** "withdraw" in Lk 5:16; and **(2)** "went aside" in Lk 9:10. See: BAGD—848c; THAYER—646a.

5299. ὑπωπιάζω {2x} **hupōpiazō**, *hoop-o-pee-ad'-zo;* from a compound of *5259* and a der. of *3700;* to hit *under* the *eye* (*buffet* or *disable* an antagonist as a pugilist), i.e. (fig.) to *tease* or *annoy* (into compliance), *subdue* (one's passions):—keep under {1x}, weary {1x}.

Hupopiazo, lit., "to strike under the eye" (from *hupopion*, "the part of the face below the eye"; *hupo*, "under," *ops*, "an eye"), hence, to beat the face black and blue (to give a black eye), is used metaphorically, and translated **(1)** "keep under" in 1 Cor 9:27, of Paul's suppressive treatment of his body, in order to keep himself spiritually fit; and **(2)** in Lk 18:5, of the persistent widow, "weary." See: TDNT—8:590, 1239; BAGD—848d; THAYER—646a.

5300. ὗς {1x} **hus**, *hoos;* appar. a primary word; a *hog* ("*swine*"):—sow {1x}. See: BAGD—848d; THAYER—646a.

5301. ὕσσωπος {2x} **hussōpŏs**, *hoos'-so-pos;* of for. or. [231]; "*hyssop*":—hyssop {2x}. See: BAGD—848d; THAYER—646a.

5302. ὑστερέω {16x} **hustĕrĕō**, *hoos-ter-eh'-o;* from *5306;* to *be later,* i.e. (by impl.) to *be inferior;* gen. to *fall short* (be *deficient*):—lack {3x}, be behind {2x}, want {2x}, come short {1x}, be in want {1x}, fail {1x}, come behind {1x}, be destitute {1x}, misc. {4x} = suffer need, be the worse. See: TDNT—8:592, 1240; BAGD—849a; THAYER—646b.

5303. ὑστέρημα {9x} **hustĕrēma**, *hoos-ter'-ay-mah;* from *5302;* a *deficit;* spec. *poverty:*—which is lacking {3x}, want {3x}, which is behind {1x}, lack {1x}, penury {1x}.

Husterema denotes **(1)** "that which is lacking, deficiency, shortcoming" (akin to *hustereo*, "to be behind, in want"), 1 Cor 16:17; Phil 2:30; Col 1:24, "that which is behind" (of the afflictions of Christ)], where the reference is not to the vicarious sufferings of Christ but to those which He endured previously, and those which must be endured by His faithful servants; **(2)** 1 Th

3:10, where "that which is lacking" means that which Paul had not been able to impart to them, owing to the interruption of his spiritual instruction among them; **(3)** "need, want, poverty," Lk 21:4, "penury"; 2 Cor 8:14 (twice) "want;" 2 Cor 9:12, "want"; 11:9, "that which was lacking (to me)." See: TDNT—8:592, 1240; BAGD—849b; THAYER—646c.

5304. ὑστέρησις {2x} **hustĕrēsis**, *hoos-ter'-ay-sis* from *5302;* a *falling short,* i.e. (spec.) *penury:*—want {2x}. Cf. Mk 12:14 and Phil 4:11. See: TDNT—8:592, 1240; BAGD—849c; THAYER—646c.

5305. ὕστερον {12x} **hustĕrŏn**, *hoos'-ter-on;* neut. of *5306* as adv.; *more lately,* i.e. *eventually:*—afterward {8x}, last {2x}, at the last {1x}, last of all {1x}.

Husterion, "afterwards," with the suggestion of at length, is found in Mt 4:2; 21:29, 32, 37, "last of all"); 22:27; 25:11; 26:60, "at the last", Mk 16:14; Lk 4:2; 20:32, "last", Jn 13:36; Heb 12:11. See: TDNT—8:592, 1240; BAGD—849c; THAYER—646c.

5306. ὕστερος {1x} **hustĕrŏs**, *hoos'-ter-os;* comparative from *5259* (in the sense of *behind*); *later:*—latter {1x}. See: TDNT—8:592, 1240; BAGD—849c; THAYER—646c.

5307. ὑφαντός {1x} **huphantŏs**, *hoo-fan-tos';* from ὑφαίνω **huphainō**, to *weave; woven,* i.e. (perh.) *knitted:*—woven {1x}. See: BAGD—849d; THAYER—646d.

5308. ὑψηλός {11x} **hupsēlŏs**, *hoop-say-los';* from *5311; lofty* (in place or character):—high {8x}, higher {1x}, highly esteemed {1x}, high things {1x}.

Hupselos, "high, lofty," is used **(1)** naturally, **(1a)** of mountains, Mt 4:8; 17:1; Mk 9:2; Rev 21:10; **(1b)** of a wall, Rev 21:12; **(2)** figuratively, **(2a)** of the arm of God, Acts 13:17; **(2b)** of heaven, "on high," plural, lit., "in high (places)," Heb 1:3; **(3)** metaphorically, **(3a)** Lk 16:15, "highly esteemed"; **(3b)** Rom 12:16, "high things." See: BAGD—849d; THAYER—646d.

5309. ὑψηλοφρονέω {2x} **hupsēlŏphrŏnĕō**, *hoop-say-lo-fron-eh'-o;* from a compound of *5308* and *5424;* to be *lofty in mind,* i.e. *arrogant:*—be highminded {2x}. See: BAGD—850a; THAYER—646d.

5310. ὕψιστος {13x} **hupsistŏs**, *hoop'-sis-tos;* superl. from the base of *5311; highest,* i.e. (masc. sing.) the *Supreme* (God), or (neut. plur.) the *heavens:*—most high {5x}, highest {8x}.

Hupistos is used in the plural in the phrase

(1) "in the highest," i.e., in the "highest" regions, the abode of God, Mt 21:9; Mk 11:10; Lk omits the article, Lk 2:14; 19:38; **(2)** for its use as a title of God, **(2a)** "most high," is a superlative degree, the positive not being in use; **(2b)** it is used of God in Lk 1:32, 35, 76; 6:35, "the highest", see also Mk 5:7; Lk 8:28; Acts 7:48; 16:17; Heb 7:1. See: TDNT—8:614, 1241; BAGD—850b; THAYER—647a.

5311. ὕψος {6x} **hupsŏs,** *hoop'-sos;* from a der. of *5228; elevation,* i.e. (abstr.) *altitude,* (spec.) the *sky,* or (fig.) *dignity:*—on high {2x}, height {2x}, high {1x}, be exalted {1x}.

Hupsos, signifying "height," is rendered **(1)** in Jas 1:9, "in that he is exalted"; **(2)** "on high," Lk 1:78; 24:49; Eph 4:8; **(3)** "height" in Eph 3:18; Rev 21:16. See: TDNT—8:602, 1241; BAGD—850c; THAYER—647a.

5312. ὑψόω {20x} **hupsŏō,** *hoop-sŏ'-o;* from *5311;* to *elevate* (lit. or fig.):—exalt {14x}, lift up {6x}.

Hupsoo, "to lift up" (akin to *hupsos,* "height"), is used **(1)** literally **(1a)** of the "lifting" up of Christ in His crucifixion, Jn 3:14; 8:28; 12:32, 34; **(1b)** illustratively, of the serpent of brass, Jn 3:14; **(2)** figuratively, "to exalt" **(2a)** of spiritual privileges bestowed on a city, Mt 11:23; Lk 10:15; **(2b)** of "raising" to dignity and happiness, Lk 1:52; Acts 13:17; **(2c)** of haughty self-exaltation, and, contrastingly, of being "raised" to honor, as a result of self-humbling, Mt 23:12; Lk 14:11; 18:14; **(2d)** of spiritual "uplifting" and revival, Jas 4:10; 1 Pet 5:6; **(2e)** of bringing into the blessings of salvation through the gospel, 2 Cor 11:7; **(3)** with a combination of the literal and metaphorical, of the "exaltation" of Christ by God the Father, Acts 2:33; 5:31. See: TDNT—8:606, 1241; BAGD—850d; THAYER—647a.

5313. ὕψωμα {2x} **hupsōma,** *hoop'-so-mah;* from *5312;* an *elevated* place or thing, i.e. (abstr.) *altitude,* or (by impl.) a *barrier* (fig.):—height {1x}, high thing {1x}.

Hupsoma is used **(1)** of "a height," as a mountain or anything definitely termed a "height," Rom 8:39 (metaphorically); **(2)** of "a high thing" lifted up as a barrier or in antagonistic exaltation, 2 Cor 10:5. See: TDNT—8:613, 1241; BAGD—851c; THAYER—647c.

Φ

5314. φάγος {2x} **phagŏs,** *fag'-os;* from *5315;* a *glutton:*—gluttonous {2x}. Cf. Mt 11:19; Lk 7:34. See: BAGD—851a; THAYER—647b.

5315. φάγω {97x} **phagō,** *fag'-o;* a primary verb (used as an alt. of *2068* in certain tenses); to *eat* (lit. or fig.):—eat {94x}, meat {3x}. See: BAGD—851a; 312b; THAYER—647b.

φαιλόνης **phailŏnēs,** *fahee-lohn'-ace;* an alt. spelling of *5341* which see; found only in 2 Ti 4:13.

5316. φαίνω {31x} **phainō,** *fah'-ee-no;* prol. for the base of *5457;* to *lighten* (*shine*), i.e. *show* (tran. or intr., lit. or fig.):— appear {17x}, seem {1x}, be seen {2x}, shine {10x}, × think {1x}.

(1) *Phaino* refers to the actual external appearance, generally correct, but possibly deceptive. **(2)** It signifies, in the active voice, "to shine"; in the passive, "to be brought forth into light, to become evident, to appear." **(3)** In Rom 7:13, concerning sin, "appear." **(4)** It is used of the "appearance" of Christ to the disciples, Mk 16:9; **(5)** of His future "appearing" in glory as the Son of Man, spoken of as a sign to the world, Mt 24:30; there the genitive is subjective, the sign being the "appearing" of Christ Himself; **(6)** of Christ as the light, Jn 1:5; **(7)** of John the Baptist, Jn 5:35; **(8)** of the "appearing" of an angel of the Lord, either **(8a)** visibly, Mt 1:20, or **(8b)** in a dream, Mt 2:13; **(9)** of a star, Mt 2:7; **(10)** of men who make an outward show, Matt. 6:5; 6:18; 23:27–28; 2 Cor 13:7; **(11)** of tares, Mt 13:26; **(12)** of a vapor, Jas 4:14; **(13)** of things physical in general, Heb 11:3; **(14)** used impersonally **(14a)** in Mt 9:33, "it was never so seen"; **(14b)** also of what appears to the mind, and so in the sense of to think, Mk 14:64, or **(14c)** to seem, Lk 24:11. Syn.: **(A)** *Hegeomai* (*2233*) and **(B)** *nomizo* (*3543*) denote a belief resting not on one's inner feeling or sentiment, but on the due consideration of external grounds, and the weighing and comparing of facts. **(C)** *Dokeo* (*1380*) and **(D)** *oiomai* (*3633*) on the other hand, describe a subjective judgment growing out of inclination or a view of facts in their relation to us. *Hegeomai* (*2233*) denotes a more deliberate and careful judgment than *nomizo* (*3543*); *oiomai* (*3633*) is a subjective judgment which has feeling rather than thought (*dokeo*—*1380*) for its ground. See: TDNT—9:1, 1244; BAGD—851b; THAYER—647d.

5317. Φάλεκ {1x} **Phalĕk,** *fal'-ek;* of Heb. or. [6389]; *Phalek* (i.e. *Peleg*), a patriarch:—Phalec {1x}. See: BAGD—852b; THAYER—648b.

5318. φανερός {21x} **phanĕrŏs,** *fan-er-os';* from *5316; shining,* i.e. *apparent* (lit. or fig.); neut. (as adv.) *publicly, extern.:*— manifest {9x}, openly + *1722* + *3588* {3x}, known {3x}, abroad + *1519* {2x}, spread abroad {1x}, outwardly + *1722* + *3588* {1x}, outward {1x}, appear {1x}.

Phaneros, "open to sight, visible, manifest"

(the root *phan*, signifying "shining"), is translated **(1)** "manifest" in Lk 8:17 first part; Acts 4:16; Rom 1:19; 1 Cor. 3:13; 11:19; 14:25; Gal 5:19; Phil 1:13; 1 Jn 3:10; **(2)** "known" in Mt 12:26; Mk 3:12; Acts 7:13; **(3)** "appear" in 1 Ti 4:15; **(4)** "openly" in Mt 6:4, 6, 18; **(5)** "abroad" in Mk 4:22; Lk 8:17 second part; **(6)** "spread abroad" in Mk 6:14; **(7)** "outwardly" in Rom 2:28 first part; and **(8)** "outward" in Rom 2:28 second part. See: TDNT—9:2, 1244; BAGD—852b; THAYER—648b.

5319. **φανερόω** {49x} **phanĕrŏō**, *fan-er-ŏ'-o;* from *5318;* to *render apparent* (lit. or fig.):—make manifest {19x}, appear {12x}, manifest {9x}, show {3x}, be manifest {2x}, show (one's) self {2x}, manifestly declare {1x}, manifest forth {1x}.

(1) *Phaneroo* means manifest, as opp. to what is concealed and invisible. **(2)** It signifies, in the active voice, "to manifest"; in the passive voice, "to be manifested." **(3)** It is translated "to appear" in 2 Cor 7:12; Col 3:4; Heb 9:26; 1 Pet 5:4; 1 Jn 2:28; 3:2; Rev 3:18. **(4)** To be manifested, in the scriptural sense of the word, is more than to "appear." **(4a)** A person may "appear" in a false guise or without a disclosure of what he truly is; **(4b)** to be manifested is to be revealed in one's true character; **(4c)** this is especially the meaning of *phaneroo*, see, e.g., Jn 3:21; 1 Cor 4:5; 2 Cor 5:10–11; Eph 5:13. Syn.: **(A)** *Phaneroo* (*5319*) is thought to describe an external manifestation, to the senses, hence open to all, single or isolated. **(B)** *Apokalupto* (*601*) is an internal disclosure, to the thinking believer, and abiding. The *apolalupto* (*601*) or unveiling precedes and produces the *phaneroo* (*5319*) or manifestation; the former looks toward the object revealed, the latter toward the persons to whom the revelation is made. **(C)** *Delos* (*1212*) means what is evident, what is known and understood and points rather to inner perception; whereas *phaneroo* (*5319*) points to outward appearance. See: TDNT—9:3, 1244; BAGD—852d; THAYER—648b.

5320. **φανερῶς** {3x} **phanĕrōs**, *fan-er-oce';* adv. from *5318; plainly*, i.e. *clearly* or *publicly:*—evidently {1x}, openly {2x}.

Phaneros, manifestly, is rendered **(1)** "openly" in Mk 1:45; Jn 7:10; and **(2)** "evidently" in Acts 10:3. See: BAGD—853a; THAYER—649a.

5321. **φανέρωσις** {2x} **phanĕrōsis**, *fan-er'-o-sis;* from *5319; exhibition*, i.e. (fig.) *expression*, (by extens.) a *bestowment:*—manifestation {2x}. Cf. 1 Cor 12:7

and 2 Cor 4:2. See: TDNT—9:6, 1244; BAGD—853b; THAYER—649a.

5322. **φανός** {1x} **phanŏs**, *fan-os';* from *5316;* a *lightener,* i.e. *light; lantern:*—lantern {1x}. See: BAGD—853b; THAYER—649a.

5323. **Φανουήλ** {1x} **Phanŏuēl**, *fan-oo-ale';* of Heb. or. [6439]; *Phanuël* (i.e. *Penuël*), an Isr.:—Phanuel {1x}. See: BAGD—853b; THAYER—649a.

5324. **φαντάζω** {1x} **phantazō**, *fan-tad'-zo;* from a der. of *5316;* to *make apparent* i.e. (pass.) to *appear* (neut. part. as noun, a *spectacle*):—a sight {1x}.

Phantazo, as a verb, means "to make visible" and is used in the present participle as a noun, with the article, translated "(the) sight": "And so terrible was the sight, that Moses said, I exceedingly fear and quake" (Heb 12:21). See: TDNT—9:6, 1244; BAGD—853b; THAYER—649a.

5325. **φαντασία** {1x} **phantasia**, *fan-tas-ee'-ah;* from a der. of *5324;* (prop. abstr.) a (vain) *show* ("fantasy"):—pomp {1x}.

Phantasia, as a philosophic term, denoted an imagination; then, an appearance, an apparition; later, a show, display, pomp (Acts 25:23). See: BAGD—853b; THAYER—649a.

5326. **φάντασμα** {2x} **phantasma**, *fan'-tas-mah;* from *5324;* (prop. concr.) a (mere) *show* ("phantasm"), i.e. *spectre:*—spirit {2x}. Cf. Mt 14:26 and Mk 6:49. See: TDNT—9:6, 1244; BAGD—853c; THAYER—649b.

5327. **φάραγξ** {1x} **pharagx**, *far'-anx;* prop. streng. from the base of *4008* or rather of *4486;* a *gap* or *chasm*, i.e. *ravine* (*winter-torrent*):—valley {1x}. See: BAGD—853c; THAYER—649b.

5328. **Φαραώ** {5x} **Pharaō**, *far-ah-o';* of for. or. [6547]; *Pharaō* (i.e. *Pharoh*), an Eg. king:—Pharaoh {5x}. See: BAGD—853c; THAYER—649b.

5329. **Φαρές** {3x} **Pharĕs**, *far-es';* of Heb. or. [6557]; *Phares* (i.e. *Perets*), an Isr.:—*Phares* {3x}. See: BAGD—853c; THAYER—649b.

5330. **Φαρισαῖος** {100x} **Pharisaiŏs**, *far-is-ah'-yos;* of Heb. or. [comp. 6567]; a *separatist*, i.e. exclusively *relig.*; a *Pharisœan*, i.e. Jewish sectary:—Pharisee {100x}.

Pharisaios comes from an Aramaic word *peras* (found in Dan 5:28) and signifies to separate, owing to a different manner of life from that of the general public. The Pharisees and

Sadducees appear as distinct parties in the latter half of the 2nd cent. B.C., though they represent tendencies traceable much earlier in Jewish history, tendencies which became pronounced after the return from Babylon (537 B.C.). The immediate progenitors of the two parties were, respectively, the Hasidaeans and the Hellenizers; the latter, the antecedents of the Sadducees, aimed at removing Judaism from its narrowness and sharing in the advantages of Greek life and culture. The Hasidaeans, a transcription of the Hebrew *chasidim*, i.e., "pious ones," were a society of men zealous for religion, who acted under the guidance of the scribes, in opposition to the godless hellenizing party; they scrupled to oppose the legitimate high priest even when he was on the Greek side.

Thus the Hellenizers were a political sect, while the Hasidaeans, whose fundamental principle was complete separation from non-Jewish elements, were the strictly legal party among the Jews, and were ultimately the more popular and influential party. In their zeal for the Law they almost deified it and their attitude became merely external, formal, and mechanical. They laid stress, not upon the righteousness of an action, but upon its formal correctness. Consequently their opposition to Christ was inevitable; His manner of life and teaching was essentially a condemnation of theirs; hence His denunciation of them, e.g., Mt 6:2, 5, 16; 15:7 and chapter 23. See: TDNT—9:11, 1246; BAGD—853b; THAYER—649b.

5331. φαρμακεία {3x} **pharmakĕia**, *far-mak-i'-ah*; from *5332; medication* ("pharmacy"), i.e. (by extens.) *magic* (lit. or fig.):—sorcery {2x}, witchcraft {1x}.

Primarily *pharmakeia* signified the use of medicine, drugs, spells; then, poisoning; then, witchcraft (Gal 5:20; Rev 9:21; 18:23). In sorcery the use of drugs, whether simple or potent, was generally accompanied by incantations and appeals to occult powers, with the provision of various charms, amulets, etc., professedly designed to keep the applicant or patient from the attention and power of devils, but actually to impress the applicant with the mysterious resources and powers of the sorcerer. See: BAGD—854a; THAYER—649d.

5332. φαρμακεύς {1x} **pharmakĕus**, *far-mak-yoos'*; from φάρμακον **pharmakŏn**, (a *drug*, i.e. spell-giving *potion*); a *druggist* ("pharmacist") or *poisoner*, i.e. (by extens.) a *magician:*—sorcerer {1x}. See: BAGD—854a; THAYER—649d.

5333. φαρμακός {1x} **pharmakŏs**, *far-mak-os'*; the same as *5332:*—sorcerer {1x}. See: BAGD—854b; THAYER—650a.

5334. φάσις {1x} **phasis**, *fas'-is;* from *5346* (not the same as "phase", which is from *5316*); a *saying*, i.e. *report:*—tidings {1x}.

Phasis denotes "information," especially against fraud or other delinquency, and is rendered "tidings" in Acts 21:31. See: BAGD—854b; THAYER—650a.

5335. φάσκω {4x} **phaskō**, *fas'-ko;* prol. from the same as *5346;* to *assert:*—affirm {1x}, profess {1x}, say {2x}.

Phasko denotes "to allege, to affirm by way of alleging or professing," and is translated **(1)** "saying" in Acts 24:9; Rev 2:2, "say"; **(2)** "affirm" in Acts 25:19; and **(3)** "professing" in Rom 1:22. See: BAGD—854b; THAYER—650a.

5336. φάτνη {4x} **phatnē**, *fat'-nay;* from πατέομαι **patĕŏmai** (to *eat*); a *crib* (for fodder):—manger {3x}, stall {1x}.

Phatne is **(1)** "a manger," Lk 2:7, 12, 16; and also denotes **(2)** "a stall," Lk 13:15. See: TDNT—9:49, 1251; BAGD—854b; THAYER—650a.

5337. φαῦλος {4x} **phaulŏs**, *fŏw'-los;* appar. a primary word; "*foul*" or "*flawy*", i.e. (fig.) *wicked:*—evil {4x}.

(1) This word means slight, ordinary, mean, worthless, of no account and ethically, bad, base, wicked. **(2)** It primarily denotes "slight, trivial, blown about by every wind"; then, "mean, common, bad," in the sense of being worthless, paltry or contemptible, belonging to a low order of things; **(3)** in Jn 5:29, those who have practiced "evil" things (*phaula*) are set in contrast to those who have done good things (*agatha*); **(4)** he who practices "evil" things hates the light, Jn 3:20; **(5)** jealousy and strife are accompanied by "every evil work," Jas 3:16. **(6)** It is also in Titus 2:8 of an evil report. See: BAGD—854c; THAYER—650a.

5338. φέγγος {3x} **phĕggŏs**, *feng'-gos;* prob. akin to the base of *5457* [comp. *5350*]; *brilliancy:*—light {3x}.

Pheggos, "brightness, luster," is used of **(1)** the "light" of the moon, Mt 24:29; Mk 13:24; **(2)** of a lamp, Lk 11:33. Syn.: **(A)** *Phos* (*5457*) is the general term for light: light of a fire. **(B)** *Pheggos* (*5338*) is a more concrete and emphatic term: the bright sunshine, the beam of light. **(C)** *Auge* (*827*) is a still stronger term, suggesting the fiery nature of light; used of shooting, heating rays. See: BAGD—854c; THAYER—650b.

5339. φείδομαι {10x} phĕidŏmai, *fi'-dom-ahee;* of uncert. aff.; to *be chary* of, i.e. (subj.) to *abstain* or (obj.) to *treat leniently:*—forbear {1x}, spare {9x}.

Pheidomai, as a verb, means "to spare" (its usual meaning), "to refrain from doing something," is rendered **(1)** "I forbear" in 2 Cor 12:6; and **(2)** "to spare," i.e., "to forego" the infliction of that evil or retribution which was designed, is **(2a)** used with a negative, in Acts 20:29, Rom 8:32; 11:21 (twice); 2 Cor 13:2; 2 Pet 2:4, 5; **(2b)** positively, in 1 Cor 7:28; 2 Cor 1:3. See: BAGD—854d; THAYER—650b.

5340. φειδομένως {2x} phĕidŏmĕnōs, *fi-dom-en'-oce;* adv. from part. of *5339; abstemiously,* i.e. *stingily:*—sparingly {2x}.

This word occurs in 2 Cor 9:6 twice. See: BAGD—854d; THAYER—650b.

5341. φελόνης {1x} phĕlŏnēs, *fel-on'-ace* or

φαιλόνης phailŏnēs, *fayl-on'-ace;* by transp. for a der. prob. of *5316* (as *showing* outside the other garments); a *mantle* (*surtout*):—cloke {1x}.

This garment is a traveling *cloak,* used for protection against stormy weather, 2 Ti 4:13. See: BAGD—854d; 851b; THAYER—650c.

5342. φέρω {64x} phĕrō, *fer'-o;* a primary verb (for which other and appar. not cognate ones are used in certain tenses only; namely,

οἴω ŏiō, *oy'-o;* and

ἐνέγκω ĕnĕgkō, *en-eng'-ko;* to *"bear"* or *carry* (in a very wide application, lit. and fig. as follows):—bring {34x}, bear {8x}, bring forth {5x}, come {3x}, reach {2x}, endure {2x}, carry {1x}, be {1x}, + let her drive {1x}, be driven {1x}, go on {1x}, lay {1x}, lead {1x}, move {1x}, rushing {1x}, uphold {1x}.

Phero, as a verb, means **(1)** "to bear, carry," and is rendered "being moved" in 2 Pet 1:21, signifying that they were "borne along," or impelled, by the Holy Spirit's power, not acting according to their own wills, or simply expressing their own thoughts, but expressing the mind of God in words provided and ministered by Him. **(2)** It is used also of "bearing or bringing forth fruit": "And other fell on good ground, and did yield fruit that sprang up and increased; and brought forth, some thirty, and some sixty, and some an hundred" (Mk 4:8; cf. Jn 15:5). Syn.: 277, 383, 761, 2795, 2796, 3334, 4525, 4531, 4579, 4787. See: TDNT—9:56, 1252; BAGD—854d; THAYER—650c.

5343. φεύγω {31x} phĕugō, *fyoo'-go;* appar. a primary verb; to *run away* (lit.

or fig.); by impl. to *shun;* by anal. to *vanish:*—escape {3x}, flee {26x}, flee away {2x}.

Pheugo, "to flee from or away" (Eng., "fugitive"), besides its literal significance, is used metaphorically, **(1)** transitively, **(1a)** of "fleeing" fornication, 1 Cor 6:18; **(1b)** idolatry, 1 Cor 10:14; **(1c)** evil doctrine, questionings, disputes of words, envy, strife, railings, evil surmisings, wranglings, and the love of money, 1 Ti 6:11; **(1d)** youthful lusts, 2 Ti 2:22; **(2)** intransitively, of the "flight" **(2a)** of physical matter, Rev 16:20; 20:11; **(2b)** of death, Rev 9:6. **(3)** It is also rendered "escape" in Mt 23:33; Heb 11:34; 12:25. See: BAGD—855d; THAYER—651a.

5344. Φῆλιξ {9x} Phēlix, *fay'-lix;* of Lat. or.; *happy; Phelix* (i.e. *Felix*), a Rom.:—Felix {9x}. See: BAGD—856a; THAYER—651b.

5345. φήμη {2x} phēmē, *fay'-may;* from *5346;* a *saying,* i.e. *rumor* ("fame"):—fame {2x}.

Pheme originally denoted "a divine voice, an oracle"; hence, "a saying or report" (akin to *phemi,* "to say," from a root meaning "to shine, to be clear"; hence, Lat., *fama,* Eng., "fame"), is rendered "fame" in Mt 9:26 and Lk 4:14. See: BAGD—856b; THAYER—651c.

5346. φημί {58x} phēmi, *fay-mee';* prop. the same as the base of *5457* and *5316;* to *show* or *make known* one's thoughts, i.e. *speak* or *say:*—affirm {1x}, say {57x}. See: BAGD—856b; THAYER—651c. comp. *3004.*

5347. Φῆστος {13x} Phēstŏs, *face'-tos;* of Lat. der.; *festal; Phestus* (i.e. *Festus*), a Rom.:—Festus {13x}. See: BAGD—856c; THAYER—651d.

5348. φθάνω {7x} phthanō, *fthan'-o;* appar. a primary verb; to *be beforehand,* i.e. *anticipate* or *precede;* by extens. to *have arrived* at:—already attain {1x}, attain {1x}, come {4x}, prevent {1x}.

Phthano denotes "to anticipate, to come sooner than expected," and is translated **(1)** "come": **(1a)** "is come upon" 1 Th 2:16, of divine wrath; **(1b)** or the kingdom is to "come" in a different manner from what was expected, Mt 12:28; Lk 11:20; **(1c)** "are come" in 2 Cor 10:14; **(2)** "already attain" in Phil 3:16; **(3)** "attain" in Rom 9:31; and **(4)** "prevent" in 1 Th 415. See: TDNT—9:88, 1258; BAGD—856d; THAYER—652a.

5349. φθαρτός {6x} phthartŏs, *fthar-tos';* from *5351; decayed,* i.e. (by impl.) *perishable:*—corruptible {6x}.

Phthartos, "corruptible", is used **(1)** of man as being mortal, liable to decay (in contrast to

God), Rom 1:23; **(2)** of man's body as death-doomed, 1 Cor 15:53–54; **(3)** of a crown of reward at the Greek games, 1 Cor 9:25; **(4)** of silver and gold, as specimens or "corruptible" things, 1 Pet 1:18; **(5)** of natural seed, 1 Pet 1:23. See: TDNT—9:93, 1259; BAGD—857a; THAYER—652b.

5350. φθέγγομαι {3x} **phthĕggŏmai,** *ftheng'-gom-ahee;* prob. akin to *5338* and thus to *5346;* to *utter* a clear sound, i.e. (gen.) to *proclaim:*—speak {3x}.

Phtheggomai, "to utter a clear, authoritative sound or voice with an intention of swaying the hearer," is translated "to speak" in Acts 4:18; 2 Pet 2:16, 18. See: BAGD—857a; THAYER—652b.

5351. φθείρω {8x} **phthĕirō,** *fthi'-ro;* probably strengthened from φθίω **phthiō** (to *pine* or *waste*); prop. to *shrivel,* or *wither,* i.e. to *spoil* (by any process) or (gen.) to *ruin* (espec. fig., by mor. influences, to *deprave*):—corrupt {4x}, corrupt (one's) self {1x}, be corrupt {1x}, defile {1x}, destroy {1x}.

Phtheiro signifies **(1)** "to destroy by means of corrupting," and so "bringing into a worse state"; **(1a)** with this significance it is used of the effect of evil company upon the manners of believers, and so of the effect of association with those who deny the truth and hold false doctrine, 1 Cor 15:33; **(1b)** in 2 Cor 7:2, of the effects of dishonorable dealing by bringing people to want (a charge made against the apostle); **(1c)** in 2 Cor 11:3, of the effects upon the minds (or thoughts) of believers by "corrupting" them "from the simplicity and the purity that is toward Christ"; **(1d)** in Eph 4:22, intransitively, of the old nature in waxing "corrupt," morally decaying, on the way to final ruin", "after the lusts of deceit"; **(1e)** in Rev 19:2, metaphorically, of the Babylonish harlot, in "corrupting" the inhabitants of the earth by her false religion. **(2)** With the significance of destroying, it is used **(2a)** of marring a local church **(2a1)** by leading it away from that condition of holiness of life and purity of doctrine in which it should abide, 1 Cor 3:17, "defile", and **(2a2)** of God's retributive destruction of the offender who is guilty of this sin (id.); **(2b)** of the effects of the work of false and abominable teachers upon themselves, Jude 10, "corrupt themselves." See: TDNT—9:93, 1259; BAGD—857b; THAYER—652b.

5352. φθινοπωρινός {1x} **phthinŏpōrinŏs,** *fthin-op-o-ree-nos';* from der. of φθίνω **phthinō** (to *wane;* akin to the base of *5351*) and *3703* (mean. *late autumn*); *autumnal* (as *stripped* of leaves):—whose fruit withereth {1x}.

Phthinoporinos, "autumnal," in Jude 12, "autumn trees," bearing no "fruit" when "fruit" should be expected: "These are spots in your feasts of charity, when they feast with you, feeding themselves without fear: clouds they are without water, carried about of winds; trees whose fruit withereth, without fruit, twice dead, plucked up by the roots." Syn.: 175, 2590, 2592, 2593, 3703. See: BAGD—857c; THAYER—652c.

5353. φθόγγος {2x} **phthŏggŏs,** *fthong'-gos;* from *5350; utterance,* i.e. a *musical* note (vocal or instrumental):—sound {2x}.

Phthoggos, "to utter a voice," occurs in Rom 10:18; 1 Cor 14:7. See: BAGD—857c; THAYER—652d.

5354. φθονέω {1x} **phthŏnĕō,** *fthon-eh'-o;* from *5355;* to *be jealous* of:—envy {1x}. See: BAGD—857c; THAYER—652d.

5355. φθόνος {9x} **phthŏnŏs,** *fthon'-os;* prob. akin to the base of *5351; illwill* (as *detraction*), i.e. *jealousy* (*spite*):—envy {8x}, envying {1x}.

Envy is the feeling of displeasure produced by witnessing or hearing of the advantage or prosperity of others; an evil sense always attaches to this word (Mt. 27:18; Mk 15:10; Rom 1:29; Gal 5:21; Phil 1:15; 1 Ti 6:4; Titus 3:3; 1 Pet 2:1). See: BAGD—857d; THAYER—652d.

5356. φθορά {9x} **phthŏra,** *fthor-ah';* from *5351; decay,* i.e. *ruin* (spontaneous or inflicted, lit. or fig.):—corruption {7x}, destroy {1x}, perish + *1519* {1x}.

Phthora, connected with *phtheiro,* signifies "a bringing or being brought into an inferior or worse condition, a destruction or corruption." It is used **(1)** physically, **(1a)** of the condition of creation, as under bondage, Rom 8:21; **(1b)** of the effect of the withdrawal of life, and so of the condition of the human body in burial, 1 Cor 15:42; **(1c)** by metonymy, of anything which is liable to "corruption," 1 Cor 15:50; **(1d)** of the physical effects of merely gratifying the natural desires and ministering to one's own needs or lusts, Gal 6:8, to the flesh in contrast to the Spirit, "corruption" being antithetic to "eternal life"; **(1e)** of that which is naturally short-lived and transient, Col 2:22, "perish"; **(2)** of the death and decay of beasts, 2 Pet 2:12, "destroyed" (first part of verse; lit., "unto . . . destruction"); **(3)** ethically, with a moral significance, **(3a)** of the effect of lusts, 2 Pet 1:4; **(3b)** of the effect upon themselves of the work of false and immoral teachers, 2 Pet 2:12, "corruption," and v. 19. See: TDNT—9:93, 1259; BAGD—858a; THAYER—652d.

5357. **φιάλη** {12x} **phialē**, *fee-al'-ay;* of uncert. aff.; a broad shallow *cup* ("phial"):—vial {12x}.

Phiale denotes **(1)** "a vial" in Rev 5:8; 15:7; 16:1–4, 8, 10, 12, 17; 17:1; 21:9; **(2)** the word is suggestive of rapidity in the emptying of the contents. **(3)** While the seals (ch. 6) give a general view of the events of the last "week" or *"hebdomad,"* in the vision given to Daniel, Dan 9:23–27, **(3a)** the "trumpets" refer to the judgments which, in a more or less extended period, are destined to fall especially, though not only, upon apostate Christendom and apostate Jews. **(3b)** The emptying of the "vials" betokens the final series of judgments in which this exercise of the wrath of God is "filled up" (Rev 15:1). **(3c)** These are introduced by the 7th trumpet. **(3d)** See Rev 11:15 and the successive order in v. 18, "the nations were wroth, and Thy wrath came"; see also 6:17; 14:19, 20; 19:11–12. See: BAGD—858b; THAYER—653a.

5358. **φιλάγαθος** {1x} **philagathŏs**, *fil-ag'-ath-os;* from *5384* and *18; fond to good,* i.e. a *promoter of virtue:*—lover of good men {1x}. See: TDNT—1:18, 3; BAGD—858b; THAYER—653a.

5359. **Φιλαδέλφεια** {2x} **Philadĕlphĕia**, *fil-ad-el'-fee-ah;* from Φι-λάδελφος **Philadĕlphŏs** (the same as *5361*), a king of Pergamos; *Philadelphia,* a place in Asia Minor:—Philadelphia {2x}. See: TDNT—1:144,*; BAGD—858b; THAYER—653a.

5360. **φιλαδελφία** {6x} **philadĕlphia**, *fil-ad-el-fee'-ah;* from *5361; fraternal affection:*—brotherly love {3x}, brotherly kindness {2x}, love of the brethren {1x}.

Philadelphia is translated **(1)** "brotherly love" in Rom 12:10; 1 Th 4:9; Heb 13:1; **(2)** "love of the brethren," 1 Pet 1:22; and **(3)** "brother kindness" in 2 Pet 1:7 twice. See: TDNT—1:144, 22; BAGD—858c; THAYER—653b.

5361. **φιλάδελφος** {1x} **philadĕlphŏs**, *fil-ad'-el-fos;* from *5384* and *80; fond of brethren,* i.e. *fraternal:*—love as brethren {1x}. See: TDNT—1:144, 22; BAGD—858c; THAYER—653b.

5362. **φίλανδρος** {1x} **philandrŏs**, *fil'-an-dros;* from *5384* and *435; fond of man,* i.e. *affectionate* as a wife:—love their husbands {1x}. See: BAGD—858c; THAYER—653b.

5363. **φιλανθρωπία** {2x} **philanthrōpia**, *fil-an-thro-pee'-ah;* from the same as *5364; fondness of mankind,* i.e. *benevolence* ("philanthropy"):—kindness {1x}, love toward man {1x}.

Philanthropia (from *philos* "loving," *an-*

thropos, "man", Eng., "philanthropy"), denotes **(1)** "kindness," and is so translated in Acts 28:2, of that which was shown by the inhabitants of Melita to the shipwrecked voyagers; **(2)** in Titus 3:4, of the "kindness" of God, translated "(His) love toward man." See: TDNT—9:107, 1261; BAGD—858d; THAYER—653b.

5364. **φιλανθρώπως** {1x} **philanthrōpōs**, *fil-an-thro'-poce;* adv. from a compound of *5384* and *444; fondly to man* ("philanthropically"), i.e. *humanely:*—courteously {1x}. See: TDNT—9:107, 1261; BAGD—858d; THAYER—653b.

5365. **φιλαργυρία** {1x} **philarguria**, *fil-ar-goo-ree'-ah;* from *5366; avarice:*—love of money {1x}.

Syn.: The main distinction between *pleonexia* (*4124*) and *philarguria* (*5365*) is being that between "covetousness" and avarice, the former having a much wider and deeper sense, being "the genus of which *philarguria* is the species." The "covetous" man is often cruel as well as grasping, while the avaricious man is simply miserly and stinting. See: BAGD—859a; THAYER—653b.

5366. **φιλάργυρος** {2x} **philargurŏs**, *fil-ar'-goo-ros;* from *5384* and *696; fond of silver (money),* i.e. *avaricious:*—covetous {2x}.

Philarguros, lit., "money-loving," is rendered "covetous" in Lk 16:14 and 2 Ti 3:2. See: BAGD—859a; THAYER—653b.

5367. **φίλαυτος** {1x} **philautŏs**, *fil'-ŏw-tos;* from *5384* and *846; fond of self,* i.e. *selfish:*—lover of (one's) own self {1x}. See: BAGD—859a; THAYER—653b.

5368. **φιλέω** {25x} **philĕō**, *fil-eh'-o;* from *5384; to be a friend to (fond of* [an indiv. or an obj.]), i.e. *have affection* for (denoting *personal* attachment, as a matter of sentiment or feeling; while *25* is wider, embracing espec. the judgment and the *deliberate* assent of the will as a matter of principle, duty and propriety: the two thus stand related very much as *2309* and *1014,* or as *2372* and *3563* respectively; the former being chiefly of the *heart* and the latter of the *head;* spec. to *kiss* (as a mark of tenderness):—kiss {2x}, love {23x}.

(1) *Phileo* is never used in a command to men to "love" God; **(1a)** it is, however, used as a warning in 1 Cor 16:22; **(1b)** *agapao* is used instead, e.g., Mt 22:37; Lk 10:27; Rom 8:28; 1 Cor 8:3; 1 Pet 1:8; 1 Jn 4:21. **(1c)** The distinction between the two verbs finds a conspicuous instance in the narrative of Jn 21:15–17. **(1d)** The context itself indicates that *agapao* in the first two questions suggests the "love" that

values and esteems (cf. Rev 12:11). It is an unselfish "love," ready to serve. (1e) The use of *phileo* in Peter's answers and the Lord's third question conveys the thought of cherishing the Object above all else, of manifesting an affection characterized by constancy, from the motive of the highest veneration. (2) Again, to "love" (*phileo*) life, from an undue desire to preserve it, forgetful of the real object of living, meets with the Lord's reproof, Jn 12:25.

(3) On the contrary, to "love" life (*agapao*) as used in 1 Pet 3:10 is to consult the true interests of living. Here the word *phileo* would be quite inappropriate, is to be distinguished from *agapao* in this, that *phileo* more nearly represents "tender affection." (4) The two words are used for the "love" of the Father (4a) for the Son, Jn 3:35, and (4b) Jn 5:20, for the believer; (4c) Jn 14:21 and 16:27, both, of Christ's "love" for a certain disciple, 13:23, and 20:2. (5) Yet the distinction between the two verbs remains, and they are never used indiscriminately in the same passage; if each is used with reference to the same objects, as just mentioned, each word retains its distinctive and essential character. Syn.: See 25 for discussion. See: TDNT—9:114, 1262; BAGD—859b; THAYER—653c.

5369. φιλήδονος {1x} **philēdŏnŏs**, *fil-ay'-don-os;* from *5384* and *2237;* *fond of pleasure*, i.e. *voluptuous:*—lover of pleasure {1x}. See: TDNT—2:909, 303; BAGD—859c; THAYER—654a.

5370. φίλημα {7x} **philēma**, *fil'-ay-mah;* from *5368;* a *kiss:*—kiss {7x}.

(1) *Philema*, "a kiss", Lk 7:45; 22:48, (1a) was a token of Christian brotherhood, whether by way of welcome or farewell, (1a1) "a holy kiss," Rom 16:16; 1 Cor 16:20; 2 Cor 13:12; 1 Th 5:26, "holy" (*hagios*), as free from anything inconsistent with their calling as saints (*hagioi*); (1b) "a kiss of charity," 1 Pet 5:14. There was to be an absence of formality and hypocrisy, a freedom from prejudice arising from social distinctions, from discrimination against the poor, from partiality toward the well-to-do. (1c) In the churches masters and servants would thus salute one another without any attitude of condescension on the one part or disrespect on the other. (1d) The "kiss" took place thus between persons of the same sex. See: TDNT—9:114, 1262; BAGD—859c; THAYER—654a.

5371. Φιλήμων {2x} **Philēmōn**, *fil-ay'-mone;* from *5368; friendly; Philemon,* a Chr.:—Philemon {2x}. See: BAGD—859d; THAYER—654a.

5372. Φιλητός {1x} **Philētŏs**, *fil-ay-tos';* from *5368; amiable; Philetus,* an opposer of Christianity:—Philetus {1x}. See: BAGD—859d; THAYER—654a.

5373. φιλία {1x} **philia**, *fil-ee'-ah;* from *5384; fondness:*—friendship {1x}.

Philia, akin to *philos*, "a friend", is rendered in Jas 4:4, "the friendship (of the world)." It involves "the idea of loving as well as being loved." See: TDNT—9:146, 1262; BAGD—859d; THAYER—654a.

5374. Φιλιππήσιος {2x} **Philippēsiŏs**, *fil-ip-pay'-see-os;* from *5375;* a *Philippesian* (*Philippian*), i.e. native of Philippi:—Philippian {2x}. See: BAGD—859d; THAYER—654b.

5375. Φίλιπποι {6x} **Philippŏi**, *fil'-ip-poy;* plur. of *5376; Philippi,* a place in Macedonia:—Philippi {6x}. See: BAGD—860a; THAYER—654b.

5376. Φίλιππος {38x} **Philippŏs**, *fil'-ip-pos;* from *5384* and *2462; fond of horses; Philippus,* the name of four Isr.:—Philip (the apostle) {16x}, Philip (the evangelist) {16x}, Philip (Herod) {3x}, Philippi (an adjunct of Caesarea) {2x}, Philip (the tetrarch) {1x}. See: BAGD—860a; THAYER—654b.

5377. φιλόθεος {1x} **philŏthĕŏs**, *fil-oth'-eh-os;* from *5384* and *2316; fond of God,* i.e. *pious:*—lover of God {1x}. See: BAGD—860c; THAYER—654c.

5378. Φιλόλογος {1x} **Philŏlŏgŏs**, *fil-ol'-og-os;* from *5384* and *3056; fond of words,* i.e. *talkative* (*argumentative, learned, "philological"); Philologus,* a Chr.:—Philologus {1x}. See: BAGD—860c; THAYER—654c.

5379. φιλονεικία {1x} **philŏnĕikia**, *fil-on-i-kee'-ah;* lit. to love strife, from *5380; quarrelsomeness,* i.e. a *dispute:*—strife {1x}.

Philoneikia, lit., "love of strife" (*phileo*, "to love," *neikos*, "strife"), signifies "eagerness to contend"; hence, a "contention," said of the disciples, Lk 22:24. See: BAGD—860c; THAYER—654c.

5380. φιλόνεικος {1x} **philŏnĕikŏs**, *fil-on'-i-kos;* from *5384* and νεῖκος *nĕikŏs* (a *quarrel;* prob. akin to *3534*); *fond of strife,* i.e. *disputatious:*—contentious {1x}. See: BAGD—860d; THAYER—654d.

5381. φιλονεξία {2x} **philŏnĕxia**, *fil-on-ex-ee'-ah;* from *5382; hospitableness:*—entertain strangers {1x}, hospitality {1x}.

Greek

Philonexia, "love of strangers" (*philos,* "loving," *xenos,* "a stranger"), is used in Rom 12:13; Heb 13:2, lit. "be not forgetful of hospitality. See: TDNT—5:1,*; BAGD—860d; THAYER—654d.

5382. φιλόξενος {3x} **philŏxĕnŏs,** *fil-ox'-en-os;* from 5384 and 3581; *fond of guests,* i.e. *hospitable:*—given to hospitality {1x}, lover of hospitality {1x}, use hospitality {1x}.

Plioxenos, "hospitable," occurs in **(1)** 1 Ti 3:2, "given to hospitality"; **(2)** Titus 1:8, "lover of hospitality"; and **(3)** 1 Pet 4:9, "use hospitality." See: TDNT—5:1, 661; BAGD—860d; THAYER—654d.

5383. φιλοπρωτεύω {1x} **philŏprōtĕuō,** *fil-op-rote-yoo'-o;* from a compound of 5384 and 4413; *to be fond of being first,* i.e. *ambitious* of distinction:—love to have the pre-eminence {1x}. See: BAGD—860d; THAYER—654d.

5384. φίλος {29x} **philŏs,** *fee'-los;* prop. *dear,* i.e. a *friend;* act. *fond,* i.e. *friendly* (still as a noun, an *associate, neighbor,* etc.):—friend {29x}.

Philos, primarily an adjective, denoting "loved, dear, or friendly," became used as a noun, **(1)** masculine, **(1a)** Mt 11:19; **(1b)** fourteen times in Lk (once feminine, 15:9); **(1c)** six in John; **(1d)** three in Acts; **(1e)** two in James, **(1e1)** 2:23, "the friend of God"; **(1e2)** 4:4, "a friend of the world"; **(1f)** 3 Jn 14 (twice); **(2)** feminine, Lk 15:9, "her friends." See: TDNT—9:146, 1262; BAGD—861a; THAYER—654d.

5385. φιλοσοφία {1x} **philŏsŏphia,** *fil-os-of-ee'-ah;* from 5386; *"philosophy",* i.e. (spec.) Jewish *sophistry:*—philosophy {1x}.

Used once in the NT of the theology, or rather theosophy, of certain Jewish Christian ascetics, which busied itself with refined and speculative enquiries into the nature and classes of angels, into the ritual of the Mosaic law and the regulations of Jewish tradition respecting practical life (Col 2:8). See: TDNT—9:172, 1269; BAGD—861b; THAYER—655a.

5386. φιλόσοφος {1x} **philŏsŏphŏs,** *fil-os'-of-os;* from 5384 and 4680; *fond of wise* things, i.e. a *"philosopher":*—philosopher {1x}.

This word denotes a philosopher, one given to the pursuit of wisdom or learning and in a narrower sense, one who investigates and discusses the cause of things and the highest good (Acts 17:18). See: TDNT—9:172, 1269; BAGD—861b; THAYER—655a.

5387. φιλόστοργος {1x} **philŏstŏrgŏs,** *fil-os'-tor-gos;* from 5384 and στοργή **stŏrgē** (*cherishing* one's kindred, espec. parents or children); *fond of* natural *relatives,* i.e. *fraternal* toward fellow Chr.:—kindly affectioned {1x}. See: BAGD—861c; THAYER—655b.

5388. φιλότεκνος {1x} **philŏtĕknŏs,** *fil-ot'-ek-nos;* from 5384 and 5043; *fond of* one's *children,* i.e. *maternal:*—love their children {1x}. See: BAGD—861c; THAYER—655b.

5389. φιλοτιμέομαι {3x} **philŏtimĕŏmai,** *fil-ot-im-eh'-om-ahee;* mid. voice from a compound of 5384 and 5092; *to* be *fond of honor,* i.e. *emulous* (*eager* or *earnest* to do something):—labour {1x}, strive {1x}, study {1x}.

Literally, this word means to be fond of honor, and so, actuated by this motive, to strive to bring something to pass; hence, to be ambitious, to make it one's aim: **(1)** Rom 15:20, of Paul's striving in gospel pioneering; **(2)** 2 Cor 5:9, of the labor of believers to be well-pleasing unto the Lord; and **(3)** in 1 Th 4:11, of the studying of believers to be quiet, do their own business and work with their own hands. See: BAGD—861c; THAYER—655b.

5390. φιλοφρόνως {1x} **philŏphrŏnōs,** *fil-of-ron'-oce;* adv. from 5391; *with friendliness of mind,* i.e. *kindly:*—courteously {1x}.

Philophronos, lit., "friendly," or, more fully, "with friendly thoughtfulness" (*philos,* "friend," *phren,* "the mind"), is found in Acts 28:7, of the hospitality showed by Publius to Paul and his fellow-shipwrecked travelers. See: BAGD—861d; THAYER—655b.

5391. φιλόφρων {1x} **philŏphrōn,** *fil-of'-rone;* from 5384 and 5424; *friendly of mind,* i.e. *kind:*—courteous {1x}. See: BAGD—861d; THAYER—655b.

5392. φιμόω {8x} **phimŏō,** *fee-mŏ'-o;* from φιμός **phimŏs,** (a *muzzle*); *to muzzle:*—put to silence {2x}, hold (one's) peace {2x}, muzzle {2x}, be speechless {1x}, be still {1x}.

Phimoo, "to close the mouth with a muzzle" (*phimos*), is used **(1)** of "muzzling the mouth of" the ox when it treads out the corn, with the lesson that those upon whom spiritual labor is bestowed should not refrain from ministering to the material needs of those who labor on their behalf, 1 Cor 9:9; 1 Ti 5:18; **(2)** metaphorically, of putting to silence, or subduing to stillness: **(2a)** Mt 22:12, "speechless"; **(2b)** Mt 22:34; 1 Pet 2:15, "put to silence"; **(2c)** Mk 1:25; Lk 4:35, "hold thy peace"; and **(2d)** Mk 4:39,

"be still"; Lk 4:35; 1 Pet 2:15. See: BAGD—
861d; THAYER—655b.

5393. Φλέγων {1x} **Phlĕgōn,** *fleg'-one;* act.
part. of the base of *5395; blaz-*
ing; Phlegon, a Chr.:—*Phlegon* {1x}. See:
BAGD—862a; THAYER—655c.

5394. φλογίζω {2x} **phlŏgizō,** *flog-id'-zo;* from
5395; to *cause a blaze,* i.e. *ig-*
nite (fig. to *inflame* with passion):—set on
fire {2x}.

Phlogizo, "to set on fire, burn up," is used
figuratively, in both active and passive voices,
in Jas 3:6, of the tongue, firstly of its disastrous
effects upon the whole round of the circumstances of life; secondly, of satanic agency in using the tongue for this purpose. See: BAGD—
862a; THAYER—655c.

5395. φλόξ {7x} **phlŏx,** *flox;* from a primary
φλέγω **phlĕgō,** (to *"flash"* or
"flame"); a *blaze:* —flame {6x}, flaming {1x}.

Phlego, "to shine," is used apart from *pur,*
"fire," **(1)** in Lk 16:24; with *pur,* it signifies "a
fiery flame," lit., "a flame of fire," (cf. Acts 7:30;
2 Th 1:8 ("flaming), where the fire is to be understood as the instrument of divine judgment);
(2) Heb 1:7, where the meaning probably is that
God makes His angels as active and powerful
as a "flame" of fire; **(3)** in Rev 1:14; 2:18; 19:12,
of the eyes of the Lord Jesus as emblematic of
penetrating judgment, searching out evil. See:
BAGD—862b; THAYER—655c.

5396. φλυαρέω {1x} **phluarĕō,** *floo-ar-eh'-o;*
from *5397;* to *be a babbler* or
trifler, i.e. (by impl.) to *berate* idly or mischie-
vously:—prate against {1x}.

This word means to utter nonsense, talk idly
(1 Jn 1:10). See: BAGD—862b; THAYER—
655c.

5397. φλύαρος {1x} **phluarŏs,** *floo'-ar-os;* from
φλύω **phluō,** (to *bubble*); a
garrulous person, i.e. *prater:*—tattler {1x}. See:
BAGD—862b; THAYER—655d.

5398. φοβερός {3x} **phŏbĕrŏs,** *fob-er-os';* from
5401; frightful, i.e. (obj.) *for-*
midable:—fearful {2x}, terrible {1x}.

(1) *Phoberos* denotes inspiring fear, terrible,
formidable, used in a good or bad sense. *Pho-*
beros, "fearful", is used **(2)** only in the active
sense in the NT, i.e., causing "fear," terrible,
and is translated **(2a)** "fearful" in Heb 10:27,
31; **(2b)** "terrible" [terror causing] in Heb 12:21.
Syn.: **(A)** *Deilia* (*1167*) denotes timidity, fearfulness, cowardice and is always used in a bad
sense. **(B)** *Eulabeia* (*2124*) is usually used in a
good sense and means caution, circumspection,
discretion, avoidance, a reasonable shunning;

used of reverence toward God, godly fear, piety.
See: BAGD—862b; THAYER—655d.

5399. φοβέω {93x} **phŏbĕō,** *fob-eh'-o;* from
5401; to *frighten,* i.e. (pass.) to
be alarmed; by anal. to *be in awe* of, i.e. *re-*
vere:—fear {62x}, be afraid {23x}, be afraid of
{5x}, reverence {1x}, misc. {2x}.

Phobeo, in the NT is always in the passive
voice, has the meanings either **(1)** "to fear, be
afraid," its most frequent use, e.g., Mt 1:20;
17:6; or **(2)** "to show reverential fear", **(2a)** of
men, Mk 6:20; Eph 5:33, "reverence"; **(2b)** of
God, e.g., Acts 10:2, 22; 13:16, 26; Col 3:22;
1 Pet 2:17; Rev 14:7; 15:4; 19:5; **(2c)** (2a) and
(2b) are combined in Lk 12:4, 5, where Christ
warns His followers not to be afraid of
men, but to "fear" God. Syn.: **(A)** *Ekplesso*
(*1605*) means "to be astonished", prop. to be
struck with terror, of a sudden and startling
alarm; but like our "astonish" in popular use,
often employed on comparatively slight occasions. **(B)** *Ptoeo* (*4422*) signifies "to terrify", to
agitate with fear. **(C)** *Tremo* (*5141*) "to tremble", predominately physical; and **(D)** *phobeo*
(*5399*) denotes "to fear", the general term; often used of a protracted state. See: BAGD—
862b; THAYER—655d.

5400. φόβητρον {1x} **phŏbētrŏn,** *fob'-ay-tron;*
neut. of a der. of *5399;* a
frightening thing, i.e. *terrific* portent:—fearful
sight {1x}.

Phobetron, as a noun, in the plural, is translated "fearful sights": "And great earthquakes
shall be in divers places, and famines, and pestilences; and fearful sights and great signs
shall there be from heaven" (Lk 21:11). See:
BAGD—863c; THAYER—656b.

5401. φόβος {47x} **phŏbŏs,** *fob'-os;* from a
primary φέβομαι **phĕbŏmai** (to
be put in fear); *alarm,* or *fright:*—fear {41x},
terror {3x}, misc. {3x} = be afraid, + exceedingly.

Phobos first had the meaning of "flight,"
that which is caused by being scared; then,
"that which may cause flight," **(1)** "fear, dread,
terror," **(1a)** always with this significance in the
four Gospels; also e.g., in Acts 2:43; 19:17;
1 Cor 2:3; 1 Ti 5:20 (lit., "may have fear"); Heb
2:15; 1 Jn 4:18; Rev 11:11; 18:10, 15; **(1b)** by
metonymy, that which causes "fear," Rom 13:3;
1 Pet 3:14, "(their) terror," an adaptation of Is
8:12, "fear not their fear"; hence some take it
to mean, as there, "what they fear," but in view
of Mt 10:28, e.g., it seems best to understand it
as that which is caused by the intimidation
of adversaries;

(2) "reverential fear," **(2a)** of God, **(2a1)** as a
controlling motive of the life, in matters spiritual and moral, **(2a2)** not a mere "fear" of His

power and righteous retribution, **(2a3)** but a wholesome dread of displeasing Him, a "fear" which banishes the terror that shrinks from His presence, Rom 8:15, and **(2a4)** which influences the disposition and attitude of one whose circumstances are guided by trust in God, **(2a5)** through the indwelling Spirit of God, Acts 9:31; Rom 3:18; 2 Cor 7:1; Eph 5:21; Phil 2:12; 1 Pet 1:17 (a comprehensive phrase: the reverential "fear" of God will inspire a constant carefulness in dealing with others in His "fear"); 3:2, 15; **(2a6)** the association of "fear and trembling," as, e.g., in Phil 2:12, (cf. Gen 9:2; Ex 15:16; Deut 2:25; 11:25; Ps 55:5; Is 19:16); **(2b)** of superiors, e.g., Rom 13:7; 1 Pet 2:18. See: TDNT—9:189, 1272; BAGD—863c; THAYER—656b.

5402. Φοίβη {2x} **Phŏibē,** *foy'-bay;* fem. of φοῖβος **phŏibŏs,** *(bright;* prob. akin to the base of 5457); *Phœbe,* a Chr. woman:—Phebe {2x}. See: BAGD—864a; THAYER—656d.

5403. Φοινίκη {3x} **Phŏinikē,** *foy-nee'-kay;* from *5404; palm*-country; *Phœnice* (or *Phœnicia*), a region of Pal.:—Phenice {2x}, Phenicia {1x}. See: BAGD—864a; THAYER—656d.

5404. φοῖνιξ {2x} **phŏinix,** *foy'-nix;* of uncert. der.; a *palm*-tree:—palm {1x}, palm tree {1x}.

Phoinix denotes "the date palm"; it is used of **(1)** "palm" trees in Jn 12:13, from which branches were taken; **(2)** of the branches themselves in Rev 7:9. See: BAGD—864b; THAYER—656d.

5405. Φοῖνιξ {1x} **Phŏinix,** *foy'-nix;* prob. the same as *5404; Phœnix,* a place in Crete:—Phenice {1x}. See: BAGD—864c; THAYER—not listed.

5406. φονεύς {7x} **phŏneus,** *fon-yooce';* from *5408;* a *murderer* (always of *criminal* [or at least *intentional*] homicide; which *443* does not necessarily imply; while *4607* is a special term for a *public* bandit):—murderer {7x}.

Phoneus is used **(1)** in a general sense, **(1a)** in the singular, 1 Pet 4:15; **(1b)** in the plural, Rev 21:8; 22:15; **(2)** of those guilty of particular acts, Mt 22:7; Acts 3:14, lit. "a man (*aner*), a murderer"; 7:52; 28:4. See: BAGD—864c; THAYER—657a.

5407. φονεύω {12x} **phŏneuō,** *fon-yoo'-o;* from *5406;* to *be a murderer* (of):—kill {10x}, do murder {1x}, slay {1x}.

Phoneuo, "to murder," akin to *phoneus,* "a murderer," is rendered by the verb **(1)** "to kill", Mt 5:21 (twice); 23:31; Mk 10:19; Lk 18:20; Rom

13:9; Jas 2:11 (twice); 4:2; 5:6; **(2)** "do . . . murder" in Mt 19:18; and **(3)** "ye slew" in Mt 23:35. See: BAGD—864c; THAYER—657a.

5408. φόνος {10x} **phŏnŏs,** *fon'-os;* from an obs. primary φένω **phēnō** (to *slay*); *murder:*—murder {8x}, be slain with + 599 {1x}, slaughter {1x}.

Phonos is used **(1)** of a special act, Mk 15:7; Lk 23:19, 25; **(2)** of "murders" in general, **(2a)** in the plural, Mt 15:19; Mk 7:21; Gal 5:21; Rev 9:21; **(2b)** in the singular, Rom 1:29; **(3)** in the sense of "slaughter," **(3a)** Heb 11:37, "they were slain with the sword," lit., "(they died by) slaughter (of the sword)"; **(3b)** in Acts 9:1, "slaughter." See: BAGD—864d; THAYER—657a.

5409. φορέω {6x} **phŏrēō,** *for-eh'-o;* from *5411;* to *have a burden,* i.e. (by anal.) to *wear* as clothing or a constant accompaniment:—bear {3x}, wear {3x}.

(1) This word stresses not a simple act of bearing, but a continuous or habitual condition. **(2)** A frequentative form of *phero* (5342, "to bear") and denoting "repeated or habitual action," is chiefly used **(2a)** of clothing, **(2a1)** of soft raiment, Mt 11:8; **(2a2)** fine clothing, Jas 2:3; **(2a3)** the crown of thorns, Jn 19:5; **(2b)** of weapons, of the civil authority in "bearing" the sword as symbolic of execution, Rom 13:4; **(2c)** of a natural state of bodily existence in this life, spoken of as "the image of the earthy," and the spiritual body of the believer hereafter, "the image of the heavenly," 1 Cor 15:49, the word "image" denoting the actual form and not a mere similitude. See: TDNT—9:83, 1252; BAGD—864d; THAYER—657a.

5410. Φόρον {1x} **Phŏrŏn,** *for'-on;* of Lat. or.; a *forum* or market-place; only in comparison with *675;* a *station* on the Appian road:—forum {1x}.

Appius Forum, a town in Italy, 43 Roman miles (70 km) from Rome on the Appian Way, Acts 28:15. See: BAGD—865a; 102b [675]; THAYER—657b.

5411. φόρος {5x} **phŏrŏs,** *for'-os;* from *5342;* a *load* (as *borne*), i.e. (fig.) a *tax* (prop. an indiv. *assessment* on persons or property; whereas *5056* is usually a gen. *toll* on goods or travel):—tribute {5x}.

Phoros denotes tribute paid by a subjugated nation (Lk 20:22; 23:2; Rom 13:6, 7). See: TDNT—9:78, 1252; BAGD—865a; THAYER—657b.

5412. φορτίζω {2x} **phŏrtizō,** *for-tid'-zo;* from *5414;* to *load* up (prop. as a vessel or animal), i.e. (fig.) to *overburden* with cerem. (or spiritual anxiety):—lade {1x}, be heavy laden {1x}.

Phortizo, "to load" (akin to *phero,* 5342, "to bear"), is used **(1)** in the active voice in Lk 11:46, "ye lade"; **(2)** in the passive voice, metaphorically, in Mt 11:28, "heavy laden." See: TDNT—9:86, 1252; BAGD—865a; THAYER—657b.

5413. φορτίον {5x} **phŏrtiŏn,** *for-tee′-on;* dimin. of *5414;* an *invoice* (as part of *freight*), i.e. (fig.) a *task* or *service:*—burden {5x}.

Phortion literally, is something carried and is used metaphorically (except in Acts 27:10, of the lading of a ship); **(1)** of that which, though light, is involved in discipleship of Christ (Mt 11:30); **(2)** of tasks imposed by the scribes, Pharisees and lawyers (Mt 23:4; Lk 11:46); **(3)** of that which will be the result, at the judgment-seat of Christ, of each believer's work (Gal 6:5). Syn.: **(A)** *Baros* (922) refers to weight, **(B)** *ogkos* (3591) to bulk, and either may be oppressive; *baros* (922) is a load in so far as it is heavy, *phortion* (5413) a burden in so far as it is borne; hence *phortion* (5413) may be either heavy or light. See: TDNT—9:84, 1252; BAGD—865a; THAYER—657b.

5414. φόρτος {1x} **phŏrtŏs,** *for′-tos;* from *5342;* something *carried,* i.e. the *cargo* of a ship:—lading {1x}. See: BAGD—865b; THAYER—657c.

5415. Φορτουνᾶτος {2x} **Phŏrtŏunatŏs,** *for-too-nat′-os;* of Lat. or.; "*fortunate,*" *Fortunatus,* a Chr.:—Fortunatus {2x}. See: BAGD—865b; THAYER—657c.

5416. φραγέλλιον {1x} **phragĕlliŏn,** *frag-el′-le-on;* neut. of a der. from the base of *5417;* a *whip,* i.e. Rom. *lash* as a public punishment:—scourge {1x}.

Phragellion, "a whip" (from Latin, *flagellum*), is used of the "scourge" of small cords which the Lord made and employed before cleansing the Temple, Jn 2:15. However He actually used it, the whip was in itself a sign of authority and judgment. See: BAGD—865b; THAYER—657c.

5417. φραγελλόω {2x} **phragĕllŏō,** *frag-el-lŏ′-o;* from a presumed equiv. of the Lat. *flagellum;* to *whip,* i.e. *lash* as a public punishment:—scourge {2x}.

Phragello is the word used in Mt 27:26 and Mk 15:15 of the scourging endured by Christ and administered by the order of Pilate. Under the Roman method of scourging the person was stripped and tied in a bending posture to a pillar, or stretched on a frame. The scourge was made of leather thongs, weighted with sharp pieces of bone or lead, which tore the flesh of both the back and the breast (cf. Ps 22:17).

Eusebius (*Chron.*) records his having witnessed the suffering of martyrs who died under this treatment. See: BAGD—865b; THAYER—657c.

5418. φραγμός {4x} **phragmŏs,** *frag-mos′;* from *5420;* a *fence,* or *inclosing barrier* (lit. or fig.):—hedge {2x}, hedge around about + 4060 {1x}, partition {1x}.

Phragmos denotes any sort of fence, hedge, palings or wall (akin to *phrasso,* "to fence in, stop"). It is used **(1)** in its literal sense, in Mt 21:33, lit. "(he put) a hedge (around)"; Mk 12:1; Lk 14:23; **(2)** metaphorically, of the "partition" which separated Gentile from Jew, which was broken down by Christ through the efficacy of His expiatory sacrifice, Eph 2:14. See: BAGD—865c; THAYER—657c.

5419. φράζω {2x} **phrazō,** *frad′-zo;* prob. akin to *5420* through the idea of *defining;* to *indicate* (by word or act), i.e. (spec.) to *expound:*—declare {2x}.

Phrazo means to indicate plainly, make known, declare, whether by gesture or by writing or speaking, or in some other ways, to explain, Mt 13:36; 15:15. See: BAGD—865c; THAYER—657c.

5420. φράσσω {3x} **phrassō,** *fras′-so;* appar. a streng. form of the base of *5424;* to *fence* or *enclose,* i.e. (spec.) to *block up* (fig. to *silence*):—stop {3x}.

Phrasso, "to fence in" (akin to *phragmos,* "a fence"), "close, stop," is used **(1)** metaphorically, passive voice, **(1a)** in Rom 3:19, of "preventing" all excuse from Jew and Gentile, as sinners; **(1b)** in 2 Cor 11:10, lit., "this boasting shall not be stopped to me"; **(2)** physically, active voice, of the mouths of lions, Heb 11:33. See: BAGD—865c; THAYER—657d.

5421. φρέαρ {7x} **phrĕar,** *freh′-ar;* of uncert. der.; a *hole* in the ground (dug for obtaining or holding water or other purposes), i.e. a *cistern* or *well;* fig. an *abyss* (as a *prison*):—well {2x}, pit {5x}.

Phrear, "a well, dug for water" (distinct from *pege,* "a fountain"), denotes **(1)** "a pit", **(1a)** in Rev 9:1, 2, thrice, "(bottomless) pit", "the pit (of the abyss)," "the pit," i.e., the shaft leading down to the abyss; **(1b)** in Lk 14:5; and **(2)** in Jn 4:11, 12, "well." See: BAGD—865d; THAYER—657d.

5422. φρεναπατάω {1x} **phrĕnapataō,** *fren-ap-at-ah′-o;* from *5423;* to *be a mind-misleader,* i.e. *delude:*—deceive {1x}.

Literally, this word means to deceive in one's mind, to deceive by fancies, and is used in Gal 6:3 with reference to self-conceit, which is self-

deceit, a sin against common sense. See: BAGD—865d; THAYER—657d.

5423. **φρεναπάτης** {1x} **phrĕnapatēs**, *fren-ap-at'-ace;* from *5424* and *539; a mind-misleader,* i.e. *seducer:*—deceiver {1x}. See: BAGD-865d; THAYER—658a.

5424. **φρήν** {2x} **phrēn**, *frane;* prob. from an obs. φράω **phraō** (to *rein* in or *curb;* comp. *5420);* the *midrif* (as a *partition* of the body), i.e. (fig. and by impl. of sympathy) the *feelings* (or sensitive nature; by extens. [also in the plur.] the *mind* or cognitive faculties):—understanding {2x}. See: TDNT—9:220, 1277; BAGD—865d; THAYER—658a.

5425. **φρίσσω** {1x} **phrissō**, *fris'-so;* appar. a primary verb; to *"bristle"* or *chill,* i.e. *shudder (fear):*—tremble {1x}.

Phrisso, primarily, "to be rough, to bristle," then, "to shiver, shudder, tremble," is said of devils, Jas 2:19, "tremble." See: BAGD—866a; THAYER—658a.

5426. **φρονέω** {29x} **phrŏnĕō**, *fron-eh'-o;* from *5424;* to *exercise* the *mind,* i.e. *entertain* or *have* a *sentiment* or *opinion;* by impl. to *be* (mentally) *disposed* (more or less earnestly in a certain direction); intens. to *interest oneself* in (with concern or obedience):—think {5x}, regard {4x}, mind {3x}, be minded {3x}, savour {2x}, be of the same mind + 846 {2x}, be like minded + 846 {2x}, misc. {8x} = set the affection on, (be) care (-ful), (+ be of one, + let this) mind (-ed).

Phroneo, "to be minded in a certain way" *(phren,* "the mind"), is rendered **(1)** "to think," **(1a)** in Rom 12:3 (2nd and 3rd occurrences), "not to think of himself more highly *(huperphroneo)* than he ought to think *(phroneo);* but to think *(phroneo)* soberly"; the play on words may be expressed by a literal rendering somewhat as follows: "not to over-think beyond what it behoves him to think, but to think unto sober-thinking"; **(1b)** in 1 Cor 4:6, "to think"; lit., the sentence is "that ye might learn the (i.e., the rule) not beyond what things have been written"; "not to go beyond the terms of a teacher's commission, thinking more of himself than the character of his commission allows"; this accords with the context and the whole passage, 3:1—4:5. **(2)** It is also means "to think, set the mind on," implying moral interest and reflection, and is translated "to regard" in Rom 14:6 (twice).

(3) It also signifies **(3a)** "to think, to be minded in a certain way"; implying moral interest or reflection, not mere unreasoning opinion. It is rendered by the verb "to mind" in the following: **(3b)** Rom 8:5, "(they that are after the flesh) do mind (the things of the

flesh)"; **(3c)** Rom 12:16, "be of (the same) mind," lit., "minding the same," and "set (not) your mind on", "mind (not)"; **(3d)** Rom 15:5, "to be like-minded"); **(3e)** 2 Cor 13:11, "be of (one) mind"; **(3f)** Gal 5:10, "ye will be (none otherwise) minded"; **(3g)** in Phil **(3g1)** Phil 1:7, "to think (this)"; **(3g2)** Phil 2:2, "be like-minded," and "being . . . of (one) mind," lit., "minding (the one thing)"; **(3g3)** Phil 2:5, "let (this) mind be," lit., "mind this"; **(3g4)** Phil 3:15, "let us . . . be (thus) minded," and "(if) . . . ye are (otherwise) minded"; **(3g5)** Phil 3:16, "let us mind"; **(3g6)** Phil 3:19, "(who) mind (earthly things)"; **(3g7)** Phil 4:2, "be of (the same) mind"; **(3h)** Col 3:2, "set your affection." See: TDNT—9:220, 1277; BAGD—866a; THAYER—658a.

5427. **φρόνημα** {4x} **phrŏnēma**, *fron'-ay-mah;* from *5426;* (mental) *inclination* or *purpose:* —mind {2x}, carnally minded + 4561 {1x}, spiritually minded + 4151 {1x}.

Phronema denotes "what one has in the mind, the thought" (the content of the process expressed in *phroneo,* "to have in mind, to think"); or "an object of thought"; and is translated **(1)** in Rom 8:6, "to be carnally minded" and "to be spiritually minded", in vv. 6 and 7, and "the mind of the spirit," in v. 6. **(2)** In Rom 8:27 the word is used of the "mind" of the Holy Spirit. See: TDNT—9:220, 1277; BAGD—866c; THAYER—658c.

5428. **φρόνησις** {2x} **phrŏnēsis**, *fron'-ay-sis;* from *5426;* mental *action* or *activity,* i.e. intellectual or mor. *insight:*—prudence {1x}, wisdom {1x}.

Phronesis means to have understanding and denotes practical wisdom, prudence in the management of affairs. It is translated **(1)** wisdom in Lk 1:17 and **(2)** prudence in Eph 1:8. See: TDNT—9:220, 1277; BAGD—866c; THAYER—658c.

5429. **φρόνιμος** {14x} **phrŏnimŏs**, *fron'-ee-mos;* from *5424; thoughtful,* i.e. *sagacious* or *discreet* (implying a *cautious* character; while *4680* denotes *practical* skill or acumen; and *4908* indicates rather *intelligence* or mental *acquirement*); in a bad sense *conceited* (also in the comparative):—wise {13x}, wiser {1x}.

Phronimos, means "prudent, sensible, practically wise," and is **(1)** found in Mt 7:24; 10:16; 24:45; 25:2, 4, 8, 9; Lk 12:42; 16:8 ("wiser", comparative degree, *phronimoteros*); 1 Cor 10:15; **(2)** in an evil sense, "wise (in your own conceits)," lit., "wise (in yourselves)," i.e., "judged by the standard of your self-complacency," Rom 11:25; 12:16; **(3)** ironically,

1 Cor 4:10; 2 Cor 11:19. See: TDNT—9:220, 1277; BAGD—866d; THAYER—658c.

5430. φρονίμως {1x} **phrŏnimōs**, *fron-im'-oce;* adv. from *5429; prudently:—* wisely {1x}. See: BAGD—866d; THAYER—658d.

5431. φροντίζω {1x} **phrŏntizo**, *fron-tid'-zo;* from a der. of *5424;* to *exercise thought,* i.e. *be anxious:*—be careful {1x}. See: BAGD—866d; THAYER—658d.

5432. φρουρέω {4x} **phrŏurĕō**, *froo-reh'-o;* from a compound of *4253* and *3708;* to *be a watcher in advance,* i.e. to *mount guard* as a sentinel (*post spies* at gates); fig. to *hem in, protect:*—keep {3x}, keep with a garrison {1x}.

Phroureo is a military term meaning to keep by guarding, to keep under guard as with a garrison. It is used **(1)** of blocking up every way of escape, as in a siege; **(2)** of providing protection against the enemy, as a garrison does (2 Cor 11:32). **(3)** It is used of the security of the Christian until the end (1 Pet 1:5); and of the sense of that security that is his when he puts all his matters into the hand of God (Phil 4:7). In these passages the idea is not merely that of protection, but of inward garrisoning as by the Holy Spirit (Gal 3:23; it means rather a benevolent custody and watchful guardianship in view of worldwide idolatry. See: BAGD—867b; THAYER—658d. comp. *5083.*

5433. φρυάσσω {1x} **phruasso**, *froo-as'-so;* akin to *1032, 1031;* to *snort* (as a spirited horse), i.e. (fig.) to *make a tumult:*—rage {1x}.

This word was primarily used of the snorting, neighing and prancing of horses; hence, metaphorically, of the haughtiness and insolence of men (Acts 4:25). See: BAGD—867b; THAYER—658d.

5434. φρύγανον {1x} **phruganŏn**, *froo'-gan-on;* neut. of a presumed der. of φρύγω **phrugō** (to *roast* or *parch;* akin to the base of *5395*); something *desiccated,* i.e. a dry *twig:*—a stick {1x}. See: BAGD—867b; THAYER—659a.

5435. Φρυγία {4x} **Phrugia**, *froog-ee'-ah;* prob. of for. or.; *Phrygia,* a region of Asia Minor:—Phrygia {4x}. See: BAGD—867c; THAYER—659a.

5436. Φύγελλος {1x} **Phugĕllŏs**, *foog'-el-los;* prob. from *5343; fugitive; Phygellus,* an apostate Chr.:—Phygellus {1x}. See: BAGD—867c; THAYER—659a.

5437. φυγή {2x} **phugē**, *foog-ay';* from *5343;* a *fleeing,* i.e. *escape:*—flight {2x}.

Cf. Mt 24:20; Mk 13:18. See: BAGD—867c; THAYER—659a.

5438. φυλακή {47x} **phulakē**, *foo-lak-ay';* from *5442;* a *guarding* or (concr. *guard*), the act, the person; fig. the place, the condition, or (spec.) the time (as a division of day or night), lit. or fig.:—prison {36x}, watch {6x}, imprisonment {2x}, hold {1x}, cage {1x}, ward {1x}.

Phulake, from *phulasso,* "to guard," denotes **(1)** "a watching, keeping watch," Lk 2:8; **(2)** "persons keeping watch, a guard," Acts 12:10; **(3)** "a period during which watch is kept," e.g., Mt 24:43. **(4)** The word is almost invariably translated prison, e.g., Mt 14:10; Mk 6:17; Acts 5:19; 2 Cor 11:23; **(4a)** in 2 Cor 6:5 and Heb 11:36 it stands for the condition of imprisonment; **(4b)** "a prison, a hold", Rev 2:10, Babylon is described figuratively, first as a "hold" and then as a "cage" (Rev 18:2) of every unclean and hateful bird. See: TDNT—9:241, 1280; BAGD—867d; THAYER—659a.

5439. φυλακίζω {1x} **phulakizo**, *foo-lak-id'-zo;* from *5441;* to *incarcerate:*—to imprison {1x}. See: BAGD—868a; THAYER—659c.

5440. φυλακτήριον {1x} **phulaktēriŏn**, *foo-lak-tay'-ree-on;* neut. of a der. of *5442;* a *guard-case,* i.e. "*phylactery*" for wearing slips of Scripture texts:—phylactery {1x}.

This word primarily means an outpost or fortification; then, any kind of safeguard and became used especially to denote an amulet. In the NT it denotes a prayer fillet, a *phylactery,* a small strip of parchment, with portions of the Law written on it; it was fastened by a leather strap either to the forehead or to the left arm over against the heart, to remind the wearer of the duty of keeping the commandments of God in the head and in the heart (cf. Ex 13:16; Deut 6:8; 11:18). It was supposed to have potency as a charm against evils and demons. The Pharisees broadened their phylacteries to render conspicuous their superior eagerness to be mindful of God's Law (Mt 23:5). See: BAGD—868a; THAYER—659c.

5441. φύλαξ {3x} **phulax**, *foo'-lax;* from *5442;* a *watcher* or *sentry:*—keeper {3x}. Cf. Acts 5:23; 12:6, 19. See: BAGD—868b; THAYER—659d.

5442. φυλάσσω {30x} **phulassō**, *foo-las'-so;* prob. from *5443* through the idea of *isolation;* to *watch,* i.e. *be on guard* (lit. or fig.); by impl. to *preserve, obey, avoid:*—keep {23x}, observe {2x}, beware {2x}, keep (one's) self {1x}, save {1x}, be . . . ware {1x}.

Phulasso denotes "to guard, watch, keep watch," e.g., Lk 2:8; **(1)** in the passive voice, **(1a)** Lk 8:29; **(1b)** "to keep by way of protection," e.g., Lk 11:21; Jn 12:25; 17:12, 2nd part; **(2)** metaphorically, "to keep a law or precept," etc., e.g., Mt 19:20 and Lk 18:21, "have observed"; Lk 11:28; Acts 7:53; 16:4; 21:24; Rom 2:26; Gal 6:13; 1 Ti 5:21, "observe"; **(3)** in the middle voice, Mk 10:20, "have observed"; **(4)** in the middle voice, "to keep oneself from," Acts 21:25. **(5)** It is also translated by the verb "to beware": **(5a)** in the middle voice, of being "on one's guard against" (the middle voice stressing personal interest in the action), **(5a1)** Lk 12:15, "beware of", **(5a2)** as in Acts 21:25; **(5b)** in 2 Ti 4:15, "be thou ware"; and **(5c)** in 2 Pet 3:17, "beware." Syn.: *Tereo* (*5083*) means to watch or keep and expresses watchful care and is suggestive of present possession; whereas, *phulasso* (*5442*) indicates safe custody and often implies assault from without. *Tereo* (*5083*) may mark the result of which *phulasso* (*5442*) is the means. See: TDNT—9:236, 1280; BAGD—868b; THAYER—659d.

5443. φυλή {31x} **phulē**, *foo-lay'*; from *5453* (comp. *5444*); an *offshoot*, i.e. *race* or *clan:*—kindred {6x}, tribe {25x}.

Phule, "a company of people united by kinship or habitation, a clan, tribe," is used **(1)** of the peoples of the earth, Mt 24:30; **(2)** of "kindred(-s)": Rev 1:7; 5:9; 7:9; 11:9; 13:7; 14:6; **(3)** of the "tribes" of Israel, Mt 19:28; Lk 2:36; 22:30; Acts 13:21; Rom 11:1; Phil 3:5; Heb 7:13, 14; Jas 1:1; Rev 5:5; 7:4–8; 21:12. See: TDNT—9:245, 1280; BAGD—868d; THAYER—660b.

5444. φύλλον {6x} **phullŏn**, *fool'-lon;* from the same as *5443;* a *sprout*, i.e. *leaf:*—leaf {6x}. Cf. Mt 21:19; 24:32; Mk 11:13 (twice); 13:28; Rev 22:2. See: BAGD—869a; THAYER—660b.

5445. φύραμα {5x} **phurama**, *foo'-ram-ah;* from a prol. form of φύρω **phurō** (to *mix* a liquid with a solid; perh. akin to *5453* through the idea of *swelling* in bulk), mean to *knead;* a *mass* of dough:—lump {5x}.

Phurama denotes "that which is mixed or kneaded" (*phurao,* "to mix") hence, "a lump," either **(1)** of dough, Rom 11:16 (cf. Num 15:21); 1 Cor 5:6, 7; Gal 5:9; or **(2)** of potter's clay, Rom 9:21. See: BAGD—869a; THAYER—660b.

5446. φυσικός {3x} **phusikŏs**, *foo-see-kos';* from *5449;* "*physical*", i.e. (by impl.) *instinctive:*—natural {3x}.

Phuskios originally signified produced by nature, inborn but in the NT denotes **(1)** according to nature (Rom 1:26, 27); **(2)** governed by mere natural instincts (2 Pet 2:12). See:

TDNT—9:251, 1283; BAGD—869b; THAYER—660b. comp. *5591.*

5447. φυσικῶς {1x} **phusikōs**, *foo-see-koce';* adv. from *5446;* "*physically*", i.e. (by impl.) *instinctively:*—naturally {1x}. See: TDNT—9:251, 1283; BAGD—869b; THAYER—660c.

5448. φυσιόω {7x} **phusiŏō**, *foo-see-ŏ'-o;* from *5449* in the primary sense of *blowing;* to *inflate*, i.e. (fig.) *make proud* (*haughty*):—puff up {7x}.

Phusioo means to puff up, blow up, inflate and is used metaphorically of being puffed up with pride (1 Cor 4:6, 18, 19; 5:2; 8:1; 13:4; Col 2:18). See: BAGD—869b; THAYER—660c.

5449. φύσις {14x} **phusis**, *foo'-sis;* from *5453;* *growth* (by *germination* or *expansion*), i.e. (by impl.) natural *production* (lineal *descent*); by extens. a *genus* or *sort;* fig. native *disposition, constitution* or *usage:*—nature {10x}, natural + 2596 {2x}, kind {1x}, mankind + 442 {1x}.

Phusis, (from *phuo,* "to bring forth, produce"), signifies **(1)** "the nature" (i.e., the natural powers or constitution) of a person or thing, Eph 2:3; Jas 3:7 ("kind"); 2 Pet 1:4; **(2)** "origin, birth," Rom 2:27, one who by birth is a Gentile, uncircumcised, in contrast to one who, though circumcised, has become spiritually uncircumcised by his iniquity; Gal 2:15; **(3)** "the regular law or order of nature," **(3a)** Rom 1:26, against "nature" (*para,* "against"); **(3b)** Rom 2:14, adverbially, "by nature", (cf. 11:21 "natural", and 11:24, "by nature" twice, "natural" once); 1 Cor 11:14; **(3c)** Gal 4:8, "by nature (are no gods)," here "nature" is the emphatic word, and the phrase includes devils, men regarded as deified, and idols; these are gods only in name (the negative, *me,* denies not simply that they were gods, but the possibility that they could be). See: TDNT—9:251, 1283; BAGD—869b; THAYER—660c.

5450. φυσίωσις {1x} **phusiōsis**, *foo-see'-o-sis;* from *5448;* *inflation,* i.e. (fig.) *haughtiness, swelling with pride:*—swelling {1x}. See: BAGD—870a; THAYER—661a.

5451. φυτεία {1x} **phutĕia**, *foo-ti'-ah;* from *5452;* trans-*planting*, i.e. (concr.) a *shrub* or *vegetable:*—plant {1x}. See: BAGD—870a; THAYER—661a.

5452. φυτεύω {11x} **phutĕuō**, *foot-yoo'-o;* from a der. of *5453;* to *set out* in the earth, i.e. *implant;* fig. to *instil* doctrine:—to plant {11x}.

Phuteuo "to plant," is used **(1)** literally, Mt 21:33; Mk 12:1; Lk 13:6; 17:6, 28; 20:9; 1 Cor 9:7; **(2)** metaphorically, Mt 15:13; 1 Cor 3:6, 7, 8. See: BAGD—870a; THAYER—661a.

5453. **φύω** {3x} **phuō**, *foo'-o;* a primary verb; prob. orig. to *"puff"* or *blow,* i.e. to *swell* up; but only used in the impl. sense, to *germinate* or *grow* (*sprout, produce*), lit. or fig.:—spring up {1x}, spring {1x}, as soon as it be sprung up {1x}.

Phuo, used transitively, "to bring forth, produce," denotes, **(1)** in the passive voice, "to spring up, grow," of seed, Lk 8:6, 8, "was sprung up" and "sprang up"; **(2)** in the active voice, intransitively, in Heb 12:15, of a root of bitterness. See: BAGD—870b; THAYER—661b.

5454. **φωλεός** {2x} **phōlĕŏs**, *fo-leh-os';* of uncert. der.; a *burrow* or *lurking-place:*—hole {2x}.

Pholeos, "a lair, burrow, den or hole," is used of foxes in Mt 8:20 and Lk 9:58. See: BAGD—870b; THAYER—661b.

5455. **φωνέω** {42x} **phōnĕō**, *fo-neh'-o;* from *5456;* to emit a *sound* (animal, human or instrumental); by impl. to *address* in words or by name, also in imitation:—call {23x}, crow {12x}, cry {5x}, call for {2x}.

Phoneo, as a verb, means "to sound" (Eng., "phone"), is used **(1)** of the crowing of a cock, e.g., Mt 26:34; Jn 13:38; **(2)** of "calling" out with a clear or loud voice, to cry out, Acts 16:28; **(3)** of "calling" to come to oneself, e.g., Mt 20:32; Lk 19:15; **(4)** of "calling" forth, as of Christ's call to Lazarus to come forth from the tomb, Jn 12:17; **(5)** of inviting, e.g., Lk 14:12; **(6)** of "calling" by name, with the implication of the pleasure taken in the possession of those "called," e.g., Jn 10:3; 13:13; **(7)** of animals, Mt 26:34; or **(8)** persons, Lk 8:8; 16:24. **(9)** This is the word which Luke uses to describe the "cry" of the Lord at the close of His sufferings on the cross (Lk 23:46). Syn.: 310, 349, 994, 995, 1916, 2019, 2896, 2905, 2906. See: TDNT—9:301, 1287; BAGD—870b; THAYER—661b.

5456. **φωνή** {141x} **phōnē**, *fo-nay';* prob. akin to *5316* through the idea of *disclosure;* a *tone* (articulate, bestial or artif.); by impl. an *address* (for any purpose), *saying* or *language:*—voice {131x}, sound {8x}, be noised abroad + 1096 {1x}, noise {1x}.

Phone, most frequently **(1)** "a voice," it is also translated **(2)** "sound" in Mt 24:31; Jn 3:8; 1 Cor 14:7 (1st part), 8; Rev 1:15; 9:9 (twice); 18:22 (2nd part); and **(3)** in Acts 2:6, "(this) was noised abroad." See: TDNT—9:278, 1287; BAGD—870c; THAYER—661c.

5457. **φῶς** {70x} **phōs**, *foce;* from an obs. φάω **phaō** (to *shine,* or make *manifest,* espec. by *rays;* comp. *5316, 5346*); *luminousness* (in the widest application, nat. or artif., abstr. or concr., lit. or fig.):—fire {2x}, light {68x}.

Phos, (akin to *phao,* "to give light", from

roots *pha*— and *phan*—, expressing "light as seen by the eye," and, metaphorically, as "reaching the mind," whence *phaino,* "to make to appear," *phaneros,* "evident," etc.; cf. Eng., "phosphorus", lit., "light-bearing"), is usually used of light. **(1)** Primarily light is a luminous emanation, probably of force, from certain bodies, which enables the eye to discern form and color. **(1a)** Light requires an organ adapted for its reception (Mt 6:22). **(1b)** Where the eye is absent, or where it has become impaired from any cause, light is useless. **(1c)** Man, naturally, is incapable of receiving spiritual light inasmuch as he lacks the capacity for spiritual things, 1 Cor 2:14. **(2)** Hence believers are called "sons of light," Lk 16:8, not merely because they have received a revelation from God, but because in the new birth they have received the spiritual capacity for it.

(3) Apart from natural phenomena, light is used in Scripture of **(3a)** the glory of God's dwelling-place, 1 Ti 6:16; **(3b)** the nature of God, 1 Jn 1:5; **(3c)** the impartiality of God, Jas 1:17; **(3d)** the favor **(3d1)** of God, cf. Ps 4:6; **(3d2)** of the King, cf. Prov 16:15; **(3d3)** of an influential man, cf. Job 29:24; **(3e)** God, as the illuminator of His people, cf. Is 60:19, 20; **(3f)** the Lord Jesus as the illuminator of men, Jn 1:4, 5, 9; 3:19; 8:12; 9:5; 12:35, 36, 46; Acts 13:47; **(3g)** the illuminating power of the Scriptures, **(3g1)** Ps 119:105; **(3g2)** and of the judgments and commandments of God, cf. Is 51:4; Prov 6:23, Ps 43:3; **(3h)** the guidance **(3h1)** of God, cf. Job 29:3; Ps 112:4; Is 58:10; and, **(3h2)** ironically, of the guidance of man, Rom 2:19; **(3i)** salvation, 1 Pet 2:9; **(3j)** righteousness, Rom 13:12; 2 Cor 11:14, 15; 1 Jn 2:9, 10; **(3k)** witness for God, Mt 5:14, 16; Jn 5:35; **(3l)** prosperity and general well-being, cf. Est 8:16; Job 18:18; Is 58:8–10. See: TDNT—9:310, 1293; BAGD—871c.

5458. **φωστήρ** {2x} **phōstēr**, *foce-tare';* from *5457;* an *illuminator,* i.e. (concr.) a *luminary,* or (abstr.) *brilliancy:*—light {2x}.

Phoster denotes "a luminary, light," or "light-giver"; it is used **(1)** figuratively of believers, as shining in the spiritual darkness of the world, Phil 2:15; and **(2)** in Rev 21:11 it is used of Christ as the "Light" reflected in and shining through the heavenly city (cf. v. 23). See: TDNT—9:310, 1293; BAGD—872c; THAYER—663a.

5459. **φωσφόρος** {1x} **phōsphŏrŏs**, *foce-for'-os;* from *5457* and *5342;* *light-bearing* ("phosphorus"), i.e. (spec.) the *morning-star* (fig.):—day star {1x}.

Phosphoros, (Eng., "phosphorus," lit., "light-bearing" *phos,* "light," *phero,* "to bear"),

is used of the morning star, as the light-bringer, 2 Pet 1:19, where it indicates the arising of the light of Christ as the personal fulfillment, in the hearts of believers, of the prophetic Scriptures concerning His coming to receive them to Himself. See: TDNT—9:310, 1293; BAGD—872d; THAYER—663a.

5460. φωτεινός {5x} **phōtĕinŏs**, *fo-ti-nos';* from *5457; lustrous*, i.e. *transparent* or *well-illuminated* (fig.):—bright {1x}, full of light {4x}.

Photeinos, (from *phos*, "bright"), is rendered **(1)** literally, "full of light" in Mt 6:22; Lk 11:34, 36 (twice); **(2)** figuratively, of the single-mindedness of the eye, which acts as the lamp of the body; and **(3)** in Mt 17:5, "bright," of a cloud. See: TDNT—9:310, 1293; BAGD—872d; THAYER—663a.

5461. φωτίζω {11x} **phōtizō**, *fo-tid'-zo;* from *5457;* to *shed rays*, i.e. to *shine* or (tran.) to *brighten* up (lit. or fig.):—give light {2x}, bring to light {2x}, lighten {2x}, enlighten {2x}, light {1x}, illuminate {1x}, make to see {1x}.

Photizo, from *phos*, "light," used **(1)** intransitively, signifies "to shine, give light," Rev 22:5; **(2)** transitively, **(2a)** "to illumine, to light, enlighten, to be lightened," Lk 11:36; Rev 21:23; **(2a1)** in the passive voice, Rev 18:1; **(2a2)** metaphorically, of spiritual enlightenment, Jn 1:9; Eph 1:18; 3:9, "to make . . . see;" Heb 6:4; 10:32, "ye were illuminated"; **(2b)** "to bring to light," **(2b1)** 1 Cor 4:5 (of God's act in the future); **(2b2)** 2 Ti 1:10 (of God's act in the past). See: TDNT—9:310, 1293; BAGD—872d; THAYER—663b.

5462. φωτισμός {2x} **phōtismŏs**, *fo-tis-mos';* from *5461; illumination* (fig.):—light {2x}.

Photismos, "an illumination, light," is used metaphorically in **(1)** 2 Cor 4:4, of the "light" of the gospel, and in **(2)** 2 Cor 4:6, of the knowledge of the glory of God. See: TDNT—9:310, 1293; BAGD—873c; THAYER—663c.

X

5463. χαίρω {74x} **chairō**, *khah'-ee-ro;* a primary verb; to be *"cheer"ful*, i.e. calmly *happy* or well-off; impers. espec. as salutation (on meeting or parting), *be well:*—rejoice {42x}, be glad {14x}, joy {5x}, hail {5x}, greeting {3x}, God speed {2x}, all hail {1x}, joyfully 1, farewell {1x}.

Chairo, "to rejoice," is most frequently so translated. **(1)** As to this verb, the following are grounds and occasions for "rejoicing," on the part of believers: **(1a)** in the Lord, Phil 3:1; 4:4; **(1b)** His incarnation, Lk 1:14; **(1c)** His power,

Lk 13:17; **(1d)** His presence with the Father, Jn 14:28; **(1e)** His presence with them, Jn 16:22; 20:20; **(1f)** His ultimate triumph, Jn 8:56; **(1g)** hearing the gospel, Acts 13:48; **(1h)** their salvation, Acts 8:39; **(1i)** receiving the Lord, Lk 19:6; **(1j)** their enrollment in heaven, Lk 10:20; **(1k)** their liberty in Christ, Acts 15:31; **(1l)** their hope, Rom 12:12 (cf. Rom 5:2; Rev 19:7); **(1m)** their prospect of reward, Mt 5:12; **(1n)** the obedience and godly conduct of fellow believers, 2 Cor 7:7, 9; 13:9; Col 2:5; 1 Th 3:9; 2 Jn 4; 3 Jn 3; **(1o)** the proclamation of Christ, Phil 1:18; **(1p)** the gospel harvest, Jn 4:36; **(1q)** suffering with Christ, Acts 5:41; 1 Pet 4:13; **(1r)** suffering in the cause of the gospel, 2 Cor 13:9 (1st part); Phil 2:17 (1st part); Col 1:24; **(1s)** in persecutions, trials and afflictions, Mt 5:12; Lk 6:23; 2 Cor 6:10; **(1t)** the manifestation of grace, Acts 11:23; **(1u)** meeting with fellow believers, 1 Cor 16:17; Phil 2:28; **(1v)** receiving tokens of love and fellowship, Phil 4:10; **(1w)** the "rejoicing" of others, Rom 12:15; 2 Cor 7:13; **(1x)** learning of the well-being of others, 2 Cor 7:16.

(2) It is also the usual word for "being glad" and is so rendered in Mk 14:11; Lk 15:32; 22:5; 23:8; Jn 8:56; 11:15; 20:20; Acts 11:23; 13:48; Rom 16:19; 1 Cor 16:17; 2 Cor 13:9; 1 Pet 4:13; Rev 19:7. Syn.: 21, 2165. See: TDNT—9:359, 1298; BAGD—873b; THAYER—663b.

5464. χάλαζα {4x} **chalaza**, *khal'-ad-zah;* prob. from *5465; hail:*—hail {4x}.

Chalaza, akin to *chalao*, "to let loose, let fall," is always used as an instrument of divine judgment, translated "hail" [balls of frozen rain] and is found in the NT in Rev 8:7; 11:19; 16:21. See: BAGD—874b; THAYER—664a.

5465. χαλάω {7x} **chalaō**, *khal-ah'-o;* from the base of *5490;* to *lower* (as into a *void*):—let down {6x}, strike {1x}.

Chalao, "to slacken, loosen, let loose," **(1)** denotes "to let down, to lower"; it is used with reference to **(1a)** the paralytic, in Mk 2:4; **(1b)** Paul/Saul: **(1b1)** Saul of Tarsus, Acts 9:25; **(1b2)** Paul, 2 Cor 11:33, "was I let down" (passive voice); **(1c)** "nets" in Lk 5:4, and "a net" in 5:5; **(1d)** a ship's boat, Acts 27:30, "let down." **(2)** In Acts 27:17, "they strake (sail)"; i.e. they lowered the sail, unfurling it; thus, "striking" out into the wind. See: BAGD—874b; THAYER—664b.

5466. Χαλδαῖος {1x} **Chaldaiŏs**, *khal-dah'-yos;* prob. of Heb. or [3778]; a *Chaldæan* (i.e. *Kasdi*), or native or the region of the lower Euphrates:—Chaldæan {1x}. See: BAGD—874c; THAYER—664b.

5467. χαλεπός {2x} **chalĕpŏs**, *khal-ep-os';* perh. from *5465* through the

Greek

idea of *reducing* the strength; *difficult*, i.e. *dangerous*, or (by impl.) *furious:*—fierce {1x}, perilous {1x}.

This word means hard to do or deal with, difficult, fierce, perilous and is said **(1)** of the Gadarene devils (Mt 8:28); and **(2)** of the last times (2 Ti 3:1). See: BAGD—874c; THAYER—664b.

5468. χαλιναγωγέω {2x} **chalinagōgĕō**, *khal-in-ag-ogue-eh'-o;* from a compound of *5469* and the redupl. form of *71;* to *be* a *bit-leader,* i.e. to *curb* (fig.):—bridle {2x}.

Chalinagogeo, from *chalinos* and *ago,* "to lead," signifies "to lead by a bridle, to bridle, to hold in check, restrain"; it is used metaphorically of the tongue and of the body in Jas 1:26 and 3:2. See: BAGD—874c; THAYER—664b.

5469. χαλινός {2x} **chalinŏs**, *khal-ee-nos';* from *5465;* a *curb* or *headstall* (as *curbing* the spirit):—bit {1x}, bridle {1x}.

Chalinos, **(1)** "bits" is used in Jas 3:3, and "bridles" in Rev 14:20. The primitive bridle was simply a loop on the haltercord passed round the lower jaw of the horse. See: BAGD—874d; THAYER—664b.

5470. χάλκεος {1x} **chalkĕŏs**, *khal'-keh-os;* from *5475;* *coppery:*—brass {1x}. See: BAGD—875b; THAYER—664c.

5471. χαλκεύς {1x} **chalkĕus**, *khalk-yooce';* from *5475;* a *copper-worker* or *brazier:*—coppersmith {1x}. See: BAGD—874d; THAYER—664c.

5472. χαλκηδών {1x} **chalkēdōn**, *khal-kay-dōhn';* from *5475* and perh. *1491; copper-like,* i.e. "*chalcedony*":—chalcedony {1x}.

Chalcedony is a precious stone of misty grey colour, or green, clouded with blue, yellow, or purple. See: BAGD—874d; THAYER—664c.

5473. χαλκίον {1x} **chalkiŏn**, *khal-kee'-on;* dimin. from *5475;* a *brazen dish:*—brazen vessel {1x}. See: BAGD—874d; THAYER—664c.

5474. χαλκολίβανον {2x} **chalkŏlibanŏn**, *khal-kol-ib'-an-on;* neut. of a compound of *5475* and *3030* (in the impl. mean of *whiteness* or *brilliancy*); *burnished copper,* an alloy of copper (or gold) and silver having a brilliant lustre:—fine brass {2x}.

Chalkolibanon is used of "white or shining copper or bronze," and describes the feet of the Lord, in Rev 1:15 and 2:18. See: BAGD—875a; THAYER—664c.

5475. χαλκός {5x} **chalkŏs**, *khal-kos';* perh. from *5465* through the idea of *hollowing* out as a vessel (this metal being chiefly used for that purpose); *copper* (the substance, or some implement or coin made of it):—brass {3x}, money {2x}.

Chalkos, primarily "brass," became used for metals in general, later was applied to bronze, a mixture of copper and tin, then, by metonymy, to any article made of these metals, e.g., **(1)** money, Mt 10:9, ["brass" used for money]; Mk 6:8; 12:41; **(2)** a sounding instrument, 1 Cor 13:1, figurative of a person destitute of love; and **(3)** the metal itself in Rev 18:12. See: BAGD—875a; THAYER—664d.

5476. χαμαί {2x} **chamai**, *kham-ah'-ee;* adv. perh. from the base of *5490* through the idea of a *fissure* in the soil; *earthward,* i.e. *prostrate:*—on the ground {1x}, to the ground {1x}.

Chamai, signifies "on the ground," **(1)** Jn 9:6, of the act of Christ in spitting on the "ground" before anointing the eyes of a blind man; and **(2)** in Jn 18:6, "to the ground," of the fall of the rabble that had come to seize Christ in Gethsemane. See: BAGD—875b; THAYER—664d.

5477. Χανάαν {2x} **Chanaan**, *khan-ah'-an;* of Heb. or. [3667]; *Chanaan* (i.e. *Kenaan*), the early name of Pal.:—*Chanaan* {2x}. See: BAGD—875b; THAYER—664d.

5478. Χαναναῖος {1x} **Chanaanaiŏs**, *khan-ah-an-ah'-yos;* from *5477;* a *Chanaanœan* (i.e. *Kenaanite*), or native of Gentile Pal.:—of Canaan {1x}. See: BAGD—875b; THAYER—664d.

5479. χαρά {59x} **chara**, *khar-ah';* from *5463; cheerfulness,* i.e. calm *delight:*—joy {51x}, gladness {3x}, joyful {1x}, joyous {1x}, joyfulness {1x}, joyfully + *3326* {1x}, greatly {1x}.

Chara, "joy, delight," is akin to *chairo,* "to rejoice." **(1)** The word is sometimes used, by metonymy, of the occasion or cause of "joy": **(1a)** Lk 2:10 (lit., "I announce to you a great joy"); **(1b)** Phil 4:1, where the readers are called the apostle's "joy"; so 1 Th 2:19, 20; **(1c)** Heb 12:2, of the object of Christ's "joy"; **(1d)** Jas 1:2, where it is connected with falling into trials; **(1e)** perhaps also in Mt 25:21, 23, where some regard it as signifying, concretely, the circumstances attending cooperation in the authority of the Lord. **(2)** In Heb 12:11, "joyous" represents the phrase *meta,* "with," followed by *chara,* lit., "with joy", so in Heb 10:34, "joyfully"; **(3)** in 2 Cor 7:4 the noun is used with the middle voice of *huperperisseuo,* "to abound more exceedingly," and translated "(I am exceeding joyful"). See: TDNT—9:359, 1298; BAGD—875c; THAYER—664d.

5480. χάραγμα {9x} **charagma,** *khar'-ag-mah;* from the same as *5482;* a *scratch* or *etching,* i.e. *stamp* (as a *badge* of servitude), or *sculptured* figure (*statue*):— graven {1x}, mark {8x}.

Charagma, "to engrave", denotes **(1)** "a mark" or "stamp," e.g., Rev 13:16, 17; 14:9, 11; 15:2; 16:2; 19:20; 20:4; **(2)** "a thing graven," Acts 17:29. See: TDNT—9:416, 1308; BAGD—876a; THAYER—665b.

5481. χαρακτήρ {1x} **charaktēr,** *khar-ak-tare';* from the same as *5482;* a *graver* (the tool or the person), i.e. (by impl.) *engraving* (["*character*"], the *figure* stamped, i.e. an exact *copy* or [fig.] *representation*):— express image {1x}.

Charakter denotes, firstly, **(1)** "a tool for graving" (from *charasso,* "to cut into, to engross"; cf. Eng., "character," "characteristic"); then, "a stamp" or "impress," as on a coin or a seal, in which case the seal or die which makes an impression bears the "image" produced by it, and, *vice versa,* all the features of the "image" correspond respectively with those of the instrument producing it. **(2)** In the NT it is used metaphorically in Heb 1:3, of the Son of God as "the express image of His substance." The phrase expresses the fact that the Son "is both personally distinct from, and yet literally equal to, Him of whose essence He is the imprint. The Son of God is not merely his "image" (His *charakter*), He is the "image" or impress of His substance, or essence. It is the fact of complete similarity which this word stresses. See: TDNT—9:418, 1308; BAGD—876b; THAYER—665b.

5482. χάραξ {1x} **charax,** *khar'-ax;* from χαράσσω **charassō** (to *sharpen,* to a point; akin to *1125* through the idea of *scratching*); a *stake,* i.e. (by impl.) a *palisade* or *rampart* (military *mound* for circumvallation in a siege):—trench {1x}.

The dirt for making the siege mound came from digging a trench. See: BAGD—876b; THAYER—665c.

5483. χαρίζομαι {23x} **charizŏmai,** *khar-id'-zom-ahee;* mid. voice from *5485;* to grant as a *favor,* i.e. gratuitously, in kindness, pardon or rescue:—forgive {11x}, give {6x}, freely give {2x}, deliver {2x}, grant {1x}, frankly forgive {1x}.

Charizomai, as a verb, means "to bestow a favor unconditionally," is used **(1)** of the act of "forgiveness," whether **(1a)** divine, Eph 4:32; Col 2:13; 3:13; or **(1b)** human, Lk 7:42, 43 (debt); 2 Cor 2:7, 10; 12:13; Eph 4:32 (1st mention). **(2)** It also means "to gratify, to do what is pleasing to anyone" and is translated "deliver": "For if I be an offender, or have committed any thing

worthy of death, I refuse not to die: but if there be none of these things whereof these accuse me, no man may deliver me unto them. I appeal unto Caesar" (Acts 25:11 to give Paul over to the Jews so as to gratify their wishes; cf. 25:16). Syn.: 325, 525, 629, 591, 859, 1325, 1560, 1659, 1807, 1929, 3086, 3860, 4506. See: TDNT—9:372, 1298; BAGD—876c; THAYER—665c.

5484. χάριν {9x} **charin,** *khar'-in;* acc. of *5485* as prep.; through *favor* of, i.e. *on account* of:—for this cause + 5127 {3x}, because of {2x}, wherefore + 3739 {1x}, wherefore 5101 {1x}, for . . . sake {1x}, to speak reproachfully + 3059 {1x}. Cf. Lk 7:47; Gal 3:19; Eph 3:1; 3:14; 1 Ti 5:14; Titus 1:5, 11; 1 Jn 3:12; Jude 16. See: BAGD—877a; THAYER—665d.

5485. χάρις {156x} **charis,** *khar'-ece;* from *5463; graciousness* (as *gratifying*), of manner or act (abstr. or concr.; lit., fig., or spiritual; espec. the divine influence upon the heart, and its reflection in the life; incl. *gratitude*):—grace {130x}, favour {6x}, thanks {4x}, thank {4x}, thank + 2192 {3x}, pleasure {2x}, misc. {7x} = acceptable, benefit, gift, gracious, joy, liberality.

(1) Grace indicates favor on the part of the giver, thanks on the part of the receiver. **(2)** Although *charis* is related to sins and is the attribute of God that they evoke, God's *eleos* (*1656*), the free gift for the forgiveness of sins, is related to the misery that sin brings. **(3)** God's tender sense of our misery displays itself in his efforts to lessen and entirely remove it—efforts that are hindered and defeated only by man's continued perverseness. **(4)** Grace removes guilt; mercy removes misery. It has various uses, **(5)** objective, that which bestows or occasions pleasure, delight, or causes favorable regard; it is applied, e.g., **(5a)** to beauty, or gracefulness of person, Lk 2:40; **(5b)** an act, 2 Cor 8:6, or **(5c)** speech, Lk 4:22, "gracious words"; Col 4:6;

(6) subjective, **(6a)** on the part of the bestower, **(6a1)** the friendly disposition from which the kindly act proceeds, graciousness, loving-kindness, goodwill generally, e.g., Acts 7:10; **(6a2)** especially with reference to the divine favor or "grace," e.g., Acts 14:26; **(6a3)** in this respect there is stress on its freeness and universality, its spontaneous character, as in the case of God's redemptive mercy, and the pleasure or joy He designs for the recipient; **(6a4)** thus it is set in contrast with debt, Rom 4:4, 16, with works, 11:6, and with law, Jn 1:17; see also, e.g., Rom 6:14, 15; Gal 5:4; **(6b)** on the part of the receiver, **(6b1)** a sense of the favor bestowed, a feeling of gratitude, e.g., Rom 6:17 ("thanks"); **(6b2)** in this respect it sometimes

signifies "to be thankful," e.g., Lk 17:9 ("doth he thank the servant?" lit., "hath he thanks to"); 1 Ti 1:12; **(6c)** in another objective sense, the effect of "grace," the spiritual state of those who have experienced its exercise, whether **(6c1)** a state of "grace," e.g., Rom 5:2; 1 Pet 5:12; 2 Pet 3:18, or **(6c2)** a proof thereof in practical effects, deeds of "grace," e.g., 1 Cor 16:3, "liberality"; 2 Cor 8:6, 19; **(6c3)** in 2 Cor 9:8 it means the sum of earthly blessings; **(6c4)** the power and equipment for ministry, e.g., Rom 1:5; 12:6; 15:15; 1 Cor 3:10; Gal 2:9; Eph 3:2, 7.

(7) To be in favor with is to find "grace" with, e.g., Acts 2:47; **(7a)** hence it appears in this sense at the beginning and the end of several epistles, where the writer desires "grace" from God for the readers, e.g., Rom 1:7; 1 Cor 1:3; **(8)** in this respect it is connected with the imperative mood of the word *chairo,* "to rejoice," a mode of greeting among Greeks, e.g., Acts 15:23; 2 Jn 10, 11, "God speed." **(9)** The fact that "grace" is received **(9a)** both from God the Father, 2 Cor 1:12, and from Christ, Gal 1:6; Rom 5:15 (where both are mentioned), is a testimony to the deity of Christ. **(9b)** See also 2 Th 1:12, where the phrase "according to the grace of our God and the Lord Jesus Christ" is to be taken with each of the preceding clauses, "in you," "and ye in Him." **(10)** In Jas 4:6, "But He giveth more grace", the statement is to be taken in connection with the preceding verse, which contains two remonstrating, rhetorical questions, "Think ye that the Scripture speaketh in vain?" and "Doth the Spirit (the Holy Spirit) which He made to dwell in us long unto envying?" The implied answer to each is "it cannot be so." Accordingly, if those who are acting so flagrantly, as if it were so, will listen to the Scripture instead of letting it speak in vain, and will act so that the Holy Spirit may have His way within, God will give even "a greater grace," namely, all that follows from humbleness and from turning away from the world. See: TDNT—9:372, 1298; BAGD—877b; THAYER—665d.

5486. χάρισμα {17x} **charisma,** *khar'-is-mah;* from *5483;* a (divine) *gratuity,* i.e. *deliverance* (from danger or passion); (spec.) a (spiritual) *endowment,* i.e. (subj.) relig. *qualification,* or (obj.) miraculous *faculty:*—free gift {2x}, gift {15x}.

(1) *Charisma* is a favor which one receives without any merit of his own. **(2)** It is "a gift of grace, a gift involving grace" (*charis*) on the part of God as the donor, is used **(3)** of His free bestowments upon sinners, Rom 5:15, 16; 6:23; 11:29; **(4)** of His endowments upon believers by the operation of the Holy Spirit in the churches, Rom 12:6; 1 Cor 1:7; 12:4, 9, 28, 30, 31; 1 Ti

4:14; 2 Ti 1:6; 1 Pet 4:10; **(5)** of that which is imparted through human instruction, Rom 1:11; **(6)** of the natural "gift" of continence, consequent upon the grace of God as Creator, 1 Cor 7:7; **(7)** of gracious deliverances granted in answer to the prayers of fellow believers, 2 Cor 1:11. See: TDNT—9:402, 1298; BAGD—878d; THAYER—667a.

5487. χαριτόω {2x} **charitŏō,** *khar-ee-tŏ'-o;* from *5485;* to *grace,* i.e. indue with special *honor:*—make accepted {1x}, be highly favoured {1x}.

Charitoo, to endow with *charis,* primarily signified "to make graceful or gracious," and came to denote, "to cause to find favor," **(1)** Lk 1:28, "highly favored" (i.e., "endued with grace"); **(2)** in Eph 1:6, it is translated "freely bestowed"; it does not here mean to endue with grace. Grace implies more than favor; grace is a free gift, favor may be deserved or gained. See: TDNT—9:372, 1298; BAGD—879a; THAYER—667a.

5488. Χαρράν {2x} **Charrhan,** *khar-hran';* of Heb. or. [2771]; *Charrhan* (i.e. *Charan*), a place in Mesopotamia:—Charran {2x}. See: BAGD—879b; THAYER—667b.

5489. χάρτης {1x} **chartēs,** *khar'-tace;* from the same as *5482;* a *sheet* ("chart") of writing-material (as to be *scribbled* over):—paper {1x}.

Chartes, "a sheet of paper made of strips of papyrus" (whence Eng., "paper", Eng., "chart," "charter," etc.), the word is used in 2 Jn 12. The papyrus reed grew in ancient times in great profusion in the Nile and was used as a material for writing. From Egypt its use spread to other countries and it was the universal material for writing in general in Greece and Italy during the most flourishing periods of their literature. The pith of the stem of the plant was cut into thin strips, placed side by side to form a sheath. Another layer was laid upon this at right angles to it. The two layers were united by moisture and pressure and frequently with the addition of glue. The sheets, after being dried and polished, were ready for use. Normally, the writing is on that side of the papyrus on which the fibers lie horizontally, parallel to the length of the roll, but where the material was scarce the writer used the other side also (cf. Rev 5:1). Papyrus continued to be used until the seventh cent. A.D., when the conquest of Egypt by the Arabs led to the disuse of the material for literary purposes and the use of vellum till the 12th century. See: BAGD—879b; THAYER—667b.

5490. χάσμα {1x} **chasma,** *khas'-mah;* from a form of an obs. primary χάω

chaō, (to *"gape"* or *"yawn"*); a *"chasm"* or *vacancy* (impassable *interval*):—gulf {1x}. See: BAGD—879b; THAYER—667b.

5491. **χεῖλος** {7x} **chĕilŏs**, *khi'-los;* from a form of the same as *5490;* a *lip* (as a *pouring* place); fig. a *margin* (of water):—lip {6x}, shore {1x}.

Cheilos is used **(1)** of the organ of speech, **(1a)** Mt 15:8 and Mk 7:6, where "honoring with the lips," besides meaning empty words, may have reference to a Jewish custom of putting to the mouth the tassel of the *tallith* (the woollen scarf wound round the head and neck during prayer), as a sign of acceptance of the Law from the heart; **(1b)** Rom 3:13; 1 Cor 14:21 (from Is 28:11, 12, speaking of the Assyrian foe as God's message to disobedient Israel); Heb 13:15; 1 Pet 3:10; **(2)** metaphorically, of "the brink or edge of things," as of the sea shore, Heb 11:12, lit., "the shore (of the sea)." See: BAGD—879c; THAYER—667b.

5492. **χειμάζω** {1x} **chĕimazō**, *khi-mad'-zo;* from the same as *5494;* to *storm*, i.e. (pass.) to *labor under a gale:*—be tossed with tempest {1x}.

Cheimazo, from *cheima*, "winter cold," primarily, "to expose to winter cold," signifies "to drive with a storm"; in the passive voice, "to be driven with storm, to be tempest-tossed," Acts 27:18, "being . . . tossed with a tempest." See: BAGD—879c; THAYER—667c.

5493. **χείμαρρος** {1x} **chĕimarrhŏs**, *khi'-mar-hros;* from the base of *5494* and *4482;* a *storm-runlet*, i.e. *winter-torrent:*—brook {1x}.

Cheimarrhos, lit., "winter-flowing" (from *cheima*, "winter," and *rheo*, "to flow"), a stream which runs only in winter or when swollen with rains, a "brook" Jn 18:1. See: BAGD—879c; THAYER—667c.

5494. **χειμών** {6x} **chĕimōn**, *khi-mone';* from a der. of χέω **chĕō**, (to *pour;* akin to the base of *5490* through the idea of a *channel*), mean. a *storm* (as *pouring* rain); by impl. the *rainy* season, i.e. *winter:*—tempest {1x}, foul weather {1x}, winter {4x}.

Cheimon denotes "winter," in Mt 24:20; Mk 13:18; Jn 10:22; 2 Ti 4:21. See: BAGD—879d; THAYER—667c.

5495. **χείρ** {179x} **chĕir**, *khire;* perh. from the base of *5494* in the sense of its congener the base of *5490* (through the idea of *hollowness* for grasping); the *hand* (lit. or fig. [*power*]; espec. [by Heb.] a *means* or *instrument*):—hand {179x}.

Cheir is used, besides its ordinary significance, **(1)** in the idiomatic phrases, "by the hand of," "at the hand of," etc., to signify "by the agency of," Acts 5:12; 7:35; 17:25; 14:3; Gal 3:19 (cf. Lev 26:46); Rev 19:2; **(2)** metaphorically, for the power of God, e.g., Lk 1:66; 23:46; Jn 10:28, 29; Acts 11:21; 13:11; Heb 1:10; 2:7; 10:31; **(3)** by metonymy, for power, e.g., Mt 17:22; Lk 24:7; Jn 10:39; Acts 12:11. See: TDNT—9:424, 1309; BAGD—879d; THAYER—667c.

5496. **χειραγωγέω** {2x} **chĕiragōgĕō**, *khi-rag-ogue-eh'-o;* from *5497;* to be a *hand-leader*, i.e. to *guide* (a blind person):—lead by the hand {2x}. Cf. Acts 9:8; 22:11. See: TDNT—9:435, 1309; BAGD—880d; THAYER—668a.

5497. **χειραγωγός** {1x} **chĕiragōgŏs**, *khi-rag-o-gos';* from *5495* and a redupl. form of *71;* a *hand-leader*, i.e. personal *conductor* (of a blind person):—some to lead by the hand {1x}. See: TDNT—9:435, 1309; BAGD—880d; THAYER—668a.

5498. **χειρόγραφον** {1x} **chĕirŏgraphŏn**, *khi-rog'-raf-on;* neut. of a compound of *5495* and *1125;* something *hand-written* ("chirograph"), i.e. a *manuscript* (spec. a legal *document* or *bond* [fig.]):—handwriting {1x}. See: TDNT—9:435, 1309; BAGD—880d; THAYER—668.

5499. **χειροποίητος** {6x} **chĕirŏpŏiētŏs**, *khi-rop-oy'-ay-tos;* from *5495* and a der. of *4160; manufactured*, i.e. of *human construction:*—made by hands {1x}, made with hands {6x}

Cheiropoietos, "made by hand," of human handiwork (*cheir*, and *poieo*, "to make"), is said **(1)** of the temple in Jerusalem, Mk 14:58; **(2)** temples in general, Acts 7:48; 17:24; **(3)** negatively, of the heavenly and spiritual tabernacle, Heb 9:11; **(4)** of the holy place in the earthly tabernacle, Heb 9:24; **(5)** of circumcision, Eph 2:11. See: TDNT—9:436, 1309; BAGD—880d; THAYER—668b.

5500. **χειροτονέω** {4x} **chĕirŏtŏnĕō**, *khi-rot-on-eh'-o;* from a comp. of *5495* and τείνω **tĕinō** (to *stretch*); to be a *hand-reacher*, or *voter* (by raising the hand), i.e. (gen.) to *select* or *appoint:*—choose {1x}, ordain {3x}.

Cheirotoneo, as a verb, **(1)** primarily used of voting in the Athenian legislative assembly and meaning "to stretch forth the hands" [*cheir*, "the hand," *teino*, "to stretch"], is not to be taken in its literal sense. **(2)** *Cheirotoneo* is said of "the appointment, the ordaining" of elders by apostolic missionaries in the various churches which they revisited, Acts 14:23, "had appointed," i.e., by the recognition of those who had been manifesting themselves as gifted of

God to discharge the functions of elders. **(3)** It is also said of those who were "appointed" (not by voting, but with general approbation) by the churches in Greece to accompany the apostle in conveying their gifts to the poor saints in Judea, 2 Cor 8:19. **(4)** The KJV of 1611 had an addendum added to the books detailing the theme or date of the letter. This word is so used in the ending to 2 Timothy and Titus. See: TDNT—9:437, 1309; BAGD—881a; THAYER—668b.

5501. χείρων {11x} **chĕirōn,** *khi'-rone;* irreg. comp. of *2556;* from an obs. equiv. χέρης **chĕrēs** (of uncert. der.); *more evil* or *aggravated* (phys., ment. or mor.):—worse {7x}, sorer {1x}, worse + 1519 + 3588 {1x}, worse and worse + 1909 + 3588 {1x}, a worse thing + 5100 {1x}.

Cheiron, used as the comparative degree of *kakos,* "evil," describes **(1)** the condition of certain men, Mt 12:45; Lk 11:26; 2 Pet 2:20; **(2)** evil men themselves and seducers, 2 Ti. 3:13; **(3)** indolent men who refuse to provide for their own households, and are worse than unbelievers, 1 Ti 5:8; **(4)** a rent in a garment, Mt 9:16; Mk 2:21; **(5)** an error, Mt 27:64; **(6)** a person suffering from a malady, Mk 5:26; **(7)** a possible physical affliction, Jn 5:14; **(8)** a punishment, Heb 10:29, "sorer." See: BAGD—881b; THAYER—668c.

5502. χερουβίμ {1x} **chĕrŏubim,** *kher-oo-beem';* plur. of Heb. or. [3742]; "*cherubim*" (i.e. cherubs or *kerubim*):—cherubims {1x}.

Cherubim are regarded by some as the ideal representatives of redeemed animate creation. In the tabernacle and temple they were represented by the two golden figures of two-winged living creatures. They were all of one piece with the golden lid of the ark of the covenant in the Holy of Holies signifying that the prospect of approaching the living God by any human means other than through a blood sacrifice was protected by the angels just as the angels protected sinful man from approaching the tree of life in the Garden of Eden after he and Eve sinned. The *cherubim* faces were toward this mercy seat, suggesting a longing on their behalf to "look into" this salvation, 1 Pet 1:12.

The first reference to the "*cherubim*" is in Gen 3:24, which should read "at the East of the Garden of Eden He caused to dwell in a tabernacle the *cherubim,* and the flaming sword which turned itself to keep the way of the Tree of Life." This was not simply to keep fallen human beings out; the presence of the "*cherubim*" suggests that redeemed men, restored to God on God's conditions, would have access to the Tree of Life. (See Rev 22:14.) In the NT the word is found in Heb 9:5, where the

reference is to the ark in the tabernacle, and the thought is suggested of those who minister to the manifestation of the glory of God. Between these figures God was regarded as having fixed his dwelling place. See: TDNT—9:438, 1312; BAGD—881b; THAYER—668c.

5503. χήρα {27x} **chēra,** *khay'-rah;* fem. of a presumed der. appar. from the base of *5490* through the idea of *deficiency;* a *widow* (as *lacking* a husband), lit. or fig.:—widow {27x}.

Chera is a widow, one whose husband is dead. **(1)** It is found in Mk 12:40, 42, 43; Lk 2:37; 4:25, 26, lit., "a woman a widow"; 7:12; 18:3, 5; 20:47; 21:2, 3; Acts 6:1; 9:39, 41; 1 Ti 5:3 (twice), 4, 5, 11, 16 (twice); Jas 1:27. **(2)** 1 Ti 5:9 refers to elderly "widows" (not an ecclesiastical "order"), recognized, for relief or maintenance by the church (cf. vv. 3, 16), as those who had fulfilled the conditions mentioned; where relief could be ministered by those who had relatives that were "widows" (a likely circumstance in large families), the church was not to be responsible; there is an intimation of the tendency to shelve individual responsibility at the expense of church funds. **(3)** In Rev 18:7, it is used figuratively of a city forsaken. See: TDNT—9:440, 1313; BAGD—881c; THAYER—668d.

5504. χθές {3x} **chthĕs,** *khthes;* of uncert. der.; "*yesterday*"; by extens. *in time past* or *hitherto:*—yesterday {3x}. Cf. John 4:52; Acts 7:28; Heb. 13:8. See: BAGD—881d; THAYER—668d.

5505. χιλιάς {23x} **chilias,** *khil-ee-as';* from *5507;* one *thousand* ("*chiliad*"):—thousand {23x}. See: TDNT—9:466, 1316; BAGD—882a; THAYER—669a.

5506. χιλίαρχος {22x} **chiliarchŏs,** *khil-ee'-ar-khos;* from *5507* and *757;* the *commander of a thousand* soldiers ("*chiliarch*"), i.e. *colonel:*—chief captain {19x}, captain {2x}, high captain {1x}.

Chiliarchos, **(1)** denoting "a commander of 1000 soldiers" (from *chilios,* "a thousand," and *archo,* "to rule"), was the Greek word for the Persian vizier, and for the Roman military tribune, the commander of a Roman cohort, e.g., Jn 18:12; Acts 21:31–33, 37. **(2)** One such commander was constantly in charge of the Roman garrison in Jerusalem. **(3)** The word became used also for any military commander, e.g., a "captain" or "chief captain," Mk 6:21; Rev 6:15; 19:18. See: BAGD—881d; THAYER—668d.

5507. χίλιοι {11x} **chiliŏi,** *khil'-ee-oy;* plur. of uncert. aff.; a *thousand:*—thousand {11x}. See: TDNT—9:466, 1316; BAGD—882a; THAYER—669a.

5508. **Χίος** {1x} **Chiŏs,** *khee'-os;* of uncert. der.; *Chios,* an island in the Mediterranean:—*Chios* {1x}. See: BAGD—882b; THAYER—669a.

5509. **χιτών** {11x} **chiton,** *khee-tone';* of for. or. [3801]; a *tunic* or *shirt:*—clothes {1x}, coat {9x}, garment {1x}.

(1) A *chiton* was a tunic, an undergarment, usually worn next to the skin, a garment, a vestment. **(2)** It denotes "the inner vest or undergarment," and is to be distinguished, as such, from the *himation.* **(2a)** The distinction is made, for instance, in the Lord's command in Mt 5:40: "If any man would go to law with thee, and take away thy coat (*chiton*), (*himation*) also." **(2b)** The order is reversed in Lk 6:29, and the difference lies in this, that in Mt 5:40 the Lord is referring to a legal process, so the claimant is supposed to claim the inner garment, the less costly. The defendant is to be willing to let him have the more valuable one too. In the passage in Luke an act of violence is in view, and there is no mention of going to law. So the outer garment is the first one which would be seized. When the soldiers had crucified Jesus they took His garments (*himation,* in the plural), His outer garments, and the "coat," the *chiton,* the inner garment, which was without seam, woven from the top throughout, Jn 19:23. The outer garments were easily divisible among the four soldiers, but they could not divide the *chiton* without splitting it, so they cast lots for it.

(3) Dorcas was accustomed to make coats (*chiton*) and garments (*himation*), Acts 9:39, that is, the close fitting undergarments and the long, flowing outer robes. **(4)** A person was said to be "naked" (*gumnos*), whether he was without clothing, or had thrown off his outer garment, e.g., his *ependutes,* (*1903*), and was clad in a light undergarment, as was the case with Peter, in Jn 21:7 and the young man in Mk 14:51–52, (Mark himself?). **(5)** The high priest, in rending his clothes after the reply the Lord gave him in answer to his challenge, rent his undergarments (*chiton*), the more forcibly to express his assumed horror and indignation, Mk 14:63. **(6)** In Jude 23, "the garment spotted by the flesh" is the *chiton,* the metaphor of the undergarment being appropriate; for it would be that which was brought into touch with the pollution of the flesh.

Syn.: **(A)** *Himation* (*2440*) refers to garments in a general sense (Mt 11:8; 26:65); or when used specifically, it refers to the large outer garment that a man could sleep in (cf. Ex 22:26). **(B)** The *chlamys* (*5511*) refers to a garment of dignity and office. **(C)** A *stole* (*4749*) is any stately robe, especially a long sweeping garment that reaches to the feet or a garment that has a train that sweeps the ground; a garment of special solemnity, richness, and beauty. **(D)** *Poderes* (*4158*) refers, like stole, to a long garment reaching the ankles. With reference to the high priestly garments, the *poderes* only refers to the robe; *stole* refers to the whole array. See: BAGD—882b; THAYER—669a.

5510. **χιών** {3x} **chiōn,** *khee-one';* perh. akin to the base of *5490* (*5465*) or *5494* (as *descending* or *empty*); *snow:*—snow {3x}. Cf. Mt 28:3; Mk 9:3; Rev 1:14. See: BAGD—882b; THAYER—669a.

5511. **χλαμύς** {2x} **chlamus,** *khlam-ooce';* of uncert. der.; a military *cloak:*—robe {2x}.

A *chlamus* was an outer garment usually worn over the tunic (Mt 27: 28, 31). Syn.: cf. 5509 for discussion. See: BAGD—882b; THAYER—669b.

5512. **χλευάζω** {2x} **chlĕuazō,** *khlyoo-ad'-zo;* from a der. prob. of *5491;* to *throw out* the *lip,* i.e. *jeer* at:—mock {2x}. See: BAGD—882c; THAYER—669b.

5513. **χλιαρός** {1x} **chliarŏs,** *khlee-ar-os';* from χλίω **chliō,** (to *warm*); *tepid:*—lukewarm {1x}. See: TDNT—2:876, 296; BAGD—882c; THAYER—669b.

5514. **Χλόη** {1x} **Chlŏē,** *khlŏ'-ay;* fem. of appar. a primary word; "*green*"; *Chloë,* a Chr. female:—*Chloe* {1x}. See: BAGD—882c; THAYER—669b.

5515. **χλωρός** {4x} **chlōrŏs,** *khlo-ros';* from the same as *5514; greenish,* i.e. *verdant, dun-colored:*—green {3x}, pale {1x}.

Chloros, (akin to *chloe,* "tender foliage", cf. the name "Chloe," 1 Cor 1:11, and Eng., "chlorine"), denotes **(1)** "pale green," the color of young grass, Mk 6:39; Rev 8:7; 9:4, "green thing"; hence, **(2)** "pale," Rev 6:8, the color of the horse whose rider's name is Death. See: BAGD—882d; THAYER—669b.

5516. **χξϛ** {1x} **chi xi stigma,** *khee xee stig'-ma;* the 22nd, 14th and an obs. letter (*4742* as a *cross*) of the Greek alphabet (intermediate between the 5th and 6th), used as numbers; denoting respectively 600, 60 and 6; 666 as a numeral:—six hundred threescore and six {1x}. See: BAGD—882d; THAYER—669b.

5517. **χοϊκός** {4x} **chŏïkŏs,** *khŏ-ik-os';* from *5522; dusty* or *dirty* (*soil*-like), i.e. (by impl.) *terrene:*—earthy {4x}.

Choikos denotes "earthy," made of earth, from *chous,* "soil, earth thrown down or heaped up," 1 Cor 15:47–49. See: TDNT—9:472, 1318; BAGD—883a; THAYER—669c.

5518. χοῖνιξ {2x} **chŏinix**, *khoy'-nix;* of uncertain der.; a *chœnix* or certain dry measure:—measure {2x}.

Choinix, as a noun, means a dry "measure" of rather less than a quart, about "as much as would support a person of moderate appetite for a day," occurs in Rev 6:6 (twice). Usually eight *choenixes* could be bought for a *denarius* (about 9 1/2d.); this passage predicts circumstances in which the *denarius* is the price of one *choenix.* Syn.: 280, 488, 943, 2884, 3313, 3354, 3358, 4057, 4568, 5234, 5249. See: BAGD— 883b; THAYER—669c.

5519. χοῖρος {14x} **chŏirŏs**, *khoy'-ros;* of uncert. der.; a *hog:*—swine {14x}.

Choiros, "a swine," is used in the plural, in the Synoptic Gospels only, Mt 7:6; 8:30, 31, 32; Mk 5:11, 13, 16; Lk 8:32, 33; 15:15, 16. See: BAGD—883b; THAYER—669c.

5520. χολάω {1x} **chŏlaō**, *khol-ah'-o;* from *5521;* to *be bilious,* i.e. (by impl.) *irritable* (*enraged,* "choleric"):—be angry {1x}.

Cholao, connected with *chole,* "gall, bile," which became used metaphorically to signify bitter anger, means "to be enraged," Jn 7:23, in the Lord's remonstrance with the Jews on account of their indignation at His having made a man whole on the Sabbath Day. See: BAGD—883b; THAYER—669c.

5521. χολή {2x} **chŏlē**, *khol-ay';* fem. of an equiv. perh. akin to the same as *5514* (from the *greenish* hue); "*gall*" or *bile,* i.e. (by anal.) *poison* or an *anodyne* (wormwood, poppy, etc.):—gall {2x}.

Chole, a word probably connected with *chloe,* "yellow," denotes "gall," **(1)** literal, Mt 27:34 (cf. Ps 69:21); some regard the word here as referring to myrrh, on account of Mk 15:23; **(2)** metaphorical, Acts 8:23, where "gall of bitterness" stands for extreme wickedness, productive of evil fruit. See: BAGD—883b; THAYER—669c.

5522. χόος {2x} **chŏos**, *khŏ'-os;* from the base of *5494;* a *heap* (as *poured* out), i.e. *rubbish;* loose *dirt:*—dust {2x}. Cf. Mk 6:11 and Rev 18:19. See: BAGD—883c, 884b; THAYER—669d.

5523. Χοραζίν {2x} **Chŏrazin**, *khor-ad-zin';* of uncert. der.; *Chorazin,* a place in Pal.:—Chorazin {2x}. See: BAGD—883c; THAYER—883c; THAYER—669d.

5524. χορηγέω {2x} **chŏrēgĕō**, *khor-ayg-eh'-o;* from a compound of *5525* and *71;* to be a *dance-leader,* i.e. (gen.) to *furnish:*—give {1x}, minister {1x}.

Choregeo, primarily, among the Greeks, signified **(1)** "to lead a stage chorus or dance" (*choros,* and *hegeomai,* "to lead"), then, **(2)** "to

defray the expenses of a chorus"; hence, later, **(3)** metaphorically, "to supply," **(3a)** 2 Cor 9:10 (2nd part, "to minister"); **(3b)** 1 Pet 4:11, "giveth." See: BAGD—883d; THAYER—670a.

5525. χορός {1x} **chŏrŏs**, *khor-os';* of uncert. der.; a *ring,* i.e. round *dance* ("choir"):—dancing {1x}. See: BAGD—883d; THAYER—670a.

5526. χορτάζω {15x} **chŏrtazō**, *khor-tad'-zo;* from *5528;* to *fodder,* i.e. (gen.) to *gorge* (*supply food* in abundance):— feed {1x}, be full {1x}, fill {12x}, satisfy {1x}. See: BAGD—883d; THAYER—670a.

5527. χόρτασμα {1x} **chŏrtasma**, *khor'-tasmah;* from *5526; forage,* i.e. *food:*—sustenance {1x}.

Chortasma refers to food, (vegetable) sustenance, whether for men or flocks, Acts 7:11. See: BAGD—884a; THAYER—670b.

5528. χόρτος {15x} **chŏrtŏs**, *khor'-tos;* appar. a primary word; a "*court*" or "*garden*", i.e. (by impl. of *pasture*) *herbage* or *vegetation:*—blade {2x}, grass {12x}, hay {1x}.

Chortos primarily denoted "a feeding enclosure"; then, "food," especially grass for feeding cattle; it is translated **(1)** "grass" in Mt 6:30; 14:19; Mk 6:39 (where "the green grass" is the first evidence of early spring); Lk 12:28; Jn 6:10; Jas 1:10, 11; 1 Pet 1:24; Rev 8:7; 9:4; **(2)** "blade" in Mt 13:26; Mk 4:28; **(3)** "hay" in 1 Cor 3:12, used figuratively. See: BAGD— 884a; THAYER—670b.

5529. Χουζᾶς {1x} **Chŏuzas**, *khood-zas';* of uncert. or.: *Chuzas,* an officer of Herod:—Chuza {1x}. See: BAGD—884b; THAYER—670b.

5530. χράομαι {11x} **chraŏmai**, *khrah'-om-ahee;* mid. voice of a primary verb (perh. rather from *5495,* to *handle*); to *furnish* what is needed; (give an *oracle,* "graze" [touch slightly], *light* upon, etc.), i.e. (by impl.) to *employ* or (by extens.) to *act toward* one in a given manner:—entreat {1x}, use {10x}.

Chraomai, denotes **(1)** "to use," Acts 27:17; 1 Cor 7:21, where "use it rather" means "use your bond-service rather"; 7:31, where "they that use (this world)" is followed by the strengthened form *katachraomai,* rendered "abusing," or "using to the full"; 9:12, 15; 2 Cor 1:17; 3:12; 13:10; 1 Ti 1:8, of "using" the Law lawfully, i.e., agreeably to its designs; 1 Ti 5:23; **(2)** "deal with," Acts 27:3. See: BAGD—884b; THAYER—670c. comp. *5531; 5534.*

5531. χράω {1x} **chraō**, *khrah'-o;* prob. the same as the base of *5530;* to *loan:*—lend {1x}. Syn.: *Daneizo (1155)* means

to lend on interest, as a business transaction; whereas, *chrao* means to lend, grant the use of, as a friendly act. See: BAGD—884d, 433a; THAYER—670d.

5532. χρεία {49x} **chrĕia**, *khri'-ah;* from the base of *5530* or *5534; employment,* i.e. an *affair;* also (by impl.) *occasion, demand, requirement* or *destitution:*—need {25x}, need + *2192* {14x}, necessity {3x}, use {2x}, needful {1x}, necessary {1x}, business {1x}, lack {1x}, wants {1x}. See: BAGD—884d; THAYER—670d.

5533. χρεωφειλέτης {2x} **chrĕōphĕilĕtēs**, *khreh-o-fi-let'-ace;* from a der. of *5531* and *3781;* a *loan-ower,* i.e. *indebted* person:—debtor {2x}. Cf. Lk 7:41; 16:5. See: BAGD—885b; THAYER—671b.

5534. χρή {1x} **chrē**, *khray;* third pers. sing. of the same as *5530* or *5531* used impers.; it *needs* (*must* or *should*) be:—ought {1x}.
Syn.: *Dei* (*1165*) expresses a logical necessity, *opheilo* (*3784*), a moral obligation; cf. *chre* (*5534*), Jas 3:10, "ought," which expresses a need resulting from the fitness of things. See: BAGD—885b; THAYER—671b.

5535. χρῄζω {5x} **chrēzō**, *khrade'-zo;* from *5532;* to *make* (i.e. *have*) *necessity,* i.e. *be in want* of:—need {2x}, have need {3x}.
Chrezo, "to need, to have need of" (akin to *chre,* "it is necessary, fitting"), is used in Mt 6:32; Lk 11:8; 12:30; Rom 16:2, "hath need"; 2 Cor 3:1. See: BAGD—885b; THAYER—671b.

5536. χρῆμα {7x} **chrēma**, *khray'-mah;* something *useful* or *needed,* i.e. *wealth, price:*—money {4x}, riches {3x}.
Chrema, "what one uses or needs" (*chraomai,* "to use"), "a matter, business," hence denotes (1) "riches," Mk 10:23, 24; Lk 18:24. It also means lit., "a thing that one uses", hence, (2) "money," (2a) Acts 4:37, singular number, "a sum of money"; (2b) plural in Acts 8:18, 20; 24:26. See: TDNT—9:480, 1319; BAGD—885c; THAYER—671b.

5537. χρηματίζω {9x} **chrēmatizō**, *khray-mat-id'-zo;* from *5536;* to *utter an oracle* (comp. the orig. sense of *5530*), i.e. divinely *intimate;* by impl. (comp. the secular sense of *5532*) to constitute a *firm* for business, i.e. (gen.) *bear* as a *title:*—be warned of God {3x}, call {2x}, be admonished of God {1x}, reveal {1x}, speak {1x}, be warned from God {1x}.
Chrematizo means primarily, "to transact business," then, "to give advice to enquirers" (especially of official pronouncements of magistrates), or "a response to those consulting an oracle," came to signify the giving of a divine "admonition" or instruction or warning, in a general way;

translated (1) "admonished" in Heb 8:5. Elsewhere it is translated (2) by the verb "to warn" in Mt 2:12, 22; Acts 10:22; 11:7. (3) It is also translated "spake" in Acts 12:25. (4) Occasionally it means "to be called or named", (4a) Rom 7:3; and (4b) Acts 11:26, of the name "Christians." Its primary significance, "to have business dealings with," led to this. They "were (publicly) called" Christians, because this was their chief business, following the Christ. See: TDNT—9:480, 1319; BAGD—885c; THAYER—671b.

5538. χρηματισμός {1x} **chrēmatismŏs**, *khray-mat-is-mos';* from *5537;* a divine *response* or *revelation:*—answer of God {1x}.
Chrematismos, "a divine response, an oracle," is used in Rom 11:4, of the answer given by God to Elijah's complaint against Israel. See: TDNT—9:482, 1319; BAGD—885d; THAYER—671c.

5539. χρήσιμος {1x} **chrēsimŏs**, *khray'-see-mos;* from *5540; serviceable:*—profit {1x}.
Chresimos means fit for use, useful, 2 Ti 2:14. See: BAGD—885d; THAYER—671d.

5540. χρῆσις {2x} **chrēsis**, *khray'-sis;* from *5530; employment,* i.e. (spec.) sexual *intercourse* (as an *occupation* of the body):—use {2x}. Cf. Rom 1:26, 27. See: BAGD—885d; THAYER—671d.

5541. χρηστεύομαι {1x} **chrēstĕuŏmai**, *khraste-yoo'-om-ahee;* mid. voice from *5543;* to *show oneself useful,* i.e. *act benevolently:*—be kind {1x}.
To be kind is to treat one as one's kin, one's own family, 1 Cor 13:4. See: TDNT—9:491, 1320; BAGD—886a; THAYER—671d.

5542. χρηστολογία {1x} **chrēstŏlŏgia**, *khrase-tol-og-ee'-ah;* from a compound of *5543* and *3004; fair speech,* i.e. *plausibility:*—good words {1x}.
This word means fair speaking, the smooth and plausible address which sounds good, easily received; yet deceptive. See: TDNT—9:492, 1320; BAGD—886a; THAYER—671d.

5543. χρηστός {7x} **chrēstŏs**, *khrase-tos';* from *5530; employed,* i.e. (by impl.) *useful* (in manner or morals):—better {1x}, easy {1x}, good {1x}, goodness {1x}, gracious {1x}, kind {2x}.
Chrestos, as an adjective, is said (1) of things, (1a) Mt 11:30, Christ's yoke being "easy"; (1b) of things, as wine, Lk 5:39, "better"; (2) of believers, Eph 4:32, "kind"; (3) of manners, "good", 1 Cor 15:33; (4) "goodness", Rom 2:4, of God. It is said (5) of the character of God as "kind",

Lk 6:35, and "gracious", 1 Pet 2:3. See: TDNT—
9:483, 1320; BAGD—886a; THAYER—671d.

5544. χρηστότης {10x} **chrēstŏtēs**, *khray-
stot'-ace;* from *5543;* use-
fulness*, i.e. mor. *excellence* (in character or
demeanor):—gentleness {1x}, good {1x}, goodness {4x}, kindness {4x}.

This word refers not to a virtue of a person
that encompasses only to a person's words and
countenance; it refers to the virtue that per-
vades and penetrates the whole nature, that mel-
lows anything harsh and austere. It is that virtue
that is gentle, charming, and calm, suited to
the company of all good people, attracting their
friendship, delightful in encouragement and
moderate in manners. *Chrestotes*, as a noun,
denotes **(1)** "good" **(1a)** in the sense of what is
upright, righteous: "They are all gone out of
the way, they are together become unprofitable; there is none that doeth good (*chrestotes*),
no, not one" (Rom 3:12); **(1b)** in the sense of
goodness of heart or act, said of God: "Behold
therefore the goodness (*chrestotes*) and severity of God: on them which fell, severity; but
toward thee, goodness (*chrestotes*), if thou continue in his goodness (*chrestotes*): otherwise thou
also shalt be cut off" (Rom 11:22); **(2)** "kindness" (Eph 2:7; Titus 3:4; 2 Cor 6:6; Col 3:12;
Gal 5:22). **(3)** It signifies "not merely goodness
as a quality, rather it is goodness in action, goodness expressing itself in deeds; yet not goodness expressing itself in indignation against
sin, for it is contrasted with severity in Rom
11:22, but in grace and tenderness and compassion." Syn.: 19. See: TDNT—9:489, 1320;
BAGD—886b.

5545. χρῖσμα {3x} **chrisma**, *khris'-mah;* from
5548; an *unguent* or *smearing,*
i.e. (fig.) the spec. *endowment* ("chrism") of the
Holy Spirit:—anointing {2x}, unction {1x}.

Chrisma, as a verb, signifies "an unguent,
or an anointing." **(1)** It was prepared from oil
and aromatic herbs. **(2)** It is used only metaphorically in the NT; by metonymy, of the Holy
Spirit: **(2a)** "But ye have an unction from the
Holy One, and ye know all things" (1 Jn 2:20)
and **(2b)** "But the anointing which ye have received of Him abideth in you, and ye need not
that any man teach you: but as the same
anointing teacheth you of all things, and is
truth, and is no lie, and even as it hath taught
you, ye shall abide in Him" (1 Jn 2:27). **(2b1)**
That believers have "an anointing from the
Holy One" indicates that this anointing renders them holy, separating them to God. **(2b2)**
The passage teaches that the gift of the Holy
Spirit is the all efficient means of enabling believers to possess a knowledge of the truth.

Syn.: 218, 1472, 2025, 3462, 5548. See: TDNT—
9:493, 1322; BAGD—886c; THAYER—672a.

5546. Χριστιανός {3x} **Christianŏs**, *khris-
tee-an-os';* from *5547;* a
Christian, i.e. follower of Christ:—Christian
{3x}. See: TDNT—9:493, 1322; BAGD—886c;
THAYER—672b.

5547. Χριστός {569x} **Christŏs**, *khris-tos';* from
5548; anointed, i.e. the *Messiah,*
an epithet of Jesus:—Christ {569x}. See: TDNT—
9:493, 1322; BAGD—886d; THAYER—672b.

5548. χρίω {5x} **chriō**, *khree'-o;* prob. akin to
5530 through the idea of *contact;*
to *smear* or *rub* with oil, i.e. (by impl.) to *consecrate* to an office or relig. service:—anoint {5x}.

Chrio, as a verb, is **(1)** more limited in its
use than *aleipho* (*218*); **(2)** it is confined to "sacred and symbolical anointings"; **(2a)** of Christ
as the "Anointed" of God (Lk 4:18; cf. Acts
4:27; 10:38), and **(2b)** Heb 1:9, where it is used
metaphorically in connection with "the oil of
gladness." **(3)** The title Christ signifies "The
Anointed One." The word (*Christos*) is rendered **(3a)** "(His) Christ" (Acts 4:26). **(3b)** Once
it is said of believers: "Now He which stablisheth us with you in Christ, and hath anointed
us, is God" (2 Cor 1:21). Syn.: 218, 1472, 1637,
2025, 3462, 3464, 5545. See: TDNT—9:493,
1322; BAGD—887c; THAYER—673a.

5549. χρονίζω {5x} **chrŏnizō**, *khron-id'-zo;*
from *5550;* to *take time,* i.e. *lin-
ger:*—delay {2x}, tarry {2x}, tarry so long {1x}.

Chronizo, as a verb, means literally "to
while away time" i.e., by way of "lingering,
tarrying, delaying" and is translated **(1)** "delayeth" in Mt 24:48; Lk 12:45; or **(2)** "tarry, tarried" in **(2a)** Mt 25:5, "tarried"; **(2b)** Lk 1:21,
"tarried so long"; **(2c)** Heb 10:37, "will (not)
tarry"). Syn.: 311, 3635. See: BAGD—887d;
THAYER—673b.

5550. χρόνος {53x} **chrŏnŏs**, *khron'-os;* of
uncert. der.; a *space* of *time* (in
gen., and thus prop. distinguished from *2540,*
which designates a *fixed* or special occasion;
and from *165,* which denotes a particular *period*) or *interval;* by extens. an indiv. *opportunity;* by impl. *delay:*—time {33x}, season {4x},
while {2x}, a while {2x}, space {2x}, oftentimes
+ 4183 {1x}, not tr {5x}, misc. {4x}.

Chronos (*5550*), whence Eng. words beginning with "chron"—, as a noun, **(1)** denotes "a
space of time," whether long or short: **(1a)** it
implies duration, whether longer: **(1a1)** Acts
1:21, "(all the) time"; **(1a2)** Acts 13:18; 20:18,
"at all seasons"; or **(1b)** shorter: Lk 4:5; **(1c)** It
sometimes refers to the date of an occurrence,
(1c1) whether past (Mt 2:7), or **(1c2)** future (Acts

3:21; 7:17). Syn.: **(A)** Broadly speaking, *chronos* expresses the duration of a period, *kairos* (*2540*) stresses it as marked by certain features; **(A1)** thus in Acts 1:7, "the Father has set within His own authority" both the times (*chronos*), the lengths of the periods, and the "seasons" (*kairos*), epochs characterized in certain events; **(A2)** in 1 Th 5:1, "times" refers to the length of the interval before the *Parousia* takes place (the presence of Christ with the saints when He comes to receive them to Himself at the Rapture), and to the length of time the *Parousia* will occupy; **(B)** "seasons" refers to the special features of the period before, during, and after the *Parousia*. **(C)** *Chronos* marks quantity, *kairos*, quality. **(D)** *Kairos* (*2540*) means a definitely limited portion of time with the added notion of suitableness; whereas, *chronos* refers to time in general. See also: 171, 2122, 2540, 3641, 4340, 5610. See: TDNT—9:581, 1337; BAGD—887d.

5551. **χρονοτριβέω** {1x} **chrŏnŏtribĕō**, *khron-ot-rib-eh'-o;* from a presumed compound of *5550* and the base of *5147;* to be a *time-wearer,* i.e. to *procrastinate* (*linger*):—spend time {1x}. See: BAGD—888c; THAYER—673d.

5552. **χρύσεος** {15x} **chrusĕŏs**, *khroo'-seh-os;* from *5557;* made of *gold:*—of gold {15x}, golden {3x}. See: BAGD—888c, 888d; THAYER—673d.

5553. **χρυσίον** {9x} **chrusiŏn**, *khroo-see'-on;* dimin. of *5557;* a *golden* article, i.e. gold plating, ornament, or coin:—gold {9x}. *Chrusion,* a diminutive of *chrusos,* (*5557*), is used **(1)** of "coin," primarily small but valuable coins, Acts 3:6; 20:33; 1 Pet 1:18; **(2)** of "ornaments," 1 Pet 3:3; **(3)** of "the metal in general," Heb 9:4; 1 Pet 1:7; Rev 21:18, 21; **(4)** metaphorically, **(4a)** of "sound doctrine and its effects," 1 Cor 3:12; **(4b)** of "righteousness of life and conduct," Rev 3:18. See: BAGD—888c; THAYER—673d.

5554. **χρυσοδακτύλιος** {1x} **chrusŏdaktuliŏs**, *khroo-sod-ak-too'-lee-os;* from *5557* and *1146; gold-ringed,* i.e. *wearing* a golden finger-ring or similar *jewelry:*—with a gold ring {1x}. See: BAGD—888c; THAYER—674a.

5555. **χρυσόλιθος** {1x} **chrusŏlithŏs**, *khroo-sol'-ee-thos;* from *5557* and *3037; gold-stone,* i.e. now called a topaz, a *yellow gem* ("chrysolite"):—chrysolite {1x}. *Chrusolithos,* lit., "a gold stone" (*chrusos,* "gold," *lithos,* "a stone"), is the name of a precious stone of a gold color, now called "a topaz," Rev 21:20. See: BAGD—888c; THAYER—674a.

5556. **χρυσόπρασος** {1x} **chrusŏprasŏs**, *khroo-sop'-ras-os;* from *5557* and πράσον **prasŏn** (a *leek*); a *greenish-yellow* gem ("chrysoprase"):—chrysoprase {1x}. *Chrusoprasos,* from (*chrusos,* "gold," and *prasos,* "a leek"), is a precious stone like a leek in color, a translucent, golden green. The word occurs in Rev 21:20. See: BAGD—888d; THAYER—674a.

5557. **χρυσός** {13x} **chrusŏs**, *khroo-sos';* perh. from the base of *5530* (through the idea of the *utility* of the metal); *gold;* by extens. a *golden* article, as an ornament or coin:—gold {13x}. *Chrusos* is used **(1)** of "coin," Mt 10:9; Jas 5:3; **(2)** of "ornaments," Mt 23:16, 17; 1 Cor 3:12; Jas 5:3 (perhaps both coin and ornaments); Rev 18:12; **(3)** of "images," Acts 17:29; **(4)** of "the metal in general," Mt 2:11; Rev 9:7; Rev 18:16. See: BAGD—888d; THAYER—674a.

5558. **χρυσόω** {2x} **chrusŏō**, *khroo-sŏ'-o;* from *5557;* to *gild,* i.e. *bespangle* with golden ornaments:—deck {2x}. *Chrusoo,* lit., "to gild with gold" (*chrusos,* "gold"), is used in Rev 17:4; 18:16. See: BAGD—889a; THAYER—674a.

5559. **χρώς** {1x} **chrōs**, *khroce;* prob. akin to the base of *5530* through the idea of *handling;* the *body* (prop. its *surface* or *skin*):—body {1x}. *Chros* signifies "the surface of a body," especially of the human body, Acts 19:12, with reference to the handkerchiefs carried from Paul's body to the sick. See: BAGD—889b; THAYER—674b.

5560. **χωλός** {15x} **chōlŏs**, *kho-los';* appar. a primary word; "*halt,*" i.e. *limping:*—cripple {1x}, halt {4x}, lame {10x}. *Cholos,* "lame," is translated **(1)** "halt" in Mt 18:8; Mk 9:45; Lk 14:21; Jn 5:3; **(2)** in Acts 14:8, "cripple"; and **(3)** "lame" in Mt 11:5; 15:30, 31; 21:14; Lk 7:22; 14:13; Acts 3:2; 3:11, "the lame man"; 8:7; Heb 12:13. See: BAGD—889a; THAYER—674b.

5561. **χώρα** {27x} **chōra**, *kho'-rah;* fem. of a der. of the base of *5490* through the idea of *empty* expanse; *room,* i.e. a space of *territory* (more or less extens.; often incl. its inhab.):—country {15x}, region {5x}, land {3x}, field {2x}, ground {1x}, coast {1x}. *Chora* properly denotes "the space lying between two limits or places"; accordingly it has a variety of meanings: **(1)** "country," Mt 2:12; 8:28; Mk 5:1, 10; Lk 2:8; 8:26; 15:15; 19:12; 21:21; Acts 12:20; 18:23; 27:27; **(2)** "land," Mk 1:5; Lk 15:13–14; Acts 10:39; **(3)** "coast," Acts 26:20; **(4)** "region," Mk 6:55. Syn.: **(A)** *Topos* (*5117*) is a

place, indefinite; a portion of space viewed in reference to its occupancy, or as appropriated to itself. **(B)** *Chora* (*5561*) is region, country, an extensive; space, yet unbounded. **(C)** *Chorion* (*5564*) is a parcel of ground, circumscribed; a definite portion of space viewed as enclosed or complete in itself. See: BAGD–889b; THAYER–674b.

5562. χωρέω {10x} **chōrĕō**, *kho-reh'-o;* from *5561;* to *be* in (*give*) *space,* i.e. (intr.) to *pass, enter,* or (tran.) to *hold, admit* (lit. or fig.):—receive {3x}, contain {2x}, come {1x}, go {1x}, have place {1x}, cannot receive + 3756 {1x}, be room to receive {1x}.

   Choreo, as a verb, means "to give space, make room for" [*chora,* "a place"], and is used metaphorically, of **(1)** "receiving" **(1a)** cannot with the mind, Mt 19:11, 12; **(1b)** into the heart, 2 Cor 7:2. It is also translated **(2)** "contain" Jn 2:6; 21:25; **(3)** "come" 2 Pet 3:9; **(4)** "go" in Mt 15:17; **(5)** "have place" Jn 8:37; and **(6)** "be room to receive" in Mk 2:2. Syn.: **(A)** *Bathmos* (*898*) primarily signifies to walk, take steps, picturing the mode of motion; to go away. **(B)** *Erchomai* (*2064*) denotes motion or progress generally, and of any sort; hence to come and arrive at, as well as to go. **(C)** *Poreuomai* (*4198*) expresses motion in general, often confined within certain limits, or giving prominence to the bearing; hence the regular word for the march of an army. **(D)** *Choreo* (*5562*) always emphasizes the idea of separation, change of place, and does not, like e.g. 4198, note the external and perceptible motion; it is more internal. See also: 324, 353, 354, 568, 588, 618, 1209, 1523, 1926, 2210, 2865, 2975, 2983, 3028, 3335, 3336, 3858, 3880, 3970, 4327, 4355, 4356, 4380, 4381, 4382, 5264, 5274. See: BAGD–889c; THAYER–674c.

5563. χωρίζω {13x} **chōrizō**, *kho-rid'-zo;* from *5561;* to *place room* between, i.e. *part;* refl. to *go away:*—depart {8x}, put asunder {2x}, separate {3x}.

   Chorizo is translated **(1)** "to separate" in Rom 8:35, 39; Heb 7:26; **(2)** "to depart" in Acts 1:4; 18:1, 2; 1 Cor 7:10, 11, 15 twice; Philem 15; and **(3)** "put asunder" in Mt 19:6; Mk 10:9. See: BAGD–890a; THAYER–674d.

5564. χωρίον {10x} **chōriŏn**, *kho-ree'-on;* dimin. of *5561;* a *spot* or *plot* of ground:—field {3x}, land {3x}, place {2x}, parcel of ground {1x}, possession {1x}.

   Chorion, as a noun, means "a region" (a diminutive of *chora* (*5561*), "a land, country"), and is translated **(1)** "field" in Acts 1:18, 19 twice; **(2)** "land" in Acts 4:34; 5:3, 8; **(3)** "place" in Mt 26:36; Mk 14:32, used of Gethsemane; **(4)** "parcel of ground" in Jn 4:5; and **(5)** "possession" in Acts 28:7. Syn.: 201, 402, 1096, 1502,

3837, 4042, 5117, 5247, 5602. See also: 5561 for discussion. See: BAGD–890b; THAYER–674d.

5565. χωρίς {39x} **chōris**, *kho-rece';* adv. from *5561;* at a *space,* i.e. *separately* or *apart* from (often as prep.):—beside {3x}, by itself {1x}, without {35x}. See: BAGD–890c; THAYER–675a.

5566. χῶρος {1x} **chŏrŏs**, *kho'-ros;* of Lat. or.; the *north-west* wind:—north west {1x}. See: BAGD–891c; THAYER–675c.

Ψ

5567. ψάλλω {5x} **psallō**, *psal'-lo;* probably strengthened from ψάω **psaō**, (to *rub* or *touch* the surface; comp. *5597*); to *twitch* or *twang,* i.e. to *play* on a stringed instrument (*celebrate* the divine worship *with* music and accompanying odes):—make melody {1x}, sing {3x}, sing psalms {1x}.

   Psallo, primarily "to twitch, twang," then, "to play a stringed instrument with the fingers," and hence, "to sing with a harp, sing psalms," denotes, in the NT, "to sing a hymn, sing praise" and is translated **(1)** "making melody" in Eph 5:19; **(2)** "sing" in Rom 15:9; 1 Cor 14:15 twice; and **(3)** "let him sing psalms" in Jas 5:13. See: TDNT–8:489, 1225; BAGD–891a; THAYER–675b.

5568. ψαλμός {7x} **psalmŏs**, *psal-mos';* from *5567;* a *set piece* of *music,* i.e. a sacred *ode* (accompanied with the voice, harp or other instrument; a "*psalm*"); collect. the book of the *Psalms:*—psalm {5x}, Psalm {2x}.

   Psalmos primarily denoted "a striking or twitching with the fingers (on musical strings)"; then, "a sacred song, sung to musical accompaniment, a psalm." It is used **(1)** of the OT book of "Psalms," Lk 20:42; 24:44; Acts 1:20; **(2)** of a particular "psalm," Acts 13:33 (cf. v. 35); **(3)** of "psalms" in general, 1 Cor 14:26; Eph 5:19; Col 3:16. Syn.: **(A)** *Ode* (*5603*) is the generic term containing praises, exhortations and other admonitions. **(B)** *Psalmos* (*5568*) and **(C)** *humnos* (*5215*) are specific, the former designating a song which took its general character from the OT Psalms and is usually accompanied by some musical instrument, although not restricted to them; the later a song of praise with or without instrumental accompaniment. See: TDNT–8:489, 1225; BAGD–891b; THAYER–675b.

5569. ψευδάδελφος {2x} **psĕudadĕlphŏs**, *psyoo-dad'-el-fos;* from *5571* and *80;* a *spurious brother,* i.e. *pretended* associate:—false brethren {2x}. Cf. 2 Cor 11:26; Gal 2:4. See: TDNT–1:144, 22; BAGD–891b; THAYER–675d.

5570. ψευδαπόστολος {1x} psĕudapŏstŏlŏs, *psyoo-dap-os'-tol-os;* from 5571 and 652; a *spurious apostle,* i.e. *pretended preacher:*—false apostles {1x}. See: TDNT—1:445, 67; BAGD—891b; THAYER—675d.

5571. ψευδής {3x} psĕudēs, *psyoo-dace';* from 5574; *untrue,* i.e. *erroneous, deceitful, wicked:*—false {1x}, liar {2x}.

Pseudes is used of (1) "false witnesses," Acts 6:13; (2) "liars," Rev 2:2; Rev 21:8. See: TDNT—9:594, 1339; BAGD—891c; THAYER—675d.

5572. ψευδοδιδάσκαλος {1x} psĕudŏdidaskalŏs, *psyoo-dod-id-as'-kal-os;* from 5571 and 1320; a *spurious teacher,* i.e. *propagator of erroneous* Chr. *doctrine:*—false teacher {1x}. See: TDNT—2:160, 161; BAGD—891d; THAYER—675d.

5573. ψευδολόγος {1x} psĕudŏlŏgŏs, *psyoo-dol-og'-os;* from 5571 and 3004; *mendacious,* i.e. *promulgating erroneous* Chr. *doctrine:*—speaking lies {1x}.

Pseudologos denotes "speaking falsely" (*pseudes,* "false," *logos,* "a word") in 1 Ti 4:2, where the adjective is translated "speaking lies", and is applied to "devils," the actual utterances being by their human agents. See: BAGD—891d; THAYER—675d.

5574. ψεύδομαι {11x} psĕudŏmai, *psyoo'-dom-ahee;* mid. voice of an appar. primary verb; to *utter an untruth* or attempt to *deceive* by falsehood:—falsely {1x}, lie {11x}.

Pseudomai, "to deceive by lies," is used (1) in the middle voice, translated "to say . . . falsely" in Mt 5:11; and is elsewhere rendered (2) "to lie" in Acts 5:3–4; Rom 9:1; 2 Cor 11:31; Gal 1:20; Col 3:9; 1 Ti 2:7; Heb 6:8; Jas 3:14; 1 Jn 1:6; Rev 3:9. See: TDNT—9:594, 1339; BAGD—891d; THAYER—675d.

5575. ψευδομάρτυρ {3x} psĕudŏmartur, *psyoo-dom-ar'-toor;* from 5571 and a kindred form of 3144; a *spurious witness,* i.e. *bearer of untrue testimony:*—false witness {3x}.

Pseudomartu, as a noun, denotes "a false witness" in Mt 26:60 twice; 1 Cor 15:15. Syn.: 267, 2649, 3140, 3141, 3142, 3143, 3144, 4828, 4901, 5576, 5577.See: TDNT—4:513,*; BAGD—892a; THAYER—676a.

5576. ψευδομαρτυρέω {6x} psĕudŏmarturĕō, *psyoo-dom-ar-too-reh'-o;* from 5575; to *be an untrue testifier,* i.e. offer *falsehood in evidence:*—bear false witness {6x}.

Pseudomartureo, as a verb, means "to bear false witness" in Mt 19:18; Mk 10:19; 14:56, 57;

Lk 18:20; Rom 13:9. Syn.: 267, 2649, 3140, 3141, 3142, 3143, 3144, 4828, 4901, 5576, 5577. See: TDNT—4:513, 564; BAGD—891d; THAYER—676a.

5577. ψευδομαρτυρία {2x} psĕudŏmarturia, *psyoo-dom-ar-too-ree'-ah;* from 5575; *untrue testimony:*—false witness {2x}.

Pseudomarturia, as a noun, means "false witness" in Mt 15:19; 26:59. Syn.: 267, 2649, 3140, 3141, 3142, 3143, 3144, 4828, 4901, 5571, 5576. See: TDNT—4:513, 564; BAGD—892a; THAYER—676a.

5578. ψευδοπροφήτης {11x} psĕudŏprŏphētēs, *psyoo-dop-rof-ay'-tace;* from 5571 and 4396; a *spurious prophet,* i.e. *pretended foreteller* or relig. *impostor:*—false prophet {11x}.

This word means "a false prophet," and is used of such (1) in OT times, Lk 6:26; 2 Pet 2:1; (2) in the present period since Pentecost, Mt 7:15; 24:11, 24; Mk 13:22; Acts 13:6; 1 Jn 4:1; (3) with reference to a false "prophet" destined to arise as the supporter of the "Beast" at the close of this age, Rev 16:13; 19:20; 20:10 (himself described as "another beast," 13:11. See: TDNT—6:781, 952; BAGD—892a; THAYER—676b.

5579. ψεῦδος {9x} psĕudŏs, *psyoo'-dos;* from 5574; a *falsehood:*—lie {7x}, lying {2x}.

Pseudos, "a falsehood", is so translated in (1) Eph 4:25, "lying"; 2 Th 2:9, "lying wonders" is lit. "wonders of falsehood," i.e., wonders calculated to deceive; (2) it is elsewhere rendered "lie" in Jn 8:44; Rom 1:25; 2 Th 2:11; 1 Jn 2:21, 27; Rev 21:27; 22:15. See: TDNT—9:594, 1339; BAGD—892b; THAYER—676b.

5580. ψευδόχριστος {2x} psĕudŏchristŏs, *psyoo-dokh'-ris-tos;* from 5571 and 5547; a *spurious Messiah:*—false Christ {2x}.

Pseudochristos denotes "one who falsely lays claim to the name and office of the Messiah," Mt 24:24; Mk 13:22. Syn.: (A) The *antichristos* (500) denies that there is a Christ; (B) the *pseudochristos* affirms himself to be the Christ. Both make war against Christ, and though under different pretenses, each would set himself on the throne of glory. See: TDNT—9:594, 1339; BAGD—892b; THAYER—676b.

5581. ψευδώνυμος {1x} psĕudōnumŏs, *psyoo-do'-noo-mos;* from 5571 and 3686; *untruly named:*—falsely so called {1x}.

Pseudonumos, "under a false name" (*pseudo* and *onoma,* "a name"; Eng., "pseudonym"), is said of the knowledge professed by the propagandists of various heretical cults, 1 Ti 6:20. See:

Greek

TDNT—5:282, 694; BAGD—892c; THAYER—676b.

5582. ψεῦσμα {1x} **psĕusma**, *psyoos'-mah;* from 5574; a *fabrication,* i.e. *falsehood:*—lie {1x}.

Pseusma is a falsehood or an acted lie (Rom 3:7), where "my lie" is not idolatry, but the universal false attitude of man toward God. See: TDNT—9:594, 1339; BAGD—892c; THAYER—676c.

5583. ψεύστης {10x} **psĕustēs**, *psyoos-tace';* from 5574; a *falsifier:*—liar {10x}.

Pseustes, "a liar," occurs in Jn 8:44, 55; Rom 3:4; 1 Ti 1:10; Titus 1:12; 1 Jn 1:10; 2:4, 22; 4:20; 5:10. See: TDNT—9:594, 1339; BAGD—892c; THAYER—676c.

5584. ψηλαφάω {4x} **psēlaphaō**, *psay-laf-ah'-o;* from the base of 5567 (comp. 5586); to *manipulate,* i.e. *verify* by contact; fig. to *search* for:—feel after {1x}, handle {2x}, touch {1x}.

Literally, this word means to feel or grope about and expresses the motion of the hands over a surface, so as to feel it. It is used **(1)** metaphorically, of seeking after God (Acts 17:27); **(2)** literally, of physical handling or touching (Lk 24:39; 1 Jn 1:1; Heb 12:18). Syn.: **(A)** *Pselaphao* never refers to handling an object in order to mold or modify it but either to feeling an object's surface (Lk 24:39; 1 Jn 1:1) perhaps to learn its composition or to feeling for or after an object without actually touching it. **(B)** *Haptomai* (680) appropriately describes the self-conscious effort of the sculptor; to touch in order to change. **(C)** *Thingano* (2345) lacks the mental effort; it refers to touching in general. See: BAGD—892c; THAYER—676c.

5585. ψηφίζω {2x} **psēphizō**, *psay-fid'-zo;* from 5586; to *use pebbles* in enumeration, i.e. (gen.) to *compute:*—count {2x}.

Literally, *psephizo* means to count with pebbles, to compute, calculate, reckon, Lk 14:28; Rev 13:18. See: TDNT—9:604, 1341; BAGD—892d; THAYER—676c.

5586. ψῆφος {3x} **psēphŏs**, *psay'-fos;* from the same as 5584; a *pebble* (as worn smooth by *handling*), i.e. (by impl. of use as a *counter* or *ballot*) a *verdict* (of acquittal) or *ticket* (of admission); a *vote:*—stone {2x}, voice {1x}.

Psephos, "a smooth stone, a pebble," worn smooth as by water, or polished (akin to *psao,* "to rub"), denotes **(1)** by metonymy, a vote (from the use of "pebbles" for this purpose; cf. *psephizo,* "to count"), Acts 26:10, "voice" implying one's "voice" is heard by his vote; and

(2) a (white) "stone" to be given to the overcomer in the church at Pergamum, Rev 2:17 (twice). A white "stone" was often used in the social life and judicial customs of the ancients; festal days were noted by a white "stone," days of calamity by a black; in the courts a white "stone" indicated acquittal, a black condemnation. A host's appreciation of a special guest was indicated by a white "stone" with the name or a message written on it; this is probably the allusion here. See: TDNT—9:604, 1341; BAGD—892d; THAYER—676d.

5587. ψιθυρισμός {1x} **psithurismŏs**, *psith-oo-ris-mos';* from a der. of ψίθος **psithŏs** (a *whisper;* by impl. a *slander;* prob. akin to 5574); *whispering,* i.e. secret *detraction:*—whispering {1x}.

Psithurismos, "a whispering," is used of "secret slander" in 2 Cor 12:20. See: BAGD—892d; THAYER—676d.

5588. ψιθυριστής {1x} **psithuristēs**, *psith-oo-ris-tace';* from the same as 5587; a secret *calumniator:*—whisperer {1x}.

Psithuristes, "a whisperer," occurs in an evil sense in Rom 1:29. See: BAGD—893a; THAYER—676d.

5589. ψιχίον {3x} **psichiŏn**, *psikh-ee'-on;* dimin. from a der. of the base of 5567 (mean. a *crumb*); a *little bit* or *morsel:*—crumb {3x}.

Psichion, "a small morsel," a diminutive of *psix,* "a bit, or crumb", of bread or meat, is used in Mt 15:27; Mk 7:28; Lk 16:21. See: BAGD—893a; THAYER—677a.

5590. ψυχή {105x} **psuchē**, *psoo-khay';* from 5594; *breath,* i.e. (by impl.) *spirit,* abstr. or concr. (the *animal* sentient principle only; thus distinguished on the one hand from 4151, which is the rational and immortal *soul;* and on the other from 2222, which is mere *vitality,* even of plants: these terms thus exactly correspond respectively to the Heb. 5315, 7307 and 2416):—soul {58x}, life {40x}, mind {3x}, heart {1x}, heartily + 1537 {1x}, not tr {2x}.

Psuche refers to **(1)** breath, **(1a)** the breath of life, that vital force which animates the body and shows itself in breathing (Acts 20:10), **(1a1)** of animals (Rev 8:9), or **(1a2)** of men (1 Th 5:23); **(1b)** life (Mt 6:25); **(1c)** that in which there is life, a living being, a living soul (1 Cor 15:45); **(2)** the soul, **(2a)** the seat of the feelings, desires, affections, aversions (Lk 1: 46; 2:35); **(2b)** the (human) soul in so far as it is constituted that by the right use of the aids offered it by God it can attain its highest end and secure eternal blessedness, the soul regarded as a moral being designed for everlasting life (3 Jn 2; 1 Pet 2:11); **(2c)** the soul as an essence which differs from

the body and is not dissolved by death (distinguished from other parts of the body), Mt 10:28; Rev 6:9. See: TDNT—9:608, 1342; BAGD—890b; THAYER—893b.

5591. ψυχικός {6x} **psuchikŏs**, *psoo-khee-kos'*; from *5590; sensitive*, i.e. *animate* (in distinction on the one hand from *4152*, which is the higher or *renovated* nature; and on the other from *5446*, which is the lower or *bestial* nature):—natural {4x}, sensual {2x}.

(1) The *psychikos* person is one who yields in everything to the human reasonings of the *soul* (*5590*), not thinking there is need for help from above. (2) It describes the man in Adam and what pertains to him (set in contrast to *pneumatikos* "spiritual"), and is (3) translated **(3a)** "natural", 1 Cor 2:14; 15:44 twice, 46 used as a noun; and **(3b)** "sensual" in Jas 3:15 and Jude 19, here relating perhaps more especially to the mind, a wisdom in accordance with, or springing from, the corrupt desires and affections. See: TDNT—9:661, 1342; BAGD—894b; THAYER—677d.

5592. ψῦχος {3x} **psuchŏs**, *psoo'-khos;* from *5594; coolness:*—cold {3x}.

Psuchos, "coldness, cold," appears in Jn 18:18; Acts 28:2; 2 Cor 11:27. Syn.: 5593. See: BAGD—894c; THAYER—678a.

5593. ψυχρός {4x} **psuchrŏs**, *psoo-chros';* from *5592; chilly* (lit. or fig.):—cold {4x}.

Psuchros, "cool, fresh, cold, chilly" (fuller in expression than *psuchos*, 5592), is used in the **(1)** natural sense in Mt 10:42, "cold water"; **(2)** metaphorically in Rev 3:15–16. Syn.: 5592. See: TDNT—2:876, 296; BAGD—894c; THAYER—678a.

5594. ψύχω {1x} **psuchō**, *psoo'-kho;* a primary verb; to *breathe* (*voluntarily* but *gently*, thus differing on the one hand from *4154*, which denotes prop. a *forcible* respiration; and on the other from the base of *109*, which refers prop. to an inanimate *breeze*), i.e. (by impl. of reduction of temperature by evaporation) to *chill* (fig.):—wax cold {1x}.

Psucho, "to breathe, blow, cool by blowing," passive voice, "grow cool slowly," is used metaphorically in Mt 24:12, in the sense of waning zeal or love. See: BAGD—894d; THAYER—678c.

5595. ψωμίζω {2x} **psōmizō**, *pso-mid'-zo;* from the base of *5596; to supply* with *bits*, i.e. (gen.) to *nourish:*—bestow to feed {1x}, feed {1x}.

Primarily, *psomizo* means to feed by putting little bits into the mouths of infants or animals and came to denote simply to give out food, to

feed (1 Cor 13:3; Rom 12:20). See: BAGD—894d; THAYER—678c.

5596. ψωμίον {4x} **psōmiŏn**, *pso-mee'-on;* dimin. from a der. of *5597;* a *crumb* or *morsel* (as if *rubbed* off), i.e. a *mouthful:*—sop {4x}.

Psomion, a diminutive of *psomos*, "a morsel," denotes "a fragment, a sop", Jn 13:26 (twice), 27, 30. It had no connection with the modern meaning of "sop," something given to pacify. See: BAGD—894d; THAYER—678c.

5597. ψώχω {1x} **psōchō**, *pso'-kho;* prol. from the same base as *5567;* to *triturate*, i.e. (by anal.) to *rub* out (kernels from husks with the fingers or hand):—rub {1x}.

Psocho, "to rub, to rub to pieces," is used in Luke 6:1. See: BAGD—894d; THAYER—678c.

Ω

5598. Ω {4x} **w** —, i.e. ὦμεγα **ōměga**, *o'-meg-ah;* the last letter of the Greek alphabet, i.e. (fig.) the *finality:*—Omega {4x}. Cf. Rev 1:8, 11; 21:6; 22:13. See: TDNT—1:1,*; BAGD—895a; THAYER—678b.

5599. ὦ {15x} **ō**, *o;* a primary interj.; as a sign of the voc. *O;* as a note of exclamation, *oh:*—O {15x}. See: BAGD—895a; THAYER—678b.

5600. ὦ {66x} **ō**, *o;* incl. the oblique forms, as well as ἦς **ēs**, *ace;* ἦ **ē**, *ay;* etc.; the subjunctive of *1510;* (*may, might, can, could, would, should, must*, etc.; also with *1487* and its comp., as well as with other particles) *be:*—be {22x}, may be {22x}, should be {6x}, is {5x}, might be {2x}, were {1x}, not tr {4x}, appear {1x}, have {1x}, + pass the flower of her age {1x}, should stand {1x}. See: BAGD—222d [1510] + 219a [1487]; THAYER—678b, 175c [1510].

5601. νΩβήδ {3x} **Obēd**, *o-bade'*or 'Ιωβήδ **Iōbēd**, *yo-bade';* of Heb. or. [5744]; *Obed*, an Isr.:—Obed {3x}. See: BAGD—895b, 385b; THAYER—678b.

5602. ὧδε {60x} **hōdě**, *ho'-deh;* from an adv. form of *3592; in this* same spot, i.e. *here* or *hither:*—here {44x}, hither {13x}, in this place {1x}, this place {1x}, there {1x}. Syn.: 201, 402, 1096, 1502, 3837, 4042, 5117, 5247, 5564. See: BAGD—895b; THAYER—678c.

5603. ᾠδή {7x} **ōdē**, *o-day';* from *103;* a *chant* or *"ode"* (the gen. term for any words sung; while *5215* denotes espec. a *relig.* metrical composition, and *5568* still more spec. a *Heb.* cantillation):—song {7x}.

Ode, "an ode, song," is **(1)** always used in the NT in praise of God or Christ; **(2)** in Eph

5:19 and Col 3:16 the adjective "spiritual" is added, because the word in itself is generic and might be used of songs anything but spiritual; **(3)** in Rev 5:9 and 14:3 (1st part) the descriptive word is "new" (*kainos*, "new," in reference to character and form), a "song," the significance of which was confined to those mentioned (v. 3, and 2nd part); **(4)** in Rev 15:3 (twice), "the song of Moses . . . and the song of the Lamb," the former as celebrating the deliverance of God's people by His power, the latter as celebrating redemption by atoning sacrifice. Syn.: **(A)** *Ode* (5603) is the generic term containing praises, exhortations and other admonitions. **(B)** *Psalmos* (5568) and **(C)** *humnos* (5215) are specific, the former designating a song which took its general character from the OT Psalms and is usually accompanied by some musical instrument, although not restricted to them; the later a song of praise with or without instrumental accompaniment. See: TDNT—1:164, 24; BAGD—895c; THAYER—679a.

5604. ὠδίν {4x} **ōdin**, *o-deen';* akin to *3601;* a *pang* or *throe*, espec. of childbirth:—pain {1x}, sorrow {2x}, travail {1x}.

Odin, as a noun, "a birth pang, travail pain," is rendered **(1)** "sorrows," metaphorically, in Mt 24:8 and Mk 13:8; **(2)** "travail" in 1 Th 5:3; and **(3)** "pains (of death)," Acts 2:24. Syn.: 253, 3076, 3077, 3600, 3601, 3997, 4036. See: TDNT—9:667, 1353; BAGD—895c; THAYER—679a.

5605. ὠδίνω {3x} **ōdinō**, *o-dee'-no;* from *5604;* to *experience* the *pains* of parturition (lit. or fig.):—travail {1x}, travail in birth {2x}.

Odino is used **(1)** negatively in Gal 4:27, "(thou) that travailest (not)," **(1a)** quoted from Is 54:1; **(1b)** the apostle applies the circumstances of Sarah and Hagar (which doubtless Isaiah was recalling) to show that, whereas the promise by grace had temporarily been replaced by the works of the Law (see Gal 3:17), this was now reversed, and, in the fulfillment of the promise to Abraham, the number of those saved by the gospel would far exceed those who owned allegiance to the Law. **(1c)** Is 54 has primary reference to the future prosperity of Israel restored to God's favor, but frequently the principles underlying events recorded in the OT extend beyond their immediate application.

(2) In Gal 4:19 the apostle uses it metaphorically of a second travailing on his part regarding the churches of Galatia; **(2a)** his first was for their deliverance from idolatry (v. 8), **(2b)** now it was for their deliverance from bondage to Judaism. **(2c)** There is no suggestion here of a second regeneration necessitated by defection.

(2d) There is a hint of reproach, as if he was enquiring whether they had ever heard of a mother experiencing second birth pangs for her children. **(3)** In Rev 12:2 the woman is figurative of Israel; the circumstances of her birth pangs are mentioned in Is 66:7 (see also Mic 5:2, 3). **(3a)** Historically the natural order is reversed. **(3b)** The manchild, Christ, was brought forth at His first advent; the travail is destined to take place in "the time of Jacob's trouble," the "great tribulation," Mt 24:21; Rev 7:14. **(3c)** The object in Rev 12:2 in referring to the birth of Christ is to connect Him with His earthly people Israel in their future time of trouble, from which the godly remnant, the nucleus of the restored nation, is to be delivered (Jer 30:7). See: TDNT—9:667, 1353; BAGD—895d; THAYER—679a.

5606. ὦμος {2x} **ōmŏs**, *o'-mos;* perh. from the alt. of *5342;* the *shoulder* (as that on which burdens are *borne*):—shoulder {2x}.

Omos occurs in Mt 23:4 and Lk 15:5, and is suggestive (as in the latter passage) of strength and safety. See: BAGD—895d; THAYER—679b.

5607. ὤν {154x} **ōn**, *oan;* incl. the fem.

οὖσα **ŏusa**, *oo'-sah;* and the neut.

ὄν **ŏn**, *on;* pres. part. of *1510; being:*—being {36x}, when . . . was {8x}, which is {12x}, that is {8x}, not tr {10x}, misc. {80x} = be, come, have. See: TDNT—2:398,*; BAGD—224d [1510]; THAYER—175c [1510].

5608. ὠνέομαι {1x} **ōnĕŏmai**, *o-neh'-om-ahee;* mid. voice from an appar. primary **ὦνος** **ōnŏs** (a *sum* or *price*); to *purchase*, (synonymous with the earlier *4092*):—buy {1x}.

Oneomai "to buy, in contradistinction to selling," is used in Acts 7:16, of the purchase by Abraham of a burying place. See: BAGD—895d; THAYER—679b.

5609. ὠόν {1x} **ōŏn**, *o-on';* appar. a primary word; an "*egg*":—egg {1x}. See: BAGD—896a; THAYER—679b.

5610. ὥρα {108x} **hōra**, *ho'-rah;* appar. a primary word; an "*hour*" (lit. or fig.):—hour {89x}, time {11x}, season {3x}, day {1x}, instant {1x}, × short {1x}, eventide {1x}, even {1x}.

Hora, whence Lat., *hora*, Eng., "hour," primarily denoted any time or period, especially a season. In the NT it is used to denote **(1)** "a part of the day," especially a twelfth part of day or night, an "hour," e.g., Mt 8:13; Acts 10:3, 9; 23:23; Rev 9:15; **(2)** in 1 Cor 15:30, "every hour" stands for "all the time"; **(3)** in some passages it expresses duration, e.g., Mt 20:12; 26:40; Lk 22:59; **(4)** inexactly, in such phrases as "for a season," Jn 5:35; 2 Cor 7:8; **(5)** "for an

hour," Gal 2:5; **(6)** "for a short time," lit., "for the time of an hour"; 1 Th 2:17; **(7)** "a period more or less extended," e.g., 1 Jn 2:18, "it is the last time"; **(8)** "a definite point of time," **(8a)** e.g., Mt 26:45, "the hour is at hand"; **(8b)** Lk 1:10; 10:21; 14:17, lit., "at the hour of supper"; Acts 16:18; 22:13; Rev 3:3; 11:13; 14:7; **(9)** a point of time when an appointed action is to begin, Rev 14:15; **(10)** in Rom 13:11, "it is high time," lit., "it is already an hour," indicating that a point of time has come later than would have been the case had responsibility been realized. **(11)** In 1 Cor 4:11, it indicates a point of time previous to which certain circumstances have existed. Syn.: 171, 2122, 2540, 3641, 4340, 5550. See: TDNT—9:675, 1355; BAGD—896a; THAYER—679b.

5611. **ὡραῖος** {4x} **hōraiŏs,** *ho-rah'-yos;* from *5610; belonging* to the right *hour* or *season* (timely), i.e. (by impl.) *flourishing* (beauteous [fig.]):—beautiful {4x}.

Horaios describes "that which is seasonable, produced at the right time," as of the prime of life, or the time when anything is at its loveliest and best (from *hora,* "a season," a period fixed by natural laws and revolutions, and so the best season of the year). **(1)** It is used of the outward appearance of whited sepulchres in contrast to the corruption within Mt 23:27; **(2)** of the Jerusalem gate called "Beautiful," Acts 3:2, 10; **(3)** of the feet of those that bring glad tidings, Rom 10:15. See: BAGD—896d; THAYER—680a.

5612. **ὠρύομαι** {1x} **ōruŏmai,** *o-roo'-om-ahee;* mid. voice of an appar. primary verb; to "*roar*":—roar {1x}.

Oruomai, "to howl" or "roar," onomatopoeic, of animals or men, is used of a lion, 1 Pet 5:8, as a simile of Satan. See: BAGD—897a; THAYER—680a.

5613. **ὡς** {492x} **hōs,** *hoce;* prob. adv. of comparison from *3739; which how,* i.e. *in that manner* (very variously used, as follows):—as {342x}, when {42x}, how {18x}, as it were {20x}, about {14x}, misc. {56x} = after (that), for, like unto, since, so (that), that, to wit, unto, while, × with all speed. See: BAGD—897a; THAYER—680a.

5614. **ὡσαννά** {6x} **hōsanna,** *ho-san-nah';* of Heb. or. [3467 and 4994]; *oh save!; hosanna* (i.e. *hoshia-na*), an exclamation of adoration:—Hosanna {6x}.

Hosanna, in the Hebrew, means "save, we pray." The word seems to have become an utterance of praise rather than of prayer, though originally, probably, a cry for help. The people's cry at the Lord's triumphal entry into Jerusalem (Mt 21:9, 15; Mk 11:9, 10; Jn 12:13) was

taken from Ps 118, which was recited at the Feast of Tabernacles in the great Hallel (Ps 113 to 118) in responses with the priest, accompanied by the waving of palm and willow branches. "The last day of the feast" was called "the great Hosanna"; the boughs also were called "hosannas." See: TDNT—9:682, 1356; BAGD—899a; THAYER—682c.

5615. **ὡσαύτως** {17x} **hōsautōs,** *ho-sŏw'-toce;* from *5613* and an adv. from *846;* as *thus,* i.e. *in the same way:*—likewise {13x}, in like manner {2x}, even so {1x}, after the same manner {1x}.

Hosautos, a strengthened form of *hos* (5613), "thus," signifies "just so, likewise, in like manner" (1 Ti 2:9; Mk 14:31; Lk 22:20; Rom 8:26; 1 Ti 3:8; 5:25). Syn.: 195, 1485, 2239, 3634, 3668, 3697, 3779, 4169, 4187, 4217, 4459, 5158, 5159, 5179. See: BAGD—899b; THAYER—682c.

5616. **ὡσεί** {34x} **hōsĕi,** *ho-si';* from *5613* and *1487; as if:*—about {18x}, as {7x}, like {5x}, as it had been {2x}, as it were {1x}, like as {1x}. See: BAGD—899c, 595c [3775]; THAYER—682c.

5617. **Ὡσηέ** {1x} **Hōsĕĕ,** *ho-say-eh';* of Heb. or. [1954]; *Hoseë* (i.e. *Hosheä*), an Isr.:—Osee {1x}. See: BAGD—899c; THAYER—682d.

5618. **ὥσπερ** {42x} **hōspĕr,** *hoce'-per;* from *5613* and *4007; just as,* i.e. *exactly like:*—as {39x}, even as {2x}, like as {1x}. See: BAGD—899c; THAYER—682d.

5619. **ὡσπερεί** {1x} **hōspĕrĕi,** *hoce-per-i';* from *5618* and *1487; just as if,* i.e. *as it were:*—as {1x}. See: BAGD—899d; THAYER—683b.

5620. **ὥστε** {83x} **hōstĕ,** *hoce'-teh;* from *5613* and *5037; so too,* i.e. *thus therefore* (in various relations of *consecution,* as follow):—so that {25x}, wherefore {17x}, insomuch that {16x}, therefore {9x}, that {6x}, so then {5x}, to {3x}, as {1x}, insomuch as {1x}. See: BAGD—899d; THAYER—683b.

5621. **ὠτίον** {5x} **ōtiŏn,** *o-tee'-on;* dimin. of *3775;* an *earlet,* i.e. *one* of the ears, or perh. the *lobe* of the ear:—ear {5x}.

Otion, a diminutive of 3775, but without the diminutive force, it being a common tendency in everyday speech to apply a diminutive form to most parts of the body: the ear of Malchus (Mt 26:51; Mk 14:47; Lk 22:51; Jn 18:10, 26). Syn.: 189, 3775. See: TDNT—5:558, 744; BAGD—900b; THAYER—683c.

5622. **ὠφέλεια** {2x} **ōphĕlĕia,** *o-fel'-i-ah;* from a der. of the base of *5624; usefulness,* i.e. *benefit:*—advantage {1x}, profit {1x}.

Opheleia is found in **(1)** Rom 3:1, "profit," and **(2)** Jude 16, "advantage," i.e., they shew respect of persons for the sake of what they may gain from them. See: BAGD—900b; THAYER—683d.

5623. ὠφελέω {15x} **ōphĕlĕō**, *o-fel-eh'-o;* from the same as *5622;* to *be useful,* i.e. to *benefit:*—advantage {1x}, better {1x}, prevail {2x}, profit {11x}.

Opheleo signifies "to be useful, do good, profit," and is translated **(1)** "advantage" in Lk 9:25; **(2)** "better" in Mk 5:26; **(3)** "prevail" in Mt 27:24; Jn 12:19; and **(4)** "profit" in Mt 15:5;

16:26; Mk 7:11; 8:36; Jn 6:63; Rom 2:25; 1 Cor 13:3; 14:6; Gal 5:2; Heb 4:2; 13:9. See: BAGD—900c; THAYER—683d.

5624. ὠφέλιμος {4x} **ōphĕlimŏs**, *o-fel'-ee-mos;* from a form of *3786; helpful* or *serviceable,* i.e. *advantageous:*—profitable {3x}, profit + 2076 {1x}.

Ophelimos, "useful, profitable", is translated **(1)** "profitable" (of godliness) in 1 Ti 4:8, second time; "profiteth" in the 1st part, of physical exercise; **(2)** "profitable" in 2 Ti 3:16 of the God-breathed Scriptures; **(3)** "profitable" in Titus 3:8, of maintaining good works. See: BAGD—900d; THAYER—683d.

NOTES

NOTES

NOTES

NOTES

NOTES

NOTES

NOTES

NOTES

NOTES